PS 3529 .N5 Z793 V.3

Reaver, J. Russell 1915-

An O'Neill concordance

AN

O'NEILL

CONCORDANCE

AN O'NEILL CONCORDANCE

In Three Volumes

VOLUME III

PORTA–Z

Compiled by

J. RUSSELL REAVER

The Florida State University

GALE RESEARCH COMPANY BOOK TOWER DETROIT, MICHIGAN 48226

CARROLL COLLEGE LIBRARY
HELENA, MONTANA 59601

Copyright © 1969 by Gale Research Co.

Library of Congress Catalog Card Number
73-75960

PORTAL

ON THE RIGHT, AN OPEN PORTAL WITH A SENTRY PACING 358 MARCOM UP AND DOWN, SPEAR IN HAND.

(THE KNIGHT HURRIES TO THE PORTAL.) 361 MARCOM

PORTALS

SUCH COOLING MY HEELS BEFORE THE SACRED PORTALS. 96 MANSNS

PORTENTIOUSLY

(THEN FROWNING PORTENTIOUSLY) 194 AHWILD

PORTENTOUS

HIS MANNER AND VOICE HAVE BECOME GRAVE AND 394 MARCOM PORTENTOUS)

HE IS STIFFLY CORRECT IN DRESS AND MANNER, DRYLY 116 POET PORTENTOUS IN SPEECH,

PORTENTOUSNESS

(REACTS--WITH AN EXTREME PROFESSIONAL 37 MANSNS PORTENTOUSNESS.)

PORTER

(JOHNNY DRAWS THE LAGER AND PORTER AND SETS THE 4 ANNA BIG.

GIMME A SCOOP THIS TIME--LAGER AND PORTER. 4 ANNA SHO' I WAS DAT WHEN I WAS PORTER ON DE PULLMANS 185 EJONES REMINDS ME OF DAMN FOOL ARGUMENT ME AND MOSE 584 ICEMAN PORTER HAS DE UDDER NIGHT.

I BRIBED THE PORTER TO TAKE A MESSAGE TO HER 149 MISBEG

PORTER'S

IS DRESSED IN A PULLMAN PORTER'S UNIFORM AND CAP. 191 EJONES

PORTHOLE

SHE LIFTS UP ONE OF THE CURTAINS AND LOOKS THROUGH540 'ILE

A PORTHOLE.)

(SHE GOES TO LEFT AND LIFTS THE CURTAINS FROM THE 546 'ILE PORTHOLE AND LOOKS OUT--

(HE GOES TO THE PORTHOLE, LEFT FORWARD) 569 CROSS

(NAT PEERS THROUGH THE PORTHOLE AND STARTS BACK, 569 CROSS

SUE TURNS FROM THE PORTHOLE. 569 CROSS

(SHE GOES TO THE PORTHOLE.' 569 CROSS

(POINTING TO THE PORTHOLE) THERE'S NOTHING THERE,570 CROSS NAT.

(SHE GOES OVER TO THE PORTHOLE AGAIN) 570 CROSS

AND SLAMS THE PORTHOLE SHUT) 514 INZONE

(SOURLY) WHAT PORTHOLES 521 INZONE

(EXCITEDLY) AN' NOW I COME TO THINK OF IT, 521 INZONE THERE'S THE PORTHOLE.

PORTHOLES

OVER THE BENCH, SEVERAL CURTAINED PORTHOLES. 535 'ILE

IN THE RIGHT WALL, FIVE PORTHOLES. 555 CROSS

HOUSE, CREEPS WEARILY IN THROUGH THE PORTHOLES 555 CROSS

STILL FARTHER, TWO MORE PORTHOLES. 555 CROSS

CLEAR MOONLIGHT FLOODS THROUGH THE PORTHOLES. 572 CROSS

BELOW THE DECK THE PORTHOLES SHOW A FAINT LIGHT 102 ELECTR FROM THE INTERIOR OF THE CABIN.

THREE OR FOUR PORTHOLES COVERED WITH BLACK CLOTH 513 INZONE CAN BE SEEN.

I'LL THROW UT OUT WAN AV THE PORTHOLES AN' BE DONE524 INZONE WID UT.

PORTICO

AT THIS MOMENT, SMITHERS APPEARS BENEATH THE 173 EJONES PORTICO.

FOR BEYOND THE PORTICO NOTHING CAN BE SEEN BUT A 173 EJONES VISTA OF DISTANT HILLS.

A WIDE ARCHWAY GIVING OUT ON A PORTICO WITH WHITE 173 EJONES PILLARS.

IT IS LATE AFTERNOON BUT THE SUNLIGHT STILL BLAZES173 EJONES

YELLOWLY BEYOND THE PORTICO 2 ELECTR

BEFORE THE DOORWAY A FLIGHT OF FOUR STEPS LEADS 2 ELECTR FROM THE GROUND TO THE PORTICO.

A WHITE WOODEN PORTICO WITH SIX TALL COLUMNS 2 ELECTR

CONTRASTS

BEHIND THE DRIVEWAY THE WHITE GRECIAN TEMPLE 5 ELECTR PORTICO WITH ITS SIX TALL COLUMNS

IN STRIKING CONTRAST TO THE WHITE COLUMNS OF THE 5 ELECTR PORTICO.

THE TEMPLE PORTICO IS LIKE AN INCONGRUOUS WHITE 5 ELECTR MASK

SHIMMERING IN A LUMINOUS MIST ON THE WHITE PORTICO 5 ELECTR AND THE GRAY STONE WALL

THE PORTICO AT THE TOP OF THE STEPS. 8 ELECTR

LAVINIA IS SITTING ON THE TOP OF THE STEPS TO THE 43 ELECTR PORTICO.

THE WHITE COLUMNS OF THE PORTICO CAST BLACK BARS 43 ELECTR OF SHADOW ON THE GRAY WALL

BEHIND HER MOTHER, IN THE PORTICO, SHE STOPS AND 51 ELECTR TURNS)

(THE DOOR BEHIND HIM IS OPENED AND LAVINIA APPEARS 56 ELECTR AT THE EDGE OF THE PORTICO

ITS WHITE PORTICO LIKE A MASK IN THE MOONLIGHT, AS 67 ELECTR IT HAD ON THAT NIGHT.

CHRISTINE IS DISCOVERED WALKING BACK AND FORTH ON 117 ELECTR THE DRIVE BEFORE THE PORTICO,

BETWEEN THE TWO COLUMNS OF THE PORTICO BEFORE THE 123 ELECTR FRONT DOOR.

STILL BATHES THE WHITE TEMPLE PORTICO IN A CRIMSON129 ELECTR LIGHT.

(HE GOES TOWARD THE PORTICO, SMALL FOLLOWING HIM, 131 ELECTR

(FROM THE PORTICO) WE'LL ALL JINE IN, JOE. 132 ELECTR

AND DOWN THE PORTICO STEPS, HIS FACE CHALKY WHITE 134 ELECTR AND HIS EYES POPPING.)

(SHE WALKS UP THE STEPS TO THE PORTICO. 137 ELECTR

SOFT GOLDEN SUNLIGHT SHIMMERS IN A LUMINOUS MIST 169 ELECTR ON THE GREEK TEMPLE PORTICO.

(HE SITS ON THE EDGE OF THE PORTICO BESIDE HER. 174 ELECTR

SHE ASCENDS TO THE PORTICO-- 179 ELECTR

WITHIN THE PORTICO ON ROWS OF CHAIRS PLACED ON A 312 LAZARU SERIES OF WIDE STEPS WHICH ARE

STANDS IN THE REAR AT THE EDGE OF THE PORTICO, 312 LAZARU ,CENTER,

PORTICO (CONT'D.)

IN THE FOREGROUND IS THE PORTICO OF A TEMPLE 312 LAZARU BETWEEN WHOSE MASSIVE COLUMNS ONE

MIRIAM HAS CRAWLED ON HER KNEES TO THE EDGE OF THE318 LAZARU PORTICO WHERE HER BLACK

PORTIERES

WITH SLIDING DOORS AND PORTIERES, 185 AHWILD

IN THE REAR WALL, LEFT, IS A DOUBLE DOORWAY WITH 185 AHWILD SLIDING DOORS AND PORTIERES,

AND PORTIERES LEADING INTO THE BACK PARLOR. 210 AHWILD

AT REAR ARE TWO DOUBLE DOORWAYS WITH PORTIERES. 11 JOURNE

PORTION

IF IT WERE, I SAY, THERE'D BE HALF FOR YOU FOR 566 CROSS YOUR WEDDING PORTION.

I THINK THEY HAVE NO PORTION IN US AFTER WE PASS 130 JOURNE THE GATE.

PORTRAIT

IS A LARGE PORTRAIT OF EZRA MANNON HIMSELF, 28 ELECTR PAINTED TEN YEARS PREVIOUSLY.

SHE TURNS SLOWLY TO HER FATHER'S PORTRAIT AND FOR 28 ELECTR A MOMENT STARES AT IT FIXEDLY.

(STARTS, LOOKS AT THE PORTRAIT AND QUICKLY DROPS 29 ELECTR HER EYES.

(INDICATING THE PORTRAIT--QUIETLY) 29 ELECTR

(HORRIFIED--WITH A GLANCE AT THE PORTRAIT) 30 ELECTR

IN THE PORTRAIT OVER THE FIREPLACE. 35 ELECTR

AND THAT OF THE PORTRAIT OF EZRA MANNON.) 36 ELECTR

(SEES THE PORTRAIT FOR THE FIRST TIME. 36 ELECTR

(HIS EYES STILL FIXED ON THE PORTRAIT-- 36 ELECTR

(SHE GLANCES AT THE PORTRAIT--THEN TURNS BACK TO 37 ELECTR BRANT WITH A LITTLE SHIVER--

SHE IS STARING AT THE PORTRAIT.) 37 ELECTR

(HE STOPS AND GLANCES WITH SAVAGE HATRED AT THE 38 ELECTR PORTRAIT.)

HER EYES ARE CAUGHT BY THE EYES OF HER HUSBAND IN 42 ELECTR THE PORTRAIT AND FOR A MOMENT

HE IS EXACTLY LIKE THE PORTRAIT IN HIS STUDY, 46 ELECTR WHICH WE HAVE SEEN IN ACT TWO.

DIRECTLY BEFORE THE PORTRAIT OF HIM OVER THE 93 ELECTR FIREPLACE.

HIS FACE IN THE CANDLELIGHT BEARS A STRIKING 93 ELECTR RESEMBLANCE TO THAT OF THE PORTRAIT

THROWING THEIR LIGHT ABOVE ON THE PORTRAIT AND 93 ELECTR BELOW ON THE DEAD MAN.

HIS MASK-LIKE FACE IS A STARTLING REPRODUCTION OF 93 ELECTR THE FACE IN THE PORTRAIT ABOVE

CANDLES ON THE MANTEL ABOVE THE FIREPLACE LIGHT UP149 ELECTR

THE PORTRAIT OF EZRA MANNON

THEN HE PUTS THE SHEET DOWN AND STARES UP AT THE 149 ELECTR PORTRAIT,

HE LOOKS ALMOST AS OLD NOW AS HIS FATHER IN THE 149 ELECTR PORTRAIT.

(SARDONICALLY, ADDRESSING THE PORTRAIT) 149 ELECTR

AT HIS EARNEST SOLICITATION--(HE WAVES A HAND TO 152 ELECTR THE PORTRAIT MOCKINGLY)

PORTRAIT AND A MALICIOUS CHUCKLE) 153 ELECTR

SHEDDING THEIR FLICKERING LIGHT ON THE PORTRAIT OF157 ELECTR ABE MANNON ABOVE.

THERE IS AN ASPECT ABOUT HER OF AN OLD PORTRAIT OF161 MANSNS A BYGONE AGE.

ON THE WALL, A FRAMED PORTRAIT STUDY OF ELEANOR. 462 WELDED

PORTRAITS

FLANKED BY SMALLER PORTRAITS OF ALEXANDER HAMILTON 28 ELECTR AND JOHN MARSHALL.

ALL THE FACES IN THE PORTRAITS HAVE THE SAME MASK 79 ELECTR QUALITY

OF THE THREE PORTRAITS ON THE OTHER WALLS, TWO ARE 79 ELECTR OF WOMEN--

PORTRAITS OF ANCESTORS HANG ON THE WALLS. 79 ELECTR

THE EYES OF THE MANNON PORTRAITS STARE WITH A GRIM139 ELECTR FORBIDDINGNESS.

IT'S ONLY THEY--(HE POINTS TO THE PORTRAITS) 140 ELECTR

(HE TURNS TO THE PORTRAITS MOCKINGLY) 141 ELECTR

(POINTS TO THE PORTRAITS MOCKINGLY) 145 ELECTR

(SHE LOOKS AT THE PORTRAITS DEFIANTLY) 146 ELECTR

THE EYES OF THE PORTRAITS SEEM TO POSSESS AN 157 ELECTR INTENSE BITTER LIFE,

HER EYES UNCONSCIOUSLY SEEKING THE MANNON 157 ELECTR PORTRAITS ON THE RIGHT WALL,

(TURNS AND ADDRESSES THE PORTRAITS ON THE WALL 165 ELECTR WITH A CRAZY MOCKERY)

(SHE TURNS TO GO AND HER EYES CATCH THE EYES OF 168 ELECTR THE MANNONS IN THE PORTRAITS

THE PORTRAITS OF THE MANNONS WILL ROT ON THE WALLS171 ELECTR

PORTRAYED

A STRONG RESEMBLANCE TO THE TYPE ANARCHIST AS 574 ICEMAN PORTRAYED, BOMB IN HAND,

PORTS

BUT DIVIL A WOMAN IN ALL THE PORTS OF THE WORLD 34 ANNA HAS IVER MADE A GREAT FOOL OF ME

THE ONLY WOMEN YOU'D MEET IN THE PORTS OF THE 37 ANNA WORLD WOULDN'D BE WILLING TO SPEAK

IN SOME OF THOSE FOREIGN PORTS OR OTHER. 85 BEYOND

AND THEN, S'FAR AS PORTS GO, WE DIDN'T TECH AT ONE497 DIFRNT THE LAST YEAR--

BUT THERE'S PLENTY OF DIVERSION GOING ON IN THE 497 DIFRNT PORTS YOU TOUCHED,

WHAT'S THE USE O' BLINDIN' THE PORTS 514 INZONE

AN' WE S'POSED TO HAVE ALL THE PORTS BLINDED/ 521 INZONE

AN' THERE'S A LOT O' THINGS A SAILOR'LL SEE IN THE522 INZONE PORTS HE PUTS IN

(THEN BRISKLY) AND HAVE WE YOUR PERMISSION TO 398 MARCOM TRADE IN THE PORTS ALONG THE WAYS

PORTSIDE

THE PORTSIDE RAIL IS IN THE REAR, THE CURVE OF THE158 STRANG STERN AT LEFT,

PORTUGAL

PORTUGAL
AND HE HAD THE CHANCE HE WANTED IN PORTUGAL AND 13 POET
SPAIN WHERE A BRITISH OFFICER
THERE WASN'T ONE COULD RESIST HIM IN PORTUGAL AND 13 POET
SPAIN.
(HIS BOASTFULLY.) BUT IT'S TRUE, IN THOSE DAYS 39 POET
IN PORTUGAL AND SPAIN--

PORTUGUESE
SILVA IS A PORTUGUESE FISHING CAPTAIN-- 129 ELECTR

PUSE
(RICHARD, PRESERVING THE POSE OF THE BITTER, 221 AHWILD
DISILLUSIONED PESSIMIST,
AND, ALL POSE GONE, HE CALLS TO HIS 261 AHWILD
(UNABLE TO RESIST FALLING INTO HIS TRAGIC LITERARY279 AHWILD
POSE FOR A MOMENT)
ALL THE POSE HAS DROPPED FROM HIM NOW 284 AHWILD
HE HAS TO, YOU SEE, TO KEEP UP HIS POSE OF 526 DAYS
FRIENDLY UNDERSTANDING--
AND WALTER WILL HAVE TO TELL THAT TO EVERY ONE, 527 DAYS
TOO--TO LIVE UP TO HIS POSE/
BUT ONE SENSES AN UNEASY WARINESS BENEATH HER 16 ELECTR
POSE)
IT ISN'T BECOMING TO YOU, REALLY--EXCEPT AS AN 219 HA APE
OBVIOUS POSE.
FOR MY PART YOU ARE QUITE FREE TO INDULGE ANY POSE219 HA APE
OF ECCENTRICITY THAT BEGUILES
YES, FOR A FRESH POSE I HAVE NO DOUBT YOU WOULD 222 HA APE
DRAG THE NAME OF DOUGLAS IN THE
SHE STARTS, TURNS PALE, HER POSE IS CRUMBLING, 225 HA APE
IT'S JUST A PUSE YOU GET OUT OF BOOKS/ 90 JOURNE
THAT WAS HIS GRAND POSE, TO DRINK ONLY CHAMPAGNE. 137 JOURNE
FACING FRONT, HER HANDS FOLDED IN HER LAP, IN A 174 JOURNE
DEMURE SCHOOL-GIRLISH POSE.)
(KEEPING HIS ABSURD MAJESTIC POSE, TURNS AND 369 LAZARU
ADDRESSES
STANDS ON IT AND STRIKES A GRANDIOSE POSE) 369 LAZARU
OH SHOULD I SAY, POSE, AS WELL AS MAY BE. 86 POET
HE ASSUMES HIS ARROGANT, BYRONIC POSE AGAIN. 116 POET
(HE STRIKES A POSE WHICH IS A VULGAR BURLESQUE OF 176 POET
HIS OLD BEFORE-THE-MIRROR ONE
OUR IMPOTENT POSE OF TODAY TO BEAT THE LOUD DRUM 5 STRANG
ON FORNICATION.....
BUT I HELD HIM TO HIS ALOOF DOCTOR'S POSE AND SENT 91 STRANG
HIM AWAY,
BEHIND A POSE OF CYNICAL INDIFFERENCE.) 138 STRANG

POSED
SITTING IN STIFF, POSED ATTITUDES THAT SUGGEST THE 46 ELECTR
STATUES OF MILITARY HEROES.

POSER
POSER/ 222 HA APE
(SCREAMS AFTER HER) I SAID POSER/ 222 HA APE
(SCORNFULLY) POSER/ 222 HA APE
(IN THE SAME TUNE) POSER/ 222 HA APE

POSES
STERN-LOOKING PEOPLE IN UNCOMFORTABLE POSES ARE 493 DIFRNT
HUNG ON THE WALLS.
OR BECAUSE HE POSES AS ARTISTIC AND 289 GGBROW
TEMPERAMENTAL--OR BECAUSE HE'S SO WILD--
AT FIRST, HE POSES TO HIMSELF, STRIKING AN 57 POET
ATTITUDE--

POSEY
AND A POSEY ACTOR SOLEMNLY PLAYING A ROLE. 193 AHWILD

POSING
AT LAST YOU ACCEPT THE TRUE END/ AT LAST YOU SEE 561 DAYS
THE EMPTY POSING
HIS WHOLE ATTITUDE WOODEN AND FIXED AS IF HE WERE 494 DIFRNT
POSING FOR A PHOTOGRAPH.
OF HIS IMPERIAL POSING. 339 LAZARU
HE WILL DEAL WITH THE FACTS, IF YOU PLEASE, 99 MANSNS
MOTHER, NOT WITH SENTIMENTAL POSING.

POSITION
HE'S IN A BETTER POSITION TO GET MARRIED THAN HE 213 AHWILD
EVER WAS.
AND SITS IN A SELF-CONSCIOUS, UNNATURAL POSITION. 293 AHWILD
(WITH DIFFICULTY RISING TO A SITTING POSITION-- 33 ANNA
SCORNFULLY)
YOU'VE ASKED ME NOT TO TALK---AND I WON'T AFTER 160 BEYOND
I'VE MADE MY POSITION CLEAR.
(TRYING TO RAISE HIMSELF TO A SITTING POSITION AS 167 BEYOND
THEY HASTEN TO HIS SIDE--
(TO PAUL, WHO HAS RETURNED TO HIS POSITION BY THE 458 CARIBE
BULWARK.
AND I FULLY APPRECIATE YOUR POSITION. 562 CROSS
LOVING TAKING UP A POSITION DIRECTLY BEHIND HIM 555 DAYS
(STARTS UP FROM HIS HALF-KNEELING POSITION, UNDER 559 DAYS
THE INFLUENCE OF THIS MEMORY)
IN SPITE OF STILLWELL, SPRINGS UP TO A HALF- 563 DAYS
SITTING POSITION IN BED.
AND STRUGGLES TO A SITTING POSITION.) 256 DESIRE
ABBIE HAS SUNK BACK LIFELESSLY INTO HER FORMER 264 DESIRE
POSITION.
HE SLOWLY TURNS, SLUMPING INTO A SITTING POSITION 268 DESIRE
ON THE FLOOR,
ASHAMED OF HER POSITION AND AFRAID SHE WILL BE 435 DYNAMO
DISCOVERED.)
STRETCHING HER ARMS UP IN THE SAME POSITION AS THE485 DYNAMO
SWITCH ARMS.)
JONES REMAINS FIXED IN HIS POSITION, LISTENING 190 EJONES
INTENTLY.
AND SITS DOWN IN A TENSE POSITION, READY FOR 195 EJONES
INSTANT FLIGHT.
HALF-SQUATTING POSITION AND 200 EJONES
TO A POSITION IN THE CLEAR GROUND BETWEEN JONES 200 EJONES
AND THE ALTAR.
(SHE SITS AGAIN IN THE SAME POSITION AS BEFORE. 59 ELECTR
HE PUSHES HIS BACK UP AGAINST THE HEAD OF THE BED 59 ELECTR
IN A HALF-SITTING POSITION.
STRAIGHTENS UP IN A SITTING POSITION IN LAVINIA'S 63 ELECTR
ARMS.

POSITION (CONT'D.)
AND HOLD A POSITION UNTIL HELL FROZE OVER/ 94 ELECTR
AND WITH DIFFICULTY RAISES HIMSELF TO A SITTING 102 ELECTR
POSITION
(HE STRUGGLES TO A SITTING POSITION) 103 ELECTR
AND I CAN GET THAT POSITION IN THE LIBRARY-- 272 GGBROW
(WITH A CERTAIN DOGGEDNESS) THERE'S A RUMOR THAT 276 GGBROW
YOU'VE APPLIED FOR A POSITION
AS IF AFRAID HER FACE ALONE WOULD NEVER INDICATE 218 HA APE
HER POSITION IN LIFE.
WHO HAVE FOLLOWED HIS MOVEMENTS OF GETTING INTO 223 HA APE
POSITION,
PUTTING HIS TWO FEET UP AGAINST THE OTHERS SO THAT244 HA APE
HIS POSITION IS PARALLEL TO
AS HE CAN GET IN HIS POSITION.) 250 HA APE
(THE NIGHT CLERK SHIFTS HIS POSITION SO HE CAN 13 HUGHIE
LEAN MORE ON THE DESK.
AND THEY'D OFFER ME THE POSITION. 604 ICEMAN
NEXT TO HIM, ON HIS LEFT, HUGO IS IN HIS HABITUAL 629 ICEMAN
POSITION, PASSED OUT,
HUGO SEEMS ASLEEP IN HIS HABITUAL POSITION) 651 ICEMAN
THE ONE AT LEFT, FRONT, BEFORE THE WINDOW TO THE 695 ICEMAN
YARD, IS IN THE SAME POSITION.
HUGO SITS AT REAR, FACING FRONT, HIS HEAD ON HIS 696 ICEMAN
ARMS IN HIS HABITUAL POSITION,
NATURALLY, THEY WOULD NEVER GIVE ME MY POSITION 707 ICEMAN
BACK.
WHO IS STILL IN THE SAME POSITION, HEAD ON HANDS, 516 INZONE
BECAUSE THEY KNOW IT ISN'T A PERMANENT POSITION. 61 JOURNE
TO REGAIN A SOUND POSITION BY MAKING A QUICK 32 MANSNS
PROFIT IN WESTERN LANDS.
YOUR POSITION IS--ER--PRECARIOUS, UNLESS--WHAT 33 MANSNS
HENRY SUGGESTED IS THIS...
AND WHEN THE TIME COMES HE WILL BE IN A POSITION 48 MANSNS
BEFORE I GO-- YOU WILL, OF COURSE, WISH ME TO 60 MANSNS
RESIGN FROM MY POSITION--
I WILL KEEP MY POSITION ONLY BECAUSE I FEEL IT MY 60 MANSNS
DUTY TO FATHER'S MEMORY TO DO
AS BECOMING TO HIS POSITION AND NOT HIMSELF. 69 MANSNS
I THOUGHT, CONSIDERING HIS POSITION, I HAD BETTER 140 MANSNS
ANNOUNCE HIM MYSELF.
HIS POSITION: 140 MANSNS
HIS POSITION NOW IS UNDER SIMON'S FEET, AND UNDER 140 MANSNS
MY FEET!
BUT ONCE LET HIS ENEMIES SEE HIS TRUE POSITION-- 142 MANSNS
YOU HAVE APPLIED TO VARIOUS BANKS FOR A POSITION. 152 MANSNS
OF COURSE, I ACCEPT THE POSITION GLADLY. 153 MANSNS
I ACCEPT THE POSITION, MADAM--AND THANK YOU 155 MANSNS
AGAIN--FOR YOUR--CHARITY!
AND OPEN HIS MOUTH CAREFULLY IN POSITION ONE OF 389 MARCOM
THE FIVE PHONETIC EXERCISES--
THE MEN SINK TO THE CROSS-LEGGED POSITION OF 433 MARCOM
PRAYER, THEIR HEADS BOWED.
(WITH ONE MOTION ALL SINK TO THE POSITION OF 435 MARCOM
PRAYER)
(HE HIMSELF SINKS TO THE POSITION OF PRAYER-- 435 MARCOM
HER BODY STIFF FROM SITTING LONG IN THE SAME 71 MISBEG
POSITION.
DON'T YOU REALIZE WHAT A LOUSY POSITION YOU'VE PUT136 MISBEG
HIM IN WITH YOUR
JOSIE SITS IN THE SAME POSITION ON THE STEPS, AS 157 MISBEG
IF SHE HAD NOT MOVED,
PLEASE REMEMBER I HAVE MY OWN POSITION TO 50 POET
MAINTAIN.
THIS WOULD BE THE FRENCH POSITION ON A RISE OF 96 POET
GROUND.
AND I SHALL INSIST IT BE A GENEROUS ONE, BEFITTING111 POET
YOUR POSITION AS MY DAUGHTER.
AND THERE WAS A TIME WHEN I POSSESSED WEALTH AND 112 POET
POSITION,
MAN'S HEAD BECAUSE HIS FAMILY HAPPENS TO POSSESS 4113 POET
LITTLE WEALTH AND POSITION.
AND BEGUN TO ESTABLISH HIS POSITION IN THE WORLD. 11 STRANG
I'M SORRY BUT I'M IN NO POSITION TO SAY. 38 STRANG
(SHE REMAINS IN A SITTING POSITION, STARING 108 STRANG
BLANKLY BEFORE HER.
JANE'S HUSBAND WASN'T MUCH--NO FAMILY OR POSITION 114 STRANG
OR ABILITY--
AND HER FOLKS HAVE GOT MONEY AND POSITION, TOO... 161 STRANG
(HE SLUMPS CLUMSILY DOWN TO A SITTING POSITION ON 175 STRANG
THE DECK BY HER CHAIR AND
JOES GETS INTO POSITION BEHIND THE BAR, ASSUMING 496 VOYAGE
HIS MOST OILY SMILE.

POSITIONS
THIS SEEMS TO RELEASE THEM FROM THEIR FIXED 291 LAZARU
POSITIONS.

POSITIVE
(SHARPLY) AND I'M POSITIVE HE HAS. 201 AHWILD
THAT'S POSITIVE. 558 CROSS
NOT IN A NEGATIVE BUT IN A POSITIVE, SELF- 12 ELECTR
POSSESSED WAY.
HIS COUNTENANCE NOW MIGHT WELL BE THAT OF THE 307 LAZARU
POSITIVE MASCULINE DIONYSUS.
(WITH A MOCKING SMILE) BUT PERHAPS WE'LL BECOME 197 STRANG
PART OF COSMIC POSITIVE AND

POSITIVELY
(CANNOT RESTRAIN A SHUDDER) SOMETIMES WHEN YOU'RE297 GGBROW
DRUNK YOU'RE POSITIVELY EVIL.
HE WAS POSITIVELY THE ONLY DOCTOR IN THE WORLD WHO626 ICEMAN
CLAIMED THAT RATTLESNAKE OIL
HER EYES POSITIVELY GLEAMED/....) 8 STRANG
I POSITIVELY MUST RUN HOME AT ONCE... 45 STRANG
(POSITIVELY BRISTLING) HER AGES 73 STRANG
(IT'S POSITIVELY BESTIAL/....!) 187 STRANG
IT'S POSITIVELY IMMORAL FOR AN OLD MARRIED COUPLE 444 WELDED
TO ACT THIS WAY.

POSSESS

WHEN IT IS THEIR COURAGE TO POSSESS THEIR OWN 542 DAYS
SOULS WHICH IS DEAD--AND STINKING/
THEY ARE APPARENTLY ALL EAGER TO POSSESS JONES. 197 EJONES
THE EYES OF THE PORTRAITS SEEM TO POSSESS AN 157 ELECTR
INTENSE BITTER LIFE.
WHAT FIRST AROUSED HIS PASSION TO POSSESS YOU 287 GGBROW
EXCLUSIVELY, DO YOU THINK?
YET TO THEM, SUCH IS MY ART, IT WILL APPEAR TO 313 GGBROW
POSSESS A PURE COMMON-SENSE,
THEN DARE TO LOVE ETERNITY WITHOUT YOUR FEAR 352 LAZARU
DESIRING TO POSSESS HER/
AND IMPLORE IT TO POSSESS YOU, 40 MANSNS
I DO NOT POSSESS THE ENTIRE CONFIDENCE IN THIS 67 MANSNS
SUDDEN FRIENDSHIP
AND AT THE OTHER END OF YOUR CHAIN YOU SHOULD 101 MANSNS
POSSESS PLANTATIONS IN THE SOUTH
YOU HAVE ABOUT ALL I POSSESS ALREADY. 146 MANSNS
NOW THAT YOU'LL SOON POSSESS A BANK, TOO, YOU CAN 148 MANSNS
AFFORD TO ADD STILL MORE.
SINCE YOU POSSESS ETERNAL LIFE, IT CAN DO YOU NO 380 MARCOM
HARM TO CUT OFF YOUR HEAD.
DO YOU STILL POSSESS YOUR IMMORTAL SOUL, MARCO 393 MARCOM
POLO?
WHICH IS THE GREATEST EVIL, TO POSSESS OR TO BE 434 MARCOM
WITHOUT?
POSSESS LIFE AS A LOVER--THEN SLEEP 435 MARCOM
AND TO POSSESS, AND ROAM ALONG, THE WORLD'S TIRED 101 POET
DENIZEN,
MAN'S HEAD BECAUSE HIS FAMILY HAPPENS TO POSSESS ALL3 POET
LITTLE WEALTH AND POSITION.
THAT HE CAN NEVER POSSESS/ 469 WELDED

POSSESSED
(SNAPPILY) IT WOULDN'T IF YOU POSSESSED A BIT OF 117 BEYOND
SPUNK.
WHAT EVIL SPIRIT OF HATE POSSESSED ME TO MAKE ME--495 DAYS
IT WAS SOME EVIL SPIRIT THAT POSSESSED YOU/ 513 DAYS
TO THINK OF HIMSELF AS POSSESSED BY A DAMNED SOUL/535 DAYS
EVERY DAY THESE EVIL VISIONS POSSESSED HIM. 536 DAYS
THAT MY HERO'S SILLY IDEA THAT HE WAS POSSESSED BY538 DAYS
A DEMON MUST STRIKE YOU AS AN
NOT IN A NEGATIVE BUT IN A POSITIVE, SELF- 12 ELECTR
POSSESSED WAY.
HER MOTHER'S HAD POSSESSED. 139 ELECTR
SO THAT THEY CAN NEVER BE POSSESSED BY HATE AND 147 ELECTR
DEATH/
(AT THE MENTION OF BROWN, DION TREMBLES AS IF 285 GGBROW
SUDDENLY POSSESSED,
HE LOVES ME BECAUSE I HAVE ALWAYS POSSESSED THE 298 GGBROW
POWER HE NEEDED FOR LOVE.
AMIABLE, IGNORANT, CLUMSY, AND POSSESSED BY A 51 JOURNE
DENSE, WELL-MEANING STUPIDITY.
DEFEATED OLD MAN, POSSESSED BY HOPELESS 125 JOURNE
RESIGNATION.
BUT THEY SEEMED AS HAPPY AS IF HIS LAUGHTER HAD 342 LAZARU
POSSESSED THEM/
COULD NOT POSSIBLY HAVE POSSESSED ANY MAGIC POWER 343 LAZARU
HIMSELF.
BE BRAVE ENOUGH TO BE POSSESSED/ 352 LAZARU
I HAVE DISCIPLINED MY WILL TO BE POSSESSED BY 29 MANSNS
FACTS--LIKE A WHORE IN A BROTHEL/
(THINKING.) WHAT THE DEVIL POSSESSED ME TO ASK 120 MANSNS
SARA TO COME TO THE OFFICES
I WOULD MAKE HIM PAY FOR ME UNTIL I HAD TAKEN 133 MANSNS
EVERYTHING HE POSSESSED/
BECAUSE IT POSSESSED YOU AND YOU WANTED TO BE 183 MANSNS
FREE/
AND I KNOW FOR A FACT THAT PEOPLE ARE SOMETIMES 349 MARCOM
POSSESSED BY DEVILS.
ARE YOU SUDDENLY POSSESSED BY A DEVIL-- 360 MARCOM
MY SOUL HE HAS ALREADY POSSESSED. 423 MARCOM
(COOLLY SELF-POSSESSED--PLEASANTLY.) 72 POET
CATO WAS ALWAYS A SELF-POSSESSED FREE MAN EVEN 86 POET
WHEN HE WAS A SLAVE.
THAN I THOUGHT SHE POSSESSED. 109 POET
AND THERE WAS A TIME WHEN I POSSESSED WEALTH AND 112 POET
POSITION.
HE APPEARS COMPLETELY POSSESSED BY A PARALYZING 164 POET
STUPOR.)
(THEN VIOLENTLY) BUT GORDON NEVER POSSESSED ME/ 19 STRANG
FORGIVE US OUR POSSESSING AS WE FORGIVE THOSE WHO 21 STRANG
POSSESSED BEFORE US...
HOW CAN YOU LOSE WHAT YOU NEVER POSSESSED?... 52 STRANG

POSSESSES
IN THE CYNICAL LEER OF ONE WHO POSSESSES SUPERIOR, 9 HUGHIE
INSIDE INFORMATION.
HIS PERSONALITY POSSESSES THE REMNANT OF A 19 JOURNE
HUMOROUS, ROMANTIC
HIS MOUTH HAS THE SAME QUALITY OF 20 JOURNE
HYPERSENSITIVENESS HERS POSSESSES.
POSSESSES THE QUALIFICATIONS I DESIRE IS A YOUNG 97 MANSNS
AND VERY BEAUTIFUL WOMAN.
THE MURDERER POSSESSES THE TRUE QUALITY OF MERCY. 180 MANSNS
COULD HE BELIEVE THIS YOUTH POSSESSES THAT THING 379 MARCOM
CALLED SOUL
HER LOVE ALREADY POSSESSES HIM/... 160 STRANG
HE POSSESSES THE RARE VIRTUE OF GRATITUDE. 166 STRANG

POSSESSING
HOPE BEING A FORMER MINOR TAMMANYITE AND STILL 571 ICEMAN
POSSESSING FRIENDS,
BUT POSSESSING AN ATMOSPHERE OF ALOOF DIGNITY AND 384 MARCOM
SIMPLICITY
POSSESSING NOW A GENUINE QUALITY HE HAS NOT HAD 88 POET
BEFORE.
EYES SO MUCH LIKE HIS, POSSESSING EYES SO HAPPY IN 19 STRANG
POSSESSING YOU/
FORGIVE US OUR POSSESSING AS WE FORGIVE THOSE WHO 21 STRANG
POSSESSED BEFORE US...
POSSESSING IT SO IT'S NO LONGER MY BODY-- 453 WELDED

POSSESSION

A STRANGE FEELING OF FEAR TOOK POSSESSION OF ME-- 507 DAYS
A HIDDEN SPIRIT OF EVIL, TOOK POSSESSION OF HIM. 538 DAYS
(HER VOICE TAKING POSSESSION) 222 DESIRE
(SHE KISSES HIS HEAD, PRESSING IT TO HER WITH A 266 DESIRE
FIERCE PASSION OF POSSESSION.)
MORE AND MORE THE SPIRIT OF TERROR GAINS 201 EJONES
POSSESSION OF HIM.
EXCEPT WHAT SHE EARNS DAY BY DAY, WHAT SHE CAN 72 MANSNS
MAKE YOU PAY FOR POSSESSION.
IT IS AS THOUGH SHE HAD SLOWLY TAKEN POSSESSION OF 73 MANSNS
SARA.
THE POSSESSION OF POWER IS THE ONLY FREEDOM, 74 MANSNS
SHE HAS MANAGED TO KEEP IN POSSESSION. 77 MANSNS
(HIS FACE HAPPY NOW WITH CONFIDENT POSSESSION AND 81 MANSNS
AROUSED DESIRE--
WHOSE BEAUTIFUL BODY WAS SO GREEDILY HUNGRY FOR 87 MANSNS
LUST AND POSSESSION.
IT MUST ATTAIN THE ALL-EMBRACING SECURITY OF 101 MANSNS
COMPLETE SELF-POSSESSION--
BUT YOU ARE BLIND OR YOU WOULD HAVE SEEN IT WAS I 105 MANSNS
WHO TOOK POSSESSION OF HER
I THOUGHT THAT WAS THE CHEAPEST WAY TO TAKE 152 MANSNS
POSSESSION OF YOUR BANK.
BEFORE THEIR DUEL FOR POSSESSION DESTROYS IT. 182 MANSNS
MARCO HAS GAINED POSSESSION OF HER TWO HANDS NOW 356 MARCOM
A TERRIBLE TENSION OF WILL ALONE MAINTAINING SELF- 13 STRANG
POSSESSION.
A DOCTOR MUST BE IN FULL POSSESSION OF THE FACTS, 85 STRANG
IF HE IS TO ADVISE.
LOVE AND HATE AND PASSION AND POSSESSION/... 100 STRANG
LOOKING FROM ONE TO THE OTHER WITH TRIUMPHANT 133 STRANG
POSSESSION
POSSESSION TO WITHER THE HEART WITH BITTER 187 STRANG
POISONS...
PROTECTIVE WARDING OFF AND AT THE SAME TIME A 480 WELDED
SEEKING POSSESSION.

POSSESSIONS
COMPETITORS IN THE RACE FOR POWER AND WEALTH AND 46 MANSNS
POSSESSIONS/

POSSESSIVE
EBEN STOPS BY THE GATE AND STARES AROUND HIM WITH 217 DESIRE
GLOWING, POSSESSIVE EYES.
THEN IN POSSESSIVE TONES) 224 DESIRE
HIMSELF, HERS GLOWINGLY POSSESSIVE. 229 DESIRE
YOU KNOW HOW POSSESSIVE VINNIE IS WITH ORIN. 72 ELECTR
(SQUEEZING HIS HAND--WITH POSSESSIVE TENDERNESS) 270 GGBROW
WELL, A WOMAN'S LOVE IS JEALOUSLY POSSESSIVE--OR 7 MANSNS
SO I HAVE READ--
WE MUST PROTECT MAN FROM HIS STUPID POSSESSIVE 8 MANSNS
INSTINCTS
(SHE GRASPS HIS HAND AND PRESSES IT--TENDERLY 45 MANSNS
POSSESSIVE.)
HE COMES AND PUTS A PROTECTING, POSSESSIVE HAND ON 57 MANSNS
HIS MOTHER'S SHOULDER.)
AS IF I REALLY DESIRED TWO DAMNED POSSESSIVE WOMEN 74 MANSNS
(HE GIVES HER A LOVING, POSSESSIVE HUG.) 87 MANSNS
TAKE A POSSESSIVE GRATIFICATION IN TEASING A YOUNG128 MANSNS
BASHFUL SON.
BOTH THEIR EXPRESSIONS CHANGE TO A TRIUMPHANT 137 MANSNS
POSSESSIVE TENDERNESS.)
(WITH A FIERCE, PASSIONATE, POSSESSIVE 194 MANSNS
TENDERNESS.)
AND STARES DOWN AT HIS FACE WITH A PASSIONATE, 103 MISBEG
POSSESSIVE TENDERNESS.
WITH FIERCE, POSSESSIVE, MATERNAL TENDERNESS) 141 MISBEG
AND POSSESSIVE AMBITION, AND UPHELD THE VIRTUE OF 84 POET
FREEING ONESELF
POSSESSIVE NATURE CAN BE--WHEN SUDDENLY ONE IS 86 POET
ATTACKED BY IT.
(WITH A POSSESSIVE SMILE OF TOLERANCE) 101 STRANG

POSSESSIVELY
(LOOKING AROUND HIM POSSESSIVELY) 245 DESIRE
(NINA LAUGHS SOFTLY, POSSESSIVELY. 103 STRANG

POSSESSIVENESS
SHE STARES AT HIM WITH A STRANGE EAGER 143 ELECTR
POSSESSIVENESS.
(THEN TAKING HIM IN WITH A SMILING APPRECIATIVE 143 ELECTR
POSSESSIVENESS)
AND BECOME ENTIRELY MATERNAL, COMPLACENT IN 75 MANSNS
POSSESSIVENESS--
I HAVE RESERVED HER INTERFERENCE AND 105 MANSAS
POSSESSIVENESS--
OF THE INSATIABLE AMBITION OF FEMALE 173 MANSNS
POSSESSIVENESS, DON'T YOU THINK?

POSSIBILITY

POSSIBILITIES
A NEW APPRECIATION FOR HER ESCORT'S POSSIBILITIES 239 AHWILD
IN HER VOICE)
KITCHEN OF A--BUT THE POSSIBILITIES ARE HEARSOME-218 HA APE
(THINK IT OVER, YOUR MAJESTY, AND LET THE ENDLESS 394 MARCOM
POSSIBILITIES DAWN ON YOU/
CREATIVE IMAGINATION ENOUGH TO VISUALIZE THE 395 MARCOM
ENORMOUS POSSIBILITIES...
PEOPLE WHO ARE AFRAID TO FACE UNPLEASANT 77 STRANG
POSSIBILITIES UNTIL IT'S TOO LATE

POSSIBILITY
TO BELIEVE IN THE POSSIBILITY OF NOBILITY OF 543 DAYS
SPIRIT IN OURSELVES/
THERE I WAS AT NIGHT IN MY STUDY TRYING TO 46 MANSNS
CONVINCE MYSELF OF THE POSSIBILITY OF
AND WE'D BE DAMNED FOOLS IF WE DIDN'T FEAR THE 34 MISBEG
POSSIBILITY, HOWEVER SMALL IT IS,
THERE'S NO POSSIBILITY 34 MISBEG
(DOESN'T BELIEVE THIS THREAT BUT IS FRIGHTENED BY 17 POET
THE POSSIBILITY.)
IN THE FLYING SERVICE RATHER MORE THAN A 10 STRANG
POSSIBILITY, WHICH NEEDLESS TO SAY,
THERE WAS THE POSSIBILITY HE MIGHT BE KILLED, 10 STRANG

POSSIBILITY

POSSIBILITY (CONT'D.)
BUT I THINK WHAT I'VE SAID HAS PLANTED IT IN HER 38 STRANG
MIND AS A POSSIBILITY.

POSSIBLE
SHE'S THAT THICK, YOU HONESTLY WOULDN'T BELIEVE IT2I1 AHWILD
POSSIBLE.
AS IF SHE WANTED TO REMAIN AS MUCH ISOLATED AS 30 ANNA
POSSIBLE.
HE'S BEEN MAKING AS PUBLIC AN ASS OF HIMSELF AS 528 DAYS
POSSIBLE.
TO GET AS FAR AWAY FROM THEM AS POSSIBLE. 197 EJONES
I WANTED YOU EVERY POSSIBLE MOMENT WE COULD STEAL/ 37 ELECTR
UH, I DON'T BELIEVE HE'LL COME, BUT IT'S POSSIBLE 44 ELECTR
HE MIGHT.
IS IT POSSIBLE SHE DOES& 291 GGBROW
TO PLAY THE GHOUL ON EVERY POSSIBLE OCCASION, 218 HA APE
EXCAVATING OLD BONES&
THERE IS ONLY ONE POSSIBLE ESCAPE. 31 HUGHIE
AS LITTLE AS POSSIBLE. 593 ICEMAN
I THINK THERE IS ONLY ONE POSSIBLE WAY OUT YOU CAN642 ICEMAN
HELP HIM TO TAKE.
THEY TURN THEIR BACKS ON EACH OTHER AS FAR AS 650 ICEMAN
POSSIBLE.
I SAW WHAT HAD HAPPENED WAS THE ONLY POSSIBLE WAY 693 ICEMAN
THEN YOU SEE IT WAS THE ONLY POSSIBLE WAY TO 695 ICEMAN
PEACE.
BEFORE I FACED THE TRUTH AND SAW THE ONE POSSIBLE 705 ICEMAN
WAY TO FREE POOR EVELYN AND
THE ONE POSSIBLE WAY TO MAKE UP TO HER FOR ALL I'D705 ICEMAN
MADE HER GO THROUGH.
BUT AS IT WAS, THERE WAS ONLY ONE POSSIBLE WAY. 706 ICEMAN
YOU'LL SEE THERE WASN'T ANY OTHER POSSIBLE WAY OUT709 ICEMAN
OF IT, FOR HER SAKE.
AND THEN IT CAME TO ME--THE ONLY POSSIBLE WAY OUT,715 ICEMAN
FOR HER SAKE.
(OBLIVIOUSLY) AND THEN I SAW I'D ALWAYS KNOWN 716 ICEMAN
THAT WAS THE ONLY POSSIBLE WAY TO
I CAN SEE NOW IT'S THE ONLY POSSIBLE WAY I CAN 720 ICEMAN
EVER GET FREE FROM HER.
THERE IS NO POSSIBLE DOUBT, HE SAID. 79 JOURNE
SO MY WAIST WOULD BE AS SMALL AS POSSIBLE. 115 JOURNE
WHERE HE CROUCHES ON HIS HAUNCHES AS 340 LAZARU
INCONSPICUOUSLY AS POSSIBLE.
TO MAKE HIS PROPOSAL AS EQUITABLE AS POSSIBLE FOR 35 MANSNS
SIMON AND HIS--ER--FAMILY.
AS A WOMAN OF BREEDING AND HONOR, YOU HAVE NO 37 MANSNS
POSSIBLE CHOICE.
THERE IS ONLY ONE POSSIBLE CHANCE FOR ME TO LIVE 53 MANSNS
AGAIN, SARA.
AND A FINER BARGAIN THAN I WOULD HAVE DREAMED 63 MANSNS
POSSIBLE, THANKS TO MOTHER.
WILLING TO GAMBLE WITH THE HIGHEST POSSIBLE STAKE, 88 MANSNS
ALL SHE HAS,
ON THIS END, THE STORES ARE THE LAST POSSIBLE 157 MANSNS
LINE--
THAT APPEARS TO ME NOW TO BE THE ONE POSSIBLE WAY 173 MANSNS
HE CAN END THE CONFLICT AND
WHY, IT ISN'T HUMANLY POSSIBLE/ 392 MARCOM
THERE IS NO OTHER ADVICE POSSIBLE FROM ONE HUMAN 401 MARCOM
BEING TO ANOTHER.
IF IT WERE POSSIBLE FOR A SON WHO LOVED A NOBLE 418 MARCOM
FATHER,
WITHOUT PREJUDICE, TRYING TO BE FAIR TO YOU AND 113 POET
MAKE EVERY POSSIBLE ALLOWANCE--
WHAT POSSIBLE REASON--& 10 STRANG
IT WOULD BE POSSIBLE TO CONSULT-- 77 STRANG
(BRUTALLY) IT'S POSSIBLE. 77 STRANG
ONLY ONE POSSIBLE THING TO DO NOW. 84 STRANG
IS IT POSSIBLE HE LOVES ME&... 119 STRANG
AND BE A BIGGER STAR THAN GORDON EVER WAS, IF 120 STRANG
THAT'S POSSIBLE.
DARRELL MOVES AS FAR AWAY FROM HIM AS POSSIBLE, 124 STRANG
THERE WAS NO POSSIBLE REASON FOR HER STAYING WITH 129 STRANG
SAM, WHEN SHE LOVED DARRELL.
(WITH FINALITY) THAT'S THE ONLY POSSIBLE 132 STRANG
SOLUTION, NED, FOR ALL OUR SAKES,
IS IT POSSIBLE YOU CAN STILL LOVE ME, NED& 144 STRANG
(WITH A WRY SMILE) IT'S POSSIBLE. 146 STRANG
WHAT POSSIBLE REASON COULD I HAVE FOR HOPING FOR 170 STRANG
SAM'S DEATH&

IS POSSIBLE FOR A WOMAN WITHOUT HER BEING LOW. 459 WELDED

POSSIBLY
ARTHUR HANGS BACK, AS IF THE DESIGNATION «KIDS» 264 AHWILD
COULDN'T POSSIBLY APPLY TO HIM.
(KISSES HER--PITYINGLY) I'LL BE AS QUICK AS I 119 ELECTR
POSSIBLY CAN.
THERE COULDN'T POSSIBLY BE ANY OTHER REASON/ 680 ICEMAN
I COULDN'T POSSIBLY EAT ANYTHING. 123 JOURNE
COULD NOT POSSIBLY HAVE POSSESSED ANY MAGIC POWER 343 LAZARU
HIMSELF.
CAN YOU POSSIBLY IMAGINE--& 33 MANSNS
I WOULD STILL LIKE TO DISCOVER IF YOU COULD 111 MANSNS
POSSIBLY IMAGINE
YOU COULD NOT POSSIBLY HAVE HEARD US IN YOUR 174 MANSNS
STUDY.
I UNDERSTAND EVERYTHING A WOMAN'S LOVE COULD 192 MANSNS
POSSIBLY COMPEL HER TO DESIRE.
IS AS LOW AS I CAN POSSIBLY MAKE IT OUT OF MY DEEP396 MARCOM
AFFECTION FOR YOUR MAJESTY--
I DON'T LIKE TO BRING UP THE MONEY CONSIDERATION 17 STRANG
BUT I COULDN'T POSSIBLY AFFORD--
(AMUSED--DRYLY) POSSIBLY SHE EATS TOO MUCH. 77 STRANG
(WINCING--THINKING) (SHE CAN'T BELIEVE ANY WOMAN114 STRANG
COULD POSSIBLY LOVE ME/.....))

POST
A THICK NECK IS JAMMED LIKE A POST INTO THE HEAVY 5 ANNA
TRUNK OF HIS BODY.

POST (CONT'D.)
A ROOM ERECTED AS A LOOKOUT POST AT THE TOP OF HIS555 CROSS
HOUSE
DEN DE REVOLUTION IS AT DE POST. 182 EJONES
BETWEEN YOU 'N' ME 'N' THE LAMP POST, IT AIN'T 135 ELECTR
SECH A JOKE AS IT SOUNDS--
POST ON THE CORNER AND TRIES TO PULL IT UP FOR A 239 HA APE
CLUB.
HE PROMISED ANY TIME I FELT AN ENERGETIC FIT HE'D 675 ICEMAN
GET ME A POST WITH THE CUNARD--
AS A MATTER OF FACT, ROCKY, I ONLY WISH A POST 676 ICEMAN
TEMPORARILY.
(SCOTTY RESUMES HIS POST AT THE DOOR.) 525 INZONE
EVEN SCOTTY LEAVES HIS POST TO TAKE A LOOK) 528 INZONE
(BITTERLY.) DRIVEN FROM PILLAR TO POST IN MY OWN 66 POET
HOME/

POSTAL
A POSTAL CARD EVERY MONTH OR SO... 456 DYNAMO

POSTCARDS
I NEVER WROTE, EXCEPT SOME POSTCARDS TO MOTHER I 461 DYNAMO
SENT TO GET HER GOAT--AND HIS.
AND YOUR HORRIBLE BLASPHEMOUS POSTCARDS KEPT 465 DYNAMO
COMING/

POSTER
IN THE MIDDLE OF THE REAR WALL IS FASTENED A BIG 206 DESIRE
ADVERTISING POSTER WITH A SHIP
BED, AN OLD FOUR-POSTER WITH FEATHER MATTRESS. 235 DESIRE
A BIG FOUR-POSTER BED IS AT REAR, CENTER, THE FOOT 58 ELECTR

POSTMAN
THE POSTMAN ENTERS AS THEY LEAVE. 4 ANNA
(THE POSTMAN GOES OUT. 5 ANNA

POSTMARK
LOOK AT THE POSTMARK, DRISC--ON THE ENVELOPE. 530 INZONE
LOOK AT THE POSTMARK. 530 INZONE
(LOOKING AT THE POSTMARK) 531 INZONE

POSTPONE
DIDN'T YOU THINK IT WOULD BE BETTER TO POSTPONE 96 ELECTR
OUR TALK UNTIL--
I'M SORRY WE HAD TO POSTPONE OUR TRIP AGAIN THIS 605 ICEMAN
APRIL, PIET.
YOU'D ONLY POSTPONE IT. AND I'M NOT YOUR JAILOR. 75 JOURNE

POSTPONING
NO EXCUSE WHATEVER FOR POSTPONING-- 684 ICEMAN

POSTURE
(HE LOWERS HIMSELF CAREFULLY TO A WOODEN POSTURE 514 DIFRNT
ON THE EDGE OF A ROCKER NEAR
AS THEIR CHORUS LIFTS HE KISSES TO A SITTING 199 EJONES
POSTURE SIMILAR TO THE OTHERS,
HE SINKS INTO A KNEELING, DEVOTIONAL POSTURE 200 EJONES
BEFORE THE ALTAR.
THIS ACCENTUATES THE NATURAL STOOPING POSTURE 207 HA APE
WHICH SHOVELING COAL AND THE
EACH MEMBER OF THE MOB REMAINS FROZEN IN A 289 LAZARU
DISTORTED POSTURE.
(HE ASSUMES THE ABSURD GRANDIOSE POSTURE 338 LAZARU
KUBLAI SITS AT THE TOP OF HIS THRONE, CROSS-LEGGED432 MARCOM
IN THE POSTURE OF AN IDOL.

POSTURING
(WITH THE SUDDEN GRANDIOSE POSTURING OF A BAD 301 LAZARU
ACTOR
(HE LAUGHS GRATINGLY, POSTURING AND GESTICULATING 357 LAZARU
UP AT LAZARUS)

POSTURINGS
TEMPERAMENTAL POSTURINGS OF THE STAGE STAR. 13 JOURNE

PUT
WELL, HOW'S MY FELLOW RUM POT, AS GOOD OLD DOWIE 271 AHWILD
CALLS US&
A MAN CAN'T TAKE DE POT ON A BOB-TAILED FLUSH ALL 182 EJONES
DE TIME.
THE LAST POT EVERYONE WOULD DROP OUT BUT HIM AND 32 HUGHIE
ME.
CARRYING A LARGE STEAMING COFFEE-POT IN HIS HAND, 513 INZONE
DAVIS ENTERS THE FORECASTLE, PLACES THE COFFEE-POT513 INZONE
BESIDE THE LANTERN.
THE COFFEE-POT IS PASSED AROUND. 514 INZONE
(BRUSQUELY) NINA'S GONE TO POT AGAIN/ 34 STRANG
WOULD SHE RATHER FACE THE PROSPECT OF GOING TO POT 87 STRANG
MENTALLY, MORALLY,

POTATO
PUTATO BUGS, SNAKES AND SKUNKS ON HIS FARM, 24 JOURNE
WHISKEY, AND THERE'S POISON IVY, AND TICKS AND 63 MISBEG
POTATO BUGS.

POTATOES
EBEN TAKES BOILED POTATOES AND BACON FROM THE 206 DESIRE
STOVE AND PUTS THEM ON THE TABLE.
SHE'D COME BACK T' HELP--COME BACK T' BILE 209 DESIRE
PUTATOES--COME BACK T' FRY BACON--

POTBELLY
WITH A POTBELLY AND SHORT ARMS LUMPY WITH MUSCLE. 51 POET

POTIONS
HE DISGUISED HIS GREED WITH SABBATH POTIONS OF 101 MANSNS
GUD-FEARING UNCTION

POTTERIN'
TO SEE FOLKS THAT GOD GAVE ALL THE USE OF THEIR 113 BEYOND
LIMBS TO PUTTERIN' ROUND AND

PUTTERING
(HE LOOKS AWAY AND BEGINS POTTERING ABOUT AGAIN, 170 ELECTR
AND MUTTERS GRIMLY)

POTTERS
HE HAS A PAIR OF GRASS CLIPPERS AND POTTERS ALONG 169 ELECTR

POUCH
(HE OSTENTATIOUSLY TAKES FROM HIS POCKET A TOBACCO187 AHWILD
POUCH WITH A BIG Y AND CLASS
(DRISCOLL TAKES A BLACK RUBBER BAG RESEMBLING A 528 INZONE
LARGE TOBACCO POUCH FROM THE BOX

POUCHES

HIS BLUE EYES HAVE DROOPING LIDS AND PUFFY POUCHES 8 HUGHIE UNDER THEM.

POULTICE

YOUR HAND IS A COOL MUD POULTICE ON THE STING OF 279 GGBROW THOUGHT/

POUNCE

TO TELL ALL OUR ENEMIES AND COMBINE WITH THEM TO 191 MANSNS POUNCE DOWN AND RUIN US/

POUNCES

HE POUNCES ON IT AND FORCING THE CLENCHED FINGERS 573 CROSS OPEN WITH A GREAT EFFORT,

POUND

OR, BY THE ETERNAL, I'LL COME DOWN AND POUND SOME 105 ELECTR SENSE IN YOUR HEAD/

SEIZED BY THE SAME FIT AND POUND WITH THEIR 707 ICEMAN GLASSES, EVEN HUGO,

POUND WITH THEIR GLASSES AND GRUMBLE IN CHORUS.. 715 ICEMAN (THEY POUND THEIR GLASSES ON THE TABLE, ROARING 728 ICEMAN WITH LAUGHTER,

SHE MADE ME PAY TWO-FOLD THE VALUE OF EVERY POUND 178 MANSNS OF FLESH--

AND HAD EATEN A POUND OF SEN-SEN TO KILL THE GIN 39 MISBEG ON HER BREATH,

I'D LAY A POUND, IF I HAD ONE, 173 POET TRYING TO POUND 69 STRANG

POUNDED

HUGO, WHO HAS AWAKENED AND RAISED HIS HEAD WHEN 672 ICEMAN LARRY POUNDED ON THE TABLE,

POUNDIN'

POUNDIN' SIDEWALKS FOR A DOUBLE-CROSSIN' 669 ICEMAN BARTENDER,

POUNDING

(POUNDING THE TABLE) THE SEA'S THE ONLY LIFE FOR 48 ANNA A MAN WITH GUTS IN HIM ISN'T

AND POUNDING ON THE TABLE WITH HER HANDS) 61 ANNA NAT IS STILL POUNDING) 572 CROSS

DRUNKEN MIRTH, ROARING WITH LAUGHTER, POUNDING 134 ELECTR EACH OTHER ON THE BACK.)

POUNDING ON THE BENCHES WITH FISTS,) 211 HA APE THE BLOODY ENGINES POUNDING AND THROBBING AND 214 HA APE SHAKING--

POUNDING ON HIS CHEST, GORILLA-LIKE, WITH THE 225 HA APE OTHER, SHOUTING)

SWELLING OUT HIS CHEST AND POUNDING ON IT WITH HIS252 HA APE FIST.

POUNDING THE TABLE WITH HIS GLASS) 634 ICEMAN (BURSTS OUT, POUNDING HIS GLASS ON THE TABLE) 707 ICEMAN (TRIES TO WARD THIS OFF BY POUNDING WITH HIS GLASS715 ICEMAN ON THE TABLE--

BEJEES, I'LL HAVE HIM BACK IN UNIFORM POUNDING A 718 ICEMAN BEAT

WHILE HUGO JUMPS TO HIS FEET AND, POUNDING ON THE 727 ICEMAN TABLE WITH HIS FIST,

SINGS HOARSELY AN OLD CAMP SONG OF THE PUNIC WARS,313 LAZARU POUNDING WITH HIS GOBLET)

(POUNDING HIS TEMPLES WITH HIS FISTS--TORTURED) 352 LAZARU POUNDING OF GLASSES ON BAR AND TABLES, 180 POET

(MY HEART POUNDING/... 12 STRANG (POUNDING HIS FIST ON THE RAIL--LETTING HIS PENT- 161 STRANG UP FEELINGS EXPLODE)

(POUNDING ON THE RAIL) COME ON, GORDON BOY/ 176 STRANG

POUNDS

THEN SUDDENLY POUNDS HIS FIST ON THE TABLE WITH 8 ANNA HAPPY EXCITEMENT)

(HE POUNDS THE TABLE WITH HIS FISTS IN 103 BEYOND EXASPERATION.)

(HE POUNDS ON THE TABLE, ATTEMPTING TO COVER UP 103 BEYOND THIS CONFESSION OF WEAKNESS.)

ANDREW POUNDS ON THE TABLE WITH HIS FIST) 155 BEYOND HE POUNDS AGAINST THE SLIDE, WHICH SEEMS TO HAVE 572 CROSS BEEN SHUT DOWN ON HIM.)

HE POUNDS HIS KNEE WITH HIS FIST) 236 DESIRE IN SPITE OF HER TWO HUNDRED AND MORE POUNDS SHE IS506 DIFRNT SURPRISINGLY ACTIVE.

MRS. FIFE POUNDS THE STEEL BODY OF THE GENERATOR 489 DYNAMO IN A FIT OF CHILDISH ANGER)

(SHE POUNDS ON THE DOOR VIOLENTLY.) 100 ELECTR WILL YOU STOP AT THE BUTCHERS' AND HAVE THEM SEND 273 GGBROW TWO POUNDS OF PORK CHOPS$

(AS HE SAYS THIS HE POUNDS WITH HIS FIST AGAINST 216 HA APE THE STEEL BUNKS.

(HE POUNDS ON THE RAIL WITH HIS FIST. 253 HA APE AND HE POUNDS HIS FIST LIKE A HAM ON DE DESK, AND 601 ICEMAN HE SHOUTS--

AND HE POUNDS THE TABLE WITH A SMALL FIST) 627 ICEMAN (HE POUNDS HIS SCHOONER ON THE TABLE) 659 ICEMAN AT THIS MOMENT LARRY POUNDS ON THE TABLE WITH HIS 672 ICEMAN FIST

POUNDS ON THE TABLE FRIGHTENEDLY WITH HIS SMALL 694 ICEMAN FISTS)

YOU'RE A FINE ARMFUL NOW, MARY, WITH THOSE TWENTY 14 JOURNE POUNDS YOU'VE GAINED.

CALIGULA, HIS HAND CLUTCHING HIS HEAD, POUNDS IT 349 LAZARU AGAINST THE EDGE OF THE STEPS..

HIS SPARE FRAME HAS PUT ON TEN POUNDS OR SO, 43 MANSNS HIS BODY HAS PUT ON TWENTY POUNDS OR MORE OF SOLID 69 MANSNS FLESH,

NOW JUST PICTURE THIS LITTLE BALL MAGNIFIED INTO 395 MARCOM ONE WEIGHING TWENTY POUNDS OR

(HE POUNDS ON THE DOOR WITH HIS FIST) 73 MISBEG AND POUNDS OUT A FEW WORDS WITH A SORT OF AIMLESS 67 STRANG DESPERATION--

HE RUSHES UP TO NED HILARIOUSLY, SHAKES HIS HAND 132 STRANG AND POUNDS HIS BACK,

(SUDDENLY EXPLODING, POUNDS HIS FIST ON THE RAIL) 163 STRANG

POUR

WHERE THE CROSS IS MADE (HE GULPS AND THE WORDS 566 CROSS POUR OUT INCOHERENTLY)

POUR (CONT'D.)

(HE DOES SO--GETS TWO GLASSES--THEY POUR OUT 217 DESIRE DRINKS OF WHISKY)

THE GIRLS POUR DRINKS. 612 ICEMAN (THEY ALL POUR OUT DRINKS.) 621 ICEMAN (THEY START AND GULP DOWN THEIR WHISKIES AND POUR 625 ICEMAN ANOTHER.

LOOKS 'S IF IT'D POUR DOWN CATS AND DOGS ANY 687 ICEMAN MINUTE.

(THEY POUR DRINKS. 722 ICEMAN (THEY POUR OUT DRINKS. 724 ICEMAN (HE WALKS AWAY FROM HER TO POUR HIMSELF A BIG 69 JOURNE DRINK.)

JUST MEASURE A FEW DRINKS OF WATER AND POUR THEM 100 JOURNE IN.

SHALL I POUR A DRINK FOR YOU? 109 JOURNE (HE LETS EDMUND'S HAND GO TO POUR A BIG DRINK, AND165 JOURNE GULPS IT DOWN.

THEY POUR IN A LAUGHING ROUT FROM THE DOORWAY ONTO285 LAZARU THE TERRACE.

POUR IN FROM EACH SIDE OF THE ROCK AND DANCE 362 LAZARU FORWARD TO GROUP THEMSELVES AROUND

LED BY THE CHORUS, THEY POUR DOWN FROM THE BANKED 368 LAZARU WALLS OF THE AMPHITHEATRE AND

LET POUR FROM THEM A PERFECT STREAM OF PRECIOUS 429 MARCOM STONES

THAT'LL TEACH YOU TO POUR OUT BATHS INSTEAD OF 113 MISBEG DRINKS.

(ANGRILY) YOU'LL POUR ME A DRINK, IF YOU PLEASE, 121 MISBEG JIM TYRONE, OR--

I'LL POUR YOU ANOTHER. 122 MISBEG WHY DON'T YOU POUR YOURSELF A DRINK AND SIT DOWN$ 126 MISBEG POUR THE WHOLE BOTTLE DOWN YOUR THROAT, IF YOU 139 MISBEG LIKE/

YOU COULD HAVE ALL THE WHISKEY YOU COULD POUR DOWN 10 POET YOU.

DESPITE HIS TREMBLING HAND HE MANAGES TO POUR A 37 POET DRINK

(BEFORE HE CAN POUR A DRINK, 161 POET (CHANTS) =POUR OUT THY FURY UPON THE HEATHEN THATS82 ROPE KNOW THEE NOT,

POURED

WINE IS POURED AND ALL RAISE THEIR GOBLETS TOWARD 278 LAZARU LAZARUS--

THE SMOKE POURED FROM THE WINDOWS' THE NEIGHBORS 346 LAZARU THOUGHT THE HOUSE WAS BURNING/

POURIN'

POURIN' IT DOWN HIS NECK/ 208 HA APE

POURING

(POURING OUT THEIR GLASSES) I'LL GET A LITTLE 77 ANNA HOUSE SOMEWHERE AND I'LL MAKE A

POURING. 947 DAYS A MOMENT LATER HURRIES IN EXCITEDLY, HER WORDS 445 DYNAMO POURING OUT)

(RETURNING AND POURING OUT A BIG DRINK IN THE 295 GGBROW TUMBLER)

(POURING A DRINK) I'M GOIN' TO GET STINKO, SEE/ 690 ICEMAN (POURING HIS) DIVIL A BIT UT WUD MATTHER WHERE YES17 INZONE ARRE.

ARE YOU POURING COALS OF FIRE ON MY HEAD FOR 29 JOURNE TEASING YOU ABOUT SNORING$

(POURING A BIG DRINK--A BIT DRUNKENLY.) 130 JOURNE BLACK SMOKE POURING FROM THE FUNNELS BEHIND AND 153 JOURNE BENEATH ME.

YOU'RE NOT POLITE, POURING YOUR OWN FIRST. 120 MISBEG (ANGRILY, POURING HIMSELF ANOTHER DRINK.) 156 POET

POURS

(POURS OUT MORE BEER INTO HIS GLASS AND FILLS ONE 78 ANNA FOR HERSELF--

AND THE WHOLE MOB, LED BY DRISCOLL, POURS OUT ON 470 CARINE DECK.

(OPENS BAG AND POURS OUT PILE OF TWENTY-DOLLAR 219 DESIRE GOLD PIECES)

(HE POURS WHISKEY FOR HIMSELF AND FIDDLER. 251 DESIRE THE POURS OUT ANOTHER BIG DRINK.) 296 GGBROW HEAT POURS FULL UPON THE MEN WHO ARE OUTLINED IN 223 HA APE SILHOUETTE IN THE CROUCHING.

(LARRY POURS A DRINK AND GULPS IT DOWN. 577 ICEMAN LARRY POURS A DRINK FROM THE BOTTLE ON WILLIE'S 580 ICEMAN TABLE AND GULPS IT DOWN.

HE POURS A BRIMFUL DRINK AND TOSSES IT DOWN HIS 586 ICEMAN THROAT.

THEN GRABS IT DEFIANTLY AND POURS A BIG DRINK) 637 ICEMAN (HE DRINKS AND POURS OUT ANOTHER) 637 ICEMAN JOE POURS A BRIMFUL DRINK--SULLENLY) 673 ICEMAN (LARRY DOWNS A DRINK AND POURS ANOTHER.) 681 ICEMAN (HE SLOPS A GLASS FULL AND DRAINS IT AND POURS 690 ICEMAN ANOTHER--

(HE POURS A DRINK AND GULPS IT DOWN.) 691 ICEMAN (HE DRINKS HIS DRINK MECHANICALLY AND POURS 692 ICEMAN ANOTHER.)

HE POURS ANOTHER AND THEY DO THE SAME. 711 ICEMAN (HE SITS IN THE CHAIR BY CHUCK AND POURS A DRINK 719 ICEMAN AND TOSSES IT DOWN.

(HE POURS A DRINK AND GULPS IT DOWN.) 721 ICEMAN (HE POURS OUT COFFEE.) 516 INZONE (HE GRABS THE BOTTLE AND POURS A DRINK, ADDS ICE 53 JOURNE WATER AND DRINKS.

AND POURS THEM IN THE WHISKEY BOTTLE AND SHAKES IT 54 JOURNE UP.)

(HE POURS WATER IN THE GLASS AND SETS IT ON THE 54 JOURNE TABLE BY EDMUND.)

HE POURS A BIG DRINK. 65 JOURNE (IGNORING THE HINT, JAMIE POURS A BIG DRINK. HIS 65 JOURNE FATHER SCOWLS--

(HE POURS HIS OWN DRINK AND PASSES THE BOTTLE TO 65 JOURNE JAMIE, GRUMBLING.)

POURS

POURS (CONT'D.)
(SHE POURS A DRINK.) HERE'S YOUR GOOD HEALTH, 100 JOURNE
MA'AM.
(SHE POURS OUT A BIG DRINK AND STARTS FOR THE BACK106 JOURNE
PARLOR WITH IT.)
(SHE POURS A DRINK FOR HIM. 109 JOURNE
AND POURS HIMSELF A BIG DRINK AND DRINKS IT. 122 JOURNE
THEN WITH A STRAINED CASUALNESS, AS HIS FATHER 136 JOURNE
POURS A DRINK.)
(HE REACHES OUT AND GETS THE BOTTLE, POURS A DRINK136 JOURNE
AND HANDS IT BACK.
(GRABS THE BOTTLE AND POURS HIS GLASS BRIMFULL-- 146 JOURNE
NEARLY.)
(POURS HIMSELF A BIG DRINK, WHICH EMPTIES THE 146 JOURNE
BOTTLE, AND DRINKS IT.
(HE REACHES OUT AND POURS A DRINK. 152 JOURNE
(HE POURS A DRINK.) HERE'S HOW. 157 JOURNE
(HE GRABS THE BOTTLE AND POURS ANOTHER DRINK, 158 JOURNE
APPEARING VERY DRUNK AGAIN.)
(POURS A DRINK.) A WASTE/ 168 JOURNE
HE POURS A DRINK WITHOUT DISARRANGING THE WEDDING 175 JOURNE
GOWN HE HOLDS CAREFULLY OVER
JAMIE POURS HIS AND PASSES THE BOTTLE TO EDMUND, 175 JOURNE
WHO, IN TURN, POURS ONE.
AND POURS SOME BLACK POWDER OUT OF IT ON HIS PALM)395 MARCOM
(AS TYRONE POURS A BIG DRINK, GRINNING AT HIM, 53 MISBEG
(SHE POURS THE OTHER TUMBLER HALF FULL.) 112 MISBEG
(SHE POURS A TUMBLER HALF FULL OF WHISKEY AND 112 MISBEG
HANDS IT TO HIM)
HE POURS WATER IN HER GLASS. 113 MISBEG
(SHE POURS OUT DRINKS AS SHE SPEAKS, A HALF 115 MISBEG
TUMBLERFUL FOR HIM.
HE PICKS UP HIS TUMBLER AND POURS A BIG DRINK. 120 MISBEG
(HE POURS A DRINK INTO HER TUMBLER.) 121 MISBEG
(HE GULPS DOWN THE DRINK AND POURS ANOTHER 122 MISBEG
MECHANICALLY, AS IF HE DIDN'T KNOW WHAT HE WAS 122 MISBEG
DOING. HE POURS ANOTHER.
TYRONE POURS A DRINK AND SETS THE BOTTLE ON THE 126 MISBEG
GROUND.
HE SHRUGS HIS SHOULDERS, POURS OUT A BIG DRINK 139 MISBEG
MECHANICALLY)
(SHE PICKS UP THE BOTTLE AND GLASS AND POURS HIM A166 MISBEG
DRINK)
(POURS OUT A BIG DRINK.) LAVE IT TO CON NEVER TO 9 POET
BE CAUGHT DRY.
(HE POURS OUT A DRINK AND GULPS IT DOWN--WITH A 11 POET
CAUTIOUS LOOK AT MALOY.)
(CREGAN POURS OUT A DRINK.) DRINK HEARTY. 15 POET
HE REACHES OUT WITH HIS RIGHT AND POURS A GLASS OF 35 POET
WATER
(HE POURS OUT ANOTHER BIG DRINK AND THIS TIME HIS 37 POET
HAND IS STEADIER.
(HE REACHES FOR THE DECANTER AND SHAKINGLY POURS A 42 POET
DRINK.
BUT IF YOU INSIST--(HE POURS A DRINK--A SMALL 46 POET
ONE--HIS HAND QUITE STEADY NOW.)
HE POURS A DRINK.) 93 POET
(HE POURS A DRINK AND RAISES HIS GLASS.) 93 POET
(HE DRINKS THE REST OF HIS WINE, POURS ANOTHER 100 POET
GLASS.
(HE POURS A SMALL DRINK AND HANDS IT TO HER.) 134 POET
(POURS OUT A BIG DRINK AND PUTS IT BEFORE MELODY--153 POET
CUXINGLY.)
(HE DOWNS THE WHISKEY, AND POURS OUT ANOTHER--TO 154 POET
NORA AND SARA.)
(HE POURS OUT A DRINK AND DOWNS IT. 160 POET
TURNING THE BAG UPSIDE DOWN, POURS ITS CONTENTS IN601 HOPE
HER LAP.
(JOE POURS THE CONTENTS OF THE LITTLE BOTTLE INTO 505 VOYAGE
OLSON'S GLASS OF GINGER BEER.)
(HE POURS OUT HER DRINK AND BRINGS IT TO THE 505 VOYAGE
TABLE)

POUTS
SHE POUTS. 469 CARIBE

POVERTY
IS ONE OF AN HABITUAL POVERTY TOO HOPELESSLY 144 BEYOND
RESIGNED
(HIS EYES SEEMED TO TAKE IN THE POVERTY-STRICKEN 155 BEYOND
APPEARANCE
THAN GO THROUGH THE POVERTY AND HUMILIATION I'VE 423 DYNAMO
HAD TO FACE/....
HE MADE HIS WAY UP FROM IGNORANCE AND POVERTY TO 60 JOURNE
THE TOP OF HIS PROFESSION/
EXCEPT MONEY AND PROPERTY AND THE FEAR HE'LL END 101 JOURNE
HIS DAYS IN POVERTY.
HIS PEOPLE WERE THE MOST IGNORANT KIND OF POVERTY-111 JOURNE
STRICKEN IRISH.
DO YOU THINK I FEAR POVERTY5 36 MANSNS
WHEN I'M SO RICH AND YOU SO POVERTY-STRICKEN. 55 MANSNS
TO SUPPORT YOUR FAMILY EXCEPT IN A SHAMEFUL 153 MANSNS
MUST REMEMBER THE OLD ADAGE--STICKS AND STONES-- 155 MANSNS
AND POVERTY--BREAK--
AS IF YOU WERE SOME POVERTY-STRICKEN PEASANT'S 50 POET
DAUGHTER6

POWDER
(SEVERELY) BE THAT PAINT AND POWDER YOU GOT ON 536 DIFRNT
YOUR FACE, EMMERS
PAINT AND POWDER/
I STUCK IT TILL I WAS EIGHTEEN BEFORE I TOOK A 238 HA APE
RUN-OUT POWDER. 14 HUGHIE
(TRIES TO IGNORE THIS.) I HAVE TO GET TOOTH 86 JOURNE
POWDER AND TOILET SOAP AND COLD
OR IS IT A POWDER YOU DISSOLVE IN WINES 354 LAZARU
IT'S THE SAME POWDER THEY'VE BEEN USING HERE IN 395 MARCOM
CHILDREN'S FIRE WORKS.
AND POURS SOME BLACK POWDER OUT OF IT ON HIS PALM)395 MARCOM

POWDER (CONT'D.)
PRETTY VICIOUS FACE UNDER CAKED POWDER AND 6 STRANG
ROUGE....
YOU'LL WANT TO GO UPSTAIRS AND POWDER YOUR NOSE. 469 WELDED

POWDERED
HER FACE IS PROFUSELY POWDERED--WITH NERVOUS 531 DIFRNT
EXCITEMENT)
SO IS HIS THINNING BROWN HAIR, POWDERED WITH 8 HUGHIE
DANDRUFF.
WELL, WHO COULD DOPE OUT A NOVEL AD ON ANOTHER 67 STRANG
POWDERED MILK, ANYWAYS...
HER FACE NEWLY ROUGED AND POWDERED, 125 STRANG
HER FACE, ROUGED, POWDERED, PENCILED, IS BROAD AND471 WELDED
STUPID.

POWDERS
POWDERS HER NOSE, ETC. 515 DAYS

POWER
MUST BE FISHERMAN'S POWER BOAT. 29 ANNA
HE IS ABOUT THIRTY, IN THE FULL POWER OF HIS 30 ANNA
HEAVY-MUSCLED, IMMENSE STRENGTH.
BUT, GLORY BE, IT'S A POWER OF STRENGTH IS IN THEM 33 ANNA
TWO FINE ARMS OF YOURS.
IT'S GREAT POWER I HAVE IN MY HAND AND ARM, AND I 35 ANNA
DU BE FORGETTING IT AT TIMES.
AND A DIVIL TO BE MAKING A POWER OF TROUBLE IF YOU 46 ANNA
HAD YOUR WAY.
WHERE I'D BE GIVING A POWER OF LOVE TO A WOMAN IS 60 ANNA
THE SAME AS OTHERS YOU'D MEET
(SIMPLY) FOR I'VE A POWER OF STRENGTH IN ME TO 74 ANNA
LEAD MEN THE WAY I WANT.
AND I'M TELLING YOU THERE'S GREAT POWER IN IT, 75 ANNA
AS IF ALL POWER OF WILLING HAD DESERTED HER. 112 BEYOND
IN WHICH HE FELT HE REALLY HAD GIVEN HIS SOUL TO 534 DAYS
SOME EVIL POWER.
HE WANTED TO DELIVER HIMSELF FROM ITS POWER AND BE538 DAYS
FREE AGAIN.
A NEW DISCIPLINE FOR LIFE WILL SPRING INTO BEING, 542 DAYS
A NEW WILL AND POWER TO LIVE,
THE POWER STILL TO SAVE-- 558 DAYS
AND WHY SHOULD YOU WAIT FOR AN END YOU KNOW WHEN 562 DAYS
IT IS IN YOUR POWER TO GRASP
CABOT IS SEVENTY-FIVE, TALL AND GAUNT, WITH GREAT,221 DESIRE
WIRY, CONCENTRATED POWER.
(WITH A SCORNFUL SENSE OF POWER) 225 DESIRE
OF RESERVE POWER AND HEALTH. 494 DIFRNT
I'M GETTING A JOB IN FIFE'S POWER HOUSE. 467 DYNAMO
EXTERIOR OF THE LIGHT AND POWER COMPANY'S HYDRO- 473 DYNAMO
ELECTRIC PLANT
(SAME AS ACT TWO, SCENE THREE--EXTERIOR OF THE 476 DYNAMO
POWER HOUSE FOUR MONTHS LATER.
HER POWER HOUSES ARE THE NEW CHURCHES/ 477 DYNAMO
WITH A SOMBER PULSATION, A BAFFLED BUT REVENGEFUL 202 EJONES
POWER.)
BUT IT IS EVIDENT LAVINIA DOES ALL IN HER POWER TO 10 ELECTR
EMPHASIZE THE DISSIMILARITY
YOU CAN FORGET THERE ALL MEN'S DIRTY DREAMS OF 24 ELECTR
GREED AND POWER/
HE WAS A POWER FOR GOOD. 69 ELECTR
HE LOVES ME BECAUSE I HAVE ALWAYS POSSESSED THE 298 GGBROW
POWER HE NEEDED FOR LOVE,
ALL ARE HAIRY-CHESTED, WITH LONG ARMS OF 207 HA APE
TREMENDOUS POWER, AND LOW,
UH, TO BE SCOOTING SOUTH AGAIN WID THE POWER OF 214 HA APE
THE TRADE WIND
AS STUPIDLY GREEDY FOR POWER AS THE WORST 588 ICEMAN
CAPITALIST THEY ATTACK,
SHE HAS THE WILL POWER NOW/ 37 JOURNE
AND DELIVERS SERMONS ON WILL POWER/ 74 JOURNE
ALL HE KNOWS ABOUT MEDICINE IS TO LOOK SOLEMN AND 92 JOURNE
PREACH WILL POWER/
YOU'VE GOT THE WILL POWER/ 92 JOURNE
I'LL BET YOU TOLD HER ALL SHE HAD TO DO WAS USE A 141 JOURNE
LITTLE WILL POWER/
HIS LAUGHTER RISES WITH MORE AND MORE SUMMONING 333 LAZARU
POWER.
COULD NOT POSSIBLY HAVE POSSESSED ANY MAGIC POWER 343 LAZARU
HIMSELF,
BAFFLED, YET FEELING HIS POWER AS CAESAR 348 LAZARU
TRIUMPHANT NEVERTHELESS)
HIS VOICE RINGING MORE AND MORE WITH A TERRIBLE 349 LAZARU
UNBEARABLE POWER AND BEAUTY THAT
AND WAS IT THY POWER THAT RECALLED LIFE TO HER 350 LAZARU
BODY FOR THAT MOMENT5
I DID NOT KILL HER, IT IS TRUE, BUT I DEPRIVED HER355 LAZARU
OF HER POWER AND SHE DIED,
WHEN I AM CAESAR, I WILL DEVOTE MY POWER TO YOUR 360 LAZARU
TRUTH.
GREEDY FOR LUST AND POWER/ 3 MANSNS
JACKSON IN POWER--AND EVEN YOUR FATHER ADMITS HE 8 MANSNS
IS SURE OF RE-ELECTION--
STAND IN THE WAY OF THE FINAL GOAL OF POWER SHE 13 MANSNS
HAS SET FOR HERSELF--
I PREFER TO BE THE SECRET POWER BEHIND THE 13 MANSNS
THRONE--
THAT I DID NOT DESIRE IT AND DID ALL IN MY POWER 37 MANSNS
TO REJECT ITS
COMPETITORS IN THE RACE FOR POWER AND WEALTH AND 46 MANSNS
POSSESSIONS/
YOUR RIGHT HAS NO POWER. 70 MANSNS
HAVE SEEMED, THROUGH THE SUBTLE POWER OF MOTHER'S 73 MANSNS
FANTASTIC WILL,
AS IF SOME LONG PATIENT TENSION HAD SNAPPED-- AS IF 74 MANSNS
I NO LONGER HAD THE POWER TO
THE POSSESSION OF POWER IS THE ONLY FREEDOM, 74 MANSNS
THEY HAD IT WHEN THEY HAD POWER. 94 MANSNS
WHO'D HAVE DREAMED IT, SARA MELODY--YOU IN YOUR 143 MANSNS
BEAUTY TO HAVE SUCH POWER/
BUT IT GAVE ME A FEELING OF POWER AND HAPPINESS 145 MANSNS

1237

POWER

POWER (CONT'D.)
HAVEN'T I ALWAYS SAID YOU'VE THE STRENGTH AND THE 158 MANSNS
POWER
AND SPRANG UP INTO THIS MIGHTY TREE TO TESTIFY 349 MARCOM
FOREVER TO HIS MIRACULOUS POWERS
(TEDALOO, WITH A SIMPLE DIGNITY AND POWER, BLESSES362 MARCOM
THEM,
WHEN HE CAME TO MANHOOD, RENOUNCED WIFE AND CHILD,372 MARCOM
RICHES AND POWER,
HAS HE NOT BY HIS WILL-POWER AND DETERMINATION 387 MARCOM
RISEN
OF YOUR GROSS ABUSE OF POWER/ 392 MARCOM
THE WHOLE PROCESS IS A MAN-POWER ORIGINAL OF THE 400 MARCOM
MODERN DEVICES
(REBELLIOUSLY) YET I WISH SOME POWER COULD GIVE 400 MARCOM
ME ASSURANCE
BEFORE THEY MAKE TOO MANY ENGINES TO WEAKEN THE 422 MARCOM
POWER OF MEN,
MY PRIDE, MY POWERS 437 MARCOM
IT WAS THE TRUTH OF POWER. 437 MARCOM
IF I WAS MAD AT CON, AND ME BLIND DRUNK, I MUST 11 POET
HAVE TOLD YOU A POWER OF LIES.
HE'S DONE A POWER AV BOASTIN' ABOUT HIS DUELS, BUT 12 POET
I THOUGHT HE WAS LYIN'.
ONCE YOU'VE THE MONEY AND THE POWER GOES WITH IT. 27 POET
THERE'S A POWER AV TALK ABOUT THE TWO AV YOU 32 POET
ALREADY.
(THEN DEFIANTLY.) BUT BY THE ETERNAL GOD, NO 66 POET
POWER ON EARTH,
AND ONCE HE'D DONE THAT NO POWER ON EARTH COULD 78 POET
CHANGE HIM.
IF HE LOVES YOU NO POWER CAN CHANGE HIM, ANYWAY. 78 POET
FROM THE LUST FOR POWER AND SAVING OUR SOULS BY 85 POET
BEING CONTENT WITH LITTLE.
I HAD FORGOTTEN HOW COMPELLING THE BRUTAL POWER OF 86 POET
PRIMITIVE,
(SUDDENLY WITH A FLASH OF HER STRANGE, FIERCE 131 POET
PRIDE IN THE POWER OF LOVE.)
HE AND JAMIE WOULD TAKE A POWER AV DRINKS TO 141 POET
CELEBRATE.
BUT HE'LL SING AND LAUGH AND DRINK A POWER AV 180 POET
WHISKEY AND SLAPE SOUND AFTER.
DESIRE FOR SPEECH HAD PARALYZED ALL POWER OF 594 ROPE
ARTICULATION.
HER POWER TO ENSLAVE MEN'S SENSES... 74 STRANG
PROUD OF HIS WILL POWER... 91 STRANG
FLOWERS REALLY HAVE THE POWER TO SOOTHE GRIEF. 188 STRANG
I HATE THAT UNKNOWN POWER IN YOU WHICH WOULD 453 WELDED
DESTROY ME.
YOU HAVE THE POWER--AND THE RIGHT--TO MURDER LOVE/473 WELDED

POWERFUL
HE IS A POWERFUL, BROAD-CHESTED SIX-FOOTER, 30 ANNA
HE IS A SQUAT, BOW-LEGGED, POWERFUL MAN, ALMOST A513 DIFRNT
BROAD AS HE IS LONG--
WHICH IS BRILLIANTLY LIGHTED BY A ROW OF POWERFUL 473 DYNAMO
BULBS IN WHITE GLOBES SET IN
IN FIGURE HE IS TALL, BROAD-SHOULDERED AND 21 ELECTR
POWERFUL.
HE SEEMS BROADER, FIERCER, MORE TRUCULENT, MORE 208 HA APE
POWERFUL,
THE SLEEVES OF HIS COLLARLESS SHIRT ARE ROLLED UP 577 ICEMAN
ON HIS THICK, POWERFUL ARMS
IN APPEARANCE LAZARUS IS TALL AND POWERFUL, ABOUT 274 LAZARU
FIFTY YEARS OF AGE,
IN DEPTHS OF SKY, PROUD AND POWERFUL, INFECTIOUS 280 LAZARU
WITH LOVE,
POWERFUL SHOULDERS AND LONG ARMS AND HANDS, AND 299 LAZARU
SHORT, SKINNY,
SURELY, CAESAR, THIS MAGICIAN MUST HAVE POWERFUL 343 LAZARU
CHARMS
AS I KNEW SHE MUST, THAT POWERFUL WOMAN WHO BORE 355 LAZARU
ME AS A WEAPON/
WHICH GIVES HIM A FORMIDABLY POWERFUL APPEARANCE, 69 MANSNS
YOU MUST BE BECOMING RICHER AND MORE POWERFUL ALL 100 MANSNS
THE TIME.
BUDDHA, ALL-POWERFUL ONE/ 352 MARCOM
SHE IS MORE POWERFUL THAN ANY BUT AN EXCEPTIONALLY 3 MISBEG
STRONG MAN.
(GRABS IT AND TEARS IT FROM HIS HAND WITH ONE 61 MISBEG
POWERFUL TWIST--FIERCELY)
AND POWERFUL, WITH LONG MUSCULAR ARMS, BIG FEET, 33 POET
AND LARGE HAIRY HANDS.
IN HIS BIG, POWERFUL HANDS IN AN EFFORT TO CONTROL 92 POET
HIMSELF.

POWERFULLY
DRISCOLL IS A TALL, POWERFUL IRISHMAN. 496 VOYAGE
ONE FEELS A POWERFUL IMAGINATION TINGED WITH 443 WELDED
SOMBER SADNESS--

POWERFULLY
(A POWERFULLY BUILT IRISHMAN WHO IS SITTING ON THE456 CARIBE
EDGE OF THE HATCH, FRONT--
CALEB WILLIAMS IS TALL AND POWERFULLY BUILT, ABOUT494 DIFRNT
THIRTY.
HE IS A TALL, POWERFULLY-BUILT, FULL-BLOODED NEGRO175 EJONES
OF MIDDLE AGE.

POWERLESS
AND ME POWERLESS TO HELP AND AT THEIR MERCY, YOU 113 BEYOND
MIGHT SAY.
ALL GODS ARE POWERLESS. 436 MARCOM
AGAINST DEATH ALL GODS ARE POWERLESS. 436 MARCOM

POWERS
HE IS A MAN OF SIXTY BUT STILL IN THE FULL PRIME 377 MARCOM
OF HIS POWERS,
BY THE POWERS, I'M GLAD YOU'RE HERE, JAMIE. 92 POET
IT'S WITH HIS MASTER I HAVE TO DEAL, AND, BY THE 124 POET
POWERS, I'LL DEAL WITH HIM/
BUT, BE THE POWERS, WE WINT DOWN FIGHTIN' TO THE 158 POET
LAST

PRAISED

PUY
GUOT PUY, YANK/ 224 HA APE

PRACTICAL
(FORCED TO LAUGH) I'VE NEVER CONSIDERED THAT 85 BEYOND
PRACTICAL SIDE OF IT FOR A MINUTE,
BUT ANDY GAVE ME AN OVERDUSE OF THE PRACTICAL 88 BEYOND
CONSIDERATIONS.
MORE BOVINE AND HOMELIEK IN FACE, SHREWDER AND 203 DESIRE
MORE PRACTICAL
WITH THE UNCONSCIOUSLY MALICIOUS HUMOR OF THE BORN498 DIFRNT
PRACTICAL JOKER,
HIS THIN MOUTH IS FULL OF THE MALICIOUS HUMOR OF 428 DYNAMO
THE PRACTICAL JOKER.
AND ONE OF US HAS GOT TO BE PRACTICAL, SO WHY NOT 276 GGBROW
ME?
A SLY FAT BOY, CONGENITALLY INDOLENT, A PRACTICAL 576 ICEMAN
JOKER,
AND THE PRACTICAL WISDOM OF THE WORLD IN THAT 585 ICEMAN
LITTLE PARABLE.
I WISH TO SAY I SEE YOUR POINT ABOUT POLICY OF 155 MANSNS
BANK--ONLY PRACTICAL VIEWPOINT--
(WITH AN ABRUPT CHANGE TO PRACTICAL CALCULATION.) 191 MANSNS
NOT NEGLECTING THE PRACTICAL SIDE, OF COURSE-- 379 MARCOM
WELL, YOU WILL FIND ME A PRACTICAL MAN, TOO-- 380 MARCOM
A PRACTICAL WAR OF FEW WORDS, AS THAT POLU YOU 422 MARCOM
ADMIRE WOULD SAY.
WHEN HIS DREAM IS FLOUTED, AND VERY PRACTICAL IN 82 POET
HIS METHODS OF DEFENDING IT.
WHERE PRACTICAL PRESENT-DAY CONSIDERATIONS ARE 6 STRANG
CONCERNED
I SEE YOU'RE A PRACTICAL PERSON. 474 WELDED

PRACTICALLY
(PRACTICALLY) HOW DO YOU KNOW WHAT YOU DID IF YOU285 AHWILD
DRANK SO MUCH CHAMPAGNES
(SITTING DOWN AGAIN) PRACTICALLY. 157 BEYOND
WELL, AS I'VE PRACTICALLY FINISHED IT---I SUPPOSE 1152 ELECTR
MIGHT AS WELL TELL YOU.
(PRACTICALLY) I'D PIN HIM DOWN IF I COULD. 311 GGBROW
AND THAT'S PRACTICALLY UNHEARD OF. 23 JOURNE
THAT IS, FOR NOTHING, OR PRACTICALLY NOTHING. 145 JOURNE
(PRACTICALLY) BUT HE COULD NOT BLAME BAD LUCK FOR276 LAZARU
EVERYTHING.
(PRACTICALLY) SHE HAS ONLY FAINTED. 283 LAZARU
THAT WE WILL BE GETTING SOMETHING FOR PRACTICALLY 63 MANSNS
NOTHING.
(PRACTICALLY) YES, I THINK SO, TOO. 356 MARCOM
SIN IS PRACTICALLY UNSEEN. 393 MARCOM
(THEN PRACTICALLY) THEN, OF COURSE, 404 MARCOM
PRACTICALLY A STRANGER. 147 MISBEG
AFTER YOU'VE PRACTICALLY ADMITTED YOU'VE 118 STRANG

PRACTICE
AND I NEEDED A LITTLE PRACTICE TO KEEP MY HAND IN.608 ICEMAN
I'M BUM AT IT NOW FOR LACK OF PRACTICE, 609 ICEMAN
I GOT TO PRACTICE. 644 ICEMAN
I'LL PRACTICE EVERY DAY FROM NOW ON. 171 JOURNE
I PLAY SO BADLY NOW. I'M ALL OUT OF PRACTICE. 171 JOURNE
A CAESAR GETS MUCH PRACTICE--FROM CHILDHOOD ON-- 341 LAZARU
TOO MUCH/
OR PROHIBITING THE PRACTICE OF THE LAWS OF BIOLOGY390 MARCOM
WITHIN A TWELVE-MILE LIMIT.
IT WASN'T BAD STUFF EITHER, CONSIDERING I'D HAD NO399 MARCOM
PRACTICE.
I WAS OUT OF PRACTICE, TOO. 412 MARCOM
THERE IS NO DECENT LIVING TO BE GAINED BY ITS 111 PUET
PRACTICE.
HIS PRACTICE IS ALL DRIBBLED AWAY FROM HIM LATELY 585 ROPE
ON ACCOUNT OF THE DRINK.
(GIVING ME THE FISHY, DIAGNOSING EYE THEY 34 STRANG
PRACTICE AT MEDICAL SCHOOL...

PRACTICED
I'VE NEVER PRACTICED BUT I WAS ONE OF THE MOST 607 ICEMAN
BRILLIANT STUDENTS IN LAW SCHOOL.
HE PRACTICED ON STREET CORNERS UNDER A TORCHLIGHT.626 ICEMAN

PRACTICING
THERE SHOULD BE A LAW TO KEEP MEN LIKE HIM FROM 74 JOURNE
PRACTICING.
AS IF AN AWKWARD SCHOOLGIRL WERE PRACTICING IT FOR170 JOURNE
THE FIRST TIME.

PRACTISES
HE PRACTISES WHEN YOU'RE NOT AT HOME. 255 AHWILD

PRACTISING
(DISAPPOINTEDLY) BUT, AUNT LILY, THAT'S JUST WHAT250 AHWILD
I WAS PRACTISING HARDEST ON.
I'VE BEEN PRACTISING A NEW WAY OF WRITING MY NAME.250 AHWILD

PRAISE
WE CAN GIVE PRAISE TO GOD THEN THAT HE'LL BE BACK 115 BEYOND
IN THE NICK OF TIME.
HE'S NOT DEAD YET AND, PRAISE GOD, HE'LL HAVE MANY479 CARDIF
A LONG DAY YET BEFORE HIM.
THAT LETTER WAS FULL OF MORE ARDENT HYMNS OF 504 DAYS
PRAISE FOR A MERE LIVING WOMAN THAN
(HE PAUSES--THEN SADLY.) THE PRAISE EDWIN BOOTH 152 JOURNE
GAVE MY OTHELLO.
PRAISE BE TO ALLAH/ 365 MARCOM
AND EVERYWHERE WHERE SONGS ARE SUNG THEY SHALL BE 418 MARCOM
IN PRAISE OF YOUR BEAUTY/
PRAISE BE TO GOD/ 54 MISBEG
(THEN GRATEFULLY.) PRAISE BE, YOU'VE COME AT 136 POET
LAST/
PRAISE BE TO THE SA'NTS, YOU'RE BACK, JAMIE/ 151 POET
(SOBS WITH RELIEF. OH, PRAISE GUD YOU'RE ALIVE/ 164 POET
NO MORE GOROON, G ADON, GOROON, LOVE AND PRAISE 22 STRANG
AND TEARS, AL' FOR GORDON/...
I WOULD PRAISE H..S JUSTICE/... 129 STRANG

PRAISED
GUD BE PRAISED/ 52 ANNA
GOD BE PRAISED/ 563 DAYS
BUT GOD BE PRAISED I'M BACK IN TIME/ 185 MANSNS
GUD BE PRAISED/ 154 POET

PRAISES

PRAISES
AND EVER SINCE THEN I'VE HEARD NOTHING BUT THE 504 DAYS
PRAISES OF ELSA--
PRAISEWORTHY
(WITH THE AIR OF ONE FRANKLY ADMITTING A 70 POET
PRAISEWORTHY WEAKNESS.)
PRAISING
THE TRUTH--TALAVERA--THE DUKE PRAISING YOUR 178 POET
BRAVERY--AN OFFICER IN HIS ARMY--
PRANCE
TO PRANCE AROUND ON AND SHOW HIMSELF OFF/ 23 POET
PRANCES
HE PRANCES INTO THE MIDST OF THE DANCERS, 250 DESIRE
SCATTERING THEM,
THE WITCH DOCTOR PRANCES UP TO HIM, TOUCHES HIM 201 EJONES
WITH HIS WAND,
PRANCING
PRANCING AROUND IN A CIRCLE WITH BODY BENT IN AN 251 DESIRE
INDIAN WAR DANCE,
HE STRUTS NOISELESSLY WITH A QUEER PRANCING STEP 200 EJONES
(WITH A QUICK PRANCING MOVEMENT, HE HAS OPENED THE318 GGBROW
DOOR, GONE THROUGH,
DANCING ROUND ME IN THE DARKNESS, PRANCING TO THE 353 LAZARU
DRUM BEAT OF MY HEART/
PRANCING AROUND DRUNK ON HIS BEAUTIFUL 168 POET
THOROUGHBRED MARE--
PRAT
HUBBED ON THE PRAT, WOULD CURE HEART FAILURE IN 626 ICEMAN
THREE DAYS.
PRATE
YOU CAN HOLD YOUR PRATE/ 81 MANSNS
WHEN YOU PRATE ABOUT IF'S AND WANT-TO'S. 25 POET
HOWLD YOUR PRATE/ 25 POET
HOLD YOUR PRATE/ 52 POET
HOOLD YOUR PRATE, NOW/ 61 POET
PRATES
DIVIL MEND HIM, HE ALWAYS PRATES AS IF HE HAD ALL 139 POET
THE HONOR THERE IS,
PRATIES
OH IN A DITCH WITH HIM, AND STEAL PRATIES FROM THE 20 MANSNS
FARMERS TO FEED HIM,
THE PRATIES THEY GROW SMALL OVER HERE. 72 MISBEG
OH THE PRATIES THEY GROW SMALL OVER HERE, OVER 72 MISBEG
HERE, OH,
OH THE PRATIES THEY GROW SMALL AND WE DIG THEM IN 72 MISBEG
THE FALL AND WE EAT THEM SKINS
*UH, THE PRATIES THEY GROW SMALL, OVER HERE, OVER 101 MISBEG
HERE,* ETC.
*UH, THE PRATIES THEY GROW SMALL, OVER HERE, OVER 103 MISBEG
HERE.*
PRATING
(THEN EXASPERATEDLY.) DAMN YOUR PRIESTS' PRATING 61 POET
ABOUT YOUR SIN/
PRAU
THE KANAKAS WENT OVER THE PRAU-- 560 CROSS
PRAY
*WORK AND PRAY WHILE YOU MAY. 233 AHWILD
HE'S AT PEACE, POOR MAN, AND FORGIVEN, LET'S PRAY.114 BEYOND
HE WOULD FEEL A TORTURED LONGING TO PRAY AND BEG 334 DAYS
FOR FORGIVENESS.
HE FEELS AT TIMES AN ABSURD IMPULSE TO PRAY. 544 DAYS
NOT FAR FROM WHERE HE NOW LIVES, IN WHICH HE USED 544 DAYS
TO PRAY AS A BOY.
HE BOWS HIS HEAD WITH A SIMPLE DIGNITY AND BEGINS 551 DAYS
TO PRAY SILENTLY.)
PRAY FOR HIS FORGIVENESS, AND HE WILL HAVE 559 DAYS
COMPASSION ON YOU/
PRAY FOR YOUR LOST FAITH AND IT WILL BE GIVEN YOU/559 DAYS
PRAY TO HIM WHO IS LOVE. 559 DAYS
(INTENSELY) PRAY WITH ME, JACK. 559 DAYS
IF YOU WOULD ONLY PRAY/ 559 DAYS
(HE SINKS TO HIS KNEES) PRAY THAT ELSA'S LIFE MAY 559 DAYS
BE SPARED TO YOU/
IF I COULD ONLY PRAY/ 562 DAYS
WHERE I USED TO BELIEVE, WHERE I USED TO PRAY/ 562 DAYS
TO PRAY, ONE MUST BELIEVE/ 565 DAYS
I PRAY HE'S DIED. 205 DESIRE
WAAL--DON'T YEW PRAY ITS 206 DESIRE
PRAY FUR HIM TO HEARKEN/ 235 DESIRE
PRAY, ABBIE/ 235 DESIRE
PRAY T' THE LORD AGEN, ABBIE. 235 DESIRE
(BITTERLY) PRAY AGEN--FUR UNDERSTANDIN'/ 238 DESIRE
I'LL PRAY MAM T' COME BACK T' HELP ME--T' PUT HER 257 DESIRE
CUSS ON YEW AN' HIM/
MOTHER USED TO MAKE HIM PRAY FOR ELECTRIC LIGHTS 462 DYNAMO
IN THE HOUSE....)
AND THEN SUDDENLY IT HIT ME THAT THERE WAS NOTHING470 DYNAMO
TO PRAY TO.
YOU CAN'T PRAY TO ELECTRICITY UNLESS YOU'RE 470 DYNAMO
FOOLISH IN THE HEAD, CAN YOU?
I FEEL THERE IS SOMETHING IN HER TO PRAY TO/... 474 DYNAMO
AND I'VE GOT TO PRAY TO HER. 478 DYNAMO
MAKE HER PRAY TO YOU.....) 482 DYNAMO
I WANT YOU TO PRAY TO HER--UP THERE WHERE I PRAY 484 DYNAMO
SOMETIMES--UNDER HER ARMS--
YOU MUST PRAY THAT SHE MAY FIND ME WORTHY. 485 DYNAMO
YOU MUST PRAY FOR ME, IF YOU LOVE ME/ 485 DYNAMO
LOVE, HATE, CURSE AND PRAY IN THEM/ 287 GGBROW
(IN HER STRANGE VOICE) CYBEL'S GONE OUT TO DIG IN288 GGBROW
THE EARTH AND PRAY.
PRAY/ 315 GGBROW
AS THEY PRAY SILENTLY IN THEIR AGONIZED 319 GGBROW
SUPPLICATION.
DON'T PRAY TOO HARD THAT I MAY FALL INTO THE FIERY222 HA APE
FURNACE.
BE GOD, IT'S NOT TO BAKUNIN'S GHOST YOU OUGHT TO 634 ICEMAN
PRAY IN YOUR DREAMS,
GOD, I USED TO PRAY SOMETIMES SHE'D-- 714 ICEMAN

PRAY (CONT'D.)
I GET ON MY KNEES AND PRAY/ 77 JOURNE
(BITTINGLY.) DID YOU PRAY FOR MAMAS 77 JOURNE
AND I CAN PRAY TO HER AGAIN-- 94 JOURNE
IN THE CONVENT WHEN YOU USED TO PRAY TO THE 107 JOURNE
BLESSED VIRGIN.
(LONGINGLY.) IF I COULD ONLY FIND THE FAITH I 107 JOURNE
LOST, SO I COULD PRAY AGAIN/
IF YOU'D GET ON YOUR KNEES AND PRAY, 134 JOURNE
AND TELL ME TO PRAY TO THE BLESSED VIRGIN, AND 171 JOURNE
THEY'LL BE WELL AGAIN IN NO TIME.
WHEN I AM CAESAR YOU SHALL SCREAM AND PRAY FOR IT/317 LAZARU
ON THE HILLS NEAR BETHANY YOU MIGHT PRAY AT NOON 330 LAZARU
AND LAUGH YOUR BOY'S LAUGHTER
I SHALL MAKE YOU PRAY FOR DEATH/ 348 LAZARU
I WHO PRAY THE SECOND FLOOD MAY COME 9 MANSNS
PRAY, WHAT HAS YOUR BROTHER TO DO WITH THIS? 33 MANSNS
PRAY DO SO. 96 MANSNS
PRAY CONTINUE. 127 MANSNS
(KNEELING DOWN TO PRAY) ALLAH, BE PITIFUL/ 352 MARCOM
I MUST PRAY TO GOD FOR STRENGTH--FOR GUIDANCE/ 362 MARCOM
A GOD OF HEAVEN TO WHOM THEY PRAY FOR HEALTH OF 373 MARCOM
MIND, AND A GOD OF EARTH,
THEY PRAY TO HIM ALSO AND DO MANY OTHER STUPID 374 MARCOM
THINGS.
(WITH IMPOTENT ANGER) HE SHALL PRAY FOR HIS SOUL 401 MARCOM
ON HIS KNEES BEFORE YOU/
PRAY TO THE SEA. 409 MARCOM
THEN I COMMAND THE WORLD TO PRAY/ 435 MARCOM
PRAY THUS/ 435 MARCOM
THE FOUR PRIESTS GO FIRST, BEGINNING TO PRAY 436 MARCOM
SILENTLY AGAIN.
(VINDICTIVELY) I'LL PRAY YOU'LL FIND A WAY TO NAB 10 MISBEG
HIM, JOSIE,
MADEMOISELLE--(THE SEES HER WEDDING RING.) PRAY 69 POET
FORGIVE ME, I SEE IT IS MADAME--
(PASSIONATELY.) ALL I PRAY TO GOD IS THAT SOMEDAY105 POET
WHEN YOU'RE ADMIRING YOURSELF
PRAY BE SEATED, SIR. 117 POET
I USED TO LIE AWAKE AND PRAY FOR HIM 130 POET
IF YOU'VE A MIND TO PRAY, IT'S DOWN IN THE MEDDER 580 ROPE
YOU OUGHT TO GO,
NO--EXCEPT WAIT ANY PRAY THAT YOUNG THIEF IS DEAD 586 ROPE
AN' WON'T COME BACK,,
I TRIED HARD TO PRAY TO THE MODERN SCIENCE GOD. 41 STRANG
I WAS TRYING TO PRAY. 41 STRANG
PRAYED
THEN, AS I PRAYED, SUDDENLY AS IF BY SOME WILL 507 DAYS
OUTSIDE ME,
THE BOY HAD PRAYED WITH PERFECT FAITH THAT HIS 510 DAYS
FATHER'S LIFE MIGHT BE SPARED.
BUT EVEN THEN HE HOPED AND PRAYED FOR A MIRACLE. 511 DAYS
SO THE POOR FOOL PRAYED AND PRAYED AND VOWED HIS 511 DAYS
LIFE OF PIETY AND GOOD WORKS.)
(SNEERINGLY) YOU FORGET I ONCE PRAYED TO YOUR GOD559 DAYS
YES, I PRAYED THEN. 559 DAYS
YE PRAYED HED DIED. 206 DESIRE
(RESENTFULLY) I'VE PRAYED, HAIN'T IS 238 DESIRE
LIKE THE OLD STONE STATUES OF GODS PEOPLE PRAYED 474 DYNAMO
TO....
I PRAYED THAT HE SHOULD BE KILLED IN THE WAR SO 37 ELECTR
INTENSELY THAT I FINALLY
I'VE PRAYED TO GOD THESE MANY YEARS FOR HER. 77 JOURNE
(IGNORES THIS.) IF YOUR MOTHER HAD PRAYED, TOO-- 78 JOURNE
I GOT ON MY KNEES AND PRAYED THAT NOTHING HAD 113 JOURNE
HAPPENED TO YOU--
THAT I HAD PRAYED TO THE BLESSED VIRGIN TO MAKE MELTS JOURNE
SURE, AND TO FIND ME WORTHY.
SO I WENT TO THE SHRINE AND PRAYED TO THE BLESSED 176 JOURNE
VIRGIN AND FOUND PEACE AGAIN
OH, IF YOU KNEW HOW I HAVE PRAYED FOR RESURRECTION 38 MANSNS
I PRAYED SAMMY'D BE BORN DEAD, AND SAMMY'S FATHER 58 STRANG
PRAYED,
PRAYER
HIS LIPS MOVE IN SOME HALF-REMEMBERED PRAYER.) 490 CARDIF
I TRIED TO LOSE MY DREAD IN PRAYER--AND MY GUILT. 507 DAYS
SPEAKS AS IF IN ANSWER TO FATHER BAIRD'S PRAYER.) 558 DAYS
SAW THERE THE ANSWER TO HIS PRAYER--IN A VOICE 565 DAYS
(TREMBLING WITH HOPE AND JOY)
(IMPLORINGLY) O GOD OF LOVE, HEAR MY PRAYER/ 565 DAYS
AT WHAT HE SEES THERE HE BOWS HIS HEAD AND HIS 566 DAYS
LIPS MOVE IN GRATEFUL PRAYER.
THERE ISN'T A DAMN PRAYER EVER GOT HIM A THING... 462 DYNAMO
BEFORE I THOUGHT, I STARTED TO DO A PRAYER ACT-- 470 DYNAMO
TO SAY A PRAYER....)
THE OLD PRAYER STUFF/....) 474 DYNAMO
U DYNAMO, WHO GIVES LIFE TO THINGS, HEAR MY 480 DYNAMO
PRAYER/
HIS VOICE CATCHES IN A CHOKING PRAYER.) 194 EJONES
(HE GETS TO HIS FEET, EVIDENTLY SLIGHTLY REASSURED196 EJONES
BY HIS PRAYER--
LAWD JESUS, HEAR MY PRAYER/ 196 EJONES
(IMMEDIATELY IN ANSWER TO HIS PRAYER COMES THE 202 EJONES
THOUGHT OF THE ONE BULLET LEFT
LAWD JESUS, HEAR MY PRAYER/ 202 EJONES
(WINN COMES IN FROM THE STATEROOM AND OVERHEARS 115 ELECTR
THE LAST OF HER PRAYER.)
WHAT WAS THE PRAYER, BILLY? 299 GGBROW
(THIS IS ALMOST A PRAYER--THEN FIERCELY DEFIANT) 305 GGBROW
WHAT'S THE PRAYER YOU TAUGHT ME--OUR FATHER--$ 322 GGBROW
LET US JOIN IN PRAYER THAT HICKEY, THE GREAT 596 ICEMAN
SALESMAN,
BECAUSE I KNEW SHE HEARD MY PRAYER AND WOULD 176 JOURNE
ALWAYS LOVE ME AND SEE NO HARM EVER
WE MAKE PRAYER BEADS. 348 MARCOM
I AM GOING TO OFFER A PRAYER FOR PROTECTION TO 349 MARCOM
THIS TREE SACRED TO BUDDHA.

PRAYER (CONT'D.)
EVERYONE SINKS INTO THE ATTITUDE OF PRAYER EXCEPT 369 MARCOM
THE POLOS
(SUDDENLY THE CALL TO PRAYER SOUNDS FROM MUEZZINS 369 MARCOM
IN THE MINARETS OF THE MOSQUE.
LAST EASTER SUNDAY WHEN FATHER AND UNCLE READ A 394 MARCOM
PRAYER
THE MEN SINK TO THE CROSS-LEGGED POSITION OF 433 MARCOM
PRAYER, THEIR HEADS BOWED.
SHE WAS A PRAYER/ 434 MARCOM
OF THE CATAFALQUE AND SINK INTO ATTITUDES OF 434 MARCOM
PRAYER.
(WITH ONE MOTION ALL SINK TO THE POSITION OF 435 MARCOM
PRAYER)
(HE HIMSELF SINKS TO THE POSITION OF PRAYER-- 435 MARCOM
THEN I SHOULD KNOW A PRAYER. 435 MARCOM
PRAYER IS BEYOND WORDS/ 435 MARCOM
OH, CHU-YIN, MY WISE FRIEND, WAS THE PRAYER I 437 MARCOM
TAUGHT THEM WISDOM/
FAITH, ME DARLIN' SON NEVER LEARNT THAT FROM HIS 22 MISBEG
PRAYER BOOK/
OH, MOTHER GOD, GRANT MY PRAYER THAT SOME DAY WE 156 STRANG
MAY TELL OUR SON THE TRUTH AND

PRAYERS
AND DON'T FORGET YOUR PRAYERS. 253 AHWILD
MIND IF I DON'T SAY MY PRAYERS TONIGHT, ESSIE$ 298 AHWILD
AND I'LL BE SAYING PRAYERS OF THANKS ON MY TWO 71 ANNA
KNEES TO THE ALMIGHTY GOD/
(MOCKINGLY) SAYIN' 'IS PRAYERS/ 490 CARDIF
TWO PRAYERS AIN BETTER NOR ONE. 235 DESIRE
HE'S DOWN T' THE CHURCH OFFERIN' UP PRAYERS O' 248 DESIRE
THANKSGIVIN'.
WE DON'T NEED ANY OLD FOOL OF A MINISTER SAYING 470 DYNAMO
PRAYERS OVER US/
FOLKS SAY MORE THAN THEIR PRAYERS/. 15 ELECTR
I'LL SHOW YOU THE HANDIEST PLACE TO SAY YOUR 132 ELECTR
PRAYERS.
(LIKE A PRIEST, OFFERING UP PRAYERS FOR THE 290 GGBROW
DYING.)
AND OPPRESSIVE SILENCE IN WHICH ONLY THE MURMURED 313 LAZARU
PRAYERS OF MIRIAM ARE HEARD.)
SHE DOES NOT NEED YOUR PRAYERS. 434 MARCOM
TO HELL WITH YOUR PRAYERS/ 6 MISBEG
I MUST HAVE SAID MORE THAN MY PRAYERS, WITH THE 10 POET
LASHINGS OF WHISKEY IN ME.
(WITH A GRIN.) MORE THAN YOUR PRAYERS IS THE 10 POET
TRUTH.
(THEN GUILTILY.) BUT I'M SAYIN' MORE THAN MY 12 POET
PRAYERS AGAIN.
THEY WERE REALLY MORE LIKE COMMANDS, OR PRAYERS. 50 STRANG

PRAYIN'
AY-EH--AN' I BEEN PRAYIN' IT'D HAPPEN, TOO. 234 DESIRE
YE BEEN PRAYIN', ABBIE$ 234 DESIRE

PRAYING
WE ARE PRAYING FOR A BOY. 232 AHWILD
AND PRAYING ALMIGHTY GOD AND THE SAINTS TO PUT A 75 ANNA
GREAT CURSE ON YOU IF SHE'D
AND PRAYING YOU WAS COMING HOME TO STAY, 138 BEYOND
IT HAPPENED ONE NIGHT WHILE I WAS PRAYING FOR YOU 507 DAYS
IN MY CHURCH.
ON HIS KNEES, WHEN EVERY ONE THOUGHT HE WAS 511 DAYS
PRAYING/
AS IF HE SUDDENLY SENSED A PRESENCE THERE THE 551 DAYS
PRIEST IS PRAYING TO.
(JEERINGLY) IS IT YOUR OLD DEMON YOU ARE PRAYING 552 DAYS
TO FOR MERCY$
HE BOWS HIS HEAD AND BEGINS PRAYING SILENTLY TO 561 DAYS
HIMSELF.
THERE'S NO USE PRAYING/... 444 DYNAMO
ARE YOU PRAYING TO IT FOR MERCY$ 452 DYNAMO
PRAYING AS USUAL.... 462 DYNAMO
SAY, HERE'S ONE ON ME, ADA--SPEAKING OF PRAYING. 470 DYNAMO
(EXCITEDLY) IT'I FEEL LIKE PRAYING NOW/.... 474 DYNAMO
OR HEAR MYSELF WHINING AND PRAYING.. 689 ICEMAN
I TOLD MOTHER I HAD HAD A TRUE VISION WHEN I WAS 175 JOURNE
PRAYING IN THE SHRINE OF OUR
HER FACE UPTURNED, HER LIPS PRAYING. 288 LAZARU
PRAYING SILENTLY WITH MOVING LIPS 313 LAZARU
I WAITED. PRAYING HE WOULDN'T. 20 MANSNS
(UNWILLINGLY) HE'S PRAYING. 362 MARCOM
ARE THEY PRAYING$ 369 MARCOM
AND I'LL KEEP ON PRAYING FOR HIM. 6 MISBEG
AS IF YOU WAS PRAYING ALMIGHTY GCD TO FORGIVE A 93 MISBEG
POOR DRUNKARD.
PRAYING YOUR BABY WOULD BE BORN DEAD/ 59 STRANG
PERHAPS I'M PRAYING. 489 WELDED

PRAYS
THEN HE PRAYS.) 558 DAYS
(HE GETS DOWN ON HIS KNEES AND PRAYS ALOUD TO THE 474 DYNAMO
DYNAMO)
PRAYS COLDLY, AS IF CARRYING OUT A DUTY) 115 ELECTR
HE PRAYS LIKE A SAINT IN THE DESERT, EXORCIZING A 273 GGBROW
DEMON)
AND PRAYS WITH AN ASCETIC FERVOR) 286 GGBROW
(HE MAKES OBEISANCE AND PRAYS TO THE TREE AS DO 350 MARCOM
THE SOLDIERS.

PREACH
I AIN'T NEVER TOOK MUCH STOCK IN THE TRUCK THEM 486 CARDIF
SKYPILOTS PREACH.
ALL HE KNOWS ABOUT MEDICINE IS TO LOOK SOLEMN AND 92 JOURNE
PREACH WILL POWER/
AND THEN HE STARTED TO PREACH ABOUT MY SINS--AND 17 MISBEG
YOURS.
WHAT DID THAT DONKEY, MIKE, PREACH TO YOU ABOUT$ 18 MISBEG
ME, PREACH$ 19 MISBEG
THAT'S WHAT YOU OUGHT TO PREACH 'STEAD OF PUTTIN' 580 ROPE
CURSES ON ME.

PREACHED
ABOUT THE RADICALS, MY DEAR--AND THE FALSE 237 HA APE
DOCTRINES THAT ARE BEING PREACHED.

PREACHER
THE PREACHER FROM NEW DOVER, HE BRUNG THE NEWS-- 212 DESIRE
TOLD IT T'OUR PREACHER
LIKE A REVIVALIST PREACHER ABOUT RELIGION. 589 ICEMAN
HUGO IS THE ONLY LICENSED PREACHER UF THAT GOSPEL 590 ICEMAN
HERE.
HE WAS A PREACHER IN THE STICKS OF INDIANA, LIKE 622 ICEMAN
I'VE TOLD YOU.
I GUESS THAT DID SOUND TOO MUCH LIKE A LOUSY 639 ICEMAN
PREACHER.
ABOUT BRINGING US PEACE--LIKE A BUGHOUSE PREACHER 718 ICEMAN
ESCAPED FROM AN ASYLUM/

PREACHER'S
DECLAIMING IN A QUEER CAMP MEETING PREACHER'S 232 DESIRE
TEMPO)

PREACHERS
(HALF-MOCKINGLY) THEN IT'LL BE GAWD'S WILL, LIKE 29 ANNA
THE PREACHERS SAY--

PREACHIN'
WHEN HE FORGETS DE BUGHOUSE PREACHIN', AND QUITS 638 ICEMAN
TELLIN' YUH WHERE YUH GET OFF.

PREACHING
(HIS VOICE A MOCKING SNEER) AND WHAT SALVATION 501 DAYS
FOR US ARE YOU PREACHING$
DID YOU HEAR HIM THROW THE WURD PREACHING IN MY 501 DAYS
FACE, MR. ELIOT--
IF YOU KNEW WHAT A BURDEN HE MADE MY LIFE FOR 501 DAYS
YEARS WITH HIS PREACHING.
(SHARPLY) NOW DON'T YOU GO PREACHING AT HIM 426 DYNAMO
AGAIN.
(IMPATIENTLY) DON'T START PREACHING, LIKE YOU 8 MISBEG
LOVE TO, OR YOU'LL NEVER GO.
THEY WAS TOO BUSY PREACHING TEMPERANCE TO HAVE 17 MISBEG
TIME FOR A DRINK.
SO DON'T YOU START PREACHING TOO. 19 MISBEG
OR EVEN A GOOD MAN PREACHING THE SIMPLE PLATITUDES 41 STRANG
OF TRUTH, THOSE GOSPEL WORDS

PRECARIOUS
YOUR POSITION IS--ER--PRECARIOUS, UNLESS--WHAT 33 MANSNS
HENRY SUGGESTED IS THIS..

PRECAUTIONS
(EPOUF SAM, IF HE ONLY KNEW THE PRECAUTIONS... 72 STRANG

PRECEDE
(HE TURNS AND OPENS THE STUDY DOOR AND BOWS CURTLY 52 MANSNS
TO JOEL TO PRECEDE HIM.
THE TWO ELDER PRECEDE MARCO. 428 MARCOM
(SHE GOES TO THE DOOR AT RIGHT, AND STEPS ASIDE TO 75 POET
LET DEBORAH PRECEDE HER.)

PRECEDED
PRECEDED BY A BAND OF MASKED MUSICIANS AND BY 306 LAZARU
THEIR CHORUS.
A MOMENT LATER, PRECEDED BY SHOUTS, A CRACKING OF 350 MARCOM
WHIPS,
(HE GOES GRANDLY, PRECEDED HURRIEDLY BY THE 383 MARCOM
TREMBLING NICOLO AND MAFFEO.
THEN JUST AT THE RIGHT MOMENT, PRECEDED BY A 390 MARCOM
CONSCIOUS COUGH,
AND DANCE THEIR PATTERN OUT BACKWARD, PRECEDED BY 437 MARCOM
THE MUSICIANS.
WHAT OF THE YEARS THAT PRECEDE0$ 455 WELDED

PRECEDENT
THE PRECEDENT WILL BE IRREVOCABLY SET. 8 MANSNS

PRECEDES
(SHE PRECEDES HIM INTO THE CABIN, 30 ANNA
THE TIME OF THE OPENING OF THIS ACT PRECEDES BY A 93 ELECTR
FEW MOMENTS THAT OF THE END OF

PRECEDING
WHICH HAS RECEDED A BIT FROM THE EXTREME OF 186 AHWILD
PRECEDING YEARS, BUT STILL RUNS TO
AS IF IT HAD BEEN ALLOWED TO REMAIN FALLOW THE 166 BEYOND
PRECEDING SUMMER.
THE STUDY IS SHOWN AS IN PRECEDING SCENE. 553 DAYS
IT IS A FEW MINUTES AFTER THE CLOSE OF THE 564 DAYS
PRECEDING SCENE.
(THE CLAP OF THUNDER FROM THE PRECEDING FLASH 441 DYNAMO
COMES WITH A GREAT RUMBLE.)
IN THIS DARKNESS THE CLAP OF THUNDER FROM THE 443 DYNAMO
PRECEDING FLASH COMES.
THE ROLL OF THE THUNDER FROM THE PRECEDING FLASH 446 DYNAMO
COMES CRASHING AND RUMBLING.
THEIR MOVEMENTS, LIKE THOSE OF JEFF IN THE 194 EJONES
PRECEDING SCENE.
THE OPENING OF THIS SCENE FOLLOWS IMMEDIATELY THE 79 ELECTR
CLOSE OF THE PRECEDING ONE.
AS AT THE CLOSE OF THE PRECEDING ACT.) 80 ELECTR
THE HAUNTED EXTERIOR OF THE MANNON HOUSE AS IN 129 ELECTR
THE TWO PRECEDING PLAYS
NO TIME HAS ELAPSED SINCE THE PRECEDING ACT. 157 ELECTR
AND HE LOOKS AS HE APPEARED AT THE CLOSE OF THE 125 JOURNE
PRECEDING ACT, A SAD,
IN THE SAME PERIOD AND TYPE AS IN THE PRECEDING 306 LAZARU
SCENE, EXCEPT THAT
THE FOLLOWERS ARE COSTUMED AND MASKED AS IN THE 306 LAZARU
PRECEDING SCENE.
AND THIS ACT FOLLOWS THE PRECEDING WITHOUT ANY 111 MISBEG
LAPSE OF TIME.
BUT, AS IN THE TWO PRECEDING ACTS, THE MIRROR 116 POET
ATTRACTS HIM.
THE ARRANGEMENT OF THE FURNITURE FOLLOWS THE SAME 90 STRANG
PATTERN AS IN PRECEDING
NINA LOOKS MUCH OLDER THAN IN THE PRECEDING ACT. 189 STRANG

PRECEPTS
FOR HOW COULD I FORGET THE PRE--PRECEPTS TAUGHT ME232 AHWILD
AT MOTHER'S DYING KNEE.

PRECIOUS

PRECIOUS
BUT HOW FOOLISH OF US TO WASTE PRECIOUS MOMENTS 5 MANSNS
(MOCKINGLY) A PRECIOUS JEWEL. 368 MARCOM
LET POUR FROM THEM A PERFECT STREAM OF PRECIOUS 429 MACOM
STONES

PRECIPITATE
HIM THAT SUCH A PRECIPITATE MARRIAGE WOULD BE 10 STRANG
UNFAIR TO NINA,

PRECISE
HE ANSWERS IN A PRECISE, COMPLETELY LIFELESS 707 ICEMAN
VOICE.

PRECISELY
WHAT IS IT PRECISELY THAT SAM'S WIFE HAS THOUGHT 85 STRANG
SO MUCH OF DOINGS

PRECISION
PLACED WITH PRECISION IN FRONT OF THE TWO DOORS 519 DIFRNT
AND UNDER THE TABLE.
THE FURNITURE IS STATIONED ABOUT WITH EXACT 79 ELECTR
PRECISION.
MOVES WITH MECHANICAL PRECISION ACROSS THE WHARF, 400 MARCOM
DISAPPEARS INTO THE JUNK.

PREDESTINED
THE GARBAGE MEN HAVE GONE THEIR PREDESTINED WAY. 19 HUGHIE

PREDICAMENT
(GETTING JAUNTILY DRUNK) PICTURE MY PREDICAMENT 723 ICEMAN
IF I HAD GONE TO THE CONSULATE.

PREDICT
FATE IS IN STORE FOR US, VINNIE--BUT I HAVEN'T 153 ELECTR
DARED PREDICT THAT--NOT YET--
THAT'S THE EVIL DESTINY OUT OF THE PAST I HAVEN'T 155 ELECTR
DARED PREDICT/
BUT HE WILL BE THE NEXT PRESIDENT, I PREDICT, 37 POET

PREDICTED
THEY PREDICTED A WONDERFUL FUTURE FOR HIM 110 JOURNE
HE PREDICTED YOU'D BE BACK ANY MOMENT, SO HE WENT 483 WELDED
RIGHT HOME AGAIN.

PREDOMINANT
EACH TYPE HAS A DISTINCT PREDOMINANT COLOR FOR ITS274 LAZARU
CUSTUMES

PREENING
PREENING HIMSELF, BUT YOU CAN BLAME THE BAD LIGHT 44 POET
IN MY ROOM.
(PREENING HIMSELF.) I FLATTER MYSELF I DO NOT 89 POET
LOOK TOO UNWORTHY

PREFER
(WITH GREAT DIGNITY) BUT I PREFER THE SHELLS. 231 AHWILD
ALL FAMOUS EPICURES PREFER THE SHELLS--TO THE LESS231 AHWILD
(DELICATE, COARSER MEAT.
(COOLLY) I WOULD PREFER NOT TO DISCUSS THIS UNTIL 50 ELECTR
WE ARE ALONE, EZRA--
I PREFER THE DARK. 59 ELECTR
I PREFER TO BE THE SECRET POWER BEHIND THE 13 MANSNS
THRONE--
DO YOU IMAGINE I'D PREFER TO HAVE YOU AT EACH 76 MANSNS
OTHER'S THROATS?
OR WOULD YOU PREFER I SHOULD GO INSANE--AND SO BE 182 MANSNS
RIC OF ME AGAINS
THEY WHAT MAN OF HONORABLE MIND WOULD NOT PREFER 185 MANSNS
TO BE CONSIDERED LUNATIC?
I'D PREFER GOLD, IF YOU DON'T MIND. 396 MARCOM
I PREFER MONKEYS BECAUSE THEY ARE SO MUCH LESS 403 MARCOM
NOISY.
AFTER ALL, HE IS MY SON AND I'D PREFER HE DIDN'T 144 STRANG
SMASH IT BEFORE MY EYES/

PREFERENCE
HE IS BY NATURE AND PREFERENCE A SIMPLE 13 JOURNE
UNPRETENTIOUS MAN,

PREFERRED
SHE SOON FOUND I MUCH PREFERRED DRINKING ALL NIGHT708 ICEMAN
WITH MY PALS
BUT, OF COURSE, I MUCH PREFERRED THE NEAREST PUB. 708 ICEMAN
YOU'VE ALWAYS PREFERRED THE CLUB OR A BARROOM, 72 JOURNE
YES, UNE WOULD THINK HE PREFERRED US TO BE JEALOUS 67 MANSNS
ENEMIES--
WHO PREFERRED DEATH TO DEFEAT. 395 MARCOM
I PREFERRED HIM THE OLD WAY. 113 STRANG

PREGNANCY
IN SPITE OF IT, HER PREGNANCY, NOW SIX MONTHS 2 MANSNS
ALONG, IS APPARENT.
SHE IS MUCH BETTER LOOKING THAN SHE HAD BEEN IN 44 MANSNS
HER PREGNANCY.
DISCUSS NINA'S PREGNANCY, I SUPPOSE... 53 STRANG

PREGNANT
AND NOW I AM LONELY AND NOT PREGNANT WITH ANYTHING 19 STRANG
AT ALL, BUT--BUT LOATHING/
PREGNANT... 52 STRANG
STRAIN OF WAITING AND HOPING SHE'D GET PREGNANT... 68 STRANG
(HE'LL BE HAPPY UNTIL HE BEGINS TO FEEL GUILTY 72 STRANG
AGAIN BECAUSE I'M NOT PREGNANT.
SHE IS AGAIN THE PREGNANT WOMAN OF ACT THREE BUT 90 STRANG
THIS TIME THERE IS A TRIUMPHANT
WHY DOESN'T SHE TELL HIM SHE'S PREGNANTS... 96 STRANG
I AM PREGNANT WITH THE THREE/... 135 STRANG

PREHISTORIC
YOU SHOULD HAVE HIM PUT IN THE MUSEUM AMONG THE 117 STRANG
PREHISTORIC MAMMALS/....

PREJUDICE
FORGETTING PREJUDICE, YOU MUST ADMIT SHE HAS BEEN 39 MANSNS
AN ESTIMABLE WIFE AND MOTHER.
WITHOUT PREJUDICE, TRYING TO BE FAIR TO YOU AND 113 POET
MAKE EVERY POSSIBLE ALLOWANCE--

PREJUDICED
THEIR EVIDENCE IS PREJUDICED. 397 MARCOM
SHE'S PREJUDICED, BEING IN LOVE. 52 MISBEG
I AM AFRAID I MAY BE PREJUDICED. 114 POET

PREJUDICES
THE EVIL REPUTATION OF RECENT FAILURE PREJUDICES 152 MANSNS
THEM AGAINST YOU.

PRELIMINARY
THEN WITH A PRELIMINARY, SUMMONING STAMP OF HIS 200 EJONES
FOOT ON THE EARTH.
(HE BEGINS THE PRELIMINARY QUAVERS ON HIS PIPES.) 101 POET

PREMATURE
(JEERINGLY) I'M AFRAID YOUR REJCICING IS A BIT 545 DAYS
PREMATURE--
THE SIGNS OF PREMATURE DISINTEGRATION ARE ON HIM. 19 JOURNE

PREMATURELY
HE IS ABOUT FORTY, STOUT, WITH A PREMATURELY BALD 496 DAYS
HEAD, A ROUND FACE.
DION IS NOW PREMATURELY GRAY. 284 GGBROW
THIS MASK ACCENTUATES HIS BULGING, PREMATURELY 299 LAZARU
WRINKLED FOREHEAD.
HIS VOICE IS DRY--PREMATURELY OLD. 26 MANSNS
WHERE SHE HAD SEEMED A PREMATURELY OLD, MIDDLE- 95 MANSNS
AGED WOMAN THEN,

PREMISES
THAT THE NIGHT CLERK'S MIND HAS LEFT THE PREMISES 22 HUGHIE
IN HIS SOLE CUSTODY.)
SO WOULD MARKER KINDLY REMOVE HIS DIRTY FEET FROM 25 JOURNE
THE PREMISES
YOU'D TELL HIM YOU'D VACATE THE PREMISES 25 MISBEG

PREMONITION
SPEAKS WITH SOMBER PREMONITION AS ANNA RE-ENTERS 78 ANNA
FROM THE LEFT)
THE TWO, SUDDENLY STRUCK BY THE SAME PREMONITION, 128 BEYOND
LISTEN TO IT BREATHLESSLY.
HE TOLD THEM HE HAD A PREMONITION HE WOULD DIE 117 JOURNE
SOON.
(FAIRLY) WHEN I SAID GOOD-BYE THAT NIGHT I HAD A 27 STRANG
PREMONITION I'D NEVER SEE HIM

PREMONITIONS
BURKE BANISHES HIS SUPERSTITIOUS PREMONITIONS WITH 78 ANNA
A DEFIANT JERK OF HIS HEAD.
(HER MIND IS FILLED WITH PREMONITIONS BY THE FIRST137 BEYOND
PART OF HIS STATEMENT)
MYSTIC PREMONITIONS OF LIFE'S BEAUTY. 198 STRANG

PREEMPTORIALLY
MRS. MILLER GOES TO THE ENTRANCE TO THE BACK 221 AHWILD
PARLOR AND CALLS PREEMPTORIALLY)

PREOCCUPATION
SEIZING ON THE OPPORTUNITY TO PLAY UP HIS 193 AHWILD
PREOCCUPATION--WITH APOLOGETIC
(SINKS BACK INTO PREOCCUPATION--SCANNING THE 250 AHWILD
PAPER--VAGUELY)
(PULLED OUT OF HER PREOCCUPATION) 250 AHWILD
MILLER'S FACE HAS ALSO LOST ITS LOOK OF HARASSED 288 AHWILD
PREOCCUPATIONS
(LOOKING OUT INTO THE NIGHT--LOST IN HIS SOMBER 78 ANNA
PREOCCUPATION--
HE COMES FORWARD, HIS EYES FIXED WITH A STRANGE 144 ELECTR
PREOCCUPATION.
AN UNDERCURRENT OF NERVOUS IRRITATION AND 629 ICEMAN
PREOCCUPATION.)
(BREAKS IN WITH HIS OWN PREOCCUPATION) 636 ICEMAN
(SPEAKS UP FROM HIS OWN PREOCCUPATION--STRANGELY) 668 ICEMAN
LARRY IS DEEP IN HIS OWN BITTER PREOCCUPATION AND 670 ICEMAN
HASN'T LISTENED TO HIM.
A BACKGROUND WHICH DOES NOT TOUCH HER 171 JOURNE
PREOCCUPATION.
(BUT IT CANNOT PENETRATE HER PREOCCUPATION. 172 JOURNE
WHAT A PREOCCUPATION FOR A NAPOLEON OF FACTS/ 111 MANSNS
HE SEEMS TO BE LAPSING AGAIN INTO VAGUE 115 MISBEG
PREOCCUPATION.)
(ANSWERS VAGUELY FROM HER PREOCCUPATION WITH THE 146 POET
POLICE--
(ABRUPTLY COMES OUT OF HER PREOCCUPATION, STARTLED148 POET
AND UNEASY.)
(SEEING HER PREOCCUPATION NOW--DEEPLY HURT-- 54 STRANG
TESTILY)

PREOCCUPIED
HER MIND IS PREOCCUPIED 249 AHWILD
BUT HIS MIND IS PLAINLY PREOCCUPIED AND WORRIED, 249 AHWILD
ONLY MRS. MILLER REMAINS DOLEFULLY PREOCCUPIED, AS259 AHWILD
IF SHE HADN'T HEARD.)
(PREOCCUPIED) LARRY BRING HIM. 8 ANNA
(MOODILY PREOCCUPIED WITH HIS OWN THOUGHTS-- 78 ANNA
STARING AT THE CARPET, PREOCCUPIED AND FROWNING. 96 BEYOND
HIS MIND IS PREOCCUPIED, HIS EXPRESSION SAD AND 545 DAYS
TROUBLED.
(PREOCCUPIED WITH HIS OWN THOUGHTS--GOING TO THE 501 DIFRNT
DOOR IN REAR)
(PREOCCUPIED WITH HER OWN THOUGHTS) 458 DYNAMO
WHEN HE SPEAKS IT IS JERKILY, WITH A STRANGE, 74 ELECTR
VAGUE, PREOCCUPIED AIR.
(ALREADY PREOCCUPIED WITH ANOTHER THOUGHT--COMES 270 GGBROW
AND SITS IN CHAIR ON LEFT)
(PREOCCUPIED.) YEAH, SURE, WHEN I GOT SCRATCH TO 34 HUGHIE
PUT UP.
(PREOCCUPIED WITH HIS OWN THOUGHTS) EHS SURE. 600 ICEMAN
BUT ARE TOO PREOCCUPIED WITH DRINKS TO PAY MUCH 726 ICEMAN
ATTENTION.)
SHARE IS TOO PREOCCUPIED TO NOTICE.) 170 JOURNE
AS HE COMES INTO THE ROOM, HE IS FROWNING, HIS 43 MANSNS
EYES PREOCCUPIED.
I'VE BEEN TOO PREOCCUPIED WITH THE COMPANY'S 85 MANSNS
AFFAIRS.
I WAS PREOCCUPIED WITH MY THOUGHTS. 121 MANSNS
(PREOCCUPIED--UNEASILY.) DON'T COUNT YOUR 31 POET
CHICKENS BEFORE THEY'RE HATCHED.
(WHO HAS BEEN WATCHING THE DOOR AT LEFT FRONT, 87 POET
PREOCCUPIED BY HER OWN WORRY--
(PREOCCUPIED WITH HER OWN THOUGHTS.) 181 POET
TOO PREOCCUPIED WITH HER RESOLVE TO REMEMBER OR 13 STRANG
SEE MARSDEN.
IN HER COOL, PREOCCUPIED VOICE) 13 STRANG
THE LATTER'S MANNER IS PREOCCUPIED AND NERVOUS. 73 STRANG

1241

PRESENT

PREOCCUPIED (CONT'D.)
(SHE IS LOOKING DOWN, PREOCCUPIED WITH HER OWN THOUGHTS. 467 WELDED
WITH AN UNNATURAL PREOCCUPIED CONCENTRATION.) 471 WELDED
PREOCCUPIEDLY
(PREOCCUPIEDLY) SURE I WILL. 469 DYNAMI
HE COMES TO THE TABLE AND STANDS STARING DOWN AT 43 MANSNS
IT PREOCCUPIEDLY.
HIS EYES CEASE READING AND STARE AT THE BOOK 119 MANSNS
PREOCCUPIEDLY.)
(THEN TO CHU-YIN--PREOCCUPIEDLY) 386 MARCOM
PREP
HE IS DRESSED IN PREP SCHOOL REFLECTION OF THE 193 AHWILD
COLLEGE STYLE OF ARTHUR.)
ALL ARE DRESSED IN THE HEIGHT OF CORRECT PREP- 323 GGBROW
SCHOOL ELEGANCE.
EVEN BEFORE THAT WHEN HE WAS IN PREP SCHOOL, 33 JOURNE
YOU NEVER KNEW WHAT WAS REALLY WRONG UNTIL YOU 57 JOURNE
WERE IN PREP SCHOOL.
PREP SCHOOL... 6 STRANG
PREPARATION
SOU'WESTERS, SEA-BOOTS, ETC. IN PREPARATION FOR 481 CARDIF
THE WATCH ON DECK.
REGARD IT AS AN INTERLUDE, OF TRIAL AND 199 STRANG
PREPARATION, SAY.
PREPARATIONS
(BUT I'LL HAVE TO INTERRUPT THEIR BIOLOGICAL 187 STRANG
PREPARATIONS...
PREPARE
=YESTERDAY THIS DAY'S MADNESS DID PREPARE 261 AHWILD
TOMORROW'S SILENCE, TRIUMPH,
(THEN MOODILY) BUT AFTER THREE SCORE AND TEN THE 232 DESIRE
LORD WARNS YE T' PREPARE.
THEY YAWN AND PREPARE TO LIE DOWN.) 374 MARCOM
TO PREPARE YOUR LORDSHIP'S BANQUETS 106 POET
PREPARED
YOU BETTER BE PREPARED FOR A BIT OF A BLOW. 208 AHWILD
YOU'D BETTER BE PREPARED FOR ANY STUPID FOLLY. 498 DAYS
I'M ALL PREPARED T' HAVE YE AGIN ME--AT FUST. 225 DESIRE
(GRUFFLY) IF IT WAS SERIOUS, I'D TELL YOU, SO 49 ELECTR
YOU'D BE PREPARED.
CHRISTINE IS PREPARED AND REMAINS UNMOVED 50 ELECTR
(PREPARED FOR THIS--WITH WELL-FEIGNED 85 ELECTR
ASTONISHMENT)
THE BACK ROOM HAS BEEN PREPARED FOR A FESTIVITY. 628 ICEMAN
(HESITATES--THEN SLOWLY.) I'M GLAD YOU'VE GOT 55 JOURNE
YOUR MIND PREPARED FOR BAD NEWS.
YOUR OLD WICKED WITCHES LIKE ME ALWAYS TO BE 13 MANSNS
PREPARED FOR THE WORST
WHERE MY ONLY CHILD'S HAPPINESS IS AT STAKE, I AM 120 POET
PREPARED TO MAKE EVERY POSSIBL
OBVIOUSLY, I MEAN THE SETTLEMENT I AM PREPARED TO 121 POET
MAKE ON MY DAUGHTER.
MR. HARFORD IS PREPARED TO PAY YOU THE SUM OF 122 POET
THREE THOUSAND DOLLARS--
PREPARING
PREPARING FOR WHAT'S GOING TO HAPPEN. 137 BEYOND
(HE CLOSES HIS EYES AND SETTLES CN HIS CHAIR AS IF610 ICEMAN
PREPARING FOR SLEEP.
PREPATORY
(JUST AS DRISCOLL IS CLEARING HIS THROAT PREPATORY460 CARIBE
TO STARTING THE NEXT VERSE)
PREPOSSESSING
HIS FACE, PREPOSSESSING IN SPITE OF ITS TOO-SMALL, 6 STRANG
OVER-REFINED FEATURES.
PREPOSSESSION
BLOOD-STIRRING CALL TO THAT ULTIMATE ATTAINMENT IN318 LAZARU
WHICH ALL PREPOSSESSION WITH
PREPOSTEROUS
(SHE FORCES A LAUGH) I SUPPOSE ALL THIS SOUNDS 522 DAYS
TOO PREPOSTEROUS.
IT IS PREPOSTEROUS, MOTHER--AN INSULT TO FATHER'S 59 MANSNS
MEMORY/
THE IDEA IS PREPOSTEROUS. 122 POET
PRESCRIBE
IT ISN'T EASY TO PRESCRIBE-- 85 STRANG
PRESCRIBED
SHE'D GIVEN HIM HIS MEDICINE-- IT WAS WHAT I WOULD 70 ELECTR
HAVE PRESCRIBED MYSELF--
HIS FACE IS SET IN THE PRESCRIBED PATTERN OF 9 HUGHIE
GAMBLER'S DEAD PAN.
I PRESCRIBED CHILD FOR THEM... 96 STRANG
PRESCRIBING
IF I WERE SERIOUS SHE WOULDN'T LISTEN, SHE'D SAY I 38 STRANG
WAS PRESCRIBING.
(WITH A SLIGHT SMILE) I'M PRESCRIBING FOR SAM, 38 STRANG
TOO, WHEN I BOOST THIS WEDDING.
ARE YOU PRESCRIBING FOR ME AGAIN, NED$ 41 STRANG
LET US DO THE PRESCRIBING THIS TIME/ 132 STRANG
PRESCRIPTION
GO TO BED AND STAY THERE--THAT'S HIS ONLY 145 BEYOND
PRESCRIPTION.
AS LONG AS HE FILLED THE PRESCRIPTION. 103 JOURNE
WHAT DRUGSTORES WHAT PRESCRIPTIONS 103 JOURNE
THE WAY THE MAN IN THE DRUGSTORE ACTED WHEN I TOOK103 JOURNE
IN THE PRESCRIPTION FOR YOU.
AND SENT HER TO GET MY PRESCRIPTION FILLED. 116 JOURNE
WRITING A PRESCRIPTION... 33 STRANG
GOES TO THE TABLE AND TAKING A PRESCRIPTION PAD 33 STRANG
FROM HIS POCKET.
PRESCRIPTIONS
AND PRESCRIPTIONS FOR MORE/ 86 JOURNE
PRESENCE
(THE FIRST TO REGAIN PRESENCE OF MIND--WITH A 261 AHWILD
GRIN)
IN YOUR PRESENCE IF YOU'RE WILLING. 50 ANNA
(SEEING ROBERT HAS NOT NOTICED HIS PRESENCE--IN A 82 BEYOND
LOUD SHOUT)

PRESENCE (CONT'D.)
THAT HE DOES NOT NOTICE ANDREW'S PRESENCE) 99 BEYOND
AND IN THE PRESENCE OF THE OTHERS TOLD ME THE 560 CROSS
DREAM.
ALTHOUGH AT TIMES ONE OR ANOTHER MAY SUBTLY SENSE 496 DAYS
HIS PRESENCE.
AS IF HE SUDDENLY SENSED A PRESENCE THERE THE 551 DAYS
PRIEST IS PRAYING TO.
AS IF HE WERE TRYING TO SEE SOME PRESENCE HE FEELS558 DAYS
THERE)
JOHN LOVING IS OBLIVIOUS TO HIS PRESENCE.) 566 DAYS
SUDDENLY HE BECOMES CONSCIOUS OF HER PRESENCE AND 225 DESIRE
LOOKS UP.
EDEN SEEMS TO FEEL HER PRESENCE, 228 DESIRE
(TO THE PRESENCE HE FEELS IN THE ROOM) 243 DESIRE
THEN SEES SHE HAS NOT NOTICED THEIR PRESENCE, AND 10 ELECTR
STOPS AND STANDS WAITING.
LAVINIA SENSES HER PRESENCE AND WHIRLS AROUND. 15 ELECTR
(THEN SHE SEES PETER, WHO IS VISIBLY EMBARRASSED 16 ELECTR
BY HER PRESENCE)
CHRISTINE AT ONCE SENSES HER PRESENCE BEHIND HER 71 ELECTR
(IMMEDIATELY SENSES HER PRESENCE--CONTROLLING A 91 ELECTR
START, HARSHLY)
SHE GIVES NO SIGN OF BEING AWARE OF HER DAUGHTER'S122 ELECTR
PRESENCE.
AS IF HE WERE UNAWARE OF THEIR PRESENCE. 144 ELECTR
THEN TO CALL HER ATTENTION TO HIS PRESENCE, 178 ELECTR
(AWKWARD IN HER PRESENCE, SHAKES HER HAND. 274 GGBROW
(STARING AT HER--FASCINATED--WITH GREAT PEACE AS 320 GGBROW
IF HER PRESENCE COMFORTED HIM)
THE PRESENCE OF A KING OF AMERICA. 23 JOURNE
JAMIE HAS BECOME RESTLESS, SENSING HIS FATHER'S 168 JOURNE
PRESENCE.
BUT THE TWO MEN REMAIN UNMINDFUL OF HER PRESENCE. 342 LAZARU
SARA: I WOULD LIKE TO UTTER A WORD OF WARNING--IN 67 MANSNS
MOTHER'S PRESENCE.
SIMON DELIBERATELY IGNORES HIS PRESENCE-- 70 MANSNS
SHE STANDS LOOKING AT SIMON BUT HE IS OBLIVIOUS OF 75 MANSNS
HER PRESENCE.
HE HAD MADE MY BEAUTY GROTESQUELY UGLY BY HIS 122 MANSNS
PRESENCE, BLOATED AND MISSHAPEN--
THIS HATE WAS BECOMING A LIVING PRESENCE IN THE 123 MANSNS
ROOM--AND IN MY MIND--
I STILL FEEL HATRED LIKE A LIVING PRESENCE IN THIS125 MANSNS
ROOM--STRANGE--DRAWING CLOSE--
SHE IS CONSCIOUS OF HIS PRESENCE BUT IGNORES HIM. 140 MANSNS
DISMISS YOUR FOLLOWERS, AND REPAIR TO HIS PRESENCE389 MARCOM
AT ONCE/
I'LL HAVE NO FOUL LANGUAGE IN MY PRESENCE. 59 MISBEG
ARE YOU LAYING PLOTS IN MY PRESENCE TO SEDUCE MY 67 MISBEG
ONLY DAUGHTER$
(SENSING HIS PRESENCE, STOPS CRYING AND LIFTS HER 174 MISBEG
HEAD--DULLY)
I MAY TOLERATE THEIR PRESENCE OUT OF CHARITY, 39 POET
MELODY SENSES HER PRESENCE. 44 POET
HE SUDDENLY FEELS HER PRESENCE AND TURNS HIS HEAD.103 POET
KEEP YOUR THICK WRISTS AND UGLY, PEASANT PAWS OFF 107 POET
THE TABLE IN MY PRESENCE.
BUT NORA SENSES HER PRESENCE AND LOOKS UP.) 136 POET
WHENEVER HE IS IN HER PRESENCE) 69 STRANG
(SUDDENLY FEELING HER PRESENCE, JERKS HIMSELF TO 69 STRANG
HIS FEET--
DARRELL IMMEDIATELY SENSES HER PRESENCE, AND, 79 STRANG
LOOKING UP,
HE DOES NOT SEEM CONSCIOUS OF DARRELL'S PRESENCE 98 STRANG
AT FIRST.
BUT SHE SUDDENLY BECOMES AWARE OF SOME PRESENCE IN444 WELDED
THE ROOM
I FEEL A CRUEL PRESENCE IN YOU PARALYZING ME, 453 WELDED
CREEPING OVER MY BODY,
PRESENT
(SARCASTICALLY) OF COURSE, THERE WON'T BE ANY 191 AHWILD
BOYS PRESENT/
AT PRESENT, HOWEVER, HIS EXPRESSION IS ONE OF 153 BEYOND
TENSE ANXIETY.
REMOVED FROM PRESENT ACTUALITY YOU MAKE YOUR 495 DAYS
ENDING, THE BETTER IT WILL BE.
PROBABLY WANTS MY ADVICE ON WHAT TO GIVE WALTER 498 DAYS
FOR A BIRTHDAY PRESENT.
I'D SPARE HER, FOR THE PRESENT, AT LEAST. 540 DAYS
IT IS THE MONTH OF MAY OF THE PRESENT DAY. ~0 DYNAMI
BUT WE'LL LET THAT PASS FOR THE PRESENT-- 154 ELECTR
FOR THEY REPRESENT AN EVER-PRESENT DAGGER POINTED 243 HA APE
AT THE HEART OF THE GREATEST
NOW THAT HE IS PRESENT, 638 ICEMAN
I GUESS THAT'LL BE ABOUT ALL FROM ME, BOYS AND 661 ICEMAN
GIRLS--FOR THE PRESENT.
THE PAST IS THE PRESENT, ISN'T IT$ IT'S THE 87 JOURNE
FUTURE, TOO.
WHERE PRESENT REALITY IS BUT AN APPEARANCE TO BE 97 JOURNE
ACCEPTED AND DISMISSED
FOR A PRESENT, AND ON THE WAY HOME SHE SPENT IT 148 JOURNE
ALL ON FOOD.
FOR THE PRESENT. 8 MANSNS
AS THE FALSE ARISTOCRACY OF OUR PRESENT SOCIETY 9 MANSNS
PRETENDS TO BE/
HE THOUGHT, AS THEY WOULD HAVE TO SELL THEIR 35 MANSNS
PRESENT HOME AND COME TO THE CITY.
THE OPPORTUNITY THEY PRESENT TO YOU. 39 MANSNS
BECOME THE FOUNDATION OF A NEW MORALITY WHICH 47 MANSNS
WOULD DESTROY ALL OUR PRESENT
THE COMPANY, I BELIEVE, IS AT PRESENT IN NEED OF 55 MANSNS
CASH--
YOU ARE WRONG TO THINK MY PRESENT FEELING IS ONE 61 MANSNS
OF ANTAGONISM.
YOU MUST ALLOW FOR YOUR PRESENT STATE OF MIND-- 74 MANSNS
AND SEE HOW MUCH OF THE OLD GREEDY SARA STILL LIES 74 MANSNS
BEHIND HER PRESENT SELF--

PRESENT

PRESENT (CONT'D.)
SHE CAN SEE QUITE ENOUGH OF THEM WHEN YOU AND I 86 MANSNS
ARE PRESENT.
THE PAST IS THE PRESENT. 99 MANSNS
EXCEPT IN THE HOUSE WHEN EITHER SHE OR I ARE 104 MANSNS
PRESENT TO PROTECT THEM.
YOU WILL RUN NO RISK OF ANYTHING WORSE THAN YOUR 111 MANSNS
PRESENT UNHAPPY EXILE.
ABOUT HIS PRESENT CIRCUMSTANCES. 150 MANSNS
AND I TO THE COURT OF GHAZAN KHAN TO PRESENT THIS 350 MARCOM
LETTER
UNDER YOUR PRESENT SYSTEM, WITH BATTERING RAMS, 394 MARCOM
(WITH RAGE) SHALL I ASK AS MY FIRST WEDDING 416 MARCOM
PRESENT FROM GHAZAN KHAN THAT HE
IT HAS BEEN MOVED TO ITS PRESENT SITE, AND LOOKS 1 MISBEG
IT.
HERE'S A LITTLE PRESENT OVER YOUR FARE. 7 MISBEG
THERE IS NO PRESENT OR FUTURE--ONLY THE PAST 128 MISBEG
HAPPENING OVER AND OVER AGAIN--NOW.
(HE DECIDES IT'S BETTER FOR THE PRESENT TO ASK NO 158 MISBEG
QUESTIONS.
OF COURSE, IT IS A BIT DIFFICULT AT PRESENT. 50 POET
HOPING YOU MIGHT KNOW THE PRESENT WHEREABOUTS OF 72 POET
MY SON, SIMON.
SHE IS SUNK IN MEMORIES OF OLD FEARS AND HER 131 POET
PRESENT WORRY ABOUT THE DUEL.
I'LL START HER ON HER WAY BY MAKING HER A WEDDING 173 POET
PRESENT AT THE MAJOR'S PLACE
AND I GIVE HER THAT AS A PRESENT TO BUY CANDY 588 ROPE
WITH.
A FUGITIVE FROM REALITY CAN VIEW THE PRESENT 3 STRANG
SAFELY FROM A DISTANCE,
WHERE PRACTICAL PRESENT-DAY CONSIDERATIONS ARE 6 STRANG
CONCERNED
BUT IN THE PRESENT STATE OF HER MIND THE REAL AND 11 STRANG
THE UNREAL BECOME CONFUSED--
BUT THERE IS ALSO AN EXPRESSION OF PRESENT 111 STRANG
CONTENTMENT AND CALM.
IT'S GOOD FOR HIM HE DIDN'T BRING ME ANY BIRTHDAY 138 STRANG
PRESENT
(INDIFFERENT AND CYNICAL) BUT YOU MEANT MY 140 STRANG
PRESENT DABBLING ABOUT.
(WITH BITTER SADNESS) I DID BRING HIM A PRESENT. 144 STRANG
YOU NEVER EVEN BROUGHT HIM A PRESENT. 144 STRANG
AS HE'S SMASHED EVERY PRESENT OF MINE IN THE PAST!144 STRANG
IS THIS--YOUR PRESENTS 150 STRANG
HIS PRESENT GRIEF, HOWEVER, IS MORE RESIGNED TO 159 STRANG
ITS FATE THAN THE OLD.
THE PRESENT IS AN INTERLUDE... 165 STRANG
OF COURSE, I REALIZE YOU'VE GOT A HUSBAND AT 175 STRANG
PRESENT BUT, NEVER MIND,

PRESENTABLE
I MEAN THEY HAVE DECENT, PRESENTABLE HOMES THEY 44 JOURNE
DON'T HAVE TO BE ASHAMED OF.
AND WENT TO THE HOTEL TO MAKE OURSELVES 51 MANSNS
PRESENTABLE.

PRESENTLY
(BUT THE DISH OF OLIVES SEEMS TO FASCINATE HIM AND217 AHWILD
PRESENTLY HE HAS APPROACHED
PRESENTLY SHE CASTS A CURIOUS GLANCE AT HER 129 BEYOND
FATHER, AND,
I'LL RETURN PRESENTLY. 562 CROSS
I'LL JOIN YOU PRESENTLY. 104 POET

PRESENTS
HER VOICE PRESENTS THE GREATEST CONTRAST TO HER 187 AHWILD
APPEARANCE--
(EXCITEDLY) WHAT DO I CARE ABOUT YOUR OLD 282 AHWILD
PRESENTS!
STANDS ON THE TABLE, PRESENTS AN APPEARANCE OF 144 BEYOND
DECAY, OF DISSOLUTION.
MARGIE AND PEARL ARE ARRANGING THE CAKE AND 629 ICEMAN
PRESENTS, AND ROCKY STANDS BY THEM.
AND MY PRESENTS, AND YOURS, GIRLS, AND CHUCK'S, 643 ICEMAN
AND ROCKY'S.
AND TURNS HIM TO FACE THE TABLE WITH THE CAKE AND 659 ICEMAN
PRESENTS)
JEES, HE AIN'T EVEN GOIN' TO LOOK AT OUR PRESENTS.656 ICEMAN
YUH AIN'T SEEN DE PRESENTS FROM MARGIE AND ME AND 656 ICEMAN
CORA AND CHUCK AND ROCKY.
HE KNEELS, PRESENTS THE BASKET TO MARCO, 391 MAHCOM
(HE JERKS THE LOCKET OUT OF AN UNDER POCKET AND 416 MARCOM
PRESENTS IT TO HER PROUDLY)
IN HIS BRILLIANT UNIFORM HE PRESENTS MORE THAN 95 POET
EVER AN IMPRESSIVELY COLORFUL
HOW'D YOU LIKE YOUR PRESENTS! 153 STRANG

PRESERVATION
IN SELF-PRESERVATION THE DEVIL MUST BELIEVE/ 297 GGB4OW

PRESERVE
GOD BLESS YOU--AND PRESERVE YOUR HAPPINESS! 524 DAYS
DE LAWD'LL PRESERVE ME FROM DEM HA'NTS AFTER DIS. 196 EJONES
STILL, HE MANAGES TO PRESERVE AN ATMOSPHERE OF 575 ICEMAN
WATTINESS
THAT OUR SILK-MAKERS MAY PRESERVE THEIR SHARE OF 422 MARCOM
THE ETERNAL SUNLIGHT/
(FRIGHTENEDLY.) GOD PRESERVE US, IT'S CRAZED HE 157 POET
IS!

PRESERVED
AND THE ROOM IS REVEALED IN ALL ITS PRESERVED 241 DESIRE
UGLINESS.
IT IS TRUE, I AM WELL PRESERVED. 5 MANSNS
MIDDLE-AGED MATRON, BUT I FLATTER MYSELF I HAVE 86 POET
PRESERVED A PHILOSOPHIC POISE.
THE UNIFORM HAS BEEN PRESERVED WITH THE GREATEST 88 POET
CARE.

PRESERVES
ONLY THE OLD BIBLE, WHICH STILL PRESERVES ITS 519 DIFRNT
PLACE OF HONOR ON THE TABLE,

PRESERVES (CONT'D.)
I SHALL OFFER HER THE FRUIT CAESAR PRESERVES FOR 342 LAZARU
THOSE HE FEARS.
HER BODY WAS ANOINTED BY EGYPTIANS SO THAT SHE 351 MARCOM
PRESERVES THE APPEARANCE OF LIFE.

PRESERVING
(RICHARD, PRESERVING THE POSE OF THE BITTER, 221 AHWILD
DISILLUSIONED PESSIMIST,
(STARTLED TO ALERTNESS, BUT PRESERVING THE SAME 182 EJONES
CARELESS TONE)

PRESIDENT
THEY'RE RUNNING ME FOR PRESIDENT OF THE W.C.T.U. 190 AHWILD
AND THIS TIME IS DROWNIN' MY SORROW FOR THE 44 ELECTR
PRESIDENT GITTIN' SHOT/
PRESIDENT BROWN/ 313 GGBROW
SO I HAD TO TELL THEM THAT MY FATHER, THE 220 HA APE
PRESIDENT OF NAZARETH STEEL,
THAT'S THE PRESIDENT OF THE STEEL TRUST, I BET. 242 HA APE
SURE--HERE--HER OLD MAN--PRESIDENT UF DE STEEL 244 HA APE
TRUST--
PRESIDENT OF THE STEEL TRUST, YOU MEANS 249 HA APE
BEEN ELECTED PRESIDENT OF THE M. C. T. U. 620 ICEMAN
YOUR FATHER IS MUCH TOO WORRIED ABOUT WHAT 10 MANSNS
PRESIDENT JACKSON WILL DO OR SAY
HAS PRESIDENT JACKSON'S FEUD WITH THE BANK OF THE 29 MANSNS
UNITED STATES
BUT HE WILL BE THE NEXT PRESIDENT, I PREDICT, 37 POET
WHERE'S TO OUR NEXT PRESIDENT, ANDY JACKSON/ 180 PUET
THE PRESIDENT WILL SPEAK AT THE FUNERAL... 23 STRANG

PRESIDENT'S
THE PRESIDENT'S ASSASSINATION IS A FRIGHTFUL 48 ELECTR
CALAMITY.

PRESS
DON'T PRESS AGAINST ME, I TELL YOU/ 484 DYNAMO
WHILE HIS SISTERS AND FATHER KISS AND PRESS HIS 278 LAZARU
HANDS.
THINKING OF ME, SCRIBBLING IN PRESS BUREAU... 14 STRANG

PRESSED
AND LISTENS WITH HIS EAR PRESSED TO THE CRACK. 536 'ILE
NEVER FEEL YE PRESSED AGIN ME AGEN--AN' YE SAID YE261 DESIRE
HATED ME FUR HAVIN' HIM--
(KEEPING THE HAND WITH THE POISON PRESSED AGAINST 63 ELECTR
HER BACK)
HER ARMS HELD STIFFLY TO HER SIDES, HER LEGS AND 170 ELECTR
FEET PRESSED TOGETHER,
(HE SUBSIDES WEAKLY ON HIS CHAIR, HIS HAND PRESSED287 GGBROW
TO HIS HEART.)
THEN SINKS DOWN IN HIS CHAIR, GASPING, HIS HANDS 297 GGBROW
PRESSED TO HIS HEART.)
I MUST HAVE THIS SUIT CLEANED AND PRESSED. 600 ICEMAN
TO GET HIS LAUNDRY AND HIS CLOTHES PRESSED SO HE 665 ICEMAN
WOULDN'T HAVE NO EXCUSES
JIMMY'S CLOTHES ARE PRESSED, HIS SHOES SHINED, HIS683 ICEMAN
WHITE LINEN IMMACULATE.
WHO HOLDS ONE OF HIS HANDS IN BOTH OF HERS, AND 274 LAZARU
KEEPS HER LIPS PRESSED TO IT.
HIS FISTS PRESSED TO HIS TEMPLES. 350 LAZARU
AS THE DOOR OPENS, HER BODY, PRESSED AGAINST IT, 27 MANSNS
DONATA'S FACE APPEARS PRESSED AGAINST THE BARS. 355 MARCOM
I AM TEMPORARILY HARD PRESSED. 50 POET
THE BONY FACE OF HIS BULLET HEAD HAS A PRESSED-IN 582 ROPE
APPEARANCE EXCEPT FOR HIS

PRESSES
(HE PRESSES HER TO HIM AND ATTEMPTS TO KISS HER,) 33 ANNA
(HE PRESSES HER CLOSE TO HIM--SLOWLY AND TENDERLY) 91 BEYOND
(HE PRESSES HER TO HIM, STROKING HER HAIR 92 BEYOND
TENDERLY.
(HE PRESSES THE CHILD IN HIS ARMS.) 130 BEYOND
HE PRESSES HIS HAND TO HIS 483 CARDIF
(HE SUDDENLY LAUGHS WILDLY AND PUT HIS ARM AROUND 469 CARIBE
HER WAIST AND PRESSES HER TO
AS SHE COMES IN, SHE PRESSES A BUTTON BY THE DOOR 514 DAYS
CAGOT GETS ONE HAND ON HIS THROAT AND PRESSES HIM 255 DESIRE
BACK ACROSS THE STONE WALL.
(HE PRESSES HIS LIPS TIGHTLY TOGETHER AN EFFORT TO423 DYNAMO
APPEAR IMPLACABLE THAT GIVES
(HE GIVES A SHUDDER AND PRESSES HER TO HIM.) 484 DYNAMO
HE PRESSES HER FIERCELY IN HIS ARMS--PASSIONATELY) 56 ELECTR
SHE PUTS THE PELLET ON HIS TONGUE AND PRESSES THE 62 ELECTR
GLASS OF WATER TO HIS LIPS.)
(PRESSES HER CONVULSIVELY--THEN WITH FORCED 287 GGBROW
HARSHNESS)
OUTSIDE, THE SPELL UF ABNORMAL QUIET PRESSES 31 HUGHIE
SUFFOCATINGLY UPON THE STREET,
(HE PRESSES A BUTTON AT REAR WHICH SWITCHES OFF 610 ICEMAN
THE LIGHTS.
HE PRESSES HIS HAND OVER HIS MOUTH CONVULSIVELY.) 286 LAZARU
(HE PRESSES HER CLOSER TO HIM) 361 LAZARU
(SHE PRESSES BOTH HANDS TO HER TEMPLES.) 30 MANSNS
(SHE GRASPS HIS HAND AND PRESSES IT--TENDERLY 45 MANSNS
POSSESSIVE.)
(HE PRESSES HER TO HIM PASSIONATELY.) 87 MANSNS
(PRESSES HER HAND AND KEEPS IT IN HERS.) 124 MANSNS
HIS EXPRESSION CHANGES AND HE PRESSES HER BODY TO 145 MANSNS
HIS
AND MY CHILDREN-- (SHE PRESSES AGAINST HIM.) AND 157 MANSNS
BEST OF ALL, FOR MY LOVER.
(SHE SUDDENLY STOPS AND PRESSES HER HANDS TO HER 163 MANSNS
HEAD TORTUREDLY.)
PULLS OUT A LITTLE ROLL OF ONE-DOLLAR BILLS AND 7 MISBEG
PRESSES IT IN HIS HAND)
AND PRESSES HIS BODY TO HERS) 137 MISBEG
(HE MOANS IN HIS SLEEP AND PRESSES MORE CLOSELY 165 MISBEG
AGAINST HER.
(MARY PRESSES THE DOLLAR TO HER BREAST 588 ROPE
(SHE PRESSES MRS. EVANS' HAND--SIMPLY) YES, 57 STRANG
MOTHER.

PRETENDING

PRESSES (CONT'D.)
(PRESSES HIS HEAD ON HER BREAST, AVOIDING HIS 70 STRANG EYES; KISSES HIM ON THE FOREHEAD)
(PRESSES HIS HEAD DOWN ON HER BREAST SO HE CANNOT 71 STRANG SEE HER EYES--GENTLY)
(SHE TAKES HIS HEAD AND PRESSES IT TO HER BREAST 109 STRANG AND BEGINS TO WEEP.
HE PRESSES HIS HANDS TO HIS FOREHEAD) 472 WELDED

PRESSING
(PRESSING ONE OF HER HANDS IN BOTH OF HIS) 22 ANNA
(SHE KISSES HIS HEAD, PRESSING IT TO HER WITH A 266 DESIRE FIERCE PASSION OF POSSESSION.)
(REASSURED--PRESSING ONE OF HIS HANDS GRATEFULLY) 537 DIFRNT
PRESSING CLOSE TO HIM AS IF SHE WERE AFRAID OF HIS468 DYNAMO
LEAVING HER.
(PRESSING HER HAND IN BOTH OF HIS--INTENSELY) 86 ELECTR
(IN AN OUTBURST OF GRATEFUL JOY--PRESSING HIM TO 89 ELECTR HER AND KISSING HIM)
(PRESSING HER HAND TO HER OWN HEART--WITH A 358 LAZARU SHUDDER)
PRESSING HIS FACE AGAINST HER BREAST AS IF FOR 161 MISBEG PROTECTION.
THEY NEED PRESSING AND LOOK TOO BIG FOR HIM.) 67 STRANG
(INTENSELY, PRESSING HER HAND) 127 STRANG
(TURNS TO NERO, GRATEFULLY TAKING HIS HAND AND 196 STRANG PRESSING IT)
(IMPULSIVELY PRESSING HIS HAND) 447 WELDED
(MOVED--PRESSING HER HANDS) ALL RIGHT. 456 WELDED

PRESSURE
FULL PRESSURE/ 245 HA APE
AND PUTS UNRELIEVED PRESSURE ON HIMSELF. 43 MANSNS
IT'S BAD FOR YOUR HIGH BLOOD PRESSURE. 163 STRANG
SAM DOES LOOK AS IF HE MIGHT HAVE A BAD 163 STRANG PRESSURE...
HE LOOKS AS THOUGH HIS BLOOD PRESSURE MIGHT BE 170 STRANG HIGHER THAN IT OUGHT TO BE.

PRESTIGE
I HAVE NEVER NEEDED THAT PRESTIGE. 59 MANSNS
FATHER, IN HIS BLIND VANITY, OVER-ESTIMATED THE 59 MANSNS PRESTIGE OF HIS NAME.

PRESUME
(HARSHLY) YOU PRESUME, JEWESS/ 329 LAZARU
BECAUSE I LOVE YOU, DO YOU PRESUME-- 359 LAZARU
(WITH ARROGANT DISDAIN.) DO YOU PRESUME TO THINK 21 MANSNS
I PRESUME YOU WONDER WHY I WISHED TO SEE YOU, MR. 151 MANSNS TENARD.
DO NOT PRESUME TO TOUCH ME/ 193 MANSNS
IF I MAY PRESUME. 68 POET
(CURTLY IGNORING THIS.) I PRESUME YOU ARE THE 90 POET INNKEEPER, MELODY$
FOR THOSE WHO CAN PRESUME THEY KNOW WHAT THEIR 86 POET DUTY TO OTHERS IS.
YOU AND TO HIMSELF--AND I PRESUME SHE ALSO MEANT 109 POET TO BOTH FAMILIES CONCERNED--

PRESUMING
(ARROGANTLY THREATENING.) ARE YOU PRESUMING TO 99 POET QUESTION MY CONDUCT

PRESUMPTUOUS
I HAVE FORGOTTEN MY OLD SILLY PRESUMPTUOUS 61 MANSNS COWARDLY DISDAIN

PRETENCE
(WITH A GREAT PRETENCE OF GRIEF, TAKING ONE OF HER531 DIFRNT HANDS IN HIS)

PRETENCES
I AM ALIVE TO LIFE AS IT IS BEHIND OUR 179 MANSNS HYPOCRITICAL PRETENCES

PRETEND
DON'T PRETEND TO NOTICE, EH$ 223 AHWILD
LILY FORGETS TO PRETEND TO READ HER BOOK BUT LOOKS257 AHWILD OVER IT.
AND YOU PRETEND TO BE IN LOVE/ 273 AHWILD
I HAD TO PRETEND, SO I'D GET A CHANCE TO SEE YOU. 286 AHWILD
WELL, I'LL LEAVE YOU TWO ALONE AND PRETEND TO BE 500 DAYS BUSY.
NOW, DON'T PRETEND. 529 DAYS
(WORRIEDLY, BUT TRYING TO PRETEND TO TREAT IT 550 DAYS LIGHTLY, REASSURINGLY)
I DON'T WANT T' PRETEND PLAYIN' MAW T' YE, EBEN. 225 DESIRE
DON'T PRETEND YOU DON'T 542 DIFRNT
AND I HAD TO SLINK BY AND PRETEND NOT TO HEAR/. 423 DYNAMO
(GRINNING) I WON'T PRETEND I'M THE SORT OF HERO 13 ELECTR THAT WANTS TO GO BACK, EITHER/.
DON'T YOU DARE PRETEND--/ 63 ELECTR
I WON'T PRETEND TO YOU I'M SORRY HE'S DEAD/ 86 ELECTR
YOU PRETEND TO LOVE ME/ 88 ELECTR
PRETEND YOU THINK I'M OUT OF MY MIND, AS SHE 100 ELECTR WANTED YOU TO.
WHY MUST I PRETEND TO SCORN IN ORDER TO PITY$ 264 GGBROW
WHAT MAKES YOU PRETEND YOU THINK LOVE IS SO 285 GGBROW IMPORTANT, ANYWAYS
I'D WISE THEM UP TO KID HIM ALONG AND PRETEND 16 HUGHIE THEY'D FELL FOR HIM.
WE'D PRETEND A CENT WAS A BUCK, AND A NICKEL WAS A 21 HUGHIE FIN AND SO ON.
WAITING FOR ANY EXCUSE TO SHY AND PRETEND TO TAKE 576 ICEMAN THE BIT IN ITS TEETH.
YOU PRETEND A BITTER, CYNIC PHILOSOPHY, 600 ICEMAN
WE'LL PRETEND TO LET HIM KID US, SEE$ 618 ICEMAN
YOU PRETEND TO BE SUCH A FOOL, LARRY. 636 ICEMAN
SHE WOULDN'T BELIEVE THE GOSSIP--OR SHE'D PRETEND 710 ICEMAN SHE DIDN'T.
JEES, ALL DE BUSY JOKES I'VE HAD TO LISTEN TO AND712 ICEMAN PRETEND WAS FUNNY/
OF COURSE, I'D PRETEND I WAS KIDDING-- 714 ICEMAN
WE DON'T PRETEND, AT ANY RATE. 77 JOURNE
HE'LL PRETEND HE'S FOUND SOMETHING SERIOUS THE 92 JOURNE MATTER

PRETEND (CONT'D.)
PRETEND NOT TO NOTICE AND SHE'LL SOON GO UP AGAIN.139 JOURNE
ALTHOUGH I CANNOT PRETEND TO VIRTUE IN MYSELF 332 LAZARU
SURE, WHAT MAN DOESN'T COMPLAIN OF HIS WORK, AND 20 MANSNS PRETEND HE'S A SLAVE$
I TALK AS IF I WERE PLANNING TO PRETEND AND PLAY A 39 MANSNS PART/
SHE KNEW FATHER WOULDN'T HAVE WISHED ME TO COME 45 MANSNS AND PRETEND GRIEF
YOU HAVE MADE YOURSELF PRETEND TO BE- 99 MANSNS
YOU ARE NOT REALLY AS EXERCISED BY THE LOSS OF THE105 MANSNS CHILDREN AS YOU PRETEND.
SHE PRETENDS TO BE JEALOUS OF YOU, JUST AS YOU 159 MANSNS PRETEND--
(SCORNFULLY) I'M TO PRETEND I'M A PURE VIRGIN, I 34 MISBEG SUPPOSE$
PRETEND NOT TO NOTICE HIM. 55 MISBEG
I'LL RAISE A SCENE AND PRETEND I'M IN A RAGE 92 MISBEG BECAUSE HE FORGOT HIS DATE.
PRETEND WE'RE FIGHTING AND I'M DRIVING YOU OFF 99 MISBEG TELL YOU'RE SOBER.
PRETEND YOU'RE AS DRUNK AS WHEN YOU CAME. 99 MISBEG
TO HAVE ME PRETEND I'M AN INNOCENT VIRGIN TONIGHT.114 MISBEG
YOU PRETEND TOO MUCH. 114 MISBEG
I'LL HAVE TO PRETEND I'M-- 135 MISBEG
BUT I'D SPOTTED ONE PASSENGER WHO WAS USED TO 149 MISBEG DRUNKS AND COULD PRETEND TO LIKE
BUT IT'S CRAZY FOR YOU TO PRETEND TO ME. 24 POET
BUT HE'LL NEVER MAKE ME PRETEND TO HIM I DON'T 24 POET KNOW THE TRUTH.
TO PRETEND TO THE WORLD WE BELIEVE THAT LIE. 24 POET
I'LL WAGER YOU WASN'T AS BRAZEN AS YOU PRETEND. 65 POET
I'LL HAVE TO PRETEND I LIKED HER AND I'D RESPECT 88 POET WHATEVER ADVICE SHE GAVE HIM.
SHE WAS NOT AS OUTRAGED BY HALF AS HER CONSCIENCE 90 POET MADE HER PRETEND,
SHE HAD TO PRETEND-- 106 POET
WHILE HE SPOUTED BYRON TO PRETEND HIMSELF WAS A 176 POET LORD WID A TOUCH AV THE POET--
PRETEND I DIDN'T SEE HER/... 145 STRANG
I CAN PRETEND I'M FORCED TO TELL HER... 177 STRANG
YOU'D LIKE TO PRETEND I WAS AS MUCH A DEPENDENT ON458 WELDED JOHN AS YOU WERE/

PRETENDED
I PRETENDED TO BE ASLEEP AND SHE WENT DOWN 280 AHWILD AGAIN.
I PRETENDED TO BE DREADFULLY WORRIED, 39 ELECTR
(WITH A MALICIOUS CHUCKLE) OH, I WASN'T AS BLIND 145 ELECTR AS I PRETENDED TO BE/
(WITH PRETENDED CARELESSNESS) 248 HA APE
I TOLD YOU YOU WEREN'T HALF AS SICK AS YOU 684 ICEMAN PRETENDED.
I PRETENDED TO BE ASLEEP. 38 JOURNE
SO YOU PRETENDED TO BE ASLEEP IN ORDER TO SPY ON 47 JOURNE ME/
(SNEERINGLY) BUT YOUR PRETENDED MESSIAH DID NOT 283 LAZARU SCORN HIM
THE PRETENDED MESSIAH IS DEAD/ 290 LAZARU
FEIGNED CYNICAL AMUSEMENT OR A PRETENDED 337 LAZARU SUPERCILIOUS INDIFFERENCE.
AND YOUR PRETENDED DISGUST WITH IT IS A LIE. 74 MANSNS
AND YOU HE'D PRETENDED TO LIKE SO MUCH. 86 MISBEG
HERE THE CHANCE WAS BEFORE HIM TO MAKE HIMSELF ALL 27 POET HIS LIES PRETENDED TO BE.
I'VE PRETENDED TO BE DONE UP EVERY NIGHT SO THEY 52 STRANG COULD...

PRETENDIN'
AND I AIN'T PRETENDIN' I CAN REG'LATE LOVE FOR 102 BEYOND YOUNG FOLKS.
I'SE GONE OUT IN DAT BIG FOREST, PRETENDIN' TO 183 EJONES HUNT,
AN' DEN HER PRETENDIN'--BUT IT GIVES ME A PAIN TO 614 ICEMAN TALK ABOUT IT.
YEAH, STILL PRETENDIN' HE'S DE ONE EXCEPTION, LIKE635 ICEMAN HICKEY TOLD HIM.
DON'T YOU GET IT IN YOUR HEADS I'S PRETENDIN' TO 637 ICEMAN BE WHAT I AIN'T.
PRETENDIN' HE WAS ASLEEP/ MIND/ 520 INZONE
WHAT'S THE USE PRETENDIN'$ 139 POET
HE'S CRAFTY AT PRETENDIN'. 596 ROPE

PRETENDING
OR PRETENDING TO WRITE ONE. 192 AHWILD
SHE IS PRETENDING TO READ A NOVEL, BUT HER 249 AHWILD ATTENTION WANDERS, TOO.
(PRETENDING AN ASSURANCE HE IS FAR FROM FEELING) 254 AHWILD
(WORRIEDLY IMPRESSED BY THIS THREAT--BUT 271 AHWILD PRETENDING SCORN)
PRETENDING TO BE ASLEEP BY TEN O'CLOCK. 280 AHWILD
PRETENDING TO READ THEM OUT OF DUTY TO RICHARD, 288 AHWILD
(THEN PRETENDING TO FLY INTO A RAGE, HER EYES 11 ANNA ENJOYING CHRIS' MISERY)
THE OTHERS ARE PRETENDING AN INTEREST WHICH IS 94 BEYOND BELIED BY THE ABSENT-MINDED
TIRED OF PRETENDING TO MYSELF I HAVE TO GO ON FOR 519 DAYS THE CHILDREN'S SAKES,
AND I'M TIRED OF PRETENDING I DON'T MIND, TIRED OF519 DAYS REALLY MINDING UNDERNEATH,
(PRETENDING TO BE HURT) NOBODY IN THIS HOUSE KIN 507 DIFRNT TAKE A JOKE.
PRETENDING TO DISMISS THE SUBJECT) 523 DIFRNT
I'LL BEGIN TO THINK YOU'RE ONLY PRETENDING TO LIKE524 DIFRNT ME.
(ALARMED BUT PRETENDING SCORN) 528 DIFRNT
HIS WIFE IS PRETENDING TO READ, BUT HER THOUGHTS 422 DYNAMO ARE ACTIVELY ELSEWHERE.
(PRETENDING TO BE SUNK IN THOUGHT HAS BEEN STARING439 DYNAMO CALCULATINGLY AT REUBEN--
(STUNG BUT PRETENDING INDIFFERENCE--WITH A WINK) 176 EJONES

CARROLL COLLEGE LIBRARY
HELENA, MONTANA 59601

PRETENDING

PRETENDING (CONT'D.)
YOU WERE ONLY PRETENDING LOVE/ 60 ELECTR
PRETENDING TO TRIM THE EDGE OF THE LAWN ALONG THE 169 ELECTR DRIVE.
(PRETENDING TO SEARCH THE GROUND AGAIN) 178 ELECTR
PRETENDING HE'S STILL HERE--AND BROWN'S HELPING 304 GGBROW HIM.
(BEWILDEREDLY, NOT KNOWING HOW MUCH IS PRETENDING,311 GGBROW PUTS AN ARM ABOUT HIM)
(PRETENDING BOREDOM BUT (IRRITATED) 218 HA APE
WHERE THEY'D NEVER LOOK FOR A WOBBLY, PRETENDING 1588 ICEMAN WAS A SPORT.
PRETENDING HE HASN'T HEARD THEM. 650 ICEMAN
HE KNOWS I'M HERE, ALL RIGHT, ALTHOUGH HE'S 700 ICEMAN PRETENDING NOT TO/
I CAN'T HAVE HIM PRETENDING THERE'S SOMETHING IN 706 ICEMAN COMMON BETWEEN HIM AND ME.
BY PRETENDING IT WAS MY WIFE'S ADULTERY THAT 707 ICEMAN RUINED MY LIFE.
PRETENDING YOU BELIEVED WHAT THEY WANTED TO 711 ICEMAN BELIEVE ABOUT THEMSELVES.
LOOK AT ME PRETENDING TO START FOR A WALK JUST TO 721 ICEMAN KEEP HIM QUIET.
PRETENDING YOU BELIEVE THEM, 721 ICEMAN
JAMIE WAS PRETENDING TO BE ASLEEP, TOO, I'M SURE, 47 JOURNE AND I SUPPOSE YOUR FATHER--
UH, I'M SO SICK AND TIRED OF PRETENDING THIS IS A 67 JOURNE HOME/
SHE'S BEEN TERRIBLY FRIGHTENED ABOUT YOUR ILLNESS,139 JOURNE FOR ALL HER PRETENDING.
AND HERE WE SIT PRETENDING TO FORGET. 152 JOURNE
BUT WHAT'S THE USE OF PRETENDING WE HAVE 78 MANSNS EVERYTHING IN COMMON ANY MORE&
(PRETENDING TO GIVE IN.) I MUST ADMIT SHE SEEMS 84 MANSNS SINCERE.
SARA IS PRETENDING TO WORK ON A PIECE OF NEEDLE- 117 MANSNS POINT.
(THINKING.) SHE IS ONLY PRETENDING TO WORK ON HER118 MANSNS NEEDLE-POINT--
(THINKING.) HE ISN'T READING--JUST PRETENDING 119 MANSNS TO--SMILING TO HIMSELF--SLY--
(SMILING GLOATINGLY.) SEE, SARA, HE IS NOT EVEN 126 MANSNS PRETENDING TO READ NOW.
YOU'RE PRETENDING TO LOVE YOUR WOMEN AND CHILDREN 154 MANSNS
FOR THE LOVE OF GOD, DEBORAH, TELL ME YOU'RE NOT 193 MANSNS JUST PRETENDING NOW--
AND YOU'VE KNOWN IT RIGHT ALONG, TOO, SO THERE'S 355 MARCOM NO PRETENDING.
(PROUD BUT PRETENDING QUERULOUSNESS) 427 MARCOM
YOU HAVE SET YOUR LIPS IN A SMILE SO REMOTE--YOU 437 MARCOM ARE PRETENDING EVEN
YOU ARE PRETENDING. 437 MARCOM
HOGAN REFILLS HIS PIPE, PRETENDING HE DOESN'T 36 MISBEG NOTICE TYRONE APPROACHING.
PRETENDING NOT TO SEE HIM. 37 MISBEG
(HE MUMBLES) PRETENDING HE'S OUR FRIEND/ 78 MISBEG
BOASTING AND PRETENDING, AM I 88 MISBEG
HE THINKS IT'S ALL BOASTING AND PRETENDING YOU'VE 88 MISBEG DONE ABOUT BEING A SLUT.
AND DON'T LET ME GET AWAY WITH PRETENDING I'M SO 126 MISBEG SOUSED I DON'T KNOW WHAT I'M
THE ONLY ONE LEFT TO BRING THE TWO OF YOU TO STOP 175 MISBEG YOUR DAMNED PRETENDING.
TIME GIVE HAPPINESS TO VARIOUS FELLOW WAR-VICTIMS 35 STRANG BY PRETENDING TO LOVE THEM.
TO GO ON LIVING WITH SAM, PRETENDING... 129 STRANG
(PRETENDING AN INTEREST IN THE ROSES) 188 STRANG
(PRETENDING GREAT DELIGHT) UH, AIN'T THAT FUNNY/ 502 VOYAGE

PRETENDS
(REALLY HURT, FORCES A FEEBLE SMILE TO HIS LIPS 230 AHWILD AND PRETENDS TO BE A GOOD SPORT.
HE PRETENDS TO BE ENGAGED IN SETTING THINGS SHIP- 41 ANNA SHAPE.
MAYO PRETENDS TO READ HIS PAPER. 95 BEYOND
JOHN IMMEDIATELY PRETENDS TO BE WRITING. 495 DAYS
SHE PRETENDS TO DO LIKEWISE BUT GIVES HIM A SIDE 235 DESIRE GLANCE OF SCORN AND TRIUMPH.)
WHEN I SLEEPS, DEY SNEAKS A SLEEP, TOO, AND I 181 EJONES PRETENDS I NEVER SUSPICIONS IT.
SHO' I PRETENDS/ 185 EJONES
(VEHEMENTLY.) I PRETENDS TO/ 185 EJONES
(SHE PRETENDS TO TAKE SOMETHING FROM THE STAND BY 62 ELECTR THE HEAD OF THE BED--
SHE'S ALWAYS CUDDLING FATHER AND HE LIKES IT, 81 ELECTR ALTHOUGH HE PRETENDS--
SHE KISSES YOU AND PRETENDS SHE LOVES YOU-- 98 ELECTR
AND PRETENDS TO BE GLANCING THROUGH A BOOK ON THE 157 ELECTR TABLE.
(SETH PRETENDS NOT TO HEAR THE QUESTION, AVOIDING 171 ELECTR HER EYES)
UION PRETENDS TO BE ENGROSSED IN HIS PAPER. 270 GGBROW
HE IS A LITTLE DEAF, BUT NOT HALF AS DEAF AS HE 577 ICEMAN SOMETIMES PRETENDS.
LARRY PRETENDS NOT TO NOTICE HIS COMING. 645 ICEMAN
(HE PRETENDS TO NOTICE WETJOEN FOR THE FIRST TIME 677 ICEMAN AND STEPS AWAY FROM THE DOOR--
LARRY'S FACE HAS TAUTENED, BUT HE PRETENDS HE 701 ICEMAN DOESN'T HEAR.
EDMUND PRETENDS TO BE SO ABSORBED IN HIS BOOK HE 51 JOURNE DOES NOT NOTICE HER.
AS THE FALSE ARISTOCRACY OF OUR PRESENT SOCIETY 9 MANSNS PRETENDS TO BE/
A FRANK STUDY OF THE TRUE NATURE OF MAN AS HE 47 MANSNS REALLY IS AND NOT AS HE PRETENDS
SHE PRETENDS TO BE JEALOUS OF YOU, JUST AS YOU 159 MANSNS PRETEND--
(BUT HE PRETENDS NOT TO HEAR. 428 MARCOM
(PRETENDS TO YAWN BOREDLY) MAYBE NOT. 42 MISBEG

PRETENDS (CONT'D.)
HOLDING A BOOK WHICH HE PRETENDS TO BE LOOKING 111 STRANG THROUGH.

PRETENSE
RESEMBLING HER FATHER TO THE COMPLETE EFFACING OF 186 AHWILD ANY PRETENSE AT PRETTINESS.
(DROPPING ALL PRETENSE--DEFIANTLY) 274 AHWILD
THAT'S THE HARDEST JOB WE HAVE NOW, FATHER-- 501 DAYS KEEPING UP THE PRETENSE OF WORK.
HE SAW THAT UNDERNEATH ALL HIS HYPOCRITICAL 538 DAYS PRETENSE HE REALLY HATED LOVE.
HE MAKES A BEWILDERED PRETENSE OF RESISTANCE. 243 DESIRE
(WITH A GREAT PRETENSE OF GUILT-STRICKEN PROTEST) 440 DYNAMO
(WITH A GREAT PRETENSE OF UNEASINESS) 441 DYNAMO
(WITH A GREAT PRETENSE OF INDIFFERENCE SHE GETS A 443 DYNAMO BOOK FROM THE TABLE AND SITS
(NUDGING ADA--WITH A GREAT PRETENSE OF GUILT) 451 DYNAMO
YOU KNOW DAMNED WELL THAT BEHIND ALL YOUR PRETENSE154 ELECTR ABOUT MOTHER'S MURDER BEING
IT HAD GIVEN UP ALL PRETENSE OF RESPECTABILITY, 7 HUGHIE
(SMITTY YAWNS LOUDLY WITH A GREAT PRETENSE OF 514 INZONE HAVING BEEN DEAD ASLEEP.
AND WHAT'S THE USE OF FAKE PRIDE AND PRETENSE. 149 JOURNE
CAST ASIDE IS OUR PITIABLE PRETENSE, OUR IMMORTAL 324 LAZARU EGOHOOD,
(TREMBLING BUT WITH A PRETENSE OF CARELESSNESS) 340 LAZARU WHAT A PRETENSE/... 147 STRANG

PRETENSES
YOU CAN'T SAY I GOT YOU UNDER NO FALSE PRETENSES. 496 DIFRNT
HYPOCRITICAL PRETENSES AND VIRTUOUS LIES ABOUT 47 MANSNS OURSELVES.
MAYBE SHE LIKED IT, FOR ALL HER PRETENSES. 77 POET
TO LAUGH UP HER SLEEVE AT YOUR PRETENSES& 91 POET

PRETENSIONS
HE WAS A DRUNKEN FOOL, FULL OF LYING PRETENSIONS-- 21 MANSNS
THERE WAS FEW DIDN'T SNEER BEHIND HIS BACK AT HIS 12 POET PRETENSIONS.

PRETENTIOUS
HE IS GRAVELY SELF-IMPORTANT AND PRETENTIOUS IN 25 MANSNS MANNER AND SPEECH.
IN PERSPECTIVE OF A PRETENTIOUS, NOUVEAU-RICHE 139 MANSNS COUNTRY ESTATE ON THE SHORE OF A
CLOSELY RESEMBLES THE FRONT OF A PRETENTIOUS 428 MARCOM DELICATESSEN STORE.
ON THE RIGHT IS A SIDE ENTRANCE OF THE PRETENTIOUS184 STRANG VILLA.

PRETENTIOUSLY
SHE IS DRESSED PRETENTIOUSLY, 218 HA APE

PRETEXT
I HAVE TO REBEL WITH ALL MY STRENGTH--SEIZE ANY 453 WELDED PRETEXT/

PRETINDIN'
HE'LL NIVIR AGAIN HURT YOU WITH HIS SNEERS, AND 168 POET HIS PRETINDIN' HE'S A GINTLEMAN,

PRETTIER
MURIEL'S A MILLION TIMES PRETTIER ANYWAY. 276 AHWILD
(QUICKLY.) AND THAT MADE IT PRETTIER THAN EVER. 28 JOURNE
DUNATA'S PRETTIER. 366 MARCOM
SHE IS MUCH PRETTIER THAN SHE HAS EVER BEEN 136 POET BEFORE.
SHE IS PRETTIER IN A CONVENTIONAL WAY AND LESS 48 STRANG STRIKING AND UNUSUAL..
MAKING HER APPEAR A YOUNGER, PRETTIER PERSON FOR 79 STRANG THE MOMENT.

PRETTIEST
ALICE BRIGGS WAS THE PRETTIEST GIRL BEFORE SHE 290 AHWILD MARRIED.
AND I'LL SHOW YOU THE PRETTIEST (RAP, RAP, RAP) 597 ICEMAN THAT EVER YOU DID SEE.»
AND I'LL SHOW YOU THE PRETTIEST (RAP, RAP, RAP ON 607 ICEMAN TABLE) THAT EVER YOU DID SEE.»
«AND I'LL SHOW YOU THE PRETTIEST (RAP, RAP, RAP) 662 ICEMAN THAT EVER YOU DID SEE/»
I TELL YOU I WOULDN'T HAVE MARRIED THE PRETTIEST 430 MARCOM GIRL IN CATHAY/
WEREN'T YOU THE PRETTIEST GIRL IN ALL IRELAND& 62 POET

PRETTINESS
RESEMBLING HER FATHER TO THE COMPLETE EFFACING OF 186 AHWILD ANY PRETENSE AT PRETTINESS.
HER FACE, IN SPITE OF ITS PLAIN FEATURES, GIVES AN494 DIFRNT IMPRESSION OF PRETTINESS.
BOTH ARE PLUMP AND HAVE A CERTAIN PRETTINESS 611 ICEMAN BUT STILL WITH TRACES OF A DOLL-LIKE PRETTINESS. 615 ICEMAN

PRETTY
WHO MUST HAVE BEEN DECIDEDLY PRETTY AS A GIRL 187 AHWILD
(PLEASED) I THOUGHT IT WAS PRETTY FAIR MYSELF. 188 AHWILD
WE SWAM AND SWAM AND WERE PRETTY EVENLY MATCHED. 230 AHWILD
BELLE IS TWENTY, A RATHER PRETTY PEROXIDE BLONDE, 236 AHWILD
(RUFFLING HIS HAIR) GEE, YOU'VE GOT PRETTY HAIR, 240 AHWILD DO YOU KNOW ITS
NO, YOU'RE--YOU'RE PRETTY. 240 AHWILD
SEEMS TO ME YOU WOKE UP PRETTY QUICK--JUST AFTER 269 AHWILD YOUR PA LEFT THE HOUSE/
EVEN IF SHE WAS PRETTY. 276 AHWILD
AH, SHE WASN'T PRETTY. 276 AHWILD
SHE IS A PRETTY GIRL WITH A PLUMP, GRACEFUL LITTLE277 AHWILD FIGURE, FLUFFY,
GOSH, YOU'RE PRETTY TONIGHT, MURIEL/ 279 AHWILD
SHE WASN'T EVEN PRETTY/ 285 AHWILD
SO I'M PRETTY SURE ANYTHING I COULD SAY TO YOU 294 AHWILD YOU'VE ALREADY SAID TO YOURSELF.
AND LOTS OF 'EM ARE PRETTY, AND IT'S HUMAN NATURE 295 AHWILD IF YOU--
HER FACE, THOUGH INCLINED TO ROUNDNESS, IS 87 BEYOND UNDENIABLY PRETTY.
SEEMS TO ME IT'S A PRETTY SLICK PLACE RIGHT NOW. 97 BEYOND
(SEVERELY) SEEMS TO ME IT'S A PRETTY LATE HOUR IN100 BEYOND THE DAY FOR YOU TO BE

PRETTY

(CONT'D.)
SHE'LL HAVE TO BE A PRETTY ONE, TOO, TO MATCH IT. 104 BEYOND
A PRETTY BUT SICKLY AND ANEMIC-LOOKING CHILD WITH 116 BEYOND
A TEAR-STAINED FACE.
WHO'S THIS PRETTY YOUNG LADYS 130 BEYOND
SHE LOOKS PRETTY, FLUSHED AND FULL OF LIFE. 135 BEYOND
(FAINTLY) A PRETTY LADY DRESSED IN BLACK. 489 CARDIF
A PRETTY YOUNG MAIDEN I CHANCED FOR TO MEET. 460 CARIBE
A PRETTY YOUNG MAIDEN I CHANCED FOR TO MEET. 460 CARIBE
A PRETTY YOUNG MAIDEN I CHANCED FOR TO MEET. 460 CARIBE
COME AHN IN, PRETTY BOY. 466 CARIBE
SOUNDS KINDER PRETTY TO ME--LOW AN' MOURNFUL-- 466 CARIBE
ULLO, PRETTY BOY. 468 CARIBE
YOU OUGHTN'T DRINK SO MUCH, PRETTY BOY. 468 CARIBE
DON' YOU LIKE ME PRETTY BOYS 469 CARIBE
(COOXINGLY) WHY YOU RUN 'WAY FROM ME, PRETTY BOYS 469 CARIBE
A PRETTY, SENTIMENTAL ENDING--BUT A BIT TOO 494 DAYS
POINTED, DON'T YOU THINK$
HER ROUND FACE IS PRETTY BUT MARRED BY ITS RATHER 221 DESIRE
GROSS SENSUALITY.
SHE MUST HAVE BEEN PRETTY AS A GIRL. 422 DYNAMO
HER FACE MUST HAVE ONCE BEEN ONE OF THOSE ROSY- 428 DYNAMO
CHEEKED PRETTY DULL-LIKE FACES
HER PRETTY FACE, WITH HER MOTHER'S BIG BLUE EYES, 428 DYNAMO
IS ALIVE AND KEEN.
GOSH, ADA---YOU'RE PRETTY IN THE MOONLIGHT. 433 DYNAMO
I'D FORGOTTEN HOW PRETTY YOU WERE/ 460 DYNAMO
GOSH, YOU'RE PRETTY/ 460 DYNAMO
HER FACE IS FLUSHED WITH EXCITEMENT, HAPPY AND 467 DYNAMO
PRETTY NOW.
GEE, YOU'RE PRETTY ADA/ 469 DYNAMO
(DREARILY) THAT'S AWFUL PRETTY, REUBEN. 477 DYNAMO
YOU'RE SO DARNED PRETTY/ 482 DYNAMO
GOD, YOU'RE PRETTY/ 485 DYNAMO
DON'T SHE SHINE PRETTYS 179 EJONCS
HAZEL IS A PRETTY, HEALTHY GIRL OF NINETEEN, WITH 12 ELECTR
DARK HAIR AND EYES.
I MUST SAY YOU TREAT YOUR ONE DEVOTED SWAIN PRETTY 16 ELECTR
RUDELY.
YOU SEEM TO TAKE GIVING HIM UP PRETTY EASILY/ 34 ELECTR
HE ALWAYS LIKED ME TO BE PRETTY. 72 ELECTR
I DON'T MEAN UGLY. HOW PRETTY YOU'VE GOTTEN-- 141 ELECTR
DO YOU REALLY THINK I'M AS PRETTY NOW AS SHE WAS, 141 ELECTR
ORINS
(THEN WITH ENTHUSIASM) GOSH, YOU LOOK SO DARNED 143 ELECTR
PRETTY--AND HEALTHY.
IT WAS THEN YOU FINALLY BECAME PRETTY--LIKE 154 ELECTR
MOTHER/
PETER IS COMING, AND I WANT EVERYTHING TO BE 170 ELECTR
PRETTY AND CHEERFUL.
(TO THE AIR) I HAD A PRETTY VOICE, WHEN I WAS A 257 GGBROW
GIRL.
SHE IS ALMOST SEVENTEEN, PRETTY AND VIVACIOUS, 262 GGBROW
BLONDE, WITH BIG ROMANTIC EYES.
HER FACE IS CONCEALED BEHIND THE MASK OF THE 274 GGBROW
PRETTY YOUNG MATRON.
SHE'S A GAME SPORT, BUT IT'S PRETTY DAMN TOUGH ON 277 GGBROW
HER/
IT'S PRETTY LATE. 282 GGBROW
IT'S PRETTY TOUGH ON HER. 289 GGBROW
HER OWN FACE IS STILL SWEET AND PRETTY BUT LINED, 291 GGBROW
I'D GOTTEN PRETTY RESIGNED TO--AND SAD HOPELESS, 309 GGBROW
TOO--
PRETTY FACE MARRED BY A SELF-CONSCIOUS EXPRESSION 217 HA APE
OF DISDAINFUL SUPERIORITY.
(WITH NAIVE ADMIRATION) SAY, DEM TINGS IS PRETTY,235 HA APE
HUH$
DAT WAS PRETTY, TOO--ALL RED AND PINK AND GREEN. 252 HA APE
THEY'D MAKE HIM PRETTY RAW PROPOSITIONS. 16 HUGHIE
=WITH A PRETTY NURSE TAKING CARE OF HIM= 26 HUGHIE
=PROBABLY NOT PRETTY.= 26 HUGHIE
TEN, TWENTY--THOSE ARE PRETTY SHOES YOU GOT ON, 609 ICEMAN
BESS=
(A BIT HURT AT THIS) THAT'S GOING PRETTY STRONG, 609 ICEMAN
HARRY.
PRETTY GOOD. 612 ICEMAN
YUH CAN SEE DEY'RE PRETTY, CAN'T YUH, YUH BIG 629 ICEMAN
DUMMYS
A GUY WHAT CAN'T SEE FLOWERS IS PRETTY MUST BE 630 ICEMAN
SOME DUMBBELL.
(SCOWLING) YEAHS HARRY'S PRETTY DARNED GOOD TO 637 ICEMAN
YOU.
(TRYING TO BRIGHTEN UP) SAY, THAT'S PRETTY. 655 ICEMAN
YOU'LL CONFESS YOU WERE PRETTY SICK OF HER HATING 657 ICEMAN
YOU FOR GETTING DRUNK.
I CAN'T EVEN REMEMBER NOW IF SHE WAS PRETTY. 707 ICEMAN
I GOT ALL WORKED UP. SHE WAS SO PRETTY AND SWEET 710 ICEMAN
AND GOOD.
IT MUST ONCE HAVE BEEN EXTREMELY PRETTY, AND IS 12 JOURNE
STILL STRIKING.
WHATEVER BULL THEY HAND YOU, THEY TELL ME HE'S A 36 JOURNE
PRETTY BUM REPORTER.
I WAS REALLY VERY PRETTY THEN, CATHLEEN. 105 JOURNE
YOU'RE JUST AS PRETTY AS ANY ACTRESS HE'S EVER 115 JOURNE
MET.
IT'S PRETTY HARD TO TAKE AT TIMES, HAVING A DOPE 120 JOURNE
FIEND FOR A MOTHER/
IT'S PRETTY HORRIBLE TO SEE HER THE WAY SHE MUST 139 JOURNE
BE NOW.
MARY IS YOUNG AND PRETTY, NERVOUS AND HIGH-STRUNG.275 LAZARU
THERE'S PRETTY GIRLS IN CARTHAGE AND WINE TO SWILL314 LAZARU
IN CARTHAGE.
I THINK YOU, PRETTY LADY. 346 LAZARU
SHE IS TWENTY-FIVE, EXCEEDINGLY PRETTY IN A 1 MANSNS
TYPICALLY IRISH FASHION.
YOU'RE AS YOUNG AND PRETTY AS EVER. 5 MANSNS
IS SHE PRETTY STILLS 7 MANSNS

PREVENTING

PRETTY (CONT'D.)
IS STILL EXCEEDINGLY PRETTY, STRONG AND HEALTHY, 75 MANSNS
WITH THE SAME FIRM,
AND ONE DAY SOON I WILL BE HATING HER YOUNG BODY 181 MANSNS
AND HER PRETTY FACE.
SHE IS A GIRL OF TWELVE, HER FACE PALE AND PRETTY 355 MARCOM
IN THE MOONLIGHT.)
HIS INSTRUCTIONS TO US WERE PRETTY EMPHATIC. 359 MARCOM
SHE'S PRETTY. 366 MARCOM
DON'T YOU THINK SHE'S PRETTYS 366 MARCOM
SHE'S PRETTY. 371 MARCOM
I'M SURE I'D MAKE A PRETTY DULL PERSON TO HAVE 398 MARCOM
AROUND
PRETTY, ISN'T SHES 416 MARCOM
BUT HER FACE IS UNLINED AND STILL PRETTY IN A 427 MARCOM
BOVINE, GOOD-NATURED WAY.
WHY, YOU'RE STILL AS PRETTY AS A PICTURE AND YOU 430 MARCOM
DON'T LOOK A DAY OLDER/
IT IS NOT A PRETTY FACE, BUT HER LARGE DARK-BLUE 3 MISBEG
EYES GIVE IT A NOTE OF BEAUTY.
SURE, ALL THE PRETTY LITTLE TARTS ON BROADWAY, NEW 21 MISBEG
YURK,
JIM CAN HAVE ALL THE PRETTY, PAINTED LITTLE 28 MISBEG
BROADWAY GIRLS HE WANTS--
AND BY THE TIME THE PRETTY LITTLE TARTS, 30 MISBEG
AND ALL THE PRETTY WHORES OF BROADWAY HE CAN BUY 85 MISBEG
WITH IT.
IF I WAS A DAINTY, PRETTY TART HE'D BE PROUD I'D 92 MISBEG
RAISE A RUMPUS ABOUT HIM.
HIM, NO MATTER HOW DAINTY AND PRETTY/ 95 MISBEG
THEN YOU'LL HAVE ALL THE PRETTY LITTLE TARTS TO 106 MISBEG
COMFORT YOU
DON'T ALL THE PRETTY LITTLE BROADWAY TARTS GET 116 MISBEG
SOUSED WITH YOUS
AS SMALL AND DAINTY AND PRETTY-- 117 MISBEG
SHE LOOKED YOUNG AND PRETTY LIKE SOMEONE I 147 MISBEG
REMEMBERED MEETING LONG AGO.
EXCEPT I'VE PULLED SOME PRETTY ROTTEN STUFF WHEN 1173 MISBEG
WAS DRAWING A BLANK.
NORA WAS AS PRETTY A GIRL AS YOU'D FIND IN A 14 POET
YEAR'S TRAVEL.
SARA IS TWENTY, AN EXCEEDINGLY PRETTY GIRL WITH A 15 POET
MASS OF BLACK HAIR.
PRETTY, IF YOU LIKE THAT KIND. 18 POET
SHE MUST HAVE BEEN AS PRETTY AS A GIRL AS SARA IS 19 POET
NOW.
I WAS ABOUT TO TELL YOU HOW EXCEEDINGLY CHARMING 45 POET
AND PRETTY YOU LOOK, MY DEAR.
I SHOULD GRANT IT IS A PRETTY WOMAN'S PRIVILEGE TO 76 POET
BE ALWAYS RIGHT
AN ABSURD TAUNT, WHEN YOU REALLY HAVE SUCH PRETTY 107 POET
HANDS AND FEET, MY DEAR.
SO WAS YOUR MOTHER PRETTY ONCE. 114 POET
YOU ARE PRETTY. 114 POET
(WITH AFFECTED CASUALNESS.) A PRETTY YOUNG WOMAN.118 POET
MUSHA BUT IT'S PLEASED AND PRETTY YOU LOOK, 140 POET
PRETTY VICIOUS FACE UNDER CAKED POWDER AND 6 STRANG
ROUGE....
HER FACE IS STRIKING, HANDSOME RATHER THAN PRETTY, 12 STRANG
THE BONE STRUCTURE PROMINENT,
IT'S A PRETTY IDEA BUT IT HASN'T WORKED OUT. 36 STRANG
SHE'S SO PRETTY AND SWEET/ 56 STRANG
BUT THEN LIFE DOESN'T SEEM TO BE PRETTY, DOES ITS 82 STRANG
(WEARILY) I WARN YOU IT ISN'T PRETTY, DOCTOR/ 82 STRANG
HE'S PRETTY SURE THERE'S AN OPENING--(WITH A 95 STRANG
CONDESCENSION HE CAN'T HELP)
SHE LOOKS EXTREMELY PRETTY 125 STRANG
HE LOOKS PRETTY DISSIPATED.... 134 STRANG
THIS BOAT IS SO PRETTY.... 149 STRANG
(SOBBING MISERABLY) IT WAS AWFUL PRETTY/ 150 STRANG
HE TAKES HIS HUBBY PRETTY SERIOUSLY/....) 152 STRANG
MADELINE ARNOLD IS A PRETTY GIRL OF NINETEEN, WITH159 STRANG
DARK HAIR AND EYES.
PRETTY LATE IN THE DAY.... 161 STRANG
THINGS HAVE GONE PRETTY FAR.... 163 STRANG
HOW I'VE COME TO DETEST HER PRETTY FACE/...) 168 STRANG
WHY, SHE'S HARDLY EVEN PRETTY AND SHE'S DEADLY 168 STRANG
STUPID.
SHE'S PRETTY, THAT MADELINE/... 168 STRANG
THAT MADELINE IS PRETTY, ISN'T SHES 175 STRANG
DON'T WORRY YOUR PRETTY HEAD/ 175 STRANG
THEY'RE PRETTY. 188 STRANG
(WITH A SMIRKING WINK) PRETTY, 'ULESOME GELS THEY499 VOYAGE
BE, AIN'T THEY, NICKS
SEEING SPOOKS, THAT'S PRETTY FAR GONE, ISN'T ITS 466 WELDED
YET SHE IS NOT UGLY--RATHER PRETTY FOR HER BOVINE,471 WELDED
STOLID TYPE--

PREVAILS
AND AN AWED AND FRIGHTENED STILLNESS PREVAILS, FOR278 LAZARU
LAZARUS IS A STRANGE,

PREVENT
(SMILING CONFIDENTLY) IS IT ANNA YOU THINK WILL 45 ANNA
PREVENT MES
AND IT'S THAT YOU'LL BE HAVING, NO MATTER WHAT 49 ANNA
YOU'LL DO TO PREVENT.
AND I CAN'T DO NOTHING TO PREVENT. 114 BEYOND
BUT REUBEN'LL NEVER BECOME A MINISTER IF I CAN 423 DYNAMO
PREVENT IT.
AND AS FOR HER GOING TO THE POLICE--DO YOU SUPPOSE 88 ELECTR
I WOULDN'T PREVENT THAT--
(BEFORE HE CAN PREVENT IT, 100 ELECTR
I'LL BE DRUNK AT THE INN, SO HOW COULD I PREVENT 67 MISBEG
IT$
FOR ALL WE OTHERS CAN DO TO PREVENT. 37 POET
I DID MY BEST TO PREVENT YOUR MARRIAGE. 20 STRANG

PREVENTING
WHAT IS IT THAT'S PREVENTING YOU WEDDING ME WHEN 54 ANNA
THE TWO OF US HAS LOVE$

PREVIOUS

PREVIOUS
THE EFFECT ON HIS AUDIENCE IS THAT OF THE PREVIOUS258 AHWILD
SONG, INTENSIFIED--
HIS EXPRESSION AS INNOCENT AS IF NOTHING HAD 263 AHWILD
OCCURRED THE PREVIOUS DAY THAT
FATHER BAIRD SITS IN THE SAME ATTITUDE AS HE HAD 541 DAYS
IN THE PREVIOUS SCENE.
THERE IS A DIM LIGHT ABOVE IN THE SWITCH GALLERIES476 DYNAMO
AS IN THE PREVIOUS SCENE.
WHICH IS A TRIFLE LOUDER AND QUICKER THAN AT THE 190 EJONES
CLOSE OF THE PREVIOUS
THE PREVIOUS ACT.) 93 ELECTR
THE ARRANGEMENT OF FURNITURE IN EACH ROOM IS THE 302 GGBROW
SAME AS IN PREVIOUS SCENES.
HE LOOKS THE SAME AS IN THE PREVIOUS ACT, 638 ICEMAN
AND HE LOOKS MORE SICKLY THAN IN THE PREVIOUS ACT. 51 JOURNE
AS IT WAS IN THE PRE-LUNCHEON SCENE OF THE 97 JOURNE
PREVIOUS SCENE.
THEY ARE NOT DIVIDED ACCORDING TO SEX AS IN THE 282 LAZARU
PREVIOUS SCENE.
THEIR MASKS ARE THE SAME AS THE LEGIONARY CHORUS 326 LAZARU
OF THE PREVIOUS SCENE.
THE SAME AS PREVIOUS SCENE--THE SAME NIGHT A SHORT350 LAZARU
WHILE LATER.
THE OAIS AS IN THE PREVIOUS SCENE, STARING AT 362 LAZARU
LAZARUS, LAUGHING CRUELLY.
SHE APPEARS GREATLY CHANGED FROM THE PREVIOUS ACT. 95 MANSNS
AS WITH THE ALI BROTHERS IN THE PREVIOUS SCENE, 370 MARCOM
BETWEEN THEM AND THE POLOS AS WITH THE BUDDHIST 374 MARCOM
MERCHANTS IN THE PREVIOUS SCENE.
PLAYING THE SAME MARTIAL AIR AS IN THE PREVIOUS 402 MARCOM
SCENE.
SHE APPEARS OLDER THAN IN THE PREVIOUS SCENE, HER 26 STRANG
FACE IS PALE AND MUCH THINNER.
PLACE AS MARSDEN HAD OCCUPIED IN THE PREVIOUS 39 STRANG
SCENE WHILE MARSDEN IS IN HER
EVAN'S MOTHER IN THE PREVIOUS ACT) 82 STRANG
THE ARRANGEMENT OF THE FURNITURE SHOWN IS AS IN 137 STRANG
PREVIOUS SCENES
SHE IS SLIMMER THAN IN THE PREVIOUS SCENE. 137 STRANG
CONDITIONS, THE PUFFINESS AND JOWLS OF THE 159 STRANG
PREVIOUS ACT ARE GONE.
MADELINE IS MUCH THE SAME AS IN THE PREVIOUS ACT 184 STRANG
EXCEPT THAT THERE IS NOW A
I ALSO HAD HEARD A LOT OF RUMORS ABOUT YOUR 446 WELDED
PREVIOUS--

PREVIOUSLY
INTO CONSIDERATION PREVIOUSLY BECAUSE I HADN'T 100 BEYOND
DARED TO HOPE
THE NEAREST DYNAMO, WHICH WE HAVE SEEN PREVIOUSLY 484 DYNAMO
THROUGH THE DOORWAY,
IS A LARGE PORTRAIT OF EZRA MANNON HIMSELF, 28 ELECTR
PAINTED TEN YEARS PREVIOUSLY.
AS THOSE OF THE JEWS SEEN PREVIOUSLY, 291 LAZARU
MASKED AS ALL THE ROMAN SOLDIERS PREVIOUSLY, ENTER326 LAZARU
FROM THE LEFT, FRONT.

PREY
RICHARD STANDS, A PREY TO FEELINGS OF BITTEREST 217 AHWILD
HUMILIATION AND SEETHING REVOLT
NERVOUS, SICK, A PREY TO GLOOMY REMORSE 256 AHWILD
(A PREY TO KEEN CURIOSITY NOW) 273 AHWILD
ALTHOUGH HE STILL IS A PREY TO CERTAIN MISGIVINGS,288 AHWILD
WHO PREY ON THE RICH SUMMER PEOPLE-- 31 JOURNE
YET AT THE SAME TIME SHE IS A PREY TO A PASSIONATE161 MANSNS

AND EACH EXPERIENCE OF THIS KIND HAS ONLY LEFT HER 36 STRANG
MORE A PREY TO A GUILTY
HE SEEMS A PREY TO SOME INNER FEAR HE IS TRYING TO 73 STRANG
HIDE EVEN FROM HIMSELF AND IS

PREYED
AND IT PREYED ON HIS MIND UNTIL HE BLAMES HIMSELF 148 ELECTR
FOR HER DEATH.

PRICE
DOWN AND THE PRICE BESIDE UT AND SIGN YOUR NAME. 463 CARIBE
THREE SHILLIN'S IS THE PRICE. 465 CARIBE
THE MORTGAGE--THE PRICE OF THAT SHIP--IS TO BE 562 CROSS
FORECLOSED.
ANY THE PRICE HE'S PAYIN' YE--THIS FARM--WAS MY 226 DESIRE
MAN'S, DAMN YE!
YOU CAN'T BEAR THAT THOUGH, EVEN AT THE PRICE OF 33 ELECTR
MY DISGRACE, CAN YOUS
(THEN INSULTINGLY) I AIN'T GOT THE PRICE OF A 106 ELECTR
DRINK. THAT'S WHY I'M HERE.
YOU'VE BROUGHT LOVE--AND THE REST IS ONLY THE 111 ELECTR

NO PRICE IS TOO GREAT, IS ITS 167 ELECTR
BEGGING AT ALL DOORS FOR LIFE AT ANY PRICE/ 266 GGBROW
AND HIS SHIFTY ONCE-OVER GLANCES NEVER MISS THE 9 HUGHIE
PRICE TAGS HE DETECTS ON
AND THEY'LL NEVER PAY THAT PRICE FOR LIBERTY. 579 ICEMAN
BUT WHAT WOULD HE DO WID BEAUTIFUL DOLLS, EVEN IF 635 ICEMAN
HE HAD DE PRICE, DE OLD GOAT!
SO I'M KEEPING DRUNK AND HANGING ON TO LIFE AT ANY641 ICEMAN
PRICE, AND WHAT OF ITS
BELOVED CHRIST, LET ME LIVE A LITTLE LONGER AT ANY689 ICEMAN
PRICE/
THIS JEWEL BEYOND PRICE, THE DIRTY, 689 ICEMAN
BUT, OF COURSE, HE'LL NEVER COME HOME SO LONG AS 109 JOURNE
HE HAS THE PRICE OF A DRINK.
I SUPPOSE I, TOO, HAVE MY PRICE--IF THEY WERE ONLY301 LAZARU
CLEVER ENOUGH TO DISCOVER IT/
YES, ONE SHOULD NEVER COMPLAIN OF THE PRICE ONE 77 MANSNS
MUST PAY FOR WHAT ONE WANTS FROM
NO PRICE IS TOO HIGH FOR ME TO PAY MY MISTRESS FOR 93 MANSNS
HER LOVE, EH!
THAT SHE WOULD SELL ANYTHING IF OFFERED THE RIGHT 98 MANSNS
PRICE.
AND ASK HER PRICE/ 121 MANSNS

PRICE (CONT'D.)
WHY DO YOU THINK I PAY SUCH AN OUTLANDISH PRICE TO159 MANSNS
KEEP A MISTRESS$
IT WAS PART OF THE PRICE I MADE HIM PAY FOR ME 167 MANSNS
WHEN HE CAME BACK FROM THE HILLS.
SHE IS SO BEAUTIFUL AND SHE DEMANDED IT AS PART OF178 MANSNS
HER PRICE.
FOR YOUR PRIDE PAID A PRICE FOR LOVE MY PRIDE 190 MANSNS
WOULD NEVER DARE TO PAY/
AND IT'S NO PRICE AT ALL I'LL BE PAYING TO MATCH 191 MANSNS
YOURS, DEBORAH.
THAT WOULD BE TOO GREAT A PRICE-- 193 MANSNS
YOUR INITIAL EXPENSE--MY PRICE-- 396 MARCOM
AT THE SMALL PRICE YOU OFFERED$ 31 MISBEG
AND EVERYTHING AND ANYONE CAN BE BOUGHT IF THE 33 MISBEG
PRICE IS BIG ENOUGH.
BUT WE'RE NOT WORRYING YOU'D EVER FORGET YOUR 66 MISBEG
PROMISE TO US FOR ANY PRICE.
WHO'D SELL HIS SOUL FOR A PRICE, 82 MISBEG
YOU FOR THE PRICE YOU OFFERED, AND NOT TO HARDER. 94 MISBEG
I WANTED TO BELIEVE IN ANY GOD AT ANY PRICE-- 41 STRANG
EVEN OUR NEW GOD HAS HIS PRICE/... 123 STRANG
(FORCING A SMILE) PERHAPS THAT'S THE PRICE. 446 WELDED
ONCE WHEN YOU WERE WILLING TO ENDURE IT AS THE 468 WELDED
PRICE OF A CAREER--

PRICED
A MEDIUM-PRICED, INOFFENSIVE RUG COVERS MOST OF 185 AHWILD
THE FLOOR.
FURNISHED WITH SCRUPULOUS MEDIUM-PRICED 185 AHWILD
TASTELESSNESS OF THE PERIOD.
THE ROOM IS MUCH TOO SMALL FOR THE MEDIUM-PRICED, 210 AHWILD
FORMIDABLE DINING-ROOM SET,

PRICES
INTERMITTENT ELECTRIC LIGHTS WINK OUT THE 233 HA APE
INCREDIBLE PRICES.
JUST LOOK AT THE BLEEDIN' PRICES ON 'EM-- 235 HA APE
THEY'LL CUT UNDER OUR PRICES WITH THEIR CHEAP JUNK365 MARCOM
AS USUAL.

PRICK
RUCKY AND CHUCK PRICK UP THEIR EARS AND GATHER 651 ICEMAN
ROUND.

PRICKED
YOU ARE A BUBBLE PRICKED BY DEATH INTO A VOID AND 309 LAZARU
A MOCKING SILENCE/
(WHO HAVE PRICKED UP THEIR EARS AT THIS LAST, RUSH417 MARCOM
TO THE PRINCESS,

PRICKING
(PRICKING UP HIS EARS--INQUISITIVELY) 506 DIFRNT

PRICKLY
AND GETS PRICKLY HEAT AND THEN HE'S TERRIBLE 429 DYNAMO
CROSS...!)

PRIDE
I GOT TO PROVE A MAN TO BE A GOOD HUSBAND FOR YE 550 'ILE
TO TAKE PRIDE IN.
(WITH PRIDE) RICHARD'LL STAND UP TO HIS GUNS, NO 206 AHWILD
MATTER WHAT.
(WITH A CERTAIN PRIDE) DEV VAS ALL SMART SEAMAN, 27 ANNA
TOO--A ONE.
BREAKING HIS HEART JUST ON ACCOUNT OF HIS STUBBORN116 BEYOND
PRIDE.
AND NOW THAT ANDY'S COMING BACK--I'M GOING TO SINK149 BEYOND
MY FOOLISH PRIDE, RUTH/
AND ALL-COUNT OF HIS PIGHEADED PRIDE 152 BEYOND
IN HIS AWAKENED PRIDE HE CURSED HIS GOD AND DENIED511 DAYS
HIM, AND, IN REVENGE,
MY PRIDE WAS SO HURT I WANTED TO REVENGE MYSELF 521 DAYS
NOT TO DELIBERATELY DISFIGURE MYSELF OUT OF 521 DAYS
WOUNDED PRIDE AND SPITE.
(SHE SMILES--THEN WITH QUIET PRIDE) 524 DAYS
AND VERY SOON HE HAD AN EXAMPLE OF WHAT HER PRIDE 537 DAYS
HAD TO ENDURE,
AND AT THE LAST MOMENT HIS WILL AND PRIDE REVIVE 545 DAYS
IN HIM AGAIN/
ADDRESSING THE CROSS NOT WITHOUT A FINAL TOUCH OF 566 DAYS
PRIDE IN HIS HUMILITY)
YET THERE IS A WEAKNESS IN IT, A PETTY PRIDE IN 221 DESIRE
ITS OWN NARROW STRENGTH.
(HIS FACE GROWING FULL OF JOYOUS PRIDE AND A SORT 234 DESIRE
OF RELIGIOUS ECSTASY)
(HE GOES WITH A CERTAIN QUEER PRIDE) 260 DESIRE
= PRIDE GOETH BEFORE A FALL.= 499 DIFRNT
(WITH PRIDE) FROM STOWAWAY TO EMPEROR IN TWO 177 EJONES
YEARS/
SHE'D SUNK HER LAST SHRED OF PRIDE AND WRITTEN TO 26 ELECTR
YOUR FATHER ASKING FOR A LOAN.
OH, I'M NOT DENYING YOU WANT TO SAVE HIS PRIDE-- 33 ELECTR
(DRAWING HIMSELF UP WITH A STERN PRIDE AND DIGNITY 55 ELECTR
SOME DAY GOD WOULD HUMBLE THEM IN THEIR SINFUL 69 ELECTR
PRIDE.
YOU'VE ALWAYS SAID ABOUT THE MANNONS THAT PRIDE 69 ELECTR
GOETH BEFORE A FALL AND THAT
IT FILLED YOU WITH PRIDE/ 154 ELECTR
(THEN WITH A GRIM PRIDE) BUT VINNIE'S ABLE FUR 170 ELECTR
PRIDE/ 272 GGBROW
PRIDE IS DYING/ 272 GGBROW
PRIDE IN MY FAILURE/ 272 GGBROW
OLD MAN BROWN PERISHES OF PATERNAL PRIDE-- 272 GGBROW
(MORE AND MORE DESPERATELY) THE PRIDE WHICH CAME 272 GGBROW
AFTER MAN'S FALL--
(WITH TERRIBLE DESPAIR) PRIDE/ 272 GGBROW
PRIDE WITHOUT WHICH THE GODS ARE WORMS/ 272 GGBROW
PRIDE IS DEAD/ 273 GGBROW
(THEN, WITH AN ABASHED PRIDE) 275 GGBROW
A MAN HAS SOME PRIDE/ 281 GGBROW
WITH THE SHY PRIDE OF ONE WHO HAS LENGTHENED HER 282 GGBROW
DRESS AND PUT UP HER HAIR.

PRIDE

(CONT'D.)
(HE LAUGHS) BUT PRIDE IS A SIN--EVEN IN A MEMORY 287 GGBROW
OF THE LONG DECEASED/
PEACE, POOR TORTURED ONE, BRAVE PITIFUL PRIDE OF 291 GGBROW
MAN.
O WOMAN--MY LOVE--THAT I HAVE SINNED AGAINST IN MY292 GGBROW
SICK PRIDE AND CRUELTY--
(WITH A GREAT HARD PRIDE IN THEM) 212 HA APE
IN THE VERY HEART OF HIS PRIDE. 226 HA APE
(HE SWELLS WITH PRIDE.) THAT WAS SOME DISPLAY, 31 HUGHIE
PAL.
(HE CHUCKLES WITH PRIC.) DEM OLD DAYS/ 601 ICEMAN
(WITH PATHETIC BOASTFUL PRIDE) 644 ICEMAN
SO I SIT HERE, WITH MY PRIDE DROWNED ON THE BOTTOM689 ICEMAN
OF A BOTTLE.
AND HE TAKES GREAT PRIDE IN IT. 13 JOURNE
HAVE TO HUMBLE MY PRIDE AND BEG FOR YOU, SAYING 32 JOURNE
YOU'VE TURNED OVER A NEW LEAF.
(WITH A TOUCH OF PRIDE.) WHATEVER EDMUND'S DONE, 35 JOURNE
REALLY, HE OUGHT TO HAVE MORE PRIDE THAN TO MAKE 43 JOURNE
SUCH A SHOW OF HIMSELF.
JESUS, PAPA, HAVEN'T YOU ANY PRIDE OR SHAME& 145 JOURNE
AND WHAT'S THE USE OF FAKE PRIDE AND PRETENSE. 149 JOURNE
WITH PRIDE/ 289 LAZARU
HER PRIDE IN CHAINS/ 302 LAZARU
CRY IN YOUR PRIDE, =I AM 310 LAZARU
CRY WITH PRIDE, =TAKE BACK, O GOD, AND ACCEPT IN 324 LAZARU
TURN A GIFT FROM ME,
I WILL LAUGH WITH THE PRIDE OF A BEGGAR SET UPON 328 LAZARU
THE THRONE OF MAN/
(WITH A GRANDIOSE PRIDE. 331 LAZARU
AND THE PRIDE OF A NEW TRIUMPH. 349 LAZARU
THEN LET IT BE MY PRIDE AS MAN TO RECREATE THE GOD352 LAZARU
IN ME/=
AND THOUGH I BURST WITH PRIDE, I CANNOT LAUGH WITH352 LAZARU
JOY/
(HE LAUGHS SOFTLY BUT WITH EXULTANT PRIDE.) 352 LAZARU
I HAVE FOUND NOTHING IN LIFE THAT MERITS PRIDE. 352 LAZARU
=IT IS MY PRIDE AS GOD TO BECOME MAN. 352 LAZARU
(HE SUDDENLY STARTS TO HIS FEET--WITH HARSH 356 LAZARU
ARROGANCE AND PRIDE, THREATENINGLY)
(CRUELLY AND GRIMLY AGAIN) SO MUCH THE MORE 357 LAZARU
REASON WHY MY PRIDE SHOULD KILL
IT IS SUCH A FINE GESTURE OF DISDAINFUL PRIDE TO 12 MANSNS
JILT IT.
YOU THINK IN YOUR YANKEE PRIDE AND IGNORANCE, 21 MANSNS
AND ONE'S PRIDE TO CHOOSE OF ONE'S OWN FREE WILL, 28 MANSNS
AND ONE CAN CHEAT LIFE.
OH NO, YOU WILL FIND SHE HAS NEVER FORGIVEN HENRY 35 MANSNS
FOR HUMILIATING HER PRIDE.
SATISFACTION AND SENSE OF SELF-FULFILLMENT AND 46 MANSNS
PRIDE OUT OF BEATING MY
YES, YOU CONSOLED YOUR PRIDE WITH THAT LIE. 99 MANSNS
IT'S HER GREAT-LADY PRIDE WON'T GIVE ME THE 118 MANSNS
SATISFACTION TO KNOW SHE'S HURT.
HE MUST HUMOR HIS MANLY PRIDE, SARA. 128 MANSNS
YOU PRIDE YOURSELF YOU HAVE CUNNINGLY SWINDLED 141 MANSNS
HIM.
HIS FACE AS HE ENTERS IS FLUSHED WITH HUMILIATED 150 MANSNS
PRIDE.)
I WARN YOU YOUR PRIDE WILL PROBABLY BE IMPELLED TO153 MANSNS
REJECT THEM.
YES, I DIDN'T LEAVE HIM ONE LAST SHRED OF HIS 155 MANSNS
PRIDE, DID I&
WHILE WE WATCHED WITH GRATIFIED WOMANLY PRIDE AND 171 MANSNS
LAUGHED AND GUARDED HIM ON/
WHILE HE STANDS APART AND WATCHES AND SNEERS AND 171 MANSNS
LAUGHS WITH GREEDY PRIDE
AS MY PRIDE AND DISDAIN HAVE ALWAYS WILLED I BE/ 185 MANSNS
FOR YOUR PATED PAID A PRICE FOR LOVE MY PRIDE 190 MANSNS
WOULD NEVER DARE TO PAY/
(A FLASH OF INSULTED PRIDE COMES TO HER EYES AND 193 MANSNS
FOR A SECOND SHE SEEMS
(BLUSTERING--BUT HIS EYES BEAMING WITH PATERNAL 381 MARCOM
PRIDE)
YOU MUST NOT ASK THAT--IF YOU RESPECT MY PRIDE/ 386 MARCOM
MY PRIDE, MY POWERS 437 MARCOM
IS WAS THE WISDOM OF PRIDE. 437 MARCOM
NOT THAT I NEED IT, BUT IT SAVES HIS PRIDE. 11 MISBEG
LIKE A POOR SHEEP WITHOUT PRIDE OR SPIRIT-- 79 MISBEG
SURE, THAT'S ALWAYS BEEN YOUR PRIDE-- 81 MISBEG
GREAT STRENGTH YOU HAD, AND GREAT PRIDE, HE SAID-- 88 MISBEG
AND GREAT GOODNESS, NO, I'LL SAY--
I'LL HUMBLE MY PRIDE AND GO DOWN TO THE INN FOR 91 MISBEG
HIM/
AND HIS BROADWAY PRIDE HE'S SO WISE NO WOMAN COULD 96 MISBEG
FOOL HIM.
I OUGHTN'T TO SPEAK TO YOU, IF I HAD ANY PRIDE. 102 MISBEG
(STARES AT HER CURIOUSLY) YOU'VE GOT TOO DAMN 102 MISBEG
MUCH PRIDE, JOSIE.
=PRIDE IS THE SIN BY WHICH THE ANGELS FELL.= 134 MISBEG
IT'S TO GIVE YOU THE LOVE YOU NEED, AND IT'LL BE 142 MISBEG
MY PRIDE AND MY JOY.
BUT THERE'S PRIDE IN MY HEART, TOO. 161 MISBEG
IT GAVE HIS PRIDE THE TASTE FOR REVENGE AND AFTER 12 POET
THAT HE WAS ALWAYS LOOKIN' FOR
BUT HE WAS ASHAMED OF HER IN HIS PRIDE AT THE SAME 14 POET
TIME
SHE'S HIS GREATEST PRIDE. 22 POET
BECAUSE IF HE HADN'T THE PRIDE OR LOVE FOR YOU 23 POET
NOT TO LIVE ON YOUR SLAVING YOUR HEART OUT, I HAD 23 POET
THAT PRIDE AND LOVE/
(EXASPERATED.) IT'S YOU OUGHT TO BE ASHAMED, FOR 24 POET
NOT HAVIN' MORE PRIDE/
UCH, MOTHER, IT'S ALL RIGHT FOR THE TWO OF US, OUT 24 POET
OF OUR OWN PRIDE.
YOU'D LEAVE HIM TODAY, IF YOU HAD ANY PRIDE/ 25 POET
I'VE PRIDE IN MY LOVE FOR HIM/ 25 POET

PRIEST

PRIDE (CONT'D.)
FOR THERE'S THE SAME CIVIL OF PRIDE IN YOU THAT'S 25 POET
IN HIM.
FOR THE LOVE OF GOD, DON'T TAKE THE PRIDE OF MY 26 POET
LOVE FROM ME, SARA.
THERE IS A LOOK OF WRECKED DISTINCTION ABOUT IT, 34 POET
OF BROODING, HUMILIATED PRIDE.
= AS IF IT WERE AN INCANTATION BY WHICH HE SUMMONS 43 POET
PRIDE TO JUSTIFY HIS LIFE TO
THOUGH IT IS DIFFICULT AT TIMES FOR MY PRIDE TO 48 POET
REMEMBER
IT WOULD BE A GREAT PRIDE TO HER, I'M SURE, TO 49 POET
KNOW YOU FOUND HER SUITABLE/
I HAVE A PRIDE UNDULY SENSITIVE TO ANY FANCIED 70 POET
SLIGHT.
IF I COULD ABJURE PRIDE AND FORGET THE PAST. 71 POET
SEETHING NOW IN A FURY OF HUMILIATED PRIDE. 72 POET
YOU SHOULD HAVE MORE PRIDE/ 79 POET
SURELY YOU CAN'T BELIEVE I COULD HAVE LOOKED 91 POET
FORWARD TO HUMBLING MY PRIDE,
REMARKING WITH CARELESS PRIDE.) 119 POET
AND THERE ARE TEARS OF HUMILIATED PRIDE IN HER 123 POET
EYES.)
WHERE IS YOUR PRIDE THAT YOU'D DIRTY YOUR HANDS ON123 POET
THE LIKE OF HIM&
SARA WITH A STRANGE LOOK OF SATISFIED PRIDE.) 124 POET
YOU'D SELL YOUR PRIDE AS MY DAUGHTER--/ 128 POET
(WITH A QUEER PRIDE.) THE DIVIL HIMSELF COULON'T 130 POET
KAPE CON MELODY FROM A DUEL/
(SUDDENLY WITH A FLASH OF HER STRANGE, FIERCE 131 POET
PRIDE IN THE POWER OF LOVE.)
HAS HE EVEN CARED FOR ANYONE EXCEPT HIMSELF AND 138 POET
HIS PRIDE&
HIS PRIDE, INDADE/ WHAT IS IT BUT A LIES 138 POET
THE PRIDE IN HER OWN LOVE/ 147 POET
I KNEW NOTHING OF LOVE, OR THE PRIDE A WOMAN CAN 147 POET
TAKE IN GIVING EVERYTHING--
HAVEN'T YOU TOLD ME OF THE PRIDE IN YOUR LOVE& 148 POET
YOUR LOVE IN HIM, AND TO KEEP THAT YOUR PRIDE WILL150 POET
DO ANYTHING.
AND HIS PRIDE AND HONOR AND HISMARE THE NEXT. 158 POET
(STANDS TENSELY--BURSTS OUT WITH A STRANGE 162 POET
TRIUMPHANT PRIDE.)
BUT HE'S DEAD NOW, AND HIS LAST BIT AV LYIN' PRIDE168 POET
IS MURDHERED AND STINKIN'.
BLATHERIN' ABOUT PRIDE AND HONOR, 168 POET
WITH NO FEAR IN THEM--PROUD, UNDERSTANDING PRIDE--169 POET
LOVING ME--
THERE WASN'T MUCH PRIDE LEFT IN THE AULD LUNATIC, 169 POET
ANYWAY,
EVEN THE LADIES IN SPAIN--DEEP DOWN THAT'S BEEN MY178 POET
PRIDE, TOO--
IT'S MY PRIDE, TOO/ 178 POET
I MUST HAVE HIS CRAZY PRIDE IN ME. 180 POET
I MEAN, THE LATE MAJOR MELODY'S PRIDE. 180 POET
GOD PITY HIM, HE'S HAD TO LIVE ALL HIS LIFE ALONE 181 POET
IN THE HELL AV PRIDE.
(SHE SMILES.) SURE, I HAVE NO PRIDE AT ALL-- 182 POET
EXCEPT THAT.
(THEN WITH A FLASH OF HUMBLE PRIDE) 29 STRANG
PRIDE... 62 STRANG
SHE'D HATE ME FOR SWALLOWING MY PRIDE AFTER HE'S 68 STRANG
NEVER BEEN TO SEE US...
(THE WORDS AND THE TONE SHOCK HIS PRIDE TO LIFE-- 99 STRANG
(THINKING TENDERLY) (ILET HIS PRIDE PUT ALL THE 102 STRANG
BLAME ON ME/...
(WITH A MATERNAL PRIDE AND AMUSEMENT) 113 STRANG
(CONTEMPLATING HIMSELF WITH PRIDE) 122 STRANG
TO HELL WITH PRIDE/...!) 125 STRANG
(GOOD-NATUREDLY, WITH A TRACE OF PRIDE) 163 STRANG
SO MANY OLD WOUNDS MAY HAVE TO BE UNBOUND, AND OLD188 STRANG
SCARS POINTED TO WITH PRIDE.
(WITH A SUDDEN QUEER, EXULTANT PRIDE) 469 WELDED
SHE TURNS TO HIM, SMILING WITH CHILDISH PRIDE) 474 WELDED
FAIL WITH PRIDE--WITH JOY/ 488 WELDED

PRIDED
WHICH HE HAD PRIDED HIMSELF HIS REASON HAD KILLED,544 DAYS

PRIED
(HE COMES TO HER) I'VE PRIED OPEN EVERYTHING I 115 ELECTR
COULD FIND.

PRIES
AS HE PRIES OPEN A DRAWER.) 114 ELECTR
(SETH PRIES OFF THE BOARD DOOR AND UNLOCKS THE 132 ELECTR
INNER DOOR.)

PRIEST
=JOHNNY-THE-PRIEST= DESERVES HIS NICKNAME. 3 ANNA
(LAUGHS) MY GOD, THINK OF YOU HAVING A PRIEST FOR499 DAYS
AN UNCLE/
A PRIEST& 499 DAYS
IT'S A PRIEST. 499 DAYS
(GIVES THE PRIEST AN AMUSED SMILE) 504 DAYS
WHILE THE PRIEST SITS IN THE ONE AT RIGHT, CENTER,505 DAYS
HE EVEN DREAMED OF BECOMING A PRIEST. 510 DAYS
(THE PRIEST GIVES A SWIFT, REPROACHFUL LOOK AT 510 DAYS
JOHN, SEEMS ABOUT TO PROTEST,
ENTERTAINING A STRANGE PRIEST-UNCLE FOR THE FIRST 530 DAYS
TIME.
THE PRIEST IS SITTING ON THE CHAISE-LONGUE, JOHN 541 DAYS
IN THE CHAIR AT FRONT OF TABLE,
AS IF HE SUDDENLY SENSED A PRESENCE THERE THE 551 DAYS
PRIEST IS PRAYING TO.
(HIS EYES TURN TO THE PRIEST. 551 DAYS
AND THE PRIEST CONTINUES, THE NURSE WATCHING AND 554 DAYS
LISTENING.
THE PRIEST NODS AND COMES AROUND THE CORNER OF THE554 DAYS
BED TOWARD JOHN.

PRIEST 1248

PRIEST (CONT'D.)
(HE FLASHES A SIGNAL TO THE PRIEST AND THEY BOTH 555 DAYS LIFT JOHN TO HIS FEET)
LIKE A PRIEST, OFFERING UP PRAYERS FOR THE 290 GGBROW DYING,
THE PRIEST GOES ON TAUNTINGLY) 283 LAZARU
ON THE RIGHT, THE INEVITABLE WARRIOR--ON HIS LEFT,364 MARCOM THE INEVITABLE PRIEST--
(TO THE BUDDHIST PRIEST) WORSHIPER OF BUDDHA, 434 MARCOM
(TO THE PRIESTS OF TAO) PRIEST OF TAO, 434 MARCOM
(WEARILY) AND YOUR ANSWER, PRIEST OF ISLAM, 435 MARCOM
NO, ONLY A PRIEST OF ALMIGHTY GOD--(WITH A ROUSED 139 POET REBELLION AGAIN,)
THAT'S KEPT ME FROM EVER CONFESSIN' TO A PRIEST. 138 POET
UP THE PRIEST TO HEAR MY CONFESSION AND GIVE ME 138 POET GOD'S FORGIVENESS THAT'D BRING
(HE MAKES A MOTION OVER THE BODY LIKE A PRIEST 183 STRANG BLESSING)

PRIEST'S
SCENE--JOHNNY-THE-PRIEST'S= SALOON NEAR SOUTH 3 ANNA STREET, NEW YORK CITY.
OF A PITYING BUT WEARY OLD PRIEST'S. 574 ICEMAN
PARTICULARLY THE TIME I TRIED TO COMMIT SUICIDE AT147 JOURNE JIMMIE THE PRIEST'S,
(SHE SIGHS REGRETFULLY) AH, WELL, MIKE, YOU WAS 5 MISBEG BORN A PRIEST'S PET,
I'M GOING TO THE PRIEST'S, SARA. 139 POET

PRIESTESS
AS IF IT WERE SOME SECRET TEMPLE OF WHICH YOU WERE109 MANSNS HIGH PRIESTESS/

PRIESTS
(HARSHLY) I DON'T KNOW ANY PRIESTS/ 499 DAYS
A FINE LORD WHOM OUR HIGH PRIESTS HAVE HAD 284 LAZARU ARRESTED LIKE A THIEF/
ACCOMPANYING THE BIER, ONE AT EACH CORNER, ARE 433 MARCOM FOUR PRIESTS--
KUBLAI SPEAKS TO THE PRIESTS IN A VOICE OF COMMAND434 MARCOM
(TO THE PRIESTS OF TAO) PRIEST OF TAO, 434 MARCOM
THE FOUR PRIESTS GO FIRST, BEGINNING TO PRAY 436 MARCOM SILENTLY AGAIN.
HE TELLS HER IT WAS THE PRIESTS TRICKED HIM INTO 14 POET MARRYING HER.
HE HATES PRIESTS. 14 POET
SHE STILL HAS A SECRET FONDNESS FOR PRIESTS. 97 POET
DERISIVELY.) OCH, LAVE IT TO THE PRIESTS, DIVIL 97 POET MEND THIM/

PRIESTS'
(THEN EXASPERATEDLY.) DAMN YOUR PRIESTS' PRATING 61 POET ABOUT YOUR SIN/

PRIM
HE IS DRESSED WITH A PRIM NEATNESS IN SHINY OLD 201 AHWILD BLACK CLOTHES,)
RATHER PRIM-LOOKING WOMAN OF FIFTY-FIVE WHO HAD 94 BEYOND ONCE BEEN A SCHOOL TEACHER.
THERE IS A QUALITY ABOUT HIM OF A PRIM, VICTORIAN 575 ICEMAN OLD MAID,
(WHO HAS BEEN DREAMING, A LOOK OF PRIM RESOLUTION 603 ICEMAN ON HIS FACE,
HIS WHOLE CHARACTER HAS SOMETHING ARIDLY PRIM AND 26 MANSNS PURITANICAL ABOUT IT.
THIS DEFENSE IS STRENGTHENED BY A NATURAL TENDENCY 6 STRANG TOWARD A PRIM PROVINCIALISM
(DESPERATELY PUTTING ON HIS PRIM SEVERE MANNER 15 STRANG TOWARD AN UNRULY PUPIL)
(HE FORCES A PRIM PLAYFUL SMILE) 16 STRANG

PRIME
PRIME MANURE, BY GOD, THAT'S WHAT I BEEN T' YE/ 218 DESIRE
A PRIME CHIP O' YER MAN YE BE/ 265 DESIRE
SIXTY YEARS OLD BUT STILL IN THE PRIME OF HEALTH 513 DIFRNT AND STRENGTH,
GET SOME FUN OUT OF WHAT PA'D LEFT ME WHILE I WAS 536 DIFRNT STILL IN THE PRIME OF LIFE,
HE'LL STILL BE IN HIS PRIME WHEN YOU'RE AN OLD 34 ELECTR WOMAN WITH ALL YOUR LOOKS GONE/
(FLATTERINGLY) IT'S THE PRIME OF LIFE, HARRY. 604 ICEMAN
IT'S STAYING SOBER AND WORKING THAT CUTS MEN OFF 626 ICEMAN IN THEIR PRIME.=
HE SEEMS TEN YEARS YOUNGER, AT THE PRIME OF FORTY.288 LAZARU
HE IS A MAN OF SIXTY BUT STILL IN THE FULL PRIME 377 MARCOM OF HIS POWERS.

PRIMITIVE
I HAD FORGOTTEN HOW COMPELLING THE BRUTAL POWER OF 86 POET PRIMITIVE,

PRIMLY
(RATHER PRIMLY) THEY WAS TOO SPORTY FOR THEIR 522 DIFRNT GOOD.
(PRIMLY) YOU SAID A LOT THAT IT'S BETTER TO 538 DIFRNT FORGET, IF YOU ASK ME.
(SUDDENLY PRIMLY VIRTUOUS.) I'D NEVER SUGGEST A 52 JOURNE MAN OR A WOMAN TOUCH DRINK,
OR PRIMLY SELF-RIGHTEOUS. 4 MISBEG
(HE SMILES) (PRIMLY CLASSICAL... 4 STRANG

PRIMNESS
THERE IS NO SUGGESTION OF PRIMNESS ABOUT THE 94 BEYOND WHOLE.

PRIMPING
SHE'S PRIMPING UP BEFORE MY MIRROR... 429 DYNAMO
SHE IS DRESSED AS IN SCENE ONE BUT WITH AN ADDED 274 GGBROW TOUCH OF EFFECTIVE PRIMPING
YOU'LL SOON SPEND HALF THE DAY PRIMPING BEFORE THE 27 JOURNE MIRROR.

PRINCE
AND BECAME PRINCE OF DARKNESS. 297 GGBROW
THE MEN ARE IN PRINCE ALBERTS, HIGH HATS, SPATS, 236 HA APE CANES, ETC.
THAT WHEN MEETING A PRINCE THE CUSTOMARY 595 ICEMAN SALUTATION IS =WHAT'LL YOU HAVE=
IF IT AIN'T PRINCE WILLIE/ 644 ICEMAN

PRINCE (CONT'D.)
BE THE AIRS 'E PUTS ON YOU'D THINK 'E WAS THE 517 INZONE PRINCE OF WALES.
I CURSE THESE DEVILS AND THAT PRINCE OF DEVILS, 285 LAZARU THAT FALSE PROPHET, JESUS/
CAESAR IS CAESAR THE AUGUST ONE PRINCE OF THE 315 LAZARU SENATE TRIBUNE OVER TRIBUNES
SHE POISONED PRINCE MARCELLUS AND YOUNG GAIUS AND 355 LAZARU LUCIUS THAT THE MAY MIGHT BE
MADE UP THE FAIRY TALE ABOUT THE EXILED PRINCE AND 75 MANSNS THE MAGIC DOOR--
WHICH SPOKE OF OUR LORD AS THE PRINCE OF PEACE. 394 MARCOM
BUDDHA, THE PRINCE OF PEACE, 422 MARCOM
(EXALTEDLY) MY BELOVED PRINCE/ 430 MARCOM
(JOKINGLY) NO, IF I WAS A PRINCE 430 MARCOM

PRINCES
EIGHT PRINCES OF THE BLOOD IN BLACK ARMOR. 433 MARCOM
THE PRINCES LIFT THE BIER OF KUKACHIN TO THE TOP 434 MARCOM OF THE CATAFALQUE.

PRINCESS
OR THE POOR ABUSED LITTLE PRINCESS--THAT WAS 12 MANSNS WONDERFUL,
AND THE COMFORT AND RICHES AND LUXURY THAT'S DUE 191 MANSNS THE GREAT PRINCESS
LOOKS LIKE A FAIRY PRINCESS AS BEAUTIFUL AS A ROSE 53 POET IN THE MORNIN' DEW.

PRINCESS'S
TO LOOK CAREFULLY AND DEEPLY INTO THE PRINCESS'S 404 MARCOM EYES

PRINCESSES
REMEMBER AGAIN, PRINCESSES MAY NOT WEEP/ 390 MARCOM

PRINCETON
THERE WASN'T ANYONE THERE BUT A PRINCETON SENIOR 1282 AHWILD KNOW--HE BELONGS
WHY DIDN'T THE PRINCETON FULLBACK WHO'D BROUGHT 283 AHWILD THEM THERE/

PRINCIPALLY
I KNOW HIS LEAVING ME WAS YOUR DOING PRINCIPALLY, 32 ELECTR VINNIE/
FOR THE BENEFIT OF THEIR WORKERS PRINCIPALLY, 149 JOURNE
THESE ARE PACKED WITH BOOKS, PRINCIPALLY EDITIONS, 3 STRANG MANY OF THEM OLD AND RARE,
BUT IT IS PRINCIPALLY HER MOOD THAT HAS CHANGED 79 STRANG HER,

PRINCIPLE
THE CELESTIAL, MALE PRINCIPLE OF THE COSMOS. 389 MARCOM

PRINT
I'M GOING TO REFUSE TO PRINT YOUR DAMNED AD AFTER 203 AHWILD TOMORROW/

PRINTED
EVEN IF HIS IDEAS ARE SO CRAZY THEY OUGHTN'T TO 288 AHWILD ALLOW THEM TO BE PRINTED,
AND AROUND THE TOP PRINTED IN FORGET-ME-NOTS WAS 31 HUGHIE =GOOD-BY, OLD PAL.=
(GLOOMILY) AND I, FOR MY SINS, AM HAWKING A 348 MARCOM NOVELTY, A BLOCK-PRINTED BOOK,
TAKES A PIECE OF PRINTED PAPER LIKE A DOLLAR BILL 393 MARCOM FROM HIS POCKET)

PRINTS
SEVERAL FRAMED PRINTS OF SCENES FROM THE BIBLE 421 DYNAMO HANG ON THE WALLS.

PRIS'NER
I 'EARD IT FROM A BLOKE WHAT WAS CAPTURED PRIS'NER4S7 CARIBBE BY 'EM

PRISON
AND THIS TERRIBLE SHIP, AND THIS PRISON OF A ROOM,545 'ILE AND THE ICE ALL AROUND,
THEY'RE LIKE THE WALLS OF A NARROW PRISON YARD 126 BEYOND SHUTTING ME IN
(A PAUSE) I WANT T' SHARE WITH YE, ABBIE--PRISON 267 DESIRE 'R DEATH 'R HELL 'R ANYTHIN'/
MAYBE I GITS IN 'NOTHER ARGUMENT WID DE PRISON 181 EJONES GUARD
THEY ARE FOLLOWED BY A WHITE MAN DRESSED IN THE 194 EJONES UNIFORM OF A PRISON GUARD.
THE PRISON GUARD POINTS STERNLY AT JONES WITH HIS 194 EJONES WHIP.
(THE PRISON GUARD CRACKS HIS WHIP--NOISELESSLY-- 194 EJONES LIVING ALONE HERE WITH THE DEAD IS A WORSE ACT OF 178 ELECTR JUSTICE THAN DEATH OR PRISON/
A ROW OF CELLS IN THE PRISON ON BLACKWELLS ISLAND.239 HA APE JUST AT THIS MOMENT THE PRISON GUARD RUSHES IN, 245 HA APE DRAGGING A HOSE BEHIND HIM.)
HE ROTTED TEN YEARS IN PRISON FOR HIS FAITH/ 641 ICEMAN
THIS ISN'T A PRISON. 75 JOURNE
I WEPT WHEN HE WAS THROWN IN PRISON-- 105 JOURNE
AND SAW THE CITY AS FROM A TOWER, HOSPITAL, 133 JOURNE BROTHEL, PRISON, AND SUCH HELLS,
A LORD WHO IS IN THE COMMON PRISON AT JERUSALEM, 1284 LAZARU HEARD TODAY
A VERY FRIGHTENING PRISON IT BECOMES AT LAST, FULL 28 MANSNS OF GHOSTS AND CORPSES.
BUT YOU KEEP TRYING TO ESCAPE AS IF IT WERE A 453 WELDED PRISON.

PRISONER
I WON'T STAND IT--I CAN'T STAND IT--PENT UP BY 546 'ILE THESE WALLS LIKE A PRISONER.
AS IF YOU WERE A JUDGE AGAIN AND IWERE THE 51 ELECTR PRISONER,
LIKE A PRISONER AT THE BAR, FACING THE JUDGE. 258 GGBROW
LOOKING AS IF HE'D LIKE TO FORGET HIS PRISONER AND718 ICEMAN START CLEANING OUT THE PLACE.
WHO HAD TAKEN LAZARUS PRISONER, MARCH IN WITH 306 LAZARU DANCERS=STEPS,
HER BIG DARK EYES ARE GRIM WITH THE PRISONER-PAIN 53 STRANG OF A WALLED-IN SOUL.

PRISONER'S
LIKE A PRISONER'S LOCKSTEP. 217 HA APE

PROBLEM

PRISONS
CITIES ARE PRISONS WHEREIN MAN LOCKS HIMSELF FROM 310 LAZARU LIFE.

PRITIND
I'LL PRITIND TO MAKE FRIENDS WITH HIM, GOD ROAST 590 ROPE HIS SOUL/
HE'S FOXY TO PRITIND HE'S LOONY, BUT HE'S HIS WITS592 ROPE WITH HIM ALL THE TIME.

PRIVACY
THE COMFORT SHE LOVED, THE PROTECTED PRIVACY, HER 47 MANSNS FANCIFUL WALLED-IN GARDEN,
CAN I NEVER HAVE A MOMENT'S PRIVACY IN MY OWN 130 MANSNS HOMES

PRIVATE
JOHN LOVING'S PRIVATE OFFICE IN THE OFFICES OF 493 DAYS ELIOT AND COMPANY, NEW YORK CITY.
HE IS DRESSED IN THE KHAKI UNIFORM OF A PRIVATE INS19 DIFRNT THE UNITED STATES ARMY.
THAT EVERAT EVERYTHING SHOULD BE PRIVATE AND 69 ELECTR QUIET.
SCENE--THE DRAFTING ROOM AND PRIVATE OFFICE OF 302 GGBROW BROWN ARE BOTH SHOWN.
(HE THROWS OPEN THE DOOR AND USHERS HER INTO HIS 304 GGBROW PRIVATE OFFICE.)
THIS YEAR'S THEIR BLEEDIN' PRIVATE LANE, AS YER 233 HA APE MIGHT SAY.
YUH REMEMBER DEY USED TO SEND DOWN A PRIVATE DICK 581 ICEMAN AND YOU THOUGHT A WOMAN YOU LOVED WAS A PIECE OF 647 ICEMAN PRIVATE PROPERTY YOU OWNED.
I'LL GO AND HAVE A PRIVATE CHIN WITH THE 652 ICEMAN COMMISSIONER,
WHO WAS NOT ONLY INTERFERING IN YOUR PRIVATE 660 ICEMAN BUSINESS,
PRIVATE B'LONGINGS/ 526 INZONE
THAT'S ONLY--HOW DARE--WHAT ARE YOU DOING WITH MY 526 INZONE PRIVATE BELONGINGSS
THE STATE HAS THE MONEY TO MAKE A BETTER PLACE 144 JOURNE THAN ANY PRIVATE SANATORIUM.
IN A FREE SOCIETY THERE MUST BE NO PRIVATE 8 MANSNS PROPERTY
IN GOING OVER HENRYY'S PRIVATE PAPERS, WE MADE THE 31 MANSNS ASTOUNDING DISCOVERY--
(SCENE SIMON'S PRIVATE OFFICE IN THE OFFICES OF 69 MANSNS SIMON HARFORD INC.
PRYING AND INTERFERING IN MY PRIVATE BUSINESS/ 74 MANSNS
I FIND IT ADVISABLE TO ADD A PRIVATE SECRETARY TO 97 MANSNS MY EMPLOY.
(--I AM AFRAID I INTERRUPTED A PRIVATE DISCUSSION.127 MANSNS
(SCENE SAME AS SCENE ONE OF ACT TWO--SIMON'S 139 MANSNS PRIVATE OFFICE.
TOWARD EVERY SECRET PRIVATE CORNER OF MY SOUL. 184 MANSNS
(INTERPOSING EAGERLY) IF I MIGHT SPEAK TO THE BOY380 MARCOM IN PRIVATE A MINUTE--
IT'S THE SAME YOU WAS DRINKING LAST NIGHT--HIS 9 POET PRIVATE DEW.
I CAME HERE TO SEEK A PRIVATE INTERVIEW WITH THE 117 POET PROPRIETOR OF THIS TAVERN.
HOME? IS THAT YOUR PRIVATE BRAND OF REVENGE--TO 472 WELDED GO WITH MEN WITH HOMES$

PRIVATEERING
HAD TO MAKE A LARGE, GREEDY FORTUNE OUT OF 83 POET PRIVATEERING AND THE NORTHWEST TRADE,

PRIVATELY
I CAME PRIVATELY FROM HER. 424 MARCOM

PRIVILEGE
BUT I FEEL I'VE HAD THE PRIVILEGE OF YOUR 500 DAYS ACQUAINTANCE ALREADY
HE THINKS IT GIVES HIM THE PRIVILEGE TO BE A 540 DIFRNT BULLY?
DOES IT GIVE THEM THE PRIVILEGE OF TRESPASSING. 16 ELECTR
MAKES THE ESTABLISHMENT LEGALLY A HOTEL AND GIVES 571 ICEMAN IT THE PRIVILEGE OF SERVING
THAT'S A HUSBAND'S PRIVILEGE. 414 MARCOM
IT HAS BEEN A PRIVILEGE TO BE ABLE TO CONVERSE 48 POET WITH A CULTURED GENTLEMAN AGAIN.
I SHOULD GRANT IT IS A PRETTY WOMAN'S PRIVILEGE TO 76 POET BE ALWAYS RIGHT

PRIVILEGES
I WILL STILL HAVE ALL THE PRIVILEGES OF MY HOME 66 MANSNS

PRIZE
GOSH, YOU DO TAKE THE PRIZE FOR DAY-DREAMING/ 82 BEYOND
YOU AIN'T NO BLEEDIN' BEAUTY PRIZE YESELF, ME MAN.461 CARIBE
(PROUDLY.) HAIN'T WE RAISED 'EM T' BE FUST-RATE, 218 DESIRE NUMBER ONE PRIZE STUCKS
YE LOOK ALL SLICKED UP LIKE A PRIZE BULL. 228 DESIRE
I'M THE PRIZE ROOSTER OF THIS ROOST. 246 DESIRE
OH, IF YOU'D ONLY MAKE A PRIZE JACKASS OF THAT 432 DYNAMO YELLOW NANCY SON OF HIS/
AND EVERYBODY'S GETTIN' A PRIZE GROUCH ON. 631 ICEMAN
DAT LOUSE HICKEY'S COITINLY MADE A PRIZE COUPLA 670 ICEMAN SUCKERS OUTA YOUSE.
WHAT A PRIZE SAP YOU BEEN, 697 ICEMAN
ALL PRIZE PIGS, TOO/ 63 MISBEG
(THICKLY) HE'S ONE AND A PRIZE ONE, BUT I DON'T 78 MISBEG MEAN HIM.
FAITH, YOU'RE A PRIZE DUNCE/ 78 MISBEG
YOU'VE MADE A PRIZE DAMNED FOOL OF HIM AND THAT'S 87 MISBEG SOME SATISFACTION/
BUT HERE'S WHERE YOU'VE MADE A PRIZE JACKASS OF 88 MISBEG HIM, LIKE I SAID.
BE GOD, YOU'LL MAKE HIM THE PRIZE SUCKER OF THE 95 MISBEG WORLD/
IF MY POOR OLD FATHER HAD SEEN YOU KNOCKING HIS 123 MISBEG PRIZE WHISKEY ON THE GROUND--
PHIL CERTAINLY HAS A PRIZE BUN ON TONIGHT. 132 MISBEG
((WHAT A PRIZE/... 120 STRANG
NINA'S CERTAINLY BECOME THE PRIZE BUM SPORT/... 160 STRANG

PRIZEFIGHTER
(A BRAWNY IRISHMAN WITH THE BATTERED FEATURES OF A478 CARDIF PRIZEFIGHTER)

PRIZES
PARADE WITH PRIZES FOR THE FATTEST-- 296 GGBROW

PROBABLE
AND THAT IT IS PROBABLE I MALICIOUSLY LIED AND 111 MANSNS GAVE YOU A FALSE HOPE.

PROBABLY
(SOUTHINGLY) HE PROBABLY COULDN'T GET A SEAT, THE251 AHWILD TRULLEYS ARE SO JAMMED.
PSHAW, WHY, RICHARD'LL PROBABLY FORGET ALL ABOUT 291 AHWILD HER BEFORE HE'S AWAY SIX
BUT THEY'RE PROBABLY LYING AROUND SOMEWHERES. 86 BEYOND
RUTH TOLD ME I'D PROBABLY FIND YOU UP TOP-SIDE 130 BEYOND HERE.
I'M NOT THE RICH MAN YOU'VE PROBABLY BEEN LED TO 156 BEYOND BELIEVE BY MY LETTERS--NOT NOW.
OH, THEY FORGOT A LOT, AND LUCKY FOR THEM THEY 560 CROSS DID, PROBABLY.
OH, I'LL PROBABLY NEVER WRITE IT, BUT IT'S AMUSING497 DAYS TO DOPE OUT.
PROBABLY WANTS MY ADVICE ON WHAT TO GIVE WALTER 498 DAYS FOR A BIRTHDAY PRESENT.
IN THIRTY YEARS WE'LL BOTH BE DEAD AND GONE, 518 DIFRNT PROBABLY.
BUT PROBABLY THAT'S BECAUSE YOU'RE SO TIRED. 49 ELECTR
PROBABLY HE'D LIVED WITH ONE OF THE NATIVE WOMEN/ 154 ELECTR
HE WAS PROBABLY HITTING IT UP ON THE Q.T. ALL THE 314 GGBROW TIME.
«PROBABLY NOT PRETTY.» 26 HUGHIE
BUT HE'LL PROBABLY BE HIS NATURAL SELF AGAIN 625 ICEMAN TOMORROW--
IT PROBABLY IS WHEN YOU LIVE IN A HOVEL ON A BOG, 34 JOURNE BUT OVER HERE,
YOU'LL PROBABLY MEET SOME OF YOUR FRIENDS UPTOWN 90 JOURNE
PROBABLY IN ONE OF THE OLD TRUNKS IN THE ATTIC. 115 JOURNE
THEN IT DOESN'T TAKE A SOUTHSAYER TO TELL HE'S 129 JOURNE PROBABLY IN THE WHOREHOUSE.
PROBABLY GIVE YOU A CASE TO TAKE WITH YOU TO THE 157 JOURNE STATE FARM FOR PAUPER PATIENTS.
AND SO I'M PROBABLY HOPING-- 163 JOURNE
PROBABLY HAVEN'T GOT CONSUMPTION AT ALL. 164 JOURNE
PROBABLY THE LEGIONS ARE TO BUTCHER THEM IN THEIR 315 LAZARU SLEEP.
YOU PROBABLY THINK I MUST BE SECRETLY KEEPING SOME 80 MANSNS BEAUTIFUL MISTRESS
SARA HAS PROBABLY TOLD YOU OF HER VISIT TO MY 96 MANSNS OFFICE THIS MORNING.
I WARN YOU YOUR PRIDE WILL PROBABLY BE IMPELLED TO153 MANSNS REJECT THEM.
THE KHAN PROBABLY MEANT WHENEVER YOU WERE WILLING.411 MARCOM
I THINK PROBABLY HER SPLEEN IS OUT OF ORDER. 420 MARCOM
PROBABLY SNORING, AS YOU WATCHED THE DAWN COME. 124 MISBEG
HE'S PROBABLY DEAD ANYWAY BY THIS. 581 ROPE
THEN, THE MOST MODERN PROBABLY BEING THACKERAY. 3 STRANG
YOU PROBABLY DON'T KNOW, 10 STRANG
IT'S PROBABLY A REFLECTION OF HER OWN SILLY FIXED 38 STRANG IDEA ABOUT HIM.
WHEN IT'S PROBABLY NOTHING....) 74 STRANG
(CYNICALLY) ((PROBABLY WHY.... 79 STRANG
(PROBABLY LUCKY FOR ME I DON'T KNOW/...)) 93 STRANG
(INDIFFERENTLY) HE'LL PROBABLY COME WITHOUT 94 STRANG BOTHERING TO WRITE.
SHE'LL PROBABLY BE ONLY TOO GLAD...) 113 STRANG
IF HE DID COME, HE'D PROBABLY AVOID ME....) 118 STRANG
THEY'LL PROBABLY ALL SHARE EQUALLY... 125 STRANG
AND YOU TWO PROBABLY HAVE A LOT TO TALK OVER. 129 STRANG
RIGHT AT THE MOMENT WHEN HE'S PROBABLY GETTING 163 STRANG INTO THE SHELL--
YOU'VE PROBABLY WONDERED WHY I OBJECTED. 178 STRANG
(MOCKINGLY) PROBABLY/ 181 STRANG
I THOUGHT NELLY'D PROBABLY HAVE HEARD FROM YOU. 450 WELDED

PROBATE
I'VE BEEN AFRAID LATELY THE MINUTE THE ESTATE IS 31 MISBEG OUT OF PROBATE,
THEY SAID THE ESTATE WOULD BE OUT OF PROBATE 131 MISBEG WITHIN A FEW DAYS.
YOU KNEW THE ESTATE WOULD BE OUT OF PROBATE IN A 163 MISBEG FEW DAYS.

PROBE
(SUDDENLY HOLDING HER AWAY FROM HIM AND STARING 76 ANNA INTO HER EYES AS IF TO PROBE
(HIS VOICE LIKE A PROBE) WHY HAS NO WOMAN EVER 298 GGBROW LOVED HIM$

PROBING
YOUR EYES HAVE BEEN PROBING ME, 51 ELECTR
REGARDING HER WITH AN UNEASY, PROBING LOOK. 20 JOURNE
ON THE OTHER HAND, JAMIE KNOWS AFTER ONE PROBING 58 JOURNE LOOK AT HER
EACH SNEAKS A SUSPICIOUS, PROBING GLANCE AT THE 136 MANSNS
(GIVES HER A QUICK, PROBING SIDE GLANCE--CASUALLY) 21 MISBEG
HIS EYES FIX ON JOSIE'S FACE IN A LONG, PROBING 157 MISBEG STARE.)
THE TWO MEN STARE AT EACH OTHER FOR A MOMENT, 34 STRANG DARRELL WITH A FRANK PROBING,

PROBINGLY
THE STOPS ABRUPTLY, STARING PROBINGLY AT THE 35 HUGHIE CLERK.

PROBITY
THE LIPS OF AN ABLE SOLDIER-STATESMAN OF RIGID 337 LAZARU PROBITY.

PROBLEM
THAT IT WOULD BE INTERESTING TO WORK OUT YOUR 495 DAYS HERO'S ANSWER TO HIS PROBLEM,
I--I WAS TRYING TO CONCENTRATE MY THOUGHTS ON THE 172 MANSNS FINAL SOLUTION OF THE PROBLEM.

PROBLEM

PROBLEM (CONT'D.)
I ATTEMPT TO EXPLAIN AN ABSTRACT PROBLEM OF THE 173 MANSNS
NATURE OF MAN.
I KNOW THE ONE PROBLEM THAT INTERESTS YOU. 174 MANSNS
EXCLUSIVE INVENTION TO SOLVE THIS PROBLEM. 395 MARCOM

PROBLEMS
STRANGE, ISN'T IT, WHAT DIFFICULT PROBLEMS YOUR 528 DAYS
LITTLE DABBLE IN FICTION HAS

PROCEED
(WITH JUBILANT HAPPINESS--AS THEY PROCEED TOWARD 39 ANNA
THE CABIN)
BUT THE POLOS PROCEED SPEEDILY ON THEIR JOURNEY 364 MARCOM
WITH YOUR PERMISSION, WE WILL PROCEED AT ONCE TO 119 POET
THE MATTER IN HAND.

PROCEEDED
I MUST SAY YOU PROCEEDED VERY UNSCIENTIFICALLY, 82 STRANG
DOCTOR/

PROCEEDING
(HAS WATCHED THIS PROCEEDING WITH AN AWAKENED 128 JOURNE
SENSE OF HUMOR--
I WAS PROCEEDING WESTWARD ON A BUSINESS VENTURE, 350 MARCOM
GOOD SIR.

PROCEEDINGS
SHE TURNS HER BACK ON THE PROCEEDINGS AND STARES 30 ANNA
OUT INTO THE FOG.

PROCEEDS
WE CAN DEVOTE THE PROCEEDS TO REHABILITATING THE 237 HA APE
VEIL OF THE TEMPLE.
AND DIVIDE THE PROCEEDS AMONG YOURSELVES/ 428 MARCOM
MELODY PROCEEDS WITH HIS ATTACK, FULL OF 70 POET
CONFIDENCE NOW.

PROCESS
IC EFFORTS TO SPEED UP AND THE MUSIC SUFFERS IN 471 CARIBE
THE PROCESS.)
I'M A WASTE PRODUCT IN THE BESSEMER PROCESS--LIKE 219 HA APE
THE MILLIONS.
WHICH IS IN PROCESS OF CONSTRUCTION-WITH BRAVADO) 238 HA APE
REVERSED THE NATURAL PROCESS AND GROWS YOUNGER& 354 LAZARU
THE WHOLE PROCESS IS A MAN-POWER ORIGINAL OF THE 400 MARCOM
MODERN DEVICES

PROCESSES
OF LIVING AND DYING AS PROCESSES IN ETERNAL 307 LAZARU
GROWTH.

PROCESSION
JOIN THE PROCESSION/ 267 GGBROW
AND HE'S STILL BEING WHEELED ALONG IN THE 296 GGBROW
PROCESSION.
A PROCESSION OF GAUDY MARIONETTES, 236 HA APE
THE PASSIVE =YES= WELCOMING THE PEACEFUL 171 MANSNS
PROCESSION OF DEMANDING DAYS/
IN A GORGEOUS UNIFORM ENTERS AND STANDS AT 427 MARCOM
ATTENTION AS THE PROCESSION BEGINS.
(A PROCESSION OF SERVANTS BEGINS TO FILE ONE BY 428 MARCOM
ONE THROUGH THE RANKS OF
A MOMENT LATER THE FUNERAL PROCESSION ENTERS. 433 MARCOM

PROCLAIM
IF THOU DIDST, I WOULD PROCLAIM THE AWFUL WARNING 423 DYNAMO
OF IT ALL OVER AMERICA/...

PROCRASTINATING
I MEAN, THERE'S NO USE IN PROCRASTINATING 295 AHWILD
FURTHER--SO, HERE GOES.

PROCURED
I PROCURED HIM AT GREAT COST--I MEAN HE'S EXTRA 391 MARCOM
WELL-BRED.

PRODIGAL
YOUR COMPLACENT ASSUMPTION THAT LIKE THE PRODIGAL 507 DAYS
OF HIS FAIRY TALE, I--
THE PRODIGAL RETURNS/... 457 DYNAMO
WELL, THIS PRODIGAL GETS THE FATTED KISS EVEN IF =459 DYNAMO
THERE AIN'T NO CALF.=

PRODIGALITY
WHAT PRODIGALITY/ 429 MARCOM

PRODIGIOUS
IT'S LIGHT, EASY TO CARRY,--(HERE HE GIVES A 393 MARCOM
PRODIGIOUS WINK)

PRODIGY
YOU HAVE BEEN A PRODIGY OF HEROIC ACCOMPLISHMENT/ 411 MARCOM

PRODS
LOUISA PRODS HER COUSIN AND WHISPERS EXCITEDLY) 8 ELECTR
SHE PRODS MARCO, WHO IS STILL COLLECTING THE 419 MARCOM
PIECES OF THE LOCKET WITH HER FOOT)

PRODUCES
(HE PRODUCES A PAIR OF DICE-CARELESSLY.) 37 HUGHIE

PRODUCING
(PRODUCING A SOVEREIGN) HO THERE, YOU FATTY/ 497 VOYAGE

PRODUCT
YOU'RE AS MUCH A PRODUCT OF IT AS AN EAR OF CORN 84 BEYOND
IS, OR A TREE.
OR RATHER, I INHERIT THE ACQUIRED TRAIT OF THE BY-219 HA APE
PRODUCT, WEALTH.
I'M A WASTE PRODUCT IN THE BESSEMER PROCESS--LIKE 219 HA APE
THE MILLIONS.
THE FLESH AND BLOOD PRODUCT OF OUR CHRISTIAN 379 MARCOM
CIVILIZATION.
TO OBTAIN THE BEST RESULTS IN THE WEAVING AND 431 MARCOM
DYEING OF THE FINISHED PRODUCT,

PRODUCTION
BESIDE THE ASTOUNDING FACT THAT ALL IN THE 431 MARCOM
PRODUCTION OF THE RAW MATERIAL
THE ROOM IS A TYPICAL SITTING ROOM OF THE 90 STRANG
QUANTITY-PRODUCTION BUNGALOW TYPE.

PROFANE
RIOTOUSLY PROFANE LACK OF ANY APPARENT DESIGN. 284 GGBROW

PROFESSION
OUTWARD EVIDENCES OF BELONGING TO THE WORLD'S 13 ANNA
OLDEST PROFESSION.
AFTER HE'S THROUGH COLLEGE, BILLY MUST STUDY FOR A258 GGBROW
PROFESSION OF SOME SORT,

PROFESSION (CONT'D.)
ERIE--BUT DID I UNDERSTAND YOU TO SAY YOU ARE A 32 HUGHIE
GAMBLER BY PROFESSIONS
THE STAMP OF HIS PROFESSION IS UNMISTAKABLY ON 13 JOURNE
HIM.
SNEER AT MY PRUFESSION, SNEER AT EVERY DAMNED 32 JOURNE
THING IN THE WORLD--
HE MADE HIS WAY UP FROM IGNORANCE AND POVERTY TO 60 JOURNE
THE TOP OF HIS PROFESSION/
WHAT RUBBISH THOUGHTS FOR A MAN OF MY YEARS AND 37 MANSNS
PROFESSION/
PROFESSION, JOSIE& 42 MISBEG
I HAVE SMALL LIKING FOR YOUR PROFESSION, SIR, 118 POET
THEN ACCEPT MY APOLOGIES, SIR, FOR MY 119 POET
ANIMADVERSIONS AGAINST YOUR PROFESSION.
(INDIGNANT AT MELODY'S INSULTS TO HIS PROFESSION--119 POET
WITH A THINLY VEILED SNEER.)

PROFESSIONAL
DRESSED WITH CHEAP NATTINESS, WITH THE 244 AHWILD
PROFESSIONAL BREEZINESS AND JOCULAR,
(WITH PROFESSIONAL AIR) WHAT'S YOUR PLEASURE, 6 ANNA
GENTLEMEN&
HE IS A SLIGHT, MEDIUM-SIZED PROFESSIONAL-LOOKING 556 CROSS
MAN OF ABOUT THIRTY-FIVE.
(WITH A PROFESSIONAL AIR) THAT WAS NOTHING NEW. 557 CROSS
(STILLWELL, HIS AIR CURTLY PROFESSIONAL AGAIN 563 DAYS
TURNS.
MAYBE HE'S A PROFESSIONAL GAMBLER. 31 HUGHIE
AND ADDRESSES HIM IN A PROFESSIONAL CHANT) 611 ICEMAN
EXTREMELY CONSCIOUS OF THE RESPECT DUE HIS 25 MANSNS
PROFESSIONAL DIGNITY.
AND NOW ATTEMPTS TO REGAIN A BRISK, PROFESSIONAL 30 MANSNS
AIR.
(REACTS--WITH AN EXTREME PROFESSIONAL 37 MANSNS
PORTENTOUSNESS.)
FRANKNESS, PLAINLY AN IMITATION AND DISTORTION OF 139 MANSNS
SIMON'S PROFESSIONAL MANNER,
HE WAS A BIT SUSPICIOUS AT FIRST, BUT DUTCH 39 MISBEG
MAISIE--HER PROFESSIONAL NAME--
AND EXTREMELY CONSCIOUS OF HIS PROFESSIONAL 116 POET
AUTHORITY AND DIGNITY.
(UNEASY UNDER HIS GLANCE) (I) HATE THAT 79 STRANG
PROFESSIONAL LOOK IN HIS EYES...
(IN A COLD, EMOTIONLESS PROFESSIONAL VOICE, HIS 85 STRANG
FACE LIKE A MASK OF A DOCTOR)
(IN HIS ULTRA-PROFESSIONAL MANNER--LIKE AN 85 STRANG
AUTOMATON OF A DOCTOR)
(SHARPLY PROFESSIONAL) NONSENSE/ 86 STRANG
(PUTTING ON HIS BEST PROFESSIONAL AIR, GOING TO 97 STRANG
HER)
WITH A CHANGE TO A STRICTLY PROFESSIONAL MANNER) 183 STRANG

PROFESSIONALLY
(WITH A PROFESSIONALLY ARCH GRIN AT HIM) 237 AHWILD
(HE GETS UP--PROFESSIONALLY) ANY CRAMPS& 413 MARCOM
TO GIVE HER THE NURSE'S PROFESSIONALLY CALLOUS 26 STRANG
ATTITUDE.
(THEN MOCKINGLY) WELL, SINCE YOU'RE OUT HERE 82 STRANG
PROFESSIONALLY,
(PROFESSIONALLY, STARING AT HER COLDLY) 183 STRANG

PROFESSOR
THE LIBRARY OF PROFESSOR LEEDS' HOME IN A SMALL 3 STRANG
UNIVERSITY TOWN IN NEW ENGLAND.
I'D LIKE TO USE THE PROFESSOR IN A NOVEL 5 STRANG
SOMETIME...
POOR PROFESSOR/. 5 STRANG
PROFESSOR LEEDS ENTERS, 6 STRANG
AND PARTICULARLY THE PROFESSOR HIMSELF--SUBTLY 7 STRANG
EMBARRASSED.
HERE I AM AGAIN, PROFESSOR/. 7 STRANG
BUT EUROPE, PROFESSOR, 7 STRANG
(WITH CONCERN) JUST WHAT DO YOU MEAN BY CHANGED, 8 STRANG
PROFESSOR&
(THE PROFESSOR GETS TO HIS FEET, 12 STRANG
THE PROFESSOR LAUGHS NERVOUSLY. 14 STRANG
(THE PROFESSOR FORCES A SNICKER.) 14 STRANG
(THE PROFESSOR OF DEAD LANGUAGES IS TALKING 15 STRANG
AGAIN...
(THEN WATCHING THE PROFESSOR WITH A PITYING 15 STRANG
SHUDDER)
(QUITE RIGHT, PROFESSOR/... 17 STRANG
(FLURRIEDLY--GOING TO HIM) DON'T TAKE HER 20 STRANG
SERIOUSLY, PROFESSOR/
NINA WILL BE BACK WITH US IN A MONTH, PROFESSOR, 21 STRANG
(PROPHETIC PROFESSOR/... 24 STRANG
THE SAME AS SCENE ONE, PROFESSOR LEEDS' STUDY. 24 STRANG
(SMILING GRIMLY) (POOR PROFESSOR/ 24 STRANG
POOR PROFESSOR/... 25 STRANG
IT ISN'T THE PROFESSOR/... 28 STRANG
(POOR OLD PROFESSOR/...) (THEN SUDDENLY JEERING 28 STRANG
AT HIMSELF)
POOR PROFESSOR/... 74 STRANG
WHOM THE PROFESSOR HATED/...= 74 STRANG
PROFESSOR'S
THE TABLE, WITH THE PROFESSOR'S ARMCHAIR AT ITS 3 STRANG
LEFT.
(HOW PERFECTLY THE PROFESSOR'S UNIQUE 4 STRANG
HAVEN/....))
(CONTINUING IN HIS PROFESSOR'S SUPERIOR MANNER) 15 STRANG
(HE'S ON THE WRONG TACK WITH HIS PROFESSOR'S 15 STRANG
MANNER...
I BEGIN TO APPRECIATE THE PROFESSOR'S 29 STRANG
VIEWPOINT....))
MARSDEN UNCONSCIOUSLY TAKES THE PROFESSOR'S PLACE 34 STRANG
BEHIND THE TABLE.
WELL, THERE THEY WERE STUCK IN THE PROFESSOR'S 52 STRANG
HOUSE...
EVANS IS SEATED IN THE PROFESSOR'S OLD CHAIR. 66 STRANG

PROFESSOR'S (CONT'D.)
THE TABLE, ALTHOUGH IT IS THE SAME, IS NO LONGER 66 STRANG
THE PROFESSOR'S TABLE,
THE PROFESSOR'S STUDY AGAIN. 66 STRANG
BETRAYS THAT THE PROFESSOR'S WELL-ORDERED MIND 66 STRANG
AS WAS THE PROFESSOR'S STUDY IN THE LAST ACT. 90 STRANG

PROFILE
A BIG, FINELY SHAPED HEAD, A HANDSOME PROFILE, 13 JOURNE
DEEP-SET LIGHT-BROWN EYES.
BUT HIS NOSE IS HIS FATHER'S AND HIS FACE IN 20 JOURNE
PROFILE RECALLS TYRONE'S.
HER BACK PROPPED AGAINST THE RIGHT SIDE OF THE 578 ROPE
DOORWAY, HER FACE IN PROFILE.

PROFIT
AND I MADE A QUICK TURNOVER UN IT FOR A FINE 15 JOURNE
PROFIT.
THIRTY-FIVE TO FORTY THOUSAND DOLLARS NET PROFIT A150 JOURNE
SEASON
AT FROM THIRTY-FIVE TO FORTY THOUSAND NET PROFIT A150 JOURNE
SEASON/
I THINK HE TRIED ONCE TO FIND ME LISTED ON THE 11 MANSNS
PROFIT SIDE OF THE LEDGER.
TO REGAIN A SOUND POSITION BY MAKING A QUICK 32 MANSNS
PROFIT IN WESTERN LANDS.
WON'T YOU LET THE PROFIT ADD UP, AND PAY OFF WHAT 157 MANSNS
YOU OWE?
IMAGINE A PROFIT BEING EXCESS/ 392 MARCOM
AND YIELDS ENORMOUS PROFIT. 393 MARCOM

PROFITABLE
HE HAS TRAINED TO DO A PROFITABLE ACT UNDER HIS 611 ICEMAN
MANAGEMENT.
ACCEPT, IF IT STRIKES YOU AS A PROFITABLE 58 MANSNS
OPPORTUNITY.

PROFITABLY
I HAVE FIVE MILLS NOW, ALL RUNNING PROFITABLY, 70 MANSNS
INSTEAD OF ONE.

PROFITS
ABOUT SHARING THE PROFITS NEXT TIME. 609 ICEMAN
MERCHANTS MAKE GREAT PROFITS. 365 MARCOM
THE MERCHANTS MAKE GREAT PROFITS. 370 MARCOM
FOR ONE THING I FOUND THEY HAD A HIGH TAX ON 392 MARCOM
EXCESS PROFITS.
WAR IS A WASTE OF MONEY WHICH EATS INTO THE 394 MARCOM
PROFITS OF LIFE LIKE THUNDER/
IF ITS PROFITS YOU'RE LOOKING FOR, YOU WON'T FIND 16 POET
THEM--
AND FINALLY WERE EVEN DRIVEN TO EMBRACE THE 83 POET
PROFITS OF THE SLAVE TRADE--

PROFOUND
IN THE MIDDLE OF PROFOUND MEDITATION) 278 AHWILD
HER LARGE EYES DREAMY WITH THE REFLECTED STIRRING 278 GGBROW
OF PROFOUND INSTINCTS.
BUT HER FACE IS STILL UNMARKED AND FRESH, HER CALM284 GGBROW
MORE PROFOUND.
WITH A PROFOUND PAIN) 322 GGBROW
(LIGHT DAWNING--CONTRITELY) MY PROFOUND 599 ICEMAN
APOLOGIES, JOSEPH, OLD CHUM.
(SHAKES HIS HEAD WITH PROFOUND DISGUST) 616 ICEMAN
A PROFOUND ASSERTION OF JOY IN LIVING, 279 LAZARU
(SPEAKS AND A PROFOUND SILENCE. 289 LAZARU
(AT HIS FIRST WORD THERE IS A PROFOUND SILENCE 369 LAZARU
I CANNOT CONTEST THE PROFOUND INTUITIONS OF 397 MARCOM
VIRGINS AND MYSTICS.

PROFOUNDLY
THE LAUGHTER OF GOD IS MORE PROFOUNDLY TENDER/ 362 LAZARU
YOUR GENEROUS AND WHOLE-HEARTED WELCOME TOUCHES ME431 MARCOM
PROFOUNDLY.
HE IS PROFOUNDLY MOVED BUT IMMEDIATELY BECOMES 172 MISBEG
SELF-CONSCIOUS
(WHO HAS LISTENED WITH AMAZED HORROR--PROFOUNDLY 83 STRANG
SHOCKED AND STUNNED)

PROFUSELY
HER FACE IS PROFUSELY POWDERED--WITH NERVOUS 531 DIFRNT
EXCITEMENT)

PROGRESS
THE NOISY LAUGHTER AND MUSIC FROM BELOW WHERE A 247 DESIRE
KITCHEN DANCE IS IN PROGRESS
EDMUND WATCHES WITH AMUSEMENT JAMIE'S WAVERING 154 JOURNE
PROGRESS THROUGH THE FRONT
IN VIEW OF THE COMPANY'S PROGRESS SINCE YOU LAST 93 MANSNS
DREAMED OF IT.
HE HAS BEEN TOO THOROUGHLY TRAINED TO PROGRESS 184 STRANG
ALONG A CERTAIN GROOVE TO SUCCESS

PROGRESSED
AS HIS THOUGHTS HAVE PROGRESSED THE EXPRESSIONS ON126 MANSNS
THE TWO WOMEN'S FACES

PROGRESSES
THIS FADES GRADUALLY AS THE ACTION OF THE SCENE 81 BEYOND
PROGRESSES.
IT IS NOT YET DAWN, BUT AS THE ACTION PROGRESSES 144 BEYOND
THE DARKNESS OUTSIDE THE
AS THE ACTION PROGRESSES THIS BECOMES BRIGHTER, 28 ELECTR
THEN TURNS TO CRIMSON.
AS THE SCENE PROGRESSES, HE FINISHES HIS 664 ICEMAN
SAWDUSTING JOB,
AS THE ACTION PROGRESSES THIS REFLECTED 577 ROPE

PROGRESSING
HOW IS YOUR BUSINESS PROGRESSING THESE DAYS? 14 MANSNS
I SEE WORK ON THE RAILROAD AT BALTIMORE IS 40 POET
PROGRESSING.

PROHIBITED
(A BIT HELPLESSLY NOW) THEY COMPLAIN THAT YOU 392 MARCOM
HAVE ENTIRELY PROHIBITED

PROHIBITING
OR PROHIBITING THE PRACTICE OF THE LAWS OF BIOLOGY390 MARCOM
WITHIN A TWELVE-MILE LIMIT.

PROHIBITION
FOLLOWING THE FIRST WORLD WAR AND PROHIBITION, 7 HUGHIE

PROHIBITION (CONT'D.)
MEAN I'M GOING PROHIBITION. 621 ICEMAN
IF I HAD A DOLLAR FOR EVERY DRINK OF IT I HAD 126 MISBEG
BEFORE PROHIBITION.

PROHIBITIONIST
AND IN A FEW WEEKS YOU'D HAVE HIM A DIRTY 29 MISBEG
PROHIBITIONIST.

PROHIBITIVE
THIS MAKES THE COST OF BREACHING PROHIBITIVE. 394 MARCOM

PROJECTS
THE FLOOR AND AN OBSERVATION BALCONY WHICH 486 DYNAMO
PROJECTS INTO THE DYNAMO ROOM FROM
BUT THERE IS A NOTICEABLE CHANGE IN THE IMPRESSION 43 MANSNS
HIS PERSONALITY PROJECTS--

PROLETARIAN
(WITH HIS SILLY GIGGLE) HELLO, HARRY, STUPID 691 ICEMAN
PROLETARIAN MONKEY-FACE/
(WITH GUTTURAL RAGE) GOTTAMNED STUPID PROLETARIAN695 ICEMAN
SLAVES/

PROLETARIANS
PROLETARIANS KEEP ORF THE GRASS/ 233 HA APE
THE VOTES OF THE ON-MARCHING PROLETARIANS OF THE 236 HA APE
BLOODY WORLD/
SOON, LEEDLE PROLETARIANS, VE VILL HAVE FREE 635 ICEMAN
PICNIC IN THE COOL SHADE.

PROLETARIAT
I LOVE ONLY THE PROLETARIAT/ 672 ICEMAN
MOTHER OF THE REVOLUTION, WHOSE ONLY CHILD IS THE 720 ICEMAN
PROLETARIAT.

PROLOGUE
THE SAME SPOT ON THE SAME DOCK AS IN PROLOGUE 323 GGBROW

PROLONGED
THAT MIGHT HAVE PROLONGED HIS LIFE SIX MONTHS AGO.158 BEYOND
THEIR VOICES ATTAIN A PROLONGED NOTE OF UNBEARABLE433 MARCOM
POIGNANCY.

PROM
A PROM WITH GORDON SHAW. 29 STRANG

PROMENADE
PROMENADE/ 250 DESIRE
A SECTION OF THE PROMENADE DECK. 217 HA APE

PROMINENT
BUT IS THIN AND PALE WITH THE BONE STRUCTURE 12 JOURNE
PROMINENT.
HER FACE IS STRIKING, HANDSOME RATHER THAN PRETTY, 12 STRANG
THE BONE STRUCTURE PROMINENT,
HER FACE, WITH ITS HIGH, PROMINENT CHEEK-BONES, 443 WELDED
LACKS HARMONY.

PROMISCUITY
CAN'T TELL HIM THE RAW TRUTH ABOUT HER 35 STRANG
PROMISCUITY...

PROMISE
NOT UNLESS YOU APOLOGIZE IN WRITING AND PROMISE TO203 AHWILD
PUNISH--
(AGITATEDLY) I DON'T THINK HE WILL--THIS TIME-- 212 AHWILD
NOT AFTER HIS PROMISE.
I PROMISE 273 AHWILD
YOU PROMISE TO KEEP YOUR FACE SHUT, MID---UNTIL 274 AHWILD
AFTER I'VE LEFT--
PROMISE-- 280 AHWILD
I PROMISE--MAYBE/ 280 AHWILD
ONE GLASS DON'T GO TO YOUR HEAD, AY PROMISE. 274 ANNA
THEN PROMISE ME YOU'LL CUT OUT SAYING NASTY THINGS 44 ANNA
ABOUT MAT BURKE EVERY CHANCE
I S'POSE YOU REMEMBER YOUR PROMISE, MATS 59 ANNA
(SOFTLY) WILL YOU PROMISE ME THATS 89 BEYOND
MY MAKING THIS TRIP IS ONLY KEEPING THAT PROMISE 89 BEYOND
OF LONG AGO.
AND I'D PROMISE MYSELF THAT WHEN I GREW UP AND WAS 89 BEYOND
STRONG, I'D FOLLOW THAT ROAD,
YOU'LL PROMISE NOT TO BE ANGRY--WHATEVER IT IS? 90 BEYOND
YES, I PROMISE. 90 BEYOND
I WON'T GO, RUTH. I PROMISE YOU. THERE/ DON'T 92 BEYOND
CRY/
AND NOW WILL YOU PROMISE TO GO RIGHT TO SLEEP IF 121 BEYOND
DADA TAKES YOU TO BED?
AND I'LL PROMISE TO BE HERE WHEN THE CLOCK 123 BEYOND
STRIKES--
SO YOU PROMISE THAT, 123 BEYOND
HONEST I WILL, ROB, I PROMISE/ 149 BEYOND
I'LL ONLY LET YOU SIT DOWN IF YOU'LL PROMISE THAT.159 BEYOND
REMEMBER.
I'LL PROMISE ANYTHING, AS GOD IS MY JUDGE/ 162 BEYOND
I WANT YOU TO PROMISE ME TO DO ONE THING, ANDY, 162 BEYOND
AFTER--
WHY DO YOU SUPPOSE HE WANTED US TO PROMISE WE'D-- 163 BEYOND
HE ASKED ME TO PROMISE--WHAT AM I GOING TO DO? 165 BEYOND
YOU CAN PROMISE--SO'S IT'LL EASE HIS MIND--AND NOT165 BEYOND
MEAN ANYTHING.
THAT'S A PROMISE. REMEMBER-- 497 DAYS
I AM THINKING THAT SUCH LOVE NEEDS THE HOPE AND 508 DAYS
PROMISE OF ETERNITY TO FULFILL
AND WILL YOU PROMISE--TO FORGIVE 529 DAYS
AND NOW PROMISE ME YOU'LL FORGET IT AND NOT WORRY 530 DAYS
ANY MORE?
WALL--IN A MANNER O' SPEAKIN'--THAT'S THE PROMISE.204 DESIRE
YE'LL HAVE A SON OUT O' ME, I PROMISE YE. 238 DESIRE
HOW KIN YE PROMISE? 238 DESIRE
AN' MAKIN' HIM PROMISE HE'D GIVE YE THE FARM AND 257 DESIRE
LET ME EAT DUST.
PROMISE ME, CALEB, THAT YOU'LL ALWAYS STAY 495 DIFRNT
DIFF'RENT FROM THEM--
(EMBARRASSED) WHY--I PROMISE TO DO MY BEST BY 495 DIFRNT
YOU, EMMA.
THEN YOU WON'T PROMISE ME TO STAY DIFF'RENT FOR MY496 DIFRNT
SAKE?
I BEEN THINKING THINGS OVER, TELL HIM--AND I TAKE 504 DIFRNT
BACK MY PROMISE--

PROMISE

PROMISE (CONT'D.)
YOU WOULDN'T WANT ME TO KEEP MY PROMISE TO CALEB 511 DIFRNT
IF YOU KNEW I'D BE UNHAPPY,
AND SURE I'LL PROMISE NOT TO SEE TILLY NO MORE. 526 DIFRNT
I WANT YOU TO PROMISE YOU WON'T GO TO SEE HER NO 526 DIFRNT
MORE.
(VINDICTIVELY) I PROMISE I WON'T STAND BETWEEN 445 DYNAMO
HIM AND PUNISHMENT THIS TIME/
(STAMMERS) I'LL TELL YOU, MOTHER--IF YOU PROMISE 446 DYNAMO
TO KEEP IT A SECRET--
I'LL PROMISE. 447 DYNAMO
AND PROMISE TO BE A DUTIFUL WIFE TO FATHER AND 32 ELECTR
MAKE UP FOR THE WRONG YOU'VE DONE
I PROMISE YOU I'LL NEVER SEE ADAM AGAIN AFTER HE 34 ELECTR
CALLS THIS EVENING.
AND BREAK THE PROMISE YOU'VE JUST MADE/ 34 ELECTR
I PROMISE. 42 ELECTR
PROMISE ME/ 42 ELECTR
PROMISE ME, NO MORE COWARDLY ROMANTIC SCRUPLES/ 42 ELECTR
WILL YOU PROMISE ME$ 76 ELECTR
I PROMISE YOU THAT/ 87 ELECTR
OH, ADAM, YOU MUST PROMISE ME TO BE ON YOUR GUARD 111 ELECTR
EVERY MINUTE/
IF YOU SEE ME FALLING ASLEEP YOU MUST PROMISE TO 119 ELECTR
WAKE ME/
(DETERMINEDLY) BUT I'M GOING TO MAKE HIM PROMISE 159 ELECTR
TO COME OVER TOMORROW.
WILL YOU PROMISE$ 160 ELECTR
AND YOU MUST PROMISE NEVER TO OPEN IT--UNLESS 160 ELECTR
SOMETHING HAPPENS TO ME.
YOU REALIZE THE PROMISE YOU MADE MEANS GIVING UP 164 ELECTR
PETER$
THAT I'LL BE CONTENT WITH A PROMISE I'VE FORCED 164 ELECTR
OUT OF YOU,
THAT'S A LARGE PROMISE, VINNIE--ANYTHING/ 165 ELECTR
(WITH DEEP GRIEF) HE WILL NEVER SEE ME AGAIN, I 290 GGBROW
PROMISE YOU.
PLEASE PROMISE ME YOU WON'T SEE DION ANTHONY 290 GGBROW
AGAIN/
THEN IT'S DEAD, I PROMISE/ 312 GGBROW
PROMISE ME FAITHFULLY NEVER TO FORGET YOUR FATHER/323 GGBROW
TILL I HAD TO PROMISE HER A DIAMOND ENGAGEMENT 22 HUGHIE
RING TO SOBER HER UP.+
AND I KNOW MY FELLOW INMATES WILL PROMISE THE 578 ICEMAN
SAME.
A PROMISE IS A PROMISE--AS I'VE OFTEN DISCOVERED. 602 ICEMAN
I PROMISE I WON'T MENTION HER AGAIN/ 648 ICEMAN
AND I PROMISE YOU, BY THE TIME THIS DAY IS OVER, 661 ICEMAN
AT LIMEY CONSULATE THEY PROMISE ANYTHING TO GET 675 ICEMAN
RID OF HIM
AND BENNY FROM DE MARKET HE PROMISE ME SAME. 676 ICEMAN
I PROMISE YOU THEY'LL BOTH COME THROUGH ALL RIGHT.692 ICEMAN
I'D HAVE TO PROMISE. SHE WAS SO SWEET AND GOOD, 710 ICEMAN
THOUGH I KNEW DARNED WELL--
SO I'D PROMISE I WOULDN'T. 710 ICEMAN
I'D PROMISE EVELYN, AND I'D PROMISE MYSELF, AND 712 ICEMAN
I'D BELIEVE IT.
OF COURSE, I PROMISE YOU. 48 JOURNE
I WANT YOU TO PROMISE ME THAT EVEN IF IT SHOULD 48 JOURNE
TURN OUT TO BE SOMETHING WORSE,
(COAXINGLY MATERNAL.) PROMISE ME YOU WILL, DEAR, 72 JOURNE
FOR MY SAKE.
PROMISE ME, DEAR. YOU WON'T BELIEVE I MADE YOU AN 93 JOURNE
EXCUSE.
PROMISE ME YOU WON'T DRINK/ IT'S SO DANGEROUS/ 94 JOURNE
THEY DON'T KNOW THAT NOT ONE IN A MILLION WHO 138 JOURNE
SHOWS PROMISE
A GREAT MONEY SUCCESS--IT RUINED ME WITH ITS 149 JOURNE
PROMISE OF AN EASY FORTUNE.
YOUNG ACTORS WITH THE GREATEST ARTISTIC PROMISE IN150 JOURNE
AMERICA.
WHO SHOWED SUCH BRILLIANT PROMISE/ 167 JOURNE
(SURILY) I WOULD LIKE TO, I PROMISE YOU/ 301 LAZARU
I PROMISE NOT TO BE TOO HORRIFIED. 13 MANSNS
I PROMISE YOU I WON'T CONFESS THAT. 21 MANSNS
I PROMISE YOU, IN TURN, I NEVER INTEND TO SEE YOUR 21 MANSNS
HUSBAND AGAIN.
I PROMISE NOT TO BEWILDER YOU WITH OPPOSITES EVER 49 MANSNS
AGAIN.
I THINK I CAN PROMISE I'LL SOON WIN BACK FOR YOU 57 MANSNS
ALL HIS STUPID FOLLY HAS LOST.
BUT PROMISE ME YOU WON'T BE CRUEL TO HER, SIMON. 87 MANSNS
I PROMISE YOU YOU WILL. 92 MANSNS
HE WISHED TO TELL YOU AND MADE ME PROMISE I 131 MANSNS
WOULDN'T.
I'LL PROMISE ANYTHING YOU WANT/ 169 MANSNS
THAT HUMAN LIFE IS A SILLY DISAPPOINTMENT, A 180 MANSNS
LIAR'S PROMISE.
PROMISE ME YOU WILL NOT-- 181 MANSNS
AND YOU'LL PROMISE TO MARRY ME WHEN I COME BACK$ 356 MARCOM
I PROMISE. EVERY CHANCE I GET. 357 MARCOM
SMILING YOUR THANKS AS I PROMISE YOU A LARGE 360 MARCOM
FORTUNE IF YOU WILL BE TRUE,
(AS HE HESITATES) FORGET YOUR PROMISE. 371 MARCOM
BUT PROMISE ME YOU WILL NOT HARM HIM/ 389 MARCOM
(BOWING LOW) I'LL PROMISE IT WON'T DISTURB YOU. 398 MARCOM
I COULD PROMISE YOU A RECORD PASSAGE, 398 MARCOM
AND WILL YOU PROMISE ME THAT AFTERWARDS YOU'LL LIE414 MARCOM
DOWN$
HOW'S THAT FOR KEEPING MY PROMISE$ 430 MARCOM
ALL RIGHT, IF YOU'LL PROMISE TO GO AHEAD AND EAT 431 MARCOM
AND NOT WAIT FOR ME.
HE MIGHT FORGET A PROMISE AS EASY WHEN HE'S DRUNK 32 MISBEG
ENOUGH.
PROMISE$ 66 MISBEG
BUT WE'RE NOT WORRYING YOU'D EVER FORGET YOUR 66 MISBEG
PROMISE TO US FOR ANY PRICE.
WHAT PROMISE$ 66 MISBEG

PROMISE (CONT'D.)
THERE'S NEVER A PROMISE OF GOD OR MAN GOES NORTH 66 MISBEG
OF TEN THOUSAND BUCKS.
PROMISE ME YOU'LL EAT SOMETHING, JIM. 68 MISBEG
I TOLD YOU THIS MORNING IF HE EVER BROKE HIS 92 MISBEG
PROMISE TO US I'D DO ANYTHING AND
(FROWNS--THEN KIDDINGLY) THAT'S A PROMISE. 115 MISBEG
AND I HOPE THAT'S ANOTHER PROMISE, LIKE THE KISS 116 MISBEG
YOU OWE ME.
DID YOU PROMISE THAT, IF ALL YOU WANTED WAS WHAT 140 MISBEG
ALL THE OTHERS WANT,
REMEMBER THAT'S A PROMISE/ 146 MISBEG
LIKE A PROMISE OF GOD'S PEACE IN THE SOUL'S DARK 153 MISBEG
SADNESS.
SHE'D MAKE HIM PROMISE TO WAIT. 87 POET
DID SHE GET HIM TO PROMISE HER HE'D WAITS 110 POET
I DON'T THINK I'LL NEED IT BUT IF THE WORST COMES 115 POET
TO THE WORST I PROMISE YOU
AND THE PROMISE HE MADE ME MAKE TO LEAVE THE 138 POET
CHURCH.
IT WOULD SERVE CUN RIGHT IF I TOOK THE CHANCE NOW 138 POET
AND BROKE MY PROMISE AND WOKE
AND SHE ONLY SUGGESTED HE WAIT A YEAR, SHE DIDN'T 144 POET
MAKE HIM PROMISE.
BUT I'LL NEVER, NEVER DO IT AGAIN, I PROMISE-- 46 STRANG
NEVER, NEVER/
I'LL PROMISE TO LOVE SAM IF HE KILLS HIM/...)) 108 STRANG
(THEN SERIOUSLY) AND WILL YOU PROMISE TO STAY 145 STRANG
AWAY TWO YEARS--
AND MADE HIM PROMISE ME HE WOULDN'T RETURN FOR TWO155 STRANG
YEARS.
DO YOU PROMISE$ 178 STRANG
I PROMISE YOU THAT, DAD/...)) 189 STRANG
(SMILING--QUICKLY) OH, I'LL PROMISE TO BE GOOD-- 446 WELDED
IF YOU WILL.
WE'RE NOT STARTING SOMETHING+ NOW, ARE WE--AFTER 447 WELDED
OUR PROMISE$
AND I WILL--I KNOW--SOME DAY--I PROMISE/ 467 WELDED
WILL YOU PROMISE ME THIS, YOU$ 474 WELDED
SURE I'LL PROMISE ANYTHING. 474 WELDED
PROMISED
NOTHING I KNEW--EXCEPT HE'D PROMISED TO TAKE HER 234 AHWILD
TO THE FIREWORKS.
ANYWAY YOU HAVEN'T PROMISED YET. 273 AHWILD
YOU REMEMBER YOU'VE PROMISED. 280 AHWILD
TELL ME ABOUT THE WRECK, LIKE YOU PROMISED ME YOU 35 ANNA
WOULD.
YOU AIN'T BEEN FIGHTING WITH HIM, MAT--AFTER YOU 50 ANNA
PROMISED
AND THEY PROMISED TO SHOW ME ALL OF THEM, IF I'D 90 BEYOND
ONLY COME, COME/
UH, THOSE CURSED HILLS OUT THERE THAT I USED TO 125 BEYOND
THINK PROMISED ME SO MUCH/
AND I'D PROMISED YOU FOLKS TO COME HOME. 133 BEYOND
YOU PROMISED/ 507 DAYS
PROMISED HIS SOUL TO THE DEVIL-- 511 DAYS
(THEN WITH KINDLY REPROOF) DIDN'T YOU TAKE A NAP 515 DAYS
LIKE YOU PROMISED YOU WOULD$
I THOUGHT YOU PROMISED ME IF I LET YOU STAY IN 555 DAYS
(HERE YOU'D KEEP QUIET.
(THEN QUICKLY) AND NOW I'VE SATISFIED YOU ON 556 DAYS
THAT, LIE DOWN AS YOU PROMISED.
(EXULTANTLY) REMEMBER YE'VE PROMISED/ 259 DESIRE
I PROMISED HIM I WOULDN'T. 446 DYNAMO
HAL, I PROMISED AMOS I'D HELP SHOW YE THE SIGHTS 7 ELECTR
WHEN YOU CAME TO VISIT HIM.
REMEMBER YOU PROMISED NOT TO LOSE YOUR HEAD. 113 ELECTR
(SHARPLY) YOU PROMISED YOU WEREN'T GOING TO TALK 141 ELECTR
ANY MORE MORBID NONSENSE.
MUSINGLY) WHEN YOU PROPOSED, I THOUGHT YOUR 259 GGBROW
FUTURE PROMISED SUCCESS--MY FUTURE--
SHE GIVES ME AN ARGUMENT I PROMISED HER TEN BUCKS. 26 HUGHIE
ANYWAY, I'VE PROMISED YOU YOU'LL COME THROUGH ALL 654 ICEMAN
RIGHT, HAVEN'T I$
I'VE PROMISED I'LL HELP YOU. 655 ICEMAN
HE PROMISED ANY TIME I FELT AN ENERGETIC FIT HE'D 675 ICEMAN
GET ME A POST WITH THE CUNARD--
THEY'D BLOODY WELL HAVE PROMISED HIM THE MOON. 676 ICEMAN
I'VE PROMISED HIM THAT. 686 ICEMAN
YOU PROMISED US PEACE/ 704 ICEMAN
AND YOU PROMISED US PEACE. 704 ICEMAN
BUT I SUPPOSE YOU'RE REMEMBERING I'VE PROMISED 48 JOURNE
BEFORE ON MY WORD OF HONOR.
AND SHE PROMISED ON HER SACRED WORD OF HONOR-- 57 JOURNE
THEY PROMISED ME IN SIX MONTHS HE'D BE CURED. 122 JOURNE
BOTH THE DOCTORS PROMISED ME, IF YOU OBEY ORDERS 143 JOURNE
AT THIS PLACE YOU'RE GOING,
A LOVER KEEPING A LIFE-LONG PROMISED TRYST$ 30 MANSNS
WE PROMISED OURSELVES-- 48 MANSNS
AND SHE PROMISED SHE WOULD TRY. 62 MANSNS
BUT I HAVE PROMISED MYSELF THAT AS SOON AS I HAD 72 MANSNS
TIME,
YOU REMEMBER I PROMISED MYSELF I WOULD. 76 MANSNS
YOU PROMISED TO REMEMBER/ 134 MANSNS
YOU PROMISED TO UNDERSTAND. 134 MANSNS
(STRUGGLING TO RESIST.) BUT I PROMISED HER-- 147 MANSNS
YOU'LL REMEMBER YOU PROMISED ME YOU'D FORGET HER 159 MANSNS
AND LET HER WAIT.
I DON'T KNOW--I MEAN, I'M SORRY BUT--YOU SEE I 368 MARCOM
PROMISED SOMEONE I'D NEVER--
BUT HE PROMISED THAT YOU WOULD REWARD ME NOBLY. 425 MARCOM
HASN'T HE TOLD US AND PROMISED YOU CAN BUY IT ON 31 MISBEG
EASY TIME PAYMENTS
SETTLE IT, AND JIM PROMISED SIMPSON HE WOULD. 84 MISBEG
AND TWO WAS WHAT YOU OFFERED THAT JIM PROMISED-- 84 MISBEG
YOU PROMISED YOU'D CAN IT TONIGHT. 106 MISBEG
YOU PROMISED YOU'D BE YOURSELF. 127 MISBEG

PROMISED (CONT'D.)
I PROMISED THIS PLACE WOULDN'T BE SOLD EXCEPT TO 133 MISBEG
HIM.
AND YOU PROMISED TONIGHT WOULD BE DIFFERENT. 139 MISBEG
YOU'RE A FINE ONE, WANTING TO LEAVE ME WHEN THE 153 MISBEG
NIGHT I PROMISED I'D GIVE YOU
HELP ME. NOW, LIKE YOUR PROMISED, 66 POET
(THINKING SADLY) (II PROMISED HER... 71 STRANG
I'VE PROMISED SAM'S MOTHER I'D MAKE HIM HAPPY/ 84 STRANG
I HOPE NED BRINGS THAT LETTER HE PROMISED ME 93 STRANG
I PROMISED... 101 STRANG
I PROMISED... 147 STRANG
FINALLY HE PROMISED-- 155 STRANG
THEY PROMISED FAITHFUL THEY'D 'APPEN IN TONIGHT'--494 VOYAGE
THEM AS WHOSE TIME WAS DONE.
(AFTER A PAUSE) I PROMISED THE CAPT'N FAITHFUL 495 VOYAGE
I'D GET 'IM ONE. AND TER-NIGHT.
THEY PROMISED FAITHFUL THEY'D COME, I TELLS YER. 499 VOYAGE
YOU KNOW YOU PROMISED NOT TO RETURN UNTIL YOU DID.445 WELDED
HE PROMISED.

PROMISES
IN SPITE OF YOUR PROMISES, 271 GGBROW
WASN'T THAT DION I JUST SAW GOING OUT--AFTER ALL 289 GGBROW
YOUR PROMISES NEVER TO SEE HIM/
PROMISES ARE ALL RIGHT, BUT--(SHE HESITATES) I 311 GGBROW
DON'T TRUST HIM.
AND PROMISES FULFILLED AND CLEAN SLATES AND NEW 578 ICEMAN
LEASES/
AND FORGIVE HIM IF HE PROMISES NOT TO DO IT AGAIN.127 MANSNS
JIM PROMISES WHATEVER YOU LIKE WHEN HE'S FULL OF 31 MISBEG
WHISKEY.
(TENSELY) YOU'RE A FINE ONE TO TALK OF PROMISES/ 106 MISBEG

PROMISIN'
HIM PROMISIN' HE'D CUT OUT DE BUGHOUSE BULL ABOUT 665 ICEMAN
PEACE--
(TO NICK) WHERE'S THE TUNE YE WAS PROMISIN' TO 501 VOYAGE
GIVE US/

PROMISING
HE CAN HEAR HER PROMISING TO FORGIVE 544 DAYS
JUST BECAUSE YOU WERE FORCED INTO PROMISING NOT T0446 DYNAMO
BY THAT ATHEIST5
I SHOULD HAVE SWINDLED HER INTO GIVING HERSELF BY 74 MANSNS
PROMISING MARRIAGE--
BUT I HAVE FINE REPORTS TO GIVE YOU OF A PROMISING 40 MISBEG
HARVEST.

PROMOTED
RIGHT AFTER HE'D BEEN PROMOTED TO MAJOR. 12 POET

PROMPT
TO PROMPT SHAUGHNESSY WITH A FEW NASTIER INSULTS. 26 JOURNE
I KNOW THE DESIRABILITY OF PROMPT OBEDIENCE. 154 MANSNS

PROMPTED
THAT THE OFFICER'S CAUTION WAS PROMPTED BY A 677 ICEMAN
DESIRE TO MAKE HIS PERSONAL ESCAPE.

(PUTS ASIDE HIS PIPE AND GETS UP PROMPTLY) 256 AHWILD
(PROMPTLY) I'LL TAKE A--(THEN SUDDENLY REMINDED-- 23 ANNA
CONFUSEDLY)
(PROMPTLY) I DID THAT/ 36 ANNA
WHO PROMPTLY KNOCKS HIM DOWN. 472 CARIBE
YOU CAN SERVE DINNER PROMPTLY AT HALF PAST SIX. 100 JOURNE
(PROMPTLY) I'D LIKE TO BE APPOINTED A COMMISSION-382 MARCOM
AGENT OF THE SECOND CLASS.

PRONE
STRIVING TO RAISE THEMSELVES ON END, FAILING AND 189 EJONES
SINKING PRONE AGAIN.
HE HAS THE FACE OF AN OLD FAMILY HORSE, PRONE TO 576 ICEMAN
TANTRUMS.

PRONOUNCE
(WARNINGLY) AND UNTIL I PRONOUNCE YOU GRADUATED, 374 MARCOM
MUM'S THE WORD, UNDERSTAND/

PRONOUNCED
IF ANYTHING, HER MOONY DREAMINESS IS MORE 476 DYNAMO
PRONOUNCED.
HER BLACK EYEBROWS MEET IN A PRONOUNCED STRAIGHT 9 ELECTR
LINE ABOVE HER STRONG NOSE.
MORE PRONOUNCED IN HIM THAN IN THE OTHERS. 46 ELECTR
IS MORE PRONOUNCED THAN EVER. 137 ELECTR
BENEATH PRONOUNCED BROWS THAT MEET ABOVE HER NOSE. 3 MANSNS
THE STOOP IN HIS SHOULDERS IS MORE PRONOUNCED, 70 MANSNS
HIS VOICE IS HIGH-PITCHED WITH A PRONOUNCED 11 MISBEG
BROGUE.)
NERVOUS TENSION PRONOUNCED... 79 STRANG

PRONOUNCEDLY
PRONOUNCEDLY AQUILINE. 19 JOURNE
MASKS OF THESE JEWS OF THE FIRST TWO SCENES OF THE275 LAZARU
PLAY ARE PRONOUNCEDLY SEMITIC
PRONOUNCEDLY FEMALE FIGURE. 75 MANSNS

PRONOUNCES
(HE PRONOUNCES IT READING GOAL--AS IN GOALPOST--.)197 AHWILD
AND PRONOUNCES LIKE A CRUEL MALIGNANT 297 GGBROW
CONDEMNATION)
(GLOOMILY PRONOUNCES AN OBITUARY) 683 ICEMAN
(HIS WORDS ARE LIKE A BENEDICTION HE PRONOUNCES 353 LAZARU
UPON THEM.
(PRONOUNCES WITH BOYISH SOLEMNITY) 31 STRANG

PRONOUNCING
(IN A COLD VOICE, AS IF HE WERE PRONOUNCING A 539 DAYS
DEATH SENTENCE)

PROOF
I HAVE PROOF OF EVERYTHING IN HIS OWN HANDWRITING/201 AHWILD
IF HE GAVE ME PROOF HE'D--BUT EVEN THEN I DON'T 213 AHWILD
BELIEVE I COULD.
SAY WHAT YOU'VE A MIND TO, KATE, THE PROOF OF THE 114 BEYOND
PUDDIN'S IN THE EATIN'.
SO, AS FINAL PROOF, HE GAVE ME A THING HE HAD KEPT561 CROSS
HIDDEN FROM THEM ALL--
HAPPINESS IS PROOF, ISN'T IT/ 524 DAYS
YE'D NEED PROOF. 205 DESIRE

PROPERTY

PROOF (CONT'D.)
THIRTY O' THE BEST YEARS OF A MAN'S LIFE OUGHT TO 538 DIFRNT
BE PROOF ENOUGH
I GOT PROOF IT'S TRUE. 541 DIFRNT
SHE GOT THAT OUT OF ME--THE PROOF OF IT, AT ANY 36 ELECTR
RATE.
YOU CAN'T DOUBT THE ABSOLUTE PROOF/ 96 ELECTR
WATCH HER WHEN SHE SEES THAT--IF YOU WANT PROOF/ 100 ELECTR
(GRIMLY) YOU WANTED PROOF/ 113 ELECTR
THAT AIN'T NO PROOF. 521 INZONE
(HEATEDLY) IS UT MORE PROOF YE'D BE NEEDIN' 524 INZONE
AFTHER WHAT WE'VE SEEN AN' HEARD5
AIN'T THAT PROOF ENOUGHS 529 INZONE
IF I NEEDED ANY FURTHER PROOF THAT OUR RULING 24 JOURNE
PLUTOCRATS/
THAT'S THE PROOF/ 83 JOURNE
WELL HE WASN'T, AND THERE'S NO PROOF OF IT IN HIS 127 JOURNE
PLAYS, EXCEPT TO YOU/
THE PROOF IS IN THE BILLS I HAVE TO PAY/ 127 JOURNE
THE PROOF IS IN HIS PLAYS. 17 JOURNE
UH, I'M OPEN TO PROOF. 65 MANSNS
IS THAT NOT A PROOF THAT FROM BIRTH TO DEATH 402 MARCOM
HERE'S PROOF FOR YOU/ 430 MARCOM
THAT'S PROOF. 159 MISBEG
LIVING PROOF/....)) 55 STRANG
WHO WOULD BE FOR HIM A LIVING PROOF THAT HIS WIFE 85 STRANG
LOVED HIM.
THE PROOF OF A GUTLESS VANITY THAT RUINED YOUR 166 STRANG
CAREER/...
THAT'S PROOF ENOUGH, ISN'T IT5 175 STRANG
(AFTER A PAUSE--SOMBERLY) YOU MENTIONED OUR YEARS455 WELDED
TOGETHER AS PROOF.
THAT'S THE PROOF. 457 WELDED

PROOFS
I THOUGHT YOU'D GET AROUND TO THAT, SO I BROUGHT 201 AHWILD
SOME OF THE PROOFS WITH ME.
(ROUGHLY) NEVER MIND WHAT YOU CALL PROOFS/ 96 ELECTR

PROP
AND I HAD TO PROP HIM UP OR HE'D FELL ON HIS NOSE.616 ICEMAN

PROPELLED
PROPELLED BY SEVERAL PARTING KICKS, 250 HA APE

PROPER
I'M THE PROPER LAD FOR YOU, IF IT'S A MESELF DO BE 33 ANNA
SAYING IT.
I'M CLUMSY IN MY WITS WHEN IT COMES TO TALKING 37 ANNA
PROPER WITH A GIRL THE LIKE OF
I'M THINKING IF IT'S A STUKEHOLD OF A PROPER 38 ANNA
LINER,
'TIL I DO BE THINKING A MADHOUSE IS THE PROPER 70 ANNA
PLACE FOR ME.
IF YOUR OATH IS NO PROPER OATH AT ALL, 76 ANNA
COUNTIN' THE STARS TO SEE IF THEY ALL COME OUT 99 BEYOND
RIGHT AND PROPER
A PROPER WAR*PRAU SUCH AS THE PIRATES USED TO USE.560 CROSS
I HAVE MY DUTY OF DENOUNCING THAT MURDERER TO THE 449 DYNAMO
PROPER AUTHORITIES.
WITH THE HALL OF THE HOUSE PROPER WHICH IS OF GRAY 2 ELECTR
CUT STONE.
TREAT YER WIV THE PROPER CONTEMPT. 236 HA APE
THERE IS A TABLE AT LEFT, FRONT, OF BARROOM 664 ICEMAN
PROPER, WITH FOUR CHAIRS.
BY APPLYING MY NATURAL GOD-GIVEN TALENTS IN THEIR 160 JOURNE
PROPER SPHERE.
SHE MUST BE TAUGHT TO CONFINE HER ACTIVITIES TO 94 MANSNS
THEIR PROPER SPHERE--
ALL I ASK IS THAT EACH OF YOU KEEP YOUR PROPER 131 MANSNS
PLACE IN MY MIND--
THE LIGHT GROWS DIMMER ON THE STAGE PROPER 426 MARCOM
BY THE WAY, WHAT AMOUNT DOES MR. HARFORD THINK 120 POET
PROPER/ ANYTHING IN REASON--
BUT ENJOY LIFE IN MY PROPER STATION AS AULD NICK 169 POET
MELODY'S SON.
BUT I'LL BE CONTENT TO STAY MESELF IN THE PROPER 170 POET
STATION I WAS BORN TO.
I KNOW IT'S HARDLY THE PROPER TIME-- 32 STRANG
SHE WAS SAYING IT TO SURPRISE YOU WITH AT HER OWN 106 STRANG
PROPER TIME--

PROPERLY
IT HAS NOT PROPERLY BEEN ICED. 658 ICEMAN
HER HOUSE WOULDN'T BE PROPERLY FURNISHED UNLESS 661 ICEMAN
SHE BOUGHT ANOTHER WASH BOILER.
THE CHAMPAGNE WAS NOT PROPERLY ICED. 672 ICEMAN
BUT THE SLAVES MUST ICE IT PROPERLY/ 691 ICEMAN
IT IS NOT PROPERLY ICED/ 694 ICEMAN
IT'S HARD FOR ME TO DO IT UP PROPERLY NOW. 20 JOURNE
THEN HE MIGHT PROPERLY EXPECT ITS END TO HAVE AS 30 MANSNS
MUCH SIGNIFICANCE AS--
NOW LET ME SEE YOU TAKE IT PROPERLY. 98 POET
AND HAS THE BREEDING TO KNOW HOW THESE MATTERS ARE120 POET
PROPERLY ARRANGED.

PROPERTIES
MARKING THE BOUNDARY-LINE BETWEEN THE TWO -0 DYNAMO
PROPERTIES.
I CONCLUDED A DEAL TODAY WHICH ADDS A RAILROAD TO 100 MANSNS
THE COMPANY'S PROPERTIES.
IF YOU HAD TO PAY THE DEBTS ON THE PROPERTIES HE 142 MANSNS
HAS MADE OVER TO YOU TOMORROW--

PROPERTY
THE VALUE OF THE PROPERTY--OUR HOME WHICH IS HIS, 564 CROSS
SMITH'S.
OLD SMITH IS AFRAID OF HIS PROPERTY. 564 CROSS
THE PROPERTY IS ENCLOSED BY A WHITE PICKET FENCE 2 ELECTR
AND A TALL HEDGE.
YOU ACTED AS IF I WERE YOUR WIFE--YOUR PROPERTY-- 60 ELECTR
NOT SO LONG AGO/
I'M NOT YOUR PROPERTY/ 155 ELECTR
BY PUTTING A PROPERTY SANDWICH IN THE MIDDLE OF 571 ICEMAN
EACH TABLE.

PROPERTY

PROPERTY (CONT'D.)
AND YOU THOUGHT A WOMAN YOU LOVED WAS A PIECE OF 647 ICEMAN
PRIVATE PROPERTY YOU OWNED.
THAT FAMILY-RESPECT STUFF IS ALL BOURGEOIS, 648 ICEMAN
PROPERTY-OWNING CRAP.
(A TRIFLE ACIDLY.) I HOPE HE DIDN'T PUT YOU ON TO IS JOURNE
ANY NEW PIECE OF PROPERTY AT
YOU'RE ONE OF THE BIGGEST PROPERTY OWNERS AROUND 31 JOURNE
HERE.
BUT IT'S ALWAYS SEEMED TO ME YOUR FATHER COULD 73 JOURNE
AFFORD TO KEEP ON BUYING PROPERTY
HE MUST HAVE ANOTHER PIECE OF PROPERTY ON HIS LIST 73 JOURNE
THAT
FLANNEL-MOUTH, GOLD-BRICK MERCHANT STING YOU WITH 80 JOURNE
ANOTHER PIECE OF BUM PROPERTY/
EXCEPT MONEY AND PROPERTY AND THE FEAR HE'LL END 101 JOURNE
HIS DAYS IN POVERTY.
SPEND MONEY TO MAKE THIS LOOK DECENT, WHILE YOU 141 JOURNE
KEEP BUYING MORE PROPERTY,
(WITH BITTER IRONY.) YES, ON PROPERTY VALUED AT A1&4 JOURNE
QUARTER OF A MILLION.
IT'S MY RIGHT--AND YOURS. WE'RE RESIDENTS. I'M A1&4 JOURNE
PROPERTY OWNER.
WITH ANOTHER BUM PIECE OF PROPERTY/ 144 JOURNE
A FEW LOUSY DOLLARS TO BUY MORE BUM PROPERTY WITH/145 JOURNE
BUT STILL, THE MORE PROPERTY YOU OWN, THE SAFER 146 JOURNE
YOU THINK YOU ARE.
IN A FREE SOCIETY THERE MUST BE NO PRIVATE 8 MANSNS
PROPERTY
YES. IT IS REALLY A VERY BEAUTIFUL AND VALUABLE 56 MANSNS
PROPERTY, SARA.
AND DEED THE WHOLE PROPERTY OVER TO YOU. 56 MANSNS
(WITH FORCED INDIFFERENCE.) I IMAGINE IT 96 MANSNS
CONCERNED PROPERTY OF YOURS--
SARA'S PROPERTY. 96 MANSNS
THIS IS YOUR PROPERTY. 96 MANSNS
ALTHOUGH, OF COURSE, IT DID CONCERN PROPERTY. 97 MANSNS
EVEN MY BEDROOM, HERE YOUR FATHER'S PROPERTY. 110 MANSNS
WHOSE PROPERTY IS IT, I'D LIKE TC KNOWS 165 MANSNS
THE DESTRUCTION OF PROPERTY AND LOSS OF LIFE WOULD395 MARCOM
BE TREMENDOUS/
LET US PAUSE TO TAKE A LOOK AT THIS VERY VALUABLE 65 MISBEG
PROPERTY.
TO SEE ABOUT SELLING A PIECE OF PROPERTY THE OLD 147 MISBEG
MAN HAD BOUGHT THERE YEARS AGO.
(LAUGHING.) WELL, WHY SHOULDN'T I TAKE WALKS ON 30 POET
OUR OWN PROPERTY$
THAT MY PROPHECY IS COMING TRUE--HER END IN MY 554 DAYS
STORY.

PROPHESY
BANKS ARE BEGINNING TO FAIL RIGHT AND LEFT 49 MANSNS
ALREADY, AND BEFORE LONG I PROPHESY--

PROPHET
IT'S A BETTER WEATHER PROPHET THAN YOU ARE, JAMES. 41 JOURNE
YOU'RE NOT MUCH OF A WEATHER PROPHET, DEAR. 82 JOURNE
I CURSE THESE DEVILS AND THAT PRINCE OF DEVILS, 285 LAZARU
THAT FALSE PROPHET, JESUS/
THE FALSE PROPHET IS DEAD/ 290 LAZARU
PROPHET THAT WAS BORN AND THEY CARRIED WITH THEM 368 MARCOM
THREE MANNER OF OFFERINGS--
YOUR JESUS WAS A GREAT PROPHET. 368 MARCOM

PROPHETIC
(PROPHETIC PROFESSOR/... 24 STRANG

PROPHETS
LIKE THE PROPHETS DONE. 210 DESIRE
*I'M RIDIN' OUT T' LEARN GOD'S MESSAGE T' ME IN 215 DESIRE
THE SPRING LIKE THE PROPHETS

PROPISQUE
PROPISQUE ADSPECTAT OLYMPUM INQUIRITQUE IOVEM,... 23 STRANG

PROPORTIONAL
RUNNING AT A SPEED OF ROTATION N, IS THEORETICALLY429 DYNAMO
PROPORTIONAL TO D4 LN2*...

PROPORTIONED
HER FIGURE IS BUXOM, BUT BEAUTIFULLY PROPORTIONED, 44 MANSNS
THE ROOM IS SMALL, WELL-PROPORTIONED, PANELLED IN 69 MANSNS
DARK WOOD.
A HIGH-CEILINGED, FINELY-PROPORTIONED ROOM 117 MANSNS

PROPORTIONS
ON ACCOUNT OF THE ENORMOUS PROPORTIONS OF HIS 538 *ILE
SHOULDERS AND CHEST,
AND A GOLD WATCH-CHAIN OF CABLE-LIKE PROPORTIONS 493 VOYAGE

PROPOSAL
(MOVED IN SPITE OF HERSELF AND TROUBLED BY THIS 38 ANNA
HALF-CONCEALED PROPOSAL--
TO MAKE HIS PROPOSAL AS EQUITABLE AS POSSIBLE FOR 35 MANSNS
SIMON AND HIS---ER--FAMILY.
HOW DARE YOU MAKE SUCH A SHAMELESS PROPOSAL/ 36 MANSNS
FATHER'S PROPOSAL IS IMMENSELY TO YOUR ADVANTAGE. 52 MANSNS
SO NOW YOU MUST CONSIDER YOUR FATHER'S AND MY 58 MANSNS
PROPOSAL.
AM I TO UNDERSTAND YOU ACCEPT YOUR FATHER'S 58 MANSNS
PROPOSAL$
AS I HAVE TOLD JOEL, I WILL ACCEPT FATHER'S 59 MANSNS
PROPOSAL, ONLY ON ONE CONDITION.
(THINKING.) HIS PROPOSAL TO VISIT ME EACH 121 MANSNS
EVENING--
PROPOSALS.... 32 STRANG

PROPOSE
(CALCULATINGLY REPROACHFUL) I DON'T THINK YOU'D 38 ELECTR
PROPOSE THAT, ADAM,
AND DID YOU HAVE ANY SPECIAL JOB IN THAT LINE YOU 248 HA APE
WANTED TO PROPOSE TO US$
BUT I WANT TO BE SOCIABLE AND PROPOSE A TOAST IN 658 ICEMAN
HONOR OF OUR OLD FRIEND, HARRY.
BUT HE DESIRED ME TO ASK WHETHER YOU PROPOSE TO 333 LAZARU
LAUGH HERE--IN CAESAR'S PALACES
I PROPOSE TO RETIRE AS SOON AS WE HAVE ENOUGH. 16 MANSNS

PROPOSE (CONT'D.)
ABOUT TO PROPOSE AN AMENDMENT TO THE CONSTITUTION 390 MARCOM
CONTEMPTUOUSLY SO I'M LEADING JIM ON TO 9 MISBEG
PROPOSE, AM I$
(THEN WITH A GENIAL GRIN) I'LL HAVE TC PROPOSE, 21 STRANG
NINA.
PROPOSE WHILE WE PACK. 22 STRANG
BUT FOR GORDON TO TAKE HER SERIOUSLY, AND PROPOSE 168 STRANG
MARRIAGE.
DON'T GROW FATALISTIC--JUST WHEN I WAS ABOUT TO 446 WELDED
PROPOSE REFORM.

PROPOSED
I PROPOSED QUITE FRANKLY THAT WE SHOULD SIMPLY 523 DAYS
LIVE TOGETHER AND EACH KEEP
MUSINGLY WHEN YOU PROPOSED, I THOUGHT YOUR 259 GGBROW
FUTURE PROMISED SUCCESS--MY FUTURE--
IT WAS HERE ON A NIGHT JUST LIKE THIS YOUR FATHER 323 GGBROW
FIRST--PROPOSED TO ME.
SHE PROPOSED AND SAID YES* FOR HIM, 23 HUGHIE
MY HUSBAND PROPOSED THAT I MAKE OVER TO YOU, AS 56 MANSNS
PART OF THE BARGAIN,
HARDER PROPOSED THAT HE MEET WITH JIM AND THE 84 MISBEG
EXECUTORS IN THE MORNING AND
I WISHED TIME TO REFLECT ON A FURTHER ASPECT OF 112 POET
THIS PROPOSED MARRIAGE.
WONDER WHAT HE'D SAY IF I PROPOSED THAT HE BACK 113 STRANG
ME....
HE'D'S JUST PROPOSED TO ME. 197 STRANG

PROPOSES
IT IS FATHER WHO PROPOSES IT, MOTHER. 36 MANSNS
CERTAIN LAST WISHES OF YOUR FATHER'S, AND A 52 MANSNS
BARGAIN HE PROPOSES.

PROPOSING
PROPOSING--TO ME/ 38 ANNA

PROPOSITION
IT SHOWED ME THE WORLD IS A LARGER PROPOSITION 138 BEYOND
THAT'S MY PROPOSITION/ 258 GGBROW
I'VE GOT A PROPOSITION TO MAKE TO DION--IF I COULD277 GGBROW
EVER GET HOLD OF HIM.
I'VE A PROPOSITION TO MAKE THAT I HOPE YOU'LL 280 GGBROW
CONSIDER FAVORABLY
THAT'LL KEEP MY PROPOSITION PINNED UP IN HIS 122 STRANG
MIND/....)

PROPOSITIONS
THEY'D MAKE HIM PRETTY RAW PROPOSITIONS. 16 HUGHIE

PROPPED
HE FACES FRONT, BROODING MOODILY, HIS CHIN PROPPED235 DESIRE
ON HIS HANDS.
HIS CHIN PROPPED ON HIS FISTS, 247 DESIRE
HIS CHIN PROPPED ON HIS HANDS, HIS DRAWN FACE 259 DESIRE
BLANK AND EXPRESSIONLESS.
AND PROPPED HIM AGAINST A WALL AND GAVE HIM A 617 ICEMAN
FRISK.
IT IS PROPPED UP ABOUT TWO FEET ABOVE GROUND BY 1 MISBEG
LAYERS OF TIMBER BLOCKS.
WITH THE BROOM HANDLE PROPPED AGAINST THE STEPS 11 MISBEG
NEAR HER RIGHT HAND.
HER BACK PROPPED AGAINST THE RIGHT SIDE OF THE 578 ROPE
DOORWAY, HER FACE IN PROFILE.
SHE IS STARING FIXEDLY AT A RAG DOLL WHICH SHE HAS578 ROPE
PROPPED UP AGAINST THE
GORDON EVANS IS SITTING ON THE STONE BENCH, HIS 184 STRANG
CHIN PROPPED ON HIS HANDS,

PROPPING
PROPPING HER DOLL UP AGAINST THE TREE, COMES OVER 129 BEYOND
AND CLAMBERS TO HIS SIDE.)

PROPRIETOR
THE SECOND FLOOR A FLAT OCCUPIED BY THE 571 ICEMAN
PROPRIETOR.
AT THE TABLE AT RIGHT, FRONT, HARRY HOPE, THE 576 ICEMAN
PROPRIETOR, SITS IN THE MIDDLE.
I ASKED THE HOTEL PROPRIETOR TO RECOMMEND THE 140 JOURNE
BEST--
IF I COULD RECONCILE MYSELF TO BEING THE 70 POET
PROPRIETOR OF A TAWDRY TAVERN,
I CAME HERE TO SEEK A PRIVATE INTERVIEW WITH THE 117 POET
PROPRIETOR OF THIS TAVERN,
AT THE FAR END OF THE BAR STANDS FAT JOE, THE 493 VOYAGE
PROPRIETOR,

PROPRIETOR'S
HE FEELS A PROUD PROPRIETOR'S AFFECTION FOR THEM, 611 ICEMAN

PROPRIETORSHIP
GRINNING WITH PROUD PROPRIETORSHIP. 726 ICEMAN
A SMILE THAT TAKES ITS PROPRIETORSHIP FOR GRANTED. 75 MANSNS

PROPRIETY
HE IS DRESSED WITH A FASTIDIOUS PROPRIETY IN WELL- 25 MANSNS
TAILORED MOURNING BLACK.
THAT I WILL OUTRAGE YOUR SENSE OF PROPRIETY BY 29 MANSNS
SUICIDE.

PROS
THEN, UNDER THE CIRCUMSTANCES, HAVING WEIGHED THE 46 STRANG
PROS AND CONS, SO TO SPEAK,

PROSE
THIS IS PROSE. 196 AHWILD
THE SYMONS' TRANSLATION OF BAUDELAIRE'S PROSE 132 JOURNE
POEM,

PROSPECT
PROSPECT OF SEEING YOUR FATHER AGAIN. 22 ELECTR
ALREADY AT THE MERE PROSPECT OF ESCAPE, I FEEL A 40 MANSNS
REBIRTH STIRRING IN ME/
WOULD SHE RATHER FACE THE PROSPECT OF GOING TO POT 87 STRANG
MENTALLY, MORALLY,

PROSPER
BUT STILL IT DOES NOT PROSPER. 7 HUGHIE

PROSPERED
IN BRIEF, I MARRIED THE WHORE, SHE TORTURED ME, MY356 LAZARU
MOTHER'S SCHEMING PROSPERED--

PROSPERITY

HARD-EARNED PROSPERITY, ENJOYED AND MAINTAINED BY 94 BEYOND THE FAMILY AS A UNIT.
THE ATMOSPHERE IS ONE OF COMFORT AND A MODERATE 43 MANSNS PROSPERITY.
OF FINANCIAL PROSPERITY STILL STAMPED ON HIM FROM 150 MANSNS LONG HABIT.
IT HAS A PROUD AIR OF MODEST PROSPERITY. 111 STRANG

PROSPEROUS

HILLS IS THE TYPE OF WELL-FED MINISTER OF A 67 ELECTR PROSPEROUS SMALL-TOWN CONGREGATION--
THE THIRD HAS THE APPEARANCE OF A PROSPEROUS 79 ELECTR SHIPOWNER OF COLONIAL DAYS.
IT LOOKS SO PROSPEROUS-- 274 GGBROW
A BACKDROP OF CAREFULLY PAINTED, PROSPEROUS, 294 GGBROW BOURGEOIS CULTURE.
HE WAS PROSPEROUS ENOUGH, TOO, IN HIS WHOLESALE 137 JOURNE GROCERY BUSINESS, AN ABLE MAN.
THERE CAN BE NO QUESTION OF MY GIVING UP MY 59 MANSNS PROSPEROUS BUSINESS HERE
IT HAD ONCE BEEN PROSPEROUS, A BREAKFAST STOP FOR 7 POET THE STAGECOACH.
THE TAPROOM OF THE TAVERN IN ITS PROSPEROUS DAYS, 7 POET

PROSTITUTE

TAWDRY FINERY OF PEASANT STOCK TURNED PROSTITUTE. 14 ANNA
I AM NO BETTER THAN A PROSTITUTE IN YOUR SISTER'S 87 ELECTR EYES/
THE MASK IS THE ROUGED AND EYE-BLACKENED 279 GGBROW COUNTENANCE OF THE HARDENED PROSTITUTE.
(THE PROSTITUTE ENTERS FROM THE RIGHT. 367 MARCOM
(SLAPPING THE PROSTITUTE ON THE BARE SHOULDER) 368 MARCOM
(THE PROSTITUTE, THE SAME BUT NOW IN INDIAN GARB, 371 MARCOM
(THE PROSTITUTE ENTERS DRESSED NOW AS A TARTAR. 374 MARCOM
THE PROSTITUTE, WALKING AWAY, CALLS BACK OVER HIS 375 MARCOM SHOULDER)
AS THOUGH I'D LOOKED INTO THE EYES OF A 25 STRANG PROSTITUTE...

PROSTITUTES

THE REST, SOLDIERS, SLAVES AND THE PROSTITUTES OF 349 LAZARU BOTH SEXES,
THE CALCULATING COQUETRY OF TWO PROSTITUTES TRYING128 MANSNS TO ENTICE A MAN.)

PROSTRATE

ESCAPE OVER YOUR PROSTRATE SOULS/ 321 GGBROW
THEY PROSTRATE THEMSELVES) 307 LAZARU
(THEY PROSTRATE THEMSELVES, THEIR FACES TO THE 350 MARCOM GROUND.
EVERYONE IS PROSTRATE. 352 MARCOM
ALL EXCEPT THE POLOS PROSTRATE THEMSELVES BEFORE 372 MARCOM THE BUDDHA.)
(THEN THEY ALL PROSTRATE THEMSELVES ON THE GROUND 376 MARCOM AS HE CHANTS)
THEY PROSTRATE THEMSELVES AT THE FOOT OF THE 390 MARCOM THRONE.
WITH ONE MOVEMENT THEY PROSTRATE THEMSELVES AS THE405 MARCOM PRINCESS COMES FROM THE CABIN
DRAGGING THEIR BOX BETWEEN THEM AND PROSTRATE 417 MARCOM THEMSELVES AT HER FEET)
WITH ONE MOTION, THE WOMEN THROW THEMSELVES 433 MARCOM PROSTRATE ON THE FLOOR.
A MUFFLED SOUND OF SOBBING COMES FROM THE 435 MARCOM PROSTRATE WOMEN.

PROSTRATED

WHO WAS SO PROSTRATED BY HIS MOTHER'S DEATH. 159 STRANG

PROSTRATES

AND PROSTRATES HIMSELF BEFORE THE KAAN. 390 MARCOM
(ENTERS HURRIEDLY AND PROSTRATES HIMSELF) 423 MARCOM

PROTECT

TO PROTECT OTHER PEOPLE'S CHILDREN/ 203 AHWILD
OR I'LL HAVE TO TELL ON YOU TO PROTECT ME GOOD 217 AHWILD NAME/
YOU WON'T DO ANYTHING TO HER--NOT WHILE I'M HERE TO246 AHWILD PROTECT HER/
THAT'LL PROTECT HIM MORE THAN A THOUSAND 289 AHWILD LECTURES--
THEY APPEAR TO PROTECT AND AT THE SAME TIME 202 DESIRE SUBDUE.
THERE IS NOTHING I WOULDN'T DO--TO PROTECT HIM 22 ELECTR FROM HURT.
IT'S MY FIRST DUTY TO PROTECT HIM FROM YOU/ 32 ELECTR
REMEMBER YOU'RE ALL I HAVE TO PROTECT ME/ 88 ELECTR
EVEN IF HE KNEW I HAD KILLED HIM, HE'D PROTECT ME/ 92 ELECTR
YOU SAID YOU LOVED ME--YOU'D PROTECT ME--PROTECT 121 ELECTR YOUR MOTHER--
LIVE AND REBEL AGAINST THAT OTHER BOY'S GOD AND 295 GGBROW PROTECT MYSELF FROM HIS CRUELTY.
(PROUDLY) I'M GLAD TO HAVE THREE SUCH STRONG BOYS300 GGBROW TO PROTECT ME.
TO SHUT OUT THE SIGHT OF HIS FACE, TO PROTECT HER 226 HA APE OWN.
SINCE LAZARUS WILL NOT HELP HIMSELF, YOU MUST 331 LAZARU PROTECT HIM.
TO PROTECT AND COMFORT HIM, TO MAKE HIM A HOME AND351 LAZARU BEAR HIS CHILDREN/
WE MUST PROTECT MAN FROM HIS STUPID POSSESSIVE 8 MANSNS INSTINCTS
I SHALL ENGAGE AN ATTORNEY TO PROTECT THAT 60 MANSNS INTEREST.
EXCEPT IN THE HOUSE WHEN EITHER SHE OR I ARE 104 MANSNS PRESENT TO PROTECT THEM.
ISN'T IT TIME TO PROTECT YOUR SOVEREIGNTY BY 392 MARCOM STRONG MEASURES?
IT'S MY DUTY TO PROTECT SAM...!) 125 STRANG
IT'S MY DUTY TO PROTECT NINA FROM HERSELF... 125 STRANG
O MOTHER GOD, PROTECT MY SON/... 181 STRANG

PROTECTED

IF YOU'D ALWAYS BEEN A LITTLE INNOCENT, PROTECTED 517 DAYS FROM ALL UGLY CONTACTS--
BUT WE PROTECTED HER. 142 ELECTR

PROTEST

PROTECTED (CONT'D.)

SO SEDULOUSLY PROTECTED AND ALOOF FROM ALL LIFE'S 14 MANSNS SORDIDNESS.
THE COMFORT SHE LOVED, THE PROTECTED PRIVACY, HER 47 MANSNS FANCIFUL WALLED-IN GARDEN,
IN HER EYES? MIRROR I WATCHED MYSELF LIVE 437 MARCOM PROTECTED FROM LIFE BY HER AFFECTION--

PROTECTING

YET HIS EYES ARE EXPRESSIVELY TENDER AND 494 DIFRNT PROTECTING WHEN HE GLANCES DOWN AT HER
WITH A LOVING, PROTECTING GESTURE. 29 ELECTR
THEY LOOM UP AROUND THE SLIGHT FIGURE OF THEIR 323 GGBROW MOTHER LIKE PROTECTING GIANTS.
(SHE PUTS A PROTECTING ARM AROUND HOPE 655 ICEMAN
HE COMES AND PUTS A PROTECTING, POSSESSIVE HAND ON 57 MANSNS HIS MOTHER'S SHOULDER.)
WHEN YOU THINK OF GAZAN PROTECTING ME AND NURSING414 MARCOM
ME WHEN I AM SICK--AND--
A PASSIONATE TENSION, A SELF-PROTECTING, ARROGANT 444 WELDED DEFIANCE OF LIFE AND HIS OWN

PROTECTINGLY

HE PUTS HIS ARM PROTECTINGLY OVER HER SHOULDERS) 546 'ILE
(RUSHING TO ANDY AND PUTTING HER ARMS ABOUT HIM 106 BEYOND PROTECTINGLY)
HE INSTINCTIVELY IMITATES HIS FATHER'S TONE, 422 DYNAMO BOOMING SELF-PROTECTINGLY.
HER MASK BEFORE HER FACE PROTECTINGLY.) 268 GGBROW
(IMMEDIATELY PUTS HIS ARMS AROUND HER 327 LAZARU PROTECTINGLY)
(DEBORAH MOVES SO THAT SHE STANDS PROTECTINGLY 185 MANSNS BEFORE SIMON.
(SHE STEPS BETWEEN THEM PROTECTINGLY) 13 STRANG

PROTECTION

A SENSE OF PROTECTION, MAYBE/ 53 ELECTR
SHE THROWS HER ARMS AROUND ORIN AS IF SEEKING 100 ELECTR PROTECTION FROM HIM)
HE HURRIES TO HER AS IF SEEKING PROTECTION. 139 ELECTR
AS IF FOR PROTECTION AGAINST HERSELF 167 ELECTR
AND HER GRABBIN' AT THE SECOND'S ARM FOR 230 HA APE PROTECTION.
I REMEMBERED I'D GIVEN HER A GUN FOR PROTECTION 715 ICEMAN WHILE I WAS AWAY
HE SHRINKS AGAINST CRASSUS FOR PROTECTION--WITH 303 LAZARU BOYISH PLEADING)
HOLDING LAZARUS' ARM AS IF FOR PROTECTION AND IN 307 LAZARU PROTECTION.
AS IF FOR PROTECTION. 348 LAZARU
I AM GOING TO OFFER A PRAYER FOR PROTECTION TO 349 MARCOM THIS TREE SACRED TO BUDDHA.
I QUITE REALIZE THAT IN SELF-PROTECTION I'VE GOT 396 MARCOM TO BUY THEM--OR KILL YOU/
PRESSING HIS FACE AGAINST HER BREAST AS IF FOR 161 MISBEG PROTECTION.

PROTECTIVE

HE'S PILED ON LAYERS OF PROTECTIVE FAT, BUT 296 GGBROW VAGUELY,
PROTECTIVE TENDERNESS.) 48 JOURNE
PROTECTIVE GENTLENESS.) 173 JOURNE
(SHE GLANCES AT TYRONE PROVOKINGLY--THEN SUDDENLY 54 MISBEG WORRIED AND PROTECTIVE)
THERE IS PASSION IN HER KISS BUT IT IS A TENDER, 141 MISBEG PROTECTIVE MATERNAL PASSION,
(HER HORROR EBBING AS HER LOVE AND PROTECTIVE 151 MISBEG COMPASSION RETURNS--
AND A FLOOD OF PROTECTIVE AFFECTION FOR HER) 83 STRANG
PROTECTIVE WARDING OFF AND AT THE SAME TIME A 480 WELDED SEEKING POSSESSION.

PROTECTIVELY

(SHE HUGS HIM PROTECTIVELY) DON'T TALK LIKE THAT/144 MISBEG

PROTECTOR

I AM HIS PROTECTOR. 342 LAZARU

PROTECTS

SHE PROTECTS ME/ 266 GGBROW

PROTEST

(STARTS TO HIS FEET WITH FIERCE PROTEST) 29 ANNA
(THE PRIEST GIVES A SWIFT, REPROACHFUL LOOK AT 510 DAYS JOHN, SEEMS ABOUT TO PROTEST.
(WITH A GREAT PRETENSE OF GUILT-STRICKEN PROTEST) 440 DYNAMO
THAT GRANDFATHER WAS SICK--(AS CHRISTINE IS ABOUT 29 ELECTR TO PROTEST INDIGNANTLY)
THEN HOPE BREAKS INTO DULLY EXASPERATED, BRUTALLY 711 ICEMAN CALLOUS PROTEST.)
(A CHORUS OF DULL, RESENTFUL PROTEST FROM ALL THE 711 ICEMAN GROUP.
THERE IS A MUFFLED GROAN OF RAGE AND PROTEST FROM 529 INZONE SMITTY.)
(AS TYRONE STARTS TO PROTEST.) 87 JOURNE
(TYRONE STARTS TO PROTEST, THEN GIVES IT UP. 152 JOURNE
(THIS PROVOKES A FURIOUS PROTEST FROM THE 283 LAZARU NAZARENES AND INSULTING HOOTS AND
I MUST PROTEST AGAINST YOUR ACTING SO CHILDISHLY, 37 MANSNS DEBORAH.
I DO PROTEST/ 142 MANSNS
ALL THE TIME THE THREE SET UP MISERABLE SCREAMS OF353 MARCOM PROTEST.
AND ANNIE'S WHINING VOICE RAISED IN ANGRY 594 ROPE PROTEST.)
(AS MARSDEN SEEMS AGAIN ABOUT TO PROTEST) 35 STRANG
(AS NINA MAKES A MOTION OF PROTEST--GRIMLY AND 64 STRANG INEXORABLY)
(TORTUREDLY--TRYING INCOHERENTLY TO FORCE OUT A 182 STRANG LAST DESPAIRING PROTEST)
(WITH A LAST TORTURED PROTEST) 198 STRANG
(IVAN BLUBBERS SOME INCOHERENT PROTEST--THEN 498 VOYAGE SUDDENLY FALLS ASLEEP.)
(SUDDENLY EXPLODES IN FURIOUS PROTEST) 451 WELDED
(IN WILD PROTEST) NELLY, WHAT ARE YOU OFFERING 452 WELDED ME--A SACRIFICE$

PROTESTANTS

PROTESTANTS
COMPOSED OF PROTESTANTS AND BAD CATHOLICS. 4 MISBEG
PROTESTED
YOU HAVE PROTESTED IN EVERY LETTER HOW HAPPY YOU 6 MANSNS
WERE.
PROTESTING
(ADVANCING TOWARD THE TABLE--PROTESTING TO BURKE) 51 ANNA
(PROTESTING PETULANTLY TO HIS GOD) 423 DYNAMO
(PROTESTING VIOLENTLY) NO! 175 ELECTR
(PROTESTING WITH A TRACE OF GENUINE EARNESTNESS) 219 HA APE
IRRITATED, PROTESTING EXCLAMATIONS FROM THOSE 244 HA APE
AWAKENED
HICKEY'S VOICE KEEPS ON PROTESTING.) 719 ICEMAN
(THEN PROTESTING UNEASILY.) BUT THAT'S MORBID 154 JOURNE
CRAZINESS ABOUT NOT BEING WANTED
(PROTESTING FEEBLY) (BUT I DON'T KNOW FOR 92 STRANG
CERTAIN.
(PITIFULLY PROTESTING) BUT I DO, JOHN/ 466 WELDED
(PROTESTING) NELLY/ 486 WELDED
PROTESTINGLY
(PROTESTINGLY) I DONE MY BEST TO MAKE IT AS COZY 546 'ILE
AND COMFORTABLE AS COULD BE.
(PROTESTINGLY) I WASN'T MEANING IT THAT WAY AT 57 ANNA
ALL AND WELL YOU KNOW IT.
(PROTESTINGLY) AND THE *SUNDA* AIN'T AN OLD 96 BEYOND
SHIP--LEASTWAYS, NOT VERY OLD--
(PROTESTINGLY) PA/ 107 BEYOND
(PROTESTINGLY) YES, DADA/ 129 BEYOND
(PROTESTINGLY) YOU OBSTINATE OLD SON OF A GUN/ 134 BEYOND
(PROTESTINGLY) BLIMEY BUT YOU'RE A CHEERFUL 482 CARDIF
BLIGHTER, DRISCOLL/
(PROTESTINGLY) AW, PUP, LAY OFF RELIGION, CAN'T 438 DYNAMO
YOU/
(PROTESTINGLY) DINNA BE A LOON, SWANSON/ 514 INZONE
(PROTESTINGLY) 516 INZONE
(PROTESTINGLY) WHY DO YOU WISH TO HURT YOURSELF 426 MARCOM
FURTHER$
(PROTESTINGLY) WELL--BUT--HOLD ON--I'M SURE NINA 42 STRANG
WOULD RATHER--
(WITH A GUILTY START--PROTESTINGLY) 54 STRANG
(FLUSHING GUILTILY--PROTESTINGLY) 95 STRANG
(WITH A GLARE AT MARSDEN--PROTESTINGLY) 126 STRANG
(PROTESTINGLY) OW, YOU AIN'T GOINTER LEAVE ME, 504 VOYAGE
ARE YERS

PROTESTS
(PROTESTS HALF-HEARTEDLY) BUT HE'S ALWAYS SWORN 213 AHWILD
HE GOT RAKED INTO THAT PARTY
(WAVING THEIR PROTESTS ASIDE)
(PROTESTS CONFUSEDLY) NO--THAT'S NOT RIGHT---I-- 106 BEYOND
(COCKY PROTESTS) 545 DAYS
(PROTESTS DULLY.) OH, FOR PETE'S SAKE, MAMA. 520 DAYS
(PROTESTS PENITENTLY.) SHE DOESN'T/ 117 JOURNE
THERE ARE MUTTERED CURSES, GROANS, PROTESTS, 142 JOURNE
IS THIS ANOTHER OF YOUR PERIODICAL DUTY-TO-THE- 301 LAZARU
COMPANY PROTESTS 70 MANSNS
PERPETRATED BY UNSCRUPULOUS JAPANESE TRADE-PIRATES422 MARCOM
WHO, IN SPITE OF HIS PROTESTS.
(PROTESTS MISERABLY.) IT WAS THE DRINK TALKIN', 24 POET
NOT HIM.

PROTONS
AND ATOMS ARE ONLY PROTONS AND ELECTRONS-- 477 DYNAMO

PROTRUDING
WITH PROTRUDING EARS AND LITTLE ROUND EYES, 576 ICEMAN
HIS FACE IS FLAT WITH A BIG MOUTH, PROTRUDING 51 JOURNE
EARS,

PROTUBERANT
THE EYES ARE PROTUBERANT, LEERING, CYNICAL SLITS, 337 LAZARU
THE LONG NOSE,

PROUD
I'M PROUD TO BE A CYNIC. 216 AHWILD
(HE PUSHES HIS PLATE AWAY FROM HIM WITH PROUD 228 AHWILD
RENUNCIATION)
BUT AT THE SAME TIME THRILLED AND PROUD OF 236 AHWILD
MINGLING WITH THE PACE THAT KILLS.
(PROUD OF HIMSELF--WITH A SHY SMILE) 240 AHWILD
BUT THE GIN IS RISING TO HIS HEAD AND HE FEELS 240 AHWILD
PROUD OF HIMSELF AND DEVILISH
BY GOD, I'M PROUD OF YOU WHEN YOU TALK LIKE THAT/ 296 AHWILD
I WAS TOO PROUD TO LET YOU SEE I CARED BECAUSE I 91 BEYOND
THOUGHT THE YEAR YOU HAD AWAY
I S'POSE YOU THINK I OUGHT TO BE PROUD TO BE YOUR 127 BEYOND
WIFE--
YOU BOTH GOT A RIGHT TO FEEL PROUD OF HER. 140 BEYOND
PROUD TO ASK ME$ 154 BEYOND
HE WAS TOO PROUD TO ASK ANYTHING, HE SAID. 154 BEYOND
(OU PROUD TO ASK HELP OF ME/ 155 BEYOND
I'M PROUD ENOUGH OF THE FIRST FOUR YEARS. 161 BEYOND
THE ONLY CONSTANT FAITH I'VE FOUND IN HIM BEFORE 304 DAYS
WAS HIS PROUD BELIEF IN HIMSELF
(WITH A PROUD ASSERTIVENESS) 542 DAYS
I'LL TELL HIM THE TRUTH 'BOUT THE SON HE'S SO 297 DESIRE
PROUD O'/
HE'S THE SMARTEST SKIPPER OUT O' THIS PORT AND 513 DIFRNT
YOU'D OUGHT TO BE PROUD YOU'D GOT
THIS TOWN'S REAL PROUD OF EZRA. 8 ELECTR
SETH IS SO PROUD OF HIS DURNED OLD MANNONS/. 8 ELECTR
HIS NAME WOULD BE MANNUN AND HE'D BE ONLY TOO 20 ELECTR
PROUD OF IT.
I'M PROUD TO BE/ 25 ELECTR
(WITH GRIM PROUD SATISFACTION) 48 ELECTR
WHEN I THINK OF HOW PROUD OF YOU HE WAS WHEN HE 94 ELECTR
CAME HOME/
BE PROUD, THEN/ 96 ELECTR
I'M PROUD OF YOU, TOO. 96 ELECTR
YOU OUGHT TO FEEL PROUD. 142 ELECTR
WHY MUST I BE SO ASHAMED OF MY STRENGTH, SO PROUD 264 GGBROW
OF MY WEAKNESS$
NOT PROUD/ 297 GGBROW

PROUD (CONT'D.)
SENSITIVE AND SELF-CONSCIOUS AND PROUD AND 297 GGBROW
REVENGEFUL--
SEEING TO GROW TALL AND PROUD--THEN WITH A LAUGH 308 GGBROW
OF BOLD SELF-ASSURANCE)
IT REALLY MAKES ME PROUD TO HAVE YOU SO AMBITIOUS.310 GGBROW
SHE WEARS HER MASK OF THE PROUD, INDULGENT MOTHER.323 GGBROW
HER AUNT IS A POMPOUS AND PROUD--AND FAT---OLD 218 HA APE
LADY.
SHE'S ALWAYS BEEN PROUD OF THAT. 589 ICEMAN
I'VE BEEN A PHILOSOPHICAL DRUNKEN BUM, AND PROUD 591 ICEMAN
OF IT.
PROUD TO CALL YOU MY FRIEND. 599 ICEMAN
BESSIE WANTED IT AND SHE WAS SO PROUD. 603 ICEMAN
HE FEELS A PROUD PROPRIETOR'S AFFECTION FOR THEM, 611 ICEMAN
OR DAT I AIN'T PROUD TO BE WHAT I IS, GET ME$ 637 ICEMAN
AND YOU'S PROUD TO DRINK WID ME OR YOU DON'T GET 673 ICEMAN
NO DRINK.
GRINNING WITH PROUD PROPRIETORSHIP. 726 ICEMAN
WE'RE ALL SO PROUD OF YOU, MAMA, SO DARNED HAPPY. 41 JOURNE
YOU OUGHT TO BE PROUD YOU'RE HIS SON/ 60 JOURNE
HE'S EVEN PROUD OF HAVING THIS SHABBY PLACE. 61 JOURNE
YOU'VE DONE SPLENDIDLY. I'M PROUD OF YOU. 89 JOURNE
HE'S PROUD YOU'RE HIS MOTHER/ 122 JOURNE
(DRUNKENLY ASSERTIVE.) WHY SHOULDN'T I BE PROUD$ 164 JOURNE
AND SO PROUD OF ME. 171 JOURNE
THE PROUD, SELF-RELIANT,. 273 LAZARU
IN DEPTHS OF SKY, PROUD AND POWERFUL, INFECTIOUS 280 LAZARU
WITH LOVE.
THEY ARE ALL OF THE PROUD SELF-RELIANT TYPE, IN 298 LAZARU
THE PERIOD OF YOUNG MANHOOD.
LIKE A PROUD GUARD OF HONOR NOW, LAUGHING, 307 LAZARU
BE PROUD, O DUST/ 309 LAZARU
INTROSPECTIVE, PROUD, SELF-RELIANT,. THE 312 LAZARU
SERVILE, HYPOCRITICAL,
(WITH MORE AND MORE OF A PASSIONATE, PROUD 324 LAZARU
EXULTATION)
IN THE PERIOD OF WOMANHOOD IN THE PROUD, SELF- 336 LAZARU
RELIANT TYPE.
HIS FACE IS STRONG AND PROUD 350 LAZARU
IF FOOLS KNEEL AND WORSHIP ME BECAUSE THEY FEAR 352 LAZARU
ME, SHOULD I BE PROUD$
I AM NOT PROUD OF BEING CAESAR--AND WHAT IS A GOD 352 LAZARU
BUT A CAESAR OVER CAESARS$
I SHALL BE PROUD/ 352 LAZARU
SHE MADE ME FEEL, IN THE PROUD QUESTIONING OF HER 355 LAZARU
SCORNFUL EYES,
THEN THAT PROUD WOMAN, MOTHER, SAW MY HAPPINESS. 356 LAZARU
I AM TOO PROUD/ 359 LAZARU
(SMILING) YOU ARE SO PROUD OF BEING EVIL/ 359 LAZARU
SHE IS VERY SENSITIVE AND PROUD-- 8 MANSNS
SO PROUD AND HAPPY BECAUSE HE'S BEAT SOMEONE ON A 20 MANSNS
SALE,
I WANT TO BE PROUD OF WHAT YOU ARE, OF THE GREAT 61 MANSNS
SUCCESS I SEE BEFORE YOU.
(SMILING.) I'M ALL THE TIME TELLING HIM HOW PROUD 64 MANSNS
I AM.
AND HAVE YOU SAY YOU'RE PROUD OF HIM. 64 MANSNS
STILL SO PROUD/ 106 MANSNS
BEAUTIFUL AND COLDLY REMOTE AND PROUD--WITH A 125 MANSNS
SMILE DELIBERATELY AMUSED BY
(TO SARA.) WELL, SINCE THE MOUNTAIN IS TOO PROUD 128 MANSNS
TO COME TO MAHOMET--
I'M PROUD OF YOU. 155 MANSNS
I'M GLAD YOU'RE PROUD. 155 MANSNS
I COULD NOT RESPECT MYSELF UNLESS YOU WERE PROUD 158 MANSNS
OF ME.
AND I AM PROUD/ 158 MANSNS
I'M DIRT UNDER YOUR FEET AND PROUD TO BE/ 158 MANSNS
LOVE IS PROUD, NOT PITIFUL/ 187 MANSNS
TO MAKE ME PROUD OF HIM/ 190 MANSNS
BUT HER FACE IS PROUD, SELF-ASSURED, ARROGANT AND 191 MANSNS
HAPPY.
I KNOW SHE CAN EVEN KILL HERSELF TO PROVE HER 193 MANSNS
LOVE, SO PROUD CAN SHE BE OF IT.
HIS FACE PROUD AND NOBLE, 377 MARCOM
ABLE TO DARE THE PROUD DESTINY OF OUR BLOOD. 385 MARCOM
(SHE BOWS WITH A PROUD HUMILITY AND WALKS OFF 388 MARCOM
LEFT.
THEY ARE ABSURDLY CONSCIOUS AND PROUD OF THIS GET-390 MARCOM
UP--
(PROUD BUT PRETENDING QUERULOUSNESS) 427 MARCOM
IN SILENCE--FOR ONE CONCENTRATED MOMENT--BE PROUD 435 MARCOM
OF LIFE/
BE HUMBLY PROUD/ 435 MARCOM
(GOOD-NATUREDLY) I'M PROUD OF IT. 5 MISBEG
YOU'VE ALWAYS BEEN BRAZEN AS BRASS AND PROUD OF 9 MISBEG
YOUR DISGRACE.
(WITH A PROUD TOSS OF HER HEAD--BOASTFULLY) 20 MISBEG
A GREAT PROUD SLUT WHO'S PLAYED GAMES WITH HALF 80 MISBEG
THE MEN AROUND HERE,
IF I WAS A DAINTY, PRETTY TART HE'D BE PROUD I'D 92 MISBEG
RAISE A RUMPUS ABOUT HIM.
BE GOD, YOU'VE GOT THE PROUD, FIGHTING SPIRIT IN 96 MISBEG
YOU THAT NEVER SAYS DIE,
AND I'M PROUD YOU CAME TO ME AS THE ONE IN THE 152 MISBEG
WORLD YOU KNOW LOVES YOU ENOUGH
YOU OUGHT TO BE PROUD/ 163 MISBEG
WHEN I'M SO PROUD I COULD GIVE IT. 175 MISBEG
THAT'S LOVE, AND I'M PROUD I'VE KNOWN THE GREAT 25 POET
SORROW AND JOY OF IT/
AND REMEMBER WHAT HE SAID, AND BE PROUD OF 61 POET
HIMSELF.
IT WAS LOVE AND JOY AND GLORY IN YOU AND YOU WERE 62 POET
PROUD/
(HER EYES SHINING.) I'M STILL PROUD AND WILL BE 62 POET
TO THE DAY I DIE/

1257

PROUD

(CONT'D.)
HE'LL BE ON HIS BEST BEHAVIOR NOW, AND HE'LL FEEL 76 POET
PROUD AGAIN IN HIS UNIFORM.
(IMPULSIVELY, WITH A PROUD TOSS OF HER HEAD.) 112 POET
(THEN SPIRITEDLY, WITH A PROUD TOSS OF HER HEAD.) 139 POET
BUT I'VE MINE, TOO, AS PROUD AS HIS. 139 POET
AND YOU'RE PROUD YOU'VE GIVEN THEM TO LOVE. 149 POET
YOU WERE PROUD LIKE ME/ 149 POET
HOW YOU CAN STILL LOVE FATHER AND BE PROUD OF IT, 150 POET
IN SPITE OF WHAT HE IS.
WITH NO FEAR IN THEM--PROUD, UNDERSTANDING PRIDE--169 POET
LOVING ME--
BE THE LIVING GOD, IT'S ME SHOULD BE PROUD THIS 171 POET
NIGHT THAT
BE GOD, WE OUGHT TO BE PROUD AV OUR DAUGHTER, 172 POET
NORA.
AND WON'T WE BE PROUD WATCHIN' HER RISE IN THE 173 POET
WORLD TILL SHE'S A GRAND LADY/
HE'S SET IN HIS PROUD, NOBLE WAYS, BUT SHE'LL FIND173 POET
THE RIGHT TRICK/
ONLY THE MAJOR, DAMN HIM, HAD ME UNDER HIS PROUD 174 POET
THUMB.
I'M TOO PROUD TO MARRY A YANKEE COWARD'S SON/ 178 POET
THAT'LL TEACH YOU, ME PROUD SARA/ 179 POET
GORDON'S PROUD SPOT, FAIRNESS AND HONOR/... 10 STRANG
AND I AM PROUD... 43 STRANG
HE'D FEEL SO PROUD OF HIMSELF, POOR DEAR... 49 STRANG
HOW PROUD I AM YOU'RE DOING SO WONDERFUL WELL/ 54 STRANG
(THEN PROUDLY) BUT I CAN SAY I FEEL PROUD OF 62 STRANG
HAVING LIVED FAIR TO THEM THAT
PROUD OF HIS WILL POWER... 91 STRANG
IT HAS A PROUD AIR OF MODEST PROSPERITY. 111 STRANG
I WAS PROUD TO BE ABLE TO WRITE HER THAT... 112 STRANG
I DON'T SEE ANYTHING TO BE SO PROUD OF/... 114 STRANG
(THINKING PROUDLY) (IT'M PROUD OF THAT... 116 STRANG
HE'S SO PROUD OF BEING THOUGHT A DON JUAN/.... 117 STRANG
(COMES BACK FROM THE RIGHT, A BEAMING LOOK OF 120 STRANG
PROUD PARENTHOOD ON HIS FACE)
I WASN'T MUCH FOR NINA TO FEEL PROUD ABOUT HAVING 121 STRANG
AROUND THE HOUSE
AND I'M PROUD/ 131 STRANG
SHE'S PROUD... 134 STRANG
PROUD WITHOUT BEING PROUD ENOUGH/... 138 STRANG
ON THE PROUD ASSURANCE THAT HE IS SELF-MADE/ 141 STRANG
AND NO MATTER WHAT I MAY SAY OR DO IN BITTERNESS, 145 STRANG
I'M PROUD--AND GRATEFUL, NINA/
(WITH PROUD AFFECTION) HE'S A FINE BOY, NINA/ 166 STRANG
THEN LET'S BE PROUD OF OUR FIGHT/ 448 WELDED
SHE CONFESSED. SHE WAS PROUD OF HER HATE/ SHE 475 WELDED
WAS PROUD OF MY TORTURE.

PROUDER

NO ONE IS PROUDER YOU'VE STARTED TO MAKE GOOD. 164 JOURNE

PROUDEST

SAM IS THE PROUDEST PARENT I'VE EVER SEEN/ 128 STRANG
(WHY, I SHOULD BE THE PROUDEST WOMAN ON EARTH/...135 STRANG

PROUDLY

(PROUDLY) =THE QUINTESSENCE OF IBSENISM.= 197 AHWILD
(SHE KISSES HIM AND HE GRINS PROUDLY, A HERO TO 242 AHWILD
HIMSELF NOW ON MANY COUNTS)
(PERKING UP PROUDLY) ARTHUR HAS A REAL NICE 255 AHWILD
VOICE.
(SIMPLY AND PROUDLY) RICHARD WON'T LIE. 267 AHWILD
(PROUDLY) YOU OUGHT 283 AHWILD
(PROUDLY) DAT VAS ANNA, LARRY. 24 ANNA
(DELIGHTED--PROUDLY) AH, IT WAS NOTHING-- 31 ANNA
(THEN SIMPLY--GLANCING DOWN HIS ARM PROUDLY) 35 ANNA
(PROUDLY) AND IF 'TWASN'T FOR ME AND MY GREAT 36 ANNA
STRENGTH, I'M TELLING YOU--
(PROUDLY) ISN'T IT MYSELF THE SEA HAS MORE NEARLY 48 ANNA
DROWNED.
(PROUDLY) AND I'VE MANAGED TO KEEP THINGS GOING, 148 BEYOND
THANK GOD.
(PROUDLY) I KNOW HE LOVES ME. 523 DAYS
(PROUDLY) AND HE DID GO ON/ 535 DAYS
(PROUDLY) YES, SIRREE/ 215 DESIRE
(PROUDLY.) HAIN'T WE RAISED 'EM T' BE FUST-RATE, 218 DESIRE
NUMBER ONE PRIZE STOCKS
(SHE LOOKS AT THE TABLE, PROUDLY) 227 DESIRE
(HE TIP TOES TO THE CRADLE AND PEERS DOWN-- 263 DESIRE
PROUDLY)
(PROUDLY) YES, I AM DIFF'RENT--AND THAT'S JUST 508 DIFRNT
WHAT I THOUGHT CALEB WAS, TOO--
(THEN PROUDLY) AND I FOUND THE STRENGTH TO DO IT.478 DYNAMO
(PROUDLY) I GOT BRAINS AND I USES 'EM QUICK. 178 EJONES
(PROUDLY) AYEN. 7 ELECTR
(PROUDLY) YOU DON'T KNOW ME, THAT'S PLAIN/ 105 ELECTR
(TO THE AIR, PROUDLY) BILLY USED TO DRAW HOUSES 259 GGBROW
WHEN HE WAS LITTLE.
(PROUDLY) HE'S MY BOY/ 261 GGBROW
(PROUDLY) I KNOW. 275 GGBROW
(PROUDLY) I'M GLAD TO HAVE THREE SUCH STRONG BOYS300 GGBROW
TO PROTECT ME.
(PROUDLY) I'M SURE HE CAN DO IT. 304 GGBROW
(PROUDLY) I RUNNED AWAY FROM MINE WHEN I WAS A 211 HA APE
KID.
(THE GORILLA GROWLS PROUDLY) 253 HA APE
(PROUDLY.) THAT FROM BOOTH, THE GREATEST ACTOR OF150 JOURNE
HIS DAY OR ANY OTHER/
(LAUGHING WITH HIM--PROUDLY) 352 LAZARU
THEY BECOME PROUDLY ARROGANT AND COLDLY 126 MANSNS
INDIFFERENT TO HIM.
(THEN PROUDLY) NO, SIR/ 379 MARCOM
(SUDDENLY STEPS FORWARD--FLUSHED BUT PROUDLY) 397 MARCOM
(PROUDLY) THE BEST LITTLE GIRL IN THE WORLD/ 404 MARCOM
(PROUDLY AND FUSSILY) YOU CAN'T HAVE WOMEN AROUND406 MARCOM
(THEN AS SHE STARES AT THE MINIATURE-PROUDLY) 416 MARCOM
(HE JERKS THE LOCKET OUT OF AN UNDER POCKET AND 416 MARCOM
PRESENTS IT TO HER PROUDLY)

PROVE

PROUDLY (CONT'D.)
(PROUDLY) WE WOULD RIDE THEIR ARMIES DOWN INTO 421 MARCOM
THE SEA/
(PROUDLY) I AM A MONGOL--A MAN OF ACTION/ 421 MARCOM
I KEPT MY NOSE TO THE GRINDSTONE EVERY MINUTE. 430 MARCOM
(PROUDLY)
BE PROUDLY GRATEFUL/ 435 MARCOM
(PROUDLY.) I GOT THIS CUT FROM A SABER AT 10 POET
TALAVERA, BAD LUCK TO IT/
(PROUDLY.) DON'T I KNOW/ 78 POET
HE SPEAKS PROUDLY.) 116 POET
(DEFIANTLY AND PROUDLY.) THERE WAS NO LETTING 148 POET
ABOUT IT.
(PROUDLY.) ASHAMED! 148 POET
(PROUDLY.) AND I'LL PLAY ANY GAME HE LIKES AND 181 POET
GIVE HIM LOVE IN IT.
(PROUDLY) SURE THING/ 29 STRANG
(PROUDLY) HOW'S THATS 54 STRANG
(THEN PROUDLY) BUT I CAN SAY I FEEL PROUD OF 62 STRANG
HAVING LIVED FAIR TO THEM THAT
(RAISING HER HEAD--THINKING--PROUDLY TRIUMPHANT) 89 STRANG
(THINKING PROUDLY) (I'M PROUD OF THAT.... 116 STRANG
(THINKING--PROUDLY) (THANK GOD FOR SAMMY/.... 116 STRANG
(PROUDLY) THAT'S EASY. 165 STRANG
(THEN PROUDLY) OH, HE'LL BEAT THEM/ 171 STRANG
(CONSOLED--PROUDLY) YES, SHE SURE WAS WONDERFUL 185 STRANG
TO HIM, ALL RIGHT/
(PROUDLY) AS PASSENGER/ 502 VOYAGE
(PROUDLY) I DON'T TAKE NOTHIN' FOR NOTHIN'--NOT 474 WELDED
FROM YOU, SEE/

PROVE

I GOT TO PROVE A MAN TO BE A GOOD HUSBAND FOR YE 550 'ILE
TO TAKE PRIDE IN.
(THEN MORE SHARPLY) WELL, I KNEW YOU'D PROVE 202 AHWILD
OBSTINATE,
WON'T BE THE PUBLIC SWINDLE I CAN PROVE YOURS IS/ 204 AHWILD
HOW'RE WE EVER GOING TO PROVE ITS 267 AHWILD
SHE CAN PROVE IT. 279 AHWILD
I'LL DO ANYTHING, ANYTHING YOU WANT TO PROVE I'M 74 ANNA
NOT LYING/
I'LL PROVE TO YOU, PA, THAT I'M AS GOOD A MAYO AS 102 BEYOND
YOU ARE--
I'LL PROVE TO YOU THE READING I'VE DONE CAN BE PUT149 BEYOND
TO SOME USE.
TO PROVE OURSELVES WORTHY OF A FINER REALIZATION. 150 BEYOND
IF YOU HEARD ALL THE DOCTOR SAID THAT OUGHT TO 160 BEYOND
PROVE IT TO YOU.
YES, YES--BUT STILL I DON'T--IS HE LIABLE TO PROVE558 CROSS
VIOLENT5
WHY, I REMEMBER ONE ARTICLE WHERE YOU ACTUALLY 497 DAYS
TRIED TO PROVE
(THEN SMILING TEASINGLY) WELL, IF YOU LOVE ME SO 529 DAYS
MUCH, PROVE IT BY TELLING ME.
A MAN WHO WILL PROVE THAT MAN'S FLEETING LIFE IN 543 DAYS
TIME AND SPACE CAN BE NOBLE.
LET HIM PROVE TO ME HIS LOVE EXISTS/ 559 DAYS
IF I COULD PROVE T' YE I WA'N'T SCHEMIN' T' STEAL 258 DESIRE
FROM YE--
I'LL PROVE T' YE.../ 258 DESIRE
(CALLS AFTER HIM INTENSELY) I'LL PROVE T' YE/ 259 DESIRE
I'LL PROVE I LOVE YE BETTER'N.... 259 DESIRE
WE KIN PROVE BY 'EM ALL HOW DRUNK HE GOT. 260 DESIRE
WHAT YOU TOLD ONLY GOES TO PROVE I WAS WRONG ABOUT504 DIFRNT
IT.
WHEN FIFE TOOK OUT HIS WATCH AND SAID IF THERE'S A424 DYNAMO
GOD LET HIM PROVE IT BY
POP TOLD YOU TO PROVE YOUR WERE YELLOW/ 451 DYNAMO
SHE WANTED TO PROVE I'VE CONQUERED THE FLESH/...)1481 DYNAMO
I WANT TO EXPLAIN EVERYTHING TO YOU--TO PROVE 482 DYNAMO
EVERYTHING/
SHE WANTS ME TO--AS A FINAL TEST--TO PROVE I'M 485 DYNAMO
PURIFIED--
AND NOW I CAN PROVE IT, ISN'T/ 29 ELECTR
ARE YOU GOING TO PROVE, THE FIRST TIME YOUR LOVE 41 ELECTR
IS PUT TO A REAL TEST,
HER AS IF INSTINCTIVELY IMPELLED TO PROVE TO HIM 62 ELECTR
SHE HAS NOTHING--
ALL I ASK IS A CHANCE TO PROVE IT/ 99 ELECTR
SO YOU PROVE IT--OR BY GOD, I'LL--/ 99 ELECTR
NOW YOU'VE GOT TO PROVE IT OR ELSE--/ 99 ELECTR
BUT YOU'VE GOT TO PROVE IT/ 99 ELECTR
THEY CAN'T PROVE WHERE I WENT. 109 ELECTR
AN' I'M SAYIN' YOU'RE SCARED TO PROVE THERE AIN'T.131 ELECTR
BUT IT WILL PROVE A STRANGE REASON, I'M CERTAIN OF144 ELECTR
THAT, WHEN I DO DISCOVER IT/
I CAN PROVE WHAT HAPPENED. 171 ELECTR
OH, I KNOW I CAN'T PROVE IT-- 172 ELECTR
ANY MORE THAN I CAN PROVE A LOT OF THINGS ORIN 172 ELECTR
HINTED AT/
COPS DESTROYED THEM, AND I REMEMBER A LOT OF 608 ICEMAN
PEOPLE, EVEN IF I CAN'T PROVE--
YOU'VE BEEN DAMNED KIND TO ME, JIMMY, AND I WANT 623 ICEMAN
TO PROVE HOW GRATEFUL I AM.
SHE JUST HAD TO KEEP ON HAVING LOVERS TO PROVE TO 647 ICEMAN
HERSELF
TO PROVE I'M NOT TEETOTAL 658 ICEMAN
DOES THAT PROVE I WANT TO BE ARISTOCRATS 672 ICEMAN
AND PROVE MY BRILLIANT RECORD IN LAW SCHOOL WAS NO679 ICEMAN
FLASH IN THE PAN.
HE'LL HAVE TO PROVE TO US-- 703 ICEMAN
BUT HOW COULD I PROVE IT, LARRYS 720 ICEMAN
YUH CAN'T PROVE NOTHIN' TILL YOU FIND OUT WHAT'S 524 INZONE
IN THERE.
YOU MUST PROVE TO ME THAT THE BLACK SHADOW-- 530 INZONE
MAYBE NOT, BUT HE CAN'T PROVE IT. 54 JOURNE
PROVE I'M A LIAR. 80 JOURNE
I KEPT WISHING I'D PAID OVER THE BET WITHOUT 136 JOURNE
MAKING YOU PROVE IT.

PROVE

1258

PROVE (CONT'D.)
AND I STAYED WITH HER TO PROVE IT, AND THAT 160 JOURNE
CHEERED HER UP.
THAT I MUST PROVE IT WASN'T SIMPLY MY IMAGINATION.175 JOURNE
(THEN THREATENINGLY) YOU SHALL BE GIVEN FULL 340 LAZARU
OPPORTUNITY TO PROVE IT/
(ECHOING) PROVE THERE IS NO DEATH/ 344 LAZARU
(WITH INDIGNANT SCORN) LET HIM PROVE THERE IS NO 344 LAZARU
DEATH, CAESAR/
(CHANT DEMANDINGLY) LET HIM PROVE THERE IS NO 344 LAZARU
DEATH/
IN MY BOOK I WILL PROVE THIS CAN EASILY BE DONE IF 9 MANSNS
ONLY MEN--
I CAN PROVE-- 15 MANSNS
MUST SORDID FACTS, TO PROVE HOW THOROUGHLY I WAS 29 MANSNS
RESIGNED TO REALITY.
AND TO PROVE MY ESCAPE--AS A SYMBOL--WATCH AND 40 MANSNS
BEAR WITNESS, NICHOLAS/
IT WAS NONSENSE WAS TO MAKE ME ATTEMPT IT AND THEN 46 MANSNS
PROVE TO MYSELF--
YES, HE WILL PROVE IT TO HIM. 62 MANSNS
ALL HE WANTS IS TO PROVE TO YOU HOW CLEVER HE HAS 64 MANSNS
BEEN FOR YOUR SAKE.
WHEN YOU PROVE YOU WANT ME THAT MUCH/ 89 MANSNS
I'LL PROVE TO YOU I CAN LEAD THE COMPANY TO A 101 MANSNS
GLORIOUS, FINAL TRIUMPH--
HAVEN'T YOU LEARNED BY THIS TIME THAT MY GREATEST 146 MANSNS
HAPPINESS IS TO PROVE TO YOU--
I'D LIKE TO SEE YOU PROVE THAT NO MATTER WHAT 149 MANSNS
HAPPENED TO ME,
WHEN YOU PROVE YOU WANT ME TO BE YOURS ENOUGH THAT159 MANSNS
YOU HAVE THE COURAGE TO--
GOD KNOWS I HAVE PAID YOU ENOUGH TO PROVE IT TO 160 MANSNS
YOU/
BUT I'LL PROVE TO YOU WHO IS THE FINAL VICTOR 189 MANSNS
BETWEEN US.
TO PROVE MY LOVE FOR YOU AND SET YOU FREE FROM THE191 MANSNS
GREED OF IT/
I KNOW SHE CAN EVEN KILL HERSELF TO PROVE HER 193 MANSNS
LOVE, SO PROUD CAN SHE BE OF IT.
CAN YOU PROVE IT TO ME? 379 MARCOM
HE RELIED ON ME TO PROVE EQUAL TO THE TASK 411 MARCOM
MAYBE HE THINKS IF HE CAUGHT YOU WITH JIM AND HAD 9 MISBEG
WITNESSES TO PROVE IT,
TO PROVE THERE'S NO HARD FEELINGS, HOW WOULD YOU 106 MISBEG
LIKE A DRINK
TO PROVE HIMSELF THE EQUAL OF ANY GENTLEMAN'S SON. 12 POET
HE WANTED TO PROVE HIS INDEPENDENCE BY LIVING 29 POET
ALONE IN THE WILDS,
TO PROVE YOU'RE STILL A GENTLEMAN/ 49 POET
YES, BY GOD, THAT I WILL PROVE TO HER-- 76 POET
IT ASTONISHES HIM THAT SIMON HAS TO PROVE THAT 86 POET
HE--I MEAN SIMON--IS FREE.
HAPPINESS--BUT THEN SHE'D SAY HE OUGHT TO WAIT AND 87 POET
PROVE HE'S SURE--
AND PROVE I HAD THAT ONE TRAIT AT LEAST IN COMMON/ 41 STRANG
TO PROVE TO OURSELVES WE HAVE BEEN BRAVE AND 188 STRANG
NOBLE/...}

PROVED
HE'S PROVED IT BY THE WAY HE LIKES TO READ 290 AHWILD
BUT SOCIALISM PROVED TOO WEAK-KNEED A MATE, 302 DAYS
I'VE PROVED I LOVE YE--BETTER'N EVERYTHIN'-- 260 DESIRE
AND NOW YOU'VE PROVED YOU AIN'T. 516 DIFFNT
AND I'VE PROVED IT WITH MORE THAN ONE FEMALE. 458 DYNAMO
I'VE PROVED TO YOU I DON'T-- 470 DYNAMO
BUT YOU HAVEN'T PROVED ANYTHING YET/ 99 ELECTR
AND IT'S KEPT GROWIN' THERE EVER SINCE, AS WHAT'S 136 ELECTR
HAPPENED THERE HAS PROVED.
AND I'D HAVE PROVED IT LONG AGO IF YOU'D ONLY 281 GGBROW
GIVEN ME HALF A CHANCE/
(HE ADDS CAUSTICALLY.) AS IF IT PROVED ANYTHING 65 JOURNE
WITH YOU AROUND.
AND IT PROVED HOW MUCH YOU LOVED ME, IN YOUR WAY. 85 JOURNE
I KNEW I'D PROVED BY THE WAY I'D LEFT EUGENE THAT 88 JOURNE
I WASN'T WORTHY TO HAVE.
I KNOW YOU HATE TO, BUT EDMUND HAS PROVED TO YOU 117 JOURNE
THAT
I'VE PROVED BY FIGURES IF YOU LEFT THE LIGHT BULB 126 JOURNE
ON ALL NIGHT
BUT HE WAS DEAD--THAT MUCH HAS BEEN PROVED-- 351 LAZARU
ALL THE SAME, I KILLED HIM AND I PROVED THERE IS 371 LAZARU
DEATH/
TO MAKE MYSELF UNEASY--AFTER HE'S PROVED SO 119 MANSNS
CONCLUSIVELY--
(EAGERLY) AND HE PROVED IT TO ME, TOO. 364 MARCOM
YOU HAVEN'T YET PROVED YOU HAVE AN IMMORTAL SOUL/ 396 MARCOM
BUT, AS I'VE PROVED TO YOU PEOPLE IN CATHAY TIME 404 MARCOM
AND AGAIN,
(BLURTS OUT BITTERLY) YES, YOU'VE PROVED THAT 103 MISBEG
TONIGHT, HAVEN'T YOUS
HE MAY AT FIRST, BUT WHEN I'VE PROVED WHAT A GOOD 31 POET
WIFE I'LL BE--
BUT I HAVE TO ADMIT HE'S PROVED IT... 113 STRANG
I HOPE MY EXPERIMENT HAS PROVED SOMETHING/... 139 STRANG
I'VE PROVED THAT, AT LEAST/ 174 STRANG

PROVEN
YOU'VE PROVEN YOU CAN LAUGH AT YOUR GHOSTS FROM 142 ELECTR
NOW ON.
(SMILING) BUT I BELIEVE THAT WHAT CAN BE PROVEN 397 MARCOM
CANNOT BE TRUE.

PROVERB
» BEHOLD, EVERY ONE THAT USETH PROVERBS SHALL USE 579 ROPE
THIS PROVERB AGAINST THEE,

PROVERBS
» BEHOLD, EVERY ONE THAT USETH PROVERBS SHALL USE 579 ROPE
THIS PROVERB AGAINST THEE,

PROVES
AND HER SMOKING CIGARETTES PROVES IT/ 283 AHWILD

PROVES (CONT'D.)
LOVE TO CREATE PROVES HOW FAR ASTRAY--SO YOU'LL BE162 BEYOND
PUNISHED.
AS THE HISTORY OF THE WORLD PROVES, THE TRUTH HAS 578 ICEMAN
NO BEARING ON ANYTHING.
AS HISTOR HISTORY PROVES, TO BE A WORLDLY SUCCESS 590 ICEMAN
AT ANY THING, ESPECIALLY REVOL
THAT PROVES I KNOW HE'S LOVABLE AT HEART AND CAN'T101 JOURNE
HELP BEING WHAT HE IS
MY SAYING WHAT I'M TELLING YOU NOW PROVES IT. 166 JOURNE
IT'S BECAUSE HE'S JEALOUS, AND THAT PROVES HOW 126 MANSNS
MUCH HE LOVES US.
I SHOULD BE GLAD--IT PROVES HOW HE LOVES ME--HOW 163 MANSNS
MUCH HE NEEDS MY LOVE--
THAT PROVES YOU IN THE EAST AREN'T RESPONSIBLE, 404 MARCOM
IT'S THAT HAREM NOTION.
(QUICKLY) WELL, IT PROVES HE CAN'T KEEP AWAY FROM 98 MISBEG
YOU,
FAIR, IT PROVES HOW LITTLE OF LOVE YOU KNOW 25 POET
PROVES CONCLUSIVELY THAT YOU'RE NOT YOURSELF/ 18 STRANG
TO EXPECT COMMON SENSE OF PEOPLE PROVES YOU'RE 79 STRANG
LACKING IN IT YOURSELF/...})

PROVIDE
WELL, I HOPE WHITECHAPEL WILL PROVIDE THE NEEDED 219 HA APE
NERVE TONIC.
I CAN OFFER YOU A SALARY THAT WILL ENABLE YOU TO 154 MANSNS
PROVIDE VERY MODERATE COMFORT

PROVIDED
THAT IS, PROVIDED HE LOVES HER AS MUCH AS HE 498 DAYS
BOASTS TO HIMSELF HE DOES--
I WON'T TELL HIM, PROVIDED YOU GIVE UP BRANT AND 32 ELECTR
NEVER SEE HIM AGAIN--
(WATCHING THEM) AT LEAST I AM LEAVING HER WELL 293 GGBROW
PROVIDED FOR.
PROVIDED A MEAL IS SERVED WITH THE BOOZE, 571 ICEMAN
PROVIDED THAT YOU DO ALSO. 651 ICEMAN
THEN THE MATTER IS SETTLED--PROVIDED, OF COURSE, 59 MANSNS
SARA CONSENTS.
PROVIDED HE DON'T PERMIT MOTHER TO POISON THEIR 85 MANSNS
MINDS WITH NONSENSE.
ALLAN HAS PROVIDED/ 353 MARCOM
A GENTLEMAN DRINKS AS HE PLEASES--PROVIDED HE CAN 46 POET
HOLD HIS LIQUOR AS HE SHOULD.
PROVIDED HIS FATHER AND I CAN AGREE ON THE AMOUNT 63 POET
OF HER SETTLEMENT.
AND ALSO PROVIDED YOU AGREE TO LEAVE THIS PART OF 122 POET
THE COUNTRY
PROVIDED, MARK YOU, THAT YOU AND YOUR DAUGHTER 122 POET
SIGN AN AGREEMENT I HAVE DRAWN UP

PROVIDENCE
BUT IT WAS AN ACT OF PROVIDENCE I DID GO. 134 BEYOND

PROVIDIN'
PROVIDIN' SHE'LL WANT COMFORTIN', WHICH AIN'T 132 ELECTR
LIKELY.

PROVIN'
HE'S PROVIN' IT TO US, POLL. 633 ICEMAN

PROVINCETOWN
»SIMON WINTHROP» AT ANCHOR IN THE OUTER HARBOR OF 25 ANNA
PROVINCETOWN, MASS.

PROVINCIAL
PROVINCIAL BUSINESS MAN, STOUT AND HEARTY IN HIS 257 GGBROW
EVENING DRESS.
SUCCESSFUL PROVINCIAL AMERICAN OF FORTY. 288 GGBROW

PROVINCIALISM
THIS DEFENSE IS STRENGTHENED BY A NATURAL TENDENCY 6 STRANG
TOWARD A PRIM PROVINCIALISM

PROVING
BUT IT'S NOT PROVING TO ME HOW YOU CAN BE SO 523 DAYS
CERTAIN THAT NEVER SINCE THEN--
AH, IT'S A GREAT NOBLE LADY YOU COULDN'T HELP 190 MANSNS
PROVING YOURSELF IN THE END.
IT DOESN'T NEED PROVING. 396 MARCOM
BUT THERE YOU STAND PROVING ME A LIAR BY 51 STRANG

PROVISION
THIS FOOD PROVISION WAS GENERALLY CIRCUMVENTED 571 ICEMAN
BUT THERE IS ONE PROVISION THAT IS PECULIAR, TO 191 STRANG
SAY THE LEAST.

PROVISIONALLY
IT'S JUST BEEN ACCEPTED--PROVISIONALLY--BY THE 275 GGBROW
PROVITEE.

PROVISO
BUT I'VE STILL GOT ONE PROVISO--THAT YOU GIVE US 396 MARCOM
PERMISSION TO GO HOME.

PROVOCATIVE
(MORE AND MORE WITH A DELIBERATE, PROVOCATIVE 662 ICEMAN
TAUNTING)
MADE MORE EFFECTIVE BY A PROVOCATIVE HINT OF 114 MANSNS
TAUNTING BEHIND IT.)

PROVOCATIVELY
(PROVOCATIVELY) DON'T LET THEM SCARE YOU, DICK. 195 AHWILD
(GRINS AT HIS FATHER PROVOCATIVELY.) 23 JOURNE
(HE GRINS AT HIS FATHER PROVOCATIVELY.) 133 JOURNE
(GRINS PROVOCATIVELY.) HE ALSO WROTE A POEM 133 JOURNE
(PROVOCATIVELY.) THEY SAY HE WAS A SOUSE, TOO. 135 JOURNE
(STILL PROVOCATIVELY UNCONVINCING, HUGGING HER 80 MANSNS
AGAIN.)
BUT STILL PROVOCATIVELY.) 81 MANSNS
HER BODY HAS GROWN STRIKINGLY VOLUPTUOUS AND 139 MANSNS
PROVOCATIVELY FEMALE.

PROVOCATOR
WELL, YOU DIRTY SPY, YOU ROTTEN AGENT PROVOCATOR, 249 HA APE

PROVOKE
YOUR MOTHER WARNED ME YOU ONLY DID IT TO PROVOKE 45 POET
ME.
(HE AGAIN SHAKES HIS HEAD AT SARA, AS IF TO SAY, 104 POET
DON'T PROVOKE HIM.

PROVOKED
BUT YOU NEEDN'T BE PROVOKED AT BEING AN ISLAND 90 ELECTR
BECAUSE
(PROVOKED) WHY, OF COURSE, TO COME HERE--AS HE 303 GGBROW
DOES EVERY DAY/
THEN IRRITABLY AS IF SUDDENLY PROVOKED AT HIMSELF 590 ICEMAN
FOR TALKING SO MUCH)
(SHE TURNS TO THE DOOR.) CATO WILL BE PROVOKED AT 86 POET
ME FOR KEEPING HIM WAITING.

PROVOKES
(THIS PROVOKES A FURIOUS PROTEST FROM THE 283 LAZARU
NAZARENES AND INSULTING HOOTS AND

PROVOKIN'
HE HAS GREAT LOVE FOR YOU, EVEN IF YOU DO BE 23 POET
PROVOKIN' HIM ALL THE TIME.

PROVOKING
(WITH A PROVOKING GRIN AT HIS BROTHER 82 BEYOND
TOUCHING THE LION WITH INTENTIONAL PROVOKING 328 LAZARU
BRUTALITY)
(WITH PROVOKING CALM) DON'T BE CALLING ME NAMES, 12 MISBEG
YOU BAD-TEMPERED OLD HORNET.
IT'S YOUR FAULT, FOR PROVOKING HIM. 61 POET
THERE IS A QUALITY ABOUT HIM, PROVOKING AND 33 STRANG
DISTURBING TO WOMEN.
(WITH PROVOKING CALM) I LOVED GORDON. 102 STRANG

PROVOKINGLY
(LAUGHING PROVOKINGLY AT HER BROTHER) 103 BEYOND
(PROVOKINGLY) 499 DIFRNT
(HE GRINS PROVOKINGLY.) 525 DIFRNT

PROVOKINGLY UNCONVENTIONAL. 26 MANSNS
(SHE GLANCES AT TYRONE PROVOKINGLY--THEN SUDDENLY 54 MISBEG
WORRIED AND PROTECTIVE)

PROWESS
FOR THE BOY, FOR ALL HIS GOOD LOOKS AND PROWESS IN 9 STRANG
SPORT AND HIS COURSES,
RATTLING ON IN THE COCKSURE BOASTFUL WAY OF ABOY 54 STRANG
SHOWING OFF HIS PROWESS BEFORE

PROWL
HIS EYES PROWL THE LOBBY AND FINALLY COME TO REST 27 HUGHIE

PROXIMITY
WHEN HE MAKES OUT ANNA IN SUCH INTIMATE PROXIMITY 38 ANNA
TO THIS STRANGE SAILOR,

PROXY
AFRAID TO FACE YOUR GHOSTS--EVEN BY PROXYS 495 DAYS
YOU'LL SEE THAT I FACE IT--BY PROXY, AT LEAST--IN 509 DAYS
MY NOVEL.
BY PROXY, I LOVE YOU. 268 GGBROW
(HE LAUGHS HARSHLY) PARADISE BY PROXY/ 305 GGBROW

PRUDENCE
(THEN RAGE AT THE INSULT TO HIS MOTHER OVERCOMING 24 ELECTR
ALL PRUDENCE--

PRUDENT
(AT LAST INSULTED BEYOND ALL PRUDENT SUBMISSION.) 154 MANSNS
IT WAS PRUDENT TO WAIT... 91 STRANG

PRUNIN'
*R PRUNIN'. 208 DESIRE

PRURIENT
YES, IF YOU SAY PRURIENT PURITY/... 100 STRANG

PRY
I'LL TROUBLE YOU NOT TO PRY INTO MY AFFAIRS, 468 CARIBE
DONKEYMAN.
ERIE GIVES HIM UP AND AGAIN ATTEMPTS TO PRY 28 HUGHIE
HIMSELF FROM THE DESK,
I HELPED TO PRY AWAY THE STONE SO I WAS RIGHT 277 LAZARU
BESIDE HIM.

PRYIN'
IT WAS ALWAYS LIKE PRYIN' OPEN A SAFE FOR ME TO 522 DIFRNT
SEPARATE HIM FROM A CENT.

PRYING
SHARP EYES STILL PEER AT LIFE WITH A SHREWD PRYING 6 ELECTR
AVIDITY AND HIS LOOSE MOUTH
GRIN CAN BE HEARD IN THE STATEROOM PRYING OPEN 114 ELECTR
BRANT'S DESK
I KNOW SOMETHING IS WORRYING YOU--AND I DON'T WANT160 ELECTR
TO SEEM PRYING--BUT
PRYING AND INTERFERING IN MY PRIVATE BUSINESS/ 74 MANSNS
HOURS SINCE SUPPER EVEN--THE CHILDREN WATCHING, 162 MANSNS
THEIR PRYING EYES SNEERING--
AS RESTLESS, PRYING, RECORDING INSTRUMENTS. 39 STRANG

PSEUDO
I'LL GRANT YOU THE PSEUDO-NIETZSCHEAN SAVIOR I 543 DAYS
JUST EVOKED OUT OF MY PAST IS AN

PSYCHE
THERE IS SOMETHING WRONG WITH ITS PSYCHE, I'M 49 STRANG
SURE.

PSYCHIC
DON'T YOU GO PSYCHIC ON US/ 517 DAYS
DON'T USUALLY GO IN FOR PSYCHIC NONSENSE. 557 DAYS
THERE ARE PSYCHIC AFFINITIES... 74 STRANG

PSYCHOANALYST
I HOPE NOT PSYCHOANALYST... 34 STRANG

PUB
BUT, OF COURSE, I MUCH PREFERRED THE NEAREST PUB. 708 ICEMAN

PUBLIC
WON'T BE THE PUBLIC SWINDLE I CAN PROVE YOURS IS/ 204 AHWILD
HE'S BEEN MAKING AS PUBLIC AN ASS OF HIMSELF AS 528 DAYS
POSSIBLE.
AND HAD A BIG PUBLIC FUNERAL TOMORROW. 69 ELECTR
SUCH A PUBLIC DISGRACE AS A MURDER TRIAL WOULD BE/ 91 ELECTR
AS IF FOR SOME PUBLIC FESTIVAL. 298 LAZARU
FOR PUBLIC OPINION'S SAKE. 45 MANSNS
COULD CONCEIVE A SCHEME BY WHICH THE PUBLIC COULD 158 MANSNS
BE COMPELLED TO BUY YOUR
DO YOU WANT TO CREATE A PUBLIC SCANDAL, CURSING 174 MANSNS
AND THREATENING EACH OTHER'S
I MADE SUCH A PUBLIC NUISANCE OF MYSELF THAT THE 149 MISBEG
CONDUCTOR THREATENED IF I
AND IF YOU GO RAISING A DRUNKEN ROW AT THEIR 127 POET
HOUSE, AND MAKE A PUBLIC SCANDAL,

PUBLIC (CONT'D.)
(BITTERLY.) NOTHING'S HAPPENED EXCEPT HE'S MADE A 150 POET
PUBLIC DISGRACE OF HIMSELF.
(THEN SELF-REASSURINGLY) (BUT THERE IS A PUBLIC 5 STRANG
TO CHERISH THEM, EVIDENTLY...
MY PUBLIC WILL BE FORGETTING ME/.... 112 STRANG

PUBLICITY
THE DISTRICT ATTORNEY GAVE HIM SC MUCH UNWELCOME 595 ICEMAN
PUBLICITY,
HE SAID, "JIMMY, THE PUBLICITY DEPARTMENT'S NEVER 604 ICEMAN
BEEN THE SAME

PUBLICLY
(SOLEMNLY OFFENDED) ARE YOU--PUBLICLY REBUKING ME225 AHWILD
BEFORE ASSEMBLED--S
WHO DEFIES THEE PUBLICLY TO STRIKE HIM DEAD,... 423 DYNAMO
AND FATHER WOULD DISOWN YOU PUBLICLY, NO MATTER 32 ELECTR
HOW MUCH THE SCANDAL COST HIM/
I TAKE THIS OPPORTUNITY TO PUBLICLY ANNOUNCE THE 430 MARCUM
BETROTHAL OF MY DAUGHTER,
AND APOLOGIZE PUBLICLY TO MY DAUGHTER, OR ELSE HE 124 POET
MEETS ME IN THE MORNING/

PUCKERED
HER FOREHEAD PUCKERED PUZZLEDLY, 170 JOURNE
SHE GLANCES AROUND VAGUELY, HER FOREHEAD PUCKERED 171 JOURNE
AGAIN.)
(SHE LOOKS AROUND THE ROOM, HER FOREHEAD PUCKERED 172 JOURNE
AGAIN.)

PUCKERS
THE NIGHT CLERK'S FOREHEAD PUCKERS PERSPIRINGLY AS 30 HUGHIE
HE TRIES TO REMEMBER.

PUCKISH
WITH THE PUCKISH FACE OF A PECK'S BAD BOY WHO HAS 188 AHWILD
NEVER GROWN UP.
HIS SHINY FAT FACE IS ONE BROAD, BLURRED, PUCKISH 223 AHWILD
NAUGHTY-BOY GRIN.
RESTORE TO ITS NATURAL PUCKISH EXPRESSION) 259 AHWILD

PUDDIN'S
SAY WHAT YOU'VE A MIND TO, KATE, THE PROOF OF THE 114 BEYOND
PUDDIN'S IN THE EATIN'..

PUDDING
OF A COLD PORK PUDDING AGAINST A BACKGROUND OF 218 HA APE
LINOLEUM TABLECLOTH IN THE
IS AS OBVIOUSLY ENGLISH AS YORKSHIRE PUDDING 575 ICEMAN

PUDDLE
BIG FROGS IN A SMALL PUDDLE. 43 JOURNE
OR LIKE THE DREARY TEARS OF A TRCLOP SPATTERING 152 JOURNE
IN A PUDDLE OF STALE BEER ON A

PUDDLER
GRANDFATHER STARTED AS A PUDDLER. 220 HA APE
MY GRANDFATHER WAS A PUDDLER. 221 HA APE

PUFF
(THEY DRINK--PUFF RESOLUTELY--SIGH--TAKE THEIR 217 DESIRE
FEET DOWN FROM THE TABLE.)

PUFFED
HIS EYES ARE BLOODSHOT AND PUFFED, HIS FACE 256 AHWILD
BLOATED.
HIS FACE IS BATTERED, NOSE RED AND SWOLLEN, LIPS 151 POET
CUT AND PUFFED,

PUFFINESS
BUT HIS FACE IS STILL GOOD-LOOKING DESPITE ITS 37 MISBEG
UNHEALTHY PUFFINESS
CONDITIONED, THE PUFFINESS AND JOWLS OF THE 159 STRANG
PREVIOUS ACT ARE GONE.

PUFFING
COMES THE SOUND OF STEAMERS' WHISTLES AND THE 41 ANNA
PUFFING SNORT OF THE DONKEY
HE IS PUFFING AND BREATHLESS FROM HIS CLIMB 140 BEYOND
(PUFFING AT HIS PIPE) 468 CARIBE
(PUFFING) LET ME GO. 471 CARIBE
AND PUFFING DEFIANTLY.) 217 DESIRE
(DREAMILY) WITH HER PIPE BESIDE HER--PUFFING IN 218 HA APE
PARADISE.
A BUDDHIST, A KASHMIRI TRAVELING MERCHANT COMES 347 MARCOM
IN, PUFFING AND SWEATING.
(AFTER A PAUSE OF PUFFING ON HIS PIPE) 18 MISBEG
(HE BEGINS PACING UP AND DOWN THE ROOM, PUFFING AT 67 STRANG
HIS PIPE.
(PUFFING) GAWD, 'E AIN'T 'ARF 'EAVY/ 503 VOYAGE

PUFFS
HE LIGHTS HIS CIGARETTE WITH ELABORATE 239 AHWILD
NONCHALANCE, PUFFS, BUT DOES NOT INHALE--
PUFFS AND BEGINS TO SNORE PEACEFULLY.) 275 AHWILD
(SHE PUFFS, STARING AT THE TABLE TOP. 15 ANNA
(AFTER A PAUSE, DURING WHICH ANDREN PUFFS AT HIS 157 BEYOND
CIGAR ABSTRACTEDLY,
(AFTER A FEW PUFFS AT HIS PIPE) 467 CARIBE
BORNE ON THE LIGHT PUFFS OF WIND THIS MUSIC IS AT 5 ELECTR
TIMES QUITE LOUD.
WHICH IS HIS CHAIR, AND PUFFS CONTENTEDLY.) 15 JOURNE
(PUFFS RUMINATIVELY) THEY ALL TAKE AFTER YOUR 16 MISBEG
MOTHER'S FAMILY.
(PUFFS ON HIS PIPE) WHAT ELSE DID MY BEAUTIFUL 20 MISBEG
SON, MIKE, SAY TO YOU/
AS HE PUFFS HE CONTINUES BOASTFULLY) 593 ROPE
HIS WORDS ARISING FROM THE TOMB CF A SOUL IN PUFFS 16 STRANG
OF ASHES...))
AND OUT AND PUFFS AT NERVOUSLY. 67 STRANG

PUFFY
HIS BLUE EYES HAVE DROOPING LIDS AND PUFFY POUCHES 8 HUGHIE
UNDER THEM.
PUFFS SHADOWS OF DISSIPATION AND SLEEPLESSNESS 124 STRANG
UNDER HIS RESTLESS, HARRIED EYES.
HIS FACE IS A BIT JOWLY AND PUFFY UNDER THE EYES. 137 STRANG

PUG
CRINKLY LONG BLACK HAIR STREAKED WITH GRAY, A 574 ICEMAN
SQUARE FACE WITH A PUG NOSE.

PUGILIST

PUGILIST

HE ADORED GOROUN AS A NEWSBOY DOES A CHAMPION 75 STRANG PUGILIST/...

PUGNACIOUS

THE LURCHES OUT INTO THE MOONLIGHT--SUDDENLY 104 ELECTR PUGNACIOUS!

I HOPE THE EFFECT IS APPARENT ONLY IN A 654 ICEMAN BRISTLING, TOUCHY, PUGNACIOUS ATTITUDE.

PUGNACIOUSLY

THEN GLARES AT HIM PUGNACIOUSLY) 237 HA APE HOPE GOES ON PUGNACIOUSLY) 718 ICEMAN FOR A SECOND JAMIE REACTS PUGNACIOUSLY AND HALF 162 JOURNE RISES FROM HIS CHAIR TO DO HEAVY JAW, WHICH STICKS OUT PUGNACIOUSLY. 582 ROPE

PUGNACIOUSNESS

(THEN DRUNKEN PUGNACIOUSNESS COMES OVER HIM AGAIN)105 ELECTR

PUKE

IT MAKES ME WANT TO PUKE/ 145 JOURNE

PUKING

PUKING IN THE GUTTER/ 158 POET

PULL

THE MEN PULL OUT SHEATH-KNIVES AND START A RUSH, 544 *ILE BUT STOP

IF I COULD PULL HIM TO THAT, I COULD HANG ON TO 230 AHWILD HIM TILL SOMEONE'D NOTICE US.

I JUST PULL MY FREIGHT. 244 AHWILD

THE MEN I KNOW DON'T PULL THAT ROUGH STUFF WHEN 32 ANNA LADIES ARE AROUND.

SAID HE DIDN'T KNOW HOW HE'D PULL THROUGH 'TIL 115 BEYOND HARVEST WITHOUT IT.

AND I'VE GOT TO PULL THINGS THROUGH SOMEHOW. 383 BEYOND

WHY CAN'T WE PULL TOGETHER? WE USED TO. 123 BEYOND

WE'LL PULL YOU THROUGH ALL RIGHT--AND--HM--WELL-- 485 CARDIFCOMING, ROBINSONS

THE TAKES ANOTHER PULL AT THE BOTTLE.) 466 CARIBE

I KIN ALLUS PULL THE WOOL OVER HIS EYES. 249 DESIRE

AND A BOOKCASE WITH THE GLASS DOORS THAT PULL UP AND 519 DIFRNT SLIDE IN FLANKS THE FIREPLACE.

STOPS AS SHE IS ABOUT TO PULL THE DOOR CLOSED 479 DYNAMO AGAIN.

(IS EVIDENTLY TRYING TO PULL HIMSELF TOGETHER. 44 ELECTR THEN SEES LAVINIA AND IMMEDIATELY MAKES AN EFFORT 174 ELECTR TO PULL HIMSELF TOGETHER AND

POSTS ON THE CORNER AND TRIES TO PULL IT UP FOR A 239 HA APE CLUB.

HE'S GOIN' TO PULL DAT SLAVE-GIRL STUFF ON ME ONCE579 ICEMAN TOO OFTEN.

(THEY BOTH PULL UP THEIR SKIRTS TO GET THE MONEY 613 ICEMAN FROM THEIR STOCKINGS.

HE'S FIXED SOME NEW GAG TO PULL ON US. 618 ICEMAN

(THEY PULL OFF A COVERING BURLAP BAG. 640 ICEMAN

AW, DON'T PULL THAT PITIFUL OLD-MAN JUNK ON ME/ 649 ICEMAN

WE'VE HEARD HARRY PULL THAT BLUFF ABOUT TAKING A 652 ICEMAN WALK EVERY BIRTHDAY

APOLOGIZE FOR SOME OF THE ROUGH STUFF I'VE HAD TO 660 ICEMAN PULL ON YOU.

I'LL HELP PULL ON THE ROPE. 691 ICEMAN

(ROCKY LOOKS GRATEFUL) BUT, BEJEES, DON'T PULL 722 ICEMAN THAT HONEST JUNK/

AND COMMENCE TO PULL ON THEIR SHOES. 514 INZONE

I HEARD HIM PULL THAT TOUCH OF MALARIA STUFF. 29 JOURNE

(STUNG.) DON'T PULL THAT/ 38 JOURNE

PULL AWAY THE FIRE FROM HIM/ 365 LAZARU

(INSTINCTIVELY SHE STARTS TO PULL HER HAND AWAY.) 134 MANSNS

YOU PULL BACK THE CLOTH THEN, SINCE THAT IS YOUR 351 MARCOM CUSTOM.

AFTER I SWEATED BLOOD TO PULL YOU THROUGH ONCE 412 MARCOM ALREADY/

AS IF SHE WERE GOING TO PULL IT DOWN TO HERS. 414 MARCOM

AND SEEN THE FOOTPRINTS WHERE YOU HAD SNEAKED UP 62 MISBEG IN THE NIGHT TO PULL IT DOWN

BUT AT THE SAME TIME ARE ABLE TO PULL THEMSELVES 72 MISBEG TOGETHER WHEN THEY WISH AND BE

DON'T LET ME PULL THAT STUFF. 119 MISBEG

(UNCONSCIOUSLY SHE TRIES TO PULL HER HAND AWAY.) 130 MISBEG

WHAT OTHER BUNK DID I PULL ON YOU--OR I MEAN, DID 170 MISBEG OLD JOHN BARLEYCORN PULL?

WHY DO I HAVE TO PULL THAT LOUSY STUFF? 172 MISBEG

(RESISTING MARY'S EFFORTS TO PULL HIM OUT. 584 ROPE

(SHE GRABS HIM BY THE HAND AND STARTS TO PULL HIM 21 STRANG AWAY.

TRYING TO PULL THE WOOL OVER MY EYES.... 38 STRANG

PULLED

(PULLED OUT OF HER PREOCCUPATION) 250 AHWILD

(HE HAS PULLED HIS WATCH OUT OF HIS VEST POCKET-- 250 AHWILD WITH FORCED CARELESSNESS)

PULLED SIDEWAYS ON THEIR HEADS AT AN AGGRESSIVE 4 ANNA ANGLE.

WONDER YOU WASN'T PULLED IN. 70 ANNA

I'VE SEEN MANY WORSE CASES WHERE THE PATIENT 557 DAYS PULLED THROUGH--

THE HAS PULLED UP THE BOARD. 268 DESIRE

SHE WEARS HER HAIR PULLED TIGHTLY BACK, AS IF TO 10 ELECTR CONCEAL ITS NATURAL CURLINESS).

MY MOTHER PULLED ME BACK AND GAVE ME A HIDING. 26 ELECTR

AND HAS A SLOUCH HAT PULLED DOWN OVER HIS EYES. 109 ELECTR

TWO MEN ABOUT TO FIGHT ARE PULLED APART.) 208 HA APE

I NOTICE HICKEY AIN'T PULLED DAT OLD ICEMAN GAG. 436 ICEMAN DIS TIME.

HE AIN'T PULLED DAT GAG OR SHOWED HER PHOTO AROUND636 ICEMAN BECAUSE HE AIN'T DRUNK.

(LARRY LETS HIMSELF BE PULLED DOWN ON HIS CHAIR. 648 ICEMAN

STINKS, AND HE PULLED A GAT AND SAID HE'D PLUG 699 ICEMAN HICKEY FOR INSULTIN' HIM.

WHAT HE'S PULLED DON'T MEAN NUTTIN'. 725 ICEMAN

WHAT HAD I TO DO WITH ALL THE CRAZY STUNTS HE'S 35 JOURNE PULLED IN THE LAST FEW YEARS--

WHEN I REMEMBER ALL THE ROTTEN STUFF I'VE PULLED/ 145 JOURNE

PULLED (CONT'D.)

(DEBORAH NEARLY LETS HERSELF BE PULLED DOWN BESIDE181 MANSNS HIM.)

THE WAGON IS PULLED SWIFTLY AWAY. 354 MARCOM

HIS FANGS HAVE BEEN PULLED OUT. 370 MARCOM

EXCEPT I'VE PULLED SOME PRETTY ROTTEN STUFF WHEN 1173 MISBEG WAS DRAWING A BLANK.

I CANTERED THE MARE BY THE RIVER AND SHE PULLED UP108 POET LAME.

HIS SCARLET UNIFORM IS FILTHY AND TORN AND PULLED 152 POET AWRY.

(PERMITTING HIMSELF TO BE PULLED OUT THE DOORWAY) 601 ROPE

THE ROCKING CHAIR IS NO LONGER AT CENTER BUT HAS 66 STRANG BEEN PULLED NEARER THE TABLE.

THE HAS PULLED OUT HIS PEN AND A CARD AND IS 77 STRANG WRITING.

WITH CAPS PULLED DOWN OVER THEIR EYES. 506 VOYAGE

IN THE LEFT WALL, CENTER, A SMALL WINDOW WITH A 470 WELDED TORN DARK SHADE PULLED DOWN.

PULLIN'

WHAT'RE YOU PULLIN' THAT LONG FACE FUR, EMMERS 504 DIFRNT HERE'S EMMER TELLIN' YOU THE TRUTH AFTER YOU HAIR-513 DIFRNT PULLIN' ME ALL THESE YEARS

ALL DAT TRIPE YOU BEEN PULLIN'--AW, DAT'S ALL 215 HA APE RIGHT.

PULLIN' DAT WHISTLE ON ME, HUH$ 229 HA APE

I WAS BAWLIN' HIM OUT FOR PULLIN' DE WHISTLE ON 230 HA APE US.

(HIS EYES ON THE ROPE) I'LL BE PULLIN' THAT THING583 ROPE DOWN, SO I WILL..

PULLING

(PULLING AWAY--EMBARRASSEDLY, ALMOST BLUSHING) 222 AHWILD

AND EVERYONE STARTS IN PULLING THE CRACKED SHELLS 228 AHWILD APART.)

(PULLING HER BACK) IT'S TIME FOR YOUR NAP. 117 BEYOND

(PULLING AT HIS HAND--SOLICITOUSLY) 129 BEYOND

FOUR OF THE MEN ARE PULLING ON PIPES 477 CARDIF

THE SINKS TO HIS KNEES PULLING HER DOWN WITH HIM. 235 DESIRE

THROWS BACK THE COVERS AND BEGINS HURRIEDLY 263 DESIRE PULLING ON HIS CLOTHES.

PULLING HIS ARM BACK--BRUSQUELY) 47 ELECTR

(WHO HAS BEEN WATCHING HIM JEALOUSLY--SUDDENLY 49 ELECTR PULLING HIM BY THE ARM--

(DELIGHTED BUT PULLING HER HAND AWAY SHYLY) 84 ELECTR

(SHE ARRANGES HIM AS A MOTHER WOULD A BOY, PULLING145 ELECTR DOWN HIS COAT,

(WITH DELIGHT, PULLING OFF HER MASK) 267 GOBROH

PULLING IT INTO MORE ACCESSIBLE HEAPS. 223 HA APE

I ADMIT I ASKED FOR IT BY ALWAYS PULLING THAT 663 ICEMAN ICEMAN GAG IN THE OLD DAYS.

IT WAS HER PULLING SHERRY FLIPS CN ME WOKE ME UP. 697 ICEMAN

BEJEES, IF YOU'D HEARD ALL THE CRAZY BULL HE WAS 718 ICEMAN PULLING

AND PULLING THEIR BLANKETS UP OVER THEIR 532 INZONE SHOULDERS.

(PULLING BOTTLE CLOSER TO HIM.) 156 JOURNE

(PULLING MARY AWAY) MARY/ 284 LAZARU

PULLING A CHARIOT IN WHICH LAZARUS STANDS DRESSED 307 LAZARU IN A TUNIC OF WHITE AND GOLD.

(PULLING AWAY FROM HIM.) NO. 5 MANSNS

(PULLING AWAY.) I WISH YOU WOULDN'T TALK AS IF 93 MANSNS LOVE--

(PULLING AWAY, STARES AT HIM WITH A PUZZLED 115 MANSNS FRIGHTENED DREAD.)

PULLING THEIR HANDS AWAY SO THEY NO LONGER TOUCH 129 MANSNS ON HIS CHEST.

PULLING HER HAND FROM THE DOOR, AND STANDS DAZED 165 MANSNS AND TREMBLING.

(PULLING AT HER HAND.) LET ME GO/ 181 MANSNS

THEY ARE PULLING A CHARIOT/ 350 MARCOM

SHE SITS ON THE TOP STEP, PULLING HIM DOWN BESIDE 119 MISBEG HER BUT ON THE ONE BELOW.

WHY ARE YOU PULLING YOUR HAND AWAY$ 130 MISBEG

(SHE GETS TO HER FEET, PULLING AT HIS ARM--WITH A 137 MISBEG LITTLE SELF-MOCKING LAUGH)

(PULLING AT LUKE'S ARM AS HE COMES BACK TO THE 590 ROPE DOORWAY)

PULLING IT BACK AND SETTING IT ON ITS LEGS 601 ROPE

PUTTING AN ARM AROUND HIS NECK AND PULLING HIS 70 STRANG HEAD ON TO HER BREAST)

(TAKING HIS OTHER HAND AND SLOWLY PULLING HIM 87 STRANG AROUND TO FACE HER.

(PULLING OUT HIS WATCH) SOON BE TIME FOR THE 160 STRANG START.

YOU MIGHT THINK THERE WAS NO ONE ELSE PULLING THE 168 STRANG SHELL/...

SHE HAS BEEN PULLING THE PINS OUT OF HER HAIR AND,474 WELDED AS SHE KISSES,

PULLMAN

(REMINISCENTLY) IF DEY'S ONE THING I LEARNS IN 178 EJONES TEN YEARS ON DE PULLMAN CA'S

IS DRESSED IN A PULLMAN PORTER'S UNIFORM AND CAP. 191 EJONES

PULLMANS

SHOR I WAS DAT WHEN I WAS PORTER ON DE PULLMANS 185 EJONES WITH WEEK AFTER WEEK OF ONE-NIGHT STANDS, IN 87 JOURNE TRAINS WITHOUT PULLMANS.

PULLS

THE PULLS HER TO HIM AND GIVES HER A SMACKING KISS221 AHWILD ON THE EAR

(WITH A QUICK LOOK TOWARD THE BAR, SHE STEALTHILY 239 AHWILD PULLS UP HER DRESS--

(PULLS OUT HIS ROLL AND HANDS A DOLLAR BILL OVER--239 AHWILD WITH EXAGGERATED CARELESSNESS)

(HE HAS BEEN FUMBLING IN HIS POCKET AND PULLS OUT 242 AHWILD HIS TEN-DOLLAR ROLL

HIS MOUTH PULLS DOWN AT THE CORNERS AND HE SEEMS 257 AHWILD ABOUT TO CRY.

PULLS (CONT'D.)
(HE PUTS THE STRAW HAT ON THE SEAT AMIDSHIPS AND 275 AHWILD
PULLS THE FOLDED LETTER OUT OF
THEN, WITH A PUZZLED EXPRESSION, PULLS IT WIDE. 13 ANNA
(HE PULLS AT HER SLEEVE SHYLY) 35 ANNA
(SHE LEANS OVER AND PULLS HIS HANDS FROM HIS 58 ANNA
EARS--WITH HYSTERICAL KAGE)
(SHE REACHES DOWN, TAKES THE COAT AND PULLS OUT A 66 ANNA
REVOLVER--
(HE PULLS ROBERT'S HAND FROM HIS SIDE AND GRIPS IT 86 BEYOND
TENSELY.
(HE GENTLY PULLS ONE OF RUTH'S HANDS AWAY FROM HER 91 BEYOND
FACE)
PULLS THE CURTAINS ASIDE, AND LOCKS OUT) 152 BEYOND
(HE SITS DOWN IN HIS CHAIR AND PULLS IT CLOSE TO 155 BEYOND
RUTH'S IMPULSIVELY)
AND THEN REACHES INSIDE HIS SHIRT AND PULLS OUT A 462 CARIBE
PINT BOTTLE)
EACH PULLS OUT A PINT BOTTLE. 465 CARIBE
(HE PULLS HIS ARM BACK QUICKLY WITH A SHUDDER OF 469 CARIBE
DISGUST AND TAKES A DRINK.
(HE PULLS HER TO THE ENTRANCE 470 CARIBE
(HE REACHES INTO THE POCKET OF HIS MACKINAW AND 560 CROSS
PULLS OUT A CRUMPLED PAPER)
(BUT ELSA PULLS HER TO HER AND SHE BREAKS DOWN 520 DAYS
FINALLY, SOBBING.
(PULLS THEM AWAY FROM HIM--COLDLY, WITHOUT LOOKING548 DAYS
AT HIM.
(HE PULLS OPEN THE DOOR IN REAR VIOLENTLY.) 211 DESIRE
COMES BACK AND PULLS UP A STRIP OF FLOORING IN 219 DESIRE
UNDER STOVE.
HE SITS DOWN AT THE TABLE, FACES THE STOVE AND 220 DESIRE
PULLS OUT THE PAPER.
AND PULLS BACK HER HEAD SLOWLY AND SHUTS THE 224 DESIRE
WINDOW.
(HE PULLS ON HIS TROUSERS, TUCKING IN HIS NIGHT 238 DESIRE
SHIRT, AND PULLS ON HIS BOOTS.)
SHE PULLS HIS HEAD BACK AND COVERS HIS MOUTH WITH 239 DESIRE
KISSES.
(SHE PULLS HIS HEAD AROUND. 243 DESIRE
(SHE KISSES HIM AND PULLS HIS HEAD OVER AGAINST 266 DESIRE
HER BREAST.)
(HE GETS TO HIS FEET ABRUPTLY AND PULLS 497 DIFRNT
PUSHES AND PULLS AT IT, TRYING TO FORCE IT OPEN.) 450 DYNAMO
(PULLS HER HEAD DOWN AND KISSES HER. 459 DYNAMO
AND PULLS HER THROUGH THE DOOR FROM THE ROOF TO 483 DYNAMO
THE GALLERIES.)
(HE PUTS AN ARM AROUND HER AND PULLS HER TO HIM.) 484 DYNAMO
(HE REACHES BELOW THE THRONE AND PULLS OUT A BIG, 182 EJONES
(HE PULLS OUT A GOLD WATCH AND LOOKS AT IT) 182 EJONES
(HE REACHES IN UNDER THE THRONE AND PULLS OUT AN 185 EJONES
EXPENSIVE PANAMA HAT
(HE PULLS A BANDANA HANDKERCHIEF FROM HIS HIP 187 EJONES
POCKET
(HE UNLACES THEM AND PULLS THEM OFF-- 196 EJONES
BUT AT HIS TOUCH SHE PULLS AWAY AND SPRINGS TO HER 24 ELECTR
FEET.)
(PULLS HER HAND AWAY FROM HIM AND SPRINGS TO HER 56 ELECTR
FEET WILDLY)
(HE GOES BACK IN THE BEDROOM AND PULLS THE SHUTTER 57 ELECTR
CLOSED.
TEN DOLLARS IN THIS POCKET--(HE PULLS THE POCKET 103 ELECTR
INSIDE OUT--
ON THE DECK ABOVE ORIN PULLS A REVOLVER FROM UNDER113 ELECTR
HIS CLOAK AND MAKES A MOVE.
(SHE PULLS HIM AWAY FORCIBLY.) 116 ELECTR
(PULLS HIMSELF UP SHARPLY--CONFUSEDLY, FORCING A 148 ELECTR
SICKLY SMILE)
ORIN UNLOCKS THE TABLE DRAWER, PULLS OUT HIS 156 ELECTR
MANUSCRIPT, AND TAKES UP HIS PEN.)
SHE PULLS VIOLENTLY AWAY. 165 ELECTR
AND PULLS THE SHUTTERS CLOSED WITH A DECISIVE 179 ELECTR
BANG.
(AS IF HE WERE SUFFOCATING, HE PULLS THE MASK FROM272 GGBROW
HIS RESIGNED, PALE,
(HE PULLS HIS CHAIR CLOSER TO HERS) 289 GGBROW
(HE CHUCKLES AT A MEMORY) REMEMBER THAT GAG HE 610 ICEMAN
ALWAYS PULLS ABOUT HIS WIFE AND
(HE PULLS A BIG ROLL FROM HIS POCKET AND PEELS OFF621 ICEMAN
A TEN-DOLLAR BILL.
(STUNG--PULLS BACK A FIST THREATENINGLY) 653 ICEMAN
(PULLS HIS FROM HIS POCKET) AND HERE'S MINE. 682 ICEMAN
(HE PULLS HIS KEY FROM HIS POCKET AND SLAPS IT ON 682 ICEMAN
THE BAR.)
IF YOU OBJECTS TO MY SITTIN' HERE, CAPTAIN, JUST 700 ICEMAN
TELL ME AND I PULLS MY FREIGHT.
MORAN PULLS BACK HIS COAT TO SHOW HIS BADGE.) 708 ICEMAN
IF HE PULLS ANY RUBBER-HOSE TRICKS, YOU LET ME 718 ICEMAN
KNOW/
REASSURED, HE LEANS DOWN AND CAUTIOUSLY PULLS OUT 513 INZONE
A SUITCASE
(HE GETS UP BUT DRISCOLL PULLS HIM DOWN AGAIN. 520 INZONE
(HE PULLS UP SMITTY'S MATTRESS AND LOOKS DOWN. 520 INZONE
(HE GOES TO HIS BUNK AND PULLS OUT A BIG WAD OF 527 INZONE
WASTE AND COMES BACK TO SMITTY.)
(HE PULLS OUT A SMALL ROLL OF BILLS FROM HIS PANTS 89 JOURNE
POCKET AND CAREFULLY SELECTS
(RATHER SHAMEFACEDLY PULLS HIMSELF TOGETHER--THEN 303 LAZARU
BROODINGLY)
(HE REACHES OUT AND PULLS BACK THE TOGA FROM HIS 339 LAZARU
FACE.
SHE RUSHES OVER, PULLS OPEN THE DOOR IN THE WALL 162 MANSNS
AT RIGHT.
(SHE REACHES DOWN INSIDE HER BODICE AND PULLS OUT 164 MANSNS
A KEY ON A CORD AROUND HER
(INSTINCTIVELY MAKES A GRAB FOR HER AND PULLS HER 167 MANSNS
AWAY--
(HE PULLS HER GENTLY BACK--QUIETLY.) 181 MANSNS

PULLS (CONT'D.)
(PULLS HER HAND VIOLENTLY FROM HIS.) 190 MANSNS
AND GINGERLY PULLS BACK THE PALL FROM THE HEAD OF 351 MARCOM
THE COFFIN.
(PULLS THE COVERING OVER THE HEAD OF THE COFFIN 353 MARCOM
WITH INDECENT HASTE)
(HE PULLS HER WILLING HAND DOWN TOWARD HIS LIPS.) 355 MARCOM
(HE FUMBLES AND PULLS OUT THE LOCKET WHICH IS HUNG366 MARCOM
AROUND HIS NECK ON A RIBBON)
WHO LIFT THE COVER AND PULLS OUT A SMALL CHOW 391 MARCOM
PUPPY
(WITH WILD DESPAIR PULLS OUT A SMALL DAGGER FROM 415 MARCOM
THE BOSOM OF HER DRESS)
MARCU MANAGES TO GET SEPARATED AND PULLS DONATA 429 MACUM
DOWN FRONT TO THE FOREGROUND.)
(HE PULLS THE PIECES OF THE MINIATURE WRAPPED IN 430 MARCOM
THE HANDKERCHIEF
PULLS OUT A LITTLE ROLL OF ONE-DOLLAR BILLS AND 7 MISBEG
PRESSES IT IN HIS HAND)
HE PULLS ON HIS PIPE REFLECTIVELY) 17 MISBEG
(SHE PULLS TRONE'S HEAD BACK AND LAUGHINGLY 51 MISBEG
KISSES HIM ON THE LIPS.
SHE SITS ON THE TOP STEP AND PULLS HIM DOWN ON THE102 MISBEG
STEP BENEATH HER.
(SHE PULLS HIS HEAD BACK AND KISSES HIM ON THE 118 MISBEG
LIPS--A QUICK, SHY KISS)
SHE PULLS BACK FRIGHTENEDLY FOR A SECOND--THEN 119 MISBEG
RETURNS HIS KISS.
HE PULLS HER HEAD DOWN AND STARES INTO HER EYES) 119 MISBEG
(HE TURNS AND PULLS HER HEAD DOWN AND KISSES HER 136 MISBEG
ON THE LIPS)
(SHE PULLS HIS ARMS AWAY SO VIOLENTLY THAT HE 137 MISBEG
STAGGERS BACK AND WOULD FALL DOWN
THE TOP STEP AND PULLS HIM DOWN ON THE STEP BELOW 142 MISBEG
HER)
(THROWS HER ARMS AROUND HIM AND PULLS HIM BACK-- 152 MISBEG
TENSELY)
THEN PULLS HIS HAND BACK.) 46 POET
(HER MOUTH PULLS DOWN PITIABLY. 130 POET
(SHE PULLS SARA'S HEAD BACK SO SHE CAN LOOK DOWN 148 POET
IN HER FACE--FALTERINGLY.)
(HE PULLS HER OVER AND KISSES HER HAIR.) 174 POET
MARY PULLS AT HIS HAND IN A SUDDEN FIT OF IMPISH 584 ROPE
GLEE, AND LAUGHS SHRILLY)
(PULLS THE BOTTLE FROM HIS COAT POCKET--WITH A 591 ROPE
WINK)
HE PULLS OUT TOBACCO AND A PAPER AND ROLLS A 593 ROPE
CIGARETTE AND LIGHTS IT.
SQUARES HIS SHOULDERS, PULLS HIS COAT DOWN IN 22 STRANG
FRONT, SETS HIS TIE STRAIGHT,
(HE TURNS TO THE BOOKCASE AND PULLS OUT THE FIRST 23 STRANG
VOLUME HIS HANDS COME ON AND
THEN HE PULLS OUT HIS WATCH MECHANICALLY AND 25 STRANG
STARES AT IT.
AND HE PULLS OUT HIS HANDKERCHIEF AND WIPES THEM, 28 STRANG
MUTTERING HUSKILY)
AND WHICH HE BITES AND SHIFTS ABOUT AND PULLS IN 66 STRANG
PULLS HIS HAND FROM NINA'S AS IF IT WERE A HOT 104 STRANG
COAL--
WITH HER OTHER HAND SHE GENTLY PULLS HIM AROUND 104 STRANG
(WITH SUDDEN RESISTANCE PULLS AWAY--DETERMINEDLY) 122 STRANG
DARRELL PULLS HIMSELF UP SHORT-- 150 STRANG
EVANS PULLS HIM UP ON HIS LAP) 153 STRANG
(HE PULLS A SOVEREIGN OUT OF HIS POCKET AND SLAMS 497 VOYAGE
IT ON THE BAR.)
DRISCOLL PULLS THE BATTERED REMNANTS OF THE DERBY 500 VOYAGE
OFF IVAN'S HEAD
(HE STOOPS DOWN AND FUMBLES IN HER BOSGM AND PULLS508 VOYAGE
OUT THE BANKNOTE,
(HE SUDDENLY PULLS HER HEAD DOWN AND KISSES HER 446 WELDED
IMPULSIVELY)
(HE PULLS HER TO HER FEET) MY WIFE/ **8 WELDED

PULP
IF IT WEREN'T FOR MY CLOTH I'D HAVE BEATEN HIS 423 DYNAMO
FACE TO A BLOODY PULP/

PULSATION
THE TOM-TOM BEATS LOUDER, QUICKER, WITH A MORE 199 EJONES
INSISTENT, TRIUMPHANT PULSATION.)
WITH A SOMBER PULSATION, A BAFFLED BUT REVENGEFUL 202 EJONES
POWER.)

PULSE
OHO, NO, OF COURSE NOT, DIVIL FEAR YOU, YOU WAS 217 AHWILD
ONLY FEELING THEIR PULSE/
(TAKING OUT HIS WATCH AND FEELING YANK'S PULSE) 484 CARDIF
RHYTHMICALLY AS IF TO THE PULSE OF LONG SWELLS OF 572 CROSS
THE DEEP SEA.)
AND FEELS ELSA'S PULSE. 554 DAYS
HE SITS IN THE CHAIR BY THE BED AND FEELS ELSA'S 558 DAYS
PULSE.
BUT AS HE FEELS HER PULSE HIS EXPRESSION CHANGES 563 DAYS
TO ONE OF EXCITED SURPRISE.)
IT STARTS AT A RATE EXACTLY CORRESPONDING TO 184 EJONES
NORMAL PULSE BEAT--
(FRIGHTENEDLY SHE FEELS FOR HIS PULSE. 63 ELECTR
SHE AUTOMATICALLY BENDS ON ONE KNEE BESIDE HER AND 64 ELECTR
HASTILY FEELS FOR HER PULSE.
LET ME FEEL YOUR PULSE/ 412 MARCOM
I OBSERVE MY PULSE IS HIGH, FOR EXAMPLE. 85 STRANG
(HE TAKES HER HAND AS IF TO FEEL HER PULSE. 97 STRANG
(HE KNEELS DOWN, FEELS OF HIS HEART, PULSE, LOOKS 183 STRANG
INTO HIS FACE--

PULSING
EMPHASIZING THE PULSING RHYTHM OF THE DANCE. 281 LAZARU

PUMP
FORGIVE ME TRYING TO PUMP YOU. 517 DAYS
PUMP HIM WHILE I HAVE A CHANCE...)) 31 STRANG

PUMP'S
I GUESS MY OLD PUMP'S BUSTED. 483 CARDIF

PUMPING

PUMPING
PUMPING HIM FULL OF WHAT YOU CONSIDER WORLDLY 34 JOURNE
WISDOM,
AND CHARGES AROUND THE CORNER OF THE HOUSE, HIS 11 MISBEG
ARMS PUMPING UP AND DOWN, HIS FI

PUMPKINS
YOU MAY FOOL 'EM INTO BELIEVING YOU'RE SOME 499 DIFRNT
PUMPKINS

PUMPS
(SMITTY TAKES HIS HAND AND HE PUMPS IT UP AND 469 CARIBE
DOWN)
SO ARE THE HIGH-HEELED PUMPS AND CLUCKED SILK 520 DIFRNT
STOCKINGS.
HICKEY GRABS HOPE'S HAND AND PUMPS IT UP AND DOWN.654 ICEMAN
LUKE SEIZES IT AND PUMPS IT UP AND DOWN.) 595 ROPE

PUNCH
YOU OUGHT TO GET A PUNCH IN THE NOSE FOR TALKING 195 AHWILD
THAT WAY ON THE FOURTH/
(THREATENINGLY) I'LL GIVE YOU A GOOD PUNCH IN THE246 AHWILD
SNOOT, THAT'S WHAT/
(RICHARD TURNS FURIOUSLY AND TRIES TO PUNCH THE 247 AHWILD
BARTENDER.)
(AVOIDS THE PUNCH) OHO, YOU WOULD WOULD YOU/ 247 AHWILD
I'LL GET YOU IF I HADN'T BEEN DRUNK I'D HAVE GIVEN276 AHWILD
HIM ONE GOOD PUNCH IN THE
HE AIN'T WORTH A PUNCH. 213 HA APE
I'M UP MUSCLES IN STEEL, DE PUNCH BEHIND IT/ 216 HA APE
DE PUNCH, DAT'S ME EVERY TIME, SEE/ 236 HA APE
AS IF HE HAD RECEIVED A PUNCH FULL IN THE FACE-- 238 HA APE
RAGING)
I BET YOU GOT A PUNCH IN EIDER FIST DAT'D KNOCK 252 HA APE
'EM ALL SILLY/
I'D LIKE AN EXCUSE TO GIVE YUH A GOOD PUNCH IN DE 669 ICEMAN
SNOOT.
DAT EVERYONE'D BEEN KICKIN' TILL DEY WAS TOO 699 ICEMAN
PUNCH-DRUNK TO FEEL IT NO MORE.
I TRIED TO PUNCH HIM IN THE NOSE, 118 JOURNE
AND BOTH OF YOU PLEASED AS PUNCH/ 46 MISBEG
HE NEVER TOOK A PUNCH AT ME BEFORE. 132 MISBEG
NUT TO PUNCH DIRT AND MILK COWS. 599 ROPE
THEN ONE NIGHT WE'D BOTH GONE TO A DANCE, WE'D 60 STRANG
BOTH HAD A LITTLE PUNCH TO DRINK,
GOIN' TO BUY FARM AN' PUNCH THE BLARSTED DIRT, 498 VOYAGE
THAT'S WUT 'E IS/

PUNCHED
THEN THE THIRD MAN PUNCHED CON AND I GAVE HIM A 156 POET
KICK WHERE IT'D DO HIM LEAST

PUNCHER
BLARSTED COAL-PUNCHER/ 462 CARIBE
I AIN'T MADE TO BE NO DAMNED DIRT-PUNCHER--NOT ME/599 ROPE

PUNCHES
TAKIN' ALL DE WOIST PUNCHES FROM BOT' OF 'EM. 253 HA APE
THE PUNCHES HIS BROTHER IN THE FACE, A BLOW THAT 162 JOURNE
GLANCES OFF THE CHEEKBONE.

PUNCHING
SINCE THE DAY I LEFT HOME FOR TO GO TO SEA 37 ANNA
PUNCHING COAL,
THEY'RE ALL THE SAME, THE BIBLE-PUNCHING BREED/ 431 DYNAMO

PUNCTUATE
(AS IF TO PUNCTUATE THIS REMARK, 189 AHWILD
(AS IF TO PUNCTUATE THIS 440 DYNAMO

PUNCTUATED
PUNCTUATED BY EXPLOSIONS OF HOARSE LAUGHTER. 7 ANNA
HIS CROON, RISING TO INTENSITY, IS PUNCTUATED BY 201 EJUNES
SHRILL CRIES.
PUNCTUATED BY NASTY, JEERING LAUGHTER.) 662 ICEMAN
PUNCTUATED BY NASTY, JEERING LAUGHTER.) 326 LAZARU
HEARD ABOVE A CONFUSED DRUNKEN CLAMOR OF VOICES, 326 LAZARU
PUNCTUATED BY THE HIGH,
PUNCTUATED BY THE BLOWS AND KICKS THEY RECEIVE. 353 MARCON

PUNCTUATION.
BUT SUFFICIENTLY EMPHATIC TO FORM A DISTURBING 189 AHWILD
PUNCTUATION TO THE CONVERSATION.)

PUNIC
SINGS HOARSELY AN OLD CAMP SONG OF THE PUNIC WARS,313 LAZARU
POUNDING WITH HIS GOBLET)

PUNISH
NOT UNLESS YOU APOLOGIZE IN WRITING AND PROMISE TO203 AHWILD
PUNISH--
I WARN YOU BEFOREHAND IF THE ANSWER IS *YES* I'M 206 AHWILD
GOING TO PUNISH YOU AND PUNISH
ALL THE BITTER HURT AND STEELY RESOLVE TO IGNORE 258 AHWILD
AND PUNISH HIM VANISH IN A
AND THAT'S JUST WHAT IT'S YOUR DUTY TO DO--PUNISH 265 AHWILD
HIM GOOD AND HARD/
TO PUNISH HIM--AND I THOUGHT HE OUGHT TO, ANYWAY, 265 AHWILD
AFTER BEING SO SICK.
I THOUGHT YOU WEREN'T GOING TO GIVE HIM ANY 265 AHWILD
DINNER--TO PUNISH HIM.
BUT IT'S HAD ENOUGH, GOODNESS KNOWS--AND YOU 266 AHWILD
PUNISH HIM GOOD JUST THE SAME.
HOW WERE YOU FIGURING TO PUNISH HIM FOR HIS SINS/ 268 AHWILD
YOU'D THINK YOU COULDN'T BEAR WAITING TO PUNISH 268 AHWILD
HIM/
HOW DID PA PUNISH YOUS 272 AHWILD
AND SHE LOVES ME AND ONLY ME AND ALWAYS WILL, NO 273 AHWILD
MATTER HOW THEY PUNISH HER/
DO YOU THINK HE'LL PUNISH YOU AWFUL5 287 AHWILD
(WITH A CONCILIATING SMILE) THEN PUNISH ME, RUTH.122 BEYOND
I SHOULD THINK HE'D HAVE TO PUNISH ADULTERY AND 444 DYNAMO
MURDER...
YOU PUNISH HIM GOOD, HUTCHINS/ 448 DYNAMO
I WANTED TO PUNISH YOU. 466 DYNAMO
I'LL FIND A WAY TO PUNISH YOU/ 64 ELECTR
IF YOU WON'T HELP ME PUNISH HER, 98 ELECTR
I'LL HELP YOU PUNISH HER/ 99 ELECTR
(THEN INTENSELY) BUT WHEN I DO, WILL YOU HELP ME 99 ELECTR
PUNISH FATHER'S MURDERERS/

PUNISH (CONT'D.)
YOU--YOU'RE JUST TELLING ME THAT--TO PUNISH ME, 120 ELECTR
AREN'T YOUS
I'VE GOT TO PUNISH MYSELF/ 178 ELECTR
AND THERE'S NO ONE LEFT TO PUNISH ME. 178 ELECTR
IT TAKES THE MANNONS TO PUNISH THEMSELVES FOR 178 ELECTR
BEING BORN/
THEN PUNISH ME WITH SELF-LOATHING AND LIFE-HATRED/314 GGBROW
ANOTHER BABY, AND THAT GOD WOULD PUNISH ME IF I 88 JOURNE
DID.
THE LORD GOD WILL PUNISH YOU/ 282 LAZARU
I SHALL PUNISH YOU/ 361 LAZARU
PUNISH ME, IF YOU WILL/ 389 MARCOM
I ONLY SAID IT TO PUNISH YOU FOR A WHILE. 175 MISBEG
GOD WILL PUNISH YOU-- 149 POET
I HATED HIM AS ONE HATES A THIEF ONE MAY NOT 20 STRANG
ACCUSE NOR PUNISH.
CONSCIENCE THAN BEFORE AND MORE DETERMINED TO 36 STRANG
PUNISH HERSELF/
YOU WILL, WON'T YOU--OR TELL ME HOW TO PUNISH 44 STRANG
MYSELF.
SO BE KIND AND PUNISH ME/ 45 STRANG
THEN I COULD PUNISH/ 46 STRANG
I MUST PUNISH HER SOME OTHER WAY....) 100 STRANG
PUNISH NINAS... 100 STRANG

PUNISHED
(THEN DEFENSIVELY) BUT YOU NEEDN'T THINK I 265 AHWILD
HAVEN'T PUNISHED HIM.
IF YOU REMEMBER, I WAS ALWAYS GETTING PUNISHED-- 268 AHWILD
I DON'T CARE HOW I'M PUNISHED AFTER/ 274 AHWILD
DICK, YOU DON'T REALIZE HOW I'VE BEEN PUNISHED 281 AHWILD
FOR YOUR SAKE.
NO, HE'S GOT TO BE PUNISHED, IF ONLY TO MAKE THE 289 AHWILD
LESSON STICK IN HIS MIND.
I THINK AFTER THE WAY I PUNISHED HIM ALL DAY, 289 AHWILD
HE'S STILL GOT TO BE PUNISHED FOR THAT. 289 AHWILD
AND THE WAY I KNOW HE'S PUNISHED HIMSELF, HE'S HAD289 AHWILD
ABOUT ALL HE DESERVES.
LOVE TO CREATE PROVES HOW FAR ASTRAY--SO YOU'LL BE162 BEYOND
PUNISHED.
HE'LL BE PUNISHED GOOD FOR THIS/....) 435 DYNAMO
AND I'D LIKE TO SEE YOU PUNISHED FOR YOUR 32 ELECTR
WICKEDNESS/
LIKE A LITTLE BOY WHO'S BEEN PUNISHED FOR 148 ELECTR
SOMETHING HE DIDN'T DO.
SHE'S GOT TO BE PUNISHED/ 160 ELECTR
YOU WILL BE PUNISHED IF YOU DO/ 173 ELECTR
NO WONDER ORIN KILLED HIMSELF--GOD, I--I HOPE 177 ELECTR
YOU'LL BE PUNISHED--I--/
BECAUSE HE HAS TO BE PUNISHED, SO HE CAN FORGIVE 642 ICEMAN
HIMSELF.
THE UNLY MORAL LAW HERE IS THE STRONG ARE 71 MANSNS
REWARDED, THE WEAK ARE PUNISHED.
HE HAS A GUILTY CONSCIENCE AND HE KNOWS HE OUGHT 127 MANSNS
TO BE PUNISHED.
YOU'VE PUNISHED YOURSELF. 148 MISBEG
YOU HAD ME PUNISHED, THAT'S SURE. 175 MISBEG
YOU PUNISHED THAT LAWYER FOR THE INSULT. 126 POET
(THEN IN A FLAT VOICE) WHAT DO YOU WANT TO BE 44 STRANG
PUNISHED FOR, NINAS
OH, I'VE GOT TO BE PUNISHED, CHARLIE, CUT OF MERCY 44 STRANG
FOR ME.
I'VE WANTED TO RUN HOME AND 'FESS UP, TELL HOW BAD 44 STRANG
I'VE BEEN, AND BE PUNISHED/
I DON'T FEEL AS IF YOU'D PUNISHED ME HARDLY AT 46 STRANG
ALL.
AND ME BEING PUNISHED WITH THEM FOR NO SIN BUT 64 STRANG
LOVING MUCH.
BUT I GOT RICHLY OVER IT LIVING HERE WITH POOR 64 STRANG
FOLKS THAT WAS BEING PUNISHED FOR
NOT ANOTHER WORD OR YOU'LL BE PUNISHED, WHETHER 142 STRANG
IT'S YOUR BIRTHDAY OR NOT/

PUNISHING
I'M PUNISHING MURIEL. 203 AHWILD
YOU KNOW PA'S PUNISHING ME BY SENDING ME TO BED AT280 AHWILD
EIGHT SHARP/

PUNISHMENT
AYE, IT'S THE PUNISHMENT O' GOD ON HIM. 537 'ILE
EVEN TO SAVE YOURSELF FROM PUNISHMENT, YOU'D LIE 206 AHWILD
TO ME NOW, WOULD YOUS
AND I'VE KEPT REMINDING HIM HIS REAL PUNISHMENT 265 AHWILD
WAS STILL TO COME--
REMEMBER, YOU'RE NOT ALLOWED OUT TODAY--FOR A 271 AHWILD
PUNISHMENT.
OR TO REMEMBER THE THREATENED PUNISHMENT. 292 AHWILD
THAT ISN'T ANY PUNISHMENT. 296 AHWILD
(TRIUMPHANTLY) IT WAS GOD'S PUNISHMENT ON JAMES 114 BEYOND
MAYO FOR THE BLASPHEMY AND
(GRIMLY) AYE, NOW'S YOUR PUNISHMENT, JUDAS. 568 CROSS
LATER, AT SCHOOL, HE LEARNED OF THE GOD OF 510 DAYS
PUNISHMENT, AND HE WONDERED.
A PUNISHMENT FOR THE DOUBT INSPIRED IN HIM BY HIS 511 DAYS
FATHER'S DEATH.
(SHAKING HER HEAD) I GOT T' TAKE MY PUNISHMENT-- 266 DESIRE
IT' PAY FUR MY SIN.
IT WOULD HAVE BEEN ONLY HER JUST PUNISHMENT IF 440 DYNAMO
THAT FELLOW HAD KILLED HER/
(VINDICTIVELY) I PROMISE I WON'T STAND BETWEEN 445 DYNAMO
HIM AND PUNISHMENT THIS TIME/
REUBEN'S PUNISHMENT CAN WAIT. 449 DYNAMO
YOU KNOW YOU DESERVE THE WORST PUNISHMENT YOU 32 ELECTR
COULD GET.
YOU AND I, WHO ARE INNOCENT, WOULD SUFFER A WORSE 97 ELECTR
PUNISHMENT THAN THE GUILTY--
BUT SHE CHOSE TO KILL HERSELF AS A PUNISHMENT FOR 142 ELECTR
HER CRIME--
(MOCKINGLY) STUDYING THE LAW OF CRIME AND 150 ELECTR
PUNISHMENT, AS YOU SAW.

PUNISHMENT (CONT'D.)
THAT'S ESCAPING PUNISHMENT. 178 ELECTR
DAY WAS WHERE I LOINED TO TAKE PUNISHMENT. 234 HA APE
I MIGHT REMEMBER THE THING THEY CALL JUSTICE 649 ICEMAN
THERE, AND THE PUNISHMENT FOR--
DO YOU NOT KNOW THERE IS A TERRIBLE PUNISHMENT FOR192 MANSNS
TRESPASSING IN MY DOMAINS
BUT IF YOU'RE SUCH A GLUTTON FOR PUNISHMENT-- 145 MISBEG
IT'S BECAUSE I'M AFRAID IT'S GOD'S PUNISHMENT, 138 POET
-THE PUNISHMENT OF THINE INIQUITY IS ACCOMPLISHED,579 ROPE
O DAUGHTER OF ZION..
PUNISHMENT TO FIT HIS CRIMES, 34 STRANG

PUNK
AND AFTER THE DAMES OVER THERE THESE BIRDS HERE 526 DIFRNT
LOOK SOME PUNK.
SOME PUNK BURGS/ 14 HUGHIE
SOME PUNK JOB/ 14 HUGHIE
SHE WAS A SALES GIRL IN SOME PUNK DEPARTMENT 23 HUGHIE
STORE,
IT WOULDA BEEN A PUNK SHOWING FOR POOR OLD HUGHIE, 31 HUGHIE
(TURNS ON HIM) YOU LYING PUNK/ 666 ICEMAN
THIS GABBY YOUNG PUNK WAS TALKING MY EAR OFF, 668 ICEMAN
THAT'S ALL.
AND NOT STAND FOR NO PUNK IMITATION/ 669 ICEMAN
HE'S PUNK COMPANY. 112 MISBEG

PUNKS
ONE OF THEM FRESH WISE PUNKS. 10 HUGHIE

PUNY
HE IS STURDILY BUILT, BUT SEEMS ALMOST PUNY 3 MISBEG

PUP
(BOASTFULLY) HE'S A GENUINE, PEDIGREED PUP. 391 MARCOM
THAN ALL THE MOONS SINCE RAMESES WAS A PUP. 130 MISBEG

PUPIL
(DESPERATELY PUTTING ON HIS PRIM SEVERE MANNER 15 STRANG
TOWARD AN UNRULY PUPIL)
PUPIL-DAUGHTER NINA... 15 STRANG

PUPPET
I FELT LIKE ONE OF THOSE FIGURES IN A PUPPET SHOW 415 MARCOM

PUPPY
(KISSES HER HAND HUMBLY, LIKE A BIG PUPPY LICKING 259 AHWILD
IT)
WHO LIFT THE COVER AND PULLS OUT A SMALL CHOW 391 MARCOM
PUPPY
(SHE CUDDLES THE PUPPY IN HER ARMS.) 391 MAHCOM
WHERE SHE STANDS FONDLING THE PUPPY AND WATCHING 392 MARCOM
MARCO.)

PURCHASE
FOR YOUR FAMILY, AND SO CONTINUE TO PURCHASE, IN 154 MANSNS
PART AT LEAST,

PURCHASER
PLANTERS--GLARING FROM HIM TO THE PURCHASER) 197 EJONES

PURE
PURE AS THE DRIVEN SNOW, THAT'S ME. 190 AHWILD
HE LAUGHS WITH THE PURE LOVE OF BATTLE. 49 ANNA
HIS MASS OF HAIR IS PURE WHITE, HIS BRISTLY 567 CROSS
MUSTACHE THE SAME.
I'LL KISS YE PURE. EBEN--SAME 'S IF I WAS A MAW T'243 DESIRE
YE--
THE PURE WHITE TEMPLE FRONT SEEMS MORE THAN EVER 43 ELECTR
LIKE AN INCONGRUOUS MASK
IS A TYPICAL NEW ENGLAND WOMAN OF PURE ENGLISH 67 ELECTR
ANCESTRY, WITH A HORSE FACE,
STRANGELY, YOU ARE GENUINELY GOOD AND PURE OF 73 ELECTR
HEART, AREN'T YOU5
I USED TO HEAR YOU SINGING AT THE QUEEREST TIMES-- 83 ELECTR
SO SWEET AND CLEAR AND PURE/
CAN'T YOU BE SIMPLE AND PURE5 176 ELECTR
(BITTERLY) HE HAS KEPT YOU DOWN TO HIS LEVEL--OUT258 GGBROW
OF PURE JEALOUSY.
HIS PALE FACE IS SINGULARLY PURE, SPIRITUAL AND 278 GGBROW
SAD.
I CAN IMAGINE HOW THE PLATONIC MUST APPEAL TO 289 GGBROW
DION'S PURE, INNOCENT TYPE/
WHICH IS RADIANT WITH A GREAT PURE LOVE FOR HER 292 GGBROW
YET TO THEM, SUCH IS MY ART, IT WILL APPEAR TO 313 GGBROW
POSSESS A PURE COMMON-SENSE,
HE WOULD HAVE GOT ME A JOB OUT OF PURE SPITE. 723 ICEMAN
HER HIGH FOREHEAD IS FRAMED BY THICK, PURE WHITE 12 JOURNE
HAIR.
THE MASK IS THE PURE PALLOR OF MARBLE, THE 274 LAZARU
EXPRESSION THAT OF A STATUE OF PURE
IN THE REAR, PURE AND BEAUTIFUL IN THE LIGHT OF A 298 LAZARU
FULL MOON,
ARE THE STARS TOO PURE FOR YOUR SICK PASSIONS5 310 LAZARU
LOVE IS PURE/ 363 LAZARU
WE--YOU AND I--IN PARTNERSHIP IN A NEW COMPANY OF 103 MANSNS
THE PURE SPIRIT.
(SCORNFULLY) I'M TO PRETEND I'M A PURE VIRGIN, I 34 MISBEG
SUPPOSE5
YOU'RE A PURE VIRGIN TO HIM, 89 MISBEG
SHE WAS SIMPLE AND KIND AND PURE OF HEART. 151 MISBEG
THAT THE POETRY HE HOPED THE PURE FREEDOM OF 81 POET
NATURE WOULD INSPIRE HIM TO WRITE I
HIS WAS A PERSONAL WAR, I AM SURE--FOR PURE 82 POET
FREEDOM.
A FANATIC IN THE CAUSE OF PURE FREEDOM, HE BECAME 83 POET
SCORNFUL OF OUR REVOLUTION.
PURE LOVE/... 33 STRANG
AND I AM BRAVE BECAUSE OF HER LITTLE GIRL'S PURE 43 STRANG
LOVE...
NO MORE ASHAMED OF BEING PURE/....) 44 STRANG
A PURE AND SIMPLE SOUL/ 183 STRANG

PURELY
PURELY AS AN OBSERVER, HE THOUGHT--THE POOR IDIOT/537 DAYS
SHE WANTS SOME ONE MAN TO LOVE HER PURELY AND WHEN477 DYNAMO
SHE FINDS HIM WORTHY SHE WILL
I'VE BEEN LOOKING YOU UP FOR PURELY SELFISH 280 GGBROW
REASONS.

PURELY (CONT'D.)
HELL, IT'S PURELY SELFISH. 164 JOURNE
PURELY AND SIMPLY AS A BUSINESS DEAL. 58 MANSNS
IF OUR MARRIAGE SHOULD BE PURELY THE PLACING OF 148 STRANG
OUR ASHES IN THE SAME TURN...
YOU'D KNOW THAT HIS LOVE HAS BECOME PURELY THAT OF455 WELDED
AN OLD FRIEND.

PURER
BECOME PURER IN OUTLINE, MORE DISTINCTLY GRECIAN. 288 LAZARU
LOVE HAS GROWN PURER/ 362 LAZAKU

PUREST
ALWAYS WRONG--BUT HEART OF GOLD, HEART OF PUREST 225 AHWILD
GULD.

PURGED
(HIS SOUL IS PURGED OF GRIEF, HIS CONFIDENCE 38 HUGHIE
RESTORED.)

PURIFIED
UNTIL I'D GIVEN UP THE FLESH AND PURIFIED MYSELF/ 478 DYNAMO
SHE WANTS ME TU--AS A FINAL TEST--TO PROVE I'M 485 DYNAMO
PURIFIED--

PURIFY
THAT WOULD PURIFY MY HEART. 358 LAZARU

PURITAN
PAGAN TEMPLE FRONT STUCK LIKE A MASK ON PURITAN 17 ELECTR
GRAY UGLINESS/
PURITAN MAIDENS SHOULDN'T PEER TOO INQUISITIVELY 49 ELECTR
INTO SPRING/
THE LIVID PURITAN TOUCH, OBVIOUSLY, AND IT GROWS 597 ICEMAN
MORE MARKED AS WE GO ON.
IN BRIEF, MIKE IS A NEW ENGLAND IRISH CATHOLIC 4 MISBEG
PURITAN, GRADE B.
IT MUST BE THEIR DAMNED NARROW PURITAN BACKGROUND. 90 POET

PURITANICAL
HIS WHOLE CHARACTER HAS SOMETHING ARIDLY PRIM AND 26 MANSNS
PURITANICAL ABOUT IT.

PURITY
AND YET I FEEL SO DRAWN TO HER PURITY/ 151 ELECTR
I WANT TO CONFESS TO YOUR PURITY/ 161 ELECTR
THAT LAST TIME I LOOKED, HER PURITY HAD FORGOTTEN 282 GGBROW
ME,
I WANT YOUTH AGAIN BECAUSE I LOATHE AND LUST AND LONG 354 LAZARU
FOR PURITY/
AND THE INSULT THEY ARE TO MY PURITY. 32 POET
PURITY5... 100 STRANG
MY PURITY/... 100 STRANG
YES, IF YOU SAY PRURIENT PURITY/... 100 STRANG

PURPLE
IS STREAKED WITH INTERLACING PURPLE VEINS. 7 ANNA
ON WHICH CRIMSON AND PURPLE FLOWERS AND FRUITS 284 GGBROW
TUMBLE OVER ONE ANOTHER IN A
I WAS BORN IN THE PURPLE, THE SON, BUT 595 ICEMAN
UNFORTUNATELY NOT THE HEIR,
THE WINDOWS OF THE PALACE GLOW CRIMSON-PURPLE 326 LAZARU
THE CRIMSON-PURPLE LIGHTS OF THE MANY WINDOWS OF 334 LAZARU
THE PALACE GO OUT ONE BY ONE AS
DYED EITHER DEEP PURPLE OR CRIMSON. 336 LAZARU
THE WOMEN ARE DRESSED AS MALES IN CRIMSON OR DEEP 336 LAZARU
PURPLE.
GOLD LAMPS WITH SHADES OF CRIMSON-PURPLE ARE 336 LAZARU
PLACED.
THOSE WITH CRIMSON HAIR ARE DRESSED IN PURPLE, AND336 LAZARU
VICE VERSA.
TIBERIUS CAESAR STANDS ON THE DAIS, DRESSED IN 337 LAZARU
DEEP PURPLE,
HER WIG AND DRESS ARE PURPLE. 337 LAZARU
THIS MASK IS A PALLID PURPLE BLOTCHED WITH DARKER 337 LAZARU
COLOR,
PURPLE AND RED AND GOLD MINGLED WITH THE DEEP 1 MANSNS
GREEN OF THE CONIFERS.
(BOUNDING BACK TO THE DECK, HIS FACE CONGESTED AND182 STRANG
PURPLE WITH A FRENZY OF JOY,

PURPLES
THE CRIMSONS AND PURPLES IN THE WINDOWS WILL STAIN197 STRANG
OUR

PURPLISH
HE WEARS A HALF-MASK OF CRIMSON, DARK WITH A 299 LAZARU
PURPLISH TINGE,
WITH THE PURPLISH-CRIMSON GLOW FROM ALL THE LAMPS)340 LAZARU

PURPOSE
HE DID IT ON PURPOSE TO SCARE US/ 189 AHWILD
(EMBARRASSEDLY) I LET IT GET THAT WAY ON PURPOSE.237 AHWILD
THAT YOU WERE COMING HOME TO DINNER ON PURPOSE-- 265 AHWILD
AN UNDERLYING, STUBBORN FIXITY OF PURPOSE. 87 BEYOND
I COULDN'T TAKE INTEREST IN THE WORK ANY MORE, 110 BEYOND
WORK WITH NO PURPOSE IN SIGHT.
SEEMS AS IF SHE CRIES ALL THE TIME ON PURPOSE TO 116 BEYOND
SET A BODY'S NERVES ON EDGE.
SINISTER PURPOSE BEHIND MY SUGGESTION. 495 DAYS
(SMILING) I'LL SAY FENCE LYING A-PURPOSE--AN'-- 226 DESIRE
HE'LL DRIVE YE OFF THE PLACE/
I UN'Y WANTED YE FUR A PURPOSE O' MY OWN-- 240 DESIRE
IT'S HIM--YEW HAVIN' HIM--A-PURPOSE T' STEAL-- 257 DESIRE
THAT'S CHANGED EVERYTHIN'5
A-PURPOSE/ 257 DESIRE
AND ACCOMPLISH ITS VEILED PURPOSE. 192 EJONES
YOU DID IT ON PURPOSE/ 63 ELECTR
KNOWS HER LIFE PURPOSE WELL ACCOMPLISHED BUT IS AT323 GGBROW
THE SAME TIME A BIT EMPTY AND
(SHARPLY) WHAT'S YOUR NOTION OF THE PURPOSE OF 247 HA APE
THE INN5
I SWITCHED THE SUBJECT ON HUGHIE, SEE, ON PURPOSE. 26 HUGHIE
I GUT SO SOMETIMES WHEN SHE'D KISS ME IT WAS LIKE 715 ICEMAN
SHE DID IT ON PURPOSE
PURPOSE TO GIVE HIS PIGS A FREE WALLOW. 23 JOURNE
(HER FACE HARDENING.) I'VE ALWAYS BELIEVED JAMIE 87 JOURNE
DID IT ON PURPOSE.
DID ON PURPOSE TO MAKE A BUM OF YOU. 165 JOURNE
AND WORST OF IT IS, I DID IT ON PURPOSE. 165 JOURNE

PURPOSE

PURPOSE (CONT'D.)
I CAME ON PURPOSE TO LISTEN. 18 MANSNS
IT REMINDS ME OF MY REAL PURPOSE IN COMING HERE. 104 MANSNS
I HAVE SERVED MY PURPOSE--SHE HAS RUTHLESSLY GOT 126 MANSNS
RID OF ME--SHE IS FREE--
SHE KEEPS HIM DREAMING IN HER GARDEN TO MAKE HIM 144 MANSNS
LATE ON PURPOSE TO TORMENT ME/
SHE DID IT ON PURPOSE/ 147 MANSNS
WHICH CREATES AND DESTROYS WITHOUT OTHER PURPOSE 426 MARCOM
WHAT PURPOSE CAN IT SERVES 426 MARCOM
IS NOT YOUR PURPOSE IN COMING HERE TO ARRANGE, ON 121 POET
MR. HARFORD'S BEHALF,
I CAN BE FOR THE PURPOSE OF THIS EXPERIMENT. 85 STRANG
NO WOMAN CAN MAKE A MAN HAPPY WHO HAS NO PURPOSE 139 STRANG
IN LIFE/...

PURPOSEFUL
(GUILTILY, PASSING HIS HAND OVER HIS FACE--FORCING 95 STRANG
A BRISK, PURPOSEFUL AIR)

PURPOSEFULLY
(CONFUSEDLY, STRANGELY AND PURPOSEFULLY) 85 STRANG

PURPOSELY
WHICH HAS BEEN PURPOSELY LEFT AT THE VERY CENTER 429 MARCOM
OF THE TABLE AT THE FRONT.

PURPOSES
HE KNOWS THE PLACE IS HIS--TO ALL PURPOSES. 563 CRUSS
ARE BREEDING AND MAINTAINING SILKWORMS FOR 422 MARCOM
PURPOSES OF AGGRESSION/
I CANNOT FOR THE LIFE OF ME SEE--I FEAR WE ARE 121 POET
DEALING AT CROSS-PURPOSES.

PURR
AN IMITATION OF THE WHIRRING PURR OF THE DYNAMO.) 436 DYNAMO
(SHE HUMS HER IMITATION OF A DYNAMO'S WHIRRING 458 DYNAMO
PURR.)
PENETRATED DOMINATINGLY BY THE HARSH, THROATY, 473 DYNAMO
METALLIC PURR OF THE DYNAMO.
ITS HYPNOTIC, METALLIC PURR WHICH FLOWS 486 DYNAMO
INSISTENTLY THROUGH THE EARS,
(THE DYNAMO'S PURR HAS REGAINED ITS ACCUSTOMED 489 DYNAMO
PITCH NOW.
THE DYNAMO'S THROATY METALLIC PURR RISES SLOWLY IN489 DYNAMO
VOLUME
(IN A MOCKING TONE) PURR, LITTLE LEOPARD. 220 HA APE
PURR, SCRATCH, TEAR, KILL, GORGE YOURSELF AND BE 220 HA APE
HAPPY--

PURRING
AND THE NOISE OF THE DYNAMO DIES UNTIL IT IS THE 488 DYNAMO
FAINTEST PURRING HUM.

PURRINGLY
(PURRINGLY) COME NOW, LIEUTENANT. 606 ICEMAN

PURSE
GOTA THE LITTLE WOMAN'S PURSE, HLHS 22 HUGHIE
WELL, ANYWAY, HUGHIE SNEAKED THE TWO BUCKS BACK IN 22 HUGHIE
THE LITTLE WOMAN'S PURSE
=THEREFORE PUT MONEY IN THY PURSE.= 165 JOURNE
GOD HIMSELF CANNOT TRANSFORM A SOW'S EAR INTO A 114 POET
SILK PURSE/

PURSED
AND A ROUND MOUTH PURSED OUT TO DRINK IN GOSSIP. 6 ELECTR
A BUTTON NOSE, A SMALL, PURSED MOUTH. 618 ICEMAN

PURSES
IT WILL BE TIME ENOUGH TO DREAM OF SILK PURSES. 590 ICEMAN

PURSING
(PURSING HIS LIPS) SLOW. I COME FROM DELHI. 348 MARCOM

PURSUE
PHILOSOPHER, WHICH HIS SON HAS CHOSEN TO PURSUE. 111 POET

PURSUED
HE FLEES, HE IS PURSUED BY DEVILS, HE HIDES, HE 201 EJONES
FLEES AGAIN.
I MUSTN'T FORGET I'M A DESPERATE CRIMINAL, PURSUED308 GGROW
BY GOD, AND BY MYSELF/

PURSUES
TO THE THREAT OF NIGHT AND SILENCE AS IT PURSUES 32 HUGHIE
AN IDEAL OF FAME AND GLORY

PURSUING
(PURSUING HER TRAIN OF THOUGHT) 98 BEYOND
NEARER AND NEARER DRAWS THE PURSUING EVIL. 201 EJONES

PURSUIT
IT WOULD HAVE SAVED HIM SO MUCH SILLY ROMANTIC 534 DAYS
PURSUIT OF MEANINGLESS ILLUSIONS.
(SARDONICALLY) IT'S A GREAT GAME, THE PURSUIT OF 581 ICEMAN
HAPPINESS.
THE HARFORD PURSUIT OF FREEDOM IMPOSED UPON THE 83 POET
WOMEN WHO SHARED THEIR LIVES.

PURSY
HIS SMALL, PURSY MOUTH IS ALWAYS CROOKED 9 HUGHIE

PURTIER'N
(WITH A TANTALIZING SNEER) SHE'S PURTIER'N YEW 230 DESIRE
BE/
MY ON'Y JOY--THE ON'Y JOY I EVER KNOWED--LIKE 258 DESIRE
HEAVEN T' ME--PURTIER'N HEAVEN--

PURTIEST
AND ONE O' THEM GALS-- THE PURTIEST ON 'EM 502 DIFRNT

PURTY
PURTY. 203 DESIRE
(GRUDGINGLY) PURTY. 204 DESIRE
(GAZING UP AT THE SKY) SUN'S DOWN'N' PURTY. 205 DESIRE
WAAL--SHE'S PURTY/ 210 DESIRE
SHE'S BEEN PURTY FUR TWENTY YEAR/ 210 DESIRE
BY GLC A'MIGHTY SHE'S PURTY, 211 DESIRE
SINCE 'EM WITH, MY SIN'S AS PURTY AS ANY ONE ON 211 DESIRE
'EM/
SHE'S PURTY... 211 DESIRE
MEBBE--BUT THE NIGHT'S WA'M--PURTY-- 211 DESIRE
GOT HIMSELF HITCHED TO A FEMALE 'BOUT THIRTY- 212 DESIRE
FIVE--AN' PURTY, THEY SAYS...
IT'S CANNED PURTY/ 217 DESIRE
IT'S PURTY/ 217 DESIRE
PURTY/ 218 DESIRE

PURTY (CONT'D.)
IT'S PURTY--PURTY/ 221 DESIRE
(WITH A SNEER) WAAL--YE HAIN'T SO DURNED PURTY 228 DESIRE
YERSELF, BE YES
TRYIN' T' TELL YERSELF I HAIN'T PURTY T'YE 229 DESIRE
(CROSSLY) I DON'T SEE NOTHIN' PURTY. 231 DESIRE
PURTY, HAIN'T ITS 231 DESIRE
SHE WAS PURTY--BUT SOFT. 237 DESIRE
PURTY HAIN'T ITS 245 DESIRE
IT'S A DURNED PURTY FARM. 245 DESIRE
AIN'T HE PURTYS 252 DESIRE
THEY'S A HULL PASSEL O' PURTY GALS. 254 DESIRE
HE WAS SO PURTY--DEAD SPIT 'N' IMAGE O' YEW. 261 DESIRE
PURTY, HAIN'T ITS 269 DESIRE
PURTY GOOD--FUR YEW/ 269 DESIRE
THEM BROWN GALS WAS PURTY AS THE DEVIL, JIM SAYS--502 DIFRNT
THEY'RE PURTY AS PICTURES, BENSON SAYS. 510 DIFRNT
BUT IT'S PURTY THERE ALL THE TIME-- 515 DIFRNT
BUT THEY'RE PURTY--IN THEIR FASHION--AND AT NIGHT 515 DIFRNT
THEY SINGS--
IT'S PURTY HEREABOUTS SOMETIMES--LIKE NOW, IN 515 DIFRNT
SPRING--
(AGAIN DULLY) OH, PURTY FAIR. 536 DIFRNT
WHAT A PURTY HUUSE/. 7 ELECTR
SHE LOOKS LIKE HER MOTHER IN FACE--QUEER LOOKIN'-- 11 ELECTR
BUT SHE AIN'T PURTY LIKE HER.
PURTY SHE WAS, TOO/ 44 ELECTR
PURTY SLICK YOU BE, ABNER. 130 ELECTR
THEY'LL FIGHT PURTY SHY OF HER NOW. 170 ELECTR

PURTY'S
(NODDING VAGUELY) AY-EH--BORN TWO WEEKS BACK-- 248 DESIRE
PURTY'S A PICTER.
PURTY'S A PICTER. 263 DESIRE

PUSH
(GIVES HIM A PUSH) GO TO YOUR PLACE AND SIT DOWN 221 AHWILD
AND NOT ANOTHER WORD OUT OF
(HE GIVES HIM ANOTHER PUSH THAT ALMOST SENDS HIM 247 AHWILD
SPRAWLING.)
(HE TURNS TO RICHARD ANGRILY AND GIVES HIM A PUSH)247 AHWILD
(HE GIVES HER CHAIR A PUSH THAT ALMOST THROWS HER 248 AHWILD
TO THE FLOOR)
(HE GIVES HER A PUSH THAT LANDS HER AGAINST THE 248 AHWILD
FAMILY-ENTRANCE DOOR)
(HE GIVES CHRIS A PUSH WITH THE FLAT OF HIS HAND 50 ANNA
WHICH SENDS THE OLD SWEDE
PUTS HER HANDS ON HIS SHOULDERS AS THOUGH TO TRY 107 BEYOND
TO PUSH HIM BACK IN THE CHAIR
FATHER BAIRD, RECOVERING FROM THE PUSH WHICH HAS 560 DAYS
SENT HIM BACK AGAINST THE
(GIVES HIM A FURIOUS PUSH WHICH SENDS HIM 264 DESIRE
STAGGERING BACK
(GIVES HIM A PUSH AWAY THAT SENDS HIM SPRAWLING-- 265 DESIRE
AND FINALLY HE GETS SICK OF IT AND HAS THE BOYS 503 DIFRNT
PUSH HER OFF WITH OARS
THEN SHE GIVES THE BIG DOOR A PUSH THAT SLIDES IT 479 DYNAMO
OPEN TO ITS FULL WIDTH AND
WHEN I USED TO COME TO YOU--WITH LOVE--BUT YOU 31 ELECTR
WOULD ALWAYS PUSH ME AWAY/
(CONTROLS A FURIOUS JEALOUS IMPULSE TO PUSH HER 100 ELECTR
VIOLENTLY AWAY FROM HIM--
(SAVAGELY--GIVING HIM A PUSH THAT SENDS HIM 237 HA APE
SPRAWLING)
(GIVING HIM A PUSH--WITH A GRIN, INDIFFERENTLY) 251 HA APE
DEN I TOINED HIM 'ROUND AND GIVE HIM A PUSH TO 617 ICEMAN
START HIM.
HE LETS CHUCK PUSH HIM INTO THE CHAIR ON MOSHER'S653 ICEMAN
(HE LETS ROCKY PUSH HIM IN A CHAIR, AT THE RIGHT 653 ICEMAN
END OF THE TABLE, REAR.)
BUT CHRIS, HIS HAND ABOUT TO PUSH THE SWINGING 677 ICEMAN
DOORS OPEN, HESITATES,
THEY PUSH HIS ARMS AWAY, REGARDING HIM WITH AMAZED725 ICEMAN
SUSPICION.)
(THEY PUSH MOTTV OVER TO THE BUCKET) 525 INZONE
DRISCOLL LEAPS FORWARD AND HELPS THEM PUSH HIM 526 INZONE
AWAY)
THE CROWDS OF MEN AND WOMEN ON EACH SIDE PUSH INTO278 LAZARU
THE ROOM TO STARE AT HIM.
THEY STIR AND PUSH ABOUT RESTLESSLY WITH AN EAGER 298 LAZARU
CURIOSITY AND IMPATIENCE.
THEY PUSH FORWARD AGGRESSIVELY AND ALMOST SWEEP 300 LAZARU
THE SOLDIERS FROM THEIR FEET.)
(THE CROWD PUSH BACK TO THEIR FORMER LINE. 301 LAZARU
(THERE IS A NEW STIR FROM THE CROWD WHO AGAIN PUSH 303 LAZARU
FORWARD.)
THEY CONTINUE TO PUSH FORWARD, HOOTING AND 305 LAZARU
JEERING.)
(SHE GIVES HIM A LITTLE PUSH.) 17 MANSNS
AND PUSH HER BACK WHERE SHE BELONGS--IN THERE--IN 40 MANSNS
PERPETUAL DARKNESS.
(SHE ADVANCES UP THE STEPS--WITH A FINAL PUSH.) 40 MANSNS
PUSH OPEN THE DOOR TO MADNESS WHERE I COULD AT 102 MANSNS
LEAST BELIEVE IN A DREAM AGAIN/
PUSH ME INSIDE ALONE WITH THAT MAD WOMAN I LOCKED 163 MANSNS
IN THERE--
(WITH EXTRAORDINARY STRENGTH SHE GIVES HIM A PUSH 190 MANSNS
IN THE CHEST THAT DRIVES HIM
THE SENTINEL AND KNIGHT ADMIT THE MESSENGER BUT 361 MARCOM
PUSH BACK THE OTHERS.)
(GIVING THE UNWILLING MARCO A PUSH) 362 MARCOM
IT IS MORE OF A PLAYFUL PUSH THAN A BLOW. 179 POET
(BEWILDERED AND TERROR-STRICKEN, TRYING FEEBLY TO 107 STRANG
PUSH HIM AWAY--THINKING)
IF I COULD HAVE GIVEN YOU A PUSH, MENTAL, MORAL, 470 WELDED
PHYSICAL---S
(SHE SUDDENLY GIVES HIM A FURIOUS PUSH 477 WELDED

PUSHED

(THE SCREEN DOOR IS PUSHED VIOLENTLY OPEN AND 260 AHWILD
RICHARD LURCHES IN AND STANDS
IT IS PUSHED OPEN AND CHRISTOPHER CHRISTOPHERSON 5 ANNA
ENTERS.
THE CABIN DOOR IS PUSHED OPEN AND CHRIS APPEARS. 25 ANNA
THE DOOR ON THE LEFT IS PUSHED OPEN AND CHRIS 76 ANNA
APPEARS IN THE DOORWAY.
HE IS DRESSED IN GRAY CORDUROY TROUSERS PUSHED 81 BEYOND
INTO HIGH LACED BOOTS.
AND A SOFT, MUD-STAINED HAT PUSHED BACK ON HIS 82 BEYOND
HEAD.
CONDEMNED TO BE PUSHED FROM DAY TO DAY OF HER LIFE113 BEYOND
IN A WHEEL CHAIR.
AND WEARS A BROAD-BRIMMED HAT OF COARSE STRAW 123 BEYOND
PUSHED BACK ON HIS HEAD)
BUT HE PUSHED ME AWAY, AS IF HE WERE DISGUSTED 522 DAYS
WITH HIMSELF AND ME.
THE OUTER DOORS BEYOND THE ARCHED DOORWAY ARE 564 DAYS
SUDDENLY PUSHED OPEN WITH A CRASH
A MOMENT LATER THE KITCHEN DOOR IS SLOWLY PUSHED 225 DESIRE
OPEN AND ABBIE ENTERS.
THE CHAIRS, WITH WOODEN BENCHES ADDED, HAVE BEEN 247 DESIRE
PUSHED BACK AGAINST THE WALLS.
AND A YELLOW SOU'WESTER PUSHED JAUNTILY ON THE 498 DIFRNT
BACK OF HIS HEAD.
HIS WIFE IS LYING BACK IN A CHAISE LONGUE THAT SHE428 DYNAMO
HAS PUSHED CLOSE TO THE
PUSHED BACK CARELESSLY FROM HIS FOREHEAD AS A 21 ELECTR
POET'S MIGHT BE.
(THE SHUTTER OF THE BEDROOM IS PUSHED OPEN AND 57 ELECTR
MANNION LEANS OUT.)
A MAN GOT KNIFED AND PUSHED OVERBOARD. 132 ELECTR
(ORIN CLOSES THE SHUTTER HE HAS PUSHED OPEN AND 144 ELECTR
TURNS BACK FROM THE WINDOW.
(THERE IS A SOUND OF A DOOR BEING PUSHED VIOLENTLY)319 GGRBOW
OPEN.
CHRIST, YUH COULDA PUSHED ME OVER WITH A FINGER/ 230 HA APE
AT CENTER, FRONT, FOUR OF THE CIRCULAR TABLES ARE 628 ICEMAN
PUSHED TOGETHER TO FORM ONE
(THE SWINGING DOORS ARE PUSHED OPEN AND WILLIE 674 ICEMAN
OBAN ENTERS FROM THE STREET.
TIME I PUSHED OFF. 685 ICEMAN
HAS BEEN PUSHED TOWARD RIGHT SO THAT IT AND 695 ICEMAN
WHO HAS GIVEN UP THE FIGHT AND IS PUSHED BACK 526 INZONE
AGAINST THE WALL NEAR THE DOORWAY
THE ROMAN SOLDIERS IN SPITE OF THEIR EFFORTS ARE 304 LAZARU
PUSHED BACKWARD STEP BY STEP.)
HE PUSHED IT BACK ON HIM AND LEFT IN THE HALL. 155 POET
RUMIN' MAD--
HE PUSHED ME AWAY LIKE HE DIDN'T SEE ME. 161 POET
WHICH IS PUSHED BACK, SETTING THE RUG ASKEW. 66 STRANG
HE CAN'T GET STARTED ON ANYTHING UNLESS HE'S 155 STRANG
PUSHED.

PUSHES

HE'S ALWAYS BEST WHEN HE'S PUSHED TO THE LIMIT/ 177 STRANG
(HE PUSHES HER BACK ON THE SOFA AND TICKLES HER 194 AHWILD
WITH FREE HAND.
(HE PUSHES THE SLIPS OF PAPER ACROSS THE TABLE 202 AHWILD
CONTEMPTUOUSLY)
(HE PUSHES HIS PLATE AWAY FROM HIM WITH PROUD 228 AHWILD
RENUNCIATION)
THEN HE FORCES HIMSELF TO A BOLD DECISION, PUSHES 20 ANNA
OPEN THE DOOR AND WALKS IN.
(SHE PUSHES IN AWAY WITH ALL HER MIGHT. 33 ANNA
(PUSHES HER AWAY FROM HIM.-- 107 BEYOND
(GRABS ROBERT'S ARM AND PUSHES HIM ASIDE-- 108 BEYOND
(SHE PUSHES THE DAMP HAIR BACK FROM HER FOREHEAD.)116 BEYOND
(HE GOES TO THE DOOR AND GENTLY PUSHES THE 128 BEYOND
TREMBLING RUTH AWAY FROM IT.
(HE PUSHES A CHAIR BETWEEN HIS OWN AND RUTH'S) 157 BEYOND
(SMITTY PUSHES HER HAND AWAY COLDLY) 468 CARIBE
(HE PUSHES HER AWAY FROM HIM DISGUSTEDLY. 469 CARIBE
(HE PUSHES THEM ROUGHLY AWAY. 250 DESIRE
(SHE TRIES TO KISS HIM BUT HE PUSHES HER VIOLENTLY256 DESIRE
AWAY
BUT HE PUSHES HER AWAY. 256 DESIRE
(SHE PUSHES EMMA GENTLY INTO A ROCKER-- 507 DIFRNT
AND PUSHES BACK HER HAIR FROM HER FLUSHED FACE AS 526 DIFRNT
IF IT WERE STIFLING HER)
HE PUSHES HER FIRMLY BUT GENTLY ASIDE. 543 DIFRNT
PUSHES THE RUGS TO THE PILE WITH HER FEET. 548 DIFRNT
(HE PUSHES THE PAPER INTO HER HANDS) 434 DYNAMO
(SHE PUSHES HIM AWAY, BUT, HOLDING HIS SHOULDERS, 446 DYNAMO
STARES DOWN INTO HIS FACE)
PUSHES AND PULLS AT IT, TRYING TC FORCE IT OPEN.) 450 DYNAMO
THEN HE PUSHES HER A LITTLE AWAY FROM HIM AND 459 DYNAMO
LAUGHS QUIETLY.
(THEN WITH A START, HE PUSHES HER AWAY FROM HIM 484 DYNAMO
ROUGHLY)
(HE CONTROLS HIMSELF WITH A VIOLENT EFFORT AND 485 DYNAMO
PUSHES HER AWAY FROM HIM KEEPING
PUSHES LAVINIA AWAY--BRUSQUELY) 51 ELECTR
HE PUSHES HIS BACK UP AGAINST THE HEAD OF THE BED 59 ELECTR
IN A HALF-SITTING POSITION.
AND PUSHES THEM OUT IN A GESTURE OF BLOTTING 123 ELECTR
LAVINIA FOREVER FROM HER SIGHT.
AND PUSHES BACK A SHUTTER AND STANDS STARING OUT. 143 ELECTR
(PUSHES HER AWAY--WITH A ROUGH BROTHERLY 166 ELECTR
IRRITATION)
HE PUSHES MOST OF IT ACROSS TO THE CLERK.) 37 HUGHIE
(HE PUSHES A BOTTLE TOWARD HIM.) 674 ICEMAN
(HE PUSHES BACK HIS CHAIR AND SPRINGS TO HIS FEET)680 ICEMAN
(HE PUSHES THE BOTTLE AWAY.) NO. 681 ICEMAN
(HE PUSHES THE SWINGING DOORS OPEN AND MAKES A 685 ICEMAN
BRAVE EXIT.
(HE PUSHES THE DOOR OPEN AND LUMBERS THROUGH IT 685 ICEMAN
HE PUSHES THE DOOR OPEN AND STRIDES BLINDLY OUT 688 ICEMAN
INTO THE STREET

PUSHING

(CONT'D.)
(ROCKY PUSHES THE BOTTLE TOWARD HIM APATHETICALLY)699 ICEMAN
(STARES AT HIM STUPIDLY--THEN PUSHES HIS CHAIR 703 ICEMAN
BACK AND GETS UP, GRUMBLING)
DRISCOLL PUSHES HIM TO ONE SIDE.) 526 INZONE
HE CAREFULLY PUSHES THE COVER BACK ON ITS HINGES 528 INZONE
(TAKES HER HANDS AND GENTLY PUSHES THEM DOWN.) 41 JOURNE
(JAMIE PUSHES THE BOTTLE TOWARD HIM. 175 JOURNE
WHICH STEADILY PUSHES THEM BACK INTO THE STREET. 304 LAZARU
(SUDDENLY PUSHES FORWARD IMPUDENTLY AND STRIKES A 321 LAZARU
GRANDIOSE ATTITUDE)
GENTLY PUSHES THE LION'S HAIR OUT OF ITS EYES-- 329 LAZARU
TENDERLY)
(SHE KISSES HIM--THEN PUSHES HIM AWAY DOWN THE 17 MANSNS
PATH--SHARPLY COMMANDING.)
PUSHES THE DOOR BACK AGAINST THE HOUSE, WIDE OPEN, 27 MANSNS
AND FACES FRONT.
(SHE KISSES HIM--THEN SUDDENLY EMBARRASSED AND 88 MANSNS
SHY, PUSHES BACK FROM HIM.)
(WITH SUDDEN REVULSION, PUSHES BACK FROM HIM.) 149 MANSNS
PUSHES HIS SNAKE BACK INTO THE BOX AND CARRIES IT 370 MARCOM
OFF.
(THEY KISS, THEN HE PUSHES HER AWAY) 430 MARCOM
(PUTS A HAND ON HIS SHOULDER AND PUSHES HIM DOWN) 40 MISBEG
(GOES TO THE SCREEN DOOR AND PUSHES IT OPEN 98 MISBEG
(PUSHES PAST HER DOWN THE STEPS--PEERING OFF LEFT- 98 MISBEG
FRONT--
(HE PUSHES HER BACK IN THE DOORWAY.) 137 MISBEG
(SUDDENLY SHE PUSHES HIM AWAY FROM HER AND SHAKES 166 MISBEG
HIM ROUGHLY)
(SHE PUSHES HIM) GET UP NOW, SO YOU WON'T FALL 166 MISBEG
ASLEEP AGAIN.
MALOY PUSHES THE DECANTER TOWARD HIM.) 10 POET
(HE PUSHES THE BOTTLE TOWARD CREGAN.) 15 POET
(TAKES A SIP, THEN PUTS THE GLASS ON THE TABLE AND134 POET
PUSHES IT AWAY LISTLESSLY.)
(HE PUSHES HER AWAY WITHOUT LOOKING AT HER. 152 POET
CREGAN HAS HIM BY THE SHOULDER AND PUSHES HIM 164 POET
ROUGHLY INTO THE ROOM.
(PUSHES HER BACK ON HER CHAIR.) 175 POET
(SHE RUNS TO HER MOTHER, WHO PUSHES HER AWAY 588 ROPE
ANGRILY)
(SWEENEY PUSHES THE BOTTLE TOWARD HIM. 592 ROPE
(HE PUSHES HIS HAND AWAY, BUT NOT ROUGHLY) 595 ROPE
(HE SLAPS LUKE ON THE SHOULDER AND PUSHES THE 598 ROPE
BOTTLE TOWARD HIM)
HE RAISES HIS HEAD AND HALF-PUSHES HER AWAY-- 99 STRANG
RESENTFULLY, THINKING)
(HE PUSHES OFF HER LAP AND BACKS AWAY FROM HER.) 156 STRANG
PUSHES NINA AWAY FROM HIM.) 174 STRANG
(SHE SUDDENLY PUSHES HIM AWAY AND GLARES AT HIM AT460 WELDED
ARMS' LENGTH.
FINALLY WITH A GROAN HE PUSHES HER AWAY, 475 WELDED
SHUDDERING WITH LOATHING.

PUSHING

MRS. MILLER LEANS FORWARD TO LOOK, PUSHING HER 292 AHWILD
SPECS UP.)
(PUSHING HIM AWAY FROM HER--FORCING A BROKEN 52 ANNA
LAUGH)
(PUSHING HER FATHER AWAY BRUSQUELY, HER EYES STILL 60 ANNA
HOLDING BURKE'S)
USED TO GET ME OUT OF THE WAY BY PUSHING MY 89 BEYOND
CHAIR TO THE WEST WINDOW AND
AND PUSHING THE CURTAINS ASIDE, STANDS LOOKING 150 BEYOND
OUT.
(PUSHING PADDY BACK) VOT'S THE MATTER VIT YOU, 461 CARIBE
PADDY.
(PUSHING HER AWAY FROM HIM ROUGHLY) 570 CROSS
(PUSHING HIM ROUGHLY AWAY) LEAVE ME ALONE/ 560 DAYS
(WITHOUT TOUCHING HIM, MAKES A MOTION OF PUSHING 563 DAYS
HIM ASIDE)
(PUSHING OPEN THE DOOR AND COMING IN, A LIGHTED 212 DESIRE
CANDLE IN HIS HAND.
(PUSHING HER AWAY VIOLENTLY) 233 DESIRE
(PUSHING HER AWAY FROM HIM--ANGRILY) 238 DESIRE
(FORCED TO SMILE--PUSHING HIM AWAY) 499 DIFRNT
(PUSHING HIM TOWARD THE CLOSET IN REAR) 445 DYNAMO
(PUSHING HER AWAY FROM HIM--FURIOUSLY) 452 DYNAMO
(PUSHING HER AWAY FROM--IN A STAMMERING PANIC) 482 DYNAMO
PUSHING IT SO SHE SITS FACING LEFT, FRONT, 59 ELECTR
(THEN ALMOST ROUGHLY, PUSHING HER BACK AND STARING 76 ELECTR
AT HER)
(ALMOST PUSHING HER HAND AWAY--BITTERLY) 82 ELECTR
(HARSHLY, PUSHING HER AWAY) YOU COULD MURDER 121 ELFCTR
FATHER, COULDN'T YOU!
AND BEGINS PUSHING THE BLACK CURTAIN ALONG THE ROD610 ICEMAN
TO THE REAR WALL.)
(PUSHING A BOTTLE AND GLASS AT LARRY) 681 ICEMAN
THE SOUNDS OF BLOWS AS THEY MEET IN A PUSHING, 290 LAZARU
WHIRLING, STRUGGLING MASS.
(THEY HAVE BEEN PUSHING FORWARD, MORE AND MORE 304 LAZARU
FIERCELY AND DEFIANTLY.
LIKE PUSHING OPEN A DOOR IN THE MIND AND THEN 28 MANSNS
PASSING THROUGH
HE BURSTS OUT WITH DISGUST, PUSHING HER AWAY FROM 42 POET
HIM.)
(HE MARKS THE TABLECLOTH.) THAT WERE PUSHING BACK 99 POET
THE GUARDS.
(PUSHING SARA AWAY--WITH NERVOUS PEEVISHNESS.) 137 POET
(PUSHING HIM TOWARD THE DOOR. 584 ROPE
(PUSHING THE BOTTLE TOWARD HIM) 593 ROPE
(THEN PUSHING HIM TOWARD DOOR) 56 STRANG
PUSHING HIS CHAIR BACK AND JUMPING TO HIS FEET) 67 STRANG
(THEN SUDDENLY RESISTING AND PUSHING HIM AWAY) 130 STRANG
(PUSHING HIM AWAY--TENDERLY) 195 STRANG
(PUSHING HIM BACK ON HIS CHAIR WITH A THUD) 498 VOYAGE
(SUDDENLY PUSHING HIM AT ARMS' LENGTH--WITH A 444 WELDED
HAPPY LAUGH)

PUSHING

PUSHING (CONT'D.)
BUT NOT EXACTLY KNOWING BY WHAT OR HOW TO RESENT 473 WELDED
IT--ANGRILY, PUSHING HIM AWAY)
(PUSHING HIM AWAY--VIOLENTLY) 485 WELDED

PUSS
(STROKING HER HAIR) PUSS, PUSS, PUSS/ 498 DIFRNT
NICE PUSS/ 507 DIFRNT
WITH HER PUSS AND FIGURE, 13 HUGHIE
(UNGUARDEDLY) YEAH. I'D LIKE TC GIVE HIM ONE 670 ICEMAN
SOCK IN DE PUSS--
IF YOU DON'T WANT A SOCK IN DE PUSS/ 683 ICEMAN
NO ONE WANTS TO ADMIT ALL HE GOT WAS A SLAP IN THEI39 MISBEG
PUSS.

PUSSON
AND IT'S IN A FOREIGN BANK WHERE NO PUSSON DON'T 177 EJONES
EVER GIT IT OUT BUT ME

PUTTEES
HE IS DRESSED IN A WORN RIDING SLIT OF DIRTY WHITEI74 EJONES
DRILL, PUTTEES, SPURS,

PUTTIN'
(THEN ANGRILY) HO--THE BLEEDIN' NIGGER--PUTTIN' ONI87 EJONES
'TS BLOODY AIRS/
WHAT'D THEY WANT PUTTIN' A SPY ON THIS OLD TUB 522 INZONE
FOR$
NO MAN AT ALL CUD BE PUTTIN' UP WID THE LOIKE AV 523 INZONE
THIS--
PUTTIN' ON THE BROGUE TO TORMENT US. 167 POET
AND I'M NOT PUTTIN' ON BROGUE TO TORMINT YOU, ME 168 POET
DARLIN'T.
PUTTIN' ON THE BROGUE AND ACTIN' LIKE ONE AV THIM 181 POET
IS THERE.
THAT'S WHAT YOU OUGHT TO PREACH 'STEAD OF PUTTIN' 580 ROPE
CURSES ON ME.

PUTTING
(PUTTING AN ARM AROUND HER SHOULDER--WITH GRUFF 545 'ILE
TENDERNESS)
(PUTTING A HAND TO HIS MOUTH TO CONCEAL A GRIN) 194 AHWILD
PUTTING THE CURB BIT ON WOULD MAKE HIM WORSE. 205 AHWILD
FOR PUTTING AN END TO HIS NONSENSE 216 AHWILD
THEN SUDDENLY COMICALLY ANGRY, PUTTING THE SPOON 224 AHWILD
DOWN WITH A BANG)
(EDGING HER CHAIR CLOSER AND PUTTING A HAND OVER 237 AHWILD
ONE OF HIS)
PUTTING ON A BLASE AIR) 237 AHWILD
(PUTTING HIS ARM AROUND HIS WIFE) 262 AHWILD
DAMN IT, I'D OUGHT TO BE BACK AT THE OFFICE 263 AHWILD
PUTTING IN SOME GOOD LICKS/
(THEN SOLICITOUSLY, PUTTING HER HAND ON HIS 271 AHWILD
FOREHEAD)
AND I THINK YOU'VE BEEN PUTTING ON WEIGHT LATELY, 291 AHWILD
TOO.
(PUTTING MONEY ON THE BAR) GIVE US ANOTHER. 4 ANNA
(PUTTING HIS OVERCOAT ON, HE COMES AROUND THE END 5 ANNA
OF THE BAR)
(PUTTING HIS HAND IN HIS POCKET) 6 ANNA
(GETTING THE DRINKS AND PUTTING THEM ON THE BAR) 12 ANNA
(PUTTING DOWN HIS PAPER AS CHRIS COMES UP--WITH A 24 ANNA
GRIN)
STARING AT IT STUPIDLY FOR A SECOND, THEN 41 ANNA
AIMLESSLY PUTTING IT DOWN AGAIN.
(PUTTING ONE HAND ON TOP OF ANDREW'S WITH A 83 BEYOND
GESTURE ALMOST OF SHYNESS)
(RUSHING TO ANDY AND PUTTING HER ARMS ABOUT HIM 106 BEYOND
PROTECTINGLY)
(PUTTING A HAND ON HIS BROTHER'S ARM) 110 BEYOND
(PUTTING HER HANDS OVER HER EARS--IN EXASPERATION)118 BEYOND
HE NEVER UNDERSTOOD, THAT'S A KINDER WAY OF 134 BEYOND
PUTTING IT.
(TAKING A THERMOMETER FROM HIS POCKET AND PUTTING 484 CARDIF
IT INTO YANK'S MOUTH)
(PUTTING HIS HANDS OVER HIS EARS) 488 CARDIF
(PUTTING A HUGE PAW OVER COCKY'S MOUTH) 463 CARIBBE
(GRINNING AT THE THREE AND PUTTING HIS FINGER TO 572 CROSS
HIS LIPS)
(PUTTING HIS MUDDY BOOTS UP ON THE TABLE, TILTING 217 DESIRE
BACK HIS CHAIR,
(HOLDING HIS EYES AND PUTTING ALL HER WILL INTO 240 DESIRE
HER WORDS
(PUTTING ONE ARM OVER HIS SHOULDER. 242 DESIRE
(PUTTING HER FINGER ON HIS LIPS) 253 DESIRE
(MOANING--PUTTING HER HANDS OVER HER EARS) 261 DESIRE
(PUTTING HIS ARM ABOUT HER WAIST) 498 DIFRNT
(RISING ALSO AND PUTTING HER HANDS ON HIS 498 DIFRNT
SHOULDERS)
(PUTTING HER ARMS ABOUT EMMA) 506 DIFRNT
(PUTTING HIS ARM ABOUT HER WAIST AND GIVING HER A 506 DIFRNT
SQUEEZE--GRINNING)
(REPENTANTLY, COMING AND PUTTING HER ARMS AROUND 510 DIFRNT
EMMA AND KISSING HER)
(GETTING UP AND PUTTING A HAND ON HIS ARM-- 527 DIFRNT
FEVERISHLY)
WHO IS UPSTAIRS IN THE BEDROOM PUTTING ON A HEAVY 428 DYNAMO
MAKE-UP ROUGE AND MASCARA,
IT'S LIKE PUTTING MY LIFE IN YOUR HANDS. 440 DYNAMO
PUTTING ON AIRS, THE STINKING NIGGER/ 175 EJONES
(PUTTING ON HIS SUAVEST MANNER, 176 EJONES
(TRYING TO BREAK AWAY FROM HER, HALF PUTTING HER 31 ELECTR
HANDS UP TO HER EARS)
(GOING TO HIM AND PUTTING AN ARM AROUND HIS 36 ELECTR
SHOULDER)
GRIMNESS--PUTTING THE PAPER IN HIS POCKET) 42 ELECTR
(PUTTING AN ARM AROUND HER--IN A STRAINED TONE) 72 ELECTR
(WITH A BOYISH BROTHERLY AIR--PUTTING AN ARM 74 ELECTR
AROUND HER)
(IMMEDIATELY ASHAMED OF HIMSELF--TENDERLY, PUTTING 80 ELECTR
HIS ARM AROUND HER)
(PUTTING IT IN HIS POCKET) WE'VE GOT TO GO 115 ELECTR
THROUGH HIS POCKETS

PUTTING (CONT'D.)
(HASTILY LOCKING THE DRAWER AND PUTTING THE KEY IN149 ELECTR
HIS POCKET)
(PUTTING HER HANDS OVER HER EARS) 155 ELECTR
WHY DOES HE KEEP PUTTING HIS DEATH IN MY HEADS 157 ELECTR
WHICH IS ON THE TABLE AND, PUTTING A FINGER IN IT AT 269 GGBROW
RANDOM,
(PUTTING THE DRAWING BACK ON HIS DESK. 275 GGBROW
(HE COMES FORWARD, PUTTING ONE ARM AROUND HER 291 GGBROW
BOWED SHOULDERS, AND THEY KISS.)
DION MUST BE PUTTING OVER SOME BLUFF ON HER. 304 GGBROW
(TURNING AWAY SLOWLY AND PUTTING ON HIS MASK-- 305 GGBROW
DULLY)
PUTTING BOTH HANDS UP BEFORE HER EYES 226 HA APE
PUTTING HIS TWO FEET UP AGAINST THE OTHERS SO THAT244 HA APE
HIS POSITION IS PARALLEL TO
BY PUTTING A PROPERTY SANDWICH IN THE MIDDLE OF 571 ICEMAN
EACH TABLE,
WHY, I WAS JUST PUTTING YOU RIGHT. 585 ICEMAN
(MARGIE AND PEARL START TAKING THEM FROM HIS ARMS 638 ICEMAN
AND PUTTING THEM ON THE TABLE.
AND PUTTING A HAND ON HIS SHOULDER) 641 ICEMAN
I REMEMBER HER PUTTING ON THE HIGH-AND-MIGHTY 647 ICEMAN
FREE-WOMAN STUFF,
(PUTTING UP HIS FISTS) YES$ 653 ICEMAN
(TO LEWIS--DISGUSTEDLY PUTTING THE KEY ON THE 675 ICEMAN
SHELF IN BACK OF THE BAR)
HOPE AND JIMMY ARE BOTH PUTTING UP A FRONT OF 683 ICEMAN
SELF-ASSURANCE,
(PUTTING ON HIS DEAF MANNER) 684 ICEMAN
YOU'RE PUTTING ON THIS ROTTEN HALF-DEAD ACT JUST 705 ICEMAN
TO GET BACK AT ME/
AND I'M NOT PUTTING UP ANY BLUFF, EITHER, 720 ICEMAN
IT'S PUTTING LIFE BACK IN ME/ 721 ICEMAN
(PUTTING A HAND OVER ONE OF HER NERVOUSLY PLAYING 17 JOURNE
ONES.)
(HE QUOTES, PUTTING ON A HAM-ACTOR MANNER.) 21 JOURNE
(PUTTING ON HIS COLLAR AND TIE.) 54 JOURNE
HE IS PUTTING ON HIS COAT.) 65 JOURNE
(WITH A WORRIED LOOK AT HIM--PUTTING ON A FAKE 65 JOURNE
HEARTINESS.)
(PUTTING HER ARM AROUND EDMUND'S SHOULDER--- 67 JOURNE
I WAS MERELY PUTTING BLUNTLY WHAT WE ALL KNOW, AND 76 JOURNE
HAVE TO LIVE WITH NOW, AGAIN.
(CYNICALLY.) HE'S BEEN PUTTING ON THE OLD SOB ACT157 JOURNE
FOR YOU, EH$
MY PUTTING YOU WISE SO YOU'D LEARN FROM MY 165 JOURNE
MISTAKES.
THEN I WOULDN'T MIND PUTTING MYSELF TO A TEST BY 175 JOURNE
GOING HOME AFTER I GRADUATED,
(THEN SUDDENLY PUTTING ON A BRAVE FRONT, HE 333 LAZARU
STIRS UP BEHIND LAZARUS)
AS THE CURTAIN RISES, SLAVES ARE HURRIEDLY PUTTING337 LAZARU
OUT THE MANY LAMPS.
(THEN IN A MORE CONVERSATIONAL TONE, PUTTING ASIDE370 LAZARU
HIS GRANDIOSE AIRS,
THEY KNEEL AT EACH SIDE OF HIM, PUTTING AN ARM 175 MANSNS
AROUND HIM,
PUTTING ON EXPRESSIONS OF THE UTMOST CORDIALITY) 365 MARCOM
(PUTTING HER HANDS ON HIS SHOULDERS AND LIFTING 368 MARCOM
HER LIPS)
PUTTING ON AIRS AS IF HE WAS TOO GOOD TO WIPE HIS 10 MISBEG
SHOES ON ME.
(LAUGHS AND SITS ON THE STEPS, PUTTING THE CLUB 15 MISBEG
AWAY)
YOU WERE ONLY PUTTING IT ON AS PART OF YOUR 162 MISBEG
SCHEME--
GOD SEEMS TO BE PUTTING ON QUITE A DISPLAY. 172 MISBEG
(PUTTING THE DECANTER AND GLASS BEFORE HIM.) 9 POET
THANK GOD, IF HE'S PUTTING ON HIS UNIFORM, HE'LL 80 POET
BE HOURS BEFORE THE MIRROR.
(PUTTING THE DECANTER AND GLASS ON THE TABLE.) 133 POET
(DESPERATELY PUTTING ON HIS PRIM SEVERE MANNER 15 STRANG
TOWARD AN UNRULY PUPIL)
PUTTING AN ARM AROUND HIS NECK AND PULLING HIS 70 STRANG
HEAD ON TO HER BREASTS)
(PUTTING ON HIS BEST PROFESSIONAL AIR, GOING TO 97 STRANG
HER)
(THEN PUTTING A BRAKE ON THIS EXUBERANCE--MATTER- 121 STRANG
OF-FACTLY)
(LOOKING AT MARSDEN KEENLY BUT PUTTING ON A JOKING121 STRANG
TONE)
(COMING TO NINA AND PUTTING HIS HAND ON HER 160 STRANG
SHOULDER)
(PUTTING DOWN THE GLASSES--WITH A GROAN) 171 STRANG
(PUTTING HER HANDS ON HIS ARM.) 172 STRANG
(PUTTING ON A TONE OF JOKING ANNOYANCE) 190 STRANG
(PUTTING HIS ARM AROUND HER--AFFECTIONATELY) 199 STRANG
(VAGUELY TAKING OFF HIS DERBY HAT AND PUTTING IT 497 VOYAGE
ON AGAIN--PLAINTIVELY)
(PUTTING HIS ARM AROUND HER) 499 VOYAGE
(GREATLY PLEASED--PUTTING HIS HAND IN HIS POCKET) 500 VOYAGE
ONLY PUTTING OUT HER HAND ON THE FLOOR TO SUPPORT 460 WELDED

PUTTINGHER
(THEN PUTTINGHER HAND ON HIS ARM--SEDUCTIVELY) 227 DESIRE

PUTTY
AND THE PUTTY THEY CALL BREAD/ 480 CARDIF
HER FACE LIKE GRAY PUTTY.... 8 STRANG
YOU'RE SOFT AS PUTTY. 122 STRANG

PUZZELED
(WITH PUZZELED GOOD NATURE) I DO NOT UNDERSTAND. 322 LAZARU

PUZZLE
WONDERING LOOK, AS IF SOME DEEP PUZZLE WERE 224 AHWILD
CONFRONTING HIM.
BUT CAN I BE ASKING YOU ONE QUESTION, MISS, HAS MY 35 ANNA
HEAD IN A PUZZLE$

PUZZLE (CONT'D.)
MERELY TRYING TO WORK OUT THE ANSWER TO A PUZZLE--496 DAYS
A HUMAN PUZZLE.
WELL, THAT'S A PUZZLE, SURELY. 59 MISBEG

PUZZLED
(AFTER A PAUSE DURING WHICH HE LOOKS DOWN AT HER 545 'ILE
WITH A PUZZLED FROWN)
MILDRED STARES AT HIM IN PUZZLED WONDERMENT, 195 AHWILD
THEN, WITH A PUZZLED EXPRESSION, PULLS IT WIDE. 13 ANNA
BUT PUZZLED AND SUSPICIOUS) 46 ANNA
(PUZZLED AND BEGINNING TO BE IRRITATED AT HER TOO) 54 ANNA
(SLOWLY, PUZZLED) WELL, THEN, IF IT ISN'T-- 88 BEYOND
(LOOKS FROM ONE TO THE OTHER OF THEM WITH A 95 BEYOND
PUZZLED AIR.
PEARL LOOKS AT HIM CURIOUSLY, PUZZLED BY HIS 469 CARIBE
STRANGE ACTIONS.
FATHER BAIRD GIVES HIM A PUZZLED, CONCERNED LOOK, 505 DAYS
HE GLANCES AT JOHN AGAIN WITH A CURIOUS PUZZLED 506 DAYS
FIXITY.
(SHE GIVES LUCY A PUZZLED GLANCE. 516 DAYS
HE SIGHS WITH A PUZZLED AWE AND BLURTS OUT WITH 203 DESIRE
HALTING APPRECIATION.)
(PUZZLED) IT'S PLUMB ONNATURAL. 220 DESIRE
(PUZZLED AND A BIT UNEASY) SAILORS AIN'T PLASTER 495 DIFRNT
SAINTS, EMMER--
(PUZZLED--UNCERTAINLY) WAAL-- 496 DIFRNT
(PUZZLED) I DON'T KNOW EXACTLY, BUT THERE'S A 537 DIFRNT
CLOCK IN THE NEXT ROOM.
THERE IS AN EXPRESSION OF PUZZLED UNEASINESS ON 462 DYNAMO
HIS FACE
(PUZZLED) WHAT'S DAT YOU SAYS 181 EJONES
(LOOKS AFTER HIM WITH A PUZZLED ADMIRATION) 187 EJONES
WITH A VAGUE GESTURE OF PUZZLED BEWILDERMENT. 200 EJONES
THEY WATCH HIM, WITH QUEER, PUZZLED EYES.) 260 GGBROW
I NEVER PUZZLED THEM WITH MYSELF. 284 GGBROW
(THEY ARE SILENT, PUZZLED BY HIS SUDDEN RESENTMENT227 HA APE
(STARES AT HIM, PUZZLED AND REPELLED--SHARPLY) 590 ICEMAN
(LARRY IS MOVED TO A PUZZLED PITY IN SPITE OF 590 ICEMAN
HIMSELF.
AND PUZZLED BY SOMETHING HE FEELS ABOUT PARRITT 592 ICEMAN
THAT ISN'T RIGHT.
(AS LARRY FLASHES HIM A PUZZLED GLANCE, HE ADDS 594 ICEMAN
CONFUSEDLY)
(REGARDS HIM WITH SURPRISE AT FIRST, THEN WITH A 623 ICEMAN
PUZZLED INTEREST)
(FROWNINGLY PUZZLED AGAIN) BUT I DON'T SEE-- 624 ICEMAN
(SUDDENLY BREEZILY GOOD-NATURED)
THEY STARE AT HIM WITH PUZZLED UNEASY 625 ICEMAN
FASCINATION.)
THEY ALL STARE AT HIM, THEIR FACES AGAIN PUZZLED, 628 ICEMAN
RESENTFUL AND UNEASY.)
(PUZZLED) SOMEONE ELSE? 693 ICEMAN
A PUZZLED EXPRESSION COMES OVER HIS FACE, FOLLOWED513 INZONE
BY ONE OF SUSPICION.
(THEY ALL LOOK AT HIM WITH PUZZLED GLANCES FULL OF518 INZONE
A VAGUE APPREHENSION.)
HE SIGHS WITH A PUZZLED EXPRESSION AND GETS UP AND523 INZONE
WALKS OUT OF THE DOORWAY.
AND LOOKS AT WHAT HE SEES INSIDE WITH AN 528 INZONE
EXPRESSION OF PUZZLED ASTONISHMENT.
AND SIGHS FREQUENTLY WITH A PUZZLED FROWN.) 531 INZONE
(CATHLEEN STARES AT HER, STUPIDLY PUZZLED. 100 JOURNE
(THEN, STUPIDLY PUZZLED.) GOOD EXCUSE! 101 JOURNE
(STUPIDLY PUZZLED.) YOU'VE TAKEN SOME OF THE 104 JOURNE
MEDICINES
(SHE REGARDS THE WEDDING GOWN WITH A PUZZLED 172 JOURNE
INTEREST.)
(PUZZLED BUT SMILING.) OF COURSE YOU CAN. 17 MANSNS
SARA SUSPICIOUS, PUZZLED.) 53 MANSNS
(PULLING AWAY, STARES AT HIM WITH A PUZZLED 115 MANSNS
FRIGHTENED DREAD.)
AND A PUZZLED EXPRESSION OF INTEREST COMES OVER 378 MARCOM
HIS FACE.)
(MARCO STANDS PUZZLED, IRRITATED, LOOKING 397 MARCOM
STUBBORN, FRIGHTENED AND FOOLISH.
(PUZZLED AND SEVERE) HUH? 412 MARCOM
(PUZZLED) WHAT, YOUR MAJESTY$ 422 MARCOM
(PUZZLED, AND NOT A LITTLE IRRITATED AS 439 MARCOM
HIS THOUGHTS,
PUZZLED AND UNEASY) 77 MISBEG
(SHE COMES TO TYRONE, WHO STANDS STARING AFTER 101 MISBEG
HOGAN WITH A PUZZLED LOOK.)
MEETING HIS EYES, WHICH ARE REGARDING HER WITH 113 MISBEG
PUZZLED
HE KEEPS STARING AT HER WITH A PUZZLED FROWN.) 113 MISBEG
(PUZZLED) YOU SAID YOU'D TELL ME ABOUT THE BLONDE145 MISBEG
ON THE TRAIN.
SHE STANDS THINKING, HER EXPRESSION PUZZLED, 87 POET
APPREHENSIVE, AND RESENTFUL.
(GIVES HER FATHER A PUZZLED, UNEASY GLANCE.) 153 POET
BUT STILL WITH THE LOOK OF PUZZLED UNEASINESS AT 154 POET
HER FATHER.)
(AS EVANS LOOKS PUZZLED AND STARTLED HE ADDS WITH 47 STRANG
AN IRONICAL)
(PUZZLED AND IRRITATED--THINKING CONFUSEDLY) 128 STRANG
PUZZLED GLANCE AS IF HE WERE AWARE OF HIS 471 WELDED
SURROUNDINGS FOR THE FIRST TIME.)
(WITH A PUZZLED GRIN) SAY? 474 WELDED

PUZZLEDLY
(STANDS LOOKING AT HIM PUZZLEDLY--THEN GIVES IT UP271 AHWILD
WITH A SIGH)
(THEN PUZZLEDLY) BUT WHY SHOULD YOU BE AFRAID 524 DAYS
THAT ANYONE--
(HER FATHER STARES AT HER PUZZLEDLY. 443 DYNAMO
(SURPRISED--SIZING HER UP PUZZLEDLY) 24 ELECTR
PETER STARES AFTER HIM PUZZLEDLY.) 167 ELECTR
(LARRY REGARDS HIM PUZZLEDLY.) 585 ICEMAN
(WATCHING HIM PUZZLEDLY) UNDERSTAND WHATS 587 ICEMAN

PUZZLEDLY (CONT'D.)
(HE LOOKS AWAY. LARRY STARES AT HIM PUZZLEDLY. 591 ICEMAN
(THEN PUZZLEDLY) SOBERS 618 ICEMAN
(CONTINUING TO STARE--PUZZLEDLY) 624 ICEMAN
(SHE PAUSES--THEN ADDS PUZZLEDLY) 637 ICEMAN
(THEN PUZZLEDLY) BUT HOW CAN YOU BE SORRY FOR HIM669 ICEMAN
RUCKY LOOKS FROM PARRITT TO LARRY PUZZLEDLY. 701 ICEMAN
(STARES AT HIM PUZZLEDLY, THEN QUOTES 32 JOURNE
MECHANICALLY.)
HER FOREHEAD PUCKERED PUZZLEDLY, 170 JOURNE
(SOMEWHAT TAKEN ABACK, PUZZLEDLY) 382 MARCOM
(REGARDS HIM FOR A SECOND PUZZLEDLY. 69 POET
CREGAN SCRATCHES HIS HEAD PUZZLEDLY.) 153 POET
(HE SUDDENLY TURNS TO EVANS WHO HAS BEEN STARING 106 STRANG
AT HIM, PUZZLEDLY--

PUZZLEMENT
(SCRATCHING HIS HEAD IN PUZZLEMENT) 101 BEYOND
(SHE LIFTS HER HANDS TO EXAMINE THEM WITH A 171 JOURNE
FRIGHTENED PUZZLEMENT.)

PUZZLES
THE GARISH STRANGENESS OF EVERYTHING EVIDENTLY 535 DIFRNT
REPELS AND PUZZLES HIM.
WITH QUEER APPALLED WONDER THAT PUZZLES HIM 395 MARCOM
SAM'S FEELING TOWARD HER PUZZLES ME. 50 STRANG

PUZZLING
YOU'RE PUZZLING TODAY, MISS LAVINIA. 22 ELECTR
BEGINNING TO DO A LOT OF PUZZLING ABOUT ME, AREN'T639 ICEMAN
YOU, LARRY$

PYRAMIDS
FACT ONE DAY--WHEN I WAS BUILDING THE PYRAMIDS-- 231 AHWILD

PYTHAGORAS
AND FOUND A BRIEF SHELTER IN PYTHAGORAS AND 503 DAYS
NUMEROLOGY.

PYTHIAS
UNIFORMS OF OUR MODERN KNIGHTS TEMPLAR, OF 390 MARCOM
COLUMBUS, OF PYTHIAS,

QUACK
AND NO THANKS TO THAT OLD FOOL OF A COUNTRY QUACK,145 BEYOND
WITHOUT ANYONE TO ATTEND TO HIM BUT A COUNTRY 154 BEYOND
QUACK?
THE QUACK I WENT TO GOT ALL MY DOUGH AND THEN TOLD713 ICEMAN
ME I WAS CURED
HE'S A CHEAP OLD QUACK! 30 JOURNE
FROM WHAT MAMA'S SAID, HE WAS ANOTHER CHEAP QUACK 39 JOURNE
LIKE HARDY/
AND YET IT WAS EXACTLY THE SAME TYPE OF CHEAP 74 JOURNE
QUACK WHO FIRST GAVE YOU THE
I WAS SO SICK AFTERWARDS, AND THAT IGNORANT QUACK 87 JOURNE
OF A CHEAP HOTEL DOCTOR--
THAT LYING OLD QUACK/ I WARNED YOU HE'D INVENT--/118 JOURNE
INSTEAD YOU PUT HER IN THE HANDS OF A HOTEL QUACK 140 JOURNE
WHO WOULDN'T ADMIT HIS

QUACKLIN'
SHUT YOUR LOUD QUACKLIN'/ 584 ROPE

QUAILS
(SHE SEES HE HAS GUESSED HER SECRET AND AT FIRST 387 MARCOM
SHE QUAILS AND SHRINKS AWAY.

QUAINT
ABOUT DEAR OLD LADIES AND WITTY, CYNICAL BACHELORS176 STRANG
AND QUAINT CHARACTERS WITH

QUAKING
QUAKING WITH TERROR NOW AS IF THIS LAUGH WAS MEANT339 LAZARU
FOR HIM, DROPS TO HIS KNEES,

QUALIFICATION
(AT THIS QUALIFICATION, A GRIN TWITCHES EDMUND'S 149 JOURNE
LIPS.

QUALIFICATIONS
POSSESSES THE QUALIFICATIONS I DESIRE IS A YOUNG 97 MANSNS
AND VERY BEAUTIFUL WOMAN.
(BITINGLY) I'M NOT ACQUAINTED WITH THEIR SOCIAL 38 STRANG
QUALIFICATIONS,

QUALIFIED
UNTIL THEY DISCOVERED I WASN'T QUALIFIED 38 MISBEG

QUALITY
CONFIDENTIAL HALF-WHISPER WITH SOMETHING VAGUELY 5 ANNA
PLAINTIVE IN ITS QUALITY.
HIS VOICE IS LOW AND DEEP WITH A PENETRATING, 556 CRUSS
HOLLOW, METALLIC QUALITY.
NO, THEIR PIETY HAD A GENUINE, GENTLE, MYSTIC 510 DAYS
QUALITY TO IT.
(HIS VOICE WITH SURPRISING SUDDENNESS TAKES ON A 545 DAYS
SAVAGE VINDICTIVE QUALITY)
THEIR STARE HAVING A STRAINING, INGROWING QUALITY.221 DESIRE
DESPERATE QUALITY WHICH IS SO APPARENT IN EBEN.) 221 DESIRE
HIS EYES HAVE TAKEN ON A STRANGE, INCONGRUOUS 230 DESIRE
DREAMY QUALITY.
DUE TO HER LARGE, SOFT BLUE EYES WHICH HAVE AN 494 DIFRNT
INCONGRUOUS QUALITY OF
SEACAPES, OF THE PAINTED-TO-ORDER QUALITY, FOUR INS19 DIFRNT
NUMBER, IN GILDED FRAMES,
(GLANCES AT HIM AND SPEAKS IN A GENTLE TONE THAT 423 DYNAMO
CARRIES A CHALLENGING QUALITY)
SHE HAS HIS ALERT QUALITY. 428 DYNAMO
LISTENING TO DE WHITE QUALITY TALK, IT'S DAT SAME 178 EJONES
FACT,
ONE IS STRUCK AT A GLANCE BY THE PECULIAR QUALITY 20 ELECTR
HIS FACE IN REPOSE HAS OF
GIVING IT AN UNREAL, DETACHED, EERIE QUALITY. 43 ELECTR
WHEN HE SPEAKS, HIS DEEP VOICE HAS A HOLLOW 46 ELECTR
REPRESSED QUALITY.
THERE IS THE SAME LIFELIKE MASK QUALITY OF HIS 73 ELECTR
FACE IN REPOSE,
ALL THE FACES IN THE PORTRAITS HAVE THE SAME MASK 79 ELECTR
QUALITY
A QUEER TROUBADOUR- OF-THE-SEA QUALITY ABOUT HIM.J103 ELECTR
HIS MOVEMENTS AND ATTITUDES HAVE THE STATUE-LIKE 137 ELECTR
QUALITY

QUALITY

QUALITY (CONT'D.)
BUT GIVING HER THE ABSTRACT QUALITY OF A GIRL 262 GGBROW
INSTEAD OF THE INDIVIDUAL.
ITS PAN QUALITY BECOMING MEPHISTOPHELEAN. 269 GGBROW
ALL OF ITS PAN QUALITY HAS CHANGED 285 GGBROW
WITH MUCH THE SAME QUALITY AS BILLY BROWN'S IN ACT293 GGBROW
ONE, SCENE ONE.
THE QUALITY OF UNQUESTIONING FAITH IN THE FINALITY294 GGBROW
OF ITS ACHIEVEMENT.
(THECHOUSED WORD HAS A BRAZEN METALLIC QUALITY 210 HA APE
AS IF THEIR THROATS WERE
METALLIC QUALITY AS IF THEIR THROATS WERE 227 HA APE
PHONOGRAPH HORNS.
(THE WORD HAS A BRAZEN, METALLIC QUALITY AS IF 227 HA APE
THEIR THROATS WERE
(THE WORD HAS A BRAZE METALLIC QUALITY 228 HA APE
(THE WORD HAS A BRAZE. METALLIC QUALITY 229 HA APE
(THE WORD HAS A BRAZEN METALLIC QUALITY 229 HA APE
AN EXPRESSION OF TIRED TOLERANCE GIVING HIS FACE 574 ICEMAN
THE QUALITY
THERE IS A QUALITY ABOUT HIM OF A PRIM, VICTORIAN 575 ICEMAN
OLD MAID.
BUT THIS TIME HIS HABITUAL PASS-CUT HAS A QUALITY 641 ICEMAN
OF HIDING.)
AND A QUALITY OF INSENSIBILITY ABOUT ALL THE 696 ICEMAN
PEOPLE IN THIS GROUP AT RIGHT.
HER MOST APPEALING QUALITY IS THE SIMPLE, 13 JOURNE
WHICH HAS A SOLIDFRLY QUALITY OF HEAD UP, CHEST 13 JOURNE
OUT, STOMACH IN,
THESE HAVE THE QUALITY OF BELONGING TO A STUDIED 13 JOURNE
TECHNIQUE.
IT IS IN THE QUALITY OF EXTREME NERVOUS 20 JOURNE
SENSIBILITY THAT THE LIKENESS OF EDMUND
HIS MOUTH HAS THE SAME QUALITY OF 20 JOURNE
HYPERSENSITIVENESS HERS POSSESSES.
(WITH A RESENTMENT THAT HAS A QUALITY OF BEING 61 JOURNE
AUTOMATIC AND ON THE SURFACE
REGAINS THE QUALITY OF STRANGE DETACHMENT-- 64 JOURNE
CALMLY.)
(STARTS AND AT ONCE THE QUALITY OF UNNATURAL 67 JOURNE
DETACHMENT SETTLES ON HER FACE
BUT THERE IS THE STRANGE QUALITY OF DETACHMENT IN 72 JOURNE
IT.)
AND THE QUALITY OF UNCANNY DETACHMENT IS IN HER 75 JOURNE
VOICE AND MANNER.)
BUT IN A STRANGE WAY THE REACTION HAS A MECHANICA101 JOURNE
QUALITY.
THERE IS A QUALITY OF AN INNOCENT CONVENT GIRL 105 JOURNE
ABOUT HER, AND SHE SMILES SHYLY.)
SHE SUDDENLY LOSES ALL THE GIRLISH QUALITY 107 JOURNE
(HER MANNER AND QUALITY DRIFT BACK TO THE SHY 112 JOURNE
CONVENT GIRL AGAIN.)
LOOKING OUT, A BLANK, FAR-OFF QUALITY IN HER 121 JOURNE
VOICE.)
IN ITS GENERAL STRUCTURE AND PARTICULARLY IN ITS 274 LAZARU
QUALITY OF DETACHED SERENITY.
CLEAR QUALITY OF BOYHOOD, GAILY MOCKING WITH LIFE)365 LAZARU
WITH A QUALITY OF MASCULINE OBSTINACY AND 2 MANSNS
DETERMINATION ABOUT IT.
THERE IS THE QUALITY OF A DEATH'S HEAD ABOUT HER 28 MANSNS
FACE.
IN A LOW VOICE THAT HAS LOST ITS OLD MUSICAL 28 MANSNS
QUALITY
A QUALITY OF NERVOUS TENSION. 43 MANSNS
SUDDENLY HE HAS THE BEATEN QUALITY OF ONE BEGGING 131 MANSNS
FOR PITY.
THE MURDERER POSSESSES THE TRUE QUALITY OF MERCY. 180 MANSNS
BUT THERE IS NO MANNISH QUALITY ABOUT HER. 3 MISBEG
GIVES HIS FACE A CERTAIN MEPHISTOPHELIAN QUALITY 37 MISBEG
WHICH IS ACCENTUATED BY HIS
AND THERE IS A CERTAIN VAGUE QUALITY IN HIS MANNER100 MISBEG
AND SPEECH.
YOU SAID HIS FATHER WASN'T OF THE QUALITY OF 11 POET
GALWAY LIKE HE MAKES OUT,
BUT HER SPEECH HAS AT TIMES A SELF-CONSCIOUS, 16 POET
STILTED QUALITY ABOUT IT.
BUT I WARN YOU IT IS A QUALITY DIFFICULT FOR A 82 POET
WOMAN TO KEEP ON ADMIRING.
SIMON'S GRANDFATHER, EVAN HARFORD, HAD THE QUALITY 83 POET
TOO.
THE QUALITY OF THE FORMIDABLY STRONG, 88 POET
POSSESSING NOW A GENUINE QUALITY HE HAS NOT HAD 88 POET
BEFORE.
BUT I DO OWE YOU AN APOLOGY FOR THE QUALITY OF THE 98 POET
SERVICE.
THERE IS AN INDEFINABLE FEMININE QUALITY ABOUT 4 STRANG
HIM.
THE MAIN POINT ABOUT HIS PERSONALITY IS A QUIET 4 STRANG
CHARM, A QUALITY OF APPEALING,
(HIS VOICE TAKES ON A MONOTONOUS MUSING QUALITY, 4 STRANG
THERE IS AN UNCONVINCING QUALITY ABOUT IT THAT 7 STRANG
LEAVES HIS LARGER AUDIENCE--
SINCE GORDON'S DEATH THEY HAVE A QUALITY OF 12 STRANG
CONTINUALLY SHUDDERING
(BEGINNING TO BE TAKEN BY HIS LIKABLE BOYISH 28 STRANG
QUALITY)
LIKABLE QUALITY THOUGH...!) 29 STRANG
THERE IS A QUALITY ABOUT HIM, PROVOKING AND 33 STRANG
DISTURBING TO WOMEN,
GIVING THEM A BLURRED GHOSTLY QUALITY. 66 STRANG
FUTILE BUT HE HAD A SENSITIVE QUALITY... 119 STRANG
HIS VOICE TAKING ON A PLEADING UNCERTAIN QUALITY) 126 STRANG
IT IS A STRONG FACE BUT OF A STRENGTH WHOLLY 184 STRANG
MATERIAL IN QUALITY.

QUALMS
I WOULDN'T HAVE QUALMS ABOUT WHICH WAS OR WASN'T 41 ELECTR
THE WAY TO KILL HER/
(BEGINNING TO HAVE QUALMS) LISTEN, PHIL. 52 MISBEG

QUAMVIS
QUAMVIS LAPIS OMNIA NUDUS.= 37 MISBEG

QUANDARY
(SCRATCHING HIS HEAD IN A QUANDARY) 10 ANNA

QUANE
A QUANE AV THE NAYGURS SHE MUSTA BEEN SURELY. 478 CARDIF
FOR THE QUANE AV THE CANNIBAL ISLES WAD A DIED AV 478 CARDIF
THE BELLYACHE THE DAY AFTHER
(GRABBING HER) DANCE WID ME, ME CANNIBAL QUANE. 471 CARIBE
FINE LADY, DRESSED LIKE A WHITE QUANE, 228 HA APE

QUANTITY
HE IS AN EXQUISITE JUDGE OF QUANTITY. 418 MARCOM
THE ROOM IS A TYPICAL SITTING ROOM OF THE 90 STRANG
QUANTITY-PRODUCTION BUNGALOW TYPE.

QUARE
IT'S QUARE YOU'D BE THE ONE TO BE MAKING GREAT 47 ANNA
TROUBLE ABOUT HER LEAVING YOU
TIS A QUARE TIME TO JOKE WITH ME, AND DON'T BE 53 ANNA
DOING IT, FOR THE LOVE OF GOD.
'TIS QUARE, ROUGH TALK, THAT--FOR A DACENT GIRL 57 ANNA
THE LIKE OF YOU!

QUARREL
(THERE IS SOMETHING IN HER TONE THAT MAKES THEM 56 ANNA
FORGET THEIR QUARREL
WITH NARY A QUARREL I KIN REMEMBER. 98 BEYOND
(CUTTINGLY) IF YOU ARE DETERMINED TO QUARREL, LET 18 ELECTR
US GO INTO THE HOUSE.
YOU SEE, HE'D HAD A QUARREL WITH HER THAT LAST 148 ELECTR
NIGHT.
ABOUT YOUR HAVING A QUARREL WITH YOUR POOR MOTHER 161 ELECTR
THAT NIGHT BEFORE SHE--
IF WE DID QUARREL, IT WAS BECAUSE I TOLD HER I'D 589 ICEMAN
BECOME CONVINCED
AS IF THEIR OWN QUARREL WAS FORGOTTEN 672 ICEMAN
(HAS STOPPED CUTTING WHEN THE QUARREL STARTED-- 672 ICEMAN
EXPOSTULATING)
(HE STOPS, BORED WITH THEIR QUARREL, AND SHRUGS 33 JOURNE
HIS SHOULDERS.)
THEY FORGET THEIR QUARREL AND ARE AS ONE AGAINST 77 JOURNE
HIM ON THIS ISSUE.)
(FORGETTING HIS QUARREL) YES, GO WITH HIM, 81 JOURNE
JAMIE.
BUT I HOPE YOU DIDN'T ASK ME HERE JUST TO QUARREL 79 MANSNS
WITH ME.
SO YOU HAVE NEVER FORGOTTEN THAT OLD QUARRELS 99 MANSNS
WE'VE UNDERSTOOD EACH OTHER AND WHAT MIGHT HAVE 124 MANSNS
DEVELOPED INTO A STUPID QUARREL
BUT IT TAKES TWO TO MAKE A QUARREL AND I DON'T 45 POET
FEEL QUARRELSOME.
I WISH NO QUARREL WITH YOU, SIR. 121 POET
NO QUARREL-- 147 STRANG
WE'VE MADE UP OUR MINDS NOT TO QUARREL. 455 WELDED

QUARRELED
YOU'VE QUARRELED WITH YOUR MOTHER AND HAZEL 175 ELECTR
WE'VE QUARRELED, BUT NEVER LIKE THIS BEFORE. 467 WELDED

QUARRELIN'
(WILDLY) WAR YEN AN' EBEN QUARRELIN' AGENS 230 DESIRE
(DEFIANTLY) HE WAS TRYIN' T' MAKE LOVE T' ME-- 233 DESIRE
WHEN YE HEERD US QUARRELIN'.

QUARRELING
I HEARD YOU FROM MY STUDY QUARRELING OUT HERE, 174 MANSNS
OUR SPIES REPORT THEIR MANY PETTY STATES ARE 421 MARCOM
ALWAYS QUARRELING.

QUARRELSOME
BUT IT TAKES TWO TO MAKE A QUARREL AND I DON'T 45 POET
FEEL QUARRELSOME.

QUART
JEES, WOULD I LIKE TO GET A QUART OF DIS REDEYE 671 ICEMAN
UNDER MY BELT!
WITH A MOON IN THE SKY TO FILL HIM WITH POETRY AND 21 MISBEG
A QUART OF BAD HOOTCH INSIDE
SHE HAS A QUART OF WHISKEY UNDER HER ARM, TWO 111 MISBEG
TUMBLERS, AND A PITCHER OF WATER.
(HE TAKES A FULL QUART FLASK OF WHISKEY FROM THE 587 ROPE
POCKET OF HIS COAT

QUARTER
OFF THE STAR*B'D QUARTER 'BOUT FIVE MILES AWAY-- 551 'ILE
BIG ONES?
(LOOKING AT HER WATCH) QUARTER PAST SIX. 212 AHWILD
(GUILTILY) WELL, IT'S QUARTER TO ELEVEN--BUT 251 AHWILD
THAT'S NOT SO LATE.
(COMES OUT OF THE CABIN WITH A TUMBLER QUARTER- 31 ANNA
FULL OF WHISKY IN HER HAND.
AGAINST A SKY PALE WITH THE LIGHT OF A QUARTER- 421 DYNAMO
MOON.
IT IS AROUND QUARTER TO ONE. 51 JOURNE
(WITH BITTER IRONY.) YES, ON PROPERTY VALUED AT A144 JOURNE
QUARTER OF A MILLION.
I ASK NO QUARTER. 71 MANSNS
AND IT'S LESS THAN A QUARTER MILE FROM THE INN 45 MISBEG
HERE.

QUARTERMASTER'S
AND YOU KNOW DURNED WELL HE WAS ONLY IN THE 541 DIFRNT
QUARTERMASTER'S DEPARTMENT UNLOADIN'

QUARTERS
AND PAST THE OFFICERS' QUARTERS TO THE MAIN DECK, 535 'ILE
IN THE REAR, LEFT, A DOOR LEADING TO THE CAPTAIN'S535 'ILE
SLEEPING QUARTERS.
(SHE GOES SLOWLY OUT, REAR, AND LEAVES THE DOOR 541 'ILE
THREE-QUARTERS SHUT BEHIND HER.)
IN THE REAR ON THE LEFT, A DOOR LEADING TO THE 41 ANNA
SLEEPING QUARTERS.
ON EITHER SIDE OF THE DOORWAY ARE TWO CLOSED DOORS455 CARIBE
OPENING ON THE QUARTERS OF
THE BOTTLE IS THREE-QUARTERS EMPTY.) 468 CARIBE
A SMALLER ARCHED DOORWAY LEADING TO THE LIVING 173 EJONES
QUARTERS OF THE PALACE.
WITH HER FACE TURNED THREE-QUARTERS AWAY FROM HIM. 59 ELECTR

QUARTERS (CONT'D.)
THE WHISKEY BOTTLE ON THE TRAY IS THREE-QUARTERS 125 JOURNE
EMPTY.

QUARTET
FROM THE CASINO COMES THE SOUND OF THE SCHOOL 257 GGBROW
QUARTET RENDERING =SWEET ADELINE=

QUARTS
THE BASKET IS PILED WITH QUARTS OF CHAMPAGNE.) 640 ICEMAN
EVEN WHEN I HAD TWO QUARTS OF ROTGUT UNDER MY BELT661 ICEMAN
AND JUKED AND SANG =SWEET

QUAVER
(HE LAUGHS AND COMMENCES TO SING IN A NASAL, HIGH- 6 ANNA
PITCHED QUAVER.)

QUAVERING
YANKING OUT HIS REVOLVER AS HE DOES SO--IN A 190 EJONES
QUAVERING VOICE)
(IN A QUAVERING, RISING AND FALLING CHANT-- 275 LAZARU
(TRYING TO CONCEAL HIS FEAR UNDER A QUAVERING, 380 MARCOM
JOKING TONE)
HIS VOICE THE QUAVERING GHOST OF A TENOR BUT STILL 96 POET
TRUE--

QUAVERS
WITH MANY ULTRA-SENTIMENTAL BARBER-SHOP QUAVERS. 257 GGBROW
PATCH RILEY GIVES A FEW TUNING-UP QUAVERS ON HIS 96 POET
PIPES.)
(HE BEGINS THE PRELIMINARY QUAVERS ON HIS PIPES.) 101 POET
HE LOOKS TOWARD THE SEA AND HIS VOICE QUAVERS IN A579 ROPE
DOLEFUL CHANT)

QUEEN
CAPTAIN KEENEY'S CABIN ON BOARD THE STEAM WHALING 535 *ILE
SHIP =ATLANTIC QUEEN=--
IT'S FROM A SPEECH MADE IN THE SENATE BY A GUY 242 HA APE
NAMED SENATOR QUEEN.
GIVE THAT QUEEN SENATOR GUY THE BARK/ 243 HA APE
(JEERINGLY.) AND THE POOR FAT BURLESQUE QUEEN 134 JOURNE
DOESN'T GET A WORD OF IT,
BUT THE NEXT MOMENT YOU'D BE THE EVIL QUEEN, OR 12 MANSNS
THE BAD FAIRY.
ONE MOMENT YOU'D BE THE GOOD FAIRY, OR THE GOOD 12 MANSNS
QUEEN.
ARE YOU AN EVIL QUEEN OF FRANCE'S 13 MANSNS
BEAUTIFUL QUEEN. 103 MANSNS
AND HOW'S MY VIRGIN QUEEN OF IRELAND'S 41 MISBEG

QUEENS
(HE PAUSES--BOASTFULLY.) SOME QUEENS I'VE BROUGHT 16 HUGHIE
HERE IN MY TIME, BROTHER--
DEAD QUEENS IN THE WEST USUALLY LIE IN STATE. 351 MARCOM
WELL, I BELIEVE IN LOVE MATCHES MYSELF, EVEN FOR 404 MARCOM
KINGS AND QUEENS.

QUEER
(SHE SHAKES HER HEAD) HE'S A QUEER BOY. 209 AHWILD
BUT SHE SEEMS TO GET SOME QUEER SATISFACTION OUT 291 AHWILD
OF FUSSING OVER HIM LIKE A HEN
GOODNESS, HE ACTS QUEER/ 293 AHWILD
WELL, HE'S GOT QUEER NOTIONS ON SOME THINGS. 18 ANNA
THINK OF THAT NOW, AND ISN'T IT QUEER-- 39 ANNA
IT'S QUEER, YES--YOU AND ME SHIPPING ON SAME BOAT 78 ANNA
DAT VAY.
DID YOU NOTICE, JAMES, HOW QUEER EVERYONE WAS AT 98 BEYOND
SUPPERS
THAT'S A QUEER REASON FOR LEAVING ME FLAT. 124 BEYOND
D'YUH WANTA QUEER ALL OF US& 464 CARIBE
(SPITTING PLACIDLY) QUEER THINGS, MEM'RIES. 467 CARIBE
(HE SPITS LEISURELY) QUEER THING, LOVE, AIN'T IT& 467 CARIBE
I THOUGHT THEIR BREATHS SMELLED DAMN QUEER. 473 CARIBE
THEY LOOK AT HIM WITH A QUEER INDIFFERENT 209 DESIRE
CURIOSITY.)
I DIDN'T SAY NOTHIN' AND HE SAYS, LOOKIN' KINDER 210 DESIRE
QUEER AN' SICK..
(WITH QUEER EXCITEMENT) IT'S MAW'S FARM AGEN/ 217 DESIRE
(AS THEY ENTER--A QUEER STRANGLED EMOTION IN HIS 221 DESIRE
DRY CRACKING VOICE)
(AS IF SHE HADN'T HEARD--WITH A QUEER SMILE) 225 DESIRE
(WALKS UP TO HIM--A QUEER COARSE EXPRESSION OF 226 DESIRE
DESIRE IN HER FACE AND BODY--
HE SEEMS IN SOME QUEER WAY SOFTENED, MELLOWED. 230 DESIRE
(AFTER A PAUSE) EBEN'S QUEER. 231 DESIRE
(A PAUSE) COWS IS QUEER. 231 DESIRE
(A PAUSE--THEN HE ADDS WITH A QUEER AFFECTION) 232 DESIRE
DECLAIMING IN A QUEER CAMP MEETING PREACHER'S 232 DESIRE
TEMPO)
(WITH A QUEER SMILE) YE'D BE TURNED FREE, TOO. 233 DESIRE
HE IS STILL IN THE QUEER, 235 DESIRE
(SHE GIVES A QUEER SMILE.) 238 DESIRE
(HE ADDS WITH A CERTAIN QUEER PRIDE) 260 DESIRE
(MORE AND MORE UNEASY) THAT'S ALL YOUR QUEER 512 DIFRNT
NOTIONS.
(AFTER A PAUSE) YOU GOT QUEER, STRICT NOTIONS, 516 DIFRNT
EMMA.
WHEN YOU ACT SO QUEER ABOUT IT. 525 DIFRNT
(WITH QUEER, STUPID INSISTENCE) 527 DIFRNT
(A BIT FRIGHTENEDLY) I JUST HEARD A LOT OF QUEER 547 DIFRNT
NOISES DOWN TO THE BARN.
(LOOKS AFTER HER--FROWNING) ((SHE ACTS QUEER 432 DYNAMO
ABOUT HIM....
AND YET THEY BURN IN THEIR DEPTHS WITH A QUEER 457 DYNAMO
DEVOURING INTENSITY.
(WITH A LAUGH, A QUEER EXPRESSION COMING INTO HIS 458 DYNAMO
EYES)
((BUT HIS EYES ARE SO QUEER... 462 DYNAMO
THAT'S DAMN QUEER...)) 464 DYNAMO
THERE'S A QUEER LOOK IN THOSE COLD EYES OF HIS 478 DYNAMO
LATELY/...
IN A QUEER, DETACHED TONE) 481 DYNAMO
SEEM LIKE QUEER HINDU IDOLS TORTURED INTO 483 DYNAMO
SCIENTIFIC SUPPLICATIONS.
(SERIOUSLY) IT'S A BLEEDIN' QUEER PLACE, THAT 185 EJONES
STINKIN' FOREST,

QUEER (CONT'D.)
IT'S MIGHTY QUEER/ 189 EJONES
(WITH MOURNFUL FOREBODING) IT'S MIGHTY QUEER/ 189 EJONES
WHAT'S DAT ODDER QUEER CLICKETY SOUND I HEAHS 191 EJONES
SCENE, THERE IS SILENCE, BROKEN EVERY FEW SECONDS 191 EJONES
BY A QUEER, CLICKING SOUND.
HE STRUTS NOISELESSLY WITH A QUEER PRANCING STEP 200 EJECTR
FURKIN LOOKIN' AND QUEER. 8 ELECTR
THERE'S SOMETHIN' QUEER LOOKIN' ABOUT HER FACE. 9 ELECTR
SHE LOOKS LIKE HER MOTHER IN FACE--QUEER LOOKIN'-- 11 ELECTR
BUT SHE AIN'T PURTY LIKE HER.
BRANT'S SORT OF QUEER FUR A NAME. 20 ELECTR
IT WOULD BE DAMNED QUEER IF YOU FELL IN LOVE WITH 36 ELECTR
ME BECAUSE I RECALLED EZRA
IT'S DAMNED QUEER, ISN'T IT& 37 ELECTR
(AWKWARDLY MOVED) TEARS ARE QUEER TOKENS OF 47 ELECTR
HAPPINESS/
QUEER, ISN'T IT& 53 ELECTR
BUT LISTEN, ME AS YOUR HUSBAND AND BEING KILLED, 54 ELECTR
THAT SEEMED QUEER AND WRONG--
SOMETHING QUEER IN ME KEEPS ME MUM ABOUT THE 55 ELECTR
THINGS I'D LIKE MOST TO SAY--
QUEER, THE DIFFERENCE IN HER AND LAVINIA-- THE WAY 68 ELECTR
THEY TAKE HIS DEATH.
THERE'S SOMETHING QUEER ABOUT HER. 68 ELECTR
WHO'D EVER SUSPECT--IT'S QUEER. 69 ELECTR
HAVEN'T YOU NOTICED HOW QUEER SHE'S BECOME& 72 ELECTR
EVERYTHING HAS SEEMED QUEER SINCE I CAME BACK TO 74 ELECTR
EARTH.
(STRANGELY) EVERYTHING IS CHANGED--IN SOME QUEER 81 ELECTR
WAY--
(STARING AT HER--IN A QUEER TONE OF GRATITUDE) 81 ELECTR
(HE CHUCKLES TO HIMSELF WITH A QUEER AFFECTIONATE 94 ELECTR
AMUSEMENT)
I HAD A QUEER FEELING THAT WAR MEANT MURDERING THE 95 ELECTR
SAME MAN OVER AND OVER.
MY HEAD WAS QUEER. 95 ELECTR
A QUEER TROUBADOUR- OF-THE-SEA QUALITY ABOUT HIM.)103 ELECTR
A QUEER FASCINATED EXPRESSION IN HIS EYES.) 119 ELECTR
IT'S QUEER/ 116 ELECTR
EZRA EZRA' SUDDEN HIS FIRST NIGHT TO HUM--THAT WAS133 ELECTR
DURNED QUEER.
(ANGRILY) IT'S DURNED QUEER OLD FOOLS LIKE YOU 133 ELECTR
WITH ONE FOOT IN THE GRAVE
THAT'S WHAT'S QUEER. 133 ELECTR
THERE'D HAVE BEEN QUEER DOIN'S COME OUT. 133 ELECTR
THERE IS SOMETHING QUEER ABOUT THIS HOUSE. 136 ELECTR
(TURNING TO HAZEL--WITH QUEER FURTIVE EXCITEMENT) 160 ELECTR
A DURN QUEER THIN' FUR A SODGER TO KILL HIMSELF 170 ELECTR
CLEANIN' HIS GUN.
HE ACTED SO QUEER ABOUT--WHAT HAPPENED TO YOU ON 177 ELECTR
THE ISLANDS.
THEY WATCH HIM, WITH QUEER, PUZZLED EYES.) 260 GGBROW
BUT AT THE SAME TIME, IN SOME QUEER WAY, MORE 269 GGBROW
SELFLESS AND ASCETIC.
(AFTER A PAUSE--WITH A QUEER BROKEN LAUGH) 286 GGBROW
(WITH QUEER AGONY) YOU MEAN YOU WON'T& 289 GGBROW
IS GETTING A BIT QUEER AND IT'S TIME HE TOOK A 311 GGBROW
VACATION.
(GIVING HIM A QUEER LOOK) I'M SERIOUS. 315 GGBROW
(WITH A QUEER LOOK) WHY, DION, THAT ISN'T YOUR 316 GGBROW
SUIT.
NOW THAT'S A QUEER WISH FROM THE UGLY LIKE OF YOU,210 HA APE
GOD HELP YOU.
THEN STOPS, FIGHTING SOME QUEER STRUGGLE WITHIN 215 HA APE
HIMSELF--
THE COAL DUST STICKS LIKE BLACK MAKE-UP, GIVING 226 HA APE
THEM A QUEER,
IN THIS CAGE IS A QUEER KIND OF BABOON THAN EVER 229 HA APE
YOU'D FIND IN DARKEST AFRICY.
(WHO HAS BEEN STARING AT SOMETHING INSIDE--WITH 236 HA APE
QUEER EXCITEMENT)
I'M TELLING YOU THIS SO YOU'LL KNOW WHY IF DON 584 ICEMAN
ACTS A BIT QUEER.
IT'S STRANGE THE QUEER WAY HE SEEMED TO RECOGNIZE 638 ICEMAN
HIM.
IT'S THAT QUEER FEELING HE GIVES ME THAT I'M MIXE0666 ICEMAN
UP WITH HIM SOME WAY.
BEJEES, IT DOES QUEER THINGS TO YOU, 721 ICEMAN
HE'S A QUEER GUY. 516 INZONE
I SEEN RIGHT AWAY SOMETHIN' ON THE QUEER WAS UP SO519 INZONE
I SLIDES BACK INTO THE
STILL, UT'S DAMN QUEER, THE LOOKS AV UT. 520 INZONE
AIN'T THAT QUEER IN ITSELF& 522 INZONE
YOU GO THROUGH THE OTHERS, DRISC, AND SING OUT IF 531 INZONE
YOU SEES ANYTHIN' QUEER.
IT'S A QUEER MEDICINE IF IT TAKES AWAY YOUR 106 JOURNE
APPETITE.
APPARENT FIRST IN THIS CHORUS, A QUEER EXCITEMENT 287 LAZARU
BEGINS TO PERVADE THIS MOB.
IN A QUEER WHISPER) 305 LAZARU
(TREMBLING, IN A QUEER AGITATION) 308 LAZARU
(IN A QUEER STATE OF MINGLED EXALTATION AND FEAR--319 LAZARU
HE IS IN A STATE OF QUEER CONFLICTING EMOTION, 326 LAZARU
(FLYING INTO A QUEER RAGE) YOU LIE/ 331 LAZARU
(THEN IN A QUEER AWED WHISPER) 334 LAZARU
(SHE LAUGHS--A QUEER, VAGUE LITTLE INWARD LAUGH) 346 LAZARU
THAT YOU'VE BEEN CHANGING IN SOME QUEER WAY INSIDE 80 MANSNS
YOU.
(FORCES A SMILE.) THAT'S A QUEER CRAZY NOTION FOR 82 MANSNS
YOU TO HAVE, SIMON--
THERE'S A QUEER THING IN THE AIR HERE, THAT MAKES 88 MANSNS
YOU--
I DON'T KNOW WHAT YOU MEAN BY THAT QUEER TALK OF 92 MANSNS
MARKED CARDS AND LOADED DICE.
(WITH QUEER, HESITATING EMBARRASSMENT.) 106 MANSNS
THIS COSTUME IS A QUEER JUMBLE OF STUNNING EFFECTS390 MARCOM
THAT RECALL THE PARADE

QUEER

QUEER (CONT'D.)
WITH QUEER APPALLED WONDER THAT PUZZLES HIM 395 MARCOM
I'VE GOT QUEER NEWS FOR YOU, 410 MARCOM
HIS ATTITUDE A QUEER MIXTURE OF FAMILIARITY AND AN410 MARCOM
UNCERTAIN AWE.)
IN A QUEER HYSTERICAL STATE WHERE SHE DELIGHTS IN413 MARCOM
SELF-HUMILIATION)
I SAW SOMETHING QUEER/ 415 MARCOM
THAT WAS THEIR QUEER CLOTHES. 427 MARCOM
CRACKED VOICES ACCOMPANYING THE MUSIC IN QUEER, 433 MARCOM
BREAKING WAVES OF LAMENTATION,
OR TAKE THE OTHER KIND OF QUEER DRUNK HE GETS ON 33 MISBEG
SOMETIMES WHEN,
ALL I'VE SAID IS, WHEN A MAN GETS AS QUEER DRUNK 34 MISBEG
AS JIM,
FENCES ARE QUEER THINGS. 50 MISBEG
THOUGHT SOMETHING MUST BE QUEER, YOU COMING HOME 75 MISBEG
BEFORE THE INN CLOSED,
HE HAD ONE OF HIS QUEER FITS WHEN YOU CAN'T TELL. 82 MISBEG
IT WAS AFTER HE'D TURNED QUEER--EARLY IN THE NIGHT 87 MISBEG
BEFORE SIMPSON CAME.
BE GOD, JOSIE, DAMNED IF I DON'T THINK HE'S SO 99 MISBEG
QUEER DRUNK HIMSELF HE DON'T
DON'T GET IN ONE OF YOUR QUEER SPELLS, NOW. 120 MISBEG
(UNEASILY) STOP TALKING SO QUEER. 160 MISBEG
SHE MUST BE A QUEER CREATURE, FROM ALL HE'S TOLD 31 POET
ME.
I FEEL SHE'S STRANGE AND QUEER BEHIND HER LADY'S 80 POET
AIRS.
QUEER BLATHER ABOUT SIMON'S ANCESTORS, AND 87 POET
HERSELF, AND NAPOLEON, AND NATURE.
(WITH A QUEER PRIDE.) THE DIVIL HIMSELF COULDN'T 130 POET
KAPE CON MELODY FROM A DUSLY
YOU'VE A QUEER WAY OF TALKING. 141 POET
MOTHER SAID SHE'S BECOME QUITE QUEER LATELY... 5 STRANG
SHE KNOWS IN SOME QUEER WAY. 11 STRANG
SHE STARES AT MARSDEN BLANKLY AND SPEAKS IN QUEER 26 STRANG
FLAT TONES)
SHE LOOKS FROM ONE TO THE OTHER WITH A QUEER, 39 STRANG
QUICK, INQUISITIVE STARE.
(IN A QUEER FLAT VOICE) YES, HE'S DEAD--MY 39 STRANG
FATHER--WHOSE PASSION CREATED ME--
DO I SEEM QUEER? 40 STRANG
(IT'S A QUEER HOUSE, NED. 49 STRANG
OK SAID SOMETHING QUEER LIKE CHILDREN DO 60 STRANG
NATURALLY.
(SHE LAUGHS A QUEER GENTLE LAUGH FULL OF AMUSED 62 STRANG
BITTERNESS.)
(QUEER FELLOW, MARSDEN... 78 STRANG
(THINKING IN A QUEER STATE OF JEALOUS CONFUSION) 116 STRANG
CHARLIE HAS ALWAYS LOVED ME IN SOME QUEER WAY OF 117 STRANG
HIS OWN...
A QUEER EXPRESSION CAME OVER HER FACE... 119 STRANG
(THEN IN A QUEER, FUTILE RAGE) 132 STRANG
(SHE'S THE OLD QUEER NINA NOW... 134 STRANG
QUEER... 134 STRANG
QUEER KIND OF LOVE, MAYBE... 135 STRANG
BUT I KNOW THERE WAS SOMETHING QUEER IN HIS MIND 146 STRANG
AND THAT HE DID IT
LIFE AND SHE'S MORBIDLY JEALOUS OF YOU AND SUBJECT179 STRANG
TO QUEER DELUSIONS/
I ALWAYS HAD A QUEER FEELING SHE WAS DOING IT AS A185 STRANG
DUTY.
(THINKING IN AMAZEMENT, BUT NOT WITHOUT A QUEER 186 STRANG
SATISFACTION)
(WITH A BITTER GLOOMY AIR) LIFE IS DAMN QUEER, 186 STRANG
THAT'S ALL I'VE GOT TO SAY/
A QUEER AGITATION COMING COMING INTO HIS FACE.) 187 STRANG
(THINKING SUSPICIOUSLY) (WHAT A QUEER 188 STRANG
CREATURE/...
A QUEER STRUGGLE IS APPARENT IN HER FACE, HER 465 WELDED
WHOLE BODY.
(WITH A SUDDEN QUEER, EXULTANT PRIDE) 469 WELDED
(AGAIN STARING AT HER WITH STRANGE INTENSITY-- 473 WELDED
SUDDENLY WITH A QUEER LAUGH)
(THEN WITH A QUEER SORT OF SAVAGE TRIUMPH) 475 WELDED
(THEY SMILE WITH A QUEER UNDERSTANDING, THEIR ARMS480 WELDED
MOVE ABOUT EACH OTHER.
(IN A QUEER FAR-AWAY VOICE) NO. 487 WELDED

QUEERER
AN' HE'S LIABLE TO TURN OUT QUEERER THAN ANY OF US516 INZONE
THINK IF WE AIN'T CAREFUL.

QUEEREST
WELL, ALL I CAN SAY IS YOU'RE THE QUEEREST BOY I 271 AHWILD
EVER DID HEAR OF/
DESE WOODS IS SHO' FULL O' DE QUEEREST THINGS AT 193 EJONES
NIGHT.
I USED TO HEAR YOU SINGING AT THE QUEEREST TIMES-- 83 ELECTR
SO SWEET AND CLEAR AND PURE/
I HAD THE QUEEREST FEELING JUST THEN THAT 145 STRANG
SOMEONE--

QUEERLY
(LOOKING QUEERLY AT HIM, PERPLEXED AND WORRIED, 34 ANNA
(LOOKING AT HER QUEERLY) DO YOU MEAN TO SAY 156 BEYOND
YOU'RE USED TO IT?
(QUEERLY INTERESTED) D'YE THINK SO, ABBIE? 231 DESIRE
(QUEERLY) DOWN WHAR IT'S RESTFUL--WHAR IT'S 238 DESIRE
WARM--DOWN T' TH' BARN.
(ADDRESSING THE AIR--QUEERLY) 242 DESIRE
(QUEERLY) DIDN'T YE FEEL HER PASSIN'--GOIN' BACK 246 DESIRE
T' HER GRAVE?
HAVEN'T YOU NOTICED HOW QUEERLY SHE ACTS? 86 ELECTR
(HE LAUGHS QUEERLY AND APPROACHES THEM. 261 GGBROW
(QUEERLY) I LIKE TO WATCH MEN DIE. 301 LAZARU
QUEERLY) THE MISTAKE BEGAN WHEN GOD WAS CREATED 42 STRANG
IN A MALE IMAGE.
HOW QUEERLY THINGS WORK OUT/.... 112 STRANG

1270

QUEERLY (CONT'D.)
MY LIFE QUEERLY IDENTIFIED WITH SAM'S AND 135 STRANG
DARRELL'S....
(LOOKING UP AT HIM QUEERLY) SAY, YOU TALK NUTTY. 473 WELDED

QUELLS
HE QUELLS THE UPROAR WITH A SHOUT) 216 HA APE

QUERULOUS
DRAWN AND CAREWORN FOR ITS YEARS, AND SAD, 291 GGBROW
RESIGNED, BUT A BIT QUERULOUS.)

QUERULOUSLY
(QUERULOUSLY) WELL, 582 ICEMAN

QUERULOUSNESS
(PROUD BUT PRETENDING QUERULOUSNESS) 427 MARCOM

QUEST
IN QUEST OF THE SECRET WHICH IS HIDDEN OVER THERE, 85 BEYOND
BEYOND THE HORIZONS
SO NOW I'LL HAVE TO FORESWEAR MY QUEST FOR HIM AND282 GGBROW
GO IN FUR THE OMNIPRESENT
THE PEACE, THE END OF THE QUEST, THE LAST HARBOR, 153 JOURNE
AND THE WISH IN HIS HEART TOLD HIM HIS QUEST WAS 111 MANSNS
ENDED.

QUESTION
WHY'D YOU ASK ME SUCH A QUESTION, ANNIE? 549 'ILE
(IGNORING THIS QUESTION--COMMANDINGLY) 550 'ILE
I'M GOING TO ASK YOU A QUESTION, AND I WANT AN 206 AHWILD
HONEST ANSWER.
BUT CAN I BE ASKING YOU ONE QUESTION, MISS, HAS MY 35 ANNA
HEAD IN A PUZZLES
(NOT SEEMING TO HAVE HEARD HER QUESTION--SADLY) 64 ANNA
AIN'T THAT JUST LIKE A FOOL WOMAN'S QUESTIONS 94 BEYOND
"MA'AM," SAYS I, "I COULDN'T RIGHTLY ANSWER THAT 94 BEYOND
QUESTION.
(TURNING TO THIS UNCLE) YOU HAVEN'T ANSWERED BY 104 BEYOND
QUESTION, UNCLE DICK.
DON'T BE SO SILLY. THERE'S NO QUESTION OF RIGHT. 120 BEYOND
(HE LEANS OVER AND ASKS HER A QUESTION.) 465 CARIBE
FOOLISH QUESTION, BILL. 496 DAYS
FIRST ANSWER ME FRANKLY ONE QUESTION. 507 DAYS
I'M SORRY I BUTTED IN WITH A SILLY QUESTION. 534 DAYS
YOU SAID THE QUESTION OF HER FORGIVING DOESN'T 539 DAYS
COME UP IN YOUR NOVEL.
THE QUESTION DOESN'T COME UP IN MY STORY, AS 539 DAYS
YOU'LL SEE, BUT--
THE NURSE SHAKES HER HEAD, ANSWERING HIS QUESTION.556 DAYS
THERE'S NO QUESTION OF-- 556 DAYS
WHAT RIGHT HEY YE T' QUESTION ME 'BOUT HIMS 264 DESIRE
(SHAKING HER HEAD--SLOWLY) IT AIN'T A QUESTION OF517 DIFRNT
TIME, CALEB.
IT'S A QUESTION OF SOMETHING BEING DEAD. 517 DIFRNT
(EMBARRASSED BY THIS DIRECT QUESTION) 536 DIFRNT
(IGNORING HER QUESTION) I SEED WHAT HE WAS COMIN'540 DIFRNT
TO YEARS BACK.
IT ISN'T A QUESTION OF RUBE... 455 DYNAMO
BUT NOW ARE YOU, VINNIE, THAT'S THE QUESTIONS. 13 ELECTR
(THEN, AS IF SHE WERE AFRAID OF AN ANSWER TO THIS 16 ELECTR
QUESTION,
(THEN AS IF SHE FELT SHE MUST DEFEND HER QUESTION 18 ELECTR
(BUT HE AT ONCE ATTRIBUTES THE QUESTION TO HER 23 ELECTR
NAIVETE--LAUGHINGLY)
IF IT WAS A QUESTION OF SOME WOMAN TAKING YOU FROM 41 ELECTR
ME,
THERE'S NO QUESTION OF ACCUSING YOU OF THAT. 51 ELECTR
IT ISN'T FOR ME TO QUESTION THE ARRANGEMENTS SHE'S 69 ELECTR
MADE, JOE.
AND YET YOU QUESTION ME AS IF YOU SUSPECTED ME, 88 ELECTR
TOO/
WHAT A FOOLISH QUESTION, DEAR/ 89 ELECTR
IT'S A QUESTION OF-- 96 ELECTR
(THEN, WITHOUT GIVING HER TIME TO ANSWER HIS 108 ELECTR
QUESTION,
WHY DO YOU ASK SUCH A FOOL QUESTIONS 159 ELECTR
I HOPE YOU REALIZE THERE'S NO MORE QUESTION OF ANY163 ELECTR
FRIENDSHIP BETWEEN US.
(SER* PRETENDS NOT TO HEAR THE QUESTION, AVOIDING 171 ELECTR
HER EYES)
AND I'M INTERESTED IN THAT GERM WHICH WRIGGLES 296 GGBROW
LIKE A QUESTION MARK OF
HE DOESN'T HEAR UNLESS A DIRECT QUESTION IS PUT TO 12 HUGHIE
HIM.
A QUESTION IS TREMBLING ON HIS PARTED LIPS, 35 HUGHIE
I WAS BORN CONDEMNED TO BE ONE OF THOSE WHO HAS TO590 ICEMAN
SEE ALL SIDES OF A QUESTION.
THE QUESTIONS MULTIPLY FOR YOU UNTIL IN THE END 590 ICEMAN
IT'S ALL QUESTION AND NO ANSWER.
AND DON'T THINK WE WILL QUESTION HOW YOU GOT IT. 596 ICEMAN
BUT HIS REPLY IS NOT TO HARRY'S QUESTION, 707 ICEMAN
IT'S NOT A QUESTION OF MY BEING MISERLY, AS YOU'D 33 JOURNE
LIKE TO MAKE OUT.
HE GLANCES AWAY, IGNORING HER QUESTION BUT SHE 81 JOURNE
DOESN'T SEEM TO EXPECT AN ANSWER.
THAT IS THE ONLY QUESTION. 132 JOURNE
BUT TO THINK WHEN IT'S A QUESTION OF YOUR SON 145 JOURNE
HAVING CONSUMPTION.
SUDDENLY LAZARUS SAID "YES" AS IF HE WERE 277 LAZARU
ANSWERING A QUESTION IN JESUS' EYES.
(CARRYING THE QUESTION FALTERINGLY BACK INTO 279 LAZARU
SILENCE)
(SUDDENLY BLURTS OUT THE QUESTION WHICH IS IN THE 279 LAZARU
MINDS OF ALL)
THEN HE LOOKS UP TO THE STARS AND, AS IF ANSWERING293 LAZARU
A QUESTION,
(THEN GRUFFLY, ASHAMED OF HIS QUESTION) 293 LAZARU
PUT YOURSELF THAT QUESTION--AS A JESTER/ 308 LAZARU
I HAVE A MIND TO QUESTION HIM. 316 LAZARU
I WOULD QUESTION YOU ABOUT YOUR MAGIC. 340 LAZARU
NOW QUESTION, AND SNEER AND LAUGH AT YOUR DREAMS, 40 MANSNS
AND SLEEP WITH UGLINESS,

QUICK

QUESTION (CONT'D.)

THERE CAN BE NO QUESTION OF MY GIVING UP MY PROSPEROUS BUSINESS HERE — 59 MANSNS

I TOLD YOU THERE COULD BE NO QUESTION OF OBLIGATIONS. — 65 MANSNS

THERE'S NO QUESTION ABOUT THE DANGER. — 156 MANSNS

ONE MORE QUESTION. — 173 MISBEG

(ARROGANTLY THREATENING.) ARE YOU PRESUMING TO QUESTION MY CONDUCT — 99 POET

LITTLE YANKEE CLIQUE THERE WOULD BE NO QUESTION — 110 POET OF A HASTY MARRIAGE.

IT'S A QUESTION OF MY HONOR/ — 127 POET

IT'S A QUESTION OF MY HAPPINESS, AND I WON'T HAVE 127 POET YOUR MAD INTERFERING--/

YOU DARE TO THINK THERE CAN BE ANY QUESTION NOW OF127 POET YOUR MARRYING

HOW ANSWER THE FIERCE QUESTION OF ALL THOSE DEAD AND MAIMED..... — 5 STRANG

SUDDENLY ASKING A NECESSARY QUESTION IN HER NURSE'S COOL, EFFICIENT TONES) — 28 STRANG

SHE ANSWERS AS IF THEY HAD ASKED A QUESTION.) — 39 STRANG

AND IT'S ONLY A QUESTION OF TIME WHEN--WHY, TO SHOW YOU, COLE-- — 54 STRANG

THERE'S NO QUESTION OF IMPOSITION, CHARLIE. — 98 STRANG

HE ASKED FOR MORE MONEY AND THEY GAVE IT WITHOUT — 113 STRANG QUESTION....

THINKING A FIERCE QUESTION) — 125 STRANG

IT WAS A TACTLESS QUESTION. — 127 STRANG

(LOOKING ABOUT HER IN THE AIR--WITH A DAZED QUESTION) — 179 STRANG

EVER TO QUESTION IT OR BE DISSATISFIED WITH ITS REWARDS. — 184 STRANG

FIRSTLY, LET ME ASK GORDON A QUESTION. — 195 STRANG

(DULLY, WITH NO MEANING TO HIS QUESTION--LIKE AN AUTOMATON) — 473 WELDED

QUESTIONING

(HE GOES AND PICKS UP THE CHAIR, THEN TURNING ON THE STILL-QUESTIONING ANNA-- — 50 ANNA

(WITH SUDDEN FIERCE QUESTIONING) — 76 ANNA

(THEN FRIGHTENEDLY QUESTIONING) — 562 DAYS

WITH A RAPT, QUESTIONING, LISTENING LOOK) — 484 DYNAMO

(STARING AT HER WITH A QUESTIONING DREAD--FORCING A SCORNFUL SMILE) — 18 ELECTR

ORIN IS QUESTIONING HER SUSPICIOUSLY.) — 80 ELECTR

SHE MADE ME FEEL, IN THE PROUD QUESTIONING OF HER 355 LAZARU SCORNFUL EYES,

(QUESTIONING HESITATINGLY) YOU'VE WANTED ME, — 44 STRANG

NINAS

(SHE EXCHANGES A QUICK, QUESTIONING GLANCE WITH — 501 VOYAGE

JOEL, WHO NODS BACK AT HER--

STARING INTO EACH OTHER'S EYES WITH AN APPREHENSIVE QUESTIONING. — 480 WELDED

QUESTIONINGLY

HE LOOKS QUESTIONINGLY AT HER AVERTED FACE — 276 GGBROW

HE TURNS THESE OVER IN HIS HANDS AND LOOKS AT THE 528 INZONE OTHERS QUESTIONINGLY.)

THEN ALL REPEAT AFTER HIM QUESTIONINGLY AND FRIGHTENEDLY.) — 279 LAZARU

(LOOKS AROUND AT HIM QUESTIONINGLY) — 382 MARCOM

QUESTIONS

AND TACTFULLY REFRAINS FROM ALL QUESTIONS.) — 296 AHWILD

(HE IS ANSWERING ROBERT'S QUESTIONS WITH GREAT RELUCTANCE.) — 161 BEYOND

(SNAPPISHLY) IF YE HEERD US THEY HAIN'T NO NEED — 231 DESIRE ASKIN' QUESTIONS.

ASK ME NO QUESTIONS AND I'LL TELL YOU NO LIES. — 527 DIFNRT

I HAVEN'T ASKED CHRISTINE MANNON ANY EMBARRASSING — 71 ELECTR QUESTIONS.

(LONG AGO HE GAVE UP CARING WHETHER QUESTIONS WERE 12 HUGHIE PERSONAL OR NOT.)

(FROWNS) DON'T ASK QUESTIONS. — 584 ICEMAN

YOU'D ASK ME QUESTIONS AND TAKE WHAT I SAID SERIOUSLY. — 588 ICEMAN

THE QUESTIONS MULTIPLY FOR YOU UNTIL IN THE END IT'S ALL QUESTION AND NO ANSWER. — 590 ICEMAN

QUESTIONS OF A STRANGER, FOR THAT'S ALL YOU ARE TO591 ICEMAN ME.

I AM ASKING THE QUESTIONS. — 606 ICEMAN

HE'S AFRAID I MIGHT ASK HIM A FEW QUESTIONS. — 665 ICEMAN

WHAT QUESTIONS? — 668 ICEMAN

SAY, LISTEN, WHAT D'YUH MEAN ABOUT HIM BEIN' SCARED YOU'D ASK HIM QUESTIONS? — 668 ICEMAN

DON'T ASK QUESTIONS, YOU DUMB MOP? — 694 ICEMAN

I DARE NOT SPEAK BEFORE HE QUESTIONS ME. — 327 LAZARU

IF ONE OF THEM WAS AWAKE AND SAW YOU HE'D BE SO EXCITED AND FULL OF QUESTIONS-- — 57 MANSNS

(HE DECIDES IT'S BETTER FOR THE PRESENT TO ASK NO 158 MISBEG QUESTIONS.

I DIDN'T CALL YOU HERE TO ANSWER QUESTIONS ABOUT WHAT'S NONE OF YOUR BUSINESS. — 162 MISBEG

DON'T TORMENT ME WITH YOUR SINFUL QUESTIONS/ — 149 POET

IT IS THE INTERLUDE THAT GENTLY QUESTIONS... — 5 STRANG

QUESTIONS DIE IN THE SILENCE OF THIS PEACE... — 91 STRANG

DAMN HIS QUESTIONS/.... — 125 STRANG

HIDE THE BOAT OR HE'LL ASK QUESTIONS. — 151 STRANG

JOHN QUESTIONS HER WITH FIERCE DISAPPOINTMENT) — 466 WELDED

QUICK

UP THE PLATES AND CASTS A QUICK GLANCE UPWARD AT THE SKYLIGHT.. — 536 *ILE

THEN SPEAK YOUR SAY AND BE QUICK ABOUT IT. — 544 *ILE

QUICK/ — 545 *ILE

(AFTER A QUICK UNDERSTANDING GLANCE AT HIM) — 196 AHWILD

AND GET OUT QUICK, IF YOU DON'T WANT A KICK IN THE203 AHWILD REAR TO HELP YOU/

AND ONE CAME AND HE WASN'T QUICK ENOUGH, AND IT WENT OFF ALMOST ON TOP OF-- — 206 AHWILD

RICHARD GIVES HIM A QUICK SIDE GLANCE AND GROWS MORE GUILTILY SELF-CONSCIOUS.) — 206 AHWILD

QUICK (CONT'D.)

MRS. MILLER GIVES HER A QUICK SIDE GLANCE) — 212 AHWILD

LET'S HAVE DINNER QUICK/ — 220 AHWILD

(WITH A QUICK LOOK TOWARD THE BAR, SHE STEALTHILY 239 AHWILD PULLS UP HER DRESS--

BEAT IT, YOU AND BEAT IT QUICK-- — 248 AHWILD

SEEMS TO ME YOU WOKE UP PRETTY QUICK--JUST AFTER YOUR PA LEFT THE HOUSE/ — 269 AHWILD

I LIKE TO THE QUICK BETTER MYSELF--MORE STYLISH. — 272 AHWILD

(THE AFTER A QUICK FURTIVE GLANCE AT RICHARD, — 294 AHWILD

YOU TAL ME LIE FOR TAL MARTHY, LARRY, SO'S SHE GAT 10 ANNA OFF BARGE QUICK.

SHE DIE POOTY QUICK AFTER THAT--ALL'LONE. — 27 ANNA

(WITH A QUICK MOVEMENT HE PUTS HIS ARMS ABOUT HER — 33 ANNA WAIST)

QUICK AND CLANE. — 36 ANNA

CHRIS WANDERS ABOUT THE ROOM, CASTING QUICK, UNEASY SIDE GLANCES AT HER FACE, — 41 ANNA

I'D GET THE HELL OUT OF THIS BARGE SO QUICK YOU COULDN'T SEE ME FOR THE DUST. — 42 ANNA

WELL, THEN, I'LL MAKE UP YOUR MIND FOR YOU BLOODY — 55 ANNA QUICK.

AND THEN SHE CALLS ME A FOOL REAL SPITEFUL AND TACKS AWAY FROM ME QUICK. — 95 BEYOND

ROBERT CASTS A QUICK GLANCE AT ANDREW, NOTICING THE LATTER'S DISCOMFITED LOOK, — 140 BEYOND

I DIDN'T KNOW IF YOU'D WANT TO SHIP AWAY AGEN SO QUICK AN' I TOLD HIM SO. — 141 BEYOND

FROM NOW ON I'LL PICK UP SO QUICK I'LL SURPRISE YOU-- — 145 BEYOND

ANDREW CASTS A QUICK GLANCE ABOUT THE ROOM) — 154 BEYOND

(WITH A QUICK GLANCE AT RUTH) — 161 BEYOND

(CASTING A QUICK GLANCE OVER HER SHOULDER) — 464 CARIBEE

(TUMBLE OVER THE SIDE DAMN QUICK/ — 473 CARIBEE

HE CASTS A QUICK GLANCE ABOUT THE ROOM, AND SEEING555 CROSS NO ONE THERE,

(WITH QUICK INTUITION) YOU BROUGHT HIM UP HERE-- 563 CROSS SO THAT I WOULDN'T KNOW/

FATHER BAIRD GIVES JOHN A QUICK GLANCE AGAIN--THEN905 DAYS CASUALLY)

JOHN FROWNS AND GIVES HIS UNCLE A QUICK UNEASY GLANCE.) — 905 DAYS

(HE BREAKS OFF AND GIVES JOHN A QUICK GLANCE, — 907 DAYS

HE CASTS CASTS A QUICK GLANCE AT ELSA, THEN LOOKS537 DAYS AS QUICKLY AWAY.

(GIVES A QUICK ANXIOUS LOOK AT ELSA-- — 538 DAYS

(HE GIVES A QUICK GLANCE AT ELSA, AS IF TO CATCH HER REACTION TO THIS, — 539 DAYS

HEARS WHAT SHE HAS TO REPORT, GIVES HER SOME QUICK558 DAYS INSTRUCTIONS.

BUT WE GUT T' DO SOMETHIN' QUICK — 260 DESIRE

ALTHOUGH HER BODY IS SLIGHT AND THIN, THERE IS A — 494 DIFNRT QUICK.

(WITH QUICK RESENTFUL RESOLUTION) — 506 DIFNRT

(AFTER A QUICK GLANCE AT HER FACE--SOOTHINGLY) — 507 DIFNRT

HER QUICK, EFFICIENT MOVEMENTS. — 507 DIFNRT

COME DOWN QUICK/ — 531 DIFNRT

(WOUNDED TO THE QUICK-- FURIOUSLY) — 542 DIFNRT

AND LET'S SEE HOW QUICK HE'D TURN HIS BACK ON YE543 DIFNRT

HE MUST HAVE KICKED IN THAT QUICK/ — 548 DIFNRT

TAKING DOWN ALL THE CURTAINS WITH QUICK MECHANICAL548 DIFNRT MOVEMENTS.

I'VE GOT TO FIX UP A SCHEME ON HIM QUICK.... — 432 DYNAMO

GET OUT OF HERE QUICK/ — 434 DYNAMO

GIVING A QUICK SIDE GLANCE AT ADA TO SEE IF SHE'S 440 DYNAMO

COME QUICK, ADA/ — 450 DYNAMO

GET IN THERE/ QUICK/ — 487 DYNAMO

GREAT FATHER (SHE TOUCHES HER FOREHEAD TO THE FLOOR WITH QUICK MECHANICAL JERK) — 175 EJONES

(PROUDLY) I GUT BRAINS AND I USES 'EM QUICK. — 178 EJONES

AND I'SE GOT ALL DE MONEY IN SIGHT, I RESIGNS ON — 180 EJONES DE SPOT AND BEATS IT QUICK.

REPEATS ONE WURD OF IT, I ENDS YO' STEALIN' UN DIS181 EJONES YEARTH MIGHTY DAMN QUICK/

WHY IT COME DARK SO QUICK LIKE OATS — 189 EJONES

(FRIGHTENEDLY) I BETTER BEAT IT QUICK WHEN — 191 EJONES

HE MAKES A QUICK SIGNAL WITH HIS HAND. — 203 EJONES

(IN A QUICK WHISPER TO MINNIE) — 11 ELECTR

(GASPINGLY) QUICK--MEDICINE/ — 62 ELECTR

(IN A QUICK WHISPER) DON'T LET HER KNOW YOU SUSPECT HER. — 100 ELECTR

QUIET/ — 113 ELECTR

QUICK/ — 114 ELECTR

QUICK. — 115 ELECTR

(KISSES HER--PITYINGLY) I'LL BE AS QUICK AS I — 119 ELECTR POSSIBLY CAN.

(THEN AFTER A QUICK LOOK AT HIM--IN A CONFIDING TONE) — 148 ELECTR

QUICK/ — 160 ELECTR

(THEN WITH A QUICK, MEANING, MOCKING GLANCE AT LAVINIA) — 167 ELECTR

FUNNY HOW IT'S GOT HOLD OF BROWN SO QUICK/ — 314 GGBROW

(WITH A QUICK PRANCING MOVEMENT, HE HAS OPENED THE318 GGBROW DOOR, GONE THROUGH,

HE TRIED TO APOLOGIZE, BUT I SHUT HIM UP QUICK. — 26 HUGHIE

I WANT QUICK ACTION FOR MY DOUGH.* — 32 HUGHIF

GET IT OUT OF YOUR HEAD QUICK, CHARLIE, — 33 HUGHIE

(HE DARTS A QUICK GLANCE AT THE CLERK'S FACE AND BEGINS TO HEDGE HASTILY. — 36 HUGHIE

HE FLASHED IT LIKE HE FORGOT AND DEN TRIED TO HIDE583 ICEMAN IT QUICK.

GIMME DE BOTTLE QUICK, ROCKY, BEFORE HE CHANGES HIS MIND/ — 586 ICEMAN

(GRINS GENIALLY) YES, DEAR OLD BESS HAD A QUICK — 608 ICEMAN TEMPER.

SO MOVE QUICK/ — 669 ICEMAN

BEJEES, GIVE ME A DRINK QUICK/ — 690 ICEMAN

QUICK

QUICK (CONT'D.)

IT WAS LIKE A GAME, SIZING PEOPLE UP QUICK, 711 ICEMAN
AND WE WANT A DRINK QUICK/ 725 ICEMAN
WITH QUICK LOOKS OUT OF THE CORNERS OF THEIR EYES,523 INZONE
WE GOTTER DO SOMETHIN' QUICK OR-- 523 INZONE
'IS YOU'LL DO THE EXPLAININ'--AN' DAMN QUICK, OR 525 INZONE
WE'LL KNOW THE REASON WHY.
QUICK, DRISCL 525 INZONE
I ONLY PUT THAT BOX THERE SO I COULD GET IT QUICK 527 INZONE
IN CASE WE WERE TORPEDOED.
AND I MADE A QUICK TURNOVER ON IT FOR A FINE 15 JOURNE
PROFIT.
(HE GIVES HER A QUICK, WORRIED LOOK.) 16 JOURNE
SHE GIVES A QUICK, SUSPICIOUS GLANCE FROM ONE TO 39 JOURNE
THE OTHER.
(WITH A QUICK, STRANGE, CALCULATING, ALMOST SLY 49 JOURNE
GLANCE AT HIM.)
HE STOPS COUGHING AND GIVES HER A QUICK 58 JOURNE
APPREHENSIVE GLANCE.
HE COMES TO THE TABLE WITH A QUICK MEASURING LOOK 65 JOURNE
AT THE BOTTLE OF WHISKEY.
THAT SHUT HIM UP QUICK. 103 JOURNE
WELL, IT FINISHED HIM QUICK--THAT AND THE 137 JOURNE
CONSUMPTION--
OR ANY KIND OF GET-RICH-QUICK SWINDLE/ 141 JOURNE
COME TRAMPING UP AT THE DOUBLE-QUICK, 291 LAZARU
AND ARE SULKY AND QUICK-TEMPERED WITH THE GREEKS. 298 LAZARU
(WHO HAS MOVED TO LAZARUS' SIDE DEFENSIVELY--IN A 332 LAZARU
QUICK WHISPER)
QUICK/ 338 LAZARU
QUICK, LAZARUS/ 367 LAZARU
TO REGAIN A SOUND POSITION BY MAKING A QUICK 32 MANSNS
PROFIT IN WESTERN LANDS.
(SHE GIVES A QUICK BITTER LOOK UP AT HIS FACE AND 57 MANSNS
MOVES HER SHOULDER AWAY.)
(WITH A QUICK RESENTFUL LOOK AT SIMON.) 124 MANSNS
(GIVES HER A QUICK RESENTFUL JEALOUS LOOK.) 129 MANSNS
(AFTER A QUICK GLANCE AT THE PAD.) 151 MANSNS
QUICK/ 187 MANSNS
(WITH A QUICK MOVEMENT OF HIS OWN HAND, CAPTURES 355 MARCOM
HERS THROUGH THE BARS)
MARK IS SURPRISINGLY QUICK AT FIGURES. 360 MARCOM
I'LL BET ANYTHING IT WAS SOME QUICK-THINKER WHO'D 394 MARCOM
JUST DISCOVERED A GOLD MINE/
(GIVES HER A QUICK, PROBING SIDE GLANCE--CASUALLY) 21 MISBEG
(AGAIN WITH A QUICK SIDE GLANCE--CASUALLY) 21 MISBEG
(HE GIVES HER A QUICK, CURIOUS SIDE GLANCE WHICH 33 MISBEG
SHE DOESN'T NOTICE.)
YOU WON'T BE ABLE TO DRAG OUT THE OLD BOTTLE QUICK 46 MISBEG
ENOUGH.
(SNEERINGLY) A LEADING ARISTOCRAT IN OUR LAND OF 47 MISBEG
THE FREE AND GET-RICH-QUICK.
(WITH A QUICK CHANGE OF PACE TO A WHEEDLING 63 MISBEG
CONFIDENTIAL TONE)
(THREATENINGLY) IF YOU'RE GOING TO YOUR ROOM, 80 MISBEG
YOU'D BETTER GO QUICK/
WE'VE GOT TO THINK OF A NEW SCHEME QUICK TO GET ME 99 MISBEG
AWAY--
(WITH A QUICK GLANCE AT HER FACE) 105 MISBEG
SHE TAKES A QUICK GLANCE AT HIS FACE--STARTLEDLY) 112 MISBEG
(SHE PULLS HIS HEAD BACK AND KISSES HIM ON THE 118 MISBEG
LIPS--A QUICK, SHY KISS)
AND YOU HAD TO DO SOMETHING QUICK 163 MISBEG
(GIVING HIM A QUICK GLANCE) 166 MISBEG
(WITH A QUICK GLANCE AT HIM) 10 POET
(WITH A QUICK CHANGE OF MANNER--EAGERLY,) 38 POET
(THEN WITH A QUICK CHANGE OF MOOD, HEARTILY,) 101 POET
(WITH A QUICK MOVEMENT PINS HERS DOWN WITH ONE OF 107 POET
HIS.)
(AFTER A QUICK GLANCE AT HER.) 129 POET
BUT CON WAS TOO QUICK. 155 POET
(WITH A QUICK MOVEMENT HE HITS HER VICIOUSLY OVER 581 ROPE
THE ARM WITH HIS STICK.
QUICK NOW/ 584 ROPE
AND GORDON WAS QUICK TO AGREE WITH ME/ 11 STRANG
(SHE TURNS TO MARSDEN WITH A QUICK SMILE) 15 STRANG
SHE LOOKS FROM ONE TO THE OTHER WITH A QUEER, 39 STRANG
QUICK, INQUISITIVE STARE.
(AFTER A QUICK, KEEN GLANCE, THINKING) 81 STRANG
GET THAT OUT OF YOUR HEAD QUICK/ 103 STRANG
HIS EYES ARE FULL OF A QUICK-TEMPERED 137 STRANG
SENSITIVENESS.
QUICK, GORDON--- 181 STRANG
(ALSO AFTER A QUICK KEEN GLANCE AT GORDON'S FACE--190 STRANG
THINKING)
(SHE EXCHANGES A QUICK, QUESTIONING GLANCE WITH 501 VOYAGE
JOE, WHO NODS BACK AT HER--
(FROM BEHIND THE BAR) QUICK, NAH/ 508 VOYAGE
(ENTWINING HER HANDS FROM HIS WITH A QUICK 457 WELDED
MOVEMENT--SARCASTICALLY)
(HE LAUGHS HARSHLY AND TURNS WITH A QUICK MOVEMENT476 WELDED
TOWARD THE DOOR)

QUICKENED
(TO CHRIS WHO HAS QUICKENED TO INSTANT ATTENTION 52 ANNA
AT HIS DAUGHTER'S GOOD-BY AND
THE SILENCE BROKEN ONLY BY THE FAR-OFF QUICKENED 190 EJONFS
THROB OF THE TOM-TOM.
CRYING WITH FEAR--AND BY THE QUICKENED, EVER 198 EJONES
LOUDER BEAT OF THE TOM-TOM.)

QUICKENS
AND HE'LL NEVER LIVE UNTIL HIS LIBERATED DUST 296 GGBROW
QUICKENS INTO EARTH/

QUICKER
THAT'LL MAKE THE TIME PASS QUICKER. 276 AHWILD
(HE SPRINGS TOWARD THE PORCH BUT CABOT IS QUICKER 255 DESIRE
AND GETS IN BETWEEN.)
WHICH IS A TRIFLE LOUDER AND QUICKER THAN AT THE 190 EJONES
CLOSE OF THE PREVIOUS

QUICKER (CONT'D.)
THE TOM-TOM BEATS LOUDER, QUICKER, WITH A MORE 199 EJONES
INSISTENT, TRIUMPHANT PULSATION.)
EDMUND IS QUICKER. 170 JOURNE
HER WORDS COMING QUICKER AND QUICKER AS HER VOICE 346 LAZARU
BECOMES FAINTER AND FAINTER)

QUICKER'N
(DARKLY) YOU SEE IF AY'M MAN--MAYBE QUICKER'N YOU 48 ANNA

QUICKLY
HE QUICKLY SHOVES THE LETTER INTO THE INSIDE 208 AHWILD
POCKET OF HIS COAT
(SHE QUICKLY LIGHTS THE OTHER TWO BULBS.) 211 AHWILD
(THEN QUICKLY) THAT WAS A GOOD NOTION OF NAT'S, 212 AHWILD
(THEN QUICKLY) I'M NOT TRYING TO LEAD YOU ASTRAY,218 AHWILD
UNDERSTAND.
(QUICKLY INTERPOSING, TRYING TO STAVE OFF THE 229 AHWILD
STORY)
AS IF AFRAID OF MEETING HER EYE, LOOKS QUICKLY 250 AHWILD
BACK AT HIS PAPER AGAIN.)
(COMES TO HER QUICKLY AND PUTS HER ARM AROUND HER)260 AHWILD
(THEN QUICKLY AND INDIGNANTLY) 266 AHWILD
(QUICKLY) AT LEAST, SO I'VE BEEN TOLD. 267 AHWILD
(STOPPED FOR A MOMENT--THEN QUICKLY) 283 AHWILD
(QUICKLY, AFRAID HE'D GONE TOO FAR) 284 AHWILD
HE LETS GO INSTINCTIVELY AND SHE JUMPS QUICKLY OUT284 AHWILD
OF THE BOAT
SHE GLANCES QUICKLY FROM SON TO HUSBAND AND 296 AHWILD
IMMEDIATELY KNOWS THAT ALL IS WELL
THEN QUICKLY FROM HIS FATHER TO HIS MOTHER AND 297 AHWILD
BACK AGAIN, STRANGELY,
(QUICKLY--TAKING IT) OH, DEIN IT COMES FROM MY 8 ANNA
DAUGHTER, ANNA.
(MARTHY GOES QUICKLY OUT OF THE FAMILY ENTRANCE.) 19 ANNA
(HE GETS TO HIS FEET QUICKLY AND PICKS UP HER BAG) 22 ANNA
(THEN SEEING HIS HURT EXPRESSION--QUICKLY) 37 ANNA
BURKE SPRINGS TO HIS FEET QUICKLY IN TIME TO MEET 49 ANNA
THE ATTACK.
(QUICKLY) AY DON'T. 67 ANNA
(QUICKLY) IT'S ALL RIGHT, MAT. 77 ANNA
(TURNING TO HER QUICKLY, IN SURPRISE--SLOWLY) 88 BEYOND
(SWALLOWING HARD, LOOKS QUICKLY FROM ONE TO THE 99 BEYOND
OTHER OF THEM.
(TURNING TO HIM QUICKLY) ANDY/ 104 BEYOND
QUICKLY TURNING AWAY AGAIN FROM THE OTHERS. 140 BEYOND
(SHE TURNS QUICKLY AWAY AGAIN. 141 BEYOND
(SHE WIPES HER EYES QUICKLY AND WITHOUT LOOKING AT143 BEYOND
ROBERT.
(HE GOES QUICKLY TO THE WINDOW IN THE REAR LEFT, 150 BEYOND
RUTH SPRINGS TO HER FEET AND COMES QUICKLY TO THE 150 BEYOND
TABLE, LEFT.
(QUICKLY) NO. 151 BEYOND
(SHE CLOSES THE DOOR AND GOES QUICKLY TO HER 151 BEYOND
MOTHER AND SHAKES HER BY THE
(GLANCING UP QUICKLY--IN A HARSH VOICE) 154 BEYOND
(HE PULLS HIS ARM BACK QUICKLY WITH A SHUDDER OF 469 CARIBE
DISGUST AND TAKES A DRINK.
(QUICKLY--IN A LOW VOICE) WHO KNIFED HIMS 472 CARIBE
(THEY WALK QUICKLY--ALMOST RUN--OFF TO THE LEFT. 473 CARIBE
(HE FLASHES IT ON HER TERROR-STRICKEN FACE, THEN 572 CROSS
QUICKLY AROUND THE ROOM.
(QUICKLY--CHANGING THE SUBJECT) 506 DAYS
(QUICKLY) BUT NOT THE IGNORANT, BIGOTED SORT, 510 DAYS
PLEASE UNDERSTAND.
(QUICKLY-- 511 DAYS
(QUICKLY, RAISING HIS VOICE TO A CONVERSATIONAL 527 DAYS
TONE)
HE CASTS A QUICK GLANCE AT ELSA, THEN LOOKS AS 537 DAYS
QUICKLY AWAY.
COMES QUICKLY AROUND THE END OF THE BED TO JOHN.) 554 DAYS
(THEN QUICKLY) AND NOW I'VE SATISFIED YOU ON 556 DAYS
THAT, LIE DOWN AS YOU PROMISED.
TABLE, FRONT. COMES QUICKLY TO THE DOORWAY. 560 DAYS
(HE TURNS AND WALKS QUICKLY OFF LEFT, REAR, TOWARD217 DESIRE
THE BARN.
(THEN QUICKLY) WHY HAIN'T YE T' WUK$ 227 DESIRE
ABBIE SEES HIM AND TURNS AWAY QUICKLY WITH 230 DESIRE
UNCONCEALED AVERSION.
(QUICKLY) NOT AS I KNOW ON. 500 DIFRNT
FINALLY SHE MAKES A DECISION. GOES QUICKLY TO THE 501 DIFRNT
DOOR ON THE RIGHT AND CALLS)
(QUICKLY) OH, THAT'S ALL SETTLED, JOHN. 513 DIFRNT
(CATCHING HERSELF QUICKLY) NOT SO AWFUL LONG 521 DIFRNT
REALLY.
(BRIDLING QUICKLY) I NEVER DID. 521 DIFRNT
(THIS ACT--A PAIL OF COLD WATER ON EMMA WHO 527 DIFRNT
MOVES AWAY FROM BENNY QUICKLY.)
(HE CHUCKLES AND GOES QUICKLY TO THE DOOR ON RIGHT531 DIFRNT
AND CALLS UP TO THE FLOOR
(HE CALLS QUICKLY) COME DOWN/ 531 DIFRNT
(QUICKLY) HELL, I DON'T MEAN THAT KIND O' TIME. 537 DIFRNT
THEN, AS IF SUDDENLY AFRAID OF WHAT HER ANSWER 538 DIFRNT
WILL BE, HE BREAKS OUT QUICKLY)
(SHE DRAWS BACK QUICKLY FROM THE WINDOW 434 DYNAMO
AND SHE MOVES QUICKLY BACK INTO THE SHADOW.) 435 DYNAMO
(SHE SLINKS BACK ALONG THE HEDGE AND THEN QUICKLY 444 DYNAMO
ACROSS THE LAWN AROUND THE
HER EYES GLANCE QUICKLY ON ALL SIDES AS IF 459 DYNAMO
SEARCHING FOR SOMEONE.)
(THEN QUICKLY) I SUPPOSE YOU THINK I'M DOING IT 467 DYNAMO
TO SPITE YOU, BUT I'M NOT.
(QUICKLY) YES, I JUST HAD TO COME/ 481 DYNAMO
THEN, MAKING UP HIS MIND, HE STEPS QUICKLY ON 174 EJONES
TIPTOE INTO THE ROOM.
HE STOPS AS HE NEARS THE EDGE OF THE FOREST, LOOKS187 EJONES
AROUND HIM QUICKLY.
(TURNING AWAY FROM THEM QUICKLY AND LOOKING DOWN 188 EJONES
AT HIS FEET.

1273 QUID

QUICKLY (CONT'D.)
(HE WALKS QUICKLY INTO THE CLEAR SPACE--THEN 192 EJONES
STANDS TRANSFIXED AS HE SEES JEFF--
HIS FOLLOWERS CREEP QUICKLY INTO THE FOREST, 203 EJONES
THE VOICE GROWS QUICKLY NEARER. 6 ELECTR
(BUT HE WHISPERS QUICKLY TO MINNIE) 9 ELECTR
(WITH AN OBVIOUS EAGERNESS TO GET HIM OFF-- 16 ELECTR
QUICKLY)
BUT CHRISTINE QUICKLY RECOVERS HERSELF AND HER AIR 16 ELECTR
RESUMES ITS DISDAINFUL
(STARTS, LOOKS AT THE PORTRAIT AND QUICKLY DROPS 29 ELECTR
HER EYES.
(QUICKLY) NOTHING. 35 ELECTR
TURNS AND WALKS QUICKLY FROM THE ROOM AND CLOSES 42 ELECTR
THE DOOR BEHIND HER.)
HE IS APPROACHING THE HOUSE AND THE SONG DRAWS 43 ELECTR
QUICKLY NEARER..
(THEN QUICKLY) HE OUGHT TO BE SUCH A COMFORT TO 72 ELECTR
YOU IN YOUR GRIEF.
(SEEING HAZEL'S LOOK, CATCHES HERSELF--QUICKLY) 73 ELECTR
(QUICKLY) FATHER TOLD YOU THAT, TOO? 76 ELECTR
(THEN QUICKLY) BUT I WAS GOING TO GIVE YOU AN 87 ELECTR
EXAMPLE OF HER INSANE SUSPICIONS
HE WANTS TO GET OVER QUICKLY AND CLOSES THE DOOR 91 ELECTR
WITH A BANG BEHIND HIM.
(THEN QUICKLY--WITH A BITTER, JOKING TONE) 95 ELECTR
HE LOOKS AROUND HIM QUICKLY WITH AN UNEASY 104 ELECTR
SUSPICIOUS AIR.
(THEN QUICKLY) GO BACK TO THE GANGPLANK. 107 ELECTR
(GOES TO THE DOOR--THEN QUICKLY) 114 ELECTR
(HE QUICKLY TURNS BRANT'S POCKETS INSIDE OUT AND 115 ELECTR
PUTS THE REVOLVER HE FINDS..
(THEN QUICKLY) I MEAN THEY SHOULD HAVE BEEN HOME 118 ELECTR
BEFORE THIS.
(QUICKLY, URGING HIM ON COMMANDINGLY) 138 ELECTR
HE GLANCES AT THEM, THEN QUICKLY AROUND THE ROOM 159 ELECTR
TO SEE IF LAVINIA IS THERE.
SHE QUICKLY SENSES SOMETHING IN THE ATMOSPHERE 162 ELECTR
QUICKLY) 174 ELECTR
(SHE GOES QUICKLY BEHIND THE LILACS AND AROUND THEI74 ELECTR
HOUSE TO THE REAR.)
(THEN QUICKLY, MOCKING AGAIN) 261 GGBROW
HE WALKS QUICKLY TO THE BENCH AT CENTER AND THROWS264 GGBROW
HIMSELF ON IT.
(QUICKLY) HE ALWAYS TELLS PEOPLE THAT. 276 GGBROW
-QUICKLY MUST THOU BE GONE FROM HENCE, SEE THEN 290 GGBROW
HOW MATTERS STAND WITH THEE.
(QUICKLY AND MALEVOLENTLY) NO? 296 GGBROW
THEN HE PICKS IT UP AGAIN QUICKLY, TAKES THE DEAD 299 GGBROW
BODY AND CARRIES IT OFF LEFT.
(TURNING QUICKLY TO THE DRAFTSMEN) 303 GGBROW
HE COMES QUICKLY TO THE OTHER DOOR AND UNLOCKS 314 GGBROW
IT.)
ALL THIS HAPPENS QUICKLY WHILE THE MEN HAVE THEIR 225 HA APE
BACKS TURNED.)
THEY CARRY HER QUICKLY BACK, DISAPPEARING IN THE 226 HA APE
DARKNESS AT THE LEFT, REAR.
(HE CATCHES ROCKY'S AND JOE'S CONTEMPTUOUS 585 ICEMAN
GLANCES--QUICKLY)
(ROCKY COUNTS THE MONEY QUICKLY AND SHOVES IT IN 613 ICEMAN
HIS POCKET.)
LARRY GIVES HIM A PITYING LOOK, THEN QUICKLY 635 ICEMAN
DRINKS HIS DRINK.)
SCOWLING AT THEM AND THEN QUICKLY LOOKING AWAY.) 650 ICEMAN
BUT HIS MANNER AS HE TURNS HIS BACK AND DUCKS 704 ICEMAN
QUICKLY ACROSS TO THE BAR ENTRANCE.
(THEN QUICKLY) WELL, NATURALLY, HER FAMILY FORBID710 ICEMAN
HER SEEING ME.
(HE SHRINKS QUICKLY PAST THE TABLE WHERE HICKEY 724 ICEMAN
HAD SAT TO THE REAR OF THE GROUP
RUNNING HIS EYES QUICKLY DOWN THE PAGES. 531 INZONE
(QUICKLY.) OH, I'M NOT. 16 JOURNE
(QUICKLY.) I'M NOT UPSET. 16 JOURNE
(QUICKLY.) AND THAT MADE IT PRETTIER THAN EVER. 28 JOURNE
(QUICKLY.) OH, THAT. 40 JOURNE
AND GOES QUICKLY TO THE WINDOWS AT RIGHT. 42 JOURNE
THEN, ASHAMED OF HIMSELF, LOOKS QUICKLY AWAY. 49 JOURNE
(HE GOES QUICKLY TO THE WINDOW AT RIGHT.) 54 JOURNE
JAMIE TURNS TO HER--THEN LOOKS QUICKLY OUT OF THE 61 JOURNE
WINDOW AGAIN.)
(QUICKLY CASUAL--PATTING HIS CHEEK.) 62 JOURNE
(SHE ADDS QUICKLY WITH A DETACHED CONTRITION.) 75 JOURNE
(QUICKLY.) YOU CAN TELEPHONE AND SAY YOU DON'T 92 JOURNE
FEEL WELL ENOUGH.
(INTERRUPTING QUICKLY.) NOW, NOW/ 92 JOURNE
(SHE TURNS QUICKLY AWAY FROM HIM TO THE WINDOWS AT122 JOURNE
RIGHT.
(THEN AS HIS FATHER STARES AT HIM, HE ADDS 152 JOURNE
QUICKLY.)
THE DOOR IS SHUT AGAIN QUICKLY. 331 LAZARU
RISING CLEAR AND PASSIONATELY WITH THAT OF 367 LAZARU
LAZARUS, THEN DYING QUICKLY OUT.)
DEBORAH STARTS QUICKLY AND OPENS HER EYES 4 MANSNS
(QUICKLY.) I HAD BEGUN TO THINK PERHAPS SARA MIGHT
NOT PERMIT YOU TO COME--
HE GOES ON QUICKLY.) 13 MANSNS
(SHE LAUGHS SOFTLY--THEN QUICKLY, SEEING HE IS 39 MANSNS
HURT.)
(GIVES HER A SHARP, CALCULATING GLANCE--QUICKLY.) 78 MANSNS
THEY BOTH LOOK QUICKLY AWAY.) 119 MANSNS
(SHE GIVES SIMON A BITTER HOSTILE LOOK--THEN 124 MANSNS
QUICKLY TO SARA.)
HE TURNS QUICKLY, GOES INTO HIS STUDY, AND LOCKS 131 MANSNS
THE DOOR.
(QUICKLY AND LIGHTLY.) OF HOW FOOLISH MEN CAN BE.136 MANSNS
MOTHER.
DEBORAH SPEAKS QUICKLY AND LIGHTLY.) 136 MANSNS
(QUICKLY.) YES, OF COURSE-- 177 MANSNS

QUICKLY (CONT'D.)
WITH A LAST GESTURE HE TURNS, GOING QUICKLY OUT 363 MARCOM
THE DOOR IN REAR.)
(THEY GO QUICKLY OUT RIGHT, MARCO FOLLOWING WITH 369 MARCOM
THE SAMPLE CASES.
THE SCENE FADES QUICKLY INTO DARKNESS AS THE CALL 369 MARCOM
OF THE MUEZZINS IS HEARD
PASSES QUICKLY BY THE OLD PEOPLE WITH A GLANCE OF 371 MARCOM
AVERSION
YOU LEARN QUICKLY, DON'T YOUS 381 MARCOM
(THEN AS PEOPLE ARE HEARD APPROACHING--QUICKLY) 390 MARCOM
WEARS OUT QUICKLY, CAN BE MADE AT VERY SLIGHT 393 MARCOM
EXPENSE
(QUICKLY) IN PAPERS. 396 MARCOM
(HE TURNS QUICKLY AND GOES.) 401 MARCOM
THE MUSIC QUICKLY GROWS LOUDER. 402 MARCOM
(QUICKLY) THANK YOU, PRINCESS. 412 MARCOM
(SHE MOVES QUICKLY TO PEEK AROUND THE CORNER OF 5 MISBEG
THE HOUSE AT LEFT.
(QUICKLY) MIND YOU, I DON'T SAY JIM WOULD EVER DO 31 MISBEG
IT, RENT OR NO RENT.
SHE GOES ON QUICKLY) 41 MISBEG
(THEN QUICKLY) BUT I'VE NO TIME NOW TO LISTEN TO 68 MISBEG
YOUR KIDDING.
(QUICKLY) WELL, I'M GLAD. 96 MISBEG
(QUICKLY) WELL, IT PROVES HE CAN'T KEEP AWAY FROM 98 MISBEG
YOU.
(QUICKLY) I KNOW HOW. 99 MISBEG
(LOWERING HER VOICE--QUICKLY) 99 MISBEG
(QUICKLY) HOW WOULD I KNOW, IF YOU DON'TS 104 MISBEG
(QUICKLY) I'M NOT. 106 MISBEG
(QUICKLY) I'M NOT. 115 MISBEG
(STARTS--QUICKLY.) I'M NOT. 116 MISBEG
(QUICKLY) I MEAN, THE GREATEST KIDDER. 119 MISBEG
(QUICKLY) OH--THAT'S RIGHT--I DID SAY--(VAGUELY) 127 MISBEG
WHAT BLONDES
(QUICKLY) BUT I'VE BEEN TO THE COAST A LOT OF 128 MISBEG
TIMES
(QUICKLY) HE DIDN'T TELL ME. 131 MISBEG
(QUICKLY) IT'S THE MOONLIGHT. 142 MISBEG
(QUICKLY, FORCING HIS CYNICAL SMILE) 144 MISBEG
(QUICKLY) BUT YOU MIGHT. 145 MISBEG
(HER FACE HAS FALLEN INTO LINES OF BITTER HURT, 172 MISBEG
BUT HE ADDS QUICKLY AND ANGRILY)
(HE TURNS AWAY AND WALKS QUICKLY DOWN THE ROAD OFF174 MISBEG
LEFT WITHOUT LOOKING BACK.
(SHE ADDS QUICKLY.) BUT NOT TOO MUCH. 31 POET
THEN YOU WILL SEE HOW QUICKLY AMERICA WILL BECOME 40 POET
RICH AND GREAT/
HE STARTS AND TURNS QUICKLY AWAY FROM THE MIRROR. 44 POET
(THEN QUICKLY.) NOT THAT I DON'T APPROVE OF YOUNG 63 POET
HARTFORD, MIND YOU.
(QUICKLY.) BUT IT WAS MY FAULT HE DIDN'T. 65 POET
SHE HURRIES TOWARD THEM QUICKLY. 72 POET
A MOMENT LATER SARA ENTERS QUICKLY FROM RIGHT AND 76 POET
COMES TO HER.)
(NORA SIGHS AND GOES OUT QUICKLY, RIGHT. 81 POET
MELODY STARTS GUILTILY AND STEPS QUICKLY AWAY FROM116 POET
THE MIRROR.
(THEN QUICKLY.) YES, I'M SURE IT ENDED HOURS AGO.141 POET
(THEN QUICKLY.) BUT IT SERVES YOU RIGHT/ 155 POET
(SHE GOES QUICKLY TO THE DOOR AND DISAPPEARS. 160 POET
(SHE RETREATS QUICKLY INTO THE ROOM AND BACKS 163 POET
AROUND THE TABLE AT LEFT FRONT
SLAMMING THE DOOR QUICKLY BEHIND HIM. 165 POET
AND QUICKLY SNATCHES UP THE DOLL, WHICH SHE HUGS 578 ROPE
FIERCELY TO HER BREAST.
(HE GIVES IT TO THE OLD MAN AS THEY COME TO THE 584 ROPE
DOORWAY AND QUICKLY STEPS BACK
MARY, DISCOVERING SHE IS UNHURT, GLANCES QUICKLY 601 ROPE
AROUND AND SEES THE BAY.
THEN SHE QUICKLY PICKS UP FOUR OR FIVE AND RUNS 602 ROPE
OUT TO THE EDGE OF THE CLIFF.
(HE HEARS SOMEONE COMING QUICKLY FROM THE RIGHT 6 STRANG
AND TURNS EXPECTANTLY.
(QUICKLY) I CAN ANSWER THAT, I THINK. 10 STRANG
(QUICKLY) YOU'RE QUITE RIGHT. 36 STRANG
(KISSES HIM QUICKLY) YOU DESERVE ONE FOR THAT/ 51 STRANG
(SEEING THIS IS HER CHANCE--QUICKLY--FORCING A 55 STRANG
SMILE)
(STARTLED--FORCING A SMILE, QUICKLY) 57 STRANG
(QUICKLY AVERTING HIS EYES--SITS DOWN--JOKINGLY) 79 STRANG
SHE COMES QUICKLY OVER TO HIM SAYING WITH FRANK 79 STRANG
PLEASURE)
(SIGHING) I WISH THAT COULD BE SAID OF MORE OF 80 STRANG
US--(THEN QUICKLY)--
(QUICKLY) NO, LEAVE NED WITH ME. 164 STRANG
(STEPS QUICKLY TO HER SIDE) I'M SORRY, NINA, BUT 179 STRANG
I WARNED YOU NOT TO MEDDLE.
FREDA MOVES QUICKLY FOR THE DOOR ON THE LEFT 508 VOYAGE
(SMILING--QUICKLY) OH, I'LL PROMISE TO BE GOOD-- 446 WELDED
IF YOU WILL.
SHE RECOILS FROM IT, TURNING QUICKLY AWAY FROM 450 WELDED
HIM, VISIBLY SHAKEN.
SHE GLANCES QUICKLY AT HIS FACE, THEN SPEAKS WITH 451 WELDED
A KIND OF DULL REMORSE)
SHE COMES QUICKLY TO THE COUCH AND FLINGS HERSELF 462 WELDED
DOWN IN ONE CORNER.
(QUICKLY RECOVERING HERSELF--IN A COLD, HARD 463 WELDED
VOICE) THAT'S--DEAD/
(SHE BENDS DOWN SWIFTLY AND KISSES HIS HEAD, TURNS487 WELDED
AWAY QUICKLY)
SHE GRABS HER CLOAK FROM THE CHAIR, GOES QUICKLY 487 WELDED
TO THE DOOR.

QUID I'D RISK A QUID UP MY NEXT PAY DAY THAT HIS REAL 522 INZONE
NAME IS SCHMIDT.

QUID

QUID (CONT'D.)
BLOKE'S ADVANCE--FULL MONTH'S PAY--FIVE QUID, 508 VOYAGE
C'YER 'EARS

QUIET
AND THE QUIET SO THICK YOU'RE AFRAID TO HEAR YOUR 538 'ILE
OWN VOICE.
KEEP IT QUIET, KID. 218 AHWILD
THE SNICKERS) NOW, DO BE QUIET, TOMMY/ 220 AHWILD
YOU BE QUIET/ 221 AHWILD
YOU KIDS GO OUT IN THE YARD AND TRY TO KEEP QUIET 234 AHWILD
FOR A WHILE.
I'LL SEE HE KEEPS QUIET, PA. 234 AHWILD
THE CHILDREN QUIET AND A BIT AWED) 234 AHWILD
QUIET NOW--OR I'LL PIN A MARY ANN ON YOUR JAW 247 AHWILD
(HAPPILY QUIET! YOU/
(SNAPPILY) YOU BE QUIET/ 251 AHWILD
MILLER MOTIONS SID TO BE QUIET) 257 AHWILD
MILLER SIZES HIM UP KEENLY--THEN SUDDENLY SMILES 293 AHWILD
AND ASKS WITH QUIET MOCKERY)
I GUESS I WAS ALWAYS QUIET. 89 BEYOND
TELLING ME TO LOOK OUT AND BE QUIET. 89 BEYOND
PUT HER DOWN AND LET HER PLAY WITH THE DOLL IF 117 BEYOND
IT'LL QUIET HER.
I WAS AFRAID. HE TALKED SO CRAZY. I COULDN'T 151 BEYOND
QUIET HIM.
I'LL SHUT THIS DOOR SO'S YOU'LL BE QUIET. 151 BEYOND
KEEP HIM QUIET AND WE'LL HOPE FOR THE BEST. 485 CARDIF
(TO DRISCOLL) YOU UND ME, VE KEEP DEM QUIET, 458 CARIBE
DRISE.
(WARNINGLY) REMEMBER YE MUST BE QUIET ABOUT UT. 458 CARIBE
YE SCUTS--
AN' DON'T FORGIT WHAT I SAID ABOUT BEIN' QUIET W10463 CARIBE
THE DHRINK.
(LOOKING AT HIM FIXEDLY FOR A MOMENT--WITH QUIET 467 CARIBE
SCORN)
SHE TRIES IN VAIN TO KEEP THE MEN QUIET. 470 CARIBE
THEN BE QUIET NOW THEY ARE OUT) 471 CARIBE
HE'S ALWAYS QUIET--TOO QUIET.. 558 CROSS
(SOMBERLY) HE IS QUIET ALWAYS--TOO QUIET. 562 CROSS
THAT FATHER IS QUIET, ALWAYS QUIET. 565 CROSS
BE QUIET. 568 CROSS
BE QUIET, DEAR, IT'S NOTHING. 571 CROSS
(SHE SMILES--THEN WITH QUIET PRIDE) 524 DAYS
(AFTER A WORRIED GLANCE AT HER--AN UNDERCURRENT UF540 DAYS
WARNING IN HIS QUIET TONE)
YOU MUST BE QUIET. 554 DAYS
THE GIVES DOWN A FURIOUS LOOK AND MOTIONS FATHER 554 DAYS
BAIRD TO KEEP HIM QUIET.)
I THOUGHT YOU PROMISED ME IF I LET YOU STAY IN 555 DAYS
HERE YOU'D KEEP QUIET.
IT'S HER VENGEANCE ON HIM--SO'S SHE KIN REST QUIET244 DESIRE
IN HER GRAVE/
BE QUIET/ 61 ELECTR
BE QUIET, CHRISTINE/ 61 ELECTR
SHE SPEAKS TO ORIN AND HER VOICE IS TENSELY QUIET 78 ELECTR
AND NORMAL)
BE QUIET/ 99 ELECTR
FOR GOD'S SAKE, BE QUIET/ 101 ELECTR
BE QUIET/ 113 ELECTR
BE QUIET/ 124 ELECTR
FOR GOD'S SAKE, WILL YOU BE QUIETS 124 ELECTR
WILL YOU BE QUIET/ 140 ELECTR
USUALLY HE'S LIKE HIMSELF, ONLY QUIET AND SAD-- 148 ELECTR
BE QUIET/ 151 ELECTR
(WITH A QUIET MAD INSISTENCE) 155 ELECTR
YOU BE QUIET/ 156 ELECTR
HE'LL BE VERY SICK AND NERVOUS AND HE'LL WANT TO 301 GGBROW
BE QUIET.
THEY'VE GOT TO QUIET THEIR FEARS, TO CAST OUT 320 GGBROW
THEIR DEVILS.
ALL DIS IS TOO CLEAN AND QUIET AND DOLLED-UP, GET 234 HA APE
ME/
(FROM A DISTANCE) QUIET THERE, YOUSE--OR I'LL GIT243 HA APE
THE HOSE.
THEY WAS QUIET LIKE HUGHIE. 25 HUGHIE
"I'M AFRAID NUT, BUT HE'LL HAVE TO BE ABSOLUTELY 26 HUGHIE
QUIET FOR MONTHS AND MONTHS."
OUTSIDE, THE SPELL OF ABNORMAL QUIET PRESSES 31 HUGHIE
SUFFOCATINGLY UPON THE STREET.
WHY DON'T YOU GIVE THE POOR FELLER A DRINK AND 582 ICEMAN
KEEP HIM QUIET/
LEAST YOU COULD DO--KEEP THINGS QUIET-- (HE FALLS 582 ICEMAN
ASLEEP)
BEADES, CAN'T YOU KEEP THAT CRAZY BASTARD QUIETS 597 ICEMAN
LEAVE HIM ALONE, LONG AS HE'S QUIET. 598 ICEMAN
I'LL BE QUIET/ 598 ICEMAN
DEN HE SITS DOWN AND SAYS QUIET AGAIN, =ALL RIGHT.601 ICEMAN
YOU CAN OPEN.
HE SAYS SLOW AND QUIET LIKE DERE WASN'T NO HARM IN601 ICEMAN
HIM.
PLEASE, HARRY/ I'LL BE QUIET/ 607 ICEMAN
(SOURLY DISAPPOINTED) YOU KEEP THEM DUMB BROADS 610 ICEMAN
QUIET.
(MORAN MAKES A PEREMPTORY SIGN TC BE QUIET. 708 ICEMAN
LOOK AT ME PRETENDING TO START FOR A WALK JUST TO 721 ICEMAN
KEEP HIM QUIET.
JAMES, DO BE QUIET. 22 JOURNE
IF SHE DON'T USE SOMETHING TO QUIET HER TEMPER, 106 JOURNE
THERE IS A PAUSE OF DEAD QUIET. 107 JOURNE
YOUR REMEDY WAS TO GIVE HIM A TEASPOONFUL OF 111 JOURNE
WHISKEY TO QUIET HIM.
(HIS FACE WORKS AND HE BLINKS BACK TEARS--WITH 112 JOURNE
QUIET INTENSITY.)
(STUNG--ANGRILY.) BE QUIET/ 140 JOURNE
BE QUIET/ 145 JOURNE
(HOARSELY.) KEEP QUIET, CAN'T YOU, PAPA/ 166 JOURNE
(SUDDENLY, IN A QUIET BUT COMPELLING VOICE) 359 LAZARU
BUT STILL KEEPING HER VOICE QUIET.) 18 MANSNS

QUIET (CONT'D.)
(WITH AN ABRUPT CHANGE TO HER QUIET POLITE MANNER 19 MANSNS
AND BROGUELESS ENGLISH.
THEN SARA'S VOICE TRYING TO QUIET THEM AND, FOR 43 MANSNS
THE MOMENT, SUCCEEDING.
WITH JUST THE CORRECT TOUCH OF QUIET RESIGNATION 50 MANSNS
IN HER BEARING
I HAD FORGOTTEN THE QUIET AND THE PEACE HERE. 99 MANSNS
A MOMENT AFTER THE CURTAIN RISES THERE IS AN 117 MANSNS
ATMOSPHERE OF TENSE QUIET
HOW TENSE THE QUIET IS IN THIS HOUSE TONIGHT-- 120 MANSNS
(GETTING UP--WITH A QUIET SMILE.) 123 MANSNS
HOW QUIET WE ARE. 136 MANSNS
SIT THERE AND BE QUIET NOW/ 167 MANSNS
(HIS TENSE QUIET BEGINNING TO SNAP.) 172 MANSNS
AND THEN WHEN YOU FINALLY DID BECOME QUIET, 174 MANSNS
(GOES ON IN THE SAME TONE OF TENSE QUIET.) 179 MANSNS
(WITH A QUIET SMILE) I SHALL STUDY THIS 379 MARCOM
APOTHEOSIS WITH UNWEARIED INTEREST,
BECAUSE HE'S EDUCATED AND QUIET-SPOKEN AND HAS 27 MISBEG
POLITENESS EVEN WHEN HE'S
=CHRIST, FATHER, IT'S NICE AND QUIET OUT HERE 39 MISBEG
I'VE PINED TO HAVE A QUIET WORD WITH MR. HARDER 51 MISBEG
FOR YEARS.
SURE, ALL WE WANT IS A QUIET CHAT WITH HIM. 53 MISBEG
THE QUIET OF THE NIGHT IS SHATTERED BY A BURST OF 71 MISBEG
MELANCHOLY SONG.
AND HE'LL GIVE ANYTHING TO KEEP US QUIET, I TELL 96 MISBEG
YOU.
HOGAN'S MOURNFUL SONG DRIFTS BACK THROUGH THE 103 MISBEG
MOONLIGHT QUIET.
COME HERE, AND BE QUIET ABOUT IT. 157 MISBEG
YOU WERE MOSTLY QUIET AND SAD-- 170 MISBEG
(GRIMLY.) YOU'D BETTER KAPE QUIET FOR FEAR OF 15 POET
HIM, TOO.
(TURNS ON HIM--WITH QUIET ANGER.) 17 POET
BE QUIET/ 45 POET
I HAVE WANTED A QUIET CHAT WITH YOU FOR SOME TIME. 46 POET
BE QUIET, DAMN YOU/ 51 POET
I WISH TO BE ALONE IN QUIET WITH MY MEMORIES. 57 POET
(TENSELY.) BE QUIET/ 75 POET
BE QUIET, PATCH. 97 POET
(SMILING OBEDIENT.) QUIET IT IS, YER HONOR. 97 POET
I KNOW THE DEVIL THAT'S IN YOU WHEN YOU'RE QUIET 105 POET
LIKE THIS
QUIET, GENTLEMANLY TONE. 105 POET
HIS VOICE QUIVERS BUT IS DEADLY QUIET.) 114 POET
THEN SHE CONTROLS HERSELF AND SPEAKS WITH QUIET, 115 POET
BITING SARCASM.)
(ADDRESSING HIM--IN HIS QUIET, THREATENING TONE 123 POET
NOW.
BE QUIET, WOMAN/ 125 POET
(THEN WITH QUIET INTENSITY.) 128 POET
BE QUIET, MOTHER. 152 POET
BE QUIET, MOTHER. 154 POET
THEN QUIET AS IF HE HAD RAISED A HAND FOR SILENCE.180 POET
LAWN BETWEEN THE HOUSE AND THE QUIET RESIDENTIAL 3 STRANG
STREET
THE MAIN POINT ABOUT HIS PERSONALITY IS A QUIET 4 STRANG
CHARM, A QUALITY OF APPEALING.
YOU MUST ALL SIT DOWN AND BE VERY QUIET. 133 STRANG
(WITH STRANGE QUIET) I THINK I STILL LOVE YOU A 170 STRANG
LITTLE, NED.
(STERNLY) IN HIS CONDITION, MR. EVANS MUST HAVE 183 STRANG
ABSOLUTE QUIET
QUIETER
(QUIETER BUT STILL GRIM AND CRUEL) 233 DESIRE
(AS HIS SOBBING GROWS QUIETER--HELPFULLY) 475 WELDED
QUIETING
(IN A QUIETING TONE) LISTEN, EPHRAIM. 233 DESIRE
QUIETLY
(QUIETLY) NO. 191 AHWILD
(SUDDENLY PUTS BOTH HANDS ON HIS SHOULDERS-- 206 AHWILD
QUIETLY)
(QUIETLY) NO. 213 AHWILD
SHE GOES QUIETLY AND SITS DOWN IN HER CHAIR AGAIN.259 AHWILD
(QUIETLY BUT FIRMLY NOW) YOU BETTER LEAVE RICHARD293 AHWILD
AND ME ALONE FOR A WHILE.
(AFTER A PAUSE--QUIETLY) ALL RIGHT. 294 AHWILD
(WATCHING HIS SON--AFTER A PAUSE--QUIETLY) 296 AHWILD
(SHE KISSES HIM AND THEY MOVE QUIETLY OUT OF THE 298 AHWILD
MOONLIGHT.
LARRY MOVES QUIETLY CLOSE TO THE PARTITION TO 10 ANNA
LISTEN, GRINNING WITH EXPECTATION.
(QUIETLY--COMING FORWARD TO THEM) 53 ANNA
(AS HE BEGINS TO TALK ANDREW ENTERS QUIETLY FROM 99 BEYOND
THE REAR.
ROBERT WALKS UP THE PATH AND OPENS THE SCREEN DOOR119 BEYOND
QUIETLY
(QUIETLY) YOU'LL BOTH BE HERE FCR DINNER, WON'T 142 BEYOND
YOU.
HE CLOSES THE DOOR QUIETLY BEHIND HIM AND COMES 157 BEYOND
FORWARD.
THE COMES BACK QUIETLY AND SITS DOWN. 479 CARDIF
RIGHT-O (COCKY, DAVIS, AND SCOTTY GO OUT QUIETLY.)482 CARDIF
(QUIETLY) SEEMS NICE AND SLEEPY-LIKE. 466 CARIBE
(QUIETLY) I'D GIT DRUNK, SAME'S YOU'RE DOIN'. 467 CARIBE
THE DONKEYMAN QUIETLY SMOKING ON HIS STOOL.. 472 CARIBE
FATHER BAIRD SAYS QUIETLY, WITHOUT ANY SIGN OF 501 DAYS
TAKING OFFENSE)
(WITHOUT TURNING--QUIETLY) NO. 502 DAYS
(WITHOUT TURNING--QUIETLY) DON'T YOU KNOW, JACKS 503 DAYS
(QUIETLY REBUKING) JACK/ 505 DAYS
(STARES AT HIM, TAKES ABACK--THEN QUIETLY) 506 DAYS
(THEN, AFTER A PAUSE, QUIETLY) 508 DAYS
(QUIETLY) WOULD YOU TALK THAT WAY IF ELSA SHOULD 509 DAYS
DIES
(RECOVERED NOW--STARING AT HIM--QUIETLY) 512 DAYS

QUITE

QUIETLY (CONT'D.)
(REGARDING HIM--QUIETLY) THEN, BY ALL MEANS. 512 DAYS
(QUIETLY) VERY WELL. 513 DAYS
(QUIETLY) I HAVE MY SHARE OF SCARS. 517 DAYS
(THEN AS LUCY GROWS CALMER--QUIETLY) 520 DAYS
SHE COMES QUIETLY TO THE RIGHT END OF THE SOFA. 528 DAYS
(QUIETLY) YES. 533 DAYS
(QUIETLY) I CANNOT SEE THE BEAUTY AND COMFORT. 534 DAYS
(WITHOUT LIFTING HIS EYES--QUIETLY) 538 DAYS
THEN QUIETLY, AN UNDERCURRENT OF STERNNESS IN HIS 538 DAYS
VOICE)
(QUIETLY) I CAN WELL BELIEVE THAT, JACK. 539 DAYS
(QUIETLY, WITHOUT LOOKING UP) 542 DAYS
(FINALLY SPEAKS QUIETLY) JACK, EVER SINCE WE CAME543 DAYS
UPSTAIRS,
(IGNORING THIS--QUIETLY) YOU ARE FORGETTING THAT 543 DAYS
MEN HAVE SUCH A SAVIOR, JACK.
(DROPPING HIS EYES--QUIETLY) 544 DAYS
(QUIETLY) OF COURSE, JACK. 545 DAYS
(HAS IMMEDIATELY CONTROLLED HIMSELF--QUIETLY) 545 DAYS
THEN MOVES QUIETLY TO THE OTHER SIDE OF THE ROOM, 556 DAYS
BY THE DOOR TO ELSA'S BEDROOM.
SHE'S RESTING QUIETLY. 556 DAYS
(RECOVERING HIMSELF--QUIETLY) 559 DAYS
THEN COMES QUIETLY UP BESIDE HIM AND STARES 566 DAYS
SEARCHINGLY INTO HIS FACE.
(THEN QUIETLY) I'LL TELL EBEN. 222 DESIRE
(HE GOES QUIETLY OUT THE DOOR IN REAR--A FEW 263 DESIRE
MOMENTS LATER ENTERS KITCHEN--
THEN HE PUSHES HER A LITTLE AWAY FROM HIM AND 459 DYNAMO
LAUGHS QUIETLY.
(INDICATING THE PORTRAIT--QUIETLY) 29 ELECTR
(QUIETLY) YOU NEEDN'T HOPE TO GET RID OF ME THAT 45 ELECTR

YOU SLUNK OUT OF BED SO QUIETLY. 59 ELECTR
HAZEL GOES QUIETLY BACK TO HER CHAIR AT CENTER. 81 ELECTR
(AUTOMATICALLY REACTS TO THE VOICE OF AUTHORITY-- 105 ELECTR
QUIETLY)
TO THE COMPANIONWAY STAIRS AND CLOSES IT QUIETLY 109 ELECTR
BEHIND THEM.
(QUIETLY) 'TAIN'T BOSH, PETER. 136 ELECTR
(QUIETLY--WITH SIMPLE DIGNITY NOW) 154 ELECTR
(WITH A MOCKING DIABOLICAL SNEER--QUIETLY) 155 ELECTR
(QUIETLY) IT WON'T TAKE ME LONG TO SAY WHAT I'VE 171 ELECTR
COME TO SAY, VINNIE.
(PUTS ON HIS MASK AGAIN--QUIETLY AND BITTERLY) 268 GGBROW
AT THE SAME MOMENT BROWN ENTERS QUIETLY FROM THE 288 GGBROW
LEFT.
BUT WILLIE HAS CLOSED HIS EYES AND IS SITTING 583 ICEMAN
QUIETLY, SHUDDERING.
HE BOWS HIS HEAD A LITTLE AND SAYS QUIETLY) 663 ICEMAN
(HE SLIPS OUT OF HIS CHAIR AND GOES QUIETLY OVER 680 ICEMAN
TO SIT IN THE CHAIR BESIDE
(QUIETLY) OH, THAT'S ALL RIGHT, LARRY. 693 ICEMAN
(GOES ON QUIETLY NOW) DON'T WORRY ABOUT THE 706 ICEMAN
CHAIR, LARRY.
TWO MEN COME QUIETLY FORWARD. 708 ICEMAN
HE STARES BEFORE HIM, HIS HAND FALLING BACK-- 714 ICEMAN
QUIETLY)
MOVES QUIETLY FROM THE ENTRANCE IN THE CURTAIN 716 ICEMAN
ACROSS THE BACK OF THE ROOM TO
TYRONE COMES IN QUIETLY THROUGH THE SCREEN DOOR 167 JOURNE
FROM THE PORCH.
HE SPEAKS QUIETLY, IN A DEEP VOICE WITH A SLIGHT 5 MANSNS
DRAWL.)
(SPEAKS QUIETLY IN A POLITE, CAREFULLY CONSIDERED 18 MANSNS
AND ARTICULATED ENGLISH.)
SARA GOES ON MORE QUIETLY.) 19 MANSNS
CLOSING THE DOOR QUIETLY BEHIND HIM. 70 MANSNS
(CHECKS HERSELF--QUIETLY CASUAL.) 100 MANSNS
QUIETLY, WITH A MOCKING IRONY TINGED WITH A 148 MANSNS
BITTER, TRAGIC SADNESS.)
(QUIETLY.) WHAT HAS YOUR RACE AND FASTIDIOUS, 178 MANSNS
(QUIETLY AGAIN. REGARDED SENSIBLY. 180 MANSNS
(HE PULLS HER GENTLY BACK--QUIETLY.) 181 MANSNS
(KEEPS HOLD OF HER HAND--QUIETLY.) 181 MANSNS
(LEERING QUIETLY.) YES. 185 MANSNS
(QUIETLY AND EXHAUSTEDLY.) I'VE TOLD YOU I'M 189 MANSNS
BEYOND SCHEMING.
(SHE GOES IN QUIETLY AND SHUTS THE DOOR.) 190 MANSNS
(QUIETLY.) I AM SURE YOU KNOW THAT, MY LADY. 193 MANSNS
AN USHER OF THE PALACE COMES QUIETLY TO MARCO 378 MARCOM
KUBLAI LAUGHS QUIETLY) 382 MARCOM
KUKACHIN'S SHOULDERS QUIVER AS, HER HEAD BOWED IN 420 MARCOM
HER HANDS, SHE SOBS QUIETLY.
(QUIETLY) THEN KEEP YOUR TONGUE OFF HIM. 4 MISBEG
(SHE PAUSES--THEN QUIETLY) HE DID NOTHING TO 161 MISBEG
BRING ME SORROW.
(QUIETLY) I WASN'T DRUNK, NO. 162 MISBEG
CLOSING THE DOOR QUIETLY AFTER HIM. 164 MISBEG
HE SAYS QUIETLY AND WITH GENUINE CONTRITION.) 37 POET
(STARES AT HER--AGAIN HE IS MOVED--QUIETLY.) 41 POET
SHE BEGINS TO SOB QUIETLY.) 57 POET
HE GOES ON QUIETLY, A BITTER, SNEERING ANTAGONISM 60 POET
UNDERNEATH.)
(QUIETLY.) ALL RIGHT, MOTHER. 61 POET
SIMON'S MOTHER, ENTERS, CLOSING THE DOOR QUIETLY 67 POET
BEHIND HER.
HE READS THE VERSE WELL, QUIETLY, WITH A BITTER 101 POET
ELOQUENCE.)
(QUIETLY.) A DAUGHTER WHO TAKES SATISFACTION IN 104 POET
LETTING EVEN THE SCUM SEE
(A LOOK OF VINDICTIVE CRUELTY COMES INTO HIS 107 POET
EYES--QUIETLY.)
HE SPEAKS QUIETLY.) 107 POET
(QUIETLY.) MAY I ASK WHAT YOU FIND SO RIDICULOUS 111 POET
IN AN OLD ESTABLISHED CUSTOMS
(HE SPEAKS QUIETLY, BUT AS HE GOES ON 112 POET

QUIETLY (CONT'D.)
(THEN QUIETLY.) THERE ARE THINGS I SAID WHICH I 115 POET
REGRET--EVEN NOW.
SARA TURNS AND GOES QUIETLY OUT RIGHT. 115 POET
(QUIETLY CONTEMPTUOUS. 154 POET
(QUIETLY.) NO. 132 STRANG
(QUIETLY AND CALMLY NOW) ALL RIGHT, DEAR. 136 STRANG
(SHE TURNS AND WALKS QUIETLY OUT OF THE ROOM. 136 STRANG
AND THEN YOU AND I'LL BE QUIETLY MARRIED/ 175 STRANG
HE SMILES QUIETLY) 188 STRANG
(QUIETLY) I'VE ALWAYS ENVIED MICHAEL. 465 WELDED
QUIETNESS
IN YOUR MIND UNDER ALL YOUR QUIETNESS/ 85 BEYOND
HIS QUIETNESS FOOLS PEOPLE INTO THINKING THEY CAN 35 JOURNE
DO WHAT THEY LIKE WITH HIM.
QUININE
IF IT IS, QUININE WILL SOON CURE IT. 27 JOURNE
QUINTESSENCE
(PROUDLY) =THE QUINTESSENCE OF IBSENISM.= 197 AHWILD
QUIT
AND NOW YOU QUIT ON ME/ 242 AHWILD
AH, QUIT THE KIDDIN'/ 19 ANNA
QUIT THE KIDDING NOW. 77 ANNA
THAT YOU KIN GIVE ME YOUR NOTICE TO QUIT LIKE 105 BEYOND
YOU'VE DONE.
I'VE EARNED MY RIGHT TO QUIT WHEN I WANT TO. 107 BEYOND
HE QUIT LAST NIGHT. 152 BEYOND
THIS LAST YEAR HAS SEEMED ROTTEN, AND I'VE HAD A 487 CARDIF
HUNCH I'D QUIT--
I COULDN'T QUIT. 28 HUGHIE
Y'KNOW, IT'S TIME I QUIT CARRYIN' THE TORCH FOR 38 HUGHIE
HUGHIE.
WELL, THAT'S WHY I QUIT THE MOVEMENT, IF IT LEAVES590 ICEMAN
YOU ANY WISER.
YOU ASKED ME WHY I QUIT THE MOVEMENT. 590 ICEMAN
HE SAYS, =QUIT TICKLIN' ME.= 617 ICEMAN
THE ONLY REASON I'VE QUIT IS-- 621 ICEMAN
AND QUIT BATTLING HIMSELF, AND FIND PEACE FOR THE 641 ICEMAN
REST OF HIS LIFE.
IT'S TIME I QUIT FOR A WHILE. 652 ICEMAN
HEY, YOU DUMB TART, QUIT BANGING THAT BOX/ 654 ICEMAN
SO QUIT WORRYING/ 654 ICEMAN
YUH JUST QUIT COLD/ 690 ICEMAN
QUIT IT/ 168 JOURNE
FOR CHRIST SAKE, QUIT THE SMUT STUFF, CAN'T YOU/ 127 MISBEG
SO I QUIT. 146 MISBEG
DIDN'T QUIT, HE'D KEEP ME LOCKED IN THE DRAWING 149 MISBEG
ROOM.
(TO HARRY, CONSOLINGLY) QUIT BAWLIN', KID. 589 ROPE
BUT I NEVER QUIT TRYING, ANYWAY/ 29 STRANG
DON'T QUIT/....) 30 STRANG
DON'T QUIT NOW/... 379 STRANG
QUIT IT. 475 WELDED

QUITE
(GRAVELY--AND QUITE TIPSILY) 242 AHWILD
HE CARRIES HIS STRAW HAT DANGLING IN HIS HAND, 292 AHWILD
QUITE UNAWARE OF ITS EXISTENCE.
HE TOOK QUITE A FANCY TO ME, AND WHAT'S MORE 133 BEYOND
IMPORTANT,
I'LL HAVE TO WAIT FOR A SHIP SAILING THERE FOR 137 BEYOND
QUITE A WHILE, LIKELY.
IT'S QUITE A TRIP. 137 BEYOND
QUITE A FEW ARE IN THEIR BARE FEET AND 455 CAKIBE
THEY ARE QUITE UNAWARE OF LOVING'S EXISTENCE, 496 DAYS
QUITE COZY, TOO, THEY SAY. 496 DAYS
I FEEL QUITE AT HOME WITH YOU NOW. 901 DAYS
OH, I'M REALLY QUITE WELL AGAIN. 515 DAYS
SHE TOOK IT QUITE PHILOSOPHICALLY-- 519 DAYS
OH, YOU'RE QUITE SURE OF THAT, ARE YOU& 519 DAYS
AND I HAD TO DO ALL THE SEDUCING--BECAUSE HE'S 521 DAYS
QUITE HAPPY.
I PROPOSED QUITE FRANKLY THAT WE SHOULD SIMPLY 523 DAYS
LIVE TOGETHER AND EACH KEEP
(SHE LAUGHS) OH, I WAS QUITE ULTRA-MODERN ABOUT 523 DAYS
IT/
QUITE UNFIT FOR LIFE, I THINK. 531 DAYS
UH, BUT I'M QUITE ALL RIGHT NOW, JOHN. 533 DAYS
OH, HE HAD IT ALL ANALYZED QUITE CORRECTLY, 537 DAYS
CONSIDERING THE KNOWN ELEMENTS.
QUITE CREDIBLE TO ME, JACK. 538 DAYS
(QUITE CONFIDENT NOW) I HAIN'T A MITE AFEERO. 240 DESIRE
EBEN GOES NOT NOTICE HER UNTIL QUITE NEAR.) 252 DESIRE
BORNE ON THE LIGHT PUFFS OF WIND THIS MUSIC IS AT 5 ELECTR
TIMES QUITE LOUD.
WELL--IF YOU'RE QUITE READY, PERHAPS YOU WILL 29 ELECTR
EXPLAIN.
YOU ARE QUITE RIGHT, DOCTOR. 70 ELECTR
QUITE FOREIGN TO THE GENERAL'S, AND HIS CHIN IS A 73 ELECTR
REFINED,
I APPRECIATE YOUR GRIEF HAS MADE YOU--NOT QUITE 77 ELECTR
NORMAL--AND I MAKE ALLOWANCES.
I HAPPEN TO FEEL QUITE WELL/ 151 ELECTR
BUT NOW I FEEL YOU'VE BECOME QUITE HUMAN--LIKE 309 GGBROW
ME--AND I'M SO HAPPY, DEAR/
I WAS QUITE FURIOUS UNTIL HE CONVINCED ME IT WAS 310 GGBROW
ALL FOR THE BEST.
FOR MY PART YOU ARE QUITE FREE TC INDULGE ANY POSE219 HA APE
OF ECCENTRICITY THAT BEGUILES
YOU'RE QUITE RIGHT. 679 ICEMAN
QUITE RIGHT. 707 ICEMAN
YOU'RE QUITE RIGHT, EDMUND. 43 JOURNE
BUT I'M QUITE ALL RIGHT, DEAR. 49 JOURNE
(THEN SLIPPING AWAY INTO HER STRANGE DETACHMENT-- 69 JOURNE
QUITE CASUALLY.)
(STARTS TO BLURT OUT THE APPEAL HE NOW FEELS IS 92 JOURNE
QUITE HOPELESS.)
I BECAME QUITE USED TO IT. 113 JOURNE
IT WAS NEVER QUITE GOOD ENOUGH. 115 JOURNE

QUITE

QUITE (CONT'D.)

I'VE THOUGHT YOU WEREN'T QUITE RIGHT IN YOUR HEAD.127 JOURNE
SHE'S QUITE RIGHT, IT ISN'T FAIR, WHEN HE'S SO 171 JOURNE
GOOD AND GENEROUS,
AND QUITE AS I HAD EXPECTED. 6 MANSNS
MY DEAR BOY, I HOPE YOU DON'T THINK YOUR POOR 14 MA/SNS
MOTHER HAS GONE QUITE INSANE/
BUT YOU'RE QUITE RIGHT. 46 MANSNS
THE THING YOU MUST BEAR IN MIND IS THAT SHE HAS 86 MANSNS
NEVER BEEN QUITE NORMAL.
SHE CAN SEE QUITE ENOUGH OF THEM WHEN YOU AND I 86 MANSNS
ARE PRESENT.
YES, THAT IS QUITE TRUE. 96 MANSNS
YES, QUITE AS FRIGHTENED AS SIMON AND I HAD 118 MANSNS
HOPED--
YES, I QUITE REALIZE YOU ARE--WHAT YOU ARE. 141 MANSNS
I ONLY WISH TO SAY--I'VE QUITE DECIDED TO SELL MY 143 MANSNS
INTEREST IN THE BUSINESS--
AS THOUGH NOT QUITE REALIZING YET WHERE HE IS OR 145 MANSNS
HOW HE GOT THERE.)
PERHAPS. I CONSIDERED THE METHODS USED NOT QUITE 152 MANSNS
ETHICAL--NOT TO SAY RUTHLESS.
QUITE THE CONTRARY. 179 MANSNS
THAT IS QUITE SUFFICIENT TO CONVERT A TARTAR 363 MARCOM
BARBARIAN/
I QUITE REALIZE THAT IN SELF-PROTECTION I'VE GOT 396 MARCOM
TO BUY THEM--OR KILL YOU/
THIS GROWS INTO QUITE A BLARE AS THE MUSICIANS 428 MARCOM
ENTER FROM THE RIGHT.
LOOSE TARTAR TRAVELING DRESS AND LOOK QUITE 429 MARCOM
SHABBY.
HE APPEARS QUITE UNAWARE OF BEING UNUSUAL 439 MARCOM
THERE WAS QUITE A CELEBRATION. 131 MISBEG
GOD SEEMS TO BE PUTTING ON QUITE A DISPLAY. 172 MISBEG
QUITE THE CONTRARY. 45 POET
BUT IF YOU INSIST--{HE POURS A DRINK--A SMALL 46 POET
ONE--HIS HAND QUITE STEADY NOW.)
MOTHER SAID SHE'S BECOME QUITE QUEER LATELY... 5 STRANG
HE CANNOT QUITE CARRY OFF OUTSIDE THE CLASSROOM, 7 STRANG
AND QUITE RIGHTLY... 12 STRANG
IN FACT, YOU'VE LED ME TO BELIEVE THAT YOU WERE 15 STRANG
QUITE CONTENTED HERE--
{WITH ASPERITY} BUT I TELL YOU IT'S QUITE 17 STRANG
IMPOSSIBLE/
{QUITE RIGHT, PROFESSOR/... 17 STRANG
QUITE SO, YOU TWO. 21 STRANG
MOTHER THINKS SHE'S BEHAVED QUITE INEXCUSABLY...) 25 STRANG
SHE'S HAD QUITE A LOT THE MATTER WITH HER SINCE 31 STRANG
HER BREAKDOWN.
{QUICKLY} YOU'RE QUITE RIGHT. 36 STRANG
I CAN QUITE APPRECIATE YOUR FEELING ABOUT GORDON. 39 STRANG
AS IF HE COULD NOT QUITE BELIEVE IN HIS GOOD 53 STRANG
FORTUNE AND HAD CONSTANTLY TO
{INDIGNANTLY} YOU'RE QUITE OUT THERE/ 74 STRANG
I DON'T UNDERSTAND--QUITE. 77 STRANG
AND YET I CAN'T QUITE CONVINCE SOMETHING IN ME 84 STRANG
THAT'S AFRAID OF SOMETHING.
QUITE SOUND. 86 STRANG
I SAID, +YOU'RE QUITE RIGHT, NED, 91 STRANG
QUITE ALL RIGHT NOW, THANK YOU. 99 STRANG
THAT'S QUITE ENOUGH FOR ONE HUMAN BEING TO THINK 104 STRANG
OF, DEAR, ISN'T IT/
I CAN'T QUITE BELIEVE IN THIS SELF-CONFIDENT 113 STRANG
BUSINESS MAN YET...
QUITE BEAUTIFUL, IF YOU LIKE THAT TYPE. 115 STRANG
UH, I WASN'T QUITE AS BAD AS ALL THAT, SAM/. 117 STRANG
I'M QUITE SURE OF THAT. 121 STRANG
HIS HEAD HAS GROWN QUITE BALD ON TOP. 159 STRANG
{COLDLY} I'M QUITE AWARE MY SON ISN'T A 160 STRANG
WEAKLING--
I HAVEN'T QUITE BURIED ALL MY BITTERNESS, I'M 167 STRANG
AFRAID.
I FIND HER QUITE CHARMING. 168 STRANG
{MORE AND MORE CONFIDENTLY} BESIDES, I'M QUITE 174 STRANG
SURE GORDON ISN'T MY SON.
{SHARPLY} I'M QUITE AWARE OF THAT. 454 WELDED
YOU SEEM TO TAKE IT QUITE CASUALLY THAT MEN MUST 473 WELDED
BE EITHER DRUNK OR DOPED--

QUITS

SHE'S QUITS WITH YE. 246 DESIRE
YEW 'N' ME IS QUITS. 246 DESIRE
DIS BABY PLAYS OUT HIS STRING TO DE END AND WHEN 184 EJONES
HE QUITS.
HE QUITS WID A BANG DE WAY HE OUGHT. 184 EJONES
WHEN HE FORGETS DE BUGHOUSE PREACHIN', AND QUITS 638 ICEMAN
TELLIN' YOU WHERE YUH GET OFF,
GIVE ME A HORSE TO LOVE AND I'LL CRY QUITS TO MEN/102 POET

QUITTER

HE'S ALL QUITTER, ROCKY. 666 ICEMAN

QUITTIN'

I'M QUITTIN' YUH, GET ME/ 11 ANNA
THAT'S FOR YOU TO FIGGER. I'M QUITTIN'. 124 BEYOND
AN' I'M QUITTIN' HERE. 124 BEYOND
I'M QUITTIN'. 124 BEYOND
SO I'M QUITTIN' YOU. 125 BEYOND
I'M QUITTIN' HERE TODAY/ 267 DESIRE
NO QUITTIN', GET ME/ 254 HA APE
{DISGUSTEDLY} AW, HE'S QUITTIN'/ 689 ICEMAN
I'M GOIN' TO TELL HARRY I'M QUITTIN'. 697 ICEMAN
WELL, I'M QUITTIN', TOO. 697 ICEMAN

QUITTING

BUT WHY ARE YOU QUITTING NOW, BEN, WHEN YOU KNOW 124 BEYOND
I'VE SO MUCH WORK ON HANDS
{DEFIANTLY} BECAUSE IT'D BE A COWARD'S QUITTING, 666 ICEMAN
THAT'S WHY/

QUIVER

HER SHOULDERS QUIVER ONCE OR TWICE AS IF SHE WERE 52 ANNA
FIGHTING BACK HER SOBS.

QUIVER (CONT'D.)

AND RISING ABOVE ALL, MAKING THE AIR HUM WITH THE 223 HA APE
QUIVER OF LIBERATED ENERGY,
{HER LIPS QUIVER AND SHE KEEPS HER HEAD TURNED 45 JOURNE
AWAY.)
THEIR LIPS QUIVER, THEIR MOUTHS OPEN AS IF TO 286 LAZARU
LAUGH.
KUKACHIN'S SHOULDERS QUIVER AS, HER HEAD BOWED IN 420 MARCOM
HER HANDS, SHE SOBS QUIETLY.
AN HYSTERICAL, SNEERING GRIN MAKING HER LIPS 166 POET
QUIVER AND TWITCH.)

QUIVERING

{HIS VOICE RAISED AND QUIVERING WITH ANGER} 106 BEYOND
QUIVERING LINE OF FLAME IS SPREADING SLOWLY 166 BEYOND
THEIR PHYSICAL ATTRACTION BECOMES A PALPABLE FORCE229 DESIRE
QUIVERING IN THE HOT AIR.
{TWITCHING AND QUIVERING AGAIN.) 598 ICEMAN
HIS QUIVERING VOICE HAS A CONDEMNING COMMAND IN 720 ICEMAN
IT)
{WINCING--HER LIPS QUIVERING PITIFULLY.) 45 JOURNE
{HIS VOICE QUIVERING.) HUSH, MARY, FOR THE LOVE 122 JOURNE
OF GOD/ HE LOVES YOU.
ONCE AS QUIVERING FLECKS OF RHYTHM WE BEAT DOWN 324 LAZARU
FROM THE SUN.
{HIS VOICE QUIVERING} NELLY/ 463 WELDED

QUIVERS

REUBEN QUIVERS BUT NOT A SOUND COMES FROM HIS 448 DYNAMO
LIPS.
HIS VOICE QUIVERS BUT IS DEADLY QUIET.) 114 POET

QUIZZICALLY

{WATCHING LARRY QUIZZICALLY} 639 ICEMAN
{QUIZZICALLY} HELLO, WHAT'S THISS 641 ICEMAN
{WINKS AT HIM QUIZZICALLY} I SEE. 643 ICEMAN
LAUGHING AFFECTIONATELY--THEN QUIZZICALLY} 333 LAZARU
{LOOKS UP AT THE CEILING QUIZZICALLY} 422 MARCOM

QUIZZING

{WITH A PERSUASIVE QUIZZING TONE} 17 STRANG

QUOTATION

{HE DECLAIMS HIS FAVORITE QUOTATION} 627 ICEMAN
{ENRAGED BY THE REPETITION OF THIS QUOTATION} 580 ROPE

QUOTE

AND THEN THE FAVORITE QUOTE FROM BYRON, RECITED 67 POET
ALOUD TO HIS OWN IMAGE.)

QUOTES

{HE QUOTES RHETORICALLY} =OH THOU, 198 AHWILD
{SUDDENLY--WITH A SAD PATHOS, QUOTES AWKWARDLY AND198 AHWILD
SHYLY}
{QUOTES FROM =CANDIDA= IN A HOLLOW VOICE} 216 AHWILD
{STANDS INSIDE THE DOOR, LOOKING AFTER THEM-- 217 AHWILD
QUOTES BITTERLY}
{QUOTES BITTERLY} =DRINK FOR YOU KNOW NOT WHENCE 235 AHWILD
YOU COME NOR WHY.
{FORCES A WICKED LEER TO HIS LIPS AND QUOTES WITH 261 AHWILD
PONDEROUS MOCKERY}
{QUOTES IN A LOW VOICE BUT WITH DEEP FEELING} 508 DAYS
COME SOON--SOON {HE QUOTES THIS LAST WITH A 286 GGBROW
MOCKING LONGING.}
{HE QUOTES A TRANSLATION OF THE CLOSING COUPLET 591 ICEMAN
SARDONICALLY}
{QUOTES ALOUD TO HIMSELF IN A GUTTURAL DECLAMATORY592 ICEMAN
STYLE}
{HE QUOTES} =DEAR COLLEGE DAYS, WITH PLEASURE 595 ICEMAN
RIFE=
HE QUOTES WITH GREAT SENTIMENT, IF WITH SLIGHT 599 ICEMAN
APPLICATION}
{HE QUOTES, PUTTING ON A HAM-ACTOR MANNER,} 21 JOURNE
{STARES AT HIM PUZZLEDLY, THEN QUOTES 32 JOURNE
MECHANICALLY.}
{HE QUOTES FROM THUS SPAKE ZARATHUSTRA.} 78 JOURNE
{HE QUOTES.) =HOW SHARPER THAN A SERPENT'S TOOTH 89 JOURNE
IT IS--=
{HE QUOTES FROM DOWSON SARDONICALLY.} 130 JOURNE
{HE QUOTES, USING HIS FINE VOICE.} 131 JOURNE
{HE QUOTES.) =THE FAULT, DEAR BRUTUS, IS NOT IN 152 JOURNE
OUR STARS, BUT IN OURSELVES
{QUOTES WITH GUSTO FROM OSCAR WILDE'S =THE 159 JOURNE
HARLOT'S HOUSE.=
{QUOTES DERISIVELY.} =HARLOTS AND HUNTED HAVE 160 JOURNE
PLEASURES OF THEIR OWN TO GIVE,
THEN SUDDENLY HE LOOKS UP, HIS FACE HARD, AND 161 JOURNE
QUOTES JEERINGLY.}
{HE QUOTES FROM KIPLING'S =SESTINA OF THE TRAMP- 161 JOURNE
ROYAL.=
{HE QUOTES FROM =THE CHAMBERED NAUTILUS.= 148 MANSNS
{HE QUOTES} =NOW MORE THAN EVER SEEMS IT RICH TO 104 MISBEG
DIE.=
{HE QUOTES DROWSILY} =BUT I WAS DESOLATE AND SICK 165 MISBEG
OF AN OLD PASSION.
HE STARTS HIS FAMILIAR INCANTATION QUOTES FROM 116 POET
BYRON.}

QUOTIN'

WITH HIS QUOTIN' LATIN AND HIS HIGH-TONED JESUIT 10 MISBEG
COLLEGE EDUCATION,
YOU QUOTIN' SCRIPTURE/ 580 ROPE

QUOTING

{WHO, BORED TO DEATH BY ALL THIS POETRY QUOTING, 199 AHWILD
SAY, DID YOU GET ME QUOTING FROM THE BIBLE, ADAS 481 DYNAMO

R*AL

IT'S A R*AL NICE BED. 224 DESIRE

R*ALLY

I CAN'T B*LIEVE IT'S R*ALLY MINE. 221 DESIRE
DID YE R*ALLY GO& 240 DESIRE
{THEN A BIT ANXIOUSLY} D'YE R*ALLY LOVE ME, EBENS 244 DESIRE
{SHUDDERS--THEN HUMBLY} AN* DID YE R*ALLY LOVE ME258 DESIRE
AFORE&

RABBIT

BUCK TEETH IN A SMALL RABBIT MOUTH. 575 ICEMAN
I'LL BET YOU'RE A MILE AWAY BY NOW, YOU RABBIT/ 10 MISBEG

RABBIT'S
SHE'S MY RABBIT'S FOOT. 180 EJONES

RABBLE
IF YOU CALL THE LEADERS OF A RABBLE OF FARMERS 677 ICEMAN
OFFICERS--
IF THEY ARE RABBLE, THEY'RE FULL OF DROLL HUMOR AT 38 POET
TIMES.

RABID
HE WENT TO FRANCE AND BECAME A RABID JACOBIN, A 83 POET
WORSHIPER OF ROBESPIERRE.

RACE
AND HE DARED ME TO RACE HIM OUT TO THE STAKE AND 230 AHWILD
BACK.
I AM SIRED BY GOLD AND DAMNED BY IT, AS THEY SAY 219 HA APE
AT THE RACE TRACK--
(THIS LAST IN THE CHANTING FORMULA OF THE GALLERY 224 HA APE
GODS AT THE SIX-DAY BIKE RACE.
AND HE'D NEVER SEEN A RACE HORSE, 21 HUGHIE
THIS OLD TURTLE NEVER WINS A RACE, BUT HE WAS AS 25 HUGHIE
FOXY AS TEN GUYS
ABOUT A RACE HORSE A GUY OWNED ONCE. 25 HUGHIE
AND FIRST THING YOU KNOW I'D BE LOUSY WITH JACK, 29 HUGHIE
BETTIN' A GRAND A RACE.
HELL, I ONCE WIN TWENTY GRAND ON A SINGLE RACE. 36 HUGHIE
THAT'S ACTION/
(HE WATCHES EXCITEDLY, AS IF IT WERE A RACE HE HAD688 ICEMAN
A BET ON.
OUR RACE WILL PERISH/ 287 LAZARU
OUR RACE WILL PERISH/ 287 LAZARU
HEAVY, DOMINEERING, SELF-COMPLACENT, THE FACE OF A291 LAZARU
CONFIDENT DOMINANT RACE.
(LAUGHS PITYINGLY) SO SAY THE RACE OF MEN, WHOSE 352 LAZARU
LIVES ARE LONG DYINGS/
SLOWLY ARISES FROM THE PAST OF THE RACE OF MEN 360 LAZARU
THAT WAS HIS TOMB OF DEATH/
AND RID THE WORLD OF THIS STUPID RACE OF MEN AND 9 MANSNS
WASH THE EARTH CLEAN/
COMPETITORS IN THE RACE FOR POWER AND WEALTH AND 46 MANSNS
POSSESSIONS/
(QUIETLY.) WHAT HAS YOUR RACE AND FASTIDIOUS, 178 MANSNS
IN AGE AND APPEARANCE, MAKING ALLOWANCE FOR THE 347 MARCOM
DIFFERENCE IN RACE.
FROM THE TIME I WAS A KID, I LOVED RACE-HORSES. 143 MISBEG
I FOUND THAT EVERY DAY I WAS GLAD WHEN THE LAST 143 MISBEG
RACE WAS OVER.
SO THAT WHEN THE RACE WAS OVER AND THEY'D WON 153 STRANG
GORDON FAINTED
BRAND NEW ONE I HAD INSTALLED ESPECIALLY FOR THIS 160 STRANG
RACE, TOO/
WHAT DO I CARE ABOUT THIS STUPID RACES... 162 STRANG
WHEN IT'S GORDON'S LAST RACE, HIS LAST APPEARANCE 162 STRANG
ON A VARSITY/
I'M NOT THE SLIGHTEST BIT INTERESTED IN THIS RACE 167 STRANG
TODAY, FOR EXAMPLE/
THERE'S A RACE GOING ON, DON'T YOU KNOW ITS 171 STRANG
AND I'VE GOTTEN INTERESTED IN THIS RACE NOW. 175 STRANG
NAVY HAS DRAWN AHEAD--HALF A LENGTH--LOOKS LIKE 177 STRANG
NAVY'S RACE, HE SAID--
COULDN'T YOU TELL ME LATER, MRS. EVANS--AFTER THE 178 STRANG
RACE/
(HE SMILES KINDLY AT HER) SO GET BACK TO THE 179 STRANG
RACE/
ALL THE SAME, I CAN'T HELP HOPING HE'LL BE BEATEN 179 STRANG
IN THIS RACE.
(FORGETTING EVERYTHING ELSE, TURNS BACK TO THE 181 STRANG
RACE)
AS IF SOME RACE OF LIFE AND DEATH WERE HAPPENING 181 STRANG
THERE FOR HER.)
GREATEST RACE IN THE HISTORY OF ROWING/ 182 STRANG
GREAT RACE YOU STROKED LAST JUNE-- 194 STRANG

RACES
THOUGH AFTER HE'S THROUGH WITH HIS BETTING ON 213 AHWILD
HORSE RACES, AND DICE,
ALL THE CIVILIZED WHITE RACES ARE REPRESENTED, 207 HA APE
AND BETTIN' ON HORSE RACES, YOU DON'T GET NO 22 HUGHIE
ASSIST FROM ME.+
THEY ACT FOR THE MOMENT LIKE TWO PERSONS OF 480 WELDED
DIFFERENT RACES,

RACETRACK
AND THE BARROOM SPONGES AND RACETRACK TOUTS AND 30 MISBEG
GAMBLERS ARE THROUGH WITH HIM

RACHEL
+AN' GOD HEARKENED UNTO RACHEL+/ 235 DESIRE

RACIAL
HERE THE MASK OF EACH MEMBER OF THE CHORUS HAS A 306 LAZARU
DIFFERENT RACIAL BASIS--

RACIALLY
RACIALLY THERE ARE MANY NATIONS REPRESENTED. 306 LAZARU

RACK
NOT ON'Y YOUR PLACE BUT MINE TOO IS DRIFTIN' TO 114 BEYOND
RACK AND RUIN,

RACKED
(HE IS RACKED BY A VIOLENT FIT OF COUGHING 148 BEYOND
IT IS STRAINED, NERVE-RACKED, HECTIC, 13 STRANG

RACKET
WELL, I SUPPOSE MARRIAGE AIN'T SUCH A BUM RACKET, 12 HUGHIE
IF YOU'RE MADE FOR IT.
+THAT'S WORSE,+ I SAID, +NO GUY CAN BEAT THAT 22 HUGHIE
RACKET.
AND HE HAD KIDS AND A WIFE, AND THE FAMILY RACKET 25 HUGHIE
IS OUT OF MY LINE.
HE LIKED TO KID HIMSELF I'M MIXED UP IN THE 28 HUGHIE
RACKET.
HE'S OUT OF THE RACKET. 33 HUGHIE
YES, IT IS A GODDAMNED RACKET WHEN YOU STOP TO 33 HUGHIE
THINK, ISN'T IT, 4925
I MEAN, THE WHOLE GODDAMNED RACKET. 33 HUGHIE
IT'S ALL IN THE RACKET, HUH5 38 HUGHIE

RACKET
(CONT'D.)
HE'S ELECTED HIMSELF BOSS OF DIS BOITHDAY RACKET. 630 ICEMAN
OBLIVIOUS TO THEIR RACKET.) 728 ICEMAN
GOSH, WHAT A RACKET/ 21 JOURNE
OUT OF A BUM RACKET. 129 MISBEG

RACKET'S
HER RACKET'S ENOUGH TO SPLIT A BODY'S EARS. 117 BEYOND

RACKETS
LIVING HAND TO MOUTH ON THE FRINGE OF THE RACKETS. 9 HUGHIE

RACKINGLY
HE HIDES IT ON HER BREAST AND SOBS RACKINGLY. 152 MISBEG

RACKS
(HE HAS A FIT OF COUGHING WHICH RACKS HIS BODY). 167 BEYOND

RADIANCE
AND THE FACE OF THE CHRIST SHINE WITH THIS 566 DAYS
RADIANCE.)
AND HIS BODY ILLUMINED BY A SOFT RADIANCE AS OF 274 LAZARU
TINY PHOSPHORESCENT FLAMES.

RADIANT
(HE RAISES HIMSELF ON HIS ELBOW, HIS FACE RADIANT,167 BEYOND
AND POINTS TO THE HORIZON)
HIS FACE SEEMED ALIVE AS A LIVING MAN'S WOULD BE, 507 DAYS
BUT RADIANT WITH ETERNAL LIFE,
WHICH IS RADIANT WITH A GREAT PURE LOVE FOR HER 292 GGBROW
HIS BRONZED FACE AND LIPS RADIANT IN THE HALO OF 307 LAZARU
HIS OWN GLOWING LIGHT.
HIS FIGURE RADIANT AND UNEARTHLY IN HIS OWN LIGHT,335 LAZARU
HIS FACE IS RADIANT WITH NEW FAITH AND JOY. 348 LAZARU

RADIATE
HIS APPEARANCE AND PERSONALITY RADIATE HEALTH AND 500 DAYS
OBSERVANT KINDLINESS--

RADIATES
HE RADIATES LOVE AND DEVOTION AND BOYISH 53 STRANG
ADORATION.

RADICAL
AND SO HE GRABS AT EVERYTHING RADICAL TO READ AND 202 AHWILD
WANTS TO PASS IT ON TO HIS
AND IT SHOCKED JOHN TERRIBLY, POOR DEAR--IN SPITE 523 DAYS
OF ALL HIS OLD RADICAL IDEAS.
THERE IS A FOREIGN ATMOSPHERE ABOUT HIM, THE STAMP574 ICEMAN
OF AN ALIEN RADICAL.
(THOUGH HE IS MOST LIBERAL--EVEN RADICAL--IN HIS 7 STRANG
TOLERANT UNDERSTANDING

RADICALS
ABOUT THE RADICALS, MY DEAR--AND THE FALSE 237 HA APE
DOCTRINES THAT ARE BEING PREACHED.
THAT'S THE WORK OF A MERE HANDFUL OF RADICALS-- 392 MARCOM

RADIO
I'M THINKN THINKIN' HE WOULDN'T USE THE TELEGRAPH 437 DYNAMO
OR TELEPHONE OR RADIO
OF COURSE, THE DAMNED RADIO HAS TO PICK OUT THIS 160 STRANG
TIME TO GO DEAD/
(WITH ANGRY DISGUST) IF ONLY THAT DAMNED RADIO 162 STRANG
WAS WORKING/
WE'LL SEE IF MCCABE'S GETTING THE DAMNED RADIO 164 STRANG
FIXED.

RAFT
HE'S A BORN DREAMER WITH A RAFT OF GREAT DREAMS, 29 POET
HE CAN GIVE YOU A RAFT OF PEASANT BRATS TO SQUEAL 114 POET
AND FIGHT/

RAG
HIS SOLDIERS ARE IN DIFFERENT DEGREES OF RAG-- 202 EJONES
CONCEALED NAKEDNESS.
(SNEERING JEALOUSLY AGAIN.) A HICK TOWN RAG/ 36 JOURNE
SHE IS STARING FIXEDLY AT A RAG DOLL WHICH SHE HAS578 ROPE
PROPPED UP AGAINST THE
WE'LL SHOVE A RAG IN HER MOUTH SC'S SHE CAN'T 600 ROPE
YELL.

RAGE
(IN A SUDDEN RAGE, SHAKING HIS FIST AT THE 536 'ILE
SKYLIGHT)
(SUDDENLY SPRINGING TO HIS FEET AND SMASHING HIS 9 ANNA
FIST ON THE TABLE IN A RAGE)
(THEN PRETENDING TO FLY INTO A RAGE, HER EYES 11 ANNA
ENJOYING CHRIS' MISERY)
(GETTING UNSTEADILY TO HIS FEET AGAIN--IN A RAGE) 32 ANNA
(THEN IN A FRENZY OF RAGE) BUT, PY GOD, YOU DON'T 40 ANNA
OU DAT/
(SPUTTERING WITH RAGE) YOU VAS CRAZY FOOL, AY 48 ANNA
TALL YOU/
(HALF RISING FROM HIS CHAIR--IN A VOICE CHOKED 49 ANNA
WITH RAGE)
(HIS FACE WORKING WITH RAGE, HIS HAND GOING BACK 49 ANNA
TO THE SHEATH-KNIFE ON HIS HIP)
BURKE'S FACE IS LIVID WITH THE RAGE THAT IS EATING 58 ANNA
HIM UP.
(SHE LEANS OVER AND PULLS HIS HANDS FROM HIS 58 ANNA
EARS--WITH HYSTERICAL RAGE)
HIS FACE TENSE WITH THE EFFORT TO SUPPRESS HIS 58 ANNA
GRIEF AND RAGE.)
(BLAZING OUT--TURNING ON HER IN A PERFECT FRENZY 60 ANNA
OF RAGE--
HE BURSTS INTO RAGE) 62 ANNA
OF IMPOTENT ANIMAL RAGE BAFFLED BY ITS OWN ABJECT 68 ANNA
MISERY.)
(HIS FACE SUDDENLY CONVULSED WITH GRIEF AND RAGE) 68 ANNA
(TURNING ON HER--OVERCOME BY RAGE AGAIN) 71 ANNA
(SHAKING HIS FINGER AT ANDY, IN A COLD RAGE) 106 BEYOND
(TEARS OF RAGE STARTING TO HIS EYES--HOARSELY) 107 BEYOND
(HER EYES FLASHING--BURSTING INTO UNCONTROLLABLE 126 BEYOND
RAGE)
(SHE STUTTERS INCOHERENTLY, OVERCOME BY RAGE.) 127 BEYOND
(WORKING HERSELF INTO A FIT OF RAGE) 152 BEYOND
(WITH IMPOTENT RAGE) GOD, WHAT A SHAME/ 162 BEYOND
(HE GROANS WITH ANGUISHED RAGE. 165 BEYOND
(HE CLENCHES HIS FISTS IN AN IMPOTENT RAGE AGAINST167 BEYOND
FATE)
(STARES AT HER FOR A MOMENT, HIS RAGE EBBING AWAY,168 BEYOND

RAGE

RAGE (CONT'D.)
(POINTING TO THE BODY--TREMBLING WITH THE VIOLENCE168 BEYOND OF HIS RAGE)
COCKY RISES TO HIS FEET, HIS FACE LIVID WITH RAGE,472 CARIBE AND SPRINGS AT PADDY,
HIS HAPPINESS FILLED ME WITH RAGE--THE THOUGHT 521 DAYS THAT HE MADE OTHERS HAPPY.
(THEN BREAKING INTO A COLD, VICIOUS RAGE) 552 DAYS
(IN IMPOTENT RAGE) NO/ 563 DAYS
RAGE AND THE FEAR THAT THEY ARE INSANE.) 223 DESIRE
(SUDDENLY ROARING WITH RAGE) 223 DESIRE
CABOT COMES BACK, PANTING WITH IMPOTENT RAGE. 224 DESIRE
HE STANDS GLOWERING, HIS FIST CLENCHED, HIS FACE 226 DESIRE GRIM WITH RAGE.)
(STARES AT HER--THEN A TERRIBLE EXPRESSION OF RAGE233 DESIRE COMES OVER HIS FACE--
CABOT'S RAGE GROWS) 254 DESIRE
(HAS BEEN LISTENING, PETRIFIED WITH GRIEF AND 255 DESIRE RAGE--
(IS CONFRONTING HIM, CHOKING WITH RAGE) 255 DESIRE
(RAGE BEGINNING TO MINGLE WITH GRIEF) 261 DESIRE
AND SPRINGS TO HER FEET--WITH WILD RAGE AND 264 DESIRE HATRED)
(STAMMERING BETWEEN FEAR AND RAGE--SHOUTING AFTER 530 DIFRNT HER)
(KEEPING HIS RAGE IN CONTROL--HEAVILY) 537 DIFRNT
(OVERCOME BY REMORSE--FORGETTING HIS RAGE 537 DIFRNT INSTANTLY--
(THEN HIS HORROR TURNING TO A CONFUSED RAGE) 440 DYNAMO
(STOPS SHORT AND STARES AT FIFE WITH A RAGE THAT 450 DYNAMO CHOKES HIM
THE JOKE HAS THROWN HIM--BURSTING INTO A FATUOUS 452 DYNAMO RAGE--TO HIS WIFE)
(HE JERKS OUT HIS REVOLVER IN A FRENZY OF 192 EJONES TERRIFIED RAGE)
HE CURSES UNDER HIS BREATH WITH RAGE AND HATRED.) 194 EJONES
JONES BELLOWS WITH BAFFLED, TERRIFIED RAGE, 195 EJONES
(THEN RAGE AT THE INSULT TO HIS MOTHER OVERCOMING 24 ELECTR ALL PRUDENCE--
(SHE CANNOT RESTRAIN HER RAGE--THREATENINGLY) 35 ELECTR
(THEN WITHOUT WAITING FOR A REPLY, BURSTING INTO 76 ELECTR JEALOUS RAGE)
(THEN IN A BURST OF RAGE) GOD DAMN HIM, I'LL 99 ELECTR
(IN A BURST OF MURDEROUS RAGE) 99 ELECTR
ORIN IS HOLDING IN A SAVAGE, REVENGEFUL RAGE. 109 ELECTR
HE GLARES AT THEM WITH JEALOUS RAGE 148 ELECTR
(THEN SUDDENLY HER HORROR TURNING INTO A VIOLENT 156 ELECTR RAGE--
(HER CONTROL SNAPPING--TURNING ON HIM NOW IN A 166 ELECTR BURST OF FRANTIC HATRED AND RAGE)
(HER RAGE PASSES, LEAVING HER WEAK AND SHAKEN. 173 ELECTR
(THEN GLARING AT HER--WITH A BURST OF RAGE) 173 ELECTR
(THERE IS A GROWL OF CURSING RAGE FROM ALL SIDES.) 224 HA APE
RAGE AND BEWILDERED FURY RUSH BACK ON YANK. 226 HA APE
(THERE IS A ROAR OF RAGE FROM ALL SIDES.) 228 HA APE
(BURSTING INTO RAGE--AS IF SHE WERE STILL IN FRONT)230 HA APE OF HIM)
(STUNG--WITH A GROWL OF RAGE) 230 HA APE
(IN A FRENZY OF RAGE) I'LL FIX HER/ 232 HA APE
HIS FACE GROWING PALE WITH RAGE 236 HA APE
(HE TURNS IN A RAGE ON THE MEN, 238 HA APF
(THEN WITH SUDDEN RAGE, RATTLING HIS CELL BARS) 240 HA APE
(THICK WITH RAGE) I'LL SHOW YUH WHO'S A APE, YUH 241 HA APE BUM/
(WITH GROWLING RAGE) I'D LIKE TO CATCH DAT 243 HA APE SENATOR GUY ALONE FOR A SECOND.
(SNARLING WITH RAGE, 672 ICEMAN
(WITH GUILTY RAGE) ALL LIES/ 677 ICEMAN
(TURNS WITH HUMILIATED RAGE--WITH AN ATTEMPT AT 685 ICEMAN JAUNTY CASUALNESS)
(THE MOMENTUM OF HIS FIT OF RAGE DOES IT. 688 ICEMAN
(WITH GUTTURAL RAGE) GOTTAMNED HICKEY/ 691 ICEMAN
(WITH GUTTURAL RAGE) GOTTAMNED STUPID PROLETARIAN695 ICEMAN SLAVES/
DRISCOLL FLIES INTO AN UNREASONABLE RAGE) 517 INZONE
(TRYING TO RESTRAIN HIS GROWING RAGE) 526 INZONE
(HIS VOICE TREMBLING WITH RAGE. 527 INZONE
THERE IS A MUFFLED GROAN OF RAGE AND PROTEST FROM 529 INZONE SMITTY.)
(HIS RAGE STILL SMOULDERING.) 80 JOURNE
BUT HE ALWAYS MANAGES TO DRIVE YOU INTO A RAGE, 83 JOURNE ESPECIALLY IF YOU'RE DRUNK, TOO.
WON'T BRIDGET BE IN A RAGE/ 123 JOURNE
(THEN IN A RAGE.) HOW DARE YOU TALK TO YOUR 141 JOURNE FATHER LIKE THAT,
I ONLY SAID THAT BECAUSE YOU PUT ME IN SUCH A GOD-142 JOURNE DAMNED RAGE.
(HE CHOKES HUSKILY, HIS VOICE TREMBLING WITH RAGE,145 JOURNE
(BURSTING WITH RAGE.) AND DON'T THINK I'LL LET 145 JOURNE YOU GET AWAY WITH IT/
THEN IN A BURST OF RAGE HE SPRINGS FROM HIS 162 JOURNE CHAIR.)
(STUNG, TURNS ON HIM IN A RAGE.) 169 JOURNE
HA--HA--(TEARING HIS BEARD AND STAMPING WITH RAGE)282 LAZARU
HA-- (THEN FRANTICALLY--HALF-WEEPING WITH 282 LAZARU INDIGNANT RAGE--TO THE NAZARENES)
(HE CHOKES WITH EXASPERATED RAGE.) 287 LAZARU
(WITH CRIES OF RAGE THE TWO GROUPS RUSH ON ONE 290 LAZARU ANOTHER,
(THEIR FRENZY OF GRIEF TURNED INTO RAGE, 290 LAZARU
(INSANE WITH RAGE NOW) THEY HAVE MURDERED HIM/ 290 LAZARU
(IN A RAGE) HO, BARBARIAN CUR, TURN ROUND/ 316 LAZARU
(WORKING HIMSELF INTO A RAGE) 319 LAZARU
(FLYING INTO A QUEER RAGE) YOU LIE/ 331 LAZARU
(THEN HIS FEAR TURNING TO RAGE) 341 LAZARU
HIM IN A CONFUSED RAGE-- 343 LAZARU
(IN A FRENZY OF DESPAIRING RAGE, HOPPING UP AND 346 LAZARU DOWN)

RAGE (CONT'D.)
IN A SINISTER COLD RAGE, THE CRUELER BECAUSE HIS 348 LAZARU DREAM OF A CURE FOR DEATH IS
(HE STUTTERS AND STAMMERS WITH RAGE, HOPPING UP 359 LAZARU AND DOWN GROTESQUELY,
BEWILDERED PAIN WHICH SPEEDILY TURNS TO RAGE AND 361 LAZARU REVENGEFUL HATRED)
(HALF HYSTERICAL WITH RAGE, PAIN AND GRIEF, 361 LAZARU
(TRIUMPHANT YET DISAPPOINTED--WITH SCORN AND RAGE)366 LAZARU
(WITH RESENTFUL JEALOUSY AND RAGE--IN A VOICE 368 LAZARU RISING TO A SCREAM)
(THEN THERE IS A FIERCE CRY OF RAGE FROM CALIGULA 369 LAZARU AND LAZARUS' LAUGHTER CEASES,
HALF-LAUGHING IN SPITE OF HIMSELF, HALF-WEEPING 369 LAZARU WITH RAGE)
(THIS CHANGES TO RAGE AGAINST DEBORAH.) 185 MANSNS
(HIS TERROR GOING AND RAGE TAKING ITS PLACE, LEAPS352 MARCOM TO HIS FEET)
SHE CONFRONTS HIM DEFIANTLY, HER EYES WILD WITH 415 MARCOM GRIEF AND RAGE.
(WITH RAGE) SHALL I ASK AS MY FIRST WEDDING 416 MARCOM PRESENT FROM GHAZAN KHAN THAT HE
AND AS FULL OF RAGE AS A NEST OF WASPS/ 10 MISBEG
(WITH SUDDEN RAGE) GOD'S CURSE ON HIM, 83 MISBEG
I'LL RAISE A SCENE AND PRETEND I'M IN A RAGE 92 MISBEG BECAUSE HE FORGOT HIS DATE.
(HE BURSTS OUT IN A FIT OF SMOLDERING RAGE) 176 MISBEG
MOST OF THEM IS IN A RAGE AT HIM BECAUSE HE'S COME 26 POET OUT
(BUT INSTANTLY HIS PAIN IS TRANSFORMED INTO RAGE. 51 POET
I'VE KNOWN TOO MANY WOMEN-- (IN A RAGE.) *ABSURD 75 POET PERFORMANCE.* WAS IT'S
I DON'T WANT IT TO REMIND ME-- (WITH HUMILIATED 76 POET RAGE AGAIN.)
AND GIVE HIM TIME TO GET OVER HIS RAGE. 87 POET
RAGE.) 91 POET
WELL, IT WAS ME LET HER GO, SO DON'T TAKE OUT YOUR 91 POET RAGE ON POOR MOTHER.
(HIS PENT-UP RAGE BURSTS OUT--SMASHING HIS FIST ON122 POET THE TABLE.)
(HIS RAGE WELLING AGAIN, AS HIS MIND DWELLS ON HIS124 POET HUMILIATION--
(BELLIGERENTLY.) A LOT CON MELODY CARES FOR 145 POET POLICE, AND HIM IN A RAGE/
I COULD SEE CON'S RAGE RISIN' BUT HE KEPT POLITE. 155 POET
ROARIN' WID RAGE AND CURSIN' LIKE A TROOPER-- 157 POET
(BURSTING INTO SENILE RAGE) NONE O' MINE/ 581 ROPE
BENTLEY WAVES HIS STICK FRANTICALLY IN THE AIR, 583 ROPE AND GROANS WITH RAGE.)
(GLARING AT HIM BUT RESTRAINING HER RAGE) 591 ROPE
(HE RAISES HIS CLENCHED FISTS OVER HIS HEAD IN A 597 ROPE FRENZY OF RAGE.)
(IN A STRANGE RAGE, THREATENINGLY) 120 STRANG
(THEN IN A QUEER, FUTILE RAGE) 132 STRANG
(TREMBLING WITH RAGE, STAMMERS) 142 STRANG
JEALOUSY AND RAGE AND GRIEF, WATCHING THEM.) 145 STRANG
(IN A RAGE--TREMBLINGLY) THEN--HERE'S WHAT--I 150 STRANG THINK OF YOU/
(WITH A SNEER OF RAGE) AND I SUPPOSE YOU WERES 457 WELDED
(TREMBLING WITH RAGE) I'LL NEVER FORGET YOU SAID 458 WELDED THAT/
(BROKENLY--WITH MINGLED GRIEF AND RAGE) 458 WELDED
(IN A TERRIBLE STATE, SOBBING WITH RAGE AND 460 WELDED ANGUISH)
WITH PAIN WHICH TURNS TO HATRED AND RAGE. 462 WELDED
(WITH DULL IMPOTENT RAGE) I CAN'T/ 476 WELDED

RAGGED
YOU'VE SEEMED WORN RAGGED LATELY. 496 DAYS
HIS UNIFORM IS RAGGED AND TORN. 192 EJONES
LOVE IS A WORD--A SHAMELESS RAGGED GHOST OF A 266 GUKROW WORD--
ON HIS LOWER LEFT SHOULDER IS THE BIG RAGGED SCAR 576 ICEMAN OF AN OLD WOUND.
HE'S GOT HARRY AND JIMMY TOMORROW RUN RAGGED, 631 ICEMAN

RAGGEDLY
WORN LONG AND RAGGEDLY CUT. 574 ICEMAN

RAGGEDY
WHAT GOOD IS GITTIN' MONEY IF YOU STAYS BACK IN 180 EJONES DIS RAGGEDY COUNTRYS

RAGING
(RAGING) AYE, DAMN HIM, AND DAMN THE ARCTIC SEAS,536 'ILE
(HE COMES TOWARD THEM, RAGING, HIS FISTS CLENCHED) 39 ANNA
RAGING TRIUMPHANTLY BEFORE ANNA HAS A CHANCE TO 54 ANNA GET IN A WORD)
(THEN RAGING. 60 ANNA
(RAGING) I'LL WAIT 'TILL SHE COMES AND CHOKE HER 68 ANNA DIRTY LIFE OUT.
(RAGING) FOOL/ 565 DAYS
(RAGING) THEN YE'RE A DOG, EBEN CABOT/ 240 DESIRE
(SUDDENLY RAGING) HA/ 262 DESIRE
(SUDDENLY CONVULSED WITH RAGING HATRED AND FEAR) 197 EJONES
(RAGING AND WHO'S TER BLAME, I ARSKS YERS 211 HA APE
AS IF HE HAD RECEIVED A PUNCH FULL IN THE FACE-- 238 HA APE RAGING)
WHEN HE CAN START THE BOER WAR RAGING AGAIN/ 677 ICEMAN
(RAGING) COWARDS/ 527 INZONE
THE DAMP IS IN BRIDGET'S RHEUMATISM AND SHE'S LIKE 99 JOURNE A RAGING DIVIL.
(RAGING) LASH THEM/ 353 MARCOM
(THEN SUDDENLY RAGING) OUT OF MY SIGHT, DOG, 425 MARCOM BEFORE I HAVE YOU IMPALED/
OLD MEN SHOULON'T RUN AROUND RAGING IN THE NOON 12 MISBEG SUN.
NOW DON'T START RAGING AGAIN, FATHER. 13 MISBEG
(RAGING.) THAT DAMNED, INSOLENT YANKEE BITCH/ 127 POET
(SUDDENLY RAGING) I'LL PAY HIM BACK AN RIGHT/ 600 ROPE
(SUDDENLY RAGING) (THEIR HONOR/... 129 STRANG
(RAGING) YOU--/ 181 STRANG

RAGINGLY

(RAGINGLY) BUT I'LL GIT MY VENGEANCE TOO/ 257 DESIRE

RAGLAN

SHE IS DRESSED IN A NURSE'S UNIFORM WITH CAP, A 26 STRANG RAGLAN COAT OVER IT.

RAGS

WITH COLORED RAGS AROUND THEIR MIDDLES AND FLOWERS145 ELECTR STUCK OVER THEIR EARS/

AND GETS DESE RAGS TO PUT ON. 581 ICEMAN

YOU'VE NOTICED MY GLAD RAGS. 588 ICEMAN

THEIR CLAWS RENDED SAILS INTO RAGS, FIERCE WERE 408 MARCOM THE WINDS/

HIS SKINNY BODY IS CLOTHED IN RAGS AND THERE IS 52 POET NOTHING UNDER HIS TATTERED COAT

AND THE SONGS AT THE SAILOR'S OPERA HOUSE WHERE 487 CARDIF THE GUY PLAYED RAGTIME--

RAH

AND THEY'RE GIVEN TO RAH-RAH EXAGGERATION AT NEW 595 ICEMAN HAVEN.

TO BE LIKE THAT RAH-RAH HERO/ 141 STRANG

RAIDED

THE JOINT I WAS IN OUT IN ST. PAUL GOT RAIDED. 16 ANNA SHE'D NEVER MAKE NO ONE EXCEPT SHE RAIDED A BLIND 13 HUGHIE ASYLUM.

RAIL

THEN CLIMBS TO THE FENCE RAIL AGAIN, AND LOOKS OUT B6 BEYOND OVER THE HILLS.

HE COMES TO THE RAIL AND STARES EXPECTANTLY UP THE104 ELECTR WHARF, OFF LEFT.

BRANT LEAPS BACK FROM THE RAIL STARTLEDLY, 104 ELECTR

THEN LEANS OVER THE RAIL AGAIN AND CALLS 104 ELECTR THREATENINGLY.)

(BRANT, STANDING BY THE RAIL LOOKING AFTER HIM, 107 ELECTR A RAIL ENCLOSES THE ENTIRE WHARF AT THE BACK. 257 GGBROW THEN STANDS AT THE LEFT CORNER, FORWARD, HIS HAND258 GGBROW BILLY STANDS AT THE LEFT CORNER, FORWARD, HIS HAND258 GGBROW ON THE RAIL.

TAKES HIS PLACE AT THE RAIL, WHERE YOUNG BROWN HAD260 GGBROW STOOD.

(HE POUNDS ON THE RAIL WITH HIS FIST. 253 HA APE HER CHIN RESTING ON HER HANDS ON TOP OF THE MARBLE363 LAZARU RAIL.

(SHE BOWS HER HEAD ON THE RAIL AND WEEPS.) 401 MARCOM DRESSED IN A ROBE OF SILVER AND STANDS AT THE RAIL405 MARCOM LOOKING DOWN.)

AS MARCO LEANS OVER THE RAIL AND BAWLS AFTER HIM) 407 MARCOM EVANS IS LEANING OVER THE RAIL DIRECTLY BACK OF 158 STRANG NINA.

THE PORTSIDE RAIL IS IN THE REAR, THE CURVE OF THE158 STRANG STERN AT LEFT.

(THIS LAST WITH A RESENTFUL LOOK DOWN AT HER AS HE160 STRANG MOVES BACK TO THE RAIL.)

(POUNDING HIS FIST ON THE RAIL--LETTING HIS PENT- 161 STRANG

OF FEELINGS EXPLODE)

(SUDDENLY EXPLODING, POUNDS HIS FIST ON THE RAIL) 163 STRANG (DARRELL GETS UP AND TAKES THE GLASSES AND GOES TO171 STRANG THE RAIL AND BEGINS ADJUSTING

(RAISING THE BINOCULARS AS HE GOES TO THE RAIL, HE171 STRANG LOOKS UP THE RIVER.)

THEY RUN TO THE RAIL AND TRAIN THEIR GLASSES UP 176 STRANG THE RIVER.)

(POUNDING ON THE RAIL) COME ON, GORDON BOY/ 176 STRANG (MOVES FROM THE RAIL TOWARD THEM--THINKING KEENLY)178 STRANG (SHE HURRIES BACK TO THE RAIL, RAISING HER 179 STRANG GLASSES.)

(HE TURNS AWAY AND RAISES HIS GLASSES, GOING BACK 179 STRANG TO THE RAIL.

ALL THREE ARE LEANING OVER THE RAIL, THEIR GLASSES180 STRANG GLUED TO THEIR EYES.

(SHE REMAINS STANDING ON THE RAIL, LEANING OUT 182 STRANG DANGEROUSLY.

(STILL STANDING ON THE RAIL, STARING AFTER 183 STRANG GORDON'S SHELL)

RAILING

CAGE AND, LEANING OVER THE RAILING, STARES IN AT 252 HA APE ITS OCCUPANT.

IN FRONT OF THE THRONE IS A MARBLE RAILING 363 LAZARU

RAILROAD

THEN I GAVE UP HOPE WHEN YOU DIDN'T SHOW UP AND I 71 ANNA WENT TO THE RAILROAD STATION.

THE RAILROAD IS JAMMED UP. 47 ELECTR

THE HITCH WAS HOW TO GET THE RAILROAD FARE TO THE 710 ICEMAN BIG TOWN.

IT HAS BEEN A STRAIN GETTING THIS AFFAIR OF THE 71 MANSNS RAILROAD SETTLED.

I REFER NOW TO THE DEAL FOR THE RAILROAD YOU ARE 71 MANSNS TO CONCLUDE THIS MORNING.

AND NOW THE RAILROAD DEAL IS COMPLETED-- 72 MANSNS

I'VE GOT THE RAILROAD NOW. 76 MANSNS

THIS RAILROAD DEAL HAS BEEN A STRAIN. 79 MANSNS

WHICH WE WILL OWN BEFORE LONG, JONATHAN AS OUR 84 MANSNS RAILROAD EXECUTIVE,

THE RAILROAD DIRECTORS WILL BE HERE IN A FEW 92 MANSNS MINUTES.

TO MY MILLS TO BE MADE INTO MY CLOTH AND SHIPPED 100 MANSNS ON MY RAILROAD.

I CONCLUDED A DEAL TODAY WHICH ADDS A RAILROAD TO 100 MANSNS THE COMPANY'S PROPERTIES.

--HAVE WORKED TOO HARD ON THIS RAILROAD DEAL-- 131 MANSNS SELL HIM THE RAILROAD FOR THE SIX. 16 MISBEG

I SEE WORK ON THE RAILROAD AT BALTIMORE IS 40 POET PROGRESSING.

RAILROADING

YOU KNOW NOTHING OF RAILROADING. 71 MANSNS

RAILROADS

WE MUST HAVE RAILROADS. 40 POET

RAIN

IS HE SEASONIN' HIS HAY WITH RAIN THIS YEAR, SAME 124 BEYOND AS LAST? THEY SHOUTS.

RIGHT AS RAIN, DARLIN'. 464 CARIBE

I WANT TO GET TO THE POLICE STATION BEFORE THE 449 DYNAMO RAIN.

THE SOUND OF WIND AND RAIN SWEEPING DOWN ON THE 454 DYNAMO TOWN FORM THE HILLS IS HEARD.)

AND IT'S THE SEA RISING UP IN CLOUDS, FALLING ON 477 DYNAMO THE EARTH IN RAIN,

I'LL CLOSE IT UP AND LEAVE IT IN THE SUN AND RAIN 171 ELECTR TO DIE.

THE LAUGHTER OF HEAVEN SOWS EARTH WITH A RAIN OF 322 GGBROW TEARS.

RIGHT AS RAIN, I'M TELLIN' YE/ 519 INZONE

A DIRTY BARN OF A PLACE WHERE RAIN DRIPPED THROUGH148 JOURNE THE ROOF,

AND THUNDER RUMBLES AND CRASHES BUT THERE IS NO 312 LAZARU RAIN.

LIKE RAIN INTO THE SEA/ 359 LAZARU

DRINK THIS NOW, MAJOR, AND YOU'LL BE RIGHT AS 153 POEFRT RAIN/

RAINCOAT

HE IS BUTTONED UP TO THE NECK IN AN OLD RAINCOAT 450 DYNAMO AND CARRIES AN UMBRELLA.)

(HE JUMPS TO HIS FATHER'S SIDE AND GRABS HIS 453 DYNAMO RAINCOAT BY THE LAPEL--

RAINES

THE RENTING OF ROOMS ON THE UPPER FLOORS, UNDER 571 ICEMAN THE RAINES-LAW LOOPHOLES.

(HARRY HOPE'S IS A RAINES-LAW HOTEL OF THE PERIOD,571 ICEMAN

RAINING

REMEMBER IT'S COLD AND RAINING OUT. 540 DAYS

IT'S RAININGS 540 DAYS

BUT IT'S STILL RAINING, ISN'T IT5 547 DAYS

AND WHEN HE REMINDED ME IT WAS RAINING, IT ALL 550 DAYS SEEMED TO FIT IN SO PERFECTLY--

RAINS

AND WHEN IT RAINS THEIR TEARS TRICKLE DOWN 202 DESIRE MONOTONOUSLY AND ROT ON THE SHINGLES.

RAINY

RAINY DAY OUT AND EVEN INDOORS YOU CAN'T BE TOO 533 DAYS CAREFUL.

(SHE LOOKS AROUND) JEES, DE MORGUE ON A RAINY 615 ICEMAN SUNDAY NIGHT/

RAISE

MARTHY RAISE HELL, TOO, FOR GOD, PY GOLLY/ 10 ANNA

ANNA RAISE HELL IF SHE FIND OAT CUT. 10 ANNA

AND I'VE BEEN ROWING THE BOAT WITH THEM LYING IN 32 ANNA THE BOTTOM NOT ABLE TO RAISE A

YOU'RE HER OLD MAN AND I'D NOT RAISE A FIST TO YOU 39 ANNA FOR THE WORLD.

(TRYING TO RAISE HIMSELF TO A SITTING POSITION AS 167 BEYOND THEY HASTEN TO HIS SIDE--

AN' HIM UPSTAIRS, I'LL RAISE HIM T' BE LIKE ME/ 256 DESIRE TO RAISE CAIN ONCE IN A WHILE--BEFORE HE MARRIED 509 DIFRNT ME, I MEAN.

HE'LL RAISE THE ROOF/. 424 DYNAMO

STRIVING TO RAISE THEMSELVES ON END, FAILING AND 189 EJONES SINKING PRONE AGAIN.

THE PLANTERS RAISE THEIR FINGERS, MAKE THEIR BIDS.197 EJONES AND MANAGES TO RAISE HIS ARM AND POINT AN ACCUSING 63 ELECTR FINGER AT HER.)

HE MAKES AN EFFORT TO RAISE HIMSELF TOWARD HER AND322 GGBROW SHE HELPS HIM.

I'D SAY, =OKAY, ARNOLD, THE SKY'S THE LIMIT,= AND 32 HUGHIE I'D RAISE HIM FIVE GRAND.

EVEN HUGO COMES OUT OF HIS COMA TO RAISE HIS HEAD 618 ICEMAN AND BLINK THROUGH HIS THICK

MANAGING TO RAISE HIS HEAD A LITTLE AND FORCE HIS 628 ICEMAN EYES HALF OPEN.

THEY RAISE THEIR SCHOONERS WITH AN ENTHUSIASTIC 659 ICEMAN CHORUS OF =HERE'S HOW, HARRY/=

OR ELSE DEY'D RAISE HELL UPSTAIRS, LAUGHIN' AND 669 ICEMAN SINGIN'.

BE GOD, YOU CAN'T SAY HICKEY HASN'T THE MIRACULOUS677 ICEMAN TOUCH TO RAISE THE DEAD.

BEING CAREFUL NOT TO RAISE A NOISE, MIND/ 519 INZONE

I DID PUT EDMUND WISE TO THINGS, BUT NOT UNTIL I 34 JOURNE SAW HE'D STARTED TO RAISE HELL.

WINE IS POURED AND ALL RAISE THEIR GOBLETS TOWARD 278 LAZARU LAZARUS--

THEY RAISE CLENCHED FISTS OR HANDS DISTENDED INTO 287 LAZARU THREATENING TALONS.

TO RAISE FROM THE DEAD OUR FREEDOM TO FREE US FROM304 LAZARU ROME/

RAISE FROM THE DEAD OUR FREEDOM/ 304 LAZARU

HIS SOLDIERS RAISE THEIR SWORDS. 305 LAZARU

RAISE THE DEAD/ 344 LAZARU

LET HIM RAISE SOMEONE FROM THE DEAD/ 344 LAZARU

RAISE THE DEAD/ 345 LAZARU

I WAS AFRAID YOU MIGHT RAISE OBJECTIONS. 90 MANSNS

(DEBORAH IS STILL NOW AND LISTENING TENSELY, BUT 167 MANSNS SHE DOES NOT RAISE HER HEAD.)

RAISE YOURSELF. 194 MANSNS

ONE ACCORD THEY RAISE THEIR ARMS AND EYES TO THE 376 MARCOM SKY.

RAISE THEIR HEADS AND STARE BEFORE THEM IN 434 MARCOM SILENCE.

IF I WAS A DAINTY, PRETTY TART HE'D BE PROUD I'D 92 MISBEG RAISE A RUMPUS ABOUT HIM.

I'LL RAISE A SCENE AND PRETEND I'M IN A RAGE 92 MISBEG BECAUSE HE FORGOT HIS DATE.

AND I RAISE THE ROOF AND THREATEN HIM IF HE DON'T 94 MISBEG MARRY YOU--

(SHE DRAWS BACK AGAIN SO HE HAS TO RAISE HIS HEAD 149 MISBEG FROM HER BREAST.

HIS HAND TREMBLES SO VIOLENTLY THAT WHEN HE 35 POET ATTEMPTS TO RAISE THE GLASS

RAISE

RAISE (CONT'D.)

I'LL RAISE A TUNE FOR YOU. 53 POET

I KNO* YOU'D RAISE A BEAUTIFUL TUNE, BUT I HAVE TO 54 POET GO OUT.

AND WOULD RAISE TO A JUMP OVER HELL IF I GAVE THE 102 POET WORD/

IF YE KAPE ON TRYING TO RAISE THE DEAD/ 176 POET

IF YE KEPT ON INTERFERIN' AND TRYIN' TO RAISE THE 179 POET DEAD.

RAISED

THEN MRS. MILLER'S VOICE, RAISED COMMANDINGLY, 186 AHWILD «TOMMY/

RAISED AS THEY COME IN AND FOR A MOMENT AFTER, 221 AHWILD THEN SUDDENLY CAUTIOUSLY LOWERED.

HIS VOICE, WHEN NOT RAISED IN A HOLLOW BOOM, IS 5 ANNA TUNED DOWN TO A SLY,

AND WHEN WE WAS RAISED HIGH ON A GREAT WAVE I TOOK 36 ANNA A LOOK ABOUT

(HIS VOICE RAISED AND QUIVERING WITH ANGER) 106 BEYOND

(HIS VOICE RAISED LOUDLY) AND NOW--I'M FINDING 127 BEYOND OUT WHAT YOU'RE REALLY LIKE--

(UNCONSCIOUSLY THEY HAVE ALL RAISED THEIR VOICES, 481 CARDIF

RAISE SQUARE OF THE NUMBER ONE MATCH, COVERED 455 CARIBE WITH CANVAS,

(PROUDLY.) HAIN'T HE RAISED 'EM T' BE FUST-RATE, 218 DESIRE NUMBER ONE PRIZE STOCKS

(IN THE MEANTIME, THE WINDOW OF THE UPPER BEDROOM 224 DESIRE ON RIGHT IS RAISED

AND WHEN SHE SAW THE SHIP WAS GITTIN' READY TO 503 DIFRNT SAIL SHE RAISED RUCTIONS,

(FROM HER HIDING PLACE BY THE HEDGE HAS CAUGHT 437 DYNAMO REUBEN'S RAISED VOICE--

BELOW THE DISCONNECTING SWITCHES IS A RAISED 483 DYNAMO PLATFORM.

THE RAISED RIVER BANK IS IN THE NEARER BACKGROUND.199 EJONES

CREW BUT NARY A LICK COULD THEY GIT INTO 'EM TILL 105 ELECTR I RAISED A TUNE--

SETH'S THIN WRAITH OF A BARITONE IS RAISED IN HIS 123 ELECTR FAVORITE MOURNFUL «SHENANDOAH,

(WHO HAS RAISED HER HEAD AND HAS BEEN STARING AT 166 ELECTR HIM WITH DREAD

ON THE GROUND FLOOR, THE UPPER PART OF THE 169 ELECTR WINDOWS, RAISED FROM THE BOTTOM,

KEEP THY HEART FREE AND RAISED UPWARDS TO GOD 291 GGBROW

DION'S VOICE CAN BE HEARD, RAISED MOCKINGLY. 294 GGBROW

BORN AND RAISED IN THE STICKS, WASN'T YOUS 13 HUGHIE

SAWBUCK THERE UNTIL I RAISED IT. 34 HUGHIE

HUGO, WHO HAS AWAKENED AND RAISED HIS HEAD WHEN 672 ICEMAN LARRY POUNCED ON THE TABLE,

ON A RAISED PLATFORM AT THE MIDDLE OF THE ONE 274 LAZARU TABLE PLACED LENGTHWISE

BETWEEN THIS AND THE HOUSE IS A SMALL RAISED 281 LAZARU TERRACE.

ACCORDING TO YOUR STUPID LIES, HE RAISED HIM FROM 283 LAZARU THE DEAD/

THE CROWD HAVE RAISED WHATEVER WEAPONS THEY HAVE 305 LAZARU FOUND--

HER ARMS RAISED OUTWARD LIKE THE ARMS OF A CROSS.)318 LAZARU

OVER THE BONES THAT RAISED THEM UNTIL BOTH ARE 330 LAZARU DUST.

HIS LAUGHTER DIES AND IS FORGOTTEN, AND THE HOPE 364 LAZARU IT RAISED DIES--

TIBERIUS STANDS ON THE RAISED DAIS LAUGHING GREAT 368 LAZARU SHOUTS OF GLEAM.

(HAS FLUNG HERSELF ON HER KNEES BESIDE SIMON AND 190 MANSNS RAISED HIS HEAD.

I ONLY RAISED MY HAND TO HER ONCE-- 18 MISBEG

I'VE RAISED A DAUGHTER SO COWARDLY SHE HAS TO USE 74 MISBEG A CLUB.

WASN'T I RAISED ON HIS ESTATES 14 POET

THEN HE RAISED WHAT MONEY HE STILL WAS ABLE, 14 POET

IT'S THE DIRTY HUT IN WHICH YOUR FATHER WAS BORN 114 POET AND RAISED YOU'RE REMEMBERING,

THEN QUIET AS IF HE HAD RAISED A HAND FOR SILENCE,180 POET

AND ANNIE'S WHINING VOICE RAISED IN ANGRY 594 ROPE PROTEST.)

RAISES

(HE RAISES HIS SOUP PLATE AND DECLAIMS) 224 AHWILD

THEN SHE KNEELS DOWN BESIDE HIM AND RAISES HIS 33 ANNA HEAD TO HER KNEE.

(HE RAISES HIMSELF ON HIS ELBOW, HIS FACE RADIANT,167 BEYOND AND POINTS TO THE HORIZON)

(HE SUDDENLY RAISES HIMSELF WITH HIS LAST 168 BEYOND REMAINING STRENGTH AND POINTS TO THE

(PADDY DEFIANTLY RAISES HIS BOTTLE AND GULPS DOWN 465 CARIBE A DRINK IN THE FULL MOONLIGHT.

AND RAISES HIS HANDS UP TO THE FIGURE OF CHRIST IN564 DAYS SUPPLICATION)

(SUDDENLY RAISES HIS HEAD AND LOOKS AT HER-- 236 DESIRE SCORNFULLY)

(HE RAISES HIS CLENCHED FISTS THREATENINGLY.) 255 DESIRE

(SHE SUDDENLY RAISES HERSELF ON TIPTOE AND KISSES 433 DYNAMO HIM--WITH A LITTLE LAUGH)

(RAISES HERSELF TO HER FEET PLACIDLY, WITHOUT A 434 DYNAMO TRACE OF RESENTMENT)

SMITHERS RAISES HIS WHIP THREATENINGLY) 174 EJONES

HE RAISES HIS WHIP AND LASHES JONES VICIOUSLY 194 EJONES ACROSS THE SHOULDERS WITH IT.

AND DOWN HEAH WHAR DESE FOOL BUSH NIGGERS RAISES 196 EJONES ME UP TO THE SEAT O' DE MIGHTY,

AND RAISES HIS CLASPED HANDS TO THE SKY--IN A 196 EJONES VOICE OF AGONIZED PLEADING)

AND WITH DIFFICULTY RAISES HIMSELF TO A SITTING 102 ELECTR POSITION

RAISES HER HANDS BETWEEN HER FACE AND HER DAUGHTER123 ELECTR

(RAISES HIS HEAD AS IF STARTING TO REMOVE THE 287 GGBROW MASK)

RAISES (CONT'D.)

(HE RAISES HIS HAND OVER THE MASK AS IF HE WERE 291 GGBROW BLESSING IT.

HE RAISES THE MASK IN HIS HANDS AND STARES AT IT 291 GGBROW WITH A PITYING TENDERNESS.

(HE RAISES HIS VOICE) COME RIGHT IN, GENTLEMEN. 316 GGBROW

(RAISES HIS HEAD AND PEERS AT ROCKY BLEARILY 579 ICEMAN THROUGH HIS THICK SPECTACLES--

HUGO SUDDENLY RAISES HIS HEAD FROM HIS ARMS 592 ICEMAN

(HE RAISES HIS GLASS, AND ALL THE OTHERS EXCEPT 620 ICEMAN PARRITT DO LIKEWISE)

AND HUGO RAISES HIS HEAD TO BLINK AT IT.) 640 ICEMAN

AND RAISES IT ABOVE HIS HEAD TO HURL AT JOE. 672 ICEMAN

(SUDDENLY RAISES HIS HEAD FROM HIS ARMS AND, 694 ICEMAN LOOKING STRAIGHT IN FRONT OF HIM,

THE RAISES HIS FIST) I'LL CHOKE HIS ROTTEN HEART524 INZONE OUT WID ME OWN HANDS.

(SHE RAISES HER HANDS AND REGARDS THEM WITH 103 JOURNE MELANCHOLY SYMPATHY.

THE RAISES HIS GLASS.) HERE'S HOW. 130 JOURNE

HE HEALS THE SICK, HE RAISES THE DEAD, BY 300 LAZARU LAUGHTER.

MIRIAM ROCKS TO AND FRO AND RAISES A LOW WAIL OF 320 LAZARU LAMENTATION.

(PUTS HIS ARM AROUND HER AND RAISES HER TO HER 325 LAZARU FEET--TENDERLY)

(HE RAISES HIS HAND TO STAB LAZARUS IN THE BACK. 333 LAZARU

RAISES HIS HAND AS IF BLESSING THE DEAD LION, THEN333 LAZARU PASSES BELOW IT,

(RAISES HIS HEAD UNEASILY, LOOKS BACK TOWARD THE 335 LAZARU PALACE,

(SHE RAISES THE PEACH TOWARD HER MOUTH. 346 LAZARU

(KISSES MIRIAM AGAIN AND RAISES HIS HEAD. 348 LAZARU

(HE RAISES HIS HAND IN AN IMPERIAL AUTOCRATIC 360 LAZARU GESTURE.)

(DEBORAH RAISES HER EYES FOR A SECOND TO STARE AT 20 MANSNS HER

(RAISES HIS HEAD, A CONFUSED, DREAMY WONDERING 175 MANSNS PEACE IN HIS FACE--DAZEDLY.)

(SHE RAISES HER LIPS) WILL YOU KISS ME NOW$ 371 MARCOM

SHE RAISES HER HANDS SLOWLY ABOVE HIS HEAD 414 MARCOM

(HE RAISES HIS RIDING CROP.) 61 MISBEG

SHE RAISES HER GLASS) 115 MISBEG

(SHE RAISES HER GLASS--MUCKINGLY) 121 MISBEG

(HE RAISES THE PAPER AGAIN. 36 POET

(HE POURS A DRINK AND RAISES HIS GLASS.) 93 POET

AND RAISES HIS GLASS OF WINE WITH THE OTHER-- 98 POET IGNORING HER.)

(AWAKENED FROM HIS DREAM, MECHANICALLY RAISES HIS 101 POET GLASS.)

HE RAISES IT TOWARD THE ROPE) 592 ROPE

(THE RAISES HIS CLENCHED FISTS OVER HIS HEAD IN A 597 ROPE FRENZY OF RAGE.)

(HIS HANDS GRASPING HER ARMS HE HALF RAISES HER TO 43 STRANG HER FEET, BUT,

HE RAISES HIS HEAD AND HALF-PUSHES HER AWAY-- 99 STRANG RESENTFULLY, THINKING)

(HE RAISES HIS GLASSES AND LOOKS UP THE RIVER-- 174 STRANG THINKING EXULTANTLY)

(HE TURNS AWAY AND RAISES HIS GLASSES, GOING BACK 179 STRANG TO THE RAIL.

COCKY GETS UNSTEADILY TO HIS FEET AND RAISES HIS 501 VOYAGE GLASS IN THE AIR.)

(SHE RAISES HER GLASS. 507 VOYAGE

(SHE RAISES HER FIST THREATENINGLY OVER HIS HEAD.)477 WELDED

FINALLY SHE RAISES HER HAND AND KNOCKS ON THE DOOR487 WELDED SOFTLY--

FIGHT--FAIL AND HATE AGAIN--(HE RAISES HIS VOICE 488 WELDED IN AGGRESSIVE TRIUMPH)

RAISIN'

(GRINNING) I FEEL LIKE RAISIN' FUN. 220 DESIRE

I KNOW YOU WON'T TRY RAISIN' THE DEAD ANY MORE. 179 POET

RAISING

NOT THE ATHLETIC BUT THE HELL-RAISING SPORT TYPE. 218 AHWILD

(THEN RAISING HIS EYES TO HERS--SIMPLY) 38 ANNA

YOU'VE NO CALL TO BE RAISING THIS RUMPUS WITH ME. 57 ANNA

(RAISING HER HEAD AT THE SOUND OF HIS VOICE--WITH 59 ANNA EXTREME MOCKING BITTERNESS)

(RAISING HIS HEAD--PLEADINGLY) 64 ANNA

(RAISING HER FACE--FORCING A WAN SMILE) 67 ANNA

(SHARPLY--RAISING THE REVOLVER IN HER HAND) 69 ANNA

(RAISING HIS FIST THREATENINGLY) 70 ANNA

(RAISING HIS HAND AS IF TO COMMAND SILENCE) 158 BEYOND

(RAISING HIS EYES DEFIANTLY) 563 CROSS

(QUICKLY, RAISING HIS VOICE TO A CONVERSATIONAL 527 DAYS TONE)

(WITHOUT RAISING HIS HEAD) YES. 937 DAYS

(RAISING HIS ARMS TO HEAVEN IN THE FURY HE CAN NO 227 DESIRE LONGER CONTROL)

(RAISING HIS VOICE) BET I KIN TELL YE, ABBIE, 248 DESIRE WHAT EBEN'S DOIN'/

AW, THESE SMALL TOWN BOOBS THINK YOU'RE RAISING 525 DIFRNT HELL IF YOU'RE UP AFTER ELEVEN.

(RAISING HER FACE TO LOOK AT HIM FOR A SECOND) 544 DIFRNT

(RAISING HER ABSURD, BESMEARED FACE TO HIS, AS IF 544 DIFRNT EXPECTING HIM TO KISS HER)

(THEN RAISING HIS VOICE DEFIANTLY) 437 DYNAMO

(WHO HAS BEEN STARING AT HIM WITH TERROR, RAISING 292 GGBROW HER MASK TO WARD OFF HIS FACE)

THE LOOKOUT WOULD BE RAISING LAND MAYBE, 214 HA APE

WHAT THE HELL YOU TRYING TO DO, YELLING AND 654 ICEMAN RAISING THE ROOF?

HER--FLURRIEDLY, RAISING HER HANDS.) 41 JOURNE

THEN, GIVING IT UP, RESUMES HIS HEARTY AIR, 66 JOURNE RAISING HIS GLASS.)

(RAISING HER VOICE UNNECESSARILY.) 123 JOURNE

(ABRUPTLY RAISING HIS GLASS.) 136 JOURNE

RAISING THEIR ARMS TO HIM) 307 LAZARU

RAISING (CONT'D.)
(RAISING HIS HANDS FOR SILENCE---WITH A PLAYFUL SMILE) 309 LAZARU
(RAISING HIS HAND) SILENCE/ 321 LAZARU
RAISING HIS RIGHT ARM) 321 LAZARU
(AS ONE MAN--RAISING THEIR ARMS.) 321 LAZARU
RAISING THEIR SPEARS ALOFT AND SALUTING LAZARUS 334 LAZARU
(SHE STARES UP INTO HIS EYES DOUBTINGLY, RAISING 361 LAZARU
HER FACE TOWARD HIS)
WITH EACH PARTY CONTINUALLY RAISING THE BIDS, 72 MANSNS
(RAISING HIS HANDS TO HEAVEN--DAZEDLY) 362 MARCOM
(HE LAUGHS GAILY, RAISING HIS HAND OVER MARCO'S 363 MARCOM
HEAD)
(RAISING HIS VOICE--WITH REVENGEFUL ANGER) 161 MISBEG
(RAISING HIS GLASS.) YOUR HEALTH AND 9 POET
INCLINATIONS--IF THEY'RE VIRTUOUS/
RAISING HER HAND AS IF SHE WERE GOING TO SLAP HIS 115 POET
FACE.
AND IT'LL BE IN THE PAPERS ABOUT ANOTHER DRUNKEN 126 POET
MICK RAISING A CRAZY ROW/
AND IF YOU GO RAISING A DRUNKEN ROW AT THEIR 127 POET
HOUSE, AND MAKE A PUBLIC SCANDAL,
(RAISING HER HEAD--THINKING--PROUDLY TRIUMPHANT) 89 STRANG
(SUDDENLY WITH AN INSULTING, UGLY SNEER, RAISING 101 STRANG
HIS VOICE)
(RAISING THE BINOCULARS AS HE GOES TO THE RAIL, HE171 STRANG
LOOKS UP THE RIVER)
(SHE HURRIES BACK TO THE RAIL, RAISING HER 179 STRANG
GLASSES.)
(RAISING HIS VOICE) HO, YOU NICK/ 493 VOYAGE

RAKE
DIVIL-MAY-CARE RAKE AV A MAN THE LOIKE AV COCKY$ 478 CARDIF
AS THE SOLDIERS RAKE BACK THE FIRE FROM THE STAKE.366 LAZARU
WHY DO YOU ALWAYS HAVE TO RAKE UP THE PAST$ 456 WELDED

RAKED
(PROTESTS HALF-HEARTEDLY) BUT HE'S ALWAYS SWORN 213 AHWILD
HE GOT RAKED INTO THAT PARTY

RAKIN'
NO USE'N YOU RAKIN' UP OLE TIMES. 177 EJONES

RAKING
FOUR DAYS WE WAS IN IT WITH GREEN SEAS RAKING OVER 36 ANNA
HER FROM BOW TO STERN.
RAKING UP THE PAST, AND SAYING YOU HATE ME-- 142 JOURNE
I HEARD HIM AGAIN LAST NIGHT, RAKING UP THE PAST, 24 POET

RALE
AISY FOR A RALE MAN WITH GUTS TO HIM, THE LIKE OF 31 ANNA
ME.
AYE, RALE FLESH AND BLOOD, DIVIL A LESS. 31 ANNA
THIS IS THE FIRST TIME I'VE HAD A WORD WITH A 37 ANNA
RALE, DACENT WOMAN.
IT'S ONLY ON THE SEA YOU'D FIND RALE MEN WITH GUTS 37 ANNA
IS FIT TO WED WITH FINE,
THERE'S HARDLY A RALE DEEPWATER SAILOR LIFT ON THE459 CARIBE
SEAS, MORE'S THE PITY.
'TIS FOINE RUM, THE RALE STUFF. 462 CARIBE
A RALE, GOD-FOR-SAKEN SON AV A TURKEY TROT WID 470 CARIBE
GUTS TO UT.
WIDOUT ONE DROP OF RALE BLOOD IN HER$ 232 HA APE
AN' HOW SHE HOPES HE'LL SETTLE DOWN TO RALE WORRK 530 INZONE
AN' NOT BE SKYLARKIN' AROUND

RALLYING
(RALLYING HERSELF AND FORCING A SMILE) 72 ELECTR
(RALLYING HIM.) NO, NO, YOU MUSTN'T. 38 POET
(THEN RALLYING HIMSELF) (HEY, YOU/... 30 STRANG
(THEN RALLYING HIMSELF) (BBOSH/... 52 STRANG

RAMBLE
WHAT MAKES YOU RAMBLE ON LIKE THAT, MAMAS 62 JOURNE

RAMBLES
WITH THE AIR OF A HOST WHOSE PARTY IS A HUGE 726 ICEMAN
SUCCESS, AND RAMBLES ON HAPPILY)
AS MARCO RAMBLES ON.) 416 MARCOM

RAMBLING
(APPEARS DRUNKER, HIS HEAD WAGGING, HIS VOICE 74 MISBEG
THICK, HIS TALK RAMBLING)
(RAMBLING TENDERLY) MICHAEL--I--I WAS AFRAID-- 480 WELDED

RAMBLINGLY
(TO PARRITT--RAMBLINGLY) EDUCATED AT HARVARD, 594 ICEMAN
TOO.

RAMESES
THAN ALL THE MOONS SINCE RAMESES WAS A PUP. 130 MISBEG

RAMPAGE
IT'S THE DIVIL'S OWN RAMPAGE WE'VE HAD. 154 POET

RAMPAGIN'
(LOWERING HIS VOICE.) TELL ME, HAS HE DONE ANY 13 POET
RAMPAGIN' WID WOMEN HERE$

RAMROD
DON'T STAND LIKE A RAMROD. 145 ELECTR

RAMS
UNDER YOUR PRESENT SYSTEM, WITH BATTERING RAMS, 394 MARCOM

RAN
WELL, I RAN INTO A COUPLE OF SWIFT BABIES FROM NEW218 AHWILD
HAVEN THIS AFTER--
I RAN INTO HIM UPSTREET THIS AFTERNOON AND HE WAS 292 AHWILD
MEEK AS PIE.
TWO WEEKS OUT WE RAN 35 ANNA
HE RAN INTO ME BEFORE HE GOT TO MISS SIMS AND 499 DAYS
ASKED YOU.
BUT AFTERWARDS HE RAN ON TO BUDDHA, 503 DAYS
BUT I FOOLED 'EM WITH THE HELP OF THE GIRL AND 441 DYNAMO
ESCAPED AND WE BOTH RAN OFF TO
HE GOT TWENTY YEARS BUT HE ESCAPED AND RAN AWAY TO447 DYNAMO
CALIFORNIA/
AT SEVENTEEN I RAN AWAY TO SEA-- 26 ELECTR
I TOLD YOU MYSELF I RAN INTO HIM BY ACCIDENT-- 30 ELECTR
I WENT MAD, WANTED TO KILL AND RAN ON, YELLING. 95 ELECTR
RAN AWAY TO JOIN CHARLIE DARWIN'S CIRCUS/ 268 GGBROW
(SURPRISED) THE ONE TIME I RAN INTO HIM, I 275 GGBROW
THOUGHT HE TOLD ME

RAN (CONT'D.)
I RAN HERE TO WARN--SOMEONE/ 320 GGBROW
THEY DO NOT STOP, BUT DISAPPEAR IN THE DARK 239 HA APE
BACKGROUND AS IF THEY RAN ON,
HE RAN A COLORED GAMBLING HOUSE THEN AND WAS A 594 ICEMAN
HELL OF A SPORT, SO THEY SAY.
BUT, BEJEESS, SOMETHING RAN OVER ME/ 691 ICEMAN
NEAR RAN OVER ME. 722 ICEMAN
AND RAN OUT OF THE HOUSE IN YOUR NIGHTDRESS HALF 86 JOURNE
CRAZY,
OF OUR HOTEL ROOM, AND KNOCKED AND THEN RAN AWAY 113 JOURNE
BEFORE I CAME TO THE DOOR.
THAT TIME I RAN DOWN IN MY NIGHTDRESS TO THROW 118 JOURNE
MYSELF OFF THE DOCK.
LASHED TILL THE BLOOD RAN DOWN YOUR FAT WHITE 165 MANSNS
SHOULDERS/
DIDN'T HAVE THE STRENGTH TO WANT THEM BUT RAN AND 167 MANSNS
HID IN HER GARDEN.
THEY WERE GETTING THE BEST OF YOU TILL I RAN OUT 14 MISBEG
SHE RAN IN THE HOUSE TO MAKE HERSELF BEAUTIFUL FOR 40 MISBEG
YOU.
I RAN INTO HIM AT THE INN. 48 MISBEG
YOU WERE USED TO IN THE OLD COUNTRY WHERE THE PIGS 53 POET
RAN IN AND OUT THE DOORS
AND THE END WAS I RAN FROM THE ROOM, BLUSHING AS 65 POET
RED AS A BEET--
AND THEN WHEN SHE GOT SICK OF YOU AND RAN AWAY-- 580 ROPE
STOLE YOUR MONEY AND RAN OFF AND LEFT YOU 581 ROPE
BUT THE THOUSAND DOLLARS PAN GOT FOR THE MORTGAGE 585 ROPE
JUST BEFORE THAT WOMAN RAN
D'YOU SUPPOSE THAT HARLOT RAN OFF WITH ITS 586 ROPE
YE WAS ONLY A LAD WHEN YE RAN AWAY AN' NOT TO BE 591 ROPE
BLAMED FOR IT.
(FORCING A JOKING TONE) LITTLE YOU KNOW THE 14 STRANG
DEADLY RISKS I RAN, NINA/
TO VISIT A FELLOW WHO'D BEEN IN MY OUTFIT I RAN 30 STRANG
INTO HIM AGAIN.
(+BUT WHEN THE GIRLS BEGAN TO PLAY *FRAID-CAT 52 STRANG
CHARLIE RAN AWAY/*
I HAVE NO USE FOR HIM BUT I DID PITY HIM WHEN I 112 STRANG
RAN ACROSS HIM IN MUNICH...
DID I TELL YOU I RAN INTO DOCTOR DARRELL IN 115 STRANG
MUNICH$
FROM HERE, RAN AWAY... 124 STRANG

RANCID
AND THE AIR IS HEAVY WITH RANCID TOBACCO SMOKE. 477 CARDIF

RANCOR
HE CUTS THE PLUG AND STUFFS HIS PIPE--WITHOUT 15 MISBEG
RANCOR)
(WITH DESPERATE RANCOR--THINKING) 173 STRANG

RANDOM
(HE HURRIEDLY STRAIGHTENS UP THE TABLE AND GRABS A149 ELECTR
BOOK AT RANDOM FROM THE
WHICH IS ON THE TABLE AND, PUTTING A FINGER IN AT 269 GGBROW
RANDOM,
HE SPEAKS IN A TONE OF RANDOM CURIOSITY) 129 MISBEG
OPENS IT AT RANDOM AND BEGINS TO READ ALOUD 23 STRANG
SONOROUSLY LIKE A CHILD WHISTLING TO

RANDS
JUST LIKE THE RANDS TO PUT ON AIRS BEFORE YOU/ 255 AHWILD

RANDS'
AND THIS EVENING I'M STAYING AT THE RANDS' FOR 191 AHWILD
DINNER.
(SMILING) OFF TO THE RANDS', I SUPPOSE. 191 AHWILD
HE'S UP AT THE RANDS'--WON'T BE HOME BEFORE TEN, 218 AHWILD
ANYWAY.
NO I'VE BEEN AT THE RANDS' EVER SINCE DINNER. 254 AHWILD
(IMPORTANTLY) WE HAD A CORKING DINNER AT THE 254 AHWILD
RANDS'.

RANG
I RANG IN A JOKE IN ONE OF MY STORIES THAT TICKLED188 AHWILD
THE FOLKS THERE PINK.
I WAS ON THE POINT OF LEAVING WHEN YOU RANG. 76 STRANG

RANGE
(AS THEY SEAT THEMSELVES AT THE BAR) 4 ANNA
(ABOUT THE TABLE WITHIN READING-LIGHT RANGE ARE 12 JOURNE
FOUR CHAIRS.
(COMES OVER TO HER FATHER BUT WARILY KEEPS OUT OF 579 ROPE
RANGE OF HIS STICK)
WE'D TEND OUR FLAME ON AN ALTAR, NOT IN A KITCHEN 448 WELDED
RANGE/

RANGY
A RANGY SIX-FOOTER WITH A LEAN WEATHER-BEATEN 539 'ILE
FACE.

RANK
THE GIRLS IN TOWN HERE ARE JUST RANK AMATEURS. 527 DIFRNT
THE SECOND RANK CROUCHING OVER THEM, THE THIRD 345 LAZARU
LEANING OVER THE SECOND.
IT IS PLACED IN A SMALL CLEARING, OVERGROWN WITH 1 MANSNS
RANK, MATTED GRASS.
I HAVE NOT FLATTERED ITS RANK BREATH,--- 107 MANSNS
TO THE HIGHEST RANK IN YOUR SERVICES 387 MARCOM
I HAVE NOT FLATTERED ITS RANK BREATH, 43 POET
I HAVE NOT FLATTERED ITS RANK BREATH, 67 POET
I HAVE NOT FLATTERED ITS RANK BREATH, 116 POET
I HAVE NOT FLATTERED ITS RANK BREATH, 176 POET
STRAGGLY WISPS FROM THE PILE OF RANK HAY FALL 601 ROPE
SILENTLY TO THE FLOOR
HEAVY AND RANK/... 99 STRANG

RANKER
I'M MERELY--A RANKER. 469 CARIBE

RANKS
BUT SHE IS A FAIRLY RECENT RECRUIT TO THE RANKS, 236 AHWILD
(A LARGE CIRCULAR CLEARING ENCLOSED BY THE SERRIED195 EJONES
RANKS OF GIGANTIC TRUNKS OF
THEY FORM IN THREE RANKS. 344 LAZARU
(A PROCESSION OF SERVANTS BEGINS TO FILE ONE BY 428 MARCOM
ONE THROUGH THE RANKS OF

RANKS

RANKS (CONT'D.)
I'M VERY MUCH A WORKER IN THE RANKS. 165 STRANG

RANSOM
A KING'S RANSOM/ 429 MARCOM

RANTING
DOES NOT HIS FOUL RANTING BEGIN TO TRY THY PATIENCES.... 423 DYNAMO

RAP
I DON'T GIVE A RAP IF IT NEVER LIFTS/ 26 ANNA
THE SOUND OF FOOTSTEPS ON THE PATH IS HEARD--THEN 153 BEYOND A SHARP RAP ON THE DOOR.
HE RAPPED AND HE RAPPED WITH A (RAP, RAP, RAP) BUT596 ICEMAN NEVER A SOUL SEEMED IN.»
AND I'LL SHOW YOU THE PRETTIEST (RAP, RAP, RAP) 597 ICEMAN THAT EVER YOU DID SEE.»
TILL HE HEARD A DAMSEL (RAP, RAP, RAP) 597 ICEMAN
AND I'LL SHOW YOU THE PRETTIEST (RAP, RAP, RAP ON 607 ICEMAN TABLE) THAT EVER YOU DID SEE.»
RAP THEIR SCHOONERS ON THE TABLE, CALL »SPEECH, 659 ICEMAN
»AND I'LL SHOW YOU THE PRETTIEST (RAP, RAP, RAP) 662 ICEMAN THAT EVER YOU DID SEE/»
THEN THERE IS A SHARP RAP OF THE KNOCKER ON THE 95 MANSNS DOOR.

RAPE
AN* RAPE YER NEW WOMAN/ 223 DESIRE
WAS I TRYING TO RAPE YOU, JOSIE$ 138 MISBEG

RAPID
(THE BEAT OF THE FAR-OFF TOM-TOM IS PERCEPTIBLY 192 EJONES LOUDER AND MORE RAPID.
(HE BEGINS A COUNT WHICH GROWS MORE RAPID AS HE 608 ICEMAN GOES ON)
(AGAINST HER WILL, HAS BECOME A BIT HYPNOTIZED BY 84 POET DEBORAH'S RAPID, LOW,
HE IS TWENTY-SEVEN, SHORT, DARK, WIRY, HIS 33 STRANG MOVEMENTS RAPID AND SURE,

RAPIDITY
BUT INCREASED IN VOLUME OF SOUND AND RAPIDITY OF 195 EJONES BEAT.)
WITH SUCH RAPIDITY THAT THE TWO SHOTS ARE ALMOST 198 EJONES SIMULTANEOUS.
HE GOES FROM ONE LETTER TO THE NEXT WITH 70 MANSNS ASTONISHING RAPIDITY.
(IN HER BLUNT FLAT TONES--WITH A MECHANICAL 57 STRANG RAPIDITY TO HER WORDS)

RAPIDLY
RAPIDLY, BUT WITH NO APPARENT EFFORT. 548 DIFRNT
JONES ENTERS FROM THE LEFT, WALKING RAPIDLY. 187 EJONES
THEY BEGIN RAPIDLY TO GET DRUNK NOW. 722 ICEMAN
WHICH RAPIDLY CHANGES TO ONE OF ANGUISH.) 525 INZONE
MARY'S FINGERS PLAY MORE RAPIDLY ON THE TABLE TOP. 73 JOURNE
RAPIDLY APPROACHING FROM THE LEFT 290 LAZARU
HE SPEAKS RAPIDLY AND INCISIVELY. 69 MANSNS
(LISTENS WITH A PLEASED, IRONICAL SMILE AS THE 402 MARCOM BAND GETS RAPIDLY NEARER.
GOT RAPIDLY WORSE. 147 MISBEG
SHE SPEAKS RAPIDLY IN A REMOTE, DETACHED WAY, 81 POET
(VAGUELY SURPRISED--SPEAKS RAPIDLY AGAIN.) 82 POET
(THEN TALKING RAPIDLY AGAIN IN HER STRANGE 86 POET DETACHED WAY.)

RAPPED
AND A COIN IS RAPPED ON THE BAR) 239 AHWILD
HE RAPPED AND HE RAPPED WITH A (RAP, RAP, RAP) BUT596 ICEMAN NEVER A SOUL SEEMED IN.»
(HE SINGS.) HE RAPPED AND RAPPED, 597 ICEMAN

RAPPING
RAPPING ON THE TABLE WITH HIS KNUCKLES AT THE 596 ICEMAN INDICATED SPOTS IN THE SONG..)
(RAPPING ON THE TABLE FOR ORDER WHEN THERE IS 658 ICEMAN NOTHING BUT A DEAD SILENCE)
RAPPING WITH KNUCKLES OR GLASSES ON THE TABLE 662 ICEMAN

RAPS
ON WHICH HE RAPS SHARPLY 305 GGBROW
(SHE RAPS HIM SMARTLY, BUT LIGHTLY, 73 MISBEG
(SHE RAPS WITH BOTH KNUCKLES IN A FIERCE TATTOO ON)35 STRANG THE TABLE)

RAPT
(COUNTS ON HER FINGERS--THEN MURMURS WITH A RAPT 548 *ILE SMILE)
(HE STANDS STARING AT THE MOON WITH A RAPT FACE. 277 AHWILD
AND THEY BOTH SIT IN A RAPT TRANCE, STARING AT THE287 AHWILD MOON.
HE LOOKS AROUND HIM WITH THE RAPT EXPRESSION OF 482 DYNAMO ONE IN A TRANCE)
WITH A RAPT, QUESTIONING, LISTENING LOOK) 484 DYNAMO
BEGIN TO OPEN--(SHE LOOKS AROUND HER WITH A RAPT 323 GGBROW SMILE)
(THE NIGHT CLERK DREAMS, A RAPT HERO WORSHIP 32 HUGHIE TRANSFIGURING HIS PIMPLY FACE..
AND A RAPT, TENDER, GIRLISH SMILE.) 105 JOURNE
(HE STARES UP AT THE STARS, RAPT IN CONTEMPLATION,290 LAZARU

RAPTLY
(RAPTLY) AH, SIGHT FOR SORE EYES, MY BEAUTIFUL 226 AHWILD MAKUSHLA.
(THEY BOTH STAND FOR A MOMENT LOOKING UP RAPTLY 269 DESIRE
(HE STARES AT IT RAPTLY NOW) 474 DYNAMO
(RAPTLY) MARGARET/ 266 GGBROW
HE STARES AT THE SKY RAPTLY) 266 GGBROW
(GETS TO HIS KNEES AND WITH CLASPED HANDS LOOKS UP286 GGBROW RAPTLY

RAPTUROUS
HER UPTURNED UNMASKED FACE LIKE THAT OF A 264 GGBROW RAPTUROUS VISIONARY.

RARE
'TWAS A RARE TREAT TO 'EAR 'IM TELL WHAT 'APPENED 457 CARIBE TO 'IM AMONG 'EM.
BUT A RARE AND THREATENING PAUSE OF SILENCE HAS 29 HUGHIE FALLEN ON THE CITY,

RARE (CONT'D.)
IT WAS ONE OF THOSE RARE OCCASIONS WHEN THE BOER 676 ICEMAN THAT WALKS LIKE A MAN--
AND RARE FLASHES OF INTUITIVE SENSIBILITY. 14 JOURNE
BUT ON THE RARE OCCASIONS WHEN HE SMILES WITHOUT 19 JOURNE SNEERING,
IT WAS A RARE SHADE OF REDDISH BROWN AND SO LONG 28 JOURNE IT CAME DOWN BELOW MY KNEES.
IT IS A RARE PLEASURE INDEED TO SEE YOU IN MY 31 MANSNS GARDEN, JOEL.
LITTLE DAUGHTER, ALL RARE THINGS ARE SECRET WHICH 400 MARCOM CANNOT BE REVEALED TO ANYONE.
THESE ARE PACKED WITH BOOKS, PRINCIPALLY EDITIONS, 3 STRANG MANY OF THEM OLD AND RARE,
THEY ARE RARE. 127 STRANG
HE POSSESSES THE RARE VIRTUE OF GRATITUDE. 166 STRANG
(WITH ASSERTIVE LOYALTY) A RARE SPIRIT/ 183 STRANG
(WITH BITTER DESPONDENCY) RUINED NOW--GONE--A 452 WELDED RARE MOMENT OF BEAUTY/

RARELY
SET APPEARANCE OF A ROOM RARELY OCCUPIED. 11 JOURNE
THAT COLLEGE HEROES RARELY SHINE BRILLIANTLY IN 9 STRANG AFTER LIFE.
SO VERY RARELY NOW, THOSE INTERLUDES OF PASSION...138 STRANG

RASCALS
(READING) »I REFER TO THAT DEVIL'S BREW OF 242 HA APE RASCALS, JAILBIRDS,
YOU OLD RASCALS$ 365 MARCOM

RASH
BUT DON'T BE RASH/ 411 MARCOM
YOU KEEP HER FROM DOING ANYTHING RASH UNTIL HE 417 MARCOM GETS HERE.

RASHERS
AN* WE HAD RASHERS OF THEM, AN* I PAYIN* FOR IT. 585 ROPE

RASPBERRY
GIVE HIM THE BUID, FELLERS--THE RASPBERRY/ 243 HA APE

RASPING
RASPING NASAL VOICE, AND LITTLE SHARP EYES. 67 ELECTR
RUDDY COMPLEXION, AND A SHRILL RASPING VOICE. 129 ELECTR

RASPY
(IN A RASPY VOICE) 'ULLO, MATES. 499 VOYAGE

RAT
I USED TO BE A REGULAR WATER RAT WHEN I WAS A BOY.228 AHWILD
YOUR OLD MAN WASN'T ONLY A BARGE RAT--BEGGING YOUR 36 ANNA PARDON--
YOU'RE A YELLOW RAT/ 451 DYNAMO
(HE YELLS AT THE WINDOW) IT'S YOU WHO'RE THE RAT,452 DYNAMO ADA/
SHE CALLED ME A YELLOW RAT--AND SHE HAD THE RIGHT 458 DYNAMO DOPE.
EVEN WHEN YOU WERE BAWLING ME OUT FOR A YELLOW 460 DYNAMO RAT.
NOW SHE'S PEDDLING THE NEWS ALONG BROADWAY I'M A 26 HUGHIE RAT AND A CHISELER,
BRING ON THE RAT POISON/ 619 ICEMAN
AND BE DROWNED LIKE A RAT IN A TRAP IN THE 517 INZONE BARGAIN, MAYBE.
HE MISTOOK RAT POISON FOR FLOUR, OR SUGAR, OR 147 JOURNE SOMETHING.
THE WATER'S DEEP DOWN THERE, AND YOU'D BE A 589 ROPE DROWNED RAT IF YOU SLIPPED.

RAT'D
THIS WAS A BIG THUMPIN' NOISE NO RAT'D MAKE. 548 DIFRNT

RAT'S
*AN THE SAME DAMN RAT'S-HOLE, SURE ENOUGH. 496 VOYAGE

RATE
(AS THEY APPEAR) OH, I LIKE THE JOB FIRST RATE, 188 AHWILD NAT.
AT ANY RATE IT WAS GOD'S WORK---AND HIS WILL BE 116 BEYOND DONE.
I'M SICK OF THE DAMNED THING--NOW, AT ANY RATE. 543 DAYS
(PROUDLY.) HAIN'T WE RAISED 'EM T' BE FUST-RATE, 218 DESIRE NUMBER ONE PRIZE STOCKS
WE GOT ALONG FUST RATE. 500 DIFRNT
AND CONTINUES AT A GRADUALLY ACCELERATING RATE 184 EJONES
FROM THIS POINT UNINTERRUPTEDLY
IT STARTS AT A RATE EXACTLY CORRESPONDING TO 184 EJONES NORMAL PULSE BEAT--
THE RATE OF THE BEAT OF THE FAR-OFF TOM-TOM 189 EJONES INCREASES PERCEPTIBLY AS HE DOES SO.
WELL, I HASN'T BROUGHT UP THAT STRICTLY AND, 23 ELECTR SHOULD OR SHOULDN'T, AT ANY RATE,
SHE GOT THAT OUT OF ME--THE PROOF OF IT, AT ANY 36 ELECTR RATE.
BILLY A FIRST-RATE, NUMBER-ONE ARCHITECT/ 258 GGBROW
WELL, DION, AT ANY RATE, I'M SATISFIED. 296 GGBROW
AT ANY RATE, YOU SEE IT HAD NOTHING TO DO WITH 590 ICEMAN YOUR MOTHER.
NOT UNTIL WE GET INTO THE WAR ZONE, AT ANY RATE. 514 INZONE
YOU WOULDN'T PAY FOR A FIRST-RATE-- 39 JOURNE
SECOND-RATE HOTEL$. 61 JOURNE
YOU SHOULD HAVE REMAINED A BACHELOR AND LIVED IN 67 JOURNE SECOND-RATE HOTELS AND
YOUR SEASON WILL OPEN AGAIN AND WE CAN GO BACK TO 72 JOURNE SECOND-RATE HOTELS AND TRAINS.
WE DON'T PRETEND, AT ANY RATE. 77 JOURNE
AT ANY RATE, NOW YOU HAVE NO LETTER/ 353 MARCOM
DURING MY CAREER AS A THIRD-RATE HAM. 128 MISBEG

RATED
EVEN IN THIS HICK BURG HE'S RATED THIRD CLASS/ 30 JOURNE

RATERS
THIRD-RATERS. 131 JOURNE

RATHER
BELLE IS TWENTY, A RATHER PRETTY PEROXIDE BLONDE, 236 AHWILD
(GIVING RICHARD A RATHER CONTEMPTUOUS LOOK) 244 AHWILD
AND I'D RATHER HAVE SOME FLESH ON MY BONES THAN BE291 AHWILD BUILT LIKE A STRING BEAN AND

RATTLESNAKE

RATHER (CONT'D.)

I WAS TELLING HER I'D RATHER YOU GAVE ME A JOB ON 296 AHWILD THE PAPER BECAUSE THEN SHE AND

HE IS A BOYISH, RED-CHEEKED, RATHER GOOD-LOOKING 4 ANNA YOUNG FELLOW OF TWENTY OR SO.)

(THEN TURNING TO MARTHA, RATHER 8 ANNA (DECIDEDLY) I'D RATHER HAVE ONE DROP OF OCEAN 27 ANNA THAN ALL THE FARMS IN THE WORLD/

(RATHER REMORSEFULLY) FORGET IT. 33 ANNA (PASSIONATELY) I'M THINKING I'D RATHER BE FRIENDS 34 ANNA WITH YOU THAN HAVE MY WISH

BUT EVEN IF HE DID, I'D RATHER HAVE HIM COME THAN 64 ANNA NOT TO SHOW UP AT ALL.

(HANDING IT TO HIM RATHER RELUCTANTLY) 82 BEYOND RATHER THE ATMOSPHERE IS ONE UF THE ORDERLY 94 BEYOND COMFORT OF A SIMPLE,

RATHER PRIM--LOOKING WOMAN OF FIFTY-FIVE WHO HAD 94 BEYOND ONCE BEEN A SCHOOL TEACHER.

I'D RATHER GO THROUGH A TYPHOON AGAIN THAN WRITE A131 BEYOND LETTER.

(EXCITEDLY--IN A RATHER BOASTFUL TONE) 138 BEYOND (A RATHER GOOD-LOOKING ROUGH WHO IS SITTING BESIDE456 CARIBE DRISCOLL)

HIS FACE IS FLUSHED AND HE TALKS RATHER WILDLY) 467 CARIBE HIS FACE IS HANDSOME, WITH THE RATHER HEAVY, 493 DAYS RATHER WEAK MOUTH IS DRAWN DOWN BY SHARP LINES AT 515 DAYS THE CORNERS.

I'D RATHER YOU HATED ME/ 520 DAYS RATHER A JOKE ON YOU, ISN'T ITS 549 DAYS RATHER THAN THAT OF A HOME. 206 DESIRE (GLANCING AT HIM RATHER IRRITABLY) 216 DESIRE HER ROUND FACE IS PRETTY BUT MARRED BY ITS RATHER 221 DESIRE GROSS SENSUALITY.

RATHER HE LOOKS MORE ROBUST AND YOUNGER. 230 DESIRE (RATHER GUILTILY) HE'S A SINNER--NATURAL-BORN. 233 DESIRE EMMA IS A SLENDER GIRL OF TWENTY, RATHER UNDER THE494 DIFRNT MEDIUM HEIGHT.

(RATHER PRIMLY) THEY WAS TOO SPORTY FOR THEIR 522 DIFRNT GOOD.

I'D RATHER SEE HIM DEAD 423 DYNAMO IT SUGGESTS, RATHER, AN INERT STRENGTH. 428 DYNAMO I'D RATHER LOOK AT THE MOON...) 435 DYNAMO I'LL DO WITHOUT A MOTHER RATHER THAN HAVE YOUR 450 DYNAMO KIND/

RATHER THAN THE MEANING OF THE WORDS.) 476 DYNAMO *E'D RATHER DO FOR YOU THAN EAT 'IS DINNER, 'E 183 EJONES WOULD/

THESE LAST THREE ARE TYPES OF TOWNSFOLK RATHER 6 ELECTR THAN INDIVIDUALS, A

HER FACE IS UNUSUAL, HANDSOME RATHER THAN 9 ELECTR BEAUTIFUL.

RATHER THAN THE RESEMBLANCE TO HER PARENT. 10 ELECTR RATHER THAN LIVING FLESH. 21 ELECTR I WOULD RATHER REST HERE FOR A SPELL. 47 ELECTR I WOULD RATHER WAIT FOR ORIN INSIDE. 73 ELECTR BUT I'D RATHER SUFFER THAT THAN LET THE MURDER OF 97 ELECTR OUR RATHER GO UNPUNISHED/

(THE OTHERS LAUGH, THEIR MIRTH A BIT FORCED, BUT 131 ELECTR SMALL LOOKS RATHER SICK.)

OR, RATHER IT HAS RENOUNCED US. 150 ELECTR OR, RATHER, OLD GRAYBEARD, WHY THE DEVIL WAS I 265 GGBROW EVER BORN AT ALL&

(RATHER TAUNTINGLY) GO EASY. 296 GGBROW OR RATHER, I INHERIT THE ACQUIRED TRAIT OF THE BY-219 HA APE PRODUCT, WEALTH,

WHEN A LEOPARD COMPLAINS OF ITS SPOTS, IT MUST 220 HA APE SOUND RATHER GROTESQUE.

RATHER IT IS HE WHO RECOILS AFTER EACH COLLISION. 238 HA APE I TELL YOU, PAL, I'D RATHER SLEEP IN THE SAME 21 HUGHIE STALL WITH OLD MAN OF WAR

I WAS THINKING. I'D RATHER BE SHOT. 25 HUGHIE IT SEEMED RATHER POINTLESS TO DISCUSS MY OTHER 601 ICEMAN SUBJECT.

THEY'D RATHER STAY HIDING UP THERE, KIDDING EACH 653 ICEMAN OTHER ALONG.

(HE TOSSES IT TO ROCKY) I'D RATHER SLEEP IN THE 682 ICEMAN GUTTER THAN PASS ANOTHER NIGHT

IF THERE WAS A MAD DOG OUTSIDE I'D GO AND SHAKE 688 ICEMAN HANDS WITH IT RATHER THAN STAY

CORA SPEAKS WITH A TIRED WONDER AT HERSELF RATHER 700 ICEMAN THAN RESENTMENT TOWARD HIM)

ALTHOUGH JAMIE RESEMBLES HIM RATHER THAN HIS 19 JOURNE MOTHER.

OR RATHER HE IS TRYING TO CONCENTRATE ON IT BUT 51 JOURNE CANNOT.

AS IF SHE WERE NOW TALKING ALOUD TO HERSELF RATHER 67 JOURNE THAN TO TYRONE.)

I'D RATHER WALK ANY DAY, OR TAKE A TROLLEY. 84 JOURNE SURE, WOULDN'T I RATHER RIDE IN A FINE AUTOMOBILE 102 JOURNE THAN STAY HERE AND LISTEN TO

AND I'D MUCH RATHER BE ALONE. 108 JOURNE (RATHER SHAMEFACEDLY PULLS HIMSELF TOGETHER--THEN 303 LAZARU BROODINGLY)

OR RATHER I SHOULD SAY, UNNATURALLY/ 314 LAZARU I WOULD RATHER BEG IN THE GUTTER--/ 33 MANSNS (SMILINGLY EVASIVE.) I'D RATHER NOT, SARA, IF YOU 55 MANSNS DON'T MIND.

FATHER WOULD RATHER HAVE FACED RUIN A THOUSAND 59 MANSNS TIMES--

I'D RATHER STARVE IN THE GUTTER LIKE A DOG/ 154 MANSNS (THEN RATHER IMPATIENTLY) THEN, 359 MARCOM RATHER BE GRATEFUL IF A THISTLE CAN BRING FORTH 360 MARCOM FIGS.

(MARCO TURNS RATHER FRIGHTENEDLY AND COMES TO THE 382 MARCOM THRONE AND KNEELS)

I WOULD SAY, RATHER THAT EVER SINCE YOU WERE OLD 385 MARCOM ENOUGH TO TALK,

RATHER (CONT'D.)

WHEN I NOTICED A RATHER STRAINED EXPRESSION BUT 425 MARCOM THIS I TOOK TO BE FEVER DUE TO

(RATHER MUFFLED BY ROAST PIG) 431 MARCOM I'D RATHER BE A COW THAN AN UGLY LITTLE BUCK GOAT. 12 MISBEG OR RATHER, HE IS ONE OF THOSE PEOPLE WHO CAN DRINK 72 MISBEG AN ENORMOUS AMOUNT AND BE

I'D RATHER HAVE ONE LIGHT ON BROADWAY 130 MISBEG I'D RATHER HAVE FREE WHISKEY GO DOWN HIS GULLET 59 POET THAN THE OTHERS'.

I KNOW SHE DIDN'T LET SIMON GUESS SHE'D RATHER 87 POET HAVE HIM DEAD THAN MARRIED TO ME.

I'D RATHER STAY ALONE. 137 POET (UGLY--ALOUD TO HERSELF RATHER THAN TO HER 180 POET MOTHER.)

RATHER HANDSOME FACE BRONZED BY THE SUN. 587 ROPE IN THE FLYING SERVICE RATHER MORE THAN A 10 STRANG POSSIBILITY, WHICH NEEDLESS TO SAY,

(THEN RATHER IRONICALLY) AND SO GORDON TOLD NINA 11 STRANG HE'D SUDDENLY REALIZED IT

HER FACE IS STRIKING, HANDSOME RATHER THAN PRETTY, 12 STRANG THE BONE STRUCTURE PROMINENT,

THE LIPS OF HER RATHER LARGE MOUTH CLEARLY 12 STRANG MODELED ABOVE THE FIRM JAW.

THIS IS RATHER A SUDDEN DECISION, ISN'T ITS 15 STRANG RATHER A MILD WORD FOR HER AFFAIRS... 36 STRANG I'D RATHER IMITATE HIS INDIFFERENCE. 41 STRANG (PROTESTINGLY) WELL--BUT--HOLD ON--I'M SURE NINA 42 STRANG WOULD RATHER--

OR RATHER HE SLEPT, I COULDN'T. 49 STRANG HIS ATTITUDE RATHER SHOCKED ME. 50 STRANG AS IF I WOULDN'T DIE RATHER THAN TAKE THE 72 STRANG SLIGHTEST CHANCE OF THAT HAPPENING/...

(WITH A RATHER FORCED WELCOMING NOTE) 73 STRANG MOTHER IS RATHER DIFFICULT TO LIVE WITH THESE 74 STRANG DAYS, GETTING ME WORRIED TO DEATH,

IT'S EVEN RATHER TOUCHING. 82 STRANG WOULD SHE RATHER SEE HER HUSBAND WIND UP IN AN 87 STRANG ASYLUM&

WOULD SHE RATHER FACE THE PROSPECT OF GOING TO POT 87 STRANG MENTALLY, MORALLY,

I'D MUCH RATHER HAVE HIM (POINTING TO GORDON) 141 STRANG (AFTER A PAUSE--RATHER IRRITABLY) 455 WELDED I'D RATHER STAY UP AND SIT WITH YOU. 464 WELDED IT'S THE FIRST DOOR UPSTAIRS ON YOUR RIGHT--IF 465 WELDED YOU'D RATHER GO ALONE.

I THINK YOUR TREATMENT HAS BEEN RATHER HARD TO 469 WELDED TAKE, NELLY--

YET SHE IS NOT UGLY--RATHER PRETTY FOR HER BOVINE,471 WELDED STOLID TYPE--

(EXALTED BY HIS EXULTATION RATHER THAN BY HIS 488 WELDED WORDS)

RATHSKELLER

IT'S BEDROCK BAR, THE END OF THE LINE CAFE, THE 587 ICEMAN BOTTOM OF THE SEA RATHSKELLER/

RATIONAL

TO MAKE MY ROMANTIC HERO COME FINALLY TO A 539 DAYS RATIONAL CONCLUSION ABOUT HIS LIFE/

THERE IS A MOCKING RATIONAL SOMETHING IN HIM THAT 545 DAYS LAUGHS WITH SCORN--

FOR THERE MUST BE A CAUSE AND A RATIONAL 353 LAZARU EXPLANATION/

SO YOU SEE IT IS ALL PERFECTLY RATIONAL AND 183 MANSNS LOGICAL.

YES, IT IS CLEARLY THE RATIONAL THING TO DO... 86 STRANG

RATIONALISM

AND IN AFTER YEARS, EVEN AT THE HEIGHT OF HIS 535 DAYS RATIONALISM,

RATIONALISTIC

HE TAUGHT HIMSELF TO TAKE A RATIONALISTIC 534 DAYS ATTITUDE.

RATIONALLY

HE ANALYZES IT RATIONALLY. 544 DAYS

RATS

(DISGUSTEDLY) OH, RATS/ 27 ANNA ONLY THE RATS RUNNING ABOUT. 571 CROSS (CARELESSLY) IT'S ONLY THE RATS. 547 DIFRNT THE BLOODY SHIP IS SINKIN' AN' THE BLEEDIN' RATS 182 EJONES 'AS SLUNG THEIR 'OOKS.

AND OF COURSE ALL THE RATS AND CHISELERS BELIEVE 26 HUGHIE HER.

A FINE BUNCH OF RATS/ 718 ICEMAN TERRIFIED RATS, THEIR VOICES SQUEAKY NOW WITH 369 LAZARU FRIGHT)

I BEGIN TO SMELL ALL THE RATS IN CATHAY/ 382 MARCOM OUR CHRISTIAN MAYOR IS EXTERMINATING OUR PLEASURES387 MARCOM AND OUR RATS

RATTERS

YOU OUGHT TO BE ABLE TO SELL SKUNKS FOR GOOD 710 ICEMAN RATTERS/=

RATTLE

IN ONE HAND HE CARRIES A BONE RATTLE, 200 EJONES HIS BONE RATTLE CLICKING THE TIME. 201 EJONES KNIVES AND FORKS AND SPOONS RATTLE AGAINST PLATES.431 MARCOM

RATTLED

NOTHING'S EVER GUT HIM RATTLED YET. 160 STRANG

RATTLES

AND THE STACK OF DISHES RATTLES IN HIS TREMBLING 539 'ILE HANDS.

(HE RATTLES THE BARS OF HIS CELL FURIOUSLY) 241 HA APE THE GORILLA RATTLES THE BARS OF HIS CAGE AND 253 HA APE SNARLS.

THEN IT ROARS AND ROCKS AND RATTLES PAST THE 19 HUGHIE NEARBY CORNER,

HE RATTLES ON) 106 STRANG

RATTLESNAKE

HE WAS POSITIVELY THE ONLY DOCTOR IN THE WORLD WHO626 ICEMAN CLAIMED THAT RATTLESNAKE OIL,

RATTLING

RATTLING
(WITH AN IMPATIENT GLANCE AT HER ESCORT--RATTLING 237 AHWILD
THE ICE IN HER GLASS)
A RATTLING NOISE THROBS FROM HIS THROAT. 168 BEYOND
ANOTHER DOOM COMES, REVERBERATING, RATTLING THE 42 ELECTR
WINDOWS.
(THEN WITH SUDDEN RAGE, RATTLING HIS CELL BARS) 240 HA APE
THEN A FURIOUS RATTLING OF BARS FROM DOWN THE 240 HA APE
CORRIDOR.)
* IS HEARD REPLYING AND THEN A GREAT SPLASH AND A 407 MARCOM
LONG RATTLING OF CHAINS.
RATTLING ON IN THE COCKSURE BOASTFUL WAY OF ABOY 54 STRANG
SHOWING OFF HIS PROWESS BEFORE

RAUCOUSLY
(HE SINGS RAUCOUSLY) "UH, WE'LL ROW, ROW, ROW, 175 STRANG
RIGHT DOWN THE RIVER/

RAVAGED
THE MASK IS NOW TERRIBLY RAVAGED. 285 GGBROW
(HE TEARS OFF HIS MASK AND REVEALS A SUFFERING 305 GGBROW
FACE THAT IS RAVAGED AND HAGGARD,

RAVAGES
IT HAS ALREADY BEGUN TO SHOW THE RAVAGES OF 269 GGBROW
DISSIPATION.
IT IS HIS FACE THAT REVEALS THE RAVAGES OF 33 POET
DISSIPATION--

RAVE
(HE LAUGHS) AND AS FOR THE EAST YOU USED TO RAVE 132 BEYOND
ABOUT--
(GRUFFLY) RAVE ON/ 296 GGBROW
LET HIM RAVE. 241 HA APE
USED TO RAVE ABOUT HIM. 105 JOURNE

RAVED
THEN HE RAVED ON SOME NONSENSE ABOUT HE'D ALWAYS 311 GGBROW
LOVED ME.

RAVENOUS
AND SHE EATS WITH A RAVENOUS APPETITE. 8 STRANG

RAVENOUSLY
(HE BEGINS TO ABSORB HIS SOUP RAVENOUSLY) 223 AHWILD

RAVES
I'LL KNOW HOW TO HUMOR HIM WHEN HE RAVES ABOUT 562 CROSS
TREASURE.

RAVING
I'M RAVING LIKE A REAL LUNATIC, I'M THINKING, 70 ANNA
YOU WERE RAVING ON ABOUT SOME CATHEDRAL PLANS. 287 GGBROW
BE GUG, THIS BUGHOUSE WILL DRIVE ME STARK, RAVING 605 ICEMAN
LOONY YET?
(PITYINGLY) YOU'RE RAVING DRUNK, HUGO. 672 ICEMAN
I WAS A RAVING ROTTEN LUNATIC OR I COULDN'T HAVE 719 ICEMAN
SAID--
RAVING WHAT A GRAND, BEAUTIFUL LADY SHE IS, 161 POET

RAW
ANOTHER OVER ONE CHEEKBONE, HIS KNUCKLES ARE 68 ANNA
SKINNED AND RAW--
RAW-BONED AND STOUP-SHOULDERED, HIS JOINTS 6 ELECTR
STIFFENED BY RHEUMATISM,
THEY'D MAKE HIM PRETTY RAW PROPOSITIONS. 16 HUGHIE
SOME OF THEM DOLLS WAS RAW BABIES. 16 HUGHIE
HE IS TALL, RAW-BONED, WITH COARSE STRAIGHT WHITE 574 ICEMAN
HAIR,
HIS KNUCKLES ARE RAW AND THERE IS A MOUSE UNDER 697 ICEMAN
ONE EYE.
BESIDE THE ASTOUNDING FACT THAT ALL IN THE 431 MARCOM
PRODUCTION OF THE RAW MATERIAL.
(IRRITABLY) NIX ON THE RAW STUFF, JOSIE. 114 MISBEG
FROM A BIG RAW BRUISE ON HIS FOREHEAD, NEAR THE 152 POET
TEMPLE.
CAN'T TELL HIM THE RAW TRUTH ABOUT HER 35 STRANG
PROMISCUITY...
LIKE A BRUTAL, HAIRY HAND, RAW AND RED, AT MY 99 STRANG
THROAT/...

RAY
A BRILLIANT LIGHT FLOODS DOWN UPON HIM IN ONE 432 MARCOM
CONCENTRATED RAY.

RAYS
THE WINDOWS OF THE LOWER FLOOR REFLECT THE SUN'S 5 ELECTR
RAYS IN A RESENTFUL GLARE.

RAZOR
DEY TOL' ME YOU DONE DIED FROM DAT RAZOR CUT I 192 EJONES
GIVES YOU.

RAZORS
FOR GETTIN' IN AN ARGUMENT WID RAZORS OVAH A CRAP 181 EJONES
GAME.

REACH
HOW LONG WOULD IT TAKE US TO REACH HOME--IF WE 548 'ILE
STARTED NOW5
(SHE STRETCHES AWKWARDLY OVER THE TABLE TO REACH 210 AHWILD
THE CHANDELIER THAT IS
(BUT IN MOVING AROUND TO REACH THE NEXT BULB 210 AHWILD
(AFTER A PAUSE) WE WON'T REACH CARDIFF FOR A WEEK488 CARDIF
AT LEAST.
(PADDY TRIES TO REACH HIM BUT THE OTHERS KEEP THEM461 CARIBE
APART.)
(THE GIRLS REACH DOWN IN THEIR BASKETS IN UNDER 465 CARIBE
THE FRUIT WHICH IS ON TOP AND
YANK AND PEARL ARE THE LAST TO REACH THE DOORWAY. 466 CARIBE
HE AND SIX OTHERS MANAGED TO REACH A SMALL ISLAND 559 CROSS
ON THE FRINGE OF THE
DAMNED WITH DISTRUST, CURSED WITH THE INABILITY 534 DAYS
EVER TO REACH A
REACH DOWN THE JUG THAR/ 217 DESIRE
HIS TWITCHING FINGERS SEEMING TO REACH OUT FOR HER261 DESIRE
THROAT)
UNTIL SHE IS NOW WITHIN ARM'S REACH OF HER. 16 ELECTR
NOT ABLE TO WORK, NOT KNOWING WHERE TO REACH MC, 26 ELECTR
GET THIS AT SOME DRUGGIST'S DOWN BY THE WATERFRONT 40 ELECTR
THE MINUTE YOU REACH THERE.
ONCE WE'RE OUT OF HER REACH, SHE CAN'T DO 111 ELECTR
ANYTHING.

REACH (CONT'D.)
IF WE DON'T GET OUT OF VINNIE'S REACH RIGHT AWAY 111 ELECTR
WHEN THEY REACH THE SPOT WHERE HIS MOTHER HAD SAT 138 ELECTR
MUANING,
HE'D STEAL ANYTHING IN REACH THAT WASN'T NAILED 25 HUGHIE
DOWN--WELL, I DIDN'T GET FAR.
BOTTLES OF BAR WHISKEY ARE PLACED AT INTERVALS 628 ICEMAN
WITHIN REACH OF ANY SITTER.
IF YOU PUT ALL DE GUYS SHE'S STAYED WID SIDE BY 698 ICEMAN
SIDE, DEY'D REACH TO CHICAGO.
THAT I HAPPEN TO KNOW WHERE TO REACH YOU. 531 INZONE
YOU GO BACK UNTIL AT LAST YOU ARE BEYOND ITS 104 JOURNE
REACH.
TO GET BEYOND OUR REACH, TO BE RID OF US, TO 139 JOURNE
FORGET WE'RE ALIVE/
DEALING OUT BLOWS WITH THEIR STAVES AT EVERYONE IN304 LAZARU
REACH,
AS THEY REACH THE MIDDLE OF THE SHADE THEY STOP. 350 MARCOM
WHICH THE PAINTING MEN REACH OUT FOR AVIDLY, THEN 351 MARCOM
SINK BACK.
WAITE ME WHEN YOU REACH PERSIA. 401 MARCOM
(OUT OF HER REACH--SULLENLY) 5 MISBEG
AND HE'D REACH IN HIS POCKET AND TAKE OUT A HALF 25 MISBEG
DOLLAR,
(REBUKINGLY.) HIMSELF WENT IN THE BAR TO BE OUT 64 POET
OF REACH OF YOUR TONGUE.
OUT OF REACH)
KEEP HIDDEN UNTIL BOAT SAILS SO SHE CAN'T REACH 584 ROPE
ME/...)) 105 STRANG
YOU WON'T BE ABLE TO REACH ME AGAIN. 106 STRANG
HE SAID WE COULDN'T REACH HIM, 108 MARCOM
THEY INSTINCTIVELY REACH OUT THEIR HANDS IN A 480 WELDED
STRANGE CONFLICTING GESTURE OF A
(HE MOVES CLOSE TO HER AND HIS HANDS REACH OUT FOR489 WELDED
HERS.

REACHED
(SURPRISED) HAVE YOU REALLY, HONESTLY REACHED 161 BEYOND
THAT CONCLUSIONS
THE FOUR OF THEM. THESE FOUR MEN FINALLY REACHED 559 CROSS
FRISCO.
OF THE SIX WHO REACHED THE ISLAND WITH MY FATHER 559 CROSS
ONLY THREE WERE ALIVE WHEN A
HIM WHEN HE REACHED EIGHTEEN. 502 DAYS
TO THE RIGHT OF THIS WINDOW IS THE FRONT DOOR, 493 DIFRNT
REACHED BY A DIRT PATH
IS REACHED--ESPECIALLY ON AMMUNITION SHIPS LIKE 515 INZONE
THIS.
TALK TO THEMSELVES, FOR THEY HAVE REACHED THAT 354 LAZARU
HOPELESS WISDOM OF EXPERIENCE
YES, IN THE END--AND I HAVE REACHED THE END-- 28 MANSNS
(TENSELY.) I HAD ONCE REACHED A POINT WHERE I HAD102 MANSNS
GROWN SO LOST,
WHEN I REACHED THE LAST VILLAGE WITH MY CAMELS 351 MARCOM
FOUNDERING,
OH I SUPPOSE I'D BETTER SAY MAJESTY NOW THAT WE'VE410 MARCOM
REACHED PERSIA--
I CALLED UP THE EXECUTORS WHEN WE REACHED THE INN 131 MISBEG
AFTER LEAVING HERE.

REACHES
MRS. MILLER SIGHS AND REACHES UP WITH DIFFICULTY 211 AHWILD
(HE REACHES HIS HAND OUT TO JOHNNY.) 6 ANNA
(HE REACHES OUT TO FEEL OF HER ARM) 31 ANNA
(SHE REACHES DOWN, TAKES THE COAT AND PULLS OUT A 66 ANNA
REVOLVER--
(HE REACHES FOR THE BOOK) LET ME SEE. 82 BEYOND
(REACHES IN UNDER A BUNK AND YANKS OUT A PAIR OF 481 CARDIF
SEA-BOOTS, WHICH HE PUTS ON)
(DRISCOLL REACHES OUT AND GRASPS HIS HAND. 489 CARDIF
AND THEN REACHES INSIDE HIS SHIRT AND PULLS OUT A 462 CARIBE
PINT BOTTLE)
(HE REACHES INTO THE POCKET OF HIS MACKINAW AND 560 CROSS
PULLS OUT A CRUMPLED PAPER)
(SHE REACHES FOR A CIGARETTE--RETURNING TO HER 522 DAYS
HARD FLIPPANCY)
(HE TURNS AND REACHES FOR HIS COFFEE, FORGETTING 534 DAYS
HE HAS DRUNK IT--
STILLWELL REACHES FOR HER WRIST IN ALARM, 563 DAYS
REACHES THE FIDDLER. 248 DESIRE
AT THE SAME MOMENT THAT HE REACHES THE CRADLE 251 DESIRE
(SHE REACHES OVER AND TAKES ONE OF HER DAUGHTER'S 508 DIFRNT
HANDS IN HERS)
(HE SEES THE NEWSPAPER ON THE TABLE AND REACHES 430 DYNAMO
FOR IT.
(ALMOST AS SOON AS HE REACHES HIS OLD HIDING PLACE459 DYNAMO
IS OVERCOME BY SHAME)
(HE GOES TO HER AND REACHES UP AS IF TO KISS HER--468 DYNAMO
(REACHES OUT HIS HAND FOR IT.) 179 EJONES
(HE REACHES BELOW THE THRONE AND PULLS OUT A BIG, 182 EJONES
(HE REACHES IN UNDER THE THRONE AND PULLS OUT AN 185 EJONES
EXPENSIVE PANAMA HAT
HIS VOICE REACHES THE HIGHEST PITCH OF SORROW, OF 199 EJONES
DESOLATION.
TREMULOUS WAIL OF DESPAIR THAT REACHES A CERTAIN 199 EJONES
PITCH, UNBEARABLY ACUTE,
JONES LOOKS UP, STARTS TO SPRING TO HIS FEET, 200 EJONES
REACHES A HALF-KNEELING,
GOES TO THE DOOR AND REACHES IT JUST AS BRANT 36 ELECTR
APPEARS FROM THE HALL.
(SHE REACHES IN THE SLEEVE OF HER DRESS 40 ELECTR
(SUDDENLY HE REACHES OVER AND TAKES HER HAND) 95 ELECTR
(HE REACHES UP AND TOUCHES HER HAIR CARESSINGLY. 90 ELECTR
SHE REACHES IN HIS POCKET AND GETS POSSESSION OF 100 ELECTR
THE BOX
LAVINIA REACHES OUT STEALTHILY AND SNATCHES UP THE 101 ELECTR
BOX.
(REACHES IN HIS POCKET AND TOSSES HIM DOWN A 106 ELECTR
SILVER DOLLAR)
(HE REACHES OUT FOR IT.) 130 ELECTR

1285 REACTS

REACHES (CONT'D.)
(THE JUG REACHES HIM, 131 ELECTR
AND PASSES IT AROUND UNTIL IT FINALLY REACHES SETHI31 ELECTR
AGAIN.
(AS HE REACHES THEM--TERRIFIEDLY) 134 ELECTR
(SUDDENLY REACHES OUT AND TAKES UP A COPY OF THE 269 GGBROW
NEW TESTAMENT
(SHE REACHES OUT AND TAKES HIS HAND--TENDERLY) 272 GGBROW
(IMPULSIVELY REACHES OUT AND TAKES HER HAND-- 276 GGBROW
AWKWARDLY)
(HE REACHES FOR THE PHONE.) 277 GGBROW
(HE REACHES FOR HIS MASK AND CLAPS IT ON 278 GGBROW
DEFENSIVELY.)
(REACHES OUT AND TAKES HIS HAND) 287 GGBROW
(SHE STARTS, JAMS OFF THE MUSIC AND REACHES FOR 288 GGBROW
HER MASK BUT HAS NO TIME TO PUT
HE REACHES OUT FOR THE MASK OF DION LIKE A DOPE 307 GGBROW
FIEND AFTER A DRUG.
(HE REACHES OUT HIS HANDS AS IF TO TAKE THE MASK 307 GGBROW
BY THE THROAT.
(HE TAKES OFF THE DION MASK AND REACHES OUT FOR 314 GGBROW
THE WILLIAM BROWN ONE--
REACHES OUT AND SHAKES THE BARS-ALOUD TO HIMSELF, 240 HA APE
WONDERINGLY) STEEL.
(HE CHUCKLES AT HIS OWN FANCY--REACHES OVER AND 579 ICEMAN
SHAKES HUGO'S SHOULDER.
(HE REACHES ON THE TABLE AS IF HE EXPECTED A GLASS606 ICEMAN
TO BE THERE--
(SHE HIKES HER SKIRT UP AND REACHES INSIDE THE TOP683 ICEMAN
OF HER STOCKING)
SNEAKS TO THE BAR AND FURTIVELY REACHES FOR 686 ICEMAN
LARRY'S GLASS OF WHISKEY.)
NOW HE REACHES IT) 687 ICEMAN
(HE REACHES MECHANICALLY FOR THE INSIDE POCKET OF 714 ICEMAN
HIS COAT)
HOPE REACHES FOR HIS DRINK) 719 ICEMAN
BUT REACHES OUT FUMBLINGLY AND PATS LARRY'S ARM 721 ICEMAN
AND STAMMERS)
(HE CACKLES AND REACHES FOR THE BOTTLE) 722 ICEMAN
HE BENDS DOWN AND REACHES OUT HIS HAND SORT O' 519 INZONE
SCARED-LIKE,
(HE REACHES TOWARD THE MATTRESS.) 524 INZONE
(HE SELECTS ONE AND GINGERLY REACHES HIS HAND IN 527 INZONE
THE WATER.)
AS HE REACHES HER SHE BURSTS OUT PITEOUSLY.) 69 JOURNE
BUT WITH A SWIFT IMPULSIVE MOVEMENT SHE REACHES 82 JOURNE
OUT AND CLASPS HIS ARM.)
(AGAIN SHE REACHES OUT AND GRASPS HIS ARM-- 83 JOURNE
PLEADINGLY.)
(SHE REACHES OUT AND CLASPS HER HUSBAND'S HAND-- 109 JOURNE
SADLY.)
(HE REACHES OUT BLINDLY AND TAKES HER HAND-- 119 JOURNE
(HE REACHES OUT AND GETS THE BOTTLE, POURS A DRINK136 JOURNE
AND HANDS IT BACK.
(HE REACHES OUT AND POURS A DRINK. 152 JOURNE
(HE REACHES OUT FUMBLINGLY AND GRABS IT.) 156 JOURNE
(REACHES OUT AND PATS HIS ARM.) 163 JOURNE
(HE REACHES OUT WITH A FOOLISH GRIN OF DOTING 164 JOURNE
AFFECTION
(HE REACHES OUT AND PULLS BACK THE TOGA FROM HIS 339 LAZARU
FACE.
INVOLUNTARILY ONE OF LAZARUS' HANDS HALF-REACHES 346 LAZARU
OUT AS IF TO STOP HER.)
(SHE REACHES FOR DEBORAH'S HAND AGAIN.) 133 MANSNS
(SHE REACHES DOWN INSIDE HER BODICE AND PULLS OUT 164 MANSNS
A KEY ON A CORD AROUND HER.
HE REACHES OUT AND TAKES ONE OF HER HANDS AND SHE 177 MANSNS
STOPS, TREMBLING,
(WORRIEDLY, SUDDENLY REACHES OUT TO TAKE HER HAND)412 MARCOM
(SHE REACHES IN HER BEDROOM CORNER BY THE DOOR 11 MISBEG
(SHE REACHES OUT TO TURN DOWN THE LAMP.) 76 MISBEG
(SHE REACHES FOR THE LAMP AGAIN.) 77 MISBEG
HE REACHES OUT WITH HIS RIGHT AND POURS A GLASS OF 35 POET
WATER
HE REACHES OUT A SHAKING HAND TO PAT HER SHOULDER 37 POET
WITH AN ODD,
(HE REACHES FOR THE DECANTER AND SHAKINGLY POURS A 42 POET
DRINK.
(UNCONSCIOUSLY HE REACHES OUT FOR THE DECANTER ON 45 POET
THE TABLE--
(WHO HAS BEEN WATCHING HIM DISDAINFULLY, REACHES 97 POET
OUT TO TAKE HIS PLATE--
(SHE REACHES OUT AND TOUCHES ONE OF HIS HANDS ON 167 POET
THE TABLE TOP WITH A FURTIVE
AS HE REACHES THE TABLE AND LEANS ONE HAND ON IT 578 ROPE
FOR SUPPORT,
(HE REACHES UP FOR THE ROPE AS IF TO TRY AND YANK 583 ROPE
IT DOWN.
(HE REACHES OUT HIS HAND FOR THE BOTTLE. 594 ROPE
LUKE REACHES FOR THE BOTTLE) 595 ROPE
(THEN SHE REACHES OUT AND TURNS HIS HEAD UNTIL HIS 88 STRANG
FACE FACES HERS BUT HE KEEPS
(SHE REACHES OUT AND TAKES HIS HAND. 104 STRANG
NOW IN DEATH HE REACHES OUT TO STEAL PRESTON/... 192 STRANG
(WITHOUT LOOKING AF HER HE REACHES OUT AND CLASPS 482 WELDED
HER HAND.)
(MOVES, WITHOUT LOOKING AT HIM, REACHES AND CLASPS483 WELDED
HIS HAND)
(SHE REACHES OUT HER HAND AND CLASPS HIS 486 WELDED
COMFORTINGLY)
(SHE REACHES THE TOP OF THE STAIRWAY AND STANDS 489 WELDED
THERE LOOKING DOWN AT HIM--

REACHING
HE IS JUST REACHING OUT FOR MORE WHEN THE PANTRY 217 AHWILD
DOOR IS OPENED SLIGHTLY AND
YOU HAVE ME REACHING FOR MY WATCH EVERY COUPLE OF 250 AHWILD
MINUTES.
(REACHING OUT FOR IT) YES. 75 ANNA

REACHING (CONT'D.)
REACHING FOR ANOTHER CIGARETTE--DRYLY) 519 DAYS
(REACHING OUT AND TAKING HIS HAND) 233 DESIRE
SHE IS BENDING OVER HIM IN A TENDER ATTITUDE, ONE 486 DYNAMO
HAND REACHING DOWN.
SMITHERS GOES AFTER HER, REACHING FOR HIS 175 EJONES
REVOLVER)
THE INTERLOCKED HOPES OF CREEPERS REACHING UPWARD 198 EJONES
TO ENTWINE THE TREE TRUNKS
(REACHING OUT AND TAKING HIS HAND) 85 ELECTR
(WITH AN UNEASY GLANCE AROUND, REACHING FOR THE 133 ELECTR
JUG)
FRIGHTENED CHILD REACHING OUT FOR ITS NURSE'S 319 GGBROW
HAND--
(REACHING OUT) TANKS. 244 HA APE
(REACHING FOR HIS HIP POCKET) 671 ICEMAN
(REACHING FOR THE BOTTLE.) WELL, MAYBE ONE MORE 100 JOURNE
WON'T HARM.
THEN HUMBLY, REACHING OUT FOR THE FRUIT) 345 LAZARU
AS REAL AS THE DOOR I HAVE JUST OPENED, AND I WAS 29 MANSNS
REACHING OUT MY HAND TO--
I CAN STILL FEEL HIS THOUGHTS REACHING OUT-- 136 MANSNS
OF EMBROIDERED CRIMSON SATIN REACHING ALMOST TO 428 MARCOM
THE GROUND.
HER HAIR IS DOWN OVER HER SHOULDERS, REACHING TO 136 POET
HER WAIST.
(HE SHRINKS SUPERSTITIOUSLY--THEN ANGRILY, 161 POET
REACHING FOR THE DECANTER.)
(REACHING OUT HER HAND TENDERLY, TRYING TO TOUCH 58 STRANG
NINA)
(HURRIEDLY REACHING IN HIS COAT POCKET) 95 STRANG
SHE SWAYS IRRESOLUTELY TOWARD HIM, AGAIN REACHING 449 WELDED
TO THE BANNISTER FOR SUPPORT.
(REACHING OVER AND GRASPING HIS HANDS--EARNESTLY) 456 WELDED
(SHE STANDS SWAYING, REACHING OUT HER HAND 465 WELDED

REACT
(THEN BEFORE HIS FATHER CAN REACT TO THIS INSULT 80 JOURNE
TO THE OLD SOD, HE ADDS DRYLY,
AND HOW SHE SHOULD REACT--WITH AN UNDERCURRENT OF 82 POET
RESENTMENT.)
ABSURD FOR ME TO REACT AS IF I LOVED... 12 STRANG

REACTED
FOR SHE REACTED TO IT IN A WAY THAT AT FIRST 937 DAYS
SHOCKED HIM

REACTING
(MECHANICALLY, REACTING INSTINCTIVELY FOR A MOMENT459 DYNAMO
AS THE TIMID BOY OF FORMERLY,
(REACTING AS HIS FATHER HAD--HIS FACE GROWN 155 ELECTR
LIVID--
(REACTING AUTOMATICALLY AND WINCING WITH PAIN-- 200 STRANG
THINKING MECHANICALLY)

REACTION
ONLY ARTHUR BETRAYS THE OUTRAGED REACTION OF A 195 AHWILD
PATRIOT.)
(HE GIVES A QUICK GLANCE AT ELSA, AS IF TO CATCH 539 DAYS
HER REACTION TO THIS.
HIM, HER IMMEDIATE REACTION ONE OF MATERNAL 446 DYNAMO
TENDERNESS.
BUT HER REACTION IS THE DIRECT OPPOSITE TO WHAT 11 ELECTR
HER MOTHER'S HAD BEEN.
AND THE REACTION WERE TOO MUCH FOR HIS WEAK HEART/ 41 ELECTR
(HER FIRST INSTINCTIVE REACTION ONE OF HURT 177 ELECTR
INSULT)
THIS STARTLES YANK TO A REACTION. 226 HA APE
THIS IS EVIDENTLY THEIR CUSTOMARY REACTION. 627 ICEMAN
ALL THEIR ATTITUDES SHOW THE REACTION CORA HAS 638 ICEMAN
EXPRESSED.
(BURSTS OUT WITH HIS TRUE REACTION BEFORE HE 679 ICEMAN
THINKS TO IGNORE HIM)
HER FIRST REACTION IS ONE OF RELIEF. 49 JOURNE
OUT IN A STRANGE WAY THE REACTION HAS A MECHANICA101 JOURNE
QUALITY.
IT IS AS IF THIS REACTION WERE TRANSMITTED THROUGH286 LAZARU
THE CHORUS TO THE CROWD.)
EVERY REACTION, FROM THE EXTREME OF PANIC FEAR OR 337 LAZARU
HYPNOTIZED ECSTASY TO A
THE REACTION OF EMPTINESS AFTER SUCCESS--YOU'VE 74 MANSNS
ALWAYS FELT IT--
(STARTS--HER FIRST INSTINCTIVE REACTION 97 MANSNS
(ABRUPTLY AND GUILTILY HER REACTION CHANGES 97 MANSNS
HIS FIRST REACTION ONE OF LOATHING FOR THE DRINK 173 MISBEG
WHICH BROUGHT BACK MEMORY.
(FORCING HER USUAL REACTION TO HIS THREATS) 177 MISBEG
(AFTER A CUNNING GLANCE AT MELODY'S FACE TO SEE 97 POET
WHAT HIS REACTION IS--
(BUT MELODY SUPPRESSES ANY ANGRY REACTION. 103 POET
DETERMINED NOT TO LET HIM KNOW HER REACTION.) 108 POET
(AT FIRST HER ONLY REACTION IS PLEASED 142 POET
SATISFACTION.)
NORA'S FIRST REACTION IS A CRY OF RELIEF.) 151 POET
AND HIS REACTION IS TO MAKE HIM DRUNKENLY ANGRY AT164 POET
MELODY.
(BEFORE SHE CAN STIFLE HEX IMMEDIATE REACTION OF 69 STRANG
CONTEMPT AND DISLIKE)
DESIRE IS A NATURAL MALE REACTION TO THE BEAUTY OF 85 STRANG
THE FEMALE...
(EASILY) REACTION. 451 WELDED

REACTIONS
AND HE WAS CURIOUS NOW TO WATCH HER REACTIONS. 937 DAYS
HIS FACE IS AS VAGUE AS HIS REACTIONS ARE 251 DESIRE
CONFUSED.
SATISFIED BY HER REACTIONS TO HIS FIRST ATTACK, 69 POET
AND HASTENS TO APOLOGIZE.)
ONLY FOR THE OBJECTIVE SATISFACTION OF STUDYING 33 STRANG
HIS OWN AND THEIR REACTIONS..

REACTS
(AUTOMATICALLY REACTS TO THE VOICE OF AUTHORITY-- 105 ELECTR
QUIETLY)

CARROLL COLLEGE LIBRARY
HELENA, MONTANA 59601

REACTS

REACTS (CONT'D.)		
HIS FATHER AGAIN REACTS CUSTOMARILY--	89	JOURNE
SARCASTICALLY.)		
(HAS BEGUN TO DRIFT INTO DREAMS AGAIN--REACTS	106	JOURNE
MECHANICALLY.)		
(REACTS MECHANICALLY.) I NEVER CLAIMED ONE BULB	117	JOURNE
COST MUCH/		
FOR A SECOND JAMIE REACTS PUGNACIOUSLY AND HALF	162	JOURNE
RISES FROM HIS CHAIR TO DO		
(REACTS--WITH AN EXTREME PROFESSIONAL	37	MANSNS
PORTENTOUSNESS.)		
HER BODY REACTS AS IF SHE WERE THROWING OFF A	449	WELDED
LOAD.)		

READ

YEARS--BOOKS THE FAMILY REALLY HAVE READ.	185	AHWILD
(CAUSTICALLY) HE READ HIS SCHOOL BOOKS, TOO,	192	AHWILD
STRANGE AS THAT MAY SEEM TO YOU.		
WHEN I THINK OF THE BOOKS I USED TO SNEAK OFF AND	193	AHWILD
READ WHEN I WAS A KID.		
I READ ABOUT THEM MYSELF, IN THE PAPERS AND IN	196	AHWILD
OTHER BOOKS.		
WHAT, HAVE YOU READ ITS	196	AHWILD
UH, I'VE READ THAT, ESSIE--GOT A COPY DOWN AT THE	198	AHWILD
OFFICE.		
WHY, NAT, I DON'T SEE HOW YOU--IT LOOKED TERRIBLE	198	AHWILD
BLASPHEMOUS--PARTS I READ.		
SOME OF THE THINGS I SIMPLY COULDN'T READ, THEY	198	AHWILD
WERE SO INDECENT--ALL ABOUT--		
(WITH SHY EXCITEMENT) I--I'VE READ IT, TOO--AT	198	AHWILD
THE LIBRARY.		
YOU READ THEM AND THEN SAY I'M A LIAR.	202	AHWILD
ABOUT RICHARD'S BRINGING UP OR WHAT HE'S ALLOWED	202	AHWILD
TO READ--		
AND SO HE GRABS AT EVERYTHING RADICAL TO READ AND	202	AHWILD
WANTS TO PASS IT ON TO HIS		
(HE PICKS THEM UP AND STARTS TO READ.)	204	AHWILD
I'VE NEVER READ HIM, BUT I'VE HEARD SOMETHING LIKE205		AHWILD
THAT WAS THE MATTER WITH HIM.		
WHEN YOU READ THROUGH THAT LITERATURE YOU WISHED	207	AHWILD
ON HIS INNOCENT DAUGHTERS		
WELL, IT'LL DO HIM GOOD TO READ THE TRUTH ABOUT	207	AHWILD
LIFE FOR ONCE		
THEN GIRDS UP HIS COURAGE AND TEARS IT OPEN AND	208	AHWILD
BEGINS TO READ SWIFTLY.		
SHE IS PRETENDING TO READ A NOVEL, BUT HER	249	AHWILD
ATTENTION WANDERS, TOO.		
LILY, YOU JUST SIT DOWN AND READ YOUR BOOK AND	256	AHWILD
DON'T PAY ANY ATTENTION TO HIM.		
LILY FORGETS TO PRETEND TO READ HER BOOK BUT LOOKS257		AHWILD
OVER IT.		
YOU READ IN THE PAPERS EVERY DAY ABOUT BOYS	259	AHWILD
GETTING RUN OVER BY AUTOMOBILES.		
AFTER I'D READ THAT I DIDN'T WANT TO LIVE ANY	281	AHWILD
MORE.		
PRETENDING TO READ THEM OUT OF DUTY TO RICHARD,	288	AHWILD
NOW I READ THAT OVER AGAIN AND LIKED IT EVEN	289	AHWILD
BETTER THAN I HAD BEFORE--		
HE'S PROVED IT BY THE WAY HE LIKES TO READ	290	AHWILD
I'M NOT GOING TO READ YOU ANY TEMPERANCE LECTURE.	294	AHWILD
BY GULLY, AT TANK AYT'M TOO DRUNK FOR READ DIS	8	ANNA
LETTER FROM ANNA.		
SLOWLY OPENS IT, AND, SQUINTING HIS EYES,	8	ANNA
COMMENCES TO READ LABORIOUSLY.		
(AFTER A PAUSE) YOU BETTER GO IN CABIN READ BOOK.	26	ANNA
HIS EYES READ SOMETHING AND HE GIVES AN	82	BEYOND
EXCLAMATION OF DISGUST)		
THE MYSTERY AND SPELL OF THE EAST WHICH LURES ME	85	BEYOND
IN THE BOOKS I'VE READ.		
MAYO PRETENDS TO READ HIS PAPER..	95	BEYOND
I'VE GOT A RIGHT TO READ IT, HAVEN'T IS	120	BEYOND
ROBERT CONTINUES TO READ, OBLIVIOUS TO THE FOOD ON121		BEYOND
THE TABLE.)		
HIS LETTERS READ LIKE THE DIARY OF A--OF A FARMER/126		BEYOND
LET ME READ THEM AGAIN.	146	BEYOND
I'LL READ THE MATTER UP AND SEND HIM SOME	485	CARDIF
MEDICINE.		
THEN TAKES THE THERMOMETER FROM YANK'S MOUTH AND	485	CARDIF
GOES TO THE LAMP TO READ IT.		
THEY SENT A BOAT OUT TO READ HER NAME.	558	CRUSS
I USED TO READ HIS ARTICLES, AS I WAS REMINDING	503	DAYS
HIM JUST BEFORE YOU CAME.		
(THEN SNEERINGLY) BUT, OF COURSE, YOU WOULD READ	504	DAYS
THAT INTO IT.		
HE READ ALL SORTS OF SCIENTIFIC BOOKS.	534	DAYS
(HIS EYES ARE ON STILLWELL'S FACE, DESPERATELY	554	DAYS
TRYING TO READ SOME ANSWER THERE.		
YE KIN READ THE YEARS OF MY LIFE IN THEM WALLS,	237	DESIRE
EVERY DAY A HEFTED STONE.		
HIS LIFE IS PRETENDING TO READ, BUT HER THOUGHTS	422	DYNAMO
ARE ACTIVELY ELSEWHERE.		
BEGINS TO READ IN A DETERMINED EFFORT TO GET HIS	426	DYNAMO
MIND OFF THE SUBJECT.)		
(AS ADA BEGINS TO READ, HE SPEAKS TO HIS WIFE)	431	DYNAMO
READ THIS AND YOU WON'T JOKE ABOUT IT/	431	DYNAMO
I'LL GO UPSTAIRS AND READ THE PAPER.	434	DYNAMO
(I DON'T WANT TO READ THE PAPER...	435	DYNAMO
I'VE LIVED A LOT AND READ A LOT TO FIND OUT FOR	458	DYNAMO
MYSELF WHAT'S REALLY WHAT--		
SOMETIMES I'VE GONE WITHOUT EATING TO BUY BOOKS--	458	DYNAMO
AND OFTEN I'VE READ ALL NIGHT--		
YOU CAN TELL HER I'VE READ UP ON LOVE IN BIOLOGY,	458	DYNAMO
AND I KNOW WHAT IT IS NOW.		
NO RIGHT EVEN TO READ THEM...	465	DYNAMO
I'D LIKE TO HAVE READ--	465	DYNAMO
SHE COULDN'T MAIL THEM, SHE KNEW YOU'D NEVER READ	465	DYNAMO
THEM.		
WHEN I READ THEM I REALIZED THAT AMELIA HAD BEEN	465	DYNAMO
THINKING OF YOU ALL THE TIME.		

READ (CONT'D.)

HOW I WISH I'D NEVER READ THEM/....)	465	DYNAMO
YOU USUALLY READ LONG AFTER THAT.	16	ELECTR
THEN YOU DID READ ITS	89	ELECTR
HAVE YOU EVER READ A BOOK CALLED =TYPES=--ABOUT	89	ELECTR
THE SOUTH SEA ISLANDERS		
I READ IT AND REREAD IT UNTIL	89	ELECTR
(THEN, AS IF SHE READ SOME ANSWER IN THE DEAD	101	ELECTR
MAN'S FACE.		
I CAN READ THAT IN YOUR FACE/	108	ELECTR
NOT KNOWING ANYTHING BUT WHAT I READ IN THE	108	ELECTR
PAPERS--THAT HE WAS DEAD.		
READ THAT, IF YOU DON'T BELIEVE ME/	121	ELECTR
TO BE READ IN CASE YOU TRY TO MARRY HIM--OR IF I	156	ELECTR
SHOULD DIE--		
THE DAY BEFORE THE WEDDING--I WANT YOU TO MAKE	160	ELECTR
PETER READ WHAT'S INSIDE.		
ORIN ASKED ME TO MAKE HIM READ IT BEFORE HE	173	ELECTR
MARRIED YOU.		
AT LEAST YOU OWE IT TO PETER TO LET HIM READ WHAT	173	ELECTR
ORIN HAD IN THAT ENVELOPE.		
SHE IS TRYING TO READ A BOOK.	308	GGBROW
WAIT'LL I SEE IF I GOT LIGHT ENOUGH AND I'LL	242	HA APE
READ YOU.		
I CAN'T READ MUCH BUT I KIN MANAGE.	244	HA APE
HE'D READ SOMEWHERE--IN THE SUCKERS' ALMANAC, I	23	HUGHIE
GUESS--		
I READ A STORY ABOUT HIM.	32	HUGHIE
YOU'VE READ IN THE PAPERS ABOUT THAT BOMBING ON	583	ICEMAN
THE COAST		
DID YE NEVERR READ OF THE GERMAN SPIES	515	INZONE
I READ IT IN THE PAPER MANY TIME.	515	INZONE
AIN'T YOU READ HOW THEY GETS CAUGHT DOIN' IT IN	521	INZONE
LUNDON AND ON THE COASTS		
AIN'T YOU READ IN THE PAPERS HOW ALL THEM GERMAN	521	INZONE
SPIES THEY BEEN CATCHIN' IN		
(SITTING DOWN AGAIN) WELL, READ 'EM AND FIND OUT.529		INZONE
READ ONE OF 'EM, DRISC.	529	INZONE
TO READ 'EM YOU WOULDN'T S'PECT NOTHIN'--JUST MUSH529		INZONE
AND ALL--		
THEY AIN'T AS INNERECENT AS THEY LOOKS, I'LL TAKE	529	INZONE
ME OATH, WHEN YOU READ 'EM.		
THE MARK'S BLURRED SO IT'S HARD TO READ.	530	INZONE
(EAGERLY) READ IT.	531	INZONE
HAVING BEEN READ AND REREAD.	12	JOURNE
WHAT ARE YOU GOING TO DO READ HERES	49	JOURNE
NOW THE STUFF YOU READ AND CLAIM YOU ADMIRE.	76	JOURNE
YOU HAVEN'T READ HIM.	77	JOURNE
IT'S THE BOOKS YOU READ/ NOTHING BUT SADNESS AND	90	JOURNE
DEATH/		
YOU COULD READ.	135	JOURNE
I READ ALL THE PLAYS EVER WRITTEN.	150	JOURNE
I USED TO READ IT EVERY ONCE IN A WHILE UNTIL	152	JOURNE
FINALLY IT MADE ME FEEL SO BAD I		
JUST BECAUSE YOU'VE READ A LOT OF HIGHBROW JUNK,	163	JOURNE
DON'T THINK YOU CAN FOOL ME/		
I HAVE LEARNED TO READ THE LIES IN FACES.	341	LAZARU
WITH THE LOVE I FELT FOR HER BEFORE I LEARNED TO	355	LAZARU
READ HER EYES/		
I WANT TO READ HIS EYES WHEN THEY SEE DEATH/	364	LAZARU
OR SO I HAVE READ IN THE POETS.	7	MANSNS
WELL, A WOMAN'S LOVE IS JEALOUSLY POSSESSIVE--OR	7	MANSNS
SO I HAVE READ--		
WHEN YOU'D READ ME FAIRY STORIES.	12	MANSNS
NO, ALL YOU HAVE TO DO IS READ YOUR DAILY	47	MANSNS
NEWSPAPER		
THE ADVERSARY ACROSS THE TABLE IN WHOSE EYES ONE	92	MANSNS
CAN READ		
AND I'D ASK YOU TO READ ALOUD TO ME--S	107	MANSNS
AND YOU WOULD READ TALES ALOUD TO ME, HERE.	109	MANSNS
I'LL BE SENSIBLE NOW AND READ MY BOOK--	119	MANSNS
(HE SMILES TO HIMSELF GLOATINGLY AND BEGINS TO	119	MANSNS
READ.		
(SHE BEGINS TO READ DETERMINEDLY.	119	MANSNS
SHE CAN'T READ--SHE'S THINKING HOW SHE'LL MISS THE122		MANSNS
CHILDREN--ALONE ALL DAY--		
(SMILING GLOATINGLY.) SEE, SARA, HE IS NOT EVEN	126	MANSNS
PRETENDING TO READ NOW.		
AND I WILL READ MY BOOK.	136	MANSNS
THERE IS A POEM BY DOCTOR HOLMES YOU SHOULD READ	148	MANSNS
SOMETIME--		
I CANNOT READ BUT I THINK YOU ARE LYING.	353	MARCON
A MODERN BUSINESSMAN'S DATE-BOOK AND READ)	365	MARCON
WE BETTER READ FROM THE NOTES WE MADE ON OUR LAST	365	MARCON
TRIP ALL THERE IS TO REMEMBER		
(BEGINS TO READ FROM HIS NOTEBOOK)	370	MARCON
AND BEGINS TO READ IN THE MONOTONE OF A BORING	373	MARCON
FORMULA)		
BECAUSE I'VE NEVER READ MUCH IN A ANY HISTORY	394	MARCON
ABOUT HEROES WHO WAGED PEACE.		
LAST EASTER SUNDAY WHEN FATHER AND UNCLE READ A	394	MARCON
PRAYER		
WISDOM/ NO, DO NOT READ/	423	MARCOM
HE BEGINS TO READ AT ONCE.	423	MARCOM
HAS WATCHED ALL THIS WITH FASCINATED DISGUST WHILE432		MARCOM
CHU-YIN HAS SAT DOWN TO READ		
I'M BEGINNING TO READ SOME SENSE INTO THIS.	61	MISBEG
SHE TRIES TO READ HIS FACE WITHOUT HIS NOTICING.	115	MISBEG
(TRYING TO READ HIS FACE--UNEASILY)	120	MISBEG
I DESIRE NOTHING--EXCEPT A LITTLE PEACE IN WHICH	35	POET
TO READ THE NEWS.		
HE WAS TRYING TO READ A BOOK OF POETRY,	143	POET
YOU CAN SIT 'N' READ YOUR BIBLE.	581	ROPE
(WITH A STRANGE SMILE) BUT SOME DAY I'LL READ IT	21	STRANG
ALL IN ONE OF YOUR BOOKS.		
OPENS IT AT RANDOM AND BEGINS TO READ ALOUD	23	STRANG
SONOROUSLY LIKE A CHILD WHISTLING TO		
READ HIS BOOKS...	34	STRANG

1287

READS

READ (CONT'D.)
AND IT'S ONE OF THOSE UNSELFISH LOVES YOU READ 37 STRANG
ABOUT.
WRITTEN AFTER WE READ OF YOUR APPOINTMENTS 49 STRANG
THEN I WANTED TO WRITE TO YOU BUT I WAS SCARED HE 61 STRANG
MIGHT READ IT.
SHE HAS BEEN TRYING TO READ A BOOK BUT HAS LET 90 STRANG
THIS DROP LISTLESSLY ON HER LAP.
I'LL TRY TO READ.....)) 123 STRANG
I'D WATCH HIM AND READ SYMPTOMS OF INSANITY INTO 139 STRANG
EVERY MOVE HE MADE...
((HE READ MY THOUGHTS?... 157 STRANG
DO YOU MEAN TO SAY YOU STILL READ THEM OVER--AFTER444 WELDED
FIVE YEARS OF HE*
(ENTHUSIASTICALLY) YOU'LL SEE WHEN I READ YOU-- 445 WELDED
(IMPETUOUSLY) YOU'VE SIMPLY GOT TO READ ME THAT 445 WELDED
LAST ACT RIGHT NOW/
WHY DON'T YOU READ US THE LAST ACT NOW, MICHAEL* 451 WELDED
(SHE STARES INTO HIS EYES AND SEEMS TO READ SOME 459 WELDED
CONFIRMATION OF HER STATEMENT
YOU DEVIL, YOU, YOU READ THOUGHTS INTO MY MIND/

READER
LOOK WELL INTO MY EYES, OLD READER OF LIES, 341 LAZARU

READING
(TURNING BACK--SCORNFULLY) GOSH, HE'S ALWAYS 192 AHWILD
READING NOW.

READIN'
I BIN A-READIN' 'EM. 568 CROSS
READIN' ABOUT IN THEM BOOKS. 496 DIFRNT
OUT O' THEM STORY BOOKS YOU'RE ALWAYS READIN', 499 DIFRNT
AIN'T HE*
I BEEN READIN' ABOUT 'EM TODAY IN THE PAPER. 242 HA APE
I WAS READIN' IN SOME MAGAZINE IN NEW YORK ON'Y 529 INZONE
TWO WEEKS AGO HOW SOME GERMAN
I'M NO HAND TO BE READIN' BUT I'LL TRY UT. 529 INZONE
WHAT'S THE USE OF READIN' THAT STUFF EVEN IF-- 530 INZONE

READING
AT CENTER IS A BIG, ROUND TABLE WITH A GREEN- 185 AHWILD
SHADED READING LAMP,
READING IS A GOOD HABIT. 192 AHWILD
HE'S STILL IN THE DINING-ROOM, READING A BOOK. 192 AHWILD
I'VE BEEN MEANING TO SPEAK TO YOU ABOUT THOSE 192 AHWILD
AWFUL BOOKS RICHARD IS READING.
THE BOOK HE HAS BEEN READING IN ONE HAND, A FINGER193 AHWILD
MARKING HIS PLACE.
SOMETHING FROM THAT BOOK YOU'RE READINGS 195 AHWILD
(THEN SERIOUSLY) GLAD YOU'RE READING IT, RICHARD.196 AHWILD
WELL, YOU SEE, EVEN A NEWSPAPER OWNER CAN'T GET 196 AHWILD
OUT OF READING A BOOK EVERY NOW
=THE BALLAD OF READING GAOL= ONE OF THE GREATEST 197 AHWILD
POEMS EVER WRITTEN.
(HE PRONOUNCES IT READING GOAL--AS IN GOALPOST--)197 AHWILD
WELL, ALL I CAN SAY IS, FROM READING HERE AND 198 AHWILD
THERE,
EVERYBODY'S READING THAT NOW, ESSIE-- 198 AHWILD
AFTER READING THOSE PAPERS, TO CLAIM YOUR SON WAS 202 AHWILD
INNOCENT OF ALL WRONGDOING/
JUDGING FROM HIS CHOICE OF READING MATTER, IS AS 202 AHWILD
FOOL
(MILLER HAS TAKEN THE SLIPS AND IS READING THEM 202 AHWILD
FROWNINGLY.
(HAS BEEN READING THE SLIPS, A BROAD GRIN ON HIS 205 AHWILD
FACE--SUDDENLY HE WHISTLES)
I THOUGHT, MAYBE, READING THOSE THINGS--THEY'RE 207 AHWILD
BEAUTIFUL, AREN'T THEY, PA*
THAT THEY'RE HARDLY FIT READING FOR A YOUNG GIRL. 207 AHWILD
HE HAS HIS READING SPECS ON AND IS RUNNING OVER 249 AHWILD
ITEMS IN A NEWSPAPER.
SHE HAS JUST ONE OF THOSE BOOKS HE'S BEEN READING.266 AHWILD
RECITING THE BALLAD OF READING GAOL TO THOSE 276 AHWILD
LOWBROWS/
ONLY THE GREENSHADED READING LAMP IS LIT AND BY 288 AHWILD
ITS LIGHT MILLER, HIS SPECS ON,
IS READING A BOOK WHILE HIS WIFE, SEWING BASKET IN288 AHWILD
LAP,
(SHE PUTS HER HAND ON THE READING-LAMP SWITCH) 298 AHWILD
READING AN EVENING PAPER. 3 ANNA
SHE IS NOT READING BUT STARING STRAIGHT IN FRONT 41 ANNA
OF HER.
HE IS READING A BOOK BY THE FADING SUNSET LIGHT. 82 BEYOND
IMAGINE ME READING POETRY AND PLOWING AT THE SAME 82 BEYOND
TIME.
JUST BECAUSE YOU SEE ME READING BOOKS ALL THE 83 BEYOND
TIME.
YOU WERE ALWAYS READING AN OLD BOOK, AND NOT 91 BEYOND
PAYING ANY ATTENTION TO ME.
IN THE CENTER OF THE TABLE, A LARGE OIL READING 93 BEYOND
LAMP,
AND A FARM JOURNAL WHICH HE HAS BEEN READING LIES 94 BEYOND
IN HIS LAP.
READING ANDY'S LETTER AGAIN* 119 BEYOND
HE SITS DOWN AND IMMEDIATELY BECOMES ABSORBED IN 121 BEYOND
READING.
(AS RUTH DOESN'T ANSWER OR SMILE HE OPENS HIS BOOK122 BEYOND
AND RESUMES HIS READING.
(SPITEFULLY) WORK YOU'LL NEVER GET DONE BY 122 BEYOND
READING BOOKS ALL THE TIME.
WHY DO YOU PERSIST IN NAGGING AT ME FOR GETTING 122 BEYOND
PLEASURE OUT OF READINGS
AND ALWAYS READING YOUR STUPID BOOKS INSTEAD OF 127 BEYOND
WORKING.
I'VE BEEN READING UP A LOT ON IT, TOO, LATELY. 133 BEYOND
I'LL PROVE TO YOU THE READING I'VE DONE CAN BE PUT149 BEYOND
TO SOME USE.
JUST STAYED INDOORS AND TOOK TO READING BOOKS 155 BEYOND
AGAIN.
AND I COULDN'T BEAR WITH HIS BLUNDERING AND BOOK- 163 BEYOND
READING--

READING (CONT'D.)
(COMES TO THE TABLE) I WAS READING. 563 CROSS
GOING TO A CONCERT NOW AND THEN, READING A LOT, 516 DAYS
KEEPING HOUSE.
BY THE HEAD OF THE BED IS A SMALL STAND ON WHICH 553 DAYS
IS A READING LAMP
ON IT ARE PILES OF FASHION MAGAZINES AND AN 519 DIFRNT
ELECTRIC READING LAMP.
ON THE TABLE AT CENTER ARE A CHEAP OIL READING 421 DYNAMO
LAMP, A BIBLE,
(READING--DISGUSTEDLY) ((=HYDRO-ELECTRIC 429 DYNAMO
ENGINEERING=...
AND SETTLES DOWN TO READING WITH A GRUNT OF 430 DYNAMO
AWAKENED INTEREST.)
(WHO HAS FINISHED READING THE STORY) 431 DYNAMO
SITTING AS BEFORE IN THE SITTING ROOM OF THE OTHER443 DYNAMO
HOUSE READING THE BIBLE.
I'VE BEEN READING A BOOK IN FATHER'S MEDICAL 40 ELECTR
LIBRARY.
BOOKCASE AND LAYS IT OPEN ON THE TABLE AS IF HE 149 ELECTR
HAD BEEN READING.
READING. 150 ELECTR
READING ALOUD FROM THE =IMITATION OF CHRIST= BY 290 GGBROW
THOMAS A KEMPIS TO HIS MASK,
THE READING LAMP ON THE TABLE IS THE ONLY LIGHT. 294 GGBROW
BROWN SITS IN THE CHAIR AT LEFT READING AN 294 GGBROW
ARCHITECTURAL PERIODICAL.
HE SWITCHES ON THE READING LAMP ON THE TABLE. 306 GGBROW
(READING) =I REFER TO THAT DEVIL'S BREW OF 242 HA APE
RASCALS, JAILBIRDS,
(READING) =THIS FIENDISH ORGANIZATION IS A FOUL 243 HA APE
ULCER
(READING) =LIKE CATO I SAY TO THIS SENATE, THE 243 HA APE
I WE MUST BE DESTROYED/
AND READING ROOM, RESEMBLES SOME DINGY SETTLEMENT 245 HA APE
BOYS' CLUB.
THE READING, MAKES A MUFFLED SOUND LIKE A SOB 530 INZONE
AROUND THE TABLE WITHIN READING-LIGHT RANGE ARE 12 JOURNE
FOUR CHAIRS,
AT CENTER IS A ROUND TABLE WITH A GREEN SHADED 12 JOURNE
READING LAMP.
EDMUND SITS IN THE ARMCHAIR AT LEFT OF TABLE, 51 JOURNE
READING A BOOK.
EDMUND LOOKS UP AS IF HIS READING WAS INTERRUPTED. 53 JOURNE
I'VE BEEN READING HERE. 56 JOURNE
(HE GETS UP AND TURNS ON THE READING LAMP-- 117 JOURNE
ROUGHLY.)
(THEN READING ACCUSATION IN HIS EYE.) 123 JOURNE
IN THE LIVING ROOM ONLY THE READING LAMP ON THE 125 JOURNE
TABLE IS LIGHTED.
(HE TURNS OUT THE THIRD BULB, SO ONLY THE READING 151 JOURNE
LAMP IS ON.
AND WHO STEERED YOU ON TO READING POETRY FIRSTS 164 JOURNE
OSCAR WILDE'S =READING GAOL= HAS THE DUPE 166 JOURNE
TWISTED.
(SHE STARES--THEN AS IF READING ADMISSION IN HIS 361 LAZARU
EYES, SHE SPRINGS TO HER FEET)
INSTEAD OF READING AND DREAMING ABOUT IT/ 3 MANSNS
(TOO CASUALLY.) WHAT PAPER IS IT YOU'VE BEEN 44 MANSNS
READINGS
AS THE CURTAIN RISES, DEBORAH IS READING FROM A 95 MANSNS
VOLUME OF BYRON'S POEMS.
AT LEFT-REAR OF THE FIREPLACE IS A LONG SOFA WITH 117 MANSNS
A SMALL TABLE AND READING-LAMP
(THINKING). HE ISN'T READING--JUST PRETENDING 119 MANSNS
TO--SMILING TO HIMSELF--SLY--
HIS EYES CEASE READING AND STARE AT THE BOOK 119 MANSNS
PREOCCUPIEDLY.)
(HAS STOPPED READING--THINKING.) 120 MANSNS
(TAKING UP THE READING FROM HIS BOOK IN THE SAME 370 MARCOM
TONE)
(READING FROM HIS BOOK) THEY HAVE TWO GODS-- 373 MARCOM
UN KUBLAI'S LEFT STANDS CHU-YIN, WHO IS READING. 421 MARCOM
(GOES BACK TO KUBLAI WHO HAS FINISHED READING THE 423 MARCOM
SHORT NOTE
EACH WALKS WITH BENT HEAD READING ALOUD TO HIMSELFA36 MARCOM
FROM HIS HOLY BOOK.
IN THEIR MANSION, READING BOOKS, OR IN HER GARDEN. 31 POET
YOU'VE BEEN READING BOOKS. 19 STRANG
THE READING LAMP ON THE TABLE IS LIT. 24 STRANG
(READING WHAT SHE HAS JUST WRITTEN OVER TO 49 STRANG
HERSELF)
(EVANS NODS HELPLESSLY AND BEGINS READING THE 74 STRANG
SHEETS.
YOU WERE ALWAYS READING DIAGNOSIS INTO ME, 79 STRANG
GLANCING THROUGH A NEWSPAPER AT HEADLINES AND 111 STRANG
READING AN ARTICLE HERE AND THERE.
(HE SEES THE BOOK HE HAS BEEN READING ON THE COUCH123 STRANG
AND GETS UP TO GET IT.
WERE YOU READING MY LETTERS 444 WELDED
(HER EYES READING HIS--AFTER A PAUSE--A BIT DRYLY)482 WELDED

READS
AS HE READS HIS FACE GROWS MORE AND MORE WOUNDED 208 AHWILD
AND TRAGIC,
AND HE IS NOT PAYING MUCH ATTENTION TO WHAT HE 249 AHWILD
READS.
(HE HAS OPENED THE LETTER AND READS) 267 AHWILD
RICHARD OPENS IT WITH A TREMBLING EAGERNESS AND 273 AHWILD
READS.
(CHUCKLES AT SOMETHING HE READS--THEN CLOSES THE 288 AHWILD
BOOK AND PUTS IN ON THE TABLE.
JOHNNY READS VERY SLOWLY) 4 ANNA
AS HE READS HIS FACE LIGHTS UP 8 ANNA
(READS THROUGH THE LETTER HURRIEDLY) 9 ANNA
HE READS ALOUD IN A DOLEFUL, SING-SONG VOICE) 82 BEYOND
SHE OPENS THE ENVELOPE AND READS THE LETTER WITH 119 BEYOND
GREAT INTEREST,
(HE READS) =HOPE YOU ARE ALL WELL. 146 BEYOND

READS

READS (CONT'D.)

(HE READS) =LEAVE FOR HOME ON MIDNIGHT TRAIN. 147 BEYOND
AS HE STOPS KNITTING AND READS OVER THE PARAGRAPH 149 ELECTR
HE HAS JUST FINISHED.
OPENS AND READS ALOUD THE TEXT AT WHICH IT POINTS)269 GGBROW
(HE READS) = THERE IS A MENACE EXISTING IN THIS 242 HA APE
COUNTRY TODAY WHICH THREATENS
(READS) =THEY PLOT WITH FIRE IN ONE HAND AND 243 HA APE
DYNAMITE IN THE OTHER.
(READS SLOWLY--HIS VOICE BECOMING LOWER AND LOWER 531 INZONE
AS HE GOES ON)
(HE READS) =FROM THE EAST, LAND OF THE FALSE GODS328 LAZARU
AND SUPERSTITION.
AS HE READS IT, HIS FACE BECOMES HARD AND BITTER. 44 MANSNS
NICOLE READS, A SCORNFUL GRIN COMING TO HIS LIPS.)360 MARCOM
FEUDALO READS--FROWNS-- 360 MARCOM
(HE READS AMUSEDLY AS MARCO SQUIRMS). 360 MARCOM
(SHE UNFOLDS IT AND READS) =I'LL HAVE A MILLION TO375 MARCOM
MY CREDIT
HE READS ALOUD) 423 MARCOM
HE READS THE VERSE WELL, QUIETLY, WITH A BITTER 101 POET
ELOQUENCE.)
(THEN TRIUMPHANTLY AS SHE READS HIM) 126 STRANG
SHE PICKS UP A LETTER FROM THE TABLE, WHICH SHE 443 WELDED
OPENS AND READS.
(SHUDDERS INSTINCTIVELY AS SHE READS HIS MEANING) 486 WELDED

READY

THEN GET HER READY AND WE'LL DRIVE HER THROUGH. 550 'ILE
ALL READY, SIR. 552 'ILE
I'LL BEAT IT AND LEAVE YOU ALONE--SEE IF THE WOMEN206 AHWILD
FOLKS ARE READY UPSTAIRS.
WELL, WE'RE ABOUT READY TO START AT LAST, THANK 208 AHWILD
GOODNESS/
(CALLS) WELL, DON'T YOU GO FAR, 'CAUSE DINNER'LL 216 AHWILD
BE READY IN A MINUTE,
ALL READY$ 298 AHWILD
GRANDPA HAS YOUR DINNER 'MUST READY FOR YOU. 136 BEYOND
IN WHICH I KNOW I'LL BE READY TO JOIN AFTER I'VE 504 DAYS
MET HER.
SUPPER'S READY. 205 DESIRE
I'VE HAD IT WRIT OUT AN' READY IN CASE YE'D EVER 213 DESIRE
GO.
I HAIN'T A-GOING TO STIR OUTA BED TILL BREAKFAST'S215 DESIRE
READY.
SHE LOOKS AWED AND FRIGHTENED NOW, READY TO RUN 241 DESIRE
AWAY.
AND WHEN SHE SAW THE SHIP WAS GITTIN' READY TO 503 DIFRNT
SAIL SHE RAISED RUCTIONS.
HE HAS CHANGED TO A DARK SUIT, IS READY FOR = UP 507 DIFRNT
STREET.=
YOU'RE ALWAYS SO READY TO BELIEVE THE WORST OF 426 DYNAMO
HIM.
AND SITS DOWN IN A TENSE POSITION, READY FOR 195 EJONES
INSTANT FLIGHT.
WELL--IF YOU'RE QUITE READY, PERHAPS YOU WILL 29 ELECTR
EXPLAIN.
READY TO FIRE AGAIN.) 114 ELECTR
WE'LL EXPECT YOU TOMORROW, AND HAVE YOUR ROOM 163 ELECTR
READY.
ARE WE ALL READY TO START$ 221 HA APE
WHEN I GIT READY, WE MOVE. 224 HA APE
WHEN I GIT READY, GOT ME? 224 HA APE
AND GET THE GRUB READY SO IT CAN BE BROUGHT RIGHT 643 ICEMAN
IN.
GET THAT WINE READY, CHUCK AND ROCKY/ 653 ICEMAN
GET READY TO PLAY, CORA/ 653 ICEMAN
I GOT IT ALL READY. 700 ICEMAN
SO I'LL WAIT, AND WHEN YOU'RE READY YOU SEND FOR 711 ICEMAN
ME AND WE'LL BE MARRIED.
(ANXIOUSLY) IS THE BOATS ALL READY$ 516 INZONE
HE WEARS A THREADBARE, READY-MADE, GREY SACK SUIT 13 JOURNE
AND SHINELESS BLACK SHOES.
(VOLUBLY.) LUNCH IS READY, MA'AM, I WENT DOWN TO 62 JOURNE
MISTER TYRONE.
I THOUGHT LUNCH WAS READY. 66 JOURNE
HE HAS CHANGED TO A READY-MADE BLUE SERGE SUIT, 89 JOURNE
HIGH STIFF COLLAR AND TIE.
DINNER WON'T BE READY FOR A MINUTE. 108 JOURNE
READY FOR A WEEP ON ANY OLD WOMANLY BOSOM. 159 JOURNE
THE DISAPPEARS TOWARD THE FLAMES, HIS SPEAR HELD 369 LAZARU
READY TO STAB.)
WE'VE A FINE ROOM ALWAYS READY. 51 MANSNS
READY TO SAIL FOR PERSIA WITHIN TEN DAYS. 388 MARCOM
I'M CONFIDENT THERE'S A READY MARKET FOR THEM 396 MARCOM
ELSEWHERE.
AND BE READY TO CAST OFF WHEN I SIGNAL. 403 MARCOM
ALL READY$ 431 MARCOM
I'D BETTER BE READY. 11 MISBEG
BUT HAVE YOU YOUR BAR BOOK READY FOR ME TO LOOK 16 POET
OVER$
WELL, I'M READY FOR HER. 80 POET
HERE. I AM ARGYIN' WITH YOUR LUNATIC NOTIONS AND 581 ROPE
THE SUPPER NOT READY.
READY, NOW/ 589 ROPE
MA SAYS SUPPER'S READY. 600 ROPE
AND I'LL HAVE TO GET THE SPARE ROOM READY. 72 STRANG
HE'S GOT SO MUCH TO DO GETTING READY TO SAIL. 107 STRANG
LUNCH IS READY. 107 STRANG
(SITTING DOWN AT LEFT) I HOPE LUNCH IS READY 153 STRANG
SOON.
I WANT TO SEE IF LUNCH IS NEARLY READY. 157 STRANG

REAL

HE TELLS THE TRUTH ABOUT REAL LOVE/ 198 AHWILD
HE'S EASILY LED--BUT THERE'S NO REAL HARM IN HIM, 212 AHWILD
YOU KNOW THAT.
I MEAN REAL SHIFT ONES THAT THERE'S SOMETHING 219 AHWILD
DOING WITH,
(TO THE BARTENDER) AND MAKE IT A REAL ONE. 238 AHWILD

REAL

REAL (CONT'D.)

WITH SOME REAL LIVE ONE--IF THERE IS SUCH A THING 241 AHWILD
IN THIS BURG/
DON'T YOU THINK IT'S THE REAL GOODS$ 250 AHWILD
(PERKING UP PROUDLY) ARTHUR HAS A REAL NICE 255 AHWILD
VOICE.
AND NO REAL NOURISHMENT TO THEM. 255 AHWILD
AND I'VE KEPT REMINDING HIM HIS REAL PUNISHMENT 265 AHWILD
WAS STILL TO COME--
(THEN WITH REAL FEELING) ONLY IT ISN'T PAST, I 281 AHWILD
CAN TELL YOU/
AND MURIEL'S REAL CUTE-LOOKING, I HAVE TO ADMIT 290 AHWILD
THAT.
I DON'T SEE BUT WHAT ITMIGHT WORK OUT REAL WELL. 290 AHWILD
IT'S REAL SINFUL. 298 AHWILD
ANNA CHRISTOPHERSON--THAT'S MY REAL NAME-- 17 ANNA
AND, ANNA, DIS AIN'T REAL SAILOR YOB. 21 ANNA
DIS AIN'T REAL BOAT ON SEA. 21 ANNA
AND DIS AIN'T REAL SEA. 26 ANNA
YOU BELONG ON A REAL SHIP, SAILING ALL OVER THE 27 ANNA
WORLD.
SHIPS VAS SHIPS DEN--AND MEN DAT SAIL ON DEM VAS 49 ANNA
REAL MEN.
I'M RAVING LIKE A REAL LUNATIC, I'M THINKING, 70 ANNA
ANYWAY, IN THOSE DAYS THEY WERE REAL ENOUGH, 90 BEYOND
AND THEN SHE CALLS ME A FOOL REAL SPITEFUL AND 95 BEYOND
TACKS AWAY FROM ME QUICK.
AND I TAKE A REAL INTEREST IN THE FARM, AND DO MY 102 BEYOND
SHARE.
'S IF I DIDN'T KNOW YOUR REAL REASON FOR RUNNIN' 106 BEYOND
AWAY.
(DOGGEDLY) I'D KNOWN YOUR REAL REASON FOR LEAVING164 BEYOND
HOME THE FIRST TIME--
REAL JEWELS$ 561 CROSS
I WANT TO GET AT THE REAL TRUTH AND UNDERSTAND 495 DAYS
WHAT WAS BEHIND--
THAT'S THE REAL REASON I DECIDED TO TAKE MY 508 DAYS
VACATION IN THE EAST, JACK.
YOU CAN'T ADMIT THAT OUR MARRIAGE IS A REAL IDEAL 523 DAYS
MARRIAGE.
FUR HE ADDS REAL SPRY AND VICIOUS.. 210 DESIRE
(WITH REAL SOLICITATION) AIR YE ABLE FUR THE 252 DESIRE
STAIRS$
THERE IS REAL MERRIMENT NOW. 253 DESIRE
(WITH REAL RESENTMENT) HE'S BETTER'N WHAT YOU 499 DIFRNT
ARE. IF THAT'S WHAT YOU MEAN.
HELL, EMMER, YOU AIN'T A REAL CROSSBY IF YOU TAKES 513 DIFRNT
A JOKE LIKE THAT SERIOUS.
HE'S TOO MEAN EVER TO GET REAL SICK. 522 DIFRNT
AND YOU AIN'T ANY OF MY REAL FOLKS, EITHER, AND 524 DIFRNT
AIN'T GOT ANY REASON.
AND I THINK IT'S REAL MEAN OF YOU, CALEB-- 537 DIFRNT
(WITH A TICKLED CHUCKLE) GOSH, THAT'D BE THE REAL545 DIFRNT
STUNT AW RIGHT, AW RIGHT.
IF HE'S WILLIN' TO DIG IN HIS JEANS FOR SOME REAL 545 DIFRNT
COIN--REAL DOUGH, THIS TIME/
AND IF THERE WAS ANY REAL JUSTICE HIS GIRL'D BE 450 DYNAMO
PUT ALONG WITH HIM
I'LL SHOW HIM WHAT A REAL WHIPPING IS/ 452 DYNAMO
THEN YOU'D KNOW THE REAL GOD....)) 474 DYNAMO
(WITH REAL ADMIRATION) BLIMEY, BUT YOU'RE A COOL 182 EJONES
BIRD, AND NO MISTAKE.
YOU WAS REAL, A-ONE PATIN' LEATHER, TOO. 196 EJONES
I AIN'T SKEERED O' REAL MEN. 196 EJONES
THIS TOWN'S REAL PROUD OF EZRA. 8 ELECTR
BUT I'VE SUSPECTED LATELY THAT WASN'T THE REAL 29 ELECTR
REASON--
BUT ALL THE SAME, THAT'S NOT YOUR REAL REASON FOR 33 ELECTR
SPARING ME/
ARE YOU GOING TO PROVE, THE FIRST TIME YOUR LOVE 41 ELECTR
IS PUT TO A REAL TEST,
HIS DEATH IS A REAL LOSS TO EVERYONE IN THIS 69 ELECTR
COMMUNITY.
HER MOTHER SEEMED REAL ANGRY ABOUT IT. 69 ELECTR
BUT SHE IS SO CRAZY I KNOW SHE THINKS--(THEN, WITH 88 ELECTR
REAL TERROR, CLINGING TO HIM)
HE'S A REAL SPORT. 258 GGBROW
HIS REAL FACE IS REVEALED IN THE BRIGHT MOONLIGHT,264 GGBROW
SHRINKING, SHY AND GENTLE,
HIS REAL FACE HAS AGED GREATLY, GROWN MORE 269 GGBROW
STRAINED AND TORTURED,
AND ON BOTH SIDES WE WERE ABLE TO KEEP OUR REAL 284 GGBROW
VIRTUE. IF YOU GET ME.
A REAL DEMON, TORTURED INTO TORTURING OTHERS) 294 GGBROW
(HE STARES AT DION'S REAL FACE CONTEMPTUOUSLY) 299 GGBROW
THE REAL NAME OF WHICH IS SMELLED READY/ 302 GGBROW
WHO WAS A REAL SHARK ON THESE DETAILS BUT THAT 306 GGBROW
YOU'VE FIRED HIM--
HIS REAL FACE IS NOW SICK, GHASTLY, TORTURED, 314 GGBROW
HOLLOW-CHEEKED AND FEVERISH-EYED)
TILL YOU'D BELIEVE 'TWAS NO REAL SHIP AT ALL YOU 214 HA APE
WAS ON BUT A GHOST SHIP LIKE
DEN WHEN I COME TO AND SEEN IT WAS A REAL SKOIT 231 HA APE
AND SEEN DE WAY SHE WAS LOOKIN'
HER HANDS--DEY WAS SKINNY AND WHITE LIKE DEY 241 HA APE
WASN'T REAL BUT PAINTED ON SOMEP'N.
BUT YUH'RE DE FOIST REAL ONE I EVER SEEN. 252 HA APE
HE AND HIS KIND IMAGINE THEY ARE IN THE REAL KNOW, 9 HUGHIE
A BROADWAY GUY LIKE ME NAMED SMITH AND IT'S MY 14 HUGHIE
REAL NAME.
SMITH IS MY REAL NAME. 14 HUGHIE
HIS CHECKING OUT WAS A REAL K. O. FOR ME. 18 HUGHIE
NOT THAT I WAS EVER REAL PALS WITH HIM, YOU 18 HUGHIE
UNDERSTAND.
BUY, IF THEY'D EVER LET ME THROW 'EM THAT WAY IN A 20 HUGHIE
REAL GAME,
WE'D PLAY WITH REAL JACK, JUST TO MAKE IT LOOK 21 HUGHIE
REAL, BUT IT WAS ALL MY JACK.

1289

REALIZATION

REAL (CONT'D.)

I MEAN A REAL HORSE. 22 HUGHIE
IS IT A REAL GOOD ONE THIS TIMES 27 HUGHIE
HELL, I'VE BEEN IN GAMES WHERE THERE WAS A HUNDRED 36 HUGHIE
GRAND IN REAL FOLDING MONEY
WE GOTTA USE REAL JACK OR IT DON'T LOOK REAL. 37 HUGHIE
WHERE WOULD I GET A REAL ROLLS 585 ICEMAN
IT DOESN'T SEEM REAL. 590 ICEMAN
(SENTIMENTALLY, WITH REAL YEARNING) 605 ICEMAN
EVERYONE KNOWS THERE WAS NO REAL EVIDENCE AGAINST 607 ICEMAN
ME.
BUT THERE WAS NO REAL HARM IN HER. 608 ICEMAN
WE STEERED DEM TO A REAL HOTEL. 612 ICEMAN
YOU GET THE IMPRESSION, TOO, THAT HE MUST HAVE 618 ICEMAN
REAL ABILITY IN HIS LINE.
BEFORE YOU'LL EVER KNOW WHAT REAL PEACE MEANS. 622 ICEMAN
NO, BOYS AND GIRLS, I'VE NEVER KNOWN WHAT REAL 625 ICEMAN
PEACE UNTIL NOW.
BUT YOU'D BETTER MAKE SURE FIRST IT'S THE REAL 626 ICEMAN
MCCOY AND NOT POISON.
HADN'T NO REAL INTENTIONS OF GETTIN' MARRIED. 631 ICEMAN
THEN YOU'LL KNOW WHAT REAL PEACE MEANS, LARRY, 641 ICEMAN
I MEAN THE OLD REAL LOVE STUFF THAT CRUCIFIES YOU.643 ICEMAN
THEN WITH A REAL INDIFFERENCE THAT COMES FROM 649 ICEMAN
EXHAUSTION
(WITH FORCED CHEERINESS) REAL CHAMPAGNE, BUMS/ 658 ICEMAN
THIS PEACE IS REAL/ IT'S A FACT/ I KNOW/ BECAUSE 661 ICEMAN
I'VE GOT IT HERE/ NOW/
OF ONE WHO GIVES AN EXCUSE WHICH EXONERATES HIM 667 ICEMAN
FROM ANY REAL GUILT.)
HE'S LOST HIS CONFIDENCE THAT THE PEACE HE'S SOLD 703 ICEMAN
US IS THE REAL MCCOY,
UNTIL I'D MADE IT A REAL FINAL TEST TO MYSELF--AND71S ICEMAN
TO HER.
BE GOD, I'M THE ONLY REAL CONVERT TO DEATH HICKEY 727 ICEMAN
MADE HERE.
I'D RISK A QUID OF MY NEXT PAY DAY THAT HIS REAL 522 INZONE
NAME IS SCHMIDT.
AN' IF IT IS ANY SATISFACTION TO YOU I LAVE YOU 532 INZONE
THE REAL-I-ZATION THAT YOU HAVE
HIS REAL ESTATE BARGAINS DON'T WORK OUT SO WELL. 15 JOURNE
YOU'RE NOT A CUNNING REAL ESTATE SPECULATOR. 15 JOURNE
IT MIGHT NEVER HAVE HAPPENED IF YOU'D SENT HIM TO 30 JOURNE
A REAL DOCTOR
THAT'S THE REAL REASON/ 47 JOURNE
(HE COUGHS NERVOUSLY AND THIS BRINGS ON A REAL FIT 58 JOURNE
OF COUGHING.
IN A REAL HOME ONE IS NEVER LONELY. 72 JOURNE
IF HE'D BEEN BROUGHT UP IN A REAL HOME, I'M SURE 82 JOURNE
HE WOULD HAVE BEEN DIFFERENT.
OH, I REALIZE HIS WAGES ARE LESS THAN A REAL 84 JOURNE
CHAUFFEUR'S.
AS IF IT DID NOT PENETRATE TO REAL EMOTION.) 101 JOURNE
ONLY THE PAST WHEN YOU WERE HAPPY IS REAL. 106 JOURNE
(MOVED.) I'M GLAD I CAME, MARY, WHEN YOU ACT LIKE112 JOURNE
YOUR REAL SELF.
AND WE'LL HAVE A REAL DRINK. 117 JOURNE
(THEY BOTH CHUCKLE WITH REAL, IF ALCOHOLIC, 143 JOURNE
AFFECTION.
BY GOD, IT'S 156 JOURNE
SHOOT THE REAL CALIGULA--THEN I MIGHT HAVE FAITH 359 LAZARU
IN CALIGULA MYSELF--
THIS IS REAL LIFE, EVEN THOUGH IT BE PAST. 13 MANSNS
AS REAL AS THE DOOR I HAVE JUST OPENED, AND I WAS 29 MANSNS
REACHING OUT MY HAND TO--
BUT I HAVE TRIED TO MAKE IT REAL TO MYSELF. 29 MANSNS
MY ONLY REAL INTEREST IS THE CHANCE FOR A NEW 55 MANSNS
LIFE.
BUT I COULDN'T HELP FEARING THE REAL REASON WAS 83 MANSNS
YOU DIDN'T WANT ME.
IT REMINDS ME OF MY REAL PURPOSE IN COMING HERE. 104 MANSNS
THEY SEEMED SO MUCH MORE REAL THAN THE BOOK ONES. 109 MANSNS
BUT I WAS VERY IMPRESSIONABLE THEN AND YOUR STORY 111 MANSNS
WAS VERY REAL TO ME.
THE REAL REASON I CAME HERE WAS TO HAVE A SENSIBLE167
TALK WITH YOU.
NOW IT BECOMES REAL--WHEN YOU PUT IT IN MY MIND. 181 MANSNS
IS THE BEST SCHOOLING FOR A REAL MERCHANT AND 396 MARCUM
FATHER HAS A SAYING THAT WHERE
REAL RICE/ 370 MARCOM
YOU NEED ONLY ME NOW TO MAKE YOU INTO A REAL MAN--371 MARCOM
FOR TEN PIECES OF GOLD.
WHERE HE MISTOOK ONE OF THE FEMALE STATUES FOR A 374 MARCOM
REAL WOMAN AND--
IT IS THE FACE OF A WOMAN WHO HAS KNOWN REAL 407 MARCOM
SORROW AND SUFFERING.
(SHE GOES LEFT TO PEER AROUND THE CORNER OF THE 10 MISBEG
HOUSE--WITH REAL ALARM)
THAT WAS THE REAL TRICK. 26 MISBEG
IT CAME THROUGH A REAL-ESTATE MAN WHO WOULDN'T 32 MISBEG
TELL WHO HIS CLIENT WAS.
I'D COME TO LOVE HIM LIKE A SON--A REAL SON OF MY 85 MISBEG
HEART/
(FORCING A PLAYFUL AIR) I SHOULD THINK, IF YOU 101 MISBEG
WERE A REAL GENTLEMAN,
YOU'RE REAL AND HEALTHY AND CLEAN AND FINE AND 118 MISBEG
WARM AND STRONG AND KIND--
(A BIT MAUDLIN) THE ONLY REAL FRIEND I'VE GOT 123 MISBEG
LEFT--EXCEPT YOU.
REAL BONDED BOURBON. 124 MISBEG
REAL BONDED BOURBON. 126 MISBEG
(GOES ON WITHOUT REAL INTEREST, TALKING TO KEEP 132 MISBEG
FROM THINKING)
REAL BOURBON. 173 MISBEG
THAT'S REAL, HONEST-TO-GOD BONDED BOURBON. 173 MISBEG
WHICH HAS BECOME MORE REAL THAN HIS REAL SELF TO 34 POET
HIM.

REAL (CONT'D.)
(HIS EXPRESSION CHANGES AND A LOOK OF REAL 37 POET
AFFECTION COMES INTO HIS EYES.
WHERE ONLY DREAMS ARE REAL TO YOU. 50 POET
HOPELESSNESS AND DEFEAT BRINGING A TRACE OF REAL 57 POET
TRAGEDY
(TRUTH WITH A REAL, LONELY YEARNING,) 66 POET
ROUGHLY BUT WITH A STRANGE REAL TENDERNESS.) AND 174 POET
I LOVE YOU.
I'LL BE A REAL HUSBAND TO YOU, AND HELP YE RUN 174 POET
THIS SHEBEEN.
AN' AFTER IT HE'LL BE A REAL LUNATIC WITH NO LEGAL587 ROPE
CLAIMS TO ANYTHIN'.
IT'S REAL STUFF. 591 ROPE
YUH WANTED TO SEE ME HANGIN' THERE IN REAL 597 ROPE
EARNEST, DIDN'T YUHS
I WANT TO SHOW THE GANG A REAL TIME, 599 ROPE
A REAL DOLLAR, TOO/ 599 ROPE
BRIGHT THINGS YUH CHUCKED IN THE OCEAN--AND YUH 601 ROPE
KIN BE A REAL SPORT.
BUT IN THE PRESENT STATE OF HER MIND THE REAL AND 11 STRANG
THE UNREAL BECOME CONFUSED--
SHE KNOWS SHE HAS NO REAL GROUNDS, 11 STRANG
(WHILE SHE FEEL ANY REAL GRIEF OVER HIS DEATH, I 25 STRANG
WONDER,
UNDERSTANDING OF ITS REAL SEXUAL NATURE. 33 STRANG
NINA HAS A REAL AFFECTION FOR YOU AND I IMAGINE 35 STRANG
YOU HAVE FOR HER.
BUT I THINK HIS UNSELFISH LOVE, COMBINED WITH HER 37 STRANG
REAL LIKING FOR HIM,
(THEN PLACING HIM--WITH REAL AFFECTION THAT IS 40 STRANG
LIKE A GALLING GOAD TO HIM)
HE IS A SPLENDID CHAP, CLEAN AND BOYISH, WITH REAL 46 STRANG
STUFF IN HIM, TOO,
THAT JOKING TONE HIDES HER REAL CONTEMPT....) 52 STRANG
AND HE THOUGHT I HAD THE MAKINGS OF A REAL FIND. 54 STRANG
SEEMED TO TAKE A REAL PERSONAL INTEREST-- 54 STRANG
IT'S A REAL FINE DAY, ISN'T IT! 56 STRANG
MY HUSBAND KEPT REAL WELL UP TO THEN. 59 STRANG
I THOUGHT YOU WERE A REAL FIND, BUT YOUR WORK'S 67 STRANG
FALLEN OFF TO NOTHING....)
AND BESIDES, HE NEVER APPRECIATED THE REAL GORDON. 80 STRANG
(THINKING IN A REAL PANIC OF HORROR-- 83 STRANG
I LOVED IT SO IT SEEMED AT TIMES THAT GORDON MUST 83 STRANG
BE ITS REAL FATHER.
SAY YOU'RE WILLING TO GIVE HER A DIVORCE SO SHE 92 STRANG
CAN MARRY SOME REAL GUY WHO CAN
I HADN'T SEEN HER IN SURE TIME, SO HER DEATH WAS 101 STRANG
NEVER VERY REAL TO ME...
(LOOKING AT HIM--WITH REAL GRATITUDE) 116 STRANG
THEN IMPULSIVELY TURNS BACK AND KISSES MARSDEN 119 STRANG
WITH REAL AFFECTION)
AND I SEE MY REAL CHANCE, CHARLIE--LYING RIGHT 121 STRANG
AHEAD, WAITING FOR ME TO GRAB IT--
A REAL FRIEND IF THERE EVER WAS ONE-- 134 STRANG
AND WE WANT HIM TO GROW UP A REAL HE-MAN AND NOT 157 STRANG
AN OLD LADY LIKE CHARLIE.
I CAN'T THINK UP THESE THINGS AS REAL ANY MORE... 165 STRANG
(WITH BITTER EMPHASIS) EXCEPT YOUR REAL SON--AND 166 STRANG
ME--
BUT SHE MUST HAVE NO REAL CLAIM TO DISPUTE YOUR 168 STRANG
OWNERSHIP, EH$...
IF THE REAL DEEP CORE OF THE TRUTH WERE KNOWN/ 174 STRANG
AFTER WE'RE MARRIED I'M GOING TO WRITE A NOVEL--MY176 STRANG
FIRST REAL NOVEL/
HE HAS WORKED HIMSELF INTO A REAL ANGER.) 191 STRANG
WHOEVER IS IN REAL CHARGE DOWN THERE WILL BE ONLY 192 STRANG
TOO GLAD TO ACCEPT IT.
(HE LAUGHS HARSHLY AND TURNS AWAY TO CONCEAL HIS 469 WELDED
REAL HURT.)
REALISM
WELL, IT WILL BE FAITHFUL REALISM, AT LEAST. 154 JOURNE
REALISTIC
WITH THE INTOLERABLE LIFELESS REALISTIC DETAIL OF 269 GGBROW
THE STEREOTYPED PAINTINGS
REALITY
BUT IN REALITY HE IS MERELY KILLING TIME, CHEWING 169 ELECTR
TOBACCO,
WHERE PRESENT REALITY IS BUT AN APPEARANCE TO BE 97 JOURNE
ACCEPTED AND DISMISSED
MOST SORDID FACTS; TO PROVE HOW THOROUGHLY I WAS 29 MANSNS
RESIGNED TO REALITY.
WE WANT THEM TRAINED TO LIVE WITH REALITY 84 MANSNS
YOU NOW HAVE THE COURAGE TO FACE SOME OF THE 101 MANSNS
THINGS THAT HAVE REALITY.
THAT WHAT YOU ARE IS GOOD BECAUSE IT IS FACT AND 172 MANSNS
REALITY--
IN THIS GARDEN SO HIDDEN FROM THE UGLINESS OF 176 MANSNS
REALITY.
WE WILL GO TOGETHER SO FAR AWAY FROM THE REALITY 181 MANSNS
BUT IN THE DEEPER REALITY INSIDE US, IT HAS THE 183 MANSNS
MEANING OUR MINDS HAVE GIVEN IT.
GOD, IF THE REALITY OF DOG-EAT-DOG AND LUST-- 185 MANSNS
DEVOUR-LOVE IS SANE,
A FUGITIVE FROM REALITY CAN VIEW THE PRESENT 3 STRANG
SAFELY FROM A DISTANCE.
HE ISN'T BUILT TO FACE REALITY... 35 STRANG
REALIZATION
BUT THE REALIZATION NEVER CAME 'TIL I AGREED TO GO 91 BEYOND
AWAY WITH UNCLE DICK.
TO PROVE OURSELVES WORTHY OF A FINER REALIZATION. 150 BEYOND
SO IT CAME HARD AT FIRST--THE REALIZATION. 160 BEYOND
OVER HIS FACE ABJECT TERROR GIVE WAY TO 197 EJONES
MYSTIFICATION, TO GRADUAL REALIZATION--
TO HAVE AN UNCERTAIN REALIZATION OF WHAT HE IS 200 EJONES
DOING.
(YEARNING FOR THE REALIZATION OF A DREAM) 258 GGBROW

REALIZATION

REALIZATION (CONT'D.)
BATTLE, BUT SUDDENLY HE SEEMS TO SOBER UP TO A 162 JOURNE
SHOCKED REALIZATION OF WHAT HE
REALIZE
AND YOU DON'T REALIZE WHAT I'VE BEEN THROUGH FOR 281 AHWILD
YOU--AND WHAT I'M IN FOR--
I GUESS I REALIZE THAT YOU'VE GOT YOUR OWN ANGLE 84 BEYOND
OF LOOKING AT THINGS.
YOU DON'T REALIZE HOW I'VE BUCKED UP IN THE PAST 84 BEYOND
FEW YEARS.
I REALIZE HOW IMPOSSIBLE IT ALL IS--AND I 91 BEYOND
UNDERSTAND.
COULDN'T YOU REALIZE--WHY, I NEARLY DROPPED IN MY 155 BEYOND
TRACKS WHEN I SAW HIM/
I DIDN'T REALIZE--THE SIGHT OF ROB LYING IN RED 156 BEYOND
THERE, SO GONE TO PIECES--
WELL, I HOPE YOU REALIZE I'M ONLY TRYING TO 495 DAYS
ENCOURAGE YOU TO MAKE SOMETHING OF
YOU REALIZE I WASN'T, DON'T YOU, ELSA& 521 DAYS
AND HE KNEW HE COULD REALIZE THAT IDEAL. 523 DAYS
IF YOU ONLY COULD REALIZE HOW MUCH THAT MEANT TO 523 DAYS
ME--ESPECIALLY AT THAT TIME.
DON'T YOU REALIZE YOU'RE ONLY HARMING HER& 556 DAYS
(THEY BOTH PLOD MECHANICALLY TOWARD THE DOOR 216 DESIRE
BEFORE THEY REALIZE.
SINCE YOU WAS OLD ENOUGH TO KNOW, YOU'D OUGHT TO 509 DIFRNT
REALIZE WHAT MEN BE.
AND SOME DAY WHEN YOU REALIZE MEN WAS NEVER CUT 518 DIFRNT
OUT FOR ANGELS YOU'LL--
HE BOTH GOT TO REALIZE NOW AND THEN THAT WE'RE 537 DIFRNT
GETTIN' OLD.
(DAZEDLY--AS IF SHE COULD NOT REALIZE THE 545 DIFRNT
SIGNIFICANCE OF HIS WORDS)
HUTCHINS: DO YOU REALIZE REUBEN WILL GRADUATE FROM423 DYNAMO
SCHOOL IN LESS THAN A MONTHS.
CONVINCED NOW OF THE TRUTH AND TRYING TO MAKE 464 DYNAMO
HIMSELF REALIZE IT AND ACCEPT IT)
SHE WANTS US TO REALIZE THE SECRET DWELLS IN HER/ 477 DYNAMO
DON'T YOU REALIZE WE'RE IN HER TEMPLE NOW/ 484 DYNAMO
I REALIZE THAT. 32 ELECTR
WELL, I HOPE YOU REALIZE I NEVER WOULD HAVE FALLEN 32 ELECTR
IN LOVE WITH ADAM IF I'D HAD
DON'T YOU REALIZE HE WOULD NEVER DIVORCE ME, OUT 38 ELECTR
OF SPITE&
YES, I REALIZE THAT. 45 ELECTR
YOU CAN'T REALIZE WHAT A STRAIN I'VE BEEN UNDER-- 52 ELECTR
I SIMPLY CAN'T REALIZE HE'S DEAD YET. 74 ELECTR
I TELL YOU, ORIN, YOU CAN'T REALIZE HOW SHE'S 86 ELECTR
CHANGED WHILE YOU'VE BEEN AWAY/
(SHE FORCES A LAUGH) YOU DON'T SEEM TO REALIZE 87 ELECTR
I'M AN OLD MARRIED WOMAN
DON'T YOU REALIZE HE WAS YOU FATHER AND HE IS 94 ELECTR
DEAD&
(THUS HUMORINGLY) BUT I REALIZE YOU'RE NOT 96 ELECTR
YOURSELF.
I REALIZE ONLY TOO WELL/ 97 ELECTR
DO YOU REALIZE WHAT IT WOULD MEAN--& 97 ELECTR
DO YOU REALIZE YOU'RE DELIBERATELY ACCUSING YOUR 97 ELECTR
OWN MOTHER--
I CAN'T REALIZE IT'S YOU/ 143 ELECTR
LAVINIA SEES THE MOVEMENT BUT DOESN'T FOR A MOMENT5 ELECTR
REALIZE THE MEANING OF IT.
I HOPE YOU REALIZE THERE'S NO MORE QUESTION OF ANY163 ELECTR
FRIENDSHIP BETWEEN US.
YOU REALIZE THE PROMISE YOU MADE MEANS GIVING UP 164 ELECTR
PETER.
UH, I REALIZE MR. BROWN HAS GIVEN STRICT ORDERS 303 GGBROW
DICK IS NOT TO BE DISTURBED.
OH, I REALIZE MR. 303 GGBROW
(AMAZED) BILLY BROWN, DO YOU REALIZE WHAT YOU'RE 305 GGBROW
SAYINGS
DO YOU REALIZE WHAT THE PENALTY FOR PERJURY IS& 606 ICEMAN
SO YOU'LL REALIZE HOW CONTENTED AND CAREFREE YOU 707 ICEMAN
OUGHT TO FEEL.
WELL, I'M NOT LYING, AND IF YOU'D EVER SEEN HER, 714 ICEMAN
YOU'D REALIZE I WASN'T.
THEY'RE DONE BEFORE YOU REALIZE IT, 61 JOURNE
(MORE EXCITEDLY.) OH, ME ALL REALIZE WHY YOU LIKE 74 JOURNE
HIM, JAMES/
OH, I REALIZE HIS WAGES ARE LESS THAN A REAL 84 JOURNE
CHAUFFEUR'S.
I'M GLAD YOU REALIZE THAT, JAMES/ 117 JOURNE
UH, I REALIZE I AM HARDLY AS BAD AS THAT YET. BUT 12 MANSNS
I WILL BE.
YOU DIDN'T REALIZE WHAT EXTRAORDINARY OPPORTUNITIES 48 MANSNS
THERE WILL BE, SARA.
(EAGERLY.) YOU CAN'T REALIZE WHAT AN OPPORTUNITY 66 MANSNS
THIS IS FOR ME, SARA.
BUT SHE DOESN'T REALIZE THERE ARE FUNDAMENTAL 73 MANSNS
WEAKNESSES IN HER PLAN.
YES, I QUITE REALIZE YOU ARE--WHAT YOU ARE. 141 MANSNS
YOU REALIZE THAT ANY TIME I CHOOSE I CAN TAKE 168 MANSNS
SIMON AWAY WITH ME/
YOU KNOW HER TRUE NATURE WELL ENOUGH TO REALIZE IT179 MANSNS
WAS SHE WHO MADE ME LAUGH
TO MAKE ME REALIZE YOU HATED YOUR LOVE FOR ME 183 MANSNS
I QUITE REALIZE THAT IN SELF-PROTECTION I'VE GOT 396 MARCOM
TO BUY THEN--OR KILL YOU/
BUT I REALIZE YOU'RE NOT YOURSELF. 419 MARCOM
DON'T YOU REALIZE WHAT A LOUSY POSITION YOU'VE PUT136 MISBEG
HIM IN WITH YOUR
I SAID HE MUST REALIZE THAT EVEN BEFORE YOU BEGAN 108 POET
NURSING HIM HERE AND GOING
HE WILL REALIZE, TOO. 111 POET
HARMFUL. YOU WOULD REALIZE HE WOULD NEVER 122 POET
COUNTENANCE--
(IRRITABLY) I REALIZE THAT. 9 STRANG
TO REALIZE HIS EXISTENCE) 93 STRANG

REALIZE (CONT'D.)
(IRRITABLY) OF COURSE, I REALIZE I'VE BEEN TO 102 STRANG
BLAME, TOO.
YOU'VE GOT TO REALIZE THAT. 131 STRANG
BUT HE'LL SOON REALIZE I'M NOT THE OLD SAM HE 134 STRANG
KNEW...
OF COURSE, I REALIZE YOU'VE GOT A HUSBAND AT 175 STRANG
PRESENT BUT, NEVER MIND.
(HIS VOICE TREMBLING) I DIDN'T REALLY REALIZE HE 184 STRANG
WAS GONE.
I REALIZE YOU'VE ACTED LIKE A CUR/ 193 STRANG
HE DOESN'T REALIZE-- 193 STRANG
(MADDENED, COMES CLOSER) I REALIZE A LOT/ 193 STRANG
I'VE GOT TO MAKE HIM REALIZE I'M HIS FATHER,...)) 195 STRANG
YOU REALIZE THAT/ 453 WELDED
(SCORNFULLY) CAN'T YOU REALIZE HOW ABSURD YOU 455 WELDED
ARE&
REALIZED
DICK, YOU DON'T REALIZED HOW I'VE BEEN PUNISHED 281 AHWILD
FOR YOUR SAKE.
I NEVER REALIZED HOW HARD IT WAS GOING TO BE FOR 96 BEYOND
ME TO HAVE ROBBIE GO--
ARRANGED, AND I REALIZED IT WOULD MEAN--LEAVING 100 BEYOND
HERE.
AND REALIZED HE WAS IN LOVE WITH HER, IT THREW HIM535 DAYS
INTO A PANIC OF FEAR.
(HURRIEDLY) BUT, OF COURSE, HE REALIZED THIS WAS 536 DAYS
ALL MORBID AND RIDICULOUS--
REALIZED THE VILENESS HE HAD BEEN GUILTY OF. 539 DAYS
WHEN I READ THEN I REALIZED THAT AMELIA HAD BEEN 465 DYNAMO
THINKING OF YOU ALL THE TIME.
SOMETHING I'VE BEEN THINKING OF EVER SINCE I 40 ELECTR
REALIZED HE MIGHT SOON COME HOME.
ME AND HE REALIZED SHE'D TELL ANY LIE SHE COULD 85 ELECTR
TO--
FROM THE TIME I REALIZED IT WASN'T IN ME TO BE AN 271 GGBROW
ARTIST--EXCEPT IN LIVING--
YOU SAID YOU REALIZED WHAT I'D BEEN UP AGAINST AS 146 JOURNE
A BOY.
(AS IF HE REALIZED SOMETHING WAS HAPPENING THAT 366 LAZARU
WAS AGAINST HIS WILL--
(WITH COLD INDIFFERENCE.) I HAVE LONG REALIZED I 33 MANSNS
BORE YOU, MOTHER.
HE REALIZED THAT JOEL HAS NOT HAD THE REQUISITE 33 MANSNS
EXECUTIVE EXPERIENCE
EVEN THAT DULL FOOL REALIZED I WAS REALLY 74 MANSNS
ADDRESSING MYSELF.
I REALIZED IT WOULD HAVE NO EFFECT. 82 POET
I DID NOT POINT OUT, BUT WHICH GORDON UNDOUBTEDLY 10 STRANG
REALIZED, POOR BOY/
(THEN RATHER IRONICALLY) AND SO GORDON TOLD NINA 11 STRANG
HE'D SUDDENLY REALIZED IT
(BITTERLY) IF HE REALIZED HOW LITTLE YOU LOVE ME 143 STRANG
ANY MORE, HE WOULDN'T BOTHER/
AND IT WAS DONE SO GRADUALLY THAT, ALTHOUGH I 167 STRANG
REALIZED WHAT WAS HAPPENING,
(INSISTENTLY) BUT HAVEN'T WE REALIZED THE IDEAL 447 WELDED
OF OUR MARRIAGE.
I REALIZED I HATED HIM/ 467 WELDED
REALIZES
AND REALIZES IMMEDIATELY THE REASON FOR IT--IN 104 BEYOND
CONSTERNATION)
HE REALIZES HE CAN NEVER BELIEVE IN HIS LOST FAITH545 DAYS
AGAIN.
EDMUND AT ONCE REALIZES HOW MUCH THE WHISKEY HAS 111 JOURNE
BEEN WATERED.
(ABRUPTLY HE REALIZES WHAT HE IS SAYING. 122 MISBEG
THEN SHE REALIZES AND WHISPERS SOFTLY) 153 MISBEG
(THEN AS THEY BOTH LOOK AT HIM IN SURPRISE HE 99 STRANG
REALIZES WHAT HE HAS SAID--
(SARDONICALLY) PERHAPS HE REALIZES SUBCONSCIOUSLY143 STRANG
THAT I AM HIS FATHER.
REALIZING
(SUBSIDING AS IF REALIZING THE USELESSNESS OF THIS537 'ILE
OUTBURST--SHAKING HIS HEAD--
(SUDDENLY REALIZING THAT HIS ARM IS AROUND HER, 90 BEYOND
BUT MY FATHER REALIZING, AS HE TOLD ME, WHAT WAS 560 CROSS
HAPPENING TO THEM.
(THEN SUDDENLY REALIZING THE CAUSE OF HIS 535 DIFRNT
DISCOMFITURE, SHE SMILES PITYINGLY.
AS THOUGH NOT QUITE REALIZING YET WHERE HE IS OR 145 MANSNS
HOW HE GOT THERE.)
(IMMEDIATELY REALIZING WHAT IS COMING--THINKING 150 STRANG
WITH SOMBER ANGUISH)
REALM
HAD BEEN DISPOSSESSED OF HIS REALM AND BANISHED TOIL0 MANSNS
WANDER OVER THE WORLD,
YOUR OLD HAPPY REALM BUT A BARREN DESERT, WHERE IT111 MANSNS
IS ALWAYS NIGHT.
WHO WISHES TO DESTROY YOUR CLAIM TO HER REALM, 111 MANSNS
REAPPEAR
THEY REAPPEAR, CARRYING CAPTAIN BARTLETT'S BODY.) 573 CROSS
TO REAPPEAR AS ONE WOMAN--A WOMAN RECALLING MOTHER125 MANSNS
BUT A STRANGE WOMAN--
REAPPEARS
INTO THE BEDROOM--REAPPEARS IMMEDIATELY WITH THE 77 ANNA
TIN CAN OF BEER IN HIS HAND--
A MOMENT LATER SHE REAPPEARS) 123 BEYOND
A MOMENT LATER SHE REAPPEARS CALLING BACK) 151 BEYOND
RUTH REAPPEARS ALMOST IMMEDIATELY CLOSING THE DOOR154 BEYOND
BEHIND HER.
(ANDREW REAPPEARS AND SHUTS THE DOOR SOFTLY. 162 BEYOND
SMITTY REAPPEARS AND CLOSES THE DOOR TO THE 466 CARIBE
FORECASTLE AFTER HIM.
(REAPPEARS IN THE WINDOW BESIDE ADA. 456 DYNAMO
HE REAPPEARS IMMEDIATELY AND GOES TO THE FRONT 299 GGBROW
DOOR AS THE KNOCKING RECOMMENCES-

REASON

REAPPEARS (CONT'D.)
(HE REAPPEARS, HAVING CHANGED HIS COAT AND TROUSERS) 308 GGBROW
A MOMENT LATER HE REAPPEARS IN THE MASK OF DION. 315 GGBROW
(HE DISAPPEARS, BUT REAPPEARS ALMOST IMMEDIATELY 318 GGBROW
IN THE MASK OF DION.
AND REAPPEARS A MOMENT LATER HAVING DUMPED ITS 400 MARCOM
LOAD

REARING
AND HAVE A HOME TO CALL HIS OWN AND BE REARING UP 46 ANNA
CHILDREN IN IT.
WITH LUXURY AND SECURITY FOR THE REARING OF 130 MANSNS
CHILDREN/

REARWALL
IN THE FAR REARWALL, WITHIN A DEEP RECESS LIKE THE377 MAKCOM
SHRINE OF AN IDOL.

REASON
(WILDLY) BECAUSE IT'S A STUPID, STUBBORN REASON. 547 'ILE
I GOT A GOOD REASON--AND THAT'S ALL YOU NEED TO 56 ANNA
KNOW.
MATTERING TO YOU WHAT OTHER REASON I GOT SO LONG 56 ANNA
AS I WASN'T MARRIED TO NO ONE
NO OTHER REASON WAS TO COUNT WITH YOU SO LONG AS I 59 ANNA
WASN'T MARRIED ALREADY.
SUPPOSE I TOLD YOU THAT WAS THE ONE AND ONLY 85 BEYOND
REASON FOR MY GOING?
BUT YOU HAVEN'T TOLD ME YOUR REASON FOR LEAVING 89 BEYOND
YET?
IT'S FOR THAT REASON--THAT AND ONE OTHER. 90 BEYOND
THAT'S THE OTHER REASON. 91 BEYOND
IN THIS MATCH YOU CAN'T OVERLOOK IN REASON. 98 BEYOND
AND REALIZES IMMEDIATELY THE REASON FOR IT--IN 104 BEYOND
CONSTERNATION)
BUT NOW ROB'S STAYING ON HERE, THERE ISN'T ANY 105 BEYOND
REASON FOR ME NOT TO GO.
(BREATHING HARD) NO REASONS 105 BEYOND
'S IF I DIDN'T KNOW YOUR REAL REASON FOR RUNNIN' 106 BEYOND
AWAY/
WANTING TO LEAVE THIS BLESSED FARM EXCEPT FOR SOME107 BEYOND
OUTSIDE REASON LIKE THAT.
BUT WHAT'S YOUR REASONS 124 BEYOND
THAT'S A QUEER REASON FOR LEAVING ME FLAT. 124 BEYOND
IT ISN'T THE REASON--(SHE LOWERS HER EYES AND HALF139 BEYOND
TURNS AWAY FROM HIM)
THE SAME REASON THAT MADE YOU GO LAST TIME THAT'S 139 BEYOND
DRIVING YOU AWAY AGAIN?
BECAUSE I'M DYING IS NO REASON YOU SHOULD TREAT ME160 BEYOND
AS AN IMBECILE OR A COWARD.
(DOGGEDLY) I'D KNOW YOUR REAL REASON FOR LEAVING164 BEYOND
HOME THE FIRST TIME--
IT'S THE BEASTLY MEMORIES THE DAMN THING BRINGS 466 CARIBE
UP--FOR SOME REASON.
TO LIE AND ESCAPE ADMITTING THE OBVIOUS NATURAL 495 DAYS
REASON FOR--
(UNCONVINCED--LOOKING AWAY) THE REASON I ASKED-- 507 DAYS
THAT'S THE REAL REASON I DECIDED TO TAKE MY 508 DAYS
VACATION IN THE EAST, JACK.
AND THE BOY HAD EVERY REASON TO BELIEVE IN SUCH A 510 DAYS
DIVINITY OF LOVE AS THE
BUT AFTERWARD HE HAD GOOD REASON TO-- 510 DAYS
WHICH HE HAD PRIDED HIMSELF HIS REASON HAD KILLED,544 DAYS
RETURN TO PLAGUE HIM.
THAT COWARDLY SOMETHING IN HIM HE DESPISES AS 544 DAYS
SUPERSTITION SEDUCES HIS REASON
HE SEES CLEARLY BY THE LIGHT OF REASON THE 545 DAYS
DEGRADATION OF HIS PITIABLE SURRENDER
CALE'LL KNOW WHAT I'M DRIVING AT AND SEE MY 508 DIFRNT
REASON--
BUT THAT AIN'T NO GOOD REASON FOR TELLIN' IT. 515 DIFRNT
(AFTER A PAUSE--INTENSELY) OH, I WISH I COULD 516 DIFRNT
MAKE YOU SEE--MY REASON.
THERE'S NO REASON YOU CAN'T. 517 DIFRNT
AND YOU AIN'T ANY OF MY REAL FOLKS, EITHER, AND 524 DIFRNT
AIN'T GOT ANY REASON.
(COQUETTISHLY) OH, YES, I HAVE A REASON. 524 DIFRNT
(COYLY) I HAVEN'T GIVEN HIM THE SLIGHTEST REASON 533 DIFRNT
TO HOPE IN THIRTY YEARS.
DON'T HURT HIM-- JUST BECAUSE YOU THINK I'M AN OLD543 DIFRNT
WOMAN AIN'T NO REASON--
BUT A MINISTER'S SON HAS REASON TO WORRY, MAYBE, 437 DYNAMO
I'VE GOOD REASON FOR KEEPING IT DARK. 440 DYNAMO
HE HAD A GOOD REASON TO TELL ME/ 447 DYNAMO
AND I WAS WITH MONEY TO YOU, DAT'S DE REASON. 177 EJONES
HE'D HAVE GOOD REASON NOT TO USE THE NAME OF 20 ELECTR
MANNON WHEN HE CAME CALLIN' HERE.
BUT I'VE SUSPECTED LATELY THAT WASN'T THE REAL 29 ELECTR
REASON--
BUT ALL THE SAME, THAT'S NOT YOUR REAL REASON FOR 33 ELECTR
SPARING ME/
THERE'LL BE NO REASON FOR HER TO SUSPECT. 40 ELECTR
FATHER HAS TAKEN A FANCY TO HIM FOR SOME REASON. 52 ELECTR
I MUST CONFESS I DIDN'T MIND HIS COMING AS MUCH AS 52 ELECTR
I MIGHT HAVE--FOR ONE REASON.
AN' I'M ONLY TELLIN' YOU FUR ONE REASON-- 136 ELECTR
BUT IT WILL PROVE A STRANGE REASON, I'M CERTAIN OF144 ELECTR
THAT, WHEN I DO DISCOVER IT/
(THEN WITH A BITTER SMILE) BUT I KNOW THE REASON 151 ELECTR
WELL ENOUGH.
SPEAKING OF MARRIAGE, THAT WAS THE BIG REASON I 14 HUGHIE
DUCKED.
MAYBE THERE'S A GOOD REASON. 584 ICEMAN
I HOPE YOU'VE DEDUCED THAT I'VE MY OWN REASON FOR 591 ICEMAN
ANSWERING THE IMPERTINENT
THE ONLY REASON I'VE QUIT IS-- 621 ICEMAN
I WANT YOU TO UNDERSTAND THE REASON. 648 ICEMAN
THERE'S NO REASON--YOU SEE, I DON'T FEEL ANY 663 ICEMAN
GRIEF.

REASON (CONT'D.)
BUT HERE'S THE TRUE REASON, LARRY--THE ONLY 667 ICEMAN
REASON/
YOU'VE GOT TO SEE WHAT MY ONLY REASON WAS/ 667 ICEMAN
NO OTHER REASON, HONEST/ 680 ICEMAN
THERE COULDN'T POSSIBLY BE ANY OTHER REASON/ 680 ICEMAN
YOU'VE KEPT THAT A DEEP SECRET, I NOTICE--FOR SOME693 ICEMAN
REASON/
BUT, IF YOU INSIST ON KNOWING NOW, THERE'S NO 693 ICEMAN
REASON YOU SHOULDN'T.
THE ONLY REASON I CAN THINK OF IS, 705 ICEMAN
'TIS YOU'LL DO THE EXPLAININ'--AN' DAMN QUICK, OR 329 INZONE
WE'LL KNOW THE REASON WHY.
THERE'S NO REASON TO SCOLD JAMIE. 26 JOURNE
THAT'S THE REAL REASON/ 47 JOURNE
THERE'S ABSOLUTELY NO REASON TO TALK AS IF YOU 48 JOURNE
EXPECTED SOMETHING DREADFUL/
REASONS 83 JOURNE
NO MAN HAS EVER HAD A BETTER REASON. 83 JOURNE
WHAT REASONS 83 JOURNE
OH, I KNOW IT'S FOOLISH TO IMAGINE DREADFUL THINGS 88 JOURNE
WHEN THERE'S NO REASON FOR
MAYBE I GUESSED THERE WAS A GOOD REASON NOT TO 110 JOURNE
LAUGH.
BUT I'M A FOOL TO TALK REASON TO YOU. 117 JOURNE
THERE'S NO REASON TO HAVE THE HOUSE ABLAZE WITH 126 JOURNE
ELECTRICITY
BUT THAT'S NO REASON TO TAKE IT FOR GRANTED SHE 138 JOURNE
COULD HAVE--
ANY PLACE YOU LIKE--WITHIN REASON. 149 JOURNE
AND YOU STUMBLE ON TOWARD NOWHERE, FOR NO GOOD 153 JOURNE
REASON/
WITHIN REASON, OF COURSE. 158 JOURNE
ANYTHING WITHIN REASON. 158 JOURNE
ONLY REASON SHE'D KEPT HER WAS SHE COULD PLAY THE 159 JOURNE
PIANO.
(CRUELLY AND GRIMLY AGAIN) SO MUCH THE MORE 357 LAZARU
REASON WHY MY PRIDE SHOULD KILL
I'VE HAD GOOD REASON TO HAVE. 20 MANSNS
WELL, PERHAPS I AM--NOW--WITH GOOD REASON--BUT IF 66 MANSNS
I AM, WHOSE WISH WAS IT---
IS THAT YOUR REASON FOR INVITING ME HERE-- 78 MANSNS
BUT I COULDN'T HELP FEARING THE REAL REASON WAS 83 MANSNS
YOU DIDN'T WANT ME.
WITHOUT GIVING HIM ANY SENSIBLE REASON-- 110 MANSNS
I KNOW YOUR TRUE REASON FOR COMING. 152 MANSNS
YOU CAME HERE HOPING AGAINST HOPE THAT THE REASON 153 MANSNS
I HAD SENT FOR YOU--
I AM PLEASED TO TELL YOU THAT IS THE REASON. 153 MANSNS
WHO HAVE SUCH GOOD REASON TO ENVY AND HATE YOU-- 156 MANSNS
REASON TO HATE ME? 156 MANSNS
THE REAL REASON I CAME HERE WAS TO HAVE A SENSIBLE167 MANSNS
TALK WITH YOU.
YOU'VE REASON FOR THE LAST. 23 MISBEG
WITHOUT ANY REASON, YOU CAN SEE, HE'LL SUDDENLY 33 MISBEG
TURN STRANGE, AND LOOK SAD,
BUT WHAT'S HARDER'S REASON, JIMS 49 MISBEG
WHAT'S THE REASON MR. HARDER DECIDED TO NOTICE 49 MISBEG
POOR, HUMBLE SCUM THE LIKE OF US?
I AGREE, BUT FOR SOME STRANGE REASON HARDER 51 MISBEG
DOESN'T LOOK FORWARD TO THE TASTE OF
HE AS MUCH AS TOLD ME HIS REASON, THOUGH HE 89 MISBEG
WOULDN'T COME OUT WITH IT PLAIN.
(HER VOICE TREMBLES) SO THAT WAS HIS REASON-- 90 MISBEG
EVERYONE ELSE BELIEVES IT--INCLUDING MYSELF--FOR A133 MISBEG
DAMNED GOOD REASON.
AND THEN SUDDENLY, FOR NO REASON, ALL THE FUN WENT170 MISBEG
OUT OF IT.
I KNOW YOU'LL UNDERSTAND THE REASON, AND NOT THINK172 MISBEG
I'M TIRED OF YOUR COMPANY.
BECAUSE SHE HATES ME, MOTHER--FOR ONE REASON. 78 POET
FURTHERED MY INTERESTS BY GIVING HER ANOTHER 91 POET
REASON.
ANOTHER REASON WAS-- 110 POET
THERE WAS ANOTHER REASON WHY I TOLD YOUNG HARFORD 112 POET
BY THE WAY, WHAT AMOUNT DOES MR. HARFORD THINK 120 POET
PROPER, ANYTHING IN REASON--
SHE'S ALL THE MORE REASON. 127 POET
(DESPERATELY FORCING HERSELF TO REASON WITH HIM 127 POET
AGAIN.)
SHE HAS A REASON. 10 STRANG
WHAT POSSIBLE REASON--? 10 STRANG
(WITH A TOUCH OF ASPERITY) YES, I SAID IT, AND I 10 STRANG
GAVE HIM MY REASON.
AND THERE'S NOT THE SLIGHTEST REASON TO WORRY 17 STRANG
ABOUT ME.
THE REASON FOR IT IS OBVIOUS. 35 STRANG
AND I'M SURE YOU HAVE EVERY REASON TO HOPE. 47 STRANG
ONE REASON WHY SHE MARRIED ME.... 55 STRANG
WHAT REASON COULD I GIVE, WITHOUT TELLING HIM 61 STRANG
EVERYTHING?
ONE REASON I'VE STEERED CLEAR SINCE.... 78 STRANG
I NEED THE COURAGE OF SOMEONE WHO CAN STAND 84 STRANG
OUTSIDE AND REASON IT OUT
AND THIS IS BEYOND REASON.... 91 STRANG
LOSE HIS REASON.... 128 STRANG
IF ANYTHING HAPPENED TO THAT CHILD I ACTUALLY 128 STRANG
BELIEVE SAM WOULD LOSE HIS REASON/
THERE WAS NO POSSIBLE REASON FOR HER STAYING WITH 129 STRANG
SAM, WHEN SHE LOVED DARRELL.
THERE'S NO EARTHLY REASON WHY HE SHOULD LIKE YOU, 144 STRANG
WHAT POSSIBLE REASON COULD I HAVE FOR HOPING FOR 170 STRANG
SAM'S DEATH?
THERE'S NO REASON FOR HIS NOT KNOWING NOW....) 191 STRANG
REASON I ARST YER ABOUT THE DROPS WAS 'CAUSE I 495 VOYAGE
SEEN THE CAPT'N OF THE *AMINDRA*

REASONABLE

REASONABLE
(CONTROLLING HERSELF--IN A FORCED REASONABLE 4 MANSNS
TONE.)
(HUMILIATED, BUT FORCING A REASONABLE TONE.) 153 MANSNS
SURE, IT ISN'T REASONABLE FOR A STANDARD OIL MAN 63 MISREG
TO HATE HOGS.
(WATCHING HIM UNEASILY, ATTEMPTS A REASONABLE, 122 POET
PERSUASIVE TONE.)
(TRYING TO BE MORE REASONABLE) 167 STRANG

REASONABLENESS
(WITH AN ATTEMPT AT OPEN-MINDED REASONABLENESS) 625 ICEMAN

REASONABLY
GOOD-NATURED AND REASONABLY CONTENTED WITH LIFE. 611 ICEMAN
(AVOIDING LOOKING AT HER, TRYING TO ARGUE 102 STRANG
REASONABLY--COLDLY)

REASONED
AND I REASONED, WHO KNOWS BUT SOME DAY THIS MARCU 388 MARCOM
MAY SEE INTO HER EYES
I REASONED, LOVE COMES LIKE THE BREATH OF WIND ON 388 MARCOM
WATER
I REASONED, BUT THIS IS AN ENCHANTED MOMENT FOR 388 MARCOM
HER

REASONING
(THE GIRLS NOD, CONVINCED BY THIS REASONING.) 636 ICEMAN
(GULLILY) I'VE BEEN CONSIDERING WHAT SAM'S WIFE 86 STRANG
TOLD ME AND HER REASONING IS

REASONS
A WOMAN COULDN'T RIGHTLY UNDERSTAND MY REASONS. 547 TILE
(REGAINING HIS COURAGE) TO THE DIVIL WITH ALL 55 ANNA
OTHER REASONS THEN.
FOR A HUNDRED REASONS--THE FAMILY'S SAKE-- 88 ELECTR
IF ONLY FOR SELFISH REASONS. 159 ELECTR
I'VE BEEN LOOKING YOU UP FOR PURELY SELFISH 280 GGBROW
REASONS.
HE'S STILL WITH ME BUT, FOR REASONS OF HIS OWN, 306 GGBROW
DOESN'T WISH IT KNOWN.
I HAD A LOT OF GOOD REASONS. 590 ICEMAN
BUT I KNOW YOU APPRECIATE MY REASONS FOR THAT, 66 MANSNS
SARA.
THE REASONS SHE GAVE HIM ARE SOUND AND SHOW A 109 POET
CONSIDERATION FOR YOUR GOOD NAME
ALTHOUGH, AS YOU KNOW, I WAS OPPOSED AT FIRST, AND .9 STRANG
FOR FAIR REASONS, I THINK.
BUT THERE MIGHT BE MANY REASONS WHY HE'D WISH TO 36 STRANG
GET RID OF HER...)
(STRANGELY) THERE ARE SO MANY CURIOUS REASONS WE 170 STRANG
DARE NOT THINK ABOUT FOR
WHY DO YOU ASK FOR REASONS? 465 WELDED

REASSURANCE
(HASTILY, IN A FORCED TONE OF REASSURANCE) 555 DAYS
(THEN WITH A SUDDEN FORCED REASSURANCE.) 234 DESIRE
JONES STANDS TREMBLING--THEN WITH A CERTAIN 192 EJONES
REASSURANCE)
(HE LOOKS AT THE NIGHT CLERK EXPECTING 16 HUGHIE
REASSURANCE.)
(THEN WITH FORCED REASSURANCE) 652 ICEMAN
THEN WITH GROWING REASSURANCE, 339 LAZARU
SEEKING THE SATISFYING REASSURANCE OF HIS 67 POET
DEFLECTION THERE.
(WITH PITIFULLY WELL-MEANT REASSURANCE.) 172 POET

REASSURE
(TRYING UNCONVINCINGLY TO REASSURE HIMSELF) 466 DYNAMO
AT THE SAME TIME TRYING TO REASSURE HERSELF) 471 DYNAMO
(HE LOOKS AT HER STILL FACE AND CLOSED EYES, 54 ELECTR
IMPLORING HER TO REASSURE HIM)
(HE DRINKS) BROWN WELL STILL NEED ME--TO REASSURE296 GGBROW
HIM HE'S ALIVE/
(AS IF TO REASSURE HIMSELF--TIMIDLY) 40 STRANG
REASSURE HIMSELF ABOUT IT, YET HE IS RIDING THE 53 STRANG
CREST OF THE WAVE.

REASSURED
(ONLY PARTLY REASSURED--SHARPLY) 293 AHWILD
(REASSURED--PRESSING ONE OF HIS HANDS GRATEFULLY) 537 OFFRNT
(HE GETS TO HIS FEET, EVIDENTLY SLIGHTLY REASSURED196 EJONES
BY HIS PRAYER--
THEN SEES THE SIGNBOARD ON THE WALL AND IS 246 HA APE
REASSURED.)
(REASSURED) NO. 624 ICEMAN
REASSURED, HE LEANS DOWN AND CAUTIOUSLY PULLS OUT 513 INZONE
A SUITCASE
(SHE IS REASSURED AND SMILES AT HIM LOVINGLY. 21 JOURNE
(HALF REASSURED.) I REALLY SHOULD HAVE NEW 27 JOURNE
GLASSES.
(HAZILY REASSURED.) THAT'S RIGHT, MA'AM. 101 JOURNE
(REASSURED AND PLEASANT.) I AM NOT MAJESTY, MY 192 MANSNS
POOR WOMAN.
BUT AT ONCE SHE IS REASSURED AS HE SHIFTS HIS 69 POET
GAZE.

REASSURING
(GRINNING CHEERFULLY, GIVES LILY A REASSURING PAT 226 AHWILD
ON THE BACK)
(WITH A REASSURING SMILE) NO. 293 AHWILD
WITH A REASSURING SMILE) 50 ANNA
(AS IF HE WERE REASSURING A CHILD) 158 BEYOND
HE STARTS GUILTILY AND HASTILY MAKES A REASSURING 424 DYNAMO
DECLARATION OF FAITH)
THE SOUND OF THE SHOT, THE REASSURING FEEL OF THE 190 EJONES
REVOLVER IN HIS HAND,
(LOOKING AROUND AT THEM--IN A KINDLY, REASSURING 663 ICEMAN
TONE)
(IN A VOICE MEANT TO BE REASSURING) 520 INZONE
(A HAPPY YOUTH--WITH REASSURING CONVICTION) 275 LAZARU
(REASSURING HERSELF--THINKING.) 118 MANSNS
(REASSURING HERSELF) (IND, IT ISN'T A LIE... 57 STRANG

REASSURINGLY
(REASSURINGLY STOICAL NOW) YOU NEEDN'T WORRY, MA.271 AHWILD
(HILLER NODS REASSURINGLY. 293 AHWILD
(WORRIEDLY, BUT TRYING TO PRETEND TO TREAT IT 550 DAYS
LIGHTLY, REASSURINGLY)

REASSURINGLY (CONT'D.)
ALL THE TIME MUTTERING REASSURINGLY) 188 EJONES
REASSURINGLY.) YOU KNOW THAT I WILL MAKE NO 52 MANSNS
DECISION WITHOUT YOUR CONSENT.
(REASSURINGLY, BECAUSE HE IS NOW EXTREMELY 351 MARCOM
CURIOUS)
(REASSURINGLY.) SHE'S HIS MOTHER, 78 POET
(THEN DEFIANTLY SELF-REASSURINGLY.) 137 POET
(THEN SELF-REASSURINGLY) (BUT THERE IS A PUBLIC 5 STRANG
TO CHERISH THEM, EVIDENTLY...
(REASSURINGLY) NO GIRL COULD FORGET GORDON IN A 9 STRANG
HURRY.
(REASSURINGLY) CERTAINLY, YOU CAN/ 70 STRANG
(HE COMES TO CAPE AND SLAPS HIM ON THE BACK 451 WELDED
REASSURINGLY)
(AS IF TO HIMSELF--REASSURINGLY) 469 WELDED

REAWAKENED
(SHARPLY, TO CONCEAL HIS OWN REAWAKENED 260 AHWILD
APPREHENSION)

REAWAKENING
THEN WITH REAWAKENING PASSION) 469 DYNAMO

REB
AFRAID OLD JOHNNY REB WOULD PICK ME OFF, WERE YOUS 52 ELECTR
I MET A REB CRAWLING TOWARD OUR LINES. 95 ELECTR

REBEL
REBEL AGAINST ALL AUTHORITY, 202 AHWILD
LIVE AND REBEL AGAINST THAT OTHER BOY'S GOD AND 295 GGBROW
PROTECT MYSELF FROM HIS CRUELTY.
I HAVE TO REBEL WITH ALL MY STRENGTH--SEIZE ANY 453 WELDED
PRETEXT/

REBELLING
(THEN REBELLING FURIOUSLY) 129 STRANG

REBELLION
FOR A MOMENT, A LOOK OF BITTER, DEFIANT REBELLION 220 AHWILD
COMING OVER HIS FACE.
NO, ONLY A PRIEST OF ALMIGHTY GOD--(WITH A ROUSED 138 POET
REBELLION AGAIN.)
(WORKING HERSELF TO REBELLION AGAIN.) 138 POET

REBELLIOUSLY
(REBELLIOUSLY) YET I WISH SOME POWER COULD GIVE 400 MARCOM
ME ASSURANCE

REBELLIOUS
EVEN HIS FATHER TURNED ENEMY, HIS FACE GROWING 235 AHWILD
MORE AND MORE REBELLIOUS.
ONLY HER MOUTH IS REBELLIOUS. 422 DYNAMO
BUT EVEN WHEN HE WAS LITTLE I SENSED IN HIM HIS 426 DYNAMO
MOTHER'S REBELLIOUS SPIRIT...
(SHE GIVES A LITTLE REBELLIOUS TOSS OF HER HEAD-- 175 JOURNE
WITH GIRLISH PIQUE.)

REBELLIOUSLY
(NODS HER HEAD, AND THEN BREAKS FORTH 87 BEYOND
REBELLIOUSLY)
(REBELLIOUSLY) WELL, I DO WISH HE WASN'T/ 96 BEYOND
PLOWED 'EM UNDER IN THE GROUND--(HE STAMPS 204 DESIRE
REBELLIOUSLY) --ROTTIN'--
EDEN STRETCHES HIS ARMS UP TO THE SKY-- 211 DESIRE
REBELLIOUSLY.)
(HE GOES TO THE DOOR--THEN TURNS--REBELLIOUSLY) 214 DESIRE
(REBELLIOUSLY) GIVE THAT BACK/ 360 MARCOM
(TURNS TO HIM--ON THE VERGE OF TEARS-- 387 MARCOM
REBELLIOUSLY)
(THEN REBELLIOUSLY) IS THE GRANDDAUGHTER OF THE 411 MALKUM
GREAT KUBLAI
(REBELLIOUSLY) HE'S NOT MY UNCLE/ 142 STRANG
(REBELLIOUSLY) DAMN IT, I DON'T SEE WHY HE HAD TO1BS STRANG
DIE!

REBELS
DISCIPLINE MY WILL TO KEEP MYSELF UNITED--ANOTHER 74 MANSNS
SELF REBELS--SECEDES--

REBIRTH
ALREADY AT THE MERE PROSPECT OF ESCAPE, I FEEL A 40 MANSNS
REBIRTH STIRRING IN ME/

REBORN
MY SON IS REBORN TO ME/ 278 LAZARU
AND MY HEART REBORN TO LOVE OF LIFE CRIED +YES/+ 279 LAZARU
I AM WILLING TO BEG HER ON MY KNEES TO GIVE ME 39 MANSNS
THIS CHANCE TO BE REBORN/

REBUFF
(THEN AS HE TURNS AWAY, HURT AND RESENTFUL AT THIS 52 ELECTR
REBUFF--HASTILY)
(THEN AFRAID SHE MAY LOSE HIS TRADE BY THIS 473 WELDED
REBUFF)

REBUFFED
(REBUFFED AND HURT, SHRUGS HIS SHOULDERS.) 42 JOURNE
MARCU IS REBUFFED, GRINS EMBARRASSED, TURNS AWAY 366 MARCOM
TO THE CHILDREN, WHO,
(HE PASSES ON, REBUFFED AGAIN, STOPS FASCINATEDLY 366 MARCOM
BEFORE THE COFFIN.

REBUFFS
(HE AGAIN STARES AT THE NIGHT CLERK APPEALINGLY, 29 HUGHIE
FORGETTING PAST REBUFFS.

REBUKE
SHOCKED REBUKE. 561 DAYS
(WITH BLEERY BENEVOLENCE, SHAKING HIS HEAD IN MILD600 ICEMAN
REBUKE)
SO HARKER CAME IN PERSON TO REBUKE SHAUGHNESSY. 24 JOURNE
YOUR REBUKE IS WELL TAKEN, NICHOLAS. 31 MANSNS
(WITH COLD REBUKE.) I SAID, TO THE DAY AND YOUR 93 POET
GOOD HEALTH, CORPORAL CREGAN.
(HELPLESSLY RESIGNED ALREADY BUT FEELING IT HER 148 POET
DUTY TO REBUKE.)
(APPREHENSIVELY, FORCING A TONE OF ANNOYED REBUKE)102 STRANG

REBUKING
(TARTLY--GIVING HER SON A REBUKING LOOK) 216 AHWILD
(REBUKING HIM FAMILIARLY) ARRAH NOW, 222 AHWILD
(SOLEMNLY OFFENDED) ARE YOU--PUBLICLY REBUKING ME225 AHWILD
BEFORE ASSEMBLED--S
(QUIETLY REBUKING) JACK/ 505 DAYS

REBUKING (CONT'D.)
(THEN TENDERLY REBUKING) YE OUGHTN'T T' TALK O' 245 DESIRE
SAD THIN'S--THIS MORNIN'.
IN A STRANGE, ARROGANTLY DISDAINFUL TONE, AS IF HE658 ICEMAN
WERE REBUKING A BUTLER)
(MECHANICALLY REBUKING.) DON'T CALL YOUR FATHER 44 JOURNE
THE OLD MAN.
(AS SHE STARTS THROUGH THE DOORWAY--PLEADING AND 75 JOURNE
REBUKING.)
(THEN REBUKING AGAIN.) WERE YOU THE WAY YOU ARE, 143 POET
IN ONLY A NIGHTGOWN AND

REBUKINGLY
(HIS FACE CLOUDING--REBUKINGLY BUT NOT SEVERELY) 542 'ILE
(REBUKINGLY) ARTHUR/ 192 AHWILD
(THEN REBUKINGLY) AND YOU OUGHT TO. 272 AHWILD
(THEN REBUKINGLY) BUT YOU AIN'T GOT NO KICK AGIN 177 EJONES
ME, SMITHERS.
(REBUKINGLY) YUH OUGHTN'T TO CALL CORA DAT. 614 ICEMAN
RUCKY.
(WITH A FLASH OF HIS USUAL HUMOR--REBUKINGLY) 651 ICEMAN
(REBUKINGLY) AW, LAY OFF DAT. 668 ICEMAN
(ASTONISHED AT HER BOLDNESS--REBUKINGLY) 397 MARCOM
O'DOWD OFFICIOUSLY SNATCHES IT OFF FOR HIM-- 53 POET
REBUKINGLY.)
(REBUKINGLY.) HIMSELF WENT IN THE BAR TO BE OUT 64 POET
OF REACH OF YOUR TONGUE.
(REBUKINGLY.) ALL THIS TIME--IN THE DEAD OF THE 142 POET
NIGHT?
(REBUKINGLY.) I'M GLAD YOU HAD THE DACENCY TO 144 POET
BLUSH.
(LOOKING REBUKINGLY AT DARRELL) 147 STRANG
(AFTER A PAUSE--REBUKINGLY) JOHN IS A GOOD MAN. 483 WELDED

REC'LECT
I REC'LECT--NOW AN' AGIN. 204 DESIRE

RECALL
DON'T TAX YOUR MEMORY TRYING TO RECALL THOSE 254 AHWILD
ANCIENT DAYS OF YOUR YOUTH.
WOULD LIKE HER TO RECALL, AT HIS MOMENT--GENTLY 259 AHWILD
DISENGAGING HER HAND FROM HIS--
TIBERIUS' DEATH, A KIND FROM WHICH NO MIRACLES CAN331 LAZARU
RECALL ONE/
TO BE ABLE TO RECALL THE PAST SO DISTINCTLY. 145 MANSNS
THIS COSTUME IS A QUEER JUMBLE OF STUNNING EFFECTS390 MARCOM
THAT RECALL THE PARADE
CAN WORDS RECALL LIFE TO HER BEAUTYS 434 MARCOM
THE NOISE, THE LIGHTS OF THE STREETS, RECALL HIM 439 MARCOM
AT ONCE TO HIMSELF.

RECALLED
IT WOULD BE DAMNED QUEER IF YOU FELL IN LOVE WITH 36 ELECTR
ME BECAUSE I RECALLED EZRA
AND WAS IT THY POWER THAT RECALLED LIFE TO HER 350 LAZARU
BODY FOR THAT MOMENTS

RECALLING
TO REAPPEAR AS ONE WOMAN--A WOMAN RECALLING MOTHER125 MANSNS
BUT A STRANGE WOMAN--
(THEN SUDDENLY STARTS HER STORY IN A DULL 82 STRANG
MONOTONOUS TONE RECALLING THAT OF
RECALLING EVERY WORD YOU SAID, EACH MOVEMENT, EACH130 STRANG
EXPRESSION ON YOUR FACE.

RECALLS
LAVINIA SPEAKS AGAIN IN CURT COMMANDING TONE THAT 122 ELECTR
RECALLS HER FATHER)
THAT RECALLS HER MOTHER IN THE LAST ACT OF 155 ELECTR
*HOMECOMING.
WRINGING MOVEMENT WHICH RECALLS HER MOTHER IN THE 157 ELECTR
LAST ACT OF *THE HUNTED.*
BUT HIS NOSE IS HIS FATHER'S AND HIS FACE IN 20 JOURNE
PROFILE RECALLS TYRONE'S.
HIS FACE RECALLS THAT OF A STATUE OF A DIVINITY UF274 LAZARU
ANCIENT GREECE
(HASTILY RECALLS MELODY TO THE BATTLEFIELD.) 98 POET
HER GENERAL MANNER RECALLS INSTANTLY THE NINA OF 158 STRANG
ACT FOUR, NEUROTIC.
AS AN OARSMAN HE RECALLS HIS FATHER, GORDON SHAW, 179 STRANG
TO ME.

RECAPTURE
(THEY TRY TO RECAPTURE THEIR MOMENTARY ENTHUSIASM,659 ICEMAN

RECEDE
(HIS MIND HAS BEEN COUNTING THE FOOTFALLS OF THE 24 HUGHIE
COP ON THE BEAT AS THEY RECEDE,
THE DRUM BEAT AND THE CHANTING RECEDE INTO THE 376 MARCOM
DISTANCE.)
RECEDE ALONG THE STREET BEYOND THE HIGH WALL. 86 POET

RECEDED
WHICH HAS RECEDED A BIT FROM THE EXTREME OF 186 AHWILD
PRECEDING YEARS, BUT STILL RUNS TO

RECEDES
IT RECEDES AND THEN GROWS LOUDER AS THEY CROSS 482 DYNAMO
FROM THE DAM
AND EACH ONE PASSING LEAVES ONE LESS TO PASS, SO 19 HUGHIE
THE NIGHT RECEDES, TOO.
THEN IT RECEDES AND DIES, AND THERE IS SOMETHING 19 HUGHIE
MELANCHOLY ABOUT THAT.
THE LAUGHTER OF THE SOLDIERS RECEDES. 295 LAZARU
THE NOISE OF THEIR PASSING RECEDES. 311 LAZARU
THE LAUGHTER RECEDES HEAVENWARD AND DIES AS THE 392 MARCOM
HALO OF LIGHT AROUND HER FACE

RECEDING
THEY LISTEN TO HIS STEPS RECEDING.) 215 DESIRE
HIS VOICE SINKING DOWN THE SCALE AND RECEDING 199 EJONES
HE BURSTS AGAIN INTO HIS MOURNFUL DIRGE, HIS VOICE107 ELECTR
RECEDING)
SMALL'S EXCITED VOICE CAN BE HEARD RECEDING 134 ELECTR
RECEDING BROWS ABOVE THEIR SMALL FIERCE, RESENTFUL207 HA APE
EYES.
(HER BITTERNESS RECEDING INTO A RESIGNED 48 JOURNE
HELPLESSNESS.)

RECEDING (CONT'D.)
STRAIN OF MUSIC RECEDING INTO THE SILENCE OVER 324 LAZARU
STILL WATERS.)
THEY HAVE STOPPED RECEDING. 40 MANSNS
THE SOUND GRADUALLY GROWS FAINTER AND FAINTER, 358 MARCOM
RECEDING INTO THE DISTANCE,
INTERVALS, RECEDING AS HE GETS FARTHER OFF ON HIS 101 MISBEG
WAY TO THE INN.
HER THOUGHTS ARE ON THE RECEDING FIGURE OF TYRONE 176 MISBEG
AGAIN.

RECEIVE
(ANGRILY TO CHRISTINE) A FINE GUEST TO RECEIVE IN 50 ELECTR
MY ABSENCE/
(KISSING HIM, COAXINGLY) YOU RECEIVE THEM. 316 GGROW
PUNCTUATED BY THE BLOWS AND KICKS THEY RECEIVE. 353 MARCOM
YOU WILL RECEIVE YOUR AGENT'S COMMISSION AT ONCE. 382 MARCOM
BY THE TIME YOU RECEIVE THIS THEY WILL BE MARRIED 424 MARCOM
IN VENICE.
BUT IT'S HORRIBLY HARD TO GIVE ANYTHING, AND 45 STRANG
FRIGHTFUL TO RECEIVE/
(FORGIVING EVANS, GETS TO HER FEET AS IF TO 95 STRANG
RECEIVE DARRELL IN HER ARMS--

RECEIVED
JUST RECEIVED YOUR WIRE. 147 BEYOND
(THIS ANNOUNCEMENT IS RECEIVED WITH GREAT 458 CARINE
ENTHUSIASM BY ALL HANDS.)
I RECEIVED ALL OF HAZEL'S LETTERS--AND VINNIE'S. 85 ELECTR
AS IF HE HAD RECEIVED A PUNCH FULL IN THE FACE-- 238 HA APE
RAGING)
GUCKY HOVERS UN THE OUTSKIRTS OF THE BATTLE, 527 INZONE
MINDFUL OF THE KICK HE RECEIVED.)
HE RECEIVED SUCH GLOWING REPORTS. EVERYONE LIKED 110 JOURNE
HIM.
YANG-CHAU, ACCORDING TO THE PETITION FOR MERCY YOU386 MARCOM
HAVE RECEIVED
(WITH A CHILLING AIR) I HAVE RECEIVED A PETITION 392 MARCOM
ANY SUGGESTION YOU CAN MAKE, CHARLIE, WILL BE 122 STRANG
GRATEFULLY RECEIVED.

RECEIVES
(THEN AS HE RECEIVES NO REPLY--WITH VAGUE 722 ICEMAN
UNEASINESS)
(THE CHRISTIAN SETS UP A WAILING CRY AND RECEIVES 354 MARCOM
A BLOW.

RECEIVING
(RECEIVING NO REPLY, HE CALLS AGAIN, THIS TIME 25 ANNA
WITH APPARENT APPREHENSION)
(RECEIVING NO ANSWER, HE 482 CARDIF
HE HATES CALLING ON PEOPLE, OR RECEIVING THEM. 44 JOURNE

RECENT
BUT SHE IS A FAIRLY RECENT RECRUIT TO THE RANKS, 236 AHWILD
ESPECIALLY IN THE LIGHT OF YOUR RECENT MYSTIC 509 DAYS
VISION.
THIS BEAUTY IS A TRIFLE DIMMED NOW BY TRACES OF 514 DAYS
RECENT ILLNESS.
THE EVIL REPUTATION OF RECENT FAILURE PREJUDICES 152 MANSNS
THEM AGAINST YOU.
I HOPE YOU APPRECIATE FROM YOUR RECENT EXPERIENCE 154 MANSNS
WITH MY METHODS

RECENTLY
RECENTLY BUILT, IS AT LEFT. -0 DYNAMO
YOU MEAN TO THE HUGHES WHO HAD THIS JOB SO LONG 11 HUGHIE
AND DIED RECENTLY?
HE RESEMBLES A HOLY SAINT, RECENTLY ELECTED TO 32 HUGHIF
PARADISE.
I TALKED RECENTLY WITH A POET WHO HAD FLED FROM 386 MARCOM
THERE IN HORROR.

RECEPTIVE
HIS EXPRESSION IS COMPOSED AND GRAVELY RECEPTIVE. 294 GGROW

RECESS
GENTLEMEN OF THE JURY, COURT WILL NOW RECESS 607 ICEMAN
IN THE FAR REARWALL, WITHIN A DEEP RECESS LIKE THE377 MARCOM
SHRINE OF AN IDOL.

RECIPES
MY MOTHER'S #RECIPES. 412 MARCOM

RECITAL
SHE HAS BEEN SINCERELY MOVED BY THE RECITAL OF HER226 DESIRE
TROUBLES.

RECITE
WHY, LILY I NEVER KNEW YOU TO RECITE POETRY 199 AHWILD
BEFORE/
(BEGINS TO RECITE SEPULCHRALLY) 244 AHWILD
I HEARD A GUY RECITE IT AT POLI'S. 246 AHWILD
RECITE SOMETHING. 276 AHWILD
I'LL HAVE TO MEMORIZE THE REST AND RECITE IT TO 277 AHWILD
MURIEL THE NEXT TIME.
DION CAN RECITE LOTS OF SHELLEY'S POEMS BY HEART. 262 GGBROW
(SHE PAUSES--THEN BEGINS TO RECITE THE HAIL MARY 107 JOURNE
IN A FLAT, EMPTY TONE.)
AND THERE WILL BE POETS TO RECITE THEIR POEMS-- 399 MARCOM
RECITE WITH DISCORDANT VIGOR) 435 MARCOM
(INTERRUPTS HIM RUDELY.) WAS IT TO LISTEN TO YOU 47 POET
RECITE BYAOO-'S
ABRUPTLY MELODY BEGINS TO RECITE FROM BYRON. 101 POET
LIKE A SCHOOLBOY WHO HAS BEEN CALLED ON TO RECITE 69 STRANG
AND CANNOT AND IS BEING

RECITED
(THEN APPRECIATIVELY.) BUT YOU RECITED IT WELL, 133 JOURNE
LAC.
I LEARNED MACBETH AND RECITED IT LETTER PERFECT, 136 JOURNE
WITH YOU GIVING ME THE CUES.
SAID SHE WAS BETTER THAN A DRUNKEN BUM WHO RECITED160 JOURNE
POETRY.
I'LL BET YOU RECITED KIPLING AND SWINBURNE AND 160 JOURNE
DOWSON AND GAVE HER
HE DETERMINEDLY RECITED IMPECCABLE PLATITUDES, 11 MANSNS
(HE HAS RECITED THIS WITH DEEP FEELING. 104 MISBEG
AND THEN THE FAVOURITE QUOTE FROM BYRON, RECITED 67 POET
ALOUD TO HIS OWN IMAGE.)

RECITES

RECITES
(HE RECITES THREATENINGLY) =THE DAYS GROW HOT, O 195 AHWILD
BABYLON/
(HE RECITES WITH A JOKING INTENSITY) 205 AHWILD
(HE RECITES WITH ADDED COMIC INTENSITY) 205 AHWILD
(SUDDENLY RECITES SENTIMENTALLY) 244 AHWILD
THE RECITES SCORNFULLY) =FOR A WOMAN'S ONLY A 245 AHWILD
WORM=
RECITES WITH DRAMATIC EMPHASIS)
THEN RECITES DRAMATICALLY TO HIMSELF, HIS EYES ON 277 AHWILD
THE APPROACHING FIGURE)
(HE RECITES DRAMATICALLY) = SOMETHING WAS DEAD IN279 AHWILD
EACH OF US,
(HE RECITES, AND RECITES WELL, WITH BITTER, 132 JOURNE
IRONICAL PASSION,
(HE RECITES THE SYMONS' TRANSLATION OF 133 JOURNE
BAUDELAIRE'S =EPILOGUE=
(HE RECITES UNRESERVEDLY BUT WITH DEEP FEELING.) 134 JOURNE
(HE RECITES SARDONICALLY FROM ROSSETTI.) 168 JOURNE
(SUDDENLY POINTS A FINGER AT HIM AND RECITES WITH 168 JOURNE
DRAMATIC EMPHASIS.)
(HE RECITES FROM SWINBURNE'S =A LEAVE-TAKING= AND 173 JOURNE
GOES IT WELL.
(HE RECITES FROM =A LEAVE-TAKING= AGAIN WITH 173 JOURNE
INCREASED BITTERNESS.)
(HE RECITES AGAIN FROM THE SWINBURNE POEM.) 174 JOURNE
(SHE RECITES--WITH GROWING ARROGANCE.) 107 MANSNS
KUKACHIN RECITES IN A LOW TONE. 304 MARCOM
(FROM BELOW, RECITES IN A CALM, SOOTHING TONE) 401 MARCOM
(TYRONE RECITES WITH FEELING) 37 MISBEG
(HE RECITES MOCKINGLY) =IT IS THE VERY ERROR OF 151 MISBEG
THE MOON.
HE STARES INTO HIS EYES IN THE GLASS AND RECITES 43 POET
FROM BYRON'S =CHILDE HAROLD.
(HE RECITES.) =BUT SWEETER STILL THAN THIS, THAN 47 POET
THESE, THAN ALL,
AND RECITES IN MOCKING BROGUE.) 176 POET
AND HIS AMUSED VOICE RECITES THE WORDS WITH A 4 STRANG
RHETORICAL RESONANCE)

RECITIN'
HE USED TO BE DOWN THERE A LOT RECITIN' SCRIPTURE 986 ROPE

RECITING
RECITING THE BALLAD OF READING GAOL TO THOSE 276 AHWILD
(NARROW)
HIS LIPS MOVE AS IF HE WERE RECITING SOMETHING TO 82 BEYOND
HIMSELF.
BY A LYING DOPE FIEND RECITING WORDS/ 107 JOURNE
RECITING DOWSON'S CYNARA TO HER. 134 JOURNE
(HE SWAYS FORWARD TO THE TABLE, RECITING KIPLING.)155 JOURNE
AND STOP RECITING THAT DAMNED MORBID POETRY. 175 JOURNE
RECITING ALWAYS MAKES ME WANT TO CRY ABOUT 405 MARCOM
SOMETHING.
WAS I RECITING POETRY TO YOUR 170 MISBEG
DO YOU THINK FATHER'S A POET BECAUSE HE SHOWS OFF 30 POET
RECITING LORD BYRON'S

RECKLESS
INTO THE EXPRESSION OF A MOCKING, RECKLESS, 260 GGBROW
DEFIANT,
IN A RECKLESS, ARROGANT FASHION. 33 POET

RECKLESSLY
I WOULD GAMBLE RECKLESSLY ON THE CHANCE-- 111 MANSNS
(RECKLESSLY) AND HOW ABOUT YOUR 355 MARCOM

RECKLESSNESS
CHRISTINE SEEMS DRUNK WITH HER OWN DEFIANT 92 ELECTR
RECKLESSNESS)
A CERTAIN DEVIL-MAY-CARE RECKLESSNESS 587 ROPE

RECKON
AND WILL HAVE TILL MY DYIN' DAY, I RECKON. 541 'ILE
(FROWNING) 'BOUT TWO MONTHS, I RECKON, ANNIE, 948 'ILE
WITH FAIR LUCK.
SAID, THERE WAS THE UNKNOWN TO RECKON WITH. 538 DAYS
RECKON, IT'S THE LIKERS 220 DESIRE
(SMILING.) I RECKON YOU'LL DO, JACK. 499 DIFRNT
(WITH A SNIFF) I RECKON YOU DON'T PLAY MUCH 499 DIFRNT
BROTHER WITH--THE KIND YOU KNOWS.
MAKIN' UP FOOLISHNESS FOR A JOKE, I RECKON. 500 DIFRNT
SHE THOUGHT ON'Y THE SKIPPER WAS GOOD ENOUGH FOR 503 DIFRNT
HER, I RECKON.
AND I RECKON HE'S AS LIKELY TO SIN THAT WAY AS ANYSO9 DIFRNT
OTHER MAN.
RECKON I'LL TAKE TO WHALIN' 'STEAD O' FISHIN' 510 DIFRNT
AFTER THIS.
MEN IS MEN THE WORLD OVER, I RECKON. 512 DIFRNT
RECKON HE WAS JOSHIN', WA'N'T HE? 513 DIFRNT
HE WON'T TELL NO MORE TALES, I RECKON. 514 DIFRNT
AND I RECKON SHE WOULDN'T HAVE SEED MY P'INT 515 DIFRNT
ANYHOW, HER BEIN' A NATIVE.
I RECKON THERE AIN'T NO USE SAYIN' NOTHIN' MORE. 517 DIFRNT
(GRIMLY) I RECKON THEY DID, TOO. 535 DIFRNT
(FROWNING--HESITATINGLY) WHY--IT'S--ALL RIGHT, I 535 DIFRNT
RECKON.
YOU'RE NOT THE SAME AS ME, I RECKON. 536 DIFRNT
AND I RECKON I BE OLD-FASHIONED AND SOT IN MY 537 DIFRNT
IDEAS.
AND I RECKON NOW THAT IF YOU PUT A COWARD IN ONE 540 DIFRNT
OF THEM THERE UNIFORMS,
RECKON I OVERPLAYS MY HAND DIS ONCE/ 182 EJUNES
DEY WAS UNLY LITTLE ANIMALS--LITTLE WILD PIGS, I 190 EJUNES
RECKON.

RECKONED
THEY RECKONED GOD WAS EASY. 236 DESIRE
AI' I NEVER RECKONED YEW HAD IT IN YE NUTHER, 249 DESIRE
EPHRAIM.

RECLINE
COUCHES FOR HIM TO RECLINE ON AT EITHER SIDE. 335 LAZARU

RECLINER
THERE IS A STONE BENCH AT CENTER, A RECLINER AT 184 STRANG
RIGHT,
DARRELL SITS ON SIDE OF THE RECLINER AT RIGHT.) 190 STRANG

RECLINES
THE KAAN RECLINES COMFORTABLY ON HIS CUSHIONED 384 MARCOM
BAMBOO THRONE.

RECLINING
MOST OF THE SEAMEN AND FIREMEN ARE RECLINING OR 455 CARIBB
SITTING ON THE HATCH.
MILDRED DOUGLAS AND HER AUNT ARE DISCOVERED 217 HA APE
RECLINING IN DECK CHAIRS.
RECLINING ON THE COUCHES ON THE RIGHT ARE YOUNG 336 LAZARU
WOMEN AND GIRLS.
=INA IS RECLINING ON THE CHAISE LONGUE WATCHING 137 STRANG
GORDON WHO IS SITTING ON THE

RECOGNITION
AND HE AND SHE EXCHANGE A GLANCE OF COMPLETE 244 AHWILD
RECOGNITION.
HE AND MARTHY EXCHANGE NODS OF RECOGNITION. 8 ANNA
LOOKING OVER THE HEAD OF LIFE WITHOUT A SIGN OF 94 ELECTR
RECOGNITION--
(PARRITT TURNS STARTLEDLY AS HUGO PEERS MUZZILY 592 ICEMAN
WITHOUT RECOGNITION AT HIM.
WITHOUT RECOGNITION, WITHOUT EITHER AFFECTION OR 172 JOURNE
ANIMOSITY.)
(TURNS HIS HEAD TO STARE AT SARA WITHOUT 186 MANSNS
RECOGNITION.
A LOOK OF RECOGNITION COMES OVER HER FACE--WITH A 192 MANSNS
REGAL GRACIOUS CONDESCENSION.)
WITH WHAT TERRIBLE RECOGNITION/.... 15 STRANG
(HE LOOKS ABOUT THE PLACE WITH AN AIR OF 496 VOYAGE
RECOGNITION)

RECOGNIZABLE
HE IS HARDLY RECOGNIZABLE AS THE REUBEN OF ACT 457 DYNAMO

RECOGNIZABLY
WHILE RECOGNIZABLY JEWISH, IS A LAZARUS MASK, 285 LAZARU
(THIS VOICE COMES, RECOGNIZABLY THE VOICE OF 365 LAZARU
LAZARUS, YET WITH A STRANGE, FRESH,

RECOGNIZE
SEE IF YOU RECOGNIZE THE HANDWRITING. 267 AHWILD
SHE APPEARS TO RECOGNIZE THESE AND HER FACE LIGHTS 68 ANNA
UP WITH JOY.
(CHUCKLING) I RECOGNIZE ALL THIS, FATHER. 503 DAYS
I RECOGNIZE HIM NOW/... 463 DYNAMO
ONE GETS TO RECOGNIZE EVERYTHING--AND TO SEE 291 GGBROW
NOTHING?
I DID NOT RECOGNIZE YOU. 592 ICEMAN
IT'S STRANGE THE QUEER WAY HE SEEMED TO RECOGNIZE 638 ICEMAN
HIM.
I RECOGNIZE THE SYMPTOMS. 643 ICEMAN
FOR A MOMENT, I DIDN'T RECOGNIZE WHO IT WAS. 75 MANSNS
UNTIL I COULD HARDLY RECOGNIZE MY SON IN THE 97 MANSNS
UNSCRUPULOUS GREEDY TRADER.
HE WOULD RECOGNIZE IT WHEN HE CAME TO IT, 111 MANSNS
CANNOT RECOGNIZE A COMPLETE VICTORY AND A CRUSHING114 MANSNS
DEFEAT WHEN HE SEES THEM?
I DO NOT MEAN--I DO NOT RECOGNIZE MYSELF. 143 MANSNS
I NO LONGER RECOGNIZE THIS AS MY FATHER'S OFFICE--143 MANSNS
OR MYSELF AS MY FATHER'S SON.
BALL, DISGUISED SO THAT NO ONE CAN FAIL TO 390 MARCOM
RECOGNIZE HIM.
I DIDN'T RECOGNIZE YOU BEFORE, YOU'VE GOTTEN SO 391 MARCOM
GROWN UP.
THE ADMIRAL POLO WILL NOT RECOGNIZE YOU. 402 MARCOM
IN SPITE OF THAT, I THOUGHT I COULD RECOGNIZE 427 MARCOM
MAFFEO.
WHAT'S MORE TO THE POINT, WILL HE RECOGNIZE HER? 427 MARCOM
I COULDN'T HARDLY RECOGNIZE HER. 147 MISBEG
HE STARES AT HIS WIFE AND DAUGHTER AS IF HE DID 152 POET
NOT RECOGNIZE THEM.)
HE SHAKES HER HAND OFF ROUGHLY AS IF HE DID NOT 159 POET
RECOGNIZE HER.)
RECOGNIZE IT, CHARLIE, LET ALONE UNDERSTAND IT? 21 STRANG
SHE LOOKS AT MARSDEN FOR A MOMENT STARTLEDLY AS IF 40 STRANG
SHE COULDN'T RECOGNIZE HIM.)
(MEEKLY) I RECOGNIZE MY ARGUMENTS. 81 STRANG
GORDON'S BECOME SO LIKE SAM, NED, YOU WON'T 162 STRANG
RECOGNIZE HIM?

RECOGNIZED
WHEN YOU FIRST CAME BACK FROM FRANCE I NEVER WOULD524 DIFRNT
HAVE RECOGNIZED YOU AS
HE HAD HIRED THE ROOM UNDER ANOTHER NAME, BUT SHE 30 ELECTR
RECOGNIZED HIS DESCRIPTION.
I HARDLY RECOGNIZED HIM, DID YOU? 136 ELECTR
BUT STILL I KNOW DAMNED WELL I RECOGNIZED 624 ICEMAN
SOMETHING ABOUT YOU.
I RECOGNIZED WAS THE BEGINNING OF THE END.= 627 ICEMAN
I KNEW DAMNED WELL JUST BEFORE SHE DIED SHE 147 MISBEG
RECOGNIZED ME.
IT IS AS IF NOW BY A SUDDEN FLASH FROM WITHIN THEY487 WELDED
RECOGNIZED THEMSELVES.

RECOGNIZES
THEN AS HE RECOGNIZES THE OWNER OF THE VOICE, 217 AHWILD
EMMA RECOGNIZES THEM 514 DIFRNT
MRS. FIFE TURNS AND GIVES A STARTLED EXCLAMATION 457 DYNAMO
AS SHE RECOGNIZES HIM.
MAFFEO RECOGNIZES THEM IMMEDIATELY--IN A SWIFT 365 MARCOM
ASIDE TO HIS BROTHER.)

RECOGNIZING
(IGNORES THIS--RECOGNIZING HIM NOW, BURSTS INTO 592 ICEMAN
HIS CHILDISH TEASING GIGGLE)
(RECOGNIZING MARTHA AND MARY) 283 LAZARU
AT LEAST I MAY CLAIM THE MERIT OF RECOGNIZING IT 332 LAZARU
IN OTHERS.
(THEY ALL TURN, AND, RECOGNIZING HER, LAUGH WITH 367 MARCOM
COARSE FAMILIARITY.)

RECOILING
(RECOILING) OH/ 173 ELECTR

RECOILS
IN SPITE OF HER FROZEN SELF-CONTROL, LAVINIA 122 ELECTR
RECOILS BEFORE THIS.
(AS HE RECOILS WITH A SORT OF GUILT--LAUGHINGLY) 308 GGBROW
RATHER IT IS HE WHO RECOILS AFTER EACH COLLISION. 238 HA APE
SHE RECOILS FROM IT, TURNING QUICKLY AWAY FROM 450 WELDED
HIM, VISIBLY SHAKEN.

RECOLLECTION
I KNOW YOU HAVE THE MOST VIVID RECOLLECTION OF HIS494 DAYS
TERRIBLE SIN.
IT STANDS ALONE, LIKE ADAM'S RECOLLECTION OF HIS 47 POET
FALL...
WITHOUT ONE BACKWARD GLANCE OF REGRET OR 49 STRANG
RECOLLECTION.

RECOMMENCES
HE REAPPEARS IMMEDIATELY AND GOES TO THE FRONT 299 GGBROW
DOOR AS THE KNOCKING RECOMMENCES--

RECOMMEND
BUT NOT THE TREATMENT I'D RECOMMEND FOR ANGINA. 71 ELECTR
I ASKED THE HOTEL PROPRIETOR TO RECOMMEND THE 140 JOURNE
BEST--
IT'S YOUR HAPPINESS I'M CONSIDERING WHEN I 27 MISBEG
RECOMMEND YOUR USING YOUR WITS TO
I'M THE DOCTOR AND I HIGHLY RECOMMEND A DROP 134 POET

RECOMMENDED
THERE WAS ANOTHER SANATORIUM THE SPECIALIST 149 JOURNE
RECOMMENDED.
WHAT HENRY RECOMMENDED IS A STRAIGHT BUSINESS 34 MANSNS
DEAL.

RECOMPENSE
I OWE YOU A RECOMPENSE, PERHAPS--FOR AN INJURY, 362 MARCOM
AND IT WILL REMAIN A POIGNANT MEMORY TO RECOMPENSE388 MARCOM
HER
BY WAY OF RECOMPENSE. AS I MIGHT HAVE KNOWN HE 82 POET
WOULD.
«RENDER UNTO THEM A RECOMPENSE, O LORD, ACCORDING 584 ROPE
TO THE WORK OF THEIR HANDS.»

RECONCILE
HE COULDN'T RECONCILE HIM WITH HIS PARENTS' FAITH.510 DAYS
IF I COULD RECONCILE MYSELF TO BEING THE 70 POET
PROPRIETOR OF A TAWDRY TAVERN,

RECONCILED
HAIRY HANDS, HE IS LOUSY AND RECONCILED TO BEING 574 ICEMAN
SO.
I'D BECOME SO RECONCILED TO NINA'S LOVE FOR HIM-- 9 STRANG

RECONCILEMENT
AND THEN TO HEAR OF YOUR RECONCILEMENT--BUT IT IS 176 MANSNS
MY DEAREST WISH--

RECONCILIATION
IT NEEDED ONLY YOUR RECONCILIATION TO COMPLETE MY 67 MANSNS
HAPPINESS

RECONSIDER
WHETHER YOU WANT TO RECONSIDER YOUR DECISION OR 203 AHWILD
NOT.

RECONSIDERED
I HAVE RECONSIDERED/ 425 MARCOM

RECORD
(AS THE RECORD STOPS--SWITCHES OFF THE MACHINE) 520 DIFRNT
(IADA SAID SHE'D PUT A RECORD ON THE VICTROLA AS 424 DYNAMO
SOON AS SHE WAS FREE...
(FROM THE FIRE HOUSE COMES THE SOUND OF A VICTROLA426 DYNAMO
STARTING A JAZZ RECORD.)
GOSH, HOW LONG IS IT SINCE I PUT ON THAT 430 DYNAMO
RECORDS...
ALL THE PIOUS FOLKS IN THIS TOWN THINK I'VE A BAD 434 DYNAMO
RECORD BEHIND ME--
(EAGERLY) I'VE GOT THAT RECORD--JOHN MCCORMACK. 262 GGBROW
AND PROVE MY BRILLIANT RECORD IN LAW SCHOOL WAS NO679 ICEMAN
FLASH IN THE PAN.
HE SAID IT HAD A RECORD AS GOOD AS ANY PLACE IN 149 JOURNE
THE COUNTRY.
(THEN SUDDENLY--CONSOLED) WELL, IT'S A NEW 359 MARCOM
WORLD'S RECORD, ANYWAY.
I COULD PROMISE YOU A RECORD PASSAGE, 398 MARCOM
IF IT WASN'T FOR HIS FINE RECORD FOR BRAVERY IN 12 POET
BATTLE.

RECORDING
AS RESTLESS, PRYING, RECORDING INSTRUMENTS. 39 STRANG

RECORDS
(TURNING TO HER) SAY, YOU'RE A REGULAR FELLER-- 520 DIFRNT
GETTIN' THEM RECORDS FOR ME.

RECOVER
(HE BEGINS TO RECOVER. 268 DESIRE
THE YOUNGER DRAFTSMAN IS THE FIRST TO RECOVER.) 318 GGBROW
(WHO HAS BEEN THE LEAST IMPRESSED BY HICKEY'S TALK626 ICEMAN
AND IS THE FIRST TO RECOVER)
(THE FIRST TO RECOVER--BEWILDEREDLY) 352 MARCOM
(HE HAS HAD ENOUGH PICK-ME-UPS TO RECOVER FROM 37 MISBEG
MORNING-AFTER NAUSEA
(BEGINNING TO RECOVER HIS APLOMB--SHORTLY.) 117 POET

RECOVERED
(RECOVERED NOW--STARING AT HIM--QUIETLY) 512 DAYS
(HAS RECOVERED HIS POISE AS SHE HAS WEAKENED-- 113 MANSNS
CURTLY.)
AND EVEN IF YOU HAD COMPLETELY RECOVERED FROM YOUR 17 STRANG
NERVOUS BREAKDOWN,

RECOVERING
(THEN RECOVERING HERSELF--TARTLY) 222 AHWILD
(RECOVERING FROM HER MIRTH--CHUCKLING SCORNFULLY) 11 ANNA
(RECOVERING, ANGRY AT HIMSELF AND FURIOUS WITH 559 DAYS
JOHN--
(RECOVERING HIMSELF--QUIETLY) 559 DAYS
FATHER BAIRD, RECOVERING FROM THE PUSH WHICH HAS 560 DAYS
SENT HIM BACK AGAINST THE
(RECOVERING FROM HIS ASTONISHMENT--SAVAGELY) 260 DESIRE
(RECOVERING HIS COMPOSURE--AND WITH IT HIS MALICE)181 EJONES
(THEN RECOVERING HIMSELF--SCORNFULLY) 204 EJONES

RECOVERING (CONT'D.)
(RECOVERING HERSELF--CURTLY) 12 ELECTR
(STUNG INTO RECOVERING ALL HIS OLD FUMING 718 ICEMAN
TRUCULENCE)
(RECOVERING HERSELF--RESOLUTELY) 386 MARCOM
(RECOVERING A BI--WITH A SICKLY SMILE) 415 MARCOM
(RECOVERING HIMSELF) FINE/ 120 MISBEG
(RECOVERING A LITTLE FROM HER CONFUSION.) 73 POET
(THE« RECOVERING--COMMISERATINGLY) 59 STRANG
(THE« RECOVERING HERSELF, SCORNFULLY) 98 STRANG
(RECOVERING HIS GOOD NATURE--WITH A GRIN, TAKING 164 STRANG
HIS ARM)
(QUICKLY RECOVERING HERSELF--IN A COLD, HARD 463 WELDED
VOICE) THAT'S--DEAD/

RECOVERS
AS THEY DO SO, LUCY RECOVERS HER POISE AND CLLLS 525 DAYS
TO HIM.)
BUT CHRISTINE QUICKLY RECOVERS HERSELF AND HER AIR 16 CLECTR
RESUMES ITS DISDAINFUL
CHRISTINE RECOVERS HERSELF.) 42 ELECTR
IMMEDIATELY RECOVERS HER POISE--TO ORIN, AS IF 77 ELECTR
LAVINIA HADN'T SPOKEN)
(ORIN RECOVERS FROM HIS SPASM WITH A START 297 GGBROW
HE WAS STILL WEAK, AS ONE WHO RECOVERS FROM A LONG309 LAZARU
ILLNESS--
(RECOVERS HERSELF) HE COULDN'T, INDEED. 43 MISBEG
(IN A FLASH MELODY RECOVERS AND IS THE LEERING 179 POET
PEASANT AGAIN.)

RECOVERY
UH, HE'S ON THE ROAD TO RECOVERY NOW, 28 POET

RECREATE
THEN LET IT BE MY PRIDE AS MAN TC RECREATE THE GOD352 LAZARU
IN ME/«

RECREATION
AND YET, BY STAYING HOME AND RESTING AND FINDING 16 STRANG
HEALTHY OUTDOOR RECREATION

RECRUIT
BUT SHE IS A FAIRLY RECENT RECRUIT TO THE RANKS, 236 AHWILD

RECTANGULAR
IS A RECTANGULAR SPACE WITH BENCHES ON THE THREE 257 GGBROW
SIDES.

RECURRENCE
BUT THERE IS ORDER IN IT, RHYTHM, A MECHANICAL 223 HA APE
REGULATED RECURRENCE, A TEMPO.
AND THAT'S OBVIOUSLY BECAUSE I AM STRICKEN WITH A 85 STRANG
RECURRENCE OF AN OLD DESIRE...

RECURRENT
THE RECURRENT DREAD THAT SHE MIGHT DIE AND HE 536 DAYS
WOULD BE LEFT ALONE AGAIN,

RECURRING
THE SOUL OF THE RECURRING SEASONS, 307 LAZARU

RED
HER EYES ARE RED FROM WEEPING AND HER FACE DRAWN 534 'ILE
AND PALE.
POETRY'S HIS RED MEAT NOWADAYS, I THINK--LOVE-- 193 AHWILD
POETRY--
THE WALLS ARE PAPERED IN A SOMBER BROWN AND DARK- 210 AHWILD
RED DESIGN.
WHOSE LIPS ARE FIREWORKS, WHOSE EYES ARE RED-HOT 228 AHWILD
SPARKS--
WELL, AS I WAS SAYING, RED AND I WENT SWIMMING 229 AHWILD
THAT DAY.
RED SKIN--HIS FATHER KEPT A BLACKSMITH SHOP WHERE 229 AHWILD
THE UNION MARKET IS NOW--
WE KIDS CALLED HIM RED BECAUSE HE HAD THE DARNDEST229 AHWILD
REDDEST CROP OF HAIR--
RED WAS FOURTEEN, BIGGER AND OLDER THAN ME, I WAS 229 AHWILD
ONLY TWELVE--
I NEVER GO DOWN TO THAT BEACH BUT WHAT IT CALLS TO229 AHWILD
MIND THE DAY I AND RED SISK
WELL, AS I WAS SAYING, THERE WAS I AND RED, 230 AHWILD
WHY DIDN'T YOU LET THAT RED DROWN, ANYWAY, NATS 230 AHWILD
AND I TURNED AND THERE WAS RED, HIS FACE ALL 230 AHWILD
PINCHED AND WHITE.
I SUPPOSE YOU'LL HAVE HIM OUT WITH YOU PAINTING 269 AHWILD
THE TOWN RED THE NEXT THING!
NOT IF I'D HAD TO CRAWL OVER RED-HOT COALS/ 287 AHWILD
HE IS A BOYISH, RED-CHEEKED, RATHER GOOD-LOOKING 4 ANNA
YOUNG FELLOW OF TWENTY OR SO.)
WEATHER-BEATEN, RED FACE FROM WHICH HIS LIGHT BLUE 5 ANNA
EYES PEER SHORTSIGHTEDLY.
HER JOWLY, MUTTLED FACE, WITH ITS THICK RED NOSE, 7 ANNA
WITH RED GOWNS ON THEM AND PAINT ON THEIR GRINNING 60 ANNA
MUGS.
THERE IS A RED BRUISE ON HIS FOREHEAD OVER ONE OF 68 ANNA
HIS EYES.
AN OAK DINING-ROOM TABLE WITH A RED COVER. 93 BEYONU
THE WALLS ARE PAPERED A DARK RED WITH A SCROLLY- 93 BEYONU
FIGURED PATTERN.
YOU KNOW FANNY THE BARMAID AT THE RED STORK IN 489 CARDIF

CARDIFF,
WITH A PALE, SAD FACE FRAMED IN A MASS OF DARK RED562 CROSS
HAIR.
(SLOWLY) A RED AND A GREEN LIGHT AT THE MAINMAST-569 CROSS
HEAD,
(SLOWLY) A RED AND A GREEN AT THE MAINMAST-HEAD. 569 CROSS
WITH THE RED AND THE GREEN SIGNAL-LIGHTS. 576 CROSS
INTO A RED-HOT ARTICLE OF YOURS DENOUNCING 497 DAYS
CAPITALISM OR RELIGION OR SOMETHING.
YER HEARTS AIR PINK, NOT RED/ 251 DESIRE
HE HAS EVIDENTLY BEEN WASHING UP, FOR HIS FACE IS 301 DIFRNT
RED AND SHINY.
WITH A GREAT, RED, WEATHER-BEATEN FACE SEAMED BY 513 DIFRNT
SUN WRINKLES.
HER FACE IS FROZEN INTO AN EXPRESSIONLESS MASK, 547 DIFRNT
HER EYES ARE RED-RIMMED,
THE BUILDING IS RED BRICK. 473 DYNAMO

RED

RED (CONT'D.)
A DEEP BUT NARROW COMPARTMENT WITH RED BRICK 483 DYNAMO WALLS.
THE DYNAMO ROOM IS HIGH AND WIDE WITH RED BRICK 486 DYNAMO WALLS.
A RED BANDANA HANDKERCHIEF COVERING ALL BUT A FEW 173 EJONES STRAY WISPS OF WHITE HAIR.
HIS LITTLE WASHY-BLUE EYES ARE RED-RIMMED AND DART174 EJONES ABOUT HIM LIKE A FERRET'S.
AND NATIVE RUM HAS PAINTED HIS POINTED NOSE TO A 174 EJONES STARTLING RED.
HIS PANTS ARE BRIGHT RED WITH A LIGHT BLUE STRIPE 175 EJONES DOWN THE SIDE.
HIS BODY IS STAINED ALL OVER A BRIGHT RED. 200 EJONES
AND WE'D SEE THE MOUNTAINS OF SOUTH AMERICY WID 214 HA APE THE RED FIRE OF THE SETTING SUN.
DAT WAS PRETTY, TOO--ALL RED AND PINK AND GREEN. 252 HA APE
IN A SHADE OF BLUE THAT SETS TEETH ON EDGE, AND A 9 HUGHIE GAY RED AND BLUE FOURLARD TIE.
HE CARRIES A PANAMA HAT AND MOPS HIS FACE WITH A 9 HUGHIE RED AND BLUE SILK HANDKERCHIEF.
HIS FACE'D BE RED AND HE'D LOOK LIKE HE WANTED TO 16 HUGHIE CRAWL UNDER THE DESK AND HIDE.
A BIG HORSESHOE OF RED ROSES/ 31 HUGHIE
HE WAS CAUGHT RED-HANDED AND THROWN OFF THE FORCE.594 ICEMAN
THE ELECTRIC-LIGHT BRACKETS ARE ADORNED WITH 629 ICEMAN FESTOONS OF RED RIBBON.
AND I'LL SOON BE RIDIN' AROUND IN A BIG RED 653 ICEMAN AUTOMOBILE--
SUNBLEACHED TO RED AT THE ENDS, BRUSHED STRAIGHT 20 JOURNE BACK FROM IT.
WITH A RED-CHEEKED COMELY FACE, BLACK HAIR AND 51 JOURNE BLUE EYES--
BECAUSE I WAS AFRAID MY EYES AND NOSE WOULD BE 105 JOURNE RED.
(COQUETTISHLY.) I GUESS MY EYES AND NOSE COULDN'T105 JOURNE HAVE BEEN RED, AFTER ALL.
SURELY THE KISSES OF HER BOUGHT RED MOUTH WERE 134 JOURNE SWEET.
HIS COMPLEXION IS THE RED-BROWN OF RICH EARTH, 288 LAZARU
HIS MOUTH ALSO IS CHILDISH, THE RED LIPS SOFT AND 299 LAZARU FEMININE IN OUTLINE.
OLIVE-COLORED WITH THE RED OF BLOOD SMOLDERING 336 LAZARU THROUGH, WITH GREAT, DARK,
IF IS ALL A RED BLOT/ 355 LAZARU
I USED TO SEE THEIR BLOOD DANCE IN RED SPECKS 355 LAZARU BEFORE MY EYES
PURPLE AND RED AND GOLD MINGLED WITH THE DEEP 1 MANSNS GREEN OF THE CONIFERS.
PAINTED A CHINESE LACQUER RED. 25 MANSNS
WITH A ROUND RED FACE, AND SHREWD LITTLE GREY 29 MANSNS EYES.
AND THE UPPER PART OF THE ARCHED LACQUER-RED DOOR 95 MANSNS
YOUR EYES ARE RED FROM WEEPING AND YOUR NOSE IS 401 MARCOM RED.
MY EYES SHALL BE EVER RED WITH WEEPING, MY HEART 405 MARCOM BLEEDING.
LIKE A RED EMBER FLARING UP FOR THE LAST TIME 413 MARCOM
FIRST COME THE MUSICIANS, NINE IN NUMBER, MEN IN 433 MARCOM NUBES OF BRIGHT RED.
A SOUR AFTERTASTE IN YOUR MOUTH OF DAGO RED INK/ 140 MISBEG
HER RED HANDS ARE KNOTTED BY RHEUMATISM. 20 POET
AND RED-RIMMED LITTLE PIG'S EYES. 51 POET
AND THE END WAS, I RAN FROM THE ROOM, BLUSHING AS 65 POET RED AS A BEET--
FRAMED BY THICK, WAVY, RED-BROWN HAIR. 67 POET
AIN'T HE THE LUNATIC, SITTIN' LIKE A PLAY-ACTOR IN100 POET HIS RED COAT.
HE'D OUGHT TO BE SHAMED HE IVIR WORE THE BLOODY 100 POET RED AV ENGLAND.
THE GRAND GENTLEMAN IN HIS RED LIVERY AV BLOODY 138 POET CWLAND.
AND SIMON LIKED MY COSTUME, IF YOU DON'T, ALTHOUGH143 POET HE TURNED RED AS A BEET WHEN
I GOT AS RED AS HE WAS. 144 POET
HIS FACE IS BATTERED, NOSE RED AND SWOLLEN, LIPS 151 POET CUT AND PUFFED.
I'LL BURY HIS MAJOR'S DAMNED RED LIVERY AV BLOODY 169 POET ENGLAND DEEP IN THE GROUND AND
WE'LL JUST SHOVE THIS INTO THE STOVE TILL IT'S 600 ROPE RED-HOT.
HIS FACE IS FRESH AND RED-CHEEKED, HANDSOME IN A 28 STRANG BOYISH FASHION.
THE FLOOR IS CARPETED IN A SMEARY BROWN WITH A 48 STRANG DARK RED DESIGN BLURRED INTO IT.
LIKE A BRUTAL, HAIRY HAND, RAW AND RED, AT MY 99 STRANG THROAT....
(HE STOPS, TRYING TO CONTROL HIMSELF, PANTING, HIS163 STRANG FACE RED.)
HIS FACE IS RED AND BLOATED, 493 VOYAGE
WID THE BIG RED NOSE AV YE ALL SCREWED UP IN A 498 VOYAGE KNOT.

RED'S
I'VE TAKEN DOWN THE DISTANCE EVERY TIME YOU'VE 230 AHWILD SAVED RED'S LIFE FOR THIRTY YEARS

REDDEN
LOOK AT HER REDDEN UP, WILL YCS 250 DESIRE

REDDER
HER MOUTH SEEMS LARGER, ITS FULL LIPS REDDER, 139 MANSNS

REDDEST
WE KIDS CALLED HIM RED BECAUSE HE HAD THE DARNDEST229 AHWILD REDDEST CROP OF HAIR--
HE WAS BIGGER 'N' OLDER THAN ME AND HAD THE 231 AHWILD DARNDEST REDDEST CROP OF HAIR BUT I

REDDISH
THE EYES SMALL AND BLUE-GRAY, THE REDDISH HAIR 422 DYNAMO GRIZZLED AND BUSHY,

REDDISH (CONT'D.)
HIS JAW IS STUBBORN, HIS THICK HAIR CURLY AND 422 DYNAMO REDDISH-BLOND.
HIS FAIR SKIN IS SUNBURNED A REDDISH, FRECKLED 19 JOURNE TAN.
IT WAS A RARE SHADE OF REDDISH BROWN AND SO LONG 28 JOURNE IT CAME DOWN BELOW MY KNEES.
A WIDE DOOR IS FLUNG OPEN AND A STREAM OF REDDISH 331 LAZARU LIGHT COMES OUT AGAINST WHICH

REDEEM
IF YC DON'T HEV A SON T' REDEEM YE.... 238 DESIRE

REDEEMER
REDEEMER AND SAVIOR/ 299 LAZARU
REDEEMER AND SAVIOR/ 299 LAZARU
HASTEN, REDEEMER/ 302 LAZARU
HASTEN, REDEEMER/ 302 LAZARU
HE COMES THE REDEEMER AND SAVIOR/ 303 LAZARU
REDEEMER/ 304 LAZARU
REDEEMER/ 307 LAZARU
REDEEMER/ 307 LAZARU
WITH HIS INCORRUPTIBLE REDEEMER, BUT HE WAS TOO 83 POET UNIMPORTANT.

REDEYE
JEES, MIXIN' CHAMPAGNE WID HARRY'S REDEYE WILL 658 ICEMAN KNOCK YUH PARALYZED/
JEES, WOULD I LIKE TO GET A QUART OF DIS REDEYE 671 ICEMAN UNDER MY BELT/
I SEE YOU BEEN HITTIN' DE REDEYE, TOO. 699 ICEMAN
BUT DOCTOR HARDY WAS RIGHT WHEN HE TOLD YOU TO CUT 55 JOURNE OUT THE REDEYE.

REDOUBT
HERE IS OUR REDOUBT WITH THE FOURTH DIVISION AND 96 POET THE GUARDS.

REDUCE
I REALLY OUGHT TO REDUCE. 14 JOURNE

REDUCING
HE'LL HAVE NO TALK OF REDUCING. 14 JOURNE

REEF
NOT A REEF IN 'EM--MAKIN' PORT, BOY, AS I SWORE 569 CROSS
SHE MUST--
AND ALWAYS THE SURF ON THE BARRIER REEF 24 ELECTR
THE SURF ON THE BARRIER REEF SINGING A CROON IN 112 ELECTR YOUR EARS LIKE A LULLABY/
THE TRADE WIND IN THE COCO PALMS--THE SURF ON THE 147 ELECTR REEF--

REEK
YOU REEK OF WHISKEY/ 72 POET

REEL
PLAYING A REEL AND THE STAMP OF DANCING FEET. 133 POET
(IN THE BAR, RILEY STARTS PLAYING A REEL ON HIS 182 POET PIPES

REELING
WHICH SENDS HIM REELING BACK AGAINST THE WALL) 477 WELDED

REELS
YOU ARE LIKE A CLOUD, YOU CAN FLY, YOUR MIND REELS300 LAZARU WITH LAUGHTER,
AND REELS AWAY. 101 MISBEG

REFER
(READING) =I REFER TO THAT DEVIL'S BREW OF 242 HA APE RASCALS, JAILBIRDS.
I REFER NOW TO THE DEAL FOR THE RAILROAD YOU ARE 71 MANSNS TO CONCLUDE THIS MORNING.
I REFER TO THE BREEDING OF WORMS/ 431 MARCOM
IN SHORT, I REFER TO YOUR GOOD NEIGHBOR, T. 47 MISBEG STEDMAN HARDER.

REFERRING
I WAS, PERHAPS WRONGLY, REFERRING TO MRS. MANNON. 70 ELECTR
(IN BLANK DENIAL NOW.) ANYWAY, I DON'T KNOW WHAT 93 JOURNE YOU'RE REFERRING TO.

REFILLED
THOLUS OUT HIS GOBLET TO BE REFILLED. 314 LAZARU

REFILLS
HOGAN REFILLS HIS PIPE, PRETENDING HE DOESN'T 36 MISBEG NOTICE TYRONE APPROACHING.
CREGAN DRAINS HIS GLASS AND REFILLS IT.) 100 POET

REFINED
HIS FEATURES ARE DELICATE AND REFINED, 81 BEYOND
QUITE FOREIGN TO THE GENERAL'S, AND HIS CHIN IS A 73 ELECTR REFINED,
REFINED IN THEM BY NOBILITY OF BLOOD BUT AT THE 312 LAZARU SAME TIME WITH STRENGTH
HIS FACE, PREPOSSESSING IN SPITE OF ITS TOO-SMALL, 6 STRANG OVER-REFINED FEATURES,

REFINEMENT
AND SHE RETAINS A CERTAIN REFINEMENT OF MOVEMENT 94 BEYOND AND EXPRESSION FOREIGN TO THE

REFLECT
THE WINDOWS OF THE LOWER FLOOR REFLECT THE SUN'S 5 ELECTR RAYS IN A RESENTFUL GLARE.
REFLECT THE SUN IN A SMOULDERING STARE, AS OF 169 ELECTR BROODING REVENGEFUL EYES.
YOU REFLECT CREDIT ON ME. 164 JOURNE
I WISHED TIME TO REFLECT ON A FURTHER ASPECT OF 112 POET THIS PROPOSED MARRIAGE.

REFLECTED
HER LARGE EYES DREAMY WITH THE REFLECTED STIRRING 278 GGBROW OF PROFOUND INSTINCTS.
THEIR BILLOWING RISE AND FALL IS REFLECTED ON THE 363 LAZARU MASKED FACES OF THE MULTITUDE
AS THE ACTION PROGRESSES THIS REFLECTED 577 ROPE
I HAVE REFLECTED AND I AM GOING/ 16 STRANG
SURELY, YOU CAN'T HAVE REFLECTED/ 16 STRANG

REFLECTING
A LAMP REFLECTING DOWNWARD HAS BEEN FIXED AT THE 326 LAZARU TOP OF THE CROSS TO LIGHT UP AN
WELL, I HAVE BEEN REFLECTING, WATCHING YOU AND 112 POET EXAMINING YOUR CONDUCT.

REFLECTION

HE IS DRESSED IN PREP SCHOOL REFLECTION OF THE 193 AHWILD COLLEGE STYLE OF ARTHUR.)
(AS CHRIS REMAINS SUNK IN GLOOMY REFLECTION) 9 ANNA
THE ONLY LIGHT IS THE REFLECTION OF THE DAWN, 564 DAYS WHICH,
SHE HURRIES ON SO AS NOT TO GIVE HIM TIME FOR 40 ELECTR REFLECTION)
WITH THE REFLECTION OF MANY SHADED LAMPS, 326 LAZARU
DANCE IN THE FLARING REFLECTION OF THE FLAMES 368 LAZARU
AND IS GONE LEAVING CALM AND REFLECTION. 388 MARCOM
HE CATCHES HIS REFLECTION IN THE MIRROR ON THE 43 POET WALL AT LEFT AND STOPS BEFORE IT,
SEEKING THE SATISFYING REASSURANCE OF HIS 67 POET REFLECTION THERE.
IT'S PROBABLY A REFLECTION OF HER OWN SILLY FIXED 38 STRANG IDEA ABOUT HIM.

REFLECTIONS

(THEN AS IF TO DISTRACT HIS MIND FROM THESE 93 ELECTR REFLECTIONS,
(THE FLAMING REFLECTIONS IN THE BANKED, MASSED 365 LAZARU FACES DANCE MADLY
THERE IS THE BLARE OF A TRUMPET, THE REFLECTIONS 417 MARCOM OF LATERNS AND TORCHES,

REFLECTIVE

(WITH A SURPRISED, REFLECTIVE AIR.) 21 HUGHIE
(HER MANNER BECOMES REFLECTIVE, 81 POET

REFLECTIVELY

MARTHA SIPS WHAT IS LEFT OF HER SCHOONER 13 ANNA REFLECTIVELY.
HE PULLS ON HIS PIPE REFLECTIVELY) 17 MISBEG
(SLOWLY--COOLLY AND REFLECTIVELY) 14 STRANG

REFORM

LILY, WHY DON'T YOU CHANGE YOUR MIND AND MARRY SID213 AHWILD AND REFORM HIM.
YOU CAN DO A LOT WITH ME FOR FIVE DOLLARS--BUT YOU243 AHWILD CAN'T REFORM ME, SEE.
WHY DON'T YOU REFORM 243 AHWILD
EXCEPT DURING THE FLEETING ALARMS OF REFORM 571 ICEMAN AGITATION,
BUT HE GOT TOO GREEDY AND WHEN THE USUAL REFORM 594 ICEMAN INVESTIGATION CAME
HE'S GOT HIS REFORM WAVE GOIN' STRONG DIS MORNIN'/665 ICEMAN
I'D WANT TO REFORM AND MEAN IT, 712 ICEMAN
SURE, YOU'RE STRONG ENOUGH TO REFORM HIM, 29 MISBEG
I WON'T WASTE WORDS TRYING TO REFORM A BORN CROOK.62 MISBEG
DON'T GROW FATALISTIC--JUST WHEN I WAS ABOUT TO 446 WELDED PROPOSE REFORM.

REFORMED

SID'S A REFORMED CHARACTER SINCE HE'S BEEN ON THE 190 AHWILD PAPER IN WATERBURY.

REFORMIN'

SHE'S REFORMIN' YOU ALREADY. 24 ANNA

REFORMING

OR LIE TO YOURSELVES ABOUT REFORMING TOMORROW5 705 ICEMAN

REFRAIN

BORNE ON THE WIND THE MELANCHOLY REFRAIN OF THE 102 ELECTR CAPSTAN CHANTY *SHENANDOAH*,
(A WHOLE CHORUS OF VOICES HAS TAKEN UP THIS 211 HA APE REFRAIN, STAMPING ON THE FLOOR,
ROCHE, AND O'DOWD, AND ALL BELLOW THE REFRAIN, 102 POET *OH, MODIDEROO, AROO, AROO/*

REFRAINS

AND TACTFULLY REFRAINS FROM ALL QUESTIONS.) 296 AHWILD

REFRESH

(IRONICALLY) NO DOUBT HE COMES TO REFRESH YOUR 386 MARCOM HUMOR.

REFRESHING

I DROWSED OFF AND HAD A NICE REFRESHING NAP. 68 JOURNE

REFUGE

THE WOMEN SHRIEK AND TAKE REFUGE ON TOP OF THE 472 CARIBE HATCH,
(THEN HE TURNS AWAY AGAIN IN CONFUSION AND TAKES 143 ELECTR REFUGE IN A BURST OF TALK)
SHE HAS HIDDEN DEEPER WITHIN HERSELF AND FOUND 97 JOURNE REFUGE AND RELEASE IN A DREAM

REFUSAL

OR TAKE YOUR SILENCE AS A REFUSAL/ 333 LAZARU
YOUR REFUSAL WOULD INSULT HIM, 386 MARCOM
WHEN A REFUSAL LIKE THAT WOULD HAVE RUINED MY 203 STRANG CONFIDENCE FOR SIX MONTHS/))

REFUSE

I'M GOING TO REFUSE TO PRINT YOUR DAMNED AD AFTER 203 AHWILD TOMORROW
DO YOU MEAN TO SAY YOU REFUSE TO TELL YOUR OWN 446 DYNAMO MOTHER,
SUPPOSE I REFUSE/ 33 ELECTR
HE DRAWS HIS HAND BACK AS IF HE WERE GOING TO 637 ICEMAN REFUSE--
I REFUSE TO BE INDEBTED--TO YOU--FOR ANYTHING. 58 MANSNS
DID YOU THINK I WOULD REFUSE TO SAVE YOU FROM 58 MANSNS BEING RUINED8
BUT HOW DO I KNOW YOU MIGHTN'T REFUSE TO SIGN 146 MANSNS AFTER--S
EVEN NOW I CAN REFUSE YOUR HAND TO ARGHUN. 400 MARCOM
I COULD NOT REFUSE MY CONSENT. 115 POET
I ABSOLUTELY REFUSE... 12 STRANG
AND YET I DID REFUSE/ 19 STRANG
WHY DID I REFUSE8 19 STRANG
I'LL ADVISE PRESTON TO REFUSE IT/ 192 STRANG
HE HAS NO RIGHT TO REFUSE/... 192 STRANG
AND I REFUSE TO GIVE UP HIS FRIENDSHIP FOR YOUR 456 WELDED SILLY WHIMS.

REFUSED

IF I'D REFUSED, IT WOULD ONLY HAVE MADE EVERYTHING286 AHWILD WORSE.
NEVER REFUSED A DRINK TO ANYONE NEEDED IT BAD IN 582 ICEMAN MY LIFE/

REFUSED (CONT'D.)

I'VE REFUSED TO BECOME A USEFUL MEMBER OF ITS 591 ICEMAN SOCIETY.
AT LAST SHE SAID SHE REFUSED TO TOUCH IT ANY MORE 115 JOURNE OR SHE MIGHT SPOIL IT,
NO HOME EXCEPT THIS SUMMER DUMP IN A PLACE SHE 141 JOURNE HATES AND YOU'VE REFUSED EVEN TO
CAESAR REFUSED TO LET THEM ENTER THE CITY. 316 LAZARU
WE SHOULD FEEL VERY OFFENDED IF YOU REFUSED US, 51 MANSNS MRS. HARFORD.
IT'S JUST THAT YOU STUBBORNLY REFUSED TO BELIEVE 110 MANSNS THAT
IF I REFUSED HIM, HE'D ONLY BUY ANOTHER WOMAN. 133 MANSNS
SHE NEVER REFUSED TO HEED MY ADVICE FOR HER 424 MARCOM WELFARE
AND IF THERE WAS AN OFFER, JIM'S REFUSED IT, AND 32 MISBEG THAT ENDS IT.
BY THE ETERNAL, IF HE'D REFUSED, I'D HAVE--/ 60 POET
IT'S YOU REFUSED. 174 POET
I'VE REFUSED TO BELIEVE IT, 10 STRANG
THAT HAPPINESS WAS CALLING ME, NEVER TO CALL AGAIN 19 STRANG IF I REFUSED/
I REFUSED HIM, CHARLIE. 197 STRANG

REFUSES

SHE STILL REFUSES TO NOTICE HIM AND HE IS FORCED 89 POET TO SPEAK.
REFUSES TO BE SERIOUS/. 6 STRANG

REFUSING

IF YOU KEPT ON REFUSING TO REST OR TAKE 556 DAYS NOURISHMENT.
(HAZEL FLUSHES GUILTILY, BUT REFUSING TO LIE, SAYS163 ELECTR NOTHING.
(REFUSING TO ADMIT ANYTHING TO HIS BROTHER YET-- 64 JOURNE WEAKLY DEFIANT.)
BY REFUSING ME WHEN I ASK YOU TO MARRY ME/ 196 STRANG

REG'LAR

I AIN'T GOT NO MISSUS--REG'LAR MARRIED, I MEANS. 463 CARIBE
I'M REG'LAR, 268 HA APE
YOU'RE REG'LAR, 253 HA APE
=DE BULL MOOSERS IS DE ON'Y REG'LAR GUYS,= ONE GUY612 ICEMAN SAYS.
(SOOTHINGLY) WE KNOW YUH GOT A REG'LAR JOB. 613 ICEMAN
ANYWAY, WE WOULDN'T KEEP NO PIMP, LIKE WE WAS 613 ICEMAN REG'LAR OLD WHORES.
=IF WE'RE WHORES WE GOTTA MIGHT TO HAVE A REG'LAR 669 ICEMAN PIMP
YUH DON'T WANTA SEE ME GET MARRIED AND SETTLE DOWNh71 ICEMAN LIKE A REG'LAR GUY/
WELL, I SAY WE STOP AT DE FOIST REG'LAR DUMP 682 ICEMAN
I WAS TINKIN' HOW YOU WAS BUT' REG'LAR GUYS, 702 ICEMAN
ON'Y A BIT NOW AN' AGEN WHEN THERE AIN'T NO 494 VOYAGE REG'LAR TRADE.

REG'LATE

AND I AIN'T PRETENDIN' I CAN REG'LATE LOVE FOR 102 BEYOND YOUNG FOLKS.

REGAIN

(THE FIRST TO REGAIN PRESENCE OF MIND--WITH A 261 AHWILD GRIN)
(TRYING TO REGAIN HER ASCENDANCY--SEDUCTIVELY) 229 DESIRE
THEN HE ASKS, WITH AN ATTEMPT TO REGAIN HIS MOST 184 EJONES CASUAL MANNER)
AND NOW ATTEMPTS TO REGAIN A BRISK, PROFESSIONAL 30 MANSNS AIR.
TO REGAIN A SOUND POSITION BY MAKING A QUICK 32 MANSNS PROFIT IN WESTERN LANDS.
REVEALED TO HIM THAT THERE WAS A WAY IN WHICH HE 110 MANSNS MIGHT REGAIN HIS LUST KINGDOM.
SHUDDERING WITH THE EFFORT TO REGAIN SOME SORT OF 128 POET POISE.
IN HER FIGHT TO REGAIN CONTROL OF HER NERVES SHE 26 STRANG HAS OVER-STRIVEN AFTER THE COOL

REGAINED

(WHO HAS REGAINED HIS COMPOSURE--SHEEPISHLY) 29 ANNA
(WHO HAS REGAINED CONTROL OVER HIMSELF) 107 BEYOND
(THE DYNAMO'S PURR HAS REGAINED ITS ACCUSTOMED 489 DYNAMO PITCH NOW.
REGAINED THE SELF-CONFIDENT SPIRIT OF ITS YOUTH, 303 GGBROW HER EYES SHINE WITH HAPPINESS.)

REGAINING

(REGAINING HIS COURAGE) TO THE CIVIL WITH ALL 55 ANNA OTHER REASONS THEN.
(REGAINING COMMAND OF HERSELF--SLOWLY) 21 ELECTR
(HURRIEDLY REGAINING HER PLAYFUL TONE) 103 MISBEG
(REGAINING CONTROL--SHAMEFACEDLY) 170 STRANG

REGAINS

BUT HE SOON REGAINS HIS APLOMB.) 254 AHWILD
BUT HE INSTANTLY REGAINS HIS IRON CONTROL) 516 DIFRNT
(SHE DRIES HER EYES AND REGAINS HER COMPOSURE. 537 DIFRNT
AND REGAINS HER TENSE CONTROL OF HERSELF.) 71 ELECTR
CHRISTINE STARTS AND IMMEDIATELY BY AN EFFORT OF 78 ELECTR WILL REGAINS CONTROL OVER
REGAINS THE QUALITY OF STRANGE DETACHMENT-- 64 JOURNE CALMLY.)
KUBLAI REGAINS CONTROL OVER HIS WEAKNESS AND RISES435 MARCOM TO HIS FEET--

REGAL

A LOOK OF RECOGNITION COMES OVER HER FACE--WITH A 192 MANSNS REGAL GRACIOUS CONDESCENSION.)

REGALE

BUT FIRST, BEFORE WE REGALE OURSELVES WITH YOUR 431 MARCOM CHEER,
IF YOU REGALE ALL YOUR GUESTS OF MY SEX WITH THIS 72 POET ABSURD PERFORMANCE/

REGALES

AFFECTIONATE WINK WITH WHICH A WISE GUY REGALES A 38 HUGHIE SUCKER.)

REGALIA

REGALIA
HE WEARS OVER HIS MAYOR'S UNIFORM THE REGALIA OF 388 MARCOM
COCK OF PARADISE
HE WEARS HIS GHOULISHLY FANTASTIC REGALIA 390 MARCOM
THEY WEAR THE REGALIA OF OFFICERS IN THE MYSTIC 390 MARCOM
KNIGHTS OF CONFUCIUS

REGALLY
THEN STIFFENS REGALLY AND RETURNS HIS GAZE 387 MARCOM
UNFLINCHINGLY.
(REGALLY) GIVE THOSE TO THE MUSICIANS/ 429 MARCOM

REGARD
(STANDING BACK FROM THE PIANO TO REGARD THE FLOWER629 ICEMAN
EFFECT)
CAESAR WISHED ME TO BID YOU WELCOME, TO TELL YOU 333 LAZARU
HOW MUCH REGARD HE HAS FOR YOU,
FOR NATURALLY I COULD NOT REGARD-- (HE STOPS 73 MANSNS
ABRUPTLY--
AND I WAS HAPPY TO REGARD HER AS MY DAUGHTER-- 122 MANSNS
AND LAST THAT ONE'S JUDGMENT SHOULD REGARD 372 MARCOM
KUBLET AND CHUPTIN REGARD THEM WITH AMUSED 390 MARCOM
ASTONISHMENT.
YOUR LONG-STANDING HIGH REGARD FOR ME/ 393 MARCOM
AND SHE STOPS TO REGARD HIM SEARCHINGLY. 58 POET
I FEEL, WITH REGARD TO NINA, 135 STRANG
REGARD IT AS AN INTERLUDE, OF TRIAL AND 199 STRANG
PREPARATION, SAY,

REGARDED
EVER REGARDED AS ANYTHING BUT A NOISOME TABLE 571 ICEMAN
DECORATION.
TO KEEP ANYONE FROM TAKING WHAT SHE REGARDED AS 88 MANSNS
HERS.
I HAVE REGARDED THE MATTER AS NONE OF MY BUSINESS.100 MANSNS
(QUIETLY AGAIN.) REGARDED SENSIBLY, 180 MANSNS
LIFE IS PERHAPS MOST WISELY REGARDED AS A BAD 402 MARCOM
DREAM BETWEEN TWO AWAKENINGS,
AND HAS ALWAYS BEEN REGARDED AS OF DELICATE 4 STRANG
CONSTITUTION.

REGARDING
(REGARDING HER BROTHER WITH SMILING SUSPICION) 189 AHWILD
(THEN REGARDING RICHARD'S ARM ABOUT HER WAIST) 242 AHWILD
LOVING SITS MOTIONLESSLY REGARDING HIM WITH 496 DAYS
SCORNFUL EYES.)
THAT I HAD A MENTAL VIEW OF HIM REGARDING HIS 503 DAYS
NAVEL FRENZIEDLY BY THE HOUR AND
(REGARDING HIM--QUIETLY) THEN, BY ALL MEANS. 512 DAYS
AS A FATHER I WANT TO KNOW WHAT YOUR INTENTIONS 438 DYNAMO
ARE REGARDING MY DAUGHTER?
(REGARDING HIM BITTERLY) POOR FATHER/ 97 ELECTR
AND STANDS REGARDING THE HOUSE. 137 ELECTR
(STANDS HOLDING THE FLOWERS AND REGARDING HER 170 ELECTR
WORRIEDLY)
(REGARDING HUGO WITH PITY) NO. 579 ICEMAN
(HE TURNS TO LARRY, WHO IS REGARDING HIM NOW 593 ICEMAN
FIXEDLY WITH AN UNEASY EXPRESSION
(IS REGARDING PARRIT ACROSS THE TABLE FROM HIM 677 ICEMAN
WITH AN EAGER, CALCULATING EYE.
TO ROCKY, WHO IS REGARDING HIM WITH SCORN-- 690 ICEMAN
APPRAISINGLY)
ROCKY IS STANDING BEHIND HIS CHAIR, REGARDING HIM 696 ICEMAN
WITH DULL HOSTILITY.
THEY PUSH HIS ARMS AWAY, REGARDING HIM WITH AMAZED725 ICEMAN
SUSPICION.)
REGARDING HER WITH AN UNEASY, PROBING LOOK. 20 JOURNE
(SHE PAUSES, REGARDING HER HANDS FIXEDLY. 104 JOURNE
(SHE LETS HIM TAKE IT, REGARDING HIM FROM 172 JOURNE
SOMEWHERE FAR AWAY WITHIN HERSELF.
SHE STANDS REGARDING DEBORAH WITH A CRUEL MOCKING 164 MANSNS
LEER OF SATISFACTION.
(APPROACHES AND STANDS REGARDING HOGAN WITH 37 MISBEG
SARDONIC RELISH.
MEETING HIS EYES, WHICH ARE REGARDING HER WITH 113 MISBEG
PUZZLED WONDER,
(REGARDING HER AS IF SHE HADN'T REALLY SEEN HER 140 POET
BEFORE--RESENTFULLY.)
(REGARDING THEM BOTH WITH AN AMUSED GRIN) 988 ROPE
(WHO HAS BEEN REGARDING HIM WITH WANING 28 STRANG
RESENTMENT.
(REGARDING HIS SUN BITTERLY) 141 STRANG
REGARDING HIMSELF AND THE PEOPLE AROUND HIM AS 158 STRANG
INTERESTING PHENOMENA.

REGARDLESS
(BLUNDERING ON REGARDLESS NOW) 32 STRANG

REGARDS
KEENEY REGARDS HER ANXIOUSLY. 549 'ILE
(AGAIN REGARDS HIS SOUP WITH ASTONISHMENT) 224 AHWILD
FINALLY HE LOOKS UP AND REGARDS HIS SISTER AND 224 AHWILD
ASKS WITH WONDERING AMAZEMENT)
(REGARDS HER BITTERLY--THEN STARTS TO HIS FEET 246 AHWILD
BELLICOSELY--TO THE SALESMAN)
(REGARDS HER BROTHER SEVERELY) 265 AHWILD
ROBERT REGARDS HIM WITH AN AFFECTIONATE SMILE.) 160 BEYOND
HOLDS THE WICKS OF THE SHOES IN HIS HANDS AND 196 EJONES
REGARDS THEM MOURNFULLY)
HE REGARDS HER UNDERSTANDINGLY.) 18 ELECTR
AS HE REGARDS HER GRIM, SET EXPRESSION) 23 ELECTR
LAVINIA REGARDS HER WITH BLEAK, CONDEMNING EYES.) 122 ELECTR
THE NIGHT CLERK REGARDS HIM WITH VACANT, 19 HUGHIE
(LARRY REGARDS HIM PUZZLEDLY.) 585 ICEMAN
(REGARDS HIM WITH SURPRISE AT FIRST, THEN WITH A 623 ICEMAN
PUZZLED INTEREST)
CHUCK REGARDS HER RESENTFULLY) 699 ICEMAN
(HIS FATHER REGARDS HIM WITH DISLIKE. 65 JOURNE
(SHE RAISES HER HANDS AND REGARDS THEM WITH 103 JOURNE
MELANCHOLY SYMPATHY.
(EDMUND REMAINS SILENT. TYRONE REGARDS HIM--THEN 167 JOURNE
GOES ON.)
(SHE REGARDS THE WEDDING GOWN WITH A PUZZLED 172 JOURNE
INTEREST.)

REGARDS (CONT'D.)
(REGARDS HIM CALCULATINGLY--THEN WITH A 106 MANSNS
CARESSINGLY GENTLE AIR.)
(SHE REGARDS HIM SUSPICIOUSLY, BUT HIS FACE IS 22 MISBEG
BLANK.
(HE REGARDS HARDER WITH PITYING CONTEMPT) 60 MISBEG
(TYRONE REGARDS HIM WITH VAGUE SURPRISE.) 101 MISBEG
(REGARDS HIM FOR A SECOND PUZZLEDLY. 69 POET
(THEN SUDDENLY REMINDED OF SOMETHING SHE REGARDS 474 WELDED
HIM CALCULATINGLY--

REGIMENT
BUT THEY FOUND OUT IT VAS REGIMENT MONEY, TOO, HE 677 ICEMAN
LOST--
DIDN'T ME AND JAMIE LICK A WHOLE REGIMENT AV 173 POET
POLICE THIS NIGHT&

REGIMENTAL
(MAKING A SIGN TO THE REGIMENTAL MUSICIANS 323 LAZARU
JUVIALLY)

REGIMENTS
IN ONE OF WELLINGTON'S DRAGOON REGIMENTS. 88 POET

REGIONS
FROM THE DIM REGIONS ABOVE THE ELECTRIC LIGHT. 224 HA APE
(SUDDENLY) MANY WONDERS HAVE COME TO PASS IN 368 MARCOM
THESE REGIONS.

REGISTER
(HE PUTS THE LETTER ON THE CASH REGISTER) 5 ANNA
I CAN STILL SEE A CASH REGISTER, BEJEES/ 582 ICEMAN

REGRET
I REGRET TO SAY IT'S SOMETHING DISAGREEABLE-- 201 AHWILD
AND DON'T THINK I'M NOT GOING TO MAKE YOU REGRET 203 AHWILD
THE INSULTS YOU'VE HEAPED ON
AND DRUNK AGAIN. I REGRET TO NOTE. 225 AHWILD
YES, I REGRET TO SAY, 227 AHWILD
OR YOU'RE GOING TO REGRET IT/ 235 AHWILD
(THEN ANGRILY) BY GOD, I'LL MAKE WHOEVER IT WAS 266 AHWILD
REGRET IT/
CHRISTINE--I DEEPLY REGRET--HAVING BEEN UNJUST THE 52 ELECTR
KISSES HER HAND IMPULSIVELY--
TRY NOT TO REGRET YOUR SHIP TOO MUCH, ADAM/ 112 ELECTR
OH, ADAM, TELL ME YOU DON'T REGRET/ 112 ELECTR
UNLESS YOU REGRET YOUR LOST POET'S DREAM OF A 15 MANSNS
PERFECT SOCIETY.
I REGRET THAT PARADISE IN WHICH YOU WERE THE GOOD,103 MANSNS
KIND, BELOVED,
YOU WILL NEVER REGRET IT. 383 MARCOM
WITH DEEP REGRET FOR THE LOSS OF YOUR UNIQUE AND 393 MARCOM
EXTRAORDINARY SERVICES.
THERE'S NOTHING YOU SAID OR DID LAST NIGHT FOR YOU'71 MISBEG
TO REGRET.
AND THERE ARE FEW THINGS IN IT THAT DO NOT CALL 40 POET
FOR BITTER REGRET--
IF I HAVE ONE REGRET FOR THE PAST-- 40 POET
I REGRET YOUR HAVING GONE TO SO MUCH TROUBLE. 56 POET
IF I'D KNOWN--NO, BE DAMNED IF I REGRET/ 75 POET
(THEN QUIETLY.) THERE ARE THINGS I SAID WHICH I 115 POET
REGRET--EVEN NOW.
WITHOUT ONE BACKWARD GLANCE OF REGRET OR 49 STRANG
RECOLLECTION.
SHOUT THAT THIS IS LIFE AND THIS IS SEX, AND HERE ARE 176 STRANG
PASSION AND HATRED AND REGRET
(WITH PASSIONATE EXULTANCE) WHY DO YOU REGRET OUR448 WELDED
FIRST DAYS/

REGRETFULLY
(REGRETFULLY) THEN WAS GOOD TIMES, THOSE DAYS. 467 CARIBE
(AFTER A LONG PAUSE--REGRETFULLY) 515 DFFANT
(THINKING--REGRETFULLY.) I HAVE GROWN TO LEAN 120 MANSNS
UPON HER HEALTH AND STRENGTH--
(UNCONSCIOUSLY SHE SIGHS REGRETFULLY.) 120 MANSNS
(UNCONSCIOUSLY SHE SIGHS REGRETFULLY. 120 MANSNS
REGRETFULLY.) HE'S A FOOL TO THINK SHE COULD EVER120 MANSNS
HAVE TAKEN MY CHILDREN--
(SHE SIGHS REGRETFULLY) AH, WELL, MIKE, YOU WAS 5 MISBEG
BURN A PRIEST'S PET.

REGRETS
THERE WILL REMAIN ONLY THE ANGUISH OF ENDLESS 561 DAYS
MEMORIES, ENDLESS REGRETS--
(THEN HARSHLY) IT'S TOO LATE FOR REGRETS NOW. 111 ELECTR
ANYWAY.
THEIR SHIPS WILL COME IN, LOADED TO THE GUNWALES 578 ICEMAN
WITH CANCELLED REGRETS
IT'S A LATE DAY FOR REGRETS. 150 JOURNE
A LONG INSOMNIA OF MEMORIES AND REGRETS 393 LAZARU
HAVE NO REGRETS/ 17 MANSNS
ITS REGRETS ARE DEAD... 191 STRANG

REGRETTED
HE OFTEN REGRETTED AFTERWARDS HE HAD NOT HAD THE 534 DAYS
COURAGE TO DIE THEN.

REGRETTING
AND HE OFTEN FOUND HIMSELF REGRETTING-- 536 DAYS
I SUPPOSE YOU'RE REGRETTING YOU WEREN'T THERE 26 JOURNE
(UNEASY, AS IF ALREADY REGRETTING HER CONSENT.) 55 MANSNS

REGULAR
I USED TO BE A REGULAR WATER RAT WHEN I WAS A BOY.228 AHWILD
GEE, YOU IRE A REGULAR PEACH/ 242 AHWILD
THAT'S THE TIME PA AND MA COME UP TO BED, AS 280 AHWILD
REGULAR AS CLOCK WORK.
ON SHIPS AT ANCHOR BREAKS AT REGULAR INTERVALS. 25 ANNA
HE'S A REGULAR MAN, NO MATTER WHAT FAULTS HE'S 44 ANNA
GOT.
IF YOU'D EVEN HAD BEEN A REGULAR FATHER AND HAD ME 58 ANNA
WITH YOU--
REGULAR PLACE FOR YOU TWO TO COME BACK TO,--WAIT 77 ANNA
AND SEE.
HER SMALL, REGULAR FEATURES ARE MARKED BY A 87 BEYOND
CERTAIN STRENGTH--
AT REGULAR INTERVALS OF A MINUTE OR SO 477 CARDIF
YOU'RE A REGULAR, UP-TO-DATE SPORT--THE ONLY LIVE 520 DIFRNT
ONE IN THIS DEAD DUMP.

REGULAR (CONT'D.)
(TURNING TO HER) SAY, YOU'RE A REGULAR FELLER-- 520 DIFRNT
GETTIN' THEM RECORDS FOR ME.
523 DIFRNT
YOU'RE REGULAR
SHAKING THEM, CASTING THEM OUT WITH THE REGULAR, 191 EJONES
RIGID,
(THE CANNON AT THE FORT KEEP BOOMING AT REGULAR 42 ELECTR
INTERVALS UNTIL THE END OF THE
146 ELECTR
HE'S BECOME A REGULAR BIGOTED MANNON.
I'M GABBING ON LIKE A REGULAR CHATTERBOX. 147 ELECTR
(TO HER) MINE IS A REGULAR FOG HORN! 257 GGBROW
WELL, IF YOU SIMPLY GOT TO BE A REGULAR DEVIL LIKE279 GGBROW
ALL THE OTHER VISITING SPORTS
300 GGBROW
HE'S A REGULAR FELLOW.
WHY, HE'S A REGULAR SPORT WHEN HE GETS STARTED/* 310 GGBROW
HE'S A REGULAR GUY. 240 HA APE
HE'S A REGULAR GUY. 247 HA APE
I'M REGULAR.
HIS FACE IS GOOD-LOOKING, WITH BLOND CURLY HAIR 389 ICEMAN
AND LARGE REGULAR FEATURES.
YOUSE REGULAR, IF YOU IS A LIMEY. 599 ICEMAN
THE GRANDEST CROWD OF REGULAR GUYS EVER GATHERED 609 ICEMAN
UNDER ONE TENT/
ONE REGULAR GUY AND ONE ALL-RIGHT TART GONE TO 683 ICEMAN
HELL/
A FOGHORN IS HEARD AT REGULAR INTERVALS, MOANING 97 JOURNE
LIKE A MOURNFUL WHALE IN LABOR,
BUT YOU WOULD SEND ME INTO MY STUDY TO WORK ON IT 46 MANSNS
LIKE A REGULAR SLAVE-DRIVER/
HIS REGULAR, GOOD-LOOKING, 390 MARCOM
WHAT I WANTS IS CASH--REGULAR COIN YUH KIN SPEND--599 ROPE
NOT DIRT.
SINCE MOTHER'S DEATH I'VE BECOME A REGULAR 120 STRANG
IDIOT/....)

REGULARLY
HE COMES HERE TWICE A YEAR REGULARLY ON A 586 ICEMAN
PERIODICAL DRUNK
SHE HAS BEEN WRITING SAM REGULARLY ONCE A WEEK 50 STRANG
EVER SINCE SHE'S KNOWN WE WERE

REGULATED
BUT THERE IS ORDER IN IT, RHYTHM, A MECHANICAL 223 HA APE
REGULATED RECURRENCE, A TEMPO.

INHERENT REGULATIONS... 429 DYNAMO

REHABILITATING
WE CAN DEVOTE THE PROCEEDS TO REHABILITATING THE 237 HA APE
VEIL OF THE TEMPLE.

REHEARSAL
(WITH A TENDER SMILE) OF THE FIRST TIME WE MET-- 446 WELDED
AT REHEARSAL, REMEMBER$

REINCARNATION
THAT LAZARUS MAY BE THE REINCARNATION OF THIS 298 LAZARU
DEITY.
THEY HAVE ALREADY CONVINCED THEMSELVES THIS 302 LAZARU
LAZARUS IS A REINCARNATION OF

REINSTATED
OF COURSE, YOU'LL BE REINSTATED, MAC. 607 ICEMAN
I'LL BE FOUND INNOCENT THIS TIME AND REINSTATED. 607 ICEMAN
WELL, I'M SICKER OF YOUR KIDDING ME ABOUT GETTING 652 ICEMAN
REINSTATED ON THE FORCE.
YOU KNOW HOW GETTING REINSTATED IS. 724 ICEMAN

REITERATES
(REITERATES STUPIDLY) WHAT'S MATTER, LARRYS 724 ICEMAN

REITERATING
I'D HAD A LETTER FROM YOU ONLY THAT DAY, 507 DAYS
REITERATING HOW HAPPY YOU WERE.
(IN THE VOICE OF ONE REITERATING MECHANICALLY A 704 ICEMAN
HOPELESS COMPLAINT)

REJECT
THAT I DID NOT DESIRE IT AND DID ALL IN MY POWER 37 MANSNS
TO REJECT IT$
I WARN YOU YOUR PRIDE WILL PROBABLY BE IMPELLED TO153 MANSNS
REJECT THEM.

REJECTS
TO OLD GHOSTLY COMFORTS--AND HE REJECTS THEM/ 545 DAYS

REJOICE
LET US REJOICE/ 278 LAZARU
I WANT EVEN TO BECOME A LOVING MOTHER-IN-LAW WHO 54 MANSNS
CAN REJOICE
TO REJOICE AT THAT FATHER'S DEATH, THEN I SHOULD 418 MARCOM
BE THAT GUILTY SON/
THAT WE COULD CRUSH EACH SINGLY AND THE REST WOULD421 MARCOM
REJOICE.

REJOICING
(JEERINGLY) I'M AFRAID YOUR REJOICING IS A BIT 545 DAYS
PREMATURE--

RELAPSE
(THE OTHERS SMILE BUT IMMEDIATELY RELAPSE INTO 95 BEYOND
EXPRESSIONS OF GLOOM AGAIN.)
THERE'D BE THE DEVIL TO PAY IF YOU SHOULD SUFFER A412 MARCOM
RELAPSE EVER.

RELAPSED
(TO CAPTAIN LEWIS WHO HAS RELAPSED INTO A SLEEPY 600 ICEMAN
DAZE AND IS LISTENING TO HIM

RELAPSES
SHE RELAPSES INTO THE FAMILIAR FORM AND FLASHES 23 ANNA
ONE OF HER WINNING TRADE SMILES
(HE RELAPSES INTO AN ATTITUDE OF SOMBER BROODING.) 28 ANNA
(CHRIS RELAPSES INTO INJURED SILENCE. 65 ANNA
AS SOON AS SHE IS GONE BURKE RELAPSES INTO AN 77 ANNA
ATTITUDE OF GLOOMY THOUGHT.
HER FEAR PASSES AND SHE RELAPSES INTO DULL 151 BEYOND
INDIFFERENCE.
(HE RELAPSES AND SMILES DREAMILY.) 145 MANSNS
(SHE FINISHES AND RELAPSES INTO HER ATTITUDE OF 384 MARCOM
BROKEN RESIGNATION.
HIS BREAKING IN ON US LIKE THAT--IHE RELAPSES INTO455 WELDED
FROWNING BROODING AGAIN.

RELAPSING
(HE SITS DOWN AGAIN, RELAPSING INTO A BROODING 209 DESIRE
SILENCE.

RELATE
THEY RELATE THAT IN OLD TIMES THREE KINGS FROM 368 MARCOM
THIS COUNTRY WENT TO WORSHIP A
BUT EACH TIME YOU RETURN FROM A JOURNEY YOU MUST 382 MARCOM
RELATE TO ME ALL THE
HE SAID TELL THE GREAT KAAN THAT *IN SPITE OF 424 MARCOM
PERILS TOO NUMEROUS TO RELATE,
ALL I WISH IS TO RELATE SOMETHING WHICH HAPPENED 106 PORT
THIS AFTERNOON.
DEFINITE AIM OR AMBITION TO WHICH HE CAN RELATE 138 STRANG
HIS LIVING.

RELATED
WELL, I MEAN IF YOU WAS RELATED TO ME IN SOME WAY,534 DIFRNT
YOU AIN'T BY ANY CHANCE RELATED$ 11 HUGHIE
TO BELIEVE HUMAN LIVES ARE VALUABLE, AND RELATED 180 MANSNS
TO SOME GOD-INSPIRED MEANING.

RELATION
I WAS ONLY A POOR RELATION, 18 ANNA
THE RELATION OF SOME SEA EPISODE. 94 BEYOND
NO RELATION. 11 HUGHIE
ON THE OTHER SIDE, PLACED SIMILARLY IN RELATION TO313 LAZARU
LAZARUS AND FACING MIRIAM,
HE'S A RELATION, TOO. 59 POET
JUST BECAUSE YOU'RE A RELATION-- 160 POET
NO ONE VOLUME IS PLACED WITH ANY RELATION TO THE 66 STRANG
ONE BENEATH IT--

RELATIONS
BUT HAVE YOU NO RELATIONS AT ALL TO CALL YOUR OWN$489 CARDIF
HUGHIE TOLD ME HE DIDN'T HAVE NO RELATIONS LEFT-- 11 HUGHIE
THERE WASN'T NOBODY BUT A COUPLA HIS WIFE'S 31 HUGHIE
RELATIONS.
MY RELATIONS WILL SO SURPRISED BE. 605 ICEMAN
HE'S SURE TO CALL ON BESSIE'S RELATIONS TO DO A 651 ICEMAN
LITTLE CRYIN' OVER DEAR BESSIE.
(DELIGHTEDLY) YES, ONCE BESSIE'S RELATIONS GET 652 ICEMAN
THEIR HOOKS IN HIM,
BRIDGET'S LIES ABOUT HER RELATIONS$ 102 JOURNE
AND SHE DIDN'T WANT HER POOR IRISH RELATIONS 49 MANSNS
SHAMING HER BEFORE THE NOTABLES/
(WHAT ARE DARRELL'S RELATIONS WITH NINA$... 31 STRANG

RELATIONSHIP
THAT RELATIONSHIP HAS NO MEANING BETWEEN US/ 31 ELECTR
AND ALL THE HYPOCRITICAL VALUES WE SET ON THE 79 MANSNS
RELATIONSHIP ARE MERE STUPIDITY.
WHATEVER THE NATURE OF THAT RELATIONSHIP IN THE 121 POET
PAST,
TO ANY FURTHER RELATIONSHIP BETWEEN HIS SON AND 121 POET
YOUR DAUGHTER.
(VERY PALE--TENSELY) WHAT RELATIONSHIPS 458 WELDED
TO DRAG THAT RELATIONSHIP OUT OF THE PAST AND 458 WELDED
THROW IT IN MY FACE/

RELATIONSHIPS
AND FOR ALL THE CONFUSION IN OUR RELATIONSHIPS 172 MANSNS
WITH ONE ANOTHER,

RELATIVE
SHE WAS TOO DISTANT A RELATIVE TC BE VULGAR. 21H HA APE

RELATIVELY
BUT I DON'T HESITATE TO STATE THAT ALL THIS 431 MARCOM
ACTIVITY IS RELATIVELY UNIMPORTANT
DARRELL MOVES BACK AND TO ONE SIDE UNTIL HE IS 39 STRANG
STANDING IN RELATIVELY THE SAME

RELATIVES
BUT IF YOU THINK MY LOVING RELATIVES WILL HAVE 651 ICEMAN
TIME TO DISCUSS YOU,
NOR DELIGHTED RELATIVES MAKING THE VELDT RING WITH677 ICEMAN
THEIR HAPPY CRIES--
SHE BEGINS TELLING ME ABOUT HER RELATIVES 29 JOURNE

RELAX
AS HER HAND STRIKES THE FLOOR THE FINGERS RELAX 64 ELECTR
RELAX/ 267 GGBROW
SHE APPEARS TO RELAX. 49 JOURNE
NEVER RELAX MY VIGILANCE-- 119 MANSNS
WEAKNESS, A DEEP NEED FOR LOVE AS A FAITH IN WHICH444 WELDED
TO RELAX.

RELAXATION
THERE IS, HOWEVER, A STRANGE EXPRESSION OF PEACE 144 MANSNS
AND RELAXATION ON HIS FACE AS
I'VE PLAYED WITH CONCUBINES AT ODD MOMENTS WHEN MY406 MARCOM
MIND NEEDED RELAXATION.

RELAXED
HER BIG BODY RELAXED AS IF SHE HAD GIVEN HERSELF 486 DYNAMO
UP COMPLETELY TO THE SPELL OF
LEANING ON THEIR SHOVELS IN RELAXED ATTITUDES OF 223 HA APE
EXHAUSTION.
THEN SHE SETTLES BACK IN RELAXED DREAMINESS, 106 JOURNE
STARING FIXEDLY AT NOTHING.
HIS WHOLE BODY IS NOW RELAXED, AT REST, A DREAMY 342 LAZARU
SMILE SOFTENS HIS THIN,
HIS EXPRESSION BECOMES RELAXED AND DREAMY.) 94 MANSNS
HER HANDS FLUTTER AIMLESSLY IN RELAXED, FLABBY 578 ROPE
GESTURES.

RELAXES
ABBIE RELAXES WITH A FAINT SIGH BUT HER EYES 236 DESIRE
REMAIN FIXED ON THE WALL.
HIS CONTROL RELAXES. 265 DESIRE
(HE STARTS TO GET UP BUT RELAXES AGAIN. 625 ICEMAN
(SUDDENLY GIVES UP AND RELAXES LIMPLY IN THE 716 ICEMAN
CHAIR--
(TIBERIUS' BODY RELAXES IN HIS HANDS, DEAD, AND 369 LAZARU
SLIPS FROM THE CHAIR.
(SHE RELAXES, HER HEAD BACK, HER EYES SHUT. 4 MANSNS
(GRADUALLY ALL TENSION RELAXES, HER EYES BECOME 21 MANSNS
DREAMY.
(HE RELAXES WITH A DREAMY SMILE OF CONTENT IN 129 MANSNS
THEIR ARMS
SHE RELAXES SLOWLY AND MURMURS DREAMILY.) 164 MANSNS

RELAXES

RELAXES (CONT'D.)
(RELAXES--SIMPLY AND GRATEFULLY) 103 MISBEG
(SHE SITS AT THE END OF CENTER TABLE RIGHT AND 76 POET
RELAXES WEARILY.
RELAXING
(RELAXING AT LAST--AVOIDING HER EYES--SHEEPISHLY) 50 ANNA
(HIS TENSE, SUPPLICATING ATTITUDE SUDDENLY 480 DYNAMO
RELAXING DEJECTEDLY)
(SUDDENLY RELAXING) SHOT YOU HAS--AND YOU BETTER 181 EJONES
GO.
RELAYING
(MARGARET DISAPPEARS AND IS HEARD RELAYING THIS 515 DAYS
INSTRUCTION.
RELEASE
I'VE WON TO MY TRIP--THE RIGHT OF RELEASE--BEYOND 168 BEYOND
THE HORIZON?
THAT DEATH IS FINAL RELEASE, THE WARM, DARK PEACE 534 DAYS
OF ANNIHILATION.
HER FINGERS RELEASE THE BOX ON THE TABLE TOP AND 62 ELECTR
SHE BRINGS HER HAND IN FRONT OF
SAUNTERING LONGINGLY TOWARD THE DAWN'S RELEASE. 24 HUGHIE
SHE HAS HIDDEN DEEPER WITHIN HERSELF AND FOUND 97 JOURNE
REFUGE AND RELEASE IN A DREAM
THIS SEEMS TO RELEASE THEM FROM THEIR FIXED 291 LAZARU
POSITIONS.
WHATEVER THE COST OF RELEASE-- 31 MANSNS
STRUGGLES TO RELEASE HER HAND. 71 POET
SUCH A WILD FEELING OF RELEASE AND FRESH 86 POET
ENSLAVEMENT.
I WILL THIS AS A SYMBOL OF RELEASE--OF THE END OF 472 WELDED
ALL THINGS?
RELEASED
LIKE A SPRINTER RELEASED BY THE STARTING SHOT.) 186 AHWILD
AS IF IN SPIRIT SHE WERE RELEASED TO BECOME AGAIN. 97 JOURNE
SUDDENLY HIS LAUGHTER IS RELEASED) 334 LAZARU
AND FOR A TIME I ACTUALLY FELT RELEASED/.... 9 STRANG
RELEASES
(THEN, AS, BROUGHT BACK TO HIMSELF HE RELEASES HER433 DYNAMO
IN SHAMEFACED CONFUSION.
HE RELEASES HER HAND AND STARES AT HER, MORBIDLY 86 ELECTR
SUSPICIOUS)
(THIS RELEASES A CHORUS OF SHAMEFACED MUMBLES FROM663 ICEMAN
THE CROWD.
HIS VOICE RELEASES HIS OWN DANCERS AND THE MOB 289 LAZARU
FROM THEIR FIXED ATTITUDES.
THAT RELEASES ME? 104 MANSNS
HOGAN RELEASES HIS HOLD ON HARDER'S COAT) 61 MISBEG
(SMILING GENTLY RELEASES HER HAND) 119 STRANG
RELEASING
THE TURNS AWAY, SUDDENLY RELEASING ROBERT'S HAND) 86 BEYOND
RELEASES ALL HIS PENT-UP PASSION) 244 DESIRE
(CONFUSEDLY, SINKING BACK ON HIS COUCH AND 343 LAZARU
RELEASING HER)
BY RELEASING EACH OTHER. 486 WELDED
RELECTED
FLARE UPWARD AND ARE RELECTED ON THEIR MASKS IN 367 LAZARU
DANCING WAVES OF LIGHT)
RELEGATED
THE HORSEHAIR SOFA HAS BEEN RELEGATED TO THE 519 DIFRNT
ATTIC.
RELENT
(SEIZING ON THIS TO RELENT A BIT) 270 AHWILD
BUT APPRECIATES SHE HAD THE UPPER HAND NOW AND 279 AHWILD
DOESN'T RELENT AT ONCE)
RELENTING
(AS SHE THINKS SHE SEES A RELENTING SOFTNESS COME 543 DIFRNT
INTO HIS FACE AS HE LOOKS DOWN
(RELENTING) HE TOLD ME YOU'D AGREED TO ASK ME AND304 GGROW
THE BOYS NOT TO COME HERE--
(RUCKY, AT A RELENTING GLANCE FROM HOPE, RETURNS 607 ICEMAN
TO THE BAR.)
(RELENTING) STILL, A DROP NOW AND THEN IS NO 52 JOURNE
HARM
RELENTINGLY
HE ROTS RELENTINGLY) 221 DESIRE
RELENTLESS
YET THIS SOUND SERVES BUT TO INTENSIFY THE 187 EJONES
IMPRESSION OF THE FOREST'S RELENTLESS
YET WITH SOMETHING OF THE RELENTLESS HORROR OF 236 HA APE
FRANKENSTEINS
(WITH AN EVEN MORE BLUNTED FLAT RELENTLESS 59 STRANG
TONELESSNESS)
(TEASINGLY) BUT YOU'RE SUCH A RELENTLESS 447 WELDED
IDEALIST.
RELENTLESSLY
(RELENTLESSLY) WHY? 178 STRANG
RELENTS
(IMMEDIATELY RELENTS--INDIGNANTLY) 598 ICEMAN
RELIABLE
AIN'T I IN LOVE AND AIN'T I AS RELIABLE AS AN OLD 906 DIFRNT
HUSSY
IF YOU COULD ONLY BRING FORWARD ONE RELIABLE 396 MARCOM
WITNESS.
(SHE LAUGHS WILDLY) I'D BE SAFE THEN, WOULDN'T 459 WELDED
I --RELIABLE, GUARANTEED NOT TO--
RELIANCE
BY A LONG RELIANCE ON CLENCHED TEETH. 53 STRANG
RELIANT
A HARDY SELF-RELIANT CONFIDENCE IN HIMSELF THAT 175 EJONES
INSPIRES RESPECT.
THE PROUD, SELF-RELIANT,. 273 LAZARU
THEY ARE ALL OF THE PROUD SELF-RELIANT TYPE, IN 298 LAZARU
THE PERIOD OF YOUNG MANHOOD.
INTRUSPECTIVE,. PROUD, SELF-RELIANT,. THE 312 LAZARU
SERVILE, HYPOCRITICAL,.
IN THE PERIOD OF WOMANHOOD IN THE PROUD, SELF- 336 LAZARU
RELIANT TYPE.

RELIED
HE--ER--EVIDENTLY RELIED ON YOUR TACT AND 35 MANSNS
DIPLOMACY, DEBORAH, TO CONVINCE HER.
HE RELIED ON ME TO PROVE EQUAL TO THE TASK 411 MARCOM
DAD RELIED ON ME TO CARRY ON WHERE HE LEFT OFF... 189 STRANG
RELIEF
(GIVES A SIGH OF RELIEF--HER HANDS DROP TO HER 544 'ILE
SIDES.
(WITH GREAT RELIEF) ALL RIGHT. 207 AHWILD
(SHE THUMPS DOWN THE DISH IN FRONT OF HIM WITH A 226 AHWILD
SIGH OF RELIEF.)
(SEIZES ON THIS INTERRUPTION WITH RELIEF) 251 AHWILD
(CONCEALING A RELIEF OF WHICH HE IS ASHAMED-- 268 AHWILD
EXASPERATEDLY)
(COVERING HIS EVIDENT RELIEF AT THIS RESPITE WITH 269 AHWILD
A FUMING MANNER)
THE HEAVES A HUGE SIGH OF RELIEF-- 277 AHWILD
WITH A DEEP SIGH OF RELIEF) 289 AHWILD
(THEN AS IF SEEKING RELIEF FROM THE TENSION IN A 20 ANNA
VOLUBLE CHATTER)
RISING TO HER FEET WITH A SIGH OF RELIEF) 33 ANNA
(CHRIS' FACE LIGHTS UP WITH RELIEF. 44 ANNA
THEN A LOOK OF RESIGNATION AND RELIEF TAKES ITS 76 ANNA
PLACE.
(WITH A SHARP SIGH OF JOYFUL RELIEF) 100 BEYOND
(IN RELIEF) THERE? 105 BEYOND
(HE HEAVES A GREAT SIGH OF RELIEF) 134 BEYOND
(HE GIVES A COMIC SIGH OF RELIEF) 501 DAYS
(STARTS BACK TO HIMSELF--STAMMERS WITH A CONFUSED 552 DAYS
AIR OF RELIEF)
(WITH IMMENSE RELIEF) LET'S GIT A BREATH O' AIR. 218 DESIRE
SHE LOOKS DOWN AT CABOT--WITH A SIGH OF RELIEF.) 224 DESIRE
(HEAVING A SIGH OF RELIEF) (SURE.... 464 DYNAMO
THERE IS A LOOK OF CALM AND RELIEF ON HIS FACE 475 DYNAMO
NOW.
IMMOBILITY, TO FORM A BACKGROUND THROWING INTO 187 EJONES
RELIEF ITS BROODING.
MAN THAT HE SEES--IN A TONE OF HAPPY RELIEF) 192 EJONES
(WITH EXASPERATED RELIEF) GOOD NIGHT. 107 ELECTR
(WITH A CRY OF RELIEF) ADAM? 107 ELECTR
(STRIVING TO CONCEAL HER EAGERNESS AND RELIEF-- 277 GGROW
JUDICIALLY)
(LOOKING DOWN THE DECK--WITH A SIGH OF RELIEF) 222 HA APE
(WITH EAGER RELIEF) SURE, I'LL BUY YOU A DRINK. 592 ICEMAN
HUGO.
(THEY HAVE ALL CAUGHT HIS SINCERITY WITH EAGER 659 ICEMAN
RELIEF.
IN A LOW VOICE IN WHICH THERE IS A STRANGE 716 ICEMAN
EXHAUSTED RELIEF)
BUT THERE IS MORE RELIEF THAN HORROR IN IT. 725 ICEMAN
SMITTY DRAWS HIS HAND AWAY SLOWLY AND UTTERS A 523 INZONE
SIGH OF RELIEF.)
(THEY ALL SIT DOWN WITH GREAT SIGHS OF RELIEF) 524 INZONE
WELL, NO MATTER WHAT THE JOKE IS ABOUT, IT'S A 18 JOURNE
RELIEF TO HEAR EDMUND LAUGH.
HER FIRST REACTION IS ONE OF RELIEF. 49 JOURNE
(WITH RELIEF.) THANK YOU, MAMA. 106 JOURNE
(STARING THROUGH THE FRONT PARLOR--WITH RELIEF.) 139 JOURNE
THE FIVE ARE HALF HYSTERICAL WITH RELIEF AND JOY, 278 LAZARU
SOBBING AND LAUGHING.)
(THEN WITH RELIEF) HOW HE IS DEAD? 329 LAZARU
(SEEING LAZARUS WHERE HE HAD BEEN--WITH RELIEF-- 340 LAZARU
(THINKING--WITH CONTEMPTUOUS RELIEF.) 123 MANSNS
(AS IF SUDDENLY EMERGING FROM A SPELL--WITH AN 127 MANSNS
IMPULSIVE GRATEFUL RELIEF.)
WITH A CRY OF HAPPY RELIEF, SARA RUSHES TO HIM AND144 MANSNS
HUGS HIM PASSIONATELY.)
(GIVES WAY TO RELIEF AND GRATITUDE.) 153 MANSNS
(WITH RELIEF) PHOO! (THEN BREAKING THE ICE) THE 348 MARCOM
SUN WOULD COOK YOU?
HE STARES AT THEM AND LAUGHS COARSELY WITH RELIEF)350 MARCOM
(JOSIE IS SMILING WITH RELIEF NOW.) 67 MISBEG
(WITH STRANGE RELIEF) OH. 104 MISBEG
HE, TURNS WITH A LOOK OF RELIEF AND ESCAPE) 111 MISBEG
(GIVING AWAY AT LAST TO HER RELIEF AND JOY) 133 MISBEG
(HE DRINKS AND SIGHS WITH RELIEF.) 9 POET
AFTER A PAUSE HE SIGHS WITH RELIEF.) 37 POET
(NEVERTHELESS, IT WILL BE A RELIEF TO RETURN TO MY 86 POET
GARDEN AND BOOKS AND
MY DEAR SARA, ALL I FEEL IS RELIEF. 91 POET
NORA'S FIRST REACTION IS A CRY OF RELIEF.) 151 POET
(SHE RUSHES TO THE DOOR AND STANDS LISTENING--WITH159 POET
RELIEF.)
(SOBS. WITH RELIEF.) OH, PRAISE GOD YOU'RE ALIVE! 164 POET
(MAKING THE SIGN OF THE CROSS--FURTIVELY--WITH A 584 ROPE
SIGH OF RELIEF)
HIS FACE NOW FULL OF SELFISH RELIEF AS HE THINKS) 7 STRANG
(THINKING WITH WEARY RELIEF) 15 STRANG
(WITH RELIEF) AH. 32 STRANG
(WITH RELIEF) SURE. 34 STRANG
(THINKING WITH GRIM RELIEF) (HE DON'T KNOW.... 55 STRANG
(WITH MARKED RELIEF) THEN BY ALL MEANS DON'T 73 STRANG
DISTURB HER.
(HAS GOTTEN UP FROM HIS CHAIR--WITH RELIEF-- 99 STRANG
THINKING)
(THINKING--DAZEDLY STILL, BUT IN A TONE OF RELIEF)174 STRANG
(THEN WITH A SORT OF DEFIANT RELIEF) 193 STRANG
SHE GIVES A SORT OF GASP OF RELIEF) 449 WELDED
(WITH A SIGH OF RELIEF) YOU GAVE ME A SCARE. 465 WELDED
RELIEVE
I'VE HAD SUCH A STRONG FEELING AT TIMES THAT IT 161 ELECTR
WOULD RELIEVE YOUR MIND
YUH SAID IF I'D TAKE YOUR DAY, YUH'D RELIEVE ME AT697 ICEMAN
SIX.
BUT RELIEVE YOUR CONSCIENCE, IF YOU MUST. 70 MANSNS
(SMILING BUT EARNESTLY) IT'LL RELIEVE YOUR MIND, 467 WELDED
NELLY--
RELIEVED
(IN RELIEVED TONES--SEEING WHO IT IS) 536 'ILE

RELIEVED (CONT'D.)

(RELIEVED AND CHEERFUL AGAIN) 211 AHWILD
(HER ANXIETY IMMEDIATELY TURNING TO RELIEVED 253 AHWILD
ANGER)
AND I CAN TELL YOU IT RELIEVED MY MIND MORE'N 266 AHWILD
ANYTHING.
(HAPPILY RELIEVED-- 279 AHWILD
(IMMENSELY RELIEVED--ENTHUSIASTICALLY) 296 AHWILD
(WITH A RELIEVED SMILE) OH--THE OLD STUFF, EH& 50 ANNA
WHILE HE IS DOING THIS THE MAN WHOSE TURN AT THE 483 CARDIF
WHEEL HAS BEEN RELIEVED ENTERS.
(WITH A RELIEVED SMILE CARRIES OVER THE LANTERN) 557 CROSS
(RELIEVED--WITH A BOYISH GRIN) 505 DAYS
(RELIEVED) OH. 563 DAYS
(RELIEVED) WAAL--IT WA'N'T NOTHIN' T' SPEAK ON. 231 DESIRE
THEN EVIDENTLY SATISFIED, TURNS TO ADA WITH A 484 DYNAMO
RELIEVED AIR)
(IMPRESSED AND RELIEVED--PLACATINGLY) 51 ELECTR
(RELIEVED) SO THAT'S WHAT HE'S UP TO. IS IT& 288 GGBROW
(IN A TONE OF ONE WHO IS WEARILY RELIEVED 10 HUGHIE
AND HOW DAMNED RELIEVED AND CONTENTED WITH 625 ICEMAN
YOURSELF YOU FEEL
(RELIEVED) DERE. 633 ICEMAN
(THEY LOOK RELIEVED.) 639 ICEMAN
(WITH A CALCULATING RELIEVED LOOK AT HIM-- 643 ICEMAN
ENCOURAGING HIM ALONG THIS LINE)
HE LOOKS RELIEVED WHEN HE SEES LARRY 645 ICEMAN
I'LL BET YOU WERE REALLY DAMNED RELIEVED WHEN SHE 657 ICEMAN
GAVE YOU SUCH A GOOD EXCUSE.
RELIEVED AND NOT GUILTY ANY MORE& 693 ICEMAN
(SHE LAUGHS--THEN WITH A PLEASED, RELIEVED AIR.) 18 JOURNE
SHE BECOMES PATHETICALLY RELIEVED AND EAGER. 108 JOURNE
I WAS SO RELIEVED AND HAPPY WHEN YOU CAME, AND 112 JOURNE
GRATEFUL TO YOU.
TYRONE SPEAKS, AT FIRST WITH A WARM, RELIEVED 126 JOURNE
WELCOME.)
(RELIEVED, GRINS SHEEPISHLY.) 14 MANSNS
(SUDDENLY CALM AND RELIEVED AND A BIT GUILTY.) 113 MANSNS
AND SMILE AT EACH OTHER WITH A RELIEVED 123 MANSNS
UNDERSTANDING.
THE TWO WOMEN SIT WITH CLASPED HANDS, THEIR FACES 124 MANSNS
RELIEVED.
(IN A PANIC SHE PUTS HER HAND OVER HIS HEART-- 190 MANSNS
RELIEVED.)
THE KAAN STUDIES HIS SULLEN BUT RELIEVED FACE WITH380 MARCOM
AMUSEMENT)
(LOOKING UP AND STRAIGHTENING HIS CRAMPED BACK-- 408 MARCOM
WITH A RELIEVED SIGH)
I SUPPOSE YOU ARE RELIEVED TO GET ME HERE ALIVE 413 MARCOM
AND DELIVER ME--LIKE A COW/
(HIS VOICE COMES FROM OVER THE WATER CHEERY AND 420 MARCOM
RELIEVED)
(KNOWS HE IS TELLING THE TRUTH--SO RELIEVED SHE 132 MISBEG
CAN ONLY STAMMER STUPIDLY)
(SHE LOOKS RELIEVED.) WELL, IF THE YOUNG LAD SAID140 POET
THAT, MAYBE IT'S TRUE.
(THE OLD MAN SINKS BACK INTO A RELIEVED 583 ROPE
IMMOBILITY.
A PLEASED RELIEVED EXPRESSION FIGHTING THE 6 STRANG
FLURRIED WORRY ON HIS FACE.
(WITH SUDDEN RELIEVED EXCITEMENT) 68 STRANG
(RELIEVED) WELL, IT'S TRUE. 94 STRANG
(HECTICALLY RELIEVED) (OF COURSE/... 129 STRANG
(RELIEVED) OH, SURE, THAT'S RIGHT/ 171 STRANG
(AS SHE SEES WHO IT IS--IN A RELIEVED TONE OF 450 WELDED
SURPRISE)

RELIEVER

BEEN PLAYIN' DE OLD RELIEVER GAME. 581 ICEMAN

RELIEVES

WHO RELIEVES HER OF A BUNDLE.) 172 JOURNE
(HE RELIEVES HER OF THE PITCHER AND TUMBLERS AS 111 MISBEG
SHE COMES DOWN THE STEPS.)

RELIGHTING

HE SMOKES A PIPE, WHICH HE IS ALWAYS RELIGHTING 66 STRANG
WHETHER IT NEEDS IT OR NOT,

RELIGION

IS IT ANY RELIGION AT ALL YOU HAVE, YOU AND YOUR 77 ANNA
ANNAS
I AIN'T NEVER HAD RELIGION. 486 CARDIF
ON SUCH A DEAD ISSUE AS RELIGION. 497 DAYS
INTO A RED-HOT ARTICLE OF YOURS DENOUNCING 497 DAYS
CAPITALISM OR RELIGION OR SOMETHING.
(THEN HURRIEDLY) BUT, FOR PETE'S SAKE, LET'S NOT 497 DAYS
GET STARTED ON RELIGION.
RELIGION, NO LESS--BUT AS FAR AWAY AS HE COULD RUNSO3 DAYS
FROM HOME--
(WITH A WINK AT ELIOT) HE SEEMS TO BE FIXED IN 504 DAYS
HIS LAST RELIGION.
AN ABSURD OBSESSION WITH RELIGION. 509 DAYS
IF SHE EVER GOT RELIGION THAT BAD, 514 DIFRNT
HE ISN'T TO BLAME BECAUSE HIS FATHER BELIEVES IN 435 DYNAMO
RELIGION...
(PROTESTINGLY) AW, POP, LAY OFF RELIGION, CAN'T 438 DYNAMO
YOU/
WHY CAN'T HIS RELIGION BUCK HIM UP NOW&... 464 DYNAMO
AND THE BROTHERHOOD OF MAN ARE A RELIGION ABSORBED243 HA APE
WITH ONE'S MOTHER'S MILK.
HAVE YOU NO RESPECT FOR RELIGION, YOU UNREGENERATE578 ICEMAN
WOPS
HE'S BOUND BY HIS RELIGION TO SPLIT FIFTY-FIFTY 584 ICEMAN
WID YOU.
LIKE A REVIVALIST PREACHER ABOUT RELIGION. 589 ICEMAN
THIS TREE IS SACRED TO THE FOUNDER OF THE ONE TRUE349 MARCOM
RELIGION, ZOROASTER,
WHICH RELIGION IN THE WORLD IS BEST. 359 MARCOM
YOU GITTIN' RELIGION ALL UF A MOMENT JUST FOR 580 ROPE
SPITE ON ME 'CAUSE I'D LEFT--

RELIGIOUS

HE WAS STILL TOO RELIGIOUS-MINDED, YOU SEE, 534 DAYS
A CREDULOUS RELIGIOUS-MINDED FOOL, AS I'VE 535 DAYS
POINTED OUT/
(HIS FACE GROWING FULL OF JOYOUS PRIDE AND A SORT 234 DESIRE
OF RELIGIOUS ECSTASY)
(WITH A SMILE) OH, I HAVEN'T NO STRICT RELIGIOUS 495 DIFRNT
NOTIONS ABOUT IT.
EXCEPT WHERE THE RELIGIOUS BIGOTRY OF HIS ATHEISM 428 DYNAMO
IS CONCERNED.
AND THEY'RE THERE 'HOLDIN THEIR 'EATHEN RELIGIOUS 184 EJONES
SERVICE-MAKIN' NO END UF UEVIL
HELPLESSLY UNPROTECTED IN, ITS CHILDLIKE, RELIGIOUS260 GGBROW
FAITH IN LIFE--
(WITH A SORT OF RELIGIOUS EXALTATION) 214 HA APE
I DIDN'T FALL FOR THE RELIGIOUS BUNK. 707 ICEMAN
THIS MASK IS THAT OF A RELIGIOUS FANATIC. 282 LAZARU
IT IS RELIGIOUS BELIEF THAT YOU DEVIDES THEM. 282 LAZARU
NO MATTER HOW IT SHOCKS OUR SENTIMENTAL MORAL AND 47 MANSNS
RELIGIOUS DELUSIONS ABOUT HIM,

RELINQUISH

WHICH SPECIFICS THAT YOU RELINQUISH ALL CLAIMS, OF122 POET
WHATEVER NATURE.

RELINQUISHED

ALTHOUGH MOTHER HAS RELINQUISHED ALL OUTWARD SHOW 77 MANSNS
OF OWNERSHIP AND AUTHORITY,

RELISH

(HE GIVES A SARDONIC LAUGH OF RELISH AT THIS 214 DESIRE
IDEA.)
MA, I DON'T RELISH ROOSTIN' ON MY FEET. 507 DIFRNT
HE BEGINS TO DESCRIBE THE SLEEPERS WITH SARDONIC 593 ICEMAN
RELISH
(SEIZING ON THIS WITH VINDICTIVE RELISH) 657 ICEMAN
(APPLAUDS AND STANDS REGARDING HOGAN WITH 37 MISBEG
SARDONIC RELISH.
THEN SHE SMILES WITH AN AMUSED AND MOCKING RELISH, 67 POET
WITH AN APPRECIATIVE RELISH FOR THE FAMILIAR 4 STRANG
SIGNIFICANCE OF THE BOOKS.

RELISHING

(PLAINLY NOT RELISHING WHATEVER IS COMING--TO SID,192 AHWILD
GRUMBLINGLY)

RELUCTANCE

(HE IS ANSWERING ROBERT'S QUESTIONS WITH GREAT 161 BEYOND
RELUCTANCE.)
(WITH EVIDENT RELUCTANCE) YOU WANT TO DO IT 136 ELECTR
TONIGHT&
(AVOIDING HER EYES--CALCULATINGLY, WITH FEIGNED 87 MANSNS
RELUCTANCE.)

RELUCTANT

(HE HESITATES, AS IF RELUCTANT TO GO ON, AS IF 545 DAYS
THIS WERE THE END.)
STARING DOWN AT THE SHOES IN HIS HANDS AS IF 196 EJONES
RELUCTANT TO THROW THEM AWAY.
(HE PUTS A RELUCTANT HAND ON THE SWINGING DOOR) 687 ICEMAN
(WITH AN INDEFINABLE GUILTY AIR--AS IF HE WERE 55 STRANG
RELUCTANT TO ADMIT IT)

RELUCTANTLY

RELUCTANTLY CALLED BACK TO EARTH FROM ANOTHER 193 AHWILD
WORLD.
(HANDING IT TO HIM RATHER RELUCTANTLY) 82 BEYOND
(SHE RELUCTANTLY LEAVES HIM AND TAKES UP HER DOLL 130 BEYOND
AGAIN.
(THINKS A MOMENT--THEN RELUCTANTLY) 232 DESIRE
(HE MOVES RELUCTANTLY TOWARD THE DOOR.) 100 ELECTR
HOPE GETS TO HIS FEET RELUCTANTLY, WITH A FORCED 694 ICEMAN
SMILE.
(RELUCTANTLY.) HE "AID IT MIGHT BE. 30 JOURNE
(RELUCTANTLY.) YES I TOLD HIM I WOULDN'T GO 158 JOURNE
THERE.
(HE TURNS RELUCTANTLY.) 17 MANSNS
(RELUCTANTLY.) YES. 82 MANSNS
(RELUCTANTLY.) I DO. 14 POET
(RELUCTANTLY MOVES AWAY) IT LOOKS UGLY HANGIN' 583 ROPE
THERE OPEN LIKE A MOUTH.

RELY

RELY ON ME NOT TO TELL HIM, THEN. 558 CROSS
I THINK YOU CAN RELY ON HIS HELP IN THE END. 646 ICEMAN
I RELY ON YOU TO HELP ME KEEP HER IN HER RIGHTFUL 106 MANSNS
PLACE HEREAFTER.
YOU CAN RELY ON ME. 153 MANSNS

REMAIN

STILL REMAIN ON IT AFTER THE CAPTAIN'S DINNER. 535 'ILE
(HE KISSES HER TREMBLINGLY AND FOR A MOMENT THEIR 287 AHWILD
LIPS REMAIN TOGETHER.
AS IF SHE WANTED TO REMAIN AS MUCH ISOLATED AS 30 ANNA
POSSIBLE.
(THEY REMAIN MOTIONLESS AND SILENT FOR A MOMENT, 69 ANNA
HOLDING EACH OTHER'S EYES)
THE TWO BROTHERS REMAIN SILENT FOR A MOMENT. 109 BEYOND
(THE TWO WOMEN REMAIN SILENT FOR A TIME STARING 152 BEYOND
DEJECTEDLY AT THE STOVE.)
AS IF IT HAD BEEN ALLOWED TO REMAIN FALLOW THE 166 BEYOND
PRECEDING SUMMER.
HIS EYES REMAIN FIXED ON HER AS SHE COMES FORWARD.528 DAYS
ONE MAY NOT GIVE ONE'S SOUL TO A DEVIL OF HATE-- 538 DAYS
AND REMAIN FOREVER SCATHELESS.
THERE WILL REMAIN ONLY THE ANGUISH OF ENDLESS 561 DAYS
MEMORIES, ENDLESS REGRETS--
ABBIE RELAXES WITH A FAINT SIGH BUT HER EYES 236 DESIRE
REMAIN FIXED ON THE WALL.
THEY BOTH REMAIN RIGID, LOOKING STRAIGHT AHEAD 241 DESIRE
WITH EYES FULL OF FEAR.
THEY REMAIN IN EACH OTHER'S ARMS.) 253 DESIRE
HE AND HIS COMPANIONS REMAIN IN THE DOORWAY.) 269 DESIRE
OR DO YOU REMAIN TRUE TO YOUR ONE AND ONLY BEAU, 17 ELECTR
PETERS.
I WANT YOU TO REMAIN MY LITTLE GIRL--FOR A WHILE 51 ELECTR
LONGER, AT LEAST.

REMAIN

REMAIN (CONT'D.)

WHY CAN'T ALL OF US REMAIN INNOCENT AND LOVING AND 79 ELECTR

TRUSTINGS
(TO THE OTHERS WHO REMAIN WHERE THEY ARE) 132 ELECTR
THE TURNS AND HIS EYES REMAIN FIXED ON HERS FROM 142 ELECTR
NOW ON.

BILLY WANTS TO REMAIN BY HER SIDE/ 266 GGBROW
HIS EYES REMAIN EMPTY BUT HIS GUMMY LIPS PART 8 HUGHTE
AUTOMATICALLY

BUT THEY REMAIN SILENT AND MOTIONLESS. 685 ICEMAN
(STANDERS, HIS EYES ON LARRY, WHOSE EYES IN TURN 694 ICEMAN
REMAIN FIXED ON HICKEY)

SO ABSORBED IN HOPEFUL EXPECTANCY THAT THEY REMAIN19 ICEMAN
OBLIVIOUS TO WHAT HAPPENS AT

THE THREE IN THE ROOM REMAIN SILENT. 75 JOURNE
THEY HAVE TOO GOOD A EXCUSE TO REMAIN IN THE 100 JOURNE
BARROOMS WHERE THEY FEEL AT HOME.

ELMORE AND JAMIE REMAIN MOTIONLESS.) 176 JOURNE
AND THE CHORUS OF OLD MEN REMAIN IN THEIR 278 LAZARU
FORMATION AT THE REAR.

THE PEOPLE REMAIN WITH GOBLETS UPLIFTED, STARING 279 LAZARU
AT HIM.

HIS FOLLOWERS REMAIN FIXED IN THEIR DANCING 289 LAZARU
ATTITUDES LIKE FIGURES IN A FRIEZE.

LAZARUS AND HIS FOLLOWERS REMAIN OBLIVIOUS TO MEN.290 LAZARU
WHAT BETTER DISGUISE IF HE WISHES TO REMAIN 300 LAZARU
UNKNOWN

(THE SOLDIERS AND GREEKS REMAIN FROZEN IN THEIR 306 LAZARU
ATTITUDES OF MURDEROUS HATE.

(LAZARUS, MIRIAM AND CALIGULA REMAIN.) 323 LAZARU
(MOTIONING HER TO REMAIN WHERE SHE IS--GENTLY) 332 LAZARU
BUT THE TWO MEN REMAIN UNMINDFUL OF HER PRESENCE. 342 LAZARU
HIS EYES REMAIN ON CAESAR. 343 LAZARU

THE MATERIAL SECURITY WHICH GAVE HER THE CHANCE TO 47 MANSNS
REMAIN ALOOF AND SCORNFUL/

TO REMAIN BACK WHERE SHE BELONGS-- 94 MANSNS
AND WOULD ALWAYS REMAIN, WAITING TO SEE IF HE 111 MANSNS
WOULD DARE OPEN THE DOOR.

BUT IT MEANS I MUST ALWAYS REMAIN IN THE GAME 119 MANSNS
MYSELF--

BUT THEY REMAIN STARING AS ONE AT HIM, THEIR EYES 131 MANSNS
HARD AND UNFORGIVING.)

THEY REMAIN GREEDY LITTLE BOYS DEMANDING THE MOON.136 MANSNS
DEBORAH'S EYES REMAIN FIXED ON HER AND ABRUPTLY 136 MANSNS
HER EXPRESSION CHANGES

BUT THERE WILL BE NO PEACE AS LONG AS WE BOTH 179 MANSNS
REMAIN ALIVE/

I CANNOT REMAIN BACK HERE MUCH LONGER/ 189 MANSNS
ALL THESE MANHATTAN FIGURES REMAIN MOTIONLESS. 364 MARCOM
(BOTH REMAIN SILENT AND MOTIONLESS, 366 MARCOM
AND IT WILL REMAIN A POIGNANT MEMORY TO RECOMPENSE388 MARCOM
HER

YOU REMAIN--SEE HIM--BRING ME WORD--(HE TURNS HIS 401 MARCOM
HEAD UP TO KUKACHIN)

I BE ALLOWED TO REMAIN ON BOARD ALONE WITH MY 419 MARCOM
WOMEN.

KEEPING HEALS THE WOUNDS OF SORROW TILL ONLY THE 420 MARCOM
SCARS REMAIN

AND UP THE CITY OF VENICE NOT ONE VESTIGE SHALL 425 MARCOM
REMAIN/

ONLY THE CHORUS REMAIN, GROUPED IN A SEMI-CIRCLE 437 MARCOM
BEHIND THE CATAFALQUE.

AND SO I WILL REMAIN TO THE END, IN SPITE OF ALL 43 POET
FATE CAN DO TO CRUSH MY SPIRIT/

BUT HIS EYES REMAIN FIXED ON THE TABLE TOP.) 166 POET
A HEALTHY GUINEA PIG MYSELF AND STILL REMAIN AN 85 STRANG
OBSERVER....

(MEANINGLY) HE HAS NO TIE OVER HERE TO REMAIN 116 STRANG
FAITHFUL TO, HAS HE?

OLSON AND FREDA REMAIN SEATED.) 501 VOYAGE
BUT DURING THE FOLLOWING SCENE THEY STARE STRAIGHT452 WELDED
AHEAD AND REMAIN MOTIONLESS.

(FOR A LONG MOMENT THEY REMAIN THERE, 466 WELDED
FOR A LONG, TENSE MOMENT THEY REMAIN FIXED, 480 WELDED

REMAINDER

THE REMAINDER OF THE REAR SPACE IN FRONT OF THE 3 ANNA
LARGE MIRRORS IS OCCUPIED BY

(HE DRAINS THE REMAINDER OF HIS DRINK, BUT THIS 659 ICEMAN
TIME HE DRINKS ALONE.

MUMBLING WITH A LAST PITIFUL REMAINDER OF 308 LAZARU
DEFIANCE)

REMAINED

(LUCY HAS REMAINED STANDING BY THE LEFT CORNER OF 525 DAYS
THE SOFA, IN A STIFF,

THERE ALWAYS REMAINED SOMETHING IN HIM THAT FELT 534 DAYS
ITSELF DAMNED BY LIFE.

FATHER BAIRD HAS REMAINED MOTIONLESS, HIS EYES ON 537 DAYS
THE FLOOR.

(WHO HAS REMAINED DETACHED) KAPE HIM DOWN TIL 232 HA APE
HE'S COOLED OFF.

BUT HICKEY HAS REMAINED UNMOVED BY ALL THIS 662 ICEMAN
TAUNTING.

YOU SHOULD HAVE REMAINED A BACHELOR AND LIVED IN 67 JOURNE
SECOND-RATE HOTELS AND

THAT MUCH REMAINED HIDDEN IN ME OF THE SAD OLD 348 LAZARU
LAZARUS WHO DIED OF SELF-PITY--

POMPEIA, WHOSE GAZE HAS REMAINED FIXED ON LAZARUS 358 LAZARU
THROUGHOUT,

SO HE REMAINED FOR THE REST OF HIS LIFE STANDING 111 MANSNS
BEFORE THE DOOR.

SHE DID NOT SPEAK AGAIN, ALTHOUGH HE KNEW SHE 111 MANSNS
REMAINED THERE.

SHE WILL NOT NOTICE WE HAVE REMAINED OUT HERE. 177 MANSNS
(HE HAS REMAINED TENSE AND MOTIONLESS, 188 MANSNS
THAT WAS UNWISE, FOR THUS HE HAS REMAINED A 388 MARCOM
STRANGER.

I'D NEVER HAVE REMAINED SINGLE ALL THESE YEARS IN 430 MARCOM
THE EAST/

REMAINED (CONT'D.)

(WHO HAS REMAINED IN THE BACKGROUND, NOW COMES 73 POET
FORWARD--

HE HAVE REMAINED LOVERS, HAVEN'T WE? 446 WELDED
THE OTHER WOMEN HE HELPED COULD HARDLY CLAIM HE 456 WELDED
HAD REMAINED--

REMAINING

MY ONE REMAINING HOPE IS THAT NIVIR IN GOD'S 532 INZONE
WORLD WILL I IVIR SEE YOUR FACE

REMAINING.

EXTENDS ALONG THE REMAINING LENGTH OF WALL. 185 AHWILD
(HE SUDDENLY RAISES HIMSELF WITH HIS LAST 168 BEYOND
REMAINING STRENGTH AND POINTS TO THE

ASCENDS THE REMAINING STEPS AND ENTERS. 555 CROSS
LOVING, HIS EYES REMAINING FIXED ON ELSA WITH THE 550 DAYS
SAME STRANGE LOOK,

THEN HE STARTS BACKWARD SLOWLY, HIS ARMS REMAINING201 EJONES
OUT.

GRAB THE LAST TWO THEMSELVES AND SIT DOWN IN THE 658 ICEMAN
TWO VACANT CHAIRS REMAINING.

CUTS OFF ALL THE REMAINING WITH ONE STROKE) 312 LAZARU
WITH NO TRACE OF THEIR ANCIENT NOBILITY OR COURAGE315 LAZARU
REMAINING--THAT AND NO MORE/

(TO THE SLAVES WHO ARE TURNING OUT THE FEW 338 LAZARU
REMAINING LAMPS)

SWIFTLY FROM LAZARUS, REMAINING HUDDLED ONE 348 LAZARU
AGAINST THE OTHER.

(STIFFENING--COLDLY.) I AM NOT REMAINING HERE. 177 MANSNS
FORGETTING TO CLEAR THE FEW REMAINING DISHES ON 115 POET
THE CENTER TABLE.

HIS EXPRESSION CHANGES SO THAT HIS FACE LOSES ALL 167 POET
ITS REMAINING DISTINCTION AND

REMAINS

ONLY LILY REMAINS STIFF AND SILENT.) 225 AHWILD
RICHARD REMAINS STANDING, SUNK IN BITTER, GLOOMY 234 AHWILD
(BUT LILY REMAINS IMPLACABLY SILENT. 257 AHWILD
ONLY MRS. MILLER REMAINS DOLEFULLY PREOCCUPIED, AS259 AHWILD
IF SHE HASN'T HEARD.)

RICHARD REMAINS STANDING BY THE DOOR, STARING OUT 296 AHWILD
AT THE MOON.

(AS CHRIS REMAINS SUNK IN GLOOMY REFLECTION) 9 ANNA
STAGGERING BACK AGAINST THE CABIN WALL, WHERE HE 50 ANNA
REMAINS STANDING.

(AS ROBERT REMAINS SILENT SHE BURSTS INTO SOBS 92 BEYOND
AGAIN)

HE REMAINS STANDING BY THE DOOR, HIS ARMS FOLDED, 99 BEYOND
ANDREW REMAINS STANDING MOTIONLESS, HIS FACE PALE 108 BEYOND
AND SET.)

(ROBERT NODS BUT REMAINS SILENT.) 142 BEYOND
WHERE SHE REMAINS WATCHING ROBERT IN A TENSE, 150 BEYOND
EXPECTANT ATTITUDE.

SHE REMAINS LIKE THIS ALL DURING THE SCENE BETWEEN160 BEYOND
THE TWO BROTHERS.)

SHE REMAINS STANDING THERE FOR A MINUTE. 166 BEYOND
(HE REMAINS WITH HIS EYES FIXED ON IT FOR A 168 BEYOND
MOMENT.

SHE REMAINS SILENT, GAZING AT HIM DULLY WITH THE 169 BEYOND
SAD HUMILITY OF EXHAUSTION,

NO ONE REMAINS ON DECK BUT THE DONKEYMAN, 466 CARIBE
AND REMAINS FOR A MOMENT LISTENING FOR SOME SOUND 562 CROSS
FROM ABOVE.

LOVING REMAINS IN HIS CHAIR, HIS EYES FIXED BEFORE500 DAYS
HIM IN A HOSTILE STARE.

LOVING REMAINS STANDING AT RIGHT, REAR, OF JOHN.) 528 DAYS
BUT, FIRST, IT STILL REMAINS TO DECIDE WHAT IS TO 528 DAYS
BE YOUR HERO'S END.

LOVING REMAINS STANDING BEHIND HIM, 530 DAYS
FOR A SECOND LOVING REMAINS LOOKING AFTER HER. 541 DAYS
LOVING REMAINING, HIS GAZE CONCENTRATED ON THE BACK 541 DAYS
OF ELSA'S HEAD

LOVING REMAINS WHERE HE IS, STANDING MOTIONLESSLY 547 DAYS
BY THE BOOKCASE.)

AND REMAINS STANDING BY THE BOOKCASE AT LEFT OF 547 DAYS
DOORWAY.)

FATHER BAIRD REMAINS FOR A MOMENT STARING SADLY AT557 DAYS
THE FLOOR.

REMAINS STANDING WITH HIS ARMS STRETCHED UP TO THE566 DAYS
CROSS,

ONLY ABBIE REMAINS APATHETIC, 250 DESIRE
SHE REMAINS STANDING WHERE SHE IS, LOOKING AFTER 259 DESIRE
HIM--

HE HARDENS HIMSELF, HE REMAINS UNMOVED AND COLD, 259 DESIRE
(AS EMMA REMAINS SILENT) YES, HARRIET, THAT'S IT.508 DIFRNT
FINALLY SHE SITS DOWN HELPLESSLY AND REMAINS FIXED514 DIFRNT
IN A STRAINED ATTITUDE)

(REMAINS STANDING BELOW--THINKING CONFUSEDLY) 485 DYNAMO
JONES REMAINS FIXED IN HIS POSITION, LISTENING 190 EJONES
INTENTLY.

(HE SIGHS DEJECTEDLY AND REMAINS WITH BOWED 196 EJONES
SHOULDERS,

ONLY BLACKNESS, REMAINS AND SILENCE BROKEN BY JONES198 EJONES
AS HE RUSHES OFF,

REMAINS RIGIDLY FIXED THERE, 201 EJONES
LEM REMAINS SITTING WITH AN IMPERTURBABLE 203 EJONES
EXPRESSION, BUT LISTENING INTENTLY.

(LAVINIA STARES AT HER BUT REMAINS SILENT. 17 ELECTR
(SHE REMAINS SILENT. 38 ELECTR
CHRISTINE IS PREPARED AND REMAINS UNMOVED 50 ELECTR
LAVINIA REMAINS BY THE FOOT OF THE STEPS, STARING 77 ELECTR
AFTER THEM.

(THEN, AS LAVINIA REMAINS SILENT, 78 ELECTR
SHE ENTERS BUT REMAINS STANDING JUST INSIDE THE 82 ELECTR
DOORWAY

LAVINIA IS TREMBLING BUT HER FACE REMAINS HARD AND 92 ELECTR
EMOTIONLESS.

HE STILL REMAINS STOOPING OVER THE BODY AND STARES115 ELECTR
INTO BRANT'S FACE.

REMEMBER

REMAINS (CONT'D.)
SHE REMAINS AS BEFORE EXCEPT THAT HER MOANING HAS 121 ELECTR
BEGUN TO EXHAUST ITSELF.
ORIN COMES BACK TO LAVINIA WHO REMAINS KNEELING BY164 ELECTR
THE CHAIR.
BROWN REMAINS IN A STUPUR FOR A MOMENT-- 299 GGBROW
MARGARET REMAINS, STUNNED WITH HORROR. 318 GGBROW
(BITTERLY) I AM THE REMAINS OF WILLIAM BROWN/ 320 GGBROW
SHE REMAINS, SOBBING WITH DEEP, SILENT GRIEF.) 321 GGBROW
THE CLERK'S MIND REMAINS IN THE STREET TO GREET 19 HUGHIE
THE NOISE OF A FAR-OFF EL TRAIN.
BUT FALLS AND REMAINS WEARILY GLUED TO IT. 27 HUGHIE
THE CLERK'S MIND STILL CANNOT MAKE A GETAWAY 30 HUGHIE
BECAUSE THE CITY REMAINS SILENT.
(LARRY REMAINS INERT. 647 ICEMAN
(BUT JOE REMAINS INERT. 697 ICEMAN
AS HIS NAILS DIG INTO HIS PALMS, BUT HE REMAINS 701 ICEMAN
SILENT.
HE REMAINS RIGID AND UNYIELDING. 91 JOURNE
(THEN AS EDMUND REMAINS HOPELESSLY SILENT, SHE 94 JOURNE
ADDS SADLY.)
(EDMUND DRINKS BUT TYRONE REMAINS STARING AT THE 111 JOURNE
GLASS IN HIS HAND.
(EDMUND REMAINS SILENT. TYRONE REGARDS HIM--THEN 167 JOURNE
GOES ON.)
BUT LAZARUS REMAINS STANDING. 278 LAZARU
EACH MEMBER OF THE MOB REMAINS FROZEN IN A 289 LAZARU
DISTORTED POSTURE.
LAZARUS REMAINS, HIS EYES FIXED ON THE CROSS, 330 LAZARU
DIRECTLY IN FRONT OF IT.
MY HEART REMAINS A LITTLE DEAD WITH LAZARUS IN 331 LAZARU
BETHANY.
(A PAUSE. MARCELLUS REMAINS BEHIND LAZARUS' BACK, 333 LAZARU
LAZARUS REMAINS WHERE HE IS, MIRIAM BESIDE AND TO 339 LAZARU
THE REAR OF HIM.
MIRIAM REMAINS STANDING AT THE FOOT. 340 LAZARU
MAN REMAINS/ 359 LAZARU
THE SEA REMAINS/ 359 LAZARU
REMAINS LOOKING INTO HIS EYES A LONG TIME, 361 LAZARU
SHRINKING BACK FROM HIM WITH
IN WHICH EACH DANCER REMAINS FROZEN IN THE LAST 369 LAZARU
MOVEMENT)
DEBORAH'S REMAINS TEASINGLY MOCKING.) 69 MANSNS
DEBORAH REMAINS STILL. 168 MANSNS
BUT DEBORAH DOES NOT TURN TO IT AND REMAINS 187 MANSNS
CONFRONTING SARA.)
(MARCO REMAINS SULLENLY APART, SHAMEFACED AND 360 MARCOM
ANGRY, HIS FISTS CLENCHED.
STANDS THERE FOR A MOMENT AWKWARDLY AS TEDALDO 362 MARCOM
REMAINS OBLIVIOUS--
SHE REMAINS RIGID, GIVING NO SIGN.) 417 MARCOM
FOR ME THERE REMAINS ONLY--HER TRUTH/ 437 MARCOM
UNTIL ONLY A DIM LIGHT REMAINS. 111 MISBEG
(REMAINS ON ONE KNEE--CONFUSEDLY, AS IF HE DIDN'T 138 MISBEG
KNOW WHAT HAD HAPPENED)
SOMETHING BUT SHE REMAINS SILENT. 139 MISBEG
IT AND HE REMAINS UNEASILY SILENT. 159 MISBEG
(THEN AS SHE REMAINS SILENT--MISERABLY) 176 MISBEG
IS REMOVING DISHES AND THE REMAINS OF THE DINNER. 95 POET
(HE PAUSES, AS IF HE EXPECTS HER TO BE FURIOUS, 108 POET
BUT SHE REMAINS TENSELY SILENT.
IT REMAINS FOR MY OWN DAUGHTER--/ 125 POET
SHE PATS HER MOTHER'S HAND, BUT REMAINS SILENT, 137 POET
HER EXPRESSION DREAMILY HAPPY.
HIS EXPRESSION REMAINS BLANK AND DEAD. 153 POET
SARA REMAINS STANDING BY THE SIDE OF THE CENTER 180 POET
TABLE, HER SHOULDERS BOWED.
AND REMAINS STANDING BY THE DOORWAY IN STUBBORN 588 ROPE
SILENCE.)
SHE REMAINS STRIKINGLY HANDSOME AND HER PHYSICAL 26 STRANG
APPEAL IS ENHANCED BY HER
NOTHING REMAINS OF THE STRANGE FASCINATION OF HER 48 STRANG
FACE EXCEPT HER UNCHANGEABLY
DARRELL REMAINS STANDING NEAR THE TABLE LOOKING 78 STRANG
AFTER THEM.
(THEN AS SHE REMAINS SILENT--GOGGINGLY) 82 STRANG
THEN REMAINS FIXED FOR A MOMENT IN THAT ATTITUDE, 89 STRANG
(SHE REMAINS IN A SITTING POSITION, STARING 108 STRANG
BLANKLY BEFORE HER.
(DARRELL REMAINS STANDING LOOKING UP THE STAIRS IN124 STRANG
A SORT OF JOYOUS STUPUR.
DARELL REMAINS STANDING.) 127 STRANG
NINA REMAINS STANDING, DOMINATING THEM, 133 STRANG
DARRELL REMAINS STANDING AND SEEMS TO BE A LITTLE 165 STRANG
UNEASY.)
(SHE REMAINS STANDING ON THE RAIL, LEANING OUT 182 STRANG
DANGEROUSLY.
MARSDEN REMAINS OBLIVIOUS.) 198 STRANG
(AS SHE REMAINS OBLIVIOUS, STARING AFTER THE 199 STRANG
PLANE--THINKING FATALISTICALLY)
UT'S NO HARD SHIFT TO TAKE THE REMAINS HOME. 504 VOYAGE
SHE REMAINS THERE FOR A MOMENT STARING AT THE 451 WELDED
CLOSED DOOR.
SHE REMAINS WHERE SHE IS, 460 WELDED
SHE DOES NOT TURN BUT REMAINS STARING AT THE DOOR 487 WELDED
IN FRONT OF HER.

REMARK
(AS IF TO PUNCTUATE THIS REMARK, 189 AHWILD
(IGNORING THIS REMARK) WHAT I WAS SAYIN' WAS THAT114 BEYOND
SINCE ROBERT'S BEEN IN CHARGE
(WAVING HER REMARK ASIDE) YOU NEEDN'T DENY IT. 148 BEYOND
(NOT SEEMING TO NOTICE THIS REMARK) 557 CROSS
(HER REMARK IS REPEATED DOWN THE LINE WITH MANY A 248 DESIRE
GUFFAW AND TITTER UNTIL IT
(EMMA LOOKS DISPLEASED AT THIS REMARK AND BENNY 521 DIFRNT
HASTENS TO ADD CAJOLINGLY)
(JAMIE IS ABOUT TO MAKE SOME SNEERING REMARK TO 26 JOURNE
HIS FATHER,

REMARK (CONT'D.)
(THINKING, OBLIVIOUS TO THIS REMARK) 8 STRANG

REMARKABLE
REMARKABLE/ 229 AHWILD
THE THREE DAYS THAT HAVE INTERVENED HAVE EFFECTED 170 ELECTR
A REMARKABLE CHANGE IN HER.
THERE IS ALSO, WHAT IS MORE REMARKABLE, A DECIDED 111 STRANG
LOOK OF SOLIDITY ABOUT HIM.
IT'S REALLY REMARKABLE. 127 STRANG
HE'S DOING REMARKABLE WORK ALREADY, AND HE'S STILL140 STRANG
IN HIS TWENTIES.

REMARKABLY
OH, HE WAS A REMARKABLY SUPERSTITIOUS YOUNG FOOL/ 510 DAYS
HIS FACE HAS BEGUN TO BREAK DOWN BUT HE IS STILL 13 JOURNE
REMARKABLY GOOD LOOKING--
HIS VOICE IS REMARKABLY FINE, RESONANT AND 13 JOURNE
FLEXIBLE,

REMARKED
AS VESPASIAN REMARKED, THE SMELL OF ALL WHISKEY IS596 ICEMAN
SWEET.

REMARKING
REMARKING WITH CARELESS PRIDE.) 119 POET

REMARKS
PERSONAL REMARKS TO THE DANCERS THEMSELVES. 250 DESIRE
THE DANDIES POINT WITH THEIR FINGERS AND MAKE 197 EJONES
WITTY REMARKS.
THEN REMARKS EVENLY) 83 ELECTR
(THEN HE GROWLS.) KEEP YOUR DAMNED ANARCHIST 24 JOURNE
REMARKS TO YOURSELF.
LUCIUS REMARKS WITH A WEARY SMILE) 316 LAZARU
CHU-YIN BOWS GRAVELY AND REMARKS AS IF ANSWERING 402 MARCOM
AN ARGUMENT IN HIS OWN MIND)
HE REMARKS WITH INSULTING DERISIVENESS.) 101 POET
(COOLLY, STRUGGLING TO KEEP CONTROL, IGNORING 17 STRANG
THESE REMARKS)
EVERYONE REMARKS THAT/ 74 STRANG

REMBLANCE
THE MANNON REMBLANCE OF HIS FACE IN REPOSE TO A 137 ELECTR
MASK

REMEDIES
SIMPLE HOME REMEDIES--FROM THE BEST FRIEND I EVER 412 MARCOM
HAD/

REMEDY
YOUR REMEDY WAS TO GIVE HIM A TEASPOONFUL OF 111 JOURNE
WHISKEY TO QUIET HIM.

REMEMBER
AND TROUBLE I'VE HAD BY LAND AND BY SEA'S LONG AS 941 'ILE
I KIN REMEMBER,
AND REMEMBER THE 944 'ILE
REMEMBER, I WARN'T HANKERIN' TO HAVE YOU COME ON 945 'ILE
THIS VOYAGE, ANNIE.
DON'T YOU REMEMBER 548 'ILE
(SHOUTS AFTER HIM) BUT YOU SET OFF YOUR CRACKERS 186 AHWILD
AWAY FROM THE HOUSE, REMEMBER?
(SMILING) WELL, YOU CAN'T EXPECT A BOY TO 188 AHWILD
REMEMBER TO SHUT DOORS ON THE FOURTH
I REMEMBER. 197 AHWILD
REMEMBER THIS ONE. 198 AHWILD
REMEMBER, I'M NEXT ON THAT ONE, DICK. 198 AHWILD
TAKE AND GIVE HIM A HIDING HE'D REMEMBER TO THE 203 AHWILD
LAST DAY OF HIS LIFE/
NOW YOU WILL TRY TO REMEMBER, WON'T YOUS 211 AHWILD
YOU REMEMBER WHAT I TOLD YOU ABOUT THAT FISH. 220 AHWILD
I NEVER REMEMBER SEEING--MORE BEAUTIFUL SUNSET. 224 AHWILD
ALWAYS AIM AT HIS HEAD, REMEMBER--SO AS NOT TO 226 AHWILD
WORRY US.
REMEMBER YOU'RE AT HOME. 231 AHWILD
WHEN YOU REMEMBER IT'S FOURTH OF JULY, 251 AHWILD
I WASN'T, FOURTH OR NO FOURTH--IF I REMEMBER. 254 AHWILD
HE SINGS THAT OLD SENTIMENTAL FAVORITE, *THEN 257 AHWILD
YOU'LL REMEMBER ME.*
YES, I REMEMBER, SID. 259 AHWILD
YOU OUGHT TO HEAR VESTA VICTORIA--YOU REMEMBER 259 AHWILD
THAT TRIP I MADE TO NEW YORK.
REMEMBER HE'S LIKE YOU INSIDE--TOO SENSITIVE FOR 265 AHWILD
HIS OWN GOOD.
WHY, I REMEMBER WHEN I COULD COME DOWN ON THE 265 AHWILD
MORNING AFTER, FRESH AS A DAISY.
(WORRIEDLY) NOW YOU KEEP YOUR TEMPER, NAT, 266 AHWILD
REMEMBER/
WELL, DON'T BLAME HIM IF HE DON'T REMEMBER 267 AHWILD
EVERYTHING THAT HAPPENED LAST NIGHT.
IF YOU REMEMBER, I WAS ALWAYS GETTING PUNISHED-- 268 AHWILD
REMEMBER, YOU'RE NOT ALLOWED OUT TODAY--FOR A 271 AHWILD
PUNISHMENT.
SEE IF YOU REMEMBER. 276 AHWILD
YOU REMEMBER YOU'VE PROMISED. 280 AHWILD
I'D NEVER REMEMBER--ANYTHING BUT IT--NEVER WANT 287 AHWILD
ANYTHING BUT IT--EVER AGAIN.
WELL, ANYWAY HE'LL HAVE IT TO REMEMBER--NO MATTER 291 AHWILD
WHAT HAPPENS AFTER--
UR TO REMEMBER THE THREATENED PUNISHMENT. 292 AHWILD
(THEN A BIT PLEADINGLY) BUT YOU'LL REMEMBER ALL I 293 AHWILD
SAID, NAT, WON'T YOU?
I CAN ONLY REMEMBER A FEW NIGHTS THAT WERE AS 296 AHWILD
BEAUTIFUL AT THIS--AND THEY WERE
LETTERS COME HERE FOR HIM SOMETIMES BEFORE, I 5 ANNA
REMEMBER NOW.
ONLY--IT'S FUNNY TO SEE YOU AND NOT REMEMBER 20 ANNA
NOTHING.
YOU DON'T REMEMBER DATS 21 ANNA
(IMPRESSED--SLOWLY) I DON'T REMEMBER NOTHING 22 ANNA
ABOUT HER.
I S'POSE YOU REMEMBER YOUR PROMISE, MATS 59 ANNA
AND I'LL BE GETTING DEAD RUTTEN DRUNK SO I'LL NOT 61 ANNA
REMEMBER IF I WAS IVER BORN
I CAN REMEMBER BEING CONSCIOUS OF IT FIRST WHEN I 89 BEYOND
WAS ONLY A KID--

REMEMBER

REMEMBER (CONT'D.)		
THAT I LOVED YOU, HAD LOVED YOU AS LONG AS I COULD	91 BEYOND	
REMEMBER,		
WITH NARY A QUARREL I KIN REMEMBER,	98 BEYOND	
I ASKED YOU TO REMEMBER THAT UNTIL THIS EVENING I	100 BEYOND	
DIDN'T KNOW MYSELF,		
(APPEALINGLY) YOU MUST ALL REMEMBER THAT FACT,	100 BEYOND	
WON'T YOUS		
YOU'RE OUT OF THIS, REMEMBER,	104 BEYOND	
PUT YOURSELF IN MY PLACE, AND REMEMBER I HAVEN'T	110 BEYOND	
STOPPED LOVING HER,		
I CAN REMEMBER HOW YOU USED TO COME UP HERE TO	131 BEYOND	
HOPE AND DREAM IN THE OLD DAYS,		
AND IS WHAT YOU'VE TOLD ME ALL YOU REMEMBER ABOUT	132 BEYOND	
IT,		
I REMEMBER THINKING ABOUT YOU AT THE WORST OF IT,	132 BEYOND	
AND SAYING TO MYSELF,		
(SURPRISED) NO, HE DIDN'T MENTION YOU, I CAN	138 BEYOND	
REMEMBER,		
REMEMBER THAT, RUTH/	157 BEYOND	
I'LL ONLY LET YOU SIT DOWN IF YOU'LL PROMISE THAT,159 BEYOND		
REMEMBER,		
REMEMBER, ANDY, RUTH HAS SUFFERED DOUBLE HER	162 BEYOND	
SHARE,		
FORGIVE ME, RUTH---FOR HIS SAKE--AND I'LL	168 BEYOND	
REMEMBER--		
HE TOLD YOU--TO REMEMBER,	168 BEYOND	
RUTH HAS SUFFERED--REMEMBER, ANDY--ONLY THROUGH	168 BEYOND	
SACRIFICE--		
(ANDY'S BENDS DOWN TO HIM) REMEMBER RUTH--	168 BEYOND	
HE MUMBLES) REMEMBER/ (AND FALLS BACK AND IS	168 BEYOND	
STILL,		
AN' YOU BLOKES REMEMBER WHEN WE 'AULED 'IM IN	479 CARDIF	
'ERE$		
REMEMBER THE TIME WE WAS THERE ON THE BEACH	487 CARDIF	
D'YUH REMEMBER THE TIMES WE HAD IN BUENOS AIRESS	487 CARDIF	
D'YUH REMEMBER THEM$	487 CARDIF	
SOME CLASS TU THEM, D'YUH REMEMBERS	487 CARDIF	
REMEMBER THE NIGHT I WENT CRAZY WITH THE HEAT IN	488 CARDIF	
SINGAPORES		
HOW DRUNK WE USED TO GET ON THAT, REMEMBERS	488 CARDIF	
DON'T YOU BOYS FORGET TO MARK DOWN CIGARETTES OR	465 CARIBE	
TOBACCO OR FRUIT, REMEMBER/		
CERTAINLY, I REMEMBER--BUT I DON'T SEE--	558 CROSS	
I SHOULD THINK YOU COULD REMEMBER THAT--ONLY YOU	496 DAYS	
WELL,		
THAT'S A PROMISE, REMEMBER--	497 DAYS	
WHY, I REMEMBER ONE ARTICLE WHERE YOU ACTUALLY	497 DAYS	
TRIED TO PROVE		
I CAN REMEMBER WHEN I COULDN'T PICK UP AN	497 DAYS	
ADVANCED-THINKER ORGAN WITHOUT RUNNING		
THE FIRST COMING IS ENOUGH, JACK--FOR THOSE WHO	501 DAYS	
REMEMBER IT,		
YES, I REMEMBER HIS WRITING TO BOAST ABOUT THAT,	502 DAYS	
I'LL REMEMBER, JACK,	512 DAYS	
ONLY REMEMBER, THE WORLD IS FULL OF SPITEFUL LIARS524 DAYS		
WHO WOULD DO ANYTHING TO		
BUT REMEMBER, WE HAD BARELY ENOUGH TO GET ALONG ONS29 DAYS		
WHEN WE WERE MARRIED--		
REMEMBER IT'S A ROTTEN, CHILLY,	533 DAYS	
WELL, YOU WILL REMEMBER MY FIRST PART ENDED WHEN	534 DAYS	
THE BOY'S PARENTS HAD DIED,		
REMEMBER, ALL THIS TIME HE SAW THROUGH HER,	537 DAYS	
REMEMBER IT'S COLD AND RAINING OUT,	540 DAYS	
ALL THEY NEED IS TO REMEMBER HIM,	543 DAYS	
BUT REMEMBER THAT IS NOT THE END/	560 DAYS	
BUT WHAT SUPERSTITIOUS NONSENSE YOU MAKE ME	562 DAYS	
REMEMBER,		
I REMEMBER TOO WELL/	562 DAYS	
I REMEMBER IT RIGHT WELL,	209 DESIRE	
I DON'T REMEMBER HER NONE,	225 DESIRE	
LISTEN, ABBIE--IF YE EVER GIT TIRED O' EBEN,	248 DESIRE	
REMEMBER ME/		
HE NEEDS YE, REMEMBER--OUR SON DOES/	252 DESIRE	
(EXULTANTLY) REMEMBER YE'VE PROMISED/	259 DESIRE	
(SIMPLY) SHE WENT BACK T' HER GRAVE THAT NIGHT WE261 DESIRE		
FUST DONE IT, REMEMBERS		
(WITH A LAUGH) REMEMBER, I'M WARNIN' YOU, EMMER,	496 DIFRNT	
IT AIN'T NO USE DEPENDIN' ON A MAN TO REMEMBER	506 DIFRNT	
NOTHIN' WHEN HE'S IN LOVE,		
YOU'D OUGHT TO REMEMBER ALL HE'S BEEN TO YOU AND	512 DIFRNT	
FORGET THIS ONE LITTLE WRONG		
YOU'LL REMEMBER WHAT I TOLD YE 'BOUT WAITIN',	518 DIFRNT	
EMMERS		
(PLEASED--CONDESCENDINGLY) YOUR UNCLE CALEB'S AN	522 DIFRNT	
OLE MAN, REMEMBER,		
BUT I REMEMBER ENOUGH ABOUT 'EM TO KNOW THEY WAS	522 DIFRNT	
GOOD SPORTS,		
YOU'D REMEMBER YOUR UNCLE CALEB'S BEEN IN LOVE	530 DIFRNT	
WITH EMMA ALL HIS LIFE AND WAITED		
I KIN REMEMBER THE OLD CUSS MARCHIN' OVER HERE	533 DIFRNT	
EVERY EVENIN' HE WAS TU HOME		
D'YOU REMEMBER WHAT HAPPENED THIRTY YEARS BACKS	538 DIFRNT	
IF YOU REMEMBER WHAT I SAID THAT DAYS	538 DIFRNT	
DO YOU REMEMBER OUR FIRST SPRING HERES	425 DYNAMO	
I REMEMBER THAT IT'S SPRING--AND I'VE JUST	425 DYNAMO	
REMEMBERED THAT FIFE HAS A DAUGHTER/		
REMEMBER, MOTHER/	447 DYNAMO	
(PLEADINGLY) REMEMBER YOU SWORE ON THE BIBLE	447 DYNAMO	
YOU'D NEVER TELL/		
I MUST REMEMBER TO GET IT FIXED OR THEY'LL BE	457 DYNAMO	
FLYING IN KEEPING HER AWAKE....))		
EVER SINCE I CAN REMEMBER THE CELLARS LEAKED LIKE464 DYNAMO		
A SIEVE,		
AND I CAN REMEMBER THE CEILING IN MY ROOM,	464 DYNAMO	
YOU ARE MY SON AS WELL AS HERS, REMEMBER,	466 DYNAMO	
REMEMBER YOU DONE GOT A LONG JOURNEY YIT BEFO'	188 EJONES	
YOU,		

REMEMBER (CONT'D.)		
I REMEMBER--SEEMS LIKE I BEEN HEAH BEFO',	200 EJONES	
REMEMBER WHAT THAT CANUCK GIRL'S NAME WAS, DO YOU,	20 ELECTR	
VINNIE, MARIE BRANTOME/		
THAT NIGHT WE WENT WALKING IN THE MOONLIGHT, DO	21 ELECTR	
YOU REMEMBERS		
(IN A DRY, BRITTLE TONE) I REMEMBER YOUR	23 ELECTR	
ADMIRATION FOR		
WHENEVER I REMEMBER THOSE ISLANDS NOW, I WILL	24 ELECTR	
ALWAYS THINK OF YOU,		
SO YOU REMEMBER THAT, DO YOUS	24 ELECTR	
I CAN REMEMBER WHEN MEN FROM THE CORNER SALOON	25 ELECTR	
WOULD DRAG HIM HOME		
I'VE FELT IT EVER SINCE I CAN REMEMBER--YOUR	31 ELECTR	
DISGUST/		
I REMEMBER THAT NIGHT WE WERE INTRODUCED AND I	36 ELECTR	
HEARD THE NAME MRS, EZRA MANNON/		
(KISSES HIM) REMEMBER THAT OATH/	37 ELECTR	
(THEN TURNING AWAY AGAIN) YOU REMEMBER MY TELLING	39 ELECTR	
YOU HE HAD WRITTEN		
REMEMBER YOUR MOTHER'S DEATH/	42 ELECTR	
REMEMBER YOUR DREAM OF YOUR OWN SHIP/	42 ELECTR	
ABOVE ALL, REMEMBER YOU'LL HAVE ME/	42 ELECTR	
I DON'T REMEMBER,	59 ELECTR	
YOU DON'T WANT TO REMEMBER YOU EVER LOVED ME/	59 ELECTR	
(FLUSTEREDLY) I DON'T REMEMBER EVER SAYING--	69 ELECTR	
YOU REMEMBER, EVERETT,	69 ELECTR	
I REMEMBER YOU SAID YOU WERE AFRAID HIS HEART WAS	70 ELECTR	
BAD,		
I REMEMBER YOU DID TOO,	70 ELECTR	
THAT'S WHAT MOTHER USED TO SAY IT REMINDED HER OF,	74 ELECTR	
I REMEMBER,		
REMEMBER, ORIN/	77 ELECTR	
DO YOU REMEMBER HOW YOU WAVED YOUR HANDKERCHIEF,	82 ELECTR	
HAZEL,		
ONLY REMEMBER WHAT I SAID, ORIN,	83 ELECTR	
NO MANNONS ALLOWED WAS OUR PASSWORD, REMEMBER/	85 ELECTR	
REMEMBER YOU'VE ALL I HAVE TO PROTECT ME/	88 ELECTR	
(WITH A BOYISH GRIN) YOU BET I REMEMBER/	90 ELECTR	
DO YOU REMEMBERS	90 ELECTR	
AND YOU REMEMBER HOW YOU USED TO LET ME BRUSH	90 ELECTR	
YOUR HAIR AND HOW I LOVED TOS		
I AM HIS SON, TOO, REMEMBER THAT/	100 ELECTR	
NO---REMEMBER YOUR FATHER WOULDN'T WANT--ANY	101 ELECTR	
SCANDAL--		
I HAD IT IN THIS POCKET--I REMEMBER I PUT IT THERE103 ELECTR		
PARTICULAR--		
AYE, I REMEMBER/	103 ELECTR	
REMEMBER YOU PROMISED NOT TO LOSE YOUR HEAD,	113 ELECTR	
WE MUST MAKE IT LOOK AS IF THIEVES KILLED HIM,	114 ELECTR	
REMEMBER/		
DO YOU REMEMBER ME TELLING YOU HOW THE FACES OF	115 ELECTR	
THE MEN I KILLED CAME BACK AND		
I SAW YOU WEREN'T YOURSELF THE MINUTE I GOT HOME,	121 ELECTR	
REMEMBERS		
WILL YOU REMEMBER TO TELL HIM THATS	125 ELECTR	
REMEMBER ALL I'VE GONE THROUGH ON YOUR ACCOUNT,	141 ELECTR	
AND REMEMBER THIS HOMECOMING IS WHAT YOU WANTED,	141 ELECTR	
YOU BET I REMEMBER/	144 ELECTR	
VINNIE IS THE SAME OLD BUSSY FUSS-BUZZER--YOU	144 ELECTR	
REMEMBER,		
DO YOU REMEMBER AVAHANNI$	145 ELECTR	
BUT REMEMBER I'M ONLY HALF MANNON,	146 ELECTR	
YOU WEREN'T TO TALK NONSENSE, REMEMBER/	146 ELECTR	
HE WANTED ME TO, IF YOU REMEMBER,	150 ELECTR	
REMEMBER/	151 ELECTR	
FOR ONE EXAMPLE, DO YOU REMEMBER THE FIRST MATE,	153 ELECTR	
WILKINS,		
HE HAD BEEN THERE TOO, IF YOU'LL REMEMBERS	154 ELECTR	
(VINDICTIVELY) YOU REMEMBER WHAT I'VE GIVEN YOU,	161 ELECTR	
HAZEL,		
(WITH A TWISTED SMILE) REMEMBER ONLY THAT DEAD	164 ELECTR	
HERO AND NOT HIS ROTTING GHOST/		
DO YOU REMEMBER, FATHERS	259 GGBROW	
I REMEMBER THE JUNE WHEN I WAS CARRYING YOU,	261 GGBROW	
DION--		
AND REMEMBER I'LL ALWAYS BE YOUR BEST FRIEND/	263 GGBROW	
REMEMBER SHE'S WAITING/	266 GGBROW	
I REMEMBER A SWEET, STRANGE GIRL, WITH	282 GGBROW	
AFFECTIONATE, BEWILDERED EYES		
(TURNS AWAY--EMBARRASSED) I--I DON'T REALLY	282 GGBROW	
REMEMBER, DION--I'LL LOOK IT UP,		
WELL, REMEMBER HE'S PAYING, HE'LL PAY--IN SOME WAY287 GGBROW		
OR OTHER,		
REMEMBER, IT'S ALL A GAME, AND AFTER YOU'RE ASLEEP288 GGBROW		
I'LL TUCK YOU IN,		
PLEASE FORGIVE MY INTRUSION, AND REMEMBER ME TO	290 GGBROW	
CYBEL WHEN YOU WRITE,		
WE DIMLY REMEMBER SO MUCH IT WILL TAKE US SO MANY	291 GGBROW	
MILLION YEARS TO FORGET/		
(SHAMEFACEDLY) I REMEMBER NOW,	295 GGBROW	
IT'S FOR HIS OWN GOOD, REMEMBERS	304 GGBROW	
(SUBTLY) REMEMBER THE SCHOOL COMMENCEMENT DANCE--	309 GGBROW	
I REMEMBER THE JONES WHEN I WAS CARRYING YOU	323 GGBROW	
BOYS--IA PAUSE,		
REMEMBER FORCE DEFEATS ITSELF,	236 HA APE	
WHEN HE DOES NOT HAVE TO REMEMBER ANYTHING--HE	10 HUGHIE	
PLUCKS OUT THE KEY,)		
I DON'T REMEMBER NOTHING MUCH ABOUT ERIE, P-A, YOU	14 HUGHIE	
UNDERSTAND--OR WANT TO,		
PUT ABOUT A THOUSAND GUYS' NAMES IN A HAT--ALL SHE	15 HUGHIE	
COULD REMEMBER--		
IT'S TOO BAD I CAN'T REMEMBER NO OTHERS,	22 HUGHIE	
REMEMBER THAT DOLL I BRUNG HOME NIGHT BEFORE LASTS	26 HUGHIE	
THE NIGHT CLERK'S FOREHEAD PUCKERS PERSPIRINGLY AS	30 HUGHIE	
HE TRIES TO REMEMBER,		
THE MANAGER WOULDN'T LIKE YOU TO REMEMBER	37 HUGHIE	
SOMETHING HE AIN'T HEARD OF YET,		

REMEMBER

REMEMBER (CONT'D.)
REMEMBER HOW HE WOKES UP DAT GAG ABOUT HIS WIFE, 580 ICEMAN
WHEN HE'S COCKEYED.
YUH REMEMBER DEY USED TO SEND DOWN A PRIVATE DICK 581 ICEMAN
I SUPPOSE YOU DON'T REMEMBER A DAMNED THING ABOUT 588 ICEMAN
IT.
(MOVED IN SPITE OF HIMSELF) I REMEMBER WELL. 588 ICEMAN
WHY, NOTHING--EXCEPT I REMEMBER WHAT A FIGHT YOU 589 ICEMAN
HAD WITH HER BEFORE YOU LEFT.
(WITH A STRANGE SMILE) I DON'T REMEMBER IT THAT 590 ICEMAN
WAY.
I REMEMBER NOW. 602 ICEMAN
BESSIE MADE ME MAKE FRIENDS WITH EVERYONE, HELPED 603 ICEMAN
ME REMEMBER ALL THEIR NAMES.
YOU REMEMBER, ED, YOU, TOO, MAC-- 603 ICEMAN
(HE CHUCKLES REMINISCENTLY) REMEMBER THE TIME SHE608 ICEMAN
SENT ME DOWN TO THE BAR TO
CUPS DESTROYED THEM, AND I REMEMBER A LOT OF 608 ICEMAN
PEOPLE, EVEN IF I CAN'T PROVE--
(HE CHUCKLES AT A MEMORY) REMEMBER THAT GAG HE 610 ICEMAN
ALWAYS PULLS ABOUT HIS WIFE AND
(SHARPLY) I'M GLAD YOU REMEMBER IT. 616 ICEMAN
I REMEMBER WELL HIS SAYING TO ME, =YOU ARE 626 ICEMAN
NATURALLY DELICATE, ED.
REMEMBER DAT, OR YOU'LL WAKE UP IN A HOSPITAL-- 636 ICEMAN
I'VE BEEN WISE, EVER SINCE I CAN REMEMBER, TO ALL 646 ICEMAN
THE GUYS SHE'S HAD.
I REMEMBER THAT LAST FIGHT YOU HAD WITH HER. 647 ICEMAN
I REMEMBER HER PUTTING ON HER HIGH-AND-MIGHTY 647 ICEMAN
FREE-WOMAN STUFF,
I REMEMBER THAT YOU GOT MAD AND YOU TOLD HER, =I 647 ICEMAN
DON'T LIKE LIVING WITH A WHORE.
I MIGHT REMEMBER THE THING THEY CALL JUSTICE 649 ICEMAN
THERE, AND THE PUNISHMENT FOR--
REMEMBER, LIEUTENANT, YOU ARE SPEAKING OF MY 651 ICEMAN
SISTER/
(HE CHUCKLES) HARRY DON'T EVEN WANT TO REMEMBER 653 ICEMAN
IT'S HIS BIRTHDAY NOW/
KINDLY REMEMBER I'M FULLY CAPABLE OF SETTLING MY 655 ICEMAN
OWN AFFAIRS/
YOU REMEMBER HOW I USED TO BE/ 661 ICEMAN
REMEMBER WHAT I WARNED YOU--/ 666 ICEMAN
YOU REMEMBER HE GAVE A DEMONSTRATION OF HIS 676 ICEMAN
EXTRAORDINARY MUSCLES LAST NIGHT
YOU REMEMBER, ROCKY, 676 ICEMAN
BUT REMEMBER, THEY GET YOU IN THE END. 679 ICEMAN
BUT I REMEMBER THE ONLY BREATH-KILLER IN THIS DUMP801 ICEMAN
IS COFFEE BEANS.
I REMEMBER NOW CLEAR AS DAY THE LAST TIME BEFORE 688 ICEMAN
SHE--
I REMEMBER I HAD SOMETHING ON MY MIND TO TELL YUH. 701 ICEMAN
BUT WE REMEMBER THE OLD TIMES, TOO, 706 ICEMAN
I CAN'T EVEN REMEMBER NOW IF SHE WAS PRETTY. 707 ICEMAN
YES, SIR, AS FAR BACK AS I CAN REMEMBER, EVELYN 709 ICEMAN
AND I LOVED EACH OTHER.
WROTE HER A KIDDING LETTER, I REMEMBER, 710 ICEMAN
I REMEMBER I STOOD BY THE BED AND SUDDENLY I HAD 716 ICEMAN
TO LAUGH.
I REMEMBER I HEARD MYSELF SPEAKING TO HER, 716 ICEMAN
YOU REMEMBER WHAT MOTHER'S LIKE, LARRY. 719 ICEMAN
WE'LL FORGET THAT AND ONLY REMEMBER HIM THE WAY 722 ICEMAN
WE'VE ALWAYS KNOWN HIM BEFORE--
REMEMBER, YOU'VE GOT TO TAKE CARE OF YOURSELF, 16 JOURNE
TOO.
(SCATHINGLY.) IF IT TAKES MY SNORING TO MAKE YOU 21 JOURNE
REMEMBER SHAKESPEARE INSTEAD
AND YOU REMEMBER SHAUGHNESSY KEEPS PIGS. 23 JOURNE
WELL, YOU REMEMBER, PAPA, 23 JOURNE
REMEMBER HE ISN'T WELL. 26 JOURNE
YOU OUGHT TO REMEMBER IT, TOO, JAMIE. 28 JOURNE
YOU MUSTN'T MAKE EDMUND WORK ON THE GROUNDS WITH 29 JOURNE
YOU, JAMES, REMEMBER.
THE RIGHT WAY IS TO REMEMBER. 45 JOURNE
BUT DON'T GET OVERHEATED, REMEMBER. 49 JOURNE
BUT REMEMBER I'VE SEEN A LOT MORE OF THIS GAME 57 JOURNE
THAN YOU HAVE.
REMEMBER YOUR FATHER IS GETTING OLD, JAMIE. 60 JOURNE
DON'T YOU REMEMBER MY FATHERS 67 JOURNE
LET'S REMEMBER ONLY THAT, AND NOT TRY TO 85 JOURNE
UNDERSTAND WHAT WE CANNOT UNDERSTAND,
YOU MUSTN'T REMEMBER/ YOU MUSTN'T HUMILIATE ME 86 JOURNE
SO/
YOU REMEMBER, JAMES, 87 JOURNE
HE HAS SNORED EVER SINCE I CAN REMEMBER, 99 JOURNE
DO YOU REMEMBER WHAT A HEALTHY, HAPPY BABY HE WAS,109 JOURNE
JAMES
YOU REMEMBER, JAMES, FOR YEARS AFTER HE WENT TO 110 JOURNE
BOARDING SCHOOL,
I CAN REMEMBER THAT TEASPOONFUL OF BOOZE EVERY 111 JOURNE
TIME I WOKE UP WITH A NIGHTMARE.
DO YOU REMEMBER$ 112 JOURNE
(WITH GUILTY VEHEMENCE.) I DON'T REMEMBER/ 113 JOURNE
WE WERE STILL ON OUR HONEYMOON, DO YOU REMEMBER$ 113 JOURNE
I REMEMBER THE FIRST NIGHT YOUR BARROOM FRIENDS 113 JOURNE
HAD TO HELP YOU UP TO THE DOOR
DO YOU REMEMBER OUR WEDDING, DEAR$ 114 JOURNE
I WANT TO REMEMBER ONLY THE HAPPY PART OF THE 114 JOURNE
PAST.
I REMEMBER I HELD MY BREATH WHEN IT WAS FITTED, 115 JOURNE
YOU REMEMBER THAT, DON'T YOU$ 118 JOURNE
(BITTERLY.) I REMEMBER, ALL RIGHT. 118 JOURNE
(HE SIGHS.) WHY CAN'T YOU REMEMBER YOUR 131 JOURNE
SHAKESPEARE AND FORGET THE
IT WAS A TERRIBLE ORDEAL, I REMEMBER, HEARING YOU 136 JOURNE
MURDER THE LINES.
REMEMBER SHE'S NOT RESPONSIBLE. 139 JOURNE
WHEN I REMEMBER ALL THE ROTTEN STUFF I'VE PULLED/ 145 JOURNE

REMEMBER (CONT'D.)
WELL I REMEMBER ONE THANKSGIVING, OR MAYBE IT WAS 148 JOURNE
CHRISTMAS,
I CAN REMEMBER HER HUGGING AND KISSING US AND 148 JOURNE
SAYING WITH TEARS OF JOY RUNNING
I REMEMBER I PUT IT AWAY CAREFULLY-- 152 JOURNE
REMEMBER DOCTOR'S ORDERS. 158 JOURNE
REMEMBER I WARNED YOU--FOR YOUR SAKE. GIVE ME 167 JOURNE
CREDIT.
I REMEMBER NOW. I FOUND IT IN THE ATTIC HIDDEN IN172 JOURNE
A TRUNK.
YES, I REMEMBER. 176 JOURNE
(WITH WONDERING AWE) DO YOU REMEMBER HIM, 276 LAZARU
NEIGHBORS, BEFORE HE DIED$
REMEMBER HE IS OUR FATHER/ 284 LAZARU
REMEMBER TIBERIUS NEVER LAUGHS/ 294 LAZARU
THEIR LOVE MUST REMEMBER--OR IT MUST FORGET. 294 LAZARU
WE REMEMBER FEAR/ 296 LAZARU
WE REMEMBER DEATH/ 296 LAZARU
WE REMEMBER FEAR/ 296 LAZARU
WE REMEMBER DEATH/ 296 LAZARU
WE REMEMBER ONLY DEATH/ 296 LAZARU
BUT I HAVE HEARD THAT WHEN HE HAS GONE PEOPLE 300 LAZARU
CANNOT REMEMBER HIS LAUGHTER,
REMEMBER CAESAR/ 311 LAZARU
REMEMBER HOME/ 311 LAZARU
I CAN REMEMBER-- 315 LAZARU
WELL, NEVER MIND NOW, REMEMBER OUR OFFER. 322 LAZARU
WHEN YOU AWAKE TOMORROW, TRY TO REMEMBER/ 323 LAZARU
REMEMBER THAT DEATH IS DEAD/ 323 LAZARU
REMEMBER TO LAUGH/ 323 LAZARU
(WITH A GREAT YEARNING) IF MEN WOULD REMEMBER/ 323 LAZARU
WE WILL REMEMBER, LAZARUS/ 323 LAZARU
REMEMBER THAT/ 357 LAZARU
AND REMEMBER THERE SHALL BE NO DEATH WHILE I AM 357 LAZARU
CAESAR/
NOW I REMEMBER THE PITY IN YOUR EYES WHEN YOU 361 LAZARU
LOOKED AT ME/
I WILL REMEMBER/ 371 LAZARU
I DON'T REMEMBER EVER SEEING YOU CRY. 5 MANSNS
I AM GLAD YOU STILL REMEMBER, DEAR. 7 MANSNS
JOEL WILL REMEMBER OUR NIGHT AT SUPPER WHEN I 29 MANSNS
ACTUALLY ASKED MY HUSBAND..
I REMEMBER HOW DEVOTED YOU ONCE WERE TO SIMON. 39 MANSNS
(WARNINGLY.) SIMON, REMEMBER-- 52 MANSNS
I REMEMBER SIMON-- 57 MANSNS
AND REMEMBER I HAVE THE RIGHT TO EXPECT A PEACEFUL 67 MANSNS
ATMOSPHERE IN MY HOME.
YOU REMEMBER I PROMISED MYSELF I WOULD. 76 MANSNS
I REMEMBER MY OWN EXPERIENCE. 84 MANSNS
SO YOU SHOULDN'T REMEMBER IT AGAINST ME. 88 MANSNS
BUT REMEMBER I'VE HAD NO EXPERIENCE. 92 MANSNS
BUT IS NOT KIND TO MAKE ME REMEMBER-- (WITH DREAD.) 98 MANSNS
OH, WHY DID YOU COME HERE$
I REMEMBER NOW I USED TO BE OF THE OPINION IT WAS 99 MANSNS
I BEGAN TO REMEMBER LATELY--AND LONG FOR THIS 103 MANSNS
GARDEN--
DO YOU REMEMBER, MOTHER, WE WOULD BE SITTING HERE 107 MANSNS
JUST AS WE ARE NOW,
(SOFTLY.) I REMEMBER, DEAR, AS CLEARLY AS IF IT 107 MANSNS
WERE YESTERDAY.
I REMEMBER SO WELL NOW, MOTHER/ 108 MANSNS
(WITH A SHIVER--HURRIEDLY.) WHY DO YOU REMEMBER 110 MANSNS
THAT SO WELL$
YOU WERE STARTING TO REMEMBER A FAIRY TALE. 110 MANSNS
I AM SURE I NEVER--I REMEMBER THE STORY AS AN 111 MANSNS
IRONICALLY HUMOROUS TALE.
=AND REMEMBER THAT AS LONG AS YOU STAY WHERE YOU 111 MANSNS
ARE
BEFORE YOU OPEN I MUST WARN YOU TO REMEMBER HOW 111 MANSNS
EVIL I CAN BE.
YES, I CAN REMEMBER HOW RESENTFUL YOU WERE AT THE 111 MANSNS
ENDING.
REMEMBER SHE IS STRONG, TOO. 114 MANSNS
AND REMEMBER I WASN'T REALLY THE ONE WHO TOOK THEM124 MANSNS
AWAY FROM YOU.
BUT I MUST REMEMBER THEY WILL ONLY SEEM TO BECOME ONE--129 MANSNS
BUT I FEEL HER ARMS AROUND ME-- 132 MANSNS
WHATEVER IT IS, I WILL REMEMBER IT IS HIS DOING, 132 MANSNS
AND I WILL UNDERSTAND.
YOU PROMISED TO REMEMBER/ 134 MANSNS
(SHE PAUSES--TRYING TO REMEMBER.) 135 MANSNS
YOU BETTER REMEMBER, IF YOU WANT TO KEEP YOUR JOB/140 MANSNS
(HARSHLY DOMINEERING.) SO YOU'LL FORGET HER AND 147 MANSNS
ONLY REMEMBER ME/
YES, I SUPPOSE, ENTIRELY SELFISH--NO TIME TO 155 MANSNS
REMEMBER SELF.
MUST REMEMBER THE OLD ADAGE--STICKS AND STONES-- 155 MANSNS
AND POVERTY--BREAK--
WHY DO YOU MAKE ME REMEMBER$ 159 MANSNS
YOU'LL REMEMBER YOU PROMISED ME YOU'D FORGET HER 159 MANSNS
AND LET HER WAIT.
I REMEMBER WHEN I WAITED FOR HIM AT THE CABIN THAT163 MANSNS
AFTERNOON,
IN A NUTSHELL, ALL ONE NEEDS TO REMEMBER IS THAT 172 MANSNS
GOOD IS EVIL, AND EVIL, GOOD.
SO HOW COULD I WISH TO REMEMBER YOUR$ 178 MANSNS
AND YOU MUST REMEMBER THAT THERE, WITH HER, MY 178 MANSNS
LIFE LIVES IN HER LIFE,
OR I WILL REMEMBER THAT THE GARDENER KEEPS ARSENIC181 MANSNS
IN THE CELLAR
MY LOVE, YOU NO LONGER REMEMBER THIS WOMAN, DO 186 MANSNS
YOU$
WHAT IS SHE TRYING TO MAKE ME REMEMBER$ 187 MANSNS
HUM--OH, YES--I REMEMBER. 349 MARCOM
I'VE LOVED YOU EVER SINCE I CAN REMEMBER 355 MARCOM

REMEMBER

REMEMBER (CONT'D.)
WE BETTER READ FROM THE NOTES WE MADE ON OUR LAST 365 MARCOM
TRIP ALL THERE IS TO REMEMBER
I REMEMBER IT--WHEN I WAS A KID. 366 MARCOM
REMEMBER ANY CLIMATE IS HEALTHY WHERE TRADE IS 370 MARCOM
BRISK.
I KISSED IT SO YOU'D REMEMBER MY KISS WHENEVER YOU375 MARCOM
KISS HER/
AND ALSO REMEMBER THAT ON EACH OCCASION HE 388 MARCOM
RETURNED IN TRIUMPH,
REMEMBER AGAIN, PRINCESSES MAY NOT WEEP/ 390 MARCOM
LET ME SEE IF I CAN REMEMBER ANY--OH, YES-- 399 MARCOM
I DON'T REMEMBER THE REST. 399 MARCOM
AND REMEMBER THIS IS YOUR LAST CHANCE/ 414 MARCOM
REMEMBER HOW THAT CHRISTIAN, PULCI, INVENTED THE 422 MARCOM
ENGINE TO BATTER DOWN WALLS$
BUT DANCING MAKES ME REMEMBER KUKACHIN WHOSE 423 MARCOM
LITTLE DANCING FEET--/
AND REMEMBER THEY'VE BEEN GONE TWENTY-ODD YEARS. 427 MARCOM
AND DO YOU REMEMBER THE TWO CRAWLEYS CAME BACK TO 14 MISBEG
GIVE ME A BEATING,
DO YOU REMEMBER HER, JOSIE$ 18 MISBEG
I REMEMBER HER WELL. 18 MISBEG
I REMEMBER WHEN I WAS A SLIP OF A GIRL, 24 MISBEG
BUT THE NEXT DAY YOU FIND HIS BRAIN WAS SO 33 MISBEG
PARALYZED HE DON'T REMEMBER A THING
I DON'T REMEMBER INVITING YOU, 44 MISBEG
REMEMBER HE'S DELICATE, JOSIE, AND LEAVE YOUR CLUB 51 MISBEG
IN THE HOUSE.
REMEMBER, NOW. 55 MISBEG
AND YOU, JOSIE, PLEASE REMEMBER WHEN I KEEP THAT 67 MISBEG
MOONLIGHT DATE TONIGHT
AND I KNEW ALL ALONG HE'D NEVER REMEMBER TO KEEP 79 MISBEG
HIS DATE AFTER HE GOT DRUNK.
(DESPERATELY) MAYBE HE'LL GET SO DRUNK HE'LL 84 MISBEG
NEVER REMEMBER--
MAKE HIM BELIEVE YOU'RE SO DRUNK YOU DON'T 99 MISBEG
REMEMBER WHAT HE'S DONE.
REMEMBER, OH HE'D NEVER COME HERE. 99 MISBEG
DE GUIL, I'M TOO DRUNK TO REMEMBER. 100 MISBEG
I REMEMBER I HAD SOME NUTTY IDEA I'D GET IN BED 103 MISBEG
WITH YOU--
REMEMBER YOU SAID-- 114 MISBEG
I KEEP FORGETTING THE THING I'VE GOT TO REMEMBER. 123 MISBEG
YOU'D BETTER REMEMBER I SAID YOU HAD BEAUTIFUL 126 MISBEG
EYES AND HAIR--AND BREASTS.
I REMEMBER YOU DID. 126 MISBEG
I DON'T REMEMBER WHICH TIME--OH ANYTHING MUCH-- 128 MISBEG
HE WAS TOO DRUNK TO REMEMBER ANYTHING. 131 MISBEG
FUNNY, PHIL WOULDN'T REMEMBER THAT. 131 MISBEG
BUT UNLESS-- I REMEMBER I DID TRY TO GET HIS GOAT. 132 MISBEG
YOU REMEMBER AFTER HARKER LEFT HERE I SAID THE 132 MISBEG
JOKE WAS ON YOU,
WHY, I REMEMBER TELLING HIM TONIGHT I'D EVEN 133 MISBEG
WAITING MY BROTHER
I'LL HAVE HAD TONIGHT AND YOUR LOVE TO REMEMBER 137 MISBEG
FOR THE REST OF MY DAYS/
REMEMBER THAT'S A PROMISE/ 146 MISBEG
DEAR GOD, LET HIM REMEMBER THAT ONE THING AND 165 MISBEG
FORGET THE REST.
TUNE WITH HIM, BUT ALL THE TIME WAITING TO SEE HOW166 MISBEG
MUCH HE WILL REMEMBER)
I REMEMBER NOW I WAS SITTING ALONE AT A TABLE IN 167 MISBEG
THE INN,
YES, I CAN REMEMBER WHAT A BEAUTIFUL NIGHT IT WAS.168 MISBEG
I REMEMBER I WAS HAVING A GRAND TIME AT THE INN, 170 MISBEG
CELEBRATING WITH PHIL,
I MAY NOT REMEMBER MUCH, 171 MISBEG
I REMEMBER NOW YOU SAID A BOOTLEGGER GAVE IT TO 173 MISBEG
PHIL.
I DO REMEMBER/ 174 MISBEG
I WANT YOU TO REMEMBER MY LOVE FOR YOU GAVE YOU 174 MISBEG
PEACE FOR A WHILE.
I DON'T REMEMBER-- 174 MISBEG
I'M GLAD I REMEMBER/ 174 MISBEG
REMEMBER, BUT NO, YOU DO, 174 MISBEG
I DON'T REMEMBER LEAVING. 8 POET
THIS HOUSE, HE ASKED YOU TO REMEMBER, ONLY GIVES 10 POET
CREDIT TO GENTLEMEN.
I CAN'T REMEMBER ALL OF IT. 29 POET
(HASTILY.) UH, AIN'T I STUPID NOT TO REMEMBER, 38 POET
THOUGH IT IS DIFFICULT AT TIMES FOR MY PRIDE TO 48 POET
REMEMBER
PLEASE REMEMBER I HAVE MY OWN POSITION TO 50 POET
MAINTAIN.
REMEMBER WHAT I SAY. 57 POET
I REMEMBER THE OTHER CELEBRATIONS-- 58 POET
AND REMEMBER WHAT HE SAID, AND BE PROUD OF 61 POET
HIMSELF.
I REMEMBER WELL. 61 POET
YOU HAD NO SHAME THEN, I REMEMBER. 62 POET
IF SHE CAN REMEMBER SHE'S A GENTLEWOMAN AND STOP 63 POET
ACTING LIKE A BOGTROTTING
I REMEMBER HIM WELL. 83 POET
FOR SHAME, YOU DOGS--NOT TO REMEMBER TALAVERA, 93 POET
BE THE MORTAL, I REMEMBER, IT, AND YOU'VE A RIGHT 93 POET
TO CELEBRATE.
AND HERE'S OUR CAVALRY BRIGADE IN A VALLEY TOWARD 96 POET
OUR LEFT, IF YOU'LL REMEMBER,
(EXCITEDLY.) REMEMBERS 96 POET
TALAVERA WAS A DEVILISH THIRSTY DAY, IF YOU'LL 98 POET
REMEMBER,
BUT I HAD THIS TOKEN ON MY CHEEK TO REMEMBER A 99 POET
FRENCH SABER BY.
I'LL REMEMBER-- 115 POET
NO, MY GOD, EVEN THEN, WHEN I REMEMBER MY OWN 115 POET
EXPERIENCE.
AND I DIDN'T REMEMBER A THING FOR HOURS, 161 POET

REMEMBER (CONT'D.)
I REMEMBER AT A FAIR IN THE AULD COUNTRY I WAS 161 POET
CLOUTED WITH THE BUTT AV A WHIP
I'LL TALK OF OUR FIGHT IN THE CITY ONLY, BECAUSE 165 POET
IT'S ALL I WANT TO REMEMBER.
HE WAS A TERRIBLE LIAR, AS I REMEMBER HIM. 170 POET
REMEMBER THE BLOOD IN YOUR VEINS AND BE YOUR 170 POET
GRANDFATHER'S TRUE DESCENDENT.
SO REMEMBER IT'S TO HELL WID HONOR IF YE WANT TO 170 POET
RISE IN THIS WORLD.
(LEERING CUNNINGLY.) WELL, I OFFERED, REMEMBER. 174 POET
AND DON'T REMEMBER WHAT THE MAJOR USED TO TELL 174 POET
YOU.
IT WAS IN TWENTY-DOLLAR GOLD PIECES HE GOT IT, I 586 ROPE
REMEMBER MA.
D'YOU NOT REMEMBER THE LETTER SHE WROTE TELLIN' 586 ROPE
HIM HE COULD SUPPORT LUKE ON THE
I REMEMBER YOU AND ME USED TO GIT ON FINE 588 ROPE
TOGETHER--LIKE HELL/
AND CHUCK SOME STONES IN THE OCEAN SAME'S WE 589 ROPE
USTER, REMEMBERS
REMEMBER HOW HUT HE WAS THAT DAY WHEN HE HUNG THATS92 ROPE
ROPE UP
=REMEMBER, WHEN YOU COME HOME AGAIN THERE'S A ROPE593 ROPE
WAITIN' FOR YOU,
AND I NEVER SEEN HIM GRIN IN MY LIFE, I C'N 595 ROPE
REMEMBER.
SAME'S YOUR KID CHUCKED THAT DOLLAR OF MINE 599 ROPE
OVERBOARD, REMEMBERS
IF YOU'LL REMEMBER, I WAS AS BROKEN UP AS ANYONE 9 STRANG
OVER GORDON'S DEATH.
YOU PREOCCUPIED WITH HER RESOLVE TO REMEMBER OR 13 STRANG
SEE MARSDEN,
I REMEMBER HE ONCE SAID... 24 STRANG
THE BEAUTIFUL THINGS WE HAVE TO KEEP DIARIES TO 25 STRANG
REMEMBER,...))
GUESS YOU DON'T REMEMBER ME, MR. 28 STRANG
BUT I CAN'T EVEN REMEMBER A TITLE OF ONE...)) 29 STRANG
THEY'RE ONLY WORDS, REMEMBER/ 41 STRANG
THEY WERE IMPORTANT TO THEMSELVES, IF I REMEMBER 45 STRANG
RIGHTLY.
BUT I REMEMBER WHEN SHE WAS ALL RIGHT, SHE WAS 59 STRANG
ALWAYS UNHAPPY,
ONLY REMEMBER IT'S A FAMILY SECRET, AND NOW YOU'RE 59 STRANG
ONE OF THE FAMILY.
I REMEMBER WHEN I WAS CARRYING SAM, SOMETIMES I'D 63 STRANG
FORGET I WAS A WIFE.
I'D ONLY REMEMBER THE CHILD IN ME. 63 STRANG
SO'S YOU WILL REMEMBER IT WHEN YOU NEED TO, AFTER 65 STRANG
YOU'VE FORGOTTEN--THIS ONE.
YOU REMEMBER DARNELL$ 75 STRANG
(AWKWARDLY) NED, YOU REMEMBER CHARLIE MARSDEN$ 76 STRANG
IT'S HARD TO REMEMBER THAT... 93 STRANG
YOU REMEMBER HOW FOND SHE ALWAYS WAS OF GORDON. 100 STRANG
OH, WHY DID CHARLIE HAVE TO REMEMBER HER$...) 101 STRANG
(THEN RESOLUTELY) (I CAN'T REMEMBER HER NOW/... 101 STRANG
YES, I REMEMBER WHAT SAM'S MOTHER SAID. 103 STRANG
BUT LET ME REMEMBER.... 113 STRANG
NOT REMEMBER EVEN ONE/. 117 STRANG
(IN CONFUSION NOW) I--I REALLY DON'T REMEMBER, 117 STRANG
NINA/.
(GETS I HAVE CHANGED ALL RIGHT/ I CAN REMEMBER 122 STRANG
UH, I DON'T REMEMBER--(THINKING APPREHENSIVELY 127 STRANG
WITH A BITTER RESENTMENT)
REMEMBER,...)) 147 STRANG
YOU MAY REMEMBER I USED TO WRITE YOU ABOUT HIM 166 STRANG
WITH ENTHUSIASM.
(WELL, AFTER ALL, HOW DO I REMEMBER OUR LOVES... 166 STRANG
(THINKING DESPERATELY) (I MUST MAKE HIM REMEMBER166 STRANG
GORDON IS HIS CHILD OR I CAN
YOU REMEMBER OUR LOVE... 166 STRANG
YOU MUST WHEN YOU REMEMBER THE HAPPINESS WE'VE 173 STRANG
KNOWN IN EACH OTHER'S ARMS/
BECAUSE YOU REMEMBER OUR AFTERNOONS--OUR MAD 174 STRANG
HAPPINESS/
AND WELL'S ROW, RUM, ROW-- REMEMBER THAT OLD 175 STRANG
TUNE--
I CAN REMEMBER THAT DAY SEEING HER KISS HIM... 189 STRANG
REMEMBER HIM/ 196 STRANG
I REMEMBER HEARING MYSELF CRY IT--ONCE--IT MUST 198 STRANG
HAVE BEEN LONG AGO/
WHY DON'T YOU SLEEP NOW--AS YOU USED TO, REMEMBER$200 STRANG
(WITH A TENDER SMILE) OF THE FIRST TIME WE MET-- 446 WELDED
AT REHEARSAL, REMEMBERS
(SOFTLY) AND DO YOU REMEMBER THE DAWN CREEPING 447 WELDED
IN--
WAS ONLY OUR PAST TOGETHER I WANTED TO REMEMBER. 447 WELDED
(SHE KISSES HIM) DO YOU REMEMBER--OUR FIRST NIGHT447 WELDED
TOGETHER
THE ORDINARY FAMILY RITE, YOU'LL REMEMBER/ 448 WELDED
IF I HAVE--BUT PLEASE REMEMBER THERE ARE OTHER 457 WELDED
PLAYWRIGHTS IN THE WORLD/
(WILDLY RESENTFUL) WHY DO YOU MAKE ME REMEMBERS 464 WELDED
JUST AS HE WAS STANDING WHEN YOU KNOCKED AT OUR 466 WELDED
DOOR, REMEMBERS
REMEMBER KISSING ME ON THE CORNER WITH A WHOLE MOB471 WELDED
PIPIN' US OFF$
(A PAUSE) I REMEMBER STREETS--LIGHTS--DEAD FACES--472 WELDED
THEN YOU--YOUR FACE
REMEMBERS 472 WELDED
DON'T YOU REMEMBERS 474 WELDED
REMEMBERED
AND HE SAID HE REMEMBERED ONCE HIS MOTHER ASKED 197 AHWILD
HIS FATHER ABOUT IT
HIS LIPS MOVE IN SOME HALF-REMEMBERED PRAYER.) 490 CARDIF
HE'D NEVER REMEMBERED IT AGAIN. 509 DIFANT
I REMEMBER THAT IT'S SPRING--AND I'VE JUST 425 DYNAMO
REMEMBERED THAT FIFE HAS A DAUGHTER/

REMEMBERED (CONT'D.)

(STAMMERS LAMELY) I--I--REMEMBERED I FORGOT TO 57 ELECTR SAY GOOD NIGHT, FATHER.
MY WIFE SHOULD HAVE REMEMBERED-- 70 ELECTR
IF YOU EVER REMEMBERED, WHICH YOU NEVER SEEMED TO/140 ELECTR
I OUGHT TO HAVE REMEMBERED WHEN YOU'RE SOUSED YOU 592 ICEMAN CALL EVERYONE A STOOL PIGEON.
AND PEANUTS FROM EVERY ELEPHANT THAT REMEMBERED 609 ICEMAN YOU?
(HE GRINS TAUNTINGLY) YOU SHOULD HAVE REMEMBERED 657 ICEMAN
WHEN SHE REMEMBERED ME. 667 ICEMAN
I REMEMBERED I'D GIVEN HER A GUN FOR PROTECTION 715 ICEMAN WHILE I WAS AWAY
BOTH SAID I HAD MORE TALENT THAN ANY STUDENT THEY 104 JOURNE REMEMBERED.
I'M SORRY I REMEMBERED OUT LOUD. 114 JOURNE
FOR HE HAD BEEN DEAD ONLY A LITTLE WHILE AND HE 309 LAZARU STILL REMEMBERED.
THEY ONLY REMEMBERED--TO GO OUT AND PICK UP THEIR 328 LAZARU SWORDS/
IT HAS BEEN CRUELER FOR YOU THAN I REMEMBERED. 346 LAZARU
YOU CAN'T HAVE FORGOTTEN THE ONE I JUST 109 MANSNS REMEMBERED.
THAT, I SUPPOSE, CONSTITUTES THE HUMOROUS IRONY 111 MANSNS YOU REMEMBEREDS
(PIQUED--RESENTFULLY.) YOU'VE ALWAYS REMEMBERED 135 MANSNS BEFORE
I SUDDENLY REMEMBERED SOMETHING I HAD NEVER 145 MANSNS REMEMBERED BEFORE.
I REMEMBERED SOMETHING. 87 MISBEG
(CHUCKLING DRUNKENLY) OH, BE GOD, I'VE JUST 88 MISBEG REMEMBERED ANOTHER THING, JOSIE.
HE REMEMBERED WELL ENOUGH, FOR HE TALKED ABOUT 89 MISBEG IT--
SHE LOOKED YOUNG AND PRETTY LIKE SOMEONE I 147 MISBEG REMEMBERED MEETING LONG AGO.
I REMEMBERED THE LAST TWO LINES OF A LOUSY TEAR- 150 MISBEG JERKER SONG I'D HEARD WHEN I WAS
HAVING REMEMBERED THE DISHES. 118 POET
WHEN I REMEMBERED GORDON AND LOOKED AT HIS FATHER 75 STRANG I HAD EITHER TO SUSPECT A
REMEMBERING
I THEN REMEMBERING, HE TAKES THE LETTER FROM IN 8 ANNA BACK OF THE BAR)
(REMEMBERING HIS INSTRUCTIONS, FORCES HIMSELF TO 100 ELECTR BLURT OUT)
YOU'LL LOVE ME AND KEEP ME FROM REMEMBERINGS 174 ELECTR
(WITH A HAPPY SIGH) I DON'T MIND REMEMBERING--NOW309 GGBROW I'M HAPPY.
ALL I CAN SAY IS THANKS TO EVERYBODY AGAIN FOR 659 ICEMAN REMEMBERING ME ON MY BIRTHDAY.
THE OTHERS, WITH AN AIR OF REMEMBERING SOMETHING 518 INZONE THEY HAD FORGOTTEN,
I COULDN'T HELP REMEMBERING THAT WHEN SHE STARTS 38 JOURNE SLEEPING ALONE IN THERE,
BUT I SUPPOSE YOU'RE REMEMBERING I'VE PROMISED 48 JOURNE BEFORE ON MY WORD OF HONOR.
AND NOW, EVER SINCE HE'S BEEN SO SICK I'VE KEPT 88 JOURNE REMEMBERING EUGENE AND MY FATHER
SURELY SHE, SHE TOO, REMEMBERING DAYS AND WORDS 174 JOURNE THAT WERE,
I WAS REMEMBERING HOW YOU USED TO ACT OUT EACH 12 MANSNS PART
YOU COULDN'T, REMEMBERING HOW HE'D LAUGHED. 53 MANSNS
REMEMBERING THE LAST TIME I WAS IN THERE--AND I 113 MANSNS WAS AFRAID--
REMEMBERING WITH LOVE THE LOVE OF MY PEOPLE. 405 MARCOM
REMEMBERING ME. 176 MISBEG
AND YOU CAN'T HELP REMEMBERING MY SIN WITH YOU. 61 POET
REMEMBERING THE MAN I WAS THEN/ 61 POET
THEN, REMEMBERING MELODY'S ORDERS, GLANCES TOWARD 80 POET THE DOOR AT LEFT FRONT
IT'S THE DIRTY HUT IN WHICH YOUR FATHER WAS BORN 114 POET AND RAISED YOU'RE REMEMBERING,
BUT MEN SHOULD HAVE BEEN GENTLEMEN ENOUGH, 42 STRANG REMEMBERING THEIR MOTHERS,
(NOT REMEMBERING TO HIDE HER CONTEMPT) 80 STRANG
BUT I CAN'T HELP REMEMBERING HOW UNREASONABLY 189 STRANG SHE'S ACTED ABOUT OUR ENGAGEMENT.

REMEMBERS
REMEMBERS, HE SAYS. 36 ANNA
HOW COME ALL DESE WHITE STONES COME HEAH WHEN I 189 EJONES ONLY REMEMBERS ONES
I NEVER REMEMBERS SEEIN' IT BEFO'. 193 EJONES
AND NOW THAT HE REMEMBERS, HIS FEET ARE GIVING HIM 30 HUGHIE HELL.
SUDDENLY HE REMEMBERS EDMUND'S ILLNESS AND 128 JOURNE INSTANTLY BECOMES GUILTY AND
AS ONE WHO FROM A DISTANCE OF YEARS OF SORROW 277 LAZARU REMEMBERS HAPPINESS.
THAT ONE REMEMBERS THERE AS HERE AND CANNOT SLEEP,353 LAZARU
I THINK LIFE REMEMBERS HE HAD FORGOTTEN ME AND IS 40 MANSNS TURNING BACK.
HE ONLY REMEMBERS ONE VERSE OF THE SONG AND HE HAS 72 MISBEG BEEN REPEATING IT.)
(THIS CLICKS IN HIS MIND AND SUDDENLY HE REMEMBERS173 MISBEG EVERYTHING AND JOSIE SEES
(HER FACE DROPS AS SHE REMEMBERS.) 39 POET

REMEMBRANCE
GOOD GOD, BUT I NEVER THOUGHT---(HE STOPS, 164 BEYOND SHUDDERING AT HIS REMEMBRANCE)
REMEMBRANCE WOULD IMPLY THE HIGH DUTY TO LIVE AS A289 LAZARU SON OF GOD--GENEROUSLY/

REMINDER
(WARNINGLY) REMEMBER YE MUST BE QUIET ABOUT UT, 458 CARIBE YE SCUTS--
I REMINDER FOIVE OR SIX YEARS BACK 496 VOYAGE

REMINDS

REMIND
FAMILIAR PLACE TO REMIND US EVERY MINUTE OF THE 88 BEYOND DAY.
HIS DEFIANT, DARK EYES REMIND ONE OF A WILD 203 DESIRE ANIMAL'S IN CAPTIVITY.
(IN A WHISPER) SEEMS LIKE MAW DIDN'T WANT ME T' 242 DESIRE REMIND YE.
I DON'T WANT TO REMIND YOU BUT-- 163 ELECTR
(LOOKING AT HER CRITICALLY) DO YOU KNOW WHAT YOU 218 HA APE REMIND ME OF?
BUT YOU REMIND ME OF HIM SOMEHOW. 11 HUGHIE
SAY, YOU DO REMIND ME OF HUGHIE SOMEHOW, PAL. 19 HUGHIE
(SMILES.) YOU REMIND ME A LOT OF HUGHIE, PAL. 38 HUGHIE
IT IS TIME I GOT MY JOB BACK--ALTHOUGH I HARDLY 626 ICEMAN NEED HIM TO REMIND ME.
I CAN'T BEAR HAVING YOU REMIND ME. 45 JOURNE
(MISERABLY.) GOD, MAMA, YOU KNOW I HATE TO REMIND 45 JOURNE YOU.
WHY YOU FELT YOU HAD TO REMIND ME-- 46 JOURNE
IT DOESN'T REMIND ME OF ANYTHING. 99 JOURNE
NOW PERHAPS YOU'LL GIVE UP TRYING TO REMIND ME, 117 JOURNE YOU AND EDMUND/
I FORBID YOU TO REMIND ME OF MY FATHER'S DEATH, DO120 JOURNE YOU HEAR ME!
BUT I REMIND MYSELF THAT WHAT I AM DOING IS MERELY 16 MANSNS A MEANS.
I CAME TO REMIND YOU, SARA, 176 MANSNS
WOULD YOU REMIND ME OF PITY NOW, YOU SCHEMING 187 MANSNS SLUT!
AND EYEBROWS THAT REMIND ONE OF A WHITE PIG'S. 11 MISBEG
UNTIL YOU REMIND HIM. 33 MISBEG
DON'T REMIND ME OF THAT NOW, JOSIE. 171 MISBEG
I DON'T WANT IT TO REMIND ME-- (WITH HUMILIATED 76 POET RAGE AGAIN.)
I WOULD REMIND HIM THAT YOU, MY DAUGHTER, WERE 112 POET BORN IN A CASTLE/
I WOULD REMIND HIM THAT I WAS BORN IN A CASTLE 112 POET
FOR HEAVEN'S SAKE, DON'T REMIND HER/ 9 STRANG
JUST WANTED TO REMIND YOU TO CALL FOR A TAXI IN 22 STRANG GOOD TIME.
ALL I WANT WAS THAT GHOSTS REMIND ME OF MEN'S 51 STRANG SMART CRACK ABOUT WOMEN,
HE DOES REMIND ME OF GORDON... 111 STRANG

REMINDED
(PROMPTLY) I'LL TAKE A--(THEN SUDDENLY REMINDED-- 23 ANNA CONFUSEDLY)
I'D GO CRAZY HERE, BEIN' REMINDED EVERY SECOND OF 110 BEYOND THE DAY
OH, YOU MEAN SHE WOULDN'T WANT TO BE REMINDED OF 135 BEYOND MY FOOLISHNESS?
AND WHEN HE REMINDED ME IT WAS RAINING, IT ALL 550 DAYS SEEMED TO FIT IN SO PERFECTLY--
(HE SUDDENLY IS REMINDED OF SOMETHING--THINKING 450 DYNAMO WILDLY)
HE REMINDED ME OF SOMEONE. 15 ELECTR
THAT'S WHAT MOTHER USED TO SAY IT REMINDED HER OF, 74 ELECTR I REMEMBER.
AND THE NATIVES ON THE ISLANDS REMINDED ME OF YOU 146 ELECTR TOO.
WILKINS REMINDED YOU OF BRANT-- 153 ELECTR
(SHE STARTS TO GO--THEN, AS IF REMINDED OF 280 GGBROW SOMETHING--TO DION)
YOU MEAN YOU DON'T WANT TO BE REMINDED THAT WE'RE 309 GGBROW GETTING OLD?
(AS IF REMINDED OF SOMETHING-- 600 ICEMAN
I TOLD SHAUGHNESSY HE SHOULD HAVE REMINDED HARKER 25 JOURNE THAT A STANDARD OIL
THIS PLACE REMINDED ME, I SUPPOSE. 8 MANSNS
I NEED TO BE REMINDED THAT LIFE IS NOT THE LONG 54 MANSNS DYING OF DEATH
(BANTERINGLY) AS I'VE OFTEN REMINDED YOU, 14 STRANG
(SUDDENLY REMINDED OF THE DEAD MAN--IN PENITENTLY 39 STRANG SAD TONES)
(THEN SUDDENLY REMINDED OF SOMETHING SHE REGARDS 474 WELDED HIM CALCULATINGLY--

REMINDER
(NOT LIKING THE REMINDER--PETTISHLY) 229 AHWILD
YOU'VE NEVER LET A LETTER PASS WITHOUT SOME PIOUS 507 DAYS REMINDER OF MY FALL--
MERELY A CONSOLING REMINDER--IN CASE YOU'VE 531 DAYS FORGOTTEN/
WASN'T SHE THE LIVIN' REMINDER, SO TO SPAKE, 168 POET
SOME REMINDER OF THE LIFE OUTSIDE WHICH CALLS YOU 453 WELDED AWAY FROM ME.

REMINDIN'
REMINDIN', KATE, I SHOULDN'T BE REMINDIN' YOU, I KNOW.114 BEYONU
AND HERE YOU GO REMINDIN' ME OF IT/ 538 DIFRNT

REMINDING
AND I'VE KEPT REMINDING HIM HIS REAL PUNISHMENT 265 AHWILD WAS STILL TO COME--
I USED TO READ HIS ARTICLES, AS I WAS REMINDING 503 DAYS HIM JUST BEFORE YOU CAME.
THINGS WERE ALWAYS REMINDING ME OF YOU--THE SHIP 146 ELECTR AND THE SEA--
THANKS BE TO BROWN FOR REMINDING ME. 295 GGBROW
IT KEEPS REMINDING YOU, AND WARNING YOU, AND 99 JOURNE CALLING YOU BACK.
THEY'RE WORSE THAN THE FOGHORN FOR REMINDING ME-- 104 JOURNE
SHE WAS ALWAYS REMINDING YOU ABOUT YOUR BOOK. 45 MANSNS
THANK YOU, MADAM, FOR REMINDING ME OF MY DUTY. 155 MANSNS
THANK YOU FOR REMINDING ME. 403 MARCOM
THANK YOU FOR REMINDING ME OF MY DUTY TO SARA. 76 POET
I HAVE JUST BEEN REMINDING SIMON THAT HIS FATHER 82 POET IS RIGIDLY UNFORGIVING
REMINDING ONE OF NINA'S WHEN WE FIRST SAW HER. 159 STRANG

REMINDS
(SHARPLY) THAT REMINDS ME, NAT. 192 AHWILD
AND THAT REMINDS ME, I BETTER GO AND PAY MY LITTLE461 DYNAMO VISIT.

REMINDS

REMINDS (CONT'D.)
AIN'T YOU NOTICED THIS BRANT REMINDS YOU OF 19 ELECTR
SOMEONE IN LOUISA
AND THE NIGHT VAGUELY REMINDS HIM OF DEATH, AND HE 30 HUGHIE
IS VAGUELY FRIGHTENED.
REMINDS ME OF DAMN FOOL ARGUMENT ME AND MUSE 584 ICEMAN
PORTER HAS DE UDDER NIGHT.
AND, I HOPE, REMINDS YOU-- 595 ICEMAN
(ABRUPTLY TO PARRITT) SPEAKING OF WHISKEY, SIR, 595 ICEMAN
REMINDS ME--
SAY, CHUCK'S KIDDIN' ABOUT DE ICEMAN A MINUTE AGO 617 ICEMAN
REMINDS ME.
WHICH REMINDS ME, HERE'S MY KEY. 675 ICEMAN
IT REMINDS ME OF MY REAL PURPOSE IN COMING HERE. 104 MANSNS
THAT REMINDS ME, BEFORE I START THE WHISPER, 191 MANSNS
AND THAT REMINDS ME, ADMIRAL POLLY 414 MARCOM
BE JAYSUS, THAT REMINDS ME I OWE YOU A SWIPE ON 100 MISBEG
THE JAW FOR SOMETHING.
(HE LICKS HIS LIPS.) BE JAYSUS, THAT REMINDS ME. 175 POET
WHICH REMINDS ME, NEO, 49 STRANG
HE REMINDS ME A GREAT DEAL OF HIS NAMESAKE. 141 STRANG
REMINDS ME OF WHEN I FIRST KNEW HER...) 161 STRANG

REMINISCENCE
(THEN ABRUPTLY MINDFUL OF HIS PAINFUL EXPERIENCE 255 AHWILD
WITH REMINISCENCE AT DINNER,
(INSPIRED TO A BOASTFUL REMINISCENCE) 999 ICEMAN
GOES ON IN A TONE OF FOND, SENTIMENTAL 709 ICEMAN
REMINISCENCE)

REMINISCENCES
SHE DIDN'T NOTICE THEM BECAUSE I'VE NEVER BORED 512 DAYS
HER WITH BOYHOOD REMINISCENCES.
FORGIVE THESE REMINISCENCES. 595 ICEMAN

REMINISCENT
(THE REMINISCENT LOOK COMES 228 AHWILD
(GLARES AT HIM--BUT IMMEDIATELY IS OVERCOME BY THE229 AHWILD
REMINISCENT MOOD AGAIN)
(FALLEN INTO REMINISCENT OBSESSION AGAIN) 230 AHWILD
(HE STARTS HIS STORY, HIS TONE AGAIN BECOMING 709 ICEMAN
MUSINGLY REMINISCENT)
(IN A DETACHED REMINISCENT TONE.) 111 JOURNE

REMINISCENTLY
(REMINISCENTLY) SHE WAS GOOD I' SIM 'N' ME. 207 DESIRE
(REMINISCENTLY) IF DEY'S ONE THING I LEARNS IN 178 EJONES
TEN YEARS ON DE PULLMA CA'S
(HE CHUCKLES--REMINISCENTLY) 584 ICEMAN
(HE CHUCKLES REMINISCENTLY) REMEMBER THE TIME SHE608 ICEMAN
SENT ME DOWN TO THE BAR TO
(HE BECOMES REMINISCENTLY MELANCHOLY) 609 ICEMAN
(HIS EYES GLISTENING REMINISCENTLY) 404 MARCOM
(FORGETS HIS ANGER TO GRIN REMINISCENTLY) 14 MISBEG
SHE ISS FIGHY-TWO (THE SMILES REMINISCENTLY) YOU 506 VOYAGE
KNOW, MISS FREDA,

REMNANT
(A REMNANT OF CAUTION COMING TO HIM) 242 AHWILD
HIS PERSONALITY POSSESSES THE REMNANT OF A 19 JOURNE
HUMOROUS, ROMANTIC,

REMNANTS
DRISCOLL PULLS THE BATTERED REMNANTS OF THE DERBY 500 VOYAGE
OFF IVAN'S HEAD

REMODELED
WHICH LOOK AS IF THEY HAD BEEN REMODELED AND SEEN 270 GGBROW
SERVICE.

REMONSTRATES
(REMONSTRATES GENTLY.) NOW, NOW, LAD. 139 JOURNE

REMONSTRATING
(REMONSTRATING GENTLY, 239 AHWILD
(GENTLY REMONSTRATING TO HER SON) 260 GGBROW
(HIS VOICE GENTLY REMONSTRATING) 366 LAZARU

REMORSE
NERVOUS, SICK, A PREY TO GLOOMY REMORSE 256 AHWILD
IF IT DROVE THE YOUNG IDIOT INTO A PANIC OF 511 DAYS
SUPERSTITIOUS REMORSE.
A TORTURING REMORSE FOR MURDERED HAPPINESS/ 561 DAYS
(OVERCOME BY REMORSE--FORGETTING HIS RAGE 537 DIFFNT
INSTANTLY--
OVERWHELMS HIM WITH GUILTY REMORSE. 466 DYNAMO
AS IF HE DIDN'T KNOW WHERE TO HIDE, HIS THOUGHTS 487 DYNAMO
HOUNDED BY REMORSE)
(OVERCOME AT ONCE BY REMORSE AND LOVE) 88 ELECTR
TURNS BY REMORSE, RUNS AFTER HIM AND THROWS HER 166 ELECTR
ARMS AROUND HIM)
AND THE REMORSE THAT NAGS AT YOU 661 ICEMAN
WITHOUT HAVING TO FEEL REMORSE OR GUILT, 705 ICEMAN
(TORTURED WITH REMORSE) NOT 334 LAZARU
HE IS LAUGHING WITH GRIEF AND REMORSE. 349 LAZARU
WHY DO I FEEL REMORSE? 364 LAZARU
(IMMEDIATELY OVERCOME BY REMORSE, GROVELING AND 371 LAZARU
BEATING HIMSELF)
NOW THE ENCHANTRESS, IT APPEARED, HAD IN A LAST 110 MANSNS
MOMENT OF REMORSE,
DIDN'T YOU COUNT ON HIS HONOR AND REMORSE, AND HIS164 MISBEG
LOVING ME IN HIS FASHION,
THE DAMNED SICK REMORSE THAT MAKES YOU WISH YOU'D 171 MISBEG
DIED IN YOUR SLEEP SO YOU
(THEN IN A PASSION OF REMORSE) 40 STRANG
(TORMENTED BY LOVE AND PITY AND REMORSE) 144 STRANG
(SUDDENLY OVERCOME BY A WAVE OF CONSCIENCE-- 156 STRANG
STRICKEN REMORSE AND PITY)
(CRUSHED, OVERCOME BY REMORSE FOR HIS BLOW) 193 STRANG
SHE GLANCES QUICKLY AT HIS FACE, THEN SPEAKS WITH 451 WELDED
A KIND OF DULL REMORSE)
(THEN SUDDENLY WITH ANGUISHED REMORSE) 458 WELDED

REMORSEFUL
AND IS STILL A BIT REMORSEFUL BEHIND HER MAKE-UP 236 AHWILD
AND DEFIANTLY CARELESS MANNER.
AS FOR SID, HE IS MOVED TO HIS REMORSEFUL, GUILT- 257 AHWILD
STRICKEN DEPTHS.
(THEN IN A FRENZY OF REMORSEFUL ANGUISH, 157 ELECTR

REMORSEFUL (CONT'D.)
(WITH FIERCE REMORSEFUL GRIEF) 295 LAZARU
(HER ANTAGONISM GIVING WAY TO REMORSEFUL PITY) 70 STRANG
(WITH REMORSEFUL TENDERNESS) 145 STRANG
(THEN SUDDENLY REMORSEFUL, CATCHING HER HAND AND 487 WELDED
COVERING IT WITH KISSES)

REMORSEFULLY
(RATHER REMORSEFULLY) FORGET IT. 33 ANNA
(REMORSEFULLY NOW) (THES RIGHT... 465 DYNAMO
THEN CHECKS HIMSELF, THINKING REMORSEFULLY) 468 DYNAMO
HE LEANS DOWN AND PICKS IT UP, POLISHING IT ON HIS375 MARCOM
SLEEVE REMORSEFULLY.
(REMORSEFULLY) GOD FORGIVE ME, IT'S BITTER 97 MISBEG
MEDICINE.
(CHECKING HERSELF--REMORSEFULLY) 69 STRANG
(REMORSEFULLY) (WHATS... 100 STRANG
(THEN REMORSEFULLY) 113 STRANG
(THINKING REMORSEFULLY) (ITS MY FAULTS... 142 STRANG
(THEN STRUGGLING WITH HIMSELF--REMORSEFULLY) 147 STRANG
(THEN REMORSEFULLY) 161 STRANG

REMORSELESS
HIS EYES COLD AND REMORSELESS IN HIS MASK OF 541 DAYS
SINISTER MOCKERY.
(COLDLY REMORSELESS--SNEERINGLY) 561 DAYS

REMORSELESSLY
(REMORSELESSLY) YE CAN'T TAKE IT WITH YE. 232 DESIRE

REMOTE
HIM, BUT GRIMLY REMOTE AND AUSTERE IN DEATH, LIKE 93 ELECTR
THE CARVEN FACE OF A STATUE.
(WITH A REMOTE, AMUSED SMILE.) 62 JOURNE
WITH A FOND SOLICITUDE WHICH IS AT THE SAME TIME 67 JOURNE
REMOTE.)
(HER MANNER BECOMING MORE AND MORE REMOTE.) 86 JOURNE
(SLOWLY TAKES HER ARM AWAY--HER MANNER REMOTE AND 93 JOURNE
OBJECTIVE AGAIN.)
(COMES TO HIM--HER FACE IS COMPOSED IN PLASTER 123 JOURNE
AGAIN AND HER TONE IS REMOTE.)
(BUT THE LAUGHTER OF LAZARUS IS AS REMOTE NOW AS 349 LAZARU
THE LAUGHTER OF A GOD.)
SO DELICATE AND FASTIDIOUS AND SPIRITUALLY 14 MANSNS
REMOTE--
BEAUTIFUL AND COLDLY REMOTE AND PROUD--WITH A 125 MANSNS
SMILE DELIBERATELY AMUSED BY
YOU HAVE SET YOUR LIPS IN A SMILE SO REMOTE--YOU 437 MARCOM
ARE PRETENDING EVEN
SHE SPEAKS RAPIDLY IN A REMOTE, DETACHED WAY, 81 POET

REMOTELY
REMOTELY CONCERNED HIM. 263 AHWILD

REMOTENESS
SMILE WITH INFINITE REMOTENESS UPON OUR SORROW, 435 MARCOM
SMILE AS A STAR SMILES/

REMOVE
(SHE LOOKS AT HIM AS IF WAITING FOR HIM TO REMOVE 279 GGBROW
HIS MASK--
(RAISES HIS HEAD AS IF STARTING TO REMOVE THE 287 GGBROW
MASK)
SO WOULD HARKER KINDLY REMOVE HIS DIRTY FEET FROM 25 JOURNE
THE PREMISES

REMOVED
BETTER PUT HER IN INSTITUTION WHERE SHE'LL BE 232 AHWILD
REMOVED FROM TEMPTATION/
REMOVED FROM PRESENT ACTUALITY YOU MAKE YOUR 495 DAYS
ENDING, THE BETTER IT WILL BE.
THE FRONT WALLS OF THESE ROOMS ARE REMOVED TO SHOW -0 DYNAMO
THE DIFFERENT INTERIORS.
A SECTION OF THE SHIP HAS BEEN REMOVED TO REVEAL 109 ELECTR
THE INTERIOR OF THE CABIN.
WOULD HAVE BEEN REMOVED FROM HIS FETID KRAAL ON 723 ICEMAN
THE VELDT
THE TRAY WITH THE BOTTLE OF WHISKEY HAS BEEN 71 JOURNE
REMOVED FROM THE TABLE.
UNREAL, A GHOST INHUMANLY REMOVED FROM LIVING, 125 MANSNS
(SCENE-- THE SAME, WITH THE WALL OF THE LIVING 71 MISBEG
ROOM REMOVED.
HIS TALL, THIN BODY STOOPS AS IF A PART OF ITS 73 STRANG
SUSTAINING WILL HAD BEEN REMOVED.
(HAVING REMOVED HER HAT AND PUT IT ON THE 471 WELDED
WASHSTAND, TURNS TO HIM IMPATIENTLY)

REMOVES
(REMOVES HIS HAND AND FLINGS EBEN SIDEWAYS FULL 255 DESIRE
LENGTH ON
(HE SLOWLY REMOVES HIS MASK. 266 GGBROW
(SLOWLY REMOVES HIS MASK. 279 GGBROW
(SHE REMOVES HIS MASK) HAVEN'T I TOLD YOU TO TAKE 280 GGBROW
OFF YOUR MASK IN THE HOUSE)
(SLOWLY REMOVES HER MASK, LAYING IT ON THE BENCH, 323 GGBROW
(GRAVELY MARKS KNEELS, REMOVES A SLIPPER, AND 413 MARCOM
FEELS THE SOLE OF HER FOOT--
(HE REMOVES THE ROPE GINGERLY FROM HIS NECK. 596 ROPE
SHE TAKES OFF HER COAT, HANGS IT ON A HOOK, AND 471 WELDED
REMOVES HER HAT.

REMOVING
REMOVING HIS FUR CAP AS HE DOES SO. 538 TILE
IS REMOVING DISHES AND THE REMAINS OF THE DINNER. 95 POET

RENDED
THEIR CLAWS RENDED SAILS INTO RAGS, FIERCE WERE 408 MARCOM
THE WINDS/

RENDER
"RENDER UNTO THEM A RECOMPENSE, O LORD, ACCORDING 584 ROPE
TO THE WORK OF THEIR HANDS."

RENDERED
AS LONG AS THEY'VE GUT HEALTH, AND AIN'T RENDERED 113 BEYOND
HELPLESS LIKE ME--

RENDERING
FROM THE CASINO COMES THE SOUND OF THE SCHOOL 257 GGBROW
QUARTET RENDERING "SWEET ADELINE"

RENDING

THIS CLASH OF SOUNDS STUNS ONE'S EARS WITH ITS 223 HA APE RENDING DISSONANCE.

ALL THE NAZARENES DO LIKEWISE, WAILING, RENDING 290 LAZARU THEIR GARMENTS,

RENEG

HE WOULDN'T WANT TO RENEG ON THAT TO YOU-- 254 AHWILD

RENEGADE

YOU, LARRY/ RENEGADE/ TRAITOR/ I WILL HAVE YOU 634 ICEMAN SHOT/

HE WAS A RENEGADE BUT A CATHOLIC JUST THE SAME. 127 JOURNE

THESE RENEGADE NAZARENES WILL SOON DENY THEY ARE 283 LAZARU JEWS AT ALL/

RENEW

(TRYING TO RENEW HIS JOKING TONE) 401 MARCOM

THEN I DECIDED TO STOP AND RENEW OUR ACQUAINTANCE. 76 STRANG

RENEWAL

(HE GOES ON TO ELIOT WITH A RENEWAL OF HIS 502 DAYS HUMOROUSLY COMPLAINING TONE)

SHE IS BEAUTIFUL WITH THAT INDIAN SUMMER RENEWAL 514 DAYS OF PHYSICAL CHARM WHICH COMES

(THEN WITH A RENEWAL OF HOPE) 517 DIFRNT

(WITH A SUDDEN RENEWAL OF HIS UNNATURAL 477 DYNAMO EXCITEMENT, BREAKS AWAY FROM HER)

RENEWED

CABOT PEERS AT HIM WITH RENEWED SUSPICION) 254 DESIRE

HE ADDRESSES HIMSELF WITH RENEWED CONFIDENCE.) 190 EJUNES

TO BE RENEWED BY FAITH INTO THE FUTURE. 309 LAZARU

RENEWING

BUT TIBERIUS BELIEVES THIS LAZARUS MAY KNOW A CURE302 LAZARU FOR DEATH OR FOR RENEWING

RENEWS

(HE RENEWS HIS CHANT) *THEY HUNT OUR STEPS THAT WE579 ROPE CANNOT GO IN OUR STREETS..

RENOUNCE

BUT IF HIS SUSPICIONS ARE AROUSED HER TENDERNESS 58 JOURNE MAKES HIM RENOUNCE THEM AND HE

SHE WAS NEVER MADE TO RENOUNCE THE WORLD. 138 JOURNE

RENOUNCED

NO, WE'VE RENOUNCED THE DAY, IN WHICH NORMAL 150 ELECTR PEOPLE LIVE--

OR RATHER IT HAS RENOUNCED US. 150 ELECTR

WHEN HE CAME TO MANHOOD, RENOUNCED WIFE AND CHILD,372 MARCOM RICHES AND POWER,

RENOVATED

IF YOU'D EATEN SOME OF THE FOOD THEY GAVE ME ON MY 14 STRANG RENOVATED TRANSPORT.

RENOVATING

HE WILL DEVOTE HIS LIFE TO RENOVATING THE HOUSE OF297 GGBROW MY CYBEL INTO A HOME FOR MY

RENOVATION

HAVE SURVIVED THE RENOVATION AND SERVE TO 519 DIFRNT EMPHASIZE IT ALL THE MORE BY CONTRAST.

RENT

ONLY I'VE GOT TO LIVE AND I OWE MY ROOM RENT IN 241 AHWILD NEW HAVEN--

IF YOU NEED THE FIVE DOLLARS SO BAD--FOR YOUR ROOM242 AHWILD RENT--

AND HE WOULD LET ME STAY, RENT-FREE, AS CARETAKER.565 CROSS

>AND ALL DESE BUMS GOT TO PAY UP DEIR ROOM RENT. 578 ICEMAN

HAD A ROLL WHEN HE PAID YOU HIS ROOM RENT, DIDN'T 583 ICEMAN HE, ROCKY?

HOW MUCH ROOM RENT DO YOU OWE ME, TELL ME THATS 602 ICEMAN

PAY THEIR RENT, TOO, WHICH IS MORE THAN I CAN SAY 610 ICEMAN FUR--

I SUPPOSE HE WANTS HIS RENT LOWERED. 22 JOURNE

WE WILL RENT A HOUSE FIRST, AND LATER BUY OUR OWN 65 MANSNS HOME.

RENT, IN TWAIN BY YOUR TEARING GREEDY CLAWS& 174 MANSNS

RENT, AND HE'D BE DAMNED IF HE'D STAND FOR IT, 24 MISBEG

UNLESS HE LOWERED THE RENT AND PAINTED THE HOUSE. 25 MISBEG

WE WERE BOTH TOO BUSY CURSING ENGLAND TO WORRY 26 MISBEG OVER THE RENT.

(QUICKLY) MIND YOU, I DON'T SAY JIM WOULD EVER DO 31 MISBEG IT, RENT OR NO RENT.

I WOULD BE, IF YOU'D PAY UP YOUR BACK RENT. 40 MISBEG

WE MUST HAVE A SERIOUS CHAT ABOUT WHEN YOU'RE 67 MISBEG GOING TO PAY THAT BACK RENT.

YOU HAVE THE BEST ROOM IN THE HOUSE, THAT WE OUGHT 45 POET TO RENT TO GUESTS.

RENTED

CAME TO LOOK YOU UP LAST NIGHT AND RENTED A ROOMS 583 ICEMAN

THE SITTING ROOM OF A SMALL HOUSE EVANS HAS RENTED 90 STRANG

RENTING

THE RENTING OF ROOMS ON THE UPPER FLOORS, UNDER 571 ICEMAN THE RAINES-LAW LOOPHOLES,

RENTS

HIS FACE IS SCRATCHED, HIS BRILLIANT UNIFORM SHOWS191 EJUNES SEVERAL LARGE RENTS)

RENUNCIATION

(HE PUSHES HIS PLATE AWAY FROM HIM WITH PROUD 228 AHWILD RENUNCIATION)

IN A VOICE WHICH IS A FINAL, COMPLETE 420 MARCOM RENUNCIATION CALLS)

REOPEN

(DARKLY) DON'T WORRY ABOUT MY NOT FORCING THE D. 607 ICEMAN A. TO REOPEN YOUR CASE.

I'M GOING TO MAKE THEM REOPEN MY CASE. 607 ICEMAN

REOPENED

THEY WELL FROM HIS LIPS LIKE CLOTS OF BLOOD FROM A357 LAZARU REOPENED WOUND.

REORGANIZATION

ALL THIS REORGANIZATION OF MY HOME IS MY AFFAIR 115 MANSNS

REORGANIZE

MIGHT REORGANIZE YOUR BANKRUPTCY--IF I MAY PUT IT 103 MANSNS IN TERMS YOU UNDERSTAND.

REORGANIZING

I SHALL HAVE TO CONCENTRATE ALL MY ATTENTION ON 66 MANSNS REORGANIZING MY COMPANY.

REPACK

I'LL GO TO THE HOUSE AND REPACK MY BAG RIGHT AWAY.142 BEYOND

REPAIR

BY THE GRAFT HE GETS FROM THE GARAGE ON REPAIR 84 JOURNE BILLS.

DISMISS YOUR FOLLOWERS, AND REPAIR TO HIS PRESENCE389 MARCOM AT ONCE/

REPAIRED

AND EVEN BROKEN HEARTS MAY BE REPAIRED TO DO 318 GGBROW YEOMAN SERVICE/

SIMPSON SAYS HE'S HAD IT REPAIRED A DOZEN TIMES, 50 MISBEG

REPAIRS

AND HAD TO BEAT BACK TO HUNG-KONG FOR REPAIRS. 131 BEYOND

IT MANAGES TO KEEP RUNNING BY CUTTING THE OVERHEAD 7 HUGHIE FOR SERVICE, REPAIRS,

REPEALED

I REPEALED IT. 392 MARCOM

AND I REPEALED THE TAX ON LUXURIES. 392 MARCOM

REPEAT

YOU'D BETTER NOT REPEAT SUCH SENTIMENTS OUTSIDE 194 AHWILD THE BOSOM OF THE FAMILY OR

GETTING OLD, I GUESS, MOTHER--GETTING TO REPEAT 231 AHWILD MYSELF.

I AIN'T GOIN' TO REPEAT 'EM TO YCU BUT YOU KIN 533 DIFRNT GUESS, CAN'T YOU.

SHE WON'T REPEAT SUCH FOOLISHNESS AFTER THE PIECE 539 DIFRNT O' MY MIND I GAVE HER.

THAT YOU'LL NEVER REPEAT WHAT I'M SAYING TO 439 DYNAMO ANYONE.

THEN ALL REPEAT AFTER HIM QUESTIONINGLY AND 279 LAZARU FRIGHTENEDLY.)

ONE OF US MIGHT REPEAT YOUR OPINION TO HIM. 316 LAZARU

SOOTHED IN A MYSTERIOUS, CHILDLIKE WAY, THEY 353 LAZARU REPEAT THE WORD AFTER HIM,

(TERRIFIED) BUT, YOUR HOLINESS, WE DARE NOT 363 MARCOM REPEAT--HE'D HAVE US KILLED/

REPEAT/ 424 MARCOM

(SO OFF BALANCE NOW HE CAN ONLY REPEAT ANGRILY) 59 MISBEG

FAITH, I'LL HAVE YOU REPEAT IT FOR MY WIFE'S 97 POET BENEFIT WHEN SHE JOINS US.

REPEATED

THE KNOCK IS REPEATED-- 45 ANNA

AND THIS MOCKING SCORN IS REPEATED IN THE 494 DAYS EXPRESSION OF THE EYES WHICH STARE

(HER REMARK IS REPEATED DOWN THE LINE WITH MANY A 248 DESIRE GUFFAW AND TITTER UNTIL IT

THE KNOCK IS REPEATED. 534 DIFRNT

THE KNOCK IS REPEATED MORE SHARPLY. 547 DIFRNT

THESE WINDOWS ARE REPEATED IN THE SAME SERIES IN 428 DYNAMO THE BEDROOM ABOVE.

(IN A REPEATED CHORUS WHICH FINALLY INCLUDES EVEN 307 LAZARU THE HUMAN SOLDIERS,

(THE KNOCK ON THE DOOR IS REPEATED MORE LOUDLY. 116 POET

THE KNOCK IS REPEATED, THIS TIME WITH AUTHORITY, 449 WELDED ASSURANCE.

REPEATIN'

AIN'T NO GOOD REPEATIN' SECH THINGS. 508 DIFRNT

REPEATING

GOOD NEWS CAN STAND REPEATING, CAN'T IT& 222 AHWILD

UNCONSCIOUSLY REPEATING THE EXACT THREAT 156 ELECTR

(REPEATING THE WORD AFTER HIM AS ONE WITH THE SAME210 HA APE

CYNICAL AMUSED MOCKERY)

(REPEATING THE WORD AFTER HIM AS ONE WITH CYNICAL 227 HA APE MOCKERY)

(REPEATING THE WORD AFTER HIM AS ONE WITH CYNICAL 227 HA APE MOCKERY)

(REPEATING THE WORD AFTER HIM AS ONE WITH CYNICAL 228 HA APE MOCKERY)

(REPEATING THE WORD AFTER HIM AS ONE WITH CYNICAL 229 HA APE MOCKERY)

(REPEATING THE WORD AFTER HIM AS ONE WITH CYNICAL 229 HA APE MOCKERY)

WILL YOU STOP REPEATING YOUR MOTHER'S CRAZY 142 JOURNE ACCUSATIONS,

I'M SIMPLY REPEATING WHAT I WAS TOLD. 149 JOURNE

HE ONLY REMEMBERS ONE VERSE OF THE SONG AND HE HAS 72 MISBEG BEEN REPEATING IT.)

THINKING AS IF SHE WERE REPEATING THE WORDS OF 109 STRANG SOME INNER VOICE OF LIFE)

REPEATS

(HE REPEATS IRONICALLY) =HOPE YOU ARE ALL WELL/= 146 BEYOND

(STARING BEFORE HER STRANGELY--REPEATS 540 DAYS FASCINATEDLY)

REPEATS ONE WORD OF IT, I ENDS YC' STEALIN' ON DIS181 EJUNES YEARTH MIGHTY DAMN QUICK/

(REPEATS MECHANICALLY) DEADS 63 ELECTR

(REPEATS PITIFULLY) I'D PLANNED IT SO CAREFULLY--110 ELECTR

(HE PAUSES, THEN REPEATS.. 44 POET

(STARTLED; REPEATS STUPIDLY.) 92 POET

HE REPEATS IN EACH DETAIL HIS PANTOMIME BEFORE THE116 POET MIRROR.

(REPEATS HIS WORDS AS IF SHE WERE MEMORIZING A 71 STRANG LESSON)

STARING AT HER BOWED HEAD AS SHE REPEATS 89 STRANG SUBMISSIVELY)

REPELLED

(REPELLED--HARSHLY) CUT IT/ 20 ANNA

SHE DRAWS AWAY FROM HIM, INSTINCTIVELY REPELLED BY 55 ANNA HIS TONE,

(REALLY REPELLED) SHUT UP, DONK. 468 CARIBE

(REPELLED) DON'T TALK IN THAT DISGUSTING WAY. 519 DAYS

WHEN SHE THREW HERSELF INTO HIS ARMS, HE WAS 537 DAYS REPELLED.

AND YET SHOCKED AND REPELLED BY HER DISPLAY OF 177 ELECTR PASSION)

(REPELLED-SHARPLY) ON THE CONTRARY, I HAD TO BEG 281 GGBROW HER TO BEG YOU TO TAKE IT/

(REPELLED BUT CAJOLING) SHUT UP, YOU NUT/ 282 GGBROW

REPELLED

REPELLED (CONT'D.)
(STARES AT HIM, PUZZLED AND REPELLED--SHARPLY) 590 ICEMAN
(STARTLED AND REPELLED.) MOTHER/ 13 MANSNS
(STARTLED AND REPELLED.) SIMON/ 80 MANSNS
(REPELLED) YOU OUGHT TO BE ASHAMED/ 129 MISBEG
(DEBORAH IS REPELLED BY NORA'S SLOVENLY APPEARANCE, 74 POET
SHE IS STARTLED AND REPELLED BY HIS BRGQUE. 166 POET
(REPELLED--WITH A SUPERIOR SNEER) 19 STRANG
(INSTANTLY REPELLED--THINKING WITH SCORNFUL 83 STRANG
JEALOUSY)
(REPELLED BY THIS IDEA--STIFFLY) 190 STRANG

REPELLENT
(A HOSTILE, REPELLENT NOTE IN HIS VOICE) 534 DAYS

REPELLENTLY
ITS STUBBORN CHARACTER BECOME REPELLENTLY SENSUAL.139 MANSNS
RUTHLESSLY CRUEL AND GREEDY.

REPELS
THE GARISH STRANGENESS OF EVERYTHING EVIDENTLY 535 DIFNT
REPELS AND PUZZLES HIM.

REPENT
I DON'T REPENT THAT SIN/ 266 DESIRE
TAKE CARE, SIN, AND WATCH YOUR WORDS OR I WARN YOU120 POET
YOU WILL REPENT THEM.

REPENTANCE
SHE WROTE TO DENOUNCE ME AND TRY TO BRING THE 589 ICEMAN
SINNER TO REPENTANCE
BUT THE SOUND OF YOURSELF CRYING YOUR HEART'S 152 MISBEG
REPENTANCE AGAINST HER BREAST.

REPENTANT
=ONCE, LONG AGO-- (THEN, SUDDENLY WITH REPENTANT 517 DAYS
SHAMEFACEDNESS)
(CONFUSEDLY REPENTANT--IN A LOW VOICE) 554 DAYS
(THEN IMMEDIATELY REPENTANT HE KISSES HER--WITH 108 ELECTR
ROUGH TENDERNESS)
(A PAUSE--SMILINGLY.) IT WAS SIMON WHO FELT GUILTY149 POET
AND REPENTANT.

REPENTANTLY
(REPENTANTLY, COMING AND PUTTING HER ARMS AROUND 510 DIFNT
EMMA AND KISSING HER)

REPENTED
(LAUGHING) AND SHE'S REPENTED AND BEEN FORGIVEN. 525 DAYS
BUT I REPENTED AND PUT HIM OUT OF MY LIFE. 77 ELECTR

REPENTENTLY
(IN A CHANGED TONE--REPENTENTLY.) 112 JOURNE

REPETITION
I'D LOST THE GREAT TALENT I ONCE HAD THROUGH YEARS150 JOURNE
OF EASY REPETITION.
WHAT FOLLOWS IS AN EXACT REPETITION OF HIS SCENE 67 POET
BEFORE THE MIRROR IN ACT ONE.
(ENRAGED BY THE REPETITION OF THIS QUOTATION) 580 ROPE

REPINING
TO HELL WITH REPINING/ 161 JOURNE

REPLACE
A CROW TO REPLACE AN EAGLE/ 418 MARCOM

REPLACED
THE PLUSH-COVERED CHAIRS ARE GONE, REPLACED BY A 519 DIFNT
SET OF VARNISHED OAK.
HAVE BEEN REPLACED, WHILE THE INTERIORS OF THE 427 DYNAMO
FIFE SITTING ROOM AND THE
(WHEN THE LIGHT COMES ON AGAIN, THE WALL OF THE 435 DYNAMO
FIFE BEDROOM HAS BEEN REPLACED.
THE WALLS OF THE FIFE AND LIGHT SITTING ROOMS HAVE443 DYNAMO
BEEN REPLACED WHILE THE
WHILE THE WALL OF THE SITTING ROOM HAS BEEN 468 DYNAMO
REPLACED.
(SCENE. THE LIVING-ROOM WALL HAS BEEN REPLACED 111 MISBEG

REPLACES
(HE REPLACES IT IN THE CHAMBER AND PUTS THE 179 EJONES
REVOLVER BACK ON HIS HIP.)
HE REPLACES THE BAG IN THE BOX, 532 INZONE
A SCOWL SLOWLY REPLACES HIS GOOD-NATURED GRIN) 596 ROPE

REPLICA
HE IS A YOUNG FELLOW OF TWENTY-THREE, A REPLICA OF519 DIFNT
OF HIS FATHER IN ACT ONE,

REPLIES
BUT HE REPLIES VIRTUOUSLY.) 36 POET
SHE REPLIES COLDLY, OBVIOUSLY DOING SO 74 POET
(MISUNDERSTANDING HIM, REPLIES IN A TONE ALMOST 120 POET
OPENLY CONTEMPTUOUS.)

REPLY
(SHE KEEPS ON PLAYING THE ORGAN, BUT MAKES NO 552 *ILE
REPLY.
YET FINDS IT BENEATH HIS DIGNITY TO REPLY. 187 AHWILD
(CUTTING OFF MRS. MILLER'S REPLY) 213 AHWILD
(DEEPLY OFFENDED, RICHARD DISDAINS TO REPLY BUT 216 AHWILD
STALKS WOUNDEDLY TO THE SCREEN.
(RICHARD IS DISGUSTED AND DISDAINS TO REPLY. 272 AHWILD
(BY WAY OF REPLY, GRINS FOOLISHLY AND BEGINS TO 13 ANNA
SING)
(RECEIVING NO REPLY, HE CALLS AGAIN, THIS TIME 25 ANNA
WITH APPARENT APPREHENSION)
(THEN AS HE DOESN'T REPLY--BITTERLY) 60 ANNA
JUST WHAT DID YOU SAY IN YOUR REPLYS 146 BEYOND
IVANK DOES NOT REPLY. 475 CARDIF
(SMITTY DOES NOT DEIGN TO REPLY TO THIS BUT SINKS 468 CARIBE
INTO A SCORNFUL SILENCE.
(SMITTY MAKES NO REPLY BUT LAUGHS HARSHLY AND 470 CARIBE
TAKES ANOTHER DRINK.
THEN, SUDDENLY, AS IF IN REPLY, LOVING GIVES A 535 DAYS
LITTLE MOCKING LAUGH.
(AS EMMA MAKES NO REPLY) JACK SAYS AS YOU'VE 508 DIFNT
SWORN YOU WAS BREAKIN' WITH CALEB.
BEFORE SHE HAS A CHANCE TO REPLY A ROAR OF 510 DIFNT
LAUGHTER COMES FROM THE NEXT ROOM AS
(SHE IS GONE, MAKES NO REPLY. 518 DIFNT
(BEFORE SHE CAN REPLY, HARRIETT'S VOICE IS HEARD 527 DIFNT
CALLING.)
(THEN AS HE DOESN'T REPLY,--RESENTFULLY) 535 DIFNT

REPLY (CONT'D.)
(LAVINIA DOESN'T REPLY. 16 ELECTR
(THEN WITHOUT WAITING FOR A REPLY, BURSTING INTO 76 ELECTR
JEALOUS RAGE)
(THEN ANXIOUSLY AS HE MAKES NO REPLY) 138 ELECTR
I'VE GOT TO BE SURE-- (SHE DOESN'T REPLY OR LOOK 164 ELECTR
AT HIM.
(THEN AS ORIN DOESN'T REPLY-- 281 GGBROW
BUT BEFORE HE CAN REPLY, 592 ICEMAN
HIS HEAD NODDING, AND HE DOESN'T REPLY, SO HOPE 611 ICEMAN
CLOSES HIS EYES.
BUT HIS REPLY IS NOT TO HARRY'S QUESTION, 707 ICEMAN
(THEN AS HE RECEIVES NO REPLY--WITH VAGUE 722 ICEMAN
UNEASINESS)
(THEN AS LARRY DOESN'T REPLY HE IMMEDIATELY 727 ICEMAN
FORGETS HIM AND TURNS TO THE PARTY.
(WITHOUT WAITING FOR A REPLY SHE DOES SO.) 109 JOURNE
(LAZARUS DOES NOT REPLY) IF THOU DOST NOT TELL 350 LAZARU
ME, I MUST ALWAYS DOUBT THEE.
(AS SHE MAKES NO REPLY) YOU HAVE HEARD& 418 MARCOM
(THEN AS HE DOESN'T REPLY--SCORNFULLY) 81 MISBEG
(SHE DOESN'T REPLY. 104 MISBEG
(HE DOESN'T REPLY. 126 MISBEG
(AS GATSBY IS ABOUT TO REPLY, SARA ENTERS FROM 117 POET
RIGHT.
HE DOESN'T LOOK UP OR REPLY.) 167 POET
(THE ONLY REPLY TO THIS IS A SNORE. 500 VOYAGE

REPLYING
(AS IF REPLYING TO THIS, WILLIE COMES TO A CRISIS 581 ICEMAN
OF JERKS AND MOANS.
= IS HEARD REPLYING AND THEN A GREAT SPLASH AND A 407 MARCOM
LONG RATTLING OF CHAINS.

REPORT
HEARS WHAT SHE HAS TO REPORT, GIVES HER SOME QUICK558 DAYS
INSTRUCTIONS.
THERE IS A FLASH, A LOUD REPORT, 190 EJONES
THIS REPORT HASN'T BEEN CONFIRMED YET, HAS ITS 18 ELECTR
REALLY, THIS UNCONFIRMED REPORT MUST HAVE TURNED 29 ELECTR
YOUR HEAD--
(THERE IS THE SHARP REPORT OF A PISTOL FROM THE 123 ELECTR
LEFT GROUND FLOOR OF THE HOUSE
WHEN SHALL I REPORT& 281 GGBROW
I GOT TO HAVE A CLEAN REPORT. 321 GGBROW
I'LL NOT REPORT THIS WATCH. 217 HA APE
INTERRUPTS PADDY WITH A SLAP ON THE BARE BACK LIKE217 HA APE
A REPORT)
I GOT A GOOD NOTION TO REPORT HIM. 514 INZONE
AFT AND REPORT, DUKE/ 516 INZONE
THIS OTHER JEW, THE REPORT STATES, 343 LAZARU
THE REPORT OF HIS FUNERAL MEANS NOTHING. 45 MANSNS
(DISMISSING THE MESSENGER, HAVING HEARD HIS 378 MARCOM
REPORT--ADDRESSES THE PULOS COLDLY)
AS HE LISTENS TO THE REPORT OF THEIR MESSENGER 378 MARCOM
ESCORT.
THIS IS ONE PART OF YOUR DUTY IN WHICH I SHALL 414 MARCOM
HAVE TO REPORT YOU INCOMPETENT.
OUR SPIES REPORT THEIR MANY PETTY STATES ARE 421 MARCOM
ALWAYS QUARRELING.
AND SHATTER INTO BITS WITH A LOUD REPORT. 432 MARCOM

REPORTER
WHATEVER BULL THEY HAND YOU, THEY TELL ME HE'S A 36 JOURNE
PRETTY BUM REPORTER.

REPORTS
(SMILING) THEN, FROM ALL REPORTS, WE SEEM TO BE 292 AHWILD
COMPLETELY SURROUNDED BY LOVE/
(THE REPORTS OF SEVERAL RIFLES SOUND FROM THE 203 EJONES
FOREST.
WE RECEIVED SUCH GLOWING REPORTS. EVERYONE LIKED 110 JOURNE
HIM.
I KNOW THAT BECAUSE THE REPORTS WERE MADE THROUGH 34 MANSNS
ME.
BUT I HAVE FINE REPORTS TO GIVE YOU OF A PROMISING 40 MISBEG
HARVEST.

REPOSE
THAT IN REPOSE GIVES ONE THE STRANGE IMPRESSION OF 6 ELECTR
A LIFE-LIKE MASK.
ONE IS STRUCK AT ONCE BY THE STRANGE IMPRESSION IT 9 ELECTR
GIVES IN REPOSE OF BEING NOT
LIFELIKE MASK IMPRESSION HER FACE GIVES IN REPOSE. 10 ELECTR
ONE IS STRUCK AT A GLANCE BY THE PECULIAR QUALITY 20 ELECTR
HIS FACE IN REPOSE HAS OF
ONE IS IMMEDIATELY STRUCK BY THE MASK-LIKE LOOK OF 46 ELECTR
HIS FACE IN REPOSE.
THERE IS THE SAME LIFELIKE MASK QUALITY OF HIS 73 ELECTR
FACE IN REPOSE,
THE MANNION REMBLANCE OF HIS FACE IN REPOSE TO A 137 ELECTR
MASK.
THE SAME HEIGHT AS YOUNG BROWN BUT LEAN AND WIRY, 260 GGBROW
WITHOUT REPOSE.
THERE IS SOMETHING OF REPOSE AND CONTENTMENT IN 95 MANSNS
HER EXPRESSION.
IN THIS SAFE HAVEN, WHERE WE COULD REPOSE OUR 103 MANSNS
SOULS IN FANTASY--
HIS FACE HAS THE SAME EXHAUSTED, DEATH-LIKE 157 MISBEG
REPOSE.
HER EYES ARE TRAGICALLY SAD IN REPOSE AND HER 137 STRANG
EXPRESSION IS SET AND MASKLIKE.

REPRESENT
FOR THEY REPRESENT AN EVER-PRESENT DAGGER POINTED 243 HA APE
AT THE HEART OF THE GREATEST
DO YOU HAPPEN BY ANY CHANCE TO REPRESENT THE 119 POET
FATHER OF YOUNG SIMON HARFORDS
I DO REPRESENT MR. HENRY HARFORD, SIR. 119 POET
NO MATTER WHOM YOU REPRESENT/ 120 POET

REPRESENTATION
IN ITS OVER-METICULOUS REPRESENTATION OF DETAIL. 274 GGBROW

REPUTATION

REPRESENTATIVE
I WANTS TO CONVINCE YER SHE WAS CN'Y A 235 HA APE
REPRESENTATIVE OF 'ER CLARSS.
AND HONEY OUR REPRESENTATIVE IN POLITICS. 84 MANSNS
SIMON'S FATHER OR HIS LEGAL REPRESENTATIVE WILL 50 POET
WISH TO DISCUSS WITH ME.

REPRESENTED
ALL THE CIVILIZED WHITE RACES ARE REPRESENTED, 207 HA APE
AND EACH OF THESE PERIODS IS REPRESENTED BY SEVEN 273 LAZARU
DIFFERENT MASKS OF GENERAL
RACIALLY THERE ARE MANY NATIONS REPRESENTED. 306 LAZARU
MATURING AND OLD AGE ARE REPRESENTED IN THE TYPES 312 LAZARU
OF THE SELF-TORTURED.
THE MALES IN THE PERIOD OF YOUTH, ONE IN EACH OF 336 LAZARU
THE TYPES REPRESENTED, AND
IS REPRESENTED IN THEIR FROZEN ATTITUDES. 337 LAZARU
IN THE PLACING OF ITS PEOPLE AND THE CHARACTERS 369 MARCOM
AND TYPES REPRESENTED.

REPRESENTING
CHORUS REPRESENTING THE TOWN COME TO LOOK AND 7 ELECTR
LISTEN
A CHORUS REPRESENTING AS THOSE OTHERS HAD, 67 ELECTR
= A CHORUS OF TYPES REPRESENTING THE TOWN AS A 129 ELECTR
HUMAN BACKGROUND

REPRESENTS
THEN, TOO, HE REPRESENTS TO THEM A SELF- 208 HA APE
EXPRESSION.

REPRESS
(THEN WITH A SHUDDER SHE CANNOT REPRESS) 462 DYNAMO
(UNABLE TO REPRESS THE GENUINE ADMIRATION OF THE 178 EJONES
SMALL FRY FOR THE LARGE)
LAVINIA CANNOT REPRESS A START, 21 ELECTR
THEN SHE JERKS HER GLANCE AWAY AND, WITH A LITTLE 42 ELECTR
SHUDDER SHE CANNOT REPRESS,
EVEN LUCIUS CANNOT REPRESS A SHUDDER OF HORROR AT 317 LAZARU
THE FACE GLARING AT HIM.
HE TRIES TO REPRESS, WHICH FASCINATES AND AT THE 140 MANSNS
SAME TIME HUMILIATES HIM.

REPRESSED
LISTENING TO ROBERT WITH A REPRESSED EXPRESSION OF 99 BEYOND
PAIN ON HIS FACE.
(IN A LOW, REPRESSED VOICE--HER EYES SMOLDERING) 126 BEYOND
(HER REPRESSED VOICE TREMBLING) 126 BEYOND
THERE IS A FIERCE REPRESSED VITALITY ABOUT HIM. 203 DESIRE
A GRIM, REPRESSED ROOM LIKE A TOMB IN WHICH THE 241 DESIRE
FAMILY HAS BEEN INTERRED ALIVE.
WHEN HE SPEAKS, HIS DEEP VOICE HAS A HOLLOW 46 ELECTR
REPRESSED QUALITY.
(GROANS RIGID--HIS VOICE TREMBLING WITH REPRESSED 677 ICEMAN
ANGER)
AS THOUGH HIS LIFE, SO LONG REPRESSED IN HIM BY 309 LAZARU
FEAR,
CALLING IN A TONE OF REPRESSED UNEASINESS... 108 MANSNS
(WITH STRANGE REPRESSED FURY.) 189 MANSNS

REPRESSES
HE HEARS SARA COMING DOWN THE STAIRS IN THE HALL 44 MANSNS
AND AT ONCE REPRESSES HIS

REPRESSING
SIMON IS REPRESSING A FEELING OF GLOATING 57 MANSNS
SATISFACTION AND EXCITED CALCULATION.

REPROACH
SPEAKS SOBBINGLY IN A STRANGE HUMBLE TONE OF 565 DAYS
BROKEN REPROACH)
(HE CRIES OUT IN A PASSION OF REPROACH) 448 DYNAMO
THE KIND THAT MAKES HIS LYING HOPES NAG AT HIM AND641 ICEMAN
REPROACH HIM
(HE MOVES AWAY--THEN ADDS WITH BITTER REPROACH) 659 ICEMAN
(HE NOTICES SHE IS WEEPING--IN SELF-REPROACH) 409 MARCOM
BUT, IN GOD'S NAME, WHO AM I TO REPROACH ANYONE 41 POET
WITH ANYTHING.
(AN APPEAL FORCED OUT OF HER THAT IS BOTH PLEADING 90 POET
AND A BITTER REPROACH.)
AND SPEAKS AS THOUGH SHE WERE HIDING A HURT 118 STRANG
REPROACH BENEATH A JOKING TONE)
(SPEAKING WITH GENTLE REPROACH) 167 STRANG

REPROACHES
I CAN'T STAND HEARING THOSE SAME REPROACHES I'VE 143 STRANG
HEARD A THOUSAND TIMES BEFORE/

REPROACHFUL
(WITH A REPROACHFUL LOOK) NAT, 267 AHWILD
(HE GIVES JOHN A SIDE GLANCE, HALF SMILING AND 504 DAYS
HALF REPROACHFUL)
(THE PRIEST GIVES A SWIFT, REPROACHFUL LOOK AT 510 DAYS
JOHN, SEEMS ABOUT TO PROTEST,
(CALCULATINGLY REPROACHFUL) I DON'T THINK YOU'D 38 ELECTR
PROPOSE THAT, ADAM,
(CONCEALING A START OF FEAR--CHANGING TO A FORCED 172 ELECTR
REPROACHFUL TONE)
(PLAYS MECHANICALLY--GENTLY REPROACHFUL.) 139 JOURNE
POOR REPROACHFUL GHOST/...) 71 STRANG
(LOOKING OVER AT HER--TENDERLY REPROACHFUL) 116 STRANG
(GENTLY REPROACHFUL) DO YOU THINK I ENJOY 446 WELDED
FIGHTING WITH YOU?

REPROACHFULLY
(TURNING ON BURKE REPROACHFULLY) 50 ANNA
(HURT--REPROACHFULLY) MAT/ 76 ANNA
(A BIT REPROACHFULLY) WHY DIDN'T YOU WHEEL MRS. 96 BEYOND
(REPROACHFULLY) YOU MIGHT'VE EVEN NOT WASTED TIME 99 BEYOND
LOOKIN' FOR THAT ONE--
(REPROACHFULLY) MA'S BEEN GETTING DINNER 142 BEYOND
ESPECIALLY FOR YOU, ANDY.
(REPROACHFULLY) YOU DON'T, NAT. 563 CROSS
(REPROACHFULLY) IT IS A TOMB--JUST NOW, ORIN. 74 ELECTR
(THEN, AS SHE LOOKS AT HIM REPROACHFULLY, HE TAKES 75 ELECTR
AWAY HIS ARM--
SHE PUTS AN ARM AROUND HIM REPROACHFULLY) 140 ELECTR
SHE GOES ON REPROACHFULLY) 141 ELECTR
(HE GLANCES REPROACHFULLY AT HOPE.) 667 ICEMAN
(REPROACHFULLY) NOW, HARRY/ 654 ICEMAN

REPROACHFULLY (CONT'D.)
(THEY LOOK AT HIM REPROACHFULLY, THEIR EYES HURT. 684 ICEMAN
(REPROACHFULLY) YOU'RE NOT VERY CONSIDERATE, 693 ICEMAN
LARRY.
(GUILTILY.) AH, DON'T SAY-- (REPROACHFULLY,) YOU 88 MANSNS
LOVED ME FOR IT/
(REPROACHFULLY.) 136 MANSNS
AND LOOKS INTO HIS EYES GENTLY AND REPROACHFULLY,)118 STRANG
(REPROACHFULLY) SO YOU HAVE FOUND A SON WHILE I 166 STRANG
WAS LOSING MINE--
(THEN DETERMINEDLY THROWING OFF THIS MOOD-- 447 WELDED
REPROACHFULLY FORCING A JOKING TONE)

REPROACHIN'
LISTEN TO HER, NORA, REPROACHIN' ME BECAUSE I'M 177 POET
NOT DRUNK.

REPROACHING
OF THEM--WONDERING AND SAD, BUT STILL TRUSTFUL, 169 POET
NOT REPROACHING ME--

REPROBATE
AN OLD REPROBATE, THAT'S WHAT YOU BE/. 7 ELECTR

REPRODUCE
FOR LOVING'S FACE IS A MASK WHOSE FEATURES 493 DAYS
REPRODUCE EXACTLY THE FEATURES OF
WHICH BROADLY REPRODUCE THEIR OWN CHARACTERS. 275 LAZARU

REPRODUCTION
HIS MASK-LIKE FACE IS A STARTLING REPRODUCTION OF 93 ELECTR
THE FACE IN THE PORTRAIT ABOVE
ON HER ENTRANCE HER FACE IS MASKED WITH AN EXACT 262 GGBROW
ALMOST TRANSPARENT REPRODUCTION

REPROOF
(THEN A TRACE OF SHOCKED REPROOF SHOWING IN HIS 205 AHWILD
VOICE)
(THEN WITH KINDLY REPROOF) DIDN'T YOU TAKE A NAP 515 DAYS
LIKE YOU PROMISED YOU WOULD?
(THEN WITH PLAYFUL REPROOF) YOU REALLY SHOULDN'T 288 GGBROW
ENCOURAGE HIM.

REPROVING
(GENTLY REPROVING) YOU OUGHTN'T TO SAY THAT. 285 AHWILD
(WEARILY REPROVING) THANK GOODNESS I'VE FOUND 291 GGBROW
YOU/
(REPROVING AND PITYING.) NOW, NOW, LAD. 110 JOURNE

REPROVINGLY
(THEN AFTER A SECOND'S PAUSE, REPROVINGLY) 42 ANNA
(REPROVINGLY) YOU CAN'T BLAME HIM. 136 BEYOND
(REPROVINGLY,) YOUR FATHER WASN'T FINDING FAULT 21 JOURNE
WITH YOU.
(REPROVINGLY BUT SHOWING SHE SHARES HIS FEELING) 185 STRANG

REPUBLIC
THE VITALS OF OUR FAIR REPUBLIC-AS FOUL A MENACE 242 HA APE
AGAINST THE VERY LIFE-BLOOD OF
ONE OF THE KINGS OF OUR REPUBLIC BY DIVINE RIGHT 47 MISBEG
OF INHERITED SWAG.

REPUBLICAN
AND I'M A REPUBLICAN/= 612 ICEMAN
HIS OLD UNIFORM OF THE FRENCH REPUBLICAN NATIONAL 83 POET
GUARD.

REPUDIATE
NOW YOU MUST EITHER CHOOSE TO REPUDIATE THAT OLD 182 MANSNS
CHOICE,

REPULSED
(MOVING AWAY FROM HER--REPULSED) 57 STRANG
(REPULSED) NINA/ 132 STRANG

REPULSES
I'M JEALOUS OF YOU--THE SOMETHING IN YOU THAT 455 WELDED
REPULSES OUR LOVE--

REPULSION
THEN, OVERCOMING WHAT IS EVIDENTLY A FEELING OF 31 ANNA
REPULSION,
(SHRINKING FROM HER FATHER WITH REPULSION-- 51 ANNA
RESENTFULLY)
(WITH A LITTLE SHIVER OF REPULSION) 522 DAYS
A LOOK OF SICK REPULSION COMING OVER HER FACE) 538 DAYS
(STEPPING AWAY WITH AN EXPRESSION OF REPULSION) 527 DIFRNT
(SHE BREAKS AWAY, SHRINKING FROM HER MOTHER WITH A 31 ELECTR
LOOK OF SICK REPULSION.
(WITH A START OF REPULSION, SHRINKING FROM HIS 52 ELECTR
HAND.)
SHE GIVES A LITTLE SHUDDER OF REPULSION 90 ELECTR
(THEN WITH SUDDEN ANGER AS HE SEES THE GROWING 165 ELECTR
HORRIFIED REPULSION ON HER FACE)
STARES AT HER WITH A STRICKEN LOOK OF HORRIFIED 177 ELECTR
REPULSION--
BUT HE INSTINCTIVELY SHRINKS WITH REPULSION. 645 ICEMAN
THEN WITH A BITTER REPULSION) 647 ICEMAN
(DISTURBED--WITH A MOVEMENT OF REPULSION) 706 ICEMAN
(SHE STARES AT HER HANDS WITH FASCINATED 41 JOURNE
REPULSION.)
(SHRINKING WITH REPULSION.) MOTHER/ 12 MANSNS
TO ONE OF ARROGANT DISDAINFUL REPULSION AND 136 MANSNS
HATRED.
(SHE SUDDENLY SHIVERS WITH REPULSION AND TEARS HER144 MANSNS
EYES FROM THE MIRROR)
(HIS VOICE HARD WITH REPULSION) 121 MISBEG
(THINKING WITH NERVOUS REPULSION) 20 STRANG
I CAN GIVE MYSELF WITHOUT REPULSION... 112 STRANG
(HE TURNS HIS BACK ON MARSDEN WITH A GLANCE OF 148 STRANG
REPULSION AND WALKS TO THE WINDOW
(STARING AT HIM WITH REPULSION--WITH COOL DISDAIN)163 STRANG

REPULSIVE
THE HOUSE HAD ONCE BEEN PAINTED A REPULSIVE YELLOW 1 MISBEG
WITH BROWN TRIM.
THE WALL PAPER, A REPULSIVE BROWN, 48 STRANG
THERE'S SOMETHING REPULSIVE ABOUT IT/ 101 STRANG

REPUTATION
YOU WANT TO LIVE UP TO YOUR SILLY REPUTATION EVEN 547 'ILE
IF YOU DO HAVE TO BEAT AND
WHY, EVEN AT HARVARD I DISCOVERED MY FATHER WAS 595 ICEMAN
WELL KNOWN BY REPUTATION.

REPUTATION

REPUTATION (CONT'D.)
(SOOTHINGLY) SURE I WILL AND IT'LL MAKE YOUR 608 ICEMAN
REPUTATION, WILLIE.
YOUR REPUTATION STINKS SO. 31 JOURNE
HE HAD THE REPUTATION OF BEING ONE OF THE BEST 105 JOURNE
LOOKING MEN IN THE COUNTRY.
HE HAD A GOOD REPUTATION-- 140 JOURNE
THE EVIL REPUTATION OF RECENT FAILURE PREJUDICES 152 MANSNS
THEM AGAINST YOU.
YOU'LL RUIN MY REPUTATION, IF YOU SPREAD THAT LIE 41 MISBEG
ABOUT ME.
YOUR REPUTATION AS A GENEROUS HOST-- 45 MISBEG
WITHOUT GRAVELY COMPROMISING YOUR REPUTATION. 108 POET
ONLY TOO GLAD--PLEASED TO MEET YOU--KNOW YOU BY 194 STRANG
REPUTATION--THE FAMOUS OAKSMAN--

REQUEST
TO REQUEST THE POPE TO SEND HIM A HUNDRED WISE MEN359 MARCOM
OF THE WEST
OR HE COULD NEVER MAKE SUCH A REQUEST. 363 MARCOM
(BOLDLY NOW) AND MAY I HUMBLY REQUEST, SINCE HIS 397 MARCOM
HONOR.
(BITTERLY) I CANNOT DENY YOUR LAST REQUEST, 398 MARCOM
MY FIRST REQUEST OF YOU, MY LORD, 418 MARCOM
I SUPPOSE I MAY EXPECT THE YOUNG MAN TO REQUEST AN 49 POET
INTERVIEW WITH ME
I HAVE ABOUT MADE UP MY MIND TO DECLINE FOR YOU 113 POET
SIMON HARFORD'S REQUEST

REQUESTING
(TO LAZARUS--REQUESTING MEEKLY BUT LONGINGLY) 345 LAZARU

REQUESTS
YOU'VE GOT TO CREATE HER OR SHE REQUESTS YOU TO 296 GGBROW
DESTROY YOURSELF.
SO I ADVISE YOU TO LISTEN TO MR. GADSBY, AS HE 33 MANSNS
REQUESTS.
LATE OF HIS MAJESTY'S SEVENTH DRAGOONS, 154 POET
RESPECTFULLY REQUESTS A WORD WITH HIM."

REQUIEM
FAITH, PATCH RILEY DON'T KNOW IT BUT HE'S PLAYING 182 POET
A REQUIEM FOR THE DEAD.

REQUIRE
AS THE SEPARATE SCENES REQUIRE, -0 DYNAMO

REQUIRED
NOT REQUIRED, ROCKY, OLD CHUM. 675 ICEMAN
NO APOLOGY REQUIRED, OLD CHAP. 700 ICEMAN

REQUIRES
BRIEFLY, CAESAR REQUIRES YOUR PLEDGE THAT YOU WILL333 LAZARU
NOT LAUGH.

REQUISITE
HE REALIZED THAT JOEL HAS NOT HAD THE REQUISITE 33 MANSNS
EXECUTIVE EXPERIENCE

REQUISITION
HAD DRIVEN OFF THEIR BEASTS TO ESCAPE REQUISITION.351 MARCOM

REQUIRED
REQUIRED IN THE ARMS OF DEATH/ 436 MARCOM
REQUIRED LOVE IS THE GREATEST BLESSING LIFE CAN 47 POET
BESTOW ON US POOR MORTALS.
(SHE KISSES HIM--THEN SHUTS HER EYES WITH A DEEP 200 STRANG
SIGH OF REQUITED WEAKNESS)

REREAD
I READ IT AND REREAD IT UNTIL 89 ELECTR
HAVING BEEN READ AND REREAD. 12 JOURNE

RE-ARISEN
MANY WHO NY WHO HAVE SEEN HIM SWEAR HE IS 300 LAZARU
DIONYSUS, RE-ARISEN FROM HADES/

RE-ELECTION
JACKSON ICKSON IN POWER--AND EVEN YOUR FATHER 8 MANSNS
ADMITS HE IS SURE OF RE-ELECTION--

RE-ENTER
FEELING AELING AS THE FLOW OF BLOOD IN HIS OWN 309 LAZARU
VEINS THE PAST RE-ENTER THE HEART
NOW HE RE-ENTER THE SUN/ 324 LAZARU
ARE YOU, E YUU, TOO, THINKING IN TERMS OF TIME, 360 LAZARU
OLD FOOL SO SOON TO RE-ENTER INF
BEGGING YOUNG YOU TO LET ME RE-ENTER THAT LOST 182 MANSNS
LIFE

RE-ENTERS
KEENEY REENEY RE-ENTERS FROM THE DOORWAY TO THE 551 *ILE
DECK AND STANDS LOOKING AT HER A
SPEAKS WIEAKS WITH SOMBER PREMONITION AS ANNA RE- 78 ANNA
ENTERS FROM THE LEFT)
A MOMENT MOMENT LATER ROBERT RE-ENTERS. 121 BEYOND
A MOMENT MOMENT LATER ANDREW RE-ENTERS, CLOSING 154 BEYOND
THE DOOR SOFTLY.
(HE LAUGHS LAUGHS AGAIN--THEN TURNS TO FACE THE 528 DAYS
DOORWAY AS ELSA RE-ENTERS THE RO
SWEENEY REENEY RE-ENTERS FROM REAR. 597 ROPE

RESCUE
(SENSING THE HURT IN HIS TONE, COMES TO HIS 230 AHWILD
RESCUE)
(COMES TO STOP'S RESCUE) SSSHHH/ 258 AHWILD
HIS FATHER COMES TO HIS RESCUE.) 297 AHWILD
SO DOES ORIN WHO UNEASILY COMES TO HAZEL'S 162 ELECTR
RESCUE.)
TO THE RESCUE/ 371 LAZARU
(HASTILY COMING TO THE RESCUE AS NICOLO CANNOT 367 MARCOM
HIDE HIS CHAGRIN-BOASTFULLY)

RESEARCH
NOW THAT YOU'VE GOT THE CHANCE YOU'VE ALWAYS 49 STRANG
WANTED TO DO RESEARCH WORK.
A HALF-MILLION FOR YOUR STATION TO BE USED IN 192 STRANG
BIOLOGICAL RESEARCH WORK.

RESEMBLANCE
WHATEVER OF RESEMBLANCE ROBERT HAS TO HIS PARENTS 94 BEYOND
MAY BE TRACED TO HER.
HE BEARS A STRIKING RESEMBLANCE TO HIS SON, 567 CROSS
THERE IS A CLEAR RESEMBLANCE TO JOHN AND LOVING IN500 DAYS
THE GENERAL CAST OF HIS

RESEMBLANCE (CONT'D.)
OH, I ADMIT THERE ARE CERTAIN POINTS OF 512 DAYS
RESEMBLANCE BETWEEN SOME OF HIS BOYHOOD
INTO A CURIOUS RESEMBLANCE TO AN AUCTION BLOCK. 195 EJONCS
RATHER THAN THE RESEMBLANCE TO HER PARENT. 10 ELECTR
ONE IS IMMEDIATELY STRUCK BY HER FACIAL 10 ELECTR
RESEMBLANCE TO HER MOTHER.
THE FACIAL RESEMBLANCE, AS THEY STAND THERE, IS 16 ELECTR
EXTRAORDINARY.
SHE MUST HAVE NOTICED YOUR RESEMBLANCE TO ORIN. 36 ELECTR
ONE IS IMMEDIATELY STRUCK BY THE RESEMBLANCE 36 ELECTR
BETWEEN HIS FACE
ACCENTUATES STRANGELY THE RESEMBLANCE BETWEEN 45 ELECTR
THEIR FACES AND AT THE SAME TIME
ONE IS AT ONCE STRUCK BY HIS STARTLING FAMILY 73 ELECTR
RESEMBLANCE TO EZRA MANNON AND
WHICH SERVES TO INCREASE THEIR RESEMBLANCE TO EACH 74 ELECTR
OTHER.
THE RESEMBLANCE BETWEEN MOTHER AND DAUGHTER AS 91 ELECTR
THEY STAND CONFRONTING EACH OTHER
HIS FACE IN THE CANDLELIGHT BEARS A STRIKING 93 ELECTR
RESEMBLANCE TO THAT OF THE PORTRAIT
AND THIS ACCENTUATES HIS RESEMBLANCE TO HIS 137 ELECTR
FATHER.
SHE NOW BEARS A STRIKING RESEMBLANCE TO HER MOTHER137 ELECTR
IN EVERY RESPECT.
HE IS DRESSED IN BLACK AND THE RESEMBLANCE BETWEEN149 ELECTR
THE TWO IS UNCANNY.
THERE THE RESEMBLANCE ENDS. 8 HUGHIE
MAYBE THAT'S THE RESEMBLANCE. 12 HUGHIE
A STRONG RESEMBLANCE TO THE TYPE ANARCHIST AS 574 ICEMAN
PORTRAYED, BOMB IN HAND,
BUT THE RESEMBLANCE CEASES THERE. 575 ICEMAN
WHERE JAMIE TAKES AFTER HIS FATHER, WITH LITTLE 19 JOURNE
RESEMBLANCE TO HIS MOTHER.
THERE IS A STRONG GENERAL RESEMBLANCE BETWEEN BOTH358 MARCOM
OF THEM AND MARCO.
I SEEMED TO DETECT A RESEMBLANCE-- 118 POET
RESEMBLANCE TO HIS 118 POET
BUT THERE THE RESEMBLANCE CEASES. 163 STRANG

RESEMBLANCES
YOUR SILLY TALK ABOUT RESEMBLANCES--DON'T SIT 37 ELECTR
THERE.
A LONG YANKEE FACE, WITH INDIAN RESEMBLANCES, 4 MANSNS
SWARTHY, WITH A BIG STRAIGHT NOSE,

RESEMBLE
DOES ORIN BY ANY CHANCE RESEMBLE HIS FATHERS 36 ELECTR
THE MEN THEMSELVES SHOULD RESEMBLE THOSE PICTURES 207 HA APE
IN WHICH THE APPEARANCE OF
DOES HE TRULY RESEMBLE A GODS 300 LAZARU
WHICH CURIOUSLY RESEMBLE MODERN SAMPLE CASES. 364 MARCOM
EVERY DAY YOU RESEMBLE YOUR MOTHER MORE, AS SHE 45 POET
LOOKED WHEN I FIRST KNEW HER.
I BEGIN TO RESEMBLE CASSANDRA WITH ALL MY 85 POET
WARNINGS.
HE DOES NOT NOTICEABLY RESEMBLE HIS MOTHER. 137 STRANG

RESEMBLES
SHE RESEMBLES SOME PASSE STOCK ACTRESS OF FIFTY 520 DIFFRNT
MADE UP FOR A HEROINE OF TWENTY.
RESEMBLES HER FATHER MORE THAN HER MOTHER. 428 DYNAMO
AND READING ROOM, RESEMBLES SOME DINGY SETTLEMENT 245 HA APE
BOYS' CLUB.
HE RESEMBLES A HOLY SAINT, RECENTLY ELECTED TO 32 HUGHIE
PARADISE.
HE HUPES RESEMBLES ARNOLD ROTHSTEIN'S.) 38 HUGHIE
ALTHOUGH JAMIE RESEMBLES HIM RATHER THAN HIS 19 JOURNE
MOTHER.
HER BEAUTIFUL WHITE HAIR IS PILED UP ON HER HEAD 161 MANSNS
IN CURLS SO THAT IT RESEMBLES
HE RESEMBLES THE OTHER TWO 347 MARCOM
THAT RESEMBLES A MODERN SAMPLE CASE, PLODS WEARILY347 MARCOM
TO THE FOOT OF THE TREE.
HE CLOSELY RESEMBLES THE CHRISTIAN. 347 MARCOM
HE GREATLY RESEMBLES A YOUTH I SAW BACK ON THE 367 MARCOM
ROAD
CLOSELY RESEMBLES THE FRONT OF A PRETENTIOUS 428 MARCOM
DELICATESSEN STORE.
(RESENTFULLY) I DON'T THINK GORDON RESEMBLES SAM 141 STRANG
AT ALL.
MERELY THAT GORDON RESEMBLES YOU IN CHARACTER. 163 STRANG

RESEMBLING
RESEMBLING HER FATHER TO THE COMPLETE EFFACING OF 186 AHWILD
ANY PRETENCE AT PRETTINESS.
RESEMBLING A BLURRED IMPRESSION OF A FALLOW FIELD 278 GGBROW
IN EARLY SPRING.
(DRISCOLL TAKES A BLACK RUBBER BAG RESEMBLING A 528 INZONE
LARGE TOBACCO POUCH FROM THE BOX
RESEMBLING HIM IN ITS EXPRESSION OF FEARLESS FAITH285 LAZARU
IN LIFE.
A FASCINATING GAME--RESEMBLING LOVE, I THINK A 91 MANSNS
WOMAN WILL FIND.
(THEY TAKE OUT NOTE-BOOKS CLOSELY RESEMBLING 365 MARCOM

RESENT
I RESENT THE IMPLICATION THAT I CORRESPOND WITH 267 AHWILD
ALL THE TRAMPS AROUND THIS TOWN.
I MUST SAY I RESENT YOUR ATTITUDE, JOHN. 527 DAYS
UH, I KNOW HOW YOU RESENT THE WAY I HAVE TO SHOW 641 ICEMAN
YOU UP TO YOURSELF.
THEY RESENT THIS DUTY, WHICH HAS ALREADY KEPT THEM298 LAZARU
THERE FOR A LONG TIME.
I BITTERLY RESENT YOUR INTRUDING HERE AND 98 MANSNS
ATTEMPTING TO CREATE SUSPICION.
I BEGIN TO RESENT LIFE AS THE INSULT OF AN IGNOBLE426 MARCOM
INFERIOR
HUH SHE MUST RESENT MY LIVING/... 14 STRANG
EVERY WORD OR ACTION OF MINE WHICH AFFECTS YOU, 453 WELDED
YOU RESENT.
BECAUSE I RESENT YOUR SUPERIOR ATTITUDE 456 WELDED

RESENTFULLY

RESENT (CONT'D.)
BECAUSE I RESENT THAT MAN'S BEING HERE--LATE AT 458 WELDED
NIGHT--WHEN I WAS AWAY
BUT NOT EXACTLY KNOWING BY WHAT OR HOW TO RESENT 473 WELDED
IT--ANGRILY, PUSHING HIM AWAY)

RESENTED
ERIE AVOIDS LOOKING AT THE NIGHT CLERK, AS IF HE 9 HUGHIE
RESENTED HIM.)
I HAVE RESENTED HER INTERFERENCE AND 105 MANSNS
POSSESSIVENESS--

RESENTFUL
(RESENTFUL AGAIN FOR A SECOND) 34 ANNA
(TURNS ON HER IN A FLASH OF RESENTFUL 522 DAYS
VINDICTIVENESS)
BUT ITS EXPRESSION IS RESENTFUL AND DEFENSIVE. 203 DESIRE
(THEN RESENTFUL OBSTINACY) 232 DESIRE
(SHE HAS TURNED A BLANK FACE, RESENTFUL EYES TO 238 DESIRE
HIS.
(WITH QUICK RESENTFUL RESOLUTION) 506 DIFRNT
SHE STARES AT HER SON WITH RESENTFUL ANNOYANCE.) 528 DIFRNT
HE STARES BEFORE HIM WITH THE RESENTFUL AIR OF ONE422 DYNAMO
BROODING OVER A WRONG DONE
(HE GRINS WITH RESENTFUL ANTICIPATION.) 461 DYNAMO
(IMMEDIATELY BECOMES RESENTFUL) 463 DYNAMO
(IMMEDIATELY RESENTFUL--WITH HIS COLD SMILE) 467 DYNAMO
THE WINDOWS OF THE LOWER FLOOR REFLECT THE SUN'S 5 ELECTR
RAYS IN A RESENTFUL GLARE.
(WITH RESENTFUL BITTERNESS) ALL RIGHT, THEN/ 86 ELECTR
(GUILTY AND RESENTFUL) YOU FOLKS AT HOME TAKE 94 ELECTR
DEATH SO SOLEMNLY/
SHE SUDDENLY ADDRESSES THEM IN A HARSH RESENTFUL 139 ELECTR
VOICE.)
(UNHEEDING--WITH A SUDDEN TURN TO BITTER RESENTFUL440 ELECTR
DEFIANCE)
(WITH RESENTFUL BITTERNESS) BUT THEY TURNED OUT 145 ELECTR
TO BE VINNIE'S ISLANDS.
(ALARMED AND RESENTFUL--COLDLY) 162 ELECTR
(A BITTER RESENTFUL NOTE COMING INTO HIS VOICE) 174 ELECTR
(BITTERLY RESENTFUL) WHAT ELSE, INDEED/ 262 GGBROW
RECEDING BROWS ABOVE THEIR SMALL FIERCE, RESENTFUL207 HA APE
EYES.
HE HAS NOT SHAVED FOR DAYS AND AROUND HIS FIERCE, 233 HA APE
RESENTFUL EYES--
(THEN MADE A BIT RESENTFUL BY THE SUSPICIOUS 247 HA APE
GLANCES FROM ALL SIDES)
(SURPRISED AND RESENTFUL) HE DID, DID HE$ 583 ICEMAN
(ABRUPTLY HIS TONE SHARPENS WITH RESENTFUL 591 ICEMAN
WARNING)
AND RESENTFUL AT BEING DISTURBED, 592 ICEMAN
(THEN WITH A RESENTFUL SNEER) 615 ICEMAN
THEY ALL STARE AT HIM, THEIR FACES AGAIN PUZZLED, 628 ICEMAN
RESENTFUL AND UNEASY.)
(SHARPLY RESENTFUL) --/ (THEN ABRUPTLY HE IS 635 ICEMAN
DRUNKENLY GOOD-NATURED,
WITH FASCINATED RESENTFUL UNEASINESS.) 639 ICEMAN
HIS EXPRESSION IS UNEASY, BAFFLED AND RESENTFUL. 703 ICEMAN
(BURSTS INTO RESENTFUL EXASPERATION) 704 ICEMAN
(WITHOUT LOOKING AT HICKEY--WITH THE DULL, RESENTFUL 705 ICEMAN
VICIOUSNESS)
(THERE IS A DULL, RESENTFUL CHORUS OF ASSENT, =WE 705 ICEMAN
DON'T GIVE A DAMN.=
(A CHORUS OF DULL, RESENTFUL PROTEST FROM ALL THE 711 ICEMAN
GROUP.
(THEN, AS HOPE'S EXPRESSION TURNS TO RESENTFUL 717 ICEMAN
CALLOUSNESS AGAIN AND HE LOOKS
(HE GIVES WAY TO A BURST OF RESENTFUL ANGER.) 38 JOURNE
(WITH A STUBBORN, BITTERLY RESENTFUL LOOK.) 42 JOURNE
(VAGUELY RESENTFUL.) HELL, HE'S A FINE, HANDSOME,101 JOURNE
KIND GENTLEMAN JUST THE SAME.
(THEN DRUNKENLY RESENTFUL.) WHAT ARE YOU TRYING 163 JOURNE
TO DO, ACCUSE ME$
THIS IS TAKEN UP BY THE CROWD-- UNPLEASANT, 300 LAZARU
RESENTFUL LAUGHTER.
(WITH RESENTFUL JEALOUSY AND RAGE--IN A VOICE 368 LAZARU
RISING TO A SCREAM)
(FLASHES HIM A RESENTFUL GLANCE--THEN FORCING A 5 MANSNS
LAUGH.)
(SHE STOPS ABRUPTLY, HER EXPRESSION SUDDENLY 57 MANSNS
BITTERLY RESENTFUL.)
(SIMON STARES AT HER IN RESENTFUL SURPRISE.) 58 MANSNS
(WITH A FLASH OF RESENTFUL ANGER.) 85 MANSNS
(STARTLED--RESENTFUL AND UNEASY.) 104 MANSNS
(WITH A RESENTFUL INTENSITY.) 105 MANSNS
YES, I CAN REMEMBER HOW RESENTFUL YOU WERE AT THE 111 MANSNS
ENDING.
HER VOICE SUDDENLY TAKES ON A RESENTFUL COMMANDING114 MANSNS
TONE.
(WITH A QUICK RESENTFUL LOOK AT SIMON.) 124 MANSNS
(SHE CASTS A RESENTFUL LOOK AT SIMON.) 124 MANSNS
(GIVES HER A QUICK RESENTFUL JEALOUS LOOK.) 129 MANSNS
(STARES AT HIM--FRIGHTENED AND RESENTFUL.) 145 MANSNS
(SUDDENLY RESENTFUL AND ANGRY HERSELF.) 159 MANSNS
(SCORNFULLY RESENTFUL.) SO HE'LL CHOOSE, WILL HE,173 MANSNS
THE GREAT MAN$
(GIVES HER FATHER A BITTER, RESENTFUL LOOK) 93 MISBEG
(SHE AGAIN GIVES HIM A BITTER RESENTFUL GLANCE) 94 MISBEG
(THEN WITH RESENTFUL BITTERNESS--ROUGHLY) 119 MISBEG
HE BECOMES RESENTFUL.) 16 POET
SHE STANDS THINKING, HER EXPRESSION PUZZLED, 87 POET
APPREHENSIVE, AND RESENTFUL.
HIS EMBARRASSMENT IS TRANSFORMED INTO RESENTFUL 116 POET
ANGER.
SHE NOTICES HIM STARING AT HER AND GIVES HIM A 118 POET
RESENTFUL, SUSPICIOUS GLANCE.
(RESENTFUL NOW AT MELODY.) 138 POET
BEING WOUNDED TO THEIR DEPTHS AND MADE DEFIANT AND 13 STRANG
RESENTFUL BY THEIR PAIN.
BUT WHY AM I SO RESENTFUL$... 25 STRANG

RESENTFUL (CONT'D.)
EXAMINING LOOK THAT RUFFLES MARSDEN AND MAKES HIM 34 STRANG
ALL THE MORE RESENTFUL TOWARD
(HYSTERICALLY RESENTFUL) WHAT DO YOU MEAN$ 59 STRANG
(HE GOES, CASTING A RESENTFUL GLANCE AT MARSDEN.) 76 STRANG
(WITH RESENTFUL MOCKERY) WELL, 79 STRANG
RESIGNATION RESENTFUL OF ITSELF. 111 STRANG
(WITH RESENTFUL SCORN) (ING, 139 STRANG
(THIS LAST WITH A RESENTFUL LOOK DOWN AT HER AS HE160 STRANG
MOVES BACK TO THE HALL.)
(WITH RESENTFUL DISAPPOINTMENT) 172 STRANG
(WITH A RESENTFUL LOOK AT DARRELL) 191 STRANG
EYES, STARING BACK WITH RESENTFUL ACCUSATION. 454 WELDED
(WILDLY RESENTFUL) WHY DO YOU MAKE ME REMEMBER$ 464 WELDED

RESENTFULLY
(RESENTFULLY) I DON'T SEE HOW YOU CAN TAKE IT SO 253 AHWILD
CALM/
(RESENTFULLY) I SEE THIS IS GOING TO WORK AROUND 265 AHWILD
TO WHERE IT'S ALL MY FAULT/
ANNA SUDDENLY BECOMES CONSCIOUS OF THIS APPRAISING 15 ANNA
STARE--RESENTFULLY)
(RESENTFULLY) WHAT D'YUH KNOW ABOUT BARGES, HUHS 17 ANNA
(RESENTFULLY) BUT WHY DIDN'T YOU NEVER COME HOME 21 AN4A
THEM DAYS$
(HALF TO HERSELF--RESENTFULLY) 29 ANNA
(WITH CHEST OUT AND HEAD THROWN BACK--RESENTFULLY) 32 ANNA
(SHRINKING FROM HER FATHER WITH REPULSION-- 51 ANNA
RESENTFULLY)
(RESENTFULLY) IT SERVES YOU RIGHT. 64 ANNA
(RESENTFULLY) THEN GET OUT. 70 ANNA
(RESENTFULLY) ANDY'S NOT LIKE YOU. 125 BEYOND
(RESENTFULLY) ROB'S TOO GOOD A CHUM TO TRY AND 137 BEYOND
STOP ME
(RESENTFULLY) YOU MIGHT HAVE. 148 BEYOND
(STARES AT HER RESENTFULLY FOR A SECOND, THEN 519 DAYS
TURNS AWAY.
HE IS CONFUSED. HE TURNS AWAY AND SLAMS THE DOOR 228 DESIRE
RESENTFULLY.
(STOPS--RESENTFULLY) WHAT D'YE WANT$ 229 DESIRE
(RESENTFULLY) BUT WE'VE MADE SUCH A DAMNED 10JIT 229 DESIRE
OUT O' THE OLD DEVIL--
(RESENTFULLY) THEY'S ME, HAIN'T THEY$ 232 DESIRE
(RESENTFULLY) I'VE PRAYED, HAIN'T IS 238 DESIRE
(RESENTFULLY) I KNOWED WELL IT WAS ON'Y PART O' 240 DESIRE
YER PLAN T' SWALLER EVERYTHIN'/
THEY CROWD BACK TOWARD THE WALLS, MUTTERING, 250 DESIRE
LOOKING AT HIM RESENTFULLY.)
(RESENTFULLY) GO TO THE DEVIL, THEN/ 505 DIFRNT
(RESENTFULLY) IT AIN'T FOOLISHNESS, MA. 507 DIFRNT
(RESENTFULLY) AND YOU NEVER TOLD ME/ 508 DIFRNT
(A BIT RESENTFULLY) I HOPE YOU AIN'T GOT IT I4 509 DIFRNT
YOUR HEAD MY BROTHER CALEB WOULD
(RESENTFULLY) MAYBE SHE IS, MA, FROM HER SIDE. 510 DIFRNT
(THEN RESENTFULLY) EMMA$, 512 DIFRNT
(RESENTFULLY) DON'T TRY TO PUT THE BLAME ON JACK.515 DIFRNT
(RESENTFULLY) I CAN'T FIGURE HOW ANYBODY'D EVER 521 DIFRNT
LIKE HIM ANYWAY.
(THEN AS HE DOESN'T REPLY,--RESENTFULLY) 535 DIFRNT
(RESENTFULLY) WELL, I HOPE YOU THINK IT'S FOR THE536 DIFRNT
BEST.
(RESENTFULLY) THINK I'M BLUFFINS 545 DIFRNT
(THEN RESENTFULLY ((WHAT DO I CARE ABOUT HIM 424 DYNAMO
ANYWAYS
ADA STARES BEFORE HER, THINKING RESENTFULLY) 455 DYNAMO
(RESENTFULLY) OH, IS HE$ 456 DYNAMO
(RESENTFULLY) I'M SORRY/ 75 ELECTR
(ORIN TURNS TO LOOK AT HIS SISTER RESENTFULLY.) 91 ELECTR
HE SAYS RESENTFULLY) 96 ELECTR
(THEN RESENTFULLY) I SEE YE AIN'T GOT MUCH EAR 107 ELECTR
FUR MUSIC.
(WITH A START--RESENTFULLY) WHY MUST SHE LIE$ 261 GGBROW
WHEN HE SEES DION, HE STOPS ABRUTLY AND GLOWERS 265 GGBROW
RESENTFULLY--
(RESENTFULLY--CLAPPING ON HIS MASK AGAIN AND 273 GGBROW
SPRINGING TO HIS FEET--DERISIVELY)
(BLINKING ABOUT HIM, STARTS TO HIS FEET 210 HA APE
RESENTFULLY, SNARLING.
(TO YANK RESENTFULLY) 'TWAS THEM DAYS MEN 214 HA APE
BELONGED TO SHIPS, NOT NOW.
(RESENTFULLY) AH SAY, YOUSE GUYS. 227 HA APE
(THEN RESENTFULLY AGAIN) AH, SAY/ 249 HA APE
(RESENTFULLY.) WELL, TO HELL WITH IT. 26 HUGHIE
(RESENTFULLY.) WELL, IF YOU DO, I DON'T. 589 ICEMAN
AT LARRY'S TABLE, PARRITT IS GLARING RESENTFULLY 615 ICEMAN
TOWARD THE GIRLS.)
HOPE STIFFENS RESENTFULLY FOR A SECOND. 622 ICEMAN
(RESENTFULLY) YOU NEEDN'T BE, THEN. 652 ICEMAN
(RESENTFULLY PUTS HIS STRAW HAT ON HIS HEAD AT A 670 ICEMAN
DEFIANT TILT)
(THEY BOTH TURN ON HIM RESENTFULLY, 682 ICEMAN
(RESENTFULLY) WELL, DIS IS DE TIME I DO TOUCH IT/690 ICEMAN
CHUCK REGARDS HIM RESENTFULLY.) 699 ICEMAN
THEY GLARE AT HIM RESENTFULLY.) 717 ICEMAN
(RESENTFULLY) IF HE'S DONE WHAT YUH THINK I'LL 524 INZONE
COCKAN HIMSELF.
(IGNORING THIS--RESENTFULLY.) 18 JOURNE
(ALMOST RESENTFULLY.) OH. 42 JOURNE
(TURNS ON JAMIE RESENTFULLY.) 66 JOURNE
(HE SIGHS--GLOOMILY AND RESENTFULLY.) 79 JOURNE
(RESENTFULLY.) I WON'T. 83 JOURNE
(RESENTFULLY.) IS 102 JOURNE
HER FACE SETS IN STUBBORN DEFENSIVENESS-- 108 JOURNE
RESENTFULLY.)
(THEN, RESENTFULLY.) ANYWAY IT'S TRUE. 111 JOURNE
(THEN RESENTFULLY.) YOU'RE A FINE ONE TO RUN AWAY 126 JOURNE
AND LEAVE ME TO SIT ALONE HERE
(THEN RESENTFULLY.) WHAT THE HELL ARE YOU STARING168 JOURNE
AT$

RESENTFULLY

RESENTFULLY (CONT'D.)
(RESENTFULLY.) I CAN'T UNDERSTAND YOUR MOTHER NOT 45 MANSNS
INVITING YOU TO THE FUNERAL.
(RESENTFULLY.) IT'S NONE OF HER BUSINESS. 91 MANSNS
(HE SUDDENLY FROWNS RESENTFULLY.) 94 MANSNS
(SHE TURNS TO SIMON--RESENTFULLY AND DERISIVELY.) 103 MANSNS
THE TWO START RESENTFULLY. 108 MANSNS
(HE TURNS TO HER RESENTFULLY.) 109 MANSNS
(HE TURNS TO STARE AT HER--FORCING A SMILE, 111 MANSNS
RESENTFULLY.)
(THINKING--RESENTFULLY.) BY THAT LIE I'VE PUT 121 MANSNS
MOTHER BACK IN MY MIND--
(THINKING--RESENTFULLY.) HE LIED--HE SAID THAT TOIZI MANSNS
HURT HER--
(THINKING--RESENTFULLY.) POOR WOMAN/ 122 MANSNS
(GLANCING AT SIMON RESENTFULLY--LOWERING HER VOICE125 MANSNS
TO A WHISPER.)
(PIQUED--RESENTFULLY.) YOU'VE ALWAYS REMEMBERED 135 MANSNS
BEFORE.
(RESENTFULLY.) AH, DON'T I KNOW HOW HE'S DRIVEN 170 MANSNS
ME?
(RESENTFULLY) YOU'RE ALL WRONG/ 349 MARCOM
(STARING AT HIM RESENTFULLY) 23 MISBEG
(RESENTFULLY) WELL, I HAVEN'T/ 27 MISBEG
(RESENTFULLY) AH, I'VE BEEN WAITING FOR THAT. 30 MISBEG
(RESENTFULLY) I WON'T HAVE YOU SUSPECTING JIM 34 MISBEG
WITHOUT ANY CAUSE. D'YOU HEAR ME?
(RESENTFULLY) I DON'T WANT TO MEET HIM. 36 MISBEG
(STARES AT HIM STARTLEDLY--THEN RESENTFULLY) 42 MISBEG
(THEN RESENTFULLY) YOU THINK I'D STARVE AT IT, 42 MISBEG
DON'T YOU.
(BRISTLES RESENTFULLY) IS IT JIM TYRONE YOU'RE 78 MISBEG
CALLING HARD NAMES?
SHE SURVEYS HIM RESENTFULLY) 96 MISBEG
(RESENTFULLY) IF I WAS, IT'D BE TO MAKE YOU FEEL 116 MISBEG
AT HOME.
(RESENTFULLY) OH, I DO, DO IS 120 MISBEG
(AGAIN HE DOESN'T SEEM TO HAVE HEARD--RESENTFULLY)126 MISBEG
(RESENTFULLY.) SO SHE ASKED FOR THE WAITRESS, DID 18 POET
SHE?
(RESENTFULLY, BUT MORE CAREFUL OF HER SPEECH.) 23 POET
(RESENTFULLY.) IT'S A WONDER SHE WOULDN'T HAVE 135 POET
MORE THOUGHT FOR YOU
(REGARDING HER AS IF SHE HADN'T REALLY SEEN HER 140 POET
BEFORE--RESENTFULLY.)
(HE THINKS RESENTFULLY) 7 STRANG
(SUDDENLY BLURTING OUT RESENTFULLY) 8 STRANG
(THINKING RESENTFULLY) 9 STRANG
(RESENTFULLY) I THINK YOU'RE MISTAKEN. 35 STRANG
WHY DOES HE SPEAK SO RESENTFULLY OF GORDON'S 39 STRANG
MEMORY...
(DULLY AND RESENTFULLY AGAIN NOW) 63 STRANG
(GLARING AT EVANS RESENTFULLY AS IF HE WERE TO 75 STRANG
BLAME)
(THINKING RESENTFULLY) (WHAT A BOOR/... 76 STRANG
(RESENTFULLY) I WON'T COME OUT HERE AGAIN/ 96 STRANG
HE RAISES HIS HEAD AND HALF-PUSHES HER AWAY-- 99 STRANG
RESENTFULLY, THINKING)
(RESENTFULLY) (SHE CAN'T HELP LETTING THE TRUTH 120 STRANG
ESCAPE HER/....
THEN HE CAN BE HEARD SAYING RESENTFULLY) 123 STRANG
(HE BLURTS OUT RESENTFULLY AT NINA) 127 STRANG
(THINKING AS HE PLAYS--RESENTFULLY) 138 STRANG
(THINKING RESENTFULLY) (HE'S ALWAYS MAKING FUN 141 STRANG
OF MY FATHER/...
(RESENTFULLY) I DON'T THINK GORDON RESEMBLES SAM 141 STRANG
AT ALL.
(RESENTFULLY) YOU KNOW WELL ENOUGH WHAT I'VE 146 STRANG
ALWAYS HELD AGAINST HIM/
(THINKING RESENTFULLY) (IS SHE TRYING TO 147 STRANG
HUMILIATE ME BEFORE HIM?...
SHE COMES FORWARD SLOWLY--THINKING RESENTFULLY) 154 STRANG
(MOVING AWAY FROM HIS FATHER AGAIN--RESENTFULLY-- 155 STRANG
THINKING)
(LOOKING BACK AT NINA RESENTFULLY--THINKING) 160 STRANG
(RESENTFULLY) I'M SORRY. 161 STRANG
(TURNING BACK TO NINA--RESENTFULLY) 162 STRANG
(THINKING RESENTFULLY) (ISHE TAKES A FINE DU- 164 STRANG
THIS-LITTLE-GIRL TONE TOWARD
(THINKING RESENTFULLY) (HE'S SNEERING AT HIS OWN167 STRANG
SON/...))
(RESENTFULLY) I CAN'T AGREE WITH YOU. 168 STRANG
(THEN LOOKING FROM ONE TO THE OTHER--RESENTFULLY) 171 STRANG
(WHO HAS COME CLOSER--RESENTFULLY THINKING) 178 STRANG
THINKING RESENTFULLY) 189 STRANG
(STARING AT GORDON'S BACK RESENTFULLY) 191 STRANG
(THINKING RESENTFULLY) (WHAT A TENDER TONE SHE 192 STRANG
TAKES TOWARD HIM/...
(RESENTFULLY) I HAVE TO FIGHT. 453 WELDED
(RESENTFULLY) I DON'T SEE ANYTHING STRANGE ABOUT 454 WELDED
IT.
(AFTER A PAUSE IN WHICH THEY EACH BROOD 456 WELDED
RESENTFULLY--SARCASTICALLY)
SHE STARES AT HIM AND MUTTERS RESENTFULLY) 473 WELDED
(TURNING TO HER RESENTFULLY) 484 WELDED

RESENTFULNESS
WITH ANGRY BOYISH RESENTFULNESS THAT IS CLOSE TO 332 LAZARU
TEARS)

RESENTING
(THEN RESENTING BEING MOVED, CHANGES THE SUBJECT) 588 ICEMAN

RESENTMENT
(A TOUCH OF RESENTMENT IN HIS VOICE) 540 'ILE
(ALL HER EMOTIONS IMMEDIATELY TRANSFORMED INTO 39 ANNA
RESENTMENT AT HIS BULLYING TONE)
A TRACE OF RESENTMENT IN HER VOICE) 55 ANNA
(WITHOUT RESENTMENT) YES, ANDY'LL SEE THE RIGHT 125 BEYOND
THING TO DO IN A JIFFY.

RESENTMENT (CONT'D.)
(TURNING TO LOOK AT ANDREW--IN A TONE OF FIERCE 141 BEYOND
RESENTMENT)
(WITH DOGGED RESENTMENT) I KNOW WHAT YOU MEAN, 158 BEYOND
DOCTOR.
(STIFFENING IN HIS CHAIR--WITH ANGRY RESENTMENT) 503 DAYS
(WITH A SIDE GLANCE OF FRANK ENVY--UNABLE TO KEEP 517 DAYS
RESENTMENT OUT OF HER VOICE)
(A GRUMBLE OF RESENTMENT GOES AROUND 249 DESIRE
(WITH REAL RESENTMENT) HE'S BETTER'N WHAT YOU 499 DIFRNT
ARE. IF THAT'S WHAT YOU MEAN.
(FROWNING--WITH A TRACE OF RESENTMENT) 539 DIFRNT
(RAISES HERSELF TO HER FEET PLACIDLY, WITHOUT A 436 DYNAMO
TRACE OF RESENTMENT)
(THEN HIS RESENTMENT SMOLDERING UP) 435 DYNAMO
(SHE TURNS WITH CHILDISH BEWILDERED RESENTMENT AND489 DYNAMO
HURT TO THE DYNAMO)
(A TRACE OF RESENTMENT HAS CREPT INTO HIS TONE) 74 ELECTR
(A JEALOUS RESENTMENT CREEPING INTO HIS VOICE) 81 ELECTR
HE STARTS TO PACE UP AND DOWN AGAIN--WITH SAVAGE 121 ELECTR
RESENTMENT)
(THEN WITH A TRACE OF RESENTMENT) 295 GGBROW
(THERE HAD BEEN A GRADUAL MURMUR OF CONTEMPTUOUS 212 HA APE
RESENTMENT RISING AMONG THE MEN
YANK CURSES WITHOUT RESENTMENT) 223 HA APE
(THEY ARE SILENT, PUZZLED BY HIS SUDDEN RESENTMENT227 HA APE
HE APPEARS NOT UNFAVORABLY IMPRESSED BUT HIS TONE 10 HUGHIE
STILL HOLDS RESENTMENT.)
ERIE, HAVING SOOTHED RESENTMENT WITH HIS WISE- 25 HUGHIE
CRACKS)
(HIDING RESENTMENT) OH, I'M THE EXCEPTION. 587 ICEMAN
(WITH DEFENSIVE RESENTMENT) NIX/ 595 ICEMAN
THEIR EYES ARE FIXED ON HIM WITH UNEASY 622 ICEMAN
RESENTMENT.
(THEIR FACES AT ONCE CLEAR OF RESENTMENT AGAINST 637 ICEMAN
HIM.)
(WITH BITTER RESENTMENT) 645 ICEMAN
A SMOLDERING RESENTMENT BEGINNING TO SHOW IN HIS 659 ICEMAN
MANNER.)
CORA SPEAKS WITH A TIRED WONDER AT HERSELF RATHER 700 ICEMAN
THAN RESENTMENT TOWARD HIM)
(DULLY, WITHOUT RESENTMENT) YEAH. 713 ICEMAN
(JOKINGLY BUT WITH AN UNDERCURRENT OF RESENTMENT.) 15 JOURNE
(WITH FRIGHTENED RESENTMENT.) 56 JOURNE
(SHARPLY--LETTING HER RESENTMENT TOWARD HIM COME 60 JOURNE
OUT.)
(WITH A RESENTMENT THAT HAS A QUALITY OF BEING 61 JOURNE
AUTOMATIC AND ON THE SURFACE
(WITH GROWING RESENTMENT.) I HAD IT HERE WAITING 84 JOURNE
FOR YOU
(WITH GUILTY RESENTMENT.) FOR GOD'S SAKE, DON'T 86 JOURNE
DIG UP WHAT'S LONG FORGOTTEN.
TEASING TONE BUT WITH AN INCREASING UNDERCURRENT 120 JOURNE
OF RESENTMENT.)
(JEALOUS RESENTMENT IN HIS BITTERNESS.) 137 JOURNE
(HE GOES ON DULLY, WITHOUT RESENTMENT.) 146 JOURNE
HIS RESENTMENT HAS GONE. 149 JOURNE
(HE ADDS, SMILING WITHOUT RESENTMENT.) 158 JOURNE
(MUMBLES GUILTILY, WITHOUT RESENTMENT.) 171 JOURNE
(WITH FIERCE, HAUGHTY RESENTMENT) 303 LAZARU
HER EXPRESSION IS A MIXTURE OF DEFIANT RESENTMENT 2 MANSNS
AND GUILT.
HE KNEW THAT SIMON STILL FEELS A RESENTMENT-- 35 MANSNS
(A SHADOW OF RESENTMENT SHOWS IN HER FACE.) 84 MANSNS
THE TWO WOMEN TURN TO STARE AT HIM, WITH A 119 MANSNS
STIRRING OF SUSPICION AND RESENTMENT.
(HE STOPS ABRUPTLY AND HIS EXPRESSION CHANGES TO 159 MANSNS
BITTER RESENTMENT.)
(AGAIN WITH ILLOGICAL RESENTMENT) 95 MISBEG
AND BITTER RESENTMENT. 114 MISBEG
(RESENTMENT IN HER KIDDING) I'D BE DIFFERENT! 115 MISBEG
SHE CONQUERS HER BITTER RESENTMENT AND PUTS ON HER166 MISBEG
OLD FREE-AND-EASY KIDDING
(CONCEALING DISCOMFITURE AND RESENTMENT-- 47 POET
PLEASANTLY.)
AND HOW SHE SHOULD REACT--WITH AN UNDERCURRENT OF 82 POET
RESENTMENT.)
HER MOOD CHANGES TO RESENTMENT AND SHE SPEAKS AS 137 POET
IF SARA HAD SPOKEN.)
(WHO HAS BEEN REGARDING HIM WITH WANING 28 STRANG
RESENTMENT.
THERE IS AN EXPRESSION OF DEFENSIVE BITTERNESS AND 95 STRANG
SELF-RESENTMENT ABOUT HIS
(THEN WITH FURIOUS RESENTMENT) 98 STRANG
(SHOWING HIS JEALOUS RESENTMENT IN SPITE OF 102 STRANG
HIMSELF)
OH, I DON'T REMEMBER--(THINKING APPREHENSIVELY 127 STRANG
WITH A BITTER RESENTMENT)
HIS EYES ARE EMBITTERED AND THEY HIDE HIS INNER 138 STRANG
SELF-RESENTMENT
WHILE SHE GUILTILY AVOIDS HER EYES--IN FEAR AND 156 STRANG
RESENTMENT.
(A PAUSE--THEN WITH A TRACE OF SCORNFUL 447 WELDED
RESENTMENT)

RESERVE
I WAS GOING ALONG EASY, WITH LOTS IN RESERVE, NOT 230 AHWILD
A BIT TIRED,
OF RESERVE POWER AND HEALTH. 494 DIFRNT
WHICH HE HAS BROUGHT FROM THE CELLAR SO THERE WILL125 JOURNE
BE AN AMPLE RESERVE AT HAND.
IT'S NOTHING TO THE BIG SURPRISE I'VE GOT IN 393 MARCOM
RESERVE FOR YOU.

RESERVEDLY
(HARDLY TAKING IT--RESERVEDLY) 303 GGBROW
(RESERVEDLY) HELLO. 246 HA APE

RESET
WE'LL HAVE TO RESET IT. 211 AHWILD

RESIDENCE
TAKES PLACE IN OR IMMEDIATELY OUTSIDE THE MANNON 2 ELECTR
RESIDENCE.

RESIDENT
BUT YOU'RE ELIGIBLE TO GO THERE BECAUSE YOU'RE A 149 JOURNE
RESIDENT.

RESIDENTIAL
LAWN BETWEEN THE HOUSE AND THE QUIET RESIDENTIAL 3 STRANG
STREET.

RESIDENTS
IT'S MY RIGHT--AND YOURS. WE'RE RESIDENTS. I'M A144 JOURNE
PROPERTY OWNER.

RESIGN
(WARNINGLY) MAYBE IT'S GETTIN' TIME FOR YOU TO 181 EJONES
RESIGN--
I DIDN'T RESIGN. 707 ICEMAN
RESIGN MYSELF TO BE A GRANDMOTHER/ 39 MANSNS
BEFORE I GO-- YOU WILL, OF COURSE, WISH ME TO 60 MANSNS
RESIGN FROM MY POSITION--
(HESITATINGLY) BUT, TO TELL THE TRUTH, I WANT TO 393 MARCOM
RESIGN ANYHOW.
THE SCANDAL WAS HUSHED UP BUT CON HAD TO RESIGN 12 POET
FROM THE ARMY.
YOU'D BETTER RESIGN FROM THE WHOLE GAME... 92 STRANG

RESIGNATION
(WITH A COMIC AIR OF RESIGNATION) 195 AHWILD
THEN A LOOK OF RESIGNATION AND RELIEF TAKES ITS 76 ANNA
PLACE.
(THEN WITH A GRIM RESIGNATION, 77 ANNA
HER EXPRESSION IS ONE OF VIRTUOUS RESIGNATION. 422 DYNAMO
A LITTLE DAB OF PASTY RESIGNATION HERE AND THERE--318 GGBROW
MINGLED NOW WITH THE BEGINNING OF AN OLD WEARY, 71 JOURNE
HELPLESS RESIGNATION.
DEFEATED OLD MAN, POSSESSED BY HOPELESS 125 JOURNE
RESIGNATION.
ENDURED WITH A GRIM FORTITUDE THAT HAD NEVER 274 LAZARU
SOFTENED INTO RESIGNATION.
TO WHIMPER YOUR FEAR TO HER RESIGNED HEART AND BE 289 LAZARU
COMFORTED BY HER RESIGNATION/
(WITH BORED RESIGNATION) AH, WELL. 315 LAZARU
THEIR DISEASE TRIUMPHS OVER DEATH--A NOBLE VICTORY352 LAZARU
CALLED RESIGNATION/
WITH JUST THE CORRECT TOUCH OF QUIET RESIGNATION 50 MANSNS
IN HER BEARING
WITH A SUGGESTION OF WEARINESS AND RESIGNATION NOW 70 MANSNS
(SHE FINISHES AND RELAPSES INTO HER ATTITUDE OF 384 MARCOM
BROKEN RESIGNATION.
I ACCEPT YOUR RESIGNATION, 393 MARCOM
(BOWS HER HEAD IN RESIGNATION. 410 MARCOM
RESIGNATION RESENTFUL OF ITSELF. 111 STRANG
RESIGNATION HAS COME INTO HER FACE, A RESIGNATION 189 STRANG
THAT USES NO MAKE-UP.
IF THERE'S NOTHING LEFT BUT--RESIGNATION/ 486 WELDED

RESIGNED
ALTHOUGH NOW IT HAS LOST ALL ITS BITTERNESS AND 249 AHWILD
BECOME SUBMISSIVE AND RESIGNED.
HIS LIPS DRAWN DOWN AT THE CORNERS GIVE HIM A 119 BEYOND
HOPELESS, RESIGNED EXPRESSION.
IS ONE OF AN HABITUAL POVERTY TOO HOPELESSLY 144 BEYOND
RESIGNED/
(A PAUSE) I'M GITTIN' T' FEEL RESIGNED T' EBEN-- 231 DESIRE
HE WAS MAYOR WHEN THIS WAR BROKE OUT BUT HE 8 ELECTR
RESIGNED TO ONCE AND JOINED THE ARMY
BECAUSE BY THEN I HAD FORCED MYSELF TO BECOME 31 ELECTR
RESIGNED IN ORDER TO LIVE/
AND NOW--WELL, YOU WANTED ME TO BE A HERO IN BLUE, 75 ELECTR
SO YOU BETTER BE RESIGNED/
(AS IF HE WERE SUFFOCATING, HE PULLS THE MASK FROM272 GGBROW
HIS RESIGNED, PALE,
DRAWN AND CAREWORN FOR ITS YEARS, AND SAD, 291 GGBROW
RESIGNED, BUT A BIT QUERULOUS.)
I'D GOTTEN PRETTY RESIGNED TO--AND SAD HOPELESS, 309 GGBROW
TOO--
AND STARES UP AT THE MOON WITH A WISTFUL, RESIGNED323 GGBROW
SWEETNESS)
RESIGNED COMES NEARER, AS IF EACH WAS GIVIN' THE 24 HUGHIE
OTHER A BREAK BY THINKING,
ERIE BREAKS THE SILENCE--BITTERLY RESIGNED.) 33 HUGHIE
SINCE YOU GOT--RESIGNED. 604 ICEMAN
(HER BITTERNESS RECEDING INTO A RESIGNED 48 JOURNE
HELPLESSNESS.)
(THEN DULLY RESIGNED.) BUT WHAT'S THE GOOD OF 78 JOURNE
TALK&
ALL HE CAN DO IS TRY TO BE RESIGNED--AGAIN. 132 JOURNE
THE SORROWFUL, RESIGNED. 273 LAZARU
THEY ARE ALL SEVEN IN THE SORROWFUL, RESIGNED TYPE274 LAZARU
OF OLD AGE.)
TO WHIMPER YOUR FEAR TO HER RESIGNED HEART AND BE 289 LAZARU
COMFORTED BY HER RESIGNATION/
(WITH DULL, RESIGNED TERROR NOW) 296 LAZARU
THE CRUEL, REVENGEFUL. AND THE RESIGNED, 312 LAZARU
SORROWFUL.
SEEMS MORE THAN EVER A FIGURE OF A SAD, RESIGNED 327 LAZARU
MOTHER OF THE DEAD.
AT YOUR AGE, A WOMAN MUST BECOME RESIGNED TO WAIT 3 MANSNS
UPON EVERY MAN'S PLEASURE.
WHEN YOU RESIGNED IN DISGUST FROM YOUR FATHER'S 8 MANSNS
BUSINESS AND CAME OUT HERE TO
I WILL FACE CHANGE AND UGLINESS, AND TIME AND 22 MANSNS
DEATH, AND MAKE MYSELF RESIGNED/
MOST SORDID FACTS, TO PROVE HOW THOROUGHLY I WAS 29 MANSNS
RESIGNED TO REALITY.
MADE MYSELF A DECENTLY RESIGNED OLD WOMAN. 29 MANSNS
RESIGNED OLD WOMAN WHOSE LIFE IS ONLY IN THE MINDS 36 MANSNS
JOSIE'S FACE IS SET IN AN EXPRESSION OF NUMBED, 157 MISBEG
RESIGNED SADNESS.
SHE STANDS GAZING AT HIM WITH A RESIGNED SADNESS, 36 POET
(HELPLESSLY RESIGNED ALREADY BUT FEELING IT HER 148 POET
DUTY TO REBUKE.)

RESIGNED (CONT'D.)
I FEEL IT HAS LOST ITS SOUL AND GROWN RESIGNED TO 49 STRANG
DOING WITHOUT IT.
HE IS SPRUCE, DRESSED IMMACULATELY, HIS FACE A BIT 50 STRANG
TIRED AND RESIGNED.
SHE THINKS WITH RESIGNED FINALITY) 71 STRANG
HIS PRESENT GRIEF, HOWEVER, IS MORE RESIGNED TO 159 STRANG
ITS FATE THAN THE OLD.
(TURNING TO DARRELL, WHO IS STANDING WITH A SAD 195 STRANG
RESIGNED EXPRESSION--
TEACH ME TO BE RESIGNED TO BE AN ATOM/...)) 199 STRANG
(FORCING A LIGHT TONE) WELL, I'LL BE RESIGNED TO 467 WELDED
WAIT AND HOPE THEN--
(AFTER A PAUSE--WITH RESIGNED DULLNESS) 467 WELDED

RESIGNEDLY
(TOMMY ACCEPTS HIS FATE RESIGNEDLY 252 AHWILD
(THEN RESIGNEDLY) BUT I AIN'T EXPECTING MUCH FROM 16 ANNA
HIM.
(RESIGNEDLY) IF IT HAS TO BE-- 115 BEYOND
(THEN RESIGNEDLY) WAAL, LET'S GO HELP EBEN A 219 DESIRE
SPELL AN' GIT WAKED UP.
(RESIGNEDLY) AND ARGHUN IS AS ACCEPTABLE AS ANY 386 MARCOM
OTHER.
(RESIGNEDLY) WELL, IT ISN'T TOO LATE YET, IS IT& 414 MARCOM
(WAITING RESIGNEDLY UNTIL HE HAS FINISHED-- 579 ROPE
WEARILY)
(RESIGNEDLY) THERE AIN'T NOTHIN' WE CAN DO THEN. 586 ROPE
(THINKING RESIGNEDLY) 190 STRANG

RESIGNS
AND I'SE GOT ALL DE MONEY IN SIGHT, I RESIGNS ON 180 EJONES
DE SPOT AND BEATS IT QUICK.
I CASHES IN AND RESIGNS DE JOB OF EMPEROR RIGHT 182 EJONES
DIS MINUTE.

RESIST
COULDN'T RESIST IT/ 222 AHWILD
JUST SIMPLY COULDN'T RESIST IT/ 222 AHWILD
- HE CAN NO LONGER RESIST, BUT JOINS IN A SHAKY 259 AHWILD
BAWL)
(UNABLE TO RESIST FALLING INTO HIS TRAGIC LITERARY279 AHWILD
POSE FOR A MOMENT)
(CAN'T RESIST THIS) WELL, ALL RIGHT--CNLY I CAN'T280 AHWILD
STAY ONLY A FEW MINUTES.
YOU COULDN'T RESIST--WATCHING HIM SQUIRM/ 526 DAYS
(THEN BITTERLY) AND HOW LONG DO YOU THINK YOU'LL 527 DAYS
BE ABLE TO RESIST TELLING
(STARTS TO RESIST FEEBLY) LET ME GO/ 555 DAYS
I HAVEN'T THE STRENGTH TO RESIST EVIL. 466 DYNAMO
WHO TRIES TO RESIST AND KICKS OUT AT THE BUCKET. 526 DAYS
(STRUGGLING TO RESIST.) BUT I PROMISED HER-- 147 MANSNS
NO ONE COULD RESIST YOU/ 195 MARCOM
AND MY BODY MAY RESIST DEATH FOR A LONG TIME YET. 423 MARCOM
THERE WASN'T ONE COULD RESIST HIM IN PORTUGAL AND 13 POET
SPAIN
SURE, YOU WAS THAT HANDSOME, NO WOMAN COULD RESIST 61 POET
YOU.
MY UNIFORM SO INVITINGLY THAT I COULD NOT RESIST 89 POET
THE TEMPTATION TO PUT IT ON
BE GOD, HE'LL NIVIR RESIST THAT, IF I KNOW HIM, 171 POET
FOR HE'S A YOUNG FOOL,
BENTLEY TRIES TO RESIST. 584 ROPE

RESISTANCE
HE MAKES A BEWILDERED PRETENSE OF RESISTANCE. 243 DESIRE
(WITH SUDDEN RESISTANCE PULLS AWAY--DETERMINEDLY) 122 STRANG
(WITH A CROWNING INTENSITY TO BREAK DOWN HIS LAST 174 STRANG
RESISTANCE)

RESISTING
(RESISTING HIS ATTEMPTS TO GUIDE HER TO THE DOOR 547 'ILE
IN REAR)
(THEN RESISTING MORE VIOLENTLY THAN BEFORE-- 36 MANSNS
FURIOUSLY.)
(RESISTING MARY'S EFFORTS TO PULL HIM OUT, 584 ROPE
(THEN SUDDENLY RESISTING AND PUSHING HIM AWAY) 130 STRANG

RESOLUTE
MORE FIXED IN ITS RESOLUTE WITHDRAWAL FROM LIFE. 269 GGBROW

RESOLUTELY
THEN RESOLUTELY TURNS HIS MIND AWAY FROM THESE 276 AHWILD
IMPROPER,
BUT HE RESOLUTELY GOES ON WHISTLING WITH BACK 278 AHWILD
TURNED,
(THEN SHAKING HIS HEAD RESOLUTELY)
(RESOLUTELY) I CAN'T TELL YOU--AND I WON'T. 10 ANNA
(THEN SUMMONING HER COURAGE--MORE RESOLUTELY) 54 ANNA
(HE HESITATES FOR A SECOND--THEN RESOLUTELY) 63 ANNA
(THEY DRINK--PUFF RESOLUTELY--SIGH--TAKE THEIR 486 CARDIF
FEET DOWN FROM THE TABLE.) 217 DESIRE
HE ACTS AS IF HE SAW EVERY MOVE SHE WAS MAKING, HE239 DESIRE
BECOMES RESOLUTELY STILL.
(THEN RESOLUTELY) (I'LL BE DAMNED IF I'M GOING 449 DYNAMO
TO LET HIM BEAT ME/....)
(SHE TURNS AWAY FROM HIM RESOLUTELY-- 115 ELECTR
(THEN CONQUERING HER HORROR--RESOLUTELY TENDER AND160 ELECTR
SOOTHING)
(BACKING HIM UP RESOLUTELY) YES, 162 ELECTR
(RECOVERING HERSELF--RESOLUTELY) 386 MARCOM
RESOLUTELY WARDING OFF FROM HIS CONSCIOUSNESS. 73 STRANG
(THEN RESOLUTELY) (II CAN'T REMEMBER HER NOW/... 101 STRANG

RESOLUTION
THE SAME LOOK OF OBSESSED RESOLUTION IN HIS EYES, 584 DAYS
HE FORCES LOVING BACK.)
(WITH A GRIM RESOLUTION) I WANT A SON NOW. 234 DESIRE
(WITH QUICK RESENTFUL RESOLUTION) 506 DIFNAT
(THEN URGING HIMSELF IN WITH MANFUL RESOLUTION) 190 EJONES
BUT THERE IS AN AIR OF STUBBORN RESOLUTION ABOUT 171 ELECTR
HER AS SHE MAKES UP HER MIND
(WHO HAS BEEN DREAMING, A LOOK OF PRIM RESOLUTION 603 ICEMAN
ON HIS FACE.

RESOLVE

RESOLVE
ALL THE BITTER HURT AND STEELY RESOLVE TO IGNORE 258 AHWILD
AND PUNISH HIM VANISH IN A
SHE SEES AT ONCE THE FIXED RESOLVE IN HIS 104 BEYOND
BROTHER'S EYES.
(PLEASANTLY AGAIN.) I HESITATED BECAUSE I HAD 46 POET
MADE A GOOD RESOLVE TO BE
DEFIANT EYES, HER FACE SET IN AN EXPRESSION OF 12 STRANG
STUBBORN RESOLVE.
TOO PREOCCUPIED WITH HER RESOLVE TO REMEMBER OR 13 STRANG
SEE MARSDEN.

RESOLVED
RESOLVED TO FIND OUT WHAT IS BACK OF ALL THIS BY 502 DIFRNT
HOOK OR CROOK--FORCING A SMILE)
(SHE FOLLOWS HIM OFF LEFT, FRIGHTENED BUT PITYING 482 DYNAMO
AND RESOLVED TO HUMOR HIM.
(THEN HER VOICE CHANGES, AS IF SHE HAD SUDDENLY 61 ELECTR
RESOLVED ON A COURSE OF ACTION.

RESOLVES
(GLANCES AT HIM--THEN RESOLVES ON A NEW TACK-- 238 AHWILD
PATTING HIS HAND)

RESOLVING
(THEN FILLED WITH UNEASINESS AND RESOLVING HE MUST 22 ELECTR
ESTABLISH HIMSELF ON AN

RESONANCE
AND HIS AMUSED VOICE RECITES THE WORDS WITH A 4 STRANG
RHETORICAL RESONANCE)

RESONANT
HIS VOICE IS REMARKABLY FINE, RESONANT AND 13 JOURNE
FLEXIBLE.

RESORT
AS A LAST RESORT I WILL--IF YOU FORCE ME TO/ 96 ELECTR
A CHEAP GINMILL OF THE FIVE-CENT WHISKEY, LAST- 571 ICEMAN
RESORT VARIETY

RESOUNDING
(HE SHAKES WITH LAUGHTER AND KISSES HIS WIFE A 513 DIFRNT
RESOUNDING SMACK.)
FOLLOWED BY A RESOUNDING THUMP AND A CHORUS OF 43 MANSNS
LAUGHTER.
(SUDDENLY, SLAPPING A STACK OF COINS INTO THE CHEST415 MARCOM
WITH A RESOUNDING CLANK)

RESOUNDS
ABSORBED IN EATING AND A PERFECT CLAMOR OF KNIVES 432 MARCOM
AND FORKS RESOUNDS.

RESOURCES
IT APPEARS HE HAD OVERREACHED HIS RESOURCES DURING 32 MANSNS
THE PAST FEW YEARS--
THE BATTLE FOR THIS BANK HAS STRAINED YOUR 157 MANSNS
RESOURCES TO THE BREAKING POINT.
OF GREAT UNDEVELOPED NATURAL RESOURCES, 359 MARCOM
WITH NO RESOURCES, SINCE HE WAS PENNILESS, EXCEPT 10 STRANG

RESPECT
(RESPECT IN HIS VOICE) THANK YOU, SIR. 239 AHWILD
I'M LOSIN' MY RESPECT FOR YOUR EYESIGHT, KATEY. 99 BEYOND
I FELT I OWED IT TO HIM AND TO MY OWN SELF-RESPECT521 DAYS
CABOT IS ESPECIALLY ACTIVE IN THIS RESPECT. 250 DESIRE
I RESPECT ADA JUST AS MUCH AS I DO MY MOTHER/ 438 DYNAMO
RESPECT HER LIKE HE DOES ME/... 439 DYNAMO
A HARDY SELF-RELIANT CONFIDENCE IN HIMSELF THAT 175 EJONES
INSPIRES RESPECT.
I WOULDN'T BELIEVE YOU COULD HAVE GROWN SO CALLOUS 94 ELECTR
TO ALL FEELING OF RESPECT--
SHE NOW BEARS A STRIKING RESEMBLANCE TO HER MOTHER137 ELECTR
IN EVERY RESPECT.
IT WOULDN'T LOOK RIGHT THE DAY ORIN--OUT OF 176 ELECTR
RESPECT FOR HIM.
THEY RESPECT HIS SUPERIOR STRENGTH--THE GRUDGING 208 HA APE
RESPECT OF FEAR.
AND SHE'LL HAVE SOME RESPECT FOR YOU." 16 HUGHIE
HAVE YOU NO RESPECT FOR RELIGION, YOU UNREGENERATES78 ICEMAN
WOPS
I'VE ALWAYS HAD A LOT OF RESPECT FOR HUGO. 593 ICEMAN
THAT FAMILY-RESPECT STUFF IS ALL BOURGEOIS, 648 ICEMAN
PROPERTY-OWNING CRAP.
YOU SHOULD HAVE MORE RESPECT. 45 JOURNE
IT'S YOU WHO SHOULD HAVE MORE RESPECT/ 66 JOURNE
SHE SHOULD HAVE MORE RESPECT. 60 JOURNE
AND I RESPECT YOU FOR IT. 147 JOURNE
THEY HAVE NO RESPECT FOR LIFE/ 286 LAZARU
LET THE SCUM LOOK AT THEIR DEAD AND LEARN RESPECT 300 LAZARU
FOR US/
(POMPOUSLY) RESPECT, SIR/ 316 LAZARU
MORE RESPECT FOR CAESAR/ 316 LAZARU
EXTREMELY CONSCIOUS OF THE RESPECT DUE HIS 25 MANSNS
PROFESSIONAL DIGNITY.
THERE ARE TIMES WHEN I ALMOST RESPECT YOU, JOEL. 34 MANSNS
I AM GLAD TO FIND YOU CHANGED IN ONE RESPECT, 101 MANSNS
MOTHER.
THEIR FORMER LOVE AND RESPECT. 154 MANSNS
I COULD NOT RESPECT MYSELF UNLESS YOU WERE PROUD 158 MANSNS
OF ME.
YOU MUST NOT ASK THAT--IF YOU RESPECT MY PRIDE/ 386 MARCOM
BOWING WITH HUMBLE RESPECT) 391 MARCOM
THEIR EYES ARE KEPT ON HIM WITH THE ARDENT 433 MARCOM
HUMILITY AND RESPECT OF WORSHIP.
WITH A FAINT TRACE OF GRUDGING RESPECT) 13 MISBEG
(DETERMINED TO BE AUTHORITATIVE AND COMMAND 57 MISBEG
RESPECT--CURTLY)
THERE'S RESPECT FOR YOU/ 73 MISBEG
(CANNOT HELP BEING IMPRESSED--LOOKS AT HER MOTHER 25 POET
WITH WONDERING RESPECT.)
BY GOD, I'D HAVE MORE RESPECT FOR YOU/ 36 POET
TO RESPECT THE MASTER/ 54 POET
ANYONE IN AMERICA WOULD PAY HER RESPECT. 77 POET
I'LL HAVE TO PRETEND I LIKED HER AND I'D RESPECT 88 POET
WHATEVER ADVICE SHE GAVE HIM.
FAIX, I'LL GIVE YOU A BOX ON THE EAR THAT'LL TEACH175 POET
YOU RESPECT.

RESPECT
(CONT'D.)
WHO KEPT COMMANDING FROM HIS BRAIN, NO, YOU 19 STRANG
MUSTN'T, YOU MUST RESPECT HER.
NEITHER DESIRE NOR RESPECT. 88 STRANG
I DON'T RESPECT YOU/ 103 STRANG
I HAVE A GENUINE RESPECT FOR HIM NOW... 112 STRANG
I COULDN'T RESPECT A WOMAN WHO HADN'T RESPECTED 115 STRANG
HERSELF/
DIALECTS, AND MARRIED FOLK WHO ALWAYS ADMIRE AND 176 STRANG
RESPECT EACH OTHER.
AND IF YOU HAD ANY RESPECT FOR ME-- 458 WELDED

RESPECTABILITY
DRESSED WITH AN AWKWARD ATTEMPT AT SOBER 188 AHWILD
RESPECTABILITY
IT HAD GIVEN UP ALL PRETENSE OF RESPECTABILITY, 7 HUGHIE

RESPECTABLE
TIME TO BECOME RESPECTABLE AGAIN/ 314 GGBROW
WHICH BEGAN AS A RESPECTABLE SECOND CLASS 7 HUGHIE
YOU'D NEVER HAVE DISGRACED YOURSELVES AS YOU HAVE, 44 JOURNE
SO THAT NOW NO RESPECTABLE
I WAS BROUGHT UP IN A RESPECTABLE HOME 102 JOURNE
DREAM YOURSELF BACK UNTIL YOU BECOME NOT THE 3 MANSNS
RESPECTABLE, IF A TRIFLE MAD,
RESPECTABLE CONSERVATISM OF THE OLD OFFICE. 139 MANSNS

RESPECTABLY
(A SILENCE AS IF HE HAD RESPECTABLY SQUELCHED 25 STRANG
HIMSELF--

RESPECTED
I'VE ALWAYS RESPECTED HER A LOT. 406 MARCOM
EVEN THE HUNS RESPECTED HIM/ 30 STRANG
I COULDN'T RESPECT A WOMAN WHO HADN'T RESPECTED 115 STRANG
HERSELF/
SHE LIKED HIM AND RESPECTED HIM. 185 STRANG

RESPECTER
AND ANGINA IS NO RESPECTER OF TIME AND PLACE. 70 ELECTR

RESPECTFUL
(FAINT RESPECTFUL. 207 AHWILD
HIS OWN AS HE ANSWERS BECOMES RESPECTFUL AND 217 AHWILD
ADMIRING.)
THE OLD RESPECTFUL BOW, HE WON'T SEE YOU. 23 JOURNE
(SMILES WITH RESPECTFUL UNDERSTANDING. 327 LAZARU
HE'S THAT RESPECTFUL YOU'D THINK I WAS A HOLY 32 POET
IMAGE.

RESPECTFULLY
HE KEEPS STANDING RESPECTFULLY IN BACK OF HER, 262 GGBROW
(HE CALLS UP--VERY RESPECTFULLY) 406 MARCOM
LATE OF HIS MAJESTY'S SEVENTH DRAGONS, 154 POET
RESPECTFULLY REQUESTS A WORD WITH HIM."
EXPLAINING FAMILIARLY BUT RESPECTFULLY FROM THE 3 STRANG
RIGHT, AND MARSDEN ENTERS.
(GRINNING RESPECTFULLY) HERE'S THE--(AS HE SEES 47 STRANG
NINA) OH/

RESPECTIVELY
AT LEFT-FRONT AND RIGHT-FRONT OF HER, 31 MANSNS
RESPECTIVELY.)

RESPECTS
WHOLE TOWN COULD HAVE PAID THEIR RESPECTS TO HIM, 69 ELECTR
I THINK THAT'S WHY SHE STILL RESPECTS YOU, BECAUSE647 ICEMAN
IT WAS YOU WHO LEFT HER.
YOU'RE THE ONLY PERSON SHE STILL RESPECTS--AND 36 STRANG
REALLY LOVES.

RESPITE
(COVERING HIS EVIDENT RELIEF AT THIS RESPITE WITH 269 AHWILD
A FUMING MANNER)
COME ON, JACK, AND GIVE YOUR POOR WIFE A RESPITE 540 DAYS
FROM THE HORRORS OF AUTHORSHIP.

RESPLENDENTLY
A BRAND NEW PIANO SHINES RESPLENDENTLY IN THE FAR 519 DIFRNT
RIGHT CORNER BY THE DOOR.

RESPOND
THEY ALL RESPOND WITH SMILES THAT ARE STILL A 722 ICEMAN
LITTLE FORCED AND UNEASY.)
(DOES NOT RESPOND TO HIS HUMOR-- 40 JOURNE

RESPONDING
AS IF RESPONDING IN KIND TO A CHALLENGE.) 50 MANSNS
(RESPONDING PASSIONATELY.) DON'T EVER DREAM OF 85 MANSNS
HAVING ANOTHER/
(RESPONDING TO A VICIOUS NUDGE FROM JOE'S ELBOW) 505 VOYAGE

RESPONDS
SHE RESPONDS TO ELSA'S GREETING WITH A NERVOUS 516 DAYS
CONSTRAINT)
(SHE KISSES HIM AND HE RESPONDS, HUGGING HER TO 83 MANSNS
HIM WITH A PASSIONATE DESIRE,
SOMBER AND THREATENING--AND SOMETHING IN MY NATURE163 MANSNS
RESPONDS--
WHICH HE RESPONDS TO WITH AN INSTANT GRATEFUL 141 MISBEG
YIELDING.)
RESPONDS TO HIS APPEAL--THEN SHE SPRINGS UP AND 141 MISBEG
RUNS TO HIM--

RESPONSE
AS IF IN RESPONSE TO HIS SUMMONS THE BEATING OF 200 EJONES
THE TOM-TOM GROWS TO A FIERCE,
(SHE PAUSES, WAITING FOR SOME RESPONSE. 77 ELECTR
DRAINED OF ALL EMOTIONAL RESPONSE TO HUMAN 39 STRANG
CONTACTS.

RESPONSIBILITIES
AND NONE OF THE RESPONSIBILITIES OF ACTUAL 66 MANSNS
OWNERSHIP.
THE RESPONSIBILITIES OF MARRIAGE AND THE DUTIES OF424 MARCOM
MOTHERHOOD

RESPONSIBILITY
JUST SKULKIN' OUT O' YOUR RIGHTFUL RESPONSIBILITY.105 BEYOND
INCREDIBLE SUPERSTITIOUS EXCUSE TO LIE OUT OF HIS 538 DAYS
RESPONSIBILITY.
YOU DON'T DARE DO THAT ON YOUR OWN 78 ELECTR
RESPONSIBILITY--BUT IF YOU CAN MAKE ORIN--
(WITH A SCORNFUL SMILE) YOU DON'T CARE TO 221 HA APE
SHOULDER THIS RESPONSIBILITY ALONE.

RESPONSIBILITY (CONT'D.)
HER FULL RESPONSIBILITY FOR WHAT I HAVE BECOME. 74 MANSNS
WELL, THAT HALF OF MY DOMESTIC RESPONSIBILITY-- 94 MANSNS
SHARING SCHEME
TRUTH AMONG YOUR ENEMIES--TO THROW OFF THE BURDEN 157 MANSNS
OF RESPONSIBILITY AND GUILT--
(INQUISITIVELY) I SUPPOSE YOU FEEL YOUR HEAVY 403 MARCOM
RESPONSIBILITY
WANTS TO EVADE ALL RESPONSIBILITY FOR HER, I 37 STRANG
SUPPOSE--
BUT ALL HE NEEDS IS A LITTLE SELF-CONFIDENCE AND A 38 STRANG
SENSE OF RESPONSIBILITY.

RESPONSIBLE
AND YOU, SID, IF YOU WERE IN ANY RESPONSIBLE 231 AHWILD
STATE,
AND HE'S GONE ON--AND WE'RE ALL RESPONSIBLE-- 233 AHWILD
MAKING IT EASY FOR HIM--
NO ONE CAN SAY I'M RESPONSIBLE FOR THAT. 125 BEYOND
THAT I MIGHT BE IN PART RESPONSIBLE 507 DAYS
I KNOW IT JUST GETS TO BE PART OF THEIR NATURES 495 DIFRNT
AND THEY AIN'T RESPONSIBLE.
AS FOR EMMER, I DON'T HOLD HER RESPONSIBLE. 529 DIFRNT
YOU'LL BE RESPONSIBLE IF--/ 35 ELECTR
AND YOUR FEELING OF BEING RESPONSIBLE FOR HER 142 ELECTR
DEATH
YOU'LL BE RESPONSIBLE IF--/ 156 ELECTR
HE SIMPLY WASN'T RESPONSIBLE. 311 GGBROW
AND NOT BE RESPONSIBLE FOR ALL DE CRAZY STUNTS 669 ICEMAN
HE'S STAGIN' HERE.
WE MUSTN'T HOLD HIM RESPONSIBLE FOR ANYTHING HE'S 722 ICEMAN
DONE.
HE AIN'T RESPONSIBLE. 725 ICEMAN
YOU'RE MORE RESPONSIBLE THAN ANYONE/ 34 JOURNE
REMEMBER SHE'S NOT RESPONSIBLE. 139 JOURNE
WELL, LET THOSE WHO ARE RESPONSIBLE FOR THE 74 MANSNS
CHALLENGE BEWARE.
YOU MEAN BECAUSE YOUR HUSBAND IS RESPONSIBLE FOR 151 MANSNS
RUINING ME$
IT IS THAT IDEALISTIC FALLACY WHICH IS RESPONSIBLE172 MANSNS
THEY'RE NOT RESPONSIBLE. 372 MARCOM
WELL-GROOMED FACE IS CAREFULLY ARRANGED INTO THE 390 MARCOM
GRAVE RESPONSIBLE EXPRESSION
THAT PROVES YOU IN THE EAST AREN'T RESPONSIBLE, 404 MARCOM
IT'S THAT HAREM NOTION--
I'M DRUNK--NOT RESPONSIBLE. 138 MISBEG
I AM AFRAID YOU'RE NOT RESPONSIBLE FOR WHAT YOU'RE 18 STRANG
SAYING.
I FEEL RESPONSIBLE. 82 STRANG
(TEASINGLY) WELL, IF I'M RESPONSIBLE, CHARLIE, 114 STRANG

RESPONSIVE
THE SOUND OF THE SINGING SEEMS TO STRIKE A 102 ELECTR
RESPONSIVE CHORD IN HIS BRAIN,
AS IF THIS SENTIMENT STRUCK A RESPONSIVE CHORD IN 701 ICEMAN
THEIR NUMBED MINDS.
TERRIFIC FLASHES OF LIGHTNING AND CRASHES OF 318 LAZARU
THUNDER SEEM A RESPONSIVE

REST
TIBBOTS 'N' HARRIS 'N' SIMMS AND THE REST--AND ALL542 'ILE
O' HOMEPORT MAKIN FUN O' ME$
US, AND YOU CAN TELL THE REST THE SAME. 545 'ILE
(DISTURBED) GO IN AND REST, ANNIE. 548 'ILE
WELL, I THOUGHT WE'D JUST SIT AROUND AND REST AND 191 AHWILD
TALK.
FOR THE REST OF THE DAY. 195 AHWILD
THESE ARE GOOD SAMPLES OF THE REST. 201 AHWILD
NEVER MIND THE REST OF THE LIGHTS. 211 AHWILD
YOU NEED REST AFTER TEACHING A PACK OF WILD 212 AHWILD
INDIANS OF KIDS ALL YEAR.
YOU'RE A GOOD WOMAN, LILY--TOO GOOD FOR THE REST 214 AHWILD
OF US.
(HE DRINKS THE REST OF HIS SOUP IN A GULP AND 225 AHWILD
BEAMS AROUND AT THE COMPANY.
GIVE US A REST, YOU DARNED FOOL/ 227 AHWILD
SO'S YOUR UNCLE SID'LL GET TO SLEEP AND YOUR AUNT 234 AHWILD
LILY CAN REST.
(BUT HE HASTILY GULPS DOWN THE REST OF HIS GLASS, 237 AHWILD
GIVE US A REST FROM THAT BUNK/ 246 AHWILD
GIVE US A REST/ 255 AHWILD
SHE HAS EVIDENTLY HAD NO REST YET FROM A 263 AHWILD
SLEEPLESS, TEARFUL NIGHT.
I'LL HAVE TO MEMORIZE THE REST AND RECITE IT TO 277 AHWILD
MURIEL THE NEXT TIME.
(WEARILY) GEE, I SURE NEED THAT REST/ 1A ANNA
AND I DON'T EXPECT HE'LL TURN OUT NO BETTER THAN 16 ANNA
THE REST.
THEN YOU THINK'S HE'LL STAKE ME TO THAT REST CURE 17 ANNA
I'M AFTER$
THAT PUTS MY IDEA OF HIS GIVING ME A REST ON THE 17 ANNA
BUM.
YOU REST ALL YOU WANT, PY YIMINY/ 22 ANNA
I NEED A LONG REST AND I DON'T SEE MUCH CHANCE OF 22 ANNA
GETTING IT.
I COULD VISIT A WHILE AND REST UP-- 22 ANNA
YOU NEED LIE DOWN, GAT REST. 23 ANNA
YOU NEED TAKE REST LIKE DAT. 23 ANNA
VELL, AY MAKE YOU TAKE GOOD LONG REST NOW. 24 ANNA
YOU NEED GAT REST, ANNA. 39 ANNA
BUT LIE THERE FOR THE REST OF YOUR LIFE HOWLING 48 ANNA
BLOODY MURDER.
YOU'RE JUST LIKE ALL THE REST OF THEM--YOU TWO/ 56 ANNA
YOU SOUNDED--YUST LIKE ALL THE REST. 57 ANNA
YOU'RE LIKE ALL THE REST OF 'EM. 57 ANNA
YOU'RE LIKE ALL THE REST/ 58 ANNA
AND I SEEN YOU WAS THE SAME AS ALL THE REST. 59 ANNA
THE REST, IS IT$ 60 ANNA
YOU'RE LIKE ALL THE REST/ 60 ANNA
AY VANT FOR YOU BE HAPPY ALL REST OF YOUR LIFE FOR 65 ANNA
MAKE UP/

REST (CONT'D.)
I COULD BE FORGETTING THE REST, MAYBE. 74 ANNA
(HOLDING IT AWAY) IT'S A CROSS WAS GIVEN ME BY MY 75 ANNA
MOTHER, GOD REST HER SOUL.
AND IT'LL GIVE HIM A TRADE FOR THE REST OF HIS 96 BEYOND
LIFE, IF HE WANTS TO TRAVEL.
YOU'RE LIKE THE REST, KATE. 113 BEYOND
WELL, AT LEAST I CAN GO TO MY ETERNAL REST WITH A 114 BEYOND
CLEAR CONSCIENCE.
AND BILL EVANS DOWN TO MEADE'S, AND ALL THE REST 124 BEYOND
ON 'EM.
BUT WON'T YOU GO BACK TO BED NOW AND REST$ 150 BEYOND
I WANTED IT TO COME EASIER, SO LIKE ALL THE REST 156 BEYOND
OF THE IDIOTS,
(WITH SATISFACTION) I NEED A REST, 157 BEYOND
AND THE KIND OF REST I NEED IS HARD WORK IN THE 157 BEYOND
OPEN.
(HE SIGHS WITH EXHAUSTION) YES, I'LL GO AND REST 162 BEYOND
A WHILE.
YOU BETTER LIE DOWN AND REST A WHILE, DON'T YOU 162 BEYOND
THINK$
REST A WHILE AND THEN WE'LL CARRY YOU-- 167 BEYOND
SURE IT'S HARD ENOUGH ON THE REST AV US WID 480 CARDIF
NUTHIN' THE MATTHER WID OUR INSIDES
WHATEVER PAY'S COMIN' TO ME YUH CAN DIVVY UP WITH 489 CARDIF
THE REST OF THE BOYS.
THE REST OF THE WHALING CREW WERE NEVER HEARD FROM559 CROSS
AGAIN--GONE TO THE SHARKS.
THEY BEGAN TO GO MAD--HUNGER, THIRST, AND THE 560 CROSS
REST--AND THEY BEGAN TO FORGET.
THEY LANDED IT AND--YOU CAN GUESS THE REST, TOO-- 560 CROSS
LET US REST IN PEACE AT LAST/ 509 DAYS
SHE'S BEEN WANTING TO HEAR THE REST OF IT, TOO. 512 DAYS
WHEN WILL YOU TELL ME THE REST OF IT$ 512 DAYS
YOU CAN'T LIVE THERE WITHOUT BECOMING LIKE THE 521 DAYS
REST OF THE CROWD/
YOU HAD BETTER MAKE UP YOUR MIND NOW TO TELL THE 528 DAYS
REST OF YOUR NOVEL TONIGHT--
TELL ME, HAVE YOU BEEN DOING ANYTHING MORE ON THE 530 DAYS
REST OF YOUR IDEA FOR A NOVEL$
SO I THREATENED HIM I MIGHT GIVE YOU BOTH AN 530 DAYS
OUTLINE OF THE REST TONIGHT.
(NERVOUSLY) WELL--(HE HESITATES--GULPS DOWN THE 533 DAYS
REST OF HIS COFFEE.)
TO GET OUT OF TELLING US THE REST OF HIS NOVEL. 533 DAYS
AND REST FOR A WHILE. 540 DAYS
AND TELL HIM THE REST OF YOUR STORY THERE. 540 DAYS
IF YOU KEPT ON REFUSING TO REST OR TAKE 556 DAYS
NOURISHMENT.
I'LL SEE T' IT MY MAW GITS SOME REST AN' SLEEP IN 209 DESIRE
HER GRAVE/
(EXCITEDLY) BY GOD, WE'VE 'ARNED A REST/ 215 DESIRE
IT'S HER VENGEANCE ON HIM--SO'S SHE KIN REST QUIET244 DESIRE
IN HER GRAVE/
MAY SHE REST IN PEACE/ 245 DESIRE
SHE KIN REST NOW AN' SLEEP CONTENT. 246 DESIRE
(WITH A DEEP SIGH) I'LL GO T' THE BARN AN' REST 4253 DESIRE
SPELL.
THEY'S NO PEACE IN HOUSES, THEY'S NO REST LIVIN' 253 DESIRE
WITH FOLKS.
YOU JUST GOT TO BE DIFF'RENT FROM THE REST. 495 DIFRNT
ON'Y DON'T GIT THE NOTION IN YOUR HEAD I'M ANY 495 DIFRNT
BETTER'N THE REST.
COUPLE--DIFF'RENT FROM THE REST--NOT THAT THEY 496 DIFRNT
AIN'T ALL RIGHT IN THEIR WAY.
NOW YOU KNOW WHAT YOU'LL BE UP AGAINST FOR THE 499 DIFRNT
REST OF YOUR NATURAL DAYS.
AND YOU'D HEAR ABOUT IT FROM SOMEONE SOONER OR 502 DIFRNT
LATER 'CAUSE JIM AND THE REST O'
YOU'RE GETTIN' TO THINK YOU'RE BETTER'N THE REST 510 DIFRNT
OF US.
IF IT WAS ONE OF THE REST--LIKE JIM BENSON OR 512 DIFRNT
JACK, EVEN--
I'M HUMAN LIKE THE REST AND ALWAYS WAS. 517 DIFRNT
YOU'RE DIFF'RENT FROM THE REST. 523 DIFRNT
AW, GIVE US A REST/ 529 DIFRNT
(ANGRILY) YOUR UNCLE CALEB'LL GIVE YOU A REST 529 DIFRNT
WHEN HE SEES YOU/
YOU USED TO SAY YOU WAS DIFF'RENT FROM THE REST O'543 DIFRNT
FOLKS.
I WASN'T AFRAID TO 'IRE YOU LIKE THE REST WAS-- 177 EJONES
IT'S TIME YOU GIT A REST. 188 EJONES
REST/ 193 EJONES
(THEN CAUTIOUSLY) REST/ 193 EJONES
I GOTTA LIE DOWN AN' REST. 198 EJONES
I GOTTA REST. 198 EJONES
(MOVING TO THE STEPS) I AM GOING IN AND REST A 18 ELECTR
WHILE.
HE'D HAVE BEEN SORRY THE REST OF HIS LIFE IF HE 32 ELECTR
HADN'T/
AND I'LL BE UNDER YOUR THUMB FOR THE REST OF MY 35 ELECTR
LIFE/
I WOULD RATHER REST HERE FOR A SPELL. 47 ELECTR
THE DOCTOR ADVISED A FEW MORE DAYS' REST. 48 ELECTR
AND IF HE DIDN'T REST HE'D BREAK DOWN. 70 ELECTR
YOU SIT DOWN AND REST. 80 ELECTR
(GRUFFLY) GIVE IT A REST, ORIN/ 82 ELECTR
(ANGRILY TO LAVINIA) CAN'T YOU LET YOUR BROTHER 83 ELECTR
HAVE A MINUTE TO REST$
REST UP AND TAKE IT EASY. 84 ELECTR
(GIVING HER HAND TO ORIN) YOU MUST REST ALL YOU 84 ELECTR
CAN NOW, ORIN--
THE REST IS ALL A JOKE/ 95 ELECTR
HE MUSTN'T BE WORRIED, HE SAID-- HE NEEDS REST AND101 ELECTR
PEACE--
YOU'VE BROUGHT LOVE--AND THE REST IS ONLY THE 111 ELECTR
PRICE.
(HARSHLY) REST IN HELL, YOU MEAN/ 115 ELECTR

REST

REST (CONT'D.)
MAY THE SOUL OF OUR COUSIN, ADAM MANNON, REST IN 115 ELECTR
PEACE/
AS NAKED AS THE REST/ 145 ELECTR
SHE NEEDS A REST FROM HIM, TOO. 159 ELECTR
YOU REST THERE IN PEACE/ 160 ELECTR
YOU KNOW THERE'S NO REST IN THIS HOUSE 171 ELECTR
REST/ 267 GGBROW
"COME UNTO ME ALL YE WHO ARE HEAVY LADEN AND I 269 GGBROW
WILL GIVE YOU REST.
THE REST IS EARTH. 286 GGBROW
YOU MUST REST/ 316 GGBROW
(CONTROLLING HIMSELF) I'LL REST IN PEACE--WHEN 316 GGBROW
HE'S GONE/
MORE SURE OF HIMSELF THAN THE REST. 208 HA APE
GIVE US A REST. 210 HA APE
ALL DAT CRAZY TRIPE ABOUT SUNS AND WINDS, FRESH 215 HA APE
AIR AND DE REST OF IT--
DE ENGINES AND DE COAL AND DE SMCKE AND ALL DE 215 HA APE
REST OF IT/
WHY NOT LET YOUR GREAT-GRANDMOTHER REST IN HER 218 HA APE
GRAVES
WE HAD A REST. 224 HA APE
DE REST WAS NUTHIN'. 234 HA APE
I'M STEEL AND STEAM AND SMOKE AND DE REST OF IT/ 238 HA APE
(FILLS OUT THE REST OF THE CARD) 246 HA APE
GIMME DE STUFF, DE OLD BUTTER--AND WATCH ME DO DE 249 HA APE
REST/
DE JUNGLE AND DE REST OF IT. 253 HA APE
I HOPE YOU HAVE A GOOD REST. 17 HUGHIE
HIS EYES PROWL THE LOBBY AND FINALLY COME TO REST 27 HUGHIE
HOW IS IT THEY DIDN'T PICK YOU UP WHEN THEY GOT 588 ICEMAN
YOUR MOTHER AND THE RESTS
FOR THE REST, THEY LIVE ON FREE LUNCH AND THEIR 593 ICEMAN
OLD FRIEND, HARRY
AND ALL THE REST OF YOU, LADIES INCLUDED, ARE IN 623 ICEMAN
THE SAME BOAT.
REST IN PEACE. 625 ICEMAN
AND DE REST IS HIDIN' IN DEIR ROOMS SO DEY WON'T 631 ICEMAN
HAVE TO LISTEN TO HIM.
ALL I CAN DO IS HELP YOU, AND THE REST OF THE 639 ICEMAN
GANG,
AND QUIT BATTLING HIMSELF, AND FIND PEACE FOR THE 641 ICEMAN
REST OF HIS LIFE.
I'M GOIN' TO REST MY FANNY. 665 ICEMAN
AND ALL DE REST BEEN BRUSHIN' AND SHAVIN' 665 ICEMAN
DEMSELVES WID DE SHAKES--
SHE DON'T GIMME A MINUTE'S REST ALL NIGHT. 671 ICEMAN
I JUST CAME BACK HERE TO REST A FEW MINUTES, NOT 674 ICEMAN
BECAUSE I NEEDED ANY BOOZE.
SORRY TO BE LEAVING GOOD OLD HARRY AND THE REST OF675 ICEMAN
YOU, OF COURSE.
THE REST OF HIS DAYS/ 691 ICEMAN
I TRIED TO WISE DE REST OF DEM UP TO STAY CLEAR OF698 ICEMAN
HIM.
ALL WE WANT OUTA YOU IS KEEP DE HELL AWAY FROM US 705 ICEMAN
AND GIVE US A REST.
GIVE US A REST, FOR THE LOVE OF CHRIST/ 715 ICEMAN
GOD REST HIS SOUL IN PEACE. 726 ICEMAN
ALL THE REST OF THE MEN TUMBLE OUT OF THEIR BUNKS, 435 INZONE
STRETCHING AND GAPING.
(POINTING) LOOKIN' AROUND SNEAKIN-LIKE AT IVAN 518 INZONE
AND SWANSON AND THE REST 'S IF
GIVE IT A REST, CAN'T YOUS 21 JOURNE
AND SPONGE ON ME FOR THE REST OF YOUR LIFE/ 32 JOURNE
YOU NEED TO REST ALL YOU CAN. 42 JOURNE
YOU WENT IN THE SPARE ROOM FOR THE REST OF THE 47 JOURNE
NIGHT.
CAN'T YOU LET OUR DEAD BABY REST IN PEACE$ 88 JOURNE
LEAN BACK AND REST. 92 JOURNE
ARMS REST LIMPLY ALONG THE ARMS OF THE CHAIR, HER 107 JOURNE
HANDS WITH LONG, WARPED,
I THINK THE BEST THING FOR ME IS TO GO TO BED AND 123 JOURNE
REST.
"WITH HEART AT REST I CLIMBED THE CITADEL'S STEEP 133 JOURNE
HEIGHT.
IN THE REAR WALL, RIGHT, A DOOR LEADING INTO THE 273 LAZARU
REST OF THE HOUSE.
IN COMBINATION WITH THE REST OF THE FACE 299 LAZARU
REST ON LAZARUS. HE GIVES A START OF GENUINE 332 LAZARU
ASTONISHMENT.
HIS WHOLE BODY IS NOW RELAXED, AT REST, A DREAMY 342 LAZARU
SMILE SOFTENS HIS THIN,
THE REST; SOLDIERS, SLAVES AND THE PROSTITUTES OF 349 LAZARU
BOTH SEXES,
(THEN GRIMLY) BUT OUR BET CAN REST. 351 LAZARU
AND I FEAR THERE IS NO REST BEYOND THERE, 353 LAZARU
DEEP REST AND FORGETFULNESS OF ALL I HAVE EVER 353 LAZARU
SEEN
TIGHT LIPS, AND HER JAW IS A LITTLE TOO LONG AND 2 MANSNS
HEAVY FOR THE REST OF HER FACE,
YOU MUST REST A WHILE. 19 MANSNS
EVADE, ESCAPE, FORGET, REST IN PEACE/ 103 MANSNS
A LITTLE REST HERE EACH DAY WILL RESTORE THE 106 MANSNS
SOUL--THE CHANGE I SO BADLY NEED--
SO HE REMAINED FOR THE REST OF HIS LIFE STANDING 111 MANSNS
BEFORE THE DOOR.
BUT WAIT TILL YOU HEAR THE REST. 133 MANSNS
OR I MIGHT SIMPLY GO AWAY--FOR A LONG, MUCH-NEEDED149 MANSNS
REST.
THE REST I LEAVE IN YOUR CAPABLE HANDS, MY 150 MANSNS
BEAUTIFUL.
TO BE ABLE TO WE STILL, OR TO TURN BACK TO REST/ 157 MANSNS
LET US SIT DOWN AND REST FOR A MOMENT TOGETHER 176 MANSNS
THEN,
LETTING SIMON'S HEAD REST BACK ON THE GRASS. 192 MANSNS
(AS THEY ALL SIT DOWN TO REST, LOOKS FROM ONE TO 348 MARCOM
THE OTHER--JOVIALLY)

REST (CONT'D.)
THE GOES ON TELLING THE REST OF THE STORY WITH 366 MARCOM
MUCH EXAGGERATED JEWISH PANTOMIME
I DON'T REMEMBER THE REST. 399 MARCOM
THERE ARE HARBORS AT EVERY VOYAGE-END WHERE WE 410 MARCOM
REST FROM THE SORROWS OF THE SEA.
THAT WE COULD CRUSH EACH SINGLY AND THE REST WOULD421 MARCOM
REJOICE.
(BUT THE REST ARE ALL 431 MARCOM
HIS EYES REST IN LOVING CONTEMPLATION ON THE BODY 435 MARCOM
OF KUKACHIN.
IF YOU SLEEP ON, REST IN PEACE/ 436 MARCOM
CATCH ME IF I TOOK A MINUTE'S REST, THE WAY HE 4 MISBEG
ALWAYS DOES$
ONE IN IT HAD SPIRIT, GOD REST HER SOUL. 17 MISBEG
THE REST OF THEM WAS A PIOUS LOUSY LOT. 17 MISBEG
(WITH ADMIRING AFFECTION) GOD REST HIM, HE WAS A 24 MISBEG
TRUE IRISH GENTLEMAN.
HASN'T A POOR MAN A RIGHT TO HIS NOON REST 39 MISBEG
SO REST AISY. 76 MISBEG
I'LL HAVE HAD TONIGHT AND YOUR LOVE TO REMEMBER 137 MISBEG
FOR THE REST OF MY DAYS/
YOU'D HATE ME AND YOURSELF--NOT FOR A DAY OR TWO 140 MISBEG
BUT FOR THE REST OF YOUR LIFE.
FOR GOD'S SAKE, CAN'T YOU LET HER REST IN PEACE$= 148 MISBEG
REST IN PEACE A WHILE LONGER. 161 MISBEG
DEAR GOD, LET HIM REMEMBER THAT ONE THING AND 165 MISBEG
FORGET THE REST.
MAY YOU REST FOREVER IN FORGIVENESS AND PEACE. 177 MISBEG
A BIT OF FARM LAND NO ONE WOULD WORK ANY MORE, AND 30 POET
THE REST ALL WILDERNESS/
(HE DRINKS THE REST OF HIS WINE, POURS ANOTHER 100 POET
GLASS.)
GO ON NOW IN THE KITCHEN AND SIT DOWN AND REST, 125 POET
MOTHER.
I DIDN'T SAY SLEEP, BUT I CAN LIE DOWN AND TRY TO 131 POET
REST.
SOON WE'D GET MARRIED, AND NOW HAPPY WE'D BE THE 147 POET
REST OF OUR LIVES TOGETHER.
GOD REST HIS SOUL IN THE FLAMES AV TORMINT/ 177 POET
THE MAJOR'S PASSIN' TO HIS ETERNAL REST HAS SET ME178 POET
FREE TO JINE THE DEMOCRATS.
(HER VOICE TREMBLES.) MAY THE HERO OF TALAVERA 182 POET
REST IN PEACE.
SAY, GIVE US A REST ON THAT STUFF, WILL YUHS 595 ROPE
A LITTLE MORE INCLINED TO DEAFNESS THAN THE REST-- 15 STRANG
LET ME BE JUST--
THE REST IS JUST TALK/ 64 STRANG
THE REST OF THE TABLE IS LITTERED WITH AN INK 66 STRANG
BOTTLE, PENS, PENCILS, ERASERS,
ON TOP OF ALL THE REST/... 83 STRANG
LIE DOWN AND REST. 108 STRANG
I SUPPOSED HE'S NO BETTER THAN THE REST OF YOU. 116 STRANG
I GUESS I DO NEED TO REST. 136 STRANG
(EXCITEDLY) AND ALL THE REST IS GUTLESS EGOTISM/ 170 STRANG
BUT YOU'LL REST IN MY ARMS... 183 STRANG
(WITH A SERENE PEACE) REST, DEAR NINA. 200 STRANG
AN' IRISH WHISKEY FOR THE REST AV US-- 500 VOYAGE
SIT DOWN AND REST FOR TIME, DRISCOLL. 504 VOYAGE
WELL---(HE GULPS DOWN THE REST) DERE/ 507 VOYAGE
SO CHEER UP--AND GET A GOOD NIGHT'S REST. 451 WELDFD
THE REST IS LOST INCOHERENTLY. 462 WELDED
TRY AND REST. 466 WELDED
RESTAURANT
I HAD A DOLL CRY ON ME ONCE IN A RESTAURANT FULL 22 HUGHIE
OF PEOPLE
THUS MAKING A BACK ROOM LEGALLY A HOTEL 571 ICEMAN
RESTAURANT.
RESTAURANTS
INFESTING CORNERS, DOORWAYS, CHEAP RESTAURANTS, 9 HUGHIE
THE BARS OF MINOR SPEAKEASIES,
RESTED
HE MIGHT BE WILLING TO STAKE ME TO A ROOM AND EATS 16 ANNA
TILL I GET RESTED UP.
BUT I DO FEEL RESTED, SO DON'T BEGIN TO SCOLD ME. 515 DAYS
(CONFUSEDLY) I RESTED. 246 DESIRE
DO YOU FEEL RESTED$ 39 JOURNE
IN THE DARK PEACE OF THE GRAVE THE MAN CALLED 309 LAZARU
LAZARUS RESTED.
RESTFUL
AND I FEEL AS IF I COULD SLEEP NOW--(CHEERFULLY) 151 BEYOND
A GOOD, SOUND, RESTFUL SLEEP.
(QUEERLY) DOWN WHAR IT'S RESTFUL--WHAR IT'S 238 DESIRE
WARM--DOWN T' THE BARN.
(STIFFLY.) YES, IT IS VERY RESTFUL HERE. 106 MANSNS
IT IS VERY RESTFUL HERE. 175 MANSNS
A GRAY IVIED CHAPEL, FULL OF RESTFUL SHADOW, 197 STRANG
YOU'RE SO RESTFUL, CHARLIE. 199 STRANG
(SHE SIGHS AGAIN, THIS TIME WITH A SORT OF RESTFUL471 WELDED
CONTENT)
RESTIN'
SHE CAN'T FIND IT NATERAL SLEEPIN' AN' RESTIN' IN 209 DESIRE
PEACE.
RESTING
AND THAT HER HEAD IS RESTING ON HIS SHOULDER, 90 BEYOND
GENTLY TAKES HIS ARM AWAY.
ROBERT IS DISCOVERED SITTING ON THE BOULDER, HIS 129 BEYOND
CHIN RESTING ON HIS HANDS,
HER CHIN RESTING ON HER HANDS AS SHE STARES OUT 140 BEYOND
SEAWARD.)
RESTING HIS ELBOW, HIS CHIN ON HIS HAND, STARING 562 CROSS
SOMBERLY BEFORE HIM.
SHE'S RESTING QUIETLY. 556 DAYS
RESTING THEIR SAGGING BREASTS AND HANDS AND HAIR 202 DESIRE
ON ITS ROOF,
WHEN YOU KNEW I WAS RESTING. 29 ELECTR
HIS HEAD RESTING SIDEWAYS ON HIS ARMS. 574 ICEMAN

RESTING — RESURRECTION

RESTING (CONT'D.)

HER CHIN RESTING ON HER HANDS ON TOP OF THE MARBLE363 LAZARU

RAIL,

HIS EYES WANDER ABOUT THE ROOM, FINALLY RESTING 397 MARCOM

APPEALINGLY ON KUKACHIN.)

AND YET, BY STAYING HOME AND RESTING AND FINDING 16 STRANG

HEALTHY OUTDOOR RECREATION

(RESTING HER HEAD ON HIS SHOULDER) 199 STRANG

BENT OVER WEARILY, HIS SHOULDERS BOWED, HIS LONG 462 WELDED

ARMS RESTING ON HIS KNEES,

RESTLESS

A RESTLESS, APPREHENSIVE, DEFIANT, SHY, DREAMY, 193 AHWILD

THEY BECOME VERY RESTLESS.) 218 DESIRE

BUT HIS EYES ARE RESTLESS 468 DYNAMO

HE'S ALWAYS BEEN RESTLESS. 48 ELECTR

CONTINUALLY IN RESTLESS NERVOUS MOVEMENT. 260 GGBROW

I WAS GETTING MORE RESTLESS. 709 ICEMAN

IT'S WHAT I NEEDED AFTER SUCH A RESTLESS NIGHT. 59 JOURNE

JAMIE HAS BECOME RESTLESS, SENSING HIS FATHER'S 168 JOURNE

PRESENCE.

AND I BECOME EMPTY, BUT AT THE SAME TIME RESTLESS 72 MANSNS

AND AIMLESS.

AND YOU ARE BECOMING RESTLESS$ 421 MARCOM

TYRONE CONTINUES TO STARE AT NOTHING, BUT BECOMES 107 MISBEG

RESTLESS.

AS RESTLESS, PRYING, RECORDING INSTRUMENTS. 39 STRANG

PUFFY SHADOWS OF DISSIPATION AND SLEEPLESSNESS 124 STRANG

UNDER HIS RESTLESS, HARRIED EYES.

RESTLESSLY

SHE SIGHS, MOVES RESTLESSLY, THEN FINALLY ASKS) 253 AHWILD

(WHO HAS BEEN FIDGITING RESTLESSLY--UNABLE TO BEAR264 AHWILD

THE SUSPENSE A MOMENT LONGER)

KICKING AT THE SAND RESTLESSLY, TWIRLING HIS STRAW275 AHWILD

(HE JUMPS TO HIS FEET RESTLESSLY) 276 AHWILD

ROBERT MOVES HIS HEAD RESTLESSLY ON RUTH'S LAP) 167 BEYOND

(THE SICK MAN IN THE LOWER BUNK IN THE REAR GROANS478 CARDIF

AND MOVES RESTLESSLY.

THEN ELSA STIRS RESTLESSLY AND MOANS. 554 DAYS

(A PAUSE--RESTLESSLY, SPEAKING O' MILK, WONDER 218 DESIRE

HOW EBEN'S MANAGIN'S

BUT THE OLD MAN TURNS RESTLESSLY, GROANING IN HIS 259 DESIRE

SLEEP.

HER HANDS APPEAR ON THE TABLE TOP, MOVING 15 JOURNE

RESTLESSLY.

(SHE GETS UP RESTLESSLY AND GOES TO THE WINDOWS AT 17 JOURNE

RIGHT.)

HER HANDS PLAY RESTLESSLY OVER THE TABLE TOP. 62 JOURNE

THEY STIR AND PUSH ABOUT RESTLESSLY WITH AN EAGER 298 LAZARU

CURIOSITY AND IMPATIENCE.

HOPPING RESTLESSLY ABOUT FROM FOOT TO FOOT-- 319 LAZARU

SHOUTING)

RESTLESSNESS

JOHN STARTS TO PACE UP AND DOWN WITH NERVOUS 545 DAYS

RESTLESSNESS--THEN STOPS ABRUPTLY)

YOU HAD A STRANGE WAY OF SHOWING YOUR 17 JOURNE

RESTLESSNESS.

RESTORE

RESTORE TO ITS NATURAL PUCKISH EXPRESSION) 259 AHWILD

A LITTLE REST HERE EACH DAY WILL RESTORE THE 106 MANSNS

SOUL--THE CHANGE I SO BADLY NEED--

IN A VERY SHORT TIME HE WILL BEG US ON HIS KNEES 135 MANSNS

TO RESTORE THAT PEACE

RESTORED

SHE ADDS TARTLY, HER CONFIDENCE RESTORED AND HER 433 DYNAMO

TEMPER A BIT RUFFLED)

HIS CONFIDENCE IN HIMSELF COMPLETELY RESTORED) 459 DYNAMO

HAVE SOMEWHAT RESTORED HIS SHAKEN NERVE. 190 EJONES

(HIS SOUL IS PURGED OF GRIEF, HIS CONFIDENCE 38 HUGHIE

RESTORED.)

AND THEN RESTORED HIMSELF TO LIFE BY MAGIC. 316 LAZARU

WHAT WAS IT RESTORED YOUR YOUTHS 354 LAZARU

(HE TURNS TO NORA, HIS SELF-CONFIDENCE PARTLY 76 POET

RESTORED.)

BEING IN IT HAS NOTABLY RESTORED HIS SELF- 88 POET

CONFIDENT ARROGANCE.

HAVE BEEN RESTORED TO HEALTH AND NORMAL 134 STRANG

FUNCTION.--

RESTORES

(THIS COMPLIMENT COMPLETELY RESTORES HIM TO HIS 93 POET

ARROGANT SELF.)

RESTRAIN

EXCEPT FOR MILDRED WHO CAN'T RESTRAIN A GIGGLE 192 AHWILD

(THEN SUDDENLY, UNABLE TO RESTRAIN HIMSELF ANY 250 DESIRE

LONGER,

(UNABLE TO RESTRAIN HIS MIRTH) 502 DIFRNT

THEN HE AND ROGERS ROAR WITH LAUGHTER AND HARRIET 507 DIFRNT

CANNOT RESTRAIN A GIGGLE AND

(HE CANNOT RESTRAIN A PARTING SHOT) 467 DYNAMO

(SHE CANNOT RESTRAIN HER RAGE--THREATENINGLY) 95 ELECTR

(CANNOT RESTRAIN A SHUDDER SOMETIMES WHEN YOU'RE297 GGBROW

DRUNK YOU'RE POSITIVELY EVIL.

HE CANNOT RESTRAIN A SARDONIC GUFFAW. 604 ICEMAN

(TRYING TO RESTRAIN HIS GROWING RAGE) 526 INZONE

AS HE SEES HER FACE, GADSBY CANNOT RESTRAIN A 27 MANSNS

STARTLED EXCLAMATION.

STOPS BEFORE THE OLD COUPLE AND CANNOT RESTRAIN 366 MARCOM

HIS CURIOSITY)

EVEN KUKACHIN CANNOT RESTRAIN A SMILE. 390 MARCOM

(LOOKS AFTER HIM FOR A MOMENT--THEN CANNOT 47 STRANG

RESTRAIN A JOYFUL, COLTISH CAPER--

(SHARPLY, BEFORE SHE CAN RESTRAIN THE IMPULSE) 94 STRANG

(CANNOT RESTRAIN HERSELF--BREAKS OUT) 115 STRANG

I COULDN'T RESTRAIN MY HATE/ 467 WELDED

(THEN UNABLE TO RESTRAIN HIS TRIUMPHANT EXULTANCE)488 WELDED

RESTRAINED

(THEY KISS IN RESTRAINED FASHION. 243 DESIRE

RESTRAINED (CONT'D.)

RESTRAINED BY A HIGH FOREHEAD FROM WHICH 443 WELDED

RESTRAINING

(RESTRAINING A GIGGLE--SEVERLY) 225 AHWILD

(TOMMY WHO HAS BEEN HAVING DIFFICULTY RESTRAINING 229 AHWILD

HIMSELF,

(RESTRAINING HIS ANGER WITH AN EFFORT) 105 BEYOND

(THEN WITH A TWITCH OF THE LIPS, AS IF SHE WERE 52 ELECTR

RESTRAINING A DERISIVE SMILE)

(TURNING AWAY AND RESTRAINING A SHUDDER) 81 ELECTR

LAVINIA PUTS A RESTRAINING HAND ON HIS ARM. 109 ELECTR

LAVINIA GRIPS HIS ARM, RESTRAINING HIM.) 112 ELECTR

DUE TO HER RESTRAINING A TENDENCY TO LAPSE INTO 16 POET

BROGUE.

(GLARING AT HIM BUT RESTRAINING HER RAGE) 591 KOPE

(RESTRAINING HIS ANGER WITH DIFFICULTY--THINKING) 163 STRANG

RESTRAINT

ITS EXPRESSION ALREADY INDICATING A DISCIPLINED 257 GGBROW

RESTRAINT.

THE PEOPLE IN THE CROWD ARE HOLDING THEMSELVES IN 298 LAZARU

RESTRAINT WITH DIFFICULTY.

(HE SITS IN ANGUISH, IN A TORTURED RESTRAINT. 487 WELDED

RESTRICTING

RESTRICTING THE MIGRATION OF NON-NORDIC BIRDS INTO390 MARCOM

TEXAS.

RESTS

(HE RESTS ONE HAND ON THE BACK OF HER CHAIR) 150 BEYOND

LISTEN.

AND RESTS LIKE TIRED DUST IN CIRCULAR PATCHES UPON555 CRUSS

THE FLOOR AND TABLE.

THE FIDDLER RESTS. 251 DESIRE

I HOPE--HE RESTS IN PEACE. 63 ELECTR

THE MASK OF WILLIAM BROWN RESTS ON THE DESK BESIDE313 GGBROW

HIM.

AND THE MOON RESTS IN THE SEA/ 323 GGBROW

GENTLY HE LETS HER BUOY SINK UNTIL IT RESTS 347 LAZARU

AGAINST THE STEPS OF THE DAIS.

(HE RESTS HIS HEAD ON HIS ARMS AND GOES TO SLEEP.)374 MARCOM

THE OTHER HAND RESTS UPON--AND PATS-- 389 MARCOM

AND, ABOVE ALL, HE RESTS SO COMPLACENTLY 141 STRANG

RESULT

STOPPING EACH TIME TO SURVEY THE RESULT 249 AHWILD

CRITICALLY, BITING HER TONGUE,

THE RESULT OF SOME SNIDE NEUTRALIZING OF LIFE 296 GGBROW

FORCES--A SPINELESS CACTUS--

ALTHOUGH THE RESULT IS ONLY TO HEIGHTEN THEIR 629 ICEMAN

SPLOTCHY LEPRPUS LOOK.

(HE APPEALS TO ROCKY, AFRAID OF THE RESULT, BUT 722 ICEMAN

DARING IT)

AS A RESULT, MOTHER, THE COMPANY STANDS ON THE 32 MANSNS

BRINK OF BANKRUPTCY.

AND HERE'S THE GRATIFYING RESULT/ 395 MARCOM

THE RESULT OF THOSE BREAKS IN THE FENCE IS THAT 50 MISBEG

YOUR PIGS STROLL--

AS A RESULT OF THE RURAL TASTE FOR GRANDEUR IN THE 48 STRANG

EIGHTIES.

THE RESULT IS A ROOM AS DISORGANIZED IN 90 STRANG

CHARACTER

RESULTANT

RESULTANT OVER-DEVELOPMENT OF BACK AND SHOULDER 207 HA APE

MUSCLES HAVE GIVEN THEM.

RESULTED

I ENDED IT WITH AN EXPERIMENT WHICH RESULTED SO 140 STRANG

SUCCESSFULLY THAT ANY FURTHER

RESULTING

ANY EMOTION RESULTING FROM HER INTERVIEW WITH HER 81 POET

SON.

RESULTS

BUT BEYOND THESE APPEARANCES--THE RESULTS OF HEAVY 68 ANNA

DRINKING--

THEY MAY BRING RESULTS. 247 HA APE

THE KIND OF PITY I FEEL NOW IS AFTER FINAL RESULTS641 ICEMAN

A WEIRD CACOPHONY RESULTS FROM THIS MIXTURE 727 ICEMAN

THAT GOT SUCH WONDERFUL RESULTS IS SIMPLICITY 392 MARCOM

ITSELF.

AND I GOT RESULTS/ 392 MARCOM

CREATING RESULTS WHERE THERE WEREN'T ANY BEFORE, 398 MARCOM

GOING AFTER THE IMPOSSIBLE--

A FRENZIED CATARACT OF SOUND RESULTS. 407 MARCOM

A MAD SCRAMBLE RESULTS. 429 MARCOM

AND I GOT RESULTS. 430 MARCOM

TO OBTAIN THE BEST RESULTS IN THE WEAVING AND 431 MARCOM

DYEING OF THE FINISHED PRODUCT,

RESUMES

(LARRY GOES BACK TO THE BAR AND RESUMES HIS 13 ANNA

NEWSPAPER.

(SHE RESUMES HER KNITTING. 95 BEYOND

(AS RUIN DOESN'T ANSWER OK SMILE HE OPENS HIS BOOK122 BEYOND

AND RESUMES HIS READING.

WAIT. THE RESUMES DELIBERATELY) ONE DAY MY 560 CROSS

FATHER SENT FOR ME

BUT CHRISTINE QUICKLY RECOVERS HERSELF AND HER AIR 16 ELECTR

RESUMES ITS DISDAINFUL

(SCUTTY RESUMES HIS POST AT THE DOOR.) 525 INZONE

THEN, GIVING IT UP, RESUMES HIS HEARTY AIR, 66 JOURNE

RAISING HIS GLASS.)

WITH A SATISFIED SIGH AT THE SHEER COMFORT OF IT 439 MARCOM

ALL, RESUMES HIS LIFE.)

RESUMING

RESUMING HIS LAWYER-LIKE MANNER) 354 LAZARU

(THEN RESUMING HIS TONE OF TENDER TEASING) 385 MARCOM

RESURRECTION

THE RESURRECTION AND THE LIFE, AND HE THAT 566 DAYS

BELIEVETH IN THY LOVE,

YOU'RE DEAD, WILLIAM BROWN, DEAD BEYOND HOPE OF 305 GGBROW

RESURRECTION/

OH, IF YOU KNEW HOW I HAVE PRAYED FOR RESURRECTION 38 MANSNS

FROM THE DEATH IN MYSELF/

RETAIL

RETAIL
(SHE TURNS AWAY TO RETAIL THIS BIT OF GOSSIP TO 248 DESIRE
HER MOTHER SITTING NEXT TO HER.
YOU STILL HAVE TO HAVE STORES TO RETAIL YOUR 157 MANSNS
COTTON GOODS--
RETAIN
SO WHY NOT RETAIN ME AS YOUR ATTORNEYS 679 ICEMAN
BUT HER BEAUTIFUL DARK EYES AND HER SMILE STILL 95 MANSNS
RETAIN THEIR OLD IMAGINATIVE,
(CAN'T RETAIN HIS ANXIETY ANY LONGER) 160 MISBEG
RETAINERS
IT'S WELL TRAINED YOU'VE GOT THE POOR RETAINERS ON 54 POET
YOUR AMERICAN ESTATE
RETAINING
BUT AT THE SAME TIME RETAINING THE ALOOF SERENITY 350 LAZARU
OF THE STATUE OF A GOD,
FULL OF HEALTH AND VITALITY, AND RETAINING ITS 2 MANSNS
GRACE DESPITE HER CONDITION.
RETAINS
AND SHE RETAINS A CERTAIN REFINEMENT OF MOVEMENT 94 BEYOND
AND EXPRESSION FOREIGN TO THE
RETAINS ITS ATTRACTIVENESS ALTHOUGH IT HAS GROWN 422 DYNAMO
FLESHY.
EACH RETAINS A VESTIGE OF YOUTHFUL FRESHNESS, 611 ICEMAN
HE IS THE SAME IN APPEARANCE, RETAINS THE 139 MANSNS
HER SKIN STILL RETAINS A TRACE OF SUMMER TAN 137 STRANG
RETALIATING
IF YOU THINK I WILL HEAR YOUR INSULTS WITHOUT 162 MANSNS
RETALIATING/
RETCHING
(HIS MOUTH GROWS CONVULSED, AS IF HE WERE RETCHING166 ELECTR
UP POISON)
WITH NAUSEA RETCHING YOUR MEMORY, AND THE WINE OF 140 MISBEG
PASSION POETS BLAB ABOUT,
RETINUE
(BOWING HIS HEAD AS DO ALL HIS RETINUE) 422 MARCOM
RETIRE
BUT HE'S TO MEAN EVEN TOO RETIRE FROM WHALIN' 522 DIFRIT
HIMSELF--
AND THE SENATORS TURN TO RETIRE, HE STOPS THEM ALL322 LAZARU
FOR A MOMENT WITH A
I PROPOSE TO RETIRE AS SOON AS WE HAVE ENOUGH. 16 MANSNS
I HEARD YOU, WHEN HE SAID HE'D RETIRE TO WRITE HIS 20 MANSNS
BOOK WHEN HE HAD ENOUGH.
ALL I'M DREAMING OF IS TO MAKE HIM RETIRE, A 21 MANSNS
LANDED GENTLEMAN.
YOU USED TO DREAM ABOUT WHERE WE ARE GOING TO 92 MANSNS
RETIRE WHEN WE HAVE ENOUGH.
(THEY BOW HUMBLY AND RETIRE BACKWARD. 359 MARCOM
YOU MAY RETIRE. 388 MARCOM
I'VE APPOINTED FIVE HUNDRED COMMITTEES TO CARRY ON393 MARCOM
MY WORK AND I RETIRE
THEY RETIRE TOWARD THE LEFT, 419 MARCOM
RETIRED
YOU'RE RETIRED FROM THE CIRCUS. 623 ICEMAN
RETIREMENT
FOUND A PLACE OF RETIREMENT HERE 589 ICEMAN
RETIRES
(CUCKY GRUMBLES AND RETIRES TO A BENCH, NURSING 526 INZONE
HIS SURE SHIN.)
(SHE BOWS AND RETIRES BACKWARD TO THE LEFT SIDE OF390 MARCOM
THE THRONE.
(SHE BOWS AND RETIRES TO LEFT, REAR, 391 MARCOM
RETIRING
WOULD YOU MIND RETIRING TO YOUR CABINS 406 MARCOM
IS THAT OF A RETIRING, STUDIOUS NATURE. 6 STRANG
RETORT
(THERE IS LOUD FEMININE LAUGHTER AT THIS RETORT.) 461 CARIBE
HE GIVES CABOT NO CHANCE TO RETORT BUT ROARS) 250 DESIRE
THEN OPENS HIS MOUTH TO MAKE SOME RETORT TO FIFE 437 DYNAMO
(STARTS AS IF TO RETORT DEFIANTLY--THEN SAYS 45 ELECTR
CALMLY)
(STARTS TO MAKE A BITTER RETORT, GLANCES AT PETER 83 ELECTR
AND HAZEL.
(STARTS AN EXASPERATED RETORT.) 135 POET
RETREAT
(BUT THEY BEAT A CAPERING RETREAT BEFORE HIM, 224 DESIRE
KEPT ADVISING CRUNJE TO RETREAT AND NOT STAND AND 677 ICEMAN
FIGHT--
ABOUT TO RETREAT ANGRILY--THEN IMPULSIVELY SHE 193 MANSNS
KNEELS AND KISSES HER HAND.)
I MUST FLY IN RETREAT FROM WHAT I CAN NEITHER 401 MARCOM
LAUGH AWAY NOR KILL.
(HARDERY'S RETREAT BECOMES A ROUT. 64 MISBEG
THE ARMY IS BACK, MAJOR, WITH THE FOE FLYING IN 129 POET
RETREAT.
SHE HAD HALF A MIND TO RETREAT BEFORE HER MOTHER 136 POET
DISCOVERED HER.
THE ATMOSPHERE OF THE ROOM IS THAT OF A COSY, 3 STRANG
CULTURED RETREAT.
RETREATING
LIVING COMES FIRST, RETREATING BACKWARD BEFORE 564 DAYS
JOHN WHOM HE DESPERATELY,
A FAINT STRAIN OF THEIR RETREATING VOICES IS 226 DESIRE
HEARD.--
SHE FOLLOWS HIS RETREATING FIGURE WITH 230 DESIRE
CONCENTRATED HATE.
SHE SPEAKS TO HIS RETREATING FIGURE WITH A STRANGE 42 ELECTR
SINISTER AIR OF ELATION)
RETREATS
(AS HE RETREATS WITH THE GLASS SHE GUFFAWS AFTER 10 ANNA
HIM DERISIVELY.)
A PIGEON-HOLE AND RETREATS SWIFTLY TO HER CHAIR 119 BEYOND
WITH IT.
(HE RETREATS BACK BEYOND THE VISION OF THE OLD MAN223 DESIRE
AND TAKES THE BAG OF MONEY
(SHE RETREATS INTO THE HOUSE.) 456 DYNAMO
AND HE RETREATS FARTHER BACK IN THE ALLEYWAY, 513 INZONE

RETREATS (CONT'D.)
KEEPING HER FACE TURNED TOWARD SOMETHING FROM 27 MANSNS
WHICH SHE RETREATS.
THEN RETREATS WITH AN EXCLAMATION AS KUKACHIN'S 351 MARCOM
FACE.
FITTING TO THE PHILOSOPHER RULER WHO RETREATS HERE384 MARCOM
(SHE RETREATS QUICKLY INTO THE ROOM AND BACKS 163 POET
AROUND THE TABLE AT LEFT FRONT
RETRIBUTION
BUT GOD WAS SIMPLY USING REUBEN TO BRING 451 DYNAMO
RETRIBUTION ON YOUR HEAD/
(HARSHLY) WERE YOU HOPING YOU COULD ESCAPE 152 ELECTR
RETRIBUTIONS
RETRIBUTION'S
WHERE I CAN, I KILL LOVE--FOR RETRIBUTION'S SAKE--356 LAZARU
BUT MUCH OF IT ESCAPES ME.
RETRIEVED
(HE TAKES THE CANNON BALL FROM HIS FATHER WHO HAS 395 MARCOM
RETRIEVED IT)
RETRIEVES
HE RETRIEVES THEM WITH DIFFICULTY, AND STARTS TO 125 JOURNE
SHUFFLE AGAIN.
RETURN
I'LL RETURN PRESENTLY. 562 CROSS
LET'S RETURN TO YOUR PLOT. 513 DAYS
(WITH A RETURN OF HER FLIPPANT TONE) 520 DAYS
WHICH HE HAD PRIDED HIMSELF HIS REASON HAD KILLED,544 DAYS
RETURN TO PLAGUE HIM.
(THEN WITH A RETURN OF HER DEFIANT COOLNESS) 30 ELECTR
PATH LEFT HIM ANY PERCEPTION, HE COULD NOT NOTICE 62 ELECTR
HER DEPARTURE AND RETURN,
WITH A RETURN OF THE ABRUPT MILITARY MOVEMENT 168 ELECTR
THEY RETURN IN A MOMENT, CARRYING THE MASK OF 318 GGBROWN
WILLIAM BROWN, TWO ON EACH SIDE)
(ATTEMPTING A RETURN OF HIS JAUNTY MANNER, AS IF 677 ICEMAN
NOTHING HAD HAPPENED)
SHE GOES ON WITH A RETURN OF HER DETACHED AIR.) 72 JOURNE
(GRINS A BIT DRUNKENLY IN RETURN.) 143 JOURNE
BUT WHY SHOULD THE GOD RETURN IN THE BODY OF A 300 LAZARU
JEW,
NOW WE RETURN TO THE SEA/ 324 LAZARU
AND IN THE DAWN AT YOUR GOING OUT, AND IN THE 330 LAZARU
EVENING ON YOUR RETURN,
I WILL EVEN LAUGH AT THEE IN RETURN. 339 LAZARU
(THEN SUDDENLY, WITH A RETURN TO GROTESQUENESS-- 371 LAZARU
HARSHLY)
WE MUST RETURN TO NATURE AND SIMPLICITY AND THEN 9 MANSNS
WE'LL FIND THAT THE PEOPLE--
AND RETURN TO COMMON SENSE IN THE LITTLE TIME LEFT 14 MANSNS
US.
(TAKES HER HAND, SMILING IN RETURN--A BIT 50 MANSNS
STILTEDLY.)
SO I CAN RETURN ON THE FIRST STAGE TOMORROW. 51 MANSNS
ALL I ASK IN RETURN IS THAT YOU ALLOW ME TO LIVE 56 MANSNS
THERE WITH YOU--
ON YOUR RETURN FROM WORK, I KNOW THE CHILDREN 103 MANSNS
WOULD BE PLEASED TO SEE YOU.
AND RETURN WHERE YOU BELONG-- 130 MANSNS
IS IT TOO MUCH TO ASK IN RETURN 130 MANSNS
WILL YOU BE GOOD ENOUGH TO RETURN TO THE HOUSE 169 MANSNS
WHERE YOU BELONG.
SEE THAT YOU TAKE YOUR LOVER AWAY AT ONCE AND 193 MANSNS
NEVER RETURN HERE/
BUT EACH TIME YOU RETURN FROM A JOURNEY YOU MUST 382 MARCOM
RELATE TO ME ALL THE
I HAVE GIVEN NO ORDERS FOR HIM TO RETURN. 386 MARCOM
WILL YOU RETURN TO THIS--SOW AND BOAST THAT A 416 MARCOM
PRINCESS AND A QUEEN--
ALL BOW AND THEY RETURN THIS SALUTATION.) 427 MARCOM
THEY COULD NOT KEEP YOU--YOU WERE TOO HOMESICK-- 438 MARCOM
YOU WANTED TO RETURN--
AND YOU RETURN HIS LOVE-- I SURMISE. 47 POET
HE GLANCES TOWARD THE BAR AS IF HE LONGED TO 59 POET
RETURN THERE TO ESCAPE HER.
I'VE WASTED SO MUCH OF THE MORNING AND I HAVE TO 74 POET
RETURN TO THE CITY.
KINDLY KEEP HER HERE ON SOME EXCUSE UNTIL I 76 POET
RETURN--
NEVERTHELESS, IT WILL BE A RELIEF TO RETURN TO MY 86 POET
GARDEN AND BOOKS AND
NO ONE NOTICED MY RETURN AND WHEN I WENT UPSTAIRS 108 POET
IT OCCURRED TO ME
(HIS EYES FOLLOW HER FOR A SECOND, THEN RETURN TO 4 STRANG
GAZE AROUND THE ROOM SLOWLY
(HER EYES IMMEDIATELY RETURN TO HER FATHER) 13 STRANG
AND I WOULDN'T ASK FOR ANYTHING IN RETURN EXCEPT 32 STRANG
THE RIGHT TO TAKE CARE OF HER.
I GIVE HIM SO LITTLE IN RETURN... 69 STRANG
HER SOMETHING IN RETURN... 85 STRANG
NINA AND DARRELL RETURN TO THEIR CHAIRS. 99 STRANG
AND MADE HIM PROMISE ME HE WOULDN'T RETURN FOR TWO155 STRANG
YEARS.
YOU KNOW YOU PROMISED NOT TO RETURN UNTIL YOU DID.445 WELDED
(WITH A RETURN TO HER NATURAL TONE--BUT 449 WELDED
HYSTERICALLY)
FOR A MOMENT SHE SUBMITS, APPEARS EVEN TO RETURN 460 WELDED
HIS KISSES IN SPITE OF HERSELF.
(HE TRIES TO FORCE HER EYES TO RETURN TO HIS.) 485 WELDED
RETURNED
(TO PAUL, WHO HAS RETURNED TO HIS POSITION BY THE 458 CARIBE
BULWARK
A DEITY WHO RETURNED HATE FOR LOVE AND REVENGED 511 DAYS
HIMSELF UPON THOSE WHO TRUSTED
WHEN I RETURNED FROM NEW YORK LAST NIGHT YOU 16 ELECTR
SEEMED TO HAVE GONE TO BED.
AND SHE SAID I WAS TO KEEP YOU COMPANY UNTIL SHE 21 ELECTR
RETURNED.

RETURNED

(CONT'D.)

AS IF BY THE VERY ACT OF DISOWNING THE MANNONS SHE168 ELECTR HAD RETURNED TO THE FOLD--
RIGHT AFTER I RETURNED FROM THE SANATORIUM, YOU 93 JOURNE
BEGAN TO BE ILL.
THAT DAY I RETURNED DID I NOT TELL YOU YOUR FEAR 289 LAZARU
WAS NO MORE.
THEY SAY YOU DIED AND HAVE RETURNED FROM DEATH'S 340 LAZARU
BUT THEN IT GREW YOUNGER AND I FELT AT LAST IT HAD345 LAZARU
RETURNED TO MY HOME--
I WOULD HAVE FORGOTTEN HER AND RETURNED TO MOTHER, 74 MANSNS
WAITING FOR ME IN HER GARDEN--
THAT DOES NOT EXPLAIN WHY SHE HAS NOT RETURNED 162 MANSNS
HOME EITHER--HE MUST BE WITH HER/
AND ALSO REMEMBER THAT ON EACH OCCASION HE 388 MARCOM
RETURNED IN TRIUMPH,
IT WAS AFTER I RETURNED FROM MY RIDE. 107 POET

RETURNING
RETURNING FROM HIS WORK IN THE FIELDS. 82 BEYOND
(RETURNING TO HER AIR OF HARD CYNICISM) 520 DAYS
(SHE REACHES FOR A CIGARETTE--RETURNING TO HER 522 DAYS
HARD FLIPPANCY)
(CABOT APPEARS RETURNING FROM THE BARN. 226 DESIRE
(RETURNING HER GLANCE IN KIND) 230 DESIRE
CABOT APPEARS, RETURNING FROM THE BARN, WALKING 253 DESIRE
WEARILY, HIS EYES ON THE GROUND.
(HIS COURAGE RETURNING, COMES FORWARD INTO THE 544 DIFRNT
ROOM)
(HIS SENSE OF HUMOR RETURNING--WITH A MALICIOUS 432 DYNAMO
GRIN)
RETURNING FROM HIS NIGHTLY VISIT TO THE SALOON.) 123 ELECTR
(RETURNING AND POURING OUT A BIG DRINK IN THE 295 GGBROW
TUMBLER)
(RETURNING THROUGH THE BACK PARLOR, CALLS.) 66 JOURNE
THE FAMILY ARE RETURNING FROM LUNCH AS THE CURTAIN 71 JOURNE
RISES.
(SHE HEARS TYRONE RETURNING AND TURNS AS HE COMES 121 JOURNE
IN, THROUGH THE BACK PARLOR,
THE RETURNING LEGIONS BURST THROUGH AND GATHER IN 320 LAZARU
A DENSE MOB IN THE STREET
(RETURNING HIS LOOK--SIMPLY 397 MARCOM
(JOSIE CAN BE SEEN THROUGH THE WINDOWS, RETURNING 111 MISBEG
FROM THE KITCHEN.
(HE HEARS SARA RETURNING DOWNSTAIRS.) 63 POET
HE BOWS A BIT STIFFLY, AND GADSBY FINDS HIMSELF 117 POET
RETURNING THE BOW.)
AND I NEVER DREAMED OF RETURNING SO SOON. 7 STRANG
(BUT RETURNING TO HIS BITTER TONE) 185 STRANG

RETURNS
(THEN WITH A SIGH AS HE RETURNS TO THE BAR) 248 AHWILD
(HE RETURNS TO THE BAR) LAGER AND ALE FOR MARTHY, 8 ANNA
LARRY.
(HE RETURNS TO THE BAR, WHISTLING. 9 ANNA
(LARRY RETURNS TO THE BAR.) 11 ANNA
LARRY COMES BACK WITH THE DRINK WHICH HE SETS 14 ANNA
BEFORE ANNA AND RETURNS TO THE BAR.
RUTH RETURNS FROM THE KITCHEN 121 BEYOND
RUTH RETURNS FROM THE KITCHEN WITH A LIGHTED LAMP 153 BEYOND
IN HER HAND
THEN SHE SHUTS THE DOOR AND RETURNS TO HER CHAIR 154 BEYOND
BY THE STOVE.
HE RUSHES INTO THE BEDROOM AND RETURNS IMMEDIATELY166 BEYOND
(LAMPS GOES TO HIS ROOM AND RETURNS WITH A CANDLE.465 CARIBE
SHE RETURNS THEIR STARE OF COLD APPRAISING 222 DESIRE
CONTEMPT WITH INTEREST--SLOWLY)
THEN HE PUTS HIS ARMS ABOUT HER NECK AND RETURNS 239 DESIRE
HER KISSES, BUT FINALLY,
RETURNS HER KISSES. 243 DESIRE
(HE STUMBLES OUT THE DOOR--IN A SHORT WHILE 264 DESIRE
RETURNS TO THE KITCHEN--
THE EXCITEMENT RETURNS TO HIS FACE, HIS EYES SNAP,267 DESIRE
HE LOOKS A BIT CRAZY)
THE PRODIGAL RETURNS/... 457 DYNAMO
UNTIL SHE GIVES UP AND RETURNS HIS KISS-- 459 DYNAMO
AND IMMEDIATELY RETURNS WITH A SMALL BOX IN HER 61 ELECTR
HAND.
HER ANGUISHED HATRED IMMEDIATELY RETURNS 64 ELECTR
CHRISTINE RETURNS FROM THE HALL, CLOSING THE 84 ELECTR
SLIDING DOORS BEHIND HER SILENTLY.
HE RETURNS IT, AROUSED AND AT THE SAME TIME A 147 ELECTR
LITTLE SHOCKED BY HER BOLDNESS.
THEN THE OBSESSED WILD LOOK RETURNS TO HIS EYES-- 166 ELECTR
WITH HARSH MOCKERY)
CYBEL RETURNS, FOLLOWED BY BILLY BROWN. 280 GGBROW
AND OUT OF EARTH'S TRANSFIGURED BIRTH-PAIN THE 322 GGBROW
LAUGHTER OF MAN RETURNS TO BLESS
BUT IMMEDIATELY RETURNS WITH A BOTTLE OF BAR 577 ICEMAN
WHISKEY AND A GLASS.
(ROCKY, AT A RELENTING GLANCE FROM HOPE, RETURNS 607 ICEMAN
TO THE BAR.)
AND IF YOU'LL ONLY WAIT UNTIL THE FINAL RETURNS 691 ICEMAN
ARE IN.
(A LONG-FORGOTTEN FAITH RETURNS TO HIM FOR A 726 ICEMAN
MOMENT AND HE MUMBLES)
(TOUCHED, RETURNS HIS HUG.) YOU'RE WELCOME, LAD. 90 JOURNE
(THE SHADOW VANISHES AND HER SHY, GIRLISH 114 JOURNE
EXPRESSION RETURNS.)
AS HE RETURNS TO THE GROUP AT CENTER, PAFFEO HAS 371 MARCOM
JUST FINISHED HIS STORY.
AND SINCE THEN, ON HIS RETURNS, TO SPEAK WITH 387 MARCOM
YOU--A PRINCESS/
THEN STIFFENS REGALLY AND RETURNS HIS GAZE 387 MARCOM
UNFLINCHINGLY.
(THE CHAMME CHAMBERLAIN RETURNS WITH THE CRYSTAL. 426 MARCOM
AND RETURNS CARRYING AN OLD COAT AND A CHEAP 5 MISBEG
BULGING SATCHEL.
(SHE GOES INTO HER BEDROOM AND RETURNS WITH HER 72 MISBEG
BROOMSTICK CLUB.

REVEALING

ETURNS (CONT'D.)
SHE PULLS BACK FRIGHTENEDLY FOR A SECOND--THEN 119 MISBEG
RETURNS HIS KISS.
(HER HORROR EBBING AS HER LOVE AND PROTECTIVE 151 MISBEG
COMPASSION RETURNS--
(HE RETURNS TO HIS NEWSPAPER, DISDAINING FURTHER 40 POET
INTEREST IN MONEY MATTERS.)
WHEN CORPORAL CREGAN RETURNS, MICKEY, SEND HIM IN 57 POET
TO ME.
BUT SHE FEELS HER SIMPLE CHARM AND GENTLENESS, AND 74 POET
RETURNS HER SMILE.)
HE SEES EVANS AND MARSDEN, NODS AT MARSDEN 33 STRANG
SILENTLY, WHO RETURNS IT COLDLY.
(HE GOES OUT TO THE OUTER DOOR--RETURNS A MOMENT 73 STRANG
LATER WITH MARSDEN.
JOE RETURNS TO HIS PLACE BEHIND THE BAR.) 505 VOYAGE

REUNION
A REUNION WITH HER 544 DAYS
MEANWHILE, KEEPING AN EYE ON THEM TO MAKE SURE 123 MANSNS
THIS SENTIMENTAL REUNION
HE DOESN'T DRINK MUCH EXCEPT WHEN HE ATTENDS HIS 55 MISBEG
CLASS REUNION EVERY SPRING--
AND WE WOULD FEEL THAT DEATH MEANT REUNION WITH 43 STRANG
HER.

REVEAL
WHO WILL REVEAL TO US HOW WE CAN BE SAVED FROM 543 DAYS
OURSELVES.
A SECTION OF THE SHIP HAS BEEN REMOVED TO REVEAL 109 ELECTR
THE INTERIOR OF THE CABIN.
AND THEN FINALLY I'LL REVEAL, MYSELF TO HER, 307 GGBROW
ONLY TO ME WILL THAT POMPOUS FACADE REVEAL ITSELF 313 GGBROW
AS THE WEARILY IRONIC GRIN OF
IN ORDER THAT YOU MIGHT BE THE MORE IMPRESSED WHEN317 GGBROW
I REVEAL IT.
THE COAT OPEN TO REVEAL AN OLD AND FADED BUT 9 HUGHIE
EXPENSIVE SILK SHIRT
WHAT IF THIS LAZARUS HAS REALLY DISCOVERED A CURE 303 LAZARU
FOR OLD AGE AND SHOULD REVEAL
TO SAY THE THING ONE HAS ALWAYS KEPT HIDDEN, TO 354 LAZARU
REVEAL ONE'S UNIQUE TRUTH--
AND IT IS MY COMMAND THAT YOU REVEAL THE SECRET OF356 LAZARU
YOUR YOUTH TO ME WHEN I
IN WHICH ONLY THE FOOLS WHO ARE FATED TO LOSE 91 MANSNS
REVEAL THEIR TRUE AIMS OR MOTIVES--
WHICH THE WEST DREAMS LIVES AFTER DEATH--AND MIGHT379 MARCOM
REVEAL IT TO ME?
THERE ARE SECRETS ONE MUST NOT REVEAL... 133 STRANG
GIVE ME YOUR WORD OF HONOR THAT YOU'LL NEVER 178 STRANG
REVEAL A WORD OF WHAT I'M GOING TO

REVEALED
AND THE PAIN OF THAT THOUGHT REVEALED TO ME IN A 91 BEYOND
FLASH--
MY EXAMINATION REVEALED THAT BOTH OF HIS LUNGS ARE158 BEYOND
TERRIBLY AFFECTED.
THEN CAME A LETTER WHICH REVEALED HIM 503 DAYS
THE TRUTH YOU HAVE YOURSELF REVEALED IN YOUR STORY560 DAYS
THE BEDROOM OF THE BROTHERS IS REVEALED. 212 DESIRE
AND HER ROOM IS REVEALED IN ALL ITS PRESERVED 241 DESIRE
UGLINESS.
HARRIET IS REVEALED STANDING OUTSIDE.) 547 DIFRNT
THE LIGHT SITTING ROOM AND REUBEN'S BEDROOM ARE 421 DYNAMO
REVEALED.
COUPLE'S BEDROOM ABOVE IT ARE NOW REVEALED. 427 DYNAMO
THEIR SITTING ROOM IS REVEALED AS BEFORE 435 DYNAMO
INTERIOR OF REUBEN'S BEDROOM IS NOW REVEALED. 443 DYNAMO
THE INTERIOR OF THE LIGHT SITTING ROOM IS 454 DYNAMO
REVEALED.
(THE SAME EXCEPT THAT REUBEN'S BEDROOM IS NOW 468 DYNAMO
REVEALED
THE INTERIORS OF THE UPPER AND LOWER SWITCH 483 DYNAMO
GALLERIES ARE REVEALED.
THE INTERIORS OF THE DYNAMO AND SWITCHBOARD ROOMS 486 DYNAMO
ARE NOW ALSO REVEALED.
THE NEAREST TREE TRUNKS ARE DIMLY REVEALED 202 EJONES
WHOLE TENSE ATTITUDES IS CLEARLY REVEALED THE 16 ELECTR
BITTER ANTAGONISM BETWEEN THEM.
HIS REAL FACE IS REVEALED IN THE BRIGHT MOONLIGHT,264 GGBROW
SHRINKING, SHY AND GENTLE.
TURN ALMIGHTY GOD'S REVEALED PLAN FOR THE WORLD 244 HA APE
TOPSY-TURVY,
EYES AND NOSE, BUT LEAVES HER MOUTH REVEALED. 274 LAZARU
HIS OWN MASKED FACE CLEARLY REVEALED NOW IN THE 339 LAZARU
LIGHT FROM LAZARUS.)
REVEALED TO HIM THAT THERE WAS A WAY IN WHICH HE 110 MANSNS
MIGHT REGAIN HIS LOST KINGDOM.
IS REVEALED INSIDE THE GLASS. 352 MARCOM
THEN THE INTERIOR OF THE PAPAL LEGATE'S PALACE AT 358 MARCOM
ACRE IS REVEALED--
THE SCENE IS REVEALED AS THE GRAND THRONE ROOM IN 377 MARCOM
THE PALACE OF KUBLAI.
LITTLE DAUGHTER, ALL RARE THINGS ARE SECRET WHICH 400 MARCOM
CANNOT BE REVEALED TO ANYONE.
(THE LIGHTS COME UP AGAIN ON THE BACK STAGE AS THE426 MARCOM
FORESTAGE IS FULLY REVEALED.
(THEY ARE REVEALED NOW IN THEIR OLD DIRTY, 429 MARCOM
(AGAIN AS IF HE WERE ASHAMED, OR AFRAID HE HAD 105 MISBEG
REVEALED SOME WEAKNESS--

REVEALING
(THE DOOR SWINGS WIDE OPEN, REVEALING SUE 562 CROSS
BARTLETT.
TRAGIC AND REVEALING TO ME. 533 DAYS
REVEALING HIS DISHEVELED, CURLY BLOND HAIR. 498 DIFRNT
REVEALING HIMSELF STRIPPED TO THE WAIST) 193 EJONES
(SCENE--LIGHT COMES, GRADUALLY REVEALING THE 364 MARCOM
SCENE
AND HER SMILE, REVEALING EVEN WHITE TEETH, GIVES 3 MISBEG
IT CHARM.

REVEALS 1322

REVEALS
CHURCH REVEALS ABOUT THE LONGING OF YOUR OWN 545 DAYS SOUL--
BUT THIS SCENE ALSO REVEALS THE INTERIOR OF ELSA'S553 DAYS BEDROOM AT LEFT OF STUDY.)
NERVOUS VITALITY ABOUT ALL HER MOVEMENTS THAT 494 DIFRNT REVEALS AN UNDERLYING CONSTITUTION
THAT SUDDENLY REVEALS REUBEN IN HIS HIDING PLACE 427 DYNAMO BY THE HEDGE.
THIS CURTAIN REVEALS THE EXTENSIVE GROUNDS--ABOUT 2 ELECTR THIRTY ACRES--
(HE TEARS OFF HIS MASK AND REVEALS A SUFFERING 305 GGBROW FACE THAT IS RAVAGED AND HAGGARD,
AND REVEALS PART OF THE INTERIOR. 239 HA APE
TYRONE'S VOICE, TRYING TO CONCEAL, REVEALS THAT HE 73 JOURNE IS HEARING BAD NEWS.)
THE LIGHT SLOWLY REVEALS THE EXTERIOR OF DONATA'S 355 MARCOM HOME ON A CANAL, VENICE.
THE SLOWLY-RISING LIGHT REVEALS AN INDIAN SNAKE- 369 MARCOM CHARMER
REVEALS A SECTION OF THE BEDROOM FRAMED IN THE 107 MISBEG DOORWAY BEHIND TYRONE.
IT IS HIS FACE THAT REVEALS THE RAVAGES OF 33 POET DISSIPATION--
THEN A CIRCLE OF LIGHT REVEALS ELEANOR LYING BACK 443 WELDED ON A CHAISE LONGUE.
IT REVEALS A BEGINNING IN UNITY THAT I MAY HAVE 488 WELDED FAITH IN THE UNITY OF THE END/

REVELATION
FOR THE REVELATION OF MY OWN LOVE SEEMED TO OPEN 91 BEYOND MY EYES TO THE LOVE OF OTHERS.
SUDDENLY HIS FACE LIGHTS UP WITH A SAVING 35 HUGHIE REVELATION.
MAYBE HE'S SAVING THE GREAT REVELATION FOR HARRY'S636 ICEMAN PARTY.
DID THIS GREAT REVELATION OF THE EVIL HABIT OF 662 ICEMAN DREAMING ABOUT TOMORROW
LIKE AN AMAZING REVELATION-- 39 MANSNS
THIS REVELATION OF AN UNSEEN AUDIENCE STARTLES 58 MISBEG HARDER.
IT WAS REVELATION THEN--A MIRACLE OUT OF THE SKY/ 447 WELDED
SOMETHING EXTRAORDINARY HAPPENED TO ME--A 485 WELDED REVELATION/

REVELATIONS
STORY, FAIRLY BURSTING TO BREAK IN WITH HIS OWN 519 INZONE REVELATIONS.)

REVELING
OBVIOUSLY REVELING IN BEING CODDLED.) 81 ELECTR

REVELLING
(REALLY REVELLING IN HIS DAUGHTER'S CODDLING BUT 47 ELECTR EMBARRASSED BEFORE HIS WIFE--

REVENGE
BUT I DEDUCE THAT THE LADY HAD A RUN-IN WITH THE 267 AHWILD BARKEEP AND WANTS REVENGE.
IN HIS AWAKENED PRIDE HE CURSED HIS GOD AND DENIED511 DAYS HIM, AND, IN REVENGE,
MY PRIDE WAS SO HURT I WANTED TO REVENGE MYSELF 521 DAYS
DO YOU IMAGINE I EVER THOUGHT IT WAS ANYTHING BUT 526 DAYS REVENGE ON YOUR PART$
WHY SHOULD I REVENGE MYSELF ON HER$ 527 DAYS
EVEN IF I'D BEEN SEIZED BY ANY PECULIAR IMPULSE OF549 DAYS HATRED AND REVENGE ON YOU.
DYING IS LIFE, ITS LAST REVENGE UPON ITSELF. 562 DAYS
(INSPIRED BY ALARM AND DESIRE FOR REVENGE SUDDENLY934 DIFRNT BLURTS OUT)
HIM AND UNSUCCESSFULLY PLOTTING REVENGE. 422 DYNAMO
IT WAS HIS JEALOUS REVENGE MADE HIM DISOWN MY 25 ELECTR FATHER
SHE IS ONLY YOUR MEANS OF REVENGE ON FATHER, IS 27 ELECTR THAT IT$
THAT I SWORE ON MY MOTHER'S BODY I'D REVENGE HER 27 ELECTR DEATH ON HIM.
YOU'RE ONLY HIS REVENGE ON FATHER/ 32 ELECTR
I THOUGHT, BY GOD, I'LL TAKE HER FROM HIM AND 36 ELECTR THAT'LL BE PART OF MY REVENGE/
IT WOULD BE A POOR REVENGE FOR YOUR MOTHER'S DEATH 38 ELECTR
IF YOU STOPPED THINKING OF YOUR REVENGE FOR A 38 ELECTR MOMENT AND THOUGHT OF ME/
TO TAKE THE SNEAKING REVENGE ON HIM OF BEING A 41 ELECTR BACKSTAIRS LOVER/
I TOLD HIM HOW YOU LIED ABOUT MY TRIPS TO NEW 91 ELECTR YORK--FOR REVENGE/
IT WASN'T THAT KIND OF REVENGE I HAD SWORN ON MY 110 ELECTR MOTHER'S BODY/
HE GOT YOU UNDER HIS INFLUENCE TO REVENGE HIMSELF/121 ELECTR
(FALTERINGLY) BRANT DID--FOR REVENGE BECAUSE-- 142 ELECTR
ISN'T IT OUT OF REVENGE--AND ENVY$ 298 GGBROW
A DIRTY TRICK ON MY CLASSMATES, INSPIRED BY 595 ICEMAN REVENGE, I FEAR.
AS IF ALL AT ONCE THEY SAW A CHANCE TO REVENGE 662 ICEMAN THEMSELVES.
GOT TO TAKE REVENGE. ON EVERYONE ELSE. 166 JOURNE ESPECIALLY YOU.
(HARSHLY) FOR THEIR JOY I WILL REVENGE MYSELF 317 LAZARU UPON THEM/
AND IN REVENGE AND SELF-TORTURE HIS LOVE HAS BEEN 352 LAZARU FAITHLESS/
(WITH MALIGNANT CRUELTY) I WILL HAVE TO REVENGE 356 LAZARU THE DEATH OF A HOPE ON YOU--
REVENGE FOR WHAT$ 99 MANSNS
I KNOW THIS IS SOME INSANE PLOT TO REVENGE 99 MANSNS YOURSELF ON ME/
AND I WOULD REVENGE MYSELF BY BECOMING WHAT HE 133 MANSNS WISHED ME TO BE/
HE'LL BE CRAZY TO REVENGE HIMSELF NOW/ 156 MANSNS
WHEN I KNOW IT IS HE WHO HAS FORCED ME TO CARRY 163 MANSNS OUT HIS EVIL SCHEME OF REVENGE--
(WITH A GLOATING SMILE.) I CAN HEAR THE REVENGE 191 MANSNS IN HIS HEART LAUGHING OUT

REVENGE (CONT'D.)
TO REVENGE EQUALLY THE WRONG OF AN EQUAL PERHAPS, 425 MARCOM BUT THIS--$
(DISTRACTEDLY) TO REVENGE ONESELF--THAT BRINGS A 425 MARCOM KIND OF PEACE/
AFTER WHAT WE DID TO HIM, ALL HE WANTS IS REVENGE. 84 MISBEG
A HELL OF A REVENGE/ 90 MISBEG
I ONLY THOUGHT YOU'D LIKE TO KNOW YOU'D HAD THAT 90 MISBEG MUCH REVENGE.
HE'D KNOW YOU WERE AFTER REVENGE. 99 MISBEG
IT WAS AS IF I WANTED REVENGE--BECAUSE I'D BEEN 150 MISBEG LEFT ALONE--
IT GAVE HIS PRIDE THE TASTE FOR REVENGE AND AFTER 12 POET THAT HE WAS ALWAYS LOOKIN' FOR
HIS REVENGE IS TO DRAW HIMSELF UP HAUGHTILY 68 POET
THAT WILL BE REVENGE IN FULL FOR ALL YOU'VE DONE 105 POET TO MOTHER AND ME/
IF SHE WANTED REVENGE ON HIM, I'M SURE SHE'S HAD 150 POET HER FILL OF IT.
OH GOD, MAYBE HE'LL TAKE REVENGE ON SIMON-- 159 POET
I CAN REVENGE MY OWN INSULTS, AND I HAVE/ 160 POET
WASN'T HE FIGHTIN' TO REVENGE THE INSULTS TO YOUR 160 POET
GOING OUT TO REVENGE AN INSULT TO YOU, WOULD SPOIL171 POET YOUR SCHEMES.
THAT IT SATISFIES COME CRAVING IN YOU--FOR 455 WELDED REVENGE/
I HAD TO REVENGE MYSELF/ 468 WELDED
THEY WOULDN'T BE VILE ENOUGH--FOR HIS BEAUTIFUL 468 WELDED REVENGE ON ME/
HOME/ IS THAT YOUR PRIVATE BRAND OF REVENGE--TO 472 WELDED GO WITH MEN WITH HOME$$
HE TURNS BACK TO HER, OVERCOME BY A CRAVING FOR 484 WELDED REVENGE)
I WANTED REVENGE AS MUCH AS YOU. 484 WELDED
AND I HAD THOUGHT OF HER ONLY AS REVENGE--THE 485 WELDED LOWEST OF THE LOW/

REVENGED
A DEITY WHO RETURNED HATE FOR LOVE AND REVENGED 511 DAYS HIMSELF UPON THOSE WHO TRUSTED
WHEN HE HAD GONE THERE WAS NOTHING LEFT--BUT HATE 32 ELECTR AND A DESIRE TO BE REVENGED--
HE COULD DIE HAPPY, KNOWING HE'D REVENGED HIMSELF 114 ELECTR ON US.
MOREOVER, YOU WOULD NOT BE REVENGED ON ME, FOR I 316 LAZARU LONG FOR DEATH.
MY MOTHER--HER BLOOD IS IN THAT BLOT, FOR I 355 LAZARU REVENGED MYSELF ON HER.
AND SHE SIMPLY WANTED TO BE REVENGED, I'M SURE. 172 STRANG

REVENGEFUL
THERE WAS SOMETHING AS EVIL AND REVENGEFUL AS I 522 DAYS WAS.
(WITH REVENGEFUL TRIUMPH) SHE'LL NEVER MARRY THE 530 DIFRNT OLD CUSS--I'LL FIX THAT/
(THINKING WITH A FIERCE, REVENGEFUL JOY) 447 DYNAMO
WITH A SOMBER PULSATION, A BAFFLED BUT REVENGEFUL 202 EJONES POWER.)
THERE'S NOTHING TO TELL--EXCEPT IN VINNIE'S MORBID 86 ELECTR REVENGEFUL MIND/
ORIN IS HOLDING IN A SAVAGE, REVENGEFUL RAGE. 109 ELECTR
REFLECT THE SUN IN A SMOULDERING STARE, AS OF 169 ELECTR BROODING REVENGEFUL EYES.
SENSITIVE AND SELF-CONSCIOUS AND PROUD AND 297 GGBROW REVENGEFUL--
(TURNS ON EDMUND WITH A HARD, ACCUSING 116 JOURNE ANTAGONISM--ALMOST A REVENGEFUL ENMITY.)
THE REVENGEFUL, CRUEL,. 273 LAZARU
THE CRUEL, REVENGEFUL,. 312 LAZARU
THE CRUEL, REVENGEFUL,. AND THE RESIGNED, 312 LAZARU SORROWFUL.
AND THE CRUEL, REVENGEFUL-- 336 LAZARU
(WITH REVENGEFUL FURY) BUT DEATH IS, AND DEATH IS349 LAZARU MINE/
IN GROWING FULL OF HATE AND REVENGEFUL AMBITION T0356 LAZARU BE CAESAR.
BEWILDERED PAIN WHICH SPEEDILY TURNS TO RAGE AND 361 LAZARU REVENGEFUL HATRED)
(SHE TURNS AWAY WITH CONTEMPT AND FACES LAZARUS 361 LAZARU WITH REVENGEFUL HATRED)
(CHANTING WITH REVENGEFUL MOCKERY) 364 LAZARU
(WITH A CRUEL REVENGEFUL SATISFACTION.) 53 MANSNS
A MAN---A DUEL TO THE DEATH-- (WITH REVENGEFUL 74 MANSNS BITTERNESS.)
(SHE TURNS TO STARE AT HIM WITH A REVENGEFUL 121 MANSNS HOSTILITY.
SHE IS REVENGEFUL AND EVIL--A CANNIBAL WITCH WHOSE126 MANSNS GREED WILL DEVOUR/
(THEIR EXPRESSIONS HAVE CHANGED TO REVENGEFUL, 126 MANSNS
(RAISING HIS VOICE--WITH REVENGEFUL ANGER) 161 MISBEG
BUT THE POINT IS, YOU CAN HAVE NO IDEA WHAT 83 POET REVENGEFUL HATE

REVENGEFULLY
(NOT HEEDING HIS INTERRUPTION--REVENGEFULLY) 57 ANNA
SOMETHING SLIP--THEN REVENGEFULLY) 635 ICEMAN
(REVENGEFULLY) YOU DROVE YOUR POOR WIFE TO 693 ICEMAN SUICIDE/
(REVENGEFULLY.) 156 MANSNS
KUBLAI STANDS UP WITH FLASHING EYES-- 425 MARCOM REVENGEFULLY.)
(REVENGEFULLY) 124 STRANG

REVENGEFULNESS
SUDDENLY A STRANGE UNDERCURRENT OF REVENGEFULNESS 47 JOURNE COMES INTO HER VOICE.)

REVENGING
AND WHOM WERE YOU REVENGING YOURSELF ON, JOHN$ 526 DAYS
(ANGRILY) WHAT DO YOU MEAN BY SAYING I WAS 527 DAYS REVENGING MYSELF$
(REVENGING HIMSELF NOW--GRINNING AT HER) 230 DESIRE

REVERBERATE
THE WALLS AND MASSIVE COLUMNS SEEM TO REVERBERATE 337 LAZARU
WITH THE SOUND.
REVERBERATING
ANOTHER BOOM COMES, REVERBERATING, RATTLING THE 42 ELECTR
WINDOWS.
REVERENCE
(HE KISSES HER HAIR WITH A GREAT REVERENCE) 43 STRANG
REVERENT
(DROPPING HIS VOICE TO A REVERENT, HUSHED TONE. 22 ELECTR
REVERENTIALLY
THEN HE KISSES HIS BROTHER REVERENTIALLY ON THE 168 BEYOND
FOREHEAD AND STANDS UP.)
HE THINKS REVERENTIALLY) 475 DYNAMO
REVERIE
(SITS AT HIS DESK AGAIN, LOOKING AHEAD IN A NOT 277 GGBROW
UNSATISFYING MELANCHOLY REVERIE.
LOST IN A SENTIMENTAL REVERIE. 443 WELDED
REVERSAL
(AGAIN WITH AN ABRUPT REVERSAL OF FEELING.) 77 POET
(WITH A SUDDEN REVERSAL UF FEELING--ALMOST 77 POET
VINDICTIVELY.)
REVERSED
REVERSED THE NATURAL PROCESS AND GROWS YOUNGERS 354 LAZARU
I SIMPLY REVERSED THE OLD SYSTEM. 392 MARCOM
REVERTED
HAS REVERTED TO UNEASY, SUSPICIOUS DEFENSIVENESS.1659 ICEMAN
REVERTING
(REVERTING TO A TEASING TONE) 135 MISBEG
REVITALIZE
OR AN UNGUENT YOU RUB INTO THE SKIN TO REVITALIZE 354 LAZARU
THE OLD BONES AND TISSUES$
REVIVAL
PUT ON REVIVAL OF «THE BELLS» THIS SEASON. 168 JOURNE
REVIVALIST
LIKE A REVIVALIST PREACHER ABOUT RELIGION. 589 ICEMAN
REVIVE
AND AT THE LAST MOMENT HIS WILL AND PRIDE REVIVE 545 DAYS
IN HIM AGAIN/
THE MIRACLE COULD NOT REVIVE ALL HIS OLD HUSBAND'S331 LAZARU
LIFE IN MY WIFE'S HEART.
BUT INSTEAD WE LET HIM REVIVE A DEAD HATE OF THE 170 MANSNS
PAST
WATER TO REVIVE THEM/ 351 MARCOM
IT MIGHT REVIVE MY SENSE UF HUMOR ABOUT MYSELF, AT123 STRANG
LEAST...
REVIVED
THE COURIER IS REVIVED AND GETS TO HIS KNEES, 423 MARCOM
WAITING HUMBLY.)
REVOKE
I REVOKE MY DECLARATION OF WAR--UNLESS YOU LEARN 423 MARCOM
TO DANCE AND BE SILENT/
REVOLT
RICHARD STANDS, A PREY TO FEELINGS OF BITTEREST 217 AHWILD
HUMILIATION AND SEETHING REVOLT
A JESTER INSPIRES MIRTH ONLY SO LONG AS HIS 387 MARCOM
DEFORMITY DOES NOT REVOLT ONE.
REVOLTED
(REVOLTED) OH/ 545 DIFRNT
(IMPRESSED AND AT THE SAME TIME REVOLTED.) 131 JOURNE
(REVOLTED AND ANGRY HALF-SPRINGS TO HIS FEET) 35 STRANG
LOOK HERE, DARRELL*
(REVOLTED) MICHAEL/ 452 WELDED
REVOLTING
OH, IT'S TOO REVOLTING, ORIN/ 88 ELECTR
IT'S TOO REVOLTING/...)) 17 STRANG
NOW, NOTHING ABOUT LOVE SEEMS IMPORTANT ENOUGH TO 149 STRANG
BE REVOLTING...
THE IDEA USED TO BE REVOLTING... 149 STRANG
REVOLTINGLY
BUT THERE IS SOMETHING REVOLTINGLY INCONGRUOUS 520 DIFRNT
ABOUT HER, A PITIABLE SHAM.
REVOLUTION
(IMPORTANTLY) CARLYLE'S «FRENCH REVOLUTION.» 196 AHWILD
THE TIME OF THE REVOLUTION, WASN'T IT$ 178 EJONES
DEN DE REVOLUTION IS AT DE POST. 182 EJONES
AS HISTOR HISTORY PROVES, TO BE A WORLDLY SUCCESS 590 ICEMAN
AT ANY THING, ESPECIALLY REVOLT
A REVOLUTION DEPOSED HIM, CONDUCTED BY THE 595 ICEMAN
DISTRICT ATTORNEY.
BEJEES, YOU'LL PAY UP TOMORROW, OR I'LL START A 605 ICEMAN
HARRY HOPE REVOLUTION/
HERE'S THE REVOLUTION STARTING ON ALL SIDES OF YOU634 ICEMAN
AND YOU'RE SLEEPING THROUGH
LONG LIVE THE REVOLUTION/ 720 ICEMAN
MOTHER OF THE REVOLUTION, WHOSE ONLY CHILD IS THE 720 ICEMAN
PROLETARIAT.
IT WAS A PLAY ABOUT THE FRENCH REVOLUTION AND THE 105 JOURNE
LEADING PART WAS A NOBLEMAN.
A MOMENT MORE AND THERE WOULD HAVE BEEN A 370 LAZARU
REVOLUTION--NO MORE CAESARS--
A FANATIC IN THE CAUSE OF PURE FREEDOM, HE BECAME 83 POET
SCORNFUL OF OUR REVOLUTION.
REVOLUTIONARY
BELLOWS IN HIS GUTTURAL BASSO THE FRENCH 727 ICEMAN
REVOLUTIONARY «CARMAGNOLE.»
REVOLVER
(TAKES A REVOLVER FROM THE POCKET OF HIS COAT AND 541 *ILE
EXAMINES IT)
AND PUTS HIS REVOLVER BACK IN HIS POCKET) 545 *ILE
(SHE REACHES DOWN, TAKES THE COAT AND PULLS OUT A 66 ANNA
REVOLVER.
TAKES THE REVOLVER OUT OF DRAWER AND CROUCHES DOWN 68 ANNA
IN THE CORNER, LEFT,
(WHO HAS COME SO CLOSE THAT THE REVOLVER IS ALMOST 69 ANNA
TOUCHING HIS CHEST)
(SHARPLY--RAISING THE REVOLVER IN HER HAND) 69 ANNA
(OVERCOME--LETTING THE REVOLVER DROP TO THE FLOOR, 69 ANNA
(NOTICING THE REVOLVER FOR THE FIRST TIME) 69 ANNA

REVOLVER (CONT'D.)
SHE STEPS INTO THE ROOM, THE REVOLVER IN HER RIGHT 69 ANNA
HAND BY HER SIDE.)
ONCE HE EVEN TOOK HIS FATHER'S REVOLVER-- 534 DAYS
TEARS OUT A DRAWER AND GETS THE REVOLVER 487 DYNAMO
(SHE SEES THE REVOLVER AIMED AT HER BREAST AS HE 488 DYNAMO
STEPS DIRECTLY BENEATH HER--
A CARTRIDGE BELT WITH AN AUTOMATIC REVOLVER IS 174 EJONES
AROUND HIS WAIST.
SMITHERS GOES AFTER HER, REACHING FOR HIS 175 EJONES
REVOLVER)
PEARL-HANDLED REVOLVER IN A HOLSTER COMPLETE HIS 175 EJONES
MAKE UP.
(HIS HAND GOING TO HIS REVOLVER LIKE A FLASH-- 176 EJONES
MENACINGLY)
FALL FROM HIS REVOLVER) 177 EJONES
(HE REPLACES IT IN THE CHAMBER AND PUTS THE 179 EJONES
REVOLVER BACK ON HIS HIP.)
(HE TAKES OUT HIS REVOLVER, BREAKS IT, 179 EJONES
(HE STARES AT THE PLAIN BEHIND HIM APPREHENSIVELY,189 EJONES
HIS HAND ON HIS REVOLVER)
THE SOUND OF THE SHOT, THE REASSURING FEEL OF THE 190 EJONES
REVOLVER IN HIS HAND,
YANKING OUT HIS REVOLVER AS HE DOES SO--IN A 190 EJONES
QUAVERING VOICE)
(HE JERKS OUT HIS REVOLVER IN A FRENZY OF 192 EJONES
TERRIFIED RAGE)
TUGGING FRANTICALLY AT HIS REVOLVER.) 195 EJONES
(HE FREES THE REVOLVER AND FIRES POINT BLANK AT 195 EJONES
THE GUARD'S BACK.
(JERKING OUT HIS REVOLVER JUST AS THE AUCTIONEER 197 EJONES
KNOCKS HIM DOWN TO ONE OF THE
A REVOLVERREVOLVER AND A CARTRIDGE BELT ARE ABOUT 202 EJONES
HIS WAIST.
JERKING A REVOLVER FROM HIS COAT POCKET-- 104 ELECTR
IMMEDIATELY HIS REVOLVER IS IN HIS HAND 107 ELECTR
ON THE DECK ABOVE ORIN PULLS A REVOLVER FROM UNDERL13 ELECTR
HIS CLOAK AND MAKES A MOVE.
(ORIN PUTS HIS REVOLVER ON THE TABLE AND TAKES A 114 ELECTR
CHISEL.
(HE QUICKLY TURNS BRANT'S POCKETS INSIDE OUT AND 115 ELECTR
PUTS THE REVOLVER HE FINDS,
ROCKY SLIPS THE REVOLVER BACK IN HIS POCKET. 672 ICEMAN
ROCKY JERKS A SHORT-BARRELED NICKEL-PLATED 672 ICEMAN
REVOLVER FROM HIS HIP POCKET.
REVOLVERS
WHEN THEY FIND THEMSELVES CONFRONTED BY THE 544 *ILE
REVOLVERS OF KEENEY AND THE MATE.)
A SQUAD OF POLICE WITH DRAWN REVOLVERS, LED BY A 321 GGBROW
GRIZZLY, BRUTAL-FACED CAPTAIN,
REVOLVES
FORM AN ENDLESS CHAIN WHICH REVOLVES MECHANICALLY,399 MARCOM
AS IT WERE,
REVULSION
(THEN WITH A SHIVER OF SHAMEFACED REVULSION AND 276 AHWILD
SELF-DISGUST)
EMMA SHUDDERS WITH REVULSION.) 511 DIFRNT
(WITH SUDDEN STRONG «REVULSION») (AND TO THINK 446 DYNAMO
(WITH SUDDEN REVULSION, PUSHES BACK FROM HIM.) 145 MANSNS
(WITH SUDDEN REVULSION) FOR GOD'S SAKE, CUT OUT 42 MISBEG
THAT KIND OF TALK, JOSIE/
(HER FACE FULL OF REVULSION--STAMMERS) 149 MISBEG
(WITH REVULSION) GOD, DON'T MAKE ME THINK OF 171 MISBEG
THOSE TRAMPS NOW/
(HE MOVES HIS ARM AWAY WITH INSTINCTIVE REVULSION 35 POET
A SUDDEN REVULSION OF FEELING CONVULSES HIS FACE. 42 POET
(SUDDENLY SHE IS OVERCOME BY A BITTER, TORTURED 162 POET
REVULSION OF FEELING.)
(THINKING WITH INDIGNANT REVULSION) 17 STRANG
HE SUSPECTS MY REVULSION... 69 STRANG
(WITH REVULSION) (THAT'S SHAMEFUL/. 93 STRANG
(THEN WITH SUDDEN SCORNFUL REVULSION) 149 STRANG
REWARD
AND, IN REWARD FOR HIS SICKENING HUMILIATION, SAW 511 DAYS
THAT NO MIRACLE WOULD HAPPEN.
OCEANS O' TROUBLE AN' NUTHIN' BUT WUK FUR REWARD. 226 DESIRE
HE WOULD NOT REWARD YOU. 316 LAZARU
IS THAT YOU REWARD THIS CHRISTIAN WHO HAS BROUGHT 418 MARCOM
ME HERE IN SAFETY.
BUT HE PROMISED THAT YOU WOULD REWARD ME NOBLY. 423 MARCOM
LITTLE DID I DREAM THEN THE DISGRACE THAT WAS TO 99 POET
BE MY REWARD LATER ON.
REWARDED
I'M DRUNK--BUT YOU WILL BE REWARDED IN HEAVEN/ 279 GGBROW
THE ONLY MORAL LAW HERE IS THE STRONG ARE 71 MANSNS
REWARDED, THE WEAK ARE PUNISHED.
REWARDING
AND SUITABLY REWARDING, ANYONE WHO SHOULD MURDER 180 MANSNS
US.
REWARDS
EVER TO QUESTION IT OR BE DISSATISFIED WITH ITS 184 STRANG
REWARDS.
RHETORIC
(SMILING--DISTRACTEDLY) WAR WITHOUT RHETORIC, 423 MARCOM
PLEASE/
RHETORICAL
WITH RHETORICAL INTONING, AND FLOWING GESTURES, 370 LAZARU
THE BODY OF LAZARUS,
AND HIS AMUSED VOICE RECITES THE WORDS WITH A 4 STRANG
RHETORICAL RESONANCE)
(WITH AN AWKWARD SENSE OF HAVING BECOME RHETORICAL448 WELDED
HE ADDS SELF-MOCKINGLY)
RHETORICALLY
(HE QUOTES RHETORICALLY) «OH THOU, 198 AHWILD
(GOADING HIM--GOES ON MORE RHETORICALLY) 245 AHWILD
(WITH IRONIC MASTERY--RHETORICALLY) 267 GGBROW
(HE LAUGHS WITH A WILD TRIUMPHANT MADNESS AND 370 LAZARU
AGAIN RHETORICALLY,

RHETORICALLY

RHETORICALLY (CONT'D.)
(HE PATS THE PAPER MONEY--RHETORICALLY) 396 MAKCOM
RHEUMATICS.
IN JEST--RHEUMATICS--GETTING OLD, VINA. 44 STRANG
RHEUMATISM
HERE'S ANNIE'S MOTHER'S RHEUMATISM, MILDRED'S 230 AHWILD
RAW-BONED AND STOOP-SHOULDERED, HIS JOINTS 6 ELECTR
STIFFENED BY RHEUMATISM,
(WITH A GRUFF) I CAN FEEL IT'S BRINGING ON MY 261 GGBROW
RHEUMATISM,
I'VE HAD RHEUMATISM ON AND OFF FOR TWENTY YEARS. 684 ICEMAN
YOU FOUND YOUR RHEUMATISM DIDN'T BOTHER YOU COMI4G684 ICEMAN
DOWN-STAIRS, DIDN'T YOUR
YES, WE KNOW IT'S THE KING OF RHEUMATISM YOU TURN 684 ICEMAN
ON AND OFF/
MY RHEUMATISM--(HE CATCHES HIMSELF) NO, MUST RE 687 ICEMAN
MY EYES.
BUT RHEUMATISM HAS KNOTTED THE JOINTS AND WARPED 12 JOURNE
THE FINGERS,
OR I SHOULD SAY, THE RHEUMATISM IN MY HANDS KNOWS. 41 JOURNE
HER LONG FINGERS, WARPED AND KNOTTED BY 49 JOURNE
RHEUMATISM,
THE DAMP IS IN BRIDGET'S RHEUMATISM AND SHE'S LIKE 99 JOURNE
A RAGING DIVIL.
THE MEDICINE FOR THE RHEUMATISM IN MY HANDS. 103 JOURNE
I NEVER KNEW WHAT RHEUMATISM WAS BEFORE YOU WERE 116 JOURNE
BORN/
THAT I SUFFER FROM RHEUMATISM IN MY HANDS 116 JOURNE
HER OLD HANDS ARE KNOTTED BY RHEUMATISM, 20 POET
HAD CESS TO THE RHEUMATISM, 21 POET
TO DRIVE OUT BLACK THOUGHTS AND RHEUMATISM. 134 POET
SURE, WHAT'S RHEUMATISM BUT A PAIN IN YOUR BODYS 138 POET
(SHE PAUSES--DULLY.) GO TO A DOCTOR, YOU SAY, TO 138 POET
CURE THE RHEUMATISM/
HIS THIN LEGS, TWISTED BY RHEUMATISM, 978 ROPE

RHYME
(GOING TO HIM--LAUGHING) A RHYME/ 360 MAKCOM
(PARAPHRASING THE *RHYME OF THE THREE SEALERS*) 66 MISBEG

RHYMES
ONE THING ABOUT IT---IT RHYMES WITH DRINK/ 211 HA APE

RHYTHM
HER BODY SWAYING A LITTLE FROM SIDE TO SIDE TO THE552 *ILE
RHYTHM OF THE HYMN,
KEEPING HIS HANDS IN THE RHYTHM OF THE MUSIC AND 250 DESIRE
INTERSPERSING THEM WITH JOCULAR
IN ITS RHYTHM OF UNBROKEN, ETERNAL CONTINUITY. 486 DYNAMO
EXULTANT ROOM WHOSE THROBS SEEM TO FILL THE AIR 200 EJONES
WITH VIBRATING RHYTHM.
BROODING RHYTHM OF THE SEA. 6 ELECTR
I WHO LOVE MUSIC AND RHYTHM AND GRACE AND SONG AND264 GGBROW
LAUGHTER/
BUT THERE IS ORDER IN IT, RHYTHM, A MECHANICAL 223 HA APE
REGULATED RECURRENCE, A TEMPO.
WITH A STRANGE, AWKWARD, SWINGING RHYTHM. 223 HA APE
HIS SPEECH IS EDUCATED, WITH THE GHOST OF A SCOTCH575 ICEMAN
RHYTHM IN IT.
BECAME DRUNK WITH THE BEAUTY AND SINGING RHYTHM 153 JOURNE
OF IT,
BECAME BEAUTY AND RHYTHM, 153 JOURNE
HAVE NOW ALL BEGUN TO LAUGH IN RHYTHM WITH THE 280 LAZARU
CHORUS--
EMPHASIZING THE PULSING RHYTHM OF THE DANCE. 281 LAZARU
THEN THEY AGAIN BEGIN TO FEEL IMPELLED BY THE 286 LAZARU
RHYTHM AND LAUGHTER.
THE RHYTHM OF THE LAUGHTER AND MUSIC AS DOES THAT 293 LAZARU
OF THE MOURNERS.)
ONCE AS QUIVERING FLECKS OF RHYTHM WE BEAT DOWN 324 LAZARU
FROM THE SUN.
ALTHOUGH THE RHYTHM OF IRISH SPEECH STILL 75 MANSNS
UNDERLIES IT.
MAKING THE RHYTHM FOR A CROONING, NASAL VOICE, 173 MARCOM
SLAVES; A FOUR-BEAT RHYTHM, THREE BEATS OF THE 400 MARCOM
DRUM,
EVERY MOVEMENT BEING CARRIED OUT IN UNISON WITH A 407 MARCOM
MACHINE-LIKE RHYTHM.
FOR WE WOULD KNOW THAT OUR LIFE'S RHYTHM BEATS FUR 43 STRANG
HER GREAT HEART,
RHYTHM OF OUR LIVES BEATING AGAINST EACH OTHER, 448 WELDED
FORMING SLOWLY THE ONE RHYTHM--

RHYTHMIC
A DENSE GREEN GLOW FLOODS SLOWLY IN RHYTHMIC WAVES570 CROSS
LIKE A LIQUID IN THE ROOM--
HE SITS IN A WEARY ATTITUDE, LISTENING TO THE 188 EJONES
RHYTHMIC BEATING OF THE TOM-TCMI
INCREASING GRADUALLY BY THE RHYTHMIC DEGREES WHICH199 EJONES
SEEM TO BE DIRECTED AND
CHARGED SLAVES, TO THE RHYTHMIC BEAT OF THE TOM- 200 EJONES
TOM.
THE MEN SHOVEL WITH A RHYTHMIC MOTION, 223 HA APE
(THEY LAUGH IN A RHYTHMIC CADENCE DOMINATED HY THE280 LAZARU
LAUGHTER OF LAZARUS.)
WITH THE RHYTHMIC BEAT OF THEIR LIBERATED 281 LAZARU
LAUGHTER--
(IN A RHYTHMIC ECHO) LAUGH/ 281 LAZARU
STRESSES THE RHYTHMIC FLOW OF THE DANCE.) 285 LAZARU
(CHANTING IN A DEEP, RHYTHMIC MONOTONE 303 LAZARU
(HE LAUGHS AND AGAIN HIS VOICE LEADS AND DOMINATES311 LAZARU
THE RHYTHMIC CHORUS OF
THE CROWDS LAUGH WITH HIM IN A FRENZIED RHYTHMIC 360 LAZARU
CHORUS.
THEIR VOICES RISE TOGETHER IN A LONG, RHYTHMIC 433 MARCOM
WAIL OF MOURNING.

RHYTHMICALLY
RHYTHMICALLY AS IF TO THE PULSE OF LONG SWELLS OF 572 CROSS
THE DEEP SEA.)
AND BY THE CHORUS WHO SWAY RHYTHMICALLY 436 MARCOM

RIBALD
(THEN AS SID SMOTHERS A BURST OF RIBALD LAUGHTER) 197 AHWILD

RIBALD (CONT'D.)
HAS A STRONG SUGGESTION OF RIBALD HUMOR. 6 ELECTR

RIBBED
HIS FACE IS SQUARE, RIBBED WITH WRINKLES, THE 422 DYNAMO
FOREHEAD LOW, THE NOSE HEAVY,

RIBBON
AND CAN BE SEEN IN THE DISTANCE WINDING TOWARD THE 81 BEYOND
HORIZON LIKE A PALE RIBBON
SEVERAL PACKAGES, TIED WITH RIBBON, ARE ALSO ON 629 ICEMAN
THE TABLE.
THE ELECTRIC-LIGHT BRACKETS ARE ADORNED WITH 629 ICEMAN
FESTOONS OF RED RIBBON.
THE FUMBLES AND PULLS OUT THE LOCKET WHICH IS HUNG366 MARCOM
AROUND HIS NECK ON A RIBBON)
I KNOW I HAD IT ON A RIBBON AROUND MY NECK LAST 375 MARCOM
NIGHT/
WITH A PINK RIBBON TIED AROUND ITS NECK. 391 MARCOM
YOU'D MAKE ME DRESS UP, WITH MY HAIR BRUSHED AND A 24 MISBEG
RIBBON IN IT,

RIBS
(HE DIGS HIS BROTHER IN THE RIBS AFFECTIONATELY) 130 BEYOND
YE'LL NEED SOMETHIN' THAT'LL STICK T' YER RIBS. 214 DESIRE
THERE IS A CRACKING SNAP OF CRUSHED RIBS-- 256 HA APE
HE DIGS HIM IN THE RIBS WITH HIS ELBOW PLAYFULLY) 655 ICEMAN
HE GIVES HOPE A PLAYFUL NUDGE IN THE RIBS) 684 ICEMAN
(THEN WITH A CRAFTY LOOK AND A NUDGE IN THE RIBS) 381 MARCOM

RICE
REAL RICE/ 370 MARCOM
PAUSES BEFORE THE MIDDLE-AGED COUPLE WHO HAVE A 370 MARCOM
BOWL OF RICE BETWEEN THEM--
(SUDDENLY) I SAW TWO OF THEM WITH A BOWL OF 372 MARCOM
RICE--

RICH
(GRINNING) SAY, THIS IS RICH/ 245 AHWILD
YOU MUST BE PLANNING TO CATCH A RICH HUSBAND. 251 AHWILD
I'M NOT THE RICH MAN YOU'VE PROBABLY BEEN LED TO 156 BEYOND
BELIEVE BY MY LETTERS--NOT NOW.
BUT YOU'RE RICH, AREN'T YOUS 161 BEYOND
THAT'S TOO RICH/ 499 DAYS
WE'LL PLAY RICH FOR A CHANGE. 215 DESIRE
I COULD O' BEEN A RICH MAN--BUT SOMETHIN' IN ME 237 DESIRE
FIT ME AN' FIT ME--
WE COME T' BROAD MEDDORS, PLAINS, WHAR THE SOIL 237 DESIRE
WAS BLACK AN' RICH AS GOLD.
I'LL GIT RICH THAR AN' COME BACK AN' FIGHT HIM FUR257 DESIRE
THE FARM HE STOLE--
AND SPY ON THE RICH AND EXCLUSIVE MANNONS. 7 ELECTR
THEY MUST BE RICH/, 7 ELECTR
HOW'D HE COME TO JINE THE ARMY IF HE'S SO RICH. 8 ELECTR
OW, THAT'S TOO RICH/ 96 ELECTR
OURS IS THE LIVING CREAM, I SAY, LIVING RICH AND 285 GGBROW
HIGH/
HE'S AWFUL RICH. 301 GGBROW
ALL OF RICH GUYS DAT TINK DEY'RE SOMEP'N, THEY 216 HA APE
AIN'T NOTHIN'/
RICH FURS OF ALL VARIETIES HANG THERE BATHED IN A 233 HA APE
DOWNPOUR OF ARTIFICIAL LIGHT.
YOU DON'T GET RICH DOING WHAT I'VE BEEN DOING. 585 ICEMAN
AND I'M NOT GETTING RICH HERE, 607 ICEMAN
THEY WERE ONE OF THE TOWN'S BEST, RICH FOR THAT 710 ICEMAN
HICK BURG.
WHO PREY ON THE RICH SUMMER PEOPLE-- 31 JOURNE
THAT DOESN'T MEAN I'M RICH. 31 JOURNE
THAT MAKES THE ELECTRIC LIGHT COMPANY RICH. 117 JOURNE
OR ANY KIND OF GET-RICH-QUICK SWINDLE/ 141 JOURNE
WE DON'T NEED THEM, AND THERE'S NO USE MAKING THE 151 JOURNE
ELECTRIC COMPANY RICH.
THE COLOR OF RICH EARTH UPTURNED BY THE PLOW, 274 LAZARU
(HER VOICE, RICH WITH SORROW, EXULTANT NOW) 277 LAZARU
HIS COMPLEXION IS THE RED-BROWN OF RICH EARTH, 288 LAZARU
LIVE ALONE--YOUR PLAN FOR A NEW SOCIETY WHERE 8 MANSNS
THERE WOULD BE NO RICH NOR POOR.
WHEN I'M SO RICH AND YOU SO POVERTY-STRICKEN. 55 MANSNS
WITHOUT A CARE IN THE WORLD, WATCHING MY SONS GROW148 MANSNS
UP HANDSOME RICH GENTLEMEN,
THE CLOTHES OF THE RULER AND HIS COURT ARE OF RICH373 MARCOM
SILK STUFFS.
OVER THEIR RICH MERCHANT'S ROBES. 390 MARCOM
HE MUST BE TERRIBLY RICH--IF IT'S REALLY HIM. 427 MARCOM
MY GOLD MEN, YOU MAY SELL THESE RICH ROBES 428 MARCOM
AND HE'LL BE RICH WHEN 8 MISBEG
FOR HIS OLD MAN WHO'D WORKED UP FROM NOTHING TO BE 24 MISBEG
RICH AND FAMOUS
RICH IS GOOD 40 MISBEG
WITHOUT BEING SNEERED AT BY HIS RICH LANDLORDS 40 MISBEG
(SNEERINGLY) A LEADING ARISTOCRAT IN OUR LAND OF 47 MISBEG
THE FREE AND GET-RICH-QUICK,
IF THAT AIN'T RICH/ 90 MISBEG
(HE QUOTES) *NOW MORE THAN EVER SEEMS IT RICH TO 104 MISBEG
DIE,*
BUT A THIEVIN' SHEBEEN KEEPER WHO GOT RICH 11 POET
(SMILES--HER VOICE IS SOFT, WITH A RICH BROGUE,) 20 POET
WASN'T HE BORN RICH IN A CASTLE ON A GRAND ESTATE 24 POET
AND EDUCATED IN COLLEGE,
LIVING LIKE A TRAMP OR A TINKER, AND HIM A RICH 29 POET
GENTLEMAN'S SON.
THEN YOU WILL SEE HOW QUICKLY AMERICA WILL BECOME 40 POET
RICH AND GREAT/
AND I'D BECOME RICH. 40 POET
ALWAYS TAKIN' SIDES WITH THE RICH YANKS AGAINST 157 POET
THE POOR IRISH/
FOR HE'S RICH AND HAS INFLUENCE. 159 POET
AN' IN A FEW YEARS WE'D BE RICH,.. 587 ROPE
SOONER WE STARTS THE SOONER WE'RE RICH. 600 ROPE
SHE MAY MEET RICH FELLOW THERE... 22 STRANG
IN SPITE OF THEIR BEING RICH FOR HEREABOUTS. 59 STRANG
AND WE'LL BE SO RICH, WE CAN BUY OFF THE DELUGE 123 STRANG
ANYWAY/...

1325 RIDICULOUS

RICH (CONT'D.)
RICH, I'VE HEARD...)) 125 STRANG
HIS OLD MAN WAS RICH... 134 STRANG
WE'VE MADE HIM RICH AND HAPPY/ 173 STRANG

RICHARD
OVER THE MIRROR BEHIND THE BAR ARE FRAMED 664 ICEMAN
PHOTOGRAPHS OF RICHARD CROKER

PEDDLER PIMP FOR NOUVEAU-RICHE CAPITALISM/ 691 ICEMAN
IN PERSPECTIVE OF A PRETENTIOUS, NOUVEAU-RICHE 139 MANSNS
COUNTRY ESTATE ON THE SHORE OF A

RICHER
YOU MUST BE BECOMING RICHER AND MORE POWERFUL ALL 100 MANSNS
THE TIME.

RICHES
AND THE COMFORT AND RICHES AND LUXURY THAT'S DUE 191 MANSNS
THE GREAT PRINCESS
WHEN HE CAME TO MANHOOD, RENOUNCED WIFE AND CHILD,372 MARCOM
RICHES AND POWER,
WITH ALL MY CRAZY DREAMS OF RICHES AND A GRAND 147 POET
ESTATE AND ME A HAUGHTY LADY

RICHEST
A SAMPLE OF THE RICHEST OF THE TREASURE... 561 CROSS
HE'S THE RICHEST KING IN THE WORLD 396 MARCOM
HE'S THE RICHEST KING IN THE WORLD. 359 MARCOM

RICHIN'
BLOOD AN' BONE AN' SWEAT--ROTTED AWAY--FERTILIZIN'218 DESIRE
YE--RICHIN' YER SOUL--

RICHLY
ALL ABOUT SOMEONE WHO MURDERED HIS WIFE AND GOT 197 AHWILD
HUNG, AS HE RICHLY DESERVED.
CLAD RICHLY, WEARING BEAUTIFULLY WROUGHT ARMOR AND298 LAZARU
HELMET.
HE IS DRESSED RICHLY. 332 LAZARU
A FILE OF SOLDIERS, ACCOMPANYING A RICHLY-DRESSED 376 MARCOM
COURT MESSENGER, COME THROUGH.
BUT I GOT RICHLY OVER IT LIVING HERE WITH POOR 64 STRANG
FOLKS THAT WAS BEING PUNISHED FOR

RICHNESS
HE IS DRESSED WITH FOPPISH RICHNESS IN EXTREME 313 LAZARU
BRIGHT COLORS.

RICKEY
BELLE HAS AN EMPTY GIN-RICKEY GLASS BEFORE HER, 236 AHWILD
MINE'S A GIN RICKEY. 245 AHWILD

RICKS
ON THE RIGHT OF THE DOORWAY, THREE STALLS WITH 577 ROPE
MANGERS AND HAY-RICKS.

RID
NAT, YOU GET RID OF HIM THE FIRST SECOND YOU CAN/ 199 AHWILD
AND GET RID OF HIS OLD-FOGY IDEAS. 207 AHWILD
HOW WAS THAT FOR SLICK WAY OF GETTING RID OF HIMS 247 AHWILD
YUH WANT TO GET RID O' ME HUH 11 ANNA
YOU'LL BE RID O' ME FOR GOOD--AND ME O' YOU--GOOD 11 ANNA
RIDDANCE FOR BOTH OF US.
SO I GOT RID OF HER THAT WAY. 95 BEYOND
I'LL BE GLAD TO GET RID OF YOU/ 127 BEYOND
AND HIM MAKIN' THEM FIRE SHOTS ROUND HER TO SCARE 509 DIFRNT
HER BACK TO LAND AND GET RID
HE WAS GLAD WHEN I ENLISTED, 'CAUSE THAT GOT HIM 523 DIFRNT
RID OF ME.
AND DON'T NEVER COME TO SEE US AGAIN TILL YOU'VE 530 DIFRNT
GOT RID OF THE MEANNESS AND
(THEN SHAKING HIMSELF LIKE A WET DOG TO GET RID OF188 EJONES
THESE DEPRESSING THOUGHTS)
I GITS RID O' DEM FRIPPETY EMPEROR TRAPPIN'S AN' 1193 EJONES
TRAVELS LIGHTER.
I'LL GIT RID OF 'EM FUR YOU. 12 ELECTR
(FORCING BACK HER ANGER) AND SEE THAT YOU GET RID 35 ELECTR
OF HIM RIGHT NOW/
I SHOULD THINK THAT WOULD RID YOU OF ANY SCRUPLES/ 41 ELECTR
(QUIETLY) YOU NEEDN'T HOPE TO GET RID OF ME THAT 45 ELECTR
WAY.
NO MORE IMPORTANT THAN RUBBISH TO BE GOT RID OF. 54 ELECTR
I'M GLAD YOU GOT RID OF HIM. 74 ELECTR
YOU MUST BE DAMNED ANXIOUS TO GET RID OF ME AGAIN/ 84 ELECTR
I JUST GOT RID OF HIM. 107 ELECTR
YOU KNEW YOU COULD RID YOURSELF FOREVER OF YOUR 141 ELECTR
SILLY GUILT ABOUT THE PAST.
YOU SEEM DAMNED ANXIOUS TO GET RID OF ME. 146 ELECTR
I WANT TO BE RID OF THE PAST. 148 ELECTR
SO I'M AFRAID YOU CAN'T HOPE TO GET RID OF ME 151 ELECTR
THROUGH HAZEL.
WHEN YOU'RE RID OF IT. 625 ICEMAN
AFTER YOU'RE RID OF THE DAMNED GUILT 661 ICEMAN
SHE'S RID OF ME AT LAST. 663 ICEMAN
(GETS UP--TO LARRY) IF YOU THINK MOVING TO 669 ICEMAN
ANOTHER TABLE WILL GET RID OF ME/
AT LIMEY CONSULATE THEY PROMISE ANYTHING TO GET 675 ICEMAN
RID OF HIM
YOU'RE RID OF ALL THAT NAGGING DREAM STUFF NOW. 690 ICEMAN
I'D ALMOST DO AS MUCH MYSELF TO BE RID OF YOU/ 693 ICEMAN
AND GET HER RID OF ME SO I COULDN'T MAKE HER 705 ICEMAN
SUFFER ANY MORE.
YOU'RE RID OF IT FOREVER/ 705 ICEMAN
I WISH YOU'D GET RID OF THAT BASTARD, LARRY. 706 ICEMAN
NOW I'VE MADE YOU GET RID OF YOUR PIPE DREAMS, 707 ICEMAN
YOU WANTED TO GET RID OF THEM. 95 JOURNE
TO GET BEYOND OUR REACH, TO BE RID OF US, TO 139 JOURNE
FORGET WE'RE ALIVE/
I GOT RID OF AN IRISH BROGUE YOU COULD CUT WITH A 150 JOURNE
KNIFE.
SHE HAS RID HER SPEECH OF BROGUE, EXCEPT IN 2 MANSNS
MOMENTS OF EXTREME EMOTION.
AND RID THE WORLD OF THIS STUPID RACE OF MEN AND 9 MANSNS
WASH THE EARTH CLEAN/
I WAS GLAD TO BE RID OF HIM WHEN HE WAS BORN-- 122 MANSNS
I HAVE SERVED MY PURPOSE--SHE HAS RUTHLESSLY GOT 126 MANSNS
RID OF ME--SHE IS FREE--

RID (CONT'D.)
BUT I KNOW YOU HATE ME MORE AND HAVE DETERMINED TO159 MANSNS
GET RID OF ME/
CAN'T YOU RID OUR LIFE OF THAT DAMNED GREEDY EVIL 160 MANSNS
WITCH
I KNOW SO WELL THE SCHEME SHE HAS IN MIND TO GET 162 MANSNS
RID OF ME--TO DRIVE ME INSANE--
UNTIL AT LAST WE'D FINALLY BE RID OF HIM. 171 MANSNS
YOU MUST ADMIT I GOT RID OF HER VERY SUCCESSFULLY.172 MANSNS
ALL I WANT NOW IS TO GET RID OF HER FOREVER. 178 MANSNS
OR WOULD YOU PREFER I SHOULD GO INSANE--AND SO HE 182 MANSNS
RID OF ME AGAIN$
I'M TOO ANXIOUS TO BE RID OF YOU. 10 MISBEG
AND HE THINKS THE BEST WAY TO GET RID OF YOU WOULD 66 MISBEG
BE TO BECOME YOUR LANDLORD.
SHE'S RID OF ME AT LAST. 148 MISBEG
(GRASPING AT THIS CHANCE TO GET RID OF HER-- 43 POET
IMPATIENTLY.)
YOUR MOTHER GOT RID OF IT ALL I'M THINKIN'. 592 ROPE
BUT THERE MIGHT BE MANY REASONS WHY HE'D WISH TO 36 STRANG
GET RID OF HER...))
STILL, NINA INSISTED ON GOING THAT SAME DAY AND 68 STRANG
MOTHER SEEMED ANXIOUS TO GET RID
COME UP AND TELL ME IF IT'S WED--AND GET RID OF 73 STRANG
CHARLIE.
GOT RID OF EVEN THAT SLIGHT SUSPICION... 78 STRANG
(BUT YOU WON'T GET RID OF ME SO EASILY, NINA...))120 STRANG
WE'LL HAVE TO GET RID OF HIM SOON/...)) 120 STRANG
YOU'D BETTER TELL HIM YOU KISSED ME GOOD-BY TO GET146 STRANG
RID OF ME/
SO I KISSED HIM TO GET RID OF HIM/ 155 STRANG
SHE WAS TRYING TO GET RID OF THE LAST OF THE 188 STRANG
PEOPLE.

RIDDANCE
IF I HAD ANY GUTS I'D KILL MYSELF, AND GOOD 258 AHWILD
RIDDANCE/
YOU'LL BE RID O' ME FOR GOOD--AND ME O' YOU--GOOD 11 ANNA
RIDDANCE FOR BOTH OF US.
GOOD RIDDANCE, BEJEES/ 610 ICEMAN
WELL, IT'S COME TO A PARTING OF THE WAYS NOW, AND 675 ICEMAN
GOOD RIDDANCE.
WELL, THAT'S THE LAST OF YOU, MIKE, AND GOOD 11 MISBEG
RIDDANCE.
THAT'S GOOD RIDDANCE. 101 MISBEG
AN' GOOD RIDDANCE/ 582 ROPE
GOOD RIDDANCE/... 92 STRANG

RIDDLE
(TRYING TO SOLVE A RIDDLE IN HIS OWN MIND-- 379 MARCOM
MUSINGLY)

RIDDLES
I'M IN NO MOOD TO PLAY RIDDLES WITH KIDS/ 273 AHWILD
NOW YOU'RE TALKING IN RIDDLES LIKE JAMIE. 64 JOURNE
TO START IN ON RIDDLES JUST AT THE LAST MOMENT/ 406 MARCOM
HOLY JOSEPH, YOU'RE FULL OF RIDDLES TONIGHT. 102 MISBEG

RIDE
WHAT DO YOU SAY TO AN AUTOMOBILE RIDE$ 191 AHWILD
'TIS HIMSELF HERE WILL BE HAVING A GRANDCHILD TO 77 ANNA
RIDE ON HIS FOOT.
WAAL, IF YE SIGN THIS YE KIN RIDE ON A BOAT. 213 DESIRE
BUT YE KIN RIDE ON A BOAT IF YE'LL SWAP. 214 DESIRE
I'D LIKE T' RIDE T' CALIFORNI-A--BUT-- 219 DESIRE
THANK YEW FUR THE RIDE. 220 DESIRE
LET HER RIDE/ 224 HA APE
*LET THIS RIDE ON THE NOSE OF WHATEVER HORSE 22 HUGHIE
YOU'RE BETTING ON TOMORROW.
SHE PUT ME DOWN AS A BAD INFLUENCE, AND LET HER 24 HUGHIE
CHIPS RIDE.
YOU USED TO RIDE IN IT EVERY DAY, BUT YOU'VE 84 JOURNE
HARDLY USED IT AT ALL LATELY.
SURE, WOULDN'T I RATHER RIDE IN A FINE AUTOMOBILE 102 JOURNE
THAN STAY HERE AND LISTEN TO
EVEN WITH YOU WHO USED TO RIDE ME ON YOUR KNEE, 301 LAZARU
(PROUDLY) WE WOULD RIDE THEIR ARMIES DOWN INTO 421 MARCOM
THE SEA/
ON HIS WAY BACK TO LUNCH FROM A HORSEBACK RIDE. 48 MISBEG
WATCHING HIM RIDE PAST IN HIS BIG SHINY AUTOMOBILE 51 MISBEG
WITH HIS SNOUT IN THE AIR.
THE GRAND GENTLEMAN MUST HAVE HIS THOROUGHBRED TO 22 POET
RIDE OUT IN STATE/
FOR LOUD AS YOU CRY, AND HIGH AS YOU RIDE, AND 102 POET
LITTLE YOU FEEL MY SORROW,
IT WAS AFTER I RETURNED FROM MY RIDE. 107 POET
IF THE MARE WASN'T LAME, I'D RIDE ALONE-- 128 POET
OR DONE MORE THAN MAKE HIM A BOW WHEN HE'D RIDE 130 POET
PAST ON HIS HUNTER.
HE'LL RIDE THE MARE BACK TO HARFCRD'S/ 162 POET

RIDERS
(LOOKING OFF LEFT) THERE'S TWO HORSEBACK RIDERS 54 MISBEG
ON THE COUNTY ROAD NOW.

RIDES
HIS MIND RIDES THE ENGINE, AND ASKS A FIREMAN WITH 27 HUGHIE
DISINTERESTED EAGERNESS...

RIDGE
WHICH SURROUND THE HOUSE, A HEAVILY WOODED RIDGE 2 ELECTR
IN THE BACKGROUND,
RIDGE AFTER RIDGE TO THE RIM OF THE WORLD/ 408 MARCOM

RIDICULING
SIT THERE FOR HOURS IN WISDOM-RIDICULING 102 MANSNS
CONTEMPLATION OF MYSELF.

RIDICULOUS
IS YOUR HERO'S RIDICULOUS CONSCIENCE, WHAT 494 DAYS
HAPPENS THEN$
(SNEERINGLY) BUT THERE WAS ONE RIDICULOUS 509 DAYS
WEAKNESS IN HER CHARACTER.
(HURRIEDLY) BUT, OF COURSE, HE REALIZED THIS WAS 536 DAYS
ALL MORBID AND RIDICULOUS--
(SNEERINGLY) AND UNDER THE INFLUENCE OF HIS 944 DAYS
RIDICULOUS GUILTY CONSCIENCE,

RIDICULOUS 1326

RIDICULOUS (CONT'D.)
YET THERE IS SOMETHING NOT ALTOGETHER RIDICULOUS 175 EJONES
ABOUT HIS GRANDEUR.
TO ANNOY YOU WITH SUCH RIDICULOUS NONSENSE/ 50 ELECTR
I'D BE VERY ANGRY WITH YOU IF IT WEREN'T SO 87 ELECTR
RIDICULOUS/
IT'S RIDICULOUS SNOBBERY FOR HIM TO SNEER AT THE 8 MANSNS
COMMON PEOPLE.
RIDICULOUS/ 26 MANSNS
RIDICULOUS/ 37 MANSNS
DON'T BE RIDICULOUS/ 78 MANSNS
MY DEAR BOY, YOUR CHILDISH FANCIES ARE RIDICULOUS.103 MANSNS
THAT IS RIDICULOUS/ 104 MANSNS
SO RIDICULOUS, ISN'T IT& 167 MANSNS
RIDICULOUS/ 174 MANSNS
(QUIETLY.) MAY I ASK WHAT YOU FIND SO RIDICULOUS 111 POET
IN AN OLD ESTABLISHED CUSTOM&
(DITTERLY) YES. HOW RIDICULOUS/ 19 STRANG
(CURTLY--WITH AUTHORITY) HOW DO YOU KNOW IT'S 35 STRANG
RIDICULOUS&
I'LL BE DAMNED IF I'LL LISTEN TO SUCH A RIDICULOUS 35 STRANG
STATEMENT/
HOW RIDICULOUS/.... 117 STRANG
PLEASE DON'T BE SO RIDICULOUS, MICHAEL. 454 WELDED
BUT IT SEEMS TO ME YOUR BRAND OF IT IS MUCH MORE 457 WELDED
RIDICULOUS.
(SHE LAUGHS) REALLY, IT WAS TOO RIDICULOUS--SO 466 WELDED
PLAIN--

RIDIN'
PLENTY O' WORK AND NO FOOD--AND THE OWNERS RIDIN' 480 CARDIF
AROUND IN CARRIAGES/
AN' NOW I'M RIDIN' OUT T' LEARN GOD'S MESSAGE T' 210 DESIRE
ME IN THE SPRING.
YE'D LIKE RIDIN' BETTER--ON A BOAT, WOULDN'T YE& 213 DESIRE
--I'M RIDIN' OUT T' LEARN GOD'S MESSAGE T' ME IN 215 DESIRE
THE SPRING LIKE THE PROPHETS
I GOT SOME DOUGH RIDIN' ON THE NOSE OF A TURTLE IN 37 HUGHIE
THE 4TH AT SARATOGA.
HE'S RIDIN' SOMEONE EVERY MINUTE. 631 ICEMAN
AND I'LL SOON BE RIDIN' AROUND IN A BIG RED 653 ICEMAN
AUTOMOBILE--

RIDING
(HE TAPS HER BUNDLE WITH HIS RIDING WHIP 174 EJONES
SIGNIFICANTLY.)
HE CARRIES A RIDING WHIP IN HIS HAND. 174 EJONES
HE IS DRESSED IN A WORN RIDING SUIT OF DIRTY WHITE174 EJONES
DRILL, PUTTEES, SPURS,
IT'S THAT LOUSY DRUMMER RIDING ME THAT'S GOT MY 655 ICEMAN
GOAT.
I'M SORRY FOR RIDING YOU, LARRY. 666 ICEMAN
I WAS SCARED OUT OF MY WITS RIDING BACK FROM TOWN. 98 JOURNE
OF THE CAPTAIN AND A CORPORAL WHO ARE RIDING ON 350 MAKCOM
THE WAGON, THE CAPTAIN DRIVING.
HE IS RIDING ON A VERY FAT WHITE HORSE. 388 MARCOM
BREECHES, IMMACULATELY POLISHED ENGLISH RIDING 56 MISBEG
BOOTS WITH SPURS.
HE IS DRESSED IN A BEAUTIFULLY TAILORED ENGLISH 56 MISBEG
TWEED COAT AND WHIPCORD RIDING
AND CARRIES A RIDING CROP IN HIS HAND. 56 MISBEG
(HE RAISES HIS RIDING CROP.) 61 MISBEG
DRESSED IN SILKS AND SATINS, AND RIDING IN A 63 POET
CARRIAGE WITH COACHMAN AND FOOTMAN.
WHEN YOU WENT RIDING ON YOUR BEAUTIFUL 106 POET
THOROUGHBRED MARE
RIDING AROUND IN A CARRIAGE WITH COACHMAN AND 147 POET
FOOTMAN/
REASSURE HIMSELF ABOUT IT, YET HE IS RIDING THE 53 STRANG
CREST OF THE WAVE,

RIFE
(HE QUOTES) «DEAR COLLEGE DAYS, WITH PLEASURE 595 ICEMAN
RIFE/

RIFFRAFF
OF THAT IDOL OF THE RIFFRAFF, ANDREW JACKSON. 37 POET
WHEN I CALLED, I THOUGHT IT WAS ONE OF THE DAMNED 117 POET
RIFFRAFF

RIFLE
A WINCHESTER RIFLE IS SLUNG ACROSS HIS SHOULDERS 194 EJONES
AND HE CARRIES A HEAVY WHIP.
EACH ONE CARRIES A RIFLE. 202 EJONES
LET THEM HATTER EACH OTHER'S BRAINS OUT WITH RIFLE 82 ELECTR
BUTTS
WITH ONE RIFLE I SHOOT DAMN FOOL LIMEY OFFICERS PY599 ICEMAN
THE DOZEN, BUT HIM I MISS.
AND I KILL THEM WITH MY RIFLE SO EASY/ 677 ICEMAN
RIFLES
THE SOLDIERS JUMP TO THEIR FEET, COCKING THEIR 203 EJONES
RIFLES ALERTLY.
(THE REPORTS OF SEVERAL RIFLES SOUND FROM THE 203 EJONES
FOREST)

RIG
(PLEASED, GLANCING UP AT HIS SHIP'S LOFTY RIG) 106 ELECTR
BUT WE CAN GET A RIG AT THE LIVERY STABLE. 128 POET
HIS COACHMAN HAD TO HELP HIM IN HIS RIG AT THE 129 POET
CORNER--
(IN A WHISPER.) I'VE GOT HIM IN A RIG OUTSIDE, 151 POET
I SAIL ON HER ONCE LONG TIME AGO--THREE MASTS, 507 VOYAGE
FULL RIG, SKY'S'L-YARDS&

RIGGED
I BETTER GO UPSTAIRS AND GET RIGGED OUT OR I NEVER208 AHWILD
WILL GET TO THAT PICNIC.
THEN HE HAS THE ROOF TOO RIGGED UP LIKE A SHIP& 557 CRUSS
BLOOD* HINDAMMER--SKY'S'L-YARDER--FULL-RIGGED-- 495 VOYAGE
PAINTED WHITE--

RIGGER
WHEN I WAS ON THE SQUAREHEAD SQUARE RIGGER, BOUND 153 JOURNE
FOR BUENOS AIRES.

RIGGING
TEARS THE RIGGING OFF AND THROWS THE DISMANTLED 150 STRANG
HULL AT DARRELL'S FEET)

RIGHTEOUS
*GOT A STERN, SELF-RIGHTEOUS BEING WHO CONDEMNED 510 DAYS
SINNERS TO TORMENT,
=THAT'S RIGHTEOUS. 206 DESIRE
(LORD GOD OF RIGHTEOUS VENGEANCE, I THANK 447 DYNAMO
THEE/...
AND IT WOULD BE A RIGHTEOUS WAR/ 422 MARCOM
OR PRIMLY SELF-RIGHTEOUS. 4 MISBEG

RIGHTEOUSLY
HE'D LIKE TO STEAL IT AS HE STEALS MY IDEAS-- 287 GGBROW
COMPLACENTLY-RIGHTEOUSLY.
(RIGHTEOUSLY INDIGNANT) (WHAT HAS BROUGHT HIM 124 STRANG
BACKS...

RIGHTEOUSNESS
(THEN HIS VOICE BOOMING LIKE HIS FATHER'S WITH 438 DYNAMO
MORAL SELF-RIGHTEOUSNESS)

RIGHTER
PERHAPS AFTER ALL ANDY WAS RIGHT--RIGHTER THAN HE 92 BEYOND
KNEW--

RIGHTFUL
INSTEAD OF DOIN' YOUR RIGHTFUL WORK, 539 'ILE
JUST SKULKIN' OUT O' YOUR RIGHTFUL RESPONSIBILITY.105 BEYOND
I ACFOLY GIVE UP WHAT WAS RIGHTFUL MINE/ 237 DESIRE
I RELY ON YOU TO HELP ME KEEP HER IN HER RIGHTFUL 106 MANSNS
PLACE HEREAFTER.
IT'S YOUR RIGHTFUL DUTY/ 64 STRANG
IT'S YOUR RIGHTFUL DUTY*... 72 STRANG

RIGHTFULLY
AND GETS WHAT'S RIGHTFULLY COMING TO HIM/ 381 MARCOM
WHEN I FEEL SOMEONE'S TRYING TO STEAL WHAT'S 411 MARCOM
RIGHTFULLY MINE, FOR INSTANCE.
IT'S RIGHTFULLY MINE. 7 MISBEG

RIGHTLY
A WOMAN COULDN'T RIGHTLY UNDERSTAND MY REASONS, 947 'ILE
=MA'M,= SAYS I, =I COULDN'T RIGHTLY ANSWER THAT 94 BEYOND
QUESTION.
NO, 'NOTHIN' A MAN'D RIGHTLY CALL WRONG. 500 DIFRNT
IT AIN'T RIGHTLY NONE O' YOUR BUSINESS WHAT HE 505 DIFRNT
DOES ON A VIGE.
HUM-- I DON'T SEE YOUR MEANIN' RIGHTLY. 542 DIFRNT
AND QUITE RIGHTLY.... 12 STRANG
THEY WERE IMPORTANT TO THEMSELVES, IF I REMEMBER 45 STRANG
RIGHTLY.

RIGHTO
(GRATEFULLY) RIGHTO--AND THANKS TER YER. 186 EJONES
(THEY ALL SAY LAUGHINGLY, =SURE, HARRY,= =RIGHTO,=618 ICEMAN
=THAT'S THE STUFF,

RIGHTS
AND ONLY FOR ME, I'M TELLING YOU, AND THE GREAT 32 ANNA
STRENGTH AND RIGHTS.
WE'D ALL OUGHT TO BE WITH DAVY JONES AT THE BOTTOM 32 ANNA
OF THE SEA, BE RIGHTS.
(WITH A GRIM SMILE) A DYING MAN HAS SOME RIGHTS, 159 BEYOND
HASN'T HE&
IT'S MY MONEY BY RIGHTS NOW. 213 DESIRE
I'M FIGHTIN' HIM--FIGHTIN' YEW--FIGHTIN' FUR MAW'S229 DESIRE
RIGHTS T' HER HUM/
WE'D OUGHT, BY ALL RIGHTS, TO MAKE ALLOWANCES FOR 539 DIFRNT
HER.
YOU'VE GOT NO RIGHTS OVER ME/ 105 ELECTR
TREE SQUARE A DAY, AND CAULIFLOWERS IN DE FRONT 250 HA APE
YARD--EKAL RIGHTS--
THE PAPERS SAY THE COPS GOT THEM ALL DEAD TO 588 ICEMAN
RIGHTS,
BY RIGHTS YOU SHOULD BE CONTENTED NOW, 704 ICEMAN
YOU STAND UP FOR YOUR RIGHTS, BEJEES, HICKEY/ 718 ICEMAN
HE WAS A KING OF IRELAND, IF HE HAD HIS RIGHTS, 24 JOURNE
AND SCUM WAS SCUM TO HIM.
GOOD HEAVENS, DID I COME HERE TO DISCUSS THE 9 MANSNS
NATURAL RIGHTS OF MAN--
I MEANT SHE HAS NO SENSE OF THE RIGHTS TO FREEDOM 86 MANSNS
OF OTHERS.

RIGID
HER EYES ARE FIXED ON HER BOOK, HER BODY TENSE AND257 AHWILD
RIGID.)
(HE STANDS IN AN ATTITUDE OF RIGID ATTENTION. 570 CROSS
THEY BOTH REMAIN RIGID, LOOKING STRAIGHT AHEAD 241 DESIRE
WITH EYES FULL OF FEAR.)
(WITH A CONCENTRATED EFFORT THAT STIFFENS HIS BODY264 DESIRE
INTO A RIGID LINE
SHAKING THEM, CASTING THEM OUT WITH THE REGULAR, 191 EJONES
RIGID
ARE THOSE OF AUTOMATONS,--RIGID, SLOW, AND 194 EJONES
MECHANICAL.
THERE IS SOMETHING STIFF, RIGID, UNREAL, 196 EJONES
MARIONETTISH ABOUT THEIR MOVEMENTS.
(SUDDENLY BECOMING RIGID AND COLD AGAIN--SLOWLY) 32 ELECTR
(LAVINIA KEEPS HER BODY RIGID, HER EYES STARING 78 ELECTR
INTO HER MOTHER'S.
TURNS, RIGID AND SQUARE-SHOULDERED, AND WALKS 101 ELECTR
WOODENLY FROM THE ROOM.)
LAVINIA STANDS AT THE LEFT OF THE STEPS, RIGID AND121 ELECTR
ERECT, HER FACE MASK-LIKE.)
LARRY IS RIGID ON HIS CHAIR, STARING BEFORE HIM. 646 ICEMAN
(GROWS RIGID--HIS VOICE TREMBLING WITH REPRESSED 677 ICEMAN
ANGER)
HE REMAINS RIGID AND UNYIELDING. 91 JOURNE
THE LIPS OF AN ABLE SOLDIER-STATESMAN OF RIGID 337 LAZARU
PROBITY.
NOT WITHOUT DETERMINATION AND A RIGID INTEGRITY, 26 MANSNS
(TO CHU-YIN--COMPLACENTLY) YOU'VE GOT TO IMPOSE 403 MARCOM
RIGID DISCIPLINE ON SHIPBOARD.
SHE REMAINS RIGID, GIVING NO SIGN.) 417 MARCOM
(UNDER HIS KISSES HER FACE AGAIN BECOMES MASK- 465 WELDED
LIKE, HER BODY RIGID,

RIGIDITY

BENEATH THE UNCOMPROMISING RIGIDITY OF HIS 70 MANSNS HABITUAL POISE.

RIGIDLY

RICHARD HOLDS RIGIDLY ALOOF 221 AHWILD
(SUDDENLY GETS UP FROM HER CHAIR AND STANDS 233 AHWILD
RIGIDLY, HER FACE WORKING--JERKILY)
(ROBERT STANDS RIGIDLY, HIS HANDS CLENCHED, HIS 106 BEYOND
FACE CONTRACTED BY PAIN.
ANDREW STANDS RIGIDLY LOOKING STRAIGHT IN FRONT OF108 BEYOND
HIM.
THEN STRAIGHTENS OUT RIGIDLY.) 489 CARDIF
HE STARES BEFORE HIM RIGIDLY, 494 DIFRNT
REMAINS RIGIDLY FIXED THERE. 201 EJONES
(SHE IS SILENT, STARING BEFORE HER WITH HARD EYES, 22 ELECTR
RIGIDLY UPRIGHT.
HIS FACE IS RIGIDLY COMPOSED, BUT HIS SUPERIOR 280 GGBROW
DISGUST FOR OION CAN BE SEEN.
SHE WAITS RIGIDLY UNTIL HE DISAPPEARS DOWN THE 42 JOURNE
STEPS.
HER FACE RIGIDLY CALM AND EMOTIONLESS. 390 MARCOM
I HAVE JUST BEEN REMINDING SIMON THAT HIS FATHER 82 POET
IS RIGIDLY UNFORGIVING
A RIGIDLY CONSERVATIVE, BEST-FAMILY ATTORNEY, 116 POET
IT PENETRATES MELODY'S STUPOR AND HE STIFFENS 166 POET
RIGIDLY ON HIS CHAIR.
OF INTENSE PASSION WHICH HE HAS RIGIDLY TRAINED 33 STRANG
HIMSELF TO CONTROL AND SET FREE

RILE

ATTENTION TO HIS TRYING TO RILE YOUS 425 DYNAMO
BUT YOU'RE ONLY TRYING TO RILE ME--AND I'M NOT 151 ELECTR
GOING TO LET YOU.

RILED

YOU'RE RUNNIN' AWAY 'CAUSE YOU'RE PUT OUT AND 106 BEYOND
RILED
(WITH A CHUCKLE) I'LL BET YE HE'S RILED/ 220 DESIRE
I OUGHTN'T T' GIT RILED SO--AT THAT 'ERE FOOL 234 DESIRE
CALF.
DON'T GIT RILED THINKIN' O' HIM. 242 DESIRE
IT SEEMED TO GET CALEB ALL RILED UP. 501 DIFRNT
ONLY IT GITS ME RILED TO THINK OF HOW AWFUL BROKE 510 DIFRNT
UP CALEB'D BE IF--
BUT IT RILED ME JEST THE SAME. 539 DIFRNT
NO NEED GETTIN' RILED AT ME. 20 ELECTR

RILEY'S

(HE TAKES RILEY'S ARM.) COME ON, PATCH. 54 POET
FROM THE BAR COMES THE SOUND OF PATCH RILEY'S 133 POET
PIPES
AND OTHER ROARS OF ACCLAIM MINGLED WITH THE MUSIC 180 POET
OF RILEY'S PIPES.

RIM

A RIM OF MILK VISIBLE ABOUT HIS LIPS. 186 AHWILD
THE SECRET THAT CALLED TO ME FROM OVER THE WORLD'S 92 BEYOND
RIM--
TO PUT THE WHOLE RIM OF THE WORLD BETWEEN ME AND 126 BEYOND
THOSE HILLS.
ALL I CAN SEE IS THE BLACK RIM OF THE DAMNED HILLS151 BEYOND
ALONG THE HORIZON RIM OF THE DARK HILLS. 166 BEYOND
HORIZON WHERE THE EDGE OF THE SUN'S DISC IS RISING168 BEYOND
FROM THE RIM OF THE HILLS)
RIDGE AFTER RIDGE TO THE RIM OF THE WORLD/ 408 MARCOM

RIMEMBER

AN' RIMEMBER THIS.. 463 CARIBE

RIMMED

THE HORIZON HILLS ARE STILL RIMMED BY A FAINT LINE 81 BEYOND
OF FLAME.
A HUMOROUS, GOOD-NATURED MOUTH, SMALL EYES BEHIND 496 DAYS
HORN-RIMMED SPECTACLES.)
HER FACE IS FROZEN INTO AN EXPRESSIONLESS MASK, 547 DIFRNT
HER EYES ARE RED-RIMMED.
HIS LITTLE WASHY-BLUE EYES ARE RED-RIMMED AND DART174 EJONES
ABOUT HIM LIKE A FERRET'S.
BEHIND HORN-RIMMED SPECTACLES, 8 HUGHIE
AND RED-RIMMED LITTLE PIG'S EYES. 51 POET

RING

YOU MIGHT AS WELL GO OUT IN THE KITCHEN AND WAIT 211 AHWILD
TILL I RING.
STOP SPINNING YOUR NAPKIN RING/ 222 AHWILD
(THERE IS AN INSISTENT RING FROM THE DOORBELL 7 ANNA
THERE IS THE RING OF THE FAMILY-ENTRANCE BELL. 13 ANNA
AND HE CAN HAVE BACK HIS RING--AND I AIN'T GOING 504 DIFRNT
TO MARRY HIM.
ALL I GOT TO DO IS TO RING DE BELL AND DEY COME 181 EJONES
FLYING.
RING THE BELL NOW AN' YOU'LL BLOODY WELL SEE WHAT 182 EJONES
I MEANS.
THEN A RING FROM THE FRONT-DOOR BELL. 158 ELECTR
THERE IS A RING AT THE OUTSIDE-DOOR BELL. 280 GGBROW
THERE IS ANOTHER RING.) 280 GGBROW
NOT THAT I'D EVER RING IN NO PHONEYS ON A PAL. 20 HUGHIE
TILL I HAD TO PROMISE HER A DIAMOND ENGAGEMENT 22 HUGHIE
RING TO SOBER HER UP.=
= BUT THERE IS A HOLLOW RING IN IT. 659 ICEMAN
AND GENTLEMAN JIM CORBETT IN RING COSTUME. 664 ICEMAN
NOR DELIGHTED RELATIVES MAKING THE VELDT RING WITH677 ICEMAN
THEIR HAPPY CRIES--
WHAT WON'T SHE WANT WHEN SHE GETS DE RING ON HER 697 ICEMAN
FINGER AND I'M HOOKED8
(STUPIDLY) I DON'T HEAR BELL RING. 516 INZONE
NO, AND YOU WON'T HEAR ANY RING, YOU BOOB-- 516 INZONE
(LOWERING HIS VOICE UNCONSCIOUSLY)
THE BELLS OF THE CHURCHES BEGIN TO RING.) 362 MARCOM
(THE TEMPLE BELLS BEGIN TO RING IN CHORUS. 372 MARCOM
MADEMOISELLE--THE SEES HER WEDDING RING.) PRAY 69 POET
FORGIVE ME. I SEE IT IS MADAME--
AND PUT A RING IN HIS HAND, AND SHOES ON HIS 594 ROPE
FEET.
(THE MAID HAS ANSWERED THE RING AND UPENED THE 94 STRANG
OUTER DOOR.

RING (CONT'D.)

(THERE IS A RING FROM THE FRONT DOOR BELL. 97 STRANG
THERE IS A RING FROM THE FRONT DOOR. 123 STRANG
EXCLAIMING IRRITABLY AS THE BELL CONTINUES TO 462 WELDED
RING--ALL RIGHT, DAMN IT/

RINGER

HE'S A DEAD RINGER FOR GORDON SHAW AT HIS BEST. 163 STRANG
OF COURSE HE'S YOURS, DEAR--AND A DEAD RINGER FOR 182 STRANG
GORDON SHAW, TOO/

RINGING

(IN A VOICE WHICH IS SUDDENLY RINGING WITH THE 167 BEYOND
HAPPINESS OF HOPE)
THERE IS A SUDDEN LOUD THUMPING ON THE FRONT DOOR 294 GGBROW
AND THE RINGING OF THE BELL.
COMES THE WARNING RINGING OF BELLS ON YACHTS AT 97 JOURNE
ANCHOR.
(LOOKS DOWN UPON THE STRUGGLING MASS AND CRIES IN 291 LAZARU
A RINGING VOICE)
AT THIS MOMENT THE VOICE OF LAZARUS COMES RINGING 305 LAZARU
THROUGH THE AIR
HIS VOICE RINGING MORE AND MORE WITH A TERRIBLE 349 LAZARU
UNBEARABLE POWER AND BEAUTY THAT
HE BEGINS TO LAUGH, HIS LAUGHTER CLEAR AND 349 LAZARU
RINGING--
FOR A TIME THE CHURCH BELLS, WHICH HAVE NEVER 363 MARCOM
CEASED RINGING,
A RINGING OF THE DOORBELL SOUNDS FROM SOMEWHERE 462 WELDED
BACK IN THE HOUSE.

RINGS

HIS VOICE RINGS WITH HOPEFUL STRENGTH AND ENERGY) 142 BEYOND
(THE TELEPHONE ON THE TABLE RINGS. 513 DAYS
(CALLS BACK IN A VOICE WHOSE BREEZINESS RINGS A 515 DAYS
BIT STRAINED)
(THE TELEPHONE IN THE HALL RINGS AND MARGARET GUESS) DAYS
TOWARD THE DOOR IN REAR TO
HE RINGS THIS VIGOROUSLY--THEN STOPS TO LISTEN. 182 EJONES
THEN HE GOES TO BOTH DOORS, RINGS AGAIN, AND LOOKS182 EJONES
OUT.)
SHO' I RINGS. 182 EJONES
THE TELEPHONE RINGS. 274 GGBROW
HE WEARS PHONY RINGS AND A HEAVY BRASS WATCH- 576 ICEMAN
CHAIN--NOT CONNECTED TO A WATCH--.
THEN THE TELEPHONE IN THE FRONT HALL RINGS AND ALL 73 JOURNE
OF THE STIFFEN STARTLEDLY.)
(HIS VOICE RINGS FROM WITHIN THE HOUSE IN EXULTANT285 LAZARU
DENIAL)
IT IS THE HAND ON WHICH HE WEARS FIVE LARGE JADE 389 MARCOM
RINGS.
(A BELL RINGS INSISTENTLY FROM THE BACK OF THE 26 STRANG
HOUSE.
(THE BELL RINGS AGAIN) (II MUST GIVE NED A GOOD 73 STRANG
CHANCE TO TALK TO HER....)
(THE DOORBELL RINGS--EXCITEDLY) 73 STRANG
YOU KNOW I DIDN'T MEAN--THE BELL RINGS. 75 STRANG
THE THICK FINGERS OF HIS BIG HANDS ARE LOADED WITH493 VOYAGE
CHEAP RINGS.

RINSING

(RINSING GLASSES BEHIND THE BAR) 613 ICEMAN

RIO

+RIO GRANDE+, ORISC. 459 CARIBE

RIOT

THAT'LL TEACH YOU TO SMUGGLE RUM ON A SHIP AND 473 CARIBE
START A RIOT.
DOLLS DIDN'T CALL HIM NO RIOT. 24 HUGHIE
JEES, AIN'T DE OLD BASTARD A RIOT WHEN HE STARTS 578 ICEMAN
DAT BULL

RIOTOUSLY

RIOTOUSLY PROFANE LACK OF ANY APPARENT DESIGN. 284 GGBROW

RIP

LET 'ER RIP/ 470 CARIBE
AND RIP EACH OTHER'S GUTS WITH BAYONETS/ 82 ELECTR
I'LL RIP YOUR GUTS OUT/ 672 ICEMAN

RIPE

I TELL YOU, I FEEL RIPE FOR BIGGER THINGS THAN 134 BEYOND
SETTLING DOWN HERE.
I'M GITTIN' RIPE ON THE BOUGH. 231 DESIRE
I'M GITTIN' OLD--RIPE ON THE BOUGH. 234 DESIRE
GROWIN' RIPE UN THE BOUGH. 238 DESIRE
GROWIN' RIPE ON THE BOUGH--... 264 DESIRE
AN' I'M GITTIN' OLD, LUMP--RIPE ON THE BOUGH..... 268 DESIRE
IS 'GUT THE TIME RIPE TO SMITE THIS BLASPHEMER 423 DYNAMO
HE'LL BE GOOD AND RIPE FOR MY BIRTHDAY PARTY 618 ICEMAN
TONIGHT AT TWELVE
AND NEVER WORK IF YOU CAN HELP IT, YOU MAY LIVE TO626 ICEMAN
A RIPE OLD AGE.
THE TIMES ARE RIPE FOR SUCH A BOOK. 8 MANSNS
IN FACT, I'M SO CONFIDENT HE IS THAT AS SOON AS HE128 STRANG
THINKS THE TIME IS RIPE TO

RIPELY

YOU ARE A MELLOW FRUIT OF HAPPINESS RIPELY 197 STRANG
FALLING/....)

RIPENED

HE IS JUST MELLOW AND BENIGNLY RIPENED. 221 AHWILD

RIPPED

LIKE A DOG WITH ITS GUTS RIPPED CUT YOU'D PUT OUT 726 ICEMAN
OF MISERY/
UNTIL MY MIND WOULD BE RIPPED APART/ 174 MANSNS

RIPPLE

A RIPPLE OF SOFT LAUGHTER FROM THE MOTIONLESS 341 LAZARU
FIGURES ABOUT THE ROOM ECHOES HIS.

RIPPLES

BUT THE LAPPING OF RIPPLES AGAINST THE PILES AND 257 GGBROW
THEIR SWISHING ON THE BEACH--

RISE

AT THE RISE OF THE CURTAIN THERE IS A MOMENT OF 535 'ILE
INTENSE SILENCE.
WHY SHOULDN'T THE WORKERS OF THE WORLD UNITE AND 195 AHWILD
RISE?

RISE

1328

RISE (CONT'D.)
AT THE RISE OF THE CURTAIN, ALBERT MAYO IS 81 BEYOND
DISCOVERED SITTING ON THE FENCE.
AT THE RISE OF THE CURTAIN MRS. MAYO AND MRS. 112 BEYOND
ATKINS ARE DISCOVERED
AT THE RISE OF THE CURTAIN RUTH IS DISCOVERED 144 BEYOND
SITTING BY THE STOVE.
I'M GOING TO SEE THE SUN RISE. 150 BEYOND
WHERE HE CAN SEE THE SUN RISE, AND COLLAPSES 166 BEYOND
WEAKLY.
IN A DITCH BY THE OPEN ROAD--WATCHING THE SUN 167 BEYOND
RISE.
THE MAKES A FEEBLE ATTEMPT TO RISE BUT SINKS BACK 482 CARDIF
WITH A SHARP GROAN.
FRINGED WITH COCU PALMS WHOSE TOPS RISE CLEAR OF 455 CARIBB
THE HORIZON.
AND JIMMY KANAKA RISE NOISELESSLY INTO THE ROOM 571 CROSS
FROM THE STAIRS.
AT THE RISE OF THE CURTAIN. 493 DAYS
I WAS ONLY TRYING TO GET A RISE OUT OF YOU. 524 DAYS
I ONLY SAID THAT--AS A JOKE--TO GET A RISE OUT OF 538 DAYS
UNCLE.
(HE STARTS TO RISE.) 517 DIFRNT
THE HOUSE IS PLACED BACK ON A SLIGHT RISE OF 2 ELECTR
GROUND ABOUT THREE HUNDRED FEET
THEN ALL THE YEARS WE'VE BEEN MAN AND WIFE WOULD 54 ELECTR
RISE UP IN MY MIND
IT WOULD RISE ABOUT THE SCREAMS OF THE DYING-- 83 ELECTR
(OUT HE CAN'T GET A RISE OUT OF THEM AND HE 598 ICEMAN
SUBSIDES INTO A FUMING MUMBLE.
WELL, WELL, YOU DID MANAGE TO GET A RISE OUT OF ME692 ICEMAN
THAT TIME.
+LET US RISE UP AND PART. SHE WILL NOT KNOW. 173 JOURNE
THE MUSIC AND LAUGHTER, RISE ABOVE THEIR HOOTING. 286 LAZARU
THE LEVEL FROM WHICH THE COLUMNS RISE IS THE 312 LAZARU
CHORUS OF SENATORS.
MIRIAM'S BODY IS SEEN TO RISE IN A WRITHING 348 LAZARU
TORTURED LAST EFFORT.)
(THE BELLOWING RISE AND FALL IS REFLECTED ON THE 363 LAZARU
MASKED FACES OF THE MULTITUDE
(SHE TAKES SARA'S HAND AND THEY RISE. 128 MANSNS
(TENSELY--MAKING A FUTILE MOVEMENT TO RISE.) 178 MANSNS
THE POLOS RISE AND STRETCH SLEEPILY.) 376 MARCOM
RISE.
RISE, MY OLD FRIEND, IT IS I WHO SHOULD BE AT YOUR425 MARCOM
FEET, NOT YOU AT MINE/
THEIR VOICES RISE TOGETHER IN A LONG, RHYTHMIC 433 MARCOM
WAIL OF MOURNING.
BUT I'LL HAVE TO MAKE YOU LEAVE BEFORE SUN-RISE. 137 MISBEG
RISE OF CURTAIN. ACT-FOUR STUFF. 172 MISBEG
AND THIS IS A COUNTRY WHERE YOU CAN RISE AS HIGH 27 POET
AS YOU LIKE.
IT'S MY CHANCE TO RISE IN THE WORLD AND NOTHING 31 POET
WILL KEEP ME FROM IT.
AND I'LL GIVE HER A CHANCE TO RISE IN THE WORLD. 63 POET
THIS WOULD BE THE FRENCH POSITION ON A RISE OF 96 POET
GROUND
(SHE PUTS HER HANDS ON THE TABLE AND STARTS TO 107 POET
RISE.)
SO REMEMBER IT'S TO HELL WID HONOR IF YE WANT TO 170 POET
RISE IN THIS WORLD.
(STILL KEEPING HIS EYES FIXED ON HERS, HE BEGINS 172 POET
TO RISE FROM HIS CHAIR.
AND WON'T HE PROUD WATCHIN' HER RISE IN THE 173 POET
WORLD TILL SHE'S A GRAND LADY/
(STARTS TO RISE.) I'LL GET YOU-- 175 POET
BUT I USED TO THINK THERE WAS A FINE CHANCE TO 70 STRANG
RISE THERE--

RISEN
MRS. MILLER, ALMOST EQUALLY MOVED, HAS HALF RISEN 258 AHWILD
TO GO TO HER BROTHER TOO
FROM WHICH HE HAS RISEN) 107 BEYOND
AS IF THE SUN HAD RISEN. 566 DAYS
THE MOON HAS JUST RISEN. 190 EJONES
(HIS VOICE HAS RISEN TO A SHOUT. 105 ELECTR
THE MOON HAS JUST RISEN. 117 ELECTR
(MARY HAS RISEN FROM THE ARM OF THE CHAIR. 62 JOURNE
(HE HAS RISEN TO A NOTE OF DRUNKEN ARROGANCE. 164 JOURNE
(HIS VOICE HAS RISEN TO A WAILING LAMENT) 285 LAZARU
THIS SOUND HAS RISEN TO ITS GREATEST VOLUME AS THE364 LAZARU
CURTAIN RISES.)
(HIS VOICE HAS RISEN TO A PASSIONATE ENTREATY.) 367 LAZARU
A GREEDY ADVENTURESS WHO HAS RISEN FROM THE GUTTER 13 MANSNS
TO NOBILITY
AND NOT AN OLD OVE RISEN FROM MY DEAD. 38 MANSNS
AS HE NOT BY HIS WILL-POWER AND DETERMINATION 387 MARCOM
RISEN
YOU MUST HAVE RISEN THE WRONG SIDE OF THE BED THIS 45 POET
MORNING.
THE TWO MEN HAVE RISEN AND STARE AT HER ANXIOUSLY. 39 STRANG

RISES
HER EYE MISTILY AND RISES TO HIS FEET, MAKING HER 226 AHWILD
A DEEP, UNCERTAIN BOW.
AS THE CURTAIN RISES, THE FAMILY WITH THE 263 AHWILD
EXCEPTION OF RICHARD.
AS THE CURTAIN RISES, JOHNNY IS DISCOVERED. 3 ANNA
(HALF RISES TO HER FEET, THEN SITS DOWN AGAIN) 23 ANNA
THE CHIMNEY OF THE CABIN STOVE RISES A FEW FEET 25 ANNA
ABOVE THE ROOF.
(BURKE RISES AND SITS ON BENCH. 33 ANNA
AS THE CURTAIN RISES, CHRIS AND ANNA ARE 41 ANNA
DISCOVERED.
AS THE CURTAIN RISES THE CAPTAIN IS JUST FINISHING 94 BEYOND
THE CHILD'S CRYING RISES TO A LOUDER PITCH) 128 BEYOND
FROM THE FORECASTLE HEAD ABOVE THE VOICE OF THE 482 CARDIF
LOOKOUT RISES IN A LONG WAIL.
IN THE SEPARATE GROUPS AS THE CURTAIN RISES. 456 CARIBB

RISES (CONT'D.)
GUCKY RISES TO HIS FEET, HIS FACE LIVID WITH RAGE,472 CARIBB
AND SPRINGS AT PADDY,
AFTER THE CURTAIN RISES THE DOOR IN THE REAR IS 555 CROSS
OPENED SLOWLY AND
THEN HE RISES, SHAKING HIS HEAD). 573 CROSS
SHE RISES SLOWLY TO HER FEET AND WALKS SLOWLY AND 541 DAYS
WUDDENLY BACK PAST HIM AND
FOR A MOMENT AFTER THE CURTAIN RISES THE WHISPERED554 DAYS
PANTOMIME BETWEEN STILLWELL
JOHN RISES FROM HIS KNEES AND STANDS WITH ARMS 566 DAYS
STRETCHED UP AND OUT,
SWIFTLY RISES TO A BRILLIANT INTENSITY OF CRIMSON 566 DAYS
AND GREEN AND GOLD.
UNCONSCIOUSLY HE STRETCHES OUT HIS ARMS FOR HER 236 DESIRE
AND SHE HALF RISES.
AS THE CURTAIN RISES, EMMA CROSBY AND CALEB 494 DIFRNT
WILLIAMS ARE DISCOVERED.
THE RISES TO HIS FEET AS HE IS SPEAKING THIS 518 DIFRNT
LAST.)
AS THE CURTAIN RISES, EMMA AND BENNY ROGERS ARE 519 DIFRNT
DISCOVERED.
EMMA RISES LIKE A WEARY AUTOMATON AND GOES TO THE 547 DIFRNI
DOOR AND OPENS IT.
HE GIVES A START AND HALF RISES FROM HIS CHAIR, 437 DYNAMC
SIMULTANEOUSLY REUBEN'S VOICE RISES 488 DYNAMO
THE DYNAMO'S THROATY METALLIC PURR RISES SLOWLY IN489 DYNAMO
VOLUME
AS THE CURTAIN RISES, 173 EJONES
AS THEIR CHORUS LIFTS HE RISES TO A SITTING 199 EJONES
POSTURE SIMILAR TO THE OTHERS.
AT THE SAME TIME, A LOW MELANCHOLY MURMUR RISES 199 EJONES
AMONG THEM.
A SHUDDER OF TERROR SHAKES HIS WHOLE BODY AS THE 199 EJONES
WAIL RISES UP ABOUT HIM AGAIN.
HIS VOICE RISES AND FALLS IN A WEIRD, MONOTONOUS 201 EJONES
CHOON.
(CHRISTINE SLOWLY RISES. 46 ELECTR
THE SHIP IS UNLOADED AND HER BLACK SIDE RISES NINE102 ELECTR
OR TEN FEET
THE CURTAIN RISES ON A TUMULT OF SOUND. 207 HA APE
AS THE CURTAIN RISES, THE FURNACE DOORS ARE SHUT. 223 HA APE
THE NIGHT CLERK RISES WEARILY. 8 HUGHIE
LARRY RISES FROM HIS CHAIR TO LOCK AT HOPE AND 577 ICEMAN
NUGS TO ROCKY.
AS THE CURTAIN RISES, ROCKY, THE NIGHT BARTENDER, 577 ICEMAN
AS THE CURTAIN RISES, CORA, CHUCK, HUGO, LARRY, 629 ICEMAN
MARGIE,
AS THEY DO SO, HICKEY RISES, A SCHOONER IN HIS 658 ICEMAN
HAND.)
(RISES TO HIS FEET AGAIN. 660 ICEMAN
AS THE CURTAIN RISES, ROCKY FINISHES HIS WORK 665 ICEMAN
BEHIND THE BAR.
THE HALF RISES FROM HIS CHAIR JUST AS FROM OUTSIDE726 ICEMAN
THE WINDOW COMES THE SOUND OF
AS THE CURTAIN RISES, THE FAMILY HAVE JUST 12 JOURNE
FINISHED BREAKFAST.
JAMIE RISES FROM HIS CHAIR AND, TAKING OFF HIS 41 JOURNE
COAT, GOES TO THE DOOR.
THE FAMILY ARE RETURNING FROM LUNCH AS THE CURTAIN 71 JOURNE
RISES.
(SHE RISES FROM THE ARM OF HIS CHAIR AND GOES TO 94 JOURNE
STARE OUT THE WINDOWS AT RIGHT
AS THE CURTAIN RISES, SHE IS STANDING BY THE 98 JOURNE
SCREEN DOOR LOOKING OUT.
(RISES FROM HER CHAIR, HER FACE LIGHTING UP 108 JOURNE
LOVINGLY--WITH EXCITED EAGERNESS.)
AS THE CURTAIN RISES, THE FOGHORN IS HEARD, 125 JOURNE
AS THE CURTAIN RISES, HE FINISHES A GAME AND 125 JOURNE
SWEEPS THE CARDS TOGETHER.
EVEN RISES TO CONCERT PLAYING. 138 JOURNE
FOR A SECOND JAMIE REACTS PUGNACIOUSLY AND HALF 162 JOURNE
RISES FROM HIS CHAIR TO DO
(IN THE MIDST OF A SILENCE MORE AWKWARD THAN 278 LAZARU
BEFORE HE RISES TO HIS FEET,
IN A GREAT, FULL-THROATED PAEAN AS THE LAUGHTER OF280 LAZARU
LAZARUS RISES HIGHER AND
THE WAIL OF LAMENTATION RISES AND FALLS. 292 LAZARU
HIS LAUGHTER RISES WITH MORE AND MORE SUMMONING 333 LAZARU
POWER.
FROM OUTSIDE, THE LAUGHTER OF LAZARUS RISES 337 LAZARU
AS THE CURTAIN RISES, SLAVES ARE HURRIEDLY PUTTING337 LAZARU
OUT THE MANY LAMPS.
HIS SHINY WHITE CRANIUM RISES LIKE A POLISHED 337 LAZARU
SHELL ABOVE HIS HALF-MASKED FACE.
TIBERIUS RISES FROM HIS COUCH TO BEND OVER WITH 347 LAZARU
CRUEL GLOATING.
THIS SOUND HAS RISEN TO ITS GREATEST VOLUME AS THE364 LAZARU
CURTAIN RISES.)
THEN AS HIS LAUGHTER RISES, THEY BEGIN TO LAUGH 366 LAZARU
WITH HIM.)
FOLLOWED BY A FAINT DYING NOTE OF LAUGHTER THAT 371 LAZARU
RISES AND IS LOST IN THE SKY
(LIFTS HIS HEAD AT THE FIRST SOUND AND RISES WITH 371 LAZARU
THE LAUGHTER TO HIS FEET.
AS THE CURTAIN RISES, SARA (MRS. 1 MANSNS
AS THE CURTAIN RISES, 43 MANSNS
AS THE CURTAIN RISES, SIMON ENTERS AT REAR AND 69 MANSNS
COMES TO HIS TABLE.
AS THE CURTAIN RISES, DEBORAH IS READING FROM A 95 MANSNS
VOLUME OF BYRON'S POEMS.
HE ALSO RISES. 114 MANSNS
AS THE CURTAIN RISES, SARA IS SITTING IN THE CHAIR117 MANSNS
AT LEFT-FRONT OF THE TABLE,
FOR A MOMENT AFTER THE CURTAIN RISES THERE IS AN 117 MANSNS
ATMOSPHERE OF TENSE QUIET
SARA'S ANGER RISES.) 168 MANSNS

RISES (CONT'D.)

IT RISES SOFTLY AND AS SOFTLY DIES AWAY UNTIL IT 354 MARCOM
IS NOTHING BUT A FAINT SOUND OF
SUDDENLY A SHOUT RISES FROM THE LIPS OF ALL THE 375 MARCOM
TARTARS.
IT RISES IN THREE TIERS, THREE STEPS TO A TIER. 377 MARCOM
THE CURTAIN THEN RISES DISCOVERING THE SCENE AS 407 MARCOM
ABOVE.
COMES FROM THE LEFT JUST BEFORE THE CURTAIN RISES)407 MARCOM
(AFTER A BROODING PAUSE SHE RISES AND CHANTS IN A 409 MARCOM
LOW VOICE)
(EVERYONE IN THE ROOM RISES WITH ONE MOTION OF 435 MARCOM
ASSERTION.)
KUBLAI REGAINS CONTROL OVER HIS WEAKNESS AND RISES435 MARCOM
TO HIS FEET--
HE RISES TO HIS FEET. 436 MARCOM
IN AN AISLE SEAT IN THE FIRST ROW A MAN RISES, 439 MARCOM
CONCEALS A YAWN IN HIS PALM.
(RISES FROM THE STEPS WITH THE BROOM HANDLE IN HER 15 MISBEG
RIGHT HAND)
(HE RISES FROM THE BOULDER THREATENINGLY) 15 MISBEG
EVERYWHERE THE SCUM RISES TO THE TOP. 37 POET
(SHE SHRINKS AWAY AND RISES TO HER FEET. 51 POET
HE HALF RISES FROM HIS CHAIR THREATENINGLY.) 51 POET
DEBORAH RISES TO HER FEET, IGNORING HIM 72 POET
DISDAINFULLY.
SHE SMILES PLEASANTLY AT SARA, WHO RISES 81 POET
GRACIOUSLY FROM HER CHAIR.)
HE RISES TO HIS FEET, A BIT STIFFLY AND CAREFULLY.103 POET
AND BOWS.
(SHE RISES SUDDENLY FROM HER CHAIR--WITH BRAVE 139 POET
DEFIANCE.)
(THE NOISE IN THE BAR RISES TO AN UPROAR OF 177 POET
LAUGHTER
BEYOND THE ROAD, THE EDGE OF A CLIFF WHICH RISES 577 ROPE
SHEER FROM THE SEA BELOW.
AS THE CURTAIN RISES MARY IS DISCOVERED SQUATTING 578 ROPE
CROSS-LEGGED ON THE FLOOR,
(LUKE RISES TO HIS FEET AND STANDS, WAITING IN A 594 ROPE
DEFENSIVE ATTITUDE.
(HIS VOICE RISES TO A THREATENING ROAR) 597 ROPE
(SWEENEY RISES. 600 ROPE
(HE RISES TO HIS FEET WITH NINA SLEEPING 46 STRANG
PEACEFULLY IN HIS ARMS.
AS THE CURTAIN RISES, JOHN CAN BE DIMLY 462 WELDED
DISTINGUISHED SITTING.
WHEN THE CURTAIN RISES. 470 WELDED
SHE HAS BEEN PULLING THE PINS OUT OF HER HAIR AND,474 WELDED
AS SHE RISES,

RISIN'
I COULD SEE CON'S RAGE RISIN' BUT HE KEPT POLITE. 155 POET

RISING
BUT THE GIN IS RISING TO HIS HEAD AND HE FEELS 240 AHWILD
PROUD OF HIMSELF AND DEVILISH
(RISING TO THE OCCASION) SURE/ 24 ANNA
AT THE RISING OF THE CURTAIN. 25 ANNA
(HER VOICE RISING ANGRILY) SAY, WHAT'RE YOU 26 ANNA
TRYING TO DO--MAKE THINGS ROTTEN8
(STUNG, RISING UNSTEADILY TO HIS FEET 32 ANNA
(WITH DIFFICULTY RISING TO A SITTING POSITION-- 33 ANNA
SCORNFULLY)
RISING TO HER FEET WITH A SIGH OF RELIEF) 33 ANNA
(RISING--PEERING AT HER FACE) 34 ANNA
(HER FACE AVERTED--RISING TO HER FEET--AGITATEDLY) 37 ANNA
WITH RISING ANGER) 42 ANNA
(WITH RISING IRRITATION) SOME DAY YOU'RE GOING TO 43 ANNA
GET ME SO MAD WITH THAT TALK,
(RISING TO HER FEET--BRUSQUELY) 43 ANNA
(HALF RISING FROM HIS CHAIR--IN A VOICE CHOKED 49 ANNA
WITH RAGE)
WITH RISING INTENSITY) 107 BEYOND
(RISING AND THROWING HER ARMS AROUND HIM-- 108 BEYOND
HYSTERICALLY)
HORIZON WHERE THE EDGE OF THE SUN'S DISC IS RISING168 BEYOND
FROM THE RIM OF THE HILLS)
(RISING TO HIS FEET WITH DRUNKEN DIGNITY) 467 CARIBE
(HIS VOICE RISING EXULTANTLY, HIS EYES ON THE FACE566 DAYS
OF THE CRUCIFIED)
(RISING ALSO AND PUTTING HER HANDS ON HIS 498 DIFRNT
SHOULDERS)
(THINKING MORE CLEARLY NOW--AN UNSTRUNG FURY 463 DYNAMO
RISING WITHIN HIM)
AND IT'S THE SEA RISING UP IN CLOUDS, FALLING ON 477 DYNAMO
THE EARTH IN RAIN.
RISING SHEER ON BOTH SIDES THE FOREST WALLS IT IN.192 EJONES
JONES' VOICE IS HEARD FROM THE LEFT RISING AND 199 EJONES
FALLING IN THE LONG
HIS CROON, RISING TO INTENSITY, IS PUNCTUATED BY 201 EJONES
SHRILL CRIES.
(TAKING HIS HANDS OFF HER SHOULDERS AND RISING) 99 ELECTR
THE MOON IS RISING ABOVE THE HORIZON OFF LEFT 102 ELECTR
REAR.
(THEN HER VOICE RISING AS IF IT WERE ABOUT TO 167 ELECTR
BREAK HYSTERICALLY--
THE SUN WILL BE RISING AGAIN. 322 GGBROW
(THERE HAD BEEN A GRADUAL MURMUR OF CONTEMPTUOUS 212 HA APE
RESENTMENT RISING AMONG THE MEN
AND RISING ABOVE ALL, MAKING THE AIR HUM WITH THE 223 HA APE
QUIVER OF LIBERATED ENERGY,
ONE--TWO--TREE--(HIS VOICE RISING EXULTANTLY IN 224 HA APE
THE JOY OF BATTLE)
WITH RISING VOLUME) WELL/ WELL// WELL/// (THEY 638 ICEMAN
ALL JUMP STARTLEDLY.
(WITH RISING ANGER, TO THE OTHERS) 654 ICEMAN
(WITH RISING ANGER.) NO, YOU CAN'T. 31 JOURNE
(IN A QUAVERING RISING AND FALLING CHANT-- 275 LAZARU
(RISING AND LOOKING AROUND HIM AT EVERYONE AND 278 LAZARU
EVERYTHING--

RISING (CONT'D.)
(THREATENINGLY, GRADUALLY RISING TO HATRED) 288 LAZARU
LIKE THE RISING AND FALLING CADENCES OF WAVES ON A303 LAZARU
BEACH)
IS HEARD RISING FROM HIS LIPS LIKE A SONG.) 308 LAZARU
(SUDDENLY RISING TO HIS FEET HE CALLS IMPLORINGLY)364 LAZARU
(RISING TO HER FEET LIKE ONE IN A TRANCE, STARING 366 LAZARU
TOWARD LAZARUS)
RISING CLEAR AND PASSIONATELY WITH THAT OF 367 LAZARU
LAZARUS, THEN DYING QUICKLY OUT.)
(WITH RESENTFUL JEALOUSY AND RAGE--IN A VOICE 368 LAZARU
RISING TO A SCREAM)
(RISING--IN A TONE OF ARROGANT PLEASURE.) 5 MANSNS
(RISING TO HER FEET.) NO/ 36 MANSNS
(RISING AS SHE ENTERS--SMILINGLY.) 44 MANSNS
(ABRUPTLY SHE TURNS ON SIMON--WITH RISING BITTER 155 MANSNS
ANGER.)
(LAUGHS SOFTLY AND SEDUCTIVELY, RISING TO HER 164 MANSNS
FEET.)
(RISING--PALE AND TREMBLING) 361 MARCOM
THE SLOWLY-RISING LIGHT REVEALS AN INDIAN SNAKE- 369 MARCOM
CHARMER
RISING AND FALLING IN A WORDLESS CHANT. 373 MARCOM
AND HUM A RISING AND FALLING MOURNING 436 MARCOM
ACCOMPANIMENT.)
(HIS TEMPER RISING AGAIN) AND I KNOW DAMNED WELL 13 MISBEG
HE HADN'T.
(SO OVERCOME BY A RISING TIDE OF SAVAGE, 122 POET
HUMILIATED FURY,
(IN SPITE OF HERSELF HER TEMPER HAS BEEN RISING. 155 POET
AT THE RISING OF THE CURTAIN SOME TRAILING CLOUDS 577 ROPE
NEAR THE HORIZON.
(AGAIN--HALF-RISING--FRIGHTENEDLY) 42 STRANG
THEY KISS EACH OTHER WITH RISING PASSION. 187 STRANG

RISK
YOU MIGHT THINK OF ME FOR A CHANGE, AFTER ALL THE 278 AHWILD
RISK I'VE RUN TO SEE YOU/
DO YOU WANT TO TAKE THE RISK OF DRIVING PETER TO 173 ELECTR
DO WHAT ORIN DIDS
I DIDN'T WANT TO RUN ANY RISK GETTING INTO MORE 278 GGBROW
I'D RISK A QUID OF MY NEXT PAY DAY THAT HIS REAL 522 INZONE
NAME IS SCHMIDT.
YOU SHOULD HAVE MORE SENSE THAN TO RISK-- 130 JOURNE
I RUN THE RISK YOU'LL HATE ME--AND YOU'RE ALL I'VE166 JOURNE
GOT LEFT.
I HAVE SAVED YOU, LAZARUS--AT THE RISK OF MY OWN 338 LAZARU
LIFE--
YOU WILL RUN NO RISK OF ANYTHING WORSE THAN YOUR 111 MANSNS
PRESENT UNHAPPY EXILE.
HE SAVED MY LIFE THREE TIMES AT THE RISK OF HIS 424 MARCOM
OWN.
UH, I'D GET DOWN ON MY KNEES TO YOU, DON'T MAKE MY 62 STRANG
BUY RUN THAT RISKY
(HOLDING ON TO A STANCHION AND LEANING FAR OUT AT 181 STRANG
THE IMMINENT RISK OF FALLING

RISKED
THERE'S NOTHING RISKED, THERE'S NOTHING GAINED. 356 MARCOM

RISKIN'
HERE I'M SWEATIN' BLOOD IN THE ARMY AFTER RISKIN' 523 DIFRNT
MY LIFE IN FRANCE

RISKS
I DO THINK YOU'VE GOT AN AWFUL NERVE TO SAY THAT 278 AHWILD
AFTER ALL THE RISKS I'VE RUN
(FORCING A JOKING TONE) LITTLE YOU KNOW THE 14 STRANG
DEADLY RISKS I RAN, NINA/

RIST
THE RIST OF THIN'LL BE COMIN' FOR'ARD WHIN SHE 463 CARIBE
COMES.
LUKE THE RIST AV USS 517 INZONE
YOU'RE AS LOONY AS THE RIST OF YOUR BREED. 590 ROPE
YE'D NEVER SHED A TEAR THE RIST AV YOUR LOIFE. 498 VOYAGE

RITE
AS IF HE WERE GUESSING AT THE PASSWORD TO SOME 246 HA APE
SECRET RITE.
THE ORDINARY FAMILY RITE, YOU'LL REMEMBER/ 448 WELDED

RITUAL
WITH THE OLD SURFACE RITUAL OF COVETING OUR 170 STRANG
NEIGHBOR'S ASS)

RIVRANCE
THAT HIS RIVRANCE LIKED WHEN THE WEATHER WAS 96 POET
COULD.

RIVAL
I NEVER KNEW YOU WENC MY HATED RIVAL, CHARLIE/. 114 STRANG
HIS RIVAL IN YOUR LOVE. 143 STRANG

RIVER
WE'LL TAKE IT WITH US FUR LUCK AN' LET 'ER SAIL 221 DESIRE
FREE DOWN SOME RIVER.
A SOFT OVERTONE OF RUSHING WATER FROM THE DAM AND 473 DYNAMO
THE RIVER BED BELOW,
MADE THAT RIVER THAT DRIVES THE TURBINES THAT 477 DYNAMO
DRIVE DYNAMO/
THE RAISED RIVER BANK IS IN THE NEARER BACKGROUND.199 EJONES
BEYOND THIS THE SURFACE OF THE RIVER SPREADS OUT, 199 EJONES
(THE FOOT OF A GIGANTIC TREE BY THE EDGE OF A 199 EJONES
GREAT RIVER.
SEEMS LIKE I KNOW DAT TREE--AN' DEM STONES--AN' * 200 EJONES
DE RIVER.
THE MOONLIT SURFACE OF THE RIVER BEYOND AND PASSES200 EJONES
HIS HAND OVER HIS HEAD
(THE WITCH DOCTOR SPRINGS TO THE RIVER BANK. 201 EJONES
THE WITCH DOCTOR POINTS WITH HIS WAND TO THE 201 EJONES
SACRED TREE, TO THE RIVER BEYOND,
THE HEAD OF THE CROCODILE SLVKS BACK BEHIND THE 202 EJONES
RIVER BANK.
"UH, SHENANDOAH, I LUNG TO HEAR YOUR A-WAY, MY 6 ELECTR
ROLLING RIVER OH, SHENANDOAH,
"UH, SHENANDOAH, I LONG TO HEAR YOU A-WAY, MY 43 ELECTR
ROLLING RIVER.

RIVER

RIVER (CONT'D.)
= OH, SHENANDOAH, I LOVE YOUR DAUGHTER A-WAY, MY 43 ELECTR
ROLLING RIVER.=
A-WAY, MY ROLLING RIVER/ 103 ELECTR
= OH, SHENANDOAH, I LOVE YOUR DAUGHTER A-WAY, MY 103 ELECTR
ROLLING RIVER/
=OH, SHENANDOAH, I LONG TO HEAR YOU A-WAY, MY 123 ELECTR
ROLLING RIVER/
=OH, SHENANDOAH, I LOVE YOUR DAUGHTER A-WAY, YOU 169 ELECTR
ROLLING RIVER.=
=OH, SHENANDOAH, I LONG TO HEAR YOU A-WAY, MY 169 ELECTR
ROLLING RIVER. OH, SHENANDOAH.
A GREAT MISTAKE I MISSED HIM AT THE BATTLE OF 598 ICEMAN
MODDER RIVER.
OR DERE'S A LITTLE IRON ROOM UP DE RIVER WAITIN' 601 ICEMAN
FOR YOU/
HE MUST BE SWIMMIN' IN DE NORTH RIVER YET/ 617 ICEMAN
I SAW THEM COME BEFORE--AT MODDER RIVER, 677 ICEMAN
MAGERSFONTEIN, SPION KOP--
COME ON, NOW, SHOW US A LITTLE OF THAT GOOD OLD 685 ICEMAN
BATTLE OF MODDER RIVER SPIRIT
NEXT TIME I SHIP ON WINDJAMMER BOSTON TO RIVER 515 INZONE
PLATE,
AN' THEY WILL SURELY GUIDE YOU 'CROSS THE FORD O' 155 JOURNE
KABUL RIVER IN THE DARK.=
=FORD, FORD, FORD O' KABUL RIVER, FORD O' KABUL 155 JOURNE
RIVER IN THE DARK/
(WITH DEEP EMOTION) YOU HAVE BEEN A GOLDEN BIRD 385 MARCOM
SINGING BESIDE A BLACK RIVER.
THE RIVER WAS NOT SO BLACK--THE RIVER OF MAN'S 385 MARCOM
LIFE SO DEEP AND SILENT--
THE RIVER SEEMS BLACK INDEED/ 386 MARCOM
HERE, YOUR MAJESTY, IS THE LINE OF THE RIVER. 421 MARCOM
DANUBE
HERE'S THE RIVER TAGUS. 96 POET
I CANTERED THE MARE BY THE RIVER AND SHE PULLED UP108 POET
LAKE.
CHARLIE SITS BESIDE THE FIERCE RIVER, IMMACULATELY 13 STRANG
TIMID, COOL AND CLOTHED.
LOOKING UP THE RIVER THROUGH A PAIR OF BINOCULARS.158 STRANG
THAT GLOWS ON THE RIVER. 158 STRANG
THERE'S A DAMNED HAZE ON THE RIVER/ 159 STRANG
(SHE LOOKS UP THE RIVER THROUGH THE GLASSES.) 159 STRANG
(RAISING THE BINOCULARS AS HE GOES TO THE RAIL, HE171 STRANG
LOOKS UP THE RIVER)
(LOOKING UP THE RIVER--WITH VINDICTIVE 171 STRANG
BITTERNESS--THINKING)
(HE RAISES HIS GLASSES AND LOOKS UP THE RIVER-- 174 STRANG
THINKING EXULTANTLY)
(HE SINGS RAUCOUSLY) =OH, WE'LL ROW, ROW, ROW, 175 STRANG
RIGHT DOWN THE RIVER/
THEY RUN TO THE RAIL AND TRAIN THEIR GLASSES UP 176 STRANG
THE RIVER.)
(THE WHISTLES AND SIRENS FROM THE YACHTS UP THE 176 STRANG
RIVER BEGIN TO BE HEARD.
(SHE HURRIES OVER TO HER, GLANCING EAGERLY OVER 178 STRANG
HER SHOULDER TOWARDS THE RIVER)
LOOKING UP THE RIVER. 180 STRANG

RIVERS
YOU'RE SETTING NO RIVERS ON FIRE/ 164 JOURNE
THE CLIMATE IS SO HOT IF YOU PUT AN EGG IN THEIR 370 MARCOM
RIVERS IT WILL BE BOILED.

RIVETED
WHOSE EYES ARE RIVETED ON THE PRINCESS, WHO HAS 419 MARCOM
TURNED AWAY FROM THEM.

RIVETS
MY BELLY FEELS LOIKE I'D SWALLEYED A DOZEN RIVETS 480 CARDIF
AT THE THOUGHT AV UT/

RIVULETS
RIVULETS OF SOOTY SWEAT HAVE TRACED MAPS ON THEIR 224 HA APE
BACKS.

RIZ
LOOKS 'S IF THE SUN WAS FULL RIZ A'MOST. 263 DESIRE
YIT CAN'T BE, WHEN DE MOON'S JES' RIZ. 191 EJONES
AND NOW HE'S RIZ TO BE GENERAL. 8 ELECTR

RIZEN
DE MOON'S RIZEN. 191 EJONES

RIZIN'
SUN'S A-RIZIN'. 269 DESIRE

ROAD
I'LL TAKE THE AUTO AND DRIVE OUT THE BEACH ROAD-- 260 AHWILD
ON THE ROAD TO MANDALAY/ 288 AHWILD
THE ROAD RUNS DIAGONALLY FROM THE LEFT, FORWARD, 81 BEYOND
TO THE RIGHT, REAR.
THE FORWARD TRIANGLE CUT OFF BY THE ROAD IS A 81 BEYOND
SECTION OF A FIELD FROM THE DARK
TO THE REAR OF THE ROAD IS A DITCH WITH A SLOPING, 81 BEYOND
GRASSY BANK ON THE FAR SIDE.
SEPARATES THIS FIELD FROM THE ROAD. 81 BEYOND
HIS BROTHER ANDREW COMES ALONG THE ROAD FROM THE 82 BEYOND
RIGHT.
(HE STEPS OVER THE DITCH TO THE ROAD WHILE HE IS 86 BEYOND
TALKING.)
(HE WALKS OFF DOWN THE ROAD TO THE LEFT. 86 BEYOND
I KNOW. I MET HIM ON THE ROAD A SECOND AGO. 87 BEYOND
I WOULDN'T TAKE A VOYAGE ACROSS THE ROAD 88 BEYOND
(AFTER A SLIGHT PAUSE) AND OTHER TIMES MY EYES 89 BEYOND
WOULD FOLLOW THIS ROAD,
AND I'D PROMISE MYSELF THAT WHEN I GREW UP AND WAS 89 BEYOND
STRONG, I'D FOLLOW THAT ROAD,
THEM, DANCE WITH THEM DOWN THE ROAD IN THE DUSK IN 90 BEYOND
A GAME OF HIDE-AND-SEEK TO
LIFTING RUTH IN HIS ARMS AND CARRYING HER TO THE 92 BEYOND
ROAD WHERE HE PUTS HER DOWN.)
A WINDOW LOOKING OUT ON THE ROAD. 93 BEYOND
GATE IN THE WHITE PICKET FENCE WHICH BORDERS THE 112 BEYOND
ROAD.

ROAD (CONT'D.)
LITTLE MARY, I'D CHUCK EVERYTHING UP AND WALK DOWN126 BEYOND
THE ROAD
YOU WERE SAYING YOU'D GO OUT ON THE ROAD IF IT 127 BEYOND
WASN'T FOR ME.
THE NOISE OF A HORSE AND CARRIAGE COMES FROM THE 128 BEYOND
ROAD BEFORE THE HOUSE.
THEY HEAR ANDY'S VOICE FROM THE ROAD SHOUTING A 128 BEYOND
LONG HAIL--AHOY THERE/=
HE'S WAITING FOR YOU AT THE ROAD. 135 BEYOND
AS THE CAR STOPS ON THE ROAD BEFORE THE FARMHOUSE.153 BEYOND
RUTH AND ANDREW COME HURRIEDLY ALONG THE ROAD FROM167 BEYOND
THE LEFT.)
IN A DITCH BY THE OPEN ROAD--WATCHING THE SUN 167 BEYOND
RISE.
THEY PASS BY ON THE ROAD AT NIGHTS COMING BACK TO 564 CROSS
THEIR FARMS FROM TOWN.
AH WELL, IT'S A ROCKY ROAD, FULL OF TWISTS AND 504 DAYS
BLIND ALLEYS, ISN'T IT, JACK--
I MEAN, UNTIL THE ROAD FINALLY TURNS BACK TOWARD 504 DAYS
HOME.
WITH A WOODEN GATE AT CENTER OPENING ON A COUNTRY 202 DESIRE
ROAD.
DOWN THE ROAD TO THE RIGHT. 203 DESIRE
I'M GOIN' OUT FUR A SPELL--UP THE ROAD. 210 DESIRE
ROAD--IN THE SAME NIGHT. 211 DESIRE
(HE STRIDES OFF DOWN THE ROAD TO THE LEFT.) 212 DESIRE
WE'LL BE KICKIN' UP AN' TEARIN' AWAY DOWN THE 221 DESIRE
ROAD/
(HE PICKS A STONE FROM THE ROAD. 224 DESIRE
HE COMES TO THE GATE AND LOOKS DOWN THE ROAD THE 226 DESIRE
BROTHERS HAVE GONE.
TO THE ROAD WITH A GRAND SWAGGER OF IGNORING HER 228 DESIRE
EXISTENCE.
OH--UP THE ROAD A SPELL-- 229 DESIRE
(HE TURNS AND STRIDES OFF UP THE ROAD. 230 DESIRE
AN' TALK O' TURNIN' ME OUT IN THE ROAD. 233 DESIRE
GIT OUT O' MY ROAD/ 250 DESIRE
AN' THE DUST O' THE ROAD--THAT'S YOU'RN/ 255 DESIRE
GIT OUT O' MY ROAD/ 255 DESIRE
AN' I'LL KICK YE BOTH OUT IN THE ROAD--T' BEG AN' 257 DESIRE
SLEEP IN THE WOODS--
AND BREAKS INTO A SWERVING SPRINT DOWN THE ROAD.) 262 DESIRE
THE SHERIFF WITH TWO MEN COMES UP THE ROAD FROM 268 DESIRE
THE LEFT.
PEERING DOWN THE ROAD, 435 DYNAMO
HAS OVERSEER OVAH US WHEN WE'RE LUKIN' DE ROAD. 181 EJONES
IT IS AS IF THE FOREST HAD STOOD ASIDE MOMENTARILY192 EJONES
TO LET THE ROAD PASS THROUGH
A WIDE DIRT ROAD RUNS DIAGONALLY FROM RIGHT, 192 EJONES
FRONT, TO LEFT, REAR.
AND THE ROAD WILL BE NO MORE. 192 EJONES
UNDER ITS LIGHT THE ROAD GLIMMERS GHASTLY AND 192 EJONES
UNREAL.
HO'D IS ROAD EVAH GIT HEAH? 193 EJONES
GOOD LEVEL ROAD, TOO. 193 EJONES
ABOUT HIM WITH NUMBED SURPRISE WHEN HE SEES THE 193 EJONES
ROAD.
AND AT THAT SIGNAL ALL THE CONVICTS START TO WORK 194 EJONES
ON THE ROAD.
UN THE ROAD OPPOSITE WHERE JONES IS SITTING. 194 EJONES
THE ROAD AND THE FIGURES OF THE CONVICT GANG ARE 195 EJONES
BLOTTED OUT.
CAPTAIN LEWIS'S, =THE OLD KENT ROAD.= 727 ICEMAN
YOU'RE TALKIN' MORE THAN A PAIR AV AULD WOMEN 518 INZONE
WOULD BE STANDIN' IN THE ROAD.
IF I HADN'T LEFT HIM WITH MY MOTHER TO JOIN YOU ON 87 JOURNE
THE ROAD.
I CAN'T SEE THE ROAD. 102 JOURNE
THE POORHOUSE IS THE END UF THE ROAD, AND IT MIGHT128 JOURNE
AS WELL BE SOONER AS LATER.
OUT BEYOND THE HARBOR, WHERE THE ROAD RUNS ALONG 131 JOURNE
THE BEACH.
YOU'VE DRAGGED HER AROUND ON THE ROAD, SEASON 141 JOURNE
AFTER SEASON, ON ONE-NIGHT STANDS,
I NEVER DRAGGED HER ON THE ROAD AGAINST HER WILL. 142 JOURNE
UN THE LEFT, A DOORWAY OPENING ON A ROAD WHERE A 271 LAZARU
CROWD OF MEN HAS GATHERED.
AT THE EXTREME FRONT IS A ROAD. 281 LAZARU
ON THE ROAD IN THE FOREGROUND, AT LEFT AND RIGHT, 282 LAZARU
COMES DOWN THE PATH TO THE ROAD. 293 LAZARU
(BEWILDEREDLY.) BUT WHY DUN'T WE WALK TOGETHER AS 17 MANSNS
FAR AS THE ROADS.
AND BEG PENNIES WITH MY CHILDREN, ON THE ROAD, 20 MANSNS
HE GREATLY RESEMBLES A YOUTH I SAW BACK ON THE 367 MARCOM
ROAD
THE SAME PATH ALSO EXTENDS LEFT TO JOIN A DIRT 1 MISBEG
ROAD WHICH LEADS UP FROM THE
(GLANCING DOWN THE ROAD, OFF LEFT-FRONT) 35 MISBEG
JIM TYRONE ENTERS ALONG THE ROAD FROM THE HIGHWAY, 36 MISBEG
LEFT.)
AND THE ROAD IS HARD MACADAM WITH DIVIL A SPEC OF 44 MISBEG
DUST.
HOGAN PEERS AT THE ROAD OFF LEFT) 52 MISBEG
(LOOKING OFF LEFT) THERE'S TWO HORSEBACK RIDERS 54 MISBEG
ON THE COUNTY ROAD NOW.
JOSIE TAKES HER STAND WHERE THE PATH MEETS THE 61 MISBEG
ROAD.
(FROM DOWN THE ROAD. 71 MISBEG
AND IF I WAS SINGING COMING ALONG THE ROAD, 75 MISBEG
AND I MADE MYSELF SING ON THE ROAD SO HE'D HEAR, 86 MISBEG
AND THEY'D ALL HEAR IN THE INN,
THERE'S SOMEONE ON THE ROAD-- 98 MISBEG
(HE STARTS OFF DOWN THE ROAD, LEFT-FRONT, WITH A 101 MISBEG
LAST WORD OVER HIS SHOULDER)
FROM FAR-OFF ON THE ROAD TO THE INN, 103 MISBEG
(HE SHRUGS HIS SHOULDERS HOPELESSLY AND TURNS 139 MISBEG
TOWARD THE ROAD.)

ROAD (CONT'D.)
(HE TURNS TOWARD THE ROAD--BITTERLY) 140 MISBEG
(HE TURNS TOWARD THE ROAD.) 173 MISBEG
(HE TURNS AWAY AND WALKS QUICKLY DOWN THE ROAD OFFL75 MISBEG
LEFT WITHOUT LOOKING BACK.
SHE FOLLOWS HIM AS FAR AS THE DOOR--THEN TURNS FORI77 MISBEG
A LAST LOOK DOWN THE ROAD.)
SHE ASKED ME WHAT ROAD WOULD TAKE HER NEAR THE 18 POET
LAKE--
FATHER FLYNN STOPPED ME ON THE ROAD YESTERDAY AND 26 POET
TOLD ME
OH, HE'S ON THE ROAD TO RECOVERY NOW, 28 POET
YOU MUST BE PARCHED AFTER WALKING FROM THE ROAD TO 85 POET
SIMON'S CABIN AND BACK ON
BEYOND THE ROAD, THE EDGE OF A CLIFF WHICH RISES 577 ROPE
SHEER FROM THE SEA BELOW.
THE FAINT TRACE OF WHAT WAS ONCE A ROAD LEADING TO577 ROPE
THE BARN.
MARY IS ABOUT SIX FEET BEYOND HIM ON THE OTHER 589 ROPE
SIDE OF THE ROAD.

ROADS
HAPPY ROADS IS BUNK. WEARY ROADS IS RIGHT. 161 JOURNE
THE HAPPY ROADS THAT TAKE YOU O'ER THE WORLD,* 161 JOURNE
MY LOVE HAS FOLLOWED YOU OVER LONG ROADS AMONG 345 LAZARU
STRANGERS
AND WENT OUT AS A BEGGAR ON THE ROADS TO SEEK THE 372 MARCOM
SUPREME ENLIGHTENMENT

ROADSIDE
THE ROADSIDE, HOWEVER, IS STILL STEEPED IN THE 166 BEYOND
GRAYNESS OF THE DAWN.
MECHANICAL GESTURES OF DIGGING UP DIRT, AND 194 EJONES
THROWING IT TO THE ROADSIDE.

ROADSTERS
I'D TELL HIM I BOUGHT ONE OF THOSE MERCEDES SPORT 32 HUGHIE
ROADSTERS

ROAM
AND TO POSSESS, AND ROAM ALONG, THE WORLD'S TIRED 101 POET
DENIZEN,

ROAMIN'
AS I WAS A-ROAMIN' DOWN PARADISE STREET-- 459 CARIBE
AS I WAS A-ROAMIN' DOWN PARADISE STREET--GIVE US 460 CARIBE
SOME TIME TO BLOW THE MAN DOWN/
(TO ANNIE) WHAT'S GOT INTO HIM TO BE ROAMIN' UP 582 ROPE
HERE'S

ROAMING
BUT FOR THE LIKE OF US DOES BE ROAMING THE SEAS, A 36 ANNA
GOOD END, I'M TELLING YOU--
WAS IT FOR THIS HE'D HAVE ME ROAMING THE EARTH 60 ANNA
SINCE I WAS A LAD ONLY,
AND 'TIS GREAT BAD LUCK IT'S SAVED ME FROM AND ME 75 ANNA
ROAMING THE SEAS,
THE FLYING DUTCHMAN THEY SAY DOES BE ROAMING THE 214 HA APE
SEAS FOREVERMORE

ROAR
TOMMY AND MILDRED ROAR WITH GLEE. 222 AHWILD
(THE CHILDREN ROAR. 231 AHWILD
(HE IS INTERRUPTED BY A ROAR OF LAUGHTER FROM THE 478 CARDIF
OTHERS.)
THERE IS A ROAR OF VOICES FROM INSIDE. 468 CARIBE
A ROAR OF LAUGHTER GOES UP. 472 CARIBE
(THEY BOTH ROAR WITH COARSE LAUGHTER. 211 DESIRE
(A ROAR OF LAUGHTER. 248 DESIRE
(A ROAR OF LAUGHTER.) 249 DESIRE
(A ROAR OF LAUGHTER IN WHICH CABOT JOINS 249 DESIRE
UPROARIOUSLY.)
THEN HE AND ROGERS ROAR WITH LAUGHTER AND HARRIET 507 DIFRNT
CANNOT RESTRAIN A GIGGLE AND
BEFORE SHE HAS A CHANCE TO REPLY A ROAR OF 510 DIFRNT
LAUGHTER COMES FROM THE NEXT ROOM AS
(HE AND ROGERS ROAR DELIGHTEDLY. 511 DIFRNT
(THEY ALL ROAR WITH LAUGHTER. 132 ELECTR
THERE IS A DEAFENING METALLIC ROAR, 216 HA APE
IT'S ME MAKES IT ROAR/ 216 HA APE
THE ROAR OF LEAPING FLAMES IN THE FURNACES, 223 HA APE
(THERE IS A ROAR OF RAGE FROM ALL SIDES.) 228 HA APE
(ANOTHER ROAR OF LAUGHTER.) 230 HA APE
(THERE IS A ROAR OF LAUGHTER FROM ALL.) 230 HA APE
(SEEING A FIGHT--WITH A ROAR OF JOY AS HE SPRINGS 239 HA APE
TO HIS FEET)
(THEY ALL ROAR WITH LAUGHTER AT THIS BURLESQUE 619 ICEMAN
THEY ARE LONGING TO LAUGH, AND AS HE FINISHES THEY627 ICEMAN
ROAR.
(THERE IS A ROAR OF LAUGHTER. 628 ICEMAN
(THERE IS ANOTHER ROAR OF LAUGHTER. 628 ICEMAN
(A ROAR OF DERISIVE, DIRTY LAUGHTER. 662 ICEMAN
AND THEY STOP SINGING TO ROAR WITH LAUGHTER. 727 ICEMAN
(THERE IS A ROAR OF MOCKING LAUGHTER FROM THE 321 LAZARU
LEGIONARIES.)
AN EXAMPLE FOR OTHER LIONS--NOT TO ROAR--OR 320 LAZARU
LAUGH--AT CAESAR/
(THERE IS A ROAR OF LAUGHTER IN WHICH TEDALDO 361 MARCOM
JOINS.
(A ROAR OF COARSE TAUNTING LAUGHTER FROM THE MEN. 368 MARCOM
THERE IS A ROAR OF LAUGHTER.) 371 MARCOM
DRUNKEST, AND DOESN'T ROAR AROUND CURSING AND 27 MISBEG
SINGING, LIKE SOME I COULD NAME.
(HE BURSTS INTO AN EXTRAVAGANT ROAR OF LAUGHTER, 58 MISBEG
SLAPPING HIS THIGH.
WON'T A ROAR INSIDE ME WHEN I SEE HIS FACE IN THE 95 MISBEG
MORNING/
(ROCHE AND O'DOWD ROAR AFTER HIM, BEATING TIME ON 96 POET
THE TABLE WITH THEIR GLASSES--
A ROAR OF WELCOME IS HEARD AS THE CROWD GREETS HIS165 POET
ARRIVAL.
THAT'LL MAKE THEM ROAR THE HOUSE DOWN. 178 POET
(AS ANOTHER ROAR IS HEARD FROM THE BAR.) 178 POET.
THERE IS A ROAR OF WELCOMING DRUNKEN SHOUTS, 180 POET
(HIS VOICE RISES TO A THREATENING ROAR) 597 ROPE

ROAR (CONT'D.)
(THE ROAR OF THE ENGINE GROWS STEADILY NEARER NOW)198 STRANG
(THERE IS A ROAR OF LAUGHTER.) 500 VOYAGE

ROARIN'
ROARIN' MAD WID THE THIRST. 482 CARDIF
AND THERE WAS YANK ROARIN' CURSES AND TURNING 229 HA APE
AROUND WID HIS SHOVEL TO BRAIN HER--
HE PUSHED IT BACK ON HIM AND LEPT IN THE HALL, 155 POET
ROARIN' MAD,
ROARIN' WID RAGE AND CURSIN' LIKE A TROOPER-- 157 POET
I'M ROARIN' MESELF INSIDE ME. 166 POET
DON'T BE ROARIN'/ 597 ROPE

ROARING
(MILLER AND HIS WIFE AND THE CHILDREN ARE ALL 233 AHWILD
ROARING WITH LAUGHTER.
I'LL BE ROARING IT OUT LIKE A FOG HORN OVER THE 39 ANNA
SEA
ROARING AND NEVER A GROAN OUT OF ME TILL THE SEA 48 ANNA
GAVE UP AND IT SEEING THE GREAT
(SUDDENLY ROARING WITH RAGE) 223 DESIRE
DRUNKEN MIRTH, ROARING WITH LAUGHTER, POUNDING 134 ELECTR
EACH OTHER ON THE BACK.)
(THEY POUND THEIR GLASSES ON THE TABLE, ROARING 728 ICEMAN
WITH LAUGHTER.
GOING TO THE MERCHANT GROUP WHO ARE ROARING WITH 367 MARCOM
LAUGHTER
(FROM THE BAY BELOW COMES THE ROARING HUM OF AN 198 STRANG
AIRPLANE MOTOR.
(ROARING INTO SONG) 498 VOYAGE

ROARS
(HE SUITS THE ACTION TO THE WORD AND ROARS WITH 470 CARIBE
MEANINGLESS LAUGHTER.)
HE GIVES CABOT NO CHANCE TO RETORT BUT ROARS) 250 DESIRE
HE ROARS *GOD DAMN YUH/* 226 HA APE
(THE GORILLA ROARS ANGRILY) SURE/ 253 HA APE
(THE GORILLA ROARS AN EMPHATIC AFFIRMATIVE.253 HA APE
THEN IT ROARS AND ROCKS AND RATTLES PAST THE 19 HUGHIE
NEARBY CORNER,
AND OTHER ROARS OF ACCLAIM MINGLED WITH THE MUSIC 180 POET
OF RILEY'S PIPES.
(HE ROARS WITH CHILDISH LAUGHTER, THEN SUDDENLY 506 VOYAGE
BECOMES SERIOUS)

ROAST
I'M WISHING THE WHOLE LOT OF THEM WILL ROAST IN 71 ANNA
HELL 'TIL THE JUDGMENT DAY--
WE ROAST THEM IN THEIR OWN SWEAT-- 229 HA APE
(RATHER MUFFLED BY ROAST PIG) 431 MARCOM
HELL ROAST HIS SOUL FOR SAYING IT. 18 MISBEG
MAY HE ROAST IN HELL AND HIS LIMEY SUPERINTENDENT 32 MISBEG
WITH HIM/
SPEAKIN' AV THE DEPARTED, MAY HIS SOUL ROAST IN 173 POET
HELL.
I'LL PRITIND TO MAKE FRIENDS WITH HIM, GOD ROAST 590 ROPE
HIS SOUL/
HELL ROAST THAT DIVIL AV A BO'SUN/ 497 VOYAGE

ROASTED
WHERE YOU ROASTED IN SUMMER, AND THERE WAS NO 148 JOURNE
STOVE IN WINTER,

ROASTING
I'D SEE HER ROASTING IN HELL FIRST/ 61 ANNA
WHICH HE DID SOON ENOUGH, AND DESERVED TO, AND I 147 JOURNE
HOPE HE'S ROASTING IN HELL.

TOASTS
ON WHICH ARE WHOLE PIGS, FOWL OF ALL VARIETIES, 428 MARCOM
ROASTS,

ROBBED
GAT DRUNK, GAT ROBBED, SHIP AVAY AGAIN ON ODER 28 ANNA
VOYAGE.
THE SEA THAT ROBBED ME OF MY ARM AND MADE ME THE 564 CROSS
BROKEN THING THAT I AM/
I BEEN ROBBED ONCE TONIGHT/ 104 ELECTR
BUT I WAS ROBBED, SIR--AYE--AN' I KNOW WHO DONE 106 ELECTR
IT--
SHE ROBBED ME ASLAPE--- 208 HA APE
AND DIVIL A CARE HOW YOU GOT IT, OR WHO YOU ROBBED163 MISBEG
OR MADE SUFFER/

ROBBER
I'LL GO TO THE POLICE STATION AND TELL 'EM THERE'S104 ELECTR
A ROBBER HERE--
HE HAS ME IN A CORNER, THE ROBBER/...)) 12 STRANG

ROBBERS
I HEER'D TELL ROBBERS BROKE IN THE 104 ELECTR

ROBBERY
WHO HASTENS TO ACQUIESCE IN THIS ROBBERY BY 209 HA APE
SAYING)

ROBBIE'LL
MAYBE ROBBIE'LL MANAGE TILL ANDY GETS BACK AND 115 BEYOND
SEES TO THINGS.

ROBBIE'S
(DULLY) ROBBIE'S ALWAYS LATE FOR THINGS. 113 BEYOND
ROBBIE'S HAD BAD LUCK AGAINST HIM. 116 BEYOND

ROBBING
WELL, IF YOU COULD SHAKE THE CRADLE-ROBBING ACT, 244 AHWILD
THERE WOULDN'T BE NO FUN ROBBING THE DEAD. 609 ICEMAN

ROBE
WEARING HIS BLACK JUDGE'S ROBE. 28 ELECTR
SHE IS DRESSED IN A BLACK KIMONO ROBE AND WEARS 320 GGBROW
SLIPPERS OVER HER BARE FEET.
THE TALL FIGURE OF LAZARUS, DRESSED IN A WHITE 288 LAZARU
ROBE.
FINGERS LAZARUS' ROBE INQUISITIVELY 308 LAZARU
LAZARUS, IN HIS ROBE OF WHITE AND GOLD, 312 LAZARU
PLUCKS AT HIS ROBE HUMBLY) 323 LAZARU
(HE FREES HIS DAGGER FROM UNDER HIS ROBE. 333 LAZARU
A VENERABLE OLD MAN WITH WHITE HAIR, DRESSED IN A 377 MARCOM
SIMPLE BLACK ROBE.
DRESSED IN A ROBE OF SILVER AND STANDS AT THE RAIL405 MARCOM
LOOKING DOWN.)

ROBE

RURE (CONT'D.)

DRESSED IN A GORGEOUS GOLDEN ROBE OF CEREMONY, 407 MARCOM
(HE SLITS UP THE WIDE SLEEVES OF HIS OWN ROBE, AS 429 MARCOM
DO HIS FATHER AND UNCLE,
HE WEARS A SIMPLE WHITE ROBE WITHOUT ADORNMENT OF 432 MARCOM
ANY SORT,
GOING FURTH THE BEST ROBE, AND PUT IT ON HIM.. 594 ROPE

RUBED

WITH BOWED HEAD THE BLACK-ROBED FIGURE OF MIRIAM 333 LAZARU
FOLLOWS HIM,

ROBERT

(WRITING) ROBERT SMITH, 246 HA APE

RUBES

IN HIS JUDGE'S ROBES, 149 ELECTR
THEY ARE DRESSD IN BRIGHT-COLORED DIAPHANOUS 285 LAZARU
ROBES,
ON EACH SIDE, MEMBERS OF THE SENATE ARE SEATED IN 312 LAZARU
THEIR WHITE ROBES,
MIRIAM IS KNEELING IN HER BLACK RUBES, SWAYING 313 LAZARU
BACKWARD AND FORWARD,
THEY ARE DRESSED IN WOMEN'S ROBES OF PALE 336 LAZARU
HELIOTROPE,
THE SQUATTING FIGURES OF THE PEOPLE ARE CLOTHED IN373 MARCOM
ROUGH ROBES,
DRESSED IN HIS HEAVY GOLD ROBES OF STATE, 377 MARCOM
OVER THEIR RICH MERCHANT'S ROBES, 390 MARCOM
HE GIVES A SIGN AT WHICH THE THREE TAKE OFF THEIR 428 MARCOM
ROBES
BUT SUCH ROBES/ 428 MARCOM
ALL THREE ARE DRESSED IN LONG ROBES 428 MARCOM
MY GOOD MEN, YOU MAY SELL THESE RICH ROBES 428 MARCOM
(AT ANOTHER SIGNAL THE THREE POLOS TAKE OFF THEIR 429 MARCOM
BLUE ROBES.)
ALL ARE DRESSED IN DEEP BLACK WITH WHITE EDGING TO433 MARCOM
THEIR ROBES,
FIRST COME THE MUSICIANS, NINE IN NUMBER, MEN IN 433 MARCOM
ROBES OF BRIGHT RED.

ROBESPIERRE

THAT PART ABOUT MIRABEAU--AND ABOUT MARAT AND 196 AHWILD
ROBESPIERRE--
NEVER YOU MIND ROBESPIERRE, YOUNG MAN/ 196 AHWILD
(TIPSILY) WELL, NOW THAT OUR LITTLE ROBESPIERRE 627 ICEMAN
HAS GOT THE DAILY BIT OF
HE WENT TO FRANCE AND BECAME A RABID JACOBIN, A 83 POET
WORSHIPER OF ROBESPIERRE,

ROBUST

HIS FORM MORE ROBUST, ERECT AND MUSCULAR, 567 CRUSS
HE IS SEVENTY, ABOUT JOHN AND LOVING'S HEIGHT, 500 DAYS
ERECT, ROBUST,
RATHER HE LOOKS MORE ROBUST AND YOUNGER, 230 DESIRE

RUCK

(SHE PICKS UP A MAGAZINE FROM THE TABLE AND BEGINS188 AHWILD
TO ROCK, FANNING HERSELF,)
(SHE WALKS TOWARD THE ROCK AND ADDRESSES ROBERT 135 BEYOND
COOLLY)
(SHE JUMPS LIGHTLY TO THE TOP OF A ROCK AND SITS 136 BEYOND
DOWN)
ANYBODY THAT WANTS THIS STINKIN' OLD ROCK-PILE OF 221 DESIRE
A FARM KIN HEV IT,
BUILD MY CHURCH ON A ROCK--OUT O' STONES AN' I'LL 237 DESIRE
BE IN THEM/
I GOT IT BE--LIKE A STONE--A ROCK IN JROUNDM'NT/ 264 DESIRE
BECAME THE SUN, THE HUT SAND, GREEN SEAWEED 153 JOURNE
ANCHORED TO A ROCK,
BY THE ROCK OF CASHEL, 36 POET
BE THE ROCK AV CASHEL, I'VE NIVIR ENGAGED IN A 154 POET
LIVELIER SHINDY/

ROCKER

(SHE SINKS IN ROCKER AT RIGHT OF TABLE) 188 AHWILD
HIS WIFE IN THE ROCKER AT RIGHT, FRONT, OF TABLE, 288 AHWILD
MILLER IS SITTING IN HIS ROCKER AT LEFT, FRONT, OF288 AHWILD
TABLE,
(CASUALLY, INDICATING MRS. MILLER'S ROCKER) SIT 239 DESIRE
DOWN, RICHARD,
A DILAPIDATED WICKER ROCKER, PAINTED BROWN, IS 41 ANNA
ALSO BY THE TABLE,
SHE SITS IN THE ROCKER IN FRONT OF THE TABLE AND 116 BEYOND
SIGHS WEARILY,
THE RUNG OF ONE ROCKER HAS BEEN CLUMSILY MENDED 144 BEYOND
WITH A PIECE OF PLAIN BOARD,
(HE WALKS WEAKLY TO A ROCKER BY THE SIDE OF THE 145 BEYOND
TABLE
HE COMES FORWARD AND SINKS DOWN IN THE ROCKER ON 154 BEYOND
THE RIGHT OF TABLE,
IS DISCOVERED SITTING IN A ROCKER AT THE END OF 228 DESIRE
THE PORCH,
(SHE PUSHES EMMA GENTLY INTO A ROCKER-- 507 DIFRNT
MRS, CROSBY HAS EFFICIENTLY BUSTLED ANOTHER ROCKER508 DIFRNT
BESIDE HER DAUGHTER'S
(HE LOWERS HIMSELF CAREFULLY TO A WOODEN PUSTURE 514 DIFRNT
ON THE EDGE OF A ROCKER NEAR
SHE IS SEATED IN A ROCKER BY THE TABLE, 519 DIFRNT
(SHE SITS IN A ROCKER BY THE TABLE,) 531 DIFRNT
(SHE PLUMPS HERSELF INTO A ROCKER BY THE TABLE-- 535 DIFRNT
HIS WIFE'S ROCKER IS AT THE RIGHT OF THE TABLE, 421 DYNAMO
THE REVEREND HUTCHINS LIGHT IS SEATED IN HIS 421 DYNAMO
ARMCHAIR, HIS WIFE IN HER ROCKER,
A VARNISHED OAK ROCKER WITH LEATHER BOTTOM, 12 JOURNE
HE LIGHTS HIS CIGAR AND SITS DOWN IN THE ROCKER AT 15 JOURNE
RIGHT OF TABLE,
(SHE SITS IN THE ROCKER AT RIGHT OF TABLE,) 99 JOURNE
AND TYRONE IN THE ROCKER AT RIGHT OF IT,) 108 JOURNE
THERE IS A FAIR-SIZED TABLE, A HEAVY ARMCHAIR, A 3 STRANG
ROCKER,
IS ARRANGED TOWARD THE LEFT OF THE ROOM, THE 3 STRANG
ROCKER IS AT CENTER,
ROCKER,) 7 STRANG

RUCKER (CONT'D.)

(HE SITS IN THE RUCKER AT CENTER AS EVANS GOES TO 28 STRANG
THE BENCH AT RIGHT,
(SHE TURNS FROM HIM AND SITS DOWN IN THE ROCKER AT 79 STRANG
CENTER,)

ROCKERS

FIVE CHAIRS ARE GROUPED ABOUT THE TABLE--THREE 185 AHWILD
ROCKERS AT LEFT, RIGHT,
FOUR CHAIRS, THREE ROCKERS WITH CROCHETED TIDIES 93 BEYOND
ON THEIR BACKS,
NEAR THE TABLE, THREE PLUSH-COVERED CHAIRS, TWO OF493 DIFRNT
WHICH ARE ROCKERS,
SHE SITS IN ONE OF THE ROCKERS BY THE TABLE, HER 501 DIFRNT
FACE GREATLY TROUBLED,

ROCKING

(HE POINTS TO THE ROCKING CHAIR AT THE RIGHT OF 193 AHWILD
TABLE NEAR HIS,)
MILLER IS SITTING IN HIS FAVORITE ROCKING CHAIR AT249 AHWILD
LEFT OF TABLE, FRONT,
(HE SITS DOWN IN THE ROCKING-CHAIR AT RIGHT, REAR,264 AHWILD
ANNA IS SEATED IN THE ROCKING-CHAIR BY THE TABLE, 41 ANNA
WITH A NEWSPAPER IN HER HANDS,
AND SITS DOWN IN THE ROCKING-CHAIR, 44 ANNA
ANNA IS SITTING IN THE ROCKING-CHAIR, 63 ANNA
HE THROWS HIMSELF INTO THE ROCKING-CHAIR-- 68 ANNA
DESPONDENTLY)
(SHE PASSES HIM AND SINKS DOWN IN THE ROCKING- 69 ANNA
CHAIR,)
(ROCKING WITH WILD LAUGHTER,) 223 DESIRE
SHE STOPS ROCKING, HER FACE GROWS ANIMATED AND 228 DESIRE
EAGER, SHE WAITS ATTENTIVELY,
ABBIE IS SITTING IN A ROCKING CHAIR, A SHAWL 247 DESIRE
WRAPPED ABOUT HER SHOULDERS,
(HE SITS DOWN IN THE ROCKING CHAIR AND SHE PUTS A 42 JOURNE
PILLOW BEHIND HIS BACK,)
(ROCKING BACK AND FORTH ON HIS HAUNCHES-- 345 LAZARU
A PUNCH ROCKING-CHAIR, PAINTED GREEN, WITH A HOLE 71 MISBEG
IN ITS CANE BUTTOM,
THE ROCKING CHAIR IS NO LONGER AT CENTER BUT HAS 66 STRANG
BEEN PULLED NEARER THE TABLE,
(HE SINKS DOWN IN THE ROCKING CHAIR DESPONDENTLY) 68 STRANG

ROCKPILE

YOU OUGHT TO PAY ME, INSTEAD, FOR OCCUPYING THIS 40 MISBEG
ROCKPILE, MISCALLED A FARM,

ROCKS

A STRAGGLING LINE OF PILED ROCKS, TOO LOW TO BE 81 BEYOND
CALLED A WALL,
SHE ROCKS LISTLESSLY, ENERVATED BY THE HEAT, 228 DESIRE
STARING IN FRONT OF HER WITH BORED,
(AFTER A PAUSE IN WHICH SHE ROCKS BACK AND FORTH 511 DIFRNT
STUDYING HER DAUGHTER'S FACE--
THEN HE HOLDS HIS HEAD IN HIS HANDS AND ROCKS BACK195 EJONES
AND FORTH,
HIS VOICE RUNS INTO THE WAIL OF A KEEN, HE ROCKS 213 HA APE
BACK AND FORTH ON HIS BENCH,
THEN IT ROARS AND ROCKS AND RATTLES PAST THE 19 HUGHIE
NEARBY CORNER,
OR OF THE CLOCK, OF WHATEVER FLIES, OR SIGHS, UR 132 JOURNE
RUCKS, OR SINGS, OR SPEAKS,
(THE ROOM ROCKS, THE AIR OUTSIDE THROBS 281 LAZARU
MIRIAM ROCKS TO AND FRO AND RAISES A LOW WAIL OF 320 LAZARU
LAMENTATION,
IF IT IS FULL OF NUDE ROCKS,. 38 MISBEG
I LIKE THAT PART ABOUT THE ROCKS, 38 MISBEG
FROM THE ROCKS BELOW THE HEADLAND SOUNDS THE 578 ROPE
MUFFLED MONOTONE OF BREAKING WAVES,
NOW WATCH HIM, FAN, I KIN CHUCK ROCKS, 590 ROPE
(SHAKING HER AWAY) THERE'S LOTS OF ROCKS, KID, 591 ROPE
I DON' WANTER THROW ROCKS, 591 ROPE

ROCKY

AH WELL, IT'S A ROCKY ROAD, FULL OF TWISTS AND 504 DAYS
BLIND ALLEYS, ISN'T IT, JACK--
(HARRY RISES FROM HIS CHAIR TO LOOK AT HOPE AND 577 ICEMAN
RODS TO ROCKY,
AS THE CURTAIN RISES, ROCKY, THE NIGHT BARTENDER, 577 ICEMAN

ROD

AND BEGINS PUSHING THE BLACK CURTAIN ALONG THE ROD610 ICEMAN
TO THE REAR WALL,)
MY OLD MAN USED TO WHALE SALVATION INTO MY HEINIE 622 ICEMAN
WITH A BIRCH ROD,
FORCE INTO HIS RIGHT HAND THE MYSTIC ROD OF 307 LAZARU
DIONYSUS WITH A PINE CONE ON TOP,

RODE

BUT THEY KNOCKED US SENSELESS AND RODE US TO THE 159 POET
STATION AND LOCKED US UP,

RODIN'S

HE IS SEATED FORWARD ON A BENCH IN THE EXACT 226 HA APE
ATTITUDE OF RODIN'S «THE THINKER.»
CROUCHED ON THE EDGE OF HIS COT IN THE ATTITUDE OF239 HA APE
RODIN'S «THE THINKER,»
IN THE ATTITUDE OF RODIN'S «THE THINKER.» 244 HA APE
IN AS NEAR TU THE ATTITUDE OF RODIN'S «THE 250 HA APE
THINKER»
THE SAME ATTITUDE AS RODIN'S «THE THINKER.» 251 HA APE

RODS

THE RODS AND SCOURGES ARE UPLIFTED OVER HIS BACK 346 LAZARU
TO STRIKE,
A FADED GINGERBREAD WITH URANGE FIXIN'S AND 49 STRANG
NUMEROUS LIGHTNING RODS,

RUGUE

SHE WAS A BIT OF A ROGUE AND A COQUETTE, GOD BLESS138 JOURNE
HER,

ROGUISH

(WITH A LAUGH AND A ROGUISH 505 DIFRNT

ROGUISHLY

(SHAKING HER HEAD ROGUISHLY) 524 DIFRNT

1333 ROMANS

ROISTERING
THERE IS A MOMENT'S PAUSE IN WHICH THE SOUND OF 163 POET
DRUNKEN ROISTERING IN THE BAR

ROLE
AND A POSEY ACTOR SOLEMNLY PLAYING A ROLE. 193 AHWILD
(JOCULARLY) YOU DON'T FIT THE ROLE OF PAN, DION. 297 GGBROW
WHAT ROLE DO YOU PLAY NOWADAYS, NOTHING'S 13 MANSNS
SO I AM CAST IN THE ROLE OF CHIEF BEGGAR/ 39 MANSNS
THE ROLE OF A SLAVISH LOVING MOTHER CONVINCINGLY 58 MANSNS
AGAIN.
I AM GLAD YOU ADMIT IT WAS JUST A ROLE. 58 MANSNS
BUT NEITHER ONE CONCLUDING A FINAL ROLE. 72 MANSNS
HE OVERDOES IT AND ONE SOON FEELS THAT HE IS 34 POET
OVERPLAYING A ROLE

ROLL
WHY DON'T YOU GET A NEW ROLL FOR THAT OLD BOX& 237 AHWILD
(PULLS OUT HIS ROLL AND HANDS A DOLLAR BILL OVER--239 AHWILD
WITH EXAGGERATED CARELESSNESS)
(HE HAS BEEN FUMBLING IN HIS POCKET AND PULLS OUT 242 AHWILD
HIS NINE-DOLLAR ROLL
HE'D GIVE ME ONE LOOK AND THEN PUT A DOUBLE 523 DIFRNT
PADLOCK ON HIS ROLL.
THE ROLL OF THE THUNDER FROM THE PRECEDING FLASH 446 DYNAMO
COMES CRASHING AND RUMBLING.
(GLOOMILY) YOU KIN BET YOU WHOLE ROLL ON ONE 184 EJONES
THING, WHITE MAN.
LISTEN TO DAT ROLL-CALL, WILL YOU& 186 EJONES
JONES'S EYES BEGIN TO ROLL WILDLY. 192 EJONES
UNISON AS IF THEY WERE LAXLY LETTING THEMSELVES 199 EJONES
FOLLOW THE LONG ROLL OF A SHIP
SHE'S BEGINNING TO ROLL TO IT. 209 HA APE
HE WAS ALWAYS WAITING FOR ME TO ROLL IN. 15 HUGHIE
JUST A ROLL ON THE DESK HERE. 20 HUGHIE
BUT AFTER HE'D SEEN ME ROLL IN HERE THE LAST ONE 23 HUGHIE
EVERY NIGHT,
SO IF I ROLL IN HERE WITH A BLONDE THAT'LL KNOCK 37 HUGHIE
YOUR EYES OUT,
HAD A ROLL WHEN HE PAID YOU HIS ROOM RENT, DIDN'T 383 ICEMAN
HE, ROCKY'S
OH, I KNOW YOU GUYS SAW-- YOU THINK I'VE GOT A 585 ICEMAN
ROLL.
WHERE WOULD I GET A REAL ROLL& 585 ICEMAN
(SHE HOLDS OUT A LITTLE ROLL OF BILLS TO ROCKY) 613 ICEMAN
WHILE I WAS FRISKIN' HIM FOR HIS ROLL/ 617 ICEMAN
JEES, A ROLL DAT'D CHOKE A HIPPOPOTAMUS/ 621 ICEMAN
(HE PULLS A BIG ROLL FROM HIS POCKET AND PEELS OFF621 ICEMAN
A TEN-DOLLAR BILL.
(SHE PASSES A SMALL ROLL OF BILLS SHE HAS IN HER 700 ICEMAN
HAND OVER HER SHOULDER.
CORA'S, =THE OCEANA ROLL=. 727 ICEMAN
(HE PULLS OUT A SMALL ROLE OF BILLS FROM HIS PANTS BY JOURNE
POCKET AND CAREFULLY SELECTS
ONLY A LAZY GROUND SWELL AND A SLOW DROWSY ROLL OF153 JOURNE
THE SHIP.
=BUILD THEE MORE STATELY MANSIONS, O MY SOUL, AS 148 MANSNS
THE SWIFT SEASONS ROLL/
PULLS OUT A LITTLE ROLL OF ONE-DOLLAR BILLS AND 7 MISBEG
PRESSES IT IN HIS HAND)
HAD AN IDEA SHE COULD ROLL ME, I GUESS. 126 MISBEG
I HOPE YOU DON'T THINK I'M SCHEMING TO ROLL YOU. 127 MISBEG
I'LL TELL HIM WHAT HE CAN DO WITH HIMSELF, HIS 132 MISBEG
BANK-ROLL, AND TIN OIL TANKS.
(HE TAKES OUT A ROLL OF NOTES FROM HIS INSIDE 500 VOYAGE
POCKET AND LAYS ONE ON THE TABLE.
SHE HANDS THE ROLL TO JOE, WHO POCKETS IT. 508 VOYAGE
AND HAS TAKEN THE ROLL OF MONEY FROM HIS INSIDE 508 VOYAGE
POCKET.

ROLLED.
SO'S THEY COULDN'T FALL OUT NO MATTER HOW SHE 103 BEYOND
ROLLED.
HE IS CARRYING A ROLLED-UP PLAN IN HIS HAND. 305 GGBROW
(GOES AND TAKES A ROLLED-UP PLAN FROM THE TABLE 310 GGBROW
DRAWER--DULLY)
I'D JUST ROLLED IN FROM TIA JUANA. 22 HUGHIE
THE SLEEVES OF HIS COLLARLESS SHIRT ARE ROLLED UP 577 ICEMAN
ON HIS THICK, POWERFUL ARMS
I ROLLED HIM. 616 ICEMAN
HE WEARS HIS WORKING CLOTHES, SLEEVES ROLLED UP. 664 ICEMAN
AN EARLY DUSK DUE TO THE FOG WHICH HAS ROLLED IN 97 JOURNE
FROM THE SOUND AND IS LIKE A
AND YOU GAVE HIM A SWEET SMILE AND ROLLED YOUR 82 MISBEG
BIG BEAUTIFUL COW'S EYES AT HIM,
GOOD, AND HE ROLLED ON THE FLOOR, GRABBIN' HIS 156 POET
GUTS.

ROLLICKING
(BURSTS INTO A ROLLICKING SONG, ACCOMPANYING 96 POET
HIMSELF ON THE PIPES.

ROLLICKINGLY
(IN THE FRONT PARLOR, ARTHUR BEGINS TO SING 259 AHWILD
ROLLICKINGLY =WAITING AT THE CHURCH,

ROLLIN'
IT'S EASY AS ROLLIN' OFF A LOG. 183 EJONES

ROLLING
THERE IS NO ROLLING OF THE SHIP, 535 'ILE
ESPECIALLY WHEN IT WAS WINDY AND THE BREAKERS WERE940 'ILE
ROLLING IN.
HONESTLY, HE HAD THAT CROWD JUST ROLLING ON THE 223 AHWILD
GROUND
HE WALKS WITH A CLUMSY, ROLLING GAIT. 5 ANNA
BETWEEN THE LOW, ROLLING HILLS WITH THEIR FRESHLY 81 BEYOND
PLOWED FIELDS CLEARLY DIVIDED
=OH, SHENANDOAH, I LONG TO HEAR YOUR A-WAY, MY 6 ELECTR
ROLLING RIVER OH, SHENANDOAH,
=OH, SHENANDOAH, I LONG TO HEAR YOU A-WAY, MY 43 ELECTR
ROLLING RIVER,
= OH, SHENANDOAH, I LOVE YOUR DAUGHTER A-WAY, MY 43 ELECTR
ROLLING RIVER.=
A-WAY, MY ROLLING RIVER/ 103 ELECTR

ROLLING (CONT'D.)
= OH, SHENANDOAH, I LOVE YOUR DAUGHTER A-WAY, MY 103 ELECTR
ROLLING RIVER/
=OH, SHENANDOAH, I LONG TO HEAR YOU A-WAY, MY 123 ELECTR
ROLLING RIVER/
=OH, SHENANDOAH, I LOVE YOUR DAUGHTER A-WAY, YOU 169 ELECTR
ROLLING RIVER.=
=OH, SHENANDOAH, I LONG TO HEAR YOU A-WAY, MY 169 ELECTR
ROLLING RIVER, OH, SHENANDOAH,
LET'S START THE PARTY ROLLING/ 657 ICEMAN
WHO'LL START THE BALL ROLLING& 685 ICEMAN
TUSSING AND ROLLING AROUND. 715 ICEMAN
ALL THE STUDENTS WERE WISE AND I HAD THEM ROLL,NG 39 MISBEG
IN THE AISLES AS I SHOWED

ROLLS
(HE ROLLS OVER ON HIS SIDE AND FALLS ASLEEP 483 CARDIF
IMMEDIATELY.)
(THE MATE ROLLS PADDY OVER AND SEES A KNIFE WOUND 472 CAKIBE
ON HIS SHOULDER.)
(HE SLUMPS FORWARD TO THE FLOOR AND ROLLS OVER ON 566 DAYS
HIS BACK, DEAD.
BRANT PITCHES FORWARD TO THE FLOOR BY THE TABLE, 114 ELECTR
ROLLS OVER,
HIS HEAD ROLLS FORWARD IN A SUDDEN SLUMBER. 696 ICEMAN
(THEN, AS THE BODY OF FLAVIUS FALLS HEAVILY AND 338 LAZARU
ROLLS DOWN THE STEPS AT RIGHT,
HE PULLS OUT TOBACCO AND A PAPER AND ROLLS A 593 KOPE
CIGARETTE AND LIGHTS IT.
HIS LITTLE PIGGISH EYES ALMOST CONCEALED BY ROLLS 493 VOYAGE
OF FAT,
ROLLS TO THE FLOOR, AND LIES THERE UNCONSCIOUS.) 508 VOYAGE
RULY-POLY
HE IS ABO IS ABOUT FIFTY, A LITTLE UNDER MEDIUM 618 ICEMAN
HEIGHT, WITH A STOUT, RULY-POLY

ROMAN
(MOURNFULLY) AIN'T WE GOING TO SET OFF THE 234 AHWILD
SKYROCKETS AND ROMAN CANDLES, PA&
IN OUTLINE, HIS FACE SUGGESTS A ROMAN CONSUL ON AN294 GGBROW
OLD COIN.
GIBBON'S ROMAN EMPIRE AND MISCELLANEOUS VOLUMES OF 11 JOURNE
OLD PLAYS, POETRY,
EVEN THE ROMAN SOLDIERS AND THE CENTURION HIMSELF.291 LAZARU
EXCEPT THAT THE BASIS OF EACH FACE IS ROMAN-- 291 LAZARU
AS THE FIGHT IS AT ITS HEIGHT A ROMAN CENTURION 291 LAZARU
AND A SQUAD OF EIGHT SOLDIERS
THESE ROMAN MASKS NOW AND HENCEFORTH IN THE PLAY 291 LAZARU
ARE CARRIED OUT ACCORDING TO
AT FRONT, PACING IMPATIENTLY UP AND DOWN, IS A 298 LAZARU
YOUNG ROMAN NOBLE OF TWENTY-ONE,
ACTING AS POLICE, A NUMBER OF ROMAN LEGIONARIES-- 298 LAZARU
WALKING WITH CALIGULA IS CNEIUS CRASSUS, A ROMAN 299 LAZARU
GENERAL--
THEY ARE BEGINNING TO CLAIM HE IS A ROMAN/ 300 LAZARU
THAT SMACKS OF ROMAN BLOOD/ 302 LAZARU
THE ROMAN SOLDIERS IN SPITE OF THEIR EFFORTS ARE 304 LAZARU
PUSHED BACKWARD STEP BY STEP.)
(THE SQUAD OF ROMAN SOLDIERS LED BY THE CENTURION,306 LAZARU
(IN A REPEATED CHORUS WHICH FINALLY INCLUDES EVEN 307 LAZARU
THE ROMAN SOLDIERS,
NOW AUGMENTED BY ALL THE GREEKS, AND THE ROMAN 311 LAZARU
SOLDIERS WHO HAD AWAITED HIM,
THEY ARE ALL MASKED IN THE ROMAN MASK, 312 LAZARU
A ROMAN EAGLE WAS MY DADDY. 313 LAZARU
THE ROMAN SENATE IS THE ROMAN SENATE 313 LAZARU
THE MIGHTY VOICE OF THE ROMAN PEOPLE AS LONG AS 313 LAZARU
ROME IS ROME.
HE MAY MISTREAT INDIVIDUAL SENATORS, BUT THE ROMAN315 LAZARU
SENATE IS THE ROMAN SENATE/
THE MIGHTY VOICE OF THE ROMAN PEOPLE. 315 LAZARU
I, THIS JEW, THIS ROMAN, THIS NOBLE OR THIS SLAVE,324 LAZARU
MASKED AS ALL THE ROMAN SOLDIERS PREVIOUSLY, ENTER326 LAZARU
FROM THE LEFT FRONT.
THIS ROMAN WORLD IS FULL OF EVIL. 329 LAZARU
WEARING THE TYPE MASK OF A ROMAN PATRICIAN 332 LAZARU
POMPEIA, A ROMAN NOBLEWOMAN, THE FAVORITE MISTRESS336 LAZARU
OF CAESAR, SITS AT FRONT,
THE MASKS ARE BASED ON THE ROMAN MASKS OF THE 336 LAZARU
PERIODS OF BOYHOOD--OR GIRLHOOD--
A ROMAN EAGLE WAS MY DADDY 357 LAZARU
HE IS A TALL, FULL-CHESTED MAN IN HIS SIXTIES, 150 MANSNS
WITH A FINE-LOOKING ROMAN FACE,

ROMANCE
BUT MARRIAGE SOON TURNED HIS ROMANCE INTO-- 31 ELECTR
DISGUST/
A DON JUAN INSPIRED TO ROMANCE BY A MONKEY'S 296 GGBROW
GLANDS--
BUT IT WAS A GAME OF ROMANCE AND ADVENTURE TO YOU,147 JOURNE
WHAT A ROMANCE// 430 MARCOM
=WHAT A ROMANCE/ 430 MARCOM
LET'S SIT DOWN WHERE THE MOON WILL BE IN OUR EYES 115 MISBEG
AND WE'LL SEE ROMANCE.
OUR MOONLIGHT ROMANCE SEEMS TO BE A FLOP, JOSIE. 139 MISBEG
IT WAS ALL ABOUT BEAUTIFUL NIGHTS AND THE ROMANCE 170 MISBEG
OF THE MOON.

ROMANS
SURE THEY WILL MAKE HIM A GOD, AS THE ROMANS DO 284 LAZARU
THEIR CAESARS/
MERCY, ROMANS/ 291 LAZARU
THE FOOLS OF ROMANS WILL NEVER SUSPECT HIM/ 300 LAZARU
(HE TURNS TOWARD THE ROMANS AND LAUGHS SNEERINGLY.300 LAZARU
DEATH TO THE ROMANS/ 304 LAZARU
(ROMANS AND GREEKS ALIKE AS ONE GREAT VOICE) 305 LAZARU
THE ROMANS AND GREEKS SEEM TO LEAN BACK FROM ONE 305 LAZARU
ANOTHER
WE WOULD ADOPT CHILDREN WHOSE PARENTS THE ROMANS 330 LAZARU
HAVE BUTCHERED.

ROMANTIC

ROMANTIC
AND MAKES THIS TART A ROMANTIC EVIL VAMPIRE IN HIS241 AHWILD
EYES.
YOU DON'T KNOW WHAT AN OLD-FASHIONED ROMANTIC 522 DAYS
IDEALIST HE IS AT HEART
IT WOULD HAVE SAVED HIM SO MUCH SILLY ROMANTIC 534 DAYS
PURSUIT OF MEANINGLESS ILLUSIONS.
(SNEERINGLY) SO ROMANTIC, YOU SEE-- 535 DAYS
TO MAKE MY ROMANTIC HERO COME FINALLY TO A 539 DAYS
RATIONAL CONCLUSION ABOUT HIS LIFE/
FREEDOM WAS MERELY OUR ROMANTIC DELUSION. 542 DAYS
(JEERINGLY) THE ROMANTIC IDEALIST AGAIN SPEAKS/ 545 DAYS
ABSENT-MINDED ROMANTIC DREAMINESS ABOUT THEM. 494 DFRNT
HE WAS SO ROMANTIC LOOKING WITH THOSE STEEL 430 DYNAMO
CLIMBING THINGS ON HIS LEGS...
HE'S SUCH A DARNED ROMANTIC-LOOKING CUSS. 15 ELECTR
OH, HE DID TELL ME THE STORY OF HIS LIFE TO MAKE 15 ELECTR
HIMSELF OUT ROMANTIC.
(GRUMPILY) HE SEEMS TO HAVE HAD PLENTY OF 15 ELECTR
ROMANTIC EXPERIENCE.
(BITTERLY) THAT'S HIS TRADE--BEING ROMANTIC/. 15 ELECTR
AS IF A ROMANTIC BYRONIC APPEARANCE WERE THE IDEAL 21 ELECTR
IN MIND.
BUT I SUPPOSE IT WOULD BE FOOLISH TO EXPECT 24 ELECTR
ANYTHING BUT CHEAP ROMANTIC LIES
HE WAS SILENT AND MYSTERIOUS AND ROMANTIC/ 31 ELECTR
PROMISE ME. NO MORE COWARDLY ROMANTIC SCRUPLES/ 42 ELECTR
BUT THERE IS SOMETHING ROMANTIC, 102 ELECTR
AND SHE'S BECOME ROMANTIC? 144 ELECTR
MORE LIKE A ROMANTIC CLIPPER CAPTAIN, IS THAT ITS 145 ELECTR
(JEERINGLY) HANDSOME AND ROMANTIC-LOOKING, 145 ELECTR
WEREN'T THEY, VINNIES
SHE IS ALMOST SEVENTEEN, PRETTY AND VIVACIOUS, 262 GGBROW
BLONDE, WITH BIG ROMANTIC EYES,
(HE KISSES HER WITH HIS MASKED FACE WITH A 267 GGBROW
ROMANTIC ACTOR'S PASSION AGAIN AND
HE THOUGHT GAMBLING WAS ROMANTIC. 28 HUGHIE
THE THOUGHT GANGSTERS WAS ROMANTIC. 28 HUGHIE
HIS CLOTHES, ASSUREDLY, DO NOT COSTUME ANY 13 JOURNE
ROMANTIC PART.
HIS PERSONALITY POSSESSES THE REMNANT OF A 19 JOURNE
HUMOROUS, ROMANTIC,
WHAT IS SO WONDERFUL ABOUT THAT FIRST MEETING 107 JOURNE
BETWEEN A SILLY ROMANTIC
IT WAS A GREAT ROMANTIC PART I KNEW I COULD PLAY 150 JOURNE
BETTER THAN ANYONE.
MADE GETTING DRUNK ROMANTIC. 165 JOURNE
ONE DAY YOU MAY LOSE YOURSELF SO DEEPLY IN THAT 3 MANSNS
ROMANTIC EVIL,
WITH ROMANTIC INIQUITY OUT OF SCANDALOUS FRENCH 14 MANSNS
MEMOIRS/
I HAVE DONE WITH THAT INSANE ROMANTIC VAPORING/ 22 MANSNS
SO THIS IS WHAT YOUR GREAT ROMANTIC LOVE COMES TO 97 MANSNS
IN THE END/
HOW ROMANTIC/ 427 MARCOM
THAT OF THE BEGUILING NE'ER-DO-WELL, SENTIMENTAL 37 MISBEG
AND ROMANTIC.
COME ON NOW AND WE'LL SIT ON MY BEDROOM STEPS AND 102 MISBEG
BE ROMANTIC IN THE MOONLIGHT,
(HE BECOMES SENTIMENTALLY ROMANTIC.) 47 POET
THERE IS A ROMANTIC TOUCH OF THE POET BEHIND HIS 48 POET
YANKEE PHLEGM.
THEY HAVE NO ROMANTIC FIRE/ 63 POET
HE BECOMES A ROMANTIC, TRAGIC FIGURE, 70 POET
(SHE SMILES.) BUT EVIDENTLY HE HAS FOUND A NEW 82 POET
ROMANTIC DREAM
A STARTLING, COLORFUL, ROMANTIC FIGURE, 88 POET
MUST HAVE ONCE BEEN OF A ROMANTIC, TENDER, 53 STRANG
CLINGING-VINE BEAUTY,
YOU'RE SIMPLY LETTING YOUR ROMANTIC IMAGINATION 102 STRANG
RUNAWAY WITH YOU--
ROMANTIC IMAGINATION/ 102 STRANG
MY ROMANTIC IMAGINATIONS... 111 STRANG
ROMANTIC IMAGINATION/... 128 STRANG
ROMANTICALLY
(THEN ROMANTICALLY) AYE/ 24 ELECTR
ROMANTICISM
(WITH PASSIONATE ROMANTICISM) 287 AHWILD
ROME
AGAINST THE EAGLES OF ANCIENT ROME/-- 242 HA APE
OF THE MANNERS AND MORALS OF GREECE AND IMPERIAL 7 STRANG
ROME/.)
ROMEO
A FOINE ROMEO YOU'D MAKE IN YOUR CONDISHUN. 498 VOYAGE
ROOF
THE CHIMNEY OF THE CABIN STOVE RISES A FEW FEET 25 ANNA
ABOVE THE ROOF.
I'LL ASK YOUR PARDON FOR BRINGING YOU TO THIS ROOM556 CROSS
ON THE ROOF--BUT--
THEN HE HAS THE ROOF TOO RIGGED UP LIKE A SHIPS 557 CROSS
(WITH A TERRIFIED GLANCE AT THE ROOF ABOVE) 566 CROSS
THEY BEND THEIR TRAILING BRANCHES DOWN OVER THE 202 DESIRE
ROOF.
RESTING THEIR SAGGING BREASTS AND HANDS AND HAIR 202 DESIRE
ON ITS ROOF.
THE SKY ABOVE THE ROOF IS SUFFUSED WITH DEEP 203 DESIRE
COLORS.
ITS CEILING IS THE SLOPING ROOF. 212 DESIRE
YE KIN FEEL IT DROPPIN' OFF THE ELUMS, CLIMBIN' UP253 DESIRE
THE ROOF,
HE'LL RAISE THE ROOF/. 424 DYNAMO
AND OTHER EQUIPMENT STRETCHING UP THROUGH THE ROOF473 DYNAMO
TO THE OUTGOING FEEDERS
IT IS A LITTLE AFTER SUNSET AND THE EQUIPMENT ON 476 DYNAMO
THE ROOF IS OUTLINED BLACKLY
(PERSUASIVELY) I'M SCARED ON THIS ROOF, RUBE. 482 DYNAMO
TO THE DYNAMO-ROOM ROOF, AND A MOMENT LATER HE IS 482 DYNAMO
SEEN THERE.

ROOF (CONT'D.)
GALLERY, AND FROM THENCE UP TO THE DOOR FROM THE 483 DYNAMO
ROOF OF THE DYNAMO ROOM.
STEEL WORK, INSULATORS, BUSSES, SWITCHES, ETC. 483 DYNAMO
STRETCHING UPWARD TO THE ROOF.
AND PULLS HER THROUGH THE DOOR FROM THE ROOF TO 483 DYNAMO
THE GALLERIES.)
JUST INSIDE THE DOOR TO THE DYNAMO-ROOM ROOF AT 484 DYNAMO
THE TOP OF THE STAIRWAY.)
WHAT THE HELL YOU TRYING TO DO, YELLING AND 654 ICEMAN
RAISING THE ROOFS
BUT I CAN'T CONTINUE TO LIVE UNDER THE SAME ROOF 675 ICEMAN
WITH THAT FELLOW.
UNDER THE SAME ROOF WITH THAT LOON, HICKEY, AND A 682 ICEMAN
LYING CIRCUS GRIFTER/
A DIRTY BARN OF A PLACE WHERE RAIN DRIPPED THROUGH148 JOURNE
THE ROOF.
AND TO THE LEFT OF DOOR A FLIGHT OF STAIRS GOES UP281 LAZARU
TO THE BALUSTRADED ROOF.
AT THE SAME MOMENT THE CHORUS OF FOLLOWERS APPEARS285 LAZARU
ON THE ROOF
SUDDENLY APPEARS ON THE ROOF OF THE HOUSE. 288 LAZARU
THEY HUDDLE INTO GROUPS ON THE ROOF AND ON THE 295 LAZARU
TERRACE.
MADE OF LOGS WITH A ROOF OF WARPED, HAND-HEWN 1 MANSNS
SHINGLES.
ITS WALLS AND POINTED ROOF ENTIRELY COVERED BY 25 MANSNS
IVY.
LATE AFTERNOON SUNLIGHT FROM BEYOND THE WALL AT 95 MANSNS
RIGHT FALLS ON THE POINTED ROOF
AN OLD BOX-LIKE, CLAPBOARDED AFFAIR, WITH A 1 MISBEG
SHINGLED ROOF AND BRICK CHIMNEY,
ITS WALLS AND SLOPING ROOF ARE COVERED WITH TAR 1 MISBEG
PAPER FADED TO DARK GRAY.
AND I RAISE THE ROOF AND THREATEN HIM IF HE DON'T 94 MISBEG
MARRY YOU--
OR SLEEP IN THE GRASS OF A FIELD WITHOUT A ROOF TO146 POET
OUR HEADS,
ROOM
IN THE CENTER OF THE ROOM, A STOVE. 535 'ILE
CLEAN UP THE CHART-ROOM. 539 'ILE
AND THIS TERRIBLE SHIP, AND THIS PRISON OF A ROOM,545 'ILE
AND THE ICE ALL AROUND,
THE ROOM IS FAIRLY LARGE, HOMELY LOOKING AND 185 AHWILD
CHEERFUL IN THE MORNING SUNLIGHT,
VOICES ARE HEARD IN A CONVERSATIONAL TONE FROM THE185 AHWILD
DINING-ROOM BEYOND THE BACK.
(SCENE--SITTING-ROOM OF THE MILLER HOME IN A LARGE185 AHWILD
SMALL-TOWN IN CONNECTICUT--
COMING FROM THE DINING-ROOM. 186 AHWILD
(LOOKING BACK TOWARD THE DINING-ROOM) 192 AHWILD
HE'S STILL IN THE DINING-ROOM, READING A BOOK. 192 AHWILD
(FROM THE DINING ROOM) ALL RIGHT. 193 AHWILD
THE ROOM IS MUCH TOO SMALL FOR THE MEDIUM-PRICED, 210 AHWILD
FORMIDABLE DINING-ROOM SET,
(SCENE--DINING-ROOM OF THE MILLER HOME-- 210 AHWILD
IT'S GETTING SO CLOUDY OUT, AND THIS PESKY ROOM IS210 AHWILD
SO DARK ANYWAY.
IN THE SITTING-ROOMS 214 AHWILD
BACK TOWARD THE SITTING-ROOM WHEN SHE SPEAKS TO 215 AHWILD
HIM PITYINGLY)
WE MIGHT AS WELL GO IN THE SITTING-ROOM AND BE 217 AHWILD
COMFORTABLE.
RICHARD COMES BACK IN THE ROOM.) 217 AHWILD
(SURLILY) IN THE SITTING-ROOM. 220 AHWILD
A SMALL, DINGY ROOM, DIMLY LIGHTED BY TWO FLY- 236 AHWILD
SPECKED GLOBES
(SCENE--THE BACK ROOM OF A BAR IN A SMALL HOTEL-- 236 AHWILD
(LOOKS AROUND THE ROOM--IRRITABLY) 238 AHWILD
ONLY I'VE GOT TO LIVE AND I OWE MY ROOM RENT IN 241 AHWILD
NEW HAVEN--
WHAT, ARE YOU TOO BASHFUL TO ASK FOR A ROOMS 241 AHWILD
GO OUT AND TELL THE BARTENDER YOU WANT A ROOM. 241 AHWILD
A ROOM ONLY COSTS TWO DOLLARS. 241 AHWILD
IF YOU NEED THE FIVE DOLLARS SO BAD--FOR YOUR ROOM242 AHWILD
RENT--
THE SALESMAN GRINS AND COMES INTO THE ROOM, 244 AHWILD
CARRYING HIS HIGHBALL IN HIS HAND.
HE SNIFFS AND LOOKS AWAY FROM HIM AROUND THE 252 AHWILD
ROOM.
UNCLE SID WAS SNORING LIKE A FOG HORN--AND HE'S 253 AHWILD
RIGHT NEXT TO MY ROOM.
HE SIDLES INTO THE ROOM GUILTILY, HIS EYES 256 AHWILD
SHIFTING ABOUT,
(AS THE SONG FINISHES, THE TWO IN THE OTHER ROOM 259 AHWILD
LAUGH.
THEY FILE INTO THE SITTING-ROOM IN SILENCE AND 263 AHWILD
THEN STAND AROUND UNCERTAINLY,
ARE DISCOVERED COMING IN THROUGH THE BACK PARLOR 263 AHWILD
FROM DINNER IN THE DINING-ROOM.
(SCENE--THE SAME--SITTING-ROOM OF THE MILLER 263 AHWILD
HOUSE--
(AS SHE IS TALKING, RICHARD APPEARS IN THE DOORWAY269 AHWILD
FROM THE SITTING-ROOM.
(THEN FUSSING ABOUT THE ROOM, SETTING THIS AND 269 AHWILD
THAT IN PLACE.
I HEARD YOU IN THE ROOM. 270 AHWILD
AND MA ALWAYS LOOKS INTO MY ROOM. 280 AHWILD
AND THEY LET ME INTO A SECRET ROOM BEHIND THE 282 AHWILD
BARROOM.
IN THE BACK ROOM ARE FOUR ROUND WOODEN TABLES WITH 3 ANNA
FIVE CHAIRS GROUPED ABOUT
THE STAGE IS DIVIDED INTO TWO SECTIONS, SHOWING A 3 ANNA
SMALL BACK ROOM ON THE RIGHT.
ON THE RIGHT IS AN OPEN DOORWAY LEADING TO THE 3 ANNA
BACK ROOM.
(HE GOES INTO THE BACK ROOM.) 7 ANNA
AT THE FAMILY ENTRANCE IN THE BACK ROOM. 7 ANNA

1335

ROOM

(CONT'D.)

(HE GOES INTO THE ROOM ON RIGHT.)

	8	ANNA
YOU BRING DRINKS IN BACK ROOM, LARRY.

	8	ANNA
(SHOUTS FROM NEXT ROOM) DON'T I GET THAT BUCKET

	10	ANNA
O' SUDS, DUTCHYS

AND WALKS UNSTEADILY INTO BACK ROOM SINGING) | 12 | ANNA
HE MIGHT BE WILLING TO STAKE ME TO A ROOM AND EATS | 16 | ANNA
TILL I GET RESTED UP.

(CHRIS STARTS FOR THE ENTRANCE TO THE BACK ROOM.) | 19 | ANNA
(SHE GOES INTO THE BACK ROOM--TO ANNA) | 19 | ANNA
(HE STANDS BEFORE THE DOOR TO THE BACK ROOM IN AN | 20 | ANNA
AGONY OF EMBARRASSED EMOTION.

CHRIS WANDERS ABOUT THE ROOM, CASTING QUICK, | 41 | ANNA
UNEASY SIDE GLANCES AT HER FACE.

HE THROWS THE KNIFE INTO A FAR CORNER OF THE | 49 | ANNA
ROOM--TAUNTINGLY.

LET YOU BE GOING INTO YOUR ROOM NOW AND BE | 55 | ANNA
DRESSING IN YOUR BEST AND WE'LL BE

(THROWING THE CHAIR AWAY INTO A CORNER OF THE | 60 | ANNA
ROOM--HELPLESSLY)

(GOES INTO ROOM ON LEFT AND GETS HIS CAP. | 62 | ANNA
(HE PICKS UP THE CAN OF BEER AND SLOWLY GOES TO | 67 | ANNA
ROOM ON LEFT.

SHE STEPS INTO THE ROOM, THE REVOLVER IN HER RIGHT | 69 | ANNA
HAND BY HER SIDE.)

(SHE PICKS UP HER BAG AND GOES INTO THE ROOM ON | 77 | ANNA
LEFT.

AN OAK DINING-ROOM TABLE WITH A RED COVER. | 93 | BEYOND
(THE SMALL SITTING ROOM OF THE MAYO FARMHOUSE | 93 | BEYOND
ABOUT NINE O'CLOCK SAME NIGHT.

EVERYTHING IN THE ROOM IS CLEAN, WELL-KEPT, AND IN | 93 | BEYOND
ITS EXACT PLACE, YET

WITH PLENTY O' ROOM TO WORK IN. | 98 | BEYOND
BUT AS HE COMES INTO THE ROOM | 99 | BEYOND
SITTING ROOM OF THE FARMHOUSE ABOUT HALF PAST | 112 | BEYOND
TWELVE IN THE AFTERNOON OF A HOT,

THE ROOM HAS CHANGED, | 112 | BEYOND
AND COMES INTO THE ROOM. | 119 | BEYOND
SHE HEARS THE VOICE FROM THE ROOM AND TIPTOES TO | 121 | BEYOND
THE DOOR TO LOOK IN.

(HE TURNS BACK TO THE ROOM WITH A GESTURE OF | 126 | BEYOND
LOATHING)

WHO MOVES TO ONE SIDE TO MAKE ROOM FOR HIM) | 130 | BEYOND
THE WHOLE ATMOSPHERE OF THE ROOM, CONTRASTED WITH | 144 | BEYOND
THAT OF FORMER YEARS,

AS IF THE AIR IN THE ROOM WERE DAMP AND COLD. | 144 | BEYOND
THE SITTING ROOM OF THE FARM HOUSE ABOUT SIX | 144 | BEYOND
O'CLOCK IN THE MORNING OF A DAY

THE ROOM, SEEN BY THE LIGHT OF THE SHADELESS OIL | 144 | BEYOND
LAMP WITH A SMOKY CHIMNEY WHICH

LOOK AT THE STATE OF THIS ROOM/ | 153 | BEYOND
I'LL LAY DOWN IN THE ROOM THE OTHER SIDE. | 153 | BEYOND
ANDREW CASTS A QUICK GLANCE ABOUT THE ROOM) | 154 | BEYOND
OF THE ROOM FOR THE FIRST TIME) | 155 | BEYOND
SHE OPENS THE DOOR AND STEPS INSIDE THE ROOM. | 166 | BEYOND
IT SEEMED AS IF ALL MY LIFE--I'D BEEN COOPED IN A | 167 | BEYOND
ROOM.

I COULDN'T STAND IT BACK THERE IN THE ROOM. | 167 | BEYOND
(LAMPS GOES TO HIS ROOM AND RETURNS WITH A CANDLE. | 465 | CARIBE
 | 471 | CARIBE
ROOM.

HE CASTS A QUICK GLANCE ABOUT THE ROOM, AND SEEING | 555 | CROSS
NO ONE THERE,

DOCTOR HIGGINS FOLLOWS HIM INTO THE ROOM AND, | 555 | CROSS
A ROOM ERECTED AS A LOOKOUT POST AT THE TOP OF HIS | 555 | CROSS
HOUSE

AND STEPS DOWN INTO THE ROOM. | 555 | CROSS
I'LL ASK YOUR PARDON FOR BRINGING YOU TO THIS ROOM | 556 | CROSS
ON THE ROOF--BUT--

SHE ASCENDS INTO THE ROOM AND SHUTS THE DOOR | 562 | CROSS
BEHIND HER.

I DIDN'T KNOW--I THOUGHT YOU WERE IN YOUR ROOM. | 563 | CROSS
CAPTAIN BARTLETT COMES INTO THE ROOM. | 567 | CROSS
A GUST OF AIR TEARS DOWN INTO THE ROOM. | 567 | CROSS
A DENSE GREEN GLOW FLOODS SLOWLY IN RHYTHMIC WAVES | 570 | CROSS
LIKE A LIQUID IN THE ROOM--

THEIR EYES. AS THEY GLIDE SILENTLY INTO THE ROOM, | 571 | CROSS
AND JIMMY KANAKA RISE NOISELESSLY INTO THE ROOM | 571 | CROSS
FROM THE STAIRS.

(HE FLASHES IT ON HER TERROR-STRICKEN FACE, THEN | 572 | CROSS
QUICKLY AROUND THE ROOM.

IT HAS PENETRATED TO ALL PARTS OF THE ROOM. | 493 | DAYS
AT CENTER OF THE ROOM, TOWARD RIGHT, ANOTHER | 493 | DAYS
CHAIR.

I ONLY WISH I COULD HAVE YOU STAY WITH US, BUT | 506 | DAYS
THERE'S NO ROOM.

A MOMENT LATER MARGARET, THE MAID, APPEARS FROM | 514 | DAYS
THE DINING-ROOM AT LEFT,

AT RIGHT OF TABLE, IN THE CENTER OF THE ROOM, A | 514 | DAYS
SOFA.

IN THE LEFT WALL IS A DOOR LEADING TO THE DINING- | 514 | DAYS
ROOM.

(SCENE--THE LIVING ROOM OF THE LOVINGS' DUPLEX | 514 | DAYS
APARTMENT.

(SHE DISAPPEARS THROUGH THE DINING-ROOM DOOR. | 526 | DAYS
(SHE MOVES TOWARD THE DINING ROOM AT LEFT.) | 526 | DAYS
ROOM) | 528 | DAYS
(HE LAUGHS AGAIN--THEN TURNS TO FACE THE DOORWAY | 528 | DAYS
AS ELSA RE-ENTERS THE ROOM.

SHE GOES OUT THROUGH THE DINING-ROOM DOOR.) | 532 | DAYS
(SCENE--THE LIVING ROOM AGAIN. | 532 | DAYS
(SHE STARTS AS IF TO RUN FROM THE ROOM.) | 550 | DAYS
FATHER BAIRD MAKES A MOVEMENT AS IF HE WERE GOING | 551 | DAYS
TO FOLLOW ELSA INTO HER ROOM.

(THEN DULLY) I'LL GO--TO MY ROOM. | 551 | DAYS
A CHAISE-LONGUE IS AT RIGHT, FRONT, OF THE ROOM. | 553 | DAYS
THEN MOVES QUIETLY TO THE OTHER SIDE OF THE ROOM, | 556 | DAYS
BY THE DOOR TO ELSA'S BEDROOM,

YOU'LL STAY OUT OF HER ROOM-- | 556 | DAYS

ROOM

(CONT'D.)

JOHN, AS SOON AS HE ENTERS, FALLS UNDER THE | 560 | DAYS
ATMOSPHERE OF THE SICK-ROOM,

THERE IS A PAUSE OF SILENT IMMOBILITY IN THE ROOM. | 561 | DAYS
FATHER BAIRD, AFTER A LOOK INTO THE ROOM TO SEE IF | 561 | DAYS
HIS HELP IS NEEDED,

EBEN STICKS HIS HEAD OUT OF THE DINING-ROOM | 205 | DESIRE
WINDOW, LISTENING.)

IS IT MY ROOM, EPHRAIM? | 224 | DESIRE
THEN WITHDRAWS BACK INTO THE ROOM. | 228 | DESIRE
EBEN IS SITTING ON THE SIDE OF HIS BED IN THE ROOM | 235 | DESIRE
ON THE LEFT.

IN THE OTHER ROOM CABOT AND ABBIE ARE SITTING SIDE | 235 | DESIRE
BY SIDE ON THE EDGE OF THEIR

(IN THE NEXT ROOM EBEN GETS UP AND PACES UP AND | 236 | DESIRE
DOWN DISTRACTEDLY.

THEN AS THE DOOR OF HIS ROOM IS OPENED SOFTLY, HE | 239 | DESIRE
TURNS AWAY.

THIS AIN MY ROOM AN' YE'RE ON'Y HIRED HELP/ | 240 | DESIRE
(FURIOUS) GIT OUT O' MY ROOM/ | 240 | DESIRE
THEY 'S ONE ROOM HAIN'T MINE YET, BUT IT'S A-GOIN' | 240 | DESIRE
T' BE TONIGHT.

A GRIM, REPRESSED ROOM LIKE A TOMB IN WHICH THE | 241 | DESIRE
FAMILY HAS BEEN INTERRED ALIVE.

AND THE ROOM IS REVEALED IN ALL ITS PRESERVED | 241 | DESIRE
UGLINESS.

(TO THE PRESENCE HE FEELS IN THE ROOM) | 243 | DESIRE
NOW IT'S GOIN' T' BE MY ROOM/ | 245 | DESIRE
(HASTILY) I MEANT--OUR ROOM. | 245 | DESIRE
THE STOVE HAS BEEN TAKEN DOWN TO GIVE MORE ROOM TO | 247 | DESIRE
THE DANCERS.

IN THE NEXT ROOM A CRADLE STANDS BESIDE THE DOUBLE | 247 | DESIRE
BED.

EBEN IS SITTING ON THE SIDE OF THE BED IN HIS | 247 | DESIRE
ROOM,

STARING AT THE DOOR AS IF SHE WERE ALONE IN A | 250 | DESIRE
SILENT ROOM.)

GIVE ME ROOM/ | 250 | DESIRE
I KIN KICK THE CEILIN' OFF THE ROOM/ | 251 | DESIRE
IN THE ROOM ABOVE, EBEN GETS TO HIS FEET AND | 251 | DESIRE
TIPTOES OUT THE DOOR IN REAR,

A NOISE AS OF DEAD LEAVES IN THE WIND COMES FROM | 252 | DESIRE
THE ROOM.

ABBIE COMES ACROSS THE ROOM SILENTLY. | 252 | DESIRE
A WHISPER GOES AROUND THE ROOM. | 252 | DESIRE
IN THE MEANTIME THE SHERIFF AND MEN HAVE COME INTO | 264 | DESIRE
THE ROOM.)

THE ROOM IS SMALL AND LOW-CEILINGED. | 493 | DIFRNT
NEAR THE PIANO ON THE RIGHT, A DOOR LEADING TO THE | 493 | DIFRNT
NEXT ROOM.

IN THE CENTER OF THE ROOM THERE IS A CLUMSY, | 493 | DIFRNT
MARBLE-TOPPED TABLE.

ON THIS SIDE OF THE ROOM ARE ALSO A SMALL BOOKCASE | 493 | DIFRNT
HALF FILLED WITH OLD VOLUMES,

JACK FOLLOWS HER INTO THE ROOM. | 507 | DIFRNT
(THE GRINNING ROGERS FOLLOWS HIM INTO THE NEXT | 507 | DIFRNT
ROOM WHERE THEY CAN BE HEARD

(FROM THE NEXT ROOM) GOSH, I WISHED I'D BEEN | 510 | DIFRNT
THERE/

BEFORE SHE HAS A CHANCE TO REPLY A ROAR OF | 510 | DIFRNT
LAUGHTER COMES FROM THE NEXT ROOM AS

(HE FOLLOWS JACK INTO THE ROOM. | 510 | DIFRNT
LOOKING AROUND THE ROOM AS IF SHE LONGED TO ESCAPE | 514 | DIFRNT
FROM IT.

THE ROOM HAS A GROTESQUE ASPECT OF OLD AGE TURNED | 519 | DIFRNT
FLIGHTY AND MASQUERADING AS

(HE STANDS IN THE MIDDLE OF THE ROOM HESITATING | 530 | DIFRNT
WHETHER TO RUN AWAY OR STAY.

(HE COMES BACK TO THE CENTER OF THE ROOM WHERE HE | 531 | DIFRNT
STANDS WAITING.

(ONCE INSIDE THE DOOR, HE STANDS STARING ABOUT THE | 535 | DIFRNT
ROOM, FROWNING.

YOU AIN'T SEEN THIS ROOM SINCE, HAVE YOUS | 535 | DIFRNT
(PUZZLED) I DON'T KNOW EXACTLY, BUT THERE'S A | 537 | DIFRNT
CLOCK IN THE NEXT ROOM.

(HIS COURAGE RETURNING, COMES FORWARD INTO THE | 544 | DIFRNT
ROOM)

(HE SWAGGERS ABOUT THE ROOM--FINALLY STOPPING | 545 | DIFRNT
BESIDE HER.

(HE SCURRIES INTO THE ROOM ON RIGHT. | 547 | DIFRNT
(COMES FROM THE NEXT ROOM) AW RIGHT. | 547 | DIFRNT
AND BENNY BURSTS INTO THE ROOM PANTING FOR BREATH. | 549 | DIFRNT
(WHERE THE CURTAINING THE FIRE SITTING ROOM, | -0 | DYNAMO
AND THE SECTION OF THE LIGHT'S HOME IN WHICH ARE | -0 | DYNAMO
SITTING ROOM

IN THE SITTING ROOM BELOW THERE IS A TABLE AT | 421 | DYNAMO
CENTER, FRONT.

THE LIGHT SITTING ROOM AND REUBEN'S BEDROOM ARE | 421 | DYNAMO
REVEALED.

JUMPS TO HIS FEET AND STARES DOWN TOWARD THE ROOM | 424 | DYNAMO
LIGHT DRAWS BACK INTO THE ROOM, MUTTERING | 425 | DYNAMO
VICIOUSLY)

(FROM THE OPEN, CURTAINED WINDOWS OF THE FIFE | 425 | DYNAMO
LIVING ROOM

HAVE BEEN REPLACED, WHILE THE INTERIORS OF THE | 427 | DYNAMO
FIFE SITTING ROOM AND THE

THERE IS A TABLE AT CENTER, FRONT, IN THE SITTING | 428 | DYNAMO
ROOM.

(LOOKING UP FROM HIS PAPER WITH A SNORT OF DISGUST | 431 | DYNAMO
JUST AS ADA ENTERS THE ROOM)

HOW CAN I THINK IN THE SAME ROOM WITH YOUS | 434 | DYNAMO
AND NOW THE INTERIOR OF THE LIGHT SITTING ROOM IS | 435 | DYNAMO
AGAIN SHOWN

THEIR SITTING ROOM IS REVEALED AS BEFORE | 435 | DYNAMO
(ADA COMES IN THE DOORWAY OF THE SITTING ROOM, | 436 | DYNAMO
LEFT, FOLLOWED BY REUBEN.)

CONTROLLING AN IMPULSE TO RUN FROM THE ROOM. | 437 | DYNAMO

ROOM

ROOM (CONT'D.)
SITTING AS BEFORE IN THE SITTING ROOM OF THE OTHER443 DYNAMO
HOUSE READING THE BIBLE.
(SHE SLOWLY RACKS HERSELF INTO HER ROOM.) 444 DYNAMO
IS ALARM AT FINDING THE ROOM DARK AND EMPTY--CALLS445 DYNAMO
UNEASILY)
AND FIFE STICKS HIS HEAD OUT OF HIS SITTING ROOM 445 DYNAMO
WINDOW.
(STILL LEANING OUT OF HIS SITTING-ROOM WINDOW, 450 DYNAMO
CATCHES SIGHT OF LIGHT--
(SHE BREAKS DOWN, WEEPING, AND RUSHES BACK INTO 452 DYNAMO
THE ROOM.
MRS. FIFE IS LEANING OUT OF ONE OF THE WINDOWS OF 454 DYNAMO
THEIR SITTING ROOM,
(AT A NOISE IN THE ROOM BEHIND HER SHE HALF TURNS 454 DYNAMO
HER HEAD--
THE INTERIOR OF THE LIGHT SITTING ROOM IS 454 DYNAMO
REVEALED.
(IN THE SITTING ROOM OF THE LIGHT HOME, HUTCHINS 455 DYNAMO
LIGHT ENTERS FROM THE REAR,
YOUR POP TOLD ME TO GET OUT OF THE ROOM 456 DYNAMO
THE SCREEN UP IN HER ROOM HAS A HOLE RUSTED IN 456 DYNAMO
IT....
(THEN SHE HALF TURNS AROUND AT SOME SOUND IN THE 459 DYNAMO
ROOM BEHIND HER--
(SHE GOES BACK INTO THE ROOM.) 460 DYNAMO
JUST AS REUBEN SLOWLY OPENS THE DOOR OF THE LIGHT 462 DYNAMO
SITTING ROOM.
(HE HAS STEPPED ON TIPTOE INTO THE ROOM AND NOW 462 DYNAMO
SUDDENLY
AND I CAN REMEMBER THE CEILING IN MY ROOM, 464 DYNAMO
IT ISN'T MY ROOM NOW. 467 DYNAMO
(DULLY) SHALL I HAVE YOUR ROOM PUT IN ORDER FOR 467 DYNAMO
YOU?
AFTER THAT I'M GOING TO GET A ROOM OUT NEAR THE 467 DYNAMO
PLANT.
(STICKS HER HEAD OUT OF THEIR SITTING ROOM WINDOW 467 DYNAMO
AS HE PASSES THE LILAC HEDGE.
WHILE THE WALL OF THE SITTING ROOM HAS BEEN 468 DYNAMO
REPLACED.
ARE IN THE LOWER PART OF THE DYNAMO-ROOM WALL, 473 DYNAMO
THE SECTION ON THE LEFT, THE DYNAMO ROOM, 473 DYNAMO
THROUGH THE WINDOW AND THE OPEN DOOR OF THE DYNAMO473 DYNAMO
ROOM.
THE DOOR OF THE DYNAMO ROOM IS SHUT BUT THE 476 DYNAMO
INTERIOR IS BRILLIANTLY LIGHTED AND
A MOMENT LATER THE DOOR FROM THE DYNAMO ROOM IS 478 DYNAMO
OPENED AGAIN.
(REUBEN SLIDES BACK THE DYNAMO ROOM DOOR A FEW 478 DYNAMO
FEET AND ENTERS.
TO THE DYNAMO-ROOM ROOF, AND A MOMENT LATER HE IS 482 DYNAMO
SEEN THERE.
GALLERY, AND FROM THENCE UP TO THE DOOR FROM THE 483 DYNAMO
ROOF OF THE DYNAMO ROOM.
IT IS OF DOUBLE WIDTH AND EXTENDS OVER THE 483 DYNAMO
SWITCHBOARD ROOM ALSO.
JUST INSIDE THE DOOR TO THE DYNAMO-ROOM ROOF AT 484 DYNAMO
THE TOP OF THE STAIRWAY.)
THE SWITCHBOARD ROOM ON THE RIGHT--ONE STORY UP-- 486 DYNAMO
ARE OF CONCRETE.
THE SWITCHBOARD ROOM IS A SMALL COMPARTMENT TO THFAR4 DYNAMO
RIGHT OF THE DYNAMO ROOM.
MRS. FIFE IS SITTING IN THE DYNAMO ROOM 486 DYNAMO
THE DYNAMO ROOM IS HIGH AND WIDE WITH RED BRICK 486 DYNAMO
WALLS.
THE FLOOR AND AN OBSERVATION BALCONY WHICH 486 DYNAMO
PROJECTS INTO THE DYNAMO ROOM FROM
THE DASHES OVER INTO THE SWITCHBOARD ROOM 487 DYNAMO
I SEE SWITCHBOARD ROOM.-- 487 DYNAMO
AND DOWN THE STAIRS TO THE DYNAMO-ROOM FLOOR, 488 DYNAMO
(HE TURNS AND RUNS HEADLONG THROUGH THE 488 DYNAMO
SWITCHBOARD ROOM.
THE ROOM IS BARE OF FURNITURE WITH THE EXCEPTION 173 EJONES
OF ONE HUGE CHAIR
A SPACIOUS, HIGH-CEILINGED ROOM WITH BARE, 173 EJONES
WHITEWASHED WALLS.
THEN, MAKING UP HIS MIND, HE STEPS QUICKLY ON 174 EJONES
TIPTOE INTO THE ROOM.
AND ITS GLOW FILLS THE ROOM WITH A GOLDEN MIST. 28 ELECTR
THE STUDY IS A LARGE ROOM WITH A STIFF, AUSTERE 28 ELECTR
ATMOSPHERE.
(LOOKING AROUND THE ROOM WITH AVERSION) 29 ELECTR
OUT WHY IN THIS MUSTY ROOM, OF ALL PLACES? 29 ELECTR
BECAUSE IT'S FATHER'S ROOM. 29 ELECTR
YOU WENT TO HIS ROOM? 30 ELECTR
HE HAD HIRED THE ROOM UNDER ANOTHER NAME, BUT SHE 30 ELECTR
RECOGNIZED HIS DESCRIPTION.
(CHRISTINE SMILES MOCKINGLY AND TURNS AWAY, AS IF 34 ELECTR
TO GO OUT OF THE ROOM.
(GLANCING UNEASILY AT HER, AS THEY COME TO THE 36 ELECTR
CENTER OF THE ROOM)
SHE TAKES HIS HAND AND DRAWS HIM INTO THE ROOM, 36 ELECTR
CLOSING THE DOOR BEHIND HIM.
(SLOWLY) I WAS THINKING--PERHAPS WE HAD BETTER GO 37 ELECTR
TO THE SITTING-ROOM.
TURNS AND WALKS QUICKLY FROM THE ROOM AND CLOSES 42 ELECTR
THE DOOR BEHIND HER.)
TO THE LEFT OF THE STAND IS A DOOR LEADING INTO 58 ELECTR
CHRISTINE'S ROOM.
NONE OF THESE DETAILS CAN BE DISCERNED AT FIRST 58 ELECTR
BECAUSE THE ROOM IS IN DARKNESS.
IF YOU ARE GOING TO SAY STUPID THINGS, I'LL GO IN 59 ELECTR
MY OWN ROOM.
(SHE MOVES AS IF TO GO INTO HER OWN ROOM.) 60 ELECTR
THIS IS NOT MY ROOM NOR MY BED. 60 ELECTR
(SHE HURRIES THROUGH THE DOORWAY INTO HER ROOM 61 ELECTR
I--(SHE TURNS AS IF TO RUN INTO THE ROOM, TAKES A 64 ELECTR
TOTTERING STEP--

ROOM (CONT'D.)
IT IS A BLEAK ROOM WITHOUT INTIMACY, 79 ELECTR
ON THE LEFT, FRONT, IS A DOORWAY LEADING TO THE 79 ELECTR
DINING-ROOM.
AT THE LEFT CENTER OF THE ROOM, FRONT, IS A TABLE 79 ELECTR
WITH TWO CHAIRS.
(SCENE--THE SITTING-ROOM OF THE MANNON HOUSE. 79 ELECTR
AND GONE TO HIS ROOM/ 87 ELECTR
I DON'T WANT TO SHOUT ACROSS THE ROOM. 91 ELECTR
AND WALKS WITH JERKY STEPS FROM THE ROOM LIKE SOME 92 ELECTR
TRAGIC MECHANICAL DOLL.
(SHE TAKES THE LITTLE BOX SHE HAS FOUND IN 97 ELECTR
CHRISTINE'S ROOM RIGHT AFTER THE
I TELL YOU SHE WENT TO HIS ROOM/ 99 ELECTR
TURNS, RIGID AND SQUARE-SHOULDERED, AND WALKS 101 ELECTR
WOODENLY FROM THE ROOM.)
(HE TURNS AND STUMBLES BLINDLY FROM THE ROOM. 101 ELECTR
AT LEFT IS THE CHART ROOM AND THE ENTRANCE TO THE 102 ELECTR
COMPANIONWAY STAIRS LEADING
SHE CAME INTO THE ROOM WHEN HE WAS DYING/ 108 ELECTR
LURIN'S VOICE IS HEARD CALLING FROM THE SITTING- 123 ELECTR
ROOM AT RIGHT «WHAT'S THAT?»
I HEARD 'EM COMIN' AFTER ME, AND I RUN IN THE ROOM134 ELECTR
OPPOSITE.
I SEE A LIGHT THROUGH THE SHUTTERS OF THE SITTING-138 ELECTR
ROOM.
IT HAS THE DEAD APPEARANCE OF A ROOM LONG SHUT UP.139 ELECTR
IN THE LIGHTED ROOM, THE CHANGE IN HER IS 139 ELECTR
STRIKINGLY APPARENT.
(SAME AS ACT TWO OF «THE HUNTED»--THE SITTING-ROOM)139 ELECTR
IN THE MANNON HOUSE.
BECOMES AWARE THAT ORIN HAS NOT FOLLOWED HER INTO 139 ELECTR
THE ROOM.
IN THIS DIM, SPOTTY LIGHT THE ROOM IS FULL OF 139 ELECTR
SHADOWS.
TURNS, AND STALKS STIFFLY WITH HURT DIGNITY 146 ELECTR
FROM THE ROOM.
IT ISN'T GOOD FOR YOU STAYING IN THIS STUFFY ROOM 150 ELECTR
IN THIS WEATHER.
IT'S A SYMBOL OF HIS LIFE--A LAMP BURNING OUT IN ALSO ELECTR
ROOM OF WAITING SHADOWS/
(SCENE--SAME AS ACT ONE, SCENE TWO--THE SITTING- 157 ELECTR
ROOM.
AND FOLLOWS THEM IN AS THEY ENTER THE ROOM.) 158 ELECTR
HE GLANCES AT THEM, THEN QUICKLY AROUND THE ROOM 159 ELECTR
TO SEE IF LAVINIA IS THERE.
AND GLANCES SHARPLY FROM ONE TO THE OTHER AS SHE 162 ELECTR
COMES INTO THE ROOM.)
WE'LL EXPECT YOU TOMORROW, AND HAVE YOUR ROOM 163 ELECTR
READY.
(HAZEL BEGINS TO SOB AND HURRIES BLINDLY FROM THE 164 ELECTR
ROOM.
(HE STEPS BACK IN THE ROOM AS PETER APPEARS IN THE167 ELECTR
DOORWAY.)
AND MARCHES STIFFLY FROM THE ROOM.) 168 ELECTR
ROOM IN THE HOUSE FULL OF FEN ALREADY. 170 ELECTR
SAY, LET'S YOU AND ME ROOM TOGETHER AT COLLEGE-- 260 GGBROW
THE SITTING ROOM OF MRS. DION ANTHONY'S HALF OF A 269 GGBROW
TWO-FAMILY HOUSE
SCENE--THE DRAFTING ROOM IN BROWN'S OFFICE. 290 GGBROW
RUSH INTO THE ROOM. 293 GGBROW
SCENE--THE DRAFTING ROOM AND PRIVATE OFFICE OF 302 GGBROW
BROWN ARE BOTH SHOWN.
THE ARRANGEMENT OF FURNITURE IN EACH ROOM IS THE 302 GGBROW
SAME AS IN PREVIOUS SCENES.
(AS HE IS SPEAKING, A WELL-DRESSED IMPORTANT STOUT305 GGBROW
MAN ENTERS THE DRAFTING ROOM.
SCENE--THE SAME AS SCENE ONE OF ACT ONE--THE 308 GGBROW
SITTING-ROOM OF MARGARET'S HOME.
I'LL GO INTO THE NEXT ROOM AND ANYTHING YOU WANT, 312 GGBROW
JUST CALL.
(THE TWO DRAFTSMEN IN THE NEXT ROOM HAVE STOPPED 313 GGBROW
WORK AND ARE LISTENING.)
SCENE--SAME AS SCENE ONE OF ACT THREE--THE 313 GGBROW
DRAFTING ROOM AND BROWN'S OFFICE.
(HE GRABS UP BOTH MASKS AND GOES INTO ROOM OFF 314 GGBROW
RIGHT)
(BROWN DISAPPEARS INTO THE ROOM OFF RIGHT. 315 GGBROW
COME INTO THE DRAFTING-ROOM.) 316 GGBROW
(RUSHING INTO THE NEXT ROOM, SHOUTS IN TERRIFIED 318 GGBROW
TONES)
THEY WILL FIND HIM IN THE LITTLE ROOM. 318 GGBROW
(THEY ALL RUN INTO THE LITTLE ROOM OFF RIGHT. 318 GGBROW
HER MASK, RUNS INTO THE ROOM. 320 GGBROW
RUN INTO THE ROOM. 321 GGBROW
THE ROOM IS CRINGED WITH MEN, SHOUTING, CURSING, 207 HA APE
LAUGHING, SINGING---
SAY, AIN'T DERE A BACK ROOM AROUND DIS DUMPS 234 HA APE
COMMONPLACE AND UNMYSTERIOUS AS A ROOM COULD WELL 245 HA APE
BE.
AND READING ROOM, RESEMBLES SOME DINGY SETTLEMENT 245 HA APE
BOYS' CLUB.
THE INTERIOR OF THE ROOM, WHICH IS GENERAL 245 HA APE
ASSEMBLY ROOM, OFFICE,
SHOWING THE INTERIOR OF A FRONT ROOM ON THE GROUND245 HA APE
FLOOR,
IS TAKEN ABACK BY THE COMMONPLACENESS OF THE ROOM 246 HA APE
AND THE MEN IN IT.
(ALL THE MEN IN THE ROOM LOOK UP. 246 HA APE
JUGGLING THE ROOM KEY IN HIS HAND.) 17 HUGHIE
(ENCOURAGED, LEANS ON THE DESK, CLACKING HIS ROOM 20 HUGHIE
KEY LIKE A CASTANET.)
CAME ALL THE WAY IN A DRAWING ROOM, AND I WASN'T 23 HUGHIE
LUCKY IN IT NEITHER.
HE STARES AT THE FLOOR, TWIRLING HIS ROOM KEY--TO 27 HUGHIE
HIMSELF.)
AWAKE WHEN EVERYONE ELSE IN THE WORLD IS ASLEEP, 29 HUGHIE
EXCEPT ROOM 492,

ROOM

ROOM (CONT'D.)
FOR A WHILE HE IS TOO DEFEATED EVEN TO TWIRL HIS 30 HUGHIE
ROOM KEY.
EVEN HOPE'S BACK ROOM IS NOT A SEPARATE ROOM, 571 ICEMAN
THUS MAKING A BACK ROOM LEGALLY A HOTEL 571 ICEMAN
RESTAURANT.
LIQUOR IN THE BACK ROOM OF THE BAR AFTER CLOSING 571 ICEMAN
HOURS AND ON SUNDAYS,
THE BACK ROOM AND A SECTION OF THE BAR OF HARRY 573 ICEMAN
HOPE'S SALOON
THE BACK ROOM IS CRAMMED WITH ROUND TABLES AND 573 ICEMAN
CHAIRS PLACED SO CLOSE TOGETHER
IN THE LEFT CORNER, BUILT OUT INTO THE ROOM, 573 ICEMAN
BY DRAWING A DIRTY BLACK CURTAIN ACROSS THE ROOM,)573 ICEMAN
THE RIGHT WALL OF THE BACK ROOM IS A DIRTY BLACK 573 ICEMAN
CURTAIN
IN THE BACK ROOM, LARRY SLADE AND HUGO KALMAR ARE 574 ICEMAN
AT THE TABLE AT LEFT-FRONT,
HE IS THE ONLY OCCUPANT OF THE ROOM WHO IS NOT 574 ICEMAN
COMES FROM THE BAR THROUGH THE CURTAIN AND STANDS 577 ICEMAN
LOOKING OVER THE BACK ROOM.
=AND ALL DESE BUMS GOT TO PAY UP DEIR ROOM RENT. 578 ICEMAN
ROCKY GLANCES AROUND THE ROOM) 580 ICEMAN
(ALL THE OCCUPANTS OF THE ROOM STIR ON THEIR 581 ICEMAN
CHAIRS
BEJEES, CAN'T I GET A WINK OF SLEEP IN MY OWN BACK582 ICEMAN
ROOMS
HAD A ROLL WHEN HE PAID YOU HIS ROOM RENT, DIDN'T 583 ICEMAN
HE, ROCKY$
CAME TO LOOK YOU UP LAST NIGHT AND RENTED A ROOMS 583 ICEMAN
UP IN HIS ROOM, ASLEEP. 583 ICEMAN
HE LOOKS AS THOUGH HE BELONGED IN A POOL ROOM 585 ICEMAN
PATRONIZED BY WOULD-BE SPORTS.
THREE LADIES OF THE PAVEMENT THAT ROOM ON THE 594 ICEMAN
THIRD FLOOR.
AND STARTS BACK FOR THE ENTRANCE TO THE BACK ROOM.596 ICEMAN
LOCK HIM IN HIS ROOM/ 597 ICEMAN
NUT PLEASE, ROCKY! I'LL GO CRAZY UP IN THAT ROOM 597 ICEMAN
ALONE! IT'S HAUNTED/
OR DERE'S A LITTLE IRON ROOM UP DE RIVER WAITIN' 601 ICEMAN
FOR YOUSE
HOW MUCH ROOM RENT DO YOU OWE ME, TELL ME THATS 602 ICEMAN
I COULD ALMOST SEE HER IN EVERY ROOM JUST AS SHE 602 ICEMAN
USED TO BE--
A SUITABLE SENTIMENTAL HUSH FALLS ON THE ROOM.) 603 ICEMAN
THE BACK ROOM BECOMES DRABBER AND DINGIER THAN 610 ICEMAN
EVER IN THE GRAY DAYLIGHT THAT
CORA LOOKS AROUND THE ROOM) 617 ICEMAN
SAME OLD ROOM. 620 ICEMAN
THE BACK ROOM HAS BEEN PREPARED FOR A FESTIVITY. 628 ICEMAN
THE OTHER TABLES AND CHAIRS THAT HAD BEEN IN THE 628 ICEMAN
ROOM HAVE BEEN MOVED OUT.
(SCENE--THE BACK ROOM ONLY. 628 ICEMAN
IT'S BEEN HELL UP IN THAT DAMNED ROOM, LARRY/ 644 ICEMAN
WHY DIDN'T YOU COME UP TO MY ROOM, LIKE I ASKED 649 ICEMAN
YOUS
THERE IS A TENSE STILLNESS IN THE ROOM. 663 ICEMAN
AT LEFT, IN WHAT HAD BEEN THE BACK ROOM, WITH THE 664 ICEMAN
DIVIDING CURTAIN DRAWN,
INCLUDING A PART OF WHAT HAD BEEN THE BACK ROOM IN664 ICEMAN
ACTS ONE AND TWO.
BUT IT DOES NOT HIT THE WINDOWS AND THE LIGHT IN 664 ICEMAN
THE BACK-ROOM SECTION IS DIM.
(DEFIANTLY) HE DIDN'T COME TO MY ROOM/ 665 ICEMAN
HE'S BEEN HOPPIN' FROM ROOM TO ROOM ALL NIGHT. 665 ICEMAN
DEY PINCHED A COUPLA BOTTLES AND BRUNG DEM UP DEIR669 ICEMAN
ROOM AND GOT STINKO.
HERE'S DE KEY TO MY ROOM. 673 ICEMAN
HE'LL BE BACK TONIGHT ASKIN' HARRY FOR HIS ROOM 674 ICEMAN
AND BUMMIN' ME FOR A GALL.
HIS BACK TO THE ROOM. 677 ICEMAN
MCGLOIN STARTS INTO THE BACK-ROOM SECTION.) 681 ICEMAN
THE BACK ROOM WITH THE CURTAIN SEPARATING IT FROM 695 ICEMAN
THE SECTION OF THE BARROOM
THE TABLES IN THE BACK ROOM HAVE A NEW 695 ICEMAN
ARRANGEMENT.
THERE IS AN ATMOSPHERE OF OPPRESSIVE STAGNATION IN696 ICEMAN
THE ROOM.
BEAT IT IN DE BACK ROOM/ 697 ICEMAN
MY PIG'S IN DE BACK ROOM, AIN'T SHES 699 ICEMAN
AS ROCKY ENTERS THE BACK ROOM AND STARTS OVER 700 ICEMAN
TOWARD LARRY'S TABLE.)
HE KEPT HIMSELF LOCKED IN HIS ROOM UNTIL A WHILE 700 ICEMAN
AGO.
THEN THE SUDDEN SILENCE DESCENDS AGAIN ON THE 701 ICEMAN
ROOM.
SUNK IN THE SAME STUPOR AS THE OTHER OCCUPANTS OF 701 ICEMAN
THE ROOM.
ROOM. 708 ICEMAN
IN THE CURTAIN LEADING TO THE BACK ROOM. 708 ICEMAN
(IN A LOW VOICE) GUY NAMED HICKMAN IN THE BACK 708 ICEMAN
ROOMS
(GRUMPILY) IN DE BACK ROOM IF YUH WANTA DRINK. 708 ICEMAN
THE SILENCE IS LIKE THAT IN THE ROOM OF A DYING 714 ICEMAN
MAN
MOVES QUIETLY FROM THE ENTRANCE IN THE CURTAIN 716 ICEMAN
ACROSS THE BACK OF THE ROOM TO.
SET APPEARANCE OF A ROOM RARELY OCCUPIED. 11 JOURNE
NEVER USED EXCEPT AS A PASSAGE FROM LIVING ROOM TO 11 JOURNE
DINING ROOM.
(SCENE LIVING ROOM OF JAMES TYRONE'S SUMMER HOME 11 JOURNE
ON A MORNING IN AUGUST, 1912.
COMING FROM THE DINING ROOM. 12 JOURNE
ENTERING THE LIVING ROOM HE GIVES HER A PLAYFUL 14 JOURNE
HUG.
FROM THE DINING ROOM JAMIE'S AND EDMUND'S VOICES 15 JOURNE
ARE HEARD.

ROOM (CONT'D.)
WHY DID THE BOYS STAY IN THE DINING ROOM, I 15 JOURNE
WONDERS
ARE THEY GOING TO STAY IN THE DINING ROOM ALL DAYS 18 JOURNE
(A BURST OF LAUGHTER COMES FROM THE DINING ROOM. 18 JOURNE
COME IN THE LIVING ROOM AND GIVE CATHLEEN A CHANCE 18 JOURNE
TO CLEAR THE TABLE.
I'LL STICK TO BROADWAY, AND A ROOM WITH A BATH, 35 JOURNE
GOING TO HIS ROOM TO SEE HOW HE WAS. 38 JOURNE
(EAGERLY.) YES, THAT'S RIGHT, SHE DID STOP TO 38 JOURNE
LISTEN OUTSIDE HIS ROOM.
I WOKE UP AND HEARD HER MOVING AROUND IN THE SPARE 38 JOURNE
ROOM.
(HESITANTLY AGAIN.) IT WAS HER BEING IN THE SPARE 38 JOURNE
ROOM THAT SCARED ME.
(WARNINGLY AS HE HEARS HIS MOTHER IN THE DINING 39 JOURNE
ROOM.)
YOU WENT IN THE SPARE ROOM FOR THE REST OF THE 47 JOURNE
NIGHT.
YOU DIDN'T GO BACK TO YOUR AND PAPA'S ROOM. 47 JOURNE
FOR HEAVEN'S SAKE, HAVEN'T I OFTEN USED THE SPARE 47 JOURNE
ROOM AS MY BEDROOMS
IT'S JUST THAT I WASN'T ASLEEP WHEN YOU CAME IN MY 47 JOURNE
ROOM LAST NIGHT.
NO SUNLIGHT COMES INTO THE ROOM NOW THROUGH THE 51 JOURNE
WINDOWS AT RIGHT.
SHE WAS LYING DOWN IN THE SPARE ROOM WITH HER EYES 53 JOURNE
WIDE OPEN.
IN THE SPARE ROOMS 57 JOURNE
AS A DIRTY ROOM IN A ONE-NIGHT STAND HOTEL. 72 JOURNE
THE THREE IN THE ROOM REMAIN SILENT. 75 JOURNE
TO GO IN THE BABY'S ROOM. 87 JOURNE
SHE STARES ABOUT THE ROOM WITH FRIGHTENED, 95 JOURNE
DUSK IS GATHERING IN THE LIVING ROOM. 97 JOURNE
MY FATHER HAD SAID HE'D GO BACKSTAGE TO HIS 105 JOURNE
DRESSING ROOM RIGHT AFTER THE PLAY.
IT IS GROWING DARK IN THE ROOM. 107 JOURNE
I'M HERE, DEAR. IN THE LIVING ROOM. 108 JOURNE
ABOUT THE NIGHT MY FATHER TOOK ME TO YOUR DRESSING112 JOURNE
ROOM
OF OUR HOTEL ROOM, AND KNOCKED AND THEN RAN AWAY 113 JOURNE
BEFORE I CAME TO THE DOOR.
I HAD WAITED IN THAT UGLY HOTEL ROOM HOUR AFTER 113 JOURNE
HOUR.
HE WALKS WEARILY OFF THROUGH THE BACK PARLOR 125 JOURNE
TOWARD THE DINING ROOM.)
IN THE LIVING ROOM ONLY THE READING LAMP ON THE 125 JOURNE
TABLE IS LIGHTED.
OR IN THE DREARY SOLITUDE OF YOUR OWN ROOM, 132 JOURNE
HIDING IN A BROADWAY HOTEL ROOM WITH SOME FAT 134 JOURNE
TART--SHE LIKES THEN FAT--
LIKE SOMEONE WHO HAS COME TO A ROOM TO GET 170 JOURNE
SOMETHING BUT HAS BECOME
SHE SEEMS AWARE OF THEM MERELY AS SHE IS AWARE OF 170 JOURNE
OTHER OBJECTS IN THE ROOM.
SHE HESITATES IN THE DOORWAY, GLANCING ROUND THE 170 JOURNE
ROOM.
IT IS SIMPLY A PART OF THE FAMILIAR ATMOSPHERE OF 171 JOURNE
THE ROOM.
(SHE FORGETS HER HANDS AND COMES INTO THE ROOM, 171 JOURNE
(SHE LOOKS AROUND THE ROOM, HER FOREHEAD PUCKERED 172 JOURNE
AGAIN.)
THE MAIN ROOM AT THE FRONT END OF THE HOUSE IS 273 LAZARU
SHOWN--
ROOM, AROUND WHICH MANY CHAIRS FOR GUESTS HAVE 273 LAZARU
BEEN PLACED.
THE CROWDS OF MEN AND WOMEN ON EACH SIDE PUSH INTO278 LAZARU
THE ROOM TO STARE AT HIM.
(MUSIC BEGINS IN THE ROOM OFF RIGHT, REAR--A 278 LAZARU
FESTIVE DANCE TUNE.
(HIS FAMILY AND THE GUESTS IN THE ROOM NOW THRONG 278 LAZARU
ABOUT LAZARUS TO EMBRACE HIM.
(THE GUESTS IN THE ROOM, 278 LAZARU
THE CROWD IN THE ROOM ARE CAUGHT BY IT. 280 LAZARU
(THE ROOM ROCKS, THE AIR OUTSIDE THROBS 281 LAZARU
IN THE CENTER OF THE ROOM ON A HIGH DAIS IS THE 335 LAZARU
IVORY AND GOLD CHAIR OF CAESAR,
THE BANQUET HALL IN THE PALACE OF TIBERIUS--AN 335 LAZARU
IMMENSE HIGH-CEILINGED ROOM.
IN THE BANQUET ROOM ALL ARE LISTENING 337 LAZARU
FASCINATEDLY.
LAZARUS CASTS A LUMINOUS GLOW OVER THE WHOLE ROOM 338 LAZARU
FLOURISHING HIS SWORD AND COMES RUNNING INTO THE 338 LAZARU
ROOM, SHOUTING)
STARING AT HIS FACE NOW THAT THE ROOM IS FLOODED 340 LAZARU
A RIPPLE OF SOFT LAUGHTER FROM THE MUTIONLESS 341 LAZARU
FIGURES ABOUT THE ROOM ECHOES HIS.
BEATS THOSE IN THE ROOM INTO AN ABJECT SUBMISSIVE 349 LAZARU
PANIC.
IN THE HALF-DARKNESS, THE WALLS ARE LOST IN 350 LAZARU
SHADOW, THE ROOM SEEMS IMMENSE.
ONLY THESE FOUR PEOPLE ARE IN THE ROOM NOW.) 350 LAZARU
POUR IN FROM EACH SIDE OF THE ROOM AND DANCE 362 LAZARU
FORWARD TO GROUP THEMSELVES AROUND
DID I EXPECT DEATH TO OPEN THE DOOR AND ENTER THE 30 MANSNS
ROOM, VISIBLE TO ME,
THE ROOM IS SMALL, A TYPICAL ROOM OF THE PERIOD, 43 MANSNS
(SCENE SITTING-ROOM OF SARA HARFORD'S HOME 43 MANSNS
AS HE COMES INTO THE ROOM, HE IS FROWNING, HIS 43 MANSNS
EYES PREOCCUPIED.
wE HAVE A ROOM FOR YOU, IF NOT FOR JOEL-- 51 MANSNS
WE'VE A FINE ROOM ALWAYS READY. 51 MANSNS
THE ROOM IS SMALL, WELL-PROPORTIONED, PANELLED IN 69 MANSNS
DARK WOOD.
YOU STARTED SLEEPING IN YOUR OWN ROOM AWAY FROM 80 MANSNS
ME--
THE SARA WHO CAME TO MY ROOM ON THAT NIGHT LONG 88 MANSNS
AGO,

ROOM

ROOM (CONT'D.)

IN THE ROOM, AN EAVESDROPPING SILENCE THAT WAITS, 117 MANSNS
A HIGH-CEILINGED, FINELY-PROPORTIONED ROOM 117 MANSNS
AS THOUGH A HUMP WERE CONCEALED IN THE ROOM WITH A1ZO MANSNS
FUSE SLOWLY SPUTTERING
THIS HATE WAS BECOMING A LIVING PRESENCE IN THE 123 MANSNS
ROOM--AND IN MY MIND--
I STILL FEEL HATRED LIKE A LIVING PRESENCE IN THIS125 MANSNS
ROOM--STRANGE--DRAWING CLOSE--
IN HORROR FROM THE ROOM.)
YES, AND IT'S A HELP TO HAVE HIM OUT OF THE ROOM. 126 MANSNS 135 MANSNS
PLACED AT FRONT-CENTER, IT IS TOO LARGE FOR THE 139 MANSNS
ROOM.
THE DOOR FROM THE BOOKKEEPER'S ROOM AT RIGHT IS 139 MANSNS
OPENED NOISELESSLY
FOR A MOMENT HE STANDS GLANCING ABOUT THE ROOM 140 MANSNS
VAGUELY, HIS GAZE AVOIDING SARA.
HE WRENCHES OPEN THE DOOR AND FLINGS HIMSELF INTO 143 MANSNS
THE BOOKKEEPER'S ROOM.
(SHE IS MOVING TOWARDS THE BOOKKEEPER'S ROOM 144 MANSNS
ON THE LEFT OF THE ROOM IS AN ALTAR WITH CANDLES 398 MARCOM
BURNING.
THE SCENE IS REVEALED AS THE GRAND THRONE ROOM IN 377 MARCOM
THE PALACE OF KUBLAI.
AN IMMENSE OCTAGONAL ROOM, THE LOFTY WALLS ADORNED377 MARCOM
IN GOLD AND SILVER.
ALL THE PEOPLE IN THE ROOM ARE STARING AT HIM. 378 MARCOM
THE LITTLE THRONE ROOM IN THE BAMBOO SUMMER PALACE384 MARCOM
OF THE KAAN AT XANADU.
HIS EYES WANDER ABOUT THE ROOM, FINALLY RESTING 397 MARCOM
APPEALINGLY ON KUKACHIN.)
FROM THE ROOM ON THE RIGHT, THE BALLROOM, 421 MARCOM
THE GRAND THRONE ROOM IN THE IMPERIAL PALACE AT 421 MARCOM
CAMBALUC.
WHICH STANDS IN THE CENTER OF THE ROOM, 432 MARCOM
GRAND THRONE ROOM IN THE IMPERIAL PALACE AT 432 MARCOM
CAMBALUC. ABOUT TWO YEARS LATER.
ROOM IS AS MOTIONLESS AS THE KAAN HIMSELF. 433 MARCOM
(EVERYONE IN THE ROOM RISES WITH ONE MOTION OF 435 MARCOM
ASSERTION.)
ONE-ROOM ADDITION HAS BEEN TACKED ON AT RIGHT. 1 MISBEG
ABOUT TWELVE FEET LONG BY SIX HIGH, THIS ROOM, 1 MISBEG
WHICH IS JOSIE HOGAN'S BEDROOM,
IT'S INSIDE THE DOOR OF MY ROOM WITH YOUR COAT 5 MISBEG
LAID OVER IT.
HE GOES UP THE STEPS INTO HER ROOM 5 MISBEG
I'LL BET HE'S IN YOUR ROOM UNDER THE BED, THE 13 MISBEG
COWARDLY LUMP!
SHE GOES INTO THE LIVING ROOM, FUMBLES AROUND FOR 71 MISBEG
THE BOX OF MATCHES.
(SCENE, THE SAME, WITH THE WALL OF THE LIVING 71 MISBEG
ROOM REMOVED.
THE LIVING ROOM IS SMALL, LOW-CEILINGED, WITH 71 MISBEG
FADED, FLY-SPECKED WALLPAPER.
I HAVE NO PATIENCE LEFT, SO GET UP FROM THAT 74 MISBEG
CHAIR, AND GO IN YOUR ROOM.
GO TO YOUR ROOM, I'M SAYING, BEFORE-- 76 MISBEG
I'LL STAY HERE IN THIS CHAIR, AND YOU GO TO YOUR 76 MISBEG
ROOM AND LET ME BE.
(THREATENINGLY) IF YOU'RE GOING TO YOUR ROOM, 80 MISBEG
YOU'D BETTER GO QUICKLY
(SHE HURRIES BACK ACROSS THE ROOM INTO HER BEDROOM 97 MISBEG
AND CLOSES THE DOOR.
I'LL GET A ROOM AND TWO BOTTLES AND STAY DRUNK AS 100 MISBEG
LONG AS I PLEASE!
SHE OPENS THE DOOR FROM HER ROOM TO THE LIGHTED 107 MISBEG
LIVING ROOM.
THE FOOT OF THE BED WHICH OCCUPIES MOST OF THE 107 MISBEG
ROOM CAN BE SEEN,
SHE HAS LEFT THE DOOR FROM THE LIVING ROOM TO HER 107 MISBEG
BEDROOM OPEN AND THE LIGHT
JOSIE STOPS BY THE TABLE IN THE LIVING ROOM TO 111 MISBEG
TURN DOWN THE LAMP
(SCENE. THE LIVING-ROOM WALL HAS BEEN REPLACED 111 MISBEG
EXCEPT I WAS PIE-EYED IN A DRAWING ROOM THE WHOLE 128 MISBEG
FOUR DAYS.
AND I COULD GO BACK TO THE HOTEL--AND THE BOTTLE 143 MISBEG
IN MY ROOM.
I TOOK A DRAWING ROOM AND HID IN IT WITH A CASE OF148 MISBEG
BOOZE.
I FOUND I COULDN'T STAY ALONE IN THE DRAWING ROOM.149 MISBEG
DIDN'T QUIT, HE'D KEEP ME LOCKED IN THE DRAWING 149 MISBEG
ROOM.
AND THAT NIGHT SHE SNEAKED INTO MY DRAWING ROOM. 149 MISBEG
AND NOW HE STARES TORTUREDIY THROUGH THE MOONLIGHT149 MISBEG
INTO THE DRAWING ROOM.)
HOGAN COMES OUT OF HER ROOM AND STANDS ON TOP OF 174 MISBEG
THE STEPS.
(HE GOES IN THE HOUSE THROUGH HER ROOM. 177 MISBEG
(SCENE THE DINING ROOM OF MELODY'S TAVERN, IN A 7 POET
VILLAGE A FEW MILES FROM BOSTON.
THE DINING ROOM AND BARROOM WERE ONCE A SINGLE 7 POET
SPACIOUS ROOM, LOW-CEILINGED.
I USED TO HAVE MY ROOM HERE. 13 POET
I DON'T KNOW IF IT'S RIGHT, YOU TO BE IN HIS ROOM 32 POET
SO MUCH, EVEN IF HE IS SICK.
(ADVANCING INTO THE ROOM--BOWS FORMALLY TO HIS 34 POET
WIFE.)
THE GLANCES AROUND THE ROOM WITH LOATHING.) 38 POET
PREENING HIMSELF, BUT YOU CAN BLAME THE BAD LIGHT 44 POET
IN MY ROOM.
YOU HAVE THE BEST ROOM IN THE HOUSE, THAT WE OUGHT 45 POET
TO RENT TO GUESTS.
AND THE END WAS I RAN FROM THE ROOM, BLUSHING AS 65 POET
RED AS A BEET--
GO ON UP TO YOUR ROOM NOW AND YOU'LL FIND 75 POET
SOMETHING TO TAKE YOUR MIND OFF.

ROOM (CONT'D.)

WHEN HE DISCOVERS DEBORAH IS NOT IN THE ROOM, HE 88 POET
IS MILDLY DISAPPOINTED
SLOWLY BECAUSE MELODY, HEARING VOICES IN THE ROOM 88 POET
AND HOPING DEBORAH IS THERE,
I HAPPENED TO GO TO MY ROOM AND FOUND YOU AND YOUR 89 POET
MOTHER HAD LAID OUT
MELODY DRAWS HIM INTO THE ROOM.) 92 POET
FIGURE IN THE ROOM, WHICH APPEARS SMALLER AND 95 POET
DINGIER IN THE CANDLELIGHT.
AND A NATE LITTLE ROOM FOR THE FATHER CONFESSOR. 96 POET
AND CREGAN CROWD INTO THE ROOM. 123 POET
THE ROOM IS IN DARKNESS EXCEPT FOR ONE CANDLE ON 133 POET
THE TABLE, CENTER.
AND HE MUST HAVE TAKEN A ROOM IN THE CITY SO HE'LL137 POET
BE NEAR THE GROUND.
YOU'VE BEEN IN HIS ROOM EVER SINCE YOU WENT UP, 142 POET
HERE I'D GONE TO HIS ROOM WITH MY MIND MADE UP TO 144 POET
BE AS BOLD AS ANY STREET WOMAN
AND JAMIE CREGAN STICKS HIS HEAD IN CAUTIOUSLY TO 151 POET
PEER AROUND THE ROOM.
NO, HE'S GONE TO HIS ROOM. 159 POET
I HEARD HIM OPENIN' THE CLOSET IN HIS ROOM WHERE 162 POET
HE KEEPS HIS AULD SET
(SHE RETREATS QUICKLY INTO THE ROOM AND BACKS 163 POET
AROUND THE TABLE AT LEFT FRONT
CREGAN HAS HIM BY THE SHOULDER AND PUSHES HIM 164 POET
ROUGHLY INTO THE ROOM.
(SHE COMES INTO THE ROOM AND JUMPS UP, TRYING TO 600 ROPE
GRAB HOLD OF THE ROPE)
FILLS THE ROOM WITH A SOOTHING LIGHT. 3 STRANG
IS ARRANGED TOWARD THE LEFT OF THE ROOM, THE 3 STRANG
ROCKER IS AT CENTER.
THIS ROOM IS AT THE FRONT PART OF HIS HOUSE WITH 3 STRANG
4 WINDOWS OPENING ON THE STRIP OF
IT IS A SMALL ROOM WITH A LOW CEILING. 3 STRANG
THE ATMOSPHERE OF THE ROOM IS THAT OF A COSY, 3 STRANG
CULTURED RETREAT.
(HIS EYES FOLLOW HER FOR A SECOND, THEN RETURN TO 4 STRANG
GAZE AROUND THE ROOM SLOWLY
AND MAKES HIMSELF WALK ABOUT THE ROOM) 5 STRANG
(THINKING PITYINGLY) (WANDERING FROM ROOM TO 8 STRANG
ROOM...
OH, HOW I LOATHE THIS ROOM/....) 15 STRANG
AND STARTS TO TAKE A BRISK TURN ABOUT THE ROOM. 22 STRANG
(THERE IS NO ANSWER) (IN OTHER ROOM... 23 STRANG
THE APPEARANCE OF THE ROOM IS UNCHANGED EXCEPT 24 STRANG
THAT ALL THE SHADES,
GIVING THE WINDOWS A SUGGESTION OF LIFELESS CLOSED 24 STRANG
EYES AND MAKING THE ROOM SEEM
(SHE PAUSES AND LOOKS ABOUT THE ROOM--THINKING 27 STRANG
CONFUSEDLY)
I'LL CARRY HER UP TO HER ROOM. 46 STRANG
COVERED SIDE PORCH, SO THAT NO SUNLIGHT EVER GETS 48 STRANG
TO THIS ROOM AND THE LIGHT
THE ROOM IS ONE OF THOSE BIG, MISPROPORTIONED 48 STRANG
DINING ROOMS
THE DINING ROOM OF THE EVANS' HOMESTEAD IN 48 STRANG
NORTHERN NEW YORK STATE--
WE SLEPT LAST NIGHT IN THE ROOM HE WAS BORN IN. 49 STRANG
A MOMENT LATER EVANS AND HIS MOTHER ENTER THE 53 STRANG
DINING ROOM.
SHE LIVES ON THE TOP FLOOR OF THIS HOUSE, HASN'T 59 STRANG
BEEN OUT OF HER ROOM IN YEARS,
JUST AS THE OTHER FURNITURE IN THE ROOM BY ITS 66 STRANG
DISARRANGEMENT.
(HE BEGINS PACING UP AND DOWN THE ROOM, PUFFING AT 67 STRANG
HIS PIPE,
NOT BE HERE IN MY FATHER'S ROOM... 69 STRANG
GORDON'S SPIRIT FOLLOWED ME FROM ROOM TO ROOM... 71 STRANG
AND I'LL HAVE TO GET THE SPARE ROOM READY. 72 STRANG
(HE COMES BACK TO THE MIDDLE OF THE ROOM, FRONT, 76 STRANG
THE ROOM IS A TYPICAL SITTING ROOM OF THE 90 STRANG
QUANTITY-PRODUCTION BUNGALOW TYPE.
THE SITTING ROOM OF A SMALL HOUSE EVANS HAS RENTED 90 STRANG
A DOOR ON RIGHT, TO THE DINING ROOM. 90 STRANG
AND THE RESULT IS A ROOM AS DISORGANIZED IN 90 STRANG
CHARACTER
BANAL NEWNESS OFF THE ROOM WITH SOME OF HER OWN 90 STRANG
THINGS FROM HER OLD HOME BUT THE
WALKS SLOWLY AND WOODENLY LIKE A MAN IN A TRANCE 98 STRANG
INTO THE ROOM.
THERE'S SOMETHING IN THIS ROOM/... 99 STRANG
THAT DARRELL IN THIS ROOM/... 100 STRANG
LOST IN THIS ROOM/... 100 STRANG
SOMETHING HUMAN AND UNNATURAL IN THIS ROOM/... 100 STRANG
NO LONGER ANY LOVE FOR ME IN ANY ROOM/... 100 STRANG
IT'S THIS ROOM/ 101 STRANG
I CAN'T STAND THIS ROOM/ 101 STRANG
(HE GETS UP FORCEFULLY AND BEGINS TO PACE ABOUT 102 STRANG
THE ROOM.
THE ROOM HAS UNDERGONE A SIGNIFICANT CHANGE. 111 STRANG
(THINKING) (I WONDER IF THERE'S A DRAFT IN THE 111 STRANG
BOYS' ROOM...
(DARRELL STARTS, COMES INTO THE ROOM, PLAINLY 124 STRANG
GETTING A GRIP ON HIMSELF.
HIS EYES WANDER ABOUT THE ROOM, GREEDILY TAKING IT124 STRANG
IN.)
I LEAVE SAM AND HIS BABY IN THIS ROOM WITH THEM...129 STRANG
EVANS' VOICE IS IMMEDIATELY HEARD, EVEN BEFORE HE 132 STRANG
BOUNDS INTO THE ROOM.
(SHE TURNS AND WALKS QUIETLY OUT OF THE ROOM. 136 STRANG
THE SITTING ROOM OF THE EVANS' APARTMENT ON PARK 137 STRANG
AVENUE, NEW YORK CITY--
IT IS A LARGE, SUNNY ROOM, THE FURNITURE EXPENSIVE137 STRANG
BUT EXTREMELY SIMPLE.
NINA AND DARRELL AND THEIR SON, GORDON, ARE IN THE137 STRANG
ROOM.

ROOM (CONT'D.)
A ROOM THAT IS A TRIBUTE TO NINA'S GOOD TASTE. 137 STRANG
(PEREMPTORILY) LEAVE THE ROOM/ 142 STRANG
IN FRONT OF IT, A DOOR LEADING TO A SIDE ROOM. 493 VOYAGE
A SQUALID, DINGY ROOM DIMLY LIGHTED 493 VOYAGE
(HIS SHIFTY EYES PEER ABOUT THE ROOM SEARCHINGLY. 495 VOYAGE
NICK SLINKS INTO THE ROOM AFTER THEM AND SITS DOWN496 VOYAGE
AT A TABLE IN REAR.
AN' YER CAN 'AVE A DANCE IN THE SIDE ROOM 'ERE. 499 VOYAGE
FROM THE SIDE ROOM COMES THE SOUND OF AN ACCORDION501 VOYAGE
AND A BOISTEROUS WHOOP FROM
(THERE IS A CRASH FROM THE ROOM ON LEFT AND THE 503 VOYAGE
MUSIC ABRUPTLY STOPS.
IKATE CARRIES FREDA INTO THE NEXT ROOM. 508 VOYAGE
THE ROOM IS IN DARKNESS. 443 WELDED
(A CIRCLE OF LIGHT APPEARS WITH HIM, FOLLOWS HIM 443 WELDED
INTO THE ROOM.
BUT SHE SUDDENLY BECOMES AWARE OF SOME PRESENCE IN444 WELDED
THE ROOM.
(JOHN STEPS INTO THE ROOM. 450 WELDED
AT FIRST THE ROOM IS IN DARKNESS. 462 WELDED
HE FOLLOWS HER INTO THE ROOM. 462 WELDED
HE STEPS PAST HER BACK INTO THE ROOM, 465 WELDED
THEN SHE WAVERS AND SUDDENLY BOLTS BACK INTO THE 466 WELDED
ROOM, GROPINGLY.
THE ROOM IS IN DARKNESS EXCEPT FOR A FAINT GLOW 470 WELDED
THEN LOOKS FROM HER AROUND THE ROOM WITH A 471 WELDED
FRIGHTENED,
THROUGH SEPARATE WAYS LOVE HAS BROUGHT US BOTH TO 477 WELDED
THIS ROOM.

ROOM'S
THIS ROOM'S BEEN DEAD LONG ENUF. 245 DESIRE

ROOMED
ROOMED IN THE SAME DORM WITH ME AT COLLEGE. 30 STRANG

ROOMING
NEVER THOUGHT I'D SEE THE DAY WHEN HARRY HOPE'S 610 ICEMAN
WOULD HAVE TARTS ROOMING IN IT.

ROOMS
AND THE STAIRWAY TO THE UPSTAIRS ROOMS. 236 AHWILD
GIRLS ARE ONLY ALLOWED TO SMOKE UPSTAIRS IN THE 239 AHWILD
ROOMS, HE SAID.
AT RIGHT OF BEDROOM, FRONT, IS THE DOOR BETWEEN 553 DAYS
THE TWO ROOMS.
BOTH ROOMS ARE LIGHTED DIMLY AND FLICKERINGLY BY 235 DESIRE
TALLOW CANDLES.)
ALL THESE ROOMS ARE SMALL, THE ONES IN THE LIGHT -0 DYNAMO
HOME PARTICULARLY SO.
THE FRONT WALLS OF THESE ROOMS ARE REMOVED TO SHOW -0 DYNAMO
THE DIFFERENT INTERIORS.
THE CEILINGS OF BOTH ROOMS ARE LOW, 421 DYNAMO
(WHEN IT GROWS LIGHT AGAIN THE OUTER WALLS OF THE 427 DYNAMO
TWO ROOMS IN THE LIGHT HOME
THE TWO ROOMS IN THE FIFE HOME, BRIGHT WITH ALL 428 DYNAMO
THEIR ELECTRIC LIGHTS ON,
THE WALLS OF THE FIFE AND LIGHT SITTING ROOMS HAVE443 DYNAMO
BEEN REPLACED WHILE THE
THE INTERIORS OF THE DYNAMO AND SWITCHBOARD ROOMS 486 DYNAMO
ARE NOW ALSO REVEALED.
WE CAN AT LEAST TIDY UP THE ROOMS A LITTLE AND GET136 ELECTR
THE FURNITURE COVERS OFF.
IN THE DOWNSTAIRS ROOMS. 137 ELECTR
WHICH USUALLY ADORN THE SITTING ROOMS OF SUCH 269 GGBROW
HOUSES.
THE BACKDROP FOR BOTH ROOMS IS OF PLAIN WALL WITH 302 GGBROW
A FEW TACKED-UP DESIGNS AND
THE PEOPLE IN THE TWO ROOMS STARE. 318 GGBROW
THE RENTING OF ROOMS ON THE UPPER FLOORS, UNDER 571 ICEMAN
THE RAINES-LAW LOOPHOLES,
I HUNG AROUND POOL ROOMS AND GAMBLING JOINTS AND 588 ICEMAN
HOOKER SHOPS,
BUT I DON'T LET 'EM USE MY ROOMS FOR BUSINESS. 610 ICEMAN
AND DE REST IS HIDIN' IN DEIR ROOMS SO DEY WON'T 631 ICEMAN
HAVE TO LISTEN TO HIM.
THE ONLY PLACE I LIKED WAS THE POOL ROOMS, WHERE I709 ICEMAN
COULD SMOKE SWEET CAPORALS,
THE DAMNED HOTEL ROOMS. 712 ICEMAN
IN DIRTY ROOMS OF FILTHY HOTELS, EATING BAD FOOD, 87 JOURNE
BEARING CHILDREN IN HOTEL ROOMS, I STILL KEPT 87 JOURNE
HEALTHY.
ALWAYS A BOTTLE ON THE BUREAU IN THE CHEAP HOTEL 110 JOURNE
ROOMS/
HOW MANY TIMES I WAS TO WAIT IN UGLY HOTEL ROOMS. 113 JOURNE
WAITING NIGHT AFTER NIGHT IN DIRTY HOTEL ROOMS FOR141 JOURNE
YOU TO COME BACK
SMALLER ARCHES IN THE MIDDLE OF THE SIDE WALLS 335 LAZARU
LEAD INTO OTHER ROOMS.
THE CHILDREN MUST BE FORBIDDEN TO GO TO HER GARDEN 86 MANSNS
OR HER ROOMS IN FUTURE.
I EXPLAINED OVER AND OVER AGAIN THAT I FELT ALL 110 MANSNS
THE ROOMS IN THE HOUSE,
NOW DIVIDED INTO TWO ROOMS BY A FLIMSY PARTITION, 7 POET
THE BARROOM BEING OFF LEFT.
THE ROOM IS ONE OF THOSE BIG, MISPROPORTIONED 48 STRANG
DINING ROOMS
ALL THE ROOMS GO ROUND AND ROUND 507 VOYAGE
THE TWO OTHER PEOPLE AND THE ROOMS ARE 443 WELDED
DISTINGUISHABLE ONLY BY THE LIGHT OF

ROOSHAN
YE ROOSHAN BABOON/ 498 VOYAGE

ROOSHUN
D'YOU HEAR THE LADY TALKIN' TO YE, YE ROOSHUN 500 VOYAGE
SWABS

ROOST
I'M THE PRIZE ROOSTER O' THIS ROOST. 246 DESIRE
YOUR ICEMAN JOKE FINALLY CAME HOME TO ROOST, DID 657 ICEMAN
IT$
SO I STROLLED ABOUT AND FINALLY CAME TO ROOST IN 723 ICEMAN
THE PARK.

ROOSTER
I'M THE PRIZE ROUSTER O' THIS ROGST. 246 DESIRE

ROOSTERS
=I BEEN HEARIN' THE HENS CLUCKIN' AN' THE ROOSTERS210 DESIRE
CROWIN' ALL THE DURN DAY.
(COMES BETWEEN THEM) HERE, YOU OLD ROOSTERS. 133 ELECTR
BARKING, CROWING LIKE ROOSTERS, HOWLING, 366 LAZARU

ROOSTIN'
ME, I DON'T RELISH ROOSTIN' ON MY FEET. 507 DIFKNT

ROOT
SO THAT I WON'T TAKE ROOT IN ANY ONE PLACE. 83 BEYOND
THE ROOT OF BELIEF IS IN YOU, TOC/ 560 CROSS
NOW AND ROOT EVERYONE OUT. 644 ICEMAN
AND SWINE SHALL ROOT WHERE THY TEMPLE STOOD/ 292 LAZARU
TO CLEANSE HIS TEETH, AND THEN THROWING IT AWAY, 349 MARCOM
IT TOOK ROOT,
WAS BURIED IN THE GRAVE OF ABU ABDALLAH WHERE IT 350 MARCOM
STRUCK ROOT
ROOT OF HER TROUBLE STILL...)) 80 STRANG

ROOTED
DEYAE MAYBE ROOTED OUT YO' GRUB AN' EAT IT, 190 EJONES
AS ONE LEANS AGAINST A TREE, DEEP-ROOTED IN THE 120 MANSNS
COMMON EARTH--

ROOTED TO THE SPOT. 177 MANSNS
THAT IT APPEARS A HARMONIOUS PART OF THE 1 MISBEG
LANDSCAPE, ROOTED IN THE EARTH.

ROOTIN'
SHE'LL HAVE SOME TROUBLE, ROOTIN' OUT HIS DREAMS. 173 POET

ROPE
AT THE END OF A ROPE. 539 'ILE
ANNA IS DISCOVERED STANDING NEAR THE COIL OF ROPE 25 ANNA
(SHE POINTS TO THE COIL OF ROPE. 26 ANNA
HEAVE A ROPE WHEN WE COME ALONGSIDE. 29 ANNA
(HE PICKS UP A COIL OF ROPE AND HURRIES OFF TOWARD 30 ANNA
THE BOW.
HE GOT A HALTER AND MADE A NOOSE OF THE ROPE FOR 548 DIFRNT
HIS NECK AND CLIMBED UP IN THE
HE'S AS GUILTY OF MURDER AS ANYONE HE EVER SENT TO 27 ELECTR
THE ROPE WHEN HE WAS A JUDGE/
MAYBE--IF THEY'VE GOT A ROPE HANDY/ 652 ICEMAN
I'LL HELP PULL ON THE ROPE. 691 ICEMAN
DAVIS SNATCHES A SMALL COIL OF ROPE FROM ONE OF 525 INZONE
THE UPPER BUNKS)
IT'S LIKE WALKING A TIGHT-ROPE OVER AN ABYSS-- 156 MANSNS
A ROPE ABOUT FIVE FEET LONG WITH AN OPEN RUNNING 577 ROPE
NOOSE AT THE END, IS HANGING.
(HE STANDS STARING UP AT THE ROPE AND TAPS IT 579 ROPE
TESTINGLY SEVERAL TIMES WITH HIS
SO YOU MIGHT 'S WELL TAKE DOWN THAT UGLY ROPE 581 ROPE
YOU'VE HAD TIED THERE SINCE HE RUN
AND HE ONLY LAUGHED HARDER WHEN YOU HUNG UP THAT 581 ROPE
SILLY ROPE THERE (SHE POINTS)
YOU CAN SEE NO ONE AIN'T TOUCHED YOUR OLD ROPE. 581 ROPE
HE WANTED TO MAKE SURE THE ROPE WAS STILL HERE. 582 ROPE
(POINTING TO THE ROPE WITH HIS STICK) 582 ROPE
(HE REACHES UP FOR THE ROPE AS IF TO TRY AND YANK 583 ROPE
IT DOWN.
(HIS EYES ON THE ROPE)) I'LL BE PULLIN' THAT THINGS83 ROPE
DOWN, SO I WILL.
LEAVE HIS ROPE BE. 583 ROPE
UNTIL HE STANDS DIRECTLY UNDER THE ROPE. 587 ROPE
HE STOOD THERE WITHE THE NOOSE OF THE ROPE ALMOST 590 ROPE
TOUCHIN' HIS HEAD.
REMEMBER HOW HOT HE WAS THAT DAY WHEN HE HUNG THAT592 ROPE
ROPE UP
THAT ROPE. 592 ROPE
(HE TURNS AROUND AND HIS EYES FIX THEMSELVES ON 592 ROPE
THE ROPE)
HE RAISES IT TOWARD THE ROPE) 592 ROPE
=REMEMBER, WHEN YOU COME HOME AGAIN THERE'S A ROPE593 ROPE
WAITIN' FOR YUH
(BENTLEY POINTS WITH HIS STICK TO THE ROPE. 596 ROPE
(MUMBLING INCOHERENTLY) LUKE--LUKE--ROPE--LUKE-- 596 ROPE
HANG.
(HE TAKES THE CHAIR FROM LEFT AND PLACES IT UNDER 596 ROPE
THE ROPE.
(HE REMOVES THE ROPE GINGERLY FROM HIS NECK. 596 ROPE
(SHE COMES INTO THE ROOM AND JUMPS UP, TRYING TO 600 ROPE
GRAB HOLD OF THE ROPE)
(SEVERELY) DON'T YUH DARE TOUCH THAT ROPE, D'YUH 600 ROPE
HEAR$
THE ROPE SEEMS TO PART WHERE IT IS FIXED TO THE 601 ROPE
BEAM.
DIRECTLY UNDERNEATH THE NOOSE OF THE ROPE. 601 ROPE
A DIRTY GRAY BAG TIED TO THE END OF THE ROPE FALLS601 ROPE

ROPE'S
BUT THE ROPE'S THERE YET, AIN'T IT$ 593 ROPE

ROPES
WATERBURY'S NIFTY OLD TOWN WITH THE LID OFF, WHEN 188 AHWILD
YOU GET TO KNOW THE ROPES.
THE INTERLOCKED ROPES OF CREEPERS REACHING UPWARD 198 EJONES
TO ENTWINE THE TREE TRUNKS
IN TWO MINUTES, THEY'D HAVE HIM HANGING ON THE 16 HUGHIE
ROPES.
(HE SIGNS EXPLOSIVELY) JEES, SHE'S GOT ME HANGIN'671 ICEMAN
ON DE ROPES/
HE STEPS SOFTLY OVER TO SMITTY AND CUTS THE ROPES 532 INZONE
ABOUT HIS ARMS AND ANKLES WITH

ROSE
(GRINS AND SINGS) =DUNNO WHAT TER CALL'IM BUT HE'S189 AHWILD
MIGHTY LIKE A ROSE-VELT.=
=YET AH, THAT SPRING SHOULD VANISH WITH THE ROSE/ 298 AHWILD
(TURNING TO THE LEFT) THIS WAY, ROSE, OR PANSY, 468 CARIBE
OR JESSAMINE, OR BLACK TULIP,
YEW AIR MY ROSE O' SHARON/ 232 DESIRE
YEW AIR MY ROSE U' SHARUN/ 238 DESIRE
SOMETHING ROSE UP IN ME--LIKE AN EVIL SPIRIT/ 155 ELECTR

ROSE

ROSE (CONT'D.)
(SLOWLY) A BIT AV A DRIED-UP FLOWER--A ROSE, 532 INZONE
MAYBE.
DO YOU NOT KNOW THIS LAZARUS DIED AND THEN BY HIS 343 LAZARU
MAGIC ROSE FROM HIS TOMB?
AND NO ONE BUT THE FOOLS WHO ENVY YOU CARE WHAT 27 POET
YOU ROSE FROM,
LOOKS LIKE A FAIRY PRINCESS AS BEAUTIFUL AS A ROSE 53 POET
IN THE MORNIN' DEW.
NINA IS A ROSE, MY MUSE, EXHAUSTED BY THE LONG, 187 STRANG
HOT DAY,
HERE, MADELINE, HERE'S A ROSE FOR YOU. 188 STRANG
(HE HANDS A ROSE TO MADELINE) 188 STRANG
SHE TAKES THE ROSE AUTOMATICALLY, STARING AT HIM 188 STRANG
UNCOMPREHENDINGLY.)

ROSES
AND THE CLIMBING ROSES ON THE TRELLIS TO THE SIDE 548 *ILE
OF THE HOUSE--THEY'RE BUDDING.
A BIG HORSESHOE OF RED ROSES/ 31 HUGHIE
THEY ARE NOT LONG, THE DAYS OF WINE AND ROSES.. 130 JOURNE
IT WILL BRING FRESH ROSES TO YOUR CHEEKS. 44 POET
I DON'T KNOW ABOUT ROSES, BUT IT WILL BRING A 44 POET
BLUSH OF SHAME TO MY CHEEKS.
ROSES HEAVY WITH AFTER-BLOOMING OF THE LONG DAY, 187 STRANG
DESIRING EVENING....
THE KISSES ONE OF THE ROSES WITH A SIMPLE 187 STRANG
SENTIMENTAL SMILE--
MY LIFE GATHERS ROSES, COOLLY CRIMSON, IN 187 STRANG
SHELTERED GARDENS,
A BUNCH OF ROSES AND A PAIR OF SHEARS IN HIS 187 STRANG
HANDS.
(PRETENDING AN INTEREST IN THE ROSES) 188 STRANG
I'VE BEEN PICKING SOME ROSES FOR YOUR MOTHER, 188 STRANG
GORDON.

ROSSETTI
AND YOUR DANTE GABRIEL ROSSETTI WHO WAS A DOPE 135 JOURNE
FIEND/
(HE RECITES SARDONICALLY FROM ROSSETTI.) 168 JOURNE
"SLEEPLESS WITH PALE COMMEMORATIVE EYES," AS 135 MISBEG
ROSSETTI WROTE.

ROSY
HER FACE MUST HAVE ONCE BEEN ONE OF THOSE ROSY- 428 DYNAMO
CHEEKED PRETTY DULL-LIKE FACES
WITH A MASS OF BLACK HAIR, A FAIR SKIN WITH ROSY 1 MANSNS
CHEEKS,
FAIR SKIN WITH ROSY CHEEKS, AND BEAUTIFUL, DEEP- 15 POET
BLUE EYES.

ROT
SO DON'T MOCK ME WITH FAIRY TALES ABOUT ARIZONA, 160 BEYOND
OR ANY SUCH ROT AS THAT.
AND ROT-TEN PO-TAY-TOES/ 481 CARDIF
PLEASE FORGET THE STUPID ROT I'VE SAID. 524 DAYS
ROT/ 545 DAYS
AND WHEN IT RAINS THEIR TEARS TRICKLE DOWN 202 DESIRE
MONOTONOUSLY AND ROT ON THE SHINGLES.
AN' ROT--A WARNIN' T' OLD FOOLS LIKE ME T' B'AR 267 DESIRE
THEIR LONESOMENESS ALONE--
THE PORTRAITS OF THE MANNUNS WILL ROT ON THE WALLS171 ELECTR
(VIOLENTLY) ROT/ 298 GGBROW
AND THAT'S ENOUGH PHILOSOPHIC WISDOM TO GIVE YOU 578 ICEMAN
FOR ONE DRINK OF ROT-GUT.
AND IN THE END THEY ROT INTO DUST IN THE SAME 649 ICEMAN
GRAVE.
BESIDES IT'S DAMNED ROT/ 35 JOURNE
"THERE SHALL HE ROT--AMBITION'S DISHONORED FOOL/ 37 POET
IT'S A FAR CRY FROM THIS DUNGHILL ON WHICH I ROT 38 POET
TO THAT GLORIOUS DAY
BUT, OF COURSE, THAT'S PERFECT ROT. 77 STRANG
WHAT DAMNED ROT I'M THINKING/...!) 85 STRANG
ANYTHING ELSE IS ROT/ 87 STRANG
HE'LL LET IT ROT IN GOVERNMENT BONDS... 113 STRANG
(INTENSELY) (I) WANT TO ROT AWAY IN PEACE/... 138 STRANG
(SADLY--THINKING) (I)D ROT AWAY IN PEACE.... 140 STRANG
THAT NOW I AM FREE AT LAST TO ROT AWAY IN PEACE..191 STRANG
(SHE KISSES HIM--WISTFULLY) WILL YOU LET ME ROT 197 STRANG
AWAY IN PEACE?
YOU'RE TALKING ROT/ 486 WELDED

ROTATION
RUNNING AT A SPEED OF ROTATION N, IS THEORETICALLY429 DYNAMO
PROPORTIONAL TO D4 $LN2$....

ROTGUT
RUINING MY STOMACH WITH ROTGUT. 652 ICEMAN
EVEN WHEN I HAD TWO QUARTS OF ROTGUT UNDER MY BELT661 ICEMAN
AND JOKED AND SANG "SWEET
LIKE A DRINK OF NICKEL ROTGUT THAT WON'T STAY 680 ICEMAN
DOWN/
OR LIVING IN FILTHY DIVES, DRINKING ROTGUT, CAN 35 JOURNE
YOU?
THAT ISN'T PHIL'S ROTGUT. 173 MISBEG

ROTHSTEIN
LIKE ARNOLD ROTHSTEIN.* 31 HUGHIE
DO YOU, BY ANY CHANCE, KNOW THE BIG SHOT, ARNOLD 32 HUGHIE
ROTHSTEIN?
*ARNOLD ROTHSTEIN/ HE MUST BE SOME GUY/ 32 HUGHIE
WITHIN ITSELF CALLED ARNOLD ROTHSTEIN.) 32 HUGHIE
YOU BY ANY CHANCE KNOW--ARNOLD ROTHSTEINS 34 HUGHIE
(WITH AWE.) SO YOU'RE AN OLD FRIEND OF ARNOLD 35 HUGHIE
ROTHSTEIN/
WOULD YOU MIND TELLING ME IF IT'S REALLY TRUE WHEN 35 HUGHIE
ARNOLD ROTHSTEIN PLAYS POKER,
(THEN INSISTENTLY, IS IT TRUE WHEN ARNOLD 36 HUGHIE
RUTHSTEIN PLAYS POKER,
AS THE GAMBLER IN 492, THE FRIEND OF ARNOLD 37 HUGHIE
ROTHSTEIN--
ROTHSTEIN'S
HE HOPES RESEMBLES ARNOLD ROTHSTEIN'S.) 38 HUGHIE

ROTOR

=THE KINETIC ENERGY OF A ROTOR OF DIAMETER D AND 429 DYNAMO
AXIAL LENGTH L,

ROTS
I HOPE HIS SOUL ROTS IN HELL, WHOEVER IT IS/ 588 ICEMAN
MY CORPSE NO LONGER ROTS IN MY HEART/ 360 LAZARU
SHE ROTS AWAY IN PEACE/...)) 138 STRANG

ROTTED
BLOOD AN' BONE AN' SWEAT--ROTTED AWAY--FERTILIZIN'218 DESIRE
YE--RICHIN' YER SOUL--
HE ROTTED TEN YEARS IN PRISON FOR HIS FAITH/ 641 ICEMAN

ROTTEN
AND THE HANDS HALF STARVED WITH THE FOOD RUNNIN' 537 *ILE
LOW, ROTTEN AS IT IS.
UN A STINKIN' WHALIN' SHIP TO THE ARCTIC SEAS TO 537 *ILE
BE LOCKED IN BY THE ROTTEN ICE
THE GRUB WE'RE GETTIN' NOW IS ROTTEN. 544 *ILE
I'M A DIRTY, ROTTEN DRUNK/ 258 AHWILD
I FEEL--ROTTEN/ 262 AHWILD
SHE MADE EVERYTHING SEEM ROTTEN AND DIRTY--AND-- 294 AHWILD
GUESS I DO LOOK ROTTEN--YUST OUT OF THE HOSPITAL 14 ANNA
TWO WEEKS.
MY NERVES IS ON EDGE AFTER THAT ROTTEN TRIP. 16 ANNA
(HER VOICE RISING ANGRILY) SAY, WHAT'RE YOU 26 ANNA
TRYING TO DO--MAKE THINGS ROTTEN?
IT'S ROTTEN, AT TAL YOU, FOR GO TO SEA. 28 ANNA
DEY ALL VORK ROTTEN YOB UN SEA FOR NUTTING, 28 ANNA
BUT IF YOU HONESTLY THINK THE SEA'S SUCH A ROTTEN 37 ANNA
LIFE,
(GROWLING) 'TIS A ROTTEN BAD LOSER YOU ARE, DIVIL 52 ANNA
MEND YOU/
DIDN'T I WRITE YOU YEAR AFTER YEAR HOW ROTTEN IT 57 ANNA
WAS
TO SMASH YOUR SKULL LIKE A ROTTEN EGG. 60 ANNA
AND I'LL BE GETTING DEAD ROTTEN DRUNK SO I'LL NOT 61 ANNA
REMEMBER IT I'WAS IVER BORN
(DARKLY) WHAT WOULD SHE BE DOING ASHORE ON THIS 68 ANNA
ROTTEN NIGHT?
FOR IT'S A ROTTEN DOG'S LIFE I'VE LIVED THE PAST 69 ANNA
TWO DAYS SINCE I'VE KNOWN WHAT
ALTHOUGH TACKING BACK AND FORTH IN THESE 126 BEYOND
BLISTERING SEAS IS A ROTTEN JOB TOO/--
THIS ROTTEN HEADACHE HAS MY NERVES SHOT TO PIECES.135 BEYOND
AND HE SOLD US ROTTEN OILSKINS AND SEA-BOOTS FULL 487 CARDIF
OF HOLES.
THIS LAST YEAR HAS SEEMED ROTTEN, AND I'VE HAD A 487 CARDIF
HUNCH I'D QUIT--
(FRETFULLY) WHY SHOULD IT BE A ROTTEN NIGHT LIKE 489 CARDIF
THIS
IT'S JUST SOMETHING ABOUT THE ROTTEN THING WHICH 466 CARIBE
MAKES ME THINK--OF--
THEY DISCOVERED IN A SHELTERED INLET THE ROTTEN, 560 CROSS
WATER DRIPS FROM THEIR SOAKED AND ROTTEN CLOTHES. 571 CROSS
WELL, IT'S ROTTEN TO KEEP HIM COOLING HIS HEELS. 500 DAYS
I'M ROTTEN TO BE FLIP ABOUT THAT. 517 DAYS
HE SAID NO MATTER IF EVERY OTHER MARRIAGE ON EARTH523 DAYS
WERE ROTTEN AND A LIE,
I'VE BEEN ACCUSED OF SO MANY ROTTEN THINGS I NEVER524 DAYS
DIE.
AND EVEN IF I WERE ROTTEN ENOUGH TO COME RIGHT OUT526 DAYS
AND TELL HER,
OH, I KNOW YOU THINK I'M A ROTTEN LIAR, BUT I LOVE527 DAYS
ELSA/
YOU GOD-DAMNED ROTTEN SWINE/ 531 DAYS
REMEMBER IT'S A ROTTEN, CHILLY, 533 DAYS
FUCKS BE ALL CRAZY AND ROTTEN TO THE CORE AND I'M 543 DIFRNT
DONE WITH THE WHOLE KIT AND
THIS IS A ROTTEN BREAK...!) 464 DYNAMO
YOU ROTTEN SON OF A---(HE CHOKES IT BACK--THEN 465 DYNAMO
HELPLESSLY, WITH A WOUNDED LOOK)
YER DON'T KNOW WHAT MIGHT 'APPEN IN THERE, IT'S 185 EJONES
THAT ROTTEN STILL.
THAT WAS ROTTEN OF ME. 83 ELECTR
I AM A ROTTEN SWINE TO--DAMN VINNIE/ 93 ELECTR
SHE TULD ME YOUR ROTTEN LIES--ABOUT HIM--ABOUT 98 ELECTR
FOLLOWING HER TO NEW YORK.
(WITH BITTER SELF-CONTEMPT) I HAVE MY FATHER'S 110 ELECTR
ROTTEN COWARD BLOOD IN ME.
IT'S A ROTTEN DIRTY JOKE ON SOMEONE/ 116 ELECTR
HE KEEPS SAYING THEY'RE ROTTEN--WHEN THEY'RE 276 GGBROW
REALLY TOO BEAUTIFUL/
BUT, DAMN IT, I SUPPOSE YOU'RE TOO MUCH OF A 281 GGBROW
ROTTEN CYNIC TO BELIEVE I MEAN WHAT
(MUSINGLY) I LOVE THOSE ROTTEN OLD SOB TUNES. 284 GGBROW
JENKINS---THE FIRST---HE'S A ROTTEN SWINE--- 208 HA APE
WE WASN'T BORN THIS ROTTEN WAY. 211 HA APE
WELL, YOU DIRTY SPY, YOU ROTTEN AGENT PROVOCATOR, 249 HA APE
UNTIL HE'S A ROTTEN SKUNK IN HIS OWN EYES. 641 ICEMAN
(NAUSEATED--TURNS ON HIM) YOU STINKING ROTTEN 649 ICEMAN
LIAR/
I'M A ROTTEN LOUSE TO THROW THAT IN YOUR FACE. 693 ICEMAN
OH, I KNOW I USED TO HATE EVERYONE IN THE WORLD 705 ICEMAN
WHO WASN'T AS ROTTEN A BASTARD
YOU'RE PUTTING ON THIS ROTTEN HALF-DEAD ACT JUST 705 ICEMAN
TO GET BACK AT ME/
GOD DAMN YOU, STOP SHOVING YOUR ROTTEN SOUL IN MY 706 ICEMAN
LAP/
THAT'S WHAT MADE ME FEEL SUCH A ROTTEN SKUNK--HER 712 ICEMAN
ALWAYS FORGIVING ME.
BUT ALL THE TIME I SAW HOW CRAZY AND ROTTEN OF ME 715 ICEMAN
THAT WAS.
I WAS A RAVING ROTTEN LUNATIC OR I COULDN'T HAVE 719 ICEMAN
SAID--
I TELL YOU DIS ROTTEN COFFEE GIVE ME BELLY-ACHE/ 515 INZONE
(HE RAISES HIS FIST) I'LL CHOKE HIS ROTTEN HEART524 INZONE
OUT WID ME OWN HANDS,
BLOODY, BLEEDIN', ROTTEN DUTCH 'GG/ 526 INZONE
ROTTEN CUNS/ 527 INZONE
ROTTEN 'OUND/ 530 INZONE

1341 ROUGHLY

ROTTEN (CONT'D.)
THAT'S A ROTTEN ACCUSATION, PAPA. 35 JOURNE
I FEEL TOO ROTTEN. 42 JOURNE
JUST BECAUSE I FEEL ROTTEN AND BLUE, I SUPPOSE. 45 JOURNE
I KNOW HOW ROTTEN I FEEL, AND THE FEVER AND CHILLS 55 JOURNE
I GET AT NIGHT ARE NO JOKE.
I KNOW HOW ROTTEN IT MUST BE FOR HER. 57 JOURNE
IT'S A ROTTEN TRICK THE WAY HE KEEPS MEALS 61 JOURNE
WAITING,
HOLD YOUR FOUL TONGUE AND YOUR ROTTEN BROADWAY 76 JOURNE
LOAFER'S LINGO/
THEY'RE BOTH ROTTEN TO THE CORE. 77 JOURNE
THAT'S A ROTTEN THING TO SAY, PAPA/ 78 JOURNE
THAT'S A ROTTEN CRACK. 90 JOURNE
GOD, IT MADE EVERYTHING IN LIFE SEEM ROTTEN/ 118 JOURNE
WHEN I REMEMBER ALL THE ROTTEN STUFF I'VE PULLED/ 145 JOURNE
NOT BECAUSE OF THE ROTTEN WAY YOU'RE TREATING ME. 145 JOURNE
BEEFED HOW ROTTEN BUSINESS WAS, AND SHE WAS GOING 159 JOURNE
TO GIVE FAT VIOLET THE GATE.
I'VE BEEN ROTTEN BAD INFLUENCE. 165 JOURNE
TO CRUSH THESE ROTTEN MEN AND THEN TO CRUMBLE 330 LAZARU
HIM DARING TO ACCUSE US OF PLANNING A ROTTEN 22 MISBEG
(BURSTS OUT) WELL YOU SHUT UP YOUR ROTTEN 67 MISBEG
BROADWAY BLATHER/
YOU ROTTEN BASTARD/ 107 MISBEG
I MEAN, FOR NOT BELIEVING I'M A ROTTEN LOUSE. 133 MISBEG
AND BECAUSE YOU'RE THE ONLY WOMAN I'VE EVER MET 145 MISBEG
WHO UNDERSTANDS THE LOUSY ROTTEN
WOULDN'T HAVE TO FACE THE ROTTEN THINGS YOU'RE 171 MISBEG
AFRAID YOU SAID AND DID THE NIGHT
EXCEPT I'VE PULLED SOME PRETTY ROTTEN STUFF WHEN 1173 MISBEG
WAS DRAWING A BLANK.
WITH THEIR COWARDLY HEARTS ROTTEN 102 POET
BACK AFTER FIVE YEARS OF BUMMIN' ROUND THE ROTTEN 588 ROPE
OLD EARTH IN SHIPS AND THINGS.
(DISAPPROVINGLY) YUH'RE STILL SPOUTIN' THE ROTTEN595 ROPE
OLD WORD OY GOD SAKES'S EVER.
AFTER ME BUMMIN' AND STARVIN' ROUND THE ROTTEN 598 ROPE
EARTH.
THE ROTTEN SON-OF-A-GUN./ 598 ROPE
YOU KIN HAVE THE ROTTEN FARM FOR ALL OF ME. 599 ROPE
I DON'T WANT NO TRUCK WITH THIS ROTTEN FARM. 599 ROPE
HALFS, AND YUH KIN START THE ROTTEN FARM GOIN' 600 ROPE
AGEN
IT WAS ROTTEN OF ME TO SAY THAT/ 27 STRANG
OUT ROTTEN ADS. 70 STRANG
(HANGING HIS HEAD) I FEEL ROTTEN, LIVING ON YOU 94 STRANG
WHEN YOU'VE GOT SO LITTLE.
(WHAT A ROTTEN LIAR I'VE BECOME/... 96 STRANG
SHE'S ACTING ROTTEN.... 162 STRANG
BUT--THIS MAY SOUND ROTTEN OF ME-- 185 STRANG
(IT SEEMS ROTTEN AND SELFISH TO BE HAPPY... 189 STRANG
IT WAS A ROTTEN, DIRTY TRICK/ 194 STRANG
MOTHER, WHAT DO YOU THINK I AM--AS ROTTEN-MINDED 195 STRANG
AS THAT/
THEY'LL COME, AN' THEY'LL ALL BE ROTTEN DRUNK, 496 VOYAGE
WAIT AN' SEE.
ROTTEN. 499 VOYAGE
ROTTEN GRUB AND DEY MAKE YOU WORK ALL TIME-- 507 VOYAGE
IT'S ROTTEN/ 451 WELDED
ROTTENER
YOU'RE A ROTTENER ACTOR THAN I AM. 53 JOURNE
ROTTENLY
I'VE TREATED YOU ROTTENLY, IN MY WAY, MORE THAN 145 JOURNE
ONCE.
ROTTENNESS
WAS THERE IVER A WOMAN IN THE WORLD HAD THE 60 ANNA
ROTTENNESS IN HER THAT YOU HAVE,
IF YOU EVER GAVE HIM ADVICE EXCEPT IN THE WAYS OF 34 JOURNE
ROTTENNESS,
ROTTER
(HE ADDS BITTERLY) AND A ROTTER. 469 CARIBE
ROTTIN'
PLOWED 'EM UNDER IN THE GROUND--(HE STAMPS 204 DESIRE
REBELLIOUSLY) --ROTTIN'--
LIKE SOMETHIN' ROTTIN' IN THE WALLS. 136 ELECTR
ROTTING
SHE HAD BEEN THERE ROTTING--GOD KNOWS HOW LONG. 560 CROSS
WITH ALL THAT WAS ELSA ROTTING IN HER GRAVE BEHIND561 DAYS
YOU/
I'VE SEEN TOO MANY ROTTING IN THE SUN TO MAKE 60 ELECTR
GRASS GREENER/
(WITH A TWISTED SMILE) REMEMBER ONLY THAT DEAD 164 ELECTR
HERO AND NOT HIS ROTTING GHOST/
ROUES
AS ELDERLY SUITORS FOR MY BODY, ROUES IN THEIR 29 MANSNS
BORED, WITHERED HEARTS.
ROUGE
THERE IS AN ABSURD SUGGESTION OF ROUGE ON HER 520 DIFRNT
TIGHT CHEEKS AND THIN LIPS,
WHO IS UPSTAIRS IN THE BEDROOM PUTTING ON A HEAVY 428 DYNAMO
MAKE-UP OF ROUGE AND MASCARA,
THERE IS NO ROUGE ON HER FACE AND 454 DYNAMO
ALTHOUGH SHE HAS MADE A DEFIANT EFFORT WITH ROUGE 480 DYNAMU
AND MASCARA TO HIDE THIS.)
THE ELDER LIKE A GRAY LUMP OF DOUGH TOUCHED UP 218 HA APE
WITH ROUGE,
HER FACE PLASTERED WITH ROUGE AND MASCARA, HER 682 ICEMAN
HAIR A BIT DISHEVELED,
SHE USES NO ROUGE OR ANY SORT OF MAKE-UP. 12 JOURNE
PRETTY VICIOUS FACE UNDER CAKED POWDER AND 6 STRANG
ROUGE....
(STARES FROM THE BILL TO HIM, FLUSHING BENEATH HER474 WELDED
ROUGE)
ROUGED
THE MASK IS THE ROUGED AND EYE-BLACKENED 279 GGBROW
COUNTENANCE OF THE HARDENED PROSTITUTE.

ROUGED (CONT'D.)
THE WOMEN ARE ROUGED, CALCIMINED, DYED, 236 HA APE
OVERDRESSED TO THE NTH DEGREE.
HER WITHERED LIPS ARE ROUGED AND THERE IS A 161 MANSNS
BEAUTY-SPOT ON EACH ROUGED CHEEK.
SHE HAS FIXED HERSELF UP, PUT ON HER BEST DRESS, 79 STRANG
ARRANGED HER HAIR, ROUGED, ETC.
HER FACE NEWLY ROUGED AND POWDERED, 125 STRANG
HER FACE, ROUGED, POWDERED, PENCILED, IS BROAD AND471 WELDED
STUPID.
ROUGH
A LONG BENCH WITH ROUGH CUSHIONS IS BUILT IN 535 'ILE
AGAINST A WALL.
(WITH ROUGH TENDERNESS) WELL, ANNIE$ 540 'ILE
HIS FACE HANDSOME IN A HARD, ROUGH, BOLD, DEFIANT 30 ANNA
WAY.
THE MEN I KNOW DON'T PULL THAT ROUGH STUFF WHEN 32 ANNA
LADIES ARE AROUND.
I'M A HARD, ROUGH MAN AND I'M NOT FIT, I'M 34 ANNA
THINKING.
ROUGH GANG OF NO GOOD FALLARS IN VORLD/ 43 ANNA
'TIS QUARE, ROUGH TALK, THAT--FOR A DACENT GIRL 57 ANNA
THE LIKE OF YOU/
BY THE LINES OF STONE WALLS AND ROUGH SNAKE 81 BEYOND
FENCES.
IN FRONT OF THE BUNKS, ROUGH WOODEN BENCHES. 477 CARDIF
(A RATHER GOOD-LOOKING ROUGH WHO IS SITTING BESIDE456 CARIBE
DRISCOLL)
THEY ACT TOO ROUGH. 469 CARIBE
YOU AIN'T ROUGH. 469 CARIBE
HE IS DRESSED IN ROUGH FARM CLOTHES. 203 DESIRE
FOUR ROUGH WOODEN CHAIRS, A TALLOW CANDLE ON THE 206 DESIRE
TABLE
(WITH ROUGH TENDERNESS) OH, HELL, EMMER, 496 DIFRNT
HE'S KIND AT BOTTOM, SPITE OF HIS ROUGH WAYS, AND 521 DIFRNT
HE'S BROUGHT YOU UP.
I TOLD HER TO CUT THE ROUGH WORK AND BEHAVE--AND 4525 DIFRNT
NICE TIME WAS HAD BY ALL.
GETS UP AND PATS HER ON THE SHOULDER--WITH ROUGH 537 DIFRNT
TENDERNESS)
ALL RIGHT, ONLY DON'T GET ROUGH AGAIN. 434 DYNAMO
TELL HER I'M SORRY FOR ACTING SO ROUGH TO HER THAT464 DYNAMO
NIGHT....)
A ROUGH STRUCTURE OF BOULDERS, LIKE AN ALTAR, IS 199 EJONES
BY THE TREE.
HE LOOKS AROUND AT THE TREE, THE ROUGH STONE 200 EJONES
ALTAR.
(THEN IMMEDIATELY REPENTANT HE KISSES HER--WITH 108 ELECTR
ROUGH TENDERNESS)
(PUSHES HER AWAY--WITH A ROUGH BROTHERLY 166 ELECTR
IRRITATION)
TREAT 'EM ROUGH, DAT'S ME. 211 HA APE
(HE GIVES HER A ROUGH HUG) DAT'S ON DE LEVEL, 616 ICEMAN
BABY.
(DOING THE SAME TO PEARL) NIX ON DE ROUGH STUFF, 632 ICEMAN
POIL.
WELL, SIT DOWN, DE BOT' OF YUH, AND CUT OUT DE 650 ICEMAN
ROUGH STUFF.
APOLOGIZE FOR SOME OF THE ROUGH STUFF I'VE HAD TO 660 ICEMAN
PULL ON YOU.
(WITH A GROWL) NIX ON THE ROUGH TALK, SEE/ 527 INZONE
(WITH ROUGH FAMILIARITY) I WAGER NO ONE WILL MAKE301 LAZARU
THAT COMPLAINT AGAINST YOU
COVERING HER GUILTY FEAR WITH A ROUGH ANGER.) 167 MANSNS
THE SQUATTING FIGURES OF THE PEOPLE ARE CLOTHED IN373 MARCOM
ROUGH ROBES.
(SHE COMES TO HIM) DON'T MIND MY ROUGH TONGUE, 6 MISBEG
I'VE NOTICED WHEN YOU TALK ROUGH AND BRAZEN LIKE 34 MISBEG
YOU DO TO OTHER MEN,
I TOLD YOU NOT TO ANNOY THE GENTLEMAN WITH YOUR 42 MISBEG
ROUGH TONGUE.
OH, TO HELL WITH THE ROUGH STUFF, JOSIE/ 106 MISBEG
(AS IF HE HADN'T SPOKEN) WHILE I'M ONLY A BIG, 118 MISBEG
ROUGH, UGLY COW OF A WOMAN.
CUT OUT THE ROUGH STUFF, KID. 166 MISBEG
(WITH ROUGH GOOD NATURE.) SHUT UP, DARLINT. 179 POET
HE WEARS A DARK BLUE JERSEY, PATCHED BLUE PANTS, 587 ROPE
ROUGH SAILOR SHOES.
THE TERRACE IS PAVED WITH ROUGH STONE. 184 STRANG
FOLLOWED BY TWO ROUGH-LOOKING, SHABBILY-DRESSED 506 VOYAGE
MEN, WEARING MUFFLERS,
ROUGHHOUSE
NO MORE ROUGHHOUSE. 194 AHWILD
ROUGHLY
HE COMES OVER AND GRABS HER ROUGHLY BY THE 551 'ILE
SHOULDER.)
(ROUGHLY) NEVER MIND THE GIRLS. 466 CARIBE
(PUSHING HER AWAY FROM HIM ROUGHLY) 570 CROSS
(PUSHING HIM ROUGHLY AWAY) LEAVE ME ALONE/ 560 DAYS
(HE PUSHES THEM ROUGHLY AWAY. 250 DESIRE
(ROUGHLY) YOU NEEDN'T WORRY. 522 DIFRNT
(ROUGHLY) WELL, HE'S STILL STUCK ON YOU, AIN'T 532 DIFRNT
HE$
(ROUGHLY) YOU KNOW DAMNED WELL IT AIN'T, YOU 540 DIFRNT
MEAN/
HE IS DRESSED ROUGHLY IN BATTERED SHOES, 457 DYNAMO
(ROUGHLY) AND A LOT THAT GOT ME, DIDN'T ITS 470 DYNAMO
(THEN WITH A START, HE PUSHES HER AWAY FROM HIM 486 DYNAMO
ROUGHLY)
(TIGHTENING HIS GRASP--ROUGHLY) EASY/ 174 EJONES
(THEN ALMOST ROUGHLY, PUSHING HER BACK AND STARING 76 ELECTR
AT HER)
(ROUGHLY) NEVER MIND WHAT YOU CALL PROUFS/ 96 ELECTR
(TRYING A BULLYING TONE--ROUGHLY) 281 GGBROW
(BUT HERE ROCKY SHAKES HIM ROUGHLY BY THE 397 ICEMAN
SHOULDER.)
JACK SLAPS HIM ROUGHLY ON THE SHOULDER AND HE 516 INZONE
COMES TO WITH A START)

ROUGHLY 1342

ROUGHLY (CONT'D.)
(ROUGHLY) YE'LL FIND UT'S NO JOKE, ME BUCKO, 525 INZONE
B'FORE WE'RE DONE WID YOU.
(AS SMITTY ENTERS THE FORECASTLE HE IS SEIZED 525 INZONE
ROUGHLY FROM BOTH SIDES AND HIS
(ROUGHLY, TO HIDE HIS TENSE NERVES.) 68 JOURNE
TYRONE SCOWLS AND LOOKS AT HIS WIFE WITH SHARP 116 JOURNE
SUSPICION--ROUGHLY.)
(HE GETS UP AND TURNS ON THE READING LAMP-- 117 JOURNE
ROUGHLY.)
SARA GRABS HER BY THE SHOULDERS AND SHAKES HER 165 MANSNS
ROUGHLY.)
(ROUGHLY) OCH/ 6 MISBEG
(ROUGHLY) GET OUT OF HERE, NOW/ 10 MISBEG
(ROUGHLY) THE LIGHT IN ME FOOT/ 27 MISBEG
(THE, ROUGHLY) FAITH, HE MUST HAVE A HANGOVER. 35 MISBEG
(BREAKS IN ROUGHLY) YOU'RE A LIAR. 40 MISBEG
(ROUGHLY) MY MODESTY$ 105 MISBEG
(THEN WITH RESENTFUL BITTERNESS--ROUGHLY) 119 MISBEG
(ROUGHLY) NO, I'M A FOOL. 127 MISBEG
HE KISSES HER ROUGHLY) 137 MISBEG
(SUDDENLY SHE PUSHES HIM AWAY FROM HER AND SHAKES 166 MISBEG
HIM ROUGHLY)
(ROUGHLY, WITH COARSE BROGUE.) 103 POET
HE SHAKES HER HAND OFF ROUGHLY AS IF HE DID NOT 159 POET
RECOGNIZE HER.)
(ROUGHLY.) STAY HERE, UNLESS YOU'RE A FOOL, SARA.160 POET
ROUGHLY, HIS VOICE TREMBLING.) 164 POET
CREGAN HAS HIM BY THE SHOULDER AND PUSHES HIM 164 POET
ROUGHLY INTO THE ROOM.
(ROUGHLY.) GAME, IS IT$ 170 POET
ROUGHLY BUT WITH A STRANGE REAL TENDERNESS.) AND 174 POET
I LOVE YOU.
(ROUGHLY.) TO HELL WID TALAVERA/ 176 POET
(ROUGHLY.) BUT TO HELL WID THE DEAD. 177 POET
(ROUGHLY.) WHY CAN'T YOU, YE MEAN. 179 POET
ROUGHLY CONSTRUCTED CARPENTER'S TABLE, EVIDENTLY 577 ROPE
HOME-MADE.
SWEENEY GRABS HER ROUGHLY BY THE ARM. 583 ROPE
(HE PUSHES HIS HAND AWAY, BUT NOT ROUGHLY) 595 ROPE
(KEEPING HIS BACK TURNED TO HER--ROUGHLY) 103 STRANG
JUMPING TO HIS FEET AND FLINGING HER HAND OFF-- 186 STRANG
ROUGHLY)
(ROUGHLY) STOP YER GRIZZLIN'/ 494 VOYAGE

ROUGHNESS
(WITH FORCED ROUGHNESS) AND, BE GOD, THE NIGHT'S 162 MISBEG
OVER.

ROUGHS
(THE TWO ROUGHS COME FORWARD) 508 VOYAGE

ROUND
(SHE TURNS ROUND TO THEM, HER FACE TRANSFIGURED 540 'ILE
WITH JOY)
AT CENTER IS A BIG, ROUND TABLE WITH A GREEN- 185 AHWILD
SHADED READING LAMP,
IN A ROUND-FACED, CUTE, SMALL-FEATURED, WIDE-EYED 187 AHWILD
FASHION.
BRING US ANOTHER ROUND--THE SAME/ 242 AHWILD
FACE IN HANDS, HIS ROUND EYES CHILDISHLY WOUNDED 258 AHWILD
AND WOE-BEGONE.
LIGHT-BROWN HAIR, BIG NAIVE WONDERING DARK EYES, A277 AHWILD
ROUND DIMPLED FACE.
CARELESSLY) OH, WE JUST KEPT DRINKING 283 AHWILD
CHAMPAGNE--I BOUGHT A ROUND--
IN THE BACK ROOM ARE FOUR ROUND WOODEN TABLES WITH 3 ANNA
FIVE CHAIRS GROUPED ABOUT
HE IS A SHORT, SQUAT, BROAD-SHOULDERED MAN OF 5 ANNA
ABOUT FIFTY, WITH A ROUND,
HER THICK, GRAY HAIR IS PILED ANYHOW IN A GREASY 7 ANNA
MOP ON TOP OF HER ROUND HEAD.
HE'LL COME ROUND ALL RIGHT WITH SOME GRUB IN HIM. 13 ANNA
GO ROUND THE CORNER. 13 ANNA
JUST WATER ALL ROUND, AND SUN, AND FRESH AIR, 23 ANNA
(AT THE SOUND OF HER NAME ANNA HAS TURNED ROUND TO 53 ANNA
THEM.
AND I HAVING IT TIED ROUND MY NECK WHEN MY LAST 75 ANNA
SHIP SUNK.
MRS. MAYO IS A SLIGHT, ROUND-FACED, 94 BEYOND
TO SEE FOLKS THAT GOD GAVE ALL THE USE OF THEIR 113 BEYOND
LIMBS TO POTTERIN' ROUND AND
SHE MUST FEEL KIND OF FUNNY HAVING ME ROUND--AFTER135 BEYOND
WHAT USED TO BE--
YOU KNOW THE DOCTOR TOLD YOU NOT TO GET UP AND 145 BEYOND
MOVE ROUND.
(HE CALCULATES) WHAT TIME IS IT NOW$ ROUND SIX, 147 BEYOND
MUST BE.
AND WE ALL SITTIN' ROUND IN THE FOC'S'TLE, YANK 481 CARDIF
BESIDE ME,
HE IS A DARK BURLY FELLOW WITH A ROUND STUPID 483 CARDIF
FACE.
AND SHIPPED US ON A SKYSAIL-YARDER ROUND THE HORN,487 CARDIF
WITH THAT DAMNED WHISTLE BLOWIN' AND PEOPLE 489 CARDIF
SWARMIN' ALL ROUND$
HE IS ABOUT FORTY, STOUT, WITH A PREMATURELY BALD 496 DAYS
HEAD, A ROUND FACE,
ALL THEY WANT IS TO START THE MERRY-GO-ROUND OF 542 DAYS
BLIND GREED ALL OVER AGAIN.
WHAT DO I CARE FOR HER--CEPTIN' SHE'S ROUND AN' 214 DESIRE
WARM$
HER ROUND FACE IS PRETTY BUT MARRED BY ITS RATHER 221 DESIRE
GROSS SENSUALITY.
YER NAVEL BE LIKE A ROUND GOBLET, 232 DESIRE
THAT WAS IT--WHAT I FELT--POKIN' ROUND THE 264 DESIRE
CORNERS--WHILE YE LIED--
WAAL, I GOT T' ROUND UP THE STOCK. 269 DESIRE
IT TOOK 'EM A WEEK TO ROUND UP ALL HANDS FROM 502 DIFRNT
WHERE THEY WAS FOOLIN' ABOUT WITH
NATIVE BROWN WOMEN, ALL NAKED A'MOST, COME ROUND 502 DIFRNT
TO MEET 'EM

ROUND (CONT'D.)
SHE KEEPS SWIMMIN' ROUND AND YELLIN' FOR CALEB. 503 DIFRNT
AND THE PASSIVE, LAZY EXPRESSION OF HER ROUND MOON506 DIFRNT
FACE IS BELIED BY
AND HIM MAKIN' THEM FIRE SHOTS ROUND HER TO SCARE 509 DIFRNT
HER BACK TO LAND AND GET RID
EVER SINCE YOU WAS CHILDREN YOU BEEN LIVIN' SIDE 512 DIFRNT
BY SIDE, GOIN' ROUND TOGETHER,
(A PAUSE) AND THEN I WAS AFEERED SHE'D CATCH COLD 515 DIFRNT
GOIN' ROUND ALL NAKED AND WET
IN THE MOONLIGHT--THOUGH IT WAS WARM--AND I WANTED515 DIFRNT
TO WRAP A BLANKET ROUND HER.
WITH LARGE BREASTS AND BROAD, ROUND HIPS. 422 DYNAMO
HER EYES ARE ROUND AND DARK BLUE. 428 DYNAMO
AND HE WORE A COLORED HANDKERCHIEF ROUND HIS NECK 430 DYNAMO
JUST LIKE A COWBOY...
THE SKY--DRIVEN TO LOVE BY WHAT MAKES THE EARTH GO461 DYNAMO
ROUND--
GUESS I'LL GO ROUND BY THE BACK. 461 DYNAMO
ROUND LIKE A WOMAN'S... 474 DYNAMO
DRIVING THROUGH SPACE, ROUND AND ROUND, JUST LIKE 477 DYNAMO
THE ELECTRONS IN THE ATOM/
GURRY, NOTHIN' ROUND HEAH LOOKS LIKE I EVAN SEED 189 EJONES
IT BEFO'.
EAGER-LISTENER TYPE, WITH A SMALL ROUND FACE, 6 ELECTR
ROUND STUPID EYES,
AND A ROUND MOUTH PURSED OUT TO DRINK IN GOSSIP. 6 ELECTR
YOU TELL HER I GOT PERMISSION FROM VINNIE TO SHOW 8 ELECTR
YOU ROUND.
I'M GOIN' ROUND BY THE KITCHEN. 8 ELECTR
HIS BIG ROUND BLUE EYES ARE BLOODSHOT, DREAMY AND 102 ELECTR
DRUNKEN.
I WAS AIMIN' TO STOP THE DURNED GABBIN' THAT'S 135 ELECTR
BEEN GOIN' ROUND TOWN
OH, DON'T GIT IT IN YOUR HEADS I TAKE STOCK IN 135 ELECTR
SPIRITS TRESPASSIN' ROUND.
AN' WHEN I GIT THROUGH TELLIN' MY STORY OF IT 135 ELECTR
ROUND TOWN TOMORROW
WE'D BE SAILING OUT, BOUND DOWN ROUND THE HORN 213 HA APE
MAYBE.
THEN FROM THESE FIERY ROUND HOLES IN THE BLACK A 223 HA APE
FLOOD OF TERRIFIC LIGHT AND
THE FIERY LIGHT FLOODS OVER THEIR SHOULDERS AS 224 HA APE
THEY BEND ROUND FOR THE COAL.
AND THERE WAS YANK ROARIN' CURSES AND TURNING 229 HA APE
ROUND WID HIS SHOVEL TO BRAIN HER--
UP IN BACK OF ME, AND I HUPPED ROUND TO KNOCK HIM 230 HA APE
DEAD WIT DE SHOVEL.
DEY TURN TINGS ROUND, DO DEY$ 244 HA APE
HIS FACE IS ROUND, HIS SNUB NOSE FLATTENED AT THE 8 HUGHIE
TIP.
AND HER PA COME ROUND LOOKING FOR ME. 15 HUGHIE
OR SOMETHING THAT ANY BLONDE 'D GO ROUND-HEELED 28 HUGHIE
ABOUT.
THAT REALLY HAPPENED SINCE I'VE BEEN HANGIN' 29 HUGHIE
ROUND.
THE BACK ROOM IS CRAMMED WITH ROUND TABLES AND 573 ICEMAN
CHAIRS PLACED SO CLOSE TOGETHER
HE HAS A ROUND KEWPIE'S FACE--A KEWPIE WHO IS AN 576 ICEMAN
UNSHAVEN HABITUAL DRUNKARD,
WITH PROTRUDING EARS AND LITTLE ROUND EYES. 576 ICEMAN
WE OUGHT TO PHONE DE BOOBY HATCH TO SEND ROUND DE 614 ICEMAN
WAGON FOR 'EM.
HER ROUND FACE SHOWING MORE OF THE WEAR AND TEAR 615 ICEMAN
OF HER TRADE THAN THEIRS,
HIS FACE IS ROUND AND SMOOTH AND BIG-BOYISH WITH 618 ICEMAN
BRIGHT BLUE EYES.
YEAH, HE'S BEEN HINTIN' ROUND TO ME AND CHUCK, 631 ICEMAN
TOO.
HUCKY AND CHUCK PRICK UP THEIR EARS AND GATHER 651 ICEMAN
ROUND.
(JERKS ROUND TO LOOK AT LARRY--SNEERINGLY) 666 ICEMAN
IT'S SICK AND TIRED OF MESSIN' ROUND WID WHITE MEN.673 ICEMAN
HEJEES, WHAT ARE ALL YOU BUMS HANGING ROUND 684 ICEMAN
STARING AT ME FOR$
ROCKY'S ROUND EYES ARE POPPING. 694 ICEMAN
I TINKS, AIN'T TWO GUYS LIKE DEM SAPS TO BE 702 ICEMAN
HANGIN' ROUND
(HIS BLACK BULLET EYES SENTIMENTAL, HIS ROUND MOP 725 ICEMAN
FACE GRINNING WELCOME)
LIKE IT WAS SOMETHIN' DANG'ROUS HE WAS AFTER, AN' 519 INZONE
FEELS ROUND IN UNDER HIS DUDS--
HE LOOKS ROUND TO SEE IF ANYONE'S WOKE UP--- 520 INZONE
I CLAPPED MY EYES SHUT WHEN HE TURNED ROUND. 520 INZONE
AT CENTER IS A ROUND TABLE WITH A GREEN SHADED 12 JOURNE
READING LAMP,
AND WORKED IN WITH THE FOLDS THAT WERE DRAPED 115 JOURNE
SHE HESITATES IN THE DOORWAY, GLANCING ROUND THE 170 JOURNE
(IN A RAGE) HO, BARBARIAN CUR, TURN ROUND/ 316 LAZARU
JEW, TURN ROUND/ 316 LAZARU
DANCING ROUND ME IN THE DARKNESS, PRANCING TO THE 353 LAZARU
DRUM BEAT OF MY HEART/
WITH A ROUND RED FACE, AND SHREWD LITTLE GREY 25 MANSNS
EYES.
ONE COMING ROUND ONE SIDE OF THE POOL, THE OTHER 175 MANSNS
ROUND THE OTHER.
BUT HE IS TALL AND STOUT WITH A ROUND, JOVIAL FACE358 MARCOM
AND SMALL, CUNNING EYES.
(ROUND-EYED) A MAN TOLD ME THAT NOAH'S ARK IS 364 MARCOM
STILL SOMEWHERE AROUND HERE
(ANOTHER WILD ROUND OF CONGRATULATIONS, KISSES, 430 MARCOM
ETC.)
HOW COULD I SNEAK HERE SOONEK WITH HIM PEEKING 4 MISBEG
ROUND THE CORNER OF THE BARN TO
HIS HEAD IS ROUND WITH THINNING SANDY HAIR. 11 MISBEG
OR IS THIS THE FINAL ROUND$ 100 MISBEG

ROUND (CONT'D.)
LOOSE A ROUND-HOUSE SWING THAT MISSES TYRONE BY A 101 MISBEG COUPLE OF FEET.
(A PAUSE--WORRIEDLY.) NEILAN SENT ROUND A NOTE TO 21 POET ME ABOUT HIS BILL.
I'LL WET A CLOTH IN COLD WATER TO PUT ROUND YOUR 35 POET HEAD.
NORA ROVERS ROUND HIM.) 35 POET
PADDY O'DOWD IS THIN, ROUND-SHOULDERED, FLAT- 51 POET CHESTED, WITH A PIMPLY COMPLEXION.
(HE TWISTS ROUND TO FACE MELODY. HOLDS UP HIS 100 POET GLASS AND BAWLS.)
GADSBY IS IN HIS LATE FORTIES, SHORT, STOUT, WITH 116 POET A BIG, BALD HEAD. ROUND.
THE WORD HAS GOT ROUND AMONG THE BOYS. 134 POET
HE SAID YOU WAS TO KEEP STILL AND NOT GO A-WALKIN'579 ROPE ROUND.
AND HIS SMALL, ROUND, BLUE EYES. 582 ROPE
BACK AFTER FIVE YEARS OF BUMMIN' ROUND THE ROTTEN 588 ROPE OLD EARTH IN SHIPS AND THINGS.
AN' HE NEEDS TO BE BLARNEYED ROUND TO FOOL HIM AN'590 ROPE FIND OUT WHAT HE'S WANTIN'.
(VICIOUSLY) I WAS WISHIN' IT WAS ROUND HIS NECK 590 ROPE CHOKIN' HIM, THAT'S WHAT I WAS--
AND WHEN I TURNED ROUND AND BEAT IT HE SHOUTED 593 ROPE AFTER ME..
I WAS GREEN AS GRASS WHEN I LEFT HERE, BUT BUMMIN'593 ROPE ROUND THE WORLD,
AFTER ME BUMMIN' AND STARVIN' ROUND THE ROTTEN 598 ROPE EARTH.
AND I AIN'T GOIN' TO LOAF ROUND HERE MORE'N I GOT 599 ROPE TO.
(ROUND AND ROUND... 52 STRANG
BUT I WAS OUT GALLIVANTING ROUND THE PLACE WITH 56 STRANG SAMMY.
THERE IS A MORRIS CHAIR AND A ROUND GOLDEN OAK 90 STRANG TABLE AT LEFT OF CENTER.
I CAN ALWAYS TWIST HIM ROUND MY FINGER/....) 118 STRANG
AT ONE OF THE TABLES, FRONT, A ROUND-SHOULDERED 493 VOYAGE YOUNG FELLOW IS SITTING.
AN' THEY'RE ROUND DOWN ROUND THE 'ORN. 495 VOYAGE
OLSON, A STOCKY, MIDDLE-AGED SWEDE WITH ROUND, 496 VOYAGE CHILDISH BLUE EYES.
(TURNS ROUND, SWAYING A BIT, AND PEERS AT HIM 496 VOYAGE ACROSS THE BAR)
AND THEN COMES ROUND THE BAR AND GOES OUT THE DOOR497 VOYAGE ON LEFT.)
I TANK I GO ROUND TO BOARDING HOUSE. 507 VOYAGE
PY YINGO, I PITY POOR FALLERS MAKE DAT TRIP ROUND 507 VOYAGE CAPE STIFF DIS TIME YEAR.
ROUND CAPE 'ORN--SAILS AT DAYBREAK. 507 VOYAGE
ALL THE ROOMS GO ROUND AND ROUND 507 VOYAGE
HIS EYES ARE ROUND AND CHILD-LIKE. 450 WELDED
SPOSIN' I GO ROUND THE CORNER, HUH& 475 WELDED
ROUND'S
NO, DIS ROUND'S ON ME. 616 ICEMAN
ROUNDED
OBLONG EYES ABOVE A GROSS, ROUNDED TORSO. 473 DYNAMO
AND OUR LITTLE LIFE IS ROUNDED WITH A SLEEP.= 131 JOURNE
ROUNDNESS
HER FACE, THOUGH INCLINED TO ROUNDNESS, IS 87 BEYOND UNDENIABLY PRETTY.
ROUNDS
HE'LL SOON BE GOING THE ROUNDS TO HIS PATIENTS 17 ELECTR AGAIN, HE HOPES.
ROUSE
THEN, AFTER A MOMENT, AS THE ALCOHOL BEGINS TO 14 ANNA ROUSE HER,
YE MIGHT'VE TUK THE TROUBLE T' ROUSE ME, ABBIE. 263 DESIRE
EXCEPT HUGO AND PARRITT, BEGINS TO ROUSE UP 617 ICEMAN HOPEFULLY.
GOD BLESS YOU, WHISKEY, IT'S YOU CAN ROUSE THE 9 POET DEAD/
WE'VE GOT TO ROUSE HIM FIRST. 153 POET
(TRYING TO ROUSE HER--IN A TEASING TONE.) 182 POET
GABRIEL'S TRUMPET ITSELF CUDN'T ROUSE HIM. 503 VOYAGE
ROUSED
(ROUSED) PY YIMINY, AY FORGAT. 9 ANNA
WELL, IF HE AIN'T THE DEVIL HIMSELF WHEN HE'S 108 BEYOND ROUSED/
(ROUSED) NO, I HAIN'T, YEW BET--NOT BY A HELL OF 232 DESIRE A SIGHT--
ALL THE MEN, ROUSED TO A PITCH 216 HA APE
(HUGO IS ROUSED BY THIS. 720 ICEMAN
BUT THREE CANNOT BE ROUSED. 353 MARCOM
(ROUSED TO INTEREST IMMEDIATELY.) 101 POET
(ROUSED BY MENTION OF HIS PET--DISDAINFULLY.) 106 POET
I'M GLAD TO SEE YOU ROUSED FROM YOUR WORRYIN'. 135 POET
NO, ONLY A PRIEST OF ALMIGHTY GOD--(WITH A ROUSED 138 POET REBELLION AGAIN.)
ROUSES
(HE SUDDENLY ROUSES HIMSELF AND THERE IS SOMETHING 34 HUGHIE
(ROUSES HIMSELF--WITH FORCED HEARTINESS) 656 ICEMAN
AND HE SETS THE BOTTLE ON THE TABLE WITH A JAR 691 ICEMAN THAT ROUSES HUGO.
(AT LAST ROUSES HIMSELF--HARSHLY TO THE COURIER) 424 MARCOM
TYRONE ROUSES HIMSELF AND STRAIGHTENS UP. 103 MISBEG
ROUSING
(ROUSING HERSELF--AFFECTIONATELY PITYING) 257 AHWILD
(ROUSING A BIT--DEFENSIVELY) 545 DAYS
(ROUSING HIMSELF--DESPERATELY FIGHTING BACK HIS 555 DAYS DROWSINESS)
(ROUSING HERSELF--FORCING A CARELESS TONE) 538 DIFRNT
(ROUSING HERSELF--TURNS TO FORCE A SMILE AT HIM) 81 ELECTR
(ROUSING HIMSELF--SHAMEFACEDLY) 110 ELECTR
(ROUSING HIMSELF GUILTILY--PATS HER HAND--WITH 111 ELECTR GRUFF TENDERNESS)
(ROUSING HERSELF--FORCING A SMILE) 118 ELECTR

ROUSING (CONT'D.)
(ROUSING HIMSELF, FORCES A SMILE 144 ELECTR
(ROUSING HIMSELF) 704 ICEMAN
(ROUSING HIMSELF) YOU CAN, IF THERE'S ANY CHANCE. 91 MISBEG
(THEN ROUSING HERSELF AS IF CONQUERING A GROWING 445 WELDED DEPRESSION)
ROUSSEAU
VOLTAIRE, ROUSSEAU, SCHOPENHAUER, NIETZSCHE, 135 JOURNE IBSEN/
I STILL BELIEVE WITH ROUSSEAU, AS FIRMLY AS EVER, 9 MANSNS
ROUSSEAU WAS SIMPLY HIDING FROM HIMSELF IN A 47 MANSNS SUPERIOR, IDEALISTIC DREAM--
ROUT
THEY POUR IN A LAUGHING ROUT FROM THE DOORWAY ONTO285 LAZARU THE TERRACE.
(HARDER'S RETREAT BECOMES A ROUT. 64 MISBEG
ROUTINE
OH, THE SAME PEACEFUL ROUTINE-- 516 DAYS
IN A ROUTINE OF FAMILY CONVERSATION, FROM HER 71 JOURNE MOUTH,
AND KEEPING YOUR MIND OCCUPIED WITH THE ROUTINE OF 16 STRANG MANAGING THE HOUSEHOLD--
ROVER
(IN ANGUISH) ((DEAR OLD ROVER, NICE OLD DOGGIE, 120 STRANG WE'VE HAD HIM FOR YEARS.
ROVING
*TIS NO MORE DRINKING AND ROVING ABOUT I'D BE 38 ANNA DOING THEN.
TIS ONLY ON THE SEA HE'S FREE, AND HIM ROVING THE 48 ANNA FACE OF THE WORLD.
(HIS EYES ROVING FROM ROBERT TO RUTH AND BACK 141 BEYOND AGAIN--UNCERTAINLY)
HE WAS THE ROVING KIND... 430 DYNAMO
HER HANDS ROVING OVER THE TABLE TOP, AIMLESSLY 42 JOURNE MOVING OBJECTS AROUND.
ROW
BUT WHAT WAS YUH SO SCARED ABOUT--THAT I'D KICK UP 12 ANNA A ROW&
(TALKING ALOUD TO HIMSELF) ROW, YE DIVIL/ 31 ANNA
AND A ROW OF TALL MAPLES IN THE BACKGROUND BEHIND -0 DYNAMO THE YARDS AND THE TWO HOUSES.
WHICH IS BRILLIANTLY LIGHTED BY A ROW OF POWERFUL 473 DYNAMO BULBS IN WHITE GLOBES SET IN
THESE SWITCHES EXTEND IN A STRAIGHT ROW BACKWARD 483 DYNAMO DOWN THE MIDDLE OF THE GALLERY,
AND A ROW OF GREAT WINDOWS IN THE LEFT WALL. 486 DYNAMO
AND WHAT A ROW THERE WAS WHEN FATHER CAUGHT ME/ 90 ELECTR
THEY STOP SHORT AND STIFFEN ALL IN A ROW, 293 GGBROW
A ROW OF CELLS IN THE PRISON ON BLACKWELLS ISLAND.239 HA APE
THE THIRD ROW OF TABLES, FOUR CHAIRS TO ONE AND 573 ICEMAN SIX TO THE OTHER.
IS A TABLE OF THE SECOND ROW WITH FIVE CHAIRS. 573 ICEMAN
AT THE FRONT OF THE TABLE IN THE SECOND ROW WHICH 619 ICEMAN IS HALF BETWEEN HOPE'S TABLE
NEAR THE MIDDLE OF THE ROW OF CHAIRS BEHIND THE 629 ICEMAN TABLE, LARRY SITS, FACING FRONT.
OF THESE, WE SEE ONE IN THE FRONT ROW WITH FIVE 664 ICEMAN CHAIRS,
SO IS THE ONE AT THE RIGHT, REAR, OF IT IN THE 695 ICEMAN SECOND ROW.
THE TABLE AT RIGHT, REAR, OF IT IN THE SECOND ROW,696 ICEMAN
AND THE LAST TABLE AT RIGHT IN THE FRONT ROW, 696 ICEMAN
DO YOU WANT TO START A ROW THAT WILL BRING MAMA 169 JOURNE DOWNS
IN AN AISLE SEAT IN THE FIRST ROW A MAN RISES, 439 MARCOM CONCEALS A YAWN IN HIS PALM,
AND IT'LL BE IN THE PAPERS ABOUT ANOTHER DRUNKEN 126 POET MICK RAISING A CRAZY ROW/
AND IF YOU GO RAISING A DRUNKEN ROW AT THEIR 127 POET HOUSE, AND MAKE A PUBLIC SCANDAL,
A CRAZY ROW--AND NOW HE'S PARALYZED DRUNK. 152 POET
HE WAS AFRAID THE ROW WOULD GET IN THE PAPER AND 159 POET PUT SHAME ON HIM.
IF WHEN YOU GO TO COLLEGE YOU CAN PLAY FOOTBALL OR153 STRANG ROW LIKE GORDON OLIO, I'LL--
(SINGS) =ROW, ROW, ROW.= 175 STRANG
AND WE'LL ROW, ROW, ROW--- REMEMBER THAT OLD 175 STRANG TUNE--
(HE SINGS RAUCOUSLY) =OH, WE'LL ROW, ROW, ROW, 175 STRANG RIGHT DOWN THE RIVER/
I NEVER COULD ROW WORTH A DAMN/ 182 STRANG
ROWBOAT
(LEFT OF CENTER) OF THE ROWBOAT IS IN THE DEEP 275 AHWILD SHADOW CAST BY THE WILLOW.
ON THE BEACH, AT CENTER, FRONT, A WHITE, FLAT- 275 AHWILD BOTTOMED ROWBOAT IS DRAWN UP.
RICHARD IS DISCOVERED SITTING SIDEWAYS ON THE 275 AHWILD GUNWALE OF THE ROWBOAT
ROWIN'
THEY'RE A-ROWIN' ASHORE. 570 CROSS
AN' SHE CAN'T FORGET THE ROWIN' YOU AN' HER USED 591 ROPE TO BE HAVIN'--
ROWING
AY HEAR DEM ROWING. 29 ANNA
AND I'VE BEEN ROWING THE BOAT WITH THEM LYING IN 32 ANNA THE BOTTOM NOT ABLE TO RAISE A
GREATEST RACE IN THE HISTORY OF ROWING/ 182 STRANG
ROWS
GRADUALLY IT SEEMS TO GROW LIGHTER IN THE ENCLOSED198 EJONES SPACE AND TWO ROWS OF SEATED
THERE ARE THREE ROWS OF TABLES, FROM FRONT TO 573 ICEMAN BACK.
WITHIN THE PORTICO ON ROWS OF CHAIRS PLACED ON A 312 LAZARU SERIES OF WIDE STEPS WHICH ARE
ROYAL
AND HE'D CALL, AND I'D HAVE A ROYAL FLUSH TO HIS 32 HUGHIE FOUR ACES.

ROYAL

ROYAL (CONT'D.)
AN UNPARDONABLE SLIGHT, ESPECIALLY AS I AM THE ONLY INMATE OF ROYAL BLOOD. 594 ICEMAN
(HE QUOTES FROM KIPLING'S =SESTINA OF THE TRAMP-ROYAL.= 161 JOURNE
(SHE HOLDS OUT HER HAND AND CLASPS THAT OF HER ROYAL DREAM LOVER, 164 MANSNS
POOP DECK OF THE ROYAL JUNK OF THE PRINCESS KUKACHIN AT ANCHOR 407 MARCOM
LISTEN. I JUST NOTICED THE ROYAL BARGE COMING. 417 MARCOM

RUB
(THINKING IT WELL TO RUB IN THIS ASPECT--DISGUSTEDLY) 294 AHWILD
BUT DON'T RUB IT IN. 72 ANNA
DON'T RUB IT IN. 544 DIFRNT
(WHY DOES HE RUB IT IN... 442 DYNAMO
(THEY RUN TO HER SIDE, KNEEL AND RUB HER WRISTS. 293 GGBROW
YOU'LL LIKELY RUB AGAINST OIL AND DIRT. 221 HA APE
ALL SET FOR AN ALCOHOL RUB? 686 ICEMAN
SHE'LL GIVE ME SOMETHING TO RUB ON MY HANDS, 171 JOURNE
OR AN UNGUENT YOU RUB INTO THE SKIN TO REVITALIZE 354 LAZARU
THE OLD BONES AND TISSUES
THERE'S THE RUB/.... 5 STRANG
RUB IT IN/ 41 STRANG

RUBAIYAT
=THE RUBAIYAT OF OMAR KHAYYAM,= 198 AHWILD
THAT RUBAIYAT OF OMAR KHAYYAM, 289 AHWILD
WHAT'S IT THAT RUBAIYAT SAYS.. 298 AHWILD

RUBAIYATS
I THINK THE =RUBAIYAT'S= GREAT STUFF, DON'T YOU$ 262 GGBROW

RUBAY
AND LAST THERE WAS A POEM--A LONG ONE--THE RUBAY--198 AHWILD
WHAT IS IT, RICHARDS

RUBBED
OR GOT RUBBED OUT, BUT I ALWAYS TOOK IT AS PART OF 18 HUGHIE
THE GAME.
RUBBED ON THE PRAT, WOULD CURE HEART FAILURE IN 626 ICEMAN
THREE DAYS.

RUBBER
AND RUBBER BOOTS TURNED DOWN FROM THE KNEE,) 568 CRUSS
IF HE PULLS ANY RUBBER-HOSE TRICKS, YOU LET ME 718 ICEMAN
KNOW/
SOMETHIN' SQUARE TIED UP IN A RUBBER BAG. 528 INZONE
(DRISCOLL TAKES A BLACK RUBBER BAG RESEMBLING A 528 INZONE
LARGE TOBACCO POUCH FROM THE BOX
DRISCOLL HOLDS THE RUBBER BAG LIMPLY IN HIS HAND 532 INZONE
AND SOME SMALL WHITE OBJECT
AND THE RUBBER COVER FOR THE TYPEWRITER LIKE A 66 STRANG
COLLAPSED TENT.

RUBBING
BEN IS VIOLENTLY RUBBING OFF THE ORGAN 538 'ILE
(AGGRIEVED--RUBBING HIS ARM AS HE GOES TO HIS 221 AHWILD
PLACE)
RUBBING HIS HANDS TOGETHER GENIALLY) 223 AHWILD
(RUBBING HIS HEAD--GOOD-NATUREDLY) 226 AHWILD
(THEN RUBBING IT IN) HER NAME WAS BELLE. 283 AHWILD
(THEN RUBBING HIS HANDS TOGETHER--WITH A BOYISH 292 AHWILD
GRIN OF PLEASURE)
SMITTY, STILL DAZEDLY RUBBING HIS CHEEK.. 472 CARIBE
THEIR BODIES BUMPING AND RUBBING TOGETHER AS THEY 206 DESIRE
HURRY CLUMSILY TO THEIR FOOD.

RUBBISH
NO MORE IMPORTANT THAN RUBBISH TO BE GOT RID OF. 54 ELECTR
WHAT FANTASTIC RUBBISH, DEBORAH/ 43 MANSNS
RUBBISH/ 74 MANSNS

RUBBISHY
WHAT RUBBISHY THOUGHTS FOR A MAN OF MY YEARS AND 37 MANSNS
PROFESSION/
WHAT RUBBISHY FANTASIES/ 74 MANSNS

RUBE
(BOASTFULLY) AW, WHAT DO YOU THINK I AM--RUBES 218 AHWILD
THE FIRST RUBE THAT CAME TO MY WAGON FOR A TICKET 608 ICEMAN

RUBE'S
(THEN DEFENSIVELY AGAIN) BUT RUBE'S A GOOD 432 DYNAMO
SCOUT---IN HIS WAY.
RUBE'S LOOKING PALE BEHIND THE GILLS, POOR GUY/...439 DYNAMO

RUBES
THE BOYS TELL ME THE RUBES ARE WASTING ALL THEIR 724 ICEMAN
MONEY BUYING FOOD

RUBIES
WITH GLITTERING DIAMONDS, EMERALOS, RUBIES, 233 HA APE
PEARLS, ETC.
RUBIES/ 429 MARCOM

RUBS
(HE RUBS HIS KNEE.) I DAMNED NEAR BUSTED MY KNEE 126 JOURNE
ON THE HAT STAND.
(HIS ANGER EVAPORATES AND HE RUBS THE TOP OF HIS 73 MISBEG
HEAD
(SHE STRETCHES AND RUBS HER NUMBED ARMS, GROANING 166 MISBEG
COMICALLY)

RUBY
I KISS YOUR RUBY LIPS AND YOU SWOON, 360 MARCOM

RUCTIONS
AFTER LAST NIGHT'S RUCTIONS/ 268 AHWILD
(THEN FROWNING) BUT DON'T LET'S TALK ABOUT THAT 497 DIFRNT
SORT O' RUCTIONS.
AND WHEN SHE SAW THE SHIP WAS GITTIN' READY TO 503 DIFRNT
SAIL SHE RAISED RUCTIONS,

RUDDY
WITH THICK WHITE HAIR, RUDDY COMPLEXION, 500 DAYS
RUDDY COMPLEXION, AND A SHRILL RASPING VOICE. 129 ELECTR
IT IS DARK-COMPLECTED, RUDDY AND BROWN, 274 LAZARU

RUDE
I DIDN'T MEAN TO BE RUDE, YOU KNOW, REALLY. 469 CARIBE
SO WHEN HE CALLED HERE I COULDN'T BE RUDE, COULD 52 ELECTR
I
YOU MUSTN'T BE SO RUDE. 144 ELECTR
IT WOULD BE RUDE TO TALK ABOUT ANYTHING TO YOU. 220 HA APE

RUDE (CONT'D.)
I--I BEG YOUR PARDON FOR BEING RUDE--I AM WORN OUT130 MANSNS
IMMEDIATELY BEFORE THE GATE IS A RUDE THRONE ON 373 MARCOM
WHICH SITS A MONGOL RULER WITH
DID I SEEM RUDE, CHARLIE$ 13 STRANG
(WITH A SILLY GIGGLE) REALLY, NINA, YOU'RE 13 STRANG
ABSOLUTELY RUDE/
14 STRANG
(TEASINGLY) BY THE WAY, IF IT ISN'T TOO RUDE TO 81 STRANG
INQUIRE, AREN'T YOU GETTING
WITHOUT BEING TOO RUDE, I URGED HIM TO GET BACK TO155 STRANG
HIS WORK,

RUDELY
I MUST SAY YOU TREAT YOUR ONE DEVOTED SWAIN PRETTY 16 ELECTR
RUDELY.
(THEN CURTLY AND RUDELY.) 130 MANSNS
(INTERRUPTS HIM RUDELY.) WAS IT TO LISTEN TO YOU 47 POET
RECITE BYRON--=
RUDELY IN MOCKING BROGUE.) 97 POET
(THEN RUDELY DEFENSIVE) DON'T BE SILLY/ 146 STRANG
(RUDELY) THINKING DOESN'T MATTER A DAMN/ 170 STRANG

RUEFUL
(SHE ADDS WITH A RUEFUL LITTLE LAUGH) 123 MISBEG

RUEFULLY
(GOES ON A BIT RUEFULLY, AS IF OPPRESSED BY A 188 AHWILD
SECRET SORROW)
(RUEFULLY) THOUGH IT'S A GREAT JACKASS I AM TO BE 34 ANNA
MISTAKING YOU,
(HASTILY DROPPING HER HAND--RUEFULLY) 35 ANNA
(RUEFULLY) SEEMS IF I PUT MY FOOT IN IT WHENEVER139 BEYOND
I OPEN MY MOUTH TODAY.

RUEFULLY--WITH BITTER COMPLAINT) 74 MISBEG
HE IS ALMOST HIMSELF AGAIN--RUEFULLY) 175 MISBEG
(RUEFULLY.) IT'S TRUE, MOTHER. 65 POET

RUFFIANS
YOU DRUNKEN RUFFIANS/ 123 POET

RUFFLED
MILLER LOOKS AROUND AT THEM WITH A WEAK SMILE, HIS227 AHWILD
DIGNITY NOW RUFFLED A BIT.)
(MORE AND MORE RUFFLED) THEN ALL I GOT TO SAY IS,102 BEYOND
YOU'RE A SOFTY,
(VERY MUCH RUFFLED) THAT'S LIKE THEY TALK$, 125 BEYOND
(HIS DIGNITY RUFFLED, TURNS HIS BACK ON HER AND 424 DYNAMO
GOES TO THE WINDOW)
SHE ADDS TARTLY. HER CONFIDENCE RESTORED AND HER 433 DYNAMO
TEMPER A BIT RUFFLED)
(A BIT RUFFLED) I AND ANTHONY CAN BUILD ANYTHING 258 GGBROW
YOUR PET CAN DRAW--
(RUFFLED BUT AMUSED IN SPITE OF IT) 41 STRANG

RUFFLES
IN TINY RUFFLES AROUND THE NECK AND SLEEVES; 115 JOURNE
EXAMINING LOOK THAT RUFFLES MARSDEN AND MAKES HIM 34 STRANG
ALL THE MORE RESENTFUL TOWARD

RUFFLING
(RUFFLING HIS HAIR) GEE, YOU'VE GOT PRETTY HAIR, 240 AHWILD
DO YOU KNOW IT$
(RUFFLING) VULGAR/ 218 HA APE
(WITH A TEASING LAUGH, RUFFLING HIS HAIR 106 MANSNS
PLAYFULLY.)

RUG
A MEDIUM-PRICED, INOFFENSIVE RUG COVERS MOST OF 185 AHWILD
THE FLOOR.
A DARK RUG COVERS MOST OF THE FLOUR. 210 AHWILD
A CHEAP, DARK-COLORED RUG IS ON THE FLOOR. 555 CROSS
(SHE IS STARTING TO HER FEET WHEN HER EYES FALL ON 64 ELECTR
THE LITTLE BOX ON THE RUG.
THE HARDWOOD FLOOR IS NEARLY COVERED BY A RUG, 12 JOURNE
(INOFFENSIVE IN DESIGN AND COLOR.
A DARK RUG IS ON THE FLOOR OF POLISHED OAK BOARDS. 69 MANSNS
A RUG COVERS MOST OF THE FLOOR OF WAXED DARK WOOD.117 MANSNS
WHICH IS PUSHED BACK, SETTING THE RUG ASKEW. 66 STRANG

RUGGED
BLACK HAIR, KEEN, DARK EYES, FACE RUGGED AND 494 DIFRNT
BRONZED.

RUGS
ITS GLASSY SURFACE SET OFF BY THREE SMALL, GARISH-519 DIFRNT
COLORED RUGS,
PUSHES THE RUGS TO THE PILE WITH HER FEET, 548 DIFRNT
THREE SMALL HOOKED RUGS ARE ON THE FLOOR. 421 DYNAMO
THERE ARE HOOKED RUGS ON THE FLOOR. 28 ELECTR
AND THE BOX SLIPS OUT ONTO ONE OF THE HOOKED 64 ELECTR
RUGS.)
(THROWING OFF HER RUGS AND GETTING TO HER FEET) 221 HA APE

RUIN
AND EGGS HIM ON AND RUINS HIS LIFE--LIKE ALL WOMEN235 AHWILD
LOVE TO RUIN MEN'S LIVES/
IT'S AUNT LILY'S FAULT, UNCLE SID'S GOING TO RUIN.235 AHWILD
NOT ONLY YOUR PLACE BUT MINE TOO IS DRIFTIN' TO 114 BEYOND
RACK AND RUIN,
I'VE DONE ALL A BODY COULD DO TO AVERT RUIN FROM 114 BEYOND
THIS HOUSE.
EXCEPT HE DID RUIN ME... 430 DYNAMO
SHE BLAMED HERSELF FOR YOUR RUIN AND SHE WROTE 465 DYNAMO
LONG LETTERS BEGGING YOUR
FOR ALL THE RUIN AND SUFFERING YOU HAD BROUGHT ON 466 DYNAMO
HER--AND ON ME/
MY LIFE WOULD BE RUINED AND I WOULD RUIN YOURS/ 38 ELECTR
YOU'RE NOT GOING TO MARRY PETER AND RUIN HIS LIFE/172 ELECTR
AN OLD DESICCATED RUIN OF DUST-LADEN BREAD AND 571 ICEMAN
MUMMIFIED HAM OR CHEESE
THEY'RE THE THINGS THAT REALLY POISON AND RUIN A 622 ICEMAN
GUY'S LIFE/
I SAID, MOTHER, THAT THE COMPANY IS FACED WITH 32 MANSNS
RUIN.
THAT IS ONLY JUST IF HE SAVES IT FROM RUIN. 34 MANSNS
AND FORESEE THE PANIC AND RUIN WHICH IS GATHERING 35 MANSNS
AROUND US.
WELL, HE CAN'T RUIN US. 48 MANSNS

1345 RUMORS

RUIN (CONT'D.)

FATHER WOULD RATHER HAVE FACED RUIN A THOUSAND 59 MANSNS TIMES--

WE KNOW THAT BECAUSE IT MADE HIM SO EASY TO RUIN. 150 MANSNS TO TELL ALL OUR ENEMIES AND COMBINE WITH THEM TO 191 MANSNS POUNCE DOWN AND RUIN US/

AND IT'S LUCKY THEY'RE NOT OR YANG-CHAU WOULD SOON393 MARCOM BE A RUIN/

YOU'LL RUIN MY REPUTATION, IF YOU SPREAD THAT LIE 41 MISBEG ABOUT ME.

MIGHT RUIN ME, GOD DAMN HIM/ 92 MISBEG

WITH NO WOMAN'S COMPANY BUT THE WHORES WAS HELPIN' 14 POET HIM RUIN THE ESTATE.

AND BLAMING HIS RUIN ON HIS HAVING TO MARRY YOU. 24 POET (WITH BYRONIC GLOOM.) I AM BUT A GHOST HAUNTING A 62 POET RUIN.

HARDLY, JAMIE--BUT NOT A TOTAL RUIN YET, I HOPE. 93 POET BRING HIM DISGUST AND BITTERNESS, AND RUIN TO ALL 113 POET HIS DREAMS.

RUIN MY CAREER/...)) 103 STRANG

RUIN MY CAREER/.....)) 105 STRANG

((SHE WANTS TO RUIN MY SON'S LIFE AS SHE RUINED 178 STRANG MINE/...))

RUINED

HAD RUINED YOUR IRON CONSTITUTION/ 265 AHWILD

I THOUGHT, WHEN I'M DEAD, SHE'LL BE SORRY SHE 282 AHWILD RUINED MY LIFE/

THEY'RE APT TO BE WHITED SEPULCHRES--I MEAN, YOUR 295 AHWILD WHOLE LIFE MIGHT BE RUINED IF--

AFTER THE WAY YOU'VE RUINED EVERYTHING WITH YOUR 126 BEYOND LAZY LOAFING/

AND HOW THE FARM'LL BE RUINED IF YOU LEAVE IT TO 138 BEYOND ROB TO LOOK AFTER.

IT'S THE FARM THAT'S RUINED OUR LIVES, DAMN IT/ 149 BEYOND

THEY JUST RUINED YOU AND WENT THEIR WAY... 430 DYNAMO

MY LIFE WOULD BE RUINED AND I WOULD RUIN YOURS/ 38 ELECTR

OFF, OUR LIVES WOULD BE RUINED/ 114 ELECTR

HE'D HAVE HAD US RUINED LONG AGO/ 260 GGBROW

AND GET HIS EYES RUINED IN SOLITARY. 593 ICEMAN

WILL YOU KINDLY KEEP OUT OF--{WITH A PITIFUL 657 ICEMAN DEFIANCE} MY LIFE IS NOT RUINED/

AND RUINED YOUR LIFE. 657 ICEMAN

BY PRETENDING IT WAS MY WIFE'S ADULTERY THAT 707 ICEMAN RUINED MY LIFE.

AFTER HE'S DELIBERATELY RUINED HIS HEALTH BY THE 33 JOURNE MAD LIFE HE'S LED

AND THE TIME CAME WHEN THAT MISTAKE RUINED MY 149 JOURNE CAREER AS A FINE ACTOR.

A GREAT MONEY SUCCESS--IT RUINED ME WITH ITS 149 JOURNE PROMISE OF AN EASY FORTUNE.

BECAUSE MY FATHER RUINED HIMSELF WITH DRINK AND 21 MANSNS GAMBLING IN IRELAND.

SIMON WILL NOT WISH YOU TO BE RUINED, MOTHER. 35 MANSNS

LET IT BE RUINED/ 36 MANSNS

DID YOU THINK I WOULD REFUSE TO SAVE YOU FROM 58 MANSNS BEING RUINED5

LET TENARD WAIT OUTSIDE THE DOOR FOR A WHILE LIKE 149 MANSNS THE RUINED BEGGAR HE IS.

WE'VE RUINED HIM. 150 MANSNS

A RUINED FACE, WHICH WAS ONCE EXTRAORDINARILY 33 POET HANDSOME

TO HIS RUINED, HANDSOME FACE. 57 POET

WHEN I THOUGHT THERE WAS DANGER THEY'D BE RUINED 143 POET FOREVER5

IT HAS RUINED MORE LIVES THAN ALL THE DISEASES/ 102 STRANG

WHEN A REFUSAL LIKE THAT WOULD HAVE RUINED MY 122 STRANG CONFIDENCE FOR SIX MONTHS/))

THE PROOF OF A GUTLESS VANITY THAT RUINED YOUR 166 STRANG CAREER/...

((SHE WANTS TO RUIN MY SON'S LIFE AS SHE RUINED 178 STRANG MINE/...))

(WITH BITTER DESPONDENCY) RUINED NOW--GONE--A 452 WELDED RARE MOMENT OF BEAUTY/

RUININ'

AN' HIMSELF RUININ' IT YEARS AGO 586 ROPE

RUINING

UNLESS YOU'RE A SCOUNDREL AND GO AROUND RUINING 295 AHWILD DECENT GIRLS--

RUINING MY STOMACH WITH ROTGUT. 652 ICEMAN

HIS INSANE BANKING POLICY IS RUINING THE COUNTRY/ 48 MANSNS

YOU MEAN BECAUSE YOUR HUSBAND IS RESPONSIBLE FOR 151 MANSNS RUINING ME5

(UNHEEDINGLY) YOU MUST KEEP HIM FROM RUINING HIS 169 STRANG LIFE.

RUINOUS

NO MATTER HOW RUINOUS THE INTEREST DEMANDED BY THE120 POET SCOUNDRELLY MONEYLENDERS.

RUINS

AND EGGS HIM ON AND RUINS HIS LIFE--LIKE ALL WOMEN235 AHWILD LOVE TO RUIN MEN'S LIVES/

IT'S FALLEN TO RUINS NOW. 132 ELECTR

RULE

BUT I GUESS IT NEVER REALLY AMOUNTED TO MORE THAN 134 BEYOND A KID IDEA I WAS LETTING RULE

BUT I SHOULD THINK YOU OUGHT TO BE A BORN 22 ELECTR EXCEPTION TO THAT RULE.

THAT'S THE LEADEN RULE FOR THE SAFE AND SANE. 294 GGBROW

NOTHING FOR NOTHING IS THE RULE HERE, YOU KNOW. 89 MANSNS

WHY DID YOU MAKE THAT SILLY RULE THAT NO ONE WAS 109 MANSNS EVER ALLOWED

(SUDDENLY EXPLODES, SLAMMING HER RULE ON THE 140 MANSNS DESK.)

FOR IT'S A GREAT JOKE TO HEAR HIM SHOUT AGAINST 26 POET MOB RULE,

WHEN IT COMES TO NOT LETTING OTHERS RULE HIM, 32 POET

I WON'T LET MY HEART RULE MY HEAD AND MAKE A SLAVE 65 POET OF ME/

RULED

AND NO LIFE THAT WASN'T RULED BY HER LIFE. 82 MANSNS

HAUNTED BY TERRIBLE GHOSTS AND RULED OVER BY A 111 MANSNS HIDEOUS OLD WITCH.

RULER

BUT THE OPPOSITES OF THE SAME STUPIDITY WHICH IS 649 ICEMAN RULER AND KING OF LIFE.

WORKING WITH A RULER AND DRAFTING INSTRUMENTS ON A139 MANSNS PLAN.

BEFORE THE MOSQUE IS A THRONE ON WHICH SITS A 364 MARCOM MAHOMETAN RULER.

IMMEDIATELY BEFORE THE GATE IS A RUDE THRONE ON 373 MARCOM WHICH SITS A MONGUL RULER WITH

THE CLOTHES OF THE RULER AND HIS COURT ARE OF RICH373 MARCOM SILK STUFFS,

DID THEIR POPE MEAN THAT A FOOL IS A WISER STUDY 381 MARCOM FOR A RULER OF FOOLS

FITTING TO THE PHILOSOPHER RULER WHO RETREATS HERE384 MARCOM

THE RULER OF EARTH, AS THEY INNOCENTLY CALL YOUR 385 MARCOM GRANDFATHER,

FUR KUKACHIN, AND HER GRANDFATHER, THE SON OF 388 MARCOM HEAVEN AND RULER OF THE WORLD/

THE GREAT KAAN, RULER OF THE WORLD, MAY NOT WEEP. 401 MARCOM

(BROKENLY) RULERS 401 MARCOM

MARCO, THE TRUE RULER OF THE WORLD, WILL HAVE COME426 MARCOM TO VENICE BY THIS TIME.

RULER OVER LIFE AND DEATH/ 435 MARCOM

RULER'S

AT THE RULER'S FEET HIS WIVES CROUCH LIKE SLAVES. 364 MARCOM

LOOMING DIRECTLY ABOVE AND IN BACK OF THE RULER'S 369 MARCOM THRONE IS AN IMMENSE BUDDHA.

THE BACKGROUND FOR THE RULER'S THRONE IS NOW A 369 MARCOM BUDDHIST TEMPLE

RULES

I'LL FORGET THE HOUSE RULES, ERIE. 37 HUGHIE

THE RULES OF THE HOUSE ARE THAT DRINKS MAY BE 585 ICEMAN SERVED AT ALL HOURS.

HE RULES OVER MILLIONS OF SUBJECTS, 359 MARCOM

IT SHALL NOT BE I WHO RULES, BUT YOU/ 418 MARCOM

RULING

IF I NEEDED ANY FURTHER PROOF THAT OUR RULING 24 JOURNE PLUTOCRATS,

RUM

SO FINE A WOMAN UNCE--AN NOW SUCH A SLAVE TO RUM/ 232 AHWILD

WELL, HOW'S MY FELLOW RUM POT, AS GOOD OLD DOWLE 271 AHWILD CALLS US5

AN' THAT BLARSTED BUMBOAT NAYGUR WOMAN TOOK HER 457 CARIBE OATH SHE'D BRING BACK RUM ENOUGH

WE'LL BE 'AVIN' OUR RUM IN ARF A MO', DUKE. 459 CARIBE

RUM, FOINE WEST INDY RUM WID A KICK IN UT LOIKE A 460 CARIBE MULE'S HOIND LEG.

'TIS FOINE RUM, THE RALE STUFF. 462 CARIBE

(STERNLY) YOU KNOW THE AGREEMENT--RUM--NO MONEY. 473 CARIBE

RUM, BY GOD/ 473 CARIBE

THAT'LL TEACH YOU TO SMUGGLE RUM ON A SHIP AND 473 CARIBE START A RIOT.

BEING DRUNK ON NATIVE RUM THEY'D STOLE, 503 DIFRNT

AND NATIVE RUM HAS PAINTED HIS POINTED NOSE TO A 174 EJONES STARTLING RED.

DRINKIN' RUM AND TALKIN' BIG DOWN IN DE TOWN. 176 EJONES

IT'S RUM AND OLD AGE. 136 ELECTR

IT SOUNDS TO ME LIKE BACCHUS, ALIAS THE DEMON RUM,297 GGBROW DOING THE TALKING.

LIKE A RUM-SOAKED TROOPER, BRAWLING BEFORE A 158 POET BROTHEL ON A SATURDAY NIGHT,

TO LET HER KNOW WE'VE NOT ALL BEEN MURDERED BY 50 STRANG RUM-BANDITS.

RUMBLE

AND A LOW RUMBLE OF THUNDER. 421 DYNAMO

(THE CLAP OF THUNDER FROM THE PRECEDING FLASH 441 DYNAMO COMES WITH A GREAT RUMBLE.)

RUMBLES

AND THUNDER RUMBLES AND CRASHES BUT THERE IS NO 312 LAZARU RAIN.

RUMBLING

THE ROLL OF THE THUNDER FROM THE PRECEDING FLASH 446 DYNAMO COMES CRASHING AND RUMBLING.

JUST AT THAT MOMENT A BUS IS HEARD RUMBLING UP. 239 HA APE

RUMINATING

MILLER GAZES BEFORE HIM WITH A RUMINATING 257 AHWILD MELANCHOLY,

BUT IN THEIR DEPTHS RUMINATING AND CONTEMPLATIVE. 4 MANSNS

(AFTER A PAUSE, RUMINATINGLY) 231 DESIRE

RUMINATIVELY

(PUFFS RUMINATIVELY) THEY ALL TAKE AFTER YOUR 16 MISBEG MOTHER'S FAMILY.

RUMMY

RUMMY GO, WHATS 459 CARIBE

RUMOR

(WITH A CERTAIN DOGGEENESS) THERE'S A RUMOR THAT 276 GGBROW YOU'VE APPLIED FOR A POSITION

(IN THE VAGUE TONE OF A CORPSE WHICH ADMITS IT 18 HUGHIE ONCE OVERHEARD A FAVORABLE RUMOR

THERE WAS A RUMOR IN SOUTH AFRICA, ROCKY, THAT A 677 ICEMAN CERTAIN BOER OFFICER--

RUMOR HAS LED THEM TO HOPE AND BELIEVE 298 LAZARU

IT WOULD TAKE ONLY A RUMOR--A WHISPER SPOKEN IN 142 MANSNS THE RIGHT EAR.

A RUMOR STARTED AMONG THE MANY DEFEATED ENEMIES 156 MANSNS

I KNOW ONLY TOO WELL HOW TEMPTED YOU ARE TO 157 MANSNS WHISPER AND START THE RUMOR OF THE

RUMORS

RUMORS LATELY. 18 ELECTR

I'VE HEARD RUMORS THE MANAGEMENT WERE AT THEIR 604 ICEMAN WITS' END

I ALSO HAF HEARD RUMORS OF A LIMEY OFFICER WHO, 677 ICEMAN AFTER THE WAR,

RUMORS

RUMORS (CONT'D.)
THEN, BECAUSE YOU MUST HAVE HEARD RUMORS OF MY 354 LAZARU
DEPRAVITY,
YES, I HAVE HEARD RUMORS THAT YOU ADVISE HIM. 152 MANSNS
I'VE HEARD THOSE RUMORS. 349 MARCOM
I ALSO HAD HEARD A LOT OF RUMORS ABOUT YOUR 446 WELDED
PREVIOUS--

RUMPUS
THEY'RE WHAT STARTED THE RUMPUS. 204 AHWILD
YOU'VE NO CALL TO BE RAISING THIS RUMPUS WITH ME. 57 ANNA
IF I WAS A DAINTY, PRETTY TART HE'D BE PROUD I'D 92 MISBEG
RAISE A RUMPUS ABOUT HIM.

RUN
LILY, YOU RUN UP THE BACK STAIRS AND GET YOUR 199 AHWILD
THINGS ON.
OR I'LL CALL SULLIVAN FROM THE CORNER AND HAVE YOU248 AHWILD
RUN IN FUR STREET-WALKING/
IF HE EVER FINDS OUT I SERVED HIS KID, HE'LL RUN 248 AHWILD
ME OUT OF TOWN.
YOU RUN UP TO BED THIS MINUTE/ 252 AHWILD
YOU RUN ALONG NOW. 253 AHWILD
YOU DIDN'T RUN INTO HIM ANYWHERE DID YOU5 254 AHWILD
YOU READ IN THE PAPERS EVERY DAY ABOUT BOYS 259 AHWILD
GETTING RUN OVER BY AUTOMOBILES.
MILDRED KEEPS STARTING TO RUN OVER POPULAR TUNES 259 AHWILD
IF YOU HAVE ANY GUTS YOU WILL RUN THAT BASTARD OUT267 AHWILD
OF TOWN.
BUT I DEDUCE THAT THE LADY HAD A RUN-IN WITH THE 267 AHWILD
BARKEEP AND WANTS REVENGE.
EVEN HAVING A RUN-IN WITH YOUR PA BECAUSE-- 270 AHWILD
I DO THINK YOU'VE GOT AN AWFUL NERVE TO SAY THAT 278 AHWILD
AFTER ALL THE RISKS I'VE RUN
YOU MIGHT THINK OF ME FOR A CHANGE, AFTER ALL THE 278 AHWILD
RISK I'VE RUN TO SEE YOU/
VIKING-DAUGHTER FASHION BUT NOW RUN DOWN IN HEALTH 13 ANNA
AND PLAINLY SHOWING ALL THE
SO I RUN AWAY--TO ST. PAUL. 18 ANNA
YOU'VE JUST HAD A RUN OF BAD LUCK WITH 'EM, THAT'S 18 ANNA
ALL.
THAT WAS WHY I RAN AWAY FROM THE FARM. 58 ANNA
ANNA LOOKS AFTER HIM WILDLY, STARTS TO RUN AFTER 61 ANNA
HIM,
THE TEAM'D RUN AWAY, I'LL BET. 82 BEYOND
(HE JUMPS DOWN FROM FENCE) I'D BETTER RUN ALONG. 86 BEYOND
(THEY RUN OFF LAUGHING AS THE CURTAIN FALLS.) 93 BEYOND
WE'LL RUN THEN. 93 BEYOND
AN I B'LIEVE IN LETTIN' YOUNG FOLKS RUN THEIR 98 BEYOND
AFFAIRS TO SUIT THEMSELVES..
YOU KNOW'S WELL AS I DO THAT IT WOULDN'T BE FAIR 105 BEYOND
OF YOU TO RUN OFF AT A MOMENT'S
HAD TO RUN BEFORE IT UNDER BARE POLES FOR TWO 131 BEYOND
DAYS.
ONE OF US IS ENOUGH TO RUN THIS LITTLE PLACE. 133 BEYOND
(EVASIVELY) I COULD SEE THE PLACE HAD RUN DOWN.. 133 BEYOND
(WITH A FROWN) THINGS ARE RUN DOWN, THAT'S A 136 BEYOND
FACT/
BUT I RUN ACROSS A BIT O' NEWS DOWN TO THE 141 BEYOND
SEAMEN'S HOME MADE ME 'BOUT SHIP AND
NOW STREAKED WITH GRAY, HER MUDDIED SHOES RUN DOWN144 BEYOND
AT THE HEEL.
WHY DIDN'T YOU RUN AND GET JAKE5 152 BEYOND
(JUMPING TO HIS FEET) I'LL RUN FOR THE CAPTAIN. 484 CARDIF
(COAXINGLY) WHY YOU RUN 'WAY FROM ME, PRETTY BOYS 469 CARIBE
(THEY WALK QUICKLY--ALMOST RUN--OFF TO THE LEFT. 473 CARIBE
HE'S RUN AWAY AS FAR AS HE CAN GET IN THAT 503 DAYS
DIRECTION.
RUN AWAY5 503 DAYS
RELIGION, NO LESS--BUT AS FAR AWAY AS HE COULD RUN503 DAYS
FROM HOME--
WE WON'T LET HIM RUN AWAY IN A FEW DAYS, NOW WE'VE504 DAYS
GOT HIM HERE.
(AS IF HE HADN'T HEARD) WHY DO YOU RUN AND HIDE 508 DAYS
FROM HIM, AS FROM AN ENEMY5
I DON'T WANT TO RUN INTO HIM. 516 DAYS
(THEN ABRUPTLY) GOT TO RUN NOW, ELSA-- 524 DAYS
SORRY I'VE GOT TO RUN, JOHN. 525 DAYS
(AS IF HIS CONVERSATION HAD RUN DRY, HE FALLS INTO529 DAYS
AN UNEASY SILENCE.
HE WANTED TO RUN AWAY FROM HER--BUT FOUND HE 535 DAYS
COULDN'T.
SHE WAS RUN OVER BY A CAR. 536 DAYS
AFRAID FOR A MOMENT I LET AN AUTHOR'S CRAVING FOR 545 DAYS
A DRAMATIC MOMENT RUN AWAY
(SHE STARTS AS IF TO RUN FROM THE ROOM.) 550 DAYS
AN' HE SAYS WITH A MULE'S GRIN.. *DON'T YE RUN 209 DESIRE
AWAY TILL I COME BACK/*
THEN I GOT T' THE VILLAGE AN' HEERD THE NEWS AN' 1214 DESIRE
GUT MADDER'N HELL AN' RUN ALL
SHE LOOKS AWED AND FRIGHTENED NOW, READY TO RUN 241 DESIRE
AWAY.
I WANTED T' YELL AN' RUN. 242 DESIRE
I THOUGHT YE MIGHT HAVE TIME T' RUN AWAY--WITH 266 DESIRE
ME--AN'...
I BEGUN T' RUN BACK. 266 DESIRE
MUST O' THE WHALIN' MEN HEREABOUT HAVE RUN UP 502 DIFRNT
AGAINST IT IN THEIR TIME.
NO, I JEST RUN OVER FROM THE HOUSE A SECOND TO SEE505 DIFRNT
IF--WHERE'S CALEB, EMMA5
NO, ALL KIDDIN' ASIDE, I KNOW HE'LL RUN ME DOWN 523 DIFRNT
FIRST SECOND HE SEES YOU.
LAND SAKES, I HARDLY GET A SIGHT OF YOU BEFORE YOU524 DIFRNT
WANT TO RUN AWAY AGAIN.
I GOT TO RUN UPSTAIRS AND TIDY MYSELF A LITTLE. 527 DIFRNT
(HE STANDS IN THE MIDDLE OF THE ROOM HESITATING 530 DIFRNT
WHETHER TO RUN AWAY OR STAY.
(EMMA STARTS) HARRIET LETS HER TONGUE RUN AWAY 539 DIFRNT
WITH HER AND SAYS DUMB FOOL
CONTROLLING AN IMPULSE TO RUN FROM THE ROOM. 437 DYNAMO

RUN (CONT'D.)
I SUPPOSE YOU WANT TO RUN OVER AND WARN YOUR FINE 450 DYNAMO
FRIENDS/
I DON'T WANT TO RUN INTO HIM UNLESS I HAVE TO. 461 DYNAMO
SHE LOOKS WORRIED AND RUN DOWN. 480 DYNAMO
RUN AWAY--TO THE FILLS5 175 EJONES
DEY'VE ALL RUN OFF TO DE HILLS, AIN'T DEYS 182 EJONES
I KIN OUTGUESS, OUT RUN, OUTFIGHT, 184 EJONES
UH, GORRY, I'SE GOT TO RUN. 192 EJONES
AND IF EBEN'S WIFE STARTS TO RUN YOU OFF FUR 8 ELECTR
TRESPASSIN',
YOU RUN IN. 12 ELECTR
WELL, I MUST RUN. 13 ELECTR
I GUESS I BETTER RUN ALONG NOW, VINNIE. 16 ELECTR
I HAPPENED TO RUN INTO CAPTAIN BRANT ON THE STREET 17 ELECTR
IN NEW YORK.
I--(SHE TURNS AS IF TO RUN INTO THE ROOM, TAKES A 64 ELECTR
TOTTERING STEP--
I WANTED TO DESERT AND RUN HOME--OR ELSE GET 89 ELECTR
KILLED/
TO KEEP ME FROM DOING ANYTHING, SO SHE'LL GET A 98 ELECTR
CHANCE TO RUN OFF AND MARRY HIM/
I'LL HAVE TO RUN HOME AND TELL MOTHER, SO SHE 119 ELECTR
WON'T WORRY.
I HEARD 'EM COMIN' AFTER ME, AND I RUN IN THE ROOM134 ELECTR
OPPOSITE,
AND, BY GOD, I RUN. 134 ELECTR
NOW RUN ALONG TO HAZEL. 146 ELECTR
I'LL HAVE TO RUN ALONG SOON AND DROP IN AT THE 158 ELECTR
COUNCIL MEETING.
SHE STARTS TO RUN AFTER HIM, STOPS HER SELF, 167 ELECTR
(SHE SPRINGS UP AS IF SHE WERE GOING TO RUN IN THE171 ELECTR
HOUSE,
AND I'D LOVE TO RUN MY FINGERS THROUGH HIS HAIR-- 263 GGBROW
AND I LOVE HIM/
BUT MY MIND DOESN'T SEEM TO RUN THAT WAY. 275 GGBROW
BUSINESS HAS BEEN PILING UP ON ME--A RUN OF LUCK- 277 GGBROW
---BUT I'M SHORT-HANDED.
I DIDN'T WANT TO RUN ANY RISK GETTING INTO MORE 278 GGBROW
THAT I'D LIKE TO RUN OUT NAKED INTO THE STREET AND286 GGBROW
LOVE THE WHOLE MOB TO DEATH.
(THEY RUN TO HER SIDE, KNEEL AND RUB HER WRISTS. 293 GGBROW
TOO FAT NOW TO LEARN TO WALK, LET ALONE TO DANCE 296 GGBROW
OR RUN.
SO RUN ALONG/ 301 GGBROW
(THEY'LL ALL RUN INTO THE LITTLE ROOM OFF RIGHT. 318 GGBROW
WE MUST TAKE STEPS AT ONCE TO RUN ANTHONY TO 319 GGBROW
EARTH/
THEN RUN BILLY, RUN/ 320 GGBROW
RUN, BILLY, RUN/ 320 GGBROW
SO RUN AWAY IF YOU WANT TO LIVE/ 320 GGBROW
RUN INTO THE ROOM. 321 GGBROW
I HAVE BEEN ADVISED TO RUN FROM YOU BUT IT IS MY 321 GGBROW
ALREADY WHEN TO DANCE INTO
AND THE COPPERS NABBED HIM--AND I RUN-- 208 HA APE
WHO MAKES DIS OLD TUS RUN5 212 HA APE
WE RUN DE WHOLE WOIKS.. 216 HA APE
(SURPRISED BUT ADMIRINGLY) YUH MEAN TO SAY YUH 248 HA APE
ALWAYS RUN WIDE OPEN--LIKE DIS5
I'D RUN YOU IN BUT IT'S TOO LONG A WALK TO THE 251 HA APE
STATION.
I STUCK IT TILL I WAS EIGHTEEN BEFORE I TOOK A 14 HUGHIE
RUN-OUT POWDER.
WHEN THE HORSES WON'T RUN FOR ME, THERE'S DRAW OR 15 HUGHIE
STUD.
HE DIDN'T RUN IN MY CLASS. 18 HUGHIE
WHEN, NO MATTER HOW MUCH HE'D WIN ON A RUN OF LUCK 20 HUGHIE
LIKE SUCKERS HAVE SOMETIMES,
I RUN ERRANDS FOR 'EM SOMETIMES, BECAUSE 28 HUGHIE
EXCEPT ONE OR TWO FROM WAY BACK WHEN I HAD A RUN 29 HUGHIE
OF BIG LUCK.
HE USES ME TO RUN ERRANDS WHEN THERE AIN'T NO ONE 34 HUGHIE
ELSE HANDY.
MY BIG WORRY IS THE RUN OF BAD LUCK I'VE HAD 35 HUGHIE
(HE SEEMS TO RUN DOWN, AND IS OVERCOME BY 579 ICEMAN
DROWSINESS.
DAT WELL DONE RUN DRY. 586 ICEMAN
'CAUSE I RUN WIDE OPEN FOR YEARS AND PAYS MY SUGAR601 ICEMAN
ON DE DOT,
AND WOULD BE ONLY TOO GLAD TO HAVE ME RUN IT FOR 604 ICEMAN
THEM AGAIN.
I'VE RUN INTO SOME NUTTY SOUSES, BUT DIS GUY WAS 616 ICEMAN
DE NUTTIEST.
I RAN INTO LUCK. 616 ICEMAN
HE'S GOT HARRY AND JIMMY TOMORROW RUN RAGGED, 631 ICEMAN
WHAT GETS MY GOAT IS DE WAY HE'S TRYIN' TO RUN DE 631 ICEMAN
WHOLE DUMP AND EVERYONE IN IT.
(ROCKY AND CHUCK RUN FROM BEHIND THE BAR CURTAIN 650 ICEMAN
AND RUSH INTO THE HALL.
THIS DUMP HAS GOT TO BE RUN LIKE OTHER DUMPS, 659 ICEMAN
NO MAN CAN RUN A CIRCUS SUCCESSFULLY WHO BELIEVES 681 ICEMAN
GUYS CHEW COFFEE BEANS BECAUSE
THEY'D RUN OVER YOU AS SOON AS LOOK AT YOU. 687 ICEMAN
PANIC-STRICKEN RUN. 689 ICEMAN
HE'D RUN RIGHT OVER ME IF I HADN'T JUMPED. 690 ICEMAN
OR I COULDN'T JUST RUN AWAY FROM HER. 706 ICEMAN
(HE STOPS LIKE A MECHANICAL DOLL THAT HAS RUN 708 ICEMAN
DOWN.
WE COULDN'T RUN AWAY OR FIGHT IF WE WANTED TO. 516 INZONE
SO YOU HAVE RUN AWAY TO SEA LOIKE THE COWARD YOU 531 INZONE
ARE
RUN DOWN EVERYBODY/ 30 JOURNE
THAT'S RIGHT/ RUN HIM DOWN/ 30 JOURNE
SHE SPRINGS TO HER FEET, AS IF SHE WANTED TO RUN 42 JOURNE
AWAY FROM THE SOUND.
(THEN RESENTFULLY,) YOU'RE A FINE ONE TO RUN AWAY 126 JOURNE
AND LEAVE ME TO SIT ALONE HERE
WHAT MADE YOU RUN AWAY5 136 JOURNE

RUNS

RUN (CONT'D.)

WHAT IF IT IS RUN BY THE STATES 144 JOURNE
AND SHE COULDN'T AFFORD TO RUN A HOME FOR FAT 159 JOURNE
TARTS.
I RUN THE RISK YOU'LL HATE ME--AND YOU'RE ALL I'VE166 JOURNE
GOT LEFT.
WITH FRIGHTENED CRIES MARTHA AND MARY RUN FROM THE283 LAZARU
GROUP OF NAZARENES AND KNEEL
WHEN YOU LAID IT, THE LAST TIME, WE ALL HAD TO RUN 346 LAZARU
FOR OUR LIVES, CHOKING,
AND THEN, TO HEAR THE OLD HOWLING OF MOB LUST, AND370 LAZARU
TO RUN HERE--
YOU'VE THE WISH FOR LIFE BUT YOU HAVEN'T THE 19 MANSNS
STRENGTH EXCEPT TO RUN AND HIDE
YOU WILL RUN NO RISK OF ANYTHING WORSE THAN YOUR 111 MANSNS
PRESENT UNHAPPY EXILE.
BUT I HAVE TO RUN DOWN TO THE MILLS TODAY. 146 MANSNS
HOW MANY TIMES NOW HAVE I RUN TO OPEN THE DOOR, 162 MANSNS
HOPING EACH TIME--S
BUT YOU BETTER RUN AHEAD, SARA, AND SEE HONEY. 177 MANSNS
AND THEN THERE WILL BE NO CHOICE LEFT TO YOU BUT 182 MANSNS
TO RUN AND HIDE IN THERE AGAIN,
OF TWO SOLDIERS WHO RUN BESIDE THEM AND THE LONG 350 MARCOM
WHIPS
MARCO STARTS AS IF TO RUN AFTER HER ANGRILY. 375 MARCOM
YOU'D BETTER RUN FOR YOUR LIFE/ 10 MISBEG
OLD MEN SHOULDN'T RUN AROUND RAGING IN THE NOON 12 MISBEG
SUN.
YOU MEAN HE'S RUN OFF TO MAKE HIS OWN WAY IN THE 13 MISBEG
WORLDS
SURE, YOU COULD GIVE JACK DEMPSEY HIMSELF A RUN 14 MISBEG
FOR HIS MONEY.
SO RUN ALONG NOW AND PLAY WITH YOUR HORSE, AND 56 MISBEG
DON'T BOTHER ME.
PITTINGLY) RUN HOME, THAT'S A GOOD LAD, BEFORE 60 MISBEG
YOUR KEEPER MISSES YOU.
NO MATTER WHAT WE DO--NOR ESCAPE OURSELVES NO 135 MISBEG
MATTER WHERE WE RUN AWAY.
WELL, I'LL RUN ALONG AND LET YOU DO YOUR WORK. 173 MISBEG
BE DAMNED IF I'LL RUN FROM HER. 15 POET
WILL YOU KEEP AN EYE ON THE BAR WHILE I RUN TO THE 20 POET
STORE FOR A BIT AV BACCYS
CRACKED WORKING SHOES, RUN DOWN AT THE HEEL, ARE 20 POET
ON HER BARE FEET.
BUT SARA HAS RUN FROM THE DOOR AT RIGHT AND SHE 123 POET
GRABS HIS ARM.
(HE AND O'DOWD RUN GADSBY TO THE DOOR AT REAR. 124 POET
TRICKLES OF DRIED BLOOD RUN DOWN TO HIS JAW. 152 POET
I'LL BE A REAL HUSBAND TO YOU, AND HELP YE RUN 174 POET
THIS SHEBEEN.
SO YOU MIGHT 'S WELL TAKE DOWN THAT UGLY ROPE 581 ROPE
YOU'VE HAD TIED THERE SINCE HE RUN
AN' DO YOU RUN TO THE HOUSE AN' BREAK THE NEWS TO 590 ROPE
THE AULD MAN.
(SHE COMMENCES TO CRY) RUN HELP YOUR MOTHER NOW 591 ROPE
OR I'LL GIVE YE A GOOD HIDIN'.
RUN ALONG UP THE STREET AND GET THIS FILLED. 34 STRANG
I'VE WANTED TO RUN HOME AND 'FESS UP, TELL HOW BAD 44 STRANG
I'VE BEEN, AND BE PUNISHED/
I POSITIVELY MUST RUN HOME AT ONCE... 45 STRANG
I LOVE IT TOO MUCH TO MAKE IT RUN THAT CHANCE/ 61 STRANG
OH, I'D GET DOWN ON MY KNEES TO YOU, DON'T MAKE MY 62 STRANG
BOY RUN THAT RISKY
I HAPPENED TO RUN INTO HIM THE OTHER DAY AND 72 STRANG
INVITED HIM
I'LL RUN UPSTAIRS. 73 STRANG
RUN ALONG. 78 STRANG
(THEN SUDDENLY) I'VE JUST THOUGHT--SAM SAID HE 82 STRANG
HAPPENED TO RUN INTO YOU.
AND NOW I'VE GOT TO RUN. 106 STRANG
WHY DID DARRELL RUN AWAYS... 112 STRANG
(CASUALLY) YES, I CHANCED TO RUN INTO HIM. 115 STRANG
I COULDN'T RUN OVER TO EUROPE AND GET AWAY WITH 117 STRANG
MURDER THE WAY YOU HAVE/.
AN AGENCY THAT'S BEEN ALLOWED TO RUN DOWN AND GO 121 STRANG
TO SEED.
OR IF YOU THINK I'LL RUN AWAY WITH YOU AND LEAVE 128 STRANG
MY BABY...)
WHEN HE KNOWS YOU'RE HERE HE'LL COME ON THE RUN, 129 STRANG
DARRELL.
(THEN IN ANGUISH) OH, NED, WHY DID YOU RUN AWAYS 130 STRANG
WHY COULDN'T MOTHER LET ME RUN MY OWN BIRTHDAYS...138 STRANG
I'VE BROKEN WITH HER, RUN AWAY, TRIED TO FORGET 139 STRANG
HER---
AND THEN THERE'LL BE THE SAME OLD TERRIBLE SCENE 143 STRANG
OF HATE AND YOU'LL RUN AWAY--
THEY RUN TO THE RAIL AND TRAIN THEIR GLASSES UP 176 STRANG
THE RIVER.)
I'LL RUN ALONG. 451 WELDED
TREMBLINGLY UNCERTAIN WHETHER TO RUN AND HIDE 480 WELDED
FROM,
OR RUN FORWARD AND GREET CAPE, WHO IS STANDING IN 480 WELDED
THE DOORWAY.

RUNAWAY

YOU'RE SIMPLY LETTING YOUR ROMANTIC IMAGINATION 102 STRANG
RUNAWAY WITH YOU--

RUNDOWN

HE WAS IN A RUNDOWN CONDITION, THEY SAY AT THE 48 ELECTR
HOSPITAL.
HEARING THE FOG DRIP FROM THE EAVES LIKE THE 152 JOURNE
UNEVEN TICK OF A RUNDOWN.

RUNG

I'VE RUNG FOR THE LOBSTER. 228 AHWILD
THE RUNG OF ONE ROCKER HAS BEEN CLUMSILY MENDED 144 BEYOND
WITH A PIECE OF PLAIN BOARD.

RUNGS

WHERE HE LUNGES FOR THE RUNGS ON THE DYNAMO'S SIDE488 DYNAMO
AND CLAMBERS UP FRENZIEDLY.

RUNNED

(PROUDLY) I RUNNED AWAY FROM MINE WHEN I WAS A 211 HA APE
KID.
I RUNNED AWAY WHEN ME OLD LADY CROAKED WIT DE 234 HA APE
TREMENS.

RUNNIN'

AND THE HANDS HALF STARVED WITH THE FOOD RUNNIN' 537 'ILE
LOW, ROTTEN AS IT IS,.
'S IF I DIDN'T KNOW YOUR REAL REASON FOR RUNNIN' 106 BEYOND
AWAY/
AND RUNNIN' AWAY'S THE ONLY WORDS TO FIT IT. 106 BEYOND
YOU'RE RUNNIN' AGAINST YOUR OWN NATURE, 106 BEYOND
YOU'RE RUNNIN' AWAY 'CAUSE YOU'RE PUT OUT AND 106 BEYOND
RILED
DOES HE SUPPOSE YOU'RE RUNNIN' A HOTEL--WITH NO 113 BEYOND
ONE TO HELP WITH THINGS#
I'LL COME A-RUNNIN' AN' BY THE ETARNAL, 256 DESIRE
I MUST 'A' PUT SOME DISTANCE BETWEEN MYSELF AN' 193 EJONES
DEM--RUNNIN' LIKE DAT--AND YIT--
RUNNIN' AN' RUNNIN' AN' RUNNIN'/ 193 EJONES
DON'T WANT YOU RUNNIN' INTO FURNITURE AN' BREAKIN'131 ELECTR
THINGS
HE'LL COME RUNNIN' OUT HELL FUR LEATHER AFORE 133 ELECTR
LONG.
WHO D'YUH TINK'S RUNNIN' DIS GAME, ME OR YOUS 224 HA APE
YUH'LL COME RUNNIN' IN HERE SOME NIGHT YELLIN' FOR670 ICEMAN
A SHOT OF BOOZE

RUNNING

THE CORD OF THE LAMP RUNNING UP TO ONE OF FIVE 185 AHWILD
SOCKETS IN THE CHANDELIER ABOVE.
THEY'RE RUNNING ME FOR PRESIDENT OF THE W.C.T.U. 190 AHWILD
YOU KNOW WHAT THOSE PICNICS ARE, AND SID'D BE 212 AHWILD
RUNNING INTO ALL HIS OLD FRIENDS.
AND I'M NOT COMING RUNNING AFTER YOU/ 216 AHWILD
HE HAS HIS READING SPECS ON AND IS RUNNING OVER 249 AHWILD
ITEMS IN A NEWSPAPER.
AT LEFT, A BANK OF DARK EARTH RUNNING HALF- 275 AHWILD
DIAGONALLY BACK ALONG THE BEACH,
AND STARTS RUNNING TOWARDS THE PATH. 285 AHWILD
(GOES OVER AND PATS HER ON THE SHOULDER, THE TEARS 62 ANNA
RUNNING DOWN HIS FACE)
(RUNNING TO HER MOTHER) MAMA/ 135 BEYOND
YOU'VE SPENT EIGHT YEARS RUNNING AWAY FROM 161 BEYOND
YOURSELF.
ONLY THE RATS RUNNING ABOUT. 571 CROSS
I CAN REMEMBER WHEN I COULDN'T PICK UP AN 497 DAYS
ADVANCED-THINKER ORGAN WITHOUT RUNNING
AND HE WAS RUNNING THROUGH GREEK PHILOSOPHY 503 DAYS
THIS RUNNING AWAY FROM TRUTH IN ORDER TO FIND ITS 504 DAYS
THERE IS A PATH RUNNING FROM THE GATE 202 DESIRE
A MOMENT LATER SHE COMES INTO THE KITCHEN AND, 259 DESIRE
RUNNING TO EBEN,
(HE HEARS RUNNING FOOTSTEPS FROM THE LEFT, 265 DESIRE
IMMEDIATELY IS HIMSELF AGAIN.
THERE IS THE NOISE OF RUNNING FOOTSTEPS FROM 548 DIFRNT
OUTSIDE
RUNNING AT A SPEED OF ROTATION N, IS THEORETICALLY429 DYNAMO
PROPORTIONAL TO DA LINE---
JONES CAN BE HEARD SCRAMBLING TO HIS FEET AND 199 EJONES
RUNNING OFF,
(BREAKING FROM HER AND RUNNING FOR THE DOOR) 167 ELECTR
(SHE COMES RUNNING IN, HER MASK IN HER HANDS. 266 GGBROW
THINK WE WERE RUNNING A CRAP GAMES 247 HA APE
IT MANAGES TO KEEP RUNNING BY CUTTING THE OVERHEAD 7 HUGHIE
FOR SERVICES, REPAIRS,
CORA, AT THE PIANO, KEEPS RUNNING THROUGH THE 651 ICEMAN
TUNE, WITH SOFT PEDAL.
I'M NOT RUNNING A DAMNED ORPHAN ASYLUM FOR BUMS 659 ICEMAN
AND CROOKS/
(HE BEGINS EAGERLY IN A STRANGE RUNNING NARRATIVE 707 ICEMAN
MANNER)
RUNNING HIS EYES QUICKLY DOWN THE PAGES. 531 INZONE
I CAN REMEMBER HER HUGGING AND KISSING US AND 148 JOURNE
SAYING WITH TEARS OF JOY RUNNING
FLOURISHING HIS SWORD AND COMES RUNNING INTO THE 336 LAZARU
ROOM, SHOUTING
(RUNNING TO SOLDIERS--FIERCELY) 348 LAZARU
(RUNNING TO THE SOLDIERS--HYSTERICALLY) 348 LAZARU
HE IS PANTING AS IF EXHAUSTED BY RUNNING. 368 LAZARU
I HAVE FIVE MILLS NOW, ALL RUNNING PROFITABLY, 70 MANSNS
INSTEAD OF ONE.
SOMEONE IS RUNNING HERE, AND A CROWD BEHIND. 361 MARCOM
THE SOUND OF RUNNING ABOUT ON DECK AND MARCO'S 417 MARCOM
VOICE GIVING COMMANDS.
IF HE CATCHES YOU RUNNING AWAY, HE'LL BEAT YOU 5 MISBEG
HALF TO DEATH.
HE'S RUNNING DOWN THERE. 10 MISBEG
A MOMENT LATER, HER FATHER, PHIL HOGAN, COMES 11 MISBEG
RUNNING UP FROM LEFT-REAR
ARE YOU RUNNING AWAY FROM HIMS 36 MISBEG
DON'T TRY RUNNING AWAY OR MY DAUGHTER WILL KNOCK 61 MISBEG
YOU SENSELESS.
RUNNING HIS TONGUE OVER HIS DRY LIPS, SHE SAYS 54 POET
ACIDLY, WITH NO TRACE OF BROGUE.)
A ROPE ABOUT FIVE FEET LONG WITH AN OPEN RUNNING 577 ROPE
NOOSE AT THE END, IS HANGING.
IT KEEPS RUNNING AWAY TO HER... 85 STRANG
(THEN GLOOMILY) (MY RUNNING AWAY WAS ABOUT AS 112 STRANG
SUCCESSFUL AS HIS...
RUNNING AWAY TO COME BACK EACH TIME MORE 139 STRANG
ABJECTLY...

RUNS

(SHE RUNS OVER TO HIM AND THROWS HER ARMS AROUND 546 'ILE
HIM, WEEPING.
WHICH HAS RECEDED A BIT FROM THE EXTREME OF 186 AHWILD
PRECEDING YEARS, BUT STILL RUNS TO
(MILDRED RUNS IN THROUGH THE BACK PARLOR. 220 AHWILD
KNOW NAT MILLER WHO RUNS THE GLOBES 248 AHWILD

RUNS

RUNS (CONT'D.)

HIS OLD MAN RUNS A PAPER IN THIS ONE-HORSE BURG, 1248 AHWILD THINK HE SAID.

AS MILDRED RUNS OVER THE SCALES. 256 AHWILD

SHE RUNS AND PUTS HER ARM AROUND HIM-- 258 AHWILD

THE BAR RUNS FROM LEFT TO RIGHT NEARLY THE WHOLE 3 ANNA LENGTH OF THE REAR WALL.

AND AS FOR ME BEING ALONE, THAT RUNS IN THE 77 ANNA FAMILY, AND I'LL GET USED TO IT.

THE ROAD RUNS DIAGONALLY FROM THE LEFT, FORWARD, 81 BEYOND TO THE RIGHT, REAR.

(THROWING ASIDE HER DOLL, RUNS TO HIM WITH A HAPPY119 BEYOND CRY)

(ROBERT PUTS HER DOWN AND SHE RUNS TO HER MOTHER. 140 BEYOND (HYSTERICALLY--RUNS WILDLY TO THE DOOR IN REAR) 572 CROSS AND RUNS HIS EYES OVER THE TITLES OF BOOKS. 545 DAYS (A CHILL RUNS THROUGH HER BODY.) 548 DAYS (A SHUDDER RUNS OVER HIM AND HE STARTS AS IF 562 DAYS AWAKENING FROM SLEEP)

A SIDE WALL RUNS DIAGONALLY BACK FROM LEFT, FRONT,564 DAYS

EDEN APPEARS IN THE KITCHEN, RUNS TO WINDOW, PEERS219 DESIRE OUT.

(HE ALMOST RUNS OFF DOWN TOWARD THE BARN. 225 DESIRE

THEN WITH A LITTLE CRY SHE RUNS OVER AND THROWS 239 DESIRE HER ARMS ABOUT HIS NECK.

WITH A STIFLED CRY SHE RUNS TOWARD THEM.) 255 DESIRE

(STRUGGLING TO HER FEET, RUNS TO THE DOOR, CALLING262 DESIRE AFTER HIM)

(HE TURNS AND RUNS OUT, AROUND THE CORNER OF 262 DESIRE HOUSE, PANTING AND SOBBING,

EDEN RUNS IN, PANTING EXHAUSTEDLY, WILD-EYED AND 265 DESIRE MAD LOOKING.

HE RUNS TO THE DOOR AND COMES INTO THE KITCHEN. 266 DESIRE

(HE RUNS OFF RIGHT, FORGETTING THAT HE HAS SNEAKED445 DYNAMO OUT BY THE BACK.

(A SECOND LATER HE RUNS IN AND, TOO DISTRACTED TO 445 DYNAMO NOTICE HER EXPRESSION,

(AS SHE SPEAKS REUBEN RUNS IN FROM THE RIGHT. 451 DYNAMO

SHE RUNS TO HIM AND TRIES TO PUT HER ARMS AROUND 452 DYNAMO HIM)

AND RUNS PANIC-STRICKEN OFF RIGHT, DRAGGING HIS 453 DYNAMO MOANING WIFE BY THE ARM.

HE RUNS TO THE GAP IN THE LILAC BUSHES AND HIDES 459 DYNAMO IN THE OLD PLACE.

A STEEL LADDER RUNS UP ITS SIDE ON THE RIGHT TO A 486 DYNAMO PLATFORM AROUND THE EXCITER.

RUNS DOWN THE STAIRS TO THE LOWER OIL SWITCH 487 DYNAMO GALLERY.

(HE TURNS AND RUNS HEADLONG THROUGH THE 488 DYNAMO SWITCHBOARD ROOM,

THERE IS A STARTLED CRY FROM MRS. FIFE AS SHE RUNS489 DYNAMO TO THE BODY.

WELL, I KNOW BLOODY WELL WOT'S IN THE AIR--WHEN 175 EJONES THEY RUNS ORF TO THE 'ILLS.

THE OLD WOMAN SPRINGS TO HER FEET AND RUNS OUT OF 175 EJONES THE DOORWAY, REAR.

(IMPERTURBABLY) WHERE DEY MOSTLY RUNS TO MINUTE 1176 EJONES CLOSES MY EYES--

MAYBE HE HITS ME WID A WHIP AND I SPLITS HIS HEAU 181 EJONES WID A SHOVEL AND RUNS AWAY AND

A WIDE DIRT ROAD RUNS DIAGONALLY FROM RIGHT, 192 EJONES FRONT, TO LEFT, REAR.

(SHE RUNS TO HIM AND THROWS HER ARMS AROUND HIM 47 ELECTR AND KISSES HIM)

(SHE RUNS DOWN THE STEPS AND FLINGS HER ARMS 76 ELECTR AROUND HIM.)

(SHE TURNS, SEIZED BY PANIC, AND RUNS TO THE 119 ELECTR HOUSE--

TORN BY REMORSE, RUNS AFTER HIM AND THROWS HER 166 ELECTR ARMS AROUND HIM)

(AS THE TUNE RUNS OUT, GLANCES AT THE CLOCK, WHICH278 GGBROW INDICATES MIDNIGHT.

SHE LEAPS UP AND RUNS BACK TO THROW HER ARMS 308 GGBROW AROUND BROWN

MARGARET RUNS FORWARD.) 317 GGBROW

HER MASK, RUNS INTO THE ROOM. 320 GGBROW

(RUNS TO HIS SIDE, LIFTS HIM ON TO THE COUCH AND 321 GGBROW TAKES OFF THE MASK OF DION)

IT RUNS DIS TUB. 212 HA APE

(HIS VOICE RUNS INTO THE WAIL OF A KEEN, HE ROCKS 213 HA APE BACK AND FORTH ON HIS BENCH,

AND RUNS FULL TILT INTO THE BENDING, STRAINING 239 HA APE YANK.

A FAT, HIGH-HATTED, SPATTED GENTLEMAN RUNS OUT 239 HA APE FROM THE SIDE STREET.

RUNS BACK DOWN THE TIER, AND ABRUPTLY CEASES.) 240 HA APE

AND IF I CAN'T FIND HER I'LL TAKE IT OUT ON DE 242 HA APE GANG SHE RUNS WIT.

A SCAR FROM A KNIFE SLASH RUNS FROM HIS LEFT 575 ICEMAN CHEEK-BONE TO JAW.

HE NEVER RUNS INTO ANYONE HE KNOWS IN HIS BUSINESS586 ICEMAN HERE.

(BOASTFULLY) MAN, WHEN I RUNS MY GAMBLIN' HOUSE, 640 ICEMAN HARBURN AND THE AVENUE THAT RUNS ALONG THE WATER 11 JOURNE FRONT.

OUT BEYOND THE HARBOR, WHERE THE ROAD RUNS ALONG 131 JOURNE THE BEACH,

FROM THE LINE OF THE STREET THAT RUNS FROM LEFT TO298 LAZARU RIGHT, FRONT.

JUMPS TO HIS FEET IN A PANIC OF TERROR, AND RUNS 335 LAZARU TOWARD TH PALACE DOOR, CALLING)

ONE RUNS TO HIM WITH A LANTERN. 340 LAZARU

CALIGULA RUNS TO HER AND CROUCHES BESIDE AND 348 LAZARU BENEATH HER.)

POMPEIA RUNS TO THE FEET OF TIBERIUS AND CROUCHES 348 LAZARU DOWN ON THE STEPS BELOW HIM.

HE RUNS OUT THROUGH THE ARCHED DOORWAY AT REAR.) 360 LAZARU

SUDDENLY A LITTLE SHUDDER RUNS OVER HER. 27 MANSNS

RUNS (CONT'D.)

(SHE RUNS FROM HER CHAIR AND DEBORAH GETS UP, 56 MANSNS TUG.)

(SHE RUNS TO HER WILDLY AND GRABS HER ARM-- 169 MANSNS STAMMERING WITH TERROR.)

EASILY RUNS INTO MILLIONS, OF MILLIONS/ 359 MARCOM

PICKS IT UP, CRAMS IT INTO HIS DOUBLET AND RUNS 363 MARCOM WILDLY OUT THE DOOR.

A DERVISH OF THE DESERT RUNS IN SHRIEKING AND 368 MARCOM BEGINS TO WHIRL.

MARCO RUNS AWAY, OFF LEFT.) 368 MARCOM

SOUND COMMON SENSE AND A HOME WHERE EVERTHING RUNS416 MARCOM SMOOTH,

(SUDDENLY RUNS UP TO THE UPPER DECK AND STANDS 420 MARCOM OUTLINED AGAINST THE SKY.

I WANT TO SEE THE MAN WHO RUNS THIS FARM. 56 MISBEG

RESPONDS TO HIS APPEAL--THEN SHE SPRINGS UP AND 141 MISBEG RUNS TO HIM--

SHE RUNS TO THE CARPENTER'S TABLE AND CRAWLS UNDER578 ROPE IT.

(SHE RUNS TO HER MOTHER, WHO PUSHES HER AWAY 588 ROPE ANGRILY.)

(MARY RUNS OUT OF THE DOOR, WHIMPERING. 591 ROPE

SHE SETS THE CHAIR IN UNDER THE LOFT AND RUNS OVER601 ROPE TO IT.

THEN SHE QUICKLY PICKS UP FOUR OR FIVE AND RUNS 602 ROPE OUT TO THE EDGE OF THE CLIFF.

(SHE TURNS AND RUNS OUT TO THROW THEM AS THE 602 ROPE CURTAIN FALLS.)

(A SHIVER RUNS OVER HER BODY.) 44 STRANG

(SHE RUNS TO THE KITCHEN DOOR) 52 STRANG

(HE RUNS OUT THROUGH THE KITCHEN DOOR.) 56 STRANG

(SHE RUNS HER HAND THROUGH HIS HAIR, 118 STRANG

(GORDON RUNS AND HIDES THE BOAT UNDER THE SOFA. 151 STRANG

WHEN EVANS ENTERS, GORDON IS ENTIRELY COMPOSED AND151 STRANG RUNS TO HIM JOYFULLY.

(HE TURNS ABRUPTLY AND RUNS OUT.) 157 STRANG

IT RUNS IN MY FAMILY/ 181 STRANG

(SHE RUNS HER FINGERS THROUGH HIS HAIR 186 STRANG CARESSINGLY--COMFORTINGLY)

RUNT

ON A STUMPY RUNT OF A MAN LIKE THE OLD SWEDE, 33 ANNA

GLORY BE TO GOD, IT'S BOLD TALK YOU HAVE FOR A 47 ANNA STUMPY RUNT OF A MAN/

(A WEAZENED RUNT OF A MAN. 478 CARDIF

(A WIZENED RUNT OF A MAN WITH A STRAGGLING GRAY 456 CARIBE MUSTACHE--

YE'LL BE LUCKY IF ANY OF THIM LOOKS AT YE, YE 461 CARIBE SQUINT-EYED RUNT.

BUT FOR A SHRIVELED RUNT LIKE SMYTHE--/ 99 JOURNE

THERE'S STEW ON THE STOVE, YOU BAD-TEMPERED RUNT. 35 MISBEG

COCKY, A WIZENED RUNT OF A MAN WITH A STRAGGLING 496 VOYAGE GRAY MUSTACHE.

=FORTUNATE SENEX, ERGO TUA RURA MANEBUNT, ET TIBI 37 MISBEG MAGNA SATIS,

RURAL

AS A RESULT OF THE RURAL TASTE FOR GRANDEUR IN THE 48 STRANG EIGHTIES.

RUSH

THE MEN PULL OUT SHEATH-KNIVES AND START A RUSH, 944 'ILE BUT STOP

(CALLOUSLY) GIVE HIM THE BUM'S RUSH/ 247 AHWILD

GIMME THE BUM'S RUSH ASHORE, HUH$ 11 ANNA

WHAT'S THE RUSH$ 23 ANNA

WITH A SUDDEN RUSH OF ANGER, DRAWING BACK HIS 49 ANNA FIST)

AS IF HE WERE ONLY COLLECTING HIS STRENGTH TO RUSH 50 ANNA AT HIM AGAIN.)

(THEY ALL RUSH TO THE SIDE AND LOOK TOWARD THE 460 CARIBE LAND.)

(THERE IS A GENERAL RUSH FOR THE FORECASTLE. 472 CARIBE

HE MAKES A RUSH PAST HER FOR THE DOOR--THEN 262 DESIRE TURNS--

HE WENT TO SEA WHEN HE WAS YOUNG AND WAS IN 15 ELECTR CALIFORNIA FOR THE GOLD RUSH.

AS IF TO RUSH OFF DOWN TO THE MAIN DECK AFTER113 ELECTR THEM.

RUSH INTO THE ROOM, 293 GGBROW

RAGE AND BEWILDERED FURY RUSH BACK ON YANK. 226 HA APE

(HE MAKES A RUSH FOR THE DOOR.) 232 HA APE

DEY SPOTTED ME AND GIMME DE BUM'S RUSH. 235 HA APE

TO GIVE HIM THE RUSH TO A CURE, BUT DE LAWYER 581 ICEMAN TELLS HARRY N'T.

GIVE HIM THE BUM'S RUSH UPSTAIRS/ 597 ICEMAN

(WITH A RUSH OF ANGER) YOU'RE A LIAR/ 641 ICEMAN

(ROCKY AND CHUCK RUN FROM BEHIND THE BAR CURTAIN 650 ICEMAN AND RUSH INTO THE HALL.

NUTTIN' NOW TILL DE NOON RUSH FROM DE MARKET. 665 ICEMAN

SHALL I GIVE HIM DE BUM'S RUSH, LARRY$ 666 ICEMAN

AND TURN AS IF THEY WERE GOING TO RUSH FOR THE 523 INCOME DECK.

(WITH CRIES OF RAGE THE TWO GROUPS RUSH ON ONE 290 LAZARU ANOTHER.

(HE IS SEEN TO RUSH PAST LAZARUS, 338 LAZARU

(WHO HAVE PRICKED UP THEIR EARS AT THIS LAST, RUSH417 MARCOM TO THE PRINCESS.

THEN WHY DIDN'T YOU GIVE ME THE BUM'S RUSH$ 168 MISBEG

(STRUGGLING FUTILELY AS THEY RUSH HIM THROUGH THE 124 POET DOOR.)

(THEN OVERCOME BY A RUSH OF BEWILDERED JOY-- 463 WELDED STAMMERING)

(THEN HIS BITTER MEMORIES RUSH BACK AGONIZINGLY. 475 WELDED

RUSHED

AND HE RUSHED OUT WITH A KNIFE AT THEM BOTH, 440 DYNAMO

I SUDDENLY FELT AS IF I WERE GOING TO FAINT, SO I 80 ELECTR RUSHED OUT IN THE FRESH AIR.

1349

S'POSE

RUSHED (CONT'D.)
I DON'T BELIEVE WHEN VINNIE RUSHED HIM OFF ON THIS136 ELECTR
TRIP TO THE EAST
(BUT THE CLERK*S MIND HAS RUSHED OUT TO FOLLOW THE 27 HUGHIE
SIREN WAIL OF A FIRE ENGINE.
HONESTLY, NINA, I'VE BEEN SO RUSHED WITH WORK 80 STRANG

RUSHES
THAT BOY/ (SHE RUSHES TO THE SCREEN DOOR AND OUT 189 AHWILD
ON THE PORCH, CALLING) TOMMY/
(SHE RUSHES INTO THE BACK PARLOR.) 200 AHWILD
(HE RUSHES OUT THROUGH THE BACK PARLOR, CALLING) 220 AHWILD
SHE RUSHES TO HER MOTHER.) 220 AHWILD
AND A MOMENT LATER TOMMY RUSHES IN FROM THE BACK 220 AHWILD
PARLOR.)
(HE RUSHES HIM THROUGH THE SCREEN DOOR 247 AHWILD
CHRIS RUSHES FORWARD WITH A CRY OF ALARM, 60 ANNA
SHE RUSHES TO THE TABLE. 68 ANNA
(RUSHES OVER AND THROWS HER ARMS ABOUT HIM.) 100 BEYOND
(SHE RUSHES AND GRABS THE KNOB OF THE SCREEN DOOR,128 BEYOND
ABOUT TO FLING IT OPEN.)
HE RUSHES INTO THE BEDROOM AND RETURNS IMMEDIATELY166 BEYOND
(HE FLINGS HER AWAY FROM HIM AND RUSHES UP THE 572 CROSS
COMPANIONWAY.
(AS IF HE HADN'T HEARD) ONE NIGHT WHEN HE IS 544 DAYS
HOUNDED BEYOND ENDURANCE HE RUSHES
EBEN RUSHES OUT AND SLAMS THE DOOR--THEN THE 211 DESIRE
OUTSIDE FRONT DOOR--
(HE RUSHES OUT THE DOOR.) 227 DESIRE
AND RUSHES INTO THE BEDROOM AND OVER TO THE 263 DESIRE
CRADLE.
(HE RUSHES OUT REAR, SLAMMING THE DOOR BEHIND 549 DIFRNT
HIM.)
(HIS VOICE COMES FROM THE HALL AS HE RUSHES 445 DYNAMO
UPSTAIRS)
((HE'S LEAVING/...)) (HE RUSHES TO THE DOOR BUT 450 DYNAMO
FINDS IT LOCKED--
(SHE BREAKS DOWN, WEEPING, AND RUSHES BACK INTO 452 DYNAMO
THE ROOM.)
ONLY BLACKNESS REMAINS AND SILENCE BROKEN BY JONES198 EJONES
AS HE RUSHES OFF,
CHRISTINE GIVES WAY TO FURY AND RUSHES DOWN THE 78 ELECTR
STEPS AND GRABS HER BY THE ARM
(THE WHOLE MEMORY OF WHAT HIS MOTHER HAD SAID 96 ELECTR
RUSHES OVER HIM)
BACKS TO THE DOOR AND RUSHES OUT.) 101 ELECTR
THEN SHE TURNS AND RUSHES INTO THE HOUSE. 123 ELECTR
AND A MOMENT LATER HE RUSHES OUT FRANTICALLY TO 124 ELECTR
LAVINIA.)
(HE RUSHES OUT AND CAN BE HEARD GOING ACROSS THE 160 ELECTR
HALL TO THE STUDY.
(HE RUSHES INTO THE HALL.) 167 ELECTR
HE HOLDS OUT HIS ARMS AND MARGARET RUSHES INTO 315 GGBROW
THEM.
(HE RUSHES TO THE PHONE.) 319 GGBROW
AND A WHOLE PLATOON OF POLICEMEN RUSHES IN ON YANK239 HA APE
FROM ALL SIDES.
JUST AT THIS MOMENT THE PRISON GUARD RUSHES IN, 245 HA APE
DRAGGING A HOSE BEHIND HIM.)
(THE THIRD GUEST OF SCENE ONE RUSHES IN 290 LAZARU
BREATHLESSLY, SHOUTING)
(HE RUSHES TO THE EDGE AND, MAKING A MEGAPHONE OF 319 LAZARU
HIS HANDS, BELLOWS)
CALIGULA RUSHES MADLY DOWN THE STAIRS 369 LAZARU
WITH A CRY OF HAPPY RELIEF, SARA RUSHES TO HIM AND144 MANSNS
HUGS HIM PASSIONATELY.)
SHE RUSHES OVER, PULLS OPEN THE DOOR IN THE WALL 162 MANSNS
AT RIGHT.
(RUSHES UP AND GRABS DEBORAH'S SKIRT AND FALLS ON 187 MANSNS
HER KNEES BEFORE HER.)
FADES AND NOON-DAY RUSHES BACK IN A BLAZE OF 352 MARCOM
BAKING PLAIN.
AN OUTRAGED CHAMBERLAIN RUSHES OVER TO MARCO AND 378 MARCOM
MOTIONS HIM TO KNEEL DOWN.)
(RUSHES AND PUTS HER ARM AROUND HIM.) 152 POET
(SHE RUSHES TO THE DOOR AND STANDS LISTENING--WITH159 POET
RELIEF.)
I'VE GOT TO KNOW-- (SHE RUSHES TO THE DOOR AT LEFT)63 POET
FRONT--
(RUSHES TO HIM AND GRABS HIS ARM.) 178 POET
AND A MOMENT LATER MARY RUSHES BREATHLESSLY INTO 583 ROPE
THE BARN.
(SWEENEY RUSHES OVER AND PICKS THE TERRIFIED OLD 597 ROPE
MAN UP)
AFTER THE LAST ONE IS THROWN SHE RUSHES BACK INTO 602 ROPE
THE BARN TO GET MORE.)
(RUSHES TO HER, SUPPORTS HER TO SOFA AT RIGHT) 108 STRANG
HE RUSHES UP TO NED HILARIOUSLY, SHAKES HIS HAND 132 STRANG
AND POUNDS HIS BACK.
THEN RUSHES TO FREDA AND LIFTS HER HEAD UP IN HER 508 VOYAGE
ARMS.)

RUSHING
(RUSHING OUT TO SHUT IT) I'VE TOLD HIM AGAIN AND 188 AHWILD
AGAIN--
(HIS ANGER RUSHING BACK ON HIM) 61 ANNA
(RUSHING TO ANDY AND PUTTING HER ARMS ABOUT HIM 106 BEYOND
PROTECTINGLY)
(RUSHING TO THE DOOR AND THROWING IT OPEN) 571 CROSS
(IN A FURY NOW, RUSHING TOWARD THEM) 224 DESIRE
A SOFT OVERTONE OF RUSHING WATER FROM THE DAM AND 473 DYNAMO
THE RIVER BED BELOW,
AND LISTEN TO THE WATER RUSHING OVER THE DAM/ LIKE476 DYNAMO
MUSIC/
THE OVERTONE OF RUSHING WATER FROM THE DAM SOUNDS 476 DYNAMO
LOUDER BECAUSE OF THE CLOSED
(RUSHING INTO THE NEXT ROOM, SHOUTS IN TERRIFIED 318 GGBROW
TONES)
(RUSHING UP AND GRABBING YANK'S ARM) 237 HA APE
(RUSHING TO LAZARUS' CAR) HAIL, DIONYSUS/ 307 LAZARU

RUSHING (CONT'D.)
(OASHES BACK AMONG THEM WAVING HIS BLOODY SPEAR 369 LAZARU
AND RUSHING UP TO THE THRONE
(EVANS AND MADELINE AND DARRELL COME RUSHING OUT 176 STRANG
OF THE CABIN.
(COMES RUSHING OUT IN WILD ALARM) 177 STRANG
(RUSHING DOWN THE STAIRS--FRANTICALLY) 449 WELDED

RUSSET
OH, RUSSET-GOLDEN AFTERNOON, 197 STRANG

RUSHA
(LAUGHING AT HIM) CHEERO, OLE CHUM, 'OWS RUSSHAS 500 VOYAGE

RUSSIA
IT'LL BE THE CZAR OF RUSSIA NEXT/ 166 MANSNS

RUSSIAN
THE RUSSIAN COMES TO IN A FLASH, SPUTTERING. 500 VOYAGE

RUSSIANS
I SAW THAT ALL THE IDEAS BEHIND THE MOVEMENT CAME 649 ICEMAN
FROM A LOT OF RUSSIANS LIKE

RUST
A BROWN COATING OF RUST COVERS THE UNBLACKED 144 BEYOND
STOVE.
IT'S CHIPPIN' RUST ON DECK YOU'LL BE IN A DAY OR 483 CARDIF
TWO KID THE BEST AV US.
AND A SHREDDED WHITE SAILOR'S BLOUSE, STAINED WITH571 CROSS
IRON-RUST.
(LOOKING AT HER MEANINGLY) MY LIFE WORK IS TO 140 STRANG
RUST--NICELY AND UNOBTRUSIVELY/

RUSTED
THE SCREEN UP IN HER ROOM HAS A HOLE RUSTED IN 456 DYNAMO
IT....

RUSTLING
A THINNY GALE OF LOW MOCKING LAUGHTER LIKE A 190 EJONES
RUSTLING OF LEAVES.
THE WARM EARTH IN THE MOONLIGHT, THE TRADE WINDS 112 ELECTR
RUSTLING THE COCO PALMS,
THERE IS A RUSTLING OF PAPER) 242 HA APE
WIND RUSTLING THE LEAVES. 355 MARCOM

RUSTY
THOUGH I'D BE RUSTY, NOT HAVING BEEN IN ALL THESE 228 AHWILD
YEARS.
TO BE STOMACHIN' THE SKOFF ON THIS RUSTY LIME- 480 CARDIF
JUICER.
DARN THING'S GUTTEN SO RUSTY. 167 ELECTR
A RUSTY PLOW AND VARIOUS UTHER FARMING IMPLEMENTS,577 ROPE
DON'T YOU GROW RUSTYS 140 STRANG

RUT
ALL HE EVER NEEDED WAS TO GET AWAY FROM THE RUT HE212 AHWILD
WAS IN HERE.

RUTHLESS
THERE IS EVEN A SUGGESTION OF RUTHLESS CUNNING 153 BEYOND
ABOUT THEM.
WHO USES LOVE BUT LOVES ONLY HERSELF, WHO IS 13 MANSNS
ENTIRELY RUTHLESS AND LETS NOTHING
SHE WAS JUST AS RUTHLESS AND UNSCRUPULOUS ABOUT 75 MANSNS
DISCARDING YOU
AT ONCE SIMON BECOMES THE FORMIDABLE, RUTHLESS 94 MANSNS
HEAD OF THE COMPANY.)
(HIS FACE HARDENING INTO HIS OFFICE MASK OF THE 107 MANSNS
RUTHLESS EXECUTIVE.)
PERHAPS, I CONSIDERED THE METHODS USED NOT QUITE 152 MANSNS
ETHICAL--NOT TO SAY RUTHLESS.
STRENGTH ABOUT HER EXPRESSION, A RUTHLESS SELF- 90 STRANG
CONFIDENCE IN HER EYES.

RUTHLESSLY
(HE ADDS RUTHLESSLY) AND I'LL SAY YOU LOOK IT, 546 DIFRNT
TOO/
RUTHLESSLY DETERMINED TO DEVOUR AND LIVE AS THE 88 MANSNS
SPIRIT OF LIFE ITSELF/
I HAVE SERVED MY PURPOSE--SHE HAS RUTHLESSLY GOT 126 MANSNS
RID OF ME--SHE IS FREE--
ITS STUBBORN CHARACTER BECOME REPELLENTLY SENSUAL,139 MANSNS
RUTHLESSLY CRUEL AND GREEDY.

RUTHLESSNESS
AND HIS FACE SETS INTO A MASK OF CALCULATING 75 MANSNS
RUTHLESSNESS.

RYE
EARTH OF WHICH MYRIAD BRIGHT-GREEN BLADES OF FALL- 81 BEYOND
SOWN RYE ARE SPROUTING.

S'CUSE
S'CUSE ME, EMMER, IT JUMPED OUT O' MY MOUTH AFORE 494 DIFRNT
I THOUGHT.
NO, YOU DIN'T HAVE NO S'CUSE TO LOOK DOWN ON ME 177 EJONES
FU' DAT.

S'ELP
'E'S GOT 'IS BLOOMIN' NERVE WITH 'IM, S'ELP ME/ 187 EJONES

S'LONG'S
I HAIN'T BEAT--S'LONG'S I GOT YE/ 267 DESIRE

S'PECT
AN' YOU SEEN THE TWO, I S'PECT, AIN'T YOUS 456 CARBEE
DOES YOT S'PECT I'SE SILLY ENUFF TO B'LIEVE IN 189 EJONES
GHOSTS AN' HA'NTS
TO READ 'EM YOU WOULDN'T S'PECT NOTHIN'--JUST MUSH529 INZONE
AND ALL.

S'PECTED
HE'D HANG YOU MORE LIKELY IF HE S'PECTED YOU HAD 581 ROPE
ANY MONEY.

S'PECTS
ENUFF TO KNOW DEIR OWN NAMES EVEN CAN CATCH BRUTUS183 EJONES
JONES, HUH, I S'PECTS NOT/

S'PICIOUS
THEN WHY DOES HE ACT SO S'PICIOUS$ 520 INZONE

S'POSE
(SLOWLY) THEY WANTS TO GIT BACK TO THEIR FOLKS 542 'ILE
AN' THINGS, I S'POSE.
(SCORNFULLY) AND D'YOU S'POSE ANY OF 'EM WOULD 542 'ILE
BELIEVE THAT--
SHE'LL MAYBE BE COMIN' HERE TO LOOK FOR YOU, I 9 ANNA
S'POSE.

S'POSE

S'POSE (CONT'D.)

I S'POSE HE LIVES ON THE BOAT, DON'T HE$ 17 ANNA
(SADLY) AY S'POSE. 21 ANNA
(PERSISTENTLY) BUT WHY D'YOU S'POSE I FEEL SO-- 28 ANNA
MARRY ME, I S'POSE. 58 ANNA
I S'POSE YOU REMEMBER YOUR PROMISE, MAT$ 59 ANNA
SO I S'POSE YOU WANT ME TO GET DRESSED AND GO 59 ANNA
ASHORE, DON'T YOU$
I S'POSE IF I TRIED TO TELL YOU I WASN'T--THAT-- 59 ANNA
(MOCKINGLY) AND I S'POSE YOU WANT ME TO BEAT IT, 61 ANNA
DON'T YOU$
I S'POSE YOU WANT TO GET DRUNK SO'S YOU CAN 61 ANNA
FURGET--LIKE HIM$
YOU DON'T WANT ME HERE DISGRACING YOU, I S'POSE$ 62 ANNA
(SUBBING) YES, YES--OF COURSE I DO--WHAT D'YOU 91 BEYOND
S'POSE$
IT'S 'COUNT O' ROBERT LEAVIN', I S'POSE. 97 BEYOND
BUT D'YOU S'POSE HE TAKES ANY NOTICE OF WHAT I 113 BEYOND
SAYS
(WEARILY) I S'POSE SO. 117 BEYOND
(SIGHING) I S'POSE IT ISN'T ROB'S FAULT THINGS GO11B BEYOND
WRONG WITH HIM.
(SHORTLY) YOU'VE GOT TO GET BACK TO YOUR WORK, I 119 BEYOND
S'POSE.
I S'POSE YOU WERE GOING TO SAY. 122 BEYOND
(DULLY) I S'POSE SO. 123 BEYOND
(BITTERLY) I S'POSE YOU'RE SORRY NOW YOU DIDN'T 125 BEYOND
GO$
I S'POSE YOU THINK I OUGHT TO BE PROUD TO BE YOUR 127 BEYOND
WIFE--
(DUMBLY) I S'POSE. 137 BEYOND
(ABSENT-MINDEDLY) YES, I S'POSE. 137 BEYOND
(DULLY) YES--I S'POSE I OUGHT. 138 BEYOND
(DULLY) HE DID THE BEST HE KNEW, I S'POSE. 145 BEYOND
IT'S BEEN MY FAULT TOO, I S'POSE. 148 BEYOND
(DULLY) HE DIDN'T THINK ABOUT IT, I S'POSE. 152 BEYOND
IT'S ANDY, I S'POSE. 153 BEYOND
BUT HE'S USED TO HER BEING GONE BY THIS, I S'POSE.156 BEYOND
YES, I S'POSE SO. 161 BEYOND
(DULLY) HIS MIND WAS WANDERING, I S'POSE. 163 BEYOND
IT'S AS GOOD A PLACE AS ANY OTHER, I S'POSE-- 489 CARDIF
MAKIN' ARRANGEMENTS ABOUT THE MONEY, I S'POSE. 462 CARIBE
(AFTER A PAUSE) S'POSE THERE'S A GEL MIXED UP IN 467 CARIBE
IT SOME PLACE, AIN'T THERE$
(PHILOSOPHICALLY) ALL DEPENDS ON HOW YOU WAS 468 CARIBE
BRUNG UP, I S'POSE.
I DON'T S'POSE YOU EVER TRIED THAT$ 468 CARIBE
(AFTER A PAUSE) WHAT IN TARNATION D'YE S'POSE HE 209 DESIRE
WENT, SIM$
I S'POSE HE'S MANAGIN'. 218 DESIRE
(EXCITEDLY) I SEE THAT MIN, I S'POSE$ 230 DESIRE
(A PAUSE) I S'POSE IT'S OLD AGE A-CREEPIN' IN MY 232 DESIRE
BONES.
AND THE OTHERS ARE ALL RIGHT IN THEIR WAY, TOO, I 495 DIFRNT
S'POSE.
MY FUST VIGE AS SKIPPER, YOU DON'T S'POSE I HAD 497 DIFRNT
TIME FOR NO MONEY-SHININ'.
HE WASN'T MARRIED THEN AND I S'POSE HE THOUGHT HE
WAS FREE TO DO AS HE'D A MIND
YOU DON'T S'POSE CALEB TOOK IT SERIOUS, DO YOU, 509 DIFRNT
BUT D'YOU S'POSE HE'S EVER GIVE HER ANOTHER 509 DIFRNT
THOUGHT$
YOU'LL MAKE UP WITH HIM, AND I S'POSE I'M A FOOL 510 DIFRNT
TO BE TAKIN' IT SO SERIOUS.
WHEN I WAS YOUR AGE, D'YOU S'POSE YOU'D EVER BE 512 DIFRNT
SETTIN' THERE NOW$
D'YOU S'POSE IF I'D HAD YOUR HIGH-FANGLED NOTIONS 512 DIFRNT
O' WHAT MEN OUGHT TO BE
I S'POSE POOR MA AND PA TURNED OVER IN THEIR 524 DIFRNT
GRAVES WHEN I ORDERED IT DONE.
(IN A SNARLING TONE) I S'POSE YOU'VE BEEN GIVIN' 528 DIFRNT
HIM AN EARFUL OF LIES ABOUT
I S'POSE SHE AIN'T GOT NOTHIN' TO DO ABOUT IT. 529 DIFRNT
(DULLY) NO. I S'POSE IT WOULDN'T. 535 DIFRNT
D'YOU S'POSE THE OLD MISER REALLY WAS SERIOUS 545 DIFRNT
ABOUT THAT$
BEEN STEALIN' A BIT, I S'POSE. 174 EJONES
YOU DIDN'T S'POSE I WAS HOLDIN' DOWN DIS EMPEROR 177 EJONES
JOB FOR DE GLORY IN IT,
DON'T YOU S'POSE I'SE LOOKED AHEAD AND MADE SHO' 183 EJONES
OF ALL DE CHANCES$
I S'POSE I GUT TO PLAY WITH YOU. 279 GGBROW
AND I S'POSE 235 HA APE
(A PAUSE) I S'POSE YUH WANTER KNOW WHAT I'M DOIN'252 HA APE
HERE, HUH$
I S'POSE YOU DON'T FALL FOR NO PIPE DREAMS 578 ICEMAN
HE GUT DRUNK PANHANDLIN' DRINKS IN NIGGER JOINTS, 699 ICEMAN
I S'POSE.
HOW D'YOU S'POSE SPIES GETS THEIR ORDERS AND SENDS529 INZONE
BACK WHAT THEY FINDS OUT IF
I S'POSE I'M A BIGGER FOUL THAN YOU BE TO ARGY 581 ROPE
WITH A HALF-WITTED BODY.
(LOWERING HER VOICE) D'YOU S'POSE HE KNOWS ABOUT 590 ROPE
THE FARM BEIN' LEFT TO HIM$
I S'POSE YUH'RE TICKLED TO PIECES TO SEE ME--LIKE 594 ROPE
HELL/
AN' YOU'RE A BLEEDIN' ANGEL, I S'POSE$ 497 VOYAGE
I S'POSE YOU'LL BE GITTIN' MARRIED, TOO$ 503 VOYAGE
S'POSED
AN' WE S'POSED TO HAVE ALL THE PORTS BLINDED/ 521 INZONE
S'POSES
MAYBE, FROM THE WAY HE WENT ON, HE S'POSES I CARE 165 BEYOND
FOR YOU YET.
S'POSIN'
(MALICIOUSLY) BUT S'PUSIN' SOMETHIN' 'APPENS 184 EJONES
WRONG AN' THEY DO NAB YER$
S'POSIN' HE DID FERGET HIS CUP--WHAT'S THE DIFFS 517 INZONE
S'POSIN' I GO ROUND THE CORNER, HUH$ 475 WELDED

S'PRISE

SHE CAUGHT ME BY S'PRISE. 515 DIFRNT
(AS THEY ARE GOING OUT) THIS SILLY BLOKE'LL 'AVE 508 VOYAGE
THE S'PRISE OF 'IS LIFE WHEN
S'PRISED
SAY, NAT, I'M S'PRISED AT YOU. 54 ANNA
S'PRISED, AIN'T YOU$ 525 INZONE
S'UTH
MR. SLOCUM, DID YOU EVER HEAR O' ME POINTIN' S'UTH541 'ILE
FOR HOME
S'UTH'ARD
THE ICE IS ALL BROKE UP TO S'UTH'ARD. 537 'ILE
S'WELL
(THEN WITH DECISION) S'WELL FUST'S LAST/ 213 DESIRE
SABBATH
DISGRACIN' YEW AN' ME--ON THE SABBATH, TOO/ 233 DESIRE
IT'S THE SABBATH/ 235 DESIRE
HE DISGUISED HIS GREED WITH SABBATH POTIONS OF 101 MANSNS
GOD-FEARING UNCTION
SABBATHS
THEY WENT TO THE WHITE MEETING-HOUSE ON SABBATHS 54 ELECTR
AND MEDITATED ON DEATH.
SABER
THERE IS A SCAR OF A SABER CUT OVER ONE CHEEKBONE. 8 POET
(PROUDLY) I GOT THIS CUT FROM A SABER AT 10 POET
TALAVERA, BAD LUCK TO IT!
WHERE I GOT MY SABER CUT. 93 POET
BUT I HAD THIS TOKEN ON MY CHEEK TO REMEMBER A 99 POET
FRENCH SABER BY.
SACHEM
SID, YOU'RE COMING TO THE SACHEM CLUB WITH ME, OF 189 AHWILD
COURSE.
I KNOW WHAT THAT SACHEM CLUB PICNIC'S ALWAYS 189 AHWILD
MEANT/
BUT I'VE KNOWN YOU TO COME BACK FROM THIS DARNED 190 AHWILD
SACHEM CLUB PICNIC--
(SHE SIGHS) BUT I SUPPOSE WITH THAT DARNED SACHEM212 AHWILD
CLUB PICNIC IT'S MORE LIKELY
SACK
WHEN I LEAD THE JACKASS MOB TO THE SACK OF 691 ICEMAN
BABYLON.
HE WEARS A THREADBARE, READY-MADE, GREY SACK SUIT 13 JOURNE
AND SHINELESS BLACK SHOES.
HE IS DRESSED IN AN OLD SACK SUIT, NOT AS SHABBY 19 JOURNE
AS TYRONE'S.
SACRAMENT
OUR LOVE COULD MAKE OURS INTO A TRUE SACRAMENT-- 523 DAYS
SACRAMENT WAS THE WORD HE USED--
A SACRAMENT OF FAITH IN WHICH EACH OF US 523 DAYS
WE SWORE TO HAVE A TRUE SACRAMENT--OR NOTHING/ 448 WELDED
SACRED
BUT HOLY AND MOST SACRED NIGHT, NOT AS I LOVE AND 82 BEYOND
HAVE LOVED THEE.
THE WITCH DOCTOR POINTS WITH HIS WAND TO THE 201 EJONES
SACRED TREE, THE RIVER BEYOND.
THE WITCH DOCTOR SPRINGS BEHIND THE SACRED TREE 202 EJONES
AND DISAPPEARS.
SHE CHEWS GUM LIKE A SACRED COW FORGETTING TIME 278 GGBROW
WITH AN ETERNAL END.
(JEERINGLY) ARE YOU FALLING IN LOVE WITH YOUR 285 GGBROW
KEEPER, OLD SACRED COW$
AND IT'S NOT SACRED--ONLY THE YOU INSIDE IS. 286 GGBROW
I GIVE YOU MY SACRED WORD OF HONOR/ 48 JOURNE
AND SHE PROMISED ON HER SACRED WORD OF HONOR-- 57 JOURNE
THE SACRED FIRE/ 299 LAZARU
SUCH COOLING OF HEELS BEFORE THE SACRED PORTALS. 96 MANSNS
(SCENE--A SACRED TREE ON A VAST PLAIN IN PERSIA 347 MARCOM
NEAR THE CONFINES OF INDIA.
AND EVER SINCE THIS TREE HAS BEEN SACRED TO HIM/ 349 MARCOM
THIS TREE IS SACRED TO THE FOUNDER OF THE ONE TRUE349 MARCOM
RELIGION, ZOROASTER.
I AM GOING TO OFFER A PRAYER FOR PROTECTION TO 349 MARCOM
THIS TREE SACRED TO BUDDHA.
(IN CHORUS--IRRITABLY) SACRED TO BUDDHA$ 349 MARCOM
ON THE GROUND UNDER THE SACRED TREE THREE BODIES 354 MARCOM
LIE IN CRUMPLED HEAPS.
BUT WHERE ARE THE HUNDRED WISE MEN OF THE SACRED 378 BEYOND
TEACHINGS OF LAO-TSEU AND
KEPT SACRED AS THE OUTWARD FORM OF OUR INNER 448 WELDED
HARMONY/
SACRIFICE
RUTH HAS SUFFERED--REMEMBER, ANDY--ONLY THROUGH 168 BEYOND
SACRIFICE--
IT IS HE WHO MUST OFFER HIMSELF FOR SACRIFICE. 201 EJONES
THE FORCES OF EVIL DEMAND SACRIFICE. 201 EJONES
A CHARM TO ALLAY THE FIERCENESS OF SOME IMPLACABLE201 EJONES
DEITY DEMANDING SACRIFICE.
WILL YOU NOT SACRIFICE IN MY HONOR$ 301 LAZARU
FEAST AND SACRIFICE OF LIFE, THE ETERNAL. 368 LAZARU
THEN SHE BEGAN TO BLAME HERSELF AND TO WANT TO 35 STRANG
SACRIFICE HERSELF AND AT THE SAME
SHE'S GOT TO FIND NORMAL OUTLETS FOR HER CRAVING 37 STRANG
FOR SACRIFICE.
THE THANKS I GET FOR SAVING SAM AT THE SACRIFICE 171 STRANG
OF MY OWN HAPPINESS/....
(IN WILD PROTEST) NELLY, WHAT ARE YOU OFFERING 452 WELDED
ME--A SACRIFICE$
SACRIFICED
I'VE SACRIFICED ENOUGH OF MY LIFE.... 93 STRANG
SACRIFICIAL
THEIR ARMS STRETCHED OUT AS IF DEMANDING LAZARUS 288 LAZARU
FOR A SACRIFICIAL VICTIM.
SAD
(SUDDENLY--WITH A SAD PATHOS, QUOTES AWKWARDLY AND198 AHWILD
SHYLY)
HER FACE GROWS SAD AND SHE AGAIN GLANCES NERVOUSLY214 AHWILD
AT HER WATCH.
(WITH A SAD, SELF-PITYING SMILE AT HIS WIFE) 231 AHWILD

SADLY

SAD (CONT'D.)
AND HER EXPRESSION IS SAD, 249 AHWILD
HER FACE GROWING TRAGICALLY SAD. 257 AHWILD
(DOLEFULLY) YES--BUT IT'S SAD--TERRIBLE SAD. 257 AHWILD
(DOLEFULLY) YES--BUT I WISH HE WOULDN'T SING SUCH258 AHWILD
SAD SONGS.
(HER FACE SUDDENLY SAD AND TIRED AGAIN-- 259 AHWILD
LILY IS GENTLY SAD AND DEPRESSED. 263 AHWILD
IT DIDN'T MAKE HIM FEEL HAPPY LIKE SID, ONLY SAD 289 AHWILD
AND SICK.
(WITH A SMILE THAT IS HALF SAD) 85 BEYOND
SHE REMAINS SILENT, GAZING AT HIM DULLY WITH THE 169 BEYOND
SAD HUMILITY OF EXHAUSTION,
WITH A PALE, SAD FACE FRAMED IN A MASS OF DARK RED562 CROSS
HAIR.
TOO, ESPECIALLY THE SAD, PITYING EYES. 507 DAYS
(WITH SAD BITTERNESS) YOU HIT IT WHEN YOU SAY 521 DAYS
DISFIGURE.
HIS EYES ON THE FLOOR, HIS EXPRESSION SAD AND A 541 DAYS
BIT STERN.
HIS MIND IS PREOCCUPIED, HIS EXPRESSION SAD AND 545 DAYS
TROUBLED.
FATHER BAIRD STARES AT HER SEARCHINGLY, HIS FACE 548 DAYS
SAD AND PITYING.)
(NODS WITH SAD UNDERSTANDING) 557 DAYS
(THEN TENDERLY REBUKING) YE OUGHTN'T T' TALK O' 245 DESIRE
SAD THIN'S--THIS MORNIN'.
(WITH A SAD SMILE OF SCORN FOR HERSELF) 455 DYNAMO
AND BIG, DEEP, SAD EYES THAT WERE BLUE AS THE 22 ELECTR
CARIBBEAN SEA/
(THEY ALL SHAKE THEIR HEADS AND LOOK SAD. 70 ELECTR
IT'S SAD AS DEATH/ 107 ELECTR
(HE HUGS HER TO HIM, STARING OVER HER HEAD WITH 111 ELECTR
SAD BLANK EYES.)
I FEEL SO STRANGE--SO SAD--AS IF I'D NEVER SEE YOU112 ELECTR
AGAIN/
I WAS FEELING SO TERRIBLY SAD--AND NERVOUS HERE. 117 ELECTR
USUALLY HE'S LIKE HIMSELF, ONLY QUIET AND SAD-- 148 ELECTR
SO SAD IT BREAKS MY HEART TO SEE HIM-- 148 ELECTR
HER FACE IS SAD AND PALE, HER EYES SHOW EVIDENCE 171 ELECTR
OF MUCH WEEPING.
BUT HE'S SAD AND SHY, TOO, JUST LIKE A BABY 263 GGBROW
SOMETIMES,
HIS PALE FACE IS SINGULARLY PURE, SPIRITUAL AND 278 GGBROW
SAD.
HIS FACE IS GENTLE AND SAD--HUMBLY) 279 GGBROW
DRAWN AND CAREWORN FOR ITS YEARS, AND SAD, 291 GGBROW
RESIGNED, BUT A BIT QUERULOUS.)
HE SEEMS TO GAIN STRENGTH AND IS ABLE TO FORCE A 307 GGBROW
SAD LAUGH)
I'D GOTTEN PRETTY RESIGNED TO--AND SAD HOPELESS, 309 GGBROW
TOO--
THERE IS ABOUT HER MANNER AND VOICE THE SAD BUT 323 GGBROW
CONTENTED FEELING OF ONE WHO
(WITH A SAD LITTLE LAUGH) EACH OF YOU IS RIGHT. 323 GGBROW
HIS FACE IS EXTREMELY MONKEY-LIKE WITH ALL THE 210 HA APE
SAD,
(WITH A SORT OF SAD CONTEMPT) 210 HA APE
YES, TELL US YOUR SAD STORY. 240 HA APE
(HIS FACE INSTANTLY BECOMING LONG AND SAD AND 602 ICEMAN
SENTIMENTAL--MOURNFULLY)
THE TOMORROW MOVEMENT IS A SAD AND BEAUTIFUL 603 ICEMAN
THING, TOO/
SHE WOULDN'T WANT ME TO FEEL SAD. 663 ICEMAN
SO WHY SHOULD I FEEL SAD$ 663 ICEMAN
(ALL THE GROUP AROUND HIM ARE SAD AND SYMPATHETIC,719 ICEMAN
TOO.
(THEN WITH A SAD BITTERNESS.) 48 JOURNE
HE SUDDENLY LOOKS A TIRED, BITTERLY SAD OLD MAN. 67 JOURNE
TYRONE'S EYES ARE ON HER, SAD AND CONDEMNING. 68 JOURNE
AND IS AN AGING, CYNICALLY SAD, EMBITTERED WOMAN.)107 JOURNE
(SHE PAUSES--THEN ADDS WITH A STRANGE, SAD 110 JOURNE
DETACHMENT.)
IT'S VERY DREARY AND SAD TO BE HERE ALONE IN THE 112 JOURNE
FOG WITH NIGHT FALLING.
(EDMUND LOOKS AWAY FROM THEM, SAD AND 112 JOURNE
EMBARRASSED.)
(SHE GIVES A LITTLE, SAD SIGH.) 113 JOURNE
I DON'T WANT TO BE SAD, OR TO MAKE YOU SAD. 114 JOURNE
WHY IS IT FOG MAKES EVERYTHING SOUND SO SAD AND 121 JOURNE
LOST, I WONDER$
HE IS A SAD, BEWILDERED, BROKEN OLD MAN. 123 JOURNE
AND HE LOOKS AS HE APPEARED AT THE CLOSE OF THE 125 JOURNE
PRECEDING ACT, A SAD,
BUT LIKE AN OLD SAD FAITHFUL LECHER, 133 JOURNE
BY THE TIME I HIT MAMIE'S DUMP I FELT VERY SAD 159 JOURNE
(SHE STARES BEFORE HER IN A SAD DREAM. 176 JOURNE
THE MOUTH OF MIRIAM IS SENSITIVE AND SAD, TENDER 274 LAZARU
WITH AN EAGER,
(SIMPLY, WITH A TRACE OF A SAD STERNNESS) 294 LAZARU
THAT THE DEAD ARE DEAD AGAIN AND THE SICK DIE, AND300 LAZARU
THE SAD GROW MORE SORROWFUL.
MIRIAM IS BESIDE HIM, DRESSED IN BLACK, SMILING 307 LAZARU
THE SAME SAD TENDER SMILE,
FOR LIVING. HE HAD BELIEVED HIS LIFE A SAD ONE/ 309 LAZARU
SEEMS MORE THAN EVER A FIGURE OF A SAD, RESIGNED 327 LAZARU
MOTHER OF THE DEAD.
(SMILING WITHOUT BITTERNESS--WITH A SAD 328 LAZARU
COMPREHENSION)
(THEN DISGUSTEDLY) BUT SHE IS SAD AND OLD. 345 LAZARU
SMILE, MY SAD ONE/ 347 LAZARU
THAT MUCH REMAINED HIDDEN IN ME OF THE SAD OLD 348 LAZARU
LAZARUS WHO DIED OF SELF-PITY--
AND BEFORE HE DIED HE WAS OLD AND SAD. 351 LAZARU
HIS MOUTH IS SILENT--AND A LITTLE SAD, I THINK. 355 LAZARU
YES, IT IS ALWAYS SAD TO CONTEMPLATE THE CORPSE OF 6 MANSNS
A DREAM.
IT IS A SAD CITY NOW. 348 MARCOM

SAD (CONT'D.)
FROM THE BRANCHES OF THE TREE COMES A SOUND OF 352 MARCOM
SWEET SAD MUSIC
THE SAME SWEET SAD MUSIC COMES FROM THE TREE AGAIN354 MARCOM
AS IF ITS SPIRIT WERE PLAYING
MY THOUGHTS IN THIS AUTUMN ARE LONELY AND SAD, 384 MARCOM
(CHIDINGLY) THAT IS A SAD POEM, LITTLE FLOWER. 385 MARCOM
ARE YOU SAD BECAUSE YOU MUST SOON BECOME QUEEN OF 385 MARCOM
PERSIA$
(KUKLA LOOKS AT HER WITH A SAD WONDERMENT, CHU- 397 MARCOM
YIN SMILINGLY,
(LOOKING UP AND CONTROLLING HERSELF--WITH A SAD 400 MARCOM
FINALITY)
ONE SHOULD BE EITHER SAD OR JOYFUL. 400 MARCOM
KUBLAI SQUATS ON HIS THRONE, AGED AND SAD, 421 MARCOM
SITTING ALONE IN A GARDEN, BEAUTIFUL AND SAD, 426 MARCOM
APART FROM LIFE, WAITING--
FINALLY HE SPEAKS TENDERLY TO HER WITH A SAD 435 MARCOM
SMILE)
HE SPEAKS WITH A SURPRISING SAD GENTLENESS) 17 MISBEG
(WITH A TEASING SMILE WHICH IS HALF SAD) 18 MISBEG
WITHOUT ANY REASON YOU CAN SEE, HE'LL SUDDENLY 33 MISBEG
TURN STRANGE, AND LOOK SAD,
(STARES AT HER WITH A HURT AND SAD EXPRESSION-- 138 MISBEG
DULLY)
(MISERABLY HURT AND SAD FOR A SECOND--APPEALINGLY)140 MISBEG
SHE LOOKS WEARY AND STRICKEN AND SAD. 153 MISBEG
YOU WERE MOSTLY QUIET AND SAD-- 170 MISBEG
(HE PAUSES) HOPE I DIDN'T TELL YOU THE SAD STORY 170 MISBEG
OF MY LIFE
I'M ONLY SAD FOR HIM. 176 MISBEG
HUGAN LOOKS AT HER SAD FACE WORRIEDLY-GENTLY) 176 MISBEG
(GENTLY) DON'T BE SAD, FATHER. 177 MISBEG
(HER FACE SAD, TENDER AND PITYING--GENTLY) 177 MISBEG
SOMETHING GENTLE AND SAD AND, SOMEHOW, DAUNTLESS.) 20 POET
(A SAD SCORN COMES INTO HER VOICE.) 20 POET
HE LOOKS SAD AND HOPELESS AND BITTER AND OLD, HIS 116 POET
EYES WANDERING DULLY.
OF THEM--WONDERING AND SAD, BUT STILL TRUSTFUL, 169 POET
NOT REPROACHING ME--
HIS THIN LIPS IRONICAL AND A BIT SAD, 4 STRANG
(HIS FACE HAS BECOME SAD WITH A MEMORY OF THE 4 STRANG
BEWILDERED SUFFERING
(SUDDENLY REMINDED OF THE DEAD MAN--IN PENITENTLY 39 STRANG
SAD TONES)
OUT OF THE SKY IN FLAMES AND HE LOOKED AT ME WITH 45 STRANG
SUCH SAD BURNING EYES,
(WITH A SAD LITTLE LAUGH) GOD KNOWS, CHARLIE/ 45 STRANG
(WITH A SAD SMILE) NO. 51 STRANG
AND YOU'RE ON YOUR HONEYMOON, AND OLD AGE IS 56 STRANG
ALWAYS SAD TO YOUNG FOLKS.
WHAT SAD EYES/...) 57 STRANG
(THINKING--WITH A SAD BITTER IRONY) 128 STRANG
HER EYES ARE TRAGICALLY SAD IN REPOSE AND HER 137 STRANG
EXPRESSION IS SET AND MASKLIKE.
(WITH A SAD SMILE) SIT DOWN, NEO. 165 STRANG
HOW SAD AND IDIOTIC THIS ALL IS/...) 190 STRANG
HIS EXPRESSION IS SAD AND BITTER.) 190 STRANG
I AM SAD BUT THERE'S COMFORT IN THE THOUGHT 191 STRANG
(TURNING TO DARRELL, WHO IS STANDING WITH A SAD 195 STRANG
RESIGNED EXPRESSION--
(WITH A SAD SMILE) NO. 196 STRANG
(AMUSED--WITH A SAD SMILE) BLESS YOU, MY 197 STRANG
CHILDREN/
JUHN IS WATCHING HER KEENLY NOW, A SAD FOREBODING 465 WELDED
COMING INTO HIS EYES.
(WITH A SAD SMILE) YOU SEE$ 467 WELDED
(SUDDENLY TURNS AND ADDRESSES HIM DIRECTLY IN A 481 WELDED
SAD, SYMPATHETIC TONE)
SUDDENLY SHE LAUGHS WITH A SAD SELF-MOCKERY) 482 WELDED

SADDEN
OUR LAMENTATIONS SADDEN THE WIND FROM THE WEST. 436 MARCOM

SADDENED
BRODEN ONLY BY THE HAUNTED, SADDENED VOICE OF THAT473 CARIBE
BROODING MUSIC,

SADDER
(IGNORING HIM) IT ONLY MAKES ME SADDER AND SICK--270 AHWILD

SADDEST
THE SADDEST PART WAS THAT HE KNEW HE WAS DOOMEU. 627 ICEMAN
ITS GOING TO BE THE SADDEST MEMORY OF MY LIFE I 21 MISBEG
DIDN'T GET ONE LAST SWIPE AT
HER EYES ARE THE SADDEST... 53 STRANG

SADDLE
WOULD YOU SADDLE YOUR YOUNG HUSBAND WITH A MADMAN 564 CROSS
AND
COUNTRY GENTLEMAN, MILDLY INTERESTED IN SADDLE 55 MISBEG
HORSES AND SPORT MODELS OF
HE CAN HARDLY STAY IN THE SADDLE FOR LAUGHING/ 64 MISBEG

SADLY
(SADLY) SHE USETER BE AWFUL NICE TO ME BEFORE-- 538 'ILE
(PEERS AT HIM BLURREDLY AND SHAKES HIS HEAD SADLY)225 AHWILD
(THEN SADLY) BUT YOU'RE RIGHT. 272 AHWILD
(SADLY) AT S'POSE. 21 ANNA
(HE SINKS DOWN IN THE CHAIR OPPOSITE HER
DEJECTEDLY--THEN TURNS TO HER--SADLY) 27 ANNA
(HE PAUSES SADLY) TWO MY BRO'DER DEY GAT LOST ON 27 ANNA
FISHING BOAT
(NOT SEEMING TO HAVE HEARD HER QUESTION--SADLY) 64 ANNA
(SADLY) TOO LATE. 487 CARDIF
SHE SHAKES HER HEAD SADLY. 569 CROSS
FATHER BAIRD REMAINS FOR A MOMENT STARING SADLY AT557 DAYS
THE FLOOR.
(A PAUSE--THEN HE MUTTERS SADLY) 268 DESIRE
SADLY) AYE, BUT IT AIN'T FUR LONG, STEAM IS 105 ELECTR
COMIN' IN, THE SEA IS FULL
HE LOOKS AROUND THE CABIN SADLY.) 114 ELECTR
(THEN SADLY) POOR ORINE/ 136 ELECTR
(SADLY) YOU'VE GIVEN ME STRENGTH TO DIE. 286 GGBROW

SADLY

SADLY (CONT'D.)
(SADLY) IT WAS SO LONG AGO. 309 GGBROW
(SADLY) YOU COULDN'T-- THEN. 310 GGBROW
AND HE WONDERS SADLY WHY HE TOOK THE TROUBLE TO 14 HUGHIE
MAKE IT.)
(HE ADDS SADLY.) AND SO HE WAS, AT THAT--EVEN IF 31 HUGHIE
HE WAS A SUCKER.
(SADLY) NO, I FANCIED YOU WOULDN'T. 601 ICEMAN
BOOZE IS THE ONLY THING YOU EVER TALK ABOUT/ 601 ICEMAN
(SADLY) TRUE.
(WARMING TO HIS SUBJECT, SHAKES HIS HEAD SADLY) 627 ICEMAN
HE WAITS FOR IT TO DIE AND THEN GOES ON SADLY) 628 ICEMAN
THEN SADLY) 712 ICEMAN
(SADLY.) I KNOW. 38 JOURNE
(THEN AS EDMUND REMAINS HOPELESSLY SILENT, SHE 94 JOURNE
ADDS SADLY.)
(SHE REACHES OUT AND CLASPS HER HUSBAND'S HAND-- 109 JOURNE
SADLY.)
(AS IF SHE HADN'T HEARD--SADLY AGAIN.) 110 JOURNE
(SADLY.) YOU MIGHT HAVE GUESSED, DEAR, THAT AFTER119 JOURNE
I KNEW YOU KNEW--ABOUT ME--
(SIGHS SADLY.) NO. 137 JOURNE
(SADLY.) I'VE NEVER ADMITTED THIS TO ANYONE 149 JOURNE
BEFORE, LAD.
(HE PAUSES--THEN SADLY.) THE PRAISE EDWIN BOOTH 152 JOURNE
GAVE MY OTHELLO.
THEN JESUS SMILED SADLY BUT WITH TENDERNESS, 277 LAZARU
(HE PAUSES--THEN SADLY) THAT IS YOUR TRAGEDY/ 289 LAZARU
(SADLY) THEY WERE LIKE YOUR CHILDREN--AND THEY 325 LAZARU
HAVE DIED.
(SADLY) THEY ARE GONE FROM US. 325 LAZARU
(SHAKING HER HEAD AND TURNING AWAY SADLY) 331 LAZARU
(HE SIGHS SADLY--THEN AFTER A STRUGGLE OVERCOMING 343 LAZARU
HIMSELF--WITH EXULTANCE)
(STOPS LAUGHING--SHAKING HIS HEAD, ALMOST SADLY) 360 LAZARU
(THEN SADLY) BUT NOW YOU IN YOUR TURN MUST LEAVE 386 MARCOM
ME.
(LOOKING DOWN AT HER--SADLY) 389 MARCOM
(MOCKINGLY BUT SADLY) 397 MARCOM
(CHANTS THE LAST LINE AFTER THEM--SADLY) 409 MARCOM
AFTER A PAUSE, SADLY) 426 MARCOM
KUBELAI CONTINUES--SADLY) 434 MARCOM
(ECHOING SADLY) THY WISDOM. 437 MARCOM
(SADLY--HIS EYES AGAIN ON KUKACHIN) 437 MARCOM
(SADLY) I NEVER KNEW YOU WERE SUCH A BLACK 25 MISBEG
TRAITOR, AND YOU ONLY A CHILD.
HER FACE SOFTENS WITH A MATERNAL TENDERNESS-- 165 MISBEG
SADLY)
(SADLY) ALL RIGHT, JIM. 174 MISBEG
(SADLY.) I KNOW WHAT MADE YOU SAY IT. 61 POET
(SADLY) OH, I FORGIVE YOU. 21 STRANG
THE CHIN ALMOST TOUCHING HIS CHEST, HIS EYES STARE 24 STRANG
SADLY AT NOTHING.)
(VERY SADLY AND BITTERLY) 62 STRANG
(SADLY) I KNOW THAT. 63 STRANG
(THINKING SADLY) (I PROMISED HER... 71 STRANG
(SADLY BUT DETERMINEDLY) HE WOULD BE. 131 STRANG
(SADLY) AND SAMS 131 STRANG
(WATCHING HIM--BROODING WITH LOVING TENDERNESS-- 138 STRANG
SADLY)
(WATCHING NINA--SADLY) (ALWAYS THINKING OF HER 139 STRANG
SON...
(SADLY--THINKING) (TO ROT AWAY IN PEACE... 140 STRANG
(SADLY) YOU'D BETTER FORGET THAT, FOR HIS SAKE 144 STRANG
AND YOUR OWN.
I'VE BEEN SADLY DISILLUSIONED/ 165 STRANG
(THINKING SADLY) (MY OLD LOVER... 165 STRANG
(SPEAKING SADLY) I'VE LOST MY SON, NED/ 167 STRANG
(THINKING SADLY, LOOKING AT HIS BACK) 190 STRANG
(GLANCING AT GORDON SEARCHINGLY--THINKING SADLY) 190 STRANG
(HE LAUGHS SOFTLY AND SADLY) 196 STRANG
(SADLY SMILING) YOU, CHARLIE, I SUPPOSE. 197 STRANG
(SMILING SADLY) AGAIN. 197 STRANG
(SADLY TEASING) IF YOU'VE WAITED THAT LONG, 197 STRANG
CHARLIE.
(SADLY) WISH I 'AD/ 502 VOYAGE
(A PAUSE--THEN SHE GOES ON SADLY) 446 WELDED
(SADLY) SOMETIMES I THINK WE'VE DEMANDED TOO 448 WELDED
MUCH.
(AFTER A PAUSE--LOOKING BEFORE HER--SADLY) 485 WELDED
THEN HE ASKS SADLY) 485 WELDED
(THEN SHE SPEAKS SADLY BUT FIRMLY AS IF SHE HAD 486 WELDED
COME TO A DECISION)

SADNESS
ANNA CONTINUES SLOWLY, A TRACE OF SADNESS IN HER 44 ANNA
VOICE)
FULL OF A DEEP SADNESS.) 264 GGBROW
(WITH BITTER SADNESS.) IT'S YOU WHO ARE LEAVING 83 JOURNE
US, MARY.
(WITH BITTER SADNESS.) ARE YOU BACK WITH EUGENE 87 JOURNE
NOW$
IT'S THE BOOKS YOU READ/ NOTHING BUT SADNESS AND 90 JOURNE
DEATH/
(WITH A WRY IRONICAL SADNESS.) 152 JOURNE
(HE LOOKS DOWN ON JAMIE WITH A BITTER SADNESS.) 167 JOURNE
SIMPLY BUT WITH A BITTER SADNESS.) 173 JOURNE
QUIETLY, WITH A MOCKING IRONY TINGED WITH A 148 MANSNS
BITTER, TRAGIC SADNESS.)
(WITH A CALM SADNESS) DO I WANT A SLAVE$ 401 MARCOM
(IN AN ECHO OF VAST SADNESS) 434 MARCOM
A LOOK OF SADNESS AND LONELINESS AND HUMILIATION. 71 MISBEG
LIKE AN OLD MANGY HOUND IN HIS SADNESS IF I KNEW 76 MISBEG
HOW, BUT I DON'T.
(WITH DRUNKEN SADNESS) I WAS TOO DRUNK--TOO 85 MISBEG
DRUNK--TOO DRUNK--
UGLY TO GET YOU FEELING HAPPY, SO YOU'LL FORGET 116 MISBEG
ALL SADNESS.

SADNESS (CONT'D.)
LIKE A PROMISE OF GOD'S PEACE IN THE SOUL'S DARK 153 MISBEG
SADNESS.
JOSIE'S FACE IS SET IN AN EXPRESSION OF NUMBED, 157 MISBEG
RESIGNED SADNESS.
IF YOU COULD SEE THE SADNESS IN YOUR FACE-- 161 MISBEG
SHE STANDS GAZING AT HIM WITH A RESIGNED SADNESS. 36 POET
THE SADNESS OF SPRING... 99 STRANG
(WITH BITTER SADNESS) I DID BRING HIM A PRESENT. 144 STRANG
(THEN WITH A WONDERING SADNESS) 190 STRANG
ONE FEELS A POWERFUL IMAGINATION TINGED WITH 443 WELDED
SOMBER SADNESS--

SAFE
YOU'VE FOUND OUT IT AIN'T SAFE TO MUTINY ON THIS 544 *ILE
SHIP, AIN'T YOU$
AND I DON'T THINK WE'LL EVER HAVE TO WORRY ABOUT 297 AHWILD
HIS BEING SAFE--FROM HIMSELF--
WHERE YUH'D BE SAFE--GAW0/ 17 ANNA
WELL, WE'RE SAFE ANYWAY--WITH THE HELP OF GOD. 31 ANNA
I'M TELLING YOU THERE'S THE WILL OF GOD IN IT THAT 39 ANNA
BROUGHT ME SAFE THROUGH THE
GET MY GOAT WITH HIS BULL ABOUT KEEPING ME SAFE 56 ANNA
INLAND.
YOU--KEEPING ME SAFE INLAND--I WASN'T NO NURSE 58 ANNA
GIRL THE LAST TWO YEARS--
AND IT BRINGING ME SAFE TO LAND WHEN THE OTHERS 75 ANNA
WENT TO THEIR DEATH.
WHEN I GET A MAN TO DIRECT THINGS THE FARM'LL BE 138 BEYOND
SAFE ENOUGH.
AND WHY IN THE END I HAD TO ASK YOU TO TAKE HIM 562 CROSS
AWAY WHERE HE'LL BE SAFE.
IT WAS ONLY A SILLY GESTURE HE FELT SAFE IN MAKING520 DAYS
BECAUSE HE WAS SO DAMNED SURE
YOU'RE PERFECTLY SAFE. 526 DAYS
I GOT 'EM SAFE HERE. 268 DESIRE
IT WAS ALWAYS LIKE PRAYIN' OPEN A SAFE FOR ME TO 522 DIFRNT
SEPARATE HIM FROM A CENT.
AND TRUCKIN' GROCERIES, AS SAFE FROM A GUN AS YOU 541 DIFRNT
ARE ME THIS MINUTE.
HE KNEW IT'D BE SAFE WITH ME WHEN I GAVE HIM MY 447 DYNAMO
WORD--
(WITH CURIOSITY) AND I BET YOU GOT YER PILE O' 177 EJONES
MONEY 'ID SAFE SOME PLACE.
FILES DE CHAINS OFF MY LEG AND GITS AWAY SAFE. 181 EJONES
AND DERE I IS SAFE WID A MIGHTY BIG BANKROLL IN MY183 EJONES
JEANS.
AND WHEN YOU GITS DAR SAFE AND HAS DAT BANKROLL IN191 EJONES
YO' HANDS YOU LAUGHS AT ALL
DEM YOU'S ALL SAFE. 194 EJONES
AN' SAFE TO THE COAST, DAMN 'S *IDE/ 203 EJONES
AND WE WILL BE HAPPY--ONCE WE'RE SAFE ON YOUR 112 ELECTR
BLESSED ISLANDS/
I'M GOING TO PUT THIS CONFESSION I'VE WRITTEN IN 156 ELECTR
SAFE HANDS--
I WANT YOU TO KEEP IT IN A SAFE PLACE AND NEVER 160 ELECTR
LET ANYONE KNOW YOU HAVE IT/
THAT'S THE LEADIN RULE FOR THE SAFE AND SANE. 294 GGBROW
BUT YOU'RE SAFE HERE. 587 ICEMAN
YOU FEEL SAFE HERE, AND MAYBE YOU ARE, FOR A 679 ICEMAN
WHILE.
BEJEES, IT AIN'T SAFE TO WALK IN THE STREETS/ 690 ICEMAN
SATISFIED THE BOX IS SAFE, 523 INZONE
IN THIS SAFE HAVEN, WHERE WE COULD REPOSE OUR 103 MANSNS
SOULS IN FANTASY--
OF BRINGING YOU SAFE AND SOUND TO YOUR HUSBAND. 411 MARCOM
COMING BACK SAFE FROM EUROPE ISN'T SUCH AN UNUSUAL 14 STRANG
FEAT NOW. IS IT$
WARM IN HIS LOVE, SAFE-DRIFTING INTO SLEEP...= 27 STRANG
I DON'T FEEL SAFE....) 118 STRANG
TO BE ON THE SAFE SIDE. 146 STRANG
I'LL SEE YOU GET HOME SAFE, MR. 164 STRANG
'APPY TO SEE YER 'OME SAFE AN' SOUND. 496 VOYAGE
(SHE LAUGHS WILDLY) I'D BE SAFE THEN, WOULDN'T 459 WELDED
I--RELIABLE, GUARANTEED NOT TO--

SAFE'S
I TELLS YOU I'SE SAFE'S *F I WAS IN NEW YORK CITY.186 EJONES
SAFELY
MR. BROWN IS NOW SAFELY IN HELL. FORGET HIM/ 312 GGBROW
NO, THAT IS WHY I CAN SAFELY TELL YOU ALL MY 39 MANSNS
SECRETS, NICHOLAS.
YES, MAKE YOURSELF BELIEVE THAT, MOTHER, AND YOU 115 MANSNS
CAN SAFELY DEFY HER.
THEN I THINK WE CAN NOW SAFELY TELL EACH OTHER 131 MANSNS
I HAVE DELIVERED MY CHARGE SAFELY TO GHAZAN KHAN. 424 MARCOM
A FUGITIVE FROM REALITY CAN VIEW THE PRESENT 3 STRANG
SAFELY FROM A DISTANCE.
HE'LL BE ONLY TOO ANXIOUS TO GET HER SAFELY 37 STRANG
MARRIED....)

SAFER
NO ONE COULD HAVE FELT SAFER THAN HE DID. 679 ICEMAN
AN' YOU WON'T BE FEELIN' NO SAFER, NEITHER. 518 INZONE
AND IT'S SAFER THAN THE STOCKS AND BONDS OF WALL 16 JOURNE
STREET SWINDLERS.
BUT STILL, THE MORE PROPERTY YOU OWN, THE SAFER 146 JOURNE
YOU THINK YOU ARE.

SAFETY
ALMOST FRIGHTENEDLY, AS IF HE FEARED FOR HER 75 ANNA
SAFETY)
THAT THEY BE APPOINTED, FOR MY GREATER SAFETY, 397 MARCOM
IS THAT YOU REWARD THIS CHRISTIAN WHO HAS BROUGHT 418 MARCOM
ME HERE IN SAFETY.

SAFFRON
THE HIDEOUS SAFFRON-COLORED WALL-PAPER IS BLOTCHED236 AHWILD
AND SPOTTED.

SAG
FOR A MOMENT HIS SHOULDERS SAG, HE BECOMES OLD, 549 *ILE
(HIS KNEES SAG, HE WAVERS AND SEEMS ABOUT TO FALL. 39 ANNA

1353

SAG

(CONT'D.)

AS HE PEERS OUT HIS BODY SEEMS GRADUALLY TO SAG, 150 BEYOND
TO GROW LIMP AND TIRED.

(AS IF THIS WERE A MORTAL BLOW, SEEMS TO SAG AND 566 DAYS
COLLAPSE--WITH A CHOKING CRY)

HE HAS GROWN VERY THIN, HIS DUNGAREES SAG ABOUT 476 DYNAMO
HIS ANGULAR FRAME.

THE CROWD SAG BACK MOMENTARILY WITH EXCLAMATIONS 305 LAZARU
OF FEAR.)

HIS SHOULDERS SAG AND HE STARES AT THE TABLE TOP, 57 POET

SAGACIOUSLY

(SAGACIOUSLY) THAT'S WHAT MADE CHARLIE LIKE HE 157 STRANG
IS, I'LL BET.

SAGE

ON HIS LEFT CHU-YIN, THE CATHAYAN SAGE AND ADVISER377 MARCOM
TO THE KAAN,

SAGELY

(SHAKING HIS HEAD SAGELY) THEY'RE DEEP ONES, 522 INZONE

SAGGING

RESTING THEIR SAGGING BREASTS AND HANDS AND HAIR 202 DESIRE
ON ITS ROOF,

HER BODY IS DUMPY, WITH SAGGING BREASTS, 20 POET

SAGINAW

I COME ORIGINALLY FROM SAGINAW, MICHIGAN, 13 HUGHIE

SAGS

BURKE SAGS FORWARD WEARILY) 31 ANNA

(SAGS WEAKLY AND SUPPORTS HERSELF AGAINST THE 167 ELECTR
TABLE--

HIS CHIN SAGS TO HIS CHEST. 625 ICEMAN

HIS EYES CLOSE, HIS CHIN SAGS, 169 JOURNE

HER BODY SAGS TIREDLY. 157 MISBEG

FOR A SECOND HE CRUMBLES, HIS SOLDIERLY ERECTNESS 116 POET
SAGS AND HIS FACE FALLS.

HIS TALL, THIN BODY SAGS WEARILY IN THE CHAIR, HIS 24 STRANG
HEAD IS SUNK FORWARD,

SAIDY

WHISHT, NOW, ME SAIDY/ 33 ANNA

SAIL

YOU MUST SAIL BACK. 546 'ILE

GO SOUTH AMERICA, GO AUSTRALIA, GO ABOARD SHIP 21 ANNA
SAIL FOR SVEDEN.

SEE SCHOONER MAKE SAIL--SEE EVERYTANG DAT'S POOTTY. 23 ANNA

(WITH A SIGH) AY'M GLAD WHEN VE SAIL AGAIN, TOO. 42 ANNA

SHIPS VAS SHIPS DEN--AND MEN DAT SAIL ON DEM VAS 49 ANNA
REAL MEN.

AY SIGN ON STEAMER SAIL TOMORROW. 65 ANNA

HE SAYS HE CAN'T CALCULATE EXACTLY ON ACCOUNT O' 115 BEYOND
THE «SUNDA» BEING A SAIL BOAT.

I'LL BE DAMN GLAD WHEN WE SAIL AGAIN, 126 BEYOND

WHEN DOES SHE SAIL$ 141 BEYOND

SET ALL SAIL BACK HERE TO FIND YOU. 141 BEYOND

SET SAIL TO BRING BACK THE TREASURE. 561 CROSS

(THERE IS A LOUD, MUFFLED CRY FROM ABOVE, WHICH 567 CROSS
SOUNDS LIKE «SAIL-HO»,

IN FULL SAIL AND THE WORD «CALIFORNIA» IN BIG 206 DESIRE
LETTERS.

WE'LL TAKE IT WITH US FUR LUCK AN' LET 'ER SAIL 221 DESIRE
FREE DOWN SOME RIVER.

AN' I'LL SAIL THAR ON ONE O' THE FINEST CLIPPERS 1268 DESIRE
KIN FIND/

AND I WON'T WHEN YOU SAIL AWAY AGAIN, NEITHER, 497 DIFRNT

AND WHEN SHE SAW THE SHIP WAS GITTIN' READY TO 503 DIFRNT
SAIL SHE RAISED RUCTIONS,

YOU SAIL TO BOSTON TOMORROW, TO WAIT FOR CARGO$ 40 ELECTR

AND THEN THERE'D BE FULL SAIL ON HER AFORE YE 105 ELECTR
KNOWED IT/

AN' YOU'RE THE KIND TO CRACK SAIL ON, I KIN TELL 106 ELECTR
BY YOUR CUT.

CRACK SAIL ON HER AND SHE'LL BEAT MOST OF 'EM-- 106 ELECTR

WE'D BE MAKING SAIL IN THE DAWN, WITH A FAIR 213 HA APE
BREEZE,

FULL SAIL ON HER/ 214 HA APE

THE MASTS WITH EVERY SAIL WHITE IN THE MOONLIGHT, 153 JOURNE
TOWERING HIGH ABOVE ME.

READY TO SAIL FOR PERSIA WITHIN TEN DAYS. 388 MARCOM

YOU SAIL AT SUNRISE$ 403 MARCOM

CALL ALL HANDS ON DECK AND STAND BY TO PUT SAIL ONO03 MARCOM
HER.

I SHALL KNOW THE LONG SORROW OF AN EXILE AS I SAIL405 MARCOM
OVER THE GREEN WATER

THE SAIL IS FRAYED AND FULL OF JAGGED HOLES AND 407 MARCOM
PATCHES.

ON THE HIGHEST DECK IN REAR SAILORS LOWER AND FURL407 MARCOM
THE SAIL OF THE MIZZENMAST,

(THEY LOWER THE SAIL, AND BEGIN TO TIE IT UP 408 MARCOM
TRIMLY.)

SAIL$ 107 STRANG

HE'S GOT SO MUCH TO DO GETTING READY TO SAIL. 107 STRANG

SAIL ON SATURDAY... 149 STRANG

YES--UNTIL STEAMER SAIL FOR STOCKHOLM--IN TWO DAY.506 VOYAGE

(ANGRILY) I KNOW DAT DAMN SHIP--WORST SHIP DAT 507 VOYAGE
SAIL TO SEA.

I SAIL ON HER ONCE LONG TIME AGO--THREE MASTS, 507 VOYAGE
FULL RIG, SKY'S'L-YARDER$

SAILED

HE'S A HARD MAN--AS HARD A MAN AS EVER SAILED THE 537 'ILE
SEAS.

THE DAY BEFORE THE STEAMER SAILED 156 BEYOND

'MEMBER WHEN WE SAILED FROM 'OME 'OW 'E STANDS ON 463 CARIBE
THE BRIDGE

THE OTHER THREE MEN SAILED AWAY ON HER. 561 CROSS

SO ONE NIGHT JEST AFORE THEY SAILED SOME O' THE 503 DIFRNT
BOYS,

HE'S SAILED ALL OVER THE WORLD--HE LIVED ON A 15 ELECTR
SOUTH SEA ISLAND ONCE, SO HE SAYS.

I'VE SAILED ON NANNON HOOKERS AN' BEEN WORKED T' 106 ELECTR
DEATH

A MONTH AFTER VINNIE AND ORIN SAILED STARTED IT. 135 ELECTR

SAILOR

SAILED (CONT'D.)

FOR MONTHS AFTER WE SAILED YOU DIDN'T KNOW WHAT 141 ELECTR
YOU WERE DOING.

I'VE WATCHED IT EVER SINCE WE SAILED FOR THE EAST.141 ELECTR

BUT JUST BEFORE HE SAILED FOR THE FRONT 10 STRANG

THAT LAST NIGHT BEFORE HE SAILED--IN HIS ARMS 19 STRANG
UNTIL MY BODY ACHED--

THAT HE'D BE VISITING FRIENDS OUT OF TOWN UNTIL HE108 STRANG
SAILED.

SAILIN'

AND ALL DE SHIPS COMIN' IN, SAILIN' OUT, ALL OVER 252 HA APE
DE OITH--

SAILING

I USED TO DREAM OF SAILING ON THE GREAT, WIDE, 545 'ILE
GLORIOUS OCEAN.

YOU BELONG ON A REAL SHIP, SAILING ALL OVER THE 27 ANNA
WORLD

NO, HE WAS BO'SUN ON SAILING SHIPS FOR YEARS. 36 ANNA

I SIGNED ON TODAY AT NOON, DRUNK AS I WAS--AND 72 ANNA
SHE'S SAILING TOMORROW.

(IT SUDDENLY COMES TO HER THAT THIS IS THE SAME 72 ANNA
SHIP HER FATHER IS SAILING ON)

AND THAT'S A LONG VOYAGE ON A SAILING SHIP,. 83 BEYOND

LAST LETTER HE GOT WAS FROM ENGLAND, THE DAY THEY 115 BEYOND
WERE SAILING FOR HOME.

I'LL HAVE TO WAIT FOR A SHIP SAILING THERE FOR 137 BEYOND
QUITE A WHILE, LIKELY.

LIKE THE CAPTAIN'S CABIN OF A DEEP-SEA SAILING 555 CROSS
VESSEL.

AS FOR MY SAILING ON YOUR SHIP, YOU'LL FIND YOU 39 ELECTR
WON'T HAVE A SHIP/

I'M NOT SAILING FOR A MONTH YET. 105 ELECTR

THE «FLYING TRADES» WON'T BE SAILING FOR A MONTH 111 ELECTR
OR MORE.

THE «ATLANTIS» IS SAILING ON FRIDAY FOR CHINA. 111 ELECTR

AN HOUR AFTER SAILING FROM NEW YORK FOR THE VOYAGE207 HA APE
ACROSS.

MIX ON DAT OLD SAILING SHIP STUFF/ 210 HA APE

WE'D BE SAILING OUT, BOUND DOWN ROUND THE HORN 213 HA APE
MAYBE.

HE'S SAILING BACK TO HOME, SWEET HOME/ 676 ICEMAN

WE'LL BE SAILING AT ONCE. 406 MARCOM

(SURPRISED) YOURSELF SAILING$ 106 STRANG

I'M SAILING FOR EUROPE IN A FEW DAYS. 106 STRANG

DIDN'T HE TELL YOU HE WAS SAILING FOR EUROPE$ 107 STRANG

NED IS SAILING THIS WEEK, CHARLIE. 147 STRANG

MUST BE BECAUSE HE SAID HE'S SAILING AND I'M 152 STRANG
GLAD....)

I'M SAILING IN A FEW DAYS--LOTS TO DO--SEE YOU 152 STRANG
LATER, SAM.

(DEFIANTLY) YES--AND HE'S NOT COMING BACK--AND 155 STRANG
HE'S SAILING SOON/

SAILOR

(TURNING TO GO) SAILOR, EH$ 5 ANNA

(FORCING A SMILE) SAILOR VAS ALL RIGHT FALLAR, 9 ANNA
BUT NOT FOR MARRY GEL.

AY'M FOOL SAILOR FALLAR. 9 ANNA

AIN'T YOU A SAILOR YOURSELF NOW, AND ALWAYS BEEN$ 9 ANNA

(WITH A WINK AT MARTHY) DIS GIRL, NOW, 'LL BE 9 ANNA
MARRYIN' A SAILOR HERSELF.

HE'S YANITOR OF SOME BUILDING HERE NOW--USED TO BE 16 ANNA
A SAILOR.

(HE SIGHS) AY DON'T KNOW WHY BUT DAT'S VAY WITH 21 ANNA
MOST SAILOR FALLAR, ANNA.

AND, ANNA, DIS AIN'T REAL SAILOR YOB. 21 ANNA

ONLY NO GOOD SAILOR FALLAR COME HERE FOR GAT 22 ANNA
DRUNK.

I DON'T WONDER YOU ALWAYS BEEN A SAILOR. 26 ANNA

(VEHEMENTLY) AY AIN'T A SAILOR, ANNA. 26 ANNA

(VEHEMENTLY) ANY GEL MARRY SAILOR, SHE'S CRAZY 28 ANNA
FOOL/

SAILOR FALLARS, 30 ANNA

WHEN HE MAKES OUT ANNA IN SUCH INTIMATE PROXIMITY 38 ANNA
TO THIS STRANGE SAILOR,

WHAT YOU DOING HERE, YOU SAILOR FALLAR$ 39 ANNA

IT'S DAT DAMN SAILOR FALLAR LEARN YOU BAD TANGS. 43 ANNA

HE AIN'T A SAILOR. 43 ANNA

DAT'S YUST WHAT YOU ARE--NO GOOD SAILOR FALLAR/ 47 ANNA

YOU'D OUGHT TO BE 'SHAMED TO BE SAYING THE LIKE, 47 ANNA
AND YOU AN OLD SAILOR YOURSELF.

THIS SAILOR LIFE AIN'T MUCH TO CRY ABOUT LEAVIN'--486 CARDIF

NEVER GITTIN' OUTA SAILOR-TOWN, HARDLY, IN ANY 486 CARDIF
PORT.

THERE'S HARDLY A RALF DEFFWATER SAILOR LIFT ON THE459 CARIBE
SEAS, MORE'S THE PITY.

SAILOR-TOWN DIVES, MADE MORE GROTESQUE BY THE FACT471 CARIBE
THAT ALL THE COUPLES ARE

WHAT WOULD I HAVE BEEN NOW BUT AN IGNORANT SAILOR 564 CROSS
LIKE HIM

(SCORNFULLY) EMMA'D OUGHT TO HAVE FALLEN IN LOVE 509 DIFRNT
WITH A MINISTER, NOT A SAILOR.

SO EARLY IN THE MORNING THE SAILOR LIKES HIS 103 ELECTR
BOTTLE OH/$

SO EARLY IN THE MORNING A SAILOR LIKES HIS BOTTLE 130 ELECTR
OH,»

«JACK, OH, JACK, WAS A SAILOR LAD AND HE CAME TO A596 ICEMAN
TAVERN FOR GIN.

(HE SINGS..) «OH, COME UP,» SHE CRIED, «MY SAILOR 597 ICEMAN
LAD, AND YOU AND I'LL AGREE.

(HE SINGS..) «OH, COME UP,» SHE CRIED, «MY SAILOR 607 ICEMAN
LAD, AND YOU AND I'LL AGREE.

IT WAS A SAILOR.. 616 ICEMAN

(SINGS TO HIS SAILOR LAD TUNE) 662 ICEMAN

WILLIE OBAN'S, THE SAILOR LAD DITTY HE SANG IN ACT727 ICEMAN
ONE.

'E AIN'T NO GOOD AS A SAILOR, IS 'E$ 517 INZONE

WORKING HIS WAY ALL OVER THE MAP AS A SAILOR AND 35 JOURNE
ALL THAT STUFF.

SAILOR

SAILOR (CONT'D.)
HE WEARS A DARK BLUE JERSEY, PATCHED BLUE PANTS, 587 ROPE
ROUGH SAILOR SHOES,
BUT IF YOU AIN'T GOINTER BE A SAILOR NO MORE, 502 VOYAGE
WHATI'LL YER DUS
YOU BEEN A SAILOR ALL YER LIFE, AIN'T YERS 503 VOYAGE
NICK GOES SO AND STANDS SO THAT THE SAILOR CANNOT 505 VOYAGE
SEE WHAT JOE IS DOING.)
NO SAILOR WHO KNOW ANYTING EVER SHIP ON HER. 507 VOYAGE

SAILORLL
AV' THERE'S A LOT O' THINGS A SAILOR'LL SEE IN THES22 INZONE
PORTS HE PUTS IN

SAILOR'S
AND THE SUNGS AT THE SAILOR'S OPERA HOUSE WHERE 487 CARDIF
THE GUY PLAYED RAGTIME--
AND A SHREUDED WHITE SAILOR'S BLOUSE, STAINED WITHS71 CROSS
IRON-RUST.

SAILORMAN
(SPITTING DISGUSTEDLY) THERE'S A FUNNY BIRD OF A 498 VOYAGE
SAILORMAN FUR YER,
I BANE POOR DEVIL SAILURMAN, DAT'S ALL. 502 VOYAGE

SAILORMEN
THEY'RE NOT FUR SAILORMEN LIKE YOU AN' ME, 'LESS 106 ELECTR
WE'RE LOOKIN' FUR SORROW/
WHERE'S ALL THE SAILORMEN, I'D LIKE TO KNOWS 493 VOYAGE

SAILORS
WEKE ALL OF 'EM YUST PLAIN SAILORSS 27 ANNA
WAS THE MEN IN OUR FAMILY ALWAYS SAILORS--AS FAR 27 ANNA
BACK AS YOU KNOW ABOUTS
(THEN HASTILY) BUT SAY--LISTEN--DID ALL THE WOMEN 28 ANNA
OF THE FAMILY MARRY SAILORSS
(THOUGHTFULLY) SAILORS NEVER DO GO HOME HARDLY, 37 ANNA
DO THEYS
ALL THE WOMEN HAVE MARRIED SAILORS, TOO. 37 ANNA
YES, THAT KIND OF A HOUSE--THE KIND SAILORS LIKE 58 ANNA
YOU AND MAT GOES TO IN PORT--
WUD BE SAILORS ENOUGH TO KNOW THE MAIN FROM THE 459 CARIBE
MIZZEN ON A WINDJAMMER.
(PUZZLED AND A BIT UNEASY) SAILORS AIN'T PLASTER 495 DIFRNT
SAINTS, EMMER--
NOT LE DE STREETS WAS BLOCKED WID SAILORS/ 669 ICEMAN
ON THE HIGHEST DECK IN REAR SAILORS LOWER AND FURL407 MARCOM
THE SAIL OF THE MIZZENMAST,
(WITH THE SAILORS) AYE-AYE, SIR/ 408 MARCOM

SAILORS'
FORGETTING THE SICK MAN IN THEIR SAILORS' DELIGHT 481 CARDIF

SAILS
YOU KNOW THE =SUNDA= SAILS AROUND THE HORN FOR 83 BEYOND
YOKOHAMA FIRST,
SHE SAILS AT DAYBREAK FRIDAY. 111 ELECTR
HER SAILS STRETCHING ALOFT ALL SILVER AND WHITE, 214 HA APE
NOT A SOUND ON THE DECK,
I DISSOLVED IN THE SEA, BECAME WHITE SAILS AND 153 JOURNE
FLYING SPRAY,
A FOREST OF MASTS, SPARS, SAILS OF WOVEN BAMBOO 400 MARCOM
LATHS,
THEIR CLAWS RENDED SAILS INTO RAGS, FIERCE WERE 408 MARCOM
THE WINDS/
KEEP HIDDEN UNTIL BOAT SAILS SO SHE CAN'T REACH 105 STRANG
ME/....!)
HE CARRIES A SMALL, EXPENSIVE YACHT'S MODEL OF A 149 STRANG
SLOOP WITH THE SAILS SET--
THEY SAILS AT DAY-BREAK TER-MORRER. 495 VOYAGE
ROUND CAPE 'ORN--SAILS AT DAYBREAK. 507 VOYAGE

SAIME
THE SAIME, MATESS 497 VOYAGE

SAINT
'TWAS ENOUGH TO MAKE A SAINT SHWEAR TO SEE HIM WID479 CARDIF
HIS GOLD WATCH IN HIS HAND,
CALEB'S A SUNDAY GO-TO-MEETIN' SAINT, AIN'T HES 499 DIFRNT
CALEB AIN'T NO PLASTER SAINT 509 DIFRNT
I KNOW FROM WHAT I CAN GUESS FROM HIS OWN STORIES 512 DIFRNT
PA NEVER WAS NO SAINT.
YOU'D THINK I WAS A SAINT IF YOU DID. 529 DIFRNT
HE PRAYS LIKE A SAINT IN THE DESERT, EXORCIZING A 273 GGBROW
DEMON)
HE RESEMBLES A HOLY SAINT, RECENTLY ELECTED TO 32 HUGHIE
PARADISE.
WHEN SAINT PATRICK DROVE THE SNAKES OUT OF IRELAND718 ICEMAN
THEY SANK TO NEW YORK AND
SHE IS SO SWEET AND GOOD. A SAINT ON EARTH. 1 175 JOURNE
LOVE HER DEARLY.
I'M NO SAINT, GOD KNOWS, BUT I'M DECENT AND 30 MISBEG
DESERVING COMPARED TO THOSE SCUM.

SAINT'S
LIKE A SAINT'S VISION OF BEATITUDE. 153 JOURNE

SAINTLIKE
MORE SAINTLIKE AND ASCETIC THAN EVER BEFORE. 290 GGBROW

SAINTS
AND MY CURSE ON YOU AND THE CURSE OF ALMIGHTY GOD 61 ANNA
AND ALL THE SAINTS/
AND PRAYING ALMIGHTY GOD AND THE SAINTS TO PUT A 75 ANNA
GREAT CURSE ON YOU IF SHE'D
FUR THE LOVE AV THE SAINTS DON'T BE TALKIN' LOIKE 483 CARDIF
THAT/
(PUZZLED AND A BIT UNEASY) SAILORS AIN'T PLASTER 495 DIFRNT
SAINTS, EMMER--
IF YOU'RE LOOKING FOR SAINTS, YOU GOT TO DIE FIRST509 DIFRNT
AND GO TO HEAVEN.
I SWEAR BY ALL THE SAINTS-- 162 MISBEG
BE THE SAINTS, THERE'S A BLACKSMITH AT WORK ON IT/ 8 POET
PRAISE BE TO THE SAINTS, YOU'RE BACK, JAMIE/ 151 POET
(WITH A LEERING CHUCKLE.) BE THE SAINTS, 173 POET

SAITH
(IN A BOOMING TRIUMPH) =VENGEANCE IS MINE, SAITH 451 DYNAMO
THE LORD/=
= THE FOOL SAITH IN HIS HEART-- 481 DYNAMO

SAKE

(WILDLY) THEN DO THIS THIS ONCE FOR MY SAKE, FOR 549 'ILE
GOD'S SAKE--TAKE ME HOME/
I'LL DO IT, ANNIE--FOR YOUR SAKE--IF YOU SAY IT'S 549 'ILE
NEEDFUL FOR YE.
YOU'D OUGHT TO DO IT FOR HIS SAKE, IF YOU HAD ANY 203 AHWILD
SENSE--
YOU KNOW FOR VARIETY'S SAKE. 258 AHWILD
DICK, YOU DON'T REALIZED HOW I'VE BEEN PUNISHED 281 AHWILD
FOR YOUR SAKE.
HUSH UP, FOR GOD'S SAKE/ 290 AHWILD
WHAT'S THAT YUH GOT--A LETTER, FUR GAWD'S SAKES 8 ANNA
FUR GAWD'S SAKE/ 38 ANNA
(WITH WEARY SCORN) OH, FOR HEAVEN'S SAKE, ARE YOU 42 ANNA
OFF ON THAT AGAINS
(UISATISFIEDLY) SO, FOR GAWD'S SAKE, LET'S TALK OF 54 ANNA
SOMETHING ELSE.
FOR GAWD'S SAKE/ 60 ANNA
(BITTERLY) FOR GAWD'S SAKE, 66 ANNA
(WITH A START) WHAT YOU GOT IN YOUR POCKET, FOR 66 ANNA
PETE'S SAKE--
(HER VOICE BREAKING) OH, FOR GAWD'S SAKE, MAT, 72 ANNA
LEAVE ME ALONE/
FOR GOD'S SAKE/ 108 BEYOND
(SLOWLY) PERHAPS--FOR HER SAKE--YOU'D BETTER NOT 135 BEYOND
TELL HER.
BUT FOR GOD'S SAKE, LET'S NOT TALK ABOUT IT/ 135 BEYOND
FOR HER SAKES 135 BEYOND
FOR YOUR SAKE AND THE OLD FOLKS AND THE LITTLE 136 BEYOND
GIRL.
FOR GOD'S SAKE, ANDY--WON'T YOU PLEASE STOP 139 BEYOND
TALKING/
FOR GOD'S SAKE, HAVEN'T YOU EVER HAD A BAD COLD 147 BEYOND
YOURSELF$
STOP THAT COUGHING FOR GOODNESS' SAKE/ 149 BEYOND
SIT DOWN, ROB, FOR GOODNESS' SAKE/ 150 BEYOND
(SHIVERING IRRITABLY) FOR GOODNESS' SAKE PUT SOME152 BEYOND
WOOD ON THAT FIRE.
(WITH A SHUDDER) DON'T TALK THAT WAY, FOR GOD'S 159 BEYOND
SAKE/
FOR GOD'S SAKE, RUTH/ 165 BEYOND
FORGIVE ME, RUTH--FOR HIS SAKE--AND I'LL 168 BEYOND
REMEMBER--
OH, YOU OUGHT TO BE GLAD--GLAD--FOR MY SAKE/ 168 BEYOND
FOR GOD'S SAKE DON'T LEAVE ME ALONE/ 484 CARDIF
FOR GAWD'S SAKE, DON'T STAND OUT HERE DRINKIN' IN 465 CARIBE
THE MOONLIGHT.
FOR GAWD'S SAKE, BOYS, DON'T SHOUT SO LOUD/ 471 CARIBE
THE NEIGHBORS--THEY'RE FAR AWAY BUT--FOR MY 562 CROSS
SISTER'S SAKE--YOU UNDERSTAND.
FOR OUR DEAD MOTHER'S SAKE. 565 CROSS
FOR OUR MOTHER'S SAKE/ 565 CROSS
FOR GOD'S SAKE (LISTEN TO ME/ 566 CROSS
(THEN HURRIEDLY) BUT, FOR PETE'S SAKE, LET'S NOT 497 DAYS
GET STARTED ON RELIGION.
I ONLY MEANT--DON'T GET THAT IDEA IN YOUR HEAD, 509 DAYS
FOR PETE'S SAKE.
(WITH A SHUDDER) FOR GOD'S SAKE, DON'T SPEAK 509 DAYS
ABOUT--
AND FOR HEAVEN'S SAKE, DON'T GO TELLING ELSA I'M 513 DAYS
UNHAPPY.
BUT, FOR HEAVEN'S SAKE, WHY DO YOU STAND ITS 519 DAYS
DON'T, FOR GOD'S SAKE/ 520 DAYS
I WOULDN'T FOR ELSA'S SAKE. 527 DAYS
(TORTUREDLY) FOR GOD'S SAKE/ 531 DAYS
FOR GOD'S SAKE, JOHN, DON'T LIE TO ME ANY MORE OR 549 DAYS
I-- I KNOW, I TELL YOU/
FOR GOD'S SAKE/ 550 DAYS
FOR GOD'S SAKE/ 551 DAYS
(WILDLY) FOR GOD'S SAKE, DON'T SAY THAT/ 556 DAYS
FOR GOD'S SAKE, TELL ME YUU KNOW SHE ISN'T GOING 556 DAYS
TO--
NOW, FOR ELSA'S SAKE--WHILE THERE IS STILL TIME. 558 DAYS
FOR GOD'S SAKE, HELP ME/ 558 DAYS
OF YOUR OLD IDEAL ABOUT MAN'S DUTY TO GO ON FOR 561 DAYS
LIFE'S SAKE,
FOR GOD'S SAKE, DON'T MAKE ME THINK-- 561 DAYS
(CURLY) FUR YERR SAKE, I HOPE THEY BE. 265 DESIRE
THEN YOU WON'T PROMISE ME TO STAY DIFF'RENT FOR MY496 DIFRNT
SAKES
I GOT TO DO IT FUR EMMER'S SAKE AS WELL AS HIS'N. 530 DIFRNT
(HASTILY) DON'T DO THAT, FOR GOD'S SAKE/ 532 DIFRNT
DON'T HURT HIM THEN, CALEB-- FOR MY SAKE/ 543 DIFRNT
OH, BENNY, I'M GIVING UP EVERYTHING I'VE HELD DEAR544 DIFRNT
ALL MY LIFE FOR YOUR SAKE.
(A BIT IRRITATED) WHAT'S THE USE OF BLUBBERIN', 546 DIFRNT
FOR GOD'S SAKES
FOR GOD'S SAKE, GET OUT OF HERE/ 434 DYNAMO
I WAS ONLY DOING IT FOR YOUR SAKE, ADA. 443 DYNAMO
FOR GOD'S SAKE, DON'T SAY THAT TC YOUR MOTHER/ 450 DYNAMO
FOR GOD'S SAKE, REUBEN/ 452 DYNAMO
FUR HEAVEN'S SAKE, WHAT'RE YOU DOPE-DREAMING ABOUT454 DYNAMO
NOW, MOMS
FOR PETE'S SAKE, LEAVE ME ALONE/ 455 DYNAMO
FOR GOD'S SAKE, SHUT UP/ 455 DYNAMO
(THINKING FRIGHTENEDLY) (FOR GOD'S SAKE, WHAT'S 482 DYNAMO
COME OVER HIM--.
I DID IT FOR YOUR SAKE/... 488 DYNAMO
GIVE ME CREDIT FO' HAVIN' SOME SENSE, FO' LAWD'S 183 EJONES
SAKE/
BUT, JUST FOR ARGUMENT'S SAKE--WHAT 'D YOU DOS 184 EJONES
FO' LAWD'S SAKE, USE YO' HAID. 189 EJONES
SOUND LIKE--SOUND LIKE--FO' GOD SAKE, SOUND LIKE 191 EJONES
SOME NIGGER WAS SHOOTIN' CRAPS/
GIMME A SHOVEL, ONE O' YOU, FO' GOD'S SAKE/ 195 EJONES
AND YOU'D OUGHT FUR YOUR PAW'S SAKE TO MAKE 20 ELECTR
SARTIN.
SO PLEASE UNDERSTAND THIS ISN'T FOR YOUR SAKE. 32 ELECTR
FOR HIS A SAKE. 46 ELECTR

SAKES

SAKE (CONT'D.)
FOR GOD'S SAKE, STOP TALKING. 56 ELECTR
DON'T DO THAT AGAIN, FOR HEAVEN'S SAKE/ 83 ELECTR
FOR A HUNDRED REASONS--THE FAMILY'S SAKE-- 88 ELECTR
MY OWN SAKE AND VINNIE'S, TOO, AS WELL AS YOURS-- 89 ELECTR
EVEN IF I KNEW--
FOR GOD'S SAKE/ 89 ELECTR
FOR GOD'S SAKE, DON'T TALK LIKE THAT/ 89 ELECTR
FOR GOD'S SAKE, KEEP ORIN OUT OF THIS/ 92 ELECTR
FOR HEAVEN'S SAKE, FORGET THE WAR/ 95 ELECTR
FOR GOD'S SAKE--HERE, BEFORE HIM/ 98 ELECTR
FOR GOD'S SAKE, BE QUIET/ 101 ELECTR
(SPRINGING TO HIS FEET) FOR GOD'S SAKE, WHY 110 ELECTR
DIDN'T YOU--
I WOULD HAVE LOVED HER AS HE LOVED HER--AND KILLED116 ELECTR
FATHER TOO--FOR HER SAKE/
ORIN, FOR GOD'S SAKE, WILL YOU STOP TALKING CRAZY 116 ELECTR
AND COME ALONG$
FOR GOD'S SAKE, WILL YOU BE QUIET$ 124 ELECTR
I ONLY WENT THERE FOR YOUR SAKE. 141 ELECTR
FOR GOD'S SAKE, WON'T 155 ELECTR
FOR GOD'S SAKE, TELL ME YOU'RE LYING, VINNIE/ 155 ELECTR
FOR GOD'S SAKE, HAZEL, IF YOU LOVE ME HELP ME TO 161 ELECTR
GET AWAY FROM HERE--
FOR MOTHER'S SAKE, YOU CAN'T/ 164 ELECTR
(DESPERATELY) FOR MY SAKE, THEN/ 164 ELECTR
FOR GOD'S SAKE--/ 165 ELECTR
NOT FOR MY SAKE--BUT FOR YOUR OWN--AND, ABOVE ALL,272 GGBROW
FOR THE CHILDREN'S/
NOT SO LOUD, FOR PETE'S SAKE/ 294 GGBROW
(HUMBLY) STOP, FOR GOD'S SAKE/ 299 GGBROW
HE SAID HE'D SWORN OFF TONIGHT--FOREVER--FOR YOUR 300 GGBROW
SAKE--AND THE KIDS/
THIS IS FOR HIS SAKE, MARGARET. 304 GGBROW
(DULLY EXASPERATED.) SAY, FOR CHRIST'S SAKE, 35 HUGHIE
WHAT'S IT TO YOU--$
AW, FOR CHRIST SAKE, DON'T GET DAT BUGHOUSE BUM 579 ICEMAN
STARTED/
PUT ON YOUR CLOTHES, FOR CHRIST'S SAKE/ 602 ICEMAN
FOR CHRIST SAKE/ 614 ICEMAN
CUT OUT THE ACT AND HAVE A DRINK, FOR CHRIST'S 621 ICEMAN
SAKE.
FOR HARRY'S SAKE, NOT YOURS, YUH LITTLE WOP/ 634 ICEMAN
YOU OUGHT TO, FOR MOTHER'S SAKE. 646 ICEMAN
I'VE GOT TO FEEL GLAD, FOR HER SAKE. 663 ICEMAN
WHAT AT, FOR CHRIST SAKE$ 675 ICEMAN
FOR GOTT'S SAKE, DO NOT LISTEN TO ME/ 695 ICEMAN
PLEASE FOR GOTT'S SAKE/ 695 ICEMAN
FOR GOD'S SAKE, LARRY, CAN'T YOU SAY SOMETHING$ 701 ICEMAN
FOR GOD'S SAKE, HARRY, ARE YOU STILL HARPING ON 706 ICEMAN
THAT DAMNED NONSENSE/
CAN'T YOU APPRECIATE WHAT YOU'VE GOT, FOR GOD'S 705 ICEMAN
SAKE$
YOU'LL SEE THERE WASN'T ANY OTHER POSSIBLE WAY OUT709 ICEMAN
OF IT, FOR HER SAKE.
I TOLD HER STRAIGHT, "YOU BETTER FORGET ME, 710 ICEMAN
EVELYN, FOR YOUR OWN SAKE.
AND THEN IT CAME TO ME--THE ONLY POSSIBLE WAY OUT,715 ICEMAN
FOR HER SAKE.
FOR YOUR OWN SAKE/ 720 ICEMAN
TAKE IT OUT, JACK--CAREFUL--DON'T SHAKE IT NOW, 524 INZONE
FOR CHRIST'S SAKE/
DON'T YOU SEE YOU MUST FOR MY SAKE$-- 530 INZONE
AN' MAKIN' A MAN AV HIMSELF FOR HER SAKE. 531 INZONE
(IRRITABLY.) YES, FOR PETE'S SAKE, PAPA/ 21 JOURNE
OH, FOR GOD'S SAKE, PAPA/ 28 JOURNE
OH, FOR GOD'S SAKE, DON'T DRAG UP THAT ANCIENT 32 JOURNE
HISTORY/
OH, FOR CHRIST'S SAKE, PAPA/ CAN'T YOU LAY OFF 36 JOURNE
ME/
(WITH FORCED SCORN.) FOR GOD'S SAKE, IS THAT ALL$ 38 JOURNE
FOR PETE'S SAKE, WHO EVER HEARD OF THEM OUTSIDE 43 JOURNE
THIS HICK BURG$
FOR HEAVEN'S SAKE, HAVEN'T I OFTEN USED THE SPARE 47 JOURNE
ROOM AS MY BEDROOM$
FOR PETE'S SAKE, WHAT OF IT$ 57 JOURNE
AND, FOR PETE'S SAKE, MAMA, WHY JUMP ON JAMIE ALL 61 JOURNE
OF A SUDDEN$
OH, FOR GOD'S SAKE, DO YOU THINK YOU CAN FOOL ME, 63 JOURNE
MAMA$
FOR GOD'S SAKE, LET'S EAT. 68 JOURNE
(COAXINGLY MATERNAL.) PROMISE ME YOU WILL, DEAR, 72 JOURNE
FOR MY SAKE.
FOR GOD'S SAKE, STOP TALKING. 74 JOURNE
WELL, FOR GOD'S SAKE, PICK OUT A GOOD PLACE AND 79 JOURNE
NOT SOME CHEAP DUMP/
FOR THE LOVE OF GOD, FOR MY SAKE AND THE BOYS' 85 JOURNE
SAKE AND YOUR OWN,
(WITH GUILTY RESENTMENT.) FOR GOD'S SAKE, DON'T 86 JOURNE
DIG UP WHAT'S LONG FORGOTTEN.
FOR GOD'S SAKE, FORGET THE PAST/ 87 JOURNE
I MEANT, FOR HIS SAKE. 88 JOURNE
FOR GOD'S SAKE TRY AND BE YOURSELF--AT LEAST UNTIL 88 JOURNE
HE GOES/
FOR GOD'S SAKE, MAMA/ YOU CAN'T TRUST HER/ 116 JOURNE
(PROTESTS DULLY.) OH, FOR PETE'S SAKE, MAMA. 117 JOURNE
IT WOULD HAVE BEEN BETTER FOR HIS SAKE. 122 JOURNE
IF THEY WANT TO BE WASTEFUL FOOLS, FOR THE SAKE OF126 JOURNE
SHOW, LET THEM BE/
OH, FOR PETE'S SAKE, PAPA/ 129 JOURNE
FOR GOD'S SAKE, PAPA/ 138 JOURNE
(PLEADS TENSELY.) FOR CHRIST'S SAKE, PAPA, FORGET!152 JOURNE
IT/
FOR PETE'S SAKE, IF WE'RE GOING TO PLAY CARDS, 152 JOURNE
LET'S PLAY.
REMEMBER I WARNED YOU--FOR YOUR SAKE. GIVE ME 167 JOURNE
CREDIT.
SAY NO FOR MY SAKE/ 322 LAZARU

SAKE (CONT'D.)
LAUGHING, WE GIVE OUR LIVES FOR LIFE'S SAKE/* 324 LAZARU
WHERE I CAN, I KILL LOVE--FOR RETRIBUTION'S SAKE--356 LAZARU
BUT MUCH OF IT ESCAPES ME.
DEBORAH, FOR THE SAKE OF THE COMPANY-- 33 MANSNS
FOR PUBLIC OPINION'S SAKE. 45 MANSNS
TO LIVE IN OTHERS' LIVES FOR THEIR SAKE AND NOT MY 53 MANSNS
SAKE.
ALL HE WANTS IS TO PROVE TO YOU HOW CLEVER HE HAS 64 MANSNS
BEEN FOR YOUR SAKE.
YES, FOR GOD'S SAKE/ 71 MANSNS
FOR GOD'S SAKE, WHY DU YOU STARE LIKE THAT$ 130 MANSNS
I HOPE NOT--FOR YOUR SAKE, MR. TENARD. 152 MANSNS
FOR GOD'S SAKE, HOW CAN YOU SAY SUCH THINGS TO 182 MANSNS
YOUR MOTHER/
FOR GOD'S SAKE/ 183 MANSNS
FOR HEAVEN'S SAKE, LET'S NOT TALK BUSINESS/ 366 MARCOM
(THEN PLEADINGLY) FOR HEAVEN'S SAKE, TRY AND BE 413 MARCOM
CALM, PRINESS/
(WITH SUDDEN REVULSION) FOR GOD'S SAKE, CUT OUT 42 MISBEG
THAT KIND OF TALK, JOSIE/
FOR GOD'S SAKE, DRY UP/ 76 MISBEG
OCH, FOR GOD'S SAKE, DRY UP/ 89 MISBEG
WHAT DID HE MEAN, FOR MY SAKE$ 89 MISBEG
FOR YOUR SAKE, BECAUSE HE LOVES YOU/ 89 MISBEG
FOR GOD'S SAKE, YOU'RE NOT A TART. 127 MISBEG
FOR CHRIST SAKE, QUIT THE SMUT STUFF, CAN'T YOU/ 127 MISBEG
I WANTED TO CLEAR THINGS UP, THAT'S ALL--FOR 136 MISBEG
PHIL'S SAKE AS WELL AS YOURS.
FOR HER SAKE. 146 MISBEG
FOR GOD'S SAKE, CAN'T YOU LEAVE HER ALONE EVEN 148 MISBEG
NOW$
FOR GOD'S SAKE, CAN'T YOU LET HER REST IN PEACE$ 148 MISBEG
WILL YOU WAKE UP, FOR GOD'S SAKE/ 164 MISBEG
FOR GOD'S SAKE, HOW LONG WAS I CRAMPED ON YOU LIKE168 MISBEG
THAT$
(PLEADINGLY) I HOPED, FOR YOUR SAKE, YOU WOULDN'T173 MISBEG
AND I TAKE MY OATH I'LL NIVIR BREATHE A WORD OF 15 POET
IT--FOR NORA'S SAKE, NOT HIS.
FOR GOD'S SAKE, STOP YOUR STARING/ 35 POET
FOR GOD'S SAKE, WHY DON'T YOU WASH YOUR HAIR$ 42 POET
WELL, I'LL DO IT JUST THIS ONCE MORE FOR MOTHER'S 59 POET
SAKE, ON SHE'D HAVE TO.
FORGET IT NOW, DO, FOR SARA'S SAKE. 75 POET
AND I WILL DO MY BEST, FOR THE SAKE OF YOUR 90 POET
INTERESTS, TO MAKE HONORABLE AMENDS.
FOR THE SAKE OF THE DIRTY MONEY YOU THINK YOU CAN 127 POET
BEG FROM HIS FAMILY.
IT'S NOT FOR HIS SAKE AT ALL/ 139 POET
FOR HEAVEN'S SAKE DON'T REMIND HER/ 9 STRANG
FOR HER SAKE/...!) 11 STRANG
FOR GORDON'S SAKE$... 18 STRANG
(WOUNDEDLY) LET US SAY THEN THAT I PERSUADED 20 STRANG
MYSELF IT WAS FOR YOUR SAKE.
I DID IT FOR YOUR SAKE, NINA. 20 STRANG
THIS TIME I DO SPEAK FOR HER SAKE. 21 STRANG
(FOR GOD'S SAKE, STOP ACTING/... 28 STRANG
FOR HER SAKE... 52 STRANG
HOW I MIGHT HAVE LOVED YOUR FATHER FOR YOUR 69 STRANG
SAKE/...!)
FOR PETE'S SAKE, HAVE A GOOD HEART-TO-HEART TALK 78 STRANG
WITH HER, NED/
THING I MUST DO FOR SAM'S SAKE, AND MY OWN. 84 STRANG
FOR HER SAKE.... 92 STRANG
BE SENSIBLE, FOR GOD'S SAKE/ 103 STRANG
FOR ITS SAKE...!) 129 STRANG
I'LL FIGHT FOR ITS SAKE AGAINST THESE TWO/...!) 129 STRANG
FOR GOD'S SAKE/ 131 STRANG
HE HAS SHARED ME FOR HIS COMFORT'S SAKE WITH A 138 STRANG
LITTLE GRATITUDE AND A BIG
FOR GOD'S SAKE/ 144 STRANG
(SADLY) YOU'D BETTER FORGET THAT, FOR HIS SAKE 144 STRANG
AND YOUR OWN.
I WANTED TO DO IT FOR SAM'S SAKE--BUT ESPECIALLY 146 STRANG
FOR MY CHILD'S SAKE.
FOR HEAVEN'S SAKE, SAM, DON'T ENCOURAGE HIM-- 154 STRANG
FOR MY SAKE... 156 STRANG
I'VE DONE MY BEST, FOR GORDON'S SAKE, TO BE NICE 160 STRANG
TO HER....!)
(EXASPERATEDLY) FOR HEAVEN'S SAKE, STOP SWEARING 162 STRANG
SO MUCH/
OF COLLEGE HERO--LIKE HIS NEVER-TO-BE-FORGOTTEN 166 STRANG
NAME-SAKE/
WHAT IS HE TO ME, FOR GOD'S SAKE$...!) 169 STRANG
WE'VE SUFFERED ALL OUR LIVES FOR HIS SAKE/ 173 STRANG
FOR MY SAKE/ 174 STRANG
(STERNLY) FOR THE SAKE OF YOUR FUTURE HAPPINESS 178 STRANG
AND MY SON'S I'VE GOT TO SPEAK/
DARRELL LONG AFTER SHE WAS MARRIED--AND THEN SHE 186 STRANG
SENT HIM AWAY FOR DAD'S SAKE--
SHE GAVE UP HER OWN HAPPINESS FOR HIS SAKE... 189 STRANG
IF HE ONLY KNEW WHAT SHE'S SUFFERED FOR HIS 191 STRANG
SAKE/...
(PITEOUSLY--HYSTERICALLY) FOR GOD'S SAKE, GORDON/193 STRANG
(IRRITABLY) FOR GAWD'S SAKE, SHET THAT DOOR/504 VOYAGE
(IRRITABLY) THEN LET'S STOP ARGUING, FOR HEAVEN'S$456 WELDED
SAKE/
FOR GOD'S SAKE/ 458 WELDED
FOR GOD'S SAKE, NOT THAT/ 459 WELDED
OH, JOHN, FOR GOD'S SAKE DUN'T ASK ME/ 467 WELDED

SAKEN
A RALE, GOD-FOR-SAKEN SON AV A TURKEY TROT WID 470 CARIBE
GUTS TO UT.

SAKES
(NORAH BEGINS PASSING SOUP) SIT DOWN, NAT, FOR 223 AHWILD
GOODNESS SAKES.
MERCY SAKES/ 231 AHWILU
GOODNESS SAKES/ 103 BEYOND
LAND SAKES, IF THIS ISN'T A SCORCHER/ 116 BEYOND

SAKES

SAKES (CONT'D.)
FOR GOODNESS SAKES, MA/ 118 BEYOND
FOR HEAVEN'S SAKES, PUT DOWN THAT OLD BOOK/ 122 BEYOND
GRACIOUS SAKES, RUTH-- 153 BEYOND
TIRED OF PRETENDING TO MYSELF I HAVE TO GO ON FOR 519 DAYS
THE CHILDREN'S SAKES.
LAND SAKES, WHAT A BROTHER TO HAVE/ 499 DIFRNT
GOD SAKES, EMMER, I DIDN'T THINK YOU WAS THAT BIG 504 DIFRNT
A FOOL.
GOODNESS SAKES, EMMER, ALL THE MEN THINKS THAT-- 509 DIFRNT
(WITH A COQUETTISH TITTER) LAND SAKES, BENNY, 522 DIFRNT
LAND SAKES, I HARDLY GET A SIGHT OF YOU BEFORE YOU524 DIFRNT
WANT TO RUN AWAY AGAIN.
(FLUSTERED) LAND SAKES, I CAN'T LET HER SEE ME 527 DIFRNT
THIS WAY.
GRACIOUS SAKES, WHY DON'T YOU SET, CALEB$ 535 DIFRNT
LAND SAKES, WHAT YOU STARIN' AT SU$ 536 DIFRNT
(HASTILY) LAND SAKES, DON'T LET'S TALK OF THAT. 537 DIFRNT
LAND SAKES, I FORGOT ALL ABOUT THAT LONG AGO. 538 DIFRNT
(WORRIEDLY) GH, LAND SAKES/ 547 DIFRNT
MY SAKES-- 7 ELECTR
THEY'D HAVE TO FOR THEIR OWN SAKES. 111 ELECTR
BUT, FOR ALL OUR SAKES, DON'T COME HERE AGAIN. 305 GGBROW
KISS AND MAKE UP, FOR GAWD'S SAKES/ 651 ICEMAN
THAT I THINK IT ADVISABLE, FOR OUR OWN SAKES IF 147 MANSNS
NOT FOR HERS, TO HUMOR HER.
LORD SAKES, SOON 'S EVER MY BACK IS TURNED YOU 579 ROPE
GOES SNEAKIN' OFF AGEN.
(IRRITABLY) LAND SAKES, PAW, 581 ROPE
(WITH FINALITY) THAT'S THE ONLY POSSIBLE 132 STRANG
SOLUTION, NED, FOR ALL OUR SAKES.

SAKYA
CERTAINLY/ DO YOU NOT KNOW THE LEGEND OF HOW THE 349 MARCOM
HOLY SAKYA PICKED A TWIG

SALACIOUS
(WITH A SALACIOUS SMIRK) CAN'T SAY AS I BLAME 71 ELECTR
HIM/

SALAD
(SUDDENLY) I'VE GOT A JOB FOR YOU, CHARLIE--MAKE 149 STRANG
THE SALAD DRESSING FOR LUNCH.

SALADS
VEGETABLES, SALADS, FRUITS, NUTS, DOZENS OF 428 MARCOM
BOTTLES OF WINES.

SALAMANCA
SINCE THE WAR WITH THE FRENCH IN SPAIN--AFTER THE 10 POET
BATTLE OF SALAMANCA IN '12.
JUST AFTER THE BATTLE OF SALAMANCA, AND THERE WAS 12 POET
A DUEL AND CON KILLED HIM.

SALAMANDER
I SHOULD HAVE INHERITED AN IMMUNITY TO HEAT THAT 220 HA APE
WOULD MAKE A SALAMANDER SHIVER.

SALARY
TO WORK THE PLACE ON A SALARY AND PERCENTAGE. 137 BEYOND
BUT HOW COULD HE WITH HIS WIFE KEEPIN' CASES ON 16 HUGHIE
EVERY NICKEL OF HIS SALARY$
THEN YOU CAN STRIKE THEM FOR A BIGGER SALARY THAN 604 ICEMAN
YOU GOT BEFORE, DO YOU SEE$
YOU'VE THROWN YOUR SALARY AWAY EVERY WEEK ON 31 JOURNE
WHORES AND WHISKEY/
MY SALARY/ 31 JOURNE
I EXPECT A SALARY OF AT LEAST ONE LARGE IRON MAN 40 JOURNE
AT THE END OF THE WEEK--
I CAN OFFER YOU A SALARY THAT WILL ENABLE YOU TO 154 MANSNS
PROVIDE VERY MODERATE COMFORT
AS TO EXPECT YOU TO LIVE ON YOUR SALARY$ 381 MARCOM
MY SALARY WILL GO FARTHER NOW... 22 STRANG

SALE
IS ALL THE MONEY FROM THE SALE OF THE HOUSE GONE$ 271 GGBROW
IN LIFE, YOU WANTED TO BELIEVE EVERY MAN WAS A 34 JOURNE
KNAVE WITH HIS SOUL FOR SALE.
SO PROUD AND HAPPY BECAUSE HE'S BEAT SOMEONE ON A 20 MANSNS
SALE.
WHICH IS NOT YET FOR SALE, ALTHOUGH I MIGHT 142 MANSNS
CONSIDER--
HE SAID HE TOLD THE AGENT TO TELL WHOEVER IT WAS 32 MISBEG
THE PLACE WASN'T FOR SALE.
THAT LOOKS AS IF IT HAD BEEN PICKED UP AT A FIRE 71 MISBEG
SALE.
SECOND, THE SALE IS MADE. 84 MISBEG

SALES
SHE WAS A SALES GIRL IN SOME PUNK DEPARTMENT 23 HUGHIE
STORE.
I GOT MY KNACK OF SALES GAB FROM HIM, TOO. 622 ICEMAN
BE GOD, IT LOOKS LIKE HE'S GOING TO MAKE TWO SALES626 ICEMAN
OF HIS PEACE AT LEAST/

SALESMAN
(THE VOICE OF THE SALESMAN, WHO HAS JUST COME IN 239 AHWILD
THE BAR, CALLS HEY/
THE BARTENDER NODS TOWARD BELLE, GIVING THE 244 AHWILD
SALESMAN A WINK.
(TURNS TO SCOWL AT THE SALESMAN--THEN TO BELLE) 244 AHWILD
BARTENDER AND THE SALESMAN APPEAR JUST INSIDE THE 244 AHWILD
SWINGING DOOR.
THE SALESMAN GRINS AND COMES INTO THE ROOM, 244 AHWILD
CARRYING HIS HIGHBALL IN HIS HAND.
(SHE TAKES HIS ARM FROM AROUND HER AND GOES TO SIT245 AHWILD
BY THE SALESMAN.
(REGARDS HER BITTERLY--THEN STARTS TO HIS FEET 246 AHWILD
BELLIGERENTLY--TO THE SALESMAN)
LET US JOIN IN PRAYER THAT HICKEY, THE GREAT 596 ICEMAN
SALESMAN.
I'M A GOOD SALESMAN-- 624 ICEMAN
I GUESS I TAKE AFTER HIM, AND THAT'S WHAT MADE ME 709 ICEMAN
A GOOD SALESMAN.
HE WAS SELLING DEATH TO ME, THAT CRAZY SALESMAN. 721 ICEMAN

SALESMAN'S
HIS EXPRESSION IS FIXED IN A SALESMAN'S WINNING 618 ICEMAN
SMILE

SALESMAN'S (CONT'D.)
HE HAS THE SALESMAN'S MANNERISMS OF SPEECH, AN 619 ICEMAN
EASY FLOW OF GLIB,
(TAKING ON A SALESMAN'S PERSUASIVENESS) 622 ICEMAN
(WITH A SALESMAN'S PERSUASIVENESS) 641 ICEMAN
HE HAS LOST HIS BEAMING SALESMAN'S GRIN. 703 ICEMAN

SALLOW
HIS FACE IS LONG, BONY, AND SALLOW, WITH DEEP-SET 556 CROSS
BLACK EYES.
HIS UNSHAVEN CHEEKS ARE SUNKEN AND SALLOW. 553 DAYS
HE IS IN THE FIFTIES, AS IS HIS WIFE, A SALLOW, 68 ELECTR
FLABBY,
BUT HIS BODY IS THIN AND HIS SWARTHY COMPLEXION 73 ELECTR
SALLOW.
HIS FACE IS LONG AND NARROW, GREASY WITH 8 HUGHIE
PERSPIRATION, SALLOW,
ON THE CLERK'S GLISTENING, SALLOW FACE. 27 HUGHIE
HE SEEMS MUCH THINNER, HIS FACE DRAWN AND SALLOW. 67 STRANG
HAEDA IS A LITTLE, SALLOW-FACED BLONDE. 499 VOYAGE

SALLOWNESS
HIS SKIN, IN SPITE OF BEING SUNBURNED A DEEP 20 JOURNE
BROWN, HAS A PARCHED SALLOWNESS.

SALOON
SCENE---JOHNNY-THE-PRIEST'S= SALOON NEAR SOUTH 3 ANNA
STREET, NEW YORK CITY.
I CAN REMEMBER WHEN MEN FROM THE CORNER SALOON 25 ELECTR
WOULD DRAG HIM HOME
I'D EXPECT A MAN WITH YOUR VOICE WOULD BE IN A 106 ELECTR
SALOON, SINGING AND MAKING MERRY/
RETURNING FROM HIS NIGHTLY VISIT TO THE SALOON.) 123 ELECTR
THE BACK ROOM AND A SECTION OF THE BAR OF HARRY 573 ICEMAN
HOPE'S SALOON.
IT'S THE NO CHANCE SALOON. 587 ICEMAN

SALT
SHE SAYS SALT WATER'S THE ONLY THING THAT REALLY 230 AHWILD
HELPS HER BUNION.
A TYPICAL OLD SALT, LOUD OF VOICE AND GIVEN TO 94 BEYOND
GESTURE.
TELL HIM TO SALT DE TAIL UF DAT EAGLE/ 242 HA APE
AS I'VE TOLD YOU BEFORE, YOU MUST TAKE HER 137 JOURNE
MEMORIES WITH A GRAIN OF SALT.
AS I WAS SAYING, YOU MUST TAKE HER TALES OF THE 138 JOURNE
PAST WITH A GRAIN OF SALT.

SALTCELLAR
KNIVES, SPOONS, SALTCELLAR, ETC. 96 POET

SALTINES
(AS NORAH COMES BACK WITH A DISH OF SALTINES-- 223 AHWILD

SALTS
YOU'LL TAKE A GOOD DOSE OF SALTS TOMORROW MORNING 271 AHWILD
AND NO NONSENSE ABOUT IT/
(SARDONICALLY) HE GAVE HIM A DOSE OF SALTS, NA 480 CARDIF
DOUT$
MID TEN DOCTORS AND NURSES FEEDIN' HER SALTS TO 232 HA APE
CLEAN THE FEAR OUT OF HER.

SALUTATION
THAT WHEN MEETING A PRINCE THE CUSTOMARY 595 ICEMAN
SALUTATION IS =WHAT'LL YOU HAVE$=
ALL BOW AND THEY RETURN THIS SALUTATION.) 427 MARCOM

SALUTE
I HAVEN'T HEARD THE FORT FIRING A SALUTE. 18 ELECTR
THAT'S THE SALUTE TO HIS HOMECOMING/ 42 ELECTR
(STARTS UP FROM HIS CHAIR AND MAKES AN AUTOMATIC 83 ELECTR
MOTION AS IF TO SALUTE--
(AUTOMATICALLY MAKES A CONFUSED MOTION OF MILITARY122 ELECTR
SALUTE--VAGUELY)
SALUTE/ 208 HA APE
HAIL, LOVE, WE WHO HAVE DIED, SALUTE YOU/ 188 STRANG

SALUTED
BEING SALUTED BY THE YOUNG MASTER--THEN ADDS 261 GGBROW
LIGHTLY)

SALUTES
(FLAVIUS SALUTES AND HASTENS TO THE VILLA. 327 LAZARU
(COMES UP AND SALUTES) WE CANNOT GET THREE OF 353 MARCOM
THEM UP, SIR.
MARCO HALTS AS HE SEES CHU-YIN, SALUTES 402 MARCOM
CONDESCENDINGLY,

SALUTING
(SALUTING LAZARUS) HAIL, VICTOR/ 320 LAZARU
(SALUTING CALIGULA--WITH AN AWED GLANCE AT 327 LAZARU
LAZARUS)
SALUTING HIM AS IF IN SPITE OF THEMSELVES.) 334 LAZARU
(RAISING THEIR SPEARS ALOFT AND SALUTING LAZARUS 334 LAZARU
(HE STANDS SALUTING HIMSELF WITH A CRAZY INTENSIT¥370 LAZARU
THAT IS NOT WITHOUT GRANDEUR.

SALVATION
(HE GIVES AN IMITATION OF A SALVATION ARMY DRUM) 232 AHWILD
(HIS VOICE A MOCKING SNEER) AND WHAT SALVATION 501 DAYS
FOR US ARE YOU PREACHING$
THE SALVATION FROM YOURSELF IT HOLDS OUT TO YOU$ 545 DAYS
THERE IS A SALVATION. 201 EJONES
AW NIX ON DAT SALVATION ARMY--SOCIALIST BULL. 212 HA APE
(WITHERINGLY) AW, JOIN DE SALVATION ARMY-- 229 HA APE
DEY'RE IN DE WRONG PEW--DE SAME OLD BULL--SOAP- 250 HA APE
BOXES AND SALVATION ARMY--
SALVATION ARMY, THAT'S WHAT YOU'D OUGHT T'BEEN 602 ICEMAN
GENERAL IN/
IT'S A WONDER HE DIDN'T BORRY A SALVATION ARMY 617 ICEMAN
UNIFORM AND SHOW UP IN THAT/
JOINED THE SALVATION ARMY. AIN'T YOU$ 620 ICEMAN
MY OLD MAN USED TO WHALE SALVATION INTO MY HEINIE 622 ICEMAN
WITH A BIRCH ROD.
I'D GET A LOT OF SPORT OUT OF SELLING MY LINE OF 661 ICEMAN
SALVATION
ALONG THE SAWDUST TRAIL TO SALVATION 661 ICEMAN
BE DRIVEN TO SEEK SPIRITUAL SALVATION SOMEWHERE/ 363 MARCOM
SAID I WAS HIS ONLY HOPE OF SALVATION. 59 STRANG
I SAID TO MYSELF, I'LL BE HIS SALVATION-- 59 STRANG
YOU'RE MY SALVATION/ 473 WELDED

1357 SAME

SAM

AIN'T UNCLE SAM DE SAP TO TRUST GUYS LIKE DAT WID 617 ICEMAN DOUGH/

SAM'LL

AND SAM'LL BE HAPPY/....)) 106 STRANG

SAMARITAN

SURE, THE GOOD SAMARITAN WAS A CROOL HAYTHEN 9 POET BESIDE YOU.

SAME

(THE SAME TONE OF AWE CREEPING INTO HIS VOICE) 536 'ILE AND MAYBE LOSE HER SENSES FOREVER--FOR IT'S SURE 538 'ILE SHE'LL NEVER BE THE SAME AGAIN. THE MATE IS DRESSED ABOUT THE SAME AS THE CAPTAIN.539 'ILE US, AND YOU CAN TELL THE REST THE SAME. 545 'ILE DAY AFTER GRAY DAY AND EVERY DAY THE SAME. 549 'ILE AT THE SAME MOMENT TOMMY APPEARS IN THE DOORWAY 186 AHWILD FROM THE BACK PARLOR-- (TEASINGLY) BET I KNOW, JUST THE SAME/ 187 AHWILD HE IS ABOUT THE SAME AGE AS MILLER 200 AHWILD (WITHOUT TAKING OFFENSE--IN SAME FLAT, BRITTLE 201 AHWILD VOICE) I'D SAY THE SAME ABOUT MY OWN MILDRED, WHO'S THE 202 AHWILD SAME AGE. (A BIT SHAKEN BY THIS THREAT--BUT IN THE SAME FLAT204 AHWILD TONE) A LITTLE AFTER 6 O'CLOCK IN THE EVENING OF THE 210 AHWILD SAME DAY. WE'VE BEEN OVER THIS A THOUSAND TIMES BEFORE AND 213 AHWILD I'LL ALWAYS FEEL THE SAME AS LONG AS SID'S THE SAME. 213 AHWILD AND AS FOR THE CHILDREN, I FEEL THE SAME LOVE FOR 214 AHWILD YOURS AS IF THEY WERE MINE. IT'S THE SAME WITH CLAMS. 231 AHWILD DASHED HIM OFF JUST THE SAME/ 231 AHWILD I'D DO THE SAME THING MYSELF IF I WERE IN HIS 235 AHWILD BOOTS/ BUT AT THE SAME TIME THRILLED AND PROUD OF 236 AHWILD MINGLING WITH THE PACE THAT KILLS. IT IS ABOUT 10 O'CLOCK THE SAME NIGHT. 236 AHWILD BRING US ANOTHER ROUND--THE SAME/ 242 AHWILD GIVE US SOME MORE OF THE SAME/ 246 AHWILD ABOUT 11 O'CLOCK THE SAME NIGHT. 249 AHWILD (SCENE--SAME AS ACT ONE--SITTING-ROOM OF THE 249 AHWILD MILLER HOME-- BUT HE'D WANT TO SEE THE OLD FIREWORKS JUST THE 254 AHWILD SAME. (SCENE--THE SAME--SITTING-ROOM OF THE MILLER 263 AHWILD HOUSE-- BUT IT'S BAD ENOUGH, GOODNESS KNOWS--AND YOU 266 AHWILD PUNISH HIM GOOD JUST THE SAME. (BLINKING--MECHANICALLY) I'LL TAKE THE SAME. 266 AHWILD THE BARTENDER THERE KNEW HE WAS UNDER AGE BUT 267 AHWILD SERVED HIM JUST THE SAME. IT AMOUNTS TO THE SAME THING AND YOU KNOW IT/ 270 AHWILD ABOUT 10 O'CLOCK THE SAME NIGHT. 288 AHWILD THE SAME AS HER MOTHER DID. 291 AHWILD YOU SORT OF FORGET THE MOON WAS THE SAME WAY BACK 297 AHWILD THEN--AND EVERYTHING. SAME HERE. 4 ANNA SAME HERE. 4 ANNA (WITH A LAUGH) SAME OLD YOSIE, EH CHRISS 6 ANNA (WITH A CHUCKLE) HE'S STILL GOT THAT SAME COW 7 ANNA LIVIN' WITH HIM, THE OLD FOOL/ SAME FOR BOTH. 12 ANNA SAME FOR ME. 14 ANNA SAME HERE. 14 ANNA YOU TAKE SAME AS THEY ALL DO. 20 ANNA SAME LIKE YOUR BRO'DERS VAS DROWNED. 27 ANNA YOUR MO'DER SHE TAL YOU SAME TANG IF SHE VAS 28 ANNA ALIVE. IN THIS SAME FOG. 28 ANNA TO HELL WITH THE DRINK--BUT I'LL TAKE IT JUST THE 31 ANNA SAME. THERE'S NOT A MAN IN THE WORLD CAN SAY THE SAME AS 33 ANNA YOU. AND IN AN HOUR WE'LL BE AS OLD FRIENDS AS IF WE 35 ANNA WAS BORN IN THE SAME HOUSE. (IN THE SAME TONE) WHY, SURE. 38 ANNA OH, AY TAL HIM SAME TANG. 43 ANNA BUT YOU KEEP ON TALKING YUST THE SAME. 43 ANNA SHE KNOWS I'M LOVING HER, AND SHE LOVES ME THE 46 ANNA SAME, AND I KNOW IT. (THEN WITH AN AMUSED LAUGH) WELL, TIS A BOLD OLD 50 ANNA MAN YOU ARE JUST THE SAME. HE TAL THE SAME TANG TO GEL EVERY PORT HE GO/ 51 ANNA I'LL BE COMING BACK AT YOU IN A SECOND FOR MORE OF 52 ANNA THE SAME/ SHE DON'T SAY IT YUST THE SAME. 53 ANNA AND I SEEN YOU WAS THE SAME AS ALL THE REST. 59 ANNA WHERE I'D BE GIVING A POWER OF LOVE TO A WOMAN IS 60 ANNA THE SAME AS OTHERS YOU'D MEET SCENE--SAME AS ACT THREE, ABOUT NINE O'CLOCK OF A 63 ANNA FOGGY NIGHT TWO DAYS LATER. BUT I'M GOING FIRST THING TOMORROW, SO IT'LL BE 64 ANNA THE SAME IN THE END. AY DON'T VANT MAKE YOURS DAT VAY, BUT AY DO YUST 65 ANNA SAME. DON'T YOU SEE YOU'RE DOING THE SAME THING YOU'VE 66 ANNA ALWAYS DONE! (IN THE SAME HARD VOICE) WELL, CAN'T YOU TALK! 69 ANNA IT'S THE SAME--OH, THIS IS TOO MUCH/ 72 ANNA (IT SUDDENLY COMES TO HER THAT THIS IS THE SAME 72 ANNA SHIP HER FATHER IS SAILING ON) (IN THE SAME TONE) MY BAG'S PACKED AND I GOT MY 72 ANNA TICKET. (HELPLESSLY) YOU MEAN--YOU'LL BE DOING THE SAME 72 ANNA AGAIN! YOU BEEN DOING THE SAME THING ALL YOUR LIFE. 73 ANNA

SAME

(CONT'D.) IN TALKING THE SAME OLD BULL YOU TALKED TO ME TO 73 ANNA THE FIRST ONE YOU MEET. AND I SUPPOSE 'TIS THE SAME LIES YOU TOLD THEM ALL 73 ANNA BEFORE THAT YOU TOLD TO ME. IT'S QUEER, YES--YOU AND ME SHIPPING ON SAME BOAT 78 ANNA DAT VAY. IMAGINE ME READING POETRY AND PLOWING AT THE SAME 82 BEYOND TIME. INSPIRED BY THE SAME LOVE, WILL TAKE UP THE WORK 84 BEYOND WHERE HE LEAVES OFF. FATHER IS THE SAME. 84 BEYOND SHE'S ABOUT THE SAME. 87 BEYOND (THE SMALL SITTING ROOM OF THE MAYO FARMHOUSE 93 BEYOND ABOUT NINE O'CLOCK SAME NIGHT. AT LEAST, NOT IF HE STILL FEELS THE SAME WAY ABOUT 96 BEYOND IT GUESS THEY WAS ALL THINKIN' ABOUT TOMORROW, SAME 98 BEYOND AS US. (MEANINGLY) AND WHAT YOU WERE HOPING FOR TURNS 101 BEYOND OUT JUST THE SAME ALMOST. (SLYLY AMUSED) IT'S JUST THE SAME WITH ME AS 102 BEYOND 'TWAS WITH YOU, DICK. I'D HAVE TO WAIT JUST THE SAME TC WASH UP AFTER 122 BEYOND YOU. IT'S BUST JUST THE SAME. 123 BEYOND WON'T THEY LAUGH AT YOU JUST THE SAME WHEN YOU'RE 124 BEYOND WORKING FOR TIMMS! IS HE SEASONING HIS HAY WITH RAIN THIS YEAR, SAME 124 BEYOND AS LAST-- THEY SHOUTS. (SHAKING HIS HEAD) BUT JUST THE SAME I DOUBT IF 125 BEYOND HE'LL WANT TO SETTLE DOWN TO A THE THIN, SUDDENLY STRUCK BY THE SAME PREMONITION, 128 BEYOND LISTEN TO IT BREATHLESSLY. THE SAME REASON THAT MADE YOU GO LAST TIME THAT'S 139 BEYOND DRIVING YOU AWAY AGAIN. RUB SHUT ME UP WITH ALMOST THE SAME WORDS WHEN I 139 BEYOND TRIED SPEAKING TO HIM ABOUT IT. FORCES ME TO THE SAME CONCLUSION AS MRS. MAYO'S. 158 BEYOND WE'VE LIVED IN THE SAME HOUSE. 165 BEYOND (SAME AS ACT ONE, SCENE UNE--A SECTION OF COUNTRY 166 BEYOND HIGHWAY. YANK WAS IN THE SAME BOAT WID ME, AND SIVIN MORTAL481 CARDIF DAYS WE DRIFTED PICKED UP WE WERE ON THE SAME DAY WID ONLY YANK IN482 CARDIF HIS SENSES. WHEN I'M HAVIN' THE SAME THOUGHTS MYSELF, TOIME 487 CARDIF AFTHER TOIME. SAME AS LISTENIN' TO THE ORGAN OUTSIDE O' CHURCH 466 CARIBE OF A SUNDAY. AN' PLENTY MORE O' THE SAME IN THE FO'C'S'TLE. 468 CARIBE THEY'RE ALL THE SAME--WHITE, BROWN, YELLER, 'N' 470 CARIBE BLACK. AND THEN THEY MADE A MAP--THE SAME OLD DREAM, YOU 560 CRUSS SEE-- HE WEARS A HEAVY, DOUBLE-BREASTED BLUE COAT, PANTS567 CRUSS OF THE SAME MATERIAL, HIS MASS OF HAIR IS PURE WHITE, HIS BRISTLY 567 CRUSS MUSTACHE THE SAME. FOLLOWED LIKE AN ECHO BY THE SAME HAIL FROM NAT. 569 CRUSS HIS HAIR IS THE SAME--DARK, STREAKED WITH GRAY. 493 DAYS HE IS THE SAME AGE, OF THE SAME HEIGHT AND FIGURE,493 DAYS IS THE SAME IN EVERY DETAIL EXACTLY THE SAME. 493 DAYS THIS VOICE SINGULARLY TONELESS AND COLD BUT AT THE494 DAYS SAME TIME INSISTENT) AT THE SAME TIME HIS FEATURES AUTOMATICALLY ASSUME495 DAYS THE MEANINGLESSLY AFFABLE I STILL FEEL THE SAME ON THAT SUBJECT. 497 DAYS (CONSTRAINED AND AT THE SAME TIME AFFECTIONATE) 500 DAYS I GET THE SAME TALE OF WOE FROM EVERY ONE IN OUR 501 DAYS PART OF THE COUNTRY. WE'VE BEEN THROUGH THE SAME FRIGHTFUL TRIALS. 502 DAYS AND I CAN'T GET IT OUT OF MY HEAD YOU'RE THE SAME 506 DAYS OLD JACK. IT WOULD GIVE ME A CHANCE TO GET YOUR AND ELSA'S 512 DAYS CRITICISMS AT THE SAME TIME. IT IS LATER THE SAME AFTERNOON. 514 DAYS LUCY HILLMAN IS ABOUT THE SAME AGE AS ELSA. 515 DAYS UH, THE SAME PEACEFUL ROUTINE-- 516 DAYS I FELT EXACTLY THE SAME WHEN I FOUND OUT ABOUT NED520 DAYS HOWELL. FACING FRONT, HIS EYES FIXED IN THE SAME COLD 525 DAYS STARE. I FEEL THE SAME WAY. 527 DAYS BUT YOU TELL YOUR STORY JUST THE SAME. 530 DAYS FATHER BAIRD IS THE SAME AS IN ACT ONE. 532 DAYS FATHER BAIRD SITS IN THE SAME ATTITUDE AS HE HAD 541 DAYS IN THE PREVIOUS SCENE. SHE IS STILL STARING BEFORE HER WITH THE SAME 541 DAYS STRANGE FASCINATED DREAD. AND THEY WERE THE SAME AS THOSE IN YOUR STORY. 549 DAYS LOVING, HIS EYES REMAINING FIXED ON ELSA WITH THE 550 DAYS SAME STRANGE LOOK. (STRANGELY SERIOUS AND BITTERLY MOCKING AT THE 550 DAYS SAME TIME) (HIS EYES FIXED ON JOHN'S FACE IN THE SAME STARE--558 DAYS (IN THE SAME LOW TONE, BUT WITH A COLD, DRIVING 561 DAYS INTENSITY) THE SAME LOOK OF OBSESSED RESOLUTION IN HIS EYES, 564 DAYS HE FORCES LUVING BACK.) THEY APPEAR TO PROTECT AND AT THE SAME TIME 202 DESIRE SUBDUE. (IN SAME TONE) BACON'S BACON/ 206 DESIRE ROAD--IN THE SAME NIGHT. 211 DESIRE (THE SAME) WALL..../ 213 DESIRE I BEGUN, T' BELLER LIKE A CALF AN' CUSS AT THE SAME214 DESIRE TIME. I WAS SO DURN MAD-- (SAME AS SCENE TWO-- 216 DESIRE

SAME 1358

SAME (CONT'D.)
SIMEON GOES THE SAME)
(THE SAME) AY-EH.
AND ABOUT HER WHOLE PERSONALITY THE SAME
UNSETTLED, UNTAMED,
SIMEON GOES THE SAME.)
I'D FEEL THE SAME AT ANY STRANGER COMIN' T' TAKE
MY MAW'S PLACE.
AMUSED, BUT AT THE SAME TIME PIQUED AND IRRITATED. 228 DESIRE
I'LL KISS YE PURE, EBEN--SAME 'S IF I WAS A MAW T'243 DESIRE
YE--
YE'RE RIGHT JIST THE SAME, FIDDLER.
AT THE SAME MOMENT THAT HE REACHES THE CRADLE
AT THE SAME MOMENT, ABBIE COMES OUT ON THE PORCH. 255 DESIRE
SO'S EVERYTHIN' COULD BE JEST THE SAME WITH US,
LOVIN' EACH OTHER JEST THE SAME.
I SEE YEW GAME NOW--THE SAME OLD SNEAKIN' TRICK-- 261 DESIRE
SAME AS SCENE THREE.
YE'D OUGHT T' BE BOTH HUNG ON THE SAME LIMB AN'
LEFT THAR T' SWING IN THE BREEZE
GOODNESS ME, HOW WOULD MA AND ME EVER HAVE LIVED 495 DIFRNT
IN THE SAME HOUSE WITH THEM TWO
YOU'RE DIFFERENT JUST THE SAME.
NOT JUST THE SAME AS ALL THE OTHER GIRLS
HEREABOUTS!
BUT LOTS AND LOTS OF THE OTHERS DOES THE SAME
THING WITHOUT THINKING NOTHING
SAME AS I DID YOU.
BUT THEY'D CHANGE THEIR MINDS IF THEY HAD TO LIVE 499 DIFRNT
IN THE SAME HOUSE WITH YOU
A GOOD LOT ON 'EM 'D BE ON'Y TOO DAMN GLAD TO GIT 499 DIFRNT
ME IN THE SAME HOUSE--
SAME AS THEY ALWAYS DOES--
YOU'LL FIND OUT CALEB'LL TURN OUT THE SAME.
(SOMEWHAT IMPATIENTLY) WALL, IF HE AIN'T, HE'S A 512 DIFRNT
GOOD MAN JEST THE SAME.
(IN THE SAME COLD TONE) YES.
I KNOW THAT MUST ANY MAN WOULD DO THE SAME.
(SCENE--THIRTY YEARS AFTER--THE SCENE IS THE SAME 519 DIFRNT
BUT NOT THE SAME.
AND AT THE SAME TIME IRRITATING AND DISGUSTING--
BUT IT AIN'T FAIR JUST THE SAME.
YOU'RE A WORTHLESS LOAFER, BENNY ROGERS, SAME AS
YOUR PA WAS.
YOU'VE GOT THE SAME FILTHY MIND YOUR PA HAD.
WELL, HE HOPES JUST THE SAME.
HE WEARS DARK CLOTHES, MUCH THE SAME AS HE WAS
DRESSED IN ACT ONE.)
SAME AS THEY WAS.
YOU'RE THE SAME AS ME, I RECKON.
BUT IT RILED ME JEST THE SAME.
CAN'T I CARE FOR HIM SAME AS ANY WOMAN CARES FOR A542 DIFRNT
MAN?
HIS EYES ARE LARGE, SHY AND SENSITIVE, OF THE SAME422 DYNAMO
BLUE-GRAY AS HIS FATHERS.
IN THE SAME WALL, TO THE REAR OF THE BED, IS THE 428 DYNAMO
DOOR.
THESE WINDOWS ARE REPEATED IN THE SAME SERIES IN
THE BEDROOM ABOVE.
(WITH A CHUCKLE) HIM ARGUING WITH ME AND AT THE
SAME TIME ADMITTING = FIFF,
(THEY'RE ALL THE SAME, THE FIBLE-PUNCHING BREED)
WHY DON'T WE WALK THE SAME AS--
(BUT AS HE DOES SO HIS EYE LIGHTS ON THE SAME
HEADLINE THAT HAD ATTRACTED HIS
HOW CAN I THINK IN THE SAME ROOM WITH YOUS
WOULDN'T YOU DO THE SAME IF ADA WAS THE GIRL AND
YOU WAS CLARK?
AT THE SAME MOMENT LIGHT CAN BE DIMLY MADE OUT AS 445 DYNAMO
HE ENTERS REUBEN'S BEDROOM.
HE'S HAD THOSE SAME ARMS HUGGING THAT LITTLE
FILTHPOT THIS VERY EVENING/...!)
AT THE SAME MOMENT THERE IS A GLARING FLASH OF
LIGHTNING AND LIGHT CRINGES BACK
(STARING AFTER HIM WITH THE SAME LOOK OF
DEFIANCE--CALLS JEERINGLY)
THE SAME AS ACT ONE, SCENE ONE.
EACH WITH THE SAME BLASPHEMY...
(WITH THE SAME DETACHED INTEREST)
THE SAME AS THAT NIGHT/...
(THE SAME EXCEPT THAT REUBEN'S BEDROOM IS NOW
REVEALED
IT IS ABOUT HALF PAST ELEVEN ON THE SAME NIGHT--
IF I'D STAYED THE SAME POUR BOOB I USED TO BE YOU 470 DYNAMO
MIGHT HAVE DIED AN OLD MAID.
AT THE SAME TIME TRYING TO REASSURE HERSELF)
IT'S ALL THE SAME THING/...!)
(A PAUSE--THEN HE GOES ON IN THE SAME FASCINATED
TONE)
(SAME AS ACT TWO, SCENE THREE--EXTERIOR OF THE
POWER HOUSE FOUR MONTHS LATER.
DID I TELL YOU THAT OUR BLOOD PLASM IS THE SAME
RIGHT NOW
SHE LOVES HIM THE SAME AS I DID YOU WHEN WE--
STRETCHING HER ARMS UP IN THE SAME POSITION AS THE485 DYNAMO
SWITCH ARMS.)
(IN THE SAME TONE) YES, I SWEAR.
SO I HAS--AND ME MAKIN' LAWS TO STOP IT AT DE
SAME TIME/
LISTENING TO DE WHITE QUALITY TALK, IT'S DAT SAME 178 EJONES
FACT.
BUT I AIN'T TALKIN' WILD JUST DE SAME.
(IN THE SAME TONE--SLIGHTLY BOASTFUL)
(STARTLED TO ALERTNESS, BUT PRESERVING THE SAME
CARELESS TONE)
COMMON DINNER BELL WHICH IS PAINTED THE SAME VIVID182 EJONES
SCARLET AS THE THRONE.
(IN THE SAME MOCKING TONE)

216 DESIRE
218 DESIRE
221 DESIRE

224 DESIRE
225 DESIRE

249 DESIRE
251 DESIRE

258 DESIRE

262 DESIRE
267 DESIRE

495 DIFRNT
496 DIFRNT

497 DIFRNT

498 DIFRNT

502 DIFRNT
512 DIFRNT

514 DIFRNT
516 DIFRNT

520 DIFRNT
523 DIFRNT
529 DIFRNT

529 DIFRNT
533 DIFRNT
535 DIFRNT

535 DIFRNT
536 DIFRNT
539 DIFRNT

428 DYNAMO

429 DYNAMO

431 DYNAMO
433 DYNAMO
434 DYNAMO

434 DYNAMO
440 DYNAMO

446 DYNAMO

448 DYNAMO

449 DYNAMO

454 DYNAMO
456 DYNAMO
458 DYNAMO
463 DYNAMO
468 DYNAMO

468 DYNAMO

471 DYNAMO
474 DYNAMO
474 DYNAMO

476 DYNAMO

477 DYNAMO

479 DYNAMO

485 DYNAMO
177 EJONES

179 EJONES
181 EJONES
182 EJONES

182 EJONES

SAME (CONT'D.)
BUT THERE'S WISHIN'YER LUCK JUST THE SAME.
DAT DAMN DRUM SOUNDS JES' DE SAME--NEARER, EVEN.
AT THE SAME TIME, A LOW MELANCHOLY MURMUR RISES
AMONG THEM.
SMITHERS IS THE SAME AS IN SCENE ONE.
SAME AS SCENE TWO, THE DIVIDING LINE OF THE FOREST202 EJONES
AND PLAIN.
HIS WIFE, LOUISA, IS TALLER AND STOUTER THAN HE
AND ABOUT THE SAME AGE.
WHO IS AT THE SAME TIME DEVOID OF EVIL INTENT,
ARE DIED THAT SAME YEAR
THE MANNINGS GOT SKELETONS IN THEIR CLOSETS SAME AS
OTHERS/.
SHE HAS THE SAME PECULIAR SHADE OF COPPER-GOLD
HAIR
HER HEAD IS THE SAME SIZE AS HER MOTHER'S,
THE SAME PALLOR AND DARK VIOLET-BLUE EYES,
THE SAME SENSUAL MOUTH, THE SAME HEAVY JAW.
ABOVE ALL ONE IS STRUCK BY THE SAME STRANGE,
BUT I'D FORGOTTEN HER JUST THE SAME--
IT IS COLD AND EMOTIONLESS AND HAS THE SAME
STRANGE SEMBLANCE OF A LIFELIKE MASK
BUT ALL THE SAME, THAT'S NOT YOUR REAL REASON FOR
SPARING ME/
UNCONSCIOUSLY HE TAKES THE SAME ATTITUDE AS
MANNON, SITTING ERECT,
(SCENE--THE SAME AS ACT ONE, SCENE ONE--THE
EXTERIOR OF THE MANNON HOUSE.
ACCENTUATES STRANGELY THE RESEMBLANCE BETWEEN
THEIR FACES AND AT THE SAME TIME
ONLY YOUR HAIR IS THE SAME--YOUR STRANGE BEAUTIFUL 52 ELECTR
HAIR I ALWAYS--
(SHE SITS AGAIN IN THE SAME POSITION AS BEFORE.
YOU MURDERED HIM JUST THE SAME--BY TELLING HIM/
THE HOUSE HAS THE SAME STRANGE EERIE APPEARANCE,
(SCENE--THE SAME AS ACTS ONE AND THREE OF
=HOMECOMING=--
SHE IS THE SAME AS IN =HOMECOMING=.
(STRANGELY) THE SAME TRAIN/
HIS MOUTH AND CHIN HAVE THE SAME GENERAL
CHARACTERISTICS AS HIS FATHER'S HAD.
HE IS ABOUT THE SAME HEIGHT AS MANNON AND BRANT,
THE SAME AQUILINE NOSE, HEAVY EYEBROWS, SWARTHY
COMPLEXION.
THERE IS THE SAME LIFELIKE MASK QUALITY OF HIS
FACE IN REPOSE.
ALL THE FACES IN THE PORTRAITS HAVE THE SAME MASK
QUALITY
(WORRIED AND PLEASED AT THE SAME TIME)
YOU'RE THE SAME, HAZEL--SWEET AND GOOD.
HE'S THE SAME AND ALWAYS WILL BE--HERE--THE SAME/
AND ALL THE MOTHERS AND WIVES AND SISTERS AND
GIRLS DID THE SAME/
IT'S FINE TO SEE YOU AGAIN--THE SAME AS EVER/
VINNIE MUST HAVE WRITTEN YOU THE SAME NONSENSE SHE
DID YOUR FATHER.
HE DID, JUST THE SAME/
YOU'VE STILL GOT THE SAME BEAUTIFUL HAIR, MOTHER.
THE SKY HAS THE SAME COLOR AS YOUR EYES.
AT THE SAME MOMENT LAVINIA APPEARS SILENTLY IN THE
DOORWAY FROM THE HALL AND
(SCENE--THE SAME AS ACT TWO OF =HOMECOMING=--EZRA
MANNON'S STUDY.
THE SAME FAMILIAR STRANGER I'VE NEVER KNOWN.
(GOES ON WITH THE SAME AIR)
BEFORE I'D GOTTEN BACK I HAD TO KILL ANOTHER IN
THE SAME WAY.
IT WAS LIKE MURDERING THE SAME MAN TWICE.
I HAD A QUEER FEELING THAT WAR MEANT MURDERING THE
SAME MAN OVER AND OVER.
YOU KNOW IN YOUR HEART I'M THE SAME AS I ALWAYS
WAS--YOUR SISTER--
YOU SEEM THE SAME TO ME IN DEATH, EZRA/
(SCENE--THE SAME AS ACT THREE OF =HOMECOMING=--
EXTERIOR OF THE MANNON HOUSE.
WALL, ALL THE SAME, I WOULDN'T BE IN ABNER'S BOOTS.132 ELECTR
(SAME AS ACT TWO OF =THE HUNTED=--THE SITTING-ROOM139 ELECTR
IN THE MANNON HOUSE.
(GRIMLY) MOTHER FELT THE SAME ABOUT--
AT THE SAME MOMENT SHE SEES HIM.
YOU'RE THE SAME OLD PETER/
NO, YOU'RE THE SAME, THANK GOODNESS/
VINNIE IS THE SAME OLD BOSSY FUSS-BUZZER--YOU
REMEMBER--
(IN A STRAINED VOICE) IT'S THE SAME THING--WHAT
THE WAR DID TO HIM--
(WITH AN APPREHENSIVE GLANCE AT PETER--PLEADING
AND AT THE SAME TIME WARNING)
HE RETURNS IT, AMUSED AND AT THE SAME TIME A
LITTLE SHOCKED BY HER BOLDNESS.
(SCENE--SAME AS ACT THREE OF =THE HUNTED=--EZRA
MANNON'S STUDY--
(THEN WITH A HARSH LAUGH) AND, AT THE SAME TIME, 151 ELECTR
A MILLION TIMES MORE VILE.
I HAVE NO RIGHT IN THE SAME WORLD WITH HER.
(AS IF HE HADN'T HEARD--IN THE SAME SINISTER
MOCKING TONE)
BUT YOU WERE GUILTY IN YOUR MIND JUST THE SAME/
(SCENE--SAME AS ACT ONE, SCENE TWO--THE SITTING-
ROOM.
THE SAME AS EVER, BUT HAZEL'S FACE WEARS A
(SYMPATHETIC AND AT THE SAME TIME EXASPERATED)
BUT SOME STRANGER WITH THE SAME BEAUTIFUL HAIR--
(SCENE--SAME AS ACT ONE, SCENE ONE--EXTERIOR OF
THE HOUSE.

186 EJONES
193 EJONES
199 EJONES

202 EJONES

6 ELECTR

6 ELECTR
8 ELECTR
9 ELECTR

10 ELECTR

10 ELECTR
10 ELECTR
10 ELECTR
10 ELECTR
26 ELECTR
28 ELECTR

33 ELECTR

36 ELECTR

43 ELECTR

45 ELECTR

59 ELECTR
64 ELECTR
67 ELECTR
67 ELECTR

71 ELECTR
72 ELECTR
73 ELECTR

73 ELECTR
73 ELECTR

73 ELECTR

79 ELECTR

80 ELECTR
81 ELECTR
81 ELECTR
82 ELECTR

84 ELECTR
85 ELECTR

86 ELECTR
90 ELECTR
90 ELECTR
93 ELECTR

93 ELECTR

94 ELECTR
95 ELECTR
95 ELECTR

95 ELECTR
95 ELECTR

96 ELECTR

101 ELECTR
117 ELECTR

140 ELECTR
143 ELECTR
143 ELECTR
143 ELECTR
146 ELECTR

146 ELECTR

146 ELECTR

147 ELECTR

149 ELECTR

151 ELECTR
154 ELECTR

155 ELECTR
157 ELECTR

158 ELECTR

159 ELECTR
165 ELECTR
169 ELECTR

SAME

SAME (CONT'D.)
THE MANNON HOUSE HAS MUCH THE SAME APPEARANCE AS 169 ELECTR
IT HAD
(FEELING GUILTY AND AT THE SAME TIME DEFIANT AND 172 ELECTR
SURE SHE IS RIGHT)
AT THE SAME TIME LOOKING AT THE GROUND AROUND HIM 178 ELECTR
THE SAME HEIGHT AS YOUNG BROWN BUT LEAN AND WIRY, 260 GGBROW
WITHOUT REPOSE.
THE SAME COURTROOM EFFECT OF THE ARRANGEMENT OF 269 GGBROW
BENCHES IN ACT ONE IS HELD TO
BUT AT THE SAME TIME, IN SOME QUEER WAY, MORE 269 GGBROW
SELFLESS AND ASCETIC.
BOYISH STILL AND WITH THE SAME ENGAGING 274 GGBROW
PERSONALITY.
BUT I SUPPOSE THE GOSSIPS ARE TELLING THE SAME 276 GGBROW
SILLY STORIES ABOUT HIM THEY
THE SAME SENTIMENTAL MEDLEY BEGINS TO PLAY. 279 GGBROW
THE SAME SENTIMENTAL TUNE STARTS. 280 GGBROW
THE OLD AUTOMATIC PIANO AT CENTER LOOKS EXACTLY 284 GGBROW
THE SAME.
THE ARRANGEMENT OF FURNITURE IS THE SAME 284 GGBROW
THE PIANO IS WHINING OUT ITS SAME OLD SENTIMENTAL 284 GGBROW
MEDLEY.
(IN THE SAME TONE) 285 GGBROW
AT THE SAME MOMENT BROWN ENTERS QUIETLY FROM THE 288 GGBROW
LEFT.
IT IS IN THE EVENING OF THE SAME DAY. 290 GGBROW
(IN SAME TONE) AND I LOVE MARGARET/ 291 GGBROW
WITH MUCH THE SAME QUALITY AS BILLY BROWN'S IN ACT293 GGBROW
ONE, SCENE ONE.
(IN THE SAME AWKWARD, SELF-CONSCIOUS TONE, ONE 293 GGBROW
AFTER ANOTHER)
SCENE--THE LIBRARY OF WILLIAM BROWN'S HOME--NIGHT 294 GGBROW
OF THE SAME DAY.
(MAINTAINING THE SAME INDULGENT, BIG-BROTHERLY 294 GGBROW
TONE)
THEY SAY HE FIRED ALL HIS OLD SERVANTS THAT SAME 302 GGBROW
DAY
THE ARRANGEMENT OF FURNITURE IN EACH ROOM IS THE 302 GGBROW
SAME AS IN PREVIOUS SCENES.
THE LIBRARY OF BROWN'S HOME ABOUT EIGHT THE SAME 306 GGBROW
NIGHT.
SCENE--THE SAME AS ACT TWO, SCENE THREE-- 306 GGBROW
SCENE--THE SAME AS SCENE ONE OF ACT ONE--THE 308 GGBROW
SITTING-ROOM OF MARGARET'S HOME.
AND THEN ALL AT ONCE YOU TURN RIGHT AROUND AND 309 GGBROW
EVERYTHING IS THE SAME AS WHEN WE
SCENE--SAME AS SCENE ONE OF ACT THREE--THE 313 GGBROW
DRAFTING ROOM AND BROWN'S OFFICE.
(IN SAME TONE) I CAN ALMOST HEAR HIM TALKING. 318 GGBROW
SCENE--THE SAME AS SCENE TWO OF ACT THREE--THE 319 GGBROW
LIBRARY OF WILLIAM BROWN'S HOME.
THE SAME SPOT ON THE SAME DOCK AS IN PROLOGUE. 323 GGBROW
AND YET I'M STILL THE SAME MARGARET. 323 GGBROW
KNOWS HER LIFE PURPOSE WELL ACCOMPLISHED BUT IS AT323 GGBROW
THE SAME TIME A BIT EMPTY AND
(REPEATING THE WORD AFTER HIM AS ONE WITH THE SAME210 HA APE
CYNICAL AMUSED MOCKERY)
(IN THE SAME TONE) POSER/ 222 HA APE
YANK SITS DOWN AGAIN IN THE SAME ATTITUDE OF =THE 227 HA APE
THINKER.=
AIN'T SHE DE SAME AS ME. 231 HA APE
THE SAME IN THE FURRIER'S. 233 HA APE
(THE WHOLE CROWD OF MEN AND WOMEN CHORUS AFTER HER238 HA APE
IN THE SAME TONE OF AFFECTED
WHAT WE NEED IS MEN WHO CAN HOLD THEIR JOBS--AND 247 HA APE
WORK FOR US AT THE SAME TIME.
DEY'RE IN DE WRONG PEW--DE SAME OLD BULL--SOAP- 250 HA APE
BOXES AND SALVATION ARMY--
THE SAME ATTITUDE AS RODIN'S =THE THINKER.= 251 HA APE
AIN'T WE BOTH MEMBERS OF DE SAME CLUB--DE HAIRY 252 HA APE
APES?
HE IS ABOUT THE SAME AGE AS THE CLERK 8 HUGHIE
AND HAS THE SAME PASTY, PERSPIRY, NIGHT-LIFE 8 HUGHIE
COMPLEXION.
BUT HE ATE IT UP, JUST THE SAME. 16 HUGHIE
IT AIN'T THE SAME PLACE SINCE HUGHIE WAS TOOK TO 17 HUGHIE
THE HOSPITAL.
YOU GOT THE SAME LOOK ON YOUR MAP. 19 HUGHIE
ALL THE SAME, LIKE I SAID, 20 HUGHIE
I TELL YOU, PAL, I'D RATHER SLEEP IN THE SAME 21 HUGHIE
STALL WITH OLD MAN O' WAR
I'VE SEEN THE SAME LOOK ON GUYS' FACES WHEN THEY 30 HUGHIE
KNEW THEY WAS ON THE SPOT,
IS ABOUT THE SAME SIZE AND AGE AS HUGO, A SMALL 575 ICEMAN
MAN,
AND AT THE SAME TIME OF A LIKABLE, AFFECTIONATE 575 ICEMAN
BOY WHO HAS NEVER GROWN UP.
FADED PINK SHIRT AND BRIGHT TIE BELONG TO THE SAME575 ICEMAN
VINTAGE.
AND I KNOW MY FELLOW INMATES WILL PROMISE THE 578 ICEMAN
SAME.
I SAYS, =HOLD ON, YOU TALK 'S IF ANARCHISTS AND 584 ICEMAN
SOCIALISTS WAS DE SAME.=
I'VE SAID THE SAME THING TO HER LOTS OF TIMES TO 590 ICEMAN
KID HER.
INTERESTED IN SPITE OF HIMSELF AND AT THE SAME 591 ICEMAN
TIME VAGUELY UNEASY.)
(APPEALINGLY) THE SAME AS YOU DID, LARRY. 592 ICEMAN
BUT AT THE SAME TIME SHOWING HIS AFFECTION FOR 593 ICEMAN
THEM)
THE SAME APPLIES TO HARRY HIMSELF AND HIS TWO 594 ICEMAN
CRONIES AT THE FAR TABLE.
(HE NODS AT JOE) JOE HERE HAS A YESTERDAY IN THE 594 ICEMAN
SAME FLUSH PERIOD.
GOOD GOD/ HAVE I BEEN DRINKING AT THE SAME TABLE 598 ICEMAN
WITH A BLOODY KAFFIR/

SAME (CONT'D.)
WELL, YOU CAN TAKE THAT+I'LL- HAVE-THE-SAME= LOOK 598 ICEMAN
OFF YOUR MAPS/
HE SAID, =JIMMY, THE PUBLICITY DEPARTMENT'S NEVER 604 ICEMAN
BEEN THE SAME
(BESIDES, JIMMY'S STARTED THEM OFF SMOKING THE SAME 605 ICEMAN
HOP.
THEIR FACES EXCITED WITH THE SAME EAGER 618 ICEMAN
ANTICIPATION.
HE GREETS EACH BY NAME WITH THE SAME AFFECTIONATE 619 ICEMAN
HEARTINESS.
SAME OLD ROOM. 620 ICEMAN
SAME AS I'VE ALWAYS DONE, AND HELP CELEBRATE YOUR 621 ICEMAN
BIRTHDAY TONIGHT+
I FEEL EXACTLY THE SAME AS I ALWAYS DID. 621 ICEMAN
SAME THING WITH YOU, JIMMY. 622 ICEMAN
AND ALL THE REST OF YOU, LADIES INCLUDED, ARE IN 623 ICEMAN
THE SAME BOAT.
=THE MEMBERS OF THE SAME LODGE--IN SOME WAY. 624 ICEMAN
IT IS GETTING ON TOWARD MIDNIGHT OF THE SAME DAY. 628 ICEMAN
(DOING THE SAME TO PEARL) NIX ON DE ROUGH STUFF, 632 ICEMAN
POLL.
IT'S DE SAME OLD CRAP. 632 ICEMAN
(FURIOUS AND AT THE SAME TIME BEWILDERED BY THEIR 633 ICEMAN
DEFIANCE)
HE LOOKS THE SAME AS IN THE PREVIOUS ACT, 638 ICEMAN
HE'S DE SAME OLD HICKEY. 638 ICEMAN
BUT I DO KNOW A LOT ABOUT HIM JUST THE SAME. 642 ICEMAN
BUT YOU'LL FIND I'M RIGHT JUST THE SAME. 643 ICEMAN
ALL THINGS ARE THE SAME MEANINGLESS JOKE TO ME, 649 ICEMAN
AND IN THE END THEY ROT INTO DUST IN THE SAME 649 ICEMAN
GRAVE.
BUT THE OPPOSITES OF THE SAME STUPIDITY WHICH IS 649 ICEMAN
RULER AND KING OF LIFE,
I'LL HAVE EVERY ONE OF YOU FEELING THE SAME WAY/ 661 ICEMAN
AND EVERY TIME DEY'D CRAWL MY FRAME WID DE SAME 669 ICEMAN
OLD ARGUMENT.
DE SAME OLD STUFF OVER AND OVER/ 671 ICEMAN
SUT'S GO WHITE MAN KICK ABOUT DRINKIN' FROM DE SAME673 ICEMAN
GLASS.
BUT I CAN'T CONTINUE TO LIVE UNDER THE SAME ROOF 675 ICEMAN
WITH THAT FELLOW.
AND BENNY FROM DE MARKET HE PROMISE ME SAME. 676 ICEMAN
(AT THE SAME MOMENT CHUCK GRABS WETJOEN AND YANKS 677 ICEMAN
HIM BACK.)
THE SAME CHANGE WHICH IS APPARENT IN THE MANNER 681 ICEMAN
AND APPEARANCE OF THE OTHERS
UNDER THE SAME ROOF WITH THAT LOON, HICKEY, AND A 682 ICEMAN
LYING CIRCUS GRAFTER/
UH, I'M BOUND TO, OLD CHAP, AND THE SAME TO YOU. 685 ICEMAN
OH, I KNOW IT'S TOUGH ON HIM RIGHT NOW, THE SAME 692 ICEMAN
AS IT IS ON HARRY.
THE ONE AT LEFT, FRONT, BEFORE THE WINDOW TO THE 695 ICEMAN
YARD, IS IN THE SAME POSITION.
(LAPSING INTO THE SAME MOOD) 699 ICEMAN
SUNK IN THE SAME STUPOR AS THE OTHER OCCUPANTS OF 701 ICEMAN
THE ROOM.
AND YOU'VE GOT EVERYBODY ELSE SINGING THE SAME 704 ICEMAN
CRAZY TUNE/
SEIZED BY THE SAME FIT AND POUND WITH THEIR 707 ICEMAN
GLASSES, EVEN HUGO,
HE POURS ANOTHER AND THEY DO THE SAME. 711 ICEMAN
BUT AT THE SAME TIME SICK OF HOME. 712 ICEMAN
THE SAME WAY SHE FORGAVE ME EVERY TIME I'D TURN UP713 ICEMAN
AFTER A PERIODICAL DRUNK.
IT WAS THE SAME OLD STORY, OVER AND OVER, FOR 713 ICEMAN
YEARS AND YEARS.
IF SHE'D BEEN THE SAME KIND OF WIFE I WAS A 714 ICEMAN
HUSBAND,
THE SAME WAY I USED TO JOKE HERE ABOUT HER BEING 714 ICEMAN
IN THE HAY WITH THE ICEMAN.
(AT FIRST WITH THE SAME DEFENSIVE CALLOUSNESS-- 717 ICEMAN
WITHOUT LOOKING AT HIM)
(EAGERLY) SAME WITH ME, JIMMY. 723 ICEMAN
ABOUT A JOB, I FELT THE SAME AS YOU, CECIL. 723 ICEMAN
THE SAME WAY WITH THE CIRCUS. 724 ICEMAN
BUT NOT THE SAME SONG. 727 ICEMAN
WHO IS STILL IN THE SAME POSITION, HEAD ON HANDS, 516 INZONE
DO THE SAME. 518 INZONE
WELL, I BRINGS IT DOWN HERE SAME AS USUAL 518 INZONE
MON, DIDN'T I SEE HIM DO THAT SAME THING WI' THESE519 INZONE
TWO EYES.
(WITH THE SAME ICY CONTEMPT) 525 INZONE
THEY'RE ALL THE SAME AS THE FIRST-- 531 INZONE
THE SAME TIME. 15 JOURNE
WITH THE SAME EXCEPTIONALLY LUNG FINGERS. 20 JOURNE
HIS MOUTH HAS THE SAME QUALITY OF 20 JOURNE
HYPERSENSITIVENESS HERS POSSESSES.
THEY EVEN HAVE TO A MINOR DEGREE THE SAME 20 JOURNE
NERVOUSNESS.
(ALMOST GENTLY.) I'VE FELT THE SAME WAY, PAPA. 37 JOURNE
(SHRUGS HIS SHOULDERS.) THE SAME OLD STUFF. 40 JOURNE
ALL THE SAME, YOU'VE GROWN MUCH TOO THIN. 42 JOURNE
JAMIE AND YOU ARE THE SAME WAY, BUT YOU'RE NOT TO 44 JOURNE
BLAME.
(SCENE THE SAME. 51 JOURNE
WITH A FOND SOLICITUDE WHICH IS AT THE SAME TIME 67 JOURNE
REMOTE.)
(SCENE THE SAME, ABOUT A HALF HOUR LATER. 71 JOURNE
YET AT THE SAME TIME, IN CONTRAST TO THIS, 71 JOURNE
AND YET IT WAS EXACTLY THE SAME TYPE OF CHEAP 74 JOURNE
QUACK WHO FIRST GAVE YOU THE
THERE'LL BE THE SAME DRIFTING AWAY FROM US UNTIL 78 JOURNE
BY THE END OF EACH NIGHT--
I'D BETTER DO THE SAME OR I'LL BE LATE FOR MY 82 JOURNE
APPOINTMENT AT THE CLUB.
THE SAME OLD WASTE THAT WILL LAND ME IN THE 84 JOURNE
POORHOUSE IN MY OLD AGE/

SAME

SAME (CONT'D.)
AND AT THE SAME TIME I WILL LAUGH BECAUSE I WILL 94 JOURNE
BE SO SURE OF MYSELF.
ISCENE THE SAME. 97 JOURNE
(VAGUELY RESENTFUL) WELL, HE'S A FINE, HANDSOME,101 JOURNE
KIND GENTLEMAN JUST THE SAME,
AT THE SAME TIME HE WAS SIMPLE, AND KIND, AND 105 JOURNE
UNASSUMING.
EUGENE WAS THE SAME, TOO, HAPPY AND HEALTHY, 109 JOURNE
ALL THE SAME THERE'S TRUTH IN YOUR MOTHER'S 109 JOURNE
WARNING.
(HE PAUSES--THEN GOES ON WITH THE SAME 111 JOURNE
DETACHMENT.)
YOU DID THE SAME THING WITH ME. 111 JOURNE
THEN SHE COMES BACK AND SITS IN HER CHAIR, THE 121 JOURNE
SAME BLANK LOOK ON HER FACE.)
ISCENE THE SAME. 125 JOURNE
HE WAS A RENEGADE BUT A CATHOLIC JUST THE SAME. 127 JOURNE
BUT THE FINAL CURTAIN WILL BE IN THE POORHOUSE 128 JOURNE
JUST THE SAME.
(IMPRESSED AND AT THE SAME TIME REVOLTED.) 131 JOURNE
HE KNEW HIM AND LITTLE OLD NEW YORK JUST THE SAME.133 JOURNE
I'VE DONE THE SAME DAMNED THING. 135 JOURNE
DOESN'T SHE DO THE SAME WITH ME 137 JOURNE
AT THE SAME TIME CRYING POORHOUSE AND MAKING IT 140 JOURNE
PLAIN YOU WANTED A CHEAP ONE/
I MIGHT SAY THE SAME OF YOU. 143 JOURNE
OR LYING ALONG ON A BEACH, I HAVE HAD THE SAME 151 JOURNE
EXPERIENCE.
I KNOW THAT'S NOT YOUR FAULT, BUT ALL THE SAME, 166 JOURNE
GOD DAMN YOU,
HIS FACE IS SICK AND DISGUSTED BUT AT THE SAME 167 JOURNE
TIME PITYING.
WHY DON'T YOU DO THE SAME, EDMUND? 169 JOURNE
SHE'S OLD AND A LITTLE CRANKY, BUT I LOVE HER JUST171 JOURNE
THE SAME.
ALL THE SAME, I DON'T THINK SHE WAS SO 175 JOURNE
UNDERSTANDING THIS TIME.
-AND THERE IS THE SAME ETERNAL LIFE IN YES? 279 LAZARU
(IN THE SAME MANNER) HA-HA-- 282 LAZARU
BETWEEN THE TWO HOSTILE GROUPS IS THE SAME CHORUS 282 LAZARU
OF OLD MEN.
AT THE SAME MOMENT THE CHORUS OF FOLLOWERS APPEARS285 LAZARU
ON THE ROOF
THE SAME FORMULA OF SEVEN PERIODS, SEVEN TYPES, 291 LAZARU
(WITH THE SAME SMILE) THE SWORD, MY OLD HYENA/ 301 LAZARU
MOB IS THE SAME EVERYWHERE, EAGER TO WORSHIP ANY 302 LAZARU
NEW CHARLATAN/
AT THE SAME TIME THE DISTANT SOUND OF EXULTANT 304 LAZARU
MUSIC.
IN THE SAME PERIOD AND TYPE AS IN THE PRECEDING 306 LAZARU
SCENE, EXCEPT THAT
LAZARUS LOOKS AT THEM, SEEMING TO SEE EACH AND ALL307 LAZARU
AT THE SAME TIME.
MIRIAM IS BESIDE HIM, DRESSED IN BLACK, SMILING 307 LAZARU
THE SAME SAD TENDER SMILE,
REFINED IN THEM MY NOBILITY OF BLOOD BUT AT THE 312 LAZARU
SAME TIME WITH STRENGTH
(WITH THE SAME JOYOUS INTOXICATION AS THE 322 LAZARU
SOLDIERS)
WHILE AT THE SAME TIME PERVASELY EXCITED AND 326 LAZARU
ELATED BY HIS OWN MORBID TENSION.
A SQUAD OF THE GUARD IN THE SAME UNIFORMS AS THE 326 LAZARU
CHORUS.
THEIR MASKS ARE THE SAME AS THE LEGIONARY CHORUS 326 LAZARU
OF THE PREVIOUS SCENE.
AT THE SAME INSTANT, LAZARUS BEGINS TO LAUGH, 333 LAZARU
SOFTLY AND AFFECTIONATELY.
THE SAME AS PREVIOUS SCENE--THE SAME NIGHT A SHORT350 LAZARU
WHILE LATER.
OUT AT THE SAME TIME RETAINING THE ALOOF SERENITY 350 LAZARU
OF THE STATUE OF A GOD.
OR HE WHO SEEK IT ARE, WHICH COMES TO THE SAME 351 LAZARU
THING.
THAT THE MIND GOES ON ETERNALLY THE SAME-- 353 LAZARU
THE GODS GRANT MEW DO THE SAME FOR HIM/ 357 LAZARU
HIS BREATH IN THE SAME AIR SUFFOCATES ME/ 357 LAZARU
IT IS JUST BEFORE DAWN OF THE SAME NIGHT. 363 LAZARU
IN THE SAME FRENZY OF DISAPPOINTMENT, WITH ALL 366 LAZARU
SORTS OF GROTESQUE AND OBSCENE
ALL THE SAME, I KILLED HIM AND I PROVED THERE IS 371 LAZARU
DEATH/
BUT WHAT I'VE SAID IS TRUE ALL THE SAME/ 21 MANSNS
AND AT THE SAME TIME PATHETICALLY CONFUSED.) 26 MANSNS
(FORCING A SMILE--CONTEMPTUOUS AND AT THE SAME 38 MANSNS
TIME AFFECTIONATE.)
IN HER PLACE, I WOULD FEEL THE SAME. 39 MANSNS
BUT IT STILL HAS THE SAME GENERAL EFFECT OF LOOSE- 43 MANSNS
JOINTED, BIG-BONED LEANNESS.
THE WAY HE DREADS THE THOUGHT OF LIVING IN THE 66 MANSNS
SAME HOUSE WITH ME/
HAVE TO LIVE TOGETHER IN THE SAME HOME DAY AFTER 67 MANSNS
DAY,
AND I BECOME EMPTY, BUT AT THE SAME TIME RESTLESS 72 MANSNS
AND AIMLESS.
BUT AT THE SAME TIME BY BECOMING SARA, LEAVE ME 73 MANSNS
LIFELESS.
IS STILL EXCEEDINGLY PRETTY, STRONG AND HEALTHY, 75 MANSNS
WITH THE SAME FIRM,
AND AT THE SAME TIME AMUSED AND CURIOUSLY 90 MANSNS
FASCINATED AND DELIGHTED.)
(PITYINGLY, BUT AT THE SAME TIME SCORNFULLY.) 93 MANSNS
ISCENE SAME AS SCENE TWO OF ACT ONE. 95 MANSNS
THE GARDEN HAS THE SAME APPEARANCE AS BEFORE 95 MANSNS
YET, AT THE SAME TIME, HE FELT SHE WAS NOT LYING, 111 MANSNS
AND HE WAS AFRAID.
IT IS AROUND NINE O'CLOCK AT NIGHT OF THE SAME 117 MANSNS
DAY.

SAME (CONT'D.)
I HAVE THE SAME SUSPICION MYSELF, DEBORAH. 131 MANSNS
HE DID THE SAME WITH ME. 131 MANSNS
ISCENE SAME AS SCENE ONE OF ACT TWO--SIMON'S 139 MANSNS
PRIVATE OFFICE.
HE IS THE SAME IN APPEARANCE, RETAINS THE 139 MANSNS
HE TRIES TO REPRESS, WHICH FASCINATES AND AT THE 140 MANSNS
SAME TIME HUMILIATES HIM.
YET AT THE SAME TIME SHE IS A PREY TO A PASSIONATE161 MANSNS
ANGER
IT IS AROUND NINE O'CLOCK THE SAME NIGHT. 161 MANSNS
THE SAME EXPRESSION OF HORRIFIED EAGERNESS ON HER 161 MANSNS
FACE.)
ISCENE SAME AS SCENE TWO OF ACT TWO-- 161 MANSNS
AND AT THE SAME TIME BAFFLED AND PANIC-STRICKEN.) 171 MANSNS
(GOES ON IN THE SAME TONE OF TENSE QUIET.) 179 MANSNS
(CRUELLY SCORNFUL AND AT THE SAME TIME UNEASY.) 187 MANSNS
THE SAME SWEET SAD MUSIC COMES FROM THE TREE AGAIN354 MARCOM
AS IF ITS SPIRIT WERE PLAYING
MAFFEU, MARCO'S UNCLE, IS AROUND THE SAME AGE, 358 MARCOM
EVIDENTLY OF THE SAME NATURE, PASSES BETWEEN THEM.365 MARCOM
THE SAME INTERPLAY GOES ON WITH THEM 370 MARCOM
AT THE SAME MOMENT TWO MERCHANTS, THIS TIME 370 MARCOM
BUDDHISTS, COME IN.
(TAKING UP THE READING FROM HIS BOOK IN THE SAME 370 MARCOM
TONE)
(THE PROSTITUTE, THE SAME BUT NOW IN INDIAN GARB, 371 MARCOM
THEY EAT THE SAME AS WE DO. 372 MARCOM
THE TWO TARTAR MERCHANTS ENTER AND THERE IS THE 374 MARCOM
SAME PANTOMIME OF GREETING
AS A CHILD MIGHT, BUT AT THE SAME TIME THERE IS 382 MARCOM
SOMETHING WARPED, DEFORMED--
I GRIEVE FOR THE DAYS WHEN WE LINGERED TOGETHER IN1384 MARCOM
THIS SAME GARDEN,
AT THE SAME MOMENT, NICOLO AND MAFFEO POLO ENTER 390 MARCOM
CEREMONIOUSLY FROM THE RIGHT.
(FLATTERED BUT AT THE SAME TIME NONPLUSSED) 393 MARCOM
IT'S THE SAME POWDER THEY'VE BEEN USING HERE IN 395 MARCOM
CHILDREN'S FIRE WORKS.
PLAYING THE SAME MARTIAL AIR AS IN THE PREVIOUS 402 MARCOM
SCENE.
AND LET PEOPLE KNOW SHE'S LEAVING AT THE SAME 403 MARCOM
TIME,
AND YOU'LL BE QUEEN JUST THE SAME, THAT'S THE MAIN410 MARCOM
THING.
(IN THE SAME FALSE VOICE) OUR GUESTS LOOK 429 MARCOM
THIRSTY.
HERE THE KAAN MAKES THE SAME BARELY PERCEPTIBLE 433 MARCOM
SIGN OF COMMAND AGAIN.
AT THE SAME INSTANT, FROM OUTSIDE, AT FIRST FAINT,433 MARCOM
THE SAME PATH ALSO EXTENDS LEFT TO JOIN A DIRT 1 MISBEG
ROAD WHICH LEADS UP FROM THE
THE SAME IS TRUE OF HER LEGS. 1 MISBEG
THAT'S WHY I'M HELPING YOU, THE SAME AS I HELPED 7 MISBEG
THOMAS AND JOHN.
(AMUSED) YOU'VE THE SAME BAD LUCK IN SONS I HAVE 16 MISBEG
IN BROTHERS.
THE CHUCKLES) SINCE YOU'VE GROWN UP, I'VE HAD THE 18 MISBEG
SAME TROUBLE.
UH, THE SAME AS EVER-- 18 MISBEG
I'LL KEEP THINKING IT OVER, AND YOU DO THE SAME. 30 MISBEG
YOU'RE A TERRIBLE BLARNEYING LIAR, JIM, BUT THANK 43 MISBEG
YOU JUST THE SAME.
SHE LOOKS STARTLED AND CONFUSED, STIRRED AND AT 51 MISBEG
THE SAME TIME FRIGHTENED.
HER BODY STIFF FROM SITTING LONG IN THE SAME 71 MISBEG
POSITION.
ISCENE.- THE SAME, WITH THE WALL OF THE LIVING 71 MISBEG
ROOM REMOVED.
BUT AT THE SAME TIME ARE ABLE TO PULL THEMSELVES 72 MISBEG
TOGETHER WHEN THEY WISH AND BE
BUT ALL THE SAME THERE'S THINGS BESIDES YOUR 89 MISBEG
BEAUTIFUL SOUL HE FEELS DRAWN TO.
HE SEEMS MUCH THE SAME AS IN ACT ONE. 100 MISBEG
UNEASINESS, EVERYTHING IS THE SAME, 111 MISBEG
WITH THE SAME STRANGE AIR OF ACTING UNCONSCIOUSLY1122 MISBEG
ALL THE SAME I'LL BE GOOD AND SORE, JOSIE. 133 MISBEG
BECAUSE YOU AND I BELONG TO THE SAME CLUB. 135 MISBEG
(IN THE SAME LISTLESS MONOTONE) 144 MISBEG
HIS FACE HAS THE SAME EXHAUSTED, DEATH-LIKE 157 MISBEG
REPOSE.
SHE GOES ON IN THE SAME TONE, WITHOUT LOOKING AT 157 MISBEG
HIM)
JOSIE SITS IN THE SAME POSITION ON THE STEPS, AS 157 MISBEG
IF SHE HAD NOT MOVED.
HE'D GO BACK TO BROADWAY JUST THE SAME AND NEVER 164 MISBEG
SEE ME AGAIN.
SAME OLD STUFF. 165 MISBEG
I'LL NEVER BE THE SAME. 166 MISBEG
THERE'D NEVER BE THE SAME FUN OR EXCITEMENT. 177 MISBEG
IT'S THE SAME YOU WAS DRINKING LAST NIGHT---HIS 9 POET
PRIVATE DEW.
BUT HE WAS ASHAMED OF HER IN HIS PRIDE AT THE SAME 14 POET
TIME
GIVES HER MOTHER AN IMPATIENT BUT AT THE SAME TIME 21 POET
WORRIED GLANCE.
FOR THERE'S THE SAME DIVIL OF PRIDE IN YOU THAT'S 25 POET
IN HIM.
IT'S TRUE, JUST THE SAME. 27 POET
THE SAME AS YOUR FATHER. 30 POET
BUT I'LL NOT SINK TO DINING AT THE SAME TABLE. 39 POET
ISCENE SAME AS ACT ONE. 57 POET
HE SITS IN THE SAME CHAIR AND PICKS UP THE PAPER, 59 POET
IGNORING HER.
(AFTER A PAUSE--TIMIDLY.) ALL THE SAME, YOU 62 POET
SHOULDN'T TALK TO SARA
IN THE SAME MANNER AS HE DID AT THE BEGINNING OF 66 POET
THE ACT.

SAME

SAME (CONT'D.)
THERE IS THE SAME SOUND OF VOICES FROM THE BAR 66 POET
THERE IS THE SAME SQUARING OF HIS SHOULDERS, 67 POET
ARROGANT LIFTING OF HIS HEAD,
IT IS THE SAME SORT OF PLEASURE A LOVER OF 69 POET
HORSFLESH WOULD HAVE
AND AT THE SAME TIME HOPEFUL. 85 POET
(SCENE THE SAME. 95 POET
ALL THE SAME, I THANK YOU FOR YOUR TOAST. 101 POET
HE SAID HIS MOTHER HAD TOLD HIM THE SAME THING. 108 POET
AND THE SAME WORRY AND SORROW. 130 POET
(SCENE THE SAME. 133 POET
IT LOOKS GENTLE AND CALM AND AT THE SAME TIME 136 POET
DREAMILY HAPPY AND EXULTANT.
ALL THE SAME, I WON'T STAY HERE THE HIST OF THE 138 POET
NIGHT
(SHE SITS DOWN IN THE SAME CHAIR.) 139 POET
WOULDN'T YOU HAVE SAID THE SAME-- 149 POET
IT'S THE SAME CRAZY BLATHER HE'S TALKED EVERY ONCE158 POET
IN A WHILE
ALL THE SAME, IT'S NO FUN LISTENING TO HIS MAD 161 POET
BLATHER ABOUT THE PALE BITCH,
OH, IT'S THE SAME CRAZY NOTION HE'S HAD EVER SINCE582 ROPE
LUKE LEFT.
(CAUTIOUSLY) OH, THE SAME AS IVIR--OLDER AN' 592 ROPE
UGLIER, MAYBE,
(HE SHAKES HIS HEAD DOUBTFULLY, AT THE SAME TIME 593 ROPE
FIXING LUKE WITH A KEEN GLANCE
THIS SAME NIGHT, WITH NO LONG WAITS, EITHER/ 598 ROPE
(WITH THE SAME COLD CALCULATING FINALITY) 17 STRANG
(IN THE SAME VOICE AS BEFORE) 20 STRANG
THE SAME AS SCENE ONE, PROFESSOR LEEDS' STUDY. 24 STRANG
(IN SAME TONES) IT'S TOO BAD. 27 STRANG
ROOMED IN THE SAME DORM WITH ME AT COLLEGE. 30 STRANG
THEN SHE BEGAN TO BLAME HERSELF AND TO WANT TO ' 35 STRANG
SACRIFICE HERSELF AND AT THE SAME
DARRELL MOVES BACK AND TO ONE SIDE UNTIL HE IS 39 STRANG
STANDING IN RELATIVELY THE SAME
THEY HERE ALL THE SAME. 45 STRANG
THAT LEADS TO A HALL OPENING ON THE SAME PORCH. 48 STRANG
AND, AT THE SAME TIME, THE GRIMMEST... 53 STRANG
YOU GIVE YOUR LIFE TO SAMMY, THEN YOU'LL LOVE HIM 62 STRANG
SAME AS YOU LOVE YOURSELF.
YES, SAMMY'S THE SAME. 64 STRANG
BUT I'M NOT THE SAME AS YOU. 64 STRANG
AND SAMMY'S THE SAME. 64 STRANG
THE TABLE, ALTHOUGH IT IS THE SAME, IS NO LONGER 66 STRANG
THE PROFESSOR'S TABLE,
STILL, NINA INSISTED ON GOING THAT SAME DAY AND 68 STRANG
MOTHER SEEMED ANXIOUS TO GET RID
SAME OLD UNJUST ACCUSATION/ 79 STRANG
(IN SAME TONE) KNOW WHATS 82 STRANG
(THINKING WITH THE SAME EAGERNESS TO BELIEVE 82 STRANG
SOMETHING HE HOPES)
(WITH THE SAME MONOTONOUS INSISTENCE) 84 STRANG
(IN THE SAME INSISTENT TONE) 85 STRANG
(IN SAME TONE) AND THE MAN SHOULD HAVE A MIND 88 STRANG
THAT CAN TRULY UNDERSTAND--
(IN SAME TONE) THE MAN SHOULD LIKE AND ADMIRE 88 STRANG
HER,
THE ARRANGEMENT OF THE FURNITURE FOLLOWS THE SAME 90 STRANG
PATTERN AS IN PRECEDING
A SOFA COVERED WITH THE SAME CHINTZ AT RIGHT. 90 STRANG
(STARES AFTER HIM DUMBLY IN THE SAME STATE OF 107 STRANG
HAPPY STUPEFACTION--MUMBLES)
(IN SAME TONE) NED LIED TO YOU/ 108 STRANG
THE SAME--AN EVENING A LITTLE OVER A YEAR LATER. 111 STRANG
TO THE SAME NOWHERE/... 123 STRANG
(WITH THE SAME STRANGE DRIVING INSISTENCE) 128 STRANG
I CAN'T BEAR TO HEAR MYSELF MAKING THE SAME OLD 143 STRANG
BITTER COUNTER-ACCUSATIONS.
I CAN'T STAND HEARING THOSE SAME REPROACHES I'VE 143 STRANG
HEARD A THOUSAND TIMES BEFORE/
AND THEN THERE'LL BE THE SAME OLD TERRIBLE SCENE 143 STRANG
OF HATE AND YOU'LL RUN AWAY--
IF OUR MARRIAGE SHOULD BE PURELY THE PLACING OF 148 STRANG
OUR ASHES IN THE SAME TOMB...
YOU'D LIKE TO MAKE HER THE SAME SORT OF CONVENIENTI68 STRANG
SLAVE FOR HIM THAT I WAS FOR
SHE HAS THE SAME STRANGE INFLUENCE OVER ME... 169 STRANG
ALL THE SAME, I CAN'T HELP HOPING HE'LL BE BEATEN 179 STRANG
IN THIS RACE.
(HAS BEEN SHRIEKING AT THE SAME TIME) 182 STRANG
MADELINE IS MUCH THE SAME AS IN THE PREVIOUS ACT 184 STRANG
EXCEPT THAT THERE IS NOW A
AT THE SAME TIME, ALTHOUGH ENTIRELY AN 184 STRANG
UNIMAGINATIVE CODE-BOUND GENTLEMAN OF HIS
(IN THE SAME TONE) NICE! 185 STRANG
I WONDER IS OUR OLD GARDEN THE SAME5 199 STRANG
AND THE SAME DARN RATS-HOLE, SURE ENOUGH. 496 VOYAGE
(WEARING THE SAME GOOD-NATURED GRIN) 498 VOYAGE
MY BROTHER HE WRITE SAME TING TOO. 506 VOYAGE
HE DOES THE SAME.) 507 VOYAGE
A DRIVING FORCE WHICH CAN BE SYMPATHETIC AND CRUEL443 WELDED
AT THE SAME TIME.
WHILE AT THE SAME TIME, YOU'RE JEALOUS OF ANY 453 WELDED
SEPARATENESS IN ME.
(SNEERINGLY) THE SAME INSATIABLE CURIOSITY ABOUT 454 WELDED
MY PLAYS
IT MAKES ME LOWER THAN YOU THOUGHT, BUT YOU'RE 459 WELDED
GLAD TO KNOW IT JUST THE SAME/
BUT CONTINUES TO LOOK INTO HIS EYES WITH THE SAME 460 WELDED
DEFIANT HATE.
(WITH THE SAME WRY SMILE) WHILE I BEGIN TO 469 WELDED
SUSPECT THAT IN A WAY I'M LUCKY--
(IN SAME TONE) IT'S GETTIN' LATE. 473 WELDED
(SCENE--SAME AS ACT ONE. 480 WELDED

SAME

SAME (CONT'D.)
PROTECTIVE HARDING OFF AND AT THE SAME TIME A 480 WELDED
SEEKING POSSESSION.
(IN THE SAME MECHANICAL TUNE) 483 WELDED
(IN HER SAME TUNE) YES/ 488 WELDED
SAME'S
SO'S WE THREE CAN BE TOGETHER SAME'S YEARS AGO, 134 BEYOND
(QUIETLY) I'D GIT DRUNK, SAME'S YOU'RE DOIN'. 467 CARIBE
HER EYES WEEPIN' AN' BLOODY WITH SMOKE AN' CINDERS209 DESIRE
SAME'S THEY USED THEC
KISSIN' AN' HAPPY THE SAME'S WE'VE BEEN HAPPY 258 DESIRE
AFORE HE COME--IF I COULD DO IT--
THEY'S NO CAUSE FOR YE T' GO NOW--THEY'S NO 260 DESIRE
SENSE--IT'S ALL THE SAME'S IT WAS--
YE SAID IF IT HADN'T BEEN FUR HIM COMIN' IT'D BE 261 DESIRE
THE SAME'S AFORE BETWEEN US.
ON'Y JIM BENSON'S ONE O' THEM SLICK JUKERS, SAME'S500 DIFRNT
JACK.
I WANT YOU TO BE LIKE ONE UF THE FAMILY SAME'S 517 DIFRNT
YOU'VE ALWAYS BEEN.
I LIKE YOU, CALEB, SAME'S I ALWAYS DID. 517 DIFRNT
AND CHUCK SOME STONES IN THE OCEAN SAME'S WE 989 RUPE
USTER, REMEMBER$
(DISAPPROVINGLY) YUH'RE STILL SPOUTIN' THE ROTTEN$95 ROPE
OLE WORD UV GOD SAME'S EVER.
SAME'S YOUR KID CHUCKED THAT DOLLAR OF MINE 599 ROPE
OVERBOARD, REMEMBERS
SAME'S WE DO WITH STOCK, TU GIVE THE MAN I LUVED A 63 STRANG
HEALTHY CHILD.
BUT AINT STOCKHOLM A CITY SAME'S LONDON$ 503 VOYAGE
SAMMY'D
I PRAYED SAMMY'D BE BORN DEAD, AND SAMMY'S FATHER 58 STRANG
PRAYED,
SAMMY'S
DON'T YOU THINK YOU BETTER WAIT UNTIL SAMMY'S 57 STRANG
MAKING MORE MONEYS
I PRAYED SAMMY'D BE BORN DEAD, AND SAMMY'S FATHER 58 STRANG
PRAYED.
AND MY HUSBAND'S SISTER, SAMMY'S AUNT, SHE'S OUT 59 STRANG
OF HER MIND.
AND FROM THEN ON UNTIL HIS FATHER DID REALLY DIE 60 STRANG
DURING SAMMY'S SECOND YEAR TO
(IGNORES ON) MY HUSBAND, SAMMY'S FATHER, 60 STRANG
SAMMY'S GOT TO FEEL SURE YOU LOVE HIM--TO BE 64 STRANG
HAPPY.
YES, SAMMY'S THE SAME. 64 STRANG
AND SAMMY'S THE SAME. 64 STRANG
(THERE, SAMMY'S MOTHER AND GORDON... 71 STRANG
I CAN HEAR HIS MOTHER SAYING, «SAMMY'S GOT TO FEEL 71 STRANG
SURE YOU LOVE HIM...
SAMPLE
A SAMPLE OF THE RICHEST OF THE TREASURE.. 561 CRUSS
THAT RESEMBLES A MODERN SAMPLE CASE, PLODS WEARILY347 MARCOM
TO THE FOOT OF THE TREE.
WHICH CURIOUSLY RESEMBLE MODERN SAMPLE CASES. 364 MARCOM
(THEY GO QUICKLY OUST RIGHT, MARCO FOLLOWING WITH 369 MARCOM
THE SAMPLE CASES.
THE POLOS STAND AT CENTER AS BEFORE, MARCO STILL 369 MARCOM
LUGGING THE SAMPLE CASES.
(THEY GO OUT LEFT FOLLOWED BY MARCO WITH THE 372 MARCOM
SAMPLE CASES.
THE POLOS STAND AT CENTER, MARCO STILL LUGGING THE373 MARCOM
BATTERED SAMPLE CASES.
TUGGING A SAMPLE CASE IN EACH HAND. 376 MARCOM
MARCO STANDS, A SAMPLE CASE IN EACH HAND, 377 MARCOM
BEWILDERED AND DAZZLED.
(HE SITS DOWN ON ONE OF THE SAMPLE CASES TO THE 378 MARCOM
GASPING HORROR OF ALL THE COURT.
SAMPLES
THESE ARE GOOD SAMPLES OF THE REST. 201 AHWILD
(GRIMLY) SAMPLES OF THE NEW FREEDOM--FROM THOSE 204 AHWILD
BOOKS ESSIE FOUND--
SAMSON
(SARDONICALLY) AN' YEW--BE YEW SAMSONS 210 DESIRE
SANATORIUM
BUT WE CAN'T IF HE HAS TO BE SENT TO A SANATORIUM. 37 JOURNE
HE'LL HAVE TO GO TO A SANATORIUM. 79 JOURNE
WHEN YOU CAME BACK FROM THE SANATORIUM. 84 JOURNE
RIGHT AFTER I RETURNED FROM THE SANATORIUM, YOU 93 JOURNE
BEGAN TO BE ILL.
IF YOU HEARD WHAT THE DOCTOR AT THE SANATORIUM, 118 JOURNE
WHO REALLY KNOWS SOMETHING,
I'VE GOT TO GO TO A SANATORIUM. 119 JOURNE
I KNOW WHY HE WANTS YOU SENT TO A SANATORIUM. TO 119 JOURNE
TAKE YOU FROM ME/
IT'S THE HILLTOWN SANATORIUM, THAT'S ALL I KNOW, 143 JOURNE
THE STATE HAS THE MONEY TO MAKE A BETTER PLACE 144 JOURNE
THAN ANY PRIVATE SANATORIUM.
ALL I TOLD THEM WAS I COULDN'T AFFORD ANY 144 JOURNE
MILLIONAIRE'S SANATORIUM
YOU KNOW DAMNED WELL HILLTOWN SANATORIUM IS A 144 JOURNE
STATE INSTITUTION/
IF I TOOK THIS STATE FARM SANATORIUM FCR A GOOD 148 JOURNE
BARGAIN,
THERE WAS ANOTHER SANATORIUM THE SPECIALIST 149 JOURNE
RECOMMENDED.
THIS SANATORIUM IS A CHARITY DUMPS 159 JOURNE
DON'T BE SCARED OF THIS SANATORIUM BUSINESS. 164 JOURNE
THINK IT OVER WHEN YOU'RE AWAY FROM ME IN THE 166 JOURNE
SANATORIUM.
SANCTITY
HIS ODOR OF SANCTITY FOR THAT OF A SKUNK'S AND 423 DYNAMO
FILL HIS'...
SANCTORUM
SANCTUM SANCTORUM/. 4 STRANG
SANCTUARY
SEDULOUSLY BUILT AS A SANCTUARY WHERE, 3 STRANG

SANCTUM

SANCTUM

SANCTUM SANCTORUM/. 4 STRANG

SAND

THE SAND OF THE BEACH SHIMMERS PALELY. 275 AHWILD
KICKING AT THE SAND RESTLESSLY, TWIRLING HIS STRAW275 AHWILD
HAIR.
MARKING THE LINE WHERE THE SAND OF THE BEACH ENDS 275 AHWILD
AND FERTILE LAND BEGINS.
I LOVE THE SAND AND THE TREES, AND THE GRASS, AND 277 AHWILD
THE WATER AND THE SKY.
AND I HAD SAND ENOUGH TO SNEAK OUT AND MEET YOU 286 AHWILD
TONIGHT, DIDN'T I?
I SHOVELED SAND ON A BIG WATERPOWER JOB OUT WEST. 461 DYNAMO
THE WARM SAND WAS LIKE YOUR SKIN. 90 ELECTR
A BOY SNEAKED UP BEHIND WHEN I WAS DRAWING A 295 GGBROW
PICTURE IN THE SAND HE COULDN'T
LIKE AN OSTRICH HIDING HIS HEAD IN THE SAND. 692 ICEMAN
BECAME THE SUN, THE HOT SAND, GREEN SEAWEED 153 JOURNE
ANCHORED TO A ROCK.
LET US GO SEAWARD AS THE GREAT WINDS GO, FULL OF 173 JOURNE
BLOWN SAND AND FOAM.
WITH BUCKET SCOOPS THAT DREDGE, LOAD COAL, 400 MARCOM
SAND, ETC. BY THE SIDE OF THE

SANDOW

IF I WANT TO DEVELOP MY BICEPS, I'LL BUY SANDOW 225 AHWILD
EXERCISER/

SANDWICH

BY PUTTING A PROPERTY SANDWICH IN THE MIDDLE OF 571 ICEMAN
EACH TABLE.

SANDY

SMALL BLUE EYES AND THICK SANDY HAIR. 186 AHWILD
HIS SANDY HAIR IS THICK AND DISHEVELED. 513 DIFRNT
THE FOREGROUND IS SANDY LEVEL GROUND DOTTED BY A 187 EJONES
FEW STONES AND CLUMPS OF
HIS SANDY HAIR IS FALLING OUT AND THE TOP OF HIS 8 HUGHIE
HEAD IS BALD.
HE IS IN HIS FIFTIES, SANDY-HAIRED, BULLET-HEADED,576 ICEMAN
JOWLY.
ON THE SANDY PLAIN IN THE BACKGROUND. 347 MARCOM
HIS HEAD IS ROUND WITH THINNING SANDY HAIR. 11 MISBEG
HE IS A STOCKY, MUSCULAR, SANDY-HAIRED 981 ROPE

SANE

SEE HOW I FREE MYSELF AND BECOME SANE. 567 CROSS
WITH MY SANE JUDGMENT. 545 DAYS
AND SHE WILL, TOO, I BELIEVE. IF SHE COMES OUT OF 530 DIFRNT
THIS FIT IN HER SANE MIND--
THAT'S THE LEADER RULE FOR THE SAFE AND SANE. 294 GGBROW
HELL, I'M TOO DAMNED SANE. 642 ICEMAN
SOMEONE STRONG AND HEALTHY AND SANE, WHO DARES TO 3 MANSNS
LOVE AND LIVE LIFE GREEDILY
I AM BEING EXTREMELY SANE. 179 MANSNS
GOD, IF THE REALITY OF DOG-EAT-DOG AND LUST- 185 MANSNS
DEVOUR-LOVE IS SANE,
(BEWILDEREDLY) I NEVER BELIEVED PEOPLE--SANE 415 MARCOM
PEOPLE---EVER SERIOUSLY TRIED--
AND I THOUGHT SAM WAS SO NORMAL--SO HEALTHY AND 61 STRANG
SANE--NOT LIKE ME/
SAM LOOKS SO HEALTHY AND SANE, DOESN'T HE? 83 STRANG
YOU'VE GOT TO SHOW ME WHAT'S THE SANE--THE TRULY 84 STRANG
SANE, YOU UNDERSTAND/
IT IS HER SANE DUTY TO HER HUSBAND. 86 STRANG
I FEEL SANE AGAIN...)) 99 STRANG
HAVE MADE A SANE LIFE FOR HIM OUT OF OUR 139 STRANG
MADNESS/...))
AND AS SANE... 149 STRANG
HE'S SANE AS A PIG/ 172 STRANG
HIS MIND WAS PERFECTLY SANE TO THE END... 191 STRANG

SANELY

THINK SANELY FOR A MOMENT/ 164 ELECTR

SANG

YOU SANG THAT DARNED WELL/ 258 AHWILD
THEY SANG THEIR LITTLE SONGS TO ME. 90 BEYOND
I'VE LOVED, LUSTED, WON AND LOST, SANG AND WEPT/ 296 GGBROW
EVEN WHEN I HAD TWO QUARTS OF ROTGUT UNDER MY BELT661 ICEMAN
AND JOKED AND SANG +SWEET
WILLIE OBAN'S, THE SAILOR LAD DITTY HE SANG IN ACT727 ICEMAN
ONE.
+MEN CALL THIS DEATH,+ IT SANG. 304 LAZARU
THUS SANG HIS LIFE TO LAZARUS WHILE HE LAY DEAD/ 310 LAZARU
WHERE I COUCHED AND WEAVED AND SANG. 350 LAZARU
YOU DANCED AND SANG LEWD SONGS. 348 MARCOM
IN THE SPRING WE SANG OF LOVE AND LAUGHED WITH 384 MARCOM
YOUTH BUT NOW WE ARE PARTED BY

SANITARIUM

THERE'S A DOCTOR I KNOW AT A SANITARIUM FOR 17 STRANG
CRIPPLED SOLDIERS--

SANITY

IT'S A SIGN OF SANITY, THEY SAY. 99 JOURNE
WHEN YOU DENY GOD, YOU DENY SANITY. 135 JOURNE
LET LAUGHTER BE YOUR NEW CLEAN LUST AND SANITY/ 310 LAZARU
SAVE HIS SANITY. 173 MANSNS

SANK

BEFORE THE AULD TEAKETTLE SANK. 481 CARDIF
HE SANK DOWN AND DOWN AND MY MOTHER WORKED AND 25 ELECTR
SUPPORTED HIM.
WHEN I SANK DROWNING, I LUVED DEATH. 409 MARCOM
HE NEAR SANK THROUGH THE BED WITH SHAME AT HIS 64 POET
BOLDNESS.

SANTA

+SANTA ANNA+ ISS A GOOD ONE. 459 CARIBE

SAP

NO WONDER YOUR SUN IS A SAP/ 451 DYNAMO
BE A SAP AND STAY HEALTHY. 11 HUGHIE
BUT THIS TIME I'M ON A SPOT WHERE I GOT TO, IF I 18 HUGHIE
AIN'T A SAP.
THE KIND OF SAP YOU'D TAKE TO THE CLEANERS A 20 HUGHIE
MILLION TIMES
Y'KNOW I HAD HUGHIE SIZED UP FOR A SAP THE FIRST 22 HUGHIE
TIME I SEE HIM.

(CONT'D.)

EVEN I BELIEVED THAT ONCE, AND NO ONE COULD EVER 23 HUGHIE
CALL ME A SAP.
HE WAS THAT KIND OF SAP. 28 HUGHIE
I AIN'T A SAP. 29 HUGHIE
(THEN WONDERINGLY) BUT DEN WHAT KIND OF A SAP IS 584 ICEMAN
HE
MARGIE WHISPERS) YUH SAP, DON'T YUH KNOW ENOUGH 613 ICEMAN
NOT TO KID HIM ON DATS
JEES, I AIN'T LYIN', HE BEGINS TO LAUGH, DE BIG 617 ICEMAN
SAP/
AIN'T UNCLE SAM DE SAP TO TRUST GUYS LIKE DAT WID 617 ICEMAN
DOUGH/
MY OPINION IS THE POOR SAP IS TEMPORARILY BUGHOUSE626 ICEMAN
FROM OVERWORK.
IMAGINE A SAP LIKE HIM ADVISIN' ME AND CHUCK TO 662 ICEMAN
GIT MARRIED/
(IRRITABLY) IF I AIN'T A SAP TO LET CHUCK KID ME 665 ICEMAN
INTO WORKIN' HIS TIME
(GRUESILY) YUH'RE A SOFT OLD SAP, LARRY. 666 ICEMAN
SHE SAYS, +YEAH, BUT AFTER A WEEK YUH'LL BE 671 ICEMAN
TINKIN' WHAT A SAP YOU WAS.
DAT'S RIGHT, WAIT ON HER AND SPOIL HER, YUH POOR 677 ICEMAN
SAP/
WHAT A PRIZE SAP YOU BEEN, 697 ICEMAN
YEAH, BUT I AIN'T NO SAP NOW. 697 ICEMAN
IMAGINE DE SAP I'DA BEEN, WHEN I CAN GET YOUR 700 ICEMAN
DOUGH JUST AS EASY WIDOUT IT/
WHAT A DAMNED OLD SAP YOU ARE/ 701 ICEMAN
I'M A SAP TO WASTE TIME ON YUH. 703 ICEMAN
AND DON'T BE A SAP. 109 ICEMAN
OF THE WINE OF LIFE STIRRING FOREVER IN THE SAP 307 LAZARU
AND BLOOD AND LOAM OF THINGS.

THE YOUNGER LOOKING AS IF THE VITALITY OF HER 218 HA APE
STUCK HAD BEEN SAPPED BEFORE SHE

SAPPIEST

BUT DE FARM STUFF IS DE SAPPIEST PART. 614 ICEMAN
STANDARD OIL'S SAPPIEST CHILD, WHOM I KNOW YOU 47 MISBEG
BOTH LOVE SO DEARLY.

SAPS

TELLIN' SAPS A STORY TO MAKE 'EM BET/ 22 HUGHIE
OH, HELL, MAC, WE'RE SAPS TO WORRY. 652 ICEMAN
I THINKS, AIN'T TWO GUYS LIKE DEM SAPS TO BE 702 ICEMAN
HANGIN' ROUND
THE TRUTH IS THERE IS NO CURE AND WE'VE BEEN SAPS 76 JOURNE
TO HOPE--

SARATOGA

FUR SARATOGA, TO LOOK THE BANGTAILS OVER. 15 HUGHIE
I GOT SOME DOUGH RIDIN' ON THE NOSE OF A TURTLE IN 37 HUGHIE
THE RACE AT SARATOGA.

SARCASM

(WITH GRIM SARCASM) 542 'LE
(WITH CAUSTIC SARCASM) 264 AHWILD
(WITH AN AMUSED SARCASM) I SEE. 34 ANNA
(THEN AS SHE MAKES NO COMMENT, HE GOES ON WITH A 42 ANNA
PONDEROUS ATTEMPT AT SARCASM)
(NOT NOTICING THE SARCASM IN ROBERT'S TONE) 133 BEYOND
(A SWEDE WITH A DROOPING BLOND MUSTACHE--WITH 478 CARDIF
PONDEROUSLY SARCASM)
(WITH HEAVY, BITING SARCASM) 229 HA APE
(FLATTERINGLY BUT WITH UNDERLYING SARCASM.) 100 MANSNS
(WITH HEAVY SARCASM) OH, NOTHING'S HAPPENED TO ME 77 MISBEG
AT ALL, AT ALL.
(WITH HEAVY SARCASM) IN YOUR BEST SHOES AND 79 MISBEG
STOCKINGS
THEN SHE CONTROLS HERSELF AND SPEAKS WITH QUIET, 115 POET
BITING SARCASM.)
(EXCITEDLY WITH A HECTIC SARCASM) 81 STRANG

SARCASTIC

(GRIMLY SARCASTIC) YE'RE FEELIN' RIGHT CHIPPER, 246 DESIRE
HAIN'T YES
TO MAKE A SARCASTIC CRACK. 27 HUGHIE
(DULLY SARCASTIC.) YES. 147 JOURNE
(DOES NOT LIKE HIS TONE--INSOLENTLY SARCASTIC.) 117 POET
(MORE AND MORE BITTERLY SARCASTIC) 81 STRANG
(AVERTING HIS EYES AND ADDRESSING HER DIRECTLY IN 454 WELDED
A COLD, SARCASTIC TONE)

SARCASTICALLY

(SARCASTICALLY) OF COURSE, THERE WON'T BE ANY 191 AHWILD
BOYS PRESENT/
(SARCASTICALLY) SHALL I SERVE IT IN A PAILS 14 ANNA
(SARCASTICALLY) GEE, AIN'T YOU A HARD GUY/ 32 ANNA
(TURNING TO HIM, SARCASTICALLY) 42 ANNA
(SARCASTICALLY) WITH ALL THEM NICE INLAND FELLERS 58 ANNA
YUST LOOKING FOR A CHANCE TO
(SARCASTICALLY) THAT'S RIGHT--TELL THE OLD MAN 458 CARIBE
ABOUT IT, AN' THE MATE TOO.
(SARCASTICALLY) SORROWIN' OVER HIS LUST O' THE 216 DESIRE
FLESH/
(SARCASTICALLY) AIR YEW AIMIN' T' BUY UP OVER THE231 DESIRE
FARM TUOS
(SARCASTICALLY) DON'T HURRY NONE ON OUR ACCOUNT/ 252 DESIRE
(SARCASTICALLY) I AIN'T HEARD THAT CALEB OFFERED 509 DIFRNT
TO MARRY HER, HAVE YOUS
(SARCASTICALLY) THE GENERALS AND THE CABINET 176 EJONES
MINISTERS AND ALLS
(SARCASTICALLY) HOW COME YOU DON'T KNOW DATS 176 EJONES
(SARCASTICALLY) WELL, GIVE US SOME OF YOUR 248 HA APE
VALUABLE INFORMATION.
LARRY LOOKS AWAY AND GOES ON SARCASTICALLY) 624 ICEMAN
(SARCASTICALLY) JEES, 670 ICEMAN
(FEELS SORRY FOR LEWIS AND TURNS ON WETJOEN-- 676 ICEMAN
SARCASTICALLY)
(SARCASTICALLY) A BIT OF A BLACK BOX, EHS 520 INZONE
(SARCASTICALLY) OR A MINE THAT DIDN'T GO OFF--- 523 INZONE
THAT TIME--
(SARCASTICALLY) HO YUS/ 526 INZONE

SATISFACTION

SARCASTICALLY (CONT'D.)
HIS FATHER AGAIN REACTS CUSTOMARILY-- 89 JOURNE
SARCASTICALLY.)
(SARCASTICALLY) I SUPPOSE YOU'VE NEVER THOUGHT OF 9 MISBEG
THAT?
(WITH A GLANCE AT MALOY, SARCASTICALLY.) 16 POET
SHE CONTINUES SARCASTICALLY) 41 STRANG
(SARCASTICALLY) I'M GLAD IT'S UNDERSTANDABLE/ 75 STRANG
(SARCASTICALLY) THEN YOU DON'T BELIEVE IN TAKING 81 STRANG
YOUR OWN MEDICINES
(SARCASTICALLY) IT WAS ONE OF THOSE LOVE 114 STRANG
MATCHES./
(SARCASTICALLY) HO, NOW/ 494 VOYAGE
(AFTER A PAUSE IN WHICH THEY EACH BROOD 456 WELDED
RESENTFULLY--SARCASTICALLY)
(SARCASTICALLY) IF I AM TO BELIEVE YOUR STORY, 456 WELDED
YOU DIDN'T THINK SO.
(WITHDRAWING HER HANDS FROM HIS WITH A QUICK 457 WELDED
MOVEMENT--SARCASTICALLY)
SARDONIC
(WITH SARDONIC BITTERNESS) HERE--IT'S STONES ATOP204 DESIRE
OF THE GROUND--
(WITH A SARDONIC CHUCKLE) HONOR THY FATHER/ 205 DESIRE
(HE GIVES ONE ABRUPT SARDONIC GUFFAW. 207 DESIRE
(HE GIVES ONE ABRUPT SARDONIC GUFFAW.) 212 DESIRE
(HE GIVES A SARDONIC LAUGH OF RELISH AT THIS 214 DESIRE
IDEA.)
(WITH HIS SARDONIC BURST OF LAUGHTER) 222 DESIRE
(EBEN SUDDENLY LAUGHS, ONE SHORT SARDONIC BARK.. 254 DESIRE
LAUGHS AGAIN HIS SARDONIC =HA.= 255 DESIRE
(WITH ONE SARDONIC) HA/ 268 DESIRE
FIFE'S VOICE, SARDONIC AND MALICIOUS, 425 DYNAMO
AND HIS VOICE BECOMES BITTER AND SARDONIC) 265 GGBROW
WITH A GLEAM OF SHARP SARDONIC HUMOR IN THEM. 574 ICEMAN
(WITH INNER SARDONIC AMUSEMENT--FLATTERINGLY) 580 ICEMAN
(GRINS WITH SARDONIC APPRECIATION) 584 ICEMAN
(WITH A SARDONIC GRIN) WHAT IS ITS 587 ICEMAN
HE BEGINS TO DESCRIBE THE SLEEPERS WITH SARDONIC 593 ICEMAN
RELISH
(IN A SARDONIC WHISPER TO PARRITT) 603 ICEMAN
(AS BEFORE, IN A SARDONIC ASIDE TO PARRITT) 603 ICEMAN
HE CANNOT RESTRAIN A SARDONIC GUFFAW. 604 ICEMAN
(WHO HAS BEEN LISTENING WITH SARDONIC 623 ICEMAN
APPRECIATION--
(BUT AN INTERRUPTION COMES FROM LARRY WHO BURSTS 634 ICEMAN
INTO A SARDONIC LAUGH.
(MASKING PITY BEHIND A SARDONIC TONE) 645 ICEMAN
AND BURSTS INTO A SARDONIC LAUGH.) 672 ICEMAN
(GIVES A SARDONIC GUFFAW--WITH HIS COMICALLY 677 ICEMAN
CRAZY, INTENSE WHISPER)
(WITH A SARDONIC LAUGH) WELL, BE GOD, IT FITS, 680 ICEMAN
(GLANCES AT HIM--FOR A MOMENT HE IS STIRRED TO 702 ICEMAN
SARDONIC PITY)
SARDONIC GRIN) 727 ICEMAN
(BREAKS THE CRACKING SILENCE--BITTERLY, SELF- 170 JOURNE
DEFENSIVELY SARDONIC.)
(APPROACHES AND STANDS REGARDING HOGAN WITH 37 MISBEG
SARDONIC RELISH.
(SUDDENLY--WITH SARDONIC AMUSEMENT) 65 MISBEG
SARDONICALLY
(SARDONICALLY) HE GAVE HIM A DOSE OF SALTS, NA 480 CARDIF
DOOCE
(HE LAUGHS SARDONICALLY AS IF MOCKING HIMSELF.) 560 CROSS
(HE LAUGHS SARDONICALLY) HOW COULD WE CONSIDER 543 DAYS
SUCH AN UNPATRIOTIC IDEA AS
THAN GETTING ALL FOUR FEET IN A TROUGH OF 543 DAYS
SWILL/(HE LAUGHS SARDONICALLY)
(SARDONICALLY) WHAT'S DRIVIN' YEW TO CALIFORNI-A,207 DESIRE
REBES
(SARDONICALLY) I TELL THAT T' PAW--WHEN HE COMES/208 DESIRE
(SARDONICALLY) AN' YEW--BE YEW SAMSONS 210 DESIRE
(SARDONICALLY) IF YE'D GROW WINGS ON US WE'D FLY 213 DESIRE
THAR/
(SARDONICALLY, ADDRESSING THE PORTRAIT) 149 ELECTR
(SARDONICALLY) IT'S A GREAT GAME, THE PURSUIT OF 581 ICEMAN
HAPPINESS.
(HE GRINS SARDONICALLY) ANO, BE GOD, THEY'RE 587 ICEMAN
RIGHT.
(SARDONICALLY) SHE DIDN'T, DON'T WORRY. 589 ICEMAN
(HE CHUCKLES SARDONICALLY-- 590 ICEMAN
(SARDONICALLY) NOTHING I COULD HELP DOING. 591 ICEMAN
(HE QUOTES A TRANSLATION OF THE CLOSING COUPLET 591 ICEMAN
SARDONICALLY)
(BREAKS IN SARDONICALLY) BE GOD, YOU'RE THERE 600 ICEMAN
ALREADY, JIMMY.
(SARDONICALLY) HA/ 626 ICEMAN
(HE ADDS SARDONICALLY) OR AS BAD. 643 ICEMAN
(SARDONICALLY) I DUNNA FRET ABOUT IT IVAN. 515 INZONE
(HE QUOTES FROM DOWSON SARDONICALLY.) 130 JOURNE
(AS IF HE HADN'T HEARD--SARDONICALLY.) 134 JOURNE
SARDONICALLY.) 137 JOURNE
(SARDONICALLY.) THE MAKINGS OF A POET. 154 JOURNE
(HE RECITES SARDONICALLY FROM ROSSETTI.) 168 JOURNE
(HE CHUCKLES SARDONICALLY.) SO, ALTHOUGH I KNOW 180 MANSNS
HOW YOU HAVE ALWAYS.
(THEN SARDONICALLY TO THE ELDER POLOS) 362 MARCOM
(HE LOOKS UP AT HER SARDONICALLY) 41 MISBEG
(SARDONICALLY) THAT'S RIGHT. 68 MISBEG
BUT HE GRINS AS HE GREETS MALOY SARDONICALLY.) 8 POET
(SARDONICALLY) THERE'S PEACE IN THE GREEN FIELDS 62 STRANG
OF EDEN, THEY SAY/
(SARDONICALLY) YES, INDEED, DARRELL, I CAN VOUCH 127 STRANG
FOR THEIR MISSING YOU--
(SARDONICALLY) PERHAPS HE REALIZES SUBCONSCIOUSLY143 STRANG
THAT I AM HIS FATHER.
(SARDONICALLY) I'VE HEARD THAT CRY FOR HAPPINESS 198 STRANG
BEFORE, NINA/

SARDONICALLY (CONT'D.)
(HE CHUCKLES SARDONICALLY AT HIS OWN PLAY ON 473 WELDED
WORDS.)
(LAUGHING SARDONICALLY) =O LOVE OF MINE, 474 WELDED
SARDONICISM
(HE LAUGHS WITH A DOUBLE-DYED SARDONICISM.) 261 AHWILD
SART'N
SART'N HE WILL/ 211 DESIRE
HE'S DEAD, SART'N. 264 DESIRE
SARTIN
WAAL, I DIDN'T HAVE NO MIND FOR IT, THAT'S SARTIN.497 DIFRNT
NOBODY KIN SWEAR THAT FOR SARTIN. 509 DIFRNT
(WITH A GRIN) HE'D OUGHT TO, THAT'S SARTIN/. 7 ELECTR
AND YOU'D OUGHT FUR YOUR PAW'S SAKE TO MAKE 20 ELECTR
SARTIN.
SAS
(FORCING A LAUGH) MAKE IT SAS, THEN. 23 ANNA
SAS'PRILLA
FINGER ALE--SAS'PRILLA, MAYBE. 23 ANNA
SASSY
SHE'S SO FAT AND SASSY, THERE'LL SOON BE NO 21 JOUNNE
HULDING HER.
SAT
(ARTHUR AGAIN FEELS SAT UPON.) 255 AHWILD
I SAT AND BROODED ABOUT DEATH. 281 AHWILD
FIRST SIGHT AND SHE CAME AND SAT ON MY LAP AND 284 AHWILD
KISSED ME.
AND I SUPPOSE YOU JUST SAT AND LET YOURSELF BE 285 AHWILD
KISSED/
BORE A HOLE IN A CHAIR EVERYTIME I SAT DOWN--LIKE 291 AHWILD
SOME PEOPLE/
AY TANK AY SAT DOWN FOR A MINUTE. 8 ANNA
AND ANCY SAT THERE DUMB, LOOKING AS IF HE'D LOST 98 BEYOND
HIS BEST FRIEND.
(HE SITS DOWN IN THE CHAIR AT RIGHT OF TABLE WHERE05 DAYS
FATHER BAIRD HAD SAT.
WHY, I ONLY SAT DOWN FOR A MINUTE TO GIVE YOU A 531 DIFRNT
CHANCE TO TALK TO HER.
FOR DAYS AFTER, HE SAT AND STARED AT NOTHING. 26 ELECTR
HE STARED AT ME WITH AN IDIOTIC LOOK AS IF HE'D 95 ELECTR
SAT ON A TACK--
WHEN THEY REACH THE SPOT WHERE HIS MOTHER HAD SAT 138 ELECTR
MORNING.
I SHE SITS IN THE CHAIR WHERE DION HAD SAT AND 300 GGBROW
STARES STRAIGHT BEFORE HER.
CONSIDERING IT'S A HELL OF A WAYS, AND I SAT IN 622 ICEMAN
THE PARK FOR A WHILE THINKING.
(HE SHRINKS QUICKLY PAST THE TABLE WHERE HICKEY 724 ICEMAN
HAD SAT TO THE REAR OF THE GROUP
IF IVER I SAW BLACK SHAME ON A MAN'S FACE 'TWAS ON523 INZONE
HIS WHIN HE SAT THERE/
THE DUTIFUL WIFE SAT BY HIS BEDSIDE. 30 MANSNS
I THINK WE COULD DISCUSS THIS MYSTERY MORE CALMLY 31 MANSNS
IF WE SAT DOWN.
HAS WATCHED ALL THIS WITH FASCINATED DISGUST WHILE432 MARCOM
CHU-YIN HAS SAT DOWN TO READ
SIMPSON CAME AND SAT AT THE TABLE WITH US-- 85 MISBEG
SIMPSON SAT DOWN WITH US. 132 MISBEG
HE ALWAYS SAT THERE...... 27 STRANG
YOU JUMPED OFF MY LAP AS THOUGH YOU'D SAT ON A 157 STRANG
TACK/
SATAN
ABOUT TO ENTER THE PRESENSE OF SATAN... 436 DYNAMO
(DULLY) YOU SOLD YOUR SOUL TO SATAN, REUBEN. 467 DYNAMO
YOUR SATAN IS DEAD. 467 DYNAMO
YOU MUST BE SATAN/ 320 GGBROW
THOU KNOWEST, O SATAN, PATRON OF MY PAIN, 133 JOURNE
SPAWN O' SATAN/ 578 ROPE
SATCHEL
(MIKE DROPS THE SATCHEL ON THE GROUND WHILE HE 5 MISBEG
PUTS ON THE COAT.)
AND RETURNS CARRYING AN OLD COAT AND A CHEAP 5 MISBEG
BULGING SATCHEL.
(MIKE GRABS THE SATCHEL, TERRIFIED. 10 MISBEG
(SEETHING) YOU'VE STOLEN MY SATCHEL TO GIVE HIM, 13 MISBEG
I SUPPOSE.
IT WAS MY SATCHEL, TOO. 13 MISBEG
YOU STOLE MY FINE SATCHEL FOR THAT LUMP/ 14 MISBEG
THE HORSE, WHEN YOU GOT THE CROWBARS TO THROW IN 14 MISBEG
THE SATCHEL FOR GOOD MEASURE%
SATIRDAY
ON SATIRDAY NIGHTS WHEN DEY BOT' GOT A SKINFUL 234 HA APE
SATIN
A SOFA WITH SILK AND SATIN CUSHIONS STANDS AGAINST185 AHWILD
THE WALL.
SHE WEARS A GREEN SATIN DRESS, SMARTLY CUT AND 9 ELECTR
EXPENSIVE.
IT WAS MADE OF SOFT, SHIMMERING SATIN, TRIMMED 115 JOURNE
WITH WONDERFUL OLD DUCHESSE LACE.
MY FATHER EVER LET ME HAVE DUCHESSE LACE ON MY 115 JOURNE
WHITE SATIN SLIPPERS,
IS AN OLD-FASHIONED WHITE SATIN WEDDING GOWN, 170 JOURNE
TRIMMED WITH DUCHESSE LACE.
I WEAR A GOWN OF CRIMSON SATIN AND GOLD, 4 MANSNS
EMBROIDERED IN PEARLS--
OF EMBROIDERED CRIMSON SATIN REACHING ALMOST TO 428 MARCOM
THE GROUND.
SATINS
DRESSED IN SILKS AND SATINS, AND RIDING IN A 63 POET
CARRIAGE WITH COACHMAN AND FOOTMAN.
SATIS
=FORTUNATE SENEX, ERGO TUA RURA PANEBUNT, ET TIBI 37 MISBEG
MAGNA SATIS.=
SATISFACTION
(WITH GRIM SATISFACTION) MUTINY% 537 'ILE
(WITH SATISFACTION) I WARN'T MUCH AFEARED O' 542 'ILE
THAT, TUM.
BUT HIS FACE IS ONE BROAD GRIN OF SATISFACTION.! 204 AHWILD

SATISFACTION

SATISFACTION (CONT'D.)
HAS BEGUN TO TAKE A MASOCHISTIC SATISFACTION IN 215 AHWILD
HIS GREAT SORROW.
THEN SUDDENLY HE GRINS MISTILY AND NODS WITH 224 AHWILD
SATISFACTION)
(HE DRINKS ALL OF HIS DOWN AND SIGHS WITH 243 AHWILD
EXAGGERATED SATISFACTION)
BUT SHE SEEMS TO GET SOME QUEER SATISFACTION OUT 291 AHWILD
OF FUSSING OVER HIM LIKE A HEN
(HE SIGHS WITH SATISFACTION 297 AHWILD
SATISFACTION, WIPING HER MOUTH WITH THE BACK OF 8 ANNA
HER HAND.
(WITH INTENSE SATISFACTION) DID THEY, NOWS 37 ANNA
(WITH SATISFACTION) I NEED A REST, 157 BEYONU
(WITH SATISFACTION) I DO THAT.. 487 CARDIF
AND SMACKING HIS LIPS WITH A DEEP >AA-AH= OF 462 CARIBE
SATISFACTION.)
(WICCOL APPEARS) WEARING A BROAD GRIN OF 462 CARIBE
SATISFACTION.
SATISFACTION.) 462 CARIBE
(TO HIS SON WITH FIERCE SATISFACTION) 369 CROSS
I'D DONE THAT AND FOUND IT WAS A GREAT 502 DAYS
SATISFACTION TO HIM
A LOOK OF UGLY SATISFACTION COMING INTO HER FACE) 520 DAYS
STILLWELL NODS TO FATHER HARD WITH SATISFACTION--556 DAYS
HE IS GRINNING TO HIMSELF WITH EVIDENT 244 DESIRE
SATISFACTION.
SEES ABBIE--WITH SATISFACTION) 263 DESIRE
AND HE MUTTERS TO HIMSELF WITH SAVAGE 531 DIFRNT
SATISFACTION)
(HIS EYES GLEAMING WITH SATISFACTION) 532 DIFRNT
FIFE'S KEEN EYES ARE WATCHING HIM AND HE GRINS 437 DYNAMO
WITH SATISFACTION.)
(BUT I WON'T GIVE HER THE SATISFACTION/... 448 DYNAMO
(HIS ASTONISHMENT GIVING WAY TO AN IMMENSE MEAN 175 EJONES
SATISFACTION)
(WITH SATISFACTION) I SHO' HAS/ 177 EJONES
(WATCHING HIM WITH MALICIOUS SATISFACTION, AFTER A182 EJONES
PAUSE--MOCKINGLY)
(THEN WITH MORE CONFIDENT SATISFACTION) 185 EJONES
HE SEES THE FIRST WHITE STONE AND CRAWLS TO IT 188 EJONES
WITH SATISFACTION)
LEM CLOCKS UP AT THE WHITE MAN WITH A GRIN OF 203 EJONES
SATISFACTION)
THEY CARRY HIM TO LEM, WHO EXAMINES HIS BODY WITH 204 EJONES
GREAT SATISFACTION.
HER EYES LIGHT UP WITH A GRIM SATISFACTION, 11 ELECTR
AND I SUPPOSE KNOWING WHO HE WAS GAVE YOU ALL THE 32 ELECTR
MORE SATISFACTION--
(HASTILY) DO YOU THINK I'LL EVER GIVE YOU THE 34 ELECTR
SATISFACTION OF SEEING ME GRIEVES
AND ACT GIVE VINATE THE SATISFACTION OF TELLING 38 ELECTR
HIM.
(A LOOK OF EXULTANT SATISFACTION COMES TO HER FACE 42 ELECTR
(WITH GRIM PROUD SATISFACTION) 48 ELECTR
(WITH SAVAGE SATISFACTION) AH/ 61 ELECTR
(SOMETHING LIKE A GRIM SMILE OF SATISFACTION FORMS 77 ELECTR
ON LAVINIA'S LIPS.
(HIS EYES LIGHTING UP WITH SAVAGE SATISFACTION) 110 ELECTR
A GRIM SMILE OF SATISFACTION TWITCHES HIS LIPS 149 ELECTR
(HIS ANGER TURNED TO GLOATING SATISFACTION) 152 ELECTR
(LAVINIA LOOKS AT HIM, FRIGHTENED BY THE 163 ELECTR
TRIUMPHANT SATISFACTION IN HIS VOICE.)
(HE GOES OUT RIGHT, LAUGHING WITH AMUSED 308 GGBROW
SATISFACTION.)
(WITH VENGEFUL SATISFACTION) 243 HA APE
(WITH SATISFACTION) WELCOME TO OUR CITY. 246 HA APE
(HE COCKS AN EYE OVER HIS SPECS AT MOSHER AND 610 ICEMAN
GRINS WITH SATISFACTION)
ITS WATCHING LARRY'S FACE WITH A CURIOUS SNEERING 623 ICEMAN
SATISFACTION)
(GUILTILY BUT WITH A STRANGE UNDERTONE OF 646 ICEMAN
SATISFACTION)
SOMETHING LIKE SATISFACTION IN HIS PITYING TONE) 667 ICEMAN
(FOR A SECOND THERE IS A GLEAM OF SATISFACTION IN 697 ICEMAN
HIS EYES.)
BECAUSE YOU DIDN'T WANT TO GIVE ME THE 704 ICEMAN
SATISFACTION
(HE ADDS WITH AN AIR OF SATISFACTION) 518 INZONE
(TO THE OTHERS WITH AN AIR OF SATISFACTION) 519 INZONE
AN' IF IT IS ANY SATISFACTION TO YOU I LAVE YOU 532 INZONE
THE REAL-IZATION THAT YOU HAVE
(WITH HEARTY SATISFACTION.) BUT THANK GOD, 14 JOURNE
(WITH SATISFACTION.) NO ONE.. 43 JOURNE
(WITH SATISFACTION, AS IF THIS WAS A PERPETUAL 121 JOURNE
BATTLE OF WITS WITH HIS ELDER SON
(SHE SPEAKS WITH MORE AND MORE VOLUPTUOUS 342 LAZARU
SATISFACTION)
SATISFACTION AND SENSE OF SELF-FULFILLMENT AND 46 MANSNS
PRIDE OUT OF BEATING MY
(WITH A CRUEL REVENGEFUL SATISFACTION.) 53 MANSNS
(WITH A STRANGE DERISIVE SATISFACTION.) 54 MANSNS
SIMON IS REPRESSING A FEELING OF GLOATING 57 MANSNS
SATISFACTION AND EXCITED CALCULATION.
(WITH A TRACE OF VINDICTIVE SATISFACTION.) 79 MANSNS
(HIS FACE LIGHTING UP WITH A PLEASED 80 MANSNS
SATISFACTION.)
ONE OF VINDICTIVE SATISFACTION AND GLOATING PITY.) 97 MANSNS
(WITH A VINDICTIVE SATISFACTION.) 104 MANSNS
(WITH AN EXULTANT SATISFACTION.) 105 MANSNS
(LAUGHINGLY, WITH AN UNDERCURRENT OF TAUNTING 111 MANSNS
SATISFACTION.)
IT'S HER GREAT-LADY PRIDE WON'T GIVE ME THE 118 MANSNS
SATISFACTION TO KNOW SHE'S HURT--
(HE GIVES A STRANGE CHUCKLE OF SATISFACTION, AND 129 MANSNS
CLOSES HIS EYES.)
SHE STANDS REGARDING DEBORAH WITH A CRUEL MOCKING 164 MANSNS
LEER OF SATISFACTION.

SATISFACTION (CONT'D.)
(WITH AN OBVIOUSLY FAKE AIR OF CONTRITION THINLY 184 MANSNS
MASKING A CRUEL SATISFACTION.)
(WITH AN ALMOST MASOCHISTIC SATISFACTION.) 191 MANSNS
(GLUMLY) OH. THEN AN IDEA COMES--WITH CRUEL 353 MARCOM
SATISFACTION)
MARCO SAYS WITH SATISFACTION) 405 MARCOM
UNTIL HE BECOMES HIS OWN IDEAL FIGURE, AN IDOL OF 418 MARCOM
STUFFED SELF-SATISFACTION/
(HE ADDS, NOT WITHOUT MORAL SATISFACTION) 8 MISBEG
JUST NOW, HE IS LETTING HIMSELF GO AND GETTING 72 MISBEG
GREAT SATISFACTION FROM IT.
YOU'VE MADE A PRIZE DAMNED FOOL OF HIM AND THAT'S 87 MISBEG
SOME SATISFACTION/
WITH A STRANGE HORRIBLE SATISFACTION IN HIS TONE) 150 MISBEG
AND IT'S THE LAST TIME YOU'LL EVER TAKE 104 POET
SATISFACTION IN HAVING ME WAIT ON TABLE
(QUIETLY. A DAUGHTER WHO TAKES SATISFACTION IN 104 POET
LETTING EVEN THE SCUM SEE
CONCLUDED TO OUR MUTUAL SATISFACTION. 110 POET
BUT THIS TIME, I WON'T GIVE YOU THE SATISFACTION--113 POET
(MICKEY GRINS WITH SATISFACTION AT HAVING CHEERED 136 POET
HER UP AND GOES IN THE BAR,
(AT FIRST HER ONLY REACTION IS PLEASED 142 POET
SATISFACTION.)
IT'S TIED STRONG--STRONG AS DEATH--(THE CACKLES 579 ROPE
WITH SATISFACTION)
ONLY FOR THE OBJECTIVE SATISFACTION OF STUDYING 33 STRANG
HIS OWN AND THEIR REACTIONS..
(THINKING FIERCELY--EVEN WITH SATISFACTION) 58 STRANG
(HE SUDDENLY SPEAKS TO EVANS WITH A REALLY SAVAGE 75 STRANG
SATISFACTION)
(WITH SATISFACTION--UNRUFFLEDLY) 77 STRANG
(THINKING WITH A CERTAIN SATISFACTION) 80 STRANG
(AGAIN WITH A CERTAIN SATISFACTION) 82 STRANG
I HAVE KNOWN A BIT OF HONOR AND A TRIFLE OF SELF- 86 STRANG
SATISFACTION...
(THEN, AS EVANS JUST STARES AT HIM DUMBLY IN A 106 STRANG
BLISSFUL SATISFACTION,
(WITH SATISFACTION) (YES, I'VE GOT IT STRAIGHT 112 STRANG
NOW...)
(WITH SAVAGE SATISFACTION) (THAT STRUCK 115 STRANG
HOME?
WAS IT SATISFACTIONS... 119 STRANG
I BOUGHT HIM A COSTLY DELICATE ONE SO HE COULD GET144 STRANG
FULL SATISFACTION AND YET NOT
(WITH SATISFACTION) 152 STRANG
(THINKING WITH SATISFACTION) 167 STRANG
(THINKING IN AMAZEMENT, BUT NOT WITHOUT A QUEER 186 STRANG
SATISFACTION)
(WITH SATISFACTION) RIGHTO/ 495 VOYAGE
THE LATTER NODS WITH SATISFACTION.) 499 VOYAGE
WHICH HE STUFFS INTO HIS POCKET WITH A GRUNT OF 508 VOYAGE
SATISFACTION.
(WITH A GRUNT OF SATISFACTION) 451 WELDED
I ONLY TELL YOU THIS FOR MY OWN SATISFACTION. 484 WELDED

SATISFIED
(WITH A GRIM LAUGH) I HOPE HE'S SATISFIED NOW-- 538 'ILE
SEEMS LIKE SHE AIN'T JEST SATISFIED UP HERE, 542 'ILE
AILIN' LIKE--
(FINALLY SURVEYS THE TWO WORDS SHE HAS BEEN 249 AHWILD
WRITING AND IS SATISFIED WITH THEM)
I HOPE YOU'LL BE SATISFIED AND KEEP STILL. 117 BEYOND
ARE YE SATISFIED NOW, YANKS 482 CARDIF
ARE YOU SATISFIED 549 DAYS)
(THEN QUICKLY) AND NOW I'VE SATISFIED YOU ON 556 DAYS
THAT, LIE DOWN AS YOU PROMISED.
NOW ARE YEH SATISFIED. 245 DESIRE
(DELIGHTED) AS LONG AS YOU LIKE IT, I'M 525 DIFRNT
SATISFIED.
I WON'T EVER BE SATISFIED NOW UNTIL I'VE FOUND THE469 DYNAMO
TRUTH ABOUT EVERYTHING.
THEN EVIDENTLY SATISFIED, TURNS TO ADA WITH A 484 DYNAMO
KILLIED AIR)
THEN, APPARENTLY SATISFIED THAT HE IS WHERE HE 187 EJONES
OUGHT TO BE,
ARE YOU SATISFIEDS 34 ELECTR
(THEN SATISFIED SHE HAS UNLY FAINTED, 64 ELECTR
(TURNING TO BORDEN--WITH A SELF-SATISFIED, KNOWING 70 ELECTR
AIR)
ARE YOU SATISFIED NOW, YOU JEALOUS GOOSE, YOU? 87 ELECTR
SATISFIED THAT THERE IS NO ONE ON THE DECK, 104 ELECTR
WELL, ARE YOU SATISFIED NOWS 113 ELECTR
(SEARCHES HIS FACE UNEASILY--THEN IS APPARENTLY 138 ELECTR
SATISFIED
(HE STARES AT HER FIXEDLY FOR A MOMENT--THEN 155 ELECTR
SATISFIED)
BROWN ISN'T SATISFIED/ 296 GGBROW
WELL, DION, AT ANY RATE, I'M SATISFIED. 296 GGBROW
BUT HE WASN'T SATISFIED. 23 HUGHIE
HE'S SO SATISFIED WITH LIFE HE'S NEVER SET FOOT 594 ICEMAN
OUT OF THIS PLACE
AIN'T YUH NEVER SATISFIEDS 658 ICEMAN
SATISFIED THE BOX IS SAFE, 523 INZONE
(WITH A STRANGE HAPPY SATISFIED AIR.) 87 MANSNS
THEN WITH A SATISFIED NOD.) 115 MANSNS
I'D BE SATISFIED THEN. 158 MANSNS
IF I HAVE SATISFIED YOU-- 412 MARCOM
WITH A SATISFIED SIGH AT THE SHEER COMFORT OF IT 439 MARCOM
ALL, RESUMES HIS LIFE.)
BUT TO TELL THE TRUTH, I'M WELL SATISFIED YOU'RE 20 MISBEG
WHAT YOU ARE.
SATISFIED BY HER REACTIONS TO HIS FIRST ATTACK, 69 POET
AND HASTENS TO APOLOGIZE.)
SARA WITH A STRANGE LOOK OF SATISFIED PRIDE.) 124 POET
YOUR FATHER'D BE SATISFIED WITH HARFORD'S APOLOGY 140 POET
AND THAT'D END IT.
SATISFIED, HE TURNS BACK INTO THE BARN) 578 ROPE

SATISFIED (CONT*D.)
YOU'RE GHOSTLESS AND WOMANLESS--AND AS SLEEK AND 52 STRANG
SATISFIED AS A PET SEAL/
AND BE SATISFIED WITH HIM ALONE. 61 STRANG
FROM HIS FACE, IT IS FULL AND HEALTHY AND 111 STRANG
SATISFIED.
(THINKING--SATISFIED) 122 STRANG
(WITH A TINGE OF SATISFIED SUPERIORITY) 191 STRANG
SATISFIEDLY
(LOOKS AFTER HIM SMILING SATISFIEDLY--THEN HALF TO227 DESIRE
HERSELF, MOUTHING THE WORD)
SATISFIES
THAT IT SATISFIES COME CRAVING IN YOU--FOR 455 WELDED
REVENGE/
SATISFY
I'LL HAVE A LOOK IF THAT'LL SATISFY YOU. 548 DIFRNT
YOU CAN SATISFY HATE/ 473 WELDED
SATISFYING
SEEKING THE SATISFYING REASSURANCE OF HIS 67 POET
REFLECTION THERE.
NOW WOULDN'T THAT BE MORE LOGICAL AND SATISFYING 43 STRANG
THAN HAVING GOD A MALE WHOSE
SATISFYINGLY
SO SATISFYINGLY RIGHT THAT HE BECOMES 221 AHWILD
SENTIMENTALLY MOVED EVEN TO THINK OF IT)
SATURDAY
A FLOOR MAN IS LEAVING SATURDAY. 468 DYNAMO
LIKE A RUM-SOAKED TROOPER, BRAWLING BEFORE A 158 POET
BROTHEL ON A SATURDAY NIGHT,
AND HE SAID SATURDAY EVENING. 72 STRANG
SAIL ON SATURDAY... 149 STRANG
IT WILL BE TWO MONTHS AGO SATURDAY SHE DIED...) 162 STRANG
SAUCER
HERS WERE LIKE PATENT LEATHER BUTTONS IN A SAUCER 25 STRANG
OF BLUE MILK/...))
SAUNTER
(SETH HURRIES DOWN TO THEM, TRYING TO APPEAR TO 133 ELECTR
SAUNTER.)
SAUNTERING
(THE CROWD FROM CHURCH ENTER FROM THE RIGHT, 236 HA APE
SAUNTERING SLOWLY AND AFFECTEDLY,
SAUNTERING LONGINGLY TOWARD THE DAWN'S RELEASE. 24 HUGHIE
SAUNTERS
HE SAUNTERS OUT OF THE DOORWAY AND OFF TO THE 187 EJONES
LEFT.)
HE GRINS WARMLY AND SAUNTERS CONFIDENTLY BACK TO 36 HUGHIE
THE DESK.)
HE SAUNTERS TO THE BAR BETWEEN LARRY AND THE 681 ICEMAN
STREET ENTRANCE.)
SAVAGE
MY GOODNESS, I NEVER SAW YOU SO SAVAGE-TEMPERED/ 268 AHWILD
(HIS VOICE WITH SURPRISING SUDDENNESS TAKES ON A 545 DAYS
SAVAGE VINDICTIVE QUALITY)
AND HE MUTTERS TO HIMSELF WITH SAVAGE 531 DIFRNT
SATISFACTION)
(FLINGING IT AT HIM LIKE A SAVAGE TAUNT) 541 DIFRNT
AND IS TAKEN UP AGAIN IN A NOTE OF SAVAGE HOPE. 201 EJONES
LEM IS A HEAVY-SET APE-FACED OLD SAVAGE OF THE 202 EJONES
EXTREME AFRICAN TYPE,
FOLLOWED A SECOND LATER BY SAVAGE EXULTANT YELLS. 203 EJONES
(WITH SAVAGE INTENSITY) OH, IF HE WERE ONLY DEAD/ 37 ELECTR
(HE STOPS AND GLANCES WITH SAVAGE HATRED AT THE 38 ELECTR
PORTRAIT.)
(WITH SAVAGE SATISFACTION) AH/ 61 ELECTR
(WITH SAVAGE VENGEFULNESS) BY GOD, 89 ELECTR
(THE STRAIN SNAPS FOR HIM AND HE LAUGHS WITH 101 ELECTR
SAVAGE IRONY)
ORIN IS HOLDING IN A SAVAGE, REVENGEFUL RAGE. 109 ELECTR
(HIS EYES LIGHTING UP WITH SAVAGE SATISFACTION) 110 ELECTR
HE STARTS TO PACE UP AND DOWN AGAIN--WITH SAVAGE 121 ELECTR
RESENTMENT)
IN WHICH A SAVAGE HATRED FIGHTS WITH HORROR AND 122 ELECTR
FEAR.
(HE LAUGHS--THEN IN A SAVAGE TONE) 253 HA APE
HIS COUNTRYMEN FELT EXTREMELY SAVAGE ABOUT IT, AND677 ICEMAN
HIS FAMILY DISOWNED HIM.
(LED BY THE CHORUS--SAVAGE NOW) 305 LAZARU
(HE STARTS TO LOP OFF THE FLOWERS FROM THEIR STEMS311 LAZARU
WITH A SAVAGE INTENSENESS)
(HE LAUGHS, HIS LAUGHTER FANATICALLY CRUEL AND 319 LAZARU
SAVAGE.
(KICKS HIS BODY WITH SAVAGE CRUELTY) 334 LAZARU
(HE STABS FLAVIUS WITH A SAVAGE CRY) 338 LAZARU
(WITH SAVAGE TRIUMPH, POINTING) 346 LAZARU
(WITH SAVAGE MALICE--JEERINGLY) 347 LAZARU
WHATEVER MADE YOU TAKE SUCH A SAVAGE GRUDGE 63 MISBEG
AGAINST PIGGS
(SO OVERCOME BY A RISING TIDE OF SAVAGE, 122 POET
HUMILIATED FURY,
(WITH A SAVAGE SCOWL) WE WON'T HURT HIM--MORE'N 600 ROPE
ENOUGH.
(HE SUDDENLY SPEAKS TO EVANS WITH A REALLY SAVAGE 75 STRANG
SATISFACTION)
(WITH SAVAGE SATISFACTION) ((THAT STRUCK 115 STRANG
HOME/...
(TRYING TO MOCK HIS OWN EMOTION BACK--WITH SAVAGE 144 STRANG
BITTERNESS)
(HIS FACE LIGHTS UP FOR A SECOND WITH A JOY THAT 463 WELDED
IS INCONGRUOUSLY SAVAGE--
(THEN WITH A QUEER SORT OF SAVAGE TRIUMPH) 475 WELDED
SAVAGELY
SAVAGELY CHEWING A TOOTHPICK. 263 AHWILD
(SAVAGELY) I HATED 'EM, I TELL YOU/ 73 ANNA
(SAVAGELY) HUMOR HIM 570 CROSS
(SAVAGELY SEIZING ON HIS WEAK POINT) 230 DESIRE
(RECOVERING FROM HIS ASTONISHMENT--SAVAGELY) 260 DESIRE
(HE STRIDES AWAY FROM HER, STOPS, AND TURNS BACK--543 DIFRNT
SAVAGELY)

SAVAGELY (CONT*D.)
(SAVAGELY) ((NO, BY GOD/... 459 DYNAMO
(SAVAGELY) ((NO/...I DON'T OWE HIM THE TRUTH/... 466 DYNAMO
(SAVAGELY) THE ONLY DECENT THING HE EVER DID/ 26 ELECTR
(SAVAGELY--GIVING HIM A PUSH THAT SENDS HIM 237 HA APE
SPRAWLING)
(TO HER FOLLOWERS--SAVAGELY) 290 LAZARU
(SAVAGELY) OH, IF I WERE CAESAR--/ 303 LAZARU
(THEN SAVAGELY) KNEEL DOWN/ 370 LAZARU
(THEN SAVAGELY.) NO/ 57 MANSNS
THE CAPTAIN GROWLS SAVAGELY AT THE CHRISTIAN TO 153 MARCOM
KEEP UP HIS COURAGE)
THE MOTHER LOOKS SAVAGELY DISAPPOINTED. 389 MARCUM
BUT HOGAN ACTS AS IF HE'D DENIED IT--SAVAGELY) 62 MISBEG
(SAVAGELY. 600 ROPE
(THINKING SAVAGELY) ((I HOPE GORDON IS IN 18 STRANG
HELL/...))
(SAVAGELY) AND THAT'S EXACTLY WHAT MY FATHER DID 20 STRANG
SAVE
(HE SWALLOWS HARD AS IF HE WERE CHOKING BACK A 92 STRANG
SOB--THEN SAVAGELY)
(SAVAGELY) UH, YES/ 108 STRANG
(SUDDENLY TURNS TO EVANS--SAVAGELY) 108 STRANG
THINKING SAVAGELY) 114 STRANG
(WATCHING HIM--SAVAGELY) ((NOW I KNOW/... 124 STRANG
(SAVAGELY) LIKE HELL I CAN'T/ 132 STRANG
BREAKS OUT SAVAGELY) 468 WELDED
SAVAGERY
(HE FINISHES UP WITH WELL-FEIGNED SAVAGERY) 440 DYNAMO
(WITH SUDDEN SAVAGERY) CALLS THEYSELVES 'UMAN 517 INZUNE
BEIN'S, TOO/
SAVAGES
BROWN COLORED SAVAGES THAT AIN'T EVEN CHRISTIANS. 497 DIFRNT
THE FIRST SQUATTING ON THEIR HAMS LIKE SAVAGES (AS345 LAZARU
CALIGULA DOES)
SAVE
EVEN TO SAVE YOURSELF FROM PUNISHMENT, YOU'D LIE 206 AHWILD
TO ME NOW. WOULD YOUR
(TURNING TO NAT) WHAT CAN WE DO TO SAVE HER, NATS232 AHWILD
MY OLDER BROTHER, HE SAVE MONEY, GIVE UP SEA, DEN 27 ANNA
HE DIE HOME IN BED.
I COULDN'T GET TO SLEEP TO SAVE MY SOUL. 147 BEYOND
AND WE'D SAVE OUR COIN, AND GO TO CANADA OR 487 CARDIF
ARGENTINE OR SOME PLACE
THEY EAT 'EM TO SAVE FUN*RAL EXPENSES. 456 CANIRE
YES, I SOLD HIM, IF YOU WILL--TO SAVE MY SOUL. 567 CROSS
SAVE ME/ 570 CROSS
(HYSTERICALLY) SAVE ME/ 570 CROSS
TO SAVE HER THE HUMILIATION OF HEARING IT THROUGH 527 DAYS
DIRTY GOSSIP/
NOTHING CAN SAVE HER. 558 DAYS
THE POWER STILL TO SAVE-- 558 DAYS
HUMAN SCIENCE HAS DONE ALL IT CAN TO SAVE HER. 559 DAYS
AND I'LL TRY TO SAVE UP MY PAY AND SEND YOU BACK 532 DIFRNT
ALL I'VE BORROWED NOW AND
IN APPEARANCE, HE HAS CHANGED BUT LITTLE IN THE 535 DIFRNT
THIRTY YEARS SAVE THAT HIS HAIR
WITH NO MARRIAGE LINES TO SAVE HER FROM DISGRACE/ 438 DYNAMO
BUT YOU SAVE YOUR HOLDING HANDS FUR MOM/ 459 DYNAMO
I'LL GET THEM PUT IN THE FIRST MONEY I SAVE... 463 DYNAMO
ALL THIS IN SILENCE SAVE FOR THE OMINOUS THROB OF 197 EJONES
THE TOM-TOM.
AH, LAWD, D'MY OE SILVER ONE LEFT--AN' I GOTTA 198 EJONES
SAVE DAT FO' LUCK.
ALL ARE NEGROES, NAKED SAVE FOR LOIN CLOTHS. 199 EJONES
LAWD, SAVE ME/ 202 EJONES
OH, I'M NOT DENYING YOU WANT TO SAVE HIS PRIDE-- 33 ELECTR
I'VE ALREADY TOLD HIM--SO YOU MIGHT AS WELL SAVE 91 ELECTR
YOURSELF THE TROUBLE.
WE'D HAVE BEEN ARRESTED--AND THEN I'D HAVE TO TELL113 ELECTR
THE TRUTH TO SAVE US.
SHOW ME THE WAY TO SAVE HIM/ 157 ELECTR
TO BE A GENEROUS HERO AND SAVE THE WOMAN AND HER 273 GGBROW
CHILDREN/
TO SAVE MY GRANDMOTHER FROM STREETWALKING. 34 HUGHIE
I'M JUST FINISHIN' FIGURIN' OUT DE BEST WAY TO 617 ICEMAN
SAVE DEM AND BRING DEM PEACE.*
BEJEGS, CORA SAID YOU WAS COMING TO SAVE US/ 620 ICEMAN
I MEANT SAVE YOU FROM PIPE DREAMS. 622 ICEMAN
TELL US MORE ABOUT HOW YOU'RE GOING TO SAVE US. 624 ICEMAN
THAT WILL REALLY SAVE THE POOR GUY, AND MAKE HIM 641 ICEMAN
CONTENTED WITH WHAT HE IS.
AND I NEED VUCK ONLY LEETLE VHILE TO SAVE MONEY 676 ICEMAN
FOR MY PASSAGE HOME.
SAVE UP ENOUGH FOR A FIRST-CLASS PASSAGE HOME, 676 ICEMAN
THAT'S THE BRIGHT IDEA.
SAVE IT FOR THE JURY. 717 ICEMAN
GOD SAVE ME, IT'LL BE HALF WATER. 100 JOURNE
I WON'T GO TO ANY DAMNED STATE FARM JUST TO SAVE 145 JOURNE
YOU
(THEN EXALTEDLY) BUT THE GREATNESS OF SAVIORS IS 289 LAZARU
THAT THEY MAY NOT SAVE/
THE GREATNESS OF MAN IS THAT NO GOD CAN SAVE HIM--289 LAZARU
UNTIL HE BECOMES A GOD/
WE MUST SAVE DEATH FROM HIM/ 342 LAZARU
NOW I KNOW LOVE, I MAY NOT GIVE MYSELF TO ANY MAN 351 LAZARU
SAVE HIM/
I COME TO SAVE YOU/ 368 LAZARU
SAVE ME FROM DEATH/ 371 LAZARU
IF THEY CAN BE SUCCESSFULLY NEGOTIATED, MAY SAVE 32 MANSNS
THE FIRM.
AND HENRY BELIEVED HE HAS THE MEANS TO SAVE IT. 35 MANSNS
THE GOLD WE'VE SLAVED TO SAVE/ 55 MANSNS
DID YOU THINK I WOULD REFUSE TO SAVE YOU FROM 58 MANSNS
BEING RUINED/
SAVE HIS SANITY. 173 MANSNS
YOU KNOW NO WOMAN COULD LOVE A MAN MORE THAN WHEN 188 MANSNS
SHE GIVES HIM UP TO SAVE HIM/

SAVE 1366

SAVE (CONT'D.)

I WILL--FOR LOVE OF HIM--TO SAVE HIM, 188 MANSNS
AND PLAN YOUR ROOK THAT WILL SAVE THE WORLD 191 MANSNS
FOR THE LOVE OF HIM, TO SAVE HIM AND SET HIM FREE/193 MANSNS
A QUEEN MAY NOT SORROW SAVE FOR HER KING/ 409 MARCOM
KUMACHIN WILL BE A MOTHER A MOTHER MAY NOT SORROW 410 MARCOM
SAVE FOR HER SON.
A WIFE MUST NOT SORROW SAVE FOR HER MAN. 410 MARCOM
AND DID THE LITTLE FLOWER SAVE HIS IMMORTAL SOUL* 423 MARCOM
(EXASPERATEDLY) GOD SAVE US, ARE YOU OFF ON THAT 24 MISBEG
AGAIN*
UH, JIM, JIM, MAYBE MY LOVE COULD STILL SAVE YOU, 153 MISBEG
IF YOU COULD WANT IT ENOUGH/
YOU'RE THAT CUNNING AND CLEVER, BUT YOU CAN SAVE 163 MISBEG
YOUR BREATH.
I WAITED TO SAVE HIM, AND I HOPED HE'D SEE THAT 175 MISBEG
ONLY YOUR LOVE COULD--
(WORRIED AGAIN.) MAYBE YOU OUGHT TO HAVE TOLD HER 19 POET
HE'S HERE SICK TO SAVE HER
I DON'T MIND AT ALL. IF I CAN SAVE YOU A BIT OF 28 POET
THE WORRY THAT'S KILLING YOU.
ARRAH, SAVE YOUR BLARNEY FOR THE YOUNG GIRLS/ 136 POET
WOULD YOU HAVE ME DO NOTHING TO SAVE MY HAPPINESS 143 POET
AND MY CHANCE IN LIFE.
IF HE HAD TO CALL THE POLICE TO SAVE HIM, 145 POET
GOD SAVE US, SARA, WILL YOU LISTEN/ 168 POET
WEEP GREAT TEARS AND APPEAL TO HIS HONOR TO MARRY 171 POET
YOU AND SAVE YOURS.
AH, WELL, I'LL SAVE WHAT I CAN AN* AT THE END OF 587 ROPE
TWO YEARS,
SHE'S GOT TO SHAKE AND HELP ME SAVE MY SAMMY/...1) 59 STRANG
I WANTED TO USE HIM TO SAVE MYSELF... 62 STRANG
I GOT TO SAVE HER/...1) 63 STRANG
AND I COULD SAVE HIM. 63 STRANG
SHE'S GIVING HER LIFE TO SAVE MY SAMMY... 63 STRANG
THIS WOMAN'S DUTY IS TO SAVE HER HUSBAND AND 87 STRANG
HERSELF.
YOU GAVE HIM TO SAM TO SAVE SAM/ 131 STRANG
(IN DULL ANGUISH) SAVE--AGAINS 183 STRANG
I WILL GIVE MY LIFE TO SAVE YOU/ 183 STRANG
SAVE ME, YOU/ 475 WELDED

SAVED

WENT IN SWIMMING THERE AND I SAVED HIS LIFE. 229 AHWILD
I'VE TAKEN DOWN THE DISTANCE EVERY TIME YOU'VE 230 AHWILD
SAVED RED'S LIFE FOR THIRTY YEARS
COME AND BE SAVED, BROTHERS/ 233 AHWILD
YOU KNEW I HAD ELEVEN DOLLARS SAVED UP TO BUY YOU 282 AHWILD
SUMETHING FOR YOUR BIRTHDAY,
AND *TIS GREAT BAD LUCK IT'S SAVED ME FROM AND ME 75 ANNA
ROAMING THE SEAS.
(AFTER A PAUSE) I'VE GOT OVER A THOUSAND SAVED, 134 BEYOND
AND YOU CAN HAVE THAT.
A NICE THIN* FOR ME TO HAVE TO SUPPORT HIM OUT OF 152 BEYOND
WHAT I'D SAVED
I'VE SAVED TEN THOUSAND FROM THE WRECKAGE, MAYBE 157 BEYOND
TWENTY.
THAT THEY MIGHT BE SAVED FROM THEMSELVES. 510 DAYS
ALL THAT SAVED ME FROM DOING SOMETHING STUPID WAS 521 DAYS
THE FAITH I HAD THAT SOMEWHERE
IT WOULD HAVE SAVED HIM SO MUCH SILLY ROMANTIC 534 DAYS
PURSUIT OF MEANINGLESS ILLUSIONS.
WHO WILL REVEAL TO US HOW WE CAN BE SAVED FROM 543 DAYS
OURSELVES*
AFTER WAITIN* THREE YEARS FOR ME TO GIT ENOUGH 496 DIFRNT
MONEY SAVED--
(WITH VINDICTIVE PASSION) HE COULD HAVE SAVED 26 ELECTR
HER--AND ME.
COME AND BE SAVED, HUH* 212 HA APE
I SAW MEN DIDN'T WANT TO BE SAVED FROM THEMSELVES,579 ICEMAN
I'D SAVED MY DOUGH SO I COULD START MY OWN 600 ICEMAN
GAMBLIN* HOUSE.
TELL HIM WE'RE WAITIN* TO BE SAVED/ 618 ICEMAN
SO AS SOON AS I GOT ENOUGH SAVED TO START US OFF, 711 ICEMAN
I'LL BET IT AIN'T NOTHIN* BUT SOME COIN HE'S SAVED520 INZONE
HE'S GOT LOCKED UP IN THERE.
AN* HE AIN'T SAVED NONE SINCE. 520 INZONE
YOU'VE NEVER SAVED A DOLLAR IN YOUR LIFE/ 31 JOURNE
SLIP A PIECE OF CHANGE TO THE JUDGE AND BE SAVED, 165 JOURNE
I HAVE SAVED YOU, LAZARUS--AT THE RISK OF MY OWN 338 LAZARU
LIFE--
BUT ALL OF THIS WASTE CAN BE SAVED. 394 MARCOM
BUT THE MAN I LOVE SAVED ME. 409 MARCOM
HE SAVED MY LIFE THREE TIMES AT THE RISK OF HIS 424 MARCOM
OWN.
BUT THAT I'VE SAVED, GOD BE THANKED. 22 POET
YOUNG HARFORD NEEDS TO BE SAVED FROM HIMSELF. 114 POET
SOMETHING TO LIFE AGAIN, AND ONCE SHE'S GOT THAT, 37 STRANG
SHE'LL BE SAVED/
IS HE ANY POORER, AM I ANY THE LESS HIS FRIEND 86 STRANG
BECAUSE I SAVED HIM*
HE'S SAVED ME/... 174 STRANG
YOUR LOVE SAVED ME. 447 WELDED
YOUR WORK SAVED MINE. 447 WELDED

SAVES

IT SAVES YOU HIRING A MAN. 32 JOURNE
THAT IS ONLY JUST IF HE SAVES IT FROM RUIN. 34 MANSNS
NOT THAT I NEED IT, BUT IT SAVES HIS PRIDE. 11 MISBEG
IT SAVES HIS WIFE... 86 STRANG
NO, IT SAVES HIM/... 86 STRANG

SAVETH

GREATER LOVE HATH NO MAN THAN THIS, THAT HE SAVETH167 JOURNE
HIS BROTHER FROM HIMSELF.

SAVIN'

WAAL, I'M THANKFUL FUR HIM SAVIN' ME THE TROUBLE. 265 DESIRE
(WITH SNEERING DIGNITY) I'S ON'Y SAVIN' YOU DE 673 ICEMAN
TROUBLE, WHITE BOY.
(MOCKINGLY) A-SAVIN' OF 'IS MONEY, 'E IS/ 498 VOYAGE

SAVIN'S

IF IT WASN'T FOR ME HELPIN' YOU ON THE SLY OUT OF 152 BEYOND
MY SAVIN'S,

SAVING

SEEING ALL THINGS, AND NOT GIVING A DAMN FOR 48 ANNA
SAVING UP MONEY.
SAVING MY WOMAN AND CHILDREN/ 297 GGBROW
SUDDENLY HIS FACE LIGHTS UP WITH A SAVING 35 HUGHIE
REVELATION.
OF COURSE, I WAS ONLY KIDDING CORA WITH THAT STUFF622 ICEMAN
ABOUT SAVING YOU.
MAYBE HE'S SAVING THE GREAT REVELATION FOR HARRY'S636 ICEMAN
PARTY.
SONS OF GOD WHO APPEARED ON WORLDS LIKE OURS TO 289 LAZARU
TELL THE SAVING TRUTH TO EARS
IN FACT--AND THIS IS THE BIG IDEA I'VE BEEN SAVING396 MARCOM
FOR THE LAST--
I WILL TELL THEM BOTH OF YOUR HEROIC CRUELTY IN 412 MARCOM
SAVING ME FROM DEATH/
FROM THE LUST FOR POWER AND SAVING OUR SOULS BY 85 POET
BEING CONTENT WITH LITTLE.
SHE WAS SAVING IT TO SURPRISE YOU WITH AT HER OWN 106 STRANG
PROPER TIME.
THE THANKS I GET FOR SAVING SAM AT THE SACRIFICE 171 STRANG
OF MY OWN HAPPINESS/...

SAVINGS

SHE'D BEEN GIVING ME MONEY OUT OF HER SAVINGS TILL155 BEYOND
SHE HADN'T MUCH LEFT.
HE GIVES THE BABY ONE YEN TO START A SAVINGS 389 MARCOM
ACCOUNT AND ENCOURAGES ITS THRIFT.

SAVIOR

(IGNORING THIS--QUIETLY) YOU ARE FORGETTING THAT 543 DAYS
MEN HAVE SUCH A SAVIOR, JACK.
I'LL GRANT YOU THE PSEUDO-NIETZSCHEAN SAVIOR I 543 DAYS
JUST EVOKED OUT OF MY PAST IS AN
A NEW SAVIOR MUST BE BORN-- 543 DAYS
AND I'M GOING TO BE THAT SAVIOR--THAT'S WHY I 477 DYNAMO
ASKED YOU TO COME--
AND HE WILL BECOME THE NEW SAVIOR WHO WILL BRING 477 DYNAMO
HAPPINESS AND PEACE TO MEN/
I WILL COME--BUT WHERE ARE YOU, SAVIORS/ 269 GGBROW
MERCY, SAVIOR/ 319 GGBROW
MERCY, COMPASSIONATE SAVIOR OF MAN/ 319 GGBROW
REDEEMER AND SAVIOR/ 299 LAZARU
REDEEMER AND SAVIOR/ 299 LAZARU
HE CURES, THE REDEEMER AND SAVIOR/ 303 LAZARU
SAVIOR/ 304 LAZARU
HAIL, SAVIOR/ 307 LAZARU
(APPREHENSIVELY) BLESSED SAVIOR/ 382 MARCOM

SAVIORS

(THEN EXALTEDLY) BUT THE GREATNESS OF SAVIORS IS 289 LAZARU
THAT THEY MAY NOT SAVE/
LET ALL STARS BE FOR YOU HENCEFORTH SYMBOLS OF 289 LAZARU
SAVIORS.

SAVOIR

THEY LACK SAVOIR-FAIRE. 63 POET

SAWBUCK

I HAD TO GET DOWN ON MY KNEES AND BEG EVERY GUY I 34 HUGHIE
KNOW FOR A SAWBUCK HERE AND A
SAWBUCK THERE UNTIL I RAISED IT. 34 HUGHIE

SAWDUST

HIS CLOTHES TORN AND DIRTY, COVERED WITH SAWDUST 60 ANNA
AS IF HE HAD BEEN GROVELING OR
SAWDUST BEFORE YOUR ADORING EYES RIGHT AT THE 501 DAYS
HEIGHT OF HIS DEIFICATIONS
THE FLOOR, WITH IRON SPITTOONS PLACED HERE AND 573 ICEMAN
THERE, IS COVERED WITH SAWDUST.
THE FLOOR HAS BEEN SWEPT CLEAN OF SAWDUST AND 628 ICEMAN
SCRUBBED.
ALONG THE SAWDUST TRAIL TO SALVATION 661 ICEMAN
JOE MOTT IS MOVING AROUND, A BOX OF SAWDUST UNDER 664 ICEMAN
HIS ARM,

SAWDUSTING

AS THE SCENE PROGRESSES, HE FINISHES HIS 664 ICEMAN
SAWDUSTING JOB,

SAWED

AND TAKES OUT A SAWED-OFF BROOM HANDLE) 11 MISBEG

SAWIN'

YE KNOW AS WELL AS I DO IF IT WASN'T FOR MY 586 ROPE
HAMMERIN', AN' SAWIN', AN' NAILIN',

SAWS

SAWS, A LATHE, A HAMMER, CHISEL, 577 ROPE

SAYIN'

WHA' WAS I SAYIN'S 224 AHWILD
AND WHAT YOU'RE SAYIN' YOU INTEND DOIN' IS 105 BEYOND
(IGNORING THIS REMARK) WHAT I WAS SAYIN' WAS THAT114 BEYOND
SINCE ROBERT'S BEEN IN CHARGE
AND SHOOK HIS HEAD, AND WALKED OUT WIDOUT SAYIN' A480 CARDIF
WURD.
(MOCKINGLY) SAYIN' 'IS PRAYERS/ 490 CARDIF
AND AIN'T HE TURNED TRAITOR--MUCKIN' AT ME AND 568 CROSS
SAYIN' IT'S ALL A LIE--
AN' I WAS GLAD SAYIN' NOW I'M FREE FUR ONCE, 226 DESIRE
EBEN WAS SAYIN'S 231 DESIRE
THAT'S WHAT EBEN WAS SAYIN'. 231 DESIRE
FOLKS KEPT ALLUS SAYIN' HE'S A HARD MAN 236 DESIRE
THE VOICE O' GOD SAYIN'*... 237 DESIRE
AN' YE KIN KISS ME BACK 'S IF YEW WAS MY SON--MY 243 DESIRE
BOY--SAYIN' GOOD-NIGHT T' ME/
YE DON'T KNOW WHAT YE'RE SAYIN'/ 256 DESIRE
YE'VE KEPT SAYIN' YE LOVED ME.... 256 DESIRE
HOLDIN' YERSELF FROM ME--SAYIN' YE'D A'READY 264 DESIRE
CONCEIVED--
(ECSTATICALLY) I'D FERGIVE YE ALL THE SINS IN 266 DESIRE
HELL FUR SAYIN' THAT/
WASN'T I SAYIN' THE JOKE'S ON 501 DIFRNT
AND I AIN'T SAYIN' NOTHIN' 'BOUT IT-- 503 DIFRNT
I AIN'T SAYIN' I LIKE IT BUT I DO LIKE HIM AND I 509 DIFRNT
GOT TO TAKE HIM THE WAY HE IS,

SAYING

SAYIN' (CONT'D.)
GOD A'MIGHTY, MA, I AIN'T SAYIN' NOTHIN' AGEN 514 DIFRNT
EMMER, BE IS
I RECKON THERE AIN'T NO USE SAYIN' NUTHIN' MORE. 517 DIFRNT
WHAT WAS YOU SAYIN'--IF YOU HAD A HUNDRED 523 DIFRNT
DOLLARS--$
FOLKS WOULD BE SAYIN' ALL SORTS OF BAD THINGS IN 532 DIFRNT
NO TIME.
I MEAN WHEN I WAS SAYIN' GOOD-BY, I SAID--(HE 538 DIFRNT
GASPS--THEN BLURTS IT OUT)
I DIDN'T PAY MUCH 'TENTION TO WHAT SHE WAS 539 DIFRNT
SAYIN'--
WAAL, I'M SAYIN' THIS BOY BENNY IS JUST ALF ALL 540 DIFRNT
OVER AGAIN--
YOU DON'T SUPPOSE I'D BE SAYIN' IT IF IT WASN'T 540 DIFRNT
SO?
YE DON'T KNOW WHAT YOU'RE SAYIN', DO YE$ 542 DIFRNT
AND YOU WAS JUST SAYIN' YOU'D NEVER BEEN IN JAIL. 181 EJONES
WAS I SAYIN' I'D SIT IN SIX MONTHS MO'$ 182 EJONES
IT'S HER GHOST FOLKS IS SAYIN' HAUNTS THE PLACE, 130 ELECTR
AIN'T IT$.
AN' I'M SAYIN' YOU'RE SCARED TO PROVE THERE AIN'T.131 ELECTR
YOU UNDERSTAND I AIN'T SAYIN' THIS TO NO ONE BUT 136 ELECTR
YOU TWO.
FOLKS IS SAYIN'. 170 ELECTR
AND I AIN'T HEARD A WORD YOU'VE BEEN SAYIN', 178 ELECTR
VINNIE.
IT PLOUGHS TROU ALL DE TRIPE HE'S BEEN SAYIN', 215 HA APE
DE NUTTY HARP IS SAYIN' SOMEP'N. 216 HA APE
DAT'S WHAT I'M SAYIN'. 216 HA APE
THAT'S WHAT YER BEEN SAYIN' EVERY BLOOMIN' HOUR 234 HA APE
SINCE SHE HINSULTED YER.
YUH GOT WHAT I WAS SAYIN' EVEN IF YUH MUFFED DE 178 252 HA APE
WOIDS.
WHAT WAS I SAYIN'$ 12 HUGHIE
CORA SAYIN' SHE'S SCARED TO MARRY HIM BECAUSE 614 ICEMAN
HE'LL GO ON DRUNKS AGAIN.
LIKE I WAS SAYIN' TO CHUCK, YUH BETTER KEEP AWAY 703 ICEMAN
FROM HICKEY.
HEY, DAVIS, WHAT WAS YOU SAYIN' ABOUT SMITTY WHEN 517 INZONE
THEY COME IN$
(THEN GUILTILY--) BUT I'M SAYIN' MORE THAN MY 12 POET
PRAYERS AGAIN.
WHAT ARE YOU SAYIN'$ 148 POET
HE'S ALL RIGHT. I'M SAYIN'/ 161 POET
(DISTRACTEDLY.) STOP IT, I'M SAYIN'/ 166 POET
YOU SAYIN' IT WAS A SIN TO MARRY A PAPIST, 580 ROPE
WELCOME, AS THE SAYIN' IS, AN' SIT DOWN. 499 VOYAGE

SAYING
NOT HEARING A WORD HE IS SAYING) 547 'ILE
I WAS SAYING IT'S ALL RIGHT IN ITS WAY--BUT 189 AHWILD
THERE'S NO PLACE LIKE HOME.
AFRAID OF PEOPLE SAYING THIS OR THAT ABOUT HER-- 207 AHWILD
AFRAID OF BEING IN LOVE--
WHAT'S THAT HE WAS SAYING ABOUT FISH IN THE SEAS 216 AHWILD
(THEN WARNINGLY) MIND WHAT I'M SAYING NOW. 217 AHWILD
WELL, AS I WAS SAYING, RED AND I WENT SWIMMING 229 AHWILD
THAT DAY.
WELL, AS I WAS SAYING, THERE WAS I AND RED, 230 AHWILD
EVERYONE ALWAYS SAYING WHAT A CARD HE IS, WHAT A 233 AHWILD
CASE, WHAT A CAUTION, SO FUNNY--
HEARD SAYING--BUT I ONLY KNOW THE CHORUS-- 258 AHWILD
I'M THE PROPER LAD FOR YOU, IF IT'S A MESELF DO BE 33 ANNA
SAYING IT.
DON'T GO, I'M SAYING/ 37 ANNA
THAT'S WHAT MY FATHER WAS SAYING. 37 ANNA
I THOUGHT YOU WAS SAYING-- 38 ANNA
THEN PROMISE ME YOU'LL CUT OUT SAYING NASTY THINGS 44 ANNA
ABOUT MAT BURKE EVERY CHANCE
BE SAYING TO HER, AND I'M THINKING IT'S A POOR 47 ANNA
WEAK THING YOU ARE.
YOU'D OUGHT TO BE 'SHAMED TO BE SAYING THE LIKE, 47 ANNA
AND YOU AN OLD SAILOR YOURSELF.
I'M SAYING OR I'LL FLATTEN YOU ON THE FLOOR WITH A 50 ANNA
BLOW.
NOW, MY OLD BUCKO, WHAT'LL YOU BE SAYINGS 52 ANNA
YOU WAS SAYING YOU LOVED ME-- 53 ANNA
WITH YOUR SAYING THIS ONE MINUTE AND THAT THE 54 ANNA
NEXT.
LET YOU GO GET DRESSED, I'M SAYING. 55 ANNA
LET YOU SHOOT, I'M SAYING, AND BE DONE WITH IT/ 69 ANNA
TELL ME IT'S A LIE, I'M SAYING/ 70 ANNA
AND I'LL BE SAYING PRAYERS OF THANKS ON MY TWO 71 ANNA
KNEES TO THE ALMIGHTY GOD/
(MISERABLY) YOU'D BE SAYING THAT, ANYWAY. 73 ANNA
BE CAREFUL WHAT YOU'D SWEAR, I'M SAYING. 75 ANNA
HE DON'T MEAN A WORD HE'S SAYING/ 106 BEYOND
HE DOESN'T KNOW WHAT HE'S SAYING. 107 BEYOND
(IN EXASPERATION) WHY DO YOU GOAD ME INTO SAYING 122 BEYOND
THINGS I DON'T MEAN$
I'M ONLY SAYING WHAT I'VE BEEN THINKING FOR YEARS.127 BEYOND
YOU WERE SAYING YOU'D GO OUT ON THE ROAD IF IT 127 BEYOND
WASN'T FOR ME.
I REMEMBER THINKING ABOUT YOU AT THE WORST OF IT, 132 BEYOND
AND SAYING TO MYSELF..
(STANDS STARING AT HER FOR A MOMENT--THEN WALKS 140 BEYOND
AWAY SAYING IN A HURT TONE)
YOU TELL THAT MOTHER OF YOURS SHE'S GOT TO STOP 148 BEYOND
SAYING
DO YOU KNOW WHAT YOU'RE SAYINGS 164 BEYOND
AND DIDN'T KNOW WHAT YOU WERE SAYING/ 165 BEYOND
WHAT ARE YOU SAYINGS 566 CROSS
AND SAYING TO MYSELF, CAN THIS BE MY OLD JACKS 501 DAYS
(ANGRILY) WHAT DO YOU MEAN BY SAYING I WAS 527 DAYS
REVENGING MYSELF$
(FRIGHTENEDLY) NO--I--I DON'T KNOW WHAT I'M 559 DAYS
SAYING--IT ISN'T I--
I AIN'T SAYING THAT. 512 DIFRNT

SAYING (CONT'D.)
I HEARD THEM SAYING TO THE STORE THAT YOU'D BEEN 525 DIFRNT
UP CALLIN' ON THAT TILLY SMALL.
GOOD GRACIOUS, WHAT'RE YOU SAYINGS 531 DIFRNT
HUTCHINS, PLEASE PAY ATTENTION TO WHAT I'M SAYING.423 DYNAMO
SAYING HE'S BOUND BY HIS CUNSCIENCE TO SQUEAL ON 431 DYNAMO
ME/
THAT YOU'LL NEVER REPEAT WHAT I'M SAYING TO 439 DYNAMO
ANYONE.
YOU DON'T KNOW WHAT YOU'RE SAYING/ 452 DYNAMO
SHE COULDN'T HAVE KNOWN WHAT SHE WAS SAYING...) 456 DYNAMO
=DON'T BE A FOOL.= SHE KEPT SAYING TO ME... 456 DYNAMO
YOU'RE JUST SAYING THAT TO GET MY GOAT/ 463 DYNAMO
I KNEW HE WAS ONLY SAYING THAT TO GET MY GOAT...11464 DYNAMO
=DON'T BE A FOOL.= SHE KEPT SAYING TO ME/ 466 DYNAMO
I WASN'T SAYING THERE WAS, WAS I$ 469 DYNAMO
HE DON'T NEED AN OLD FOOL OF A MINISTER SAYING 470 DYNAMO
PRAYERS OVER US/
BUT--YOU'RE NOT ANGRY AT ME FOR SAYING THAT, ARE 22 ELECTR
YOU$
STOP SAYING THAT/ 31 ELECTR
I DON'T KNOW WHAT YOU'RE SAYING. 56 ELECTR
(FLUSTERED) I DON'T REMEMBER EVER SAYING-- 69 ELECTR
AS FOR YOUR SAYING WHO'D EVER EXPECT IT-- 70 ELECTR
NO ONE IS SAYING YOU'D DELIBERATELY LIE. 96 ELECTR
YOU KNOW WHAT YOU'RE SAYING/ 99 ELECTR
(THEN HASTILY) YOU MUSTN'T MIND WHAT ORIN WAS 146 ELECTR
SAYING ABOUT THE ISLANDS.
DON'T KEEP SAYING THAT/ 156 ELECTR
YOU DON'T KNOW WHAT YOU'RE SAYING/ 165 ELECTR
YOU DON'T KNOW WHAT YOU'RE SAYING/ 177 ELECTR
(THEN TURNS AWAY, SAYING IN A LOST, EMPTY TONE) 178 ELECTR
(AS IF SHE HADN'T HEARD) ORIN CERTAINLY DRANK 275 GGBROW
WELL, BILLY BROWN WAS SAYINGS
HE KEEPS SAYING THEY'RE ROTTEN--WHEN THEY'RE 276 GGBROW
REALLY TOO BEAUTIFUL/
(AMAZED) BILLY BROWN, DO YOU REALIZE WHAT YOU'RE 305 GGBROW
SAYINGS
THE ELDEST WAS SAYING TO ME TODAY.. 310 GGBROW
WHO HASTENS TO ACQUIESCE IN THIS ROBBERY BY 209 HA APE
SAYING)
WE BELONG TO THIS, YOU'RE SAYINGS 213 HA APE
WE MAKE THE SHIP TO GO, YOU'RE SAYINGS 213 HA APE
AND BE DAMNED IF YOU WON'T HEAR SOME OF THIM 224 HA APE
SAYING THEY LIKE IT/
LIKE A MAN YOU'D HEAR IN A CIRCUS WOULD BE 229 HA APE
SAYING...
(WHILE HE HAS BEEN SAYING THIS LAST 244 HA APE
BUT LIKE HE COULDN'T THINK OF NOTHIN' ABOUT 23 HUGHIE
HIMSELF WORTH SAYING.
I KEPT SAYING TO MYSELF, =IF I CAN ONLY FIND 587 ELECTR
LARRY.
I REMEMBER WELL HIS SAYING TO ME, =YOU ARE 626 ICEMAN
NATURALLY DELICATE, ED.
SAYING YOU WERE STILL A SLAVE TO BOURGEOIS 647 ICEMAN
MORALITY AND JEALOUSY
AND SAYING HE OUGHT TO HAVE ME PUT IN SING SING/ 652 ICEMAN
HARRY'S THE GREATEST KIDDER IN THIS DUMP AND 655 ICEMAN
THAT'S SAYING SOMETHING/
HARDLY THE DECENT THING TO POP OFF WITHOUT SAYING 677 ICEMAN
GOOD-BYE TO OLD HARRY.
YOU'LL BE SAYING SOMETHING SOON THAT WILL MAKE YOU880 ICEMAN
VOMIT YOUR OWN SOUL
(FALTERINGLY) CAN'T HEAR A WORD YOU'RE SAYING. 688 ICEMAN
YOU'VE HEARD THE OLD SAYING, =MINISTERS' SONS ARE 709 ICEMAN
SONS OF GUNS.=
SAYING I WAS PEDOLING BABY CARRIAGES 710 ICEMAN
AND SHE KEPT ENCOURAGING ME AND SAYING, =I CAN SEE719 ICEMAN
YOU REALLY MEAN IT NOW.
SAYING TO EACH IN A LOW VOICE.. 513 INZONE
AND HE WOUND UP BY SAYING THAT HE HAD TO PUT UP 24 JOURNE
WITH POISON IVY, TICKS,
(HE GOES TO THE FRONT PARLOR, SAYING DISGUSTEDLY,) 26 JOURNE
THE ONE THING TO AVOID IS SAYING ANYTHING 29 JOURNE
HAVE TO HUMBLE MY PRIDE AND BEG FOR YOU, SAYING 32 JOURNE
YOU'VE TURNED OVER A NEW LEAF,
I WAS SAYING AGAIN DOC HARDY ISN'T MY IDEA OF THE 40 JOURNE
WORLD'S GREATEST PHYSICIAN.
THAT THEIR THOUGHTS ARE NOT ON WHAT SHE IS SAYING 71 JOURNE
ANY MORE THAN HER OWN ARE.
SUCH MORBID NONSENSE/ SAYING YOU'RE GOING TO DIE/ 90 JOURNE
AS YOU'LL FIND EVERYTHING ELSE WORTH SAYING. 131 JOURNE
AS I WAS SAYING, YOU MUST TAKE HER TALES OF THE 138 JOURNE
PAST WITH A GRAIN OF SALT.
I'M SAYING NO MATTER HOW YOU EXCUSE YOURSELF YOU 140 JOURNE
KNOW DAMNED WELL
RAKING UP THE PAST, AND SAYING YOU HATE ME-- 142 JOURNE
I CAN REMEMBER HER HUGGING AND KISSING US AND 148 JOURNE
SAYING WITH TEARS OF JOY RUNNING
MY SAYING WHAT I'M TELLING YOU NOW PROVES IT. 166 JOURNE
DO NOT KEEP SAYING TO YOURSELF SO BITTERLY, YOU 347 LAZARU
ARE A FAILURE IN LIFE/
SAYING YOU LOVE-- (IN A FRENZY, HE JUMPS TO HIS 359 LAZARU
FEET THREATENING LAZARUS)
AS FOR WHAT YOU'RE AFTER SAYING ABOUT MY ORIGIN-- 18 MANSNS
(ABRUPTLY SHAMEFACED.) AH, WHAT AM I SAYING/ 82 MANSNS
I AM SAYING THESE THINGS BECAUSE, IN ORDER TO 154 MANSNS
AVOID ALL FUTURE MISUNDERSTANDING,
(WHILE SHE IS SAYING THIS LAST, SARA SLINKS IN 164 MANSNS
NOISELESSLY.
WAKE UP FROM YOUR MAD DREAMS, I'M SAYING/ 165 MANSNS
(WHILE SHE HAS BEEN SAYING THIS LAST, 191 MANSNS
YOU KNOW--WITHOUT MY SAYING IT. 356 MARCOM
IS THE BEST SCHOOLING FOR A REAL MERCHANT AND 356 MARCOM
FATHER HAS A SAYING THAT WHERE
IT IS LIKE HIM NOT TO NEGLECT A PERSON IN THE CITY402 MARCUM
WHEN SAYING GOOD-BYE.
MY LIPS SPOKE WITHOUT ME SAYING A WORD. 415 MARCOM

SAYING

SAYING (CONT'D.)
HE CAN BE HEARD SAYING... 417 MARCOM
IT'S YOU THAT'S SAYING IT, NOT ME. 6 MISBEG
I'VE BEEN HOLDING MY TEMPER, BECAUSE WE'RE SAYING 9 MISBEG
GOOD-BYE.
HELL ROAST HIS SOUL FOR SAYING IT. 18 MISBEG
AND YOU'D GET A LETTER SAYING HIS AGENT TOLD HIM 24 MISBEG
YOU WERE A YEAR BEHIND IN THE
IT DIDN'T STOP HIM FROM SAYING 25 MISBEG
(SCORNFULLY) I'M IN LOVE WITH HIM, YOU'LL BE 27 MISBEG
SAYING NEXT!
ALL I'M SAYING IS, THERE MAY BE A CHANCE IN IT TO 29 MISBEG
BETTER YOURSELF.
SAYING MONEY IS THE ONLY THING IN THE WORLD, 33 MISBEG
(HE LOOKS UP AT THROAT) IS IT MASS YOU'RE SAYING, 36 MISBEG
JIMS
WHEN SHE WAS SAYING GOOD-BYE TO FATHER FULLER, SHE 39 MISBEG
ADDED INNOCENTLY.
AS I WAS SAYING, MY THROAT IS PARCHED AFTER A 44 MISBEG
LONG DUSTY WALK I TOOK JUST FOR
OPEN THIS DOOR, I'M SAYING, BEFORE I DRIVE A FIST 73 MISBEG
THROUGH IT.
GO TO YOUR ROOM, I'M SAYING, BEFORE- 76 MISBEG
AND SAYING I'D NEVER SPEAK TO HIM AGAIN. 79 MISBEG
(FURIOUSLY) STOP SAYING IT! 88 MISBEG
(ABRUPTLY HE REALIZES WHAT HE IS SAYING. 122 MISBEG
(DEFENSIVELY) THAT'S NOT SAYING MUCH. 124 MISBEG
THE HORSES WERE BEAUTIFUL, BUT I FOUND MYSELF 143 MISBEG
SAYING TO MYSELF, WHAT OF IT!
BUT ALL THE TIME I KEPT SAYING TO MYSELF, *YOU 148 MISBEG
LOUSY HAM*
YOU WERE FULL OF BLARNEY, SAYING HOW BEAUTIFUL I 169 MISBEG
WAS TO YOU.
MIND YOU, I'M NOT SAYING ANYTHING AGAINST POUR 14 POET
NUMA. A SWEETER WOMAN NEVER LIVE
DON'T BE SAYING THAT. 23 POET
BUT WHAT WAS I SAYING? 49 POET
SAYING AS IS THE MOTHER, SO IS HER DAUGHTER/* 579 ROPE
I AM AFRAID YOU'RE NOT RESPONSIBLE FOR WHAT YOU'RE 18 STRANG
SAYING.
WHAT SHE IS SAYING INTERESTS HIM AND HE FEELS 40 STRANG
TALKING IT OUT WILL DO HER GOOD.
I KNOW YOU'RE SAYING CROSSLY *SHE'S STILL MORBID* 49 STRANG
BUT I'M NOT.
(THINKING FRIGHTENEDLY) (WHAT IS BEHIND WHAT 57 STRANG
SHE'S SAYINGS...
(VIOLENTLY) I DON'T BELIEVE YOU KNOW WHAT YOU'RE 58 STRANG
SAYING!
AND I'M SAYING WHAT I SAID ABOUT A HEALTHY BABY 64 STRANG
I CAN HEAR HIS MOTHER SAYING, *SAMMY'S GOT TO FEEL 71 STRANG
SURE YOU LOVE HIM*...
SHE COMES QUICKLY OVER TO HIM SAYING WITH FRANK 79 STRANG
PLEASURE)
I THOUGHT WE'D GET SOME WORD FROM CHARLIE THIS 94 STRANG
MORNING SAYING IF HE WAS COMING
THEN HE CAN BE HEARD SAYING RESENTFULLY) 123 STRANG
BUT I WAS SAYING GOOD-BYE. 151 STRANG
WHAT WERE YOU SAYING, NEUS 170 STRANG
WHAT AM I SAYINGS... 175 STRANG
DO YOU KNOW WHAT YOU'RE SAYING! 180 STRANG
I LOVE YOU FOR SAYING *WE.* 445 WELDED
SAYING KINDLY BUT WITH A FAINT TRACE OF 465 WELDED
BITTERNESS)

SAYING*
A SLUT, I'M SAYING*! 208 HA APE

SCAFFOLD
SHE'S THE KIND WOULD BE POLITE TO THE HANGMAN, AND 78 POET
HER ON THE SCAFFOLD.

SCALE
HIS VOICE SINKING DOWN THE SCALE AND RECEDING 199 EJONES

SCALES
AS MILDRED RUNS OVER THE SCALES. 256 AHWILD

SCALLYWAG
I'M SURE HE DID, TOO, THE DIRTY SCALLYWAG. 24 JOURNE

SCALP
SURMOUNTED BY A SHINY BALD SCALP FRINGED WITH 578 ROPE
SCANTY WISPS OF WHITE HAIR.

SCAMP
YOU YOUNG SCAMP! (LAUGHING) HA-HA! GOOD BOY, 381 MARCOM
MARK!

SCANDAL
SCANDAL BEING FOR HIM MERELY THE SUBJECT MOST 6 ELECTR
POPULAR WITH HIS AUDIENCE.
OF A SIMILAR SCANDAL-BEARING TYPE, HER TONGUE IS 6 ELECTR
SHARPENED BY MALICE.
BUT WHAT HAS THAT OLD SCANDAL GOT TO DO WITH-- 19 ELECTR
AND FATHER WOULD DISOWN YOU PUBLICLY, NO MATTER 32 ELECTR
HOW MUCH THE SCANDAL COST HIM!
WHERE WILL YOU AND YOUR FATHER AND THE FAMILY NAME 33 ELECTR
BE AFTER THAT SCANDALS
AND I KNOW HOW ANXIOUS YOU ARE TO KEEP THE FAMILY 33 ELECTR
FROM MORE SCANDAL!
AND THAT'S THE WHOLE OF THE GREAT CAPTAIN BRANT 87 ELECTR
SCANDAL?
(W)--REMEMBER YOUR FATHER WOULDN'T WANT--ANY 101 ELECTR
SCANDAL--
IT WOULD SCANDAL IN THE PAPERS MAKE ABOUT A LIMEY 675 ICEMAN
OFFICER AND GENTLEMAN!
THERE WAS THE SCANDAL OF THAT WOMAN WHO HAD BEEN 86 JOURNE
YOUR MISTRESS, SUING YOU.
THERE HAS NEVER BEEN A BREATH OF SCANDAL ABOUT 105 JOURNE
HIM.
IT IS BECOMING AN OPEN SCANDAL! 143 MANSNS
GO YOU WANT TO CREATE A PUBLIC SCANDAL, CURSING 174 MANSNS
AND THREATENING EACH OTHER!
HAVING A SISTER WHO'S THE SCANDAL OF THE 6 MISBEG
NEIGHBORHOOD.
THAT I'M THE SCANDAL OF THE COUNTRY-SIDE, 19 MISBEG

SCANDAL

SCANDAL (CONT'D.)
I DON'T CARE A DAMN FOR THE SCANDAL. 19 MISBEG
THE SCANDAL WAS HUSHED UP BUT CON HAD TO RESIGN 12 POET
FROM THE ARMY.
AND IF YOU GO RAISING A DRUNKEN ROW AT THEIR 127 POET
HOUSE, AND MAKE A PUBLIC SCANDAL,
WHAT A SCANDAL... 12 STRANG
(THINKING VINDICTIVELY) (SERVE HER RIGHT, THE 73 STRANG
OLD SCANDAL-MONGER,
(UNHEEDING) BUT THERE WAS SCANDAL ENOUGH ABOUT 458 WELDED
YOU AND HIM,

SCANDALIZED
(SCANDALIZED, BUT LAUGHING) SID/ 198 AHWILD
(SCANDALIZED) NAT! 222 AHWILD
(SCANDALIZED) WHAT! 289 GGROW
(SCANDALIZED AS AN OLD MAID--THINKING) 187 STRANG

SCANDALOUS
WITH ROMANTIC INIQUITY OUT OF SCANDALOUS FRENCH 14 MANSNS
MEMOIRS/

SCANDALS
FAILURES FROM THE FOLLIES, OR THE SCANDALS, OR THE 16 HUGHIE
FROLICS.
OR IN THE SCANDALS OR FROLICS. 28 HUGHIE

SCANNING
(SINKS BACK INTO PREOCCUPATION--SCANNING THE 250 AHWILD
PAPER--VAGUELY)

SCANS
MILLIE* AS HE SCANS THE HEADLINES. 187 AHWILD
SHE SCANS HIM IMPATIENTLY--THEN HOLDS UP HER 240 AHWILD
DRINK)

SCANTY
SURMOUNTED BY A SHINY BALD SCALP FRINGED WITH 578 ROPE
SCANTY WISPS OF WHITE HAIR.
HE DOES NOT LOOK HIS AGE EXCEPT THAT HIS HAIR HAS 152 STRANG
GROWN SCANTY AND THERE IS A

SCAR
BUT HIS EXPERIENCE HAD LEFT AN INDELIBLE SCAR ON 534 DAYS
HIS SPIRIT.
A SCAR FROM A KNIFE SLASH RUNS FROM HIS LEFT 575 ICEMAN
CHEEK-BONE TO JAW.
ON HIS LOWER LEFT SHOULDER IS THE BIG RAGGED SCAR 576 ICEMAN
OF AN OLD WOUND.
HE STRIPS TO DISPLAY THAT SCAR ON HIS BACK HE GOT 593 ICEMAN
FROM A NATIVE SPEAR
THERE IS A SCAR OF A SABER CUT OVER ONE CHEEKBONE. 8 POET

SCARCELY
THE CAPTAIN SEEMS SCARCELY TO HAVE CHANGED AT ALL 140 BEYOND
*HO SCARCELY A DROP OF WATHER OR A BITE TO CHEW 482 CARDIF
ON.
SCARCELY BREATHING AND LISTENING INTENTLY.) 523 INZONE
I COULD SCARCELY HEAR HER VOICE. 424 MARCOM
AND SCARCELY HONORABLE ON HIS PART. 10 STRANG

SCARE
HE DID IT ON PURPOSE TO SCARE US! 189 AHWILD
(PROVOCATIVELY) DON'T LET THEM SCARE YOU, DICK. 195 AHWILD
BY GOLLY, DAT SCARE ME FUR MINUTE. 29 ANNA
MAYBE SKIPPER SCARE HER. 460 CARIBS
DID I SCARE YOUS 528 DAYS
YOU HAVE GIVEN US A SCARE, MY LADY. 548 DAYS
SHOUTING TO SCARE FOLKS AS IF YOU WAS A LITTLE 498 DIFRNT
BOY.
AND HIM MAKIN' THEM FIRE SHOTS ROUND HER TO SCARE 509 DIFRNT
HER BACK TO LAND AND GOT RID
WAITING TO SCARE SOME FRIEND OF HIS...!) 431 DYNAMO
I KNEW NOTHING COULD EVER SCARE ME AGAIN 460 DYNAMO
DON'T SAY THAT--NOT AFTER--YOU SCARE ME/ 469 DYNAMO
I DIDN'T MEAN TO SCARE YOU, ADA. 481 DYNAMO
(WITH COOL DEADLINESS) YOU MEAN LYNCHING'D SCARE 180 EJONES
TAKES MORE'N DAT TO SCARE DIS CHICKEN/ 185 EJONES
TINGS YOU KIN SCARE ME*. 131 ELECTR
I WAS ONLY TRYING TO SCARE YOU--FOR A JOKE! 148 ELECTR
WHY DE HELL SHOULD I SCARE HERS 231 HA APE
JUST AS DOUGH ANY DRUNK COULD SCARE CORA/ 614 ICEMAN
AND HIS SHOTGUN TO SCARE HIM-- 9 MISBEG
LOOKING LIKE SOMETHING YOU'D PUT IN THE FIELD TO 169 MISBEG
SCARE THE CROWS FROM THE CORN.
AHRAH, DON'T TRY TO SCARE ME. 17 POET
(WITH A SIGH OF RELIEF) YOU GAVE ME A SCARE. 465 WELDED

SCARECROW
THE CLOTHES HE WEARS BELONG ON A SCARECROW. 577 ICEMAN
IN CLOTHES I WOULDN'T PUT ON A SCARECROW, NOT 24 MISBEG
CARING WHO SAW HIMS
AS GRACEFUL AS A SCARECROW, AND HIS POOR HORSE 55 MISBEG
LONGING TO GIVE HIM A KICK.

SCARED
I TELL YOU SCARED THE PANTS OFF HIM. 206 AHWILD
HE'S SCARED OF YOU. 223 AHWILD
WELL, I DON'T MIND TELLING YOU I GOT MIGHTY 230 AHWILD
SCARED.
WHY IS EVERYONE SCARED TO TELL ME! 264 AHWILD
AW, THERE YOU GO AGAIN--ALWAYS SCARED OF LIFE!/ 278 AHWILD
I WAS SO SCARED, AND THEN I SNEAKED OUT THROUGH 281 AHWILD
THE BACK YARD,
BUT WHAT WAS YUH SO SCARED ABOUT--THAT I'D KICK UP 12 ANNA
A FUSS--
YOU ACT'S IF YOU WAS SCARED SOMETHING WAS GOING 29 ANNA
TO HAPPEN.
GEE, I WAS SCARED FOR A MOMENT I'D KILLED YOU. 33 ANNA
YOU DON'T GAT IT IN HEAD AY'M SCARED OF HIM YUST 43 ANNA
'CAUSE HE WAS STRONGAR'N AY
YOU'VE A YEAR'S GROWTH SCARED OUT OF ME, 69 ANNA
BUT IT'S THE TRUTH AND I AIN'T SCARED TO SWEAR. 75 ANNA
AND SCARED ME NEAR OUT OF MY WITS! 151 BEYOND
I WAS SCARED TO LOOK OVER FOR A MINUTE, 479 CARDIF
D'YUH THINK I'M SCARED TO-- 482 CARDIF
BUT I'M SCARED TO STAY HERE WITH ALL OF THEM 484 CARDIF
SLEEPIN' AND SNORIN'.

SCARED

SCARED (CONT'D.)
I AIN'T GOT A CHANCE, BUT I AIN'T SCARED. 486 CARDIF
WHY SO SCAREDS 499 DAYS
YE'RE SCARED O' HIM. 210 DESIRE
AN' SHE GOT SCARED--AN' I JEST GRABBED HOLT AN' 214 DESIRE
TUK HER/
I'M SCARED YOU'LL WANT ME TO LIVE UP TC ONE OF 496 DIFRNT
THEM HIGH-FANGLED HEROES YOU BEEN
(WITH A GRIN) YOU GOT ME SCARED, EMMER. 496 DIFRNT
WHAT YOU SCARED OF? 522 DIFRNT
YOU NEEDN'T BE SCARED--TO TALK OPEN WITH ME. 526 DIFRNT
I'VE BEEN SCARED TO DO MORE'N HINT ABOUT IT TO 530 DIFRNT
HIM.
HE HATES FIFE BECAUSE HE'S SCARED OF HIM... 424 DYNAMO
HE'S SCARED TO TAKE UP FIFE'S CHALLENGE 424 DYNAMO
OH, ALL RIGHT, CLOSE THEM IF YOU'RE GETTING 424 DYNAMO
SCARED.
HE'LL BE SCARED STIFF/... 432 DYNAMO
IT'S NOT BECAUSE I'M SCARED OF YOUR FATHER.. 433 DYNAMO
ARE YOU SCARED POP WILL EAT YOUS 433 DYNAMO
HE'S ONLY SCARED THAT 436 DYNAMO
((WHY DID THE POOR BOOB LET POP GET WISE HE WAS 438 DYNAMO
SCARED OF LIGHTNING...))
THEY'RE SCARED OF THE DARK/ 442 DYNAMO
I'M SCARED, MOTHER/ 446 DYNAMO
I'LL NEVER BE SCARED OF LIGHTNING AGAIN/...)) 449 DYNAMO
((HE LOOKS SCARED/... 449 DYNAMO
PICTURE MY BEING SCARED OF THAT BOOB ALL MY LIFE/ 449 DYNAMO
I'M NOT SCARED OF YOU OR YOUR GOD ANYMORE/ 452 DYNAMO
I'M NOT SCARED OF YOU/ 452 DYNAMO
I'LL NEVER BE SCARED AGAIN/ 453 DYNAMO
AND DIDN'T GET WHAT YOU WANTED AND WAS SO DAMNED 460 DYNAMO
SCARED TO TOUCH YOU.
WHAT ARE YOU SCARED ABOUTS 469 DYNAMO
(IRRITATEDLY) CUT OUT THAT TALK OF BEING SCARED/ 469 DYNAMO
SCARED WHAT HE DID WAS A SIN. 469 DYNAMO
THERE'S NOTHING TO BE SCARED ABOUT OR SORRY FOR. 469 DYNAMO
THEN I WON'T BE SCARED--OR SORRY. 469 DYNAMO
(PERSUASIVELY) I'M SCARED ON THIS ROOF, RUBE. 482 DYNAMO
(UNEASILY) RUBE/ I'M SCARED UP HERE/ 482 DYNAMO
YOU KNOW, ADA, THERE USED TO BE TIMES WHEN I WAS 484 DYNAMO
SCARED HERE TOO--
I KNOWS YOUSE SCARED TO STEAL FROM ME. 180 EJONES
DOES YOU THINK I'SE SCARED O' HIM 183 EJONES
YOU WAS SCARED TO PUT AFTER 'IM TILL YOU'D MOULDED203 EJONES
SILVER BULLETS, EHS
I WAS SO SCARED ANYMORE WOULD GUESS I WAS AFRAID/ 95 ELECTR
AN' I'M SAYIN' YOU'RE SCARED TO PROVE THERE AIN'T.131 ELECTR
THERE'S TIMES WHEN A MAN'S A DARN FOOL NOT TO BE 135 ELECTR
SCARED.
(THEN SCORNFULLY) HOW CAN YOU BE SO SCARED OF 161 ELECTR
VINNIES
(PATS HIS HEAD MATERNALLY) THERE, DON'T BE 286 GGBROW
SCARED.
HIS FACE SCARED ME. 311 GGBROW
I WAS SCARED, GET MES 230 HA APE
I SCARED HERS 231 HA APE
YOU SCARED HER OUT OF A YEAR'S GROWTH. 231 HA APE
(SCARED NOW--YELLING OFF LEFT) 245 HA APE
FUN OF YUH, LAUGHIN' AT YUH, GITTIN' SCARED OF 253 HA APE
YUH--DAMN 'EM/
I SHOWED HIM LOTS OF WAYS HE COULD CROSS HER UP, 16 HUGHIE
BUT HE WAS TOO SCARED.
BUT HE WAS TOO SCARED. 16 HUGHIE
I GOT SCARED HE'D PASS OUT WITH EXCITEMENT. 21 HUGHIE
SCARED IF DEY HIT THE HAY DEY WOULDN'T BE HERE 580 ICEMAN
WHEN HICKEY SHOWED UP.
YOU NEEDN'T BE SCARED OF ME/ 601 ICEMAN
(AMUSED) SCARED HE'RE HOLDIN' OUT ON HIM. 613 ICEMAN
CORA SAYIN' SHE'S SCARED TO MARRY HIM BECAUSE 614 ICEMAN
HE'LL GO ON DRUNKS AGAIN.
SHOW YOU A LITTLE WALK AROUND THE WARD IS NOTHING 621 ICEMAN
TO BE SO SCARED ABOUT.
LIKE DEY WAS SCARED IF DEY GET TOO DRUNK, 631 ICEMAN
JEES, HICKEY, YUH SCARED ME OUTA A YEAR'S GROWTH, 638 ICEMAN
SWEARIN' IN LIKE DAT.
BUT EVEN MORE SCARED OF DYING. 641 ICEMAN
YOU'LL SAY TO YOURSELF, I'M JUST AN OLD MAN WHO IS641 ICEMAN
SCARED OF LIFE.
BECAUSE YOU WON'T BE SCARED OF EITHER LIFE OR 641 ICEMAN
DEATH ANY MORE.
I'M SCARED OF HIM, HONEST. 648 ICEMAN
(HE PATS HIM ON THE BACK) DON'T BE SO SCARED/ 655 ICEMAN
HE'S YELLOW. HE AIN'T GOT THE GUTS, HE'S SCARED 660 ICEMAN
HE'LL FIND OUT--
(SCORNFULLY) YEAHS IT DON'T LOOK TO ME'S 665 ICEMAN
SCARED OF YUH.
I'M GETTING MORE AND MORE SCARED OF HIM. 666 ICEMAN
I'D SAY YOU WAS SCARED OF HIM. 666 ICEMAN
SAY, LISTEN, WHAT D'YUH MEAN ABOUT HIM BEIN' 668 ICEMAN
SCARED YOU'D ASK HIM QUESTIONSS
SO I'D GET SCARED DEY'D GET DE JOINT PINCHED 669 ICEMAN
THEY'RE SCARED TO CALL THE POLICE AND HAVE HIM 675 ICEMAN
PINCHED BECAUSE
LOOKING AS IF YOU WERE SCARED THE STREET OUTSIDE 685 ICEMAN
WOULD BITE YOU/
WHAT THE HELL'S TO BE SCARED OF, JUST TAKING A 687 ICEMAN
STROLL AROUND MY OWN YARDS
NOT THAT I'M SCARED OF 'EM. 687 ICEMAN
SCARED STIFF OF AUTOMOBILES. 688 ICEMAN
SCARED ME OUT OF A YEAR'S GROWTH/ 690 ICEMAN
THERE MUST HAVE BEEN SOMETHING THERE HE WAS EVEN 700 ICEMAN
MORE SCARED TO FACE THAN HE IS
(CONTEMPTUOUSLY) YES/ WHAT ARE YOU SO DAMNED 703 ICEMAN
SCARED OF DEATH FORS
SHE JUST SATO, LOOKING WHITE AND SCARED, *WHY, 710 ICEMAN
TEDDY*
YOU LOOK SCARED. 723 ICEMAN

SCENE

SCARED (CONT'D.)
HE BENDS DOWN AND REACHES OUT HIS HAND SORT U' 519 INZONE
SCARED-LIKE.
(HESITANTLY AGAIN.) IT WAS HER BEING IN THE SPARE 38 JOURNE
ROOM THAT SCARED ME.
I WAS SCARED OUT OF MY WITS RIDING BACK FROM TOWN. 98 JOURNE
DON'T BE SCARED OF THIS SANATORIUM BUSINESS. 164 JOURNE
(SMILING GLOATINGLY.) AS SCARED AS IF HE SAW A 126 MANSNS
GHOST.
I'LL SHOW YOU I'M NOT SCARED/ 362 MARCOM
HE GOT SCARED TO DEATH THAT HIS KISSING ME THIS 143 POET
MORNING HAD MADE ME ANGRY.
AND THEN SIMON TOLD ME HOW SCARED HE'D BEEN 145 POET
YUH NEEDN'T BE SCARED I'M A GHOST. 599 ROPE
I'D HAVE LEFT HIM CLEAN D*TY I WAS A KID AND 599 ROPE
SCARED TO PINCH MORE.
THEN I WANTED TO WRITE TO YOU BUT I WAS SCARED HE 61 STRANG
MIGHT READ IT.

SCARES
ALL THIS STUFF SCARES ME. 484 DYNAMO
HE SCARES ME AT TIMES--AND VINNIE--I'VE WATCHED 158 ELECTR
HER LOOKING AT YOU.
SCARES THEM INTO LETTING HIM IN CN EVERYTHING-- 381 MARCOM

SCARING
LISTENING TO MY OLD MAN WHOOPING UP HELL FIRE AND 709 ICEMAN
SCARING THOSE HOUSIER SUCKERS

SCARLET
(JEERINGLY) THE SCARLET WOMAN/ 210 DESIRE
YER LIPS AIR LIKE SCARLET.. 232 DESIRE
(SCARLET--BLAZING) IT'S A LIE/ 541 DIFRNT
STRIPS, OF MATTING, DYED SCARLET. 173 EJONES
IT IS PAINTED A DAZZLING, EYE-SPITTING SCARLET. 173 EJONES
COMMON DINNER BELL WHICH IS PAINTED THE SAME VIVIDI82 EJONES
SCARLET AS THE THRONE.
WEARING THE BRILLIANT SCARLET FULL-DRESS UNIFORM 88 POET
OF A MAJOR.
HIS SCARLET UNIFORM IS FILTHY AND TORN AND PULLED 152 POET
AWRY.

SCARS
(QUIETLY) I HAVE MY SHARE OF SCARS. 517 DAYS
KEEPING HEALS THE WOUNDS OF SORROW TILL ONLY THE 420 MARCOM
SCARS REMAIN.
SO MANY OLD MOUNDS MAY HAVE TO BE UNBOUND, AND OLD188 STRANG
SCARS POINTED TO WITH PRIDE.

SCATHELESS
ONE MAY NOT GIVE ONE'S SOUL TO A DEVIL OF HATE-- 938 DAYS
AND REMAIN FOREVER SCATHELESS.

SCATHINGLY
(SCATHINGLY) YOU TALKING OF YOUR DEAR SISTER/ 608 ICEMAN
(SCATHINGLY.) IF IT TAKES MY SNORING TO MAKE YOU 21 JOURNE
REMEMBER SHAKESPEARE INSTEAD
(SCATHINGLY.) FOR THE MONEY/ 144 JOURNE
(LOOKING HIM OVER SCATHINGLY) 381 MARCOM
(SCATHINGLY) AND, GOD PITY YOU, IF YOU AIN'T THAT 75 MISREG
FULL.
(SCATHINGLY) SURE, WASN'T YOU THE HERCS 86 MISREG
(SCATHINGLY) I'M SURE YOU'VE MADE UP A WHOLE NEW 163 MISRFG
SET OF LIES AND EXCUSES.
SHE ADDS SCATHINGLY:) I HOPE YOU SAW SOMETHING IN 44 POET
THE MIRROR YOU COULD ADMIRES
(SCATHINGLY) THAT'S ABSURD/ 457 WELDEO

SCATTER
AND FLOWERS IN THEIR HANDS WHICH THEY SCATTER 306 LAZARU
ABOUT.

SCATTERBRAINED
YOU MUST THINK I'VE BECOME AWFULLY SCATTERBRAINED/147 ELECTR

SCATTERED
I'VE SEEN DEAD MEN SCATTERED BOUT, 54 ELECTR
THE CLOTHES HE HAS TORN OFF IN HIS AGONY ARE 319 GGBROW
SCATTERED ON THE FLOOR.
THE LOFT IS BARE EXCEPT FOR A FEW SCATTERED MOUNDS577 ROPE
OF DARK-LOOKING HAY.
THAT ARE FOUND IN THE LARGE, JIGSAW COUNTRY HOUSES 48 STRANG
SCATTERED AROUND THE COUNTRY

SCATTERING
HE PRANCES INTO THE MIDST OF THE DANCERS, 250 DESIRE
SCATTERING THEM.
SCATTERING SO THAT EACH ENTERS AT A DIFFERENT 203 EJONES
SPOT.)
AND SCATTERING THE CONTENTS OF DRAWERS AROUND. 115 ELECTR

SCAVENGER
AND AT LAST WE DIE AND THE STARVING SCAVENGER HUGS180 MANSNS
OF LIFE DEVOUR OUR CARRIUN/

SCENE
(SCENE--SITTING-ROOM OF THE MILLER HOME IN A LARGE185 AHWILD
SMALL-TOWN IN CONNECTICUT--
AND CONTINUES AT INTERVALS THROUGHOUT THE SCENE. 189 AHWILD
(SCENE--DINING-ROOM OF THE MILLER HOME-- 210 AHWILD
(SCENE--THE BACK ROOM OF A BAR IN A SMALL HOTEL-- 236 AHWILD
(SCENE--SAME AS ACT ONE--SITTING-RKOM OF THE 249 AHWILD
MILLER HOME--
(SCENE--THE SAME--SITTING-ROOM OF THE MILLER 263 AHWILD
HOUSE--
(SCENE--A STRIP OF BEACH ALONG THE HARBOR. 275 AHWILD
CURTAIN ACT 4, SCENE 3 288 AHWILD
(SCENE THE SITTING-ROOM OF THE MILLER HOUSE 288 AHWILD
AGAIN--
SCENE--JOHNNY-THE-PRIEST'S>> SALCON NEAR SOUTH 3 ANNA
STREET, NEW YORK CITY.
SCENE--TEN DAYS LATER. 25 ANNA
SCENE-- 41 ANNA
SCENE--SAME AS ACT THREE, ABOUT NINE O'CLOCK OF A 63 ANNA
FOGGY NIGHT TWO DAYS LATER.
THIS FADES GRADUALLY AS THE ACTION OF THE SCENE 81 BEYOND
PROGRESSES.
THERE'D BE BOUND TO BE SUCH A SCENE WITH THEM ALL 92 BEYOND
TOGETHER.

SCENE

SCENE (CONT'D.)

DURING THE FOLLOWING SCENE SHE KEEPS MARY IN HER 140 BEYOND ARMS.)

SHE REMAINS LIKE THIS ALL DURING THE SCENE BETWEEN160 BEYOND THE TWO BROTHERS.)

(SAME AS ACT ONE, SCENE ONE--A SECTION OF COUNTRY 166 BEYOND HIGHWAY.

AT THE CLOSE OF THE OPENING SCENE BETWEEN JOHN AND493 DAYS LOVING.

(SCENE--THE LIVING ROOM OF THE LOVINGS' DUPLEX 514 DAYS APARTMENT.

(SCENE--THE LIVING ROOM AGAIN. 532 DAYS

FATHER BAIRD SITS IN THE SAME ATTITUDE AS HE HAD 541 DAYS IN THE PREVIOUS SCENE.

(SCENE--JOHN LOVING'S STUDY ON THE UPPER FLOOR OF 541 DAYS THE APARTMENT.

AS IF HE WERE VISUALIZING THE SCENE HE IS 544 DAYS DESCRIBING)

SCENE, IN WHICH HE FINALLY CONFRONTS HIS GHOSTS/ 544 DAYS OUT THIS SCENE ALSO REVEALS THE INTERIOR OF ELSA'S553 DAYS BEDROOM AT LEFT OF STUDY.)

THE STUDY IS SHOWN AS IN PRECEDING SCENE, 553 DAYS

(SCENE--A SECTION OF THE INTERIOR OF AN OLD 564 DAYS CHURCH.

IT IS A FEW MINUTES AFTER THE CLOSE OF THE 564 DAYS PRECEDING SCENE.

(SAME AS SCENE TWO-- 216 DESIRE

(IN HER MOST SEDUCTIVE TONES WHICH SHE USES ALL 225 DESIRE THROUGH THIS SCENE)

SAME AS SCENE THREE. 262 DESIRE

(SCENE--PARLOR OF THE CROSBY HOME. 493 DIFRNT

TALKING AND LAUGHING DURING THE FOLLOWING SCENE.) 507 DIFRNT

(SCENE--THIRTY YEARS AFTER--THE SCENE IS THE SAME 519 DIFRNT BUT NOT THE SAME.

ACT ONE, GENERAL SCENE -0 DYNAMO

TO MARK THE END OF SCENE ONE. 427 DYNAMO

WITH LIGHT SITTING AS AT THE END OF SCENE ONE. 435 DYNAMO

(THERE IS DARKNESS AGAIN FOR A MOMENT, TO MARK THE435 DYNAMO END OF SCENE TWO.

(THERE IS A PAUSE OF DARKNESS HERE TO MARK THE END443 DYNAMO OF SCENE THREE.

(THE SAME AS ACT ONE, SCENE ONE. 454 DYNAMO

THERE IS A DIM LIGHT ABOVE IN THE SWITCH GALLERIES476 DYNAMO AS IN THE PREVIOUS SCENE.

(SAME AS ACT TWO, SCENE THREE--EXTERIOR OF THE 476 DYNAMO POWER HOUSE FOUR MONTHS LATER.

(THERE IS A PAUSE OF DARKNESS HERE TO INDICATE THE483 DYNAMO END OF SCENE ONE.

(THERE IS A PAUSE OF DARKNESS TO INDICATE THE END 485 DYNAMO OF SCENE TWO.

AS THE SCENE OPENS NOTHING CAN BE DISTINCTLY MADE 190 EJONES OUT.

SCENE, THERE IS SILENCE, BROKEN EVERY FEW SECONDS 191 EJONES BY A QUEER, CLICKING SOUND.

THEIR MOVEMENTS, LIKE THOSE OF JEFF IN THE 194 EJONES PRECEDING SCENE.

SMITHERS IS THE SAME AS IN SCENE ONE. 202 EJONES

SAME AS SCENE TWO, THE DIVIDING LINE OF THE FOREST202 EJONES AND PLAIN.

(GENERAL SCENE OF THE TRILOGY THE ACTION OF THE 2 ELECTRA TRILOGY.

(SCENE--EXTERIOR OF THE MANNON HOUSE ON A LATE 5 ELECTRA AFTERNOON IN APRIL, 1865.

(UNREBDING--AS IF THE SCENE WERE STILL BEFORE HIS 26 ELECTRA EYES)

(SCENE--IN THE HOUSE--EZRA MANNON'S STUDY. 28 ELECTRA

SCENE. 42 ELECTRA

(SCENE--THE SAME AS ACT ONE, SCENE ONE--THE 43 ELECTRA EXTERIOR OF THE MANNON HOUSE.

(SCENE--EZRA MANNON'S BEDROOM. 58 ELECTRA

(SCENE--THE SAME AS ACTS ONE AND THREE OF 67 ELECTRA "HOMECOMING"--

THE OPENING OF THIS SCENE FOLLOWS IMMEDIATELY THE 79 ELECTRA CLOSE OF THE PRECEDING ONE.

(SCENE--THE SITTING-ROOM OF THE MANNON HOUSE. 79 ELECTRA

(SCENE--THE SAME AS ACT TWO OF "HOMECOMING"--EZRA 93 ELECTRA MANNON'S STUDY.

THE SCENE FADES OUT INTO DARKNESS. 109 ELECTRA

(SCENE--THE SAME AS ACT THREE OF "HOMECOMING"-- 117 ELECTRA EXTERIOR OF THE MANNON HOUSE.

(SCENE--SAME AS ACT THREE OF THE HUNTED--EZRA 149 ELECTRA MANNON'S STUDY--

(SCENE--SAME AS ACT ONE, SCENE TWO--THE SITTING- 157 ELECTRA ROOM--

(SCENE--SAME AS ACT ONE, SCENE ONE--EXTERIOR OF 169 ELECTRA THE HOUSE.

SCENE--A CROSS SECTION OF THE PIER OF THE CASINO. 257 GGBROW

SCENE--SEVEN YEARS LATER. 269 GGBROW

SCENE--BILLY BROWN'S OFFICE, AT FIVE IN THE 274 GGBROW AFTERNOON.

SHE IS DRESSED AS IN SCENE ONE BUT WITH AN ADDED 274 GGBROW TOUCH OF EFFECTIVE PRIMPING

(KEATED SIMILARLY TO THAT OF SCENE ONE 274 GGBROW

SCENE--CYBEL'S PARLOR. 276 GGBROW

SCENE--CYBEL'S PARLOR--ABOUT SUNSET IN SPRING 284 GGBROW SEVEN YEARS LATER.

SCENE--THE DRAFTING ROOM IN BROWN'S OFFICE. 290 GGBROW

WITH MUCH THE SAME QUALITY AS BILLY BROWN'S IN ACT293 GGBROW ONE, SCENE ONE.

WHICH HE TRIES TO HOLD THROUGHOUT THE SCENE) 294 GGBROW

SCENE--THE LIBRARY OF WILLIAM BROWN'S HOME--NIGHT 294 GGBROW OF THE SAME DAY.

SCENE--THE DRAFTING ROOM AND PRIVATE OFFICE OF 302 GGBROW BROWN ARE BOTH SHOWN.

LAST SCENE--THE SELF-ASSURED SUCCESS. 303 GGBROW

SCENE--THE SAME AS ACT TWO, SCENE THREE-- 306 GGBROW

SCENE--THE SAME AS SCENE ONE OF ACT ONE--THE 308 GGBROW SITTING-ROOM OF MARGARET'S HOME.

SCENE (CONT'D.)

IT IS ABOUT HALF AN HOUR AFTER THE LAST SCENE. 308 GGBROW

SCENE--SAME AS SCENE ONE OF ACT THREE--THE 313 GGBROW DRAFTING ROOM AND BROWN'S OFFICE.

SCENE--THE SAME AS SCENE TWO OF ACT THREE--THE 319 GGBROW LIBRARY OF WILLIAM BROWN'S HOME.

SCENE--FOUR YEARS LATER. 323 GGBROW

THE TREATMENT OF THIS SCENE, OR OF ANY OTHER SCENE207 HA APE IN THE PLAY.

THE IMPRESSION TO BE CONVEYED BY THIS SCENE IS ONE218 HA APE OF THE BEAUTIFUL.

HE IS DRESSED AS IN SCENE FIVE. 245 HA APE

(SCENE THE DESK AND A SECTION OF LOBBY OF A SMALL 7 HUGHIE HOTEL

THE BLACK CURTAIN DIVIDING IT FROM THE BAR IS THE 628 ICEMAN RIGHT WALL OF THE SCENE.

(SCENE--THE BACK ROOM ONLY. 628 ICEMAN

AS THE SCENE PROGRESSES, HE FINISHES HIS 664 ICEMAN SAWDUSTING JOB.

(SCENE LIVING ROOM OF JAMES TYRONE'S SUMMER HOME 11 JOURNE ON A MORNING IN AUGUST, 1912.

(SCENE THE SAME. 51 JOURNE

(SCENE THE SAME, ABOUT A HALF HOUR LATER. 71 JOURNE

THIS CHANGE BECOMES MORE MARKED AS THE SCENE GOES 81 JOURNE ON.

(SCENE THE SAME. 97 JOURNE

AS IT WAS IN THE PRE-LUNCHEON SCENE OF THE 97 JOURNE PREVIOUS ACT.

YOU LOVE TO MAKE A SCENE OUT OF NOTHING SO YOU CAN120 JOURNE BE DRAMATIC AND TRAGIC.

(SCENE THE SAME. 125 JOURNE

THE MAD SCENE. 170 JOURNE

(SCENE.. 281 LAZARU

(CURTAIN) LAZARUS LAUGHED ACT ONE SCENE TWO 281 LAZARU

THEY ARE NOT DIVIDED ACCORDING TO SEX AS IN THE 282 LAZARU PREVIOUS SCENE.

(THE FOURTH GUEST OF SCENE ONE) 283 LAZARU

(THE SEVENTH GUEST OF SCENE ONE--STARTS TO 286 LAZARU HARANGUE THE CROWD.

(SECOND GUEST OF SCENE ONE) JESUS IS DEAD/ 290 LAZARU

(THE THIRD GUEST OF SCENE ONE RUSHES IN 290 LAZARU BREATHLESSLY, SHOUTING)

MASKED LIKE THE SOLDIERS OF SCENE TWO-- 298 LAZARU

IN THE SAME PERIOD AND TYPE AS IN THE PRECEDING 306 LAZARU SCENE, EXCEPT THAT

THE FOLLOWERS ARE COSTUMED AND MASKED AS IN THE 306 LAZARU PRECEDING SCENE,

(SCENE.. 312 LAZARU

(CURTAIN) ACT TWO SCENE TWO 312 LAZARU

AT THE OPENING OF THE SCENE THERE IS HEARD THE 313 LAZARU STEADY TRAMP OF DEPARTING TROOPS.

THEIR MASKS ARE THE SAME AS THE LEGIONARY CHORUS 326 LAZARU OF THE PREVIOUS SCENE.

(SCENE.. 335 LAZARU

(CURTAIN) ACT THREE SCENE TWO 335 LAZARU

THE CHORUS IN THIS SCENE AND THE NEXT 336 LAZARU

(SCENE.. 350 LAZARU

THE SAME AS PREVIOUS SCENE--THE SAME NIGHT A SHORT350 LAZARU WHILE LATER.

THE DAIS AS IN THE PREVIOUS SCENE, STARING AT 362 LAZARU LAZARUS, LAUGHING CRUELLY,

(SCENE.. 363 LAZARU

(SCENE A LOG CABIN BY A LAKE IN THE WOODS 1 MANSNS

(SCENE A CORNER OF THE GARDEN OF DEBORAH HARFORD'S 25 MANSNS HOME

SCENE SITTING-ROOM OF SARA HARFORD'S HOME 43 MANSNS

(SCENE SIMON'S PRIVATE OFFICE IN THE OFFICES OF 69 MANSNS SIMON HARFORD INC.

(SCENE SAME AS SCENE TWO OF ACT ONE, 95 MANSNS

(SCENE PARLOR OF THE HARFORD MANSION-- 117 MANSNS

AND ALL DURING THE FOLLOWING SCENE TALK IN 125 MANSNS WHISPERS, THEIR EYES FIXED ON SIMON.)

(SCENE SAME AS SCENE ONE OF ACT TWO--SIMON'S 139 MANSNS PRIVATE OFFICE.

(SCENE SAME AS SCENE TWO OF ACT TWO-- 161 MANSNS

COME BACK TO HAUNT THE SCENE OF LONG-PAST 162 MANSNS ASSIGNATION.)

(SCENE--A SACRED TREE ON A VAST PLAIN IN PERSIA 347 MARCOM NEAR THE CONFINES OF INDIA.

(SCENE--SIX MONTHS LATER. THE TOLLING OF A CHURCH358 MARCOM BELL IS FIRST HEARD.

THE SCENE FADES INTO DARKNESS. 363 MARCOM

(SCENE--LIGHT COMES, GRADUALLY REVEALING THE 364 MARCOM SCENE

THE SCENE FADES QUICKLY INTO DARKNESS AS THE CALL 369 MARCOM OF THE MUEZZINS IS HEARD

OTHERWISE, THE SCENE. 369 MARCOM

AS WITH THE ALI BROTHERS IN THE PREVIOUS SCENE, 370 MARCOM

THE SCENE FADES INTO DARKNESS. 372 MARCOM

BETWEEN THEM AND THE POLOS AS WITH THE BUDDHIST 374 MARCOM MERCHANTS IN THE PREVIOUS SCENE.

THE SCENE IS REVEALED AS THE GRAND THRONE ROOM IN 377 MARCOM THE PALACE OF KUBLAI.

(SCENE-- 384 MARCOM

(SCENE--THE WHARVES OF THE IMPERIAL FLEET AT THE 399 MARCOM SEAPORT OF ZAYTON--

PLAYING THE SAME MARTIAL AIR AS IN THE PREVIOUS 402 MARCOM SCENE

THE CURTAIN THEN RISES DISCOVERING THE SCENE AS 407 MARCOM ABOVE.

(SCENE.. THE SAME, WITH THE WALL OF THE LIVING 71 MISBEG ROOM REMOVED.

I'LL RAISE A SCENE AND PRETEND I'M IN A RAGE 92 MISBEG BECAUSE HE FORGOT HIS DATE.

(DURING A PART OF THE FOLLOWING SCENE THE SONG 101 MISBEG CONTINUES TO BE HEARD AT

(SCENE.. THE LIVING-ROOM WALL HAS BEEN REPLACED 111 MISBEG

AS IF HE SAW THIS DEATHBED SCENE BEFORE HIM.) 147 MISBEG

SCENE

(CONT'D.)

(SCENE THE DINING ROOM OF MELODY'S TAVERN, IN A VILLAGE A FEW MILES FROM BOSTON. 7 POET

(SCENE SAME AS ACT ONE. 57 POET

WHAT FOLLOWS IS AN EXACT REPETITION OF HIS SCENE 67 POET BEFORE THE MIRROR IN ACT ONE.

THEY TAKE IN THE SCENE AT A GLANCE. 72 POET

(SCENE THE SAME. 95 POET

(SCENE THE SAME. 133 POET

(THINKING WORRIEDLY) (II HOPE SHE WON'T MAKE A 12 STRANG SCENE...

(SCENE.. 24 STRANG

THE SAME AS SCENE ONE, PROFESSOR LEEDS' STUDY. 24 STRANG

SHE APPEARS OLDER THAN IN THE PREVIOUS SCENE, HER 26 STRANG FACE IS PALE AND MUCH THINNER.

PLACE AS MARSDEN HAD OCCUPIED IN THE PREVIOUS 39 STRANG SCENE WHILE MARSDEN IS IN HER

(SCENE.. 48 STRANG

(SCENE.. 66 STRANG

(SCENE.. 90 STRANG

I APOLOGIZE FOR MAKING A SCENE. 99 STRANG

(SCENE.. 111 STRANG

(SCENE.. 137 STRANG

SHE IS SLIMMER THAN IN THE PREVIOUS SCENE. 137 STRANG

AND THEN THERE'LL BE THE SAME OLD TERRIBLE SCENE 143 STRANG OF HATE AND YOU'LL RUN AWAY--

(SCENE.. 158 STRANG

SCENE THERE IS A PERFECT PANDEMONIUM OF SOUND.) 176 STRANG

BUT DURING THE FOLLOWING SCENE THEY STARE STRAIGHT452 WELDED AHEAD AND REMAIN MOTIONLESS.

(SCENE--SAME AS ACT ONE. 480 WELDED

SCENES

AS THE SEPARATE SCENES REQUIRE, -0 DYNAMO

SEVERAL FRAMED PRINTS OF SCENES FROM THE BIBLE 421 DYNAMO HANG ON THE WALLS.

NO TIME ELAPSES BETWEEN SCENES ONE AND TWO. 427 DYNAMO

NO TIME ELAPSES BETWEEN SCENES TWO AND THREE.) 435 DYNAMO

NO TIME ELAPSES BETWEEN SCENES THREE AND FOUR.) 443 DYNAMO

NO TIME ELAPSES BETWEEN SCENES ONE AND TWO.) 483 DYNAMO

A SHORT TIME IS SUPPOSED TO ELAPSE BETWEEN SCENES 486 DYNAMO TWO AND THREE.)

THE ARRANGEMENT OF FURNITURE IN EACH ROOM IS THE 302 GGBROW SAME AS IN PREVIOUS SCENES.

MASKS OF THESE JEWS OF THE FIRST TWO SCENES OF THE275 LAZARU PLAY ARE PRONOUNCEDLY SEMITIC

SCENES. 90 STRANG

ONLY YOU MUST ADMIT THESE TRIANGULAR SCENES ARE, 96 STRANG TO SAY THE LEAST, HUMILIATING.

THE ARRANGEMENT OF THE FURNITURE SHOWN IS AS IN 137 STRANG PREVIOUS SCENES

SCENT

BUT SOMETIMES THE SCENT OF HER HAIR AND SKIN... 5 STRANG

SCENTED

THAT YOUTH'S SWEET-SCENTED MANUSCRIPT SHOULD 298 AHWILD CLOSE/*

SCENTING

(SCENTING THE OTHER'S FEELINGS--MALICIOUSLY) 185 EJONES

SKEPTICALLY

(SKEPTICALLY) YOU MUST HAVE SHARP EARS TO HAVE 277 LAZARU HEARD HIM LAUGH IN THAT UPROAR/

SCEPTICISM

(WITH A SNEER OF SCEPTICISM BUT WITH AN UNDERLYING340 LAZARU EAGERNESS)

SCHEDULE

WELL, CARGO'S ALL ABOARD, BEFORE SCHEDULE, TOO. 405 MARCOM

AND, BY GOD, I'M GOING TO SEE TO IT THEIR MARRIAGE161 STRANG GOES THROUGH ON SCHEDULE.

SCHEME

GOT SOME NEW SCHEME FOR US$ 496 DAYS

MIN MIGHT O' PUT SOME SCHEME IN HIS HEAD. 215 DESIRE

I'VE GOT TO FIX UP A SCHEME ON HIM QUICK... 432 DYNAMO

(IRRITABLY) (THAT THE DEVIL KILL ME IF I CAN 434 DYNAMO THINK UP A GOOD SCHEME....)

I SOON SAW THROUGH HIS LITTLE SCHEME AND HE'LL 87 ELECTR NEVER CALL HERE AGAIN.

I'LL BET THEY'RE COOKING UP SOME NEW SCHEME TO 15 JOURNE TOUCH THE OLD MAN.

ALL OF THESE PEOPLE ARE MASKED IN ACCORDANCE WITH 273 LAZARU THE FOLLOWING SCHEME.

THEY ARE MASKED ACCORDING TO THE SCHEME OF SEVEN 298 LAZARU PERIODS

WELL, THAT HALF OF MY DOMESTIC RESPONSIBILITY-- 94 MANSNS SHARING SCHEME

AS PART OF MY SCHEME/ 105 MANSNS

COULD CONCEIVE A SCHEME BY WHICH THE PUBLIC COULD 158 MANSNS BE COMPELLED TO BUY YOUR

I KNOW SO WELL THE SCHEME SHE HAS IN MIND TO GET 162 MANSNS RID OF ME--TO DRIVE ME INSANE--

WHEN I KNOW IT IS HE WHO HAS FORCED ME TO CARRY 163 MANSNS OUT HIS EVIL SCHEME OF REVENGE--

BUT HE MADE US DECEIVE EACH OTHER AND HATE AND 170 MANSNS SCHEME--

I BEGIN TO SEE YOUR SCHEME--YOU WANT TO MAKE ME 189 MANSNS FEEL CONTEMPTIBLE--

MY TAX SCHEME, YOUR MAJESTY, 392 MARCOM

IT'S REALLY A SCHEME TO WHILE AWAY THE HOURS, 398 MARCOM

UP SOME SCHEME TO HOOK HIM, AND THE OLD MAN PUT 9 MISBEG YOU UP TO IT.

AND THE DIRTY TICK ACCUSED YOU AND ME OF MAKING UP 21 MISBEG A FOXY SCHEME TO TRAP JIM.

(TURNS ON HIM ANGRILY) ARE YOU TAKING MIKE'S 22 MISBEG SCHEME SERIOUSLY, YOU OLD GOAT$

MIKE SAID MAYBE HE HAD A SCHEME THAT I'D GET JIM 22 MISBEG IN BED WITH ME AND YOU'D COME

SURE, THAT'S EVERY WOMAN'S SCHEME SINCE THE WORLD 28 MISBEG WAS CREATED.

NO MATTER HOW DRUNK HE WAS, I'D BE WITH YOU IN ANY 35 MISBEG SCHEME YOU MADE AGAINST HIM.

SCHEME

(CONT'D.)

MIKE'S FIRST SCHEME ON HIM, IF YOU GOT HIM ALONE 87 MISBEG IN THE MOONLIGHT,

THEN IT'S MIKE'S SECOND SCHEME YOU'RE THINKING 92 MISBEG ABOUT$

AND I'VE NO FAITH IN YOUR SCHEME BECAUSE YOU'LL BE 93 MISBEG TOO FULL OF SCRUPLES.

WE'VE GOT TO THINK OF A NEW SCHEME QUICK TO GET ME 99 MISBEG AWAY--

SURE, I GOT SO BLIND DRUNK AT THE INN I FORGOT ALL158 MISBEG ABOUT OUR SCHEME AND CAME

AND THEN CAME SNEAKING HERE TO SEE IF THE SCHEME 159 MISBEG BEHIND YOUR SCHEME HAD WORKED/

YOU WERE ONLY PUTTING IT UN AS PART OF YOUR 162 MISBEG SCHEME--

I DON'T WANT YOU AROUND TO START SOME NEW SCHEME. 164 MISBEG

AND I CONFESSED THAT I WAS UP TO EVERY SCHEME TO 147 POET GET HIM,

SCHEMED

YOU'VE ALWAYS SCHEMED TO STEAL MY PLACE/ 33 ELECTR

SCHEMER

THE DAMNED OLD SCHEMER, I'LL TEACH HIM TO-- 134 MISBEG

DON'T TELL ME YOU DIDN'T COUNT ON THAT, AND YOU 164 MISBEG SUCH A CLEVER SCHEMER/

SCHEMES

HE SITTING ALONE, THINKING OUT SCHEMES FOR HIS 120 MANSNS COMPANY--NOT BOTHERING US--

IF YOU'LL SWEAR TO STOP YOUR MAD SCHEMES, I'LL 167 MANSNS MAKE PEACE WITH YOU.

THAT'S ONE OF MIKE'S DIRTY SCHEMES. 28 MISBEG

YOU CAN LIVE ALONE AND WORK ALONE YOUR CUNNING 164 MISBEG SCHEMES ON YOURSELF.

GOING OUT TO REVENGE AN INSULT TO YOU, WOULD SPOIL171 POET YOUR SCHEMES.

SCHEMIN'

IF I COULD PROVE T' YE I WA'N'T SCHEMIN' T' STEAL 258 DESIRE FROM YE--

SCHEMING

EXACTLY AS YOU'RE SCHEMING NOW TO LEAVE ME AND 152 ELECTR MARRY PETER/

IN BRIEF, I MARRIED THE WHORE, SHE TORTURED ME, MY356 LAZARU MOTHER'S SCHEMING PROSPERED--

AND YOU MUSTN'T DO SO MUCH PLANNING AND SCHEMING, 49 MANSNS

I WOULD PUT A STOP TO HER GREEDY SCHEMING, 72 MANSNS

WOULD YOU REMIND ME OF PITY NOW, YOU SCHEMING 187 MANSNS SLUT$

(QUIETLY AND EXHAUSTEDLY.) I'VE TOLD YOU I'M 189 MANSNS BEYOND SCHEMING.

AND HIM ALWAYS SCHEMING HOW HE'LL CHEAT PEOPLE, 8 MISBEG

I WAS GOING TO SAY I WISH YOU LUCK WITH YOUR 10 MISBEG SCHEMING, FOR ONCE.

AND YOU KEEP YOUR MAD SCHEMING TO YOURSELF. 30 MISBEG

YOU'RE STEADY ON YOUR PINS, AIN'T YOU, YOU 96 MISBEG SCHEMING OLD THIEF,

I MUST BE SCHEMING TO GET MYSELF SOUSED, TOO. 116 MISBEG

I HOPE YOU DON'T THINK I'M SCHEMING TO ROLL YOU. 127 MISBEG

HE DOESN'T CARE, EXCEPT TO USE ME IN HIS SCHEMING.136 MISBEG

SURE, IF THERE'S ONE THING I OWE YOU TONIGHT, 142 MISBEG AFTER ALL MY LYING AND SCHEMING.

GOD FORGIVE ME, IT'S A FINE END TO ALL MY 153 MISBEG SCHEMING.

YOU WORKED IT SO IT WAS ME WHO DID ALL THE DIRTY 163 MISBEG SCHEMING--

ALL YOU SAID ABOUT MY LYING AND SCHEMING, 174 MISBEG

UR MAYBE I WAS CURSING MYSELF FOR A DAMNED OLD 177 MISBEG SCHEMING FOOL, LIKE I OUGHT TO.

WITH YOU TWO SCHEMING PEASANTS LAYING SNARES TO 60 POET TRAP HIM/

ALL I CAN SEE IN YOU IS A COMMON, GREEDY, 113 POET SCHEMING, CUNNING PEASANT GIRL.

YOU TALK LIKE A SCHEMING PEASANT/ 126 POET

SCHOLARS

THEN THE COURTIERS, OFFICERS, POETS, SCHOLARS, 377 MARCOM ETC.

SCHOOL

NOT ABLE TO GO BACK TEACHING SCHOOL ON ACCOUNT OF 945 'ILE BEING DAVE KEENEY'S WIFE.

(IN GREAT EXCITEMENT) WHALES, SIR--A WHOLE SCHOOL551 'ILE OF 'EM--

SHE CONFORMS OUTWARDLY TO THE CONVENTIONAL TYPE OF187 AHWILD OLD-MAID SCHOOL TEACHER,

(CAUSTICALLY) HE READ HIS SCHOOL BOOKS, TOO, 192 AHWILD STRANGE AS THAT MAY SEEM TO YOU.

HE IS DRESSED IN PREP SCHOOL REFLECTION OF THE 193 AHWILD COLLEGE STYLE OF ARTHUR.)

THE IS GOING ON SEVENTEEN, JUST CUT OF HIGH 193 AHWILD SCHOOL.

I DON'T WANT THEM THINKING I'M TRAVELLING AROUND 219 AHWILD WITH ANY HIGH-SCHOOL KID.

I'M DARN GLAD I STOPPED AT HIGH SCHOOL, OR MAYBE 82 BEYOND I'D BEEN CRAZY TOO.

RATHER PRIM-LOOKING WOMAN OF FIFTY-FIVE WHO HAD 94 BEYOND ONCE BEEN A SCHOOL TEACHER.

HE TOOK ME FROM SCHOOL AND FORCED ME ON HIS SHIP, 564 CROSS

DIDN'T HE$

LATER, AT SCHOOL, HE LEARNED OF THE GOD OF 510 DAYS PUNISHMENT, AND HE WONDERED.

HUTCHINS, DO YOU REALIZE REUBEN WILL GRADUATE FROM423 DYNAMO SCHOOL IN LESS THAN A MONTH.

MY MOTHER SEWED FOR A LIVING AND SENT ME TO 26 ELECTR SCHOOL.

FROM THE CASINO COMES THE SOUND OF THE SCHOOL 257 GGBROW QUARTET RENDERING =SWEET ADELINE=

I NEVER GOT ABOVE GRAMMAR SCHOOL BUT I'VE MADE 260 GGBROW MONEY

TIME FOR SCHOOL/ 267 GGBROW

(SOFTLY) REMEMBER THE SCHOOL COMMENCEMENT DANCE--309 GGBROW

SCHOOL

SCHOOL (CONT'D.)
ALL ARE DRESSED IN THE HEIGHT OF CORRECT PREP- 323 GGBROW
SCHOOL ELEGANCE.
AFTER GRAMMAR SCHOOL, MY OLD MAN PUT ME TO WORK IN 14 HUGHIE
HIS STORE.
GRADUATED FROM HIGH SCHOOL. 23 HUGHIE
I WAS A BRILLIANT STUDENT AT LAW SCHOOL, TOO. 595 ICEMAN
I'VE NEVER PRACTICED BUT I WAS ONE OF THE MUST 607 ICEMAN
BRILLIANT STUDENTS IN LAW SCHOOL.
IT WAS COMPOSED IN A WANTON MOMENT BY THE DEAN OF 607 ICEMAN
THE DIVINITY SCHOOL ON A
AND DEN DEY'D MAKE UP AND CRY AND SING =SCHOOL 612 ICEMAN
DAYS=
AND CORA GIGGLIN' LIKE SHE WAS IN GRAMMAR SCHOOL 614 ICEMAN
HE WAS A GENTLEMAN OF THE OLD SCHOOL. 628 ICEMAN
AND PADDY MY BRILLIANT RECORD IN LAW SCHOOL WAS NO679 ICEMAN
FLASH IN THE PAN.
WELL, ANYWAY, AS I SAID, HOME WAS LIKE JAIL, AND 709 ICEMAN
SO WAS SCHOOL.
=OH SHE'S GONE AWAY TO SINGIN' SCHOOL-- 530 INZONE
EVEN BEFORE THAT WHEN HE WAS IN PREP SCHOOL, 33 JOURNE
YOU NEVER KNEW WHAT WAS REALLY WRONG UNTIL YOU 57 JOURNE
WERE IN PREP SCHOOL.
YOU REMEMBER, JAMES, FOR YEARS AFTER HE WENT TO 110 JOURNE
BOARDING SCHOOL,
HE NEVER WENT TO SCHOOL AFTER HE WAS TEN. 111 JOURNE
THERE WAS NO MORE SCHOOL FOR ME. 149 JOURNE
FACING FRONT, HER HANDS FOLDED IN HER LAP, IN A 174 JOURNE
DEMURE SCHOOL-GIRLISH POSE.)
BUT NOW THEY'LL BE AWAY AT SCHOOL A LOT OF THE 84 MANSNS
DAY.
THE CHILDREN WILL BE AWAY MOST OF THE DAY AT 89 MANSNS
SCHOOL FROM NOW ON.
SO HE PACKED HIM OFF TO DUBLIN TC SCHOOL, 12 POET
DIDN'T HE SEND YOU TO SCHOOL SO YOU COULD TALK 23 POET
LIKE A GENTLEMAN'S DAUGHTER?
PREP SCHOOL.... 6 STRANG
(GIVING ME THE FISHY, DIAGNOSING EYE THEY 34 STRANG
PRACTICE AT MEDICAL SCHOOL....
COLLEGE. I KEPT HIM AWAY AT SCHOOL IN WINTER AND 60 STRANG
CAMP IN SUMMERS AND I WENT TO
I SENT SAMMY RIGHT OFF TO BOARDING SCHOOL. 60 STRANG
(A PAUSE) MY MOTHER DIED WHEN I WAS AWAY AT 101 STRANG
SCHOOL.
TO ESCAPE FROM ME TO BOARDING SCHOOL AND THEN TO 167 STRANG
COLLEGE,

SCHOOL'S
I CALC'LATE IT'S 'CAUSE SCHOOL'S OUT. 220 DESIRE

SCHOOLBOY
LIKE A SCHOOLBOY WHO HAS BEEN CALLED ON TO RECITE 69 STRANG
AND CANNOT AND IS BEING

SCHOOLBOYS
THEY'D TURNED NAUGHTY SCHOOLBOYS AND WERE THROWING3O3 DAYS
SPITBALLS AT ALMIGHTY GOD AND
(ELATED, EXCITED AS A CROWD OF SCHOOLBOYS GOING ON323 LAZARU
A VACATION.

SCHOOLGIRL
=CHATTERING SCHOOLGIRL OF HER CONVENT DAYS. 97 JOURNE
SCHOOLGIRL AND A MATINEE IDOL'S 107 JOURNE
NOT THAT YOUR MOTHER DIDN'T PLAY WELL FOR A 138 JOURNE
SCHOOLGIRL.
AS IF AN AWKWARD SCHOOLGIRL WERE PRACTICING IT FOR170 JOURNE
THE FIRST TIME.

SCHOOLING
IS THE BEST SCHOOLING FOR A REAL MERCHANT AND 356 MARCOM

SCHOOLMASTER'S
FATHER HAS A SAYING THAT WHERE

FARTHER FRONT AT RIGHT, THERE IS A HIGH 7 POET
SCHOOLMASTER'S DESK WITH A STOOL.

SCHOOLS
YOU'VE HAD EVERYTHING--NURSES, SCHOOLS, COLLEGE, 146 JOURNE
THOUGH YOU DIDN'T STAY THERE.

SCHOONER
MARTHY TAKES A LONG DRAUGHT OF HER SCHOONER AND 8 ANNA
HEAVES A HUGE SIGH OF
(GRASPING HER SCHOONER HASTILY--ANGRILY) 9 ANNA
MARTHY SIPS WHAT IS LEFT OF HER SCHOONER 13 ANNA
REFLECTIVELY.
(SHE TAKES A GULP FROM HER SCHOONER.) 15 ANNA
SEE SCHOONER MAKE SAIL--SEE EVERYTANG DAT'S POOTY. 23 ANNA
THE SCHOONER MY FATHER MORTGAGED THIS HOUSE TO FIT561 CROSS
OUT.
BUT AT NIGHT--SOME OTHER SCHOONER-- 969 ICEMAN
HE WOULD AS SOON BLOW THE COLLAR OFF A SCHOONER OF596 ICEMAN
BEER AS LOOK AT YOU/
THE VASE BEING A BIG SCHOONER GLASS FROM THE BAR, 629 ICEMAN
ON TOP OF THE PIANO.
(CORA GOES BACK TO GIVE THE SCHOONER OF FLOWERS A 629 ICEMAN
FEW MORE TOUCHES.)
AS THEY DO SO, HICKEY RISES, A SCHOONER IN HIS 658 ICEMAN
HAND.)
(HE GRABS HIS SCHOONER AND TAKES A GREEDY GULP-- 658 ICEMAN
(HE POUNDS HIS SCHOONER ON THE TABLE) 659 ICEMAN

SCHOONERS
FOAMING SCHOONERS BEFORE THEM. 4 ANNA
SCHOONERS/ THAT'S THE SPIRIT FOR HARRY'S BIRTHDAY/640 ICEMAN
(HE AND CHUCK FINISH SERVING OUT THE SCHOONERS, 658 ICEMAN
TRAY LADEN WITH SCHOONERS OF CHAMPAGNE 658 ICEMAN
RAP THEIR SCHOONERS ON THE TABLE, CALL =SPEECH, 659 ICEMAN
THEY RAISE THEIR SCHOONERS WITH AN ENTHUSIASTIC 659 ICEMAN
CHORUS OF =HERE'S HOW, HARRY/=

SCHOPENHAUER
STENDHAL, PHILOSOPHICAL AND SOCIOLOGICAL WORKS BY 11 JOURNE
SCHOPENHAUER, NIETZSCHE, MARX,
VOLTAIRE, ROUSSEAU, SCHOPENHAUER, NIETZSCHE, 135 JOURNE
IBSEN/

SCHREECHIN'
IS THAT BANSHEE SCHREECHIN' FIT MUSIC FOR A SICK 481 CARDIF
MAN?

SCIENCE
HUMAN SCIENCE HAS DONE ALL IT CAN TO SAVE HER. 559 DAYS
I'M STUDYING A LOT OF SCIENCE. 458 DYNAMO
IT'S THE DEADLIEST HABIT KNOWN TO SCIENCE, A GREAT626 ICEMAN
PHYSICIAN ONCE TOLD ME.
YOU SEE BEFORE YOU A BROKEN MAN, A MARTYR TO 627 ICEMAN
MEDICAL SCIENCE.
THEN I MOST DECIDEDLY THINK YOU SHOULD FINISH OUT 17 STRANG
YOUR SCIENCE COURSE AND TAKE
I TRIED HARD TO PRAY TO THE MODERN SCIENCE GOD. 41 STRANG
IN FACT, IN THE INTEREST OF SCIENCE, 85 STRANG
IN THE INTEREST OF SCIENCES.... 85 STRANG
SO DOES SCIENCE/ 86 STRANG
IT'S FOR SCIENCE, NED. 192 STRANG
(THINKING TORTUREDLY) (BUT IT'S FOR SCIENCE/... 192 STRANG

SCIENTIFIC
BUBBLED DOWN IN EVOLUTIONARY SCIENTIFIC TRUTH 503 DAYS
AGAIN--
HE READ ALL SORTS OF SCIENTIFIC BOOKS. 534 DAYS
THAT'S SCIENTIFIC FACT.... 472 DYNAMO
SEEM LIKE QUEER HINDU IDOLS TORTURED INTO 483 DYNAMO
SCIENTIFIC SUPPLICATIONS.
AND SO HE HAS COME TO CONSIDER HIMSELF AS IMMUNE 33 STRANG
TO LOVE THROUGH HIS SCIENTIFIC
I NEED YOUR ADVICE--YOUR SCIENTIFIC ADVICE THIS 84 STRANG
TIME, IF YOU PLEASE, DOCTOR.
A SCIENTIFIC MIND SUPERIOR TO THE MORAL SCRUPLES 88 STRANG
(STUNG--MOCKINGLY) IT WAS YOU WHO TAUGHT ME THE 132 STRANG
SCIENTIFIC APPROACH, DOCTOR/
A SCIENTIFIC DILLETANTE/... 147 STRANG

SCIENTIFICALLY
SO SCIENTIFICALLY/...)) 91 STRANG

SCIENTIST
DID YOU EVER KNOW A YOUNG SCIENTIST, CHARLIES 41 STRANG
METCHNIKOFF, EMINENT SCIENTIST... 67 STRANG
HE HAS AGAIN THE AIR OF THE COOL, DETACHED 158 STRANG
SCIENTIST
A SCIENTIST SHOULDN'T BELIEVE IN GHOSTS. 197 STRANG

SCOFF
LET THEM--SCOFF/ 228 AHWILD
ONE OF THESE 'ERE WOULD BUY SCOFF FOR A STARVIN' 235 HA APE
FAMILY FOR A YEAR/

SCOFFED
AND GUTS IS IN ME, WE'D BE BEING SCOFFED BY THE 32 ANNA
FISHES THIS MINUTE/

SCOFFING
WAVLY SCOFFING AND SENSUAL YOUNG PAN. 260 GGBROW

SCOLD
BUT I DO FEEL RESTED, SO DON'T BEGIN TO SCOLD ME. 515 DAYS
JAMES, IT'S EDMUND YOU OUGHT TO SCOLD FOR NOT 16 JOURNE
EATING ENOUGH.
THERE'S NO REASON TO SCOLD JAMIE. 26 JOURNE
SO I CAN'T GET A WORD IN EDGEWAYS AND SCOLD HER. 29 JOURNE
YOUR MOTHER'S RIGHT TO SCOLD US. 41 JOURNE
SHE USED TO SCOLD MY FATHER. 114 JOURNE

SCOLDING
FORGIVE ME FOR SCOLDING YOU, JAMES. 68 JOURNE
YOU'RE FOREVER SCOLDING ME FOR BEING LATE, BUT NOW115 JOURNE
I'M ON TIME FOR ONCE.
SISTER THERESA WILL GIVE ME A DREADFUL SCOLDING. 171 JOURNE
(SCOLDING HIM AS THOUGH HE WERE A SMALL BOY.) 49 MANSNS

SCOLDINGLY
(SHE GOES ON SCOLDINGLY) 293 AHWILD

SCOOP
GIMME A SCOOP THIS TIME--LAGER AND PORTER. 4 ANNA
(APPEASED) GIMME A SCOOP OF LAGER AN' ALE. 8 ANNA
BLOW ME TO ANOTHER SCOOP, HUH? 12 ANNA
WITH BUCKTH BUCKET SCOOPS THAT DREDGE, LOAD COAL, 400 MARCOM
SAND, ETC. BY THE SIDE OF THE

SCORCHED
DETECTED THROUGH THE BLEACHED, SUN-SCORCHED GRASS.129 BEYOND

SCORCHER
THIS IS GOING TO BE A SCORCHER. 188 AHWILD
LAND SAKES, IF THIS ISN'T A SCORCHER/ 116 BEYOND

SCORCHING
THE NOON ENERVATION OF THE SULTRY, SCORCHING DAY 112 BEYOND
MY LIFE IS COOL GREEN SHADE WHEREIN COMES NO 187 STRANG
SCORCHING ZENITH SUN OF PASSION AND

SCORE
(THEN MOODILY) BUT AFTER THREE SCORE AND TEN THE 232 DESIRE
LORD WARNS YE T' PREPARE.
(ANXIOUS TO SCORE HER POINT AND KEEP ORIN'S MIND 163 ELECTR
ON IT)
(UNHEEDING) AND NOW YOUR APPEARANCE IS OF ONE 353 LAZARU
YOUNGER BY A SCORE.
I SHOULDN'T LET SCORE SO EASILY. 45 POET

SCORN
(MRS. KEENEY LOOKS AROUND HER IN WILD SCORN) 546 'ILE
(WITH HIGH SCORN) OH, YALE/ 195 AHWILD
(WORRIEDLY IMPRESSED BY THIS THREAT--BUT 271 AHWILD
PRETENDING SCORN)
WITH A TRACE OF SCORN IN HER VOICE) 21 ANNA
(WITH WEARY SCORN) OH, FOR HEAVEN'S SAKE, ARE YOU 42 ANNA
OFF ON THAT AGAIN?
(WITH BITTER SCORN) SO--YOU WANT TO GO OUT INTO 106 BEYOND
THE WORLD AND SEE THIN'S$
(HE SINKS DOWN INTO HIS CHAIR AND SMILES WITH 126 BEYOND
BITTER SELF-SCORN)
(WITH A TRACE OF SCORN) 132 BEYOND
(WITH FIERCE SCORN) I SUPPOSE YCU'RE SO USED TO 155 BEYOND
THE IDEA
(LOOKING AT HIM FIXEDLY FOR A MOMENT--WITH QUIET 467 CARIBE
SCORN)
AND THIS MOCKING SCORN IS REPEATED IN THE 494 DAYS
EXPRESSION OF THE EYES WHICH STARE

SCORN

(CONT*D.)

(WITH MOCKING SCORN) MY FAITHS 507 DAYS
(IN WHAT IS CLOSE TO A SNARL OF SCORN) 508 DAYS
SOMETHING THAT LAUGHED WITH MOCKING SCORN/ 535 DAYS
(BREAKS IN--WITH BORED SCORN) 542 DAYS
THERE IS A MOCKING RATIONAL SOMETHING IN HIM THAT 545 DAYS
LAUGHS WITH SCORN--
AT WHICH SOMETHING LAUGHS WITH A WEARY SCORN/ 561 DAYS
THERE IS ONLY SCORN/ 565 DAYS
(WITH LOFTY SCORN) LOVE/ 214 DESIRE
(WITH BITTER SCORN) HA/ 225 DESIRE
SHE PRETENDS TO DO LIKEWISE BUT GIVES HIM A SIDE 235 DESIRE
GLANCE OF SCORN AND TRIUMPH.)
(ALARMED BUT PRETENDING SCORN) 528 DIFRNT
(WITH HEAVY SCORN) IF HE SHED ANY BLOOD, HE MUST 541 DIFRNT
HAVE GOT A NOSE BLEED.
(WITH A SAD SMILE OF SCORN FOR HERSELF) 455 DYNAMO
(THEN TRYING TO PASS IT OFF BY AN ATTEMPT AT 177 EJONES
SCORN)
(WITH INDIGNANT SCORN) LOOK-A-HEAH, WHITE MAN/ 183 EJONES
TO FOLLOW SETH'S ADVICE--STARING AT HIM WITH 24 ELECTR
DELIBERATELY INSULTING SCORN)
CHRISTINE SAYS WITH FORCED SCORN) 29 ELECTR
(WITH TAUNTING SCORN) HE DOESN'T LOVE YOU/ 32 ELECTR
(STILL SUSPICIOUSLY--WITH A TOUCH OF SCORN) 34 ELECTR
(WITH FIERCE SCORN NOW, SEEING THE NECESSITY OF 41 ELECTR
GOADING HIM.
(PITYINGLY--WITH A TINGE OF SCORN IN HER VOICE) 49 ELECTR
(WITH BITTER SCORN) YOUR BODYS 60 ELECTR
(SHE ADDRESSES THE DEAD MAN DIRECTLY IN A STRANGE 101 ELECTR
TONE OF DEFIANT SCORN)
(WITH BITTER SCORN) ORIN/ 122 ELECTR
WHY MUST I PRETEND TO SCORN IN ORDER TO PITYS 264 GGRBON
(FROM THEROM THE CENTER OF THE LINE--WITH 223 HA APE
EXUBERANT SCORN)
(WITH A BITTER, IRONICAL SCORN, INCREASING AS HE 228 HA APE
GOES ON)
(GLARING FROM ONE TO THE OTHER OF THEM--WITH AN 237 HA APE
INSULTING SNORT OF SCORN)
(WITH ABYSMAL SCORN) AW, HELL/ 243 HA APE
(WITH FORCED SCORN) A LOT YOU KNOW ABOUT HIM/ 642 ICEMAN
TO ROCKY, WHO IS REGARDING HIM WITH SCORN-- 690 ICEMAN
APPEALINGLY)
(WITH ANGRY SCORN) AH, SHUT UP, YOU YELLOW FAKER/706 ICEMAN
(WITH FORCED SCORN.) FOR GOD'S SAKE, IS THAT ALL'S 38 JOURNE
HE SCORN HIM) 283 LAZARU
(SNEERINGLY) BUT YOUR PRETENDED MESSIAH DID NOT 283 LAZARU
SCORN HIM
(WITH INSULTING SCORN) I, CALIGULA, COMMAND YOU/ 316 LAZARU
EYE TO EYE WITH THE FEAR OF DEATH, DID THEY NOT 324 LAZARU
LAUGH WITH SCORNS
(WITH INDIGNANT SCORN) LET HIM PROVE THERE IS NO 344 LAZARU
DEATH, CAESAR/
(TRIUMPHANT YET DISAPPOINTED--WITH SCORN AND RAGE)366 LAZARU
A LITTLE SMILE OF GLOATING SCORN COMES TO 95 MANSNS
DEBORAH'S LIPS.
(TURNING ON HIM WITH FORCED SCORN.) 113 MANSNS
THREATENING SCORN IN HER TONE.) 131 MANSNS
(WITH STRANGE SCORN.) YOU ARE A FOOL/ 180 MANSNS
FINALLY SPITS WITH EXAGGERATED SCORN) 370 MARCOM
MARCO SITS ON ONE OF THE CASES AND GLANCES ABOUT 370 MARCOM
WITH A FORCED SCORN.
HIS FACE WEARS AN EXPRESSION OF HUMOROUS SCORN. 410 MARCOM
SPEAKING WITH A PITYING SCORN.) 432 MARCOM
DON'T SCORN ME JUST BECAUSE YOU HAVE ON YOUR 64 MISBEG
JOCKEY'S PANTS.
(WITH BITING SCORN) DREAMS, IS ITS 162 MISBEG
(WITH BITTER SCORN.) WE CAN'T AFFORD A WAITRESS, 23 POET
(WITH A STRANGE SUPERIOR SCORN.) 25 POET
(SHE LAUGHS WITH BITTER SCORN.) 26 POET
SHE STIFFENS INTO HOSTILITY AND HER MOUTH SETS IN 33 POET
SCORN.
EVERYWHERE IGNORANCE--OR THE SCORN OF MY OWN 66 POET
DAUGHTER/
(A SAD SCORN COMES INTO HER VOICE.) 90 POET
(WHO HAS BEEN STARING AT HIM WITH SCORN UNTIL HE 91 POET
SAYS THIS LAST--
(WITH ANGRY SCORN, LAPSING INTO BROAD BROGUE.) 92 POET
AND FOR ALL HIS SCORN, 139 POET
SHE LOOKS AT MELODY WITH ANGRY SCORN.) 155 POET
(TO MELODY WITH BITING SCORN.) 156 POET
(THINKING WITH WEARY SCORN) 15 STRANG
HER CHEEK BONES STAND OUT, HER MOUTH IS TAUT IN 26 STRANG
HARD LINES OF A CYNICAL SCORN.
(SHE SMILES AT HIM WITH A PITYING SCORN.) 41 STRANG
(SUDDENLY, WITH PITY YET WITH SCORN) 42 STRANG
(SHE STICKS OUT HER TONGUE AT HIM AND MAKES A FACE 52 STRANG
OF SUPERIOR SCORN)
HE FEELS I'M ALWAYS WATCHING HIM WITH SCORN... 69 STRANG
(WITH RESENTFUL SCORN) (INO. 139 STRANG
(SUBMISSIVELY--BUT WITH A LOOK OF BITTER SCORN AT 157 STRANG
HIM)
(THINKING WITH A SORT OF TENDER, LOVING SCORN FOR 186 STRANG
HIS BOYISH NAIVETE)
(CAPE STARES AT HER WITH A HOT GLANCE OF SCORN. 450 WELDED
(WITH WILD HYSTERICAL SCORN) 460 WELDED
(STARTING--WITH WILD SCORN) DO YOU THINK I--/ 473 WELDED
(WITH PASSIONATE SELF-SCORN) 486 WELDED

SCORNED

HE STERNLY SCORNED MY OFFER. 523 DAYS

SCORNFUL

THEN HE FORCES A SCORNFUL SMILE TO HIS LIPS.) 235 AHWILD
(HE GIVES HIS SISTER A SUPERIOR SCORNFUL GLANCE) 274 AHWILD
(GLARING AT HIM WITH HATRED AND FORCING A SCORNFUL 45 ANNA
LAUGH)
(WITH SCORNFUL PITY) GOD HELP YOU/ 45 ANNA
(TRYING TO BE SCORNFUL AND SELF-CONVINCING) 52 ANNA
(WITH SCORNFUL BITTERNESS/) LOVE 'EM/ 73 ANNA

SCORNFULLY

SCORNFUL (CONT'D.)
(SMITTY DOES NOT DEIGN TO REPLY TO THIS BUT SINKS 468 CARIBE
INTO A SCORNFUL SILENCE.
SNEER OF SCORNFUL MOCKERY ON HIS LIPS. 494 DAYS
LOVING SITS MOTIONLESSLY REGARDING HIM WITH 496 DAYS
SCORNFUL EYES.)
OH, DON'T BE SO SUPERIOR AND SCORNFUL, ELSA. 519 DAYS
STARING DOWN AT HIM WITH COLD, SCORNFUL EYES. 530 DAYS
(HE GIVES A LOW, SCORNFUL LAUGH) 561 DAYS
(WITH A SCORNFUL SENSE OF POWER) 225 DESIRE
(LOOKS AFTER HIM WITH SCORNFUL PITY) 246 DESIRE
THEN WITH SCORNFUL CONFIDENCE) 254 DESIRE
(STARING AT HER WITH A QUESTIONING DREAD--FORCING 18 ELECTR
A SCORNFUL SMILE)
SHE IS UNEASY UNDERNEATH, BUT AFFECTS A SCORNFUL 29 ELECTR
INDIGNATION.)
(THEN SUDDENLY CATCHING CHRISTINE'S SCORNFUL 51 ELECTR
GLANCE
(WITH A CALCULATED SCORNFUL CONTEMPT NOW) 98 ELECTR
(WITH A SCORNFUL SMILE) YOU DON'T CARE TO 221 HA APE
SHOULDER THIS RESPONSIBILITY ALONE,
(WITH A SCORNFUL NOD TO CORA) 619 ICEMAN
PARRITI EXAMINES HIS FACE AND BECOMES INSULTINGLY 648 ICEMAN
SCORNFUL)
(WITH A SCORNFUL SHRUG OF HIS SHOULDERS.) 31 JOURNE
(BITTERLY SCORNFUL.) LEAVE IT TO YOU TO HAVE SOME 86 JOURNE
OF THE STUFF HIDDEN.
(STIFFENS INTO SCORNFUL, DEFENSIVE STUBBORNNESS.) 118 JOURNE
SHE MADE ME FEEL, IN THE PROUD QUESTIONING OF HER 355 LAZARU
SCORNFUL EYES,
THE MATERIAL SECURITY WHICH GAVE HER THE CHANCE TO 47 MANSNS
REMAIN ALOOF AND SCORNFULLY
WITHOUT SCREAMING SCORNFUL LAUGHTER AT MYSELF. 102 MANSNS
(CRUELLY SCORNFUL AND AT THE SAME TIME UNEASY.) 187 MANSNS
NICULO HEADS, A SCORNFUL GRIN COMING TO HIS LIPS.)360 MARCOM
(WITH A SCORNFUL SMILE) AND I WITH YOU--NOW THAT 375 MARCOM
YOU'RE A MAN.
(SHE ADDS IN A HARD, SCORNFUL TONE) 21 MISBEG
(FORCING A SCORNFUL SMILE) I'M SHOCKING YOU, I 42 MISBEG
SUPPOSE/
SHE FORCES A SCORNFUL LAUGH) 51 MISBEG
(WITH A STRANGE, SCORNFUL VANITY.) 61 POET
A FANATIC IN THE CAUSE OF PURE FREEDOM, HE BECAME 83 POET
SCORNFUL OF OUR REVOLUTION.
(INSTANTLY REPELLED--THINKING WITH SCORNFUL 83 STRANG
JEALOUSY)
(WITH SCORNFUL PITY) OH, I GUESS NED WILL BRING 93 STRANG
THE LETTER.
(LOOKS AFTER HIM WITH A MIXTURE OF ANNOYANCE AND 122 STRANG
SCORNFUL AMUSEMENT)
(THINKING WITH SCORNFUL PITY) 147 STRANG
(THEN WITH SUDDEN SCORNFUL REVULSION) 149 STRANG
(A PAUSE--THEN WITH A TRACE OF SCORNFUL 447 WELDED
RESENTMENT)

SCORNFULLY

(SCORNFULLY) AND D'YOU S'POSE ANY OF 'EM WOULD 542 'ILE
BELIEVE THAT--
(FROWNING SCORNFULLY) FRESH KID/ 189 AHWILD
(TURNING BACK--SCORNFULLY) GOSH, HE'S ALWAYS 192 AHWILD
READING NOW.
(SCORNFULLY SUPERIOR) THAT SILLY SKIRT PARTY/ 194 AHWILD
(SCORNFULLY) 210 AHWILD
(SCORNFULLY) AW, I KNOW WHAT TO DO. 219 AHWILD
(NODDING AT THE PLAYER-PIANO SCORNFULLY) 237 AHWILD
(HE RECITES SCORNFULLY) +FOR A WOMAN'S ONLY A 245 AHWILD
WOMAN.
(COMING TOWARD HER--SCORNFULLY) 278 AHWILD
(SCORNFULLY, BUT DRIFTING BACK A STEP IN HIS 285 AHWILD
DIRECTION)
(SCORNFULLY) I SHOULD SAY NOT/ 285 AHWILD
(SCORNFULLY) THAT DUMP WHERE ALL THE SILLY FOOLS 287 AHWILD
GO/
(SCORNFULLY) ON A COAL BARGE/ 10 ANNA
(RECOVERING FROM HER MIRTH--CHUCKLING SCORNFULLY) 11 ANNA
(SCORNFULLY) THINK I'D BREAK MY HEART TO LOOSE 12 ANNA
YUNS
(IRRITATED BY THE OTHER'S TONE--SCORNFULLY) 15 ANNA
(SCORNFULLY) ME\ 17 ANNA
(WITH DIFFICULTY RISING TO A SITTING POSITION-- 33 ANNA
SCORNFULLY)
SCORNFULLY) 38 ANNA
(SCORNFULLY) LITTLE HOME IN THE COUNTRY/ 43 ANNA
(SNORTS SCORNFULLY) PY YIMINY, YOU GO CRAZY, AY 44 ANNA
TANK/
(SCORNFULLY) IS IT THE LIKE OF YOURSELF WILL STOP 45 ANNA
ME, ARE YOU THINKINGS
(SCORNFULLY) IS IT BLAMING THE SEA FOR YOUR 47 ANNA
TROUBLES YE ARE AGAINS
(SCORNFULLY) YES, YOU VAS HELL OF FALLAR, HEAR 48 ANNA
YOU FALL IT/
(SCORNFULLY--FORCING A LAUGH) 51 ANNA
(SCORNFULLY) NO, AND I WASN'T HEARING HER SAY THE 53 ANNA
SUN IS SHINING EITHER.
(SCORNFULLY) SORRY/ 64 ANNA
(GLANCING AT HIS HANDS AND FACE--SCORNFULLY) 70 ANNA
MARY CHUCKLES SCORNFULLY) 99 BEYOND
(SCORNFULLY) LOVE/ THEY AIN'T OLD ENOUGH TO KNOW/102 BEYOND
LOVE WHEN THEY SIGHT IT/
(SCORNFULLY) GET A MAN TO TAKE YOUR PLACE/ 105 BEYOND
(SCORNFULLY) HUMPH/ 118 BEYOND
(SCORNFULLY) BAD LUCK/ 123 BEYOND
(SCORNFULLY) THAT'S ABOUT THE WAY HE SUMMED UP 126 BEYOND
HIS IMPRESSIONS OF THE EAST.
(SCORNFULLY) IT'S HIS OWN FAULT. 136 BEYOND
(SCORNFULLY) HUMPH/ 151 BEYOND
(SCORNFULLY) HE FIDDLES IN HIS MOUTH WI' A BIT OF479 CARDIF
GLASS.

SCORNFULLY

SCORNFULLY (CONT'D.)
(SCORNFULLY) DOWN'T BE SHOWIN' YER IGERANCE BE TRYIN' TO
SHUT YOUR MOUTHS, ALL AV YOU (SCORNFULLY) A CHANTY IS UT YE WANTS
(SCORNFULLY) TWO THOUSAND/
(SCORNFULLY) SO HE WEAKLY SURRENDERED--
(THEN SCORNFULLY) SOMETHIN'/
(SCORNFULLY) NO, YE MOULDN'T/
(SCORNFULLY) AY-EH/
(SUDDENLY RAISES HIS HEAD AND LOCKS AT HER-- SCORNFULLY)
(EYEING HER SCORNFULLY) I DUNNO, MRS.
(SCORNFULLY) EMMA'D OUGHT TO HAVE FALLEN IN LOVE WITH A MINISTER, NOT A SAILOR.
(THINKS SCORNFULLY) (THE IS ALWAYS SO SURE OF WHAT GOD WILLS/.
(THE SCORNFULLY) OH, YOU MEAN 'IS BLOOMIN' MAJESTY.
(SCORNFULLY) DAT FOUL NO-COUNT NIGGER/
(THEN RECOVERING HIMSELF--SCORNFULLY)
(SHE NODS SCORNFULLY TOWARD THE HOUSE)
(SCORNFULLY) DO YOU IMAGINE YOU COULD FORCE HIM TO FIGHT A DUEL WITH YOU$
(SCORNFULLY) OUTSIDE ON DECK WHERE THE SHOT WOULD113 ELECTR BE SURE TO BE HEARD$
(THEN TURNING ON SMALL--SCORNFULLY) 134 ELECTR
(THEN SCORNFULLY) HOW CAN YOU BE SO SCARED OF VINNIES
(AGAIN TURNING AROUND SCORNFULLY) 210 HA APE
(SCORNFULLY) IS IT ONE WHO THIS YOU'D BE, YANK--- 214 HA APE
(TURNS HIS BACK ON PADDY SCORNFULLY) 217 HA APE
(SCORNFULLY) POSER/ 222 HA APE
(HE GLANCES SCORNFULLY AT YANK.) 229 HA APE
(SCORNFULLY) YERRA, YANK, YOU'RE A GREAT FOOL. 232 HA APE
(SCORNFULLY) DE GUARDS$ 241 HA APE
(SCORNFULLY) HURRAH FOR DE FORT' OF JULY/ 243 HA APE
THE GLARES SCORNFULLY AT YANK, WHO IS SUNK IN AN 250 HA APE OBLIVIOUS STUPOR)
(HER FACE HARD--SCORNFULLY) NUTTIN'. 631 ICEMAN
(SCORNFULLY) YEAHS IT DON'T LOOK TO ME HE'S 665 ICEMAN SCARED OF YUH.
(SCORNFULLY) BUT DAT'S CRAZY/ 668 ICEMAN
(SCORNFULLY) A HELL OF A LOT OF USE KEEPIN' A 516 INZONE LOOKOUT/
(SCORNFULLY) ARE YE FRIGHTENED, YE TOADS 520 INZONE
(SCORNFULLY) THAT'S LIKELY, AIN'T ITS 520 INZONE
(SCORNFULLY) LETTIN' ON BE 'IS SILLY AIRS, AND 522 INZONE ALL.
(SCORNFULLY PARODYING HIS BROTHER'S CYNICISM.) 76 JOURNE
(ABRUPTLY HIS TONE BECOMES SCORNFULLY SUPERIOR.) 146 JOURNE
(SCORNFULLY.) WHAT DO YOU KNOW OF THE VALUE OF A 147 JOURNE DOLLARS
(SCORNFULLY) DO YOU FEAR HIM NOW$ 303 LAZARU
(SCORNFULLY) TO BELIEVE THAT, I MUST HAVE SEEN 343 LAZARU IT, CAESAR.
(SHE LAUGHS SCORNFULLY.) IT'S LITTLE YOU KNOW 20 MANSNS SIMON, IF YOU ARE HIS MOTHER.
(PITYINGLY, BUT AT THE SAME TIME SCORNFULLY.) 93 MANSNS
(SCORNFULLY RESENTFUL.) SO HE'LL CHOOSE, WILL HE,173 MANSNS THE GREAT MANS
(SCORNFULLY) YOU ARE A PAIR OF SUPERSTITIOUS 349 MARCOM SHEEP/
(SCORNFULLY--TAKES THE MINIATURE FROM HER BOSOM) 375 MARCOM
(SCORNFULLY) I'M IN LOVE WITH HIM, YOU'LL BE 27 MISBEG SAYING NEXT/
(SCOANFULLY) BETTER MYSELF BY BEING TIED DOWN 29 MISBEG
(THEN SCORNFULLY) THIS LAND FOR AN ESTATES 32 MISBEG
(SCORNFULLY) WHAT DRUNK HASN'TS 34 MISBEG
(SCORNFULLY) I'M TO PRETEND I'M A PURE VIRGIN, I 34 MISBEG SUPPOSE$
(THEN AS HE DOESN'T REPLY--SCORNFULLY) 81 MISBEG
(SCORNFULLY.) GOD HELP YOU, MOTHER/ 30 POET
(SHE STARES AT HIM SCORNFULLY. 46 POET
(SHE NODS SCORNFULLY TOWARD HER FATHER.) 60 POET
(SHE SMILES A BIT SCORNFULLY.) 62 POET
(SCORNFULLY.) AND BE DAMNED TO YOUR LYING, PIOUS 62 POET SHAME/
(SCORNFULLY.) OCH, WHO CARES FOR THE LAWS 140 POET
(SCORNFULLY) A FINE ONE YOU BE TO BE SHOUTIN' 580 ROPE SCRIPTURE IN A BODY'S EARS ALL
(INSTINCTIVELY CROSSES HIMSELF--(THEN SCORNFULLY) 582 ROPE
(HE INDICATES THE CARPENTRY OUTFIT SCORNFULLY) 587 ROPE
(THEN SCORNFULLY) BUT I WAS TOO AFRAID OF GOD 63 STRANG THEN TO HAVE EVER DONE IT/
(THEN RECOVERING HERSELF, SCORNFULLY) 98 STRANG
(SCORNFULLY) MARRYS 103 STRANG
(SCORAFULLY ASHAMED OF HIMSELF--THINKING) 117 STRANG
(HE LAUGHS SCORNFULLY AND SITS DOWN IN EVANS' 123 STRANG CHAIR.
(SHAKING HER HEAD--SCORNFULLY) 163 STRANG
(A PAUSE--THEN SCORNFULLY) DON'T TELL ME YOU'RE 454 WELDED BECOMING JEALOUS OF JOHN AGAIN/
(SCORNFULLY) CAN'T YOU REALIZE HOW ABSURD YOU 455 WELDED ARE$
A VAGUE COMPREHENSION COMING INTO HER FACE-- 475 WELDED SCORNFULLY)

SCORNING
AFURE WE DONE NOTHIN'--YEW WAS SCORNIN' ME--GOIN' 257 DESIRE T' SEE MIN--

SCORNING
AS HE CALLS HER, LIKE SHE WAS A GHOST, HAUNTING 161 POET AND SCORNING HIM.

SCOT
STILL, I CAN'T LET HIM DO SUCH THINGS AND GO SCOT-289 AHWILD FREE.
BUT HE WON'T GET OFF SCOT-FREE. 123 POET

456 CARIBE
459 CARIBE
565 CRUSS
535 DAYS
207 DESIRE
210 DESIRE
231 DESIRE
236 DESIRE
248 DESIRE
509 DIFRAT
423 DYNAMO
174 EJONES
183 EJONES
204 EJONES
17 ELECTR
38 ELECTR

SCOTCH

FIFE IS A SMALL WIRY MAN OF FIFTY, OF SCOTCH-IRISH428 DYNAMO ORIGIN.
HIS SPEECH IS EDUCATED, WITH THE GHOST OF A SCOTCH575 ICEMAN RHYTHM IN IT.
HE STARTED THROWING SCOTCH INTO HIM AS IF HE WERE 171 STRANG DRINKING AGAINST TIME.

SCOTCHMAN
(A LANKY SCOTCHMAN--DERISIVELY) 457 CARIBE

SCOUNDREL
UNLESS YOU'RE A SCOUNDREL AND GO AROUND RUINING 295 AHWILD DECENT GIRLS--
(WITH KINDLY BULLYING) WELL YOU DIDN'T, YOU OLD 167 BEYOND SCOUNDREL.
THAT FOUL-MOUTHED SCOUNDREL/. 422 DYNAMO
THAT SCOUNDREL CALLED SOMETHING AT ME ON THE 425 DYNAMO STREET TODAY--
THE DAMNED OLD SCOUNDREL! 25 JOURNE
CONTEMPTIBLE, DRUNKEN SCOUNDREL/ 37 POET
DIDN'T I FORBID YOU EVER TO MENTION THAT SCOUNDREL 53 POET JACKSON'S NAME IN MY HOUSE OR
WHAT A LOW SCOUNDREL YOU ARE/... 100 STRANG

SCOUNDRELLY
NO MATTER HOW RUINOUS THE INTEREST DEMANDED BY THE120 POET SCOUNDRELLY MONEYLENDERS.

SCOUNDRELS
YUU SCOUNDRELS/ 124 POET

SCOURGE
(THEN TO HIS SOLDIERS) SCOURGE HIM/ 348 LAZARU
GIVE ME A SCOURGE/ 348 LAZARU

SCOURGES
THE RODS AND SCOURGES ARE UPLIFTED OVER HIS BACK 348 LAZARU TO STRIKE,

SCOUT
WHAT MILLER'S A GOOD SCOUT. 248 AHWILD
YOU'RE A GOOD OLD SCOUT AT THAT, D'YOU KNOW ITS 544 DIFRAT
(INSOLENTLY) SURE, I KNOW YOU'RE A GOOD SCOUT. 544 DIFRAT
(THEN DEFENSIVELY AGAIN) BUT RUBE'S A GOOD 432 DYNAMO SCOUT--IN HIS WAY.
BE A GOOD SCOUT. 297 GGBROWN
YOU'RE A GOOD SCOUT. 598 ICEMAN
=HUM'S THE OLD SCOUTS= 619 ICEMAN
=BEST SCOUT/= 722 ICEMAN
HE'S A GRAND OLD SCOUT, JOSIE. 123 MISBEG
YOU'RE GOING TO BE A FATHER, OLD SCOUT, THAT'S THE106 STRANG SECRET/
HOW WAS THE OLD SCOUTS 115 STRANG

SCOUTS
(CYNICALLY.) BOY SCOUTS GOT NOTHIN' ON ME, PAL, 22 HUGHIE WHEN IT COMES TO GOOD DEEDS.
THEY'RE THE BEST LITTLE SCOUTS IN THE WORLD, 639 ICEMAN

SCOW
AND WHAT IS A FINE HANDSOME WOMAN THE LIKE OF YOU 31 ANNA DOING ON THIS SCOWS

SCOWL
(TURNS TO SCOWL AT THE SALESMAN--THEN TO BELLE) 244 AHWILD
EDEN HAS A MIXTURE OF SILLY GRIN AND VICIOUS SCOWL212 DESIRE ON HIS FACE)
(WITH A SCOWL) YOU'RE A LIAR. 133 ELECTR
(THEN WITH A SCOWL) THREE DOGS CF UNBELIEVERS, 350 MARCOM TOO/
SET IN AN ANGRY SCOWL.) 582 ROPE
A SCOWL SLOWLY REPLACES HIS GOOD-NATURED GRIN) 596 ROPE
(WITH A SAVAGE SCOWL) WE WON'T HURT HIM--MORE'N 600 ROPE ENOUGH.

SCOWLING
RICHARD SUBSIDES INTO SCOWLING GLOOM. 243 AHWILD
(BLINKING AT HER AND SCOWLING) 245 AHWILD
(SCOWLING AND FORCING OUT THE WORDS) 44 ANNA
(CHRIS SITS DUMB, SCOWLING, HIS EYES AVERTED. 45 ANNA
(SCOWLING) YEAHS HARRY'S PRETTY DAMNED GOOD TO 637 ICEMAN YOU.
SCOWLING AT THEM AND THEN QUICKLY LOOKING AWAY.) 650 ICEMAN
WHO GIVES HIM A SCOWLING, SUSPICIOUS GLANCE AND 674 ICEMAN THEN IGNORES HIM.
(STARTS--SCOWLING DEFENSIVELY) 677 ICEMAN
(BUT LARRY IS AT THE BAR, BACK TURNED, AND ROCKY 680 ICEMAN IS SCOWLING AT HIM.
(SCOWLING.) HE'S NOT SO FUNNY WHEN YOU'RE HIS 22 JOURNE LANDLORD.
(SCOWLING.) THAT LOAFER/ 154 JOURNE
(SCOWLING.) WHAT THE HELL IS THIS, THE MORGUES 155 JOURNE
(HE TURNS TO THE SCOWLING SWEENEY) 588 ROPE

SCOWLS
(HE SCOWLS AND TURNS HIS BACK ON HER. 220 AHWILD
CHRIS SCOWLS AT THE INTRUDER 45 ANNA
HE GRINS, THEN SCOWLS) 205 DESIRE
HE SCOWLS BACK HIS THOUGHTS OF HER AND SPITS WITH 228 DESIRE EXAGGERATED DISDAIN--
HE SCOWLS, STRIDES OFF THE PORCH TO THE PATH AND 228 DESIRE STARTS TO WALK PAST HER
HE SCOWLS AT THE FLOOR. 247 DESIRE
(HE SCOWLS.) I'VE BEEN CAMPIN' HERE, OFF AND ON, 17 HUGHIE FIFTEEN YEARS.
(SCOWLS BEWILDEREDLY.) SAY, WHAT IS THIS, 33 HUGHIE
(SCOWLS AT PARRITT) YEAH, KEEP CUTTA DIS, YOU/ 666 ICEMAN
(HE SCOWLS) THAT DRUMMER SON OF A DRUMMER/ 681 ICEMAN
(HE LAUGHS--THEN STOPS ABRUPTLY AND SCOWLS.) 25 JOURNE
(IGNORING THE HINT, JAMIE POURS A BIG DRINK. HIS 65 JOURNE FATHER SCOWLS--
TYRONE SCOWLS AND LOOKS AT HIS WIFE WITH SHARP 116 JOURNE SUSPICION--ROUGHLY.)
(HE STARTS LOOKING OVER THE PAPER AGAIN--SCOWLS AT 37 POET SOMETHING--
BUT SIMPLY SHUTS THE DOOR BEHIND HIM. HE SCOWLS 66 POET WITH DISGUST.)
(SCOWLS AT THEM, THEN TURNS TO CREGAN.) 97 POET
(SCOWLS AT HIS TONE BUT, AS HE COMPLETELY 120 POET MISUNDERSTANDS GADSBY'S MEANING,

SCREEN

SCRAGGLY
AND THENCE BACK THROUGH A SCRAGGLY ORCHARD OF 1 MISBEG
APPLE TREES TO THE BARN.

SCRAMBLE
'TWAS A MAD, FIGHTIN' SCRAMBLE IN THE LAST SECONDS 36 ANNA
WITH EACH MAN FOR HIMSELF.
THEY SEEM INCLINED TO JOIN IN THE SCRAMBLE.) 429 MARCOM
A MAD SCRAMBLE RESULTS. 429 MARCOM

SCRAMBLES
EVEN SCRAMBLES TO HIS FEET. 265 DESIRE
(HE SCRAMBLES TO HIS FEET, LOOKING BACK ACROSS THE188 EJONES
PLAIN)
(HE SCRAMBLES TO THE NEXT STONE AND TURNS IT OVER)188 EJONES
(WHILE HE IS TALKING HE SCRAMBLES FROM ONE STONE 189 EJONES
TO ANOTHER.
(HE SCRAMBLES UNSTEADILY TO HIS FEET) 104 ELECTR
(THE GORILLA SCRAMBLES GINGERLY OUT OF HIS CAGE. 254 HA APE
(HE SCRAMBLES TO HIS FEET IN A CONFUSED PANIC. 692 ICEMAN
(THE TERROR-STRICKEN COURIER SCRAMBLES OUT LIKE A 425 MARCOM
FLASH.
(SCRAMBLES HASTILY TO HIS FEET.) 162 POET
(HE SCRAMBLES TO HIS FEET AND PEERS ABOUT HIM WITH177 STRANG
A HECTIC EAGERNESS.

SCRAMBLING
(SCRAMBLING TO HIS FEET AND FOLLOWING HER-- 256 DESIRE
ACCUSINGLY)
JONES CAN BE HEARD SCRAMBLING TO HIS FEET AND 199 EJONES
RUNNING OFF.
(SCRAMBLING TO HIS FEET--IRRITABLY) 91 ELECTR
HUGO IS THE LAST, SUDDENLY COMING TO AND 653 ICEMAN
SCRAMBLING TO HIS FEET.

SCRAP
I WAS LISTENING TO THE LAST OF YOUR SCRAP. 204 AHWILD
I BURNT THEM TO THE LAST SCRAP/ 465 DYNAMO
DEN DEY'D GET MAD MAKE A BLUFF DEY WAS GOIN' 612 ICEMAN
TO SCRAP.
WHAT STARTED DE SCRAPS 650 ICEMAN
YOU AND I NEVER SCRAP--THAT BAD. 162 JOURNE

SCRAPED
IN WHICH OUR SOULS HAVE BEEN SCRAPED CLEAN OF 199 STRANG
IMPURE FLESH

SCRAPERS
(WITH A GRIN) DEY WAS SCRAPPERS FOR FAIR, BOT' OF234 HA APE
DEM.

SCRAPPIN'
WHAT ARE YOU AND ME SCRAPPIN' OVERS 15 ANNA
NO SCRAPPIN' NOW/ 208 HA APE
(IGNORING THIS) ME AND DIS OVERGROWN TRAMP HAS 616 ICEMAN
BEEN SCRAPPIN' ABOUT IT.
(THEN MOLLIFYINGLY) JEES, YUH GOT YOUR SCRAPPIN' 630 ICEMAN
PANTS ON, AIN'T YUHS
BEEN SCRAPPIN', HUHS 697 ICEMAN

SCRAPPING
YOU BEEN SCRAPPING, TOO, AIN'T YOUS 70 ANNA

SCRAPS
(AFTER A PAUSE) YOU--A FARMER--TO GAMBLE IN A 161 BEYOND
WHEAT PIT WITH SCRAPS OF PAPER.

SCRATCH
THIS IS ONLY A SCRATCH. 472 CARIBE
(POINTS TO EMMA) DON'T SHE LOOK LIKE SHE'D 507 DIFRNT
SCRATCH A FELLER'S EYES OUT/
HE WAS WOUNDED IN THE HEAD--A CLOSE SHAVE BUT IT 48 ELECTR
TURNED OUT ONLY A SCRATCH.
PURR, SCRATCH, TEAR, KILL, GORGE YOURSELF AND BE 220 HA APE
HAPPY--
(PREOCCUPIED.) YEAH, SURE, WHEN I GOT SCRATCH TO 34 HUGHIE
PUT UP.
(BAFFLED, SITS ON THE BOULDER AND TAKES OFF HIS 13 MISBEG
HAT TO SCRATCH HIS HEAD--
LOOKING FOR YOU TO SCRATCH YOUR EYES OUT. 19 POET

SCRATCHED
HIS FACE IS SCRATCHED, HIS BRILLIANT UNIFORM SHOWS191 EJONES
SEVERAL LARGE RENTS)
(WRATHFULLY.) THE PADLOCK IS ALL SCRATCHED. 121 JOURNE

SCRATCHES
(HE SCRATCHES A MATCH AND LIGHTS THE LANTERN.) 557 CROSS
(ALARMED FOR A SECOND, SCRATCHES HIS HEAD, THEN 182 EJONES
PHILOSOPHICALLY)
(HE SCRATCHES A MATCH ON HIS TROUSERS AND PEERS 189 EJONES
ABOUT HIM.
FROM THE WAY HE METHODICALLY SCRATCHES HIMSELF 574 ICEMAN
WITH HIS LONG-FINGERED,
HOGAN SCRATCHES A MATCH ON THE SEAT OF HIS OVER- 37 MISBEG
ALLS AND LIGHTS HIS PIPE.
(HE TAKES OFF HIS HAT AND SCRATCHES HIS HEAD IN 59 MISBEG
COMIC BEWILDERMENT)
CREGAN SCRATCHES HIS HEAD PUZZLEDLY.) 153 POET
HASTILY SCRATCHES ON IT.) 33 STRANG

SCRATCHIN'
AIN' SCRATCHIN' DE HIDE OFF YO' LEGS IN DE BUSHES. 191 EJONES

SCRATCHING
(SCRATCHING HIS HEAD IN A QUANDARY) 10 ANNA
(SCRATCHING HIS HEAD IN PUZZLEMENT) 101 BEYOND
HE TAKES OFF HIS DRIPPING SOU'WESTER AND STANDS, 490 CARDIF
SCRATCHING HIS HEAD.)
(SCRATCHING HIS HEAD IN UNEASY PERPLEXITY) 520 INZONE
WHO AT THIS MOMENT IS SCRATCHING HIMSELF, 359 MARCOM

SCRAWNY
SCRAWNY WOMAN. 520 DIFRNT
TALL, THIN, WITH A SCRAWNY NECK AND JUTTING ADAM'S 8 HUGHIE
APPLE.

SCREAM
GEE, KID YOU ARE A SCREAM/ 240 AHWILD
THIS IS A SCREAM/ 246 AHWILD
YUH'RE A SCREAM, SQUARE-HEAD--AN HONEST-TER-GAWD 11 ANNA
KNOCKOUT/
(IN A SCREAM) DON'T, MAT/ 60 ANNA
(IN A DEFIANT SCREAM) YES, I DO MEAN IT/ 128 BEYOND

SCREAM (CONT'D.)
(THEN IN A SCREAM) GIT OUT O' MY SIGHT/ 230 DESIRE
SHE'S A SCREAM, HONEST/ 529 DIFRNT
I'LL SCREAM IN A MINUTE...)) 444 DYNAMO
(FORCING A NERVOUS LAUGH) IT GETS ON MY NERVES 73 ELECTR
UNTIL I COULD SCREAM/
SHE STARTS BACK WITH A STIFLED SCREAM AND STARES 101 ELECTR
AT IT WITH GUILTY FEAR.)
(IN A SCREAM) YUU COWARD/ 317 GGBROW
(HE CLAPS HIS HANDS AND BEGINS TO SCREAM) 239 HA APE
(SHE GIGGLES) LISTEN, IT WAS A SCREAM. 616 ICEMAN
I WILL HEAR MYSELF SCREAM WITH AGONY, 94 JOURNE
JEERS FROM THE ORTHODOX, PENETRATED BY A PIERCING 283 LAZARU
SCREAM FROM LAZARUS' MOTHER,
WHEN I AM CAESAR YOU SHALL SCREAM AND PRAY FOR IT/317 LAZARU
MIRIAM STIFLES A SCREAM. 333 LAZARU
(WITH RESENTFUL JEALOUSY AND RAGE--IN A VOICE 368 LAZARU
RISING TO A SCREAM)
AND SCREAM IN SILENCE AND BEAT ON THE WALLS UNTIL 40 MANSNS
YOU DIE OF STARVATION.
KUKACHIN GIVES A SCREAM A FRIGHT, THEN A GASP OF 399 MARCOM
DELIGHT, AND CLAPS HER HANDS.
I'LL SCREAM OUT THE TRUTH ABOUT EVERY WOMAN/ 40 STRANG
THE PEOPLE HAVE TO YELL AND SCREAM TO MAKE 181 STRANG
THEMSELVES HEARD.)

SCREAMED
THE ONE WHEN YOU SCREAMED FOR IT, 86 JOURNE
AND ALL THE WOMEN SCREAMED/ 277 LAZARU
DEMONS SCREAMED/ 408 MARCOM
OR HAD A NIGHTMARE AND SCREAMED, 60 STRANG
SHE SCREAMED.. *I'LL GO TOO.* 479 WELDED

SCREAMIN'
STANDIN' ON THE BEACH HOWLIN' AND SCREAMIN', 503 DIFRNT

SCREAMING
AND I'D HAVE TO KILL HIS SILENCE BY SCREAMING OUT 40 ELECTR
THE TRUTH/
AND YOU TWO HOOKERS, SCREAMING AT THE TOP OF YOUR 654 ICEMAN
LUNGS/
THE IDEA OF SCREAMING AS IF THIS WERE A CHEAP 60 JOURNE
BOARDINGHOUSE/
THEN CALIGULA'S VOICE IS HEARD SCREAMING ABOVE THE338 LAZARU
CHORUS OF LAUGHTER AS HE
INTO THE MIDST OF THE OBLIVIOUS, LAUGHING, DANCING369 LAZARU
CROWD, SCREAMING)
THROAT CHOKES HIM, FORCING HIM BACK ON THE 369 LAZARU
THRONE--SCREAMING)
WITHOUT SCREAMING SCORNFUL LAUGHTER AT MYSELF. 102 MANSNS
AND YOU BEAT THE WALLS, SCREAMING FOR ESCAPE AT 163 MANSNS
ANY COST/
SCREAMING LIKE A STUCK PIG/ 155 POET
(SCREAMING) NO/ 991 ROPE
I HEAR HIS SCREAMING LAUGHTER/... 181 STRANG

SCREAMS
(WITH MOCK TERROR--SCREAMS IN FALSETTO) 246 AHWILD
HIS MOTHER SCREAMS. 453 DYNAMO
SCREAMS AND LEAPS MADLY TO THE TOP OF THE STUMP 197 EJONES
IT WOULD RISE ABOUT THE SCREAMS OF THE DYING-- 83 ELECTR
(SCREAMS AFTER HER) I SAID POSER/ 222 HA APE
HE STARES TOWARD THE FLAMES STUPIDLY--THEN SCREAMS368 LAZARU
DESPAIRINGLY ABOVE THE CHANT)
ALL THE TIME THE THREE SET UP MISERABLE SCREAMS OF353 MARCOM
PROTEST.
DROWN THE GUNS AND THE SCREAMS... 14 STRANG

SCREECH
SCREECH OWLS IS OP'RY SINGERS COMPARED TO HIM/ 103 ELECTR

SCREECHING
'TIS A MAD LUNATIC, SCREECHING WITH FEAR, YOU'D BE 48 ANNA
THIS MINUTE/
(SCREECHING HAPPILY) DADA/ 119 BEYOND
IMMEDIATELY A CHORUS OF ANGRY CHATTERING AND 251 HA APE
SCREECHING BREAKS OUT.
AND I DON'T WANT NO DAMN-FOOL LAUGHING AND 610 ICEMAN
SCREECHING.

SCREEN
IN THE RIGHT WALL, REAR, A SCREEN DOOR IN THIS 185 AHWILD
WALL ARE TWO WINDOWS,
(BUT TOMMY IS ALREADY THROUGH THE SCREEN DOOR, 186 AHWILD
WHICH HE LEAVES OPEN BEHIND HIM.)
(TOMMY JUMPS FOR THE SCREEN DOOR TO THE PORCH AT 186 AHWILD
RIGHT
(SUDDENLY SHE IS AWARE OF THE SCREEN DOOR STANDING187 AHWILD
HALF OPEN)
THAT BOY/ (SHE RUSHES TO THE SCREEN DOOR AND OUT 189 AHWILD
ON THE PORCH, CALLING) TOMMY/
IN THE LEFT WALL, EXTREME FRONT, IS A SCREEN DOOR 210 AHWILD
OPENING ON A SIDE PORCH.
(DEEPLY OFFENDED, RICHARD DISJOINTS TO REPLY BUT 216 AHWILD
STALKS WOUNDEDLY TO THE SCREEN
THEY HAVE NO SOONER DISAPPEARED THAN THE SCREEN 217 AHWILD
DOOR IS OPENED CAUTIOUSLY AND
HE GOES OVER TO THE SCREEN DOOR GRUMPILY-- 217 AHWILD
THE FRONT SCREEN DOOR IS HEARD SLAMMING AND NAT'S 221 AHWILD
AND SID'S LAUGHING VOICES,
(MILDRED AND TOMMY GO OUT THROUGH THE SCREEN DOOR.234 AHWILD
(HE TURNS AND GOES OUT THE SCREEN DOOR.) 236 AHWILD
(HE RUSHES HIM THROUGH THE SCREEN DOOR 247 AHWILD
(THE SCREEN DOOR IS PUSHED VIOLENTLY OPEN AND 260 AHWILD
RICHARD LUNCHES IN AND STANDS
AND THE SCREEN DOOR IS OPENED AND MILDRED ENTERS. 272 AHWILD
MOONLIGHT SHINES THROUGH THE SCREEN DOOR AT RIGHT.288 AHWILD
REAR.
(RICHARD OPENS THE SCREEN DOOR AND CALLS * MA,* 296 AHWILD
AND A MOMENT LATER SHE COMES IN.
(RICHARD TURNS IMPULSIVELY AND KISSES HIM--THEN 297 AHWILD
HURRIES OUT THE SCREEN DOOR.
IN THROUGH THE SCREEN DOOR. WALKING TOGETHER 298 AHWILD
TOWARD THE FRONT PARLOR
A PATCHED SCREEN DOOR IS IN THE REAR. 112 BEYOND

SCREEN

SCREEN (CONT'D.)
(GOING AND HOLDING THE SCREEN DOOR OPEN FOR THEM--118 BEYOND LISTLESSLY)
AND STARTS TO WHEEL THE INVALID'S CHAIR TOWARD THE118 BEYOND SCREEN DOOR)
ROBERT WALKS UP THE PATH AND OPENS THE SCREEN DOOR119 BEYOND QUIETLY.
(SHE RUSHES AND GRABS THE KNOB OF THE SCREEN DOOR,128 BEYOND ABOUT TO FLING IT OPEN.)
BEFORE THIS DOOR IS A SCREEN. 553 DAYS
THROUGH THE WINDOW AND THE SCREEN DOOR IN THE REAR493 DIFRNT THE FRESH GREEN OF THE LAWN
JACK COMES UP THE SCREEN DOOR. 498 DIFRNT
PEEKING THROUGH THE SCREEN AND CATCHING SIGHT OF 505 DIFRNT EMMA, HARRIET CALLS)
CALEB APPEARS OUTSIDE THE SCREEN DOOR. 514 DIFRNT
THE SCREEN UP IN HER ROOM HAS A HOLE RUSTED IN 456 DYNAMO IT.
IS A SCREEN DOOR LEADING OUT ON THE PORCH 11 JOURNE
(HE OPENS THE SCREEN DOOR AND GOES OUT ON THE 41 JOURNE PORCH AND
(HE GOES TO THE SCREEN DOOR--FORCING A JOKING 49 JOURNE TONE.)
(GOES TO THE SCREEN DOOR, GRUMBLING GOOD- 53 JOURNE NATUREDLY.)
(SHE GOES OUT ON THE SIDE PORCH, LETTING THE 53 JOURNE SCREEN DOOR SLAM BEHIND HER,
THE SCREEN DOOR ON THE FRONT PORCH IS HEARD 64 JOURNE CLOSING.
TYRONE LIGHTS A CIGAR AND GOES TO THE SCREEN DOOR, 71 JOURNE STARING OUT.
(TURNS TO LOOK OUT THE SCREEN DOOR.) 81 JOURNE
(THE FRONT SCREEN DOOR IS HEARD CLOSING AFTER 95 JOURNE THEM.
AS THE CURTAIN RISES, SHE IS STANDING BY THE 98 JOURNE SCREEN DOOR LOOKING OUT.
TYRONE COMES IN QUIETLY THROUGH THE SCREEN DOOR 167 JOURNE FROM THE PORCH,
(THEN ABRUPTLY, STARTING FOR THE SCREEN DOOR AT 97 MISBEG LEFT)
(GOES TO THE SCREEN DOOR AND PUSHES IT OPEN 98 MISBEG

SCREENS
WHICH PARTLY SCREENS ANYONE SITTING ON IT FROM THE 5 ELECTR FRONT OF THE STAGE.

SCREWED
WITH HER SILLY FACE ALL SCREWED UP SERIOUS AS 94 BEYOND JUDGEMENT--
HIS BODY ALL SCREWED UP INTO AN AWKWARD INTENSITY,358 MARCOM
(HE TURNS AWAY, HIS FACE IS SCREWED UP IN HIS 133 STRANG EFFORT TO HOLD BACK HIS TEARS.
HID THE BIG RED NOSE AV YE ALL SCREWED UP IN A 498 VOYAGE KNOT.

SCREWS
I'VE TOOK THE SCREWS OUT O' THAT DOOR. 131 ELECTR

SCRIBBLING
THINKING OF ME, SCRIBBLING IN PRESS BUREAU... 14 STRANG

SCRIPT
HE HASTILY GRABS THE SCRIPT AND PUTS IT IN THE 149 ELECTR DRAWER OF THE DESK..

SCRIPTS
NEWSY, LOVELESS SCRIPTS, TELLING NOTHING WHATEVER 25 STRANG ABOUT HERSELF...

SCRIPTURE
YOU QUOTIN' SCRIPTURE/ 580 ROPE
(SCORNFULLY) A FINE ONE YOU BE TO BE SHOUTIN' 580 ROPE SCRIPTURE IN A BODY'S EARS ALL
HE USED TO BE DOWN THERE A LOT RECITIN' SCRIPTURE 586 ROPE IN HIS FITS.

SCROLLY
THE WALLS ARE PAPERED A DARK RED WITH A SCROLLY- 93 BEYOND FIGURED PATTERN.

SCRUBBED
IT STUCK IN MY MIND--CLEAN-SCRUBBED AND 54 ELECTR WHITEWASHED--A TEMPLE OF DEATH/
THE FLOOR HAS BEEN SWEPT CLEAN OF SAWDUST AND 628 ICEMAN SCRUBBED.
AND MY POOR MOTHER WASHED AND SCRUBBED FOR THE 148 JOURNE YANKS BY THE DAY,

SCRUBBIN'
(GRUMBLINGLY) I DON'T TAKE NO BACK-TALK FROM THAT462 CARIBE DECK-SCRUBBIN' SHRIMP.

SCRUBBING
DECK-SCRUBBING SCUT/ 31 ANNA
THEIR FACES AND BODIES SHINE FROM SOAP-AND-WATER 226 HA APE SCRUBBING BUT AROUND THEIR
WHEN SOME YANK IN WHOSE HOUSE MOTHER HAD BEEN 148 JOURNE SCRUBBING GAVE HER A DOLLAR EXTRA
I WAS SWEEPING AND NORA WAS SCRUBBING THE KITCHEN. 17 POET

SCRUBWOMAN
ITS MOVEMENTS JUST NOW ARE THOSE OF A TIRED 471 WELDED SCRUBWOMAN.

SCRUFF
AND GO TO BED, OR I'LL TAKE YOU BY THE SCRUFF OF 74 MISBEG YOUR NECK AND THE SEAT OF YOUR
IF I HAVE TO MARCH YE BOTH BY THE SCRUFF AV THE 179 POET NECK TO THE NEAREST CHURCH.

SCRUPLE
WHOSE WILL WAS AS DEVOID OF SCRUPLE, AS 87 MANSNS
THEN YOU CAN GO ON--SUCCESSFULLY--WITH A CLEAR 91 MANSNS VISION--WITHOUT FALSE SCRUPLE--
IF YOU CAN, DISCOVER HIS WEAKNESS AND THEN USE IT 150 MANSNS WITHOUT SCRUPLE.
WITH THAT OLD MAD DEBORAH, WHO WILL HAVE NO 163 MANSNS SCRUPLE--
BUT I GATHER HE DIDN'T TELL HER IT WAS YOUR 11 STRANG SCRUPLE ORIGINALLY$
SCRUPLE, WITHOUT FEAR, WITHOUT JOY EXCEPT IN HIS 18 STRANG JOY/

SCRUPLES
I SHOULD THINK THAT WOULD RID YOU OF ANY SCRUPLES/ 41 ELECTR
PROMISE ME, NO MORE COWARDLY ROMANTIC SCRUPLES/ 42 ELECTR
FATHER HAD SCRUPLES. 101 MANSNS
THAT YOU WILL HAVE TO FORGET ALL SCRUPLES. 154 MANSNS
BUT HOW'LL YOU GET HIM IN BED, WITH ALL HIS 92 MISBEG HONORABLE SCRUPLES,
AND I'VE NO FAITH IN YOUR SCHEME BECAUSE YOU'LL BE 93 MISBEG TOO FULL OF SCRUPLES.
TO HELL WITH YOUR HONORABLE SCRUPLES/ 137 MISBEG
A SCIENTIFIC MIND SUPERIOR TO THE MORAL SCRUPLES 88 STRANG

SCRUPULOUS
FURNISHED WITH SCRUPULOUS MEDIUM-PRICED 185 AHWILD TASTELESSNESS OF THE PERIOD.
EVERYTHING HAS AN ASPECT OF SCRUPULOUS NEATNESS. 493 DIFRNT
THEN WHAT MAKES YOU SUDDENLY SO SCRUPULOUS ABOUT 41 ELECTR HIS DEATH$

SCRUTINIZE
(SHE SMILES.) I NEED NOT WARN YOU TO SCRUTINIZE 52 MANSNS IT CLOSELY.

SCRUTINIZES
JOHNNY SCRUTINIZES THE LETTER) 5 ANNA
WITHOUT APPEARING TO NOTICE, JOHN SCRUTINIZES 450 WELDED THEIR FACES KEENLY.

SCRUTINIZING
(SCRUTINIZING HIM CAREFULLY) 246 HA APE
AND THEN SCRUTINIZING THE KEYS IN HIS HAND) 527 INZONE
(SCRUTINIZING HIM--WITH SINISTER FINALITY) 340 LAZARU

SCUDDING
OH, TO BE SCUDDING SOUTH AGAIN WID THE POWER OF 214 HA APE THE TRADE WIND

SCUFFLE
SUDDENLY THERE IS A NOISE OF ANGRY, CURSING VOICES650 ICEMAN AND A SCUFFLE FROM THE HALL.
AND THEN THE SCUFFLE STOPS AND ROCKY APPEARS 650 ICEMAN HOLDING CAPTAIN LEWIS BY THE ARM,

SCUFFLING
A MOMENT LATER THERE IS THE SOUND OF SCUFFLING 550 'ILE FEET OUTSIDE
THEN THERE IS A PAUSE--THE MURMUR OF EXCITED 30 ANNA VOICES--THEN THE SCUFFLING OF FEET.
THERE IS A SCUFFLING NOISE FROM ABOVE. 573 CROSS
(SCUFFLING--EMBARRASSED) WHY--OF COURSE-- 301 GGBROW
THE SOUND OF SCUFFLING COMING THROUGH THE CEILING, 43 MANSNS

SCUM
SCUM OF THE EARTH/ 425 DYNAMO
THEY WOULD TEAR DOWN SOCIETY, PUT THE LOWEST SCUM 244 HA APE IN THE SEATS OF THE MIGHTY,
YOU BLOODY DUTCH SCUM/ 677 ICEMAN
HE WAS A KING OF IRELAND, IF HE HAD HIS RIGHTS, 24 JOURNE AND SCUM WAS SCUM TO HIM,
LET THE SCUM LOOK AT THEIR DEAD AND LEARN RESPECT 300 LAZARU FOR US/
AND YOU ARE SCUM WHOM I WILL KILL AT HIS ORDER AS 331 LAZARU I WOULD TWO BEETLES/
O MY GOOD PEOPLE, MY FAITHFUL SCUM, MY BROTHER 370 LAZARU SWINE,
(HE SPITS DISGUSTEDLY) THE SCUM OF THE EARTH/ 17 MISBEG
I'M NO SAINT, GOD KNOWS, BUT I'M DECENT AND 30 MISBEG DESERVING COMPARED TO THOSE SCUM.
THAT ENGLISH SCUM OF A SUPERINTENDENT/ 48 MISBEG
WHAT'S THE REASON MR. HARDER DECIDED TO NOTICE 49 MISBEG POOR, HUMBLE SCUM THE LIKE OF US$
AS IF I'D DIRTY MY HANDS ON THE SCUM. 52 MISBEG
AND AS LONG AS THE NEIGHBOURING SCUM LEAVE ME 62 MISBEG ALONE, I'LL LET THEM ALONE,
AND HE CONSIDERS THE FEW IRISH AROUND HERE TO BE 13 POET SCUM BENEATH HIS NOTICE.
I'D BETTER WARN HIM NOT TO SNEER AT THE IRISH 26 POET AROUND HERE AND CALL THIN SCUM,
YOU OUGHT TO TELL THE GOOD FATHER WE AREN'T THE 27 POET IGNORANT SHANTY SCUM
EVERYWHERE THE SCUM RISES TO THE TOP. 37 POET
(QUIETLY. A DAUGHTER WHO TAKES SATISFACTION IN 104 POET LETTING EVEN THE SCUM SEE
FOR DRUNKEN SCUM LIKE O'DOWD AND-- 104 POET
THE SPRINGS TO HIS FEET.) BUT FIRST, YOU YANKEE 122 POET SCUM, I'LL DEAL WITH YOU/
DON'T GO IN WITH THOSE DRUNKEN SCUM/ 176 POET

SCUMWIPER
SCUMWIPER/ 366 LAZARU

SCURRIED
THE FORMLESS CREATURES HAVE SCURRIED BACK INTO THE190 EJONES FOREST.

SCURRIES
(HE SCURRIES INTO THE ROOM ON RIGHT. 547 DIFRNT

SCURRY
THEN AT A CRY FROM ONE OF THE WOMEN, THEY ALL 238 HA APE SCURRY TO THE FURRIER'S WINDOW.)
THEN SCURRY AROUND TO RIGHT AND LEFT, 362 LAZARU

SCURRYIN'
SCURRYIN' LIKE A FRIGHTENED HARE 597 ROPE

SCURRYING
(TURNING AND SCURRYING AWAY-- 369 LAZARU

SCURSE
A GOOD STEPMAN'S SCURSE. 207 DESIRE

SCUSE
SCUSE ME FOR LIVIN'. 699 ICEMAN
SCUSE ME, WHITE BOYS. 699 ICEMAN

SCUT
(THEN IRRITABLY) WHERE ARE YE, YE SCUTS 29 ANNA
DECK-SCRUBBING SCUT/ 31 ANNA
SCUT STINKING OF PIGS AND DUNGS 48 ANNA
I HAVE--WITH EVERY SCUT WOULD TAKE OFF HIS COAT TO 70 ANNA ME/
GOD STIFFEN YOU, YE SQUARE-HEADED SCUT/ 481 CARDIF
WHO'S THE DIRTY SCUT LEFT THIS CUP WHERE A MAN 'UDS17 INZONE SIT ON UT$

SEA

SCUT (CONT'D.)
GOOD WURHK FOR YE, DAVIS, YE SCUT/ 524 INZONE
TRYIN' TO MURROHER US ALL, THE SCUT/ 526 INZONE
HO, YE SCUT/ 498 VOYAGE
WHATTLE YE HAVE, YE LITTLE SCUTS 908 VOYAGE

SCUTS
LET YOU NOT BE THINKING I'M THE LIKE OF THEM THREE 32 ANNA
WEAK SCUTS COME IN THE BOAT
(WARNINGLY) REMEMBER YE MUST BE QUIET ABOUT UT. 458 CARIBE
YE SCUTS--
(WILDLY ELATED) HURROO, YE SCUTS/ 460 CARIBE

SCUTTLE
FARTHER FORWARD A DOUBLE-HEATER STOVE WITH COAL 93 BEYOND
SCUTTLE, ETC.

SCUTTLED
AND THEN I HEARD HIM GROAN AND I SCUTTLED DOWN 479 CARDIF
AFTER HIM.
AND THEIR SHIPS ARE LONG SINCE LOOTED AND SCUTTLED578 ICEMAN
AND SUNK ON THE BOTTOMS

SEA
THE NEXT DISH YOU BREAK, MR. STEWARD, YOU TAKE A 539 'ILE
BATH IN THE BERING SEA
HE IS DRESSED IN A HEAVY BLUE JACKET AND BLUE 539 'ILE
PANTS STUFFED INTO HIS SEA-BOOTS.
YOU AIN'T TURNIN' NO DAMNED SEA-LAWYER, BE YOU, 541 'ILE
MR. SLOCUMS
ALL ARE DRESSED ALIKE--SWEATERS, SEA-BOOTS, ETC. 543 'ILE
WE'RE AT SEA NOW, AND I'M THE LAW ON THIS SHIP. 544 'ILE
FIRST MAN OF YE I SEE SHIRKIN' I'LL SHOOT DEAD AS 545 'ILE
SURE AS THERE'S A SEA UNDER
BUT NOW--I DON'T EVER WANT TO SEE THE SEA AGAIN. 548 'ILE
I USED TO LOVE THE SEA THEN. 548 'ILE
THERE'S LOTS OF OTHER FISH IN THE SEA. 208 AHWILD
WHAT'S THAT HE WAS SAYING ABOUT FISH IN THE SEAS 216 AHWILD
THERE'S PLENTY OF OTHER FISH IN THE SEA/ 216 AHWILD
SEA-SICK TINGE, HIS EYES SEEM TO BE TURNED INWARD 261 AHWILD
UNEASILY--
AY TANK IT'S BETTER ANNA LIVE ON FARM, DEN SHE 9 ANNA
DON'T KNOW DAT OLE DAVIL, SEA,
THAT'S WHAT COMES OF HIS BRINGING YOU UP INLAND-- 17 ANNA
AWAY FROM THE OLD DEVIL SEA--
AND A LOT OF CRAZY STUFF ABOUT STAYING AWAY FROM 18 ANNA
THE SEA--
DAT OLE DAVIL SEA MAKE DEM CRAZY FOOLS WITH HER 21 ANNA
DIRTY TRICKS.
YOB ON HER AIN'T SEA YOB. 21 ANNA
DIS AIN'T REAL BOAT ON SEA. 21 ANNA
AY DON'T GAT YOB ON SEA, ANNA, IF AY DIE FIRST. 21 ANNA
(WITH A SHURT LAUGH) BEEFING ABOUT THE SEA AGAINS 26 ANNA
AND DIS AIN'T REAL SEA. 26 ANNA
FUNNY! I DON'T KNOW NOTHING ABOUT SEA TALK-- 27 ANNA
HE'S BURIED AT SEA. 27 ANNA
ALL MEN IN OUR VILLAGE ON COAST, SVEDEN, GO TO 27 ANNA
SEA.
MY DDER BRO'DER, HE SAVE MONEY, GIVE UP SEA, DEN 27 ANNA
HE DIE HOME IN BED.
(DETERMINED TO DISGUST HER WITH SEA LIFE--VOLUBLY) 28 ANNA
AND DAT OLE DAVIL, SEA, SOONER, LATER SHE SWALLOW 28 ANNA
DEM UP.
IT'S ROTTEN. AY TAL YOU, FOR GOD TO SEA. 28 ANNA
DEY ALL VORK ROTTEN YOB ON SEA FOR NUTTING, 28 ANNA
AND WHEN DEIR BOYS GROW UP, GO TO SEA, DEY SIT AND 28 ANNA
VAIT SOME MORE.
DAT OLE DAVIL, SEA, SHE AIN'T GOD/ 29 ANNA
SHE COME IN FROM OPEN SEA. 29 ANNA
I THOUGHT YOU WAS SOME MERMAID OUT OF THE SEA COME 31 ANNA
TO TORMENT ME.
WE'D ALL OUGHT TO BE WITH DAVY JONES AT THE BOTTOM 32 ANNA
OF THE SEA, BE RIGHTS.
THERE'S TOO MANY STRAPPING GREAT LADS ON THE SEA 33 ANNA
WOULD GIVE THEIR HEART'S BLOOD
BUT FEARING A CLOUT OF MY RIGHT ARM MORE THAN 36 ANNA
THEY'D FEAR THE SEA ITSELF.
AND DIVIL A SIGHT THERE WAS OF SHIP OR MEN ON TOP 36 ANNA
OF THE SEA.
AND ALL THE MEN ON BOTH SIDES OF THE FAMILY HAVE 36 ANNA
GONE TO SEA AS FAR BACK AS HE
THE SEA, YOU MEANS 36 ANNA
SINCE THE DAY I LEFT HOME FOR TO GO TO SEA 37 ANNA
PUNCHING COAL.
IT'S ONLY ON THE SEA YOU'D FIND RALE MEN WITH GUTS 37 ANNA
IS FIT TO WED WITH FINE.
(WITH SUDDEN MELANCHOLY) IT'S A HARD AND LONESOME 37 ANNA
LIFE, THE SEA IS.
(ARGUMENTATIVELY) BUT THERE'S GOOD JOBS AND BAD 38 ANNA
JOBS AT SEA,
I'LL BE ROARING IT OUT LIKE A FOG HORN OVER THE 39 ANNA
SEA/
(TURNS SUDDENLY AND SHAKES HIS FIST OUT AT THE 40 ANNA
SEA--WITH BITTER HATRED)
(MOCKINGLY) THAT'S WHAT YOUR TAKING ME TO SEA HAS 43 ANNA
DONE FOR ME.
YES, AY DO, ANNA---ONLY NOT FALLAR ON SEA. 43 ANNA
BUT DIVIL TAKE YOU, THERE'S A TIME COMES TO EVERY 46 ANNA
MAN, ON SEA OR LAND,
(CAJOLINGLY) BIG FALLAR LIKE YOU DAT'S ON SEA, HE 46 ANNA
DON'T NEED VIFE.
GROW UP INLAND WHERE SHE DON'T EVER KNOW OLE 47 ANNA
DAVIL, SEA,
(SCORNFULLY) IS IT BLAMING THE SEA FOR YOUR 47 ANNA
TROUBLES YE ARE AGAINS
AND AY DON'T VANT SHE EVER KNOW NO-GOOD FALLAR ON 47 ANNA
SEA--
IT'S SQUARE FOOL'S BLATHER YOU HAVE ABOUT THE SEA 47 ANNA
DONE THIS AND THE SEA DONE
TIS ONLY ON THE SEA HE'S FREE, AND HIM ROVING THE 48 ANNA
FACE OF THE WORLD.

SEA (CONT'D.)
(PROUDLY) ISN'T IT MYSELF THE SEA HAS WORE NEARLY 48 ANNA
DROWNED,
ROARING AND NEVER A GROAN OUT OF ME TILL THE SEA 48 ANNA
GAVE UP AND IT SEEING THE GREAT
THE SEA GIVE YOU A CLOUT ONCE, KNOCKED YOU DOWN, 48 ANNA
I'M THINKING YES OUT OF YOUR WITS YOU'VE GOT WITH 48 ANNA
FRIGHT OF THE SEA.
IF GREAT FEAR OF THE SEA HAS MADE YOU A LIAR AND 48 ANNA
COWARD ITSELF.
VE VAS TALKING ABOUT SHIPS AND FALLARS ON SEA. 50 ANNA
THAT CRAZY BULL ABOUT WANTING TO KEEP ME AWAY FROM 57 ANNA
THE SEA DON'T GO DOWN WITH
A SEA MAN AS DIFFERENT FROM THE ONES ON LAND AS 59 ANNA
WATER IS FROM MUD--
AND BEING ON THE SEA HAD CHANGED ME AND MADE ME 59 ANNA
FEEL DIFFERENT ABOUT THINGS.
IT'S DAT OLE DAVIL, SEA, DO THIS TO ME/ 62 ANNA
(SHAKING HIS FIST) IT'S DAT OLE DAVIL SEA/ 65 ANNA
DAT OLE DAVIL, SEA, SHE MAKE ME YUNAH 65 ANNA
(AFTER A HESITATING PAUSE) AY'M SHIPPING AVAY ON 65 ANNA
SEA AGAIN, ANNA.
AND AY TANK NOW IT AIN'T NO USE FIGHT WITH SEA. 66 ANNA
(THEN ANGRILY) YOU'D BE GOING BACK GO TO SEA AND 77 ANNA
LEAVE HER ALONE WOULD YOU,
ONLY DAT OLE DAVIL, SEA---SHE KNOWS/ 78 ANNA
HERE'S, TO THE SEA, NO MATTER WHAT/ 78 ANNA
AY GUNN'T KNOW--IT'S DAT FUNNY VAY OLE DAVIL SEA DO 78 ANNA
HER VORST DIRTY TRICKS, YES.
+I HAVE LOVED WIND AND LIGHT AND THE BRIGHT SEA. 82 BEYOND
WHEN I KNOW HOW YOU NEED THIS SEA TRIP TO MAKE A 84 BEYOND
NEW MAN OF YOU--
AND YOU CAN HAVE ALL THE SEA YOU WANT BY WALKING A 85 BEYOND
MILE DOWN TO THE BEACH.
WAS SEARCHING FOR THE SEA. 89 BEYOND
AND I USED TO WONDER WHAT THE SEA WAS LIKE. 89 BEYOND
I KNEW THE SEA WAS OVER BEYOND THOSE HILLS,--THE 89 BEYOND
FOLKS HAD TOLD ME--
AND IT AND I WOULD FIND THE SEA TOGETHER. 89 BEYOND
FAR-OFF SEA--AND THERE STILL IS/ 89 BEYOND
WHERE THE SEA-GULLS SLEEPS AT NIGHTS/ 94 BEYOND
I AIN'T NEVER SEED A SEA-GULL IN HIS BUNK YET. 94 BEYOND
THE RELATION OF SOME SEA EPISODE. 94 BEYOND
BUT WHEN IT COMES TO THAT, WHERE DO SEA-GULLS 95 BEYOND
SLEEP, DICKS
THERE'S THE BUY THAT WOULD MAKE A GOOD, STRONG 97 BEYOND
SEA-FARIN' MAN--
IN THE DISTANCE THE SEA CAN BE SEEN. 129 BEYOND
YES--IN THE CHINA SEA. 131 BEYOND
+THIS'D CURE 408 OF THEM IDEAS OF HIS ABOUT THE 132 BEYOND
BEAUTIFUL SEA.
(DRYLY) THE SEA DOESN'T SEEM TO HAVE IMPRESSED 132 BEYOND
YOU VERY FAVORABLY.
WHY, I'D FORGOTTEN ALL ABOUT--THAT--BEFORE I'D 134 BEYOND
BEEN AT SEA SIX MONTHS.
(LAUGHING EXCITEDLY) I FEEL SO FREE I'D LIKE TO 136 BEYOND
HAVE WINGS AND FLY OVER THE SEA.
NOT TO SEA, NO-- 137 BEYOND
I'M THROUGH WITH THE SEA FOR GOOD AS A JOB. 137 BEYOND
(AGHAST) YOU'RE GOING AWAY TO SEA/ 137 BEYOND
IV UNDER THE HUNKS A GLIMPSE CAN BE HAD OF SEA- 477 CARDIF
CHESTS, SUITCASES, SEA-BOOTS, ETC
(ANGRILY) THE DIVIL'S OWN LIFE UT IS TO BE OUT ON479 CARDIF
THE LONELY SEA AND NOTHIN'
AND SEA-BISCUIT THAT'D BREAK THE 480 CARDIF
(REACHES IN UNDER A BUNK AND YANKS OUT A PAIR OF 481 CARDIF
SEA-BOOTS, WHICH HE PUTS ON)
SOUW'WESTERS, SEA-BOOTS, ETC. IN PREPARATION FOR 481 CARDIF
THE WATCH ON DECK.
'WAY IN THE MIDDLE OF THE LAND WHERE YUH'D NEVER 496 CARDIF
SMELL THE SEA OR SEE A SHIP.
(GLOOMILY) IT'S A HELL AV A LIFE, THE SEA. 486 CARDIF
SEA-FARIN' IS ALL RIGHT WHEN YOU'RE YOUNG AND 487 CARDIF
DON'T CARE.
AND HE SOLD US ROTTEN OILSKINS AND SEA-BOOTS FULL 487 CARDIF
OF HOLES.
I'LL BE BURIED AT SEA. 488 CARDIF
THE SEA IS CALM AND THE SHIP MOTIONLESS. 455 CARIBE
(AFTER A SLIGHT PAUSE) WHAT EVER SET YOU GOIN' T0467 CARIBE
SEAS
LIKE THE CAPTAIN'S CABIN OF A DEEP-SEA SAILING 555 CROSS
VESSEL.
PERHAPS AWAY FROM THE SIGHT OF THE SEA HE MAY--- 562 CROSS
YOU KNOW HE'D DIE IF HE HADN'T THE SEA TO LIVE 563 CROSS
WITH.
I BELIEVE--IT WOULD BE BETTER FOR HIM--AWAY--WHERE563 CROSS
HE COULDN'T SEE THE SEA.
OF THE DAMNED SEA HE FORCED ME ON AS A BOY--- 564 CROSS
(VIOLENTLY) OH, HIM AND THE SEA HE CALLS TO/ 564 CROSS
NO. IT'S THE SEA I SHOULD NOT BLAME, 564 CROSS
THE SEA THAT ROBBED ME OF MY ARM AND MADE ME THE 564 CROSS
BROKEN THING THAT I AM/
HE'LL BE BETTER OFF--AWAY FROM THE SEA. 566 CROSS
POINTING OUT TO SEA--MOCKING ME WITH STUFF LIKE 566 CROSS
THIS/
AND WE'LL MOVE TO SOME LITTLE HOUSE--BY THE SEA 50566 CROSS
THAT FATHER--
AND THE ONLY OTHER MAP IS THE ONE SILAS HORNE T0K567 CROSS
TO THE BOTTOM OF THE SEA WITH
IT'S THE WIND AND SEA YOU HEAR, NAT. 570 CROSS
THE SOUND OF THE WIND AND SEA SUDDENLY CEASES AND 570 CROSS
THERE IS A HEAVY SILENCE.
AS OF GREAT DEPTHS OF THE SEA FAINTLY PENETRATED 570 CROSS
BY LIGHT.)
(HE SHIVERS) DEEP UNDER THE SEA/ 570 CROSS
THE WIND AND SEA ARE HEARD AGAIN. 572 CROSS
RHYTHMICALLY AS IF TO THE PULSE OF LONG SWELLS OF 572 CROSS
THE DEEP SEA.)

SEA

SEA (CONT'D.)

WE'LL BE VOYAGIN' ON THE SEA/ 223 DESIRE
*I JUMPED ABOARD THE LIZA SHIP, AND TRAVELED ON 224 DESIRE
THE SEA.
AIN'T I A SEA-FARIN' MAN, TOJS 495 DIFRNT
BEING SEA-FARING MEN, AWAY FROM THEIR WOMEN FOLKS 499 DIFRNT
MOST OF THE TIME.
IT WAS WHEN THEY PUT IN TO GIT WATER AT THEM SOUTHSOL DIFRNT
SEA ISLANDS.
THERE'S PLENTY OF FISH IN THE SEA. 510 DIFRNT
WHEN HE AIN'T AT SEA. 522 DIFRNT
IT SOUNDS LIKE POETRY--LIFE OUT OF THE SEA.= 476 DYNAMO
ABOUT HOW LIFE FIRST CAME OUT OF THE SEAS 476 DYNAMO
EVEN OUR BLOOD AND THE SEA ARE ONLY ELECTRICITY INA77 DYNAMO
THE END/
AND IT'S THE SEA RISING UP IN CLOUDS, FALLING ON 477 DYNAMO
THE EARTH IN RAIN.
AS THE SEA WAS WHEN LIFE CAME OUT OF ITS 477 DYNAMO
THE SEA MAKES HER HEART BEAT, TOO/ 477 DYNAMO
BUT THE SEA IS ONLY HYDROGEN AND OXYGEN AND 477 DYNAMO
MINERALS, AND THEY'RE ONLY ATOMS.
WE'VE GOT THE SEA IN OUR BLOOD STILL/ 477 DYNAMO
AT SEA.
BROODING RHYTHM OF THE SEA. 199 EJONES
HE WENT TO SEA WHEN HE WAS YOUNG AND WAS IN 15 ELECTR
CALIFORNIA FOR THE GOLD RUSH.
HE'S SAILED ALL OVER THE WORLD--HE LIVED ON A 15 ELECTR
SOUTH SEA ISLAND ONCE, SO HE SAYS.
I'VE LIVED MOST OF MY LIFE AT SEA AND IN CAMPS 22 ELECTR
AND BIG, DEEP, SAD EYES THAT WERE BLUE AS THE 22 ELECTR
CARIBBEAN SEA/
THEY ALWAYS SUSPECT THE SEA. 23 ELECTR
SHIPWRECKED MY FIRST VOYAGE AT SEA. 23 ELECTR
BY MY SEA CAMPING THAT NIGHT. 23 ELECTR
YOU CAN'T PICTURE THE GREEN BEAUTY OF THEIR LAND 24 ELECTR
SET IN THE BLUE OF THE SEA/
AS YOU WALKED BESIDE ME THAT NIGHT WITH YOUR HAIR 24 ELECTR
BLOWING IN THE SEA WIND AND
AT SEVENTEEN I RAN AWAY TO SEA-- 26 ELECTR
FOR YOUR SHIPS OR YOUR SEA OR YOUR NAKED ISLAND 42 ELECTR
GIRLS--WHEN I GROW OLD AND UGLY/
HAVE YOU EVER READ A BOOK CALLED *TYPEE*--ABOUT 89 ELECTR
THE SOUTH SEA ISLANDS$
A QUEER TROUBADOUR- OF-THE-SEA QUALITY ABOUT HIM.)103 ELECTR
SAUL$ AYE, BUT IT AIN'T FUR LONG, STEAM IS 105 ELECTR
CUMIN' IN, THE SEA IS FULL
I'VE A FOREBODING I'LL NEVER TAKE THIS SHIP TO 107 ELECTR
SEA.
THE SEA HATES A COWARD/ 107 ELECTR
(THEN FORCING A WRY SMILE) I'LL GIVE UP THE SEA. 112 ELECTR
THE SEA HATES A COWARD. 112 ELECTR
THINGS WERE ALWAYS REMINDING ME OF YOU--THE SHIP 146 ELECTR
AND THE SEA--
COMING OUT OF THE LAND AND SEA. 147 ELECTR
AND PEACE SINKS DEEP THROUGH THE SEA/ 264 GGBROW
AND THE LIVING COLORS OF EARTH AND SKY AND SEAS 264 GGBROW
I WANT TO FEEL THE MOON KISSING THE SEA. 264 GGBROW
DOWN IS THE MOON AND I'M THE SEA. 264 GGBROW
ONCE I DREAMED OF PAINTING WIND ON THE SEA AND THE287 GGBROW
SKIMMING FLIGHT OF CLOUD
AND THE MOON RESTS IN THE SEA/ 323 GGBROW
I WANT TO FEEL THE MOON AT PEACE IN THE SEA/ 323 GGBROW
*FAR AWAY IN CANADA, FAR ACROSS THE SEA, 211 HA APE
MEN THAT WAS SONS OF THE SEA AS IF 'TWAS THE 213 HA APE
MOTHER THAT BORE THEM.
'TWAS THEM DAYS A SHIP WAS PART OF THE SEA, AND A 214 HA APE
MAN WAS PART OF A SHIP.
BLACK SMOKE FROM THE FUNNELS SMUDGING THE SEA, 214 HA APE
SMUDGING THE DECKS--
AND THE SEA JOINED ALL TOGETHER AND MADE IT ONE. 214 HA APE
SUNSHINE ON THE DECK IN A GREAT FLOOD, THE FRESH 218 HA APE
SEA WIND BLOWING ACROSS IT.
VIVID LIFE OF THE SEA ALL ABOUT-- 218 HA APE
(DISTURBED BY HER EYES, GLANCES OUT TO SEA--BLURTS221 HA APE
OUT)
I WILL THROW THIS ONE INTO THE SEA WHEN I COME 221 HA APE
BACK.
(ALL AT SEA--UNEASILY) IS THAT SO$ 221 HA APE
SEA-LAWYER/ 229 HA APE
DID YER OLD MAN FOLLOW THE SEAS 234 HA APE
*CCKEL WHISKEY ON ITS BREATH, AND THEIR SEA IS A 578 ICEMAN
GROWLER OF LAGER AND ALE.
IT'S BEDROCK BAR, THE END OF THE LINE CAFE, THE 587 ICEMAN
BOTTOM OF THE SEA RATHSKELLER!
LET YOURSELF SINK DOWN TO THE BOTTOM OF THE SEA. 625 ICEMAN
NOT EVEN HERE ON THE BOTTOM OF THE SEA. 646 ICEMAN
THERE'S MANY A GOOD SHIP BLOWN UP AND AT THE 515 INZONE
BOTTOM OF THE SEA.
SO YOU HAVE RUN AWAY TO SEA LOIKE THE COWARD YOU 531 INZONE
ARE
THE FOG AND THE SEA SEEMED PART OF EACH OTHER. 131 JOURNE
IT WAS LIKE WALKING ON THE BOTTOM OF THE SEA. 131 JOURNE
AS IF I WAS A GHOST BELONGING TO THE FOG, AND THE 131 JOURNE
FOG WAS THE GHOST OF THE SEA.
EVEN SINCE I WENT TO SEA AND WAS ON MY OWN, 145 JOURNE
OVER THE SKY AND SEA WHICH SLEPT TOGETHER. 153 JOURNE
THEY'RE ALL CONNECTED WITH THE SEA. 153 JOURNE
A CALM SEA, THAT TIME. 153 JOURNE
I WOULD HAVE BEEN MUCH MORE SUCCESSFUL AS A SEA 153 JOURNE
GULL OR A FISH.
I DISSOLVED IN THE SEA, BECAME WHITE SAILS AND 153 JOURNE
FLYING SPRAY.
THE SEA LAUGHS/ 280 LAZARU
HE WILL LAUGH OUR TYRANTS INTO THE SEA/ 300 LAZARU
ONLY A SEA OF THEIR MASKS CAN BE SEEN, THEIR EYES 320 LAZARU
SHINING EXULTANTLY.
*ONCE AS SQUIRMING SPECKS WE CREPT FROM THE TIDES 324 LAZARU
OF THE SEA.

SEA (CONT'D.)

NOW WE RETURN TO THE SEA/ 324 LAZARU
THERE IS A TAINT OF BLOOD IN THE AIR THAT POISONS 329 LAZARU
THE BREATH OF THE SEA.
GRASS AND DISTANTLY FROM THE SHINING SEA. 330 LAZARU
LIKE RAIN INTO THE SEA/ 359 LAZARU
THE SEA REMAINS/ 359 LAZARU
THERE IS PEACE DEEP IN THE SEA BUT THE SURFACE IS 409 MARCOM
SORROW.
PRAY TO THE SEA. 409 MARCOM
DEATH LIVES IN A SILENT SEA, GRAY AND COLD UNDER 409 MARCOM
DULL GRAY SKY.
THERE ARE HARBORS AT EVERY VOYAGE-END WHERE WE 410 MARCOM
REST FROM THE SORROWS OF THE SEA.
SHE TURNS AWAY AND LOOKS OUT OVER THE SEA WITH A 410 MARCOM
SIGH--AFTER A PAUSE)
(THEN WILDLY TO MARCO) I WISHED TO SLEEP IN THE 413 MARCOM
DEPTHS OF THE SEA.
(PROUDLY) WE WOULD RIDE THEIR ARMIES DOWN INTO 421 MARCOM
THE SEA/
WHETHER IT'S THE BOTTOM OF A BOTTLE, OR A SOUTH 135 MISBEG
SEA ISLAND,
BEYOND THE ROAD, THE EDGE OF A CLIFF WHICH RISES 577 ROPE
SHEER FROM THE SEA BELOW.
THE SEA IS A DARK SLATE COLOR. 578 ROPE
HE LOOKS TOWARD THE SEA AND HIS VOICE QUAVERS IN A579 ROPE
DOLEFUL CHANT)
YOU AIN'T GOT YOUR SEA-LEGS WORKIN' RIGHT. 595 ROPE
AND THEN SHIP AWAY TO SEA AGEN OR GO BUMMIN' AGEN.599 ROPE
(THINKING--MORE AND MORE AT SEA) 126 STRANG
SENSIBLE UNICELLULAR LIFE THAT FLOATS IN THE SEA 198 STRANG
I GOT ALL SEA I WANT FOR MY LIFE--TOO MUCH HARD 502 VOYAGE
WORK FOR LITTLE MONEY.
I DON'T NEVER SHIP ON SEA NO MORE. 502 VOYAGE
I GOT NICE GIRL ONCE BEFORE I GO ON SEA. 503 VOYAGE
(GRINNING) NO MORE SEA, NO MORE BUM GRUB, NO MORE503 VOYAGE
STORMS--YUST NICE WORK.
(ANGRILY) I KNOW DAT DAMN SHIP--WORST SHIP DAT 507 VOYAGE
SAIL TO SEA.

SEA'S

AND TROUBLE I'VE HAD BY LAND AND BY SEA'S LONG AS 541 'ILE
I KIN REMEMBER,
THEN YOU THINK THE SEA'S TO BLAME FOR EVERYTHING, 21 ANNA
ENS
BUT IF YOU HONESTLY THINK THE SEA'S SUCH A ROTTEN 37 ANNA
LIFE,
(POUNDING THE TABLE) THE SEA'S THE ONLY LIFE FOR 48 ANNA
A MAN WITH GUTS IN HIM ISN'T

SEABOAT

BY CHRIST, I'LL GO BACK AN' GIVE HER A SEABOAT IN 104 ELECTR
HER FAT TAIL

SEABOOTS.

COAT, PANTS, SOU'WESTER AND WEARS HIGH SEABOOTS.) 25 ANNA
HE WEARS HIGH SEABOOTS TURNED DOWN FROM THE KNEE, 498 DIFRNT
DIRTY COTTON SHIRT AND PANTS.

SEACAPES

SEACAPES, OF THE PAINTED-TO-ORDER QUALITY, FOUR INS19 DIFRNT
NUMBER, IN GILDED FRAMES.

SEACOAST

THE INTERIOR OF AN OLD BARN SITUATED ON TOP OF A 577 ROPE
HIGH HEADLAND OF THE SEACOAST.

SEAL

PERFORMANCE AS A TRAINED SEAL. 168 JOURNE
THE OFFICIAL SEAL/ 362 MARCOM
YOU'RE GHOSTLESS AND WOMANLESS--AND AS SLEEK AND 52 STRANG
SATISFIED AS A PET SEAL/

SEALED

A MOMENT LATER HE HURRIES BACK WITH A BIG SEALED 160 ELECTR
ENVELOPE IN HIS HAND
MECHANICALLY SHE HIDES THE SEALED ENVELOPE IN A 167 ELECTR
DRAWER OF THE TABLE AND.
TAUGHT AT OUR FATHER'S KNEE, SEALED, SIGNED, 243 HA APE
(EXHAUSTED--FALLS ON HIS KNEES BEFORE TEDALDO, 361 MARCOM
HOLDING OUT A SEALED PAPER)
(HE HANDS HER A SEALED PAPER) 410 MARCOM

SEALERS

(PARAPHRASING THE *RHYME OF THE THREE SEALERS*) 66 MISBEG

SEALS

BCJEES, YOU'VE EVEN BORROWED FISH FROM THE TRAINED609 ICEMAN
SEALS
I SHALL GIVE THE ART OF ACTING BACK TO THE 160 JOURNE
PERFORMING SEALS.
SEALS ARE INTELLIGENT AND HONEST. 168 JOURNE

SEAMAN

(WITH A CERTAIN PRIDE) DEV VAS ALL SMART SEAMAN, 27 ANNA
TOO--A ONE.
ABLE BODY SEAMAN, MOST OF DEM. 27 ANNA
THE SEAMAN WHO HAS BEEN ON LOOKOUT, SMITTY, A 483 CARDIF
YOUNG ENGLISHMAN.
(THE STUPID-FACED SEAMAN, WHO COMES IN AFTER 483 CARDIF
SMITTY.

SEAMAN'S

THE SEAMAN'S FORECASTLE OF THE BRITISH TRAMP 477 CARDIF
STEAMER *GLENCAIRN*ON A FOGGY NIGHT
THE SEAMAN'S FORECASTLE. ON THE RIGHT ABOVE THE 513 INZONE
BUNKS

SEAMED

WITH A GREAT, RED, WEATHER-BEATEN FACE SEAMED BY 513 DIFRNT
SUN WRINKLES.

SEAMEN

MOST OF THE SEAMEN AND FIREMEN ARE RECLINING OR 455 CARIBE
SITTING ON THE HATCH.
ALTHOUGH THE GENERAL IDEA SEEMS TO BE A BATTLE 472 CARIBE
BETWEEN SEAMEN AND FIREMEN.
THE SEAMEN COME TO THE TABLE, FRONT.) 496 VOYAGE

SEAMEN'S

BUT I RUN ACROSS A BIT O' NEWS DOWN TO THE 141 BEYOND
SEAMEN'S HOME MADE ME 'BOUT SHIP AND

SEATS

SEAMEN'S (CONT'D.)
SEAMEN'S AND FIREMEN'S COMPARTMENTS. 455 CARIBE
SEAPORT
ON THE OUTSKIRTS OF ONE OF THE SMALL NEW ENGLAND 2 ELECTR
SEAPORT TOWNS.
(SCENE--THE WHARVES OF THE IMPERIAL FLEET AT THE 399 MARCOM
SEAPORT OF ZAYTON--
SEARCH
YOU CAN SEARCH ME. 208 AHWILD
(IS STARING AT HIM WITH EYES THAT SEARCH HIS FACE 460 DYNAMO
APPREHENSIVELY) RUBE/
(PRETENDING TO SEARCH THE GROUND AGAIN) 178 ELECTR
WELL, I SUPPOSE--SEARCH ME. 304 GGBROW
HE MUST SEARCH THE WORLD FOR A CERTAIN MAGIC DOOR.110 MANSNS
SEARCHER
AND MY DUTY AS AN EXPERIMENTAL SEARCHER AFTER 86 STRANG
TRUTH...
SEARCHES
SEARCHES HIS FATHER'S EXPRESSIONLESS FACE WITH 293 AHWILD
UNEASY SIDE GLANCES.
(SHE SEARCHES HIS FACE SUSPICIOUSLY. 35 ANNA
(GETS ON HIS HANDS AND KNEES AND SEARCHES THE 188 EJONES
GROUND AROUND HIM WITH HIS EYES)
(SEARCHES HIS FACE UNEASILY--THEN IS APPARENTLY 138 ELECTR
SATISFIED)
(WITH A STRANGE STERNNESS, SEARCHES HIS FACE) 280 GGBROW
HE TRIES THE DOOR--SEARCHES HIS POCKET.) 6 MANSNS
(SHE SEARCHES HIS FACE, UNEASY NOW, FEELING A 105 POET
THREAT HIDDEN BEHIND HIS COLD.
SEARCHING
(DROPPING HER EYES BEFORE HIS SEARCHING GLANCE) 88 BEYOND
WAS SEARCHING FOR THE SEA. 89 BEYOND
(GIVES HIM A SEARCHING LOOK--TO FATHER BAIRD) 555 DAYS
(SEARCHING REUBEN'S FACE--INSISTENTLY) 442 DYNAMO
HER EYES GLANCE QUICKLY ON ALL SIDES AS IF 459 DYNAMO
SEARCHING FOR SOMEONE.)
PEERING INTO THE DARK AS IF SEARCHING FOR SOME 187 EJONES
FAMILIAR LANDMARK.
BENEATH THE SEARCHING SUSPICIOUS GLANCE MANNON NOW 50 ELECTR
DIRECTS AT HER.)
(THEN WITH A STRANGE, SEARCHING GLANCE AT HER) 140 ELECTR
AS IF SEARCHING FOR SOMETHING.) 178 ELECTR
(THEY START IN SEARCHING SMITTY, 526 INZONE
WE SPEND OUR LIVES SEARCHING FOR A MAGIC DOOR AND 180 MANSNS
A LOST KINGDOM OF PEACE--
(WHOSE EYES HAVE BEEN SEARCHING HER FACE--AGHAST) 387 MARCOM
(HER EYES SEARCHING HIS FACE, LIGHTED UP BY THE 130 MISBEG
MATCH)
HIS EYES SEARCHING HER FACE, 157 MISBEG
(MOVING A LITTLE NEARER--SEARCHING HER FACE-- 155 STRANG
THINKING)
BUT I THOUGHT YOU'D UNDERSTAND--THAT I'D BEEN 458 WELDED
SEARCHING FOR SOMETHING--
THEIR HANDS CLASP AND THEY AGAIN STOP, SEARCHING 480 WELDED
EACH OTHER'S EYES.
SEARCHINGLY
(LOOKING AT HIM SEARCHINGLY) 542 *ILE
(HE SIZES RICHARD UP SEARCHINGLY--THEN SUDDENLY 294 AHWILD
SPEAKS SHARPLY)
(LOOKING AT HER SEARCHINGLY. 90 BEYOND
(TURNS AND LOOKS INTO ANDREW'S EYES SEARCHINGLY) 134 BEYOND
FATHER BAIRD LOOKS UP AND STUDIES JOHN'S FACE 543 DAYS
SEARCHINGLY, HOPEFULLY.)
FATHER BAIRD STARES AT HER SEARCHINGLY, HIS FACE 548 DAYS
SAD AND PITYING.)
THEN COMES QUIETLY UP BESIDE HIM AND STARES 566 DAYS
SEARCHINGLY INTO HIS FACE.
(STARING AT HIM SEARCHINGLY--UNEASILY) 175 ELECTR
(LOOKING SEARCHINGLY AT MARCUS'S FACE--GENTLY) 361 MARCOM
(ASTONISHED--GAZING AT HER SEARCHINGLY) 385 MARCOM
AND SHE STOPS TO REGARD HIM SEARCHINGLY. 59 POET
(GLANCING AT GORDON SEARCHINGLY--THINKING SADLY) 190 STRANG
(HIS SHIFTY EYES PEER ABOUT THE ROOM SEARCHINGLY. 495 VOYAGE
SEAS
(RAGING) AYE, DAMN HIM, AND DAMN THE ARCTIC SEAS,*936 *ILE
HE'S A HARD MAN--AS HARD A MAN AS EVER SAILED THE *937 *ILE
SEAS.
ON A STINKIN' WHALIN' SHIP TO THE ARCTIC SEAS TO 537 *ILE
BE LOCKED IN BY THE ROTTEN ICE
IT AIN'T THE DAMNED MONEY WHAT'S KEEPIN' ME UP IN 542 *ILE
THE NORTHERN SEAS, TOM.
FOUR DAYS WE WAS IN IT WITH GREEN SEAS RAKING OVER 36 ANNA
HER FROM BOW TO STERN.
BUT FOR THE LIKE OF US DOES BE ROAMING THE SEAS, A 36 ANNA
GOOD END, I'M TELLING YOU--
AND 'TIS GREAT BAD LUCK IT'S SAVED ME FROM AND ME 75 ANNA
ROAMING THE SEAS.
YOU CAN'T ORDER THE TIDES ON THE SEAS TO SUIT YOU.102 BEYOND
ALTHOUGH TACKING BACK AND FORTH IN THESE 126 BEYOND
BLISTERING SEAS IS A ROTTEN JOB TOO/*
THERE'S HARDLY A RALE DEEPWATER SAILOR LIFT ON THE459 CARIBE
SEAS, MORE'S THE PITY.
(EXPLOSIVELY) THE MARY ALLEN, YE BLIND FOOL, COME568 CROSS
BACK FROM THE SOUTHERN SEAS--
YOU WERE INTERESTED WHEN I TOLD YOU OF THE ISLANDS 23 ELECTR
IN THE SOUTH SEAS WHERE I WAS
LEAVE VINNIE HERE AND GO AWAY ON A LONG VOYAGE--TO122 ELECTR
THE SOUTH SEAS--
THE FLYING DUTCHMAN THEY SAY DOES BE ROAMING THE 214 HA APE
SEAS FOREVERMORE
ON A LONG VOYAGE IN DANGEROUS, ENCHANTED SEAS. 401 MARCOM
SEASHORE
IN A SEASHORE SUBURB NEAR NEW YORK. 90 STRANG
SEASICK
GITTIN' SEASICK, SQUARE-HEADS 209 HA APE
SEASON
BESIDES, I STILL WORKED THEN, AND THE CIRCUS 608 ICEMAN
SEASON WAS GOING TO BEGIN SOON.

SEASON (CONT'D.)
IT'S LATE IN THE SEASON BUT HE'LL BE GLAD TO TAKE 652 ICEMAN
ME ON.
AT THE END OF EACH SEASON YOU'RE PENNILESS/ 31 JOURNE
YOUR SEASON WILL OPEN AGAIN AND WE CAN GO BACK TO 72 JOURNE
SECOND-RATE HOTELS AND TRAINS.
EVEN TRAVELING WITH YOU SEASON AFTER SEASON, 87 JOURNE
YOU'VE DRAGGED HER AROUND ON THE ROAD, SEASON 141 JOURNE
AFTER SEASON, ON ONE-NIGHT STANDS.
AT FROM THIRTY-FIVE TO FORTY THOUSAND NET PROFIT A150 JOURNE
SEASON/
THIRTY-FIVE TO FORTY THOUSAND DOLLARS NET PROFIT A150 JOURNE
SEASON
PUT ON REVIVAL OF «THE BELLS» THIS SEASON. 168 JOURNE
SEASONIN'
IS HE SEASONIN' HIS HAY WITH RAIN THIS YEAR, SAME 124 BEYOND
AS LASTS» THEY SHOUTS.
SEASONS
(THE SOUL OF THE RECURRING SEASONS, 307 LAZARU
«BUILD THEE MUNE STATELY MANSIONS, O MY SOUL, AS 148 MANSNS
THE SWIFT SEASONS ROLL/
SEAT
(HE GRABS RICHARD BY THE BACK OF THE NECK AND THE 247 AHWILD
SEAT OF THE PANTS
(SOOTHINGLY) HE PROBABLY COULDN'T GET A SEAT, THE251 AHWILD
TROLLEYS ARE SO JAMMED.
(HE PUTS THE STRAW HAT ON THE SEAT AMIDSHIPS AND 275 AHWILD
PULLS THE FOLDED LETTER OUT OF
(HE HELPS HER IN AND SHE SETTLES HERSELF IN THE 280 AHWILD
STERN SEAT OF THE BOAT.
(HE TURNS FROM HER AND GOES BACK TO HIS SEAT BY 570 CROSS
THE TABLE.
HE GOES BACK TO HIS SEAT, HIS FACE GREATLY 537 DIFRNT
SOFTENED.
THERE IS A BRILLIANT ORANGE CUSHION ON THE SEAT 173 EJONES
AND DOWN HEAH WHAH DESE FOOL BUSH NIGGERS RAISES 196 EJONES
ME UP TO THE SEAT O' DE MIGHTY,
AND I TOOK A SEAT IN THE GRANDSTAND OF 579 ICEMAN
PHILOSOPHICAL DETACHMENT TO FALL ASLEEP
BUT IF HE GETS DE HOT SEAT I WON'T GO INTO NU 698 ICEMAN
MOURNIN'/
THERE'S NUTTING BETTER THAN TO SIT DOWN IN A GOOD 398 MARCOM
SEAT AT A GOOD PLAY
TAKES HIS HAT FROM UNDER THE SEAT 439 MARCOM
IN AN AISLE SEAT IN THE FIRST ROW A MAN RISES, 439 MARCOM
CONCEALS A YAWN IN HIS PALM,
(HE STRIKES A MATCH ON THE SEAT OF HIS OVERALLS 16 MISBEG
AND LIGHTS HIS PIPE)
HOGAN SCRATCHES A MATCH ON THE SEAT OF HIS OVER- 37 MISBEG
ALLS AND LIGHTS HIS PIPE,
AND GO TO BED, OR I'LL TAKE YOU BY THE SCRUFF OF 74 MISBEG
YOUR NECK AND THE SEAT OF YOUR
SEATED
ANNA IS SEATED IN THE ROCKING-CHAIR BY THE TABLE, 41 ANNA
WITH A NEWSPAPER IN HER HANDS.
(A SHORT, DARK MAN SEATED ON THE RIGHT OF HATCH) 456 CARIBE
THIS LIGHT IS CONCENTRATED AROUND THE TWO FIGURES 493 DAYS
SEATED AT THE TABLE.
JOHN IS SEATED IN THE CHAIR AT LEFT OF DESK. 493 DAYS
(THEY GET HIM SEATED ON THE CHAISE-LONGUE, 555 DAYS
ON THESE ARE SEATED, SQUEEZED IN TIGHT AGAINST ONE247 DESIRE
ANOTHER,
THE MUSICIAN IS TUNING UP HIS FIDDLE, SEATED IN 247 DESIRE
THE FAR RIGHT CORNER.
THE PEOPLE SEATED ALONG THE WALLS STAMP THEIR FEET250 DESIRE
SHE IS SEATED IN A ROCKER BY THE TABLE. 519 DIFRNT
THE REVEREND HUTCHINS LIGHT IS SEATED IN HIS 421 DYNAMO
ARMCHAIR, HIS WIFE IN HER ROCKER.
RAMSAY FIFE IS SEATED AT THE LEFT OF THE TABLE, 428 DYNAMO
JENNINGS, THE OPERATOR ON DUTY, A MAN OF THIRTY OR486 DYNAMO
SO, IS SEATED AT THE DESK.
GRADUALLY IT SEEMS TO GROW LIGHTER IN THE ENCLOSE0198 EJONES
SPACE AND TWO ROWS OF SEATED
SEATED STIFFLY IN AN ARMCHAIR, HIS HANDS ON THE 28 ELECTR
ARMS.
HER THIN FIGURE, SEATED STIFFLY UPRIGHT, ARMS 43 ELECTR
AGAINST HER SIDES,
IN THE CABIN, BRANT IS SEATED AT THE RIGHT OF 110 ELECTR
TABLE.
BILLY BROWN IS SEATED AT THE DESK LOOKING OVER A 274 GGBROW
BLUEPRINT
CYBEL IS SEATED ON THE STOOL IN FRONT OF THE 278 GGBROW
PIANO.
YANK IS SEATED IN THE FOREGROUND. 208 HA APE
HE IS SEATED FORWARD ON A BENCH IN THE EXACT 226 HA APE
ATTITUDE OF RODIN'S «THE THINKER.»
TYRONE IS SEATED AT THE TABLE. 129 JOURNE
SEATED IN THE MIDDLE OF THE LOWER OF THE THREE 312 LAZARU
HIGH BROAD STAIRS THAT LEAD TO
ON EACH SIDE, MEMBERS OF THE SENATE ARE SEATED IN 312 LAZARU
THEIR WHITE ROBES.
SARA IS DISCOVERED SEATED ON THE HIGH STOOL BEFORE139 MANSNS
HER DESK.
IS SEATED ON A SORT OF THRONE PLACED AGAINST THE 358 MARCOM
REAR WALL.
MELODY MAKES A GALLANT SHOW OF HOLDING HER CHAIR 69 POET
AND HELPING HER BE SEATED.
PRAY BE SEATED, SIR. 117 POET
MANSDEN IS SEATED ON THE CHAIR AT CENTER. 24 STRANG
NINA IS SEATED AT THE FOOT OF THE TABLE, HER BACK 48 STRANG
TO THE WINDOW.
EVANS IS SEATED IN THE PROFESSOR'S OLD CHAIR. 66 STRANG
ON SON AND FREDA REMAIN SEATED.) 501 VOYAGE
SEATING
A LARGER ONE, SEATING SIX, AT RIGHT CENTER. 7 POET
SEATS
THEY WOULD TEAR DOWN SOCIETY, PUT THE LOWEST SCUM 244 HA APE
IN THE SEATS OF THE MIGHTY,

SEATS

SEATS (CONT'D.)
WE'LL PUT UP ONE LAST STAR BOUT DAT'LL KNOCK 'EM 253 HA APE
OFFEN DEIR SEATS/
THE SENATORS LEAN FORWARD IN THEIR SEATS, 318 LAZARU
FASCINATED BY HIS FACE.

SEAWARD
(SHE MAKES A SWEEPING GESTURE SEAWARD) 27 ANNA
THERE IS A PAUSE DURING WHICH EACH OF THEM LOOKS 129 BEYOND
OUT SEAWARD.
STARING OUT TOWARD THE HORIZON SEAWARD. 129 BEYOND
HER CHIN RESTING ON HER HANDS AS SHE STARES OUT 140 BEYOND
SEAWARD.)
(HE FLINGS HIS LEFT ARM IN A WIDE GESTURE SEAWARD)557 CROSS
LET US GO SEAWARD AS THE GREAT WINDS GO, FULL OF 173 JOURNE
BLOWN SAND AND FOAM.

SEAWEED
THEIR HAIR IS MATTED, INTERTWINED WITH SLIMY 571 CROSS
STRANDS OF SEAWEED.
BECAME THE SUN, THE HOT SAND, GREEN SEAWEED 153 JOURNE
ANCHORED TO A ROCK.

SECEDE
HE WISHES MASSACHUSETTS WOULD SECEDE FROM THE 8 MANSNS
UNION.

SECEDES
DISCIPLINE MY WILL TO KEEP MYSELF UNITED--ANOTHER 74 MANSNS
SELF REBELS---SECEDES---

SECH
AN' KIN HAIN'T SECH A BAD UN. 214 DESIRE
I DON'T TAKE NO STOCK IN SECH SLOP/ 214 DESIRE
I CALC'LATE I C'D A'MOST TAKE T' HIM--IF HE WA'N'T232 DESIRE
SECH A DUMB FOOL/
I'D NEVER SUSPICION SECH WEAKNESS FROM A BOY LIKE 249 DESIRE
YEW/
ABBIE NEVER SAID NO SECH THING/ 255 DESIRE
AIN'T NO GOOD REPEATIN' SECH THINGS. 508 DIFRNT
(UNFOLDING) HOW CAN YOU SAY SECH A THING/ 509 DIFRNT
IF AIN'T IN OUR BET FOR YOU TO PUT SECH NOTIONS IN131 ELECTR
MY HEAD AFORE I GU IN.
THERE AIN'T NO SECH THING AS GHOSTS. 131 ELECTR
NO SECH THING. 131 ELECTR
BUT THERE IS SECH A THING AS EVIL SPIRIT. 135 ELECTR
INWINDUH SHEETS OR NO SECH LUNATIC DOIN'S. 135 ELECTR
BETWEEN YOU 'N' ME 'N' THE LAMP POST, IT AIN'T 135 ELECTR
SECH A JOKE AS IT SOUNDS--
A.' WE 'AVIN SECH A NICE TALK, 'N ALL. 504 VOYAGE

SECON'
I'SE GWINE AWAY FROM HEAH DIS SECON'. 185 EJONES

SECOND
HE IS FOLLOWED INTO THE CABIN BY THE SECOND MATE, 539 'ILE
THE SECOND MATE WALKS SLOWLY OVER TO THE CAPTAIN.1539 'ILE
OH, I HEARD YOU TALKING WITH THE SECOND MATE. 547 'ILE
AND THE SECOND MATE ENTERS THE CABIN.) 550 'ILE
(RICHARD FOR A SECOND, LOOKS SUDDENLY GUILTY AND 190 AHWILD
CRUSHED.
AND THE SECOND BOOK WAS POETRY. 197 AHWILD
NAT, YOU GET RID OF HIM THE FIRST SECOND YOU CAN/ 199 AHWILD
I'LL BE UP IN A SECOND. 199 AHWILD
MILLER LOOKS INTO HIS SON'S FACE A SECOND, THEN 208 AHWILD
TURNS AWAY.
MRS. MILLER IS SUPERVISING AND HELPING THE SECOND 210 AHWILD
GIRL, MIRAN.
I LIKE TO FEEL I'M A SORT OF SECOND MOTHER TO THEM214 AHWILD
AND HELPING THEM TO GROW UP
TOO FLUSTERED TO BE ANYTHING BUT GUILTY BOY FOR A 217 AHWILD
SECOND)
TELL ME I WANT TO SEE HIM A SECOND-- 218 AHWILD
WELL, IF I'M GOING TO BE INTERRUPTED EVERY SECOND 229 AHWILD
ANYWAY--
RICHARD STANDS FOR A SECOND, BITTER, HUMILIATED, 235 AHWILD
WRONGED.
(LOOKS AFTER HER WORRIEDLY FOR A SECOND--THEN 248 AHWILD
SHRUGS HIS SHOULDERS)
AND HOW DARNED HAPPY YOUR SECOND LETTER MADE ME--/279 AHWILD
(GLARES AT HIM FOR A SECOND--THEN CANNOT CONTROL A 11 ANNA
BURST OF LAUGHTER)
WAIT A SECOND. 23 ANNA
STARES AT HER FOR A SECOND ANXIOUSLY--PATTING HER 24 ANNA
HAND)
CHRIS STOPS FOR A SECOND--VOLUBLY) 30 ANNA
ANNA STANDS FOR A SECOND, LOOKING DOWN AT HIM 33 ANNA
FRIGHTENEDLY.
(RESENTFUL AGAIN FOR A SECOND) 34 ANNA
STARING AT IT STUPIDLY FOR A SECOND, THEN 41 ANNA
AIMLESSLY PUTTING IT DOWN AGAIN.
(ANGRILY FOR A SECOND) GOD STIFFEN YOU/ 46 ANNA
I'LL BE COMING BACK AT YOU IN A SECOND FOR MORE OF 52 ANNA
THE SAME/
BUT I WAS AFRAID TO EVEN GO OUT OF THE CABIN FOR A 71 ANNA
SECOND, HONEST--
(PLEASINGLY) OH, MAT, YOU MUSTN'T THINK THAT FOR 74 ANNA
A SECOND/
I KNOW. I MET HIM ON THE ROAD A SECOND AGO. 87 BEYOND
I'D GO CRAZY HERE, BEIN' REMINDED EVERY SECOND OF 110 BEYOND
THE DAY
I CAN GET A BERTH AS SECOND OFFICER, AND I'LL JUMP132 BEYOND
THE SHIP WHEN I GET THERE.
DO YOU THINK HE'D CONSIDER A BERTH AS SECOND ON A141 BEYOND
STEAMER, CAPTAIN/
A SPECIALIST WILL TELL YOU IN A SECOND 147 BEYOND
THE SECOND MATE AFTHER HIM NO WISER THAN HIMSELF, 480 CARDIF
(THE CAPTAIN AND THE SECOND MATE OF THE STEAMER 484 CARDIF
ENTER THE FORECASTLE.
(HE HESITATES FOR A SECOND--THEN RESOLUTELY) 486 CARDIF
THERE IS SILENCE FOR A SECOND OR SO. 473 CARIBE
THEIR SECOND DAY ON THE ISLAND, HE SAID, 560 CROSS
SURELY YOU DON'T NEED TO MAKE ANY MORE NOTES FOR 494 DAYS
THE SECOND PART--
THE SECOND COMINGS 501 DAYS

SECOND (CONT'D.)
DAMNED OLD FOOL WITH HIS BEDTIME TALES FOR SECOND 513 DAYS
CHILDHOOD
(STARES AT HER RESENTFULLY FOR A SECOND, THEN 519 DAYS
TURNS AWAY.
WELL--BUT I CAN'T STAY MORE THAN A SECOND. 526 DAYS
(HE PAUSES FOR A SECOND, NERVING HIMSELF TO GO IN.537 DAYS
THEN STARTS AGAIN)
FOR A SECOND LOVING REMAINS LOOKING AFTER HER. 541 DAYS
(JOHN STOPS FOR A SECOND TO LISTEN, THEN HURRIES 547 DAYS
TO THE DOOR IN REAR.
SHE MOANS AND HER BODY TWITCHES FOR A SECOND. 558 DAYS
(STARES AT THEM INDIFFERENTLY FOR A SECOND, THEN 205 DESIRE
DRAWLS)
I GOT SECOND-SIGHT MEBBE. 238 DESIRE
ABBIE STANDS FOR A SECOND STARING AT HIM, HER EYES239 DESIRE
BURNING WITH DESIRE.
(HE LOOKS AT HER UNCOMPREHENDING FACE FOR A 248 DESIRE
SECOND--THEN GRUNTS DISGUSTEDLY)
(CABOT STARES AT HER A SECOND, THEN BOLTS OUT THE 263 DESIRE
REAR DOOR.
(HESITATING FOR A SECOND--THEN FIRMLY) 500 DIFRNT
JEST A SECOND. 501 DIFRNT
NO, I JEST RUN OVER FROM THE HOUSE A SECOND TO SEE509 DIFRNT
IF--WHERE'S CALEB, EMMERS
(HIS VOICE BETRAYS HIS ANGUISH FOR A SECOND 516 DIFRNT
NO, ALL KIDDIN' ASIDE, I KNOW HE'LL RUN ME DOWN 523 DIFRNT
FIRST-SECOND HE SEES YOU.
AW MYUH-- JEST FOR A SECOND. 524 DIFRNT
(RAISING HER FACE TO LOOK AT HIM FOR A SECOND) 544 DIFRNT
THE JURY SAID IT WAS MURDER IN THE SECOND DEGREE 441 DYNAMO
AND GAVE ME TWENTY YEARS--
(A SECOND LATER HE RUNS IN AND, TOO DISTRACTED TO 445 DYNAMO
NOTICE HER EXPRESSION,
IF THERE IS HIS GOD LET HIM STRIKE ME DEAD THIS 453 DYNAMO
SECOND)
(TURNS AND LOOKS AT HER LIKE A SLEEPWALKER FOR A 482 DYNAMO
SECOND--
THIS SECOND GALLERY, DIMLY LIGHTED LIKE THE ONE 483 DYNAMO
BELOW, IS A FRETWORK OF WIRES,
(ALARMED FOR A SECOND, SCRATCHES HIS HEAD, THEN 182 EJONES
PHILOSOPHICALLY)
FOLLOWED A SECOND LATER BY SAVAGE EXULTANT YELLS. 203 EJONES
WITH THE EXCEPTION OF AN ACT OF THE SECOND PLAY, 2 ELECTR
BUT I JUST DROPPED IN FOR A SECOND TO FIND OUT IF 13 ELECTR
YOU'D HAD ANY MORE NEWS FROM
I WAS JUST PASSING AND DROPPED IN FOR A SECOND. 16 ELECTR
YOU HAD GONE TO NEW YORK--(SHE PAUSES A SECOND-- 17 ELECTR
(DISAPPROVINGLY) THIS IS THE SECOND TIME THIS 44 ELECTR
WEEK I'VE CAUGHT YOU COMING HOME
HE STOPS SHORT IN THE SHADOW FOR A SECOND AND 46 ELECTR
STANDS, ERECT AND STIFF,
IN THE BEDROOM ON THE SECOND FLOOR TO THE LEFT. 57 ELECTR
THINKS FOR A SECOND IT IS HER MOTHER'S GHOST AND 143 ELECTR
GIVES AN EXCLAMATION OF DREAD.
NEVER LEAVES HIM ALONE HARDLY A SECOND/ 158 ELECTR
I CAN CHANGE MY CLOTHES IN A SECOND AND PUT ON THE176 ELECTR
COLOR YOU LIKE/
U4 IT'S RIGHT IS A DIRTY GILT SECOND-HAND SOFA. 278 GGBRN
ONLY AT THE SECOND OF MY CONCEPTION. 282 GGBRN
THERE'S MILLIONS OF 'I BURN EVERY SECOND. 286 GGBRN
(LOVINGLY) AND CAN WE GO ON THAT SECOND 316 GGBRN
HONEYMOON, RIGHT AWAY WHEN
AND STARES FROM ONE TO THE OTHER FOR A SECOND IN 320 GGBRN
CONFUSION.
FOR A SECOND THERE IS AN EMBARRASSED SILENCE. 209 HA APE
THE SECOND ENGINEER IS TO ESCORT ME. 220 HA APE
(THE SECOND ENGINEER ENTERS. 220 HA APE
IN JUST A SECOND, MA'AM. 221 HA APE
AT THIS INSTANT THE SECOND AND FOURTH ENGINEERS 225 HA APE
ENTER FROM THE DARKNESS ON THE
AND THE SECOND POINTING AT US 229 HA APE
(WITH GROWLING RAGE) I'D LIKE TO CATCH DAT 243 HA APE
SENATOR GUY ALONE FOR A SECOND.
WHICH BEGAN AS A RESPECTABLE SECOND CLASS 7 HUGHIE
THE SECOND TIME I WENT, THEY WOULDN'T LET ME SEE 30 HUGHIE
HIM.
THE SECOND FLOOR A FLAT OCCUPIED BY THE 571 ICEMAN
PROPRIETOR.
IS A TABLE OF THE SECOND ROW WITH FIVE CHAIRS. 573 ICEMAN
IN A CHAIR FACING RIGHT AT THE TABLE IN THE SECOND577 ICEMAN
LINE.
AT THE FRONT OF THE SECOND ROW WHICH 619 ICEMAN
IS HALF BETWEEN HOPE'S TABLE
HOPE STIFFENS RESENTFULLY FOR A SECOND. 622 ICEMAN
HE PAUSES, AND FOR A SECOND THEY STARE AT HIM 639 ICEMAN
DE GUY, IT'S A SECOND FEAST OF BELSHAZZAR, 644 ICEMAN
HE STOPS ABRUPTLY AND FOR A SECOND HE SEEMS TO 657 ICEMAN
LOSE HIS SELF-ASSURANCE
(LARRY STARTS AND FOR A SECOND LOOKS 657 ICEMAN
SUPERSTITIOUSLY FRIGHTENED.
HE GOES BACK AND SITS AT THE LEFT OF THE SECOND 674 ICEMAN
TABLE, FACING PARRITT,
FOR A SECOND THEY STAND THERE, ONE BEHIND THE 677 ICEMAN
OTHER.
(PARRITT STARES INTO HIS EYES GUILTILY FOR A 679 ICEMAN
SECOND.
SO IS THE ONE AT THE RIGHT, REAR, OF IT IN THE 695 ICEMAN
SECOND ROW.
THE TABLE AT RIGHT, REAR, OF IT IN THE SECOND ROW,696 ICEMAN
(FOR A SECOND THERE IS A GLEAM OF SATISFACTION IN 697 ICEMAN
HIS EYES.)
(MURRAN WALKS UP BEHIND HIM ON ONE SIDE, WHILE THE 717 ICEMAN
SECOND DETECTIVE, LIEB,
WE CAN LOWER 'EM IN A SECOND. 516 INZONE
SHE TOLD ME ALL ABOUT HER SECOND COUSIN ON THE 41 JOURNE
POLICE FORCE IN ST. LOUIS.

SECRET

SECOND (CONT'D.)
THE SECOND GIRL, CATHLEEN, ENTERS FROM THE BACK 51 JOURNE
PARLOR.
SECOND-RATE HOTELS. 61 JOURNE
YOU SHOULD HAVE REMAINED A BACHELOR AND LIVED IN 67 JOURNE
SECOND-RATE HOTELS AND
I'LL JOIN YOU IN A SECOND. 68 JOURNE
YOUR SEASON WILL OPEN AGAIN AND WE CAN GO BACK TO 72 JOURNE
SECOND-RATE HOTELS AND TRAINS.
(STAMMERS IN GUILTY CONFUSION FOR A SECOND.) 85 JOURNE
MARY AND THE SECOND GIRL, CATHLEEN, ARE 97 JOURNE
DISCOVERED.
AS IF THE SECOND GIRL WERE AN OLD, INTIMATE 98 JOURNE
FRIEND.
HE STANDS A SECOND AS IF NOT KNOWING WHAT TO DO. 123 JOURNE
(HE STARTS AND FOR A SECOND LOOKS MISERABLE AND 135 JOURNE
FRIGHTENED.
FOR A SECOND THERE IS MEANING/ 153 JOURNE
FOR A SECOND YOU SEE---AND SEEING THE SECRET, ARE 153 JOURNE
THE SECRET.
(STARTS AND STARES AT HIS BROTHER FOR A SECOND 161 JOURNE
WITH BITTER HOSTILITY--THICKLY.)
FOR A SECOND JAMIE REACTS PUGNACIOUSLY AND HALF 162 JOURNE
RISES FROM HIS CHAIR TO DO
IT SEEMS FOR A SECOND HE IS GOING TO HIDE IN THE 169 JOURNE
BACK PARLOR.
(FOR A SECOND HE SEEMS TO HAVE BROKEN THROUGH TO 174 JOURNE
HER.
(NUDGING THE SECOND--UNEASILY) 277 LAZARU
(SECOND GUEST OF SCENE ONE) JESUS IS DEAD/ 290 LAZARU
THERE IS A SECOND OF COMPLETE, DEATH-LIKE SILENCE.295 LAZARU
(EXPLODING FOR A SECOND) BY THE GODS--/ 305 LAZARU
(AT THIS SECOND THE BLARING TRUMPETS OF THE 320 LAZARU
LEGIONS ARE HEARD APPROACHING AND
THE SECOND RANK CROUCHING OVER THEM, THE THIRD 345 LAZARU
LEANING OVER THE SECOND,
A SECOND OF DEAD SILENCE. 347 LAZARU
HE TALKS TO HIMSELF LIKE A MAN IN SECOND 357 LAZARU
CHILDHOOD.
I WHO PRAY THE SECOND FLOOD MAY COME 9 MANSNS
YOU REALLY DID SHOCK ME FOR A SECOND, MOTHER. 14 MANSNS
(DEBORAH RAISES HER EYES FOR A SECOND TO STARE AT 20 MANSNS
HER
THE DOORWAY TO THE ENTRANCE HALL---AND THE STAIRS 43 MANSNS
TO THE SECOND FLOOR--
HER EXPRESSION FRIGHTENED FOR A SECOND, THEN 50 MANSNS
HARDENING INTO HOSTILITY.
A VOYAGE TO FRANCE, SAY--WITH SARA--A SECOND 72 MANSNS
HONEYMOON.
IN ORDER TO MAKE OF MY WIFE A SECOND SELF THROUGH 73 MANSNS
WHICH SHE COULD LIVE AGAIN.
(STIFFENS, STARES AT HER WITH HATRED FOR A 104 MANSNS
SECOND--THEN COLDLY, IN A CURT TONE.)
(THINKING.) SHE HAD BEGUN TO LOOK UPON ME AS A 122 MANSNS
SECOND MOTHER--
(A FLASH OF INSULTED PRIDE COMES TO HER EYES AND 193 MANSNS
FOR A SECOND SHE SEEMS
AFTER EYEING HIM FOR AN APPRAISING SECOND, 348 MARCOM
FOR A SECOND HE IS FRAMED IN IT, OUTLINED AGAINST 376 MARCOM
THE BRILLIANT SKY.
ASK TO BE APPOINTED A SECOND CLASS GOVERNMENT 380 MARCOM
COMMISSION-AGENT.
A SECOND CLASS TRAVELS AROUND, IS ALLOWED HIS 381 MARCOM
EXPENSES.
(WITH MOCKING GRANDEUR) ARISE THEN, SECOND CLASS 382 MARCOM
MARCO/
(PROMPTLY) I'D LIKE TO BE APPOINTED A COMMISSION-382 MARCOM
AGENT OF THE SECOND CLASS.
I CAN SEE WHERE I'LL HAVE TO BE TELLING HER WHAT 406 MARCOM
TO DO EVERY SECOND.
(HIS VOICE THRILLING FOR THIS SECOND WITH 415 MARCOM
OBLIVIOUS PASSION)
THE GUESTS STARE POP-EYED, OPEN-MOUTHED, 429 MARCOM
SPEECHLESS FOR A SECOND.
(THEN AFTER STARING AT KUKACHIN FOR A SECOND, 437 MARCOM
BITTERLY)
(GRATEFULLY MOVED FOR A SECOND) 7 MISBEG
HE DISAPPEARS ON LEFT, BUT A SECOND LATER HIS 64 MISBEG
VOICE, TREMBLING WITH ANGER,
SECOND THE SALE IS MADE. 84 MISBEG
THEN IT'S MIKE'S SECOND SCHEME YOU'RE THINKING 92 MISBEG
ABOUTS
FOR A SECOND SHE STARES AT HIM, 106 MISBEG
(TRIUMPHANT FOR A SECOND) YOU MEANT IT/ 119 MISBEG
SHE PULLS BACK FRIGHTENEDLY FOR A SECOND--THEN 119 MISBEG
RETURNS HIS KISS.
(MISERABLY HURT AND SAD FOR A SECOND--APPEALINGLY)140 MISBEG
(WATCHES HIM FOR A SECOND, FIGHTING THE LOVE THAT,141 MISBEG
IN SPITE OF HER,
FOR A SECOND SHE IS FRIGHTENED. 153 MISBEG
GIVING ON A HALLWAY AND THE MAIN STAIRWAY TO THE 7 POET
SECOND FLOOR,
SHE IS EXASPERATED FOR A SECOND--THEN SHE SMILES 27 POET
PITYINGLY.)
FOR A SECOND HIS EYES WAVER AND HE LOOKS GUILTY. 33 POET
FOR A SECOND HIS EXPRESSION IS GUILTY AND 44 POET
CONFUSED.
(MELODY IS SHAKEN FOR A SECOND. 59 POET
FOR THE SECOND TIME IN ONE MORNING BEFORE THE 68 POET
MIRROR.
(REGARDS HIM FOR A SECOND PUZZLEDLY. 69 POET
FOR A SECOND IT SEEMS HE WILL KISS HER AND SHE 71 POET
CANNOT HELP HERSELF.
(LOWERING HER VOICE.) SHE STARTED TALKING THE 79 POET
SECOND SHE GOT IN THE DOOR.
FRIGHTENEDLY.) YOUR FATHER'LL BE DOWN ANY SECOND. 87 POET
(FOR A SECOND IS ANGRY--THEN HE GRINS AND MUTTERS 93 POET
ADMIRINGLY.)

SECOND (CONT'D.)
(FOR A SECOND IS ASHAMED AND REALLY CONTRITE.) 107 POET
FOR A SECOND HE BREAKS--TORTUREDLY.) 115 POET
FOR A SECOND HE CRUMBLES, HIS SOLDIERLY ERECTNESS 116 POET
SAGS AND HIS FACE FALLS.
AND FOR A SECOND HE STANDS, AS CLOSE TO GAPING AS 116 POET
HE CAN BE.
(BEWILDERED FOR A SECOND--THEN IN A THREATENING 120 POET
TONE.)
(HE BURNS HIS SECOND DRINK--BOASTFULLY.) 154 POET
FOR A SECOND THERE IS ANGRY PITY IN HER EYES. 157 POET
(MELODY STIFFENS FOR A SECOND, BUT THAT IS ALL. 167 POET
(TO PAT) I'LL STEP OUTSIDE A SECOND AND GIVE YOU 399 ROPE
TWO A CHANT.
LUKE JUMPS TO THE FLOOR AND LOOKS AT HIS FATHER 596 ROPE
FOR A SECOND.
(HIS EYES FOLLOW HER FOR A SECOND, THEN RETURN TO 4 STRANG
GAZE AROUND THE ROOM SLOWLY
(HE SMILES WITH A WRY AMUSEMENT FOR A SECOND--THEN 25 STRANG
BITTERLY)
AND FROM THEN ON UNTIL HIS FATHER DID REALLY DIE 60 STRANG
DURING SAMMY'S SECOND YEAR TO
WAIT A SECOND. 119 STRANG
IN A SECOND I'LL SEE HER/...)) 125 STRANG
ONE NOTICES THE MANY LINES IN HER FACE AT SECOND 137 STRANG
GLANCE.
IT WAS ONLY FOR A SECOND... 152 STRANG
(THINKING) (I'LL YELL THE TRUTH INTO YOUR EARS 152 STRANG
IF I STAY A SECOND LONGER...
I WAS ON MY WAY HOME FROM THE THEATER AND I 450 WELDED
THOUGHT I'D DROP IN FOR A SECOND.
I CAN'T STAY A SECOND-- 460 WELDED
(CAPE STARES AT HER ANOTHER SECOND-- 463 WELDED
HIS FACE LIGHTS UP FOR A SECOND WITH A JOY THAT
IS INCONGRUOUSLY SAVAGE--
EVERYTHING, FOR THIS SECOND, BECOMES SIMPLE FOR 488 WELDED
THEM--

SECOND'S
(AFTER A SECOND'S HESITATION, 28 ANNA
(THEN AFTER A SECOND'S PAUSE, REPROVINGLY) 42 ANNA
(AFTER A SECOND'S PAUSE-- 494 DAYS
(AFTER A SECOND'S PAUSE--TENSELY) 533 DAYS
(THEN AFTER A SECOND'S THOUGHT--WONDERINGLY) 203 EJONES
THERE IS A SECOND'S UNCOMFORTABLE SILENCE. 45 ELECTR
(A SECOND'S PAUSE OF WAITING SILENCE-- 265 GGBROW
AND HER GRABBING AT THE SECOND'S ARM FOR 240 HA APE
PROTECTION.
(THERE IS A SECOND'S TENSE SILENCE.) 693 ICEMAN
(THERE IS A SECOND'S DEAD SILENCE AS HE FINISHES--706 ICEMAN
SHE'LL NEVER HAVE A SECOND'S PEACE. 720 ICEMAN
A SECOND'S UNQUESTIONING ACCEPTANCE OF ONESELF, 28 MANSNS
THEN, AFTER A SECOND'S FEARFUL HESITATION, 578 ROPE

SECONDHAND
NOT LIKE OUR SECONDHAND PACKARD. 43 JOURNE
YOU SHOULDN'T HAVE BOUGHT A SECONDHAND AUTOMOBILE. 84 JOURNE
BECAUSE YOU INSIST ON SECONDHAND BARGAINS IN 84 JOURNE
EVERYTHING.

SECONDS
'TWAS A MAD, FIGHTIN' SCRAMBLE IN THE LAST SECONDS 36 ANNA
WITH EACH MAN FOR HIMSELF.
SCENE, THERE IS SILENCE, BROKEN EVERY FEW SECONDS 191 EJONES
BY A QUEER, CLICKING SOUND.
WE ARE WHERE CENTURIES ONLY COUNT AS SECONDS AND 323 GGBROW
AFTER A THOUSAND LIVES OUR EYES
AND KEEPS THEM BUSY FOR A FEW SECONDS. 526 INZUNE
FOR I CONSTANTLY SENSE IN THE SECONDS AND MINUTES 12 MANSNS
AND HOURS FLOWING THROUGH ME,

SECRECY
A PART OF THE SECRECY) 247 HA APE

SECRET
(GOES ON A BIT RUEFULLY, AS IF OPPRESSED BY A 188 AHWILD
SECRET SORROW)
=THEY DO NOT KNOW THE SECRET IN THE POET'S HEART.=217 AHWILD
BUT HE DOES NOT WIN WHO PLAYS WITH SIN IN THE 246 AHWILD
SECRET HOUSE OF SHAME/=
AND THEY LET ME INTO A SECRET ROOM BEHIND THE 282 AHWILD
BARROOM.
IT'S A =SECRET HOUSE OF SHAME.= 282 AHWILD
IT'S A SECRET. 73 ANNA
IN QUEST OF THE SECRET WHICH IS HIDDEN OVER THERE, 85 BEYOND
BEYOND THE HORIZONS
THE SECRET THAT CALLED TO ME FROM OVER THE WORLD'S 92 BEYOND
RIM--
THE SECRET BEYOND EVERY HORIZON,, 92 BEYOND
I THINK LOVE MUST HAVE BEEN THE SECRET-- 92 BEYOND
THE SECRET BEYOND THERE-- 168 BEYOND
I WAS TO BE HEIR TO THE SECRET. 560 CROSS
I'LL KEEP THE MAU SECRET. 561 CROSS
AS HEIR TO THE SECRET, YES. 561 CROSS
IS IT YOUR OLD SECRET WEAKNESS--THE COWARDLY 499 DAYS
YEARNING TO GO BACK--S
SECRET FEARS 536 DAYS
(MOCKINGLY) AND SECRET FEAR/ 536 DAYS
THROUGH THE SECRET LONGING OF YOUR OWN HEART FOR 560 DAYS
FAITH/
THEY EVIDENTLY HAVE SOME SECRET JOKE IN COMMON. 247 DESIRE
HE'S HONOR BOUND TO TELL HIS FUTURE SON-IN-LAW THE431 DYNAMO
SECRET OF HIS PAST,.
KNOW THE SECRET OF THE FAMILY YOU'RE WANTING TO 439 DYNAMO
MARRY INTO,
(WITH A CHUCKLE) HE'LL BE BLABBIN' MY DREADFUL 442 DYNAMO
SECRET TO HIS OLD MAN YET,
(STAMPS) I'LL TELL YOU, MOTHER--IF YOU PROMISE 446 DYNAMO
TO KEEP IT A SECRET--
YOU ALMOST GET THE SECRET... 474 DYNAMO
LOVE HIM AND GIVE HIM THE SECRET OF TRUTH 677 DYNAMO
SHE WANTS US TO REALIZE THE SECRET DWELLS IN HER/ 477 DYNAMO

SECRET

SECRET (CONT'D.)
THAT DYNAMO WOULD NEVER FIND ME WORTHY OF HER 478 DYNAMO
SECRET
DON'T YOU UNDERSTAND I CAN'T--THAT MY FINDING THE 478 DYNAMO
SECRET IS MORE IMPORTANT THAN--
(SMILING AT HIS SECRET THOUGHT) 178 EJONES
SECRET LOOKIN'--'S IF IT WAS A MASK SHE'D PUT ON. 9 ELECTR
(AGAIN STARTS--THEN SLOWLY AS IF ADMITTING A 11 ELECTR
SECRET UNDERSTANDING BETWEEN THEM)
YOU SAID THEY HAD FOUND THE SECRET OF HAPPINESS 24 ELECTR
BECAUSE THEY HAD NEVER HEARD
I TOLD YOU MY SECRET FEELINGS. 61 ELECTR
I'LL TELL YOU A SECRET, JOSIAH--STRICTLY BETWEEN 71 ELECTR
YOU AND ME.
WE'LL BE SECRET CONSPIRATORS, SHALL WE, AND I'LL 72 ELECTR
HELP YOU AND YOU'LL HELP ME$
(WITH A TENDER SMILE) WE HAD A SECRET LITTLE 85 ELECTR
WORLD OF OUR OWN IN THE OLD DAYS.
I'VE TRIED TO TRACE IT ITS SECRET HIDING PLACE IN 193 ELECTR
THE MANNON PAST
WASN'T IT THE ONLY WAY TO KEEP YOUR SECRET, TOUS 168 ELECTR
I HAVE BEEN KEEPING A SECRET FROM YOU. 317 GGBROW
THIS IS DADDY'S BEDTIME SECRET FOR TODAY.. 318 GGBROW
HE LUCKS AROUND FOR SECRET DOORS, MYSTERY, 246 HA APE
AS IF HE WERE GUESSING AT THE PASSWORD TO SOME 246 HA APE
SECRET RITE
NO, BY GUD, YOU'RE SUCH A BONEHEAD I'LL BET YOU'RE249 HA APE
I-- THE SECRET SERVICE?
SHAKIN--OR SECRET GRIP OF OUR ORDER. 254 HA APE
YOU'VE KEPT THAT A DEEP SECRET, I NOTICE--FOR SOME693 ICEMAN
REASON?
AS IF HE WERE DETERMINED TO FIGURE OUT ITS SECRET 531 INZONE
MEANING.
IT'S A SECRET CONFAB THEY DON'T WANT ME TO HEAR, I 15 JOURNE
SUPPOSE.
FOR A SECOND YOU SEE--AND SEEING THE SECRET, ARE 153 JOURNE
THE SECRET.
(DRYLY.) THANKS FOR TELLING ME YOUR GREAT SECRET.155 JOURNE
(MOCKINGLY.) THE SECRET OF MY SUCCESS/ 165 JOURNE
YOUTH, AND THE OLD LECHER HOPES HE CAN WORM THE 302 LAZARU
SECRET OUT OF HIM--
THE ONLY EARS THAT CAN EVER HEAR ONE'S SECRET ARE 355 LAZARU
ONE'S OWN/
AND IT IS MY COMMAND THAT YOU REVEAL THE SECRET OF356 LAZARU
YOUR YOUTH TO ME WHEN I
I PREFER TO BE THE SECRET POWER BEHIND THE 13 MANSNS
THRONE--
WELL, OUT WITH THE TERRIBLE SECRET, MOTHER. 13 MANSNS
BUT SIMON, I KNOW YOU'VE KEPT A SECRET GRUDGE 78 MANSNS
AGAINST HER IN YOUR HEART.
AS MY SECRETARY AND SECRET PARTNER. 89 MANSNS
A GAME OF SECRET, CUNNING STRATAGEMS, 91 MANSNS
AS IF IT WERE SOME SECRET TEMPLE OF WHICH YOU WERE109 MANSNS
HIGH PRIESTESS/
SOMETHING ABOUT HIM, TOO--SLY--LIKE THERE WAS A 118 MANSNS
SECRET BETWEEN THEM--
I WILL LEAVE YOU NOW TO INFORM EACH OTHER OF THE 131 MANSNS
SECRET
TELL ME YOUR SECRET, DAUGHTER. 132 MANSNS
I'M TO BE HIS SECRETARY AND A SECRET PARTNER. 132 MANSNS
HAVE YOU MADE A SECRET BARGAIN WITH HER TO PLAY 159 MANSNS
OUR ANOTHER'S GAMES
TOWARD EVERY SECRET PRIVATE CORNER OF MY SOUL. 184 MANSNS
AND, BEING ALWAYS IN THE SECRET, 381 MARCOM
(SHE SEES HE HAS GUESSED HER SECRET AND AT FIRST 387 MARCOM
SHE QUAILS AND SHRINKS AWAY.
IN HIS SECRET FRATERNAL ORDER OF THE MYSTIC 388 MARCOM
KNIGHTS OF CONFUCIUS?
WELL, I'LL TELL YOU THE SECRET. 393 MARCOM
I LEARNED THE FORMULA, IMPROVED ON IT, 395 MARCOM
EXPERIMENTED IN SECRET.
LITTLE DAUGHTER, ALL RARE THINGS ARE SECRET WHICH 400 MARCOM
CANNOT BE REVEALED TO ANYONE.
HIS MAJESTY GAVE ME SOME SECRET LAST INSTRUCTIONS 404 MARCOM
FOR YOU.
WHISPER YOUR SECRET IN MY EAR. 438 MARCOM
TELL ME NOW. IF IT ISN'T A SECRET, 63 MISBEG
(A GLINT OF SECRET AMUSEMENT IN HER EYES.) 81 POET
SHE STILL HAS A SECRET FONDNESS FOR PRIESTS. 97 POET
IF WE EVER LET THEM KNOW OUR SECRETS 150 POET
MY OWN SECRET... 49 STRANG
ONLY REMEMBER IT'S A FAMILY SECRET, AND NOW YOU'RE 59 STRANG
ONE OF THE FAMILY.
A SECRETS 105 STRANG
OR IS IT A SECRET, NEDS 105 STRANG
YES, YOU BET IT'S A SECRET? 105 STRANG
(THEN ELATEDLY) AND NOW FOR YOUR SECRET/ 106 STRANG
YOU'RE GOING TO BE A FATHER, OLD SCOUT, THAT'S THE106 STRANG
SECRET?
(TENDERLY) NED TOLD ME--THE SECRET--AND I'M SO 107 STRANG
HAPPY, DEAR/
WHY DID YOU WANT TO KEEP IT A SECRET FROM ME$ 107 STRANG
WE HAVE BUILT UP A SECRET LIFE OF SUBTLE 148 STRANG
SYMPATHIES AND CONFIDENCES...
(THE SECRET ESCAPING HIM) I SAW YOU KISSING 151 STRANG
MOTHER?
BUT THERE'S STILL SOME SECRET BETWEEN THEM SHE'S 164 STRANG
NEVER TOLD ME...
TELL ME YOUR SECRET. 165 STRANG
(WITH A CRY OF GRIEF) OH, NED, DID ALL OUR OLD 183 STRANG
SECRET HOPES DO THIS AT LAST$

SECRETARY
THE SECRETARY IS PERCHED ON THE STOOL MAKING 245 HA APE
ENTRIES IN A LARGE LEDGER.
(GIVES THE SECRETARY THE MONEY.) 247 HA APE
AS MY SECRETARY AND SECRET PARTNER. 89 MANSNS
I FIND IT ADVISABLE TO ADU A PRIVATE SECRETARY TO 97 MANSNS
MY EMPLOY.

SECRETARY (CONT'D.)
I HAVE NOT SAID MY SECRETARY WAS TO BE ANYTHING 98 MANSNS
MORE INTIMATE THAN MY SECRETARY.
OF THE COMPANY AND THE SECRETARY-MISTRESS HE 119 MANSNS
BOASTED OF--
I'M TO BE HIS SECRETARY AND A SECRET PARTNER. 132 MANSNS
(HER MANNER THAT OF AN EFFICIENT, OBEDIENT 147 MANSNS
SECRETARY.)
(HER ATTITUDE BECOMING AGAIN THAT OF THE EFFICIENT148 MANSNS

SECRETIVE
(HIS MANNER HAS BECOME SECRETIVE, WITH SINISTER 11 HUGHIE
UNDERTONES.
PARRITT LEANS TOWARD HIM AND SPEAKS INGRATIATINGLY645 ICEMAN
IN A LOW SECRETIVE TUNE.)

SECRETLY
AND THAT OTHER BOY, SECRETLY HE FELT ASHAMED BUT 295 GGBROW
HE COULDN'T ACKNOWLEDGE IT.
THAT HENRY HAD BEEN SECRETLY GAMBLING IN WESTERN 31 MANSNS
LANDS.
YOU PROBABLY THINK I MUST BE SECRETLY KEEPING SOME 80 MANSNS
BEAUTIFUL MISTRESS
UNLESS YOU SECRETLY BELIEVE HER TRUE NATURE IS SO 98 MANSNS
GREEDY
(SHE LAUGHS A LITTLE DETACHED LAUGH, AS IF SHE 82 POET
WERE SECRETLY AMUSED.)
HER HAPPINESS, THAT I HAD HOPED FOR GORDON'S DEATH 11 STRANG
AND BEEN SECRETLY OVERJOYED
PERHAPS I'M MORBID BUT I ALWAYS HAVE THE FEELING 190 STRANG
THAT THEY'RE SECRETLY GLAD

SECRETS
WE AIN'T GOT NO SECRETS FROM YOU. 507 DIFANT
THEY DON'T WANT FOLKS TO GUESS THEIR SECRETS. 9 ELECTR
(BREATHLESSLY EAGER) SECRETS. 9 ELECTR
I'LL LIVE ALONE WITH THE DEAD, AND KEEP THEIR 178 ELECTR
SECRETS, AND LET THEM HOUND ME.
I AGREE TO ANYTHING--EXCEPT HUMILIATION OF YELLING281 GGBROW
SECRETS AT THE DEAF/
WE GOT NO SECRETS. 248 HA APE
BECAUSE I'M AFRAID BOOZE WOULD MAKE ME SPILL MY 658 ICEMAN
SECRETS, AS YOU THINK.
YOU CAN'T KEEP ANY SECRETS FROM HER. 175 JOURNE
NO, THAT IS WHY I CAN SAFELY TELL YOU ALL MY 39 MANSNS
SECRETS, NICHOLAS.
WE HAVE NEVER HAD SECRETS FROM EACH OTHER, YOU AND386 MARCOM
I.
BUT WENT AROUND TELLIN' EVERY STRANGER ALL MY 161 POET
SECRETS.
THERE'RE ARE SECRETS ONE MUST NOT REVEAL... 133 STRANG

SECTION
THE STERN SECTION IS IN MOONLIGHT. 275 AHWILD
THE FORWARD TRIANGLE CUT OFF BY THE ROAD IS A 81 BEYOND
SECTION OF A FIELD FROM THE DARK
(A SECTION OF COUNTRY HIGHWAY. 81 BEYOND
(SAME AS ACT ONE, SCENE ONE--A SECTION OF COUNTRY 166 BEYOND
HIGHWAY.
A FORWARD SECTION OF THE MAIN DECK OF THE BRITISH 455 CARIBE
TRAMP STEAMER *GLENCAIRN*.
NEAR EACH BULWARK THERE IS ALSO A SHORT STAIRWAY, 455 CARIBE
LIKE A SECTION OF FIRE ESCAPE,
(SCENE--A SECTION OF THE INTERIOR OF AN OLD 564 DAYS
CHURCH.
AND THE SECTION OF THE LIGHT'S HOME IN WHICH ARE -0 DYNAMO
SITTING ROOM
AND THERE IS A SIMILAR WINDOW IN THE UPPER PART OF473 DYNAMO
THE SECTION ON RIGHT.
THE SECTION IN THE LEFT, THE DYNAMO ROOM, 473 DYNAMO
THROUGH THE UPPER WINDOW OF THE RIGHT SECTION OF 473 DYNAMO
THE BUILDING.
IS MUCH WIDER THAN THE RIGHT SECTION BUT IS A 473 DYNAMO
STORY LESS IN HEIGHT.
ONE STORY UP IN THE OTHER SECTION OF THE BUILDING.486 DYNAMO
(THE STERN SECTION OF A CLIPPER SHIP MOORED 102 ELECTR
ALONGSIDE A WHARF IN EAST BOSTON.
A SECTION OF THE SHIP HAS BEEN REMOVED TO REVEAL 109 ELECTR
THE INTERIOR OF THE CABIN.
SCENE-- A CROSS SECTION OF THE PIER OF THE CASINO. 257 GGBROW
14 THE HOMES SECTION OF THE TOWN-- 269 GGBROW
A SECTION OF THE PROMENADE DECK. 217 HA APE
THE DESK FACES LEFT ALONG A SECTION OF SEEDY LOBBY 7 HUGHIE
WITH SHABBY CHAIRS.
(SCENE THE DESK AND A SECTION OF LOBBY OF A SMALL 7 HUGHIE
HOTEL.
AT RIGHT OF THIS DIVIDING CURTAIN IS A SECTION OF 573 ICEMAN
THE BARROOM.
THE BACK ROOM AND A SECTION OF THE BAR OF HARRY 573 ICEMAN
HOPE'S SALOON
IN THE SECTION OF BAR AT RIGHT, 586 ICEMAN
BUT IT DOES NOT HIT THE WINDOWS AND THE LIGHT IN 664 ICEMAN
THE BACK-ROOM SECTION IS DIM.
MCGLOIN STARTS INTO THE BACK-ROOM SECTION.) 681 ICEMAN
THE BACK ROOM WITH THE CURTAIN SEPARATING IT FROM 695 ICEMAN
THE SECTION OF THE BARROOM
IN THE BAR SECTION, JOE IS SPRAWLED IN THE CHAIR 696 ICEMAN
AT RIGHT OF TABLE, FACING LEFT.
IN THE REAR IS A SECTION OF THE GREAT WALL OF 373 MARCOM
CHINA WITH AN ENORMOUS SHUT GATE.
IT WAS SECTION ONE OF A BLANKET STATUTE 392 MARCOM
REVEALS A SECTION OF THE BEDROOM FRAMED IN THE 107 MISBEG
DOORWAY BEHIND TYRONE.
THE LEFT SECTION OF THE BARN CONTAINS THE HAYLOFT,577 ROPE

SECTIONS
THE STAGE IS DIVIDED INTO TWO SECTIONS, SHOWING A 3 ANNA
SMALL BACK ROOM ON THE RIGHT.
ONLY THE HALF SECTIONS OF THE TWO HOUSES ARE -0 DYNAMO
VISIBLE WHICH ARE NEAREST TO EACH

1383

SEEING

SECTOR
BUILT IN THE DECADE 1900-10 ON THE SIDE STREETS OF 7 HUGHIE THE GREAT WHITE WAY SECTOR,

SECURE
ITSELF--ABOVE ALL, TO FEEL ITSELF SECURE, 508 DAYS
WAITING TO CATCH MEN AT ITS MERCY, IN THEIR HOUR 535 DAYS OF SECURE HAPPINESS--
SECURE WITH THE CULTURE OF THE PAST AT HIS BACK, 3 STRANG SO HE'S CONCENTRATING HIS AFFECTIONS ON SAM WHOSE 144 STRANG LOVE HE KNOWS IS SECURE,

SECURES
SECURES A CRUMPLED BALL OF PAPER.) 573 CROSS

SECURITY
AND THE MORE PEACE AND SECURITY HE FOUND IN HIS 536 DAYS WIFE'S LOVE,
SLAVERY MEANS SECURITY--OF A KIND, THE ONLY KIND 542 DAYS THEY HAVE COURAGE FOR.
AND THE OLD COMFORTING PEACE AND SECURITY AND JOY 545 DAYS STEAL BACK INTO HIS HEART,
EVERYTHING THAT WAS PEACE AND WARMTH AND SECURITY. 90 ELECTR THE MATERIAL SECURITY WHICH GAVE HER THE CHANCE TO 47 MANSNS REMAIN ALOOF AND SCORNFUL
SOMETHING OF AN INNER SECURITY AND HARMONY, 95 MANSNS IT MUST ATTAIN THE ALL-EMBRACING SECURITY OF 101 MANSNS COMPLETE SELF-POSSESSION--
A FAITH IN MY OWN LIVING--AND NOW HE DARES TO TAKE122 MANSNS THAT SECURITY AWAY FROM ME/
WITH LUXURY AND SECURITY FOR THE REARING OF 130 MANSNS CHILDREN/
SECURITY OR FAITH OR LOVE BUT ONLY DANGER AND 184 MANSNS SUSPICION AND DEVOURING GREED/
A FEW MORE AND SHE'LL DIVE FOR THE GUTTER JUST TO 35 STRANG GET THE SECURITY THAT COMES
YOU'RE CLOSELY ASSOCIATED IN HER MIND WITH THAT 36 STRANG PERIOD OF HAPPY SECURITY,
WILL GRADUALLY GIVE HER BACK A SENSE OF SECURITY 37 STRANG AND A FEELING OF BEING WORTH

SEDAN
BY THE WAY, I LOCATED THE SPOT NEAR SEDAN WHERE 9 STRANG GORDON'S MACHINE FELL.

SEDUCE
ARE YOU LAYING PLOTS IN MY PRESENCE TO SEDUCE MY 67 MISBEG ONLY DAUGHTER?
TRUST HIMSELF, AND IT'D BE A SIN ON HIS CONSCIENCE 90 MISBEG IF HE WAS TO SEDUCE YOU.

SEDUCED
TO HEAR YOU TELL IT, YOU'D THINK IT WAS YOU WHO 61 POET SEDUCED ME/
ONE AV THE YANKEE GINTRY HAS STOPPED TO BE SEDUCED172 POET BY MY SLUT AV A DAUGHTER/
YE SEDUCED HIM AND YE'LL MAKE AN HONEST GENTLEMAN 179 POET AV HIM

SEDUCER
THE SUCCESSFUL SEDUCER OF OLD. 70 POET

SEDUCES
THAT COWARDLY SOMETHING IN HIM HE DESPISES AS 544 DAYS SUPERSTITION SEDUCES HIS REASON
HE'S AN OLD MAID WHO SEDUCES HIMSELF IN HIS 76 STRANG NOVELS...

SEDUCING
AND I HAD TO DO ALL THE SEDUCING--BECAUSE HE'S 521 DAYS QUITE HAPPY.
I'LL HAVE NO YOUNG SPARK SEDUCING MY DAUGHTER-- 438 DYNAMO FAITH, IF IT CAME TO SEDUCING, IT'D BE ME THAT'D 32 POET HAVE TO DO IT.

SEDUCTIVE
IN HER MOST SEDUCTIVE TONES WHICH SHE USES ALL 225 DESIRE THROUGH THIS SCENE)
(ABRUPTLY CHANGING TO A GAY, ARROGANTLY-PLEASED, 113 MANSNS SEDUCTIVE COQUETRY.)
THERE IS SEDUCTIVE CHARM IN HIS WELCOMING SMILE 68 POET AND IN HIS VOICE.)
(WITH A SEDUCTIVE SMILE) I DOWN'T BLAME YER. 501 VOYAGE

SEDUCTIVELY
(SEDUCTIVELY) YOU SEE, IT'S THIS WAY WITH ME. 238 AHWILD
(THEN PUTTING HER HAND ON HIS ARM--SEDUCTIVELY) 227 DESIRE
(TRYING TO REGAIN HER ASCENDANCY--SEDUCTIVELY) 229 DESIRE
(COLLECTED NOW AND CALCULATING--TAKES HOLD OF HIS 56 ELECTR ARM, SEDUCTIVELY)
(AUTOMATICALLY SHE SMILES SEDUCTIVELY AT PARRITT 611 ICEMAN
(PLAINLY ENJOYING THIS, MOVES HER BODY 141 MANSNS SEDUCTIVELY--TEASINGLY.)
(LAUGHS SOFTLY AND SEDUCTIVELY, RISING TO HER 164 MANSNS FEET.)

SEDUCTIVENESS
AND A CALCULATING FEMININE SEDUCTIVENESS. 139 MANSNS

SEDULOUSLY
RICHARD SEDULOUSLY AVOIDS EVEN GLANCING AT HIM, 295 AHWILD SO SEDULOUSLY PROTECTED AND ALOOF FROM ALL LIFE'S 14 MANSNS SORDIDNESS.
SEDULOUSLY BUILT AS A SANCTUARY WHERE, 3 STRANG

SEED
I AIN'T NEVER SEED A SEA-GULL IN HIS BUNK YET. 94 BEYOND OF AN INDUSTRY GONE TO SEED. 112 BEYOND AND I RECKON SHE WOULDN'T HAVE SEED MY P'INT 515 DIFRNT ANYHOW, HER BEIN' A NATIVE.
(STERNLY) THE KIND OF WOMEN I'VE SEED IN CITIES 536 DIFRNT WEARIN' IT--
I'VE SEED HE WAS GITTIN' MORE 'N' MORE LIKE HIS 540 DIFRNT PA--
(IGNORING HER QUESTION) I SEED WHAT HE WAS COMIN'540 DIFRNT TO, YEARS BACK.
GORRY, NOTHIN' ROUND HEAH LOOKS LIKE I EVAN SEED 189 EJONES IT BEFO'.
MANY'S A TIME I'VE SEED A SKIPPER AN' MATES 105 ELECTR SWEATIN' BLOOD TO BEAT WORK OUT OF A
AN' I SEED IN THE PAPER WHERE EZRA MANNON WAS 106 ELECTR DEAD/

SEED (CONT'D.)
AN' I SEED EZRA'S GHOST DRESSED LIKE A JUDGE 134 ELECTR COMIN' THROUGH THE WALL--
I SEED YOU SETTIN' OUT HERE ON THE STEPS WHEN I 170 ELECTR GOT UP AT FIVE THIS MORNIN'--
SUW THE SEED, ONLY GO ABOUT IT RIGHT. 247 HA APE THE OLD, GROWN MELLOW WITH GOD, BURST INTO FLAMING349 LAZARU SEED/
OU THE LAST DAY ONE OF YOUR SEED 362 MARCOM AN AGENCY THAT'S BEEN ALLOWED TO RUN DOWN AND GO 121 STRANG TO SEED.

SEEDY
THE DESK FACES LEFT ALONG A SECTION OF SEEDY LOBBY 7 HUGHIE WITH SHABBY CHAIRS.

SEEIN'
AIN'T THAT A WOMAN'S WAY O' SEEIN' THINGS FOR YOUS 95 BEYOND TRAVELIN' ALL OVER THE WORLD AND NEVER SEEIN' NONE486 CARDIF OF IT.
BUT SEEIN' IT'S YOU-- 469 CARIBE
(HE TURNS AWAY) I HAIN'T SEEIN' YE AGEN. 258 DESIRE AND US NOT SEEIN' HIDE OR HAIR OF EACH OTHER THE 496 DIFRNT LAST TWO OF 'EM.
YOU JUS' GET SEEIN' DEM THINGS 'CAUSE YO' BELLY'S 193 EJONES EMPTY AND YOU'S SICK WID
I NEVER REMEMBERS SEEIN' IT BEFO'. 193 EJONES
VINNIE'S BACK SEEIN' TO SOMETHIN'. 158 ELECTR
SHE LAMPED ME LIKE SHE WAS SEEIN' SOMEP'N BROKE 241 HA APE LOOSE FROM DE MENAGERIE.
SHE HAD ME TAGGED FOR A BUM, AND SEEIN' ME MADE 26 HUGHIE HER SURE SHE WAS RIGHT.
I'D GET TO SEEIN' MYSELF LIKE HE SEEN ME. 29 HUGHIE AND YOU SEEIN' THE MARKS AV THE BATIN' WE GOT/ 154 POET

SEEING
(IN RELIEVED TONES--SEEING WHO IT IS) 536 'TLE
(TURNING AND SEEING HIM) DON'T BE STANDIN' THERE 543 'TLE LIKE A GAWK, HARPOONER.
UN SEEING HIS AUNT, HE GIVES HER A DARK LOOK AND 215 AHWILD TURNS AND IS ABOUT TO STALK.
I NEVER REMEMBER SEEING--MORE BEAUTIFUL SUNSET. 224 AHWILD AND SEEING I LIKE YOU SO MUCH, I'D ONLY TAKE FIVE 241 AHWILD DOLLARS--FROM YOU.
(ACCUSINGLY) YOU DON'T MEAN TO TELL ME YOU'RE 263 AHWILD GOING BACK WITHOUT SEEING HIM?
HE WENT BACK TO THE OFFICE WITHOUT SEEING ME. 272 AHWILD SHE SMILES ON SEEING HER UNCLE, THEN GIVES A START272 AHWILD ON SEEING RICHARD.)
(SEEING HE ISN'T FOLLOWING HER, STOPS AT THE FOOT 285 AHWILD OF THE PATH--DEFIANTLY)
NOTHING WOULD HAVE KEPT ME FROM SEEING YOU 287 AHWILD TONIGHT--
AND I'M GOING TO TELL HIM HE CAN'T GO TO YALE, 289 AHWILD SEEING HE'S SO UNDEPENDABLE.
AND I WAS THINKING MAYBE, SEEING HE AIN'T NEVER 16 ANNA DONE A THING FOR ME IN MY LIFE,
(THEN SEEING HIS CRESTFALLEN LOOK--FORCING A 23 ANNA SMILE)
(THEN SEEING HER IRRITATION, HE HASTILY ADOPTS A 26 ANNA MORE CHEERFUL TONE)
(THEN SEEING THE HURT EXPRESSION ON HER FATHER'S 26 ANNA FACE, SHE FORCES A SMILE)
(EAGERLY--SEEING A CHANCE TO DRIVE HOME HIS POINT) 28 ANNA
(SEEING THE COLD, HOSTILE EXPRESSION ON ANNA'S 32 ANNA FACE,
SEEING HIS SIMPLE FRANKNESS, SHE GOES ON 35 ANNA CONFIDENTLY.)
(THEN SEEING HIS HURT EXPRESSION--QUICKLY) 37 ANNA
BUT ONLY BE SEEING THE GOOD HERSELF PUT IN ME$ 38 ANNA AND YOU'D BE SEEING HER AFTER SO-- 47 ANNA KUARING AND NEVER A GROAN OUT OF ME TILL THE SEA 48 ANNA GAVE UP AND IT SEEING THE GREAT
SEEING ALL THINGS, AND NOT GIVING A DAMN FOR 48 ANNA SAVING UP MONEY.
(THEN TURNING TO CHRIS) WE'LL BE SEEING WHO'LL 55 ANNA WIN IN THE END--ME OR YOU.
NIGHT IN THE FOG. AND AFTERWARDS SEEING THAT YOU 59 ANNA WAS STRAIGHT GOODS STUCK ON ME,
WOULDN'T BE SEEING OR THINKING MORE OF YOU. 70 ANNA IT WASN'T HIS FACE I'D BE SEEING AT ALL, BUT 70 ANNA YOURS.
SEEING WHO IT IS, HE SMILES) 82 BEYOND
(SEEING ROBERT HAS NOT NOTICED HIS PRESENCE--IN A 82 BEYOND LOUD SHOUT)
YOU WERE SO USED TO SEEING ME LYING AROUND THE 84 BEYOND HOUSE IN THE OLD DAYS THAT YOU
(SEEING HIM) HELLO, ROB/ 87 BEYOND
(HASTILY--SEEING THE GATHERING STORM) 105 BEYOND THEN, SEEING NO ONE ABOUT, HE GOES TO THE 121 BEYOND SIDEBOARD AND SELECTS A BOOK.
(SEEING ALL FOUR ARE SERVED) 465 CARIBE HE CASTS A QUICK GLANCE ABOUT THE ROOM, AND SEEING555 CROSS NO ONE FINGER.
AND MY SEEING YOU YOURSELF 556 CROSS
(HIS EYES PASS OVER LOVING WITHOUT SEEING HIM, 496 DAYS LOOKING AT HIM AND SEEING WHAT A BIG MAN OF 501 DAYS AFFAIRS HE'D GROWN.
HE STOPS ON SEEING JOHN LOVING, 566 DAYS HE COMES AROUND CORNER, STOPS ON SEEING HIS 227 DESIRE FATHER,
(PEERING IN AND SEEING THEM--IN A JOKING BELLOW) 499 DIFRNT AND BEING LIKE THEM IS EXACTLY WHAT'LL KEEP YOU 516 DIFRNT FAUM EVER SEEING MY MEANING.
(SEEING HER EXPRESSION HE HURRIES ON) 521 DIFRNT
(SEEING HIS CALCULATIONS DEMAND IT) 524 DIFRNT
(HE BEGINS TO LOOK AT HER AS IF HE WERE SEEING HER536 DIFRNT FOR THE FIRST TIME.)
(THEN SEEING HIS ASHAMED LOOK, SHE SMILES) 424 DYNAMO WITH EYES THAT SEE YOU WITHOUT SEEING YOU... 474 DYNAMO

SEEING

SEEING (CONT'D.)
(STRANGELY) NOT LATELY--NOT SINCE I GAVE UP 478 DYNAMO
SEEING ADA.
YOU GAVE ME A START, SEEING YOU ALL OF A SUDDEN. 481 DYNAMO
(SEEING THE USELESSNESS OF STRUGGLING, GIVES WAY 174 EJONES
TO FRANTIC TERROR.
(NOT SEEING ANYONE--GREATLY IRRITATED AND BLINKING)76 EJONES
SLEEPILY--SHOUTS)
(SEEING SHE IS PAYING NO ATTENTION TO HIM BUT IS 7 ELECTR
STARING WITH OPEN-MOUTHED AWE
(SEEING HER) THERE SHE BE NOW. 10 ELECTR
HE STARTS ON SEEING LAVINIA 20 ELECTR
PROSPECT OF SEEING YOUR FATHER AGAIN. 22 ELECTR
(HASTILY) DO YOU THINK I'LL EVEN GIVE YOU THE 34 ELECTR
SATISFACTION OF SEEING ME GRIEVE?
SEEING YOU IN NEW YORK SHOULD HAVE BEEN ENOUGH FOR 37 ELECTR
ME.
SHE ADDS CALCULATINGLY SEEING HE IS BOILING 38 ELECTR
(ASIDE)
(WITH FIERCE SCORN NOW, SEEING THE NECESSITY OF 41 ELECTR
GUARDING HIM.
(SEEING THE MAN'S FIGURE STOP IN THE SHADOW--CALLS 46 ELECTR
EXCITEDLY)
(HE FORCES HIMSELF TO TURN AND, SEEING HER EYES 53 ELECTR
ARE SHUT.
IT WAS SEEING DEATH ALL THE TIME IN THIS WAY GOT 53 ELECTR
ME TO THINKING THESE THINGS.
(SEEING HAZEL'S LOOK, CATCHES HERSELF--QUICKLY) 73 ELECTR
(FORCING A WAN SMILE) THE HAPPINESS OF SEEING YOU 80 ELECTR
AGAIN.
(THEN, SEEING ORIN WAVERING, PITIFULLY) 88 ELECTR
THEY STOP IN SURPRISE ON SEEING SETH AND HIS 134 ELECTR
FRIENDS.
I CAN'T GET OVER SEEING YOU DRESSED IN COLOUR. 143 ELECTR
AND NEVER SEEING HIM AGAIN! 166 ELECTR
AND LEAD YOUR OWN LIFE--EXCEPT FOR SEEING HIM. 289 GGBROW
(AS IF HE HADN'T HEARD) IT'S MINE--AND I'M 296 GGBROW
INTERESTED IN SEEING
(SEIZING THE BOTTLE, FORCING A LAUGH) 300 GGBROW
SHE STOPS SHORT ON SEEING BROWN AND THE MASK. 320 GGBROW
(SEEING A FLIGHT--WITH A ROAR OF JOY AS HE SPRINGS 239 HA APE
TO HIS FEET)
I WILL HAVE A DRINK, NOW YOU MENTION IT, SEEING 601 ICEMAN
IT'S SO NEAR YOUR BIRTHDAY.
SEEING I GOT IT ALL SET FOR MY BIRTHDAY TOMORROW. 626 ICEMAN
(THEN QUICKLY) WELL, NATURALLY, HER FAMILY FORBID710 ICEMAN
HER SEEING ME.
I'D GET SEEING THINGS IN THE WALL PAPER. 712 ICEMAN
AT FIRST HE STRUGGLES FIERCELY, BUT SEEING THE 925 INZONE
USELESSNESS OF THIS.
(SEEING HIS AUDIENCE IS AGAIN ALL WITH HIM) 529 INZONE
(EXCITEDLY.) IT'S SIMPLY A WASTE OF TIME AND 92 JOURNE
MONEY SEEING HIM.
IT'S HARD TO BELIEVE, SEEING JAMIE AS HE IS NOW, 109 JOURNE
THAT HE WAS EVER MY BABY.
(HE STARES AT HIS WATCH WITHOUT SEEING IT. 113 JOURNE
FOR A SECOND YOU SEE--AND SEEING THE SECRET, ARE 153 JOURNE
THE SECRET.
(SEEING HE IS HURT--AFFECTIONATELY.) 157 JOURNE
NAY, AND THOUGH ALL MEN SEEING HAD PITY ON ME, SHE174 JOURNE
WOULD NOT SEE.+
IF I TELL YOU TO LAUGH IN THE MIRROR, THAT SEEING309 LAZARU
YOUR LIFE GAY.
(SEEING LAZARUS WHERE HE HAD BEEN--WITH RELIEF-- 340 LAZARU
I DON'T REMEMBER EVER SEEING YOU CRY. 5 MANSNS
(SEEING THE SKULL OF DEATH LEEK OVER ITS SHOULDER 12 MANSNS
IN THE GLASS/
(SHE LAUGHS SOFTLY--THEN QUICKLY, SEEING HE IS 39 MANSNS
HURT.)
FINALLY, SEEING SHE IS APPARENTLY ABSORBED IN HER 140 MANSNS
WORK.
YOU WERE LATE AGAIN THIS MORNING ON ACCOUNT OF 147 MANSNS
SEEING HER.
HE STOPS ON SEEING THEM. 348 MARCOM
IT WASN'T YOU I WAS SEEING AND TALKING TO, NOT A 416 MARCOM
PRINCESS AT ALL.
SURE, ALL I WANTED WAS TO GIVE HIM THE FUN OF 26 MISBEG
SEEING THROUGH THEM
BUT WHEN IT COMES TO STANDING BY AND SEEING MY 62 MISBEG
POOR PIGS MURTHERED ONE BY ONE--/
I WAS SEEING THINGS. 136 MISBEG
SEEING MALOY, HE COMES IN. 8 POET
(THEN, SEEING THE LOOK OF WONDERING HURT IN THE 54 POET
OLD MAN'S EYES.
BUT AT ONCE, SEEING SHE IS ATTRACTIVE AND A LADY, 68 POET
HIS MANNER CHANGES.
(SEIZED BY AN IDEA.) WELL, SEEING WOULD BE 76 POET
BELIEVING, EH, MY FINE LADYS
THEY CAN'T HELP SEEING SIN HIDING UNDER EVERY 90 POET
BUSH.
SEEING SARA ALONE, SHE COMES IN.) 129 POET
AND SEEING HER DIE MADE AN END AV HIM. 169 POET
(SEEING THAT SHE HAS BEEN CRYING) 582 ROPC
SEEING NINA AGAIN/... 12 STRANG
HER EYES SEEING CRUELLY THROUGH HIM... 15 STRANG
(SEEING HER PREOCCUPATION NOW--DEEPLY HURT-- 54 STRANG
TESTILY)
(SEEING THIS IS HER CHANCE--QUICKLY--FORCING A 55 STRANG
SMILE)
WITHOUT SEEING ME....) 79 STRANG
(PLACATINGLY--SEEING HE IS REALLY ANGRY) 114 STRANG
I CAN REMEMBER THAT DAY SEEING HER KISS HIM... 189 STRANG
SEEING SPOOKS, THAT'S PRETTY FAR GONE, ISN'T ITS 466 WELDED
(STARES AT HER--AN EXPRESSION COMES AS IF HE WERE 477 WELDED
SEEING HER FOR THE FIRST TIME-

SEEK
THEM, DANCE WITH THEM DOWN THE ROAD IN THE DUSK IN 90 BEYOND
A GAME OF HIDE-AND-SEEK TO

SEEK

SEEK (CONT'D.)
IN WHAT I'D CALL HIS MIDDLE HIDE-AND-GO-SEEK 503 DAYS
PERIOD.
IF HE CAN ONLY BELIEVE AGAIN IN HIS OLD GOD OF 544 DAYS
LOVE, AND SEEK HER THROUGH HIM.
I'LL GO OUT AN' SEEK AN' FIND/ 238 DESIRE
SEEK THE MONKEY IN THE MOON/ 262 GGBROW
LET'S PLAY HIDE-AND-SEEK/ 262 GGBROW
OK WE WHO SEEK IT ARE, WHICH COMES TO THE SAME 351 LAZARU
THING.
SEEK MAN IN THE BROTHERHOOD OF THE DUST?/ 368 LAZARU
BE DRIVEN TO SEEK SPIRITUAL SALVATION SOMEWHERE/ 363 MARCOM
AND WENT OUT AS A BEGGAR ON THE ROADS TO SEEK THE 372 MARCOM
SUPREME ENLIGHTENMENT
YOU ARE PLAYING HIDE AND SEEK. 437 MARCOM
I DIDN'T COME HOME TO FIGHT, BUT SEEK COMFORT IN 75 MISBEG
YOUR COMPANY.
SINCE HE LEFT HOME TO SEEK SELF-EMANCIPATION AT 81 POET
THE BREAST OF NATURE.
I CAME HERE TO SEEK A PRIVATE INTERVIEW WITH THE 117 POET
PROPRIETOR OF THIS TAVERN.
THEN INSTINCTIVELY I SEEK YOU--MY HAND TOUCHES 488 WELDED
YOU?

SEEKERS
THEIR VOICES AS THEY GO OFF TAKE UP THE SONG OF 224 DESIRE
THE GOLD-SEEKERS

SEEKEST
=AH, FONDEST, BLINDEST, WEAKEST, I AM HE WHOM THOUSOB DAYS
SEEKEST/

SEEKING
GULPS DOWN HIS WHISKEY DESPERATELY AS IF SEEKING 10 ANNA
FOR COURAGE.
(THEN AS IF SEEKING RELIEF FROM THE TENSION IN A 20 ANNA
VOLUBLE CHATTER)
(STRAIGHTENING UP AND LOOKING ABOUT AS IF HE WERE 57 ANNA
SEEKING A WAY TO ESCAPE--
WHEN HE SAID I COULD FIND ALL THE THINGS I WAS 92 BEYOND
SEEKING FOR HERE.
AND NOW--THE STOPS AS IF SEEKING VAINLY FOR WORDS1161 BEYOND
(SEEKING VAINLY FOR SOME WORD OF COMFORT) 486 CARDIF
(HE LOOKS ABOUT HIM, SEEKING A NEUTRAL SUBJECT FOR524 DIFRNT
CONVERSATION.)
SEEKING VAINLY TO DISCOVER HIS WHEREABOUTS BY 189 EJONES
THEIR CONFORMATION.)
AS IF SEEKING A HIDING PLACE. 62 ELECTR
SHE THROWS HER ARMS AROUND ORIN AS IF SEEKING 100 ELECTR
PROTECTION FROM HIM)
HE HURRIES TO HER AS IF SEEKING PROTECTION. 139 ELECTR
HER EYES UNCONSCIOUSLY SEEKING THE MANNON 157 ELECTR
PORTRAITS ON THE RIGHT WALL.
SEEKING TO HIDE BEHIND A MOULD MANNER.) 152 JOURNE
AND TWIST DISTRACTEDLY, SEEKING TO HIDE 349 LAZARU
THEIR HEADS AGAINST EACH OTHER.
SEEKING THE SATISFYING REASSURANCE OF HIS 67 POET
REFLECTION THERE.
PROTECTIVE WARDING OFF AND AT THE SAME TIME A 480 WELDED
SEEKING POSSESSION.

SEEM
I ALWAYS COME BACK--WITH A FULL SHIP--AND--IT 547 'ILE
DON'T SEEM RIGHT NOT TO--SOMEHOW.
(SHE DOESN'T ANSWER OR SEEM TO KNOW HE IS THERE. 551 'ILE
(CAUSTICALLY) HE READ HIS SCHOOL BOOKS, TOO. 192 AHWILD
STRANGE AS THAT MAY SEEM TO YOU.
AND IT DON'T SEEM TO DO THEM ANY HARM. 198 AHWILD
(TURNS TO HIM CAUSTICALLY) YOU SEEM IN A MERRY 228 AHWILD
MOOD, RICHARD.
(GOOD-NATUREDLY) YOU SEEM TO BE GETTING A LOT OF 232 AHWILD
FUN KIDDING ME.
SEA-SICK TINGE, HIS EYES SEEM TO BE TURNED INWARD 261 AHWILD
UNEASILY--
CAN'T SEEM TO KEEP AWAKE. 264 AHWILD
(SMILING) THEN, FROM ALL REPORTS, WE SEEM TO BE 292 AHWILD
COMPLETELY SURROUNDED BY LOVE/
SHE MADE EVERYTHING SEEM ROTTEN AND DIRTY--AND-- 294 AHWILD
A CASSOCK WOULD SEEM MORE SUITED TO HIM THAN THE 3 ANNA
APRON HE WEARS.
THE OTHERS DIDN'T SEEM TO MIND BEING IN THE COOLER 16 ANNA
MUCH.
AND I SEEM TO HAVE FORGOT--EVERYTHING THAT'S 28 ANNA
HAPPENED--
(A TRIFLE IMPATIENTLY) ALL OF YOU SEEM TO KEEP 84 BEYOND
HARPING ON MY HEALTH.
YOU'VE SEEN A BIT OF THE WORLD, ENOUGH TO MAKE THE 84 BEYOND
FARM SEEM SMALL.
SEEM TO TAKE INTO CONSIDERATION--THAT ROB WANTS TO 96 BEYOND
GO.
HE DOES SEEM SORT O' GLUM AND OUT OF SORTS. 97 BEYOND
YOU SEEM MIGHTY FIXED IN YOUR OPINION, KATEY. 99 BEYOND
BUT RUTH AND ROBBIE SEEM HAPPY ENOUGH TOGETHER. 116 BEYOND
HE DOESN'T SEEM TO FROM HIS LETTERS, DOES HES 125 BEYOND
THINGS DON'T SEEM TO BE-- 131 BEYOND
(DRYLY) THE SEA DOESN'T SEEM TO HAVE IMPRESSED 132 BEYOND
YOU VERY FAVORABLY.
I SUPPOSE IT DOES SEEM SMALL TO YOU NOW. 133 BEYOND
YOU CAN'T SEEM TO GET IT IN YOUR HEAD THAT 146 BEYOND
THINGS KEPT GETTING WORSE. THAT'S ALL--AND ROB 155 BEYOND
DIDN'T SEEM TO CARE.
IT'S TOO BAD--THINGS SEEM TO GO WRONG SO. 157 BEYOND
WELL, IT DOESN'T SEEM TO AMOUNT TO MUCH NOW. 161 BEYOND
SHITTY STARES BEFORE HIM AND DOES NOT SEEM TO KNOW470 CARIBE
THERE IS ANYONE ON DECK BUT
PARDON ME IF I SEEM TO INDULGE IN THE MELANCHOLY 517 DAYS
JITTERS.
YOU KNOW I WOULDN'T, EVEN IF I HATED YOU AS YOU 527 DAYS
SEEM TO HATE ME.
I SEEM TO HAVE THE NERVOUS JUMPS LATELY. 528 DAYS
I SEEM TO BE TALKING NONSENSE. 551 DAYS
SHE DOES NOT SEEM TO NOTICE. 232 DESIRE

SEEM

(CONT'D.)

THEIR HOT GLANCES SEEM TO MEET THROUGH THE WALL. 236 DESIRE
HE DOES NOT SEEM TO NOTICE--PASSIONATELY) 242 DESIRE
(CBEN DOESN'T SEEM TO HEAR. 254 DESIRE
ANY IT'LL SEEM LIKELY ANY TRUE TO 'EM, 267 DESIRE
(SUSPICIOUSLY) CALEB DIDN'T SEEM WILLING TO TELL 501 DIFRNT
ME MUCH ABOUT THEIR TOUCHING.
HE DIDN'T SEEM TO WANT TO OWN UP IT WAS ANYTHING. 501 DIFRNT
AND NEITHER YOU NOR HIM EVER DID SEEM TO CARE FOR 512 DIFRNT
NO ONE ELSE.
(HELPLESSLY) BUT YOU DON'T SEEM BAD, CALEB. 517 DIFRNT
OVER, YOU'LL SEE DIFF'RENT AND KNOW I AIN'T AS BADS17 DIFRNT
AS I SEEM TO YE NOW.
I AIN'T AS STRICT AS I SEEM--ABOUT HEARIN' THINGS.526 DIFRNT
(HAPPILY) WHY I SEEM TO GET FEELIN' YOUNGER AND 536 DIFRNT
MORE CHIPPER EVERY DAY.
(ISHE DOESN'T SEEM TO BE COMING... 431 DYNAMO
BUT HE DOESN'T SEEM LIKE REUBEN...) 463 DYNAMO
(HIS FATHER DOESN'T SEEM TO HEAR HIM. 466 DYNAMO
SEEM LIKE QUEER HINDU IDOLS TORTURED INTO 403 DYNAMO
SCIENTIFIC SUPPLICATIONS.
SOUND LOUDER, SEEM LIKE. 188 EJONES
INCREASING GRADUALLY BY THE RHYTHMIC DEGREES WHICH199 EJONES
SEEM TO BE DIRECTED AND
EXULTANT BOOM WHOSE THROBS SEEM TO FILL THE AIR 200 EJONES
WITH VIBRATING RHYTHM.
YOU SEEM TO TAKE GIVING HIM UP PRETTY EASILY/ 34 ELECTR
THAT MADE THE WHITE MEETING-HOUSE SEEM 54 ELECTR
MEANINGLESS--
SHE DOESN'T SEEM TO FEEL AS MUCH SORROW AS SHE 68 ELECTR
OUGHT.
BUT IT DOES SEEM AS IF EZRA SHOULD HAVE BEEN LAID 69 ELECTR
OUT IN THE TOWN HALL WHERE THE
IT MAY SEEM A HARD THING TO SAY ABOUT THE DEAD, 86 ELECTR
BUT HE WAS JEALOUS OF YOU.
(SHE FORCES A LAUGH) YOU DON'T SEEM TO REALIZE 87 ELECTR
I'M AN OLD MARRIED WOMAN
YOU SEEM THE SAME TO ME IN DEATH, EZRA/ 101 ELECTR
(FORCING A SMILE) THEY SEEM TO HAVE DESERTED ME. 118 ELECTR
(SLYLY) YOU SEEM A MITE SHAKY. 133 ELECTR
YOU SEEM DAMNED ANXIOUS TO GET RID OF ME. 146 ELECTR
THE EYES OF THE PORTRAITS SEEM TO POSSESS AN 157 ELECTR
INTENSE BITTER LIFE.
I KNOW SOMETHING IS WORRYING YOU--AND I DON'T WANT160 ELECTR
TO SEEM PRYING--BUT
THERE ARE THINGS NOW WHEN YOU DON'T SEEM TO BE MY 165 ELECTR
SISTER, NOR MOTHER,
YOU DON'T SEEM TO FEEL ALL YOU MEAN TO ME NOW--ALL165 ELECTR
YOU HAVE MADE YOURSELF MEAN--
BUT MY MIND DOESN'T SEEM TO RUN THAT WAY. 275 GGBROW
YOU SEEM TO BE GOING IN FOR SINCERITY TODAY. 219 HA APE
THEY DIDN'T SEEM A BIT ANXIOUS THAT I SHOULD 220 HA APE
INVESTIGATE
(BUT AS THEY SEEM NEITHER TO SEE NOR HEAR HIM, HE 238 HA APE
FLIES INTO A FURY)
YOU SEEM TO BE A WISE TO A LOT OF STUFF NONE OF US 247 HA APE
KNOWS ABOUT.
HUGHIE DIDN'T SEEM TO MIND IT MUCH, ALTHOUGH IF 12 HUGHIE
YOU WANT MY LOW-DOWN,
THEY SEEM CONSTRUCTED OF AN INFERIOR GRADE OF 577 ICEMAN
DIRTY BLOTTING PAPER.
IT DOESN'T SEEM REAL. 590 ICEMAN
ALL YOU GUYS SEEM TO THINK I'M MADE OF DOUGH. 595 ICEMAN
(WATCHING HIM) YOU SEEM DOWN ON THE LADIES. 615 ICEMAN
THAT MAKES WHAT HE SAYS SEEM DOUBLY FALSE) 648 ICEMAN
I SEEM TO BE BLOCKING YOUR WAY OUT. 677 ICEMAN
THEY SEEM ABOUT TO CURSE HIM, TO SPRING AT HIM. 685 ICEMAN
(LARRY DOESN'T SEEM TO HEAR. 700 ICEMAN
BUT IT DOES SEEM A SHAME HE SHOULD HAVE TO BE SICK 16 JOURNE
RIGHT NOW.
BUT I SEEM TO BE ALWAYS PICKING ON YOU, TELLING 58 JOURNE
YOU DON'T DO THIS
IT'S TOO BAD THEY SEEM TO BE JUST THE TIMES YOU'RE 72 JOURNE
SURE TO BE LATE, JAMES.
HE GLANCES AWAY, IGNORING HER QUESTION BUT SHE 81 JOURNE
DOESN'T SEEM TO EXPECT AN ANSWER.
BUT HE DIDN'T SEEM TO THINK I WAS A FOOL. 105 JOURNE
GOD, IT MADE EVERYTHING IN LIFE SEEM ROTTEN/ 118 JOURNE
HE DOESN'T SEEM TO HAVE ANY APPETITE THESE DAYS. 122 JOURNE
HE DON'T SEEM ABLE TO AVOID UNPLEASANT TOPICS, DO 137 JOURNE
WE?
LIKE THE VEIL OF THINGS AS THEY SEEM DRAWN BACK BY153 JOURNE
AN UNSEEN HAND.
SHE DOESN'T SEEM TO HEAR HIM. 172 JOURNE
(SHE DOES NOT SEEM TO HEAR. 173 JOURNE
(BUT NONE NEED HER OR SEEM TO SEE HER. 290 LAZARU
BUT NOW THESE BLOWS SEEM ONLY TO INFURIATE THE 304 LAZARU
CROWD
THE ROMANS AND GREEKS SEEM TO LEAN BACK FROM ONE 305 LAZARU
ANOTHER
(LAZARUS DOES NOT SEEM TO HEAR, BUT CALIGULA TURNS316 LAZARU
ON THEM FIERCELY.)
(THE SENATORS SEEM TO SHRINK BACK FROM HIM IN 316 LAZARU
FEAR, ALL BUT LUCIUS,
TERRIFIC FLASHES OF LIGHTNING AND CRASHES OF 318 LAZARU
THUNDER SEEM A RESPONSIVE
THICK WALLS SEEM WAITING TO FALL. 330 LAZARU
THE WALLS AND MASSIVE COLUMNS SEEM TO REVERBERATE 337 LAZARU
WITH THE SOUND.
BUT YOU SEEM--SOMETHING OTHER THAN MAN/ 340 LAZARU
YOU SEEM SO LONELY. 11 MANSNS
SHE WOULD TRY TO STEAL ALL IDENTITY FROM YOU-- 105 MANSNS
UNTIL THERE WAS BUT ONE WOMAN--
(HE DOES NOT SEEM TO HEAR.) STILL SO VAIN AND 128 MANSNS
STUBBORN
BUT I MUST REMEMBER THEY ONLY SEEM TO BECOME ONE--129 MANSNS
BUT I FEEL HER ARMS AROUND ME--

SEEMED

SEEM (CONT'D.)
AND NOW I HAVE IT, I SEEM TO HAVE NOTHING-- (HE 131 MANSNS
PAUSES.)
I CAN'T SEEM TO--I'M AFRAID I HAVE ENTIRELY 135 MANSNS
FORGOTTEN, SARA.
TOWARD HERS, THEIR LIPS SEEM ABOUT TO MEET IN A 415 MARCOM
KISS.
THEY SEEM INCLINED TO JOIN IN THE SCRAMBLE.) 429 MARCOM
HE DIDN'T SEEM SO LIT UP AT THE INN, BUT I GUESS 1101 MISBEG
WASN'T PAYING MUCH ATTENTION.
YOU DIDN'T SEEM SO PERISHING FOR A DRINK. 112 MISBEG
(AGAIN HE DOESN'T SEEM TO HAVE HEARD--RESENTFULLY)126 MISBEG
HE DOESN'T SEEM TO NOTICE THIS.) 149 MISBEG
BECAUSE I DIDN'T SEEM TO WANT TO FORGET. 150 MISBEG
DON'T SEEM TO WANT A DRINK. 167 MISBEG
(MELODY DOES NOT SEEM TO HEAR HER. 55 POET
THESE WOULD APPEAR LARGE IN ANY FACE, BUT IN HERS 68 POET
THEY SEEM ENORMOUS
OH, FATHER, WHY CAN'T YOU EVER BE THE THING YOU 90 POET
CAN SEEM TO BE?
WOULD SEEM TO SMILE THE LESS, OF ALL THAT 101 POET
FLATTERED--FOLLOWED--SOUGHT, AND SUED,
BUT HIS MOVEMENTS DO NOT SEEM THOSE OF 152 POET
DRUNKENNESS.
(MELODY DOES NOT SEEM TO NOTICE. 153 POET
HIS BODY IS LIMP, HIS FEET OKAY, HIS EYES SEEM TO 164 POET
HAVE NO SIGHT.
(HE DOES NOT SEEM TO HEAR OR SEE HER, 165 POET
DID I SEEM RUDE, CHARLES 13 STRANG
HE IS DRESSED CAREFULLY IN AN ENGLISH MADE SUIT OF 24 STRANG
BLUE SERGE SO DARK AS TO SEEM
GIVING THE WINDOWS A SUGGESTION OF LIFELESS CLOSED 24 STRANG
EYES AND MAKING THE ROOM SEEM
DOESN'T THAT SEEM GOOD SENSE TO YOU? 38 STRANG
DO I SEEM QUEER? 40 STRANG
BUT THEN LIFE DOESN'T SEEM TO BE PRETTY, DOES ITS 82 STRANG
HE DOES NOT SEEM CONSCIOUS OF DARRELL'S PRESENCE 98 STRANG
AT FIRST.
(SHE DOESN'T SEEM TO LIKE HIM SO MUCH... 155 STRANG
THERE IS LITTLE LEFT OF HER FACE'S CHARM EXCEPT 158 STRANG
HER EYES WHICH NOW SEEM LARGER
IT HAS THE TRAGIC EFFECT OF MAKING HER FACE SEEM 158 STRANG
OLDER
SHE DOESN'T SEEM TO CARE A DAMN ONE WAY OR THE 185 STRANG
OTHER ANY MORE/
YOU SEEM TO TAKE IT QUITE CASUALLY THAT MEN MUST 473 WELDED
BE EITHER DRUNK OR DOPED--
THEY SEEM IN A FORGETFUL, HAPPY TRANCE AT FINDING 480 WELDED
EACH OTHER AGAIN.

SEEM'S
(RUEFULLY) SEEM'S IF I PUT MY FOOT IN IT WHENEVER139 BEYOND
I OPEN MY MOUTH TODAY.

SEEMED
BECAUSE IT SEEMED SORT OF A SNEAKING TRICK, 214 AHWILD
WHY, HE SEEMED DISGUSTED WITH ME FOR HAVING SUCH A266 AHWILD
NOTION.
LIFE SEEMED LIKE A TRAGIC FARCE. 281 AHWILD
FOR THE REVELATION OF MY OWN LOVE SEEMED TO OPEN 91 BEYOND
MY EYES TO THE LOVE OF OTHERS.
BECAUSE YOU NEVER SEEMED TO WANT TO GO ANY PLACE 91 BEYOND
WITH ME.
ROBERT SEEMED STIRRED UP ABOUT SOMETHING. 98 BEYOND
(HIS EYES SEEMED TO TAKE IN THE POVERTY-STRICKEN 155 BEYOND
APPEARANCE
I'M SORRY, RUTH--IF I SEEMED TO BLAME YOU. 156 BEYOND
IT SEEMED AS IF ALL MY LIFE--I'D BEEN COOPED IN A 167 BEYOND
ROOM.
THIS LAST YEAR HAS SEEMED ROTTEN, AND I'VE HAD A 487 CARDIF
HUNCH I'D QUIT--
YOU'VE SEEMED WORN RAGGED LATELY. 496 DAYS
HIS FACE SEEMED ALIVE AS A LIVING MAN'S WOULD BE, 507 DAYS
BUT RADIANT WITH ETERNAL LIFE.
HE SEEMED TO LOOK THROUGH ME AT SOME ONE ELSE, 522 DAYS
AND I SEEMED FOR A MOMENT TO BE WATCHING SOME 522 DAYS
HIDDEN PLACE IN HIS MIND WHERE
IT SEEMED TO HIM THAT HE HAD FORSWORN ALL LOVE 534 DAYS
FOREVER--AND WAS CURSED.
AND WHEN HE REMINDED ME IT WAS RAINING, IT ALL 950 DAYS
SEEMED TO FIT IN SO PERFECTLY--
WHEN I FUST COME IN--IN THE DARK--THEY SEEMED 241 DESIRE
SOMETHIN' HERE.
IT SEEMED TO GET CALEB ALL RILED UP. 501 DIFRNT
CALEB ALWAYS SEEMED DIFF'RENT--AND I THOUGHT HE 512 DIFRNT
WAS.
HIS EYES SEEMED TO TAKE ALL THE CLOTHES OFF ME... 462 DYNAMO
WHEN ALL THESE SWITCHES AND BUSSES AND WIRES 484 DYNAMO
SEEMED LIKE THE ARMS OF A DEVIL
WHEN I RETURNED FROM NEW YORK LAST NIGHT YOU 16 ELECTR
SEEMED TO HAVE GONE TO BED.
AND WHEN ORIN WAS BORN HE SEEMED MY CHILD, ONLY 31 ELECTR
MINE, AND I LOVED HIM FOR THAT/
SEEMED TO THINK YOU WERE WITH HIM. 49 ELECTR
BUT LISTEN, ME AS YOUR HUSBAND AND BEING KILLED, 54 ELECTR
THAT SEEMED QUEER AND WRONG--
SHE'S SEEMED TO BE-- 68 ELECTR
HER MOTHER SEEMED REAL ANGRY ABOUT IT. 69 ELECTR
EVERYTHING HAS SEEMED QUEER SINCE I CAME BACK TO 74 ELECTR
EARTH.
SHE SEEMED STRANGE. 86 ELECTR
BUT YOUR LETTERS GOT FARTHER AND FARTHER BETWEEN-- 89 ELECTR
--AND THEY SEEMED SO COLD/
AND LATER ON ALL THE TIME I WAS OUT OF MY HEAD I 90 ELECTR
SEEMED REALLY TO BE THERE.
SEEMED TO ME ABNER'S BRAGGIN' GAVE ME A GOOD 135 ELECTR
CHANCE TO STOP IT
IF YOU EVER REMEMBERED, WHICH YOU NEVER SEEMED TO/140 ELECTR
AND I BELIEVED YOU, YOU SEEMED SO CERTAIN OF 141 ELECTR
YOURSELF.

SEEMED

SEEMED	(CONT'D.)	
YOU NEVER SEEMED SO MUCH LIKE MOTHER AS YOU DID JUST THEN/	155	ELECTR
DID YOU NOTICE THAT ANYTHING SEEMED LACKING IN THIS?	275	GGBROW
IT SEEMED I WAS NEVER REALLY TOUCHING YOU.	309	GGBROW
THEN HE CAME TO HIMSELF AND WAS ALL RIGHT AND	311	GGBROW
BEGGED MY PARDON AND SEEMED		
HUMBLE AND HER SEEMED HAPPY ENOUGH	24	HUGHIE
YET SHE SEEMED TO FORGIVE YOU.	589	ICEMAN
HE RAPPED AND HE RAPPED WITH A (RAP, RAP, RAP) BUTS96		ICEMAN
NEVER A SOUL SEEMED IN--		
IT SEEMED RATHER POINTLESS TO DISCUSS MY OTHER	601	ICEMAN
SUBJECT.		
WITHOUT HER, NOTHING SEEMED WORTH THE TROUBLE.	603	ICEMAN
I SEEMED TO GET HERE BEFORE I KNEW IT.	621	ICEMAN
IT'S STRANGE THE QUEER WAY HE SEEMED TO RECOGNIZE	638	ICEMAN
HIM.		
THEY SEEMED TO BE WISHING I WAS DEAD/	714	ICEMAN
WHY, NOTHING, EXCEPT YOU'VE SEEMED A BIT HIGH-	16	JOURNE
STRUNG THE PAST FEW DAYS.		
BUT IT'S ALWAYS SEEMED TO ME YOUR FATHER COULD	73	JOURNE
AFFORD TO KEEP ON BUYING PROPERTY		
YOU FEEL THAT EVERYTHING HAS CHANGED, AND NOTHING	98	JOURNE
IS WHAT IT SEEMED TO BE.		
THE FOG AND THE SEA SEEMED PART OF EACH OTHER.	131	JOURNE
JESUS LOOKED INTO HIS FACE FOR WHAT SEEMED A LONG	277	LAZARU
TIME AND		
IT SEEMED IT WAS NOT THEY WHO DIED BUT DEATH	321	LAZARU
ITSELF THEY KILLED/		
BUT THEY SEEMED AS HAPPY AS IF HIS LAUGHTER HAD	342	LAZARU
POSSESSED THEM/		
HE SEEMED NOT TO SUFFER BUT TO BE IMPATIENT AND	30	MANSNS
EXASPERATED--		
HAVE SEEMED, THROUGH THE SUBTLE POWER OF MOTHER'S	73	MANSNS
FANTASTIC WILL,		
WHERE SHE HAD SEEMED A PREMATURELY OLD, MIDDLE-	95	MANSNS
AGED WOMAN THEN,		
THEY SEEMED SO MUCH MORE REAL THAN THE BOOK ONES.	109	MANSNS
HE SEEMED SO NERVOUS AND TIRED OUT AND DISTRACTED,	132	MANSNS
IT SEEMED THERE WOULD NEVER BE A MOMENT'S PEACE IN174		MANSNS
MY LIFE AGAIN--		
IT SEEMED TO ME HE WAS A BIT FEVERISH.	177	MANSNS
IT SEEMED THAT AT ANY MOMENT SHE MUST AWAKE AND	352	MARCOM
SPEAK/		
AND SEEMED SUCH A DEVOUT GIRL THAT HE FORGOT HIS	39	MISBEG
SUSPICIONS.		
HE SEEMED TOUCHED AND GRATEFUL.	134	MISBEG
IT SEEMED THAT WOULD BE THE IDEAL LIFE--FOR ME.	143	MISBEG
I SEEMED DEAD, TOO.	148	MISBEG
YOU SEEMED TO ENJOY IT THE WHILE WE WERE SITTING	168	MISBEG
HERE TOGETHER.		
I SEEMED TO DETECT A RESEMBLANCE--	118	POET
MOTHER SEEMED JEALOUS OF MY CONCERN....	5	STRANG
BEFORE I LEFT SHE SEEMED TO BE COMING OUT OF THAT	8	STRANG
HORRIBLE NUMBED CALM.		
SHE'S SEEMED ON THE VERGE ALL DAY...	12	STRANG
HER EYES SEEMED CYNICAL....	25	STRANG
I SEEMED TO FEEL GORDON STANDING AGAINST A WALL	45	STRANG
WITH EYES BANDAGED AND THESE MEN		
SEEMED STARING OUT OF HIS EYES WITH A BURNING	45	STRANG
PAIN/ AND I WOKE UP CRYING.		
SHE SEEMED DREADFULLY UPSET TO SEE CHARLIE WITH	50	STRANG
US.		
SEEMED TO TAKE A REAL PERSONAL INTEREST--	54	STRANG
THEY SEEMED TO LIKE EACH OTHER...	68	STRANG
STILL, NINA INSISTED ON GOING THAT SAME DAY AND	68	STRANG
MOTHER SEEMED ANXIOUS TO GET RID		
THAT SEEMED RIGHT THEN...	72	STRANG
I LOVED IT SO IT SEEMED AT TIMES THAT GORDON MUST	83	STRANG
BE ITS REAL FATHER,		
SHE SEEMED LONELY.	101	STRANG
DARRELL'S LOVE MUST HAVE SEEMED LIKE TREACHERY...	112	STRANG
(MALICIOUSLY) HE SEEMED IN FINE FEATHER--SAID HE	115	STRANG
WAS HAVING A GAY TIME.		
SEEMED TO BURN INSIDE MY HEAD....	125	STRANG
I--I DIDN'T KNOW--YOU SEEMED SO COLD--DAMN	130	STRANG
MARSDEN--HE SUSPECTS, DOESN'T HE?		
WHAT SAM ADVISED SEEMED ALWAYS THE BEST THING FOR	167	STRANG
GORDON'S FUTURE.		
THE WAITING AND HOPING SEEMED EXCESS LABOR.	467	WELDED
(AFTER A PAUSE) WAS THAT WHY YOU SEEMED SO HAPPY--482		WELDED
THERE--S		

SEEMING

HIS FACE SEEMING TO BECOME GENTLY SORROWFUL AND	257	AHWILD
OLD.		
HIS VOICE SEEMING TO PLEAD FOR HER FORBEARANCE!	20	ANNA
(SUDDENLY SEEMING TO COME TO A BOLD DECISION--WITH	50	ANNA
A DEFIANT GRIN AT CHRIS)		
(TO HIM--SEEMING NOT TO HAVE HEARD THEIR	58	ANNA
INTERRUPTIONS)		
(NOT SEEMING TO HAVE HEARD HER QUESTION--SADLY)	64	ANNA
(NOT SEEMING TO NOTICE THIS REMARK)	557	CRUSS
SEEMING TO BE MORE THAN EVER SNEERING AND	525	DAYS
SINISTER.)		
(STARES BEFORE HER, NOT SEEMING TO HAVE HEARD THIS539		DAYS
LAST--HER		
SEEMING PALE AND WASHED OUT BY CONTRAST.	203	DESIRE
WITHOUT SEEMING TO SEE THE TWO STIFF FIGURES AT	221	DESIRE
THE GATE)		
(NOT SEEMING TO HEAR HER--FIERCELY)	257	DESIRE
(HE GOES IN THE DOOR, NOT SEEMING TO HEAR.	259	DESIRE
HIS TWITCHING FINGERS SEEMING TO REACH OUT FOR HER261		DESIRE
THROAT)		
(SEEMING TO SHRIVEL UP IN HIS SON'S GRIP--	466	DYNAMO
SEEMING TO GROW TALL AND PROUD--THEN WITH A LAUGH	308	GGBROW
OF BOLD SELF-ASSURANCE)		

SEEMING (CONT'D.)

(FOR THE FIRST TIME SEEMING TO TAKE NOTICE OF THE	209	HA APE
UPROAR ABOUT HIM,		
(CHANTING A COUNT AS HE SHOVELS WITHOUT SEEMING	224	HA APE
EFFORT)		
(WITHOUT SEEMING TO SEE HIM,	237	HA APE
(BUT, WITHOUT SEEMING TO SEE HIM,	238	HA APE
(GOOD-NATUREDLY BUT SEEMING A LITTLE HURT)	624	ICEMAN
ALL LIFE SEEMING TO DRAIN FROM HER FACE,	120	JOURNE
(WITHOUT LOOKING AT HIM--HIS VOICE SEEMING TO COME292		LAZARU
FROM SOME DREAM WITH HIM)		
LAZARUS LOOKS AT THEM, SEEMING TO SEE EACH AND ALL307		LAZARU
AT THE SAME TIME,		
THE AURA OF LIGHTS SURROUNDING HIS BODY SEEMING TO312		LAZARU
GLOW MORE BRIGHTLY THAN EVER,		
SEEMING TO BE FILLED WITH A NERVOUS DREAD AND	326	LAZARU
TERROR OF EVERYTHING ABOUT HIM,		
SEEMING TO TAKE IN THE CONTENTS OF EACH AT A	70	MANSNS
GLANCE.		
(WHO HAS BEEN TAKING EVERYTHING IN WITHOUT SEEMING	42	MISBEG
TO)		
SEEMING/	45	POET
I WAS MERELY EXPLAINING MY SEEMING VANITY.	45	POET
FRAMED IN IRON-GRAY HAIR, SEEMING MUCH TOO LARGE	53	STRANG
FOR HER BODY.		
SHE LOOKS DOWN AT HIM, SEEMING TO MAKE UP HER MIND452		WELDED
TO SOMETHING--		

SEEMINGLY

SEEMINGLY UNCONSCIOUS OF EVERYTHING.	516	INZONE
HE IS SEEMINGLY UNAWARE OF THE DARK GLANCES OF	522	INZONE
SUSPICION		
(SEEMINGLY UNMOVED BY THIS TAUNT--CALMLY.)	106	POET

SEEMLY

IT IS NOT SEEMLY.	341	LAZARU

SEEMS

DURING WHICH SHE SEEMS TO BE ENDEAVORING TO	540	*ILE
COLLECT HER THOUGHTS)		
SEEMS LIKE SHE AIN'T JEST SATISFIED UP HERE,	542	*ILE
AILIN' LIKE--		
IT SEEMS SO LONG AGO--AS IF I'D BEEN DEAD AND	547	*ILE
COULD NEVER GO BACK.		
HER WHOLE ATTENTION SEEMS CENTERED IN THE ORGAN.	552	*ILE
SEEMS TO HAVE BLUNTED YOUR SENSE OF HUMOR.	192	AHWILD
SEEMS TO ME SHE MIGHT WAIT UNTIL THE FOURTH IS	192	AHWILD
OVER BEFORE BRINGING UP--		
THERE'S FINE THINGS IN IT, SEEMS TO ME--TRUE	198	AHWILD
THINGS.		
(BUT THE DISH OF OLIVES SEEMS TO FASCINATE HIM AND217		AHWILD
PRESENTLY HE HAS APPROACHED		
WHY, SEEMS TO ME IT WAS ONLY YESTERDAY HE WAS	217	AHWILD
STILL A BABY.		
THE MERE SMELL OF IT SEEMS TO DRIVE HER FRANTIC/	232	AHWILD
YOU'RE GROWING A LOT TOO BIG FOR YOUR SIZE, SEEMS	235	AHWILD
TO ME/		
SEEMS TO ME YOU'VE BEEN INVENTING A NEW SIGNATURE	251	AHWILD
EVERY WEEK LATELY.		
I'M THE ONLY ONE IN THIS HOUSE SEEMS TO CARE--(HER251		AHWILD
LIPS TREMBLE.)		
HIS MOUTH PULLS DOWN AT THE CORNERS AND HE SEEMS	257	AHWILD
ABOUT TO CRY.		
SEEMS TO ME THAT YOU'VE BEEN JUST ITCHING FOR IT	264	AHWILD
LATELY/		
SEEMS TO ME YOU WOKE UP PRETTY QUICK--JUST AFTER	269	AHWILD
YOUR PA LEFT THE HOUSE/		
SEEMS TO ME I'VE HEARD SOMEONE SAY THAT BEFORE,	272	AHWILD
IT SEEMS AGES SINCE WE'VE BEEN TOGETHER/	279	AHWILD
BUT SHE SEEMS TO GET SOME QUEER SATISFACTION OUT	291	AHWILD
OF FUSSING OVER HIM LIKE A HEN		
SEEMS MUSHY AND SILLY--BUT THAT MEANT SOMETHING/	297	AHWILD
CHRIS SEEMS ON THE VERGE OF SPEAKING, HESITATES,	10	ANNA
HE SEEMS CONSIDERABLY SOBERED UP)	19	ANNA
IT ALL SEEMS LIKE I'D BEEN HERE BEFORE LOTS OF	28	ANNA
TIMES--ON BOATS--		
(HIS KNEES SAG, HE WAVERS AND SEEMS ABOUT TO FALL.	39	ANNA
CHRIS SEEMS IN A STUPOR OF DESPAIR, HIS HOUSE OF	58	ANNA
CARDS FALLEN ABOUT HIM.		
(SOFTENED) SEEMS TO ME YOU'VE CHANGED YOUR TUNE A	65	ANNA
LOT.		
(A STRANGE TERROR SEEMS SUDDENLY TO SEIZE HER.	68	ANNA
(SUDDENLY SEEMS TO HAVE A SOLUTION.	74	ANNA
SHE NEVER SEEMS TO GET ANY BETTER OR ANY WORSE.	87	BEYOND
AWAY AND YOU AND I--WHY IT SEEMS AS IF WE'D ALWAYS	85	BEYOND
BEEN TOGETHER.		
BECAUSE--FRANKLY IT SEEMS SUCH A SHAME,	88	BEYOND
(A SUDDEN UNEASINESS SEEMS TO STRIKE HIM)	96	BEYOND
SEEMS TO ME IT'S A PRETTY SLICK PLACE RIGHT NOW.	97	BEYOND
(SEVERELY) SEEMS TO ME IT'S A PRETTY LATE HOUR IN100		BEYOND
THE DAY FOR YOU TO BE		
SEEMS TO ME I'VE GOT A RIGHT TO HAVE MY SAY.	103	BEYOND
(FROWNING) SEEMS TO ME THIS AIN'T NO SUBJECT TO	105	BEYOND
JOKE OVER--NOT FOR ANDY.		
SEEMS TO HAVE PENETRATED INDOORS.	112	BEYOND
IT SEEMS MORE LIKE THREE HUNDRED.	115	BEYOND
SEEMS AS IF SHE CRIES ALL THE TIME ON PURPOSE TO	116	BEYOND
SET A BODY'S NERVES ON EDGE.		
THE OLD EASY-GOING GOOD-NATURE SEEMS TO HAVE BEEN	130	BEYOND
PARTLY LOST IN A BREEZY,		
SEEMS AS IF NOW THAT YOU'RE BACK IT WOULDN'T BE	137	BEYOND
NEEDFUL.		
IT ALL SEEMS TRIFLING, SOMEHOW.	138	BEYOND
AND NOW--IT SEEMS--WELL--AS IF YOU'D ALWAYS BEEN	139	BEYOND
MY SISTER, THAT'S WHAT, RUTH.		
EVERYBODY HEREABOUTS SEEMS TO BE ON EDGE TODAY.	140	BEYOND
THE CAPTAIN SEEMS SCARCELY TO HAVE CHANGED AT ALL	140	BEYOND
IT SEEMS HARD TO RIGHT AWAY AGAIN WHEN I'VE	141	BEYOND
JUST GOT HOME.		
AS HE PEERS OUT HIS BODY SEEMS GRADUALLY TO SAG,	150	BEYOND
TO GROW LIMP AND TIRED.		

SEEMS

SEEMS (CONT'D.)
HIS FACE SEEMS TO HAVE GROWN HIGHSTRUNG, 153 BEYOND
THE APPLE TREE IS LEAFLESS AND SEEMS DEAD. 166 BEYOND
HE SEEMS BETTER NOW. 480 CARDIF
(YANK SEEMS COMFORTED BY THIS ASSURANCE.) 483 CARDIF
STARING TOWARD THE SPOT ON SHORE WHERE THE SINGING456 CARIBE
SEEMS TO COME FROM.)
(QUIETLY) SEEMS NICE AND SLEEPY-LIKE. 466 CARIBE
ALTHOUGH THE GENERAL IDEA SEEMS TO BE A BATTLE 472 CARIBE
BETWEEN SEAMEN AND FIREMEN.
HE POUNDS AGAINST THE SLIDE, WHICH SEEMS TO HAVE 572 CROSS
BEEN SHUT DOWN ON HIM.)
(WITH A WINK AT ELIOT) HE SEEMS TO BE FIXED IN 504 DAYS
HIS LAST RELIGION.
(THE PRIEST GIVES A SWIFT, REPROACHFUL LOOK AT 510 DAYS
JOHN, SEEMS ABOUT TO PROTEST,
THERE'S NOTHING WRONG, EXCEPT WHAT SEEMS TO BE 517 DAYS
WRONG WITH EVERY ONE.
SHE SEEMS TO HAVE TAKEN HER END IN YOUR STORY VERY551 DAYS
SERIOUSLY.
DAMN IT, SHE SEEMS TO WANT TO DIE. 557 DAYS
(SUDDENLY HE SEEMS TO SEE FATHER BAIRD FUR THE 558 DAYS
FIRST TIME--WITH A CRY OF APPEAL--
(AS IF THIS WERE A MORTAL BLOW, SEEMS TO SAG AND 566 DAYS
COLLAPSE--WITH A CHOKING CRY)
A SUDDEN HORRIBLE THOUGHT SEEMS TO ENTER CABOT'S 225 DESIRE
HEAD)
EBEN SEEMS TO FEEL HER PRESENCE. 228 DESIRE
HE SEEMS IN SOME QUEER WAY SOFTENED, MELLOWED. 230 DESIRE
SHE SEEMS DRIVEN INTU A DECISION--GOES OUT THE 239 DESIRE
DOOR IN REAR DETERMINEDLY.
I BUT HER EYES ARE FIXED ON HIS SO BURNINGLY THAT 240 DESIRE
HIS WILL SEEMS TO WITHER
(THIS SEEMS TO AROUSE CONNOTATIONS. 241 DESIRE
NOW--SINCE YEW COME--SEEMS LIKE IT'S GROWIN' SOFT 242 DESIRE
AN' KIND T' ME.
(IN A WHISPER) SEEMS LIKE MAW DIDN'T WANT ME T' 242 DESIRE
REMIND YE.
HE SEEMS CHANGED. 244 DESIRE
(MEANINGILY) SEEMS LIKE HE'S SPENT MOST U' HIS 248 DESIRE
TIME T' HUM SINCE YEW COME.
ABBIE SEEMS TO SENSE SOMETHING. 252 DESIRE
WAAL, SEEMS LIKE THEY ALL WENT ASHORE ON THEM 502 DIFRNT
ISLANDS TO GIT WATER AND THE
WAAL, SEEMS 'S IF HE KEPT ABUARD MINDIN' HIS OWN 502 DIFRNT
BUSINESS.
(BITTERLY) WHICH NOBODY ELSE SEEMS TO. 508 DIFRNT
(EMMA SEEMS ABOUT TO SPEAK BUT STOPS HELPLESSLY 513 DIFRNT
AFTER ONE GLANCE AT HER FATHER.)
BUT IT'S ALL SU DEAD AND GONE IT SEEMS A LONG 521 DIFRNT
WHILE.
THE TURN THE CONVERSATION HAS TAKEN SEEMS TO HAVE 526 DIFRNT
AROUSED A HECTIC,
(A PAUSE) SEEMS TO ME, EMMER, 538 DIFRNT
(AFTER A PAUSE) SOMEHOW--SEEMS TO ME 'S IF--YOU 539 DIFRNT
MIGHT REALY NEED ME NOW.
NO MATTER HOW DREADFUL IT SEEMS TO YOU! 439 DYNAMO
YOU'RE ALWAYS HAVING TO GO OUT THESE DAYS, IT 479 DYNAMO
SEEMS!
(THE COCKNEY SEEMS ABOUT TO CHALLENGE THIS LAST 176 EJONES
STATEMENT WITH THE FACTS BUT
SEEMS LIKE FUTEYAH! 191 EJONES
THE GUARD SEEMS TO WAIT EXPECTANTLY, HIS BACK 195 EJONES
TURNED TO THE ATTACKER.
GRADUALLY IT SEEMS TO GROW LIGHTER IN THE ENCLOSED198 EJONES
SPACE AND TWO ROWS OF SEATED
I REMEMBER--SEEMS LIKE I BEEN HEAH BEFO'. 200 EJONES
SEEMS LIKE I KNOW DAT TREE--AN' DEM STONES--AN ' 200 EJONES
DE RIVER.
THEN HE SEEMS TO COME TO HIMSELF PARTLY, 200 EJONES
JONES SEEMS TO SENSE THE MEANING OF THIS. 201 EJONES
THE TOM-TOM SEEMS ON THE VERY SPOT, 202 EJONES
SEEMS AS IF WE HADN'T SEEN YOU IN AGES/. 13 ELECTR
(GRUMPILY) HE SEEMS TO HAVE HAD PLENTY OF 15 ELECTR
ROMANTIC EXPERIENCE.
HE SEEMS TO HAVE BEEN SICK SO MUCH THIS PAST YEAR. 17 ELECTR
I WANT TO KNOW ALL I CAN ABOUT HIM BECAUSE--HE 18 ELECTR
SEEMS TO BE CALLING TO COURT ME.
INCREDIBLE AS THAT SEEMS NOW/ 31 ELECTR
CHRISTINE SEEMS CONSIDERING SOMETHING. 34 ELECTR
THE PURE WHITE TEMPLE FRONT SEEMS MORE THAN EVER 43 ELECTR
LIKE AN INCONGRUOUS MASK
IT SEEMS TO ME A LATE DAY, WHEN I AM AN OLD WOMAN 51 ELECTR
WITH GROWN-UP CHILDREN,
IT SEEMS A LIFETIME/ 72 ELECTR
GOSH, IT SEEMS NATURAL TO HEAR MYSELF CALLING YOU 75 ELECTR
THAT OLD NICKNAME AGAIN.
CHRISTINE STARES AFTER HER, HER STRENGTH SEEMS TO 78 ELECTR
LEAVE HER.
IT SEEMS ONLY YESTERDAY WHEN I USED TO FIND YOU IN 90 ELECTR
YOUR NIGHTSHIRT
CHRISTINE SEEMS DRUNK WITH HER OWN DEFIANT 92 ELECTR
RECKLESSNESS)
THE SOUND OF THE SINGING SEEMS TO STRIKE A 102 ELECTR
RESPONSIVE CHORD IN HIS BRAIN.
SHE SEEMS A MATURE WOMAN, SURE OF HER FEMININE 139 ELECTR
ATTRACTIVENESS.
SHE SEEMS SUDDENLY WEAK AND FRIGHTENED.) 146 ELECTR
SEEMS HALF TO COME BACK TO HIS NATURAL SELF 156 ELECTR
(HER VOICE TREMBLES AND SHE SEEMS ABOUT TO BURST 159 ELECTR
INTO TEARS)
SHE SEEMS ABOUT TO LET HIM GO.) 287 GGBROW
HE SEEMS TO GAIN STRENGTH AND IS ABLE TO FORCE A 307 GGBROW
SAD LAUGH)
THE SEEMS TO HEAR SOME MOCKING DENIAL FROM THE 307 GGBROW
MASK.
FINALLY A VOICE SEEMS TORN OUT OF HIM. 319 GGBROW
(HE SEEMS TO WAIT FOR AN ANSWER-- 319 GGBROW

SEEMS (CONT'D.)
HE SEEMS BROADER, FIERCER, MORE TRUCULENT, MORE 208 HA APE
POWERFUL.
HIS BIG HEAD SQUATS ON A NECK WHICH SEEMS PART OF 8 HUGHIE
HIS BEEFY SHOULDERS.
(THE NIGHT CLERK SEEMS TURNED INTO A DROOPING WAX- 16 HUGHIE
WORK, DRAPED ALONG THE DESK.
THE SEEMS TO RUN DOWN, AND IS OVERCOME BY 57? ICEMAN
DRUNKENESS.
AFTER 'BOUT AN HOUR, SEEMS LIKE TO ME, 601 ICEMAN
BEJEES, HICKEY, IT SEEMS NATURAL TO SEE YOUR UGLY,619 ICEMAN
GRINNING MAP.
SEEMS TO BE DRUNK. 629 ICEMAN
HUGO SEEMS ASLEEP IN HIS HABITUAL POSITION) 651 ICEMAN
(HE STOPS ABRUPTLY AND FOR A SECOND HE SEEMS TO 657 ICEMAN
LOSE HIS SELF-ASSURANCE.
HE SEEMS GROTESQUELY LIKE A HARRIED FAMILY MAN. 670 ICEMAN
HE SEEMS SUDDENLY AT PEACE WITH HIMSELF. 720 ICEMAN
FINALLY HE SEEMS TO SENSE THE HOSTILE ATMOSPHERE 523 INZONE
OF THE FORECASTLE AND LOOKS
HE SEEMS TALLER AND SLENDERER BECAUSE OF HIS 13 JOURNE
BEARING.
WELL, IT SEEMS THERE'S A BREAK IN THE FENCE 23 JOURNE
WHY DO YOU SAY, SEEMS 37 JOURNE
(HESITANTLY.) OUTSIDE OF NERVES, SHE SEEMS 37 JOURNE
PERFECTLY ALL RIGHT THIS MORNING.
HE SEEMS TO BE LISTENING FOR SOME SOUND FROM 51 JOURNE
UPSTAIRS.
SHE SEEMS NOT TO NOTICE, BUT SHE MOVES 68 JOURNE
INSTINCTIVELY AWAY.)
WHICH SEEMS TO STAND APART FROM HER NERVES AND THE 71 JOURNE
ANXIETIES WHICH HARRY THEM.
HER VOICE SEEMS TO DRIFT FARTHER AND FARTHER 87 JOURNE
AWAY.)
SHE SEEMS TO HAVE FORGOTTEN THE TEARS WHICH ARE 91 JOURNE
STILL IN HER EYES.)
BATTLE, BUT SUDDENLY HE SEEMS TO SOBER UP TO A 162 JOURNE
SHOCKED REALIZATION OF WHAT HE
IT SEEMS FOR A SECOND HE IS GOING TO HIDE IN THE 169 JOURNE
BACK PARLOR.
EXPERIENCE SEEMS IRONED OUT OF IT. 170 JOURNE
SHE SEEMS AWARE OF THEM MERELY AS SHE IS AWARE OF 170 JOURNE
OTHER OBJECTS IN THE ROOM.
(FOR A SECOND HE SEEMS TO HAVE BROKEN THROUGH TO 174 JOURNE
HER.
THAT STRANGE LIGHT SEEMS TO COME FROM WITHIN HIM/ 275 LAZARU
NOW HE SEEMS AS BROWN AS ONE WHO HAS LABORED IN 276 LAZARU
THE EARTH ALL DAY IN A VINEYARD
MAJESTIC FIGURE WHOSE UNDERSTANDING SMILE SEEMS 278 LAZARU
TERRIBLE AND ENIGMATIC TO THEM.)
HE SEEMS TEN YEARS YOUNGER, AT THE PRIME OF FORTY.288 LAZARU
TO EACH HE SEEMS TO LOOK AT HIM OR HER ALONE. 291 LAZARU
THIS SEEMS TO RELEASE THEM FROM THEIR FIXED 291 LAZARU
POSITIONS.
LAZARUS SEEMS NOT TO HEAR HIM. 316 LAZARU
HE SEEMS NO MORE THAN THIRTY. 317 LAZARU
WHOSE LAUGHTER SEEMS NOW TO HAVE ATTAINED 320 LAZARU
THEIR LAUGHTER SEEMS TO SHAKE THE WALLS 321 LAZARU
SEEMS MORE THAN EVER A FIGURE OF A SAD, RESIGNED 327 LAZARU
MOTHER OF THE DEAD.
ONE FROM AFRICA SEEMS ALMOST GONE. 329 LAZARU
HE SEEMS ABSOLUTELY UNAWARE OF POMPEIA. 343 LAZARU
HE SEEMS MORE YOUTHFUL STILL NOW. 350 LAZARU
IN THE HALF-DARKNESS, THE WALLS ARE LOST IN 350 LAZARU
SHADOW, THE ROOM SEEMS IMMENSE.
SUDDENLY THE SILENCE SEEMS TO CRUSH DOWN UPON HIM.370 LAZARU
(SUDDENLY SEEMS TO LOOSE HERSELF--ARROGANTLY.) 13 MANSNS
THEIR DISCONTENT SEEMS MEAN AND SELFISH. 17 MANSNS
DEBORAH NOW SEEMS MUCH OLDER THAN HER FORTY-NINE 27 MANSNS
YEARS.
THAT AFTERNOON AT THE CABIN WITH SIMON SEEMS A 29 MANSNS
LIFETIME AGO.
HE SEEMS TO HAVE CAREFULLY FOLLOWED SIMON'S 34 MANSNS
CAREER.
HE SEEMS TO FEEL SO ANTAGONISTIC TO ME BECAUSE I 66 MANSNS
DIDN'T ANSWER A FEW LETTERS.
AND MORE AND MORE IT SEEMS HE IS TALKING TO 72 MANSNS
HIMSELF.)
HAS GROWN A LITTLE MORE MATRONLY, PERHAPS, BUT 75 MANSNS
SEEMS NO OLDER.
UNTIL NOTHING IS WHAT IT SEEMS TO BE, AND WE ALL 82 MANSNS
GET SUSPICIOUS OF EACH OTHER,
(PRETENDING TO GIVE IN.) I MUST ADMIT SHE SEEMS 84 MANSNS
SINCERE.
HER MOUTH SEEMS LARGER, ITS FULL LIPS REDDER, 139 MANSNS
MY BROTHER SEEMS TO BE LATE EVERY DAY NOW. 140 MANSNS
BUT THERE IS A STARTLING CHANGE IN HIS MANNER, 140 MANSNS
WHICH NOW SEEMS WEAK, INSECURE,
(ALL AT ONCE HE SEEMS TO COLLAPSE INSIDE. 155 MANSNS
AND SO PALE IT SEEMS BLOODLESS AND CORPSE-LIKE, A 161 MANSNS
MASK OF DEATH,
(BUT NEITHER WOMAN SEEMS TO HEAR.) 188 MANSNS
(A FLASH OF INSULTED PRIDE COMES TO HER EYES AND 193 MANSNS
FOR A SECOND SHE SEEMS
HER CALM EXPRESSION SEEMS TO GLOW WITH THE INTENSE352 MARCOM
PEACE OF A LIFE BEYOND DEATH,
HE SEEMS TO HAVE TAKEN A FANCY TO MARK. 162 MARCOM
IT SEEMS AN IRISHMAN GOT DRUNK IN TANGUT AND 374 MARCOM
WANDERED INTO A TEMPLE.
THE RIVER SEEMS BLACK INDEED! 386 MARCOM
HIS HONOR, MARCO POLO, MAYOR OF YANG-CHAU, SEEMS 386 MARCOM
ABOUT TO VISIT YOU IN STATE/
LOVE IS TO WISDOM WHAT WISDOM SEEMS TO LOVE--A 389 MARCOM
FOLLY.
FINALLY IT SEEMS TO TURN A CORNER NEARBY, AND A 402 MARCOM
MOMENT LATER,
(SHE SEEMS NOT TO HEAR OR TO SEE THEM BUT STARES 417 MARCOM
AHEAD STONILY.

SEEMS

SEEMS	(CONT'D.)	
BUT SHE SEEMS FUCKED TO STUF.	417 MARCU..	
HE IS STURDILY BUILT, BUT SEEMS ALMOST PUNY	3 MISBEG	
(IGNORING THIS) AND WHISKEY SEEMS TO HAVE NO	33 MISBEG	
EFFECT ON HIM.		
WHILE HE SEEMS INTENT ON HIS PIPE.)	43 MISBEG	
WELL, IT SEEMS HE HAS AN ICE POND ON HIS ESTATE.	47 MISBEG	
HE SEEMS MUCH THE SAME AS IN ACT ONE.	100 MISBEG	
THE OUTSIDE'S NOW MORE THAN EVER SEEMS IT RICH TO	104 MISBEG	
DIE.		
STILL, IT SEEMS TO BELONG TONIGHT--IN THE	104 MISBEG	
MOONLIGHT--OR IN MY MIND--		
THE SEEMS ABOUT TO BREAK DOWN AND SOB BUT HE	111 MISBEG	
FIGHTS THIS BACK)		
HE SEEMS TO BE LAPSING AGAIN INTO VAGUE	115 MISBEG	
PREOCCUPATION.)		
BUT IT SEEMS LIKE TONIGHT.	128 MISBEG	
I SUPPOSE BECAUSE IT SEEMS CRAZY FOR YOU TO HOLD	130 MISBEG	
MY BIG UGLY PAW SO TENDERLY.		
OUR MOONLIGHT ROMANCE SEEMS TO BE A FLOP, JOSIE.	139 MISBEG	
GOD SEEMS TO BE PUTTING ON QUITE A DISPLAY.	172 MISBEG	
IT SEEMS CRAZY TO ME, WHEN I THINK OF WHAT PEOPLE	29 POET	
ARE LIKE.		
YOUNG MARSDEN SEEMS A DECENT LAD.	31 POET	
(HE GETS UP--BITTERLY.) AS THE SIGHT OF ME SEEMS	63 POET	
TO IRRITATE HER.		
FOR A SECOND IT SEEMS HE WILL KISS HER AND SHE	71 POET	
CANNOT HELP HERSELF.		
SHE SEEMS A KIND LADY.	75 POET	
HE SEEMS TO SHRINK BACK GUILTILY WITHIN HIMSELF.	89 POET	
HE SEEMS OBLIVIOUS TO HIS SURROUNDINGS.	95 POET	
SEEMS LOUDER.	163 POET	
(HE PATS NORA'S HAND WITH WHAT SEEMS TO BE GENUINE168 POET		
COMFORTING AFFECTION.)		
THE OLD MAN WATCHES HER WITH EAGER EYES AND SEEMS 596 ROPE		
TO BE TRYING TO SMILE.		
THE ROPE SEEMS TO PART WHERE IT IS FIXED TO THE	601 ROPE	
MEAN.		
SEEM IMPOSSIBLE SHE'S BEEN DEAD SIX YEARS...	5 STRANG	
IT SEEMS TO ME WHEN YOU GAVE HIM YOUR LOVE,	19 STRANG	
SEEMS LIKE GOOD EGG....	29 STRANG	
(IMAGINING) (SHE CERTAINLY SEEMS ALL FOR ME...	31 STRANG	
(AS MARSDEN SEEMS AGAIN ABOUT TO PROTEST)	35 STRANG	
HER WHOLE PERSONALITY SEEMS CHANGED. HER FACE HAS	46 STRANG	
A CONTENTED EXPRESSION.		
HE SEEMS MUCH THINNER, HIS FACE DRAWN AND SALLOW.	67 STRANG	
IT SEEMS COWARDLY....	72 STRANG	
HE SEEMS A PREY TO SOME INNER FEAR HE IS TRYING TO	73 STRANG	
HIDE EVEN FROM HIMSELF AND IS		
(LOOKING AFTER HER--THINKS) (SHE SEEMS BETTER	73 STRANG	
TONIGHT....		
SHE SEEMS TO LOVE ME...	73 STRANG	
THIS TALK OF HAPPINESS SEEMS TO ME EXTRANEOUS...))	86 STRANG	
THAT SEEMS TO HER SO RIGHT AND THEN SO WRONG/	87 STRANG	
SHE SEEMS NERVELESS AND DEEPLY CALM.	90 STRANG	
(HE SEEMS ABOUT TO SUB--THEN ABRUPTLY SPRINGS TO	101 STRANG	
HIS FEET WILDLY)		
SHE SEEMS TO GROW OLDER.	109 STRANG	
IT SEEMS INSIDIOUS SOMEHOW/....	119 STRANG	
IT SEEMS TO ME YOU'RE COMPLAINING UNREASONABLY/	131 STRANG	
ONLY THE OTHER MATE, NED, SEEMS TO HAVE SUFFERED	134 STRANG	
DETERIORATION.)		
HE SEEMS TO HAVE SPRUNG FROM A LINE DISTINCT FROM	137 STRANG	
ANY OF THE PEOPLE WE HAVE		
NOW, NOTHING ABOUT LOVE SEEMS IMPORTANT ENOUGH TO	149 STRANG	
BE REVOLTING...		
MY FATE IS MERCILESS, IT SEEMS/...))	150 STRANG	
DARRELL SEEMS TO HAVE THROWN BACK/	158 STRANG	
SEEMS TO ME YOU COULD SHOW A LITTLE MORE INTEREST	162 STRANG	
WITHOUT IT HURTING YOU.		
(EVEN MARSDEN SEEMS TO HAVE LEFT HER FOR THE	162 STRANG	
DEAD....))		
DARRELL REMAINS STANDING AND SEEMS TO BE A LITTLE	165 STRANG	
UNEASY.)		
IT SEEMS TO ME IF I WERE IN GORDON'S SHOES I'D DO	168 STRANG	
EXACTLY WHAT HE HAS DONE.		
THERE'S A YOUNG LADY WHO SEEMS TO CARE A LOT	168 STRANG	
WHETHER GORDON COMES IN LAST OR		
(EXCITEDLY) THE ONE IN THE MIDDLE SEEMS TO BE	180 STRANG	
AHEAD!		
(IT SEEMS ROTTEN AND SELFISH TO BE HAPPY...	189 STRANG	
(EVAN SEEMS TO SEE THE WOMEN FOR THE FIRST TIME	500 VOYAGE	
AND GRINS FOOLISHLY.)		
SHE HEARS IT, STARTS, SEEMS SUDDENLY BROUGHT BACK	449 WELDED	
TO HERSELF.		
IT SEEMS AT TIMES AS IF SOME JEALOUS DEMON OF THE	452 WELDED	
COMMONPLACE WERE MOCKING US.		
(THIS SEEMS TO GOAD HIM TO DESPERATION)	453 WELDED	
BUT IT SEEMS TO ME YOUR BRAND OF IT IS MUCH MORE	457 WELDED	
RIDICULOUS.		
HER FACE SEEMS SUDDENLY TO CONGEAL/	459 WELDED	
(SHE STARES INTO HIS EYES AND SEEMS TO READ SOME	459 WELDED	
CONFIRMATION OF HER STATEMENT		
SHE SEEMS ABOUT TO IMPLORE HIM NOT TO SPEAK.)	484 WELDED	
HE SEEMS TO COLLECT ALL HIS FORCES AND TURNS ON	486 WELDED	
HER WITH A FIERCE CHALLENGE)		
SEEPING		
AND IT WAS SO STILL YOU COULD HEAR THE FOG SEEPING	95 ELECTR	
INTO THE GROUND.		
SEEPS		
AND SEEPS DOWN INTO THE ROOM.	555 CRUSS	
SEES		
(SEES THE SLIPS FOR THE FIRST TIME AND IS OVERCOME207 AHWILD		
BY EMBARRASSMENT.		
(AS SHE SEES MILLER ABOUT TO EXPLODE--INTERPOSES	229 AHWILD	
TACTFULLY)		
(BEAMING NOW THAT HE SEES HIS TROUBLES	11 ANNA	
DISAPPEARING)		

(CONT'D.)

SHE GIVES A START WHEN SHE SEES BURKE SO NEAR HER,	31 ANNA	
(FURIOUSLY, AS HE SEES THIS IS MAKING NO	32 ANNA	
IMPRESSION ON HER)		
(AS HE SEES CHRIS--IN A JOVIAL TONE OF MOCKERY)	45 ANNA	
(WITH PLEASED SURPRISE AS SHE SEES BURKE)	50 ANNA	
(HE SEES HER BAG AND GIVES A START)	64 ANNA	
(OUT SHE SEES THE LOOK OF OBSESSED STUBBORNNESS ON	66 ANNA	
HER FATHER'S FACE		
(HIS VOICE DIES AWAY AS HE SEES THE PAIN IN	101 BEYOND	
ANOTHER'S EYES.)		
(HE SEES AT ONCE THE FIXED RESOLVE IN HIS	104 BEYOND	
BROTHER'S EYES.		
MAYBE ROBBIE'LL MANAGE TILL ANDY GETS BACK AND	115 BEYOND	
SEES TO THINGS.		
(SEES THE DOLL UNDER THE TABLE AND STRUGGLES ON	117 BEYOND	
HER MOTHER'S LAP.		
EVEN IF HE DID TALK THEM WAY UP IN THE AIR, LIKE	163 BEYOND	
HE ALWAYS SEES THINGS.		
(MODE KINDLY AS HE SEES DRISCOLL'S GRIEF)	485 CARDIF	
THEY SAY HE SEES EVERYTHING.	488 CARDIF	
(COCKY SEES DRISCOLL AND STANDS STARING AT HIM	490 CARDIF	
WITH OPEN MOUTH.		
DOWN'T DRINK IT ALL AFORE WE SEES IT.	461 CARIBE	
OELLA SEES HIM)	465 CARIBE	
SHE SHUTS THE DOOR BEHIND HER, SEES SMITTY ON THE	466 CARIBE	
HATCH.		
HE JUMPS TO HIS FEET WITH HIS FISTS CLENCHED BUT	471 CARIBE	
SEES WHO HIT HIM AND SITS DOWN		
(HE SEES THE MAN LYING ON THE DECK)	472 CARIBE	
(THE MATE ROLLS PADDY OVER AND SEES A KNIFE WOUND	472 CARIBE	
ON HIS SHOULDER.)		
THE MATE LOOKS UP AND SEES THE WOMEN ON THE HATCH	473 CARIBE	
FOR THE FIRST TIME.)		
HE SEES AND HEARS ONLY JOHN, EVEN WHEN LOVING	496 DAYS	
SPEAKS.		
THIS IS--THE SEES ELIOT AND STOPS, A BIT	500 DAYS	
EMBARRASSED.)		
HE SEES IT CLEARLY AS A THROWBACK TO BOYHOOD	544 DAYS	
EXPERIENCES.		
HE SEES CLEARLY BY THE LIGHT OF REASON THE	545 DAYS	
DEGRADATION OF HIS PITIABLE SURRENDER		
AT WHAT HE SEES (HERE HE BOWS HIS HEAD AND HIS	566 DAYS	
LIPS MOVE IN GRATEFUL PRAYER.		
(SEES THE BROTHERS.	222 DESIRE	
ABBIE SEES HIM AND TURNS AWAY QUICKLY WITH	230 DESIRE	
UNCONCEALED AVERSION.		
SHE STARTS VIOLENTLY, LOOKS AT HIM, SEES HE IS NOT236 DESIRE		
WATCHING HER.		
I SEES WHY.	243 DESIRE	
(WITH A WINK AT THE OTHERS) YE'RE THE SPRYEST	250 DESIRE	
SEVENTY-SIX EVER I SEES, EPHRAIM/		
HE SEES EBEN AND HIS WHOLE MOOD IMMEDIATELY	253 DESIRE	
CHANGES.		
(SUDDENLY TRIUMPHANT WHEN HE SEES HOW SHAKEN EBEN	255 DESIRE	
IS)		
SEES ABBIE--WITH SATISFACTION)	263 DESIRE	
(HE TURNS--SEES NO ONE THERE--	263 DESIRE	
NO, ALL KIDDIN' ASIDE, I KNOW HE'LL RUN ME DOWN	523 DIFRNT	
FIRST SECOND HE SEES YOU.		
I WANT TO SPEAK TO HER AND FIND OUT HOW I STAND	527 DIFRNT	
BEFORE HE SEES ME.		
(ANGRILY) YOUR UNCLE CALEB'LL GIVE YOU A REST	529 DIFRNT	
WHEN HE SEES YOU/		
(AS SHE THINKS SHE SEES A RELENTING SOFTNESS COME	543 DIFRNT	
INTO HIS FACE AS HE LOOKS DOWN		
(STOPS SHORT AS HE SEES THE PILE ON THE FLOOR)	548 DIFRNT	
(HE LOOKS AT HER AND SEES SHE IS NOT LISTENING ANY429 DYNAMO		
MORE)		
(HE SEES THE NEWSPAPER ON THE TABLE AND REACHES	430 DYNAMO	
FOR IT.		
LOOKS UP AROUND THE CORNER OF THE HEDGE AND SEES	436 DYNAMO	
HER AND IMMEDIATELY DISSOLVES		
HE SEES HIS FATHER AND A SNEERING SMILE	462 DYNAMO	
IMMEDIATELY COMES TO HIS LIPS)		
(THEN, AS HE SEES REUBEN SHRINKING BACK IN HIS	466 DYNAMO	
CHAIR,		
STEPS INSIDE AND, AS SHE SEES REUBEN,	479 DYNAMO	
(SHE SEES THE REVOLVER AIMED AT HER BREAST AS HE	488 DYNAMO	
STOPS DIRECTLY BENEATH HER--		
HE SEES THE WOMAN AND STOPS TO WATCH HER	174 EJUNES	
SUSPICIOUSLY.		
AND WHEN I SEES OFSE NIGGERS GITTIN' UP DEIR NERVE180 EJONES		
TO TU'N ME OUT,		
DEN, WHEN I SEES TROUBLE COMIN', I MAKES MY	180 EJONES	
GETAWAY.		
(HE SEES THE FIRST WHITE STONE AND CRAWLS TO IT	188 EJONES	
WITH SATISFACTION)		
NOW YOU SEES WHEN YO'SE GWINE.	191 EJONES	
MAN THAT HE SEES--IN A TUNE OF HAPPY RELIEF)	192 EJONES	
(HE WALKS QUICKLY INTO THE CLEAR SPACE--THEN	192 EJONES	
STANDS TRANSFIXED AS HE SEES JEFF--		
ABOUT HIM WITH NUMBED SURPRISE WHEN HE SEES THE	193 EJONES	
ROAD.		
UNMINDFUL OF THEIR NOISELESS APPROACH, SUDDENLY	194 EJONES	
LOOKS DOWN AND SEES THEM.		
LOOKS WILDLY FOR SOME OPENING TO ESCAPE, SEES	197 EJONES	
NONE.		
JONES LOOKS UP, SEES THE FIGURES ON ALL SIDES,	197 EJONES	
JONES STARTS, LOOKS UP, SEES THE FIGURES,	199 EJONES	
THEN SEES SHE HAS NOT NOTICED THEIR PRESENCE AND	10 ELECTR	
STOPS AND STANDS WAITING.		
(THEN HASTILY AS HE SEES SOMEONE COMING UP THE	12 ELECTR	
DRIVE)		
(THEN SHE SEES PETER, WHO IS VISIBLY EMBARRASSED	16 ELECTR	
BY HER PRESENCE)		
(SHE TURNS AND SEES SETH WHO HAS JUST COME TO THE	18 ELECTR	
CORNER OF THE HOUSE, LEFT.		

SEES

(CONT'D.)

(THEN AS SHE SEES HER MOTHER'S ASTONISHMENT-- 32 ELECTR GRIMLY)

(SEES THE PORTRAIT FOR THE FIRST TIME. 36 ELECTR AS SHE SEES HE IS DEFINITELY WON OVER NOW. 42 ELECTR THEN SUDDENLY SEES LAVINIA ON THE STEPS AND STOPS 44 ELECTR ABRUPTLY, A BIT SHEEPISH--

(THEN WARNINGLY, MAKING A SURREPTITIOUS SIGNAL AS 45 ELECTR HE SEES THE FRONT DOOR OPENING BEFORE I KNEW HE'S THE KIND WHO CHASES AFTER EVERY 50 ELECTR WOMAN HE SEES.

WATCH HER WHEN SHE SEES THAT--IF YOU WANT PROOF/ 100 ELECTR (HER EYES SHIFT FROM HIS FACE AND SHE SEES THE BOX101 ELECTR OF POISON.

SHE SEES THE FIGURE ON THE DECK ABOVE HER 107 ELECTR SHE SEES SOMEONE SHE IS EVIDENTLY EXPECTING 117 ELECTR APPROACHING THE HOUSE FROM UP THE

I WANT TO BE THE ONE-- (HE SEES HIS MOTHER-- 120 ELECTR STARTLEDLY)

(SHE SEES SETH APPROACHING, WHISTLING LOUDLY, FROM137 ELECTR LEFT, REAR.

(THEN AS SHE SEES HE STILL KEEPS HIS EYES AVERTED 138 ELECTR FROM THE HOUSE)

AT THE SAME MOMENT SHE SEES HIM. 143 ELECTR (SHE SEES HIM AT THE WINDOW) 144 ELECTR I WANT YOU TO LOOK YOUR BEST WHEN SHE SEES YOU. 145 ELECTR AS SHE SEES HAZEL AND ORIN ARE ALONE. 162 ELECTR LAVINIA SEES THE MOVEMENT BUT DOESN'T FOR A MOMENT163 ELECTR REALIZE THE MEANING OF IT.

(SEES THE ENVELOPE IN PLAIN SIGHT AND CALLS TO HER163 ELECTR WARNINGLY) HAZEL/

(THEN WITH SUDDEN ANGER AS HE SEES THE GROWING 165 ELECTR HORRIFIED REPULSION ON HER FACE)

THEN SEES LAVINIA AND IMMEDIATELY MAKES AN EFFORT 174 ELECTR TO PULL HIMSELF TOGETHER AND

LOOKS AROUND HER UNCERTAINLY AND SEES SOMEONE 174 ELECTR COMING FROM OFF LEFT, FRONT--

WHEN HE SEES DION, HE STOPS ABRUTLY AND GLOWERS 265 GGBROW RESENTFULLY--

(SHE LOOKS UP AND SEES THE MASKED DION STANDING BY285 GGBROW THE PIANO--CALMLY)

NOW HE SEES HIS FACE/ 298 GGBROW WHEN HE SEES MARGARET, HE STARTS BACK 303 GGBROW APPREHENSIVELY.)

(THEN CALMING HIMSELF AS HE SEES HOW FRIGHTENED 316 GGBROW SHE IS)

YANK SEES HIS LIPS MOVING. 216 HA APE HE SEES MILDRED, LIKE A WHITE APPARITION 225 HA APE (HE TURNS AND SEES THE WINDOW DISPLAY IN THE TWO 235 HA APE STORES FOR THE FIRST TIME)

(SEES YANK) HELLO, IT'S YOU, HUHS 245 HA APE THEN SEES THE SIGNBOARD ON THE WALL AND IS 246 HA APE REASSURED.)

MAYBE THOSE SHOES HE SEES ADVERTISED FOR FALLEN 13 HUGHIE ARCHES--

THE CLERK SEES HIM NOW 36 HUGHIE HE GLANCES AROUND DEFENSIVELY, SEES LARRY AND 585 ICEMAN COMES FORWARD.)

AND SEES ROCKY APPEARING FROM THE BAR. 607 ICEMAN (HE SEES THE DRINK IN FRONT OF HIM, AND GULPS IT 634 ICEMAN DOWN.

(THEN, AS HE SEES THEY ARE SURPRISED AT HIS 636 ICEMAN VEHEMENCE, HE ADDS HASTILY)

HE LOOKS RELIEVED WHEN HE SEES LARRY 645 ICEMAN (HE SEES WHAT JIMMY IS AT AND GRABS HIS ARM 686 ICEMAN HE SEES HICKEY AND STANDS WATCHING HIM AND 708 ICEMAN LISTENING.)

HE STOPS SHORT WHEN HE SEES SMITTY. 513 INZONE AND GOT AS FAR AS THE DOOR THERE WHEN I SEES HIM. 518 INZONE AND LOOKS AT WHAT HE SEES INSIDE WITH AN 528 INZONE EXPRESSION OF PUZZLED ASTONISHMENT.

OF THE LETTER THEY SEES ON'Y THE WORDS WHAT TELLS 529 INZONE THEM WHAT THEY WANTS TO KNOW.

YOU GO THROUGH THE OTHERS, DRISC, AND SING OUT IF 531 INZONE YOU SEES ANYTHIN' QUEER.

SUDDENLY AND STARTLINGLY ONE SEES IN HER FACE THE 28 JOURNE GIRL SHE HAD ONCE BEEN.

BY GOD, HOW YOU CAN LIVE WITH A MIND THAT SEES 38 JOURNE NOTHING BUT THE WORST MOTIVES

EDMUND GLANCES AT HIS FATHER AND SEES THAT HE 67 JOURNE KNOWS.

(HE STOPS IN THE DOORWAY AS HE SEES HIS MOTHER 81 JOURNE APPROACHING FROM THE HALL,

HE SEES TO THAT. 83 JOURNE SMYTHE SEES TO THAT, I'M AFRAID. 85 JOURNE AND SEES EDMUND COMING DOWN THE STAIRS IN THE 88 JOURNE HALL.)

(THEN HE SEES HIS FATHER IS BITTERLY HURT.) 90 JOURNE WHEN SHE SEES NO ONE IN THE WORLD CAN BELIEVE IN 94 JOURNE HE EVEN FOR A MOMENT ANY MORE.

(STARTS GUILTILY WHEN SHE SEES TYRONE--WITH 122 JOURNE DIGNITY.)

(HE SEES HIS FATHER STARING AT HIM WITH MINGLED 131 JOURNE WORRY AND IRRITATED DISAPPROVAL.

(AS HE SUDDENLY SEES THE SHINING FIGURE OF LAZARUS338 LAZARU AS HE SEES HER FACE, GADSBY CANNOT RESTRAIN A 27 MANSNS STARTLED EXCLAMATION.

HE SEES THE VOLUME OF BYKON ON THE STEPS. 106 MANSNS CANNOT RECOGNIZE A COMPLETE VICTORY AND A CRUSHING114 MANSNS DEFEAT WHEN HE SEES THEM/

UNTIL NOW HE SEES HER AS THE FILTHY SLUT SHE IS-- 162 MANSNS WHEN SHE SEES THEM BOTH STILL OUTSIDE THE SUMMER- 185 MANSNS HOUSE.

HIS EYES FOLLOWING THEM LISTLESSLY, TEDALDO SEES 359 MARCOM MARCO.

(THE KAAN NOW SEES MARCO 378 MARCOM (SHE SEES HE HAS GUESSED HER SECRET AND AT FIRST 387 MARCOM SHE QUAILS AND SHRINKS AWAY.

SEIZES

SEES (CONT'D.)

HE GLANCES ABOUT--SEES THE PRINCESS-- 391 MARCOM (WITH WONDERING BITTERNESS) THE EYE SEES ONLY ITS397 MARCOM OWN SIGHT.

(HE SEES SHE IS ASLEEP--CHUCKLES) 402 MARCOM MARCO HALTS AS HE SEES CHU-YIN, SALUTES 402 MARCOM CONDESCENDINGLY

(HE SEES SOMETHING) AH--IT BEGINS. 426 MARCOM SEES YOU ON HIS DOORSTEP. 9 MISBEG HE SEES YOU'RE NOT WORKING. 10 MISBEG (SHE TURNS AND SEES HE'S GONE--CONTEMPTUOUSLY) 10 MISBEG (STOPS AS HE TURNS THE CORNER AND SEES HER-- 11 MISBEG FURIOUSLY)

(HE SEES THE PITCHFORK) THERE'S HIS PITCHFORK/ 12 MISBEG HE SEES US NOW. 35 MISBEG IF HARDEN SEES YOU HERE, HE'LL LAY THE WHOLE BLAME 54 MISBEG ON YOU.

HIS EXPRESSION BECOMING GUILTY AND MISERABLE AT 157 MISBEG WHAT HE SEES.

IT'S DIFFERENT FROM ALL THE OTHERS-- (SHE SEES HE 165 MISBEG IS ASLEEP--BITTERLY)

(THIS CLICKS IN HIS MIND AND SUDDENLY HE REMEMBERS173 MISBEG EVERYTHING AND JOSIE SEES

MADEMOISELLE--THE SEES HER WEDDING RING.) PRAY 59 POET FORGIVE ME, I SEE IT IS MADAME--

THEIR EYES MEET AND AT THE NAKEDLY PHYSICAL 69 POET APPRAISEMENT SHE SEES IN HIS,

(SEES THE DOOR AT LEFT FRONT BEGIN TO OPEN--IN A 88 POET WHISPER.)

(HE SEES MELODY IS NOT THERE--TO SARA.) 129 POET BUT WHAT SHE SEES IN HER MOTHER'S FACE STOPS HER. 130 POST SHE SEES THE CHAIR IN UNDER THE LOFT AND RUNS OVER601 ROPE TO IT.

MARY, DISCOVERING SHE IS UNHURT, GLANCES QUICKLY 601 ROPE AROUND AND SEES THE BAG,

SEES EVERYONE--BURKES, FOULUS-- 8 STRANG IMMEDIATELY, AS MARY SEES NINA, 26 STRANG (HE LAUGHS HARSHLY--THEN SUDDENLY SEES A MAN 28 STRANG OUTSIDE THE DOORWAY AND STARES--

HE SEES EVANS AND MARSDEN, NODS AT MARSDEN 33 STRANG SILENTLY, WHO RETURNS IT COLDLY,

(GRINNING RESPECTFULLY) HERE'S THE--IAS HE SEES 47 STRANG NINA) UH/

THIS VANISHES INTO ONE OF DESIRE AND JOY AS HE 95 STRANG SEES NINA.

(THEN STOPS SHORT AS HE SEES EVANS.) 95 STRANG HE SEES THEIR TWO HANDS TOGETHER BUT MISTAKES 106 STRANG THEIR MEANING.)

SHE STOPS IN AMAZEMENT WHEN SHE SEES HIM ON HIS 107 STRANG KNEES.

(HE SEES THE BOOK HE HAS BEEN READING ON THE COUCH123 STRANG AND GETS UP TO GET IT.

HE SEES LOVE IN HER YOUNG EYES/... 160 STRANG THE SUDDENLY SEES THAT OLSON IS NOT THERE, AND 90B VOYAG TURNS TO JOE)

TRYING TO CONCEAL HER ACTION, BUT JOE SEES HER. 50B VOYAGE SHE GIVES A EXCLAMATION OF DELIGHTED ASTONISHMENT444 WELDED WHEN SHE SEES MICHAEL AND

(AS SHE SEES WHO IT IS--IN A RELIEVED TONE OF 450 WELDED SURPRISE)

(HE STANDS FIXED AS HE SEES HER BEFORE THE DOOR 487 WELDED SEETHING

RICHARD STANDS, A PREY TO FEELINGS OF BITTEREST 217 AHWILD HUMILIATION AND SEETHING REVOLT

(SEETHING) YOU'VE STOLEN MY SATCHEL TO GIVE HIM, 13 MISBEG I SUPPOSE,

SEETHING NOW IN A FURY OF HUMILIATED PRIDE. 72 POET MELODY, SNUBBED AND SEETHING, GLARES AT HER.) 74 POET

SEIZE

(A STRANGE TERROR SEEMS SUDDENLY TO SEIZE HER. 68 ANNA SEIZE ON HIM, FURIES, TAKE HIM INTO TORMENT,A 168 JOURNE HE WILL SEIZE HIS KINGDOM AND ALL WHO DENY HIM 284 LAZARU SHALL BE CRUCIFIED!

SOLDIERS WITH DRAWN SWORDS LEAP FORWARD AND SEIZE 379 MARCOM HIM, TRUSSING HIM UP,

I HAVE TO REBEL WITH ALL MY STRENGTH--SEIZE ANY 453 WELDED PRETEXT/

SEIZED

HE HAS SEIZED BY FITS OF TERROR, 534 DAYS HIS FAMILIAR DREAD SEIZED HIM. 536 DAYS EVEN IF I'D BEEN SEIZED BY ANY PECULIAR IMPULSE UF549 DAYS HATRED AND REVENGE ON YOU.

JONES HAS BEEN SEIZED BY THE COURAGE OF 197 EJONES DESPERATION.

(SEIZED WITH FURY) YOU DARED--/ 61 ELECTR SEIZED BY AN HYSTERICAL TERROR, BY SOME FEAR SHE 92 ELECTR HAS KEPT HIDDEN)

(SHE TURNS, SEIZED BY PANIC, AND RUNS TO THE 119 ELECTR HOUSE--

(A HOLIDAY SPIRIT OF GAY FESTIVITY HAS SEIZED THEMO460 ICEMAN ALL.

SEIZED BY THE SAME FIT AND POUND WITH THEIR 707 ICEMAN GLASSES, EVEN HUGO.

(AS SMITTY ENTERS THE FORECASTLE HE IS SEIZED 525 INZONE ROUGHLY FROM BOTH SIDES AND HIS

HER EYES OPEN AND SHE STRAINS FORWARD, SEIZED BY A 49 JOURNE FIT OF NERVOUS PANIC,

SHE WAITS FRIGHTENEDLY, SEIZED AGAIN BY A NERVOUS 89 JOURNE PANIC.

(SEIZED BY AN IDEA.) WELL, SEEING WOULD BE 76 POET BELIEVING, EH, MY FINE LADYS

SEIZES

(SEIZES ON THIS INTERRUPTION WITH RELIEF) 251 AHWILD SEIZES THIS AS AN ESCAPE VALVE-- 264 AHWILD I'D BE KILLING THE WORLD-- (HE SEIZES HER IN HIS 76 ANNA ARMS AND KISSES HER FIERCELY.)

SEIZES HIM BY THE ARM AND FORCES HIM DOWN ON THE 355 DAYS CHAISE-LONGUE AGAIN)

SEIZES

SEIZES (CONT'D.)
THEN WITH A SUDDEN MOVEMENT HE SEIZES HER HANDS 232 DESIRE
AND SQUEEZES THEM.
SEIZES A DRINK WHICH THE OLD FARMER HOLDS OUT TO 250 DESIRE
HIM AND DRINKS IT)
(THEN AS HE STARTS BACK IN CONFUSION, SHE SEIZES 24 ELECTR
THIS OPPORTUNITY
HE COMES TO THE BREAKFAST OUT= HE SEIZES ONE 244 HA APE
BAR WITH BOTH HANDS AND,
(HE SEIZES THE KNOB.)
FOR THIS YOU GROW CONFUSED AND THE TEMPTATION 111 MANSNS
SEIZES YOU TO HURL YOURSELF-- 156 MANSNS
A FASCINATED FEAR SUDDENLY SEIZES HER.
(SHE SEIZES IT AND PUMPS IT UP AND DOWN.) 69 POET
(HE SEIZES HER HAND AND KISSES IT IN A 595 HOPE
PASSIONATELY GRATEFUL SILENCE-- 71 STRANG
THEN, WITH A SNARL OF FURY LIKE AN ANIMAL'S HE 460 WELDED
SEIZES HER ABOUT THE THROAT WITH

SEIZING
SEIZING ON THE OPPORTUNITY TO PLAY UP HIS 193 AHWILD
PREOCCUPATION--WITH APOLOGETIC
(SEIZING ON THIS TO RELENT A BIT) 270 AHWILD
(SEIZING HER HAND AND KISSING IT--BROKENLY) 65 ANNA
(SAVAGELY SEIZING ON HIS WEAK POINT) 230 DESIRE
(SEIZING HIS ARMS-- FRIGHTENEDLY) 542 DIFRNT
HIS THOUGHTS SEIZING ON THIS COINCIDENCE) 481 DYNAMO
(THEN SEIZING HER BY THE SHOULDERS AND STARING 89 ELECTR
INTO HER EYES--
(THEN SUDDENLY SEIZING ON THIS AS A WAY OUT--WITH 177 ELECTR
CALCULATED COARSENESS)
(TURNING TO THE OTHERS, BEWILDERMENT SEIZING HIM 230 HA APE
AGAIN)
(SEIZING ON THIS WITH VINDICTIVE RELISH) 657 ICEMAN
(SEIZING THE OPPORTUNITY) FRIENDS, 430 MARCOM
(SEIZING ON THIS--HOARSELY.) 128 POET

SEIZURE
(HE BEGINS TO TREMBLE ALL OVER AS IF IN A 359 LAZARU
SEIZURE--CHOKINGLY)

SELBY
SELBY IS NINETEEN. 217 AHWILD
(HE OPENS THE DOOR AND WINT SELBY ENTERS AND 217 AHWILD
STANDS JUST INSIDE THE DOOR.

SELECT
I'M SURE THE CONCLAVE OF CARDINALS MUST SOON 359 MARCOM
SELECT A POPE.
SO EACH TIME HER THOUGHTS COME TO THE MAN SHE MUST 88 STRANG
SELECT THEY ARE AFRAID TO GO

SELECTED
THE FURNITURE HAS BEEN SELECTED WITH A LOVE FOR 3 STRANG
OLD NEW ENGLAND PIECES.

SELECTS
SELECTS FIVE OR SIX SLIPS OF PAPER, AND HOLDS THEMZ01 AHWILD
OUT TO MILLER.
THEN, SEEING NO ONE ABOUT, HE GOES TO THE 121 BEYOND
SIDEBOARD AND SELECTS A BOOK.
(HE SELECTS ONE AND GINGERLY REACHES HIS HAND IN 527 INZONE
THE WATER.)
HE GOES AROUND IN BACK OF HER AND SELECTS A CIGAR 14 JOURNE
(HE PULLS OUT A SMALL ROLL OF BILLS FROM HIS PANTS 89 JOURNE
POCKET AND CAREFULLY SELECTS

SELF
SELF-CONSCIOUS INTELLIGENCE ABOUT HIM. 193 AHWILD
(SELF-CONSCIOUSLY) WELL--THERE'S-- 196 AHWILD
RICHARD GIVES HIM A QUICK SIDE GLANCE AND GROWS 206 AHWILD
MORE GUILTILY SELF-CONSCIOUS.)
(HE MOVES AWKWARDLY AND SELF-CONSCIOUSLY OFF 208 AHWILD
THROUGH THE FRONT PARLOR.
(WITH A SAD, SELF-PITYING SMILE AT HIS WIFE) 231 AHWILD
AND HITTER FEELINGS OF SELF-LOATHING AND SELF- 256 AHWILD
PITY.
HEAR MISERABLY SELF-CONSCIOUS AND ILL AT EASE 257 AHWILD
THERE
IN A PASSION OF SELF-DENUNCIATION) 258 AHWILD
ARTHUR IS SELF-CONSCIOUSLY A VIRTUOUS YOUNG MAN 263 AHWILD
(WITH SELF-CONSCIOUS UNCONCERN, IGNORING HIS 269 AHWILD
MOTHER)
(THEN WITH A SHIVER OF SHAMEFACED REVULSION AND 276 AHWILD
SELF-DISGUST)
AND SITS IN A SELF-CONSCIOUS, UNNATURAL POSITION. 293 AHWILD
AND BEGINS WITH A SHAMEFACED, SELF-CONSCIOUS 294 AHWILD
SOLEMNITY)
EMBARRASSED AND SELF-CONSCIOUS AND HIS EXPRESSIONS 295 AHWILD
MORE STILTED.
IS CHILDISHLY SELF-WILLED AND WEAK, OF AN 5 ANNA
OBSTINATE KINDLINESS.
(HIS OLD SELF AGAIN) I'VE NOT LAID A HAND ON HIM, 50 ANNA
ANNA.
(TRYING TO BE SCORNFUL AND SELF-CONVINCING) 52 ANNA
SHE'S THAT STUBBORN AND SELF-WILLED. 118 BEYOND
(HE SINKS DOWN INTO HIS CHAIR AND SMILES WITH 126 BEYOND
BITTER SELF-SCORN)
IF I COULD HAVE SEEN HOW YOU WERE IN YOUR TRUE 127 BEYOND
SELF--LIKE YOU ARE NOW--
HE MUST KNOW IT HAS DONE IN FAIR FIGHT, IN SELF- 488 CARDIF
DEFENSE, DON'T YUH THINK?
NOT A STEAM, SELF-RIGHTEOUS BEING WHO CONDEMNED 510 DAYS
SINNERS TO TORMENT?
I'M BECOMING THE DAMNDEST WHINER AND SELF-PITIER. 517 DAYS
I FELT I OWED IT TO HIM AND TO MY OWN SELF-RESPECT321 DAYS
WOULD FIND THE COMPLETEST SELF-EXPRESSION IN 524 DAYS
MAKING OUR UNION A BEAUTIFUL THING.
I'LL PROBABLY FEEL A BIT SELF-CONSCIOUS, 530 DAYS
(SUDDENLY--HIS FACE FULL OF THE BITTEREST, 531 DAYS
TORTURED SELF-LOATHING--
(STERNLY) YOU WOULD BE MORE HONEST WITH YOURSELF 547 DAYS
IF YOU SAID A SELF-DAMNED FOOL
(ANGRILY) IT IS MY TRUE SELF--MY ONLY SELF 559 DAYS

SELF (CONT'D.)
I KNOW YOU COULDN'T BLASPHEME AT SUCH A TIME--NOT 559 DAYS
YOUR TRUE SELF.
HER MOUTH AND CHIN ARE HEAVY, FULL OF A SELF- 494 DIFRNT
WILLED STUBBORNNESS.
AND IS UNCOMFORTABLY SELF-CONSCIOUS AND STIFF 494 DIFRNT
THEREIN.
BOLDLY-APPEALING VITALITY OF SELF-CONFIDENT YOUTH.505 DIFRNT
SELF-CONSCIOUSLY COQUETTISH MANNER THAT 520 DIFRNT
LAUGHABLE.
(ARGUING TORMENTEDLY WITHIN SELF) 422 DYNAMO
HE INSTINCTIVELY IMITATES HIS FATHER'S TONE, 422 DYNAMO
BURNING SELF-PROTECTINGLY.
HER SPEECH IS SELF-ASSERTIVE AND CONSCIOUSLY 429 DYNAMO
SLANGY.
(THEN HIS VOICE BOOMING LIKE HIS FATHER'S WITH 438 DYNAMO
MORAL SELF-RIGHTEOUSNESS)
HE KILLED HIM IN SELF-DEFENSE/ 440 DYNAMO
A SELF-ASSURED, INSINUATING LAUGH 460 DYNAMO
(THEN WITH BITTER SELF-CONTEMPT) 480 DYNAMO
A HARDY SELF-RELIANT CONFIDENCE IN HIMSELF THAT 175 EJONES
INSPIRES RESPECT.
NOT IN A NEGATIVE BUT IN A POSITIVE, SELF- 12 ELECTR
POSSESSED WAY.
(THEN EMBARRASSED, FORCES A SELF-CONSCIOUS LAUGH 13 ELECTR
AND GETS UP AND KISSES
I COULD LET HIM SHOOT FIRST AND THEN KILL HIM IN 38 ELECTR
SELF-DEFENSE.
THEN STARTS PACING SELF-CONSCIOUSLY UP AND DOWN AT 51 ELECTR
THE RIGHT OF STEPS.)
A STOUT SELF-IMPORTANT OLD MAN WITH A STUBBORN 68 ELECTR
OPINIONATED EXPRESSION.
SELF-EFFACING MINISTER'S WIFE. 68 ELECTR
(TURNING TO GUNDER--WITH A SELF-SATISFIED, KNOWING 70 ELECTR
AIR)
OR WITH A SELF-CONSCIOUS SQUARE-SHOULDERED 73 ELECTR
STIFFNESS
AND HAVE YOU YOUR OLD SELF AGAIN BEFORE YOU KNOW 80 ELECTR
IT.
(THEY STOP TALKING SELF-CONSCIOUSLY AS ORIN AND 80 ELECTR
CHRISTINE ENTER FROM THE REAR.
(WITH BITTER SELF-CONTEMPT) I HAVE MY FATHER'S 110 ELECTR
ROTTEN COWARD BLOOD IN ME.
IN SPITE OF HER FROZEN SELF-CONTROL, LAVINIA 122 ELECTR
RECOILS BEFORE THIS.
(WITH TORTURED SELF-ACCUSATION) 124 ELECTR
(IN A FINAL FRENZY OF SELF- DENUNCIATION) 124 ELECTR
SETH GREETS THEM SELF-CONSCIOUSLY) 134 ELECTR
SEEMS HALF TO COME BACK TO HIS NATURAL SELF 156 ELECTR
HAZEL LOOKS SELF-CONSCIOUS AND STIFF. 161 ELECTR
SHE STARTS TO RUN AFTER HIM, STOPS HER SELF, 167 ELECTR
(WITH A STRANGE CRUEL SMILE OF GLOATING OVER THE 178 ELECTR
YEARS OF SELF-TORTURE)
HIS MANNER HAS THE EASY SELF-ASSURANCE OF A NORMAL257 GGBROW
INTELLIGENCE.
WHY MUST I HIDE MYSELF IN SELF-CONTEMPT IN ORDER 264 GGBROW
TO UNDERSTAND
(SELF-MOCKINGLY--FLIPPING THE BIBLE) 270 GGBROW
SELF-CONTEMPT. 270 GGBROW
BY WHICH HE LAUGHS AS A CREATOR AT HIS SELF- 272 GGBROW
DEFEATS/
(HE COUGHS SELF-CONSCIOUSLY.) 276 GGBROW
HIS FACE IS THAT OF AN ASCETIC, A MARTYR, FURROWEOZ64 GGBROW
BY PAIN AND SELF-TORTURE.
(IN THE SAME AWKWARD, SELF-CONSCIOUS TONE, ONE 293 GGBROW
AFTER ANOTHER)
SENSITIVE AND SELF-CONSCIOUS AND PROUD AND 297 GGBROW
REVENGEFUL--
IN SELF-PRESERVATION THE DEVIL MUST BELIEVE/ 297 GGBROW
REGAINED THE SELF-CONFIDENT SPIRIT OF ITS YOUTH, 303 GGBROW
HER EYES SHINE WITH HAPPINESS.)
LAST SCENE--THE SELF-ASSURED SUCCESS. 303 GGBROW
SEEMING TO GROW TALL AND PROUD--THEN WITH A LAUGH 308 GGBROW
OR BOLD SELF-ASSURANCE)
THEN PUNISH ME WITH SELF-LOATHING AND LIFE-HATRED5314 GGBROW
THEN, TOO, HE REPRESENTS TO THEM A SELF- 208 HA APE
EXPRESSION.
UF FRENZIED SELF-GLORIFICATION BY HIS SPEECH, DO 216 HA APE
LIKEWISE.
PRETTY FACE MARRED BY A SELF-CONSCIOUS EXPRESSION 217 HA APE
OF DISDAINFUL SUPERIORITY.
ABOUT THEMSELVES HAS GIVEN HIM A FOOLPROOF 11 HUGHIE
TECHNIQUE OF SELF-DEFENSE.
HIS POKER FACE AS SELF-BETRAYING AS A HURT DOG'S-- 19 HUGHIE
APPEALINGLY.)
ERIE GOES ON WITH GATHERING WARMTH AND SELF- 36 HUGHIE
ASSURANCE.)
SELF-CONFIDENT AFFABILITY AND A HEARTY GOOD 618 ICEMAN
FELLOWSHIP.
OUT HERE PROBABLY BE HIS NATURAL SELF AGAIN 625 ICEMAN
TOMORROW--
(SELF-ASSURINGLY) OH, I KNOW I CAN MAKE GOOD. 644 ICEMAN
HE FORGETS HIS SULLENNESS AND BECOMES HIS OLD SELF644 ICEMAN
AGAIN)
PARRITT INSTANTLY SUBSIDES AND BECOMES SELF- 650 ICEMAN
CONSCIOUS AND DEFENSIVE.
WHO SPEAKS WITH MUZZY, SELF-PITYING MELANCHOLY OUT0656 ICEMAN
OF A SENTIMENTAL DREAM.
(HE STOPS ABRUPTLY AND FOR A SECOND HE SEEMS TO 657 ICEMAN
LOSE HIS SELF-ASSURANCE.
(HE SITS DOWN IN HIS OLD PLACE AND SINKS INTO A 669 ICEMAN
WOUNDED, SELF-PITYING BROODING.)
(HE STOPS IN BEWILDERED SELF-AMAZEMENT--TO LARRY 672 ICEMAN
APPEALINGLY)
HIS MANNER IS FULL OF A FORCED, JAUNTY SELF- 674 ICEMAN
ASSURANCE.
PUTS ON AN EXAGGERATEDLY SELF-CONFIDENT BEARING. 681 ICEMAN

SELF

SELF (CONT'D.)
HOPE AND JIMMY ARE BOTH PUTTING UP A FRONT OF SELF-ASSURANCE. 683 ICEMAN
(HE LAUGHS WITH A SNEERING, VINDICTIVE SELF-LOATHING. 689 ICEMAN
THE POOR MAD DEVIL--{THEN WITH ANGRY SELF-CONTEMPT) 703 ICEMAN
HIS MANNER IS NO LONGER SELF-ASSURED. 703 ICEMAN
(HIS FACE IS CONVULSED WITH SELF-LOATHING) 715 ICEMAN
(WITH DRUNKEN SELF-ASSURANCE) 723 ICEMAN
(HE OPENS HIS EYES--WITH A BITTER SELF-DERISION) 726 ICEMAN
I MEAN, IT MAKES ME SELF-CONSCIOUS. 17 JOURNE
TO SEE YOU AS YOU'VE BEEN SINCE YOU CAME BACK TO 17 JOURNE
US, YOUR DEAR OLD SELF AGAIN.
HER SMILE VANISHES AND HER MANNER BECOMES SELF-CONSCIOUS.) 20 JOURNE
(SHE STOPS SHORT, OVERCOME BY A FIT OF ACUTE SELF- 27 JOURNE
CONSCIOUSNESS AS SHE CATCHES
HER MANNER NERVOUSLY SELF-CONSCIOUS. 40 JOURNE
(SUDDENLY SHE IS SELF-CONSCIOUSLY AWARE THAT THEY 41 JOURNE
ARE BOTH STARING FIXEDLY AT
AND YOU'VE LOST YOUR TRUE SELF FOREVER. 61 JOURNE
SHE IS EXCITED AND SELF-CONSCIOUS. 66 JOURNE
AND YOUR DENIAL HAS BROUGHT NOTHING BUT SELF- 77 JOURNE
DESTRUCTION/
(THEN HER FACE HARDENS INTO BITTER SELF-CONTEMPT.) 95 JOURNE
SIMPLY AND WITHOUT SELF-CONSCIOUSNESS, THE NAIVE, 97 JOURNE
HAPPY,
(THEN WITH DEFIANT SELF-ASSURANCE.) 104 JOURNE
(MOVED.) I'M GLAD I CAME, MARY, WHEN YOU ACT LIKE112 JOURNE
YOUR REAL SELF.
BITTERLY DRAMATIC SELF-PITY.) 128 JOURNE
(WITH A LOOSE-MOUTHED SNEER OF SELF-CONTEMPT.) 146 JOURNE
(BREAKS THE CRACKING SILENCE--BITTERLY, SELF- 170 JOURNE
DEFENSIVELY SARDONIC.)
THE SELF-TORTURED, INTROSPECTIVE.. 273 LAZARU
THE PROUD, SELF-RELIANT.. 273 LAZARU
UNDERSTANDING SMILE OF SELF-FORGETFUL LOVE, THE 274 LAZARU
LIPS STILL FRESH AND YOUNG.
(A SELF-TORTURED MAN--GLOOMILY) 276 LAZARU
SO DEVOID OF ALL SELF-CONSCIOUSNESS OR FEAR, 273 LAZARU
GLANCING SIDEWAYS AT ONE ANOTHER, SMILING 280 LAZARU
FOULISHLY AND SELF-CONSCIOUSLY.
HEAVY, DOMINEERING, SELF-COMPLACENT, THE FACE OF A291 LAZARU
CONFIDENT DOMINANT RACE.
THEY ARE ALL OF THE PROUD SELF-RELIANT TYPE, IN 298 LAZARU
THE PERIOD OF YOUNG MANHOOD.
HEIR EXPRESSION IS SPOILED, PETULANT AND SELF- 299 LAZARU
OBSESSED, WEAK BUT DOMINEERING.
LET A LAUGHING AWAY OF SELF BE YOUR NEW RIGHT TO 310 LAZARU
LIVE FOREVER/
THEN, FORCING A TWISTED GRIN OF SELF-CONTEMPT-- 311 LAZARU
HARSHLY.)
MATURING AND OLD AGE ARE REPRESENTED IN THE TYPES 312 LAZARU
OF THE SELF-TORTURED,
INTROSPECTIVE.. PROUD, SELF-RELIANT,. THE 312 LAZARU
SERVILE, HYPOCRITICAL..
SELF IS LOST IN AN ECSTATIC AFFIRMATION OF LIFE. 318 LAZARU
IN THE PERIOD OF WOMANHOOD IN THE PROUD, SELF- 336 LAZARU
RELIANT TYPE.
IN EACH OF THE THREE TYPES OF THE INTROSPECTIVE, 336 LAZARU
SELF-TORTURED..
THE LIPS ARE THIN AND STERN AND SELF-CONTAINED-- 337 LAZARU
GIRLISH MOUTH IS SET IN AN EXPRESSION OF AGONIZED 337 LAZARU
SELF-LOATHING AND WEARINESS OF
THAT MUCH REMAINED HIDDEN IN ME OF THE SAD OLD 348 LAZARU
LAZARUS WHO DIED OF SELF-PITY--
SHE IS LAUGHING WITH HORROR AND SELF-LOATHING. 349 LAZARU
AND IN REVENGE AND SELF-TORTURE HIS LOVE HAS BEEN 352 LAZARU
FAITHLESS/
IN SELF-CONTEMPT OF MAN I HAVE MADE THIS MAN, 354 LAZARU
MYSELF.
(HE LAUGHS WITH JOYOUS SELF-MOCKERY.) 360 LAZARU
(LOOKS AROUND THE CLEARING--BITTERLY, FORCES A 3 MANSNS
SELF-MOCKING SMILE.)
THESE INSANE INTERMINABLE DIALOGUES WITH SELF/ 3 MANSNS
HE IS GRAVELY SELF-IMPORTANT AND PRETENTIOUS IN 25 MANSNS
MANNER AND SPEECH,
BUT LACKS ALL SELF-CONFIDENCE OR AMBITION BEYOND 26 MANSNS
THESE LIMITS.
SHE EXUDES AN ATMOSPHERE OF SELF-CONFIDENT LOVING 44 MANSNS
HAPPINESS AND CONTENTMENT,
SATISFACTION AND SENSE OF SELF-FULFILLMENT AND 46 MANSNS
PRIDE OUT OF BEATING MY
(MADE SELF-CONSCIOUS AND ILL AT EASE.) 64 MANSNS
IN ORDER TO MAKE OF MY WIFE A SECOND SELF THROUGH 73 MANSNS
WHICH SHE COULD LIVE AGAIN.
TRICK SARA INTO BEING AN ACCESSORY IN THE MURDER 73 MANSNS
OF THAT OLD SELF.
AND SEE HOW MUCH OF THE OLD GREEDY SARA STILL LIES 74 MANSNS
BEHIND HER PRESENT SELF--
DISCIPLING MY WILL TO KEEP MYSELF UNITED--ANOTHER 74 MANSNS
SELF REBELS--SECEDES--
HER MANNER HAS TAKEN ON A LOT OF DEBORAH'S WELL- 75 MANSNS
BRED, SELF-ASSURED POISE.
WELL THEN, I KNOW YOU WILL BE WILLING TO BECOME 88 MANSNS
YOUR OLD TRUE SELF AGAIN FOR ME.
BEFORE THE COMPANY CAN BE FREE AND INDEPENDENT AND 93 MANSNS
SELF-SUFFICIENT.
THE GARDEN OF YOUR OLD SELF DISOWNS THE DOTING OLD 99 MANSNS
GRANNY
TO MAKE THE COMPANY ENTIRELY SELF-SUFFICIENT. 101 MANSNS
IT MUST ATTAIN THE ALL-EMBRACING SECURITY OF 101 MANSNS
COMPLETE SELF-POSSESSION--
(COARSELY SELF-CONFIDENT.) I'D LIKE TO SEE YOU TRY149 MANSNS
TO WANT TO/
YES, I SUPPOSE, ENTIRELY SELFISH--NO TIME TO 155 MANSNS
REMEMBER SELF.

SELF (CONT'D.)
FOR ALL THE CONFUSION IN OUR MINDS, THE CONFLICTS 172 MANSNS
WITHIN THE SELF,
THEN THAT MAN IS FORCED AT LAST, IN SELF-DEFENSE, 175 MANSNS
TO CHOOSE ONE OR THE OTHER--
WITH A SELF-CONTEMPTUOUS LAUGH.) 190 MANSNS
BUT HER FACE IS PROUD, SELF-ASSURED, ARROGANT AND 191 MANSNS
HAPPY.
STARTS TO HIDE IT IN HIS JACKET, STOPS, MUTTERS 363 MARCOM
WITH BRAVE SELF-CONTEMPT)
HE IS NOW NEARLY EIGHTEEN, A BRASH, SELF-CONFIDENT373 MARCOM
YOUNG MAN.
I QUITE REALIZE THAT IN SELF-PROTECTION I'VE GOT 396 MARCOM
TO BUY THEM--OR KILL YOU/
THE NOTICES SHE IS WEEPING--IN SELF-REPROACH) 400 MARCOM
THE NOBLE MAN IGNORES SELF. 401 MARCOM
WEARING THE SELF-ASSURANCE OF AN IMMORTAL SOUL ANDWOL MARCOM
HIS NEW ADMIRAL'S UNIFORM/
HE IS DRESSED IN FULL UNIFORM, LOOKING SPICK AND 410 MARCOM
SPAN AND SELF-CONSCIOUS.
(IN A QUEER HYSTERICAL STATE WHERE SHE DELIGHTS IN413 MARCOM
SELF-HUMILIATION)
UNTIL HE BECOMES HIS OWN IDEAL FIGURE, AN IDOL OF 418 MARCOM
STUFFED SELF-SATISFACTION/
WALKING WITH BURSTING SELF-IMPORTANCE BETWEEN THE 428 MARCOM
FILES OF MUSICIANS
CAN YOUR SELF-OVERCOMING OVERCOME THAT GREATEST 434 MARCOM
OVERCOMER OF SELFS?
WITH ANGRY SELF-CONTEMPT) 435 MARCOM
AND WALKS IN THE CROWD WITHOUT SELF-CONSCIOUSNESS,439 MARCOM
VERY MUCH AS ONE OF THEM.
OR PRIMLY SELF-RIGHTEOUS. 4 MISBEG
HE USUALLY HAS THE SELF-CONFIDENT ATTITUDE OF 56 MISBEG
ACKNOWLEDGED SUPERIORITY.
(SHE GETS TO HER FEET, PULLING AT HIS ARM--WITH A 137 MISBEG
LITTLE SELF-MOCKING LAUGH)
SHE FORCES A DEFENSIVE, SELF-DERISIVE SMILE) 153 MISBEG
(SELF-MOCKINGLY) SURE, HASN'T HE TOLD ME I'M 161 MISBEG
BEAUTIFUL TO HIM AND HE LOVES ME--
AS IF ALL MY SINS HAD BEEN FORGIVEN--(HE BECOMES 171 MISBEG
SELF-CONSCIOUS--CYNICALLY)
HE IS PROFOUNDLY MOVED BUT IMMEDIATELY BECOMES 172 MISBEG
SELF-CONSCIOUS
BUT HER SPEECH HAS AT TIMES A SELF-CONSCIOUS, 16 POET
STILTED QUALITY ABOUT IT,
WHICH HAS BECOME MORE REAL THAN HIS REAL SELF TO 34 POET
HIM.
THE THIRD DRINK BEGINS TO WORK AND HIS FACE 43 POET
BECOMES ARROGANTLY SELF-ASSURED.
(COOLLY SELF-POSSESSED--PLEASANTLY.) 72 POET
HE TURNS TO AURA, HIS SELF-CONFIDENCE PARTLY 76 POET
RESTORED.)
SINCE HE LEFT HOME TO SEEK SELF-EMANCIPATION AT 81 POET
THE BREAST OF NATURE.
CATO HAS ALWAYS A SELF-POSSESSED FREE MAN EVEN 86 POET
WHEN HE WAS A SLAVE.
BEING IN IT HAS NOTABLY RESTORED HIS SELF- 88 POET
CONFIDENT ARROGANCE.
(THIS COMPLIMENT COMPLETELY RESTORES HIM TO HIS 93 POET
ARROGANT SELF.)
(THEN DEFIANTLY SELF-REASSURINGLY.) 137 POET
(SHE SMILES WITH A SELF-MOCKING HAPPINESS.) 150 POET
HIS FOREHEAD BROAD, HIS MILD BLUE EYES THOSE OF A 4 STRANG
DREAMY SELF-ANALYST,
(THEN SELF-REASSURINGLY) (BUT THERE IS A PUBLIC 5 STRANG
TO CHERISH THEM, EVIDENTLY...
(HE SIGHS--THEN SELF-MOCKINGLY) 5 STRANG
(THINKING SELF-MOCKINGLY BUT A BIT WORRIED ABOUT 12 STRANG
HIMSELF)
(HE SMILES WITH BITTER SELF-MOCKERY) 12 STRANG
A TERRIBLE TENSION OF WILL ALONE MAINTAINING SELF- 13 STRANG
POSSESSION.
(WITH FIERCE SELF-CONTEMPT) I GAVE HIM 19 STRANG
GOD'S SNEER AT OUR SELF-IMPORTANCE/...) 24 STRANG
PARTICULARLY THAT SELF-IMPORTANT YOUNG ASS OF A 29 STRANG
DOCTOR--
(SHE SMILES WITH A CYNICAL SELF-CONTEMPT) 27 STRANG
THERE IS A LACK OF SELF-CONFIDENCE, A LOST AND 29 STRANG
STRAYED APPEALING AIR ABOUT HIM.
BUT ALL HE NEEDS IS A LITTLE SELF-CONFIDENCE AND A 38 STRANG
SENSE OF RESPONSIBILITY.
SELF-MOCKING GENIALITY) 47 STRANG
(SELF-MOCKINGLY) 52 STRANG
I HAVE KNOWN A BIT OF HONOR AND A TRIFLE OF SELF- 86 STRANG
SATISFACTION....
STRENGTH ABOUT HER EXPRESSION, A RUTHLESS SELF- 90 STRANG
CONFIDENCE IN HER EYES.
THERE IS AN EXPRESSION OF DEFENSIVE BITTERNESS AND 95 STRANG
SELF-RESENTMENT ABOUT HIS
(GENIALLY--WITH A FORCED SELF-CONFIDENT AIR) 104 STRANG
AVOIDING EVAN'S EYES, MOVING AWAY FROM HER JERKILY164 STRANG
AND SELF-CONSCIOUSLY)
HE IS STOUTER, THE HAGGARD LUCK OF WORRY AND SELF-111 STRANG
CONSCIOUS INFERIORITY HAS GONE
I CAN'T QUITE BELIEVE IN THIS SELF-CONFIDENT 113 STRANG
BUSINESS MA YET...
(WITH GRIEVING SELF-PITY) (IF ONLY MOTHER HAD 115 STRANG
LIVED....
(HE LAUGHS WITH BITTER SELF-PITY--THEN BEGINS TO 123 STRANG
THINK WITH AMUSED CURIOSITY)
(WITH A STRANGE, SELF-ASSURED SMILE AT HIM) 131 STRANG
HIS EYES ARE EMBITTERED AND THEY HIDE HIS INNER 138 STRANG
SELF-RESENTMENT
(SHE LOOKS OVER AT DARRELL--SELF-MOCKINGLY) 138 STRANG
ON THE PROUD ASSURANCE THAT HE IS SELF-MADE/ 141 STRANG
(THEN SUDDENLY MISERABLY SELF-CONTEMPTUOUS) 148 STRANG
SELF TO YOU WOULD BRING YOU A MOMENT'S HAPPINESS, 149 STRANG
COULD I...

SELF

(CONT'D.)
BUT INCREASINGLY STUBBORN AND SELF-OPINIONATED, 157 STRANG
(THE, STRUGGLING WITH HIMSELF--WITH A DEFENSIVE 187 STRANG
SELF-MOCKERY)
(SUIT I'D LIKE TO JOLT HIS STUPID SELF- 191 STRANG
COMPLACENCY/...
YOU'LL MY--THE CONTROLS HIMSELF ABRUPTLY--WITH A 198 STRANG
SMILE OF CYNICAL SELF-PITY)
PARTLY IMPOSED BY YEARS OF SELF-DISCIPLINE. 443 WELDED
A PASSIONATE TENSION, A SELF-PROTECTING, ARROGANT 444 WELDED
DEFIANCE OF LIFE AND HIS OWN
I ONLY--(WITH A SMILE OF IRONICAL SELF-PITY) 445 WELDED
(WITH AN AWKWARD SENSE OF HAVING BECOME RHETORICAL448 WELDED
HE ADDS SELF-MOCKINGLY)
HER WHOLE TORTURED FACE EXPRESSES AN ABYSMAL SELF-460 WELDED
LOATHING.
(TRYING TO CONTROL HERSELF--SELF-MOCKINGLY) 466 WELDED
(AFTER A PAUSE--WITH MELANCHOLY SELF-DISGUST) 468 WELDED
SUDDENLY SHE LAUGHS WITH A SAD SELF-MOCKERY) 482 WELDED
(SELF-DEFENSIVELY) OF COURSE, I KNEW YOU MUST 482 WELDED
HAVE GONE.
(WITH PASSIONATE SELF-SCORN) 486 WELDED

SELFISH
SHE HAS DEVELOPED THE SELFISH, IRRITABLE NATURE OF113 BEYOND
THE CHRONIC INVALID.
I WAS SELFISH THEN. 84 ELECTR
IF ONLY FOR SELFISH REASONS. 159 ELECTR
I'VE BEEN LOOKIN, YOU UP FOR PURELY SELFISH 280 GGBROW
REASONS.
I WON'T BE SELFISH. 310 GGBROW
HELL, IT'S PURELY SELFISH. 106 JOURNE
THEIR DISCONTENT SEEMS MEAN AND SELFISH. 17 MANSNS
YES, I SUPPOSE, ENTIRELY SELFISH--NO TIME TO 155 MANSNS
REMEMBER SELF.
HIS FACE NOW FULL OF SELFISH RELIEF AS HE THINKS) 7 STRANG
BUT I'M SELFISH ENOUGH TO WANT TO SEE YOU HAPPY 106 STRANG
BEFORE I GO!
I'M SELFISH, YOU SEE? 144 STRANG
I'M LOW AND SELFISH/... 156 STRANG
(IT SEEMS ROTTEN AND SELFISH TO BE HAPPY... 189 STRANG

SELFISHLY
AND NOT SELFISHLY INTERESTED, THAT'S THE 165 STRANG
DIFFERENCE.

SELFISHNESS
AND, OF COURSE, IT BLEW MY PETTY MODERN 524 DAYS
SELFISHNESS RIGHT OUT THE WINDOW.
FORGIVE MY SELFISHNESS, THINKING ONLY OF MYSELF. 142 MISBEG

SELFLESS
BUT AT THE SAME TIME, IN SOME QUEER WAY, MORE 269 GGBROW
SELFLESS AND ASCETIC.
HE BEGINS TO LAUGH, AT FIRST A CLEAR LAUGHTER OF 338 LAZARU
SELFLESS JOY.

SELFLESSNESS
I FELT ETERNAL LIFE MADE NOBLER BY YOUR 362 LAZARU
SELFLESSNESS/

SELL
THEY'RE GOIN' TO BRING WID 'EM TC SELL TO US 458 CARIBC
FOR AND.
SMITH SAID HE WOULD GIVE TWO THOUSAND CASH IF I 569 CROSS
WOULD SELL THE PLACE TO HIM--
FORCED HIM TO SELL FOR ONE-TENTH ITS WORTH, YOU 25 ELECTR
KNOW.
AND CLARK AND DAWSON WOULD BE WILLING TO SELL THE 39 ELECTR
"FLYING TRADES."
DEATH SUBTRACKS ANTHONY AND I SELL OUT--BILLY 272 GGBROW
GRADUATES--
WITH CUTE ALLUREMENTS SO THAT FOOLS WILL DESIRE TO28/ GGBROW
BUY, SELL, BREED, SLEEP,
I'LL SELL OUT HERE/ 305 GGBROW
HE WAS THE GUY WHO COULD SELL THOSE HOOSIER 622 ICEMAN
HAYSEEDS BUILDING LOTS.
DON'T LOOK AT ME AS IF I WAS TRYING TO SELL YOU A 622 ICEMAN
GOLDBRICK.
(DERISIVELY) NOW YOU CAN SELL DEM BACK TO HIM 674 ICEMAN
AGAIN TOMORROW.
WHENEVER I MADE UP MY MIND TO SELL SOMEONE 703 ICEMAN
SOMETHING I KNEW THEY OUGHT TO WANT,
AND I KNEW I COULD KID PEOPLE AND SELL THINGS. 710 ICEMAN
YOU OUGHT TO BE ABLE TO SELL SKUNKS FOR GOOD 710 ICEMAN
RAITERS/-.
WHAT'S WORSE, THEY'LL SELL YOURS, 74 JOURNE
THEY'LL SELL THEIR SOULS/ 74 JOURNE
YOU WILL HAVE TO SELL THIS HOME. 33 MANSNS
HE THOUGHT, AS THEY WOULD HAVE TC SELL THEIR 35 MANSNS
PARENTS' HOME AND COME TO THE CITY,
TO SELL HER DEARLY. 88 MANSNS
AS IF I WAS SOME LOW STREET GIRL WHO CAME THAT 88 MANSNS
NIGHT TO SELL HERSELF.
THAT SHE WOULD SELL ANYTHING IF OFFERED THE RIGHT 98 MANSNS
PRICE.
AND YOU WILL WANT YOUR OWN STORES HERE IN THE CITY100 MANSNS
TO SELL YOUR GOODS.
I ONLY WISH TO SAY--I'VE QUITE DECIDED TO SELL MY 143 MANSNS
INTEREST IN THE BUSINESS--
WILL INTERRUPT GABRIEL TO SELL HIM ANOTHER 362 MARCOM
TRUMPET/
SOUVENIRS TO SELL TO CHRISTIANS$ 365 MARCOM
I SELL TO ALL NATIONS. 367 MARCOM
WHAT DO YOU SELL$ 368 MARCOM
(PETTISHLY) UNLESS YOUR JOKES IMPROVE YOU'LL 374 MARCOM
NEVER SELL ANYTHING.
DON'T SELL YOUR SOUL FOR NOTHING. 375 MARCOM
MY GOOD MEN, YOU MAY SELL THESE RICH ROBES 424 MARCOM
SELL HIM THE RAILROAD FOR THE SIX. 16 MISBEG
JIM WILL SELL THE FARM. 31 MISBEG
I'VE ALWAYS WANTED TO OWN A GOLD MINE--SO I COULD 67 MISBEG
SELL IT.
WHO'D SELL HIS SOUL FOR A PRICE. 82 MISBEG

SELL
(CONT'D.)
HE'S AGREED TO SELL THE FARM, THAT'S WHAT/ 83 MISBEG
ALL WE WANT IS A PAPER SIGNED BY HIM WITH 94 MISBEG
WITNESSES THAT HE'LL SELL THE FARM TO
HE'D BE HEARTBROKEN IF HE HAD TO SELL HER. 22 POET
YOU'D SELL YOUR PRIDE AS MY DAUGHTER--/ 128 POET
I HAD TO SELL MY FATHER'S HOME TC GET MONEY SO WE 93 STRANG
COULD MOVE NEAR HIS JOB...
AND IT WAS I WHO WANTED TO SELL THE PLACE... 93 STRANG
WITHIN A YEAR OR SO THEY'LL BE WILLING TO SELL OUT121 STRANG
CHEAP.

SELLIN'
BUT IF PAW'S HITCHED WE'D BE SELLIN' EBEN 215 DESIRE
SOMETHIN' WE'D NEVER GIT 'OOHOW/
IS YOU SELLIN' ME LIKE DEY USTER BEFO' DE WARS 197 EJONES
BY SELLIN' EVERYTHING/ TO BUY THAT SLUT NEW 586 RUPE
CLOTHES.

SELLING
CRAMMED WITH BOYS' AND GIRLS' BOOKS AND THE BEST- 185 AHWILD
SELLING NOVELS OF MANY PAST
(THEN, SELLING HIS IDEA) IT'S A GREAT CHANCE FOR 258 GGBROW
HIM.
WHAT FINISHED ME WAS THIS LAST BUSINESS OF SOMEONE592 ICEMAN
SELLING OUT.
I'D GET A LOT OF SPORT OUT OF SELLING MY LINE OF 661 ICEMAN
SALVATION
EVEN ABOUT SELLING OUT. 719 ICEMAN
HE WAS SELLING DEATH TO ME, THAT CRAZY SALESMAN, 721 ICEMAN
THE LAST I HEARD THEY WERE STILL SELLING BOOZE, 81 JOURNE
NOT GIVING IT AWAY.
HE'S MADE ME THINK THAT LIFE MEANS SELLING 144 MANSNS
YOURSELF, AND THAT LOVE IS LUST--
WHY, I WAS COUNTING ON SELLING HER AND HER HUSBAND349 MARCOM
A WHOLE FLEET OF GOODS/
(WITH A CUNNING SMILE, SELLING A BIG BILL OF 365 MARCOM
GOODS HERE--ABOUTS, I'LL WAGER,
THE WOMEN DO ALL THE BUYING AND SELLING. 373 MARCOM
SELLING THEM A BROKEN-DOWN NAG OR A SICK COW OR 8 MISBEG
FIG THAT HE'S DOCTORED UP TO
AND SELLING THE PLACES 90 MISBEG
AND GOT HIS GRAY ON SELLING THE FARM TO HIM. 133 MISBEG
TO SET ABOUT SELLING A PIECE OF PROPERTY THE OLD 147 MISBEG
MAN HAD BOUGHT THERE YEARS AGO.
YOU LIED ABOUT JIM SELLING THE FARM. 163 MISBEG

SELLS
AND YOU SELLS MES 197 EJONES
YESTERDAY HE SELLS DE BUM ONE BACK TO SOLLY FOR 581 ICEMAN
FOUR BITS

SELTZER
DO YOU WANT ME TO GET YOU SOME BROMO SELTZERS 271 AHWILD

SELVES.
AS IF AT LAST I MUST BECOME TWO SELVES FROM NOW 74 MANSNS
ON--DIVISION AND CONFUSION--
IF THE CONFLICTING SELVES WITHIN A MAN ARE TOO 172 MANSNS
EVENLY MATCHED--
AND OUR WEAK SENTIMENTAL MORAL EVASIONS OF OUR 179 MANSNS
NATURAL SELVES.
FREE OF ONE OF MY TWO SELVES, OF ONE OF THE 182 MANSNS
ENEMIES WITHIN MY MIND.

SEMBLANCE
IT IS COLD AND EMOTIONLESS AND HAS THE SAME 20 ELECTR
STRANGE SEMBLANCE OF A LIFELIKE MASK
THE MANNION MASK-SEMBLANCE OF HER FACE APPEARS 170 ELECTR
INTENSIFIED NOW.
SO THAT ONE'S WINNINGS HAVE THE SEMBLANCE OF 92 MANSNS
LOSSES.

SEMI
WHO SQUAT DOWN ON THEIR HAUNCHES IN A SEMI- 203 EJONES
CIRCLE.)
THE TWO WOMEN WEAR SEMI-FORMAL EVENING GOWNS, 117 MANSNS
DEBORAHS ALL WHITE,
FORMING A SORT OF SEMI-CIRCLE WITH THE THRONE AT 364 MARCOM
CENTER.
ONLY THE CHORUS REMAIN, GROUPED IN A SEMI-CIRCLE 437 MARCOM
BEHIND THE CATAFALQUE.

SEMICIRCLE
GROUPING IN A BIG SEMICIRCLE AS OF SPECTATORS IN A344 LAZARU
THEATRE,

SEMICIRCULAR
THEN AFTER HE HAS GONE OUT THROUGH THE ARCH, THEY 363 LAZARU
CLOSE INTO A SEMICIRCULAR

SEMITIC
MASKS OF THESE JEWS OF THE FIRST TWO SCENES OF THE275 LAZARU
PLAY ARE PRONOUNCEDLY SEMITIC

SEN
AND HAD EATEN A POUND OF SEN-SEN TO KILL THE GIN 39 MISBEG
ON HER BREATH,

SENATE
IT'S FROM A SPEECH MADE IN THE SENATE BY A GUY 242 HA APE
NAMED SENATOR QUEEN.
(READING) "LIKE CATO I SAY TO THIS SENATE, THE 243 HA APE
FOE MUST BE DESTROYED/
ON EACH SIDE, MEMBERS OF THE SENATE ARE SEATED IN 312 LAZARU
THEIR WHITE ROBES.
THE ROMAN SENATE IS THE ROMAN SENATE 313 LAZARU
(POMPOUSLY) TIBERIUS WOULD NOT DARE HARM THE 314 LAZARU
SENATE.
WITH CAESAR'S COMMAND THAT THE SENATE MEET HERE AT314 LAZARU
MIDNIGHT.
(AFTER A PAUSE--SIGHING) IN TRUTH, THE SENATE IS 315 LAZARU
NOT WHAT IT USED TO BE.
HE MAY MISTREAT INDIVIDUAL SENATORS, BUT THE ROMAN315 LAZARU
SENATE IS THE ROMAN SENATE/
WHILE ROME IS HOME THE SENATE IS THE SENATE 315 LAZARU
CAESAR IS CAESAR THE AUGUST ONE PRINCE OF THE 315 LAZARU
SENATE TRIBUNE OVER TRIBUNES
THE SENATE IS AN EMPTY NAME-- 315 LAZARU
IN THE NAME OF THE SENATE/ 316 LAZARU

SENATE

SENATE (CONT'D.)
THE SENATE COMMANDS YOU? 316 LAZARU
(APPEALING TO SENATE) AND YOU, SENATORS/ 322 LAZARU

SENATOR
SENATOR BROWN/
IT'S FROM A SPEECH MADE IN THE SENATE BY A GUY 313 GGBROW
NAMED SENATOR QUEEN. 242 HA APE
(WITH GROWLING RAGE) I'D LIKE TO CATCH DAT 243 HA APE
SENATOR GUY ALONE FOR A SECOND.
GIVE THAT QUEEN SENATOR GUY THE BARK/ 243 HA APE
OF A SENATOR FROM THE SOUTH OF THE UNITED STATES 390 MARCOM
OF AMERICA

SENATORS
THE LEVEL FROM WHICH THE COLUMNS RISE IS THE 312 LAZARU
CHORUS OF SENATORS.
THE SENATORS ARE DIVIDED INTO TWO GROUPS ON EACH 312 LAZARU
SIDE, THIRTY IN EACH.
THE SENATORS BEGIN TO TALK TO EACH OTHER IN LOW 314 LAZARU
VOICES.)
HE MAY MISTREAT INDIVIDUAL SENATORS, BUT THE ROMAN315 LAZARU
SENATE IS THE ROMAN SENATE/
(THE SENATORS SEEM TO SHRINK BACK FROM HIM IN 316 LAZARU
FEAR, ALL BUT LUCIUS.
(THE SENATORS ARE NOW TREMBLING. 317 LAZARU
EVEN THE SENATORS, ARE DRAWN INTO IT. 318 LAZARU
THE SENATORS LEAN FORWARD IN THEIR SEATS, 318 LAZARU
FASCINATED BY HIS FACE.
(THE MULTITUDE BEYOND THE WALL, ALL THE SENATORS, 319 LAZARU
THE SENATORS CHEER AND SHOUT AS AT A TRIUMPH.) 320 LAZARU
(APPEALING TO SENATE) AND YOU, SENATORS/ 322 LAZARU
AND THE SENATORS TURN TO RETIRE, HE STOPS THEM ALL322 LAZARU
FOR A MOMENT WITH A

SEND
GOD SEND HIS SOUL TO HELL FOR THE DEVIL HE IS/ 538 'ILE
THEY WANTS TO SEND A DEPITATION AFT TO HAVE A WORD543 'ILE
WITH YOU.
HE KNOWS, BECAUSE I HAD TO SEND HIM TO MARKET FOR 214 AHWILD
IT.
I'VE A GOOD MIND TO SEND YOU STRAIGHT BACK TO BED 270 AHWILD
AND MAKE YOU STAY THERE/
I GOT GOOD AND SICK AND THEY HAD TO SEND ME TO THE 16 ANNA
HOSPITAL.
WOULD SEND YOUR SOUL TO THE DIVILS IN HELL IF YOU 74 ANNA
WAS LYING
(INCONSEQUENTIALLY) I HAD TO SEND IT COLLECT. 146 BEYOND
(OURT) I WANTED TO SEND YOU WORD ONCE, BUT HE 154 BEYOND
ONLY GOT MAD WHEN I TOLD HIM.
I'LL READ THE MATTER UP AND SEND HIM SOME 485 CARDIF
MEDICINE.
SEND FATHER BAIRD IN. 500 DAYS
DIDN'T HE SEND ME EVERY ONE WITH BLUE PENCIL 503 DAYS
UNDERLININGS/
YOU JUST SEND UNCLE AND ME OFF TO MY STUDY. 533 DAYS
EVEN IF HE CAME, WE'D ONLY SEND HIM TO THE INSANE 543 DAYS
ASYLUM
WE'LL SEND YE A LUMP O' GOLD FUR CHRISTMAS. 220 DESIRE
(TAUNTINGLY) WOULDN'T YE LIKE US TO SEND YE BACK 223 DESIRE
SOME SINFUL GULD.
AND I'LL TRY TO SAVE UP MY PAY AND SEND YOU BACK 532 DIFRNT
ALL I'VE BORROWED NOW AND
(UNSUSPECTINGLY--WITH A GRIN) SEND FOR ME TO COME461 DYNAMO
HOME AND BE GOOD&
WHY, I THOUGHT-- DIDN'T THEY SEND FOR YOU& 461 DYNAMO
I HONESTLY DIDN'T SEND FOR YOU TO-- 118 ELECTR
(SUDDENLY--PLEADING) YOU SIMPLY MUST SEND HIM TO 260 GGBROW
COLLEGE/
WILL YOU STOP AT THE BUTCHERS' AND HAVE THEM SEND 273 GGBROW
TWO POUNDS OF PORK CHOPS&
IT WAS UP TO ME TO GIVE HUGHIE A BIG-TIME SEND- 33 HUGHIE
OFF.
IT SURE WAS WORTH IT TO GIVE HUGHIE THE BIG SEND- 35 HUGHIE
OFF.
YUH REMEMBER DEY USED TO SEND DOWN A PRIVATE DICK 581 ICEMAN
--I HOPE THEY SEND HIM TO SING SING FOR LIFE.= 606 ICEMAN
WE OUGHT TO PHONE DE BUDDY HATCH TO SEND ROUND DE 614 ICEMAN
MAN KNOW FER 'EM.
WE DON'T WANT TO KNOW THINGS THAT WILL MAKE US 706 ICEMAN
HELP SEND YOU TO THE CHAIR/
SO I'LL WAIT, AND WHEN YOU'RE READY YOU SEND FOR 711 ICEMAN
ME AND WE'LL BE MARRIED.
(ANGRILY) 'COS DRTSC HEARD THE FIRST SEND THE 515 INZONE
THIRD BELOW TO WAKE THE SKIPPER
(STUNG.) I'LL SEND HIM WHEREVER HARDY THINKS 79 JOURNE
BEST/
WHERE DOES HARDY WANT TO SEND HIM& 79 JOURNE
WHY DIDN'T YOU SEND HER TO A CURE THEN, AT THE 141 JOURNE
START.
WHY DIDN'T I SEND HER TO A CURE, YOU SAYS 141 JOURNE
DOCTORS GET A CUT FOR EVERY PATIENT THEY SEND. 164 JOURNE
SEND HERADS TO MAKE THEM/ 362 LAZARU
BUT YOU WOULD SEND ME INTO MY STUDY TO WORK ON IT 46 MANSNS
LIKE A REGULAR SLAVE-DRIVER/
TO REQUEST THE POPE TO SEND HIM A HUNDRED WISE MEN359 MARCOM
OF THE WEST
I WILL SEND HIM A MONK OR TWO. 363 MARCOM
I SHALL SEND HIM HOME TO HIS NATIVE WALLOW. 387 MARCOM
STUFF HIM WITH FOOD AND GOLD AND SEND HIM HOME. 419 MARCOM
SEND HIM ANOTHER MILLION. 424 MARCOM
SAY IT A THIRD TIME AND I'LL SEND MY DAUGHTER TO 59 MISBEG
TELEPHONE THE ASYLUM.
I'LL COME BACK SOMETIME WHEN YOU'RE SOBER--OR SEND 60 MISBEG
SIMPSON--
DIDN'T ME SEND YOU TO SCHOOL SO YOU COULD TALK 23 POET
LIKE A GENTLEMAN'S DAUGHTERS
WHEN CORPORAL CREGAN RETURNS, MICKEY, SEND HIM IN 57 POET
TO ME.
OR YOU'D THINK HE'D SEND JAMIE OR SOMEONE BACK 138 POET
WITH A WORD FOR ME.

SENSE

SEND (CONT'D.)
OR I'LL SEND YOU AWAY, AND THEN AFTER A TIME I'LL 149 STRANG
CALL YOU BACK.
I'LL SEND YOU A COUPLE OF MILLION CELLS YOU CAN 170 STRANG
TORTURE WITHOUT HARMING

SENDING
THAT'S NO KIND OF THING TO BE SENDING A DECENT 205 AHWILD
GIRL.
THE IDEA OF YOUR SENDING A NICE GIRL LIKE HER 216 AHWILD
YOU KNOW PA'S PUNISHING ME BY SENDING ME TO BED AT280 AHWILD
EIGHT SHARP.
EVERY MAN OF YOUR MEANS IN TOWN IS SENDING HIS 289 AHWILD
BOYS TO COLLEGE/
OTHERWISE I'D FIND IT DIFFICULT TO UNDERSTAND YOUR 29 ELECTR
SENDING ANNIE TO DISTURB ME
HE'S SENDING SILLY TO COLLEGE--MRS. BROWN JUST 260 GGBROW
TOLD ME--
THAT'S WHY YOU'RE SENDING ME TO A STATE FARM-- 149 JOURNE
I'M SENDING HIM TO THE CITY BY THE FIRST STAGE 62 MANSNS
AND THE HANDS ARE SENDING A DEPUTATION. 146 MANSNS
WELL, I WAS SENDING IN TO YOUR TREASURY THE TAXES 391 MARCOM
OF YANG-CHAU
SHE'S SENDING HIM AWAY/... 147 STRANG

SENDS
(HE GIVES HIM ANOTHER PUSH THAT ALMOST SENDS HIM 247 AHWILD
SPRAWLING.)
AND I HAD TO GET ALL UNDRESSED AND INTO BED 'CAUSE280 AHWILD
AT HALF-PAST HE SENDS MA UP
(HE GIVES CHRIS A PUSH WITH THE FLAT OF HIS HAND 50 ANNA
WHICH SENDS THE OLD SWEDE
(GIVES HIM A FURIOUS PUSH WHICH SENDS HIM 264 DESIRE
STAGGERING BACK
(GIVES HIM A PUSH AWAY THAT SENDS HIM SPRAWLING-- 265 DESIRE
ALWAYS SENDS THE COLD SHIVERS DOWN MY BACK MINUTE 189 EJOUNS
I GETS IN IT.
(SAVAGELY--GIVING HIM A PUSH THAT SENDS HIM 237 HA APE
SPRAWLING)
HOW D'YOU SPOSE SPIES GETS THEIR ORDERS AND SENDS529 INZONE
BACK WHAT THEY FINDS OUT IF
OFF BALANCE AND SENDS HIM SPINNING DOWN THE STEPS 190 MANSNS
TO FALL HEAVILY AND LIE STILL
OR IS IT ONLY THEES INFERNAL HANCEMAN FLEAS THE 360 MARCOM
ALMIGHTY SENDS US FOR OUR SINS&
(GIVING HIS FATHER ONE MORE SHAKE, WHICH SENDS HIM597 ROPE
SPRAWLING ON THE FLOOR)
WHICH SENDS HIM REELING BACK AGAINST THE WALL) 477 WELDED

SENEX
--FORTUNATE SENEX, ERGO TUA RURA MANEBUNT, ET TIBI 37 MISBEG
MAGNA SATIS.

SENILE
HE IS BECOMING SENILE. 355 LAZARU
THEY WOULD HAVE SMILED LIKE SENILE, 85 POET
(BURSTING INTO SENILE RAGE) NONE O' MINE/ 581 ROPE

SENIOR
THERE WASN'T ANYONE THERE BUT A PRINCETON SENIOR 1282 AHWILD
KNOW--HE BELONGS
THAT WAS IN THE WINTER OF SENIOR YEAR. 176 JOURNE
I MADE A BET WITH ANOTHER SENIOR I COULD GET A 30 MISBEG
TAXI FROM THE HAYMARKET TO VISIT
THE TIME HE WAS TAPPED FOR AN EXCLUSIVE SENIOR 55 MISBEG
SOCIETY
HE WAS A SENIOR WHEN I WAS A FRESHMAN. 30 STRANG

SENSATION
(DRUNKENLY GLORYING IN THE SENSATION HE IS 261 AHWILD
CREATING--
SENSATIONAL
I THINK YOU'VE TIRED ELSA OUT WITH YOUR 540 DAYS
SENSATIONAL IMAGININGS, JACK.

SENSE
SEEMS TO HAVE BLUNTED YOUR SENSE OF HUMOR. 192 AHWILD
THAT'S WHY I'M GIVING HER CREDIT FOR ORDINARY GOLU202 AHWILD
SENSE
YOU'D OUGHT TO DO IT FOR HIS SAKE, IF YOU HAD ANY 203 AHWILD
SENSE--
SO I DON'T SEE ANY SENSE IN IT. 271 AHWILD
NOW YOU'RE TALKING SENSE/ 271 AHWILD
WHY DIDN'T YOU HAVE MORE SENSE THAN TO LET HIM 286 AHWILD
MAKE YOU WRITE IT&
JUST HORSE SENSE ABOUT HIMSELF. 289 AHWILD
YOU DON'T GIVE ME CREDIT FOR EVER HAVING COMMON 291 AHWILD
SENSE, THAT'S WHY.
MURIEL'S GOT GOOD SENSE AND YOU HAVE&T/ 296 AHWILD
WHICH HARD USAGE HAS FAILED TO STIFLE, A SENSE OF 7 ANNA
HUMOR MOCKING.
THAT'S GOOD SENSE FOR YOU. 13 ANNA
(THE IRONY OF IT STRIKES HER SENSE OF HUMOR AND 17 ANNA
SHE LAUGHS HOARSELY.)
I'VE HALF A MIND TO HIT YOU A GREAT CLOUT WILL PUT 49 ANNA
SENSE IN YOUR SQUARE HEAD.
AY GAT BETTER SENSE RIGHT AWAY. 67 ANNA
(KISSING HER--GAYLY) AS YOU LIKE--LITTLE MISS 93 BEYOND
COMMON SENSE/
IT AIN'T COMMON SENSE--NO SIREE, IT AIN'T--NOT BY 102 BEYOND
A HELL OF A SIGHT/
IT SOUNDS STRANGE TO HEAR YOU, ANDY, THAT I ALWAYS105 BEYOND
THOUGHT HAD GOOD SENSE.
SHE WOULDN'T LISTEN TO SENSE. 116 BEYOND
THERE WOULDN'T BE ANY SENSE. 133 BEYOND
ALTHOUGH AT TIMES ONE ANOTHER MAY SUBTLY SENSE 449 DAYS
HIS PRESENCE.
AND ONE GETS IMMEDIATELY FROM HIM THE SENSE OF 500 DAYS
UNSHAKABLE INNER CALM AND
BUT THERE HAVE BEEN TIMES WHEN I'VE HAD THE 557 DAYS
STRONGEST SENSE OF--
(WITH A SCORNFUL SENSE OF POWER) 225 DESIRE
ABBIE SEEMS TO SENSE SOMETHING. 292 DESIRE
AN' SHE SAYS NO, THAT HAI'T SENSE, 255 DESIRE

SENSE

SENSE (CONT'D.)

THEY'S NO CAUSE FOR YE T' GO NOW--THEY'S NO 260 DESIRE SENSE--IT'S ALL THE SAME'S IT WAS-- IT'S YEW I SHOULD'VE MURDERED, IF I'D HAD GOOD 264 DESIRE SENSE/ YOU'LL NEVER GET SENSE. 499 DIFRNT YOU'LL MAYBE LISTEN TO HER AND GIT SOME SENSE. 505 DIFRNT (YOUR BETWEEN CURIOSITY AND A SENSE OF BEING ONE 507 DIFRNT TOO MANY) BUT HER--SHE OUGHT TO HAVE BETTER SENSE-- 525 DIFRNT AIN'T YOU GOT SENSE ENOUGH, YOU BIG LUMP, TO 528 DIFRNT ANSWER ME WHEN I CALL? AND TRY TO PUT SOME SENSE BACK INTO HER HEAD. 529 DIFRNT (HIS SENSE OF HUMOR RETURNING--WITH A MALICIOUS 432 DYNAMO GRIN) (THIS WITH AN EXASPERATED SENSE OF FRUSTRATION, 448 DYNAMO GAZING AT REUBEN'S SET FACE) TALK SENSE, ADA/ 470 DYNAMO HE'LL ADDLE THE LITTLE SENSE YOU'VE LEFT/ 479 DYNAMO GIVE ME CREDIT FO' HAVIN' SOME SENSE, FO' LAWD'S 183 EJONES SAKE/ JONES SEEMS TO SENSE THE MEANING OF THIS. 201 EJONES A SENSE OF PROTECTION, MAYBE/ 53 ELECTR (OVERCOME BY A SENSE OF GUILT--VIOLENTLY 98 ELECTR DEFENSIVE) OH, BY THE ETERNAL, I'LL COME DOWN AND POUND SOME 105 ELECTR SENSE IN YOUR HEAD/ A SENSE OF DREAD AND DESPERATION.) 150 ELECTR DOWN TO COMMON SENSE, WITH HIS CRAZY WILDCAT 260 GGBROW NOTIONS. YET TO THEM, SUCH IS MY ART, IT WILL APPEAR TO 313 GGBROW POSSESS A PURE COMMON-SENSE, BESS USUALLY HAD BETTER SENSE, BUT SHE WAS IN A 608 ICEMAN HURRY TO GO TO CHURCH. BY THE CHANGE THEY NOW SENSE IN HIM.) 620 ICEMAN I HAVE TO ADMIT THERE WAS SOME SENSE IN HIS 626 ICEMAN NONSENSE. I'M GLAD YOU'RE GETTIN' SOME SENSE. 697 ICEMAN FINALLY HE SEEMS TO SENSE THE HOSTILE ATMOSPHERE 923 INZONE OF THE FORECASTLE AND LOOKS SHE IS DRESSED SIMPLY BUT WITH A SURE SENSE OF 12 JOURNE WHAT BECOMES HAVEN'T YOU ANY SENSE! 29 JOURNE THERE'S NO SENSE LETTING YOUR FEAR OF THE 117 JOURNE POORHOUSE MAKE YOU TOO STINGY. I'VE GIVEN UP HOPE HE'LL EVER GET SENSE. 128 JOURNE (HAS WATCHED THIS PROCEEDING WITH AN AWAKENED 128 JOURNE SENSE OF HUMOR-- WHAT DO WE WANT WITH SENSE! 130 JOURNE TO HELL WITH SENSE/ WE'RE ALL CRAZY. 130 JOURNE YOU SHOULD HAVE MORE SENSE THAN TO RISK-- 130 JOURNE I'M TALKING SENSE. 131 JOURNE AND KEEP YOUR SENSE OF HUMOR. 157 JOURNE SURELY YOUR GOOD SENSE TELLS YOU-- 370 LAZARU FOR A CONSTANTLY SENSE, IN THE SECONDS AND MINUTES 12 MANSNS AND HOURS FLOWING THROUGH ME, AND RETURN TO COMMON SENSE IN THE LITTLE TIME LEFT 14 MANSNS US. THAT I WILL OUTRAGE YOUR SENSE OF PROPRIETY BY 29 MANSNS SUICIDE. HEARTLESSLY UNCOMPREHENDING BUT DISTURBED BECAUSE 30 MANSNS HE SENSES HER DESPAIR. YES, DEBORAH, THE ATMOSPHERE IS HARDLY CONDUCIVE 37 MANSNS TO--COMMON SENSE, SHALL I SAY! SATISFACTION AND SENSE OF SELF-FULFILLMENT AND 46 MANSNS PRIDE OUT OF BEATING MY I DO, AND I'M GRATEFUL YOU HAD THE FAIRNESS AND 66 MANSNS GOOD SENSE NOT TO-- I MEANT SHE HAS NO SENSE OF THE RIGHTS TO FREEDOM 86 MANSNS OF OTHERS. ONE FINALLY GETS A SENSE OF CONFUSION IN THE 92 MANSNS MEANING OF THE GAME. THIS FACADE MAKES ALL THE MORE PITIINGLY ACUTE THE150 MANSNS SENSE ONE IMMEDIATELY GETS MAYBE THAT WILL BRING SOME SENSE BACK IN YOUR 167 MANSNS HEAD. I HAVE NEVER FORGOTTEN THE ANGUISHED SENSE OF 184 MANSNS BEING SUDDENLY BETRAYED. HIS MILKINESS THOUGHT YOU MUST HAVE A SENSE OF 377 MARCOM HUMOR. A MAN OF YOUR COMMON SENSE. 396 MARCOM SOUND COMMON SENSE AND A HOME WHERE EVERTHING RUNS416 MARCOM SMOOTH. YOU KNOW I'LL BEAT BETTER SENSE IN YOUR SKULL IF 15 MISBEG YOU LAY A FINGER ON ME. SLOW ON THE UPTAKE, AND HAS NO SENSE OF HUMOR. 56 MISBEG I'M BEGINNING TO READ SOME SENSE INTO THIS. 61 MISBEG SLEEP IT OFF TILL YOU GET SOME SENSE. 77 MISBEG I THINK NOW MIKE'S THE ONLY ONE IN THIS HOUSE 86 MISBEG WITH SENSE. EVERYONE OUGHT TO BE, IF THEY HAVE ANY SENSE. 129 MISBEG SHE HAD THE SENSE TO SEE HE'D BEEN DRINKING AND 77 POET NOT TO MIND HIM. IN MY OPINION, THE LADY DISPLAYED MORE COMMON 109 POET SENSE AND KNOWLEDGE OF THE WORLD YOU'VE STILL GOT SOME SURE SENSE IN YOU. 126 POET IT'S SMALL SENSE YOU HAVE TO HIDE YOUR HATE FROM 590 ROPE HIM. BUT THAT HER FATHER'S DEATH IS A SHOCK IN THE 34 STRANG USUAL SENSE OF GRIEF. WILL GRADUALLY GIVE HER BACK A SENSE OF SECURITY 37 STRANG AND A FEELING OF BEING WORTH BUT ALL HE NEEDS IS A LITTLE SELF-CONFIDENCE AND A 38 STRANG SENSE OF RESPONSIBILITY. DOESN'T THAT SEEM GOOD SENSE TO YOU! 38 STRANG TO EXPECT COMMON SENSE OF PEOPLE PROVES YOU'RE 79 STRANG LACKING IN IT YOURSELF/...))

SENSE (CONT'D.)

IT MIGHT REVIVE MY SENSE OF HUMOR ABOUT MYSELF, AT123 STRANG LEAST... THERE'S NO SENSE/... 129 STRANG I WOULD LIKE TO BE HER HUSBAND AND IN A SENSE... 135 STRANG THERE IS BENEATH THIS A SENSE OF GREAT MENTAL 137 STRANG STRAIN. 'TIS A FOINE SIGHT TO SEE A MAN WID SOME SENSE IN 498 VOYAGE HIS HEAD. YOU GOT SENSE, YOU 'AVE. 501 VOYAGE (WITH AN AWKWARD SENSE OF HAVING BECOME RHETORICAL448 WELDED HE ADDS SELF-MOCKINGLY) IF YOU HAD ANY SENSE 455 WELDED NOT IN YOUR COMMERCIAL SENSE, PERHAPS, BUT-- 457 WELDED AND THIS HEIGHTENS THE SENSE OF LONELINESS ABOUT 462 WELDED HIM. NOW YOU'RE TALKING SENSE. 465 WELDED

SENSED

AS IF HE CONSTANTLY SENSED A MALIGNANT SPIRIT 535 DAYS HIDING BEHIND LIFE, AS IF HE SUDDENLY SENSED A PRESENCE THERE THE 551 DAYS PRIEST IS PRAYING TO. ABBIE HAS SENSED HIS MOVEMENT. 228 DESIRE BUT EVEN WHEN HE WAS LITTLE I SENSED IN HIM HIS 426 DYNAMO MOTHER'S REBELLIOUS SPIRIT... AS IF THEIR MINDS HAD PARTLY SENSED THE TENOR OF 119 MANSNS HIS THOUGHT.

SENSELESS

OH, THE WHOLE AFFAIR IS SO SENSELESS--AND TRAGIC. 109 BEYOND ANOTHER WORD BLURTED INTO A SENSELESS SIGH BY 353 LAZARU MEN'S LONGING/ DON'T TRY RUNNING AWAY OR MY DAUGHTER WILL KNOCK 61 MISBEG YOU SENSELESS. AND HE'LL KNOCK HIM SENSELESS WITH ONE BLOW. 146 POET THE LAST THING I SAW BEFORE I WAS KNOCKED 158 POET SENSELESS BUT THEY KNOCKED US SENSELESS AND RODE US TO THE 159 POET STATION AND LOCKED US UP.

SENSES

(SHAKING HIS HEAD) I THINK THE MAN'S MIGHTY NIGH 537 'ILE LOSIN' HIS SENSES. AND MAYBE LOSE HER SENSES FOREVER--FOR IT'S SURE 538 'ILE SHE'LL NEVER BE THE SAME AGAIN. AND EVERY TIME HE SENSES ANY OF THE FAMILY 249 AHWILD GLANCING IN HIS DIRECTION, CURING THE SOUL BY MEANS OF THE SENSES, AS OSCAR 271 AHWILD WILDE SAYS. BUT BENEATH ALL HIS MILDNESS ONE SENSES THE MAN 3 ANNA BEHIND THE MASK-- I KNEW ANDY'D COME TO HIS SENSES/ 105 BEYOND DON'T SAY A WORD TO HIM 'TIL HE'S IN HIS RIGHT 107 BEYOND SENSES AGAIN. WHERE SHE'S WORRIED NEAR OUT OF HER SENSES BY HIS 114 BEYOND GUIN'S-ON. PICKED UP HE WHERE ON THE SAME DAY WID ONLY YANK IN482 CARDIF HIS SENSES, AND I HAD FAITH, IF LET ALONE, HE'D COME BACK TO 502 DAYS HIS SENSES IN THE END. HARKER SAID YOU'D BEEN ACTIN' OUT O' YOUR RIGHT 542 DIFRNT SENSES. ONE SENSES A STRONG TRACE OF HER MOTHER'S 429 DYNAMO SENTIMENTALITY.) HASN'T MY LOVE FOR AMELIA BEEN ONE LUNG DESIRE OF 435 DYNAMO THE SENSES?... LAVINIA SENSES HER PRESENCE AND WHIRLS AROUND. 15 ELECTR BUT ONE SENSES AN UNEASY WARINESS BENEATH HER 16 ELECTR POISE) CHRISTINE AT ONCE SENSES HER PRESENCE BEHIND HER 71 ELECTR (IMMEDIATELY SENSES HER PRESENCE--CONTROLLING A 91 ELECTR START, HARSHLY) BECAUSE HE THOUGHT A CHANGE WOULD BRING HER BACK 108 ELECTR TO HER SENSES. SHE QUICKLY SENSES SOMETHING IN THE ATMOSPHERE 162 ELECTR HE IMMEDIATELY SENSES WHO IT IS--WITH ALARM) 314 GGBROW THEN DESPERATELY, AS IF TO DROWN HIS SENSES, 216 HA APE ALL UP A SUDDEN ROCKY SENSES THEY ARE DETECTIVES 708 ICEMAN AND SPRINGS UP TO FACE THEM. WITHOUT TURNING, JAMIE SENSES THIS.) 65 JOURNE BUT ONE SENSES AN INNER SENSE EXCITEMENT, A VITAL 50 MANSNS EAGER MENTAL ALIVENESS. GIVEN A FOCUS, THE WILL CAN PERHAPS OVERCOME THE 426 MARCOM LIMITS OF THE SENSES. ONE SENSES A TENSE EXPECTANCY OF SOME SIGN FROM 433 MARCOM THE THRONE. MELODY SENSES HER PRESENCE. 44 POET BUT SARA SENSES HER PRESENCE AND LOOKS UP.) 136 POET HE'S COME TO HIS SENSES FOR ONCE IN HIS LIFE/ 158 POET WHERE THERE'S MEN IN THEIR RIGHT SENSES LAUGHING 165 POET AND SINGING? THE AULD DIVIL WAS PLAIN IN HIS FULL SENSES WHEN 586 ROPE HE MADE IT.. HE'LL NOT LAST LUNG IN HIS SENSES, THE DOCTOR TOLD587 ROPE AH' HIM TAKIN' LEAVE OF HIS SENSES ALTOGETHER. 587 ROPE HER POWER TO ENSLAVE MEN'S SENSES.... 74 STRANG DARRELL IMMEDIATELY SENSES HER PRESENCE, AND, 79 STRANG LOOKING UP, I AM THE ONLY ONE WHO SENSES HIS DEEP HURT.... 148 STRANG

SENSIBILITY

AND RARE FLASHES OF INTUITIVE SENSIBILITY. 14 JOURNE IT IS IN THE QUALITY OF EXTREME NERVOUS 20 JOURNE SENSIBILITY THAT THE LIKENESS OF EDMUND

SENSIBLE

THERE CAN BE ONLY ONE SENSIBLE, LOGICAL END FOR 498 DAYS YOUR HERO. BUT THERE IS STILL ANOTHER END OF MY STORY--THE 545 DAYS ONE SENSIBLE HAPPY END/ 'TAIN'T SENSIBLE. 234 DESIRE

1395

SENTIMENTAL

SENSIBLE (CONT'D.)
AS GOOD AS ANY SENSIBLE GIRL'D WANT TO MARRY. 512 DIFERNT
HE STRIKES ME AS THE ONLY BLOODY SENSIBLE MEDICO 1627 ICEMAN
EVER HEARD OF.
(NODDING APPROVINGLY) YOU ARE SENSIBLE. 301 LAZARU
IN YOUR CONSENTING TO THE ONE SENSIBLE COURSE. 38 MANSNS
WITHOUT GIVING HIM ANY SENSIBLE REASON-- 110 MANSNS
I'LL BE SENSIBLE NOW AND READ MY BOOK-- 114 MANSNS
THE REAL REASON I CAME HERE WAS TO HAVE A SENSIBLE167 MANSNS
TALK WITH YOU.
WILL SOBER HER SPIRIT AND SHE WILL SETTLE DOWN AS 424 MARCOM
A SENSIBLE WIFE SHOULD.
IT'S SO OBVIOUSLY THE SENSIBLE THING...!) 79 STRANG
IT'S SENSIBLE AND KIND AND JUST AND GOOD. 84 STRANG
BE SENSIBLE, FOR GOD'S SAKE! 103 STRANG
(THINKING CAUTIOUSLY) I'LL MUST KEEP VERY COOL AND165 STRANG
SENSIBLE OR HE WON'T HELP.
SENSIBLE UNICELLULAR LIFE THAT FLOATS IN THE SEA 198 STRANG

SENSIBLY
(QUIETLY AGAIN.) REGARDED SENSIBLY, 180 MANSNS
(APPROVINGLY) SENSIBLY DONE, MY BOY. 361 MARCOM

SENSING
(IMMEDIATELY SENSING SOMETHING =DOWN= IN HIS 208 AHWILD
MANNER--GOING TO HIM WORRIEDLY)
(SENSING THE HURT IN HIS TONE, COMES TO HIS 230 AHWILD
RESCUE)
(SHE STOPS, LOOKING FROM ONE TO THE OTHER, SENSING 50 ANNA
IMMEDIATELY THAT SOMETHING
(SENSING SOMETHING FROM HIS MANNER--EAGERLY) 71 ELECTR
(SENSING HER UNEASINESS--MOCKINGLY) 162 ELECTR
NOT UNDERSTANDING WHAT IS BEHIND THEIR TALK BUT 164 ELECTR
SENSING SOMETHING SINISTER,
JAMIE HAS BECOME RESTLESS, SENSING HIS FATHER'S 168 JOURNE
PRESENCE.
(SENSING SOMETHING) HAS THIS MAN OFFENDED YOU8 419 MARCOM
(SENSING HIS PRESENCE, STOPS CRYING AND LIFTS HER 174 MISBEG
HEAD--DULLY)
(THEN SUDDENLY SENSING MARSDEN'S CURIOSITY-- 51 STRANG
PERFUNCTORILY)
(SENSING HER THOUGHTS, SITS UP IN HER LAP AND 156 STRANG
STARES INTO HER FACE,

SENSITIVE
REMEMBER HE'S LIKE YOU INSIDE--TOO SENSITIVE FOR 265 AHWILD
HIS OWN GOOD.
HIS EYES ARE LARGE, SHY AND SENSITIVE, OF THE SAME422 DYNAMO
BLUE-GRAY AS HIS FATHER'S.
(DIFFERENTLY.) I THOUGHT HE MIGHT BE SENSITIVE 277 GGBROW
ABOUT WORKING FOR--
SENSITIVE AND SELF-CONSCIOUS AND PROUD AND 297 GGBROW
REVENGEFUL--
I KNOW GUYS IS SENSITIVE ABOUT THEM LITTLE 27 HUGHIE
AFFLICTIONS.
HER NOSE IS LONG AND STRAIGHT, HER MOUTH WIDE WITH 12 JOURNE
FULL, SENSITIVE LIPS.
THE MORE SO BECAUSE ONE IS CONSCIOUS SHE IS 12 JOURNE
SENSITIVE ABOUT THEIR APPEARANCE AND
HE WAS BORN NERVOUS AND TOO SENSITIVE, AND THAT'S 88 JOURNE
MY FAULT.
SWOLLEN-KNUCKLED, SENSITIVE FINGERS DROOPING IN 107 JOURNE
COMPLETE CALM.
(BITTERLY.) I'M AFRAID YOU'RE NOT VERY SENSITIVE,119 JOURNE
AFTER ALL.
THE MOUTH OF MIRIAM IS SENSITIVE AND SAD, TENDER 274 LAZARU
WITH AN EAGER,
A WIDE SENSITIVE MOUTH, A FINE FOREHEAD, LARGE 4 MANSNS
EARS, THICK BROWN HAIR,
SHE IS VERY SENSITIVE AND PROUD-- 8 MANSNS
YOU WERE EXTREMELY SENSITIVE AND IMAGINATIVE--AS A 12 MANSNS
CHILD.
I HAVE A PRIDE UNDULY SENSITIVE TO ANY FANCIED 70 POET
SLIGHT.
MORBIDLY SUPER-SENSITIVE ALREADY, 45 STRANG
LUST WITH A LOATHSOME JEER TAUNTING MY SENSITIVE 100 STRANG
TIMIDITIES/...
FUTILE BUT HE HAD A SENSITIVE QUALITY... 113 STRANG

SENSITIVENESS
THERE IS SOMETHING OF EXTREME SENSITIVENESS 193 AHWILD
ADDED--
SENSITIVENESS, A BROAD FOREHEAD, BLUE EYES. 493 DAYS
HIS EYES ARE FULL OF A QUICK-TEMPERED 137 STRANG
SENSITIVENESS.

SENSUAL
HER CHIN IS HEAVY, HER MOUTH LARGE AND SENSUAL, 9 ELECTR
THE LOWER LIP FULL.
THE SAME SENSUAL MOUTH, THE SAME HEAVY JAW. 10 ELECTR
HIS WIDE MOUTH IS SENSUAL AND MOODY-- 21 ELECTR
GAYLY SCOFFING AND SENSUAL YOUNG PAN. 260 GGBROW
SHE IS A STRONG, CALM SENSUAL,BLONDE GIRL OF 278 GGBROW
TWENTY OR SO.
HIS HOLLOW TEMPLES AND HIS BULBOUS, SENSUAL NOSE. 299 LAZARU
ITS STUBBORN CHARACTER BECOME REPELLENTLY SENSUAL,139 MANSNS
RUTHLESSLY CRUEL AND GREEDY.
SHE IS PAINTED, HALF-NAKED, ALLURING IN A BRAZEN, 367 MARCOM
SENSUAL WAY.
WITH A FINELY CHISELED NOSE OVER A DOMINEERING, 34 POET
SENSUAL MOUTH SET IN DISOAIN.
HE TAKES IN ALL HER POINTS WITH SENSUAL 69 POET
APPRECIATION.
ALL FLESH NOW...LUST...WHO WOULD DREAM SHE WAS SO 20 STRANG
SENSUAL...

SENSUALIST
IS IT HIS LOOKS--OR BECAUSE HE'S SUCH A VIOLENT 289 GGBROW
SENSUALIST--
THE NOSE AND MOUTH OF A SENSUALIST. 443 WELDED

SENSUALIST'S
(HE STARES AT HER WITH A DELIBERATE SENSUALIST'S 114 MISBEG
LOOK THAT UNDRESSES HER)

SENSUALITY
HER ROUND FACE IS PRETTY BUT MARRED BY ITS RATHER 221 DESIRE
GROSS SENSUALITY.
HER MOUTH, ON THE OTHER HAND, HAS A TOUCH OF 2 MANSNS
COARSE SENSUALITY ABOUT ITS THICK,
HER MOUTH, ON THE OTHER HAND, HAS A TOUCH OF 15 POET
COARSENESS AND SENSUALITY

SENSUALLY
(SENSUALLY AROUSED--KISSING HIS HAIR.) 87 MANSNS

SENTENCE
INTERRUPTING HIM AT THE END OF EACH SENTENCE WITH 478 CAMDIF
LOUD DERISIVE GUFFAWS)
(IN A GOOD VOICE, AS IF HE WERE PRONOUNCING A 939 DAYS
DEATH SENTENCE)
THE PERIOD AT THE CLOSE OF A SIMPLE SENTENCE, SAY, 30 MANSNS
(HE TYPES A SENTENCE OR TWO, A STRAINED FROWN OF 68 STRANG
CONCENTRATION ON HIS FACE.

SENTENCED
RICHARD, KEENLY CONSCIOUS OF HIMSELF AS THE ABOUT-293 AHWILD
TO-BE-SENTENCED CRIMINAL BY

SENTENCES
WHILE THEY ARE DOING THIS HE KEEPS ON TALKING IN 48 ELECTR
HIS ABRUPT SENTENCES,

SENTENTIOUSLY
(SENTENTIOUSLY) YEAH. 612 ICEMAN
(SENTENTIOUSLY) WHOA CAESAR FEARS--DISAPPEARS/ 302 LAZARU

SENTIMENT
HE QUOTES WITH GREAT SENTIMENT, IF WITH SLIGHT 599 ICEMAN
APPLICATION)
AS IF THIS SENTIMENT STRUCK A RESPONSIVE CHORD IN 701 ICEMAN
THEIR NUMBED MINDS.
THAT THERE BE NO HYPOCRITICAL FAMILY SENTIMENT IN 58 MANSNS
THIS BARGAIN.
LET ME SAY THAT ANY SENTIMENT OF GRATITUDE ON YOUR153 MANSNS
PART IS UNCALLED FOR.

SENTIMENTAL
(SUDDENLY SENTIMENTAL) POOR KID. 247 AHWILD
HE SINGS THAT OLD SENTIMENTAL FAVORITE, =THEN 257 AHWILD
YOU'LL REMEMBER ME.=
PLAYING UP ITS SENTIMENTAL VALUE FOR ALL HE IS 258 AHWILD
WORTH.
A PRETTY, SENTIMENTAL ENDING--BUT A BIT TOO 494 DAYS
POINTED. DON'T YOU THINKS
HER VOICE IS SENTIMENTAL AND WONDERING. 428 DYNAMO
SENTIMENTAL MOURNFULNESS.) 106 ELECTR
WITH MANY ULTRA-SENTIMENTAL BARBER-SHOP QUAVERS. 257 GGBROW
THE PLAYER-PIANO IS SHRUGGILY BANGING OUT A 278 GGBRUN
SENTIMENTAL MEDLEY
THE SAME SENTIMENTAL MEDLEY BEGINS TO PLAY. 279 GGBROW
THE SAME SENTIMENTAL TUNE STARTS. 280 GGBROW
THE PIANO IS WHINING OUT ITS SAME OLD SENTIMENTAL 284 GGBROW
MEDLEY.
WHICH STARTS UP ITS OLD SENTIMENTAL TUNE. 288 GGBROW
GO TO THE DEVIL, YOU SENTIMENTAL OLD PIG/ 288 GGBROW
A VERY DRUNKEN SENTIMENTAL TENOR BEGINS TO SING)..211 HA APE
SOME SENTIMENTAL SOFTNESS BEHIND IT 9 HUGHIE
A TOUGH GUY BUT SENTIMENTAL, IN HIS WAY, AND GOOD-577 ICEMAN
NATURED.
THERE'S NOTHING SOFT OR SENTIMENTAL ABOUT MOTHER. 589 ICEMAN
(HIS FACE INSTANTLY BECOMING LONG AND SAD AND 602 ICEMAN
SENTIMENTAL--MOURNFULLY)
(WITH A HUGE SENTIMENTAL SIGH--AND A CALCULATING 603 ICEMAN
LOOK AT HOPE)
A SUITABLE SENTIMENTAL HUSH FALLS ON THE ROOM.) 603 ICEMAN
BOTH ARE SENTIMENTAL, FEATHER-BRAINED, GIGGLY, 811 ICEMAN
LAZY,
HOPE SUDDENLY BECOMES ALMOST TEARFULLY 656 ICEMAN
SENTIMENTAL)
WHO SPEAKS WITH MUZZY, SELF-PITYING MELANCHOLY OUT056 ICEMAN
OF A SENTIMENTAL DREAM.
(THEN HE DROPS HIS HAND--WITH SENTIMENTAL 687 ICEMAN
MELANCHOLY)
GOES ON IN A TUNE OF FOND, SENTIMENTAL 709 ICEMAN
REMINISCENCE)
(THEY ALL CHORUS HEARTY SENTIMENTAL ASSENT... 722 ICEMAN
HOPE BECOMES SENTIMENTAL) 722 ICEMAN
(LOOKS AROUND HIM IN AN ECSTASY OF BLEERY 724 ICEMAN
SENTIMENTAL CONTENT)
(HIS BLACK BULLET EYES SENTIMENTAL, HIS ROUND MOP 725 ICEMAN
FACE GRINNING WELCOME)
WITH STREAKS OF SENTIMENTAL MELANCHOLY 14 JOURNE
(BITTERLY.) YOU'RE A SENTIMENTAL FOOL. 107 JOURNE
ESCAPE TONIGHT TIBERIUS' MOOD IS TO PLAY 358 LAZARU
SENTIMENTAL.
NO MATTER HOW IT SHOCKS OUR SENTIMENTAL MORAL AND 47 MANSNS
RELIGIOUS DELUSIONS ABOUT HIM,
WHAT A SENTIMENTAL ASS YOU ARE, JOEL! 71 MANSNS
WE WILL DEAL WITH THE FACTS. IF YOU PLEASE, 99 MANSNS
MOTHER, NOT WITH SENTIMENTAL POSING.
WHAT MADE THEIR PETTY SENTIMENTAL WOMEN'S WORLD 120 MANSNS
MEANWHILE, KEEPING AN EYE ON THEM TO MAKE SURE 123 MANSNS
THIS SENTIMENTAL REUNION
YOU COULD REALLY HAVE WON THEN BLT YOU ARE WEAKLY 169 MANSNS
SENTIMENTAL AND PITIFUL.
AND OUR WEAK SENTIMENTAL MORAL EVASIONS OF OUR 179 MANSNS
NATURAL SELVES.
(THE SENTIMENTAL SINGING VOICES AND 357 MARCOM
(WITH SENTIMENTAL SOLEMNITY) 412 MARCOM
AN ORCHESTRA VIGOROUSLY BEGINS A FLOWERY, 428 MARCOM
SENTIMENTAL ITALIAN TUNE.
THAT OF THE BEGUILING NE'ER-DO-WELL, SENTIMENTAL 37 MISBEG
AND ROMANTIC.
HOW SENTIMENTAL... 12 STRANG
(SHORTLY AND DRYLY) WE CAN'T WASTE TIME BEING 35 STRANG
SENTIMENTAL, MARSDEN/
SENTIMENTAL NUNSENSE/... 96 STRANG
AND THEN HE BECAME SILLY AND SENTIMENTAL AND ASKED155 STRANG
ME TO KISS HIM GOOD-BYE FOR

SENTIMENTAL

SENTIMENTAL (CONT'D.)
THE KISSES ONE OF THE MUSES WITH A SIMPLE 187 STRANG
SENTIMENTAL SMILE--
LOST IN A SENTIMENTAL REVERIE. 443 WELDED
SENTIMENTALITY
HE HAS A FAIRLY DECENT VOICE BUT HIS METHOD IS 257 AHWILD
UNRAINED SENTIMENTALITY
ONE SENSES A STRONG TRACE OF HER MOTHER'S 429 DYNAMO
SENTIMENTALITY.)
(BENEATH HIS DRUNKEN SENTIMENTALITY THERE IS A 156 JOURNE
GENUINE SINCERITY.)
SENTIMENTALLY
SO SATISFYINGLY RIGHT THAT HE BECOMES 221 AHWILD
SENTIMENTALLY MOVED EVEN TO THINK OF IT)
THEN LAUGHS AND IMMEDIATELY BECOMES SENTIMENTALLY 242 AHWILD
GRATEFUL)
(SUDDENLY RECITES SENTIMENTALLY) 244 AHWILD
(SENTIMENTALLY) PALS IS PALS AND ANY PAL OF MINE 469 CARIBE
CAN HAVE ANYTHIN' I GOT, SEE?
(DREAMING SENTIMENTALLY) (IF HEAR ADA UPSTAIRS...429 DYNAMO
(HAS AGAIN FALLEN TO DREAMING SENTIMENTALLY OF THE430 DYNAMO
PAST)
(SENTIMENTALLY TOUCHED--BEAMING ON HIM) 458 DYNAMO
(SENTIMENTALLY) THAT'S RIGHT. 460 DYNAMO
(SHE PUTS HER ARM AROUND HIM--SENTIMENTALLY) 477 DYNAMO
(SENTIMENTALLY) MOST PEOPLE DON'T BELIEVE IN 478 DYNAMO
GHOSTS.
A BIT BLURRY WITH BOOZE NOW AND SENTIMENTALLY 103 ELECTR
MOURNFUL TO A DEGREE.
(SENTIMENTALLY) NOW, COME, CECIL, PIET/ 599 ICEMAN
(SENTIMENTALLY, WITH REAL YEARNING) 605 ICEMAN
(SENTIMENTALLY AGAIN BUT WITH DESPERATION) 688 ICEMAN
THAT OF THE BEGUILING NE'ER-DO-WELL, WITH A STRAIN 19 JOURNE
OF THE SENTIMENTALLY POETIC.
(FIGHTING TIPSY DROWSINESS--SENTIMENTALLY.) 106 JOURNE
(HE BECOMES SENTIMENTALLY ROMANTIC.) 47 POET
(THEN SENTIMENTALLY) POOR GUY/ 156 STRANG
HE WOULDN'T BE SOBBING SENTIMENTALLY ABOUT SAM... 191 STRANG
SENTIMENTS
YOU'D BETTER NOT REPEAT SUCH SENTIMENTS OUTSIDE 194 AHWILD
THE BOSOM OF THE FAMILY OR
(FROWNING.) KEEP YOUR DAMNED SOCIALIST ANARCHIST 25 JOURNE
SENTIMENTS OUT OF MY AFFAIRS/
KEEP SUCH SENTIMENTS TO YOURSELF. 132 JOURNE
THOSE HEROIC SENTIMENTS DO YOU A LOT OF CREDIT, 395 MARCOM
SENTINEL
STIFFLY ERECT LIKE A SENTINEL AT ATTENTION. 93 ELECTR
STANDING SQUARE-SHOULDERED AND STIFF LIKE A GRIM 123 ELECTR
SENTINEL IN BLACK.)
THE SENTINEL AND KNIGHT ADMIT THE MESSENGER BUT 361 MARCOM
PUSH BACK THE OTHERS.)
AT THE FOOT OF THE STAIRS, CHU-YIN STANDS LIKE A 400 MARCOM
SENTINEL.
SENTRY
SHE WAS PACING UP AND DOWN BEFORE THE HOUSE LIKE A 59 ELECTR
SENTRY GUARDING YOU.
SENTRY/ 319 LAZARU
LIKE A SENTRY GUARDING THE DOOR. 109 MANSNS
ON THE RIGHT, AN OPEN PORTAL WITH A SENTRY PACING 358 MARCOM
UP AND DOWN, SPEAR IN HAND.
SEPARATE
IN THE SEPARATE GROUPS AS THE CURTAIN RISES. 456 CARIBE
(THEY SEPARATE WITH STARTLED EXCLAMATIONS. 498 DIFRNT
IT WAS ALWAYS LIKE PRYIN' OPEN A SAFE FOR ME TO 522 DIFRNT
SEPARATE HIM FROM A CENT.
AS THE SEPARATE SCENES REQUIRE, -0 DYNAMO
ONLY WHEN THE EYE BECOMES ACCUSTOMED TO THE GLOOM 187 EJONES
CAN THE OUTLINES OF SEPARATE
THEY SEPARATE, STARTLED.) 56 ELECTR
I'M IN DE MIDDLE TRYIN' TO SEPARATE 'EM, 253 HA APE
EVEN HOPE'S BACK ROOM IS NOT A SEPARATE ROOM, 571 ICEMAN
BY THE SEPARATE TABLE AT RIGHT, FRONT, 629 ICEMAN
IN THE MIDDLE OF THE SEPARATE TABLE AT RIGHT, 629 ICEMAN
FRONT.
TWO SEPARATE GROUPS OF JEWS ARE GATHERED. 282 LAZARU
AS IF NOTHING HAD EVER HAPPENED TO SEPARATE THEM. 287 LAZARU
THE TWO GROUPS MECHANICALLY SEPARATE TO RIGHT AND 290 LAZARU
LEFT AGAIN.
THE NAZARENES AND THE ORTHODOX SEPARATE AND SLINK 291 LAZARU
QUIETLY APART.
TO LOSE THEIR SEPARATE IDENTITIES IN MY MIND'S 73 MANSNS
EYE--
NOW I WON'T HAVE A SEPARATE MAN'S LIFE FREE UF 120 MANSNS
WOMAN EVEN THERE/
I CANNOT KEEP THEM SEPARATE--THEY ARE TOO STRONG 129 MANSNS
HERE IN THEIR HOME--
THROUGH SEPARATE WAYS LOVE HAS BROUGHT US BOTH TO 477 WELDED
THIS ROOM.
SEPARATED
ALWAYS FIGHTING AND SEPARATED A LOT OF THE TIME, 83 BEYOND
THEY ARE SEPARATED BY NARROW STRIPS OF LAWN, -0 DYNAMO
MARCO MANAGES TO GET SEPARATED AND PULLS DONATA 429 MARCOM
DOWN FRONT TO THE FOREGROUND.)
DEEPLY IN LOVE BUT SEPARATED BY A BARRIER OF 480 WELDED
LANGUAGE.)
SEPARATENESS
WHILE, AT THE SAME TIME, YOU'RE JEALOUS OF ANY 453 WELDED
SEPARATENESS IN ME.
SEPARATES
SEPARATES THIS FIELD FROM THE ROAD. 81 BEYOND
THROUGH THE SMALL LAWN WHICH SEPARATES THE HOUSE 493 DIFRNT
FROM THE STREET.
WHICH SEPARATES IT FROM THE BAR. 573 ICEMAN
SEPARATING
WITH A SPACE OF THREE FEET SEPARATING THE UPPER 477 CARDIF
FROM THE LOWER.
THE BACK ROOM WITH THE CURTAIN SEPARATING IT FROM 695 ICEMAN
THE SECTION OF THE BARROOM

SEPARATING (CONT'D.)
(AS ONE, THEY SPRING TO THEIR FEET AND GO TO HIM, 175 MANSNS
SEPARATING.
WITH AN EMPTY CHAIR SEPARATING THEM.) 105 POET
BUT THE GLASS SEPARATING THEM FROM THE WORLD IS 66 STRANG
GRAY WITH DUST,
SEPARATION
BEYOND FEAR OF SEPARATION/ 562 DAYS
AND NEW LOVE INTO SEPARATION AND PAIN AGAIN AND 274 LAZARU
THE LONELINESS OF AGE.
SEPARATIONS
WE SHALL HAVE GONE BACK BEYOND SEPARATIONS. 185 MANSNS
SEPTEMBER
BETWEEN THE HOURS OF NOON ON A DAY IN EARLY 1 MISBEG
SEPTEMBER, 1923,
SEPULCHRALLY
(BEGINS TO RECITE SEPULCHRALLY) 245 AHWILD
SEPULCHRE
EACH TIME I COME BACK AFTER BEING AWAY IT APPEARS 17 ELECTR
MORE LIKE A SEPULCHRE/.
SEPULCHRES
THEY'RE APT TO BE WHITED SEPULCHRES--I MEAN, YOUR 295 AHWILD
WHOLE LIFE MIGHT BE RUINED IF--
SER
DOWN'T BE SER DAWHN IN THE MARF, DUKE. 456 CARIBE
SERENE
SHE LOOKS BEAUTIFUL AND SERENE, AND MANY YEARS 191 MANSNS
YOUNGER.)
(WITH A SERENE PEACE) REST, DEAR NINA. 200 STRANG
SERENELY
SERENELY UNQUESTIONABLE. 488 WELDED
SERENITY
IN ITS GENERAL STRUCTURE AND PARTICULARLY IN ITS 274 LAZARU
QUALITY OF DETACHED SERENITY.
WALKS IN A DEEP, DETACHED SERENITY. 327 LAZARU
BUT AT THE SAME TIME RETAINING THE ALOOF SERENITY 350 LAZARU
OF THE STATUE OF A GOD.
SERGE
HE WEARS AN ILL-FITTING BLUE SERGE SUIT, WHITE 8 HUGHIE
SHIRT AND COLLAR, A BLUE TIE.
HE HAS CHANGED TO A READY-MADE BLUE SERGE SUIT, 89 JOURNE
HIGH STIFF COLLAR AND TIE.
HE IS DRESSED CAREFULLY IN AN ENGLISH MADE SUIT OF 24 STRANG
BLUE SERGE SO DARK AS TO SEEM
SERGEANT
AND THE MEMORY OF VINNIE BOSSING ME AROUND LIKE A 83 ELECTR
DRILL SERGEANT.
AND HIM WAY UP IN THE WORLD, A NOBLE SERGEANT OF 5 MISBEG
THE BRIDGEPORT POLICE.
SERIES
THERE BEGINS A SERIES OF BANGS FROM JUST BEYOND 189 AHWILD
THE PORCH OUTSIDE,
THAT IS CONTAINS ONLY ONE SERIES OF BUNKS. 477 CARDIF
THESE WINDOWS ARE REPEATED IN THE SAME SERIES IN 428 DYNAMO
THE BEDROOM ABOVE.
WITH A SERIES OF ACCOMPANYING BANGS.) 224 HA APE
IN THE LEFT WALL, A SIMILAR SERIES OF WINDOWS 11 JOURNE
LOOKS OUT
FARTHER FORWARD, A SERIES OF THREE WINDOWS LOOKS 11 JOURNE
OVER THE FRONT LAWN TO THE
WITHIN THE PORTICO ON ROWS OF CHAIRS PLACED ON A 312 LAZARU
SERIES OF WIDE STEPS WHICH ARE
BEFORE THESE COUCHES, A SERIES OF NARROW TABLES 15335 LAZARU
SET.
SERIOUS
IT ISN'T AS SERIOUS AS ALL THAT. 233 AHWILD
THIS IS A DAMNED SIGHT MORE SERIOUS THAN ESSIE HAS266 AHWILD
ANY IDEA/
BUT THERE IS ANOTHER THING THAT'S MORE SERIOUS. 294 AHWILD
IT'S ABOUT TIME YOU AND I HAD A SERIOUS TALK 295 AHWILU
ABOUT--HMMM--
BUT NOT EXACTLY SURE IF HE IS SERIOUS OR NOT-- 55 ANNA
(HE TAKES HER BY THE ARMS, GRINNING TO SOFTEN HIS 55 ANNA
SERIOUS BULLYING)
I'M SERIOUS. 85 BEYOND
WITH HER SILLY FACE ALL SCREWED UP SERIOUS AS 94 BEYOND
JUDGEMENT--
AND I LOOKS AT HER SERIOUS AS I COULD. 94 BEYOND
(AFTER A PAUSE--FROWNING) I HOPE HER AND ANDY 98 BEYOND
AIN'T HAD A SERIOUS FALLIN' OUT.
(ASTOUNDED) YOU AIN'T SERIOUS, BE YOU, ROBERTS 100 BEYOND
IT'S TOO SERIOUS FOR ME. 485 CARDIF
UH, IT'S NOTHING SERIOUS. 506 DAYS
(STRANGELY SERIOUS AND BITTERLY MOCKING AT THE 550 DAYS
SAME TIME)
"TWAN'T NOTHIN' BAD--ON'Y A BOY'S FOOLIN'-- 233 DESIRE
"TWAN'T MEANT SERIOUS--
DUN'T TAKE HER SO DEAD SERIOUS, HARRIET. 506 DIFRNT
SINK SO LOW AS TO FALL IN LOVE SERIOUS WITH ONE OF509 DIFRNT
THEM CRITTERS/
YOU DON'T S'POSE CALEB TOOK IT SERIOUS, DO YOU, 509 DIFRNT
YOU'LL MAKE UP WITH HIM, AND S'POSE I'M A FOOL 510 DIFRNT
TO BE TAKIN' IT SO SERIOUS.
HELL, EMMER, YOU AIN'T A REAL CROSBY IF YOU TAKES 513 DIFRNT
A JOKE LIKE THAT SERIOUS.
THIS IS DEAD SERIOUS. 533 DIFRNT
(A PAUSE) BUT NEITHER YOU NOR ME OUGHT TO GET MAD539 DIFRNT
AT HARRIET SERIOUS.
D'YOU S'POSE THE OLD MISER REALLY WAS SERIOUS 545 DIFRNT
ABOUT THAT?
WHAT'RE YOU TAKIN' IT SO DAMNED SERIOUS FUR-- ME 546 DIFRNT
ASKIN' YOU TO MARRY ME, I MEANS
I WANT A DAMNED SERIOUS TALK WITH YOU, YOUNG MAN/ 436 DYNAMO
HE SAID IT WAS NUTHING SERIOUS. 39 ELECTR
(GRUFFLY) IF IT WAS SERIOUS, I'D TELL YOU, SO 49 ELECTR
YOU'D BE PREPARED.
I'VE BEEN SO AFRAID YOU MIGHT BE MAKING IT OUT 49 ELECTR
LESS SERIOUS THAN IT REALLY WAS

SERIOUS (CONT'D.)

HE TOLD ME THE TROUBLE HE HAD WASN'T SERIOUS. 74 ELECTR
THE GROUP OUTSIDE BECOMES SERIOUS.) 132 ELECTR
YOU'LL FIND FOLKS'LL SHUT UP AND NOT TAKE IT 135 ELECTR
SERIOUS NO MORE.
(WITHDRAWING HER HAND) I WAS SERIOUS. 270 GGBROW
I WANT TO HAVE A SERIOUS TALK WITH YOU, YOUNG MAN/271 GGBROW
SUCCESSFUL SERIOUS ONE, THE GREAT GOD MR. BROWN, 282 GGBROW
INSTEAD/
DEADLY SERIOUS/ 315 GGBROW
(GIVING HIM A QUEER LOOK) I'M SERIOUS. 315 GGBROW
(SERIOUS AND JOKING) DAT'S DE TALKIN'/ 242 HA APE
HE'S LUCKY NO LINE DON'T TAKE HIS CRACKS SERIOUS 579 ICEMAN
YOU WERE A SERIOUS LONELY LITTLE SHAVER. 588 ICEMAN
FURGET IT, IF ANYTHING I'VE SAID SOUNDS TOO 624 ICEMAN
SERIOUS.
GIGGLING AGAIN) WHY YOU SO SERIOUS, LEEDLE 635 ICEMAN
MONKEY-FACES
DE BOYS WASN'T TAKIN' YUH SERIOUS. 637 ICEMAN
I'M TELLING YOU, ED, IT'S SERIOUS THIS TIME. 651 ICEMAN
HE KIDDED HIM HE WAS SERIOUS. 723 ICEMAN
THE DIRTY BLACKGUARD/ HE'LL GET ME IN SERIOUS 25 JOURNE
TROUBLE YET.
NOT ABOUT ANYTHING SERIOUS, SIMPLY LAUGH AND 46 JOURNE
GOSSIP AND FORGET FOR A WHILE--
HE'LL PRETEND HE'S FOUND SOMETHING SERIOUS THE 92 JOURNE
MATTER
WHAT I'VE GOT IS SERIOUS, MAMA. 118 JOURNE
(HE BENDS AND SLAPS AT THE KNEES OF HIS TROUSERS.155 JOURNE
HAD SERIOUS ACCIDENT.
NO JOKE. VERY SERIOUS. 159 JOURNE
FOR A MOMENT I THOUGHT YOU WERE SERIOUS-- 14 MANSNS
IDEALLY SERIOUS.) FAR FROM IT. 100 MANSNS
THRILL OR A GOOD LAUGH AND GET YOUR MIND OFF 399 MARCOM
SERIOUS THINGS
I'M SERIOUS, AND YOU'D BETTER LISTEN. 31 MISBEG
(STARES AT HER IN SURPRISE) WHY SO SERIOUS AND 67 MISBEG
INDIGNANT, JOSIE$
WE MUST HAVE A SERIOUS CHAT ABOUT WHEN YOU'RE 67 MISBEG
GOING TO PAY THAT BACK RENT.
AND HE'S VERY SERIOUS ABOUT THEM. 29 POET
AND SIMON SAID I WAS FOOLISH TO THINK SHE WOULD 144 POET
TAKE THE DUKE CRAZINESS SERIOUS.
REFUSES TO BE SERIOUS/ 8 STRANG
IF I WERE SERIOUS SHE WOULDN'T LISTEN, SHE'D SAY I 38 STRANG
WAS PRESCRIBING.
NOTHING SERIOUS BUT IT ANNOYS HER TERRIBLY. 73 STRANG
I MEAN, NED WAS ALWAYS SO SERIOUS-MINDED IT'S HARD115 STRANG
TO IMAGINE HIM MESSED UP IN
(HE ROARS WITH CHILDISH LAUGHTER, THEN SUDDENLY 506 VOYAGE
BECOMES SERIOUS)
(AFTER A PAUSE--IN A CALMING, SERIOUS TONE) 467 WELDED

SERIOUSLY

(THEN SERIOUSLY) GLAD YOU'RE READING IT, RICHARD.196 AHWILD
YOU REALLY MUSN'T LET YOURSELF TAKE IT SO 215 AHWILD
SERIOUSLY.
AND SHE TOOK IT SERIOUSLY, LIKE A FOOL. 215 AHWILD
(TURNS TO BELLE SERIOUSLY) NO KIDDING, THAT'S A 246 AHWILD
PEACHERING.
(THEN GETS A BRIGHT IDEA FOR ELIMINATING RICHARD--247 AHWILD
SERIOUSLY TO THE BARTENDER)
YOU CAN'T TAKE A WORD HE SAYS SERIOUSLY. 272 AHWILD
YOU'RE ACTUALLY TAKING THIS MURIEL CRUSH OF 291 AHWILD
RICHARD'S SERIOUSLY, DO YOU$
BUT THAT DOESN'T MEAN TO EVER GET MIXED UP WITH 295 AHWILD
THEM SERIOUSLY/
(SERIOUSLY) AY DON'T TANK DAT. 11 ANNA
(THEN MORE SERIOUSLY BUT STILL IN A BOASTFUL TONE, 31 ANNA
(LAUGHING--GIVES HER A HUG) YOU'RE NOT TAKING ME 516 DAYS
SERIOUSLY, ARE YOU$
SHE BECOMES SERIOUSLY ILL. 539 DAYS
DON'T TAKE IT SO SERIOUSLY. 545 DAYS
FOR THE LOVE OF GOD, DON'T TELL ME YOU TOOK HIS 550 DAYS
MORBID NONSENSE SERIOUSLY/
TAKES HER IMPIETY SERIOUSLY) 551 DAYS
SHE SEEMS TO HAVE TAKEN HER END IN YOUR STORY VERY551 DAYS
SERIOUSLY.
(THEN SERIOUSLY, WITH A CALCULATING LOOK AT HER) 523 DIFRNT
(SERIOUSLY) IT'S A BLEEDIN' QUEER PLACE, THAT 185 EJONES
STINKIN' FOREST.
(MAKING A WARNING SIGN TO PETER NOT TO TAKE THIS 144 ELECTR
SERIOUSLY--FORCING A SMILE)
I SHOULD NEVER HAVE TOLD YOU-- BUT I NEVER 312 GGBROW
IMAGINED YOU'D TAKE IT SERIOUSLY.
(BUT THE NIGHT CLERK CANNOT TAKE THIS SERIOUSLY. 24 HUGHIE
(HE CHUCKLES--THEN SERIOUSLY.) 29 HUGHIE
NO ONE TAKES HIM SERIOUSLY. 579 ICEMAN
YOU'D ASK ME QUESTIONS AND TAKE WHAT I SAID 588 ICEMAN
SERIOUSLY.
(HE PAUSES--SERIOUSLY) BUT I'M TELLING YOU SOME 607 ICEMAN
DAY BEFORE LONG
(THEN SERIOUSLY) NO, I WASN'T EITHER. 622 ICEMAN
WHEN NO ONE TAKES SERIOUSLY. 654 ICEMAN
SHE'D HAVE BEEN SO HURT IF I'D SAID IT SERIOUSLY. 714 ICEMAN
I KNOW IT'S FOOLISH TO TAKE THEM SERIOUSLY BUT I 91 JOURNE
CAN'T HELP IT.
IF HE WOULD ONLY LEARN TO TAKE LIFE SERIOUSLY. 110 JOURNE
YOU BETTER TAKE IT SERIOUSLY. 165 JOURNE
(SERIOUSLY) BUT HE MUST BE EXPERT IN MAGIC. 302 LAZARU
HE KNEW YOUR MOTHER COULD NEVER TAKE A SHORT, FAT 37 MANSNS
MAN SERIOUSLY.
(VERY SERIOUSLY) YOU KNOW, DONATA. 355 MARCOM
HOW CAN ONE DEAL SERIOUSLY WITH SUCH A CHILD-- 389 MARCOM
ACTOR$
AND ALL WOMEN MUST TAKE ACTING SERIOUSLY IN ORDER 389 MARCOM
TO LOVE AT ALL.
THERE'S NOTHING SERIOUSLY WRONG. 413 MARCOM

SERIOUSLY (CONT'D.)

(BEWILDEREDLY) I NEVER BELIEVED PEOPLE--SANE 415 MARCOM
PEOPLE--EVER SERIOUSLY TRIED--
(TURNS ON HIM ANGRILY) ARE YOU TAKING MIKE'S 22 MISBEG
SCHEME SERIOUSLY, YOU OLD GOAT$
(SERIOUSLY) IT'S TRUE, IF I WAS HIS WIFE, 29 MISBEG
(YOU HE SERIOUSLY WORRIED. 67 MISBEG
YOU DON'T MEAN SERIOUSLY$ 73 POET
I CANNOT IMAGINE YOU TAKING THAT SERIOUSLY. 89 POET
SURELY YOU COULD NOT HAVE SPOKEN SERIOUSLY WHEN 122 POET
YOU TALKED OF MARRIAGE.
(SEVERELY) YOU SERIOUSLY MEAN TO TELL ME YOU, IN 17 STRANG
YOUR CONDITION,
(FLURREDLY--GOING TO HIM) DON'T TAKE HER 20 STRANG
SERIOUSLY, PROFESSOR/
(VERY SERIOUSLY--IN A CONFIDENTIAL TONE) 121 STRANG
(HE GRINS--THEN SERIOUSLY) IT WAS ABOUT TIME I GOT121 STRANG
HOLD OF MYSELF.
(THEN SERIOUSLY) AFTER ALL, 144 STRANG
(THEN, SERIOUSLY) AND WILL YOU PROMISE TO STAY 145 STRANG
AWAY TWO YEARS--
HE TAKES HIS HOBBY PRETTY SERIOUSLY/...)) 152 STRANG
BUT FOR GORDON TO TAKE HER SERIOUSLY, AND PROPOSE 168 STRANG
MARRIAGE--

SERIOUSNESS

(AMUSED BY HER SERIOUSNESS) DIFFERENT$ 449 DIFRNT
(TAKES HER HAND--WITH DEEP SERIOUSNESS.) 43 JOURNE
(WITH GREAT SERIOUSNESS.) I'M AS DRUNK AS A 155 JOURNE
FIDDLER'S BITCH.
DEADLY SERIOUSNESS AS SHE GOES ON.) 13 MANSNS
(WITH MOCK SERIOUSNESS) IN BEHALF OF THE 193 MARCOM
POPULATION OF YANG-CHAU
(HE PAUSES--THEN WITH GREAT SERIOUSNESS, TURNING 31 MISBEG
TOWARD HER)
(WITH GREAT SERIOUSNESS) DO YOU THINK SO, SAMMY$ 113 STRANG
(WITH GREAT SERIOUSNESS NOW--DEEPLY MOVED) 151 STRANG

SERMON

SERMON, BUT HIS MIND IS ABSTRACTED. 422 DYNAMO
WHAT WAS THE SERMON$ 236 HA APE
WHILE HE WAS TRYING TO WRITE A SERMON. 596 ICEMAN
HELL, THIS BEGINS TO SOUND LIKE A DAMNED SERMON$ 622 ICEMAN

SERMONIZER

HIS VOICE IS THE BULLYING ONE OF A SERMONIZER WHO 422 DYNAMO
IS THE VICTIM OF AN INNER

SERMONS

AND DELIVERS SERMONS ON WILL POWER/ 74 JOURNE

SERPENT'S

(HE QUOTES.) "HOW SHARPER THAN A SERPENT'S TOOTH 89 JOURNE
IT IS--
OR HE'LL POISON LIFE FOR YOU WITH HIS DAMNED 109 JOURNE
SNEERING SERPENT'S TONGUE/

SERPENTS

HUNGRY SERPENTS AND WELCOMED YOU INTO THEIR COILS. 83 POET

SERRIED

(A LARGE CIRCULAR CLEARING ENCLOSED BY THE SERICULYS EJONES
RANKS OF GIGANTIC TRUNKS OF

SERVANT

LIKE THE WILL O' GOD, LIKE THE SERVANT O' HIS 217 DESIRE
HAND.
YOU'RE TOO GUJU FOR THE SON OF A SERVANT, EHS 25 ELECTR
BE DAMNED IF YOU CAN ORDER ME ABOUT AS IF I WAS 27 ELECTR
YOUR SERVANT/
I THE VILEST, MOST COWARDLY WAY--LIKE THE SUN OF 27 ELECTR
A SERVANT YOU ARE/
(HE KISSES HIS MOTHER, WHO BOWS WITH A STRANGE 261 GGBROW
HUMILITY AS IF SHE WERE A SERVANT
BROWN FROWNS AND LISTENS AS A SERVANT ANSWERS. 294 GGBROW
HE TOLD THE SERVANT TO TELL ME HE WOULD COME. 4 MANSNS
A MOTHER OF CHILDREN, OUR IRISH BIDDY NURSE GIRL 118 MANSNS
AND HOUSE SERVANT)
(HAUGHTILY--AS IF ADDRESSING A SERVANT.) 169 MANSNS
(HUMORING HER--BOBS HER AN AWKWARD SERVANT-GIRL 192 MANSNS
CURTSY AND SPEAKS HUMBLY.)
A CONTRIBUTION TO YOUR BODY--FROM YOUR MOST HUMBLE 391 MARCOM
SERVANT/
HE ADDRESSES HER AS IF SHE WERE A SERVANT.) 103 POET
I WILL SUMMON A SERVANT TO INQUIRE YOUR PLEASURE. 117 POET
MELODY IGNORES HER AS HE WOULD A SERVANT. 118 POET

SERVANT'S

WHY DO YOU GRIEVE FOR THAT SERVANT'S BASTARD$ 121 ELECTR
(WITH A MOCKING, AWKWARD, SERVANT'S CURTSY--IN 45 POET
BROAD BROGUE.)

SERVANTS

AIN'T NOTICED ANY OF THE GUARDS OR SERVANTS ABOUT 181 EJONES
THE PLACE TODAY, I 'AVE'N'T.
THEY SAY HE FIXED ALL HIS OLD SERVANTS THAT SAME 302 GGBROW
DAY
SOMEONE BESIDES THE SERVANTS--THAT STUPID 46 JOURNE
CATHLEEN/
THE REALLY GOOD SERVANTS ARE ALL WITH PEOPLE WHO 61 JOURNE
HAVE HOMES
YOU DON'T HAVE TO KEEP HOUSE WITH SUMMER SERVANTS 61 JOURNE
WHO DON'T CARE.
SO THE SERVANTS WON'T SEE HIM. 117 JOURNE
IN A GRAND MANSION LIKE A CASTLE, WITH SLOOS OF 21 MANSNS
SERVANTS, AND STABLES.
AND HAND THEM TO THE SERVANTS. 428 MARCOM
THE SERVANTS ARRANGE THESE ON THE TABLE, IN 428 MARCOM
SYMMETRICAL GROUPS.
MARCO ADDRESSES THE SERVANTS IN A FALSE VOICE.) 428 MARCOM
(A PROCESSION OF SERVANTS BEGINS TO FILE ONE BY 428 MARCOM
ONE THROUGH THE RANKS OF
AND ALL THOSE SERVANTS/ 428 MARCOM
(HE TOSSES A HANDFUL OF GOLD TO THE SERVANTS AND 429 MARCOM
ANOTHER TO THE MUSICIANS.
(THE SERVANTS DO SO. 429 MARCOM
SERVANTS FLIT ABOUT NOISILY. 431 MARCOM
HIS SERVANTS WILL KEEP YOU 175 POET

SERVANTS

SERVANTS (CONT'D.)
YOU LET HARFORD'S SERVANTS INSULT YOU/ 155 POET
SERVANTS'
THE PLACE FOR THE LUIKS AV YOU IS THE SERVANTS' 155 POET ENTRANCE.

SERVE
AND SERVE HIM RIGHT AFTER THE MANNER HE'S TREATED 537 'ILE THEM--
(WITH A CHUCKLE) SERVE YE RIGHT, YE OLD DIVIL-- 10 ANNA
HAVIN' A WOMAN AT YOUR AGE/
(SARCASTICALLY) SHALL I SERVE IT IN A PAILS 14 ANNA
*IT'S NOT MUCH BUT TWILL SERVE TO TAKE THE BLACK 462 CARIBE
TASTE OUT AV YOUR MOUTHS
IT'LL SERVE T' SHOW HIM WE'RE DONE WITH HIM. 216 DESIRE
HAVE SURVIVED THE RENOVATION AND SERVE TO 519 DIFRNT
EMPHASIZE IT ALL THE MORE BY CONTRAST.
AND SERVE HIM RIGHT, THE BLOODY SNEAK/ 440 DYNAMO
IF YOU DON'T STOP YOUR BLASPHEMING, I'LL--I MEAN, 442 DYNAMO
IT'D SERVE YOU RIGHT IF I--
AND ANOTHER SMALLER ONE IS PLACED ON THE FLOOR TO 173 EJONES
SERVE AS A FOOTSTOOL.
SERVE 'IM RIGHT/ 175 EJONES
I'LL SERVE YOU HIS HEART FOR BREAKFAST/ 311 GGBROW
HE HAD THE GUTS TO SERVE TEN YEARS IN THE CAN IN 593 ICEMAN
HIS OWN COUNTRY
SERVE YUH RIGHT IF HE BEAT YUH UP/ 613 ICEMAN
IT'D SERVE ME RIGHT. 714 ICEMAN
SERVE HIM BLOODY WELL RIGHT/ 514 INZONE
AN' SERVE HIM RIGHT/ 524 INZONE
AND BARS THAT SERVE BONDED BOURBON. 35 JOURNE
IT WOULD SERVE ALL OF YOU RIGHT IF IT WAS TRUE/ 47 JOURNE
YOU CAN SERVE DINNER PROMPTLY AT HALF PAST SIX. 106 JOURNE
IT WILL SERVE HER RIGHT TO BE ALONE IN THE 159 MANSNS
TWILIGHT SHE DREADS SO
IT WOULD SERVE HIM RIGHT IF WE TURNED THE TABLES 171 MANSNS
ON HIM, SARA.
AND ANY WAY WE CAN SERVE YOUR MAJESTY-- 382 MARCOM
I WILL ALWAYS SERVE YOUR BEST INTERESTS, SO HELP 383 MARCOM
ME GOD/
WHAT PURPOSE CAN IT SERVE& 426 MARCOM
(THEN, CONTEMPTUOUSLY) YOU'RE A DIRTY TICK AND 10 MISBEG
IT'D SERVE YOU RIGHT IF I LET YOU
IT WOULD SERVE CON RIGHT IF I TOOK THE CHANCE NOW 138 POET
AND BROKE MY PROMISE AND WORE
(VIOLENTLY) SERVE HIM DAMN RIGHT IF I DONE IT. 598 ROPE
*TWILL SERVE HIM RIGHT TO HEAT UP HIS HOOFS FOR 600 ROPE
HIM, THE LIMPIN' AULD MISER/
(THINKING VINDICTIVELY) I SERVE HER RIGHT, THE 73 STRANG
OLD SCANDAL-MONGER.
YES, MORE DEEPLY THAN EITHER OF THE OTHERS SINCE 1135 STRANG
SERVE FOR NOTHING...)
(EXPLOSIVELY) IT WOULD SERVE YOU GOOD AND RIGHT--151 STRANG
AND MOTHER, TOO--

SERVED
IF HE EVER FINDS OUT I SERVED HIS KID, HE'LL RUN 248 AHWILD
ME OUT OF TOWN.
THE BARTENDER THERE KNEW HE WAS UNDER AGE BUT 267 AHWILD
SERVED HIM JUST THE SAME.
(SEEING ALL FOUR ARE SERVED) 465 CARIBE
PROVIDED A MEAL IS SERVED WITH THE BOOZE, 571 ICEMAN
THE RULES OF THE HOUSE ARE THAT DRINKS MAY BE 585 ICEMAN
SERVED AT ALL HOURS.
HIS PLAN TO MURDERER HIS OWN SHIPMATES THAT HAVE 524 INZONE
SERVED HIM FAIR--
WAITING IN THE OVEN, SHE SAID IT SERVED YOU RIGHT, 67 JOURNE
DINNER IS SERVED, SIR. 122 JOURNE
DINNER IS SERVED, MA'AM. 123 JOURNE
WHO SERVED WITH HONOUR IN SPAIN UNDER THE GREAT 21 MANSNS
DUKE OF WELLINGTON.
IT WOULD HAVE SERVED HER RIGHT TO BE BEATEN AT HER 74 MANSNS
OWN GAME--
I HAVE SERVED MY PURPOSE--SHE HAS RUTHLESSLY CUT 126 MANSNS
RID OF ME--SHE IS FREE--
WE'VE SERVED YOU FAITHFULLY, 396 MARCOM
HE SERVED UNDER ME AT TALAVERA, AS YOU KNOW. 38 POET
WHO SERVED WITH HONOUR UNDER THE DUKE OF WELLINGTONLIT 7 POET
IN SPAIN, I AM HE.

SERVES
THERE IS SILENCE FOR A MOMENT AS MILLER SERVES THE227 AHWILD
FISH AND IT IS PASSED AROUND.
LARRY SERVES HIM) 12 ANNA
(RESENTFULLY) IT SERVES YOU RIGHT. 64 ANNA
AN' SERVES HIM RIGHT/ 260 DESIRE
A CANE-BOTTOMED AFFAIR WITH FANCY CUSHIONS SERVES 319 DIFRNT
IN ITS STEAD.
YET THIS SOUND SERVES BUT TO INTENSIFY THE 187 EJONES
IMPRESSION OF THE FOREST'S RELENTLESS
WHICH SERVES TO INCREASE THEIR RESEMBLANCE TO EACH 74 ELECTR
OTHER.
IT SERVES ME RIGHT, WHAT HAS HAPPENED AND IS TO 110 ELECTR
HAPPEN/
SERVES HIM RIGHT/ 321 GGBROW
YES, IT SERVES HER RIGHT. 77 POET
(THEN QUICKLY.) BUT IT SERVES YOU RIGHT/ 159 POET
JOE SERVES CUCKY AND DRISCOLL. 504 VOYAGE

SERVICE
AS IF THEY WERE ATTENDING A FUNERAL SERVICE. 263 AHWILD
LITTLE SERVICE/ 14 ANNA
YOU HAVE TO FEEL GOD CALLING YOU TO HIS SERVICE. 437 DYNAMO
AND THEY'RE THERE HOLDIN' THEIR HEATHEN RELIGIOUS 184 EJONES
SERVICE--MAKIN' NO END OF DEVIL
WHICH LOOK AS IF THEY HAD BEEN REMODELED AND SEEN 270 GGBROW
SERVICE.
AND EVEN BROKEN HEARTS MAY BE REPAIRED TO DO 318 GGBROW
YEOMAN SERVICE/
AFTER EXHAUSTING THE MORBID THRILLS OF SOCIAL 219 HA APE
SERVICE WORK ON NEW YORK'S EAST

SERVICE (CONT'D.)
OH, THEY DIDN'T WANT TO AT FIRST, IN SPITE OF MY 220 HA APE
SOCIAL SERVICE CREDENTIALS.
NO, BY GOD, YOU'RE SUCH A BONEHEAD I'LL BET YOU'RE249 HA APE
IN THE SECRET SERVICE/
IT MANAGES TO KEEP RUNNING BY CUTTING THE OVERHEAD 7 HUGHIE
FOR SERVICE, REPAIRS,
START THE SERVICE/ 620 ICEMAN
IN MEMORY OF OLD SERVICE AND AS A DOMESTIC SLAVE 73 MANSNS
AT YOUR SERVICE. 92 MANSNS
AND FATHER AND UNCLE BOTH SAY THERE'S MILLIONS TO 356 MARCOM
BE MADE IN HIS SERVICE IF
TO THE HIGHEST RANK IN YOUR SERVICES 387 MARCOM
GARISHLY SET WITH AN ORNATE GOLD SERVICE. 426 MARCOM
IS THAT GOLD SERVICE REALLY GOLD& ABSOLUTELY. 427 MARCOM
HOW GREAT AN HONOR I WILL ESTEEM IT TO BE OF ANY 69 POET
SERVICE.
AT YOUR SERVICE. 70 POET
BUT I DO OWE YOU AN APOLOGY FOR THE QUALITY OF THE 98 POET
SERVICE.
IN THE FLYING SERVICE RATHER MORE THAN A 10 STRANG
POSSIBILITY, WHICH *NEEDLESS TO SAY,
(THINKING GLUMLY) (WON'T TELL HIM I TRIED FOR 30 STRANG
FLYING SERVICE...

SERVICES
WITH DEEP REGRET FOR THE LOSS OF YOUR UNIQUE AND 393 MARCOM
EXTRAORDINARY SERVICES.

SERVILE
THE SERVILE, HYPOCRITICAL.. 273 LAZARU
SEVEN IN NUMBER, FACING FRONT, IN DOUBLE-SIZED 312 LAZARU
MASKS OF THE SERVILE.
INTROSPECTIVE.. PROUD, SELF-RELIANT.. THE 312 LAZARU
SERVILE, HYPOCRITICAL..
THE SERVILE, HYPOCRITICAL.. 336 LAZARU
WITH THEIR CHORUS, SEVEN MEN MASKED IN MIDDLE AGE 363 LAZARU
IN THE SERVILE,
HER SMILE MADE ME FORGET THE SERVILE GRIN OF THE 437 MARCOM
FACE OF THE WORLD.

SERVILELY
(TAPS LEWIS ON THE SHOULDER--SERVILELY APOLOGETIC)700 ICEMAN

SERVILITY
WHO ANSWERS WITH A MOCKING SERVILITY.) 317 LAZARU
STAND IN ATTITUDES OF PATIENT SERVILITY BEFORE THE358 MARCOM
THRONE.

SERVING
MARGARET IS SERVING THEM THE AFTER-DINNER COFFEE. 532 DAYS
AND SERVING DRINKS TO ALL THE MEN. 247 DESIRE
MAKES THE ESTABLISHMENT LEGALLY A HOTEL AND GIVES 571 ICEMAN
IT THE PRIVILEGE OF SERVING
THE AND CHUCK FINISH SERVING OUT THE SCHOONERS, 658 ICEMAN
FOR SERVING MY SPITE UPON MANKIND& 339 LAZARU
SO WHEN THE TIME COMES THEY WILL BE CAPABLE OF 84 MANSNS
SERVING OUR COMPANY--
SERVING UNDER HIM. 10 POET

SEN-SEN
AND HAD ED HAD EATEN A POUND OF SEN-SEN TO KILL 39 MISBEG
THE GIN ON HER BREATH,

SESSION
TWO YEARS IN SESSION/ 359 MARCOM

SESTINA
THE QUOTES FROM KIPLING'S =SESTINA OF THE TRAMP- 161 JOURNE
ROYAL.=

SET
I BEGIN TO DOUBT IF EVER I'LL SET FOOT ON LAND 537 'ILE
AGAIN.
(SHAKING HIS HEAD) BUT YOU WAS SO SET ON IT-- 546 'ILE
(HIS JAW SET STUBBORNLY) IT AIN'T THAT, ANNIE. 547 'ILE
(SHOUTS AFTER HIM) BUT YOU SET OFF YOUR CRACKERS 186 AHWILD
AWAY FROM THE HOUSE, REMEMBER/
HELP TOMMY SET OFF FIRECRACKERS, EHS 194 AHWILD
SCRAWNY BRAWNY NECK, AND A LONG SOLEMN HORSE FACE 200 AHWILD
WITH DEEP-SET LITTLE BLACK EYE
THE ROOM IS MUCH TOO SMALL FOR THE MEDIUM-PRICED, 210 AHWILD
FURNISHED LIVING-ROOM SET&
HIS FACE A SET EXPRESSION OF BITTER GLOOM. 215 AHWILD
HASN'T SUN--PERFECT RIGHT TO SET& 224 AHWILD
(MOURNFULLY) AIN'T ME GOING TO SET OFF THE 234 AHWILD
SKYROCKETS AND ROMAN CANDLES, PA&
HIS FACE IS SET IN AN EXPRESSION OF FROWNING 263 AHWILD
SEVERITY.
A LANTERN SET UP ON AN IMMENSE COIL OF THICK 25 ANNA
HAWSER SHEDS A DULL,
DEY SET AND WAIT ALL 'LONE. 28 ANNA
AND IF YOU'RE SET ON TRAVELING, 85 BEYOND
ITS LARGE EYES OF A DEEP BLUE SET OFF STRIKINGLY 87 BEYOND
BY THE SUN-BRONZED COMPLEXION.
HE'S DEAD SET ON IT. 96 BEYOND
AND I GOT MY MIND SO SET ON HAVIN' HIM I'M GOIN' 103 BEYOND
TO BE DOUBLE LONESOME THIS
HIS FACE IS SET IN A LOOK OF GRIM DETERMINATION) 104 BEYOND
AUDREE REMAINS STANDING MOTIONLESS, HIS FACE PALE 108 BEYOND
AND SET.)
A PLACE IS SET AT THE END OF THE TABLE, LEFT, FOR 112 BEYOND
SOMEONE'S DINNER.
(WITH A DISAPPROVING GLANCE AT THE PLACE SET ON 113 BEYOND
THE TABLE)
SEEMS AS IF SHE CRIES ALL THE TIME ON PURPOSE TO 116 BEYOND
SET A BODY'S NERVES ON EDGE.
RUTH GLANCES AT THE PLACE SET ON THE TABLE) 117 BEYOND
I'LL NEVER SET FOOT ON A SHIP AGAIN IF I CAN HELP 132 BEYOND
IT
WHEN HE KNOWS I'M SET ON A THING. 137 BEYOND
SET ALL SAIL BACK HERE TO FIND YOU. 141 BEYOND
I JUDGE FROM THEM YOU'VE ACCOMPLISHED ALL YOU SET 160 BEYOND
OUT TO DO FIVE YEARS AGO&
(THEY ALL SET THEMSELVES TO WAIT) 458 CARIBE
(AFTER A SLIGHT PAUSE) WHAT EVER SET YOU GOIN' TO467 CARIBE
SEA&

SET

(CONT'D.)	
HIS FACE IS LONG, BONY, AND SALLOW, WITH DEEP-SET 556 CROSS	
BLACK EYES.	
SET SAIL TO BRING BACK THE TREASURE. 561 CROSS	
HE THINKS THAT HE MAY SET FIRE TO THE HOUSE--DO 564 CROSS	
ANYTHING---	
MY BOOK IS THREE-FOURTHS DONE--MY BOOK THAT WILL 565 CROSS	
SET ME FREE/	
THAT'S RIGHT, SIT ON ME THE MINUTE I SET FOOT IN 515 DAYS	
YOUR HOUSE/	
ELSA'S FACE IS PALE AND SET, HER EYES HAVE A 537 DAYS	
BEWILDERED, STRICKEN LOOK.	
BUT SHE IS STARING STRAIGHT BEFORE HER WITH A 539 DAYS	
STILL, SET FACE.	
"# IF I COULD, IN MY DYIN' HOUR, I'D SET IT AFIRE 232 DESIRE	
AN' WATCH IT BURN--	
YE'D ONT'Y TO PLOW AN' SOW AN' THEN SET AN' SMOKE 237 DESIRE	
YER PIPE AN' WATCH THIN'S GROW.	
WON'T YE SETS 241 DESIRE	
AN' THAR YE SET CACKLIN' LIKE A LOT O' WET HENS 249 DESIRE	
WITH THE PIP/	
I'LL SET FIRE T' HOUSE AN' BARN AN' WATCH 'EM 267 DESIRE	
BURN.	
SHE'S GOT HER HEAD SET 499 DIFRNT	
WON'T YOU SETS 505 DIFRNT	
SET DOWN. 507 DIFRNT	
SET DOWN, HARRIET. 507 DIFRNT	
LET'S SET DOWN AND BE COMFORTABLE. 507 DIFRNT	
HIS FACE IS SET EMOTIONLESSLY BUT HIS EYES CANNOT 514 DIFRNT	
CONCEAL A WORRIED	
KIN I SET A SPELL 514 DIFRNT	
THE PLUSH-COVERED CHAIRS ARE GONE, REPLACED BY A 519 DIFRNT	
SET OF VARNISHED OAK.	
ITS GLASSY SURFACE SET OFF BY THREE SMALL, GARISH-519 DIFRNT	
COLORED MUGS.	
HE'S SET IN HIS WAYS AND BELIEVES IN BEING STRICT 522 DIFRNT	
WITH YOU--	
DU SET DOWN A SPELL, BENNY/ 524 DIFRNT	
COME RIGHT IN AND SET. 534 DIFRNT	
GRACIOUS SAKES, WHY DON'T YOU SET, CALEB& 535 DIFRNT	
HIS FACE WEARS ITS SET EXPRESSION OF AN 535 DIFRNT	
EMOTIONLESS MASK	
ARE YOU LOOKING FOR YOUR OLD CHAIR YOU USED TO SET535 DIFRNT	
IN&	
DU SET DOWN AND MAKE 535 DIFRNT	
SHE STARES STRAIGHT BEFORE HER, HER MOUTH SET 538 DIFRNT	
THINLY.	
I'D LET YOU MARRY THE SKUNK AND SET AND WATCH WHAT'S43 DIFRNT	
HAPPENED--	
(THEN WITH AN EXASPERATED SENSE OF FRUSTRATION, 448 DYNAMO	
GAZING AT REUBEN'S SET FACE)	
HER FACE IS SET IN AN UGLY, SNEERING EXPRESSION. 450 DYNAMO	
WHICH IS BRILLIANTLY LIGHTED BY A ROW OF POWERFUL 473 DYNAMO	
BULBS IN WHITE GLOBES SET IN	
THE EXCITER SET ON THE MAIN STRUCTURE LIKE A HEAD 473 DYNAMO	
WITH BLANK,	
LEM IS A HEAVY-SET APE-FACED OLD SAVAGE OF THE 202 EJONES	
EXTREME AFRICAN TYPE.	
IT IS SET IN A GRIM EXPRESSION, BUT HIS SMALL, 6 ELFCTR	
IN WHICH ONLY THE DEEP-SET EYES, OF A DARK VIOLET 9 ELFCTR	
BLUE, ARE ALIVE.	
AS HE REGARDS HER GRIM, SET EXPRESSION) 23 ELECTR	
YOU CAN'T PICTURE THE GREEN BEAUTY OF THEIR LAND 24 ELECTR	
SET IN THE BLUE OF THE SEA/	
OUTSIDE THE SUN IS BEGINNING TO SET 28 ELECTR	
FOR DEATH--TO SET YOU FREE/ 60 ELECTR	
THE DAY I SET OFF TO BECOME A HEROS 82 ELECTR	
LAVINIA IS STIFFLY SQUARE-SHOULDERED, HER EYES 119 ELECTR	
HARD, HER MOUTH GRIM AND SET.	
(HIS FACE SET GRIMLY, HE GOES OFF RIGHT FRONT. 125 ELECTR	
HER FOLKS HAS SET ME FREE.* 130 ELECTR	
I'D LET EZRA'S WOMAN'S GHOST SET ON MY LAP. 130 ELECTR	
LET'S GIT OUR SET OUT PLAIN AFORE WITNESSES. 131 ELECTR	
YOU FEEL SOMETHING COLD GRIP YOU THE MOMENT YOU 137 ELECTR	
SET FOOT--	
HIS HAGGARD SWARTHY FACE IS SET IN A BLANK 138 ELECTR	
LIFELESS EXPRESSION.)	
AS IN HER DEATH AND SET YOU FREE--TO BECOME HER/ 141 ELECTR	
BUT I DON'T WISH TO CONVEY THAT HE APPROVES OF ALL153 ELECTR	
I'VE SET DOWN--	
YOU SET DOWN AND SHE'LL BE HERE AS SOON AS SHE 158 ELECTR	
KIN.	
TELL HER TO SET THEM AROUND INSIDE. 170 ELECTR	
I'M ALL SET/ 279 GGROW	
CYNTHI JAGS SET TO MUSIC/ 284 GGROW	
(THEN, AS HE HESITATES) WHAT SET YOU OFF ON THIS 287 GGROW	
BATS	
ALL THE OTHER MONKEYS SET UP AN ANGRY CHATTERING 253 HA APE	
IN THE DARKNESS.	
THE MONKEYS SET UP A CHATTERING, WHIMPERING WAIL. 254 HA APE	
HIS FACE IS SET IN THE PRESCRIBED PATTERN OF 9 HUGHIE	
GAMBLER'S DEAD PAN.	
TWIRLING HIS KEY FRANTICALLY AS IF IT WERE A 28 HUGHIE	
FETISH WHICH MIGHT SET HIM FREE.)	
SET ME BACK A HUNDRED BUCKS, AND NO KIDDIN'/ 31 HUGHIE	
YOU COULD SET YOUR WATCH BY HIS PERIODICALS BEFORE580 ICEMAN	
DIS.	
HE'S SO SATISFIED WITH LIFE HE'S NEVER SET FOOT 594 ICEMAN	
OUT OF THIS PLACE	
I SAY AGAIN IT WAS A GRAVE ERROR IN OUR FOREIGN 599 ICEMAN	
POLICY EVER TO SET YOU FREE.	
AND I'VE NEVER SET FOOT OUT OF THIS HOUSE SINCE 603 ICEMAN	
THE DAY I BURIED HER.	
SET 'EM UP. 617 ICEMAN	
SET 'EM UP AGAIN, ROCKY. 621 ICEMAN	
SEEING I GOT IT ALL SET FOR MY BIRTHDAY TOMORROW. 626 ICEMAN	
TRUCULENT SWAGGER AND HIS GOOD-NATURED FACE IS SET636 ICEMAN	
IN SULLEN SUSPICION.)	
(CONT'D.)	
DO YOU SUPPOSE I'D DELIBERATELY SET OUT TO GET 642 ICEMAN	
UNDER EVERYONE'S SKIN	
CAKE ALL SET. 643 ICEMAN	
MY IDEA IS TO USE THE WINE FOR THAT, SO GET IT ALL643 ICEMAN	
SET.	
EVERYTHING ALL SETS 653 ICEMAN	
CURA GETS HER HANDS SET OVER THE PIANO KEYS, 653 ICEMAN	
WATCHING OVER HER SHOULDER.	
HIS MANNER IS SULLEN, HIS FACE SET IN GLOOM. 664 ICEMAN	
SET 'EM UP, ROCKY. 680 ICEMAN	
ALL SET FOR AN ALCOHOL RUB/ 686 ICEMAN	
THEY ARE LIKE WAX FIGURES, SET STIFFLY ON THEIR 690 ICEMAN	
CHAIRS.	
ROCKY'S FACE IS SET IN AN EXPRESSION OF TIRED, 696 ICEMAN	
CALLOUS TOUGHNESS.	
IT HAS THE STUBBORN SET OF AN OBSESSED 703 ICEMAN	
DETERMINATION.	
ONCE SHE'D SET HER HEART ON ANYTHING, 713 ICEMAN	
SET APPEARANCE OF A ROOM RARELY OCCUPIED. 11 JOURNE	
A BIG, FINELY SHAPED HEAD, A HANDSOME PROFILE, 13 JOURNE	
DEEP-SET LIGHT-BROWN EYES.	
(AGAIN WITH THE STRANGE OBSTINATE SET TO HER 29 JOURNE	
FACE.)	
A FINE EXAMPLE YOU SET HIM/ 34 JOURNE	
SHE TURNS TO HIM, HER LIPS SET IN A WELCOMING, 42 JOURNE	
MOTHERLY SMILE.)	
(LOOKS DIRECTLY AT HIM NOW, HER FACE SET AGAIN 63 JOURNE	
(HER FACE INSTANTLY SET IN BLANK DENIAL.) 72 JOURNE	
I WAS SET FREE/ 153 JOURNE	
HIS FOREHEAD IS BROAD AND NOBLE, HIS EYES BLACK 274 LAZARU	
AND DEEP-SET.	
THE DISCIPLE OF THEIR JESUS, HAS SO WELL SET THEM 283 LAZARU	
THE EXAMPLE/	
IN THE EXACT CENTRE OF THE AICH ITSELF A CROSS IS 326 LAZARU	
SET UP	
I WILL LAUGH WITH THE PRIDE OF A BEGGAR SET UPON 328 LAZARU	
THE THRONE OF MAN/	
HEFUL THESE COUCHES, A SERIES OF NARROW TABLES IS335 LAZARU	
SET.	
GIRLISH MOUTH IS SET IN AN EXPRESSION OF AGONIZED 337 LAZARU	
SELF-LOATHING AND WEAKNESS OF	
SHE HAS SMALL EARS SET CLOSE TO HER HEAD, A WELL- 2 MANSNS	
SHAPED HEAD ON A SLENDER NECK.	
HER EYES ARE SO LARGE THEY LOOK ENORMOUS, BLACK, 3 MANSNS	
DEEP-SET,	
LIGHT-BROWN EYES, SET WIDE APART, THEIR EXPRESSION 4 MANSNS	
SHARPLY OBSERVANT AND SHREWD.	
THE PRECEDENT WILL BE IRREVOCABLY SET. 8 MANSNS	
STAND, IN THE WAY OF THE FINAL GOAL OF POWER SHE 13 MANSNS	
HAS SET FOR HERSELF--	
THEN, HER FACE SET AND DETERMINED, 18 MANSNS	
IT WON'T TAKE LONG FOR US TO GET THE HUNDRED 48 MANSNS	
THOUSAND WE HAVE SET AS OUR GOAL.	
AND ALL THE HYPOCRITICAL VALUES WE SET ON THE 79 MANSNS	
RELATIONSHIP ARE MERE STUPIDITY.	
ARE YOU GOING TO ASK ME TO SET YOU FREE TO BE 81 MANSNS	
HIS&--	
TO PROVE MY LOVE FOR YOU AND SET YOU FREE FROM THE191 MANSNS	
GREED OF IT/	
FOR THE LOVE OF HIM, TO SAVE HIM AND SET HIM FREE/193 MANSNS	
TO SET HIS PACK BESIDE THE BAGS OF THE OTHERS.) 349 MARCOM	
NOW SET ME FREE/ 353 MARCOM	
ALL THE TIME THE THREE SET UP MISERABLE SCREAMS OF353 MARCOM	
PROTEST.	
LET HIM SET AN EXAMPLE OF VIRTUOUS WESTERN MANHOOD363 MARCOM	
AND ALL THE LOVELIES UP	
MIGHT SET AN EXAMPLE THAT WOULD ILLUSTRATE, BETTER379 MARCOM	
THAN WISE WORDS,	
SET THAT FORESAIL/ 406 MARCOM	
DIDN'T I TELL YOU TO STRIKE UP WHEN I SET FOOT ON 406 MARCOM	
THE DECK&	
HOW WELL IT IS SET OFF ON THE BOSOM OF A SHEEP/ 419 MARCOM	
WE WOULD TEAR DOWN THEIR CHRISTIAN IDOLS AND SET 422 MARCOM	
UP THE IMAGE OF THE BUDDHA/	
GARISHLY SET WITH AN ORNATE GOLD SERVICE. 426 MARCOM	
YOU HAVE SET YOUR LIPS IN A SMILE SO REMOTE--YOU 437 MARCOM	
ARE PRETENDING EVEN	
(VINDICTIVELY) I'VE NEVER SET FOOT IN A CHURCH 17 MISBEG	
SINCE, AND NEVER WILL.	
THIS SET-UP SUGGESTS THAT HE FOLLOWS A STYLE SET 37 MISBEG	
BY WELL-GROOMED BROADWAY	
AT ONCE AND NEVER LET AN OPPONENT GET SET TO HIT 56 MISBEG	
BACK.	
BUT I COULDN'T BRING MYSELF TO SET FOOT ON LAND 61 MISBEG	
BOUGHT WITH	
SHE COMES OUT A FIXED SMILE ON HER LIPS, HER HEAD 97 MISBEG	
HIGH, HER FACE SET DEFIANTLY.	
JOSIE'S FACE IS SET IN A A+ EXPRESSION OF NUMBED, 157 MISBEG	
RESIGNED SADNESS.	
(SCATHINGLY) I'VE SURE YOU'VE MADE UP A WHOLE NEW 163 MISBEG	
SET OF LIES AND EXCUSES.	
ALL THESE TABLES ARE SET WITH WHITE TABLECLOTHS, 7 POET	
ETC.	
HIS MOUTH USUALLY SET IN A HALF-LEERING GRIN. 8 POET	
AND BOUGHT AN ESTATE WITH A PACK OF HOUNDS AND SET 11 POET	
UP AS ONE OF THE GENTRY.	
SHE HAS SMALL EARS SET CLOSE TO HER WELL-SHAPED 19 POET	
HEAD, AND A SLENDER NECK.	
WELL, YOU'VE HAD YOUR CAP SET FOR HIM 16 POET	
I'VE LOVED HIM SINCE THE DAY I SET EYES ON HIM, 25 POET	
WITH A FINELY CHISELED NOSE OVER A DOMINEERING, 34 POET	
SENSUAL MOUTH SET IN DISDAIN.	
HE BRUSHES A SLEEVE FASTIDIOUSLY, ADJUSTS THE SET 43 POET	
OF HIS COAT.	
HER FACE IS SET. 95 POET	
"AND THE FOX SET HIM DOWN, AND LOOKED ABOUT, AND 102 POET	
MANY WERE FEARED TO FOLLOW.	

SET

SCT

(CONT'D.)
THAT SHE DEIGNS TO SET HER DAINTY HOOVES IN THEIR 106 POET
PALTRY GARDENS/
AND HIT THE CLUMSY CUT WITH HIS WHIP ACROSS HIS 155 POET
UGLY MUG THAT SET HIM
I HEARD HIM OPENIN' THE CLOSET IN HIS ROOM WHERE 162 POET
HE KEEPS HIS AULD SET
HE'S SET IN HIS PROUD NOBLE WAYS, BUT SHE'LL FIND173 POET
THE RIGHT TRICK/
THE MAJOR'S PASSIN' TO HIS ETERNAL REST HAS SET ME178 POET
FREE TO JINE THE DEMOCRATS.
FARTHER FORWARD AN OLD CANE-BUTTOMED CHAIR IS SET 577 ROPE
BACK AGAINST THE WALL.
THEY SET HER TO IT. 578 ROPE
AND SET IN AN ANGRY SCOWL.) 582 ROPE
I WAS TRYIN' TO GIT HIM HOME BUT HE'S THAT SET I 582 ROPE
COULDN'T BUDGE HIM.
IS THE BIG CASUALTY THEY WERE AFRAID TO SET DOWN 7 STRANG
ON THE LIST.
DEFIANT EYES, HER FACE SET IN AN EXPRESSION OF 12 STRANG
STUBBORN RESOLVE.
OF INTENSE PASSION WHICH HE HAS RIGIDLY TRAINED 33 STRANG
HIMSELF TO CONTROL AND SET FREE
OF THE UGLY TABLE WITH ITS SET OF STRAIGHTBACKED 48 STRANG
CHAIRS
TO THE RIGHT OF DOOR A HEAVY SIDEBOARD, A PART OF 48 STRANG
THE SET.
SET BACK AT SPACED INTERVALS AGAINST THE WALLS. 48 STRANG
THAT'D SET HER FREE... 93 STRANG
AND WITH NINA FOR A MOTHER, HIS NAMESAKE OUGHT TO 121 STRANG
INHERIT A FULL SET OF BRAINS.
HER EYES ARE TRAGICALLY SAD IN REPOSE AND HER 137 STRANG
EXPRESSION IS SET AND MASKLIKE.
HE CARRIES A SMALL, EXPENSIVE YACHT'S MODEL OF A 149 STRANG
SLOOP WITH THE SAILS SET.
(THE WOMEN COME FORWARD TO THE TABLE, WEARING 499 VOYAGE
THEIR BEST SET SMILES.)

SETH'S

SETH'S GROWED IT ON, TOO, DIDN'T YOU NOTICE--FROM 9 ELECTR
BEIN' WITH HER ALL HIS LIFE.
SOME FRIENDS OF SETH'S. 16 ELECTR
TO FOLLOW SETH'S ADVICE--STARING AT HIM WITH 24 ELECTR
DELIBERATELY INSULTING SCORN)
THE SOUND OF SETH'S THIN, AGED BARITONE MOURNFULLY 43 ELECTR
SINGING
SETH'S THIN WAILFUL A BARITONE IS RAISED IN HIS 123 ELECTR
FAVORITE MOURNFUL SHENANIGOAN.
SETH'S VOICE COMES FROM THE DRIVE, RIGHT, CLOSE AT124 ELECTR
HAND.

SETS

AT REAR OF SOFA, A BOOKCASE WITH GLASS DOORS, 185 AHWILD
FILLED WITH CHEAP SETS.
(THEN, AS A LOUDER BANG COMES FROM IN BACK AS 209 AHWILD
TOMMY SETS OFF A CANNON CRACKER,
(SHE SETS THE SOUP TUREEN DOWN WITH A THUD IN 222 AHWILD
FRONT OF MRS. MILLER
WHICH SHE SETS BEFORE MILLER, AND DISAPPEARS.) 228 AHWILD
CAN'T I GO OUT ON THE PIAZZA AND SIT FOR A WHILE--297 AHWILD
UNTIL THE MOON SETS?
(JOHNNY DRAWS THE LAGER AND PORTER AND SETS THE 4 ANNA
BIER
(JOHNNY SETS TWO GLASSES OF BARREL WHISKEY BEFORE 4 ANNA
THEM.)
LARRY BRINGS IN THE DRINKS AND SETS THEM ON THE 8 ANNA
TABLE.
LARRY COMES BACK WITH THE DRINK WHICH HE SETS 14 ANNA
BEFORE ANNA AND RETURNS TO THE BAR
(SETS DOWN HER BAG IMMEDIATELY--HASTILY) 23 ANNA
CHRIS COMES IN AND SETS THE DRINKS DOWN ON THE 24 ANNA
TABLE--
THEN HE GOES TO THE TABLE, SETS THE CLOTH STRAIGHT 44 ANNA
MECHANICALLY.
SHE SETS THOSE BEFORE HIM AND SITS DOWN IN HER 121 BEYOND
FORMER PLACE.
(HE SETS HER DOWN ON THE GROUND AGAIN) 130 BEYOND
WHICH SHE SETS ON THE TABLE BESIDE THE OTHER. 153 BEYOND
(HE OPENS THE LANTERN AND SETS FIRE TO THE MAP IN 567 CROSS
HIS HAND.
SUE SETS THE LANTERN DOWN BY THE COUCH. 573 CROSS
SETS THE CUP DOWN AGAIN ABRUPTLY AND GOES ON 534 DAYS
HURRIEDLY)
THEN SETS THE FLOORBOARD BACK IN PLACE. 219 DESIRE
HIS FACE SETS IN ITS CONCEALMENT MASK OF 518 DIFRNT
GROTESQUENESS AND HE TURNS SLOWLY AND
HIS BOOKCASE IS FULL OF INSTALLMENT-PLAN SETS OF 519 DIFRNT
UNCUT VOLUMES.
WITH A BRIGHT MULTI-COLORED HAND AND SETS IT 186 EJONES
JAUNTILY ON HIS HEAD)
HE CAN DO THAT IF HE SETS ABOUT IT. 39 ELECTR
SHE IS DRESSED IN A GOWN OF GREEN VELVET THAT SETS 45 ELECTR
OFF HER HAIR.
HE TAKES A DRINK--THEN SETS IT DOWN ON THE DRIVE) 131 ELECTR
IT SETS OFF HER HAIR AND EYES. 150 ELECTR
HE KISSES IT ON THE LIPS AND SETS IT DOWN AGAIN. 291 GGBROW
BOOKCASES FILLED WITH SETS, ETC. 294 GGBROW
IN A SHADE OF BLUE THAT SETS TEETH ON EDGE, AND A 9 HUGHIE
GAY RED AND BLUE FOULAND TIE.
SETS YOU BACK A HUNDRED BUCKS? 36 HUGHIE
UNITED BENEATH THE FLAG ON WHICH THE SUN NEVER 599 ICEMAN
SETS.
THEN SETS IT BACK ON THE TABLE WITH A GRIMACE OF 658 ICEMAN
DISTASTE--
AND HE SETS THE BOTTLE ON THE TABLE WITH A JAR 691 ICEMAN
THAT ROUSES HUGO.
CUCKY IMMEDIATELY SETS DOWN THE PAIL WITH A BANG 526 INZONE
AND--
WHO AGAIN LIFTS THE BOX OUT OF THE WATER AND SETS 528 INZONE
IT CAREFULLY ON ITS KNEES.

SETS

(CONT'D.)
FARTHER BACK IS A LARGE, GLASSED-IN BOOKCASE WITH 11 JOURNE
SETS OF DUMAS, VICTOR HUGO,
CHARLES LEVER, THREE SETS OF SHAKESPEARE, 11 JOURNE
THE ASTONISHING THING ABOUT THESE SETS IS THAT ALL 11 JOURNE
THE VOLUMES HAVE THE LOOK OF
(HE POURS WATER IN THE GLASS AND SETS IT ON THE 54 JOURNE
TABLE BY EDMUND.)
HIS FACE SETS IN AN EXPRESSION OF EMBITTERED, 58 JOURNE
DEFENSIVE CYNICISM.
(HER FACE AGAIN SETS IN STUBBORN DEFIANCE.) 69 JOURNE
HER FACE SETS IN STUBBORN DEFENSIVENESS-- 108 JOURNE
RESENTFULLY.)
WHEN I'VE THREE GOOD SETS OF SHAKESPEARE THERE 135 JOURNE
AND HIS FACE SETS INTO A MASK OF CALCULATING 75 MANSNS
RUTHLESSNESS.
SETS HER DOWN BEFORE THE BENCH AT RIGHT AND FORCES167 MANSNS
HER DOWN ON IT.)
THE MAGIAN SETS DOWN HIS BAG AND WIPES HIS BROW.) 347 MARCOM
(THE CHRISTIAN SETS UP A WAILING CRY AND RECEIVES 354 MARCOM
A BLOW.
HE SETS THESE DOWN AND GAZES AROUND WITH A 364 MARCOM
BEWILDERED AWE.)
AND SETS IT UP ON THE FLOOR. 394 MARCOM
(HE SETS THE BOTTLE ON TOP OF THE BOULDER.) 54 MISBEG
TYRONE POURS A DRINK AND SETS THE BOTTLE ON THE 126 MISBEG
GROUND.
SHE STIFFENS INTO HOSTILITY AND HER MOUTH SETS IN 33 POET
SCORN.
AND HE SETS THE GLASS BACK ON THE TABLE WITH A 35 POET
BANG.
(NORA GETS THE DECANTER AND GLASS FROM THE 36 POET
CUPBOARD AND SETS THEM BEFORE HIM.
SQUARES HIS SHOULDERS, PULLS HIS COAT DOWN IN 22 STRANG
FRONT, SETS HIS TIE STRAIGHT,
(JOE BRINGS OLSON'S DRINK TO THE TABLE AND SETS IT505 VOYAGE
BEFORE HIM.)
HE HAS A SUITCASE, HAT, AND OVERCOAT WHICH HE SETS444 WELDED
INSIDE ON THE FLOOR.

SETTIN'

YOU FOLKS LOOK AS IF YOU WAS SETTIN' UP WITH A 95 BEYOND
CORPSE.
DON'T I KNOW THE MARE 'N' BUGGY, AN' TWO PEOPLE 219 DESIRE
SETTIN' IN IT?
SETTIN' IN HER PARLOR WHAR SHE WAS LAID-- 242 DESIRE
WHEN I WAS YOUR AGE, D'YOU S'POSE YOU'D EVER BE 512 DIFRNT
SETTIN' THERE NOW?
YOU WAS SETTIN' ME UP WHERE I'D NO BUSINESS TO BE,517 DIFRNT
THEY'LL SEE HIM A-SETTIN' ON THE YARDS AND HEAR HIM132 ELECTR
MORNIN' TO HIMSELF.
I SEED YOU SETTIN' OUT HERE ON THE STEPS WHEN I 170 ELECTR
GOT UP AT FIVE THIS MORNIN'--

SETTING

AS TOMMY INAUGURATES HIS CELEBRATION BY SETTING 189 AHWILD
OFF A PACKAGE OF FIRECRACKERS.
IN THE SETTING OF THE TABLE. 210 AHWILD
(SETTING THEM DOWN--WITH A WINK AT BELLE) 239 AHWILD
GLASSES BEFORE SETTING THEM DOWN) 242 AHWILD
(SETTING THEM ON THE TABLE) HERE'S YOUR PLEASURE.242 AHWILD
(THEN FUSSING ABOUT THE ROOM, SETTING THIS AND 269 AHWILD
THAT IN PLACE.)
THE MOON'S WAY DOWN LOW--ALMOST SETTING. 296 AHWILD
HE PRETENDS TO BE ENGAGED IN SETTING THINGS SHIP- 41 ANNA
SHAPE.
(HE SITS IN A CHAIR BY THE TABLE, SETTING DOWN THE 63 ANNA
CAN OF BEER.
CLOSING THE DOOR BEHIND HIM, AND SETTING THE 99 BEYOND
LIGHTED LANTERN ON THE FLOOR.
THEY FINISHED SETTING ME FREE. 147 ELECTR
AND HE'D SEE THE MOUNTAINS OF SOUTH AMERICY WID 214 HA APE
THE RED FIRE OF THE SETTING SUN
ROCKY BEGINS SETTING OUT DRINKS. WHISKEY GLASSES 619 ICEMAN
WITH CHASERS.
(HER FACE SETTING INTO THAT STUBBORN DENIAL 70 JOURNE
AGAIN.)
YOU'RE SETTING NO RIVERS ON FIRE/ 164 JOURNE
AND MAKE AN INSTANT DECISION, SETTING IT ON THE 70 MANSNS
TABLE AT HIS RIGHT.
SARA MUST BE WONDERING WHAT IS KEEPING ME, NOW THE102 MANSNS
SUN IS SETTING.
SETTING YOU FREE TO GO AGAIN THE MAN YOU WERE WHEN191 MANSNS
I FIRST MET YOU--
(SETTING DOWN THE BAGS WITH A THUMP 373 MARCOM
THE BLINDING GLARE OF THE SETTING SUN FLOODS IN 376 MARCOM
FROM BEYOND.
PLACED SO PERFECTLY IN ITS SETTING 1 MISBEG
PULLING IT BACK AND SETTING IT ON ITS LEGS 601 ROPE
I NEED A NEW SETTING FOR MY NEXT NOVEL--- 52 STRANG
WHICH IS PUSHED BACK, SETTING THE RUG ASKEW. 66 STRANG

SETTLE

AND SETTLE DOWN RIGHT HERE. 96 BEYOND
I'M GOING TO SETTLE RIGHT DOWN 102 BEYOND
AND ANXIOUS TO GET HOME AND SETTLE DOWN TO WORK 115 BEYOND
AGAIN.
(SHAKING HIS HEAD) BUT JUST THE SAME I DOUBT IF 125 BEYOND
HE'LL WANT TO SETTLE DOWN TO A
TO SETTLE DOWN ON THE FARM AND SEE TO THINGS. 138 BEYOND
AND THEN I'LL COME BACK AND SETTLE DOWN 138 BEYOND
AND SETTLE OUT IN THE COUNTRY AWAY FROM FOLKS AND 147 ELECTR
THEIR EVIL TALK.
THEN JEERINGLY) SO MY WIFE THINKS IT BEHOOVES ME 271 GGBROW
TO SETTLE DOWN AND SUPPORT MY
SETTLE WITH YOURSELF ONCE AND FOR ALL$ 655 ICEMAN
YUH DON'T WANTA SEE ME GET MARRIED AND SETTLE DOWN671 ICEMAN
LIKE A REGULAR GUY?
YES, LARRY, YOU'VE GOT TO SETTLE WITH HIM. 689 ICEMAN
AN' HUW SHE HOPES HE'LL SETTLE DOWN TO RALE WORRK 530 INZONE
AN' NOT BE SKYLARKIN' AROUND

SETTLE (CONT'D.)
WHEN IT'S GETTING NEAR BEDTIME, OR YOU'LL NEVER 49 MANSNS
SETTLE DOWN TO SLEEP.
AND THAT WILL SETTLE HER HALF OF IT. 94 MANSNS
TO OFFER MY CONGRATULATIONS--AND BEFORE I SETTLE 391 MAHCOM
DOWN TO DISCUSSING BUSINESS--
WILL SOBER HER SPIRIT AND SHE WILL SETTLE DOWN AS 424 MARCOM
A SENSIBLE WIFE SHOULD.
I OUGHT TO MARRY AND SETTLE DOWN-- 20 MISBEG
AND HE WAS COMING HERE TO SETTLE THE MATTER. 24 MISBEG
NO URGE TO DO ANYTHING EXCEPT SETTLE DOWN ON HIS 55 MISBEG
ESTATE AND LIVE THE LIFE OF A
SETTLE IT, AND JIM PROMISED SIMPSON HE WOULD. 84 MISBEG
HAVE TO SETTLE BY THE END OF THE WEEK OR WE'LL GET 22 POET
NO MORE GROCERIES.
SO NATURALLY HE WILL SETTLE AN ALLOWANCE ON SIMON,111 POET
HENRY HANFORD IS WILLING TO SETTLE ON HIS SON. 111 POET
NOW THAT SIMON HAS DECIDED TO MARRY AND SETTLE 111 POET
DOWN
(IF SHE'D SETTLE DOWN HERE... 31 STRANG
OUGHT TO GET MARRIED AND SETTLE DOWN... 134 STRANG
SETTLED
THEN, THAT'S ALL SETTLED. 191 AHWILD
IT AIN'T NO GOOD GOIN' ON THAT WAY, KATE, NOW IT'S 96 BEYOND
ALL SETTLED.
IT'S SETTLED THEN. 104 BEYOND
(GETTING TO HIS FEET) THEN, THAT'S SETTLED. 142 BEYOND
(IN A TONE OF FINALITY AS IF THIS SETTLED THE 512 DIFNNT
MATTER)
(QUICKLY) OH, THAT'S ALL SETTLED, JOHN. 513 DIFNNT
WHERE HE SETTLED DOWN UNDER ANOTHER NAME 431 DYNAMO
THE FAR WEST AND SETTLED DOWN IN NICLUM, 441 DYNAMU
CALIFORNIA.
(GETTING UP) THEN IT'S ALL SETTLED, ISN'T ITS 277 GGBROW
IN THE YEARS SINCE WE SETTLED DOWN HERE. 292 GGBROW
I HOPED THE BLASTED OLD ESTATE WOULD BE SETTLED UP605 ICEMAN
BY THEN.
BUT THERE WAS SOMETHING I HAD TO GET FINALLY 704 ICEMAN
SETTLED.
IT'S ALL SETTLED NOW. 158 JOURNE
IT'S SETTLED, THEN. 38 MANSNS
THEN THE MATTER IS SETTLED--PROVIDED, OF COURSE, 59 MANSNS
SARA CONSENTS.
IT HAS BEEN A STRAIN GETTING THIS AFFAIR OF THE 71 MANSNS
RAILROAD SETTLED.
LOVE SHOULD BE A DEAL FOREVER INCOMPLETE, NEVER 72 MANSNS
FINALLY SETTLED.
WELL, I THINK WE'VE SETTLED EVERYTHING. 92 MANSNS
THAT'S SETTLED, THEN. 135 MANSNS
WELL, THAT'S SETTLED. 158 MANSNS
I'VE HAD MY FUN AND I SUPPOSE IT'S ABOUT TIME I 404 MAHCOM
SETTLED DOWN.
HIS MOTHER'S ESTATE IS SETTLED. 9 MISBEG
(REALLY WORRIED NOW) HOW IS IT ALL SETTLES 81 MISBEG
IT'S ALL SETTLED. 81 MISBEG
JIM WON'T HAVE TO WAIT FOR HIS HALF OF THE CASH 84 MISBEG
TILL THE ESTATE'S SETTLED.
ESTATE IS SETTLED. 95 MISBEG
HE'D HARDLY GOT SETTLED WHEN HIS WIFE DIED GIVIN' 11 POET
BIRTH TO CON.
(BRISKLY) THEN IT'S ALL SETTLED! 46 STRANG
THAT'S SETTLED FOR ALL TIME/... 133 STRANG
OUR ACCOUNT WITH GOD THE FATHER IS SETTLED... 165 STRANG
SETTLEMENT
AND READING ROOM, RESEMBLES SOME DINGY SETTLEMENT 245 HA APE
BOYS' CLUB.
THE DAMNED LAWYERS CAN'T HOLD UP THE SETTLEMENT 605 ICEMAN
MUCH LONGER.
(FIRMLY.) YOUR SETTLEMENT, CERTAINLY. 50 POET
MY SETTLEMENT/ 50 POET
THE AMOUNT OF YOUR SETTLEMENT HAS TO BE AGREED 50 POET
UPON.
PROVIDED HIS FATHER AND I CAN AGREE ON THE AMOUNT 63 POET
OF HER SETTLEMENT.
THERE WAS THE AMOUNT OF SETTLEMENT TO BE AGREED 111 POET
UPON, FOR INSTANCE.
YOU HAVE COME ABOUT THE SETTLEMENTS 120 POET
THAT A SETTLEMENT WOULD BE FOREMOST IN YOUR MIND. 120 POET
WILL YOU TELL ME PLAINLY WHAT YOU MEAN BY YOUR 121 POET
TALK OF SETTLEMENTS
OBVIOUSLY, I MEAN THE SETTLEMENT I AM PREPARED TO 121 POET
MAKE ON MY DAUGHTER.
THAT IS WHAT I THOUGHT YOU WERE EXPECTING WHEN YOU122 POET
MENTIONED A SETTLEMENT.
SETTLES
THE HELPS HER IN AND SHE SETTLES HERSELF IN THE 280 AHWILD
STERN SEAT OF THE BOAT.
WELL, I BELIEVE YOU--AND I GUESS THAT SETTLES 294 AHWILD
THAT.
THEN THAT SETTLES--THE BOOZE END OF IT. 294 AHWILD
THAT SETTLES IT/ 465 CARIBE
AND SETTLES DOWN TO READING WITH A GRUNT OF 430 DYNAMO
AWAKENED INTEREST.)
(HE SETTLES HIMSELF AND IMMEDIATELY FALLS ASLEEP.1586 ICEMAN
THE SETTLES HIMSELF IN HIS CHAIR, GRUMBLING) 610 ICEMAN
(HE CLOSES HIS EYES AND SETTLES ON HIS CHAIR AS IF616 ICEMAN
PREPARING FOR SLEEP.
AND SETTLES INTO THE CHAIR AT THE NEXT TABLE WHICH692 ICEMAN
FACES LEFT.
A THICK SILENCE SETTLES OVER THE FORECASTLE. 522 INZONE
(STARTS AND AT ONCE THE QUALITY OF UNNATURAL 87 JOURNE
DETACHMENT SETTLES ON HER FACE
THEN SHE SETTLES BACK IN RELAXED DREAMINESS, 106 JOURNE
STARING FIXEDLY AT NOTHING.
SO THAT SETTLES THAT. 149 JOURNE
A GREAT SPELL OF SILENCE SETTLES UPON ALL HIS 366 LAZARU
HEARERS--

SETTLES (CONT'D.)
THE LUCK OF GUILT AND SHAME AND ANGUISH SETTLES 173 MISBEG
OVER HIS FACE.
(A RELIGIOUS GRIN SETTLES OVER HIS FACE) 607 RUPE
(SHE SETTLES BACK AND STARES DREAMILY BEFORE HER-- 91 STRANG
A PAUSE)
SETTLIN'
NO DAT OLD PIPE DREAM ABOUT GETTIN' MARRIED AND 614 ICEMAN
SETTLIN' DOWN ON A FARM.
SETTLING
I TELL YOU, I FEEL RIPE FOR BIGGER THINGS THAN 134 BEYOND
SETTLING DOWN HERE.
KINDLY REMEMBER I'M FULLY CAPABLE OF SETTLING MY 655 ICEMAN
OWN AFFAIRS/
SEVEN
HE IS TWENTY-SEVEN YEARS OLD, AN OPPOSITE TYPE TO 82 BEYOND
ROBERT--
THE LAST TRIP HE MADE WAS SEVEN YEARS AGO. 559 CRUSS
ARCHIPELAGO--A. ISLAND BARREN AS HELL, DOCTOR-- 559 CRUSS
AFTER SEVEN DAYS IN AN OPEN BOAT.
DINNER IS AT SEVEN-THIRTY. 512 DAYS
SIMEON IS THIRTY-NINE AND PETER THIRTY-SEVEN-- 203 DESIRE
ONE NIGHT WHEN I WAS SEVEN HE CAME HOME CRAZY 25 ELECTR
DRUNK--
SLEEK--SEVEN YEARS LATER. 269 GGBROW
SCENE--CYBEL'S PARLOR--ABOUT SUNSET IN SPRING 284 GGBROW
SEVEN YEARS LATER.
WE'VE BEEN FRIENDS, HAVEN'T WE, FOR SEVEN YEARS$ 285 GGBROW
YOU WERE ONLY SEVEN. 589 ICEMAN
OH, I KNOW JAMIE WAS ONLY SEVEN, BUT HE WAS NEVER 87 JOURNE
STUPID.
IT'S ONLY SEVEN DOLLARS A WEEK BUT YOU GET TEN 149 JOURNE
TIMES THAT VALUE.
AND I WAS ONLY TWENTY-SEVEN YEARS OLD/ 150 JOURNE
AND EACH OF THESE PERIODS IS REPRESENTED BY SEVEN 273 LAZARU
DIFFERENT MASKS OF GENERAL
THERE ARE SEVEN PERIODS OF LIFE SHOWN. 273 LAZARU
INSIDE THE HOUSE ON THE MEN'S SIDE, SEVEN MALE 273 LAZARU
GUESTS ARE GROUPED BY THE DOOR.
THIS INCLUDES AMONG THE MEN THE SEVEN GUESTS WHO 273 LAZARU
ARE COMPOSED OF ONE MALE OF
THE CHORUS OF OLD MEN, SEVEN IN NUMBER, IS DRAWN 273 LAZARU
UP IN A CRESCENT.
THEY ARE ALL SEVEN IN THE SORROWFUL, RESIGNED TYPE274 LAZARU
OF OLD AGE.)
TYPE TWO, AND SO ON UP TO PERIOD SEVEN--TYPE 274 LAZARU
SEVEN--
THE CHORUS OF FOLLOWERS, SEVEN IN NUMBER, ALL MEN,285 LAZARU
THE SAME FORMULA OF SEVEN PERIODS, SEVEN TYPES. 291 LAZARU
THEY ARE MASKED ACCORDING TO THE SCHEME OF SEVEN 294 LAZARU
PERIODS
IN SEVEN TYPES OF CHARACTER FOR EACH SEX. 298 LAZARU
ON THE LEFT, THE CHORUS OF GREEKS IS GROUPED, 298 LAZARU
SEVEN IN NUMBER, FACING FRONT,
THESE SEVEN ARE CLAD IN GOAT SKINS, 298 LAZARU
ABOVE IT, HIS HAIR IS THE CURLY BLOND HAIR OF A 299 LAZARU
CHILD OF SIX OR SEVEN.
SEVEN TYPES IN SEVEN PERIODS, EXCEPT THAT, AS IN 306 LAZARU
THE CHORUS,
SEVEN IN NUMBER, FACING FRONT, IN DOUBLE-SIZED 312 LAZARU
MASKS OF THE SERVILE,
AND THERE ARE SEVEN INDIVIDUALS OF EACH PERIOD AND336 LAZARU
SEX
IN THEIR CHORUS, SEVEN MEN MASKED IN MIDDLE AGE 361 LAZARU
IN THE SERVILE,
HE IS TWENTY-SEVEN, SHORT, DARK, WIRY, HIS 33 STRANG
MOVEMENTS RAPID AND SURE,
BUT I DID WITH OTHERS--OUR FOUR OR FIVE OR SIX OR 45 STRANG
SEVEN MEN, CHARLIE.
SEVEN MONTHS OR SO LATER-- 48 STRANG
AN EVENING EARLY IN THE FOLLOWING WINTER ABOUT 66 STRANG
SEVEN MONTHS LATER.
ABOUT THE TIME HE WAS STROKING THE CREW AND THE 153 STRANG
FELLOW WHO WAS NUMBER SEVEN
(BITINGLY) YOU WERE ON THE STAGE SEVEN YEARS 457 WELDED
BEFORE I MET YOU.
SEVENTEEN
(HE IS GOING ON SEVENTEEN, JUST OUT OF HIGH 193 AHWILD
SCHOOL.
HE IS SEVENTEEN, TALL AND THIN. 422 DYNAMO
AT SEVENTEEN I RAN AWAY TO SEA-- 26 ELECTR
SHE IS ALMOST SEVENTEEN, PRETTY AND VIVACIOUS, 262 GGBROW
BLONDE, WITH BIG ROMANTIC EYES,
PLATES AND CUTLERY BEFORE EACH OF THE SEVENTEEN 628 ICEMAN
CHAIRS.
HE IS SEVENTEEN NOW. 369 MARCOM
SEVENTH
(TOO MUCH IN THE SEVENTH HEAVEN OF BLISS 52 ANNA
(THE SEVENTH GUEST OF SCENE ONE--STARTS TO 286 LAZARU
HARANGUE THE CROWD.
I WAS A CORPORAL IN THE SEVENTH DRAGOONS AND HE 10 POET
WAS MAJOR.
I AM MAJOR CORNELIUS MELODY, ONE TIME OF HIS 70 POET
MAJESTY'S SEVENTH DRAGOONS.
ONE TIME OF HIS MAJESTY'S SEVENTH DRAGOONS, 117 POET
LATE OF HIS MAJESTY'S SEVENTH DRAGOONS. 154 POET
RESPECTFULLY REQUESTS A WORD WITH HIM-- 168 POET
UNALIC, MAJOR CORNELIUS MELODY, AV HIS MAJESTY'S 168 POET
SEVENTH DRAGOONS, USED TO DO.
(IN THE SEVENTH HEAVEN NOW--PASSIONATELY) 70 STRANG
SEVENTY
HE IS SEVENTY, ABOUT JOHN AND LOVING'S HEIGHT, 500 DAYS
ERECT, ROBUST,
CABOT IS SEVENTY-FIVE, TALL AND GAUNT, WITH GREAT,221 DESIRE
WIRY, CONCENTRATED POWER,
THEY HAIN'T MANY T' TOUCH YE, EPHRAIM--A SON AT 249 DESIRE
SEVENTY-SIX.

SEVENTY

SEVENTY (CONT'D.)
(WITH A WINK AT THE OTHERS) YE'RE THE SPRYEST 250 DESIRE
SEVENTY-SIX EVER I SEES, EPHRAIM/
SEVENTY-SIX, IF I'M A DAY/ 251 DESIRE
SEVENTY-SIX AN' HIM NOT THIRTY YIT-- 256 DESIRE
IS AN OLD MAN OF SEVENTY-FIVE WITH WHITE HAIR AND 6 ELECTR
BEARD, TALL,
ONY SEVENTY-FIVE/ 7 ELECTR
TEN, TWENTY, THIRTY, FORTY, FIFTY, SIXTY, SEVENTY,608 ICEMAN
EIGHTY, NINETY, A DOLLAR.
FORTY FIFTY, SEVENTY, EIGHTY, NINETY, THREE 609 ICEMAN
DOLLARS.
FIFTY, SIXTY, SEVENTY, NINETY, FOUR DOLLARS. 609 ICEMAN
TEN, TWENTY, THIRTY, FIFTY, SEVENTY, EIGHTY, 609 ICEMAN
NINETY--
AN OLD MAN OF SEVENTY-SIX, TALL, 337 LAZARU

SEVERAL
OVER THE BENCH, SEVERAL CURTAINED PORTHOLES. 535 *ILE
SEVERAL BOOKS ARE PILED ON THE TABLE BY HIS ELBOW,288 AHWILD
HER BARE FEET ARE ENCASED IN A MAN'S BROGANS 7 ANNA
SEVERAL SIZES TOO LARGE FOR HER.
SEVERAL TIMES I'VE BEEN ALMOST A MILLIONAIRE--ON 156 BEYOND
PAPER--
(DRISCOLL AND SEVERAL OF THE OTHERS SIT 464 CARIBE
THEY KISS SEVERAL TIMES. 244 DESIRE
HE SWALLOWS PAINFULLY SEVERAL TIMES--FORCES A WEAK268 DESIRE
SMILE AT LAST)
SEVERAL ENLARGED PHOTOS OF STRAINED, 493 DIFRNT
AND SEVERAL BOOKS THAT LOOK SUSPICIOUSLY LIKE 493 DIFRNT
CHEAP NOVELS.
SEVERAL FRAMED PRINTS OF SCENES FROM THE BIBLE 421 DYNAMO
HANG ON THE WALLS.
HIS FACE IS SCRATCHED, HIS BRILLIANT UNIFORM SHOWS191 EJONES
SEVERAL LARGE RENTS)
(THE REPORTS OF SEVERAL RIFLES SOUND FROM THE 203 EJONES
FOREST.
SEVERAL MINUTES ARE SUPPOSED TO ELAPSE. 109 ELECTR
(SEVERAL BOTTLES ARE EAGERLY OFFERED. 209 HA APE
SEVERAL SNORES FROM DOWN THE CORRIDOR. 244 HA APE
PROPELLED BY SEVERAL PARTING KICKS, 250 HA APE
HE KNOWS THERE ARE SEVERAL HOURS TO GO BEFORE HIS 7 HUGHIE
SHIFT IS OVER.
WHEN SEVERAL PEOPLE GOT KILLED5 583 ICEMAN
SEVERAL PACKAGES, TIED WITH RIBBON, ARE ALSO ON 629 ICEMAN
THE TABLE.
AND SEVERAL HISTORIES OF IRELAND. 11 JOURNE
AND SEVERAL OTHERS HAD BEEN TAKEN DOWN WITH 24 JOURNE
CHOLERA
SEVERAL WHISKEY GLASSES, AND A PITCHER OF ICE 51 JOURNE
WATER.
AND SEVERAL OTHER TIMES IN MY LIFE, WHEN I WAS 153 JOURNE
SWIMMING FAR OUT,
TO THE LEFT OF CENTER SEVERAL LONG TABLES PLACED 273 LAZARU
LENGTHWISE TO THE WIDTH OF THE
THEN SEVERAL AT A TIME, THEN MULTITUDES, JOIN IN 318 LAZARU
HIS LAUGHTER.
THE BLACK FIGURES OF SEVERAL MEN ARE OUTLINED. 331 LAZARU
SEVERAL SLAVES BEARING LAMPS ON POLES ESCORT THE 331 LAZARU
PATRICIAN, MARCELLUS,
I HAVE FORGOTTEN HIM SEVERAL TIMES BEFORE IN MY 133 MANSNS
LIFE--
SEVERAL WEEKS LATER. 399 MARCOM
EXPLAINING EARNESTLY WITH SEVERAL MAPS IN HIS 421 MARCOM
HAND.
BUT THERE WERE SEVERAL PEOPLE AROUND AND I KNEW 148 MISBEG
THEY EXPECTED ME TO SHOW
(HE STANDS STARING UP AT THE ROPE AND TAPS IT 579 ROPE
TESTINGLY SEVERAL TIMES WITH HIS
(NODDING HIS HEAD SEVERAL TIMES--STUPIDLY) 27 STRANG
SEVERAL MONTHS LATER. 184 STRANG
SWALLOWING HARD SEVERAL TIMES AS IF HE WERE 472 WELDED
STRIVING TO GET CONTROL OF HIS

SEVERE
(THEN ATTEMPTING A SEVERE TONE AGAIN) 34 ANNA
IT IS AN INTERIOR COMPOSED OF STRAIGHT SEVERE 79 ELECTR
LINES WITH HEAVY DETAIL.
(FLIPPANTLY) YOU ARE TOO SEVERE WITH YOURSELF, 315 LAZARU
LUCIUS/
HIS CHIN IS FORCEFUL AND SEVERE. 337 LAZARU
I KNOW YOU'VE JUST BEEN UNDER A SEVERE STRAIN. 156 MANSNS
(PUZZLED AND SEVERE) HUH? 412 MARCOM
(DESPERATELY PUTTING ON HIS PRIM SEVERE MANNER 15 STRANG
TOWARD AN UNRULY PUPIL)
(HE GETS TO HIS FEET, HIS FACE UNCONSCIOUSLY 189 STRANG
BECOMING OLDER AND COLD AND SEVERE.
YOU'RE TOO SEVERE. 453 WELDED

SEVERELY
(HIS FACE CLOUDING--REBUKINGLY BUT NOT SEVERELY) 542 *ILE
(REGARDS HER BROTHER SEVERELY) 265 AHWILD
THEN SEVERELY) 33 ANNA
(SEVERELY) SEEMS TO ME IT'S A PRETTY LATE HOUR IN100 BEYOND
THE DAY FOR YOU TO BE
(SEVERELY) AND I HOPE YOU KNOW THE KIND OF WOMAN 525 DIFRNT
SHE IS AND HAS BEEN
(THEN SEVERELY) YOUR UNCLE'S TO HUME. 528 DIFRNT
(SEVERELY) BE THAT PAINT AND POWDER YOU GOT ON 536 DIFRNT
YOUR FACE, EMMER8
(SEVERELY) LUCK/ 178 EJONES
AND THERE IS NOT A TOUCH OF FEMININE ALLUREMENT TO 10 ELECTR
HER SEVERELY PLAIN GET-UP.
SHE IS DRESSED, AS BEFORE, SEVERELY IN BLACK. 43 ELECTR
(SEVERELY, AS HE TAKES THE POEM) 360 MARCOM
(SEVERELY) MARK/ 371 MARCOM
(SEVERELY) LET YOUR UNCLE IN PEACE, YE BRAT/ 591 ROPE
(SEVERELY) DON'T YUH DARE TOUCH THAT ROPE, D'YUH 600 ROPE
HEAR8
(SEVERELY) YOU SERIOUSLY MEAN TO TELL ME YOU, IN 17 STRANG
YOUR CONDITION,

SEVEREST
IF YOU CONTINUE TO BE MY SEVEREST CRITIC, 21 STRANG

SEVERITY
(WITH FORCED SEVERITY) SID/ 225 AHWILD
HIS FACE IS SET IN AN EXPRESSION OF FROWNING 263 AHWILD
SEVERITY.
(THEN WITH A TOUCH OF SEVERITY) 431 DYNAMO
(WITH A SUDDEN CHANGE TO SEVERITY) 436 DYNAMO
(WITH MOCK SEVERITY) BUT OUGHT IS 445 DYNAMO

SEVERLY
(RESTRAINING A GIGGLE--SEVERLY) 225 AHWILD

SEW
SHE DOES NOTHIN' ALL DAY LONG BUT SIT AND SEW-- 538 *ILE

SEWED
MY MOTHER SEWED FOR A LIVING AND SENT ME TO 26 ELECTR
SCHOOL.
AND MY OLDER SISTER SEWED, AND MY TWO YOUNGER 148 JOURNE
STAYED AT HOME TO KELP THE HOUSE.

SEWERS
AND WE WON'T LAY SIDEWALKS--OR DIG SEWERS--EVER 258 GGBHOW
AGAIN5

SEWING
ON THE SIDEBOARD, A WOMAN'S SEWING BASKET. 535 *ILE
A SEWING BASKET IS ON HER LAP 249 AHWILD
MRS. MILLER LOOKS UP FROM HER SEWING) 288 AHWILD
IS READING A BOOK WHILE HIS WIFE, SEWING BASKET IN288 AHWILD
LAP,
(SHE GOES BACK TO HER SEWING.) 291 AHWILD
(HAVING THUS SQUARED MATTERS SHE TAKES UP HER 291 AHWILD
SEWING AGAIN.
(HAS STOPPED SEWING--THINKING.) 119 MANSNS
(GETTING UP FROM THE SOFA.) I'LL GET MY SEWING. 136 MANSNS
AND COME BACK TO YOU.
FIDDLES AROUND UNNECESSARILY GATHERING UP HER 137 MANSNS
SEWING THINGS.

SEX
TO PUT IT THAT WAY--I MEAN, PERTAINING TO THE 295 AHWILD
OPPOSITE SEX--
WHAT WE DID WAS JUST PLAIN SEX--AN ACT OF NATURE--469 DYNAMO
AND THAT'S ALL THERE IS TO IT/
WHAT PEOPLE CALL LOVE IS JUST SEX--AND THERE'S NO 469 DYNAMO
SIN ABOUT IT/
THEY ARE NOT DIVIDED ACCORDING TO SEX AS IN THE 282 LAZARU
PREVIOUS SCENE.
IN SEVEN TYPES OF CHARACTER FOR EACH SEX. 298 LAZARU
THERE IS A DISTINCTIVE CHARACTER TO THE MASKS OF 336 LAZARU
EACH SEX,
AND THERE ARE SEVEN INDIVIDUALS OF EACH PERIOD AND336 LAZARU
SEX.
THE WHOLE EFFECT OF THESE TWO GROUPS IS OF SEX 336 LAZARU
CORRUPTED AND WARPED.
AROUND AND TO THE SIDES OF THE DAIS, ONE SEX ON 344 LAZARU
EACH SIDE.
IF YOU RECALL ALL YOUR GUESTS OF MY SEX WITH THIS 72 PUET
ABSURD PERFORMANCE/
TO THE DEVIL WITH SEX/.... 5 STRANG
MY SEX LIFE AMONG THE PHANTOMS/....)) 5 STRANG
MORE THAN ONE CAN SAY OF THESE MODERN SEX- 5 STRANG
YAHOOS/....
SEX THE PHILOSOPHER'S STONE,... 34 STRANG
TRYING NOT TO DISCOVER WHICH SEX THEY BELONG 34 STRANG
TO/...)
SHE NEVER IMAGINES SEX COULD ENTER INTO IT/...)) 114 STRANG
A GOOD SPORT AND IS POPULAR WITH HER OWN SEX AS 159 STRANG
WELL AS SOUGHT AFTER BY MEN.
SHOUT =THIS IS LIFE AND THIS IS SEX, AND HERE ARE 176 STRANG
PASSION AND HATRED AND REGRET

SEXES
FARMERS AND THEIR WIVES AND THEIR YOUNG FOLKS OF 247 DESIRE
BOTH SEXES
COMPOSED ABOUT EQUALLY OF BOTH SEXES, WEAR A MASK 285 LAZARU
THAT,
AN EXCITED CROWD OF GREEKS OF BOTH SEXES IS 298 LAZARU
GATHERED IN THE SQUARE.
THE REST, SOLDIERS, SLAVES AND THE PROSTITUTES OF 347 LAZARU
BOTH SEXES,

SEXUAL
HE SAID I COULD HAVE EQUAL LIBERTY TO INDULGE ANY 520 DAYS
OF MY SEXUAL WHIMS.
UNDERSTANDING OF ITS REAL SEXUAL NATURE. 33 STRANG

SEXUALLY
THAT HAS GIVEN UP THE STRUGGLE TO BE SEXUALLY 189 STRANG
ATTRACTIVE AND LOOK

SH'D
'CEPTIN' YOUR GRANDPAW LET OUT TO ME ONE TIME SH'D 19 ELECTR
HAD THE BABY--A BOY.

SHABBILY
HE IS DRESSED CARELESSLY, ALMOST SHABBILY. 124 STRANG
FOLLOWED BY TWO ROUGH-LOOKING, SHABBILY-DRESSED 504 VOYAGE
MEN, WEARING MUFFLERS,

SHABBY
THE CHAIRS APPEAR SHABBY FROM LACK OF PAINT. 112 BEYOND
BUT HE THINKS THE CASE LOOKS SHABBY AND HE WANTS 285 GGBHOW
IT JUNKED.
THE DESK FACES LEFT ALONG A SECTION OF SEEDY LOBBY 7 HUGHIE
WITH SHABBY CHAIRS.
IT IS COMMONPLACE SHABBY. 13 JOURNE
HE IS DRESSED IN AN OLD SACK SUIT, NOT AS SHABBY 19 JOURNE
AS TYRONE'S,
HE'S EVEN PROUD OF HAVING THIS SHABBY PLACE. 61 JOURNE
ALL THE POLOS ARE WEARY AND THEIR CLOTHES SHABBY 373 MARCOM
AND TRAVEL-WORN.
LOOSE TARTAR TRAVELING DRESS AND LOOK QUITE 429 MARCOM
SHABBY,
SHE WEARS A SHABBY GINGHAM DRESS. 578 ROPE
SHABBY COLLEGIATE GENTILITY--AND HE HAS FORGOTTEN 92 STRANG
TO SHAVE.

SHABBY (CONT'D.)
HE IS DRESSED IN A SHABBY SUIT, WHICH MUST HAVE 493 VOYAGE ONCE BEEN CHEAPLY FLASHY,

SHACKLED
ONE LEG DRAGS LIMPINGLY, SHACKLED TO A HEAVY BALL 194 EJONES AND CHAIN.
AS IF THEY WERE SHACKLED TO THEM. 199 EJONES

SHADE
MARY IS SITTING ON THE GRASS NEAR HIM IN THE 129 BEYOND SHADE, PLAYING WITH HER DOLL,
AND BE CAREFUL TO KEEP IN THE SHADE. 130 BEYOND
TEARING THE SHADE.) 224 DESIRE
EACH SHADE DISTINCT AND YET BLENDING WITH THE 9 ELECTR OTHER.
SHE HAS THE SAME PECULIAR SHADE OF COPPER-GOLD 10 ELECTR HAIR.
THE TRUNK OF THE PINE AT RIGHT IS AN EBONY PILLAR, 43 ELECTR ITS BRANCHES A MASS OF SHADE.
AN EYE SHADE CASTS HIS FACE INTO SHADOWS. 245 HA APE
IN A SHADE OF BLUE THAT SETS TEETH ON EDGE, AND A 9 HUGHIE GAY RED AND BLUE FOULARD TIE.
SOON, LEEDLE PROLETARIANS, VE VILL HAVE FREE 635 ICEMAN PICNIC IN THE COOL SHADE.
IT WAS A RARE SHADE OF REDDISH BROWN AND SO LONG 28 JOURNE IT CAME DOWN BELOW MY KNEES.
I LOVE TO LIE IN THE SHADE AND WATCH HIM WORK. 49 JOURNE
THE MALE MASKS ARE A BLOTCHED HELIOTROPE IN SHADE.336 LAZARU
IS STILL ANOTHER SHADE OF GREEN. 99 MANSNS
BENEATH THEM IS DEEP COOL SHADE, 347 MARCOM
THIS SHADE IS GRATEFUL. 350 MARCOM
AS THEY REACH THE MIDDLE OF THE SHADE THEY STOP. 350 MARCOM
SUNSHINE, COOLED AND DIMMED IN THE SHADE OF TREES, 3 STRANG
THE AFTERDECK IS IN COOL SHADE, 158 STRANG
MY LIFE IS COOL GREEN SHADE WHEREIN COMES NO 187 STRANG SCORCHING ZENITH SUN OF PASSION AND
IN THE LEFT WALL, CENTER, A SMALL WINDOW WITH A 470 WELDED TURN DARK SHADE PULLED DOWN.
ON THE WINDOW SHADE FROM SOME STREET LAMP. 470 WELDED

SHADED
AT CENTER IS A BIG, ROUND TABLE WITH A GREEN- 185 AHWILD SHADED READING LAMP.
IT IS LIGHTED BY A SHADED DROP LIGHT OVER THE 486 DYNAMO DESK.
AT CENTER IS A ROUND TABLE WITH A GREEN SHADED 12 JOURNE READING LAMP,
WITH THE REFLECTION OF MANY SHADED LAMPS. 326 LAZARU

SHADELESS
THE ROOM, SEEN BY THE LIGHT OF THE SHADELESS OIL 144 BEYOND LAMP WITH A SMOKY CHIMNEY WHICH

SHADES
(DREAMILY, LIKE A GHOST ADDRESSING FELLOW SHADES) 292 AHWILD
ON THE RIGHT, THE PARLOR, THE SHADES OF WHICH ARE 203 DESIRE ALWAYS DRAWN DOWN.)
GOLD LAMPS WITH SHADES OF CRIMSON-PURPLE ARE 336 LAZARU PLACED.
AND THE TREES ALONG THE BRICK WALL AT REAR GLOW IN 95 MANSNS DIFFERENT SHADES OF GREEN.
THESE WINDOWS HAVE NO SHUTTERS, CURTAINS OR 1 MISBEG SHADES.
THE APPEARANCE OF THE ROOM IS UNCHANGED EXCEPT 24 STRANG THAT ALL THE SHADES,

SHADOW
(LEFT OF CENTER) OF THE ROWBOAT IS IN THE DEEP 275 AHWILD SHADOW CAST BY THE WILLOW.
(HESITATING TIMIDLY ON THE EDGE OF THE SHADOW) 278 AHWILD
SHADOW AT THE FOOT OF THE PATH, WAITING FOR 278 AHWILD RICHARD TO SEE HER.
(COMING TOWARD HIM AS FAR AS THE EDGE OF THE 278 AHWILD SHADOW--DISAPPOINTEDLY)
I CAN'T HERE IN THE SHADOW. 280 AHWILD
AFRAID OF HIS OWN SHADOW. 48 ANNA
(A SHADOW CROSSES THE CABIN WINDOWS. 50 ANNA
(A SHADOW COMING OVER HER FACE) 87 BEYOND
CASTING A VAGUE GLOBULAR SHADOW OF THE COMPASS ON 955 CRUSS THE FLOOR.
THE GREEN OF THE ELMS GLOWS, BUT THE HOUSE IS IN 203 DESIRE SHADOW.
ACROSS THE PATCH OF MOONLIT LAWN TO THE SHADOW OF 427 DYNAMO THE LILACS.
KEEPING IN THIS SHADOW HE MOVES DOWN 427 DYNAMO
CROUCHED IN THE SHADOW OF THE LILACS. 428 DYNAMO
(SHE STARTS OUT OF THE SHADOW OF THE LILACS AS IF 434 DYNAMO TO GO DOWN THE STREET
LAWN TO THE SHADOW OF THE LILACS AT THE EXTREME 434 DYNAMO EDGE OF THE HEDGE, FRONT.)
MRS. LIGHT, AS BEFORE, IS HIDING IN THE SHADOW OF 435 DYNAMO THE LILAC HEDGE.
AND SHE MOVES QUICKLY BACK INTO THE SHADOW. 435 DYNAMO
DISAPPEARS IN THE SHADOW.) 192 EJONES
BUT THE FOREST BEHIND THEM IS STILL A MASS OF 202 EJONES GLOOMING SHADOW.
THE WHITE COLUMNS CAST BLACK BARS OF SHADOW ON THE 5 ELECTR GRAY WALL BEHIND THEM.
THE WHITE COLUMNS OF THE PORTICO CAST BLACK BARS 43 ELECTR OF SHADOW ON THE GRAY WALL
(SEEING THE MAN'S FIGURE STOP IN THE SHADOW--CALLS 46 ELECTR EXCITEDLY)
HE STOPS SHORT IN THE SHADOW FOR A SECOND AND 46 ELECTR STANDS, ERECT AND STIFF,
HALF IN AND HALF OUT OF THE SHADOW OF THE 102 ELECTR WAREHOUSE.
IN THE MOONLIGHT BEYOND THE SHADOW. 102 ELECTR
(HE TAKES A STEP BUT LURCHES INTO THE SHADOW AND 104 ELECTR LEANS AGAINST THE WAREHOUSE)
PASSING FROM MOONLIGHT INTO THE SHADOW OF THE 117 ELECTR PINES AND BACK AGAIN.
THE RIGHT HALF OF THE HOUSE IS IN THE BLACK SHADOW117 ELECTR CAST BY THE PINE TREES BUT

SHADOW (CONT'D.)
THE COLUMNS CAST BLACK BARS OF SHADOW ON THE WALL 129 ELECTR BEHIND THEM.
AND DIES FOR A LIFETIME IN SHADOW. 167 ELECTR
THE COLUMNS CAST BLACK BARS OF SHADOW ON THE GRAY 169 ELECTR STONE WALL BEHIND THEM.
THE ENLARGED MUSCLES FORM BUNCHES OF HIGH LIGHT 224 HA APE AND SHADOW.)
MOONLIGHT ON THE NARROW STREET, BUILDINGS MASSED 245 HA APE IN BLACK SHADOW.
SHROUDED IN SHADOW FROM WHICH CHATTERINGS 251 HA APE
YOU MUST PROVE TO ME THAT THE BLACK SHADOW-- 530 INZONE
(THE SHADOW VANISHES AND HER SHY, GIRLISH 114 JOURNE EXPRESSION RETURNS.)
(A SHADOW OF VAGUE GUILT CROSSES HER FACE.) 114 JOURNE
IN THE HALF-DARKNESS, THE WALLS ARE LOST IN 350 LAZARU SHADOW, THE ROOM SEEMS IMMENSE,
LAUGH AT CALIGULA, THE FUNNY CLOWN WHO BEATS THE 359 LAZARU BACKSIDE OF HIS SHADOW WITH A
(A SHADOW OF RESENTMENT SHOWS IN HER FACE.) 84 MANSNS
THE GEOMETRICAL FORM OF EACH SHRUB AND ITS BLACK 161 MANSNS SHADOW ARE SHARPLY DEFINED.
14 THE SHADOW OF THE HIGHEST DECK IN REAR HER 407 MARCOM WOMEN-IN-WAITING ARE IN A GROUP,
BUT WITH YOUR EYES TO WATCH I MAY BECOME AT LEAST 418 MARCOM A SHADOW OF HIS GREATNESS.
THE WALLS TOWER MAJESTICALLY IN SHADOW. 432 MARCOM
AND, IN SPITE OF HIMSELF, A SHADOW OF A SMILE-- 432 MARCOM
I'M NOT AFRAID OF MY OWN SHADOW ANY MORE. 121 STRANG
(THINKING STRANGELY) (INOT TO BE AFRAID OF ONE'S 121 STRANG SHADOW...
A GRAY IVIED CHAPEL, FULL OF RESTFUL SHADOW, 197 STRANG

SHADOWED
A WIDE THIN-LIPPED MOUTH SHADOWED BY AN UNKEMPT 556 CRUSS BRISTLE OF MUSTACHE.
THE UPPER A THIN BOW, SHADOWED BY A LINE OF HAIR. 9 ELECTR
THE CLEARING IS PARTLY IN SUNLIGHT, PARTLY 1 MANSNS SHADOWED BY THE WOODS.

SHADOWS
(LOOKING AROUND HER FRIGHTENEDLY AT THE WEIRD 484 DYNAMO SHADOWS OF THE EQUIPMENT WAITING
AND HE PEERS DOWN INTO THE SHADOWS OF THE 107 ELECTR WAREHOUSE)
IN THIS DIM, SPOTTY LIGHT THE ROOM IS FULL OF 139 ELECTR SHADOWS.
IT'S A SYMBOL OF HIS LIFE--A LAMP BURNING OUT IN A150 ELECTR ROOM OF WAITING SHADOWS?
SHADOWS OVER THE TOPS OF TREES/ 287 GGBROW
MURKY AIR LADEN WITH COAL DUST TO PILE UP MASSES 222 HA APE OF SHADOWS EVERYWHERE.
AN EYE SHADE CASTS HIS FACE INTO SHADOWS. 245 HA APE
HER FACE HAS A BLURRED, DISSIPATED LOOK, WITH DARK139 MANSNS SHADOWS UNDER HER EYES.
FOR THE DAY GOETH AWAY, FOR THE SHADOWS OF THE 579 ROPE EVENING ARE STRETCHED OUT.*
PUFFY SHADOWS OF DISSIPATION AND SLEEPLESSNESS 124 STRANG UNDER HIS RESTLESS, HARRIED EYES.
TURN ON THE SUN INTO THE SHADOWS OF LIES-- 176 STRANG
HE WATCHES WITH CONTENTED EYES THE EVENING SHADOWS200 STRANG CLOSING IN AROUND THEM.)

SHADOWY
SHADOWY AND VAGUE. 166 BEYOND
BLINKING INTO THE SHADOWY BARN. 578 ROPE
AND SOFTENS INTO DEEP SORROW THE SHADOWY GRIMNESS 53 STRANG OF HER EYES.

SHAFT
HIS FACE, LIGHTED UP BY THE SHAFT OF SUNLIGHT FROM220 DESIRE THE WINDOW,
EMPHASIZED BY ANOTHER DOWNPOURING SHAFT OF LIGHT. 432 MARCOM

SHAGGY
(SHAKING HIS SHAGGY OX-LIKE HEAD IN AN EMPHATIC 514 INZONE AFFIRMATIVE)

SHAKE
WELL, IF YOU COULD SHAKE THE CRADLE-ROBBING ACT, 244 AHWILD
(THEY SHAKE HANDS.) 6 ANNA
(EXTENDING HER HAND) SHAKE AND FORGET IT, HUH? 15 ANNA
(HOLDS OUT HIS HAND) AND LET YOU TAKE IT AND 52 ANNA WE'LL SHAKE AND FORGET WHAT'S OVER
(WITH IMPLACABLE HATRED) AY DON'T SHAKE HANDS 52 ANNA WITH YOU FALLER--
HURRY UP NOW, AND SHAKE A LEG. 56 ANNA
HER SHOULDERS SHAKE AS IF SHE WERE SOBBING. 142 BEYOND
IF WE CAN ONLY SHAKE OFF THE CURSE OF THIS FARM/ 149 BEYOND
SHAKE A LEG, ANY COME ABOARD THIN. 461 CARLBE
(HOLDING OUT HIS HAND) SHAKE, DUKE. 469 CARLBE
I FEEL--(THEN, AS IF DESPERATELY TRYING TO SHAKE 495 DAYS OFF HIS THOUGHTS)
(THEY SHAKE HANDS) A PLEASANT SURPRISE. 525 DAYS
COME BACK ALL CRAMPED UP 'T SHAKE THE FIRE, AN' 209 DESIRE CARRY ASHES.
LET'S SHAKE HANDS. 246 DESIRE
AND NOW YOU WANT TO SHAKE ME/ 546 DIFRNT
(AS SHE HESITATES--INSISTENTLY, GIVING HER HEAD A 460 DYNAMO LITTLE SHAKE)
DAT EMPEROR JOB IS SHO' HARD TO SHAKE. 193 EJONES
(THEY ALL SHAKE THEIR HEADS AND LOOK SAD. 70 ELECTR
(THEY SHAKE HANDS. 144 ELECTR
(HE GIVES HER HAND A FINAL SHAKE--SWALLOWS HARD-- 266 GGBROW THEN MANFULLY)
(THIS HUSKILY--HE FUMBLES FOR DION'S HAND AND 265 GGBROW GIVES IT A SHAKE.)
(THEY SHAKE HANDS) SIT DOWN. 306 GGBROW
(THEY SHAKE THEIR HEADS IN SOLEMN SURPRISE) 317 GGBROW
STEP OUT AND SHAKE HANDS. 254 HA APE
SHAKE--DE SECRET GRIP OF OUR ORDER. 254 HA APE
(HE PAUSES.) MAYBE YOU THINK I AIN'T GIVING HER A 24 HUGHIE SQUARE SHAKE.

SHAKE

SHAKE (CONT'D.)
(GENEROUSLY.) NOW I SEE YOU'RE A RIGHT GUY. 36 HUGHIE
SHAKE.
I'D SURE LIKE TO SHAKE THEIR HANDS AGAIN/ 609 ICEMAN
MOVES TO THE MIDDLE TABLE TO SHAKE HANDS WITH 619 ICEMAN
LEWIS, JOE MOTT,
LEANS RIGHT TO SHAKE HANDS WITH MARGIE AND PEARL, 614 ICEMAN
HICKEY COMES FORWARD TO SHAKE HANDS WITH HOPE-- 619 ICEMAN
WITH AFFECTIONATE HEARTINESS)
(GIVES HUGO A SHAKE) HEY, HUGO, COME UP FOR AIR/ 658 ICEMAN
IT DIDN'T DO DEM NO GOOD IF DEY THOUGHT DEY'D 665 ICEMAN
SHAKE HIM.
IF THERE WAS A MAD DOG OUTSIDE I'D GO AND SHAKE 688 ICEMAN
HANDS WITH IT RATHER THAN STAY
NOTHING ON EARTH COULD SHAKE HER FAITH IN ME. 710 ICEMAN
YOU COULDN'T SHAKE HER FAITH THAT IT HAD TO COME 713 ICEMAN
TRUE--TOMORROW/
(GLARING AT ROCKY) SHAKE DE LEAD OUTA YOUR PANTS.725 ICEMAN
PIMP!
AN' WHEN I GOES TO CALL HIM I DON'T EVEN SHAKE 521 INZONE
HIM.
TAKE IT OUT, JACK--CAREFUL--DON'T SHAKE IT NOW, 524 INZONE
FOR CHRIST'S SAKE/
I'LL HAVE TO SHAKE A LEG. 91 JOURNE
(TRYING TO SHAKE OFF HIS HOPELESS STUPOR.) 174 JOURNE
(HELA LAUGHTER SEEMS TO SHAKE THE WALLS 321 LAZARU
(HE GIVES HIM A SHAKE) AND LET ME WARN YOU/ 63 MISBEG
IT'S THE FIRST TIME I EVER SAW YOU SO PARALYZED 81 MISBEG
YOU COULDN'T SHAKE THE WHISKEY
(GIVES HIM A SHAKE) KEEP HOLD OF YOUR WITS 83 MISBEG
(SHE GIVES HIM A SHAKE) GET YOUR WITS ABOUT YOU 91 MISBEG
AND ANSWER ME THIS..
(SHE GIVES HIS SHOULDER A SHAKE--FORCING A LIGHT 120 MISBEG
TONE)
(SHE GIVES HIM A GENTLE SHAKE) 165 MISBEG
(SHE GIVES HIM A MORE VIGOROUS SHAKE) 165 MISBEG
BUT HER SHOULDERS STILL SHAKE. 166 POET
DON'T YOU EVE+ WANT TO SHAKE FLIPPERS WITH YOUR 588 ROPE
DEAR, LONG-LOST BUSHIN' ANNIES
(THEY SHAKE HANDS AND SIT DOWN BY THE TABLE, 591 ROPE
COME ON AND SHAKE HANDS LIKE A GOOD SPORT. 595 ROPE
(GIVING HIS FATHER ONE MORE SHAKE, WHICH SENDS HIMS97 ROPE
SPRAWLING ON THE FLOOR)
(TURNING HER EYES TO MARSDEN, HOLDING OUT HER HAND 13 STRANG
FOR HIM TO SHAKE.
(AS THEY SHAKE HANDS--SMILING) 79 STRANG
WEAKLY STRUGGLING TO SHAKE OFF HER HANDS, WITHOUT 172 STRANG
LOWERING THE GLASSES)
SHAKE HANDS, HUN'T YOU 194 STRANG

SHAKEN
(MORE SHAKEN, HIS EYES SHIFTING ABOUT FURTIVELY) 204 AHWILD
(A BIT SHAKEN BY THIS THREAT--BUT IN THE SAME FLAT204 AHWILD
TONE)
(TERRIBLY SHAKEN--FAINTLY) I CAN'T, MAT. 71 ANNA
AND THE POOR SIMPLETON'S NAIVE FAITH WAS A BIT 510 DAYS
SHAKEN.
I CAN'T BEAR--(SHE IS SHAKEN AGAIN BY A CHILL.) 550 DAYS
(SHE IS SHAKEN AGAIN BY A WAVE OF UNCONTROLLABLE 550 DAYS
CHILLS. HER TEETH CHATTER--
(SHAKEN--THEN WITH FIERCE DEFIANCE) 562 DAYS
(SUDDENLY TRIUMPHANT WHEN HE SEES HOW SHAKEN EBEN 255 DESIRE
IS)
(TERRIBLY SHAKEN) YOU'RE A LIAR/ 463 DYNAMO
(A TINY BIT AWED AND SHAKEN, IN SPITE OF HIMSELF) 185 EJONES
HAVE SOMEWHAT RESTORED HIS SHAKEN NERVE. 190 EJONES
(SHAKEN) HE ASKED ME TO MEET A FRIEND OF HIS--A 30 ELECTR
LADY.
(SHAKEN--DEFENSIVELY) I TRIED TO LOVE YOU. 31 ELECTR
(STRANGELY SHAKEN AND TREMBLING--STAMMERS) 155 ELECTR
(HER RAGE PASSES, LEAVING HER WEAK AND SHAKEN. 173 ELECTR
HE HAS SHAKEN HIS CELL DOOR TO A CLANGING 244 HA APE
ACCOMPANIMENT.
(LEANING TOWARD LARRY CONFIDENTIALLY--IN A LOW 544 ICEMAN
SHAKEN VOICE)
(ABRUPTLY GETTING CONTROL OF HIMSELF--WITH SHAKEN 686 ICEMAN
FIRMNESS)
(TORTUREDLY ARGUING TO HIMSELF IN A SHAKEN 726 ICEMAN
WHISPER)
AND THEN IS SHAKEN BY A FIT OF COUGHING.) 145 JOURNE
(IN A STRAINED VOICE SHAKEN BY APPREHENSION AND 337 LAZARU
AWE)
(ABRUPTLY--FRIGHTENED AND SHAKEN.) 142 MANSNS
SHE MAKES A SHAKEN ATTEMPT TO DRAW HERSELF UP WITH165 MANSNS
HER OLD ARROGANCE.)
(MELODY IS SHAKES FOR A SECOND. 59 POET
SHAKE+ WITH DISGUST AND CUDDLY ANGRY. 71 POET
CREGAN IS SHAKEN BY THE EXPERIENCE HE HAS JUST 164 POET
BEEN THROUGH
SHE RECOILS FROM IT, TURNING QUICKLY AWAY FROM 450 WELDED
HIM, VISIBLY SHAKEN.

SHAKENLY
STOPS AGAIN AND STAMMERS SHAKENLY) 123 ELECTR
SHE CALLS SHAKENLY AS IF THE WORDS WERE WRUNG OUT 123 ELECTR
OF HER AGAINST HER WILL)
(SHAKENLY) THEN SHE--WAS MURDERED. 694 ICEMAN
(SHAKENLY.) YES, MARY, IT'S NO TIME-- 75 JOURNE
(SHAKENLY.) DON'T SAY THAT/ 118 JOURNE
(SHAKENLY) YOU'RE LYING. 88 MISBEG
(AFTER A PAUSE--SHAKENLY.) I--SHE MISTOOK MY 61 POET
MEANING--IT'S AS YOU SAID.
(HE SHUDDERS AND PUTS THE PISTOL ON THE TABLE. 165 POET
SHAKENLY.)
(STRUGGLING--SHAKENLY) NO, I THINK I'D BETTER-- 104 STRANG
(THINKING DESPERATELY)

SHAKES
(SHE SHAKES HER HEAD) HE'S A QUEER GUY. 209 AHWILD
MRS. MILLER SHAKES HER HEAD FOREBODINGLY-- 220 AHWILD
(SHAKES HIM BY THE ARM INDIGNANTLY) 221 AHWILD

SHAKES (CONT'D.)
(PEEKS AT HIM BLURREDLY AND SHAKES HIS HEAD SADLY)225 AHWILD
(SHE SHAKES RICHARD BY THE ARM) 244 AHWILD
BUT MILLER WINKS AND SHAKES HIS HEAD VIGOROUSLY 258 AHWILD
AND MOTIONS HER TO SIT DOWN.)
(SHAKES CHRIS BY THE HAND) SPEAK OF THE DEVIL. 6 ANNA
(THEN AS CHRIS SHAKES HIS HEAD OBSTINATELY) 13 ANNA
(SHE SHAKES HER HAND GLADLY) 15 ANNA
(TURNS SUDDENLY AND SHAKES HIS FIST OUT AT THE 40 ANNA
SEA--WITH BITTER HATRED)
SHE LEANS OVER IN EXASPERATION AND SHAKES HIM 57 ANNA
VIOLENTLY BY THE SHOULDER)
(HE SHAKES HIS FIST AT THE DOOR) 62 ANNA
(HE SHAKES HIS FIST AGAIN) DIRTY OLE DAVIL/ 62 ANNA
SHAKES HIS HEAD AND MUTTERS) 78 ANNA
(SHAKES HIS HEAD IMPATIENTLY, 93 BEYOND
MAYO SHAKES HER HEAD) 99 BEYOND
(HE GETS TO HIS FEET AND SHAKES ROBERT'S HAND, 101 BEYOND
MUTTERING A VAGUE)
(HE SHAKES HIS FINGER INDIGNANTLY) 103 BEYOND
(HE SHAKES OVER HIS MUTTERED THREAT AND STRIDES 108 BEYOND
TOWARD THE DOOR HEAR, RIGHT.)
(HE SHAKES HIS BROTHER FIERCELY BY THE SHOULDER) 110 BEYOND
(AS ROBERT SHAKES HIS HEAD) --AND IF HE DON'T-- 110 BEYOND
WELL, IT CAN'T BE HELPED.
(HE SHAKES HER VIOLENTLY) 128 BEYOND
(SHE CLOSES THE DOOR AND GOES QUICKLY TO HER 151 BEYOND
MOTHER AND SHAKES HER BY THE
(GETS UP AND SHAKES HIS FIST AT THE NORWEGIAN) 481 CARDIF
HE SHUDDERS AND SHAKES HIS SHOULDERS AS IF SHAKING466 CARIBE
OFF SOMETHING WHICH DISGUSTED
WHERE SHE SHAKES OFF HIS HAND LONG ENOUGH TO TURN 470 CARIBE
ON SMITTY FURIOUSLY.)
(HE PUTS IT BACK IN HIS POCKET AND SHAKES HIS HEAD561 CROSS
AS IF THINKING OFF A BURDEN)
SHE SHAKES HER HEAD SADLY. 569 CROSS
(SHAKES HIS HAND--A FORMAL, OLD-FASHIONED COURTESY500 DAYS
IN HIS MANNER)
(FATHER BAIRD GETS UP AND HE SHAKES HIS HAND 504 DAYS
HEARTILY
THE NURSE SHAKES HER HEAD, ANSWERING HIS QUESTION.556 DAYS
I HE SHAKES HIS HEAD SLOWLY) 236 DESIRE
THEN HIS ARMS DROP. HE SHAKES HIS HEAD AND PLODS 239 DESIRE
OFF TOWARD THE BARN.
(AS SHE DOESN'T ANSWER, HE GRABS HER VIOLENTLY BY 264 DESIRE
THE SHOULDER AND SHAKES HER)
(AS EMMA SHAKES HER HEAD) OH, YES, YOU WILL. 510 DIFFRNT
(AS EMMA SHAKES HER HEAD) PSHAW, EMMER, 511 DIFFRNT
(HE SHAKES WITH LAUGHTER AND KISSES HIS WIFE A 513 DIFFRNT
RESOUNDING SMACK.)
(HE COMES IN AND SHAKES THE HAND SHE HOLDS OUT TO 534 DIFFRNT
HIM IN A LIMP, VAGUE,
GOES UP AND SHAKES REUBEN'S HAND WITH AN 436 DYNAMO
EXAGGERATED CORDIALITY)
(SHAKES HER HANDS OFF HIS SHOULDERS-- 447 DYNAMO
(SHE STARES AT HIM, FRIGHTENED AND FASCINATED, AND461 DYNAMO
SHAKES HER HEAD)
A SHUDDER OF TERROR SHAKES HIS WHOLE BODY AS THE 199 EJONES
WAIL RISES UP ABOUT HIM AGAIN.
(SHE AND HAZEL KISS AND SHE SHAKES HANDS WITH 13 ELECTR
PETER.)
AND SHAKES HER) 78 ELECTR
(SHAKES HIS HAND) GOOD NIGHT. 84 ELECTR
(GRABS HER BY THE SHOULDER AND SHAKES HER, FORCING 99 ELECTR
HER TO HER KNEES--FRENZIEDLY)
GRIN SHAKES HER--DESPERATELY) 122 ELECTR
SHAKES HIS HEAD AND MUTTERS TO HIMSELF) 169 ELECTR
SETH STARES AT HER WORRIEDLY, SHAKES HIS HEAD AND 171 ELECTR
SPITS.
AND I GUESS I KNOW HOW TO LOSE-- (HE TAKES HER 263 GGBROW
HAND AND SHAKES IT)
(AWKWARD IN HER PRESENCE, SHAKES HER HAND. 274 GGBROW
(SHAKES HER HAND) GOOD-BY, MARGARET. 277 GGBROW
SHAKES HIS HAND OFF HIS SHOULDER AND WALKS AWAY 282 GGBROW
FROM HIM--AFTER A PAUSE)
HE STARES AHEAD. THEN SHAKES OFF HIS THOUGHTS AND 312 GGBROW
CONCENTRATES ON HIS WORK--
REACHES OUT AND SHAKES THE BARS--ALOUD TO HIMSELF, 240 HA APE
WONDERINGLY) STEEL.
(HE SHAKES THE BARS OF HIS CELL DOOR TILL THE 244 HA APE
WHOLE TIER TREMBLES.
(HE CHUCKLES AT HIS OWN FANCY--REACHES OVER AND 579 ICEMAN
SHAKES HUGO'S SHOULDER.
(GRABS HIS SHOULDER AND SHAKES HIM) HEY, YOU/ 581 ICEMAN
(BUT HER+ ROCKY SHAKES HIM ROUGHLY BY THE 597 ICEMAN
SHOULDER.)
(AT ONCE GRINS GOOD-NATUREDLY AND SHAKES HIS HAND)599 ICEMAN
(SHAKES HIS HEAD WITH PROFOUND DISGUST) 616 ICEMAN
(HICKEY SHAKES HANDS WITH MOSHER AND MCGLOIN, 619 ICEMAN
WARMING TO HIS SUBJECT, SHAKES HIS HEAD SADLY) 627 ICEMAN
(IGNORING THEM-- TURNS TO HUGO AND SHAKES HIM BY 634 ICEMAN
THE SHOULDER--
(HE SHAKES HIS HEAD) NO, IT'S MORE THAN THAT. 642 ICEMAN
(SHAKES HIS HEAD) YOU'LL FIND HE WON'T AGREE TO 642 ICEMAN
THAT.
AND ALL DE REST DEEN BRUSHIN' AND SHAVIN' 665 ICEMAN
DEMSELVES WID DE SHAKES--
(GRABS HIM BY THE SHOULDER AND SHAKES HIM) 667 ICEMAN
(HE SHAKES HIS HEAD) WHORES GOIN' ON STRIKE/ CAN 670 ICEMAN
YUH TIE DAT)
(EYES THE BOTTLE YEARNINGLY BUT SHAKES HIS HEAD-- 674 ICEMAN
DETERMINEDLY)
AND HIS NERVES IN A SHOCKING STATE OF SHAKES.) 674 ICEMAN
(HE SHAKES HIS HEAD AND AND BEGINS TO WIPE THE BAR 677 ICEMAN
MECHANICALLY.)
(AS ROCKY SHOVES A BOTTLE TOWARD HIM HE SHAKES HIS681 ICEMAN
HEAD)
(GRINS AND SHAKES HIS HEAD) NO, HARRY. 687 ICEMAN

1405

SHAKES

SHAKES (CONT*D.)
(SHAKES JOE BY THE SHOULDER) 697 ICEMAN
(GRABS HIS SHOULDER AND SHAKES HIM FURIOUSLY) 706 ICEMAN
AND GOES FROM ONE TO THE OTHER OF THE SLEEPERS AND513 INZONE
SHAKES THEM VIGOROUSLY,
AND POURS THEM IN THE WHISKEY BOTTLE AND SHAKES IT 54 JOURNE
UP.)
SHE FROWNS AND SHAKES HER HEAD MECHANICALLY 107 JOURNE
(TYRONE STARES AT HER AND SHAKES HIS HEAD 122 JOURNE
HELPLESSLY
YOU'RE NO GREAT SHAKES AS A SON. 143 JOURNE
(BUT JAMIE'S SOBBING BREAKS HIS ANGER, AND HE 171 JOURNE
TURNS AND SHAKES HIS SHOULDER.
(AS LAZARUS SMILINGLY SHAKES HIS HEAD, TIBERIUS 339 LAZARU
FROWNS)
(SMILING AFFECTIONATELY AT HIM, SHAKES HIS HEAD) 357 LAZARU
(SHE SHAKES HER HEAD SLOWLY.) 30 MANSNS
(FURIOUS AT THE THOUGHT, SHE GRABS HIS SHOULDERS 81 MANSNS
AND SHAKES HIM FIERCELY.)
(HE FROWNS AND SHAKES HIS HEAD.) 92 MANSNS
SARA GRABS HER BY THE SHOULDERS AND SHAKES HER 165 MANSNS
ROUGHLY.
HE SHAKES HANDS WITH A ONE-LEGGED VETERAN OF THE 389 MARCOM
MANZI CAMPAIGN
(SHAKES HIS HEAD) NO SIGN OF BILIOUSNESS. 413 MARCOM
(HE SHAKES HIS HEAD VIOLENTLY) 81 MISBEG
(SHAKES HIM) IF YOU DON'T KEEP AWAKE, BE GOD, I 85 MISBEG
WON'T MISS YOU!
(SHE SHAKES HER HEAD) NO. 153 MISBEG
(SUDDENLY SHE PUSHES HIM AWAY FROM HER AND SHAKES 166 MISBEG
HER ROUGHLY)
(SHAKES OFF HER HAND EXASPERATEDLY.) 88 POET
(WITH AN APPREHENSIVE GLANCE AT MELODY, SHAKES HIS103 POET
HEAD AT HER ADMONISHINGLY.)
(HE AGAIN SHAKES HIS HEAD AT SARA, AS IF TO SAY, 104 POET
DON'T PROVOKE HIM.
(AS SHE SHAKES HER HEAD.) OH, I KNOW YOU DON'T 134 POET
INDULGE.
(AS SHE AGAIN SHAKES HER HEAD--WITH KINDLY 134 POET
BULLYING.)
HE SHAKES HER HAND OFF ROUGHLY AS IF HE DID NOT 159 POET
RECOGNIZE HER.)
THERE IS A DRUNKEN CHORUS OF ANSWERING *HURROSS* 180 POET
THAT SHAKES THE WALLS.)
THEN SHAKES HIS CANE AFTER HER) 578 ROPE
HE SHAKES HER IMPATIENTLY) 583 ROPE
(HE SHAKES HIS HEAD DOUBTFULLY, AT THE SAME TIME 593 ROPE
FIXING LIKE WITH A KEEN GLANCE
(HE SHAKES THE OLD MAN MORE AND MORE FURIOUSLY.) 597 ROPE
(AS HE SHAKES HIS HEAD--WHININGLY) 601 ROPE
THEN HE SHAKES HIS HEAD, FLINGING OFF HIS 5 STRANG
THOUGHTS.
(SHE SHAKES HER HEAD) (IYES, I HEAR YOU, LITTLE 27 STRANG
NINA--
FORCES A CORDIAL SMILE AND SHAKES HANDS) 28 STRANG
(SHE SHAKES HANDS WITH DARRELL) 78 STRANG
HE RUSHES UP TO NED HILARIOUSLY, SHAKES HIS HAND 132 STRANG
AND POUNDS HIS BACK.
(HE TURNS AND SHAKES HANDS WITH DARRELL COLDLY-- 147 STRANG
GRABS DARRELL BY BOTH SHOULDERS AND SHAKES HIM) 181 STRANG
(HE TAKES DARRELL'S HAND AND SHAKES IT AGAIN. 195 STRANG
YOU'D FAIR GUY A BLOCK THE SHAKES A*WATCHIN' YER. 494 VOYAGE
(HE SHAKES HIS HEAD SORROWFULLY.) 495 VOYAGE
(HE SHAKES HIS FIST AT JOE.) 496 VOYAGE
(OLSON SHAKES HIS HEAD) DENMARK'S 502 VOYAGE
(HE COMES TO HIM AND SHAKES HIS HAND WHICH CAPE 450 WELDED
EXTENDS JEKILLY.
(HE SHAKES HIS HEAD AS IF TO DRIVE SOME THOUGHT 476 WELDED
FROM HIS MIND

SHAKESPEARE
IT'S ABOUT IBSEN, THE GREATEST PLAYWRIGHT SINCE 197 AHWILD
SHAKESPEARE/
WITH A PICTURE OF SHAKESPEARE ABOVE IT, CONTAINING 11 JOURNE
NOVELS BY BALZAC, ZOLA,
CHARLES LEVER, THREE SETS OF SHAKESPEARE, 11 JOURNE
(SCATHINGLY.) IF IT TAKES MY SNORING TO MAKE YOU 21 JOURNE
REMEMBER SHAKESPEARE INSTEAD
(DERISIVELY.) SHAKESPEARE WAS AN IRISH CATHOLIC, 127 JOURNE
FOR EXAMPLE.
(HE SIGHS.) WHY CAN'T YOU REMEMBER YOUR 131 JOURNE
SHAKESPEARE AND FORGET THE
WHAT LITTLE TRUTH IS IN IT YOU'LL FIND NOBLY SAID 133 JOURNE
IN SHAKESPEARE.
WHEN I'VE THREE GOOD SETS OF SHAKESPEARE THERE 135 JOURNE
YOU CAN'T ACCUSE ME OF NOT KNOWING SHAKESPEARE. 136 JOURNE
I LOVED SHAKESPEARE. 150 JOURNE
I STUDIED SHAKESPEARE AS YOU'D STUDY THE BIBLE. 150 JOURNE

SHAKESPEAREAN
I COULD HAVE BEEN A GREAT SHAKESPEAREAN ACTOR, IF 150 JOURNE
I'D KEPT ON.

SHAKILY
THEN SUDDENLY FORCES CONTROL ON HERSELF AND GETS 551 DAYS
SHAKILY TO HER FEET)

SHAKIN'
DERE. YOU SEE, CAPTAIN. I WEN' TO DE CHIEF, 600 ICEMAN
SHAKIN' IN MY BOOTS.
HE WAS STANDIN' THERE SHAKIN' HIS STICK AT ME, 592 ROPE

SHAKING
(IN A SUDDEN RAGE, SHAKING HIS FIST AT THE 536 *ILE
SKYLIGHT)
(SHAKING HIS HEAD) I THINK THE MAN'S MIGHTY NIGH 537 *ILE
LOSIN' HIS SENSES.
(SUBSIDING AS IF REALIZING THE USELESSNESS OF THIS537 *ILE
OUTBURST--SHAKING HIS HEAD--
(FURIOUSLY--SHAKING HIS FIST) 538 *ILE
(SHAKING HIS HEAD) BUT YOU WAS SO SET ON IT. 546 *ILE
(SHAKING HIM--FIERCELY) BUT YOU DO, DON'T YOU, 549 *ILE
DAVID*

SHAKING

SHAKING (CONT*D.)
(SHAKING HIM AGAIN--STILL MORE FIERCELY) 549 *ILE
(THEN SHAKING HIS HEAD) NIX, KID, I DON'T WANT TO218 AHWILD
BORROW YOUR MONEY.
(SHAKING HER HEAD) WILD HORSES COULDN'T DRAG HER 234 AHWILD
THERE NOW.
(SHAKING IN HIS BOOTS) PY GOLLY. 10 ANNA
(THEN SHAKING HIS HEAD RESOLUTELY) 10 ANNA
(SHAKING HER HEAD) NOT FOR MINE. 15 ANNA
(SHAKING HIS HEAD EMPHATICALLY--AFTER A PAUSE) 22 ANNA
(SHAKING HER HEAD) VO? 44 ANNA
(SHAKING CHRIS OFF--FURIOUSLY) 61 ANNA
(SHAKING HIS FIST) IT'S DAT OLE DAVIL SEA/ 65 ANNA
(SHAKING HIS HEAD) IT'S TOO SMALL. 97 BEYOND
(SHAKING HER HEAD) NO. 98 BEYOND
(SHAKING HIS FINGER AT ANDY, IN A COLD RAGE) 106 BEYOND
HE POINTS TO THE DOOR WITH A SHAKING FINGER) 108 BEYOND
(SHAKING HIS FINGER) LOOK-A-HERE. 124 BEYOND
(SHAKING HIS HEAD) BUT JUST THE SAME I DOUBT IF 125 BEYOND
HE'LL WANT TO SETTLE DOWN TO A
(SHAKING OFF HIS DEPRESSION--BRISKLY) 157 BEYOND
(SHAKING HIS HEAD) IT'S TOO LATE. 198 BEYOND
(SHAKING HIS HEAD DOUBTFULLY) 479 CARDIF
(SHAKING HIS HEAD) I'M AFRAID--HE'S VERY WEAK. 485 CARDIF
HE SHUDDERS AND SHAKES HIS SHOULDERS AS IF SHAKING466 CARIBE
OFF SOMETHING WHICH DISGUSTED
(SHAKING HIS HEAD--MOODILY) THERE ARE CASES WHERE559 CROSS
FACTS--
THEN HE RISES, SHAKING HIS HEAD. 573 CROSS
(SHAKING HIS FINGER THREATENINGLY AT HIM) 227 DESIRE
(SHAKING HIS FINGER THREATENINGLY AT HIM) 233 DESIRE
HE SPRINGS TO HIS FEET SHAKING ALL OVER) 233 DESIRE
(SHAKING HIS HEAD) NO. 236 DESIRE
(THEN SHAKING HER HAND OFF HIS ARM--WITH A BITTER 259 DESIRE
SMILE)
SHAKING BOTH FISTS AT HER, VIOLENTLY) 262 DESIRE
(SHAKING HER HEAD) I GOT T' TAKE MY PUNISHMENT-- 266 DESIRE
T' PAY FUR MY SIN.
(SHAKING HER HEAD--SLOWLY) IT AIN'T A QUESTION OF517 DIFRNT
TING CALEB--
(SHAKING HER HEAD ROGUISHLY) 524 DIFRNT
(SHAKING HER IN HIS ANXIETY) 534 DIFRNT
(SHAKING HER) STOP--NOW, EMMER/ 547 DIFRNT
(HE POINTS A SHAKING FINGER AT REUBEN) 452 DYNAMO
(SHAKING HIS HEAD) I CAN'T FORGET. 469 DYNAMO
(SHAKING HER HEAD VEHEMENTLY) 174 EJONES
(THEN SHAKING OFF HIS NERVOUSNESS--WITH A 184 EJONES
CONFIDENT LAUGH)
(THEN SHAKING HIMSELF LIKE A WET DOG TO GET RID OF188 EJONES
THOSE DEPRESSING THOUGHTS)
SHAKING THEM, CASTING THEM OUT WITH THE REGULAR, 191 EJONES
RIGID,
(SHAKING HIS HEAD APPREHENSIVELY) 193 EJONES
(SHAKING HIS HEAD WITH A DOGGED BEWILDERMENT) 54 ELECTR
(SHAKING HIS HEAD) TOO BAD. 70 ELECTR
(HE STOPS ABRUPTLY, SHAKING HIS HEAD--MOURNFULLY) 103 ELECTR
(TENSELY--SHAKING HIM BY THE ARM) 116 ELECTR
(SHAKING HIS FIST IN MACKEL'S FACE) 133 ELECTR
(SHAKING HER HEAD--SLOWLY) NO. 136 ELECTR
(FRANTICALLY GRABBING HIS ARM AND SHAKING HIM 156 ELECTR
FIERCELY)
(SHAKING HER HAND IN AN AGONY OF UNCERTAINTY) 263 GGBROW
(SUDDENLY SHAKING HIM) WHAT IN HELL HAS COME OVER281 GGBROW
YOU, ANYWAY?
AND CLOSED IT AFTER HIM SILENTLY, SHAKING WITH 318 GGBROW
SUPPRESSED LAUGHTER.
SHAKING WITH SILENT LAUGHTER. 318 GGBROW
THE BLOODY ENGINES POUNDING AND THROBBING AND 214 HA APE
SHAKING--
(SHAKING HIS FIST UPWARD--CONTEMPTUOUSLY) 224 HA APE
(SHAKING ONE FIST UPWARD AND BEATING ON HIS CHEST 232 HA APE
WITH THE OTHER)
(WATCHES WILLIE, WHO IS SHAKING IN HIS SLEEP LIKE 581 ICEMAN
AN OLD DOG)
(WITH BLEERY BENEVOLENCE, SHAKING HIS HEAD IN MILD600 ICEMAN
REBUKE)
(MOSHER WINKS AT HOPE, SHAKING HIS HEAD, 608 ICEMAN
WHERE HE SITS IN DEJECTED, SHAKING MISERY, HIS 645 ICEMAN
CHIN ON HIS CHEST.)
KEEPING DRUNK SO I WON'T SEE MYSELF SHAKING IN MY 689 ICEMAN
BRITCHES WITH FRIGHT.
HIS SHAKING HAND MISJUDGES THE DISTANCE 691 ICEMAN
BUT THERE WAS NO SHAKING EVELYN'S BELIEF IN ME, UR711 ICEMAN
HER DREAMS ABOUT THE FUTURE.
WITH THE NEIGHBORS SHAKING THEIR HEADS AND FEELING713 ICEMAN
(SHAKING HIS SHAGGY OX-LIKE HEAD IN AN EMPHATIC 514 INZONE
AFFIRMATIVE)
SHAKING HIS HEAD) 521 INZONE
(SHAKING HIS HEAD SAGELY) THEY'RE DEEP ONES, 522 INZONE
(SHAKING HIS FIST IN SMITTY'S FACE) 526 INZONE
(SHAKING HIS FIST IN SMITTY'S DIRECTION) 530 INZONE
(VAGUE SIGHS, SHAKING HIS HEAD HOPELESSLY, AND 115 JOURNE
ATTEMPTS TO CATCH HIS SON'S EYE,
(SHAKING HIS FIST AT LAZARUS' FOLLOWERS) 287 LAZARU
(SHAKING HER HEAD AND TURNING AWAY SADLY) 331 LAZARU
(HE POINTS WITH A SHAKING FINGER. 338 LAZARU
(SHAKING HIS HEAD) I WANT HOPE--FOR ME, TIBERIUS 351 LAZARU
CAESAR.
THEN TIBERIUS SIGHS HEAVILY, SHAKING HIS HEAD) 353 LAZARU
SHAKING HIS FIST AT LAZARUS, 359 LAZARU
(STOPS LAUGHING--SHAKING HIS HEAD, ALMOST SADLY) 360 LAZARU
(SHAKING HIS HEAD) THIS UNCERTAINTY IS BAD FUR 359 MARCOM
TRADE.
THEN, SHAKING AWAY THIS INTERRUPTION, BENDS TO HIS359 MARCOM
WRITING AGAIN.)
CHUFFIN COVERS HIS EARS AND MOVES AWAY, SHAKING 407 MARCOM
HIS HEAD,

SHAKING

SHAKING (CONT'D.)		
SHE TURNS HER BACK FOR A MOMENT, SHAKING WITH	61	MISBEG
SUPPRESSED LAUGHTER.		
SHAKING HIS HEAD PITYINGLY)	97	MISBEG
(TRYING IS STILL TRYING WITH SHAKING HANDS TO GET	111	MISBEG
HIS CIGARETTE LIGHTED.		
HE REACHES OUT A SHAKING HAND TO PAT HER SHOULDER	37	POET
WITH AN ODD.		
I FOUND HIM THERE SHIVERING AND SHAKING AND MADE	73	POET
HIM COME HERE		
BY SHAKING HIS HAND WHENEVER THEY MEET.	86	POET
(CONTROLS HIMSELF--HIS VOICE SHAKING.)	123	POET
(SHAKING OFF HER HAND--ANGRILY.)	126	POET
(SHE STOPS, SHAKING HER HEAD HELPLESSLY.)	130	POET
STANDS SHAKING HIS STICK AT SWEENEY AND HIS WIFE)	584	ROPE
(SHAKING HER AWAY) THERE'S LOTS OF ROCKS, KID.	591	ROPE
SHAKING ALL OVER, GASPING FOR BREATH.	596	ROPE
(SHAKING HIS HEAD) AN' HIM CURSIN' YOU DAY AN'	595	ROPE
NIGHT/		
(GRABBING BENTLEY'S SHOULDER AND SHAKING HIM--	597	ROPE
HOARSELY)		
(SHAKING HIS HAND AND PATTING HIM ON THE BACK--	7	STRANG
WITH GENUINE AFFECTION)		
(HIS VOICE IS SHAKING WITH EMOTION)	11	STRANG
(SHAKING HER HEAD--	27	STRANG
(SHAKING HIS HEAD EXASPERATEDLY)	52	STRANG
(SHAKING HER, FIERCELY) YOU CAN'T/	61	STRANG
(SHAKING HIS HAND--BRIEFLY) HELLO.	76	STRANG
(SHAKING HER HEAD--SCORNFULLY)	163	STRANG
(SHAKING HIS HEAD) NOTING DIS TIME, THANK YOU.	498	VOYAGE
(SHAKING HIS FIST AT JOE) OHO, I KNOW YOUR GAMES,S90	VOYAGE
ME SONNY BYE/		
(SHAKING ELEANOR BY THE HAND)	450	WELDED
(UNCONSCIOUSLY HE GRIPS HER TIGHTER, ALMOST	451	WELDED
SHAKING HER.)		

SHAKINGLY

THE REACHES FOR THE DECANTER AND SHAKINGLY POURS A 42 POET DRINK.

SHAKY

= HE CAN NO LONGER RESIST, BUT JOINS IN A SHAKY 259 AHWILD GRAWL.

AND, OUTSIDE OF EYES THAT ARE BLOODSHOT AND NERVES263 AHWILD THAT ARE SHAKY,

(SLYLY) YOU SEEN A MITE SHAKY.	133	ELECTR
MY LEGS ARE A BIT SHAKY YET.	674	ICEMAN
BEYOND SHAKY NERVES, IT SHOWS NO EFFECTS OF HARD	33	POET
DRINKING.		

SHALL

(WORRIEDLY) SHALL I WAKE UP THE FIRST AND FOURTH,543 'LE SIN

NOR ALL YOUR PIETY NOR WIT SHALL LURE IT BACK TO	199	AHWILD
CANCEL HALF A LINE,		
LIPS THAT TOUCH LIQUOR SHALL NEVER TOUCH YOURS/	232	AHWILD
WHAT SHALL WE DO ABOUT IT, EH$	241	AHWILD
SHALL I GO UP NOW AND TELL HIM TO GET DRESSED, YOU266	AHWILD
WANT TO SEE HIM,$		
(SARCASTICALLY) SHALL I SERVE IT IN A PAILS	14	ANNA
THIS PLOT OF YOURS MORE SIGNIFICANT--FOR YOUR	495	DAYS
SOUL, SHALL I SAY$		
SHALL I TELL YOU WHERE I WENT, AND WHY$	548	DAYS
HIS LIVE SHALL NEVER DIE/	566	DAYS
HE SHALL FOLLOW IN MY FOOTSTEPS--	423	DYNAMO
(SHALL I MAKE HIM COME IN$	432	DYNAMO
THIS DUNCE-- THIS STUPID OOLT--NOW I SHALL BE THE	452	DYNAMO
BUTT OF ALL THEIR SNEERS/		
(DULLY) SHALL I HAVE YOUR ROOM PUT IN ORDER FOR	467	DYNAMO
YOU$		
WE'LL BE SECRET CONSPIRATORS, SHALL WE, AND I'LL	72	ELECTR
HELP YOU AND YOU'LL HELP ME$		
LET'S GO IN, SHALL WE$	73	ELECTR
LET'S SIT DOWN FOR A MOMENT, SHALL WE, AND GET	140	ELECTR
USED TO BEING HOME$		
SHALL I GET IT AWAY FROM HIM$	167	ELECTR
DION ANTHONY, SHALL WE GO IN AND MAY I HAVE THE	268	GOBROW
NEXT DANCE$		
BLESSED ARE THE MEEK FOR THEY SHALL INHERIT	273	GGBROW
GRAVES/		
WHEN SHALL I REPORT$	281	GGBROW
(MOCKINGLY) WHAT SAY$ SHALL WE HAVE A DRINK$	286	GGBROW
NOR DOST THOU KNOW WHAT SHALL BEFALL THEE AFTER	290	GGBROW
DEATH.		
SHALL I PHONE FOR A DOCTOR$	305	GGBROW
=BLESSED ARE THEY THAT WEEP, FOR THEY SHALL	322	GGBROW
LAUGH/		
SHALL WE GIVE HIM WHAT'S WHAT AND PUT THE BOOTS TO249	HA APE
HIM$		
YOU SHALL BE PAID TOMORROW.	602	ICEMAN
BUT I SHALL ENJOY MORE VEN I AM HOME, TOO.	605	ICEMAN
SHALL I GIVE HIM DE BUM'S RUSH, LARRY$	666	ICEMAN
SHALL WE NOT GO INTO LUNCH, DEAR$	69	JOURNE
SHALL I POUR A DRINK FOR YOU$	109	JOURNE
I SHALL GIVE THE ART OF ACTING BACK TO THE	160	JOURNE
PERFORMING SEALS.		
I SHALL ATTAIN THE PINNACLE OF SUCCESS/	160	JOURNE
HE THAT BELIEVETH SHALL NEVER DIE/	275	LAZARU
HE THAT LIVETH, HE THAT BELIEVETH, SHALL NEVER	275	LAZARU
DIE/		
SOON I SHALL KNOW PEACE.=	276	LAZARU
HE WILL SEIZE HIS KINGDOM AND ALL WHO DENY HIM	284	LAZARU
SHALL BE CRUCIFIED/		
AND SWINE SHALL ROOT WHERE THY TEMPLE STOOD/	292	LAZARU
WELL, WE SHALL SOON SEE WITH OUR OWN EYES.	300	LAZARU
I AM IMAGINING WHAT I SHALL HAVE DONE TO YOU/	317	LAZARU
WHEN I AM CAESAR YOU SHALL SCREAM AND PRAY FOR IT/317	LAZARU
I SHALL TAKE CARE TO DIE BEFORE YOU BECOME	317	LAZARU
CAESAR--AND LIFE BECOMES TOO IDIOTIC/		
SHALL I GIVE THE SIGNAL TO KILL, LAZARUS$	319	LAZARU

SHALL

SHALL (CONT'D.)		
I SWEAR YOU SHALL NOT LAUGH AT DEATH WHEN I AM	324	LAZARU
DEATH/		
YOUR FEAR SHALL NEVER BE/	330	LAZARU
(THEN THREATENINGLY) YOU SHALL BE GIVEN FULL	340	LAZARU
OPPORTUNITY TO PROVE IT/		
(HER VOICE CRUEL) HE SHALL NOT LAUGH AT ME/	342	LAZARU
THEN I SHALL LAUGH/	342	LAZARU
I SHALL OFFER HER THE FRUIT CAESAR PRESERVES FOR	342	LAZARU
THOSE HE FEARS.		
AND MEN SHALL KEEP ON IN PANIC NAILING MAN-S SOUL	343	LAZARU
TO THE CROSS OF THEIR FEAR		
YES, I SHALL COMMAND HIM TO LAUGH/	345	LAZARU
I SHALL BE LONELY, DEAR ONE.	346	LAZARU
AND I SHALL MAKE DEATH LAUGH AT YOU/	348	LAZARU
I SHALL MAKE YOU PRAY FOR DEATH/	348	LAZARU
I SHALL BE PROUD/	352	LAZARU
YOU ARE PLEASED TO ACT THE MYSTERIOUS, JEW, BUT I	353	LAZARU
SHALL SOLVE YOU/		
OR I SHALL LOSE PATIENCE WITH YOU--AND--(WITH A	354	LAZARU
GRIM SMILE) I CAN BE TERRIBLE/		
AND I SHALL BE CAESAR.	355	LAZARU
THEN I SHALL LAUGH/	355	LAZARU
AND REMEMBER THERE SHALL BE DEATH WHILE I AM	357	LAZARU
CAESAR/		
IT SHALL LEARN TO LAUGH YOUR LAUGHTER, LAZARUS, OR360	LAZARU
I--		
HOME SHALL KNOW HAPPINESS, IT SHALL BELIEVE IN	360	LAZARU
LIFE.		
YOU SHALL BE TORTURED AS YOU HAVE TORTURED/	361	LAZARU
I SHALL PUNISH YOU/	361	LAZARU
SHALL WE CUT AWAY THE GAG$	364	LAZARU
YOU SHALL DIE, LAZARUS--DIE--HA-AH--/	369	LAZARU
AND ALL OF MEN ARE VILE AND MAD, AND I SHALL BE	370	LAZARU
THEIR MADMEN'S CAESAR/		
WE SHALL BE GOVERNED BY THE IGNORANT GREEDY MOB	8	MANSNS
FOR ALL FUTURE TIME.		
I SHALL BE, AS EVER, YOUR MOTHER CONFESSOR.	17	MANSNS
I SHALL NEVER SEE HIM AGAIN.	18	MANSNS
YES, DEBORAH, THE ATMOSPHERE IS HARDLY CONDUCIVE	37	MANSNS
TO--COMMON SENSE, SHALL I SAY$		
I SHALL ARRANGE FOR PLACES IN THE STAGE.	38	MANSNS
I SHALL HAVE TO BE VERY CUNNING.	39	MANSNS
(GETTING TO HIS FEET.) WE SHALL SEE.	52	MANSNS
I SHALL ENGAGE AN ATTORNEY TO PROTECT THAT	60	MANSNS
INTEREST.		
I SHALL GO TO THE CITY BY THE MORNING STAGE	60	MANSNS
AND I SHALL SEE THAT YOU ARE GIVEN AN INTEREST IN	60	MANSNS
MY COMPANY		
I SHALL HAVE TO CONCENTRATE ALL MY ATTENTION ON	66	MANSNS
REORGANIZING MY COMPANY.		
HADN'T I BETTER THINK OUT MORE EXACTLY HOW I SHALL	74	MANSNS
ATTACK$		
YOU SHALL HAVE YOUR ESTATE.	93	MANSNS
SHE KNOWS WITHOUT THEM I SHALL BE LOST AGAIN/	105	MANSNS
I SHALL BE DELIGHTED TO DROP IN AND KEEP YOU	106	MANSNS
COMPANY HERE		
HEREAFTER I SHALL SPEND MY EVENINGS THERE ALONE,	130	MANSNS
AND YOU MAY DO AS YOU PLEASE.		
SHALL I LET HIM IN$	149	MANSNS
I SHALL GO TO HER.	182	MANSNS
	182	MANSNS
AND I SHALL BE FREE TO BE SARA'S, BODY AND SOUL.	183	MANSNS
WE SHALL HAVE GONE BACK BEYOND SEPARATIONS.	185	MANSNS
WE SHALL BE ONE AGAIN.	185	MANSNS
SHALL I EXPECT YOU AGAIN TONIGHT$	374	MARCOM
(WITH A QUIET SMILE) I SHALL STUDY THIS	379	MARCOM
APOTHEGSIS WITH UNHURRIED INTEREST.		
YOU SHALL TELL ME ABOUT YOUR SOUL	380	MARCOM
TELL ME, WHAT SHALL I DO WITH HIM$	382	MARCOM
AT LEAST, IF HE CANNOT LEARN, WE SHALL.	382	MARCOM
MANY LEAGUES AND YEARS, AND I KEEP THAT NEVER	384	MARCOM
AGAIN SHALL I SEE YOUR FACE.		
EXCEPT THAT I SHALL BE HOMESICK FOR YOU.	386	MARCOM
I SHALL SEND HIM HOME TO HIS NATIVE WALLOW.	387	MARCOM
(THEN BRUSQUELY) I SHALL INFORM THE AMBASSADORS	387	MARCOM
YOU WILL BE		
IT IS THE LAST FAVOR I SHALL EVER ASK.	397	MARCOM
(EAGERLY) BUT WE SHALL HAVE DANCERS ON THE SHIP	398	MARCOM
I SHALL HAVE HIM KILLED/	401	MARCOM
(WITH IMPOTENT ANGER) HE SHALL PRAY FOR HIS SOUL	401	MARCOM
ON HIS KNEES BEFORE YOU/		
I SHALL KNOW THE LONG SORROW OF AN EXILE AS I SAIL405	MARCOM
OVER THE GREEN WATER		
MY EYES SHALL BE EVER RED WITH WEEPING, MY HEART	405	MARCOM
BLEEDING,		
HE SHALL LOOK INTO MY EYES AND SEE THAT I AM A	414	MARCOM
WOMAN AND BEAUTIFUL/		
THIS IS ONE PART OF YOUR DUTY IN WHICH I SHALL	414	MARCOM
HAVE TO REPORT YOU INCOMPETENT.		
I SHALL SLEEP FOREVER/	415	MARCOM
(WITH RAGE) SHALL I ASK AS MY FIRST WEDDING	416	MARCOM
PRESENT FROM GHAZAN KHAN THAT HE		
IT SHALL NOT BE I WHO RULES, BUT YOU/	418	MARCOM
I SHALL BE YOUR SLAVE/	418	MARCOM
PERSIA SHALL BE YOUR CONQUEST	418	MARCOM
YOU SHALL BE QUEEN OF LOVE--/	418	MARCOM
I SHALL OBEY THE ETERNAL WILL WHICH GOVERNS YOUR	418	MARCOM
DESTINY AND MINE.		
AND EVERYWHERE WHERE SONGS ARE SUNG THEY SHALL BE	418	MARCOM
IN PRAISE OF YOUR BEAUTY/		
SHALL HE BE KILLED/	419	MARCOM
I DOUBT IF I SHALL BE BLESSED WITH A SON.	423	MARCOM
I SHALL CONQUER THE WEST/	425	MARCOM
FAMINE SHALL FINISH WHAT I LEAVE UNDONE/	425	MARCOM
AND UF THE CITY OF VENICE NOT ONE VESTIGE SHALL	425	MARCOM
REMAIN/		

SHALL (CONT'D.)

AND OF THE BODY OF MARCO POLO THERE SHALL NOT BE A425 MARCOM FRAGMENT OF BONE NOR AN ATOM
I SHALL LEAD MY ARMIES IN PERSON/ 425 MARCOM
I SHALL NOT LEAVE ONE TEMPLE STANDING 425 MARCOM
THEIR CITIES SHALL VANISH IN FLAME, THEIR FIELDS 425 MARCOM SHALL BE WASTED/
HOW LONG BEFORE WE SHALL BE PERMITTED TO DIE, MY 426 MARCOM FRIENDS
(STARING FIXEDLY) I SHALL OBSERVE 426 MARCOM DISPASSIONATELY.
=THERE SHALL HE NOT--AMBITION'S DISHONORED FOOL/= 37 POET
OF COURSE I SHALL HONOR THE OCCASION. 58 POET
I SHALL NEVER VENTURE FORTH AGAIN TO DO MY DUTY. 86 POET
I SHALL DO THE LADY THE HONOR OF TENDERING HER MY 90 POET HUMBLE APOLOGIES
AND I SHALL INSIST IT BE A GENEROUS ONE, BEFITTINGILL POET YOUR POSITION AS MY DAUGHTER.
IF YOU WILL EXCUSE ME, I SHALL JOIN CORPORAL 115 POET CREGAN.
= BEHOLD, EVERY ONE THAT USETH PROVERBS SHALL USE 579 ROPE THIS PROVERB AGAINST THEE,
(ARGUING WITH HIMSELF) (I SHALL I TELL HIMS.... 8 STRANG
(THEN IN A SUDDEN FLURRY) (I SHALL I TELL HIMS... 31 STRANG
((I SHALL BE HAPPY FOR A WHILE/...)) 89 STRANG
((I SHALL BE HAPPY/... 89 STRANG
I SHALL MAKE MY HUSBAND HAPPY/...)) 90 STRANG
SHALL HE COME RIGHT UP$ 145 STRANG
SHALL I TELL HER YOU WANT TO SEE HER$ 188 STRANG
SHALL I BEGIN AGAIN$ 482 WELDED
SHALL I TELL YOU WHAT HAPPENED TO ME$ 484 WELDED

SHALT

BECAUSE THOU KNOWST NOT WHEN THOU SHALT DIE. 290 GGBROW
O DIVIDED HOUSE, THOU SHALT CRUMBLE TO DUST, 292 LAZARU

SHAM

BUT THERE IS SOMETHING REVOLTINGLY INCONGRUOUS 520 DIFRNT ABOUT HER, A PITIABLE SHAM.
IF YOU THINK I CAN BE TAKEN IN BY SUCH AN OBVIOUS 176 MANSNS SHAM--

SHAMBLES

AND MAKE OF OUR SWEET AND LOVELY CIVILIZATION A 244 HA APE SHAMBLES.

SHAMBLING

(HOPE PASSES THE WINDOW OUTSIDE THE FREE-LUNCH 689 ICEMAN COUNTER IN A SHAMBLING,
HE SLOUCHES AND HIS MOVEMENTS ARE SHAMBLING AND 175 POET CLUMSY.

SHAME

WHAT A SHAME--ON THE FOURTH, 208 AHWILD
IT'S A SHAME FOR YOU--A MEASLY SHAME--YOU THAT 213 AHWILD WOULD
BUT HE DOES NOT WIN WHO PLAYS WITH SIN IN THE 246 AHWILD SECRET HOUSE OF SHAME/=
(LAUGHING) WELL, I GUESS IT'S A SHAME TO KEEP YOU273 AHWILD GUESSING.
IT'S A =SECRET HOUSE OF SHAME.= 282 AHWILD
SHAME-FACEDLY) 9 ANNA
YOU'RE HER FATHER, AND WOULDN'T IT BE A SHAME FOR 46 ANNA US TO BE AT EACH OTHER'S
TO COME TO BLACK SHAME IN THE END, 60 ANNA
'TIS BLACK SHAME IS ON ME/ 70 ANNA
(THOROUGHLY EXASPERATED) IS IT NO SHAME YOU HAVE 73 ANNA AT ALL$
BECAUSE--(LAMELY) IT SEEMS SUCH A SHAME. 88 BEYOND
IT'S A SHAME YOU'RE GOING-- 88 BEYOND
AND YOU OUGHT TO BE BOWED IN SHAME TO THINK OF IT/107 BEYOND
(WITH WEARY VEXATION) IT'S A SHAME FOR HIM TO 118 BEYOND COME HOME.
(SHAME-FACEDLY) NO--NO. 122 BEYOND
IT'S A DAMNED SHAME/ 154 BEYOND
(WITH IMPOTENT RAGE) GOD, WHAT A SHAME/ 162 BEYOND
AIN'T THAT'D PUT ANY OF YEW PORE CRITTERS T' SHAME/ 249 DESIRE
(VIOLENTLY) IT'S A SHAME, THAT'S WHAT IT IS/ 528 DIFRNT
BUT SHAME AIN'T IN YOU. 529 DIFRNT
IF SHAME WAS IN YOU, 530 DIFRNT
IT'S A SHAME THE WAY THEY DENY YOU THE ORDINARY 425 DYNAMO COMFORTS OF LIFE/
INTO ABJECT SHAME AND FRIGHT) 436 DYNAMO
(THEN THINKING WITH GUILTY SHAME) 447 DYNAMO
(ALMOST AS SOON AS HE REACHES HIS OLD HIDING PLACE459 DYNAMO IS OVERCOME BY SHAME)
IT'S A SHAME TO FOOL DESE BLACK TRASH AROUND HEAH,183 EJONES DE'RE SO EASY.
IT'S A DURNED SHAME. 11 ELECTR
MY ONLY SHAME IS MY DIRTY MANNON BLOOD/ 25 ELECTR
NOW YOU SAY THAT--WITHOUT ANY SHAME/ 30 ELECTR
IT WILL SHAME THEM BACK INTO DEATH/ 176 ELECTR
AFTER THAT, WE GREW HOSTILE WITH CONCEALED SHAME. 282 GGBROW
YOU BASTARD/ SHE'S YOUR MOTHER/ HAVE YOU NO SHAME$467 ICEMAN
IF IVIR I SAW BLACK SHAME ON A MAN'S FACE 'TWAS ON523 INZONE HIS WHIN HE SAT THERE/
BUT IT DOES SEEM A SHAME HE SHOULD HAVE TO BE SICK 16 JOURNE RIGHT NOW.
(OVERWHELMED BY SHAME WHICH HE TRIES TO HIDE, 113 JOURNE FUMBLES WITH HIS WATCH.)
JESUS, PAPA, HAVEN'T YOU ANY PRIDE OR SHAME$ 145 JOURNE
OH, SHAME AND GUILT/ 295 LAZARU
FILLING THEM WITH THE SHEEPISH SHAME OF CHILDREN 306 LAZARU CAUGHT IN MISCHIEF.
FOR SHAME/ 334 LAZARU
HAVE YOU BECOME SO UTTERLY COARSE THAT YOU FEEL NO 97 MANSNS SHAME BUT ACTUALLY BOAST
SHAME ON YOU. 124 MANSNS
(GENUINELY OVERCOME BY A SUDDEN SHAME) 371 MARCOM
I NO LONGER CAN ENDURE THE SHAME OF LIVING/ 415 MARCOM
GOD FORGIVE YOU, IT'S A GREAT SHAME TO ME 76 MISBEG
(SHE BEGINS TO SOB WITH A STRANGE FORLORN SHAME 136 MISBEG AND HUMILIATION)

SHAME (CONT'D.)

(SHAME-FACEDLY) AND YOU LET ME GET AWAY WITH IT. 167 MISBEG
THE LOOK OF GUILT AND SHAME AND ANGUISH SETTLES 175 MISBEG OVER HIS FACE.
I DON'T KNOW ABOUT ROSES, BUT IT WILL BRING A 44 POET BLUSH OF SHAME TO MY CHEEKS.
(SCORNFULLY) AND BE DAMNED TO YOUR LYING, PIOUS 62 POET SHAME/
YOU HAD NO SHAME THEN, I REMEMBER. 62 POET
HE NEAR SAW THROUGH THE BED WITH SHAME AT HIS 62 POET BOLDNESS.
TRYING TO HIDE HER APPREHENSION AND ANGER AND 72 POET SHAME.
SHAME ON YOU/ 79 POET
FOR SHAME, YOU DUG, NOT TO REMEMBER TALAVERA. 93 POET
SHAME ON YOU/ 143 POET
THERE WAS NO SHAME IN IT/ 148 POET
I WAS DEAD WITH SHAME. 148 POET
AND WOULDN'T IT SHAME THEIR BOASTING AND VANITY 150 POET
HE WAS AFRAID THE ROW WOULD GET IN THE PAPER AND 159 POET PUT SHAME ON HIM.
DON'T PUT THIS FINAL SHAME ON YOURSELF. 177 POET
SHAME ON YOU TO LAY WHEN YOU HAVE LOVE. 182 POET
LEFT YOU--THE SHAME OF THE WHOLE COUNTRY/ 580 ROPE
ANCIENT SHAME... 53 STRANG
(THINKING WITH A STRANGE TORTURED SHAME) 145 STRANG
(SHAME-FACEDLY) I SHOULD HAVE KNOWN. 477 WELDED

SHAMED

YOU OUGHT TO BE SHAMED-- 24 POET
HE IS SHAMED AND HUMILIATED AND FURIOUS AT BEING 68 POET CAUGHT
HE'D OUGHT TO BE SHAMED HE IVIR WOKE THE BLOODY 100 POET RED AV ENGLAND.
IT WAS I WHO SHAMED HIM INTO TAKING UP BIOLOGY 139 STRANG

SHAMEFACED

(FROWNING--A LITTLE SHAMEFACED) 234 AHWILD
(RICHARD LOOKS SHAMEFACED. 240 AHWILD
(THEN WITH A SHIVER OF SHAMEFACED REVULSION AND 276 AHWILD SELF-DISGUST)
AND BEGINS WITH A SHAMEFACED, SELF-CONSCIOUS 294 AHWILD SOLEMNITY)
(THEN, AS, BROUGHT BACK TO HIMSELF HE RELEASES HER433 DYNAMO IN SHAMEFACED CONFUSION,
= (HE SUDDENLY CHECKS HIMSELF AND FORCES A 481 DYNAMO STRANGE, SHAMEFACED LAUGH)
(AGAIN SHAMEFACED) I DIDN'T MEAN THAT. 75 ELECTR
(IMMEDIATELY SHAMEFACED) YOU'RE RIGHT, PETER. 82 ELECTR
(A BIT SHAMEFACED) WELL, SO HAVE I LIKED YOU. 624 ICEMAN
(A BIT SHAMEFACED--SULKILY) WHO WANTS TO$ 632 ICEMAN
(SHAMEFACED) SURE HE IS. 637 ICEMAN
(LOOKING GUILTY AND SHAMEFACED NOW-- 654 ICEMAN
(THIS RELEASES A CHORUS OF SHAMEFACED MUMBLES FROM663 ICEMAN THE CROWD.
(HE IS SUDDENLY SHAMEFACED.) 35 JOURNE
SHAMEFACED.) FORGIVE ME, LAD. I FORGOT-- 128 JOURNE
(SHE LAUGHS--THEN SUDDENLY SHAMEFACED.) 44 MANSNS
(ABRUPTLY SHAMEFACED.) AH, WHAT AM I SAYING/ 82 MANSNS
(MARCO REMAINS SULLENLY APART, SHAMEFACED AND 360 MARCOM ANGRY, HIS FISTS CLENCHED.

SHAMEFACEDLY

SHE IS LAUGHING TO HERSELF A BIT SHAMEFACEDLY. 220 AHWILD
(SHAMEFACEDLY) ALL RIGHT. 238 AHWILD
HASTILY, SHEEPISH, LOOKING AROUND HIM 276 AHWILD SHAMEFACEDLY.
(TOTALLY UNPREPARED FOR THIS APPROACH-- 293 AHWILD SHAMEFACEDLY MUTTERS)
(FLUSHING--SHAMEFACEDLY) HELL/ 142 BEYOND
(TURNS TO HIM SHAMEFACEDLY) DON'T TALK THAT WAY, 505 DAYS UNCLE.
(HE GETS TO HIS FEET-- A BIT SHAMEFACEDLY) 424 DYNAMO
(SHAMEFACEDLY) I--I DON'T THINK SO. 436 DYNAMO
(HURRIEDLY--SHAMEFACEDLY) I--I'D FORGOTTEN. 74 ELECTR
(HE TRIES TO FORCE A LAUGH--THEN SHAMEFACEDLY) 93 ELECTR
(ROUSING HIMSELF--SHAMEFACEDLY) 110 ELECTR
(SHAMEFACEDLY) I DIDN'T SAY--STILL--SOMETHING'S 271 GGBROW GOT TO BE DONE.
(AWKWARDLY AND SHAMEFACEDLY) 293 GGBROW
(SHAMEFACEDLY) I REMEMBER NOW. 295 GGBROW
(SPEAKS UP SHAMEFACEDLY) LISTEN, BOYS, I'S SORRY.437 ICEMAN
(RATHER SHAMEFACEDLY PULLS HIMSELF TOGETHER--THEN 303 LAZARU BEGRUDGINGLY)
(SHE HIDES HER FACE ON HIS SHOULDER SHAMEFACEDLY-- 90 MANSNS
(A BIT SHAMEFACEDLY) FORGET THAT STUFF, JOSIE-- 104 MISBEG
(HE STOPS A LITTLE SHAMEFACEDLY, BUT NORA GIVES NO 39 POET SIGN OF OFFENSE.
(SHAMEFACEDLY) YES--INFANTRY--BUT I NEVER GOT TO 30 STRANG THE FRONT.
(A BIT SHAMEFACEDLY--CHANGING THE SUBJECT HASTILY) 38 STRANG
(COMING TO HIMSELF--WITH A GROAN--SHAMEFACEDLY) 101 STRANG
(THINKING SHAMEFACEDLY) (WHY HAVE I BEEN TRYING 118 STRANG TO HURT HER$...
(THEN CONFUSEDLY AND SHAMEFACEDLY) 120 STRANG
(REGAINING CONTROL--SHAMEFACEDLY) 170 STRANG
(A BIT SHAMEFACEDLY, CAPE LETS GO OF HER ARM. 451 WELDED

SHAMEFACEDNESS

=ONCE, LONG AGO--- (THEN, SUDDENLY WITH REPENTANT 517 DAYS SHAMEFACEDNESS)

SHAMEFUL

TO SUPPORT YOUR FAMILY EXCEPT IN A SHAMEFUL 153 MANSNS POVERTY.
(TEASINGLY) I OUGHT TO CUT YOU DEAD AFTER THE 79 STRANG SHAMEFUL WAY YOU'VE IGNORED US/
(WITH REVULSION) ((THAT'S SHAMEFUL/... 93 STRANG

SHAMELESS

YOU'RE SHAMELESS AND EVIL/ 30 ELECTR
YOU'VE CALLED ME VILE AND SHAMELESS/ 31 ELECTR
FATHER, HOW CAN YOU LOVE THAT SHAMELESS HARLOT$ 57 ELECTR
AND YOU WENT TO WATCH THEIR SHAMELESS DANCES 154 ELECTR

SHAMELESS

SHAMELESS (CONT'D.)
LOVE IS A WORD--A SHAMELESS RAGGED GHOST OF A 266 GGBROW
WORD--
BY THE TERRIFIC IMPACT OF THIS UNKNOWN, ABYSMAL 225 HA APE
BRUTALITY, NAKED AND SHAMELESS.
BY THIS SHAMELESS CONFESSION.) 680 ICEMAN
SHAMELESSLY 288 LAZARU
HOW DARE YOU MAKE SUCH A SHAMELESS PROPOSAL. 36 MANSNS
(SHE ADDS LAUGHINGLY.) OH, I ADMIT THIS IS 56 MANSNS
SHAMELESS BRIBERY ON MY PART, SARA.
AND I DON'T CARE HOW SHAMELESS I AM/ 89 MANSNS
YES, YOU WILL HAVE TO LEARN TO BE SHAMELESS HERE. 91 MANSNS
AREN'T WE THE SHAMELESS ONES/ 91 MANSNS
AND STOP YOUR SHAMELESS WAYS WITH MEN. 8 MISBEG
HE ONLY ACTS LIKE HE'S HARD AND SHAMELESS TO GET 33 MISBEG
BACK AT LIFE WHEN IT'S
MADE ME GO AFTER HIM, GET HIM DRUNK, GET DRUNK 163 MISBEG
MYSELF SO I COULD BE SHAMELESS--
LOVE HIM ALL THE MORE AND BE MORE SHAMELESS AND 164 MISBEG
KILLINGS
THEIR SHAMELESS PERFIDY HAS DISHONORED/ 40 POET
A PIECE OF THE MOST SHAMELESS EFFRONTERY. 120 POET
IF HE'S THAT CRUEL AND SHAMELESS AFTER WHAT HE'S 167 POET
DONE--
HOW SHAMELESS/...)) 93 STRANG
SHAMELESSLY
(SNEERINGLY.) HOW SHAMELESSLY HUMBLE YOU ARE/ 188 MANSNS
WHOSE ONLY THOUGHT IS MONEY AND WHO HAS 113 POET
SHAMELESSLY THROWN HERSELF AT A YOUNG
SHAMING
AND SHE DIDN'T WANT HER POOR IRISH RELATIONS 45 MANSNS
SHAMING HER BEFORE THE NOTABLES/
SHAN'T
YOU SHAN'T LEAVE HERE UNTIL--/ 163 ELECTR
(HE PUTS IT ON THE BAR) I SHAN'T BE COMING BACK. 675 ICEMAN
SHANKED
BETUNE YOU AND A GRAVE IN THE OCEAN BUT A SPINDLE-479 CARDIF
SHANKED.
(GLARES AT HARDER) WHERE'S YOUR MANNERS, YOU 57 MISBEG
SPINDLE-SHANKED JOCKEYS
SHANTY
IN ANY HOOKER-SHANTY IN PORT, 60 ANNA
NOR A GOD-DAMNED HOOKER SHANTY, EITHER/ 660 ICEMAN
HE'S A WILY SHANTY MICK, THAT ONE. 22 JOURNE
YOU OUGHT TO MARRY AND HAVE A HOME OF YOUR OWN 8 MISBEG
AWAY FROM THIS SHANTY
LIKE YOU DESERVE, INSTEAD OF IN THIS SHANTY ON A 175 MISBEG
LOUSY FARM, SLAVING FOR MES
YOU OUGHT TO TELL THE GOOD FATHER WE AREN'T THE 27 POET
IGNORANT SHANTY SCUM
SHAPE
HE PRETENDS TO BE ENGAGED IN SETTING THINGS SHIP- 41 ANNA
SHAPE.
HE IS IN BAD SHAPE-- 68 ANNA
WELL, THERE WAS SO MUCH DIRTY WORK GETTING THINGS 131 BEYOND
SHIP-SHAPE AGAIN I MUST HAVE
I'LL BE IN GOOD SHAPE TOMORROW/ 686 ICEMAN
I'VE BROUGHT YOU THROUGH IN GOOD SHAPES 411 MARCOM
WHOSE CHARACTER YOU COULD SHAPE AND WHOSE LIFE YOU 81 STRANG
COULD GUIDE AND MAKE WHAT YOU
SHAPED
AN IRREGULAR-SHAPED COMPARTMENT, 477 CARDIF
A BIG, FINELY SHAPED HEAD, A HANDSOME PROFILE, 13 JOURNE
DEEP-SET LIGHT-BROWN EYES.
THE MOUTH SHAPED BY LAUGHTER. 285 LAZARU
SHE HAS SMALL EARS SET CLOSE TO HER HEAD, A WELL- 2 MANSNS
SHAPED HEAD ON A SLENDER NECK.
SHE HAS SMALL EARS, SET CLOSE TO HER WELL-SHAPED 15 POET
HEAD, AND A SLENDER NECK.
IT IS SMALL WITH HIGH CHEEKBONES, WEDGE-SHAPED, 67 POET
NARROWING FROM A BROAD FOREHEAD
SHAPELESS
SHAPELESS AND FADED NONDESCRIPT IN CUT AND COLOR.)188 AHWILD
THEY ARE BLACK, SHAPELESS, ONLY THEIR GLITTERING 189 EJONES
LITTLE EYES CAN BE SEEN.
HE IS SLOVENLY DRESSED IN A DIRTY SHAPELESS 575 ICEMAN
PATCHED SUIT, SPOTTED BY FOOD.
SHAPES
THE SHRUBS, OF VARIOUS SIZES, ARE ALL CLIPPED INTO 25 MANSNS
GEOMETRICAL SHAPES--
SHARE
THEIR SHARE O' THE FOUR HUNDRED BARREL WOULDN'T 542 'ILE
KEEP 'EM IN CHEWIN' TOBACCO.
WE'VE HAD OUR SHARE, HAVEN'T WES 292 AHWILD
AND TAKE A REAL INTEREST IN THE FARM, AND DO MY 102 BEYOND
SHARE.
I'VE DONE MY SHARE OF WORK HERE. 107 BEYOND
HAVEN'T I GOT MY SHARE UF TROUBLES TRYING TO WORK 122 BEYOND
THIS CURSED FARM
AFTER TWO YEARS I HAD A SHARE IN IT. 161 BEYOND
REMEMBER, ANDY, RUTH HAS SUFFERED DOUBLE HER 162 BEYOND
SHARE.
NOT THAT I AIN'T HAD MY SHARE OF THINGS GOIN' 467 CARIBE
WRONG.
I DONE MY SHARE O' DRINKIN' IN MY TIME. 467 CARIBE
(QUIETLY) I HAVE MY SHARE OF SCARS. 517 DAYS
THAT I WOULDN'T HAVE TO SHARE HIM EVEN WITH THE 523 DAYS
PAST.
YE WON'T NEVER GO BECAUSE YE'LL WAIT HERE FUR YER 208 DESIRE
SHARE O' THE FARM,
YE MIGHT 'ARN A SHARE O' A FARM THAT WAY. 254 DESIRE
THEN I WANT T' SHARE IT WITH YE. 266 DESIRE
(A PAUSE) I WANT T' SHARE WITH YE, ABBIE--PRISON 267 DESIRE
'R DEATH 'R HELL 'R ANYTHIN'/
(EMOTIONLESSLY) I SWAPPED IT T' SIM AN' PETER FUR268 DESIRE
THEIR SHARE O' THE FARM--
AND CHEAT HIM OUT OF HIS SHARE OF THE BUSINESS 25 ELECTR
THEY'D INHERITED/

1408

SHARE (CONT'D.)
WE COULD BE MARRIED NOW AND I WOULD BRING YOU MY 39 ELECTR
SHARE OF THE MANNON ESTATE.
I LOVE YOU NOW WITH ALL THE GUILT IN ME--THE GUILT165 ELECTR
WE SHARE/
AND MAKE HIM SHARE ITS 172 ELECTR
AND WHATEVER STICKS TO THE CEILING IS MY SHARE/ 582 ICEMAN
(SURPRISED AND A BIT NETTLED TO HAVE TO SHARE HIS 519 INZONE
STORY WITH ANYONE)
WELL, I KNOW WHAT HE'LL DO WITH HIS SHARE. 94 JOURNE
AND HE ASKED ME WOULDN'T I PLEASE HELP HIM WITH 132 MANSNS
HIS WORK AND SHARE--
THAT OUR SILK-MAKERS MAY PRESERVE THEIR SHARE OF 422 MARCOM
THE ETERNAL SUNLIGHT/
I BORROWED SOME MONEY ON MY SHARE OF THE ESTATE, 143 MISBEG
AND STARTED GOING TO TRACKS.
YOU KIN HAVE MY SHARE OF THAT. 599 ROPE
I WOULDN'T CARE TO SHARE WITH A GHOST-LOVER 39 STRANG
MYSELF.
AND I COULDN'T SHARE A WOMAN--EVEN WITH A GHOST/ 39 STRANG
SHE'S GOT TO SHAKE AND HELP ME SAVE MY SAMMY/...) 59 STRANG
THEY'LL PROBABLY ALL SHARE EQUALLY... 125 STRANG
DIDN'T I ALWAYS GIVE YER YER SHARE, FAIR AN' 494 VOYAGE
SQUARE, AS MAN TO MAN?
SHARED
IT HAS NOT SHARED IN THE GREAT HOLLOW BOOM OF THE 7 HUGHIE
TWENTIES.
AND THIS GARDEN I SHARED WITH YOU. 110 MANSNS
THE HARFORD PURSUIT OF FREEDOM IMPOSED UPON THE 83 POET
WOMEN WHO SHARED THEIR LIVES.
HE HAS SHARED ME FOR HIS COMFORT'S SAKE WITH A 138 STRANG
LITTLE GRATITUDE AND A BIG
SHARES
YE AGREE YEWR SHARES O' THE FARM IS SOLD T' ME. 213 DESIRE
(REPROVINGLY BUT SHOWING SHE SHARES HIS FEELING) 185 STRANG
SHARIN'
IF I'M SHARIN' WITH YE, I WON'T FEEL LONESOME, 267 DESIRE
LEASTWAYS.
SHARING
ABOUT SHARING THE PROFITS NEXT TIME. 609 ICEMAN
WELL, THAT HALF OF MY DOMESTIC RESPONSIBILITY-- 94 MANSNS
SHARING SCHEME.
AND MY HANDS ARE TIED AS FAR AS SHARING THE ESTATE14 STRANG
WITH HER IS CONCERNED.
AND SHARING ME HAS CORRUPTED HIM/...) 139 STRANG
SHARK
WHO WAS A REAL SHARK ON THESE DETAILS BUT THAT 306 GGBROW
YOU'VE FIRED HIM--
IN MY GAME, TO BE A SHARK AT IT, 624 ICEMAN
SHARKS
WE'D HAVE GONE TO THE SHARKS, ALL OF US. 131 BEYOND
THE REST OF THE WHALING CREW WERE NEVER HEARD FROM559 CROSS
AGAIN--GONE TO THE SHARKS.
SHARON
YEW AIR MY ROSE O' SHARON/ 232 DESIRE
YEW AIR MY ROSE O' SHARON/ 238 DESIRE
SHARP
(THE MATE LOOKS DOWN CONFUSEDLY BEFORE HIS SHARP 542 'ILE
GAZE)
AND SHE'S TO BE IN BED EVERY NIGHT BY EIGHT SHARP.203 AHWILD
THY SHARP SIGHS DIVIDE MY FLESH AND SPIRIT WITH 205 AHWILD
SOFT SOUND--'S
I WAS GOING OUT TO LOOK--IF HE WASN'T BACK BY 260 AHWILD
TWELVE SHARP.
AND THEN YOU LOST YOUR TEMPER AND WERE SO SHARP 265 AHWILD
WITH HIM RIGHT AFTER DINNER
YOU KNOW PA'S PUNISHING ME BY SENDING ME TO BED AT280 AHWILD
EIGHT SHARP.
YOU OUGHT TO HAVE WORN YOUR COAT A SHARP NIGHT 99 BEYOND
LIKE THIS, ROBBIE.
(WITH A SHARP SIGH OF JOYFUL RELIEF) 100 BEYOND
THE SOUND OF FOOTSTEPS ON THE PATH IS HEARD--THEN 153 BEYOND
A SHARP RAP ON THE DOOR.
(HE MAKES A FEEBLE ATTEMPT TO RISE BUT SINKS BACK 482 CARDIF
WITH A SHARP GROAN.
KATH'S MEAN MOUTH IS DRAWN DOWN BY SHARP LINES AT 515 DAYS
THE CORNERS.
STILLWELL IS IN HIS EARLY FIFTIES, TALL, WITH A 553 DAYS
SHARP,
(THERE IS A SHARP KNOCK ON THE DOOR IN THE REAR, 528 DIFRNT
WITH A SHARP FACE AND KEEN BLACK EYES. 428 DYNAMO
SHARP FEATURES TO A SICKLY YELLOW, 174 EJONES
SHARP EYES STILL PEER AT LIFE WITH A SHREWD PRYING 6 ELECTR
AVIDITY AND HIS LOOSE MOUTH
RASPING NASAL VOICE, AND LITTLE SHARP EYES. 67 ELECTR
BUCK TEETH AND BIG FEET, HER MANNER DEFENSIVELY 67 ELECTR
SHARP AND ASSERTIVE.
THEN HE INTERRUPTS THE CHANTYMAN'S TIRADE BY A 105 ELECTR
SHARP COMMAND.)
(THERE IS THE SHARP REPORT OF A PISTOL FROM THE 123 ELECTR
LEFT GROUND FLOOR OF THE HOUSE
WITH A GLEAM OF SHARP SARDONIC HUMOR IN THEM. 574 ICEMAN
(OFFENSIVELY SHARP) WHAT ABOUT ITS 622 ICEMAN
(HIS FATHER GIVES HIM A SHARP WARNING LOOK BUT HE 27 JOURNE
DOESN'T SEE IT.)
TYRONE SCOWLS AND LOOKS AT HIS WIFE WITH SHARP 116 JOURNE
SUSPICION--ROUGHLY.)
(WITH SHARP IRRITATION.) I TOLD YOU TO TURN OUT 126 JOURNE
THAT LIGHT/
(SKEPTICALLY) YOU MUST HAVE SHARP EARS TO HAVE 277 LAZARU
HEARD HIM LAUGH IN THAT UPROAR/
(GIVES HER A SHARP, CALCULATING GLANCE--QUICKLY.) 78 MANSNS
THEN THERE IS A SHARP RAP OF THE KNOCKER ON THE 95 MANSNS
DOOR.
(THERE IS ANOTHER KNOCK ON THE DOOR, SHARP AND 150 MANSNS
IMPATIENT.
(WITH SHARP SUSPICION) I COULD, 14 MISBEG
(SHE GIVES HIM A SHARP BITTER GLANCE. 113 MISBEG

SHARP (CONT'D.)
IT'S HIMSELF CAN KEEP HIS HEAD CLEAR AND HIS EYES 137 POET
SHARP.
SHARPENED
OF A SIMILAR SCANDAL-BEARING TYPE, HER TONGUE IS 6 ELECTR
SHARPENED BY MALICE.
SHARPENS
(ABRUPTLY HIS TONE SHARPENS WITH RESENTFUL 591 ICEMAN
WARNING)
SHARPER
WELL, MAYBE A WOMAN'S EYES IS SHARPER IN SUCH 98 BEYOND
THINGS, BUT--
(HE QUOTES.) =HOW SHARPER THAN A SERPENT'S TOOTH 89 JOURNE
IT IS--=
BUYING A PIECE OF NOAH'S ARK FROM A WAYSIDE 367 MARCOM
SHARPER.
THEN A SHARPER KNOCK COMES AT THE DOOR. 449 WELDED
SHARPLY
(TURNING TO HIM--SHARPLY) WAIT/ 540 'ILE
(SHARPLY) ANNIE/ 541 'ILE
(GLANCING SHARPLY AT THE MATE) 541 'ILE
(SHARPLY) THAT REMINDS ME, NAT. 192 AHWILD
(SHARPLY) AND I'M POSITIVE HE HAS. 201 AHWILD
(SHARPLY) LET'S GET DOWN TO BRASS TACKS. 201 AHWILD
(THEN MORE SHARPLY) WELL, I KNEW YOU'D PROVE 202 AHWILD
OBSTINATE.
(SHARPLY) NIX ON THAT LINE OF TALK/ 243 AHWILD
(THEN SHARPLY TO TOMMY) YOU HEARD WHAT I SAID, 252 AHWILD
YOUNG MAN/
(SHARPLY) WHEN YOU WERE WHERE$ 253 AHWILD
(SHARPLY, TO CONCEAL HIS OWN REAWAKENED 260 AHWILD
APPREHENSION)
(THEN HE NOTICES THAT SID IS DOZING---SHARPLY) 266 AHWILD
(SHARPLY) I'M NOT TOO FAT AND DON'T YOU SAY IT/ 291 AHWILD
(ONLY PARTLY REASSURED--SHARPLY) 293 AHWILD
(HE SIZES RICHARD UP SEARCHINGLY--THEN SUDDENLY 294 AHWILD
SPEAKS SHARPLY)
(SHARPLY--RAISING THE REVOLVER IN HER HAND) 69 ANNA
(SHARPLY) DON'T PLAY THE DUNCE, DICK/ 95 BEYOND
(SHARPLY) DON'T YOU PUT NO SUCH FOOL NOTIONS IN 97 BEYOND
ANDY'S HEAD, DICK--
(SHARPLY) S-H-H/ 148 BEYOND
(SHARPLY) S-H-H/ LISTEN/ AIN'T THAT AN AUTO I 153 BEYOND
HEAR
IN THE REAR THE DARK OUTLINE OF THE PORT BULWARK 455 CARIBE
IS SHARPLY DEFINED AGAINST A
(SHARPLY) HERE, YOU/ 465 CARIBE
(SHARPLY) JACK/ 507 DAYS
(FROM THE DOORWAY IN REAR--SHARPLY) 540 DAYS
(COMES THROUGH THE DOORWAY AT REAR--SHARPLY) 550 DAYS
(SHARPLY) LEAVE HER ALONE, JACK. 551 DAYS
SHARPLY BUT IN A VOICE JUST ABOVE A WHISPER) 555 DAYS
(SHARPLY) YEARN'N$ 221 DESIRE
(STARING AT HER SHARPLY--AFTER A PAUSE) 539 DIFFRNT
THE KNOCK IS REPEATED MORE SHARPLY. 547 DIFFRNT
(SUDDENLY ALERT--SHARPLY) SH/ 547 DIFFRNT
(SHARPLY) NOW DON'T YOU GO PREACHING AT HIM 426 DYNAMO
AGAIN.
(AS HE GIVES A START--SHARPLY) 446 DYNAMO
(SHARPLY) YOU AIN'T 'SINUATIN' I'SE A LIAR, IS 180 EJONES
YOU$
(HIS FACE GROWING GRIM--SHARPLY) 8 ELECTR
(TURNING ON HIM SHARPLY) WHAT DO YOU MEAN, SETHS. 11 ELECTR
(THEN SHARPLY) WARN MRS. 12 ELECTR
(SHARPLY) HE NEEDS ME MORE/. 14 ELECTR
(SHARPLY) YOU SAY THAT AS IF YOU DIDN'T BELIEVE 19 ELECTR
ME.
(SHARPLY) YES. 44 ELECTR
NOW MANAGES TO WORM HERSELF BETWEEN THEM--SHARPLY) 47 ELECTR
(SHARPLY) STOP YOUR SQUABBLING, BOTH OF YOU/ 50 ELECTR
(SHARPLY) WHAT IS IT$ 57 ELECTR
LAVINIA INTERRUPTS HIM SHARPLY.) 75 ELECTR
FROM INSIDE THE HOUSE COMES THE SOUND OF ORIN'S 78 ELECTR
VOICE CALLING SHARPLY =MOTHER/
(SHARPLY) ORIN/ 87 ELECTR
(AS LAVINIA TURNS TO FACE HER--SHARPLY) 91 ELECTR
(SHARPLY) SSSH/ 99 ELECTR
(SHARPLY COMMANDING) ORIN/ 113 ELECTR
(SHARPLY) DON'T STAND THERE/ 114 ELECTR
(SHARPLY) ORIN/ 122 ELECTR
(AS HE HESITATES--MORE SHARPLY) 122 ELECTR
(SHARPLY) I WANT YOU TO GO FOR DOCTOR BLAKE. 124 ELECTR
BUT KEEPING HIS FACE EXPRESSIONLESS--MORE SHARPLY) 124 ELECTR
(SHARPLY) DON'T BE A DURNED FOOL. 133 ELECTR
(SHARPLY) WHAT'S THIS ALL ABOUT$. 134 ELECTR
(THEN SHARPLY COMMANDING) 138 ELECTR
(THEN SHARPLY) 141 ELECTR
(SHARPLY) ORIN/ 141 ELECTR
(SHARPLY) YOU PROMISED YOU WEREN'T GOING TO TALK 141 ELECTR
ANY MORE MORBID NONSENSE.
LAVINIA WATCHES HIM UNEASILY AND SPEAKS SHARPLY) 144 ELECTR
(PULLS HIMSELF UP SHARPLY--CONFUSEDLY, FORCING A 148 ELECTR
SICKLY SMILE)
(SHARPLY) PLEASE OPEN THE DOOR/ 149 ELECTR
(SHARPLY) YOUR WORKS 150 ELECTR
(SHARPLY) DON'T BE SILLY, PETER/ 158 ELECTR
(SHE GLANCES SHARPLY AT HAZEL--FORCING A JOKING 162 ELECTR
TONE)
(TURNING TO ORIN--SHARPLY) I THOUGHT YOU WERE IN 162 ELECTR
THE STUDY.
(SHARPLY) WHY NOT$ 162 ELECTR
AND GLANCES SHARPLY FROM ONE TO THE OTHER AS SHE 162 ELECTR
COMES INTO THE ROOM.)
THEN HE TURNS BACK AND SAYS SHARPLY) 166 ELECTR
LAVINIA PIVOTS SHARPLY ON HER HEEL AND MARCHES 179 ELECTR
WOODENLY INTO THE HOUSE.
(TURNS TO HIM SHARPLY) YOU GO NOW AND CLOSE THE 179 ELECTR
SHUTTERS AND NAIL THEM TIGHT.

SHARPLY

SHARPLY (CONT'D.)
(SHARPLY) BECAUSE YOU WERE THE BRAINS/ 258 GGBROW
(REPELLED--SHARPLY) ON THE CONTRARY, I HAD TO BEG 281 GGBROW
HER TO BEG YOU TO TAKE IT/
BUT SURELY...(SHARPLY) (SHARPLY) WHERE IS MY 303 GGBROW
HUSBAND, PLEASE$
ON WHICH HE RAPS SHARPLY
(WITH A START, SHARPLY) WHAT MAKES YOU SAY THAT$ 311 GGBROW
(SHARPLY) DON'T YOU KNOW YOUR OWN NAMES 246 HA APE
(SHARPLY) WHAT HAVE THE COPS GOT TO DO WITH US$ 247 HA APE
(SHARPLY) WHAT'S YOUR NOTION OF THE PURPOSE OF 247 HA APE
THE TWWS
(SHARPLY) JUST WHAT WAS IT MADE YOU WANT TO JOIN 248 HA APE
US$
(SHARPLY) WHEN/ WHEN/ (HE GRABS THE BOTTLE) I 582 ICEMAN
DIDN'T SAY, TAKE A BATH/
(STARES AT HIM, PUZZLED AND REPELLED--SHARPLY) 590 ICEMAN
(SHARPLY) I'M GLAD YOU REMEMBER IT. 616 ICEMAN
(SHARPLY RESENTFUL) I--/ (THEN ABRUPTLY HE IS 635 ICEMAN
DRUNKENLY GOOD-NATURED.)
(SHARPLY) WAIT/ (INSISTENTLY--WITH A SNEER) 661 ICEMAN
(SHARPLY) WHAT WAS IT HAPPENED$ 693 ICEMAN
(MOVING AWAY FROM HIM TOWARD RIGHT--SHARPLY) 703 ICEMAN
(ADDRESSING THE CROWD, SHARPLY) 717 ICEMAN
(INTERRUPTING HIM SHARPLY) WAIT/ 530 INZONE
(SHARPLY,) WHAT DO YOU MEAN, TOO LATE$ 53 JOURNE
(SHE TURNS ON HIM--SHARPLY.) 46 JOURNE
(LOOKS AT HIM SHARPLY.) WHEN DID SHE GO UP$ 55 JOURNE
(SHARPLY--LETTING HER RESENTMENT TOWARD HIM COME 60 JOURNE
OUT.)
(HER EYES BECOME FIXED ON THE WHISKEY GLASS ON THE 67 JOURNE
TABLE BESIDE HIM--SHARPLY.)
(SHARPLY.) PLEASE/ STOP STARING/ 68 JOURNE
SHE FEELS THEM AND TURNS SHARPLY WITHOUT MEETING 68 JOURNE
HIS STARE.)
(SHARPLY.) MARY/ 74 JOURNE
(SHARPLY, IN A LOW VOICE.) HERE'S EDMUND. 88 JOURNE
(SHARPLY.) PAPA/ 111 JOURNE
(SHARPLY.) WHY DO YOU MENTION HIM$ 120 JOURNE
(SHARPLY.) WHY DON'T YOU DEAL, IF WE'RE GOING TO 138 JOURNE
PLAY.
(SHARPLY.) NIX ON THE LOUD NOISE/ 155 JOURNE
(STEPPING BETWEEN THEM--SHARPLY) 532 LAZARU
LIGHT-BROWN EYES, SET WIDE APART, THEIR EXPRESSION 4 MANSNS
SHARPLY OBSERVANT AND SHREWD.
(SHE MISSES HIM--THEN PUSHES HIM AWAY DOWN THE
PATH--SHARPLY COMMANDING.) 17 MANSNS
AFTER ANOTHER MOMENT THERE IS A LOUDER KNOCK AND 95 MANSNS
SIMON'S VOICE CALLS SHARPLY..
(SHE GLANCES AT HIM SHARPLY, 96 MANSNS
(A BIT SHARPLY, AS IF HE WERE STILL THE LITTLE 110 MANSNS
BOY.)
(SHARPLY COMMANDING.) NO/ 115 MANSNS
(SHARPLY MATTER-OF-FACT.) I'VE EXPLAINED UNTIL 147 MANSNS
I'M TIRED.
THE GEOMETRICAL FORM OF EACH SHRUB AND ITS BLACK 161 MANSNS
SHADOW ARE SHARPLY DEFINED.
THEN SUDDENLY--SHARPLY AND SUSPICIOUSLY.) 192 MANSNS
(SHARPLY) GIVE AN ACCOUNT OF YOURSELVES/ 350 MARCOM
(SHARPLY WITH PAIN) NO/ 418 MARCOM
EXCEPT ONE THING--(AS SHE STARTS TO SHUT HIM UP-- 31 MISBEG
SHARPLY)
(SHARPLY) JOSIE/ 61 MISBEG
(STARTS--SHARPLY) TRAINS 127 MISBEG
BUT HIS LITTLE PIG'S EYES ARE SHARPLY WIDE AWAKE 157 MISBEG
AND SOBER.
(SHARPLY.) DON'T DO IT, MOTHER. 20 POET
(SHARPLY.) DON'T PUT ON THE BROGUE, NOW. 23 POET
(THEN SHARPLY.) BUT YOU NEEDN'T WASTE YOUR DREAMS 50 POET
WORRYING ABOUT MY AFFAIRS.
(AS GADSBY ONLY LOOKS MORE DUMFOUNDED, HE 121 POET
CONTINUES SHARPLY.)
(FEELING HE HAS NOW THE UPPER HAND--SHARPLY.) 121 POET
(SHARPLY, A COMMANDER ORDERING HIS SOLDIERS.) 123 POET
(SHARPLY.) WHIST, I'M TELLING YOU/ 151 POET
(SHARPLY.) HE'S NOT. 153 POET
(SHARPLY) WHO$ 584 ROPE
IN HER HAND--SHARPLY) 588 ROPE
(SHARPLY) NO, I CAN'T SEE--NOR ANYONE ELSE/ 18 STRANG
(SHARPLY) SHE MUST STAY AWAY UNTIL SHE GETS WELL. 21 STRANG
(THEN CALLS SHARPLY) 28 STRANG
(SHARPLY) AND JUST WHAT DO YOU EXPECT ME TO DO 32 STRANG
ABOUT ALL THIS$
(THEN SHARPLY DRIVING HIS WORDS IN) 35 STRANG
(SHARPLY) WHO SAID SAMMY KNEW$ 60 STRANG
(SHARPLY) UH WHAT$ 77 STRANG
(SHARPLY) SHE'S SHOWING MORE INTELLIGENCE ABOUT 77 STRANG
HER PAIN THAN YOU ARE.
(SHARPLY PROFESSIONAL NONSENSE/ 86 STRANG
(SHARPLY, BEFORE SHE CAN RESTRAIN THE IMPULSE) 94 STRANG
(WITH A START--SHARPLY) WHY$ 94 STRANG
(SHARPLY) CHARLIE/ 101 STRANG
(SHARPLY) DON'T BE STUPID/. 114 STRANG
(GLANCES AT MARSDEN SHARPLY, 121 STRANG
(SHARPLY) WHEN DID YOU GET BACK FROM EUROPE$ 124 STRANG
(SHARPLY) COME ON IN AND SIT DOWN. 124 STRANG
(SHARPLY) NED/ 141 STRANG
(SHARPLY) IF GORDON DOESN'T LOVE YOU 144 STRANG
IN APPEARANCE, HE IS ONCE MORE SHARPLY DEFINED, 158 STRANG
(TAKING HIS HAND AWAY, SHARPLY) 160 STRANG
(SHE CALLS MORE SHARPLY) MADELINE/ 177 STRANG
(STEPS UP SUDDENLY BESIDE THEM--SHARPLY AND 178 STRANG
STERNLY COMMANDING)
(SHARPLY) I THINK YOU'VE SAID ABOUT ENOUGH. 193 STRANG
GORDON/
(SHARPLY) NED/ 195 STRANG
(SHARPLY) DON'T/ 446 WELDED
(SHARPLY) I'M QUITE AWARE OF THAT. 454 WELDED

SHARPLY

SHARPLY (CONT'D.)
(SHARPLY) YOU IMAGINE I'M JEALOUS OF YOUR WORKS 457 WELDED
(SHARPLY) HOWS 486 WELDED
SHARPNESS
BUT BESS HAD A HEART OF GOLD UNDERNEATH HER 604 ICEMAN
SHARPNESS.
SHATISFIED
AW RIGHT, IF YOU'RE SHATISFIED--LET HIM GET AWAY 158 JOURNE
WITH IT.
SHATTER
THE WORDS SHATTER HER MERCIFUL NUMBNESS AND AWAKEN122 ELECTR
HER TO AGONY AGAIN.
AND SHATTER INTO BITS WITH A LOUD REPORT. 432 MARCOM
SHATTERED
HER PULSE SHATTERED FOR THE MOMENT. 30 ELECTR
HE IS SICK, HIS NERVES ARE SHATTERED, HIS EYES ARE681 ICEMAN
APPREHENSIVE, BUT HE TOO
THE QUIET OF THE NIGHT IS SHATTERED BY A BURST OF 71 MISBEG
MELANCHOLY SONG.
IT IS MORE AS IF A SUDDEN SHOCK OR STROKE HAD 152 POET
SHATTERED HIS COORDINATION
(HIS'S BLISS SHATTERED--DEJECTEDLY) 72 STRANG
SHAUGHNESSY
BUT SHAUGHNESSY, THE TENANT ON THAT FARM OF YOURS. 22 JOURNE
BAD LUCK TO SHAUGHNESSY, ANYWAY! 23 JOURNE
AND HARKER'S FOREMAN TOLD HIM HE WAS SURE 23 JOURNE
SHAUGHNESSY HAD BROKEN THE FENCE ON
AND YOU REMEMBER SHAUGHNESSY KEEPS PIGS. 23 JOURNE
THE POOR PIGS, SHAUGHNESSY YELLED, HAD CAUGHT 24 JOURNE
THEIR DEATH OF COLD.
YES, HE'D BE NO MATCH FOR SHAUGHNESSY. 24 JOURNE
SO HARKER CAME IN PERSON TO REBUKE SHAUGHNESSY. 24 JOURNE
SHAUGHNESSY GOT A FEW DRINKS UNDER HIS BELT 24 JOURNE
I TOLD SHAUGHNESSY HE SHOULD HAVE REMINDED HARKER 25 JOURNE
THAT A STANDARD OIL
SHAUGHNESSY ALMOST WEPT BECAUSE HE HADN'T THOUGHT 25 JOURNE
OF THAT ONE, BUT
TO PROMPT SHAUGHNESSY WITH A FEW NASTIER INSULTS. 26 JOURNE
SHAVE
WHY DON'T YOU SHAVES 119 BEYOND
HE WAS WOUNDED IN THE HEAD--A CLOSE SHAVE BUT IT 48 ELECTR
TURNED OUT ONLY A SCRATCH.
YOU'D BE SO HANDSOME IF YOU'D ONLY SHAVE OFF THAT 145 ELECTR
SILLY BEARD
SHABBY COLLEGIATE GENTILITY--AND HE HAS FORGOTTEN 92 STRANG
TO SHAVE.
YOU'D BETTER GO AND SHAVE, HADN'T YOU, IF YOU'RE 95 STRANG
GOING TO TOWNS
(THEN INCONSEQUENTIALLY) HE'S ALWAYS FORGETTING TO 96 STRANG
SHAVE LATELY.
SHAVED
HE HAS NOT SHAVED FOR DAYS AND AROUND HIS FIERCE, 233 HA APE
RESENTFUL EYES--
HE IS SHAVED AND WEARS AN EXPENSIVE, WELL-CUT 674 ICEMAN
SUIT, GOOD SHOES AND CLEAN LINEN.
SHAVEN
WITH HIS PALE, THIN, CLEAN-SHAVEN FACE, MILD BLUE 3 ANNA
EYES AND WHITE HAIR,
THE MATE IS CLEAN-SHAVEN AND MIDDLE-AGED. 484 CARDIF
THEY ARE DRESSED IN STRIPED CONVICT SUITS, THEIR 194 EJONES
HEADS ARE SHAVEN,
HE WEARS A MUSTACHE, BUT HIS HEAVY CLEFT CHIN IS 21 ELECTR
CLEAN-SHAVEN.
(LEWIS LOOKS SPRUCE AND CLEAN-SHAVEN. 674 ICEMAN
SHAVER
YOU WERE A SERIOUS LONELY LITTLE SHAVER. 588 ICEMAN
SHAVIN'
AND ALL DE REST BEEN BRUSHIN' AND SHAVIN' 665 ICEMAN
DEMSELVES WID DE SHAKES--
SHAW
AND THEN THERE WERE TWO BOOKS BY THAT BERNARD 197 AHWILD
SHAW--
ENGELS, KROPOTKIN, MAX STIRNER, PLAYS BY IBSEN, 11 JOURNE
SHAW, STRINDBERG,
SHAW'S
THIS SHAW'S A COMICAL CUSS-- 288 AHWILD
I ALWAYS WAS IN GORDON SHAW'S SHOES/... 168 STRANG
SHAWL
(SHE GOES AND TAKES A SHAWL FROM A HOOK NEAR THE 44 ANNA
DOOR
A HEAVY SHAWL IS WRAPPED ABOUT HER SHOULDER, 144 BEYOND
ABBIE IS SITTING IN A ROCKING CHAIR, A SHAWL 247 DESIRE
WRAPPED ABOUT HER SHOULDERS.
SHE IS HUNCHED UP IN AN OLD SHAWL, HER ARMS 133 POET
CROSSED OVER HER BREAST.
SHOCK
IT WILL ONLY MAKE THE SHOCK WORSE WHEN SHE HAS TO 29 JOURNE
FACE IT.
SHEARS
A BUNCH OF ROSES AND A PAIR OF SHEARS IN HIS 187 STRANG
HANDS.
THE LETS THE SHEARS DROP TO THE GROUND. 188 STRANG
SHEATH
THE MEN PULL OUT SHEATH-KNIVES AND START A RUSH, 544 'ILE
BUT STOP
AND HIS HAND INSTINCTIVELY GOES BACK TO THE SHEATH 45 ANNA
KNIFE ON HIS HIP.
(HIS FACE WORKING WITH RAGE, HIS HAND GOING BACK 49 ANNA
TO THE SHEATH-KNIFE ON HIS HIP)
(HIS HAND ON HIS SHEATH-KNIFE--SNARLING) 461 CARIBE
HIS SHEATH-KNIFE, AND UNTIES THE HANDKERCHIEF OVER932 INZONE
THE GAG.
SHEBEEN
SURE, MY CREDIT OUGHT TO BE GOOD IN THIS SHEBEEN/ 10 POET
BUT A THIEVIN' SHEBEEN KEEPER WHO GOT RICH 11 POET
HAVE YOU MISTAKEN THIS INN FOR THE SORT OF DIRTY 53 POET
SHEBEEN
THAN ANY NIGHT SINCE THIS SHEBEEN STARTED/ 134 POET

SHEBEEN (CONT'D.)
BUT THE BLOOD OF THIEVIN' AULD NED MELODY WHO KEPT138 POET
A DIRTY SHEBEEN
CURSING LIKE A DRUNKEN, FOUL-MOUTHED SON OF A 157 POET
THIEVING SHEBEEN KEEPER
I'LL BE A REAL HUSBAND TO YOU, AND HELP YE RUN 174 POET
THIS SHEBEEN.
SHED
(WITH HEAVY SIGHS) IF HE SHED ANY BLOOD, HE MUST 541 DIFRNT
HAVE GOT A NOSE BLEED.
THAT WENT WAY OVER TO FRANCE TO SHED HIS BLOOD FOR541 DIFRNT
YOU AND ME/
AND HAS THE LIFELESS SHEEN OF A SHED SNAKESKIN. 27 MANSNS
BY THE SIDE OF THE SHED. 400 MARCOM
AS EACH INDIVIDUAL LINK PASSES OUT OF THE SHED IT 400 MARCOM
CARRIES A BALE ON ITS HEAD.
IN THE INTERIORS OF THE SHED AND THE JUNK, 400 MARCOM
AND MOVES BACK INTO THE SHED. 400 MARCOM
(THE HUMAN CHAIN IN BACK FINISHES ITS LABORS AND 405 MARCOM
DISAPPEARS INTO THE SHED.
IT IS THAT I SHED MY BLOOD FOR A COUNTRY THAT 40 POET
THANKED ME WITH DISGRACE.
YE'D NEVER SHED A TEAR THE RIST AV YOUR LOIFE. 498 VOYAGE
SHEDDING
SHEDDING THEIR FLICKERING LIGHT ON THE PORTRAIT OF157 ELECTR
ABE MANNUN ABOVE.
SHEDS
A LANTERN SET UP ON AN IMMENSE COIL OF THICK 25 ANNA
HAWSER SHEDS A DULL,
THE LIGHT FROM THE PINNACLE SHEDS OVER THIS FROM 555 CROSS
ABOVE
HIGH OVERHEAD ONE HANGING ELECTRIC BULB SHEDS JUST222 HA APE
ENOUGH LIGHT THROUGH THE
ONE ELECTRIC BULB FROM THE LOW CEILING OF THE 239 HA APE
NARROW CORRIDOR SHEDS ITS LIGHT
SHEEN
AND HAS THE LIFELESS SHEEN OF A SHED SNAKESKIN. 27 MANSNS
SHEENY
WHAT'S DAT, YOU SHEENY BUM, YUH/ 250 HA APE
SHEEP
I COUNTED TEN MILLION SHEEP IF I COUNTED ONE. 147 BEYOND
(MOCKINGLY) NAGGIN' HIS SHEEP IT SIN/ 227 DESIRE
I AM THY SNORN, BALD, NUDE SHEEP/ 283 GGBROW
HE WAS A BAD FARMER, A POOR BREEDER OF SHEEP, 276 LAZARU
THEY ALL LISTEN, HUDDLED TOGETHER LIKE SHEEP.) 290 LAZARU
I WOULD HEAR IN THE HUSHED AIR THE BLEATING OF 330 LAZARU
SHEEP AND
AND GRASS FOR SHEEP SPRINGS UP ON THE HILLS OF 349 LAZARU
EARTH/
(SCORNFULLY) YOU ARE A PAIR OF SUPERSTITIOUS 349 MARCOM
SHEEP/
LARGEST SHEEP IN THE WORLD. 370 MARCOM
HOW WELL IT IS SET OFF ON THE BOSOM OF A SHEEP/ 419 MARCOM
LIKE A POOR SHEEP WITHOUT PRIDE OR SPIRIT-- 79 MISBEG
BE GOD, YOU OUGHT TO SEE WHAT A STUPID SHEEP THAT 88 MISBEG
MAKES HIM.
AND YOU TRUSTING HIM LIKE A POOR SHEEP, AND NEVER 99 MISBEG
SUSPECTING--
SHEEP'S
I'VE WATCHED YOU MAKING SHEEP'S EYES AT HIM. 9 MISBEG
I DON'T LIKE HIS SILLY SHEEP'S FACE, AND I'VE NO 58 MISBEG
USE FOR JOCKEYS, ANYWAY.
HE'S NO WOLF IN SHEEP'S CLOTHING. 78 MISBEG
AND SAID IN A SICK SHEEP'S VOICE. 82 MISBEG
SHEEPISH
(WILURED LAUGHS AND ARTHUR LOOKS SHEEPISH. 254 AHWILD
(WITH A SHEEPISH SMILE) DARN HIM/ 260 AHWILD
(SID LOOKS SHEEPISH AND FORCES A GRIN. 264 AHWILD
HASTILY, SHEEPISH, LOOKING AROUND HIM 276 AHWILD
SHAMEFACEDLY)
(FINALLY HE GETS UP WITH A SHEEPISH GRIN AND WALKS01 BEYOND
OVER TO ROBERT)
THEN SUDDENLY SETS LAVINIA ON THE STEPS AND STOPS 44 ELECTR
ABRUPTLY, A BIT SHEEPISH.
(WITH A SHEEPISH GRIN) I'LL BET FATHER SAID THAT 300 GGBROW
WHEN HE WAS JUST TALKING.
(LANKY LOOKS SHEEPISH. 658 ICEMAN
THEIR FIGHTING FURY SUDDENLY DIES OUT AND THEY 672 ICEMAN
APPEAR DEFLATED AND SHEEPISH.)
FILLING THEM WITH THE SHEEPISH SHAME OF CHILDREN 306 LAZARU
CAUGHT IN MISCHIEF.
THE CURIOUS, SHEEPISH, BASHFUL SMILE 333 LAZARU
(LOOKING A BIT SHEEPISH AND ANNOYED AT HIMSELF FOR 43 MISBEG
HIS INTEREST--
SHEEPISHLY
(GRINS SHEEPISHLY--ALL BOY NOW) 194 AHWILD
(STARTLED--SHEEPISHLY) AW, DON'T GO DRAGGING THAT272 AHWILD
UP, UNCLE SID.
(WHO HAS REGAINED HIS COMPOSURE--SHEEPISHLY) 29 ANNA
(RELAXING AT LAST--AVOIDING HER EYES--SHEEPISHLY) 50 ANNA
(SHEEPISHLY) AV FORGET. 66 ANNA
(CLINT LAUGHS AND JOHN CHUCKLES SHEEPISHLY IN 503 DAYS
SPITE OF HIMSELF.
EBEN AVOIDS THEIR EYES SHEEPISHLY) 210 DESIRE
THEN SHEEPISHLY BUT MORE DEFIANTLY) 214 DESIRE
(COMES THROUGH THE HEDGE TO HER SHEEPISHLY) 433 DYNAMO
(THEN SHEEPISHLY) I GUESS I'VE NEVER BOTHERED 259 GGBROW
MUCH ABOUT WHAT I'D LIKE TO DO
SITS DOWN SHEEPISHLY--GRUMBLES PATHETICALLY.) 128 JOURNE
(THE CENTURION GRINS SHEEPISHLY. 293 LAZARU
(RELIEVED, GRINS SHEEPISHLY.) 14 MANSNS
(COMING OUT OF HIS FIT--SHEEPISHLY) 360 MARCOM
(SHEEPISHLY) YOU MEAN IT WAS A TERRIBLE INSULT 415 MARCOM
WHEN I CALLED YOU--BY YOUR NAMES
(SHEEPISHLY) NOTHING. 32 STRANG
(SHEEPISHLY HE GLANCES UP AT CEILING, THEN DOWN AT 33 STRANG
FLOOR, TWIDDLING HIS HAT.)
(HE GRINS SHEEPISHLY.) 503 VOYAGE

SHEER

RISING SHEER ON BOTH SIDES THE FOREST WALLS IT IN.192 EJONES
BY SHEER WEIGHT OF NUMBERS HAVE BORNE HIM TO THE 232 HA APE
FLOOR JUST INSIDE THE DOOR.)
WITH A SATISFIED SIGH AT THE SHEER COMFORT OF IT 439 MARCOM
ALL, RESUMES HIS LIFE.)
(FEELING HERSELF BORNE DOWN WEAKLY BY THE SHEER 71 POET
FORCE OF HIS PHYSICAL STRENGTH,
BEYOND THE ROAD, THE EDGE OF A CLIFF WHICH RISES 577 ROPE
SHEER FROM THE SEA BELOW.

SHEET

(FUMBLES IN HIS POCKET AND TAKES OUT A CRUMPLED 213 DESIRE
SHEET OF FOOLSCAP)
THEN HE PUTS THE SHEET DOWN AND STARES UP AT THE 149 ELECTR
PORTRAIT,
OF THE DOPE SHEET ON THE PONIES, I HOPE I'LL KEEP 21 JOURNE
ON WITH IT.)
HER BODY IS WRAPPED IN A WINDING SHEET OF DEEP 434 MARCOM
BLUE.
OR IS ABOUT TO TYPE FOR A SHEET OF PAPER CAN BE 66 STRANG
SEEN IN THE MACHINE.
THEN TEARS THE SHEET OUT OF THE MACHINE WITH AN 67 STRANG
EXCLAMATION OF DISGUST,
PICKING UP A FRESH SHEET OF PAPER, JAMS IT INTO 68 STRANG
THE MACHINE)
(HE STOOPS AND PICKS UP ONE SHEET OF PAPER, 76 STRANG
(BENDING DOWN FOR ANOTHER SHEET, HIS VOICE 77 STRANG
TREMBLING WITH TERROR)
(AS HE BENDS AND CAREFULLY PICKS ANOTHER SHEET 77 STRANG
FROM THE FLOOR

SHEETS

MY MIDDLE NAME IS KELLY AND SHEETS/ 246 AHWILD
AS THE MEN SIGN THE SHEETS OF PAPER FOR THEIR 465 CARIBE
BOTTLES)
IN HINDLAY SHEETS OR NO SECH LUNATIC DOIN'S. 135 ELECTR
A FEW SHEETS OF PAPER 66 STRANG
(EVANS NODS HELPLESSLY AND BEGINS READING THE 74 STRANG
SHEETS.

SHEETS'N'BLANKETS

'N' NEW SHEETS'N'BLANKETS 'N' THINGS. 103 BEYOND

SHEIK

HE WANTED ME TO BE THE SHEIK OF ARABY, 28 HUGHIE

SHELF

I FOUND THEM WHERE HE'D HIDDEN THEM ON THE SHELF 192 AHWILD
IN HIS WARDROBE.
WELL NO MATTER HOW, THERE THEY WERE ON HIS SHELF.196 AHWILD
THEY WERE ON THE SHELF IN YOUR WARDRUBE AND NOW 196 AHWILD
YOU'VE GONE AND HID THEM
I'SE AFTER DE COIN, AN' I LAYS MY JESUS ON DE 185 EJONES
SHELF FOR DE TIME BEIN'.
AND A SHELF ON WHICH ARE BARRELS OF CHEAP WHISKEY 664 ICEMAN
(TO LEWIS--DISGUSTEDLY PUTTING THE KEY ON THE 675 ICEMAN
SHELF IN BACK OF THE BAR)
ROCKY TOSSES THE KEYS ON THE SHELF--DISGUSTEDLY) 682 ICEMAN

SHELL

IF I COULD GET THE OLD CUSS TO SHELL OUT THAT WAY/545 DIFRNT
A GOD-DAMNED HOLLOW SHELL. 158 JOURNE
HIS SHINY WHITE CRANIUM RISES LIKE A POLISHED 337 LAZARU
SHELL ABOVE HIS HALF-MASKED FACE.
LEAVING THINE OUTGROWN SHELL-- 148 MANSNS
RIGHT AT THE MOMENT WHEN HE'S PROBABLY GETTING 163 STRANG
INTO THE SHELL--
YOU MIGHT THINK THERE WAS NO ONE ELSE PULLING THE 168 STRANG
SHELL/...
HOLDING ON WITH ONE HAND, LOOKING DOWN LONGINGLY 182 STRANG
TOWARD HIS SHELL.)
(STILL STANDING ON THE RAIL, STARING AFTER 183 STRANG
GORDON'S SHELL)

SHELLEY

THE GREATEST POET SINCE SHELLEY/ 198 AHWILD

SHELLEY'S

OION CAN RECITE LOTS OF SHELLEY'S POEMS BY HEART. 262 GGHROW

SHELLING

INTO SHELLING OUT THEIR DOUGH ONLY HANDED ME A 709 ICEMAN
LAUGH.

SHELLS

AND EVERYONE STARTS IN PULLING THE CRACKED SHELLS 228 AHWILD
APART.)
UNLESS I EAT THE SHELLS THERE IS A CERTAIN, 231 AHWILD
(WITH GREAT DIGNITY) BUT I PREFER THE SHELLS. 231 AHWILD
HE'S EATING THAT CLAM, SHELLS AND ALL/ 231 AHWILD
ALL FAMOUS EPICURES PREFER THE SHELLS--TO THE LESS231 AHWILD
DELICATE, COARSER MEAT.
(BITINGLY) I SUPPOSE THAT WAS BEFORE EATING 265 AHWILD
LOBSTER SHELLS
THEM, THROWING THE SHELLS ON THE FLOOR WITH AN 544 DIFRNT
IMPUDENT CARELESSNESS)
TO KNOW AS THERE'S A SHIP FULL OF SHELLS LI'BLE TOST7 INZONE
GO OFF IN UNDER YOUR BLOOMIN'

SHELTER

AND FOUND A BRIEF SHELTER IN PYTHAGORAS AND 503 DAYS
NUMEROLOGY.

SHELTERED

THEY DISCOVERED IN A SHELTERED INLET THE ROTTEN, 560 CROSS
MY LIFE GATHERS ROSES, COOLLY CRIMSON, IN 187 STRANG
SHELTERED GARDENS.

SHELVES

THE WALLS ARE LINED ALMOST TO THE CEILING WITH 3 STRANG
GLASSED-IN BOOK-SHELVES.

SHENANDOAH

FROM THE LEFT REAR, A MAN'S VOICE IS HEARD SINGING 5 ELECTR
THE CHANTY «SHENANDOAH»--
«OH, SHENANDOAH, I LONG TO HEAR YOUR A-WAY, MY 6 ELECTR
ROLLING RIVER OH, SHENANDOAH,
« OH, SHENANDOAH, I LOVE YOUR DAUGHTER A-WAY, MY 43 ELECTR
ROLLING RIVER.»
«OH, SHENANDOAH, I LONG TO HEAR YOU A-WAY, MY 43 ELECTR
ROLLING RIVER.

SHENANDOAH (CONT'D.)

THE CHANTY «SHENANDOAH» IS HEARD FROM DOWN THE 43 ELECTR
DRIVE.
HE WALKS UP BY THE LILACS STARTING THE NEXT LINE 43 ELECTR
«OH, SHENANDOAH»--
UH, SHENANDOAH, I CAN'T GET NEAR YOU WAY-AY, 43 ELECTR
BORNE ON THE WIND THE MELANCHOLY REFRAIN OF THE 102 ELECTR
CAPSTAN CHANTY «SHENANDOAH,
«UH, SHENANDOAH, I LONG TO HEAR YOU-- 103 ELECTR
UH, SHENANDOAH, I CAN'T GET NEAR YOU-- 103 ELECTR
I'LL GIVE HIM A TASTE OF HOW «SHENANDOAH» OUGHT I'103 ELECTR
BE SUNG/
« UH, SHENANDOAH, I LOVE YOUR DAUGHTER A-WAY, MY 103 ELECTR
ROLLING RIVER/
SETH'S THIN WRAITH OF A BARITONE IS RAISED IN HIS 123 ELECTR
FAVORITE MOURNFUL «SHENANDOAH,
«UH, SHENANDOAH, I LONG TO HEAR YOU A-WAY, MY 123 ELECTR
ROLLING RIVER/
UH, SHENANDOAH, I CAN'T GET NEAR YOU WAY--AY, I'M 123 ELECTR
BOUND AWAY ACROSS THE WIDE---
«OH, SHENANDOAH, I LONG TO HEAR YOU A-WAY, MY 169 ELECTR
ROLLING RIVER, OH, SHENANDOAH,
«OH, SHENANDOAH, I LOVE YOUR DAUGHTER A-WAY, YOU 169 ELECTR
ROLLING RIVER.»
IN HIS AGED PLAINTIVE WRAITH OF A ONCE-GOOD 169 ELECTR
BARITONE, THE CHANTY «SHENANDOAH».
HE BEGINS SINGING HALF UNDER HIS BREATH HIS 178 ELECTR
MELANCHOLY «SHENANDOAH» CHANTY,
«UH, SHENANDOAH, I CAN'T GET NEAR YOU WAY-AY, I'M 178 ELECTR
BOUND AWAY--»

SHEPHERD

A KIND-HEARTED SHEPHERD OF THE LORD LIKE YOUS 451 DYNAMO

SHERIFF

I'LL GIT THE SHERIFF/ 262 DESIRE
I'LL GIVE YE UP T' THE SHERIFF/ 262 DESIRE
I'M A-GOIN' FUR THE SHERIFF T' COME AN' GIT YE/ 262 DESIRE
(AMAZED) EBEN--GONE FUR THE SHERIFF'S 265 DESIRE
I'LL GIT THE SHERIFF NOW. 265 DESIRE
DID YE TELL THE SHERIFF? 265 DESIRE
IF YE'D LOVED ME, I'D NEVER TOLD NO SHERIFF ON YE 265 DESIRE
--NO MATTER WHAT YE DID.
GIT OFF THIS FARM WHEN THE SHERIFF TAKES HER-- 265 DESIRE
AN' IT'S MY MURDER, TOO, I'LL TELL THE SHERIFF-- 266 DESIRE
(BROKENLY) BUT I TOLD THE SHERIFF. 266 DESIRE
THE SHERIFF WITH TWO MEN COMES UP THE ROAD FROM 268 DESIRE
THE LEFT.
THE SHERIFF KNOCKS ON IT WITH THE BUTT OF HIS 268 DESIRE
PISTOL.)
(THE SHERIFF NODS. 268 DESIRE
IN THE MEANTIME THE SHERIFF AND MEN HAVE COME INTO269 DESIRE
THE ROOM.)
IT'S THE SHERIFF AGAIN. 47 MISBEG
A MORE EMINENT GRAFTER THAN THE SHERIFF-- 47 MISBEG

SHERLOCK

I CONFESS I HAD A SNEAKING SHERLOCK HOLMES DESIRE 505 DAYS
TO HAVE A GOOD LOOK AT YOU
YOU'RE NOT SO GOOD WHEN YOU START PLAYING SHERLOCK638 ICEMAN
HOLMES.
YOU'RE A HELL OF A SHERLOCK HOLMES, AIN'T YUHS 528 INZONE

SHERRY

(TURNS INDIGNANTLY) SHERRY FLIP/ 670 ICEMAN
YEAH, I TOLD HER, WHAT WOULD WE USE FOR SHERRY, 670 ICEMAN
CORA WANTS A SHERRY FLIP. FOR HER NOIVES. 670 ICEMAN
AND YUH GOTTA BLOW ME TO A SHERRY FLIP--OR FOUR OM682 ICEMAN
FIVE, IF I WAIT TEMP
IF HAS HE PULLING SHERRY FLIPS ON ME WOKE ME UP. 697 ICEMAN

SHESHED

WITH BUCKET SCOOPS THAT DREDGE, LOAD COAL, SAND, 400 MARCOM
ETC. BY THE SIDE OF SHESHED,

SHET

WE HARRY 'BOLISHES SHET GATES, AN' OPEN GATES, AN'221 DESIRE
ALL GATES, BY THUNDER/
CAN'T KEEP THEIR MOUTHS SHET OR MIND THEIR OWN 500 DIFRNT
BUSINESS.
(VIOLENTLY) I WANT YOU TO SHET UP/ 505 DIFRNT
(ANGRILY) YOU SHET UP, ALF ROGERS/ 506 DIFRNT
(GOOD-NATUREDLY) SHET UP YOUR FOOLIN', JACK. 507 DIFRNT
THAT'S WHY I KEPT MY MOUTH SHET. 508 DIFRNT
SHET UP, CAN'T YUHS 9 ELECTR
YOU'LL FIND FOLKS'LL SHET UP AND NOT TAKE IT 135 ELECTR
SERIOUS NO MORE.
(THEN (HKITABLY) FUR GAWD'S SAKE, SHET THAT DOOR/504 VOYAGE

SHI

DE MOON, SHE SHI-I-I-INE. 6 ANNA
«DE MOON, SHE SHI-I-I-INE. 12 ANNA

SHIELD

HE THINKS HE'S FOUND A GOOD SHIELD TO COVER UP HIS541 DIFRNT
NATURAL-BORN LAZINESS--
ON HIS RIGHT A MONGOL WARRIOR IN FULL ARMOR WITH 377 MARCOM
SHIELD AND SPEAR.

SHIELDING

FOR YOU'LL BE SHIELDING ME UNLAWFULLY BY KEEPING 441 DYNAMO
SILENCE.
AND SHIELDING HIS FACE WITH ONE HAND FROM THE 487 DYNAMO
SIGHT OF HER.

SHIELDS

COVER ME WITH YOUR SHIELDS/ 338 LAZARU
THEY HOLD THEIR SHIELDS SO THAT THEY FORM A WALL 338 LAZARU
AROUND HIM AND HALF OVER HIM.
TO WHERE TIBERIUS CROUCHES BEHIND THE SHIELDS OF 339 LAZARU
THE GUARDS.

SHIFT

AND WE'LL MAKE SHORT SHIFT OF IT. 543 'ILE
EXCEPT IT WAS A HARD SHIFT TO GET THE BOATS OVER 481 CARDIF
THE SIDE
(HER EYES SHIFT FROM HIS FACE AND SHE SEES THE BOX101 ELECTR
OF POISON.

SHIFT 1412

SHIFT (CONT'D.)
HE KNOWS THERE ARE SEVERAL HOURS TO GO BEFORE HIS 7 HUGHIE SHIFT IS OVER.
HIS EXPRESSION IS DISPIRITED, HIS EYES SHIFT 67 STRANG ABOUT.
IT'S NO HARD SHIFT TO TAKE THE REMAINS HOME. 904 VOYAGE

SHIFTING
(MORE SHAKEN, HIS EYES SHIFTING ABOUT FURTIVELY) 204 AHWILD
HE SIDLES INTO THE ROOM GUILTILY, HIS EYES 256 AHWILD SHIFTING ABOUT.
THERE IS A SHIFTING DEFIANCE AND INGRATIATION IN 585 ICEMAN HIS LIGHT-BLUE EYES AND AN
(EMBARRASSED, HIS EYES SHIFTING AWAY) 623 ICEMAN
HIS FACE IS PASTY, HIS MOUTH WEAK, HIS EYES 493 VOYAGE SHIFTING AND CRUEL.

SHIFTLESS
BUT YOU'SE TOO SHIFTLESS TO TAKE DE TROUBLE. 179 EJONES

SHIFTS
THIS FACE LIGHTS UP A BIT BUT HIS GAZE SHIFTS TO 257 AHWILD LILY WITH A MUTE APPEAL.
INSTANTLY HIS BODY SHIFTS TO A FIGHTING TENSENESS) 36 ELECTR
(THE NIGHT CLERK SHIFTS HIS POSITION SO HE CAN 13 HUGHIE LEAN MORE ON THE DESK.
HIM AROUND--THEN SHIFTS HIS GRIP TO THE LAPEL OF 61 MISBEG HAYDEN'S COAT.)
BUT AT ONCE SHE IS REASSURED AS HE SHIFTS HIS 69 POET GAZE.
AND WHICH HE BITES AND SHIFTS ABOUT AND PULLS IN 66 STRANG

SHIFTY
WITH A HEAVY, STUPID FACE AND SHIFTY, CUNNING 123 BEYOND EYES.
AND HIS SHIFTY ONCE-OVER GLANCES NEVER MISS THE 9 HUGHIE PRICE TAGS HE DETECTS ON
GLARE OUT WITH A SHIFTY FEVERISH SUSPICION AT 299 LAZARU EVERYONE.
HIS BROWN EYES ARE LARGE BUT SHIFTY AND 587 RUPE ACQUISITIVE.
(HIS SHIFTY EYES PEER ABOUT THE ROOM SEARCHINGLY. 495 VOYAGE

SHILLIN'
'TWAS HERE I WAS STRIPPED AV ME LAST SHILLIN' 496 VOYAGE WHIN I WAS ASLAPE.

SHILLIN'S
THREE SHILLIN'S A BOTTLE. 462 CARIBE
(FIRMLY) FOUR SHILLIN'S. 465 CARIBE
THREE SHILLIN'S IS THE PRICE. 465 CARIBE
FOUR SHILLIN'S UT IS. 465 CARIBE

SHILLING
TO A SHILLING SHE'LL SEE THE DAY WHEN SHE'LL WEAR 173 POET FINE SILKS

SHIMMERING
SHIMMERING IN A LUMINOUS MIST ON THE WHITE PORTICO 5 ELECTR AND THE GRAY STONE WALL
IT WAS MADE OF SUFT, SHIMMERING SATIN, TRIMMED 115 JOURNE WITH WONDERFUL OLD DUCHESSE LACE.
THEY LIE THERE IN A GLITTERING PILE, SHIMMERING IN002 ROPE THE FAINT SUNSET GLOW--

SHIMMERS
THE SAND OF THE BEACH SHIMMERS PALELY. 275 AHWILD
SOFT GOLDEN SUNLIGHT SHIMMERS IN A LUMINOUS MIST 169 ELECTR ON THE GREEK TEMPLE PORTICO.

SHIN
KICKS AGAIN AT THE BUCKET BUT ONLY SUCCEEDS IN 526 INZONE HITTING COCKY ON THE SHIN.
(COCKY GRUMBLES AND RETIRES TO A BENCH, NURSING 526 INZONE HIS SORE SHIN.)

SHINDY
BE THE ROCK AV CASHEL, I'VE NIVER ENGAGED IN A 154 POET LIVELIER SHINDY!
AND HELP COUSIN JAMIE CELEBRATE CUR WONDERFUL 175 POET SHINDY WID THE PULICE.

SHINE
AND THE FACE OF THE CHRIST SHINE WITH THIS 586 DAYS RADIANCE.)
THAT BROWN GAL TOOK AN AWFUL SHINE TO CALEB 503 DIFRNT
(HIS EYES SHINE WITH A NEW ELATION) 467 DYNAMO
DON'T SHE SHINE PRETTYS 179 EJONES
DAT WHY I MAKE HAY WHEN DE SUN SHINE. 180 EJONES
REGAINED THE SELF-CONFIDENT SPIRIT OF ITS YOUTH, 303 GOBRTH HER EYES SHINE WITH HAPPINESS.)
THEIR FACES AND BODIES SHINE FROM SOAP-AND-WATER 226 HA APE SCOURING BUT AROUND THEIR
AND SHINES, SWANSUN. 514 INZONE
HAVY IS PALER THAN BEFORE AND HER EYES SHINE WITH 97 JOURNE UNNATURAL BRILLIANCE.
THE WINDOWS SHINE BRILLIANTLY WITH THE FLICKERING 281 LAZARU LIGHT OF MANY CANDLES WHICH
HIS EYES SHINE 317 LAZARU
(WITH AWE) HIS FLESH MELTS IN THE FIRE BUT HIS 364 LAZARU EYES SHINE WITH PEACE/
THAT COLLEGE HCROES RARELY SHINE BRILLIANTLY IN 9 STRANG AFTER LIFE.
ARISE AND SHINE, YE DRUNKEN SWINE/ 500 VOYAGE

SHINED
AND BLACK SHOES NEWLY SHINED. 45 ANNA
I MUST HAVE MY SHOES SOLED AND HEELED AND SHINED 603 ICEMAN FIRST THING TOMORROW MORNING.
JIMMY'S CLOTHES ARE PRESSED, HIS SHOES SHINED, HIS083 ICEMAN WHITE LINEN IMMACULATE.

SHINELESS
HE WEARS A THREADBARE, READY-MADE, GREY SACK SUIT 13 JOURNE AND SHINELESS BLACK SHOES.

SHINES
BEST WAIT FOR A DAY WHEN THE SUN SHINES. 940 'ILE
(DESPERATELY) BUT THE SUN NEVER SHINES IN THIS 940 'ILE TERRIBLE PLACE.
MOONLIGHT SHINES THROUGH THE SCREEN DOOR AT NIGHT.288 AHWILD NEAR.

SHINES (CONT'D.)
IN THE ENSUING DARKNESS THE FAINT MOONLIGHT SHINES298 AHWILD FULL
HIS FACE SHINES FROM SOAP AND WATER. 228 DESIRE
A BRAND NEW PIANO SHINES RESPLENDENTLY IN THE FAR 519 DIFRNT RIGHT CORNER BY THE DOOR.
IT IS SHORTLY BEFORE SUNSET AND THE SOFT LIGHT OF 5 ELECTR THE DECLINING SUN SHINES
THE SUIT IS OLD AND SHINES AT THE ELBOWS AS IF IT 8 HUGHIE HAD BEEN WAXED AND POLISHED.
(THE LIGHT IN THE HALL IS TURNED ON AND SHINES 108 JOURNE THROUGH THE FRONT PARLOR TO FALL
SO THAT NOW NO LIGHT SHINES THROUGH THE FRONT 125 JOURNE PARLOR.
PLACED BESIDE THE HEAD OF MIRIAM, SHINES DOWN UPON350 LAZARU THE WHITE MASK OF HER FACE.
AND SHINES CLEARLY ON THE SUMMER-HOUSE DOOR. 162 MANSNS
(THE MOON AGAIN COMES FROM BEHIND A CLOUD AND 163 MANSNS SHINES ON THE SUMMER-HOUSE.
THE SUN SHINES AGAIN. 417 MARCOM
SUNLIGHT SHINES IN THROUGH THE WINDOWS AT REAR. 8 POET
YET IN SPITE OF HER SLOVENLY APPEARANCE THERE IS A 20 POET SPIRIT WHICH SHINES THROUGH

SHINGLED
AN OLD BOX-LIKE, CLAPBOARDED AFFAIR, WITH A 1 MISBEG SHINGLED ROOF AND BRICK CHIMNEY,

SHINGLES
AND WHEN IT RAINS THEIR TEARS TRICKLE DOWN 202 DESIRE MONOTONOUSLY AND ROT ON THE SHINGLES.
MADE OF LOGS WITH A ROOF OF WARPED, HAND-HEWN 1 MANSNS SHINGLES.

SHININ'
LET THE OLD MAN SEE YE UP FUR'ARD MONKEY-SHININ' 536 'ILE WITH THE HANDS
MY FUST VIGE AS SKIPPER, YOU DON'T S'POSE I HAD 497 DIFRNT TIME FOR NO MONKEY-SHININ',

SHINING
HIS FACE IS A PASTY PALLOR, SHINING WITH 260 AHWILD
(HIS EYES SHINING) GEE, MID, DO YOU KNOW WHAT SHE273 AHWILD SAYS--
HE WALKS LIKE ONE IN A TRANCE, HIS EYES SHINING 292 AHWILD WITH A DREAMY HAPPINESS.
(SCORNFULLY) NO, AND I WASN'T HEARING HER SAY THE 53 ANNA SUN IS SHINING EITHER.
(SLOWLY--HIS EYES SHINING) AND THEN SHE CRIED AND100 BEYOND SAID IT WAS I
(SHE LAUGHS WITH HYSTERICAL MOCKERY, HER EYES 550 DAYS SHINING FEVERISHLY.)
ONLY A SEA OF THEIR MASKS CAN BE SEEN, THEIR EYES 320 LAZARU SHINING EXULTANTLY.
GRASS AND DISTANTLY FROM THE SHINING SEA. 330 LAZARU
(AS HE SUDDENLY SEES THE SHINING FIGURE OF LAZARUS338 LAZARU
(HER EYES SHINING.) I'M STILL PROUD AND WILL BE 62 POET
TO THE DAY I DIE/
EACH BUTTON IS SHINING AND THE CLOTH IS SPOTLESS. 88 POET
(MOVED BY THE SHINING HAPPINESS IN SARA'S FACE.) 144 POET
SHE LOOKS UP AT HIM WITH SHINING EYES (AND CLAPS 589 ROPE HER HANDS.)
(HE GOES TO HER AND LOOKS UP INTO HER FACE WITH 156 STRANG SHINING EYES)
(HER EYES SHINING WITH EXCITED PLEASURE) 445 WELDED
YOU WERE A SHINING EXCEPTION, IT APPEARS. 456 WELDED

SHINY
BLOND HAIR WETTED AND PLASTERED DOWN IN A PART, 186 AHWILD AND A SHINY, GOOD-NATURED FACE.
HE IS DRESSED WITH A PRIM NEATNESS IN SHINY OLD 201 AHWILD BLACK CLOTHES.)
HIS SHINY FAT FACE IS ONE BROAD, BLURRED, PUCKISH 223 AHWILD NAUGHTY-BOY GRIN.
WITH THE MARE ALL BRESHED AN' SHINY, 209 DESIRE
HE HAS EVIDENTLY BEEN WASHING UP, FOR HIS FACE IS 501 DIFRNT RED AND SHINY.
HIS SHINY WRINKLED FACE IS OBLONG WITH A SQUARE 129 ELECTR WHITE CHIN WHISKER.
AND WIND OVER THE MILES OF SHINY GREEN OCEAN LIKE 214 HA APE STRONG DRINK TO YOUR LUNGS.
HIS SHINY WHITE CRANIUM RISES LIKE A POLISHED 337 LAZARU SHELL ABOVE HIS HALF-MASKED FACE.
WATCHING HIM KIDS PAST IN HIS BIG SHINY AUTOMOBILE 51 MISBEG WITH HIS SNOOT IN THE AIR.
YOU'RE NOT IN YOUR SHINY AUTOMOBILE NOW 63 MISBEG
SURROUNDED BY A SHINY BALD SCALP FRINGED WITH 578 ROPE SCANTY WISPS OF WHITE HAIR.
AND FERMOREER MUNNIN', KID, I'LL GIVE YUH A WHOLE 601 ROPE HANDFUL OF THEM SHINY,

SHIP
THERE IS NO ROLLING OF THE SHIP, 535 'ILE
UN THE LEFT (THE STERN OF THE SHIP) 535 'ILE
CAPTAIN KEENEY'S CABIN ON BOARD THE STEAM WHALING 535 'ILE SHIP *ATLANTIC QUEEN*--
AND DAMN THIS STINKIN' WHALIN' SHIP OF HIS, AND 536 'ILE
DAMN ME FOR A FOOL
ON A STINKIN' WHALIN' SHIP TO THE ARCTIC SEAS TO 537 'ILE BE LOCKED IN BY THE ROTTEN ICE
TO EVER SHIP ON IT? 537 'ILE
'TIS A GOD'S WONDER WE'RE NOT A SHIP FULL OF 538 'ILE CRAZED PEOPLE--
I AIN'T NEVER COME BACK HOME IN ALL MY DAYS 542 'ILE WITHOUT A FULL SHIP.
WE'RE AT SEA NOW, AND I'M THE LAW ON THIS SHIP. 544 'ILE
YOU'VE FOUND OUT IT AIN'T SAFE TO MUTINY ON THIS 544 'ILE SHIP, AIN'T YOUS
AND THIS TERRIBLE SHIP, AND THIS PRISON OF A ROOM,545 'ILE AND THE ICE ALL AROUND.
IF I DON'T GET AWAY FROM HERE, OUT OF THIS 546 'ILE TERRIBLE SHIP, I'LL GO MAD!
I ALWAYS COME BACK--WITH A FULL SHIP--AND--IF 547 'ILE DON'T SEEM RIGHT NOT TO--SOMEHOW.

SHIP

SHIP (CONT'D.)
BECAUSE YOU DIDN'T COME BACK WITH A FULL SHIP. 547 'ILE
= MY YOSEPHINE, COME BOARD DE SHIP. 6 ANNA
=MY YOSEPHINE, COME BOARD DE SHIP== 12 ANNA
=MY YOSEPHINE, COME BOARD DE SHIP== 13 ANNA
GO SOUTH AMERICA, GO AUSTRALIA, GO ABOARD SHIP 21 ANNA
SAIL FOR SVEDEN.
MY FA'DER DIE ON BOARD SHIP IN INDIAN OCEAN. 27 ANNA
YOU BELONG ON A REAL SHIP, SAILING ALL OVER THE 27 ANNA
WORLD.
GAT DRUNK, GAT ROBBED, SHIP AVAY AGAIN ON ODER 28 ANNA
VOYAGE.
AND DIVIL A SIGHT THERE WAS OF SHIP OR MEN ON TOP 36 ANNA
OF THE SEA.
HE PRETENDS TO BE ENGAGED IN SETTING THINGS SHIP- 41 ANNA
SHAPE.
ENGINES OF SOME SHIP UNLOADING NEARBY. 41 ANNA
MY YOSEPHINE, COME BOARD DE SHIP. 41 ANNA
YOU SHIP AVAY AGAIN, LEAVE ANNA ALONE. 46 ANNA
YOU GAT FALLAS ON DECK DON'T KNOW SHIP FROM 49 ANNA
MUDSCOW.
(DULLY) WHERE'S THIS SHIP GOING TO$ 67 ANNA
(IT SUDDENLY COMES TO HER THAT THIS IS THE SAME 72 ANNA
SHIP HER FATHER IS SAILING ON)
WHY AIN'T YOU GOT THAT SHIP WAS GOING TO TAKE YOU 72 ANNA
TO THE OTHER SIDE OF THE EARTH
AND I HAVING IT TIED ROUND MY NECK WHEN MY LAST 75 ANNA
SHIP SUNK,
AND THAT'S A LONG VOYAGE ON A SAILING SHIP. 83 BEYOND
IF I HAD NO OTHER EXCUSE FOR GOING ON UNCLE DICK'S 84 BEYOND
SHIP BUT JUST MY HEALTH,
I KNOW YOU'RE GOING TO LEARN NAVIGATION, AND ALL 85 BEYOND
ABOUT A SHIP.
ABOUT SPELLS AND THINGS WHEN YOU'RE ON THE SHIP. 86 BEYOND
(PROTESTINGLY) AND THE =SUNDA= AIN'T AN OLD 96 BEYOND
SHIP--LEASTWAYS, NOT VERY OLD--
THEY'RE LIABLE AS NOT TO SUSPICION IT WAS A WOMAN 103 BEYOND
I'D PLANNED TO SHIP ALONG,
AND IF UNCLE DICK WON'T TAKE ME ON HIS SHIP, I'LL 107 BEYOND
FIND ANOTHER.
WELL, THERE WAS SO MUCH DIRTY WORK GETTING THINGS 131 BEYOND
SHIP-SHAPE AGAIN I MUST HAVE
I CAN GET A BERTH AS SECOND OFFICER, AND I'LL JUMP!132 BEYOND
THE SHIP WHEN I GET THERE.
I'LL NEVER SET FOOT ON A SHIP AGAIN IF I CAN HELP 132 BEYOND
IT--
JUST AS SOON AS I'VE SEEN YOU FOLKS A WHILE AND 132 BEYOND
CAN GET A SHIP.
I'LL HAVE TO GO DOWN AND TEND TO THE SHIP WHEN HE 135 BEYOND
COMES.
I'LL HAVE TO WAIT FOR A SHIP SAILING THERE FOR 137 BEYOND
QUITE A WHILE, LIKELY.
THERE MAY NOT BE ANOTHER SHIP FOR BUENOS AIRES 141 BEYOND
WITH A VACANCY IN MONTHS.
I DIDN'T KNOW IF YOU'D WANT TO SHIP AWAY AGEN SO 141 BEYOND
QUICK AN' I TOLD HIM SO.
BUT I RUN ACROSS A BIT O' NEWS DOWN TO THE 141 BEYOND
SEAMEN'S HOME MADE ME 'BOUT SHIP AND
OF COURSE I'LL STAY FOR DINNER IF I MISSED EVERY 142 BEYOND
DAMNED SHIP IN THE WORLD.
(INDIGNANTLY) IT'S A STARVATION SHIP. 480 CARDIF
AND THE SHIP HEELED OVER TILL WE WAS ALL IN A HEAP481 CARDIF
ON WAN SIDE.
JUST ONE SHIP AFTER ANOTHER, HARD WORK, SMALL PAY,486 CARDIF
AND BUM GRUB.
'WAY IN THE MIDDLE OF THE LAND WHERE YUH'D NEVER 486 CARDIF
SMELL THE SEA OR SEE A SHIP.
AND ALL YOUR MONEY GONE, AND THEN SHIP AWAY AGAIN.486 CARDIF
IT'S HARD TO SHIP ON THIS VOYAGE I'M GOIN' ON-- 489 CARDIF
ALONE/
WHAT MIGHT BE CALLED THE PETTY OFFICERS OF THE 455 CARIBE
SHIP.
THE SEA IS CALM AND THE SHIP MOTIONLESS. 455 CARIBE
OR HE WUDN'T BUY A THING OFF AV HER FOR THE SHIP. 458 CARIBE
THINKS I WANTS THE OLE CAPTAIN TO PUT ME OFF THE 464 CARIBE
SHIP, DO YOU$
IN THE SILENCE THE MOURNFUL CHANT FROM THE SHORE 472 CARIBE
CREEPS SLOWLY OUT TO THE SHIP.)
THERE IS ABSOLUTE SILENCE ON THE SHIP FOR A FEW 473 CARIBE
MOMENTS.
THAT'LL TEACH YOU TO SMUGGLE RUM ON A SHIP AND 473 CARIBE
START A RIOT.
HIS SHIP--THE MARY ALLEN--NAMED FOR MY DEAD 557 CROSS
MOTHER.
THE SHIP, OF COURSE. 557 CROSS
THEN HE HAS THE ROOF TOO RIGGED UP LIKE A SHIP$ 557 CROSS
WHAT SHIP$ 557 CROSS
BUT--I DON'T UNDERSTAND--IS THE SHIP LONG 558 CROSS
OVERDUE--OR WHAT$
HIS SHIP HAD BEEN WRECKED IN THE INDIAN OCEAN. 559 CROSS
THE SHIP HE'S STILL LOOKING FOR--THAT WAS LOST 561 CROSS
THREE YEARS AGO$
THE MORTGAGE--THE PRICE OF THAT SHIP--IS TO BE 562 CROSS
FORECLOSED.
THAT SHIP-- 562 CROSS
HE'LL FORGET HIS MAD IDEA OF WAITING FOR A LOST 563 CROSS
SHIP
HE TOOK ME FROM SCHOOL AND FORCED ME ON HIS SHIP, 564 CROSS
DIDN'T HE$
NOT KNOW MY OWN SHIP/ 569 CROSS
NOT A SHIP. 570 CROSS
THERE'S NOT A SHIP IN THE HARBOR. 570 CROSS
IN THE MIDDLE OF THE REAR WALL IS FASTENED A BIG 206 DESIRE
ADVERTISING POSTER WITH A SHIP
=I JUMPED ABOARD THE LIZA SHIP, AND TRAVELED ON 224 DESIRE
THE SEA.
WHY, I WAS THAT ANXIOUS TO BRING BACK YOUR PA'S 497 DIFRNT
SHIP WITH A FINE VIGE THAT'D

SHIP (CONT'D.)
AND WHEN SHE SAW THE SHIP WAS GITTIN' READY TO 503 DIFRNT
SAIL SHE RAISED RUCTIONS,
GIT ABOARD THE SHIP WHERE HE WAS WAITIN' FOR HER 503 DIFRNT
ALONE.
I'D SHIP HER OFF AS FEMALE MISSIONARY TO THE 514 DIFRNT
DAMNED YELLOW CHINKS.
AND I TELLS YOU, AFTER A YEAR OR MORE ABOARD SHIP,514 DIFRNT
THE BLOODY SHIP IS SINKIN' AN' THE BLEEDIN' RATS 182 EJONES
'AS SLUNG THEIR 'OOKS.
UNISON AS IF THEY WERE LAXLY LETTING THEMSELVES 199 EJONES
FOLLOW THE LONG ROLL OF A SHIP
LOOKS MORE LIKE A GAMBLER OR A POET THAN A SHIP 15 ELECTR
CAPTAIN.
HE SAID HE WAS COMING UP HERE TODAY TO TAKE OVER 17 ELECTR
HIS SHIP
THERE IS LITTLE OF THE OBVIOUS SHIP CAPTAIN ABOUT 21 ELECTR
HIM, EXCEPT HIS BIG,
SHE'S AS BEAUTIFUL A SHIP AS YOU'RE A WOMAN. 39 ELECTR
YOU COULD BUY YOUR OWN SHIP AND BE YOUR OWN 39 ELECTR
MASTER/
AS FOR MY SAILING ON YOUR SHIP, YOU'LL FIND YOU 39 ELECTR
WON'T HAVE A SHIP/
YOU CAN MAKE UP SOME STORY ABOUT A SICK DOG ON 40 ELECTR
YOUR SHIP.
AND LET HIM TAKE AWAY YOUR SHIP$ 41 ELECTR
REMEMBER YOUR DREAM OF YOUR OWN SHIP/ 42 ELECTR
TO ACCUSE ME OF FLIRTING WITH A STUPID SHIP 51 ELECTR
CAPTAIN$
A STUPID SHIP CAPTAIN I HAPPENED TO MEET AT YOUR 87 ELECTR
GRANDFATHER'S
AND USE YOUR FATHER WHEN HE CAME HOME TO GET HIM A 87 ELECTR
BETTER SHIP$
THE SHIP IS UNLOADED AND HER BLACK SIDE RISES NINE102 ELECTR
OR TEN FEET
(THE STERN SECTION OF A CLIPPER SHIP MOORED 102 ELECTR
ALONGSIDE A WHARF IN EAST BOSTON.
ITS LIGHT ACCENTUATING THE BLACK OUTLINES OF THE 102 ELECTR
SHIP.
DRIFTS OVER THE WATER FROM A SHIP THAT IS WEIGHING102 ELECTR
ANCHOR IN THE HARBOR.
I USED TO SHIP ON THE MANNON PACKETS 105 ELECTR
(THEN FLATTERINGLY) IT'S A FINE SHIP YOU'VE GOT 106 ELECTR
THERE, SIR.
I WASN'T SURE WHICH SHIP/ 107 ELECTR
MOVES STEALTHILY OUT FROM THE DARKNESS BETWEEN THE107 ELECTR
SHIP AND THE WAREHOUSE, LEFT.
(THE CHANTYMAN GOES UNSTEADILY OFF LEFT, BETWEEN 107 ELECTR
THE WAREHOUSE AND THE SHIP.
I'VE A FOREBODING I'LL NEVER TAKE THIS SHIP TO 107 ELECTR
SEA.
ON THE SHIP IN THE HARBOR COMES MOURNFULLY OVER 109 ELECTR
THE WATER.
A SECTION OF THE SHIP HAS BEEN REMOVED TO REVEAL 109 ELECTR
THE INTERIOR OF THE CABIN.
CAN'T WE GO ON ANOTHER SHIP--AS PASSENGERS--TO THE111 ELECTR
EAST--
I KNOW HOW IT HURTS TO GIVE UP YOUR SHIP. 111 ELECTR
TRY NOT TO REGRET YOUR SHIP TOO MUCH, ADAM/ 112 ELECTR
WE TOOK ADVANTAGE OF OUR BEING ON A MANNON SHIP TO144 ELECTR
THINGS WERE ALWAYS REMINDING ME OF YOU--THE SHIP 146 ELECTR
AND THE SEA--
HE WAS AN OFFICER OF THE SHIP TO ME, AND NOTHING 153 ELECTR
MORE/
THE EFFECT SOUGHT AFTER IS A CRAMPED SPACE IN THE 207 HA APE
BOWELS OF A SHIP.
NIX ON DAT OLD SAILING SHIP STUFF/ 210 HA APE
'E SAYS THIS 'ERE STINKIN' SHIP IS OUR 'OME. 211 HA APE
THEY DRAGGED US DOWN 'TIL WE'RE ONY WAGE SLAVES 212 HA APE
IN THE BOWELS OF A BLOODY SHIP.
WE MAKE THE SHIP TO GO, YOU'RE SAYINGS 213 HA APE
TILL YOU'D BELIEVE 'TWAS NO REAL SHIP AT ALL YOU 214 HA APE
WAS ON BUT A GHOST SHIP LIKE
'TWAS THEM DAYS A SHIP WAS PART OF THE SEA, AND A 214 HA APE
MAN WAS PART OF A SHIP,
IN THE HEART OF THE SHIP. 217 HA APE
HOW THE OTHER HALF LIVES AND WORKS ON A SHIP. 220 HA APE
'E'S GOT ENUF BLOODY GOLD TO SINK THIS BLEEDIN' 228 HA APE
SHIP/
TAKE SOME OF THOSE PAMPHLETS WITH YOU TO 247 HA APE
DISTRIBUTE ABOARD SHIP.
=SHIP ME SOMEWHERE EAST OF SUE2=== 599 ICEMAN
NEXT TIME I SHIP ON WINDJAMMER BOSTON TO RIVER 515 INZONE
PLATE,
THERE'S MANY A GOOD SHIP BLOWN UP AND AT THE 515 INZONE
BOTTOM OF THE SEA,
WOT'S 'E DOIN' ON A SHIP, I ARSKS YER$ 517 INZONE
TO KNOW AS THERE'S A SHIP FULL OF SHELLS LI'BLE TO517 INZONE
GO UP IN UNDER YOUR BLOOMIN'
HE'S BEEN ON SHIP NEAR TWO YEAR, AIN'T HE$ 520 INZONE
THE MAN THAT OPENED IT MEANT NO GOOD TO THIS SHIP,521 INZONE
WHEREVER HE WAS.
AN' IF HE KIN SIGNAL TO 'EM AN' THEY BLOWS US UP 522 INZONE
IT'S ONE SHIP LESS AIN'T IT$
OR A PIECE OF WRECKAGE FROM SOME SHIP THEY'VE SENT523 INZONE
TO DAVY JUNKS.
D'YOU WANT TO WAKE THE WHOLE SHIP$ 526 INZONE
HULLO/ HERE'S WAN ADDRESSED TO THIS SHIP = S. S. 531 INZONE
GLENCAIRN. UT SAYS=
ONLY A LAZY GROUND SWELL AND A SLOW DROWSY ROLL OF153 JOURNE
THE SHIP.
BECAME MOONLIGHT AND THE SHIP AND THE HIGH DIM- 153 JOURNE
STARRED SKY/
HAD ENOUGH TO SINK A SHIP, BUT CAN'T SINK. 156 JOURNE
(EAGERLY) BUT WE SHALL HAVE DANCERS ON THE SHIP 398 MARCOM
(FAMILIARLY) AND THE TROUBLE WITH ANY SHIP, FOR A 398 MARCOM
MAN OF ACTION,
(ORCAMILY) I DESIRE A CAPTAIN OF MY SHIP 401 MARCOM

SHIP

SHIP (CONT'D.)
(AS PEOPLE BEGIN TO COME IN AND STARE AT THE POOP 403 MARCOM OF THE SHIP)
HE SUDDENLY BAWLS TO SOMEONE IN THE SHIP) 403 MARCOM
THE SHIP CAN BE HEARD MAKING OFF.) 420 MARCOM
AND THEIR SHIP AWAY TO SEA AGEN OR GO BUMMIN' AGEN.599 ROPE
WOT SHIP IS THATS 495 VOYAGE
ANT NO ONE'LL DARE SHIP ON 'ER. 495 VOYAGE
(GOT FOR THIS SHIP, OLE BUCK. 495 VOYAGE
(WITH AFFECTED HEARTINESS) SHIP AHOY, MATES/ 496 VOYAGE
YUST WORK, WORK, WORK ON SHIP. 502 VOYAGE
AN' YOU'LL GIT ANOTHER SHIP UP THERE ARTER YOU'VE 502 VOYAGE 'AD A VACATIONS
I DON'T NEVER SHIP O4 SEA NO MORE. 502 VOYAGE
BUT I GO ON SHIP, AND I DON'T COME BACK, AND SHE 503 VOYAGE MARRY OTHER FALLER.
I SPEND ALL MONEY, I HAVE TO SHIP AWAY FOR ANOTHER506 VOYAGE VOYAGE.
(ANGRILY) I KNOW DAT DAMN SHIP--WORST SHIP DAT 507 VOYAGE SAIL TO SEA.
NO SAILOR WHO KNOW ANYTING EVER SHIP ON HER. 507 VOYAGE
ISS DAT SHIP YOU MEAN 507 VOYAGE
AY YOU, NICK, DON'T YER LEAVE THE BLEEDIN' SHIP 508 VOYAGE TILL THE CAPT'N GUVS YER THIS

SHIPS
MC AND MR. SLOCUM HAS BUSINESS TO TALK ABOUT-- 541 'ILE
SHIPS'S BUSINESS.
NO, AND I AIN'T AGOIM' TO TILL THIS SHIP'S FULL OFS44 'ILE ILE.
HE IS DRESSED IN THE SIMPLE BLUE UNIFORM AND CAP 130 BEYOND OF A MERCHANT SHIP'S OFFICER.)
(THE SHIP'S BELL IS HEARD HEAVILY EIGHT TIMES. 482 CARDIF
THE BO'SUN, THE SHIP'S CARPENTER, THE MESSROOM 455 CARIBE STEWARD, AND THE DONKEYMAN--
THE SHIP'S BELL TOLLS FOUR BELLS. 473 CARIBE
IN THE REAR, LEFT, A MARBLE-TOPPED SIDEBOARD WITH 555 CROSS A SHIP'S LANTERN ON IT.
IN THE RIGHT EXTREMITY OF THE SKYLIGHT IS PLACED A555 CROSS FLOATING SHIP'S COMPASS.
I SUPPOSE THIS IS ALL MEANT TO BE LIKE A SHIP'S 556 CROSS CABINS
(PLEASED, GLANCING UP AT HIS SHIP'S LOFTY RIG) 106 ELECTR
ABOVE IT, A SHIP'S CLOCK. 109 ELECTR
SUSPENDED IN THE SKYLIGHT IS A SHIP'S COMPASS. 109 ELECTR
THERE IS A LIGHTED LAMP ON THE SIDEBOARD AND A 110 ELECTR SHIP'S LANTERN, ALSO LIGHTED.
(MOCKINGLY) ADAM BRANT WAS A SHIP'S OFFICER, TOO,153 ELECTR WASN'T HES
IT AIN'T IN THE SHIP'S ARTICLES. 228 HA APE
IS THAT IN THE SHIP'S ARTICLES 228 HA APE

SHIPBOARD
(TO CHU-YIN--COMPLACENTLY) YOU'VE GOT TO IMPOSE 403 MARCOM RIGID DISCIPLINE ON SHIPBOARD.
HER HIGHNESS'S SPLEEN BEING SLUGGISH AFTER THE 425 MARCOM LONG CONFINEMENT ON SHIPBOARD.*

SHIPBUILDER
I SUPPOSE CLIPPERS ARE TOO OLD A STORY TO THE 23 ELECTR DAUGHTER OF A SHIPBUILDER.

SHIPMATE
(WARMLY) A GOOD SHIPMATE HE WAS AND IS, NONE 480 CARDIF BETTER.
(AFTER A PAUSE) YANK WAS A GOOD SHIPMATE, PURE 480 CARDIF BEGGAR.
EASY GOES, SHIPMATE/ 104 ELECTR
(HASTILY) NO TRICK, SHIPMATE/ 499 VOYAGE
*AVIN' SOMETHIN' YESELF, SHIPMATES 505 VOYAGE

SHIPMATES
(ASTOUNDED) SHIPMATES--HAS HIMSELF-- 77 ANNA
YOU'RE GOING TO BE SHIPMATES ON THE *LONDONDERRY.* 77 ANNA
DID YOU KNOW ITS
YOU AND HE HAVE BEEN SHIPMATES A LONG TIMES 485 CARDIF
HIS PLAN TO MURDHER HIS OWN SHIPMATES THAT HAVE 524 INZONE SERVED HIM FAIR--

SHIPOWNER
THE THIRD HAS THE APPEARANCE OF A PROSPEROUS 79 ELECTR SHIPOWNER OF COLONIAL DAYS.

SHIPPED
EVER SHIPPED ON A WINDBAG/ 49 ANNA
FIVE YEARS AND MORE UT IS SINCE FIRST I SHIPPED 480 CARDIF WID HIM.
AND SHIPPED US ON A SKYSAIL-YARDER ROUND THE HORN.487 CARDIF
AND HAD TO GO TO TOMMY MOORE'S BOARDING HOUSE TO 487 CARDIF GET SHIPPED
SHIPPED WIV 'IM ONE VOYAGE. 457 CARIBE
DEN I SHIPPED IN DE STOKEHOLE. 234 HA APE
TO MY HILLS TO BE MADE INTO MY CLOTH AND SHIPPED 100 MANSNS ON MY RAILROAD.

SHIPPIN'
* THEIR MAN IN CHARGE O' THE SHIPPIN' ASKED AFTER 141 BEYOND YOU *SPECIAL CURIOUS.
HE INHERITED SOME AND MADE A PILE MORE IN 7 ELECTR SHIPPIN'.
AND EZRA GIVE UP THE ARMY AND TOOK HOLT OF THE 8 ELECTR SHIPPIN' BUSINESS HERE.

SHIPPING
AND I'LL BE SHIPPING AWAY ON SOME BOAT WILL TAKE 61 ANNA ME TO THE OTHER END OF THE
I'M SHIPPING AWAY OUT OF THIS, I'M TELLING YOU/ 61 ANNA
(AFTER A HESITATING PAUSE) AY'M SHIPPING AWAY UN 65 ANNA SEA AGAIN, ANNA.
IT'S QUEER, YES--YOU AND ME SHIPPING ON SAME BOAT 78 ANNA DAT WAY.
THAT'S WHY THE SHIPPING WASN'T ENOUGH-- 55 ELECTR
JOSIAH BURDEN, THE MANAGER OF THE MANNON SHIPPING 67 ELECTR COMPANY.
AND WE CAN'T DISMISS THE SHIPPING TRADE AS 48 MANSNS SOMETHING THAT DOESN'T CONCERN US.
IN SHIPPING, FOR EXAMPLE, 48 MANSNS

SHIPPING (CONT'D.)
IF WE OWNED OUR OWN SHIPPING COMPANY, 48 MANSNS

SHIPS
AY SIGN ON ODER SHIPS-- 21 ANNA
ON SHIPS AT ANCHOR BREAKS AT REGULAR INTERVALS. 25 ANNA
I NEVER THOUGHT LIVING ON SHIPS WAS SO DIFFERENT 26 ANNA FROM LAND.
DEN MY TREE BROT'ER OLDERN ME, DEY GO ON SHIPS. 27 ANNA
IN THE STOKEHOLES OF SHIPS SINCE I WAS A LAD ONLY. 35 ANNA
NO, HE WAS BO'SUN ON SAILING SHIPS FOR YEARS. 36 ANNA
I LOVE TO WATCH THE SHIPS PASSING. 44 ANNA
SHIPS VAS SHIPS UEN--AND MEN DAT SAIL ON DEM VAS 49 ANNA REAL MEN.
VE VAS TALKING ABOUT SHIPS AND FALLARS ON SEA. 50 ANNA
THAT FOOLIN' ON SHIPS IS ALL RIGHT FOR A SPELL. 115 BEYOND
MAYBE I BORED YOU WITH MY TALK OF CLIPPER SHIPS 23 ELECTR AND MY LOVE FOR THEMS
WOMEN ARE JEALOUS OF SHIPS. 23 ELECTR
BRANT WAS SMART AND EASY ON SHIPS--AND I WOULDN'T 26 ELECTR WEAR THE NAME OF MANNON.
THERE ARE TWICE AS MANY SKIPPERS AS SHIPS THESE 39 ELECTR DAYS.
FOR YOUR SHIPS OR YOUR SEA OR YOUR NAKED ISLAND 42 ELECTR GIRLS--WHEN I GROW OLD AND UGLY/
THERE ARE PLENTY OF SHIPS--BUT THERE IS ONLY ONE 111 ELECTR YOUR CHRISTINE/
OH, THERE WAS FINE BEAUTIFUL SHIPS THEM DAYS-- 213 HA APE
(TO YANK RESENTFULLY) 'TWAS THEM DAYS MEN 214 HA APE BELONGED TO SHIPS, NOT NOW.
AND ALL DE SHIPS COMIN' IN, SAILIN' OUT, ALL OVER 252 HA APE DE OIT--
THEIR SHIPS WILL COME IN, LOADED TO THE GUNWALES 578 ICEMAN WITH CANCELLED REGRETS
AND THEIR SHIPS ARE LONG SINCE LOOTED AND SCUTTLED578 ICEMAN
AND SUN ON THE BOTTOM
IS REACHED--ESPECIALLY UN AMMUNITION SHIPS LIKE 515 INZONE THIS.
ALL WE KNOW IS HE SHIPS ON HERE IN LONDON 'BOUT A 522 INZONE YEAR B'FORE THE WAR STARTS.
SUNK TOO MUCH CAPITAL IN NEW SHIPS-- 32 MANSNS
OUR COTTON IS BROUGHT TO US IN SHIPS, ISN'T ITS 48 MANSNS
IT HAS SIGNIFICANCE AS A LINK IN THE CHAIN IN 100 MANSNS WHICH MY SHIPS BRING COTTON
AND OWN YOUR OWN SLAVES, IMPORTED IN YOUR OWN 101 MANSNS SLAVE SHIPS.
YOUR OWN SLAVE SHIPS AND YOUR OWN SLAVE DEALERS INI57 MANSNS AFRICA.
NOW IF I HAD THE KIND OF SHIPS WE BUILD IN VENICE 398 MARCOM
TO HUMP WITH
(TO HIS FATHER AND UNCLE) YOU TWO BETTER GET 403 MARCOM ABOARD YOUR SHIPS.
EVEN IF IT IS A GREAT COMPANY THAT TRADES WITH THE 29 POET WHOLE WORLD IN ITS OWN SHIPS.
AND HER GOIN' WITH THIS FARMER AND THAT, AND EVEN 980 ROPE
MEN OFF THE SHIPS, IN THE PORT.
BACK AFTER FIVE YEARS OF BUMMIN' ROUND THE ROTTEN 588 ROPE OLD EARTH IN SHIPS AND THINGS.
AND WORKIN' MYSELF TO DEATH IN SHIPS AND THINGS-- 598 ROPE
THERE'S PLENTY OF 'ANDS LYIN' ABANT WAITIN' FUR 495 VOYAGE SHIPS, I SHOULD FINK.
ARE YE GOIN' UP TO--TO STOCKHOLM B'FORE YER SHIPS 502 VOYAGE AWAY AGEN*

SHIPS'
(THERE IS A PAUSE IN WHICH THE FOGHORN AND THE 121 JOURNE SHIPS' BELLS ARE HEARD.)
FOLLOWED BY THE SHIPS' HELLS FROM THE HARBOR. 125 JOURNE

SHIPWRECKED
IT WAS IN NEW GUINEA, TIME I WAS SHIPWRECKED 457 CARIBE THERE.
SHIPWRECKED MY FIRST VOYAGE AT SEA. 23 ELECTR

SHIPWRECKS
TALKIN' ABANT SHIPWRECKS IN THIS 'ERE BLOOMIN' 482 CARDIF FUG.
THAT IN SPITE OF TYPHOONS, SHIPWRECKS, 411 MARCOM

SHIRAZ
IN THE HOUSE OF THE COURTEZANS AT SHIRAZ. 348 MARCOM

SHIRK
DON'T SHIRK/ 362 MARCOM
SHIRK/ NO ONE CAN EVER SAY----/ 414 MARCOM
YOU ARE TAKING ADVANTAGE OF THIS BEING THE LAST 414 MARCOM DAY TO SHIRK YOUR DUTY/
HE'S ALWAYS LOOKING FUR EXCUSES TO SHIRK. 21 POET

SHIRKIN'
FIRST MAN OF YE I SEE SHIRKIN' I'LL SHOOT DEAD AS 545 'ILE SURE AS THERE'S A SEA UNDER

SHIRKING
YOU'RE SIMPLY SHIRKING, CHARLIE/. 114 STRANG

SHIRT
I DON'T WANT HIM TO GET THE IDEA HE'S GOT A 289 AHWILD STUFFED SHIRT
WEARS A CHEAP BLUE SUIT, A STRIPED COTTON SHIRT 45 ANNA WITH A BLACK TIE,
AND A BLUE FLANNEL SHIRT WITH A BRIGHT COLORED 81 BEYOND TIE.
HE WEARS OVERALLS, LEATHER BOOTS, A GRAY FLANNEL 82 BEYOND SHIRT OPEN AT THE NECK.
HE IS DRESSED IN OVERALLS, LACED BOOTS, AND A 119 BEYOND FLANNEL SHIRT OPEN AT THE NECK.)
HE IS DRESSED IN CORDUROY PANTS, A FLANNEL SHIRT, 145 BEYOND
(HE CHOKES, HIS FACE CONVULSED WITH AGONY, HIS 489 CARDIF HANDS TEARING AT HIS SHIRT-FRONT,
AND THEN REACHES INSIDE HIS SHIRT AND PULLS OUT A 462 CARIBE PINT BOTTLE)
HC IS DRESSED IN A DARK SUIT, WHITE SHIRT AND 493 DAYS COLLAR, A DARK TIE.
(AFTER A GLANCE, FOLDS IT CAREFULLY AND HIDES IT 220 DESIRE UNDER HIS SHIRT--GRATEFULLY)

SHOCKED

SHIRT (CONT'D.)
(HE PUTS THEM IN BAG AND PUTS IT INSIDE HIS SHIRT 220 DESIRE CAREFULLY.)
HE IS IN HIS NIGHT SHIRT, SHE IN HER NIGHTDRESS. 235 DESIRE
(HE PULLS ON HIS TROUSERS, TUCKING IN HIS NIGHT 238 DESIRE SHIRT AND PULLS ON HIS BOOTS.)
FOR HE COMES BACK AND PUTS ON HIS WHITE SHIRT, 241 DESIRE COLLAR.
HE WEARS HIGH SEABOOTS TURNED DOWN FROM THE KNEE, 498 DIFRNT DIRTY COTTON SHIRT AND PANTS,
STRIPED COTTON SHIRT OPEN AT THE NECK. 513 DIFRNT
IS SITTING IN HIS SHIRT SLEEVES ON THE SIDE OF HIS422 DYNAMO BED.
DUNGAREE TROUSERS FADED BY MANY WASHINGS, A BLUE 457 DYNAMO FLANNEL SHIRT OPEN AT THE NECK.
GIVING A TOUCH TO HIS SHIRT AND TIE. 145 ELECTR
HE IS DRESSED IN A GRAY FLANNEL SHIRT, OPEN AT THE260 GGBROW NECK.
HE WEARS AN ILL-FITTING BLUE SERGE SUIT, WHITE 8 HUGHIE SHIRT AND COLLAR, A BLUE TIE.
THE COAT OPEN TO REVEAL AN OLD AND FADED BUT 9 HUGHIE EXPENSIVE SILK SHIRT
HIS GRAY FLANNEL SHIRT, OPEN AT THE NECK, 574 ICEMAN
AND HIS WHITE SHIRT IS FRAYED AT COLLAR AND CUFFS,574 ICEMAN
FADED PINK SHIRT AND BRIGHT TIE BELONG TO THE SAME575 ICEMAN VINTAGE.
HE IS STRIPPED TO THE WAIST, HIS COAT, SHIRT, 576 ICEMAN UNDERSHIRT,
THE SLEEVES OF HIS COLLARLESS SHIRT ARE ROLLED UP 577 ICEMAN ON HIS THICK, POWERFUL ARMS
CLEAN COLLAR AND SHIRT, 604 ICEMAN
A LOUD SUIT, TIE AND SHIRT, AND YELLOW SHOES. 615 ICEMAN
A COLLAR-LESS SHIRT WITH A THICK WHITE 13 JOURNE HANDKERCHIEF.
HE WEARS A SHIRT, COLLAR AND TIE, NO COAT, OLD 20 JOURNE FLANNEL TROUSERS, BROWN SNEAKERS.
(ENTHUSIASTICALLY, GROPING IN HIS SHIRT FRONT) 416 MARCOM
(MIKE WEARS DIRTY OVERALLS, A SWEAT-STAINED BROWN 4 MISBEG SHIRT.
DARK-BROWN MADE-TO-ORDER SHOES AND SILK SOCKS, A 37 MISBEG WHITE SILK SHIRT,
HE'D GIVE THEM HIS SHIRT. 123 MISBEG
AND A BLUE FLANNEL SHIRT. 582 ROPE

SHIRTS
THEY ARE DRESSED IN DIRTY PATCHED SUITS OF 477 CARDIF DUNGAREE, FLANNEL SHIRTS.

SHIRTWAIST
SHE IS DRESSED IN SHIRTWAIST AND SKIRT IN THE 186 AHWILD FASHION OF THE PERIOD.
SHE, ALSO, IS DRESSED IN A SHIRTWAIST AND SKIRT.) 187 AHWILD
SHE IS DRESSED IN SHIRTWAIST AND SKIRT. 187 AHWILD

SHIV
LEGGO DAT SHIV AND I'LL PUT DIS GAT AWAY. 672 ICEMAN

SHIVER--
(HE GIVES A LITTLE SHIVER OF PASSIONATE LONGING-- 276 AHWILD
(THEN WITH A SHIVER OF SHAMEFACED REVULSION AND 276 AHWILD SELF-DISGUST)
(SHE GIVES A LITTLE SHIVER OF AVERSION) 520 DAYS
(WITH A LITTLE SHIVER OF REPULSION) 522 DAYS
(SHE GLANCES AT THE PORTRAIT--THEN TURNS BACK TO 37 ELECTR BRANT WITH A LITTLE SHIVER--
(SUDDENLY WITH A LITTLE SHIVER) 158 ELECTR
(WITH A SUDDEN SHIVER) THE NIGHTS ARE SO MUCH 259 GGBROW COLDER THAN THEY USED TO BE/
(AT LAST, WITH A SHIVER) IT'S COLD. 261 GGBROW
I SHOULD HAVE INHERITED AN IMMUNITY TO HEAT THAT 220 HA APE WOULD MAKE A SALAMANDER SHIVER.
SHE WON'T SHIVER AT NOTHIN', DEY-- 232 HA APE
(WITH A SHIVER--HURRIEDLY.) WHY DO YOU REMEMBER 110 MANSNS THAT SO WELL
(WITH A LITTLE SHIVER.) I AM THERE. 113 MANSNS
(WITH A LITTLE SHIVER OF DREAD.) 136 MANSNS
THEN TURNS AWAY HASTILY WITH A SHIVER OF DREAD.) 162 MANSNS
(WITH A SHIVER) IT'S BAD, KID. 600 ROPE
(A SHIVER RUNS OVER HER BODY.) 44 STRANG
BUT THAT OLD SHIVER OF DREAD TOOK ME THE MINUTE 54 STRANG SHE STEPPED IN THE DOOR/...
(WITH A SHIVER OF FEAR SHE HURRIES OVER AND SITS 199 STRANG ON THE BENCH BESIDE MARSDEN,
A BIT BEWILDEREDLY, BREAKING AWAY FROM HIM WITH A 480 WELDED LITTLE SHIVER--STUPIDLY)

SHIVERIN'
WHAT'RE YE SHIVERIN' 'BOUTS 536 'ILE
'TIS A HELL AV A THING FUR GROWN MEN TO BE 520 INZONE SHIVERIN' LOIKE CHILDER

SHIVERING
WHERE HE STANDS FOR A MOMENT SHIVERING, BLOWING ON536 'ILE HIS HANDS.
(SHIVERING IRRITABLY) FOR GOODNESS' SAKE PUT SOME152 BEYOND WOOD ON THAT FIRE.
I FOUND HIM THERE SHIVERING AND SHAKING AND MADE 73 POET HIM COME HERE

SHIVERS
(HE SHIVERS) DEEP UNDER THE SEA/ 570 CROSS
(HE SHIVERS) IT'S COLD IN THIS HOUSE. 238 DESIRE
ALWAYS SENDS THE COLD SHIVERS DOWN MY BACK MINUTE 185 EJONES I GETS IN IT.
(SHE SHIVERS, LOOKING BEFORE HER BUT DOESN'T 81 ELECTR ANSWER.)
SHE SHIVERS WITH FRIGHT IN SPITE OF THE BLAZING 225 HA APE HEAT.
(SHE SHIVERS AND PUTS HER HANDS OVER HER FACE.) 714 ICEMAN
(SHE SUDDENLY SHIVERS WITH REPULSION AND TEARS HER144 MANSNS EYES FROM THE MIRROR
YOU GIVE ME THE SHIVERS. 160 MISBEG

SHO'T
I KNOWS DIS EMPEROR'S TIME IS SHO'T. 180 EJONES

SHOCK
GIMME A SHOCK. 4 ANNA
BY THE BURDEN OF HIS MASSIVE HEAD WITH ITS HEAVY 556 CROSS SHOCK OF TANGLED BLACK HAIR.
(BROUGHT BACK WITH A SHOCK, ASTONISHED AT HER 22 ELECTR TUNE)
BUT HE GOT BRAIN FEVER FROM THE SHOCK. 48 ELECTR
ISN'T IT A SHOCK TO YOU, ORIN? 75 ELECTR
I KNOW WHAT A SHOCK IT MUST BE TO YOU. 75 ELECTR
AND NOW, WITH THE SHOCK OF YOUR FATHER'S DEATH ON 86 ELECTR TOP OF EVERYTHING,
(MOVED) I DIDN'T MEAN--I ONLY THINK THE SHOCK OF 96 ELECTR HIS DEATH--
AND ON TOP OF THAT FATHER'S DEATH--AND THE SHOCK 146 ELECTR OF MOTHER'S SUICIDE.
THE SHOCK TO MY SYSTEM BROUGHT ON A STROKE WHICH, 627 ICEMAN AS A DOCTOR,
IT'S A SHOCK, BUT HE'S YOUNG AND HE'LL SOON FIND 643 ICEMAN ANOTHER DREAM JUST AS GOOD.
BUT THAT'S ONLY THE FIRST SHOCK. 692 ICEMAN
JUST LEAVE HARRY ALONE AND WAIT UNTIL THE SHOCK 692 ICEMAN WEARS OFF AND YOU'LL SEE.
GETTING OVER THE FIRST SHOCK. 694 ICEMAN
YOU REALLY DID SHOCK ME FOR A SECOND, MOTHER. 14 MANSNS
NATURALLY, THE SHOCK--HER GRIEF. 26 MANSNS
IT IS SUCH AN UNEXPECTED SHOCK--TO FIND SARA HERE 176 MANSNS WHERE SHE NEVER INTRUDES--
"BUT MIDST THE CROWD, THE HUM, THE SHOCK OF MEN, 101 POET TO HEAR, TO SEE, TO FEEL,
IT IS MORE AS IF A SUDDEN SHOCK OR STROKE HAD 152 POLT SHATTERED HIS COORDINATION)
ESPECIALLY AFTER THE SHOCK OF HIS TRAGIC DEATH. 9 STRANG
NOT THAT HER FATHER'S DEATH IS A SHOCK IN THE 34 STRANG USUAL SENSE OF GRIEF.
NO, IT'S A SHOCK BECAUSE IT'S FINALLY CONVINCED 34 STRANG HER
IT ACTS LIKE AN ELECTRIC SHOCK ON HIM, 97 STRANG
(THE WORDS AND THE TONE SHOCK HIS PRIDE TO LIFE. 99 STRANG
IT ACTS LIKE A GALVANIC SHOCK ON HER. 449 WELDED

SHOCKED
(SHOCKED) SID/ 195 AHWILD
LILY IS SHOCKED BUT, TAKING HER CUE FROM THEM, 195 AHWILD SMILES.
(THEN A TRACE OF SHOCKED REPROOF SHOWING IN HIS 205 AHWILD VOICE)
THEN, AS HE DOES, A LOOK OF SHOCKED INDIGNATION 207 AHWILD COMES OVER HIS FACE)
(A LITTLE SHOCKED) YOU MUSN'T TALK THAT WAY. 215 AHWILD
(REALLY SHOCKED THIS TIME) I DON'T LIKE YOU WHEN 216 AHWILD YOU SAY SUCH HORRIBLE.
MILLER GUFFAWS--THEN SUDDENLY GROWS SHOCKED.) 231 AHWILD
(WHO HAS HEARD THEM BUT IS SHOCKED AT HEARING A 237 AHWILD GIRL SAY THEM--
(RICHARD IS STARTLED AND SHOCKED BY THIS CURSE AND238 AHWILD LOOKS DOWN AT THE TABLE)
TO RICHARD'S SHOCKED FASCINATION--- 239 AHWILD
THEN, WATCHING HER, WITH SHOCKED CONCERN) 239 AHWILD
TIMIDITY, DISGUST AT THE MONEY ELEMENT, SHOCKED 241 AHWILD MODESTY,
(THEN SHOCKED AND CONDEMNING) 261 AHWILD
SHOCKED FACES.) 263 AHWILD
(SHOCKED AND DELIGHTED) SSSHH/ 287 AHWILD
(THEN SHOCKED INDIGNATION COMING INTO HIS VOICE) 295 AHWILD
HIS FACE IS DRAWN IN A SHOCKED EXPRESSION OF GREATI54 BEYOND GRIEF.
I AM AFRAID YOU WILL BE TERRIBLY SHOCKED-- 509 DAYS
(SHOCKED) YOU MEAN YOU-- 520 DAYS
HOW HORRIBLY SHOCKED YOU LOOK/ 520 DAYS
AND IT SHOCKED JOHN TERRIBLY, POOR DEAR--IN SPITE 523 DAYS OF ALL HIS OLD RADICAL IDEAS.
(FATHER BAIRD STARTS AND STARES AT HIM WITH A 536 DAYS SHOCKED EXPRESSION.)
FOR SHE REACTED TO IT IN A WAY THAT AT FIRST 537 DAYS SHOCKED HIM
SHOCKED REBUKE. 561 DAYS
(SPRINGING TO HER FEET--SHOCKED BUT PLEASED) 533 DIFRNT
SHOCKED LOOK OF STUPEFACTION. 438 DYNAMO
(EVERYONE STARES AT HER, SHOCKED AND IRRITATED.) 69 ELECTR
(SHOCKED) OH, MRS. MANNON, I CAN'T BELIEVE 72 ELECTR VINNIE--/
(HAZEL GIVES A SHOCKED EXCLAMATION.) 82 ELECTR
(SHOCKED BACK TO AWARENESS BY HER TONE--PITIFULLY 140 ELECTR CONFUSED)
OH, SHE WAS A BIT SHOCKED AT FIRST BY THEIR 145 ELECTR
(IN SHOCKED AMAZEMENT) WHAT'S COME OVER HIM$ 146 ELECTR
HE RETURNS IT, AROUSED AND AT THE SAME TIME A 147 ELECTR LITTLE SHOCKED BY HER BOLDNESS.
HAZEL IS A BIT SHOCKED, THEN SMILES HAPPILY. 148 ELECTR
(BEWILDERED AND A BIT SHOCKED) 176 ELECTR
AND YET SHOCKED AND REPELLED BY HER DISPLAY OF 177 ELECTR PASSION)
THEY LOOK AWAY FROM HIM, SHOCKED AND MISERABLY 663 ICEMAN ASHAMED OF THEMSELVES.
HE STOPS WITH A HORRIFIED START, AS IF SHOCKED 716 ICEMAN OUT OF A NIGHTMARE.
(SHOCKED AND AMUSED.) GOOD HEAVENS/ 24 JOURNE
(SHOCKED BUT GIGGLING.) HEAVENS, WHAT A TERRIBLE 25 JOURNE TONGUE THAT MAN HAS/
BATTLE, BUT SUDDENLY HE SEEMS TO SOBER UP TO A 162 JOURNE SHOCKED REALIZATION OF WHAT HE
I WAS REALLY SHOCKED. 176 JOURNE
NO, I AM NOT SHOCKED. 13 MANSNS
YOU WOULD BE HORRIBLY SHOCKED IF I SHOULD TELL YOU 13 MANSNS THE NATURE OF THE PART I PLAY
HIS MANNER IS SHOCKED AND INDIGNANT, 26 MANSNS
(SHOCKED, EMBARRASSED. 89 MANSNS
(SHOCKED) DON'T BE IMPIOUS/ 376 MARCOM
I WAS AFRAID I MIGHT HAVE SHOCKED YOUR MODESTY. 105 MISBEG

SHOCKED

SHOCKED (CONT'D.)
(SMILING, BUT A BIT SHOCKED.) 32 POET
(SHOCKED) NINA/ 19 STRANG
HIS ATTITUDE RATHER SHOCKED ME. 50 STRANG
(WHO HAS LISTENED WITH AMAZED HORROR--PROFOUNDLY 83 STRANG
SHOCKED AND STUNNED)
(SHOCKED AND INDIGNANT) GORDON/ 142 STRANG
(STARTLED, STARES AT HER--SHOCKED AND HORRIFIED-- 195 STRANG

SHOCKING
AND HIS NEAVES IN A SHOCKING STATE OF SHAKES.) 674 ICEMAN
(FUNCING A SCORNFUL SMILE) I'M SHOCKING YOU, I 42 MISBEG
SUPPOSES

SHOCKS
NO MATTER HOW IT SHOCKS OUR SENTIMENTAL MORAL AND 47 MANSNS
RELIGIOUS DELUSIONS ABOUT HIM,

SHODDY
GOD, WHAT A SHODDY, PITIFUL/... 120 STRANG

SHOE
TO BE KISSING THE SHOE-SOLES OF A FINE, DACENT 34 ANNA
GIRL THE LIKE OF YOURSELF.
THERE'S ONE OLD SHOE OFF--AND THERE'S THE OTHER 121 BEYOND
OLD SHOE--
(HE STANDS NEAR THE PATH, LEFT, KICKING AT THE 146 BEYOND
GRASS WITH THE TOE OF HIS SHOE.
THE KINDEST, BIGGEST-HEARTED GUY EVER WORE SHOE 722 ICEMAN
LEATHER.
LUST OGLING ME FOR A DOLLAR WITH OILY SHOE BUTTON 100 STRANG
ITALIAN EYES/...))

THAT THEY CANNOT BE TAKEN OFF WITH SHOES ON.) 187 AHWILD
YOU'D BETTER BEAT IT WHILE YOUR SHOES ARE GOOD/ 200 AHWILD
HE HAS DISCARDED COLLAR AND TIE, COAT AND SHOES, 249 AHWILD
AND WEARS AN OLD, WORN,
IF I WAS IN YOUR SHOES, I'D KEEP STILL/ 265 AHWILD
THAT'S HATCHED A DUCK--THOUGH LORD KNOWS I 292 AHWILD
WOULDN'T IN HER SHOES/
(LAUGHING) WHY DO YOU BOTHER UNLACING YOUR SHOES 298 AHWILD
"NOW, YOU BIG GOOSE--
AND, SITTING DOWN IN HIS CHAIR, BEGINS TO UNLACE 298 AHWILD
HIS SHOES)
AND BLACK SHOES NEWLY SHINED. 45 ANNA
(MECHANICALLY) COME AND LET ME TAKE OFF YOUR BEYOND
SHOES AND STOCKINGS, MARY,
HE COMES FORWARD AND PICKS UP THE SHOES AND 121 BEYOND
STOCKINGS WHICH HE SHOVES CARELESSLY
(TAKING OFF HER SHOES AND STOCKINGS) 121 BEYOND
DOES YOUR MOTHER TAKE OFF YOUR SHOES AND STOCKINGS121 BEYOND
BEFORE YOUR NAP?
NOW STREAKED WITH GRAY, HER MUDDIED SHOES RUN DOWN144 BEYOND
AT THE HEEL.
BLACK SHOES AND SOCKS, 493 DAYS
BUT THE LOWER PART OF HER SKIRT AND HER STOCKINGS 548 DAYS
AND SHOES ARE SOAKING WET.
LOOK AT YOUR SHOES/ 548 DAYS
(GLANCING AT HER SHOES, STOCKINGS, AND DRESS) 537 DFRNT
HE IS DRESSED ROUGHLY IN BATTERED SHOES, 457 DYNAMO
WELL, WE EATS RIGHT HEAH AN' NOW SOON'S I GITS 188 EJONES
DESE PESKY SHOES LACED UP.
(HE TAKES OFF HIS SHOES, HIS EYES STUDIOUSLY 188 EJONES
AVOIDING THE FOREST.
(HE FINISHES LACING UP HIS SHOES) 188 EJONES
(BUT HE SITS DOWN AND BEGINS TO LACE UP HIS SHOES 188 EJONES
IN GREAT HASTE.
HIS SHOES CUT AND MISSHAPEN, FLAPPING ABOUT HIS 195 EJONES
FEET.
STARING DOWN AT THE SHOES IN HIS HANDS AS IF 196 EJONES
RELUCTANT TO THROW THEM AWAY.
HOLDS THE WRECKS OF THE SHOES IN HIS HANDS AND 196 EJONES
REGARDS THEM MOURNFULLY)
THEN LOOKS DOWN AT HIS FEET, WORKING HIS TOES 196 EJONES
INSIDE THE SHOES--WITH A GROAN)
DEM SHOES AIN'T NO MORE 'CEPTIN' TO HURT. 196 EJONES
ALL ARE DRESSED IN DUNGAREE PANTS, HEAVY UGLY 207 HA APE
SHOES.
HIS SHOES ARE TAN AND WHITE, HIS SOCKS WHITE SILK. 9 HUGHIE
MAYBE THOSE SHOES HE SEES ADVERTISED FOR FALLEN 13 HUGHIE
ARCHES--
HIS POINTED TAN BUTTONED SHOES, 575 ICEMAN
HIS SHOES ARE EVEN MORE DISREPUTABLE, WRECKS OF 577 ICEMAN
IMITATION LEATHER.
SOLD HIS SUIT AND SHOES AT SULLY'S TWO DAYS AGO. 981 ICEMAN
HIS CLOTHES AND SHOES ARE NEW, COMPARATIVELY 985 ICEMAN
EXPENSIVE, SPORTY IN STYLE.
I MUST HAVE MY SHOES SOLED AND HEELED AND SHINED 603 ICEMAN
FIRST THING TOMORROW MORNING.
TEN, TWENTY--THOSE ARE PRETTY SHOES YOU GOT ON, 609 ICEMAN
BESS--
A LOUD SUIT, TIE AND SHIRT, AND YELLOW SHOES. 615 ICEMAN
HE IS SHAVED AND WEARS AN EXPENSIVE, WELL-CUT 674 ICEMAN
SUIT, GOOD SHOES AND CLEAN LINEN.
JIMMY'S CLOTHES ARE PRESSED, HIS SHOES SHINED, HIS683 ICEMAN
WHITE LINEN IMMACULATE.
HOPE IS DRESSED IN AN OLD BLACK SUNDAY SUIT, BLACK683 ICEMAN
TIE, SHOES, SOCKS.
I'M NOT WORTHY TO WIPE YOUR SHOES.* 710 ICEMAN
AND COMMENCE TO PULL ON THEIR SHOES. 514 INZONE
NO SHOES ON, MIND, SO HE WOULDN'T MAKE NO NOISE/ 519 INZONE
DUNKS'S SHOES AND ALL, TURNING THEIR FACES TO THE 532 INZONE
WALL.
HE WEARS A THREADBARE, READY-MADE, GREY SACK SUIT 13 JOURNE
AND SHINELESS BLACK SHOES,
BLACK SHOES.) 89 JOURNE
AN AFRICAN SLAVE, DRESSED IN PINK LIVERY WITH 391 MARCOM
GREEN HAT AND SHOES AND STOCKINGS
PUTTING ON AIRS AS IF HE WAS TOO GOOD TO WIPE HIS 10 MISBEG
SHOES ON ME.
DARK-BROWN MADE-TO-ORDER SHOES AND SILK SOCKS, A 37 MISBEG
WHITE SILK SHIRT,

SHOES (CONT'D.)
BLACK STOCKINGS AND SHOES. 71 MISBEG
(WITH HEAVY SARCASM, IN YOUR BEST SHOES AND 79 MISBEG
STOCKINGS)
CRACKED WORKING SHOES, RUN DOWN AT THE HEEL, ARE 20 POET
ON HER BARE FEET.
HE WEARS A DARK BLUE JERSEY, PATCHED BLUE PANTS, 587 ROPE
ROUGH SAILOR SHOES.
AND PUT A RING IN HIS HAND, AND SHOES ON HIS 594 ROPE
FEET.
AND TAKE OFF HIS SHOES AND SUCKS AND WARM THE 600 ROPE
BUTTONS OF HIS FEET FOR HIM.
HE WEARS FLANNEL PANTS, A BLUE COAT, WHITE 159 STRANG
BUCKSKIN SHOES.
BUCKSKIN SHOES. 159 STRANG
IT SEEMS TO ME IF I WERE IN GORDON'S SHOES I'D DO 168 STRANG
EXACTLY WHAT HE HAS DONE.
I ALWAYS WAS IN GORDON SHAW'S SHOES/... 168 STRANG
(IN GORDON'S SHOES/... 168 STRANG

SHOESTRING
AND I DON'T NEED BUT A SHOESTRING TO START WITH. 157 BEYOND

SHOIT
BUT YUH CAN BET YOUR SHOIT NO ONE AIN'T NEVER 211 HA APE
LICKED ME SINCE/

SHOITS
YOUSE ALL KIN BET YOUR SHOITS I'LL GIT EVEN WIT 231 HA APE
HER.

SHONE
IT IS THE ONE THAT SHONE OVER BETHLEHEM/ 289 LAZARU

SHOO
JUST SHOO ME OUT. 505 DAYS

SHOOED
THE FLURRIED WAY SHE SHOOED ME OUT OF THE KITCHEN.136 BEYOND

SHOOK
AND SHOOK HIS HEAD, AND WALKED OUT WIDOUT SAYIN' 4480 CARDIF
WORD,
AND WE ALWAYS SHOOK HANDS THE NIXT MORNIN'. 480 CARDIF
OA BOTH SIDES SUDDENLY SAW THE JOKE WAR WAS ON 95 ELECTR
THEM AND LAUGHED AND SHOOK HANDS/
AND THEN WE SHOOK HANDS. 599 ICEMAN

SHOOT
FIRST MAN OF YE I SEE SHRINKIN' I'LL SHOOT DEAD AS 545 *ILE
SURE AS THERE'S A SEA UNDER
LET YOU SHOOT, THEN/ 69 ANNA
LET YOU SHOOT, I'M SAYING, AND HE DONE WITH IT/ 69 ANNA
AND FINALLY THEY HAS TO P'INT A GUN AT HER AND 503 DFRNT
SHOUT IN THE WATER NEAR HER AFORE
SHOOT AWAY, OLD BOZO/ 452 DYNAMO
STOP OR I'LL SHOOT/ 175 EJONES
I ONLY 'OPES I'M THERE WHEN THEY TAKES 'IM OUT TO 175 EJONES
SHOOT 'IM.
SHOOT DE PIECE. 181 EJONES
I COULD LET HIM SHOOT FIRST AND THEN KILL HIM IN 38 ELECTR
SELF-DEFENSE.
COME OUT AND LET ME HAVE A LOOK AT YOU OR BY GOD 104 ELECTR
I'LL SHOOT/
SHOOT/ 279 GGBROW
SHOOT DE PIECE NOW/ 224 HA APE
LET'S GO SHOOT A BALL. 234 HA APE
I'LL SHOOT DE WOIKS FOR YOUSE. 247 HA APE
I'D GET HIM TO SHOOT CRAP WITH ME HERE ON THE 20 HUGHIE
DESK.
OF COURSE, I'D STALL HIM OFF WHEN HE'D WANT TO 21 HUGHIE
SHOOT NIGHTS
--IF HE'D ONLY SHOOT IT OUT WITH A GUNMAN SOME 24 HUGHIE
NIGHT/
I SHOOT TWO BITS. 38 HUGHIE
HE SAYS, "SOCIALIST AND ANARCHIST, WE OUGHT TO 584 ICEMAN
SHOOT DEM DEAD.
SO GO AHEAD AND SHOOT HIM. 584 ICEMAN
SO YOU DON'T SHOOT NO SOCIALISTS WHILE I'M AROUND.584 ICEMAN
VILL MINE RIFLE I SHOOT DAMN FOOL LIMEY OFFICERS PV599 ICEMAN
THE DOZEN, BUT HIM I MISS.
I SHOUT CLEAN IN THE MITTLE OF FOREHEAD AT SPTION 599 ICEMAN
KEEP--AND YOU I MISS/
THEY'D SHOOT YOU ON SIGHT. 609 ICEMAN
AND NOT JUST SHOOT OFF HIS OLD BAZOO ABOUT IT. 632 ICEMAN
AND SHOOT THE CHUTES AND MAYBE WE'LL COME BACK AND670 ICEMAN
MAYBE WE WON'T.
THEN SHOOT UP AGAIN AND POMPEIA'S LAUGHTER IS 367 LAZARU
HEARD FOR A MOMENT.
WHO BROUGHT A SHOOT OF THE TREE OF LIFE DOWN FROM 349 MARCOM
PARADISE AND PLANTED IT HERE.
AND AT THE DAWN HE'LL HAVE HAD TOO MUCH TO SHOOT 137 POET
HIS BEST AND MAYBE--
COME ON IN THE CABIN, NED, AND SHOOT A DRINK. 164 STRANG
YOU'RE COMING TO SHOOT A DRINK. 164 STRANG

SHOOTER
NOT THAT I'M SKEERED O' YOU OR YOUR SHOOTER/ 104 ELECTR

SHOOTIN'
SOUND LIKE--SOUND LIKE--FO' GOD SAKE, SOUND LIKE 191 EJONES
SOME NIGGER WAS SHOOTIN' CRAP/
AND HEAH I IS SHOOTIN' SHOTS TO LET 'EM KNOW JES' 192 EJONES
WHAH I IS/
HUH ABOUT SHOOTIN' A LITTLE CRAP, CHARLIES 37 HUGHIE

SHOOTING
AND THEN IT'LL BE LIKE SHOOTING IN THE DARK. 268 AHWILD
SHOUTING OFF THEIR LOUD TRAPS ON SOAPBOXES 592 ICEMAN
TAKING CARE OF YOU AND SHOOTING AWAY YOUR SNAKES, 610 ICEMAN
SO HE DION'T BOTHER SHOOTING HIMSELF, 169 POET

SHOOTS
KEENEY'S FIST SHOUTS OUT TO THE SIDE OF HIS JAW. 544 *ILE
HIS GUN MISSES FIRE AND I SHOOTS HIM DEAD, WHAT 178 EJONES
YOU HEAH ME SAYS
GIT AWAY FROM ME BEFO' I SHOOTS YOU UP/ 190 EJONES
IF I SHOOTS DAT ONE I'M A GONER SHO'/ 198 EJONES

SHORTLY

SHOP

RED SISK--HIS FATHER KEPT A BLACKSMITH SHOP WHERE 229 AHWILD
THE UNION MARKET IS NOW--
WITH MANY ULTRA-SENTIMENTAL BARBER-SHOP QUAVERS. 257 GGBROW
DE OUL GENT SURE MADE A PILE OF DOUGH IN DE 581 ICEMAN
BUCKET-SHOP GAME
THE FACT THAT HE WAS A CROOKED OLD BUCKET-SHOP 607 ICEMAN
BASTARD
HE HAD ONE HOOKER SHOP IN TOWN, AND, OF COURSE, I 709 ICEMAN
LIKED THAT, TOO.
YOUR FATHER HAD TO GO TO WORK IN A MACHINE SHOP 117 JOURNE
WHEN HE WAS ONLY TEN YEARS OLD.
I'VE HEARD PAPA TELL THAT MACHINE SHOP STORY TEN 117 JOURNE
THOUSAND TIMES.
I WORKED TWELVE HOURS A DAY IN A MACHINE SHOP, 148 JOURNE
LEARNING TO MAKE FILES.
IMAGINE ME SUNK TO THE FAT GIRL IN A HICK TOWN 161 JOURNE
HOOKER SHOP/

SHOPS

IN THE REAR, THE SHOW WINDOWS OF TWO SHOPS, 233 HA APE
I HUNG AROUND POOL ROOMS AND GAMBLING JOINTS AND 588 ICEMAN
HOOKER SHOPS.
OF THE LATE WORLD-FAMOUS BILL OBAN, KING OF THE 595 ICEMAN
BUCKET SHOPS.

SHORE

THE BEST SHORE DINNER YOU EVER TASTED AND I DON'T 190 AHWILD
WANT YOU COMING HOME--
IN THE SWEET BYE AND BYE WE WILL MEET ON THAT 233 AHWILD
BEAUTIFUL SHORE--
HE IS DRESSED IN A WRINKLED, ILL-FITTING DARK SUIT 5 ANNA
OF SHORE CLOTHES,
PY YINGO, AY GAT DAT MARTHY SHORE OFF BARGE BEFORE 10 ANNA
ANNA COME/
STARING TOWARD THE SPOT ON SHORE WHERE THE SINGING496 CARIBE
SEEMS TO COME FROM.)
(NODDING TOWARD THE SHORE) DON'T YUH KNOW THIS IS457 CARIBE
THE WEST INDIES,
THERE IS A SILENCE BROKEN ONLY BY THE MOURNFUL 459 CARIBE
SINGING OF THE NEGROES ON SHORE.)
THE SINGING FROM SHORE COMES CLEARLY OVER THE 466 CARIBE
MOONLIT WATER.)
CADENCE OF THE SONG FROM THE SHORE CAN AGAIN BE 466 CARIBE
FAINTLY HEARD.
IN THE SILENCE THE MOURNFUL CHANT FROM THE SHORE 472 CARIBE
CREEPS SLOWLY OUT TO THE SHIP.)
HAVE YOU FORGOTTEN THAT NIGHT WALKING ALONG THE 23 ELECTR
SHORES
LONG IS DRESSED IN SHORE CLOTHES, WEARS A BLACK 233 HA APE
WINDSOR TIE, CLOTH CAP.
WORKED ALONG SHORE. 234 HA APE
I CAN HARDLY SEE THE OTHER SHORE. 82 JOURNE
IN PERSPECTIVE OF A PRETENTIOUS, NOUVEAU-RICHE 139 MANSNS
COUNTRY ESTATE ON THE SHORE OF A
A BOAT JUST CAME FROM THE SHORE WITH AN OFFICIAL 410 MARCOM
NOTIFICATION
WHAT DO YOU SAY TO A LITTLE STROLL DOWN TO THE 122 STRANG
SHORE AND BACK
ALL ARE DRESSED IN THEIR ILL-FITTING SHORE CLOTHES496 VOYAGE
AND LOOK VERY UNCOMFORTABLE.

SHORES

STROLL THROUGH TO WALLOW HAPPILY ALONG THE SHORES 50 MISBEG
OF THE ICE POND.
TO THE GRANDEST GINTLEMAN IVIR COME FROM THE 100 POET
SHORES AV IRELAND/

SHORN

SHORN OF YOUR BOASTFUL WORDS, 561 DAYS
I AM THY SHORN, BALD, NUDE SHEEP/ 283 GGBROW
SHORN OF ALL THE IDEAS, ATTITUDES, 487 WELDED

SHORT

AND WE'LL MAKE SHORT SHIFT OF IT. 543 *ILE
KEENEY TURNS TO THE MATE WITH A SHORT LAUGH 545 *ILE
A SHORT STOUT WOMAN WITH FADING LIGHT-BROWN HAIR 187 AHWILD
SPRINKLED WITH GRAY,
(SID DAVIS, HIS BROTHER-IN-LAW, IS FORTY-FIVE, 188 AHWILD
SHORT AND FAT, BALDHEADED.
ARE AWKWARDLY SHORT AND MUSCULAR. 5 ANNA
HE IS A SHORT, SQUAT, BROAD-SHOULDERED MAN OF 5 ANNA
ABOUT FIFTY, WITH A ROUND,
IT'S SHORT LETTERS, DON'T TAL ME MUCH MORE'N DAT. 8 ANNA
(SHE CATCHES HERSELF UP SHORT--WITH A GRIN) 15 ANNA
OH, HE'S SHORT AND-- 17 ANNA
(FORCING A SHORT LAUGH) NO-- COURSE NOT. 20 ANNA
YUST SHORT TIME AGO AY GOT DIS YOB CAUSE AY VAS 21 ANNA
SICK, NEED OPEN AIR.
(WITH A SHORT LAUGH) REEFING ABOUT THE SEA AGAINS 26 ANNA
(WITH A SHORT LAUGH) YOU MUST THINK I'M OFF MY 28 ANNA
BASE.
ON SUCH SHORT ACQUAINTANCES 38 ANNA
(TURNING AWAY FROM HIM WITH A SHORT LAUGH-- 38 ANNA
UNEASILY)
HER BROTHER, THE CAPTAIN, IS SHORT AND STOCKY, 94 BEYOND
AN ANDRE SIXTY-FIVE YEARS OLD WITH A SHORT, 94 BEYOND
SQUARE, WHITE BEARD.
I'LL HAVE A HARD TIME GETTING ANOTHER MAN AT SUCH 124 BEYOND
SHORT NOTICE.
TWO OF THE CREW ARE DOWN WITH FEVER AND WE'RE 126 BEYOND
SHORT-HANDED ON THE WORK.
(WITH A SHORT LAUGH) I WAS PLANNING OUR FUTURE 149 BEYOND
WHEN I GET WELL.
DOCTOR FAWCETT IS A SHORT, DARK, MIDDLE-AGED MAN 153 BEYOND
WITH A VANDYKE BEARD.
(WITH A SHORT LAUGH) TO BE CANDID, RUTH, 156 BEYOND
NEAR EACH BULWARK THERE IS ALSO A SHORT STAIRWAY, 455 CARIBE
LIKE A SECTION OF FIRE ESCAPE.
(A SHORT, DARK MAN SEATED ON THE RIGHT OF HATCH) 456 CARIBE
WHISTLING IN THE DARK, AND I SEE HE'S STILL ONLY 501 DAYS
OUT OF SHORT PANTS A WHILE,
(HE GIVES A SHORT BITTER LAUGH) 537 DAYS
(HE GIVES A SHORT CONTEMPTUOUS LAUGH AGAIN) 537 DAYS

SHORT (CONT'D.)

THEN THEY STOP SHORT.) 216 DESIRE
WAAL, LIFE IS SHORT AN' SO'S LOVE, AS THE FELLER 250 DESIRE
SAYS.
(EBEN SUDDENLY LAUGHS, ONE SHORT SARDONIC BARK.. 254 DESIRE
(HE STUMBLES OUT THE DOOR--IN A SHORT WHILE 264 DESIRE
RETURNS TO THE KITCHEN--
(STOPS SHORT AS HE SEES THE PILE ON THE FLOOR) 548 DIFRNT
(STOPS SHORT AND STARES AT FIFE WITH A RAGE THAT 450 DYNAMO
CHOKES HIM
A SHORT TIME IS SUPPOSED TO ELAPSE BETWEEN SCENES 486 DYNAMO
TWO AND THREE.)
SOUNDS MADE UP TO ME--LIKE SHORT FUR SCMETHIN' 20 ELECTR
ELSE.
BHANT WAS SHORT AND EASY ON SHIPS--AND I WOULDN'T 26 ELECTR
WEAR THE NAME OF MANNON.
HE STOPS SHORT IN THE SHADOW FOR A SECOND AND 46 ELECTR
STANDS, ERECT AND STIFF.
OLD STICK--SHORT FOR STICK-IN-THE-MUD. 94 ELECTR
(SHE STOPS SHORT AND STARES AT LAVINIA. 171 ELECTR
BUSINESS HAS BEEN PILING UP ON ME--A RUN OF LUCK-- 277 GGBROW
---BUT I'M SHORT-HANDED--
THEY STOP SHORT AND STIFFEN ALL IN A ROW, 293 GGBROW
MR. BROWN--(THEN STOPS SHORT.) 318 GGBROW
SHE STOPS SHORT ON SEEING BROWN AND THE MASK, 320 GGBROW
AND HIS FAT LEGS ARE TOO SHORT FOR HIS BODY. 8 HUGHIE
HIS GAIT A BIT WADDLING BECAUSE OF HIS SHORT LEGS. 9 HUGHIE
SO YOU WON'T KICK AFTERWARDS I SHORT-CHANGED YOU,+608 ICEMAN
BUT IN THOSE DAYS I COULD HAVE SHORT-CHANGED THE 609 ICEMAN
KEEPER OF THE MINT.
HOW YOU SHORT-CHANGED YOUR OWN SISTER/ 609 ICEMAN
ROCKY JERKS A SHORT-BARRELED, NICKEL-PLATED 672 ICEMAN
REVOLVER FROM HIS HIP POCKET.
HE STOPS SHORT WHEN HE SEES SMITHY. 513 INCONE
(SHE STOPS SHORT, OVERCOME BY A FIT OF ACUTE SELF- 27 JOURNE
CONSCIOUSNESS AS SHE CATCHES
POWERFUL SHOULDERS AND LONG ARMS AND HANDS, AND 299 LAZARU
SHORT, SKINNY
THEY ALSO WEAR WIRE WIGS BUT OF STRAIGHT HAIR CUT 336 LAZARU
IN SHORT BOYISH MODE.
FOR PILATE CRUCIFIED HIM A SHORT TIME AFTER AND 343 LAZARU
THE SAME AS PREVIOUS SCENE--THE SAME NIGHT A SHORT350 LAZARU
WHILE LATER.
(STOPS SHORT AND STARES AT LAZARUS, CONFUSED AND 357 LAZARU
STUTTERING)
GATSBY IS A SHORT, TUBBY MAN OF FIFTY-SIX, ALMOST 25 MANSNS
COMPLETELY BALD.
HE KNEW YOUR MOTHER COULD NEVER TAKE A SHORT, FAT 37 MANSNS
MAN SERIOUSLY.
IN A VERY SHORT TIME HE WILL BEG US ON HIS KNEES 135 MANSNS
TO RESTORE THAT PEACE.
I WON'T CARE HOW SHORT IT IS IF IT'S ONLY A POEM. 357 MARCOM
IN SHORT, THE PEOPLE LIVE LIKE BEASTS. 373 MARCOM
I'LL HAVE TO GIVE MARCO SOME LESSONS IN HOW TO 374 MARCOM
TELL A SHORT STORY.
(GOES BACK TO KUBLAI WHO HAS FINISHED READING THE 423 MARCOM
SHORT NOTE
HIS ARMS ARE SHORT AND MUSCULAR, WITH LARGE HAIRY 11 MISBEG
HANDS.
HE WEARS HEAVY BROGANS, FILTHY OVERALLS, AND A 11 MISBEG
DIRTY SHORT-SLEEVED UNDERSHIRT.
IN SHORT, I REFER TO YOUR GOOD NEIGHBOR, T. 47 MISBEG
STEDMAN HARDER,
I WAS SHORT WITH HER. 18 POET
SOLELY ON CREEPING CANAL BOATS, AS SHORT-SIGHTED 40 POET
FOOLS WOULD HAVE US BELIEVE,
WITH A PUTREFLY AND SHORT ARMS LUMPY WITH MUSCLE. 51 POET
I HAVE ONLY TIME FOR A SHORT VISIT-- 74 POET
GADSBY IS IN HIS LATE FORTIES, SHORT, STOUT, WITH 116 POET
A BIG, BALD HEAD, ROUND,
BUT I MUST TELL YOU MY LINE IS SHORT. 119 POET
SHORT LEGS AND THICK ANKLES... 6 STRANG
IN SHORT, I AM A MAN WHO HAPPENS TO BE YOUR 20 STRANG
FATHER.
(THINKING TIMIDLY) (IN SHORT, 21 STRANG
HE IS TWENTY-SEVEN, SHORT, DARK, WIRY, HIS 33 STRANG
MOVEMENTS RAPID AND SURE.
(WITH A SHORT LAUGH) TRYING TO IS RIGHT/ 70 STRANG
(THEN STOPS SHORT AS HE SEES EVANS.) 95 STRANG
HE WAS ASKING ABOUT YOU ONLY A SHORT WHILE AGO-- 127 STRANG
DARRELL PULLS HIMSELF UP SHORT-- 150 STRANG
WE'LL BE COMIN' BACK IN A SHORT TIME, SURELY. 504 VOYAGE
(A PAUSE--THEN FORCING A SHORT LAUGH) 446 WELDED
(WITH A SHORT LAUGH) I SHOULD THINK AFTER FIVE 455 WELDED
YEARS--

SHORTENED

I SHORTENED MY SWORD AND LET HIM HAVE THE POINT 95 ELECTR
UNDER THE EAR.

SHORTER

AROUND FIVE-TEN IN HEIGHT BUT LOOKING MUCH SHORTER538 *ILE
IT'S SHORTER. 113 ELECTR
ERIE IS AROUND MEDIUM HEIGHT BUT APPEARS SHORTER 8 HUGHIE
BECAUSE HE IS STOUT
IS AN INCH TALLER AND WEIGHS LESS, BUT APPEARS 19 JOURNE
SHORTER AND STOUTER
(MIKE HOGAN IS TWENTY, ABOUT FOUR INCHES SHORTER 3 MISBEG
THAN HIS SISTER.

SHORTLY

(SHORTLY) NEVER MIND. 243 AHWILD
(SURVEYS HIM OVER HIS GLASSES, NOT WITH 253 AHWILD
ENTHUSIASM--SHORTLY)
(SHORTLY) YES-- 27 ANNA
(SHORTLY) SHUT UP, WILL YOUS 66 ANNA
YOU'LL BE COMING ALONG SHORTLY, WON'T YOUS 86 BEYOND
(SHORTLY) NO-- 117 BEYOND
(SHORTLY) YOU'VE GOT TO GET BACK TO YOUR WORK, I 119 BEYOND
S'POSE.

SHORTLY

SHORTLY (CONT'D.)
(HIS FACE FLUSHING--INTERRUPTS HIS BROTHER 131 BEYOND
SHORTLY)
(SHORTLY) COME, MARY/ 136 BEYOND
(SHORTLY) OF COURSE/ WHAT ELSE$ 154 BEYOND
(SHORTLY) NO. 231 DESIRE
IT IS SHORTLY BEFORE SUNSET AND THE SOFT LIGHT OF 5 ELECTR
THE DECLINING SUN SHINES
IT IS SHORTLY AFTER SUNSET BUT THE AFTERGLOW IN 129 ELECTR
THE SKY
(SHORTLY) DON'T COMPLAIN ABOUT THIS PLACE. 587 ICEMAN
(AFTER A PAUSE--SHORTLY) HOW DID YOU LOCATE ME$ 588 ICEMAN
(BEGINNING TO RECOVER HIS APLOMB--SHORTLY.) 117 POET
SHORTLY AFTER NINA WENT AWAY...." 24 STRANG
(A BIT SHORTLY) YES. 29 STRANG
(SHORTLY AND DRYLY) WE CAN'T WASTE TIME BEING 35 STRANG
SENTIMENTAL, MARSDEN/
(SHORTLY) NO, SAM, I CAN'T THINK OF ANYONE. 122 STRANG
(SHORTLY) MY FATHER DIED THREE WEEKS AGO. 125 STRANG

SHORTNESS
WE LAMENT THE SHORTNESS OF LIFE. 436 MARCOM

SHORTSIGHTEDLY
WEATHER-BEATEN, RED FACE FROM WHICH HIS LIGHT BLUE 5 ANNA
EYES PEER SHORTSIGHTEDLY.

SHOT
LIKE A SPRINTER RELEASED BY THE STARTING SHOT.) 186 AHWILD
HALF-BARRELS OF CHEAP WHISKY OF THE =NICKEL-A- 3 ANNA
SHOT= VARIETY.
LET YOU END ME WITH A SHOT AND I'LL BE THANKING 69 ANNA
YOU.
THIS ROTTEN HEADACHE HAS MY NERVES SHOT TO PIECES.135 BEYOND
(HE CANNOT RESTRAIN A PARTING SHOT) 467 DYNAMO
IT SOUNDED LIKE A SHOT. 488 DYNAMO
DAT SHOT FIX 'EM. 190 EJONES
THE SOUND OF THE SHOT, THE REASSURING FEEL OF THE 190 EJONES
REVOLVER IN HIS HAND.
(EXCITEDLY) GORRY, YOU GIVE DE GAME AWAY WHEN YOU190 EJONES
FIRE DAT SHOT.
HA'NT OR NOT HA'NT, DAT SHOT FIX HIM. 192 EJONES
I'LL BET YER IT AIN'T 'IM THEY SHOT AT ALL, YER 204 EJONES
BLEEDIN' LOONEY/
AND THIS TIME IS DROWNIN' MY SORROW FOR THE 44 ELECTR
PRESIDENT GITTIN' SHOT/
(SCORNFULLY) OUTSIDE ON DECK WHERE THE SHOT WOULDN113 ELECTR
BE SURE TO BE HEARD$
I'D HAVE SHOT HIS GUTS OUT IN FRONT OF HER/ 113 ELECTR
MUTHER--SHOT HERSELF--FATHER'S PISTOL--GET A 124 ELECTR
DOCTOR--
(APPROACHING) SAY, VINNIE, DID YOU HEAR A SHOT--$124 ELECTR
SHE SHOT HERSELF THERE. 133 ELECTR
(THERE IS A MUFFLED SHOT FROM THE STUDY ACROSS THE167 ELECTR
HALL.)
HE'LL GET SHOT/ 232 HA APE
AND HAD A SHOT AT DIFFERENT JOBS IN THE OLD HOME 23 HUGHIE
TOWN BUT COULDN'T MAKE THE
I WAS THINKING, I'D RATHER BE SHOT. 25 HUGHIE
DO YOU, BY ANY CHANCE, KNOW THE BIG SHOT, ARNOLD 32 HUGHIE
ROTHSTEIN$
BRAGGING WHAT A SHOT YOU WERE, AND, BEJEES, YOU 602 ICEMAN
MISSED HIM/
AND THE DOC GIVES YOU A SHOT IN THE ARM, AND THE 625 ICEMAN
PAIN GOES, AND YOU DRIFT OFF.
YOU, LARRY/ RENEGADE/ TRAITOR/ I VILL HAVE YOU 634 ICEMAN
SHOT/
YUH'LL COME RUNNIN' IN HERE SOME NIGHT YELLIN' FOR670 ICEMAN
A SHOT OF BOOZE
(HE WALKS STIFFLY TO THE STREET DOOR--THEN TURNS 673 ICEMAN
FOR A PARTING SHOT--BOASTFULLY)
I WOULDN'T MIND A SHOT MYSELF. 681 ICEMAN
ABOUT MY PIPE DREAMS, I'D HAVE SHOT THEM DEAD. 686 ICEMAN
BUY ME A DRINK OR I VILL HAVE YOU SHOT/ 695 ICEMAN
(CYNICALLY BRUTAL.) ANOTHER SHOT IN THE ARM/ 76 JOURNE
YOU'VE SHOT OFF YOUR MOUTH TOO MUCH ALREADY. 169 JOURNE
THERE IS A BANG, AND A LEADEN BALL IS SHOT OUT 395 MARCOM
I'LL HAVE ANOTHER SHOT-- 138 MISBEG
(HE GOES TO THE DOOR AT REAR AND OPENS IT, BURNING 20 POET
FOR A PARTING SHOT AT SARA.)
(FROM THE YARD, OFF LEFT FRONT, THERE IS THE 162 POET
MUFFLED CRACK OF A PISTOL SHOT
A SHOT/ 163 POET
A SHOT/ 163 POET
WE HEARD A SHOT. 165 POET
SO IT WAS THE MARE YOU SHOT$ 166 POET
IT WAS THE MARE HE SHOT/ 166 POET
BUT FAIR, HE SAW THE SHOT THAT KILLED HER HAD 169 POET
FINISHED HIM, TOO.
AS IF YOU'D SHOT YOURSELF ALONG WITH THE MARE/ 177 POET
I'LL WAGER SIMON NEVER HEARD THE SHOT OR ANYTHING.182 POET
THAN ANY THAT WAS EVER SHOT DOWN IN FLAMES.... 71 STRANG
SINCE THE BABY WAS BORN, I'VE FELT AS IF I HAD A 121 STRANG
SHOT OF DYNAMITE IN EACH ARM.

SHOTGUN
I'LL GIT THE SHOTGUN AN' BLOW HIS SOFT BRAINS T' 233 DESIRE
THE TOP OV THEM ELUMS/
A DOLL NEARLY HAD ME HOOKED FOR THE OLD SHOTGUN 14 HUGHIE
CEREMONY.
AND HIS SHOTGUN TO SCARE HIM-- 9 MISBEG
IF HE HAD A SHOTGUN POINTED AT YOUR HEART/ 16 MISBEG
WITH WITNESSES AND A SHOTGUN, AND CATCH HIM THERE. 22 MISBEG
(MUTTERS) IT'S THE LANDLORD AGAIN, AND MY SHOTGUN 38 MISBEG
NOT HANDY.

SHOTS
AND HIM MAKIN' THEM FIRE SHOTS ROUND HER TO SCARE 509 DIFRNT
HER BACK TO LAND AND GET RID
AND HEAR I IS SHOOTIN' SHOTS TO LET 'EM KNOW JES' 192 EJONES
WHAR I IS/
WITH SUCH RAPIDITY THAT THE TWO SHOTS ARE ALMOST 198 EJONES
SIMULTANEOUS.

SHOTS (CONT'D.)
(SHOUTS FROM THE GARDEN AND A VOLLEY OF SHOTS. 321 GGBROW
I TOLD HIM I KNEW ALL THE BIG SHOTS. 28 HUGHIE
GIT A COUPLA SHOTS IN YUH. 644 ICEMAN

SHOULD'VE
IT'S YEW I SHOULD'VE MURDERED, IF I'D HAD GOOD 264 DESIRE
SENSE/
(INTENSELY) YOU SHOULD'VE BEEN OBLIVIOUS TO 452 WELDED
EVERYTHING/

SHOULDA
YOU SHOULDA SEEN THE DOLL I MADE NIGHT BEFORE 12 HUGHIE
LAST.
I SHOULDA STAYED ON A DRUNK. 17 HUGHIE
YUH SHOULDA SEEN HIM LOOKIN' AT ME. 598 ROPE

SHOULDER
(PUTTING AN ARM AROUND HER SHOULDER--WITH GRUFF 545 'ILE
TENDERNESS)
(SHE THROWS HER ARMS AROUND HIM, WEEPING AGAINST 549 'ILE
HIS SHOULDER.
HE COMES OVER AND GRABS HER ROUGHLY BY THE 551 'ILE
SHOULDER.)
(SHE HIDES HER FACE ON MILLER'S SHOULDER AND SOBS 262 AHWILD
HEARTBROKENLY.)
THEN SHE LETS HER HEAD SINK ON HIS SHOULDER AND 287 AHWILD
SIGHS SOFTLY.)
THEN SHE LETS HER HEAD SINK ON HIS SHOULDER AGAIN 287 AHWILD
(TAKING ONE OF HIS ARMS OVER HER SHOULDER) 39 ANNA
SHE LEANS OVER IN EXASPERATION AND SHAKES HIM 57 ANNA
VIOLENTLY BY THE SHOULDER)
AND SWINGING IT HIGH OVER HIS SHOULDER, SPRINGS 60 ANNA
TOWARD HER.
(GOES OVER AND PATS HER ON THE SHOULDER, THE TEARS 62 ANNA
RUNNING DOWN HIS FACE)
(SHE COMES FORWARD AND PUTS HER ARM ABOUT HIS 78 ANNA
SHOULDER--
AND THAT HER HEAD IS RESTING ON HIS SHOULDER, 90 BEYOND
GENTLY TAKES HIS ARM AWAY.
(SHE SUDDENLY THROWS HER ARMS ABOUT HIS NECK AND 91 BEYOND
HIDES HER HEAD ON HIS SHOULDER)
(LOOKING AT ANDREW OVER HIS WIFE'S SHOULDER-- 107 BEYOND
STUBBORNLY)
(HE PATS HIS BROTHER'S SHOULDER) 110 BEYOND
(HE SHAKES HIS BROTHER FIERCELY BY THE SHOULDER) 110 BEYOND
(GETS UP AND PUTS HIS HAND ON HER SHOULDER) 123 BEYOND
(AS HE GOES OUT HE SPEAKS BACK OVER HIS SHOULDER) 125 BEYOND
ANDREW CALLS BACK OVER HIS SHOULDER) 142 BEYOND
A HEAVY SHAWL IS WRAPPED ABOUT HER SHOULDER. 144 BEYOND
SHOULDER) 151 BEYOND
(OVER HIS SHOULDER) YOU'LL BE HAVIN' YOURS, ME 461 CARIBE
SONNY BYE, DON'T FRET.
(CASTING A QUICK GLANCE OVER HER SHOULDER) 464 CARIBE
AND COMES OVER AND SITS BESIDE HIM AND PUTS HER 468 CARIBE
ARM OVER HIS SHOULDER.)
(THE MATE ROLLS PADDY OVER AND SEES A KNIFE WOUND 472 CARIBE
ON HIS SHOULDER.)
HIS RIGHT ARM HAS BEEN AMPUTATED AT THE SHOULDER 556 CROSS
AND
AT THE FOOT OF IT HORNE PUTS A SWAYING HAND ON HIS572 CROSS
SHOULDER
HER FACE BURIED AGAINST ELSA'S SHOULDER.) 520 DAYS
(FINALLY TAPS HIM GENTLY ON THE SHOULDER.) 566 DAYS
SIMEON AND PETER SHOULDER IN, SLUMP DOWN IN THEIR 206 DESIRE
CHAIRS WITHOUT A WORD.
(PUTTING ONE ARM OVER HIS SHOULDER. 242 DESIRE
(PATS HER ON SHOULDER. 263 DESIRE
(AS SHE DOESN'T ANSWER, HE GRABS HER VIOLENTLY BY 264 DESIRE
THE SHOULDER AND SHAKES HER)
CABOT GRABS HIM BY THE SHOULDER. 265 DESIRE
HER HEAD LEANING BACK AGAINST HIS SHOULDER, 494 DIFRNT
(SHE HIDES HER HEAD ON HIS SHOULDER.) 534 DIFRNT
GETS UP AND PATS HER ON THE SHOULDER--WITH ROUGH 537 DIFRNT
TENDERNESS)
(COMES AND PUTS AN ARM AROUND HIS SHOULDER-- 431 DYNAMO
TEASINGLY)
(THEN HE COMES AND PATS HER ON THE SHOULDER) 443 DYNAMO
(CALLS OVER HER SHOULDER) DO YOU HEAR THAT, 448 DYNAMO
HUTCHINS$
CALLS EXCITEDLY OVER HIS SHOULDER) 450 DYNAMO
(LEANS AGAINST HER GRATEFULLY, HIS HEAD ALMOST ON 477 DYNAMO
HER SHOULDER.
A BUGLE BOUND IN COLORED CLOTH IS CARRIED OVER 173 EJONES
HER SHOULDER
WHEN SHE DOES SMITHERS SPRINGS FORWARD AND GRABS 174 EJONES
HER FIRMLY BY THE SHOULDER.
THE WOMAN LOOKING BACK OVER HER SHOULDER 174 EJONES
CONTINUALLY.
JONES BECOMES CONSCIOUS OF IT--WITH A START, 192 EJONES
LOOKING BACK OVER HIS SHOULDER)
HE TOUCHES JONES ON THE SHOULDER PEREMPTORILY. 197 EJONES
SMITHERS LEANS OVER HIS SHOULDER--IN A TONE OF 204 EJONES
FRIGHTENED AWE)
THEN SHE TURNS PITYINGLY AND PUTS HER HAND ON HIS 14 ELECTR
SHOULDER)
(GOING TO HIM AND PUTTING AN ARM AROUND HIS 36 ELECTR
SHOULDER)
(SHE BURSTS INTO TEARS AND HIDES HER FACE AGAINST 47 ELECTR
HIS SHOULDER.)
(DOES NOT ANSWER HER BUT CALLS BACK TO HER BROTHER 83 ELECTR
OVER HER SHOULDER)
(GRABS HER BY THE SHOULDER AND SHAKES HER, FORCING 99 ELECTR
HER TO HER KNEES--FRENZIEDLY)
(SOOTHINGLY, PATTING HER SHOULDER) 159 ELECTR
(SUDDENLY CALLS BACK OVER HER SHOULDER) 259 GGBROW
(SHE THROWS HER ARMS AROUND HIM AND HIDES HER HEAD268 GGBROW
ON HIS SHOULDER.)
(SHAKES HIS HAND OFF HIS SHOULDER AND WALKS AWAY 282 GGBROW
FROM HIM--AFTER A PAUSE)

1419 SHOULDERS

SHOULDER (CONT'D.)

(THEY SIT ON THE SOFA, HIS ARM ABOUT HER, HER HEAD309 GGBROW ON HIS SHOULDER.)
THROWING HER KIMONO OVER HIS BARE BODY, DRAWING 322 GGBROW HIS HEAD ON TO HER SHOULDER.)
RESULTANT OVER-DEVELOPMENT OF BACK AND SHOULDER 207 HA APE MUSCLES HAVE GIVEN THEM.
(WITH A SCORNFUL SMILE) YOU DON'T CARE TO 221 HA APE SHOULDER THIS RESPONSIBILITY ALONE.
HIS HEAD DROPPING JERKILY TOWARD ONE SHOULDER. 576 ICEMAN
ON HIS LOWER LEFT SHOULDER IS THE BIG RAGGED SCAR 576 ICEMAN OF AN OLD WOUND.
(HE CHUCKLES AT HIS OWN FANCY--REACHES OVER AND 579 ICEMAN SHAKES HUGO'S SHOULDER.
(GRABS HIS SHOULDER AND SHAKES HIM) HEY, YOU/ 581 ICEMAN
(BUT HERE ROCKY SHAKES HIM ROUGHLY BY THE 597 ICEMAN SHOULDER.)
(HE CHUCKLES AND SLAPS LEWIS ON HIS BARE SHOULDER)599 ICEMAN
(OVER HER SHOULDER TO CHUCK--ACIDLY) 630 ICEMAN
(IGNORING THEM, TURNS TO HUGO AND SHAKES HIM BY 634 ICEMAN THE SHOULDER--
(SHE LAUGHS TEASINGLY--THEN PATS LARRY ON THE 635 ICEMAN SHOULDER AFFECTIONATELY)
AND PUTTING A HAND ON HIS SHOULDER) 641 ICEMAN
(HE PUTS AN ARM AROUND LARRY'S SHOULDER AND GIVES 643 ICEMAN HIM AN AFFECTIONATE HUG)
CORA GREETS HIM OVER HER SHOULDER KIDDINGLY) 644 ICEMAN
WHY, JUST NOW HE PATS ME ON THE SHOULDER, LIKE HE 646 ICEMAN WAS SYMPATHIZING WITH ME.
CORA GETS HER HANDS SET OVER THE PIANO KEYS, 653 ICEMAN WATCHING OVER HER SHOULDER.
NOW HE REALLY HAS A CHIP ON HIS SHOULDER. 654 ICEMAN
(GRABS HIM BY THE SHOULDER AND SHAKES HIM) 667 ICEMAN
(HE PASSES HIM TO CLAP HOPE ENCOURAGINGLY ON THE 684 ICEMAN SHOULDER)
(HE CLAPS HIM ON THE SHOULDER AGAIN, CHUCKLING.) 684 ICEMAN
AND PUTS A HAND ON HIS SHOULDER--KINDLY) 690 ICEMAN
(HE TURNS TO HOPE AND PATS HIS SHOULDER-- 691 ICEMAN COAXINGLY)
WITH AN ARM AROUND HIS SHOULDER--AFFECTIONATELY 694 ICEMAN COAXING)
(SHAKES JOE BY THE SHOULDER) 697 ICEMAN
(SHE PASSES A SMALL ROLL OF BILLS SHE HAS IN HER 700 ICEMAN HAND OVER HER SHOULDER.
(TAPS LEWIS ON THE SHOULDER--SERVILELY APOLOGETIC)700 ICEMAN
(GRABS HIS SHOULDER AND SHAKES HIM FURIOUSLY) 706 ICEMAN
(TAPS HICKEY ON THE SHOULDER) 717 ICEMAN
JACK SLAPS HIM ROUGHLY ON THE SHOULDER AND HE 516 INZONE COMES TO WITH A START)
JACK, COCKY AND SCOTTY LOOK OVER HIS SHOULDER WITH531 INZONE EAGER CURIOSITY.
(SHE PUTS AN ARM AROUND HIS SHOULDER--COAXINGLY.) 22 JOURNE
(GRABS HER SHOULDER.) MAMA/ STOP IT/ 48 JOURNE
(PUTS A HAND AFFECTIONATELY ON HIS SHOULDER.) 53 JOURNE
(HE PATS HER HAND ON HIS SHOULDER. 59 JOURNE
(PUTTING HER ARM AROUND EDMUND'S SHOULDER-- 67 JOURNE AND GRABS EDMUND'S SHOULDER.) 68 JOURNE
A LOT OF THEM GAVE ME THE COLD SHOULDER. 86 JOURNE
(SHE BREAKS AND HIDES HER FACE ON HIS SHOULDER, 91 JOURNE SOBBING.
HE PATS HER SHOULDER WITH AN AWKWARD TENDERNESS.) 91 JOURNE
CHAIR, AN ARM AROUND HIS SHOULDER, SO HE CANNOT 92 JOURNE MEET HER EYES.)
AND HIDES HER FACE ON HIS SHOULDER--SOBBINGLY.) 122 JOURNE
CHIP-ON-THE-SHOULDER AGGRESSIVENESS IN HIS MANNER.126 JOURNE
(BUT JAMIE'S SOBBING BREAKS HIS ANGER, AND HE 171 JOURNE TURNS AND SHAKES HIS SHOULDER.
GLANCING OVER HIS SHOULDER AND WHIRLING AROUND 311 LAZARU
(HE TURNS FROM HER AND PUTS HIS HAND ON LAZARUS' 317 LAZARU SHOULDER)
(STARES AT LAZARUS--THEN OVER HIS SHOULDER AT 332 LAZARU CALIGULA
CLUTCHING POMPEIA BY THE SHOULDER AND FORCING HER 343 LAZARU TO HER KNEES)
HE TALKS TO LAZARUS HALF OVER HIS SHOULDER. 350 LAZARU
SEEING THE SKULL OF DEATH LEER OVER ITS SHOULDER 12 MANSNS IN THE GLASS/
OVER HER SHOULDER INTO THE DARK INTERIOR. 27 MANSNS
HE COMES AND PUTS A PROTECTING, POSSESSIVE HAND ON 57 MANSNS HIS MOTHER'S SHOULDER.)
(SHE GIVES A QUICK BITTER LOOK UP AT HIS FACE AND 57 MANSNS MOVES HER SHOULDER AWAY.)
(SHE HIDES HER FACE ON HIS SHOULDER SHAMEFACEDLY-- 90 MANSNS
I FEEL SOMETHING IS STARING OVER MY SHOULDER--IT'S119 MANSNS STRANGE HERE
AND HIDES HER FACE AGAINST HIS SHOULDER.) 144 MANSNS
PATS HER SHOULDER MECHANICALLY--VAGUELY.) 145 MANSNS
(HE PATS HER SHOULDER.) 155 MANSNS
(ADDRESSING HIM OVER HER SHOULDER HER EYES ON 186 MANSNS SARA.)
(SHE BENDS AND PUTS HER ARM AROUND HIS SHOULDER TO194 MANSNS HELP HIM.)
A GUITAR OVER HIS SHOULDER. 355 MARCOM
(SLAPPING THE PROSTITUTE ON THE BARE SHOULDER) 368 MARCOM
THE PROSTITUTE, WALKING AWAY, CALLS BACK OVER HIS 375 MARCOM SHOULDER)
(PUTS A HAND ON HIS SHOULDER AND PUSHES HIM DOWN) 40 MISBEG
(HE TURNS EAGERLY TOWARD LEFT BUT SUDDENLY HOGAN 60 MISBEG GRABS HIS SHOULDER AND SPINS
(HANGING ON TO HER ARM AND SHOULDER--MAUDLINLY 80 MISBEG AFFECTIONATE NOW)
(HE PATS HER ON THE SHOULDER APPROVINGLY) 96 MISBEG
(HE STARTS OFF DOWN THE ROAD, LEFT-FRONT, WITH A 101 MISBEG LAST WORD OVER HIS SHOULDER)
(SHE GIVES HIS SHOULDER A SHAKE--FORCING A LIGHT 120 MISBEG TONE)
(SHE PUTS A HAND ON HIS SHOULDER.) 151 MISBEG

SHOULDER (CONT'D.)

HE REACHES OUT A SHAKING HAND TO PAT HER SHOULDER 37 POET WITH AN ODD,
SARA HIDES HER FACE ON HER SHOULDER, ON THE VERGE 65 POET OF TEARS.)
AS IF BY ACCIDENT TO BRUSH HIS HAND AGAINST HER 69 POET SHOULDER.
HE GLANCES OVER HIS SHOULDER. 116 POET
(FOLLOWING HIM, SPEAKS OVER HIS SHOULDER TO SARA.)129 POET
THEN, KEEPING HER FACE TURNED AWAY FROM HER 131 POET MUTHER, TOUCHES HER SHOULDER.)
CREGAN HAS HIM BY THE SHOULDER AND PUSHES HIM 164 POET ROUGHLY INTO THE ROOM.
HIDING HER FACE ON HER MUTHER'S SHOULDER-- 182 POET BEWILDEREDLY.)
(GRABBING BENTLEY'S SHOULDER AND SHAKING HIM-- 597 ROPE HOARSELY)
(HE SLAPS LUKE ON THE SHOULDER AND PUSHES THE 598 ROPE BUTLE TOWARD HIM)
HIDE HER FACE ON MY SHOULDER..." 27 STRANG
DEAR OLD CHARLIE IS CRYING BECAUSE SHE DIDN'T WEEP 28 STRANG ON HIS SHOULDER....
SHE SLIPS ON TO HIS LAP LIKE A LITTLE GIRL AND 43 STRANG HIDES HER FACE ON HIS SHOULDER.
(HE JUMPS FROM HIS CHAIR AND GOING TO MARSDEN PUTS 77 STRANG A HAND ON HIS SHOULDER.
HE GIVES WAY AND SOBS, HIS HEAD AGAINST HER 98 STRANG SHOULDER.)
(THEN OFFERING CONVENTIONAL CONSOLATION, PATS 134 STRANG MARSDEN'S SHOULDER)
(GLANCING FURTIVELY OVER HIS SHOULDER AT NINA-- 134 STRANG BROODINGLY THINKING)
(HE HAS PUT HIS HAND AROUND GORDON'S SHOULDER 151 STRANG IMPULSIVELY)
(COMING TO NINA AND PUTTING HIS HAND ON HER 160 STRANG SHOULDER)
(PASSING BY MARSDEN HE CLAPS HIM ON THE SHOULDER 164 STRANG EXASPERATEDLY)
(HE TOUCHES MADELINE ON THE SHOULDER) 177 STRANG
(HE TAPS MADELINE ON THE SHOULDER AND DRAWS HER 178 STRANG ASIDE.
(SHE HURRIES OVER TO HER, GLANCING EAGERLY OVER 178 STRANG HER SHOULDER TOWARDS THE RIVER)
(RESTING HER HEAD ON HIS SHOULDER) 199 STRANG
(CALLING OVER HIS SHOULDER) COME ON AN' DANCE, 501 VOYAGE OLLIE.
SHE GOES OVER AND PUTS HER ARMS AROUND OLSON'S 504 VOYAGE SHOULDER.
AS THEY GO OUT DRISCOLL SHOUTS BACK OVER HIS 504 VOYAGE SHOULDER)
(THEN AFTER A PAUSE SHE COMES OVER AND PUTS HER 452 WELDED HAND ON HIS SHOULDER)

SHOULDERED

A LITTLE STOOP SHOULDERED, MORE THAN A LITTLE 188 AHWILD BALD,
HE IS A SHORT, SQUAT, BROAD-SHOULDERED MAN OF 5 ANNA ABOUT FIFTY, WITH A ROUND,
A JERK-SHOULDERED VERSION OF THE OLD TURKEY TROT 471 CARIBE AS IT WAS DONE IN THE
BUT STOOP-SHOULDERED FROM TOIL. 221 DESIRE
SMITHERS IS A TALL, STOOP-SHOULDERED MAN ABOUT 173 EJONES FORTY.
RAW-BONED AND STOOP-SHOULDERED, HIS JOINTS 6 ELECTR STIFFENED BY RHEUMATISM,
SQUARE-SHOULDERED, MILITARY BEARING. 10 ELECTR
IN FIGURE HE IS TALL, BROAD-SHOULDERED AND 21 ELECTR POWERFUL.
SUDDENLY ERECT AND SQUARE-SHOULDERED.) 27 ELECTR
SQUARE-SHOULDERED AND STIFF, WITHOUT A BACKWARD 35 ELECTR GLANCE.
OR WITH A SELF-CONSCIOUS SQUARE-SHOULDERED 73 ELECTR STIFFNESS
TURNS, RIGID AND SQUARE-SHOULDERED, AND WALKS 101 ELECTR WOODENLY FROM THE ROOM.)
LAVINIA IS STIFFLY SQUARE-SHOULDERED, HER EYES 119 ELECTR HARD, HER MOUTH GRIM AND SET.
STANDING SQUARE-SHOULDERED AND STIFF LIKE A GRIM 123 ELECTR SENTINEL IN BLACK.)
HER MOVEMENTS HAVE LOST THEIR SQUARE-SHOULDERED 137 ELECTR STIFFNESS.
(SHE STOPS ABRUPTLY AND STIFFENS INTO HER OLD, 178 ELECTR SQUARE-SHOULDERED ATTITUDE.
AND THEN TURNS AND STANDS FOR A WHILE, STIFF AND 179 ELECTR SQUARE-SHOULDERED,
HIS LEAN FIGURE IS STILL ERECT AND SQUARE- 576 ICEMAN SHOULDERED.
HE IS EIGHTEEN, TALL AND BROAD-SHOULDERED BUT 585 ICEMAN THIN, GANGLING AND AWKWARD.
ABOUT FIVE FEET EIGHT, BROAD-SHOULDERED AND DEEP- 13 JOURNE CHESTED.
HE HAS HIS FATHER'S BROAD-SHOULDERED, DEEP-CHESTED 19 JOURNE PHYSIQUE,
BROAD-SHOULDERED AND DEEP-CHESTED. 36 MISBEG
(CORNELIUS MELODY IS FORTY-FIVE, TALL, BROAD- 33 POET SHOULDERED, DEEP-CHESTED,
PADDY O'DOWD IS THIN, ROUND-SHOULDERED, FLAT- 51 POET CHESTED, WITH A PIMPLY COMPLEXION,
HE IS A TALL, LEAN, STOOP-SHOULDERED OLD MAN OF 578 ROPE SIXTY-FIVE.
AT ONE OF THE TABLES, FRONT, A ROUND-SHOULDERED 493 VOYAGE YOUNG FELLOW IS SITTING,
HE IS A MAN OF ABOUT FIFTY, TALL, LOOSE-LIMBED, A 450 WELDED BIT STOOP-SHOULDERED.

SHOULDERING

THEY TURN, SHOULDERING EACH OTHER, 206 DESIRE

SHOULDERS

ON ACCOUNT OF THE ENORMOUS PRUPPORTIONS OF HIS 538 'ILE SHOULDERS AND CHEST.

SHOULDERS

SHOULDERS (CONT'D.)
HE PUTS HIS ARM PROTECTINGLY OVER HER SHOULDERS) 546 'ILE
FOR A MOMENT HIS SHOULDERS SAG, HE BECOMES OLD, 549 'ILE
(HE PUTS BOTH HANDS ON HER SHOULDERS 551 'ILE
PADDED SHOULDERS AND PANTS HALF-PEGGED AT THE TOP,187 AHWILD
(SUDDENLY PUTS BOTH HANDS ON HIS SHOULDERS-- 206 AHWILD
QUIETLY)
(UNIMPRESSED--WITH A CYNICAL SHRUG OF HER 243 AHWILD
SHOULDERS)
(LOOKS AFTER HER WORRIEDLY FOR A SECOND--THEN 248 AHWILD
SHRUGS HIS SHOULDERS)
LARRY COMES AND PEERS OVER HIS SHOULDERS. 4 ANNA
THE MUSCLES OF HIS ARMS AND SHOULDERS ARE LUMPED 30 ANNA
IN KNOTS AND BUNCHES.
AND THROWS IT OVER HER SHOULDERS) 44 ANNA
HER SHOULDERS QUIVER ONCE OR TWICE AS IF SHE WERE 52 ANNA
FIGHTING BACK HER SOBS.
(CHRIS IS SITTING WITH BOWED SHOULDERS, HIS HEAD 57 ANNA
IN HIS HANDS.
HIS SHOULDERS BOWED, HIS HEAD SUNK FORWARD 67 ANNA
DEJECTEDLY.
PUTS HER HANDS ON HIS SHOULDERS AS THOUGH TO TRY 107 BEYOND
TO PUSH HIM BACK IN THE CHAIR
HIS SHOULDERS ARE STOUPED AS IF UNDER TOO GREAT A 119 BEYOND
BURDEN.
WITH YOU AGAINST ME--(HE SHRUGS HIS SHOULDERS. 123 BEYOND
ROBERT GRABS HER BY THE SHOULDERS AND GLARES INTO 127 BEYOND
HER EYES)
(SHE AGAIN HIDES HER FACE IN HER HANDS, HER BOWED 139 BEYOND
SHOULDERS TREMBLING.)
HER SHOULDERS SHAKE AS IF SHE WERE SOBBING. 142 BEYOND
(SHRUGGING HIS SHOULDERS) WHAT'S THE USE OF 148 BEYOND
TALKING TO YOU?
(ANDREW GROANS) BUT NOW--(HE SHRUGS HIS SHOULDERS158 BEYOND
SIGNIFICANTLY.)
HE SHUDDERS AND SHAKES HIS SHOULDERS AS IF SHAKING466 CARIBE
OFF SOMETHING WHICH DISGUSTED
(HE GETS WEARILY TO HIS FEET AND WALKS WITH BOWED 473 CARIBE
SHOULDERS, STAGGERING A BIT.
(THEY TAKE PADDY BY THE SHOULDERS AND FEET AND 473 CARIBE
CARRY HIM OFF LEFT.
THE HEAD AND SHOULDERS OF NAT BARTLETT APPEAR OVER555 CROSS
THE SILL.
HIS SHOULDERS HAVE A WEARY STOOP AS IF WORN DOWN 556 CROSS
WAIT ME TO GET YOU SOMETHING TO PUT OVER YOUR 533 DAYS
SHOULDERS)
WEARILY TO HIS FEET, HIS SHOULDERS BOWED, LOOKING 560 DAYS
TRAGICALLY OLD AND BEATEN--
THEIR SHOULDERS STOOP A BIT FROM YEARS OF FARM 204 DESIRE
WORK.
HE STANDS STARING AT HER, HIS ARMS HANGING 241 DESIRE
DISJOINTEDLY FROM HIS SHOULDERS.
HER HAIR TUMBLES OVER HER SHOULDERS IN DISARRAY, 244 DESIRE
HER FACE IS FLUSHED,
HE GRINS--THEN SQUARES HIS SHOULDERS AND AWAITS 245 DESIRE
HIS FATHER CONFIDENTLY.
ABBIE IS SITTING IN A ROCKING CHAIR, A SHAWL 247 DESIRE
WRAPPED ABOUT HER SHOULDERS.
COMES OUT AND AROUND THE CORNER OF THE HOUSE, HIS 269 DESIRE
SHOULDERS SQUARED.
(RISING ALSO AND PUTTING HER HANDS ON HIS 498 DIFRNT
SHOULDERS STOOP, AND HER FIGURE IS FLABBY AND 528 DIFRNT
UGLY.
GRABS HER BY THE SHOULDERS AND BENDS HIS FACE 433 DYNAMO
CLOSE TO HERS) ADA/
(SHE PUSHES HIM AWAY, BUT, HOLDING HIS SHOULDERS, 446 DYNAMO
STARES DOWN INTO HIS FACE)
(SHAKES HER HANDS OFF HIS SHOULDERS-- 447 DYNAMO
SHOULDERS, STARES UNEASILY IN HIS FACE) 466 DYNAMO
HEAVY GOLD CHEVRONS ON HIS SHOULDERS, GOLD BRAID 175 EJONES
ON THE COLLAR, CUFFS, ETC.
HE RAISES HIS WHIP AND LASHES JONES VICIOUSLY 194 EJONES
ACROSS THE SHOULDERS WITH IT.
A WINCHESTER RIFLE IS SLUNG ACROSS HIS SHOULDERS 194 EJONES
AND HE CARRIES A HEAVY WHIP.
(HE SIGHS DEJECTEDLY AND REMAINS WITH BOWED 196 EJONES
SHOULDERS.
LOOK AT THOSE SHOULDERS. 197 EJONES
HIS FACE HIDDEN, HIS SHOULDERS HEAVING WITH SOBS 200 EJONES
OF HYSTERICAL FRIGHT.
BUT AT ONCE SHE SHRUGS HER SHOULDERS WITH DISDAIN 9 ELECTR
AND COMES DOWN THE STEPS AND
(STUNG, GRABBING HER BY THE SHOULDERS--FIERCELY) 41 ELECTR
THE LEGS CLOSE TOGETHER, THE SHOULDERS SQUARE, THE 43 ELECTR
HEAD UPRIGHT.
(GRABS HER BY THE SHOULDERS AND STARES INTO HER 56 ELECTR
FACE)
(GRABBING HER BY THE SHOULDERS--FIERCELY) 63 ELECTR
(THEN SEIZING HER BY THE SHOULDERS AND STARING 89 ELECTR
INTO HER EYES--
(SHE GOES TO HIM AND, GRASPING HIM BY HIS 96 ELECTR
SHOULDERS.
(TAKING HIS HANDS OFF HER SHOULDERS AND RISING) 99 ELECTR
ORIN STOPS BEFORE HER AGAIN AND GRASPS HER BY THE 121 ELECTR
SHOULDERS.
(GRABBING HIM BY THE SHOULDERS) 124 ELECTR
(SHE SQUARES HER SHOULDERS. 168 ELECTR
(HE COMES FORWARD, PUTTING ONE ARM AROUND HER 291 GGBROW
BOWED SHOULDERS, AND THEY KISS.)
AS IF THEY WERE CARRYING A BODY BY THE LEGS AND 318 GGBROW
SHOULDERS.
HER YELLOW HAIR HANGS DOWN IN A GREAT MANE OVER 320 GGBROW
HER SHOULDERS.
THE FIERY LIGHT FLOODS OVER THEIR SHOULDERS AS 224 HA APE
THEY BEND ROUND FOR THE COAL.
(WITH A JERK OF HIS HEAD BACK ON HIS SHOULDERS, 238 HA APE

SHOULDERS (CONT'D.)
HIS BIG HEAD SQUATS ON A NECK WHICH SEEMS PART OF 8 HUGHIE
HIS BEEFY SHOULDERS.
(SHRUGS HIS SHOULDERS AND SITS DOWN AGAIN) 583 ICEMAN
(SHRUGS HIS SHOULDERS--INDIFFERENTLY) 584 ICEMAN
HIS ARM AROUND HICKEY'S SHOULDERS.) 618 ICEMAN
(ROCKY SHRUGS HIS SHOULDERS AND YAWNS SLEEPILY.) 666 ICEMAN
BUT ROCKY ONLY SHRUGS HIS SHOULDERS WITH WEARY 671 ICEMAN
DISGUST
(HE SHRUGS HIS SHOULDERS) AW RIGHT, IF HE ASKED 708 ICEMAN
FOR IT.
ROCKY STANDS IN BACK OF THEM, A HAND ON EACH OF 726 ICEMAN
THEIR SHOULDERS,
AND PULLING THEIR BLANKETS UP OVER THEIR 532 INZONE
SHOULDERS.
HIS SHOULDERS CONTINUE TO HEAVE SPASMODICALLY BUT 532 INZONE
HE MAKES NO FURTHER SOUND.
SHOULDERS SQUARED. 13 JOURNE
(JAMIE SHRUGS HIS SHOULDERS AND SITS DOWN IN THE 21 JOURNE
CHAIR ON HER RIGHT.)
BUT HE SHRUGS HIS SHOULDERS.) 26 JOURNE
(SHRUGGING HIS SHOULDERS.) ALL RIGHT. HAVE IT 29 JOURNE
YOUR WAY.
(WITH A SCORNFUL SHRUG OF HIS SHOULDERS.) 31 JOURNE
(HE STOPS, BORED WITH THEIR QUARREL, AND SHRUGS 33 JOURNE
HIS SHOULDERS.)
(HE SHRUGS HIS SHOULDERS--CYNICALLY.) 35 JOURNE
(SHRUGS HIS SHOULDERS.) THE SAME OLD STUFF. 40 JOURNE
(REBUFFED AND HURT, SHRUGS HIS SHOULDERS.) 42 JOURNE
(JAMIE AGAIN SHRUGS HIS SHOULDERS. 64 JOURNE
(SHRUGGING HIS SHOULDERS.) YOU WON'T BE SINGING A 66 JOURNE
SONG YOURSELF SOON.
(STUNG FOR A MOMENT--THEN SHRUGGING HIS SHOULDERS, 76 JOURNE
DRYLY.)
(SHRUGS HIS SHOULDERS.) YOU CAN'T TALK TO HER 78 JOURNE
NOW.
(SHRUGGING HIS SHOULDERS.) 80 JOURNE
IF YOU WOULD NOT FEEL THE HORRIBLE BURDEN OF TIME 132 JOURNE
WEIGHING ON YOUR SHOULDERS AND
(SHRUGS HIS SHOULDERS--THICKLY.) 158 JOURNE
POWERFUL SHOULDERS AND LONG ARMS AND HANDS, AND 299 LAZARU
SHORT, SKINNY,
(THEY SURROUND HIM, THROW OVER HIS SHOULDERS AND 307 LAZARU
HEAD THE FINELY DRESSED HIDE OF
SHE HAS GROWN MUCH OLDER, HER HAIR IS GRAY, HER 313 LAZARU
SHOULDERS ARE BOWED,
WHOSE MASKS, HELMETS AND ARMORED SHOULDERS CAN BE 313 LAZARU
SEEN AS THEY PASS THROUGH THE
CALIGULA SHRUGS HIS SHOULDERS, TURNING AWAY-- 328 LAZARU
LIGHTLY)
(MARCELLUS SHRUGS HIS SHOULDERS AND SMILES 332 LAZARU
DEPRECATINGLY.)
(GOING TO HIM, PUTS BOTH HANDS ON HIS SHOULDERS 333 LAZARU
AND LOOKS IN HIS EYES.
(SHE PUTS HER HANDS ON HIS SHOULDERS.) 6 MANSNS
(SHE SHRUGS HER SHOULDERS.) TOO LATE, DEBORAH. 32 MANSNS
(SHRUGS HER SHOULDERS INDIFFERENTLY.) 56 MANSNS
(THEN ABRUPTLY, WITH COLD CURTNESS, SHRUGGING HIS 66 MANSNS
SHOULDERS)
MOSTLY AROUND HIS CHEST AND SHOULDERS AND ARMS, 69 MANSNS
THE STOOP IN HIS SHOULDERS IS MORE PRONOUNCED, 70 MANSNS
(FURIOUS AT THE THOUGHT, SHE GRABS HIS SHOULDERS 81 MANSNS
AND SHAKES HIM FIERCELY.)
(STOPS CRYING INSTANTLY AT THE TONE OF HIS VOICE, 145 MANSNS
HOLDS HIM BY THE SHOULDERS.
LASHED TILL THE BLOOD RAN DOWN YOUR FAT WHITE 165 MANSNS
SHOULDERS/
SARA GRABS HER BY THE SHOULDERS AND SHAKES HER 165 MANSNS
ROUGHLY.)
(PUTTING HER HANDS ON HIS SHOULDERS AND LIFTING 368 MARCOM
HER LIPS)
KUKACHIN'S SHOULDERS QUIVER AS, HER HEAD BOWED IN 420 MARCOM
HER HANDS, SHE SOBS QUIETLY.
PRINCESS KUKACHIN, CARRIED ON A BIER DIRECTLY 433 MARCOM
BEHIND THEM ON THE SHOULDERS OF
HER SLOPING SHOULDERS ARE BROAD, HER CHEST DEEP 3 MISBEG
WITH LARGE, FIRM BREASTS.
HE HAS A THICK NECK, LUMPY, SLOPING SHOULDERS, 11 MISBEG
(SHRUGS HIS SHOULDERS) MAYBE. 41 MISBEG
SHRUGS HIS SHOULDERS) 43 MISBEG
(SHRUGS HIS SHOULDERS) NOTHING. 102 MISBEG
(SHRUGS HIS SHOULDERS) ALL RIGHT. 113 MISBEG
(STARES AT HER--THEN SHRUGS HIS SHOULDERS) 121 MISBEG
HE GIVES THE CHARACTERISTIC SHRUG OF SHOULDERS-- 122 MISBEG
CYNICALLY)
(SHRUGS HIS SHOULDERS) YES. 123 MISBEG
(HE SHRUGS HIS SHOULDERS) NUTS/ 129 MISBEG
(SHRUGS HIS SHOULDERS) WELL, HE'S STEWED TO THE 131 MISBEG
EARS.
(GLANCES UP AT HER, SURPRISED--THEN SHRUGS HIS 136 MISBEG
SHOULDERS)
HE SHRUGS HIS SHOULDERS, POURS OUT A BIG DRINK 139 MISBEG
MECHANICALLY)
(HE SHRUGS HIS SHOULDERS HOPELESSLY AND TURNS 139 MISBEG
TOWARD THE ROAD.)
JOSIE--(GIVES THE CHARACTERISTIC SHRUG OF HIS 140 MISBEG
SHOULDERS--SIMPLY)
(HE SHRUGS HIS SHOULDERS MECHANICALLY) 151 MISBEG
(HE SHRUGS HIS SHOULDERS.) WELL, ANYWAYS, 14 POET
(HE SQUAKES HIS SHOULDERS DEFIANTLY. 43 POET
HIS SHOULDERS SAG AND HE STARES AT THE TABLE TOP, 57 POET
THERE IS THE SAME SQUARING OF HIS SHOULDERS, 67 POET
ARROGANT LIFTING OF HIS HEAD,
(HE SHRUGS HIS SHOULDERS.) BUT NO MATTER. 105 POET
HER HAIR IS DOWN OVER HER SHOULDERS, REACHING TO 136 POET
HER WAIST.
BUT HER SHOULDERS STILL SHAKE. 166 POET

SHOULDERS

SHOULDERS (CONT'D.)

SARA REMAINS STANDING BY THE SIDE OF THE CENTER TABLE, HER SHOULDERS BOWED, 180 POET

AND THE STOOP TO HIS SHOULDERS OF A MAN WEAK MUSCULARLY, 4 STRANG

SHE IS TWENTY, TALL WITH BROAD SQUARE SHOULDERS, 12 STRANG
(SHRUGGING HIS SHOULDERS--CONFUSEDLY) 21 STRANG
SQUAKES HIS SHOULDERS, PULLS HIS COAT DOWN IN 22 STRANG
FRONT, SETS HIS TIE STRAIGHT,

HIS SHOULDERS ARE COLLAPSED SUBMISSIVELY. 67 STRANG
HIS SHOULDERS HUNCHED-DESPONDENTLY) 67 STRANG
(THEN DISMISSING MARSDEN WITH A SHRUG OF HIS 78 STRANG
SHOULDERS)

(GETTING UP, COMES TO HER AND PUTS HIS HANDS ON 83 STRANG
HER SHOULDERS,

HIS SHOULDERS ARE BOWED, HIS WHOLE FIGURE DROOPS.) 98 STRANG
(SHE GETS UP AND PUTS HER HANDS ON HIS SHOULDERS 145 STRANG
AND LOOKS INTO HIS EYES--

GRABS DARRELL BY BOTH SHOULDERS AND SHAKES HIM) 181 STRANG
MADELINE STANDING BEHIND HIM, HER ARM ABOUT HIS 189 STRANG
SHOULDERS.

BENT OVER WEARILY, HIS SHOULDERS BOWED, HIS LONG 462 WELDED
ARMS RESTING ON HIS KNEES,

(THEN SHRUGGING HER SHOULDERS, FATALISTICALLY) 469 WELDED
IT FALLS OVER HER SHOULDERS IN A PEROXIDED FLOOD. 474 WELDED
(THEN TOUCHED, SHE COMES TO HIM AND PUTS HER ARMS 479 WELDED
AROUND HIS SHOULDERS,

SHOULON'TA

WE SHOULON'TA MADE THIS TRIP, AND THEN--HOW'D ALL 487 CARDIF
THE FOG GIT IN HERES

SHOULDST

WHAT HAVE I DONE THAT THOU SHOULDST TORTURE MES 413 MARCOM

SHOUT

(SEEING ROBERT HAS NOT NOTICED HIS PRESENCE--IN A 82 BEYOND
LOUD SHOUT)

(IN AN ANSWERING SHOUT OF FORCED CHEERINESS) 128 BEYOND
(IN A LOUDER SHOUT) AHOY THERE, ROB/ 128 BEYOND
(HIS VOICE IS A HARSH SHOUT.) 128 BEYOND
FOR GAWD'S SAKE, BOYS, DON'T SHOUT SO LOUD/ 471 CARIBE
I HEARD A SHOUT. 568 CROSS
(FLOURISHING IT ABOVE HIS HEAD WITH A SHOUT OF 573 CROSS
TRIUMPH)

DON'T SHOUT LIKE THAT/ 57 ELECTR
I DON'T WANT TO SHOUT ACROSS THE ROOM. 91 ELECTR
(HIS VOICE HAS RISEN TO A SHOUT. 105 ELECTR
HE QUELLS THE UPROAR WITH A SHOUT) 216 HA APE
(WITH HIS VOICE LEADING THEY ALL SHOUT *HAPPY 653 ICEMAN
BIRTHDAY, HARRY/*

AND ROCKY IN THE BAR, AND SHOUT IN CHORUS, *WHO 707 ICEMAN
THE HELL CARES*

(THEY ALL TAKE IT UP AND SHOUT IN ENTHUSIASTIC 727 ICEMAN
JEERING CHORUS)

GIVE A SHOUT IF HE STARTS THIS WAY. 518 INZONE
(WITH A GREAT SHOUT) HUSANNAH/ 278 LAZARU
(THE SOLDIERS FORM A WEDGE AND CHARGE WITH A 291 LAZARU
SHOUT.

THE SENATORS CHEER AND SHOUT AS AT A TRIUMPH.) 320 LAZARU
SUDDENLY A SHOUT RISES FROM THE LIPS OF ALL THE 375 MARCOM
TARTARS,

(WITH A GREAT FIERCE SHOUT AND A CLANKING OF 422 MARCOM
SWORDS) DEATH/

(THERE IS A SHOUT OF LAUGHTER FROM JOSIE'S 62 MISBEG
BEDROOM.

FOR IT'S A GREAT JOKE TO HEAR HIM SHOUT AGAINST 26 POET
MOB RULE.

SHOUT *THIS IS LIFE AND THIS IS SEX, AND HERE ARE 176 STRANG
PASSION AND HATRED AND REGRET

SHOUTED

AND WHEN I TURNED ROUND AND BEAT IT HE SHOUTED 593 ROPE
AFTER ME.

SHOUTIN'

WHEN YOU GOT TO SHOUTIN' I SNEAKED OUT O' THE 544 DIFRNT
KITCHEN INTO THERE TO HEAR WHAT

(SCORNFULLY) A FINE ONE YOU BE TO BE SHOUTIN' 580 ROPE
SCRIPTURE IN A BODY'S EARS ALL

SHOUTING

AND THE MATE'S VOICE SHOUTING ORDERS.) 550 'ILE
(HIS HEAD IS WITHDRAWN AND HE CAN BE HEARD 551 'ILE
SHOUTING ORDERS.)

(SHOUTING) HEY, DICK WAKE UP/ 193 AHWILD
(THEN SHOUTING OUT AGAIN) DIS VAY/ 29 ANNA
THE VOICE IS HEARD AGAIN SHOUTING *AHOY* AND CHRIS 30 ANNA
ANSWERING *DIS VAY.*

THEY HEAR ANDY'S VOICE FROM THE ROAD SHOUTING A 128 BEYOND
LUNG HAIL--*AHOY THERE/*

THE UPROAR OF SHOUTING LAUGHING AND SINGING 469 CARIBE
VOICES HAS INCREASED IN VIOLENCE.

SHOUTING TO SCARE FOLKS AS IF YOU WAS A LITTLE 498 DIFRNT
BOY,

AND NOT HAVE ME SHOUTING MY LUNGS OUTS 528 DIFRNT
(STAMMERING BETWEEN FEAR AND RAGE--SHOUTING AFTER 530 DIFRNT
HER)

(WHAT'S HE SHOUTING ABOUT..... 424 DYNAMO
(HE SPRINGS UP THE STAIRS TO HER, SHOUTING 488 DYNAMO
FIERCELY) HARLOT/

HE SNATCHES AT HIS HIP, SHOUTING DEFIANTLY.) 202 EJUNES
THE ROOM IS CROWDED WITH MEN, SHOUTING, CURSING, 207 HA APE
LAUGHING, SINGING---

POUNDING ON HIS CHEST, GORILLA-LIKE, WITH THE 225 HA APE
OTHER, SHOUTING)

(SHOUTING) WHAT IS UT, YE SWINES 526 INZONE
HE BEGAN BY SHOUTING THAT HE WAS NO SLAVE STANDARD 24 JOURNE
OIL COULD TRAMPLE ON.

A MOMENT LATER SHE IS HEARD SHOUTING.) 53 JOURNE
(THE THIRD GUEST OF SCENE ONE RUSHES IN 290 LAZARU
BREATHLESSLY, SHOUTING)

HOPPING RESTLESSLY ABOUT FROM FOOT TO FOOT-- 319 LAZARU
SHOUTING)

SHOVEL

SHOUTING (CONT'D.)

FLOURISHING HIS SWORD AND COMES RUNNING INTO THE 338 LAZARU
ROOM, SHOUTING)

FLAMES, LIKE A MAN HALF OVERCOME BY A POISONOUS 369 LAZARU
GAS, SHOUTING,

I HEAR THEM SHOUTING *POPE,* 361 MARCOM
(AS A NOISE OF SHOUTING COMES TOWARD THEM) 361 MARCOM
SHOUTING YOU WANT TO MURDER HIS FATHER, 127 POET
OF MARSDEN'S VOICE YELLING DRUNKENLY, OF EVANS', 174 STRANG
ALL SHOUTING, *GORDON/

SHOUTS

(SHOUTS AFTER HIM) BUT YOU SET OFF YOUR CRACKERS 186 AHWILD
AWAY FROM THE HOUSE, REMEMBER/

(SHOUTS AFTER HER) I CAN'T WAIT. 200 AHWILD
(SHOUTS FROM NEXT ROOM) DON'T I GET THAT BUCKET 10 ANNA
OF SUDS, DUTCHY/

(SHOUTS) BRING ODER DRINK, LARRY/ 13 ANNA
(HE HOLDS HIS HANDS TO HIS MOUTH, MEGAPHONE- 29 ANNA
FASHION, AND SHOUTS BACK)

CHRIS'S VOICE SHOUTS AFTER HIM) 30 ANNA
IS HE SEASONIN' HIS HAY WITH RAIN THIS YEAR, SAME 124 BEYOND
AS LAST* THEY SHOUTS.

THE FIDDLER SHOUTS DIRECTIONS FOR THE DIFFERENT 250 DESIRE
MOVEMENTS,

AND ALL THE WHILE HE INTERSPERSES HIS ANTICS WITH 291 DESIRE
SHOUTS AND DERISIVE COMMENTS)

(THIS LAST HE HALF SHOUTS, HALF CROONS 262 DESIRE
INCOHERENTLY.

HIS MOTHER AND FATHER SHRINK BACK FROM HIM AS HE 452 DYNAMO
SHOUTS UP AT THE SKY)

(NOT SEEING ANYONE---GREATLY IRRITATED AND BLINKINGLTe EJUNES
SLEEPILY--SHOUTS)

(RUSHING INTO THE NEXT ROOM, SHOUTS IN TERRIFIED 318 GGBROW
TONES)

(SHOUTS FROM THE GARDEN AND A VOLLEY OF SHOTS. 321 GGBROW
(SHOUTS) COME IN, WHY DON'T YOU/ 246 HA APE
AND HE PUNCHES HIS FIST LIKE A HAM ON DE DESK, AND 601 ICEMAN
HE SHOUTS,

(HE SHOUTS TO THE BAR) HEY, CHUCK AND ROCKY/ 657 ICEMAN
(THIS IS FOLLOWED BY AN OUTBURST OF INSULTING 283 LAZARU
SHOUTS

(SHOUTS COMMANDINGLY) DISPERSE/ 291 LAZARU
TIBERIUS STANDS ON THE RAISED DAIS LAUGHING GREAT 368 LAZARU
SHOUTS OF GLEE,

A MOMENT LATER, PRECEDED BY SHOUTS, A CRACKING OF 350 MARCOM
WHIPS,

(WITH A GREAT CRACKING OF WHIPS AND SHOUTS OF PAIN554 MARCOM
KUBLAI SHOUTS AT HIM IMPATIENTLY) 423 MARCOM
(IMMEDIATELY WITH MAD SHOUTS OF *BRAVO/* 429 MARCOM
SWITCHING SUDDENLY FROM JARRING SHOUTS TO LOW, 56 MISBEG
CONFIDENTIAL VITUPERATION.

(SHOUTS) WHATS 58 MISBEG
(SHOUTS) HOLD YOUR DIRTY TONGUE/ 59 MISBEG
(SHOUTS) WAIT/ 59 MISBEG
(SHOUTS DERISIVELY) AND I'LL PUT IT IN MY 64 MISBEG
LAWYER'S HANDS AND IN THE NEWSPAPERS/

(SHOUTS BACK) SHUT UP YOUR NOISE, YOU CRAZY OLD 73 MISBEG
BILLY GOAT/

HE SHOUTS) 93 MISBEG
THERE IS A ROAR OF WELCOMING DRUNKEN SHOUTS, 180 POET
THEN MELODY'S VOICE IS PLAINLY HEARD IN THE 180 POET
SILENCE AS HE SHOUTS A TOAST..

(VIOLENTLY--ALMOST SHOUTS AT HER) 97 STRANG
(HE SHOUTS UP AT THE SKY) YOU'RE MY SON, GORDON/ 198 STRANG
AS THEY GO OUT DRISCOLL SHOUTS BACK OVER HIS 904 VOYAGE
SHOULDER)

SHOVE

(SHE GIVES HIM A FINAL SHOVE INSIDE THE DOOR AND 445 DYNAMO
CLOSES IT.)

WHO ASKED YOU TO SHOVE IN AN OARS 626 ICEMAN
SHOVE HIM BACK TO HIS OWN TABLE, ROCKY. 668 ICEMAN
(BELLIGERENTLY) GUV 'IM A SHOVE IN THE MARF AND 524 INZONE
LEAVE 'IM OVER THE SIDE/

SHOVE OVER THE BOTTLE. 156 JOURNE
(SHE GIVES HIM A SHOVE INSIDE AND CLOSES THE 55 MISBEG
DOOR.)

(HE GIVES HARDER A SHOVE) BEAT IT NOW/ 64 MISBEG
IN THE MORNING HE'LL SIGN ALL THEY SHOVE IN FRONT 91 MISBEG
OF HIM.

A SHOVE THAT ALMOST KNOCKS HIM OFF HIS CHAIR. 97 POET
WE'LL SHOVE A RAG IN HER MOUTH SO'S SHE CAN'T 600 ROPE
YELL.

WE'LL JUST SHOVE THIS INTO THE STOVE TILL IT'S 600 ROPE
RED-HOT

GUV 'IM A SHOVE IN THE MARF, DRISC. 504 VOYAGE

SHOVEL

THE DOOR TO THE BAR IS SHOVED OPEN AND MICKEY 92 POET
CALLS IN.)

(MELODY HAS SHOVED THE DECANTER TOWARD HIM. 93 POET
IRISHMAN DRESSED IN PATCHED CORDUROY TROUSERS 582 ROPE
SHOVED DOWN INTO HIGH LACED BOOTS,

SHOVEL

AND BELOW DECK YOU GOT FALLAS YUST KNOW HOW FOR 49 ANNA
SHOVEL COAL--

MAYBE HE HITS ME WID A WHIP AND I SPLITS HIS HEAD 181 EJUNES
WID A SHOVEL AND RUNS AWAY AND

(AS IF THERE WERE A SHOVEL IN HIS HANDS HE GOES 194 EJUNES
THROUGH WEARY,

THEY SWING THEIR PICKS, THEY SHOVEL, BUT NOT A 194 EJUNES
SOUND COMES FROM THEIR LABOR.

WITH ARMS UPRAISED AS IF HIS SHOVEL WERE A CLUB IN194 EJUNES
HIS HANDS HE SPRINGS

GIMME MY SHOVEL 'TIL I SPLITS HIS DAMN HEAD/ 195 EJUNES
SHOVEL ON THE WHITE MAN'S SKULL, 195 EJUNES
GIMME A SHOVEL, ONE O' YOU, FO' GOD'S SAKE/ 195 EJUNES
WHAT'S MY SHOVEL A 195 EJUNES
THE MEN SHOVEL WITH A RHYTHMIC MOTION, 223 HA APE

SHOVEL

SHOVEL (CONT'D.)
HE BRANDISHES HIS SHOVEL MURDEROUSLY OVER HIS HEAD225 HA APE
IN ONE HAND.
AND HURLS HIS SHOVEL AFTER THEM AT THE DOOR WHICH 226 HA APE
HAS JUST CLOSED.
AND THERE WAS YANK ROARIN' CURSES AND TURNING 229 HA APE
ROUND WID HIS SHOVEL TO BRAIN HER--
UP IN BACK OF ME, AND I HOPPED ROUND TO KNOCK HIM 230 HA APE
DEAD WIT DE SHOVEL.
AND THE LOVING WAY YANK HEAVED HIS SHOVEL AT THE 230 HA APE
SKULL OF HER.
AND I FLUNG DE SHOVEL--ON'Y SHE'D BEAT IT. 231 HA APE

SHOVELED
I SHOVELED SAND ON A BIG WATERPOWER JOB OUT WEST. 461 DYNAMO

SHOVELERS
MOTIONS HIM TO TAKE HIS PLACE AMONG THE OTHER 194 EJONES
SHOVELERS.

SHOVELING
WITH ME SHOVELING A MILLION TONS OF COAL 35 ANNA
DEN FALLAHS DAT VORK BELOW SHOVELING COAL VAS DE 43 ANNA
DIRTIESS.
THIS ACCENTUATES THE NATURAL STOOPING POSTURE 207 HA APE
WHICH SHOVELING COAL AND THE

SHOVELS
SOME CARRY PICKS, THE OTHERS SHOVELS. 194 EJONES
THEY USE THE SHOVELS TO THROW OPEN THE FURNACE 223 HA APE
DOORS.
NOR LEFT, HANDLING THEIR SHOVELS AS IF THEY WERE 223 HA APE
PART OF THEIR BODIES,
LEANING ON THEIR SHOVELS IN RELAXED ATTITUDES OF 223 HA APE
EXHAUSTION.
(CHANTING A COUNT AS HE SHOVELS WITHOUT SEEMING 224 HA APE
EFFORT)

SHOVES
(MILDRED SLYLY SHOVES HER FOOT OUT SO THAT HE 193 AHWILD
TRIPS OVER IT, ALMOST FALLING.
HE QUICKLY SHOVES THE LETTER INTO THE INSIDE 208 AHWILD
POCKET OF HIS COAT
(HAS BROUGHT HER PAPER AROUND TO HER FATHER AND 251 AHWILD
NOW SHOVES IT UNDER HIS NOSE)
THEN SHOVES IT AWAY 275 AHWILD
HE COMES FORWARD AND PICKS UP THE SHOES AND 121 BEYOND
STOCKINGS WHICH HE SHOVES CARELESSLY
(GRABBING HIS HAT HE TAKES RUTH'S ARM AND SHOVES 166 BEYOND
HER TOWARD THE DOOR)
(HE SHOVES OUT HIS HAND. 10 HUGHIE
(HE SHOVES OUT HIS HAND WHICH THE CLERK CLASPS 36 HUGHIE
WITH A LIMP PLEASURE.
(ROCKY COUNTS THE MONEY QUICKLY AND SHOVES IT IN 613 ICEMAN
HIS POCKET.)
(SHOVES THE KEY IN HIS POCKET) THANKS, ROCKY. 620 ICEMAN
(ROCKY GIVES HIM A HOSTILE LOOK BUT SHOVES A 673 ICEMAN
BOTTLE AND GLASS AT HIM.
(AS ROCKY SHOVES A BOTTLE TOWARD HIM HE SHAKES HIS681 ICEMAN
HEAD)
THEN SHOVES IT IN HIS POCKET WITHOUT A WORD OF 700 ICEMAN
ACKNOWLEDGMENT.
ROCKY SHOVES A GLASS AND BOTTLE AT HIM. 724 ICEMAN
SHOVES THE SUITCASE BACK UNDER THE BUNK, CLIMBS 513 INZONE
INTO HIS BUNK AGAIN.
(HE SHOVES THE BOTTLE OVER. 157 JOURNE
HIS OTHER ARM AND ON HIS LAP, AND SHOVES THE 175 JOURNE
BOTTLE BACK.
(HE SHOVES THE MONEY INTO HIS POCKET.) 7 MISBEG
SHE STRIPS OFF A NOTE FURTIVELY AND SHOVES IT INTO508 VOYAGE
HER BOSOM.

SHOVING
WHICH THEY START SHOVING IN FRONT OF EACH MEMBER 658 ICEMAN
OF THE PARTY.)
GOD DAMN YOU, STOP SHOVING YOUR ROTTEN SOUL IN MY 706 ICEMAN
LAP!
(SHOVING AND WHACKING) BACK! 300 LAZARU
(FIERCELY, SHOVING HIS DIRTY UNSHAVEN FACE ALMOST 62 MISBEG
INTO HARDER'S)

SHOW
I'LL SHOW YOU! 194 AHWILD
THERE MUST BE SOME BOY HE KNOWS WHO'S TRYING TO 196 AHWILD
SHOW OFF AS ADVANCED AND WICKED,
I'LL HAVE HER SHOW HIM IN HERE. 199 AHWILD
ELDERS AND HIS GIRL AND BOY FRIENDS TO SHOW OFF 202 AHWILD
WHAT A YOUNG HELLION HE IS!
I'LL SHOW HER! 208 AHWILD
I'LL SHOW HER SHE CAN'T TREAT ME THE WAY SHE'S 220 AHWILD
DONE!
I'LL SHOW THEM ALL! 220 AHWILD
I'LL SHOW ALL OF YOU HOW MUCH I CARE. 228 AHWILD
(THEN SUDDENLY IN THE TONES OF A SIDE-SHOW BARKER)231 AHWILD
I'LL SHOW THEM! 235 AHWILD
(LAUGHS IRRITABLY--TO RICHARD) DON'T LET HIM KID 237 AHWILD
YOU. YOU SHOW HIM.
SHOW ME HOW MUCH! 240 AHWILD
SHOW ME YOU REALLY KNOW HOW TO DRINK. 240 AHWILD
AND THIS TIME I'LL BLOW YOU JUST TO SHOW MY 242 AHWILD
APPRECIATION.
I'LL SHOW THEM! 245 AHWILD
(SHE PASSES AROUND THE TABLE TO SHOW HER AUNT 250 AHWILD
LILY.
HE JUST WANTS TO SHOW OFF HE'S HEARTBROKEN ABOUT 251 AHWILD
THAT SILLY MURIEL--
YOU KNOW YOU'RE JUST DYING TO SHOW OFF. 256 AHWILD
IT ALL GOES TO SHOW YOU NEVER CAN TELL BY 269 AHWILD
APPEARANCES--
DARN IT, I WISH SHE'D SHOW UP/. 276 AHWILD
YUH DON'T KNOW WHAT TIME YOUR KID'S LIABLE TO SHOW 13 ANNA
UP.
(SKEPTICALLY) HE'LL HAVE TO SHOW ME. 19 ANNA
YOU GO TO MOVIES, SEE SHOW, GAT ALL KINDS FUN-- 42 ANNA

SHOW (CONT'D.)
AY'M OLE BIRD MAYBE, BUT AY BET AY SHOW HIM TRICK 43 ANNA
OR TWO.
I'LL SHOW YOU! 56 ANNA
BUT EVEN IF HE DID, I'D RATHER HAVE HIM COME THAN 64 ANNA
NOT TO SHOW UP AT ALL.
THEN I GAVE UP HOPE WHEN YOU DIDN'T SHOW UP AND I 71 ANNA
WENT TO THE RAILROAD STATION.
THOUGH HE'S BEEN TRYING NOT TO SHOW IT. 83 BEYOND
AND THEY PROMISED TO SHOW ME ALL OF THEM, IF I'D 90 BEYOND
ONLY COME. COME!
TU SORTA TALK TO AND SHOW THINGS TO, AND TEACH, 103 BEYOND
KINDA.
HOLES SHOW IN THE CURTAINS. 112 BEYOND
WE'LL SHOW MAMA YOU'RE A GOOD LITTLE GIRL, WON'T 121 BEYOND
WE?
WE'LL SHOW MAMA WE KNOW HOW TO DO THOSE THINGS, 121 BEYOND
WON'T WE?
HE'LL SHOW WHAT A MAN CAN DO! 127 BEYOND
SHOW IN THE FADED CARPET. 144 BEYOND
HE IS BEGINNING TO SHOW THE EFFECTS OF THE LIQUOR.467 CARIBE
HIS GOD OF LOVE WAS BEGINNING TO SHOW HIMSELF AS A511 DAYS
GOD OF VENGEANCE, YOU SEE?
AND INSIDE I KEPT SWEARING TO MYSELF THAT I'D SHOW521 DAYS
WALTER--
SHOW ME THE WAY! 562 DAYS
IT'LL SERVE 'M SHOW HIM WE'RE DONE WITH HIM. 216 DESIRE
STARTING EYES SHOW THE AMOUNT OF =LIKKER= HE HAS 248 DESIRE
CONSUMED.)
I'LL SHOW YE DANCIN'. 250 DESIRE
THEY'S A ARRER WOUND ON MY BACKSIDE I C'D SHOW YE/251 DESIRE
(HOPEFULLY) AND MAYBE IF I SHOW YOU WHAT I DONE 517 DIFRNT
WASN'T NATURAL TO ME--
AND HE'LL SHOW ME A GOOD TIME, AND IF I HAD A 523 DIFRNT
HUNDRED DOLLARS--
AND I COULDN'T SHOW MYSELF UP AS A CHEAP SKATE BY 523 DIFRNT
TRAVELIN' AROUND WITH HIM.
AND I'LL SHOW 'EM I'M DIFF'RENT, TOO. 532 DIFRNT
I'LL SHOW YOU SOMETIMES. 545 DIFRNT
THE FRONT WALLS OF THESE ROOMS ARE REMOVED TO SHOW -0 DYNAMO
THE DIFFERENT INTERIORS.
AND IF I DON'T SHOW HIM UP YELLOW 432 DYNAMO
(GLAD TO MAKE A SHOW OF HIS INDEPENDENCE BEFORE 437 DYNAMU
FIFE)
YOU CAN'T MAKE ME SHOW HER YOU HURT ME/....) 449 DYNAMO
I'LL SHOW HIM! 451 DYNAMO
I'LL SHOW HIM WHAT A REAL WHIPPING IS! 452 DYNAMO
I'LL SHOW YOU! 453 DYNAMO
BUT I'LL SOON SHOW ADA/... 459 DYNAMO
(HE FORCES ANOTHER LAUGH) IT JUST GOES TO SHOW 470 DYNAMO
YOU WHAT A HOLD THAT BUNK GETS
I'LL SHOW YER WHAT'S WHAT. 174 EJONES
DEY WANTS DE BIG CIRCUS SHOW FOR DEIR MONEY. 177 EJONES
AND JUST TO SHOW YER I'M YER FRIEND, 181 EJONES
IS YOU LIGHTIN' MATCHES TO SHOW DEM WHAR YOU IS? 189 EJONES
ALL EXCHANGE COURTLY GREETINGS IN DUMB SHOW AND 196 EJONES
CHAT SILENTLY TOGETHER.
WAL, I PROMISED AMOS I'D HELP SHOW YE THE SIGHTS 7 ELECTR
WHEN YOU CAME TO VISIT HIM.
YOU TELL HER I GOT PERMISSION FROM VINNIE TO SHOW 8 ELECTR
YOU ROUND.
I'LL SHOW YOU THE PEACH ORCHARD AND THEN WE'LL GO 10 ELECTR
TO MY GREENHOUSE.
I GAVE SETH PERMISSION TO SHOW THEM AROUND. 17 ELECTR
THEN EMBARRASSED BY THIS SHOW OF EMOTION, ADDS IN 52 ELECTR
A GRUFF, JOKING TONE)
KEEPS ME HIDING THE THINGS I'D LIKE TO SHOW. 55 ELECTR
WELL, IT ONLY GOES TO SHOW HOW YOU CAN MISJUDGE A 68 ELECTR
PERSON WITHOUT MEANING TO--
HE NEVER WAS ONE FOR SHOW. 69 ELECTR
I'D SHOW YOU THEN I HADN'T BEEN TAUGHT TO KILL FOR 89 ELECTR
NOTHING!
I'LL SHOW YOU TO THE WORLD AS A DAUGHTER WHO 91 ELECTR
DESIRED HER MOTHER'S LOVER AND THEN
BELOW THE DECK THE PORTHOLES SHOW A FAINT LIGHT 102 ELECTR
FROM THE INTERIOR OF THE CABIN.
COME DOWN OUT O' THAT AND I'LL SHOW YE WHO'S A 105 ELECTR
THIEF!
I'LL SHOW YOU THE HANDIEST PLACE TO SAY YOUR 132 ELECTR
PRAYERS.
SHOW ME THE WAY TO SAVE HIM! 157 ELECTR
THEY'LL NEVER GIT HER TO SHOW NOTHIN'. 170 ELECTR
HER FACE IS SAD AND PALE, HER EYES SHOW EVIDENCE 171 ELECTR
OF MUCH WEEPING.
IT HAS ALREADY BEGUN TO SHOW THE RAVAGES OF 269 GGBROW
DISSIPATION.
(TRYING NOT TO SHOW HIS ANNOYANCE) 275 GGBROW
(WITH A SHOW OF TORTURED DERISION) 311 GGBROW
I'LL SHOW YUH! 225 HA APE
I'LL SHOW YUH WHO'S A APE! 230 HA APE
I'LL SHOW HER I'M BETTER'N HER, IF SHE ON'Y KNEW 231 HA APE
IT.
I'LL SHOW HER IF SHE TINKS SHE--SHE GRINDS DE 231 HA APE
ORGAN AND I'M ON DE STRING, HUMS
IN THE REAR, THE SHOW WINDOWS OF TWO SHOPS, 233 HA APE
I'LL SHOW HER WHO'S A APE! 233 HA APE
AIN'T THAT WHY I BROUGHT YER UP 'ERE--TO SHOW YER$235 HA APE
(THICK WITH RAGE) I'LL SHOW YUH WHO'S A APE, YUH 241 HA APE
BUM!
I'LL SHOW HER WHO BELONGS! 242 HA APE
I'LL SHOW HER WHO'S IN DE MOVE AND WHO AIN'T. 242 HA APE
AFTER I'M 'NITIATED, I'LL SHOW YUH. 248 HA APE
I'LL SHOW YOUSE I'M ONE UF DE GANG. 249 HA APE
I'LL SHOW YUH! 249 HA APE
I JUST WANT TO SHOW YOU HOW I'LL TAKE YOU TO THE 37 HUGHIE
CLEANERS.
HE HAS NO SOCKS, AND HIS BARE FEET SHOW THROUGH 577 ICEMAN
HOLES IN THE SOLES,

SHOW

SHOW (CONT'D.)

I'LL SHOW YOU. 585 ICEMAN
WELL, THEY'LL GET A CHANCE NOW TO SHOW-- (HASTILY)593 ICEMAN
I DON'T MEAN--
AND I'LL SHOW YOU THE PRETTIEST (RAP, RAP, RAP) 597 ICEMAN
THAT EVER YOU DID SEE.
KEPT ME DOWN HERE WAITIN' FOR HICKEY TO SHOW UP, 602 ICEMAN
AND I'LL SHOW YOU THE PRETTIEST (RAP, RAP, RAP ON 607 ICEMAN
TABLE) THAT EVER YOU DID SEE.
THE GREATEST LIFE ON EARTH WITH THE GREATEST SHOW 609 ICEMAN
ON EARTH/
IT'S A WONDER HE DIDN'T HURRY A SALVATION ARMY 617 ICEMAN
UNIFORM AND SHOW UP IN THAT/
SHOW YOU A LITTLE WALK AROUND THE WARD IS NOTHING 621 ICEMAN
TO BE SO SCARED ABOUT.
SHOW THE OLD FAKER UP/ 623 ICEMAN
HAVE HAD PLENTY TO DRINK AND SHOW IT, BUT NO ONE, 629 ICEMAN
EXCEPT HUGO,
WE'RE GOIN' TO SHOW HIM/ 631 ICEMAN
AND IF YUH TINK WE'RE JUST KIDDIN' OURSELVES, 631 ICEMAN
WE'LL SHOW YUH/
(FURIOUSLY) I'LL SHOW YUH WHO'S A WHORE/ 632 ICEMAN
ALL THEIR ATTITUDES SHOW THE REACTION CORA HAS 638 ICEMAN
EXPRESSED.
UH, I KNOW HOW YOU RESENT THE WAY I HAVE TO SHOW 641 ICEMAN
YOU UP TO YOURSELF.
(WITH HATRED) I'LL SHOW HIM/ 645 ICEMAN
AND WON'T ALL THE OLD GANG BE TICKLED TO DEATH 652 ICEMAN
WHEN I SHOW UP ON THE LOT?
A SMOLDERING RESENTMENT BEGINNING TO SHOW IN HIS 659 ICEMAN
MANNER.)
BUT I'LL SHOW YOU, BEJEES/ 660 ICEMAN
OF COURSE YOU'LL TRY TO SHOW ME/ 660 ICEMAN
(HE GLARES AT HICKEY) I'LL SHOW YOU, TOO, 660 ICEMAN
*AND I'LL SHOW YOU THE PRETTIEST (RAP, RAP, RAP) 662 ICEMAN
THAT EVER YOU DID SEE/
WITH SPIGGOTS AND A SMALL SHOW CASE OF BOTTLED 664 ICEMAN
GOODS.
I'LL SHOW THAT CHEAP DRUMMER I DON'T HAVE TO HAVE 674 ICEMAN
ANY DUTCH COURAGE--
I'LL SHOW DOT BLOODY LIMEY CHENTLEMAN, AND DOT 676 ICEMAN
LIAR, HICKEY/
WAVING THEIR SILLY SWORDS, SO AFRAID THEY COULDN'T677 ICEMAN
SHOW OFF HOW BRAVE THEY VAS/
AND DON'T SHOW OFF YOUR LEGS TO DESE BUMS WHEN 683 ICEMAN
YOU'RE GOIN' TO BE MARRIED.
COME ON, NOW, SHOW US A LITTLE OF THAT GOOD OLD 685 ICEMAN
BATTLE OF MODDER RIVER SPIRIT
SHOW THE OLD YELLOW FAKER UP/ 689 ICEMAN
I WAS BETTIN' YUH'D MAKE IT AND SHOW DAT FOUR- 690 ICEMAN
FLUSHER UP.
IS TO SHOW YOU WHAT A PIPE DREAM DID TO ME AND 707 ICEMAN
EVELYN.
MURAN PULLS BACK HIS COAT TO SHOW HIS BADGE.) 708 ICEMAN
THEY WANTED TO BUY SOMETHING TO SHOW THEIR 711 ICEMAN
GRATITUDE.
I'LL SHOW YOU. 714 ICEMAN
I'LL SHOW YER WHAT FOR, YER BLEEDIN' SNEAK/ 526 INZONE
REALLY, HE OUGHT TO HAVE MORE PRIDE THAN TO MAKE 43 JOURNE
SUCH A SHOW OF HIMSELF.
YOU REALLY OUGHT TO SHOW MORE CONSIDERATION. 60 JOURNE
A TRACE OF BLUR IN HIS SPEECH, HE DOES NOT SHOW 108 JOURNE
IT.
IF THEY WANT TO BE WASTEFUL FOOLS, FOR THE SAKE OF126 JOURNE
SHOW, LET THEM BE/
YOU CAN SHOW YOURSELF UP BEFORE THE WHOLE TOWN AS 145 JOURNE
SUCH A STINKING OLD TIGHTWAD/
I'LL HAVE TO GO TO THE INFIRMARY AND SHOW SISTER 171 JOURNE
MARTHA.
AND HOW THESE THINGS ARE, THOUGH YE STROVE TO 173 JOURNE
SHOW, SHE WOULD NOT KNOW.=
EVEN A SON OF MAN MUST DIE TO SHOW MEN THAT MAN 293 LAZARU
MAY LIVE/
(STUNG--HER INWARD ANGER BEGINNING TO SHOW, AND 18 MANSNS
WITH IT HER BROGUE.
ALTHOUGH MOTHER HAS RELINQUISHED ALL OUTWARD SHOW 77 MANSNS
OF OWNERSHIP AND AUTHORITY,
BUT SINCE HE STARTED PLAYING NAPOLEON TO SHOW OFF 142 MANSNS
HIS GENIUS TO YOU,
I AM CONFIDENT YOU CAN SOON SHOW HIM HIS PLACE. 150 MANSNS
WITH A MOUSTACHE AND BEARD BEGINNING TO SHOW GRAY.347 MARCOM
SHOW ME YOUR LETTER AGAIN/ 353 MARCOM
I'LL SHOW YOU I'M NOT SCARED/ 362 MARCOM
I'LL MAKE HIM PAY, JUST TO SHOW HIM/ 368 MARCOM
AND NOW I WANT TO SHOW ANOTHER LITTLE AID TO 394 MARCOM
GOVERNMENT THAT I THOUGHT OUT.
I FELT LIKE ONE OF THOSE FIGURES IN A PUPPET SHOW 415 MARCOM
SHE HAS LONG SMOOTH ARMS, IMMENSELY STRONG, 3 MISBEG
ALTHOUGH NO MUSCLES SHOW.
TO SHOW THEM I DIDN'T CARE A DAMN. 86 MISBEG
THAT'LL SHOW HIM TWO CAN PLAY AT TRICKS/ 95 MISBEG
TO SHOW HIM NO MAN CAN GET THE BEST OF YOU--WHAT 97 MISBEG
ELSE?
I'LL SHOW HIM TO HIS SORROW/ 97 MISBEG
SMILES AT HIM COQUETTISHLY, BEGINNING TO SHOW THE 115 MISBEG
EFFECT OF HER REG DRUNK BY HER
AND I OUGHT TO SHOW YOU HOW PLEASED I AM. 118 MISBEG
I'LL SHOW YOU WHAT LOVE IS. 137 MISBEG
BUT THERE WERE SEVERAL PEOPLE AROUND AND I KNEW 148 MISBEG
THEY EXPECTED ME TO SHOW
TO PRANCE AROUND ON AND SHOW HIMSELF OFF/ 23 POET
MELODY MAKES A GALLANT SHOW OF HOLDING HER CHAIR 67 POET
AND HELPING HER BE SEATED.
YES, BUT IT DOESN'T SHOW SHE WANTS HIM TO MARRY 79 POET
ME.
SHOW SHE'S ON SIMON'S SIDE& 79 POET
I'LL SHOW YE/ 101 POET

SHOWING

SHOW (CONT'D.)
SURE, I HOPE YOU DIDN'T SHOW OFF AND JUMP YOUR 106 POET
BEAUTY OVER A FENCE
THE REASONS SHE GAVE HIM ARE SOUND AND SHOW A 109 POET
CONSIDERATION FOR YOUR GOOD NAME
IF YOU'LL KEEP OUT OF IT, I'LL SHOW YOU HOW I'LL 127 POET
MAKE A FOOL OF OLD HARFORD/
I'LL SHOW HIM I CAN PLAY AT THE GAME OF 131 POET
GENTLEMAN'S HONOR TOO/
(HE IS BEGINNING TO SHOW THE EFFECTS OF THE DRINK 593 ROPE
HE HAS HAD.
SWEENEY BEGINS TO SHOW SIGNS OF GETTING DRUNK. 594 ROPE
JUST WAIT TILL HE'S ASLEEP AND I'LL SHOW YUH-- 594 ROPE
TERNIGHT.
I WANT TO SHOW THE GANG A REAL TIME. 599 ROPE
I'LL SHOW YUH. 599 ROPE
WELL, IF HE DON'T ANSWER UP NICE AND EASY WE'LL 600 ROPE
SHOW HIM/
HE USED TO SHOW THEM TO ME... 25 STRANG
I'M GLAD HE DOESN'T SHOW IT/ 49 STRANG
AND IT'S ONLY A QUESTION OF TIME WHEN--WHY, TO 54 STRANG
SHOW YOU, COLE--
THEN I'D SHOW THEM ALL WHAT I COULD DO/... 68 STRANG
YOU'VE GOT TO SHOW ME WHAT'S THE SAME--THE TRULY 84 STRANG
SANE. YOU UNDERSTAND?
SEEMS TO ME YOU COULD SHOW A LITTLE MORE INTEREST 162 STRANG
WITHOUT IT HURTING YOU.
NICK'LL SHOW YER. 508 VOYAGE

SHOWCASE 3 ANNA
IN BACK OF THE BAR, A SMALL SHOWCASE DISPLAYING A
FEW BOTTLES OF CASE GOODS.

SHOWDOWN
THERE'LL BE NO SHOWDOWN/ 643 ICEMAN
WHEN YOU GET TO THE FINAL SHOWDOWN WITH HIM. 643 ICEMAN

SHOWED
AFTER WHAT I SHOWED YOU AND TOLD YOU 136 BEYOND
IT SHOWED ME THE WORLD IS A LARGER PROPOSITION 138 BEYOND
AND YET HE NEVER SAID OR SHOWED--GOD, HOW HE MUST 164 BEYOND
HAVE SUFFERED)
YOU CERTAINLY SHOWED YOU COULD WRITE IN THE OLD 497 DAYS
DAYS--ARTICLES, ANYWAY.
NOT SINCE THE LETTER I SHOWED YOU. 13 ELECTR
I GUESS I HAVEN'T SAID IT OR SHOWED IT MUCH--EVER. 55 ELECTR
I SHOWED HIM LOTS OF WAYS HE COULD CROSS HER UP, 16 HUGHIE
BUT HE WAS TOO SCARED.
I SURE TOOK HIM AROUND WITH ME IN TALES AND SHOWED 29 HUGHIE
HIM ONE HELL OF A TIME.
SCARED IF DEY HIT THE HAY DEY WOULDN'T BE HERE 580 ICEMAN
WHEN HICKEY SHOWED UP.
IT'S ABOUT TIME DEY SHOWED. 610 ICEMAN
(THEN ANGRILY) I WISH DE LOUSE NEVER SHOWED UP/ 631 ICEMAN
HE AIN'T PULLED DAT GAG OR SHOWED HER PHOTO AROUND636 ICEMAN
BECAUSE HE AIN'T DRUNK.
HE'S SHOWED YOU UP, AW RIGHT. 666 ICEMAN
I COULDN'T HELP FEELIN' SORRY FOR DE POOR BUMS 698 ICEMAN
WHEN DEY SHOWED UP TONIGHT.
AND EVERY ONE OF US NOTICED HE WAS NUTTY THE 718 ICEMAN
MINUTE HE SHOWED UP HERE/
I SHOWED THE LETTER TO ALL THE GIRLS, AND HOW 105 JOURNE
ENVIOUS THEY WERE/
WHO SHOWED SUCH BRILLIANT PROMISE? 167 JOURNE
ALL THE STUDENTS WERE WISE AND I HAD THEM ROLLING 39 MISBEG
IN THE AISLES AS I SHOWED
LIKE YOU SHOWED ALL THE OTHERS. 97 MISBEG
AND HE SHOWED IT TO HER. 78 POET

SHOWER
YOU'D SHOWER ME WITH CONGRATULATIONS/ 14 STRANG

SHOWIN'
(SCORNFULLY) DOWN'T BE SHOWIN' YER IGERANCE BE 456 CARIBE
TRYIN' TO
NOW YOU'RE SHOWIN' YOURSELF UP FOR WHAT YOU ARE/ 530 DIFRNT
I WAS JUST SHOWIN' SOME FRIENDS AROUND-- 134 ELECTR
SO WE'RE SHOWIN' DE BASTARD, AIN'T WE, HONEYS 682 ICEMAN
O'YE NO KEN THE DANGERR O' SHOWIN' A LICHT WI' A 514 INZONE
PACK OF SUBMARINES LYIN' ABOUT
AND HIS SHOWIN' OFF BEFORE THE YANKEES, AND THIM 168 POET
LAUGHIN' AT HIM,

SHOWING
(THEN A TRACE OF SHOCKED REPROOF SHOWING IN HIS 205 AHWILD
VOICE)
(HE GRINS SUPERIORLY) DIDN'T YOU HEAR HIM THIS 254 AHWILD
MORNING SHOWING OFF BAWLING OUT
AND THEN IT WAS ALL SHOWING OFF. 276 AHWILD
THE STAGE IS DIVIDED INTO TWO SECTIONS, SHOWING A 9 ANNA
SMALL BACK ROOM ON THE RIGHT.
VIKING-DAUGHTER FASHION BUT NOW RUN DOWN IN HEALTH 13 ANNA
AND PLAINLY SHOWING ALL THE
(HE SINKS SLOWLY BACK IN HIS CHAIR AGAIN, THE 57 ANNA
KNUCKLES SHOWING WHITE
BUT THAT'S A POOR SHOWING FOR FIVE YEARS' HARD 157 BEYOND
WORK.
(HIS VOICE SHOWING EMOTION IN SPITE OF HIM) 260 DESIRE
*WITH A TRACE OF SOMETHING LIKE PITY SHOWING IN HIS5946 DIFRNT
TONE)
(SHOWING HIMSELF--IN A MANNER HALF-AFRAID AND 176 EJONES
HALF-DEFIANT)
HE DID THE WORK AND LET OTHERS DO THE SHOWING-OFF. 69 ELECTR
SHOWING THAT THE HOUSE IS UNOCCUPIED. 129 ELECTR
HE'S JUST SHOWING OFF. 250 GORBOW
SHOWING THE INTERIOR OF A FRONT ROOM ON THE GROUND245 HA APE
FLOOR.
IT WOULDA BEEN A PUNK SHOWING FOR POOR OLD HUGHIE, 31 HUGHIE
(BITINGLY, BUT SHOWING HE IS COMFORTED AT HAVING 33 HUGHIE
MALE SOME SORT OF CONTACT.)
(SHOWING THE BOTTLE TO LARRY--INDIGNANTLY) JEES, 582 ICEMAN
LOOK/
BUT AT THE SAME TIME SHOWING HIS AFFECTION FOR 593 ICEMAN
THEM)

SHOWING

SHOWING (CONT'D.)
SHOWING OFF YOUR WOUNDS/   602 ICEMAN
HER ROUND FACE SHOWING MORE OF THE WEAR AND TEAR 615 ICEMAN
OF HER TRADE THAN THEIRS.
BY SHOWING YOU THE WAY TO FIND IT.   639 ICEMAN
UF SHOWING ME I'D HAD THE RIGHT DOPE.   704 ICEMAN
BUT SHOWING LITTLE EVIDENCE OF MIDDLE-AGED WAIST   12 JOURNE
AND HIPS.
YOU HAD A STRANGE WAY OF SHOWING YOUR   17 JOURNE
RESTLESSNESS.
SHOWING YOU WANTED TO WISH ME ON CHARITY/   144 JOURNE
TOO LARGE AND STRONG FOR HER FACE, SHOWING BIG,   2 MANSNS
EVEN.
RATTLING ON IN THE COCKSURE BOASTFUL WAY OF ABOY   54 STRANG
SHOWING OFF HIS PROWESS BEFORE
(SHARPLY) SHE'S SHOWING MORE INTELLIGENCE ABOUT   77 STRANG
HER PAIN THAN YOU ARE.
(SHOWING HIS JEALOUS RESENTMENT IN SPITE OF   102 STRANG
HIMSELF)
(REPROVINGLY BUT SHOWING SHE SHARES HIS FEELING) 185 STRANG
(HER FACE SHOWING A TRACE OF HURT IN SPITE OF   445 WELDED
HERSELF)
BUT SHOWING BY THEIR TONE IT IS A THINKING ALOUD 452 WELDED
TO ONESELF.

SHOWN
THERE'S ALL THE DIFFERENCE SHOWN IN JUST THE WAY   84 BEYOND
US TWO FEEL ABOUT THE FARM.
THE STUDY IS SHOWN AS IN PRECEDING SCENE.   553 DAYS
THE INTERIOR OF THE TWO BEDROOMS ON THE TOP FLOOR 235 DESIRE
IS SHOWN.
THE INTERIOR OF THE PARLOR IS SHOWN.   241 DESIRE
THE KITCHEN AND THE TWO BEDROOMS UPSTAIRS ARE   247 DESIRE
SHOWN.
ABOVE ALL THERE IS SHOWN IN HER SIMPERING,   520 DIFRNT
AND NOW THE INTERIOR OF THE LIGHT SITTING ROOM IS 435 DYNAMO
AGAIN SHOWN.
THE FOUR PIECES OF FURNITURE SHOWN ARE IN   269 GGBROW
KEEPING--
SCENE--THE DRAFTING ROOM AND PRIVATE OFFICE OF   302 GGBROW
BROWN ARE BOTH SHOWN.
WITH THE NEAREST APPROACH TO FEELING HE HAS SHOWN   17 HUGHIE
IN MANY A LONG NIGHT--
THAT HENRY WADSWORTH LONGFELLOW WOULD HAVE SHOWN A595 ICEMAN
DRUNKEN NEGRESS
I'VE NOTICED HE HASN'T SHOWN HER PICTURE AROUND   662 ICEMAN
THIS TIME/
YOU HAVE SHOWN THAT YOUR DRUNKENNESS MEANS MORE TD532 INZONE
YOU
(ABRUPTLY HER TONE AND MANNER CHANGE TO THE   64 JOURNE
STRANGE DETACHMENT SHE HAS SHOWN
IF HE'S EVER HAD A LOFTIER DREAM THAN WHORES AND 129 JOURNE
WHISKEY, HE'S NEVER SHOWN IT.
THE MAIN ROOM AT THE FRONT END OF THE HOUSE IS   273 LAZARU
SHOWN--
THERE ARE SEVEN PERIODS OF LIFE SHOWN.   273 LAZARU
BESIDES, YOU HAVE SHOWN ME CLEARLY I DO NOT NEED 106 MANSNS
HER TO TAKE BACK WHAT IS MINE.
THE ARRANGEMENT OF THE FURNITURE SHOWN IS AS IN   137 STRANG
PREVIOUS SCENES

SHOWS
HE SHOWS NO AFTER EFFECTS EXCEPT THAT HE IS   263 AHWILD
FRANKLY SLEEPY.
HE SHOWS NO ILL EFFECTS FROM HIS EXPERIENCE THE   269 AHWILD
NIGHT BEFORE.
SHE IS DRESSED IN WHITE, SHOWS SHE HAS BEEN FIXING135 BEYOND
UP.
HER AGE SHOWS, IN SPITE OF A HEAVY MAKE-UP.   515 DAYS
SHOWS THE INTERIOR OF THE KITCHEN WITH A LIGHTED   216 DESIRE
CANDLE ON TABLE.
(SHOWS PAPER IN HIS HAND) AY-EH.   219 DESIRE
(JUST BEFORE DAWN IN THE MORNING--SHOWS THE   259 DESIRE
KITCHEN AND CABOT'S BEDROOM.
SHOWS THE KITCHEN AND CABOT'S BEDROOM.   262 DESIRE
(WITH A LAUGH) SHOWS YE WHAT TRUST I PUT IN YOU. 496 DIFRNT
EMBER.
(HER VOICE SHOWS THAT SHE HOPES AGAINST HOPE FOR A515 DIFRNT
DENIAL.)
IT SHOWS YOU UP AND I CAN HATE YOU NOW/   450 DYNAMO
REUBEN'S FACE SHOWS THAT HE ALSO IS STRUGGLING   468 DYNAMO
WITH CONFLICTING EMOTIONS.
HIS FACE IS SCRATCHED, HIS BRILLIANT UNIFORM SHOWS191 EJONES
SEVERAL LARGE RENTS)
I SHOWS   197 EJONES
A SPECIAL CURTAIN SHOWS THE HOUSE AS SEEN FROM THE   2 ELECTR
STREET.
I HOPE HE SHOWS SOON.   580 ICEMAN
'LESS HICKEY SHOWS UP.   586 ICEMAN
THAT SHOWS EVEN THROUGH THEIR BLOBBY MAKE-UP.   611 ICEMAN
SHOWS IN HIM.   681 ICEMAN
BUT THE ACTOR SHOWS IN ALL HIS UNCONSCIOUS HABITS   13 JOURNE
UF SPEECH.
HER EXPRESSION SHOWS MORE OF THAT STRANGE   71 JOURNE
ALOOFNESS
HE PLAINLY SHOWS HE IS HEARTSICK AS WELL AS   71 JOURNE
PHYSICALLY ILL.
SHE SHOWS THE EFFECTS OF DRINK.   97 JOURNE
HE IS DRUNK AND SHOWS IT BY THE OWLISH,   125 JOURNE
THE LIGHT FROM HERE SHOWS IN THE HALL.   126 JOURNE
THEY DON'T KNOW THAT NOT ONE IN A MILLION WHO   138 JOURNE
SHOWS PROMISE
(A SHADOW OF RESENTMENT SHOWS IN HER FACE.)   84 MANSNS
(HE SHOWS THEM A PIECE OF WOOD)   364 MARCOM
ON THE BUREAU IS AN ALARM CLOCK WHICH SHOWS THE   71 MISBEG
TIME TO BE FIVE PAST ELEVEN.
HE DOES NOT APPEAR TO BE DRUNK--THAT IS, HE SHOWS 100 MISBEG
NONE OF THE USUAL SYMPTOMS.
(A DEEP CONFLICT SHOWS IN HIS EXPRESSION AND TONE.145 MISBEG

SHOWS (CONT'D.)
DO YOU THINK FATHER'S A POET BECAUSE HE SHOWS OFF   30 POET
RECITING LORD BYRON'S
BEYOND SHAKY NERVES, IT SHOWS NO EFFECTS OF HARD   33 POET
DRINKING.
THAT SHOWS YOU WHAT GOD THINKS OF YOUR CURSES--AN'583 ROPE
HIM DEAF TO YOU/
THEIR AUSTERE ARRAY SHOWS NO GAPS,   66 STRANG
FACE SHOWS IT....   79 STRANG
(THE IN A VOICE WHICH SHOWS SHE   123 STRANG

SHRANK
SO I SHRANK AWAY, BACK INTO LIFE, WITH NAKED   282 GGBROW
NERVES JUMPING LIKE FLEAS,
THAT SHRANK BACK, STAMPING ON ITS OWN TOES.   30 MANSNS

SHRED
SHE'D SUNK HER LAST SHRED OF PRIDE AND WRITTEN TO   26 ELECTR
YOUR FATHER ASKING FOR A LOAN.
YES, I DIDN'T LEAVE HIM ONE LAST SHRED OF HIS   155 MANSNS
PRIDE, DID I$

SHREDDED
AND A SHREDDED WHITE SAILOR'S BLOUSE, STAINED WITHS71 CROSS
IRON-RUST.

SHREDS
THEIR UNDERSHIRTS IN SHREDS, BENDING OVER THE   472 CARIBE
STILL FORM OF PADDY,

SHREWD
SHREWD HUMOROUS GRAY EYES.   188 AHWILD
A SON OF THE SOIL, INTELLIGENT IN A SHREWD WAY,   82 BEYOND
(SHE BECOMES VERY THOUGHTFUL, HER FACE GROWING   234 DESIRE
SHREWD.
IN MANNER HE IS SHREWD, SUSPICIOUS, EVASIVE.   175 EJONES
SHARP EYES STILL PEER AT LIFE WITH A SHREWD PRYING   6 ELECTR
AVIDITY AND HIS LOOSE MOUTH
IS SHREWD AND COMPETENT.   67 ELECTR
A SHREWD BUSINESS MAN, WHO DOESN'T MISS ANY   580 ICEMAN
OPPORTUNITY TO GET ON IN THE WORLD.
LIGHT-BROWN EYES, SET WIDE APART, THEIR EXPRESSION   4 MANSNS
SHARPLY OBSERVANT AND SHREWD,
WITH A ROUND RED FACE, AND SHREWD LITTLE GREY   25 MANSNS
EYES.
HE HAS BEEN SHREWD ENOUGH TO ANTICIPATE CONDITIONS 35 MANSNS
YOU ARE WONDERFULLY SHREWD AND FAR-SIGHTED,   101 MANSNS
MOTHER.
WITH A DRY, SHREWD FACE.   358 MARCOM
YOU'RE BECOMING SHREWD EVEN ABOUT KISSES.   371 MARCOM
HE IS ONLY A SHREWD AND CRAFTY GREED.   387 MARCOM
(THINKING CYNICALLY) (IA SHREWD MOVE/...   10 STRANG
WITH IRON-GRAY HAIR, AND A GAUNT, SHREWD FACE.   450 WELDED
SHREWD--HA/   483 WELDED

SHREWDER
MIKE DIVINE AND HOMELIER IN FACE, SHREWDER AND   203 DESIRE
MORE PRACTICAL

SHREWDLY
(SIZING HIM UP SHREWDLY) HELLO, SON.   293 AHWILD
SHREWDLY)   205 DESIRE
AND HIS EYES CAN TAKE YOU IN SHREWDLY AT A GLANCE.619 ICEMAN

SHREWDNESS
HENRY MUST HAVE LOST HIS FAMOUS SHREWDNESS IN MORE 35 MANSNS
WAYS THAN ONE.

SHRIEK
MRS. KEENEY GIVES A SHRIEK AND HIDES HER FACE IN 544 'ILE
HER HANDS.
(WITH A SHRIEK) JAMES/   108 BEYOND
THE WOMEN SHRIEK AND TAKE REFUGE ON TOP OF THE   472 CARIBE
HATCH.
FRIGHTENED SHRIEK AND HASTILY PUTS ON HER MASK.   266 GGBROW
IT WAS THE STILLNESS THAT FOLLOWS A SHRIEK OF   174 MANSNS
TERROR, WAITING TO BECOME AWARE--
THEN WITH A SHRIEK OF DELIGHT SHE KICKS THE CHAIR 601 ROPE
FROM UNDER HER

SHRIEKED
OF FLESH WHICH WILL NOT HAVE SHRIEKED THROUGH TEN 425 MARCOM
DAYS' TORTURE BEFORE IT DIED/

SHRIEKING
A DERVISH OF THE DESERT RUNS IN SHRIEKING AND   368 MARCOM
BEGINS TO WHIRL.
(HAS BEEN SHRIEKING AT THE SAME TIME)   182 STRANG

SHRIEKS
SHE SHRIEKS.)   194 AHWILD
SHE SHRIEKS)   543 DIFRNT
THERE IS A CONFUSED TUMULT OF YELLS, GROANS,   290 LAZARU
CURSES, THE SHRIEKS OF WOMEN,

SHRILL
(WITH A SHRILL LAUGH) CAN'T IS   240 DESIRE
(FINALLY, IN A SHRILL WHISPER)   544 DIFRNT
HIS CROON, RISING TO INTENSITY, IS PUNCTUATED BY   201 EJONES
SHRILL CRIES.
(SHE BURSTS INTO SHRILL LAUGHTER, STOPS IT   123 ELECTR
ABRUPTLY,
RUDDY COMPLEXION, AND A SHRILL RASPING VOICE.   129 ELECTR
A THIN, SHRILL NOTES FROM SOMEWHERE OVER-HEAD IN   223 HA APE
THE DARKNESS.
(MANY POLICE WHISTLES SHRILL OUT ON THE INSTANT   239 HA APE
(THE WITTICISM DELIGHTS HIM AND HE BURSTS INTO A   606 ICEMAN
SHRILL CACKLE.
DRUNKENLY SHRILL.   724 ICEMAN
SWAYING ITS HEAD TO THE THIN, SHRILL WHINE OF A   369 MARCOM
GOURD.
(TUGGING AT HIS HAND AND BURSTING AGAIN INTO   584 ROPE
SHRILL LAUGHTER)
A SHRILL BURST OF MARY'S LAUGHTER CAN BE HEARD ANDS87 ROPE
THE DEEP VOICE OF A MAN

SHRILLING
CRESCENDO OF DRUMS, GONGS, AND THE PIERCING   377 MARCOM
SHRILLING OF FLUTES.

SHRILLS
THE WITCH DOCTOR'S VOICE SHRILLS OUT IN   201 EJONES

1425 SHRUG

SHRILLY
HE IS STAGGERING A BIT AND SHE IS LAUGHING 468 CARIBE
SHRILLY.I
PEARL DRINKS FROM YANK'S BOTTLE EVERY MOMENT OR 470 CARIBE
SO, LAUGHING SHRILLY,
AND WHISTLES SHRILLY WITH HIS FINGERS IN HIS 175 EJONES
MOUTH.
SHE HUMS SHRILLY TO HERSELF. 578 ROPE
MARY PULLS AT HIS HAND IN A SUDDEN FIT OF IMPISH 584 ROPE
GLEE AND LAUGHS SHRILLY)
CLAPPING HER HANDS AND LAUGHING SHRILLY. 602 ROPE
SHRIMP
(GRUMBLINGLY) I DON'T TAKE NO BACK-TALK FROM THAT462 CARIBE
DECK-SCRUBBIN' SHRIMP.
SHRINE
LIKE A CURED CRIPPLE'S TESTIMONIAL OFFERING IN A 566 DAYS
SHRINE.)
I TOLD MOTHER I HAD HAD A TRUE VISION WHEN I WAS 175 JOURNE
PRAYING IN THE SHRINE OF OUR
SO I WENT TO THE SHRINE AND PRAYED TO THE BLESSED 176 JOURNE
VIRGIN AND FOUND PEACE AGAIN
IN THE FAR REARWALL, WITHIN A DEEP RECESS LIKE THE377 MARCOM
SHRINE OF AN IDOL.
SHRINERS
MYSTIC SHRINERS, THE KLAN, ETC. 390 MARCUM
SHRINK
HIS MOTHER AND FATHER SHRINK BACK FROM HIM AS HE 452 DYNAMO
SHOUTS UP AT THE SKY)
(PASS HIS CHECK AS HE TRIES NOT TO SHRINK AWAY.) 73 JOUNNE
(THE SENATORS SEEM TO SHRINK BACK FROM HIM IN 316 LAZARU
FEAR, ALL BUT LUCIUS.
A SHUDDERING MURMUR OF SUPERSTITIOUS FEAR COMES 348 LAZARU
FROM THEM AS THEY SHRINK BACK
THEY SHRINK BACK TO THE EDGE OF THE BENCH AT THE 172 MANSNS
RIGHT--REAR UP POOL.
HE SEEMS TO SHRINK BACK GUILTILY WITHIN HIMSELF. 89 POET
(WHY DOES SHE SHRINK AWAY... 104 STRANG
SHRINKING
(SHRINKING AWAY FROM HIM) OH, I CAN'T BEAR IT/ 545 'ILE
(SHRINKING FROM HER FATHER WITH REPULSION-- 51 ANNA
RESENTFULLY)
(SHRINKING AWAY FROM HER IN HORROR) 164 BEYOND
(SHRINKING BACK HORRIFIED) EDEN/ 256 DESIRE
SHRINKING AWAY FROM THE CRADLE WITH A GESTURE OF 259 DESIRF
HORROR.
(SHRINKING AWAY--TREMBLINGLY) 264 DESIRE
SHRINKING BACK FROM HER, STILL ON HIS KNEES) 447 DYNAMO
DESPERATE STRUGGLE TO KILL THE SHRINKING BOY IN 457 DYNAMO
HIM.
(THEN AS HE SEES REUBEN SHRINKING BACK IN HIS 466 DYNAMO
CHAIR,
SHRINKING CLOSE TO REUBEN, WHO IS STARING AT ALL 484 DYNAMO
THIS
(SHRINKING AWAY) DON'T TOUCH ME/ 487 DYNAMO
(SHE BREAKS AWAY, SHRINKING FROM HER MOTHER WITH A 31 ELECTR
LOOK OF SICK REPULSION.
(WITH A START OF REPULSION, SHRINKING FROM HIS 52 ELECTH
HAND)
(FEELING HIS DESIRE AND INSTINCTIVELY SHRINKING-- 51 ELECTR
WITHOUT OPENING HER EYES)
(FRIGHTENED, SHRINKING FROM HIM) 87 ELECTR
(SHRINKING BACK FROM HIM--FALTERINGLY) 164 ELECTR
(SHRINKING FROM HIM) WHAT DO YOU MEAN) 165 ELECTR
(SHRINKING FROM HER AGHAST--BROKENLY) 177 ELECTR
HIS REAL FACE IS REVEALED IN THE BRIGHT MOONLIGHT,264 GGBROW
SHRINKING, SHY AND GENTLE.
(SHRINKING BACK) NO. 318 GGBROW
HE IS OBVIOUSLY FRIGHTENED AND SHRINKING BACK 654 ICEMAN
WITHIN HIMSELF.
(ALOUD TO HIMSELF WITH A SUPERSTITIOUS SHRINKING) 663 ICEMAN
HE STOPS, SHRINKING BACK INTO HIMSELF HELPLESSLY, 6H0 ICEMAN
AND TURNS AWAY.
AS HE SPEAKS, THERE IS A START FROM ALL THE CROWD,703 ICEMAN
A SHRINKING AWAY FROM HIM.)
AND A GENERAL SHRINKING MOVEMENT.) 706 ICEMAN
(EDMUND LOOKS AWAY, SHRINKING INTO HIMSELF.) 116 JOURNE
HE GIVES UP HELPLESSLY, SHRINKING INTO HIMSELF. 172 JOURNE
TIBERIUS STANDS, SHRINKING BACK. 337 LAZARU
REMAINS LOOKING INTO HIS EYES A LONG TIME, 361 LAZARU
SHRINKING BACK FROM HIM WITH
(SHRINKING WITH REPULSION.) MOTHER/ 12 MANSNS
(SHE GIVES A SHRINKING, 14 MANSNS
(SHRINKING BACK TO THE FOOT OF THE STEPS-- 166 MANSNS
GUILTILY.)
(SHRINKING BACK TO THE TOP STEP--DISTRACTEDLY. 166 MANSNS
(THEN AS MARCO IS SHRINKING BACK--MORE KINDLY) 362 MARCOM
MINIONS OF SPLENDOUR SHRINKING FROM DISTRESS/ 101 POET
HIS EYES ARE SO SHRINKING/... 119 STRANG
(SHRINKING BACK FROM HER--THREATENINGLY) 132 STRANG
SHRINKINGLY
THEY SUBMIT SHRINKINGLY. 108 JOURNE
TIBERIUS LOOKS INTO HIS EYES, AT FIRST 339 LAZARU
SHRINKINGLY.
SHRINKS
(MAKES A THREATENING MOVE--BEN SHRINKS AWAY) 936 'ILE
KEENEY DRAWS BACK HIS FIST AND THE STEWARD SHRINKS939 'ILE
AWAY.
HE HESITATES, THEN KISSES HER AND AT ONCE SHRINKS 241 AHWILD
BACK)
(SHRINKS AWAY FROM HIM, HALF FRIGHTENED) WHAT'S 20 ANNA
THATA SWEDISH&
(AS ANNA SHRINKS AWAY FROM HIM AT THIS, HE HURRIES 34 ANNA
ON PLEADINGLY)
THEN SHRINKS BACK FROM HIM WITH A STRANGE, BROKEN 38 ANNA
LAUGH)
ROBERT LOOKS AT RUTH WHO SHRINKS AWAY FROM HIM IN 160 BEYOND
TERROR.
(HE SHRINKS AWAY FROM THE FUNK, MAKING THE 489 CARDIE
(AT SHRINKS BACKWARD A STEP) 568 CROSS

SHRINKS
(CONT'D.)
(SHE SHRINKS AWAY FROM HIM TO THE END OF THE SOFA 938 DAYS
NEAR FATHER BAIRD.)
(SHRINKS FROM HIS TOUCH) NO, NO, IT'S NOTHING. 940 DAYS
SHE SHRINKS FROM HIS TOUCH.) 292 DESIRE
(HIS MOOD SUDDENLY CHANGING TO HORROR, SHRINKS 263 DESIRE
AWAY FROM HER)
HE SHRINKS CLOSER TO HER AND BLURTS OUT) 446 DYNAMO
SHE SHRINKS BACK FROM THEIR EMBRACE WITH AVERSION. 56 ELECTR
(SHE SHRINKS BACK TO THE TABLE, THE HAND WITH THE 62 ELECTR
BOX HELD OUT BEHIND HER.
THEN WITH A SHUDDERING CRY SHE SHRINKS BACK ALONG 64 ELECTR
THE SIDE OF THE BED,
AND SHRINKS BACK WITH A STIFLED GASP OF FEAR. 107 ELECTR
CHRISTINE SHRINKS BACKWARD UP THE STEPS UNTIL SHE 123 ELECTR
STANDS AT THE TOP
HE SPRINGS TOWARD HER WITH OUTSTRETCHED ARMS BUT 266 GGBROW
SHE SHRINKS AWAY WITH A
THEN SHRINKS BACK WITH A SHUDDER OF HOPELESS 307 GGBROW
DESPAIR
UTTERS A LOW, CHOKING CRY AND SHRINKS AWAY FROM 226 HA APE
HIM.
(SHRINKS A BIT FRIGHTENEDLY) 591 ICEMAN
(SHRINKS AWAY--STAMMERS) WHATS 592 ICEMAN
BUT HE INSTINCTIVELY SHRINKS WITH REPULSION. 649 ICEMAN
HUGO SHRINKS BACK IN HIS CHAIR, BLINKING AT HIM. 658 ICEMAN
LARRY SHRINKS AWAY, BUT DETERMINEDLY IGNORES HIM.1666 ICEMAN
(WILLIE WINCES AND SHRINKS DOWN IN HIS CHAIR. 681 ICEMAN
(LARRY STARES AT HIM WITH GROWING HORROR AND 694 ICEMAN
SHRINKS BACK ALONG THE BAR AWAY
(HE SHRINKS QUICKLY PAST THE TABLE WHERE HICKEY 724 ICEMAN
HAL SAT TO THE REAR OF THE GROUP
(HE SHRINKS BACK INTO HIMSELF. 120 JOURNE
HE SHRINKS AGAINST CRASSUS FOR PROTECTION--WITH 303 LAZARU
BOYISH PLEADING)
HE GIVES A STARTLED GASP AND SHRINKS BACK, 340 LAZARU
CALLING)
(DEBORAH SHRINKS BACK. 19 MANSNS
(AS IF THE TOUCH OF HIS HAND ALARMED HER--SHRINKS 103 MANSNS
BACK, TURNING AWAY FROM HIM--
AND YET INSTINCTIVELY SHRINKS BACK IN HIS CHAIR, 128 MANSNS
AND SHRINKS INTO HERSELF WITH HORRIFIED DISGUST.) 144 MANSNS
(SHRINKS AS IF SHE'D BEEN STRUCK--STRICKENLY.) 186 MANSNS
DEFIANT DARING, SHUDDERS SUPERSTITIOUSLY AND 367 MARCOM
SHRINKS AWAY.
(SHE SEES HE HAS GUESSED HER SECRET AND AT FIRST 387 MARCOM
SHE QUAILS AND SHRINKS AWAY.
(SHE SHRINKS AWAY AND RISES TO HER FEET. 51 POET
SHE SHRINKS AND LOOKS UP AT HIM. 69 POET
(SHRINKS BACK FRIGHTENEDLY.) 128 POET
(HE SHRINKS SUPERSTITIOUSLY--THEN ANGRILY, 161 POET
REACHING FOR THE DECANTER.)
SHE SHRINKS AWAY, LOOKING AT HIM WITH TERRIFIED 583 ROPE
EYES)
(SHE SHRINKS BACK A STEP) YOU CHUCK IT WHEN I SAYS89 ROPE
THREE.
(THEN AS NINA SHRINKS AWAY FROM HER HAND--IN HER 58 STRANG
BLUNTED TONES)
SHE SHRINKS AWAY. 104 STRANG
THEN SHRINKS BACK WITH A SHUDDER AND FORCES A 473 WELDED
HARSH LAUGH.
SHRIVEL
(SEEMING TO SHRIVEL UP IN HIS SON'S GRIP-- 466 DYNAMO
SHRIVELED
SHRIVELED SWABS DOES BE WORKING IN CITIES) 48 ANNA
IF YOU'D SEEN THE ENDEARIN' LOOK ON HER PALE MUG 229 HA APE
WHEN SHE SHRIVELED AWAY WITH
BUT FOR A SHRIVELED RUNT LIKE SMYTHE--/ 99 JOURNE
SHROUD
JUST AS HE APPEARED IN THE OPENING OF THE TOMB, 277 LAZARU
WRAPPED IN HIS SHROUD--
---IN A SHROUD OF THOUGHTS WHICH WERE NOT THEIR 108 MANSNS
THOUGHTS---
LET DOWN YOUR HAIR AND I WILL MAKE MY SHROUD OF 474 WELDED
IT..
SHROUDED
SHROUDED IN SHADOW FROM WHICH CHATTERINGS 251 HA APE
SHROUDS
DENSE FOG SHROUDS THE BARGE ON ALL SIDES, AND SHE 25 ANNA
FLOATS MOTIONLESS IN A CALM.
SHRUB
THE LEFT ONE PASSING BEHIND A SPHERICAL SHRUB AT 25 MANSNS
LEFT--FRONT TO THE HOUSE.
THE GEOMETRICAL FORM OF EACH SHRUB AND ITS BLACK 161 MANSNS
SHADOW ARE SHARPLY DEFINED.
SHRUBBERY
A BENCH IS PLACED ON THE LAWN AT FRONT OF THIS 5 ELECTR
SHRUBBERY
THE GREEN OF THE LAWN AND SHRUBBERY, THE BLACK AND 5 ELECTR
GREEN OF THE PINE TREE,
THE GREEN OF THE SHRUBBERY, THE BLACK AND GREEN UF169 ELECTR
THE PINES.
SHRUBS
AT LEFT AND RIGHT OF THE SUMMER-HOUSE ARE SHRUBS, 25 MANSNS
THE SHRUBS, OF VARIOUS SIZES, ARE ALL CLIPPED INTO 25 MANSNS
GEOMETRICAL SHAPES--
THE SHRUBS, CLIPPED AS BEFORE IN ARBITRARY 95 MANSNS
GEOMETRICAL DESIGNS.
SHRUG
(UNIMPRESSED--WITH A CYNICAL SHRUG OF HER 243 AHWILD
SHOULDERS)
THE RUTH TURNS AWAY WITH A SHRUG OF AFFECTED 121 BEYOND
INDIFFERENCE)
(WITH A GOOD-HUMORED SHRUG) ALL RIGHT. 295 GGBROW
(WITH A SCORNFUL SHRUG OF HIS SHOULDERS.) 31 JOURNE
JAMIE TURNS HIS BACK WITH A SHRUG AND LOOKS OUT 64 JOURNE
THE WINDOW.)

SHRUG

SHRUG (CONT'D.)
(WITH A CARELESS SHRUG) YOU WILL NOT WIN HIS LOVE342 LAZARU
BY KILLING HER.
HE GIVES THE CHARACTERISTIC SHRUG OF SHOULDERS- 122 MISBEG
CYNICALLY)
JOSIE--(GIVES THE CHARACTERISTIC SHRUG OF HIS 140 MISBEG
SHOULDERS--SIMPLY)
(THEN DISMISSING MARSDEN WITH A SHRUG OF HIS 78 STRANG
SHOULDERS)

SHRUGGING
(SHRUGGING HIS SHOULDERS) WHAT'S THE USE OF 148 BEYOND
TALKING TO YOU&
(SHRUGGING HIS SHOULDERS.) ALL RIGHT. HAVE IT 29 JOURNE
YOUR WAY.
(SHRUGGING HIS SHOULDERS.) YOU WON'T BE SINGING A 66 JOURNE
SONG YOURSELF SOON.
(STUNG FOR A MOMENT--THEN SHRUGGING HIS SHOULDERS, 76 JOURNE
DRYLY.)
SHRUGGING HIS SHOULDERS.) 80 JOURNE
(THEN ABRUPTLY, WITH COLD CURTNESS, SHRUGGING HIS 66 MANSNS
SHOULDERS.)
(SHRUGGING HIS SHOULDERS--CONFUSEDLY) 21 STRANG
(THEN SHRUGGING HER SHOULDERS, FATALISTICALLY) 469 WELDED

SHRUGS
(LOOKS AFTER HER WORRIEDLY FOR A SECOND--THEN 248 AHWILD
SHRUGS HIS SHOULDERS)
WITH YOU AGAINST ME--(HE SHRUGS HIS SHOULDERS. 123 BEYOND
(ANDREW GROANS) BUT NOW--(HE SHRUGS HIS SHOULDERS158 BEYOND
SIGNIFICANTLY.)
BUT AT ONCE SHE SHRUGS HER SHOULDERS WITH DISDAIN 9 ELECTR
AND COMES DOWN THE STEPS AND
(SHRUGS HIS SHOULDERS AND SITS DOWN AGAIN) 583 ICEMAN
(SHRUGS HIS SHOULDERS--INDIFFERENTLY) 584 ICEMAN
(ROCKY SHRUGS HIS SHOULDERS AND YAWNS SLEEPILY.) 666 ICEMAN
BUT ROCKY ONLY SHRUGS HIS SHOULDERS WITH WEARY 671 ICEMAN
DISGUST
(HE SHRUGS HIS SHOULDERS) AW RIGHT, IF HE ASKED 708 ICEMAN
FOR IT.
(JAMIE SHRUGS HIS SHOULDERS AND SITS DOWN IN THE 21 JOURNE
CHAIR ON HER RIGHT.)
BUT HE SHRUGS HIS SHOULDERS.) 26 JOURNE
(HE STOPS, BORED WITH THEIR QUARREL, AND SHRUGS 33 JOURNE
HIS SHOULDERS.)
(HE SHRUGS HIS SHOULDERS--CYNICALLY.) 35 JOURNE
(SHRUGS HIS SHOULDERS.) THE SAME OLD STUFF. 40 JOURNE
(REBUFFED AND HURT, SHRUGS HIS SHOULDERS.) 42 JOURNE
(JAMIE AGAIN SHRUGS HIS SHOULDERS. 64 JOURNE
(SHRUGS HIS SHOULDERS.) YOU CAN'T TALK TO HER 78 JOURNE
NOW.
(SHRUGS HIS SHOULDERS--THICKLY.) 158 JOURNE
CALIGULA SHRUGS HIS SHOULDERS, TURNING AWAY-- 328 LAZARU
LIGHTLY
(MARCELLUS SHRUGS HIS SHOULDERS AND SMILES 332 LAZARU
DEPRECATINGLY.)
(SHE SHRUGS HER SHOULDERS.) TOO LATE, DEBORAH. 32 MANSNS
(SHRUGS HER SHOULDERS INDIFFERENTLY.) 56 MANSNS
(SHRUGS HIS SHOULDERS) MAYBE. 41 MISBEG
SHRUGS HIS SHOULDERS) 43 MISBEG
(HE SHRUGS) NUTS. 102 MISBEG
(SHRUGS HIS SHOULDERS) NOTHING. 102 MISBEG
(SHRUGS HIS SHOULDERS) ALL RIGHT. 113 MISBEG
(STARES AT HER--THEN SHRUGS HIS SHOULDERS) 121 MISBEG
(SHRUGS HIS SHOULDERS) YES. 123 MISBEG
(HE SHRUGS HIS SHOULDERS) NUTS/ 129 MISBEG
(SHRUGS HIS SHOULDERS) WELL, HE'S STEWED TO THE 131 MISBEG
EARS.
(GLANCES UP AT HER, SURPRISED--THEN SHRUGS HIS 136 MISBEG
SHOULDERS)
(HE SHRUGS HIS SHOULDERS HOPELESSLY AND TURNS 139 MISBEG
TOWARD THE ROAD.)
HE SHRUGS HIS SHOULDERS, POURS OUT A BIG DRINK 139 MISBEG
MECHANICALLY)
(HE SHRUGS HIS SHOULDERS MECHANICALLY) 151 MISBEG
(HE SHRUGS HIS SHOULDERS.) WELL, ANYWAYS, 14 POET
(HE SHRUGS HIS SHOULDERS.) BUT NO MATTER. 105 POET

SHRUNK
LARRY STANDS SHRUNK BACK AGAINST THE BAR. 695 ICEMAN
(HAS SHRUNK BACK IN HIS CHAIR UNDER THIS ATTACK, 145 JOURNE
(SHE IS AGAIN LOOKING AT HIM WITH BEWILDERED 115 MANSNS
DREAD, HAS SHRUNK BACK,

SHUCKS
SHUCKS/ 99 BEYOND
BUT SHUCKS, WHAT'S THE GOOD PAYING ANY ATTENTION 499 DIFRNT
TO YOU.
SHUCKS/ 507 DIFRNT
SHUCKS, EMMER, YOU'LL GIT ME TO LOSE PATIENCE WITH512 DIFRNT
YOU IF YOU ACT THAT STUBBORN.

SHUD
(TURNING TO HIM) SHUD UP, YOU TAWN FOOL, PADDY/ 458 CARIBE

SHUDDER
(WITH A SHUDDER) WHAT A TERRIBLE END/ 36 ANNA
(WITH A SHUDDER) SAY, YOU'RE CRAZIER THAN I 67 ANNA
THOUGHT.
(WITH A SHUDDER) LET'S NOT THINK ABOUT THEM. 89 BEYOND
CONVULSIVE SHUDDER--THEN BREAKS OUT IN A 148 BEYOND
PASSIONATE AGONY)
(WITH A SHUDDER) DON'T TALK THAT WAY, FOR GOD'S 159 BEYOND
SAKE/
(WITH A SHUDDER) I C'D SEE HIM A MINUTE AGO 488 CARDIF
(HE PULLS HIS ARM BACK QUICKLY WITH A SHUDDER OF 469 CARIBE
DISGUST AND TAKES A DRINK.
(WITH A SHUDDER) GOD/ 567 CROSS
(STARTS--WITH A SHUDDER) DAMN YOU/ 494 DAYS
(WITH A SHUDDER) FOR GOD'S SAKE, DON'T SPEAK 509 DAYS
ABOUT--
(A SHUDDER RUNS OVER HIM AND HE STARTS AS IF 562 DAYS
AWAKENING FROM SLEEP)
(WITH A SHUDDER) NO/ 562 DAYS

SHUDDER

SHUDDER (CONT'D.)
(WITH A SHUDDER--HUMBLY) HE'S YEWR SON, TOO, 257 DESIRE
EBEN.
(WITH A SHUDDER) IT AIN'T A JOKE TO ME. 508 DIFRNT
(BREAKING AWAY FROM HER WITH A SHUDDER OF DISGUST)563 DIFRNT
(THEN WITH A SHUDDER SHE CANNOT REPRESS) 462 DYNAMO
(HE GIVES A SHUDDER AND PRESSES HER TO HIM.) 484 DYNAMO
A SHUDDER OF TERROR SHAKES HIS WHOLE BODY AS THE 199 EJUNES
HATE RISES UP ABOUT HIM AGAIN.
(WITH A SHUDDER) OH/ 26 ELECTR
(GIVES A LITTLE SHUDDER--THEN FIERCELY) 34 ELECTR
(THEN SHE JERKS HER GLANCE AWAY AND, WITH A LITTLE 42 ELECTR
SHUDDER SHE CANNOT REPRESS,
(TURNING AWAY AND RESTRAINING A SHUDDER) 81 ELECTR
SHE GIVES A LITTLE SHUDDER OF REPULSION 90 ELECTR
(LAVINIA MAKES A MOVEMENT LIKE A FAINT SHUDDER 91 ELECTR
(WITH A SHUDDER) DON'T THINK OF THAT NOW/ 95 ELECTR
(THEN SUDDENLY, WITH A LITTLE SHUDDER) 112 ELECTR
(WITH A SHUDDER) PLEASE DON'T TALK ABOUT--HE IS 117 ELECTR
BURIED/
(SHE GLANCES AT THE HOUSE BEHIND HER WITH A 119 ELECTR
SHUDDER.)
(WITH A SHUDDER.) 138 ELECTR
(WITH A SHUDDER) MOTHER WAS UNDER HIS INFLUENCE--142 ELECTR
(CANNOT RESTRAIN A SHUDDER) SOMETIMES WHEN YOU'RE297 GGBROW
DRUNK YOU'RE POSITIVELY EVIL.
A SHUDDER PASSES THROUGH BOTH OF THEM. 301 GGBROW
(WITH A SHUDDER) ARE YOU CRAZY& 305 GGBROW
THEN SHRINKS BACK WITH A SHUDDER OF HOPELESS 307 GGBROW
DESPAIR)
(THEN WITH A SHUDDER) BUT HONESTLY, DION, 311 GGBROW
(TURNS AWAY WITH A SHUDDER.) 275 LAZARU
(STEPS BACK FROM HIM WITH AN UNEASY SHUDDER) 301 LAZARU
EVEN LUCIUS CANNOT REPRESS A SHUDDER OF HORROR AT 317 LAZARU
THE FACE GLARING AT HIM.
(WITH A SHUDDER) MONSTER/ 327 LAZARU
(PRESSING HER HAND TO HER OWN HEART--WITH A 358 LAZARU
SHUDDER)
(TURNING TO HIM AGAIN WITH A SHUDDER OF AGONY-- 364 LAZARU
BESEECHINGLY)
(AVERTING HER EYES WITH A SHUDDER) 364 LAZARU
SUDDENLY A LITTLE SHUDDER RUNS OVER HER. 27 MANSNS
(WITH A FRIGHTENED SHUDDER.) 29 MANSNS
(WITH A LITTLE SHUDDER--FORCING A LAUGH.) 111 MANSNS
(STARING AT HIM--CANNOT CONTROL A SHUDDER.) 174 MANSNS
SO I CANNOT SEE WHY THE THOUGHT SHOULD MAKE YOU 181 MANSNS
SHUDDER NOW.
(WITH A SHUDDER.) I KNOW/ 184 MANSNS
AGAIN, NOW TURNS AWAY WITH A SHUDDER OF LOATHING--432 MARCOM
HE TURNS AWAY WITH A COMIC SHUDDER) 53 MISBEG
(WITH A SHUDDER OF DISGUST) OF THAT PIGS 129 MISBEG
(THEN WATCHING THE PROFESSOR WITH A PITYING 15 STRANG
SHUDDER)
(WITH A SHUDDER) (WHY DOES HE CHALLENGE ME THAT 155 STRANG
WAYS.
(THINKING WITH A STRANGE SHUDDER OF MINGLED 169 STRANG
ATTRACTION AND FEAR AS SHE TOUCHES
DARRELL GIVES A VIOLENT SHUDDER AS IF HE WERE 174 STRANG
COMING OUT OF A NIGHTMARE AND
(THEN WITH A SHUDDER AT HIS THOUGHTS) 183 STRANG
AT LAST HE COMES TO HIMSELF WITH A SHUDDER AND 460 WELDED
STEPS AWAY FROM HER.
(WITH A SHUDDER--INCOHERENTLY) 464 WELDED
(WITH A SHUDDER) NO/ 464 WELDED
THEN SHRINKS BACK WITH A SHUDDER AND FORCES A 473 WELDED
HARSH LAUGH.
(WITH A SHUDDER) SAY, YOU'RE BEGINNING TO GIVE ME476 WELDED
THE CREEPS.
(WITH A SHUDDER) AH/ 485 WELDED

SHUDDERING
(SHUDDERING) MAT/ 71 ANNA
(SHUDDERING) OH, MY GOD/ 139 BEYOND
GOOD GOD, BUT I NEVER THOUGHT--(HE STOPS, 164 BEYOND
SHUDDERING AT HIS REMEMBRANCE)
RUTH GIVES A CRY OF HORROR AND SPRINGS TO HER 168 BEYOND
FEET, SHUDDERING.
SHE COVERS HER FACE WITH HER HANDS, SHUDDERING. 569 CROSS
(SHUDDERING) SSSHHH/ 571 CROSS
(SHUDDERING--CLUTCHES HIS HEAD IN BOTH HANDS AS IF551 DAYS
TO CRUSH OUT HIS THOUGHTS)
(SHUDDERING IN HIS SLEEP) NO/ 558 DAYS
THEN WITH A SHUDDERING CRY SHE SHRINKS BACK ALONG 64 ELECTR
THE SIDE OF THE BED,
LAVINIA GIVES A SHUDDERING GASP, TURNS BACK TO THE123 ELECTR
STEPS, STARTS TO GO UP THEM,
AND DRAWS A DEEP SHUDDERING BREATH.) 138 ELECTR
BUT WILLIE HAS CLOSED HIS EYES AND IS SITTING 583 ICEMAN
QUIETLY, SHUDDERING.
(PARRITT SUBSIDES, HIDING HIS FACE IN HIS HANDS 706 ICEMAN
AND SHUDDERING.)
LARRY GASPS AND DROPS BACK ON HIS CHAIR, 726 ICEMAN
SHUDDERING.
(JUMPING UP WITH A SHUDDERING START) 341 LAZARU
A SHUDDERING MURMUR OF SUPERSTITIOUS FEAR COMES 348 LAZARU
FROM THEM AS THEY SHRINK BACK.
(THEN WITH A GLANCE AT MIRIAM'S BODY AND A 356 LAZARU
SHUDDERING, AWAY FROM IT--VAGUELY)
(IN A SHUDDERING WHISPER.) SIMON/ 179 MANSNS
(SHUDDERING.) NO/ 182 MANSNS
SHUDDERING WITH THE EFFORT TO REGAIN SOME SORT OF 128 POET
PULSE.
HE DRAWS A SHUDDERING BREATH--THEN LAUGHS 172 POET
HOARSELY.)
SINCE GORDON'S DEATH THEY HAVE A QUALITY OF 12 STRANG
CONTINUALLY SHUDDERING
(HE STOPS, SHUDDERING. 472 WELDED
FINALLY WITH A GROAN HE PUSHES HER AWAY, 475 WELDED
SHUDDERING WITH LOATHING,

SHUDDERS

HE LOOKS--(HE SHUDDERS) TERRIBLE/ 155 BEYOND
YANK SHUDDERS AND OPENS HIS EYES.) 483 CARDIF
HE SHUDDERS AND SHAKES HIS SHOULDERS AS IF SHAKING466 CARIBE
OFF SOMETHING WHICH DISGUSTED
THEN A LOOK OF TERROR COMES INTO HIS FACE AND HE 531 DAYS
SHUDDERS.)
JOHN SHUDDERS. 535 DAYS
SOMETHING--(THE SHUDDERS.) 561 DAYS
(HE SHUDDERS. 225 DESIRE
(SHUDDERS--THEN HUMBLY) AN' DID YE R'ALLY LUVE ME259 DESIRE
AFORES
SHE SHUDDERS) 263 DESIRE
(SHUDDERS--THEN IN A DEAD VOICE) 263 DESIRE
EMMA SHUDDERS WITH REVULSION.) 511 DIFRNT
(THE SHUDDERS, FLINGING OFF THE MEMORY--THEN 456 DYNAMO
WONDERING BITTERLY)
(HE SHUDDERS). 466 DYNAMO
BUT DEM ODDERS--(THE SHUDDERS-- 196 EJONES
(SHE SHUDDERS) I CAN STILL SEE HER SITTING ON 136 ELECTR
THAT BENCH
(HE SHUDDERS) I THOUGHT I'D GO CRAZY. 644 ICEMAN
(CALIGULA SHUDDERS AND BACKS AWAY TO THE EXTREME 340 LAZARU
LEFT CORNER, FRONT.
(HE SHUDDERS) COME NEARER. 341 LAZARU
(HE SHUDDERS) AND I AM AFRAID, LAZARUS-- 353 LAZARU
(SHE SHUDDERS.) I SEE NOW THE PART MY GREED AND 190 MANSNS
MY FATHER'S CRAZY DREAMS IN ME
DEFIANT DARING, SHUDDERS SUPERSTITIOUSLY AND 367 MARCOM
SHRINKS AWAY.
(HE SHUDDERS AND PUTS THE PISTOL ON THE TABLE 165 POET
SHAKENLY.)
(HE SHUDDERS.) LET ME GET AWAY FROM THE SIGHT OF 165 POET
HIM
(SHE SHUDDERS--THEN SUDDENLY BURSTS OUT WILDLY) 467 WELDED
(SHUDDERS INSTINCTIVELY AS SHE READS HIS MEANING) 486 WELDED

SHUFFLE

THE THREE MEN GRIN AND SHUFFLE EMBARRASSEDLY. 269 DESIRE
HE RETRIEVES THEM WITH DIFFICULTY, AND STARTS TO 125 JOURNE
SHUFFLE AGAIN.

SHUFFLES

(SHE SHUFFLES OVER TO ANNA'S TABLE AND SITS DOWN 15 ANNA
OPPOSITE HER.
(THEN BEFORE HE CAN SPEAK, SHE SHUFFLES HURRIEDLY 19 ANNA
PAST HIM INTO THE BAR,
(AS HE SHUFFLES, DRAGGING ONE FOOT, OVER TO HIS 194 EJONES
PLACE.
AND SHUFFLES OFF MENACINGLY INTO THE DARKNESS AT 254 HA APE
LEFT.
HE SHUFFLES THEM CLUMSILY, DROPPING A COUPLE ON 125 JOURNE
THE FLOOR.
TOTTER FEEBLY UNDER HIM AS HE SHUFFLES SLOWLY 578 ROPE
ALONG BY THE AID OF A THICK CANE.

SHUFFLING

(THERE IS THE SHUFFLING OF FOOTSTEPS FROM OUTSIDE 543 'ILE
AND FIVE OF THE CREW CROWD
WHICH GIVES HER A SHUFFLING WOBBLY GAIT.) 7 ANNA
HE IS SHUFFLING ALONG DISCONSOLATELY. 265 GGBROW
(THE OTHERS LIKEWISE BETRAY THEIR UNEASINESS, 519 INZONE
SHUFFLING THEIR FEET NERVOUSLY.)
(SHUFFLING THE CARDS CLUMSILY.) 137 JOURNE
(KEEPS SHUFFLING THE CARDS FUMBLINGLY, FORGETTING 138 JOURNE
TO DEAL THEM.)
(THERE IS A NOISE OF SHUFFLING FOOTSTEPS OUTSIDE 594 ROPE
(MARY IS HEARD SHUFFLING TO THE FRONT DOOR WHICH 26 STRANG
IS OPENED.
(OVERCOME, HIS EYES ON HIS SHUFFLING FEET AND 47 STRANG
TWIDDLING CAP)

SHUN

YES, MY ADVICE TO YOU WOULD BE TO SHUN MARRIAGE 72 MANSNS
AND KEEP A WHORE INSTEAD/
PAGANISM, SHUN THE FRAILTY OF POETRY, HAVE A 363 MARCOM
MILLION TO HIS CREDIT,

SHUSH

SHUSH. 19 JOURNE

SHUT

(SHE GOES SLOWLY OUT, REAR, AND LEAVES THE DOOR 541 'ILE
THREE-QUARTERS SHUT BEHIND HER.)
(RUSHING OUT TO SHUT IT) I'VE TOLD HIM AGAIN AND 188 AHWILD
AGAIN--
(SMILING) WELL, YOU CAN'T EXPECT A BOY TO 188 AHWILD
REMEMBER TO SHUT DOORS ON THE FOURTH
(SHE SLAMS THE DOOR SHUT.) 188 AHWILD
(FLUSHING BASHFULLY) YOU SHUT UP/ 194 AHWILD
I MIGHT TELL YOU, IF YOU CAN KEEP YOUR FACE SHUT. 218 AHWILD
DO SHUT UP FOR A MINUTE/ 225 AHWILD
(SURLILY) AW, SHUT UP, MID. 228 AHWILD
EAT YOUR LOBSTER AND SHUT UP/ 229 AHWILD
CAN'T YOU SHUT UP& 231 AHWILD
YOU EAT YOUR LOBSTER AND MAYBE IT'LL KEEP YOUR 231 AHWILD
MOUTH SHUT/
SHUT UP ABOUT HER, CAN'T YOUS 243 AHWILD
HIS EYES BLINK SHUT ON HIM, HIS HEAD BEGINS TO 249 AHWILD
NOD, BUT HE ISN'T GIVING UP.
(THE FRONT DOOR IS HEARD BEING OPENED AND SHUT, 253 AHWILD
YOU KEEP YOUR MOUTH SHUT TILL YOU'RE SPOKEN TO-- 266 AHWILD
YOU PROMISE TO KEEP YOUR FACE SHUT, MID--UNTIL 274 AHWILD
AFTER I'VE LEFT--
THE SOUND OF THE FRONT DOOR BEING OPENED AND SHUT 292 AHWILD
IS HEARD.
THE DOOR IS SHUT, THEN OPENED AGAIN AS JOHNSON 30 ANNA
COMES OUT.
SHUT UP, CAN'T YOUS 51 ANNA
(HYSTERICALLY) BUT, DAMN IT, SHUT UP/ 57 ANNA
(SHORTLY) SHUT UP, WILL YOUS 66 ANNA
(HALF ANGRILY) YOU SHUT UP, ROB/ 105 BEYOND
(NODDING WITH HALF-SHUT EYES) 121 BEYOND

SHUT (CONT'D.)

ROB SHUT ME UP WITH ALMOST THE SAME WORDS WHEN I 139 BEYOND
TRIED SPEAKING TO HIM ABOUT IT.
I'LL SHUT THIS DOOR SO'S YOU'LL BE QUIET. 151 BEYOND
SHUT THE DOOR, ANDY. 162 BEYOND
(HOLDING UP HIS HAND) SHUT YOUR MOUTHS, ALL AV 481 CARDIF
YOU.
(GLOOMILY) SHUT UP, COCKY/ 456 CARIBE
SHUT YOUR MOUTHS, ALL AV YOU (SCORNFULLY) A 459 CARIBE
CHARITY IS UT YE WANTS
SHUT UP, YE INSECT/ 463 CARIBE
NOW THAT THE CLOSED DOOR HAS SHUT OFF NEARLY ALL 466 CARIBE
THE NOISE.
(REALLY REPELLED) SHUT UP, DONK. 468 CARIBE
HE POUNDS AGAINST THE SLIDE, WHICH SEEMS TO HAVE 572 CROSS
BEEN SHUT DOWN ON HIM.)
SHUT UP, DAMN YE/ 226 DESIRE
(FURIOUSLY NOW) SHUT UP, OR I'LL KILL YE/ 261 DESIRE
SHUT UP/ 529 DIFRNT
SHUT UP IN THIS HOUSE ALL HER LIFE. 529 DIFRNT
FOR GOD'S SAKE, SHUT UP/ 455 DYNAMO
THE DOOR OF THE DYNAMO ROOM IS SHUT BUT THE 476 DYNAMO
INTERIOR IS BRILLIANTLY LIGHTED AND
YOU HAVE SHUT ME FROM YOUR HEART FOREVER/....) 487 DYNAMO
I COULD GO THROUGH ON DEM TRAILS WID MY EYES SHUT.183 EJONES
THE MOONLIGHT IS ALMOST COMPLETELY SHUT OUT AND 198 EJONES
ONLY A VAGUE WAN LIGHT FILTERS
AND THROWS HIMSELF DOWN AGAIN TO SHUT OUT THE 199 EJONES
SIGHT.
(HE SITS DOWN BESIDE HER) SHUT YOUR EYES AGAIN/ 53 ELECTR
(HE FORCES HIMSELF TO TURN AND, SEEING HER EYES 53 ELECTR
ARE SHUT.
YOUR EYES ARE SHUT. 53 ELECTR
(SUDDENLY UNEASY AGAIN) DUN'T KEEP YOUR EYES SHUT 53 ELECTR
LIKE THAT/
SHUT YOUR EYES AGAIN. 96 ELECTR
SO SHUT UP BEFORE YOU START/ 96 ELECTR
I'LL ARRANGE WITH HER SKIPPER TO GIVE US PASSAGE--111 ELECTR
AND KEEP HIS MOUTH SHUT.
IT HAS THE DEAD APPEARANCE OF A ROOM LONG SHUT UP,139 ELECTR
KEEPING HIM SHUT UP HERE IS THE WORST THING VINNIE158 ELECTR
COULD DO.
SHUT UP. 166 ELECTR
(THERE IS NO ANSWER BUT THE SOUND OF THE STUDY 167 ELECTR
DOOR BEING SHUT.
(ANGRILY) SHUT UP/ 271 GGBROW
(REPELLED BUT CAJOLING) SHUT UP, YOU NUT/ 282 GGBROW
SHUT UP, WOP/ 209 HA APE
(FIERCELY CONTEMPTUUUS) SHUT UP, YUH LOUSY BOUB/ 211 HA APE
SHUT UP/ 212 HA APE
THE BRAZEN CLANG OF THE FURNACE DOORS AS THEY ARE 223 HA APE
FLUNG OPEN UR SLAMMED SHUT,
AS THE CURTAIN RISES, THE FURNACE DOORS ARE SHUT. 223 HA APE
HE SLAMS HIS FURNACE DOOR SHUT. 224 HA APE
AN IRON DOOR CLANGS SHUT. 226 HA APE
TO SHUT OUT THE SIGHT OF HIS FACE, TO PROTECT HER 226 HA APE
OWN.
SHUT UP/ 229 HA APE
HER HANDS OVER HER EYES TO SHUT OUT THE SIGHT 229 HA APE
(FRIGHTENEDLY) KEEP YER BLOUMIN' MOUTH SHUT, I 237 HA APE
TELLS YER.
WHICH THEY GIVE A GUY WHO CAN KEEP HIS CLAM SHUT. 15 HUGHIE
HE TRIED TO APOLOGIZE, BUT I SHUT HIM UP QUICK. 26 HUGHIE
BETTER BEAT IT UP TO MY CELL AND GRAB SOME SHUT 27 HUGHIE
EYE.
(HIS EYES SHUT AGAIN--MUTTERS) 582 ICEMAN
SHUT UP, YOU/ 632 ICEMAN
AW, SHUT UP, OLD CEMETERY/ ALWAYS BEEFIN'/ 644 ICEMAN
SHUT YOUR DAMNED TRAP/ 646 ICEMAN
SHUT UP, DAMN YOU/ I'LL KILL HER. 667 ICEMAN
GOD DAMN YOU, SHUT UP/ 667 ICEMAN
AW, SHUT UP. 670 ICEMAN
KEEP YOUR MOUTH SHUT. 679 ICEMAN
(WITH ANGRY SCORN) AH, SHUT UP, YOU YELLOW FAKER/706 ICEMAN
(BURSTS OUT) YOU MAO FOOL, CAN'T YOU KEEP YOUR 706 ICEMAN
MOUTH SHUT/
AT THE TABLE BY THE WINDOW LARRY HAS UNCONSCIOUSLY724 ICEMAN
SHUT HIS EYES AS HE LISTENS.
WHY YOU KEEP EYES SHUTS 724 ICEMAN
JEEZ, HE'S GOT HIS EYES SHUT. 726 ICEMAN
AND SLAMS THE PORTHOLE SHUT) 514 INZONE
I CLAPPED MY EYES SHUT WHEN HE TURNED ROUND. 520 INZONE
I FELT THE COLD AIR ON MY NECK AN' SHUT IT. 521 INZONE
(ANGRILY) SHUT YER MARF, FEAR/ 525 INZONE
SHUT YOUR MOUTH/ 526 INZONE
I'LL SHUT YOUR DIRTY MOUTH FOR YOU. 527 INZONE
MID HAS STOOD TENSELY WITH HIS EYES SHUT AS IF HE 530 INZONE
WERE UNDERGOING TORTURE DURING
SHUT UP, JAMIE. 66 JOURNE
SHUT UP, BOTH OF YOU/ 77 JOURNE
THAT SHUT HIM UP QUICK. 103 JOURNE
SHUT UP/ 110 JOURNE
SHUT UP, PAPA/ 110 JOURNE
SHUT YOUR MOUTH RIGHT NOW, OR-- 116 JOURNE
AS THE FRONT DOOR IN THE HALL BANGS SHUT BEHIND 154 JOURNE
JAMIE.
(IRRITABLY.) OH, SHUT UP, WILL YOU. 158 JOURNE
(VIOLENTLY.) SHUT UP/ 161 JOURNE
(INDIGNANTLY.) SHUT UP, YOU DAMNED FOOL/ 163 JOURNE
(UNEASILY.) SHUT UP/ 165 JOURNE
SHUT UP/ 166 JOURNE
SHUT UP, JAMIE/ 168 JOURNE
FINALLY WITH A METALLIC CLASH THE GATE IS SHUT 313 LAZARU
BEHIND THEM AND THERE IS A HEAVY
(SMILING DRUNKENLY) SHUT UP, YOURSELF, CAMP-BRAT/322 LAZARU
COVERS HER EYES WITH HER HANDS TO SHUT OUT THE 327 LAZARU
SIGHT.)

SHUT

SHUT (CONT'D.)
(THEN WITH HIS WRY SMILE) BUT I WILL TURN MY 329 LAZARU
BACK--AND SHUT MY EYES--
THE DOOR IS SHUT AGAIN QUICKLY. 331 LAZARU
(SHE RELAXES, HER HEAD BACK, HER EYES SHUT, 4 MANSNS
SHUT MY EYES AND FORGET--NOT OPEN THEM UNTIL HE 4 MANSNS
COMES--
A ND SHUT THE DOOR/ 40 MANSNS
THEY GO INSIDE AND SHUT THE DOOR. 52 MANSNS
THE SNAPS HIS BOOK SHUT AND SPRINGS TO HIS FEET-- 130 MANSNS
SHUT THEE FROM HEAVEN WITH A DOME MORE VAST, TILL 148 MANSNS
THOU AT LENGTH ART FREE.
THE EYES ARE SHUT AS IF SHE WERE ASLEEP. 152 MARCOM
(SMILING) SHUT UP. 367 MARCOM
IT THE REAR IS A SECTION OF THE GREAT WALL OF 373 MARCOM
CHINA WITH AN ENORMOUS SHUT GATE.
SHUT THE DOORS/ 423 MARCOM
(WITH ONE MOTION THEY SHUT THEIR BOOKS. 434 MARCOM
(THEN OMINOUSLY) YOU'D BETTER SHUT UP NOW. 9 MISBEG
UCH, SHUT UP. KILL YOUR 23 MISBEG
EXCEPT ONE THING--(AS SHE STARTS TO SHUT HIM UP-- 31 MISBEG
SHARPLY)
(ANGRILY) SHUT UP/ 35 MISBEG
(FULL OF CURIOSITY) SHUT UP, FATHER. 46 MISBEG
(ANGRILY) SHUT UP, YOU OLD LIAR/ 52 MISBEG
(BURSTS OUT) WILL YOU SHUT UP YOUR ROTTEN 67 MISBEG
BREAKAWAY BLATHER/
(SHOUTS BACK) SHUT UP YOUR NOISE, YOU CRAZY OLD 73 MISBEG
BILLY GOAT/
(STUNG) SHUT UP/ 79 MISBEG
SHUT UP YOUR INSULTS/ 81 MISBEG
(DISGRACEFULLY) WILL YOU SHUT UP/ 85 MISBEG
(HIS CHIN SINKS ON HIS CHEST AND HIS EYES SHUT.) 89 MISBEG
I'LL DISGRACE HIM TILL HE'LL BE GLAD TO COME WITH 92 MISBFG
ME TO SHUT ME UP.
(FURIOUSLY) SHUT UP/ 96 MISBEG
(STUNG) SHUT UP/ 97 MISBEG
SHUT UP/ 118 MISBEG
WELL--(ALMOST HYSTERICALLY) FOR THE LOVE OF GOD, 136 MISBEG
CAN'T YOU SHUT UP ABOUT HIM/
TO GET ME TO--(AS HE STARTS TO SPEAK) SHUT UP/ 162 MISBEG
SHUT UP. 163 MISBFG
KAPE YOUR MOUTH SHUT, AND LAVE ME TELL IT, AND 155 POET
YOU'LL SEE IF WE LET THEM/
THEN HE STARTED TO SHUT THE DOOR. 155 POET
SHUT YOUR MOUTH, SARA, AND DON'T BE TRYING TO 156 POET
PLAGUE HIM.
(ANGRILY.) WILL YOU SHUT YOUR GAB, SARA/ 158 POET
(DISTRACTEDLY.) WILL YOU SHUT UP, THE TWO AV YOU/162 POET
(SARA PUTS HER HAND OVER HER MOUTH TO SHUT OFF THE166 POET
SOUND OF HER LAUGHING.
(WITH ROUGH GOOD NATURE.) SHUT UP, DARLINT. 179 POET
SHUT YOUR LOUD QUACKIN'/ 584 ROPE
SHUT YOUR MOUTH/ 594 ROPE
(ROWSILY--HER EYES SHUT) YOU SOUND SO LIKE 46 STRANG
FATHER, CHARLIE.
THEN THE OUTER DOOR BEING OPENED AND SHUT AGAIN AS 53 STRANG
MARSDEN DEPARTS.
((SHUT UP/... 75 STRANG
OH, SHUT UP/ 95 STRANG
YOU--SHUT UP--MAKING FUN OF MY FATHER/ 142 STRANG
(EXASPERATEDLY) OH, NED, DO SHUT UP/ 143 STRANG
(THERE IS THE SOUND OF A DOOR BEING FLUNG OPEN AND151 STRANG
SHUT
((SHUT UP, YOU FOOL/... 169 STRANG
SHUT UP, YOU/ 193 STRANG
AND HER EYES ARE HALF SHUT AS IF SHE WERE DOZING 493 VOYAGE
ON HER FEET.
SHUT UP. 498 VOYAGE
SHUT UP, YE APE, AN' DON'T BE MAKIN' THAT 498 VOYAGE
SQUEALIN'.
AN' I'LL 'IT YOU, TOO, IF YER DON'T KEEP YER MARF 508 VOYAGE
SHUT.
SHUT THE DOOR. 471 WELDED
I'LL SHUT THE DOOR. 480 WELDED
(HER HEAD THROWN BACK, HER EYES SHUT--SLOWLY. 489 WELDED
DREAMILY)

SHUTS
(SHE GOES TO PANTRY AND SHUTS THE DOOR BEHIND HER 211 AHWILD
WITH EXAGGERATED CARE
THEN HE COMES BACK INSIDE AND SHUTS THE DOOR. 44 ANNA
HE SHUTS THIS, KEEPING A FINGER IN TO MARK THE 82 BEYOND
PLACE.
THEN SHE SHUTS THE DOOR AND RETURNS TO HER CHAIR 154 BEYOND
BY THE STOVE.
(ANDREW REAPPEARS AND SHUTS THE DOOR SOFTLY. 162 BEYOND
SHE SHUTS THE DOOR BEHIND HER, SEES SMITTY ON THE 468 CARIBE
HATCH.
(HE GOES IN AND SHUTS THE DOOR.) 473 CARIBE
SHE ASCENDS INTO THE ROOM AND SHUTS THE DOOR 562 CROSS
BEHIND HER.
WHEN HE SHUTS THE LANTERN AGAIN IT FLICKERS AND 567 CROSS
GOES OUT.
AND PULLS BACK HER HEAD SLOWLY AND SHUTS THE 224 DESIRE
WINDOW.
HE SHUTS THE DOOR BEHIND HIM AND LOCKS IT.) 449 DYNAMO
(SHE SHUTS HER EYES. 54 ELECTR
HAZEL FOLLOWS HER AND SHUTS THE DOOR. 73 ELECTR
(SHE SHUTS THE DOOR BEHIND HER. 78 ELECTR
GETS HIM INSIDE AND SHUTS THE DOCK BEHIND THEM. 113 ELECTR
THEN PICKS IT UP, THROWS IT IN THE CAGE, SHUTS THE254 HA APE
DOOR.
(HE SHUTS HIS EYE AGAIN.) 612 ICEMAN
AS THEN HE CRAWLS INTO HIS BUNK AN' SHUTS HIS 520 INZONE
EYES, AN' STARTS IN SNORIA'.
(SHE GOES IN QUIETLY AND SHUTS THE DOOR.) 190 MANSNS
THEN THE GATE SHUTS, THE LIGHT FADES OUT. 376 MARCUM

SHUTS (CONT'D.)
SHUTS OUT ALL VIEW OF THE HARBOR AT THE END OF THE400 MARCOM
WHARF.
(HE SHUTS THE DOOR CONTEMPTUOUSLY ON MICKEY'S 57 POET
EYES.
BUT SIMPLY SHUTS THE DOOR BEHIND HIM. HE SCOWLS 66 POET
WITH DISGUST.)
(HE COMES IN AND SHUTS THE DOOR.) 124 POET
(SHE KISSES HIM--THEY SHUTS HER EYES WITH A DEEP 200 STRANG
SIGN OF REQUITED WEAKNESS)
(OLSON COMES TO HIMSELF WITH A START AND SHUTS THE504 VOYAGE
DOOR.)

SHUTTER
A SHUTTER IN THE WIND. 571 CROSS
(HE GOES BACK IN THE BEDROOM AND PULLS THE SHUTTER 57 ELECTR
CLOSED.
(THE SHUTTER OF THE BEDROOM IS PUSHED OPEN AND 57 ELECTR
MANNION LEANS OUT.)
AND PUSHES BACK A SHUTTER AND STANDS STARING OUT. 143 ELECTR
(RIFE CLOSES THE SHUTTER HE HAS PUSHED OPEN AND 144 ELECTR
TURNS BACK FROM THE WINDOW.

SHUTTERS
IN THE MIDDLE OF THE RIGHT WALL IS A WINDOW WITH 236 AHWILD
CLOSED SHUTTERS.
ITS WALLS ARE A SICKLY GRAYISH, THE GREEN OF THE 202 DESIRE
SHUTTERS FADED.
THE WINDOW OF THE PARLOR IS HEARD OPENING AND THE 244 DESIRE
SHUTTERS ARE FLUNG BACK AND
I'M GOING T' LEAVE THE SHUTTERS OPEN AND LET IN 245 DESIRE
THE SUN 'N' AIR.
SHUTTERS, AT RIGHT. -0 DYNAMO
I THINK I'LL CLOSE THE SHUTTERS. 424 DYNAMO
THE WINDOW SHUTTERS ARE PAINTED A DARK GREEN. 2 ELECTR
THE SOMBER GRAYNESS OF THE WALL, THE GREEN OF THE 5 ELECTR
OPEN SHUTTERS.
ALL THE SHUTTERS ARE CLOSED. 43 ELECTR
LIGHT APPEARS BETWEEN THE CHINKS OF THE SHUTTERS 57 ELECTR
EXCEPT FOR WHAT MOONLIGHT FILTERS FEEBLY THROUGH 58 ELECTR
THE SHUTTERS.
ALL THE SHUTTERS ARE CLOSED. 67 ELECTR
ALL THE SHUTTERS OF THE WINDOWS ARE CLOSED. 117 ELECTR
WHY ARE THE SHUTTERS STILL CLOSED/ 122 ELECTR
ALL THE SHUTTERS ARE CLOSED AND THE FRONT DOOR IS 129 ELECTR
BOARDED UP.
THERE IS A PAUSE IN WHICH PETER CAN BE HEARD 137 ELECTR
OPENING WINDOWS BEHIND THE SHUTTERS
I SEE A LIGHT THROUGH THE SHUTTERS OF THE SITTING-138 ELECTR
ROOM.
THE SHUTTERS OF THE WINDOWS ARE CLOSED. 149 ELECTR
(SHE GOES TO THE WINDOW AND THROWS THE SHUTTERS 151 ELECTR
OPEN AND LOOKS OUT)
THE SHUTTERS ARE ALL FASTENED BACK, THE WINDOWS 169 ELECTR
OPEN.
INTENSIFYING THE WHITENESS OF THE COLUMNS, THE 169 ELECTR
DEEP GREEN OF THE SHUTTERS.
I'LL HAVE THE SHUTTERS NAILED CLOSED SO NO 178 ELECTR
SUNLIGHT CAN EVER GET IN.
(TURNS TO HIM SHARPLY) YOU GO NOW AND CLOSE THE 179 ELECTR
SHUTTERS AND WALL THEM TIGHT.
AND PULLS THE SHUTTERS CLOSED WITH A DECISIVE 179 ELECTR
BANG.
THESE WINDOWS HAVE NO SHUTTERS, CURTAINS OR 1 MISBEG
SHADES.

SHUTTING
(HE DISAPPEARS AND A MOMENT LATER THE FRONT DOOR 269 AHWILD
IS HEARD SHUTTING BEHIND HIM.)
(SHE IS INTERRUPTED BY THE OPENING AND SHUTTING OF 19 ANNA
THE STREET DOOR IN THE BAR
(ANDREW GOES OUT, SHUTTING THE DOOR.) 97 BEYOND
(SHUTTING THE BOOK WITH A SNAP) 122 BEYOND
THEY'RE LIKE THE WALLS OF A NARROW PRISON YARD 126 BEYOND
SHUTTING ME IN
(SHUTTING THE DOOR BEHIND HIM.) 133 ELECTR
(THE NOISE OF THE OUTER DOOR SHUTTING IS HEARD. 269 GGBROW
(SHE GRABS THE DOORKNOB, SHUTTING THE DOOR.) 40 MANSNS
AND THE NOISE OF AN OUTER DOOR SHUTTING. 130 POET
SHUTTING OUT AN UPROAR OF MUSIC AND DRUNKEN 133 POET
VOICES.

SHWEAR
'TWAS ENOUGH TO MAKE A SAINT SHWEAR TO SEE HIM WID479 CARDIF
HIS GOLD WATCH IN HIS HAND,

SHY
AND HER WHOLE ATMOSPHERE IS ONE OF SHY KINDLINESS.187 AHWILD
A RESTLESS, APPREHENSIVE, DEFIANT, SHY, DREAMY, 193 AHWILD
(WITH SHY EXCITEMENT) I--I'VE READ IT, TOO--AT 198 AHWILD
THE LIBRARY.
(PROUD OF HIMSELF--WITH A SHY SMILE) 240 AHWILD
(RICHARD ICHARO LOOKS DREADFULLY SHY AND 297 AHWILD
EMBARRASSED AT THIS.
BY A SMILE OF SHY UNDERSTANDING AND SYMPATHY. 297 AHWILD
HE STANDS THERE, CASTS A SHY GLANCE AT ANNA WHOSE 20 ANNA
BRILLIANT CLOTHES AND TO HIM
HIS EYES ARE LARGE, SHY AND SENSITIVE, OF THE SAME422 DYNAMO
BLUE-GRAY AS HIS FATHER'S.
(WITH A STRANGE SHY EAGERNESS) 141 ELECTR
THEY'LL FIGHT PURTY SHY UP HER NOW. 170 ELECTR
BUT HE'S SAD AND SHY, TOO, JUST LIKE A BABY 263 GGBROW
SOMETIMES.
HIS WEAK FACE IS REVEALED IN THE BRIGHT MOONLIGHT+264 GGBROW
SHRINKING, SHY AND GENTLE,
WITH THE SHY PRIDE OF ONE WHO HAS LENGTHENED HER 282 GGBROW
DACES AND PUT UP HER HAIR.
GO HIDE YOURSELF BEFORE DE HORSES SHY AT YUH. 238 HA APE
WAITING FOR ANY EXCUSE TO SHY AND PRETEND TO TAKE 576 ICEMAN
THE BIT IN ITS TEETH.
UNAFFECTED CHARM OF A SHY CONVENT-GIRL 13 JOURNE
YOUTHFULNESS SHE HAS NEVER LOST--

SICK

SHY (CONT'D.)
HER FACE LIGHTS UP WITH A CHARMING, SHY 28 JOURNE
EMBARRASSMENT.
(SHE GIVES A LITTLE EXCITED, SHY LAUGH.) 105 JOURNE
(HER MANNER AND QUALITY DRIFT BACK TO THE SHY 112 JOURNE
CONVENT GIRL AGAIN.)
(THE SHADOW VANISHES AND HER SHY, GIRLISH 114 JOURNE
EXPRESSION RETURNS.)
(HER MANNER DRIFTS BACK TO THE SHY, GAY CONVENT 114 JOURNE
GIRL.)
IT IS A MARBLE MASK OF GIRLISH INNOCENCE, THE 170 JOURNE
MOUTH CAUGHT IN A SHY SMILE.
(WITH THE SHY POLITENESS OF A WELL-BRED YOUNG GIRL172 JOURNE
TOWARD AN ELDERLY GENTLEMAN
THERE IS SOMETHING OF SHY WONDERING CHILD ABOUT 308 LAZARU
HIS ATTITUDE NOW.
(SHE KISSES HIM--THEN SUDDENLY EMBARRASSED AND 88 MANSNS
SHY, PUSHES BACK FROM HIM.)
(KISSES HER HAND WITH A SHY, BOYISH 109 MANSNS
IMPULSIVENESS.)
HEARING, WHILE YOU ACT SHY AS A MOUSE. 93 MISBEG
(SHE PULLS HIS HEAD BACK AND KISSES HIM ON THE 118 MISBEG
LIPS--A QUICK, SHY KISS)
HE'S THAT SHY HE'S NEVER DARED EVEN TO KISS HER 62 POET
HAND/
(SHE SMILES A SHY, GENTLE SMILE.) 130 POET
SHE STANDS LOOKING AT HER MOTHER, AND SUDDENLY SHE136 POET
BECOMES SHY AND UNCERTAIN--
(SHE PAUSES--HER TIRED, WORN FACE BECOMES SUDDENLY181 POET
SHY AND TENDER.)

SHYIN'
HE'S SHYIN' AT THE FURNITURE COVERS AN' HIS TEETH 133 ELECTR
ARE CLICKIN' A'READY.

SHYLY
(SUDDENLY--WITH A SAD PATHOS, QUOTES AWKWARDLY AND198 AHWILD
SHYLY)
(SHYLY) A SMALL ONE, PLEASE. 238 AHWILD
(SHYLY) I'M GLAD--IT MAKES YOU HAPPY. 279 AHWILD
(COMES BACK AND SITS DOWN BY HIM SHYLY) 286 AHWILD
(SHYLY LIFTING HER LIPS) THEN--ALL RIGHT--DICK. 287 AHWILD
IT WAS WONDERFUL--DOWN AT THE BEACH--{HE STOPS 296 AHWILD
ABRUPTLY, SMILING SHYLY.)
HE SPEAKS SHYLY.) 297 AHWILD
(THEN AFTER HESITATING A MOMENT--SHYLY) 27 ANNA
(HE HOLDS OUT HIS HAND TO HER SHYLY. 34 ANNA
(HE PULLS AT HER SLEEVE SHYLY) 35 ANNA
(EMBARRASSED--STAMMERS SHYLY) 72 ELECTR
(DELIGHTED BUT PULLING HER HAND AWAY SHYLY) 84 ELECTR
THERE IS A QUALITY OF AN INNOCENT CONVENT GIRL 105 JOURNE
ABOUT HER, AND SHE SMILES SHYLY.)
THE SHYLY EAGER, TRUSTING SMILE IS ON HER LIPS AS 175 JOURNE
SHE TALKS ALOUD TO HERSELF.)
(PLEASED--SHYLY) I DON'T--BUT I'M HAPPY IF YOU 68 MISBEG
THINK--
(SHE HESITATES--THEN SHYLY.) 64 POET
(GOOD MORNING--(SHE HESITATES--THEN SHYLY) MOTHER. 56 STRANG

SHYNESS
(PUTTING ONE HAND ON TOP OF ANDREW'S WITH A 83 BEYOND
GESTURE ALMOST OF SHYNESS)
BEHIND ALL HER SHYNESS AND BLUSHES. 138 JOURNE
THE WAITING FOR ME, AND THE FEAR HE'D MADE HIM144 POET
FORGET ALL HIS SHYNESS,
AND HE FORGOT WHATEVER SHYNESS WAS LEFT IN THE 147 POET
DARK.

SIBJECT
LESH HAVE SOME LIGHT ON SIBJECT. 155 JOURNE

SIC
I'M GOIN' TO TELL MA AND SIC HER ONTO YOU. 505 DIFRNT

SICH
'TAINT SICH BAD MUSIC, IS ITS 466 CARIBE
WHO'D THINK OLLIE'D BE SICH A DIVIL WID THE WIMIN$508 VOYAGE

SICK
AND LEAVES HIM LOOKING A BIT SICK AND DISGUSTED. 204 AHWILD
(DESPERATELY) I--I DON'T FEEL SO WELL--MY 208 AHWILD
STOMACH'S SICK.
(TURNING TO THE OTHERS) MAYBE I BETTER STAY HOME 209 AHWILD
WITH HIM, IF HE'S SICK.
WELL, I GUESS HE CAN'T BE SO VERY SICK--AFTER 209 AHWILD
THAT.
I'M NOT REALLY SICK. 209 AHWILD
I'M SICK OF HIS BULL/ 247 AHWILD
NERVOUS, SICK, A PREY TO GLOOMY REMORSE 256 AHWILD
(HE HIDES HIS FACE IN HIS HANDS AND BEGINS TO SOB 258 AHWILD
LIKE A SICK LITTLE BOY.
YOU'LL MAKE YOURSELF SICK/ 260 AHWILD
SEA-SICK TINGE, HIS EYES SEEM TO BE TURNED INWARD 261 AHWILD
UNEASILY--
MOTHER APPEALINGLY, LIKE A SICK LITTLE BOY) 262 AHWILD
TO PUNISH HIM--AND I THOUGHT HE OUGHT TO, ANYWAY, 265 AHWILD
AFTER BEING SO SICK.
DO YOU WANT HIM TO BE TAKEN DOWN SICK$ 268 AHWILD
(IGNORING HIM) IT ONLY MAKES ME SADDER AND SICK--270 AHWILD
HAVING TO BE PUT TO BED AND GETTING SICK/. 276 AHWILD
IT DIDN'T MAKE HIM FEEL HAPPY LIKE SID, ONLY SAD 289 AHWILD
AND SICK.
SHE GAT SICK ON YOB IN ST. 8 ANNA
I'M TELLIN' YUH I'M SICK OF STICKIN' WITH YUH, AND 11 ANNA
I'M LEAVING YUH FLAT, SEE$
I GOT GOOD AND SICK AND THEY HAD TO SEND ME TO THE 16 ANNA
HOSPITAL.
SHE'S BEEN SICK. 19 ANNA
YUST SHORT TIME AGO AY GOT DIS YOB CAUSE AY VAS 21 ANNA
SICK, NEED OPEN AIR.
(SKEPTICALLY) SICK$ 21 ANNA
(DISMISSING THE SUBJECT) SPEAKING OF BEING SICK, 22 ANNA
I BEEN THERE MYSELF--
GEE, WASN'T I SICK OF IT--AND OF THEM/ 27 ANNA
(IMPULSIVELY) BUT HE IS SICK. 39 ANNA

SICK (CONT'D.)
YOU AIN'T SICK LIKE UDDERS. 39 ANNA
THAT ISN'T A BURN FOOL, WHEN HE'S SICK OF THE LOT 46 ANNA
OF THEM COWS$
I'M SICK OF THE WHOLE GAME. 60 ANNA
FEELING SICK$ 63 ANNA
(DULLY) INSIDE MY HEAD FEEL SICK. 63 ANNA
I'D BEEN WAITING AND WAITING TILL I WAS SICK OF 64 ANNA
IT.
AY'M SICK FROM TANK TOO MUCH ABOUT YOU, ABOUT ME. 64 ANNA
BUT AY'M NOT SICK INSIDE HEAD VAY YOU MEAN. 64 ANNA
AY FEEL SICK. 67 ANNA
I'M SICK AND TIRED OF THE WHOLE DAMN BUSINESS. 107 BEYOND
I'M SICK OF DIGGING IN THE DIRT AND SWEATING 107 BEYOND
BUT I'M SICK AND TIRED OF IT--WHETHER YOU WANT TO 107 BEYOND
BELIEVE ME OR NOT--
THINKS SHE KNOWS BETTER THAN AN OLD, SICK BODY 113 BEYOND
LIKE ME.
BUT HE MUST BE RIGHT SICK OF IT BY THIS. 115 BEYOND
I'M SICK OF HEARING YOU. 117 BEYOND
I'M SICK O' BEING MADE FUN AT, THAT'S WHAT. 124 BEYOND
DADA SICK$ 129 BEYOND
DADA DOES FEEL SICK--A LITTLE. 129 BEYOND
(DULLY) HE COULDN'T KNOW YOU'D BEEN TOOK SICK 146 BEYOND
MY BRAIN MUST BE SICK, TOO. 147 BEYOND
(WITH A FLASH OF SICK JEALOUSY) 147 BEYOND
(WEARILY) YOU OUGHTN'T TO TALK ABOUT HIM NOW WHEN152 BEYOND
HE'S SICK IN HIS BED.
YOU MEAN--HOW LONG HAS HE BEEN SICK$ 154 BEYOND
TO BE SICK IN THIS OUT-OF-THE-WAY HOLE 154 BEYOND
DIDN'T YOU SEE HOW SICK HE WAS GETTING$ 155 BEYOND
I'M SICK OF IT ALL. 157 BEYOND
(THE SICK MAN IN THE LOWER BUNK IN THE REAR GROANS478 CARDIF
AND MOVES RESTLESSLY.
THE SICK MAN GIVES A GROAN OF PAIN.) 481 CARDIF
IS THAT BANSHEE SCHREECHIN' FIT MUSIC FOR A SICK 481 CARDIF
MAN$
AND A SICK MAN MAYBE DYIN' LISTENIN' TO US. 481 CARDIF
FORGETTING THE SICK MAN IN THEIR SAILORS' DELIGHT 481 CARDIF
TWISTS HIS HEAD IN THE DIRECTION OF THE SICK MAN) 483 CARDIF
AND HOW IS THE SICK MAN$ 484 CARDIF
DIDN'T I TELL YOU YOU WASN'T HALF AS SICK AS YOU 485 CARDIF
THOUGHT YOU WAS$
ABOUT--ABOUT BEIN' SO SICK. 487 CARDIF
YOU'RE SICK. 566 CROSS
I WISH I DIDN'T LOOK SO LIKE A SICK CAT. 519 DAYS
PARTICULARLY SICK OF MYSELF BECAUSE I ENDURE THE 519 DAYS
HUMILIATION OF WALTER'S OPEN
SICK OF MYSELF/ 519 DAYS
IT'S SIMPLY THAT I'VE GROWN SICK OF MY LIFE, 519 DAYS
SICK OF THE ALL THE LYING AND FAKING OF IT, SICK 519 DAYS
OF MARRIAGE AND MOTHERHOOD,
A LOOK OF SICK REPULSION COMING OVER HER FACE) 538 DAYS
YOU--YOU DON'T FEEL REALLY SICK, DO YOU, DEAREST$ 940 DAYS
I'M SICK OF THE DAMNED THING--NO*, AT ANY RATE. 943 DAYS
SICK OF THE DAMNED THING, YES. 943 DAYS
YOU LOOK SICK. 548 DAYS
I'M COLD, I'M SICK. 550 DAYS
I'M SICK OF YOUR DAMNED CROAKING/ 560 DAYS
JOHN, AS SOON AS HE ENTERS, FALLS UNDER THE 560 DAYS
ATMOSPHERE OF THE SICK-ROOM,
I DIDN'T SAY NOTHIN' AND HE SAYS, LOOKIN' KINDER 210 DESIRE
QUEER AND SICK--
AN' MY HUSBAND GUT SICK AN' DIED TOO, 226 DESIRE
(UNFEELINGLY) YE'VE MADE A FOOL O' ME--A SICK, DUMB257 DESIRE
FOOL--
YE FEELIN' SICK$ 263 DESIRE
AND FINALLY HE GITS SICK UF IT AND HAS THE BOYS 503 DIFRNT
PUSH HER UFF WITH OARS.
HE'S TOO MEAN EVER TO GET REAL SICK. 522 DIFRNT
DIDN'T YOU TELL ME YOU ENLISTED AGAIN 'CAUSE YOU 523 DIFRNT
WERE SICK UF THIS SMALL PLACE
YOU LOOK 'S IF YOU WAS GETTIN' SICK. 527 DIFRNT
(GONE TO BED...SO EARLY$...WAS HE SICK AND 427 DYNAMO
DIDN'T TELL ME....I)
I'M SICK OF THESE FRESH GUYS THAT THINK ALL THEY 430 DYNAMO
HAVE TO DO IS WINK AND YOU
YOU MAKE ME SICK, RUBE/ 433 DYNAMO
I'M SICK OF WALKING. 433 DYNAMO
I'M SICK OF HIS GROUCHES. 455 DYNAMO
BEEN SICK$ 463 DYNAMO
SHE'S MAKING HERSELF SICK WORRYING. 478 DYNAMO
NO WONDER HE'S SICK OF ME/.... 480 DYNAMO
(JUDICIALLY) OH, I'SE GOOD FOR SIX MONTHS YIT 180 EJONES
'FORE DEY GITS SICK O' MY GAME.
I'LL MAKE DEM LOOK SICK, I WILL. 183 EJONES
WONDER DEY WOULDN'T GIT SICK O' BEATIN' DAT DRUM. 186 EJONES
YOU JUS' GET SEEIN' DEM THINGS 'CAUSE YO' BELLY'S 193 EJONES
EMPTY AND YOU'S SICK WID
WELL--IF YOU CALL A PESKY COLD SICK. 13 ELECTR
YOU HAVEN'T BEEN SICK, I HOPE/. 13 ELECTR
HE SEEMS TO HAVE BEEN SICK SO MUCH THIS PAST YEAR. 17 ELECTR
THAT GRANDFATHER WAS SICK--(AS CHRISTINE IS ABOUT 29 ELECTR
TO PROTEST INDIGNANTLY)
(SHE BREAKS AWAY, SHRINKING FROM HER MOTHER WITH A 31 ELECTR
LOOK OF SICK REPULSION.
YOU CAN MAKE UP SOME STORY ABOUT A SICK DOG ON 40 ELECTR
YOUR SHIP.
FATHER'S BEEN SICK FOR THE PAST YEAR, AS I WROTE 52 ELECTR
YOU.
I'M SICK OF DEATH/ 56 ELECTR
DOCTOR BLAKE SAYS SHE WILL HAVE HERSELF IN BED 68 ELECTR
SICK IF SHE DOESN'T LOOK OUT.
I'M SO AFRAID YOU WILL MAKE YOURSELF SICK. 72 ELECTR
HOW SICK AND CHANGED HE LOOKS, DOESN'T HE, PETER$ 80 ELECTR
SHE EVEN FOLLOWED ME TO NEW YORK, WHEN I WENT TO 88 ELECTR
SEE YOUR SICK GRANDFATHER/
HE'S STILL SICK/ 92 ELECTR

SICK

SICK	(CONT'D.)

HE'S SICK, YOU KNOW, 118 ELECTR
(AURREDLY) PERHAPS ORIN GOT SO SICK HE WASN'T 119 ELECTR
ABLE TO.
(THE OTHERS LAUGH, THEIR MIRTH A BIT FORCED, BUT 131 ELECTR
SMALL LOOKS RATHER SICK.)
THEY ONLY MADE ME SICK--AND THE NAKED WOMEN 145 ELECTR
DISGUSTED ME.
WHAT DID YOU DO WITH HIM THE NIGHT I WAS SICK 154 ELECTR
THAT HE'D GOTTEN SICK OF PAINTING AND COMPLETELY 276 GGBROW
GIVEN IT UP.
O WOMAN--MY LOVE--THAT I HAVE SINNED AGAINST IN MY292 GGBROW
SICK PRIDE AND CRUELTY--
SICK/ 297 GGBROW
SICK OF MYSELF AND HIM/ 297 GGBROW
HE'LL BE VERY SICK AND NERVOUS AND HE'LL WANT TO 301 GGBROW
BE QUIET.
POOR DEAR, DO YOU FEEL SICK5 301 GGBROW
YOU'RE SICK/ 305 GGBROW
HIS REAL FACE IS NOW SICK, GHASTLY, TORTURED, 314 GGBROW
HOLLOW-CHEEKED AND FEVERISH-EYED)
AW, YUH MAKE ME SICK/ 217 HA APE
AW, YUH MAKE ME SICK/ 223 HA APE
(ENRAGED) YUH TINK I MADE HER SICK, TOO, DO YUHS 232 HA APE
WELL, I'M GLAD THEY FIRED THAT YOUNG SQUIRT THEY 10 HUGHIE
TOOK ON WHEN HUGHIE GOT SICK.
SICK OF TRAVELLING. 23 HUGHIE
AND SHE WAS SICK OF STANDING ON HER DOGS ALL DAY, 23 HUGHIE
I GOT SICK OF LYING AWAKE. 985 ICEMAN
I'M SICK OF YOU AND HUGO, TOO. 605 ICEMAN
I'M SICK OF YOU/ 610 ICEMAN
I'M SICK OF HEARIN' ABOUT DAT FARM. 616 ICEMAN
LIKE WHEN YOU'RE SICK AND SUFFERING LIKE HELL 625 ICEMAN
I'M SICK OF LISTENIN' TO DEM HOP DEMSELVES UP. 631 ICEMAN
(THEN KINDLY) GEE, KID, YUH LOOK SICK. 644 ICEMAN
HAGGARD WITH SLEEPLESSNESS AND NERVES, HIS EYES 644 ICEMAN
SICK AND HAUNTED.
SHE GOT SICK OF THE OTHERS BEFORE THEY DID OF HER.647 ICEMAN
ALL I KNOW IS I'M SICK OF LIFE/ 649 ICEMAN
I'M DAMNED SICK OF THAT KIDDING/ 652 ICEMAN
YOU'LL CONFESS YOU WERE PRETTY SICK OF HER HATING 657 ICEMAN
YUH FOR GETTING DRUNK.
I'M SICK OF BEING PLAYED FOR A SUCKER/ 660 ICEMAN
I KNOW YOU ARE SICK OF MY GABBING. 660 ICEMAN
COME TO YOU AFTER YOU FOUND YOUR WIFE WAS SICK OF 662 ICEMAN
YOUS
BUT I GOT SICK OF ARGUIN' WID 'IM. 665 ICEMAN
I'M SICK OF HIM. 669 ICEMAN
WE'RE SICK OF WEARIN' OUT OUR DOGS 669 ICEMAN
IT'S SICK AND TIRED OF MESSIN' ROUND WID WHITE MEN.673 ICEMAN
(SYMPATHETICALLY) YUH LOOK SICK, WILLIE. 674 ICEMAN
BUT HE IS SICK AND RESET BY KATZENJAMMER.) 674 ICEMAN
HE IS ABSOLUTELY SOBER, BUT HIS FACE IS SICK, 674 ICEMAN
BEHIND THIS, HE IS SICK AND FEEBLY HOLDING HIS 675 ICEMAN
DUCET-SODDEN BODY TOGETHER.)
HE IS SICK, HIS NERVES ARE SHATTERED, HIS EYES ARE681 ICEMAN
APPREHENSIVE, BUT HE, TOO,
I TOLD YOU YOU WEREN'T THAT AS SICK AS YOU 684 ICEMAN
PRETENDED.
WHILE HE IS GOING SO, JIMMY, IN A SICK PANIC, 686 ICEMAN
IF HE WAS REALLY SICK OF LIFE AND ONLY HAD THE 700 ICEMAN
NERVE TO DIE/
BUT AT THE SAME TIME SICK OF HOME. 712 ICEMAN
I'M SICK AND THINKIN' AND JUMPIN' AT IVIRY BIT AV 917 INZONE
A NOISE.)
HE HAS NEVER BEEN REALLY SICK A DAY IN HIS LIFE. 13 JOURNE
BUT IT DOES SEEM A SHAME HE SHOULD HAVE TO BE SICK 16 JOURNE
RIGHT NOW.
YES, IT'S LIKE HAVING A SICK WHALE IN THE BACK 17 JOURNE
YARD.
GOSH, PAPA, I SHOULD THINK YOU'D GET SICK OF 26 JOURNE
HEARING YOURSELF-- (HE DISAPPEARS.
THE KID IS DAMNED SICK. 27 JOURNE
WHEN HE FIRST GOT SICK. 30 JOURNE
HARDY'S TREATED HIM WHENEVER HE WAS SICK UP HERE, 33 JOURNE
SINCE HE WAS KNEE HIGH.
IT'S DAMNABLE LUCK EDMUND SHOULD BE SICK RIGHT 36 JOURNE
NOW.
SHE HAS CONTROL OF HER NERVES--OR SHE HAD UNTIL 37 JOURNE
EDMUND GOT SICK.
AND EVERY NIGHT SINCE EDMUND'S BEEN SICK SHE'S 38 JOURNE
BEEN UP AND DOWN.
I'VE BEEN SO WORRIED EVER SINCE YOU'VE BEEN SICK. 46 JOURNE
AND YOU WON'T WORRY YOURSELF SICK, AND YOU'LL KEEP 48 JOURNE
ON TAKING CARE OF YOURSELF--
I MEAN, IT'S A CINCH YOU'RE REALLY SICK, 55 JOURNE
HE LOOKS SICK AND HOPELESS.) 64 JOURNE
OH, I'M SO SICK AND TIRED OF PRETENDING THIS IS A 67 JOURNE
HOME/
I WAS SO SICK AFTERWARDS, AND THAT IGNORANT QUACK 87 JOURNE
OF A CHEAP HOTEL DOCTOR--
AND NOW, EVER SINCE HE'S BEEN SO SICK I'VE KEPT 88 JOURNE
REMEMBERING EUGENE AND MY FATHER
(CHECKS HIMSELF GUILTILY, LOOKING AT HIS SON'S 89 JOURNE
SICK FACE WITH WORRIED PITY.)
YOU'RE NOT REALLY SICK AT ALL/ 90 JOURNE
AND BAD FOOD NEVER MADE HIM CROSS OR SICK. 109 JOURNE
FOR A CHILD WHO IS SICK OR FRIGHTENED. 111 JOURNE
AND YOU WON'T EVEN LISTEN WHEN I TRY TO TELL YOU 120 JOURNE
HOW SICK--
BUT I WAS DESOLATE AND SICK OF AN OLD PASSION, 134 JOURNE
IF YOU'D SPENT MONEY FOR A DECENT DOCTOR WHEN SHE 140 JOURNE
WAS SO SICK AFTER I WAS BORN.
EDMUND HAS STOPPED COUGHING. HE LOOKS SICK AND 146 JOURNE
WEAK.
HER ONE FEAR WAS SHE'D GET OLD AND SICK AND HAVE 148 JOURNE
TO DIE IN THE POORHOUSE.
SORRY TO HEAR YOU WERE SICK. 160 JOURNE

SICK (CONT'D.)
EDMUND'S FACE LOOKS STRICKEN AND SICK. 162 JOURNE
EVEN HIS OFFENSIVE DRUNKENNESS TAKEN FROM HIM, 172 JOURNE
LEAVING HIM SICK AND SOBER.
THAT THE DEAD ARE DEAD AGAIN AND THE SICK DIE, AND300 LAZARU
THE SAD GROW MORE SORROWFUL.
HE HEALS THE SICK, HE RAISES THE DEAD, BY 300 LAZARU
LAUGHTER.
THE HEIRS OF A CAESAR TAKE SICK SO MYSTERIOUSLY/ 301 LAZARU
ARE THE STARS TOO PURE FOR YOUR SICK PASSIONS 310 LAZARU
ITS WILL IS SO SICK THAT IT MUST KILL IN ORDER TO 330 LAZARU
BE AWARE OF LIFE AT ALL.
THEY EVADE THEIR FEAR OF DEATH BY BECOMING SO SICK352 LAZARU
OF LIFE
WE ARE SICK, THEY SAY, *THEREFORE THERE IS NO 352 LAZARU
GOD IN US.*
I AM SICK, LAZARUS, SICK OF CRUELTY AND LUST AND 358 LAZARU
HUMAN FLESH AND ALL THE
I'LL ADMIT I DO GET DEATHLY SICK OF THE DAILY 16 MANSNS
GRIND OF THE COUNTING-HOUSE--
OH, DARLING, AND I WAS SO AFRAID I'D BECOME UGLY 90 MANSNS
TO YOU AND YOU WERE SICK OF ME.
YOU'RE WASTING MY TIME AND I'M SICK OF YOU/ 142 MANSNS
AH, I HOPE HE'S NOT GOING TO BE SICK. 177 MANSNS
WHEN YOU THINK OF GHAZAN PROTECTING ME AND NURSING414 MARCOM
ME WHEN I AM SICK--AND--
SELLING THEM A BROKEN-DOWN NAG OR A SICK COW OR 8 MISBEG
PIG THAT HE'S DOCTORED UP TO
SURE, IT'S ONLY WHEN HE GETS SICK OF THE DRUNKS AT 27 MISBEG
THE INN.
(THEN ANGRILY) OCH, I'M SICK OF YOUR CRAZY GAB, 29 MISBEG
FATHER/
OCH, YOU MAKE ME SICK, YOU SLY MISER/ 36 MISBEG
HE WAS LAUGHING HIMSELF SICK. 48 MISBEG
AND A THOUSAND TO CURE THE SICK AND COVER FUNERAL 63 MISBEG
EXPENSES FOR THE DEAD.
(ANGRILY) OCH, YOU OLD LOON, I'M SICK OF YOU. 77 MISBEG
AND SAID IN A SICK SHEEP'S VOICE. 82 MISBEG
MIDDLE-AGED DRUNKARD AGAINST HER BREAST, AS IF HE 157 MISBEG
WERE A SICK CHILD.
(HE QUOTES DROWSILY) *BUT I WAS DESOLATE AND SICK 165 MISBEG
OF AN OLD PASSION.
THE DAMNED SICK REMORSE THAT MAKES YOU WISH YOU'D 171 MISBEG
DIED IN YOUR SLEEP SO YOU
WHEN HE'S HERE SICK AND TOO WEAK TO DEFEND 17 POET
HIMSELF.
(WORRIED AGAIN.) MAYBE YOU OUGHT TO HAVE TOLD HER 19 POET
HE'S HERE SICK TO SAVE HER
FOR WITHOUT IT WHAT AM I AT ALL BUT AN UGLY, FAT 26 POET
WOMAN GETTIN' OLD AND SICK/
I DON'T KNOW IF IT'S RIGHT, YOU TO BE IN HIS ROOM 32 POET
SO MUCH, EVEN IF HE IS SICK.
ARE YOU SICK, CON, DARLIN'S 34 POET
ARE YOU REALLY SICK OR IS IT JUST-- 58 POET
SICK5 73 POET
HE'S BEEN SICK-- 73 POET
HE'D HAVE WRITTEN YOU HE WAS SICK, BUT HE DIDN'T 75 POET
WANT TO WORRY YOU.
IF HE WASN'T SICK, I'D--BUT I'LL GET HIM OUT OF 127 POET
HERE TOMORROW/
I'M SICK WITH WORRY AND I'VE GOT TO THE PLACE 136 POET
WHERE I CAN'T BEAR WAITIN' ALONE.
HE'D NEVER HARM A SICK MAN, NO MATTER-- 159 POET
BUT SHE GOES ON CROONING TO HIM COMFORTINGLY AS IF165 POET
HE WERE A SICK CHILD.)
(SHE STARES AT HIM, SICK AND DESPERATE. 176 POET
AND THEN WHEN SHE GOT SICK OF YOU AND RAN AWAY-- 580 ROPE
THAT SHE'S A SICK GIRL...)) 8 STRANG
BUT SHE'S A SICK GIRL.... 13 STRANG
(SLOWLY AND STRANGELY) I'M NOT SICK. 18 STRANG
SHE'S A SICK GIRL/ 18 STRANG
BUT THEY ARE SICK AND I MUST GIVE MY HEALTH TO 18 STRANG
HELP THEM TO LIVE ON,
SICK WITH MEN.... 25 STRANG
THERE--THERE--DON'T--NINA, PLEASE--DON'T CRY-- 43 STRANG
YOU'LL MAKE YOURSELF SICK--
I AM SICK OF SICKNESS. 46 STRANG
(APPREHENSIVE HERSELF NOW) ((THAT SICK DEAD 57 STRANG
FEELING....
I TOLD HIM HIS FATHER WAS SICK, 60 STRANG
THINKING ANY MINUTE THE CURSE MIGHT GET HIM, EVERY 60 STRANG
TIME HE WAS SICK,
AND I HATE IT TOO, NOW, BECAUSE IT'S SICK, IT'S 61 STRANG
NOT MY BABY, IT'S HIS/
SINCE NINA GOT SICK.... 67 STRANG
(DESPERATELY) ((IF I WAS ONLY SURE IT WAS BECAUSE 68 STRANG
SHE'S REALLY SICK....
NOT JUST SICK OF ME/...)) 68 STRANG
POOR SICK BABY/.... 70 STRANG
BEING TIED TO A WIFE WHO'S TOO SICK TO BE A WIFE. 70 STRANG
BUT I WAS REALLY SICK.... 71 STRANG
TO HAVE SUCH THOUGHTS WHEN MOTHER IS SICK AND I 75 STRANG
OUGHT TO BE THINKING ONLY OF
SHE'S NEVER BEEN SICK A DAY IN HER LIFE AND-- 77 STRANG
AND SICK OF HIMSELF WITH DESIRE FOR ME/... 91 STRANG
SHE WAS NEVER SICK A DAY IN HER LIFE UNTIL--THE 100 STRANG
TURNS ON DARRELL--COLDLY)
((POOR SICK ASS THAT I AM/.... 117 STRANG
HE'D TAKE IT ON HIMSELF BUT HE'S SICK OF THE GAME.121 STRANG
SHE MAKES ME SICK/.... 138 STRANG
I'M SICK OF THE FIGHT FOR HAPPINESS/....)) 138 STRANG
I'D THINK SHE'D GET SICK OF THE OLD FOOL 138 STRANG
((THESE MEN MAKE ME SICK/.... 149 STRANG
HE'S SICK OF BEING BAITED, NINA. 157 STRANG
(((I'M GETTING SICK OF THIS/... 163 STRANG
(((WILL GORDON EVER GET OLD AND SICK LIKE THAT,... 185 STRANG
NOT SINCE YOUR FATHER WAS TAKEN SICK, SHE HASN'T, 185 STRANG
DEAR.

SICK (CONT'D.)
(COMMENCING TO SOB AGAIN) H'ABUSIN' ME LIKE A DAWG494 VOYAGE
CUS I'M SICK AN' ORF ME OATS,
GAWD KNOWS WOT'S GUIN' TO 'APPEN TO ME, I'M THAT 495 VOYAGE
SICK.
I BANE FEELING SICK. 908 VOYAGE

SICKED
BEFORE HE SICKED THE DOG ON HIM. 25 JOURNE

SICKEN
IT WOULD SICKEN YOU FOR LIFE WITH THE =WONDER AND 132 BEYOND
MYSTERY= YOU USED TO DREAM OF.

SICKENED
AS IF THE IMPERIAL BLOOD IN HIS VEINS HAD BEEN 337 LAZARU
SICKENED BY AGE AND DEBAUCHERY.
(TENSELY--SICKENED BY HIS HYPOCRISY) 123 MISBEG

SICKENING
AND, IN REWARD FOR HIS SICKENING HUMILIATION, SAW 511 DAYS
THAT NO MIRACLE WOULD HAPPEN.
WHAT A SICKENING IDEA/..... 114 STRANG

SICKENINGLY
AS SICKENINGLY CLEAR AS IF IT WERE YESTERDAY... 6 STRANG

SICKER
HE MUSTN'T THINK I'M SICKER THAN I AM. 151 BEYOND
WELL, I'M SICKER OF YOUR KIDDING ME ABOUT GETTING 652 ICEMAN
REINSTATED ON THE FORCE.

SICKING
(DOUBTFULLY) BUT HICKEY WASN'T SICKING HIM ON 652 ICEMAN
THOSE TIMES.
BUT EVEN SICKING SOME OF YOU ON TO NAG AT EACH 660 ICEMAN
OTHER.
TO CONVINCE SOME DAME, WHO WAS SICKING HER DOG ON 661 ICEMAN
ME.

SICKLY
AND THE LIGHT WHICH COMES THROUGH THE SKYLIGHT IS 535 *ILE
SICKLY AND FAINT.
(FORCING A SICKLY, TWITCHING SMILE) 256 AHWILD
YOU HAVEN'T FORGOTTEN WHAT A SICKLY SPECIMEN I WAS 89 BEYOND
THEN, IN THOSE DAYS.
SHE GETS IT RIGHT FROM HER PA--BEIN' SICKLY ALL 116 BEYOND
THE TIME.
A PRETTY BUT SICKLY AND ANEMIC-LOOKING CHILD WITH 116 BEYOND
A TEAR-STAINED FACE.
ITS WALLS ARE A SICKLY GRAYISH, THE GREEN OF THE 202 DESIRE
SHUTTERS FADED.
YEH--A SICKLY GENERATION/ 251 DESIRE
HIS FACE THE SICKLY GREEN OF AN ATTACK OF NAUSEA. 268 DESIRE
SHARP FEATURES TO A SICKLY YELLOW. 174 EJONES
PETER HAS DIFFICULTY IN HIDING HIS PAINED SURPRISE144 ELECTR
AT ORIN'S SICKLY APPEARANCE.)
(PULLS HIMSELF UP SHARPLY--CONFUSEDLY, FORCING A 148 ELECTR
SICKLY SMILE)
(WITH A SICKLY SMILE) HELL/ 523 INZONE
AND HE LOOKS MORE SICKLY THAN IN THE PREVIOUS ACT. 51 JOURNE
(RECOVERING A BIT--WITH A SICKLY SMILE) 415 MARCOM
HIS EYES ARE BLOODSHOT, HIS MANNER SICKLY, 8 POET
THE PORCH, IS CHEERLESS AND SICKLY. 48 STRANG

SICKNESS
OF HIS BEING DELICATE THAT YOU TOOK HIS SICKNESS 155 BEYOND
AS A MATTER OF COURSE.
HE IMAGINED HER SICKNESS WAS A TERRIBLE WARNING TO511 DAYS
HIM.
OF SICKNESS AND STARVATION AND I FOUND OUT THAT 26 ELECTR
WHEN SHE'D BEEN LAID UP,
FORGIVE MY SINS--FORGIVE MY SOLITUDE--FORGIVE MY 292 GGBROW
SICKNESS--FORGIVE ME/
(ACCUSINGLY.) THE LESS YOU SAY ABOUT EDMUND'S 34 JOURNE
SICKNESS--
IT WAS TO HER LONG SICKNESS AFTER BRINGING HIM 39 JOURNE
INTO THE WORLD THAT SHE FIRST--
I THOUGHT SHE'D NEVER GOT OVER HER SICKNESS. 141 JOURNE
THAT'S ALL.
ALL LAUGHTER IS MALICE, ALL GODS ARE DEAD, AND 352 LAZARU
LIFE IS A SICKNESS.
WHAT IF THERE ARE ONLY HEALTH AND SICKNESS/ 359 LAZARU
NO SICKNESS/ 360 LAZARU
I AM SICK OF SICKNESS. 46 STRANG
SOME WOMAN'S SICKNESS... 67 STRANG

SIDEBOARD
ON THE SIDEBOARD, A WOMAN'S SEWING BASKET. 535 *ILE
ON THE RIGHT, TO THE REAR, A MARBLE-TOPPED 535 *ILE
SIDEBOARD.
AND HE SMASHES HIS FIST DOWN ON THE MARBLE TOP OF 542 *ILE
THE SIDEBOARD)
UGLY SIDEBOARD WITH THREE PIECES OF OLD SILVER ON 210 AHWILD
ITS TOP.
MILLER STACKS UP AND THEN PUTS ON THE SIDEBOARD. 225 AHWILD
IN THE REAR WALL TO THE RIGHT OF THE SIDEBOARD, 93 BEYOND
IN THE LEFT CORNER, REAR, A SIDEBOARD WITH A 93 BEYOND
MIRROR.
A NUMBER OF BOOKS ARE PILED CARELESSLY ON THE 112 BEYOND
SIDEBOARD.
THEN, SEEING NO ONE ABOUT, HE GOES TO THE 121 BEYOND
SIDEBOARD AND SELECTS A BOOK.
IN THE REAR, LEFT, A MARBLE-TOPPED SIDEBOARD WITH 555 CROSS
A SHIP'S LANTERN ON IT.
THERE'S A LANTERN ON THE SIDEBOARD, THERE, DOCTOR.556 CROSS
A BIG SIDEBOARD STANDS AGAINST THE LEFT WALL, 109 ELECTR
CENTER.
THERE IS A LIGHTED LAMP ON THE SIDEBOARD AND A 110 ELECTR
SHIP'S LANTERN, ALSO LIGHTED.
SHE HURRIEDLY HIDES HERSELF BY THE SIDEBOARD AT 114 ELECTR
LEFT, FRONT.
TO THE RIGHT OF DOOR A HEAVY SIDEBOARD, A PART OF 48 STRANG
THE SET.

SIDEBOARDS
TWO UGLY SIDEBOARDS, ONE AT LEFT, THE OTHER AT 71 MISBEG
RIGHT-REAR.

SIDED
SHE'S ALWAYS SIDED WITH ME....) 424 DYNAMO
HE ALWAYS SIDED WITH YOU AGAINST MOTHER AND ME/ 97 ELECTR

SIDEKICK
I'M WISE TO YOU AND YOUR SIDEKICK, CHUCK. 982 ICEMAN

SIDELIGHTS
A DOORWAY WITH SQUARED TRANSOM AND SIDELIGHTS 2 ELECTR
FLANKED BY INTERMEDIATE COLUMNS.

SIDELONG
ORIN+ GIVES HIS MOTHER A SIDELONG GLANCE OF UNEASY 83 ELECTR
SUSPICION.

SIDERA
=STETIT UNUS IN ARCEM EAECTUS CAPITIS VICTORQUE AD 23 STRANG
SIDERA MITTIT SIDEREUS UCULOS

SIDEREUS
=STETIT UNUS IN ARCEM ERECTUS CAPITIS VICTIMQUE AD 23 STRANG
SIDERA MITTIT SIDEAFOS UCULOS

SIDES
SLAPPING THEM AGAINST HIS SIDES, ON THE VERGE OF 536 *ILE
CRYING.
(GIVES A SIGH OF RELIEF--HER HANDS DROP TO HER 344 *ILE
SIDES.
AND SPLITTING THEIR SIDES/ 223 AHWILD
UH, MY SIDES ACHE. I DECLARE/ 231 AHWILD
DENSE FOG SHROUDS THE BARGE ON ALL SIDES, AND SHE 25 ANNA
FLOATS MOTIONLESS IN A CALM.
AND ALL THE MEN ON BOTH SIDES OF THE FAMILY HAVE 36 ANNA
GONE TO SEA AS FAR BACK AS HE
HIS FISTS CLENCHED AT HIS SIDES.) 108 BEYOND
THE SIDES OF WHICH ALMOST MEET AT THE FAR END TO 477 CARDIF
FORM A TRIANGLE.
ARE BUILT AGAINST THE SIDES. 477 CARDIF
I'VE HEARD ABOUT HIM FROM ALL SIDES SINCE I FIRST 557 CROSS
CAME TO THE ASYLUM YONDER.
(HE AND PETER STOP THEIR DANCE, HOLDING THEIR 223 DESIRE
SIDES.
AND ALL HANDS SPLITTIN' THEIR SIDES/ 503 DIFRNT
HER EYES GLANCE QUICKLY ON ALL SIDES AS IF 459 DYNAMO
SEARCHING FOR SOMEONE.)
RISING SHEER ON BOTH SIDES) THE FOREST WALLS IT IN.192 EJONES
INSTANTLY THE WALLS OF THE FOREST CLOSE IN FROM 195 EJONES
BOTH SIDES.
A CROWD OF FIGURES SILENTLY ENTER THE CLEARING 196 EJONES
FROM ALL SIDES.
JONES LOOKS UP, SEES THE FIGURES ON ALL SIDES, 197 EJONES
GIVE AN ARCHED APPEARANCE TO THE SIDES. 198 EJONES
HER THIN FIGURE, SEATED STIFFLY UPRIGHT, ARMS 43 ELECTR
AGAINST HER SIDES,
HER MOUTH TWITCHES, HER EYES LOOK DESPERATELY ON 71 ELECTR
ALL SIDES.
ON BOTH SIDES SUDDENLY SAW THE JOKE WAR WAS UN 95 ELECTR
THEM AND LAUGHED AND SHOOK HANDS/
HER ARMS HELD STIFFLY TO HER SIDES, HER LEGS AND 170 ELECTR
FEET PRESSED TOGETHER,
IS A RECTANGULAR SPACE WITH BENCHES ON THE THREE 257 GGBROW
SIDES.
AND ON BOTH SIDES WE WERE ABLE TO KEEP OUR REAL 284 GGBROW
VIRTUE, IF YOU GET ME.
TIERS OF NARROW, STEEL BUNKS, THREE DEEP, ON ALL 207 HA APE
SIDES.
LETS HIS HANDS FALL TO HIS SIDES--CONTEMPTUOUSLY) 215 HA APE
(THERE IS A GROWL OF CURSING RAGE FROM ALL SIDES.) 224 HA APE
(A GROWL OF ANGER GOES UP FROM ALL SIDES.) 228 HA APE
(THERE IS A ROAR OF RAGE FROM ALL SIDES.) 228 HA APE
AND A WHOLE PLATOON OF POLICEMEN RUSHES IN ON YANK)234 HA APE
FROM ALL SIDES.
(THIS MADE A BIT RESENTFUL BY THE SUSPICIOUS 247 HA APE
GLANCES FROM ALL SIDES)
I WAS BORN CONDEMNED TO BE ONE OF THOSE WHO HAS TO590 ICEMAN
SEE ALL SIDES OF A QUESTION.
HERE'S THE REVOLUTION STARTING ON ALL SIDES OF YLU634 ICEMAN
AND YOU'RE SLEEPING THROUGH
I'LL BE A WEAK FOOL LOOKING WITH PITY AT THE TWO 726 ICEMAN
SIDES OF EVERYTHING
DIRECTED AT HIM FROM ALL SIDES. 522 INZONE
(AS SMITTY ENTERS THE FORECASTLE HE IS SEIZED 925 INZONE
ROUGHLY FROM BOTH SIDES AND HIS
OF ACCUSATION AND DENIAL FROM BOTH SIDES.) 283 LAZARU
CONCEALED SHROUDS AND KNIVES ARE BROUGHT OUT BY 290 LAZARU
BOTH SIDES.)
THEIR HANDS HANG, THEIR ARMS SINK TO THEIR SIDES. 306 LAZARU
AROUND AND TO THE SIDES OF THE DAIS, ONE SEX ON 344 LAZARU
EACH SIDE.
AT THE SIDES ARE MONGOL CIRCULAR HUTS. 373 MARCOM
AND BOWS WITH A MECHANICAL DIGNITY ON ALL SIDES. 390 MARCOM
AND JOSIE DOUBLES UP AND HOLDS HER SIDES. 62 MISBEG
O GOD, MY SIDES ARE SORE. 65 MISBEG
HE'LL SEE THE WHOLE OF BROADWAY SPLITTING THEIR 96 MISBEG
SIDES LAUGHING AT HIM--
AND ME WITH THE SIDES OF MY STOMACH KNOCKING 176 MISBEG
TOGETHER/
ALWAYS TAKIN' SIDES WITH THE RICH YANKS AGAINST 157 POET
THE POOR IRISH/
HIS BIG HAIRY HANDS DANGLING AT HIS SIDES. 175 POET
(I HATE HER TOO WHEN SHE SIDES WITH HIM/... 142 STRANG

SIDESHOW
WITH THE THRILLED APPRECIATION INSPIRED BY A FREAK369 MARCOM
IN A SIDESHOW.

SIDEWALK
ONE OF THEM TORN FROM THE SPRAWL ON THE SIDEWALK 261 AHWILD
HE HAD TAKEN.
IT'S ONE VIVID BLASPHEMY FROM SIDEWALK TO THE TIPS2497 GGBROW
OF ITS SPIRES/
WHERE HE STANDS IN THE MIDDLE OF THE SIDEWALK.) 237 HA APE

SIDEWALKS
BUT THEY TAKE THE SIDEWALKS IN AFTER NINE O'CLOCK/238 AHWILD
AND WE WON'T LAY SIDEWALKS--OR DIG SEWERS--EVER 258 GGBROW
AGAIN$

SIDEWALKS

SIDEWALKS (CONT'D.)
POUNDIN' SIDEWALKS FOR A DOUBLE-CROSSIN' 669 ICEMAN BARTENDFR.

SIDEWAY
RICHARD IS DISCOVERED SITTING SIDEWAYS ON THE 275 AHWILD GUNWALE OF THE ROWBOAT
PULLS SIDEWAYS ON THEIR HEADS AT AN AGGRESSIVE 4 ANNA ANGLE.
I'M WISE TO THE GAME, UP, DOWN, AND SIDEWAYS. 11 ANNA
(REMOVES HIS HAND AND FLINGS BEER SIDEWAYS FULL 255 DESIRE LENGTH ON
(RESULT: FIXES TWICE AND SHE JERKS BACK AND PITCHES488 DYNAMO SIDEWAYS ON THE STAIRS.)
TURNED SIDEWAYS TO FACE HER, 51 ELECTR
HIS HEAD RESTING SIDEWAYS ON HIS ARMS, 574 ICEMAN
HIS HEAD SIDEWAYS ON THIS PILLOW, FACING FRONT, 576 ICEMAN
HE IS SLUMPED SIDEWAYS ON HIS CHAIR, 576 ICEMAN
(SHE GETS HIM TO SIT AND SHE SITS SIDEWAYS ON THE 91 JOURNE ARM OF HIS
GLANCING SIDEWAYS AT ONE ANOTHER, SMILING 280 LAZARU FOOLISHLY AND SELF-CONSCIOUSLY,
(EBENEZER CRUMPLES UP AND FALLS SIDEWAYS FACE DOWN 167 MANSNS ON THE BENCH
HE KEEPS BEHIND HIS MOTHER, TURNED SIDEWAYS TO 186 MANSNS STARE.
KILEY IS AT FRONT, BUT HIS CHAIR IS TURNED 95 POET SIDEWAYS SO HE FACES RIGHT.
DRISCOLL HAS UNBUTTONED HIS STIFF COLLAR AND ITS 496 VOYAGE ENDS STICK OUT SIDEWAYS.

SIDLE
(SHE TRIPS AWKWARDLY TO SIDLE TOWARD THE DOOR.) 163 ELECTR

SIDLES
HE SIDLES INTO THE ROOM GUILTILY, HIS EYES 256 AHWILD SHIFTING ABOUT.
A SNAKE-FENCE SIDLES FROM LEFT TO RIGHT ALONG THE 81 BEYOND TOP OF THE BANK.
THEN, SUDDENLY, TERRIFIED, SLINKS AWAY AND SIDLES 324 LAZARU OFF AT RIGHT.)

SIDLIN'
SIDLIN' UP TO HER, PLAYIN' THE GREAT GENTLEMAN AND 13 POET MAKIN' COMPLIMENTS,

SIDLING
(SIDLING UP TO MARCELLUS, CRUEL AND MOCKING) 334 LAZARU

SIDNEY
AND THE TIME WE WAS BOTH LOCKED UP IN SIDNEY FOR 488 CARDIF FIGHTIN'S
THE NAME THAT'S WRITTEN IS SIDNEY DAVIDSON, WAN 530 INZONE HUNDRED AN'--
A,' HOW GLAD SHE IS THAT HER SIDNEY BYE IS 531 INZONE WORKIN' HARD
OF BEGINS WID SIMPLY THE NAME SIDNEY DAVIOSON-- 531 INZONE
I AM SORRY--FOR I LOVED YOU, SIDNEY DAVIDSON--BUT 532 INZONE THIS IS THE END.

SIEVE
EVER SINCE I CAN REMEMBER THE CELLAR'S LEAKED LIKE464 DYNAMO A SIEVE.

SIFTING
TEASING THEM, SIFTING INTO THE CROWD, THEIR CHORUS300 LAZARU IN A HALF CIRCLE.

SIGH
(GIVES A SIGH OF RELIEF--HER HANDS DROP TO HER 549 'ILE SIDES.
(SHE THUMPS DOWN THE DISH IN FRONT OF HIM WITH A 226 AHWILD SIGH OF RELIEF.)
(THEN WITH A SIGH AS HE RETURNS TO THE BAR) 248 AHWILD
(WITH ANOTHER SIGH) WHAT TIME IS IT NOW, NATS 250 AHWILD
(WITH A SIGH) WELL, I HOPE YOU'RE RIGHT. 254 AHWILD
WITH A HOPELESS SIGH) 259 AHWILD
(THEN AT A SOUND FROM THE FRONT PARLOR--WITH A 268 AHWILD SIGH)
(STARES LOOKING AT HIM PUZZLEDLY--THEN GIVES IT UP271 AHWILD WITH A SIGH)
(HE HEAVES A HUGE SIGH OF RELIEF-- 277 AHWILD
WITH A DEEP SIGH OF RELIEF) 289 AHWILD
MARTHY TAKES A LONG DRAUGHT OF HER SCHOONER AND 8 ANNA HEAVES A HUGE SIGH OF
(SITS DOWN BESIDE HER WITH A SIGH) 27 ANNA
(AS CHRIS MAKES NO COMMENT BUT A HEAVY SIGH, SHE 29 ANNA CONTINUES WONDERINGLY)
RISING TO HER FEET WITH A SIGH OF RELIEF) 33 ANNA
(WITH A SIGH) AYE, GLAD VE SAIL AGAIN, TOO. 42 ANNA
(WITH A STUPENDOUS SIGH) OH, GLORY BE TO GOD, I'M 75 ANNA AFTER BELIEVING YOU NOW!
(BURYING HIS HEAD IN GLOOMY ACQUIESCENCE--WITH A 73 ANNA GREAT SIGH)
(WITH A SIGH) I VOUGHTN'T TO TALK THAT WAY 88 BEYOND
(WITH A SHARP SIGH OF JOYFUL RELIEF) 100 BEYOND
(THE FIRST TO FIND HIS VOICE--WITH AN EXPLOSIVE 108 BEYOND SIGH)
(WITH A SIGH) THREE YEARS! 115 BEYOND
(WITH A SIGH) YES, I WAS FORGETTING. 119 BEYOND
(THROWING HIS HAT OVER ON THE SOFA--WITH A GREAT 119 BEYOND SIGH OF EXHAUSTION)
(WITH A SIGH) HARD-UPS DON'T COUNT. 122 BEYOND
(HE HEAVES A GREAT SIGH OF RELIEF) 134 BEYOND
(WITH A GREAT SIGH) IT MUST BE, SURELY.. 487 CARDIF
(HE SIGHS HEAVILY, A SIGH THAT IS HALF A SOB.) 473 CARDIF
(HE GIVES A COMIC SIGH OF RELIEF) 501 DAYS
(THEY DRINK--PUFF RESOLUTELY--SIGH--TAKE THEIR 217 DESIRE FEET DOWN FROM THE TABLE.)
UNCONSCIOUSLY THEY BOTH SIGH.) 217 DESIRE
SHE LOOKS DOWN AT CABOT--WITH A SIGH OF RELIEF.) 224 DESIRE
ABBIE RELAXES, WITH A FAINT SIGH BUT HER EYES 236 DESIRE REMAIN FIXED ON THE WALL.
(WITH A DEEP SIGH) I'LL GU T' THE BARN AN' REST A253 DESIRE SPELL.
AND SITS DOWN WITH A COMFORTABLE SIGH) 508 DIFRNT
(WITH A SIGH) 524 DIFRNT

SIGH (CONT'D.)
(WITH A SIGH) I SUPPOSE PA AND MA TURNED OVER IN 535 DIFRNT THEIR GRAVES.
(WITH A TRAGIC SIGH) THERE'S NOT A LIVING SOUL 440 DYNAMO KNOWS IT.
(LOOKS AT HER WORRIEDLY--WITH A SIGH) 454 DYNAMO
(HEAVING A SIGH OF RELIEF) (ISURE... 464 DYNAMO
(WITH A SIGH) IF ONLY MY FOOL LEGS STANDS UP. 193 EJONES
(WITH A SIGH) WELL, I SUPPOSE WE'VE BEEN 259 GGBROW COMFORTABLE.
(THEN WITH A PITYING SIGH) POOR MARGARET/ 288 GGBROW
(WITH A SIGH) I THINK YOU'D BETTER START ON 301 GGBROW BEFORE--RIGHT NOW--
(WITH A HAPPY SIGH) I DON'T MIND REMEMBERING--NOW309 GGBROW
(LOOKING DOWN THE DECK--WITH A SIGH OF RELIEF) 222 HA APE
(HE STOPS TO PAY TRIBUTE OF A SIGH TO THE MEMORY 29 HUGHIE OF BRAVE DAYS
(WITH A HUGE SENTIMENTAL SIGH--AND A CALCULATING 603 ICEMAN LOOK AT HOPE)
(WITH A SIGH) BLIMEY, IT AIN'T NO BLEEDIN' JOKE, 517 INZONE YER FIRST TRIP.
SMITTY DRAWS HIS HAND AWAY SLOWLY AND UTTERS A 523 INZONE SIGH OF RELIEF.)
(SHE GIVES A LITTLE, SAD SIGH.) 113 JOURNE
(WITH A SIGH OF BEWILDERED HAPPINESS, TURNS TO 351 LAZARU CALIGULA)
ANOTHER WORD BLURRED INTO A SENSELESS SIGH BY 353 LAZARU MEN'S LONGING/
THIS VOICE IS HEARD IN A GENTLY, EXPIRING SIGH OF 371 LAZARU COMPASSION,
(WITH A SIGH) IT'S BEAUTIFUL TONIGHT. 356 MARCOM
(WITH A SIGH) A QUEEN MAY BE ONLY A WOMEN WHO IS 385 MARCOM UNHAPPY.
(WITH A SIGH) WELL, 404 MARCOM
(LOOKING UP AND STRAIGHTENING HIS CRAMPED BACK-- 408 MARCOM WITH A RELIEVED SIGH)
SHE TURNS AWAY AND LOOKS OUT OVER THE SEA WITH A 410 MARCOM SIGH--AFTER A PAUSE)
(HE MOVES TOWARD HER WITH A SIGH OF HALF- 414 MARCOM IMPATIENCE AND HER WHIMS.)
KUBLAI TAKES HIS EYES FROM THE DEAD GIRL WITH A 437 MARCOM SIGH OF BITTER IRONY.)
WITH A SATISFIED SIGH AT THE SHEER COMFORT OF IT 439 MARCOM ALL, RESUMES HIS LIFE.)
(WITH A GREAT HAPPY SIGH) THIS IS GOING TO BE A 49 MISBEG BEAUTIFUL DAY ENTIRELY.
(WITH A SIGH) I CAN'T BLAME HIM. 22 POET
(SHE SINKS ON A CHAIR WITH A WEARY SIGH.) 131 POET
(MAKING THE SIGN OF THE CROSS--FURTIVELY--WITH A 584 ROPE SIGH OF RELIEF)
(HE TAKES ANOTHER NIP AT THE BOTTLE AND PUTS IT 587 ROPE BACK IN HIS POCKET--WITH A SIGH)
(GLANCING APPREHENSIVELY TOWARD THE DOOR--WITH A 590 ROPE GREAT SIGH)
(WITH A SIGH) IT'S A MURD'ROUS AULD LOON HE IS, 597 ROPE SURE ENOUGH.
(HE SITS DOWN WITH A FORCED SIGH OF PEACE) 22 STRANG
LIFE IS JUST A LONG DRAWN OUT LIE WITH A SNIFFLING 40 STRANG SIGH AT THE END)
(THEN WITH A HAPPY SIGH, TURNS BACK TO LETTE!) 50 STRANG
(WITH A SIGH) IT WAS HARU, GIVING UP SAMMY, 60 STRANG
(WITH A SIGH) 123 STRANG
(WITH AN IMPATIENT SIGH, LOWERING THE GLASSES) 162 STRANG
(SHE KISSES HIM--THEN SHUTS HER EYES WITH A DEEP 200 STRANG SIGH OF REQUITED WEARINESS)
(WITH A SIGH OF RELIEF) YOU GAVE ME A SCARE. 465 WELDED
(THEN WITH A SIGH OF PHYSICAL WEARINESS AS SHE 471 WELDED SITS ON THE SIDE OF THE BED)

SIGHING
(SIGHING) I S'POSE IT ISN'T RUB'S FAULT THINGS GO118 BEYOND WRONG WITH HIM.
(SIGHING HAPPILY) GOSH, I WISH WE COULD SIT THIS 494 DIFRNT WILL TURN A LITTLE TOWARD US, SIGHING. 174 JOURNE
(AFTER A PAUSE--SIGHING) IN TRUTH, THE SENATE IS 315 LAZARU (SIGHING) WHAT IT USED TO BE.
(SIGHING) ALL RIGHT, JOSIE. 52 MISBEG
(SIGHING) I WISH THAT COULD BE SAID OF MORE OF 80 STRANG US--(THEN QUICKLY)--

SIGHS
THY SHARP SIGHS DIVIDE MY FLESH AND SPIRIT WITH 205 AHWILD SOFT SOUND--
(STARES AFTER HIM WORRIEDLY--THEN SIGHS 209 AHWILD PHILOSOPHICALLY)
(DRAWS A DEEP BREATH--THEN SIGHS HELPLESSLY) 211 AHWILD
MRS. MILLER SIGHS AND REACHES UP WITH DIFFICULTY 211 AHWILD
(SHE SIGHS) BUT I SUPPOSE WITH THAT DARNED SACHEM212 AHWILD CLUB PICNIC IT'S MORE LIKELY
(LILY LOOKS WORRIED, AND SIGHS. 212 AHWILD
(SHE SIGHS--THEN BRAVELY--OR FACTLY) 217 AHWILD
(HE DRINKS ALL OF HIS DOWN AND SIGHS WITH 243 AHWILD EXAGGERATED SATISFACTION)
(STARING BEFORE HER--SIGHS WORRIEDLY) 250 AHWILD
SHE SIGHS, MOVES RESTLESSLY, THEN FINALLY ASKS) 253 AHWILD
(SIGHS WORRIEDLY AGAIN) I DO WISH THAT BOY WOULD 255 AHWILD GET HOME/
MILDRED WATCHES HIM CURIOUSLY--THEN SIGHS 273 AHWILD AFFECTEDLY)
(HE SIGHS AND STARES AROUND HIM AT THE NIGHT) 277 AHWILD
THEN SHE LETS HER HEAD SINK ON HIS SHOULDER AND 287 AHWILD SIGHS SOFTLY)
(SHE SIGHS SYMPATHETICALLY) POOR LILY/ 291 AHWILD
SHE SITS IN HER CHAIR AND SIGHS CONTENTEDLY. 296 AHWILD
(HE SIGHS WITH SATISFACTION 296 AHWILD
(THEN HE SIGHS AND SPEAKS WITH A GENTLE NOSTALGIC 298 AHWILD MELANCHOLY)

SIGHT

SIGHS (CONT'D.)
(THE SIGHS) AY DON'T KNOW WHY BUT DAT'S VAY WITH 21 ANNA
MOST SAILOR FALLAR, ANNA.
HOLDS HIS HEAD IN HIS HANDS AND SIGHS DREARILY. 44 ANNA
(SHE SIGHS) POOR MA, LORD KNOWS IT'S HARD ENOUGH 87 BEYOND
FOR HER.
(HE SIGHS UNCONSCIOUSLY) BUT YOU SEE I'VE FOUND--102 BEYOND
A BIGGER DREAM.
(SHE SIGHS HEAVILY) IT WAS A CRAZY MISTAKE FOR 116 BEYOND
THEM TWO TO GET MARRIED.
SHE SITS IN THE ROCKER IN FRONT OF THE TABLE AND 116 BEYOND
SIGHS WEARILY.
ROBERT SIGHS) 147 BEYOND
(SHE SIGHS AND WALKS TO THE WINDOW IN THE REAR, 152 BEYOND
LEFT.
HE SIGHS HEAVILY, STAKING MOURNFULLY IN FRONT OF 154 BEYOND
HIM.
(A WEARY EXPRESSION COMES OVER HIS FACE AND HE 157 BEYOND
SIGHS HEAVILY)
(HE SIGHS WITH EXHAUSTION) YES, I'LL GO AND REST 162 BEYOND
A WHILE.
YOU'LL HAVE TO SUFFER TO WIN BACK--{HIS VOICE 162 BEYOND
GROWS WEAKER AND HE SIGHS WEARILY)
(SHE SIGHS WEARILY) IT CAN'T DO NO HARM TO TELL 164 BEYOND
YOU NOW--
(HE SIGHS.) 456 CARIBE
THEN SIGHS HEAVILY, A SIGH THAT IS HALF A SOB.) 473 CARIBE
(HE SIGHS) IT HAS BEEN A LONG TIME--TOO LONG. 505 DAYS
(HE SIGHS, GIVING WAY FOR A MOMENT TO HIS OWN 557 DAYS
PHYSICAL WEARINESS)
HE SIGHS WITH A PUZZLED AWE AND BLURTS OUT WITH 203 DESIRE
HALTING APPRECIATION.)
(HE SIGHS--THEN SPITS) WAAL--NO USE'N CRYIN' UVER218 DESIRE
SPILT MILK.
(HE SIGHS HEAVILY--A PAUSE) STONES. 237 DESIRE
EBEN SIGHS HEAVILY AND ABBIE ECHOES IT. 239 DESIRE
SHE SIGHS HOPELESSLY, CLASPING AND UNCLASPING HER 514 DIFRNT
HANDS.
HE SIGHS FORLORNLY AND BLUNDERS ON) 538 DIFRNT
(SHE SIGHS CONTENTEDLY.) 430 DYNAMO
(HE SIGHS HEAVILY) (IND SLEEP AGAIN LAST NIGHT 455 DYNAMO
EXCEPT FOR A FEW MINUTES...
(HE SIGHS WITH LONGING, HIS BODY SUDDENLY GONE 477 DYNAMO
LIMP AND WEARY.)
(HE SIGHS DEJECTEDLY AND REMAINS WITH BOWED 196 EJONES
SHOULDERS,
SHE SIGHS WITH AFFECTED WEARINESS AND LEANS BACK 53 ELECTR
AND CLOSES HER EYES.)
I SUPPOSE IT WAS--BUT-- (SHE STOPS AND SIGHS--THEN137 ELECTR
WORRIEDLY)
MARGARET SIGHS WITH A TIRED INCOMPREHENSION 273 GGBROW
(STIRS, SIGHS AND MURMURS DREAMILY) 278 GGBROW
(SHE SIGHS WEARILY, TURNS, PUTS A PLUG IN THE 288 GGBROW
PIANO,
(HE SIGHS AGAIN.) BUT I SURE AM SORRY HE'S GONE. 18 HUGHIE
(BUT THIS FATALISTIC PHILOSOPHY IS NO COMFORT AND 18 HUGHIE
ERIE SIGHS.)
ERIE SIGHS AGAIN-- 19 HUGHIE
(HE SIGHS TENDERLY) DEAR OLD BESS. 609 ICEMAN
(MOSHER SIGHS AND GIVES UP AND CLOSES HIS EYES. 610 ICEMAN
(HE PAUSES--THEN SIGHS) JEES, LARRY, WHAT A NIGHT669 ICEMAN
DEM TWO PIGS GIVE ME/
THE SIGHS DEJECTEDLY. 670 ICEMAN
(HE SIGHS EXPLOSIVELY) JEES, SHE'S GOT ME HANGIN'671 ICEMAN
ON DE ROPES/
(HE SIGHS GLOOMILY) DAT KIND OF DAME, YUH CAN'T 698 ICEMAN
TRUST 'EM.
(HE SIGHS. 711 ICEMAN
HE SIGHS WITH A PUZZLED EXPRESSION AND GETS UP AND523 INZONE
WALKS OUT OF THE DOORWAY.
(THEY ALL SIT DOWN WITH GREAT SIGHS OF RELIEF) 524 INZONE
AND SIGHS FREQUENTLY WITH A PUZZLED FROWN.) 531 INZONE
(SHE GETS UP AND SIGHS WITH HUMOROUS 29 JOURNE
EXAGGERATION.)
(HE SIGHS--GLOOMILY AND RESENTFULLY.) 79 JOURNE
IT'S YOUR OWN FAULT-- (HE STOPS AND SIGHS 84 JOURNE
HELPLESSLY--PERSUASIVELY.)
(TYRONE STARES AT HER AND SIGHS HELPLESSLY. 88 JOURNE
TYRONE SIGHS, SHAKING HIS HEAD HOPELESSLY, AND 115 JOURNE
ATTEMPTS TO CATCH HIS SON'S EYE.
(SIGHS--THEN SUMMING HIS ACTOR'S HEARTINESS.) 123 JOURNE
(HE SIGHS.) WHY CAN'T YOU REMEMBER YOUR 131 JOURNE
SHAKESPEARE AND FORGET THE
OR OF THE CLOCK, OR WHATEVER FLIES, OR SIGHS, OR 132 JOURNE
ROCKS, OR SINGS, OR SPEAKS,
(HE SMILES TEASINGLY AND SIGHS.) 136 JOURNE
(SIGHS SADLY.) NO. 137 JOURNE
(HE SIGHS SADLY--THEN AFTER A STRUGGLE OVERCOMING 343 LAZARU
HIMSELF--WITH EXULTANCE)
IF IT WAS NOT FOR ME--(SHE SIGHS--THEN BRIGHTLY 346 LAZARU
AND LOVINGLY)
THEN TIBERIUS SIGHS HEAVILY, SHAKING HIS HEAD) 353 LAZARU
THEN HE SIGHS WEARILY.) 102 MANSNS
(UNCONSCIOUSLY SHE SIGHS REGRETFULLY.) 120 MANSNS
(UNCONSCIOUSLY SHE SIGHS REGRETFULLY.) 120 MANSNS
HE SIGHS, TIRED AND HOT.) 347 MARCOM
(SHE SIGHS REGRETFULLY) AH, WELL, MIKE, YOU WAS 5 MISBEG
BORN A PRIEST'S PET.
(THEN DISMISSES HIM. SHE SIGHS) WELL, HIMSELF 11 MISBEG
WILL BE HERE IN A MINUTE.
SHE SIGHS AND GETS SLUMP' TO HER FEET, 71 MISBEG
(HE DRINKS AND SIGHS WITH RELIEF.) 9 POET
NORA SIGHS.) 21 POET
(DRIES HER EYES--AFTER A PAUSE SHE SIGHS 26 POET
WORRIEDLY.)
SHE SIGHS, HER HANDS FIDDLING WITH HER APRON. 36 POET
AFTER A PAUSE HE SIGHS WITH RELIEF.) 37 POET
(SIGHS.) AH WELL, IT'S ALL RIGHT. 76 POET

SIGHS (CONT'D.)
(NORA SIGHS AND GOES OUT QUICKLY, RIGHT. 81 POET
(OVERCOME BY PHYSICAL EXHAUSTION AGAIN, SIGHS.) 180 POET
(HE SIGHS--THEN SELF-MOCKINGLY) 5 STRANG
(HE SIGHS--THINKING WITH A TRACE OF GUILTY ALARM) 7 STRANG
(BLOWS HIS NOSE, WIPES HIS EYES, SIGHS, CLEARS HIS 22 STRANG
THROAT.
(IN A MUFFLED VOICE, HER SOBBING BEGINNING TO EBB 44 STRANG
AWAY INTO SIGHS--
(SHE SIGHS HAPPILY, CLOSING HER EYES. 92 STRANG
A PAUSE--THEN THE WOMAN SIGHS AND YAWNS WEARILY-- 471 WELDED
BORED)
(SHE SIGHS AGAIN, THIS TIME WITH A SORT OF RESTFUL471 WELDED
CONTENT)
SHE SIGHS.) 481 WELDED

SIGHT
(FLUSHING) NOT BY A HELL OF A SIGHT, SIR. 942 'ILE
(RAPTLY) AH, SIGHT FOR SORE EYES, MY BEAUTIFUL 226 AHWILD
MACUSHLA.
THIS IS A DAMNED SIGHT MORE SERIOUS THAN ESSIE HAS266 AHWILD
ANY IDEA!
YOU MUST HAVE BEEN A FINE SIGHT WHEN YOU GOT HOME.276 AHWILD
AND I GOT UP AND DRESSED IN SUCH A HURRY--I MUST 281 AHWILD
LOOK A SIGHT, DON'T I?
FIRST SIGHT AND SHE CAME AND SAT ON MY LAP AND 284 AHWILD
KISSED ME.
AND UNTIL A SIGHT THERE WAS OF SHIP UR MEN UN TOP 36 ANNA
OF THE SEA.
(STOUTLY) YES, THANK GOD, THOUGH I'VE NOT SEEN A 37 ANNA
SIGHT OF IT IN FIFTEEN YEARS.
(THEY GO OUT OF SIGHT IN THE CABIN. 40 ANNA
A SIGHT MORE OFTEN THAN EVER YOU SAW HER 47 ANNA
SHE'S HERD MAKE NO MISTAKE, AND HIM HATING THE 51 ANNA
SIGHT OF ME.
YOU'RE A FINE LOOKING SIGHT/ 63 ANNA
IT AIN'T COMMON SENSE--NO SIREE, IT AIN'T--NOT BY 102 BEYOND
A HELL OF A SIGHT/
(SCORNFULLY) LOVE/ THEY AIN'T OLD ENOUGH TO KNOW102 BEYOND
LOVE WHEN THEY SIGHT IT/
I COULDN'T TAKE INTEREST IN THE WORK ANY MORE, 110 BEYOND
WITH NO PURPOSE IN SIGHT.
HOW I'VE GROWN TO HATE THE SIGHT OF THEM/ 125 BEYOND
I HATE THE SIGHT OF YOU. 127 BEYOND
I DON'T WANT HIM TO SEE ME LOOKING A SIGHT. 153 BEYOND
I DIDN'T REALIZE--THE SIGHT OF ROB LYING IN BED 156 BEYOND
THERE, SO GONE TO PIECES--
(HE CATCHES SIGHT OF THE STILL FIGURE IN THE BUNK 490 CAHITE
THERE'S LOVE AT FIRST SIGHT FOR YOU-- 468 CAXIRE
PERHAPS AWAY FROM THE SIGHT OF THE SEA HE MAY--- 562 CROSS
THE SIGHT OF IT INFURIATES HIM AND HE HURLS IT 366 CAGSS
INTO A CORNER.
THE MARY ALLEN'S THERE IN PLAIN SIGHT OF ANYONE, 570 CROSS
HAIN'T I AS FAR--SIGHT AS HE'S NEAR-SIGHTE 219 DESIRE
WAAL, YOU'LL FIND I'M A HEAP SIGHT BIGGER HUNK NOR229 DESIRE
YEW KIN CHEW/
(THEN IN A SCREAM) GIT OUT O' MY SIGHT/ 233 DESIRE
I HATE THE SIGHT O' YE/ 230 DESIRE
AY' I HATE THE SIGHT O' YEW/ 230 DESIRE
(AMUSED) NO, I HAIN'T, YEW BET--NOT BY A HELL UF 232 DESIRE
A SIGHT--
I GOT SECOND-SIGHT MEBBE. 238 DESIRE
I HATE THE SIGHT O' YE/ 239 DESIRE
NOW IF YE'D ONY GOOD EYE-SIGHT.../ 250 DESIRE
HE HAIN'T WITH HARDLY FUR--NOT BY A HELL OF A 256 DESIRE
SIGHT/
I HATE THE SIGHT O' YE AN' ALL US DID/ 264 DESIRE
PEERING THROUGH THE SCREEN AND CATCHING SIGHT OF 505 DIFRNT
EMMA, HARRIET CALLS)
HE'D FORGOT ALL ABOUT THE HULL THING BEFORE THEY 509 DIFRNT
WAS OUT OF SIGHT OF LAND.
NOT BY A HELL OF A SIGHT. 518 DIFRNT
LAND SAKES, I HARDLY GET A SIGHT OF YOU BEFORE YOU524 DIFRNT
WANT TO RUN AWAY AGAIN.
YOU KNOW A DURN SIGHT MORE ABOUT THIS GAME THAN I 429 DYNAMO
DO.*
I LOVED HIM AT FIRST SIGHT... 430 DYNAMO
AND THE DEVIL KNOWS WHAT SIN YOU'LL THINK IT IN 451 DYNAMO
THE SIGHT OF GOD/
YOU KNOW YOU'RE GUILTY IN THE SIGHT OF GOD/ 442 DYNAMO
AND A SNEAK, AND I DON'T WONDER YOU FEEL GUILTY IN446 DYNAMO
GOD'S SIGHT/
(STILL LEANING OUT OF HIS SITTING-ROOM WINDOW, 450 DYNAMO
CATCHES SIGHT OF LIGHT--
YOU WOULDN'T DO ANYTHING TO MAKE ME UNWORTHY IN 485 DYNAMO
HER SIGHT, WOULD YOU?
AND SHIELDING HIS FACE WITH ONE HAND FROM THE 487 DYNAMO
SIGHT OF HER.
AND I'SE GOT ALL DE MONEY IN SIGHT, I RESIGNS OV 180 EJONES
DE SPOT AND BEATS IT QUICK.
AND THROWS HIMSELF DOWN AGAIN TO SHUT OUT THE 199 EJONES
SIGHT.
I 'ATES THE SIGHT O' 'IM OUT I'LL SAY THAT FUR 203 EJONES
'IM.
(INTENSELY) I HATE THE SIGHT OF HIM/. 19 ELECTR
HE'D GROW TO HATE THE SIGHT OF YOU/ 34 ELECTR
YOU CERTAINLY ARE A SIGHT FOR SORE EYES, VINNIE/ 75 ELECTR
I HATE THE SIGHT OF DEATH/ 101 ELECTR
AND PUSHES THEM OUT IN A GESTURE OF BLOTTING 123 ELECTR
LAVINIA FOREVER FROM HER SIGHT.
AT THE SIGHT OF LAVINIA HE STOPS STARTLEDLY, 143 ELECTR
NOT MY A DAMNED SIGHT/ 153 ELECTR
(SEES THE ENVELOPE IN PLAIN SIGHT AND CALLS TO HER163 ELECTR
WARNINGLY, HAZEL/
(COMES JUST INTO SIGHT AT LEFT AND SPEAKS FRONT 323 GGBROW
WITHOUT LOOKING AT THEM--
CAVED IN BY STEEL FROM A SIGHT OF THE SKY LIKE 214 HA APE
MUDDY APES IN THE ZOO/

SIGHT

SIGHT (CONT'D.)
*TO GIVE A SIGHT OF SIN OR A BREATH OF CLEAN 214 HA APE
AIR..
TO SHUT OUT THE SIGHT OF HIS FACE, TO PROTECT HER 226 HA APE
ON..
(HYSTERICALLY) WE'RE FREE AND EQUAL IN THE SIGHT 229 HA APE
OF GOD--
(ELUNG SLINKS BACK OUT OF SIGHT.) 229 HA APE
HER HANDS OVER HER EYES TO SHUT OUT THE SIGHT 229 HA APE
THAN LOVE AT FIRST SIGHT, GIVE'LL A COUNT OF TIT/ 229 HA APE
SHE WASN'T WISE DAT I WAS IN A CAGE, TOO--WORSER'N252 HA APE
YUCKS--SURE--A DAMN SIGHT--
HOPE IS ONE OF THOSE MEN WHOM EVERYONE LIKES ON 576 ICEMAN
SIGHT, A SOFTHEARTED SLOB,
HIS SIGHT IS FAILING BUT IS NOT AS BAD AS HE 577 ICEMAN
COMPLAINS IT IS.
THEY'LL SHOOT YOU ON SIGHT. 609 ICEMAN
GENEROUS PERSONALITY THAT MAKES EVERYONE LIKE HIM ON ICEMAN
ON SIGHT.
AT THE SIGHT OF THEM, 650 ICEMAN
THE PASSENGERS ASLEEP AND NONE OF THE CREW IN 153 JOUNNE
SIGHT.
IT IS A FOUL SIN IN THE SIGHT OF JEHOVAH/ 282 LAZARU
BUT AT THE FIRST SIGHT OF HIS FACE HE STOPS IN HIS30R LAZARU
TRACKS, TREMBLING,
GIVES HER EYES WITH HER HANDS TO SHUT OUT THE 327 LAZARU
SIGHT.)
AT SIGHT OF HER, SARA INSTANTLY PUTS ON HER MUST 50 MANSNS
LACE-LIKE MANNERS,
BECAUSE THAT IS THE ONE SURE WAY TO MAKE HIM 137 MANSNS
LOATHE THE SIGHT OF YOU--
YOU FOLKS ARE A WELCOME SIGHT/ 365 MARCOM
(WITH WONDERING BITTERNESS) THE EYE SEES ONLY ITS597 MARCOM
OWN SIGHT.
(THEY ARE GONE FROM SIGHT. 420 MARCOM
(THE SUDDENLY RAGING) OUT OF MY SIGHT, DOG, 425 MARCOM
BEFORE I HAVE YOU IMPALED/
OUT WHEN THEY SIT THEY ARE OUT OF SIGHT.) 431 MARCOM
THERE'S NO SIGHT OF HIM. 5 MISBEG
I CAN TURN MY BACK SO THE SIGHT OF HIM DRINKING 52 MISBEG
FACE WON'T BREAK MY HEART
AND THERE AT THE BAR IN PLAIN SIGHT WAS TWO OF THE 90 MISBEG
MEN YOU'VE BEEN OUT WITH.
IT IS AS IF HE HAD TO HIDE FROM SIGHT BEFORE HE 146 MISBEG
CAN BEGIN.
AT SIGHT OF HER FATHER THEY BECOME MORE SO. 57 POET
HE GETS UP--BITTERLY.) AS THE SIGHT OF ME SEEMS 63 POET
TO IRRITATE HER,
HIS BODY IS LIMP, HIS FEET DRAG, HIS EYES SEEM TO 164 POET
HAVE NO SIGHT.
(HE SHUDDERS.) LET ME GET AWAY FROM THE SIGHT OF 165 POET
HIM
OUT OF MY SIGHT, YOU PAPIST BRAT/ 578 ROPE
IT'S FIVE YEARS HE'S BEEN GONE, AND NOT A SIGHT OF583 ROPE
HER.
AND LET YOU KNOW WHEN THEY GET IN SIGHT. 171 STRANG
'TIS A FOINE SIGHT TO SEE A MAN WID SOME SFNSE IN 498 VOYAGE
HIS HEAD

SIGHTED
SHE WAS SIGHTED BOTTOM UP, A COMPLETE WRECK, BY 558 CROSS
THE WHALER JOHN SLOCUM.
HIS EYES ARE SMALL, CLOSE TOGETHER, AND EXTREMELY 221 DESIRE
NEAR-SIGHTED.
YOU ARE WONDERFULLY SHREWD AND FAR-SIGHTED, 101 MANSNS
MOTHER,
SULLEN ON CREEPING CANAL BOATS, AS SHORT-SIGHTED 40 POET
FOOLS WOULD HAVE US BELIEVE.

SIGHTEDLY
A WALRUS MUSTACHE, BLACK EYES WHICH PEER NEAR- 574 ICEMAN
SIGHTEDLY

SIGHTLESS
HER EYES HAVE A STILL, FIXED, SIGHTLESS, TRANCE- 191 MANSNS
LIKE LOOK,

SIGHTLESSLY
THEY STARE AT HIM AND HE STARES SIGHTLESSLY AT THE153 POET
TABLE TOP.
(BUT HE IS STARING SIGHTLESSLY AT THE TABLE TOP 156 POET

SIGHTS
BUT YOU'LL HAVE NEW SIGHTS AND NEW PEOPLE TO TAKE 88 BEYOND
YOUR MIND OFF.
WAL, I PROMISED AMOS I'D HELP SHOW YE THE SIGHTS 7 ELECTR
WHEN YOU CAME TO VISIT HIM.

SIGN
AND NOT A SIGN OF HIM TURNIN' BACK FOR HOME/ 517 'ILE
AN SIGN ON THER SHIPS-- 21 ANNA
(HE MAKES THE SIGN OF THE CROSS MECHANICALLY, 31 ANNA
STARING INTO HIS FACE ANXIOUSLY FOR SOME SIGN OF 33 ANNA
LIFE.)
AY SIGN ON STEAMER SAIL TOMORROW. 65 ANNA
(HE MAKES THE SIGN OF THE CROSS MECHANICALLY) 75 ANNA
YOU DON'T MEAN TO SAY YOU'RE GOIN' TO SIGN AWAY 115 BEYOND
YOUR FARM, KATE MAYO--
BE--(BUT RUTH, IF SHE IS AWARE OF HIS WORDS, GIVES169 BEYOND
NO SIGN.
(DRISCOLL MAKES THE SIGN OF THE CROSS AGAIN.) 490 CARDIF
SIGN OF THE CROSS.. 490 CARDIF
DOWN AND THE PRICE BESIDE UT AND SIGN YOUR NAME. 463 CARIBE
DID YOU TELL 'EM THEY GOTTER SIGN FOR WHAT THEY 464 CARIBE
GETS--AND HOW TO SIGN
AS THE MEN SIGN THE SHEETS OF PAPER FOR THEIR 465 CARIBE
BOTTLES)
HE MAKES A SIGN TO SOMEONE IN THE DARKNESS 555 CROSS
BENEATH..
GOD KNOWS WHERE, FOR THERE WAS NO SIGN ON THE 560 CROSS
ISLAND THAT MAN HAD EVER TOUCHED
AND THAT SIGNS 561 CROSS
FATHER BAIRD SAYS QUIETLY, WITHOUT ANY SIGN OF 501 DAYS
TAKING OFFENSE)

SIGN (CONT'D.)
WAL, IF YE SIGN THIS YE KIN RIDE ON A BOAT. 213 DESIRE
AN' DON'T SIGN NOTHIN' TILL WE DOES/ 215 DESIRE
(WITH EXCITED JOY) YE MEAN YE'LL SIGN THE PAPERS 217 DESIRE
LET'S SEE THE COLOR O' THE OLD SKINFLINT'S MONEY 219 DESIRE
AN' WE'LL SIGN.
(ANXIOUSLY) WILL YE SIGN IT AFORE YE GOS 219 DESIRE
(GIVES NO SIGN OF HAVING HEARD HIM BUT COMES BACK 547 DIFRNT
TO HER CHAIR AND SITS DOWN.
CAN'T YOU GIVE ME SOME SIGNS 480 DYNAMO
LAVINIA DOES NOT TURN OR GIVE ANY SIGN OF KNOWING 45 ELECTR
HER MOTHER IS BEHIND HER.
LOOKING OVER THE HEAD OF LIFE WITHOUT A SIGN OF 94 ELECTR
RECOGNITION--
BUT HERE IT'S SIGHT AND NO SIGN OF THEM. 118 ELECTR
(SHE GIVES NO SIGN OF HAVING HEARD HIM. 121 ELECTR
SHE GIVES NO SIGN OF HAVING HEARD HIM. 122 ELECTR
SHE GIVES NO SIGN OF BEING AWARE OF HER DAUGHTER'S122 ELECTR
PRESENCE.
(MAKING A WARNING SIGN TO PETER NOT TO TAKE THIS 144 ELECTR
SERIOUSLY--FORCING A SMILE)
OLD WE SIGN FOR INSULTS TO OUR DIGNITY AS 'ONEST 228 HA APE
WORKERS
FROM EACH PIECE HANGS AN ENORMOUS TAG FROM WHICH A233 HA APE
DOLLAR SIGN AND NUMERALS IN
(HE MAKES A SIGN TO 248 HA APE
ON THE ONE CAGE A SIGN FROM WHICH THE WORD 251 HA APE
"GORILLA" STANDS OUT.
GRATEFUL EVEN FOR THIS SIGN OF COMPANIONSHIP, 20 HUGHIE
GROWLS.)
IS THE TOILET WITH A SIGN «THIS IS IT» ON THE 573 ICEMAN
DOOR.
WITH A SIGN.. «SPECTATORS MAY DISTINGUISH THE TRUE599 ICEMAN
BABOON BY HIS BLUE BEHIND.»
HUGO, HIS HEAD HIDDEN IN HIS ARMS, GIVES NO SIGN 694 ICEMAN
OF LIFE.)
PARRITI GIVES NO SIGN OF HAVING HEARD HIM. 702 ICEMAN
INDIAN MAKES A PEREMPTORY SIGN TO BE QUIET. 708 ICEMAN
NO ONE GIVES ANY SIGN OF HAVING HEARD HIM. 708 ICEMAN
NO ONE MOVES OR GIVES ANY SIGN EXCEPT BY THE DREAD709 ICEMAN
IN THEIR EYES THAT THEY HAVE
I WOULDN'T GIVE A DAMN IF YOU EVER DISPLAYED THE 32 JOUNNE
SLIGHTEST SIGN OF GRATITUDE.
IT HAS ALWAYS BEEN A SIGN-- 38 JOUNNE
IT'S A SIGN OF SANITY, THEY SAY. 94 JOUNNE
MARY'S FACE GIVES NO SIGN SHE HAS HEARD, 107 JOUNNE
AND GIVES LITTLE PHYSICAL SIGN OF IT EXCEPT IN HIS126 JOUNNE
EYES AND A
EDMUND GIVES NO SIGN OF HAVING HEARD. 167 JOUNNE
HE MAKES A SIGN AND THE MUSIC CEASES. 289 LAZARU
(MAKING A SIGN TO THE REGIMENTAL MUSICIANS 323 LAZARU
JOYFULLY)
(WITH A SIGH--MEEKLY) I CANNOT UNDERSTAND, 325 LAZARU
LAZARUS.
YOU WISHED HER TO SIGN. 97 MANSNS
TO GET MY BROTHER TO SIGN OVER HIS INTERESTS ONE 141 MANSNS
BY ONE TO YOU.
BUT OF COURSE I WON'T SIGN THEM UNTIL AFTER-- 146 MANSNS
BUT HOW DO I KNOW YOU MIGHTN'T REFUSE TO SIGN 146 MANSNS
AFTER--S
ISHMOA HAS NOT TURNED, GIVES NO SIGN OF HEARING 154 MANSNS
HIM.
I'LL SIGN EVERYTHING OVER TO YOU. 188 MANSNS
(AT A SIGN, THE SOLDIERS FALL UPON THE THREE 353 MARCOM
MERCHANTS.
(HE MAKES A SIGN TO A SOLDIER WHO FLOURISHES HIS 380 MARCOM
SWORD.)
AND IF HE ISN'T HAPPY, IT'S A SURE SIGN HE'S NO 392 MARCOM
GOOD TO HIMSELF OR ANYONE ELSE
(HE MAKES A SIGN TO HIS UNCLE AND FATHER. 394 MARCOM
(SHAKES HIS HEAD) NO SIGN OF BILIOUSNESS. 413 MARCOM
SHE REMAINS RIGID, GIVING NO SIGN.) 417 MARCOM
(GHAZAN MAKES A SIGN. 419 MARCOM
HE GIVES A SIGN AT WHICH THE THREE TAKE OFF THEIR 428 MARCOM
ROBES
HERE THE KAAN MAKES THE SAME BARELY PERCEPTIBLE 433 MARCOM
SIGN OF COMMAND AGAIN.
ONE SENSES A TENSE EXPECTANCY OF SOME SIGN FROM 433 MARCOM
THE THRONE.
(BOLDLY) SURE, YOU'VE NEVER GIVEN ME A SIGN OF 54 MISBEG
IT.
IN THE MORNING HE'LL SIGN ALL THEY SHOVE IN FRONT 91 MISBEG
OF HIM.
DID SIMPSON GET HIM TO SIGN A PAPERS 91 MISBEG
WE'LL MAKE HIM SIGN A PAPER HE OWES ME TEN 99 MISBEG
THOUSAND DOLLARS THE MINUTE THE
HUNGRY, AND THAT'S A GOOD SIGN. 28 POET
(HE STOPS A LITTLE SHAMEFACEDLY, BUT NORA GIVES NO 39 POET
SIGN OF OFFENSE.
(HE GIVES NO SIGN HE HEARS THIS. 44 POET
SARA'S FACE HARDENS AND SHE GIVES NO SIGN OF 89 POET
KNOWING HE IS THERE.
I WILL SIGN A NOTE OF HAND, 120 POET
PROVIDED, MARK YOU, THAT YOU AND YOUR DAUGHTER 122 POET
SIGN AN AGREEMENT I HAVE DRAWN UP
(IF HE HEARS THIS, HE GIVES NO SIGN OF IT. 129 POET
(MAKING THE SIGN OF THE CROSS--FURTIVELY--WITH A 584 ROPE
SIGN OF RELIEF)
(UDE GOES BACK OF THE BAR, MAKING A SIGN TO NICK 505 VOYAGE
TO GO TO THEIR TABLE.
SHE GIVES NO SIGN. 485 WELDED

SIGNAL
AND HEED THIS..D'YOU CALL TO MIND THE SIGNAL 569 CROSS
WITH THE RED AND THE GREEN SIGNAL-LIGHTS.
(HE FLASHES A SIGNAL TO THE PRIEST AND THEY BOTH 555 DAYS
LIFT JOHN TO HIS FEET)
((THAT'S HER SIGNAL/...)) (HE HURRIEDLY PUTS ON 426 DYNAMO
HIS COAT)

SIGNAL (CONT'D.)
AND AT THAT SIGNAL ALL THE CONVICTS START TO WORK 194 EJONES
ON THE ROAD.
AT A SIGNAL FROM THE GUARD THEY STOP 194 EJONES
AS IF THIS WERE A SIGNAL THE WALLS OF THE FOREST 198 EJONES
FOLD IN.
HE MAKES A QUICK SIGNAL WITH HIS HAND. 203 EJONES
(THEN WARNINGLY, MAKING A SURREPTITIOUS SIGNAL AS 45 ELECTR
HE SEES THE FRONT DOOR OPENING
(HE GIVES A SIGNAL. 249 HA APE
AN' IF HE KIN SIGNAL TO 'EM AN' THEY BLOWS US UP 522 INZONE
IT'S ONE SHIP LESS AIN'T ITS
I MUST SIGNAL TO THE LEGIONS/ 317 LAZARU
I MUST GIVE THE SIGNAL/ 317 LAZARU
THE SIGNAL/ 319 LAZARU
SHALL I GIVE THE SIGNAL TO KILL, LAZARUS$ 319 LAZARU
THAT A SIGNAL HONOR HAS JUST BEEN CONFERRED ON ME$382 MARCOM
(MISINTERPRETING HIS SIGNAL) 382 MARCOM
AND GET READY TO CAST OFF WHEN I SIGNAL. 403 MARCOM
(AT ANOTHER SIGNAL THE THREE POLOS TAKE OFF THEIR 429 MARCOM
BLUE ROBES.)
AND, AS THE MUSICIANS, OBEYING THIS SIGNAL, START 429 MARCOM
UP A GREAT BLARE,

SIGNALIN'
FOR ALL'S WE KNOW HE MIGHT'A BEEN SIGNALIN' WITH 521 INZONE
IT.

SIGNALING
(TAKING ONE ARM AND SIGNALING FATHER BAIRD TO TAKE555 DAYS
THE OTHER--

SIGNALS
HE SIGNALS TO LARRY WITH A CAUTIOUS =SST!= 577 ICEMAN
HICKEY SIGNALS TU CORA, 653 ICEMAN
THEY MAKE FRANTIC SIGNALS TO MARCO TO DO LIKEWISE 378 MARCOM
BUT HE IS TOO DAZED TO NOTICE.
AND SIGNALS THE BAND TO BE SILENT. 402 MARCOM
NICK SIGNALS BACK THAT HE UNDERSTANDS.) 497 VOYAGE

SIGNATURE
SEEMS TO ME YOU'VE BEEN INVENTING A NEW SIGNATURE 251 AHWILD
EVERY WEEK LATELY.

SIGNATURES
AND HERE ARE THE SIGNATURES (I SEE. 561 CROSS

SIGNBOARD
A BIG SIGNBOARD IS ON THE WALL AT THE REAR, 245 HA APE
=INDUSTRIAL WORKERS OF THE WORLD--
THEN SEES THE SIGNBOARD ON THE WALL AND IS 246 HA APE
REASSURED.)

SIGNED
THE TWO YEARS WE ALL SIGNED UP FOR ARE DONE THIS 537 'ILE
DAY.
THE TWO YEARS THEY SIGNED UP FOR IS UP TODAY. 539 'ILE
AND THE TWO YEARS THEY SIGNED ON FUR IS UP TODAY. 541 'ILE
THE TIME WE SIGNED UP FOR IS DONE TODAY. 544 'ILE
IT'S A WOMAN'S HANDWRITING--NOT SIGNED, OF COURSE.267 AHWILD
I SIGNED ON TODAY AT NOON. DRUNK AS I WAS--AND 72 ANNA
SHE'S SAILING TOMORROW.
YOU AIN'T SIGNED FOR THAT YET. 465 CARIBE
WE ALL SIGNED IT HERE THE MORNING THE MARY ALLEN, 561 CROSS
HAVE SIGNEDS
PEACE OUGHT TO BE SIGNED SOON. 219 DESIRE
PEACE OUGHT TO BE SIGNED SOON. 48 ELECTR
I AIN'T SIGNED ON YOUR OLD HOOKER/ 105 ELECTR
TAUGHT AT OUR FATHER'S KNEE, SEALED, SIGNED, 243 HA APE
UP'S SIGNED-- 930 INZONE
BUT NOTHING IS SIGNED YET. 64 MANSNS
(DRYLY) FIVE HUNDRED THOUSAND NAMES ARE SIGNED TO392 MARCOM
IT.
ALL WE WANT IS A PAPER SIGNED BY HIM WITH 94 MISBEG
WITNESSES THAT HE'LL SELL THE FARM TO
IT WASN'T SIGNED, SHE SAID. 78 POET
MONEY HE'D GOT ON THE MORTGAGE SHE'D SIGNED WITH 586 ROPE
HIM.

SIGNIFICANCE
THERE'S A SPIRITUAL SIGNIFICANCE IN THAT PICTURE, 161 BEYOND
ANDY.
(OAZEDLY--AS IF SHE COULD NOT REALIZE THE 545 DIFRNT
SIGNIFICANCE OF HIS WORDS)
THERE IS AN APPALLING MORBID SIGNIFICANCE TO HIS 299 LAZARU
MOUTH.
THEN WE MIGHT PROPERLY EXPECT ITS END TO HAVE AS 30 MANSNS
MUCH SIGNIFICANCE AS--
IT HAS SIGNIFICANCE AS A LINK IN THE CHAIN IN 100 MANSNS
WHICH MY SHIPS BRING COTTON
(WITH ANGRY SIGNIFICANCE--TO MARSDEN) 18 STRANG
THAT IN THE STATE OF MIND I HAD BEEN IN THEY HAD 459 WELDED
NO SIGNIFICANCE

SIGNIFICANT
HE AND THE MATE EXCHANGE A SIGNIFICANT GLANCE.) 540 'ILE
LITTLE SIGNIFICANT DETAILS GIVE EVIDENCE OF 112 BEYOND
CARELESSNESS, OF INEFFICIENCY.
THIS PLOT OF YOURS MORE SIGNIFICANT--FOR YOUR 495 DAYS
SOUL, SHALL I SAYS

STILLWELL, WITH A SIGNIFICANT LOOK, CALLS ON HIM 563 DAYS
FOR CONFIRMATION)
HIS FOUR UNDERGRADUATE YEARS WILL ALWAYS BE FOR 55 MISBEG
HIM THE MOST SIGNIFICANT IN HIS
THE ROOM HAS UNDERGONE A SIGNIFICANT CHANGE. 111 STRANG
AND JOE GIVES HIM A SIGNIFICANT WINK AND NODS 497 VOYAGE
TOWARD THE DOOR ON THE LEFT.

SIGNIFICANTLY
(ANDREW GROANS) BUT NOW--(HE SHRUGS HIS SHOULDERS158 BEYOND
SIGNIFICANTLY.)
(HE PAUSES SIGNIFICANTLY, 440 DYNAMO
(HE TAPS HER BUNDLE WITH HIS RIDING WHIP 174 EJONES
SIGNIFICANTLY.)
(HE PAUSES SIGNIFICANTLY, LOOKING FROM ONE TO THE 518 INZONE
OTHER OF HIS LISTENERS.

SIGNIFIGANCE
WITH AN APPRECIATIVE RELISH FOR THE FAMILIAR 4 STRANG
SIGNIFIGANCE OF THE BOOKS.

SIGNING
AND WHILE I'M SIGNING UP FOR THE BRIDAL SUITE 23 HUGHIE

SIGNS
(MAKING SIGNS TO HER TO HUMOR HIM--GENTLY) 162 BEYOND
THE SIGNS OF PREMATURE DISINTEGRATION ARE ON HIM. 19 JOURNE
SWEENEY BEGINS TO SHOW SIGNS OF GETTING DRUNK. 594 ROPE
(AS THE OLD MAN MAKES SIGNS TO HIM WITH HIS HAND) 596 ROPE
JOE MAKES VIOLENT SIGNS TO FREDA TO BRING HIM 504 VOYAGE
BACK.

SILENCE
AT THE RISE OF THE CURTAIN THERE IS A MOMENT OF 535 'ILE
INTENSE SILENCE.
THE SILENCE IS UNBROKEN EXCEPT FOR THE MEASURED 535 'ILE
TREAD OF SOMEONE WALKING UP AND
(THE MEN STAND HUDDLED TOGETHER IN A SULLEN 544 'ILE
SILENCE.
(THE MEN LEAVE IN COWED SILENCE, CARRYING JOE WITH545 'ILE
THEM.
AND THE SILENCE. 545 'ILE
(LAUGHING HYSTERICALLY) IT'S THE ICE AND THE COLD546 'ILE
AND THE SILENCE--
I FEEL AS IF THE COLD AND THE SILENCE WERE 546 'ILE
CRUSHING DOWN ON MY BRAIN.
I CAN HEAR THE SILENCE THREATENING ME-- 549 'ILE
THERE IS SILENCE FOR A MOMENT AS MILLER SERVES THE227 AHWILD
FISH AND IT IS PASSED AROUND.
(HE TURNS TO HIS LOBSTER AND CHEWS IN SILENCE FOR 229 AHWILD
A MOMENT.)
(THERE IS SILENCE FOR A MOMENT.) 255 AHWILD
=YESTERDAY THIS DAY'S MADNESS DID PREPARE 261 AHWILD
TOMORROW'S SILENCE, TRIUMPH=--
THEY FILE INTO THE SITTING-ROOM IN SILENCE AND 263 AHWILD
THEN STAND AROUND UNCERTAINLY,
SHE SITS IT IN SILENCE. 10 ANNA
(WITH A START--MAKING A GESTURE WITH HER HAND AS 25 ANNA
IF TO IMPOSE SILENCE--
(IN THE PAUSE OF SILENCE THAT COMES AFTER HIS 29 ANNA
DEFIANCE A HAIL IN A MAN'S HUSKY,
BURKE IS IRRITATED BY THIS SILENCE) 45 ANNA
THE CONDEMNATION SHE FEELS IN THEIR SILENCE GOADS 58 ANNA
ANNA INTO A HARSH,
(CHRIS RELAPSES INTO INJURED SILENCE. 65 ANNA
FINALLY HE IS UNABLE TO BEAR THE THICK SILENCE A 95 BEYOND
MINUTE LONGER, AND BLURTS OUT)
(MAKING A GESTURE TO HER TO KEEP SILENCE) 105 BEYOND
(THE TWO WOMEN SIT IN SILENCE FOR A MOMENT. 116 BEYOND
AND PLAYS WITH THE DOLL IN SILENCE.) 117 BEYOND
THERE IS A MOMENT OF EMBARRASSED SILENCE.) 141 BEYOND
(RUTH STARES AT THE STOVE IN SILENCE. 147 BEYOND
(RAISING HIS HAND AS IF TO COMMAND SILENCE) 158 BEYOND
THERE IS A HUSHED SILENCE. 478 CARDIF
THE STEAMER'S WHISTLE SOUNDS PARTICULARLY LOUD IN 481 CARDIF
THE SILENCE.)
THIS IS FOLLOWED BY A SUDDEN SILENCE 456 CARIBE
(HE SINKS INTO DIGNIFIED SILENCE.) 457 CARIBE
THERE IS A SILENCE BROKEN ONLY BY THE MOURNFUL 459 CARIBE
SINGING OF THE NEGROES ON SHORE.)
(SMITHY DOES NOT BEGIN TO REPLY TO THIS BUT SINKS 468 CARIBE
INTO A SCORNFUL SILENCE.
IN THE SILENCE THE MOURNFUL CHANT FROM THE SHORE 472 CARIBE
CREEPS SLOWLY OUT TO THE SHIP.)
THERE IS ABSOLUTE SILENCE ON THE SHIP FOR A FEW 473 CARIBE
MOMENTS.
THERE IS SILENCE FOR A SECOND OR SO. 473 CARIBE
THE SOUND OF THE WIND AND SEA SUDDENLY CEASES AND 570 CROSS
THERE IS A HEAVY SILENCE.
THEN FOLLOWED A LONG SILENCE. 503 DAYS
(A PAUSE OF SILENCE. 505 DAYS
(AS IF HIS CONVERSATION HAD RUN DRY, HE FALLS INTO529 DAYS
AN UNEASY SILENCE.
THERE IS A PAUSE OF SILENCE.) 531 DAYS
THERE IS A PAUSE OF SILENCE.) 565 DAYS
(WITH TRIUMPHANT MOCKERY) SILENCE/ 565 DAYS
THE THREE EAT IN SILENCE FOR A MOMENT. 206 DESIRE
(HE SITS DOWN AGAIN, RELAPSING INTO A BROODING 209 DESIRE
SILENCE.
(ANOTHER SILENCE. 220 DESIRE
THERE IS AN IMMEDIATE SILENCE.) 249 DESIRE
(HE LAPSES INTO CRUSHED SILENCE--THEN WITH A 264 DESIRE
STRANGE EMOTION)
A PAUSE OF DEAD SILENCE. 268 DESIRE
FOR YOU'LL BE SHIELDING ME UNLAWFULLY BY KEEPING 441 DYNAMO
SILENCE.
(UNDERSTANDING HIS FATHER'S SILENCE AS 463 DYNAMO
INTENTIONAL,
IMPLACABLE SILENCE. 187 EJONES
THEN SILENCE BROKEN ONLY BY THE FAR-OFF QUICKENED 190 EJONES
THROB OF THE TOM-TOM.
SCENE, THERE IS SILENCE, BROKEN EVERY FEW SECONDS 191 EJONES
BY A QUEER, CLICKING SOUND.
ALL THIS IN SILENCE SAVE FOR THE OMINOUS THROB OF 197 EJONES
THE TOM-TOM.
ONLY BLACKNESS REMAINS AND SILENCE BROKEN BY JONES198 EJONES
AS HE RUSHES OFF.
THEN FALLS BY SLOW GRADATIONS OF TONE INTO SILENCE199 EJONES
AND IS TAKEN UP AGAIN.
AS HIS VOICE SINKS INTO SILENCE, HE ENTERS THE 200 EJONES
OPEN SPACE.
WHIMPERING WITH FEAR AS THE THROB OF THE TOM-TOM 202 EJONES
FILLS THE SILENCE ABOUT HIM.
AND I'D HAVE TO KILL HIS SILENCE BY SCREAMING OUT 40 ELECTR
THE TRUTH/
HIS SILENCE ALWAYS CREEPS INTO MY THOUGHTS. 40 ELECTR
THERE IS A SECOND'S UNCOMFORTABLE SILENCE. 45 ELECTR
YOUR EYES WERE ALWAYS SO--SO FULL OF SILENCE/ 53 ELECTR
(THERE IS AN UNCOMFORTABLE SILENCE. 81 ELECTR
THEN SILENCE. 137 ELECTR

SILENCE

SILENCE (CONT'D.)
AGAIN: THERE IS SILENCE EXCEPT FOR THE SOUND OF THE2 GGBROW
LAPPING WAVS.
(SHE LOOKS UPWARD IN SILENCE. 262 GGBROW
THERE IS SILENCE AGAIN, IN WHICH THE DANCE MUSIC 264 GGBROW
IS HEARD.
(A SECOND'S PAUSE OF WAITING SILENCE-- 265 GGBROW
THERE IS A MOMENT OF INTENSE BLACKNESS AND 267 GGBROW
SILENCE.
INTO SILENCE--INTO NIGHT--INTO EARTH--INTO SPACE--267 GGBROW
INTO PEACE--INTO MEANING--
THERE'S A PAUSE OF SILENCE. 318 GGBROW
FOR A SECOND THERE IS AN EMBARRASSED SILENCE. 209 HA APE
(A SILENCE. 240 HA APE
TIPTOES SOFTLY UP TO IT, LISTENS, IS IMPRESSED BY 245 HA APE
THE SILENCE
(AT THE SOUND OF HIS VOICE THE CHATTERING DIES 251 HA APE
AWAY INTO AN ATTENTIVE SILENCE.
THEY YAWN, MOVES, GROANING, OPENING HIS EYES, AND 254 HA APE
THERE IS SILENCE.
UNTIL THE EXPECTANT SILENCE CRASHES HIS EARS.) 15 HUGHIE
BUT A RARE AND THREATENING PAUSE OF SILENCE HAS 29 HUGHIE
FALLEN ON THE CITY.
TO THE THREAT OF NIGHT AND SILENCE AS IT PURSUES 32 HUGHIE
AN IDEAL OF FAME AND GLORY
ERIE BREAKS THE SILENCE--BITTERLY RESIGNED. 33 HUGHIE
(RAPPING ON THE TABLE FOR ORDER WHEN THERE IS 658 ICEMAN
NOTHING BUT A DEAD SILENCE)
(THERE IS A SECOND'S TENSE SILENCE.) 693 ICEMAN
THEN THE SUDDEN SILENCE DESCENDS AGAIN ON THE 701 ICEMAN
ROOM.
(THERE IS A SUDDEN SILENCE. 705 ICEMAN
(THERE IS A SECOND'S DEAD SILENCE AS HE FINISHES--706 ICEMAN
(THERE IS A HEAVY SILENCE. 708 ICEMAN
THERE IS A SUSPENDED, WAITING SILENCE. 711 ICEMAN
THE SILENCE IS LIKE THAT IN THE ROOM OF A DYING 714 ICEMAN
MAN
(THERE IS A MOMENT OF DEAD SILENCE. 716 ICEMAN
THEY MUNCH THEIR BISCUITS AND SIP THEIR COFFEE IN 914 INZONE
DULL SILENCE.)
A THICK SILENCE SETTLES OVER THE FORECASTLE. 522 INZONE
THERE IS SILENCE FOR A MOMENT AFTER HIS DEPARTURE 523 INZONE
THERE IS A MOMENT OF SILENCE, IN WHICH EACH MAN IS532 INZONE
IN AGONY WITH THE
DEEP SILENCE, BROKEN ONLY BY SMITTY'S MUFFLED 532 INZONE
SOBBING.
(THERE IS A DEAD SILENCE. 72 JOURNE
(THERE IS ANOTHER PAUSE OF DEAD SILENCE. 73 JOURNE
(THERE IS AGAIN A PAUSE OF DEAD SILENCE. 75 JOURNE
SHE TALKS ON AS IF UNAWARE OF THEIR SILENCE.) 109 JOURNE
THERE IS A TENSE SILENCE. 162 JOURNE
(BREAKS THE CRACKING SILENCE--BITTERLY, SELF- 170 JOURNE
DEFENSIVELY SARDONIC.)
(THEN MARY SPEAKS, AND THEY FREEZE INTO SILENCE 171 JOURNE
AGAIN, STARING AT HER.
(A SIMPLE BOY--IN A FRIGHTENED WHISPER AFTER A 275 LAZARU
PAUSE OF DEAD SILENCE)
(IN THE MIDST OF A SILENCE MORE AWKWARD THAN 278 LAZARU
BEFORE HE RISES TO HIS FEET,
(A PAUSE OF SILENCE.) 279 LAZARU
(CARRYING THE QUESTION FALTERINGLY BACK INTO 279 LAZARU
SILENCE)
THEY FALL INTO SILENCE. 286 LAZARU
(SPEAKS AMID A PROFOUND SILENCE. 289 LAZARU
(THERE IS A SECOND OF COMPLETE, DEATH-LIKE SILENCE.295 LAZARU
THE CHORUISH MUHO GETS DOWN ALL SOUND INTO A 305 LAZARU
STRICKEN SILENCE.
(RAISING HIS HANDS FOR SILENCE--WITH A PLAYFUL 309 LAZARU
SMILE)
YOU ARE A BUBBLE PRICKED BY DEATH INTO A VOID AND 309 LAZARU
A MOCKING SILENCE!
HE LAY DREAMING TO THE CROWN OF SILENCE, 309 LAZARU
AND OPPRESSIVE SILENCE IN WHICH ONLY THE MURMURED 313 LAZARU
PRAYERS OF MIRIAM ARE HEARD.)
THERE IS SILENCE AGAIN. 314 LAZARU
SILENCE? 316 LAZARU
(AFTER A PAUSE OF SILENCE--DRYLY) 316 LAZARU
(RAISING HIS HAND) SILENCE! 321 LAZARU
(FRENZIED!) SILENCE, IMPIOUS TRAITOR! 322 LAZARU
STRAIN OF MUSIC RECEDING INTO THE SILENCE OVER 324 LAZARU
STILL WATERS.)
(A SILENCE. 328 LAZARU
ABRUPTLY AND THERE IS A HEAVY SILENCE.) 331 LAZARU
OR TAKE YOUR SILENCE AS A REFUSAL/ 333 LAZARU
THERE IS A PAUSE OF DEAD SILENCE.) 335 LAZARU
HE STOPS LAUGHING AND IMMEDIATELY THERE IS 338 LAZARU
SILENCE, EXCEPT FOR CALIGULA.
IN THE SILENCE THAT ENSUES POMPEIA GETS UP AND 341 LAZARU
WALKS OVER TO THE DAIS.
A SECOND OF DEAD SILENCE. 347 LAZARU
WHEN IN THE DEAD EXPECTANT SILENCE, 349 LAZARU
(FOR A LONG MOMENT THERE IS COMPLETE SILENCE. 353 LAZARU
IS SWALLOWED AT ONE GULP LIKE A WHINING GNAT BY 358 LAZARU
THE CRETIN'S SILENCE UP
(MOVED, AND IMMEDIATELY THERE IS SILENCE. 362 LAZARU
THE CROWDS AND YOUTHS AND GIRLS MAKE WAY FOR HIM 362 LAZARU
IN AWED SILENCE--
A GREAT SPELL OF SILENCE SETTLES UPON ALL HIS 366 LAZARU
HEARERS--
(AT HIS FIRST WORD THERE IS A PROFOUND SILENCE 369 LAZARU
SUDDENLY THE SILENCE SEEMS TO CRUSH DOWN UPON HIM.370 LAZARU
FOR A MOMENT THERE IS SILENCE. 2 MANSNS
DEBORAH SITS IN SILENCE, HER EYES ON THE GROUND.) 20 MANSNS
A SILENCE 29 MANSNS
AND SCREAM IN SILENCE AND BEAT ON THE WALLS UNTIL 40 MANSNS
YOU DIE OF STARVATION.
SARA ACKNOWLEDGES THE INTRODUCTION IN SILENCE, 90 MANSNS
THEN TURNS TO DEBORAH.)

SILENCE (CONT'D.)
FOR A MOMENT THERE IS A TENSE SILENCE. 95 MANSNS
AND THE SILENCE OF DEAD DREAMS. 113 MANSNS
IN THE ROOM, AN EAVESDROPPING SILENCE THAT WAITS, 117 MANSNS
THEN, AS THOUGH THE MEANING OF THE SILENCE WERE 118 MANSNS
BECOMING AUDIBLE,
TOWARD--AND THE SILENCE WAITS--HANDS CLAPPED OVER 120 MANSNS
ITS EARS--
THERE IS A MOMENT'S SILENCE. 131 MANSNS
ALL FOUR SQUAT AGAIN IN SILENCE.) 368 MARCOM
THERE IS A SUDDEN DEAD SILENCE. 377 MARCOM
(STERNLY) SILENCE! 380 MARCOM
HE WAVES ONE HAND FOR SILENCE. 389 MARCOM
UNTIL A SMALL MULTITUDE IS GATHERED STANDING IN 405 MARCOM
SILENCE STARING UP AT THE POOP.
A PAUSE OF SILENCE) 410 MARCOM
RAISE THEIR HEADS AND STARE BEFORE THEM IN 434 MARCOM
SILENCE.
IN SILENCE--FOR ONE CONCENTRATED MOMENT--BE PROUD 435 MARCOM
OF LIFE!
IN SILENCE? 435 MARCOM
SMILE WITH INFINITE SILENCE UPON OUR SPEECH, 435 MARCOM
(A PAUSE OF SILENCE. 436 MARCOM
(THEIR VOICES DIE INTO SILENCE.) 436 MARCOM
I WANT-- (HIS VOICE TRAILS OFF INTO SILENCE.) 120 MISBEG
THEN QUIET AS IF HE HAD RAISED A HAND FOR SILENCE,180 POET
AS IF SOMEONE HAD CALLED FOR SILENCE-- 180 POET
THEN MELODY'S VOICE IS PLAINLY HEARD IN THE 180 POET
SILENCE AS HE SHOUTS A TOAST--
THE GROOMS FOR A MOMENT IN SILENCE--THEN HITS THE 585 ROPE
TABLE FURIOUSLY WITH HIS FIST)
AND REMAINS STANDING BY THE DOORWAY IN STUBBORN 588 ROPE
SILENCE.)
LUKE GLARES AT HIM FOR A MOMENT IN SILENCE) 596 ROPE
I MUST GO AWAY WHERE I CAN THINK OF YOU IN 16 STRANG
SILENCE/....}
(A SILENCE AS IF HE HAD RESPECTABLY SQUELCHED 25 STRANG
HIMSELF--
(HE SEIZES HER HAND AND KISSES IT IN A 71 STRANG
PASSIONATELY GRATEFUL SILENCE--
QUESTIONS DIE IN THE SILENCE OF THIS PEACE... 91 STRANG
THEY SIT STARING BEFORE THEM IN SILENCE. 133 STRANG
WE SIT TOGETHER IN SILENCE, THINKING... 139 STRANG
HE STARES ACCUSINGLY AT THEM AS THEY COME SLOWLY 189 STRANG
TOWARD HIM IN SILENCE.

SILENCED
AND STARES AT HIM WITH SUCH A PASSION OF HATRED 27 ELECTR
THAT HE IS SILENCED.
THE VOICES ARE INSTANTLY SILENCED. 433 MARCOM
(SILENCED--WITH STIFF POLITENESS.) 85 POET

SILENCES
(SILENCES THEM WITH A MOTION OF HER HAND) 405 MARCOM
(SILENCES THEM BY AN IMPERIOUS GESTURE-- 435 MARCOM
BUT HOGAN SILENCES HIM.) 58 MISBEG

SILENT
DAVID, I--(SHE IS SILENT. 940 *ILE
THE TWO MEN STAND SILENT FOR A MOMENT, LISTENING. 543 *ILE
(AFTER A FURTIVE GLANCE AT THE STIFF AND SILENT 190 AHWILD
LILY--
LILLY KEEPS SILENT, HER EYES DOWNCAST. 212 AHWILD
(HE IS SILENT, STUDYING HIS SOUP PLATE, AS IF IT 224 AHWILD
WERE SOME STRANGE ENIGMA.
ONLY LILY REMAINS STIFF AND SILENT.) 225 AHWILD
(BUT LILY REMAINS IMPLACABLY SILENT. 257 AHWILD
BOTH ARE MOTIONLESS AND SILENT. 58 ANNA
HE IS SILENT, HIS FACE AVERTED, HIS FEATURES 59 ANNA
BEGINNING TO WORK WITH FURY.
HE GOES TO THE DOOR, SILENT AND STUPID--THEN 62 ANNA
TURNS)
(THEY REMAIN MOTIONLESS AND SILENT FOR A MOMENT, 69 ANNA
HOLDING EACH OTHER'S EYES)
(AT THIS MENTION OF THE TRIP THEY BOTH FALL 83 BEYOND
SILENT.
(AS AGENET REMAINS SILENT SHE BURSTS INTO SOBS 92 BEYOND
AGAIN)
THE TWO BROTHERS REMAIN SILENT FOR A MOMENT. 109 BEYOND
(ROBERT NODS BUT REMAINS SILENT.) 142 BEYOND
(THE TWO WOMEN REMAIN SILENT FOR A TIME STARING 152 BEYOND
DISGEFULLY AT THE STOVE.)
COULDN'T YOU HAVE KEPT SILENT! 164 BEYOND
SHE REMAINS SILENT, GAZING AT HIM DULLY WITH THE 169 BEYOND
SAD HUMILITY OF EXHAUSTION.
ALL ARE SILENT, AVOIDING EACH OTHER'S EYES.) 479 CARDIF
(WAVING HIS HAND FOR HER TO BE SILENT) 568 CROSS
(FATHER BAIRD STARES AT HIM BUT KEEPS SILENT. 545 DAYS
(FROWNING, MAKES A MOTION TO JOHN TO BE SILENT) 554 DAYS
MAKES A GESTURE FOR HIM TO BE SILENT) 560 DAYS
THERE IS A PAUSE OF SILENT IMMOBILITY IN THE ROOM.561 DAYS
THEN, EVIDENTLY UNABLE TO KEEP SILENT ABOUT HIS 236 DESIRE
THOUGHTS,
STARING AT THE DOOR AS IF SHE WERE ALONE IN A 250 DESIRE
SILENT ROOM.)
(AS EMMA REMAINS SILENT) YES, HARRIET, THAT'S IT.508 DIFFRNT
(AS EMMA KEEPS SILENT--IRRITATED) 510 DIFFRNT
THE WOMAN KEEPS SULLENLY SILENT. 174 EJONES
THE AUCTIONEER BEGINS HIS SILENT SPIEL. 197 EJONES
AT FIRST THEY ARE SILENT AND MOTIONLESS. 199 EJONES
(LAVINIA STARES AT HER BUT REMAINS SILENT. 17 ELECTR
(SHE IS SILENT, STARING BEFORE HER WITH HARD EYES, 22 ELECTR
RIGIDLY UPRIGHT.
HE WAS SILENT AND MYSTERIOUS AND ROMANTIC/ 31 ELECTR
(SHE REMAINS SILENT. 38 ELECTR
BUT LAVINIA SIMPLY STARES AT HER, FROZEN AND 77 ELECTR
SILENT.
(THEN, AS LAVINIA REMAINS SILENT, 78 ELECTR
SO I BECAME SILENT FOR LIFE AND DESIGNED A MASK OF295 GGBROW
THE BAD BOY PAL IN WHICH TO
SHAKING WITH SILENT LAUGHTER. 314 GGBROW

SILENT (CONT'D.)
SHE REMAINS, SOBBING WITH DEEP, SILENT GRIEF.) 321 GGBROW
(THEY ARE SILENT, PUZZLED BY HIS SUDDEN RESENTMENT227 HA APE
WHO STARES BACK AT HIM, SILENT AND MOTIONLESS. 252 HA APE
THE CLERK'S MIND STILL CANNOT MAKE A GETAWAY 30 HUGHIE
BECAUSE THE CITY REMAINS SILENT.
(LARRY'S FACE TIGHTENS BUT HE KEEPS SILENT. 646 ICEMAN
(LARRY REMAINS SILENT. 647 ICEMAN
BUT THEY REMAIN SILENT AND MOTIONLESS. 685 ICEMAN
AS HIS NAILS DIG INTO HIS PALMS, BUT HE REMAINS 701 ICEMAN
SILENT.
(UNABLE TO KEEP SILENT LONGER) 519 INZONE
(SHE IS SILENT ON THIS, KEEPING HER HEAD TURNED 15 JOURNE
TOWARD THEIR VOICES.
THE THREE IN THE ROOM REMAIN SILENT. 75 JOURNE
(THEN AS EDMUND REMAINS HOPELESSLY SILENT, SHE 94 JOURNE
ADDS SADLY.)
(EDMUND REMAINS SILENT. TYRONE REGARDS HIM--THEN 167 JOURNE
GOES ON.)
(STERNLY) BE SILENT/ 277 LAZARU
(THEY ARE SILENT. 307 LAZARU
BELOW LAZARUS, WHO LOOKS DOWN UPON THEM, SILENT 320 LAZARU
BUT SMILING GENTLY NOW.
HIS MOUTH IS SILENT--AND A LITTLE SAD, I THINK. 355 LAZARU
YOU WILL SOON BE SILENT/ 367 LAZARU
(OUTH REMAIN SILENT AND MOTIONLESS, 366 MARCOM
THE MINSTREL AND HIS DRUM BECOME SILENT, AND WITH 375 MARCOM
THE RIVER WAS NOT SO BLACK--THE RIVER OF MAN'S 385 MARCOM
LIFE SO DEEP AND SILENT--
AND SIGNALS THE BAND TO BE SILENT. 402 MARCOM
I'M BY NATURE A SILENT MAN, AND I LET MY ACTIONS 404 MARCOM
DO THE TALKING.
DEATH LIVES IN A SILENT SEA, GRAY AND COLD UNDER 409 MARCOM
COLD GRAY SKY.
I REVOKE MY DECLARATION OF WAR--UNLESS YOU LEARN 423 MARCOM
TO DANCE AND BE SILENT/
A SILENT MAN GIVEN TO DEEDS, NOT WORDS--THERE HE 431 MARCOM
FALTERS FITTINGLY) AND SO NOW--
SOMETHING BUT SHE REMAINS SILENT. 139 MISBEG
IT AND HE REMAINS UNEASILY SILENT. 159 MISBEG
SHE IS SILENT, AS IF SHE WERE NOT AWARE OF HIM 160 MISBEG
NOW.
(THEN AS SHE REMAINS SILENT--MISERABLY) 176 MISBEG
AND YOU, RILEY, KEEP YOUR BAGPIPE SILENT, OR OUT 57 POET
YOU GO.
(HE IS SILENT. 75 POET
(HE PAUSES, AS IF HE EXPECTS HER TO BE FURIOUS, 108 POET
BUT SHE REMAINS TENSELY SILENT.
SHE PATS HER MOTHER'S HAND, BUT REMAINS SILENT, 137 POET
HER EXPRESSION DREAMILY HAPPY.
YOU'RE COLD COMFORT, SITTING SILENT LIKE A STATUE,140 POET
AND ME MAKING TALK TO MYSELF--
(THEN AS SHE REMAINS SILENT--URGINGLY) 82 STRANG
AND BECOME HIS SILENT PARTNER. 124 STRANG
COUNTERFEITS--FAKES--SAM'S SILENT PARTNERS/ 147 STRANG

SILENTLY
(HE TURNS AWAY FROM HER SILENTLY AND WALKS TOWARD 550 'ILE
THE COMPANIONWAY.
(THEY BOW TO EACH OTHER SILENTLY. 154 BEYOND
WAS IT BECAUSE--TRUTH NODS SILENTLY. 155 BEYOND
THEIR EYES, AS THEY GLIDE SILENTLY INTO THE ROOM, 571 CROSS
DURING THE NEXT FEW SPEECHES HE MOVES SILENTLY TO 525 DAYS
THE CORNER OF THE LONG TABLE
LOVING MOVES SILENTLY OVER UNTIL HE IS STANDING 526 DAYS
JUST BEHIND JOHN BUT A STEP
LOVING FOLLOWS SILENTLY BUT STOPS 547 DAYS
HE BOWS HIS HEAD WITH A SIMPLE DIGNITY AND BEGINS 551 DAYS
TO PRAY SILENTLY.)
LOVING FOLLOWS THEM SILENTLY, MOVING BACKWARD, 555 DAYS
THE GOES INTO THE BEDROOM AND CLOSES THE DOOR 557 DAYS
SILENTLY BEHIND HIM.
HE BOWS HIS HEAD AND BEGINS PRAYING SILENTLY TO 561 DAYS
HIMSELF.
HE MOVES SILENTLY, EVEN FRIGHTENEDLY, 251 DESIRE
THE OTHERS WATCH CABOT SILENTLY WITH COLD, HOSTILE251 DESIRE
EYES.
ABBIE COMES ACROSS THE ROOM SILENTLY. 252 DESIRE
SHE STRUGGLES TO GET AWAY, FIERCELY BUT SILENTLY. 174 EJONES
ALL EXCHANGE COURTLY GREETINGS IN DUMB SHOW AND 196 EJONES
CHAT SILENTLY TOGETHER.
A GROUP OF FIGURES SILENTLY ENTER THE CLEARING 196 EJONES
FROM ALL SIDES.
SHE MOVES SO SILENTLY.) 62 ELECTR
CHRISTINE RETURNS FROM THE HALL, CLOSING THE 84 ELECTR
SLIDING DOORS BEHIND HER SILENTLY.
(THE SLIDING DOORS IN REAR ARE OPENED A LITTLE AND 91 ELECTR
LAVINIA SLIPS SILENTLY IN AND
AT THE SAME MOMENT LAVINIA APPEARS SILENTLY IN THE 93 ELECTR
DOORWAY FROM THE HALL AND
THEY APPROACH THE CABIN SKYLIGHT SILENTLY. 109 ELECTR
(HE SLIPS OUT SILENTLY. 114 ELECTR
THEY WORK SILENTLY.) 302 GGBROW
AND CLOSED IT AFTER HIM SILENTLY, SHAKING WITH 318 GGBROW
SUPPRESSED LAUGHTER.
AS THEY PRAY SILENTLY IN THEIR AGONIZED 319 GGBROW
SUPPLICATION.
FILE THROUGH THE DOOR SILENTLY CLOSE UPON EACH 217 HA APE
OTHER'S HEELS IN WHAT IS VERY
(AS HE IS SPEAKING HICKEY APPEARS SILENTLY IN THE 703 ICEMAN
DOORWAY AT REAR.
PRAYING SILENTLY WITH MOVING LIPS 313 LAZARU
(AS SHE SAYS THIS LAST THE CABIN DOOR IS SILENTLY 1H MANSNS
UNLOCKED AND OPENED AND SARA
(THEY STARE SILENTLY. 366 MARCOM
THE CROWD SILENTLY FILTERS AWAY, LEAVING ONLY THE 406 MARCOM
BAND.)
THE FOUR PRIESTS GO FIRST, BEGINNING TC PRAY 436 MARCOM
SILENTLY AGAIN.

SILENTLY (CONT'D.)
(THE COURT LEAVES SILENTLY AT HIS COMMAND IN A 436 MARCOM
FORMAL, EXPRESSIONLESS ORDER.
(HE BOWS AGAIN AND GOES OUT SILENTLY.) 437 MARCOM
(HE OBEYS MEEKLY, COMING AS FAR AS THE BOULDER 157 MISBEG
SILENTLY.
SARA APPEARS SILENTLY IN THE DOORWAY AT RIGHT. 136 POET
(AS THE CHILD CONTINUES TO STARE AT HIM SILENTLY 583 RUPE
WITH EYES STUPID FROM FEAR,
STRAGGLY WISPS FROM THE PILE OF RANK HAY FALL 601 RUPE
SILENTLY TO THE FLOOR
HE SEES EVANS AND MARSDEN, NODS AT MARSDEN 33 STRANG
SILENTLY, AND RETURNS IT COLDLY.
NINA COMES SILENTLY THROUGH THE DOOR AND STANDS 68 STRANG
JUST INSIDE IT LOOKING AT HIM.
(ENTERS SILENTLY. 79 STRANG
(HE VANISHED AS SILENTLY AS HE HAD COME.) 145 STRANG

SILENUS
THEY'LL KNEEL AND WORSHIP THE IRONIC SILENUS WHO 297 GGBROW
TELLS THEM THE BEST GOOD IS
WE'LL ADROITLY HIDE OLD SILENUS ON THE CUPOLA/ 312 GGBROW

SILHOUETTE
HEAT POURS FULL UPON THE MEN WHO ARE OUTLINED IN 223 HA APE
SILHOUETTE IN THE CROUCHING.

SILHOUETTED
THEN THE DOOR IS OPENED AND A WOMAN'S FIGURE IS 470 WELDED
SILHOUETTED

SILK
A SOFA WITH SILK AND SATIN CUSHIONS STANDS AGAINST189 AHWILD
THE WALL.
SO ARE THE HIGH-HEELED PUMPS AND CLOCKED SILK 520 DIFNIT
STOCKINGS.
THE COAT OPEN TO REVEAL AN OLD AND FADED BUT 9 HUGHIE
EXPENSIVE SILK SHIRT
HE CARRIES A PANAMA HAT AND MOPS HIS FACE WITH A 9 HUGHIE
RED AND BLUE SILK HANDKERCHIEF.
HIS SHOES ARE TAN AND WHITE, HIS SOCKS WHITE SILK. 9 HUGHIE
IT WILL BE TIME ENOUGH TO DREAM OF SILK PURSES-- 590 ICEMAN
THE CLOTHES OF THE MULCH AND HIS COURT ARE OF RICH373 MARCOM
SILK STUFFS,
IF SHE WERE A MILLION YEN WORTH OF SILK OR SPICES,403 MARCOM
IT WOULDN'T WORRY AN INSTANT.
THAT OUR SILK-MAKERS MAY PRESERVE THEIR SHARE OF 422 MARCOM
THE ETERNAL SUNLIGHT/
WHOSE SILK INDUSTRY IS BEGINNING TO THREATEN THE 422 MARCOM
SUPREMACY OF OUR OWN.
BY THE CONTINUED OUTRAGES AGAINST OUR SILK 422 MARCOM
NATIONALS
BUT I'LL BE GLAD TO LET YOU HAVE A FEW INSTRUCTIVE431 MARCOM
FACTS ABOUT THE SILK INDUSTRY
LAYING ESPECIAL EMPHASIS UPON THE KEYSTONE OF THE 431 MARCOM
WHOLE SILK BUSINESS--
HIS EYES ARE FIXED ON A CATAFALQUE, DRAPED IN 432 MARCOM
HEAVY WHITE SILK,
SILK HANDKERCHIEF IN BREAST POCKET, A DARK TIE. 37 MISBEG
DARK-BROWN MADE-TO-ORDER SHOES AND SILK SOCKS, A 37 MISBEG
WHITE SILK SHIRT,
GOD HIMSELF CANNOT TRANSFORM A SOW'S EAR INTO A 114 POET
SILK PURSE/
(HE DRINKS) THERE YOU ARE--SMOOTH AS SILK. 595 ROPE

SILKS
DRESSED IN SILKS AND SATINS, AND RIDING IN A 63 POET
CARRIAGE WITH COACHMAN AND FOOTMAN.
TO A SHILLING SHE'LL SEE THE DAY WHEN SHE'LL WEAR 173 POET
FINE SILKS

SILKWORMS
ARE BREEDING AND MAINTAINING SILKWORMS FOR 422 MARCOM
PURPOSES OF AGGRESSION/

SILL
THE HEAD AND SHOULDERS OF NAT BARTLETT APPEAR OVERS55 CROSS
THE SILL.

SILLINESS
HE'S NOT OLD ENOUGH FOR SUCH SILLINESS. 217 AHWILD

SILLY
YOU WANT TO LIVE UP TO YOUR SILLY REPUTATION EVEN 547 'ILE
IF YOU DO HAVE TO BEAT AND
I'LL BET HE'S OFF SOMEWHERE WRITING A POEM TO 192 AHWILD
MURIEL MCCUMBER, THE SILLY/
I DON'T BELIEVE IN THIS SILLY CELEBRATING THE 194 AHWILD
FOURTH OF JULY--
(SCORNFULLY SUPERIOR) THAT SILLY SKIRT PARTY/ 194 AHWILD
YOU CAN HAVE YOUR SILLY OPTIMISM, IF YOU LIKE, 215 AHWILD
AUNT LILY.
HE WAVES HIS HAND AIMLESSLY AND SPEAKS WITH A 224 AHWILD
SILLY GRAVITY.)
(TURNING TO HER BROTHER) YOU SILLY GOAT, YOU/ 228 AHWILD
I WAS TRYING SO HARD NOT TO--BUT YOU CAN'T HELP 233 AHWILD
IT, HE'S SO SILLY/
HE JUST WANTS TO SHOW OFF HE'S HEARTBROKEN ABOUT 251 AHWILD
THAT SILLY MURIEL--
BUT YOU'RE A SILLY GABBLER YOURSELF WHEN YOU TALK 271 AHWILD
THAT WAY
YOU'RE NOT ALLOWED OUT, YOU SILLY/ 274 AHWILD
AH, THAT'S SILLY. 275 AHWILD
DON'T YOU SEE, SILLY, 286 AHWILD
(SCORNFULLY) THAT DUMP WHERE ALL THE SILLY FOOLS 287 AHWILD
GO/
SEEMS MUSHY AND SILLY--BUT THAT MEANT SOMETHING/ 297 AHWILD
WITH HER SILLY FACE ALL SCREWED UP SERIOUS AS 94 BEYOND
JUDGEMENT--
GOOD GRACIOUS, DICK, YOU DO ACT SILLY, FLYING INTO103 BEYOND
A TEMPER OVER NOTHING.
DARN ALL THIS SILLY LOVIN' BUSINESS, ANYWAY. 103 BEYOND
DON'T BE SO SILLY. THERE'S NO QUESTION OF RIGHT. 120 BEYOND
IF I HADN'T BEEN SUCH A FOOL TO LISTEN TO YOUR 127 BEYOND
CHEAP, SILLY,
I WANT YOU TO BELIEVE I PUT ALL THAT SILLY 139 BEYOND
NONSENSE BACK OF ME A LONG TIME AGO--

SILLY

SILLY (CONT'D.)
YOU'RE SILLY TO WORRY. 150 BEYOND
(WITH NERVOUS IRRITATION) DON'T SIT THERE LIKE A 153 BEYOND
SILLY GOOSE.
IT WAS ONLY THE SILLY UNCERTAINTY THAT HURT. 160 BEYOND
AND WITH THAT I FETCHED 'ER A BIFF ON THE EAR WOT 478 CARDIF
KNOCKED 'ER SILLY, AN'--
THAT SILLY OL' JOSSER/ 479 CARDIF
THE SILLY LAUGHTER OF A WOMAN IS HEARD.) 463 CARIBE
BUT THAT'S SILLY. 517 DAYS
IT WAS ONLY A SILLY GESTURE HE FELT SAFE IN MAKING520 DAYS
BECAUSE HE WAS SO DAMNED SURE
YOU JUST PUT YOUR MIND ON THAT AND FORGET YOUR 530 DAYS
SILLY WORRIES.
IT WOULD HAVE SAVED HIM SO MUCH SILLY ROMANTIC 534 DAYS
PURSUIT OF MEANINGLESS ILLUSIONS.
I'M SORRY I BUTTED IN WITH A SILLY QUESTION. 534 DAYS
THAT MY HERO'S SILLY IDEA THAT HE WAS POSSESSED BY538 DAYS
A DEMON MUST STRIKE YOU AS AN
IT'S ALL SILLY TWADDLE, OF COURSE. 542 DAYS
WELL, AS HE SAID, SOMETHING--(THEN CURTLY, FEELINGS57 DAYS
THIS MAKES HIM APPEAR SILLY)
EDEN HAS A MIXTURE OF SILLY GRIN AND VICIOUS SCOWL212 DESIRE
ON HIS FACE)
(LAUGHING) I WASN'T THINKING OF WHALES, SILLY/ 497 DIFRNT
PLAYING SILLY JOKES ALL THE TIME. 499 DIFRNT
SILLY! 509 DIFRNT
(WITH A SILLY LAUGH) YOU'RE TOO YOUNG. 527 DIFRNT
THE SNEAKIN' WAY YOU'RE MAKIN' A SILLY FOOL OUT OF528 DIFRNT
POOR EMMIE CROSBY.
HER FACE IS BEAMING WITH HAPPINESS AND LOOKS 534 DIFRNT
INDESCRIBABLY SILLY.
(I I OUGHT TO CONQUER THAT SILLY FEAR IN MYSELF... 443 DYNAMO
DOES NOT EXPECT I'SE SILLY ENUFF TO B'LIEVE IN 185 EJONES
GHOSTS AN' HA'NTS
BEATIN' YER BLOODY DRUM AND CASTIN' YER SILLY 203 EJONES
SPELLS/
YOUR SILLY TALK ABOUT RESEMBLANCES--DON'T SIT 37 ELECTR
THERE.
IT WAS JUST A SILLY IDEA OF YOURS. 44 ELECTR
WHENEVER DID YOU GET THAT SILLY IDEA! 85 ELECTR
WHO TOOK IT INTO HIS SILLY HEAD TO CALL HERE A FEW 87 ELECTR
TIMES WITHOUT BEING ASKED.
THE WAR HAS GOT ME SILLY, I GUESS/ 87 ELECTR
I HEARD SOME SILLY TALK BUT DIDN'T PAY ANY 135 ELECTR
ATTENTION--
YOU KNEW YOU COULD RID YOURSELF FOREVER OF YOUR 141 ELECTR
SILLY GUILT ABOUT THE PAST.
YOU'D BE SO HANDSOME IF YOU'D ONLY SHAVE OFF THAT 145 ELECTR
SILLY BEARD
(SHARPLY) DON'T BE SILLY, PETER/ 158 ELECTR
BUT, YOU SILLY BOY, VINNIE TOLD PETER HERSELF WHATI61 ELECTR
IT IS AND TOLD HIM TO TELL
BUT I SUPPOSE THE GOSSIPS ARE TELLING THE SAME 276 GGBROW
SILLY STORIES ABOUT HIM THEY
(HESITATINGLY) WELL--IT'S REALLY TOO SILLY--HE 311 GGBROW
SUDDENLY GOT AWFULLY STRANGE.
I BET YOU GOT A PUNCH IN CIDER FIST DAT'D KNOCK 252 HA APE
'EM ALL SILLY/
CHUCK WID A SILLY GRIN ON HIS UGLY MAP, DE BIG 614 ICEMAN
BOOB.
SO DON'T BE SILLY NOW. 640 ICEMAN
(WITH HIS SILLY GIGGLE) VE VILL TRINK VINE 640 ICEMAN
BENEATH THE VILLOW TREES/
THAT WAS A SILLY STUNT FOR A FREE ANARCHIST WOMAN,646 ICEMAN
WASN'T IT,
WAVING THEIR SILLY SWORDS, SO AFRAID THEY COULDN'T677 ICEMAN
SHOW OFF HOW BRAVE THEY VAS/
(WITH HIS SILLY GIGGLE) HELLO, HARRY, STUPID 691 ICEMAN
PROLETARIAN MONKEY-FACE/
(LOOKS AT PARRITT AND BURSTS INTO HIS SILLY 721 ICEMAN
GIGGLE)
(SCORNFULLY) LETTIN' ON DE 'IS SILLY AIRS, AND 522 INZONE
ALL.
YOU MUSTN'T BE SO SILLY, JAMES. 28 JOURNE
(FRIGHTENEDLY.) I WON'T LISTEN WHEN YOU'RE SO 48 JOURNE
SILLY/
THAT'S A SILLY THING TO SAY, JAMES. 83 JOURNE
(DOES THIS--WITH A SILLY GIGGLE.) 100 JOURNE
DON'T BE SILLY, CATHLEEN. 101 JOURNE
WHAT IS SO WONDERFUL ABOUT THAT FIRST MEETING 107 JOURNE
BETWEEN A SILLY ROMANTIC
I HAVE FORGOTTEN MY OLD SILLY PRESUMPTUOUS 61 MANSNS
COWARDLY DISDAIN
DON'T BE SILLY, MOTHER. 66 MANSNS
WHY DID YOU MAKE THAT SILLY RULE THAT NO ONE WAS 109 MANSNS
EVER ALLOWED
WHAT SILLY NONSENSE, SIMON/ 111 MANSNS
JUST BECAUSE YOU ARE SUCH A SILLY JEALOUS BOY. 127 MANSNS
DON'T BE SILLY. 145 MANSNS
ONLY IN A SILLY FANCY--TO WHILE AWAY THE TIME-- 166 MANSNS
THAT HUMAN LIFE IS A SILLY DISAPPOINTMENT, A 180 MANSNS
LIAR'S PROMISE.
BUT TO CONNECT THE DOOR AND THAT SILLY TALE WITH 183 MANSNS
THE ACTUAL WOODEN DOOR--
FURGET THOSE SILLY FEARS, MOTHER. 184 MANSNS
(TENDERLY) YOU SILLY BOY/ 355 MARCOM
(IN A WHISPER) I LOVE YOU. THERE, SILLY/ 356 MARCOM
IT WAS SILLY. 361 MARCOM
HE MAKES A SILLY GESTURE TO ATTRACT THE BABY'S 370 MARCOM
ATTENTION.
HE IS NOT THE BLATANTLY SILLY. 55 MISBEG
I DON'T LIKE HIS SILLY SHEEP'S FACE, AND I'VE NO 58 MISBEG
USE FOR JOCKEYS, ANYWAY.
COME HERE TO ME, YOU GREAT FOOL, AND STOP YOUR 141 MISBEG
SILLY BLATHER.
AND THE SILLY MUG OF THE MOON GRINNING DOWN, 157 MISBEG
ENJOYING THE JOKE/

SILLY (CONT'D.)
I WAS ONLY AN IGNORANT, SILLY GIRL BOASTING, BUT 147 POET
I'M A WOMAN NOW, MOTHER.
AND HE ONLY LAUGHED HARDER WHEN YOU HUNG UP THAT 581 ROPE
SILLY ROPE THERE (SHE POINTS)
TOO SILLY... 6 STRANG
IT MIGHT SOUND SILLY... 8 STRANG
(WITH A SILLY GIGGLE) REALLY, NINA, YOU'RE 13 STRANG
ABSOLUTELY RUDE/
I'M STILL GORDON'S SILLY VIRGIN/ 19 STRANG
(HE MAKES A SILLY GESTURE TOWARD THE DOOR-- 37 STRANG
THINKING CONFUSEDLY)
IT'S PROBABLY A REFLECTION OF HER OWN SILLY FIXED 38 STRANG
IDEA ABOUT HIM.
FUR PLAYING THE SILLY SLUT, CHARLIE. 44 STRANG
SILLY ASS/... 52 STRANG
(YOU SILLY COWARD/... 98 STRANG
(STILL MORE CONFUSED--WITH A SILLY IDIOTIC SMIRK) 117 STRANG
ISN'T HE SILLY?... 141 STRANG
(THEN RUDELY DEFENSIVE) DON'T BE SILLY/ 146 STRANG
AND THEN HE BECAME SILLY AND SENTIMENTAL AND ASKED155 STRANG
ME TO KISS HIM GOOD-BYE FOR
THE SILLY FOOL/ 155 STRANG
I THINK YOUR HARD-HEADED DAD IS GETTING MUSHY AND 156 STRANG
SILLY/
SHE DIDN'T THINK HE WAS A SILLY FOOL THEN/... 156 STRANG
HE'S SILLY/ 156 STRANG
IT'S SILLY AND INDECENT... 169 STRANG
OH, DON'T BE SILLY/... 188 STRANG
(WITH A SILLY GIGGLE) OO-ER/ 501 VOYAGE
(AS THEY ARE GOING OUT) THIS SILLY BLOKE'LL 'AVE 508 VOYAGE
THE S'PRISE OF 'IS LIFE WHEN
PLEASE--DON'T BE SILLY, MICHAEL. 449 WELDED
IT'S TOO ABSOLUTELY SILLY, YOUR BEING JEALOUS OF 455 WELDED
JOHN.
AND I REFUSE TO GIVE UP HIS FRIENDSHIP FOR YOUR 456 WELDED
SILLY WHIMS.

SILVER
UGLY SIDEBOARD WITH THREE PIECES OF OLD SILVER ON 210 AHWILD
ITS TOP.
(LOOKING AT HIS BIG SILVER WATCH) 96 BEYOND
YER KNOW THEY WASN'T 'ARDLY LIABLE TO GET NO 178 EJONES
SILVER BULLETS.
I SUPPOSE YOU'LL SAY AS THAT SWANK ABOUT THE 178 EJONES
SILVER BULLET AIN'T LUCK--
(WITH A LAUGH) UH, DAT SILVER BULLET/ 178 EJONES
I HAS DE SILVER BULLET MOULDED AND I TELLS 'EM 179 EJONES
WHEN DE TIME COMES I KILLS MYSELF
FIVE LEAD AN' DIS SILVER BABY AT DE LAST. 179 EJONES
WHAT'S THIS I'VE 'EARD ABOUT YER REALLY 'AVING' A 179 EJONES
SILVER BULLET MOULDED FOR
AND TAKES THE SILVER BULLET OUT OF ONE CHAMBER) 179 EJONES
WITH THAT BLOOMIN' SILVER BULLET, WOTS 181 EJONES
(BOASTFULLY) SILVER BULLET BRING ME LUCK ANYWAY, 184 EJONES
(JEERINGLY) HO, I WAS FERGETTIN' THAT SILVER 184 EJONES
BULLET.
SPELLS AND CHARMS TO 'ELP 'EM AGAINST YOUR SILVER 184 EJONES
BULLET.
AND AFTER DAT I GOT DE SILVER BULLET LEFT TO CHEAT184 EJONES
'EM OUT O' GITTIN' ME.
SILVER BULLET AIN'T NONE TOO GOOD FOR HIM WHEN HE 184 EJONES
GO, DAT'S A FAC'/
AND I'SE GOT LITTLE SILVER BULLET O' MY OWN, DON'T185 EJONES
FORGE!/
AH, LAWD, ON'Y DE SILVER ONE LEFT--AN' I GOTTA 198 EJONES
SAVE DAT FO' LUCK.
AIN'T I GOT NO BULLET LEFT ON'Y DE SILVER ONE. 198 EJONES
DE SILVER BULLET/ 202 EJONES
MY MENS DEY GOT UM SILVER BULLETS. 203 EJONES
I COOK UM MONEY, MAKE UM SILVER BULLET, MAKE UM 203 EJONES
STRONG CHARM, TOO.
YOU WAS SCARED TO PUT AFTER 'IM TILL YOU'D MOULDED203 EJONES
SILVER BULLETS, EH!
(THEN WITH A GRIN) SILVER BULLETS/ 204 EJONES
(REACHES IN HIS POCKET AND TOSSES HIM DOWN A 106 ELECTR
SILVER DOLLAR)
SKY AND TRIMMED WITH SILVER LEAVES/ 261 GGBROW
HER SAILS STRETCHING ALOFT ALL SILVER AND WHITE, 214 HA APE
NOT A SOUND ON THE DECK,
AND PLAYING SUCKER FOR EVERY CON MAN WITH A GOLD 141 JOURNE
MINE, OR A SILVER MINE,
YOUR SKIN IS LIKE SILVER IN THE MOON YOUR EYES ARE360 MARCOM
BLACK PEARLS I HAVE WON.
WHILE I AM AWAY EARNING GOLD AND SILVER 361 MARCOM
TEN SOLD IN SILVER. 365 MARCOM
AN IMMENSE OCTAGONAL ROOM, THE LOFTY WALLS ADORNED377 MARCOM
IN GOLD AND SILVER.
ITS ADVANTAGES OVER GOLD AND SILVER COIN ARE 393 MARCOM
OBVIOUS.
DRESSED IN A ROBE OF SILVER AND STANDS AT THE RAIL405 MARCOM
(LOOKING DOWN.)
ON A SILVER THRONE AT CENTER KUKACHIN IS SITTING 407 MARCOM
THEY CARRY SILVER CENSERS WHICH THEY SWING IN 433 MARCOM
UNISON TOWARD THE CORPSE OF THE
I FEEL HER IN THE MOONLIGHT, HER SOUL WRAPPED IN 152 MISBEG
IT LIKE A SILVER MANTLE, AND I
(TO MARY, WHO IS PLAYING CATCH WITH A SILVER 588 ROPE
DOLLAR WHICH SHE HAS HAD CLUTCHED
THAT'S ON'Y A SILVER DOLLAR I GIVE HER WHEN I MET 588 ROPE
HER FRONT OF THE HOUSE.

SIMEON
=SIMEON WINTHROP= AT ANCHOR IN THE OUTER HARBOR OF 25 ANNA
PROVINCETOWN, MASS.
THE INTERIOR OF THE CABIN ON THE BARGE =SIMEON 41 ANNA
WINTHROP= AT DOCK IN BOSTON--

SIMILAR
HELPING ALONG ANOTHER EXHAUSTED MAN SIMILAR 30 ANNA
FASHION.

SIMILAR (CONT'D.)
HE WEARS A UNIFORM SIMILAR TO ANDREW'S. 140 BEYOND
IN FRONT OF TABLE A SIMILAR CHAIR. 541 DAYS
AND THERE IS A SIMILAR WINDOW IN THE UPPER PART OF473 DYNAMO
THE SECTION ON RIGHT.
AS THEIR CHORUS LIFTS HE RISES TO A SITTING 199 EJONES
POSTURE SIMILAR TO THE OTHERS,
OF A SIMILAR SCANDAL-BEARING TYPE, HER TONGUE IS 6 ELECTR
SHARPENED BY MALICE.
HE WEARS A MUSTACHE SIMILAR TO BRANT'S 74 ELECTR
GOWN SIMILAR TO THAT WORN BY CHRISTINE IN ACT 150 ELECTR
THREE OF "HOMECOMING."
UNDER A SIMILAR ARRANGEMENT TO THE ONE I'VE MADE 289 GGBROW
WITH CYBEL
(IN A SIMILAR CALCULATING MOOD) 603 ICEMAN
DRESSED IN SIMILAR STYLE, 615 ICEMAN
FOLLOWED BY CHUCK WITH A SIMILAR HOLD ON GENERAL 650 ICEMAN
WETJOEN.
LEWIS TAKES UP A SIMILAR STAND AT THE WINDOW ON 677 ICEMAN
THE LEFT OF DOOR.)
IN THE LEFT WALL, A SIMILAR SERIES OF WINDOWS 11 JOURNE
LOOKS OUT
HE IS NOT WITH HER AS HE WAS IN THE SIMILAR 71 JOURNE
ENTRANCE AFTER BREAKFAST AT THE
THREE OF THE FEMALES IN SIMILAR TYPE-PERIOD MASKS.336 LAZARU
SIMILARITY
IN CONTRAST TO THIS SIMILARITY BETWEEN THE TWO, 493 DAYS
SIMILARLY
TREATED SIMILARLY TO THAT OF SCENE ONE 274 GGBROW
A TABLE, SIMILARLY PLACED AT REAR OF FRONT TABLES 573 ICEMAN
TWO AND THREE,
ON THE OTHER SIDE, PLACED SIMILARLY IN RELATION TO313 LAZARU
LAZARUS AND FACING MIRIAM,
SIMON
WHAT A SIMPLE-SIMON/... 75 STRANG
SIMP
MAYBE HE WASN'T KIDDIN' AT THAT, THE OLD SIMP/ 545 DIFRNT
TRYIN' TO KID ME, YUH SIMP, YUH$ 234 HA APE
SIMPER
HER STUPID, GOOD-HUMORED FACE WEARS A PLEASED AND 97 JOURNE
FLATTERED SIMPER.
SIMPERING
ABOVE ALL THERE IS SHOWN IN HER SIMPERING, 520 DIFRNT
TALKING IN TONELESS, SIMPERING VOICES. 236 HA APE
SIMPLE
IN MANNER HE IS ALTERNATELY PLAIN SIMPLE BOY 193 AHWILD
TWINKLING WITH A SIMPLE GOOD HUMOR. 5 ANNA
ONLY, HE'S A SIMPLE OLD GUY, SEE$ 19 ANNA
SEEING HIS SIMPLE FRANKNESS, SHE GOES ON 35 ANNA
CONFIDENTLY.)
AND I WOULD NOW--ONLY HE'S SUCH A SIMPLE GUY--A 44 ANNA
BIG KID--
SHE WEARS A SIMPLE WHITE DRESS BUT NO HAT.) 87 BEYOND
RATHER THE ATMOSPHERE IS ONE OF THE ORDERLY 94 BEYOND
COMFORT OF A SIMPLE,
HE IS DRESSED IN THE SIMPLE BLUE UNIFORM AND CAP 130 BEYOND
OF A MERCHANT SHIP'S OFFICER.)
BOTH ARE DRESSED IN SIMPLE BLUE UNIFORMS.) 484 CARDIF
(IRONICALLY) SIMPLE, ISN'T IT$ 960 CROSS
SHE WEARS A SIMPLE NEGLIGEE. 514 DAYS
ELSA WEARS A WHITE EVENING GOWN OF EXTREMELY 532 DAYS
SIMPLE LINES.
HE BOWS HIS HEAD WITH A SIMPLE DIGNITY AND BEGINS 551 DAYS
TO PRAY SILENTLY.)
EBEN'S A DUMB FOOL--LIKE HIS MAW--SOFT AN' SIMPLE/222 DESIRE
(HER EYES MOONING AT HIM, WITH A SIMPLE, PLEASED 457 DYNAMO
SMILE)
AND TO THOSE HE WANTED TO KNOW HE WAS AS PLAIN AND 70 ELECTR
SIMPLE--
WHAT WE NEED MOST IS TO GET BACK TO SIMPLE NORMAL 140 ELECTR
THINGS AND BEGIN A NEW LIFE.
THEY WERE SO SIMPLE AND FINE-- 146 ELECTR
(AGAIN GRATEFUL FOR HIS SIMPLE GOODNESS--LOVINGLY)148 ELECTR
(QUIETLY--WITH SIMPLE DIGNITY NOW) 154 ELECTR
CAN'T YOU BE SIMPLE AND PURE$ 176 ELECTR
SHE IS IN A SIMPLE WHITE DRESS. 262 GGBROW
SIMPLE GUY LIKE HUGHIE WILL ALL OF A SUDDEN GET 21 HUGHIE
SOMETHING RIGHT.
AND THE CURE FOR THEM IS SO DAMNED SIMPLE, ONCE 622 ICEMAN
YOU HAVE THE NERVE.
(HE HAS SAID THIS WITH A SIMPLE PERSUASIVE 639 ICEMAN
EARNESTNESS.
(THEN WITH A SIMPLE EARNESTNESS, TAKING A CHAIR BY641 ICEMAN
LARRY.
NO, I GAVE YOU THE SIMPLE TRUTH ABOUT THAT. 658 ICEMAN
HE ADDRESSES THEM NOW WITH THE SIMPLE, 660 ICEMAN
(HE STOPS, LOOKING AROUND AT THEM WITH A SIMPLE, 663 ICEMAN
GENTLE FRANKNESS.
HER MOST APPEALING QUALITY IS THE SIMPLE, 13 JOURNE
HE IS BY NATURE AND PREFERENCE A SIMPLE 13 JOURNE
UNPRETENTIOUS MAN.
SHE WEARS THE DRESS INTO WHICH SHE HAD CHANGED FOR 97 JOURNE
HER DRIVE TO TOWN, A SIMPLE,
AT THE SAME TIME HE WAS SIMPLE, AND KIND, AND 105 JOURNE
UNASSUMING.
THE SIMPLE, IGNORANT... 273 LAZARU
(A SIMPLE BOY--IN A FRIGHTENED WHISPER AFTER A 275 LAZARU
PAUSE OF DEAD SILENCE)
THE MOTHER IS TALL AND STOUT, OVER SIXTY-FIVE, A 275 LAZARU
GENTLE, SIMPLE WOMAN.
ALL ARE OF THE SIMPLE, IGNORANT TYPE.) 291 LAZARU
THEY ARE IN THE PERIOD OF MANHOOD, OF THE SIMPLE, 320 LAZARU
IGNORANT TYPE.
(HE GRINS HORRIBLY) IT IS ALL VERY SIMPLE, AS YOU356 LAZARU
SEE/
THE PERIOD AT THE CLOSE OF A SIMPLE SENTENCE, SAY. 30 MANSNS
WHEREAS IT IS VERY SIMPLE--YOU WANT SARA-- 94 MANSNS

SIMPLE (CONT'D.)
AND THEN, OF COURSE, IT WOULD BE SO SIMPLE TO HAVE163 MANSNS
ME LOCKED UP IN AN ASYLUM--
(TEDALDO, WITH A SIMPLE DIGNITY AND POWER, BLESSE5362 MARCOM
THEM.
THE PEOPLE ARE SIMPLE CREATURES. 365 MARCOM
THE PEOPLE ON THE OTHER SIDE OF THAT WALL MAY LOOK374 MARCOM
SIMPLE BUT THEY'RE NOT.
A VENERABLE OLD MAN WITH WHITE HAIR, DRESSED IN A 377 MARCOM
SIMPLE BLACK ROBE.
IT'S SO SIMPLE--AND YET, WHO EVER THOUGHT OF IT 394 MARCOM
BEFORE ME$
SIMPLE HOME REMEDIES--FROM THE BEST FRIEND I EVER 412 MARCOM
HAD/
I WOULD I HAD THE GIFT OF ORATORY TO THANK YOU 431 MARCOM
FITTINGLY, BUT I AM A SIMPLE MAN,
HE WEARS A SIMPLE WHITE ROBE WITHOUT ADORNMENT OF 432 MARCOM
ANY SORT.
A SIMPLE OLD MAN DYING CONTENTEDLY A LITTLE, DAY 437 MARCOM
AFTER PLEASANT DAY.
HE SOBS LIKE A SIMPLE OLD MAN. 438 MARCOM
(AGAIN WITH A STRANGE, SIMPLE GRATITUDE) 133 MISBEG
SHE WAS SIMPLE AND KIND AND PURE OF HEART. 151 MISBEG
AND MAKES HER LOVABLE, A SIMPLE SWEETNESS AND 20 POET
CHARM,
BUT SHE FEELS HER SIMPLE CHARM AND GENTLENESS, AND 74 POET
RETURNS HER SMILE.)
(IMPATIENTLY.) DON'T BE SO SIMPLE, MOTHER. 79 POET
YOU ARE VERY SIMPLE-MINDED, MY DEAR, 106 POET
THEN YUH'RE SIMPLE-- 593 ROPE
THAT'S WHAT--SIMPLE/ 593 ROPE
AW, SAY, YOU'RE SIMPLE/ 600 ROPE
CHARLIE, AND IT'LL BE SO SIMPLE AND EASY TO 21 STRANG
UNDERSTAND THAT I WON'T BE ABLE TO
SIMPLE, HEALTHY PEOPLE. I'M SURE OF THAT ALTHOUGH 38 STRANG
I'VE NEVER MET THEM.
OR EVEN A GOOD MAN PREACHING THE SIMPLE PLATITUDES 41 STRANG
OF TRUTH, THOSE GOSPEL WORDS
(WITH SIMPLE SURPRISE) NEDS 45 STRANG
WHAT A SIMPLE-SIMON/... 75 STRANG
IT IS A LARGE, SUNNY ROOM, THE FURNITURE EXPENSIVE137 STRANG
BUT EXTREMELY SIMPLE.
WEALTH, JOVIAL AND SIMPLE AND GOOD-NATURED AS 159 STRANG
EVER.
A PURE AND SIMPLE SOUL/ 183 STRANG
(HE KISSES ONE OF THE ROSES WITH A SIMPLE 187 STRANG
SENTIMENTAL SMILE--
TOO SIMPLE FOR THE COMPLICATED,-- 476 WELDED
EVERYTHING, FOR THIS SECOND, BECOMES SIMPLE FOR 488 WELDED
THEM--
SIMPLER
BUILT ON A SQUARER, SIMPLER MODEL, FLESHIER IN 203 DESIRE
BODY,
THE OPENING OF ONE OF CHOPIN'S SIMPLER WALTZES, 169 JOURNE
DONE WITH
(TO SIMON.) BUT I THINK, DEAR, IT MIGHT BE SIMPLER186 MANSNS
FOR US TO LEAVE HER NOW.
SIMPLETON
IF SHE WERE MARRIED TO THIS SIMPLETON WOULD SHE BE 33 STRANG
FAITHFUL$...
(WHAT A POOR SIMPLETON SAM IS/...... 116 STRANG
SAM IS A SIMPLETON... 125 STRANG
SIMPLETON'S
AND THE POOR SIMPLETON'S NAIVE FAITH WAS A BIT 510 DAYS
SHAKEN,
SIMPLICITY
(WITH GREAT SIMPLICITY) 249 DESIRE
(WITH NAIVE SIMPLICITY) YES, OF COURSE IT HAS, 479 DYNAMO
RAMSAY.
SHE ASKS WITH DISARMING SIMPLICITY. 51 ELECTR
(HE ADDS WITH A STRANGE IMPRESSIVE SIMPLICITY) 706 ICEMAN
WE MUST RETURN TO NATURE AND SIMPLICITY AND THEN 9 MANSNS
WE'LL FIND THAT THE PEOPLE--
BUT POSSESSING AN ATMOSPHERE OF ALOOF DIGNITY AND 384 MARCOM
SIMPLICITY
THAT GOT SUCH WONDERFUL RESULTS IS SIMPLICITY 392 MARCOM
ITSELF.
HER SLENDER, FRAGILE BODY IS DRESSED IN WHITE WITH 68 POET
CALCULATED SIMPLICITY.
SIMPLY
(SIMPLY) I DO, ANNIE/ 549 'ILE
SOME OF THE THINGS I SIMPLY COULDN'T READ, THEY 198 AHWILD
WERE SO INDECENT--ALL ABOUT--
JUST SIMPLY COULDN'T RESIST IT/ 222 AHWILD
WHY, IT'S SIMPLY STAGGERING/ 225 AHWILD
THEIR MINDS SIMPLY DON'T KNOW WHAT LOGIC IS/ 266 AHWILn
(SIMPLY AND PROUDLY) RICHARD WON'T LIE. 267 AHWILD
(SIMPLY) YES, NAT. 298 AHWILn
(THEN SIMPLY--GLANCING DOWN HIS ARM PROUDLY) 35 ANNA
(THEN RAISING HIS EYES TO HERS--SIMPLY) 38 ANNA
BUT SIMPLY TWISTS HIS RIGHT HAND BEHIND HIS BACK 49 ANNA
(SIMPLY) FOR I'VE A POWER OF STRENGTH IN ME TO 74 ANNA
LEAD MEN THE WAY I WANT,
(SIMPLY) I LOVE YOU. 90 BEYOND
(LOOKING AT THE FLOOR--SIMPLY) 105 BEYOND
(WIPING HER EYES--SIMPLY) JAMES WAS A GOOD MAN. 114 BEYOND
(SIMPLY) NO. I'M DYING. 167 BEYOND
ADDS SIMPLY) 508 DAYS
IT'S SIMPLY THAT I'VE GROWN SICK OF MY LIFE, 519 DAYS
YOU SIMPLY DON'T KNOW JOHN, THAT'S ALL. 522 DAYS
I PROPOSED QUITE FRANKLY THAT WE SHOULD SIMPLY 523 DAYS
LIVE TOGETHER AND EACH KEEP
YOU SIMPLY MUST KEEP JOHN COMPANY FOR A FEW 525 DAYS
MINUTES.
WE'RE SIMPLY GOING TO INSIST. 533 DAYS
HE'S SIMPLY LOOKING FOR AN EXCUSE 533 DAYS
YOU FORGET I'M SIMPLY FOLLOWING WHAT THIS MAN TOLD5534 DAYS
ME.

SIMPLY

SIMPLY (CONT'D.)

I SIMPLY WENT FOR A WALK. 549 DAYS
(SIMPLY) AY-EH. 232 DESIRE
(SIMPLY) MAW. 241 DESIRE
(SIMPLY) SHE WENT BACK T' HER GRAVE THAT NIGHT WE261 DESIRE
JUST DONE IT, REMEMBERS
I'M SIMPLY HAVING FUN KIDDING HIM ALONG. 432 DYNAMO
POP SIMPLY COPIED THAT STORY-- 451 DYNAMO
BUT GOD WAS SIMPLY USING REUBEN TO BRING 451 DYNAMO
RETRIBUTION ON YOUR HEAD/
(SIMPLY) RAMSAY'LL BE GLAD. 458 DYNAMO
(SIMPLY) OF COURSE, YOU LOVE ADA--AND YOU 478 DYNAMO
SHOULDN'T ACT SO MEAN TO HER, REUBEN.
(SIMPLY) YES, YOU'VE GOT TO DO THE RIGHT THING BY480 DYNAMO
ADA, REUBEN.
OH, ADA, YOU SIMPLY CAN'T HELP BELIEVING IN HER/ 482 DYNAMO
(SIMPLY STATING A FACT) YES. 203 EJONES
AND I SIMPLY COULDN'T BELIEVE THAT HE EVER WOULD 37 ELECTR
COME HOME.
HE'D SIMPLY FEEL BOUND TO DO HIS DUTY AS A FORMER 38 ELECTR
JUDGE AND HAVE YOU ARRESTED/
I SIMPLY CAN'T REALIZE HE'S DEAD YET. 74 ELECTR
BUT LAVINIA SIMPLY STARES AT HER, FROZEN AND 77 ELECTR
SILENT.
YOU SIMPLY WOULDN'T BELIEVE IT, IF I TOLD YOU SOME 86 ELECTR
OF THE THINGS.
IT SIMPLY STRUCK ME HE LOOKS SO STRANGELY 94 ELECTR
FAMILIAR--
SIMPLY BECAUSE HE USED TO SMILE AT ME AND I SMILED147 ELECTR
BACK.
I SIMPLY THINK, AND I'D SAY IT TO HER FACE, THAT 158 ELECTR
SHE'S A BAD INFLUENCE FOR ORIN.
I LOVE EVERYTHING THAT GROWS SIMPLY--UP TOWARD THE167 ELECTR
SUN--
(SUDDENLY--PLEADING) YOU SIMPLY MUST SEND HIM TO 260 GGBROW
COLLEGE/
WELL, IF YOU SIMPLY GOT TO BE A REGULAR DEVIL LIKE279 GGBROW
ALL THE OTHER VISITING SPURTS
WHY, BELIEVE--I SIMPLY WON'T BELIEVE--AFTER ALL 305 GGBROW
THESE YEARS.
HE SIMPLY WASN'T RESPONSIBLE. 311 GGBROW
HE SIMPLY DROOPS AND STARES ACQUIESCENTLY AT 7 HUGHIE
NOTHING.
BUT SIMPLY THE REAR OF THE BARROOM DIVIDED FROM 571 ICEMAN
THE BAR
I SIMPLY HAVEN'T THE HEART. 603 ICEMAN
I KNOW IT'S HARD TO BELIEVE BUT--{HE PAUSES--THEN 620 ICEMAN
ADDS SIMPLY}
YOU SIMPLY WON'T GIVE A DAMN/ 641 ICEMAN
BUT IT SIMPLY HAD TO BE DONE/ 660 ICEMAN
{HE PAUSES--THEN ADDS SIMPLY} 706 ICEMAN
(SIMPLY) SO I KILLED HER. 716 ICEMAN
HE SPEAKS SIMPLY AND GRATEFULLY. 720 ICEMAN
UT BEGINS WID SIMPLY THE NAME SIDNEY DAVIDSON-- 531 INZONE
SHE IS DRESSED SIMPLY BUT WITH A SURE SENSE OF 12 JOURNE
WHAT BECOMES.
I KEEP TELLING HIM THAT BUT HE SAYS HE SIMPLY HAS 16 JOURNE
NO APPETITE.
YOU'RE SIMPLY DELIGHTED/ 25 JOURNE
NOT ABOUT ANYTHING SERIOUS, SIMPLY LAUGH AND 46 JOURNE
GOSSIP AND FORGET FOR A WHILE--
{EXCITEDLY.} IT'S SIMPLY A WASTE OF TIME AND 92 JOURNE
MONEY SEEING HIM.
SIMPLY AND WITHOUT SELF-CONSCIOUSNESS, THE NAIVE, 97 JOURNE
HAPPY.
I'M SIMPLY REPEATING WHAT I WAS TOLD. 149 JOURNE
IT IS SIMPLY A PART OF THE FAMILIAR ATMOSPHERE OF 171 JOURNE
THE ROOM.
SIMPLY BUT WITH A BITTER SADNESS.) 173 JOURNE
THAT I MUST PROVE IT WASN'T SIMPLY MY IMAGINATION.175 JOURNE
BUT I KNEW IT WAS SIMPLY A WASTE OF TIME. 176 JOURNE
{LOOKING DOWN AT HIM NOW--WITH A SMILE, SIMPLY} 292 LAZARU
AGAIN SAYS SIMPLY AND ACCEPTINGLY) 293 LAZARU
(SIMPLY, WITH A TRACE OF A SAD STERNNESS) 294 LAZARU
(SIMPLY) YES, CAESAR. 341 LAZARU
(SIMPLY) I HEAR, TIBERIUS. 355 LAZARU
ROUSSEAU WAS SIMPLY HIDING FROM HIMSELF IN A 47 MANSNS
SUPERIOR, IDEALISTIC DREAM--
WHO ARE SO SIMPLY AND PASSIONATELY CONSCIOUS OF 47 MANSNS
LIFE AS IT IS,
PURELY AND SIMPLY AS A BUSINESS DEAL. 58 MANSNS
I SIMPLY WANTED TO BE SURE.= 108 MANSNS
OR I MIGHT SIMPLY GO AWAY--FOR A LONG, MUCH-NEEDED149 MANSNS
REST.
OH GOD, THINK OF HOW SIMPLY CONTENTED WE COULD BE 171 MANSNS
ALONE TOGETHER.
WHY NOT SIMPLY EXPLAIN TO THE GREAT KAAN, KUBLAI, 359 MARCOM
I SIMPLY REVERSED THE OLD SYSTEM. 392 MARCOM
{RETURNING HIS LOOK--SIMPLY} 397 MARCOM
(SIMPLY) OH, NO. 416 MARCOM
WAY, SUNBURNT AND HEALTHY, BEGINNING TO TAKE ON 56 MISBEG
FAT, HE IS SIMPLY IMMATURE.
{RELAXES--SIMPLY AND GRATEFULLY} 103 MISBEG
(SIMPLY) THANKS, JOSIE. 105 MISBEG
THEN TAKES ONE OF HER HANDS IN BOTH OF HIS-- 129 MISBEG
SIMPLY)
(SIMPLY) THANKS, JOSIE. 129 MISBEG
JOSIE--{GIVES THE CHARACTERISTIC SHRUG OF HIS 140 MISBEG
SHOULDERS--SIMPLY}
(SIMPLY) THANKS, JOSIE. 141 MISBEG
(SIMPLY) YOU MEAN I LOOKED DEAD& 142 MISBEG
{LETS HIS HEAD FALL BACK ON HER BREAST--SIMPLY} 152 MISBEG
(SIMPLY) YES, I KNOW SHE--{HIS VOICE BREAKS.} 152 MISBEG
{HER FACE CLEARING--SIMPLY} I'M GLAD, JIM. 172 MISBEG
AND BUILD HIS OWN CABIN, AND DO ALL THE WORK, AND 29 POET
SUPPORT HIMSELF SIMPLY,
(SIMPLY.) I AM, MOTHER. 31 POET

SIMPLY (CONT'D.)

BUT SIMPLY SHUTS THE DOOR BEHIND HIM. HE SCOWLS 66 POET
WITH DISGUST.)
THEY SIMPLY FORGOT TO KILL HIM. 83 POET
(SIMPLY.) HE WILL, SURELY. 173 POET
I'VE THOUGHT IT ALL OUT AND DECIDED THAT I SIMPLY 14 STRANG
YOU'VE SIMPLY GOT TO. IF YOU LOVE ME/ 44 STRANG
THEREFORE YOU'D SIMPLY ADORE IT. 49 STRANG
{SHE PRESSES MRS. EVANS' HAND--SIMPLY} YES, 57 STRANG
MOTHER.
{THEN VERY SIMPLY} HE LOVED CHILDREN SO, MY POOR 63 STRANG
HUSBAND DID.
BUT SIMPLY GOT TO WORK OUT SOMETHING OR... 67 STRANG
(SIMPLY) I THINK IT IS. 80 STRANG
I SIMPLY CAN'T BELIEVE/ 83 STRANG
SHE SIMPLY DISAPPROVES....)) 99 STRANG
YOU'RE SIMPLY LETTING YOUR ROMANTIC IMAGINATION 102 STRANG
RUNAWAY WITH YOU--
YOU'RE SIMPLY SHIRKING, CHARLIE/. 114 STRANG
I'VE SIMPLY NEVER CARED TO DEGRADE MYSELF/....)) 117 STRANG
(SIMPLY, EVEN MATTER-OF-FACTLY) 131 STRANG
(SIMPLY) SAM WILL NEVER KNOW. 132 STRANG
IF I HADN'T HE'D SIMPLY HAVE HUNG AROUND ME YEAR 139 STRANG
AFTER YEAR, DOING NOTHING...))
I SIMPLY CAN'T GO HIM ANYMORE, NINA/ 146 STRANG
EVANS IS SIMPLY EVANS. 159 STRANG
I SIMPLY CAN'T BELIEVE HE REALLY LOVES HER/ 168 STRANG
(SIMPLY) I NEEDED TO BE ABLE TO HOPE THAT, THEN. 172 STRANG
AND SHE SIMPLY WANTED TO BE REVENGED, I'M SURE. 172 STRANG
{STARING BEFORE HER AS IF SHE WERE IN A TRANCE-- 179 STRANG
SIMPLY, LIKE A YOUNG GIRL}
I SIMPLY THOUGHT YOU MEANT-- 186 STRANG
{IMPLORINGLY} YOU'VE SIMPLY GOT TO READ ME THAT 445 WELDED
LAST ACT RIGHT NOW/
(SIMPLY) YES, I MEANT IT. 463 WELDED
AT ONCE CONTROLLING THIS--SIMPLY) 463 WELDED
AFTER A PAUSE HE ASKS SIMPLY) 482 WELDED
(AFTER A PAUSE--SIMPLY) I COULDN'T. 484 WELDED
(SIMPLY) SOMETHING STRONGER. 485 WELDED

SIMPS

YOUSE SIMPS DON'T MOVE. 238 HA APE
JEES, CAN YUH BEAT DEM SIMPS/ 677 ICEMAN

SIMULACRA

MOCKERY OF UNDIGNIFIED AGE SNATCHING GREEDILY AT 520 DIFRNT
THE EMPTY SIMULACRA OF YOUTH.

SIMULATION

{TURNS AROUND WITH AN ELABORATE SIMULATION OF 278 AHWILD
BEING DISTURBED
{HURRIES ON WITH A SIMULATION OF FRANKNESS} 517 DAYS
AND SPEAK WITH A SIMULATION OF OUTRAGED FEELING.} 63 ELECTR

SIMULTANEOUS

WITH SUCH RAPIDITY THAT THE TWO SHOTS ARE ALMOST 198 EJONES
SIMULTANEOUS.

SIMULTANEOUSLY

SIMULTANEOUSLY REUBEN'S VOICE RISES 488 DYNAMO
{THEY BOTH SPEAK TO EACH OTHER SIMULTANEOUSLY.. 123 MANSNS
THEN SIMULTANEOUSLY THE TWO FIRMS ADVANCE TO MEET 365 MARCOM
EACH OTHER

SIN

BUT HE DOES NOT WIN WHO PLAYS WITH SIN IN THE 246 AHWILD
SECRET HOUSE OF SHAME/=
I KNOW YOU HAVE THE MOST VIVID RECOLLECTION OF HIS494 DAYS
TERRIBLE SIN.
{SNEERINGLY} YOUR TERRIBLE SIN BEGINS TO CLOSE INS13 DAYS
ON YOU, EH&
{STRANGELY} HE KNOWS SHE KNOWS OF HIS SIN NOW. 544 DAYS
{MOCKINGLY} NAGGIN' HIS SHEEP T' SIN/ 227 DESIRE
{SHAKING HER HEAD} I GOT T' TAKE MY PUNISHMENT-- 266 DESIRE
T' PAY FUR MY SIN.
HE WAS THE CHILD O' OUR SIN. 266 DESIRE
I DON'T REPENT THAT SIN/ 266 DESIRE
I GOT T' PAY FUR MY PART O' THE SIN/ 267 DESIRE
I'M HARDENED IN SIN SO FAR'S THEY'RE CONCERNED. 495 DIFRNT
AND I RECKON HE'S AS LIKELY TO SIN THAT WAY AS ANYS09 DIFRNT
OTHER MAN.
HE DOESN'T FEEL ANY CALL TO THE MINISTRY AND I 424 DYNAMO
THINK IT WOULD BE A GREAT SIN IF--
UP ON THEN LYING IN EACH OTHER'S ARMS--IN SIN, AS 440 DYNAMO
YOU'D CALL IT--
AND THE DEVIL KNOWS WHAT SIN YOU'LL THINK IT IN 441 DYNAMO
THE SIGHT OF GOD/
I DIDN'T MEAN SIN/...)) 444 DYNAMO
{EAH, WHAT IS SIN, ANYWAYS... 444 DYNAMO
SCARED WHAT WE DID WAS A SINS 469 DYNAMO
WHAT PEOPLE CALL LOVE IS JUST SEX--AND THERE'S NO 469 DYNAMO
SIN ABOUT IT/
WASHING ALL DIRT AND SIN AWAY/ 476 DYNAMO
THAT I WAS LIVING IN SIN-- 478 DYNAMO
AND THEY LIVE IN AS NEAR THE GARDEN OF PARADISE 24 ELECTR
BEFORE SIN WAS DISCOVERED AS
THAT LOVE CAN BE A SIN. 24 ELECTR
THE NATIVES DANCING NAKED AND INNOCENT--WITHOUT 147 ELECTR
KNOWLEDGE OF SIN/
CAN'T YOU FORGET SIN AND SEE THAT ALL LOVE IS 176 ELECTR
BEAUTIFUL&
I WANTED TO LEARN LOVE FROM HIM--LOVE THAT WASN'T 177 ELECTR
A SIN/
{HE LAUGHS} BUT PRIDE IS A SIN--EVEN IN A MEMORY 287 GGBROW
OF THE LONG DECEASED/
WE DON'T WANT TO TEMPT HIM INTO SIN. 620 ICEMAN
IT IS A FOUL SIN IN THE SIGHT OF JEHOVAH/ 282 LAZARU
IS IT A SIN TO BE BORN A DREAMER& 347 LAZARU
THEN I'LL HAVE TO STEAL IT, AND THAT'S A WORSE 355 MARCOM
SIN.
{GENUELY} IT'S A SIN, I'M SURE OF IT. 355 MARCOM
SIN IS PRACTICALLY UNSEEN. 393 MARCOM
TRUST HIMSELF, AND IT'D BE A SIN ON HIS CONSCIENCE 90 MISBEG
IF HE WAS TO SEDUCE YOU.

SINCE

SIN (CONT'D.)
(FORCING A PLAYFUL TONE) FOR THE SIN OF WANTING 104 MISBEG
TO BE IN BED WITH ME.
PRIDE IS THE SIN BY WHICH THE ANGELS FELL. 134 MISBEG
NUTS WITH THAT SIN BUNK, BUT YOU KNOW WHAT I MEAN.171 MISBEG
(THEN EXASPERATEDLY.) DAMN YOUR PRIESTS' PRATING 61 POET
ABOUT YOUR SIN!
AND YOU CAN'T HELP REMEMBERING MY SIN WITH YOU. 61 POET
THEY CAN'T HELP SEEING SIN HIDING UNDER EVERY 90 POET
BUSH.
AND I HAVE THE BLACK TORMINT IN MY MIND THAT IT'S 138 POET
THE FAULT OF THE MORTAL SIN
BUT IT'S A MORTAL SIN. 149 POET
YOU SAYIN' IT WAS A SIN TO MARRY A PAPIST, 580 ROPE
IT'D BE A SIN, ADULTERY, THE WORST SIN/- 63 STRANG
AND ME BEING PUNISHED WITH THEM FOR NO SIN BUT 64 STRANG
LOVING MUCH.

SIN'S
SINNED 'EM WITH, MY SIN'S AS PURTY AS ANY ONE ON 211 DESIRE
'EM/

SINCE
THESE LAST SIX YEARS SINCE WE WERE MARRIED-- 545 'ILE
WAITING, AND WATCHING, AND FEARING--
YOU SEE--I'VE ALWAYS DONE IT--SINCE MY FIRST 547 'ILE
VOYAGE AS SKIPPER.
SID'S A REFORMED CHARACTER SINCE HE'S BEEN ON THE 190 AHWILD
PAPER IN WATERBURY.
IT'S ABOUT IBSEN, THE GREATEST PLAYWRIGHT SINCE 197 AHWILD
SHAKESPEARE/
THE GREATEST POET SINCE SHELLEY/ 198 AHWILD
IT'S BEEN SIXTEEN YEARS SINCE I BROKE OFF OUR 213 AHWILD
ENGAGEMENT.
NO I'VE BEEN AT THE RANDS' EVER SINCE DINNER. 254 AHWILD
IT SEEMS AGES SINCE WE'VE BEEN TOGETHER/ 279 AHWILD
YOU KNOW, MARTHY, AY'VE TOLE YOU AY DON'T SEE MY 9 ANNA
ANNA SINCE SHE VAS LITTLE GEL
AND I AIN'T SPOKE A WORD WITH NO ONE SINCE DAY 15 ANNA
BEFORE YESTERDAY.
NOT SINCE THIS MORNING ON THE TRAIN. 15 ANNA
I AIN'T SEEN HIM SINCE I WAS A KID--DON'T EVEN 16 ANNA
KNOW WHAT HE LOOKS LIKE--
BUT I DO BE THINKING IVER SINCE THE FIRST LOOK MY 33 ANNA
EYES TOOK AT YOU.
SINCE I WAS GROWED TO A MAN. 34 ANNA
IN THE STOKEHOLES OF SHIPS SINCE I WAS A LAD ONLY. 35 ANNA
SINCE THE DAY I LEFT HOME FOR TO GO TO SEA 37 ANNA
PUNCHING COAL.
(SHE TURNS TO BURKE) YOU TELL ME, MAT, SINCE HE 51 ANNA
DON'T WANT TO.
WAS IT FOR THIS HE'D HAVE ME ROAMING THE EARTH 60 ANNA
SINCE I WAS A LAD ONLY.
FOR IT'S A ROTTEN DOG'S LIFE I'VE LIVED THE PAST 69 ANNA
TWO DAYS SINCE I'VE KNOWN WHAT
HE'S BEEN DREAMING OVER THIS TRIP EVER SINCE IT 96 BEYOND
WAS FIRST TALKED ABOUT.
(IGNORING THIS REMARK) WHAT I WAS SAYIN' WAS THAT114 BEYOND
SINCE ROBERT'S BEEN IN CHARGE
EVER SINCE YOUR HUSBAND DIED TWO YEARS BACK. 114 BEYOND
I'VE OFTEN THOUGHT SINCE IT MIGHT HAVE BEEN BETTER116 BEYOND
THE OTHER WAY.
YOU KNOW THE ODDS I'VE BEEN UP AGAINST SINCE PA 123 BEYOND
DIED.
THERE'S BEEN A CURSE ON IT EVER SINCE YOU TOOK 127 BEYOND
HOLD.
I'VE BEEN FEELING SORT OF AWKWARD EVER SINCE I'VE 134 BEYOND
BEEN HOME.
ESPECIALLY THE LAST EIGHT MONTHS SINCE MARY--DIED.147 BEYOND
BUT HE'S BEEN AILIN' EVER SINCE MARY DIED--EIGHT 154 BEYOND
MONTHS AGO.
HE NEVER TOOK ANY INTEREST SINCE WAY BACK WHEN 155 BEYOND
YOUR MA DIED.
WE'VE NEVER SPOKE A WORD ABOUT IT SINCE THAT DAY. 165 BEYOND
IT'S YOU WHO'LL HAVE TO DO THE LYING, SINCE IT 165 BEYOND
MUST BE DONE.
AND WE'VE STUCK TOGETHER IVER SINCE THROUGH GOOD 480 CARDIF
LUCK AND BAD.
FIVE YEARS AND MORE UT IS SINCE FIRST I SHIPPED 480 CARDIF
WID HIM.
OR TIMES HAS CHANGED SINCE I PUT IN HERE LAST. 458 CARIBE
I'VE HEARD ABOUT HIM FROM ALL SIDES SINCE I FIRST 557 CROSS
CAME TO THE ASYLUM YONDER.
EVER SINCE THEM FOOLS ON THE SLOCUM TATTLED 568 CROSS
I HAVEN'T SEEN HIM SINCE I WAS A BOY. 499 DAYS
AND EVER SINCE THEN I'VE HEARD NOTHING BUT THE 504 DAYS
PRAISES OF ELSA--
AS I HAVE EVERY DAY SINCE I LEFT YOU. 507 DAYS
THE DREAD OF IT HAS HAUNTED ME EVER SINCE WE WERE 509 DAYS
MARRIED.
NOT SINCE BEFORE I WENT TO BOSTON IN FEBRUARY. 516 DAYS
THAT'S HOW I'VE FELT EVER SINCE. 521 DAYS
BUT IT'S NOT PROVING TO ME HOW YOU CAN BE SO 523 DAYS
CERTAIN THAT NEVER SINCE THEN--
AND I THINK WE'VE LIVED UP TO THAT IDEAL EVER 524 DAYS
SINCE.
BEEN A LONG TIME SINCE WE'VE HAD THIS PLEASURE. 525 DAYS
EVER SINCE I CAME BACK FROM BOSTON. 529 DAYS
HE WAS HAPPY AGAIN FOR THE FIRST TIME SINCE HIS 535 DAYS
PARENTS' DEATH--
(FINALLY SPEAKS QUIETLY) JACK, EVER SINCE WE CAME543 DAYS
UPSTAIRS.
MORE, NOT SINCE HE MARRIED EBEN'S MAW. 205 DESIRE
YE BEEN FIGHTIN' YER NATURE EVER SINCE THE DAY I 229 DESIRE
COME--
IT HAIN'T BEEN OPENED SINCE MAW DIED AN' WAS LAID 240 DESIRE
OUT THAR/
NOW--SINCE YEW COME--SEEMS LIKE IT'S GROWIN' SOFT 242 DESIRE
AN' KIND T' ME.

SINCE (CONT'D.)
I BEEN DYIN' FUR WANT O' YE--EVERY HOUR SINCE YE 244 DESIRE
COME/
(MEANINGLY) SEEMS LIKE HE'S SPENT MOST O' HIS 248 DESIRE
TIME T' HUM SINCE YEW COME.
YE'VE BEEN LYIN' T' ME EVERY WORD YE SPOKE, DAY 256 DESIRE
AN' NIGHT, SINCE WE FUST--
I HAIN'T FELT HER ABOUT SINCE. 261 DESIRE
CALEB'S SISTER AND LIVIN' RIGHT NEXT DOOR EVER 507 DIFRNT
SINCE YOU WAS ALL CHILDREN
SINCE YOU WAS OLD ENOUGH TO KNOW, YOU'D OUGHT TO 509 DIFRNT
REALIZE WHAT MEN BE.
EVER SINCE YOU WAS CHILDREN YOU BEEN LIVIN' SIDE 512 DIFRNT
BY SIDE, GOIN' ROUND TOGETHER.
EVER SINCE WE WAS LITTLE I GUESS I'VE ALWAYS HAD 516 DIFRNT
THIS IDEA THAT YOU WAS--
SINCE YOU WAS OVERSEAS. 520 DIFRNT
I'VE HATED HIM EVER SINCE PA DIED AND MA AND ME 521 DIFRNT
HAD TO GO LIVE NEXT DOOR WITH
GEE, YOU'VE HAD THIS OLD PLACE FIXED UP SWELL 524 DIFRNT
SINCE I WAS TO HOME LAST.
ESPECIALLY SINCE YOU'VE BEEN TO HOME THESE LAST 524 DIFRNT
FEW TIMES AND COME TO CALL SO
SINCE SHE WAS A GIRL. 525 DIFRNT
UH, YOU'RE LOW, YOU'RE LOW ALL THROUGH LIKE YOUR 528 DIFRNT
PA WAS--AND SINCE YOU
SINCE I WAS A KID. 533 DIFRNT
YOU AIN'T SEEN THIS ROOM SINCE, HAVE YOUR 535 DIFRNT
AIN'T I BROUGHT HIM UP IN MY OWN HOUSE SINCE HE 540 DIFRNT
WAS KNEE-HIGH
AND SINCE YOU'VE THROWED HIM OUT OF HIS HOUSE IN 542 DIFRNT
YOUR MAD JEALOUSNESS/
FIFE, HAS BEEN SINCE THE DEVIL BROUGHT HIM NEXT 423 DYNAMO
DOOR/...))
AND WE'VE ALL BEEN HAPPY EVER SINCE...)) 430 DYNAMO
GOSH, HOW LONG IS IT SINCE I PUT ON THAT 430 DYNAMO
RECORDS...
YOU'VE KEPT A GRUDGE AGAINST HIM EVER SINCE THE 455 DYNAMO
NIGHT THAT LIGHT BOY--
EVER SINCE THAT NIGHT HE HAS BEEN DEAD FOR ME... 456 DYNAMO
SHE'S BEEN SORRY ABOUT IT EVER SINCE. 458 DYNAMO
I'VE LEARNED A LOT ABOUT LOVE SINCE I LEFT--AND I 460 DYNAMO
GET YOU NOW, ALL RIGHT/
EVER SINCE I CAN REMEMBER THE CELLAR'S LEAKED LIKE464 DYNAMO
A SIEVE.
(STRANGELY) NOT LATELY--NOT SINCE I GAVE UP 478 DYNAMO
SEEING ADA.
HE HASN'T CHANGED SINCE HIS LAST APPEARANCE. 478 DYNAMO
YOU HAVEN'T GIVE MUCH 'EED TO YOUR BAPTIST CHURCH 185 EJONES
SINCE YOU'VE BEEN DOWN 'ERE.
NOT SINCE THE LETTER I SHOWED YOU. 13 ELECTR
I WOULDN'T LOSE YOU AS A BROTHER FOR ANYTHING 14 ELECTR
WE'VE BEEN LIKE THAT EVER SINCE WE
SINCE HAZEL'S TEASING STATEMENT, 14 ELECTR
AND SINCE WHEN HAVE YOU THE RIGHT WITHOUT 17 ELECTR
CONSULTING ME/
SINCE THE DAY HE LEFT-- 19 ELECTR
I HAVE--EVER SINCE I FIRST SAW HIM--BUT I'VE NEVER 19 ELECTR
BEEN ABLE TO PLACE WHO--
I HAVEN'T HAD A CHANCE TO BE ALONE WITH YOU 21 ELECTR
SINCE--
IT'S ONLY SINCE YOU SUSPECTED WHO I WAS/ 25 ELECTR
I'VE ALWAYS GUESSED THAT, MOTHER--EVER SINCE I WAS 31 ELECTR
LITTLE--
I'VE FELT IT EVER SINCE I CAN REMEMBER--YOUR 31 ELECTR
DISGUST/
IT'S YOU WHO HAVE STOLEN ALL LOVE FROM ME SINCE 33 ELECTR
THE TIME I WAS BORN/
I'VE WATCHED YOU EVER SINCE YOU WERE LITTLE, 33 ELECTR
SOMETHING I'VE BEEN THINKING OF EVER SINCE I 40 ELECTR
REALIZED HE MIGHT SOON COME HOME.
THAT IS, SINCE WE'VE BEEN MARRIED. 53 ELECTR
AS YOU'VE ALWAYS DONE SINCE OUR FIRST MARRIAGE 60 ELECTR
NIGHT/
SHE HASN'T SPOKEN A SINGLE WORD SINCE HER FATHER'S 72 ELECTR
DEATH/
EVERYTHING HAS SEEMED QUEER SINCE I CAME BACK TO 74 ELECTR
EARTH.
YOU'VE HARDLY SPOKEN A WORD SINCE YOU MET ME. 75 ELECTR
BUT SINCE YOU'VE GONE SHE HAS WORRIED AND BROODED 86 ELECTR
WHO HAS KNOWN ME EVER SINCE I WAS A BABY/ 88 ELECTR
WE HAVEN'T SEEN THEM SINCE THE FUNERAL. 118 ELECTR
THERE'S BEEN EVIL IN THAT HOUSE SINCE IT WAS FIRST136 ELECTR
BUILT IN HATE--
AND IT'S KEPT GROWIN' THERE EVER SINCE, AS WHAT'S 136 ELECTR
HAPPENED THERE HAS PROVED.
YOU HAVEN'T HAD ONE OF THESE MORBID SPELLS SINCE 141 ELECTR
WE LEFT THE ISLANDS.
I'VE WATCHED IT EVER SINCE WE SAILED FOR THE EAST.141 ELECTR
NO TIME HAS ELAPSED SINCE THE PRECEDING ACT. 157 ELECTR
SINCE WE MURDERED MOTHER/ 165 ELECTR
AND EVERY MORNIN' SINCE ORIN--AIN'T YOU BEEN 170 ELECTR
GITTIN' NO SLEEP/
WE'VE BEEN CHUMS EVER SINCE WE WERE KIDS, HAVEN'T 265 GGBROW
WE/
BUT IT IS TRUE HE HASN'T DONE SO MUCH LATELY SINCE276 GGBROW
WE'VE BEEN BACK.
WE'VE BEEN FRIENDS SINCE WE WERE KIDS. 289 GGBROW
IN THE YEARS SINCE WE SETTLED DOWN HERE. 292 GGBROW
WHY HAS HE NEVER BEEN ABLE TO LOVE--SINCE MY 298 GGBROW
MARGARET'S
YES, EVER SINCE HE FIRED DION. 302 GGBROW
NO, NOT SINCE BROWN TOLD US HE'D CANNED HIM. 302 GGBROW
I HAVEN'T SEEN DION AROUND TOWN SINCE THEN. 302 GGBROW
BUT YOU CAN BET YOUR SHIRT NO ONE AIN'T NEVER 211 HA APE
LICKED ME SINCE/
SEE WHAT'S HAPPENED SINCE YUH CROAKED. 215 HA APE
BUT SINCE I AM 218 HA APE

SINCE

SINCE (CONT'D.)

THAT'S WHAT YE BEEN SAYIN' EVERY BLOOMIN' HOUR 234 HA APE SINCE SHE HINSULTED YER.

I BEEN WARMIN' A BENCH DOWN TO DE BATTERY--EVER 252 HA APE SINCE LAST NIGHT.

I BEEN ONE EVEN SINCE. 15 HUGHIE

IT AIN'T THE SAME PLACE SINCE HUGHIE WAS TOOK TO 17 HUGHIE THE HOSPITAL.

I AIN'T WON NOTHIN' SINCE HUGHIE WAS TOOK TO THE 18 HUGHIE HOSPITAL.

IT IS YEARS SINCE HE CARED WHAT ANYONE CALLED HIM. 24 HUGHIE THAT REALLY HAPPENED SINCE I'VE BEEN HANGIN' 29 HUGHIE ROUND.

I DON'T WIN A BET SINCE HUGHIE WAS TOOK TO THE 34 HUGHIE HOSPITAL.

SINCE HUGHIE GOT TOOK TO THE HOSPITAL. NOT A WIN. 35 HUGHIE AND THEIR SHIPS ARE LONG SINCE LOOTED AND SCUTTLED578 ICEMAN AND SUNK ON THE BOTTOMS

IF I'VE BEEN THROUGH WITH THE MOVEMENT LONG SINCE,579 ICEMAN IT'S BEEN THROUGH WITH HIM.

I'M THROUGH WITH THE MOVEMENT LONG SINCE. 579 ICEMAN AND SINCE THEN IT'S BEEN NO FUN DODGING AROUND THE587 ICEMAN COUNTRY.

I HAVEN'T SEEN HIM SINCE HE WAS A KID. 587 ICEMAN IF I AM THROUGH LONG SINCE WITH ANY CONNECTION 588 ICEMAN WITH THEM.

WHAT HAVE YOU BEEN DOING ALL THE YEARS SINCE YOU 591 ICEMAN LEFT--THE COAST, LARRY$

TO HEAR NEWS OF YOUR MOTHER SINCE SHE'S BEEN IN 591 ICEMAN JAIL$

AND THEY'VE BEEN BOSOM PALS EVER SINCE. 593 ICEMAN SINCE HIS WIFE DIED TWENTY YEARS AGO. 594 ICEMAN AND IT'S TWENTY YEARS SINCE 602 ICEMAN COUPLE OF CON MEN LIVING IN MY FLAT SINCE CHRIST 602 ICEMAN KNOWS WHEN/

AND I'VE NEVER SET FOOT OUT OF THIS HOUSE SINCE 603 ICEMAN THE DAY I BURIED HER.

SINCE YOU GOT--RESIGNED. 604 ICEMAN ME, THAT'S KNOWN YOU SINCE YOU WAS KNEE-HIGH, AND,606 ICEMAN BEJEEZ,

I'VE BEEN THINKING ABOUT YOU EVER SINCE I LEFT THE621 ICEMAN HOUSE--

(BITTERLY) JEES, EVER SINCE HE WOKE UP, YUH CAN'T630 ICEMAN HOLD HIM.

I'VE BEEN WISE, EVER SINCE I CAN REMEMBER, TO ALL 646 ICEMAN THE GUYS SHE'S HAD.

I KNOW NOW, SINCE HICKEY'S BEEN AFTER ME, 648 ICEMAN AIN'T EVER HAD A CAKE SINCE BESSIE--SIX CANDLES. 656 ICEMAN ESPECIALLY SINCE HE TOLD US HIS WIFE WAS DEAD. 664 ICEMAN EVER SINCE BESSIE DIED. 684 ICEMAN (EAGERLY) AND YOU'VE BEEN CRAZY EVER SINCE$ 717 ICEMAN YES. HARRY, OF COURSE, I'VE BEEN OUT OF MY MIND 717 ICEMAN EVER SINCE/

AN' HE AIN'T SAVED NONE SINCE. 520 INZONE TO SEE YOU AS YOU'VE BEEN SINCE YOU CAME BACK TO 17 JOURNE US. YOUR DEAR OLD SELF AGAIN.

EVER SINCE HE WAS FIRED FROM COLLEGES 33 JOURNE HARRY'S TREATED HIM WHENEVER HE WAS SICK UP HERE, 33 JOURNE SINCE HE WAS KNEE HIGH.

SHE'S BEEN SO WELL IN THE TWO MONTHS SINCE SHE 36 JOURNE CAME HOME.

AND EVERY NIGHT SINCE EDMUND'S BEEN SICK SHE'S 38 JOURNE BEEN UP AND DOWN.

I'VE BEEN SO WORRIED EVER SINCE YOU'VE BEEN SICK. 48 JOURNE I'VE BEEN LYING DOWN EVER SINCE YOU WENT OUT. 59 JOURNE YOU NEVER HAVE WANTED ONE--NEVER SINCE THE DAY WE 67 JOURNE WERE MARRIED/

AND NOW, EVER SINCE HE'S BEEN SO SICK I'VE KEPT 88 JOURNE REMEMBERING EUGENE AND MY FATHER.

HE HAS SNORED EVER SINCE I CAN REMEMBER, 99 JOURNE WE'VE LOVED EACH OTHER EVER SINCE. 105 JOURNE I MEAN, WITH ANY OTHER WOMAN. NEVER SINCE HE MET 105 JOURNE ME.

SINCE HE FIRST OPENED HIS EYES, HE'S SEEN YOU 110 JOURNE DRINKING.

I HAVEN'T SEEN HIM SINCE THIS AFTERNOON. 129 JOURNE HE'S POISONED YOUR MIND AGAINST ME EVER SINCE YOU 144 JOURNE WERE OLD ENOUGH TO LISTEN/

EVEN SINCE I WENT TO SEA AND WAS ON MY OWN. 145 JOURNE ALTHOUGH ALL MY LIFE SINCE I HAD ANYTHING I'VE 146 JOURNE THROWN MONEY OVER THE BAR TO BUY

I'VE NEVER BEEN ABLE TO BELIEVE IN MY LUCK SINCE. 146 JOURNE TAKE THE LOSS OF HIS FATHER'S WEALTH SINCE HE TOOK276 LAZARU OVER THE MANAGEMENT.

(THEY EMBRACE HER, WEEPING) I HAVE NOT KISSED YOU283 LAZARU SINCE YOU LEFT HOME TO FOLLOW

HENCE THE MULTITUDE OF FOOLS WHO HAVE ACCLAIMED 302 LAZARU HIM EVERYWHERE SINCE HE LEFT HIS

SINCE LAZED THAT LADY LIED MARCH, OH MARCH ON/ 314 LAZARU SINCE LAZARUS WILL NOT HELP HIMSELF, YOU MUST 331 LAZARU PROTECT HIM.

SINCE HE DARES TO MOCK TIBERIUS TO HIS FACE/ 343 LAZARU NOW, SINCE YOUR LIFE PASSED, 362 LAZARU DREAM THEM AWAY AS YOU HAVE ALL THE OTHER YEARS 3 MANSNS SINCE SIMON DESERTED YOU$

SINCE FATHER DIED SHE HAS APPEARED--WELL, 26 MANSNS DELIBERATELY DERANGED--

I HAVE KNOWN YOUR MOTHER SINCE BEFORE YOU WERE 26 MANSNS BORN.

MY LIFE, I SUPPOSE YOU MIGHT CALL IT, SINCE I HAVE 28 MANSNS NEVER LIVED EXCEPT IN MIND.

I HAVE KNOWN HENRY SINCE WE WERE BOYS TOGETHER. 31 MANSNS SINCE HENRY'S WILL BEQUEATHES THE COMPANY JOINTLY 32 MANSNS TO YOU AND JOEL.

YOU KNOW I'VE NEVER HAD A LETTER FROM HER SINCE I 45 MANSNS SAW HER THAT TIME AT MY CABIN.

IT IS A LONG TIME SINCE OUR MEETING AT THE CABIN. 53 MANSNS AND I HAVE NOT DREAMED THAT DREAM SINCE THAT DAY. 53 MANSNS

SINCE (CONT'D.)

BUT NOW NO LONGER NEEDED SINCE THE MOTHER BY 73 MANSNS BECOMING WIFE

A LONG TIME SINCE YOU'VE GIVEN ME THE CHANCE/ 83 MANSNS IT'S A LONG TIME SINCE YOU'VE KISSED ME--LIKE 83 MANSNS THAT, DARLING.

IF YOU KNEW HOW UNHAPPY AND UGLY I'VE FELT SINCE 87 MANSNS YOU STARTED SLEEPING ALONE--

IN VIEW OF THE COMPANY'S PROGRESS SINCE YOU LAST 93 MANSNS DREAMED OF IT.

(TO SARA.) WELL, SINCE THE MOUNTAIN IS TOO PROUD 128 MANSNS TO COME TO MAHOMET--

I KNOW I HAVE, BUT--A LOT OF THINGS HAVE HAPPENED 136 MANSNS SINCE THEN TO DISTURB MY MIND.

BUT SINCE HE STARTED PLAYING NAPOLEON TO SHOW OFF 142 MANSNS HIS GENIUS TO YOU.

HOURS SINCE SUPPER EVEN--THE CHILDREN WATCHING, 162 MANSNS THEIR PRYING EYES SNEERING--

ALL MY LIFE SINCE THEN I HAVE STOOD OUTSIDE THAT 182 MANSNS DOOR IN MY MIND.

YOU ONCE DROVE ME OUT, AND ALL THAT HAS HAPPENED 182 MANSNS SINCE BEGAN.

I HAVE WAITED EVER SINCE I WAS A LITTLE BOY. 182 MANSNS SINCE THEN WE HAVE BOTH BEEN CONDEMNED TO AN 183 MANSNS INSATIABLE GREED FOR SUBSTITUTES--

AND EVER SINCE THIS TREE HAS BEEN SACRED TO HIM/ 349 MARCOM YOU PULL BACK THE CLOTH THEN, SINCE THAT IS YOUR 351 MARCOM CUSTOM.

I'VE LOVED YOU EVER SINCE I CAN REMEMBER. 355 MARCOM SINCE YOU POSSESS ETERNAL LIFE, IT CAN DO YOU NO 380 MARCOM HARM TO CUT OFF YOUR HEAD.

I WOULD SAY, RATHER THAT EVER SINCE YOU WERE OLD 385 MARCOM ENOUGH TO TALK,

AND SINCE THEN, ON HIS RETURNS, TO SPEAK WITH 387 MARCOM YOU--A PRINCESS/

WHY, SINCE SHE WAS A LITTLE GIRL, 388 MARCOM (BOLDLY NOW) AND MAY I HUMBLY REQUEST, SINCE HIS 397 MARCOM HONOR,

(VINDICTIVELY) I'VE NEVER SET FOOT IN A CHURCH 17 MISBEG SINCE, AND NEVER WILL.

(HE CHUCKLES) SINCE YOU'VE GROWN UP, I'VE HAD THE 18 MISBEG SAME TROUBLE.

I LEARNED LONG SINCE TO LET YOU GO YOUR OWN WAY 19 MISBEG BECAUSE THERE'S NO CONTROLLING

SURE, THAT'S EVERY WOMAN'S SCHEME SINCE THE WORLD 28 MISBEG WAS CREATED.

SINCE WHEN$ 41 MISBEG SINCE THAT DAY HE HAS FELT NO NEED FOR FURTHER 55 MISBEG ASPIRING.

EVER SINCE YOU SAID YOU LOVED MY BEAUTIFUL SOUL. 126 MISBEG THAN ALL THE MOONS SINCE RAMESES WAS A PUP. 130 MISBEG EVER SINCE MAMA DIED. 144 MISBEG SINCE THE WAR WITH THE FRENCH IN SPAIN--AFTER THE 10 POET BATTLE OF SALAMANCA IN '12.

SINCE YOU'VE BEEN PLAYIN' NURSE TO THE YOUNG 16 POET YANKEE UPSTAIRS.

EVER SINCE HE CAME TO LIVE BY THE LAKE, AND NOW'S 17 POET YOUR CHANCE.

WELL, SMALL BLAME TO HIM, HE HASN'T SEEN JAMIE 21 POET SINCE--

I'VE LOVED HIM SINCE THE DAY I SET EYES ON HIM, 25 POET THAT'S SINCE YOU BEGAN TO TAKE LONG WALKS BY THE 29 POET LAKE.

SINCE WHEN HAS MY CREDIT NOT BEEN GOOD$ 40 POET SINCE SO MANY MUST HAVE GIVEN THEIR HEARTS TO YOU. 71 POET HE'S FORBIDDEN HER TO SEE SIMON EVER SINCE SIMON 79 POET CAME OUT HERE TO LIVE.

SINCE HE LEFT HOME TO SEEK SELF-EMANCIPATION AT 81 POET THE BREAST OF NATURE.

OF COURSE, IT IS SOME TIME SINCE HE HAS WRITTEN. 81 POET ALTHOUGH SINCE SIMON BECAME EMANCIPATED HE HAS 86 POET EMBARRASSED CATO ACUTELY

THAN ANY NIGHT SINCE THIS SHEBEEN STARTED/ 134 POET THE YANKEE DIDN'T APOLOGIZE OR YOUR FATHER'D BEEN 137 POET BACK HERE LONG SINCE.

YOU'VE BEEN IN HIS ROOM EVER SINCE YOU WENT UP$ 142 POET NOT TO SEE HIM AT ALL SINCE HIS MOTHER LEFT. 143 POET HE'S NOT TAKEN A DROP SINCE WE LEFT HERE. 153 POET SINCE THEY BROUGHT HIM TO--ABOUT THE HARFORD 158 POET WOMAN--

IT'S THE DAMNEDEST JOKE A MAN IVIR PLAYED ON 166 POET HIMSELF SINCE TIME BEGAN.

SO YOU MIGHT 'S WELL TAKE DOWN THAT UGLY ROPE 581 ROPE YOU'VE HAD TIED THERE SINCE HE RUN

OH, IT'S THE SAME CRAZY NOTION HE'S HAD EVER SINCE582 ROPE LUKE LEFT.

I'VE SMALL DOUBT BUT THAT LUKE IS HUNG LONG 583 ROPE SINCE--BY THE POLICE.

SAY, WAS HE HAD THAT HANGIN' THERE EVER SINCE I 592 ROPE SKIPPED$

OF ALL THE ENGLISH AUTHORS WHO WROTE WHILE $ WAS 3 STRANG STILL LIKE AN F AND A FEW SINCE

SHE HAS BOSSED ME, TOO, EVER SINCE SHE WAS A 5 STRANG BABY...

I SUPPOSE YOU FOUND EVERYTHING COMPLETELY CHANGED 7 STRANG SINCE BEFORE THE WAR.

WITH NO RESOURCES, SINCE HE WAS PENNILESS, EXCEPT 10 STRANG SINCE GORDON'S DEATH THEY HAVE A QUALITY OF 12 STRANG CONTINUALLY SHUDDERING

SINCE I WAS BORN I HAVE BEEN IN HIS CLASS, LOVING- 15 STRANG ATTENTIVE,

REALLY ONLY SINCE SHE'S BEEN AT THE HOSPITAL, 29 STRANG ALTHOUGH I MET HER ONCE YEARS AGO

EVER SINCE SHE WAS A KID, HAVEN'T YOU$ 29 STRANG SHE'S HAD QUITE A LOT THE MATTER WITH HER SINCE 31 STRANG HER BREAKDOWN,

AND EVER SINCE THEN I'VE STUDIED HER CASE. 35 STRANG WHAT DO YOU KNOW OF NINA SINCE SHE LEFT HOME$ 35 STRANG

SINCE (CONT'D.)
THAT IT'S OVER SIX MONTHS SINCE SAM AND I WERE MARRIED 49 STRANG
AND WE HAVEN'T SEEN HIDE NOR HAIR OF YOU SINCE THE 49 STRANG CEREMONY.
AS IF ALL THE LIFE IN THE AIR HAD LONG SINCE BEEN 49 STRANG EXHAUSTED IN KEEPING THE DYING
SHE HAS BEEN WRITING SAM REGULARLY ONCE A WEEK 50 STRANG EVER SINCE SHE'S KNOWN WE WERE
NOT SINCE THEIR MARRIAGE... 52 STRANG
BUT I'M MAKING GOOD, ALL RIGHT, ALL RIGHT--SINCE I 54 STRANG GOT MARRIED--
SHE HASN'T SEEN YOU SINCE YOU WERE EIGHT. 56 STRANG
BUT HERE'S WHAT I'VE COME TO THINK SINCE, NINA.. 60 STRANG
BEEN GOING STALE EVER SINCE WE CAME BACK FROM THAT 67 STRANG TRIP HOME...
SINCE NINA GOT SICK... 67 STRANG
SINCE THAT VISIT HOME... 68 STRANG
SINCE THEN, I COULDN'T... 71 STRANG
AND SINCE THEN, I'VE FELT AN AVERSION... 74 STRANG
ONE REASON I'VE STEERED CLEAR SINCE... 78 STRANG
(BEEN THROUGH A LOT SINCE I SAW HER... 79 STRANG
(THEN MOCKINGLY) WELL, SINCE YOU'RE OUT HERE 82 STRANG PROFESSIONALLY,
SHE HAS CHANGED, DOCTOR, SINCE SHE BECAME SAM'S 87 STRANG
I'VE LOVED HIM EVER SINCE THAT FIRST AFTERNOON... 90 STRANG
EVERY WEEK SINCE THEN HE'S BEEN COMING OUT HERE... 91 STRANG
I KNOW IT'S AN IMPOSITION--BUT--I'VE BEEN IN SUCH 98 STRANG A TERRIBLE STATE SINCE MOTHER--
SINCE I FIRST MET YOU, I'VE ALWAYS DESIRED YOU 102 STRANG PHYSICALLY.
SINCE MOTHER'S DEATH I'VE BECOME A REGULAR 120 STRANG IDIOT/.../)
SINCE THE BABY WAS BORN, I'VE FELT AS IF I HAD A 121 STRANG SHOT OF DYNAMITE IN EACH ARM.
I ONLY INTENDED TO STAY A YEAR, AND IT'S OVER THAT126 STRANG SINCE--
YES, EVER SINCE THE BABY WAS BORN SAM'S BEEN 128 STRANG ANOTHER MAN--
IN FACT, EVER SINCE HE KNEW THERE WAS GOING TO BE 128 STRANG A BABY, ISN'T IT, NINA$
YES, MORE DEEPLY THAN EITHER OF THE OTHERS SINCE 1135 STRANG SERVE FOR NOTHING.../)
MUCH BIGGER AND STRONGER IN THE TWO MONTHS SINCE 147 STRANG I'VE SEEN HIM.
IT HAS BEEN SO LONG SINCE WE LOVED EACH OTHER WE 165 STRANG CAN BE FRIENDS AGAIN.
(WITH A FRIENDLY SMILE) I HAVEN'T SEEN YOU LOOK 165 STRANG SO YOUNG AND HANDSOME SINCE I
HOW MANY YEARS SINCE$... 169 STRANG
I DON'T LIKE HIM SINCE HE'S GROWN UP/ 175 STRANG
I'VE NEVER TOLD YOU, BUT I'VE ALWAYS FELT, EVER 185 STRANG SINCE I WAS A LITTLE KID,
I'VE FELT IT TOO STRONGLY, EVER SINCE 185 STRANG
NOT SINCE YOUR FATHER WAS TAKEN SICK, SHE HASN'T, 185 STRANG DEAR.
I'VE BEEN SURE OF IT SINCE THEN. 186 STRANG
I'VE KNOWN EVER SINCE I WAS A KID 194 STRANG
THERE WAS SOMETHING UNREAL IN ALL THAT HAS 199 STRANG HAPPENED SINCE YOU FIRST MET GORDON
AND I'VE BEEN HOPING EVER SINCE I FIRST MET YOU. 467 WELDED
(HER HEAD HAS BEEN AVERTED SINCE HE TURNED AWAY-- 481 WELDED WITHOUT LOOKING AT HIM)

SINCERE
(INTENSELY SINCERE NOW) I'LL THINK OF HER--AND 274 AHWILD DREAM/
(FRIGHTENED--IMMEDIATELY BECOMES TERRIBLY 278 AHWILD SINCERE--GRABBING HER HAND)
(THEN WITH SINCERE BOYISH FERVOR) 279 AHWILD
AND I THINK IT'S WONDERFUL AND SINCERE. 84 BEYOND
THERE IS A SINCERE MATERNAL LOVE IN HER MANNER AN0243 DESIRE VOICE--
I WOULD LIKE TO BE SINCERE, TO TOUCH LIFE 219 HA APE SOMEWHERE
HE IS SO SINCERE/ 236 HA APE
HICKEY PATS HIM ON THE BACK AGAIN--WITH SINCERE 657 ICEMAN SYMPATHY)
AND AS HE GOES ON HE BECOMES MORE MOVED AND 658 ICEMAN OBVIOUSLY SINCERE)
(TURNS ON HIM WITH A FLASH OF SINCERE INDIGNATION)690 ICEMAN
(PRETENDING TO GIVE IN.) I MUST ADMIT SHE SEEMS 84 MANSNS SINCERE
I WAS SINCERE IN THAT, NED/ 131 STRANG
(HIS VOICE SUDDENLY BREAKING WITH A SINCERE HUMAN 183 STRANG GRIEF)

SINCERELY
(THEN SINCERELY CONCERNED) I HOPE YOU'RE WRONG, 267 AHWILD NAT.
SHE HAS BEEN SINCERELY MOVED BY THE RECITAL OF HER226 DESIRE TROUBLES.
(ABRUPTLY HE BECOMES SINCERELY SYMPATHETIC AND 684 ICEMAN EARNEST)
BECAUSE SHE SINCERELY LIKES HER MISTRESS.) 98 JOURNE
I MEANT EVERY WORD SINCERELY/ 57 MANSNS
WHY SHOULDN'T THEY BE SINCERELY SORRY$ 190 STRANG

SINCERITY
(THEN FALLING BACK ON SWINBURNE--BUT WITH 287 AHWILD PASSIONATE SINCERITY)
(MOLLIFIED BY HIS VERY EVIDENT SINCERITY--SITTING 42 ANNA DOWN AGAIN)
(A BIT PLACATED, IN SPITE OF HIMSELF, BY BURKE'S 46 ANNA EVIDENT SINCERITY--
(WITH A GREAT DEPTH OF SINCERITY IN HIS HUMBLE 52 ANNA GRATITUDE)
YOU SEEM TO BE GOING IN FOR SINCERITY TODAY. 219 HA APE
THERE'S A SORT OF SINCERITY IN THAT, YOU KNOW. 219 HA APE
GIVE ME CREDIT FOR SOME SORT OF GROPING SINCERITY 219 HA APE IN THAT AT LEAST.

SINCERITY (CONT'D.)
(THEY HAVE ALL CAUGHT HIS SINCERITY WITH EAGER 659 ICEMAN RELIEF.
CONVINCING SINCERITY OF ONE MAKING A CONFESSION 660 ICEMAN
HE GOES ON WITH CONVINCING SINCERITY) 663 ICEMAN
(WITH AN INTENSE BITTER SINCERITY) 726 ICEMAN
(BENEATH HIS DRUNKEN SENTIMENTALITY THERE IS A 156 JOURNE GENUINE SINCERITY.)
CONVINCING SINCERITY.) 165 JOURNE
THEN ADDS WITH STRANGE, WONDERING SINCERITY) 103 MISBEG
(WITH A FIERCE, LUSTFUL SINCERITY.) 71 POET

SINEWY
JIMMY IS A TALL, SINEWY, BRONZED YOUNG KANAKA. 571 CROSS
HE IS TWENTY-FIVE, TALL AND SINEWY. 203 DESIRE

SINFUL
IT'S REAL SINFUL. 298 AHWILD
DENYIN' OF GOD HE DONE ALL HIS SINFUL LIFE/ 114 BEYOND
AND A SINFUL DOUBT CONCERNING THE DIVINE LOVE 511 DAYS ASSAILED HIM/
I'VE SWORN T' LIVE A HUNDRED AN' I'LL DO IT, IF 210 DESIRE ON'Y T' SPITE YER SINFUL GREED/
(EDGING AWAY) LUST FOR GOLD--FUR THE SINFUL, EASY223 DESIRE GOLD O' CALIFORNI-A/
(TAUNTINGLY) WOULDN'T YE LIKE US TO SEND YE BACK 223 DESIRE SOME SINFUL GOLD,
NOW THAT HIS CUSSED SINFUL BROTHERS IS GONE THEIR 232 DESIRE PATH T' HELL,
LIKE 'TWAS SINFUL T' BE HARD, SO'S AT LAST I SAID 237 DESIRE BACK AT 'EM...
WHERE THE SPIRIT DECAYS IN THE SINFUL SLOTH OF THE425 DYNAMO FLESH.../)
LET THIS PUT BACK THE FEAR OF GOD INTO YOUR SINFUL448 DYNAMO HEART, REUBEN/
SOME DAY GOD WOULD HUMBLE THEM IN THEIR SINFUL 69 ELECTR PRIDE.
IT MAY BE SINFUL OF ME BUT I LOVE HER BETTER THAN 175 JOURNE MY OWN MOTHER.
HE'S TERRIBLY ASHAMED OF HIS SINFUL INCLINATIONS 32 POET
YOU WICKED, SINFUL GIRL/ 148 POET
DON'T TORMENT ME WITH YOUR SINFUL QUESTIONS/ 149 POET

SINFULLER
AND SINFULLER, TOO/ 223 DESIRE

SING
(HE STARTS TO SING THE OLD ARMY HYMN) 233 AHWILD
RAND WAS TELLING ME HE LIKED NOTHING BETTER THAN 255 AHWILD TO HEAR YOU SING--
HE MAKES IT PLAIN BY THIS PANTOMIME THAT HE WANTS 256 AHWILD HIM TO SING TO DISTRACT HIS
ARTHUR'S GOING TO SING FOR US. 257 AHWILD
ARTHUR BEGINS TO SING. 257 AHWILD
(DOLEFULLY) YES--BUT I WISH HE WOULDN'T SING SUCH258 AHWILD SAD SONGS.
(IN THE FRONT PARLOR, ARTHUR BEGINS TO SING 259 AHWILD ROLLICKINGLY *WAITING AT THE CHURCH,
(HE LAUGHS AND COMMENCES TO SING IN A NASAL, HIGH- 6 ANNA PITCHED QUAVER.)
(HE DRINKS--THEN BEGINS TO SING LOUDLY) 12 ANNA
(BY WAY OF REPLY, GRINS FOOLISHLY AND BEGINS TO 13 ANNA SING)
HE CLEARS HIS THROAT AND STARTS TO SING TO HIMSELF 41 ANNA IN A LOW, DOLEFUL VOICE..*
HE READS ALOUD IN A DOLEFUL, SING-SONG VOICE) 82 BEYOND
SING SOMETHING DRISC. 459 CARIBE
WE ALL SING IN ON CHORUS. 459 CARIBE
SING *WISKEY JOHNNY.* 459 CARIBE
I'LL SING FUR YE/ 242 DESIRE
SOMETIMES SHE USED T' SING FUR ME. 242 DESIRE
(A PAUSE) SOMETIMES SHE USED TO SING FUR ME. 243 DESIRE
I'LL SING FUR YE/ 243 DESIRE
SING AN' CELEBRATE/ 256 DESIRE
YE JEST SING OUT. 256 DESIRE
THEN I'LL SING *I'M OFF TO CALIFORNI-A/= 262 DESIRE
I COULD SIT FOREVER AND LISTEN TO THEM SING... 436 DYNAMO
I LOVE TO HEAR THEM SING. 458 DYNAMO
(THEN SUDDENLY) DO YOU STILL SING, HAZEL= 83 ELECTR
(HE BEGINS TO SING IN A SURPRISINGLY GOOD TENOR 103 ELECTR VOICE.
TOLD ME HOW FINE I COULD SING/ 104 ELECTR
THE CHANTYMAN SUDDENLY BEGINS TO SING THE CHANTY 106 ELECTR =HANGING JOHNNY= WITH
I SING THE JUBILEE HURRAH. 130 ELECTR
WHY DOESN'T BILLY SING$ 257 GGBROW
SING SOME MORE. 262 GGBROW
SING US THAT WHISKY SONG, PADDY. 209 HA APE
I'M NEVER TOO DRUNK TO SING. 210 HA APE
(HE STARTS TO SING IN A THIN, NASAL, DOLEFUL 210 HA APE TONE.)
'TIS ONLY WHEN I'M DEAD TO THE WORLD I'D BE 210 HA APE WISHFUL TO SING AT ALL.
A VERY DRUNKEN SENTIMENTAL TENOR BEGINS TO SING)..211 HA APE
(BEGINS TO SING THE *MILLER OF DEE* WITH ENORMOUS 216 HA APE GOOD NATURE)
MEANWHILE, I WILL SING A SONG. 596 ICEMAN
=I HOPE THEY SEND HIM TO SING SING FOR LIFE.= 606 ICEMAN
AND DEN DEY'D MAKE UP AND CRY AND SING =SCHOOL 612 ICEMAN DAYS.=
SING A GOD-DAMNED HYMN IF YOU LIKE. 620 ICEMAN
HE BEGINS TO SING THE CARMAGNOLE IN A GUTTURAL 634 ICEMAN BASSO.
(JOE BEGINS TO HUM AND SING IN A LOW VOICE AND 644 ICEMAN CORRECT HER.
AND SAYING HE OUGHT TO HAVE ME PUT IN SING SING/ 652 ICEMAN
WHY DON'T YOU LAUGH AND SING =SWEET ADELINE=$ 705 ICEMAN
BEJEES, LET'S SING/ 727 ICEMAN
I WANT TO SING/ 727 ICEMAN
SING OUT IF HE MAKES A MOVE. 524 INZONE
(TO SCOTTY) KAPE YOUR EYES PEELED, SCOTTY, AND 525 INZONE SING OUT IF ANYONE'S COMIN'.

SING 1444

SING (CONT'D.)
YOU GO THROUGH THE OTHERS, DRISC, AND SING OUT IF 531 INZONE
YOU SEES ANYTHIN' QUEER.
SING ALL ONCE MORE TOGETHER. 174 JOURNE
THEY ARE LEAVING OUR FARMS--TO DANCE AND SING/ 286 LAZARU
THEY SING TO THE EARTH WHEN THEY ARE PLOWING/ 287 LAZARU
LET ME SING/ 305 LAZARU
(MUSINGLY) SING WHILE YOU CAN. 384 MARCOM
IT WAS ONLY BECAUSE THERE'S TIMES YOU HAVE TO SING 75 MISBEG
TO KEEP FROM CRYING.
SING, IS IT$ 76 MISBEG
AND I MADE MYSELF SING ON THE ROAD SO HE'D HEAR, 86 MISBEG
AND THEY'D ALL HEAR IN THE INN,
CAN'T PHIL SING ANYTHING BUT THAT DAMNED DIRGE, 104 MISBEG
JOSIE$
(HE BEGINS TO SING SNEERINGLY HALF UNDER HIS 111 MISBEG
BREATH
YOU'D WALK IN THEM GLADLY TO BE WITH HIM, AND SING 25 POET
WITH JOY AT YOUR OWN BURNIN',
I'D BE IN HEAVEN AND SING WITH THE JOY OF OUR 146 POET
LOVE/
HE'LL LAUGH AND SING AND HELP YOU CELEBRATE 176 POET
TALAVERA--
BUT HE'LL SING AND LAUGH AND DRINK A POWER AV 180 POET
WHISKEY AND SLAPE SOUND AFTER.
SHE TALKS IN A HIGH-PITCHED, SING-SONG WHINE. 579 ROPE

SINGA
SINGA DA SONG, CARUSO PAT/ 210 HA APE

SINGAPORE
*WE'RE IN SINGAPORE NOW. 126 BEYOND
REMEMBER THE NIGHT I WENT CRAZY WITH THE HEAT IN 488 CARDIF
SINGAPORE$

SINGER
(SITTING DOWN) AY'M GOOD SINGER, YES$ 12 ANNA
THE SINGER, SETH BECKWITH. 6 ELECTR

SINGERS
SCREECH OWLS IS UP'RY SINGERS COMPARED TO HIM/ 103 ELECTR
THEY ARE FOLLOWED BY THE CHORUS OF NINE SINGERS, 433 MARCOM
FIVE MEN AND FOUR WOMEN.
THE MUSIC AND THE SINGING CEASE AS THE DANCERS, 434 MARCOM
SINGERS.

SINGIN'
AN' HE DRUV OFF SINGIN' A HYMN. 210 DESIRE
HOW'S THAT FUR SINGIN' FUR AN OLD FELLER$. 7 ELECTR
SHE WAS ALWAYS LAUGHIN' AND SINGIN'--FRISKY AND 44 ELECTR
FULL OF LIFE--
OR ELSE DEY'D RAISE HELL UPSTAIRS, LAUGHIN' AND 669 ICEMAN
SINGIN'.
NOW SHE'S GONE AWAY TO SINGIN' SCHOOL-- 530 INZONE
LUVIN' BLARNEY, AN' HOW HER SINGIN' IS DOIN', AND 531 INZONE
THE GREAT THINGS THE DUTCH
I WANT COMPANY AND SINGIN' AND DANCIN' AND GREAT 175 POET
LAUGHTER.

SINGING
AND THOU BESIDE ME SINGING IN THE WILDERNESS-- 199 AHWILD
AS SHE DOES SO, FROM THE FRONT YARD SID'S VOICE IS220 AHWILD
HEARD SINGING *POOR JOHN*/
(HE TURNS AND MARCHES SOLEMNLY OUT THROUGH THE 233 AHWILD
BACK PARLOR, SINGING)
I DIDN'T KNOW YOU CARED FOR SINGING, NAT. 255 AHWILD
ARTHUR, WHAT'S THIS I HEAR ABOUT YOUR HAVING SUCH 255 AHWILD
A GOOD SINGING VOICE$
I'VE BEEN SINGING A LOT TONIGHT. 256 AHWILD
(THEN WITH SURLY DIGNITY) I DON'T FEEL LIKE 256 AHWILD
SINGING TONIGHT, PA.
AND WALKS UNSTEADILY INTO BACK ROOM SINGING) 12 ANNA
SINGING HAPPILY TO HERSELF. 129 BEYOND
IN WHICH THE SINGING FROM THE LAND CAN BE PLAINLY 456 CARIBE
HEARD.)
STARING TOWARD THE SPOT ON SHORE WHERE THE SINGING456 CARIBE
SEEMS TO COME FROM.)
THERE IS A SILENCE BROKEN ONLY BY THE MOURNFUL 459 CARIBE
SINGING OF THE NEGROES ON SHORE.)
THE SINGING FROM SHORE COMES CLEARLY OVER THE 466 CARIBE
MOONLIT WATER.)
THE UPROAR OF SHOUTING, LAUGHING AND SINGING 469 CARIBE
VOICES HAS INCREASED IN VIOLENCE.
(FROWNING) THEY SAID YOU HAD THE PIANO GOIN' AND 525 DIFRNT
WAS SINGING.
THEY'RE ALWAYS SINGING ABOUT EVERYTHING IN THE 436 DYNAMO
WORLD...))
((SINGING ALL THE TIME ABOUT EVERYTHING IN THE 458 DYNAMO
WORLD--
THEY'RE SINGING ALL THE TIME ABOUT EVERYTHING IN 458 DYNAMO
THE WORLD/
(LISTEN TO HER SINGING... 474 DYNAMO
ALWAYS SINGING ABOUT EVERYTHING IN THE WORLD*... 474 DYNAMO
LIKE SOME ONE SINGING ME TO SLEEP--MY MOTHER--WHEN476 DYNAMO
I WAS A KID--
WHAT ARE YOU SINGING FOR$ 489 DYNAMO
FROM THE LEFT REAR, A MAN'S VOICE IS HEARD SINGING 5 ELECTR
THE CHANT *SHENANDOAH*--
HIS SINGING HAS BEEN FOR HER BENEFIT. 7 ELECTR
SINGING A CROON IN YOUR EARS LIKE A LULLABY/ 24 ELECTR
THE SOUND OF SETH'S THIN, AGED BARITONE MOURNFULLY 43 ELECTR
SINGING
I USED TO HEAR YOU SINGING--DOWN THERE. 83 ELECTR
I USED TO HEAR YOU SINGING AT THE QUEEREST TIMES-- 83 ELECTR
SO SWEET AND CLEAR AND PURE/
THE SOUND OF THE SINGING SEEMS TO STRIKE A 102 ELECTR
RESPONSIVE CHORD IN HIS BRAIN.
(LISTENS TO THE SINGING WITH CRITICAL DISAPPROVAL)103 ELECTR
I'D EXPECT A MAN WITH YOUR VOICE WOULD BE IN A 106 ELECTR
SALOON, SINGING AND MAKING MERRY/
SOME DRUNKEN MAN CAME ALONG SINGING-- 107 ELECTR
A PAUSE IN WHICH THE SINGING OF THE CREW 109 ELECTR
THE SURF ON THE BARRIER REEF SINGING A CROON IN 112 ELECTR
YOUR EARS LIKE A LULLABY/

SINGING (CONT'D.)
AND SINGING MOURNFULLY TO HIMSELF, 169 ELECTR
(STOPS SINGING AND STANDS PEERING OFF LEFT TOWARD 169 ELECTR
THE FLOWER GARDEN--
HE BEGINS SINGING HALF UNDER HIS BREATH HIS 178 ELECTR
MELANCHOLY *SHENANDOAH* CHANTY,
SUCH SINGING/ 257 GGBROW
(LOOKING UPWARD AT THE MOON AND SINGING IN LOW 262 GGBROW
TONE AS THEY ENTER)
THE ROOM IS CROWDED WITH MEN, SHOUTING, CURSING, 207 HA APE
LAUGHING, SINGING---
SINGING A CHANTY SONG AND NO CARE TO IT. 213 HA APE
SINGING AND EVERYTHING. 598 ICEMAN
AND SINGING THE CHORUS HALF UNDER HER BREATH, 651 ICEMAN
WHO STARTS PLAYING AND SINGING IN A WHISKEY 653 ICEMAN
SOPRANO
(HE YELLS AT CORA WHO HAS STOPPED SINGING 654 ICEMAN
SHE WAS ALWAYS SINGING IT. 656 ICEMAN
AND YOU'VE GOT EVERYBODY ELSE SINGING THE SAME 704 ICEMAN
CRAZY TUNE/
JOKING AND LAUGHING AND SINGING AND SWAPPING LIES.715 ICEMAN
HE STOPS SINGING TO DENOUNCE THEM IN HIS MOST 727 ICEMAN
FIERY STYLE)
AND THEY STOP SINGING TO ROAR WITH LAUGHTER. 727 ICEMAN
(SHRUGGING HIS SHOULDERS.) YOU WON'T BE SINGING A 66 JOURNE
SONG YOURSELF SOON.
I BECAME DRUNK WITH THE BEAUTY AND SINGING RHYTHM 153 JOURNE
OF IT.
THERE IS CONTINUALLY AN OVERTONE OF SINGING 281 LAZARU
LAUGHTER
SINGING AND LAUGHTER BECOMES STEADILY LOUDER. 304 LAZARU
HAD FOUND AT LAST ITS VOICE AND A SONG FOR 309 LAZARU
SINGING.
DANCING, PLAYING, SINGING, LAUGHING, HE IS 311 LAZARU
ESCORTED OFF.
(IN A GREAT CHANTING SINGING CHORUS) 318 LAZARU
MINGLED WITH THE LAUGHING FROM BEYOND THE WALL 318 LAZARU
COMES THE SOUND OF SINGING AND
(THERE IS NOW NO SOUND OF THE SINGING OR 320 LAZARU
SINGING A VERSE OF THE LEGIONARY'S SONG) 357 LAZARU
A FRESH BOY'S VOICE IS HEARD SINGING A LOVE SONG 355 MARCOM
IN A SUBDUED TONE.
(THE SENTIMENTAL SINGING VOICES AND 357 MARCOM
(WITH DEEP EMOTION) YOU HAVE BEEN A GOLDEN BIRD 385 MARCOM
SINGING BESIDE A BLACK RIVER.
MUSIC BRINGS BACK HER VOICE SINGING/ 423 MARCOM
THE MUSIC AND THE SINGING CEASE AS THE DANCERS, 434 MARCOM
SINGERS.
JUST A SLAP BECAUSE SHE TOLD ME TO STOP SINGING, 18 MISBEG
IT WAS AFTER DAYLIGHT.
AND WE'D START DRINKING AND TELLING STORIES, AND 26 MISBEG
SINGING SONGS.
DRUNKE$T, AND DOESN'T ROAR AROUND CURSING AND 27 MISBEG
SINGING, LIKE SOME I COULD NAME.
(SHE LISTENS TO THE SINGING--GRIMLY) 72 MISBEG
OUTSIDE THE SINGING GROWS LOUDER AS HOGAN 72 MISBEG
APPROACHES THE HOUSE.
AND IF I WAS SINGING COMING ALONG THE ROAD, 75 MISBEG
(SNORTS) AND HAVE YOU SINGING AGAIN IN A MINUTE 76 MISBEG
AND SMASHING THE FURNITURE--
CELEBRATION OR NOT, I'LL HAVE NO DRUNKS CURSING 100 MISBEG
AND SINGING ALL NIGHT.
CHRIST, IN A MINUTE YOU'LL START SINGING *MOTHER 148 MISBEG
MACREE*/
A KID KEPT SINGING OVER AND OVER IN MY BRAIN. 150 MISBEG
I COULDN'T STOP IT SINGING. 150 MISBEG
WHERE THERE'S MEN IN THEIR RIGHT SENSES LAUGHING 165 POET
AND SINGING/
THEY AT LEAST WOULD HAVE DIVERTED HER IN HER LAST 100 STRANG
HOURS WITH THEIR SINGING AND
(THERE IS THE NOISE OF LOUD BOISTEROUS SINGING 496 VOYAGE
FROM THE STREET)

SINGLE
FORTY-FIVE YEARS AGO--WASN'T A SINGLE HOUSE DOWN 229 AHWILD
THERE THEN--
BUT I KNOW HE NEVER HAD A SINGLE AFFAIR IN HIS 522 DAYS
LIFE BEFORE HE MET ME.
(HE LAUGHS HIMSELF IN ONE SINGLE MIRTHLESS BARK.) 208 DESIRE
I'LL STAY SINGLE. 512 DIFRNT
I'LL STAY SINGLE. 517 DIFRNT
I AIN'T GOIN' TO STAY SINGLE. 518 DIFRNT
AND I DON'T WANT YOU TO THINK IT'S NEEDFUL FOR YOU518 DIFRNT
TO STAY SINGLE 'CAUSE I--
HIM AND ME'S AGREED NOT TO GIVE YOU ANOTHER SINGLE529 DIFRNT
PENNY
SHE HASN'T SPOKEN A SINGLE WORD SINCE HER FATHER'S 72 ELECTR
DEATH/
HELL. I ONCE WIN TWENTY GRAND ON A SINGLE RACE. 36 HUGHIE
THAT'S ACTION/
LIGHTING COMES FROM SINGLE WALL BRACKETS, TWO AT 573 ICEMAN
LEFT AND TWO AT REAR.
NOT A SINGLE DAMNED HOPE OR DREAM LEFT TO NAG YOU.625 ICEMAN
THERE WOULDN'T BE A SINGLE VACANT CEMETERY LOT 628 ICEMAN
LEFT IN THIS GLORIOUS COUNTRY.=
I HAVEN'T A SINGLE FRIEND LEFT IN THE WORLD. 646 ICEMAN
WITH ITS SINGLE TABLE AT RIGHT OF CURTAIN, FRONT. 695 ICEMAN
WITHOUT A SINGLE DAMNED HOPE OR LYING DREAM LEFT 704 ICEMAN
TO TORMENT YOU/
WHY, YOU BONEHEAD, I HAVEN'T GOT A SINGLE DAMNED 719 ICEMAN
LYING HOPE OR PIPE DREAM LEFT/
IT WASN'T UNTIL AFTER EDMUND WAS BORN THAT I HAD A 28 JOURNE
SINGLE GREY HAIR.
THEY'VE HAD IT UNDER THEIR NOSES FOR YEARS WITHOUT395 MARCOM
A SINGLE SOUL EVER HAVING
I'D NEVER HAVE REMAINED SINGLE ALL THESE YEARS IN 430 MARCOP
THE EAST/
THE DINING ROOM AND BARROOM WERE ONCE A SINGLE 7 POET
SPACIOUS ROOM, LOW-CEILINGED,

SINGLE (CONT'D.)
(THEN JEALOUSLY) (I SUPPOSE EVERY SINGLE DAMNED 25 STRANG
INMATE HAS FALLEN IN LOVE WITH
HE DON'T KNOW A SINGLE THING ABOUT IT/ 60 STRANG
(HARSHLY) ON EVERY SINGLE POINT, DOCTOR/ 81 STRANG

SINGLEHANDED
I WOULD CHARGE A SQUARE OF NAPOLEON'S OLD GUARD 71 POET
SINGLEHANDED

SINGLET
AND A SINGLET TORN OPEN ACROSS HIS HAIRY CHEST. 571 CROSS

SINGLETS
SOME WEAR SINGLETS, BUT THE MAJORITY ARE STRIPPED 207 HA APE
TO THE WAIST.

SINGLY
THAT WE COULD CRUSH EACH SINGLY AND THE REST WOULD421 MARCOM
REJOICE.

SINGS
(GRINS AND SINGS) =DUNNO WHAT TER CALL'IM BUT HE'S189 AHWILD
MIGHTY LIKE A ROSE-VEIL.=
(THEN SHE SINGS TO THE MUSIC FROM THE PIANO, HER 237 AHWILD
EYES NOW ON RICHARD)
HE SINGS THAT OLD SENTIMENTAL FAVORITE, =THEN 257 AHWILD
YOU'LL REMEMBER ME.=
ARTHUR SINGS THE POPULAR =DEARIE,= 258 AHWILD
(HE SINGS) AS I WAS A 'ROAMIN' DOWN PARADISE 459 CARIBE
STREET--
(HE SINGS THIS-- 268 DESIRE
BUT THEY'RE PURTY--IN THEIR FASHION--AND AT NIGHT 515 DIFRNT
THEY SINGS--
(HE SINGS WITH A MAUDLIN ZEST.) 103 ELECTR
AND HE PLAYS AND SINGS AND DANCES SO MARVELOUSLY. 263 GGBROW
(SHE SINGS LAUGHINGLY, ELFISHLY) 264 GGBROW
(STANDS AND SINGS) WILLIAM BROWN'S SOUL LIES 294 GGBROW
MOLDERING IN THE CRIB
(HE SINGS IN A BOISTEROUS BARITONE, 596 ICEMAN
(HE SINGS..) =HE RAPPED AND RAPPED, 597 ICEMAN
(HE SINGS..) =OH, COME UP,= SHE CRIED, =MY SAILOR 597 ICEMAN
LAD, AND YOU AND I'LL AGREE.
(HE SINGS..) =OH, HE PUT HIS ARM AROUND HER WAIST,597 ICEMAN
WHILE THE D. A. SINGS OUT A LITTLE DITTY HE 607 ICEMAN
LEARNED AT HARVARD.
(HE SINGS..) =OH, COME UP,= SHE CRIED, =MY SAILOR 607 ICEMAN
LAD, AND YOU AND I'LL AGREE.
THROWS BACK HIS HEAD, AND SINGS IN A FALSETTO 619 ICEMAN
TENOR)
(HE BEATS TIME WITH HIS FINGER AND SINGS IN A LOW 645 ICEMAN
VOICE)
(SINGS TO HIS SAILOR LAD TUNE) 662 ICEMAN
OR OF THE CLOCK, OR WHATEVER FLIES, OR SIGHS, OR 132 JOURNE
ROCKS, OR SINGS, OR SPEAKS.
(IMPRESSIVELY) ONE LOOK IN HIS EYES WHILE HIS 300 LAZARU
LAUGHTER SINGS IN YOUR EARS AND
SINGS HOARSELY AN OLD CAMP SONG OF THE PUNIC WARS,313 LAZARU
POUNDING WITH HIS GOBLET)
UPWARD IT SPRINGS LIKE A LARK FROM A FIELD, AND 345 LAZARU
SINGS!
SINGS WITH WAILING MELANCHOLY THE FIRST VERSE THAT1102 POET
COMES TO HIS MIND
MARY CLAPS HER HANDS AND SINGS TO HERSELF.= 602 ROPE
(SINGS) =ROW, ROW, ROW.= 175 STRANG
(HE SINGS RAUCOUSLY) =OH, WE'LL ROW, ROW, ROW, 175 STRANG
RIGHT DOWN THE RIVER/

SINGULAR
IT IS SINGULAR THAT SUCH A CONQUERING NAPOLEON 114 MANSNS

SINGULARLY
(HIS VOICE SINGULARLY TONELESS AND COLD BUT AT THE494 DAYS
SAME TIME INSISTENT)
HIS PALE FACE IS SINGULARLY PURE, SPIRITUAL AND 278 GGBROW
SAD.

SINISTER
(WITH A SINISTER SMILE) IT'S LUCKY THERE AREN'T 271 AHWILD
ANY OF GENERAL GABLER'S PISTOLS
IN A VOICE HE TRIES TO MAKE CASUAL BUT WHICH IS 494 DAYS
INDEFINABLY SINISTER)
SINISTER PURPOSE BEHIND MY SUGGESTION. 495 DAYS
(THE HIDDEN SINISTER NOTE AGAIN CREEPING INTO HIS 498 DAYS
COLDLY CASUAL TONE)
THEN STOPS ABRUPTLY AND CONTINUES IN HIS TONE OF 513 DAYS
COLD, SINISTER INSISTENCE)
SEEMING TO BE MORE THAN EVER SNEERING AND 525 DAYS
SINISTER.)
(WITH SINISTER MOCKERY) WHO KNOWS$ 527 DAYS
(HE GIVES A LOW, SINISTER LAUGH) 531 DAYS
I NEED HER DEATH FOR MY END. (THEN IN A SINISTER,539 DAYS
JEERING TONE)
(SLOWLY, IN HIS COLD TONE WITH ITS UNDERCURRENT OF540 DAYS
SINISTER HIDDEN MEANING)
HIS EYES COLD AND REMORSELESS IN HIS MASK OF 541 DAYS
SINISTER MOCKERY.
(THEN A SINISTER NOTE COMING INTO HIS VOICE) 545 DAYS
HIS EYES ARE FIXED ON ELSA'S FACE WITH AN EAGER, 548 DAYS
SINISTER INTENSENESS.)
HIS COLD EYES FIXED WITH A SINISTER INTENSITY 551 DAYS
THE SINISTER, MOCKING CHARACTER OF HIS MASK IS 553 DAYS
ACCENTUATED NOW.
HIS EYES FIXED WITH SINISTER GLOATING INTENTNESS 555 DAYS
ON ELSA'S FACE.
(HE GIVES A SINISTER LAUGH. 555 DAYS
THERE IS A SINISTER MATERNITY IN THEIR ASPECT, A 202 DESIRE
CRUSHING, JEALOUS ABSORPTION.
A SINISTER EXPRESSION COMES TO HER FACE. 34 ELECTR
HER FACE HAS BECOME LIKE A SINISTER EVIL MASK. 35 ELECTR
SHE SPEAKS TO HIS RETREATING FIGURE WITH A STRANGE 42 ELECTR
SINISTER AIR OF ELATION)
ALTHOUGH I CAN GUESS--(HE GIVES A SINISTER 153 ELECTR
CHUCKLE.)
(HE CHUCKLES WITH A SINISTER MOCKERY) 154 ELECTR

SINISTER (CONT'D.)
(AS IF HE HADN'T HEARD--IN THE SAME SINISTER 154 ELECTR
MOCKING TONE)
NOT UNDERSTANDING WHAT IS BEHIND THEIR TALK BUT 164 ELECTR
SENSING SOMETHING SINISTER,
SINISTER EXPRESSION. 226 HA APE
(HIS MANNER HAS BECOME SECRETIVE, WITH SINISTER 11 HUGHIE
UNDERTONES.
(IN A CASUAL TONE WHICH TO THEM SOUNDS SINISTER) 523 INZONE
(TO CALIGULA--WITH SINISTER EMPHASIS) 340 LAZARU
(SCRUTINIZING HIM--WITH SINISTER FINALITY) 340 LAZARU
IN A SINISTER COLD RAGE, THE CRUELER BECAUSE HIS 348 LAZARU
DREAM OF A CURE FOR DEATH IS

SINK
THEN SHE LETS HER HEAD SINK ON HIS SHOULDER AND 287 AHWILD
SIGHS SOFTLY)
THEN SHE LETS HER HEAD SINK ON HIS SHOULDER AGAIN 287 AHWILD
(PAUSES FOR A MOMENT, AFTER FINISHING THE LETTER, 8 ANNA
AS IF TO LET THE NEWS SINK IN--
(LETTING HIS HEAD SINK BACK ON THE DECK, 33 ANNA
AND NOW THAT ANDY'S COMING BACK--I'M GOING TO SINK149 BEYOND
MY FOOLISH PRIDE, RUTH/
SINK SO LOW AS TO FALL IN LOVE SERIOUS WITH ONE OF509 DIFRNT
THEM CRITTERS$
WE CAN SINK IT OVERBOARD AFTERWARDS/ 114 ELECTR
I'LL SINK THESE OVERBOARD FROM THE DOCK, ALONG 115 ELECTR
WITH WHAT WAS IN HIS STATEROOM.
UNTIL YOU GET SO DEEP AT THE BOTTOM OF HELL THERE 160 ELECTR
IS NO LOWER YOU CAN SINK AND
SINK INTO THE GUTTER AND DRAG MARGARET WITH YOU$ 281 GGBROW
'E'S GOT ENUF BLOODY GOLD TO SINK THIS BLEEDIN' 228 HA APE
SHIP/
LET YOURSELF SINK DOWN TO THE BOTTOM OF THE SEA. 625 ICEMAN
HAD ENOUGH TO SINK A SHIP, BUT CAN'T SINK. 156 JOURNE
THEIR HANDS HANG, THEIR ARMS SINK TO THEIR SIDES. 306 LAZARU
GENTLY HE LETS HER BODY SINK UNTIL IT RESTS 347 LAZARU
AGAINST THE STEPS OF THE DAIS.
WHICH THE PANTING MEN REACH OUT FOR AVIDLY, THEN 351 MARCOM
SINK BACK.
THE MEN SINK TO THE CROSS-LEGGED POSITION OF 433 MARCOM
PRAYER, THEIR HEADS BOWED.
OF THE CATAFALQUE AND SINK INTO ATTITUDES OF 434 MARCOM
PRAYER.
(WITH ONE MOTION ALL SINK TO THE POSITION OF 435 MARCOM
PRAYER)
(HIS VOICE BEGINS TO SINK INTO A DEJECTED 82 MISBEG
MONOTONE)
NOW DON'T SINK BACK HALF-DEAD-AND-ALIVE IN DREAMS 115 MISBEG
THE WAY YOU WERE BEFORE.
BUT I'LL NOT SINK TO DINING AT THE SAME TABLE. 39 POET
THE EFFECT OF THE DRINK ON RILEY IS MERELY TO SINK 95 POET
HIM DEEPER IN DREAMS.

SINKERS
FEEDIN' YOUR FACE--SINKERS AND COFFEE--DAT DON'T 250 HA APE
TOUCH IT.

SINKIN'
THE BLOODY SHIP IS SINKIN' AN' THE BLEEDIN' RATS 182 EJONES
'AS SLUNG THEIR 'OOKS.

SINKING
HER MIND ALREADY SINKING BACK INTO THAT SPENT CALM169 BEYOND
HE DOES SO MEEKLY, SINKING INTO THE CHAIR AT 561 DAYS
RIGHT CENTER.
(PITEOUSLY, SINKING ON HER KNEES) 261 DESIRE
(HE BREAKS DOWN ABJECTLY, SINKING ON HIS CHAIR AND464 DYNAMO
SOBBING.
STRIVING TO RAISE THEMSELVES ON END, FAILING AND 189 EJONES
SINKING PRONE AGAIN.
HIS VOICE SINKING DOWN THE SCALE AND RECEDING 199 EJONES
(THEN SINKING BACK--TENSELY) 48 ELECTR
(WITH SUDDEN WILDNESS--TORTUREDLY, SINKING ON HIS 292 GGBROW
KNEES BESIDE HER)
(SINKING IN HIS CHAIR, MORE AND MORE WEAKLY) 299 GGBROW
AND ASTERN THE LAND WOULD BE SINKING LOW AND DYING213 HA APE
OUT,
THAT ACCOUNTS FOR YOUR SINKING INTO THE DUMPS, 59 JOURNE
DOESN'T IT$
(CONFUSEDLY, SINKING BACK ON HIS COUCH AND 343 LAZARU
RELEASING HER)
(SUDDENLY THROWING HIS SPEAR AWAY AND SINKING ON 371 LAZARU
HIS KNEES.
(SINKING DOWN ON A CHAIR, HIS HEAD IN HIS HANDS) 452 WELDED

SINKS
(SHE SINKS IN ROCKER AT RIGHT OF TABLE) 188 AHWILD
(SID GIVES HER A HURT, MOURNFUL LOOK AND THEN 226 AHWILD
SINKS MEEKLY DOWN ON HIS CHAIR.)
(SINKS BACK INTO PREOCCUPATION--SCANNING THE 250 AHWILD
PAPER--VAGUELY)
SID'S CHIN SINKS ON HIS CHEST AND HE BEGINS TO 272 AHWILD
BREATHE NOISILY, FAST ASLEEP.
SHE COMES AND SINKS WEARILY IN A CHAIR BY THE 14 ANNA
TABLE, LEFT FRONT.)
(HE SINKS DOWN IN THE CHAIR OPPOSITE HER 21 ANNA
DEJECTEDLY--THEN TURNS TO HER--SADLY)
(HE SINKS SLOWLY BACK IN HIS CHAIR AGAIN, THE 57 ANNA
KNUCKLES SHOWING WHITE
(SHE PASSES HIM AND SINKS DOWN IN THE ROCKING- 69 ANNA
CHAIR.)
(SHE COVERS HER FACE WITH HER HANDS AND SINKS 108 BEYOND
WEAKLY INTO MAYO'S CHAIR.
(HE SINKS DOWN INTO HIS CHAIR AND SMILES WITH 126 BEYOND
BITTER SELF-SCORN)
(HER VOICE SINKS TO A TREMULOUS, TENDER WHISPER AS139 BEYOND
SHE FINISHES.)
AND SINKS DOWN IN IT EXHAUSTED.) 145 BEYOND
HE COMES FORWARD AND SINKS DOWN IN THE ROCKER ON 154 BEYOND
THE RIGHT OF TABLE.
(HE SINKS INTO HIS CHAIR, HIS HEAD BETWEEN HIS 165 BEYOND
HANDS)

SINKS 1446

SINKS (CONT'D.)
RUTH SINKS DOWN BESIDE HIM WITH A SOB AND PILLOWS 167 BEYOND HIS HEAD ON HER LAP.
(HE MAKES A FEEBLE ATTEMPT TO RISE BUT SINKS BACK 482 CARDIF WITH A SHARP GROAN.
HE GROWS CALMER AND SINKS BACK ON THE MATTRESS) 484 CARDIF
(HE SINKS DOWN ON HIS KNEES BESIDE THE BUNK, HIS 490 CARDIF HEAD ON HIS HANDS.
(HE SINKS INTO DIGNIFIED SILENCE.) 457 CARIBE
(SMITTY DOES NOT DEIGN TO REPLY TO THIS BUT SINKS 468 CARIBE INTO A SCORNFUL SILENCE.
(AVERTS HIS EYES AND SINKS BACK ON HIS CHAIR 563 CROSS AGAIN)
(SINKS DOWN IN THE CHAIR BY THE TABLE AND WAITS 547 DAYS TENSELY--
(JOHN SINKS DOWN HOPELESSLY ON THE CHAISE-LONGUE. 551 DAYS
(HE SINKS INTO DRUGGED SLEEP AGAIN.) 557 DAYS
(HE SINKS TO HIS KNEES) PRAY THAT ELSA'S LIFE MAY 559 DAYS BE SPARED TO YOU!
(SHE SINKS BACK AND CLOSES HER EYES. 563 DAYS
(HE SINKS TO HIS KNEES PULLING HER DOWN WITH HIM. 235 DESIRE
(SHE SINKS INTO A CHAIR BY 543 DIFRNT
(SHE SINKS DOWN TO THE GROUND, HER HANDS OVER HER 439 DYNAMO FACE)
REUBEN SINKS DOWN ON HIS KNEES BESIDE HER, HIDING 446 DYNAMO HIS FACE IN HER LAP.)
AND SINKS TO THE GROUND, EMBRACING HIS KNEES 174 EJONES SUPPLICATINGLY)
HIS EYES POP OUT, HE TRIES TO GET TO HIS FEET AND 194 EJONES FLY, BUT SINKS BACK,
HE SINKS INTO A KNEELING, DEVOTIONAL POSTURE 200 EJONES BEFORE THE ALTAR.
AS HIS VOICE SINKS INTO SILENCE, HE ENTERS THE 200 EJONES OPEN SPACE.
THE HEAD OF THE CROCODILE SINKS BACK BEHIND THE 202 EJONES RIVER BANK.
THEN SINKS INTO FAINTNESS AS THE WIND DIES. 5 ELECTR
THE BOX CLUTCHED IN HER HAND, AND SINKS ON HER 64 ELECTR KNEES BY THE HEAD OF THE BED.
(SHE SINKS IN THE CHAIR AT RIGHT OF TABLE.) 93 ELECTR
(OVERCOME BY GLOOMY DEJECTION, SINKS DOWN ON HIS 110 ELECTR CHAIR AGAIN)
SINKS DOWN ON THE LOWEST STEP AND BEGINS TO MOAN 121 ELECTR TO HERSELF.
(HE SINKS ON HIS KNEES BEFORE HER) 122 ELECTR
SHE GOES TO HER CHAIR AND SINKS ON IT.) 173 ELECTR
AND PEACE SINKS DEEP THROUGH THE SEA/ 264 GGBROW
THEN SINKS DOWN IN HIS CHAIR, GASPING, HIS HANDS 297 GGBROW PRESSED TO HIS HEART.
HIS HEAD SINKS TO THE TABLE AGAIN AND HE IS AT 579 ICEMAN ONCE FAST ASLEEP.)
(HE CLOSES HIS EYES AND SINKS BACK IN HIS CHAIR 598 ICEMAN EXHAUSTEDLY.
(LARRY SINKS BACK IN HIS CHAIR) 648 ICEMAN
(HE SITS DOWN IN HIS OLD PLACE AND SINKS INTO A 669 ICEMAN WOUNDED, SELF-PITYING BROODING.)
(HE SINKS BACK WEAKLY ON A BENCH.) 523 INZONE
THEN SHE SINKS DOWN IN THE CHAIR HE HAD OCCUPIED, 42 JOURNE
SHE SINKS DOWN IN ONE OF THE WICKER ARMCHAIRS AT 49 JOURNE REAR OF TABLE
(HAS SAID AND HE SINKS BACK LIMPLY.) 162 JOURNE
(HE SINKS BACK ON HIS CHAIR.) 162 JOURNE
HE SINKS BACK ON HIS CHAIR, 172 JOURNE
WHO, CRUSHED IN THE CROWD, SINKS FAINTING TO THE 283 LAZARU GROUND.
(HE SINKS ON HIS KNEES SOBBING. 290 LAZARU
HIS ARM SINKS TO HIS SIDE. 333 LAZARU
TIBERIUS SINKS BACK ON HIS COUCH, FIGHTING TO 341 LAZARU CONTROL HIMSELF--CONFUSEDLY.
(SHE LAUGHS AND SINKS BACK AND IS STILL. 348 LAZARU
(SINKS DOWN ON THE BENCH.) THANK YOU. 19 MANSNS
(HE SUDDENLY BREAKS AND SINKS ON THE BENCH AT LEFT)174 MANSNS OF POOL.
EVERYONE SINKS INTO THE ATTITUDE OF PRAYER EXCEPT 369 MARCOM THE POLES
(HER HEAD SINKS BACK ON HER ARMS AND SHE IS SOON 402 MARCOM ASLEEP.)
(THE PRINCESS SINKS TO HER KNEES, HER FACE HIDDEN 420 MARCOM IN HER ARMS ON THE BULWARK.)
HE SINKS INTO A HEAP BEFORE THE THRONE. 423 MARCOM
(HE SINKS DEJECTEDLY ON HIS THRONE AGAIN. 425 MARCOM
(HE HIMSELF SINKS TO THE POSITION OF PRAYER-- 435 MARCOM
(HIS CHIN SINKS ON HIS CHEST AND HIS EYES SHUT.) 85 MISBEG
THEN HE SINKS BACK IN HIS CHAIR AND STARES AT THE 37 POET TABLE.
HE FORCES CONTROL ON HIMSELF AND SINKS BACK IN HIS 51 POET CHAIR.
(SHE SINKS ON A CHAIR WITH A WEARY SIGH.) 131 POET
AS SOON AS HE IS GONE, SHE SINKS BACK INTO 136 POET APPREHENSIVE BROODING.
NORA SINKS ON THE CHAIR AT REAR OF THE TABLE. 166 POET
HE GROWS LIMP AND SINKS BACK ON HIS CHAIR 172 POET
(SHE SINKS DOWN ON HER CHAIR AT REAR OF THE CENTER172 POET TABLE
(THE OLD MAN SINKS BACK INTO A RELIEVED 583 ROPE IMMOBILITY.
(BENTLEY SINKS DOWN ON THE BENCH. 595 ROPE
(SHE SINKS DOWN ON HER KNEES AT MRS. EVANS' FEET-- 63 STRANG PITEOUSLY)
(HE SINKS DOWN IN THE ROCKING CHAIR DESPONDENTLY) 68 STRANG
(HE SINKS DOWN IN THE CHAIR BY THE TABLE AT LEFT. 97 STRANG
(SUDDENLY WITH A CRY OF PAIN, SINKS ON HER KNEES 182 STRANG BESIDE THE BODY)
(HE SINKS ON THE CHAIR WITH HIS HEAD IN HIS HANDS.472 WELDED
AND SINKS BACK ON THE CHAIR) 475 WELDED
(SHE GOES AWAY FROM HIM AND SINKS ON THE BED 478 WELDED EXHAUSTEDLY)

SINNED
SINNED 'EM WITH, MY SIN'S AS PURTY AS ANY ONE ON 211 DESIRE 'EM/
AN' I DON'T GIVE A DAMN HOW MANY SINS SHE'S SINNED211 DESIRE AFORE MINE OR WHO SHE'S
O WOMAN--MY LOVE--THAT I HAVE SINNED AGAINST IN MY292 GGBROW SICK PRIDE AND CRUELTY--

SINNER
YE OLD SINNERS 223 DESIRE
(RATHER GUILTILY) HE'S A SINNER--NATERAL-BORN. 233 DESIRE
OF BEING A CONDEMNED SINNER ALONE IN THE 444 DYNAMO THREATENING NIGHT)
FORGIVE DIS PO' SINNER/ 196 EJONES
I'SE A PO' SINNER, A PO' SINNER/ 196 EJONES
OH, LAWD, PERFECT DIS SINNER/ 200 EJONES
MERCY ON DIS PO' SINNER. 201 EJONES
WITHOUT MALICE, FEELING SUPERIOR TO NO ONE, A 576 ICEMAN SINNER AMONG SINNERS,
SHE WROTE TO DENOUNCE ME AND TRY TO BRING THE 589 ICEMAN SINNER TO REPENTANCE
IT'S NOT LIKELY THE LORD GOD'LL BE LISTENIN' TO A 582 ROPE WICKED OLD SINNER THE LIKE OF

SINNERS
NOT A STERN, SELF-RIGHTEOUS BEING WHO CONDEMNED 510 DAYS SINNERS TO TORMENT,
WITHOUT MALICE, FEELING SUPERIOR TO NO ONE, A 576 ICEMAN SINNER AMONG SINNERS,
I THINK IT WOULD HELP US POOR PIPE-DREAMING 661 ICEMAN SINNERS
AND SO IS ONE OF THE ELITE OF THE ALMIGHTY GOD IN 4 MISBEG A WORLD OF DAMNED SINNERS

SINNING
THEY HAD NO CHANCE TO DO ANY SINNING. 17 MISBEG

SINS
HOW WERE YOU FIGURING TO PUNISH HIM FOR HIS SINS 268 AHWILD
AFRAID HE'S COME TO LECTURE YOU ON YOUR SINS 499 DAYS
BUT THERE IS ALWAYS DEATH TO WASH ONE'S SINS 531 DAYS AWAY--
AN' I DON'T GIVE A DAMN HOW MANY SINS SHE'S SINNED211 DESIRE AFORE MINE OR WHO SHE'S
(ECSTATICALLY) I'D FORGIVE YE ALL THE SINS IN 266 DESIRE HELL FUN SAYIN' THAT!
MAY GOD FIND FORGIVENESS FOR YOUR SINS/ 115 ELECTR
FORGIVE MY SINS--FORGIVE MY SOLITUDE--FORGIVE MY 292 GGBROW SICKNESS--FORGIVE ME?
LIKE A NUN WHO ASKS MERCY FOR THE SINS OF THE 313 LAZARU WORLD.
(GLOOMLY) AND I, FOR MY SINS, AM HAWKING A 348 MARCOM NOVELTY, A BLOCK-PRINTED BOOK,
OR IS IT ONLY THESE INFERNAL MAHOMETAN FLEAS THE 360 MARCOM ALMIGHTY SENDS US FOR OUR SINS?
AND THEN HE STARTED TO PREACH ABOUT MY SINS--AND 17 MISBEG YOURS.
THEY SPENT SO MUCH TIME CONFESSING THEIR SINS, 17 MISBEG
AS IF ALL MY SINS HAD BEEN FORGIVEN--(HE BECOMES 171 MISBEG SELF-CONSCIOUS--CYNICALLY)
HE WILL DISCOVER THY SINS.= 579 ROPE
NO SINS OF THEIR OWN, 64 STRANG

SIP
(THE BOTTLE PASSES FROM HAND TO HAND, EACH MAN 462 CARIBE TAKING A SIP
(ACIDLY) ANY TIME YOU ONLY TAKE ONE SIP OF A 606 ICEMAN DRINK,
WHY, I'D ONLY TAKEN ONE SIP OF IT. 606 ICEMAN
THEY MUNCH THEIR BISCUITS AND SIP THEIR COFFEE IN 514 INZONE DULL SILENCE.)
(TAKES A SIP, THEN PUTS THE GLASS ON THE TABLE AND134 POET PUSHES IT AWAY LISTLESSLY.)
(THEN TAKING A SIP OF COFFEE, AND TRYING TO BE 57 STRANG PLEASANTLY CASUAL)

SIPS
(SHE SIPS.) 243 AHWILD
SHE SIPS IT IN SILENCE. 10 ANNA
MARTHY SIPS WHAT IS LEFT OF HER SCHOONER 13 ANNA REFLECTIVELY.
(HE TOSSES DOWN HIS DRINK IN ONE GULP, OLSON SIPS 497 VOYAGE HIS GINGER ALE.

SIRE
I WILL PLAY YOUR HUMBLE SLAVE, SIRE. 106 MANSNS
I--I CONFESS I AM A LITTLE FRIGHTENED, SIRE. 164 MANSNS
I HAVE THE KEY HERE, SIRE. 164 MANSNS
AT LAST YOU HAVE COME, SIRE. 164 MANSNS
GIVE ME YOUR HAND AND LET US GO WITHIN, SIRE-- 164 MANSNS

SIRED
I AM SIRED BY GOLD AND DAMNED BY IT, AS THEY SAY 219 HA APE AT THE RACE TRACK--

SIREE
IT AIN'T COMMON SENSE--NO SIREE, IT AIN'T--NOT BY 102 BEYOND A HELL OF A SIGHT/
BUTTER WON'T MELT IN YOUR MOUTH, NO SIREE/ 500 DIFRNT

SIREN
(BUT THE CLERK'S MIND HAS RUSHED OUT TO FOLLOW THE 27 HUGHIE SIREN WAIL OF A FIRE ENGINE.

SIRENS
(THE WHISTLES AND SIRENS FROM THE YACHTS UP THE 176 STRANG RIVER BEGIN TO BE HEARD.

SIRREE
(PROUDLY) YES, SIRREE/ 214 DESIRE
T'AIN'T OUR'N, NO SIRREE/ 221 DESIRE

SISSY
WHY GORDON SHOULD TAKE SUCH A FANCY TO THAT OLD 146 STRANG SISSY IS BEYOND ME/

SISTER
(MEANWHILE, THEIR MOTHER, AND THEIR AUNT LILY, 187 AHWILD THEIR FATHER'S SISTER,
LILY MILLER, HER SISTER-IN-LAW, IS FORTY-TWO, 187 AHWILD TALL, DARK AND THIN.
I HATE TO SAY IT OF YOUR SISTER. 191 AHWILD

SITS

SISTER (CONT'D.)
FINALLY HE LOOKS UP AND REGARDS HIS SISTER AND 224 AHWILD
ASKS WITH WONDERING AMAZEMENT)
SISTER, MY HEART BLEEDS FOR YOU AND YOUR POOR 225 AHWILD
FATHERLESS CHICKS/
(AS BELLE SITS BESIDE HIM) WELL, WHAT KIND OF 245 AHWILD
BEER WILL YOU HAVE, SISTERS
(HE GIVES HIS SISTER A SUPERIOR SCORNFUL GLANCE) 274 AHWILD
AND NOW--IT SEEMS--WELL--AS IF YOU'D ALWAYS BEEN 139 BEYOND
MY SISTER, THAT'S WHAT, RUTH.
MY SISTER-IN-LAW, MRS. MAYO--DOCTOR FAWCETT. 153 BEYOND
MY SISTER BRINGS HIS FOOD UP TO HIM. 556 CROSS
MY SISTER AND I WILL BE HERE--WITH HIM. 558 CROSS
WE HAVE TO MOVE, MY SISTER AND I. 562 CROSS
(HIS SISTER STARES AT HIM WITH DREAD FOREBODING. 565 CROSS
(TO HIS SISTER--EXCITEDLY) THERE/ 571 CROSS
THEN GLANCES BACK AT HIS SISTER MALICIOUSLY AND 500 DIFRNT
SAYS MEANINGLY)
CALEB'S SISTER IS A TALL, DARK GIRL OF TWENTY. 505 DIFRNT
CALEB'S SISTER AND LIVIN' RIGHT NEXT DOOR EVER 507 DIFRNT
SINCE YOU WAS ALL CHILDREN
WHO WAS TAKING CARE OF FATHER'S LITTLE SISTER WHO 19 ELECTR
DIED,
THAT THERE ISN'T ANYTHING YOUR SISTER WILL STOP 85 ELECTR
AT--
(ORIN TURNS TO LOOK AT HIS SISTER RESENTFULLY.) 91 ELECTR
YOU KNOW IN YOUR HEART I'M THE SAME AS I ALWAYS 96 ELECTR
WAS--YOUR SISTER--
DON'T YOU KNOW I'M YOUR SISTER, WHO LOVES YOU, 156 ELECTR
THERE ARE TIMES NOW WHEN YOU DON'T SEEM TO BE MY 165 ELECTR
SISTER, NOR MOTHER,
(MOCKINGLY) BLESSED ARE THE PITIFUL, SISTER/ 279 GGBROW
I'M HER SISTER. 288 GGBROW
MEN HAVE THEIR FAULTS, SISTER/ 318 GGBROW
A MAN COULDN'T WANT A BETTER SISTER THAN SHE WAS 603 ICEMAN
TO ME.
(SCATHINGLY) YOU TALKING OF YOUR DEAR SISTER/ 608 ICEMAN
BESS SOMEHOW NEVER HAD THE CONFIDENCE IN ME A 609 ICEMAN
SISTER SHOULD.
HOW YOU SHORT-CHANGED YOUR OWN SISTER/ 609 ICEMAN
REMEMBER, LIEUTENANT, YOU ARE SPEAKING OF MY 651 ICEMAN
SISTER/
AND MY OLDER SISTER SEWED, AND MY TWO YOUNGER 148 JOURNE
STAYED AT HOME TO KEEP THE HOUSE.
I'LL HAVE TO GO TO THE INFIRMARY AND SHOW SISTER 171 JOURNE
MARTHA.
SISTER THERESA WILL GIVE ME A DREADFUL SCOLDING. 171 JOURNE
HERE IS YOUR SISTER, MARTHA, LAZARUS. 292 LAZARU
SISTER AND SISTER, ONE WOMAN AND ANOTHER, WITH THE171 MANSNS
WAY SO CLEAR BEFORE US.
(MIKE HOGAN IS TWENTY, ABOUT FOUR INCHES SHORTER 3 MISBEG
THAN HIS SISTER.
HAVING A SISTER WHO'S THE SCANDAL OF THE 6 MISBEG
NEIGHBORHOOD.
ME, INTRODUCE HER TO THE JEBS AS MY SISTER--AND 38 MISBEG
GET AWAY WITH IT.
SISTER AROUND THE GROUNDS, ACCOMPANIED BY ONE OF 39 MISBEG
THE JEBS.
MAYBE IT'S HIS SISTER. 19 POET
HE HASN'T A SISTER. 19 POET
(TAKING IT--WITH A LOOK OF DISGUST AT HIS HALF- 589 ROPE
SISTER)
AND MY HUSBAND'S SISTER, SAMMY'S AUNT, SHE'S OUT 59 STRANG
OF HER MIND.
(TURNING TO NINA) I THINK I'LL WRITE TO MY SISTER113 STRANG
IN CALIFORNIA AND ASK HER TO
I HOPE YOUR SISTER IS WELL. 147 STRANG
I'VE SEEN IT IN YOU, YOUR FATHER, MY MOTHER, 177 STRANG
SISTER, GORDON, SAM,
SISTER. 478 WELDED
SISTER'S
THE NEIGHBORS--THEY'RE FAR AWAY BUT--FOR MY 562 CROSS
SISTER'S SAKE--YOU UNDERSTAND.
(CATCHING AT HIS SISTER'S HAND--CHOKINGLY) 570 CROSS
(HE LAUGHS LOUDLY--THEN NOTICING HIS SISTER'S 503 DIFRNT
STONY EXPRESSION,
I AM NO BETTER THAN A PROSTITUTE IN YOUR SISTER'S 87 ELECTR
EYES/
NOW IT IS HIS SISTER'S DEATH TWO MONTHS BEFORE 159 STRANG
SISTERS.
AYE, THE TWO OF YOU ARE LIKE SISTERS. 39 ELECTR
AND ALL THE MOTHERS AND WIVES AND SISTERS AND 82 ELECTR
GIRLS DID THE SAME/
AFFECTIONATE SISTERS TOWARD A BULLYING BROTHER 611 ICEMAN
I WOULDN'T SAY THIS UNLESS I KNEW, BROTHERS AND 661 ICEMAN
SISTERS.
KNEELING BESIDE HIM WITH BOWED HEADS ARE HIS WIFE,274 LAZARU
MIRIAM, HIS SISTERS,
WHILE HIS SISTERS AND FATHER KISS AND PRESS HIS 278 LAZARU
HANDS,
AND SISTERS AND KISSES EACH IN TURN ON THE 293 LAZARU
FOREHEAD.
THE THREE DAUGHTERS-IN-LAW OF JONATHAN, EVAN'S 83 POET
HALF-SISTERS,
THE SISTERS, AS EVERYONE CALLED THEM, 84 POET
SITE
IT HAS BEEN MOVED TO ITS PRESENT SITE, AND LOOKS 1 MISBEG
IT.
NOT BY A DAMNED SITE/ 598 ROPE
SITS
SHE SITS DOWN AND STARTS TO PLAY WILDLY AN OLD 551 'ILE
HYMN.
SHE SITS WITH HALF-CLOSED EYES, 552 'ILE
MILDRED SITS ON THE SOFA AT LEFT, FRONT.) 187 AHWILD
AS IF HE WISHED IT WERE MCCOMBER'S HEAD, AND SITS 201 AHWILD
DOWN OPPOSITE HIM.)
SITS DOWN IN HIS PLACE IN THE CHAIR AT THE RIGHT 221 AHWILD
OF THE TWO

SITS (CONT'D.)
LILY SITS IN THE ONE OF THOSE AT LEFT, BY THE HEAD221 AHWILD
UP THE TABLE.
(SHE SITS DOWN STIFFLY AT THE FOOT OF THE TABLE.) 222 AHWILD
(SITS DOWN BUT BENDS FORWARD TO CALL TO HIS WIFE 223 AHWILD
IN A CONFIDENTIAL TONE)
YES-- (SHE COMES AND SITS ON HIS LAP. 240 AHWILD
(AS BELLE SITS BESIDE HIM) WELL, WHAT KIND OF 245 AHWILD
BEER WILL YOU HAVE, SISTERS
MRS.MILLER SITS BY THE TABLE AT RIGHT, FRONT. 249 AHWILD
MILDRED SITS AT THE DESK AT RIGHT, FRONT, WRITING 249 AHWILD
TWO WORDS OVER AND OVER AGAIN.
TOMMY SITS ON THE SOFA AT LEFT, FRONT. 249 AHWILD
(HE SITS DOWN IN THE ARMCHAIR AT LEFT OF TABLE, 254 AHWILD
REAR)
(SHE SITS DOWN AGAIN AND BENDS OVER HER BOOK 256 AHWILD
TENSELY.
AND SITS AT THE END OF THE SOFA, FACING FRONT, 258 AHWILD
HUNCHED UP, ELBOWS ON KNEES,
SHE GOES QUIETLY AND SITS DOWN IN HER CHAIR AGAIN.259 AHWILD
(HE SITS DOWN IN THE ROCKING-CHAIR AT RIGHT, REAR,264 AHWILD
SID SITS DOWN AGAIN.) 268 AHWILD
RICHARD SITS IN TRAGIC GLOOM. 271 AHWILD
(COMES AND SITS IN HER FATHER'S CHAIR AT RIGHT, 272 AHWILD
FRONT OF TABLE)
(HE SITS BESIDE HER) BUT I'VE GOT TO BE HOME IN 280 AHWILD
BED AGAIN.
(COMES BACK AND SITS DOWN BY HIM SHYLY) 286 AHWILD
AND SITS IN A SELF-CONSCIOUS, UNNATURAL POSITION. 293 AHWILD
WHERE THE LIGHT IS DIMMEST, AND SITS DOWN ON THE 293 AHWILD
SOFA, AND STARES BEFORE HIM,
(SHE SITS IN HER CHAIR AND SIGHS CONTENTEDLY. 296 AHWILD
(SHE COMES FORWARD AND SITS AT THE TABLE IN THE 7 ANNA
RIGHT CORNER, FRONT).
(HE SITS DOWN OPPOSITE HER. 8 ANNA
(HE TAKES HER DRINK IN TO MARTHY AND SITS DOWN AT 10 ANNA
THE TABLE.
(SHE SHUFFLES OVER TO ANNA'S TABLE AND SITS DOWN 15 ANNA
OPPOSITE HER.
(HALF RISES TO HER FEET, THEN SITS DOWN AGAIN) 23 ANNA
(SITS DOWN BESIDE HER WITH A SIGH) 27 ANNA
HE FINDS HIS WAY TO THE COIL OF HIS HAWSER AND 30 ANNA
SITS DOWN ON IT FACING THE
(HE SITS DOWN WEAKLY) YOU'RE ALL IN, YOU MIGHT AS 32 ANNA
WELL OWN UP TO IT.
(BURKE RISES AND SITS ON BENCH. 33 ANNA
(WITH A HALF LAUGH) WELL--(SHE SITS DOWN) BUT WE 35 ANNA
WON'T TALK ABOUT ME, SEE5
AND SITS DOWN IN THE ROCKING-CHAIR. 44 ANNA
THEN THINKS BETTER OF IT AND SITS STILL. 45 ANNA
(HE SITS DOWN OPPOSITE CHRIS AT THE TABLE AND 45 ANNA
LEANS OVER TOWARD HIM)
(CHRIS SITS DUMP, SCOWLING, HIS EYES AVERTED. 45 ANNA
(HE SITS DOWN AT THE LEFT OF TABLE.) 51 ANNA
(HE SITS CRUSHED.) 52 ANNA
(HE SITS IN A CHAIR BY THE TABLE, SETTING DOWN THE 63 ANNA
CAN OF BEER.
ANNA SITS AT THE TABLE, STARING STRAIGHT IN FRONT 63 ANNA
OF HER.)
(HE CROSSES THE DITCH AND SITS ON THE FENCE NEAR 82 BEYOND
HIS BROTHER)
JAMES MAYO SITS IN FRONT OF THE TABLE. 94 BEYOND
(ANDREW SITS FORWARD IN HIS CHAIR WITH AN ABRUPT 96 BEYOND
MOVEMENT)
(ROBERT COMES FORWARD AND SITS ON ANDY'S CHAIR. 99 BEYOND
SCOTT SITS DUMBFOUNDED AND OPEN-MOUTHED. 106 BEYOND
SHE SITS IN THE ROCKER IN FRONT OF THE TABLE AND 116 BEYOND
SIGHS WEARILY.
(MARY SITS DOWN ON THE FLOOR BEFORE THE TABLE 117 BEYOND
RUTH COMES BACK AND SITS DOWN IN HER CHAIR.) 118 BEYOND
SHE IMMEDIATELY THINKS BETTER OF THIS AND SITS 119 BEYOND
WITH THE LETTER IN HER HANDS
SHE SETS THOSE BEFORE HIM AND SITS DOWN IN HER 121 BEYOND
FORMER PLACE.
HE SITS DOWN AND IMMEDIATELY BECOMES ABSORBED IN 121 BEYOND
READING.
AND SITS DOWN DEJECTEDLY IN HER OLD PLACE) 125 BEYOND
(HE WALKS OVER AND SITS DOWN ON THE BOULDER BESIDE130 BEYOND
ROBERT)
(SHE JUMPS LIGHTLY TO THE TOP OF A ROCK AND SITS 136 BEYOND
DOWN)
(HE SITS DOWN ON THE GRASS, MOPPING HIS FACE.) 141 BEYOND
AFTER A PAUSE HE OPENS HIS EYES AND SITS UP IN HIS149 BEYOND
CHAIR.
SHE SITS DOWN IN HER CHAIR AND STARES AT THE 151 BEYOND
STOVE--DULLY)
(HE SITS DOWN IN HIS CHAIR AND PULLS IT CLOSE TO 155 BEYOND
RUTH'S IMPULSIVELY)
HE COMES AND SITS DOWN ON HIS CHAIR AGAIN, 162 BEYOND
SUPPORTING HIS HEAD ON HIS HANDS.
(HE COMES BACK QUIETLY AND SITS DOWN. 479 CARDIF
(DRISCOLL, NOT KNOWING WHAT TO DO, SITS DOWN ON 484 CARDIF
THE BENCH BESIDE HIM.
WHO SITS SMOKING HIS PIPE IN FRONT OF HIS DOOR. 466 CARIBE
SMITTY SITS DOWN ON THE HATCH FACING HIM. 466 CARIBE
AND COMES OVER AND SITS BESIDE HIM AND PUTS HER 468 CARIBE
ARM OVER HIS SHOULDER.)
THEN SITS STARING BEFORE HIM. 470 CARIBE
HE JUMPS TO HIS FEET WITH HIS FISTS CLENCHED BUT 471 CARIBE
SEES WHO HIT HIM AND SITS DOWN
(BIG FRANK SITS DOWN ON THE HATCH, RIGHT. 471 CARIBE
(HE SITS DOWN IN THE CHAIR TO THE LEFT OF THE 556 CROSS
TABLE)
THEN HE GOES OVER TO THE TABLE, TURNING THE 562 CROSS
LANTERN VERY LOW, AND SITS DOWN.
LOVING SITS IN THE ARMCHAIR AT REAR OF TABLE. 493 DAYS
LOVING SITS MOTIONLESSLY REGARDING HIM WITH 496 DAYS
SCORNFUL EYES.)

SITS

SITS (CONT'D.)

FATHER BAIRD SITS DOWN. 900 DAYS
JOHN SITS IN HIS CHAIR AT LEFT. 500 DAYS
(HE SITS DOWN IN THE CHAIR AT RIGHT OF TABLE WHERE505 DAYS
FATHER BAIRD HAD SAT.
WHILE THE PRIEST SITS IN THE ONE AT RIGHT, CENTER.505 DAYS
THEN HE COMES SLOWLY BACK AND SITS DOWN IN HIS 513 DAYS
CHAIR AND STARES BEFORE HIM.
SHE COMES FORWARD AND SITS ON THE SOFA. 514 DAYS
(SHE SITS ON THE SOFA AND DRAWS LUCY DOWN BESIDE 516 DAYS
HER.)
SHE SITS DOWN BESIDE HIM--WITH A SMILE) 528 DAYS
SITS DOWN ON IT AND STARES BEFORE HIM WITH HUNTED 528 DAYS
EYES.
FATHER BAIRD SITS IN THE SAME ATTITUDE AS HE HAD 541 DAYS
IN THE PREVIOUS SCENE.
(SHE SITS IN THE CHAIR IN FRONT OF TABLE. 548 DAYS
JOHN SITS IN THE CHAIR TOWARD THE FOOT OF THE BED.553 DAYS
FRONT.
STILLWELL SITS IN THE CHAIR BY THE HEAD OF THE 554 DAYS
BED, REAR.
HE SITS, WATCHING HER FACE WORRIEDLY, HIS FINGERS 558 DAYS
ON HER WRIST.
HE SITS IN THE CHAIR BY THE BED AND FEELS ELSA'S 558 DAYS
PULSE.
AS JOHN COMES IN, STILLWELL TURNS FROM WHERE HE 560 DAYS
SITS BESIDE THE BEDSIDE.
(HE SITS DOWN IN CONFUSION.) 207 DESIRE
(HE SITS DOWN AGAIN, RELAPSING INTO A BROODING 209 DESIRE
SILENCE.
EBEN SITS BEFORE HIS PLATE OF UNTOUCHED FOOD, 216 DESIRE
BROODING FROWNINGLY.)
HE SITS DOWN AT THE TABLE, FACES THE STOVE AND 220 DESIRE
PULLS OUT THE PAPER.
(HE SITS DOWN ON THE EDGE OF PORCH.) 231 DESIRE
SHE SITS BESIDE HIM. 234 DESIRE
(HE SITS DOWN ON THE EDGE OF THE PORCH. 234 DESIRE
EBEN SITS UP WITH A START, LISTENING. 239 DESIRE
(MECHANICALLY HE PLACES HIS HAT CAREFULLY ON THE 241 DESIRE
FLOOR NEAR THE DOOR AND SITS
ABBIE SITS ON THE EDGE OF THE HORSEHAIR SOFA. 241 DESIRE
IN THE KITCHEN, ABBIE SITS AT THE TABLE, HER BODY 262 DESIRE
LIMP AND EXHAUSTED.
SHE SITS IN ONE OF THE ROCKERS BY THE TABLE, HER 501 DIFRNT
FACE GREATLY TROUBLED,
AND SITS DOWN WITH A COMFORTABLE SIGH) 508 DIFRNT
FINALLY SHE SITS DOWN HELPLESSLY AND REMAINS FIXED514 DIFRNT
IN A STRAINED ATTITUDE.
(SITS DOWN--WETTING HER LIPS) 526 DIFRNT
(SHE SITS IN A ROCKER BY THE TABLE.) 531 DIFRNT
(GIVES NO SIGN OF HAVING HEARD HIM BUT COMES BACK 547 DIFRNT
TO HER CHAIR AND SITS DOWN.
EMMA SITS STRAIGHT AND STIFF IN HER CHAIR FOR A 548 DIFRNT
WHILE.
(HE SITS DOWN BY THE TABLE AND, PICKING UP HIS 426 DYNAMO
BIBLE.
(SITS THINKING GLOOMILY) (NEVER LIED TO HER... 426 DYNAMO
ADA SITS DOWN AT RIGHT, WATCHING HER FATHER WITH A436 DYNAMO
CHALLENGING SMILE.)
(WITH A GREAT PRETENSE OF INDIFFERENCE SHE GETS A 443 DYNAMO
BOOK FROM THE TABLE AND SITS
AND MRS. LIGHT SITS CROUCHING BY THE HEDGE. 444 DYNAMO
SHE LEADS HIM FRONT AND SITS ON THE SIDE OF THE 446 DYNAMO
BED)
HE COMES AND SITS IN HIS OLD CHAIR AND 455 DYNAMO
MECHANICALLY PICKS UP HIS BIBLE FROM THE
(HE SITS DOWN ON HIS THRONE WITH EASY DIGNITY) 176 EJONES
(HE SITS IN A WEARY ATTITUDE, LISTENING TO THE 188 EJONES
RHYTHMIC BEATING OF THE TOM-TOM)
(BUT HE SITS DOWN AND BEGINS TO LACE UP HIS SHOES 188 EJONES
IN GREAT HASTE.
AND SITS DOWN IN A TENSE POSITION, READY FOR 195 EJONES
INSTANT FLIGHT.
(SITS DOWN ON THE STUMP AGAIN) 196 EJONES
(HAZEL SITS AT LEFT OF BENCH, LAVINIA BESIDE HER 13 ELECTR
IN THE MIDDLE.
PETER SITS GINGERLY ON THE RIGHT EDGE SO THAT 13 ELECTR
THERE IS AN OPEN SPACE BETWEEN HIM
AND GOES AND SITS ON THE BENCH AT LEFT. 18 ELECTR
(HE SITS ON THE BENCH AT HER RIGHT. 21 ELECTR
(CHRISTINE SITS IN THE CHAIR AT REAR CENTER. 29 ELECTR
COMES AND SITS IN MANNON'S CHAIR ON THE LEFT OF 36 ELECTR
TABLE.
(SHE SITS DOWN.) 37 ELECTR
(CHRISTINE SITS ON THE TOP STEP AT CENTER.. 47 ELECTR
HE SITS ON THE MIDDLE STEP AT RIGHT.. 47 ELECTR
(HE SITS AWKWARDLY TWO STEPS BELOW HER, ON HER 51 ELECTR
LEFT.
(HE SITS DOWN BESIDE HER) SHUT YOUR EYES AGAIN/ 53 ELECTR
CHRISTINE HASTILY SITS DOWN IN THE CHAIR BY THE 59 ELECTR
TABLE.
PUSHING IT SO SHE SITS FACING LEFT, FRONT. 59 ELECTR
(SHE SITS AGAIN IN THE SAME POSITION AS BEFORE. 59 ELECTR
(THEN, AS SHE SITS DOWN AGAIN, HE GOES ON 60 ELECTR
GLOOMILY)
CHRISTINE GOES AROUND THE TABLE TO THE CHAIR 81 ELECTR
OPPOSITE ORIN AND SITS DOWN.)
HE SITS DOWN IN THE CHAIR AT LEFT OF TABLE AND 84 ELECTR
STARES BEFORE HIM BITTERLY.
(HE SITS ON THE FLOOR AT HER FEET AND LOOKS UP 89 ELECTR
INTO HER FACE.
(THEN WITH A DRY SMILE) DEATH SITS SO NATURALLY 94 ELECTR
ON YOU/
(SHE SITS ON THE BENCH) LET'S SIT OUT HERE. 117 ELECTR
(HAZEL SITS BESIDE HER.) 117 ELECTR
(SITS IN THE CHAIR OPPOSITE HIM--WEARILY) 151 ELECTR
AND SITS ON THE SOFA AT RIGHT, ADOPTING A 161 ELECTR
SUSPICIOUSLY CARELESS ATTITUDE.

SITS (CONT'D.)
(SHE GOES AND SITS AT THE TOP OF THE STEPS, BOLT 170 ELECTR
UPRIGHT.
(HE SITS ON THE EDGE OF THE PORTICO BESIDE HER. 174 ELECTR
(SHE GOES AND SITS ON THE CENTER BENCH. 258 GGBROW
THE FATHER STRIDES TO THE CENTER BENCH AND SITS 260 GGBROW
DOWN.
(HE SITS IN HIS FATHER'S PLACE AT CENTER 261 GGBROW
(HE SITS DOWN ON THE BENCH AT RIGHT, FORCING A 265 GGBROW
JOKING TONE)
(ALREADY PREOCCUPIED WITH ANOTHER THOUGHT--COMES 270 GGBROW
AND SITS IN CHAIR ON LEFT)
(SHE SITS DOWN ON THE LOUNGE. 274 GGBROW
(SITS AT HIS DESK AGAIN, LOOKING AHEAD IN A NOT 277 GGBROW
UNSATISFYING MELANCHOLY REVERIE.
SYMPATHETICALLY AS SHE COMES BACK AND SITS DOWN ON279 GGBROW
HER STOOL.)
DION SITS IN THE CHAIR ON LEFT, CYBEL ON THE SOFA.284 GGBROW
WEARILY COMES AND SITS DOWN AT HER FEET AND LAYS 285 GGBROW
HIS HEAD IN HER LAP--
BROWN SITS IN THE CHAIR AT LEFT READING AN 294 GGBROW
ARCHITECTURAL PERIODICAL.
(SHE SITS IN THE CHAIR WHERE DION HAD SAT AND 300 GGBROW
STARES STRAIGHT BEFORE HER.
HE SITS BEHIND THE DESK.) 304 GGBROW
(SHE SITS ON THE CHAIR STIFFLY. 304 GGBROW
BROWN SITS DOWN AT HIS DESK, TAKING OFF THE MASK 305 GGBROW
AGAIN.
MARGARET SITS ON THE SOFA, WAITING WITH THE 308 GGBROW
ANXIOUS.
SHE SITS ON SOFA AND PICKS UP HER BOOK.) 310 GGBROW
FINALLY HE SITS WITH HER ON THE LOUNGE.) 315 GGBROW
CYBEL TAKES OFF HER MASK AND SITS DOWN BY BROWN'S 321 GGBROW
HEAD.
YANK SITS DOWN AGAIN IN THE SAME ATTITUDE OF =THE 227 HA APE
THINKER.=
(HE SITS, THE PAPER IN THE HAND AT HIS SIDE, 244 HA APE
HE SITS THERE, BROODING. 250 HA APE
THE NIGHT CLERK SITS ON THE STOOL, FACING FRONT, 7 HUGHIE
HIS BACK TO THE SWITCHBOARD.
JOE MOTT SITS AT LEFT-FRONT OF THE TABLE, FACING 574 ICEMAN
FRONT.
---JIMMY TOMORROW---SITS FACING FRONT. 574 ICEMAN
AT THE TABLE AT RIGHT, FRONT, HARRY HOPE, THE 576 ICEMAN
PROPRIETOR, SITS IN THE MIDDLE
BETWEEN THE FIRST TWO TABLES, SITS WILLIE OBAN, 577 ICEMAN
(HE SITS DOWN IN THE CHAIR AT LARRY'S LEFT.) 578 ICEMAN
(SHRUGS HIS SHOULDERS AND SITS DOWN AGAIN) 583 ICEMAN
(PARRITT SITS DOWN. 585 ICEMAN
HE COMES FORWARD AND SITS AT THE TABLE AND SLUMPS 586 ICEMAN
BACK.
DEN HE SITS DOWN AND SAYS QUIET AGAIN, =ALL RIGHT.601 ICEMAN
YOU CAN OPEN.
CHUCK TAKES AN EMPTY CHAIR FROM HOPE'S TABLE AND 615 ICEMAN
PUTS IT BY HERS AND SITS DOWN.
(CORA SITS DOWN BETWEEN MARGIE AND PEARL, 615 ICEMAN
NEAR THE MIDDLE OF THE ROW OF CHAIRS BEHIND THE 629 ICEMAN
TABLE, LARRY SITS, FACING FRONT.
CHUCK SITS IN A CHAIR AT THE FOOT ((LEFT)) OF THE629 ICEMAN
BANQUET TABLE.
(HE SITS DOWN WHERE HE WAS, HIS BACK TURNED TO 640 ICEMAN
THEM.)
(HE SITS DOWN WEAKLY ON LARRY'S RIGHT.) 644 ICEMAN
WHERE HE SITS IN DEJECTED, SHAKING MISERY, HIS 645 ICEMAN
CHIN ON HIS CHEST.)
(HE SITS, WITH CORA ON HIS LEFT AND JOE ON HER 657 ICEMAN
LEFT.
AT THE BARROOM TABLE, FRONT, LARRY SITS IN A 665 ICEMAN
CHAIR, FACING RIGHT-FRONT.
ON HIS RIGHT, IN A CHAIR FACING RIGHT, HUGO SITS 665 ICEMAN
SPRAWLED FORWARD.
(HE SITS DOWN IN HIS OLD PLACE AND SINKS INTO A 669 ICEMAN
WOUNDED, SELF-PITYING BROODING.)
(HE GOES BACK AND SITS AT THE LEFT OF THE SECOND 674 ICEMAN
TABLE, FACING PARRITT.
MCGLOIN GOES TO THE FIRST TABLE BEYOND HIM AND 681 ICEMAN
SITS WITH HIS BACK TO THE BAR.)
(AS IF THAT FINISHED THE SUBJECT, HE COMES FORWARD694 ICEMAN
TO HOPE AND SITS BESIDE HIM,
AT RIGHT, REAR, OF HIM, ALSO AT THIS TABLE, 696 ICEMAN
GENERAL WETJOEN SITS FACING FRONT.
AT RIGHT, REAR, OF WETJOEN, BUT BESIDE THE LAST 696 ICEMAN
TABLE OF THE GROUP, SITS WILLIE.
AT THE FIRST TABLE AT RIGHT OF CENTER, CORA SITS 696 ICEMAN
AT LEFT, FRONT, OF IT.
HUGO SITS AT REAR, FACING FRONT, HIS HEAD ON HIS 696 ICEMAN
ARMS IN HIS HABITUAL POSITION,
OF LARRY'S TABLE AND SITS IN THE ONE CHAIR THERE, 704 ICEMAN
FACING FRONT.
(HE SITS IN THE CHAIR BY CHUCK AND POURS A DRINK 719 ICEMAN
AND TOSSES IT DOWN.
HE CHANGES AGAIN, GIGGLING GOOD-NATUREDLY, AND 724 ICEMAN
SITS AT REAR OF THE MIDDLE TABLE)
(HE SITS DOWN, OVERTURNING AS HE DOES SO THE 517 INZONE
UNTOUCHED CUP OF COFFEE WHICH
(SCOTTY HURRIES OVER TO A BENCH AND SITS DOWN. 522 INZONE
SMITTY ENTERS AND SITS DOWN BESIDE HIS BUNK. 522 INZONE
(HE SITS DOWN AGAIN.) 523 INZONE
(FOR A MOMENT HE SITS STARING IN FRONT OF HIM. 523 INZONE
(HE TAKES THE PAIL AND SITS DOWN, PLACING IT ON 527 INZONE
THE FLOOR BETWEEN HIS FEET.
(SHE LAUGHS AND SITS IN THE WICKER ARMCHAIR AT 14 JOURNE
RIGHT REAR OF TABLE.
HE LIGHTS HIS CIGAR AND SITS DOWN IN THE ROCKER AT 15 JOURNE
RIGHT OF TABLE.
(JAMIE SHRUGS HIS SHOULDERS AND SITS DOWN IN THE 21 JOURNE
CHAIR ON HER RIGHT.)

SITS

(CONT'D.)

(HE SITS DOWN IN THE ROCKING CHAIR AND SHE PUTS A 42 JOURNE PILLOW BEHIND HIS BACK.)

EDMUND SITS IN THE ARMCHAIR AT LEFT OF TABLE, 51 JOURNE READING A BOOK.

HE PUTS THE GLASS HASTILY ON THE TRAY AND SITS 53 JOURNE DOWN AGAIN, OPENING HIS BOOK.

(HE SITS ACROSS THE TABLE FROM EDMUND--IRRITABLY.) 54 JOURNE

EDMUND SITS IN A CHAIR BY THE TABLE, 71 JOURNE

WHEN YOU'RE IN AGONY AND HALF INSANE, HE SITS AND 74 JOURNE HOLDS YOUR HAND

(SHE GETS HIM TO SIT AND SHE SITS SIDEWAYS ON THE 91 JOURNE ARM OF HIS

(SHE SITS IN THE ROCKER AT RIGHT OF TABLE.) 99 JOURNE

(SHE SITS IN THE ARMCHAIR AT RIGHT REAR OF TABLE. 103 JOURNE

(SHE SITS AT LEFT REAR OF TABLE, EDMUND AT LEFT OF108 JOURNE TABLE.

THEN SHE COMES BACK AND SITS IN HER CHAIR, THE 121 JOURNE SAME BLANK LOOK ON HER FACE.)

(SITS DOWN OPPOSITE HIS FATHER--CONTEMPTUOUSLY.) 127 JOURNE

(SITS DOWN SHEEPISHLY--GRUMBLES PATHETICALLY.) 128 JOURNE

AND SITS DOWN AGAIN HEAVILY. 151 JOURNE

EDMUND SITS TENSELY. 169 JOURNE

TYRONE COMES TO THE TABLE AND SITS DOWN, 169 JOURNE

THEN HE SITS DOWN AGAIN AND WAITS, HIS EYES 169 JOURNE AVERTED.

SHE MOVES LEFT TO THE FRONT END OF THE SOFA 174 JOURNE BENEATH THE WINDOWS AND SITS DOWN,

AT CENTER SITS LAZARUS, HIS HEAD HALOED 274 LAZARU

THE COMPANY SITS DOWN IN THEIR PLACES, 278 LAZARU

POMPEIA, A ROMAN NOBLEWOMAN, THE FAVORITE MISTRESS336 LAZARU OF CAESAR, SITS AT FRONT.

(HE MOUNTS THE STEPS OF THE DAIS AND SITS ON THE 340 LAZARU COUCH AT LEFT OF TABLE--

FAILING IN THIS, SHE PASSES OVER AND SITS BESIDE 341 LAZARU CALIGULA.

TIBERIUS SITS FACING FRONT, HIS ELBOWS ON HIS 350 LAZARU KNEES.

ON THE TOP STEP, POMPEIA SITS, FACING RIGHT, HER 350 LAZARU HANDS CLASPED ABOUT ONE KNEE,

LAZARUS SITS ON THE COUCH AT THE RIGHT ON THE 350 LAZARU DAIS.

TIBERIUS SITS ON THE THRONE, 363 LAZARU

(SHE SITS DOWN.) AND WHAT WILL YOU DO WITH THESE 3 MANSNS YEARS, DEBORAH?

(SHE SITS DOWN AGAIN.) IT IS I WHO AM EARLY. 4 MANSNS

(SHE SITS DOWN AGAIN.) YOU HAVEN'T TOLD ME A WORD 10 MANSNS ABOUT YOURSELF YET.

DEBORAH SITS IN SILENCE, HER EYES ON THE GROUND.) 20 MANSNS

(SHE SITS ON THE STEP OF THE SUMMER-HOUSE, 31 MANSNS

SHE SITS IN THE CHAIR AT RIGHT-FRONT, AND HE SITS 44 MANSNS WHERE HE HAD BEEN.)

SIMON SITS IN THE CHAIR AT LEFT-FRONT OF TABLE. 44 MANSNS

SARA SITS LISTENING. 49 MANSNS

SIMON SITS IN HIS OLD PLACE AT LEFT-FRONT OF 50 MANSNS TABLE.

(HE STOPS ABRUPTLY AND SITS DOWN AGAIN AS THE 57 MANSNS DOOR FROM THE STUDY IS OPENED AND

(HE SITS AT THE TABLE--JOEL BEHIND IT--CURTLY.) 59 MANSNS

HE SITS DOWN, PICKS UP THE MORNING MAIL STACKED ON 69 MANSNS HIS DESK.

HE COMES BACK AND SITS DOWN STIFFLY IN THE CHAIR.) 71 MANSNS

(THE SITS STARING BEFORE HIM, FROWNINGLY 75 MANSNS CONCENTRATED.

(SHE SITS DOWN AND HE SITS DOWN AGAIN.) 76 MANSNS

(SHE SITS DOWN ON THE ARM OF HIS CHAIR AND HUGS 81 MANSNS HIM TO HER.)

(HE SITS DOWN AT HIS DESK--WITH A STRANGE SMILE OF 94 MANSNS ANTICIPATION.

AND GOES AND OPENS THE DOOR, THEN SITS DOWN BY THE 96 MANSNS STEPS AGAIN.

(HE SITS ON THE STONE BENCH ON HER LEFT.) 96 MANSNS

(SHE SITS DOWN, CLOSE BESIDE HER, SO THEIR ARMS 123 MANSNS TOUCH.)

HE SITS IN HIS CHAIR AND STARES AT HIS BOOK 130 MANSNS AGAIN.)

SHE SITS DOWN BESIDE DEBORAH, 137 MANSNS

SHE SITS DOWN IN SIMON'S CHAIR.) 150 MANSNS

(HE NODS AT THE PLANS ON SARA'S DESK, TURNS HIS 151 MANSNS BACK ON TENARD, AND SITS DOWN.

TENARD COMES AND SITS IN THE CHAIR OPPOSITE SARA.1151 MANSNS

(SHE SITS ON THE STONE BENCH AT RIGHT-REAR OF THE 163 MANSNS POOL, CLOSING HER EYES.

BEFORE THE MOSQUE IS A THRONE ON WHICH SITS A 364 MARCOM MAHOMETAN RULER.

MARCO SITS ON ONE OF THE CASES AND GLANCES ABOUT 370 MARCOM WITH A FORCED SCORN.

IMMEDIATELY BEFORE THE GATE IS A RUDE THRONE ON 373 MARCOM WHICH SITS A MONGOL RULER WITH

ON GOLDEN CUSHIONS AT THE TOP KUBLAI SITS 377 MARCOM

(HE SITS DOWN ON ONE OF THE SAMPLE CASES TO THE 378 MARCOM GASPING HORROR OF ALL THE COURT.

KUBLAI SITS IN A SOMBER STUDY, FROWNING AND BITING388 MARCOM HIS LIPS.

A FOREMAN SITS WITH A DRUM AND GONG WITH WHICH HE 400 MARCOM MARKS A PERFECT TIME FOR THE

KUBLAI SITS AT THE TOP OF HIS THRONE, CROSS-LEGGED432 MARCOM IN THE POSTURE OF AN IDOL.

KUBLAI SITS BACK ON HIS CUSHIONS AGAIN, 436 MARCOM WITHDRAWING INTO CONTEMPLATION.

(SHE SITS ON THE STEPS 11 MISBEG

(BAFFLED, SITS ON THE BOULDER AND TAKES OFF HIS 13 MISBEG HAT TO SCRATCH HIS HEAD--

(LAUGHS AND SITS ON THE STEPS, PUTTING THE CLUB 15 MISBEG AWAY)

(HE CHUCKLES AND SITS ON THE BOULDER AGAIN.) 15 MISBEG

(SITS DOWN ON THE STEPS--WITH A CHANGE OF MANNER) 39 MISBEG

(SHE SITS ON THE TOP STEP--BANTERINGLY) 40 MISBEG

(CONT'D.)

(SHE SITS ON THE STEPS, HE ON THE BOULDER) 55 MISBEG

SHE SITS ON THE TOP STEP AND PULLS HIM DOWN ON THE102 MISBEG STEP BENEATH HER.

HE SITS HUNCHED UP ON THE STEP, STARING AT 106 MISBEG NOTHING.

(HE SITS ON THE BOULDER AND WAITS. 111 MISBEG

SHE SITS ON THE TOP STEP, PULLING HIM DOWN BESIDE 115 MISBEG HER BUT ON THE ONE BELOW.

(HE SITS DOWN BUT DOESN'T LEAN BACK) 126 MISBEG

(SHE SITS ON 141 MISBEG

JOSIE SITS IN THE SAME POSITION ON THE STEPS, AS 157 MISBEG IF SHE HAD NOT MOVED.

(HE SITS MEEKLY ON THE BOULDER. 158 MISBEG

(HE GOES AND SITS ON THE BOULDER, 167 MISBEG

(HE SITS AT RIGHT OF TABLE.) 8 POET

MICKEY MALOY SITS AT THE TABLE AT LEFT FRONT, 8 POET FACING RIGHT.

THEN HE SITS DOWN DEFIANTLY.) 15 POET

(SHE TURNS HER BACK ON HIM, SITS AT THE DESK, 16 POET

AND GOES TO THE TABLE AT CENTER FRONT, AND SITS IN 35 POET THE CHAIR SHE HAD OCCUPIED.

(EYES HIM SUSPICIOUSLY--THEN SITS DOWN.) 46 POET

HE SITS AT REAR OF THE TABLE AT LEFT FRONT. 57 POET

HE SITS IN THE SAME CHAIR AND PICKS UP THE PAPER, 59 POET IGNORING HER.

(SHE SITS AT THE END OF CENTER TABLE RIGHT AND 76 POET RELAXES WEARILY.

SARA SITS AT REAR OF THE CENTER TABLE AND WAITS, 81 POET

(HE SITS AT RIGHT OF THE TABLE AT LEFT FRONT AS MELODY 92 POET SITS AT REAR.)

MELODY SITS AT THE HEAD OF THIS TABLE. 95 POET

SHE SITS DOWN AND HE SITS AT REAR OF TABLE, 105 POET

(HE SITS DOWN ON THE CHAIR ON GADSBY'S LEFT, AT 119 POET REAR OF TABLE--

NORA SITS AT THE FOOT OF THE TABLE AT CENTER. 133 POET

(SARA SITS DOWN ON HER LEFT AT REAR OF TABLE. 137 POET

(SHE SITS DOWN IN THE SAME CHAIR.) 139 POET

(HE LABORIOUSLY CREEPS TO THE BENCH AND SITS 579 ROPE DOWN WEARILY.

(HE SITS DOWN ON THE BENCH TO THE LEFT OF TABLE) 584 ROPE

(SHE SITS DOWN ON THE BENCH IN FRONT OF TABLE. 584 ROPE

HE COMES OVER AND SITS DOWN IN HIS OLD PLACE) 597 ROPE

(HE SITS IN HIS CHAIR ON THE LEFT OF THE TABLE 7 STRANG WHILE MARSDEN SITS IN THE

CHARLIE SITS BESIDE THE FIERCE RIVER, IMMACULATELY 13 STRANG TIMID, COOL AND CLOTHED.

(HE SITS DOWN WITH A FORCED SIGH OF PEACE) 22 STRANG

AND COMES AND SITS DOWN AGAIN IN THE CHAIR-- 25 STRANG

EVANS SITS UNCOMFORTABLY HUNCHED FORWARD, 28 STRANG TWIDDLING HIS HAT IN HIS HANDS.

(HE SITS IN THE ROCKER AT CENTER AS EVANS GOES TO 28 STRANG THE BENCH AT RIGHT.

(HE SITS DOWN ABRUPTLY IN THE CHAIR AT CENTER, 34 STRANG

(SHE SITS AT CENTER. 41 STRANG

MARSDEN SITS BY THE TABLE. 41 STRANG

HE COMES AND SITS ON THE BENCH. 41 STRANG

(SHE COMES OVER AND KISSES HER--SLIPS DOWN AND 56 STRANG SITS ON THE FLOOR BESIDE HER.)

SHE JUST SITS, DOESN'T SAY A WORD, BUT SHE'S 59 STRANG HAPPY. SHE LAUGHS TO HERSELF A LOT.

(HE SITS DOWN ON THE EDGE OF THE BENCH NEARBY, 67 STRANG

(SHE COMES FORWARD TO THE CHAIR AT CENTER AND SITS 69 STRANG DOWN--FORCING A SMILE)

(SHE KISSES HIM AND SITS ON THE ARM OF HIS CHAIR, 70 STRANG

(AWKWARDLY, AS DARRELL SITS DOWN IN THE CHAIR AT 76 STRANG CENTER,

THEN SITS DOWN IN ARMCHAIR--AMUSED.) 78 STRANG

QUICKLY AVERTING HIS EYES--SITS DOWN--JOKINGLY) 79 STRANG

(SHE TURNS FROM HIM AND SITS DOWN IN THE ROCKER AT 79 STRANG CENTER.)

(HE LAUGHS SCORNFULLY AND SITS DOWN IN EVANS' 123 STRANG CHAIR,

(SHE MOVES AWAY FROM HIM AND SITS DOWN AT CENTER. 127 STRANG

(SENSING HER THOUGHTS, SITS UP IN HER LAP AND 156 STRANG STARES INTO HER FACE,

(HE SITS DOWN IN ONE OF THE CHAIRS AT LEFT, 165 STRANG DRAWING IT UP CLOSER TO HER.

(SHE SITS DOWN AGAIN.) 174 STRANG

(HE COMES AND AGAIN SITS ON THE DECK BY HER CHAIR 179 STRANG AND TAKES HER HAND)

(SHE SITS BESIDE HIM. 186 STRANG

(HE SITS DOWN ON THE BENCH AGAIN, HIS CHIN ON HIS 189 STRANG HANDS)

(SHE SITS WEARILY ON THE BENCH. 190 STRANG

DARRELL SITS ON SIDE OF THE RECLINER AT RIGHT.) 190 STRANG

(WITH A SHIVER OF FEAR SHE HURRIES OVER AND SITS 199 STRANG ON THE BENCH BESIDE MARSDEN.

THEN HE BECKONS TO JOE, WHO COMES OVER TO THE 495 VOYAGE TABLE AND SITS DOWN)

NICK SLINKS INTO THE ROOM AFTER THEM AND SITS DOWN496 VOYAGE AT A TABLE IN REAR.

(FREDA FAVORS HIM WITH A VIPERISH GLANCE AND SITS 500 VOYAGE DOWN BY OLSON)

NICK FOLLOWS THEM AND SITS DOWN AT THE TABLE IN 503 VOYAGE REAR.)

(HE PUTS A CUSHION ON THE FLOOR BESIDE THE CHAISE 444 WELDED LONGUE AND SITS DOWN)

(SHE SITS DOWN) GET A CUSHION. 444 WELDED

(HE HALF-SITS ON THE ARM OF A CHAIR. 450 WELDED

SHE SITS DOWN, THIS TIME FACING HIM, AND LOOKS AT 455 WELDED HIM UNEASILY.)

HE SITS ON THE EXTREME EDGE IN THE EXACT MIDDLE OF462 WELDED THE BIG COUCH.

SHE SITS IN A CHAIR. 464 WELDED

(THEN WITH A SIGH OF PHYSICAL WEARINESS AS SHE 471 WELDED SITS ON THE SIDE OF THE BED)

HE COMES AND SITS BESIDE HER. 480 WELDED

SITS

SITS (CONT'D.)

SHE WALKS TO HER CHAIR AND SITS DOWN. 480 WELDED

(CAPE STARES AT HER UNCERTAINLY, THEN SITS DOWN IN485 WELDED HIS CHAIR AGAIN.)

(HE SITS IN ANGUISH, IN A TORTURED RESTRAINT. 487 WELDED

SITTER

BOTTLES OF BAR WHISKEY ARE PLACED AT INTERVALS 628 ICEMAN WITHIN REACH OF ANY SITTER.

SITTIN'

AND WE ALL SITTIN' ROUND IN THE FO'C'S'TLE, YANK 481 CARDIF BESIDE ME,

I'LL BE SITTIN' HERE AT ME EASE, AND DRINKING, AND217 HA APE THINKING.

HOW D'YUH FEEL SITTIN' IN DAT PEN ALL DE TIME. 252 HA APE

AND DERE HE IS SITTIN' BEHIND A BIG DESK, LOOKIN' 600 ICEMAN AS BIG AS A FREIGHT TRAIN.

(DISGUSTEDLY) I'LL BET DEY BEEN SITTIN' AROUND 614 ICEMAN KIDDIN' DEMSELVES

SEEN HIM SITTIN' ON DE DOCK ON WEST STREET, 699 ICEMAN LOOKIN' AT DE WATER AND CRYIN'/

IF YOU OBJECTS TO MY SITTIN' HERE, CAPTAIN, JUST 700 ICEMAN TELL ME AND I PULLS MY FREIGHT.

HE'S DE FAT GUY SITTIN' ALONE. 708 ICEMAN

IT FAIR GIVES ME THE TREMBLES SITTIN' STILL IN 520 INZONE 'ERE.

(CAUTIOUSLY PEERING OUT) AYE, HE'S SITTIN' THERE 524 INZONE THE NOO.

IN FEAR OF IT, SITTIN' LONELY IN YOUR GARDEN, 19 MANSNS HEARIN' AGE CREEP UP ON YOU,

AIN'T HE THE LUNATIC, SITTIN' LIKE A PLAY-ACTOR IN100 POET HIS RED COAT,

(TO KATE) YOU'LL BE SITTIN' BY ME, DARLIN'-- 499 VOYAGE WHAT'S YOUR NAMES

SITTING

(SCENE--SITTING-ROOM OF THE MILLER HOME IN A LARGE185 AHWILD SMALL-TOWN IN CONNECTICUT--

POOR LILY NEVER HAS ANY FUN, ALWAYS SITTING HOME 191 AHWILD WITH ME.

(SITTING DOWN IN THE CHAIR AT THE RIGHT OF TABLE--201 AHWILD ACIDLY)

IN THE SITTING-ROOMS 214 AHWILD

BACK TOWARD THE SITTING-ROOM WHEN SHE SPEAKS TO 215 AHWILD HIM PITYINGLY)

WE MIGHT AS WELL GO IN THE SITTING-ROOM AND BE 217 AHWILD COMFORTABLE.

(SURLILY) IN THE SITTING-ROOM. 220 AHWILD

WELL, NO USE SITTING HERE MOURNING OVER SPILT 234 AHWILD MILK.

RICHARD AND BELLE ARE DISCOVERED SITTING AT THE 236 AHWILD TABLE AT CENTER,

(SITTING DOWN) HOPE I'M NOT BUTTING IN ON YOUR 244 AHWILD PARTY--

MILLER IS SITTING IN HIS FAVORITE ROCKING CHAIR AT249 AHWILD LEFT OF TABLE, FRONT.

(SCENE--SAME AS ACT ONE--SITTING-RROM OF THE 249 AHWILD MILLER HOME--

LILY IS SITTING IN THE ARMCHAIR BY THE TABLE AT 249 AHWILD REAR, FACING RIGHT.

THEY FILE INTO THE SITTING-ROOM IN SILENCE AND 263 AHWILD THEN STAND AROUND UNCERTAINLY.

(SCENE--THE SAME--SITTING-ROOM OF THE MILLER 263 AHWILD HOUSE--

(AS SHE IS TALKING, RICHARD APPEARS IN THE DOORWAY269 AHWILD FROM THE SITTING-ROOM.

RICHARD IS DISCOVERED SITTING SIDEWAYS ON THE 275 AHWILD GUNWALE OF THE ROWBOAT)

SITTING DEJECTEDLY IN THE STERN OF THE BOAT, 285 AHWILD APATHETIC FIGURE OF INJURED GRIEF)

(SCENE THE SITTING-RROM OF THE MILLER HOUSE 288 AHWILD AGAIN--

MILLER IS SITTING IN HIS ROCKER AT LEFT, FRONT, OF288 AHWILD TABLE.

AND, SITTING DOWN IN HIS CHAIR, BEGINS TO UNLACE 298 AHWILD HIS SHOES)

(SITTING DOWN) AY'M GOOD SINGER, YESS 12 ANNA

I COULD LICK THE THREE OF THEM SITTING DOWN WITH 32 ANNA ONE HAND TIED BEHIND ME.

(WITH DIFFICULTY RISING TO A SITTING POSITION-- 33 ANNA SCORNFULLY)

(MOLLIFIED BY HIS VERY EVIDENT SINCERITY--SITTING 42 ANNA DOWN AGAIN)

BUT TIS NOT TROUBLE I'M LOOKING FOR, AND ME 46 ANNA SITTING DOWN HERE.

(CHRIS IS SITTING WITH BOWED SHOULDERS, HIS HEAD 57 ANNA IN HIS HANDS.

(HE PICKS UP THE CHAIR ON WHICH HE HAS BEEN 60 ANNA SITTING

ANNA IS SITTING IN THE ROCKING-CHAIR. 63 ANNA

AT THE RISE OF THE CURTAIN, ROBERT MAYO IS 81 BEYOND DISCOVERED SITTING ON THE FENCE.

(THE SMALL SITTING ROOM OF THE MAYO FARMHOUSE 93 BEYOND ABOUT NINE O'CLOCK SAME NIGHT.

SITTING FACING EACH OTHER, MRS. MAYO TO THE REAR, 112 BEYOND

SITTING ROOM OF THE FARMHOUSE ABOUT HALF PAST 112 BEYOND TWELVE IN THE AFTERNOON OF A HOT,

(SITTING DOWN IN THE CHAIR ON THE LEFT OF TABLE 119 BEYOND AND CUDDLING MARY ON HIS LAP)

ROBERT IS DISCOVERED SITTING ON THE BOULDER, HIS 129 BEYOND CHIN RESTING ON HIS HANDS.

MARY IS SITTING ON THE GRASS NEAR HIM IN THE 129 BEYOND SHADE, PLAYING WITH HER DOLL.

(HALF-SITTING ON THE SIDE OF THE BOULDER) 136 BEYOND

THE SITTING ROOM OF THE FARM HOUSE ABOUT SIX 144 BEYOND O'CLOCK IN THE MORNING OF A DAY

AT THE RISE OF THE CURTAIN RUTH IS DISCOVERED 144 BEYOND SITTING BY THE STOVE.

SHE'S BEEN SITTING UP WITH ME MOST OF THE NIGHT. 147 BEYOND

(SITTING DOWN AGAIN) PRACTICALLY. 157 BEYOND

SITTING (CONT'D.)

(SITTING DOWN AND CLEARING HIS THROAT--IN A 157 BEYOND PERFUNCTORY, IMPERSONAL VOICE)

(TRYING TO RAISE HIMSELF TO A SITTING POSITION AS 167 BEYOND THEY HASTEN TO HIS SIDE--

FIVE MEN ARE SITTING ON THE BENCHES TALKING. 477 CARDIF

SITTING ON THE TOP BUNK IN THE LEFT FOREGROUND, A 477 CARDIF NORWEGIAN, PAUL,

(WITH THE EXCEPTION OF OLSON, ALL THE MEN SITTING 481 CARDIF UP PUT ON OILSKINS,

(SITTING UP IN HIS BUNK, FRANTIC WITH FEAR) 484 CARDIF

SMITTY AND COCKY ARE SITTING ON THE EDGE OF THE 455 CARIBE FORECASTLE HEAD WITH

MOST OF THE SEAMEN AND FIREMEN ARE RECLINING OR 455 CARIBE SITTING ON THE HATCH.

(A POWERFULLY BUILT IRISHMAN WHO IS SITTING ON THE456 CARIBE EDGE OF THE HATCH, FRONT--

(A RATHER GOOD-LOOKING ROUGH WHO IS SITTING BESIDE456 CARIBE DRISCOLL)

HE IS SITTING ON THE FORECASTLE HEAD LOOKING OUT 456 CARIBE OVER THE WATER

(A FAT SWEDE WHO IS SITTING ON A CAMP STOOL IN 457 CARIBE FRONT OF HIS DOOR TALKING WITH

HE IS SITTING ON A CAMP STOOL IN FRONT OF HIS 458 CARIBE DOOR, RIGHT FRONT)

PADDY PLANTS HIMSELF IN FRONT OF PEARL WHO IS 465 CARIBE SITTING BY YANK WITH HIS ARM STILL

WHO IS STILL SITTING ON THE FORECASTLE HEAD, HIS 466 CARIBE CHIN ON HIS HANDS,

WHO IS SITTING ON THE EDGE WITH BIG FRANK, 471 CARIBE

(SITTING GINGERLY ON THE CHAIR IN FRONT OF TABLE) 557 CROSS

(SITTING DOWN--INSISTENTLY) WHO WAS IT? 563 CROSS

FATHER BAIRD IS SITTING IN THE CHAIR AT LEFT, 532 DAYS FRONT, ELSA ON THE SOFA.

THE PRIEST IS SITTING ON THE CHAISE-LONGUE, JOHN 541 DAYS IN THE CHAIR AT FRONT OF TABLE,

WHO IS STILL SITTING IN THE CHAIR BY THE HEAD OF 556 DAYS THE BED, WATCHING ELSA.

IN SPITE OF STILLWELL, SPRINGS UP TO A HALF- 563 DAYS SITTING POSITION IN BED.

(SITTING DOWN ON A BED--WITH VICIOUS HATRED) 213 DESIRE

IS DISCOVERED SITTING IN A ROCKER AT THE END OF 228 DESIRE THE PORCH.

EBEN IS SITTING ON THE SIDE OF HIS BED IN THE ROOM235 DESIRE ON THE LEFT.

IN THE OTHER ROOM CABOT AND ABBIE ARE SITTING SIDE235 DESIRE BY SIDE ON THE EDGE OF THEIR

ABBIE IS SITTING IN A ROCKING CHAIR, A SHAWL 247 DESIRE WRAPPED ABOUT HER SHOULDERS.

EBEN IS SITTING ON THE SIDE OF THE BED IN HIS 247 DESIRE ROOM,

(SHE TURNS AWAY TO RETAIL THIS BIT OF GOSSIP TO 248 DESIRE HER MOTHER SITTING NEXT TO HER.

AND STRUGGLES TO A SITTING POSITION.) 256 DESIRE

IN THE KITCHEN, BY THE LIGHT OF A TALLOW CANDLE ON259 DESIRE THE TABLE, EBEN IS SITTING.

HE SLOWLY TURNS, SLUMPING INTO A SITTING POSITION 268 DESIRE ON THE FLOOR,

THEY ARE SITTING ON THE HORSEHAIR SOFA, SIDE BY 494 DIFRNT SIDE.

OTHER, THE ONE CONTAINING THE FIFE SITTING ROOM, -0 DYNAMO AND THE SECTION OF THE LIGHT'S HOME IN WHICH ARE -0 DYNAMO SITTING ROOM

IN THE SITTING ROOM BELOW THERE IS A TABLE AT 421 DYNAMO CENTER, FRONT.

THE LIGHT SITTING ROOM AND REUBEN'S BEDROOM ARE 421 DYNAMO REVEALED.

IS SITTING IN HIS SHIRT SLEEVES ON THE SIDE OF HIS422 DYNAMO BED.

HAVE BEEN REPLACED, WHILE THE INTERIORS OF THE 427 DYNAMO FIFE SITTING ROOM AND THE

THERE IS A TABLE AT CENTER, FRONT, IN THE SITTING 428 DYNAMO ROOM.

WITH FIFE STILL SITTING LOOKING EXPECTANTLY AT THE435 DYNAMO DOOR,

WITH LIGHT SITTING AS AT THE END OF SCENE ONE, 435 DYNAMO

AND NOW THE INTERIOR OF THE LIGHT SITTING ROOM IS 435 DYNAMO AGAIN SHOWN

THEIR SITTING ROOM IS REVEALED AS BEFORE 435 DYNAMO

(ADA COMES IN THE DOORWAY OF THE SITTING ROOM, 436 DYNAMO LEFT, FOLLOWED BY REUBEN.)

SITTING AS BEFORE IN THE SITTING ROOM OF THE OTHER443 DYNAMO HOUSE READING THE BIBLE.

THE WALLS OF THE FIFE AND LIGHT SITTING ROOMS HAVE443 DYNAMO BEEN REPLACED WHILE THE

AND FIFE STICKS HIS HEAD OUT OF HIS SITTING ROOM 445 DYNAMO WINDOW

(STILL LEANING OUT OF HIS SITTING-ROOM WINDOW, 450 DYNAMO CATCHES SIGHT OF LIGHT--

MRS. FIFE IS LEANING OUT OF ONE OF THE WINDOWS OF 454 DYNAMO THEIR SITTING ROOM,

THE INTERIOR OF THE LIGHT SITTING ROOM IS 454 DYNAMO REVEALED.

(IN THE SITTING ROOM OF THE LIGHT HOME, HUTCHINS 455 DYNAMO LIGHT ENTERS FROM THE REAR,

LIGHT IS STILL SITTING, HIS FACE HIDDEN IN HIS 462 DYNAMO ARMS ON THE TABLE,

JUST AS REUBEN SLOWLY OPENS THE DOOR OF THE LIGHT 462 DYNAMO SITTING ROOM.

(STICKS HER HEAD OUT OF THEIR SITTING ROOM WINDOW 467 DYNAMO AS HE PASSES THE LILAC HEDGE.

WHILE THE WALL OF THE SITTING ROOM HAS BEEN 468 DYNAMO REPLACED.

MRS. FIFE IS SITTING IN THE DYNAMO ROOM 486 DYNAMO

ON THE ROAD OPPOSITE WHERE JONES IS SITTING. 194 EJONES

AS THEIR CHORUS LIFTS HE RISES TO A SITTING 199 EJONES POSTURE SIMILAR TO THE OTHERS,

SITTING

SITTING (CONT'D.)
THEY ARE SITTING IN CRUMPLED, DESPAIRING 199 EJONES
ATTITUDES, HUNCHED,
LEM REMAINS SITTING WITH AN IMPERTURBABLE 203 EJONES
EXPRESSION, BUT LISTENING INTENTLY.
WHICH PARTLY SCREENS ANYONE SITTING ON IT FROM THE 5 ELECTR
FRONT OF THE HOUSE.
I'LL BE SITTING HERE. 12 ELECTR
UNCONSCIOUSLY HE TAKES THE SAME ATTITUDE AS 36 ELECTR
MANNION, SITTING ERECT,
I'VE SO OFTEN SEEN HIM SITTING HERE--I FORCING A 37 ELECTR
LITTLE LAUGH)
(SLOWLY) I WAS THINKING--PERHAPS WE HAD BETTER GO 37 ELECTR
TO THE SITTING-ROOM.
LAVINIA IS SITTING ON THE TOP OF THE STEPS TO THE 43 ELECTR
PORTICO.
SITTING IN STIFF, POSED ATTITUDES THAT SUGGEST THE 46 ELECTR
STATUES OF MILITARY HEROES.
SOMETHING KEEPS ME SITTING NUMB IN MY OWN HEART-- 55 ELECTR
HE PUSHES HIS BACK UP AGAINST THE HEAD OF THE BED 59 ELECTR
IN A HALF-SITTING POSITION.
STRAIGHTENS UP IN A SITTING POSITION IN LAVINIA'S 63 ELECTR
ARMS.
(SCENE--THE SITTING-ROOM OF THE MANNON HOUSE. 79 ELECTR
HAZEL IS DISCOVERED SITTING IN THE CHAIR AT 80 ELECTR
CENTER, FRONT.
PETER IS SITTING ON THE SOFA AT RIGHT. 80 ELECTR
(COMING FORWARD AND SITTING ACROSS THE TABLE FROM 84 ELECTR
HIM--
SITTING ON A CHAIR IN A PARK OR STRADDLING A HORSE 94 ELECTR
IN A TOWN SQUARE--
AND WITH DIFFICULTY RAISES HIMSELF TO A SITTING 102 ELECTR
POSITION.
(HE STRUGGLES TO A SITTING POSITION) 103 ELECTR
(ORIN'S VOICE IS HEARD CALLING FROM THE SITTING- 123 ELECTR
ROOM AT RIGHT *WHAT'S THAT?*
(SHE SHUDDERS) I CAN STILL SEE HER SITTING ON 136 ELECTR
THAT BENCH
I SEE A LIGHT THROUGH THE SHUTTERS OF THE SITTING-138 ELECTR
ROOM.
(SAME AS ACT TWO OF *THE HUNTED*--THE SITTING-ROOM139 ELECTR
IN THE MANNON HOUSE.
SITTING BACK IN HIS CHAIR.) 149 ELECTR
ORIN IS SITTING IN HIS FATHER'S CHAIR AT LEFT OF 149 ELECTR
TABLE.
(SCENE--SAME AS ACT ONE, SCENE TWO--THE SITTING- 157 ELECTR
ROOM.
(SITTING DOWN ON THE CHAIR AT CENTER) 162 ELECTR
WHAT ARE YOU SITTING HERE FOR, YOU NUT--TRYING TO 265 GGBROW
GET MORE MOONSTRUCK?
THE SITTING ROOM OF MRS. DION ANTHONY'S HALF OF A 269 GGBROW
TWO-FAMILY HOUSE
DION IS SITTING BEHIND THE TABLE, STARING BEFORE 269 GGBROW
HIM.
WHICH USUALLY ADORN THE SITTING ROOMS OF SUCH 269 GGBROW
HOUSES.
(THEN WITH A START HE OPENS HIS EYES AND, HALF 278 GGBROW
SITTING UP,
DION IS SITTING ON THE STOOL IN BACK OF THE TABLE,290 GGBROW
ARE SITTING ON STOOLS BEHIND WHAT WAS FORMERLY 302 GGBROW
DION'S TABLE.
SCENE--THE SAME AS SCENE ONE OF ACT ONE--THE 308 GGBROW
SITTING-ROOM OF MARGARET'S HOME.
(WHO HAS BEEN SITTING IN A BLINKING, MELANCHOLY 213 HA APE
DAZE--
BUT WILLIE HAS CLOSED HIS EYES AND IS SITTING 583 ICEMAN
QUIETLY, SHUDDERING.
NO MORE OF THIS SITTING AROUND AND LOAFING. 603 ICEMAN
SITTING WITH A PARCHED THROAT WAITING FOR HARRY 607 ICEMAN
HOPE TO BUY A DRINK.
AND WHATEVER YOU'D LIKE, I CAN'T SPEND MY LIFE 652 ICEMAN
SITTING HERE WITH YOU.
(SITTING DOWN--GOOD-NATUREDLY) 659 ICEMAN
PARRITT IS SITTING. 665 ICEMAN
I'D GET THINKING HOW PEACEFUL IT WAS HERE, SITTING715 ICEMAN
AROUND WITH THE OLD GANG.
THE TABLE WHERE HIS COMPANION, LIEB, IS SITTING. 716 ICEMAN
WHAT THE HELL YOU DOING, SITTING THERE? 727 ICEMAN
(SITTING DOWN AGAIN) WELL, READ 'EM AND FIND OUT.529 INZONE
(SITTING DOWN BESIDE HIM, PATS HIS HAND.) 19 JOURNE
MARY GOES ON, HALF SITTING ON THE ARM OF EDMUND'S 58 JOURNE
CHAIR, HER ARM AROUND HIM.
AS IF THE STRAIN OF SITTING THROUGH LUNCH WITH 71 JOURNE
THEM HAD BEEN TOO MUCH FOR HER.
TYRONE, WHO'S SITTING OUT IN THE AUTOMOBILE.* 103 JOURNE
I WAS SITTING HERE SO LONELY AND BLUE. 108 JOURNE
SITTING IN YOUR WALLED-IN GARDEN, DRESSED ALL IN 14 MANSNS
WHITE.
(SCENE SITTING-ROOM OF SARA HARFORD'S HOME 43 MANSNS
(SHE INDICATES THE CHAIR IN WHICH SHE HAD BEEN 50 MANSNS
SITTING.
SITTING IN MY GARDEN WITH AN EMPTY DREAMLESS MIND, 54 MANSNS
DEBORAH IS SITTING ON THE STEPS LEADING UP TO THE 95 MANSNS
SUMMER-HOUSE DOOR.
DO YOU REMEMBER, MOTHER, WE WOULD BE SITTING HERE 107 MANSNS
JUST AS WE ARE NOW.
I CAN SEE YOU SITTING THERE, AS YOU ARE NOW, 109 MANSNS
DRESSED ALL IN WHITE.
YOU WOULD BE SITTING THERE BEFORE THE SUMMER- 109 MANSNS
HOUSE.
AS THE CURTAIN RISES, SARA IS SITTING IN THE CHAIR117 MANSNS
AT LEFT-FRONT OF THE TABLE.
I HAD FORGOTTEN HIM SITTING ALONE THERE-- 120 MANSNS
SHE AND I WOULD BE SITTING TOGETHER ON THE SOFA. 120 MANSNS
HE SITTING ALONE, THINKING OUT SCHEMES FOR HIS 120 MANSNS
COMPANY--NOT BOTHERING US--
MARCO IS SITTING ON A STOOL IN THE FOREGROUND, 358 MARCOM
IS SITTING AT HIS FEET. 384 MARCOM

SIX FOOTER

SITTING (CONT'D.)
SITTING ON CUSHIONS. 407 MARCOM
ON A SILVER THRONE AT CENTER KUKACHIN IS SITTING 407 MARCOM
SITTING ALONE IN A GARDEN, BEAUTIFUL AND SAD, 426 MARCOM
APART FROM LIFE, WAITING--
JOSIE IS SITTING ON THE STEPS BEFORE THE FRONT 71 MISBEG
DOOR.
HER BODY STIFF FROM SITTING LONG IN THE SAME 71 MISBEG
POSITION.
HE'S DOWN AT THE INN SITTING ALONE, 91 MISBEG
I REMEMBER NOW I WAS SITTING ALONE AT A TABLE IN 167 MISBEG
THE INN.
YOU SEEMED TO ENJOY IT THE WHILE WE WERE SITTING 168 MISBEG
HERE TOGETHER
YOU'RE COLD COMFORT, SITTING SILENT LIKE A STATUE,140 POET
AND ME MAKING TALK TO MYSELF.
(SITTING DOWN AT REAR OF THE SMALL TABLE AT LEFT 160 POET
FRONT--ANGRILY.)
THERE WERE MILLIONS SITTING UP WITH THE CORPSE 7 STRANG
ALREADY.
THE ROOM IS A TYPICAL SITTING ROOM OF THE 90 STRANG
QUANTITY-PRODUCTION BUNGALOW TYPE.
THE SITTING ROOM OF A SMALL HOUSE EVANS HAS RENTED 90 STRANG
NINA IS SITTING IN THE CHAIR AT CENTER. 90 STRANG
(SHE REMAINS IN A SITTING POSITION, STARING 108 STRANG
BLANKLY BEFORE HER.
EVANS IS SITTING BY THE TABLE AT LEFT, 111 STRANG
MARSDEN IS SITTING ON THE SOFA AT RIGHT, 111 STRANG
SITTING DOWN ON THE SOFA AT RIGHT. 126 STRANG
DARRELL IS SITTING BY THE TABLE AT LEFT, WATCHING 137 STRANG
NINA.
NINA IS RECLINING ON THE CHAISE LONGUE WATCHING 137 STRANG
GORDON WHO IS SITTING ON THE
THE SITTING ROOM OF THE EVANS' APARTMENT ON PARK 137 STRANG
AVENUE, NEW YORK CITY--
(SITTING DOWN AT LEFT) I HOPE LUNCH IS READY 153 STRANG
SOON.
NINA IS SITTING BY THE TABLE AT CENTER, DARRELL IN158 STRANG
THE CHAIR FARTHEST LEFT,
BUT I'M PERFECTLY CONTENTED SITTING-- 164 STRANG
(HE SLUMPS CLUMSILY DOWN TO A SITTING POSITION ON 175 STRANG
THE DECK BY HER CHAIR AND
GORDON EVANS IS SITTING ON THE STONE BENCH, HIS 184 STRANG
CHIN PROPPED ON HIS HANDS,
(SITTING DOWN BESIDE HER) I SUSPECTED AS MUCH, 197 STRANG
AT ONE OF THE TABLES, FRONT, A ROUND-SHOULDERED 493 VOYAGE
YOUNG FELLOW IS SITTING.
AS THE CURTAIN RISES, JOHN CAN BE DIMLY 462 WELDED
DISTINGUISHED SITTING.

SITUATED
SITUATED ON A HIGH POINT OF LAND ON THE CALIFORNIA555 CROSS
COAST.
THE PALACE IS EVIDENTLY SITUATED ON HIGH GROUND 173 EJONES
SITUATED ON THE DOWNTOWN WEST SIDE OF NEW YORK. 571 ICEMAN
THE INTERIOR OF AN OLD BARN SITUATED ON TOP OF A 577 ROPE
HIGH HEADLAND OF THE SEACOAST.

SITUATION
(FORGETTING THE SITUATION FOR A MOMENT, 23 ANNA
AFTER ALL, THE SITUATION HAS ITS COMPENSATIONS. 520 DAYS
HE SAW CLEARLY THAT THIS SITUATION WAS THE CLIMAX 538 DAYS
OF A LONG DEATH STRUGGLE
(THINKING OUT, IN HIS TOTAL MISUNDERSTANDING OF THE119 POET
SITUATION.)
SIZING UP THE SITUATION.) 450 WELDED

SIVIN
YANK WAS IN THE SAME BOAT WID ME, AND SIVIN MORTA481 CARDIF
DAYS WE DRIFTED
WHIN HE WAS IN CAPE TOWN SIVIN MONTHS AGO-- 531 INZONE
AN' IF HE DIDN'T COME BACK BY SIVIN YEARS FROM 586 ROPE
WHEN HE'D LEFT--

SIX-FOOTER
A RANGY SIX-FOOTER WITH A LEAN WEATHER-BEATEN 539 'ILE
FACE.
JOE, THE HARPOONER, AN ENORMOUS SIX-FOOTER WITH A 543 'ILE
BATTERED, UGLY FACE.
THESE LAST SIX YEARS SINCE WE WERE MARRIED-- 545 'ILE
WAITING, AND WATCHING, AND FEARING--
SELECTS FIVE OR SIX SLIPS OF PAPER, AND HOLDS THEM201 AHWILD
OUT TO MILLER.
(LOOKING AT HER WATCH) QUARTER PAST SIX. 212 AHWILD
PSHAW, WHY, RICHARD'LL PROBABLY FORGET ALL ABOUT 291 AHWILD
HER BEFORE HE'S AWAY SIX
HE IS A POWERFUL, BROAD-CHESTED SIX-FOOTER, 30 ANNA
AND LEAVIN' HERE AT SIX BELLS MYSELF. 96 BEYOND
WHY, I'D FORGOTTEN ALL ABOUT--THAT--BEFORE I'D 134 BEYOND
BEEN AT SEA SIX MONTHS.
(EASILY) SIX THOUSAND MILES MORE OR LESS. 137 BEYOND
THE SITTING ROOM OF THE FARM HOUSE ABOUT SIX 144 BEYOND
O'CLOCK IN THE MORNING OF A DAY
(HE CALCULATES) WHAT TIME IS IT NOW? ROUND SIX, 147 BEYOND
MUST BE.
(AS A CLOCK IN THE KITCHEN STRIKES SIX) SIX 152 BEYOND
O'CLOCK.
THAT MIGHT HAVE PROLONGED HIS LIFE SIX MONTHS AGO,158 BEYOND
SIX MONTHS AGO THERE MIGHT HAVE-- 158 BEYOND
IT'S AFTER SIX. 162 BEYOND
SLEEPING BUNKS ABOUT SIX FEET LONG, ARRANGED THREE477 CARDIF
DEEP
PY VINGO, I SEE SIX IN BOAT, YES, SIR. 460 CARIBE
THERE'S FIVE OR SIX OF THEM IN IT--AND THEY PADDLE460 CARIBE
LIKE SKIRTS.
HE AND SIX OTHERS MANAGED TO REACH A SMALL ISLAND 559 CROSS
ON THE FRINGE OF THE
OF THE SIX WHO REACHED THE ISLAND WITH MY FATHER 559 CROSS
ONLY THREE WERE ALIVE WHEN A
SIX HUNDRED. 219 DESIRE
AN' THEN IT'S STILL MINE--EVEN THOUGH I BE SIX 234 DESIRE
FOOT UNDER.

SIX FOOTER

SIX-FOOTER (CONT'D.)
THEY HAIN'T MANY T' TOUCH YE, EPHRAIM--A SON AT SEVENTY-SIX. 249 DESIRE
(WITH A WINK AT THE OTHERS) YE'RE THE SPRYEST SEVENTY-SIX EVER I SEES, EPHRAIM/ 250 DESIRE
SEVENTY-SIX, IF I'M A DAY/ 251 DESIRE
SEVENTY-SIX AN' HIM NOT THIRTY YIT-- 256 DESIRE
UNDER HIS ARM HE CARRIES SIX BOOKS, BOUND TOGETHER457 DYNAMO (WITH A STRAP.)
THEIR SIX CUPPED ARMS STRETCHING UPWARD, 483 DYNAMO
(JUDICIALLY) OH, I'SE GOOD FOR SIX MONTHS YIT 180 EJONES
'FORE DEY GITS SICK O' MY GAME.
WAS I SAYIN' I 'D SIT IN SIX MONTHS MO'S 182 EJONES
SUNDOWN'S AT SIX-THUTY UR DERE-ABOUTS. 183 EJONES
A WHITE WOODEN PORTICO WITH SIX TALL COLUMNS 2 ELECTR
CONTRASTS
BEHIND THE DRIVEWAY THE WHITE GRECIAN TEMPLE 5 ELECTR
PORTICO WITH ITS SIX TALL COLUMNS
THIRTY-SIX, I THINK. 20 ELECTR
YES--SIX PAST ELEVEN. 56 ELECTR
SO LONELY YOU'VE WRITTEN ME EXACTLY TWO LETTERS IN 85 ELECTR
THE LAST SIX MONTHS/
SIX DAYS IN HELL--AND THEN SOUTHAMPTON. 209 HA APE
(THIS LAST IN THE CHANTING FORMULA OF THE GALLERY 224 HA APE
GODS AT THE SIX-DAY BIKE RACE.
THE THIRD ROW OF TABLES, FOUR CHAIRS TO ONE AND 573 ICEMAN
SIX TO THE OTHER.
ALL SIX OF US COLORED BOYS, WE WAS TOUGH AND I WAS599 ICEMAN
DE TOUGHEST.
THAT'S A SWELL NEW HAT, BESS, LOOKS VERY 609 ICEMAN
BECOMING--SIX DOLLARS.
SIX HOURS, SAY. 622 ICEMAN
LOOKIT/ SIX CANDLES. 629 ICEMAN
IS A BIRTHDAY CAKE WITH SIX CANDLES. 629 ICEMAN
AIN'T EVER HAD A CAKE SINCE BESSIE--SIX CANDLES. 656 ICEMAN
YUH SAID IF I'D TAKE YOUR DAY, YUH'D BELIEVE ME AT697 ICEMAN
SIX.
HE CLAIMS THAT IN SIX MONTHS TO A YEAR EDMOND WILL 79 JOURNE
BE CURED, IF HE OBEYS ORDERS.
IT IS AROUND HALF PAST SIX IN THE EVENING. 97 JOURNE
I'VE LOVED HIM DEARLY FOR THIRTY-SIX YEARS. 101 JOURNE
THIRTY-SIX YEARS AGO, BUT I CAN SEE IT AS CLEARLY 105 JOURNE
AS IF IT WERE TONIGHT/
AND IN ALL THOSE THIRTY-SIX YEARS, 105 JOURNE
YOU CAN SERVE DINNER PROMPTLY AT HALF PAST SIX. 106 JOURNE
HIS FATHER DESERTED HIS MUTHER AND THEIR SIX 117 JOURNE
CHILDREN.
THEY PROMISED ME IN SIX MONTHS HE'D BE CURED. 122 JOURNE
YOU'LL BE CURED IN SIX MONTHS, OR A YEAR AT MOST. 143 JOURNE
SIX MONTHS AND YOU'LL BE IN THE PINK. 164 JOURNE
ABOVE IT, HIS HAIR IS THE CURLY BLOND HAIR OF A 299 LAZARU
CHILD OF SIX OR SEVEN.
AN OLD MAN OF SEVENTY-SIX, TALL, 337 LAZARU
IN SPITE OF IT, HER PREGNANCY, NOW SIX MONTHS 2 MANSNS
ALONG, IS APPARENT.
HE IS TWENTY-SIX BUT THE POISE OF HIS BEARING 4 MANSNS
MAKES HIM APPEAR MUCH MORE MATURE.
GAUSBY IS A SHORT, TUBBY MAN OF FIFTY-SIX, ALMOST 25 MANSNS
COMPLETELY BALD.
(SCENE--SIX MONTHS LATER. THE TOLLING OF A CHURCH358 MARCOM
BELL IS FIRST HEARD.
WE KILLED SIX SLAVES BUT, BY GOD, WE DID IT/ 405 MARCOM
SIX IN NUMBER, IN BRILLIANT UNIFORMS) 428 MARCOM
ABOUT TWELVE FEET LONG BY SIX HIGH, THIS ROOM, 1 MISBEG
WHICH IS JOSIE HOGAN'S BEDROOM.
(HOGAN IS FIFTY-FIVE, ABOUT FIVE FEET SIX. 11 MISBEG
SELL HIM THE RAILROAD FOR THE SIX. 16 MISBEG
SIX DOLLARS ONLY. 16 MISBEG
I KNEW WHEN YOU'D CALMED DOWN YOU'D THINK IT WORTH 16 MISBEG
SIX DOLLARS TU SEE THE LAST
A LARGER ONE, SEATING SIX, AT RIGHT CENTER. 7 POET
MALOY IS TWENTY-SIX, WITH A STURDY PHYSIQUE AND AN 8 POET
AMIABLE, CUNNING FACE.
IT IS BETWEEN SIX AND HALF-PAST IN THE EVENING OF 577 ROPE
A DAY IN EARLY SPRING.
(INTERRUPTING) AND THE CARRYIN'S-ON YOU HAD THE 580 ROPE
SIX YEARS AT HOME AFTER I'D
MARY IS ABOUT SIX FEET BEYOND HIM ON THE OTHER 589 ROPE
SIDE OF THE ROAD.
SIX... 4 STRANG
SEEMS IMPOSSIBLE SHE'S BEEN DEAD SIX YEARS.... 5 STRANG
THAT SIX MONTHS AGO THE DOCTORS THOUGHT IT MIGHT 16 STRANG
BE YEARS BEFORE--
I'VE ALREADY HAD SIX MONTHS' TRAINING FOR A NURSE. 17 STRANG
BUT I DID WITH OTHERS--OH, FOUR OR FIVE OR SIX OR 45 STRANG
SEVEN MEN, CHARLIE.
THAT IT'S OVER SIX MONTHS SINCE SAM AND I WERE 49 STRANG
MARRIED
WHEN A REFUSAL LIKE THAT WOULD HAVE RUINED MY 122 STRANG
CONFIDENCE FOR SIX MONTHS/)
OVER SIX MONTHS.... 139 STRANG
GORDON IS OVER SIX FEET TALL WITH THE FIGURE OF A 184 STRANG
TRAINED ATHLETE.
I REMEMBER FOIVE OR SIX YEARS BACK 496 VOYAGE
I'M ONLY TWENTY-SIX, HONEST. 474 WELDED
A RANGY SHANTY SIX-FOOTER WITH A LEAN WEATHER- 539 'ILE
BEATEN FACE.
JUE, THE E, THE HARPOONER, AN ENORMOUS SIX-FOOTER 543 'ILE
WITH A BATTERED, UGLY FACE.
HE IS A P IS A POWERFUL, BROAD-CHESTED SIX-FOOTER, 30 ANNA

SIXTEEN
IT'S BEEN SIXTEEN YEARS SINCE I BROKE OFF OUR 213 AHWILD
ENGAGEMENT.
SHE IS FIFTEEN, GOING ON SIXTEEN. 277 AHWILD
IT WAS ONE OF THE SONS--THE YOUNGEST--STARTED ME-- 18 ANNA
WHEN I WAS SIXTEEN.
WHERE YOU HAD ME IN JAIL TILL I WAS SIXTEEN/ 43 ANNA
AFTER A MATTER O' SIXTEEN 237 DESIRE

SIXTEEN (CONT'D.)
ALL DOLLED UP LIKE A KID OF SIXTEEN 529 DIFRNT
THEIR DAUGHTER, ADA, SIXTEEN, 428 DYNAMO
JUST WHEN HE WAS SIXTEEN AND OLD ENOUGH TO HELP. 581 ROPE
SIXTEEN... 6 STRANG

SIXTH
(HIS MIND HAS HOPPED AN AMBULANCE CLANGING DOWN 26 HUGHIE
SIXTH.
ON SIXTH AVENOO. 612 ICEMAN
THE SIXTH IS A SQUARE JEWELER'S WATCH BOX. 629 ICEMAN
OPPOSITE CORA, IN A SIXTH CHAIR, IS CAPTAIN LEWIS,696 ICEMAN
ALSO FACING FRONT.
AWAY FROM THE DAMNED SIXTH AVENUE EL. 39 MISBEG

SIXTIES
HE IS A MAN IN HIS EARLY SIXTIES, SLIGHTLY UNDER 422 DYNAMO
MEDIUM HEIGHT.
HE IS A TALL, FULL-CHESTED MAN IN HIS SIXTIES, 150 MANSNS
WITH A FINE-LOOKING ROMAN FACE.

SIXTY
AN ANDREW SIXTY-FIVE YEARS OLD WITH A SHORT, 94 BEYOND
SQUARE, WHITE BEARD.
I BE ON'Y SIXTY-EIGHT AN' I COULDN'T DO IT. 249 DESIRE
SIXTY YEARS OLD BUT STILL IN THE PRIME OF HEALTH 513 DIFRNT
AND STRENGTH,
I DON'T GIVE A DURN HOW LONG IT'LL TAKE--TILL I'M 518 DIFRNT
SIXTY YEARS OLD--
I AIN'T BEEN WITH THE MANNONS FOR SIXTY YEARS 19 ELECTR
WITHOUT LEARNING THAT.
HE IS AROUND SIXTY, SMALL AND WIZENED, WHITE HAIR 67 ELECTR
AND BEARD.
DONE WHEN HE WAS SIXTY. 79 ELECTR
HE IS A THIN, WIRY MAN OF SIXTY-FIVE OR SO, WITH A102 ELECTR
TOUSLED MOP OF BLACK HAIR,
HE IS SIXTY. 129 ELECTR
SMALL IS A WIRY OLD MAN OF SIXTY-FIVE, A CLERK IN 129 ELECTR
A HARDWARE STORE.
THE FATHER IS A TALL LEAN MAN OF FIFTY-FIVE OR 259 GGBROW
SIXTY WITH A GRIM,
LARRY SLADE IS SIXTY. 574 ICEMAN
HE IS GOING ON SIXTY. 575 ICEMAN
HARRY HOPE IS SIXTY, WHITE-HAIRED, 576 ICEMAN
ED MOSHER IS GOING ON SIXTY. 576 ICEMAN
SIXTY. THAT AIN'T TOO OLD. 604 ICEMAN
TEN, TWENTY, THIRTY, FORTY, FIFTY, SIXTY, SEVENTY,608 ICEMAN
EIGHTY, NINETY, A DOLLAR.
FIFTY, SIXTY, SEVENTY, NINETY, FOUR DOLLARS. 609 ICEMAN
TWENTY, THIRTY, FORTY, FIFTY, SIXTY--YOU'RE 609 ICEMAN
COUNTING WITH ME, BESS, AREN'T YOUS
HICKEY WAS GOIN' TO HAVE YOU SIXTY CANDLES, BUT I 630 ICEMAN
SAYS, JEES,
(BITTERNESS COMING OUT) ONLY DON'T THINK BECAUSE 659 ICEMAN
I'M SIXTY
JAMES TYRONE IS SIXTY-FIVE BUT LOOKS TEN YEARS 13 JOURNE
YOUNGER.
IF I AM SIXTY-FIVE. 14 JOURNE
THE MOTHER IS TALL AND STOUT, OVER SIXTY-FIVE, A 275 LAZARU
GENTLE, SIMPLE WOMAN.
HE IS SIXTY OR SO/ 282 LAZARU
A SQUAT, MUSCULAR MAN OF SIXTY, 299 LAZARU
THE LEGATE, TEDALDO, A MAN OF SIXTY WITH A STRONG,358 MARCOM
INTELLIGENT FACE,
HE IS A MAN OF SIXTY BUT STILL IN THE FULL PRIME 377 MARCOM
OF HIS POWERS.
HE IS A TALL, LEAN, STOOP-SHOULDERED OLD MAN OF 578 ROPE
SIXTY-FIVE.
SHE IS ONLY ABOUT FORTY-FIVE BUT SHE LOOKS AT 53 STRANG
LEAST SIXTY.
SHE'S SIXTY-EIGHT... 73 STRANG
(SURPRISED) OVER SIXTY-FIVE, ISN'T SHE5 74 STRANG
SHE'S STILL UNDER SIXTY-FIVE-- 74 STRANG
SHE LOVED BATHING AND BOATING IN THE SUMMER EVEN 100 STRANG
AFTER SHE WAS SIXTY,

SIZE
YOU'RE GROWING A LOT TOO BIG FOR YOUR SIZE, SEEMS 235 AHWILD
TO ME/
ALL DEPENDS ON WHAT I FEEL ABOUT WHAT HE FEELS 268 AHWILD
WHEN I FIRST SIZE HIM UP--
THE TWO WOMEN SIZE EACH OTHER UP WITH FRANK 14 ANNA
STARES.
ITS BASE ABOUT FIVE FEET FROM THE FLOOR, WITH A 564 DAYS
LIFE-SIZE FIGURE OF CHRIST,
ABOUT THE SIZE OF A CREEPING CHILD. 189 EJONES
HER HEAD IS THE SAME SIZE AS HER MOTHER'S, 10 ELECTR
IS ABOUT THE SAME SIZE AND AGE AS HUGO, A SMALL 575 ICEMAN
MAN.
(THEY NOD AND SIZE HIM UP WITH EXPRESSIONLESS 585 ICEMAN
EYES.)
AND WHAT MADE ME GOOD WAS I COULD SIZE UP ANYONE. 624 ICEMAN
I CAN SIZE UP GUYS, AND TURN 'EM INSIDE OUT. 642 ICEMAN
BETTER THAN I EVER COULD.
THE MASKS OF THE CHORUS OF OLD MEN ARE DOUBLE THE 274 LAZARU
SIZE OF THE OTHERS.
HAVE IDENTICAL MASKS OF DOUBLE SIZE, AS BEFORE. 285 LAZARU
AS BEFORE THE CHORUS WEARS MASKS DOUBLE THE LIFE 298 LAZARU
SIZE OF THE CROWD MASKS.
THIS CHORUS WEARS, IN DOUBLE SIZE, THE LAUGHING 306 LAZARU
MASK OF LAZARUS/ FOLLOWERS
DIAMONDS OF GREAT SIZE. 370 MARCOM

SIZED
AND I SIZED YOU UP AS A DIFFERENT KIND OF MAN-- 59 ANNA
HE IS A SLIGHT, MEDIUM-SIZED PROFESSIONAL-LOOKING 556 CROSS
MAN OF ABOUT THIRTY-FIVE.
Y'KNOW I HAD HUGHIE SIZED UP FOR A SAP THE FIRST 22 HUGHIE
TIME I SEE HIM.
BESSIE HAD YOU SIZED UP. 608 ICEMAN
YEAH, HE'S COITINLY GOT ONE GUY I KNOW SIZED UP 638 ICEMAN
RIGHT/

SIZED (CONT'D.)
SEVEN IN NUMBER, FACING FRONT, IN DOUBLE-SIZED 312 LAZARU
MASKS OF THE SERVILE,
THEIR CHORUS OF LEGIONNAIRES IN DOUBLE-SIZED MASKS 320 LAZARU
THEY SIT, FACING FRONT IN THEIR DOUBLE-SIZED 336 LAZARU
MASKS,
THERE IS A FAIR-SIZED TABLE, A HEAVY ARMCHAIR, A 3 STRANG
ROCKER,

SIZES
MILLER SIZES HIM UP KEENLY--THEN SUDDENLY SMILES 293 AHWILD
AND ASKS WITH QUIET MOCKERY)
(HE SIZES RICHARD UP SEARCHINGLY--THEN SUDDENLY 294 AHWILD
SPEAKS SHARPLY)
HER BARE FEET ARE ENCASED IN A MAN'S BROGANS 7 ANNA
SEVERAL SIZES TOO LARGE FOR HER,
THE SHRUBS, OF VARIOUS SIZES, ARE ALL CLIPPED INTO 25 MANSNS
GEOMETRICAL SHAPES--

SIZING
(SIZING HIM UP SHREWDLY) HELLO, SON. 293 AHWILD
KEENLY SIZING HIM UP. 436 DYNAMO
(SURPRISED--SIZING HER UP PUZZLEDLY) 24 ELECTR
ERIE IS SIZING HIM UP WITH ANOTHER CYNICAL, 13 HUGHIE
FRIENDLY GLANCE.)
(HIS EYES COME BACK TO HICKEY TO FIND HIM STILL 624 ICEMAN
SIZING HIM UP--DEFENSIVELY)
IT WAS LIKE A GAME, SIZING PEOPLE UP QUICK, 711 ICEMAN
SIZING UP THE SITUATION.) 450 WELDED

SIZZCHELS
WHAT CAN THEY UNDERSTAND ABOUT GIRLS WHOSE HAIR 228 AHWILD
SIZZCHELS,

SKATE
WELL, IF YOU AREN'T THE LOUSIEST CHEAP SKATE/ 241 AHWILD
I'M NOT A CHEAP SKATE/ 241 AHWILD
AND I COULDN'T SHOW MYSELF UP AS A CHEAP SKATE BY 523 DIFRNT
TRAVELIN' 'ROUND WITH HIM
CHEAP SKATE/ 682 ICEMAN
CHRIST, DON'T BE SUCH A CHEAP SKATE/ 126 JOURNE

SKEDADDLE
(PEREMPTORILY) YOU KIDS SKEDADDLE--ALL OF YOU. 264 AHWILD

SKEER
IF MO' O' DEM HA'NTS COME AFTER ME, HOW I GWINE 198 EJONES
SKEER DEM AWAYS

SKEERED
(WITH A CHUCKLE) AND CALEB LYIN' LOW IN THE CABIN503 DIFRNT
SKEERED TO MOVE OUT,
WHAT YOU SKEERED AT$ 190 EJONES
I AIN'T SKEERED O' REAL MEN. 196 EJONES
I'SE SKEERED. 200 EJONES
(TREMBLINGLY) OH, GORRY, I'SE SKEERED IN DIS 200 EJONES
PLACE/
NOT THAT I'M SKEERED O' YOU OR YOUR SHOOTER/ 104 ELECTR
I'M SKEERED/ 583 ROPE

SKELETON
(HIS LAUGHTER IS COLD, CRUEL AND MERCILESS AS THE 339 LAZARU
GRIN OF A SKELETON.)

SKELETONS
THE MANNONS GOT SKELETONS IN THEIR CLOSETS SAME AS 9 ELECTR
OTHERS/.

SKEPTICALLY
(SKEPTICALLY) HE'LL HAVE TO SHOW ME. 19 ANNA
(SKEPTICALLY) SICK$ 21 ANNA
(KINDLY BUT SKEPTICALLY) THAT'S THE RIGHT SPIRIT,102 BEYOND
ROBERT.
(SKEPTICALLY) HO, YES/ 180 EJONES
(SKEPTICALLY) BROKE$ YOU HAVEN'T THE THIRSTY 595 ICEMAN
LOOK OF THE IMPECUNIOUS.

SKETCHING
HE KEEPS HIS SMILE FROZEN AS HE NOTICES AN ARTIST 389 MARCOM
SKETCHING HIM.

SKETCHY
(SMILING) YOUR LETTERS WERE--SKETCHY, TO SAY THE 131 BEYOND
LEAST.

SKIES
THESE SKIES THREATEN. 329 LAZARU

SKILL
SURE, YOU WORKED UNDER THE SKY AND 'TWAS WORK WID 214 HA APE
SKILL AND DARING TO IT.
WITH THOSE OTHER FIVE-DOLLARS-TO-LOOK-AT-YOUR- 31 JOURNE
TONGUE FELLOWS, NOT THEIR SKILL.

SKIMMING
ONCE I DREAMED OF PAINTING WIND ON THE SEA AND THE287 GGBRDW
SKIMMING FLIGHT OF CLOUD

SKIN
I'LL SKIN HER BLACK HOIDE OFF AV HER IF SHE GOES 460 CARIBE
BACK ON HER WORRД.
I'D LOVE TO HAVE A SKUNK-SKIN COAT NEXT WINTER..439 DYNAMO
HIS SKIN IS TANNED AND WEATHER-BEATEN. 457 DYNAMO
THE WARM SAND WAS LIKE YOUR SKIN. 90 ELECTR
STEER CLEAR O' GALS OR THEY'LL SKIN YOUR HIDE OFF 106 ELECTR
AN' USE IT FUR A CARPET/
DON'T LET HIM PLAY NO SKIN GAMES. 130 ELECTR
SWELL MY LICKER SO'S YOU KIN SKIN ME OUT O' MY 130 ELECTR
BET,
A SKIN, O GOD, THAT I MUST WEAR ARMOR IN ORDER TO 265 GGBRDW
TOUCH OR TO BE TOUCHED$
SHE IS MY SKIN/ 266 GGBRDW
BUT EXCEPT FOR THE SLIGHT DIFFERENTIATION IN COLOR207 HA APE
OF HAIR, SKIN, EYES,
IT'LL GET UNDER YOUR SKIN. 227 HA APE
AS IF THE SKIN IN THE WINDOW WERE A PERSONAL 236 HA APE
INSULT)
(WITH GRIM HUMOR) THEY WOULDN'T BLOODY WELL PAY 236 HA APE
THAT FOR A 'AIRY APE'S SKIN--
WHY SHOULD THEY GET UNDER MY SKIN NOW$ 608 ICEMAN
DO YOU SUPPOSE I'D DELIBERATELY SET OUT TO GET 642 ICEMAN
UNDER EVERYONE'S SKIN
HIS FAIR SKIN IS SUNBURNED A REDDISH, FRECKLED 19 JOURNE
TAN.

SKIN (CONT'D.)
HIS SKIN, IN SPITE OF BEING SUNBURNED A DEEP 20 JOURNE
BROWN, HAS A PARCHED SALLOWNESS.
HER SKIN, IN CONTRAST TO THE MASK, IS SUNBURNED 274 LAZARU
AND EARTH-
BELOW HIS MASK HIS OWN SKIN IS OF AN ANAEMIC 299 LAZARU
TRANSPARENT PALLOR.
THE COMPLEXION OF HIS OWN SKIN IS THAT OF A 337 LAZARU
HEALTHY OLD CAMPAIGNER.
OR AN UNGUENT YOU RUB INTO THE SKIN TO REVITALIZE 354 LAZARU
THE OLD BONES AND TISSUES$
WITH A MASS OF BLACK HAIR, A FAIR SKIN WITH ROSY 1 MANSNS
CHEEKS,
THE DRY SKIN IS STRETCHED TIGHTLY OVER THE BONES 27 MANSNS
YOUR SKIN IS LIKE SILVER IN THE MOON YOUR EYES ARE360 MARCOM
BLACK PEARLS I HAVE WON.
BLACK HAIR AS COARSE AS A HORSE'S MANE, FRECKLED, 3 MISBEG
SUNBURNED FAIR SKIN,
AND SKIN HIM OUT OF HIS LAST NICKEL/ 10 MISBEG
I'M A FOOL TO LET THIS STUFF ABOUT PHIL GET UNDER 139 MISBEG
MY SKIN, BUT--
FAIR SKIN WITH ROSY CHEEKS, AND BEAUTIFUL, DEEP- 15 POET
BLUE EYES.
(IN SPITE OF HIMSELF, THIS GETS UNDER HIS SKIN-- 45 POET
ANGRILY.)
BUT HIS BARE SKIN. 52 POET
AND YOU STAY HERE, D'YOU HEAR, YE BRAT, TILL WE 601 ROPE
CALL YE--OR I'LL SKIN YE ALIVE.
BUT SOMETIMES THE SCENT OF HER HAIR AND SKIN... 5 STRANG
TOUCH OF HER SKIN/... 97 STRANG
THE TOUCH OF HER SOFT SKIN/... 104 STRANG
HER SKIN STILL RETAINS A TRACE OF SUMMER TAN 137 STRANG
HIS SKIN IS TANNED ALMOST BLACK BY HIS YEARS IN 159 STRANG
THE TROPICS.
HER SKIN IS DEEPLY TANNED, HER FIGURE TALL AND 159 STRANG
ATHLETIC.
LEAVING HIS SKIN A MONGOLIAN YELLOW. 190 STRANG
(IT GETS UNDER MY SKIN TO SEE HIM ACT SO 191 STRANG
UNFEELINGLY TOWARD HIS MOTHER/...

SKINFLINT
THE OLD SKINFLINT HAS A GUILTY CONSCIENCE. 204 AHWILD
YE OLD SKINFLINT/ 223 DESIRE
THE OLD SKINFLINT MUST HAVE LEFT A PILE O' MONEY. 106 ELECTR
THERE'S A CRUEL SKINFLINT OF A LANDLORD WHO 63 MISBEG
SWINDLES ME OUT OF MY LAST DROP OF

SKINFLINT'S
LET'S SEE THE COLOR O' THE OLD SKINFLINT'S MONEY 219 DESIRE
AN' WE'LL SIGN.

SKINFLINTS
AND ALL THE SLAVE-DRIVIN' YANKEE SKINFLINTS LIKE 52 POET
YOU/

SKINFUL
HE'S COPPED A FINE SKINFUL--AND GEE, HE'S HARDLY 246 AHWILD
HAD ANYTHING.
ON SATIRDAY NIGHTS WHEN DEY BOT' GOT A SKINFUL 234 HA APE

SKINNED
ANOTHER OVER ONE CHEEKBONE, HIS KNUCKLES ARE 68 ANNA
SKINNED AND RAW--
HE SKINNED 'EM TOO SLICK. 205 DESIRE
JOE MOTT IS A NEGRO, ABOUT FIFTY YEARS OLD, BROWN-574 ICEMAN
SKINNED, STOCKY,
BOTH HIS HANDS ARE SWOLLEN, WITH SKINNED KNUCKLES,152 POET
AS ARE CREGAN'S.

SKINNY
WELL, YOU'RE NOT SKINNY EITHER--ONLY SLENDER-- 291 AHWILD
OR WOULD YOU HAVE HER TIED FOR LIFE TO THE LIKE OF 48 ANNA
THEM SKINNY
YUH SKINNY TART/ 230 HA APE
WHITE AND SKINNY. 231 HA APE
IS IT PAYIN' ATTENTION AT ALL YOU ARE TO THE LIKE 232 HA APE
OF THAT SKINNY SOW
HER HANDS--DEY WAS SKINNY AND WHITE LIKE DEY 241 HA APE
WASN'T REAL BUT PAINTED ON SOMEP'N.
SKINNY TARTS AND DE BOOBS WHAT MARRY 'EM--MAKIN' 252 HA APE
POWERFUL SHOULDERS AND LONG ARMS AND HANDS, AND 299 LAZARU
SHORT, SKINNY,
THE IMPRESSION OF BEING BODILESS, A LITTLE, 161 MANSNS
SKINNY, WITCH-LIKE, OLD WOMAN,
HIS SKINNY BODY IS CLOTHED IN RAGS AND THERE IS 52 POET
NOTHING UNDER HIS TATTERED COAT
I NEVER HAD AN EYE FOR SKINNY, PALE SNIPS OF 90 POET
WOMEN--
SHE IS A SKINNY, OVERGROWN GIRL OF TEN, WITH THIN,578 ROPE
UT'S FAT YE ARE, KATY DEAR, AN' I NEVER CUD ENDURE500 VOYAGE
SKINNY WIMIN.

SKINS
OH, THE CLEAN SKINS OF THEM, AND THE CLEAR EYES, 213 HA APE
SKINS OF POOR, 'ARMLESS ANIMALS SLAUGHTERED 236 HA APE
THESE SEVEN ARE CLAD IN GOAT SKINS, 298 LAZARU
OH THE PRAITIES THEY GROW SMALL AND WE DIG THEM IN 72 MISBEG
THE FALL AND WE EAT THEM SKINS

SKIP
SO I'D SKIP DOWN THE PATH TO MEET HIM, AND MAKE 24 MISBEG
HIM A COURTESY,
YOU SKIP THIS ONE. 120 MISBEG
I'LL SKIP THIS ONE. 122 MISBEG
IT'S FLAT 'N' IT'LL SKIP. 589 ROPE
SKIP/ 602 ROPE
SKIP/ 602 ROPE
SKIP--SKIP--SKIP.* 602 ROPE

SKIPPED
SAY, HAS HE HAD THAT HANGIN' THERE EVER SINCE I 592 ROPE
SKIPPED$

SKIPPER
*DAVE KEENEY WHAT BOASTS HE'S THE BEST WHALIN' 542 'ILE
SKIPPER OUT O' HOMEPORT
YOU SEE--I'VE ALWAYS DONE IT--SINCE MY FIRST 547 'ILE
VOYAGE AS SKIPPER.

SKIPPER

SKIPPER (CONT'D.)
I BEEN ALWAYS FIRST WHALIN' SKIPPER OUT O' 547 'ILE
HOMEPORT, AND--
THE SKIPPER WAS HOPING TO MAKE BOSTON BEFORE 36 ANNA
ANOTHER BLOW WOULD FINISH HER.
IF IT HADN'T BEEN FOR UNCLE DICK BEING SUCH A GOOD131 BEYOND
SKIPPER
MAYBE SKIPPER SCARE HER. 460 CARIBE
UP HAVIN' A WORRD WID THE SKIPPER. 462 CARIBE
'E AIN'T 'ARF A FUNNY OLE BIRD, THE SKIPPER. 463 CARIBE
(TO THE WOMEN, HARSHLY) YOU NEEDN'T GO TO THE 473 CARIBE
SKIPPER FOR ANY MONEY.
MY FUST VICE AS SKIPPER, YOU DON'T S'POSE I HAD 497 DIFRNT
TIME FOR NO MONKEY-SHININ'.
SHE THOUGHT ON'Y THE SKIPPER WAS GOOD ENOUGH FOR 503 DIFRNT
HER, I RECKON.
AND A DAMN GOOD MAN AND AS SMART A SKIPPER AS 505 DIFRNT
THERE BE IN THESE PARTS/
HE'S THE SMARTEST SKIPPER OUT O' THIS PORT AND 513 DIFRNT
YOU'D OUGHT TO BE PROUD YOU'D GOT
(GOING) AYE-AYE, SKIPPER/ 514 DIFRNT
I'M SKIPPER OF THIS VESSEL 104 ELECTR
MANY'S A TIME I'VE SEED A SKIPPER AN' MATES 105 ELECTR
SWEATIN' BLOOD TO BEAT WORK OUT OF A
SMASHED EVERYTHING AND STOLE TWO HUNDRED DOLLARS 105 ELECTR
OFF HER SKIPPER.
I DON'T GIVE A DAMN IF YE AIR A SKIPPER/ 105 ELECTR
I WARN YE, SKIPPER/ 106 ELECTR
I'LL ARRANGE WITH HER SKIPPER TO GIVE US PASSAGE--111 ELECTR
AND KEEP HIS MOUTH SHUT.
THEY'LL HAVE TO FIND ANOTHER SKIPPER FOR THE 111 ELECTR
"FLYING TRADES."
AND THE SKIPPER AND MATES AND ENGINEERS, THEY'RE 228 HA APE
'IS SLAVES/
FOR I'M AFEARD IN THE DARK AND ME MOTHER'S ON DECK230 HA APE
MAKIN' EYES AT THE SKIPPER/
(ANGRILY) 'CUS DRISC HEARD THE FIRST SEND THE 515 INZONE
THIRD BELOW TO WAKE THE SKIPPER
WE'D BEST BE TAKIN' THIS TO THE SKIPPER, D'YOU 528 INZONE
THINK, MAYBE$
SKIPPER'LL
WHEN SHE LAVES THE SKIPPER'LL PAY WHAT'S OWIN' ON 463 CARIBE
THE PAPER
SKIPPERS
ANY O' THEM SKIPPERS I'VE BEATEN VOYAGE AFTER 542 'ILE
VOYAGE$
THEM SKIPPERS WOULD NEVER DARE SNEER TO MY FACE. 547 'ILE
THERE ARE TWICE AS MANY SKIPPERS AS SHIPS THESE 39 ELECTR
DAYS.
SKIPPERS ARE ON'Y TOO GLAD TO GIT ME/ 105 ELECTR
SKIPPING
THE SKIPPING MARY TUGGING AT HER HAND. 143 BEYOND
SKIPS
(MARY SKIPS TO THE DOORWAY AND PEEPS AFTER THEM 601 ROPE
FOR A MOMENT.
SKIRT
SHE IS DRESSED IN SHIRTWAIST AND SKIRT IN THE 186 AHWILD
FASHION OF THE PERIOD.
SHE, ALSO, IS DRESSED IN A SHIRTWAIST AND SKIRT.) 187 AHWILD
SHE IS DRESSED IN SHIRTWAIST AND SKIRT. 187 AHWILD
(SCORNFULLY SUPERIOR) THAT SILLY SKIRT PARTY/ 194 AHWILD
SHE WEARS A MAN'S CAP, DOUBLE-BREASTED MAN'S 7 ANNA
JACKET, AND A GRIMY, CALICO SKIRT.
BUT THE LOWER PART OF HER SKIRT AND HER STOCKINGS 548 DAYS
AND SHOES ARE SOAKING WET.
(SHE HIKES HER SKIRT UP AND REACHES INSIDE THE TOP683 ICEMAN
OF HER STOCKING)
(SHE KICKS HER SKIRT FROM SARA'S HAND AND HALF 187 MANSNS
TURNS TO THE DOOR.
(RUSHES UP AND GRABS DEBORAH'S SKIRT AND FALLS ON 187 MANSNS
HER KNEES BEFORE HER.)
(WILDLY, GRABBING DEBORAH'S SKIRT AGAIN.) 188 MANSNS
SKIRTS
THERE'S FIVE OR SIX OF THEM IN IT--AND THEY PADDLE460 CARIBE
LIKE SKIRTS.
THESE SMALL TOWN SKIRTS DON'T HAND ME NOTHIN'. 526 DIFRNT
THAT PAINT FLAPPER WITH HER SKIRTS HITCHED UP OVER425 DYNAMO
HER KNEES/
SHE DOESN'T WANT ME NOW--A COWARD HIDING BEHIND A 107 ELECTR
WOMAN'S SKIRTS/
(THEY BOTH PULL UP THEIR SKIRTS TO GET THE MONEY 613 ICEMAN
FROM THEIR STOCKINGS.
BUT A TIMID LITTLE BOY HIDING FROM LIFE BEHIND MY 135 MANSNS
SKIRTS/
SKOAL
(LIFTING HIS GLASS) SKOAL/ 6 ANNA
SKOAL/ 12 ANNA
SKOAL/ 12 ANNA
SKOAL/ 15 ANNA
SKOAL/ 24 ANNA
SKOAL, ANNA/ 24 ANNA
SKOAL/ 24 ANNA
SKOAL/ 77 ANNA
SKOAL/ 295 GGBROW
SKOAL/ 208 HA APE
SKOAL/ 507 VOYAGE
SKOAL/ 507 VOYAGE
SKOFF
TO BE STOMACHIN' THE SKOFF ON THIS RUSTY LIME- 480 CARDIF
JUICER.
SKOIT
DEN WHEN I COME TO AND SEEN IT WAS A REAL SKOIT 231 HA APE
AND SEEN DE WAY SHE WAS LOOKIN'
(AGAIN BEWILDEREDLY) SAY, WHO IS DAT SKOIT, HUH$ 231 HA APE
NO GUY AND NO SKOIT NEITHER/ 231 HA APE
WHAT DOES A SKOIT LIKE HER MEAN, HUH$ 231 HA APE
DIS WAS A NEW KIND OF SKOIT. 241 HA APE

SKOIT

SKOIT (CONT'D.)
SURE DERE WAS A SKOIT IN IT-BUT NOT WHAT YOUSE 241 HA APE
MEAN, NOT DAT OLD TRIPE.
SKOITS
WHERE'S ALL DE WHITE-COLLAR STIFFS YUH SAID WAS 234 HA APE
HERE--AND DE SKOITS--HER KINDS
SKULKED
YEAR ARTER YEAR IT'S SKULKED IN YER EYE-- 208 DESIRE
SOMETHIN'.
HE SKULKED AND AVOIDED PEOPLE. 25 ELECTR
SKULKIN'
AND SEE TO IT THEY DON'T TRY NONE OF THEIR 545 'ILE
SKULKIN' TRICKS.
JUST SKULKIN' OUT O' YOUR RIGHTFUL RESPONSIBILITY.105 BEYOND
YE STABBED HIM, AND BE DAMNED TO HIM, FOR THE 488 CARDIF
SKULKIN' SWINE HE WAS,
SKULKING
THE TIME FOR SKULKING AND LYING IS OVER--AND BY 37 ELECTR
GOD I'M GLAD OF IT--
SKULL
WELL, IF HE'S REALLY GOT THAT VIEW OF IT DRIVEN 289 AHWILD
INTO HIS SKULL,
IT'D TAKE MORE THAN A BIT OF A BLOW TO CRACK MY 33 ANNA
THICK SKULL.
TO SMASH YOUR SKULL LIKE A ROTTEN EGG. 60 ANNA
I'LL SPLIT THE SKULL AV THE FIRST MAN AV YE STARTS458 CARIBE
TO FOIGHT.
THEY'S NOTHIN' IN THAT THICK SKULL O' YOUR'N BUT 254 DESIRE
NOISE--LIKE A EMPTY KEG IT BE/
BUT CLARK PICKED UP AN AX AND SPLIT HIS SKULL/ 440 DYNAMO
SHOVEL ON THE WHITE MAN'S SKULL. 195 EJONES
I'LL CRASH YER SKULL IN/ 225 HA APE
AND THE LOVING MAY YANK HEAVED HIS SHOVEL AT THE 230 HA APE
SKULL OF HER,
HIS BLOND HAIR, BADLY IN NEED OF A CUT, CLINGS IN 577 ICEMAN
A LIMP PART TO HIS SKULL.
FUR THEY GRIN AT ME FROM THE ONE SKULL OF DEATH. 649 ICEMAN
BUT TOMORROW HE WILL JEER WHILE HYENAS GNAW AT 358 LAZARU
YOUR SKULL AND LICK YOUR BRAIN.
SEEING THE SKULL OF DEATH LEER OVER ITS SHOULDER 12 MANSNS
IN THE GLASS/
OF A SKULL BEGINNING TO EMERGE FROM ITS MASK OF 28 MANSNS
FLESH.
YOU KNOW, I'LL BEAT BETTER SENSE IN YOUR SKULL IF 15 MISBEG
YOU LAY A FINGER ON ME.
HE'D HAVE HAD ME DOWN ONLY CON BROKE THE BUTT AV 156 POET
THE WHIP OVER HIS BLACK SKULL
HEAD AS IF HE WERE GOING TO CRUSH BENTLEY'S SKULL 597 ROPE
WITH IT.
SKULLS
CRACK THEIR SKULLS/ 305 LAZARU
SKULP
THE INJUNS'LL SKULP YE ON THE PLAINS. 208 DESIRE
LUCKY WE DON'T SKULP YE/ 223 DESIRE
SKULPED
I'VE KILLEED INJUNS IN THE WEST AFORE YE WAS BORN--251 DESIRE
AN' SKULPED 'EM TOO/
SKUNK
I'D AS SOON PET A SKUNK 'R KISS A SNAKE/ 214 DESIRE
(TUNING UP) LET'S CELEBRATE THE OLD SKUNK GITTIN'253 DESIRE
FOOLED/
YE LIE, YE OLD SKUNK/ 255 DESIRE
I'LL GIT SQUARE WITH THE OLD SKUNK--AN' YEW/ 257 DESIRE
I'LL MAKE IT LOOK S'IF THE OLD SKUNK 'D KILLED 260 DESIRE
HIMSELF WHEN HE WAS DRUNK.
HE'S A MEAN SKUNK FROM TRUCK TO KEELSON/ 540 DIFRNT
I'M GOIN' TO FIND THE SKUNK. 542 DIFRNT
WHERE-- WHERE IS THE SKUNK NOW$ 542 DIFRNT
I'D LET YOU MARRY THE SKUNK AND SET AND WATCH WHAT543 DIFRNT
HAPPENED--
AND WHAT DO YOU SUPPOSE THAT YOUNG SKUNK DOES$ 431 DYNAMO
I'D LOVE TO HAVE A SKUNK-SKIN COAT NEXT WINTER... 439 DYNAMO
MAYBE IT'S A SKUNK.... 439 DYNAMO
I'M NOT ANXIOUS TO BE HANGED--FOR THAT SKUNK/ 113 ELECTR
YOU CAN GO BACK AND TELL WHATEVER SKUNK IS PAYING 249 HA APE
YOU BLOOD-MONEY FOR BETRAYING
UNTIL HE'S A ROTTEN SKUNK IN HIS OWN EYES. 641 ICEMAN
ADELINE,* I STILL FELT LIKE A GUILTY SKUNK. 661 ICEMAN
THAT'S WHAT MADE ME FEEL SUCH A ROTTEN SKUNK--HER 712 ICEMAN
ALWAYS FORGIVING ME.
CHRISTI, CAN YOU IMAGINE WHAT A GUILTY SKUNK SHE 713 ICEMAN
MADE ME FEEL/
THE SNEAKING SKUNK/ 66 MISBEG
SO I ONLY CALLED HIM A DIRTY LYING SKUNK OF A 86 MISBEG
TREACHEROUS BASTARD,
I'LL GIT EVEN WITH HIM, THE OLD SKUNK/ 598 ROPE
WHAT D'YUH KNOW ABOUT HIM--THE MEAN SKUNK. 599 ROPE
SKUNK'D
THE OLD SKUNK'D JEST BE STINKIN' MEAN ENUF TO TAKE260 DESIRE
IT OUT ON THAT BABY.
SKUNK'S
HIS ODOR OF SANCTITY FOR THAT OF A SKUNK'S AND 423 DYNAMO
FILL HIS*...
SKUNKS
THE HELL OF SKUNKS LIKE MCCOMBER IS THAT AFTER 204 AHWILD
BEING WITH THEM TEN MINUTES YOU
BECOME AS BIG SKUNKS AS THEY ARE. 204 AHWILD
YOU OUGHT TO BE ABLE TO SELL SKUNKS FOR GOOD 710 ICEMAN
RATTERS/
PUTATO BUGS, SNAKES AND SKUNKS ON HIS FARM, 24 JOURNE
AND THERE'S SNAKES AND SKUNKS/ 63 MISBEG
SKY
INDICATING ONE OF THOSE GRAY DAYS OF CALM WHEN 535 'ILE
OCEAN AND SKY ALIKE ARE DEAD.
WE WILL MEET IN THE SKY BYE AND BYE.* 233 AHWILD
HALFWAY DOWN THE SKY. AT REAR, LEFT, THE CRESCENT 275 AHWILD
OF THE NEW MOON CASTS A SOFT,

1455 SKYSAIL

SKY (CONT'D.)

I LOVE THE SAND AND THE TREES, AND THE GRASS, AND 277 AHWILD THE WATER AND THE SKY,

AND THE SKY ABOVE THEM GLOWS WITH THE CRIMSON 81 BEYOND FLUSH OF THE SUNSET.

THE SKY TO THE EAST IS ALREADY ALIGHT WITH BRIGHT 166 BEYOND COLOR AND A THIN,

THE FULL MOON, HALFWAY UP THE SKY, THROWS A CLEAR 455 CARIBE LIGHT ON THE DECK.

AT AN ANG AN ANGLE OF FORTY FIVE DEGREES, BLACK 455 CARIBE AGAINST THE SKY.

THE UPPER PART OF HIS STOCKY FIGURE OUTLINED 455 CARIBE AGAINST THE SKY.

LOOKIN' LIKE A BLOODY OLE SKY PILOTS 463 CARIBE

THEY SEE HIM UP THERE WALKING BACK AND FORTH-- 564 CROSS WAVING HIS ARMS AGAINST THE SKY.

THE SKY ABOVE THE ROOF IS SUFFUSED WITH DEEP 203 DESIRE COLORS,

THEN HE PUTS HIS HANDS ON HIS HIPS AND STARES UP 203 DESIRE AT THE SKY.

(GROWING EXCITED) GOLD IN THE SKY--IN THE WEST-- 204 DESIRE GOLDEN GATE--CALIFORNI-A/.

IN THE SKYS. 204 DESIRE

(FOR A MOMENT THEY CONTINUE LOOKING UP AT THE 204 DESIRE SKY--THEN THEIR EYES DROP.)

AS IF WITH THE ONE IMPULSE, STARE DUMBLY UP AT THE204 DESIRE SKY, LEANING ON THEIR HOES.

(GAZING UP AT THE SKY) SUN'S DOWNIN' PURTY. 205 DESIRE

(THE COLOR FADES FROM THE SKY. 206 DESIRE

EBEN STRETCHES HIS ARMS UP TO THE SKY-- 211 DESIRE REBELLIOUSLY.)

STARING UP AT THE SKY.) 211 DESIRE

DEFIANT EYES AT THE SKY) 217 DESIRE

THE SKY IS BEGINNING TO GROW FLUSHED WITH SUNRISE.217 DESIRE

THEY STARE UP AT THE SKY WITH A NUMBED 218 DESIRE APPRECIATION.)

THE SKY. 231 DESIRE

HE STARES UP AT THE SKY) 231 DESIRE

BLINKING AT THE SKY. 239 DESIRE

I MEAN THE SKY. 245 DESIRE

CABOT WALKS SLOWLY UP FROM THE LEFT, STARING UP AT245 DESIRE THE SKY WITH A VAGUE FACE.)

STARING AT THE SKY BLINKINGLY. 252 DESIRE

EBEN IS STANDING BY THE GATE LOOKING UP AT THE 253 DESIRE SKY.

THE SKY IS BRILLIANT WITH THE SUNRISE. 262 DESIRE

(HE GOES OUT--COMES AROUND TO THE GATE--STARES UP 265 DESIRE AT THE SKY.

EBEN STOPS THERE AND POINTS TO THE SUNRISE SKY) 269 DESIRE

WHAT D'YOU WANT TO MARRY, ANYHOW--A MAN OR A SKY- 505 DIFRNT PILOT$

A DURNED, HE-VIRGIN, SKY-PILOTS 513 DIFRNT

AGAINST A SKY PALE WITH THE LIGHT OF A QUARTER- 421 DYNAMO MOON.

WINDOWS ON THE RIGHT SO SHE CAN STARE OUT AT THE 428 DYNAMO SKY.

GIVES A START AS A FLASH OF LIGHTNING FLICKERS 431 DYNAMO OVER THE SKY)

HIS MOTHER AND FATHER SHRINK BACK FROM HIM AS HE 452 DYNAMO SHOUTS UP AT THE SKY)

ADDRESSING THE SKY WITH INSULTING INSOLENCE) 453 DYNAMO

THE SKY--DRIVEN TO LOVE BY WHAT MAKES THE EARTH GO461 DYNAMO ROUND--

A SULTRY, HAZY SKY WITH FEW STARS VISIBLE. 468 DYNAMO

IT'S AS FAR OFF AS THE SKY AND YET IT'S ALL AROUND474 DYNAMO YOU/...

AGAINST A DARKENING CRIMSON SKY. 476 DYNAMO

JONES, WHO HAS BEEN STARING UP AT THE SKY, 194 EJONES

AND RAISES HIS CLASPED HANDS TO THE SKY--IN A 196 EJONES VOICE OF AGONIZED PLEADING)

THE SKY WAS THE SAME COLOR AS YOUR EYES. 90 ELECTR

IT IS SHORTLY AFTER SUNSET BUT THE AFTERGLOW IN 129 ELECTR THE SKY

ALL GLOW HAS FADED FROM THE SKY AND IT IS GETTING132 ELECTR DARK.)

(SHE STARES UP AT THE SKY) THE MOONLIGHT WAS 261 GGBROW WARM, THEN.

SKY AND TRIMMED WITH SILVER LEAVES/ 261 GGBROW

I WANT DION TO LEAVE THE SKY TO ME. 264 GGBROW

AND THE LIVING COLORS OF EARTH AND SKY AND SEAS 264 GGBROW

HE STARES AT THE SKY RAPTLY) 266 GGBROW

(HE STRETCHES OUT HIS ARMS TO THE SKY) 266 GGBROW

I WANT DION TO LEAVE THE SKY FOR ME/ 323 GGBROW

CLIPPERS WID TALL MASTS TOUCHING THE SKY--FINE 213 HA APE STRONG MEN IN THEM.

CAGED IN BY STEEL FROM A SIGHT OF THE SKY LIKE 214 HA APE BLOODY APES IN THE ZOO/

SURE, YOU WORKED UNDER THE SKY AND 'TWAS WORK WID 214 HA APE SKILL AND DARING TO IT.

HOW THE BLACK SMOKE SWIRLS BACK AGAINST THE SKY/ 218 HA APE

GRANDFATHER'S BLAST FURNACES, FLAMING TO THE SKY, 219 HA APE MELTING STEEL.

IF EDMUND WAS A LOUSY ACRE OF LAND YOU WANTED, THE 31 JOURNE SKY WOULD BE THE LIMIT/

BECAME MOONLIGHT AND THE SHIP AND THE HIGH DIM- 153 JOURNE STARRED SKY/

OVER THE SKY AND SEA WHICH SLEPT TOGETHER. 153 JOURNE

SHE WEARS A SKY-BLUE DRESSING GOWN OVER HER 170 JOURNE NIGHTDRESS.

A BACKGROUND OF TWILIGHT SKY. 275 LAZARU

IN DEPTHS OF SKY, PROUD AND POWERFUL, INFECTIOUS 280 LAZARU WITH LOVE.

IT IS A CLEAR, BRIGHT NIGHT, THE SKY SPARKLING 281 LAZARU WITH STARS.

(HE STRETCHES OUT HIS ARMS TO THE SKY--THEN 289 LAZARU SUDDENLY POINTS)

BUT THE COMMAND OF HIS FATE FROM THE SKY) 293 LAZARU

SKY (CONT'D.)

(THEN SUPERSTITIOUSLY LOOKING UP AT THE SKY WITH 301 LAZARU CRINGING FOREBODING)

LIKE A COMMAND FROM THE SKY.) 306 LAZARU

OUT WITH YOU UNDER THE SKY/ 310 LAZARU

IN THE SKY OVERHEAD LIGHTNING FLASHES 312 LAZARU

SKY BEYOND THE WALL. 313 LAZARU

LOOM UP WITH A STARTLING CLARITY AGAINST THE SKY. 326 LAZARU

IN THE SUN AND THERE WOULD BE ECHOING LAUGHTER 330 LAZARU FROM THE SKY AND UP FROM THE

(HE DIES, LAUGHING UP AT THE SKY.) 334 LAZARU

A CLOUD CAME FROM A DEPTH OF SKY-- 342 LAZARU

AROUND ME, SOFTLY, WARMLY, AND THE CLOUD DISSOLVED342 LAZARU INTO THE SKY.

AND THE SKY INTO PEACE/ 342 LAZARU

LIKE A BLACK FIGURE OF JOB AGAINST THE SKY/ 347 LAZARU

WHEN I LOOKED AT THE SKY. 355 LAZARU

NOW I TAKE HIM OUT UNDER THE SKY, WHERE I CAN 360 LAZARU WATCH HIS MONKEY TRICKS,

GO OUT UNDER THE SKY/ 360 LAZARU

IN DEEPER BLACK AGAINST THE DARK SKY. 363 LAZARU

FOLLOWED BY A FAINT DYING NOTE OF LAUGHTER THAT 371 LAZARU RISES AND IS LOST IN THE SKY

HIS ARMS STRAINING UPWARD TO THE SKY, A TENDER, 371 LAZARU

FOR A SECOND HE IS FRAMED IN IT, OUTLINED AGAINST 376 MARCOM THE BRILLIANT SKY.

ONE ACCORD THEY RAISE THEIR ARMS AND EYES TO THE 376 MARCOM SKY.

THE SKY IS GRAY, A SNOWFLAKE FALLS. 384 MARCOM

THE FIGURES OF KUBLAI AND KUKACHIN ARE OUTLINED 400 MARCOM AGAINST THE LIGHTENING SKY.)

AND THE BLUE WATER ALONE UNDER A STRANGE SKY AMID 405 MARCOM ALIEN FLOWERS AND FACES.

DEATH LIVES IN A SILENT SEA, GRAY AND COLD UNDER 409 MARCOM COLD GRAY SKY.

(SUDDENLY RUNS UP TO THE UPPER DECK AND STANDS 420 MARCOM OUTLINED AGAINST THE SKY,

WITH A MOON IN THE SKY TO FILL HIM WITH POETRY AND 21 MISBEG A QUART OF BAD HOOTCH INSIDE

IN FACT, I'LL BET THE SKY IS THE LIMIT NOW. 66 MISBEG

WITH A DAWN THAT WON'T CREEP OVER DIRTY 153 MISBEG WINDOWPANES BUT WILL WAKE IN THE SKY

(HER EYES LEAVE HIS FACE TO STARE UP AT THE SKY. 153 MISBEG

APPEAR IN THE EASTERN SKY AT LEFT. 157 MISBEG

HER EYES ARE FIXED ON THE WANTON SKY.) 160 MISBEG

LOOKING AT THE EASTERN SKY WHICH IS NOW GLOWING 164 MISBEG WITH COLOR)

WHERE THE SKY IS NOW GLOWING 172 MISBEG

A WIND FROM THE SOUTH, AND A SKY GRAY WITH 102 POET CLOUDS--GOOD WEATHER FOR THE HOUNDS.

OUT OF THE SKY IN FLAMES AND HE LOOKED AT ME WITH 45 STRANG SUCH SAD BURNING EYES,

OUT OF A BLUE SKY.... 58 STRANG

(SHE IS LOOKING DESPERATELY UP INTO THE SKY 181 STRANG

(THEN WITH A GRIM FATALISM--WITH A FINAL WAVE OF 198 STRANG HIS HAND AT THE SKY)

(HE SHOUTS UP AT THE SKY) YOU'RE MY SON, GORDON/ 198 STRANG

(LOOKING UP AT THE SKY--STRANGELY) 199 STRANG

(HE LAUGHS UP AT THE SKY) (10h, GOD, SO DEAF AND 199 STRANG DUMB AND BLIND/...

IT WAS REVELATION THEN--A MIRACLE OUT OF THE SKY/ 447 WELDED

SKY'D

WHEN THE SKY'D BE BLAZING AND WINKING WID STARS. 214 HA APE

SKY'S

(LOOKING AT WINDOW) SKY'S GRAYIN'. 214 DESIRE

I'D SAY, =OKAY, ARNOLD, THE SKY'S THE LIMIT,= AND 32 HUGHIE I'D RAISE HIM FIVE GRAND,

SKYLARKIN'

AN' HOW SHE HOPES HE'LL SETTLE DOWN TO RALE WORRK 530 INZONE AN' NOT BE SKYLARKIN' AROUND

SKYLIGHT

A SMALL, SQUARE COMPARTMENT ABOUT EIGHT FEET HIGH 535 *ILE WITH A SKYLIGHT IN THE CENTER

AND THE LIGHT WHICH COMES THROUGH THE SKYLIGHT IS 535 *ILE SICKLY AND FAINT.

(IN A SUDDEN RAGE, SHAKING HIS FIST AT THE 536 *ILE SKYLIGHT)

UP THE PLATES AND CASTS A QUICK GLANCE UPWARD AT 536 *ILE THE SKYLIGHT.

(A MOMENT LATER THE MATE'S FACE APPEARS THROUGH 551 *ILE THE SKYLIGHT.

THE MATE'S FACE APPEARS AGAIN THROUGH THE 552 *ILE SKYLIGHT.)

A SKYLIGHT EXTENDING FROM OPPOSITE THE DOOR TO 555 CROSS ABOVE THE LEFT EDGE OF THE TABLE.

IN THE RIGHT EXTREMITY OF THE SKYLIGHT IS PLACED A555 CROSS FLOATING SHIP'S COMPASS.

HIS FACE, IN THE LIGHT FROM THE SKYLIGHT, BECOMES 109 ELECTR DISTORTED WITH JEALOUS FURY.

SUSPENDED IN THE SKYLIGHT IS A SHIP'S COMPASS. 109 ELECTR

THE SKYLIGHT GIVING ON THE DECK ABOVE IS IN THE 109 ELECTR MIDDLE OF THE CEILING.

THEY APPROACH THE CABIN SKYLIGHT SILENTLY. 109 ELECTR

SKYPILOTS

I AIN'T NEVER TOOK MUCH STOCK IN THE TRUCK THEM 486 CARDIF SKYPILOTS PREACH.

SKYROCKETS

(MOURNFULLY) AIN'T WE GOING TO SET OFF THE 234 AHWILD SKYROCKETS AND ROMAN CANDLES, PA$

SKYS'L

IS WORSEN'N GOIN' ALOFT TO THE SKYS'L YARD IN A 140 BEYOND BLOW.

BLOODY WINDJAMMER--SKYS'L-YARDER--FULL-RIGGED-- 495 VOYAGE PAINTED WHITE--

I SAIL ON HER ONCE LONG TIME AGO--THREE MASTS, 507 VOYAGE FULL RIG, SKYS'L-YARDER$

SKYSAIL

AND SHIPPED US ON A SKYSAIL-YARDER ROUND THE HORN,487 CARDIF

SKYSCRAPER

SKYSCRAPER
(POINTING TO A SKYSCRAPER ACROSS THE STREET 238 HA APE
SKYSCRAPERS
I WAS LOOKIN' AT DE SKYSCRAPERS-STEEL-- 252 HA APE
SLACK
HIS EYES HAVE A MISTED, OILY LOOK AND HIS MOUTH IS125 JOURNE
SLACK,
HIS MOUTH SLACK LIKE HIS FATHER'S, A LEER ON HIS 154 JOURNE
LIPS,)
ONE DOESN'T ENCOUNTER SUCH FRIENDSHIP OFTEN IN 127 STRANG
THESE SLACK DAYS.
SLACKER
THAT FOR YOU, 'FRAID-CAT CHARLIE, YOU SLACKER 52 STRANG
BACHELOR/
SLAVE
IN THE BACK ROOM, LARRY SLADE AND HUGO KALMAR ARE 574 ICEMAN
AT THE TABLE AT LEFT-FRONT,
LARRY SLADE IS SIXTY. 574 ICEMAN
SLAIN
HOW COULD HE BE SLAIN, OLD FOOLS 303 LAZARU
THOU HAST SLAIN DEATH/ 320 LAZARU
THOU HAST SLAIN FEAR/ 320 LAZARU
BELIEVING NOW THAT THEY HAD SLAIN THEM/ 328 LAZARU
WELCOME IN THE NAME OF CAESAR, NOW CAESAR IS SLAIN338 LAZARU
AND I AM CAESAR/
SLAM
AND DO BE CAREFUL NOT TO LET THAT PANTRY DOOR SLAM211 AHWILD
BEHIND YOU.
(NORAH EXITS INTO THE PANTRY AND LETS THE DOOR 223 AHWILD
SLAM WITH A BANG BEHIND HER.)
THE DOOR SLAM WITH A CRASH BEHIND HER. 227 AHWILD
(HE GOES, LETTING THE DOOR SLAM TO BEHIND HIM.) 543 DIFRNT
I'LL SLAM YER NOSE TROU DE BACK OF YER HEAD/ 225 HA APE
THEN FROM THE HALL COMES THE SLAM OF THE STREET 719 ICEMAN
DOOR.
(SHE GOES OUT ON THE SIDE PORCH, LETTING THE 53 JOURNE
SCREEN DOOR SLAM BEHIND HER,
WHEN HE'D SAID THAT, THE FLUNKY TRIED TO SLAM THE 155 POET
DOOR IN OUR FACES,
SLAMMED
(THE SOUND OF A DOOR BEING HEAVILY SLAMMED IS 571 CROSS
HEARD FROM WAY DOWN IN THE HOUSE.)
THERE IS THE NOISE OF THE FRONT DOOR BEING SLAMMED445 DYNAMO
THE BRAZEN CLANG OF THE FURNACE DOORS AS THEY ARE 223 HA APE
FLUNG OPEN OR SLAMMED SHUT.
HE GETS IN BRISKLY. THE DOOR IS SLAMMED, 439 MARCOM
ITS DOOR IS SLAMMED, IT DRIVES OFF.. 462 WELDED
SLAMMING
(HE STALKS OUT, SLAMMING THE DOOR BEHIND HIM.) 216 AHWILD
(THEN THE FRONT DOOR IS HEARD SLAMMING. 220 AHWILD
THE FRONT SCREEN DOOR IS HEARD SLAMMING AND NAT'S 221 AHWILD
AND SID'S LAUGHING VOICES.
(HE DISAPPEARS AND THE SLAMMING OF THE KITCHEN 125 BEYOND
DOOR IS HEARD.)
(SHE GOES INTO THE FORECASTLE, SLAMMING THE DOOR.)470 CARIBE
(EBEN APPEARS OUTSIDE, SLAMMING THE DOOR BEHIND 227 DESIRE
HIM.
GOSH, THAT SOUNDED LIKE OUR FRONT DOOR SLAMMING. 534 DIFRNT
(HE RUSHES OUT REAR, SLAMMING THE DOOR BEHIND 549 DIFRNT
HIM.)
(THERE IS THE NOISE OF THE FRONT DOOR SLAMMING) 450 DYNAMO
(HE GOES, WHISTLING, SLAMMING THE DOOR.) 288 GGBROW
THE STREET DOOR IS HEARD SLAMMING BEHIND THEM.) 683 ICEMAN
(DRINKING THE LAST OF HIS COFFEE AND SLAMMING HIS 515 INZONE
FIST ON THE BENCH EXPLOSIVELY)
(SUDDENLY EXPLODES, SLAMMING HER RULE ON THE 140 MANSNS
DESK.)
SLAMMING THE DOOR BEHIND HIM.) 143 MANSNS
(HE WRENCHES OPEN THE DOOR AND FLINGS HIMSELF INTO155 MANSNS
THE HALL, SLAMMING THE DOOR.
(SHE GOES IN THROUGH HER BEDROOM, SLAMMING THE 36 MISBEG
DOOR BEHIND HER.
(HE DISAPPEARS, LAUGHING, SLAMMING THE DOOR BEHIND129 POET
HIM.
SLAMMING THE DOOR QUICKLY BEHIND HIM. 165 POET
(THE FRONT DOOR IS HEARD SLAMMING. 130 STRANG
SLAMS
(SHE SLAMS THE DOOR SHUT.) 188 AHWILD
(SHE GOES OUT AND SLAMS THE DOOR.) 248 AHWILD
EBEN RUSHES OUT AND SLAMS THE DOOR--THEN THE 211 DESIRE
OUTSIDE FRONT DOOR--
HE IS CONFUSED, HE TURNS AWAY AND SLAMS THE DOOR 228 DESIRE
RESENTFULLY.
I DON'T WANT TO GO-- (HE SLAMS THE DOOR BEHIND 483 DYNAMO
THEM.)
A DOOR SLAMS. 123 ELECTR
(HE GOES, THE OUTER DOOR SLAMS. 273 GGBROW
IT SLAMS DAT OFFEN DE FACE OF DE OITH/ 215 HA APE
HE SLAMS HIS FURNACE DOOR SHUT. 224 HA APE
AND SLAMS THE PORTHOLE SHUT) 514 INZONE
(HE PULLS A SOVEREIGN OUT OF HIS POCKET AND SLAMS 497 VOYAGE
IT ON THE BAR.)
SLANDER
(ABASHED ONLY FOR A MOMENT) OH, SO THEY'VE SENT 392 MARCOM
THAT VILE SLANDER TO YOU,
SLANG
DON'T TALK THAT HORRIBLE SLANG. 250 AHWILD
THAT HEART IS MORE THAN A WORD USED IN «HAVE A 27 HUGHIE
HEART,» AN OLD SLANG EXPRESSION.)
SLANGILY
(GRUFFLY AND SLANGILY) I'M OUT OF IT--SHE GAVE ME265 GGBROW
THE GATE.
SLANGY
HER SPEECH IS SELF-ASSERTIVE AND CONSCIOUSLY 429 DYNAMO
SLANGY.
SLANT
TAKE A SLANT IN THE MIRROR AND YUH'LL SEE. 11 ANNA
TAKE A SLANT AT DAT/ 236 HA APE

SLANT
(CONT'D.)
STILL, SOME GUYS GET A WRONG SLANT ON US. 247 HA APE
LADIES AND GENTS, STEP FORWARD AND TAKE A SLANT AT254 HA APE
DE ONE AND ONLY--
SLAP
FRIGHTENED TO CLOSE HER MOUTH WITH A SLAP/ 70 ANNA
INTERRUPTS PADDY WITH A SLAP ON THE BARE BACK LIKE217 HA APE
A REPORT)
(GIVES HER A SLAP, TOO) AND DAT'LL LOIN YOU/ 633 ICEMAN
I JUST GIVE DEM A SLAP, LIKE ANY GUY WOULD HIS 633 ICEMAN
WIFE, IF SHE GOT TOO GABBY.
(HE GIVES HER A SLAP ON THE SIDE OF THE FACE.) 633 ICEMAN
(HE CHUCKLES AND GIVES LARRY A FRIENDLY SLAP ON 639 ICEMAN
THE BACK.
JUST SLAP DEM. 669 ICEMAN
DEN I'D SLAP DEM. 669 ICEMAN
SHE MEANS IT TO BE ONLY A SLAP, BUT HIS HEAD JERKS 4 MISBEG
BACK AND HE STUMBLES.
JUST A SLAP BECAUSE SHE TOLD ME TO STOP SINGING, 18 MISBEG
IT WAS AFTER DAYLIGHT.
NO ONE WANTS TO ADMIT ALL HE GOT WAS A SLAP IN THE135 MISBEG
PUSS,
RAISING HER HAND AS IF SHE WERE GOING TO SLAP HIS 115 POET
FACE--
DON'T MIND HIS GIVING YOU A SLAP. 180 POET
(SHE SMILES STRANGELY.) MAYBE I DESERVED THE SLAP181 POET
FOR INTERFERING.
SLAPPED
BUT, MY GOD, YOUR FIRST MARRIAGE MUST HAVE SLAPPED517 DAYS
YOUR FACE
(THEY WINCE AS IF HE HAD SLAPPED THEM, 639 ICEMAN
AND THEN YOU SLAPPED THEM GROGGY WHEN THEY TRIED 135 MISBEG
FOR MORE.
TAKING A STEP BACK AS THOUGH HE HAD BEEN SLAPPED 72 POET
IN THE FACE.
THE ORIGINAL ARE SLAPPED HELTER-SKELTER ON TOP OF 66 STRANG
EACH OTHER ON IT.
SLAPPING
SLAPPING THEM AGAINST HIS SIDES, ON THE VERGE OF 536 'ILE
CRYING.)
(SLAPPING THE TABLE) HO/ 95 BEYOND
SLAPPING SMITH ON THE BACK) 456 CARIBE
(SLAPPING HIM ON THE BACK) CHEERO, OLE LOVE/ 459 CARIBE
(THEY LAUGH UPROARIOUSLY, SLAPPING THEIR THIGHS.) 223 DESIRE
(SLAPPING HIM ON THE BACK) I'M SORRY FUR YE, HI. 249 DESIRE
(SLAPPING HIS THIGH AND GUFFAWING) 204 EJONES
(SLAPPING HIM ON THE BACK) GOD DAMN YOU, JOE, 130 ELECTR
YOU'RE GITTIN' TO BE A POET.
(HE GRINS, SLAPPING ORIN ON THE BACK AND GOES OUT.160 ELECTR
IN A FLASH ALL IS HILARIOUS AMIABILITY AGAIN, BACK213 HA APE
SLAPPING, LOUD TALK, ETC.)
(SLAPPING HIS THIGH--ANGRILY) 522 INZONE
(SLAPPING DAVIS ON THE BACK) 524 INZONE
(SLAPPING DAVIS ON THE BACK) 528 INZONE
WAGGING THEM AT THEIR EARS, STICKING OUT THEIR 366 LAZARU
TONGUES, SLAPPING THEIR BEHINDS,
(SLAPPING THE PROSTITUTE ON THE BARE SHOULDER) 368 MARCOM
(SUDDENLY SLAPPING A STACK OF COINS INTO THE CHEST415 MARCOM
WITH A RESOUNDING CLANK)
(HE BURSTS INTO AN EXTRAVAGANT ROAR OF LAUGHTER, 58 MISBEG
SLAPPING HIS THIGH.
(SLAPPING GORDON ON THE BACK) 151 STRANG
(SLAPPING IVAN'S FACE WITH HIS FREE HAND) 503 VOYAGE
SLAPS
(HE SLAPS HER JOVIALLY ON HER FAT BUTTOCKS. 222 AHWILD
SLAPS HIM ON THE BACK) COME ON/ 78 ANNA
(HE GRINS AND SLAPS ROBERT ON THE BACK 82 BEYOND
AFFECTIONATELY)
(HE SLAPS HIS BROTHER ON THE BACK WITH A LAUGH) 85 BEYOND
(HE SLAPS THE TABLE WITH THE PALMS OF HIS HANDS 94 BEYOND
AND LAUGHS LOUDLY.)
(HE SLAPS ROBERT ON THE BACK) 133 BEYOND
DRISCOLL LAUGHS AND SLAPS HIS THIGH) 464 CARIBE
PEARL SLAPS HIM ACROSS THE SIDE OF TH 471 CARIBE
(THIS TICKLES HIS HUMOR AND HE SLAPS HIS THIGH AND245 DESIRE
LAUGHS)
HE STRIDES UP AND SLAPS EBEN ON THE BACK. 253 DESIRE
(HE SLAPS HER ON THE BACK) BUCK UP/ 946 DIFRNT
YANK SLAPS PADDY ON THE BACK) 217 HA APE
(SHE SLAPS HER AUNT INSULTINGLY ACROSS THE FACE 222 HA APE
AND WALKS OFF, LAUGHING GAILY.)
(HE CHUCKLES AND SLAPS LEWIS ON HIS BARE SHOULDER)599 ICEMAN
THE SLAPS HOPE ON THE BACK ENCOURAGINGLY. 654 ICEMAN
(JOE SULLENLY GOES BACK BEHIND THE COUNTER AND 672 ICEMAN
SLAPS THE KNIFE ON TOP OF IT.
(HE TAKES A KEY FROM HIS POCKET AND SLAPS IT ON 673 ICEMAN
THE BAR)
(HE PULLS HIS KEY FROM HIS POCKET AND SLAPS IT ON 682 ICEMAN
THE BAR)
LEWIS LEANS OVER AND SLAPS WETJOEN AFFECTIONATELY 723 ICEMAN
ON THE KNEE)
JACK SLAPS HIM ROUGHLY ON THE SHOULDER AND HE 516 INZONE
COMES TO WITH A START)
(WITH NO GENTLE HAND SLAPS THE WASTE OVER SMITTY'5527 INZONE
MOUTH)
(HE BENDS AND SLAPS AT THE KNEES OF HIS TROUSERS.1155 JOURNE
HAD SERIOUS ACCIDENT.
HE SLAPS JAMIE ACROSS THE MOUTH WITH THE BACK OF 170 JOURNE
HIS HAND.)
(HE SUDDENLY SLAPS LAZARUS VICIOUSLY ACROSS THE 348 LAZARU
FACE)
HE SLAPS A POLICEMAN ON THE BACK AND ASKS HIS 388 MARCOM
NAME/
THERE IS A CONFUSED WHIRL OF EMBRACES, KISSES, 429 MARCOM
BACK-SLAPS,
(HE SLAPS HER ON THE BACK.) 430 MARCOM
(HE SLAPS HIS THIGH) O JAYSUS, THIS IS A GREAT 64 MISBEG
DAY FOR THE POOR AND OPPRESSED/

SLAPS (CONT'D.)
(HE SLAPS HIS THIGH ENTHUSIASTICALLY) 95 MISBEG
SUDDENLY HE SLAPS AT HER HAND, KNOCKING THE GLASS 121 MISBEG
TO THE GROUND.)
WHAT THE HELL--(HE IS SUDDENLY CONVULSED WITH 592 ROPE
LAUGHTER AND SLAPS HIS THIGHS)
(HE SLAPS LUKE ON THE SHOULDER AND PUSHES THE 598 ROPE
BOTTLE TOWARD HIM)
(FACING HIM--WITH A STRANGE FRIENDLINESS) SLAPS HIM1B1 STRANG
ON THE BACK)
(HE STEPS FORWARD AND SLAPS DARRELL ACROSS THE 193 STRANG
FACE VICIOUSLY.
(HE SLAPS CAPE ON THE BACK WITH JOVIAL 450 WELDED
FAMILIARITY)
(HE COMES TO CAPE AND SLAPS HIM ON THE BACK 451 WELDED
REASSURINGLY)

SLASH
A SCAR FROM A KNIFE SLASH RUNS FROM HIS LEFT 575 ICEMAN
CHEEK-BONE TO JAW.
MEN STILL NEED THEIR SWORDS TO SLASH AT GHOSTS IN 328 LAZARU
THE DARK.

SLATE
THE SEA IS A DARK SLATE COLOR. 578 ROPE

SLATED
I'M SLATED TO LEAVE ON A TRIP. 661 ICEMAN

SLATES
AND PROMISES FULFILLED AND CLEAN SLATES AND NEW 578 ICEMAN
LEASES/

SLAUGHTERED
SKINS OF POOR, 'ARMLESS ANIMALS SLAUGHTERED 236 HA APE

SLAVE
THE WAGE SLAVE GROUND UNDER THE HEEL OF THE 194 AHWILD
CAPITALIST CLASS, STARVING.
HOME OF THE SLAVE IS WHAT THEY OUGHT TO CALL IT-- 194 AHWILD
SO FINE A WOMAN ONCE--AN NOW SUCH A SLAVE TO RUM/ 232 AHWILD
I HAD TO SLAVE FOR ALL OF 'EM. 18 ANNA
WHO D'YOU THINK YOU'RE TALKING TO--A SLAVES 39 ANNA
AND WHAT A DIRTY SLAVE THEM COUSINS MADE OF ME$ 57 ANNA
IN THE SUN LIKE A SLAVE WITHOUT GETTING A WORD OF 107 BEYOND
THANKS FOR IT.
HAD SUPPLANTED HIM WITH THE SLAVE-OWNING STATE-- 503 DAYS
DIDN'T HE SLAVE MAN T' DEATH/ 207 DESIRE
TO THE SLAVE-MARKET FOR DIVERSION. 196 EJONES
YOU'D THINK I WAS HER SLAVE/ 10 ELECTR
YOU LET ME TAKE YOU AS IF YOU WERE A NIGGER SLAVE 60 ELECTR
I'D BOUGHT AT AUCTION/
LET HIM SLAVE LIKE I HAD TO/ 260 GGBROW
THE SNIVELING, CRINGING, LIFE-DENYING CHRISTIAN 292 GGBROW
SLAVE YOU HAVE SO NOBLY IGNORED
I'M NO SLAVE THE LIKE OF YOU. 217 HA APE
BLOODY SLAVE-DRIVER/ 224 HA APE
HE'S GOIN' TO PULL DAT SLAVE-GIRL STUFF ON ME ONCE$79 ICEMAN
TOO OFTEN.
VERE IS YOUR LEEDLE SLAVE GIRLS$ 579 ICEMAN
SAYING YOU WERE STILL A SLAVE TO BOURGEOIS 647 ICEMAN
MORALITY AND JEALOUSY
HE BEGAN BY SHOUTING THAT HE WAS NO SLAVE STANDARD 24 JOURNE
OIL COULD TRAMPLE ON.
AND BY THE TIME I WOKE UP TO THE FACT I'D BECOME A149 JOURNE
SLAVE TO THE DAMNED THING AND
DEATH WOULD HAVE BEEN MY SLAVE WHEN I AM CAESAR. 308 LAZARU
THE SLAVE WEARS A BLACK NEGROID MASK. 313 LAZARU
A SLAVE WITH AN AMPHORA OF WINE CROUCHES ON THE 313 LAZARU
STEPS BY HIS CHAIR.
(CALLS AS TO A SLAVE) YOU, THERE/ 316 LAZARU
I THIS JEW, THIS ROMAN, THIS NOBLE OR THIS SLAVE,324 LAZARU
(SHE POINTS TO MIRIAM) NOT THAT UGLY SLAVES 341 LAZARU
FORGIVE YOUR LOVING SLAVE/ 343 LAZARU
THEN IT WAS ONLY MY BODY THAT WANTED A SLAVE. 351 LAZARU
WITH HIS SLAVE HE CALLS IMMORTAL SOUL/ 352 LAZARU
DO YOU THINK I AM YOUR SLAVE, DOG OF A JEW, THAT 359 LAZARU
YOU CAN--INSULT--TO MY FACE--
BECOME YOUR SLAVE, WAIT UPON YOU, GIVE YOU LOVE 361 LAZARU
AND PASSION AND BEAUTY IN
YOU TALK AS THOUGH I WERE A SLAVE. 7 MANSNS
OH, TO LOVE I AM A WILLING SLAVE. 7 MANSNS
HER SLAVE/ 13 MANSNS
SURE, WHAT MAN DOESN'T COMPLAIN OF HIS WORK, AND 20 MANSNS
PRETEND HE'S A SLAVE$
WHO'D MADE HIM A SLAVE AND KILLED HIS FINE POET'S 20 MANSNS
DREAM.
BUT YOU WOULD SEND ME INTO MY STUDY TO WORK ON IT 46 MANSNS
LIKE A REGULAR SLAVE-DRIVER/
AS IF AT THE END OF EVERY DREAM OF LIBERTY ONE DID 49 MANSNS
NOT FIND THE SLAVE, ONESELF.
IN MEMORY OF OLD SERVICE AND AS A DOMESTIC SLAVE 73 MANSNS
LUSTFUL, WANTON CREATURE AND MAKING YOU A SLAVE TO 90 MANSNS
MY BEAUTY.
AND OWN YOUR OWN SLAVES, IMPORTED IN YOUR OWN 101 MANSNS
SLAVE SHIPS.
THE RIGHT WHICH IS THE SOLE RIGHT NOT TO BE A 101 MANSNS
SLAVE/
I WILL PLAY YOUR HUMBLE SLAVE, SIRE. 106 MANSNS
I WORK LIKE A SLAVE ALL DAY TO STUFF YOUR 130 MANSNS
INSATIABLE MAWS
YOUR OWN SLAVE SHIPS AND YOUR OWN SLAVE DEALERS IN157 MANSNS
AFRICA.
SOULLESS TRADER IN THE SLAVE MARKET OF LIFE YOU 178 MANSNS
HAVE BECOME--/
HAS BEEN LITTLE BETTER THAN YOUR SLAVE. 385 MARCOM
AN AFRICAN SLAVE, DRESSED IN PINK LIVERY WITH 391 MARCOM
GREEN HAT AND SHOES AND STOCKINGS
THE FOURTH A BANG ON THE GONG AS ONE SLAVE AT EACH400 MARCOM
END LOADS AND UNLOADS.
(WITH A CALM SADNESS) DO I WANT A SLAVE$ 401 MARCOM
I AM MY SLAVE/ 401 MARCOM
NO BETTER THAN A SLAVE$ 411 MARCOM
I SHALL BE YOUR SLAVE/ 418 MARCOM

SLAVE (CONT'D.)
AND THE OLD DIVIL WOULD ALWAYS KEEP YOU A SLAVE. 7 MISBEG
HE'S GONE LIKE THOMAS AND JOHN BEFORE HIM TO 13 MISBEG
ESCAPE YOUR SLAVE-DRIVING.
I'LL NOT LET LOVE MAKE ME ANY MAN'S SLAVE. 31 POET
YOU MEAN, MAKE MOTHER SLAVE TO KEEP HER FOR YOU, 49 POET
EVEN IF SHE HAS TO STARVE/
AND ALL THE SLAVE-DRIVIN' YANKEE SKINFLINTS LIKE 52 POET
YOU/
I WON'T LET MY HEART RULE MY HEAD AND MAKE A SLAVE 65 POET
OF ME/
AND FINALLY WERE EVEN DRIVEN TO EMBRACE THE 83 POET
PROFITS OF THE SLAVE TRADE--
CATO WAS ALWAYS A SELF-POSSESSED FREE MAN EVEN 86 POET
WHEN HE WAS A SLAVE.
AND NEVER LET HIMSELF BECOME A SLAVE 146 POET
THE OLD SLAVE DRIVER/ 593 ROPE
YOU'D LIKE TO MAKE HER THE SAME SORT OF CONVENIENTI68 STRANG
SLAVE FOR HIM THAT I WAS FOR
THE CAPT'N AN' MATE ARE BLOODY SLAVE-DRIVERS, 495 VOYAGE
STILL--I'D HAVE BEEN THE POOREST SLAVE. 469 WELDED

SLAVE'S
ONCE, WHEN HE BOUND UP MY DOG'S LEG, ONCE WHEN HE 397 MARCOM
PLAYED WITH A SLAVE'S BABY,

SLAVED
HE'S SLAVED HIMSELF T' DEATH. 207 DESIRE
HE'S SLAVED SIM 'N' ME 'N' YEW T' DEATH--ON'Y NONE207 DESIRE
OF US HAIN'T DIED--YIT.
THE GOLD WE'VE SLAVED TO SAVE/ 55 MANSNS
HOW HE'S SLAVED/... 113 STRANG

SLAVERY
NOT SLAVERY OR BOREDOM BUT FREEDOM AND HARMONY 524 DAYS
WITHIN OURSELVES--AND HAPPINESS.
SLAVERY MEANS SECURITY--OF A KIND, THE ONLY KIND 542 DAYS
THEY HAVE COURAGE FOR.
BUT I'LL LOVE WHERE I'LL GAIN ME FREEDOM AND NOT 26 POET
PUT ME IN SLAVERY FOR LIFE.
THER'S NO SLAVERY IN IT WHEN YOU LOVE/ 26 POET
THANK GOD MY SLAVERY IS OVER/... 161 STRANG

SLAVES
IF WOMEN ARE TOO SURE OF YOU, THEY TREAT YOU LIKE 277 AHWILD
SLAVES.
THEY HAVE ONLY TO OBEY ORDERS FROM OWNERS WHO ARE,542 DAYS
IN TURN, THEIR SLAVES/
WE KNOW WE ARE ALL THE SLAVES OF MEANINGLESS 542 DAYS
CHANCE--
NOR NOTHIN'S SLAVES NUTHER. 218 DESIRE
(DEFIANTLY) WE HAIN'T NOBODY'S SLAVES FROM THIS 218 DESIRE
ON.
WE BEEN SLAVES T' STONE WALLS HERE. 218 DESIRE
FINALLY A BATCH OF SLAVES IS LED IN FROM THE LEFT 197 EJONES
BY AN ATTENDANT--
CHAINED SLAVES, TO THE RHYTHMIC BEAT OF THE TOM- 200 EJONES
TOM.
THEY DRAGGED US DOWN 'TIL WE'RE ON'Y WAGE SLAVES 212 HA APE
IN THE BOWELS OF A BLOODY SHIP.
ONLY SLAVES DO BE GIVING HEED TO THE DAY THAT'S 214 HA APE
GONE OR THE DAY TO COME--
SLAVES, HELL/ 216 HA APE
AND YOU AND ME, COMRADES, WE'RE HIS SLAVES/ 228 HA APE
AND SHE'S 'IS BLOODY DAUGHTER AND WE'RE ALL 'ER 228 HA APE
SLAVES, TOO/
AND THE SKIPPER AND MATES AND ENGINEERS, THEY'RE 228 HA APE
'IS SLAVES/
HAVE THE SLAVES NO RIGHT TO SLEEP EVEN$ 579 ICEMAN
AND LET THE LOUSY SLAVES DRINK VINEGAR/ 640 ICEMAN
THEY VILL BE MY SLAVES/ 672 ICEMAN
BUT THE SLAVES MUST ICE IT PROPERLY/ 691 ICEMAN
(WITH GUTTURAL RAGE) GOTTAMNED STUPID PROLETARIAN695 ICEMAN
SLAVES/
BE DRUNKEN, IF YOU WOULD NOT BE MARTYRED SLAVES UF132 JOURNE
TIME.
THE GALLEY SLAVES FORGOT THEIR FETTERS AND MADE 327 LAZARU
THEIR OARS FLY
YOU HEARD EVEN THE GALLEY SLAVES LAUGH AND CLANK 331 LAZARU
TIME WITH THEIR CHAINS/
SEVERAL SLAVES BEARING LAMPS ON POLES ESCORT THE 331 LAZARU
PATRICIAN, MARCELLUS.
AS THE CURTAIN RISES, SLAVES ARE HURRIEDLY PUTTING337 LAZARU
OUT THE MANY LAMPS.
(TO THE SLAVES WHO ARE TURNING OUT THE FEW 338 LAZARU
REMAINING LAMPS)
(A CROWD OF MASKED SLAVES OBEY HIS ORDERS. 340 LAZARU
THE REST, SOLDIERS, SLAVES AND THE PROSTITUTES OF 349 LAZARU
BOTH SEXES.
AND OWN YOUR OWN SLAVES, IMPORTED IN YOUR OWN 101 MANSNS
SLAVE SHIPS.
YOUR OWN PLANTATIONS WORKED BY YOUR OWN SLAVES-- 157 MANSNS
COTTON GOODS AND ONLY YOURS--SO YOU WOULD OWN YOUR158 MANSNS
OWN CONSUMER SLAVES, TOO.
LIKE A MASTER PICKING WHICH OF TWO SLAVES HE'D 173 MANSNS
LIKE TO OWN/
THEY MUST BE SLAVES. 350 MARCOM
AT THE RULER'S FEET HIS WIVES CROUCH LIKE SLAVES. 364 MARCOM
AT THE RIGHT IS A WAREHOUSE, FROM A DOOR IN WHICH 399 MARCOM
A LINE OF HALF-NAKED SLAVES,
SLAVES, A FOUR-BEAT RHYTHM, THREE BEATS OF THE 400 MARCOM
DRUM,
WE KILLED SIX SLAVES BUT, BY GOD, WE DID IT/ 405 MARCOM
ATTENDED BY A TRAIN OF NOBLES AND SLAVES WITH 417 MARCOM
LIGHTS.
TWO SLAVES BRING A CHEST OF GOLD COINS TO HER. 419 MARCOM
MILLIONS OF CONTENTED SLAVES LABOR UNREMITTINGLY 431 MARCOM
MILLIONS OF HOURS PER ANNUM
THE DIRTY SLAVES. 50 MISBEG
IT'S LOVE'S SLAVES WE ARE, MOTHER, NOT MEN'S-- 150 POET

SLAVIN'

SLAVIN'
WAS SLAVIN' HER TO HER GRAVE--T'PAY HER BACK FUR 208 DESIRE
THE KINDNESS SHE DONE T' YE$
AN' THAT I'VE BEEN SLAVIN' ME HANDS OFF TO PAY THES86 ROPE
INT'RIST ON/

SLAVING
SLAVING AND TOILING AS USUAL, I SEE. 39 MISBEG
LIKE YOU DESERVE, INSTEAD OF IN THIS SHANTY ON A 175 MISBEG
LOUSY FARM, SLAVING FOR ME$
NUT TO LIVE ON YOUR SLAVING YOUR HEART OUT, I HAD 23 POET
THAT PRIDE AND LOVE/
YOU KEEP ON SLAVING FOR HIM WHEN IT'S THAT HAS 24 POET
MADE YOU OLD BEFORE YOUR TIME/
SLAVING AS A WAITRESS AND CHAMBERMAID 33 POET

SLAVISH
STILL A COWARDLY SLAVISH SOMETHING IN ME, 520 DAYS
TOO POOR AND TIRED AND UGLY AND OLD TO CARE, TOO 361 LAZARU
SLAVISH--/
THE ROLE OF A SLAVISH LOVING MOTHER CONVINCINGLY 58 MANSNS
AGAIN.

SLAY
(TAUNTINGLY) THE LEGIONS DID SLAY THEM/ 328 LAZARU

SLAYER
GUD IS A SLAYER/ 297 LAZARU
SLAYER OF DEATH/ 320 LAZARU
SLAYER OF FEAR/ 320 LAZARU
AND A HOPE AT MY AGE DEMANDS A TERRIBLE EXPIATION 356 LAZARU
ON ITS SLAYER/

SLEEK
YOU'RE GHOSTLESS AND WOMANLESS--AND AS SLEEK AND 52 STRANG
SATISFIED AS A PET SEAL/

SLEEP
NO, LET THEM SLEEP. 543 'ILE
SO'S YOUR UNCLE SID'LL GET TO SLEEP AND YOUR AUNT 234 AHWILD
LILY CAN REST.
SLEEP TIGHT. 252 AHWILD
SLEEP WELL. 252 AHWILD
HOW CAN I EVER GET TO SLEEP WHILE HE'S-- 253 AHWILD
I GUESS YOU'D GET TO SLEEP ALL RIGHT IF YOU WERE 253 AHWILD
INSIDE A FOG HORN.
AND SID, HE'D SLEEP THROUGH AN EARTHQUAKE. 256 AHWILD
WELL, HE'S HAD A GOOD SLEEP AND HE'D OUGHT TO BE 256 AHWILD
SOBERED UP.
YOU KNOW AS WELL AS I DO HE NEEDS ALL THE SLEEP HE268 AHWILD
CAN GET TODAY--
SLEEP, WONDERING HOW I WAS EVER GOING TO SEE YOU 284 AHWILD
AGAIN AND CRYING MY EYES OUT.
I COULDN'T SLEEP. 297 AHWILD
IT GOT MY GOAT RIGHT--COULDN'T EAT OR SLEEP OR 16 ANNA
NOTHING.
I HAD TO SIT UP IN A DIRTY COACH ALL NIGHT-- 20 ANNA
COULDN'T GET NO SLEEP, HARDLY--
I DON'T WANT TO SLEEP. 26 ANNA
DAT PUT YOU TO SLEEP. 26 ANNA
LIE DOWN AND SLEEP. IS IT$ 32 ANNA
YOU MUST WANT TO SLEEP. 32 ANNA
YOU GO TO SLEEP. 39 ANNA
YOU GAT SLEEP. 39 ANNA
DON'T GO TO SLEEP, OLD MAN/ 57 ANNA
BUT WHEN IT COMES TO THAT, WHERE DO SEA-GULLS 95 BEYOND
SLEEP, DICK$
I AIN'T GETTIN' NO FUN OUT O' MISSING SLEEP 95 BEYOND
HIS VOICE CAN BE HEARD FAINTLY AS HE LULLS THE 121 BEYOND
CHILD TO SLEEP.
AND NOW WILL YOU PROMISE TO GO RIGHT TO SLEEP IF 121 BEYOND
DADA TAKES YOU TO BED$
I COULDN'T GET TO SLEEP TO SAVE MY SOUL. 147 BEYOND
YOUR MOTHER IS LUCKY TO BE ABLE TO SLEEP SO 147 BEYOND
SOUNDLY.
(WITH ASPERITY) AND IS THAT ALL YOU WOKE ME OUT 151 BEYOND
OF A SOUND SLEEP FOR.
AND I FEEL AS IF I COULD SLEEP NOW--(CHEERFULLY) 151 BEYOND
A GOOD, SOUND, RESTFUL SLEEP.
(COMING OUT OF HER SLEEP WITH A START) 151 BEYOND
LET HIM SLEEP IF HE CAN. 152 BEYOND
YOU DON'T NEED ME NOW AND I'M DEAD FOR SLEEP. 153 BEYOND
LOUD AND HIM TRYIN' TO HAVE A BIT AV A SLEEP. 479 CARDIF
I JUST CAN'T SLEEP WHEN WEESTLE BLOW. 481 CARDIF
SOBER--I'D NEVER GO TO SLEEP. 466 CARIBE
AND I WAS TOO EXCITED TO SLEEP. 515 DAYS
SLEEP, UNTROUBLED BY LOVE'S BETRAYING DREAM/ 531 DAYS
HE MAY BE ABLE TO SLEEP FUR A WHILE AND FORGET. 544 DAYS
GOD, HOW CAN I SLEEP WHEN--/ 555 DAYS
I WON'T SLEEP/ 555 DAYS
WHILE IF YOU'LL SLEEP FOR A WHILE-- 556 DAYS
BUT I THINK HE'LL SLEEP NOW, FOR A WHILE ANYWAY. 556 DAYS
JOHN ALMOST IMMEDIATELY DROPS OFF INTO A DRUGGED 556 DAYS
HALF-SLEEP.
YOU'VE GOT TO GET SOME SLEEP/ 556 DAYS
THE SINKS INTO DRUGGED SLEEP AGAIN.) 557 DAYS
(SHUDDERING IN HIS SLEEP) NO/ 558 DAYS
(A SHUDDER RUNS OVER HIM AND HE STARTS AS IF 562 DAYS
AWAKENING FROM SLEEP)
DUST WITHIN DUST TO SLEEP/ 562 DAYS
THE DREAM IN WHICH YOU AND ELSA MAY SLEEP AS ONE 562 DAYS
FOREVER.
I'LL SET T' IT MY MAW GITS SOME REST AN' SLEEP IN 209 DESIRE
HER GRAVE/
(ANGRILY) COULDN'T YE HOLD IT 'TIL WE'D GOT OUR 212 DESIRE
SLEEP$
LET'S US JEST SLEEP AN' EAT AN' DRINK LIKKER, 215 DESIRE
YE'D BEST GO T' SLEEP. 236 DESIRE
WAAL, I'M A-GUIN' T' STEAL A WINK O' SLEEP. 245 DESIRE
SHE KIN SLEEP NOW. 245 DESIRE
SHE KIN REST NOW AN' SLEEP CONTENT. 246 DESIRE
THEY KNOW HOW T' SLEEP. 246 DESIRE
(WITH A WINK) MEBBE HE'S DOIN' THE DUTIFUL AN' 248 DESIRE
WALKIN' THE KID T' SLEEP.

SLEEP (CONT'D.)
AN' I'LL KICK YE BOTH OUT IN THE ROAD--T' BEG AN' 257 DESIRE
SLEEP IN THE WOODS--
BUT THE OLD MAN TURNS RESTLESSLY, GROANING IN HIS 259 DESIRE
SLEEP.
I LOCKED MYSELF IN THE CABIN AND LEFT HER TO SLEEP516 DIFRNT
OUT ON DECK.
(HE SIGHS HEAVILY) (END SLEEP AGAIN LAST NIGHT 455 DYNAMO
EXCEPT FOR A FEW MINUTES...
(HE WALKS AROUND NERVOUSLY) NO USE TRYING TO GO 472 DYNAMO
TO SLEEP...
I CAN SLEEP... 475 DYNAMO
LIKE SOME ONE SINGING ME TO SLEEP--MY MOTHER--WHEN476 DYNAMO
I WAS A KID--
HIM SLEEP AFTER EAT. 175 EJONES
HIM SLEEP. 175 EJONES
WHEN I SLEEPS, DEY SNEAKS A SLEEP, TOO, AND I 181 EJONES
PRETENDS I NEVER SUSPICIONS IT.
HE MOVES WITH A STRANGE DELIBERATION LIKE A SLEEP-200 EJONES
WALKER OR ONE IN A TRANCE.
GO TO BED AND SLEEP IT OFF. 45 ELECTR
I HAVEN'T BEEN ABLE TO SLEEP EITHER. 58 ELECTR
I HAVEN'T BEEN ABLE TO SLEEP. 58 ELECTR
LET HIM SLEEP. 62 ELECTR
(HER VOICE BECOMES THICK, AS IF SHE WERE DROWSY 63 ELECTR
AND FIGHTING OFF SLEEP.
I--I'VE MISSED SOMETHING--SOME MEDICINE I TAKE TO 77 ELECTR
PUT ME TO SLEEP--
SHE FOUND SOME MEDICINE I TAKE TO MAKE ME SLEEP, 88 ELECTR
IT'S ONLY SOME STUFF SHE TAKES TO MAKE HER SLEEP/ 97 ELECTR
MEDICINE TO MAKE YOU SLEEP--WASN'T IT$ 101 ELECTR
SLEEP IT OFF/ 103 ELECTR
BUT I'D ADVISE YOU TO TURN IN AND SLEEP IT OFF. 105 ELECTR
I DON'T BELIEVE THERE'S SUCH A THING ON THIS EARTH118 ELECTR
AS SLEEP/
YOU OUGHT TO TRY AND SLEEP. 118 ELECTR
LUSING A LITTLE SLEEP WON'T HURT ME ANY. 119 ELECTR
I MUST'NT SLEEP/ 119 ELECTR
AND EVERY MORNIN' SINCE ORIN--AIN'T YOU BEEN 170 ELECTR
GITTIN' NO SLEEP$
SO I TOOK YOU IN TO SLEEP IT OFF. 279 GGBROW
I'M GOING TO SLEEP. 280 GGBROW
(LIKE AN IDOL) GO HOME AND SLEEP. 287 GGBROW
WITH CUTE ALLUREMENTS SO THAT FOOLS WILL DESIRE TO287 GGBROW
BUY, SELL, BREED, SLEEP,
COME HOME AND SLEEP/ 292 GGBROW
GO HOME AND GET SOME SLEEP. 296 GGBROW
AND ONLY USES HIS HOUSE TO SLEEP IN. 302 GGBROW
STRENGTH TO LOVE IN THIS WORLD AND DIE AND SLEEP 307 GGBROW
AND BECOME FERTILE EARTH.
OR THEY'LL NEVER SLEEP SOUNDLY AGAIN/ 320 GGBROW
YOU'VE GOT TO GO TO SLEEP ALONE. 321 GGBROW
GO TO SLEEP, BILLY. 322 GGBROW
YOU WILL SLEEP UNDER MY HEART/ 323 GGBROW
I WILL FEEL YOU STIRRING IN YOUR SLEEP, FOREVER 323 GGBROW
UNDER MY HEART/
I WANT HIM TO SLEEP IN THE TIDES OF MY HEART/ 323 GGBROW
I FEEL YOU STIRRING IN YOUR SLEEP, FOREVER UNDER 323 GGBROW
MY HEART.
YOU SLEEP BETTER. 227 HA APE
(R TRYING TO GET TO SLEEP) 244 HA APE
I TELL YOU, PAL, I'D RATHER SLEEP IN THE SAME 21 HUGHIE
STALL WITH OLD MAN O' WAR
DISTANT THE CARAVAN, AND FAR AWAY THE SLEEP. 25 HUGHIE
HE KEEPS MUTTERING AND TWITCHING IN HIS SLEEP. 577 ICEMAN
WHAT'S BEFORE ME IS THE COMFORTING FACT THAT DEATH578 ICEMAN
IS A FINE LONG SLEEP.
HAVE THE SLAVES NO RIGHT TO SLEEP EVEN$ 579 ICEMAN
(WILLIE OBAN JERKS AND TWITCHES IN HIS SLEEP AND 580 ICEMAN
BEGINS TO MUMBLE.
(WATCHES WILLIE, WHO IS SHAKING IN HIS SLEEP LIKE 581 ICEMAN
AN OLD DOG)
BEJEES, CAN'T I GET A WINK OF SLEEP IN MY OWN BACK582 ICEMAN
ROOM$
IF HICKEY AIN'T COME, IT'S TIME JOE GOES TO SLEEP 583 ICEMAN
AGAIN.
-LO, SLEEP IS GOOD, BETTER IS DEATH. 591 ICEMAN
EAT AND SLEEP AND GET DRUNK/ 598 ICEMAN
LET ME SLEEP ON A CHAIR LIKE A BUM/ 602 ICEMAN
(BUT THE THREE ARE FINISHED, THEIR EYES CLOSED 605 ICEMAN
AGAIN IN SLEEP OR A DROWSE.)
DEY DIDN'T BOTHER US MUCH DAT WAY, BUT DEY 612 ICEMAN
WOULDN'T GO TO SLEEP EITHER, SEE$
JEES, IMAGINE TRYIN' TO SLEEP WID DAT ON DE 612 ICEMAN
PHONOGRAPH/
WE FIGGERED DEY WAS TOO STINKO TO BOTHER US MUCH 612 ICEMAN
AND WE COULD COP A GOOD SLEEP
I COULDN'T SLEEP A WINK. 614 ICEMAN
(HE CLOSES HIS EYES AND SETTLES ON HIS CHAIR AS IF616 ICEMAN
PREPARING FOR SLEEP.
HAVEN'T BEEN ABLE TO SLEEP LATELY AND I'M TIRED AS620 ICEMAN
HELL.
FIRST TIME I EVER HEARD YOU WORRY ABOUT SLEEP. 620 ICEMAN
YOU'RE JUST WAITING IMPATIENTLY FOR THE END--THE 623 ICEMAN
GOOD OLD LONG SLEEP/
(THE SLEEP OF COMPLETE EXHAUSTION OVERPOWERS HIM. 625 ICEMAN
BEJEES, THAT'S A FINE STUNT, TO GO TO SLEEP ON US/625 ICEMAN
ALL I WANT IS TO SEE YOU HAPPY-- (HE SLIPS BACK 628 ICEMAN
INTO HEAVY SLEEP AGAIN.
I WANT TO SLEEP. 635 ICEMAN
YOU BETTER STICK TO THE PART OF OLD CEMETERY, THE 639 ICEMAN
BARKER FOR THE BIG SLEEP--
AND THE WAITING FOR THE BIG SLEEP STUFF IS A PIPE 641 ICEMAN
DREAM.
THEN YOU'D BETTER WATCH OUT HOW YOU KEEP CALLING 657 ICEMAN
FOR THAT OLD BIG SLEEP/
NOT A WINK OF SLEEP. 666 ICEMAN
I DON'T GET A WINK OF SLEEP, SEE$ 669 ICEMAN

SLEEP (CONT'D.)
LAY YOUR HEAD DOWN NOW AND SLEEP IT OFF. 672 ICEMAN
I SHOULD SLEEP. 672 ICEMAN
(HE TOSSES IT TO ROCKY) I'D RATHER SLEEP IN THE 682 ICEMAN
GUTTER THAN PASS ANOTHER NIGHT
HICKEY'S FACE IS A BIT DRAWN FROM LACK OF SLEEP 684 ICEMAN
AND HIS VOICE IS HOARSE FROM
AND I'LL WELCOME CLOSING MY EYES IN THE LONG SLEEP689 ICEMAN
OF DEATH--
I MUST SLEEP IT OFF. 691 ICEMAN
BUT I CAN'T SLEEP HERE WITH YOU. 692 ICEMAN
IT IS VERY NECESSARY I SLEEP. 692 ICEMAN
I CANNOT SLEEP/ 695 ICEMAN
JOE MUMBLES IN HIS SLEEP. 699 ICEMAN
AND I'D STAY UP ALONE BECAUSE I COULDN'T SLEEP AND715 ICEMAN
I DIDN'T WANT TO DISTURB HER.
SHE'LL NEVER BE ABLE TO FORGET WHAT I'VE DONE TO 720 ICEMAN
HER EVEN IN HER SLEEP.
GOD STIFFEN US, ARE WE NEVER GOIN' TO TURN IN FUR 532 INZONE
A WINK AV SLEEP!
I WASN'T ABLE TO GET MUCH SLEEP WITH THAT AWFUL 17 JOURNE
FOGHORN GOING ALL NIGHT LONG.
I DID IT BECAUSE I KNEW IF YOU FOUND OUT I WAS 47 JOURNE
FEVERISH AND COULDN'T SLEEP,
I COULDN'T SLEEP BECAUSE I WAS THINKING ABOUT YOU. 47 JOURNE
I WANTED TO GIVE HER A CHANCE TO SLEEP. 56 JOURNE
SHE DIDN'T GET MUCH SLEEP LAST NIGHT. 56 JOURNE
AND OUR LITTLE LIFE IS ROUNDED WITH A SLEEP." 131 JOURNE
WHETHER THOU SLEEP, WITH HEAVY VAPOURS FULL, 134 JOURNE
SODDEN WITH DAY, OR,
NIGHT-LONG WITHIN MINE ARMS IN LOVE AND SLEEP SHE 134 JOURNE
LAY.
I WAS HOPING SHE'D GONE TO SLEEP. 136 JOURNE
AND CAMP ON PARK BENCHES BECAUSE I HAD NO PLACE TO145 JOURNE
SLEEP,
GOD KNOWS WHEN SHE'LL GO TO SLEEP. 152 JOURNE
WHERE'S THE HOPHEADS GONE TO SLEEP! 161 JOURNE
WE'D BETTER LET HIM STAY WHERE HE IS AND SLEEP IT 167 JOURNE
OFF.
JAMIE, GO BACK TO SLEEP/ 169 JOURNE
PROBABLY THE LEGIONS ARE TO BUTCHER THEM IN THEIR 315 LAZARU
SLEEP.
THAT ONE REMEMBERS THERE AS HERE AND CANNOT SLEEP,353 LAZARU
IF I WERE SURE OF ETERNAL SLEEP BEYOND THERE, 353 LAZARU
AFRAID THAT THERE IS NO SLEEP BEYOND THERE, 353 LAZARU
EITHER/
AND NOW I MUST LIE DOWN AND TRY TO SLEEP/ 356 LAZARU
(DESCENDING THE STEPS LIKE A SLEEP-WALKER) 366 LAZARU
NO QUESTION, AND SNEER AND LAUGH AT YOUR DREAMS, 40 MANSNS
AND SLEEP WITH UGLINESS.
BUT I'LL SLEEP SOUNDLY AGAIN NOW I'VE PUT THAT 49 MANSNS
DAMNED BOOK OUT OF MY MIND.
WHEN IT'S GETTING NEAR BEDTIME, OR YOU'LL NEVER 49 MANSNS
SETTLE DOWN TO SLEEP.
BUT OUR TALKING HERE HAD WAKENED JONATHAN AND I 61 MANSNS
HAD TO GET HIM BACK TO SLEEP.
IT'S HARD TO GET HIM TO SLEEP 63 MANSNS
SLEEP WITH IT, DREAM OF IT--AND THEN SUDDENLY ONE 72 MANSNS
DAY IT IS ACCOMPLISHED--
WHEN YOU COULDN'T SLEEP BECAUSE YOUR MIND KEPT 83 MANSNS
MAKING PLANS FOR THE COMPANY.
YOU'LL SAY NEXT IT WAS I THAT WANTED YOU TO SLEEP 83 MANSNS
ALONE.
BUT MAYBE YOU'D BETTER LET HER SLEEP. 88 MANSNS
I CAN'T SLEEP, WORRYING/ 156 MANSNS
(FOLLOWING HER.) BEGGING YOU TO LET THEM SLEEP 166 MANSNS
WITH YOU!
THE HARNESSED WRETCHES IN THE EXHAUSTED ATTITUDES 352 MARCOM
OF SLEEP.
(HE RESTS HIS HEAD ON HIS ARMS AND GOES TO SLEEP.1374 MARCOM
(WEARILY AND DROWSILY) YOUR WISDOM MAKES ME 402 MARCOM
SLEEP.
A LITTLE SLEEP, PRINCESS, AND YOU WILL BE 402 MARCOM
BEAUTIFUL.
SLEEP AND AWAKE IN THE NEW. 402 MARCOM
(THEN SPECULATIVELY) YOUTH NEEDS SO MUCH SLEEP 402 MARCOM
AND OLD AGE SO LITTLE.
(CYNICALLY) MAYBE, BUT THEY LOVE THEIR SLEEP, 405 MARCOM
TOO.
SLEEP IN GREEN WATER. 409 MARCOM
(THEN WILDLY TO MARCO) I WISHED TO SLEEP IN THE 413 MARCOM
DEPTHS OF THE SEA.
IF YOU WOULD ONLY TRY TO SLEEP A WHILE-- 413 MARCOM
I ADVISE YOU TO GO TO SLEEP. 415 MARCOM
I SHALL SLEEP FOREVER/ 415 MARCOM
POSSESS LIFE AS A LOVER--THEN SLEEP 435 MARCOM
IF YOU SLEEP ON, REST IN PEACE/ 436 MARCOM
COULDN'T SLEEP. 41 MISBEG
I'VE HAD ALL I CAN BEAR THIS NIGHT, AND I WANT 74 MISBEG
SOME PEACE AND SLEEP.
I COULDN'T SLEEP WITH MY THOUGHTS TORMENTED THE 76 MISBEG
WAY THEY ARE.
SLEEP IT OFF TILL YOU GET SOME SENSE. 77 MISBEG
SLEEP IT OFF! 77 MISBEG
WE'LL SEE IF YOU'LL SLEEP IT OFF WHEN YOU KNOW-- 77 MISBEG
OR KEEP YOU UP WHEN YOU WANT SLEEP SO BAD. 77 MISBEG
HAVE A GOOD SLEEP, WHILE YOU CAN, JOSIE, DARLIN'-- 81 MISBEG
SLEEP IN PEACE, MY DARLING. 153 MISBEG
HOME AND WENT TO SLEEP IN THE HAYLOFT. 158 MISBEG
(TYRONE STIRS IN HIS SLEEP AND MOANS. 161 MISBEG
HE WANTED TO SLEEP THE WAY HE IS, AND I LET HIM 162 MISBEG
SLEEP.
(HE MOANS IN HIS SLEEP AND PRESSES MORE CLOSELY 165 MISBEG
AGAINST HER.
GO TO SLEEP, KID--AND LET ME SLEEP. 165 MISBEG
IF YOU COULD HAVE DIED IN YOUR SLEEP, THAT'S WHAT 165 MISBEG
YOU WOULD HAVE LIKED.
AS IF I'D HAD A SOUND SLEEP WITHOUT NIGHTMARES. 167 MISBEG

SLEEP (CONT'D.)
AND I SUDDENLY HAD A CRAZY NOTION I'D COME UP HERE167 MISBEG
AND SLEEP WITH MY HEAD ON
THE DAMNED SICK MEMORIES THAT MAKES YOU WISH YOU'D 171 MISBEG
DIED IN YOUR SLEEP SO YOU
MAY YOU HAVE YOUR WISH AND DIE IN YOUR SLEEP SOON,177 MISBEG
JIM, DARLING.
I DIDN'T SAY SLEEP, BUT I CAN LIE DOWN AND TRY TO 131 POET
REST.
I HOPE HE'LL SLEEP, BUT I'M FEARED HE'LL STAY UP 137 POET
DRINKIN'.
OR SLEEP IN THE GRASS OF A FIELD WITHOUT A ROOF TO146 POET
OUR HEADS.
WARM IN HIS LOVE, SAFE-DRIFTING INTO SLEEP...." 27 STRANG
SHE'S GOT TO GET SOME SLEEP TONIGHT. 34 STRANG
DO I HEAR GRAVEYARDS YAWNING FROM THEIR SLEEP-- 51 STRANG
(PEREMPTORILY) HOW DID YOU SLEEP! 51 STRANG
(STRANGELY) YOU COULDN'T SLEEP! 57 STRANG
BUT I WASN'T ABLE TO GET TO SLEEP UNTIL AFTER 57 STRANG
DAYLIGHT SOMEHOW.
HE DOESN'T SLEEP.... 69 STRANG
I MUST SLEEP WITH HIM AGAIN SOON... 69 STRANG
DOESN'T MY BOY WANT TO SLEEP WITH ME AGAIN-- 71 STRANG
SOMETIME SOON.
WHY DON'T YOU SLEEP NOW--AS YOU USED TO, REMEMBER!200 STRANG
TO SLEEP WITH PEACE TOGETHER--/ 200 STRANG
GO HUPSTAIRS AND 'AVE A SLEEP. 495 VOYAGE
(A PAUSE) AN END OF LOATHING--NO WOUNDS, NO 476 WELDED
MEMORIES--SLEEP/

SLEEP'LL
THE SLEEP'LL DO HIM GOOD. 480 CARDIF

SLEEP'S
THE SLEEP'S DONE YOU GOOD. 482 CARDIF

SLEEPERS
HE BEGINS TO DESCRIBE THE SLEEPERS WITH SARDONIC 593 ICEMAN
RELISH
LIKE SLEEPERS TALKING OUT OF A DULLY IRRITATING 701 ICEMAN
DREAM, =THE HELL WITH IT/=
THEY MUMBLE, LIKE SLEEPERS WHO CURSE A PERSON WHO 711 ICEMAN
KEEPS AWAKENING THEM,
AND GOES FROM ONE TO THE OTHER OF THE SLEEPERS AND513 INZONE
SHAKES THEM VIGOROUSLY.
CONTENTMENT IS A WARM STY FOR THE EATERS AND 400 MARCOM
SLEEPERS/

SLEEPILY
(TOMMY GIVES UP, GRINS SLEEPILY AND MOVES OFF TO 253 AHWILD
BED.
(MARY NODS SLEEPILY) THAT'S THE GOOD LITTLE GIRL.121 BEYOND
(NOT SEEING ANYONE--GREATLY IRRITATED AND BLINKING176 EJONES
SLEEPILY--SHOUTS)
(HIS EYES BLINKING SLEEPILY) 583 ICEMAN
(ADDRESSING MCGLOIN AND MOSHER, WHO ARE SLEEPILY 598 ICEMAN
AWAKE--ACCUSINGLY)
(ROCKY SHRUGS HIS SHOULDERS AND YAWNS SLEEPILY.) 666 ICEMAN
THE POLOS RISE AND STRETCH SLEEPILY. 376 MARCOM
(MOVING HIS ARMS AND LEGS GINGERLY--SLEEPILY) 166 MISBEG
(VERY SLEEPILY) THANK YOU, FATHER. 46 STRANG
(TURNING TO COCKY, WHO IS BLINKING SLEEPILY) 508 VOYAGE

SLEEPIN'
BUT I'M SCARED TO STAY HERE WITH ALL OF THEM 484 CARDIF
SLEEPIN' AND SNORIN'.
SHE CAN'T FIND IT NATERAL SLEEPIN' AN' RESTIN' IN 209 DESIRE
PEACE.
(SPITTING WITH DISGUST) HER--HERE--SLEEPIN' WITH 214 DESIRE
HIM---STEALIN' MY MAW'S FARM/
SLEEPIN' SOUND. 263 DESIRE
HE'D OUGHT T' WAKE UP WITH A GNASHIN' APPETITE, 263 DESIRE
THE SOUND WAY HE'S SLEEPIN'.
(CARELESSLY) DEY'RE ALL OUT IN DE GARDEN SLEEPIN'181 EJONES
UNDER DE TREES.
SOME OF DESE BUMS BEEN SLEEPIN' ON DE FIRE 726 ICEMAN
ESCAPES.
YOU CAN THINK OF SLEEPIN' WHEN HE'S-- 131 POET
I'LL DIG IN THE CELLAR THIS NIGHT WHEN HE'S 586 ROPE
SLEEPIN'.

SLEEPINESS
I'M HALF DEAD WITH TIREDNESS AND SLEEPINESS. 162 MISBEG

SLEEPING
IN THE REAR, LEFT, A DOOR LEADING TO THE CAPTAIN'S535 'ILE
SLEEPING QUARTERS.
SLEEPING LIKE A BABY--SO INNOCENT-LOOKING. 269 AHWILD
IN THE REAR ON THE LEFT, A DOOR LEADING TO THE 41 ANNA
SLEEPING QUARTERS.
WOULD BE SLEEPING WITH ANY MAN FOR A DOLLAR OR 60 ANNA
TWO/
SLEEPING ON BARROOM FLOORS. 68 ANNA
I WAS A LAD ONLY, AND SHE TOLD ME TO KEEP IT BY ME 75 ANNA
IF I'D BE MAKING OR SLEEPING
FINALLY ROBERT'S EYES ARE FIXED ON THE SLEEPING 147 BEYOND
MRS. ATKINS)
SLEEPING BUNKS ABOUT SIX FEET LONG, ARRANGED THREE477 CARDIF
DEEP
HE STOPS AT THE FOOT OF THE CHAISE-LONGUE AND 558 DAYS
STARES DOWN AT THE SLEEPING JOHN.
YOU'VE ONLY BEEN SLEEPING A FEW MINUTES. 558 DAYS
YOU ARE SLEEPING UNDER MY HEART/ 323 GGBROW
GET A FEW SLUGS UNDER YOUR BELT AND YOU'LL FURGET 620 ICEMAN
SLEEPING.
HERE'S THE REVOLUTION STARTING ON ALL SIDES OF YOU634 ICEMAN
AND YOU'RE SLEEPING THROUGH
(HE LEANS OVER THE UPPER BUNK IN WHICH PAUL IS 514 INZONE
SLEEPING
I COULDN'T HELP REMEMBERING THAT WHEN SHE STARTS 38 JOURNE
SLEEPING ALONE IN THERE,
I COULD WELCOME MY OWN MURDER AS AN EXCUSE FOR 314 LAZARU
SLEEPING.
YOU STARTED SLEEPING IN YOUR OWN ROOM AWAY FROM 80 MANSNS
ME--

SLEEPING

SLEEPING (CONT'D.)
IF YOU KNEW HOW UNHAPPY AND UGLY I'VE FELT SINCE 87 MANSNS
YOU STARTED SLEEPING ALONE--
AND YET, TO LOOK AT HER FACE YOU WOULD THINK HER 351 MARCOM
ONLY SLEEPING.
HE WAS SLEEPING LIKE A BABY WHEN I LEFT HIM. 182 POET
(HE RISES TO HIS FEET WITH NINA SLEEPING 46 STRANG
PEACEFULLY IN HIS ARMS.
SLEEPING IN A STRANGE BED, I SUPPOSE. 51 STRANG
SLEEPING ALONE... 67 STRANG
HE WAS SLEEPING SO SOUNDLY AN EARTHQUAKE WOULDN'T 120 STRANG
HAVE MADE HIM PEEP/
(THINKING CYNICALLY) (OH, SO YOU'LL COMPROMISE 168 STRANG
ON HIS SLEEPING WITH HER...

SLEEPLESS
SHE HAS EVIDENTLY HAD NO REST YET FROM A 263 AHWILD
SLEEPLESS, TEARFUL NIGHT.
AS IF THE TWO DAYS JUST PAST HAD BEEN ONES OF 63 ANNA
SUFFERING AND SLEEPLESS NIGHTS.
HIS FACE ALSO BEARS OBVIOUS TRACES OF SLEEPLESS 553 DAYS
STRAIN.
=SLEEPLESS WITH PALE COMMEMORATIVE EYES,= AS 135 MISBEG
ROSSETTI WROTE.

SLEEPLESSNESS
HIS DARK EYES ARE BLOODSHOT AND WILD FROM 30 ANNA
SLEEPLESSNESS.
HIS EYES, BLOODSHOT FROM SLEEPLESSNESS, 553 DAYS
IT IS DEEPLY LINED, HAGGARD WITH SLEEPLESSNESS AND170 ELECTR
STARING,
HAGGARD WITH SLEEPLESSNESS AND NERVES, HIS EYES 644 ICEMAN
SICK AND HAUNTED.
PUFFY SHADOWS OF DISSIPATION AND SLEEPLESSNESS 124 STRANG
UNDER HIS RESTLESS, HARRIED EYES.

SLEEPS
WHERE THE SEA-GULLS SLEEPS AT NIGHTS* 94 BEYOND
WHEN I SLEEPS, DEY SNEAKS A SLEEP, TOO, AND I 181 EJONES
PRETENDS I NEVER SUSPICIONS IT.
IT'S ONLY IN THE EARTH ONE SLEEPS/ 118 ELECTR
HE SLEEPS, CHIN ON CHEST, HANDS FOLDED IN HIS LAP.575 ICEMAN
HICKEY SLEEPS ON LIKE A DEAD MAN, BUT HUGO, 627 ICEMAN
HICKEY SLEEPS ON. 627 ICEMAN

SLEEPWALKER
(SHE MOVES LIKE A SLEEPWALKER TOWARD THE DOOR IN 549 DIFRNT
THE REAR AS THE CURTAIN FALLS.
(TURNS AND LOOKS AT HER LIKE A SLEEPWALKER FOR A 482 DYNAMO
SECOND--

SLEEPY
FILLING UP ON BEER WILL ONLY MAKE YOU SLEEPY. 238 AHWILD
HE HAS HAD A HARD DAY AND IS TERRIBLY SLEEPY BUT 249 AHWILD
WILL NOT ACKNOWLEDGE IT.
(VALIANTLY) I AM NOT SLEEPY/ 252 AHWILD
YOU'RE SO SLEEPY YOU COULDN'T SEE ITS 252 AHWILD
HE SHOWS NO AFTER EFFECTS EXCEPT THAT HE IS 263 AHWILD
TERRIBLY SLEEPY.
(QUIETLY) SEEMS NICE AND SLEEPY-LIKE. 466 CARIBE
(WITH A HARD LAUGH) SLEEPY/ 466 CARIBE
(THINKING WITH A SLEEPY CONTENT) 454 DYNAMO
(WODDENLY) I DIDN'T FEEL SLEEPY. 56 ELECTR
I'M GETTING SO SLEEPY. 299 GGBROW
AREN'T YOU SLEEPY$ 300 GGBROW
(FEEBLY) I'M GETTING SLEEPY. 322 GGBROW
HE IS NOT SLEEPY. 7 HUGHIE
(TO CAPTAIN LEWIS WHO HAS RELAPSED INTO A SLEEPY 600 ICEMAN
DAZE AND IS LISTENING TO HIM
(COCKS ONE SLEEPY EYE AT HER--IRRITABLY) 615 ICEMAN
I'M A BIT TIRED AND SLEEPY BUT OTHERWISE I FEEL 621 ICEMAN
GREAT.
(HE YAWNS AGAIN) GOD, I'M SLEEPY ALL OF A SUDDEN.625 ICEMAN
HE LOOKS SLEEPY, IRRITABLE AND WORRIED. 665 ICEMAN
HE LOOKS SLEEPY, HOT, UNCOMFORTABLE AND GROUCHY.) 670 ICEMAN
(YAWNING--TOO SLEEPY TO BE AROUSED BY ANYTHING-- 514 INZONE
CARELESSLY)
AT ONCE HE BECOMES SLEEPY, TOO.) 169 JOURNE
NOT LOOKING FOR ARGUMENT. TOO DAMNED SLEEPY. 169 JOURNE
IN FACT, IT IS NONE OTHER THAN MARCO POLO HIMSELF,439 MARCOM
LOOKING A BIT SLEEPY.
WISPS OF HAY STICK TO HIS CLOTHES AND HIS FACE IS 157 MISBEG
SWOLLEN AND SLEEPY.
(HE DOES SO WITH DIFFICULTY, STILL IN A SLEEPY 166 MISBEG
DAZE, HIS BODY STIFF AND CRAMPED.
AIN'T YOU GETTIN' SLEEPY$ 473 WELDED

SLEEVE
(HE PULLS AT HER SLEEVE SHYLY) 35 ANNA
THE SLEEVE ON THAT SIDE OF THE HEAVY MACKINAW HE 556 CROSS
WEARS HANGS FLABBILY.
(HE BLINKS BACK ONE TEAR, WIPING HIS SLEEVE ACROSS264 DESIRE
HIS NOSE.)
AND MOPS OFF HIS FACE ON HIS SLEEVE. 191 EJONES
SHE TUCKS THIS PAPER IN THE SLEEVE OF HER DRESS 35 ELECTR
(SHE REACHES IN THE SLEEVE OF HER DRESS 40 ELECTR
(HE BRUSHES HIS SLEEVE FASTIDIOUSLY) 600 ICEMAN
NOTHING UP MY SLEEVE, HONEST. 622 ICEMAN
(SHE SOBS AND WIPES HER EYES WITH HER SLEEVE-- 345 LAZARU
I KNOW YOU DO NOT WANT HER LAUGHING AT YOU UP HER 114 MANSNS
SLEEVE ANY MORE.
HE LEANS DOWN AND PICKS IT UP, POLISHING IT ON HIS375 MARCOM
SLEEVE REMORSEFULLY.
ANYWAY, I WANTED TO FIND OUT WHAT TRICK HE HAD UP 85 MISBEG
HIS SLEEVE.
I WISH I'D BEEN THERE TO LAUGH UP MY SLEEVE. 90 MISBEG
HE BRUSHES A SLEEVE FASTIDIOUSLY, ADJUSTS THE SET 43 POET
OF HIS COAT
TO LAUGH UP HER SLEEVE AT YOUR PRETENSES$ 91 POET
(SHE WIPES HIS MOUTH ON HIS SLEEVE WITH A SNIFFLE) 598 ROPE

SLEEVED
HE WEARS HEAVY BROGANS, FILTHY OVERALLS, AND A 11 MISBEG
DIRTY SHORT-SLEEVED UNDERSHIRT.

SLEEVELESS
SHE WEARS A CHEAP, SLEEVELESS, BLUE COTTON DRESS. 3 MISBEG

SLEEVES
IS SITTING IN HIS SHIRT SLEEVES ON THE SIDE OF HIS422 DYNAMO
BED.
THE SLEEVES OF HIS COLLARLESS SHIRT ARE ROLLED UP 577 ICEMAN
ON HIS THICK, POWERFUL ARMS
HE WEARS HIS WORKING CLOTHES, SLEEVES ROLLED UP. 664 ICEMAN
IN TINY RUFFLES AROUND THE NECK AND SLEEVES. 115 JOURNE
LOWER THEIR OPENED SLEEVES. 429 MARCOM
(HE SLITS UP THE WIDE SLEEVES OF HIS OWN ROBE, AS 429 MARCOM
DO HIS FATHER AND UNCLE.

SLENDER
MILDRED IS FIFTEEN, TALL AND SLENDER, WITH BIG, 186 AHWILD
IRREGULAR FEATURES.
WELL, YOU'RE NOT SKINNY EITHER--ONLY SLENDER-- 291 AHWILD
HE IS A TALL, SLENDER YOUNG MAN OF TWENTY-THREE. 81 BEYOND
WITH A GRACEFUL, SLENDER FIGURE. 87 BEYOND
SHE IS A TALL, SLENDER WOMAN OF TWENTY-FIVE, 562 CROSS
EMMA IS A SLENDER GIRL OF TWENTY, RATHER UNDER THE494 DIFRNT
MEDIUM HEIGHT.
THE FORMER IS A GIRL OF TWENTY, SLENDER, DELICATE,217 HA APE
WITH A PALE,
MIRIAM IS A SLENDER, DELICATE WOMAN OF THIRTY- 274 LAZARU
FIVE, DRESSED IN DEEP BLACK.
WITH THE SLENDER IMMATURE FIGURE OF A YOUNG GIRL. 2 MANSNS
SHE HAS SMALL EARS SET CLOSE TO HER HEAD, A WELL- 2 MANSNS
SHAPED HEAD ON A SLENDER NECK.
THERE ARE HOLLOWS UNDER HER CHEEKBONES AND IN HER 28 MANSNS
SLENDER NECK.
WITH FULL BREASTS AND A SLENDER WAIST.) 44 MANSNS
HER WAIST WIDE BUT SLENDER BY CONTRAST WITH HER 3 MISBEG
HIPS AND THIGHS.
SHE HAS SMALL EARS SET CLOSE TO HER WELL-SHAPED 15 POET
HEAD, AND A SLENDER NECK.
AND A SLENDER WAIST. 16 POET
HER SLENDER, FRAGILE BODY IS DRESSED IN WHITE WITH 68 POET
CALCULATED SIMPLICITY.
IS IT BECAUSE SHE HAS SUCH SLENDER ANKLES AND 107 POET
DAINTY FEET
WITH HER SLENDER ANKLES AND DAINTY FEET, 161 POET
HE IS A SMALL, SLENDER MAN OF FIFTY-FIVE, HIS HAIR 6 STRANG

SLENDERER
HE SEEMS TALLER AND SLENDERER BECAUSE OF HIS 13 JOURNE
BEARING.

SLEPT
I SLEPT GOOD--DOWN WITH THE COWS. 246 DESIRE
I HAIN'T SLEPT THIS LATE IN FIFTY YEAR/ 263 DESIRE
I HAIN'T SLEPT SO LATE IN... 263 DESIRE
I HADN'T SLEPT. 95 ELECTR
HAVEN'T YOU SLEPT$ 174 ELECTR
AS SLOVENLY AS HUGO IS NEAT, HIS CLOTHES ARE DIRTY$574 ICEMAN
AND MUCH SLEPT IN.
THOUGH CAN'T SAY I SLEPT MUCH, THANKS TO THAT 675 ICEMAN
INTERFERING ASS, HICKEY.
OVER THE SKY AND SEA WHICH SLEPT TOGETHER. 153 JOURNE
DON'T COME BACK TILL YOU'VE SLEPT IT OFF, OR I'LL 100 MISBEG
WIPE THE FLOOR WITH YOU/
I'VE SLEPT WITH DRUNKEN TRAMPS ON TOO MANY NIGHTS/121 MISBEG
THE MARE, MOTHER, AND HASN'T HE SLEPT IN HER STALL162 POET
MANY A TIME
WE SLEPT LAST NIGHT IN THE ROOM HE WAS BORN IN. 49 STRANG
OR RATHER HE SLEPT, I COULDN'T. 49 STRANG

SLEWS
BUT I'D HAD SLEWS OF DRINKS AND THEY WERE IN MY 162 MISBEG
HEAD

SLICK
HOW WAS THAT FOR SLICK WAY OF GETTING RID OF HIMS 247 AHWILD
SEEMS TO ME IT'S A PRETTY SLICK PLACE RIGHT NOW. 97 BEYOND
HE SKINNED 'EM TOO SLICK. 205 DESIRE
YE MAKE A SLICK PAIR O' MURDERIN' TURTLE DOVES/ 247 DESIRE
ON'Y JIM BENSON'S ONE O' THEM SLICK JOKERS, SAME'S500 DIFRNT
JACK.
PURTY SLICK YOU BE, ABNER. 130 ELECTR
THAT HAS A DARNED SLICK NOTION. 135 ELECTR

SLICKED
YE LOOK ALL SLICKED UP LIKE A PRIZE BULL. 228 DESIRE
HIS HAIR WET AND SLICKED IN A PART. 501 DIFRNT
WASHED AND SLICKED UP IN HIS ILL-FITTING BEST.) 505 DIFRNT

SLICKEST
(WITH PROUD CONFIDENCE) AND HE'LL MAKE THIS ONE 97 BEYOND
OF THE SLICKEST.
FUR THE SLICKEST CHANTYMAN ON THE WESTERN OR ANY 103 ELECTR
UTHER DAMN OCEANS

SLID
TOMMY HAS ALREADY SLID INTO THE END CHAIR 221 AHWILD
THE SLIDE TO THE COMPANIONWAY ABOVE IS SLID BACK 567 CROSS
WITH A BANG.

SLIDE
THE SLIDE TO THE COMPANIONWAY ABOVE IS SLID BACK 567 CROSS
WITH A BANG.
HE POUNDS AGAINST THE SLIDE, WHICH SEEMS TO HAVE 572 CROSS
BEEN SHUT DOWN ON HIM.)
AND A BOOKCASE WITH GLASS DOORS THAT PULL UP AND 519 DIFRNT
SLIDE IN FLANKS THE FIREPLACE.
LET IT SLIDE. 640 ICEMAN
PARRITT GIVES HIM A GLANCE AND THEN GETS UP AND 666 ICEMAN
SLINKS OVER TO SLIDE INTO THE
AND LETS THE PISTOL SLIDE FROM HIS FINGERS ON THE 172 POET
TABLE.

SLIDES
(REUBEN SLIDES BACK THE DYNAMO ROOM DOOR A FEW 478 DYNAMO
FEET AND ENTERS.
THEN SHE GIVES THE BIG DOOR A PUSH THAT SLIDES IT 479 DYNAMO
OPEN TO ITS FULL WIDTH AND
HE SPOTS HICKEY AND SLIDES INTO A CHAIR AT THE 708 ICEMAN
LEFT OF THE DOORWAY.

SLIDES (CONT'D.)
I SEEN RIGHT AWAY SOMETHIN' ON THE QUEER WAS UP SOS19 INZONE
I SLIDES BACK INTO THE
HE SLIDES HIS HAND BACK STEALTHILY OVER HIS 522 INZONE
MATTRESS AND HIS FINGERS MOVE.
SLIDIN'
WITH A SLIDIN' BAR FIXED ACROSS'T IT, MIND, 103 BEYOND
SLIDING
WITH SLIDING DOORS AND PORTIERES, 185 AHWILD
IN THE REAR WALL, LEFT, IS A DOUBLE DOORWAY WITH 185 AHWILD
SLIDING DOORS AND PORTIERES.
AT LEFT, TOWARD REAR, IS A DOUBLE DOORWAY WITH 210 AHWILD
SLIDING DOORS
AN IMMENSE WINDOW AND A BIG SLIDING DOOR 473 DYNAMO
(HE COMES OUT, SLIDING THE DOOR CLOSED AFTER HIM.1481 DYNAMO
CHRISTINE RETURNS FROM THE HALL, CLOSING THE 84 ELECTR
SLIDING DOORS BEHIND HER SILENTLY.
(THE SLIDING DOORS IN REAR ARE OPENED A LITTLE AND 91 ELECTR
LAVINIA SLIPS SILENTLY IN AND
SLIGHT
SHE IS A SLIGHT, SWEET-FACED LITTLE WOMAN DRESSED 539 'ILE
IN BLACK.
(AFTER A SLIGHT PAUSE DURING WHICH THE OTHERS 544 'ILE
MUMBLE ANGRILY TO ONE ANOTHER)
(AFTER A SLIGHT PAUSE) DID YUH SAY YUH GOT TO 16 ANNA
MEET SOMEONE HERE
(AFTER A SLIGHT PAUSE--CURIOUSLY) 72 ANNA
(AFTER A SLIGHT PAUSE) AND OTHER TIMES MY EYES 89 BEYOND
WOULD FOLLOW THIS ROAD.
MRS. MAYO IS A SLIGHT, ROUND-FACED, 94 BEYOND
(AFTER A SLIGHT PAUSE) IT'S NO USE TALKING ANY 105 BEYOND
MORE ABOUT IT.
(AFTER A SLIGHT PAUSE) HE SAID HE'D MADE UP HIS 152 BEYOND
MIND
(AFTER A SLIGHT PAUSE) WHAT EVER SET YOU GOIN' TO467 CARIBE
SEA?
HE IS A SLIGHT, MEDIUM-SIZED PROFESSIONAL-LOOKING 556 CROSS
MAN OF ABOUT THIRTY-FIVE.
(THEN, AFTER A SLIGHT PAUSE--CASUALLY) 517 DAYS
ALTHOUGH HER BODY IS SLIGHT AND THIN, THERE IS A 494 DIFRNT
QUICK,
THE HOUSE IS PLACED BACK ON A SLIGHT RISE OF 2 ELECTR
GROUND ABOUT THREE HUNDRED FEET
LIVING AND LOVING AND HAVING CHILDREN--(A SLIGHT 271 GGBROW
PAUSE--
THEY LOOM UP AROUND THE SLIGHT FIGURE OF THEIR 323 GGBROW
MOTHER LIKE PROTECTING GIANTS.
BUT EXCEPT FOR THE SLIGHT DIFFERENTIATION IN COLOR207 HA APE
OF HAIR, SKIN, EYES,
AN UNPARDONABLE SLIGHT, ESPECIALLY AS I AM THE 594 ICEMAN
ONLY INMATE OF ROYAL BLOOD.
HE QUOTES WITH GREAT SENTIMENT, IF WITH SLIGHT 599 ICEMAN
APPLICATION)
MAKING A SLIGHT NOISE AS HE DOES SO. 513 INZONE
HE MAKES A SLIGHT MOVEMENT, A STIRRING IN HIS 277 LAZARU
VISION.
HE SPEAKS QUIETLY, IN A DEEP VOICE WITH A SLIGHT 5 MANSNS
DRAWL.)
JOEL HARFORD IS TWENTY-NINE, TALL AND THIN, WITH A 25 MANSNS
SLIGHT STOOP IN HIS CARRIAGE.
WEARS OUT QUICKLY, CAN BE MADE AT VERY SLIGHT 393 MARCOM
EXPENSE
AT LAST, KUBLAI MAKES A SLIGHT BUT IMPERIOUS 433 MARCOM
MOTION OF COMMAND
THERE HAD BEEN A SLIGHT MISUNDERSTANDING JUST 38 MISBEG
BEFORE I WAS TO GRADUATE.
I HAVE A PRIDE UNDULY SENSITIVE TO ANY INTENDED 70 POET
SLIGHT.
THERE WAS NO INTENTION ON MY PART TO SLIGHT YOU. 70 POET
(WITH A SLIGHT SMILE) I'M PRESCRIBING FOR SAM, 38 STRANG
TOO, WHEN I BOOST THIS WEDDING.
GOT RID OF EVEN THAT SLIGHT SUSPICION... 78 STRANG
SO NEAR THAT BY A SLIGHT MOVEMENT EACH COULD TOUCH452 WELDED
THE OTHER.
(A SLIGHT PAUSE) I BEGIN TO KNOW--SOMETHING. 469 WELDED
SLIGHTEST
HIS VANITY COULDN'T ADMIT I'D EVER FEEL THE 520 DAYS
SLIGHTEST DESIRE OUTSIDE OF HIM.
HE HAD NOT THE SLIGHTEST DESIRE FOR THIS WOMAN. 537 DAYS
(DRYLY) I HAVEN'T GIVEN HIM THE SLIGHTEST REASON 533 DIFRNT
TO HOPE IN THIRTY YEARS.
NOW AFTER IT'S ALL PAST AND FORGOTTEN--WHEN THERE 152 ELECTR
ISN'T THE SLIGHTEST SUSPICION--
I WOULDN'T GIVE A DAMN IF YOU EVER DISPLAYED THE 32 JOURNE
SLIGHTEST SIGN OF GRATITUDE.
HE HASN'T THE SLIGHTEST IDEA-- 74 JOURNE
I'VE NEVER HAD THE SLIGHTEST DESIRE TO BE AN 102 JOURNE
ACTRESS.
(WITH A BELITTLING LAUGH.) IF I GAVE YOU THE 120 JOURNE
SLIGHTEST ENCOURAGEMENT.
BUT STRAINING OUR EARS LISTENING FOR THE SLIGHTEST152 JOURNE
SOUND.
IF HE HAD THE SLIGHTEST INKLING-- 142 MANSNS
AND THERE'S NOT THE SLIGHTEST REASON TO WORRY 17 STRANG
ABOUT ME.
AS IF I WOULDN'T DIE RATHER THAN TAKE THE 72 STRANG
SLIGHTEST CHANCE OF THAT HAPPENING/...
NOT THE SLIGHTEST BIT IN THE WORLD/ 141 STRANG
IT'S BECAUSE YOU'VE NEVER MADE THE SLIGHTEST 144 STRANG
ATTEMPT TO BE LOVABLE TO HIM/
HE ISN'T REALLY LIKE HIM AT ALL, NOT THE SLIGHTEST163 STRANG
BIT/
I'M NOT THE SLIGHTEST BIT INTERESTED IN THIS RACE 167 STRANG
TODAY, FOR EXAMPLE/
I DON'T FEEL THE SLIGHTEST TWINGE OF JEALOUSY. 175 STRANG
GLANCING TOWARD ELEANOR, TRYING NOT TO MAKE THE 444 WELDED
SLIGHTEST NOISE.

SLIGHTLY
HE IS JUST REACHING OUT FOR MORE WHEN THE PANTRY 217 AHWILD
DOOR IS OPENED SLIGHTLY AND
THE TOP OF THE HILL SLOPES DOWNWARD SLIGHTLY 129 BEYOND
TOWARD THE LEFT.
IT CREAKS SLIGHTLY AND NAT JUMPS TO HIS FEET--IN A562 CRUSS
THICK VOICE OF TERROR)
HE IS A MAN IN HIS EARLY SIXTIES, SLIGHTLY UNDER 422 DYNAMO
MEDIUM HEIGHT,
(IN THE SAME TONE--SLIGHTLY BOASTFUL) 181 EJONES
PITCHED ON A SLIGHTLY HIGHER KEY 191 EJONES
(HE GETS TO HIS FEET, EVIDENTLY SLIGHTLY REASSURED196 EJONES
BY HIS PRAYER--
(HIS MANNER SLIGHTLY CONTEMPTUOUS) 514 INZONE
IT HAS A SLIGHTLY DISHEVELED, LOPSIDED LOOK. 97 JOURNE
TYRONE HAS HAD A LOT TO DRINK BUT BEYOND A 108 JOURNE
SLIGHTLY GLAZED LOOK IN HIS EYES AND
SLIM
SLIM STRONG HIPS AND LONG BEAUTIFULLY DEVELOPED 12 STRANG
LEGS--
GREEN BUDS ON THE SLIM TREES... 99 STRANG
SLIMMER
SHE IS SLIMMER THAN IN THE PREVIOUS SCENE. 137 STRANG
SLIMY
THEIR HAIR IS MATTED, INTERTWINED WITH SLIMY 571 CROSS
STRANDS OF SEAWEED.
SLING
SLING IT INTO HER/ 224 HA APE
SLINGIN'
AN' I AIN'T SLINGIN' ME 'OOK ABAFT THE 'OLE 494 VOYAGE
BLEEDIN' TOWN FUR NOW MAN.
SLINK
AND I HAD TO SLINK BY AND PRETEND NOT TO HEAR/. 423 DYNAMO
DOES YOU THINK I'D SLINK OUT DE BACK DOOR LIKE A 186 EJONES
COMMON NIGGERS
THE NAZARENES AND THE ORTHODOX SEPARATE AND SLINK 291 LAZARU
GUILTILY APART.
SLINKS
SLINKS STEALTHILY AROUND THE REAR CORNER 427 DYNAMO
APPEARS AROUND THE CORNER OF HER HOUSE AND SLINKS 434 DYNAMO
HURRIEDLY ACROSS THE PATCH OF
(SHE SLINKS BACK ALONG THE HEDGE AND THEN QUICKLY 444 DYNAMO
ACROSS THE LAWN AROUND THE
AS HE PEERS AROUND THE HALF-OPENED DOOR, THEN 462 DYNAMO
SLINKS IN AS IF HE WERE A BURGLAR.
HE SLINKS CAUTIOUSLY TO THE STUMP IN THE CENTER 195 EJONES
(LONG SLINKS BACK OUT OF SIGHT.) 229 HA APE
(HE SLINKS OFF LEFT.) 237 HA APE
HE SLINKS IN FURTIVELY, AS IF HE WERE ESCAPING 645 ICEMAN
FROM SOMEONE.
(PARRITT SLINKS TO A CHAIR AT THE LEFT END OF THE 650 ICEMAN
TABLE.
PARRITT GIVES HIM A GLANCE AND THEN GETS UP AND 666 ICEMAN
SLINKS OVER TO SLIDE INTO THE
DEATH SLINKS OUT OF HIS GRAVE IN THE HEART/ 296 LAZARU
THEN SUDDENLY, TERRIFIED, SLINKS AWAY AND SIDLES 324 LAZARU
OFF AT RIGHT.)
(CALIGULA SLINKS DOWN WARILY) 339 LAZARU
HE SLINKS NOISELESSLY UP THE STEPS OF THE DAIS AND357 LAZARU
SQUATS COVERINGLY AT
(WHILE SHE IS SAYING THIS LAST, SARA SLINKS IN 164 MANSNS
NOISELESSLY
HE SLINKS SWIFTLY AROUND THE CORNER 10 MISBEG
NICK SLINKS INTO THE ROOM AFTER THEM AND SITS DOWN496 VOYAGE
AT A TABLE IN REAR.
SLIP
I THOUGHT I'D GIVEN YOU THE SLIP. 167 BEYOND
EACH GIRL'LL HAVE A SLIP AV PAPER WID HER AN' WHIN463 CARIBE
YOU BUY ANYTHIN' YOU WRITE UT
A MAN'LL NEVER LIVE UP TO 'EM--WITH NEVER ONE 516 DIFRNT
SLIP.
BUT I DIDN'T BELIEVE YOU'D LET A SLIP LIKE THAT 516 DIFRNT
MAKE--SUCH A DIFFERENCE.
TO YOU TO MAKE YOU FORGET--THAT ONE SLIP O' MINE. 538 DIFRNT
TEARS OFF A SLIP OF PAPER AND WRITES TWO WORDS ON 35 ELECTR
IT.
AND TAKES OUT THE SLIP OF PAPER SHE HAD WRITTEN 40 ELECTR
ON)
THEN SHE LETS IT SLIP THROUGH HER FINGERS, 121 ELECTR
YOU'RE AFRAID I'LL LET SOMETHING SLIP. 151 ELECTR
OH, I KNOW YOU THINK YOU KNOW WHERE YOU'RE GOING, 151 ELECTR
BUT THERE'S MANY A SLIP,
SLIP ME DE INSIDE DOPE, DE INFORMATION RIGHT FROM 250 HA APE
DE STABLE--
(THE GORILLA LETS THE CRUSHED BODY SLIP TO THE 254 HA APE
FLOOR.
AND TRY TO SLIP 'EM TO ME. 22 HUGHIE
SOMETHING SLIP--THEN REVENGEFULLY) 635 ICEMAN
COULD I HELP OUT MY HANDS SLIPS 675 ICEMAN
SLIP A PIECE OF CHANGE TO THE JUDGE AND BE SAVED, 165 JOURNE
SHE ALLOWS THE BOOK TO SLIP FROM HER HAND 95 MANSNS
(LETTING THE PAPER SLIP FROM HER HAND WITHOUT A 410 MARCOM
GLANCE--DULLY)
I REMEMBER WHEN I WAS A SLIP OF A GIRL, 24 MISBEG
SLIP OF THE TONGUE/ 181 STRANG
SLIPPED
I SLIPPED THIS WAN OUT AV WAN OF THE BASKETS WHIN 462 CARIBE
THEY WASN'T LOOKIN'.
MY FOOT SLIPPED. 521 DIFRNT
BUT THE CLERK'S MIND HAS SLIPPED AWAY 16 HUGHIE
YOU SHOULD AWAKEN AND THE DRUNKENNESS BE HALF OR 132 JOURNE
WHOLLY SLIPPED AWAY FROM YOU.
IN THE MEANTIME, MARCO HAS SLIPPED OFF, FULL OF 366 MARCOM
CURIOSITY AND WONDER.
THE WATER'S DEEP DOWN THERE, AND YOU'D BE A 589 ROPE
DROWNED RAT IF YOU SLIPPED.
SLIPPER
(GRAVELY MARCO KNEELS, REMOVES A SLIPPER, AND 413 MARCOM
FEELS THE SOLE OF HER FOOT--

SLIPPERS

SLIPPERS
BROWN DRESSING-GOWN AND DISREPUTABLE-LOOKING 249 AHWILD
CARPET SLIPPERS.
AND WEARS WORN CARPET SLIPPERS ON HIS BARE FEET.) 145 BEYOND
SHE WEARS A DARK WRAPPER AND SLIPPERS.) 562 CROSS
SHE WEARS SLIPPERS OVER HER BARE FEET 56 ELECTR
SHE IS DRESSED AS AT THE END OF ACT THREE, IN 62 ELECTR
NIGHTGOWN, WRAPPER AND SLIPPERS.
PADDING FEET IN SLIPPERS, AND CYBEL, WEARING 319 GGBROW
SHE IS DRESSED IN A BLACK KIMONO ROBE AND WEARS 320 GGBROW
SLIPPERS OVER HER BARE FEET.
MY FATHER EVEN LET ME HAVE DUCHESSE LACE ON MY 115 JOURNE
WHITE SATIN SLIPPERS.
DAINTY SLIPPERS WITH POMPONS ON HER BARE FEET. 170 JOURNE
SHE WEARS A FADED OLD WRAPPER OVER HER NIGHTGOWN. 136 POET
SLIPPERS ON HER BARE FEET.

SLIPPIN'
YOU MUST BE SLIPPIN'.= 16 HUGHIE
I AIN'T SLIPPIN'. 16 HUGHIE

SLIPPING
FATHER BAIRD OPENS THE DOOR AND THEY PASS THROUGH,555 DAYS
LOVING SLIPPING AFTER THEM.
(HALF-SLIPPING TO HIS KNEES--LONGINGLY) 559 DAYS
(FEELING THE GROUND SLIPPING FROM UNDER HIS FEET--229 HA APE
DESPERATELY)
(SLIPPING BACK INTO NARRATIVE.) 25 HUGHIE
I MUST BE SLIPPING. 31 HUGHIE
(THEN SLIPPING AWAY INTO HER STRANGE DETACHMENT-- 69 JOURNE
QUITE CASUALLY.)
(THINKING WORRIEDLY) (SLIPPING BACK INTO THAT 51 STRANG
MUXBID TONE...

SLIPS
SELECTS FIVE OR SIX SLIPS OF PAPER, AND HOLDS THEM201 AHWILD
OUT TO MILLER.
(HE PUSHES THE SLIPS OF PAPER ACROSS THE TABLE 202 AHWILD
CONTEMPTUOUSLY)
(MILLER HAS TAKEN THE SLIPS AND IS READING THEM 202 AHWILD
FROWNINGLY.
(NOTICES THE SLIPS OF PAPER ON THE TABLE) 204 AHWILD
(HAS BEEN READING THE SLIPS, A BROAD GRIN ON HIS 205 AHWILD
FACE--SUDDENLY HE WHISTLES)
(SEES THE SLIPS FOR THE FIRST TIME AND IS OVERCOME207 AHWILD
BY EMBARRASSMENT,
POINTS TO THE SLIPS OF PAPER ON THE TABLE) 207 AHWILD
TWO SWATE LITTLE SLIPS AV THINGS, NEAR AS WHITE AS462 CARIBE
YOU AN' ME ARE, FOR THAT
LOVING HAS COME AROUND BEHIND THE TABLE AND SLIPS 560 DAYS
IN AFTER HIM.
AS SHE SLIPS SLOWLY AND STEALTHILY FROM THE BED. 58 ELECTR
AND THE BOX SLIPS OUT ONTO ONE OF THE HOOKED 64 ELECTR
RUGS.)
(THE SLIDING DOORS IN REAR ARE OPENED A LITTLE AND 91 ELECTR
LAVINIA SLIPS SILENTLY IN AND
(HE SLIPS IT INTO HIS COAT POCKET.) 97 ELECTR
(HE SLIPS OUT SILENTLY. 114 ELECTR
(HE SLIPS IN A HEAP ON THE FLOOR AND DIES. 254 HA APE
ALL I WANT IS TO SEE YOU HAPPY-- (HE SLIPS BACK 628 ICEMAN
INTO HEAVY SLEEP AGAIN.
AND COMES AND SLIPS INTO THE CHAIR ON HIS RIGHT. 645 ICEMAN
ROCKY SLIPS THE REVOLVER BACK IN HIS POCKET. 672 ICEMAN
(HE SLIPS OUT OF HIS CHAIR AND GOES QUIETLY OVER 680 ICEMAN
TO SIT IN THE CHAIR BESIDE
(HE NODS TO LIEB, WHO SLIPS A PAIR OF HANDCUFFS ON717 ICEMAN
HICKEY'S WRISTS.
TO HIS BUNK AN' SLIPS THE BLACK BOX UNDER HIS 520 INZONE
MATTRESS--
MONEY SLIPS THROUGH YOUR FINGERS. 346 LAZARU
(TIBERIUS' BODY RELAXES IN HIS HANDS, DEAD, AND 369 LAZARU
SLIPS FROM THE CHAIR.
AND SLIPS TO HER KNEES AND PUTS HER ARMS ABOUT 141 POET
HER--GIVING HER A HUG.)
SHE SLIPS ON TO HIS LAP LIKE A LITTLE GIRL AND 43 STRANG
HIDES HER FACE ON HIS SHOULDER.
(HE COMES OVER AND KISSES HER--SLIPS DOWN AND. 56 STRANG
SITS ON THE FLOOR BESIDE HER.)

SLIT
A BLUNT FORMLESS NOSE AND A TINY SLIT OF A MOUTH. 200 AHWILD

SLITHERIN'
WHIN ALL AV A SUDDINT WE HEARD A GREAT SLITHERIN' 481 CARDIF
CRASH.

SLITS
THE EYES ARE PROTUBERANT, LEERING, CYNICAL SLITS, 337 LAZARU
THE LONG NOSE,
(HE SLITS UP THE WIDE SLEEVES OF HIS OWN ROBE, AS 429 MARCOM
DO HIS FATHER AND UNCLE,

SLOB
MAKING SUCH A DARNED SLOB OF YOURSELF. 276 AHWILD
HOPE IS ONE OF THOSE MEN WHOM EVERYONE LIKES ON 576 ICEMAN
SIGHT, A SOFTHEARTED SLOB.
THE KIND THAT LEAVES THE POOR SLOB WORSE OFF 641 ICEMAN
I'VE ALWAYS BEEN THE BEST-NATURED SLOB IN THE 641 ICEMAN
WORLD.
HES ALWAYS BEEN A HAPPY-GO-LUCKY SLOB. 693 ICEMAN
JEES, DE POOR OLD SLOB IS SO LICKED HE CAN'T EVEN 698 ICEMAN
GET DRUNK.
HAPPY-GO-LUCKY SLOB LIKE ME. 715 ICEMAN

SLOBS
WHAT'S DEM SLOBS IN DE FOIST CABIN GOT TO DO WIT 212 HA APE
USS
DISEASED SLOBS THEY REALLY ARE. 165 JOURNE

SLOCUM'S
THAT BOY UP TO HARRIS' AND THE NEW FELLER UP TO 124 BEYOND
SLOCUM'S.

SLOE
BEER AND SLOE-GIN FIZZ AND MANHATTANS. 219 AHWILD
BRING ME A SLOE- GIN FIZZ. 238 AHWILD

SLOGAN
WHAT AN INSPIRING SLOGAN/ 545 DAYS

SLOGAN (CONT'D.)
UNIVERSAL SLOGAN, KEEP MOVING... 122 STRANG

SLOOP
HE CARRIES A SMALL, EXPENSIVE YACHT'S MODEL OF A 149 STRANG
SLOOP WITH THE SAILS SET.

SLOOS
AND I'LL BE DRINKING SLOUS OF WHISKY 61 ANNA
IN A GRAND MANSION LIKE A CASTLE, WITH SLOOS OF 21 MANSNS
SERVANTS, AND STABLES,
AND AFTER THAT TO THE COLLEGE WITH SLOOS OF MONEY 12 POET

SLOP
I DON'T TAKE NO STOCK IN SECH SLOP/ 214 DESIRE
(JEERINGLY) WAAL--YE'RE GITTIN' SOFT NOW--SOFT AS231 DESIRE
SLOP/
WE DON'T WANTER LISTEN TO NO MORE OF THAT SLOP. 244 HA APE

SLOPES
THE TOP OF THE HILL SLOPES DOWNWARD SLIGHTLY 129 BEYOND
TOWARD THE LEFT.

SLOPING
TO THE REAR OF THE ROAD IS A DITCH WITH A SLOPING, 81 BEYOND
GRASSY BANK ON THE FAR SIDE.
ITS CEILING IS THE SLOPING ROOF. 212 DESIRE
ITS WALLS, AND SLOPING ROOF ARE COVERED WITH TAR 1 MISBEG
PAPER, FADED TO DARK GRAY.
HER SLOPING SHOULDERS ARE BROAD, HER CHEST DEEP 3 MISBEG
WITH LARGE, FIRM BREASTS,
HE HAS A THICK NECK, LUMPY, SLOPING SHOULDERS. 11 MISBEG

SLOPS
(HE SLOPS A GLASS FULL AND DRAINS IT AND POURS 690 ICEMAN
ANOTHER--
(HE SLOPS A BIG DRINK INTO A GLASS.) 156 JOURNE

SLOSHES
TO HIS LIPS THE WATER SLOSHES OVER HIS HAND 35 POET
(HE SLOSHES WHISKEY FROM THE DECANTER INTO BOTH 100 POET
THEIR GLASSES.)

SLOT
AT REAR OF DOOR, AGAINST THE WALL, IS A NICKEL-IN-236 AHWILD
THE-SLOT PLAYER-PIANO.
AN AUTOMATIC, NICKEL-IN-THE-SLOT PLAYER-PIANO IS 278 GGBROW
AT CENTER, REAR.
AGAINST THE MIDDLE OF THE LEFT WALL IS A NICKEL- 573 ICEMAN
IN-THE-SLOT PHONOGRAPH.

SLOTH
WHERE THE SPIRIT DECAYS IN THE SINFUL SLOTH OF THE425 DYNAMO
FLESH...)

SLOUCH
AND HAS A SLOUCH HAT PULLED DOWN OVER HIS EYES. 109 ELECTR

SLOUCHES
AND SLOUCHES BACK INTO THE ARMCHAIR AT LEFT REAR 187 AHWILD
OF TABLE.
(BEN SLOUCHES IN FROM THE KITCHEN. 123 BEYOND
(PADDY SLOUCHES INTO THE FORECASTLE) 465 CARIBE
BENNY SLOUCHES TO THE DOOR--SULLENLY) 547 DIFRNT
HE SLOUCHES AND HIS MOVEMENTS ARE SHAMBLING AND 175 POET
CLUMSY.

SLOUCHINESS
HE CARRIES HIMSELF BY TURNS WITH A MARKED 73 ELECTR
SLOUCHINESS

SLOVENLY
THE NEGLIGENT DISORDER OF HER DRESS, THE SLOVENLY 144 BEYOND
ARRANGEMENT OF HER HAIR,
AS SLOVENLY AS HUGO IS NEAT, HIS CLOTHES ARE DIRTY574 ICEMAN
AND MUCH SLEPT IN.
HE IS SLOVENLY DRESSED IN A DIRTY SHAPELESS 575 ICEMAN
PATCHED SUIT, SPOTTED BY FOOD.
HE WEARS OLD CLOTHES AND IS SLOVENLY. 576 ICEMAN
LIKE MCGLOIN, HE IS SLOVENLY. 576 ICEMAN
ALMOST SLOVENLY WAY SHE WEARS IT. 97 JOURNE
YET IN SPITE OF HER SLOVENLY APPEARANCE THERE IS A 20 POET
SPIRIT WHICH SHINES THROUGH
DEBORAH IS REPELLED BY NORA'S SLOVENLY APPEARANCE, 74 POET
SHE IS A THIN, SLOVENLY, WORN-OUT-LOOKING WOMAN OF579 ROPE
ABOUT FORTY WITH A DRAWN,
A SLOVENLY BARMAID WITH A STUPID FACE SODDEN WITH 493 VOYAGE
DRINK IS MOPPING OFF THE BAR.

SLOW
(THEN CONTINUES WITH SLOW INTENSITY) 548 'ILE
(CALCULATEDLY TAUNTING) SAY, HONEST, ARE THINGS 238 AHWILD
THAT SLOW UP AT HARVARD'S
VE MAKE SLOW VOYAGE--DIRTY VEDDER--YUST FOG, FOG, 7 ANNA
ALL BLOODY TIME/
SLOW STEPS SOUND FROM THE PATH IN FRONT OF THE 514 DIFRNT
HOUSE.
NOT LIKE THEM SLOW, OLD-TIMEY TUNES. 520 DIFRNT
ARE THOSE OF AUTOMATONS,--RIGID, SLOW, AND 194 EJONES
MECHANICAL.
THEN FALLS BY SLOW GRADATIONS OF TONE INTO SILENCE199 EJONES
AND IS TAKEN UP AGAIN.
SHE TWINES AND UNTWINES THE FINGERS OF HER CLASPED157 ELECTR
HANDS WITH A SLOW
HER MOVEMENTS SLOW AND SOLIDLY LANGUOROUS LIKE AN 278 GGBROW
ANIMALS,
WANTER WIND UP LIKE A SPORT 'STEAD OF CROAKIN' 253 HA APE
SLOW IN DERE'S
HE SAYS SLOW AND QUIET LIKE DERE WASN'T NO HARM IN601 ICEMAN
HIM,
OR MAYBE WORSE, WID YOUR WIFE AND DE ICEMAN 636 ICEMAN
WALKIN' SLOW BEHIND YUH.=
ONLY A LAZY GROUND SWELL AND A SLOW DROWSY ROLL OF153 JOURNE
THE SHIP.
AT FIRST THIS IS SLOW BUT IT MOMENTARILY BECOMES 287 LAZARU
MORE HECTIC AND PECULIAR.
(THEIR DANCE IS FALTERING AND SLOW NOW) 295 LAZARU
IT SOUNDED SLOW, SLOWER THAN WHEN I LAST HEARD IT.357 LAZARU
(PURSING HIS LIPS) SLOW. I COME FROM DELHI. 348 MARCOM
THE BELLS, EXCEPT FOR ONE SLOW DEEP-TONED ONE IN 433 MARCOM
THE PALACE ITSELF,

SLOWLY

SLOW (CONT'D.)
LIKE A DEAD MAN WALKING SLOW BEHIND HIS OWN COFFIN. 35 MISBEG

SLOW ON THE UPTAKE, AND HAS NO SENSE OF HUMOR. 56 MISBEG
YOU'RE SLOW. 592 ROPE
(YAWNING) BLIMEY IF BIZNESS AIN'T 'ARF SLOW TONIGHT. 493 VOYAGE

(THEN AS SHE TAKES A SLOW, MECHANICAL STEP TOWARD 449 WELDED
THE DOOR--WITH TENSE PLEADING)
HER VOICE IS HEAVY AND SLOW WITH THE STRONG TRACE 470 WELDED
OF A FOREIGN INTONATION.

SLOWER
IT SOUNDED SLOW, SLOWER THAN WHEN I LAST HEARD IT.357 LAZARU

SLOWLY
(AGAIN IN HIS FLAT, BRITTLE VOICE, SLOWLY GETTING 203 AHWILD
TO HIS FEET)
SLOWLY THE ANGER DRAINS FROM HIS FACE 204 AHWILD
CAN IT BE THIS WOMAN HAS BEEN SLOWLY POISONING YOU2Z7 AHWILD
ALL THESE YEARS$
(TOMMY GOES SLOWLY TO THE DOORWAY-- 253 AHWILD
RICHARD COMES IN SLOWLY FROM THE FRONT PARLOR. 292 AHWILD
(SLOWLY, PUZZLED) WELL, THEN, IF IT ISN'T-- 88 BEYOND
(TURNING TO HER QUICKLY, IN SURPRISE--SLOWLY) 88 BEYOND
HE PRESSES HER CLOSE TO HIM--SLOWLY AND TENDERLY) 91 BEYOND
(SLOWLY--HIS EYES SHINING) AND THEN SHE CRIED AND100 BEYOND
SAID IT WAS I
AND WALK SLOWLY INTO THE BEDROOM.) 128 BEYOND
(STARING AT HIS BROTHER--SLOWLY) 132 BEYOND
(SLOWLY) PERHAPS--FOR HER SAKE--YOU'D BETTER NOT 135 BEYOND
TELL HER.
(SLOWLY AND VINDICTIVELY) THAT'S JUST LIKE HIM-- 137 BEYOND
NOT TO--
AND THEN SLOWLY FOLLOWS AS THE CURTAIN FALLS.) 144 BEYOND
AND GOES SLOWLY TO THE OUTSIDE DOOR, WHICH SHE 154 BEYOND
OPENS.
(SLOWLY) IN THE FIRST PLACE I KNOW I'M DYING. 160 BEYOND
(SLOWLY) I THINK I KNOW WHAT YOU'RE DRIVING AT, 162 BEYOND
ROB-- AND IT'S TRUE, I GUESS.
(SLOWLY) YOU MEAN--YOU FOUND OUT YOU DIDN'T LOVE 163 BEYOND
ROB$
(SLOWLY) I WOULDN'T KNOW HOW TO FEEL LOVE, EVEN 165 BEYOND
IF I TRIED, ANY MORE.
(SHE GETS WEARILY TO HER FEET AND WALKS SLOWLY 166 BEYOND
TOWARD THE BEDROOM)
QUIVERING LINE OF FLAME IS SPREADING SLOWLY 166 BEYOND
THE SUN COMES SO SLOWLY. 167 BEYOND
AFTER THE CURTAIN RISES THE DOOR IN THE REAR IS 555 CROSS
OPENED SLOWLY AND
(WALKING SLOWLY TOWARD THE TABLE) 556 CROSS
THE DOOR IN THE REAR IS SLOWLY OPENED. 562 CROSS
(SLOWLY) A RED AND A GREEN LIGHT AT THE MAINMAST-569 CROSS
HEAD.
(SLOWLY) A RED AND A GREEN AT THE MAINMAST-HEAD. 569 CROSS
A DENSE GREEN GLOW FLOODS SLOWLY IN RHYTHMIC WAVES570 CROSS
LIKE A LIQUID IN THE ROOM--
THEY MOVE SLOWLY--SLOWLY. 571 CROSS
NAT MOVES SLOWLY TO HIS FATHER'S BODY, 573 CROSS
(NAT GOES UP SLOWLY. 573 CROSS
(AS IF TO HIMSELF--SLOWLY) I FEEL-- 506 DAYS
THEN HE COMES SLOWLY BACK AND SITS DOWN IN HIS 513 DAYS
CHAIR AND STARES BEFORE HIM.
(SLOWLY, IN HIS COLD TONE WITH ITS UNDERCURRENT OF540 DAYS
SINISTER HIDDEN MEANING)
SHE RISES SLOWLY TO HER FEET AND WALKS SLOWLY AND 541 DAYS
WOODENLY BACK PAST HIM AND
(SLOWLY) YES, PERHAPS IF WE COULD AGAIN HAVE 543 DAYS
FAITH IN--
HE STARES FIXEDLY AT JOHN NOW AND ADDS SLOWLY) 544 DAYS
AND SLOWLY HIS EXPRESSION CHANGES TO ONE OF 551 DAYS
FEARFUL, FASCINATED AWE.
(HE WALKS SLOWLY OVER TO WHERE HE HAD STOOD WITH 444 DYNAMO
ADA--DULLY)
(SHE SLOWLY BACKS HERSELF INTO HER ROOM.) 444 DYNAMO
(A PAUSE--THEN REUBEN LIGHT COMES SLOWLY IN FROM 457 DYNAMO
THE LEFT AND STANDS THERE.
JUST AS REUBEN SLOWLY OPENS THE DOOR OF THE LIGHT 462 DYNAMO
SITTING ROOM.
(HE PAUSES ON HIS KNEES FOR A MOMENT, THEN GETS 475 DYNAMO
SLOWLY TO HIS FEET.
(HE WALKS SLOWLY OFF RIGHT.) 476 DYNAMO
(AS THE LIGHT SLOWLY COMES ON AGAIN, 486 DYNAMO
THE DYNAMO'S THROATY METALLIC PURR RISES SLOWLY IN489 DYNAMO
VOLUME
(WITH A KEEN GLANCE AT HER--SLOWLY) 11 ELECTR
(AGAIN STARTS--THEN SLOWLY AS IF ADMITTING A 11 ELECTR
SECRET UNDERSTANDING BETWEEN THEM)
(SLOWLY) I CAN'T MARRY ANYONE, PETER. 14 ELECTR
THEN ADDS SLOWLY, STARING FIXEDLY AT HER MOTHER) 17 ELECTR
THEN HE ASKS SLOWLY) 19 ELECTR
(REGAINING COMMAND OF HERSELF--SLOWLY) 21 ELECTR
SHE TURNS SLOWLY TO HER FATHER'S PORTRAIT AND FOR 28 ELECTR
A MOMENT STARES AT IT FIXEDLY.
(SUDDENLY BECOMING RIGID AND COLD AGAIN--SLOWLY) 32 ELECTR
HIS HANDS ON THE ARMS OF THE CHAIR--SLOWLY) 36 ELECTR
HE SAYS SLOWLY) 36 ELECTR
(SLOWLY) I WAS THINKING--PERHAPS WE HAD BETTER GO 37 ELECTR
TO THE SITTING-ROOM.
(SLOWLY--WITHOUT LOOKING AT HIM) 37 ELECTR
(SLOWLY) YES--BUT EZRA IS ALIVE/ 39 ELECTR
(TURNING TO STARE AT HIM--SLOWLY) 39 ELECTR
(SHE HAS BEEN STARING BEFORE HER--NOW SHE SUDDENLY 40 ELECTR
TURNS ON BRANT--SLOWLY)
(CHRISTINE SLOWLY RISES. 46 ELECTR
(HAS SLOWLY DESCENDED THE STEPS, HER EYES FIXED ON 47 ELECTR
HIM--TENSELY)
AS SHE SLIPS SLOWLY AND STEALTHILY FROM THE BED. 58 ELECTR
(THEY BEGIN MOVING SLOWLY 70 ELECTR

SLOWLY (CONT'D.)
WALKS SLOWLY AND WOODENLY OFF LEFT BETWEEN THE 78 ELECTR
LILAC CLUMP AND THE HOUSE.
(LAVINIA COMES SLOWLY FORWARD UNTIL SHE IS AT 91 ELECTR
ARM'S LENGTH.
(GOES SLOWLY TO THE BODY AND STANDS LOOKING DOWN 114 ELECTR
INTO BRANT'S FACE.
(SLOWLY) AYEH. 125 ELECTR
(SHAKING HER HEAD--SLOWLY) NO. 136 ELECTR
(HE COMES SLOWLY AND HESITATINGLY IN FROM LEFT, 137 ELECTR
FRONT.
SHE COMES FORWARD SLOWLY. 139 ELECTR
(STARES AT HIM--SLOWLY) DO YOU REALLY WANT TO 159 ELECTR
MARRY HER--NOW$
HE STARES AT HER AND SLOWLY A DISTORTED 164 ELECTR
SETH APPEARS WALKING SLOWLY UP THE DRIVE FROM 169 ELECTR
RIGHT, FRONT.
(HE MOVES SLOWLY OFF BEHIND THE LILACS AS HAZEL 171 ELECTR
ENTERS FROM LEFT, FRONT--
HE WALKS SLOWLY, HIS EYES ON THE GROUND-- 174 ELECTR
THEY STARE AFTER HIM--THEN SLOWLY FOLLOW. 262 GGBROW
(SLOWLY TAKES OFF HER MASK--TO THE MOON) 262 GGBROW
THEN SLOWLY TAKES OFF HIS MASK. 264 GGBROW
(HE SLOWLY REMOVES HIS MASK. 286 GGBROW
THEN GOES SLOWLY OVER TO DION AND PUTS HER HAND 278 GGBROW
GENTLY ON HIS FOREHEAD)
(SLOWLY REMOVES HIS MASK. 279 GGBROW
(TAKING OFF HIS MASK--SLOWLY) 282 GGBROW
(SLOWLY) I LOVE MARGARET. 286 GGBROW
HE COMES SLOWLY BACK. 287 GGBROW
(HE SLOWLY STARTS TO PUT THE MASK ON. 299 GGBROW
(TURNING AWAY SLOWLY AND PUTTING ON HIS MASK-- 305 GGBROW
DULLY)
(SLOWLY REMOVES HER MASK, LAYING IT ON THE BENCH, 323 GGBROW
(SHE SLOWLY TAKES FROM UNDER HER CLOAK, FROM HER 323 GGBROW
BOSOM, AS IF FROM HER HEART,
(TURNS TO LOOK LARRY IN THE EYES--SLOWLY) 588 ICEMAN
(HIS EYES GROW HARD--SLOWLY) 613 ICEMAN
THEN SLOWLY) NO, I'M SORRY TO HAVE TO TELL YOU MY694 ICEMAN
POOR WIFE WAS KILLED.
(SLOWLY,) HE THINKS IT'S CONSUMPTION, DOESN'T HE, 30 JOURNE
PAPA$
HE SPEAKS SLOWLY WITH A SUPERSTITIOUS DREAD.) 39 JOURNE
(HESITATES--THEN SLOWLY,) I'M GLAD YOU'VE GOT 55 JOURNE
YOUR MIND PREPARED FOR BAD NEWS.
EDMUND MOVES SLOWLY TO HIS CHAIR. 64 JOURNE
(HE WALKS SLOWLY TO WHERE SHE STANDS IN THE 69 JOURNE
DOORWAY.
(SLOWLY TAKES HER ARM AWAY--HER MANNER REMOTE AND 93 JOURNE
OBJECTIVE AGAIN.)
(GOES SLOWLY TO THE WINDOWS AT RIGHT LIKE AN 121 JOURNE
AUTOMATON--
(MOVED, STARES AT HIS FATHER WITH UNDERSTANDING-- 151 JOURNE
SLOWLY.)
(THEN SLOWLY.) ALTHOUGH, IN A WAY, I DO FEEL SORRY157 JOURNE
FOR HIM ABOUT ONE THING.
BUT BEFORE THEY CAN DRINK MARY SPEAKS AND THEY 175 JOURNE
SLOWLY LOWER THEIR DRINKS TO THE
(AFTER A PAUSE--SLOWLY AND LAMENTINGLY) 329 LAZARU
MOVING SLOWLY ON TOWARD THE PALACE IN THE REAR. 333 LAZARU
(WALKS TO THE DAIS WHICH SHE ASCENDS SLOWLY UNTIL 342 LAZARU
SHE STANDS BY CAESAR'S COUCH
SLOWLY ARISES FROM THE PAST OF THE RACE OF MEN 360 LAZARU
THAT WAS HIS TOMB OF DEATH/
THEN SLOWLY DRAWS AWAY-- 361 LAZARU
(BUT EVEN AS HE IS SPEAKING THE DOOR IS SLOWLY 27 MANSNS
OPENED OUTWARDS AND DEBORAH
(SHE SHAKES HER HEAD SLOWLY.) 30 MANSNS
(STARES AT HIM WONDERINGLY--SLOWLY.) 34 MANSNS
(SLOWLY--AS IF FORCING THE WORDS OUT IN SPITE OF 38 MANSNS
HERSELF.)
IT IS AS THOUGH SHE HAD SLOWLY TAKEN POSSESSION OF 73 MANSNS
SARA.
AS THOUGH A BOMB WERE CONCEALED IN THE ROOM WITH A120 MANSNS
FUSE SLOWLY SPUTTERING
(SLOWLY, HARDLY ABOVE A WHISPER, BUT WITH A 131 MANSNS
TAUNTING.
(SARA GOES SLOWLY TOWARD HER OLD CHAIR AT LEFT-- 136 MANSNS
FRONT OF TABLE.
SHE RELAXES SLOWLY AND MURMURS DREAMILY.) 164 MANSNS
TURNS TOWARDS THE DOOR AND SLOWLY BEGINS TO ASCEND164 MANSNS
THE STEPS.)
(SHE GETS TO HER FEET SLOWLY AND EXHAUSTEDLY.) 188 MANSNS
THE DOOR OF THE SUMMER-HOUSE HAS SLOWLY OPENED AND191 MANSNS
DEBORAH HAS APPEARED.
THE LIGHT SLOWLY REVEALS THE EXTERIOR OF DONATA'S 355 MARCOM
HOME ON A CANAL, VENICE.
THEY BACK OUT SLOWLY, THE MONK AND KNIGHT LAST. 362 MARCOM
THE SLOWLY-RISING LIGHT REVEALS AN INDIAN SNAKE- 369 MARCOM
CHARMER
THE CLAMOR OF THE TEMPLE BELLS SLOWLY DIES OUT IN 372 MARCOM
THE DISTANCE.)
THE LIGHT SLOWLY COMES TO A PITCH OF BLINDING 377 MARCOM
BRIGHTNESS.
(SLOWLY AND INTENSELY) YES/ 412 MARCOM
SHE RAISES HER HANDS SLOWLY ABOVE HIS HEAD 414 MARCOM
MOVING SLOWLY BACKWARD IN A GLIDING, INTER-WEAVING433 MARCOM
DANCE PATTERN.
THEIR ARMS WITH ONE MOTION MOVE SLOWLY UP.. 433 MARCOM
(SLOWLY) BEFORE WE KNOW LIFE, HOW CAN WE KNOW 434 MARCOM
DEATH$
A PAUSE--THEN SLOWLY) 435 MARCOM
SLOWLY APPROACHES THE CATAFALQUE, 437 MARCOM
AND STARTS TO GO OUT SLOWLY WITH THE OTHERS IN THE439 MARCOM
AUDIENCE.
SHE SIGHS AND GETS SLOWLY TO HER FEET, 71 MISBEG
(HE ADDS SLOWLY) I'D LIKE TONIGHT TO BE 105 MISBEG
DIFFERENT.

SLOWLY

SLOWLY (CONT'D.)
(HE PAUSES--SLOWLY) THERE HAVE BEEN TOO MANY 120 MISBEG
NIGHTS--AND DAWNS.
(SLOWLY, STARING BEFORE HIM) 138 MISBEG
HE BECOMES AWARE OF THIS FOR THE FIRST TIME AND 151 MISBEG
TURNS SLOWLY TO STARE AT HER.)
SLOWLY) I KNEW YOU'D BE BITTER AGAINST ME, JOSIE,164 MISBEG
BUT I TOOK THE CHANCE YOU'D
(AS IF HE HADN'T HEARD--SLOWLY) 171 MISBEG
HE TURNS SLOWLY TO FACE THE EAST. 172 MISBEG
(SHE TURNS SLOWLY AND GOES INTO THE HOUSE.) 177 MISBEG
(THE DOOR AT LEFT FRONT IS SLOWLY OPENED 33 POET
SARA CLOSES THE DOOR AND COMES BACK SLOWLY TO THE 87 POET
HEAD OF THE TABLE AT CENTER.
THE DOOR AT LEFT FRONT SLOWLY OPENS-- 88 POET
SLOWLY BECAUSE MELODY, HEARING VOICES IN THE ROOM 88 POET
AND HOPING DEBORAH IS THERE.
HE COMES SLOWLY AROUND THE TABLE AT LEFT FRONT, 89 POET
(AS IF SHE HADN'T HEARD, COMES BACK SLOWLY.) 139 POET
(THE DOOR IS OPENED SLOWLY 151 POET
HE SPEAKS SLOWLY, WITH DIFFICULTY KEEPING HIS 171 POET
WORDS IN BROGUE.)
(HIS EYES FOLLOW HER FOR A SECOND, THEN RETURN TO 4 STRANG
GAZE AROUND THE ROOM SLOWLY
(SLOWLY AND CAREFULLY) YES. 8 STRANG
(SLOWLY--COOLLY AND REFLECTIVELY) 14 STRANG
(SLOWLY AND STRANGELY) I'M NOT SICK. 18 STRANG
(NINA ENTERS SLOWLY. 39 STRANG
(NODDING SLOWLY) I KNOW. 42 STRANG
(TAKING HIS OTHER HAND AND SLOWLY PULLING HIM 87 STRANG
AROUND TO FACE HER.
WALKS SLOWLY AND WOODENLY LIKE A MAN IN A TRANCE 98 STRANG
INTO THE ROOM.
SHE COMES FORWARD SLOWLY--THINKING RESENTFULLY) 154 STRANG
(STARES DOWN AT EVANS--SLOWLY, AS IF TRYING TO 182 STRANG
BRING HER MIND BACK TO HIM)
HE STARES ACCUSINGLY AT THEM AS THEY COME SLOWLY 189 STRANG
TOWARD HIM IN SILENCE.
(THEN LOOKING HER SON IN THE EYES, SLOWLY AND 195 STRANG
IMPRESSIVELY)
THEN STOPS WHEN HE IS HALF-WAY AND, HESITATING, 445 WELDED
TURNS SLOWLY AND COMES BACK.
RHYTHM OF OUR LIVES BEATING AGAINST EACH OTHER, 448 WELDED
FORMING SLOWLY THE ONE RHYTHM--
SHE LOOKS UP AT JOHN AND FORCES THE WORDS OUT 462 WELDED
SLOWLY)
(AFTER A LONG PAUSE--SLOWLY) 466 WELDED
(SLOWLY) PEACE ISN'T OUR MEANING. 481 WELDED
(LOOKS AT HIM, STRANGELY IMPRESSED--A PAUSE-- 483 WELDED
SLOWLY)
(HER HEAD THROWN BACK, HER EYES SHUT--SLOWLY, 489 WELDED
DREAMILY)
(SHE ASCENDS THE STAIRS SLOWLY) 489 WELDED

SLOWPOKE
BAD LUCK TO YOU FOR A SLOWPOKE. 4 MISBEG

SLUGGISH
MY OLD ONE LABORS WITH MEMORIES AND ITS BLOOD IS 345 LAZARU
SLUGGISH WITH THE PAST.
HER HIGHNESS'S SPLEEN BEING SLUGGISH AFTER THE 425 MARCOM
LONG CONFINEMENT ON SHIPBOARD.
(HIS THOUGHTS AT EBB, WITHOUT EMPHASIS, SLUGGISH 24 STRANG
AND MELANCHOLY)

SLUGS
GET A FEW SLUGS UNDER YOUR BELT AND YOU'LL FORGET 620 ICEMAN
SLEEPING.

SLUM
MARGIE HAS BROWN HAIR AND HAZEL EYES, A SLUM NEW 611 ICEMAN
YORKER OF MIXED BLOOD.

SLUMBER
THE CHANTYMAN LIES SPRAWLED ON HIS BACK, SNORING 102 ELECTR
IN A DRUNKEN SLUMBER.
THIS TIME IT PENETRATES HICKEY'S EXHAUSTED 628 ICEMAN
SLUMBER.
HIS HEAD ROLLS FORWARD IN A SODDEN SLUMBER. 696 ICEMAN

SLUMMING
YOU ARE NOW BENT ON MAKING YOUR SLUMMING 219 HA APE
INTERNATIONAL.

SLUMP
SIMEON AND PETER SHOULDER IN, SLUMP DOWN IN THEIR 206 DESIRE
CHAIRS WITHOUT A WORD.

SLUMPED
HE IS SLUMPED SIDEWAYS ON HIS CHAIR, 576 ICEMAN

SLUMPING
HE SLOWLY TURNS, SLUMPING INTO A SITTING POSITION 268 DESIRE
ON THE FLOOR.

SLUMPS
(RICHARD SLUMPS AWKWARDLY INTO THE CHAIR 293 AHWILD
(HE SLUMPS FORWARD TO THE FLOOR AND ROLLS OVER ON 566 DAYS
HIS BACK, DEAD.
(HIS LEGS CRUMPLE UNDER HIM, HE SLUMPS TO HIS 566 DAYS
KNEES BESIDE JOHN.
HE TURNS AND SLUMPS INTO THE CHAIR AT THE FAR SIDE464 DYNAMO
OF THE TABLE)
(HE SLUMPS DOWN IN HIS CHAIR AT LEFT OF TABLE) 151 ELECTR
(HE SLUMPS DOWN HEAVILY IN HIS FATHER'S CHAIR AND 156 ELECTR
STARES AT THE FLOOR.
SLUMPS DOWN INTO HIS CHAIR, CRUSHED, HIS FACE 272 GCBROW
AVERTED FROM HERS.
HE COMES FORWARD AND SITS AT THE TABLE AND SLUMPS 586 ICEMAN
BACK.
SLUMPS DOWN ON THE PIANO STOOL.) 637 ICEMAN
STRICKEN LOOK AND TURNS AWAY AND SLUMPS INTO THE 655 ICEMAN
CHAIR ON MOSHER'S RIGHT.)
SLUMPS DOWN IN THE CHAIR, FACING LEFT-FRONT. 691 ICEMAN
IN THE BAR HE COMES FORWARD AND SLUMPS IN A CHAIR 704 ICEMAN
AT THE TABLE, FACING FRONT.)
(HE SLUMPS DOWN IN HIS CHAIR AGAIN) 708 ICEMAN

SLUMPS (CONT'D.)
(HE SLUMPS DOWN IN THE CHAIR AT LEFT OF TABLE NEXT 21 JOURNE
TO HIS BROTHER.
(HE SLUMPS DOWN ON THE MORRIS CHAIR.) 74 MISBEG
(NORA SLUMPS ON A CHAIR AT THE REAR OF THE TABLE 56 POET
(HE SLUMPS DOWN IN THE CHAIR AT CENTER 99 STRANG
MECHANICALLY.
(HE SLUMPS CLUMSILY DOWN TO A SITTING POSITION ON 175 STRANG
THE DECK BY HER CHAIR AND
NINA SLUMPS DOWN IN HER CHAIR AGAIN.) 179 STRANG
(HE SLUMPS DOWN ON THE CHAIR AGAIN, SUNK IN A 473 WELDED
SOMBER STUPOR.

SLUMS
SLUMS OF NAPLES...* 6 STRANG

SLUNG
THE BLOODY SHIP IS SINKIN' AN' THE BLEEDIN' RATS 182 EJONES
'AS SLUNG THEIR 'OOKS.
A WINCHESTER RIFLE IS SLUNG ACROSS HIS SHOULDERS 194 EJONES
AND HE CARRIES A HEAVY WHIP.

SLUNK
YOU SLUNK OUT OF BED SO QUIETLY. 59 ELECTR

SLUSHIER
I WAS A SLUSHIER DAMN FOOL IN THOSE DAYS THAN YOU 134 BEYOND
WERE.

SLUT
YOU SLUT, YOU, I'LL BE KILLING YOU NOW/ 60 ANNA
YOU--YOU SLUT/ 128 BEYOND
AND I'M SUCH AN UNGRATEFUL LITTLE SLUT/ 517 DAYS
GO ON F' YER SLUT--DISGRACIN' YER PAW 'N' ME/ 230 DESIRE
A SLUT, I'M SAYING*/ 208 HA APE
VULGAR, COMMON SLUT/ 21 MANSNS
YOUR SLUT COMMANDS YOU NOW/ 114 MANSNS
YOU VILE DEGRADED SLUT/ 136 MANSNS
SO YOU CAN GO BACK AND SNEER WITH HER AT WHAT A 155 MANSNS
LOW, COMMON SLUT I AM IN MY HEAR
UNTIL NOW HE SEES HER AS THE FILTHY SLUT SHE IS-- 162 MANSNS
HE IS EVEN NOW LYING IN THE ARMS OF THAT SLUT, 162 MANSNS
YOU VULGAR COMMON SLUT/ 166 MANSNS
WOULD YOU REMIND ME OF PITY NOW, YOU SCHEMING 187 MANSNS
SLUTS
HAVEN'T YOU A TONGUE IN YOUR HEAD, YOU GREAT SLUT 12 MISBEG
YOUS
A GREAT PROUD SLUT WHO'S PLAYED GAMES WITH HALF 80 MISBEG
THE MEN AROUND HERE.
HE THINKS IT'S ALL BOASTING AND PRETENDING YOU'VE 88 MISBEG
DONE ABOUT BEING A SLUT.
PUT ME OUT OF MY OWN HOME, WILL YOU, YOU UNDUTIFUL100 MISBEG
SLUT/
YOU FILTHY PEASANT SLUT/ 128 POET
AND GOT CALLED A PEASANT SLUT AND A WHORE FOR MY 150 POET
PAINS.
ONE AV THE YANKEE GINTRY HAS STOPPED TO BE SEDUCED172 POET
BY MY SLUT AV A DAUGHTER
LET YOU KAPE YOUR MOUTH CLOSED, YE SLUT, 176 POET
HAVE YE NO SUPPER AT ALL MADE, YE LAZY SLUT& 582 ROPE
BY SELLIN' EVERYTHIN' TO BUY THAT SLUT NEW 586 ROPE
CLOTHES.
FOR PLAYING THE SILLY SLUT, CHARLIE. 44 STRANG

SLY
(WITH A SLY, BLURRY WINK AROUND) 229 AHWILD
I'VE BEEN SMOKING FOR THE LAST TWO YEARS--ON THE 239 AHWILD
SLY.
HIS VOICE, WHEN NOT RAISED IN A HOLLOW BOOM, IS 5 ANNA
TUNED DOWN TO A SLY,
IF IT WASN'T FOR ME HELPIN' YOU ON THE SLY OUT OF 152 BEYOND
MY SAVIN'S,
(WITH A SLY WINK) OH, IS HE& 502 DIFRNT
(WITH A SLY GRIN) WHO D'YOU HAVE IT DONE FOR, 524 DIFRNT
THEN&
(WITH A SLY GRIN--IN A WHISPER) 529 DIFRNT
HIS YELLOWISH BROWN EYES ARE SLY. 129 ELECTR
(HIS TONE BECOMING SLY, INSINUATING AND MOCKING. 144 ELECTR
(WITH A SLY CUNNING AIR) NOT LOOK SO MUCH LIKE 145 ELECTR
FATHER, EH&
A SLY FAT BOY, CONGENITALLY INDOLENT, A PRACTICAL 576 ICEMAN
JOKER,
WITH A STRANGE, SLY, CALCULATING LOOK-- 702 ICEMAN
(INGRATIATINGLY)
SHE'D SNEAK NOTES TO ME AND MEET ME ON THE SLY. 710 ICEMAN
HE'S ALWAYS HAD THAT SLY AIR ABOUT HIM *S IF HE 522 INZONE
WAS HIDIN' SOMETHIN'.
'E AIN'T ARF A SLY ONE WIV 'IS TALK OF SUBMARINES,523 INZONE
GAWD BLIND 'IM.
BRIDGET IS SO LAZY. AND SO SLY. 29 JOURNE
(WITH A QUICK, STRANGE, CALCULATING, ALMOST SLY 49 JOURNE
GLANCE AT HIM.)
SOMETHING ABOUT HIM, TOO--SLY--LIKE THERE WAS A 118 MANSNS
SECRET BETWEEN THEM--
(THINKING.) HE ISN'T READING--JUST PRETENDING 119 MANSNS
TO--SMILING TO HIMSELF--SLY--
HE STARES UP AND DOWN THE CURVES OF HER BODY WITH 140 MANSNS
A SLY DESIRE.)
(WITH A SLY GRIN) IT'S A GREAT HONOR--A VERY 381 MARCOM
GREAT HONOR.
(SUDDENLY WITH A SLY SMILE TO HIMSELF) 404 MARCOM
HE MUST HAVE IMPROVED HIS MIND ON THE SLY. 22 MISBEG
UGH, YOU MAKE ME SICK, YOU SLY MISER/ 36 MISBEG
YOU'RE FULL OF SLY ADVICE ALL OF A SUDDEN, AIN'T 93 MISBEG
YOUS
(COQUETTISHLY.) AREN'T YOU THE SLY ONE/ 28 POET
(SHE SMILES.) IT'S YOU ARE THE SLY ONE. 30 POET
HE'S A SLY OLD BIRD. 593 ROPE

SLYER
AND I'M A SLYER BIRD. 593 ROPE

SLYLY
(MILDRED SLYLY SHOVES HER FOOT OUT SO THAT HE 193 AHWILD
TRIPS OVER IT, ALMOST FALLING.
MAYO SMILES SLYLY AT HIS WIFE) 99 BEYOND

SLYLY

(CONT'D.)
(SLYLY AMUSED) IT'S JUST THE SAME WITH ME AS 102 BEYOND
'TWAS WITH YOU, DICK.
AND HE GRINS ABOUT HIM SLYLY WITH A GREEDY 247 DESIRE
MALICE.)
(SLYLY) WE'RE WAITIN' FUR EBEN. 249 DESIRE
(SLYLY) YOU SEEM A MITE SHAKY. 133 ELECTR
(THEN SLYLY FEELING HIS WAY.) 37 HUGHIE
(HE CHUCKLES, GIVING THE NIGHT CLERK THE SLYLY 38 HUGHIE
AMUSED, CONTEMPTUOUS
(ABRUPTLY HIS TONE BECOMES SLYLY TAUNTING.) 131 MANSNS
HE HAS A COMMON IRISH FACE, ITS EXPRESSION SULLEN, 4 MISBEG
OR SLYLY CUNNING.
(WINKS SLYLY.) MAYBE THEY WASN'T LIES. 11 POET
(SLYLY) IF HE HAS A CENT. 593 ROPE

SMACK
(HE SHAKES WITH LAUGHTER AND KISSES HIS WIFE A 513 DIFRNT
RESOUNDING SMACK.)

SMACKING
(HE PULLS HER TO HIM AND GIVES HER A SMACKING KISS221 AHWILD
ON THE EAR
AND SMACKING HIS LIPS WITH A DEEP »AA-AH« OF 462 CARIBE
SATISFACTION.)
(SMACKING HIS LIPS.) GOOD WINE, CORPORAL. 98 POET

SMACKS
(STARTLED--SMACKS HIS LIPS) I AIR HUNGRY/ 205 DESIRE
(HE SMACKS HIS LIPS LASCIVIOUSLY.) 130 ELECTR
THAT SMACKS OF ROMAN BLOOD/ 302 LAZARU
HE SMACKS HIS LIPS.) 37 POET

SMALL
AT RIGHT OF THIS DOORWAY, ANOTHER BOOKCASE, THIS 185 AHWILD
TIME A SMALL, OPEN ONE.
(SCENE--SITTING-ROOM OF THE MILLER HOME IN A LARGE185 AHWILD
SMALL-TOWN IN CONNECTICUT--
SMALL BLUE EYES AND THICK SANDY HAIR. 186 AHWILD
AND SO SMALL AT THEIR WIDE-CUFFED BOTTOMS 187 AHWILD
IN A ROUND-FACED, CUTE, SMALL-FEATURED, WIDE-EYED 187 AHWILD
FASHION.
HIS FEATURES ARE NEITHER LARGE NOR SMALL. 193 AHWILD
THE ROOM IS MUCH TOO SMALL FOR THE MEDIUM-PRICED, 210 AHWILD
FORMIDABLE DINING-ROOM SET,
A SMALL, DINGY ROOM, DIMLY LIGHTED BY TWO FLY- 236 AHWILD
SPECKED GLOBES
(SCENE--THE BACK ROOM OF A BAR IN A SMALL HOTEL-- 236 AHWILD
(SHYLY) A SMALL ONE, PLEASE. 238 AHWILD
YOU'VE SEEN A BIT OF THE WORLD, ENOUGH TO MAKE THE 84 BEYOND
FARM SEEM SMALL,
HER SMALL, REGULAR FEATURES ARE MARKED BY A 87 BEYOND
CERTAIN STRENGTH--
(THE SMALL SITTING ROOM OF THE MAYO FARMHOUSE 93 BEYOND
ABOUT NINE O'CLOCK SAME NIGHT.
(SHAKING HIS HEAD) ITS TOO SMALL. 97 BEYOND
ITS SMALL STRETCH OF LAWN DIVIDED BY THE DIRT PATH112 BEYOND
LEADING TO THE DOOR FROM THE
IT WASN'T THAT I HAVEN'T GUESSED HOW MEAN AND 127 BEYOND
SMALL YOU ARE--
I SUPPOSE IT DOES SEEM SMALL TO YOU NOW. 133 BEYOND
ANDREW ENTERS, FOLLOWED BY DOCTOR FAWCETT CARRYING153 BEYOND
A SMALL BLACK BAG.
HE AND SIX OTHERS MANAGED TO REACH A SMALL ISLAND 559 CROSS
ON THE FRINGE OF THE
A HUMOROUS, GOOD-NATURED MOUTH, SMALL EYES BEHIND 496 DAYS
HORN-RIMMED SPECTACLES.)
AT RIGHT OF CHAIR, A SMALL TABLE WITH A LAMP. 514 DAYS
THERE ARE WRINKLES ABOUT HER EYES, AND HER SMALL, 515 DAYS
FULL,
BY THE HEAD OF THE BED IS A SMALL STAND ON WHICH 553 DAYS
IS A READING LAMP
THE FIFE HOUSE, A SMALL BROWNISH-TINTED MODERN -0 DYNAMO
STUCCO BUNGALOW TYPE,
ALL THESE ROOMS ARE SMALL, THE ONES IN THE LIGHT -0 DYNAMO
HOME PARTICULARLY SO.
(THE EXTERIOR OF THE HOMES OF THE LIGHTS AND THE -0 DYNAMO
FIFES IN A SMALL TOWN IN
THREE SMALL HOOKED RUGS ARE ON THE FLOOR. 421 DYNAMO
A SMALL TABLE ON WHICH ARE STACKED HIS TEXTBOOKS, 421 DYNAMO
AND A CHAIR IN LEFT CORNER,
THE EYES SMALL AND BLUE-GRAY, THE REDDISH HAIR 422 DYNAMO
GRIZZLED AND BUSHY.
IT IS A THIN SMALL MOUTH, DETERMINED AND STUBBORN.422 DYNAMO
UNTIL HE COMES TO A SMALL GAP THAT IS ALMOST AT 427 DYNAMO
THE END OF THE HEDGE, FRONT.
THERE IS ONE SMALL WINDOW ON THE TOP FLOOR FRONT 427 DYNAMO
OF THE
FIFE IS A SMALL WIRY MAN OF FIFTY, OF SCOTCH-IRISH428 DYNAMO
ORIGIN,
HER MOUTH IS SMALL WITH FULL LIPS. 428 DYNAMO
THE PLANT IS COMPARATIVELY A SMALL ONE. 473 DYNAMO
THE SWITCHBOARD ROOM IS A SMALL COMPARTMENT TO THE486 DYNAMO
RIGHT OF THE DYNAMO ROOM,
ON THE OUTSKIRTS OF ONE OF THE SMALL NEW ENGLAND 2 ELECTR
SEAPORT TOWNS.
EAGER-LISTENER TYPE, WITH A SMALL ROUND FACE, 6 ELECTR
ROUND STUPID EYES.
IT IS SET IN A GRIM EXPRESSION, BUT HIS SMALL, 6 ELECTR
HER FEATURES ARE SMALL BUT CLEARLY MODELED. 12 ELECTR
A SMALL STAND, WITH A CANDLE ON IT, IS BY THE HEAD 58 ELECTR
OF THE BED ON THE LEFT.
AND IMMEDIATELY RETURNS WITH A SMALL BOX IN HER 61 ELECTR
HAND.
HILLS IS THE TYPE OF WELL-FED MINISTER OF A 67 ELECTR
PROSPEROUS SMALL-TOWN CONGREGATION--
HE IS AROUND SIXTY, SMALL AND WIZENED, WHITE HAIR 67 ELECTR
AND BEARD,
A SMALL COMPARTMENT, THE WALLS NEWLY PAINTED A 109 ELECTR
LIGHT BROWN.
THE OTHERS ARE ABNER SMALL, JOE SILVA AND IRA 129 ELECTR
MACKEL.

SMALL

(CONT'D.)
THESE FOUR--AMES, SMALL, SILVA AND MACKEL-- 129 ELECTR
SMALL IS A WIRY OLD MAN OF SIXTY-FIVE, A CLERK IN 129 ELECTR
A HARDWARE STORE.
(THE OTHERS LAUGH, THEIR MIRTH A BIT FORCED, BUT 131 ELECTR
SMALL LOOKS RATHER SICK.)
(HE GOES TOWARD THE PORTICO, SMALL FOLLOWING HIM, 131 ELECTR
(SMALL HANDS THE JUG TO HIM AND HE DRINKS 131 ELECTR
(IN THE MEANTIME SMALL TALKS TO SETH.) 131 ELECTR
SMALL LOOKS BITTER. 132 ELECTR
THE FRONT DOOR IS FLUNG OPEN AND SMALL COMES 134 ELECTR
TEARING OUT
(THEN TURNING ON SMALL--SCORNFULLY) 134 ELECTR
A SMALL PILE OF MANUSCRIPT IS STACKED BY HIS RIGHT149 ELECTR
HAND.
GIVING HER A STRANGE ASPECT OF LONELY, DETACHED, 323 GGBROW
SMALL FEMININITY.
(SCENE THE DESK AND A SECTION OF LOBBY OF A SMALL 7 HUGHIE
HOTEL
THE TYPE OF SMALL FRY GAMBLER AND HORSE PLAYER, 9 HUGHIE
HIS SMALL, PURSY MOUTH IS ALWAYS CROOKED 9 HUGHIE
LONG EXPERIENCE WITH GUESTS WHO STOP AT HIS DESK 11 HUGHIE
IN THE SMALL HOURS TO TALK
HUGO IS A SMALL MAN IN HIS LATE FIFTIES. 574 ICEMAN
IS ABOUT THE SAME SIZE AND AGE AS HUGO, A SMALL 575 ICEMAN
MAN.
BUCK TEETH IN A SMALL RABBIT MOUTH. 575 ICEMAN
HIS HAGGARD, DISSIPATED FACE HAS A SMALL NOSE, A 577 ICEMAN
POINTED CHIN,
(HE TAKES A SMALL WAD OF DOLLAR BILLS FROM HIS 585 ICEMAN
POCKET)
YOU COULD PUT ENGLAND ON IT, AND IT WOULD LOOK 605 ICEMAN
LIKE A FARMER'S SMALL GARDEN.
A BUTTON NOSE, A SMALL, PURSED MOUTH. 618 ICEMAN
CITIES AND SMALL TOWNS--NOT FLASHY BUT 619 ICEMAN
CONSPICUOUSLY SPIC AND SPAN.
AND HE POUNDS THE TABLE WITH A SMALL FIST) 627 ICEMAN
AT RIGHT, FRONT, IS A SMALL FREE-LUNCH COUNTER, 664 ICEMAN
FACING LEFT,
WITH SPIGGOTS AND A SMALL SHOW CASE OF BOTTLED 664 ICEMAN
GOODS.
POUNDS ON THE TABLE FRIGHTENEDLY WITH HIS SMALL 694 ICEMAN
FISTS)
(SHE PASSES A SMALL ROLL OF BILLS SHE HAS IN HER 700 ICEMAN
HAND OVER HER SHOULDER)
WELL, YOU KNOW WHAT A SMALL TOWN IS. 709 ICEMAN
AGAINST THE WALL BETWEEN THE DOORWAYS IS A SMALL 11 JOURNE
BOOKCASE,
A SMALL WICKER TABLE AND AN ORDINARY OAK DESK ARE 11 JOURNE
AGAINST THE WALL,
BIG FROGS IN A SMALL PUDDLE. 43 JOURNE
ONE SMALL DRINK WON'T HURT EDMUND. 68 JOURNE
(HE INDICATES THE SMALL BOOKCASE AT REAR.) 76 JOURNE
(HE PULLS OUT A SMALL ROLL OF BILLS FROM HIS PANTS 89 JOURNE
POCKET AND CAREFULLY SELECTS
SO MY WAIST WOULD BE AS SMALL AS POSSIBLE. 115 JOURNE
(HE INDICATES THE SMALL BOOKCASE AT REAR.) 135 JOURNE
(HE INDICATES THE SMALL BOOKCASE AGAIN.) 139 JOURNE
WHERE THE ONLY LIGHT CAME THROUGH TWO SMALL FILTHY149 JOURNE
WINDOWS,
GRAY IN THE FADING DAYLIGHT THAT ENTERS FROM THREE273 LAZARU
SMALL WINDOWS AT THE LEFT.
THE FATHER IS A SMALL, THIN, FEEBLE OLD MAN OF 275 LAZARU
OVER EIGHTY, MEEK AND PIOUS.
BETWEEN THIS AND THE HOUSE IS A SMALL RAISED 281 LAZARU
TERRACE,
YOU ARE SMALL AND WEAK LIKE OTHER MEN WHEN THE 319 LAZARU
TEST COMES/
IT IS PLACED IN A SMALL CLEARING, OVERGROWN WITH 1 MANSNS
RANK, MATTED GRASS.
AND A SMALL WINDOW AT LEFT OF DOOR, OVERLOOKS THE 1 MANSNS
LAKE.
HER FACE IS SMALL, ASTONISHINGLY YOUTHFUL. 2 MANSNS
SHE IS SMALL, NOT OVER FIVE FEET TALL, 2 MANSNS
SHE HAS SMALL EARS SET CLOSE TO HER HEAD, A WELL- 2 MANSNS
SHAPED HEAD ON A SLENDER NECK.
HER HANDS ARE SMALL WITH THIN, STRONG, TAPERING 3 MANSNS
FINGERS, AND SHE HAS TINY FEET.
TWO SMALL STONE BENCHES FACE RIGHT-FRONT AND LEFT- 25 MANSNS
FRONT.
THEY APPEAR MORE ENORMOUS THAN EVER IN HER SMALL 27 MANSNS
OVAL FACE.
HE KNEW THAT SIMON'S BUSINESS IS STILL A SMALL 34 MANSNS
LOCAL AFFAIR--
FROM THE HALL AT REAR THE SOUND OF SMALL BOYS' 43 MANSNS
ARGUING VOICES
THE ROOM IS SMALL, A TYPICAL ROOM OF THE PERIOD. 43 MANSNS
(SCOLDING HIM AS THOUGH HE WERE A SMALL BOY.) 49 MANSNS
THE ROOM IS SMALL, WELL-PROPORTIONED, PANELED IN 69 MANSNS
DARK WOOD.
THE WATER IN THE SMALL OVAL POOL BEFORE THE 95 MANSNS
SUMMER-HOUSE.
AT EXTREME LEFT-FRONT A SMALL TABLE AGAINST THE 117 MANSNS
WALL.
AT LEFT-REAR OF THE FIREPLACE IS A LONG SOFA WITH 117 MANSNS
A SMALL TABLE AND READING-LAMP
HER SMALL, GIRLISH FIGURE HAS GROWN SO TERRIBLY 161 MANSNS
EMACIATED THAT SHE GIVES
HER SMALL, DELICATE, OVAL FACE IS HAGGARD WITH 161 MANSNS
INNUMERABLE WRINKLES,
HE CARRIES A SMALL, SQUARE BAG. 347 MARCOM
MARCO'S FATHER, NICOLO, IS A SMALL THIN MIDDLE- 358 MARCOM
AGED MAN,
BUT HE IS TALL AND STOUT WITH A ROUND, JOVIAL FACE358 MARCOM
AND SMALL, CUNNING EYES.
FROM THE DARKNESS COMES THE SOUND OF A SMALL 373 MARCOM
TARTAR KETTLE-DRUM, ITS BEATS

SMALL

SMALL (CONT'D.)
IN THE BACK OF THE THRONE AND ABOVE IT IS A SMALL 373 MARCOM
IDOL MADE OF FELT AND CLOTH.
WHO LEFT THE COVER AND PULLS OUT A SMALL CHOW 391 MARCOM
PUPPY
IF HER HIGHNESS--MAJESTY--WILL ACCEPT A SMALL 391 MARCOM
TOKEN OF MY ESTEEM--
UNTIL A SMALL MULTITUDE IS GATHERED STANDING IN 405 MARCOM
SILENCE STARING UP AT THE POOP.
(WITH WILD DESPAIR PULLS OUT A SMALL DAGGER FROM 415 MARCOM
THE BOSOM OF HER DRESS)
AT RIGHT OF DOOR IS A SMALL WINDOW. 1 MISBEG
WITH ITS LONG UPPER LIP AND SMALL NOSE, THICK 3 MISBEG
BLACK EYEBROWS.
AT THE SMALL PRICE YOU OFFERED$ 31 MISBEG
AND WE'D BE DAMNED FOOLS IF WE DIDN'T FEAR THE 34 MISBEG
POSSIBILITY, HOWEVER SMALL IT IS,
GO GET THE BOTTLE AND ONE SMALL GLASS, OR HE'LL 52 MISBEG
NEVER STOP NAGGING ME.
I TELL YOU A SMALL GLASS AND YOU GIVE HIM A 53 MISBEG
BUCKET!
SMALL BLAME TO YOU. 64 MISBEG
THE LIVING ROOM IS SMALL, LOW-CEILINGED, WITH 71 MISBEG
FADED, FLY-SPECKED WALLPAPER.
THE PRATIES THEY GROW SMALL OVER HERE. 72 MISBEG
OH THE PRATIES THEY GROW SMALL OVER HERE, OVER 72 MISBEG
HERE. OH,
OH THE PRATIES THEY GROW SMALL AND WE DIG THEM IN 72 MISBEG
THE FALL AND WE EAT THEM SKINS
WELL, THANK GOD FOR SMALL FAVORS. 77 MISBEG
SMALL ALLOWANCE, AND HE LONGS TO GO BACK TO 84 MISBEG
BROADWAY AND HIS WHORES.
=UH, THE PRATIES THEY GROW SMALL, OVER HERE, OVER 101 MISBEG
HERE.= ETC.
=UH, THE PRATIES THEY GROW SMALL, OVER HERE, OVER 103 MISBEG
HERE.=
A SMALL ONE FOR HERSELF) 115 MISBEG
AS SMALL AND DAINTY AND PRETTY-- 117 MISBEG
BEYOND THE BAR DOOR A SMALL CABINET IS FASTENED TO 7 POET
THE WALL.
EXCEPT THE SMALL ONES IN THE FOREGROUND AT LEFT. 8 POET
SMALL WONDER. YOU'D THE DIVIL'S OWN LOAD WHEN YOU 8 POET
LEFT AT TWO THIS MORNIN'.
SHE HAS SMALL EARS SET CLOSE TO HER WELL-SHAPED 15 POET
HEAD, AND A SLENDER NECK.
TAKES A SMALL ACCOUNT BOOK FROM IT, AND BEGINS 16 POET
CHECKING FIGURES.)
WELL, SMALL BLAME TO HIM, HE HASN'T SEEN JAMIE 21 POET
SINCE--
BUT IF YOU INSIST--{HE POURS A DRINK--A SMALL 46 POET
ONE--HIS HAND QUITE STEADY NOW.)
SHE IS SMALL, A LITTLE OVER FIVE FEET TALL, WITH A 67 POET
FRAGILE, YOUTHFUL FIGURE.
IT IS SMALL, WITH HIGH CHEEKBONES, WEDGE-SHAPED, 67 POET
NARROWING FROM A BROAD FOREHEAD
FLORID FACE, AND SMALL, BLUE EYES. 116 POET
I HAVE SMALL LIKING FOR YOUR PROFESSION, SIR. 118 POET
(HE POURS A SMALL DRINK AND HANDS IT TO HER.) 134 POET
SMALL WONDER HE DID/ 143 POET
IT'S ONLY A SMALL MILL AND THAT'S WHAT TEMPTS 146 POET
SIMON.
SMALL THANKS TO HIM/ 159 POET
(SITTING DOWN AT REAR OF THE SMALL TABLE AT LEFT 160 POET
FRONT--ANGRILY.)
(DUMPS MELODY DOWN ON THE NEAREST CHAIR AT LEFT OF164 POET
THE SMALL TABLE--
THE LIBRARY OF PROFESSOR LEEDS' HOME IN A SMALL 3 STRANG
UNIVERSITY TOWN IN NEW ENGLAND.
IT IS A SMALL ROOM WITH A LOW CEILING. 3 STRANG
HIS FACE, PREPOSSESSING IN SPITE OF ITS TOO-SMALL, 6 STRANG
OVER-REFINED FEATURES.
HE IS A SMALL, SLENDER MAN OF FIFTY-FIVE, HIS HAIR 6 STRANG
GRAY.
THE SITTING ROOM OF A SMALL HOUSE EVANS HAS RENTED 90 STRANG
(INDIFFERENTLY BUT WITH AUTHORITY, LIKE A 94 STRANG
GOVERNESS TO A SMALL BOY)
HE CARRIES A SMALL, EXPENSIVE YACHT'S MODEL OF A 149 STRANG
SLOOP WITH THE SAILS SET.
WE'LL GIVE YOU A SMALL ONE. 164 STRANG
IN THE REAR, THE TERRACE OVERLOOKS A SMALL HARBOR 184 STRANG
WITH THE OCEAN BEYOND.
IN THE LEFT WALL, CENTER, A SMALL WINDOW WITH A 470 WELDED
TORN DARK SHADE PULLED DOWN.
HER SMALL EYES HAVE A GLAZED LOOK. 471 WELDED

SMALL'S
SMALL'S EXCITED VOICE CAN BE HEARD RECEDING 134 ELECTR
MANNER SMALL'S ALWAYS BRAGGIN' HOW BRAVE HE IS-- 135 ELECTR

SMALLER
AND ANOTHER SMALLER ONE IS PLACED ON THE FLOOR TO 173 EJONES
SERVE AS A FOOTSTOOL.
A SMALLER ARCHED DOORWAY LEADING TO THE LIVING 173 EJONES
QUARTERS OF THE PALACE.
FLANKED BY SMALLER PORTRAITS OF ALEXANDER HAMILTON 28 ELECTR
AND JOHN MARSHALL.
SMALLER ARCHES IN THE MIDDLE OF THE SIDE WALLS 335 LAZARU
LEAD INTO OTHER ROOMS.
SMALLER, MORE INTIMATE THAN THE ONE AT CAMBALUC, 384 MARCOM
FIGURE IN THE ROOM, WHICH APPEARS SMALLER AND 95 POET
DINGIER IN THE CANDLELIGHT.
THERE IS A SMALLER TABLE AT CENTER, AND A CHAISE 137 STRANG
LONGUE.

SMALLEST
UNLESS THE SMALLEST BET YOU COULD MAKE--ONE WHITE 32 HUGHIE
CHIP/ WAS A HUNDRED DOLLARS.

SMART
YOU'RE GETTING TOO SMART/ 221 AHWILD
(HER EYES NARROWING) AIN'T YOU SMART/ 15 ANNA

SMART (CONT'D.)
(WITH A CERTAIN PRIDE) DEY VAS ALL SMART SEAMAN, 27 ANNA
TOO--A ONE.
YOU MUST BE SMART, SURELY. 35 ANNA
(WITH A FORCED SMILE) YOU MEN FOLKS ARE TOO SMART 95 BEYOND
TO LIVE, AREN'T YOU$
YE BETTER LOOK SMART AN' GIT UPSTAIRS. 245 DESIRE
WALL, YE PLAYED SMART. 251 DESIRE
AND A DAMN GOOD MAN AND AS SMART A SKIPPER AS 505 DIFRNT
THERE BE IN THESE PARTS/
DON'T LET THIS SMART-ALECK DICK GET FUNNY WITH 718 ICEMAN
YOU.
DON'T BE SO DAMN SMART, JACK. 529 INZONE
THEY AIN'T ARF SMART BLEEDERS/ 529 INZONE
LOOKS FINALLY AT THE BUDDHA--IN A SMART-ALECK 370 MARCOM
TONE)
SHE IS DRESSED IN SMART SPORT CLOTHES. 13 STRANG
ALL I MEANT WAS THAT GHOSTS REMIND ME OF MEN'S 51 STRANG
SMART CRACK ABOUT WOMEN.

SMARTEST
HE'S THE SMARTEST SKIPPER OUT O' THIS PORT AND 513 DIFRNT
YOU'D OUGHT TO BE PROUD YOU'D GOT

SMARTLY
SHE WEARS A GREEN SATIN DRESS, SMARTLY CUT AND 9 ELECTR
EXPENSIVE.
(SHE RAPS HIM SMARTLY, BUT LIGHTLY, 73 MISBEG

SMARTY
IS THAT SO, SMARTY$ 274 AHWILD
(TENDERLY PLAYFUL) I WASN'T LOOKING FOR ANDY, 87 BEYOND
SMARTY, IF THAT'S WHAT YOU MEAN.

SMASH
TO SMASH YOUR SKULL LIKE A ROTTEN EGG. 60 ANNA
(THEN VIOLENTLY) I'LL GO SMASH MY FIST IN HER 211 DESIRE
FACE/
YOU'VE GOT TO HELP ME SMASH IT DOWN/ 55 ELECTR
SMASH OPEN EVERYTHING IN HIS STATEROOM. 114 ELECTR
I HIT HIM SMASH IN YAW, MY GOTT/ 208 HA APE
DEY SMASH TROU, DON'T DEY$ 215 HA APE
WE SPLIT DAT UP AND SMASH TROU--TWENTY-FIVE KNOTS 217 HA APE
A HOUR/
THERE IS A SPATTERING SMASH 245 HA APE
(VENGEFULLY) DEN I'LL BE DE ONE TO SMASH DE 674 ICEMAN
GLASS.
WELL, BY THE ETERNAL, I'LL SMASH IT SO THERE'LL BE191 MANSNS
NOTHING LEFT TO TEMPT ME/
THE LONGING IN YOUR HEART THAT I'D SMASH THE 191 MANSNS
COMPANY INTO SMITHEREENS
(HE DRAWS BACK HIS FIST TO SMASH GADSBY IN THE 122 POET
FACE,
I'D SMASH YOUR BRAINS OUT FOR A NICKEL/ 597 ROPE
I'LL SMASH IT UP/... 129 STRANG
I CAN SMASH YOUR CALCULATING GAME FOR YOU/ 132 STRANG
OR I'D SMASH IT FIRST CHANCE I GOT/...) 138 STRANG
AFTER ALL, HE IS MY SON AND I'D PREFER HE DIDN'T 144 STRANG
SMASH IT BEFORE MY EYES/
SHE'LL SMASH THEIR ENGAGEMENT IF SHE CAN... 161 STRANG

SMASHED
SMASHED EVERYTHING AND STOLE TWO HUNDRED DOLLARS 105 ELECTR
OFF HER SKIPPER.
YOU'RE A BIT SMASHED BUT THAT WAS DONE IN A HAND- 430 MARCOM
TO-HAND FIGHT WITH PIRATES.
STRAIN HIMSELF WHEN HE SMASHED IT, 144 STRANG
AS HE'S SMASHED EVERY PRESENT OF MINE IN THE PAST/144 STRANG

SMASHES
AND HE SMASHES HIS FIST DOWN ON THE MARBLE TOP OF 542 'ILE
THE SIDEBOARD)
(HE SMASHES HIS FIST ON THE TABLE WITH A BANG.) 13 ANNA
(SOMEONE DROPS A BOTTLE ON DECK AND IT SMASHES.) 471 CARIBE
HE DELIBERATELY THROWS HIS WHISKEY GLASS ON THE 673 ICEMAN
FLOOR AND SMASHES IT.) HEY/
AND SMASHES IT BACK AGAIN) 500 VOYAGE
(SPRINGING TO ACTION, SMASHES IVAN'S DERBY OVER 500 VOYAGE
HIS EARS)

SMASHING
(SUDDENLY SPRINGING TO HIS FEET AND SMASHING HIS 9 ANNA
FIST ON THE TABLE IN A RAGE)
(SNORTS) AND HAVE YOU SINGING AGAIN IN A MINUTE 76 MISBEG
AND SMASHING THE FURNITURE--
(HIS PENT-UP RAGE BURSTS OUT--SMASHING HIS FIST ON122 POET
THE TABLE.)

SMEARY
THE FLOOR IS CARPETED IN A SMEARY BROWN WITH A 48 STRANG
DARK RED DESIGN BLURRED INTO IT.

SMELL
THE MERE SMELL OF IT SEEMS TO DRIVE HER FRANTIC/ 232 AHWILD
WELL, YOU OUGHT TO SEE IT, AND SMELL IT/ 132 BEYOND
'WAY IN THE MIDDLE OF THE LAND WHERE YUH'D NEVER 486 CARDIF
SMELL THE SEA OR SEE A SHIP.
THEY SMELL OF EARTH. 204 DESIRE
CAN YOU SMELL THE PERFUME OF THE LILACS, AMELIAS 425 DYNAMO
(HE BREATHES IN THE SPRING) (EGEE, THOSE LILACS 425 DYNAMO
SMELL SWEET...
AS VESPASIAN REMARKED, THE SMELL OF ALL WHISKEY IS596 ICEMAN
SWEET.
I BEGIN TO SMELL ALL THE RATS IN CATHAY/ 382 MARCOM
THE GUESTS GAZE, SMELL, TASTE.) 429 MARCOM
WITH YOUR FUNNY NOSE COCKED SO YOU WON'T SMELL THE 63 MISBEG
POOR PEOPLE.
NOW THERE'S THE SMELL OF MONEY AROUND/ 96 MISBEG
THEN ABRUPTLY THE SMELL OF WHISKEY ON HIS BREATH 71 POET
BRINGS HER TO HERSELF.
SMELL OF IODOFORM IN THE COOL HALLS... 4 STRANG

SMELLED
I THOUGHT THEIR BREATHS SMELLED DAMN QUEER. 473 CARIBE
I SMELLED IT IN THE AIR FIRST THING I GOT UP THIS 174 EJONES
MORNIN'.

SMELLIN'

IT'S WA'M DOWN T' THE BARN--NICE SMELLIN' AN' 231 DESIRE
WARM--WITH THE COWS.

SMELLING

I'D HAVE NO CHANCE IF I WENT TO THE D. A.'S OFFICE674 ICEMAN
SMELLING OF BOOZE.

IS THE WARM EARTH SMELLING OF NIGHT 310 LAZARU

SMELLING YOUR HAIR, FEELING YOUR SOFT BODY-- 130 STRANG

SMELLS

HE STOOPS DOWN AND PICKS IT UP AND SMELLS OF IT.) 473 CARIBE
(SNIFFING) I SMELLS BACON/ 205 DESIRE

HER MOUTH'S WA'M, HER ARMS'RE WA'M, SHE SMELLS 211 DESIRE
LIKE A WA'M PLOWED FIELD.

THEN IT MUST BE THE AIR ITSELF SMELLS OF WHISKEY 45 MISBEG
TODAY.

SMELLS OUT LOVE... 124 STRANG

SMILE

(WITH A GRIM SMILE) HERE IT COMES, THE TROUBLE 543 'ILE
YOU SPOKE OF, MR. SLOCUM.

(COUNTS ON HER FINGERS--THEN MURMURS WITH A RAPT 548 'ILE
SMILE)

SHE STARES UP AT HIM WITH A STUPID EXPRESSION, A 551 'ILE
VAGUE SMILE ON HER LIPS.

SHE HAS VIVACITY AND A FETCHING SMILE, 186 AHWILD

EVEN LILY CANNOT SUPPRESS A SMILE.) 192 AHWILD

(HIDING A SMILE BEHIND HIS HAND) 197 AHWILD

(TARTLY, BUT EVIDENTLY SUPPRESSING HER USUAL SMILE198 AHWILD
WHERE HE IS CONCERNED)

(WITH A GRIM SMILE) HM. 205 AHWILD

MILLER ADDS WITH A KINDLY SMILE) 208 AHWILD

(FORCING A SMILE) I DON'T SEE HOW YOU STAND ME-- 212 AHWILD

AS SOON AS SHE IS GONE, THE SMILE FADES FROM 214 AHWILD
LILY'S LIPS.

(HE FORCES A CRUEL SMILE TO HIS LIPS) 215 AHWILD

(THEN WITH A TEASING SMILE AT RICHARD) 220 AHWILD

A HUMOROUS SMILE HOVERS AT THE CORNERS OF HER 220 AHWILD
LIPS)

LILY FORCES A SMILE.) 222 AHWILD

MILLER CONCEALS A SMILE. 225 AHWILD

MILLER LOOKS AROUND AT THEM WITH A WEAK SMILE, HIS227 AHWILD
DIGNITY NOW RUFFLED A BIT.)

(REALLY HURT, FORCES A FEEBLE SMILE TO HIS LIPS 230 AHWILD
AND PRETENDS TO BE A GOOD SPORT

(WITH A SAD, SELF-PITYING SMILE AT HIS WIFE) 231 AHWILD

THEN HE FORCES A SCORNING SMILE TO HIS LIPS.) 235 AHWILD

(PROUD OF HIMSELF-WITH A SHY SMILE) 240 AHWILD

(FORCING A SICKLY, TWITCHING SMILE) 256 AHWILD

(WITH A SHEEPISH SMILE) DARN HIM/ 260 AHWILD

(WITH A SINISTER SMILE) IT'S LUCKY THERE AREN'T 271 AHWILD
ANY OF GENERAL GABLER'S PISTOLS

(WITH A REASSURING SMILE) NO... 293 AHWILD

BY A SMILE OF SHY UNDERSTANDING AND SYMPATHY. 297 AHWILD

(THEN THRHEN THROWING OFF HIS MELANCHOLY, WITH A 298 AHWILD
LOVING SMILE AT HER)

(FORCING A SMILE) SAILOR VAS ALL RIGHT FALLAR, 9 ANNA
BUT NOT FOR MARRY GEL.

(MOLLIFIED--WITH A SMILE) WELL, I WOULDN'T BLAME 14 ANNA
YOU, AT THAT.

SHE TURNS TO MARTHY WITH A FRIENDLY SMILE) 14 ANNA

(THEN AS LARRY TURNS TO GO, FORCING A WINNING 14 ANNA
SMILE AT HIM)

(SURPRISED AND PLEASED BY HIS EAGERNESS--WITH A 22 ANNA
SMILE)

(THEN SEEING HIS CRESTFALLEN LOOK--FORCING A 23 ANNA
SMILE)

AS SHE HEARS HIM COMING, ANNA HASTILY DRIES HER 24 ANNA
EYES, TRIES TO SMILE.

(THEN SEEING THE HURT EXPRESSION ON HER FATHER'S 26 ANNA
FACE, SHE FORCES A SMILE)

(CONCEALING A SMILE--AMUSED BY THIS BOYISH 36 ANNA
BOASTING OF HIS)

(TURNING TO HIM AGAIN--FORCING A SMILE) 37 ANNA

(WITH A FAINT TRACE OF A SMILE) 42 ANNA

(WATCHING HIM INTENTLY--A MOCKING SMILE ON HIS 49 ANNA
LIPS)

(WITH A RELIEVED SMILE) OH--THE OLD STUFF, EH5 50 ANNA

WITH A REASSURING SMILE) 50 ANNA

LOOKING FROM ONE TO THE OTHER OF THE TWO MEN WITH 56 ANNA
HER HARD, MOCKING SMILE.

AS HE GOES ON, A BITTER SMILE COMES OVER HER FACE) 65 ANNA

(RAISING HER FACE--FORCING A WAN SMILE) 67 ANNA

(WITH A SMILE THAT IS HALF SAD) 85 BEYOND

(WITH A WRY ATTEMPT AT A SMILE) 88 BEYOND

(WITH A SMILE) THERE WAS ALL THE MYSTERY IN THE 89 BEYOND
WORLD TO ME THEN ABOUT THAT--

(WITH A SMILE) YOU SEE, 89 BEYOND

(WITH A SMILE) PERHAPS I STILL DO BELIEVE IN THEM. 90 BEYOND

(SHE LIFTS UP HER HEAD AND LOOKS INTO HIS EYES 91 BEYOND
WITH A TREMULOUS SMILE)

(THE OTHERS SMILE BUT IMMEDIATELY RELAPSE INTO 95 BEYOND
EXPRESSIONS OF GLOOM AGAIN.)

(WITH A FORCED SMILE) YOU MEN FOLKS ARE TOO SMART 95 BEYOND
TO LIVE, AREN'T YOUS

(HIS FACE TENSE AND DRAWN COMES FORWARD AND HOLDS 101 BEYOND
OUT HIS HAND, FORCING A SMILE)

(AS THE OTHERS SMILE--SULKILY) 104 BEYOND

(AS RUTH DOESN'T ANSWER OR SMILE HE OPENS HIS BOOK122 BEYOND
AND RESUMES HIS READING.

(WITH A CONCILIATING SMILE) THEN PUNISH ME, RUTH.122 BEYOND

(WITH AN AFFECTIONATE SMILE) 125 BEYOND

(LOOKING AT HER WITH A FORCED SMILE) 129 BEYOND

(KISSING HER--WITH A SMILE) THERE/ 129 BEYOND

(WITH A SMILE) I COME UP HERE NOW BECAUSE IT'S 131 BEYOND
THE COOLEST PLACE ON THE FARM.

(WITH AN EMBARRASSED SMILE) NO, ANDY, I-- 133 BEYOND

RUTH LOOKS AFTER THEM FOR A MOMENT, FROWNING--THEN136 BEYOND
TURNS TO ANDY WITH A SMILE)

(FORCING A SMILE) HE WHO HESITATES, YOU KNOW. 141 BEYOND

(AFTER A PAUSE--WITH A TENDER SMILE) 148 BEYOND

SMILE (CONT'D.)

HE MAKES A PITIFUL ATTEMPT TO SMILE) 151 BEYOND

(WITH A GRIM SMILE) A DYING MAN HAS SOME RIGHTS, 159 BEYOND
HASN'T HE5

(WITH AN AFFECTIONATE SMILE) FINE/ THANK YOU/ 160 BEYOND

ROBERT REGARDS HIM WITH AN AFFECTIONATE SMILE.) 160 BEYOND

(WITH A MOCKING SMILE) LATER ON/ 162 BEYOND

(WITH AN IRONICAL SMILE) THE DOCTOR TOLD ME TO GO167 BEYOND
TO THE FAR-OFF PLACES--

WITH A WAN SMILE) 167 BEYOND

(WITH A BITTER SMILE) 486 CARDIF

(WITH AN IRONIC SMILE) GRAND LARCENY, BY GOD/ 462 CARIBE

(WITH A FOOLISH SMILE) THEN I'LL DRINK ONE FOR 467 CARIBE
YOU.

(WITH A RELIEVED SMILE CARRIES OVER THE LANTERN) 557 CROSS

(WITH AN ANSWERING SMILE) TREASURE, OF COURSE. 560 CROSS

(WITH A TWISTED SMILE) YOU FORGET I'M HEIR TO THE560 CROSS
TREASURE, TOO.

(DUMBFOUNDED--FORCING A SMILE) 499 DAYS

(GIVES THE PRIEST AN AMUSED SMILE) 504 DAYS

YOU KNOW I WOULDN'T--(WITH A NATURAL, BOYISHLY 505 DAYS
AFFECTIONATE SMILE)

(FORCING A SMILE) IS THAT THE SUSPICIOUS GUARDIANS06 DAYS
LOOKS

(FORCING A SMILE) AND PLEASE DON'T BRING UP THOSE512 DAYS
COINCIDENCES BEFORE ELSA.

(FORCING A SMILE) YOU'RE WASTING WORRY. 512 DAYS

(WITH A TWISTED SMILE) I THOUGHT WE WEREN'T GOING517 DAYS
TO TALK ABOUT MY TROUBLES/

(THEN CONTROLLING HERSELF--FORCING A SMILE) 522 DAYS

(COMING TO HER, HIS FACE WEARING ITS MOST CORDIAL,525 DAYS
POKER-FACED SMILE)

JOHN'S CORDIAL SMILE VANISHES AND HIS FACE TAKES 526 DAYS
ON A TENSE, HARRIED LOOK.

(FORCING A SMILE) DON'T KNOW WHAT'S THE MATTER 528 DAYS
WITH ME.

SHE SITS DOWN BESIDE HIM--WITH A SMILE) 528 DAYS

(FORCING A SMILE) CONFESS/ 529 DAYS

(TURNS TO HER, FORCING A SMILE) 536 DAYS

HE FORCES A SMILE AND ADOPTS A JOKING TONE) 539 DAYS

(AS IF SHE HADN'T HEARD--WITH A QUEER SMILE) 225 DESIRE

(WITH A QUEER SMILE) YE'D BE TURNED FREE, TOO. 233 DESIRE

(WITH A CAJOLING SMILE) YE'RE A STRONG MAN YET, 234 DESIRE
HAIN'T YES

(SHE GIVES A QUEER SMILE.) 238 DESIRE

(THEN SHAKING HER HAND OFF HIS ARM--WITH A BITTER 259 DESIRE
SMILE)

(FORCING A SMILE--ADORINGLY) 267 DESIRE

(LOOKS INTO HER EYES AND FORCES A TREMBLING 267 DESIRE
SMILE)

HE SWALLOWS PAINFULLY SEVERAL TIMES--FORCES A WEAK268 DESIRE
SMILE AT LAST)

(WITH A SMILE) OH, I HAVEN'T NO STRICT RELIGIOUS 495 DIFRNT
NOTIONS ABOUT IT.

(FORCED TO SMILE--PUSHING HIM AWAY) 499 DIFRNT

RESOLVED TO FIND OUT WHAT IS BACK OF ALL THIS BY 502 DIFRNT
HOOK OR CROOK--FORCING A SMILE)

(HUSKILY, TRYING TO FORCE A SMILE) 505 DIFRNT

(TRYING TO SMILE) NOTHING. 506 DIFRNT

(FORCING A SMILE) I GUESS THERE'S WORSE THINGS 517 DIFRNT
THAN BEING AN OLD MAID.

(WITH A MOURNFUL SMILE) YOU MIGHT JUST AS WELL 518 DIFRNT
SAY FOR LIFE, CALEB.

(WITH A COY SMILE) AND BESIDES, BENNY, 533 DIFRNT

(WITH AN AFFECTIONATE SMILE) 537 DIFRNT

ADA SITS DOWN AT RIGHT, WATCHING HER FATHER WITH A430 DYNAMO
CHALLENGING SMILE.)

(WITH A SAD SMILE OF SCORN FOR HERSELF) 455 DYNAMO

(HER EYES MOONING AT HIM, WITH A SIMPLE, PLEASED 457 DYNAMO
SMILE)

(WITH A COLD SMILE) WELL, NEVER MIND WHAT--BUT 458 DYNAMO
YOU CAN TELL HER I'VE CHANGED.

(WALKS TOWARD HER, THE SMILE FROZEN ON HIS LIPS, 459 DYNAMO
HIS EYES FIXED ON HERS)

(WITH A SNAGGER AND A COLD SMILE ON HIS LIPS HE 459 DYNAMO
WALKS THROUGH THE GAP JUST AS

(WITH A TEASING SMILE) ADA, I'VE GOT A BIG 459 DYNAMO
SURPRISE FOR YOU.

HE SEES HIS FATHER AND A SNEERING SMILE 462 DYNAMO
IMMEDIATELY COMES TO HIS LIPS)

(IMMEDIATELY RESENTFUL--WITH HIS COLD SMILE) 467 DYNAMO

THERE IS A FIXED SMILE OF TRIUMPH AND GRATIFIED 468 DYNAMO
VANITY ON HIS LIPS,

THEN FORCES THE COLD SMILE TO HIS LIPS) 468 DYNAMO

(WITH HIS COLD SMILE) SURE/ 468 DYNAMO

(WITH HIS COLD SMILE) YOU MEAN FORGIVES US FOR 470 DYNAMO
WHAT WE DID TONIGHT5

MRS. FIFE LOOKS AFTER HIM WITH A PLACID SMILE-- 479 DYNAMO

(SHE FORCES A SMILE BUT HER TONE IS REALLY HURT.) 13 ELECTR

(STARING AT HER WITH A QUESTIONING DREAD--FORCING 18 ELECTR
A SCORNFUL SMILE)

(WITH A GRIM SMILE) SHE DIDN'T SUCCEED, AS YOU 26 ELECTR
NOTICE/

(WITH A GRIM SMILE) I KNOW. 36 ELECTR

(THEN WITH A MOCKING SMILE) 46 ELECTR

(WITH AN EASY SMILE.) YOU HAD BETTER ASK VINNIE/ 50 ELECTR

(THEN WITH A TWITCH OF THE LIPS, AS IF SHE WERE 52 ELECTR
RESTRAINING A DERISIVE SMILE)

(HE FORCES A STRAINED SMILE) 53 ELECTR

(RALLYING HERSELF AND FORCING A SMILE) 72 ELECTR

(FORCING A SMILE) IS IS DIFFERENT5 76 ELECTR

(SOMETHING LIKE A GRIM SMILE OF SATISFACTION FORMS 77 ELECTR
ON LAVINIA'S LIPS.

(FORCING A WAN SMILE) THE HAPPINESS OF SEEING YOU 80 ELECTR
AGAIN

(ROUSING HERSELF--TURNS TO FORCE A SMILE AT HIM) 81 ELECTR

(WITH A SMILE) I CAN'T PICTURE VINNIE BEING THAT 81 ELECTR
SOFT.

SMILE

SMILE (CONT'D.)
(WITH A WRY SMILE) WE'D ALL FORGOTTEN HE'S DEAD, 81 ELECTR
HADN'T WE$
(AVOIDING HIS EYES--FORCING A SMILE) 82 ELECTR
(WITH A TENDER SMILE) WE HAD A SECRET LITTLE 85 ELECTR
WORLD OF OUR OWN IN THE OLD DAYS.
(THEN GLANCING AT THE DEAD MAN WITH A KINDLY 94 ELECTR
AMUSED SMILE)
(THEN WITH A DAY SMILE) DEATH SITS SO NATURALLY 94 ELECTR
ON YOU/
(THEN FORCING A WRY SMILE) I'LL GIVE UP THE SEA. 112 ELECTR
(ENTERS FROM LEFT--WITH A KINDLY SMILE) 117 ELECTR
(ROUSING HERSELF--FORCING A SMILE) 118 ELECTR
(FORCING A SMILE) THEY SEEM TO HAVE DESERTED ME. 118 ELECTR
(ROUSING HIMSELF, FORCES A SMILE 144 ELECTR
(MAKING A WARNING SIGN TO PETER NOT TO TAKE THIS 144 ELECTR
SERIOUSLY--FORCING A SMILE)
(WITH A STRANGE SMILE) I WAS DEAD THEN. 144 ELECTR
SHE FORCES A SMILE AND A MOTHERLY TONE) 145 ELECTR
STARES AT HIM FRIGHTENEDLY, HE SMILES AN UGLY 146 ELECTR
TAUNTING SMILE)
SIMPLY BECAUSE HE USED TO SMILE AT ME AND I SMILED147 ELECTR
BACK.
(TURNING TO PETER AND HOLDING OUT HIS HAND, HIS 148 ELECTR
SMILE BECOMING GHASTLY)
(PULLS HIMSELF UP SHARPLY--CONFUSEDLY, FORCING A 148 ELECTR
SICKLY SMILE)
A GRIM SMILE OF SATISFACTION TWITCHES HIS LIPS 149 ELECTR
(FORCING A SMILE) GOOD GRACIOUS, WHY WOULDN'T I 150 ELECTR
BE$
(FORCING A SMILE AGAIN AND TURNING AWAY FROM HIM) 150 ELECTR
(AGAIN CONTROLLING HERSELF WITH A GREAT EFFORT, 151 ELECTR
FORCING A SMILE)
(THEN WITH A BITTER SMILE) BUT I KNOW THE REASON 151 ELECTR
WELL ENOUGH.
(WITH A TWISTED SMILE) REMEMBER ONLY THAT DEAD 164 ELECTR
HERO AND NOT HIS ROTTING GHOST/
(THEN A BIT UNEASILY--FORCING A SMILE) 175 ELECTR
WITH A GRIM WEATHER SMILE) 178 ELECTR
(WITH A STRANGE CRUEL SMILE OF GLOATING OVER THE 178 ELECTR
YEARS OF SELF-TORTURE)
HE IS BLOND AND BLUE-EYED, WITH A LIKEABLE SMILE 257 GGBROW
AND A FRANK GOOD-HUMORED FACE.
(THEN MECHANICALLY FLASHING A TRADE SMILE AT 280 GGBROW
BILLY)
(WITH A STRANGE SMILE) LET'S SAY, NEVER ANYTHING 280 GGBROW
LESS/
WITH A GRATEFUL SMILE) 285 GGBROW
(THEN WITH A TWISTED SMILE) BUT THEY WOULDN'T SEE286 GGBROW
ME.
(FORCING A TIRED SMILE) I SUPPOSE SO, DION. 291 GGBROW
(FORCING A SMILE) BUT PERHAPS I WOULD. 292 GGBROW
(THEN, WISHING TO LEAVE ON A PLEASANT CHANGE OF 305 GGBROW
SUBJECT--FORCING A SMILE)
(FORCING A SMILE) WELL, DON'T LET IT BURN YOUR 316 GGBROW
INSIDES OUT/
BEGIN TO OPEN--(SHE LOOKS AROUND HER WITH A RAPT 323 GGBROW
SMILE)
(WITH A TRIUMPHANT SMILE) I HAVE IT--BOTH HIS AND220 HA APE
THE CHIEF ENGINEER'S.
(FORCING A SMILE) TWO ARE BETTER THAN ONE. 221 HA APE
(FORCING A SMILE) WELL, YOU'LL FIND IT NOT ENOUGH221 HA APE
WHERE YOU'RE GOING.
(WITH A SCORNFUL SMILE) YOU DON'T CARE TO 221 HA APE
SHOULDER THIS RESPONSIBILITY ALONE.
MILDRED TURNS A MOCKING SMILE ON HER AUNT) 222 HA APE
IN A WELCOMING THE-PATRON-IS-ALWAYS-RIGHT GRIMACE, 8 HUGHIE
INTENDED AS A SMILE.
(WITH A COMPLIANT, UNINTERESTED SMILE.) 10 HUGHIE
BUT HE COOKED UP A SMILE AND SAID, =HELLO, ERIE, 30 HUGHIE
(FORCING A SMILE) I GET YOU. 585 ICEMAN
(WITH A STRANGE SMILE) I DON'T REMEMBER IT THAT 590 ICEMAN
WAY.
AS IF HE SUDDENLY WERE AFRAID OF HIS OWN 593 ICEMAN
THOUGHTS--FORCING A SMILE)
WITH A GENTLE DRUNKEN SMILE.) 599 ICEMAN
HIS EXPRESSION IS FIXED IN A SALESMAN'S WINNING 618 ICEMAN
SMILE.
HE SPEAKS WITH A DROWSY, AFFECTIONATELY 628 ICEMAN
ENCOURAGING SMILE.
(INSTANTLY THEY FORGIVE HIM AND SMILE 655 ICEMAN
AFFECTIONATELY.)
HOPE GETS TO HIS FEET RELUCTANTLY, WITH A FORCED 659 ICEMAN
SMILE.
(HE FORCES A FEEBLE SMILE--THEN WEARILY) 691 ICEMAN
(HE PAUSES--THEN WITH A DERISIVE SMILE) 720 ICEMAN
THEY SMILE AND EXCHANGE MATERNALLY AMUSED 725 ICEMAN
GLANCES.)
(WITH A SICKLY SMILE) HELL/ 523 INZONE
(FORCING A SMILE.) I HAVE$ 16 JOURNE
HER SMILE VANISHES AND HER MANNER BECOMES SELF- 20 JOURNE
CONSCIOUS.)
SHE FORCES A SMILE.) 27 JOURNE
AND THERE IS AN OLD BOYISH CHARM IN HIS LOVING 28 JOURNE
SMILE AT HIS MOTHER.)
(TO JAMIE, FORCING A SMILE.) 40 JOURNE
(CHANGING THE SUBJECT--FORCING A SMILE.) 41 JOURNE
SHE TURNS TO HIM, HER LIPS SET IN A WELCOMING, 42 JOURNE
MOTHERLY SMILE.)
(FORCING A SMILE.) ALL RIGHT, DEAR. 48 JOURNE
(WITH A REMOTE, AMUSED SMILE.) 62 JOURNE
(WITH A STRANGE DERISIVE SMILE.) 75 JOURNE
AND A RAPT, TENDER, GIRLISH SMILE.) 105 JOURNE
(HUSKILY, TRYING TO FORCE A SMILE.) 114 JOURNE
(TURNS ON HIM--WITH A STRANGELY TRIUMPHANT, 117 JOURNE
TAUNTING SMILE.)
(FORCING A SMILE.) DEVIL TAKE YOUR PESSIMISM. 131 JOURNE
(CONCEALING HIS SMILE--CASUALLY.) 149 JOURNE

SMILE (CONT'D.)
(WITH A LOOSE, TWISTED SMILE.) 151 JOURNE
IT IS A MARBLE MASK OF GIRLISH INNOCENCE, THE 170 JOURNE
MOUTH CAUGHT IN A SHY SMILE.
(WITH A SWEET SMILE OF AFFECTIONATE TRUST.) 171 JOURNE
(HE SHYLY EAGER, TRUSTING SMILE IS ON HER LIPS AS 175 JOURNE
SHE TALKS ALOUD TO HERSELF.)
UNDERSTANDING SMILE OF SELF-FORGETFUL LOVE, THE 274 LAZARU
LIPS STILL FRESH AND YOUNG.
IT WAS THE FIRST TIME I HAD SEEN HIM SMILE IN 276 LAZARU
YEARS.
MAJESTIC FIGURE WHOSE UNDERSTANDING SMILE SEEMS 278 LAZARU
TERRIBLE AND ENIGMATIC TO THEM.)
LISTENS TO HIS LAUGHTER WITH A TENDER SMILE OF 280 LAZARU
BEING HAPPY IN HIS HAPPINESS--
(LOOKING DOWN AT HIM NOW--WITH A SMILE, SIMPLY) 292 LAZARU
(WITH A SMILE) BUT ALL DEATH IS MEN'S INVENTION/ 294 LAZARU
(SUDDENLY WITH A DISTORTED WARPED SMILE) 300 LAZARU
(WITH THE SAME SMILE) THE SWORD, MY OLD HYENA/ 301 LAZARU
(HE TAKES OFF HIS HELMET AND SPITS IN IT--THEN 301 LAZARU
WITH A GRIM SMILE)
MIRIAM IS BESIDE HIM, DRESSED IN BLACK, SMILING 307 LAZARU
THE SAME SAD TENDER SMILE.
(RAISING HIS HANDS FOR SILENCE--WITH A PLAYFUL 309 LAZARU
SMILE)
LUCIUS REMARKS WITH A WEARY SMILE) 316 LAZARU
CALIGULA FORCES A CRUEL VINDICTIVE SMILE) 324 LAZARU
(THEN WITH AN IRONIC SMILE) BUT YOU NEED NOT TELL327 LAZARU
TIBERIUS THAT, GOOD FLAVIUS.
(THEN WITH HIS WRY SMILE) BUT I WILL TURN MY 329 LAZARU
BACK--AND SHUT MY EYES--
(HE SMILES HIS TWISTED SMILE) 331 LAZARU
HIS SMILE IS HYPOCRITICAL AND HIS EYES ARE HARD 332 LAZARU
AND COLD BUT WHEN THEY COME TO
A SMILE GRADUALLY COMING TO HIS FACE. 333 LAZARU
THE CURIOUS, SHEEPISH, BASHFUL SMILE 333 LAZARU
WITH A TWISTED ATTEMPT AT A SMILE) 339 LAZARU
HIS WHOLE BODY IS NOW RELAXED, AT REST, A DREAMY 342 LAZARU
SMILE SOFTENS HIS THIN
(LAZARUS CONTINUES TO SMILE. 343 LAZARU
(WITH A CRUEL SMILE) I HAVE THOUGHT OF A SPECIAL 345 LAZARU
TEST FOR HIM, CAESAR.
SMILE, MY SAD ONE/ 347 LAZARU
OR I SHALL LOSE PATIENCE WITH YOU--AND--(WITH A 354 LAZARU
GRIM SMILE) I CAN BE TERRIBLE/
(AGAIN MOVED AND CONFUSED--FORCING A MOCKING 355 LAZARU
SMILE)
TALKING DOWN TO HER FACE--WITH A TENDER SMILE) 362 LAZARU
(LOOKS AROUND THE CLEARING--BITTERLY, FORCES A 3 MANSNS
SELF-MOCKING SMILE.)
(WITH A FAINT SMILE.) I THOUGHT YOU WERE A FOOL. 20 MANSNS
(A BITTER IRONICAL SMILE COMES TO HER LIPS.) 22 MANSNS
SHE SMILES AT HIM--AN AMUSED, DERISIVE SMILE.) 31 MANSNS
(WITH ALMOST A GLOATING SMILE.) 35 MANSNS
(INSTINCTIVELY HER FACE LIGHTS UP WITH AN EAGER 37 MANSNS
GRATEFUL SMILE.)
(FORCING A SMILE--CONTEMPTUOUS AND AT THE SAME 38 MANSNS
TIME AFFECTIONATE.)
(COMES FORWARD WITH A GRACIOUS SMILE, HOLDING OUT 50 MANSNS
HER HAND.)
A SMILE THAT HAS LOST ITS OLD PASSIONATE 75 MANSNS
TENDERNESS.
A SMILE THAT TAKES ITS PROPRIETORSHIP FOR GRANTED. 75 MANSNS
(FORCING A SMILE--PLACATINGLY.) 79 MANSNS
(FORCES A SMILE.) THAT'S A QUEER CRAZY NOTION FOR 82 MANSNS
YOU TO HAVE, SIMON--
THIS FAMILIAR STRANGER TO WHOM WITH A TRUSTFUL 92 MANSNS
SMILE
(HE SITS DOWN AT HIS DESK--WITH A STRANGE SMILE OF 94 MANSNS
ANTICIPATION.
A LITTLE SMILE OF GLOATING SCORN COMES TO 95 MANSNS
DEBORAH'S LIPS.
BUT HER BEAUTIFUL DARK EYES AND HER SMILE STILL 95 MANSNS
RETAIN THEIR OLD IMAGINATIVE.
HE ADDS WITH A MOCKING SMILE.) 98 MANSNS
(WITH A LITTLE SMILE--CARELESSLY.) 99 MANSNS
(WITH A LITTLE MOCKING SMILE.) 100 MANSNS
(WITH A MALICIOUS SMILE.) EVEN A LITTLE 108 MANSNS
FRIGHTENED PERHAPS--
(HE TURNS TO STARE AT HER--FORCING A SMILE, 111 MANSNS
RESENTFULLY.)
(THINKING.) I KNOW THAT SMILE--WHEN HE'S MANAGED 119 MANSNS
A FOXY DEAL FOR THE COMPANY--
I HATE THAT SMUG, LUSTFUL, GREEDY TRADER'S SMILE 119 MANSNS
OF HIS/
(GETTING UP--WITH A QUIET SMILE.) 123 MANSNS
AND SMILE AT EACH OTHER WITH A RELIEVED 123 MANSNS
UNDERSTANDING.
BEAUTIFUL AND CUDDLY REMOTE AND PROUD--WITH A 125 MANSNS
SMILE DELIBERATELY AMUSED BY
(BEGINNING TO SMILE.) HE WAS ALWAYS A GREEDY, 125 MANSNS
JEALOUS BOY.
(BEGINNING TO SMILE, TOO.) AND SO WE DON'T HAVE 125 MANSNS
TO NEED HIM.
(SPEAKS TO SIMON WITH AN AMUSED, TEASING SMILE.) 127 MANSNS
(HE RELAXES WITH A DREAMY SMILE OF CONTENT IN 129 MANSNS
THEIR ARMS
THEN TRYING DESPERATELY TO BE CONFIDENTLY MATTER- 131 MANSNS
OF-FACT, AND FORCING A SMILE.)
(WITH A VINDICTIVE SMILE--STRANGELY.) 133 MANSNS
AND FORCES A HYPOCRITICALLY AFFECTIONATE, 136 MANSNS
DISARMING SMILE.
AND THEY SMILE A CONFIDENTIAL SMILE AT EACH 139 MANSNS
OTHER.)
(THEN AVOIDING HER EYE AND FORCING A SMILE.) 152 MANSNS
SHE FORCES A SMILE--MECHANICALLY.) 155 MANSNS
HE NODS HIS HEAD IN A NUMBED ACQUIESCENCE, FORCING155 MANSNS
A VACANT SMILE.)

SMILE

SMILE (CONT'D.)
(ABRUPTLY STRAIGHTENS UP AND STARES AT HER--WITH A168 MANSNS MOCKING SMILE.)
(WITH A GLOATING SMILE.) I CAN HEAR THE REVENGE 191 MANSNS IN HIS HEART LAUGHING OUT
WITH A SMILE OF GRACIOUS UNDERSTANDING AMUSEMENT.)193 MANSNS
(HERE HER LIPS PART IN A SMILE OF BEAUTIFUL PITY) 352 MARCOM
(WITH A WEARY SMILE) I BEGIN TO THINK KUBLAI IS A359 MARCOM HUMORIST, TOO.
(WITH A TRACE OF A BITING SMILE) 367 MARCOM
(TRYING TO HIDE HER PIQUE--FORCING A CYNICAL 368 MARCOM SMILE)
(WITH A SURE SMILE) LATER, THEN--WHEN WE MEET 371 MARCOM AGAIN.
(WITH A SCORNFUL SMILE) AND I WITH YOU--NOW THAT 375 MARCOM YOU'RE A MAN.
(WITH A SMILE) I BID YOU WELCOME, MASTER MARCO. 378 MARCOM
(WITH A QUIET SMILE) I SHALL STUDY THIS 379 MARCOM APOTHEOSIS WITH UNWEAKENED INTEREST.
(WITH A SMILE OF APPRECIATION) 379 MARCOM
TURNS TO CHU-YIN AND THEY BOTH SMILE.) 381 MARCOM
(THEN SUDDENLY FORCING A SMILE) 385 MARCOM
(SHE FORCES A SMILE) IT MAKES NO DIFFERENCE 386 MARCOM WHETHER I STAY OR GO.
(WITH A PITIFUL SMILE) YOU SEE--HE DOES NOT EVEN 386 MARCOM KNOW--
HE KEEPS HIS SMILE FROZEN AS HE NOTICES AN ARTIST 389 MARCOM SKETCHING HIM.
EVEN KUKACHIN CANNOT RESTRAIN A SMILE. 390 MARCOM
(CONQUERED-- SUDDENLY OVERPOWERED BY A GREAT 393 MARCOM SMILE)
(LISTENS WITH A PLEASED, IRONICAL SMILE AS THE 402 MARCOM BAND GETS RAPIDLY NEARER.
(SUDDENLY WITH A SLY SMILE TO HIMSELF) 404 MARCOM
(FORCING A SMILE) WON'T YOU MISS BEING MY 414 MARCOM GUARDIANS
(RECOVERING A BIT--WITH A SICKLY SMILE) 415 MARCOM
(THEN SUDDENLY FORCING A SMILE) 419 MARCOM
(THEN TO BAYAN WITH A CYNICAL BITTER SMILE) 422 MARCOM
AND, IN SPITE OF HIMSELF, A SHADOW OF A SMILE-- 432 MARCOM
FINALLY HE SPEAKS TENDERLY TO HER WITH A SAD 435 MARCOM SMILE)
SMILE WITH INFINITE SILENCE UPON OUR SPEECH, 435 MARCOM
SMILE WITH INFINITE FOREBEARANCE UPON OUR WISDOM, 435 MARCOM
SMILE WITH INFINITE REMOTENESS UPON OUR SORROW, 435 MARCOM SMILE AS A STAR SMILES!
YOU HAVE SET YOUR LIPS IN A SMILE SO REMOTE--YOU 437 MARCOM ARE PRETENDING EVEN
SPEAKING TO THE DEAD GIRL SOFTLY AS HE DOES SO-- 437 MARCOM WITH A TREMBLING SMILE)
HER SMILE MADE ME FORGET THE SERVILE GRIN OF THE 437 MARCOM FACE OF THE WORLD.
AND HER SMILE, REVEALING EVEN WHITE TEETH, GIVES 3 MISBEG IT CHARM.
(WITH A TEASING SMILE WHICH IS HALF SAD) 18 MISBEG
WITH BEAUTIFUL EYES AND HAIR AND TEETH AND A 29 MISBEG SMILE.
(FORCING A SCORNFUL SMILE) I'M SHOCKING YOU, I 42 MISBEG SUPPOSE5
AND EVEN TO SMILE WITH CONDESCENDING DISDAIN) 60 MISBEG
AND YOU GAVE HIM A SWEET SMILE, AND ROLLED YOUR 82 MISBEG BIG BEAUTIFUL COME EYES AT HIM.
(WITH A TWITCHING SMILE) IT MUST HAVE BEEN MAD, 90 MISBEG SURELY.
SHE COMES OUT, A FIXED SMILE ON HER LIPS, HER HEAD 97 MISBEG HIGH, HER FACE SET DEFIANTLY.
(WITH A FIXED SMILE) YOU'D THINK I'D BEEN GONE 111 MISBEG YEARS.
AND BEAUTIFUL EYES AND HAIR, AND A BEAUTIFUL SMILE119 MISBEG AND BEAUTIFUL WARM BREASTS.
(HE TURNS TO SMILE AT HER TEASINGLY) 124 MISBEG
(FORCING A SMILE) 130 MISBEG
(SHE FORCES A TREMBLING SMILE--FAINTLY) 136 MISBEG
(QUICKLY, FORCING HIS CYNICAL SMILE) 144 MISBEG
AND A COME-ON SMILE AS COLD AS A POLAR BEAR'S 149 MISBEG FEET.
SHE FORCES A DEFENSIVE, SELF-DERISIVE SMILE) 153 MISBEG
(SHE SMILES A LITTLE AMUSED SMILE) 153 MISBEG
(SHE FORCES A SMILE.) 172 MISBEG
(FORCES A TEASING SMILE AND A LITTLE OF HER OLD 175 MISBEG MANNER)
(TURNS TO HIM, FORCING A TEASING SMILE) 177 MISBEG
(WITH A TEASING SMILE.) I'M THINKIN' IT ISN'T ON 28 POET NEILAN ALONE.
(WITH A TENDER SMILE.) OH, HE ISN'T LIKE HIS 29 POET KIND, OR LIKE ANYONE ELSE AT ALL.
(WITH A PLEASED SMILE.) I'M AFRAID YOU'VE BLARNEY 39 POET ON YOUR TONGUE THIS MORNING.
(WITH A DEPRECATING SMILE.) FAITH, I WAS FAR AWAY 58 POET IN SPIRIT.
THERE IS SEDUCTIVE CHARM IN HIS WELCOMING SMILE 68 POET AND IN HIS VOICE.)
WITH HER SWEET, FRIENDLY SMILE.) 73 POET
BUT SHE FEELS HER SIMPLE CHARM AND GENTLENESS, AND 74 POET RETURNS HER SMILE.)
(STARTS, AS IF AWAKENING--WITH A PLEASANT SMILE.) 84 POET
WOULD SEEM TO SMILE THE LESS, OF ALL THAT 101 POET FLATTERED--FOLLOWED--SOUGHT, AND SUED.
(SHE SMILES A SHY, GENTLE SMILE.) 130 POET
(A SWEET SMILE OF PLEASED COQUETRY LIGHTS UP HER 136 POET DRAWN FACE.)
(A STRANGE, TENDERLY AMUSED SMILE ON HER LIPS-- 139 POET TEASINGLY.)
(SHE PAUSES. A HARD, TRIUMPHANT SMILE ON HER LIPS.160 POET IT FADES.
HE ADVANCES INTO THE STABLE WITH A MOCKING SMILE 587 ROPE ON HIS LIPS
(WITH AN INGRATIATING SMILE) 591 ROPE

SMILE (CONT'D.)
(LUKE SMILES A SUPERIOR KNOWING SMILE) HE HAS 592 ROPE ON'Y THE FARM.
THE OLD MAN WATCHES HIM WITH EAGER EYES AND SEEMS 596 ROPE TO BE TRYING TO SMILE.
HE HAS INTELLIGENT EYES AND A SMILE THAT CAN BE 6 STRANG IRONICAL.
(SHE KISSES HIM WITH A COOL, FRIENDLY SMILE) 13 STRANG
(THEN SUDDENLY EXPANDING IN A SWEET, GENUINELY 14 STRANG AFFECTIONATE SMILE)
(SHE TURNS TO MARSDEN WITH A QUICK SMILE) 15 STRANG
(HE FORCES A PRIM PLAYFUL SMILE) 16 STRANG
(WITH A STRANGE SMILE) BUT SOME DAY I'LL READ IT 21 STRANG ALL IN ONE OF YOUR BOOKS.
FORCES A CORDIAL SMILE AND SHAKES HANDS) 28 STRANG
(FORCING A SMILE) 29 STRANG
(WITH A SMILE) IF NINA WILL, SHE WILL--AND IF SHE 33 STRANG WON'T, SHE WON'T.
(WITH A SLIGHT SMILE) I'M PRESCRIBING FOR SAM, 38 STRANG TOO, WHEN I BOOST THIS WEDDING.
(THEN WITH A STRANGE TWISTED SMILE) 39 STRANG
(THEN FORCING A SMILE--SOOTHINGLY) 40 STRANG
(FORCING A SMILE) YOU LOOK FRIGHTENED, CHARLIE. 40 STRANG
(WITH A COMFORTED SMILE, CLOSING HER EYES AND 44 STRANG CUDDLING UP AGAINST HIM)
(FORCING A SMILE--IRONICALLY) 44 STRANG
(WITH A SAD SMILE) NO. 51 STRANG
(WITH A FORCED SMILE) NO, THANK YOU. 52 STRANG
(SEEING THIS IS HER CHANCE--QUICKLY--FORCING A 55 STRANG SMILE)
(STARTLED--FORCING A SMILE, QUICKLY) 57 STRANG
(THEN WITH A GRIM SMILE) WHY, I EVEN LOVE THAT 62 STRANG IDIOT UPSTAIRS.
(WITH A GRIM SMILE) AND I DON'T BELIEVE IN HIM, 64 STRANG NEITHER, NOT ANY MORE.
(SHE COMES FORWARD TO THE CHAIR AT CENTER AND SITS 69 STRANG DOWN--FORCING A SMILE)
(WITH A GRIM BITTER SMILE) 72 STRANG
(FORCING A SMILE) AND I WANTED TO ASK A FAVOR OF 76 STRANG YOU.
HIDING BEHIND HER SMILE...) 79 STRANG
GETS TO HIS FEET WITH A SMILE OF AFFECTIONATE 79 STRANG ADMIRATION)
(WITH A SMILE) WELL, YOU'RE THE TAKING KIND FOR 80 STRANG WHOM OPPORTUNITIES ARE MADE!
(FORCING A PITIFUL SMILE TO HIS LIPS) 98 STRANG
(WITH A POSSESSIVE SMILE OF TOLERANCE) 101 STRANG
(FORCING A SMILE) HOW ABOUT TRAINING HIS MIND5 120 STRANG
(WITH A STRANGE, SELF-ASSURED SMILE AT HIM) 131 STRANG
A SMILE--PUTS HER ARMS AROUND HIM AFFECTIONATELY) 136 STRANG
(THEN FORCING A SMILE) BUT I'M EXAGGERATING. 140 STRANG
(WITH A WRY SMILE) IT'S POSSIBLE. 146 STRANG
(STARTLED BUT IMMEDIATELY FORCING A SMILE) 151 STRANG
(SHE5 FORWARD TO THE CHAIR AT CENTER, FORCING154 STRANG A SMILE)
(WITH A FRIENDLY SMILE) I HAVEN'T SEEN YOU LOOK 165 STRANG SO YOUNG AND HANDSOME SINCE I
(THEN FORCING A SMILE) SO TELL ME WHAT FOUNTAIN 165 STRANG OF YOUTH YOU'VE FOUND.
(WITH A SAD SMILE) SIT DOWN, NED. 165 STRANG
(THEN FORCING A SMILE) BUT I'M NOT LAMENTING. 166 STRANG
(WITH A DEADLY SMILE OF TRIUMPH) 176 STRANG
(WITH A SMILE OF CRUEL TRIUMPH--THINKING) 177 STRANG
IRONICAL SMILE ON HIS LIPS) 182 STRANG
(HE KISSES ONE OF THE ROSES WITH A SIMPLE 187 STRANG SENTIMENTAL SMILE.)
CLOSING OUR LIFE TOGETHER WITH THAT SMILE... 191 STRANG
(FORCING A TORTURED SMILE) NOT FOR ANYTHING IN 196 STRANG THE WORLD!
(WITH AN IRONICAL SMILE--FORCING A JOKING TONE) 196 STRANG
(WITH A SAD SMILE) NO. 196 STRANG
(AMUSED--WITH A SAD SMILE) BLESS YOU, MY 197 STRANG CHILDREN!
(WITH A MOCKING SMILE) BUT PERHAPS WE'LL BECOME 197 STRANG PART OF GUSMIC POSITIVE AND
YOU'RE MY--(HE CONTROLS HIMSELF ABRUPTLY--WITH A 198 STRANG SMILE OF CYNICAL SELF-PITY)
(WITH A STRANGE SMILE) STRANGE INTERLUDE/ 199 STRANG
WITH A HAPPY SMILE) 200 STRANG
JOES GETS INTO POSITION BEHIND THE BAR, ASSUMING 496 VOYAGE HIS MOST OILY SMILE.
(WITH A SEDUCTIVE SMILE) I DOWN'T BLAME YER. 501 VOYAGE
(WITH A SMILE UP INTO HIS FACE) 501 VOYAGE
(WITH A SMILE) WE'D 'AVE A BLOOMIN' LARK OF IT IF502 VOYAGE I 'AD, WOULDN'T WE5
(TRYING TO SMILE) NO. 502 VOYAGE
(WITH A TENDER SMILE) GH--SOMETIMES. 444 WELDED
HE BENDS DOWN AND LIFTS HER FACE TO HIS--WITH A 445 WELDED SMILE)
I ONLY--(WITH A SMILE OF IRONICAL SELF-PITY) 445 WELDED
YOU'RE SURE YOU DIDN'T FORCE IT--(WITH A TENDER 445 WELDED SMILE AT HIM)
(FORCING A SMILE) PERHAPS THAT'S THE PRICE. 446 WELDED
(WITH A TENDER SMILE--MUSINGLY) 446 WELDED
(WITH A TENDER SMILE) OF THE FIRST TIME WE MET-- 446 WELDED AT REHEARSAL, REMEMBER5
SHE FORCES A SMILE, HALF TURNING AWAY.) 452 WELDED
(SHE PATS HIS HEAD WITH A FRIENDLY SMILE.) 455 WELDED
PERHAPS IT'S ALL MY SUPERSENSITIVENESS--(PATTING 456 WELDED HER HAND AND FORCING A SMILE)
(FORCING AN AWKWARD SMILE) THEN--NOW--FOREVER 463 WELDED AFTER, AHH--
(WITH A WAN, GRATEFUL SMILE) 464 WELDED
(FORCING A TWISTED SMILE--WILDLY) 466 WELDED
(WITH A WRY SMILE) THAT ISN'T ME. 466 WELDED
(HE FORCES A SMILE) YOU SEE, I'M ALREADY STARTING467 WELDED TO NURSE ALONG
(WITH A SAD SMILE) YOU SEE5 467 WELDED

SMILE

SMILE (CONT'D.)
(THEN CHECKING HIS ANGER AND FORCING A WRY SMILE) 468 WELDED
(WITH A TWISTED SMILE) THAT'S WHAT HE'S DOING 468 WELDED
NOW.
(AFTER A PAUSE, WITH A GESTURE TOWARD THE DOOR AND469 WELDED
A WEARY, BEATEN SMILE)
(WITH THE SAME WRY SMILE) WHILE I BEGIN TO 469 WELDED
SUSPECT THAT IN A WAY I'M LUCKY--
(WITH A TIRED SMILE) NO. 469 WELDED
(WITH A WRY SMILE) STUDY YOUR PART. 469 WELDED
AND SMILE FORLORNLY AT EACH OTHER.) 470 WELDED
(FORCING A TRADE SMILE--WITH AN ATTEMPT AT 471 WELDED
LIGHTNESS)
AND FORCES A TREMBLING, MOCKING SMILE) 476 WELDED
(THEY SMILE WITH A QUEER UNDERSTANDING, THEIR ARMS480 WELDED
MOVE ABOUT EACH OTHER.
(SHE FALTERS, TURNS AWAY WITH A BITTER SMILE) 484 WELDED
(CONTROLLING HIMSELF--FORCING A SMILE) 486 WELDED
(SHE OPENS THE DOOR AND TURNS TO CAPE WITH A 487 WELDED
STRANGE SMILE)

SMILED
AND SHE SMILED AND HELD OUT HER ARMS TO ME. 477 DYNAMO
(SHE GOES TOWARD HIM, SMILING AS HER MOTHER MIGHT 143 ELECTR
HAVE SMILED)
SIMPLY BECAUSE HE USED TO SMILE AT ME AND I SMILED147 ELECTR
BACK.
THAT THE BLESSED VIRGIN HAD SMILED AND BLESSED ME 175 JOURNE
WITH HER CONSENT.
AND HE SMILED. 276 LAZARU
AND THEN LAZARUS KNELT AND KISSED JESUS' FEET AND 277 LAZARU
BOTH OF THEM SMILED
THEN JESUS SMILED SADLY BUT WITH TENDERNESS, 277 LAZARU
THEY WOULD HAVE SMILED LIKE SENILE, 83 POET
SHE JUST SMILED. 32 STRANG
AND JUST BEFORE HE DIED, HE SMILED AT ME... 191 STRANG

SMILES
IT WAS SO LONG AGO (A PAUSE--THEN SHE SMILES 548 'ILE
DREAMILY)
(SHE SMILES GOOD-NATUREDLY. 190 AHWILD
LILY IS SHOCKED BUT, TAKING HER CUE FROM THEM, 195 AHWILD
SMILES.
(IS A LITTLE PIQUED, BUT SMILES) 250 AHWILD
LILY SMILES AT SID'S LAUGHTER. 259 AHWILD
(HE SMILES A LITTLE BITTERLY) 268 AHWILD
SHE SMILES ON SEEING HER UNCLE, THEN GIVES A START272 AHWILD
ON SEEING RICHARD.)
(SHE SMILES.) 292 AHWILD
MILLER SIZES HIM UP KEENLY--THEN SUDDENLY SMILES 293 AHWILD
AND ASKS WITH QUIET MOCKERY)
SHE RELAPSES INTO THE FAMILIAR FORM AND FLASHES 23 ANNA
ONE OF HER WINNING TRADE SMILES
SEEING WHO IT IS HE SMILES) 82 BEYOND
(HE SMILES AT HIS OWN IRRITATION) 88 BEYOND
THE OTHERS FORCE SMILES) 94 BEYOND
(THEN HE SMILES) YOU COULDN'T TEMPT HIM, NO WAYS. 97 BEYOND
MAYO SMILES SLYLY AT HIS WIFE) 99 BEYOND
(HE SINKS DOWN INTO HIS CHAIR AND SMILES WITH 126 BEYOND
BITTER SELF-SCORN)
(HE SMILES BITTERLY) BUSINESS FIRST WAS ALWAYS 146 BEYOND
ANDY'S MOTTO.
(HE SMILES GRIMLY, PACING UP AND DOWN, HIS HANDS 157 BEYOND
IN HIS POCKETS.)
ROBERT SMILES BITTERLY. 160 BEYOND
(HE SMILES BITTERLY) I'M A FAILURE, AND RUTH'S 161 BEYOND
ANOTHER--
(ROBERT SMILES GRATEFULLY AND STRETCHES OUT HIS 162 BEYOND
HAND.
BUT (SHE SMILES AT HIM ENTICINGLY) 469 CARIBE
(HE LEANS BACK IN HIS CHAIR AND SMILES IRONICALLY)560 CROSS
(HE SMILES) TO TELL YOU THE TRUTH, 505 DAYS
(SHE SMILES) AND MARGARET SMILES BACK. 515 DAYS
(SHE SMILES) THE TROUBLE WITH YOU IS, YOU OLD 523 DAYS
CYNIC.
(SHE SMILES LOVINGLY) YOU SEE, 524 DAYS
(SHE SMILES--THEN WITH QUIET PRIDE) 524 DAYS
(HE SMILES FAINTLY) POOR JOHN. 563 DAYS
(SHE SMILES AT HIM ADORINGLY.) 245 DESIRE
(SHE SMILES AT HIM AFFECTIONATELY.) 499 DIFRNT
MRS. CROSBY SMILES. 507 DIFRNT
(SMILES LOVINGLY AT HIS BACK) 520 DIFRNT
(THEN SUDDENLY REALIZING THE CAUSE OF HIS 535 DIFRNT
DISCOMFITURE, SHE SMILES PITYINGLY.
(THEN SEEING HIS ASHAMED LOOK, SHE SMILES) 424 DYNAMO
LOUISA SMILES IN SPITE OF HERSELF. 7 ELECTR
(CHRISTINE SMILES MOCKINGLY AND TURNS AWAY, AS IF 34 ELECTR
TO GO OUT OF THE ROOM.
BUT WHEN HE SMILES NATURALLY HIS FACE HAS A GENTLE 74 ELECTR
BOYISH CHARM WHICH MAKES
(HE SMILES WITH A DREAMY TENDERNESS) 90 ELECTR
CHRISTINE SMILES TAUNTINGLY) 91 ELECTR
(HE SMILES GRIMLY) HE LOOKS LIKE ME, TOO/ 115 ELECTR
STARES AT HIM FRIGHTENEDLY. HE SMILES AN UGLY 146 ELECTR
TAUNTING SMILE)
HAZEL IS A BIT SHOCKED, THEN SMILES HAPPILY. 148 ELECTR
THE NIGHT CLERK SMILES AT A GUEST. 12 HUGHIE
(SMILES.) YOU REMIND ME A LOT OF HUGHIE, PAL. 38 HUGHIE
(SMILES ALMOST MOCKINGLY) OH, SURE, I SEE. 590 ICEMAN
(SHE CATCHES LARRY'S EYE AND SMILES 611 ICEMAN
AFFECTIONATELY)
(AUTOMATICALLY SHE SMILES SEDUCTIVELY AT PARRITT 611 ICEMAN
(SUDDENLY SHE IS MOLLIFIED AND SMILES) 635 ICEMAN
THEN HE SMILES SNEERINGLY.) 679 ICEMAN
(SMILES AT HIM WITH AFFECTIONATE AMUSEMENT) 694 ICEMAN
THEY ALL RESPOND WITH SMILES THAT ARE STILL A 722 ICEMAN
LITTLE FORCED AND UNEASY.)
(SMILES AFFECTIONATELY.) I'VE GOTTEN TOO FAT, YOU 14 JOURNE
MEAN, DEAR.
(SMILES NOW WITH TEASING AFFECTION.) 15 JOURNE

SMILES (CONT'D.)
BUT ON THE RARE OCCASIONS WHEN HE SMILES WITHOUT 19 JOURNE
SNEERING.
(SHE IS REASSURED AND SMILES AT HIM LOVINGLY. 21 JOURNE
(SHE SMILES, HER FACE LIGHTING UP, AND KISSES HIM 41 JOURNE
GRATEFULLY.
JAMIE TAKES ONE LOOK AT THE BOTTLE AND GLASSES AND 53 JOURNE
SMILES CYNICALLY.
SHE EVEN SMILES WITH AN IRONICAL AMUSEMENT TO 67 JOURNE
HERSELF.)
(SHE SMILES STRANGELY.) BUT IT CAN'T TONIGHT. 99 JOURNE
THERE IS A QUALITY OF AN INNOCENT CONVENT GIRL 105 JOURNE
ABOUT HER, AND SHE SMILES SHYLY.)
(SMILES WITH DETACHED TENDERNESS AT EDMUND.) 110 JOURNE
(SHE SMILES AT TYRONE WITH A STRANGE, INCONGRUOUS 114 JOURNE
COQUETRY.)
(HE SMILES TEASINGLY AND SIGHS.) 136 JOURNE
(HE SUDDENLY SMILES-- 142 JOURNE
(SMILES GENTLY AND SPEAKS AS IF TO A GROUP OF 279 LAZARU
INQUISITIVE CHILDREN)
(SMILES WITH RESPECTFUL UNDERSTANDING. 327 LAZARU
I COULD SWEAR HE SMILES--WITH HIS LAST BREATH/ 329 LAZARU
(HE SMILES HIS TWISTED SMILE) 331 LAZARU
(MARCELLUS SHRUGS HIS SHOULDERS AND SMILES 332 LAZARU
DEPRECATINGLY.)
HE SMILES BACK AT LAZARUS-- 333 LAZARU
(HIS EYES FALL AGAIN TO TIBERIUS AND HE SMILES) 343 LAZARU
HE SMILES WITH HAPPINESS AND 348 LAZARU
(LAZARUS SMILES GENTLY AT HIM. 354 LAZARU
WHO SMILES AT HIM AFFECTIONATELY AS AT A CHILD IN 359 LAZARU
A TANTRUM.)
WHITE TEETH WHEN SHE SMILES. 2 MANSNS
(SHE SMILES MOCKINGLY AND GOES OFF RIGHT-REAR.) 21 MANSNS
SHE SMILES AT HIM--AN AMUSED, DERISIVE SMILE.) 31 MANSNS
(SHE SMILES WRYLY.) THERE. 39 MANSNS
HE SMILES AND CHUCKLES TO HIMSELF. 44 MANSNS
(SHE SMILES.) BUT OF COURSE THEY'RE MINE AND I'D 51 MANSNS
BE BOUND TO THINK THAT.
(SHE SMILES.) I NEED NOT WARN YOU TO SCRUTINIZE 52 MANSNS
IT CLOSELY.
(SHE SMILES STRANGELY.) THAT MAY BE THE CHANGE IN 72 MANSNS
ACTIVITY I NEED.
SHE SMILES ASSUREDLY, 75 MANSNS
(LOOKS AFTER HER AND SMILES STRANGELY-- 94 MANSNS
IRONICALLY.)
(SHE SMILES TEASINGLY.) 103 MANSNS
---NOR BOWED TO ITS IDOLATRIES A PATIENT KNEE, NOR107 MANSNS
COINED MY CHEEK TO SMILES;---
(HE SMILES WITH PLEASANT CASUALNESS.) 115 MANSNS
(HE SMILES TO HIMSELF GLOATINGLY AND BEGINS TO 119 MANSNS
READ.
(SMILES AT HIM NOW, CAJOLINGLY AFFECTIONATE.) 127 MANSNS
ENTICING SMILES. 128 MANSNS
(HE SMILES SNEERINGLY, BUT IS AFRAID TO MEET THEIR131 MANSNS
EYES.
(SHE SMILES CONTENTEDLY AND PATS SARA'S HAND.) 135 MANSNS
(HE RELAPSES AND SMILES DREAMILY.) 145 MANSNS
(SHE PAUSES--THEN SMILES WITH COLD PLEASANTRY.) 153 MANSNS
(HE SMILES AT HER WITH A SUDDEN AWKWARD 183 MANSNS
TENDERNESS.)
(SMILES CONDESCENDINGLY.) YOU ARE IMPERTINENT. 193 MANSNS
(DEBORAH SMILES AND ADDRESSES HIM IN AN 359 MARCOM
AFFECTIONATE, HUMOROUS TONE)
SMILES DOWN AT IT UNCERTAINLY, THEN BENDS DOWN TO 366 MARCOM
TAKE HOLD OF ITS HAND.)
SHE SMILES AT MARCO ENTICINGLY.) 367 MARCOM
HE IS A BIT BREATHLESS FROM HASTE BUT HIS FACE IS 386 MARCOM
WREATHED IN SMILES.)
HE SMILES. HE IS TALKING LOUDLY SO EVERYONE CAN 389 MARCOM
OVERHEAR.
CHU-YIN STARTS--THEN SMILES. 402 MARCOM
SMILE WITH INFINITE REMOTENESS UPON OUR SORROW, 435 MARCOM
SMILE AS A STAR SMILES/
(SHE SMILES MOCKINGLY) I KNOW WHAT A TRIAL IT'S 6 MISBEG
BEEN TO YOU, MIKE.
BUT WHEN HE SMILES WITHOUT SNEERING, 37 MISBEG
SHE SMILES DOWN AT JIM, HER FACE SOFTENING, 40 MISBEG
PLEASED TO HEAR HIM LAUGH.)
(HE SMILES KIDDINGLY) ANYWAY, WHO TOLD YOU I FALL 43 MISBEG
FOR THE DAINTY DOLLS$
JOSIE SMILES) 65 MISBEG
(SMILES KIDDINGLY) AFRAID YOU'LL LOSE ME$ 68 MISBEG
SMILES AT HIM COQUETTISHLY, BEGINNING TO SHOW THE 115 MISBEG
EFFECT OF HER BIG DRINK BY HER
HE SMILES AT HER CYNICALLY) 124 MISBEG
(SMILES) OF COURSE, I DID IT TO KID PHIL, TOO. 133 MISBEG
(SMILES) YOU'LL GET OUT THE OLD CLUB, EH$ 134 MISBEG
(SHE SMILES A LITTLE AMUSED SMILE) 153 MISBEG
(SHE SMILES STRANGELY) EXCEPT A GREAT MIRACLE 159 MISBEG
THEY'D NEVER BELIEVE.
(SMILES--HER VOICE IS SOFT, WITH A RICH BROGUE.) 20 POET
SHE IS EXASPERATED FOR A SECOND--THEN SHE SMILES 27 POET
PITYINGLY.)
(SHE SMILES COQUETTISHLY.) ALL HE'S WRITTEN THE 29 POET
LAST FEW MONTHS ARE LOVE POEMS.
(SHE SMILES.) IT'S YOU ARE THE SLY ONE. 30 POET
(SHE SMILES.) YOU DON'T KNOW HIM. 32 POET
NOR BOWED TO ITS IDOLATRIES A PATIENT KNEE, NOR 43 POET
COINED MY CHEEK TO SMILES;--
(CONSOLED, THE OLD MAN SMILES AT HER GRATEFULLY.) 54 POET
(SHE SMILES A BIT SCORNFULLY.) 62 POET
(SUDDENLY SHE SMILES CONFIDENTLY.) 65 POET
THEN SHE SMILES WITH AN AMUSED AND MOCKING RELISH. 67 POET
NOR BOWED TO ITS IDOLATRIES A PATIENT KNEE, NOR 67 POET
COINED MY CHEEK TO SMILES;--
(HE SMILES CONDESCENDINGLY.) 76 POET
SHE SMILES PLEASANTLY AT SARA, WHO RISES 81 POET
GRACIOUSLY FROM HER CHAIR.)

SMILES

(CONT'D.)
(SHE SMILES.) BUT EVIDENTLY HE HAS FOUND A NEW 82 POET
ROMANTIC DREAM.
(SHE SMILES AGAIN.) MY WARNING WAS THE MECHANICAL 82 POET
GESTURE OF A MOTHER'S DUTY.
(SHE SMILES.) IT HAS BEEN A MOST CONFUSING 86 POET
MORNING FOR A TIRED.
(SHE SMILES.) GOODBYE AGAIN, MISS MELODY. 86 POET
(HE SMILES.) FAITH, I DID PUT MY FOOT IN IT. 90 POET
BUT AT THE END HE SMILES WITH LORDLY 96 POET
CONDESCENSION.
(SHE SMILES A SHY, GENTLE SMILE.) 130 POET
(SHE SMILES TENDERLY.) 145 POET
(SHE SMILES WITH A SELF-MOCKING HAPPINESS.) 150 POET
NOR BOWED TO UTS IDOLATRIES A PASHUNT KNEE, NOR 176 POET
COINED ME CHEEK TO SMILES.--
(SHE SMILES STRANGELY.) MAYBE I DESERVED THE SLAP181 POET
FOR INTERFERING.
(SHE SMILES.) SURE, I HAVE NO PRIDE AT ALL-- 182 POET
EXCEPT THAT.
(SHE COMES OVER AND HUGS HER--THEN SHE SMILES 182 POET
TENDERLY.)
(LUKE SMILES A SUPERIOR (KNOWING SMILE) HE HAS 592 ROPE
ON'Y THE FARM.
(HE SMILES) (PRIMLY CLASSICAL... 4 STRANG
HE SMILES AFFECTIONATELY 4 STRANG
EUROPE HAS =GONE WEST=--(HE SMILES WHIMSICALLY) 7 STRANG
TO AMERICA. LET'S HOPE/.
(HE SMILES WITH BITTER SELF-MOCKERY) 12 STRANG
NINA SMILES PERFUNCTORILY.) 14 STRANG
(HE SMILES WITH A WRY AMUSEMENT FOR A SECOND--THEN 25 STRANG
BITTERLY)
(SHE SMILES WITH A CYNICAL SELF-CONTEMPT) 27 STRANG
(HE SMILES CASUALLY.) 31 STRANG
(SHE SMILES AT HIM WITH A PITYING SCORN.) 41 STRANG
(HE KISSES HER HAIR AGAIN TENDERLY AND SMILES AT 44 STRANG
HIMSELF--
(HE SMILES BITTERLY TO HIMSELF AS HE GOES OUT.) 47 STRANG
I HAVE WATCHED HAPPY SMILES FORM ON THE LIPS OF 86 STRANG
THE DYING...
(SHE SMILES STRANGELY) 112 STRANG
(HE SMILES MOCKINGLY) 140 STRANG
(HE SMILES GRIMLY) 144 STRANG
(HE SMILES AND SHE SMILES AND THEY KISS AGAIN. 145 STRANG
(HE SMILES KINDLY AT HER) SO GET BACK TO THE 179 STRANG
RACE/
(HE SMILES STRANGELY. 188 STRANG
HE SMILES QUIETLY) 188 STRANG
(THE WOMEN COME FORWARD TO THE TABLE, WEARING 499 VOYAGE
THEIR BEST SET SMILES.)
SHE ISS EIGHTY-TWO (HE SMILES REMINISCENTLY) YOU 506 VOYAGE
KNOW, MISS FREDA,
(OLSON SMILES) DOES SHE KNOW YER COMIN'S 506 VOYAGE
(SHE SMILES TENDERLY) AND THEN WE FIGHT/ 448 WELDED
(CAPE SMILES WITH BITTER IRONY) 451 WELDED
THEN, AS IF UNCONSCIOUSLY, FALTERINGLY, WITH 480 WELDED
TREMBLING SMILES,
SHE SMILES AT HIM AND SPEAKS WITH A TENDER 487 WELDED
WEARINESS)
SMILES TO HERSELF AND WALKS BACK TO THE FOOT OF 487 WELDED
THE STAIRWAY.

SMILING

(SMILING) WELL, YOU CAN'T EXPECT A BOY TO 188 AHWILD
REMEMBER TO SHUT DOORS ON THE FOURTH
(REGARDING HER BROTHER WITH SMILING SUSPICION) 189 AHWILD
(SMILING) OFF TO THE RANDS?, I SUPPOSE. 191 AHWILD
(SMILING) WHY, WHAT DID SHE DO NOW& 211 AHWILD
(SMILING) HE SAYS HE'S THROUGH WITH MURIEL NOW. 216 AHWILD
HIS FACE IS ONE LARGE, SMILING, HAPPY BEAM OF 221 AHWILD
UTTER APPRECIATION OF LIFE--
(SURVEYING MILDRED'S HANDIWORK--SMILING) 250 AHWILD
(SMILING TEASINGLY) I CAN SEE WHERE YOU'RE 288 AHWILD
BECOMING CORRUPTED BY THOSE BOOKS.
(SMILING) THEN, FROM ALL REPORTS, WE SEEM TO BE 292 AHWILD
COMPLETELY SURROUNDED BY LOVE/
IT WAS WONDERFUL--DOWN AT THE BEACH--(HE STOPS 296 AHWILD
ABRUPTLY, SMILING SHYLY.)
(HALF SMILING) DRINK IT ALL AND YOU'LL FIND IT 31 ANNA
AIN'T NO DREAM.
(SMILING COMFIDENTLY) IS IT ANNA YOU THINK WILL 45 ANNA
PREVENT ME&
HE IS SMILING HAPPILY, AND HUMMING A SONG TO 99 BEYOND
HIMSELF.
(SMILING) YOUR LETTERS WERE--SKETCHY, TO SAY THE 131 BEYOND
LEAST.
AGAIN SMILING BITTERLY. 471 CARIBE
(HE GETS UP SMILING) AND THANK YOU FOR THE 562 CROSS
INTERESTING STORY.
(SMILING GOOD-NATUREDLY) YOU ALWAYS DID HAVE A 497 DAYS
NEAR MEMORY, BILL.
(HE GIVES JOHN A SIDE GLANCE, HALF SMILING AND 504 DAYS
HALF REPROACHFUL)
(SMILING) BUT I'M STILL FLABBERGASTED. 505 DAYS
(SMILING WITH A STRANGE WRYNESS) 516 DAYS
(SMILING) BUT WHY& 516 DAYS
(SMILING) WELL, HE IS FOR ME. 517 DAYS
(THEN SMILING TEASINGLY) WELL, IF YOU LOVE ME SO 529 DAYS
MUCH, PROVE IT BY TELLING ME.
(SMILING AT JOHN ENCOURAGINGLY) 530 DAYS
(SMILING) I NEVER SAW YOU SO FLUSTERED BEFORE, 533 DAYS
JOHN.
(SMILING) I'LL SAY YE'RE LYIN' A-PURPOSE--AN' 226 DESIRE
HE'LL DRIVE YE OFF THE PLACE/
(LOOKS AFTER HIM SMILING SATISFIEDLY--THEN HALF TO227 DESIRE
HERSELF, MOUTHING THE WORD)
(SMILING.) I RECKON YOU'LL DO, JACK. 499 DIFRNT
(SMILING AT HARRIET AND ROGERS) 507 DIFRNT
(SMILING, PUTS HER ARMS AROUND EMMA) 507 DIFRNT

SMILING

(CONT'D.)
(SMILING AT HIM COQUETTISHLY) 534 DIFRNT
(SMILING) WALK, EVEN THAT DON'T MAKE YOU OUT NO 538 DIFRNT
SPRING CHICKEN, EMMA.
(SMILING MOCKINGLY AT REUBEN) 437 DYNAMO
SHE IS SMILING WITH A DOTING GOOD NATURE) 456 DYNAMO
(SMILING, AT HIS SECRET THOUGHT) 178 EJOINES
SHE HAS A STRONG CHIN AND A CAPABLE SMILING MOUTH. 12 ELECTR
(SMILING HAPPILY) OF COURSE WE WILL. 80 ELECTR
(AGAIN WITH TENDERNESS, STROKING HIS HAIR-- 90 ELECTR
SMILING)
(THEN TAKING HIM IN WITH A SMILING APPRECIATIVE 143 ELECTR
POSSESSIVENESS)
(SHE GOES TOWARD HIM, SMILING AS HER MOTHER MIGHT 143 ELECTR
HAVE SMILED)
(SMILING) YOUR LUCK IS UNCANNY. 285 GGBROW
(INGRATIATING PALLY, SMILING.) 37 HUGHIE
(SMILING AMIABLY) AS FOR YOU, MY BALMY BOER THAT 599 ICEMAN
WALKS LIKE A MAN.
(HIS SMILING FACE CONGEALING) 606 ICEMAN
(SMILING) SURE TING/ 635 ICEMAN
SHE TURNS HER HEAD, SMILING.) 18 JOURNE
(SMILING.) THAT DREADFUL MAN/ 22 JOURNE
HE WAS ALWAYS SMILING OR LAUGHING. 109 JOURNE
(HE ADDS, SMILING WITHOUT RESENTMENT.) 158 JOURNE
GLANCING SIDEWAYS AT ONE ANOTHER, SMILING 280 LAZARU
FOOLISHLY AND SELF-CONSCIOUSLY.
MIRIAM IS BESIDE HIM, DRESSED IN BLACK, SMILING 307 LAZARU
THE SAME SAD TENDER SMILE.
BELOW LAZARUS, WHO LOOKS DOWN UPON THEM, SILENT 320 LAZARU
BUT SMILING GENTLY NOW.
(SMILING DRUNKENLY) SHUT UP, YOURSELF, CAMP-BRAT/322 LAZARU
(SMILING WITHOUT BITTERNESS--WITH A SAD 328 LAZARU
COMPREHENSION)
(HE ADVANCES TOWARD LAZARUS, SMILING, 332 LAZARU
(SMILING GENTLY) THEN FEAR NOT FEAR, TIBERIUS/ 339 LAZARU
(SMILING--AS IF HE WERE CORRECTING A CHILD) 340 LAZARU
(SMILING) DO YOU FEAR PEACE& 343 LAZARU
(LOOKS UP, SMILING WITH IRONICAL BITTERNESS) 343 LAZARU
(SMILING MOCKINGLY) YES. 353 LAZARU
(SMILING AFFECTIONATELY AT HIM, SHAKES HIS HEAD) 357 LAZARU
(SMILING DOWN ON THEM--GENTLY) 358 LAZARU
(SMILING) YOU ARE SO PROUD OF BEING EVIL/ 359 LAZARU
(HE DOES SO, SMILING GENTLY) 361 LAZARU
(PUZZLED BUT SMILING.) OF COURSE YOU CAN. 17 MANSNS
(TAKES HER HAND, SMILING IN RETURN--A BIT 50 MANSNS
STILTEDLY.)
(SMILING.) OH, I KNOW. 57 MANSNS
(SMILING.) I'M ALL THE TIME TELLING HIM HOW PROUD 64 MANSNS
I AM.
(SMILING.) IF THAT ISN'T LIKE YOU, TO PUT THE 76 MANSNS
BLAME ON ME.
(SMILING.) MOTHER HAS ALWAYS HAD A SUBTLE TALENT 77 MANSNS
FOR CONTRIVING IT SO THAT
(SMILING FONDLY.) YES, I'M SURE I CAN GUESS-- 107 MANSNS
(SMILING.) WELL, ANYWAY, IT WOULD NOT BE A HAPPY 113 MANSNS
ENDING, WOULD IT.
(THINKING.) HE ISN'T READING--JUST PRETENDING 119 MANSNS
TO--SMILING TO HIMSELF--SLY!--
DEBORAH PATS THE SOFA ON HER LEFT, SMILING AN 123 MANSNS
AFFECTIONATE WELCOME.)
(SMILING GLOATINGLY.) SEE, SARA, HE IS NOT EVEN 126 MANSNS
PRETENDING TO READ NOW.
(SMILING GLOATINGLY.) AS SCARED AS IF HE SAW A 126 MANSNS
GHOST/
(SMILING-- 143 MANSNS
(COMES TO THE DESK--SMILING GLOATINGLY. 150 MANSNS
(SMILING WITH COLD PLEASANTNESS.) 151 MANSNS
SMILING YOUR THANKS AS I PROMISE YOU A LARGE 360 MARCOM
FORTUNE IF YOU WILL BE TRUE.
(SMILING) AND HE HAD MILLIONS OF PLATES, TOO/ 363 MARCOM
(SMILING) SHUT UP. 367 MARCOM
(SMILING) ARE YOU HIS HUNDRED WISE MENS 379 MARCOM
KUBLAI LAUGHS AND TURNS TO CHU-YIN WHO IS 383 MARCOM
SMILING.)
(THEN SMILING AT HIM) HAVE I BEEN SO BAD AS THATS385 MARCOM
YOUR LIPS DROOP EVEN IN SMILING/ 385 MARCOM
(WITH SMILING MOCKERY) BUT--WHO CAN PLAY YOUR 396 MARCOM
PARTS
(GRIMLY SMILING) OH, 396 MARCOM
(SMILING) BUT I BELIEVE THAT WHAT CAN BE PROVEN 397 MARCOM
CANNOT BE TRUE.
(SMILING AT HIM AS AT A BOY--TEASINGLY) 399 MARCOM
(SMILING BACK LIKE A BOY) YES, I DID TOO, WHEN I 399 MARCOM
WAS YOUNG AND FOOLISH.
(HALF SMILING AND HALF WEEPING AT HIS TEASING) 402 MARCOM
(SMILING--DISTRACTEDLY) WAR WITHOUT RHETORIC, 423 MARCOM
PLEASE/
(SMILING) TERRIBLE. 44 MISBEG
(JOSIE IS SMILING WITH RELIEF NOW.) 67 MISBEG
(SMILING, BUT A BIT SHOCKED.) 32 POET
(SMILING.) ARRAH, NONE OF YOUR AIRS AND GRACES 66 POET
WITH ME/
SHE SPEAKS IN A LOW, CONFIDENTIAL TONE HERSELF, 84 POET
SMILING NATURALLY.)
(SHE PAUSES, SMILING AT HER MEMORIES.) 84 POET
SMILING TOLERANTLY.) 101 POET
(SMILING) SURE. 592 ROPE
NODDING BACK AT THE MAID AND SMILING KINDLY) 5 STRANG
(WHAT MEMORIES ON SUCH A SMILING AFTERNOON/..... 5 STRANG
(SMILING GRIMLY) (POOR PROFESSOR/ 24 STRANG
(GOOD-NATUREDLY SMILING) THAT'S RIGHT/ 41 STRANG
(SMILING AT HIM SWIFTLY AND MECHANICALLY) 41 STRANG
(SMILING KINDLY AT EVANS--STILL IN HER FATHER'S 47 STRANG
TONES)
BUT SMILING KINDLY. 50 STRANG
(COMES IN FROM THE KITCHEN, A CUP OF COFFEE IN HER 56 STRANG
HAND, SMILING HAPPILY)

SMILING

SMILING (CONT'D.)
BUT SAMMY WAS BORN HEALTHY AND SMILING, AND WE 58 STRANG
JUST HAD TO LOVE HIM.
(AS THEY SHAKE HANDS--SMILING) 79 STRANG
(SMILING) OR WHAT A BECOMING ALIBI YOU COULD COOK 80 STRANG
UP/
(SMILING) WELL--MAYBE. 80 STRANG
(SMILING) I HOPE SO. 80 STRANG
(SMILING--BUT EMPHATICALLY) NOT ON YOUR LIFE/ 81 STRANG
(SMILING TENDERLY--THINKING) 102 STRANG
SMILING/... 105 STRANG
(SMILING-- 114 STRANG
(SMILING, GENTLY RELEASES HER HAND) 119 STRANG
(IMMEDIATELY URBANE AND SMILING) 129 STRANG
(HE COMES TO HER, SMILING WITH ASSURANCE.) 133 STRANG
(SMILING WITH A WRY AMUSEMENT AT HERSELF) 138 STRANG
(SMILING BACK) AND I MUST LOVE YOU. 144 STRANG
(MOURNFULLY SMILING) I MUST, OR I'D NEVER ACT 144 STRANG
THIS FOOL WAY, WOULD I?
(SMILING) SURELY--AGAIN? 145 STRANG
(MARSDEN COMES IN FROM THE REAR, SMILING, 146 STRANG
IMMACULATELY DRESSED AS USUAL.
(SMILING STRANGELY) YES. 152 STRANG
HER FACE IS THIN, HER CHEEKS TAUT, HER MOUTH DRAWN158 STRANG
WITH FORCED SMILING.
(SMILING) YES, PERHAPS UNCONSCIOUSLY PRESTON IS A166 STRANG
COMPENSATING SUBSTITUTE.
(THEN SMILING GOODNATUREDLY) 179 STRANG
THEN STILL SMILING, MAKES A GESTURE TOWARD THE TWO187 STRANG
LOVERS)
(SMILING SADLY) AGAIN. 197 STRANG
(SADLY SMILING) YOU, CHARLIE, I SUPPOSE. 197 STRANG
(SMILING--PUTS HER HAND OVER HIS ON THE TABLE) 501 VOYAGE
(SMILING) WHAT WERE YOU DREAMING ABOUT WHEN I 445 WELDED
INTRUDED?
(SMILING--QUICKLY) OH, I'LL PROMISE TO BE GOOD-- 446 WELDED
IF YOU WILL.
(SMILING BUT WITH DEEP EARNESTNESS NEVERTHELESS) 447 WELDED
(SMILING) ANOTHER GRAND IDEAL FOR OUR MARRIAGE? 447 WELDED
(SMILING TENSELY) WOULD I STILL BE WELCOME IF I'D463 WELDED
COME--TO STAY?
(SMILING BUT EARNESTLY) IT'LL RELIEVE YOUR MIND, 467 WELDED
NELLY--
SHE TURNS TO HIM, SMILING WITH CHILDISH PRIDE) 474 WELDED
(SMILING DIMLY AT HERSELF) MY ACTING--DIDN'T 488 WELDED
CONVINCE ME.
(SMILING) DEEPER AND MORE BEAUTIFUL? 489 WELDED
SMILINGLY
THE WALKS TO HER CHAIR AND BENDS DOWN TO KISS HER 150 BEYOND
SMILINGLY)
(AWARE OF HER DAUGHTER'S FEELINGS--SMILINGLY BUT 511 DIFRNT
FIRMLY)
(TURNS SMILINGLY TO THEM, IN A MERRY TONE THAT IS 20 JOURNE
A BIT FORCED.)
(SHE ADDS SMILINGLY.) THAT IS IF I CAN FIND MY 75 JOURNE
GLASSES.
MARY GOES ON SMILINGLY.) 100 JOURNE
(AS LAZARUS SMILINGLY SHAKES HIS HEAD, TIBERIUS 339 LAZARU
FROWNS)
(SMILINGLY LAZARUS ASCENDS TO WHERE TIBERIUS 340 LAZARU
POINTS AT THE TOP OF THE DAIS.
THOUGHTS AND LOOKS BACK TOWARD THE DOORWAY AT REAR 44 MANSNS
SMILINGLY.
(RISING AS SHE ENTERS--SMILINGLY.) 44 MANSNS
(STARES AT HER--SMILINGLY.) YOU OBJECTED TO THAT5 45 MANSNS
(SMILINGLY EVASIVE.) I'D RATHER NOT, SARA, IF YOU 55 MANSNS
DON'T MIND.
(THROWS OFF HER MOOD--SMILINGLY.) 57 MANSNS
(SMILINGLY, BUT WITH A THREAT UNDERNEATH.) 92 MANSNS
(SMILINGLY.) YOU WILL UNDERSTAND WHY WHEN I TELL 97 MANSNS
YOU THE ONE PERSON WHO
(SMILINGLY--COMPLACENTLY MATERNAL.) 127 MANSNS
(SHE TURNS, MAKING HER FACE SMILINGLY 137 MANSNS
EXPRESSIONLESS.
LAUGHS--THEN SMILINGLY TO NICOLO) 360 MARCOM
(SMILINGLY) YES. AND BE AMUSED. 382 MARCOM
(KUBLAI LOOKS AT HER WITH A SAD WONDERMENT, CHU- 397 MARCOM
VIN SMILINGLY.
(A PAUSE--SMILINGLY.) IT WAS SIMON WHO FELT GUILTY149 POET
AND REPENTANT.
(SMILINGLY GETS TO HIS FEET--THINKING) 129 STRANG
SMIRK
(HE LAUGHS WITH A LASCIVIOUS SMIRK.) 526 DIFRNT
(WITH A SALACIOUS SMIRK) CAN'T SAY AS I BLAME 71 ELECTR
HIM/
(WITH A COARSE, MEANING SMIRK) 303 LAZARU
EVERYONE IS GETTING TO KNOW--TO SMIRK AND WHISPER/142 MANSNS
(WITH A CUNNING SMIRK) SELLING A BIG BILL OF 365 MARCOM
GOODS HERE--ABOUT5. I'LL WAGER.
(STILL MORE CONFUSED--WITH A SILLY IDIOTIC SMIRK) 117 STRANG
SMIRKING
(SMIRKING MYSTERIOUSLY) OH, WAYS OF DRESSIN' AND 526 DIFRNT
DOIN' THEIR HAIR--
(HE APPROACHES A LADY--WITH A VICIOUS GRIN AND A 237 HA APE
SMIRKING WINK)
(WITH A SMIRKING WINK) PRETTY, 'OLESOME GELS THEY499 VOYAGE
BE, AIN'T THEY, NICKS
SMIRKINGLY
(SMIRKINGLY OBEDIENT.) QUIET IT IS, YER HONOR. 97 POET
SMIRKS
SHE SMIRKS AT RICHARD) 237 AHWILD
SMITE
LORD GOD O' HOSTS, SMITE THE UNDUTIFUL SONS WITH 227 DESIRE
THY WUST CUSS/
IS NOT THE TIME RIPE TO SMITE THIS BLASPHEMER 423 DYNAMO
MAY JEHOVAH SMITE YOU IN YOUR LIES/ 284 LAZARU

SMITH'S
THE VALUE OF THE PROPERTY--OUR HOME WHICH IS HIS, 564 CROSS
SMITH'S.
ERIE SMITH'S THE NAME. 10 HUGHIE
SMITHEREENS
YE'D BE BLOWN TO SMITHEREENS B'FORE YE CUD SAY 517 INZONE
YOUR NAME.
THE LONGING IN YOUR HEART THAT I'D SMASH THE 191 MANSNS
COMPANY INTO SMITHEREENS
SMITHERS'
(THEN CATCHING SMITHERS' EYE ON HIM, 182 EJONES
SMITING
IT IS PAINTED A DAZZLING, EYE-SMITING SCARLET. 173 EJONES
SMITTEN
CRUEL WHEN SPRING IS SMITTEN BY WINTER, WHEN BIRDS436 MARCOM
ARE STRUCK DEAD IN FULL SONG,
SMOKE
WELL, I'LL SMOKE ALONE THEN. 201 AHWILD
I NEVER SMOKE. 201 AHWILD
PUT THAT IN YOUR PIPE AND SMOKE IT/ 203 AHWILD
GIRLS ARE ONLY ALLOWED TO SMOKE UPSTAIRS IN THE 239 AHWILD
ROOMS, HE SAID.
YOU SMOKE, DON'T YOUS 239 AHWILD
BUT A GOOD CIGAR'S A SMOKE.-- 245 AHWILD
LET YOU SMOKE IN HERE, WON'T THEY5 15 ANNA
SO PUT THAT IN YOUR PIPE AND SMOKE IT/ 57 ANNA
LOOK AT THAT LAMP CHIMNEY ALL SMOKE/ 151 BEYOND
AND THE AIR IS HEAVY WITH RANCID TOBACCO SMOKE. 477 CARDIF
HER EYES WEEP'IN AN' BLOODY WITH SMOKE AN' CINDERS209 DESIRE
SAME'S THEY USED T'BE.
YE'D ON'Y TO PLOW AN' SOW AN' THEN SET AN' SMOKE 237 DESIRE
YER PIPE AN' WATCH THIN'S GROW.
WHEN THE SMOKE CLEARS WHAT JEFF HAS DISAPPEARED. 192 EJONES
BLACK SMOKE FROM THE FUNNELS SMUDGING THE SEA, 214 HA APE
SMUDGING THE DECKS--
DE ENGINES AND DE COAL AND DE SMOKE AND ALL DE 215 HA APE
REST OF IT/
DE NOISE AND SMOKE AND ALL DE ENGINES MOVIN' DE 216 HA APE
WOILD, DEY STOP.
I'M SMOKE AND EXPRESS TRAINS AND STEAMERS AND 216 HA APE
FACTORY WHISTLES.
(WITHOUT LOOKING UP) I DISLIKE SMOKE OF ANY KIND.218 HA APE
HOW THE BLACK SMOKE SWIRLS BACK AGAINST THE SKY/ 218 HA APE
WATCH HER SMOKE/ 224 HA APE
I'M STEEL AND STEAM AND SMOKE AND DE REST OF IT/ 238 HA APE
YOU WATCH MY SMOKE/ 242 HA APE
WATCH DE SMOKE AND SEE IT MOVE/ 249 HA APE
THE ONLY PLACE I LIKED WAS THE POOL ROOMS, WHERE 1709 ICEMAN
COULD SMOKE SWEET CAPORAL5.
BLACK SMOKE POURING FROM THE FUNNELS BEHIND AND 153 JOURNE
BENEATH ME.
NO, I'M AFRAID I'M LIKE THE GUY WHO IS ALWAYS 154 JOURNE
PANHANDLING FOR A SMOKE.
THE SMOKE POURED FROM THE WINDOWS' THE NEIGHBORS 346 LAZARU
THOUGHT THE HOUSE WAS BURNING/
(BLOWS OUT THE MATCH IN A CLOUD OF SMOKE) 131 MISBEG
BUT I'LL TELL YOU SOMETHING YOU CAN PUT IN YOUR 596 ROPE
PIPE AND SMOKE.
SMOKED
MY GREAT-GRANDMOTHER SMOKED A PIPE---A CLAY PIPE. 218 HA APE
SMOKES
HOLY SMOKES, 237 HA APE
HE SMOKES A PIPE, WHICH HE IS ALWAYS RELIGHTING 66 STRANG
WHETHER IT NEEDS IT OR NOT,
SMOKIN'
AND DE EMPEROR BETTER GIT HIS FEET SMOKIN' UP DE 182 EJONES
TRAIL.
SMOKING
BOTH SMOKING CIGARS. 188 AHWILD
I'VE BEEN SMOKING FOR THE LAST TWO YEARS--ON THE 239 AHWILD
SLY.
SHE KEPT SMOKING UNE CIGARETTE AFTER ANOTHER-- 283 AHWILD
AND HER SMOKING CIGARETTES PROVES IT/ 283 AHWILD
NEARLY ALL ARE SMOKING PIPES OR CIGARETTES. 455 CARIBE
WHO SITS SMOKING HIS PIPE IN FRONT OF HIS DOOR. 466 CARIBE
THE DONKEYMAN QUIETLY SMOKING ON HIS STOOL. ... 472 CARIBE
AND WID THE DAY DONEY IN THE DOG WATCH, SMOKING ME214 HA APE
PIPE AT EASE.
THE OTHERS, MOST OF THEM SMOKING PIPES, ARE 226 HA APE
STARING AT YANK HALF-APPREHENSIVELY.
MOST OF THEM ARE SMOKING PIPES. 245 HA APE
BEJEÉS, JIMMY'S STARTED THEM OFF SMOKING THE SAME 605 ICEMAN
HOP.
THE YOUNG BOYS AND GIRLS PLACE THEIR SMOKING 434 MARCOM
CENSERS ABOUT THE CATAFALQUE.
SMOKING A CIGARETTE. 493 VOYAGE
SMOKING'S
SMOKING'S AWFUL BAD FOR GIRLS, ANYWAY, EVEN IF 240 AHWILD
THEY DON'T--
SMOKY
THE ROOM, SEEN BY THE LIGHT OF THE SHADELESS OIL 144 BEYOND
LAMP WITH A SMOKY CHIMNEY WHICH
O' SMOKY TEA-KETTLES, THE OLD DAYS IS DYIN', AND 105 ELECTR
WHERE'LL YOU AN' ME BE THEN5
LIGHT GRADUALLY BECOMES BRIGHTER, AND THEN SLOWLY 578 ROPE
FADES INTO A SMOKY CRIMSON.
SMOLDERING
(WITH SMOLDERING HATRED) VELL, YUST LET HIM/ 43 ANNA
(IN A LOW, REPRESSED VOICE--HER EYES SMOLDERING) 126 BEYOND
(THEN HIS RESENTMENT SMOLDERING UP) 435 DYNAMO
WITH BALKINESS ALWAYS SMOLDERING IN ITS WALL EYES,576 ICEMAN
A SMOLDERING RESENTMENT BEGINNING TO SHOW IN HIS 659 ICEMAN
MANNER.)
OLIVE-COLORED WITH THE RED OF BLOOD SMOLDERING 336 LAZARU
THROUGH, WITH GREAT, DARK,
(HE BURSTS OUT IN A FIT OF SMOLDERING RAGE) 176 MISBEG
SMOLLETT'S
THIERS' HISTORY OF THE CONSULATE AND EMPIRE, 11 JOURNE
SMOLLETT'S HISTORY OF ENGLAND,

SMOOTH

YOU GO IN AND SMOOTH HIM DOWN, MOM, 455 DYNAMO
HIS FACE IS ROUND AND SMOOTH AND BIG-BOYISH WITH 618 ICEMAN
BRIGHT BLUE EYES,
SOUND COMMON SENSE AND A HOME WHERE EVERTHING RUNS416 MARCOM
SMOOTH,
SHE HAS LONG SMOOTH ARMS, IMMENSELY STRONG, 3 MISBEG
ALTHOUGH NO MUSCLES SHOW.
(HE DRINKS) THERE YUH ARE--SMOOTH AS SILK. 595 ROPE

SMOOTHING
SMOOTHING HIS HAIR BACK FROM HIS FOREHEAD) 208 AHWILD
(SMOOTHING MARY'S HAIR--TENDERLY) 121 BEYOND
(TENDERLY, SMOOTHING HIS HAIR) 184 STRANG

SMOOTHLY
(BUT IT DOESN'T GO SMOOTHLY AND AS HE GOES ON HE 295 AHWILD
BECOMES MORE AND MORE GUILTILY

SMOOTHS
THE ELDEST SMOOTHS BACK HER HAIR.) 293 GGBROW
SHE BENDS OVER MIRIAM AND SMOOTHS THE HAIR BACK 361 LAZARU
FROM HER FOREHEAD)

SMOTHERED
I SMOTHERED HIM. 263 DESIRE
SHE GIVES A SMOTHERED GASP, WRENCHES HER EYES FROM 27 MANSNS
THE DARKNESS INSIDE.

SMOTHERS
(THEN AS SID SMOTHERS A BURST OF RIBALD LAUGHTER) 197 AHWILD

SMOULDER
THE FLAME OF AMBITION SMOULDER INTO A CHILL 102 MANSNS
DISMAY--
AND HER EYES SMOULDER WITH A BITTER, JEALOUS 161 MANSNS
HATRED.

SMOULDERING
REFLECT THE SUN IN A SMOULDERING STARE, AS OF 169 ELECTR
BROODING REVENGEFUL EYES.
(HIS RAGE STILL SMOULDERING.) 80 JOURNE

SMUDGE
THE BLACK SMUDGE OF COAL DUST STILL STICKS LIKE 233 HA APE
MAKE-UP.

SMUDGED
STREAKS OF SWEAT HAVE SMUDGED THE LAYER OF DUST ON119 BEYOND
HIS CHEEKS.

SMUDGING
BLACK SMOKE FROM THE FUNNELS SMUDGING THE SEA, 214 HA APE
SMUDGING THE DECKS--

SMUG
I HATE THAT SMUG, LUSTFUL, GREEDY TRADER'S SMILE 119 MANSNS
OF HIS/

SMUGGLE
THAT'LL TEACH YOU TO SMUGGLE RUM ON A SHIP AND 473 CARIBE
START A RIOT.

SMUT
FOR CHRIST SAKE, QUIT THE SMUT STUFF, CAN'T YOU/ 127 MISBEG
HOW ABOUT YOUR NOT TALKING THE OLD SMUT STUFF TO 127 MISBEG
ME$

SMUTTIEST
YOU SEE, SHE WAS ONE OF THE SMUTTIEST TALKING PIGS127 MISBEG
I'VE EVER LISTENED TO.

SMUTTY
YOU MADE OUR LOVE A SMUTTY JOKE FOR HER AND EVERY 549 DAYS
ONE LIKE HER--
YOU EVEN ARE DUTY BOUND TO LAUGH AT A GUEST'S 31 HUGHIE
SMUTTY JOKES.

SNAKE
A SNAKE-FENCE SIDLES FROM LEFT TO RIGHT ALONG THE 81 BEYOND
TOP OF THE BANK,
BY THE LINES OF STONE WALLS AND ROUGH SNAKE 81 BEYOND
FENCES.
PARTS OF THE SNAKE-FENCE IN THE REAR HAVE BEEN 166 BEYOND
BROKEN DOWN.
SHE SAID SHE CUD SNAKE UT ON BOARD IN THE BOTTOMS 458 CARIBE
AV THIM BASKETS AV FRUIT
I'D AS SOON PET A SKUNK 'N KISS A SNAKE/ 214 DESIRE
KEPT HIS NOSE TO THE GRINDSTONE AND SOLD ONE 627 ICEMAN
BOTTLE OF SNAKE OIL TOO MANY.
TELLING THEM THERE'S NOTHING LIKE SNAKE OIL FOR A 628 ICEMAN
BAD BURN.
A SNAKE IS STARTING TO CRAWL FROM THE BASKET IN 369 MARCOM
FRONT OF HIM.
THE SLOW-RISING LIGHT REVEALS AN INDIAN SNAKE- 369 MARCOM
CHARMER.
THEY STARE AT THE SNAKE-CHARMER, THE TWO OLDER MEN369 MARCOM
CYNICALLY.
THE SNAKE-CHARMER GLARES AT THEM, STOPS PLAYING, 370 MARCOM
PUSHES HIS SNAKE BACK INTO THE BOX AND CARRIES IT 370 MARCOM
OFF.
LOOK AT THAT DEADLY SNAKE/ 370 MARCOM
SURE, IF YOU'VE FOUND A SNAKE WHO CAN STAB YOU 78 MISBEG
WITH A KNIFE.
NOR A TREACHEROUS SNAKE IN THE GRASS WHO STABS YOU 78 MISBEG
IN THE BACK WITH A KNIFE--
HE'S A DIRTY SNAKE/ 86 MISBEG
A HEAP OF STONES, A MUD IMAGE, A DRAWING ON A 41 STRANG
WALL, A BIRD, A FISH, A SNAKE,

SNAKE'S
HIS OLD SNAKE'S EYES WAS GLITTERIN' IN THE SUN 209 DESIRE
LIKE HE'D BEEN DRINKIN' A JUGFUL
FEELING LOWER THAN A SNAKE'S BELLY. 29 HUGHIE
WHAT A SNAKE'S TONGUE HE HAS IN HIM/ 584 ROPE

SNAKES
I'LL DROWN YOUR SNAKES FOR YUH/ 245 HA APE
TAKING CARE OF YOU AND SHOOTING AWAY YOUR SNAKES, 610 ICEMAN
WHEN SAINT PATRICK DROVE THE SNAKES OUT OF IRELAND718 ICEMAN
THEY SWAM TO NEW YORK AND
POTATO BUGS, SNAKES AND SKUNKS ON HIS FARM, 24 JOURNE
AND THERE'S SNAKES AND SKUNKS/ 63 MISBEG
WHILE INNUMERABLE PLAIN ONES TELL HIM DREAMS ABOUT 34 STRANG
SNAKES...

SNAKESKIN
AND HAS THE LIFELESS SHEEN OF A SHED SNAKESKIN. 27 MANSNS

SNAP
(SHUTTING THE BOOK WITH A SNAP) 122 BEYOND
THE EXCITEMENT RETURNS TO HIS FACE, HIS EYES SNAP,267 DESIRE
HE LOOKS A BIT CRAZY)
FROM NOW ON YOU HAS A SNAP. 191 EJONES
(BEGINNING TO SNAP UNDER THE STRAIN--JUMPS TO HER 60 ELECTR
FEET AGAIN)
THERE IS A CRACKING SNAP OF CRUSHED RIBS-- 254 HA APE
(HIS TENSE QUIET BEGINNING TO SNAP.) 172 MANSNS
YOU'VE GOT TO HELP SNAP HER OUT OF THIS. 37 STRANG
SNAP OUT OF IT/ 165 STRANG

SNAPPED
SOMETHING SNAPPED IN HIM THEN. 511 DAYS
AS IF SOME LONG PATIENT TENSION HAD SNAPPED-- AS IF 74 MANSNS
I NO LONGER HAD THE POWER TO

SNAPPILY
(SNAPPILY) YOU BE QUIET/ 251 AHWILD
(SNAPPILY) HE'S HAD THREE YEARS TO LEARN, 114 BEYOND
(SNAPPILY) IT WOULDN'T IF YOU POSSESSED A BIT OF 117 BEYOND
SPUNK.

SNAPPING
(HIS EYES AND VOICE SNAPPING) 544 *ILE
AND A HABIT OF SNAPPING OUT HER WORDS LIKE AN 10 ELECTR
OFFICER GIVING ORDERS.
(HER VOICE STRIDENT, AS IF HER WILL WERE SNAPPING)151 ELECTR
(HER CONTROL SNAPPING--TURNING ON HIM NOW IN A 166 ELECTR
BURST OF FRANTIC HATRED AND RAGE)
(SNAPPING) GOD DAMN HIS YELLOW SOUL, IF HE DOESN'T726 ICEMAN
SOON,
LIKE SNAPPING YOUR FINGERS/ 150 JOURNE
(THEN HER TENSION SNAPPING SHE BURSTS INTO SOBS 144 MANSNS
(THEN SUDDENLY SNAPPING AND BURSTING OUT IN A 63 STRANG
DESPAIRING CRY)

SNAPPISHLY
(SNAPPISHLY) IF YE HEERD US THEY HAIN'T NO NEED 231 DESIRE
ASKIN' QUESTIONS.

SNAPPY
LINEN DUSTERS, VEILS, GOGGLES, SID IN A SNAPPY 208 AHWILD
CAP.)

SNAPS
(HE SNAPS HIS FINGERS) THAT EASY/ I PLUNGED. 156 BEYOND
(HE SNAPS HIS FINGERS--THEN URGENTLY) 548 DIFRNT
(THE STRAIN SNAPS FOR HIM AND HE LAUGHS WITH 101 ELECTR
SAVAGE IRONY)
(SNAPS AND TURNS ON HIM, HIS FACE CONVULSED WITH 720 ICEMAN
DETESTATION.
(HE SNAPS HIS BOOK SHUT AND SPRINGS TO HIS FEET-- 130 MANSNS
THERE IS A CRACK AS THE CHAIR BACK SNAPS IN HALF. 92 POET

SNARES
(TRIUMPHANTLY) YOU THOUGHT YOU HAD HIM CAUGHT IN 451 DYNAMO
YOUR SNARES, DID YOU$
WITH YOU TWO SCHEMING PEASANTS LAYING SNARES TO 60 POET
TRAP HIM/

SNARL
(IN WHAT IS CLOSE TO A SNARL OF SCORN) 508 DAYS
(WITH A DEFENSIVE SNARL--HASTILY) 321 GGBROW
(DRAWING BACK HIS FIST, WITH A SNARL) 216 HA APE
THEN, WITH A SNARL OF FURY LIKE AN ANIMAL'S HE 460 WELDED
SEIZES HER ABOUT THE THROAT WITH

SNARLING
(HIS HAND ON HIS SHEATH-KNIFE--SNARLING) 461 CARIBE
(IN A SNARLING TONE) I S'POSE YOU'VE BEEN GIVIN' 528 DIFRNT
HIM AN EARFUL OF LIES ABOUT
(IN A SNARLING WHISPER) THAT'S RIGHT/ 529 DIFRNT
(SNARLING) GAWD BLIMEY/ 179 EJONES
HE WHIRLS DEFENSIVELY WITH A SNARLING, MURDEROUS 225 HA APE
GROWL, CROUCHING TO SPRING.
FOILED IN THIS, SNARLING WITH PASSION, HE LEAPS TO238 HA APE
THE LAMP--
(SNARLING) ARRH/ THINK YOU'RE FUNNY/ CAPTAIN, 602 ICEMAN
BEJESUS/
(SNARLING WITH RAGE, 672 ICEMAN

SNARLS
THE GORILLA RATTLES THE BARS OF HIS CAGE AND 253 HA APE
SNARLS.

SNATCH
I WILL BE THE ONE TO SNATCH AWAY MY HAND AND LEAVE163 MANSNS
YOU ALONE IN THERE
AND AT THE LAST MOMENT HE WILL SNATCH HIS HAND 163 MANSNS
AWAY.
(TRIES TO SNATCH IT) NO/ 375 MARCOM
A SNATCH FROM AN OLD SOB SONG, POPULAR IN THE 111 MISBEG
NINETIES)
I HAVE TRIED TO TEACH THE WAITRESS NOT TO SNATCH 98 POET
PLATES FROM THE TABLE

SNATCHED
WITH A PIECE OF CLOTH WHICH HE HAS SNATCHED FROM 538 *ILE
HIS POCKET.

SNATCHES
(HARDLY ABLE TO BELIEVE HER EYES, ALMOST SNATCHES 242 AHWILD
IT FROM HIS HAND--
HE SNATCHES HIS HAND AWAY FROM HER ANGRILY.) 256 AHWILD
(SHE HOLDS OUT A BOTTLE WHICH HE SNATCHES FROM HER465 CARIBE
HAND.
HE SNATCHES AT A CHANCE TO CHANGE THE SUBJECT-- 188 EJONES
SOLICITOUSLY)
HE SNATCHES AT HIS HIP, SHOUTING DEFIANTLY.) 202 EJONES
SNATCHES UP THE BOX FROM THE TABLE AND HOLDS IT 62 ELECTR
BEHIND HER BACK.
IMMEDIATELY SHE SNATCHES IT UP AND STARES AT IT, 64 ELECTR
LAVINIA REACHES OUT STEALTHILY AND SNATCHES UP THE 101 ELECTR
BOX.
(CHUCK SNATCHES A WHISKEY BOTTLE FROM THE BAR 672 ICEMAN
DAVIS SNATCHES A SMALL COIL OF ROPE FROM ONE OF 525 INZONE
THE UPPER BUNKS)
(AS IF HE HAD TO CUT SOMETHING, HE SNATCHES UP A 311 LAZARU
HANDFUL OF FLOWERS--

SNATCHES

SNATCHES

SNATCHES (CONT'D.)
HOPS TO HIS FEET AND SNATCHES UP HIS SWORD 311 LAZARU DEFENSIVELY.
(HE SNATCHES A SPEAR FROM A SOLDIER AND FIGHTS HIS369 LAZARU WAY DRUNKENLY TOWARD THE
(WITH SUDDEN CUNNING MOTION, HE SNATCHES IT FROM 360 MARCOM MARCOT'S HAND.)
O'DOWE OFFICIOUSLY SNATCHES IT OFF FOR HIM-- 53 POET REBUKINGLY.)
SHE SNATCHES HER HAND FROM HIS AND SPEAKS WITH 72 POET WITHERING CONTEMPT.)
THEN SNATCHES THE PLATE FROM IN FRONT OF HIM.) 98 POET AND QUICKLY SNATCHES UP THE DOLL, WHICH SHE HUGS 578 ROPE FIERCELY TO HER BREAST.

SNATCHING
MOCKERY UP UNDIGNIFIED AGE SNATCHING GREEDILY AT 520 DIFRNT THE EMPTY SIMULACRA OF YOUTH.
(SNATCHING HER HAND BACK) DON'T BE STUPID, 14 ELECTR PETER/.
AGITATEDLY SNATCHING HER HAND FROM HIS AND TURNING 21 ELECTR AWAY FROM HIM.)
(WITH HAUGHTY ANGER--SNATCHING SARA'S HAND OFF HER193 MANSNS AAM.)
(THE TWO ELDER ARE SURREPTITIOUSLY SNATCHING AT 419 MARCOM THE COINS

SNEAK
WHEN I THINK OF THE BOOKS I USED TO SNEAK OFF AND 193 AHWILD READ WHEN I WAS A KID.
AND SHE'S GOING TO TRY AND SNEAK OUT AND MEET ME 273 AHWILD TONIGHT.
I'LL SNEAK OUT THE BACK. 274 AHWILD
YOU DIDN'T TAKE THE TROUBLE TO SNEAK ANY LETTER TO278 AHWILD ME, I NOTICE/
AND I HAD SAND ENOUGH TO SNEAK OUT AND MEET YOU 286 AHWILD TONIGHT, DIDN'T IS
PUT A SNEAK IN ONE AND IT GIVES HIM THE COURAGE TO541 DIFRNT BE A THIEF/
(I BETTER SNEAK OUT THE BACK...)) 426 DYNAMO
AND SERVE HIM RIGHT, THE BLOODY SNEAK/ 440 DYNAMO
AND A SNEAK, AND I DON'T WONDER YOU FEEL GUILTY IN446 DYNAMO GOD'S SIGHT/
AND YOU BETTER GRAB ALL YOU KIN SNEAK AWAY WID 186 EJONES BEFO' DEY GITS HERE.
WHY DID YOU SNEAK AWAY LIKE THATS 80 ELECTR
(TURNS TO HER STARTLEDLY) DAMN IT, DON'T SNEAK 94 ELECTR AROUND LIKE THAT/
(FURTIVELY) I COULD SNEAK OUT WHEN SHE WASN'T 161 ELECTR LOOKING--
(ANGRILY) THE LITTLE SNEAK/ 175 ELECTR
DIDN'T I SNEAK ON DE DOCK AND WAIT FOR HER BY DE 235 HA APE GANGPLANKS
HE'S GOT NO RIGHT TO SNEAK OUT OF EVERYTHING. 623 ICEMAN
SHE'D SNEAK NOTES TO ME AND MEET ME ON THE SLY. 710 ICEMAN
I'LL SHOW YER WHAT FOR, YER BLEEDIN' SNEAK/ 526 INZONE
THAT'LL TEACH YOU TO BE MISNAMIN' A MAN, YE SNEAK.527 INZONE
THAT YOU'RE MAKING ME CALL THEM SO YOU CAN SNEAK A 52 JOURNE DRINK BEFORE THEY COME.
WHY DON'T YOU SNEAK ONE WHILE YOU'VE GOT A CHANCE5 54 JOURNE
(WITH DETACHED AMUSEMENT.) HE'LL SNEAK AROUND TO 117 JOURNE THE OUTSIDE CELLAR DOOR.
I'VE GOT TO SNEAK BACK. 357 MARCOM
HOW COULD I SNEAK HERE SOONER WITH HIM PEEKING 4 MISBEG ROUND THE CORNER OF THE BARN TO
I'VE OFTEN SUSPECTED YOU SNEAK OUT OF BED IN THE 23 MISBEG NIGHT TO PICK YOUR OWN POCKETS.
DON'T TALK NONSENSE TO SNEAK OUT OF TREATING JIM. 52 MISBEG
THEN YOU CAN SNEAK IN THE INN YOURSELF AND PICK 96 MISBEG THE WITNESSES TO STAY UP WITH
I CAN'T SNEAK AWAY OR HE'D BE SUSPICIOUS. 99 MISBEG
I HEARD YOU SNEAK UP. 157 MISBEG
LIKE A SNEAK, A COWARD/... 108 STRANG

SNEAKED
DICK ONLY SNEAKED OFF TO THE FIREWORKS AT THE 251 AHWILD BEACH. YOU WAIT AND SEE.
I SUPPOSE HE SNEAKED OFF TO WATCH THE FIREWORKS. 254 AHWILD
GEE, I'LL BET MA HAD A FIT WHEN SHE FOUND OUT I'D 275 AHWILD SNEAKED OUT....
AND THEN I SNEAKED DOWN THE BACK STAIRS. 281 AHWILD
I WAS SO SCARED, AND THEN I SNEAKED OUT THROUGH 281 AHWILD THE BACK YARD.
I SNEAKED OUT AND WENT TO A LOW DIVE I KNOW ABOUT.282 AHWILD
WHEN YOU GOT TO SHOUTIN' I SNEAKED OUT O' THE 544 DIFRNT KITCHEN INTO THERE TO HEAR WHAT
HE SNEAKED OUT/... 427 DYNAMO
BUT THIS FELLOW WHO WAS ENGAGED TO HER GOT 440 DYNAMO SUSPICIOUS AND ONE NIGHT HE SNEAKED
(HE RUNS OFF RIGHT, FORGETTING THAT HE HAS SNEAKED445 DYNAMO OUT BY THE BACK.
IT REALLY BEGAN THE NIGHT BEFORE WHEN I SNEAKED 95 ELECTR THROUGH THEIR LINES.
A BOY SNEAKED UP BEHIND WHEN I WAS DRAWING A 295 GGBROW PICTURE IN THE SAND HE COULDN'T
AND DEN I SEEN YOUSE LOOKIN' AT SOMEP'N AND I 230 HA APE TOUGHT HE'D SNEAKED DOWN TO COME
WELL, ANYWAY, HUGHIE SNEAKED THE TWO BUCKS BACK IN 22 HUGHIE THE LITTLE WOMAN'S PURSE.
I SNEAKED UP THERE ONE NIGHT AFTER SHE WAS 589 ICEMAN ARRESTED.
HE WAS IN THE MEADOW, BUT THE MINUTE I TURNED MY 12 MISBEG BACK HE SNEAKED OFF.
I'LL BET, LIKE WHEN THOMAS AND JOHN SNEAKED OFF, 14 MISBEG YOU--
AND SEEN THE FOOTPRINTS WHERE YOU HAD SNEAKED UP 62 MISBEG IN THE NIGHT TO PULL IT DOWN
AND THAT NIGHT SHE SNEAKED INTO MY DRAWING ROOM. 149 MISBEG
(AVOIDING HER EYES.) I SNEAKED BACK TO LISTEN 79 POET OUTSIDE THE DOOR.

SNEAKED (CONT'D.)
(THINKING IN A PANIC) (SHE SNEAKED INTO MY SOUL 42 STRANG TO SPY/...))

SNEAKERS
SNEAKERS OVER BARE FEET, AND SOILED WHITE FLANNEL 260 GGBROW TROUSERS.
HE WEARS A SHIRT, COLLAR AND TIE, NO COAT, OLD 20 JOURNE FLANNEL TROUSERS, BROWN SNEAKERS.

SNEAKIN
(POINTINTING) LOOKIN' AROUND SNEAKIN-LIKE AT IVAN 518 INZONE AND SWANSON AND THE REST 'S IF

SNEAKIN'
SHE DON'T GO SNEAKIN' AN' STEALIN'---WHAT'S MINE. 230 DESIRE
THE OLD CRITTER'S LIABLE T' SUSPICION AN' COME 245 DESIRE SNEAKIN' UP.
SNEAKIN' DOWN THE CHIMNEY, POKIN' IN THE CORNERS/ 253 DESIRE
SHE TOLD ME YE WAS SNEAKIN' 'ROUND TRYIN' T' MAKE 255 DESIRE LOVE T' HER
SO THAT'S HER SNEAKIN' GAME--ALL ALONG/ 255 DESIRE
YE'VE BEEN ONLY PLAYIN' YER SNEAKIN', STEALIN' 257 DESIRE GAME ALL ALONG--
I SEE YER GAME NOW--THE SAME OLD SNEAKIN' TRICK-- 261 DESIRE
THE SNEAKIN' WAY YOU'RE MAKIN' A SILLY FOOL OUT OF528 DIFRNT POUR EMMER CROSBY,
BUT WHEN HE STARTS IN HIS SNEAKIN' THIEVERY WITH 541 DIFRNT YOU, EMMER,
WHAT SNEAKIN' THIEVERY WITH MES 541 DIFRNT
WHAT ARE YOU SNEAKIN' AWAY FORS 174 EJONES
JEES, HICKEY, YUH SCARED ME OUTA A YEAR'S GROWTH, 638 ICEMAN SNEAKIN' IN LIKE DAT.
AND ALL DE GANG SNEAKIN' UPSTAIRS, 665 ICEMAN
DID YE SEE THE SNEAKIN' LOOKS HE GAVE US$ 523 INZONE
(IMPRESSIVELY) BUT THEY HAD A WAY O' DOIN' IT--A 529 INZONE DAMN SNEAKIN' WAY.
AND NOT BE SNEAKIN' UP TO THIS BARN NO MORE. 579 ROPE
LORD SAKES, SOON 'S EVER MY BACK IS TURNED YOU 579 ROPE GOES SNEAKIN' OFF AGEN.
AND I SEEN HIM MANY A TIME AT HIS SNEAKIN'. 599 ROPE
I SEEN YER A-PLAYIN' YER SNEAKIN' TRICKS, BUT YER 508 VOYAGE CAN'T FOOL JOE.

SNEAKIN-LIKE
(POINTINGOINTING) LOOKIN' AROUND SNEAKIN-LIKE AT 518 INZONE IVAN AND SWANSON AND THE REST '

SNEAKING
BECAUSE IT SEEMED SORT OF A SNEAKING TRICK, 214 AHWILD
MAKING THIS DATE AND THEN SNEAKING OUT? 278 AHWILD
FOR SNEAKING OUT--(THEN DARKLY) AND FOR WHAT I 281 AHWILD DID LAST NIGHT--
I CONFESS I HAD A SNEAKING SHERLOCK HOLMES DESIRE 505 DAYS TO HAVE A GOOD LOOK AT YOU
TO TAKE THE SNEAKING REVENGE ON HIM OF BEING A 41 ELECTR BACKSTAIRS LOVER/
IS JUST HIS OWN SNEAKING PLOTS THAT HE'S FRAMED UP249 HA APE TO PUT US IN JAIL.
AND SNEAKING AROUND BLOWING UP A LOUSY BUILDING OR592 ICEMAN A BRIDGE/
SNEAKINGS 638 ICEMAN
I KNOW YOU, BEJEES, YOU SNEAKING, LYING DRUMMER/ 654 ICEMAN
DO YOU KNOW, LARRY, I ONCE HAD A SNEAKING 667 ICEMAN SUSPICION THAT MAYBE,
SNEAKING ONE, EHS 53 JOURNE
WHAT DO YOU MEAN BY SNEAKING--/ 75 MANSNS
THE SNEAKING SKUNKS/ 66 MISBEG
AND THEM CAME SNEAKING HERE TO SEE IF THE SCHEME 159 MISBEG BEHIND YOUR SCHEME HAD WORKED/

SNEAKS
BENNY SNEAKS THROUGH THE DOOR ON RIGHT, HESITATES 544 DIFRNT FOR A WHILE.
A NATIVE NEGRO WOMAN SNEAKS IN CAUTIOUSLY FROM THE173 EJONES ENTRANCE ON THE RIGHT.
WHEN I SLEEPS, DEY SNEAKS A SLEEP, TOO, AND I 181 EJONES PRETENDS I NEVER SUSPICIONS IT.
SNEAKS TO THE BAR AND FURTIVELY REACHES FOR 686 ICEMAN LARRY'S GLASS OF WHISKEY.)
SNEAKS 519 INZONE
EACH SNEAKS A SUSPICIOUS, PROBING GLANCE AT THE 136 MANSNS OTHER.

SNEER
YOU'RE AFRAID THE OTHER CAPTAINS WILL SNEER AT YOU547 'ILE
THEM SKIPPERS WOULD NEVER DARE SNEER TO MY FACE. 547 'ILE
(WITH A TRAGIC SNEER) LIFE/ 215 AHWILD
(WITH AN UGLY SNEER) AND HOW ABOUT HERE$ 243 AHWILD
INTO THE HARDENED SNEER OF HER EXPERIENCE.) 55 ANNA
(WITH A SNEER) WHY NOT, I'D LIKE TO KNOWS 64 ANNA
(HE LOOKS AT HER WITH APPEALING EYES AS IF AFRAID 149 BEYOND SHE WILL SNEER AT HIM.
SNEER OF SCORNFUL MOCKERY ON HIS LIPS. 494 DAYS
YOUR HERO'S MANHOOD UP TO THE TIME HE (A SNEER 494 DAYS COMES INTO HIS VOICE)
(HIS VOICE A MOCKING SNEER) AND WHAT SALVATION 501 DAYS FOR US ARE YOU PREACHINGS
WITH A DIRTY SNEER IN HIS VOICES 501 DAYS
(WITH A FLIPPANT SNEER) HARDLY THE LOVER-LIKE 527 DAYS TONE, IS ITS
(WITH A CONTEMPTUOUS SNEER) YE NEEDN'T HEED EBEN.222 DESIRE
(WITH A SNEER) WAAL--YE HAIN'T SO DURNED PURTY 228 DESIRE YERSELF, BE YES
(HE TURNS FROM HER WITH A SNEER.) 229 DESIRE
(WITH A TANTALIZING SNEER) SHE'S PURTIER'N YEW 230 DESIRE BE/
(WITH A SNEER) LIKE YEW DID, YE MEANS 254 DESIRE
HOW THE GOSSIPS WOULD SNEER AT ME/....) 426 DYNAMO
(THEN HE TURNS TO HIS MOTHER WITH A SNEER-- 449 DYNAMO CONTEMPTUOUSLY)
(WITH A SNEER) WHAT GODS 452 DYNAMO
(WITH A SNEER) IT MUST BE THE MANNON IN YOU 41 ELECTR CUMMING OUT/
(WITH A MOCKING DIABOLICAL SNEER--QUIETLY) 155 ELECTR

SNEER

(CONT'D.)

IT IS OLDER, MORE DEFIANT AND MOCKING, ITS SNEER 269 GGBROW
MORE FORCED AND BITTER,
(WITH A SNEER) ARTISTIC TEMPERAMENT, MAYBE-- 302 GGBROW
(THEN WITH A SNEER) ANYWAY, THAT DOESN'T MATTER/ 307 GGBROW
(WHO HAS BEEN LISTENING WITH A CONTEMPTUOUS SNEER,215 HA APE
BARKS OUT THE ANSWER)
(THEN WITH A RESENTFUL SNEER) 615 ICEMAN
IT IS HE WHO MAKES ME SNEER, 635 ICEMAN
(WITH A SNEER) IS THAT SO$ 646 ICEMAN
(SHARPLY) WAIT/ INSISTENTLY--WITH A SNEER) 661 ICEMAN
(WITH A SNEER) LOOK AT HIM/ 525 INZONE
SNEER AT MY PROFESSION, SNEER AT EVERY DAMNED 32 JOURNE
THING IN THE WORLD--
THE ONLY THANKS IS TO HAVE YOU SNEER AT ME FOR A 32 JOURNE
DIRTY MISER,
EVERYONE ELSE ADMIRES HIM AND YOU SHOULD BE THE 60 JOURNE
LAST ONE TO SNEER--
YOU'RE A FINE ONE TO SNEER, WITH THE MAP OF IT ON 80 JOURNE
YOUR FACE/
(WITH A LOOSE-MOUTHED SNEER OF SELF-CONTEMPT.) 146 JOURNE
(WITH A SNEER--MALICIOUSLY) YOU SHOULD KNOW BEST 276 LAZARU
ABOUT THAT/
CALIGULA SPEAKS GRUFFLY TO MIRIAM WITH A SNEER) 330 LAZARU
(WITH A SNEER OF SCEPTICISM BUT WITH AN UNDERLYING340 LAZARU
EAGERNESS)
IT'S RIDICULOUS SNOBBERY FOR HIM TO SNEER AT THE 8 MANSNS
COMMON PEOPLE,
SNEER TO HIM THAT WE'D NEVER HAVE ENOUGH, 21 MANSNS
NOW QUESTION, AND SNEER AND LAUGH AT YOUR DREAMS, 40 MANSNS
AND SLEEP WITH UGLINESS,
AH NOW, YOU SHOULDN'T SNEER AT YOUR MOTHER LIKE 65 MANSNS
THAT,
SO YOU CAN GO BACK AND SNEER WITH HER AT WHAT A 155 MANSNS
LOW, COMMON SLUT I AM IN MY HEAR
(WITH A COLD CALCULATING SNEER.) 159 MANSNS
(HIS SNEER CHANGES TO A LOOK OF STRICKEN GUILT AND111 MISBEG
GRIEF)
(THEN WITH A SNEER) THEY'RE ALL GRAY, 165 MISBEG
THERE WAS FEW DIDN'T SNEER BEHIND HIS BACK AT HIS 12 POET
PRETENSIONS,
BUT CON WIPED THE SNEER OFF THEIR MUGS 12 POET
I'D BETTER WARN HIM NOT TO SNEER AT THE IRISH 26 POET
AROUND HERE AND CALL THEM SCUM,
(HER TONE CHANGES TO A SNEER.) 30 POET
(WITH A SNEER.) BUT SHE DIDN'T FOOL ME WITH HER 75 POET
INSULTED AIRS/
IMPULSIVELY, WITH A SNEER OF AGREEMENT.) 91 POET
WHEN HE CATCHES THE SNEER IN HER EYES, 103 POET
(INDIGNANT AT MELODY'S INSULTS TO HIS PROFESSION--119 POET
WITH A THINLY VEILED SNEER.)
FOR SIMON'S MOTHER TO SNEER AT-- 150 POET
WELL, THE FLUNKY PUT AN INSOLENT SNEER ON HIM, 154 POET
SHE'LL SOON SNEER FROM THE WRONG SIDE OF HER 158 POET
MOUTH/
BUT I'VE BEATEN HER AND I'LL SNEER LAST/ 160 POET
AND HE'S ONLY MADE A FOOL OF HIMSELF FOR HER TO 160 POET
SNEER AT.
(REPELLED--WITH A SUPERIOR SNEER) 19 STRANG
GOD'S SNEER AT OUR SELF-IMPORTANCE/...) 24 STRANG
(SUDDENLY WITH AN INSULTING, UGLY SNEER, RAISING 101 STRANG
HIS VOICE)
(WITH A TRACE OF A SNEER) 140 STRANG
(WITH A SNEER--TO EVANS) I'M GLAD NED'S GONE. 155 STRANG
(THEN GLANCING AT MARSDEN--WITH A TRACE OF A 162 STRANG
SNEER)
(HE GLANCES AT NINA WITH A SNEER, 162 STRANG
(WITH A SNEER) I SHOULD SAY FROM ALL I'VE BEEN 166 STRANG
HEARING THAT HE WAS YOUR IDEAL
(THINKING WITH A SNEER) ((GORDON'S THIRD/= 168 STRANG
(WITH A SNEER) OUR SONS 173 STRANG
(WITH A SNEER) YOU'D BETTER ACCEPT. 192 STRANG
A LAST SNEER OF OWNERSHIP/... 192 STRANG
(WITH A SNEER) YUS--B'CAUSE YOU 'AS TO. 494 VOYAGE
(WITH A SNEER OF RAGE) AND I SUPPOSE YOU WERE$ 497 WELDED
SNEERED
HE SNEERED THAT WE'D BETTER KEEP HIM HOME AT NIGHT426 DYNAMO
WITHOUT BEING SNEERED AT BY HIS RICH LANDLORDS 40 MISBEG
SNEERIN'
CAN'T YOU HEAR 'EM LAUGHIN' AND SNEERIN'-- 542 'ILE

SNEERING

(AN UNDERCURRENT OF ANGER IN HIS SNEERING) 498 DAYS
BUT FIRST GIVE ME YOUR WORD OF HONOR THERE WILL BE506 DAYS
NO CHEAP SNEERING,
AS IF AFRAID OF FINDING HIM SNEERING, 507 DAYS
(IN A BITTER, SNEERING TONE) 508 DAYS
(A SNEERING TAUNT IN HIS VOICE) 509 DAYS
SEEMING TO BE MORE THAN EVER SNEERING AND 525 DAYS
SINISTER.)
SNEERING TO HERSELF ABOUT MY STUPID FAITH IN YOU. 549 DAYS
AS HE PASSES HER, GIVES A SNEERING, TAUNTING 228 DESIRE
CHUCKLE.)
HER FACE IS SET IN AN UGLY, SNEERING EXPRESSION. 450 DYNAMO
(TO LIGHT WITH SNEERING CONTEMPT) 451 DYNAMO
HE SEES HIS FATHER AND A SNEERING SMILE 462 DYNAMO
IMMEDIATELY COMES TO HIS LIPS)
(SNEERING) A BLOOMIN' CHARM, WOT$ 180 EJONES
I WASN'T SNEERING, LARRY. ONLY KIDDING. 590 ICEMAN
(IS WATCHING LARRY'S FACE WITH A CURIOUS SNEERING 623 ICEMAN
SATISFACTION)
(BUT THEY ONLY STARE AT HIM WITH HARD SNEERING 633 ICEMAN
EYES.)
(SNEERING) DE OLD WISE GUY/ 635 ICEMAN
(WITH A SNEERING LOOK AT ROCKY) 638 ICEMAN
AS HE FINISHES, A CHORUS OF SNEERING TAUNTS 662 ICEMAN
BEGINS,
(WITH SNEERING DIGNITY) I'S ON'Y SAVIN' YOU DE 673 ICEMAN
TROUBLE, WHITE BOY.

SNEERINGLY

SNEERING (CONT'D.)
(HE LAUGHS WITH A SNEERING, VINDICTIVE SELF- 689 ICEMAN
LOATHING,
WITH A SNEERING, PLEADING CHALLENGE. 696 ICEMAN
HE'S FOREVER MAKING SNEERING FUN OF SOMEBODY, THAT 18 JOURNE
ONE,
BUT ON THE RARE OCCASIONS WHEN HE SMILES WITHOUT 19 JOURNE
SNEERING,
(JAMIE IS ABOUT TO MAKE SOME SNEERING REMARK TO 26 JOURNE
HIS FATHER,
(STUNG INTO SNEERING JEALOUSY,) 35 JOURNE
(SNEERING JEALOUSLY AGAIN.) A HICK TOWN RAG/ 36 JOURNE
STOP SNEERING AT YOUR FATHER/ 60 JOURNE
(BITTERLY.) BECAUSE HE'S ALWAYS SNEERING AT 61 JOURNE
SOMEONE ELSE,
(SHE GIVES A HARD SNEERING LITTLE LAUGH.) 92 JOURNE
OH HE'LL POISON LIFE FOR YOU WITH HIS DAMNED 109 JOURNE
SNEERING SERPENT'S TONGUE/
(THEN WITH SNEERING CYNICISM.) 157 JOURNE
(SNEERING.) THAT MEANS ANOTHER CHEAP DUMP. 158 JOURNE
(IN A CRUEL, SNEERING TONE WITH HATRED IN IT.) 161 JOURNE
DRAG HER FROM HER SNEERING-PLACE IN MY MIND AND 40 MANSNS
HEART,
HOURS SINCE SUPPER EVEN--THE CHILDREN WATCHING, 162 MANSNS
THEIR PRYING EYES SNEERING--
(SUSPICIOUSLY AGAIN--SNEERING AT HERSELF.) 163 MANSNS
(WITH A SNEERING CHUCKLE.) WELL, 177 MANSNS
HE MIGHT BE LED INTO IT SOMETIMES WHEN HE HAS ONE 33 MISBEG
OF HIS SNEERING BITTER DRUNKS
BUT WHEN HE SMILES WITHOUT SNEERING, 37 MISBEG
AND THERE'S A SNEERING DIVIL IN HIM, 83 MISBEG
HE LOOKS HER OVER NOW WITH A SNEERING CYNICAL 137 MISBEG
LUST.
(HE GIVES A SNEERING LAUGH.) 140 MISBEG
(HE OPENS HIS EYES AND GIVES A TORTURED, SNEERING 148 MISBEG
LAUGH,
I THOUGHT--(ABRUPTLY HIS EXPRESSION BECOMES 151 MISBEG
SNEERING AND CYNICAL--HARSHLY)
HE GOES ON QUIETLY, A BITTER, SNEERING ANTAGONISM 60 POET
UNDERNEATH.)
IN A SNEERING WHISPER.) 100 POET
WITH THAT PALE YANKEE BITCH WATCHING FROM A 157 POET
WINDOW, SNEERING WITH DISGUST/
(TO MELODY.) SO SHE WAS SNEERING, WAS SHE$ 158 POET
AN HYSTERICAL, SNEERING GRIN MAKING HER LIPS 166 POET
QUIVER AND TWITCH.)
(GROWING MORE UNEASY BUT SNEERING.) 167 POET
I KNOW IT'S MY FAULT--ALWAYS SNEERING AND 178 POET
INSULTING YOU--
IN SNEERING, CONVERSATIONAL TONES 25 STRANG
(CUTTING HIM WITH A CARELESS SNEERING TONE) 70 STRANG
(SHE LAUGHS A BITTER, SNEERING LAUGH.) 81 STRANG
(MOVING AWAY AGAIN--WITH A COLD SNEERING LAUGH OF 87 STRANG
IMPATIENCE)
(THINKING RESENTFULLY) ((HE'S SNEERING AT HIS OWN167 STRANG
SON/...))
(THINKING WITH SNEERING PITY) 188 STRANG
(COLDLY SNEERING) I THOUGHT IT MUST BE A JOKE 192 STRANG
MYSELF--BUT DAD INSISTED.
SNEERINGLY
(SNEERINGLY) AS FOR THE THIRD PART, 494 DAYS
(SNEERINGLY) TO EXCUSE YOURSELF TO YOURSELF, YOU 495 DAYS
MEAN/
(SNEERINGLY) AND HOW MISTAKEN YOU WERE IN THAT 502 DAYS
FAITH/
(THEN SNEERINGLY) BUT, OF COURSE, YOU WOULD READ 504 DAYS
THAT INTO IT.
(SNEERINGLY) OLD SUPERSTITION, BORN OF FEAR/ 508 DAYS
(SNEERINGLY) BUT THERE WAS ONE RIDICULOUS 509 DAYS
WEAKNESS IN HER CHARACTER,
(SNEERINGLY) YOUR TERRIBLE SIN BEGINS TO CLOSE IN513 DAYS
ON YOU, EH$
(SNEERINGLY) BUT HE WAS AFRAID TO FACE DEATH. 534 DAYS
(SNEERINGLY) SO ROMANTIC, YOU SEE-- 535 DAYS
(SNEERINGLY) AS FOR THE ADULTERY ITSELF, 538 DAYS
(SNEERINGLY) AND UNDER THE INFLUENCE OF HIS 544 DAYS
RIDICULOUS GUILTY CONSCIENCE,
(SNEERINGLY) YOU FORGET I ONCE PRAYED TO YOUR GOD559 DAYS
(COLDLY REMORSELESS--SNEERINGLY) 561 DAYS
(SNEERINGLY) WHAT IF IT BE$ 240 DESIRE
PARRITT STARES AT HIM SNEERINGLY. 610 ICEMAN
(LINES UP WITH MARGIE--SNEERINGLY) 632 ICEMAN
(COMING TO ROCKY'S DEFENSE--SNEERINGLY) 632 ICEMAN
(SNEERINGLY) AND YOU'RE THE BOY WHO'S NEVER 643 ICEMAN
WRONG/
(HE GRINS SNEERINGLY) HOW ABOUT IT, LARRYS 647 ICEMAN
(JERKS ROUND TO LOOK AT LARRY--SNEERINGLY) 666 ICEMAN
(SNEERINGLY) I'D TAKE THAT HOP OFF YOUR FIRE 668 ICEMAN
ESCAPE YOU'RE TOO YELLOW TO TAKE,
WETJOEN GLARES AT HIM SNEERINGLY. 675 ICEMAN
(SNEERINGLY) YES, CHUCK. 676 ICEMAN
THEN HE SMILES SNEERINGLY.) 679 ICEMAN
(SNEERINGLY) JEES, DAT CORA SURE PLAYED YOU FUR A697 ICEMAN
DOPE.
(HE PAUSES SNEERINGLY. 701 ICEMAN
(TO LARRY--SNEERINGLY) YES, THAT'S IT/ 716 ICEMAN
(SNEERINGLY.) INTERRUPTING THE FAMOUS BEAUTIFUL 60 JOURNE
VOICE/
(SNEERINGLY.) YOU EXPECT THE BLESSED VIRGIN TO BE107 JOURNE
FOOLED
(SNEERINGLY) BUT YOUR PRETENDED MESSIAH DID NOT 283 LAZARU
SCORN HIM
(HE TURNS TOWARD THE ROMANS AND LAUGHS SNEERINGLY,300 LAZARU
(SNEERINGLY) YOU BOAST. 328 LAZARU
(SUDDENLY HE STARES AT HIS MOTHER--SNEERINGLY.) 65 MANSNS
(HE SMILES SNEERINGLY, BUT IS AFRAID TO MEET THEIR131 MANSNS
EYES.
(SNEERINGLY.) I CAN. 132 MANSNS

SNEERINGLY

SNEERINGLY (CONT'D.)
SNEERINGLY.) 141 MANSNS
(SHE LAUGHS SNEERINGLY.) OH NO, MY DEAR SARA, 162 MANSNS
(SNEERINGLY.) HOW SHAMELESSLY HUMBLE YOU ARE/ 188 MANSNS
(SNEERINGLY) A LEADING ARISTOCRAT IN OUR LAND OF 47 MISBEG
THE FREE AND GET-RICH-QUICK,
(HE BEGINS TO SING SNEERINGLY HALF UNDER HIS 111 MISBEG
BREATH
(SNEERINGLY) OUTSIDE THE FAMILY, SURE. 128 MISBEG
(HE PAUSES--THEN BLURTS OUT SNEERINGLY) 145 MISBEG
(HE PAUSES--THEN SNEERINGLY) 147 MISBEG
(HE PAUSES--THEN SNEERINGLY) 148 MISBEG
(THEN SNEERINGLY.) THAT IS, 63 POET
(GIVING WAY TO BITTERNESS AT HER HUMILIATION 106 POET
AGAIN--SNEERINGLY.)
(SNEERINGLY.) OF COURSE, 126 POET
(SNEERINGLY.) BUT THERE'S DEVIL A CHANCE HE'LL 151 POET
EVER LET THAT HAPPEN.
(THINKING SNEERINGLY) (AMUSING, THESE YOUNG 33 STRANG
DOCTORS/...
(COLDLY AND SNEERINGLY) 36 STRANG
(SNEERINGLY--WITH A MEANING EMPHASIS) 115 STRANG
PICKING UP THE PAPER AND GLANCING AT IT 123 STRANG
SNEERINGLY)
(SNEERINGLY) THE SAME INSATIABLE CURIOSITY ABOUT 454 WELDED
MY PLAYS

SNEERS
THIS DUNCE-- THIS STUPID DOLT--NOW I SHALL BE THE 452 DYNAMO
BUTT OF ALL THEIR SNEERS/
AND YOUR SNEERS AGAINST DOCTOR HARDY ARE LIES/ 31 JOURNE
WITH YOUR SNEERS ABOUT PEASANTS AND BOGS AND 34 JOURNE
HOVELS/
THOSE WHOM FATHER SNEERS AT AS GREEDY MOB--ARE AS 9 MANSNS
GENUINELY NOBLE AND HONORABLE
WHILE HE STANDS APART AND WATCHES AND SNEERS AND 171 MANSNS
LAUGHS WITH GREEDY PRIDE
SNEERS AND PASSES ON, 366 MARCOM
NOW HE SNEERS) 104 MISBEG
(HE SNEERS TO HIMSELF) THE OLD POETIC BULL, EH5 135 MISBEG
I'M THE ONLY ONE IN THE WORLD HE KNOWS NIVIR 138 POET
SNEERS AT HIS DREAMS/
HE'LL NIVIR AGAIN HURT YOU WITH HIS SNEERS, AND 168 POET
HIS PRETINDIN' HE'S A GINTLEMAN.
THE GINTLEMAN'S SNEERS HE PUT ON IS BURIED WITH 174 POET
HIM.

SNICKER
(FORCING A SNICKER) GEE, PA, UNCLE SID'S A BIGGER206 AHWILD
KID THAN TOMMY IS.
(THEY SNICKER.) 214 DESIRE
SO FAR MAN HAS ONLY LEARNED TO SNICKER MEANLY AT 310 LAZARU
HIS NEIGHBOR/
(GRIMLY FORCING A HARSH SNICKER) 331 LAZARU
(THE PROFESSOR FORCES A SNICKER.) 14 STRANG

SNICKERING
ROCKING, SNICKERING--BUT FRIGHTENED, TOO-- 162 MANSNS
HE IS LEERING AT KATE AND SNICKERING TO HIMSELF INSOL VOYAGE
A MAUDLIN FASHION.

SNICKERS
(HE SNICKERS) NOW, DO BE QUIET, TOMMY/ 220 AHWILD
SNICKERS, AND MRS. 225 AHWILD
(SHE SNICKERS CONTEMPTUOUSLY.) 231 DESIRE
(HE SNICKERS.) 526 DIFRNT
(HE SNICKERS) SO YUH THINKS THE OLD MAN'S FLAT 593 ROPE
BROKE, DO YUH5

SNIDE
THE RESULT OF SOME SNIDE NEUTRALIZING OF LIFE 296 GGBROW
FORCES--A SPINELESS CACTUS--

SNIFF
(WITH A SNIFF) I HOPE I KNOW HIM BETTER THAN YOU.269 AHWILD
(WITH A SNIFF) OF COURSE YOU'D SAY THAT. 269 AHWILD
(WITH A SNIFF) I RECKON YOU DON'T PLAY MUCH 499 DIFRNT
BROTHER WITH--THE KIND YOU KNOWS.
AN' THESE BLACKS 'ERE CAN SNIFF AND FOLLOW A TRAIL183 EJONES
IN THE DARK LIKE HOUNDS.
(WITH A CONTEMPTUOUS SNIFF) I AIN'T NO CHICKEN- 185 EJONES
LIVER LIKE YOU IS.

SNIFFING
(SNIFFING) I SMELLS BACON/ 205 DESIRE

SNIFFLE
(BEGINNING TO SNIFFLE) U', YOU DO FRIGHTEN ME 494 VOYAGE
WHEN YOU 'OLLER AT ME, JOE.

SNIFFLING
LIFE IS JUST A LONG DRAWN OUT LIE WITH A SNIFFLING 40 STRANG
SIGH AT THE END/

SNIFFS
SHE SNIFFS AND LOOKS AWAY FROM HIM AROUND THE 252 AHWILD
ROOM.
(SNIFFS, BUT THINKS IT BETTER TO LET THIS PASS) 290 AHWILD
(STANDS BY THE WINDOW AND SNIFFS THE AIR) 425 DYNAMO

SNIPPY
OH, WELL, IF YOU'RE GOING TO GET SNIPPY/ 273 AHWILD

SNIPS
I NEVER HAD AN EYE FOR SKINNY, PALE SNIPS OF 90 POET
WUMEN--

SNITCH
I'D HAVE TO SNITCH ON SOMEONE--AND YOU WOULDN'T 294 AHWILD
WANT ME TO DO THAT.

SNIVELING
THE SNIVELING, CRINGING, LIFE-DENYING CHRISTIAN 292 GGBROW
SLAVE YOU HAVE SO NOBLY IGNORED

SNOBBERY
IT'S RIDICULOUS SNOBBERY FOR HIM TO SNEER AT THE 8 MANSNS
COMMON PEOPLE.
I SUPPOSE IT WOULD BE DOWNRIGHT SNOBBERY TO HOLD 48 POET
TO OLD-WORLD STANDARDS.
(HIS SNOBBERY COMING OUT) DO YOU KNOW HIS 38 STRANG
FAMILY--WHAT SORT OF PEOPLE5

SNOBBISH
STOUT AND UNCTUOUS, SNOBBISH AND INGRATIATING, 67 ELECTR
CONSCIOUS OF GODLINESS,

SNOOT
(THREATENINGLY) I'LL GIVE YOU A GOOD PUNCH IN THE246 AHWILD
SNOOT, THAT'S WHAT/
I'D LIKE AN EXCUSE TO GIVE YUH A GOOD PUNCH IN DE 669 ICEMAN
SNOOT.
WATCHING HIM RIDE PAST IN HIS BIG SHINY AUTOMOBILE 51 MISBEG
WITH HIS SNOOT IN THE AIR,

SNOOTFUL
(WITH A GRIN) YOU GOT A HALF-SNOOTFUL NOW. 6 ANNA
DIS GOITY DINGE WAS ABLE TO GET HIS SNOOTFUL AND 699 ICEMAN
PASS OUT.

SNOOZE
SORRY TO DISTURB YOUR LITTLE SNOOZE. 463 DYNAMO
I'M GOING UP IN A LITTLE WHILE AND GRAB A SNOOZE. 620 ICEMAN

SNORE
SID PUFFS AND BEGINS TO SNORE PEACEFULLY.) 275 AHWILD
CLOSES HIS EYES AND BEGINS TO SNORE LOUDLY. 513 INZONE
WELL, I SUPPOSE I SNORE AT TIMES, TOO, AND I DON'T 99 JOURNE
LIKE TO ADMIT IT.
GO ON AND SNORE LIKE A PIG TO YOUR HEART'S 76 MISBEG
CONTENT.
(SHE FALLS ASLEEP AND GIVES A SOFT LITTLE SNORE.) 46 STRANG
(ANOTHER SNORE. 500 VOYAGE
IVAN GIVES A PARTICULARLY VIOLENT SNORE.) 500 VOYAGE
(THE ONLY REPLY TO THIS IS A SNORE. 500 VOYAGE

SNORED
HE HAS SNORED EVER SINCE I CAN REMEMBER, 99 JOURNE

SNORES
(AFTER A PAUSE BROKEN ONLY BY SNORES--WITH A 483 CARDIF
BITTER LAUGH)
SEVERAL SNORES FROM DOWN THE CORRIDOR. 244 HA APE
AH, SURE, EVERYBODY HEALTHY SNORES. 99 JOURNE
EXCEPT PERHAPS, MR. TYRONE'S SNORES. 99 JOURNE

SNORIN'
SNORIN', I SAYS, +I'LL MAKE A NOTE OF WHERE HE'S 95 BEYOND
TURNED IN.
I WON'T STAY HERE ALONE WITH EVERYONE SNORIN'. 482 CARDIF
BUT I'M SCARED TO STAY HERE WITH ALL OF THEM 484 CARDIF
SLEEPIN' AND SNORIN'.
WITH THAT DAMNED WHISTLE BLOWIN' AND PEOPLE 489 CARDIF
SNORIN' ALL ROUNDS
AN' THEN HE CRAWLS INTO HIS BUNK AN' SHUTS HIS 520 INZONE
EYES AN' STARTS IN SNORIN'.
GAWD, 'OW I 'ATES TO 'EAR SNORIN'. 500 VOYAGE

SNORING
UNCLE SID WAS SNORING LIKE A FOG HORN--AND HE'S 253 AHWILD
RIGHT NEXT TO MY ROOM.
(HE TURNS HIS BACK TO THE LIGHT AND IS SOON FAST 481 CARDIF
ASLEEP AND SNORING.)
THE CHANTYNAN LIES SPRAWLED ON HIS BACK, SNORING 102 ELECTR
IN A DRUNKEN SLUMBER.
YOU WERE SNORING WHEN I LEFT/ 270 GGBROW
YOU WERE SNORING SO HARD I COULDN'T TELL WHICH WAS 17 JOURNE
THE FOGHORN/
YOU ALWAYS EXAGGERATE ABOUT MY SNORING. 17 JOURNE
I'VE BEEN TEASING YOUR FATHER ABOUT HIS SNORING. 20 JOURNE
(SCATHINGLY.) IF IT TAKES MY SNORING TO MAKE YOU 21 JOURNE
REMEMBER SHAKESPEARE INSTEAD
I'LL RACK YOU UP ABOUT PAPA'S SNORING. 21 JOURNE
ARE YOU POURING COALS OF FIRE ON MY HEAD FOR 29 JOURNE
TEASING YOU ABOUT SNORING5
WHERE ELSE COULD SHE GO LAST NIGHT TO GET AWAY 38 JOURNE
FROM MY SNORING5
BECAUSE YOUR FATHER'S SNORING WAS DRIVING ME 47 JOURNE
CRAZY/
ITS FULFILLED DESIRE A SNORING IN A STY IN THE MUD330 LAZARU
AMONG SWINE.
PROBABLY SNORING, AS YOU WATCHED THE DAWN COME. 124 MISBEG
DIRTY WINDOWPANES, WITH SOME TART SNORING BESIDE 171 MISBEG
YOU--
(INDICATING IVAN, WHO IS SNORING) 499 VOYAGE

SNORT
COMES THE SOUND OF STEAMERS' WHISTLES AND THE 41 ANNA
PUFFING SNORT OF THE DONKEY
(WITH AN ANGRY SNORT OF DISBELIEF) 107 BEYOND
(WITH A SNORT) CAN'T HELP IT/ 113 BEYOND
(WITH A SNORT) WHAT'D ROB THINK YOU AND HIM WAS 152 BEYOND
LIVIN' ON, I'D LIKE TO KNOW5
(WITH A SNORT) ANOTHER LYIN' COCKNEY, THE LOIKE 457 CARIBE
AV YOURSELF.
(WITH A SNORT) HIS HANDS AIR LIKE HOOFS/ 217 DESIRE
(WITH A SNORT) HER HOUSE/ 222 DESIRE
HE LOOKS TOWARD THE WINDOW AND GIVES A SNORT OF 262 DESIRE
SURPRISE AND IRRITATION--
(LOOKING UP FROM HIS PAPER WITH A SNORT OF DISGUST431 DYNAMO
JUST AS ADA ENTERS THE ROOM)
(WITH A CONTEMPTUOUS SNORT) LOVE, HELL/ 228 HA APE
(GLARING FROM ONE TO THE OTHER OF THEM--WITH AN 237 HA APE
INSULTING SNORT OF SCORN)

SNORTS
(SNORTS SCORNFULLY) PY YIMINY, YOU GO CRAZY, AY 44 ANNA
TANK
(HE NODS AT HICKEY--THEN SNORTS) 690 ICEMAN
(HIS FATHER SNORTS CONTEMPTUOUSLY. 35 JOURNE
(SNORTS) AND HAVE YOU SINGING AGAIN IN A MINUTE 76 MISBEG
AND SMASHING THE FURNITURE--
(HE SNORTS DISDAINFULLY.) BY THE ETERNAL, WHEN I 63 POET
WAS HIS AGE--

SNOW
PURE AS THE DRIVEN SNOW, THAT'S ME. 190 AHWILD

SNOWFLAKE
THE SKY IS GRAY, A SNOWFLAKE FALLS, 384 MARCOM

SNUB
HIS FACE IS ROUND, HIS SNUB NOSE FLATTENED AT THE 8 HUGHIE
TIP.

1477 SOBBING

SNUB (CONT*D.)
HIS FACE IS FAT WITH A SNUB NOSE, LONG UPPER LIP, 11 MISBEG
BIG MOUTH,

SNUBBED
AFTER ALL, I COULDN'T KEEP CHASING AFTER YOU AND 281 GGBROW
BE SNUBBED EVERY TIME.
MELODY, SNUBBED AND SEETHING, GLARES AT HER.) 74 POET
HE WON'T FORGET IN A HURRY HOW SHE SNUBBED HIM, 77 POET

SNUBBY
HIS FACE IS BROAD, PLAIN, WITH A SNUBBY NOSE, 12 ELECTR
CURLY BROWN HAIR,

SNUFFINGLY
(HE SOBS SNUFFINGLY--THEN BEGINS TO LAUGH AT 367 LAZARU
HIMSELF.

SNUFFLE
(HE WIPES HIS MOUTH ON HIS SLEEVE WITH A SNUFFLE) 598 ROPE

SNUGGLES
(UNCONSCIOUSLY SHE SNUGGLES CLOSE AGAINST HIS 90 BEYOND
SIDE.

SNUGGLING
(SNUGGLING AGAINST HER--GRATEFULLY) 322 GGBROW
(SNUGGLING GORDON'S HEAD AGAINST HERS--LAUGHING 156 STRANG
TEASINGLY)

SO'LL
SO'LL YE. 254 DESIRE

SOAK
BUT I DON'T WANTA BE MARRIED TO NO SOAK. 616 ICEMAN
AND DEN I'LL BE TIED FOR LIFE TO A NO-GOOD SOAK, 671 ICEMAN

SOAKED
WATER DRIPS FROM THEIR SOAKED AND ROTTEN CLOTHES. 571 CROSS
THEY'RE SOAKED/ 548 DAYS
LIKE A RUM-SOAKED TROOPER, BRAWLING BEFORE A 158 POET
BROTHEL ON A SATURDAY NIGHT.

SOAKING
BUT THE LOWER PART OF HER SKIRT AND HER STOCKINGS 548 DAYS
AND SHOES ARE SOAKING WET.

SOAP
ALWAYS TASTE LIKE SOAP TO ME. 255 AHWILD
LETTER UPON LETTER--EACH WITH A SOAP BOX INCLOSED,901 DAYS
SO TO SPEAK.
BUT I'M DENOUNCING FROM MY OLD SOAP BOX AGAIN. 542 DAYS
HIS FACE SHINES FROM SOAP AND WATER. 228 DESIRE
I TRIED MY DAMNDEST TO PUT HER OFF THE COURSE BY 37 ELECTR
GIVING HER SOME SOFT SOAP--
AND SOAP-BOX FOR THE EIGHT-HOUR NIGHT/ 280 GGBROW
THEIR FACES AND BODIES SHINE FROM SOAP-AND-WATER 226 HA APE
SCRUBBING BUT AROUND THEIR
DEY'RE IN DE WRONG PEW--DE SAME OLD BULL--SOAP-- 250 HA APE
BOXES AND SALVATION ARMY--
(TRIES TO IGNORE THIS.) I HAVE TO GET TOOTH 86 JOURNE
POWDER AND TOILET SOAP AND COLD

SOAPBOX
GIT A SOAPBOX/ 212 HA APE
(HIS TONE SUDDENLY CHANGES TO ONE OF GUTTURAL 627 ICEMAN
SOAPBOX DENUNCIATION

SOAPBOXES
SHOOTING OFF THEIR LOUD TRAPS ON SOAPBOXES 592 ICEMAN

SOARING
AND A HIGH NOTE OF LAUGHTER SOARING THROUGH CHAOS 309 LAZARU
FROM THE DEEP HEART OF GOD/
DREAMS LIKE SPARKS SOARING UP TO DIE IN THE COLD 27 STRANG
DARK...

SOB
(SHE SUDDENLY COVERS HER FACE WITH HER HANDS AND 548 'ILE
COMMENCES TO SOB.)
(SHE GIVES A LAUGH WHICH IS HALF A SOB) 548 'ILE
(HE HIDES HIS FACE IN HIS HANDS AND BEGINS TO SOB 258 AHWILD
LIKE A SICK LITTLE BOY.
AND COVERING HER FACE WITH HER HANDS, BEGINS TO 24 ANNA
SOB.)
WITH A SOB) 67 ANNA
(HE FORCES) BACK A SOB WITH A 147 BEYOND
(WITH A HOARSE SOB) ROB/ 167 BEYOND
RUTH SINKS DOWN BESIDE HIM WITH A SOB AND PILLOWS 167 BEYOND
HIS HEAD ON HER LAP.
(WITH A GREAT SOB) YANK/ 490 CARDIF
THEN SIGHS HEAVILY, A SIGH THAT IS HALF A SOB.) 473 CARIBE
(WITH A SOB) YOU'RE BITTER, NAT--AND HARD. 564 CROSS
(WITH A LAUGH THAT IS HALF SOB) 566 DAYS
(THEN ALMOST WITH A SOB, HIDING HER FACE IN HER 57 ELECTR
HANDS)
(SHE BEGINS TO SOB HYSTERICALLY) 112 ELECTR
(HAZEL BEGINS TO SOB AND HURRIES BLINDLY FROM THE 164 ELECTR
ROOM.
HER MOUTH TWITCHES AND DRAWS DOWN AT THE CORNERS 174 ELECTR
AS SHE STIFLES A SOB.
(WITH A SOB) OH, DION, I AM ASHAMED/ 268 GGBROW
(MUSINGLY) I LOVE THOSE RUTTEN OLD SOB TUNES. 284 GGBROW
HE BEGINS TO SOB. 288 GGBROW
AW, CUT DE SOB STUFF/ 235 HA APE
IT'S A GOD-DAMNED LIE/ (HE BEGINS TO SOB) OH, 581 ICEMAN
PAPA/ JESUS/
(HIS VOICE BREAKS ON A SOB.) 688 ICEMAN
(WITH A MUFFLED SOB) JEES, HICKEY/ 714 ICEMAN
HIS FACE BEGINS TO CRUMBLE AS IF HE WERE GOING TO 721 ICEMAN
BREAK DOWN AND SOB.
THE READING, MAKES A MUFFLED SOUND LIKE A SOB 530 INZONE
(CYNICALLY.) HE'S BEEN PUTTING ON THE OLD SOB ACTIS7 JOURNE
FOR YOU, EH$
(HE BEGINS TO SOB, AND THE HORRIBLE PART OF HIS 162 JOURNE
WEEPING IS THAT IT APPEARS
(HE PUTS HIS HANDS OVER HIS FACE AND BEGINS TO 171 JOURNE
SOB.)
THEN CALIGULA BREAKS INTO A CRY OF FEAR AND A SOB,320 LAZARU
AND, CASTING HIS SWORD ASIDE,
THEN, WITH A SOUND THAT IS VERY LIKE A SOB, HE 347 LAZARU
KISSES HER ON THE LIPS)
(SHE BEGINS TO SOB.) 5 MANSNS

SOB (CONT*D.)
I COULDN'T BEAR-- (SHE STARTS TO SOB.) 83 MANSNS
(SHE SUDDENLY BREAKS--WITH A SOB.) 155 MANSNS
(SHE THROWS HER ARMS AROUND SARA AND BEGINS TO SOB169 MANSNS
HYSTERICALLY.)
(HE BEGINS TO SOB EXHAUSTEDLY--THE TWO WOMEN SIT 174 MANSNS
TOGETHER.
A SNATCH FROM AN OLD SOB SONG, POPULAR IN THE 111 MISBEG
NINETIES)
(HE SEEMS ABOUT TO BREAK DOWN AND SOB BUT HE 111 MISBEG
FIGHTS THIS BACK)
(SHE BEGINS TO SOB WITH A STRANGE FORLORN SHAME 136 MISBEG
AND HUMILIATION)
(SHE CONTINUES TO SOB. 138 MISBEG
I MIGHT DEVELOP A CRYING JAG, AND SOB ON YOUR 144 MISBEG
BEAUTIFUL BREAST.
(GENTLY) YOU CAN SOB ALL YOU LIKE. 145 MISBEG
SHE BEGINS TO SOB QUIETLY.) 57 POET
SHE STARTS FOR THE BAR WITH A SOB.) 130 POET
(SHE STARTS TO SOB. 137 POET
(HE GULPS AS IF HE WERE CHOKING BACK A SOB.) 168 POET
(HE STARTS TO SOB BUT WRENCHES HIMSELF OUT OF IT 169 PUET
AND SPEAKS IN BROAD,
(HE BEGINS TO LAUGH AGAIN BUT HE CHOKES ON A 169 POET
STIFLED SOB.
(HE ENDS UP WITH A CONVULSIVE SOB.) 595 ROPE
HIS KNEES AND BEGINS TO SOB--STIFLED TORN SOUNDS.) 43 STRANG
(SHE BEGINS TO SOB, TOO, KISSING NINA'S BOWED 66 STRANG
HEAD.)
HUMBLY--WITH A SOB) 89 STRANG
(HE SWALLOWS HARD AS IF HE WERE CHOKING BACK A 92 STRANG
SOB--THEN SAVAGELY)
(HE SEEMS ABOUT TO SOB--THEN ABRUPTLY SPRINGS TO 101 STRANG
HIS FEET WILDLY)
(COMMENCING TO SOB AGAIN) H'ABUSIN' ME LIKE A DAWG494 VOYAGE
COS I'M SICK AN' ORF ME OATS.
(WITH A HALF SOB) NIX/ 478 WELDED
(SHE BEGINS TO SOB SOFTLY.) 489 WELDED

SOBBED
"I HATE TO GO BEFORE MY TASK IS COMPLETED, ED= HE 627 ICEMAN
SOBBED.
THEN SOBBED... 6 STRANG

SOBBIN'
SOBBIN' AND BEGGIN' HER FORGIVENESS AND TALKIN' OF161 POET
DISHONOR AND DEATH--

SOBBING
(THERE IS THE SOUND OF SUBDUED SOBBING FROM THE 543 'ILE
DOOR IN THE REAR.
(SOBBING) I'LL GO MAD, I KNOW I WILL. 549 'ILE
(SHE BREAKS INTO HYSTERICAL SOBBING, 59 ANNA
THEN HIDES HER FACE IN HER OUTSTRETCHED ARMS, 61 ANNA
SOBBING.
(SOBBING) YES, YES--OF COURSE I DO--WHAT D'YOU 91 BEYOND
S'POSES
MAYO BURSTS INTO NOISY SOBBING.) 108 BEYOND
HER SHOULDERS SHAKE AS IF SHE WERE SOBBING. 142 BEYOND
(SOBBING) DON'T, ANDY/ 168 BEYOND
(SOBBING) NAT/ 571 CROSS
(BUT ELSA PULLS HER TO HER AND SHE BREAKS DOWN 520 DAYS
FINALLY, SOBBING,
(HE BURSTS INTO A FIT OF SOBBING.) 243 DESIRE
(HE SUDDENLY BREAKS DOWN, SOBBING WEAKLY.) 256 DESIRE
(HE TURNS AND RUNS OUT, AROUND THE CORNER OF 262 DESIRE
HOUSE, PANTING AND SOBBING,
EBEN STUMBLES OVER AND THROWS HIMSELF ON HIS KNEES266 DESIRE
BESIDE HER SOBBING BROKENLY.)
(LAYING HER HEAD ON HIS--SOBBING) 267 DESIRE
THE TABLE SOBBING HYSTERICALLY. 546 DIFRNT
(HE BREAKS DOWN, SOBBING, AND BURIES HIS HEAD IN 456 DYNAMO
HIS ARMS ON THE TABLE)
(HE BREAKS DOWN ABJECTLY, SINKING ON HIS CHAIR AND464 DYNAMO
SOBBING.
REUBEN IS HEARD SOBBING BROKENLY FROM THE GALLERY.486 DYNAMO
(HE TURNS TO GO BACK INTO THE HOUSE, STILL SOBBING124 ELECTR
HELPLESSLY.
HE BREAKS DOWN, SOBBING WEAKLY AGAINST HER BREAST.142 ELECTR
(STILL SOBBING, HER HAND OVER EYES, 156 ELECTR
SHE REMAINS, SOBBING WITH DEEP, SILENT GRIEF.) 321 GGBROW
(HE HIDES HIS FACE ON HIS ARMS, SOBBING MUFFLEDLY)695 ICEMAN
DEEP SILENCE, BROKEN ONLY BY SMITTY'S MUFFLED 532 INZONE
SOBBING.
(SHE BREAKS AND HIDES HER FACE ON HIS SHOULDER, 91 JOURNE
SOBBING.
(BUT JAMIE'S SOBBING BREAKS HIS ANGER, AND HE 171 JOURNE
TURNS AND SHAKES HIS SHOULDER.
THE FIVE ARE HALF HYSTERICAL WITH RELIEF AND JOY, 278 LAZARU
SOBBING AND LAUGHING.)
(HE SINKS ON HIS KNEES SOBBING. 290 LAZARU
MARCELLUS HIDES HIS FACE IN HIS HANDS, HALF- 333 LAZARU
SOBBING.
(SOBBING, HIDING HER FACE IN HER HANDS.) 156 MANSNS
AND BURSTS INTO HYSTERICAL SOBBING.) 167 MANSNS
A MUFFLED SOUND OF SOBBING COMES FROM THE 435 MARCOM
PROSTRATE WOMEN.
NORA STOPS SOBBING. 137 POET
HE WAS SOBBING LIKE A SOUL IN HELL-- 165 POET
SHE BREAKS DOWN AND THERE IS THE SOUND OF HER 26 STRANG
UNCONTROLLED SOBBING AND CHOKING.
HER FACE STILL HIDDEN IN HER HANDS, SOBBING, 43 STRANG
(IN A MUFFLED VOICE, HER SOBBING BEGINNING TO EBB 44 STRANG
AWAY INTO SIGHS--
(SOBBING PITIFULLY) DON'T/ 65 STRANG
(SOBBING MISERABLY) IT WAS AWFUL PRETTY/ 150 STRANG
HE WOULDN'T BE SOBBING SENTIMENTALLY ABOUT SAM... 191 STRANG
(STUMBLING AROUND THE BAR TO THE DOOR ON LEFT-- 495 VOYAGE
SOBBING)
(IN A TERRIBLE STATE, SOBBING WITH RAGE AND 460 WELDED
ANGUISH)

SOBBING

SOBBING (CONT'D.)
AWAY AND THROWS HERSELF ON THE COUCH IN A FIT OF 467 WELOED
ABANDONED SOBBING.)
(HE FLINGS HIMSELF ON THE CHAIR IN A VIOLENT 475 WELOED
OUTBURST OF DRY SOBBING.)
(AS HIS SOBBING GROWS QUIETER--HELPFULLY) 475 WELOED
(HALF-SOBBING AS THE INTENSITY OF HIS PASSION 488 WELOED
SOBBINGLY
SPEAKS SOBBINGLY IN A STRANGE HUMBLE TONE OF 565 DAYS
BROKEN REPROACH)
AND HIDES HER FACE ON HIS SHOULDER--SOBBINGLY.) 122 JOURNE
SOBER
DRESSED WITH AN AWKWARD ATTEMPT AT SOBER 188 AHWILD
RESPECTABILITY
HE OUGHT TO BE AT THIS TABLE EATING SOMETHING TO 223 AHWILD
SOBER HIM UP.
COLD SOBER. 224 AHWILD
YUH WANT TO BE SOBER WHEN SHE COMES, DON'T YUH8 13 ANNA
IT'LL SOBER YOU UP. 13 ANNA
SOBER--I'D NEVER GO TO SLEEP. 466 CARIBE
BELLA IS THE ONLY ONE OF THE WOMEN WHO IS 470 CARIBE
ABSOLUTELY SOBER.
THERE WON'T BE A SOBER MAN IN TOWN TONIGHT. 7 ELECTR
(THEN WITH A GRIN) AN' YOU'RE SUPPOSED TO GO IN 131 ELECTR
SOBER.
BUT I WON'T MAKE IT TOO DEAD SOBER. 131 ELECTR
MAN WHO IS ONLY HONEST WHEN HE ISN'T SOBER-- 273 GGBROW
I HEARD SOMEONE HAD SEEN HIM AT HOME AND HE WAS 302 GGBROW
SOBER AND LOOKING FINE.
TILL I HAD TO PROMISE HER A DIAMOND ENGAGEMENT 22 HUGHIE
RING TO SOBER HER UP.=
TO THE WHOLE MISBEGOTTEN MAD LOT OF US, DRUNK OR 578 ICEMAN
SOBER.
WHEN YOU'RE DEALING TO SOMEONE WHO'S SOBER AND CAN609 ICEMAN
COUNT.
SURE, HE WAS SOBER, BABY. 618 ICEMAN
WELL, BEJEES, HE WON'T BE SOBER LONG/ 618 ICEMAN
(THEN PUZZLEDLY) SOBERS 618 ICEMAN
STONE COLD SOBER AND DEAD TO THE WORLD/ 626 ICEMAN
IT'S STAYING SOBER AND WORKING THAT CUTS MEN OFF 626 ICEMAN
IN THEIR PRIME.=
HE IS SOBER. 644 ICEMAN
ALTHOUGH THESE TWO HAVE BEEN DRINKING THEY ARE 650 ICEMAN
BOTH SOBER, FOR THEM.
=YEAH,= SHE'D SAY, =AND HOW LONG WILL YUH STAY 671 ICEMAN
SOBER NOW8
HE IS ABSOLUTELY SOBER, BUT HIS FACE IS SICK, 674 ICEMAN
PY GOTT, I AM SOBER, AND I DON'T JOKE, AND I SAY 677 ICEMAN
IT/
BUT HE WAS COLD SOBER. 699 ICEMAN
I DISCOVERED EARLY IN LIFE THAT LIVING FRIGHTENED 707 ICEMAN
ME WHEN I WAS SOBER.
IF I WAS SOBERS 126 JOURNE
YOU COULD SEE YOUR WAY WELL ENOUGH IF YOU WERE 126 JOURNE
SOBER.
I CAN'T FEEL THAT WAY ABOUT IT WHEN I'M SOBER IN 146 JOURNE
MY HOME.
I WAS STONE COLD SOBER. 147 JOURNE
BATTLE, BUT SUDDENLY HE SEEMS TO SOBER UP TO A 162 JOURNE
SHOCKED REALIZATION OF WHAT HE
SOBER, NOT THE MAUDLIN TEARS OF DRUNKENNESS.) 162 JOURNE
TYRONE STARTS TO WIDE-AWAKENESS AND SORER DREAD, 170 JOURNE
EVEN HIS DEFENSIVE DRUNKENNESS TAKEN FROM HIM, 172 JOURNE
LEAVING HIM SICK AND SOBER.
YOU GARNISH'T EXPENSIVE AND LUXURIOUS, IN VULGAR 139 MANSNS
CONTRAST TO THE SOBER.
WILL SOBER HER SPIRIT AND SHE WILL SETTLE DOWN AS 424 MARCOM
A SENSIBLE WIFE SHOULD.
I NEVER YET LAID HANDS ON A WOMAN--NOT WHEN I WAS 15 MISBEG
SOBER--
I'LL COME BACK SOMETIME WHEN YOU'RE SOBER--OR SEND 60 MISBEG
SIMPSON--
BE GOD, I'LL MAKE MYSELF AS SOBER AS A JUDGE FOR 91 MISBEG
YOU IN THE WINK OF AN EYE/
IS KEEPING HIMSELF HALF-SOBER. 97 MISBEG
PRETEND WE'RE FIGHTING AND I'M DRIVING YOU OFF 99 MISBEG
TILL YOU'RE SOBER.
HE IS AS STEADY ON HIS FEET AS IF HE WERE 124 MISBEG
COMPLETELY SOBER.)
HE WAS SOBER WHEN I TULD HIM. 131 MISBEG
BUT HIS LITTLE PIG'S EYES ARE SHARPLY WIDE AWAKE 157 MISBEG
AND SOBER.
TRUE, HE IS A BIT ON THE SOBER SIDE FOR ONE SO 48 POET
YOUNG.
WILL YOU NEVER LET YOURSELF WAKE UP--NOT EVEN NOW 51 POET
WHEN YOU'RE SOBER, OR NEARLYS
BUT I'D LIKE HER TO SEE HIM IN HIS UNIFORM, AT 80 POET
THAT, IF HE WAS SOBER.
YOU'VE STILL GOT SOME SOBER SENSE IN YOU. 126 POET
OLSON IS PERFECTLY SOBER. 496 VOYAGE
'TIS LUCKY HE'S SOBER OR SHE'D HAVE HIM STRIPPED 508 VOYAGE
TO HIS LAST HA'PENNY.
SOBERED
WELL, HE'S HAD A GOOD SLEEP AND HE'D OUGHT TO BE 256 AHWILD
SOBERED UP.
HE SEEMS CONSIDERABLY SOBERED UP) 19 ANNA
(AGAIN MOMENTARILY SOBERED--TOUCHING HIS FOREHEAD)104 ELECTR
(STARES UP, STARTLED IN HIS TURN AND MOMENTARILY 104 ELECTR
SOBERED--HASTILY)
HE HAS SUDDENLY SOBERED UP, TOO--DULLY.) 173 JOURNE
(HORRIFIED AND COMPLETELY SOBERED BY WHAT HE HAS 180 STRANG
HEARD--
SOBERING
MOONLIGHT NIGHT IN JULY, 1776, WHILE SOBERING UP 607 ICEMAN
IN A TURKISH BATH.
SOBERLY
(HAS GOTTEN TO HIS FEET, FROWNING--SOBERLY) 260 AHWILD
(SOBERLY) NO. 8 ANNA

SOBERLY (CONT'D.)
(THEN SOBERLY) WHERE'S HERSELFS 45 ANNA
(SOBERLY) THERE'S SOMETHING I WANT TO TALK ABOUT.133 BEYOND
RUB--THE FARM.
(SOBERLY) I DON'T BLAME YOU, RUTH, FEELING 139 BEYOND
EMBARRASSED HAVING ME AROUND AGAIN.
(SUDDENLY HOLDING OUT HIS HAND--SOBERLY) 246 DESIRE
SHE IS DRESSED SOBERLY AND NEATLY IN BLACK 494 DIFRNT
SUNDAY BEST, STYLE OF THE PERIOD.
(SOBERLY--A BIT DISTURBED) I WAS TELLIN' EMMER 499 DIFRNT
NOT TO TAKE ME THAT HIGH.
HE SUDDENLY LEANS OVER TOWARD HER AND, LOWERING 44 ELECTR
HIS VOICE, ASKS SOBERLY)
(A PAUSE--SOBERLY) NO MORE ESTATE TO FALL BACK 271 GGBROW
ON, EHS
(FIGHTING THE EFFECT OF HER LAST DRINK AND TRYING 101 JOURNE
TO BE SOBERLY CONVERSATIONAL.)
(HE LAUGHS--THEN SOBERLY, WITH GENUINE SYMPATHY.) 135 JOURNE
(SOBERLY) YES, I DO. 403 MARCOM
(SOBERLY) IT'D BE MUCH BETTER IF SHE'D TAKE HIS 31 STRANG
ADVICE.
SOBERS
(SOBERS UP MOMENTARILY AND WITH A PITYING LOOK.) 157 JOURNE
SOBS
(SHE HIDES HER FACE ON MILLER'S SHOULDER AND SOBS 262 AHWILD
HEARTBROKENLY.)
HER SHOULDERS QUIVER ONCE OR TWICE AS IF SHE WERE 52 ANNA
FIGHTING BACK HER SOBS.
(AS ROBERT REMAINS SILENT SHE BURSTS INTO SOBS 92 BEYOND
AGAIN)
(SHE WIPES HER EYES WITH HER HANDKERCHIEF AND 116 BEYOND
SOBS.)
(RUTH SOBS BROKENLY AND WIPES ROBERT'S LIPS WITH 167 BEYOND
HER HANDKERCHIEF.)
(SUE SOBS HOPELESSLY.) 565 CROSS
(HE GIVES WAY, HIS HEAD BOWED, AND SOBS 565 DAYS
HEARTBROKENLY--
(VIOLENTLY, BETWEEN SOBS AND GASPS) 256 DESIRE
SUDDENLY, SHE BREAKS DOWN AND SOBS. 259 DESIRE
(SHE SOBS UNRESTRAINEDLY.) 264 DESIRE
EMMA BURSTS INTO SOBS AND THROWS HERSELF ON A 505 DIFRNT
CHAIR.
(SHE HIDES HER FACE IN HER HANDS AND SOBS.) 537 DIFRNT
(SOBS BITTERLY.) 544 DIFRNT
(AFTER A PAUSE-- AS SHE STILL SOBS-- 546 DIFRNT
CALCULATINGLY)
(HE BREAKS DOWN AND SOBS.) 445 DYNAMO
HIS FACE HIDDEN, HIS SHOULDERS HEAVING WITH SOBS 200 EJONES
OF HYSTERICAL FRIGHT.)
HE SOBS DESPAIRINGLY) 124 ELECTR
(SHE BREAKS DOWN AND SOBS BROKENLY. 156 ELECTR
(SHE BREAKS DOWN AND SOBS HYSTERICALLY.) 166 ELECTR
SOMETHING THAT WAS DRIVING ORIN CRAZY--(SHE BREAKS172 ELECTR
DOWN AND SOBS) POOR ORIN/
AND I KNEW MY SOBS WERE UGLY AND MEANINGLESS TO 282 GGBROW
HER VIRGINITY.
SUDDENLY IT IS TOO MUCH FOR HER AND SHE BREAKS OUT122 JOURNE
AND SOBS.)
(TRYING TO CONTROL HIS SOBS.) 163 JOURNE
AND IF, ALSO, MY POOR BOY, LAZARUS--(SHE SOBS.) 284 LAZARU
(SHE SOBS AND WIPES HER EYES WITH HER SLEEVE-- 345 LAZARU
(HE HALF SOBS, BOWING HIS HEAD. 395 LAZARU
(HE SOBS SNUFFLINGLY--THEN BEGINS TO LAUGH AT 367 LAZARU
HIMSELF.
(THEN HER TENSION SNAPPING SHE BURSTS INTO SOBS 144 MANSNS
KUKACHIN'S SHOULDERS QUIVER AS, HER HEAD BOWED IN 420 MARCOM
HER HANDS, SHE SOBS QUIETLY.
OUR SOBS STIFLE US, OUR TEARS WET THE GROUND, 436 MARCOM
HE SOBS LIKE A SIMPLE OLD MAN. 438 MARCOM
(SHE COVERS HER FACE WITH HER HANDS AND SOBS 138 MISBEG
AGAIN.)
(SHE SOBS.) 138 MISBEG
I FLOPPED ON MY KNEES AND HID MY FACE IN MY HANDS 148 MISBEG
AND FAKED SOME SOBS AND CRIED.
HE HIDES IT ON HER BREAST AND SOBS RACKINGLY. 152 MISBEG
HIS SOBS BEGIN TO STOP EXHAUSTEDLY. 153 MISBEG
THEN SHE PUTS HER HANDS OVER HER FACE, HER HEAD 174 MISBEG
BENTS, AND SOBS.
(SOBS WITH RELIEF.) OH, PRAISE GOD YOU'RE ALIVE/ 164 POET
(SHE BREAKS DOWN AND SOBS. 182 POET
NINA SOBS OUT) 61 STRANG
HE GIVES WAY AND SOBS, HIS HEAD AGAINST HER 98 STRANG
SHOULDER.)
(SHE BURSTS INTO A TEMPEST OF SOBS.) 494 VOYAGE
(HER VOICE MUFFLED--BETWEEN SOBS) 467 WELOED
SOCIABLE
WHY DON'T YOU COME SIT OVER HERE, BE SOCIABLE. 14 ANNA
BUT I WANT TO BE SOCIABLE AND PROPOSE A TOAST IN 658 ICEMAN
HONOR OF OUR OLD FRIEND, HARRY,
AND YOU CAN'T HOLD YOUR END UP AND BE SOCIABLE 90 JOURNE
WITH NOTHING IN YOUR JEANS.
YOU'LL NEVER DO IT UNLESS YOU'RE MORE SOCIABLE AND 93 MISBEG
STOP LOOKING AT HIM.
SOCIAL
WHERE HE BELIEVED IN ONE SOCIAL OR PHILOSOPHICAL 535 DAYS
ISM AFTER ANOTHER.
AM I DROOLING ON ABOUT MY OLD SOCIAL IDEALS AGAINS542 DAYS
AFTER EXHAUSTING THE MORBID THRILLS OF SOCIAL 219 HA APE
SERVICE WORK ON NEW YORK'S EAST
OH, THEY DIDN'T WANT TO AT FIRST, IN SPITE OF MY 220 HA APE
SOCIAL SERVICE CREDENTIALS.
(BITINGLY) I'M NOT ACQUAINTED WITH THEIR SOCIAL 38 STRANG
QUALIFICATIONS.
THOSE STUPID PEOPLE WITH THEIR SOCIAL CONDOLENCES 190 STRANG
WERE KILLING ME.
SOCIALISM
AND SOCIALISM, TOO, I SUSPECT, FROM SOME DIRE 193 AHWILD
DECLARATIONS HE'S MADE.

SOCIALISM (CONT'D.)

BUT SOCIALISM PROVED TOO WEAK-KNEED A MATE, 502 DAYS
THEN IT WAS ATHEISM WEDDED TO SOCIALISM. 502 DAYS

SOCIALIST

AW NIX ON DAT SALVATION ARMY--SOCIALIST BULL. 212 HA APE
HE SAYS, +SOCIALIST AND ANARCHIST, WE OUGHT TO 584 ICEMAN
SHOOT DEM DEAD.
BUT DE SOCIALIST, SOMETIMES, HE'S GOT A JOB, AND 584 ICEMAN
IF HE GETS TEN BUCKS.
NEVER MIND THE SOCIALIST GABBLE. 23 JOURNE
(FROWNING.) KEEP YOUR DAMNED SOCIALIST ANARCHIST 25 JOURNE
SENTIMENTS OUT OF MY AFFAIRS/

SOCIALISTS

I SAYS, +HOLD ON, YOU TALK 'S IF ANARCHISTS AND 584 ICEMAN
SOCIALISTS WAS DE SAME.+
SO YOU DON'T SHOOT NO SOCIALISTS WHILE I'M AROUND.584 ICEMAN

SOCIALLY

I WAS ACCEPTED SOCIALLY WITH ALL THE WARM 595 ICEMAN
CORDIALITY

SOCIETY

WELL, HUMAN SOCIETY BEING ORGANIZED THE WAY IT IS,295 AHWILD
THERE'S ONLY ONE OUTLET FOR--
BUT IN A DIFFERENT STRATUM OF SOCIETY. 67 ELECTR
THEY WOULD TEAR DOWN SOCIETY, PUT THE LOWEST SCUM 244 HA APE
IN THE SEATS OF THE MIGHTY,
YOU MEAN CHANGE THE UNEQUAL CONDITIONS OF SOCIETY 248 HA APE
BY LEGITIMATE DIRECT ACTION--
THE MATERIAL THE IDEAL FREE SOCIETY MUST BE 590 ICEMAN
CONSTRUCTED FROM IS MEN THEMSELVES
I'VE REFUSED TO BECOME A USEFUL MEMBER OF ITS 591 ICEMAN
SOCIETY.
IF YOU MEAN I CAN'T AFFORD ONE OF THE FINE SOCIETY 31 JOURNE
DOCTORS
IN A FREE SOCIETY THERE MUST BE NO PRIVATE 8 MANSNS
PROPERTY
LIVE ALONE--YOUR PLAN FOR A NEW SOCIETY WHERE 8 MANSNS
THERE WOULD BE NO RICH NOR POOR.
BUT I'M AFRAID I'M BORING YOU WITH MY PERFECT 9 MANSNS
SOCIETY.
AS THE FALSE ARISTOCRACY OF OUR PRESENT SOCIETY 9 MANSNS
PRETENDS TO BE/
UNLESS YOU REGRET YOUR LOST POET'S DREAM OF A 15 MANSNS
PERFECT SOCIETY.
THE TIME HE WAS TAPPED FOR AN EXCLUSIVE SENIOR 55 MISBEG
SOCIETY

SOCIOLOGICAL

AND DISGUST WITH ALL SOCIOLOGICAL NOSTRUMS. 503 DAYS
STENDHAL, PHILOSOPHICAL AND SOCIOLOGICAL WORKS BY 11 JOURNE
SCHOPENHAUER, NIETZSCHE, MARX,

SOCIOLOGY

DID THE SOCIOLOGY YOU TOOK AT COLLEGE TEACH YOU 218 HA APE
THAT--

SOCK

OH, GOD, SOMETIMES THE TRUTH HITS ME SUCH A SOCK 286 GGBROW
BETWEEN THE EYES
(UNGUARDEDLY) YEAH. I'D LIKE TO GIVE HIM ONE 670 ICEMAN
SOCK IN DE PUSS--
IF YUH DON'T WANT A SOCK IN DE PUSS/ 683 ICEMAN
I WANT ONE GOOD SOCK AT DAT GUY--JUST ONE/ 698 ICEMAN

SOCKED

HE DIDN'T SAY IT RIGHT OUT OR I'DA SOCKED HIM ONE.631 ICEMAN

SOCKETS

THE CORD OF THE LAMP RUNNING UP TO ONE OF FIVE 185 AHWILD
SOCKETS IN THE CHANDELIER ABOVE.
(HE STARES STRAIGHT IN FRONT OF HIM WITH EYES 489 CARDIF
STARTING FROM THEIR SOCKETS)
THE CORD PLUGGED IN ONE OF THE FOUR SOCKETS IN THE 12 JOURNE
CHANDELIER ABOVE.

SOCKS

BLACK SHOES AND SOCKS. 493 DAYS
HIS SHOES ARE TAN AND WHITE, HIS SOCKS WHITE SILK. 9 HUGHIE
HE HAS NO SOCKS, AND HIS BARE FEET SHOW THROUGH 577 ICEMAN
HOLES IN THE SOLES.
IF I WASH THE ONES I'VE GOT ON ANY MORE, THEY'LL 604 ICEMAN
FALL APART. SOCKS, TOO.
HOPE IS DRESSED IN AN OLD BLACK SUNDAY SUIT, BLACK683 ICEMAN
TIE, SHOES, SOCKS,
DARK-BROWN MADE-TO-ORDER SHOES AND SILK SOCKS, A 37 MISBEG
WHITE SILK SHIRT,
AND TAKE OFF HIS SHOES AND SOCKS AND WARM THE 600 ROPE
BOTTOMS OF HIS FEET FOR HIM.

SOD

(THEN BEFORE HIS FATHER CAN REACT TO THIS INSULT 80 JOURNE
TO THE OLD SOD, HE ADDS DRYLY,

SODAS

EVER DRINK ANYTHING BESIDES SODAS? 219 AHWILD

SODDEN

AND HE'D FALL IN THE DOOR, A SODDEN CARCASS. 25 ELECTR
BUT DESPITE HIS BLUBBER MOUTH AND SODDEN BLOODSHOT575 ICEMAN
BLUE EYES,
BEHIND THIS, HE IS SICK AND FEEBLY HOLDING HIS 675 ICEMAN
BOOZE--SODDEN BODY TOGETHER.)
HIS HEAD ROLLS FORWARD IN A SODDEN SLUMBER. 696 ICEMAN
(JOE STARES AT HIM WITH SODDEN PERPLEXITY--THEN 700 ICEMAN
CLOSES HIS EYES.
THEN THE SODDEN SILENCE DESCENDS AGAIN ON THE 701 ICEMAN
ROOM.
(THERE IS A SODDEN SILENCE. 705 ICEMAN
WHETHER THOU SLEEP, WITH HEAVY VAPOURS FULL, 134 JOURNE
SODDEN WITH DAY, OR,
(WITH SODDEN MELANCHOLY.) NOT SO APT. 161 JOURNE
A SLOVENLY BARMAID WITH A STUPID FACE SODDEN WITH 493 VOYAGE
DRINK IS MOPPING OFF THE BAR.

SODGER

A DURN QUEER THIN' FUR A SODGER TO KILL HIMSELF 170 ELECTR
CLEANIN' HIS GUN.

SOFA

A SOFA WITH SILK AND SATIN CUSHIONS STANDS AGAINST185 AHWILD
THE WALL.
AT REAR OF SOFA, A BOOKCASE WITH GLASS DOORS, 185 AHWILD
FILLED WITH CHEAP SETS,
MILDRED SITS ON THE SOFA AT LEFT, FRONT.) 187 AHWILD
(HE PUSHES HER BACK ON THE SOFA AND TICKLES HER 194 AHWILD
WITH FREE HAND,
I'LL GO IN THE FRONT PARLOR AND LIE DOWN ON THE 234 AHWILD
SOFA AWHILE.
TOMMY SITS ON THE SOFA AT LEFT, FRONT. 249 AHWILD
AND SITS AT THE END OF THE SOFA, FACING FRONT, 258 AHWILD
HUNCHED UP, ELBOWS ON KNEES,
WHERE THE LIGHT IS DIMMEST, AND SITS DOWN ON THE 293 AHWILD
SOFA, AND STARES BEFORE HIM,
FARTHER RIGHT, A BLACK HORSEHAIR SOFA, AND ANOTHER 93 BEYOND
DOOR OPENING ON A BEDROOM.
(THROWING HIS HAT OVER ON THE SOFA--WITH A GREAT 119 BEYOND
SIGH OF EXHAUSTION)
AT RIGHT OF TABLE, IN THE CENTER OF THE ROOM, A 514 DAYS
SOFA.
IN FRONT OF SOFA, A LOW STAND WITH CIGARETTE BOX 514 DAYS
AND ASH TRAYS.
SHE COMES FORWARD AND SITS ON THE SOFA. 514 DAYS
(SHE SITS ON THE SOFA AND DRAWS LUCY DOWN BESIDE 516 DAYS
HER.)
(SHE GIVES A BITTER LITTLE LAUGH AND STARTS TO GO 524 DAYS
AROUND THE LEFT OF SOFA--
(SHE HURRIES AROUND THE RIGHT OF SOFA AND BACK 525 DAYS
TOWARD THE DOORWAY.)
(LUCY HAS REMAINED STANDING BY THE LEFT CORNER OF 525 DAYS
THE SOFA, IN A STIFF,
HE IS NOW STANDING BEHIND THE RIGHT END OF SOFA, 526 DAYS
LUCY BEHIND THE LEFT END.
AS SOON AS THEY HAVE GONE, JOHN TURNS AND, COMING 528 DAYS
AROUND THE SOFA,
SHE COMES QUIETLY TO THE RIGHT END OF THE SOFA. 528 DAYS
(SHE GOES AROUND THE LEFT END OF THE SOFA AND BACK530 DAYS
TOWARD THE HALL DOOR)
FATHER BAIRD IS SITTING IN THE CHAIR AT LEFT, 532 DAYS
FRONT, ELSA ON THE SOFA,
(SHE SHRINKS AWAY FROM HIM TO THE END OF THE SOFA 538 DAYS
NEAR FATHER BAIRD.)
AS HE DOES SO, LOVING COMES AND STANDS BEHIND HER,540 DAYS
AT REAR OF SOFA)
I--I THINK I'LL LIE DOWN HERE ON THE SOFA--AND 540 DAYS
TAKE SOME ASPIRIN--
STIFFLY BESIDE HER ON THE EDGE OF THE SOFA. 241 DESIRE
ABBIE SITS ON THE EDGE OF THE HORSEHAIR SOFA. 241 DESIRE
(THROWS HIMSELF ON HIS KNEES BESIDE THE SOFA AND 244 DESIRE
GRABS HER IN HIS ARMS--
A BLACK HORSEHAIR SOFA, AND ANOTHER WINDOW. 493 DIFRNT
THEY ARE SITTING ON THE HORSEHAIR SOFA, SIDE BY 494 DIFRNT
SIDE.
THE HORSEHAIR SOFA HAS BEEN RELEGATED TO THE 519 DIFRNT
ATTIC.
THERE IS ANOTHER CHAIR AT CENTER, FRONT, AND A 79 ELECTR
SOFA AT RIGHT, FRONT,
PETER IS SITTING ON THE SOFA AT RIGHT. 80 ELECTR
(LEADING HIM TO THE SOFA) HERE. 140 ELECTR
AND SITS ON THE SOFA AT RIGHT, ADOPTING A 161 ELECTR
SUSPICIOUSLY CARELESS ATTITUDE.
A SOFA AT RIGHT. 269 GGBROW
ON ITS RIGHT IS A DIRTY GILT SECOND-HAND SOFA. 278 GGBROW
DION IS SPRAWLED ON HIS BACK, FAST ASLEEP ON THE 278 GGBROW
SOFA.
BUT THE CHAIR AND SOFA ARE NEW, BRIGHT-COLORED, 284 GGBROW
COSTLY PIECES.
DION SITS IN THE CHAIR ON LEFT, CYBEL ON THE SOFA.284 GGBROW
MARGARET SITS ON THE SOFA, WAITING WITH THE 308 GGBROW
ANXIOUS.
(THEY SIT ON THE SOFA, HIS ARM ABOUT HER, HER HEAD309 GGBROW
ON HIS SHOULDER.)
SHE SITS ON SOFA AND PICKS UP HER BOOK.) 310 GGBROW
SHE MOVES LEFT TO THE FRONT END OF THE SOFA 174 JOURNE
BENEATH THE WINDOWS AND SITS DOWN,
IN THE LEFT CORNER, REAR, IS A SOFA. 43 MANSNS
AT LEFT-REAR OF THE FIREPLACE IS A LONG SOFA WITH 117 MANSNS
A SMALL TABLE AND READING-LAMP
AND DEBORAH ON THE LEFT END OF THE SOFA BY THE 117 MANSNS
LAMP.
(THINKING.) THEY DO NOT SIT TOGETHER ON THE SOFA 118 MANSNS
AS HAS BEEN THEIR WONT--
SHE AND I WOULD BE SITTING TOGETHER ON THE SOFA, 120 MANSNS
DEBORAH PATS THE SOFA ON HER LEFT, SMILING AN 123 MANSNS
AFFECTIONATE WELCOME,
AND GOES TO THE SOFA. 123 MANSNS
(SHE PATS THE SOFA INVITINGLY.) 128 MANSNS
(SHE MOVES OVER AND PATS THE SOFA BETWEEN HER AND 128 MANSNS
DEBORAH--ENTICINGLY.)
(THEY PASS BEHIND HIM TO SIT ON THE SOFA, SIDE BY 130 MANSNS
SIDE AS BEFORE.
(GETTING UP FROM THE SOFA.) I'LL GET MY SEWING. 136 MANSNS
AND COME BACK TO YOU.
AND GOES BACK TOWARD THE SOFA. 137 MANSNS
A SOFA HAS BEEN ADDED TO THE FURNITURE. 139 MANSNS
(BETRAYING AN INNER JEALOUS EXCITABILITY, HIS EYES141 MANSNS
FIXED ON THE SOFA--
A SOFA COVERED WITH THE SAME CHINTZ AT RIGHT. 90 STRANG
(RUSHES TO HER, SUPPORTS HER TO SOFA AT RIGHT) 108 STRANG
MARSDEN IS SITTING ON THE SOFA AT RIGHT, 111 STRANG
SITTING DOWN ON THE SOFA AT RIGHT. 124 STRANG
DARRELL ON THE SOFA AT RIGHT. 133 STRANG
A LARGE, MAGNIFICENTLY COMFORTABLE SOFA IS AT 137 STRANG
RIGHT.
(GORDON RUNS AND HIDES THE BOAT UNDER THE SOFA. 151 STRANG

SOFAS

HOW'D YOU LIKE IF I HAULED ONE OF THEM SOFAS OUT 170 ELECTR
FUR YOU TO LIE ON, VINNIE$

SOFT

SOFT

SOFT AND FULL OF SWEETNESS. 187 AHWILD
SHE HAS BIG BROWN EYES, SOFT AND MATERNAL-- 187 AHWILD
THY SHARP SIGHS DIVIDE MY FLESH AND SPIRIT WITH 205 AHWILD
SOFT SOUND--
HALFWAY DOWN THE SKY, AT HEAR, LEFT, THE CRESCENT 275 AHWILD
OF THE NEW MOON CASTS A SOFT,
THEY ARE SOFT AND BLAND. 3 ANNA
AND A SOFT, MUD-STAINED HAT PUSHED BACK ON HIS 82 BEYOND
HEAD.
(IN A SOFT MURMUR) YES. 93 BEYOND
(MORE AND MORE RUFFLED) THEN ALL I GOT TO SAY IS.102 BEYOND
YOU'RE A SOFT.
SHE'S LIKE T'NIGHT, SHE'S SOFT 'N' WA'M, HER EYES 211 DESIRE
KIN WINK LIKE A STAR,
EBEN'S A DUMB FOLK--LIKE HIS MAW--SOFT AN' SIMPLE/222 DESIRE
'BOUT AS SOFT AS YEW BE/ 231 DESIRE
(JEERINGLY) WAAL--YE'RE GITTIN' SOFT NOW--SOFT AS231 DESIRE
SLOP/
HE'S SO THUNDERIN' SOFT--LIKE HIS MAW. 231 DESIRE
I'LL GIT THE SHOTGUN AN' BLOW HIS SOFT BRAINS T' 233 DESIRE
THE TOP O' THEM ELUMS/
SHE HAS PURTY--BUT SOFT. 237 DESIRE
I HATED THEM 'CAUSE THEY WAS SOFT. 238 DESIRE
NOW--SINCE YEW COME--SEEMS LIKE IT'S GROWIN' SOFT 242 DESIRE
AN' KIND T' ME.
SHE WAS SOFT AN' EASY. 242 DESIRE
SOFT-HEADED. 246 DESIRE
YE'RE ALL TOO SOFT/ 250 DESIRE
DUE TO HER LARGE, SOFT BLUE EYES WHICH HAVE AN 494 DIFRNT
INCONGRUOUS QUALITY OF
THEIR SOFT GRAY-BLUE HAS BECOME CHILLED AND 457 DYNAMO
FROZEN.
A SOFT OVERTONE OF RUSHING WATER FROM THE DAM AND 473 DYNAMO
THE RIVER BED BELOW.
DAT SOFT EMPEROR JOB AIN'T NO TRAININ' FO' A LONG 187 EJONES
HIKE OVAH DAT PLAIN IN DE
IT IS SHORTLY BEFORE SUNSET AND THE SOFT LIGHT OF 5 ELECTR
THE DECLINING SUN SHINES
I TRIED MY DAMNDEST TO PUT HER OFF THE COURSE BY 37 ELECTR
GIVING HER SOME SOFT SOAP--
SHE CAN BE SOFT--ON OCCASION. 81 ELECTR
(WITH A SMILE) I CAN'T PICTURE VINNIE BEING THAT 81 ELECTR
SOFT.
SOFT GOLDEN SUNLIGHT SHIMMERS IN A LUMINOUS MIST 169 ELECTR
ON THE GREEK TEMPLE PORTICO.
THERE'S NOTHING SOFT OR SENTIMENTAL ABOUT MOTHER. 589 ICEMAN
(WITH THE SOFT PEDAL DOWN, 644 ICEMAN
CORA, AT THE PIANO, KEEPS RUNNING THROUGH THE 651 ICEMAN
TUNE, WITH SOFT PEDAL.
(DROWSILY) YUH'RE A SOFT OLD SAP, LARRY. 666 ICEMAN
HER VOICE IS SOFT AND ATTRACTIVE. 13 JOURNE
IT WAS MADE OF SOFT, SHIMMERING SATIN, TRIMMED 119 JOURNE
WITH WONDERFUL OLD DUCHESSE LACE,
YOU KNOW HOW YOU GET WHEN JOHN BARLEYCORN TURNS ON159 JOURNE
THE SOFT MUSIC INSIDE YOU.
WITH THE OLD MASTER, JOHN BARLEYCORN, PLAYING SOFT160 JOURNE
MUSIC.
AND HIS BODY ILLUMINED BY A SOFT RADIANCE AS OF 274 LAZARU
TINY PHOSPHURESCENT FLAMES.
THE MUSIC BEGINS TO PLAY AGAIN WITHIN THE HOUSE, 289 LAZARU
VERY SOFT AND BARELY AUDIBLE.
HIS MOUTH ALSO IS CHILDISH, THE RED LIPS SOFT AND 299 LAZARU
FEMININE IN OUTLINE.
(HE GIVES A SOFT, CRUEL LAUGH) 301 LAZARU
AND THE SOFT HEALING OF INNUMERABLE DAWNS AND 330 LAZARU
EVENINGS.
A RIPPLE OF SOFT LAUGHTER FROM THE MOTIONLESS 341 LAZARU
FIGURES ABOUT THE ROOM ECHOES HIS.
(IN A SOFT, DREAMY MURMUR) WE LOVE HIS LAUGHTER/ 367 LAZARU
(DEBORAH GIVES A SOFT, GRATIFIED LITTLE LAUGH. 37 MANSNS
WITH A SOFT LAUGH.) 83 MANSNS
(SHE BREAKS AWAY--WITH A SOFT HAPPY LAUGH.) 91 MANSNS
(WITH A SOFT TEASING LAUGH.) 99 MANSNS
(HER FACE HAS TAKEN ON A SOFT, DREAMY, ECSTATIC 162 MANSNS
LOOK--EXULTANTLY.)
LIKE THE GREAT SOFT FOOL YOU ARE/ 13 MISBEG
I'D NEVER GIVE IT A THOUGHT IF I DIDN'T KNOW YOU 26 MISBEG
HAD A SOFT SPOT IN YOUR HEART
HIS NATURALLY FINE PHYSIQUE HAS BECOME SOFT AND 36 MISBEG
SOGGY FROM DISSIPATION.
KEEP YOUR PLACE AND BE SOFT-SPOKEN TO YOUR 63 MISBEG
BETTERS/
DEFEND HIM, YOU BIG SOFT FOOL/ 78 MISBEG
HIM GABING LIKE A SOFT LOON ABOUT YOU-- 90 MISBEG
HER VOICE IS SOFT AND MUSICAL. 16 POET
(SMILES--HER VOICE IS SOFT, WITH A RICH BROGUE.) 20 POET
BUT THE BACON IS CRISP, AND THE EGGS NOT TOO SOFT, 55 POET
THE WAY YOU LIKE THEM.
ON A GRAND ESTATE AV STATELY WOODLAND AND SOFT 173 POET
GREEN MEADOWS AND A LAKE.
(SHE GIVES A LITTLE, SOFT LAUGH.) 181 POET
(TO HIS WIFE) IT'S SOFT-MINDED SHE IS, LIKE I'VE 583 ROPE
ALWAYS TOLD YOU, AN' STUPID..
I'M NOT SO SOFT TO LICK AS WHEN I WAS A KID.. 588 ROPE
(SHE FALLS ASLEEP AND GIVES A SOFT LITTLE SNORE.) 46 STRANG
THE TOUCH OF HER SOFT SKIN/... 104 STRANG
YOU'RE SOFT AS PUTTY. 122 STRANG
SMELLING YOUR HAIR, FEELING YOUR SOFT BODY-- 130 STRANG
CONTRASTED WITH THE SOFT GOLDEN HAZE OF LATE 158 STRANG
AFTERNOON SUNLIGHT
I'M TOO SOFT. 468 WELDED

SOFTEN

(HE TAKES HER BY THE ARMS, GRINNING TO SOFTEN HIS 55 ANNA
SERIOUS BULLYING)
IN SPITE OF ALL YOU AND ROBERT DID TO SOFTEN HIM$ 116 BEYOND
VENETIAN BLINDS SOFTEN THE LIGHT FROM A BIG WINDOW$14 DAYS
AT RIGHT.

SUFTEN (CONT'D.)
AND LEAVE ME TO SOFTEN HIS HEART BEFORE HE SAW 24 MISBEG
YOU.

SOFTENED

(SHE LOOKS UP AT HIM, SOFTENED. 62 ANNA
(SOFTENED) SEEMS TO ME YOU'VE CHANGED YOUR TUNE A 65 ANNA
LOT.
HE NEVER--SOFTENED UP, DID HE--ABOUT ME, I MEANS 134 BEYOND
HE SEEMS IN SOME QUEER WAY SOFTENED, MELLOWED. 230 DESIRE
HE GOES BACK TO HIS SEAT, HIS FACE GREATLY 537 DIFRNT
SOFTENED.
ENDURED WITH A GRIM FORTITUDE THAT HAD NEVER 274 LAZARU
SOFTENED INTO RESIGNATION.
(HER VOICE HAS SOFTENED, AND SHE BLINKS BACK 7 MISBEG
TEARS.

SOFTENING

HE HOLDS HER OUT AT ARM'S LENGTH, HIS EXPRESSION 549 'ILE
SOFTENING.
SOMETIMES. I THINK IF IT WASN'T FOR YOU, RUTH, 126 BEYOND
AND--(HIS VOICE SOFTENING) --
(HER MANNER SOFTENING) WAIT. 6 MISBEG
SHE SMILES DOWN AT JIM, HER FACE SOFTENING, 40 MISBEG
PLEASED TO HEAR HIM LAUGH.)

SOFTENS

AS THEY LOOK UPWARD, THIS SOFTENS.) 204 DESIRE
HIS GRADUALLY SOFTENS. 231 DESIRE
WITH A FAINT HAZINESS IN THE AIR WHICH SOFTENS THE 51 JOURNE
GLARE OF THE SUN.
HIS WHOLE BODY IS NOW RELAXED, AT REST, A DREAMY 342 LAZARU
SMILE SOFTENS HIS THIN,
(HER EXPRESSION SOFTENS TO A CONDESCENDING 126 MANSNS
MATERNAL TENDERNESS.)
(SHE STARES OFF--HER FACE SOFTENS AND GROWS 35 MISBEG
PITYING)
THE HARD, CALCULATING EXPRESSION ON HER FACE 106 MISBEG
SOFTENS.
HER FACE SOFTENS WITH A MATERNAL TENDERNESS-- 165 MISBEG
SADLY)
HER FACE SOFTENS.) 181 POET
AND SOFTENS INTO DEEP SORROW THE SHADOWY GRIMNESS 53 STRANG
OF HER EYES.

SOFTER

WAAL--HAIN'T IT EASIER FUR YEW WITH HIM CHANGED 229 DESIRE
SOFTER

SOFTHEARTED

HOPE IS ONE OF THOSE MEN WHOM EVERYONE LIKES ON 576 ICEMAN
SIGHT, A SOFTHEARTED SLOB.

SOFTLY

THEN CLOSES THE DOOR SOFTLY. 543 'ILE
HE STUMBLES AWAY FROM HER, AND SHE COMMENCES 551 'ILE
SOFTLY TO PLAY THE ORGAN AGAIN.)
(A MOMENT LATER ARTHUR ENTERS THROUGH THE FRONT 253 AHWILD
PARLOR, WHISTLING SOFTLY.
THEN SHE LETS HER HEAD SINK ON HIS SHOULDER AND 287 AHWILD
SIGHS SOFTLY)
(SOFTLY) WILL YOU PROMISE ME THATS 89 BEYOND
(SOFTLY, HER FACE STILL AVERTED) 90 BEYOND
(HE TURNS TO HER--SOFTLY) DO YOU UNDERSTAND NOW, 90 BEYOND
RUTH$
(MRS. MAYO BEGINS TO WEEP SOFTLY. 114 BEYOND
A MOMENT LATER ANDREW RE-ENTERS, CLOSING THE DOOR 154 BEYOND
SOFTLY.
(ANDREW REAPPEARS AND SHUTS THE DOOR SOFTLY. 162 BEYOND
IS SOFTLY PLAYING SOME FOLK-SONG ON A BATTERED 477 CARDIF
ACCORDION.
THE ENGLISHMAN STEPS SOFTLY OVER TO DRISCOLL. 483 CARDIF
HE SOFTLY CLOSES THE DOOR AGAIN.) 556 DAYS
SHE ADDS SOFTLY) 227 DESIRE
(SOFTLY) YE DON'T MEAN THAT, EBEN. 229 DESIRE
(SHE LAUGHS AGAIN SOFTLY, HOLDING HIS EYES. 229 DESIRE
THEN AS THE DOOR OF HIS ROOM IS OPENED SOFTLY, HE 239 DESIRE
TURNS AWAY.
SHE LOOKS AT EBEN WITH TENDER, LANGUOROUS EYES AND244 DESIRE
CALLS SOFTLY.)
(SHE BEGINS TO WEEP SOFTLY.) 261 DESIRE
(SOFTLY) I DO WISH YOU WOULDN'T SWEAR SO AWFUL 494 DIFRNT
MUCH, CALEB.
(NESTLING CLOSER TO HIM--SOFTLY) 498 DIFRNT
(SOFTLY) DO YOU MEAN ME, TOO, BENNY$ 523 DIFRNT
THEN TURNS BACK TOWARD HER OWN FRONT DOOR AND 470 DYNAMO
BEGINS TO CRY SOFTLY.
(THEN SHE LEAVES OFF, HAVING HURT HER HANDS, AND 489 DYNAMO
BEGINS TO CRY SOFTLY.)
(LAUGHING SOFTLY) YES. 143 ELECTR
SHE CALLS SOFTLY.) 143 ELECTR
HER ARMS ARE SOFTLY AROUND ME/ 266 GGBROW
(SOFTLY) REMEMBER THE SCHOOL COMMENCEMENT DANCE--309 GGBROW
TIPTOES SOFTLY UP TO IT, LISTENS, IS IMPRESSED BY 245 HA APE
THE SILENCE
HE STEPS SOFTLY OVER TO SMITHY AND CUTS THE ROPES 532 INZONE
ABOUT HIS ARMS AND ANKLES WITH
WHERE EVIL COMES UP SOFTLY LIKE A FLOWER. 133 JOURNE
(WHO HAS BEEN GAZING AT LAZARUS--SOFTLY) 276 LAZARU
BEGAN TO LAUGH SOFTLY LIKE A MAN IN LOVE WITH GOD/277 LAZARU
(HE BEGINS TO LAUGH, SOFTLY AT FIRST-- 279 LAZARU
(SUDDENLY LAUGHING SOFTLY OUT OF HIS VISION, AS IF279 LAZARU
TO HIMSELF,
LAZARUS' BODY IS SOFTLY ILLUMINED BY ITS INNER 288 LAZARU
LIGHT.
(HE BEGINS TO LAUGH AGAIN SOFTLY.) 308 LAZARU
(HE LAUGHS SOFTLY, AND SOFTLY THEY ALL ECHO HIS 309 LAZARU
LAUGHTER)
(FIXING HIS CRUEL, BURNING EYES ON HIM--SOFTLY) 317 LAZARU
(HE LAUGHS SOFTLY.) 328 LAZARU
(HE LAUGHS AGAIN, SOFTLY AND MUSICALLY.) 328 LAZARU
(LAUGHING SOFTLY) ESCAPE--WHATS 329 LAZARU
(SUDDENLY LAUGHS SOFTLY) WHY DO YOU DELIGHT IN 331 LAZARU
BELIEVING EVIL OF YOURSELF,

SOLDIERS

SOFTLY (CONT'D.)

AT THE SAME INSTANT, LAZARUS BEGINS TO LAUGH, 333 LAZARU
SOFTLY AND AFFECTIONATELY.
(LAZARUS, LOOKING INTO HIS EYES, BEGINS TO LAUGH 341 LAZARU
SOFTLY.
(HE LAUGHS SOFTLY. 341 LAZARU
AROUND ME, SOFTLY, WARMLY, AND THE CLOUD DISSOLVED342 LAZARU
INTO THE SKY.
(SHE LAUGHS SOFTLY AND STEPS FORWARD.) 342 LAZARU
(HE LAUGHS SOFTLY TO HIMSELF.) 344 LAZARU
(HE LAUGHS SOFTLY, GAILY, MOCKINGLY--THEN TO 352 LAZARU
TIBERIUS DIRECTLY)
(HE LAUGHS SOFTLY BUT WITH EXULTANT PRIDE.) 352 LAZARU
(LAUGHING SOFTLY AND TENDERLY. 362 LAZARU
(SHE LAUGHS SOFTLY AND PASSES SWIFTLY ACROSS THE 367 LAZARU
ARENA TOWARD LAZARUS.)
(SHE LAUGHS SOFTLY--THEN QUICKLY, SEEING HE IS 39 MANSNS
HURT.)
(SHE LAUGHS SOFTLY--TEASINGLY.) 99 MANSNS
(SOFTLY INSINUATING.) ALONES 106 MANSNS
(SOFTLY.) I REMEMBER, DEAR, AS CLEARLY AS IF IT 107 MANSNS
WERE YESTERDAY.
(SHE LAUGHS SOFTLY AND JEERINGLY. 125 MANSNS
(THEY LAUGH SOFTLY TOGETHER.) 135 MANSNS
(LAUGHS SOFTLY.) 150 MANSNS
(LAUGHS SOFTLY AND SEDUCTIVELY, RISING TO HER 164 MANSNS
FEET.)
(SHE LAUGHS SOFTLY AND SARA LAUGHS WITH HER.) 173 MANSNS
IT RISES SOFTLY AND AS SOFTLY DIES AWAY UNTIL IT 354 MARCOM
IS NOTHING BUT A FAINT SOUND OF
(SOFTLY) GO ON AND TELL ME, MARK. 355 MARCOM
(SOFTLY) I WASN'T SURE. 355 MARCOM
SOFTLY) PERHAPS ON THE VOYAGE YOU MAY BE INSPIRED399 MARCOM
TO WRITE ANOTHER.
(AFTER A PAUSE--SOFTLY) KUKACHIN/ 402 MARCOM
(WITH A SUDDEN CHANGE--SOFTLY) 412 MARCOM
(SOFTLY) ANY TIME/ (THEY HUG.) 430 MARCOM
SPEAKING TO THE DEAD GIRL SOFTLY AS HE DOES SO-- 437 MARCOM
WITH A TREMBLING SMILE)
SHE HUGS HIM MORE TIGHTLY AND SPEAKS SOFTLY, 152 MISBEG
STARING INTO THE MOONLIGHT)
THEN SHE REALIZES AND WHISPERS SOFTLY) 153 MISBEG
(CROONS SOFTLY) THERE, THERE, MY DARLING. 161 MISBEG
(SOFTLY.) YES, THE HONOR OF HER LOVE TO A WOMAN. 139 POET
(MARY STARTS TO CRY SOFTLY, BUT COMES TO LUKE AND 589 ROPE
HANDS HIM THE DOLLAR.)
BARK SOFTLY IN BOOKS AT THE DEEP NIGHT....) 14 STRANG
(HE HIDES HIS FACE IN HIS HANDS AND WEEPS SOFTLY) 20 STRANG
HIS EYES DOWN--SHE BENDS HER HEAD MEEKLY AND 88 STRANG
SUBMISSIVELY--SOFTLY)
(NINA LAUGHS SOFTLY, POSSESSIVELY. 103 STRANG
(SOFTLY) IT'S BECAUSE WE'RE GOING TO HAVE A CHILD,109 STRANG
NINA.
(SOFTLY) PERHAPS YOU'RE RIGHT, DEAR. 154 STRANG
(SOFTLY) ONLY YOU ARE ALIVE NOW, FATHER--AND 180 STRANG
GORDON.
(HE LAUGHS SOFTLY AND SADLY) 196 STRANG
(SOFTLY) AND DO YOU REMEMBER THE DAWN CREEPING 447 WELDED
IN--
FINALLY SHE RAISES HER HAND AND KNOCKS ON THE DOOR487 WELDED
SOFTLY--
(SHE BEGINS TO SOB SOFTLY.) 489 WELDED

SOFTNESS

SOFTNESS--JEST LIKE HER'N. 232 DESIRE
(AS SHE THINKS SHE SEES A RELENTING SOFTNESS COME 543 DIFRNT
INTO HIS FACE AS HE LOOKS DOWN
SOME SENTIMENTAL SOFTNESS BEHIND IT 9 HUGHIE

SOGGY

HIS NATURALLY FINE PHYSIQUE HAS BECOME SOFT AND 36 MISBEG
SOGGY FROM DISSIPATION.

SOIL

A SON OF THE SOIL, INTELLIGENT IN A SHREWD WAY, 82 BEYOND
YOU'RE WEDDED TO THE SOIL. 84 BEYOND
MAKIN' SOIL FOR HIS CROPS/. 204 DESIRE
WE COME T' BROAD MEDDERS, PLAINS, WHAR THE SOIL 237 DESIRE
WAS BLACK AN' RICH AS GOLD.
CLOSEST TO THE SOIL OF THE GRECIAN GODS, A SON OF 307 LAZARU
MAN, BORN OF A MORTAL.

SOILED

ALL THE WINDOWS ARE OPEN, BUT NO BREEZE STIRS THE 112 BEYOND
SOILED WHITE CURTAINS.
SHE WEARS A GINGHAM DRESS WITH A SOILED APRON TIED116 BEYOND
AROUND HER WAIST.)
SNEAKERS OVER BARE FEET, AND SOILED WHITE FLANNEL 260 GGBROW
TROUSERS.
AND HE WEARS A SOILED APRON. 577 ICEMAN

SOIVE

I'LL SOIVE LIFE FOR IT--AND GIVE 'EM DE LAUGH/ 249 HA APE
IT'D SOIVE YOU RIGHT IF I WOULDN'T GIVE DE KEYS 682 ICEMAN
BACK TO YUH TONIGHT.

SOIVICE

A LITTLE SOIVICE/ 725 ICEMAN

SOLD

I SOLD OUT LAST YEAR. 161 BEYOND
AND HE SOLD US ROTTEN OILSKINS AND SEA-BOOTS FULL 487 CARDIF
OF HOLES.
(DULLY) YOU'VE SOLD HIM. 566 CROSS
YOU'VE SOLD HIM. 566 CROSS
YES, I SOLD HIM, IF YOU WILL--TO SAVE MY SOUL. 567 CROSS
(WITH MAD, SOLEMN DECISION) WHEN THE HOUSE IS 573 CROSS
SOLD I'LL GO--AND I'LL FIND IT/.
YE AGREE YEW SHARES O' THE FARM IS SOLD T' ME. 213 DESIRE
I MEAN THE FARM YEW SOLD YERSELF FUR LIKE ANY 230 DESIRE
OTHER OLD WHORE--
(DULLY) YOU SOLD YOUR SOUL TO SATAN, REUBEN. 467 DYNAMO
I MEAN, WITH ME--WHEN, IF HE HADN'T SOLD OUT TO 277 GGBROW
DAD HE'D BE MY PARTNER NOW--
SOLD HIS SUIT AND SHOES AT SOLLY'S TWO DAYS AGO. 581 ICEMAN

SOLD (CONT'D.)

AND SOMEONE INSIDE THE MOVEMENT MUST HAVE SOLD OUT588 ICEMAN
AND TIPPED THEM OFF.
KEPT HIS NOSE TO THE GRINDSTONE AND SOLD ONE 627 ICEMAN
BOTTLE OF SNAKE OIL TOO MANY.
AND IT MUST BE THE FINAL KNOCKOUT FOR HER IF SHE 667 ICEMAN
KNOWS I WAS THE ONE WHO SOLD--
YOU'VE GOT TO BELIEVE ME THAT I SOLD THEM OUT 680 ICEMAN
(WITH FORCED JEERING) I SUPPOSE YOU THINK I OUGHT701 ICEMAN
TO DIE BECAUSE I SOLD OUT A
I'VE SOLD 'EM/ 703 ICEMAN
HE'S LOST HIS CONFIDENCE THAT THE PEACE HE'S SOLD 703 ICEMAN
US IS THE REAL MCCOY.
ALTHOUGH I HAD TO HAND IT TO HIM, THE WAY HE SOLD 709 ICEMAN
THEM NOTHING FOR SOMETHING.
MARK WOULD HAVE SOLD HIM THE LIONS OF ST. 367 MARCOM
I PROMISED THIS PLACE WOULDN'T BE SOLD EXCEPT TO 133 MISBEG
HIM.
OR DO YOU BELIEVE I JUST SOLD MYSELFS 459 WELDED

SOLDI

TEN SOLDI IN SILVER. 365 MARCOM

SOLDIER

OH, HE'D BEEN A SOLDIER AFORE THIS WAR. 8 ELECTR
(TERRIBLY WOUNDED, WITHDRAWN INTO HIS STIFF 56 ELECTR
SOLDIER ARMOR--
IT WAS PART OF MY TRAINING AS A SOLDIER UNDER HIM. 75 ELECTR
HE CARRIES HIMSELF WOODENLY ERECT NOW, LIKE A 137 ELECTR
SOLDIER.
AND GOT CARRY YOURSELF LIKE A TIN SOLDIER 145 ELECTR
WELL, HOMEWARD CHRISTIAN SOLDIER/ 287 GGBROW
I AM A SOLDIER. 321 LAZARU
THE LIPS OF AN ABLE SOLDIER-STATESMAN OF RIGID 337 LAZARU
PROBITY.
I HAVE BEEN A SOLDIER. 339 LAZARU
(HE SNATCHES A SPEAR FROM A SOLDIER AND FIGHTS HIS369 LAZARU
WAY DRUNKENLY TOWARD THE
(HE MAKES A SIGN TO A SOLDIER WHO FLOURISHES HIS 380 MARCOM
SWORD.)
A BRAVE SOLDIER, IF HE ISN'T A GENTLEMAN. 38 POET
I'M SORRY I NEVER KNEW THAT SOLDIER. 90 POET

SOLDIERLY

THAT INDICATES A SOLDIERLY BEARING IS UNNATURAL TO 74 ELECTR
HIM.
ORIN STRAIGHTENS WOODENLY TO A SOLDIERLY 145 ELECTR
ATTENTION.
WHICH WAS A SOLDIERLY QUALITY OF HEAD UP, CHEST 13 JOURNE
OUT, STOMACH IN,
HIS HEAVY-BONED BODY IS STILL FIRM, ERECT, AND 33 POET
SOLDIERLY.
FOR A SECOND HE CRUMBLES, HIS SOLDIERLY ERECTNESS 116 POET
SAGS AND HIS FACE FALLS.
HIS OLD SOLDIERLY BEARING IS GONE. 175 POET

SOLDIERS

ONE OF THE SOLDIERS, EVIDENTLY A TRACKER, IS 202 EJONES
PEERING ABOUT KEENLY ON THE GROUND.
HIS SOLDIERS ARE IN DIFFERENT DEGREES OF RAG- 202 EJONES
CONCEALED NAKEDNESS.
LEM ENTERS FROM THE LEFT, FOLLOWED BY A SMALL 202 EJONES
SQUAD OF HIS SOLDIERS.
THE SOLDIERS JUMP TO THEIR FEET, COCKING THEIR 203 EJONES
RIFLES ALERTLY.
(HE MAKES A MOTION TO HIS SOLDIERS 203 EJONES
(THE SOLDIERS COME OUT OF THE FOREST CARRYING 204 EJONES
JONES' LIMP BODY
EVEN THE ROMAN SOLDIERS AND THE CENTURION HIMSELF.291 LAZARU
HE IS MIDDLE-AGED, HIS SOLDIERS BELONG TO THE 291 LAZARU
PERIOD OF MANHOOD.
(THE SOLDIERS FORM A WEDGE AND CHARGE WITH A 291 LAZARU
SHOUT.
AS THE FIGHT IS AT ITS HEIGHT A ROMAN CENTURION 291 LAZARU
AND A SQUAD OF EIGHT SOLDIERS
(BUT NO ONE HEARS HIM--WITH ANGRY DISGUST TO HIS 291 LAZARU
SOLDIERS)
THE CENTURION DIFFERS FROM HIS SOLDIERS ONLY IN 291 LAZARU
BEING MORE INDIVIDUALIZED.
THE SOLDIERS CHUCKLE. 293 LAZARU
THE SOLDIERS LAUGH. 293 LAZARU
(AT FIRST IN A TUNE OF GREAT AWE--TO HIS SOLDIERS)293 LAZARU
(LAUGHING, TO HIS LAUGHING SOLDIERS) 294 LAZARU
(HE LAUGHS AND THE CENTURION AND SOLDIERS LAUGH 294 LAZARU
WITH HIM.
THE LAUGHTER OF THE SOLDIERS RECEDES. 295 LAZARU
NICKNAMED CALIGULA BY THE SOLDIERS IN WHOSE 298 LAZARU
ENCAMPMENTS HE WAS BORN AND
MASKED LIKE THE SOLDIERS OF SCENE TWO-- 298 LAZARU
THEY PUSH FORWARD AGGRESSIVELY AND ALMOST SWEEP 300 LAZARU
THE SOLDIERS FROM THEIR FEET.)
(THE SOLDIERS WORK WITH A WILL. 304 LAZARU
BOTH SOLDIERS AND CROWD ARE INSPIRED TO BATTLE BY 304 LAZARU
THESE STRAINS
FORGETFUL OF THE GROWING PLIGHT OF HIS SOLDIERS.) 304 LAZARU
THE ROMAN SOLDIERS IN SPITE OF THEIR EFFORTS ARE 304 LAZARU
PUSHED BACKWARD STEP BY STEP.)
(HIS SOLDIERS RAISE THEIR SWORDS. 305 LAZARU
KILL, SOLDIERS/ 305 LAZARU
(TO THE SOLDIERS) DRAW YOUR SWORDS/ 305 LAZARU
(THE SQUAD OF ROMAN SOLDIERS LED BY THE CENTURION,306 LAZARU
(THE SOLDIERS AND GREEKS REMAIN FROZEN IN THEIR 306 LAZARU
ATTITUDES OF MURDEROUS HATE.
THEY WHIRL IN BETWEEN THE SOLDIERS AND CROWD, 306 LAZARU
FORCING THEM BACK FROM EACH OTHER.
IN A REPEATED CHORUS WHICH FINALLY INCLUDES EVEN 307 LAZARU
THE ROMAN SOLDIERS,
NOW AUGMENTED BY ALL THE GREEKS, AND THE ROMAN 311 LAZARU
SOLDIERS WHO HAD AWAITED HIM,
HE STAMMERS AFTER THE SOLDIERS) 311 LAZARU
(HE APPEALS TO THE SOLDIERS.) 322 LAZARU

SOLDIERS

SOLDIERS (CONT'D.)
(WITH THE SAME JOYOUS INTOXICATION AS THE 322 LAZARU
SOLDIERS)
(AS THE SOLDIERS START TO MARCH AWAY BEHIND 322 LAZARU
CRASSUS,
MASKED AS ALL THE ROMAN SOLDIERS PREVIOUSLY, ENTER326 LAZARU
FROM THE LEFT, FRONT,
THE SOLDIERS FORM IN LINE WITH THE COLUMNS.) 327 LAZARU
(THEN TO HIS SOLDIERS) SCOURGE HIM/ 348 LAZARU
(RUNNING TO SOLDIERS--FIERCELY) 348 LAZARU
(HURLING TO THE SOLDIERS-HYSTERICALLY) 348 LAZARU
THE REST, SOLDIERS, SLAVES AND THE PROSTITUTES OF 349 LAZARU
BOTH SEXES,
I WAS BORN IN A CAMP AMONG SOLDIERS. 352 LAZARU
(CALLS TO THE SOLDIERS) LET HIM SPEAK/ 365 LAZARU
AS THE SOLDIERS RAKE BACK THE FIRE FROM THE STAKE.366 LAZARU
CAESAR COMMANDS--(CALLING FEEBLY TO THE SOLDIERS) 366 LAZARU
(AS THE FLAMES, PILED BACK AND FED ANEW BY THE 367 LAZARU
SOLDIERS,
THE SOLDIERS SPRAWL DOWN BESIDE THEM. 350 MARCOM
OF TWO SOLDIERS WHO RUN BESIDE THEM AND THE LONG 350 MARCOM
WHIPS
(HE MAKES OBEISANCE AND PRAYS TO THE TREE AS DO 350 MARCOM
THE SOLDIERS,
(THE SOLDIERS CARRY AROUND JUGS OF WATER 351 MARCOM
(AT A SIGN, THE SOLDIERS FALL UPON THE THREE 353 MARCOM
MERCHANTS,
(WITH BLOWS AND KICKS THE SOLDIERS GET THEIR HUMAN353 MARCOM
BEASTS TO THEIR FEET.
(TO HIS SOLDIERS) ATTENTION/ 353 MARCOM
A FILE OF SOLDIERS, ACCOMPANYING A RICHLY-DRESSED 376 MARCOM
COURT MESSENGER, COME THROUGH.
SOLDIERS WITH DRAWN SWORDS LEAP FORWARD AND SEIZE 379 MARCOM
HIM, TRUSSING HIM UP,
YOU CAN'T CONSIDER SOULS WHEN YOU'RE DEALING WITH 395 MARCOM
SOLDIERS, CAN YOUR
(SHARPLY, A COMMANDER ORDERING HIS SOLDIERS.) 123 POET
THERE'S A DOCTOR I KNOW AT A SANITARIUM FOR 17 STRANG
CRIPPLED SOLDIERS--
SOLDIERS'
WANT TO NURSE IN A SOLDIERS' HOSPITAL/ 17 STRANG
SOLE
WAAL, YE GOT T' BE SOLE HAND, TOO. 216 DESIRE
YE'RE SOLE OWNER--TILL HE COMES--THAT'S WHAT YE 216 DESIRE
WANTED.
I WAS THE SOLE DOLL OUR OGRE, HER HUSBAND, HAD 282 GGBROW
ALLOWED HER
THAT THE NIGHT CLERK'S MIND HAS LEFT THE PREMISES 22 HUGHIE
IN HIS SOLE CUSTODY.)
THE NIGHT WHICH IS THE SOLE RIGHT NOT TO BE A 101 MANSNS
SLAVE/
(GRAVELY MARCO KNEELS, REMOVES A SLIPPER, AND 413 MARCOM
FEELS THE SOLE OF HER FOOT--
SOLED
THEY CLUMP HEAVILY ALONG IN THEIR CLUMSY THICK- 204 DESIRE
SOLED BOOTS CAKED WITH EARTH.
I MUST HAVE MY SHOES SOLED AND HEELED AND SHINED 603 ICEMAN
FIRST THING TOMORROW MORNING.
SOLELY
SOLELY ON ITS MERITS AS A BUSINESS OPPORTUNITY. 52 MANSNS
I AM SOLELY CONCERNED WITH WHAT IS MINE. 153 MANSNS
SOLELY ON CREEPING CANAL BOATS, AS SHORT-SIGHTED 40 POET
FOOLS WOULD HAVE US BELIEVE.
SOLEMN
SCRAWNEY NECK, AND A LONG SOLEMN HORSE FACE WITH 200 AHWILD
DEEP-SET LITTLE BLACK EYES,
(TAKES OUT HIS PIPE AND FILLS AND LIGHTS IT WITH 254 AHWILD
SOLEMN GRAVITY)
(WITH MAD, SOLEMN DECISION) WHEN THE HOUSE IS 573 CROSS
SOLD I'LL GO--AND I'LL FIND IT/
MAKING SO MUCH SOLEMN FUSS OVER DEATH/ 54 ELECTR
DON'T BE SO SOLEMN--FUSS BUZZER/ 148 ELECTR
(THEY SHAKE THEIR HEADS IN SOLEMN SURPRISE) 317 GGBROW
ALL HE KNOWS ABOUT MEDICINE IS TO LOOK SOLEMN AND 92 JOURNE
PREACH WILL POWER/
(HE CLICKS OUT ONE BULB.) ON MY SOLEMN OATH, 151 JOURNE
EDMUND,
(TAKING IT UP IN A TONE BETWEEN CHANTING AND THEIR318 LAZARU
OLD SOLEMN INTONING)
I HEREBY TAKE A SOLEMN OATH NEVER TO COME TO YOU. 67 MANSNS
(HE STARTS WITH A SOLEMN EARNESTNESS) MR. 31 STRANG
MARSDEN, I--THERE'S
SOLEMNLY
AND BEGINS WITH A SHAMEFACED, SELF-CONSCIOUS 294 AHWILD
SOLEMNITY)
(WITH SENTIMENTAL SOLEMNITY) 412 MARCOM
(PRONOUNCES WITH BOYISH SOLEMNITY) 31 STRANG
SOLEMN,
(SOLEMNLY) AYE. 537 'ILE
HIS MANNER IS SOLEMNLY COLLEGIATE. 186 AHWILD
(AGAIN EMBARRASSED AND HUMILIATED--AGAIN JOKING IT191 AHWILD
OFF, SOLEMNLY)
AND A POSEY ACTOR SOLEMNLY PLAYING A ROLE. 193 AHWILD
(SOLEMNLY) SON, IF I DIDN'T KNOW IT WAS YOU 195 AHWILD
TALKING,
(SUDDENLY--SOLEMNLY AUTHORITATIVE) 197 AHWILD
(BOWING SOLEMNLY TO RIGHT AND LEFT) 224 AHWILD
AS HE ENTERS HE MAKES A SOLEMN INTENSE EFFORT TO224 AHWILD
APPEAR CASUAL AND DEAD,
(SOLEMNLY OFFENDED) ARE YOU--PUBLICLY REBUKING ME225 AHWILD
BEFORE ASSEMBLED--S
(HE TURNS AND MARCHES SOLEMNLY OUT THROUGH THE 233 AHWILD
BACK PARLOR, SINGING)
(THEN SOLEMNLY TRAGIC) IT'S ONLY THAT I'VE GOT A 239 AHWILD
WEIGHT ON MY MIND.
(LYING BOLDLY) I DID WANT TO--ONLY I--(THEN HE 242 AHWILD
ADDS SOLEMNLY) I'VE SWORN OFF.
(SOLEMNLY) I TOOK AN OATH I'D BE FAITHFUL. 243 AHWILD

SOLEMNLY (CONT'D.)
(WITH SURPRISED EXCITEMENT) WELL, IF YOU DON'T 272 AHWILD
SOLEMNLY SWEAR YOU WON'T--
HE FEELS IN THE POCKET OF HIS COAT AND GRASPS 74 ANNA
SOMETHING--SOLEMNLY)
(THEN SOLEMNLY) BUT HERE'S WHAT I DID HAVE YOU IN438 DYNAMO
FOR.
(SOLEMNLY) YOUNG MAN, I'LL BE HONEST WITH YOU. 439 DYNAMO
(GUILTY AND RESENTFUL) YOU FOLKS AT HOME TAKE 94 ELECTR
DEATH SO SOLEMNLY/
AND THE OTHER TWO SAID VERY SOLEMNLY.. 310 GGBROW
THEY SOLEMNLY LAY HIM DOWN ON THE COUCH AND STAND 318 GGBROW
LOOKING DOWN AT HIM.)
(INTONING SOLEMNLY) SOON THE GOD COMES/ 299 LAZARU
(SOLEMNLY) TAKE MY WORD FOR IT, HE IS INDEED A 300 LAZARU
GOD.
(SOLEMNLY) YES, I SWEAR TO, MARK. 357 MARCOM
(SOLEMNLY) DO YOU IMAGINE THE KAAN IS SUCH A NERO381 MARCOM
(THEN SOLEMNLY) BUT MY LAST OBJECTION IS 396 MARCOM
INSURMOUNTABLE.
SOLES
TO BE KISSING THE SHOE-SOLES OF A FINE, DACENT 34 ANNA
GIRL THE LIKE OF YOURSELF.
HE FEELS OF THE SOLES OF HIS FEET GINGERLY) 188 EJONES
HE HAS NO SOCKS, AND HIS BARE FEET SHOW THROUGH 577 ICEMAN
HOLES IN THE SOLES,
HER FEET ARE BARE, THE SOLES EARTH-STAINED AND 3 MISBEG
TOUGH AS LEATHER.
SOLICIT
I HAVE DELIBERATELY GONE OUT OF MY WAY TO SOLICIT 29 MANSNS
EVEN THE MEANEST,
SOLICITATION
(WITH REAL SOLICITATION) AIR YE ABLE FUR THE 252 DESIRE
STAIRS$
AT HIS EARNEST SOLICITATION--(HE WAVES A HAND TO 152 ELECTR
THE PORTRAIT MOCKINGLY)
SOLICITOUSLY
(THEN SOLICITIOUSLY) YOU MUST BE TERRIBLY TIRED. 47 ELECTR
SOLICITOUS
(SOLICITOUS EXPRESSION--PLEASANTLY TO THE STARING 314 GGBROW
DRAFTSMAN)
(CALCULATINGLY SOLICITOUS--WHISPERING TO HOPE) 608 ICEMAN
HER MANNER BECOMES TENDERLY SOLICITOUS, 72 JOURNE
(TENDERLY SOLICITOUS NOW, PUTS AN ARM AROUND HER.)131 POET
SOLICITOUSLY
(THEN SOLICITOUSLY, PUTTING HER HAND ON HIS 271 AHWILD
FOREHEAD)
(WALKS OVER TO HER SOLICITOUSLY) 25 ANNA
(PULLING AT HIS HAND--SOLICITOUSLY) 129 BEYOND
HE SNATCHES AT A CHANCE TO CHANGE THE SUBJECT-- 188 EJONES
SOLICITOUSLY)
(THEN SOLICITOUSLY) BUT YOU MUST BE WORN OUT. 301 GGBROW
(SOLICITOUSLY) WHY, DO YOU HAVE TO SEE HIM ABOUT 108 STRANG
SOMETHING IMPORTANT, NINA$
(SOLICITOUSLY) ISN'T IT TIME TO NURSE HIM AGAINS 118 STRANG
(LOOKING UP AT HER--SOLICITOUSLY) 134 STRANG
(JUMPS FROM HIS CHAIR AND GOES TO HER-- 193 STRANG
SOLICITOUSLY)
SOLICITUDE
(THEN TEASINGLY) BUT DO YOU KNOW WHAT I THINK IS 533 DAYS
BEHIND ALL THIS SOLICITUDE OF
CHRISTINE GOES ON WITH MOTHERLY SOLICITUDE) 81 ELECTR
(WITH TIRED SOLICITUDE) I SUPPOSE YOU HAVEN'T 291 GGBROW
EATEN A THING, AS USUAL.
(IMMEDIATELY, WITH A MOTHERLY SOLICITUDE) 320 GGBROW
WITH A FOND SOLICITUDE WHICH IS AT THE SAME TIME 67 JOURNE
REMOTE.)
HER MANNER IS AGAIN ONE OF DETACHED MOTHERLY 91 JOURNE
SOLICITUDE.
(WITH SUDDEN, BIG-BROTHERLY SOLICITUDE, GRABBING 156 JOURNE
THE BOTTLE.)
(TREMULOUSLY--GRATEFUL FOR HIS SOLICITUDE) 406 MARCOM
HER MANNER CHANGES TO WORRIED SOLICITUDE) 68 MISBEG
SOLID
WAAL--THIS AIR SOLID COMFORT--FUR ONCE. 217 DESIRE
HIS BODY HAS PUT ON TWENTY POUNDS OR MORE OF SOLID 69 MANSNS
FLESH,
WHY EVERY PLATE ON HIS TABLE IS SOLID GOLD/ 363 MARCOM
POLO BROTHERS AND SON--DOESN'T THAT SOUND SOLID, 381 MARCOM
EH$
EVERY BOULDER ON THE PLACE HAS TURNED TO SOLID 65 MISBEG
GOLD.
SOLIDITY
THERE IS ALSO, WHAT IS MORE REMARKABLE, A DECIDED 111 STRANG
LOOK OF SOLIDITY ABOUT HIM,
SOLIDLY
HER MOVEMENTS SLOW AND SOLIDLY LANGUOROUS LIKE AN 278 GGBROW
ANIMAL'S,
SOLITAIRE
BOTH ARE PLAYING SOLITAIRE. 284 GGBROW
HE WEARS HIS PINCE-NEZ, AND IS PLAYING SOLITAIRE. 125 JOURNE
SOLITARY
AND GET HIS EYES RUINED IN SOLITARY. 593 ICEMAN
LIFE IS FOR EACH MAN A SOLITARY CELL WHOSE WALLS 309 LAZARU
ARE MIRRORS.
SOLITUDE
FORGIVE MY SINS--FORGIVE MY SOLITUDE--FORGIVE MY 292 GGBROW
SICKNESS--FORGIVE ME/
OR IN THE DREARY SOLITUDE OF YOUR OWN ROOM, 132 JOURNE
IN THE NAME OF MAN'S SOLITUDE--HIS AGONY OF 367 LAZARU
FAREWELL--
THIS IS TO BE ALONE--THIS, THIS IS SOLITUDE/= 101 POET
SOLITUDE AND WORK. 457 WELDED
THEY HAVEN'T KILLED IT--THAT LONELY LIFE OF ONE'S 477 WELDED
OWN WHICH SUFFERS IN SOLITUDE.
SOLOMON
IN THE SOLOMON ISLANDS. 457 CARIBE

SOLOMON (CONT'D.)
I MIGHT JUST AS WELL HAVE IMPORTED SOME WITCH DOCTORS FROM THE SOLOMON ISLANDS/ 100 STRANG

SOLOMON'S
SOLOMON'S MINES, THEY SAYS. 204 DESIRE
ANY THE CABOTS'LL FIND SOLOMON'S MINES T'GETHER/ 268 DESIRE

SOLUTION
(SUDDENLY SEEMS TO HAVE A SOLUTION. 74 ANNA
AFTER ALL, THAT WOULD BE ONE SOLUTION-- 130 MANSNS
I-- I WAS TRYING TO CONCENTRATE MY THOUGHTS ON THE 172 MANSNS
FINAL SOLUTION OF THE PROBLEM.
(WITH FINALITY) THAT'S THE ONLY POSSIBLE 132 STRANG
SOLUTION, NEO. FOR ALL OUR SAKES.
(EXCITEDLY) BUT, MY GOD, WHAT A SOLUTION--$ 486 WELDED

SOLVE
YOU ARE PLEASED TO ACT THE MYSTERIOUS, JEW, BUT I 353 LAZARU
SHALL SOLVE YOU/
(TRYING TO SOLVE A RIDDLE IN HIS OWN MIND-- 379 MARCOM
MUSINGLY)
EXCLUSIVE INVENTION TO SOLVE THIS PROBLEM. 395 MARCOM
THAT WILL SOLVE EVERYTHING/... 176 STRANG

SOMBER
THE WALLS ARE PAPERED IN A SOMBER BROWN AND DARK- 210 AHWILD
RED DESIGN.
(SUDDENLY GROWING SOMBER--IN A LOW TONE) 9 ANNA
(HE RELAPSES INTO AN ATTITUDE OF SOMBER BROODING.) 28 ANNA
SPEAKS WITH SOMBER PREMONITION AS ANNA RE-ENTERS 78 ANNA
FROM THE LEFT)
(LOOKING OUT INTO THE NIGHT--LOST IN HIS SOMBER 78 ANNA
PREOCCUPATION--
ROBERT STARES AT HER WITH A GRIM, SOMBER 142 BEYOND
EXPRESSION.
A SOMBER MONOTONE OF WIND LOST IN THE LEAVES MOANS187 EJONES
IN THE AIR.
WITH A SOMBER PULSATION, A BAFFLED BUT REVENGEFUL 202 EJONES
POWER.)
FIXED ON THE HOUSE TO HIDE ITS SOMBER GRAY 5 ELECTR
UGLINESS.
THE SOMBER GRAYNESS OF THE WALL, THE GREEN OF THE 5 ELECTR
OPEN SHUTTERS,
(THEN WITH A CHANGE TO SOMBER 41 ELECTR
FIXED ON THE SOMBER STONE HOUSE. 43 ELECTR
WITH SOMBER INTENSITY) 89 ELECTR
(THEN WITH SOMBER BITTERNESS) 140 ELECTR
HIS EXPRESSION BECOMES SOMBER. 39 JOURNE
HE STARES AT LAZARUS WITH A SOMBER INTENTNESS. 314 LAZARU
TIBERIUS STARES FOR A WHILE WITH SOMBER INTENSITY 340 LAZARU
AT LAZARUS)
SOMBER AND THREATENING--AND SOMETHING IN MY NATURE163 MANSNS
RESPONDS--
KUBLAI SITS IN A SOMBER STUDY, FROWNING AND BITING388 MARCOM
HIS LIPS.
(CHOKING WITH WRATH) O GOD OF THE SOMBER HEAVENS/425 MARCOM
NO, SHE'S TOO SOMBER... 53 STRANG
(THEN WITH A SOMBER ALIEN FORCEFULNESS) 92 STRANG
(IMMEDIATELY REALIZING WHAT IS COMING--THINKING 150 STRANG
WITH SOMBER ANGUISH)
ONE FEELS A POWERFUL IMAGINATION TINGED WITH 443 WELDED
SOMBER SADNESS--
(HE SLUMPS DOWN ON THE CHAIR AGAIN, SUNK IN A 473 WELDED
SOMBER STUPOR.

SOMBERLY
(SOMBERLY) THAT'S RIGHT, LAUGH/ 195 AHWILD
(SOMBERLY) I'M ALL RIGHT, AUNT LILY. 215 AHWILD
(SOMBERLY) HELL IS THE ONLY WORD THAT CAN 281 AHWILD
DESCRIBE IT.
(AFTER A MOMENT'S HESITATION--SOMBERLY) 18 ANNA
(SOMBERLY) AY GO FOR A DRINK. 61 ANNA
RESTING HIS ELBOW, HIS CHIN ON HIS HAND, STARING 562 CROSS
SOMBERLY BEFORE HIM.
(SOMBERLY) HE IS QUIET ALWAYS--TOO QUIET. 562 CROSS
(THEN AFTER A PAUSE--SOMBERLY) 48 ELECTR
(A PAUSE--THEN HE GOES ON SOMBERLY) 60 ELECTR
(SOMBERLY) DARKNESS WITHOUT A STAR TO GUIDE US/ 151 ELECTR
(SOMBERLY) NO. 151 ELECTR
(SOMBERLY) WHEN PAN WAS FORBIDDEN THE LIGHT AND 297 GGBROW
WARMTH OF THE SUN HE GREW
THE FORMER SQUATTING ON HIS HAMS, MONKEY-WISE, AND311 LAZARU
BROODING SOMBERLY.)
(THEN SOMBERLY) YOU SHOULD NEVER HAVE COME HERE. 328 LAZARU
(THEN SOMBERLY) A LITTLE FEAR IS USEFUL EVEN FOR 329 LAZARU
LIONS--
(SOMBERLY) HE LOVES EVERYONE--BUT NO ONE--NOT EVEN351 LAZARU
ME/
SOMBERLY CONTEMPTUOUS AND THREATENING) 353 LAZARU
AND IS STARING SOMBERLY BEFORE HIM) 423 MARCOM
(AFTER A PAUSE--SOMBERLY) YOU MENTIONED OUR YEARS455 WELDED
TOGETHER AS PROOF.
(BEGINS TO FROWN SOMBERLY--LETS GO OF HER HAND) 483 WELDED

SOMBERNESS
WHICH DARKENS TO SOMBERNESS AT THE END. 28 ELECTR

SOMEBODY
SOMEBODY HAD GOT TO. 146 BEYOND
THEY BURY SOMEBODY--PY CHIMINY CHRISTMAS, I TINK 456 CARIBE
SO FROM WAY IT SOUND.
AND NOT WHAT SOMEBODY DEALS ME. 25 HUGHIE
GIVE ME A HAND WITH THESE BUNDLES, SOMEBODY. 638 ICEMAN
SOMEBODY LIGHT THE CANDLES ON THE CAKE WHEN YOU 644 ICEMAN
HEAR US COMING.
(WITH A DULL CALLOUSNESS) SOMEBODY CROAKED YOUR 694 ICEMAN
EVELYN, EH$
HE'S FOREVER MAKING SNEERING FUN OF SOMEBODY, THAT 18 JOURNE
ONE.

SOMEBODY'LL
JEES, SOMEBODY'LL HAVE TO TAKE AN AXE TO CROAK 579 ICEMAN
YOU/

SOMEBODY'S
INTO SOMEBODY'S GARDEN, LIKE YOU'VE DONE BEFORE, 106 POET

SOMEDAY
I PLANTED IT IN YOUR MIND THAT SOMEDAY YOU'D 164 JOURNE
WRITE/
NO, SOMEDAY, I WILL GIVE YOU THE COURAGE TO OPEN 113 MANSNS
THE DOOR YOURSELF
(PASSIONATELY.) ALL I PRAY TO GOD IS THAT SOMEDAY105 POET
WHEN YOU'RE ADMIRING YOURSELF

SOMEHOW
I ALWAYS COME BACK--WITH A FULL SHIP--AND--IT 547 *ILE
DON'T SEEM RIGHT NOT TO--SOMEHOW.
I--IT JUST STUCK IN MY MEMORY SOMEHOW. 199 AHWILD
(THEN LAMELY) SO SOMEHOW-- 266 AHWILD
AND I FEEL CLEAN, SOMEHOW--LIKE YOU FEEL YUST 28 ANNA
AFTER YOU'VE TOOK A BATH.
OH SOMEHOW AFTER A TIME I'D FORGET ANY PAIN I WAS 89 BEYOND
IN, AND START DREAMING.
I'LL GET AWAY SOMEWHERE, SOMEHOW. 107 BEYOND
AND I'VE GOT TO PULL THINGS THROUGH SOMEHOW. 123 BEYOND
IT ALL SEEMS TRIFLING, SOMEHOW. 138 BEYOND
BUT WE AIN'T CHICKENS NO MORE, AND SOMEHOW, I 487 CARDIF
DUNNO,
I C'D LIE OUT ON DECK AND LOOK AT THEM, AND IT'D 489 CARDIF
MAKE IT EASIER TO GO--SOMEHOW.
YOU SOMEHOW MANAGE TO LIVE IN SOME LOST WORLD 517 DAYS
I DID HELP YE--SOMEHOW. 267 DESIRE
(FEELING HIMSELF SOMEHOW MORE AND MORE HEARTENED 517 DIFRNT
BY HOPE)
(AFTER A PAUSE) SOMEHOW--SEEMS TO ME 'S IF--YOU 539 DIFRNT
MIGHT REALLY NEED ME NOW.
WHAT I MEAN IS IN THEM--SOMEHOW. 458 DYNAMO
WATCHING THEM ALWAYS HELPS ME SOMEHOW. 472 DYNAMO
GORRY, I GOTTA FIND DAT GRUB HIGH AN' LOW SOMEHOW/189 EJONES
YOU HAVE CHANGED, SOMEHOW. 47 ELECTR
YOU'RE YOUNGER, TOO, SOMEHOW. 82 ELECTR
I FEEL THERE'S SOMETHING AWFULLY WRONG--SOMEHOW. 158 ELECTR
AND THAT YOU'RE TO BLAME FOR THEM, SOMEHOW/ 172 ELECTR
WE'LL MANAGE SOMEHOW-- 272 GGBROW
THAT GETS HIM SOMEHOW. 285 GGBROW
YOU'RE BROTHERS, I GUESS, SOMEHOW. 287 GGBROW
BUT YOU REMIND ME OF HIM SOMEHOW. 11 HUGHIE
SAY, YOU DO REMIND ME OF HUGHIE SOMEHOW, PAL. 19 HUGHIE
BESS SOMEHOW NEVER HAD THE CONFIDENCE IN ME A 609 ICEMAN
SISTER SHOULD.
BUT HE WAS FUNNY, TOO, SOMEHOW. 618 ICEMAN
I'LL GIT DE MONEY FOR MY STAKE TODAY, SOMEHOW, 673 ICEMAN
SOMEHERES)
(PATHETICALLY) SOMEHOW, I CAN'T FEEL IT'S RIGHT 688 ICEMAN
FOR ME TO GO, HICKEY, EVEN NOW.
SOMEHOW, THAT TOOK HOLD OF ME. 394 MARCOM
AND SOMEHOW HARDER'S FENCE IN THAT VICINITY HAS A 50 MISBEG
HABIT OF BREAKING DOWN.
SOMETHING GENTLE AND SAD AND, SOMEHOW, DAUNTLESS.) 20 POET
SOMEHOW... 12 STRANG
BUT DO YOU UNDERSTAND NOW THAT I MUST SOMEHOW FIND 21 STRANG
A WAY TO GIVE MYSELF TO
BUT I WASN'T ABLE TO GET TO SLEEP UNTIL AFTER 57 STRANG
DAYLIGHT SOMEHOW.
SOMEHOW... 63 STRANG
(GROPING) THERE MUST BE A WAY--SOMEHOW. 63 STRANG
(HE FINISHES MISERABLY) SOMEHOW. 70 STRANG
SO I MUST HAVE ANOTHER BABY--SOMEHOW--DON'T YOU 84 STRANG
THINK, DOCTOR$
IT SEEMS INCESTUOUS SOMEHOW/..... 119 STRANG
BEGAN TO CRACK, AND HE COULDN'T SEE HIM BUT HE 153 STRANG
FELT HIM CRACKING SOMEHOW,

SOMEONE
(THEN HASTILY AS HE SEES SOMEONE COMING UP THE 12 ELECTR
DRIVE)

SOMEONE
THE SILENCE IS UNBROKEN EXCEPT FOR THE MEASURED 535 *ILE
TREAD OF SOMEONE WALKING UP AND
(THERE IS THE NOISE OF SOMEONE COMING SLOWLY DOWN 538 *ILE
THE COMPANIONWAY STAIRS.
ALL ABOUT SOMEONE WHO MURDERED HIS WIFE AND GOT 197 AHWILD
HUNG, AS HE RICHLY DESERVED,
SOMEONE OUGHT TO STOP ME. 231 AHWILD
I HEAR SOMEONE ON THE PIAZZA. 253 AHWILD
AND SOMEONE WHISTLING =WALTZ ME AROUND AGAIN, 253 AHWILD
WILLIE.=)
THERE'S SOMEONE ON THE PIAZZA NOW--COMING AROUND 260 AHWILD
TO THIS DOOR, TOO.
HE MUST HAVE BEEN INFLUENCED AND LED BY SOMEONE. 266 AHWILD
SEEMS TO ME I'VE HEARD SOMEONE SAY THAT BEFORE. 272 AHWILD
(THERE IS A SOUND OF SOMEONE ON THE PORCH. 272 AHWILD
BUT THERE MIGHT BE SOMEONE. 280 AHWILD
I'D HAVE TO SNITCH ON SOMEONE--AND YOU WOULDN'T 294 AHWILD
WANT ME TO DO THAT.
(THEN WITH EVIDENT ANXIETY) ON'Y TROW IT AWAY IF 15 ANNA
YUH HEAR SOMEONE COMIN'.
I GOT TO MEE SOMEONE TOO. 16 ANNA
(AFTER A SLIGHT PAUSE) DID YUH SAY YUH GOT TO 16 ANNA
MEET SOMEONE HERE$
IT SOUNDS GOOD TO HEAR SOMEONE--TALK TO ME THAT 22 ANNA
WAY.
(THEN FEARFULLY) IS IT MARRIED TO SOMEONE ELSE 55 ANNA
YOU ARE--IN THE WEST MAYBE$
AND I THOUGHT SHE LOVED--SOMEONE ELSE. 100 BEYOND
THERE'S SOMEONE AT THE KITCHEN DOOR. 123 BEYOND
ALL THE FARM'S EVER NEEDED WAS SOMEONE WITH THE 136 BEYOND
KNACK OF LOOKING AHEAD AND
AS IF SOMEONE WERE GETTING OUT OF BED. 145 BEYOND
IT'S ONLY RIGHT FOR SOMEONE TO MEET HIM AFTER HE'S146 BEYOND
BEEN GONE FIVE YEARS.
IT HAD TO BE BECAUSE I LOVED SOMEONE ELSE, I'D 164 BEYOND
FOUND OUT.
(SOMEONE DROPS A BOTTLE ON DECK AND IT SMASHES.) 471 CARIBE
HE MAKES A SIGN TO SOMEONE IN THE DARKNESS 555 CROSS
BENEATH...

SOMEONE

SOMEONE (CONT'D.)
THE AUTHORITIES HAVE BEEN COMPLAINED TO--NOT BY 558 CROSS
US, MIND--BUT BY SOMEONE.
THEN I HEARD SOMEONE COME DOWN THE STAIRS AND GO 563 CROSS
OUT.
YOU'VE PICKED ON SOMEONE OUT OF YOUR CLASS. 501 DAYS
ISN'T THAT SOMEONE NOW$ 547 DAYS
(THEN TAUNTINGLY) WHEN I KISSED YE BACK, MEBBE I 239 DESIRE
THOUGHT 'TWAS SOMEONE ELSE.
HER EYES ARE FIXED ANXIOUSLY ON THE OPEN DOOR IN 247 DESIRE
HEAD AS IF WAITING FOR SOMEONE.
AND YOU'D HEAR ABOUT IT FROM SOMEONE SOONER OR 502 DIFRNT
LATER 'CAUSE JIM AND THE REST O'
YOU HEARD IT FROM SOMEONE ELSE. 502 DIFRNT
IT MAKES HIM ANOTHER PERSON--NOT CALEB, BUT 512 DIFRNT
SOMEONE JUST LIKE ALL THE OTHERS.
HE NEEDS A GOOD LICKIN' FROM SOMEONE. 515 DIFRNT
I HEAR SOMEONE COMING. 547 DIFRNT
WELL, I GOT TO GET SOMEONE ELSE, THAT'S ALL. 549 DIFRNT
HER EYES GLANCE QUICKLY ON ALL SIDES AS IF 459 DYNAMO
SEARCHING FOR SOMEONE.)
(FLUSTEREDLY) (I'M SURE I HEARD SOMEONE... 459 DYNAMO
THE HEAVY, PLODDING FOOTSTEPS OF SOMEONE 191 EJONES
APPROACHING ALONG THE TRAIL FROM THE
THERE IS THE NOISE OF SOMEONE APPROACHING FROM THE198 EJONES
LEFT.
THAT IS, UNLESS IT'S BECAUSE YOU LOVE SOMEONE 14 ELECTR
ELSE--
HE REMINDED ME OF SOMEONE. 15 ELECTR
AIN'T YOU NOTICED THIS BRANT REMINDS YOU OF 19 ELECTR
SOMEONE IN LOOKS$
HERE'S SOMEONE/ 46 ELECTR
THEY ARE EMPTY--WAITING FOR SOMEONE TO MOVE IN/ 60 ELECTR
THERE'S SOMEONE ELSE WAITING WHO WILL BE SO GLAD 77 ELECTR
TO SEE YOU.
SOMEONE LOANED ME THE BOOK. 89 ELECTR
THEN SOMEONE KNOCKS LOUDLY.) 99 ELECTR
THERE'S SOMEONE IN THE HALL/ 99 ELECTR
BRANT IS ALARMED THAT THIS UPROAR WILL ATTRACT 105 ELECTR
SOMEONE.
SOMEONE MAY COME/ 115 ELECTR
IT'S A ROTTEN DIRTY JOKE ON SOMEONE/ 116 ELECTR
SHE SEES SOMEONE SHE IS EVIDENTLY EXPECTING 117 ELECTR
APPROACHING THE HOUSE FROM UP THE
SHE'S MET SOMEONE BY THE GATE/ 119 ELECTR
THERE'S SOMEONE COMIN' UP THE DRIVE. 134 ELECTR
AND THE WAY HE ACTED--LIKE SOMEONE IN A TRANCE/ 136 ELECTR
THAT IN ONE OF YOUR FITS YOU'LL SAY SOMETHING 152 ELECTR
BEFORE SOMEONE--
LOOKS AROUND HER UNCERTAINLY AND SEES SOMEONE 174 ELECTR
COMING FROM OFF LEFT, FRONT--
MARRY SOMEONE ELSE. 177 ELECTR
HE HEARD SOMEONE YELL. 293 GGBROW
I HEARD SOMEONE HAD SEEN HIM AT HOME AND HE WAS 302 GGBROW
SOBER AND LOOKING FINE.
THEY ARE HUNTING FOR SOMEONE/ 320 GGBROW
THEY'VE GOT TO KILL SOMEONE NOW, TO LIVE/ 320 GGBROW
I RAN HERE TO WARN--SOMEONE/ 320 GGBROW
(AFTER A PAUSE) I WAS TRYIN' TO GIT EVEN WIT 241 HA APE
SOMEONE SEES
SOMEONE DAT DONE ME DOIT. 241 HA APE
WHAT THE HELL IS THAT--SOMEONE KNOCKING$ 246 HA APE
FOOTSTEPS ECHO IN THE DESERTED LOBBY AS SOMEONE 8 HUGHIE
COMES IN FROM THE STREET.
AND SOMEONE INSIDE THE MOVEMENT MUST HAVE SOLD OUT588 ICEMAN
AND TIPPED THEM OFF.
WHAT FINISHED ME WAS THIS LAST BUSINESS OF SOMEONES92 ICEMAN
SELLING OUT.
WHEN YOU'RE DEALING TO SOMEONE WHO'S SOBER AND CAN609 ICEMAN
COUNT.
YUH'LL HAVE TO HIRE SOMEONE TO CROAK YUH WID AN 615 ICEMAN
AXE.
HE'S HIDIN' SOMEONE EVERY MINUTE. 631 ICEMAN
HE SLINKS IN FURTIVELY, AS IF HE WERE ESCAPING 645 ICEMAN
FROM SOMEONE.
BUT I COULD HEAR HIM THROUGH THE WALL DOING HIS 681 ICEMAN
SPIEL TO SOMEONE ALL NIGHT LONG.
BUT CHUCK HEARS SOMEONE UPSTAIRS IN THE HALL AND 683 ICEMAN
GRABS CORA'S ARM)
(PUZZLED) SOMEONE ELSE$ 693 ICEMAN
(VINDICTIVELY) I THINK IT WAS SOMETHING YOU DROVE693 ICEMAN
SOMEONE ELSE TO DO/
(HE HEARS SOMEONE AT REAR AND CALLS) 697 ICEMAN
DE MINUTE YOUR BACK IS TOINED, DEY'RE CHEATIN' WID698 ICEMAN
DE ICEMAN OR SOMEONE.
HE'D BORROWED OR GOT TO STICK UP SOMEONE, AND DEN 699 ICEMAN
DIDN'T HAVE DE GUTS.
AND MAKE SOMEONE ELSE WORK FOR YUH, IS DERE$ 702 ICEMAN
WHENEVER I MADE UP MY MIND TO SELL SOMEONE 703 ICEMAN
SOMETHING I KNEW THEY OUGHT TO WANT.
IT'S WORSE IF YOU KILL SOMEONE AND THEY HAVE TO GO706 ICEMAN
ON LIVING.
SOMEONE I COULD TELL A DIRTY JOKE TO AND SHE'D 712 ICEMAN
LAUGH.
YOU HAVE TO BEGIN BLAMING SOMEONE ELSE, TOO. 715 ICEMAN
HEJESUS, IT'S GOOD TO HEAR SOMEONE LAUGH AGAIN/ 722 ICEMAN
ALMOST NOTHING, JUST TO KEEP SOMEONE ON IT, 23 JOURNE
SOMEONE BESIDES THE SERVANTS--THAT STUPID 46 JOURNE
CATHLEEN/
AS HE DOES SO, HE HEARS SOMEONE COMING IN THE 53 JOURNE
FRONT DOOR.
(BITTERLY.) BECAUSE HE'S ALWAYS SNEERING AT 61 JOURNE
SOMEONE ELSE.
HE WAS DIFFERENT FROM ALL ORDINARY MEN, LIKE 105 JOURNE
SOMEONE FROM ANOTHER WORLD.
I WAS SO LONESOME I KEPT CATHLEEN WITH ME JUST TO 112 JOURNE
HAVE SOMEONE TO TALK TO.
WHEN HE HEARS SOMEONE ENTERING THE FRONT DOOR. 125 JOURNE

SOMEONE (CONT'D.)
AS IF SOMEONE HAD STUMBLED AND FALLEN ON THE FRONT154 JOURNE
STEPS.
A WALL SWITCH, AND A MOMENT LATER SOMEONE STARTS 169 JOURNE
PLAYING THE PIANO IN THERE--
LIKE SOMEONE WHO HAS COME TO A ROOM TO GET 170 JOURNE
SOMETHING BUT HAS BECOME
AS IF HE EXPECTED SOMEONE TO STAB HIM IN THE BACK.311 LAZARU
LET HIM RAISE SOMEONE FROM THE DEAD/ 344 LAZARU
I MUST FIND SOMEONE OUTSIDE MYSELF IN WHOM I CAN 3 MANSNS
CONFIDE, AND SO ESCAPE MYSELF--
SOMEONE STRONG AND HEALTHY AND SANE, WHO DARES TO 3 MANSNS
LOVE AND LIVE LIFE GREEDILY
SO PROUD AND HAPPY BECAUSE HE'S BEAT SOMEONE ON A 20 MANSNS
SALE.
GUSSY STARES AROUND HIM, LOOKING FOR SOMEONE. 26 MANSNS
SUPPOSING SOMEONE CAME IN/ 83 MANSNS
AND SOMEONE HAS TO HUMOR HER 147 MANSNS
AND THEN STAND OUTSIDE YOUR DOOR KNOCKING AND 151 MANSNS
KNOCKING LIKE SOMEONE--/
IF SOMEONE STUMBLED AND FELL AGAINST HER 179 MANSNS
I HEAR SOMEONE COMING/ 185 MANSNS
SOMEONE IS CALLING ME/ 189 MANSNS
THERE'S SOMEONE MOVING INSIDE. 357 MARCOM
SOMEONE IS RUNNING HERE, AND A CROWD BEHIND. 361 MARCOM
I DON'T KNOW--I MEAN, I'M SORRY BUT--YOU SEE I 368 MARCOM
PROMISED SOMEONE I'D NEVER--
HE SUDDENLY BAWLS TO SOMEONE IN THE SHIP) 403 MARCOM
WITH SOMEONE JERKING THE WIRES. 415 MARCOM
YOU'D CHANGED INTO SOMEONE ELSE, SOMEONE I'VE GOT 416 MARCOM
A GOOD RIGHT TO--JUST A GIRL--
WELL, GOD GRANT SOMEONE WITH WITS WILL SEE THAT 16 MISBEG
DOPEY GANDER AT THE DEPOT AND
SOMEONE HAS LATELY. 32 MISBEG
TO TALK TO MESELF SO I'LL KNOW SOMEONE WITH BRAINS 80 MISBEG
IS LISTENING.
THERE'S SOMEONE ON THE ROAD-- 98 MISBEG
SHE LOOKED YOUNG AND PRETTY LIKE SOMEONE I 147 MISBEG
REMEMBERED MEETING LONG AGO.
AN EXCUSE TO CHALLENGE SOMEONE. 12 POET
WHERE THERE'S A DOCTOR HANDY AND SOMEONE TO NURSE 73 POET
HIM.
(PLEASANTLY.) THE SOMEONE BEING YOU, MISS MELODY$ 73 POET
I SUPPOSE SOMEONE AROUND HERE THAT HATES FATHER-- 78 POET
AND WHO DOESN'T$
OR YOU'D THINK HE'D SEND JAMIE OR SOMEONE BACK 138 POET
WITH A WORD FOR ME.
TRYING TO WAKE UP SOMEONE WHO COULD MARRY US. 149 POET
HE'LL MURDER SOMEONE/ 162 POET
AS IF SOMEONE HAD CALLED FOR SILENCE-- 180 POET
(HER FACE HARD.) I HEARD SOMEONE. 181 POET
(THEY ARE BOTH STARTLED BY THE HEAVY FOOTSTEPS OF 587 ROPE
SOMEONE APPROACHING OUTSIDE.
(HE HEARS SOMEONE COMING QUICKLY FROM THE RIGHT 6 STRANG
AND TURNS EXPECTANTLY.
((SOMEONE WITH HEAVY... 26 STRANG
BUT THAT'S JUST WHAT SHE NEEDS NOW, SOMEONE SHE 37 STRANG
CARES ABOUT TO MOTHER AND BOSS
IT'S TOO TERRIBLE FOR YOU--SAM'S OWN MOTHER--HOW 58 STRANG
WOULD YOU HAVE FELT IF SOMEONE--
IF HE'D ONLY FALL IN LOVE WITH SOMEONE ELSE... 69 STRANG
IT'S YOU WHO OUGHT TO HAVE MARRIED SOMEONE WORTH 70 STRANG
WHILE, NOT A POOR FISH LIKE ME/
I NEED THE COURAGE OF SOMEONE WHO CAN STAND 84 STRANG
OUTSIDE AND REASON IT OUT
THE MAN MUST BE SOMEONE WHO IS NOT UNATTRACTIVE TO 88 STRANG
HER PHYSICALLY, OF COURSE.
((AW, DON'T KID YOURSELF, IF SHE'D MARRIED SOMEONE 92 STRANG
ELSE...
(STUPIDLY) SOMEONE--AT THE DOOR. 97 STRANG
SOMEONE USED TO... 109 STRANG
(THINKING ANGRILY) (SHE PICKS SOMEONE BEYOND THE114 STRANG
AGE/...
I ONLY MENTIONED IT ON THE OFF CHANCE YOU MIGHT 122 STRANG
KNOW OF SOMEONE.
(AND SOMEONE ANSWERING 'HELLO, MARSDEN' AND COMING123 STRANG
IN AND THE DOOR CLOSING.)
I HAD THE QUEEREST FEELING JUST THEN THAT 145 STRANG
SOMEONE--
SOMEONE IS DEAD-- 190 STRANG
SSSHH--LISTEN--SOMEONE--(SHE SPEAKS IN AN 449 WELDED
UNNATURAL, MECHANICAL TONE.
SHE TURNS AND SPEAKS TO SOMEONE WHO IS FOLLOWING 470 WELDED
HER.
SOMEONE'D
IF I COULD PULL HIM TO THAT, I COULD HANG ON TO 230 AHWILD
HIM TILL SOMEONE'D NOTICE US.
(PLACATINGLY) I THOUGHT SOMEONE'D BETTER STAY 171 STRANG
HERE
SOMEONE'LL
NOW SOMEONE'LL HAVE TO GO DOWN TO THE STORE. 72 STRANG
SOMEONE'S
I'M GLAD SOMEONE'S FEELING GOOD. 42 ANNA
A PLACE IS SET AT THE END OF THE TABLE, LEFT, FOR 112 BEYOND
SOMEONE'S DINNER.
SOMEONE'S IN THERE, BENNY, SURE AS I'M ALIVE. 547 DIFRNT
BUT DON'T YOU HAVE TO HAVE THE CAPTAIN'S--OR 220 HA APE
SOMEONE'S--
(STARTS AND LISTENS) SOMEONE'S COMING NOW. 610 ICEMAN
WHEN I FEEL SOMEONE'S TRYING TO STEAL WHAT'S 411 MARCOM
RIGHTFULLY MINE, FOR INSTANCE.
AND IT MAY NOT BE MARCO AFTER ALL BUT ONLY A JOKE 427 MARCOM
SOMEONE'S PUT UP ON US.
SOMEONE'S AT THE YARD DOOR. 163 POET
SUMEP'N
ME FOR SOMEP'N WIT A KICK TO IT/ 209 HA APE
DE NUTTY HARP IS SAYIN' SOMEP'N. 216 HA APE
IT CAN'T MOVE WITOUT SOMEP'N ELSE, SEE$ 216 HA APE

SOMETHING

SOMEP'N (CONT'D.)
EVERYTING ELSE DAT MAKES DE WOILD MOVE, SOMEP'N 216 HA APE
MAKES IT MOVE.
ALL DE RICH GUYS DAT TINK DEY'RE SOMEP'N, THEY 216 HA APE
AIN'T NOTHIN'/
I START SOMEP'N AND DE WOILD MOVES/ 216 HA APE
NOW YUH'RE GETTIN' WISE TO SOMEP'N. 217 HA APE
AND DEN I SEEN YOUSE LOOKIN' AT SOMEP'N AND I 230 HA APE
TOUGHT HE'D SNEAKED DOWN TO COME
TINK I WANTER LET HER PUT SOMEP'N OVER ON ME$ 231 HA APE
OR ELSE DEY BOT' JUMPED ON ME FOR SOMEP'N. 234 HA APE
YOUSE GUYS LIVE ON IT AND TINK YUH'RE SOMEP'N. 238 HA APE
SHE LAMPED ME LIKE SHE WAS SEEIN' SOMEP'N BROKE 241 HA APE
LOOSE FROM DE MENAGERIE.
HER HANDS--DEY WAS SKINNY AND WHITE LIKE DEY 241 HA APE
WASN'T REAL BUT PAINTED ON SOMEP'N.
AND DAT YUH'D WANTER GIVE ME THE ONCE-OVER TROU A 247 HA APE
PEEP-HOLE OR SOMEP'N
FOR ALL YOUSE KNOW, I MIGHT BE A PLAIN-CLOTHES 248 HA APE
DICK, OR SOMEP'N.

SOMEPLACE
I GUESS HE MUST HAVE MET ANOTHER GIRL SOMEPLACE 13 ELECTR
AND GIVEN ME THE GO BY.
GET DRUNK SOMEPLACE WHERE HE CAN BE WITH 94 JOURNE

SOMEPODY
PY YESUS, I VISH SOMEPODY TAKE MY FIRST VATCH FOR 209 HA APE
ME/

SOMERSAULTS
BEJEES, ED, I'LL BET BESSIE IS DOING SOMERSAULTS 610 ICEMAN
IN HER GRAVE/

SOMETHIN'
AND D'YOU THINK YOU'RE TELLIN' ME SOMETHIN' NEW, 539 'ILE
MR. SLOCUM$
I WAS THINKIN' OF SOMETHIN' ELSE. 14 ANNA
I WANTA TELL YUH SOMETHIN'. 19 ANNA
I'M AFRAID SOMETHIN'S HAPPENED--SOMETHIN' ELSE. 98 BEYOND
YUH'RE AS SORE AS A BOIL ABOUT SOMETHIN'. 457 CARIBE
WHIN YE BUY A BOTTLE AV DHRINK OR (WITH A WINK) 463 CARIBE
SOMETHIN' ELSE FORBID,
YE MUST WRITE DOWN TOBACCY OR FRUIT OR SOMETHIN' 463 CARIBE
THE LOIKE AV THAT.
LISTEN, BELLA, I'VE SOMETHIN' TO ASK YE 464 CARIBE
THEY ALWAYS HAD SOMETHIN' SPECIAL NICE COOKED FUR 468 CARIBE
ME TO EAT.
IT'S SOMETHIN'--DRIVIN' HIM--T' DRIVE US/ 207 DESIRE
WHAT'S SOMETHIN'$ 207 DESIRE
(THEN SCORNFULLY) SOMETHIN'/ 207 DESIRE
IT'S ALUS SOMETHIN'. 207 DESIRE
YEAR ARTER YEAR IT'S SKULKED IN YER EYE-- 208 DESIRE
SOMETHIN'.
THEY'S SOMETHIN'. 208 DESIRE
AN' PAW KIN TELL YEW SOMETHIN' TOO/ 210 DESIRE
YE'LL NEED SOMETHIN' THAT'LL STICK T' YER RIBS. 214 DESIRE
BUT IT PAWS HITCHED WE'D BE SELLIN' EBEN 215 DESIRE
SOMETHIN' WE'D NEVER GIT NOHOW/
AH'D LIKE T' CATCH US NAPPIN'--JEST T' HAVE 216 DESIRE
SOMETHIN' T' HOSS US 'ROUND OVER.
MEBBE--MEBBE THEY'VE PIEENED THE STOCK--R' 225 DESIRE
SOMETHIN'/
THEY BEEN UP TO SOMETHIN'/ 225 DESIRE
INTO SOMETHIN' ELSE--TILL YE' BE JINED WITH IT-- 229 DESIRE
AN' IT'S YOUR'N--
I COULD O' BEEN A RICH MAN--BUT SOMETHIN' IN ME 237 DESIRE
FIT ME AN' FIT ME--
WHEN I FUST COME IN--IN THE DARK--THEY SEEMED 241 DESIRE
SOMETHIN' HERE.
I KIN STILL FEEL--SOMETHIN'..... 242 DESIRE
GIVE 'EM SOMETHIN' T' DANCE T'/ 250 DESIRE
(AT THE GATE, CONFUSEDLY) EVEN THE MUSIC CAN'T 253 DESIRE
DRIVE IT OUT--SOMETHIN'.
BUT HE GOT T' DO SOMETHIN' QUICK 260 DESIRE
I MUST'VE SUSPICIONED--SOMETHIN'. 264 DESIRE
I FELT THEY WAS SOMETHIN' ONNATURAL--SOMEHWARS-- 264 DESIRE
THE HOUSE GOT SO LONESOME--
IT HURT LIKE SOMETHIN' WAS BUSTIN' IN MY CHEST AN'266 DESIRE
HEAD.
I WANT TO TALK WITH YOU 'BOUT SOMETHIN'. 514 DIFRNT
THERE'S SOMETHIN' FUNNY GOIN' ON. 174 EJONES
(MALICIOUSLY) BUT S'POSIN' SOMETHIN' 'APPENS 184 EJONES
WRONG AN' THEY DO NAB YER$
IT TAKES DEM NIGGERS FROM NOW TO DARK TO GIT UP DE186 DESIRE
NERVE TO START SOMETHIN'.
WOODS IS YOU TRYIN' TO PUT SOMETHIN' OVAH ON MES 189 EJONES
THERE'S SOMETHIN' QUEER LOOKIN' ABOUT HER FACE. 9 ELECTR
THERE'S SOMETHIN' BEEN ON MY MIND LATELY I WANT TO 12 ELECTR
WARN YOU ABOUT.
SOMETHIN' I CALCULATE NO ONE'D NOTICE 'SPECIALLY 12 ELECTR
'CEPTIN' ME, BECAUSE--
THERE'S SOMETHIN' ABOUT HIS WALK CALLS BACK DAVID 20 ELECTR
MANNION, TOO.
SOUNDS MADE UP TO ME--LIKE SHORT FUR SOMETHIN' 20 ELECTR
ELSE.
LIKE SOMETHIN' ROTTIN' IN THE WALLS. 136 ELECTR
VINNIE'S BACK SEEIN' TO SOMETHIN'. 158 ELECTR
HELL, YUH'D TINK I WUZ A PIMP OR SOMETHIN'. 580 ICEMAN
HE WAS DIFFERENT, OR SOMETHIN'. 618 ICEMAN
DEY MIGHT SPILL DEIR GUTS, OR SOMETHIN'. 631 ICEMAN
YUH'D TINK HE WAS PARALYZED OR SOMETHIN'/ 689 ICEMAN
AND I'VE SOMETHIN' MYSELF TO TELL ABOUT HIS 518 INZONE
LORDSHIP.
I SEEN RIGHT AWAY SOMETHIN' ON THE QUEER WAS UP SO519 INZONE
I SLIDES BACK INTO THE
LIKE IT WAS SOMETHIN' DANG'ROUS HE WAS AFTER, AN' 519 INZONE
FEELS ROUND IN UNDER HIS DUDS--
HE'S ALWAYS HAD THAT SLY AIR ABOUT HIM 'S IF HE 522 INZONE
WAS HIDIN' SOMETHIN'.
WE GOTTER DO SOMETHIN' QUICK OR-- 523 INZONE
SOMETHIN' SQUARE TIED UP IN A RUBBER BAG. 528 INZONE

SOMETHIN' (CONT'D.)
MAYBE IT'S DYNAMITE--OR SOMETHIN'--YOU CAN'T NEVER528 INZONE
TELL.
MAYBE I KIN MAKE SOMETHIN' OUT OF IT. 531 INZONE
TELL ME SOMETHIN' ABAHT YESELF, 502 VOYAGE
UW, TIKE SOMETHIN'. 505 VOYAGE

SOMETHING'S
I'M AFRAID SOMETHING'S HAPPENED--SOMETHIN' ELSE. 98 BEYOND
SOMETHING'S BOUND T' HAPPEN. 253 DESIRE
SOMETHING'S ALWAYS LIVIN' WITH YE. 253 DESIRE

SOMETHING
THERE IS SOMETHING OF EXTREME SENSITIVENESS 193 AHWILD
ADDED--
SOMETHING FROM THAT BOOK YOU'RE READING$ 195 AHWILD
ONE BOOK WAS CALLED THE PICTURE OF SOMETHING OR 197 AHWILD
OTHER.
AND POEMS BY SWIN SOMETHING-- 198 AHWILD
BUT IT'S TO COMPLAIN ABOUT SOMETHING. 200 AHWILD
I REGRET TO SAY IT'S SOMETHING DISAGREEABLE-- 201 AHWILD
SOMETHING HE BROUGHT$ 204 AHWILD
(THEN FROWNING) I'VE GOT TO DO SOMETHING ABOUT 204 AHWILD
THAT YOUNG ANARCHIST
I'VE NEVER READ HIM, BUT I'VE HEARD SOMETHING LIKE205 AHWILD
THAT WAS THE MATTER WITH HIM.
YOU HARD BECAUSE YOU'LL HAVE DONE SOMETHING NO BUY206 AHWILD
OF MINE OUGHT TO DO.
HAVE YOU BEEN TRYING TO HAVE SOMETHING TO DO WITH 206 AHWILD
MURIEL--
I'VE GOT SOMETHING ELSE TO TALK TO YOU ABOUT 206 AHWILD
BESIDES FIRECRACKERS.
SOMETHING YOU SHOULDN'T--YOU KNOW WHAT I MEAN. 207 AHWILD
(IMMEDIATELY SENSING SOMETHING «DOWN» IN HIS 208 AHWILD
MANNER--GOING TO HIM WORRIEDLY)
YOU KNOW, SOMETHING HAPPENS AND THINGS LIKE THAT 215 AHWILD
COME UP
WHY, THEN SOMETHING ELSE IS BOUND TO HAPPEN SOON 215 AHWILD
THAT CHANGES EVERYTHING AGAIN,
I MEAN REAL SWIFT ONES THAT THERE'S SOMETHING 219 AHWILD
DOING WITH.
(HE STARTS OUT AND IS JUST ABOUT TO CLOSE THE DOOR219 AHWILD
WHEN HE THINKS OF SOMETHING)
HE OUGHT TO BE AT THIS TABLE EATING SOMETHING TO 223 AHWILD
SOBER HIM UP.
I KNEW SOMETHING WAS WRONG WHEN HE CAME HOME. 234 AHWILD
I WAS THINKING OF SOMETHING ELSE. 237 AHWILD
SOMETHING THAT'LL WARM HIM UP, EH$ 238 AHWILD
WELL, GET IT OFF YOUR MIND AND GIVE SOMETHING ELSE239 AHWILD
A CHANCE TO WORK.
THAT'S SOMETHING LIKE/ 240 AHWILD
YOU'VE GOT SOMETHING ON THE BALL, ALL RIGHT, ALL 245 AHWILD
RIGHT/
AND WONDERING IF HE HASN'T DROWNED HIMSELF OR 251 AHWILD
SOMETHING.
(HASTILY--CALLS) GIVE US SOMETHING CHEERY, NEXT 258 AHWILD
ONE, ARTHUR.
OH, I'M GETTING WORRIED SOMETHING DREADFUL, NAT/ 259 AHWILD
WHY DON'T YOU DO SOMETHING$ 260 AHWILD
(ON THE VERGE OF HYSTERIA) OH, I KNOW SOMETHING 260 AHWILD
DREADFUL'S HAPPENED/
THEN I WON'T GIVE YOU SOMETHING I'VE GOT FOR YOU. 272 AHWILD
ONLY YOU'VE GOT TO DO SOMETHING FOR ME WHEN I ASK.274 AHWILD
THINK OF SOMETHING ELSE. 276 AHWILD
RECITE SOMETHING. 276 AHWILD
(HE SQUIRMS DISGUSTEDLY) THINK OF SOMETHING ELSE,276 AHWILD
CAN'T YOU$
(HE RECITES DRAMATICALLY) = SOMETHING WAS DEAD IN1279 AHWILD
EACH OF US.
YOU KNOW I HAD ELEVEN DOLLARS SAVED UP TO BUY YOU 282 AHWILD
SOMETHING FOR YOUR BIRTHDAY,
AND I CAN GET YOU SOMETHING NICE WITH THAT. 282 AHWILD
(CHUCKLES AT SOMETHING HE READS--THEN CLOSES THE 288 AHWILD
BOOK AND PUTS IN ON THE TABLE.
THERE'S SOMETHING TO THEM. 289 AHWILD
AND THAT'S SOMETHING. 291 AHWILD
YOU BET THAT'S SOMETHING. 291 AHWILD
I MEAN, GIRLS LIKE THAT ONE YOU--GIRLS THERE'S 295 AHWILD
SOMETHING DOING WITH--
SEEM MUSHY AND SILLY--BUT THAT MEANT SOMETHING/ 297 AHWILD
CONFIDENTIAL HALF-WHISPER WITH SOMETHING VAGUELY 5 ANNA
PLAINTIVE IN ITS QUALITY.
HAVE SOMETHING ON ME$ 14 ANNA
LET'S TALK OF SOMETHING ELSE. 26 ANNA
LIKE I'D FOUND SOMETHING I'D MISSED AND BEEN 28 ANNA
LOOKING FOR--
YOU ACT 'S IF YOU WAS SCARED SOMETHING WAS GOING 29 ANNA
TO HAPPEN.
SAY, LISTEN HERE, YOU AIN'T TRYING TO INSINUATE 42 ANNA
THAT THERE'S SOMETHING WRONG
(SHE TURNS ON CHRIS) WHY DON'T YOU SAY SOMETHING$ 50 ANNA
(SHE STOPS, LOOKING FROM ONE TO THE OTHER, SENSING 50 ANNA
IMMEDIATELY THAT SOMETHING
(ALARMED BY SOMETHING IN HER MANNER) 53 ANNA
(DISTRACTEDLY) SO, FOR GAWD'S SAKE, LET'S TALK UF 54 ANNA
SOMETHING ELSE.
I'M GOING TO TELL YOU SOMETHING--AND THEN I'M 56 ANNA
GOING TO BEAT IT.
FIRST THING IS, I WANT TO TELL YOU TWO GUYS 56 ANNA
SOMETHING.
(THERE IS SOMETHING IN HER TONE THAT MAKES THEM 56 ANNA
FORGET THEIR QUARREL.
YOU SAID A MINUTE AGO YOU'D FIXED SOMETHING UP-- 65 ANNA
ABOUT ME.
HE FEELS IN THE POCKET OF HIS COAT AND GRASPS 74 ANNA
SOMETHING--SOLEMNLY)
HIS LIPS MOVE AS IF HE WERE RECITING SOMETHING TO 82 BEYOND
HIMSELF.
HIS EYES READ SOMETHING AND HE GIVES AN 82 BEYOND
EXCLAMATION OF DISGUST)

SOMETHING

SOMETHING (CONT'D.)
THERE'S SOMETHING CALLING ME-- 84 BEYOND
THERE IS SOMETHING I WANT TO-- 86 BEYOND
(ABSENT-MINDEDLY--FEELING THAT SHE HAS TO SAY SOMETHING) 86 BEYOND
ROBERT SEEMED STIRRED UP ABOUT SOMETHING.. 98 BEYOND
YOU LOOK ALL WORKED UP OVER SOMETHING, ROBBIE. 99 BEYOND
SOMETHING I DISCOVERED ONLY THIS EVENING--VERY 99 BEYOND
BEAUTIFUL AND WONDERFUL--
SOMETHING I DID NOT TAKE 99 BEYOND
YES, THERE IS SOMETHING--SOMETHING I MUST TELL 99 BEYOND
YOU--ALL OF YOU.
(HE STANDS BESIDE ROBERT AS IF HE WANTED TO SAY 101 BEYOND
SOMETHING MORE
THEY'RE ONLY LOOKIN' TO HAVE THE LAUGH ON ME FOR 103 BEYOND
SOMETHING LIKE THAT.
THERE IS A TRACE IN HER EXPRESSION OF SOMETHING 116 BEYOND
HARD AND SPITEFUL.
(DULLY) SOMETHING MUST HAVE GONE WRONG AGAIN. 117 BEYOND
LET'S TALK OF SOMETHING PLEASANT. 117 BEYOND
(COLORING AS IF SHE'D BEEN ACCUSED OF SOMETHING-- 120 BEYOND
DEFIANTLY)
WITH SOMETHING AKIN TO HATRED IN THEIR 121 BEYOND
EXPRESSIONS.
SOMETHING CROPS UP EVERY DAY TO DELAY ME. 122 BEYOND
BUT THERE IS SOMETHING IN HIS EYES THAT MAKES HER 128 BEYOND
TURN.
LET'S TALK ABOUT SOMETHING INTERESTING. 131 BEYOND
TO GET A START AT SOMETHING IN B. A. 132 BEYOND
HAD TO DO SOMETHING OR I'D GONE MAD. 132 BEYOND
AND I WANT TO GET IN ON SOMETHING BIG BEFORE I 133 BEYOND
DIE.
I'M NO FOOL WHEN IT COMES TO FARMING, AND I KNOW 133 BEYOND
SOMETHING ABOUT GRAIN.
(SURELY) THERE'S SOMETHING I WANT TO TALK ABOUT,133 BEYOND
RUB--THE FARM.
I JUST HAPPENED TO THINK OF SOMETHING ELSE. 133 BEYOND
JAKE WANTS TO SEE YOU ABOUT SOMETHING. 135 BEYOND
THERE'S SOMETHING ABOUT HER EYES-- 140 BEYOND
I'M GLAD HE'S BRINGING A DOCTOR WHO KNOWS 147 BEYOND
SOMETHING.
(DULLY) MAKES NO DIFFERENCE. I HAD TO TELL ANDY 147 BEYOND
SOMETHING, DIDN'T I.
(VAGUELY) I'LL WRITE OR SOMETHING OF THAT SORT. 149 BEYOND
OH IF YOU KNEW HOW GLORIOUS IT FEELS TO HAVE 150 BEYOND
SOMETHING TO LOOK FORWARD TO/
YOU LOOK AS IF I WERE ACCUSING YOU OF SOMETHING. 161 BEYOND
SOMETHING HAPPENED FIVE YEARS BACK, THE TIME YOU 163 BEYOND
CAME HOME FROM THE TRIP.
(WITH CONVICTION) NO--THERE WAS SOMETHING BACK OF163 BEYOND
IT.
TELL HIM SOMETHING, ANYTHING, THAT'LL BRING HIM 165 BEYOND
PEACE/
IF HE WUD EAT SOMETHING-- 480 CARDIF
AT FINDING SOMETHING TO GRUMBLE ABOUT.) 481 CARDIF
SOMETHING TO EASE THE PAIN, ANYWAY. 485 CARDIF
SING SOMETHING, DRISC. 499 CARIBE
(BIG FRANK LEANS OVER AND SAYS SOMETHING TO HIM IN464 CARIBE
A LOW VOICE.
HE SHUDDERS AND SHAKES HIS SHOULDERS AS IF SHAKING466 CARIBE
OFF SOMETHING WHICH DISGUSTED
IT'S JUST SOMETHING ABOUT THE ROTTEN THING WHICH 466 CARIBE
MAKES ME THINK--OF--
BUT HE MIGHT DO SOMETHING--ANYTHING--IF HE KNOWS--558 CROSS
YOU'RE HOLDING SOMETHING BACK. 563 CROSS
(CLUTCHING AT HIS THROAT AS THOUGH TO STRANGLE 565 CROSS
SOMETHING WITHIN HIM--HOARSELY)
THERE'LL BE SOMETHING OVER THE MORTGAGE.. 566 CROSS
(AS IF IN A TRANCE) THERE WAS SOMETHING HORNE 573 CROSS
HANDED HIM.
HORNE HANDED HIM SOMETHING. 573 CROSS
WELL, I HOPE YOU REALIZE I'M ONLY TRYING TO 495 DAYS
ENCOURAGE YOU TO MAKE SOMETHING OF
INTO A RED-HOT ARTICLE OF YOURS DENOUNCING 497 DAYS
CAPITALISM OR RELIGION OR SOMETHING.
OH, I KNEW THERE WAS SOMETHING I'D FORGOTTEN TO 497 DAYS
TELL YOU.
WELL, I THOUGHT I MIGHT AS WELL DO SOMETHING WITH 497 DAYS
ALL THIS LEISURE.
I WAS THE HEATHEN TO HIM AND HE WAS BOUND HE'D 502 DAYS
CONVERT ME TO SOMETHING.
YOU TALK AS IF I WERE AFRAID OF SOMETHING. 503 DAYS
(COMING AROUND TO THEM) I'LL FIX UP SOMETHING 504 DAYS
WITH ELSA FOR THE FOUR OF US.
AS IF HE WERE TRYING TO FIGURE SOMETHING OUT. 505 DAYS
(THEN SUDDENLY) THERE'S SOMETHING I WANT TO TELL 506 DAYS
YOU, JACK.
SOMETHING SNAPPED IN HIM THEN. 511 DAYS
BUT I AM ABOUT SOMETHING ABOUT YOU THAT ADMITS OF 512 DAYS
NO ARGUMENT--TO ME.
THAT YOU WERE UPSET ABOUT SOMETHING AND TRYING TO 517 DAYS
HIDE IT.
STILL A COWARDLY SLAVISH SOMETHING IN ME. 520 DAYS
ALL THAT SAVED ME FROM DOING SOMETHING STUPID WAS 521 DAYS
THE FAITH I HAD THAT SOMEWHERE
THERE WAS SOMETHING AS EVIL AND REVENGEFUL AS I 522 DAYS
WAS.
SOMETHING YOU'RE KEEPING BACK BECAUSE YOU'RE 529 DAYS
AFRAID OF WORRYING ME.
I KNOW THERE'S SOMETHING THAT'S BEEN TROUBLING YOU529 DAYS
FOR WEEKS--
LET'S TALK OF SOMETHING ELSE. 530 DAYS
WANT ME TO GET YOU SOMETHING TO PUT OVER YOUR 533 DAYS
SHOULDERS?
THERE ALWAYS REMAINED SOMETHING IN HIM THAT FELT 534 DAYS
ITSELF DAMNED BY LIFE.
AS IF HE SAW THIS SOMETHING BEFORE HIM. 535 DAYS
SOMETHING THAT HATED LIFE/ 535 DAYS

SOMETHING (CONT'D.)
SOMETHING THAT LAUGHED WITH MOCKING SCORN/ 535 DAYS
HIS LOVE MADE HIM FEEL AT THE MERCY OF THAT 536 DAYS
MOCKING SOMETHING HE DREADED.
AT THE THOUGHT OF HIS WIFE, SUDDENLY IT WAS AS IF 538 DAYS
SOMETHING OUTSIDE HIM,
ELECTRICITY OR SOMETHING, WHICH WHIRLS US--ON TO 542 DAYS
HERCULES?
THAT COWARDLY SOMETHING IN HIM HE DESPISES AS 544 DAYS
SUPERSTITION SEDUCES HIS REASON
THERE IS A MOCKING RATIONAL SOMETHING IN HIM THAT 545 DAYS
LAUGHS WITH SCORN--
I FEEL THERE'S SOMETHING-- 555 DAYS
WELL, AS HE SAID, SOMETHING--(THEN CURTLY, FEELING557 DAYS
THIS MAKES HIM APPEAR SILLY)
THAT HE MUST DO SOMETHING TO THWART IT AT ONCE. 558 DAYS
THERE'S SOMETHING-- 560 DAYS
AT WHICH SOMETHING LAUGHS WITH A WEARY SCORN/ 561 DAYS
SOMETHING--(HE SHUDDERS.) 561 DAYS
ABBIE SEEMS TO SENSE SOMETHING. 252 DESIRE
(SOMETHING IN HER VOICE AROUSES HIM. 260 DESIRE
THEN THERE IS--SOMETHING/ 500 DIFRNT
(HER VOICE TREMBLING) IT'S 'COUNT OF SOMETHING I 504 DIFRNT
GOT IN MY OWN HEAD.
AND IT'S ALL DIFF'RENT LIKE SOMETHING YOU'D SEE IN515 DIFRNT
A PAINTED PICTURE.
WAS SOMETHING HAPPENING 516 DIFRNT
IT'S A QUESTION OF SOMETHING BEING DEAD. 517 DIFRNT
YOU'VE BUSTED SOMETHING WAY DOWN INSIDE ME-- 517 DIFRNT
BUT THERE IS SOMETHING REVOLTINGLY INCONGRUOUS 520 DIFRNT
ABOUT HER, A PITIABLE SHAM.
SAY, HERE'S SOMETHING I NEVER COULD MAKE OUT-- 521 DIFRNT
YOU'D GET WISE TO SOMETHING THEN. 529 DIFRNT
I'D LIKE TO SEE HIM START SOMETHING/ 544 DIFRNT
WITH A TRACE OF SOMETHING LIKE PITY SHOWING IN HIS546 DIFRNT
TONE)
(THEN WITH A SUDDEN AIR OF HAVING DECIDED 549 DIFRNT
SOMETHING IRREVOCABLY)
THAT SCOUNDREL CALLED SOMETHING AT ME ON THE 425 DYNAMO
STREET TODAY--
WHY HASN'T HE DONE SOMETHING TO FIFES... 444 DYNAMO
MOTHER'LL GUESS SOMETHING IS WRONG AS SOON AS SHE 444 DYNAMO
LOOKS AT ME...
OH, HUTCHINS, SOMETHING AWFUL HAS HAPPENED--THAT 445 DYNAMO
FIFE GIRL--
(MADE UNEASY BY SOMETHING IN HER TONE-- 447 DYNAMO
INSISTENTLY)
(HE SUDDENLY IS REMINDED OF SOMETHING--THINKING 450 DYNAMO
WILDLY)
THERE'S POP HOWLING HIS HEAD OFF ABOUT SOMETHING. 455 DYNAMO
THAT FOR HER HAS SOMETHING AT ONCE FASCINATING AND460 DYNAMO
FRIGHTENING ABOUT IT)
HE OWES IT TO RUBE TO DO SOMETHING FOR HIM... 462 DYNAMO
THEN SOMETHING HAS TO MAKE YOU UP--AND START YOU 469 DYNAMO
THINKING AGAIN.
AND WHY COULDN'T SOMETHING LIKE THAT THAT NO ONE 472 DYNAMO
UNDERSTANDS YET...
WITH SOMETHING OF A MASSIVE FEMALE IDOL ABOUT IT, 473 DYNAMO
SOMETHING THAT'LL ANSWER ME/...!) 474 DYNAMO
I FEEL THERE IS SOMETHING IN HER TO PRAY TO/... 474 DYNAMO
THERE MUST BE SOMETHING IN HER SONG THAT'D TELL 474 DYNAMO
YOU IF YOU HAD EARS TO HEAR/...
HER MANNER IS FURTIVE AS IF SHE WERE DOING 480 DYNAMO
SOMETHING SHE IS ASHAMED OF.
DO YOU THINK IT'S SOMETHING I'VE GOT TO DO ABOUT 480 DYNAMO
ADA?
THERE MUST STILL BE SOMETHING I'VE GOT TO DO...) 480 DYNAMO
DIDN'T YOU FEEL SOMETHING DRIVING YOU TO COME HERE481 DYNAMO
RIGHT NOW?
YET THERE IS SOMETHING DECIDEDLY DISTINCTIVE ABOUT175 EJONES
HIS FACE--
YET THERE IS SOMETHING NOT ALTOGETHER RIDICULOUS 175 EJONES
ABOUT HIS GRANDEUR.
SOMETHING IN THE OTHER'S EYES HOLDS AND COWS HIM.1176 EJONES
THERE IS SOMETHING STIFF, RIGID, UNREAL, 196 EJONES
MARIONETTISH ABOUT THEIR MOVEMENTS.
STRUCK BY SOMETHING IN HER MANNER. 10 ELECTR
AND HE HAS SOMETHING HE'S JUST DYING TO ASK YOU/. 14 ELECTR
SOMETHING I'D MADE UP MY MIND TO ASK YOU TODAY. 14 ELECTR
NO DOGS--SOMETHING ABOUT HIS FACE-- 19 ELECTR
FEELING SOMETHING STRANGE IN HER ATTITUDE BUT NOT 21 ELECTR
ABLE TO MAKE HER OUT--
(AT SOMETHING IN HER TONE HE STARES AT HER 21 ELECTR
SUSPICIOUSLY)
(THEN AT SOMETHING IN HER FACE HE HURRIEDLY GOES 23 ELECTR
OFF ON ANOTHER TACK)
THEN LISTEN A BIT AND YOU'LL HEAR SOMETHING ABOUT 26 ELECTR
ANOTHER OF THEM/
I'VE SUSPECTED SOMETHING LATELY-- 29 ELECTR
CHRISTINE SEEMS CONSIDERING SOMETHING. 34 ELECTR
I FELT THERE WAS SOMETHING WRONG THE MOMENT I SAW 37 ELECTR
HER.
SOMETHING I'VE BEEN THINKING OF EVER SINCE I 40 ELECTR
REALIZED HE MIGHT SOON COME HOME.
I'VE WRITTEN SOMETHING HERE. 40 ELECTR
WITH SOMETHING FREE AND WILD ABOUT HER LIKE AN 44 ELECTR
ANIMAL.
I KNOW YOU'RE PLOTTING SOMETHING/ 45 ELECTR
(TAKING HIS ARM) COME INSIDE WITH ME AND I'LL GET 47 ELECTR
YOU SOMETHING TO EAT.
HE CLEARS HIS THROAT AS IF ABOUT TO SAY 51 ELECTR
SOMETHING--
LIKE SOMETHING DYING THAT HAD NEVER LIVED. 54 ELECTR
SOMETHING KEEPS ME SITTING NUMB IN MY OWN HEART-- 55 ELECTR
SOMETHING QUEER IN ME KEEPS ME MUM ABOUT THE 55 ELECTR
THINGS I'D LIKE MOST TO SAY--
IT'S SOMETHING UNEASY TROUBLING MY MIND-- 60 ELECTR

SOMETHING

SOMETHING (CONT'D.)
AS IF SOMETHING IN ME WAS LISTENING, WATCHING, 60 ELECTR
WAITING FOR SOMETHING TO HAPPEN.
YOU ARE WAITING FOR SOMETHING/ 60 ELECTR
(SHE PRETENDS TO TAKE SOMETHING FROM THE STAND BY 62 ELECTR
THE HEAD OF THE BED--
THERE'S SOMETHING QUEER ABOUT HER. 68 ELECTR
(SENSING SOMETHING FROM HIS MANNER--EAGERLY) 71 ELECTR
AS IF SHE LONGED TO FLY FROM SOMETHING. 71 ELECTR
OR IS IT SOMETHING IN ME$ 74 ELECTR
THERE'S SOMETHING I WANT TO ASK YOU BEFORE I SEE 75 ELECTR
MOTHER.
I'VE GOT TO TELL YOU SOMETHING TOO/ 76 ELECTR
I--I'VE MISSED SOMETHING--SOME MEDICINE I TAKE TO 77 ELECTR
PUT ME TO SLEEP--
(SOMETHING LIKE A GRIM SMILE OF SATISFACTION FORMS 77 ELECTR
ON LAVINIA'S LIPS.
WE'LL TALK OF SOMETHING ELSE. 89 ELECTR
I WANT TO TELL YOU SOMETHING. 89 ELECTR
AGAIN HER PALE LIPS PART AS IF SHE WERE ABOUT TO 92 ELECTR
SAY SOMETHING
I KNOW SHE'S PLOTTING SOMETHING--CRAZY/ 100 ELECTR
BUT THERE IS SOMETHING ROMANTIC, 102 ELECTR
THERE'S SOMETHING GONE WRONG/ 108 ELECTR
BUT SOMETHING MADE THINGS HAPPEN/ 110 ELECTR
I KNOW SOMETHING HORRIBLE WILL HAPPEN/ 111 ELECTR
(HER EYES CAUGHT BY SOMETHING DOWN THE DRIVE--IN A119 ELECTR
TENSE WHISPER)
THERE IS SOMETHING QUEER ABOUT THIS HOUSE. 136 ELECTR
YOU FEEL SOMETHING COLD GRIP YOU THE MOMENT YOU 137 ELECTR
SET FOOT--
THERE WAS SOMETHING THERE MYSTERIOUS AND 147 ELECTR
BEAUTIFUL--A GOOD SPIRIT--OF LOVE--
LIKE A LITTLE BOY WHO'S BEEN PUNISHED FOR 148 ELECTR
SOMETHING HE DIDN'T DO.
YOU'RE AFRAID I'LL LET SOMETHING SLIP. 151 ELECTR
THAT IN ONE OF YOUR FITS YOU'LL SAY SOMETHING 152 ELECTR
BEFORE SOMEONE--
SOMETHING HAPPENED BETWEEN YOU/ 154 ELECTR
OH, ORIN, SOMETHING MADE ME SAY THAT TO YOU-- 155 ELECTR
AGAINST MY WILL--
SOMETHING ROSE UP IN ME--LIKE AN EVIL SPIRIT/ 155 ELECTR
I KNOW YOU'RE PLOTTING SOMETHING/ 156 ELECTR
THERE'S SOMETHING BOLD ABOUT HER. 158 ELECTR
I'VE GOT SOME RIGHT TO SAY SOMETHING ABOUT 158 ELECTR
I FEEL THERE'S SOMETHING AWFULLY WRONG--SOMEHOW. 158 ELECTR
SHE'S GONE TO SEE TO SOMETHING, SETH SAID. 159 ELECTR
I WANT YOU TO DO SOMETHING/ 160 ELECTR
AND YOU MUST PROMISE NEVER TO OPEN IT--UNLESS 160 ELECTR
SOMETHING HAPPENS TO ME.
I KNOW SOMETHING IS WORRYING YOU--AND I DON'T WANT160 ELECTR
TO SEEM PRYING--BUT
OR SOMETHING TERRIBLE WILL HAPPEN/ 161 ELECTR
YOU'RE HIDING SOMETHING. 162 ELECTR
SHE QUICKLY SENSES SOMETHING IN THE ATMOSPHERE 162 ELECTR
NOT UNDERSTANDING WHAT IS BEHIND THEIR TALK BUT 164 ELECTR
SENSING SOMETHING SINISTER,
(THEN AS IF THE WORDS STIRRED SOMETHING WITHIN HIM168 ELECTR
(THEN HE HEARS SOMETHING AND PEERS DOWN THE DRIVE, 171 ELECTR
OFF LEFT.)
BUT I KNOW THERE'S SOMETHING--AND SO DO YOU-- 172 ELECTR
SOMETHING THAT WAS DRIVING ORIN CRAZY--(SHE BREAKS172 ELECTR
DOWN AND SOBS) POOR ORIN/
(AS IF THIS WERE SOMETHING SHE HAD BEEN DREADING--172 ELECTR
HARSHLY)
YOU MAKE ME THINK THERE WAS SOMETHING-- 176 ELECTR
WAS IT SOMETHING THERE--SOMETHING TO DO WITH THAT 177 ELECTR
NATIVE--$
AS IF SEARCHING FOR SOMETHING.) 178 ELECTR
I WANTED TO ASK YOU SOMETHING, TOO. 262 GGBROW
BECAUSE I WANTED TO TELL YOU SOMETHING. 262 GGBROW
SO WAS I--ABOUT SOMETHING OR OTHER. 270 GGBROW
STILL--I HAVE DONE A LITTLE SOMETHING MYSELF. 275 GGBROW
(AROUSED BY SOMETHING IN HIS MANNER) 276 GGBROW
(SHE STARTS TO GO--THEN, AS IF REMINDED OF 280 GGBROW
SOMETHING--TO OION)
ONE MUST DO SOMETHING TO 281 GGBROW
I'VE--JUST--SEEN--SOMETHING. 288 GGBROW
WHY, OION. SOMETHING HAS HAPPENED. 301 GGBROW
(THEY STARE AT HER) I FORGOT TO TELL HIM 303 GGBROW
SOMETHING IMPORTANT THIS MORNING AND
THERE'S SOMETHING. 305 GGBROW
OH, SOMETHING THAT HAPPENED TODAY. 311 GGBROW
SOMETHING ABOUT OION, OF COURSE. 314 GGBROW
(SUDDENLY ME BECOMES CONSCIOUS OF ALL THE OTHER 225 HA APE
MEN STARING AT SOMETHING
(WHO HAS BEEN STARING AT SOMETHING INSIDE--WITH 236 HA APE
QUEER EXCITEMENT)
YET WITH SOMETHING OF THE RELENTLESS HORROR OF 236 HA APE
FRANKENSTEINS
(SOMETHING, THE TONE OF MOCKERY, PERHAPS, SUDDENLY254 HA APE
ENRAGES THE ANIMAL.
YET THERE IS SOMETHING PHONEY ABOUT HIS 9 HUGHIE
CHARACTERIZATION OF HIMSELF.
LOTS OF GUYS I'VE BEEN PALS WITH, IN A WAY, 18 HUGHIE
CROAKED FROM BOOZE OR SOMETHING.
SOMETHING ALWAYS TURNS UP FOR ME. 18 HUGHIE
THEN IT RECEDES AND DIES, AND THERE IS SOMETHING 19 HUGHIE
MELANCHOLY ABOUT THAT.
=WHAT I ALWAYS TELL JESS WHEN SHE NAGS ME TO WORRY 19 HUGHIE
ABOUT SOMETHING.=
(HE LAUGHS.) YOU'DA THOUGHT HUGHIE WOULDA GOT 20 HUGHIE
WISE SOMETHING WAS OUT OF ORDER
SIMPLE GUY LIKE HUGHIE WILL ALL OF A SUDDEN GET 21 HUGHIE
SOMETHING RIGHT.
I THOUGHT IT WAS UP TO ME TO PUT OUT SOMETHING, 25 HUGHIE
AND KIDS LIKE ANIMAL STORIES.
THERE'D ALWAYS BE SOMETHING LEFT.= 27 HUGHIE

SOMETHING (CONT'D.)
OR SOMETHING THAT ANY BLONDE 'D GO ROUND-HEELED 28 HUGHIE
ABOUT.
THAT'S SOMETHING I'VE ALWAYS WANTED TO KNOW MORE 31 HUGHIE
ABOUT, TOO.
IF HIS MIND COULD ONLY FASTEN ONTO SOMETHING 492 31 HUGHIE
HAS SAID.
WHY, TO BE FRANK, I REALLY DON'T--JUST SOMETHING 33 HUGHIE
THAT CAME INTO MY HEAD.
THERE'D ALWAYS BE SOMETHING LEFT TO START IT GOING 33 HUGHIE
AGAIN.
(HE SUDDENLY ROUSES HIMSELF AND THERE IS SOMETHING 34 HUGHIE
THE MANAGER WOULDN'T LIKE YOU TO REMEMBER 37 HUGHIE
SOMETHING HE AIN'T HEARD OF YET.
I HAVE A STRONG HUNCH YOU'VE COME HERE EXPECTING 591 ICEMAN
SOMETHING OF ME.
I FEEL YOU'RE LOOKING FOR SOME ANSWER TO 591 ICEMAN
SOMETHING.
AND PUZZLED BY SOMETHING HE FEELS ABOUT PARRITT 592 ICEMAN
THAT ISN'T RIGHT.
AS IF AVOIDING SOMETHING HE DOES NOT WISH TO SEE.1596 ICEMAN
(AS IF REMINDED OF SOMETHING-- 600 ICEMAN
BUT STILL I KNOW DAMNED WELL I RECOGNIZED 624 ICEMAN
SOMETHING ABOUT YOU.
BEJEES, LARRY, YOU'RE ALWAYS CROAKING ABOUT 626 ICEMAN
SOMETHING TO DO WITH DEATH.
BUT THERE IS SOMETHING FORCED ABOUT THEIR MANNER, 629 ICEMAN
SOMETHING SLIP--THEN REVENGEFULLY) 635 ICEMAN
THERE'S SOMETHING FAMILIAR ABOUT HIM, SOMETHING 642 ICEMAN
BETWEEN US.
THE WAY HE ACTS, YOU'D THINK HE HAD SOMETHING ON 645 ICEMAN
ME.
THERE'S SOMETHING NOT HUMAN BEHIND HIS DAMNED 648 ICEMAN
GRINNING AND KIDDING.
AS IF HE WERE TRYING TO HAMMER SOMETHING INTO HIS 649 ICEMAN
OWN BRAIN)
HARRY'S THE GREATEST KIDDER IN THIS DUMP AND 655 ICEMAN
THAT'S SAYING SOMETHING/
THAT MAKES YOU LIE TO YOURSELVES YOU'RE SOMETHING 661 ICEMAN
YOU'RE NOT.
AS IF SHE WANTED TO MAKE UP FOR SOMETHING. 667 ICEMAN
SOMETHING LIKE SATISFACTION IN HIS PITYING TONE) 667 ICEMAN
D'YUH MEAN YUH TINK SHE COMMITTED SUICIDE, 'COUNT 668 ICEMAN
OF HIS CHEATIN' OR SOMETHING$
WELL, I FEEL HE'S HIDING SOMETHING. 668 ICEMAN
CLARK IN THE OFFICE OR SOMETHING OF THE KIND. 675 ICEMAN
YOU'LL BE SAYING SOMETHING SOON THAT WILL MAKE YOU680 ICEMAN
VOMIT YOUR OWN SOUL
BUT, BEJEES, SOMETHING RAN OVER ME/ 691 ICEMAN
(VINDICTIVELY) I THINK IT WAS SOMETHING YOU DROVE693 ICEMAN
SOMEONE ELSE TO DO/
THERE MUST HAVE BEEN SOMETHING THERE HE WAS EVEN 700 ICEMAN
MORE SCARED TO FACE THAN HE IS
FOR GOD'S SAKE, LARRY, CAN'T YOU SAY SOMETHING$ 701 ICEMAN
DEY FALL FOR YUH LIKE YUH WAS DEIR UNCLE OR OLD 702 ICEMAN
MAN OR SOMETHING.
WHENEVER I MADE UP MY MIND TO SELL SOMEONE 703 ICEMAN
SOMETHING I KNEW THEY OUGHT TO WANT,
WHEN ARE YOU GOING TO DO SOMETHING ABOUT THIS 704 ICEMAN
BOOZE, HICKEY$
BUT THERE WAS SOMETHING I HAD TO GET FINALLY 704 ICEMAN
SETTLED.
BEJEES, WE ALL KNOW YOU DID SOMETHING TO TAKE THE 704 ICEMAN
LIFE OUT OF IT.
I CAN'T HAVE HIM PRETENDING THERE'S SOMETHING IN 706 ICEMAN
COMMON BETWEEN HIM AND ME.
BEJEES, YOU DONE SOMETHING. 707 ICEMAN
ALTHOUGH I HAD TO HAND IT TO HIM, THE WAY HE SOLD 709 ICEMAN
THEM NOTHING FOR SOMETHING.
CHRIST, WHY CAN'T YOU SAY SOMETHINGS 709 ICEMAN
THEY WANTED TO BUY SOMETHING TO SHOW THEIR 711 ICEMAN
GRATITUDE.
LIKE SOMETHING LYING IN THE GUTTER THAT NO ALLEY 713 ICEMAN
CAT WOULD LOWER ITSELF TO DRAG
SOMETHING THAT OUGHT TO BE DEAD AND ISN'T/ 713 ICEMAN
IN--SOMETHING THEY THREW OUT OF THE D. T. WARD IN 713 ICEMAN
BELLEVUE
AS IF IT WAS SOMETHING I'D ALWAYS WANTED TO SAY.. 716 ICEMAN
JESUS, LARRY, CAN'T YOU SAY SOMETHING$ 720 ICEMAN
SOMETHING FELL OFF DE FIRE ESCAPE. 726 ICEMAN
SOMETHING HURTLING DOWN, FOLLOWED BY A MUFFLED, 726 ICEMAN
CRUNCHING THUD.
I'VE GOT SOMETHING I WANT TO TELL THE BOYS 518 INZONE
THE OTHERS, WITH AN AIR OF REMEMBERING SOMETHING 518 INZONE
THEY HAD FORGOTTEN
HE IS INTERRUPTED BY THE SOUND OF SOMETHING 523 INZONE
HITTING AGAINST THE PORT SIDE OF
JAMES, YOU'LL REALLY HAVE TO DO SOMETHING-- 23 JOURNE
ALL JAMIE MEANT WAS EDMUND MIGHT HAVE A TOUCH OF 27 JOURNE
SOMETHING ELSE, TOO.
I HEARD YOU SAY SOMETHING ABOUT A DOCTOR, 40 JOURNE
STILL, THE CHAFFORDS AND PEOPLE LIKE THEM STAND 44 JOURNE
FOR SOMETHING.
THERE'S ABSOLUTELY NO REASON TO TALK AS IF YOU 48 JOURNE
EXPECTED SOMETHING DREADFUL/
I WANT YOU TO PROMISE ME THAT EVEN IF IT SHOULD 48 JOURNE
TURN OUT TO BE SOMETHING WORSE,
(VAGUELY.) THERE IS SOMETHING I WANTED TO SAY. 82 JOURNE
SOMETHING IS ALWAYS WRONG. 84 JOURNE
THERE'S SOMETHING I MUST GET AT THE DRUGSTORE. 86 JOURNE
I KNEW SOMETHING TERRIBLE WOULD HAPPEN. 88 JOURNE
HE'LL PRETEND HE'S FOUND SOMETHING SERIOUS THE 92 JOURNE
MATTER
PLEASE LISTEN/ I WANT TO ASK YOU SOMETHING/ 92 JOURNE
IF YOU CAN CALL IT WORK WHEN YOU DO SOMETHING YOU 103 JOURNE
LOVE.
IF SHE DON'T GET SOMETHING TO QUIET HER TEMPER, 106 JOURNE
YOU OUGHT TO EAT SOMETHING, MA'AM. 106 JOURNE

SOMETHING

SOMETHING (CONT'D.)
STARTS TO SAY SOMETHING BUT STOPS.) 112 JOURNE
YOU'D WANT HER TO PICK UP SOMETHING AT A BARGAIN. 115 JOURNE
IF YOU HEARD WHAT THE DOCTOR AT THE SANATORIUM, 118 JOURNE
WHO REALLY KNOWS SOMETHING,
(DAZEDLY, AS IF THIS WAS SOMETHING THAT HAD NEVER 119 JOURNE
OCCURRED TO HER.)
THEN HE EVIDENTLY COLLIDES WITH SOMETHING 125 JOURNE
YOU KNOW SOMETHING IN HER DOES IT DELIBERATELY-- 139 JOURNE
HOW DARE YOU TALK OF SOMETHING YOU KNOW NOTHING 140 JOURNE
ABOUT?
WHO REALLY KNOW SOMETHING ABOUT IT, HAVE TOLD YOU!141 JOURNE
HE MISTOOK RAT POISON FOR FLOUR, OR SUGAR, OR 147 JOURNE
SOMETHING.
WITHIN SOMETHING GREATER THAN MY OWN LIFE, OR THE 153 JOURNE
LIFE OF MAN, TO LIFE ITSELF/
SOMETHING I OUGHT TO HAVE TOLD YOU LONG AGO--FOR 165 JOURNE
YOUR OWN GOOD.
HE HEARS SOMETHING AND JERKS NERVOUSLY FORWARD IN 169 JOURNE
HIS CHAIR.
LIKE SOMEONE WHO HAS COME TO A ROOM TO GET 170 JOURNE
SOMETHING BUT HAS BECOME
SHE'LL GIVE ME SOMETHING TO RUB ON MY HANDS. 171 JOURNE
BUT SOMETHING HORRIBLE HAS HAPPENED TO MY HANDS. 171 JOURNE
I KNOW IT'S SOMETHING I LOST. 172 JOURNE
(LOOKING AROUND HER.) SOMETHING I MISS TERRIBLY. 173 JOURNE
THEN IN THE SPRING SOMETHING HAPPENED TO ME. 176 JOURNE
THERE IS SOMETHING OF SHY WONDERING CHILD ABOUT 308 LAZARU
HIS ATTITUDE NOW.
(AS IF HE HAD TO CUT SOMETHING, HE SNATCHES UP A 311 LAZARU
HANDFUL OF FLOWERS--
I IMAGINE IT HAS SOMETHING TO DO WITH 315 LAZARU
BUT YOU SEEM--SOMETHING OTHER THAN MAN/ 340 LAZARU
HE IS SOMETHING LIKE A GOD. 341 LAZARU
AND YET--HE MUST KNOW SOMETHING--AND IF HE WOULD--364 LAZARU
EVEN NOW HE COULD TELL--
(AS IF HE REALIZED SOMETHING WAS HAPPENING THAT 366 LAZARU
WAS AGAINST HIS WILL--
HIS WHOLE CHARACTER HAS SOMETHING ARIDLY PRIM AND 26 MANSNS
PURITANICAL ABOUT IT.
KEEPING HER FACE TURNED TOWARD SOMETHING FROM 27 MANSNS
WHICH SHE RETREATS.
THERE IS SOMETHING IN THERE THAT FRIGHTENS YOU, 28 MANSNS
DEBORAH$
SOMETHING$ 28 MANSNS
DID I THINK DEATH WOULD BE SOMETHING IN ITSELF-- 30 MANSNS
AND WE CAN'T DISMISS THE SHIPPING TRADE AS 48 MANSNS
SOMETHING THAT DOESN'T CONCERN US.
EACH OTHER AND EACH HAS SOMETHING THE OTHER LACKS 54 MANSNS
AND NEEDS--
(JOEL STARES AT HIM, IS ABOUT TO SAY SOMETHING 60 MANSNS
MORE, THEN BOWS STIFFLY.
THAT WE WILL BE GETTING SOMETHING FOR PRACTICALLY 63 MANSNS
NOTHING.
SUDDENLY SHE STOPS, AND LISTENS TO SOMETHING 95 MANSNS
BEYOND THE WALL AT RIGHT.
THERE IS SOMETHING OF REPOSE AND CONTENTMENT IN 95 MANSNS
HER EXPRESSION.
SOMETHING OF AN INNER SECURITY AND HARMONY. 95 MANSNS
I WOULD HARDLY LIE ABOUT SOMETHING YOU CAN CONFIRM104 MANSNS
AS SOON AS YOU SEE HER.
AND THERE'S SOMETHING MORE BEHIND IT-- I THOUGHT 118 MANSNS
THEY'D NEVER COME IN--
SOMETHING ABOUT HIM, TOO--SLY--LIKE THERE WAS A 118 MANSNS
SECRET BETWEEN THEM--
I FEEL SOMETHING IS STARING OVER MY SHOULDER--IT'S119 MANSNS
STRANGE HERE
YOU WERE GOING TO SAY SOMETHING$ 121 MANSNS
YOU WANTED TO SAY SOMETHING$ 122 MANSNS
BUT THERE IS SOMETHING MORE BEHIND THIS-- 128 MANSNS
I SUDDENLY REMEMBERED SOMETHING I HAD NEVER 145 MANSNS
REMEMBERED BEFORE.
YOU OWNED SOMETHING I DESIRED. 152 MANSNS
SOMBER AND THREATENING--AND SOMETHING IN MY NATURE163 MANSNS
RESPONDS--
SO I HAD TO DO SOMETHING TO WARN YOU, AND I 184 MANSNS
THOUGHT A FAIRY TALE--
I'M ONLY WRITING SOMETHING. 360 MARCOM
(MORE CONFUSED) NOTHING, SIR--JUST--SOMETHING. 360 MARCOM
AND I WILL WAGER A MILLION OF SOMETHING OR OTHER 363 MARCOM
MYSELF THAT THE KAAN WILL SOON
THERE IS CERTAINLY SOMETHING ABOUT YOU, SOMETHING 379 MARCOM
COMPLETE AND UNANSWERABLE--
AS A CHILD MIGHT, BUT AT THE SAME TIME THERE IS 382 MARCOM
SOMETHING WARPED, DEFORMED--
AN ENIGMA WITH SOMETHING ABOUT HIM OF A LIKABLE 388 MARCOM
BOY
AND THAT SOMETHING MUST BE HIS HONOR'S SOUL, MUST 397 MARCOM
IT NOT$
SOMETHING STRANGE AND DIFFERENT-- 397 MARCOM
AFTER A GOOD DAY'S WORK IN WHICH YOU KNOW YOU'VE 398 MARCOM
ACCOMPLISHED SOMETHING.
RECITING ALWAYS MAKES ME WANT TO CRY ABOUT 405 MARCOM
SOMETHING.
WHEN YOU'RE TRYING TO GET SOMETHING DONE. 406 MARCOM
BUT HERE'S SOMETHING I WANT TO ASK YOU. 411 MARCOM
THEN SOMETHING MUST HAVE DISAGREED WITH YOU. 413 MARCOM
I MYSELF FEEL THERE IS SOMETHING, SOMETHING I 414 MARCOM
CANNOT UNDERSTAND.
SOMETHING YOU MUST INTERPRET FOR ME/ 414 MARCOM
THERE MUST BE SOMETHING HE WISHED YOU TO FIND. 414 MARCOM
I SAW SOMETHING QUEER/ 415 MARCOM
(SENSING SOMETHING) HAS THIS MAN OFFENDED YOUS 419 MARCOM
(HE SEES SOMETHING) AH--IT BEGINS. 426 MARCOM
AND HERE IS A LITTLE SOMETHING EXTRA. 428 MARCOM
TRANSLATED VERY FREELY INTO IRISH ENGLISH, 38 MISBEG
SOMETHING LIKE THIS.
THAT'S SOMETHING PEOPLE WASH WITH, ISN'T IT$ 44 MISBEG

SOMETHING (CONT'D.)
THE IS GOING TO ADD "TO LISTEN TO YOUR DAMNED 58 MISBEG
JOKES" OR SOMETHING LIKE THAT.
PROMISE ME YOU'LL EAT SOMETHING, JIM. 68 MISBEG
THOUGHT SOMETHING MUST BE QUEER, YOU COMING HOME 75 MISBEG
BEFORE THE INN CLOSED.
I REMEMBERED SOMETHING. 87 MISBEG
BE JAYSUS, THAT REMINDS ME I OWE YOU A SWIPE ON 100 MISBEG
THE JAW FOR SOMETHING.
SOMETHING BUT SHE REMAINS SILENT. 139 MISBEG
AS IF HE FELT HE OUGHT TO EXPLAIN SOMETHING TO 143 MISBEG
HER--
SOMETHING WHICH NO LONGER INTERESTS HIM) 143 MISBEG
AT HER, AND SOMETHING HAPPENED TO ME. 148 MISBEG
SOMETHING. 148 MISBEG
SHE WAS ONLY SOMETHING THAT BELONGED IN THE PLOT. 150 MISBEG
AND YOU HAD TO DO SOMETHING QUICK 163 MISBEG
(HE GIVES HER A FRIGHTENED LOOK, AS IF SOMETHING 163 MISBEG
HE HAD DREADED HAS HAPPENED.
LOOKING LIKE SOMETHING YOU'D PUT IN THE FIELD TO 169 MISBEG
SCARE THE CROWS FROM THE CORN.
SOMETHING GENTLE AND SAD AND, SOMEHOW, DAUNTLESS.) 20 POET
BUT IN SPITE OF THIS, THERE IS SOMETHING 34 POET
FORMIDABLE AND IMPRESSIVE ABOUT HIM.
(AS IF THIS WERE SOMETHING HE HAD BEEN WAITING TO 36 POET
HEAR.
(HE STARTS LOOKING OVER THE PAPER AGAIN--SCOWLS AT 37 POET
SOMETHING--
I'LL GO TO THE STORE AND GET SOMETHING TASTY. 39 POET
SHE ADDS SCATHINGLY.) I HOPE YOU SAW SOMETHING IN 44 POET
THE MIRROR YOU COULD ADMIRE/
AS IF SOMETHING VITAL HAD BEEN STABBED IN HIM-- 51 POET
WITH A CRY OF TORTURED APPEAL.)
BUT SOMETHING UNUSUAL IN HIS ATTITUDE STRIKES HER 58 POET
SHE STARTS TO SAY SOMETHING BITTER--STOPS-- 58 POET
SOMETHING PERVERSELY ASSERTIVE ABOUT IT TOO, 68 POET
GO ON UP TO YOUR ROOM NOW AND YOU'LL FIND 75 POET
SOMETHING TO TAKE YOUR MIND OFF.
THAT MAYBE HIS MOTHER SAID SOMETHING. 88 POET
I WANT TO GET HIM ANXIOUS AND AFRAID MAYBE I'M MAD 88 POET
AT HIM FOR SOMETHING.
WITH A CUPBOARD AND CURTAINS, AND SOMETHING, I'M 96 POET
TOLD,
IN THE MIRROR SOMETHING WILL MAKE YOU SEE AT LAST 105 POET
WHAT YOU REALLY ARE/
ALL I WISH IS TO RELATE SOMETHING WHICH HAPPENED 106 POET
THIS AFTERNOON.
(SARA STARTS TO SAY SOMETHING BITTER 130 POET
BE JAYSUS, HE NIVIR FELT ANYTHING BENEATH HIM THAT170 POET
COULD GAIN HIM SOMETHING,
BUT I'LL TELL YUH SOMETHING YOU CAN PUT IN YOUR 598 ROPE
PIPE AND SMOKE.
SHE SAID SHE WANTED TO FINISH THINKING SOMETHING 7 STRANG
OUT--
ALWAYS FUSSING ABOUT SOMETHING... 9 STRANG
WHAT WAS THAT COWARDLY SOMETHING IN ME THAT CRIED, 19 STRANG
NO, YOU MUSTN'T,
SOMETHING IN ME KNOWING HE WOULD DIE, THAT HE 19 STRANG
WOULD NEVER KISS ME AGAIN--
SUPPOSE I OUGHT TO SAY SOMETHING ABOUT HIS BOOKS, 29 STRANG
SOMETHING I OUGHT TO TELL YOU, I THINK. 32 STRANG
SOMETHING TO MOTHER....) 32 STRANG
TRYING TO GOAD HERSELF INTO FEELING SOMETHING/ 35 STRANG
SOMETHING TO LIFE AGAIN, AND ONCE SHE'S GOT THAT, 37 STRANG
SHE'LL BE SAVED/
BUT I FEEL HE'S HIDING SOMETHING... 39 STRANG
UNLESS GOD CALLED HIM IN BECAUSE HE'D CAUGHT 41 STRANG
SOMETHING.
HE DO SOMETHING.) 42 STRANG
OH, GOD, CHARLIE, I WANT TO BELIEVE IN SOMETHING/ 43 STRANG
I'LL JUST CARRY NINA UPSTAIRS AND PUT HER ON HER 47 STRANG
BED AND THROW SOMETHING OVER
THERE IS SOMETHING WRONG WITH ITS PSYCHE, I'M 49 STRANG
SURE.
WHEN SOMETHING IS GOING TO HAPPEN... 57 STRANG
OR SAID SOMETHING QUEER LIKE CHILDREN DO 60 STRANG
NATURALLY...
FOR FEAR HE MIGHT GET TO SUSPECT SOMETHING. 61 STRANG
BUT SIMPLY GOT TO WORK OUT SOMETHING OR... 67 STRANG
SOMETHING COMES BETWEEN....) 72 STRANG
HE MIGHT SAY SOMETHING/....) 75 STRANG
THINKING WITH THE SAME EAGERNESS TO BELIEVE 82 STRANG
SOMETHING HE HOPES)
AND YET I CAN'T QUITE CONVINCE SOMETHING IN ME 84 STRANG
THAT'S AFRAID OF SOMETHING.
HER SOMETHING IN RETURN... 85 STRANG
I OWE SAM SOMETHING... 85 STRANG
(AS IF LISTENING FOR SOMETHING WITHIN HER-- 90 STRANG
JOYFULLY)
THE NEXT MINUTE SOMETHING HATEFUL URGES ME TO 94 STRANG
DRIVE HIM INTO DOING IT/...!)
SOMETHING DISGUSTING/... 99 STRANG
THERE'S SOMETHING IN THIS ROOM/... 99 STRANG
SAY SOMETHING/... 100 STRANG
SOMETHING HUMAN AND UNNATURAL IN THIS ROOM/... 100 STRANG
THERE'S SOMETHING REPULSIVE ABOUT IT/ 101 STRANG
(SOLICITOUSLY) WHY, DO YOU HAVE TO SEE HIM ABOUT 108 STRANG
SOMETHING IMPORTANT, NINA$
I TELL YOU, THE MOMENT NED TOLD ME, SOMETHING 109 STRANG
HAPPENED TO ME/
SOMETHING IN HIS EYES... 111 STRANG
I FEEL I OUGHT TO DO SOMETHING ABOUT IT. 114 STRANG
BUT I MIGHT HAVE DONE SOMETHING BIG... 120 STRANG
BUT I CAN DO SOMETHING ELSE/ 132 STRANG
HE WANTS TO TELL YOU SOMETHING, SAM. 133 STRANG
LOOKS BLUE ABOUT SOMETHING... 134 STRANG
BUT I FELT WHEN SHE SAID IT THERE WAS SOMETHING IN135 STRANG
IT...

1489

SOMEWAY

SOMETHING (CONT'D.)
I HOPE MY EXPERIMENT HAS PROVED SOMETHING/... 139 STRANG
WHEN ARE WE EVER GOING TO LEARN SOMETHING ABOUT 143 STRANG
EACH OTHERS
BUT I KNOW THERE WAS SOMETHING QUEER IN HIS MIND 146 STRANG
AND THAT HE DID IT
(STARTLED AND AFRAID SHE MAY HAVE GUESSED 146 STRANG
SOMETHING HE DOESN'T ACKNOWLEDGE TO
MR. EVANS IS GETTING SOMETHING-- 167 STRANG
A FATHER OWES SOMETHING TO HIS SON... 169 STRANG
LIFE IS SOMETHING IN ONE CELL THAT DOESN'T NEED TO170 STRANG
THINK/
(NOT HEEDING--IMPRESSIVELY) THERE'S SOMETHING I 178 STRANG
MUST TELL YOU.
SOMETHING OF INFINITE IMPORTANCE, I KNOW/...!! 179 STRANG
(OUTRAGED BY SOMETHING IN HER TONE-- 186 STRANG
AND THEN WHEN I WAS ELEVEN--SOMETHING HAPPENED. 186 STRANG
THERE'S SOMETHING UNCANNY/... 188 STRANG
IT DID SOMETHING TO ME I NEVER GOT OVER... 189 STRANG
(THERE'S SOMETHING UP... 190 STRANG
IF ONLY TO GET SOMETHING BACK FROM SAM OF ALL HE'S193 STRANG
STOLEN FROM ME/...!)
I'VE GOT TO TELL YOU SOMETHING-- 195 STRANG
DID YOU STILL WANT TO TELL GORDON SOMETHING, NEDS 196 STRANG
THERE WAS SOMETHING UNREAL IN ALL THAT HAS 199 STRANG
HAPPENED SINCE YOU FIRST MET GORDON
SHAW, SOMETHING EXTRAVAGANT AND FANTASTIC, THE 199 STRANG
SORT OF THING THAT ISN'T DONE,
(INDIGNANTLY) I TELL YOU--DOT'S SOMETHING I DON 500 VOYAGE
LI-IKE/
THERE IS SOMETHING TORTURED ABOUT HIM-- 444 WELDED
EACH PERFORMANCE OF YOURS HAS TAUGHT ME SOMETHING.445 WELDED
WITH A GROWTH OF SOMETHING DEEPER--FINER-- 447 WELDED
WE'RE NOT *STARTING SOMETHING* NOW, ARE WE--AFTER 447 WELDED
OUR PROMISES
NOW THERE'S NOTHING LEFT BUT THAT SOMETHING WHICH 448 WELDED
CAN'T GIVE ITSELF.
IT MIGHT BE--SOMETHING IMPORTANT. 449 WELDED
(STILL BEWILDEREDLY AS IF SOMETHING MYSTERIOUS 449 WELDED
WERE HAPPENING THAT HE CANNOT
SHE LOOKS DOWN AT HIM, SEEMING TO MAKE UP HER MIND452 WELDED
TO SOMETHING--
I'M JEALOUS OF YOU--THE SOMETHING IN YOU THAT 455 WELDED
REPULSES OUR LOVE--
LET'S TALK OF SOMETHING ELSE. 456 WELDED
THAT I NEEDED LOVE--SOMETHING I FOUND IN YOU/ 458 WELDED
BUT I THOUGHT YOU'D UNDERSTAND--THAT I'D BEEN 458 WELDED
SEARCHING FOR SOMETHING--
(A SLIGHT PAUSE) I BEGIN TO KNOW--SOMETHING. 469 WELDED
(THEN SUDDENLY REMINDED OF SOMETHING SHE REGARDS 474 WELDED
HIM CALCULATINGLY--
YOU'VE SOMETHING YOU WANT TO ASK ME, MICHAELS 481 WELDED
IS THERE SOMETHING YOU WANT TO ASK ME$ 482 WELDED
THEN THERE IS SOMETHING--$ 482 WELDED
HAVEN'T YOU SOMETHING YOU WANT TO TELL$ 482 WELDED
WELL, THEN--AS IF SHE WERE GOADING HIM TO 484 WELDED
SOMETHING AGAINST HIS WILL--
I SAW--SOMETHING. 484 WELDED
(SIMPLY) SOMETHING STRONGER. 485 WELDED
SOMETHING EXTRAORDINARY HAPPENED TO ME--A 485 WELDED
REVELATION/
SOMETHING IN ME--MINE--NOT YOU/ 485 WELDED
SOMETHING'D
GEE, I KNEW SOMETHING'D BE BOUND TO TURN OUT 17 ANNA
WRONG--ALWAYS DOES WITH ME.
SOMETHING'S
OR I WARN YOU SOMETHING'S GOING TO HAPPEN/ 264 AHWILD
SOMETHING'S ALWAYS GOING WRONG THESE DAYS, IT 117 BEYOND
LOOKS LIKE.
((SOMETHING'S ALL WRONG HERE... 462 DYNAMO
(SHAMEFACEDLY) I DIDN'T SAY--STILL--SOMETHING'S 271 GGBROW
GOT TO BE DONE.
SOMETHING'S HOLDING YOU UP SOMEWHERE. 695 ICEMAN
SOMETIME
I WILL--SOMETIME. 279 AHWILD
(SUPPLICATINGLY) AND YOU TANK--MAYBE--YOU FORGIVE 65 ANNA
ME SOMETIMES
I'LL SHOW YOU SOMETIME. 545 DIFRNT
THERE ISN'T A DAMN JOB IN THE GAME I HAVEN'T HAD 4429 DYNAMO
HAND AT SOMETIME OR ANOTHER.
WELL, MAYBE AFTER YOU'RE A MINISTER YOU AND ME'LL 437 DYNAMO
ARGUE IT OUT SOMETIME.
I SUPPOSE I'LL HAVE TO DIE SOMETIME... 454 DYNAMO
(WITH A GRIN) SEE YOU IN JAIL SOMETIME, MAYBE/ 186 EJONES
GOD DAMN YOU' SOUL, I GITS EVEN WID YOU YIT, 194 EJONES
SOMETIME.
CATCH HIM OFF GUARD SOMETIME AND PUT IT UP TO HIM 20 ELECTR
STRONG-- AS IF YOU KNOWED IT--
SOMETIME IN SOME WAR. 82 ELECTR
THAT A GREAT WAVE MID SUN IN THE HEART OF IT MAY 215 HA APE
SWEEP ME OVER THE SIDE SOMETIME
DEN MAYBE I COMES BACK HERE SOMETIME TO SEE DE 673 ICEMAN
BUMS.
I HOPE, SOMETIME, WITHOUT MEANING IT, I WILL TAKE 121 JOURNE
AN OVERDOSE.
THERE IS A POEM BY DOCTOR HOLMES YOU SHOULD READ 148 MANSNS
SOMETIME--
HE MIGHT BE LED INTO IT SOMETIME WHEN HE HAS ONE 33 MISBEG
OF HIS SNEERING BITTER DRUNKS
I'LL COME BACK SOMETIME WHEN YOU'RE SOBER--OR SEND 60 MISBEG
SIMPSON--
I'D LIKE TO USE THE PROFESSOR IN A NOVEL 5 STRANG
SOMETIME...
((BUT SPEAKING OF SAM'S BIRTH, YOU REALLY MUST 50 STRANG
MEET HIS MOTHER SOMETIME.
SOMETIME... 63 STRANG
YOU'VE GOT TO HAVE A HEALTHY BABY--SOMETIME--SO'S 64 STRANG
YOU CAN BOTH BE HAPPY/

SOMETIME (CONT'D.)
DOESN'T MY BOY WANT TO SLEEP WITH ME AGAIN-- 71 STRANG
SOMETIME SOON$
SOMETIME... 72 STRANG
WHY DON'T YOU WRITE A NOVEL ABOUT LIFE SOMETIME, 148 STRANG
MARSDEN$
AND SOMETIME I'M GOING TO TELL HIM I SAW YOU-- 151 STRANG
SHE'LL TELL ME SOMETIME... 164 STRANG
SOMETIMES
I SOMETIMES THINK IF WE COULD ONLY HAVE HAD A 549 'ILE
CHILD.
SOMETIMES I CAN'T MAKE HEAD OR TAIL OF HIM. 209 AHWILD
LETTERS COME HERE FOR HIM SOMETIMES BEFORE, I 5 ANNA
REMEMBER NOW.
IT'S HARD TO STAY--AND EQUALLY HARD TO GO, 87 BEYOND
SOMETIMES.
AND I USED TO CRY SOMETIMES AND MA WOULD THINK I 90 BEYOND
WAS IN PAIN.
AND SOMETIMES I COULD ACTUALLY HEAR THEM CALLING 90 BEYOND
TO ME TO COME OUT AND PLAY WITH
SOMETIMES I THINK IF IT WASN'T FOR YOU, RUTH, 126 BEYOND
AND--HIS VOICE SOFTENING)--
SOMETIMES YE AIR THE FARM AN' SOMETIMES THE FARM 236 DESIRE
BE YEW.
YE GIVE ME THE CHILLS SOMETIMES. 238 DESIRE
SOMETIMES SHE USED T' SING FUR ME. 242 DESIRE
(A PAUSE) SOMETIMES SHE USED TO SING FUR ME. 243 DESIRE
IT'S PURTY HEREABOUTS SOMETIMES--LIKE NOW, IN 515 DIFRNT
SPRING--
(WITH A WINK) YOU OUGHTER SEE HER PERFORM 529 DIFRNT
SOMETIMES.
RAMSAY SAYS AWFUL MEAN THINGS SOMETIMES... 439 DYNAMO
SOMETIMES I'VE GONE WITHOUT EATING TO BUY BOOKS-- 458 DYNAMO
AND OFTEN I'VE READ ALL NIGHT--
SOMETIMES I'D GO IN A PLANT AND GET TALKING TO THE461 DYNAMO
GUYS JUST TO HANG AROUND.
YOU KNOW WHAT SHE MEANS SOMETIMES. 480 DYNAMO
I WANT YOU TO PRAY TO HER--UP THERE WHERE I PRAY 484 DYNAMO
SOMETIMES--UNDER HER ARMS--
AND SOMETIMES IT GETS OUT BEFORE I CAN STOP IT. 59 ELECTR
BUT HE'S SAD AND SHY, TOO, JUST LIKE A BABY 263 GGBROW
SOMETIMES.
(AFTER A PAUSE) I DON'T BLAME YOUR BEING JEALOUS 286 GGBROW
OF MR. BROWN SOMETIMES.
OH, GOD, SOMETIMES THE TRUTH HITS ME SUCH A SOCK 286 GGBROW
BETWEEN THE EYES
(CANNOT RESTRAIN A SHUDDER) SOMETIMES WHEN YOU'RE297 GGBROW
DRUNK YOU'RE POSITIVELY EVIL.
AND SOMETIMES NOT EVEN THEN. 12 HUGHIE
WHEN, NO MATTER HOW MUCH HE'D WIN ON A RUN OF LUCK 20 HUGHIE
LIKE SUCKERS HAVE SOMETIMES.
WELL, SO I DO, MUST OF 'EM. TO SAY HELLO, AND 28 HUGHIE
SOMETIMES THEY HELLO BACK.
I RUN ERRANDS FOR 'EM SOMETIMES, BECAUSE 28 HUGHIE
HE IS A LITTLE DEAF, BUT NOT HALF AS DEAF AS ME 577 ICEMAN
SOMETIMES PRETENDS.
BUT DE SOCIALIST, SOMETIMES, HE'S GOT A JOB, AND 584 ICEMAN
IF HE GETS TEN BUCKS,
TO HEAR HER GO ON SOMETIMES, YOU'D THINK SHE WAS 590 ICEMAN
THE MOVEMENT.
SOMETIMES SHE DIDN'T SAY BEHIND, EITHER. 608 ICEMAN
(GOES ON BELIEVOUSLY) SOMETIMES I'D TRY SOME JOKE712 ICEMAN
I THOUGHT WAS A CORKER ON
GOD, I USED TO PRAY SOMETIMES SHE'D-- 714 ICEMAN
BECAUSE SOMETIMES I COULDN'T FORGIVE HER FOR 714 ICEMAN
FORGIVING ME.
I GOT SO SOMETIMES WHEN SHE'D KISS ME IT WAS LIKE 715 ICEMAN
SHE DID IT ON PURPOSE.
BUT SOMETIMES I FEEL SO LONELY. 45 JOURNE
AND IF SOMETIMES, ON THE STAIRS OF A PALACE, OR UNI32 JOURNE
THE GREEN SIDE OF A DITCH,
SOMETIMES IT IS HARD TO LAUGH--EVEN AT MEN/ 291 LAZARU
SOMETIMES THE TWO HAVE APPEARED 73 MANSNS
SOMETIMES AT NIGHT WHEN YOU SIT IN THE PARLOR WITH 80 MANSNS
US, ALL OF A SUDDEN,
SOMETIMES I BECOME SO INTENSELY CONSCIOUS OF YOUR 82 MANSNS
UNITY
BUT SOMETIMES LATELY, MOTHER, ALONE IN MY OFFICE, 102 MANSNS
SOMETIMES, I GO MAD WORRYING/ 142 MANSNS
AND I KNOW FOR A FACT THAT PEOPLE ARE SOMETIMES 349 MARCOM
POSSESSED BY DEVILS.
YOU MIGHT NOT BELIEVE IT, BUT WHEN I'M IDLE I 398 MARCOM
ACTUALLY GET GLOOMY SOMETIMES/
AND SOMETIMES AN OLD TRICK IS BEST 22 MISBEG
OR TAKE THE OTHER KIND OF QUEER DRUNK HE GETS ON 33 MISBEG
SOMETIMES WHEN,
(THEN STRANGELY) ONLY SOMETIMES IT DOESN'T. 131 MISBEG
NO--SOMETIMES IT DOESN'T. 132 MISBEG
I SOMETIMES BELIEVE YOU HAVE ALWAYS DELIBERATELY 36 POET
ENCOURAGED ME TO--
BUT SOMETIMES THE SCENT OF HER HAIR AND SKIN... 5 STRANG
SOMETIMES I FEEL IT'S TOO GOOD TO BE TRUE... 55 STRANG
I REMEMBER WHEN I WAS CARRYING SAM, SOMETIMES I'D 63 STRANG
FORGET I WAS A WIFE,
(THINKING BITTERLY) (SOMETIMES I ALMOST HATE 96 STRANG
HER/...
EVEN THOUGH HE DOES GO WEAK THINGS SOMETIMES. 160 STRANG
(WITH A TENDER SMILE) OH--SOMETIMES. 444 WELDED
(SADLY) SOMETIMES I THINK WE'VE DEMANDED TOO 448 WELDED
MUCH.
SOMETIN'
WANTA MAKE SOMETIN' OF IT$ 671 ICEMAN
SOMETING
BUT DIS IS SOMETING TO ME. 697 ICEMAN
I REMEMBER I HAD SOMETING ON MY MIND TO TELL YUH. 701 ICEMAN
I TANK SOMETING GO WRONG WITH DRISC AND COCKY. 507 VOYAGE
SOMEWAY
I KNEW SHE MUST BE CONNECTED SOMEWAY WITH HARFORD 18 POET

SOMEWAYS

SOMEWAYS
YE THINK YE KIN GIT 'ROUND THAT SOMEWAYS, DO YES 255 DESIRE

SOMEWHAT'S
THAT'S A STAR, AN' SOMEWHAT'S THEY'S HIM, AN' 211 DESIRE
HERE'S ME, AN' THAT'S MIN UP THE

SOMWHARS
I FELT THEY WAS SOMETHIN' ONNATURAL--SOMEWHARS-- 264 DESIRE
THE HOUSE GOT SO LONESOME--

SOMEWHAT
(SOMEWHAT IMPATIENTLY) WALL, IF HE AIN'T, HE'S A 512 DIFRNT
GOOD MAN JES' THE SAME,
HAVE SOMEWHAT RESTORED HIS SHAKEN NERVE. 190 EJONES
(KNOCKS--SOMEWHAT EMBARRASSEDLY) MR. BROWN/ 314 GGBROW
ONCE I LAUGHED SOMEWHAT LIKE THAT--SO I PARDON 339 LAZARU
THEE.
(SOMEWHAT TAKEN ABACK, PUZZLEDLY) 382 MARCOM

SOMEWHERE
I'LL BET HE'S OFF SOMEWHERE WRITING A POEM TO 192 AHWILD
MURIEL MCCUMBER, THE SILLY/
I'VE GOT TO DRAW THE LINE SOMEWHERE/ 206 AHWILD
SOMEWHERE OUT ON THE LONG TRAIL--THE TRAIL THAT IS288 AHWILD
ALWAYS NEW--
(POURING OUT THEIR GLASSES) I'LL GET A LITTLE 77 ANNA
HOUSE SOMEWHERE AND I'LL MAKE A
I'LL GET AWAY SOMEWHERE, SOMEHOW. 107 BEYOND
(SOMEWHERE/SOMEWHERE IN THE CROWD) HERE'S THE MATE 472 CARIBE
COMIN'/
SOMEWHERE. 498 DAYS
HE MUST FIND A FAITH--SOMEWHERE/ 498 DAYS
NOW I WONDER WHAT HIDES BEHIND THAT SOMEWHERES 499 DAYS
ALL THAT SAVED ME FROM DOING SOMETHING STUPID WAS 521 DAYS
THE FAITH I HAD THAT SOMEWHERE
(THEN, AS FIFE'S VOICE IS HEARD CALLING FROM 455 DYNAMO
SOMEWHERE IN THE HOUSE)
IT ALL COMES DOWN TO ELECTRICITY SOMEWHERE. 458 DYNAMO
CALLING ME BACK TO SOMEWHERE FAR OFF 476 DYNAMO
IT MADE ME FEEL LIFE MIGHT STILL BE ALIVE 83 ELECTR
SOMEWHERE--
I HOPE THERE IS A HELL FOR THE GOOD SOMEWHERE/ 174 ELECTR
PERHAPS I CAN LOCATE HIM LATER AROUND TOWN 277 GGBROW
SOMEWHERE.
I WOULD LIKE TO BE SINCERE, TO TOUCH LIFE 219 HA APE
SOMEWHERE
(FROM SOMEWHERE IN THE LINE--PLAINTIVELY) 223 HA APE
A THIN, SHRILL NOTES FROM SOMEWHERE OVER-HEAD IN 223 HA APE
THE DARKNESS.
HALF-AMUSEDLY, AS IF THEY SAW A JOKE SOMEWHERE 226 HA APE
THAT TICKLED THEM.
HE'D READ SOMEWHERE--IN THE SUCKERS' ALMANAC, I 23 HUGHIE
GUESS--
ONCE IN A WHILE ONE OF THEM MAKES A SUCCESSFUL 593 ICEMAN
TOUCH SOMEWHERE.
=SHIP ME SOMEWHERE EAST OF SUEZ-- 599 ICEMAN
SOMETHING'S HOLDING YOU UP SOMEWHERE. 695 ICEMAN
BUT HE WAS AN HONEST MAN WHO DREW THE LINE 25 JOURNE
SOMEWHERE.
SOMEWHERE IN THIS HOUSE. 152 JOURNE
(SHE LETS HIM TAKE IT, REGARDING HIM FROM 172 JOURNE
SOMEWHERE FAR AWAY WITHIN HERSELF,
BUT THERE IS A GOD IN IT SOMEWHERE/ 321 LAZARU
BUT THERE IS A GOD IN IT SOMEWHERE--A GOD OF 322 LAZARU
PEACE--A GOD OF HAPPINESS/
IS THERE HOPE OF LOVE SOMEWHERE FOR MEN ON EARTH$ 365 LAZARU
BE DRIVEN TO SEEK SPIRITUAL SALVATION SOMEWHERE/ 363 MARCOM
(ROUND-EYED) A MAN TOLD ME THAT NOAH'S ARK IS 364 MARCOM
STILL SOMEWHERE AROUND HERE
YOU'RE BOUND TO GET SOMEWHERE/ 406 MARCOM
SOMEWHERE THIS DREAM IS BEING DREAMED. 417 MARCOM
BUT, BE GOD, I DRAW THE LINE SOMEWHERE, 63 MISREG
AFRAID HE'LL MEET HIMSELF SOMEWHERE... 34 STRANG
A RINGING OF THE DOORBELL SOUNDS FROM SOMEWHERE 462 WELDED
BACK IN THE HOUSE.

SOMEWHERES
I'LL BET HE'S GOT A DATE WITH HER SOMEWHERES. 194 AHWILD
SOMEWHERES ELSE. 196 AHWILD
HE'S GOT A DAUGHTER SOMEWHERES OUT WEST, I THINK 5 ANNA
HE TOLD ME ONCE.
BUT THEY'RE PROBABLY LYING AROUND SOMEWHERES. 86 BEYOND
AND HUNT UP A WIFE SOMEWHERES FOR THAT SPICK 'N' 104 BEYOND
SPAN CABIN.
THEY'RE HIDING SOMEWHERES... 434 DYNAMO
LEFT MY CLIPPERS AROUND SOMEWHERES. 178 ELECTR
I'LL GIT DE MONEY FOR MY STAKE TCOAY, SOMEHOW, 673 ICEMAN
SOMEWHERES/
HAVEN'T I SEEN YOU SOMEWHERES BEFORE$ 348 MARCOM

SON
AND EVERY MOTHER'S SON OF YOU WHAT DON'T OBEY 544 'ILE
ORDERS GOES IN IRONS.
(SOLEMNLY) SON, IF I DIDN'T KNOW IT WAS YOU 195 AHWILD
TALKING,
DISGRACEFUL WOULD BE NEARER THE TRUTH--AND IT 201 AHWILD
CONCERNS YOUR SON, RICHARD/
AFTER READING THOSE PAPERS, TO CLAIM YOUR SON WAS 202 AHWILD
INNOCENT OF ALL WRONGDOING/
HERE'S A LETTER FROM MURIEL FOR YOUR SON (PUTS IT 203 AHWILD
ON THE TABLE) IT MAKES CLEAR,
MILLER WATCHES HIS SON FROWNINGLY. 206 AHWILD
LOOK HERE, SON. 206 AHWILD
(TARTLY--GIVING HER SON A REBUKING LOOK) 216 AHWILD
LATER, SON, LATER. 234 AHWILD
GOOD NIGHT, SON. 252 AHWILD
TURNS AND FIXES HIS YOUNGEST SON WITH A STERN 264 AHWILD
FORBIDDING EYE)
=YOUR SON GOT THE BOOZE HE DRANK LAST NIGHT AT THE267 AHWILD
PLEASANT BEACH HOUSE.
(SIZING HIM UP SHREWDLY) HELLO, SON. 293 AHWILD
SHE GLANCES QUICKLY FROM SON TO HUSBAND AND 296 AHWILD
IMMEDIATELY KNOWS THAT ALL IS WELL

SON (CONT'D.)
(WATCHING HIS SON--AFTER A PAUSE--QUIETLY) 296 AHWILD
BETTER GET TO BED EARLY TONIGHT, SON, HADN'T YOU$ 297 AHWILD
I HATE 'EM ALL, EVERY MOTHER'S SON OF 'EM/ 18 ANNA
THE YOUNGEST SON--PAUL--THAT STARTED ME WRONG. 57 ANNA
A SON OF THE SOIL, INTELLIGENT IN A SHREWD WAY, 82 BEYOND
I'D BE A NICE SON-OF-A-GUN IF I DIDN'T, WOULDN'T 84 BEYOND
I$
MAYO IS HIS SON ANDREW OVER AGAIN IN BODY AND 94 BEYOND
FACE--
YES--BETTER HAD, SON. 97 BEYOND
(FROWNING) LET'S GET TO THE POINT, SON. 100 BEYOND
WITH AN UNEASY SIDE GLANCE AT JAMES MAYO WHO IS 104 BEYOND
STARING AT HIS ELDER SON AS IF
BUT WHY, SON$ 105 BEYOND
I NEVER THOUGHT I'D LIVE TO SEE THE DAY WHEN A SON106 BEYOND
O' MINE'D LOOK ME IN THE FACE
YOU'RE NO SON O' MINE--NO SON O' MINE/ 108 BEYOND
(PROTESTINGLY) YOU OBSTINATE OLD SON OF A GUN/ 134 BEYOND
A RALE, GOD-FUR-SAKEN SON AV A TURKEY TROT WID 470 CARIBE
GUTS TO UT.
HE BEARS A STRIKING RESEMBLANCE TO HIS SON. 567 CROSS
(IN A STATE OF MAD EXULTATION STRIDES TOWARD HIS 568 CROSS
SON
(TO HIS SON WITH FIERCE SATISFACTION) 569 CROSS
(HE POINTS AT HIS SON) HE HAS NO RIGHT NOW. 572 CROSS
O SON OF MAN, I AM THOU AND THOU ART I/ 565 DAYS
A SON IS ME--MY BLOOD--MINE. 234 DESIRE
WHAT SON O' MINE'LL KEEP ON HERE T' THE FARM--WHEN234 DESIRE
THE LORD DOES CALL ME$
YE MEAN--A SON--T' ME'N' YEW$ 234 DESIRE
(WITH GRIM RESOLUTION) I WANT A SON NOW. 234 DESIRE
FUR A SON$ 234 DESIRE
(SUDDENLY) MEBBE THE LORD'LL GIVE US A SON. 234 DESIRE
THE FARM NEEDS A SON. 235 DESIRE
EXCITED MOOD INTO WHICH THE NOTION OF A SON HAS 235 DESIRE
THROWN HIM.
I NEED A SON. 236 DESIRE
ME AN' THE FARM HAS GOT T' BEGET A SON/ 236 DESIRE
IF YE DON'T HEV A SON T' REDEEM YE... 238 DESIRE
YE'LL HAVE A SON OUT O' ME, I PROMISE YE. 238 DESIRE
AN' YE KIN KISS ME BACK 'S IF YEW WAS MY SON--MY 243 DESIRE
BUY--SAYIN' GOOD-NIGHT T' ME/
THEY HAIN'T MANY T' TOUCH YE, EPHRAIM--A SON AT 249 DESIRE
SEVENTY-SIX.
I GOT A NEW SON/ 249 DESIRE
HE NEEDS YE, REMEMBER--OUR SON DOES/ 252 DESIRE
AN' THEN SHE SAYS YEW'N ME OUGHT T' HAVE A SON--I 255 DESIRE
KNOW SHE DID, SHE SAYS--
IF YE DID GIT HIM A SON/ 257 DESIRE
I'LL TELL HIM THE TRUTH 'BOUT THE SON HE'S SO 257 DESIRE
PROUD OF/
GITTIN' ME T' LIE WITH YE SO'S YE'D HEV A SON HE'D257 DESIRE
THINK WAS HIS'N,
(WITH A SHUDDER--HUMBLY) HE'S YEWR SON, TOO. 257 DESIRE
EBEN.
AN' YER SON ALONG WITH YE--T' STARVE AN' DIE/ 257 DESIRE
GITTIN' ME T' LOVE YE--LYIN' YEW LOVED ME--JEST T'258 DESIRE
GIT A SON T' STEAL/
AN' HE WAS EBEN'S SON--MINE AN' EBEN'S--NOT 264 DESIRE
YOUR'N/
THINK I'D HAVE A SON BY YEW$ 264 DESIRE
HE WAN'T YEWR SON/ 264 DESIRE
HE'D OUGHT T' BEEN MY SON, ABBIE. 265 DESIRE
SHE STARES AT HER SON WITH RESENTFUL ANNOYANCE.) 528 DIFRNT
THAT I SHOULD LIVE TO SEE THE DAY WHEN A SON OF 528 DIFRNT
MINE'D DESCEND SO LOW
=BETTER CALL IN YOUR SON UR SOME NIGHT I MIGHT 422 DYNAMO
MISTAKE
IN THE BEDROOM ABOVE, THEIR SON, REUBEN, 422 DYNAMO
BECAUSE HE HAPPENS TO BE A MINISTER'S SON-- 425 DYNAMO
ESPECIALLY WHEN IT'S SPRING$
WHAT A FEATHER IN THAT BLASPHEMER'S CAP TO CORRUPT426 DYNAMO
MY SON/..
AND DAMNED IF HIS DAUGHTER DIDN'T GET ENGAGED TO 431 DYNAMO
THE MINISTER'S SON/
HE'S HONOR BOUND TO TELL HIS FUTURE SON-IN-LAW THE431 DYNAMO
SECRET OF HIS PAST.
OH, IF YOU'D ONLY MAKE A PRIZE JACKASS OF THAT 432 DYNAMO
YELLOW NANCY SON OF HIS/
BUT A MINISTER'S SON HAS REASON TO WORRY, MAYBE, 437 DYNAMO
IN THE NAME OF GOD, HAS YOUR SON$ 451 DYNAMO
NO WONDER YOUR SON IS A SAP/ 451 DYNAMO
ESPECIALLY A MINISTER'S SON. 456 DYNAMO
GLARING AT HIS SON) 463 DYNAMO
YOU ROTTEN SON OF A---(HE CHOKES IT BACK--THEN 465 DYNAMO
HELPLESSLY, WITH A WOUNDED LOOK)
(HAS LIFTED HIS HEAD AND IS GLARING AT HIS SON) 465 DYNAMO
YOU UNNATURAL ACCUSED SON/ 465 DYNAMO
YOU ARE MY SON AS WELL AS HERS, REMEMBER. 466 DYNAMO
A DAUGHTER FEELS CLOSER TO HER FATHER AND A SON TO 22 ELECTR
HIS MOTHER/
FROM THE SON OF A LOW CANUCK NURSE GIRL/ 24 ELECTR
YOU'RE TOO GOOD FOR THE SON OF A SERVANT, EH$ 25 ELECTR
SO--IT IS TRUE--YOU ARE HER SON/ 25 ELECTR
IN THE VILEST-- MOST COWARDLY WAY--LIKE THE SON OF 27 ELECTR
A SERVANT YOU ARE/
HE'S THE SON OF THAT LOW NURSE GIRL GRANDFATHER 32 ELECTR
PUT OUT OF OUR HOUSE/
I'D GIVE MY SOUL TO SEE HIS FACE WHEN HE KNOWS YOU 38 ELECTR
LOVE MARIE BRANTOME'S SON/
THE SON OF THAT---/ 61 ELECTR
HE IS MARIE BRANTOME'S SON/ 61 ELECTR
BECAUSE HIS NAME IS BRANT, HE MUST BE THE SON OF 87 ELECTR
THAT NURSE GIRL MARIE BRANTOME$
I AM HIS SON, TOO, REMEMBER THAT/ 100 ELECTR
HE KNEW BEFORE HE DIED WHOSE SON I WAS, YOU SAID$ 110 ELECTR
I'M NOT HER SON ANY MORE/ 140 ELECTR

SON

SON (CONT'D.)

HE'S ALWAYS BEEN SUCH A WONDERFUL SON BEFORE--AND 173 ELECTR BROTHER.

ANTHONY, BROWN AND SON, ARCHITECTS AND BUILDERS-- 258 GGBROW FOLLOWING THEM, AS IF HE WERE A STRANGER, WALKING 259 GGBROW ALONE. IS THEIR SON, DION.

(GENTLY REMONSTRATING TO HER SON) 260 GGBROW (WITH BITTER HOPELESSNESS--TO HIS WIFE--INDICATING261 GGBROW THEIR SON)

THE IDENTICAL SON/ 262 GGBROW BROWN AND SON, ARCHITECTS AND BUILDERS-- 272 GGBROW EVERY DAMN MOTHER'S SON-OF-A-GUN OF YOU, 286 GGBROW DEEP FAR-OFF VOICE--AND YET LIKE A MOTHER TALKING 288 GGBROW TO HER LITTLE SON)

BECAUSE AT WHAT HOUR YOU KNOW NOT THE SON OF MAN 291 GGBROW WILL COME/AMEN.

MUCK-EATIN' SON OF A-- 225 HA APE I WAS BORN IN THE PURPLE, THE SON, BUT 595 ICEMAN UNFORTUNATELY NOT THE HEIR.

*YOU BLACK SON OF A BITCH. 601 ICEMAN (WITH AN AFFECTIONATE GRIN) HERE'S THE OLD SON OF618 ICEMAN A BITCH/

VIVE LE SON DES CANONS/= 634 ICEMAN AND SAYS, =I KNOW HOW IT IS, SON, BUT YOU CAN'T 646 ICEMAN HIDE FROM YOURSELF.

BEJEEES, HICKEY, YOU OLD SON OF A BITCH, THAT'S 659 ICEMAN WHITE OF YOU/

YOU SON OF A BITCH OF A FRYING-PAN-PEDDLING 660 ICEMAN BASTARD/

YOU DAMNED FOOL, DO YOU THINK I'D HAVE YOUR 681 ICEMAN FATHER'S SON FOR MY LAWYERS

(HE SCOWLS) THAT DRUMMER SON OF A DRUMMER/ 681 ICEMAN BEJEEES, YOU SON OF A BITCH, 688 ICEMAN WHERE IS DAT SON OF A BITCH, HICKEYS 698 ICEMAN POOR CRAZY SON OF A BITCH/ 719 ICEMAN VIVE LE SON/ 727 ICEMAN VIVE LE SON/ 727 ICEMAN VIVE LE SON DES CANONS/ 727 ICEMAN *E'S THE SON OF A BLASTED EARL OR SOMETHINK/ 522 INZONE A FINE SON YOU ARE TO HELP THAT BLACKGUARD GET ME 26 JOURNE INTO A LAWSUIT/

IF YOU WEREN'T MY SON, 31 JOURNE YOU'RE MY SON--/ 33 JOURNE (HIS SON LOOKS AT HIM, FOR THE FIRST TIME WITH AN 36 JOURNE UNDERSTANDING SYMPATHY.

IF HE WEREN'T YOUR SON-- (ASHAMED AGAIN.) NO, 36 JOURNE THAT'S NOT TRUE/

HE TURNS TO HIS SON.) 41 JOURNE YOU OUGHT TO BE PROUD YOU'RE HIS SON/ 60 JOURNE (WITH SATISFACTION, AS IF THIS WAS A PERPETUAL 121 JOURNE BATTLE OF WITS WITH HIS ELDER SON

(HE STOPS WITH A GUILTY GLANCE AT HIS SON.) 137 JOURNE SHE LOVES YOU AS DEARLY AS EVER MOTHER LOVED A 142 JOURNE SON/

YOU'RE NO GREAT SHAKES AS A SON. 143 JOURNE BUT TO THINK WHEN IT'S A QUESTION OF YOUR SON 145 JOURNE HAVING CONSUMPTION,

NO SON OF MINE WOULD EVER-- YOU WERE DRUNK. 147 JOURNE NOT ONLY DID HIS SON DIE BUT MIRIAM COULD NEVER 276 LAZARU BEAR HIM MORE CHILDREN.

(PATHETICALLY UNEASY) YOU FRIGHTEN US, MY SON. 278 LAZARU MY SON IS REBORN TO ME/ 278 LAZARU TO MY SON, LAZARUS, WHOM A BLESSED MIRACLE HAS 279 LAZARU BROUGHT BACK FROM DEATH/

IT WAS NOT MY SON WHO CAME BACK BUT A DEVIL/ 285 LAZARU MY SON IS DEAD/ 285 LAZARU I CURSE THE DAY HE CALLED MY GOOD SON, LAZARUS, 285 LAZARU REMEMBRANCE WOULD IMPLY THE HIGH DUTY TO LIVE AS A289 LAZARU SON OF GOD--GENEROUSLY/

EASIER TO FORGET, TO BECOME ONLY A MAN, THE SON OF289 LAZARU A WOMAN,

(SUDDENLY--WITH DEEP GRIEF) AND JESUS WHO WAS THE292 LAZARU SON

EVEN A SON OF MAN MUST DIE TO SHOW MEN THAT MAN 293 LAZARU MAY LIVE/

DIONYSUS, SON OF MAN AND A GOD/ 299 LAZARU HE MUST BE THE FIRE-BORN, THE SON OF ZEUS/ 299 LAZARU SON OF THE LIGHTNING/ 302 LAZARU SON OF THE LIGHTNING/ 302 LAZARU CLOSEST TO THE SOIL OF THE GRECIAN GODS, A SON OF 307 LAZARU MAN, BORN OF A MORTAL.

LAUGHTER WHICH IS TO ME AS MY SON, MY LITTLE BOY/ 330 LAZARU ONCE I KNEW YOUR LAUGHTER WAS MY CHILD, MY SON OF 345 LAZARU LAZARUS.

LIKE A YOUNG SON WHO KEEPS WATCH BY THE BODY OF 350 LAZARU HIS MOTHER.

A SON WAS BORN TO US. 356 LAZARU MAN, SON OF GOD'S LAUGHTER, IS/ 360 LAZARU AFTER ALL, YOU ARE YOUR FATHER'S SON. 19 MANSNS (SHE EMBRACES HIM AGAIN.) MY DEAR SON/ 17 MANSNS APPEARS ACCOMPANIED BY DEBORAH'S YOUNGER SON, 25 MANSNS JOEL.

(SHE LAUGHS.) I CAN SEE YOU HAVE MADE HIM YOUR 63 MANSNS ELDEST SON.

AND SO I AM LEFT ALONE, AN UNWANTED SON, A 73 MANSNS DISCARDED LOVER.

OF A MEANS TO MOTHERHOOD--A SON IN ONE CASE, A 73 MANSNS HUSBAND IN THE OTHER--

ALMOST ANY FOOL OF A WOMAN CAN HAVE A SON, 79 MANSNS UNTIL I COULD HARDLY RECOGNIZE MY SON IN THE 97 MANSNS UNSCRUPULOUS GREEDY TRADER,

I SEE YOU HAVE, MY SON. 103 MANSNS TO HAVE MY SON AGAIN/ 114 MANSNS THAT YOU ARE NOW MY OWN DEAR SON AGAIN/ 115 MANSNS THAT HE IS MY SON AGAIN-- 118 MANSNS TAKE A POSSESSIVE GRATIFICATION IN TEASING A YOUNG128 MANSNS BASHFUL SON.

NOW THAT I HAVE MY OWN SON AGAIN. 134 MANSNS

SON (CONT'D.)

(THINKING.) THEN MY BELOVED SON WILL HAVE NO ONE 137 MANSNS BUT ME/

I NO LONGER RECOGNIZE THIS AS MY FATHER'S OFFICE--143 MANSNS OR MYSELF AS MY FATHER'S SON.

MY BELOVED SON AND I--ONE AGAIN--HAPPILY EVER 162 MANSNS AFTER.

I KNOW MY SON IS WAITING FOR AN OPPORTUNITY TO SEE169 MANSNS ME ALONE.

OUR BELOVED SON/ 175 MANSNS AND BECOME AGAIN ONLY YOUR SON/ 178 MANSNS MY BELOVED SON/ 181 MANSNS OH, MY SON/ 181 MANSNS FROM THE HEAD OF MY FIRM--MARCO POLO OF POLO 348 MARCOM BROTHERS AND SON, VENICE.

WHAT ARE YOU WRITING, SONS 360 MARCOM (TURNING ON HIM--GENIALLY) WELL, SON, HERE WE ARE364 MARCOM IN ISLAM.

(TEASINGLY) YOUR SON AND YOUR MONEY ARE SOON 365 MARCOM PARTED, BROTHER.

(TO NICOLO) YOUR SONS 367 MARCOM (DEFIANTLY) HE WAS THE SON OF GOD/ 368 MARCOM THE LIGHT PASSED INTO THE WOMB OF MAYA, AND SHE 372 MARCOM BORE A SON WHO.

NICOLO STARES AT HIS SON BITTERLY, MAFFEO WITH 374 MARCOM CONTEMPTUOUS PITY.

(HESITANTLY) MY SON, MARCO, YOUR MAJESTY--STILL 378 MARCOM YOUNG AND GRACELESS.

POLO BROTHERS AND SON--DOESN'T THAT SOUND SOLID, 381 MARCOM EH?

IT WILL BE POLO BROTHERS AND SON FROM NOW ON, 382 MARCOM FOR KUKACHIN, AND HER GRANDFATHER, THE SON OF 388 MARCOM HEAVEN AND RULER OF THE WORLD/

KUKACHIN WILL BE A MOTHER A MOTHER MAY NOT SORROW 410 MARCOM SAVE FOR HER SON.

AND I'M TO HAND YOU OVER TO HIS SON, GHAZAN, TO 410 MARCOM MARRY.

(IN CHORUS) THE LOVER COMES, WHO BECOMES A 417 MARCOM HUSBAND, WHO BECOMES A SON,

YOU MUST BEAR THE HUMILIATION OF ACCEPTING HIS SON418 MARCOM FOR HUSBAND.

TO REJOICE AT THAT FATHER'S DEATH, THEN I SHOULD 418 MARCOM BE THAT GUILTY SON/

IF IT WERE POSSIBLE FOR A SON WHO LOVED A NOBLE 418 MARCOM FATHER

I AM WIFE OF HIS SON, GHAZAN. 423 MARCOM I DOUBT IF I SHALL BE BLESSED WITH A SON. 423 MARCOM SON OF HEAVEN/ 435 MARCOM THE SON OF HEAVENS 435 MARCOM (PUFFS ON HIS PIPE) WHAT ELSE DID MY BEAUTIFUL 20 MISBEG SON, MIKE, SAY TO YOUS

FAITH, ME DARLIN' SON NEVER LEARNT THAT FROM HIS 22 MISBEG PRAYER BOOK/

(MUMBLES) THE SON OF A BITCH/ 78 MISBEG I'D COME TO LOVE HIM LIKE A SON--A REAL SON OF MY 85 MISBEG HEART.

TO PROVE HIMSELF THE EQUAL OF ANY GENTLEMAN'S SON. 12 POET LIVING LIKE A TRAMP OR A TINKER, AND HIM A RICH 29 POET GENTLEMAN'S SON.

HOPING YOU MIGHT KNOW THE PRESENT WHEREABOUTS OF 72 POET MY SON, SIMON.

SURE, YOUR SON IS A GENTLE, 73 POET I AM SURE MRS. HARFORD IS WAITING TO BE TAKEN TO 74 POET HER SON.

WHAT WOMAN WOULD WANT HER SON TO MARRY THE 77 POET DAUGHTER OF A MAN LIKE--

FOR YOUR KINDNESS TO MY SON DURING HIS ILLNESS. 81 POET ANY EMOTION RESULTING FROM HER INTERVIEW WITH HER 81 POET SON.

HENRY HARFORD IS WILLING TO SETTLE ON HIS SON. 111 POET SIMON IS AN ELDER SON, THE HEIR TO HIS FATHER'S 111 POET ESTATE.

PHILOSOPHER, WHICH HIS SON HAS CHOSEN TO PURSUE, 111 POET OLD HARFORD MIGHT NOT THINK IT AN HONOR TO HAVE 112 POET HIS SON MARRY YOUR DAUGHTER.

TO ANY FURTHER RELATIONSHIP BETWEEN HIS SON AND 121 POET YOUR DAUGHTER.

FOR THE MARRIAGE OF HIS SON WITH MY DAUGHTERS 121 POET THE SON OF A MAN WHO HAS INSULTED MY HONOR-- 127 POET CURSING LIKE A DRUNKEN, FOUL-MOUTHED SON OF A 157 POET THIEVING SHEBEEN KEEPER

BUT ENJOY LIFE IN MY PROPER STATION AS AULD NICK 169 POET MELODY'S SON.

I'LL FIRE MICKEY AND TEND THE BAR MYSELF, LIKE MY 174 POET FATHER'S SON OUGHT TO.

I'M TOO PROUD TO MARRY A YANKEE COWARD'S SON/ 178 POET SHE LEAVES YOU ALONE WITH THAT--YOUR SON, LUKE, 580 ROPE SHE CALLED HIM--

*AS IS THE MOTHER, SO IS HER SON---- 580 ROPE MAD AS YOU ARE, FOR THINKIN' THAT THIEF OF A SON 582 ROPE OF YOURS WOULD

FOR THIS MY SON WAS DEAD, AND IS ALIVE AGAIN,. 595 ROPE (THICKLY) THE DAMNED SON-OF-A-GUN/ 597 ROPE YUH DAMNED SON-OF-A-GUN/ 597 ROPE THE ROTTEN SON-OF-A-GUN,/ 598 ROPE THE DAMNED SON-OF-A-GUN/ 601 ROPE WHAT SON CAN EVER UNDERSTANDS.... 4 STRANG AND MY SON/... 128 STRANG NINA CALLED MY SON AFTER GORDON/... 128 STRANG YOU OLD SON OF A GUN/ 132 STRANG NINA AND DARRELL AND THEIR SON, GORDON, ARE IN THE137 STRANG ROOM.

(WATCHING NINA--SADLY) (IALWAYS THINKING OF HER 139 STRANG SON....

(REGARDING HIS SON BITTERLY) 141 STRANG THEN DON'T BLAME HIM FOR ACTING LIKE SAM'S SON/ 143 STRANG I DON'T WANT MY SON TO BE TOO HAPPY AT MY EXPENSE.144 STRANG EVEN ON HIS BIRTHDAY/

SON

SON

(CONT'D.)

AFTER ALL, HE IS MY SON AND I'D PREFER HE DIDN'T 144 STRANG
SMASH IT BEFORE MY EYES/
YOU SHOULDN'T HAVE DONE THAT, SON. 150 STRANG
(THIS IS MY SON/... 151 STRANG
BUCK UP, SON 151 STRANG
WHERE'S MOTHER, SON$ 152 STRANG
TO SEE MY SON HIS SON/... 152 STRANG
HOW'S THE OLD SON$ 152 STRANG
UH, MOTHER GOD, GRANT MY PRAYER THAT SOME DAY WE 156 STRANG
MAY TELL OUR SON THE TRUTH AND
THIS IS THE SON OF OUR LOVE IN MY ARMS/... 156 STRANG
YOU TOLD ME TO LIE TO YOUR SON AGAINST YOU... 156 STRANG
MY SON/...) 160 STRANG
(COLDLY) I'M QUITE AWARE MY SON ISN'T A 160 STRANG
WEAKLING--
IS THERE SUCH A PERSON AS MY SONS... 165 STRANG
(WITH BITTER EMPHASIS) EXCEPT YOUR REAL SON--AND 166 STRANG
ME--
(REPROACHFULLY) SO YOU HAVE FOUND A SON WHILE I 166 STRANG
WAS LOSING MINE--
(SPEAKING SADLY) I'VE LOST MY SON, NED/ 167 STRANG
(THINKING RESENTFULLY) (HE'S SNEERING AT HIS OWN167 STRANG
SON/...)
AND YOUR SON, TOO/ 169 STRANG
MY SON, NED/ 169 STRANG
THE SON OF OUR OLD LOVE, NED/ 169 STRANG
GORDON IS MY SON, ISN'T HE$ 169 STRANG
A FATHER OWES SOMETHING TO HIS SON... 169 STRANG
HIS SON BUT MINE/... 173 STRANG
IT'S TIME HE GAVE US BACK OUR SON/ 173 STRANG
(WITH A SNEER) OUR SON) 173 STRANG
THEN HER SON, GORDON/...) 173 STRANG
(MORE AND MORE CONFIDENTLY) BESIDES, I'M QUITE 174 STRANG
SURE GORDON ISN'T MY SON.
GORDON IS REALLY GORDON'S SON/ 174 STRANG
UH, DEAD, DEAD GORDON, HELP ME TO GET BACK YOUR 174 STRANG
SON/...
SHE THINKS GORDON IS SAM'S SON.)) 176 STRANG
COME ON, SON/ 181 STRANG
O MOTHER GOD, PROTECT MY SON/... 181 STRANG
LIFT HER OUT OF THE WATER, SON/ 182 STRANG
WHAT IS SAM TO DARRELL'S SONS... 187 STRANG
AND EVEN IF HE WERE SAM'S SON, WHAT HAVE THE 187 STRANG
LIVING TO DO WITH THE DEADS...
(IS THAT MY SON$... 190 STRANG
HE'S NOT MY SON NOW, NOR GORDON'S SON, NOR SAM'S, 190 STRANG
NOR NED'S...
HAS CERTAINLY MADE MY SON AN INSENSITIVE 191 STRANG
CLOD/...)
WASN'T IT ENOUGH FOR HIM TO OWN MY WIFE, MY SON, 192 STRANG
IN HIS LIFETIME$...
THE SON SPANKS THE FATHER/...) 193 STRANG
NO--IT'S ALL RIGHT, SON--ALL RIGHT--YOU DIDN'T 193 STRANG
KNOW--
IT'S NOTHING, SON--NOTHING/ 194 STRANG
(THEN LOOKING HER SON IN THE EYES, SLOWLY AND 195 STRANG
IMPRESSIVELY)
(HOLDING GORDON'S HAND) LISTEN, SON. 195 STRANG
GOOD-BYE, SON. 196 STRANG
MY DEAR SON/ 198 STRANG
HE'S MY SON, TOO/ 198 STRANG
(HE SHOUTS UP AT THE SKY) YOU'RE MY SON, GORDON/ 198 STRANG
GOOD-BYE, GORDON'S SON/ 198 STRANG
MY HAVING A SON WAS FAILURE, WASN'T IT$ 199 STRANG
WHAT I MEAN IS, HE FLEW AWAY TO ANOTHER LIFE--MY 199 STRANG
SON, GORDON, CHARLIE.
AN' SEE WHAT THAT CRIMPIN' SON AV A CRIMP'LL BE 497 VOYAGE
WANTIN'--

SON'LL

AN' YER PAW'S SON'LL NEVER KILL WHAT HE WANTS/ 240 DESIRE
(HALF JOCULARLY) YER SON'LL BE NEEDIN' YE SOON. 263 DESIRE

SON'S

MILLER LOOKS INTO HIS SON'S FACE A SECOND, THEN 208 AHWILD
TURNS AWAY.
(NOT HEEDING HER--HIS EYES FIXED HYPNOTICALLY ON 569 CROSS
HIS SON'S)
AND STARES AT HIS SON'S FACE WITH STUPEFIED 463 DYNAMO
BEWILDERMENT)
(SEEMING TO SHRIVEL UP IN HIS SON'S GRIP-- 466 DYNAMO
(CHECKS HIMSELF GUILTILY, LOOKING AT HIS SON'S 89 JOURNE
SICK FACE WITH WORRIED PITY,
TYRONE SIGHS, SHAKING HIS HEAD HOPELESSLY, AND 115 JOURNE
ATTEMPTS TO CATCH HIS SON'S EYE,
EVEN HER SON'S. 3 MANSNS
IN YOUR HAPPINESS AS MY SON'S WIFE AND HIS 54 MANSNS
HAPPINESS AS YOUR HUSBAND.
(GLOATING--HAUGHTILY,) YOU HAVE MY SON'S ORDERS/ 186 MANSNS
I THE EVIL ONE WHO DESIRES HER SON'S LIFE/ 189 MANSNS
(WHAT UNGRATEFUL THOUGHTS OH MY SON'S 138 STRANG
BIRTHDAY/...
CONGRATULATIONS ON YOUR SON'S BIRTHDAY/ 146 STRANG
GHOST AT MY SON'S FEAST/... 149 STRANG
NINA WILL SOON BE FIGHTING SAM FOR MY SON'S 149 STRANG
LOVE/...
(STERNLY) FOR THE SAKE OF YOUR FUTURE HAPPINESS 178 STRANG
AND MY SON'S I'VE GOT TO SPEAK/
(SHE WANTS TO RUIN MY SON'S LIFE AS SHE RUINED 178 STRANG
MINE/...)

SONG

WHY NOT GIVE US A SONG OR TWO NOW$ 255 AHWILD
THE SONG COMES TO AN END. 257 AHWILD
THE EFFECT ON HIS AUDIENCE IS THAT OF THE PREVIOUS258 AHWILD
SONG, INTENSIFIED--
WE'RE GOING TO HAVE ANOTHER SONG. 258 AHWILD
(AS THE SONG FINISHES, THE TWO IN THE OTHER ROOM 259 AHWILD
LAUGH.
YOU DON'T KNOW GOOD SONG WHEN YOU HEAR HIM. 6 ANNA

SONG

(CONT'D.)

HE READS ALOUD IN A DOLEFUL, SING-SONG VOICE) 82 BEYOND
HE IS SMILING HAPPILY, AND HUMMING A SONG TO 99 BEYOND
HIMSELF.
IS SOFTLY PLAYING SOME FOLK-SONG ON A BATTERED 477 CARDIF
ACCORDION.
I WONDER NOW, DO THEY CALL THAT KEENIN' A SONG$ 456 CARIBE
I WISH THEY'D STOP THAT SONG. 459 CARIBE
CADENCE OF THE SONG FROM THE SHORE CAN AGAIN BE 466 CARIBE
FAINTLY HEARD.
DAMN THAT SONG OF THEIRS (HE TAKES ANOTHER BIG 466 CARIBE
DRINK
THE MELANCHOLY SONG OF THE NEGROES DRIFTS CROONING473 CARIBE
OVER THE WATER.
THEIR VOICES AS THEY GO OFF TAKE UP THE SONG OF 224 DESIRE
THE GOLD-SEEKERS
A LAST FAINT NOTE OF THE «CALIFORNI-A» SONG IS 227 DESIRE
HEARD FROM THE DISTANCE.
WHAT WAS THE SONG THEY SUNG$ 268 DESIRE
THERE MUST BE SOMETHING IN HER SONG THAT'D TELL 474 DYNAMO
YOU IF YOU HAD EARS TO HEAR/...
HER SONG IN THERE--DYNAMO'S--ISN'T THAT THE 476 DYNAMO
GREATEST POEM OF ALL--
HER SONG IS THE HYMN OF ETERNAL GENERATION, THE 482 DYNAMO
SONG OF ETERNAL LIFE/
A SONG THAT MORE THAN ANY OTHER HOLDS IN IT THE 5 ELECTR
HE IS APPROACHING THE HOUSE AND THE SONG DRAWS 43 ELECTR
QUICKLY NEARER..
(BURSTS INTO SONG) «A BOTTLE OF BEER AND A BOTTLE130 ELECTR
OF GIN
(BURSTS INTO SONG AGAIN) «HURRAH.. 130 ELECTR
I WHO LOVE MUSIC AND RHYTHM AND GRACE AND SONG AND264 GGBROW
LAUGHTER$
(COMPASSIONATELY) EVERY SONG IS A HYMN. 284 GGBROW
(A VOICE STARTS BAWLING A SONG.) 209 HA APE
SING US THAT WHISKY SONG, PADDY. 209 HA APE
SINGA DA SONG, CARUSO PAT/ 210 HA APE
SINGING A CHANTY SONG WID NO CARE TO IT. 213 HA APE
(COLDLY) WHAT'S DE SONG AND DANCE ABOUTS 385 ICEMAN
MEANWHILE, I WILL SING A SONG. 596 ICEMAN
RAPPING ON THE TABLE WITH HIS KNUCKLES AT THE 596 ICEMAN
INDICATED SPOTS IN THE SONG.)
WHO IS STILL CHUCKLING TO HIMSELF OVER WILLIE'S 598 ICEMAN
SONG.
MARJORIE'S FAVORITE SONG WAS «LOCK LOMOND.» 656 ICEMAN
* AND INSTANTLY THEY ALL BURST INTO SONG. 727 ICEMAN
BUT NOT THE SAME SONG. 727 ICEMAN
I WAS HALFWAY UP THE WALK WHEN CATHLEEN BURST INTO 54 JOURNE
SONG.
(SHRUGGING HIS SHOULDERS.) YOU WON'T BE SINGING A 66 JOURNE
SONG YOURSELF SOON.
WELL, DON'T GIVE HARDY YOUR OLD OVER-THE-HILLS-TO- 79 JOURNE
THE-POORHOUSE SONG
THAT GOD-DAMNED PLAY I BOUGHT FOR A SONG AND MADE 149 JOURNE
SUCH A GREAT SUCCESS IN--
THAT IT IS LIKE A GREAT BIRD SONG TRIUMPHANT 279 LAZARU
IS HEARD RISING FROM HIS LIPS LIKE A SONG.) 308 LAZARU
HAD FOUND AT LAST ITS VOICE AND A SONG FOR 309 LAZARU
SINGING.
AND HERE THE SONG OF LAZARUS' LIFE GREW PITIFUL. 310 LAZARU
SINGS HOARSELY AN OLD CAMP SONG OF THE PUNIC WARS,313 LAZARU
POUNDING WITH HIS GOBLET)
SINGING A VERSE OF THE LEGIONARY'S SONG) 357 LAZARU
THE SONG FINISHED, HE WAITS ANXIOUSLY. 355 MARCOM
A FRESH BOY'S VOICE IS HEARD SINGING A LOVE SONG 355 MARCOM
IN A SUBDUED TONE.
SURELY IT CANNOT BE A SONG HE HAS WRITTEN 360 MARCOM
WHEN THE VOICE FAILS, LISTEN TO SONG. 384 MARCOM
CRUEL WHEN SPRING IS SMITTEN BY WINTER, WHEN BIRDS436 MARCOM
ARE STRUCK DEAD IN FULL SONG.
ALAS THAT OUR PRINCESS IS DEAD, SHE WAS THE SONG 436 MARCOM
OF SONGS.
THE QUIET OF THE NIGHT IS SHATTERED BY A BURST OF 71 MISBEG
MELANCHOLY SONG.
HE ONLY REMEMBERS ONE VERSE OF THE SONG AND HE HAS 72 MISBEG
BEEN REPEATING IT.)
A MOMENT LATER HE BEGINS TO BAWL HIS MOURNFUL 101 MISBEG
IRISH SONG.
(DURING A PART OF THE FOLLOWING SCENE THE SONG 101 MISBEG
CONTINUES TO BE HEARD AT
HUGO'S MOURNFUL SONG DRIFTS BACK THROUGH THE 103 MISBEG
MOONLIGHT QUIET...
A SNATCH FROM AN OLD SOB SONG, POPULAR IN THE 111 MISBEG
NINETIES)
I REMEMBERED THE LAST TWO LINES OF A LOUSY TEAR- 150 MISBEG
JERKER SONG I'D HEARD WHEN I WAS
(BURSTS INTO A ROLLICKING SONG, ACCOMPANYING 96 POET
HIMSELF ON THE PIPES.
PLEASED BY THE IRREVERENCE OF THE SONG.) 97 POET
A SONG IN THE RIGHT SPIRIT, PIPER. 97 POET
GIVE US A HUNTING SONG, PATCH. 101 POET
OF AN OLD HUNTING SONG.) 102 POET
SHE TALKS IN A HIGH-PITCHED, SING-SONG WHINE. 579 ROPE
(ROARING INTO SONG) 498 VOYAGE
SONGED
SURE--HER OLD MAN--PRESIDENT OF DE SONGED-- 244 HA APE

SONGS

(DOLEFULLY) YES--BUT I WISH HE WOULDN'T SING SUCH258 AHWILD
SAD SONGS.
AND YOU CAN SIT THERE LISTENING TO SONGS AND 260 AHWILD
LAUGHING AS IF--
SONGS THAT TOLD OF ALL THE WONDERFUL THINGS THEY 90 BEYOND
HAD.
THEY SANG THEIR LITTLE SONGS TO ME. 90 BEYOND
AND THE SONGS AT THE SAILOR'S OPERA HOUSE WHERE 487 CARDIF
THE GUY PLAYED RAGTIME--
«LET US GO HENCE, MY SONGS. SHE WILL NOT HEAR. 173 JOURNE
YOU DANCED AND SANG LEWD SONGS. 348 MARCOM

SONGS (CONT'D.)

SONGS AND MUSIC COME FROM NEAR AND FAR-OFF IN THE 356 MARCOM NIGHT ABOUT THEM.

AND EVERYWHERE WHERE SONGS ARE SUNG THEY SHALL BE 418 MARCOM IN PRAISE OF YOUR BEAUTY/

ALAS THAT OUR PRINCESS IS DEAD, SHE WAS THE SONG 436 MARCOM OF SONGS,

AND WE'D START DRINKING AND TELLING STORIES, AND 26 MISBEG SINGING SONGS.

SONNY

(OVER HIS SHOULDER) YOU'LL BE HAVIN' YOURS, ME 461 CARIBE SONNY BYE, DON'T FRET.

(GRINNING) YE CAN TAKE UT OR LAVE UT, ME SONNY 462 CARIBE BYES.

MORNIN', SONNY. 263 DESIRE

WHIN I OPEN THIS BOX I'LL NOT BE THE MAN TO BE 527 INZONE KILT, ME SONNY BYE/

(SHAKING HIS FIST AT JOE) OHO, I KNOW YOUR GAMES,504 VOYAGE ME SONNY BYE/

SONOROUSLY

OPENS IT AT RANDOM AND BEGINS TO READ ALOUD 23 STRANG SONOROUSLY LIKE A CHILD WHISTLING TO

SONS

I DON'T BELIEVE IN KISSING BETWEEN FATHERS AND 297 AHWILD SONS AFTER A CERTAIN AGE--

THE OLD MAN OF THE FAMILY, HIS WIFE, AND FOUR 18 ANNA SONS--

IT WAS ONE OF THE SONS--THE YOUNGEST--STARTED ME-- 18 ANNA WHEN I WAS SIXTEEN.

LORD GOD O' HOSTS, SMITE THE UNDUTIFUL SONS WITH 227 DESIRE THEY MUST CUSS/

TRUE SONS O' MINE IF THEY BE DUMB FOOLS-- 268 DESIRE

HE'S MARRIED AND GOT THREE BIG SONS. 289 GGBROW

IN THE FATHER OF YOUR SONS/ 292 GGBROW

THE THREE SONS 292 GGBROW

THREE STRONG SONS/ 292 GGBROW

MR. AND MRS. BROWN AND SONS, HAPPILY EVER AFTER/ 299 GGBROW

THE SONS GROUP AROUND HER, AS IF FOR A FAMILY 300 GGBROW PHOTO.

THE THREE SONS ARE WITH HER. 300 GGBROW

MARGARET AND HER THREE SONS APPEAR FROM THE RIGHT.323 GGBROW

MEN THAT WAS SONS OF THE SEA AS IF 'TWAS THE 213 HA APE MOTHER THAT BORE THEM.

DEY'S ALL NO-GOOD SONS OF BITCHES.* 584 ICEMAN

FINE PAIR OF SONS OF BITCHES TO HAVE GLUED ON ME 598 ICEMAN FOR LIFE/

YOU WHITE SONS OF BITCHES/ 672 ICEMAN

YOU'VE HEARD THE OLD SAYING, *MINISTERS' SONS ARE 709 ICEMAN SONS OF GUNS.*

(THEIR SONS JAMES, JR. AND EDMUND ENTER TOGETHER 19 JOURNE FROM THE BACK PARLOR.

(HIS TWO SONS STARE AT HIM CONTEMPTUOUSLY. 77 JOURNE

TYRONE LIFTS HIS GLASS AND HIS SONS FOLLOW SUIT 175 JOURNE MECHANICALLY.

SONS OF GOD WHO APPEARED ON WORLDS LIKE OURS TO 289 LAZARU TELL THE SAVING TRUTH TO EARS

HAS MY FOUR SONS TO SUBSTITUTE FOR ME, AND THE 73 MANSNS WIFE HAVING THEM.

I'VE MY FOUR SONS AND I KNOW THE LOVE I FEEL FOR 79 MANSNS THEM,

AFTER ALL, THEY ARE MY SONS, TOO. 84 MANSNS

BUT WE ALREADY HAVE FOUR SONS-- 125 MANSNS

AND I'LL HAVE MY OWN SONS ALL TO MYSELF NOW. 134 MANSNS

WITHOUT A CARE IN THE WORLD, WATCHING MY SONS GROW148 MANSNS UP HANDSOME RICH GENTLEMEN,

ON THE RIGHT, THE SONS OF THE KAAN. 377 MARCOM

YOU WILL BE BLESSED WITH STRONG SONS 385 MARCOM

(AMUSED) YOU'VE THE SAME BAD LUCK IN SONS I HAVE 16 MISBEG IN BROTHERS.

ONE WOULD NEVER SUSPECT THAT SHE IS THE MIDDLE- 67 POET AGED MOTHER OF TWO GROWN SONS.

AND THESE ARE MEN AND WOMEN AND SONS AND DAUGHTERS176 STRANG WHOSE HEARTS ARE WEAK

THE SONS OF THE FATHER HAVE ALL BEEN FAILURES/ 199 STRANG

HE COULDN'T GIVE ME HAPPINESS, SONS ARE ALWAYS 199 STRANG THEIR FATHERS.

SOON'S

AND HE COULD SEE JUST AS SOON'S I TOLD HIM WHAT A 137 BEYOND GOOD CHANCE IT WAS.

TO MAKE SURE YOU'D BEST LEAVE HERE SOON'S YOU KIN.142 BEYOND

I'LL GO WITH YOU TO THE CITY--SOON'S YOU'RE WELL 149 BEYOND AGAIN.

(FORCING A DEFIANT LAUGH) MAYBE I WILL GO SOON'S 537 DIFRNT I LEARN--

WELL, HE EATS RIGHT HEAH AN' NOW SOON'S I GITS 188 EJONES DESE PESKY SHOES LACED UP.

I'S GOIN' TO DRINK IT DAT WAY AGAIN, TOO, SOON'S 1640 ICEMAN MAKE MY STAKE/

NOW YOU DON'T HAVE TO BREAK IT, SOON'S MY BACK'S 673 ICEMAN TURNED.

SOONER

THEY HAVE NO SOONER DISAPPEARED THAN THE SCREEN 217 AHWILD DOOR IS OPENED CAUTIOUSLY AND

(MUTTERS GRACIOUSLY) IMMEDIATELY--IF NOT SOONER. 232 AHWILD

I COULD GET MARRIED SOONER. 296 AHWILD

AND DAT OLE DAVIL, SEA, SOONER, LATER SHE SVALLOW 28 ANNA DEM UP.

I ALWAYS SORTER HOPED THEY'D HITCH UP TOGETHER 98 BEYOND SOONER OR LATER.

AND THE SOONER I'M IN THE GRAVE AND OUT O' THEIR 113 BEYOND WAY THE BETTER IT'D SUIT THEM.

WELL, YOU CAN GO, AND THE SOONER THE BETTER/ 127 BEYOND

THE SOONER I GO THE SOONER I'LL BE BACK, THAT'S A 142 BEYOND CERTAINTY.

I'M GOIN' TO DIE, THAT'S WHAT, AND THE SOONER THE 486 CARDIF BETTER/

YOU'RE BOUND TO SEE HIM SOONER OR LATER. 557 CROSS

SOONER (CONT'D.)

AND YOU'D HEAR ABOUT IT FROM SOMEONE SOONER UR 502 DIFRNT LATER 'CAUSE JIM AND THE REST O'

AND THE SOONER I DO IT, THE LESS SUSPICION 41 ELECTR THERE'LL BE/

I'LL BE BACK IN HALF AN HOUR--MAYBE SOONER. 158 ELECTR

FOR ONE THING, HE LIVED IN BROOKLYN, AND I'D 25 HUGHIE SOONER TAKE A TRIP TO CHINA.

WELL, THE SOONER I GET STARTED-- 687 ICEMAN

YES, AND THE SOONER THE BETTER, HARDY SAID, FOR 79 JOURNE HIM AND EVERYONE AROUND HIM.

THE POORHOUSE IS THE END OF THE ROAD, AND IT MIGHT128 JOURNE AS WELL BE SOONER AS LATER/

THE SOONER YOU KICK THE BUCKET, THE LESS EXPENSE. 157 JOURNE

THE SOONER THE BETTER. 60 MANSNS

HOW COULD I SNEAK HERE SOONER WITH HIM PEEKING 4 MISBEG ROUND THE CORNER OF THE BARN TO

I DIDN'T COME BACK HERE FUR FUN, AND THE SOONER 589 ROPE YOU GETS THAT IN YOUR BEANS,

WASN'T WISHIN' HERSELF TO SEE IT OR I'D HAVE ASKED592 ROPE YE SOONER.

AN' YOU LAUGHIN' AT HIM A MOMENT SOONER/ 598 ROPE

SOONER WE STARTS THE SOONER WE'RE RICH. 600 ROPE

HE'S NO SOONER HERE THAN I START... 134 STRANG

YOU SHOULD HAVE BEEN GENEROUS SOONER. 485 WELDED

SOONER'R

(WITH VENGEFUL PASSION) AN' SOONER'R LATER, I'LL 209 DESIRE MEUDDLE.

SOOTH

IN SOOTH, THE BEST OF ALL WERE NEVER TO BE BORN.* 591 ICEMAN

SOOTHE

(TRYING TO SOOTHE HIM) FATHER/ 568 CROSS

FLOWERS REALLY HAVE THE POWER TO SOOTHE GRIEF. 188 STRANG

SOOTHED

ERNIE, HAVING SOOTHED RESENTMENT WITH HIS WISE- 25 HUGHIE CRACK,

SOOTHED IN A MYSTERIOUS, CHILDLIKE WAY, THEY 353 LAZARU REPEAT THE WORD AFTER HIM,

SOOTHES

AND SOOTHES HIM AS IF HE WERE A LITTLE BOY. 258 AHWILD

ANDREA SOOTHES HIS MOTHER WHO IS ON THE VERGE OF 106 BEYOND TEARS.)

(SHE SOOTHES HIM IN DULL TONES) 149 BEYOND

SHE SOOTHES HIM) 142 ELECTR

SHE IS OVERCOME BY PITY AND SOOTHES HER AS SHE 169 MANSNS WOULD A CHILD.)

SOOTHES HER WITH UNCERTAIN TREMBLING WORDS) 43 STRANG

SOOTHIN'

THINKIN' IT MIGHT BE SOOTHIN' TO YE TO BE PLAYIN' 546 'ILE IT TIMES WHEN THEY WAS CALMS

SOOTHING

(A TIRED, HARASSED, DEEPLY WORRIED LOOK ON HIS 262 AHWILD FACE--SOOTHING HER)

(SHE PUTS A SOOTHING HAND ON HIS FOREHEAD.) 570 CROSS

(TENDERLY SOOTHING HER) TURN IT AGAINST YOUS 88 ELECTR

(IMMEDIATELY CONTRITE AND SOOTHING, PETTING HER) 89 ELECTR

(SOOTHING HIM NOW) I'M NOT ANGRY, DEAR-- 140 ELECTR

(THEN CONQUERING HER HORROR--RESOLUTELY TENDER AND160 ELECTR SOOTHING)

(SOOTHING HER) BE COMFORTED, BELOVED. 330 LAZARU

OH, HOW HIS SOOTHING GRAY WORDS MUST HAVE PECKED 361 LAZARU AT THE WOUND IN YOUR HEART LIKE

(FROM BELOW, RECITES IN A CALM, SOOTHING TONE) 401 MARCOM

FILLS THE ROOM WITH A SOOTHING LIGHT, 3 STRANG

(INCOHERENT WORDS DROWNING OUT NINA'S VOICE, 26 STRANG SOOTHING HER.)

AND STRONG, WHOSE BLOOD IS BLOOD AND NOT A 177 STRANG SOOTHING SYRUP/

(MAKING HER SIT DOWN AGAIN--SOOTHING HER) 194 STRANG

SOOTHINGLY

(SOOTHINGLY) IN A MONTH OR TWO, WITH GOOD LUCK, 546 'ILE THREE AT THE MOST.

(SOOTHINGLY) HE PROBABLY COULDN'T GET A SEAT, THE251 AHWILD TROLLEYS ARE SO JAMMED.

MILLER SAYS SOOTHINGLY) 256 AHWILD

(SOOTHINGLY) AY WOULDN'T NEVER DREAM-- 42 ANNA

(SOOTHINGLY) THERE, DON'T BE FRIGHTENED. 563 DAYS

(AFTER A QUICK GLANCE AT HER FACE--SOOTHINGLY) 507 DIFRNT

(SOOTHINGLY) ALL RIGHT, RUBE. 482 DYNAMO

(SOOTHINGLY) YOU MUSTN'T BE AFRAID. 484 DYNAMO

(SOOTHINGLY--HUMORING HIM) ALL RIGHT, RUBE. 485 DYNAMO

(TENDERLY AND SOOTHINGLY) WHY DID YOU SAY A 489 DYNAMO MINUTE AGO, IF I LOVED YOUS

(SOOTHINGLY, COMING TO HIM AND TAKING HIS ARM) 96 ELECTR

LAVINIA PUTS HER ARM AROUND HIM SOOTHINGLY. 124 ELECTR

(SOOTHINGLY) SSSHH/ 124 ELECTR

(SOOTHINGLY) THAT'S A GOOD BOY. 140 ELECTR

(SHE PATS HIM ON THE ARM--SOOTHINGLY) 151 ELECTR

(SOOTHINGLY, PATTING HER SHOULDER) 159 ELECTR

(SOOTHINGLY, LOOKING BEFORE HER LIKE AN IDOL) 322 GGBROW

(SOOTHINGLY) SURE I WILL AND IT'LL MAKE YOUR 608 ICEMAN REPUTATION, WILLIE.

(SOOTHINGLY) WE KNOW YUH GOT A REG'LAR JOB. 613 ICEMAN

(SOOTHINGLY) NOW, GOVERNOR. 656 ICEMAN

(SOOTHINGLY.) COME NOW/ YOU KNOW THAT'S A FIB. 46 JOURNE

(SOOTHINGLY.) THAT'S FOOLISHNESS. 48 JOURNE

(WORRIED--SOOTHINGLY) THERE/ 414 MARCOM

(SOOTHINGLY) SSSHH. 147 MISBEG

SHE LOOKS DOWN AT HIM AGAIN AND SPEAKS SOOTHINGLY 153 MISBEG AS SHE WOULD TO A CHILD)

(PUTS HER ARM AROUND HER--SOOTHINGLY.) 26 POET

(SOOTHINGLY,) HUSH, NOW. 30 POET

(SOOTHINGLY) HUSH/ 598 ROPE

(SOOTHINGLY) THAT'S JUST WHAT YOU OUGHT TO BEAR 12 STRANG IN YOUR MIND--

(THEN FORCING A SMILE--SOOTHINGLY) 40 STRANG

THEN SOOTHINGLY WITH A TEASING INCONGRUOUS GAIETY) 44 STRANG

(SOOTHINGLY--BUT PLAINLY DISTURBED) 82 STRANG

SOOTHINGLY

SOOTHINGLY (CONT'D.)
(LEADING HIM TO THE CHAIR AT CENTER, SOOTHINGLY) 98 STRANG
(SOOTHINGLY) I KNOW IT'S UGLY, CHARLIE. 101 STRANG
(LOOKING AT HER IN AMAZEMENT--SOOTHINGLY) 178 STRANG
(SOOTHINGLY, HUMORING HER--KISSING HER AGAIN) 182 STRANG
THEN HIS VOICE SOOTHINGLY----COME IN/ 462 WELDED

SOOTHSAYER
THEN IT DOESN'T TAKE A SOOTHSAYER TO TELL HE'S 129 JOURNE
PROBABLY IN THE WHOREHOUSE.

SOOTY
RIVULETS OF SOOTY SWEAT HAVE TRACED MAPS ON THEIR 224 HA APE
BACKS.

SOPRANO
WHO STARTS PLAYING AND SINGING IN A WHISKEY 653 ICEMAN
SOPRANO

SORCERER
(HE DRAWS HIS SWORD) COVER HER FACE, ACCURSED 353 MARCOM
SORCERER/
WARRIOR AND SORCERER TO RIGHT AND LEFT OF HIM. 373 MARCOM

SORDID
BUT SHE GAVE ME ALL THE SORDID DETAILS 549 DAYS
(HE HAS THE TERRIBLE GROTESQUE AIR, IN CONFESSING 667 ICEMAN
HIS SORDID BASENESS).
IT IS CHEAP AND MEAN AND SORDID LIKE LIFE. 21 MANSNS
MOST SORDID FACTS, TO PROVE HOW THOROUGHLY I WAS 29 MANSNS
RESIGNED TO REALITY.
AND GOD KNOWS I KNOW THE SORDID TRAGEDY OF SUCH A 113 POET
UNION.
IT'S ALL A SORDID MESS/... 76 STRANG

SORDIDNESS
SO SEDULOUSLY PROTECTED AND ALOOF FROM ALL LIFE'S 14 MANSNS
SORDIDNESS.

SURE
(RAPTLY) AH, SIGHT FOR SORE EYES, MY BEAUTIFUL 226 AHWILD
MACUSHLA.
PLEASE DON'T GET SURE AT ME. 238 AHWILD
I'M NOT SORE. 238 AHWILD
NOBODY'S SORE AT NOBODY. 11 ANNA
I'M NOT SORE AT YOU, HONEST. 37 ANNA
(MUMBLING) IT'S ALL RIGHT, RUB--LONG AS YOU'RE 135 BEYOND
NOT SORE AT ME.
YUH'RE AS SORE AS A BOIL ABOUT SOMETHIN'. 457 CARIBE
MA'LL TELL HIM ALL HER TALES, AND HE'LL BE SURE AT523 DIFRNT
ME RIGHT OFF.
DON'T GO GETTIN' SORE AT ME AGAIN. 548 DIFRNT
PLEASE DON'T GET SORE/ 433 DYNAMO
(LOOKING AT HIM HOPEFULLY) YOU'RE NOT SORE AT ME 481 DYNAMO
FOR COMING? ARE YOU?
YOU CERTAINLY ARE A SIGHT FOR SORE EYES, VINNIE/ 75 ELECTR
AT ME--LIKE PADDY SAID--CHRIST, I WAS SORE, GET 231 HA APE
ME?
I GOT SORE. 22 HUGHIE
THAT MADE HER SORE. 591 ICEMAN
I'M SORRY I GOT SORE. 592 ICEMAN
DON'T GET SORE. 607 ICEMAN
DON'T GET SORE. JEES, CAN'T YUH TAKE A LITTLE 613 ICEMAN
KIDDIN'S
HELL, DON'T GET SORE, LARRY. NOT AT ME. 624 ICEMAN
I GOT SORE. 631 ICEMAN
DE FUNNY TING IS, YUH CAN'T STAY SORE AT DE BUM 638 ICEMAN
WHEN HE'S AROUND.
DON'T GET SORE, BOYS AND GIRLS. 639 ICEMAN
YOU LOOK SURE. 640 ICEMAN
BUT YOU KEEP ACTING AS IF YOU WERE SURE AT ME, AND640 ICEMAN
THAT GETS MY GOAT.
DEN SHE'D BUST OUT CRYIN', AND I'D GET SORE. 671 ICEMAN
DAT'D MAKE ME SOKE AND I'D SAY, "DON'T CALL ME A 671 ICEMAN
LIAR."
I'M NOT SORE AT YOU. 679 ICEMAN
(COOKY GRUMBLES AND RETIRES TO A BENCH, NURSING 526 INZONE
HIS SORE SHIN.)
YOU DON'T WANT TU GET A SORE THROAT ON TOP OF YOUR 58 JOURNE
COLD.
THEN SHE GOT GOOD AND SORE. 160 JOURNE
U GOD, MY SIDES ARE SORE. 65 MISBEG
STILL SORE AT ME FOR BEING LATE? 106 MISBEG
ALL THE SAME, I'LL BE GOOD AND SORE, JOSIE. 133 MISBEG
YOU HAVE A HELL OF A LICENSE TO BE SURE. 136 MISBEG
I WAS SURE AT MYSELF AFTERWARDS... 41 STRANG
YOU MUSTN'T BE SORE AT HIM. 107 STRANG
(TOUCHED ON A SORE SPOT--WITH A NASTY LAUGH-- 141 STRANG
CUTTINGLY)
NINA'LL BE SORE AS THE DEVIL BUT SHE'LL HAVE TO 161 STRANG
LIKE IT...!)

SURED
YOU OUGHT TO SEE THE DOLLS GET SORED UP WHEN I 13 HUGHIE
WORK IT ON THEM/

SOREHEADS
HARRY'S PARTY BEGINS IN A MINUTE AND WE DON'T WANT651 ICEMAN
NO SOREHEADS AROUND.

SORR
(GRATEFULLY) YES, SORR. 226 AHWILD
THANK YE, SORR. 484 CARDIF
YES, SORR, BUT YANK WAS FEARIN' TO BE ALONE, AND--484 CARDIF
NOT MUCH FOR THE HOUR JUST PAST, SORR, BUT BEFORE 485 CARDIF
THAT--
NO, SORR. 485 CARDIF
PLAZE HELP HIM SOME WAY, SORR/ 485 CARDIF
YES, SORR. 485 CARDIF
YES, SORR, BUT IT DIDN'T STAY DOWN. 485 CARDIF
FIVE YEARS AND MORE, SORR. 485 CARDIF

SORROW
(GOES ON A BIT RUEFULLY, AS IF OPPRESSED BY A 188 AHWILD
SECRET SORROW)
HAS BEGUN TO TAKE A MASOCHISTIC SATISFACTION IN 215 AHWILD
HIS GREAT SORROW.
AND THE SORROW YOU PUT ON ME HAS MY BRAINS 70 ANNA
DROWNED IN GRIEF.

SORROW (CONT'D.)
HIS VOICE REACHES THE HIGHEST PITCH OF SORROW, OF 199 EJONES
DESOLATION.
AND THIS TIME IS DROWNIN' MY SORROW FOR THE 44 ELECTR
PRESIDENT GITTIN' SHOT/
SHE DOESN'T SEEM TO FEEL AS MUCH SORROW AS SHE 68 ELECTR
OUGHT.
THEY'RE NOT FUK SAILORMEN LIKE YOU AN' ME, 'LESS 106 ELECTR
WE'RE LOOKIN' FUR SORROW/
THE SORROW THAT'S AFFLICTED OUR FAMILY'S 172 ELECTR
I SUPPOSE HE'S OFF DROWNING HIS SORROW/ 302 GGBROW
(WITH AGONIZED SORROW) -- 322 GGBROW
SUDDENLY CRIES OUT IN A VOICE FULL OF OLD SORROW) 213 HA APE
(AS IF TO HIMSELF--WITH GREAT SORROW) 215 HA APE
(WITH GENTLE SORROW) YOU WERE LUCKY, HARRY. 656 ICEMAN
HOPE'S FACE FALLS--WITH GENUINE SORROW) 719 ICEMAN
CONCERNING THE INFINITE SORROW OF LIFE. 160 JOURNE
THERE IS NO LONGER ANY SORROW IN HIS EYES. 276 LAZARU
=I HAVE KNOWN MY FILL OF LIFE AND THE SORROW OF 276 LAZARU
LIVING.
THEY MUST HAVE FORGOTTEN SORROW IN THE GRAVE. 276 LAZARU
(HER VOICE, RICH WITH SORROW, EXULTANT NOW) 277 LAZARU
AS ONE WHO FROM A DISTANCE OF YEARS OF SORROW 277 LAZARU
REMEMBERS HAPPINESS.
YOU FORGET SORROW/ 300 LAZARU
YES, IN SPITE OF SORROW-- 347 LAZARU
HIS FACE EXPRESSES SORROW AND A HAPPINESS THAT 350 LAZARU
TRANSCENDS SORROW.
AND FOR YOUR EVENTUAL DELIVERANCE FROM SORROW TO 400 MARCOM
ACCEPTANCE AND PEACE.
I SHALL KNOW THE LONG SORROW OF AN EXILE AS I SAIL405 MARCOM
OVER THE GREEN WATER
IT IS THE FACE OF A WOMAN WHO HAS KNOWN REAL 407 MARCOM
SORROW AND SUFFERING.
THERE IS PEACE DEEP IN THE SEA BUT THE SURFACE IS 409 MARCOM
SORROW.
IF I WERE ASLEEP IN GREEN WATER, NO PANG COULD BE 409 MARCOM
ADDED TO MY SORROW.
WHERE THERE IS NEITHER SUN NOR WIND NOR JOY NOR 409 MARCOM
SORROW/
A QUEEN MAY NOT SORROW SAVE FOR HER KING/ 409 MARCOM
KUKACHIN WILL BE A MOTHER A MOTHER MAY NOT SORROW 410 MARCOM
SAVE FOR HER SON.
A WIFE MUST NOT SORROW SAVE FOR HER MAN. 410 MARCOM
WEEPING HEALS THE WOUNDS OF SORROW TILL ONLY THE 420 MARCOM
SCARS REMAIN
SMILE WITH INFINITE REMOTENESS UPON OUR SORROW. 435 MARCOM
SMILE AS A STAR SMILES/
SORROW BECOMES DESPAIR WHEN DEATH COMES TO THE 436 MARCOM
YOUNG, UNTIMELY.
TOO BRIEF FOR THE WISDOM OF JOY, TOO LONG FOR THE 436 MARCOM
KNOWLEDGE OF SORROW.
THE OLD SHOULD CHERISH SORROW. 437 MARCOM
I'D GIVE A KEEN OF SORROW OR HOWL AT THE MOON 76 MISBEG
YOU'VE HAD SORROW ENOUGH THIS NIGHT. 81 MISBEG
MY HEART WAS TOO BROKEN WITH SORROW. 85 MISBEG
I WAS TOO DROWNED IN SORROW BY HIS BETRAYING ME-- 86 MISBEG
I WANT TO FORGET MY SORROW. 93 MISBEG
I'LL SHOW HIM TO HIS SORROW/ 97 MISBEG
I'VE FELT ALL ALONG IT WAS THAT SORROW WAS MAKING 144 MISBEG
YOU--(SHE PAUSES--
WHAT WOMAN DOESN'T SORROW FOR THE MAN SHE LOVED 161 MISBEG
WHO HAS DIED?
(SHE PAUSES--THEN QUIETLY) HE DID NOTHING TO 161 MISBEG
BRING ME SORROW.
IF JIM TYRONE HAS DONE ANYTHING TO BRING YOU 161 MISBEG
SORROW--
IT'S THAT YOU SEE IN MY FACE, NOT SORROW. 162 MISBEG
BUT I CAN'T BEAR TO HAVE YOU ASHAMED YOU WANTED MY173 MISBEG
LOVE TO COMFORT YOUR SORROW--
THAT'S LOVE, AND I'M PROUD I'VE KNOWN THE GREAT 25 POET
SORROW AND JOY OF IT/
FOR LOUD AS YOU CRY, AND HIGH AS YOU RIDE, AND 102 POET
LITTLE YOU FEEL, MY SORROW,
AND THE SAME WORRY AND SORROW. 130 POET
ALL THE SORROW AND TROUBLE THAT'S COME ON US, 138 POET
IT WAS A GREAT SORROW TORMENTIN' ME THAT THE DUEL 142 POET
WOULD COME BETWEEN YOU.
=GIVE THEM SORROW OF HEART, THY CURSE UNTO THEM. 584 ROPE
IT'S ONLY LATER WHEN SORROW...!) 8 STRANG
YOU KNOW--GRIEF, SORROW, LOVE, FATHER-- 40 STRANG
AND SOFTENS INTO DEEP SORROW THE SHADOWY GRIMNESS 53 STRANG
OF HER EYES.
YOU'RE LIKE THE DAUGHTER OF MY SORROW/ 65 STRANG
HER SORROW OF BIRTH CONSOLING MY SORROW OF 100 STRANG
DEATH...
NO SORROW, NO TRAGIC MEMORIES... 113 STRANG
(THINKING WITH BITTER SORROW) 166 STRANG
I'VE FORGOTTEN SORROW/ 175 STRANG

SORROWFUL
HIS FACE SEEMING TO BECOME GENTLY SORROWFUL AND 257 AHWILD
OLD.
THERE IS AN EXPRESSION OF SORROWFUL FOREBODING ON 551 DAYS
HIS FACE.
THE SORROWFUL, RESIGNED. 273 LAZARU
THEY ARE ALL SEVEN IN THE SORROWFUL, RESIGNED TYPE274 LAZARU
OF OLD AGE.)
(AN AGED, SORROWFUL MAN) AND I USED TO VISIT HIM 276 LAZARU
EVERY DAY.
THAT THE DEAD ARE DEAD AGAIN AND THE SICK DIE, AND300 LAZARU
THE SAD GROW MORE SORROWFUL.
THE CRUEL, REVENGEFUL. AND THE RESIGNED, 312 LAZARU
SORROWFUL.
WHEN YOU GET YOUR SORROWFUL SPELL ON. 106 MISBEG
THIS BIG SORROWFUL WOMAN HUGGING A HAGGARD-FACED, 157 MISBEG
(SUBSIDES, BUT HIS FACE LOOKS SORROWFUL AND OLD-- 176 MISBEG
DULLY)
(TRYING TO BE SORROWFUL AND APPEALING) 168 STRANG

SORRY

SORROWFULLY
(HE SHAKES HIS HEAD SORROWFULLY.) 495 VOYAGE
SORROWIN'
(SARCASTICALLY) SORROWIN' OVER HIS LUST O' THE 216 DESIRE FLESH/
SORROWS
I MIGHT AS WELL FORGET HER AND LEAD THE PACE THAT 282 AHWILD KILLS, AND DROWN MY SORROWS/
MORE BITTER SORROWS THAN LOSING THE WOMAN ONE 657 ICEMAN LOVES BY THE HAND OF DEATH--
HE HAS SUCH A GOOD EXCUSE, HE BELIEVES, TO DROWN 101 JOURNE HIS SORROWS.
THERE ARE HARBORS AT EVERY VOYAGE-END WHERE WE 410 MARCOM REST FROM THE SORROWS OF THE SEA.

SORRY
NOW DON'T YOU GO FEELING SORRY FOR ME. 214 AHWILD
SORRY--SORRY-. LILY--DEEPLY SORRY. 224 AHWILD
I'M SO SORRY, NAT. 226 AHWILD
(THEN CONTRITELY) I'M SORRY, NAT. 233 AHWILD
I'M SORRY, ESSIE. 233 AHWILD
YOU'VE GOT EXTRAVAGANT TASTES, I'M SORRY TO SEE. 245 AHWILD
LILY--I'M SORRY--ABOUT THE FIREWORKS. 257 AHWILD
I'M SORRY, NAT--BUT HE WAS SOUND ASLEEP AND I 268 AHWILD DIDN'T HAVE THE HEART TO WAKE HIM.
YOU TALK AS IF YOU WEREN'T SORRY FOR WHAT YOU DID 270 AHWILD LAST NIGHT/
AND IMAGINE ME STANDING THERE, AND FEELING SORRY 270 AHWILD FOR YOU, LIKE A FOOL--
I'M NOT SORRY. 270 AHWILD
(WITH BITTER DESPONDENCY) I'M NOT SORRY BECAUSE 1270 AHWILD I DON'T CARE A DARN WHAT I DID.
BUT I'M NOT SORRY I TRIED IT ONCE-- 271 AHWILD
I'M SO AWFUL SORRY, DICK--HONEST I AM/ 281 AHWILD
I THOUGHT, WHEN I'M DEAD, SHE'LL BE SORRY SHE 282 AHWILD RUINED MY LIFE/
I'M SORRY--I HURT YOUR HAND. 286 AHWILD
I'VE TOLD YOU HOW SORRY HE WAS, AND HOW HE SAID 289 AHWILD HE'D NEVER TOUCH LIQUOR AGAIN.
(MOLLIFYINGLY) AY'M SORRY, MARTHY. 7 ANNA
I WAS SORRY TO LEAVE IT, HONEST/ 16 ANNA
AND I AIN'T SORRY NEITHER. 18 ANNA
AY'M SORRY, ANNA. 23 ANNA
I'M SORRY IT HAPPENED, SEE3 33 ANNA
(PASSIONATELY) SHE'D NOT BE SORRY FOR IT, I'D 38 ANNA TAKE MY OATH/
YOU TANK AY LAT HER LIFE BE MADE SORRY BY YOU LIKE 47 ANNA HER MO'DER'S VAS BY ME/
(TURNING TO HER EARNESTLY) AND AY'M SORRY FOR YOU 64 ANNA LIKE HELL HE DON'T COME.
(SCORNFULLY) SORRY/ 64 ANNA
AY'M SORRY, ANNA. 64 ANNA
(HUMBLY) AY'M SORRY, ANNA. 64 ANNA
AY MAKE YOUR MO'DER'S LIFE SORRY. 65 ANNA
AY'M SORRY FOR EVERYTANG AY DO WRONG FOR YOU, 65 ANNA ANNA.
I'M SORRY, PA. 105 BEYOND
AND YOU'RE GOIN' TO BE A'MIGHTY SORRY FOR IT IF 106 BEYOND YOU DO.
I'M SORRY, RUTH, REALLY I AM. 122 BEYOND
(BITTERLY) I S'POSE YOU'RE SORRY NOW YOU DIDN'T 125 BEYOND GO/
YOU'LL BE SORRY FOR TALKING LIKE THAT. 127 BEYOND
I WON'T NEVER BE SORRY/ 127 BEYOND
I WAS SORRY FOR IT BEFORE WE'D BEEN TOGETHER A 127 BEYOND MONTH.
I'M SORRY, LITTLE GIRL. 130 BEYOND
(APPEALINGLY) I'M SORRY, RUTH. 147 BEYOND
I'M SORRY, RUTH-- IF I SEEMED TO BLAME YOU. 156 BEYOND
I AM SORRY I HAVE TO TELL YOU THIS. 158 BEYOND
YOU MUSN'T FEEL SORRY FOR ME. 167 BEYOND
THERE AIN'T MUCH IN ALL THAT THAT'D MAKE YUH SORRY486 CARDIF TO LOSE IT, OR IS?
I'M SORRY-- 573 CROSS
JOHN, I BEGIN TO FEEL SORRY FOR YOU. 501 DAYS
GOSH, I'M SORRY I MISSED THAT/ 503 DAYS
I'M SO SORRY, LUCY. 520 DAYS
SORRY I'VE GOT TO RUN, JOHN. 525 DAYS
(BITTERLY AGAIN) I'M SORRY I CAN'T TRUST YOU, 527 DAYS LUCY.
I'M SORRY I BUTTED IN WITH A SILLY QUESTION. 534 DAYS
I'M SO DARNED SORRY, ELSA, IF I'VE-- 540 DAYS
SORRY TO BORE YOU, UNCLE. 542 DAYS
(CONFUSEDLY--HURRIEDLY) I--I DIDN'T MEAN--I'M 545 DAYS SORRY, UNCLE.
(TENSELY) I'M SORRY, FATHER. 548 DAYS
(CONFUSEDLY) I'M SORRY. 551 DAYS
I'M SORRY. 551 DAYS
I'M SORRY. 554 DAYS
(A BIT ASHAMED) SORRY. 557 DAYS
I'M SO SORRY. 563 DAYS
(SLAPPING HIM ON THE BACK) I'M SORRY FUR YE, HI. 249 DESIRE
I'M SORRY, EMMER. 510 DIFRNT
(AFTER A PAUSE) I WAS SORRY FOR IT, AFTER. 516 DIFRNT
I'M SORRY TO PUT SUCH A LOAD ON YOUR CONSCIENCE, 442 DYNAMO MR. LIGHT.
AND WHY FEEL SORRY FOR HER, ANYWAYS 454 DYNAMO
SHE'S BEEN SORRY ABOUT IT EVER SINCE. 458 DYNAMO
SORRY TO DISTURB YOUR LITTLE SNOOZE. 463 DYNAMO
TELL HER I'M SORRY FOR ACTING SO ROUGH TO HER THAT464 DYNAMO NIGHT...)
THERE'S NOTHING TO BE SCARED ABOUT OR SORRY FOR. 469 DYNAMO
THEN I WON'T BE SCARED--OR SORRY. 469 DYNAMO
I'M SORRY SHE HATED ME SO. 470 DYNAMO
OH, I'SE SORRY I EVAH WENT IN FOR DIS. 193 EJONES
I'SE SORRY/ 196 EJONES
I'M SORRY, PETER. 14 ELECTR
HE'D HAVE BEEN SORRY THE REST OF HIS LIFE IF HE 32 ELECTR HADN'T/

SORRY (CONT'D.)
I'M SORRY, FATHER-- 47 ELECTR
I'M SORRY, EZRA. 52 ELECTR
I'M SORRY I SAID THAT. 60 ELECTR
(RESENTFULLY) I'M SORRY/ 75 ELECTR
BY GOD, IF HE DARES COME HERE AGAIN, I'LL MAKE HIM 76 ELECTR DAMNED SORRY HE DID/
I'M SORRY--LOOK HERE, THEN. 80 ELECTR
I'M SORRY, HAZEL. 82 ELECTR
I WON'T PRETEND TO YOU I'M SORRY HE'S DEAD/ 86 ELECTR
HE WAS JEALOUS AND MAD AND SAID THINGS HE WAS 149 ELECTR SORRY FOR AFTER
I'M SORRY. 151 ELECTR
I'M SORRY BEING SO LONG. 162 ELECTR
I'M SORRY. 172 ELECTR
I'M SORRY. 279 GGRDHW
AND THEN I'M SO DAMN SORRY FOR THE LOT OF YOU, 286 GGRDHW
DREADFULLY SORRY, AND I FELT SORRY FOR HIM. 311 GGRDHW
I'M SORRY/ 317 GGRDHW
I AM SORRY, LITTLE CHILDREN, BUT YOUR KINGDOM IS 319 GGRDHW EMPTY.
(BITINGLY.) SORRY IF I'M KEEPING YOU UP, SPORT. 15 HUGHIE
(HE SIGHS AGAIN.) BUT I SURE AM SORRY HE'S GONE. 18 HUGHIE
+SORRY, BROTHER, BUT THERE'S NO CHANCE. 27 HUGHIE
I HAD TO FEEL SORRY FOR HIM. 31 HUGHIE
I'M SORRY I GOT SORE. 592 ICEMAN
SORRY. ADDING HAS ALWAYS BAFFLED ME. 602 ICEMAN
I'M SORRY WE HAD TO POSTPONE OUR TRIP AGAIN THIS 605 ICEMAN APRIL, PIET.
(HE CHUCKLES) I SAID, "I'M SORRY, BESS, BUT I HAD608 ICEMAN TO TAKE IT ALL IN DIMES."
I'M SORRY TO SAY SHE DISCOVERED MY MISTAKES IN 609 ICEMAN ARITHMETIC
(SPEAKS UP SHAMEFACEDLY) LISTEN, BOYS, I'S SORRY.637 ICEMAN
I'M JUST SORRY FOR YOU, MAC. 652 ICEMAN
I WAS ONLY FEELING SORRY FOR YOU. 652 ICEMAN
WELL, I HAVE TO ADMIT THAT'S TRUE, AND I'M DAMNED 660 ICEMAN SORRY ABOUT IT.
+SORRY, HICKEY.+ I'M SORRY, HICKEY.+ +WE'RE SORRY.663 ICEMAN HICKEY.+
I'M SORRY TO TELL YOU MY DEARLY BELOVED WIFE IS 663 ICEMAN DEAD.
I'M SORRY FOR RIDING YOU, LARRY, 666 ICEMAN
JEEZ, IF SHE COMMITTED SUICIDE, YUH GOT TO FEEL 669 ICEMAN SORRY FOR HICKEY, HUH?
(THEN PUZZLEDLY) BUT HOW CAN YUH BE SORRY FOR HIM669 ICEMAN
SORRY TO BE LEAVING GOOD OLD HARRY AND THE REST OF675 ICEMAN YOU. OF COURSE.
(FEELS SORRY FOR LEWIS AND TURNS ON WETJOEN-- 676 ICEMAN SARCASTICALLY)
SORRY. 677 ICEMAN
OFTEN WHEN I AM TRUNK AND KIDDING YOU I SAY I AM 677 ICEMAN SORRY I MISSED YOU, BUT NOW,
I'M SORRY, HICKEY. 693 ICEMAN
THEN SLOWLY) NO, I'M SORRY TO HAVE TO TELL YOU MY694 ICEMAN POOR WIFE WAS KILLED.
I COULDN'T HELP FEELIN' SORRY FOR DE POOR BUMS 698 ICEMAN WHEN DEY SHOWED UP TONIGHT,
I GUESS DEY FELT SORRY FOR HIM. 699 ICEMAN
SORRY I HAD TO LEAVE YOU FOR A WHILE, 704 ICEMAN
WITH THE NEIGHBOURS SHAKING THEIR HEADS AND FEELING713 ICEMAN SORRY FOR HER OUT LOUD.
I CAN'T FEEL SORRY FOR HIM. 719 ICEMAN
I AM SORRY--FOR I LOVED YOU, SIDNEY DAVIDSON--BUT 532 INZONE THIS IS THE END.
I'M SORRY, JAMIE. 37 JOURNE
I'M SORRY I SPOKE. 42 JOURNE
TELL BRIDGET I'M SORRY BUT SHE'LL HAVE TO WAIT A 62 JOURNE FEW MINUTES UNTIL MISTER TYRONE
SORRY I'M LATE. 65 JOURNE
I'M SORRY, DEAR. 75 JOURNE
(ASHAMED.) I'M SORRY. 86 JOURNE
THEY WROTE US HOW SORRY THEY WERE, 110 JOURNE
I'M SORRY IF I SOUNDED BITTER, JAMES. 112 JOURNE
I'M SORRY I REMEMBERED OUT LOUD. 114 JOURNE
(DULLY.) I'M SORRY, MAMA. 119 JOURNE
(THEN SLOWLY.) ALTHOUGH, IN A WAY, I DO FEEL SORRY157 JOURNE FOR HIM ABOUT ONE THING.
WELL, THAT MADE ME FEEL SORRY FOR FAT VIOLET, 159 JOURNE
AND SHE FELT SORRY FOR HER BECAUSE SHE DIDN'T KNOW159 JOURNE
HUG THE HELL SHE'D MAKE A
SORRY TO HEAR YOU WERE SICK. 160 JOURNE
(HE PAUSES--MISERABLY.) I'M SORRY I HIT YOU. 162 JOURNE
THEN YOU'D BE SORRY AFTERWARDS. 172 JOURNE
PLACATINGLY) I AM SORRY, GAIUS, 332 LAZARU
BUT BEFORE THAT I WANT TO TELL YOU HOW SORRY I WAS 19 MANSNS WHEN SIMON LAUGHED.
I'M SORRY TO KEEP YOU WAITING SO LONG, DEBORAH, 61 MANSNS
I'M SORRY, SARA. 64 MANSNS
I'M SORRY, JOEL. 71 MANSNS
I AM SORRY TO HAVE TO DISILLUSION YOU, MOTHER, 98 MANSNS
I'M SORRY, MOTHER. 111 MANSNS
I'M SORRY. 131 MANSNS
SORRY TO HAVE KEPT YOU WAITING, MR. TENARD. 151 MANSNS
I'M SORRY IF I HURT YOU, BUT I HAD TO MAKE YOU-- 165 MANSNS
I AM SORRY IF I HURT YOU. 184 MANSNS
I DON'T KNOW--I MEAN, I'M SORRY BUT--YOU SEE I 368 MARCOM PROMISED SOMEONE I'D NEVER--
I'M SORRY TO SEE YOU GO, BUT IT'S THE BEST THING 7 MISBEG FOR YOU.
HE'S DONE A LOT OF MAD THINGS, WHEN HE WAS THAT 34 MISBEG WAY, HE WAS SORRY FOR AFTER.
I'M SORRY I DIDN'T GIVE HIM THAT KICK. 66 MISBEG
AND I'LL PLAY A JOKE ON HIM YET THAT'LL MAKE HIM 83 MISBEG SORRY HE--
I'M DAMNED SORRY. 102 MISBEG
I'M SORRY, FATHER. 121 MISBEG
I'M SORRY I WAS SO STUPID AND DIDN'T SEE-- 141 MISBEG

SORRY

SORRY (CONT'D.)
YOU'D BE SORRY. 145 MISBEG
SORRY. 151 MISBEG
GOD, I'M SORRY JOSIE, BUT IT'S YOUR OWN FAULT FOR 168 MISBEG
LETTING ME--
I'M SORRY TO INTERRUPT YOU WHEN YOU'RE SO BUSY, 16 POET
I AM SORRY THEY ARE DEAD AND CANNOT KNOW YOU. 83 POET
(HASTILY.) BUT WHAT I WANT TO TELL YOU IS I AM 90 POET
SORRY IT HAPPENED, SARA.
I'M SORRY I NEVER KNEW THAT SOLDIER. 90 POET
TWO YEARS IN THE UNIVERSITY, I AM SORRY TO SAY, 17 STRANG
((I'M SORRY, FATHER/... 27 STRANG
I'M SORRY BUT I'M IN NO POSITION TO SAY. 38 STRANG
BUT THERE'S NOTHING TO BE TERRIBLY SORRY ABOUT/ 69 STRANG
I'M TERRIBLY SORRY/ 69 STRANG
I FELT A BIT SORRY FOR MYSELF AT THEIR WEDDING... 78 STRANG
I'M SO DAMN SORRY/ 83 STRANG
I'M SORRY, NED. 96 STRANG
BUT NEITHER AM I SORRY....) 98 STRANG
THERE'S NOTHING TO BE SORRY ABOUT THAT I CAN 99 STRANG
DISCOVER/
I MEAN--SORRY--IS HARDLY THE RIGHT WORD--HARDLY-- 99 STRANG
IS IT.
I'M SORRY, MARSDEN. 99 STRANG
HE'LL BE SORRY FOR IT SOME DAY AFTER SHE--(HE 101 STRANG
GULPS) WELL--(HE GOES.)
I'M SORRY/... 106 STRANG
SORRY. 122 STRANG
(HEARTILY) NOTHING TO BE SORRY ABOUT, OLD MAN. 122 STRANG
MUCH AS I HATE THIS MAN I CAN'T HELP FEELING 126 STRANG
SORRY...
I'M SORRY. 145 STRANG
SORRY. 152 STRANG
(RESENTFULLY) I'M SORRY. 161 STRANG
(GENTLY) I'M SORRY YOU'RE UNHAPPY, NINA. 167 STRANG
NO, NINA--SORRY--BUT I CAN'T HELP YOU. 174 STRANG
(STEPS QUICKLY TO HER SIDE) I'M SORRY, NINA, BUT 179 STRANG
I WARNED YOU NOT TO MEDDLE.
I'M SO DAMNED SORRY/ 183 STRANG
SORRY TO DISTURB YOU. 188 STRANG
WHY SHOULDN'T THEY BE SINCERELY SORRYS 190 STRANG
I'M SORRY-- 194 STRANG
I'M DAMNED SORRY/ 194 STRANG
SORRY--YOU'RE RIGHT, MOTHER--DAD WOULD FEEL AS IF 194 STRANG
I'D HIT HIM--
I'M SORRY. 452 WELDED
I'M SORRY-- 482 WELDED

SORT
BUT STARING AT THE LETTER WITH A SORT OF 208 AHWILD
FASCINATED DREAD.
BECAUSE IT SEEMED SORT OF A SNEAKING TRICK, 214 AHWILD
I LIKE TO FEEL I'M A SORT OF SECOND MOTHER TO THEM214 AHWILD
AND HELPING THEM TO GROW UP
ESSIE--STOPS SORT OF EMBARRASSED ABOUT COMING-- 223 AHWILD
WHEN SUDDENLY I HEARD A SORT OF GASP FROM BEHIND 230 AHWILD
ME--LIKE THIS--*HELP*--
THAT'S JUST THE SORT OF DAMNED FOOL THING HE MIGHT267 AHWILD
DO TO SPITE MURIEL.
BUT, HELL, WITH RICHARD I ALWAYS GET SORT OF 268 AHWILD
ASHAMED OF MYSELF.
I WAS SORT OF FORGETTING THAT, WASN'T IS 296 AHWILD
YOU SORT OF FORGET THE MOON WAS THE SAME WAY BACK 297 AHWILD
THEN--AND EVERYTHING.
I DO FEEL SORT OF--NUTTY, TONIGHT. 28 ANNA
(WITH A SORT OF DUMB, UNCOMPREHENDING ANGUISH) 68 ANNA
(FILLED WITH A SORT OF BEWILDERED FOREBODING) 76 ANNA
YOU'RE FITTED FOR THAT SORT OF THING--JUST AS I 83 BEYOND
AIN'T.
HE DOES SEEM SORT O' GLUM AND OUT OF SORTS. 97 BEYOND
I'VE BEEN FEELING SORT OF AWKWARD EVER SINCE I'VE 134 BEYOND
BEEN HOME.
(VAGUELY) I'LL WRITE, OR SOMETHING OF THAT SORT. 149 BEYOND
IT MUST BE HARD ON HER--THIS SORT OF THING--WELL--542 CROSS
(QUICKLY) BUT NOT THE IGNORANT, BIGOTED SORT. 510 DAYS
PLEASE UNDERSTAND.
THAT SORT OF SQUELCHED ME. 520 DAYS
HE KNEW THAT THIS FRIEND WAS CONTINUALLY HAVING 537 DAYS
AFFAIRS OF THIS SORT AND THAT
(HIS FACE GROWING FULL OF JOYOUS PRIDE AND A SORT 234 DESIRE
OF RELIGIOUS ECSTASY)
I AIN'T LIKE THAT SORT. 497 DIFRNT
(THEN FROWNING) BUT DON'T LET'S TALK ABOUT THAT 497 DIFRNT
SORT OF AUCTIONS.
I WASN'T EXPECTIN' NOTHIN' O' THAT SORT. 515 DIFRNT
THEM SORT O' THINGS OUGHT TO BE KEPT AMONG MEN. 515 DIFRNT
IT SORT O' BUSTS EVERYTHIN' TO BITS FOR ME-- 546 DIFRNT
I WAS ONLY SORT OF KIDDIN' ANYWAY-- 546 DIFRNT
(GRINNING) I WON'T PRETEND I'M THE SORT OF HERO 13 ELECTR
THAT WANTS TO GO BACK, EITHER.
BRANT'S SORT OF QUEER FUR A NAME. 20 ELECTR
AFTER HE'S THROUGH COLLEGE, BILLY MUST STUDY FOR A258 GGBROW
PADESSION OF SOME SORT.
(HE STARES BEFORE HIM IN A SORT OF TRANCE, 269 GGBROW
(HE LAUGHS WITH A SORT OF DIABOLICAL, IRONICAL 273 GGBROW
GLEE NOW, AND STARTS TO GO OUT.)
(THEN ADVANCING TO THE TABLE WITH A SORT 294 GGBROW
DIRECTLY UNDER IT ON A SORT OF STAND IS THE MASK 306 GGBROW
OF DION.
(AS HE RECOILS WITH A SORT OF GUILT--LAUGHINGLY) 308 GGBROW
A CONFUSED, INCHOATE UPROAR SWELLING INTO A SORT 207 HA APE
OF UNITY, A MEANING---
(WITH A SORT OF SAD CONTEMPT) 210 HA APE
(WITH A SORT OF RELIGIOUS EXALTATION) 214 HA APE
THERE'S A SORT OF SINCERITY IN THAT, YOU KNOW. 219 HA APE
LET US PATCH UP SOME SORT OF ARMED TRUCE. 219 HA APE
GIVE ME CREDIT FOR SOME SORT OF GROPING SINCERITY 219 HA APE
IN THAT AT LEAST.
YANK GOES ON WITH A SORT OF FURIOUS EXALTATION) 253 HA APE

SORT (CONT'D.)
THE SORT OF GUY HE'D LIKE TO BE IF HE COULD TAKE A 28 HUGHIE
CHANCE.
I GUESS HE SAW ME LIKE A SORT OF DREAM GUY, 28 HUGHIE
I GUESS HE LIVED A SORT OF DOUBLE LIFE 28 HUGHIE
IRRITINGLY, BUT SHOWING HE IS COMFORTED AT HAVING 33 HUGHIE
MADE SOME SORT OF CONTACT.)
I WAS STARED TO THEM--AS A DISGUISE, SORT OF. 588 ICEMAN
HE GOES ON IN A SORT OF FURIOUS DESPERATION. 660 ICEMAN
HE BENDS DOWN AND REACHES OUT HIS HAND SORT O' 519 INZONE
SCARED-LIKE.
SHE USES NO ROUGE OR ANY SORT OF MAKE-UP. 12 JOURNE
IN A GROTESQUE SORT OF MARIONETTES' COUNTRY DANCE.287 LAZARU
CALIGULA IS SQUATTING ON HIS HAMS ON A SORT OF 313 LAZARU
THRONE-CHAIR OF IVORY AND GOLD.
(IN A SORT OF CHILDISH COMPLAINT) 367 LAZARU
(WITH A SORT OF BEWILDERED ANGUISH.) 189 MANSNS
IS SEATED ON A SORT OF THRONE PLACED AGAINST THE 358 MARCOM
REAR WALL.
FORMING A SORT OF SEMI-CIRCLE WITH THE THRONE AT 364 MARCOM
CENTER.
TO SORT OF CHEER UP THE PRINCESS, 403 MARCOM
HE WEARS A SIMPLE WHITE ROBE WITHOUT ADORNMENT OF 432 MARCOM
ANY SORT.
(HAROER TRIES TO MAKE SOME SORT OF DISDAINFULLY 64 MISBEG
DIGNIFIED EXIT.
SORT OF AT PEACE WITH MYSELF AND THIS LOUSY LIFE--171 MISBEG
HAVE YOU MISTAKEN THIS INN FOR THE SORT OF DIRTY 53 POET
SHEBEEN
IT IS THE SAME SORT OF PLEASURE A LOVER OF 69 POET
HORSEFLESH WOULD HAVE
ISN'T THERE SOME SORT OF COOLING DRINK I COULD GET 85 POET
YOU BEFORE YOU GOS
SHUDDERING WITH THE EFFORT TO REGAIN SOME SORT OF 128 POET
POISE.
HOPS UP AND DOWN IN A SORT OF GROTESQUE DANCE, 602 ROPE
(AWKWARDLY) I SORT OF FEEL I'M BUTTING IN. 28 STRANG
(HESITATINGLY) WELL, SORT OF. 30 STRANG
(IN A SORT OF PANIC--THINKING) 32 STRANG
I MEAN THE SORT OF LOVE SHE'D FEEL FOR AN UNCLE. 37 STRANG
(HIS SNOBBERY COMING OUT) DO YOU KNOW HIS 38 STRANG
FAMILY--WHAT SORT OF PEOPLES
AND GHOSTS OF SOME SORT ARE THE ONLY NORMAL LIFE A 49 STRANG
HOUSE HAS--
(WITH A SORT OF DULL STUPID WONDERMENT) 62 STRANG
AND POUNDS OUT A FEW WORDS WITH A SORT OF AIMLESS 67 STRANG
DESPERATION--
THAT SORT OF THING. 115 STRANG
(WITH A SORT OF PITY--THINKING) 120 STRANG
(DARRELL REMAINS, STANDING LOOKING UP THE STAIRS IN124 STRANG
A SORT OF JOYOUS STUPOR.
TENDERLY IN A SORT OF PLEADING) 145 STRANG
SHE EVEN KNOWS THE SORT OF LOVE IT IS....) 148 STRANG
AND HE BEGAN TALKING BACK TO HIM ALL THE TIME AND 153 STRANG
SORT OF GAVE HIM HIS STRENGTH
IT'S TRUE HE'S SORT OF LOST HIS GRIP IN A WAY BUT 155 STRANG
HE'S OUR BEST FRIEND.
YOU'D LIKE TO MAKE HER THE SAME SORT OF CONVENTION168 STRANG
SLAVE FOR HIM THAT I WAS FOR
NINA LETS GO OF HER WRIST AND STARES AFTER THEM IN178 STRANG
A SORT OF STUNNED STUPOR)
(THEN AFFECTIONATELY.) AND GORDON IS--WELL--SORT 179 STRANG
OF MY STEPSON, ISN'T HES
(THINKING--WITH A SORT OF TENDER, LOVING SCORN FOR 186 STRANG
HIS BOYISH NAIVETE)
(THEN WITH A SORT OF DEFIANT RELIEF) 193 STRANG
SHAW, SOMETHING EXTRAVAGANT AND FANTASTIC, THE 199 STRANG
SORT OF THING THAT ISN'T DONE.
SHE GIVES A SORT OF GASP OF RELIEF) 449 WELDED
(SHE SIGHS AGAIN, THIS TIME WITH A SORT OF RESTFUL471 WELDED
(THEN WITH A QUEER SORT OF SAVAGE TRIUMPH) 475 WELDED

SORTA
TO SURTA TALK TO AND SHOW THINGS TO, AND TEACH, 103 BEYOND
KINDA.

SURTER
I ALWAYS SORTER HOPED THEY'D HITCH UP TOGETHER 98 BEYOND
SOONER OR LATER.

SORTS
YOU'RE BOUND TO FIND ALL SORTS OF OPPORTUNITIES TO 88 BEYOND
GET ON, YOUR FATHER SAYS.
HE DULS SEEM SORT O' GLUM AND OUT OF SORTS. 97 BEYOND
HE READ ALL SORTS OF SCIENTIFIC BOOKS. 534 DAYS
HE BEGAN IMAGINING ALL SORTS OF CATASTROPHES. 536 DAYS
FOLKS WOULD BE SAYIN' ALL SORTS OF BAD THINGS IN 532 DIFRNT
NO TIME.
(SHE TURNS BACK.) I DO FEEL OUT OF SORTS THIS 17 JOURNE
MORNING.
I IMAGINED ALL SORTS OF HORRIBLE ACCIDENTS. 113 JOURNE
IN THE SAME FRENZY OF DISAPPOINTMENT, WITH ALL 366 LAZARU
SORTS OF GROTESQUE ABUSE AND OBSCENE
HANDSHAKES AND LOUD GREETINGS OF ALL SORTS. 429 MARCOM
TO TELL THE TRUTH, MY STOMACH IS OUT OF SORTS. 36 POET

SOT
LIKKER DON'T PEAR T' SOT RIGHT. 218 DESIRE
I WISH I'D NEVER SOT EYES ON HIM/ 257 DESIRE
I'M WANTIN' T' FORGET I EVER SOT EYES ON YE/ 258 DESIRE
WELL, YOU ALWAYS WAS A SOFT, OLD-FASHIONED CRITTER,535 DIFRNT
CALEB WILLIAMS,
AND I RECKON I BE OLD-FASHIONED AND SOT IN MY 537 DIFRNT
IDEAS.

BECAUSE THEY KNOW THAT LAZY OLD SOT, 16 ELECTR
HE WOULDN'T MIND IF A GHOST SOT ON HIS LAP. 130 ELECTR

SOU'WESTER
COAT, PANTS, SOU'WESTER AND WEARS HIGH SEABOOTS.) 25 ANNA
(ENTERS, HIS OILSKINS AND SOU'WESTER GLISTENING 490 CARDIF
WITH DROPS OF WATER)

SOUL

SOU'WESTER (CONT'D.)
HE TAKES OFF HIS DRIPPING SOU'WESTER AND STANDS, 490 CARDIF
SCRATCHING HIS HEAD.
AND A YELLOW SOU'WESTER PUSHED JAUNTILY ON THE 498 DIFRNT
BACK OF HIS HEAD,
SOU'WESTERS
SOU'WESTERS, SEA-BOOTS, ETC. IN PREPARATION FOR 481 CARDIF
THE WATCH ON DECK.
SOUGHT
I SOUGHT YE AN' I FOUND YE/ 238 DESIRE
THE EFFECT SOUGHT AFTER IS A CRAMPED SPACE IN THE 207 HA APE
BOWELS OF A SHIP,
WOULD SEEM TO SMILE THE LESS, OF ALL THAT 101 POET
FLATTERED--FOLLOWED--SOUGHT, AND SUED.
A GOOD SPORT WHO IS POPULAR WITH HER OWN SEX AS 159 STRANG
WELL AS SOUGHT AFTER BY MEN.

SOUL
GOD SEND HIS SOUL TO HELL FOR THE DEVIL HE IS/ 538 'ILE
CURING THE SOUL BY MEANS OF THE SENSES, AS OSCAR 271 AHWILD
WILDE SAYS.
= AND LO MY LOVE, MINE OWN SOUL'S HEART, MORE DEAR277 AHWILD
THAN MINE OWN SOUL.
THE DESPAIR IN MY SOUL-- 279 AHWILD
THERE ISN'T A SOUL. 280 AHWILD
YOU ARE =MY LOVE, MINE OWN SOUL'S HEART, MORE DEAR287 AHWILD
THAN MINE OWN SOUL.
WOULD SEND YOUR SOUL TO THE DIVILS IN HELL IF YOU 74 ANNA
WAS LYING$
(HOLDING IT AWAY) 'TIS A CROSS WAS GIVEN ME BY MY 75 ANNA
MOTHER, GOD REST HER SOUL.
INTO HER SOUL--SLOWLY) 76 ANNA
I COULDN'T GET TO SLEEP TO SAVE MY SOUL. 147 BEYOND
I COULD CURSE GOD FROM THE BOTTOM OF MY SOUL--IF 148 BEYOND
THERE WAS A GOD/
WOULD YOU BRING HER TIRED SOUL BACK TO HIM AGAIN 565 CROSS
TO BE BRUISED AND WOUNDED$
YES, I SOLD HIM, IF YOU WILL--TO SAVE MY SOUL. 567 CROSS
THIS PLOT OF YOURS MORE SIGNIFICANT--FOR YOUR 495 DAYS
SOUL, SHALL I SAY$
IT WAS NOT FOR THE WESTERN SOUL, HE DECIDED, 503 DAYS
PROMISED HIS SOUL TO THE DEVIL-- 511 DAYS
PERHAPS, IN MY SOUL, I HATE LOVE/ 527 DAYS
IN WHICH HE FELT HE REALLY HAD GIVEN HIS SOUL TO 534 DAYS
SOME EVIL POWER.
TO THINK OF HIMSELF AS POSSESSED BY A DAMNED SOUL/535 DAYS
ONE MAY NOT GIVE ONE'S SOUL TO A DEVIL OF HATE-- 538 DAYS
AND REMAIN FOREVER SCATHELESS.
CHURCH REVEALS ABOUT THE LONGING OF YOUR OWN 545 DAYS
SOUL--
IF YOU WOULD ONLY BE HONEST WITH YOURSELF AND 558 DAYS
ADMIT THE TRUTH IN YOUR OWN SOUL
IT'S THE HATRED YOU ONCE GAVE YOUR SOUL TO WHICH 559 DAYS
SPEAKS, NOT YOU.
(PLEADINGLY) I IMPLORE YOU TO CAST THAT EVIL FROM559 DAYS
YOUR SOUL/
AND I AM AFRAID IF YOU PERSIST IN YOUR MAD DENIAL 560 DAYS
OF HIM AND YOUR OWN SOUL,
LOOK INTO YOUR SOUL AND FORCE YOURSELF TO ADMIT 560 DAYS
THE TRUTH YOU FIND THERE--
FORGIVE--THE DAMNED SOUL--OF JOHN LOVING/ 566 DAYS
BLOOD AN' BONE AN' SWEAT--ROTTED AWAY--FERTILIZIN'218 DESIRE
YE--RICHIN' YER SOUL--
LITTLE CRITTER--YE MUST'VE SWAPPED YER SOUL T' 262 DESIRE
HELL/
(WITH A TRAGIC SIGH) THERE'S NOT A LIVING SOUL 440 DYNAMO
KNOWS IT.
EVEN HER SOUL LOST TO MES... 466 DYNAMO
(DULLY) YOU SOLD YOUR SOUL TO SATAN, REUBEN. 467 DYNAMO
GOD DAMN YOU, SOUL, I GITS EVEN WID YOU YIT, 194 EJONES
SOMETIME.
I'D GIVE MY SOUL TO SEE HIS FACE WHEN HE KNOWS YOU 38 ELECTR
LOVE MARIE BRANTOME'S SON/
I'D GIVE MY SOUL TO BELIEVE THAT--BUT--I'M AFRAID/ 56 ELECTR
MAY THE SOUL OF OUR COUSIN, ADAM MANNON, REST IN 115 ELECTR
PEACE/
I MEAN THE CHANGE IN YOUR SOUL, TOO. 141 ELECTR
LITTLE BY LITTLE IT GREW LIKE MOTHER'S SOUL--AS IF141 ELECTR
YOU WERE STEALING HERS--
I LOVE YOU WITH ALL MY SOUL/ 268 GGBROW
IS THAT THE ONLY ANSWER--TO PIN MY SOUL INTO EVERY279 GGBROW
VACANT DIAPERS
(STANDS AND SINGS) WILLIAM BROWN'S SOUL LIES 294 GGBROW
MOLDERING IN THE CRIB
MAY YOU DESIGN THE TEMPLE OF MAN'S SOUL/ 299 GGBROW
AND SOUL THROWN IN/ 236 HA APE
HELL, I DIDN'T WANT TO BUY YOUR SOUL/ 26 HUGHIE
THIS SOUL IS PURGED OF GRIEF, HIS CONFIDENCE 38 HUGHIE
RESTORED.)
I HOPE HIS SOUL ROTS IN HELL, WHOEVER IT IS/ 588 ICEMAN
WHEN MAN'S SOUL ISN'T A SOW'S EAR, 590 ICEMAN
HE RAPPED AND HE RAPPED WITH A (RAP, RAP, RAP) BUT596 ICEMAN
NEVER A SOUL SEEMED IN.*
YOU'LL BE SAYING SOMETHING SOON THAT WILL MAKE YOU680 ICEMAN
VOMIT YOUR OWN SOUL
GOD DAMN YOU, STOP SHOVING YOUR ROTTEN SOUL IN MY 706 ICEMAN
LAP/
GOD REST HIS SOUL IN PEACE. 726 ICEMAN
(SNAPPING) GOD DAMN HIS YELLOW SOUL, IF HE DOESN'T726 ICEMAN
SOON,
IN LIFE, YOU WANTED TO BELIEVE EVERY MAN WAS A 34 JOURNE
KNAVE WITH HIS SOUL FOR SALE,
EXCEPT THAT ONE DAY LONG AGO I FOUND I COULD NO 93 JOURNE
LONGER CALL MY SOUL MY OWN.
I DIDN'T MEET A SOUL. 131 JOURNE
THE SOUL LET GO/ 278 LAZARU
THE SOUL OF THE RECURRING SEASONS, 307 LAZARU
AND MEN SHALL KEEP ON IN PANIC NAILING MAN-S SOUL 343 LAZARU
TO THE CROSS OF THEIR FEAR

SOUL (CONT'D.)
WITH HIS SLAVE HE CALLS IMMORTAL SOUL/ 352 LAZARU
LIKE THE FLIGHT OF HIS SOUL BACK INTO THE WOMB OF 371 LAZARU
INFINITY)
IT IS THE SOUL, STARING INTO THE MIRROR OF ITSELF, 12 MANSNS
I HAVE MY HONOR AND IT'S A TRUE WOMAN'S HONOR THAT 18 MANSNS
YOU'D GIVE YOUR SOUL TO KNOW/
FOR THE EXPORT OF HIS SOUL, AND LIFE WAS 30 MANSNS
NEEDLESSLY DELAYING HIM.
UPON MY SOUL, I COULD NOT CREDIT THE EVIDENCE OF 31 MANSNS
MY OWN EYES/
UPON MY SOUL, DEBORAH, I---ER--- 38 MANSNS
A LITTLE REST HERE EACH DAY WILL RESTORE THE 106 MANSNS
SOUL--THE CHANGE I SO BADLY NEED--
=BUILD THEE MORE STATELY MANSIONS, O MY SOUL, AS 148 MANSNS
THE SWIFT SEASONS ROLL.
IF IT'S A WHORE YOU LOVE ME TO BE, THEN I AM IT, 158 MANSNS
BODY AND SOUL.
HE KNOWS SHE'LL NEVER HAVE STRENGTH TO CLAIM HER 171 MANSNS
BODY OR SOUL HER OWN AGAIN/
DREAMING POET'S SOUL IN COMMON WITH THAT FEMALE 178 MANSNS
ANIMALS
AND I SHALL BE FREE TO BE SARA'S, BODY AND SOUL. 183 MANSNS
TOWARD EVERY SECRET PRIVATE CORNER OF MY SOUL. 184 MANSNS
THE DREAMER WITH A TOUCH OF THE POET IN HIS SOUL, 191 MANSNS
AND THE HEART OF A BOY/
YOUR SOUL/ DEAD AND BURIED/ 375 MARCOM
DON'T SELL YOUR SOUL FOR NOTHING. 375 MARCOM
COULD HE BELIEVE THIS YOUTH POSSESSES THAT THING 379 MARCOM
CALLED SOUL
(SUDDENLY TO MARCO) HAVE YOU AN IMMORTAL SOUL$ 379 MARCOM
WHY, IF YOU DIDN'T HAVE A SOUL, WHAT WOULD HAPPEN 379 MARCOM
WHEN YOU DIE$
WELL, THEN, IF YOU WILL CONFESS THAT YOUR SOUL IS 380 MARCOM
A STUPID INVENTION OF YOUR
BUT FORGETTING THE SOUL SIDE OF IT, I'VE GOT TO 380 MARCOM
EAT.
YOU SHALL TELL ME ABOUT YOUR SOUL 380 MARCOM
OBSERVATIONS AND COMMENTS OF YOUR SOUL ON THE 382 MARCOM
EAST.
AND HE HAS A SOUL/ 387 MARCOM
HE HAS NOT EVEN A MORTAL SOUL, HE HAS ONLY AN 387 MARCOM
ACQUISITIVE INSTINCT.
YANG-CHAU USED TO HAVE A SOUL, HE SAID. 387 MARCOM
AND HIS SOUL MAY BE BORN AND THAT WILL MAKE A VERY388 MARCOM
INTERESTING STUDY--
DO YOU STILL POSSESS YOUR IMMORTAL SOUL, MARCO 393 MARCOM
POLO$
DID YOU CONQUER HIS IMMORTAL SOUL$ 395 MARCOM
THEY'VE HAD IT UNDER THEIR NOSES FOR YEARS WITHOUT395 MARCOM
A SINGLE SOUL EVER HAVING
YOU HAVEN'T YET PROVED YOU HAVE AN IMMORTAL SOUL/ 396 MARCOM
AND THAT SOMETHING MUST BE HIS HONOR'S SOUL, MUST 397 MARCOM
IT NOT$
I WILL BEAR WITNESS HE HAS A SOUL. 397 MARCOM
TELL ME--ALL YOU CAN TELL--PARTICULARLY WHAT HIS 401 MARCOM
IMMORTAL SOUL IS LIKE/
(WITH IMPOTENT ANGER) HE SHALL PRAY FOR HIS SOUL 401 MARCOM
ON HIS KNEES BEFORE YOUR
WEARING THE SELF-ASSURANCE OF AN IMMORTAL SOUL AND401 MARCOM
HIS NEW ADMIRAL'S UNIFORM/
DOES YOUR IMMORTAL SOUL$ 413 MARCOM
OR A MAN'S--A MAN WHO HAS A SOUL, 414 MARCOM
(INTENSELY) I IMPLORED AN OX TO SEE MY SOUL/ 415 MARCOM
THERE IS NO SOUL EVEN IN YOUR LOVE, WHICH IS NO 416 MARCOM
BETTER THAN A MATING OF SWINE/
MY SOUL HE HAS ALREADY POSSESSED. 423 MARCOM
AND DID THE LITTLE FLOWER SAVE HIS IMMORTAL SOUL$ 423 MARCOM
YOU WERE RIGHT ABOUT HIS SOUL. 424 MARCOM
IS THIS THE PEACE OF THE SOUL$ 425 MARCOM
SOUL WITH IT. 434 MARCOM
ONE IN IT HAD SPIRIT, GOD REST HER SOUL. 17 MISBEG
HELL ROAST HIS SOUL FOR SAYING IT. 18 MISBEG
WHO'D SELL HIS SOUL FOR A PRICE. 82 MISBEG
BUT ALL THE SAME THERE'S THINGS BESIDES YOUR 89 MISBEG
BEAUTIFUL SOUL HE FEELS DRAWN TO,
I HAVE A BEAUTIFUL SOUL, YOU MEAN$ 118 MISBEG
THAT'S FOR MY BEAUTIFUL SOUL. 119 MISBEG
EVER SINCE YOU SAID YOU LOVED MY BEAUTIFUL SOUL. 126 MISBEG
I FEEL HER IN THE MOONLIGHT, HER SOUL WRAPPED IN 152 MISBEG
IT LIKE A SILVER MANTLE, AND I
THAT IT WAS A DAMNED SOUL COMING TO ME IN THE 161 MISBEG
MOONLIGHT.
IT'S THE PAIN OF GUILT IN MY SOUL. 138 POET
MY SOUL PEACE AND COMFORT SO I WOULDN'T FEEL THE 138 POET
THREE OF US WERE DAMNED.
AND IT ISN'T HALF OF ME THAT'S IN IT BUT ALL OF 141 POET
ME, BODY AND SOUL.
WITH ALL MY HEART AND SOUL/ 147 POET
AND YOU CAN'T CALL YOUR SOUL YOUR OWN ANY MORE, 149 POET
LET ALONE YOUR BODY.
HE WAS SOBBING LIKE A SOUL IN HELL-- 165 POET
SPEAKIN' AV THE DEPARTED, MAY HIS SOUL ROAST IN 173 POET
HELL.
GOD REST HIS SOUL IN THE FLAMES AV TORMENT/ 177 POET
I'LL PRETIND TO MAKE FRIENDS WITH HIM, GOD ROAST 590 ROPE
HIS SOUL/
HIS WORDS ARISING FROM THE TOMB OF A SOUL IN PUFFS 16 STRANG
OF ASHES...))
((THEY'VE KILLED HER SOUL DOWN THERE/...)) 28 STRANG
BUT STRONG ENOUGH FOR THIS LADYLIKE SOUL....)) 36 STRANG
(THINKING IN A PANIC) ((SHE SNEAKED INTO MY SOUL 42 STRANG
TO SPY/...))
I FEEL IT HAS LOST ITS SOUL AND GROWN RESIGNED TO 49 STRANG
DOING WITHOUT IT.
SOUL--AS THE DEAD SO OFTEN LEAVE THE LIVING-- 51 STRANG
MOSQUITOES OF THE SOUL... 52 STRANG

SOUL

SOUL (CONT'D.)
HER BIG DARK EYES ARE GRIM WITH THE PRISONER-PAIN 53 STRANG
OF A WALLED-IN SOUL.
(DRYLY) FOR MY SOUL, DOCTORS 81 STRANG
GORDON REALLY SHOULD GET BEATEN TODAY--FOR THE 175 STRANG
GOOD OF HIS SOUL. HINA,
TELL YOU TO A LIVING SOUL--ABOVE ALL NOT TO 178 STRANG
GORDON/
A PURE AND SIMPLE SOUL/ 183 STRANG
OH, KELLY, I LOVE YOU WITH ALL MY SOUL/ 446 WELDED
THEN GRASPING AT SOME LAST INMOST THING WHICH 453 WELDED
MAKES ME ME--MY SOUL--
THEN I CAN REALLY GIVE YOU MY SOUL-- 486 WELDED

SOUL'S
A LITTLE COWARD THAT'S AFRAID TO SAY HER SOUL'S 216 AHWILD
HER OWN,
TO SAY HER SOUL'S HER OWN 273 AHWILD
* AND LO MY LOVE, MINE OWN SOUL'S HEART, MORE DEAR277 AHWILD
THAN MINE OWN SOUL,
YOU ARE MY LOVE, MINE OWN SOUL'S HEART, MORE DEAR287 AHWILD
THAN MINE OWN SOUL,
LIKE A PROMISE OF GOD'S PEACE IN THE SOUL'S DARK 153 MISBEG
SADNESS.

SOULLESS
SOULLESS TRADER IN THE SLAVE MARKET OF LIFE YOU 178 MANSNS
HAVE BECOME--/

SOULS
WHEN IT IS THEIR COURAGE TO POSSESS THEIR OWN 542 DAYS
SOULS WHICH IS DEAD--AND STINKING/
YOU LOSE A FREE NIGGER, DAMN YO' SOULS/ 198 EJONES
(GRIMLY) DON'T YOU BELIEVE IN SOULS ANY MORE$ 141 ELECTR
THAT'S THE ONLY WAY TO WASH THE GUILT OF OUR 152 ELECTR
MOTHER'S BLOOD FROM OUR SOULS/
ESCAPE OVER YOUR PROSTRATE SOULS/ 321 GGBROW
THEY'LL SELL THEIR SOULS/ 74 JOURNE
IN THIS SAFE HAVEN, WHERE WE COULD REPOSE OUR 103 MANSNS
SOULS IN FANTASY--
GOD OF THE HEAVEN, BE IN OUR SOULS/ 376 MARCOM
YOU CAN'T CONSIDER SOULS WHEN YOU'RE DEALING WITH 395 MARCOM
SOLDIERS, CAN YOUR
AND LOOK LIVELY, DAMN YOUR LAZY SOULS/ 403 MARCOM
WELL, I DON'T KNOW MUCH ABOUT LADIES' SOULS-- 118 MISBEG
FROM THE LUST FOR POWER AND SAVING OUR SOULS BY 85 POET
BEING CONTENT WITH LITTLE.
IN WHICH OUR SOULS HAVE BEEN SCRAPED CLEAN OF 199 STRANG
IMPURE FLESH
AND WE'LL TORTURE AND TEAR, AND CLUTCH FOR EACH 488 WELDED
OTHER'S SOULS/

SOUND

(THERE IS THE SOUND OF SUBDUED SOBBING FROM THE 543 'ILE
DOOR IN THE REAR.
A MOMENT LATER THERE IS THE SOUND OF SCUFFLING 550 'ILE
FEET OUTSIDE
(THE SOUND OF THE BELL COMES FROM THE REAR OF THE 200 AHWILD
HOUSE.
THY SHARP SIGHS DIVIDE MY FLESH AND SPIRIT WITH 205 AHWILD
SOFT SOUND---*
YOU SOUND AS IF YOU'D LOST YOUR LAST FRIEND/ 208 AHWILD
(AT THE SOUND OF VOICES FROM THE FRONT PARLOR, 208 AHWILD
ONE MORE SOUND OUT OF YOU, YOUNG MAN AND YOU'LL 229 AHWILD
LEAVE THE TABLE/
(THEY AT A SOUND FROM THE FRONT PARLOR--WITH A 268 AHWILD
SIGH)
I'M SORRY, NAT--BUT HE WAS SOUND ASLEEP AND I 268 AHWILD
DIDN'T HAVE THE HEART TO WAKE HIM.
(THERE IS A SOUND OF SOMEONE ON THE PORCH 272 AHWILD
THE SOUND OF THE FRONT DOOR BEING OPENED AND SHUT 292 AHWILD
IS HEARD.
SOUND FROM DIS SIDE. 29 ANNA
(THERE IS A MUFFLED SOUND OF OARS IN OARLOCKS.) 29 ANNA
COMES THE SOUND OF STEAMERS' WHISTLES AND THE 41 ANNA
PUFFING SNORT OF THE DONKEY
(AT THE SOUND OF HER NAME ANNA HAS TURNED ROUND TO 53 ANNA
THEM.
(RAISING HER HEAD AT THE SOUND OF HIS VOICE--WITH 59 ANNA
EXTREME MOCKING BITTERNESS)
AS SHE HEARS THE SOUND OF HEAVY FOOTSTEPS ON THE 68 ANNA
DECK OUTSIDE.
HEARING NO SOUND, HE CLOSES THE DOOR BEHIND HIM 68 ANNA
AND COMES FORWARD TO THE TABLE.
(THEY ARE INTERRUPTED BY THE SOUND OF A LOUD KNOCK123 BEYOND
AT THE KITCHEN DOOR)
AS TO A SOUND HEARD IN A DREAM. 128 BEYOND
IF DON'T SOUND WELL FOR ME, GETTING OVER THINGS SO134 BEYOND
EASY.
UH, EVERYTHING'LL BE UN A SOUND FOOTING AFTER 134 BEYOND
HARVEST.
THERE IS A SOUND FROM THE OPEN BEDROOM DOOR IN THE145 BEYOND
REAR
AND I FEEL AS IF I COULD SLEEP NOW--(CHEERFULLY) 151 BEYOND
A GOOD, SOUND, RESTFUL SLEEP.
(WITH ASPERITY) AND IS THAT ALL YOU WOKE ME OUT 151 BEYOND
OF A SOUND SLEEP FOR.
THE SOUND OF FOOTSTEPS ON THE PATH IS HEARD--THEN 153 BEYOND
A SHARP RAP ON THE DOOR.
THE SOUND OF ANDREW'S AND ROBERT'S VOICES COMES 154 BEYOND
FROM THE BEDROOM.
WE CAN GET THE FARM WORKING ON A SOUND BASIS ONCE 156 BEYOND
MORE.
THEY BURY SOMEBODY--PY CHIMINY CHRISTMAS, I TINK 456 CARIBE
SO FROM WAY IT SOUND.
(THE SOUND OF WOMEN'S VOICES CAN BE HEARD TALKING 461 CARIBE
AND LAUGHING.)
AND REMAINS FOR A MOMENT LISTENING FOR SOME SOUND 562 CROSS
FROM ABOVE.
THE SOUND OF THE WIND AND SEA SUDDENLY CEASES AND 570 CROSS
THERE IS A HEAVY SILENCE.

SOUND (CONT'D.)
(THE SOUND OF A DOOR BEING HEAVILY SLAMMED IS 571 CROSS
HEARD FROM WAY DOWN IN THE HOUSE.)
YOU SOUND DOWNHEARTED, JOHN. 496 DAYS
(MOCKINGLY) MUST SOUND LIKE MY OLD LETTERS TO 543 DAYS
YOU, UNCLE.
(HEARING A SOUND FROM BELOW) 547 DAYS
(AS A SOUND OF VOICES COMES FROM LEFT, REAR) 221 DESIRE
EVERY SOUND WITHIN THE HOUSE. 228 DESIRE
I'M SOUND 'N' TOUGH AS HICKORY/ 232 DESIRE
SLEEPIN' SOUND. 263 DESIRE
HE'D OUGHT'T WAKE UP WITH A GNASHIN' APPETITE, 263 DESIRE
THE SOUND WAY HE'S SLEEPIN'.
(HEARS THE SOUND OF FEET OUTSIDE) 267 DESIRE
SLOW STEPS SOUND FROM THE PATH IN FRONT OF THE 514 DIFRNT
HOUSE.
THAT DON'T SOUND LIKE YOU. 522 DIFRNT
I'M AS ABLE AND SOUND AS EVER. 538 DIFRNT
(FROM THE FIFE HOUSE COMES THE SOUND OF A VICTROLA426 DYNAMO
STARTING A JAZZ RECORD.)
REUBEN QUIVERS BUT NOT A SOUND COMES FROM HIS 448 DYNAMO
LIPS.
THE SOUND OF WIND AND RAIN SWEEPING DOWN ON THE 454 DYNAMO
TOWN FORM THE HILLS IS HEARD.)
SHE'S CAUGHT THE SOUND...) 458 DYNAMO
(THEN SHE HALF TURNS AROUND AT SOME SOUND IN THE 459 DYNAMO
ROOM BEHIND HER--
THE AIR IS FULL OF SOUND. 473 DYNAMO
AS IF THE SOUND OF HIS VOICE HYPNOTIZED HER 476 DYNAMO
IT'S AS IF THAT SOUND WAS COOL WATER WASHING OVER 476 DYNAMO
MY BODY/
AND THIS CRY DIES INTO A SOUND THAT IS LIKE THE 488 DYNAMO
CROONING OF A BABY AND MERGES
(JONES STARTS AT THE SOUND. 184 EJONES
YET THIS SOUND SERVES BUT TO INTENSIFY THE 187 EJONES
IMPRESSION OF THE FOREST'S RELENTLESS
SOUND LOUDER, SEEM LIKE. 188 EJONES
SOUND OF THE SHOT, THE REASSURING FEEL OF THE 190 EJONES
REVOLVER IN HIS HAND.
WHAT'S DAT ODDER QUEER CLICKETY SOUND I HEARS 191 EJONES
SCENE, THERE IS SILENCE, BROKEN EVERY FEW SECONDS 191 EJONES
BY A QUEER, CLICKING SOUND.
SOUND LIKE--SOUND LIKE-- FO' GOD SAKE, SOUND LIKE 191 EJONES
SOME NIGGER WAS SHOOTIN' CRAP/
SOUND CLOSE? 191 EJONES
SHO' GITS NEARER FROM DE SOUND. 191 EJONES
THEY SWING THEIR PICKS, THEY SHOVEL, BUT NOT A 194 EJONES
SOUND COMES FROM THEIR LABOR.
BUT INCREASED IN VOLUME OF SOUND AND RAPIDITY OF 195 EJONES
BEAT.)
DAT BEGIN TO SOUND HA'NTED, TOO. 196 EJONES
HERE IS A GOOD FIELD HAND, SOUND IN WIND AND LIMB 197 EJONES
AS THEY CAN SEE.
(A SOUND COMES FROM THE FOREST. 203 EJONES
(THE REPORTS OF SEVERAL RIFLES SOUND FROM THE 203 EJONES
FOREST.
BUT STILL SOUND AND HALE. 6 ELECTR
THE SOUND OF SETH'S THIN, AGED BARITONE MOURNFULLY 43 ELECTR
SINGING.
THERE IS THE SOUND OF FOOTSTEPS. 46 ELECTR
SHE STANDS LISTENING FOR SOME SOUND FROM THE BED. 58 ELECTR
THERE IS A SOUND OF VOICES FROM INSIDE THE HOUSE, 67 ELECTR
(AT A SOUND FROM INSIDE THE HOUSE) 76 ELECTR
FROM INSIDE THE HOUSE COMES THE SOUND OF ORIN'S 78 ELECTR
VOICE CALLING SHARPLY *MOTHER/
THE SOUND OF THE SINGING SEEMS TO STRIKE A 102 ELECTR
RESPONSIVE CHORD IN HIS BRAIN.
A MOMENT LATER THERE IS THE SOUND OF SPLINTERING 114 ELECTR
WOOD
I'M TERRIFIED AT EVERY SOUND. 119 ELECTR
OH, I KNOW IT MUST SOUND FUNNY HEARING ME TALK 146 ELECTR
LIKE THAT.
(THERE IS NO ANSWER BUT THE SOUND OF THE STUDY 167 ELECTR
DOOR BEING SHUT.
FROM THE CASINO COMES THE SOUND OF THE SCHOOL 257 GGBROW
QUARTET RENDERING *SWEET ADELINE*
FOR A MOMENT THE FAINT SOUND OF THE MUSIC AND THE 259 GGBROW
LAPPING OF THE WAVES IS HEARD.
AND ESTABLISHED A SOUND BUSINESS. 260 GGBROW
AGAIN THERE IS SILENCE EXCEPT FOR THE SOUND OF THE262 GGBROW
LAPPING WAVES.
I LOVE THE SOUND OF IT/ 263 GGBROW
YOU WAS CAMPING ON MY STEPS, SOUND ASLEEP. 278 GGBROW
THERE IS A SOUND OF HEAVY, HURRYING FOOTSTEPS ON 292 GGBROW
THE STAIRS.
AT THIS SOUND, BROWN STARTS. 314 GGBROW
YOU SOUND AS CRAZY AS HE DID--WHEN YOU LAUGH/ 316 GGBROW
THE SOUND OF HIS FEET LEAPING DOWN THE STAIRS, 318 GGBROW
FIVE AT A TIME, CAN BE HEARD.
(THERE IS A SOUND OF A DOOR BEING PUSHED VIOLENTLY319 GGBROW
OPEN.
THE SOUND OF THE WAVES AND OF DISTANT DANCE MUSIC.323 GGBROW
THE CURTAIN RISES ON A TUMULT OF SOUND. 207 HA APE
HER SAILS STRETCHING ALOFT ALL SILVER AND WHITE, 214 HA APE
NOT A SOUND ON THE DECK,
(EIGHT BELLS SOUND, MUFFLED. 217 HA APE
WHEN A LEOPARD COMPLAINS OF ITS SPOTS, IT MUST 220 HA APE
SOUND RATHER GROTESQUE.
THE GORILLA TURNS HIS EYES BUT MAKES NO SOUND OR 251 HA APE
MOVE.
(AT THE SOUND OF HIS VOICE THE CHATTERING DIES 251 HA APE
AWAY INTO AN ATTENTIVE SILENCE.
BY THE SOUND OF THAT SURFACE CAR. 25 HUGHIE
(AT A SOUND FROM THE HALL HE TURNS AS DON PARRITT 585 ICEMAN
APPEARS IN THE DOORWAY.
AND THE SOUND OF A MAN'S AND WOMAN'S ARGUING 615 ICEMAN
VOICES.)
HELL, THIS BEGINS TO SOUND LIKE A DAMNED SERMON 622 ICEMAN

SOUNDS

SOUND (CONT'D.)
I GUESS THAT DID SOUND TOO MUCH LIKE A LOUSY 639 ICEMAN
PREACHER.
SHE WAS SOUND ASLEEP. 715 ICEMAN
LISTENING FOR THE SOUND HE KNOWS IS COMING FROM 721 ICEMAN
THE BACKYARD OUTSIDE THE WINDOW.
THE SOUND OF MARGIE'S AND PEARL'S VOICES IS HEARD 724 ICEMAN
FROM THE HALL.
(HE HALF RISES FROM HIS CHAIR JUST AS FROM OUTSIDE726 ICEMAN
THE WINDOW COMES THE SOUND OF
(HE IS INTERRUPTED BY THE SOUND OF SOMETHING 523 INZONE
HITTING AGAINST THE PORT SIDE OF
AN EVEN IF THESE LETTERS OF HIS DO SOUND ALL 529 INZONE
RIGHT
THE READING, MAKES A MUFFLED SOUND LIKE A SOB 530 INZONE
(AT THE SOUND OF THE NAME SMITHY, 530 INZONE
HIS SHOULDERS CONTINUE TO HEAVE SPASMODICALLY BUT 532 INZONE
HE MAKES NO FURTHER SOUND.
SHE SPRINGS TO HER FEET, AS IF SHE WANTED TO RUN 42 JOURNE
AWAY FROM THE SOUND.
HE SEEMS TO BE LISTENING FOR SOME SOUND FROM 51 JOURNE
UPSTAIRS.
(DULLY.) THAT DIDN'T SOUND LIKE GLAD TIDINGS. 73 JOURNE
AN EARLY DUSK DUE TO THE FOG WHICH HAS ROLLED IN 97 JOURNE
FROM THE SOUND AND IS LIKE A
IT'S JUST AN UGLY SOUND. 99 JOURNE
THEN STOPS IN THE DOORWAY AS SHE HEARS THE SOUND 107 JOURNE
OF VOICES FROM THE FRONT PATH.
WHY IS IT FOG MAKES EVERYTHING SOUND SO SAD AND 121 JOURNE
LOST, I WONDER?
THEN HE STARTS AS HE HEARS A SOUND FROM UPSTAIRS--136 JOURNE
WITH DREAD.)
THEN TYRONE STOPS, LISTENING TO A SOUND UPSTAIRS.)152 JOURNE
BUT STRAINING OUR EARS LISTENING FOR THE SLIGHTEST152 JOURNE
SOUND.
NO SOUND OF MAN. 153 JOURNE
FROM WITHIN COMES THE SOUND OF FLUTES AND DANCE 281 LAZARU
MUSIC.
THEIR VOICES SOUND THICK AND HARSH AND ANIMAL-LIKE287 LAZARU
WITH ANGER AS THEY MUTTER AND
SWELLING UP AND DOWN LIKE THE SOUND OF AN ORGAN 289 LAZARU
FROM A DISTANT CHURCH)
AT THE SAME TIME THE DISTANT SOUND OF EXULTANT 304 LAZARU
MUSIC.
(THE CHORUSED WORD BEATS DOWN ALL SOUND INTO A 305 LAZARU
STRICKEN SILENCE.
BEATING WAVES OF SOUND IN THE AIR. 318 LAZARU
MINGLED WITH THE LAUGHING FROM BEYOND THE WALL 318 LAZARU
COMES THE SOUND OF SINGING AND
(THE BRAZEN TRUMPETS OF THE LEGIONS SOUND FROM 319 LAZARU
BEYOND THE WALL.
(THERE IS NOW NO SOUND OF THE SINGING OR 320 LAZARU
THE SOUND OF MUSIC IN A STRAINED THEME OF THAT 326 LAZARU
JOYLESS ABANDON WHICH IS VICE IS
(AS HE FINISHES SPEAKING ALL THE SOUND OF MUSIC 331 LAZARU
AND VOICES FROM THE HOUSE CEASES.
THE WALLS AND MASSIVE COLUMNS SEEM TO REVERBERATE 337 LAZARU
WITH THE SOUND.
THEN, WITH A SOUND THAT IS VERY LIKE A SOB, HE 347 LAZARU
KISSES HER ON THE LIPS)
(IN A FRENZY AS LAZARUS NEITHER MAKES A SOUND NOR 348 LAZARU
LOOKS UP)
THIS SOUND HAS RISEN TO ITS GREATEST VOLUME AS THE364 LAZARU
CURTAIN RISES.)
(HE BEGINS TO LAUGH, AND AT THE SOUND OF HIS 366 LAZARU
LAUGHTER,
(LIFTS HIS HEAD AT THE FIRST SOUND AND RISES WITH 371 LAZARU
THE LAUGHTER TO HIS FEET,
(THERE IS A SOUND FROM UP THE PATH AT LEFT-FRONT, 4 MANSNS
THROUGH THE WOODS.
BUT GOOD HEAVENS, I SOUND LIKE CASSANDRA/ 17 MANSNS
THERE IS A SOUND OF MEN'S VOICES FROM DOWN THE 25 MANSNS
PATH OFF LEFT.
THAT DOES NOT SOUND LIKE HENRY. 31 MANSNS
TO REGAIN A SOUND POSITION BY MAKING A QUICK 32 MANSNS
PROFIT IN WESTERN LANDS.
FROM THE HALL AT REAR THE SOUND OF SMALL BOYS' 43 MANSNS
ARGUING VOICES.
THE SOUND OF SCUFFLING COMING THROUGH THE CEILING, 43 MANSNS
(THEY ARE INTERRUPTED BY THE SOUND OF THE KNOCKER 49 MANSNS
ON THE FRONT DOOR,
(FRIGHTENEDLY.) YOU SOUND AS THOUGH YOU'D LIKE-- 142 MANSNS
YOU WOULDN'T--/
YOU SOUND--/ 145 MANSNS
FROM THE BRANCHES OF THE TREE COMES A SOUND OF 352 MARCOM
SWEET SAD MUSIC
(A SOUND OF TENDER LAUGHTER, OF AN INTOXICATING, 352 MARCOM
SUPERNATURAL GAIETY,
IT RISES SOFTLY AND AS SOFTLY DIES AWAY UNTIL IT 354 MARCOM
IS NOTHING BUT A FAINT SOUND OF
THE SOUND GRADUALLY GROWS FAINTER AND FAINTER, 358 MARCOM
RECEDING INTO THE DISTANCE,
AND THE SOUND IS SOON LEFT BEHIND THEM.) 364 MARCOM
FROM THE DARKNESS COMES THE SOUND OF A SMALL 373 MARCOM
TARTAR KETTLE-DRUM, ITS BEATS
(FROM BEHIND THE WALL COMES THE SOUND OF MARTIAL 376 MARCOM
CHINESE MUSIC.
THEN, AS LIGHT AND SOUND ATTAIN THEIR HIGHEST 377 MARCOM
POINT,
POLO BROTHERS AND SON--DOESN'T THAT SOUND SOLID, 381 MARCOM
EH?
FROM THE DISTANCE COMES THE SOUND OF POLO'S BAND 402 MARCOM
(A SOUND OF LOW WEEPING COMES FORM THE CROWD) 405 MARCOM
A FRENZIED CATARACT OF SOUND RESULTS. 407 MARCOM
OF BRINGING YOU SAFE AND SOUND TO YOUR HUSBAND. 411 MARCOM
SOUND COMMON SENSE AND A HOME WHERE EVERYTHING RUNS416 MARCOM
SMOOTH.

SOUND (CONT'D.)
THE SOUND OF RUNNING ABOUT ON DECK AND MARCO'S 417 MARCOM
VOICE GIVING COMMANDS.
A SOUND OF DANCE MUSIC AND LAUGHTER COMES THROUGH 421 MARCOM
THE CLOSED DOORS.)
BUT GROWING MOMENTARILY IN VOLUME, COMES THE SOUND433 MARCOM
OF FUNERAL MUSIC.
A MUFFLED SOUND OF SOBBING COMES FROM THE 435 MARCOM
PROSTRATE WOMEN.
YOU WON'T HEAR A SOUND FROM ME. 76 MISBEG
I SUPPOSE THAT DOES SOUND LIKE MOANING-AT-THE-BAR 123 MISBEG
STUFF.
BUT THE SOUND OF YOURSELF CRYING YOUR HEART'S 152 MISBEG
REPENTANCE AGAINST HER BREAST.
AS IF I'D HAD A SOUND SLEEP WITHOUT NIGHTMARES. 167 MISBEG
THERE IS THE SAME SOUND OF VOICES FROM THE BAR 66 POET
(THEY BOTH HEAR A SOUND FROM UPSTAIRS.) 80 POET
THE REASONS SHE GAVE HIM ARE SOUND AND SHOW A 109 POET
CONSIDERATION FOR YOUR GOOD NAME
FROM THE BAR COMES THE SOUND OF PATCH RILEY'S 133 POET
PIPES
THERE IS A MOMENT'S PAUSE IN WHICH THE SOUND OF 163 POET
DRUNKEN MUISTERING IN THE BAR
(SARA PUTS HER HAND OVER HER MOUTH TO SHUT OFF THE166 POET
SOUND OF HER LAUGHING.
BUT HE'LL SING AND LAUGH AND DRINK A POWER AV 180 POET
WHISKEY AND SLAPE SOUND AFTER.
(THE SOUND OF A MAN'S FOOTSTEPS IS HEARD FROM 581 ROPE
OUTSIDE, AND SWEENEY ENTERS.
THE SOUND OF A MAID'S VOICE--A MIDDLE-AGED WOMAN-- 3 STRANG
IT MIGHT SOUND SILLY... 8 STRANG
IT MAY SOUND INCREDIBLE, BUT NINA HAS BEGUN TO ACT 10 STRANG
AS IF SHE HATED ME/
THOSE DON'T SOUND LIKE YOUR THOUGHTS. 19 STRANG
SHE BREAKS DOWN AND THERE IS THE SOUND OF HER 26 STRANG
UNCONTROLLED SOBBING AND CHOKING.
WE LOVE THE SOUND OF BUT WHOSE MEANING WE PASS ON 42 STRANG
TO SPOOKS TO LIVE BY/
(DROWSILY--HER EYES SHUT) YOU SOUND SO LIKE 46 STRANG
FATHER, CHARLIE.
(THE SOUND OF EVANS' VOICE AND HIS MOTHER'S IS 53 STRANG
HEARD FROM THE GARDEN.
(AT THE SOUND OF STEPS FROM THE KITCHEN 56 STRANG
QUITE SOUND. 86 STRANG
(AT THE FIRST SOUND OF EVANS' VOICE, 104 STRANG
SOUND OF HER VOICE... 125 STRANG
(FROM THE HALLWAY COMES THE SOUND OF MARSDEN'S 146 STRANG
VOICE AND GORDON'S GREETING HIM
(THERE IS THE SOUND OF A DOOR BEING FLUNG OPEN AND151 STRANG
SHUT)
(THEN BLANDLY APOLOGETIC) PARDON ME IF I SOUND A 175 STRANG
BIT PIPPED--A GOOD BIT/
SCENE THERE IS A PERFECT PANDEMONIUM OF SOUND.) 176 STRANG
BUT--THIS MAY SOUND ROTTEN OF ME-- 185 STRANG
HE HEARS THE SOUND OF THE DOOR AND LOOKS AROUND. 189 STRANG
HAPPY TO SEE YER 'OME SAFE AN' SOUND. 496 VOYAGE
FROM THE SIDE ROOM COMES THE SOUND OF AN ACCORDION501 VOYAGE
AND A BOISTEROUS WHOOP FROM
IT SOUND NICE TO HEAR THE OLD TALK YUST ONCE IN A 502 VOYAGE
TIME.
SUDDENLY HE STARES AS THE SOUND OF A MOTOR COMES 462 WELDED
FROM THE DRIVEWAY.
MOVING HIS LIPS AS IF ANSWERING BUT NOT MAKING A 471 WELDED
SOUND)

SOUNDED
YOU SOUNDED--YUST LIKE ALL THE REST. 57 ANNA
ONLY THIS TIME IT SOUNDED--UNNATURAL, DON'T YOU 163 BEYOND
THINK?
IT MUST HEV SOUNDED WUSSER'N I MEANT. 233 DESIRE
YOU SOUNDED SO--WHY, WHERE'S YOUR MA? 531 DIFRNT
GUSH, THAT SOUNDED LIKE OUR FRONT DOOR SLAMMING. 534 DIFRNT
IT SOUNDED LIKE...) 459 DYNAMO
IT SOUNDED LIKE A SHOT. 488 DYNAMO
YOU SOUNDED JUST LIKE HIM. 83 ELECTR
IT SOUNDED LIKE MOTHER. 293 GGBROW
FOR A MOMENT, I THOUGHT IT WAS DION, YOUR VOICE 304 GGBROW
SOUNDED SO MUCH.
MAYBE IT SOUNDED LIKE TEN, BUT IT WAS TWO, AND 26 HUGHIE
THAT'S ALL YOU GET.
I'M SORRY IF I SOUNDED BITTER, JAMES. 112 JOURNE
EVERYTHING LOOKED AND SOUNDED UNREAL. 131 JOURNE
IT SOUNDED SLOW, SLOWER THAN WHEN I LAST HEARD IT.357 LAZARU
I THOUGHT SHE SOUNDED A LITTLE UNEASY. 108 MANSNS
(THEN WORRIEDLY) HIS VOICE SOUNDED FUNNY. 146 STRANG

SOUNDING
(THIS TIME SOUNDING NEARER BUT UP FORWARD TOWARD 29 ANNA
THE BOW)
(THE --BANJO-- COMES AGAIN THROUGH THE WALL OF FOG, 29 ANNA
SOUNDING MUCH NEARER THIS TIME.
LISTENING TO THE DYNAMO'S HUM SOUNDING FROM 484 DYNAMO
BELOW--
AND STOP DAT DRUM SOUNDING IN MY EARS/ 196 EJONES
SOUNDING STARTLINGLY INCONGRUOUS FROM HIM) 338 LAZARU
(HIS VOICE SOUNDING ABOVE THE HUBBUB) 430 MARCOM

SOUNDLY
YOUR MOTHER IS LUCKY TO BE ABLE TO SLEEP SO 147 BEYOND
SOUNDLY.
OK THEY'LL NEVER SLEEP SOUNDLY AGAIN/ 320 GGBROW
BUT I'LL SLEEP SOUNDLY AGAIN NOW I'VE PUT THAT 49 MANSNS
DAMNED BOOK OUT OF MY MIND.
HE WAS SLEEPING SO SOUNDLY AN EARTHQUAKE WOULDN'T 120 STRANG
HAVE MADE HIM PEEP/

SOUNDS
THAT SOUNDS HOPEFUL. 244 AHWILD
I ONLY MEANT--IT SOUNDS FISHY. 285 AHWILD
I KNOW THAT SOUNDS HARD AND UNFEELING, BUT WE'RE 295 AHWILD
TALKING FACTS AND--

SOUNDS

SOUNDS (CONT'D.)
IT SOUNDS GOOD TO HEAR SOMEONE--TALK TO ME THAT WAY. 22 ANNA
IT SOUNDS GOOD TO HEAR YOU TELL IT. 23 ANNA
IT SOUNDS STRANGE TO HEAR YOU, ANDY, THAT I ALWAYS105 BEYOND THOUGHT HAD GOOD SENSE.
(THE WHINING CRYING OF THE CHILD SOUNDS FROM THE 116 BEYOND KITCHEN.
A LOUD FRIGHTENED WHIMPER SOUNDS FROM THE AWAKENED128 BEYOND CHILD IN THE BEDROOM. IT CON
(THE THROBBING WHINE OF A MOTOR SOUNDS FROM THE 153 BEYOND DISTANCE OUTSIDE.)
THE BLAST OF THE STEAMER'S WHISTLE CAN BE HEARD 477 CARDIF ABOVE ALL THE OTHER SOUNDS.
THE STEAMER'S WHISTLE SOUNDS PARTICULARLY LOUD IN 481 CARDIF THE SILENCE.)
SOUNDS KINDER PRETTY TO ME--LOW AN' MOURNFUL-- 466 CARIBE
(THERE IS A LOUD, MUFFLED CRY FROM ABOVE, WHICH 567 CROSS SOUNDS LIKE --SAIL--HO!,
(THE PADDING OF BARE FEET SOUNDS FROM THE FLOOR 571 CROSS BELOW--
IF YOU KNEW HOW FAMILIAR THAT NOTE SOUNDS FROM 501 DAYS HI'M, MR. ELIOT.
(SHE FORCES A LAUGH) I SUPPOSE ALL THIS SOUNDS 522 DAYS TOO PREPOSTEROUS.
WELL, THAT SOUNDS ENCOURAGING. 530 DAYS
IT SOUNDS SO BITTER--AND FALSE--COMING FROM YOU. 534 DAYS
IT SOUNDS LIKE POETRY--"LIFE OUT OF THE SEA." 476 DYNAMO
THE OVERTONE OF RUSHING WATER FROM THE DAM SOUNDS 476 DYNAMO LOUDER BECAUSE OF THE CLOSED
DAT DAMN DRUM SOUNDS JES' DE SAME--NEARER, EVEN. 193 EJONES
THE ONLY SOUNDS ARE A CRASHING IN THE UNDERBRUSH 195 EJONES AS JONES LEAPS AWAY IN MAD
(BY THE SOUNDS HE IS FEELING HIS WAY CAUTIOUSLY 198 EJONES FORWARD)
SOUNDS MADE UP TO ME--LIKE SHORT FUR SOMETHIN' 20 ELECTR ELSE.
(THE BOOM OF A CANNON SOUNDS FROM THE FORT THAT 42 ELECTR GUARDS THE HARBOR.
BETWEEN YOU 'N ' ME 'N' THE LAMP POST, IT AIN'T 135 ELECTR SECH A JOKE AS IT SOUNDS--
AFTER COLLEGE--BUT ARCHITECTURE SOUNDS ALL RIGHT 259 GGBROW TO ME, I GUESS.
BUT ARCHITECTURE SOUNDS LESS LABORIOUS. 261 GGBROW
IT SOUNDS WONDERFUL, DOESN'T ITS 268 GGBROW
IT SOUNDS TO ME LIKE BACCHUS, ALIAS THE DEMON RUM,297 GGBROW DOING THE TALKING.
IT ACTUALLY SOUNDS YOUNGER, DO YOU KNOW ITS 301 GGBROW
THAT SOUNDS THRILLING. 222 HA APE
THIS CLASH OF SOUNDS STUNS ONE'S EARS WITH ITS 223 HA APE RENDING DISSONANCE.
THEN THE INEXORABLE WHISTLE SOUNDS AGAIN 224 HA APE
(HE IS TURNING TO GET COAL WHEN THE WHISTLE SOUNDS225 HA APE AGAIN IN A PEREMPTORY,
FROM OVERHEAD THE WHISTLE SOUNDS AGAIN IN A LONG, 226 HA APE ANGRY, INSISTENT COMMAND.)
HE CAN TELL TIME BY SOUNDS IN THE STREET. 8 HUGHIE
(EMBARRASSEDLY) BUT, HELL, THAT SOUNDS LIKE A LOTS88 ICEMAN OF MUSH.
THAT SOUNDS MORE LIKE YOU, HICKEY. 621 ICEMAN
FORGET IT, IF ANYTHING I'VE SAID SOUNDS TOO 624 ICEMAN SERIOUS.
BEJEES, I KNOW THAT SOUNDS CRAZY, 721 ICEMAN
(IN A CASUAL TONE WHICH TO THEM SOUNDS SINISTER) 523 INZONE
(FOLLOWING HER.) I HOPE I'M NOT AS BIG A GLUTTON 14 JOURNE AS THAT SOUNDS.
(HE SOUNDS MORE TIPSY AND LOOKS IT.) 130 JOURNE
TYRONE AGAIN LISTENS TO SOUNDS UPSTAIRS--WITH 136 JOURNE DREAD.)
IT SOUNDS LIKE A GOOD BARGAIN TO ME. 149 JOURNE
WELL, THAT SOUNDS LIKE THE ABSENT BROTHER. 154 JOURNE
THE SOUNDS OF BLOWS AS THEY MEET IN A PUSHING, 290 LAZARU WHIRLING, STRUGGLING MASS
FOR A MOMENT, ABOVE ALL THE CHORUS OF OTHER 320 LAZARU SOUNDS,
(SUDDENLY THE CALL TO PRAYER SOUNDS FROM MUEZZINS 369 MARCOM IN THE MINARETS OF THE MOSQUE.
THE DANCE MUSIC SOUNDS LOUDLY) 423 MARCOM
IT SOUNDS LIKE HELL. 42 MISBEG
I KNOW IT SOUNDS CRAZY BUT-- 89 MISBEG
AH, THANK GOD, THAT SOUNDS NATURAL/ 94 MISBEG
FROM THE ROCKS BELOW THE HEADLAND SOUNDS THE 578 ROPE MUFFLED MONOTONE OF BREAKING WAVES.
BUT THAT SOUNDS SPLENDID/. 8 STRANG
WE POOR MONKEYS HIDE FROM OURSELVES BEHIND THE 40 STRANG SOUNDS CALLED WORDS/
THOSE SOUNDS OUR LIPS MAKE AND OUR HANDS WRITE. 40 STRANG
IT'S BECAUSE I'VE SUDDENLY SEEN THE LIES IN THE 40 STRANG SOUNDS CALLED WORDS.
HIS KNEES AND BEGINS TO SOB--STIFLED TORN SOUNDS.) 43 STRANG
(HIS VOICE SOUNDS FROM THE HALL WITH A STRAINED 145 STRANG CASUALNESS)
SOUNDS LIKE 'EM NOW. 496 VOYAGE
A RINGING OF THE DOORBELL SOUNDS FROM SOMEWHERE 462 WELDED BACK IN THE HOUSE.

SOUP
YOU CAN BRING IN THE SOUP. 221 AHWILD
BRING THAT SOUP HERE THIS MINUTE/ 222 AHWILD
AND NORAH, WHO HAS JUST ENTERED FROM THE PANTRY 222 AHWILD WITH A HUGE TUREEN OF SOUP IN
(SHE BRINGS THE SOUP AROUND THE HEARD OF THE 222 AHWILD TABLE, PASSING MILLER.)
(SHE SETS THE SOUP TUREEN DOWN WITH A THUD IN 222 AHWILD FRONT OF MRS. MILLER
(NORAH, STILL STANDING WITH THE SOUP TUREEN HELD 222 AHWILD OUT STIFFLY IN FRONT OF HER,
YOU KNOW I'VE GIVEN UP SOUP. 223 AHWILD
(THEN TO NORAH, HANDING HER A SOUP PLATE) 223 AHWILD

SOUP (CONT'D.)
BEGINS LADLING SOUP INTO THE STACK OF PLATES 223 AHWILD BEFORE HER)
(NORAH BEGINS PASSING SOUP) SIT DOWN, NAT, FOR 223 AHWILD GOODNESS SAKES.
(HE BEGINS TO ABSORB HIS SOUP RAVENOUSLY) 223 AHWILD
GOOD SOUP/ 223 AHWILD
GOOD SOUP, ESSIE/ 223 AHWILD
SOUPS 224 AHWILD
OF COURSE, IT'S SOUP. 224 AHWILD
(AGAIN REGARDS HIS SOUP WITH ASTONISHMENT) 224 AHWILD
(HE RAISES HIS SOUP PLATE AND DECLAIMS) 224 AHWILD
(HE IS SILENT, STUDYING HIS SOUP PLATE, AS IF IT 224 AHWILD WERE SOME STRANGE ENIGMA.
SOUP BE IT/ 224 AHWILD
(HE STARTS DRINKING THE SOUP. 224 AHWILD
HURRY UP AND FINISH YOUR SOUP, AND STOP TALKING 225 AHWILD NONSENSE/
ISN'T THIS SOUP LIQUID$ 225 AHWILD
(HE DRINKS THE REST OF HIS SOUP IN A GULP AND 225 AHWILD BEAMS AROUND AT THE COMPANY,
JUST THINK OF WASTE EFFORT EATING SOUP WITH 225 AHWILD SPOONS--
(PEERS AT HER MUZZILY, LOWERING THE SOUP PLATE A 225 AHWILD LITTLE FROM HIS LIPS)
FIFTY GRUELING LIFTS PER PLATE--BILLIONS OF SOUP- 225 AHWILD EATERS ON GLOBE--
PASS ME YOU SOUP PLATES EVERYBODY. 225 AHWILD
(FROM THE ALLEYWAY) GAWD BLIMEY, THE FOG'S THICK 482 CARDIF AS SOUP.
NO THROWIN' SPITBALLS IN MY SOUP OR THEM KIND OF 25 HUGHIE GAGS.
YEAH, HUGHIE LAPPED UP MY STORIES LIKE THEY WAS 29 HUGHIE DUCK SOUP,
I KNOW ALL ABOUT THAT GAME FAUM SOUP TO NUTS. 621 ICEMAN
FOR THE DEALER TO STAND WHEN HE DISHES OUT SOUP AT664 ICEMAN THE NOON HOUR.
SOUP IS HEARD. 431 MARCOM
AS IF SHE HAD DISCOVERED A COCKROACH IN HER SOUP) 57 MISBEG
SOUP'D
MAYBE SOUP'D FIX YOU. 475 WELDED

SOUR
(TAUNTINGLY) SOUR GRAPES, AREN'T THEY, DICKS 103 BEYOND
(FORCING A SOUR GRIN) STEAL GERMS$ 296 GGBROW
A SOUR AFTERTASTE IN YOUR MOUTH OF DAGO RED INK/ 140 MISBEG

SOURLY
(SOURLY DISAPPOINTED) YOU KEEP THEM DUMB BROADS 610 ICEMAN QUIET.
(SOURLY) WHAT PORTHOLES 521 INZONE
(SOURLY, BUT WITH A TRACE OF ADMIRATION.) 24 JOURNE

SOUSE
BUT IF I WERE IN YOUR BOOTS I'D GIVE THIS YOUNG 247 AHWILD SUSE THE GATE.
HE'S A NO-GOOD SOUSE LIKE HICKEY. 666 ICEMAN
BEJEES, WE'LL GO ON A GRAND OLD SOUSE TOGETHER/ 690 ICEMAN
WRITING IT TO A DUMB BARMAID, WHO THOUGHT HE WAS A139 JOURNE POUR CRAZY SOUSE,
(PROVOCATIVELY.) THEY SAY HE WAS A SOUSE, TOO. 135 JOURNE

SOUSED
UNCLE SID'S SOUSED AGAIN. 221 AHWILD
I LIKED HIM--BEFORE HE GOT SOUSED. 247 AHWILD
HE'S ONLY SOUSED. 261 AHWILD
HE THOUGHT IT WAS A GOOD JOKE TO GET HIM SOUSED. 267 AHWILD
YOU'RE SOUSED TO THE EARS, DUTCHY. 13 ANNA
WELL, WHAT D'YOU EXPECT AFTER BEING SOUSED FOR TWO 64 ANNA DAYS
ALTHOUGH THE GOSSIPS ARE BEGINNING TO SAY I'M 315 GGBROW SOUSED ALL THE TIME/
I GUESS I'M A BIT SOUSED ON LIFE, TOO/ 316 GGBROW
SOUSED ON LIFE/ 316 GGBROW
SOUSED TO THE EARS ALL THE TIME/ 316 GGBROW
YOU'RE SOUSED. 251 HA APE
I OUGHT TO HAVE REMEMBERED WHEN YOU'RE SOUSED YOU 592 ICEMAN CALL EVERYONE A STOOL PIGEON.
I NEVER BEEN SOUSED ON CHAMPAGNE. 640 ICEMAN
THEN YOU'LL TELL YOURSELF YOU WOULDN'T STAND A 686 ICEMAN CHANCE IF YOU WENT UP SOUSED TO
I AM A BIT SOUSED, I GUESS. 128 JOURNE
IF YOU'RE SUSPICIOUS I'M TRYING TO GET YOU 116 MISBEG SOUSED--WELL, HERE GOES.
I MUST BE SCHEMING TO GET MYSELF SOUSED, TOO. 116 MISBEG
DON'T ALL THE PRETTY LITTLE BROADWAY TARTS GET 116 MISBEG SOUSED WITH YOU/
TRYING TO GET ME SOUSED, JOSIE$ 116 MISBEG
STILL TRYING TO GET ME SOUSED, JOSIE$ 124 MISBEG
AND DON'T LET ME GET AWAY WITH PRETENDING I'M SO 126 MISBEG SOUSED I DON'T KNOW WHAT I'M

SOUSES
I'VE RUN INTO SOME NUTTY SOUSES, BUT DIS GUY WAS 616 ICEMAN DE NUTTIEST.
AMONG THE SOUSES IN THE HOTEL BAR, I SUPPOSE/ 140 JOURNE

SOUSIN'
AIN'T YOU SOUSIN' WITH 'EM MOST EVERY DAYS 176 EJONES

SOUSING
WHEN EVERYONE KNOWS YOU'VE BEEN CUT EVERY NIGHT 281 GGBROW

SOUTH
THEY SAID IF HE DON'T PUT BACK SOUTH FOR HOME 537 *ILE TODAY THEY'RE GOIN' TO MUTINY.
THERE'S CLEAR WATER TO THE SOUTH NOW. 546 *ILE
SCENE----JOHNNY-THE-PRIEST'S= SALOON NEAR SOUTH 3 ANNA STREET, NEW YORK CITY.
GO SOUTH AMERICA, GO AUSTRALIA, GO ABOARD SHIP 21 ANNA SAIL FOR SWEDEN.
DAT'S, IN SOUTH AFRICA. 67 ANNA
INDIA, OR AUSTRALIA, OR SOUTH AFRICA, OR SOUTH 83 BEYOND AMERICA--

SOUTH

SOUTH (CONT'D.)

WHEN I THINKS O' YOU WANTIN' TO GET BACK DOWN 141 BEYOND
SOUTH TO THE PLATE AGEN..

THE SOUTH END OF THE HOUSE FACES FRONT TO A STONE 202 DESIRE WALL.

*CERTIN' WHEN THAT DURN TEMPEST BLOWED US SOUTH 497 DIFRNT IT WAS WHEN THEY PUT IN TO GIT WATER AT THEM SOUTH501 DIFRNT SEA ISLANDS

HE'S SAILED ALL OVER THE WORLD--HE LIVED ON A 15 ELECTR SOUTH SEA ISLAND ONCE, SO HE SAYS.

YOU WERE INTERESTED WHEN I TOLD YOU OF THE ISLANDS 23 ELECTR IN THE SOUTH SEAS WHERE I WAS

WE'D STOP AT THE SOUTH PACIFIC ISLANDS I'VE TOLD 39 ELECTR YOU ABOUT.

HAVE YOU EVER READ A BOOK CALLED «TYPEE»--ABOUT 89 ELECTR THE SOUTH SEA ISLANDS$

LEAVE VINNIE HERE AND GO AWAY ON A LONG VOYAGE--TO122 ELECTR THE SOUTH SEAS--

AND WE'D SEE THE MOUNTAINS OF SOUTH AMERICY WID 214 HA APE THE RED FIRE OF THE SETTING SUN

OH, TO BE SCUDDING SOUTH AGAIN WID THE POWER OF 214 HA APE THE TRADE WIND

USED TO FOLLOW THE HORSES SOUTH EVERY WINTER. 23 HUGHIE

THEY DREAM THE HOURS AWAY IN HAPPY DISPUTE OVER 593 ICEMAN THE BRAVE DAYS IN SOUTH AFRICA

THERE WAS A RUMOR IN SOUTH AFRICA, ROCKY, THAT A 677 ICEMAN CERTAIN BOER OFFICER--

YOU CAN'T IMAGINE HE GETTING FUN OUT OF BEING ON 35 JOURNE THE BEACH IN SOUTH AMERICA,

AND AT THE OTHER END OF YOUR CHAIN YOU SHOULD 101 MANSNS POSSESS PLANTATIONS IN THE SOUTH

OF A SENATOR FROM THE SOUTH OF THE UNITED STATES 390 MARCOM OF AMERICA

WHETHER IT'S THE BOTTOM OF A BOTTLE, OR A SOUTH 135 MISBEG SEA ISLAND,

OF BETTING ON FAVORITES, AND FOLLOW THE HORSES 143 MISBEG SOUTH IN THE WINTER,

A WIND FROM THE SOUTH, AND A SKY GRAY WITH 102 POET CLOUDS--GOOD WEATHER FOR THE HOUNDS.

SOUTHAMPTON

THEN YOU CAN TAKE THE UNION CASTLE FROM 605 ICEMAN SOUTHAMPTON TO CAPE TOWN.

SOUTHERN

(EXPLOSIVELY) THE MARY ALLEN, YE BLIND FOOL, COME568 CROSS BACK FROM THE SOUTHERN SEAS--

ALL ARE DRESSED IN SOUTHERN COSTUMES 196 EJONES

WE'VE HAD SOUTHERN PLANTERS AS OUR GUESTS, 51 MANSNS

SOUVENIRS

SOUVENIRS TO SELL TO CHRISTIANS$ 365 MARCOM

SOVEREIGN

SOVEREIGN OF THE WORLD/ 435 MARCOM

SOVEREIGN OF THE WORLD$ 435 MARCOM

(PRODUCING A SOVEREIGN) HO THERE, YOU FATTY/ 497 VOYAGE

(HE PULLS A SOVEREIGN OUT OF HIS POCKET AND SLAMS 497 VOYAGE IT ON THE BAR.)

SOVEREIGNS

FOUR TWO-YEAR MEN PAID ORF WIV THEIR BLOODY 495 VOYAGE POCKETS FULL O' SOVEREIGNS--

SOVEREIGNTY

ISN'T IT TIME TO PROTECT YOUR SOVEREIGNTY BY 392 MARCOM STRONG MEASURES$

SOW

YE'D ON'Y TO PLOW AN' SOW AN' THEN SET AN' SMOKE 237 DESIRE

YER PIPE AN' WATCH THIN'S GROW.

MY MOTHER USED TO BELIEVE THE FULL OF THE MOON WAS261 GGBROW THE TIME TO SOW.

IS IT PAYIN' ATTENTION AT ALL YOU ARE TO THE LIKE 232 HA APE OF THAT SKINNY SOW

SOW THE SEED, ONLY GO ABOUT IT RIGHT. 247 HA APE

WHILE THEY SOW, THEY DANCE/ 287 LAZARU

WILL YOU RETURN TO THIS SOW AND BOAST THAT A 416 MARCOM PRINCESS AND A QUEEN--$

SOW I NEVER KNEW SWEDISH. 502 VOYAGE

I'M SOW COLD. 505 VOYAGE

SOW'S

WHEN MAN'S SOUL ISN'T A SOW'S EAR, 590 ICEMAN

GOD HIMSELF CANNOT TRANSFORM A SOW'S EAR INTO A 114 POET SILK PURSE/

SOWL

I WISHT I HAD NOTHIN' BLACKER THAN THAT ON MY 488 CARDIF SOWL.

SOWN

EARTH OF WHICH MYRIAD BRIGHT-GREEN BLADES OF FALL- 81 BEYOND SOWN RYE ARE SPROUTING.

YOU AND I HAVE SEEN FIELDS AND HILLSIDES SOWN WITH 93 ELECTR THEM--AND THEY MEANT NOTHING/

THE FIELDS OF INFINITE SPACE ARE SOWN-- 349 LAZARU

SOWS

YE'D BETTER TURN HER IN THE PEN WITH THE OTHER 222 DESIRE SOWS.

THE LAUGHTER OF HEAVEN SOWS EARTH WITH A RAIN OF 322 GGBROW TEARS.

SPACE

THEIR BACKS TO FRONT, TAKES UP MOST OF THE 210 AHWILD AVAILABLE SPACE.

THE REMAINDER OF THE REAR SPACE IN FRONT OF THE 3 ANNA LARGE MIRRORS IS OCCUPIED BY

THERE'S WIDE SPACE ENOUGH, LORD KNOWS.. 85 BEYOND

WITH A SPACE OF THREE FEET SEPARATING THE UPPER 477 CARDIF FROM THE LOWER,

IN THE CENTER OF THE DECK, AND OCCUPYING MOST OF 455 CARIBE THE SPACE, IS THE LARGE,

A MAN WHO WILL PROVE THAT MAN'S FLEETING LIFE IN 543 DAYS TIME AND SPACE CAN BE NOBLE.

BY WHAT DRIVES THE STARS THROUGH SPACE/ 461 DYNAMO

DRIVING THROUGH SPACE, ROUND AND ROUND, JUST LIKE 477 DYNAMO THE ELECTRONS IN THE ATOM/

SPANKED

SPACE (CONT'D.)

OCCUPIES MOST OF THE FLOOR SPACE IN THE 486 DYNAMO FOREGROUND.

(HE WALKS QUICKLY INTO THE CLEAR SPACE--THEN 192 EJONES STANDS TRANSFIXED AS HE SEES JEFF--

THE SPACE THUS ENCLOSED IS LIKE THE DARK, NOISOME 198 EJONES HOLD OF SOME ANCIENT VESSEL.

(A CLEARED SPACE IN THE FOREST. 198 EJONES

DIS FEELS LIKE A CLEAR SPACE. 198 EJONES

GRADUALLY IT SEEMS TO GROW LIGHTER IN THE ENCLOSED198 EJONES SPACE AND TWO ROWS OF SEATED

AS HIS VOICE SINKS INTO SILENCE, HE ENTERS THE 200 EJONES OPEN SPACE.

PETER SITS GINGERLY ON THE RIGHT EDGE SO THAT 13 ELECTR THERE IS AN OPEN SPACE BETWEEN HIM

IS A RECTANGULAR SPACE WITH BENCHES ON THE THREE 257 GGBROW SIDES.

INTO SILENCE--INTO NIGHT--INTO EARTH--INTO SPACE--267 GGBROW INTO PEACE--INTO MEANING--

SHE BENDS DOWN AND KISSES HIM GENTLY--SHE 322 GGBROW STRAIGHTENS UP AND LOOKS INTO SPACE--

THE EFFECT SOUGHT AFTER IS A CRAMPED SPACE IN THE 207 HA APE BOWELS OF A SHIP.

PY GOTT, THERE IS SPACE TO BE FREE, THE AIR LIKE 605 ICEMAN VINE IS.

LEAVING A CLEAR FLOOR SPACE AT REAR FOR DANCING. 628 ICEMAN

WITH A SPACE BETWEEN IT AND THE WINDOW 664 ICEMAN

THERE IS GOD'S LAUGHTER ON THE HILLS OF SPACE, AND330 LAZARU THE HAPPINESS OF CHILDREN.

YOUR HOME ON THE HILLS OF SPACE IS TOO FAR AWAY. 345 LAZARU

THE FIELDS OF INFINITE SPACE ARE SOWN-- 349 LAZARU

WHERE THERE IS SPACE FOR LAUGHTER AND WHERE THIS 360 LAZARU NEW JOY, YOUR LOVE OF ME,

SPACE IS TOO FAR AWAY, YOU SAID/ 362 LAZARU

AND NOW THE THREE, STANDING BESIDE A BIG EMPTY 429 MARCOM SPACE

SPACED

ARE HUNG ON THE WALLS AT MATHEMATICALLY- SPACED 519 DIFRNT INTERVALS.

SET BACK AT SPACED INTERVALS AGAINST THE WALLS. 48 STRANG

SPACES

THE NEED OF THE FREEDOM OF GREAT WIDE SPACES, THE 85 BEYOND JOY OF WANDERING ON AND ON--

SPACIOUS

A SPACIOUS, HIGH-CEILINGED ROOM WITH BARE, 173 EJONES WHITEWASHED WALLS.

WITH A BEAUTIFUL, SPACIOUS GARDEN FOR THE CHILDREN 66 MANSNS TO PLAY IN$

THE DINING ROOM AND BARROOM WERE ONCE A SINGLE 7 POET SPACIOUS ROOM, LOW-CEILINGED,

SPADES

LITTLE MO' AN' IT'D BE BLACKER'N DE ACE OF SPADES 187 EJONES HEAHABOUTS.

HIS WIFE IS A BUM--IN SPADES/ 12 HUGHIE

AND I'D CUT THE ACE OF SPADES AND WIN AGAIN.» 32 HUGHIE

SPAIN

WHO SERVED WITH HONOR IN SPAIN UNDER THE GREAT 21 MANSNS DUKE OF WELLINGTON.

THE AMBITIOUS SARA WHO USED TO LONG TO OWN AN 74 MANSNS IRISH-CASTLE-IN-SPAIN,

SINCE THE WAR WITH THE FRENCH IN SPAIN--AFTER THE 10 POET BATTLE OF SALAMANCA IN '12.

AND HE HAD THE CHANCE HE WANTED IN PORTUGAL AND 13 POET SPAIN WHERE A BRITISH OFFICER

THERE WASN'T ONE COULD RESIST HIM IN PORTUGAL AND 13 POET SPAIN.

AND NIVIR SAW HER AGAIN TILL HE WAS SENT HOME FROM 14 POET SPAIN.

(THEN BOASTFULLY.) BUT IT'S TRUE, IN THOSE DAYS 39 POET IN PORTUGAL AND SPAIN--

LOST IN MEMORIES OF A GLORIOUS BATTLE IN SPAIN, 58 POET NINETEEN YEARS AGO TODAY.

AND YOU LOOK AS FINE A FIGURE IN IT AS EVER YOU 92 POET DID IN SPAIN.

WHO SERVED WITH HONOR UNDER THE DUKE OF WELLINGTON17 POET IN SPAIN, I AM HE.

AND THE LADIES OF SPAIN AND FIGHTIN' THE FRENCH/ 169 POET

EVEN THE LADIES IN SPAIN--DEEP DOWN THAT'S BEEN MY178 POET PRIDE, TOO--

SPAKE

(HE QUOTES FROM THUS SPAKE ZARATHUSTRA.) 78 JOURNE

SPAN

AND HUNT UP A WIFE SOMEWHERES FOR THAT SPICK 'N' 104 BEYOND SPAN CABIN.

HE DRIV OFF IN THE BUGGY, ALL SPICK AN' SPAN, 209 DESIRE

CITIES AND SMALL TOWNS--NOT FLASHY BUT 619 ICEMAN CONSPICUOUSLY SPIC AND SPAN.

YOU LOOK SPIC AND SPAN. 89 JOURNE

HE IS DRESSED IN FULL UNIFORM, LOOKING SPICK AND 410 MARCOM SPAN AND SELF-CONSCIOUS.

SPANGLES

OVERDRESSED IN BLACK LACE AND SPANGLES. 257 GGBROW

SPANISH

HE GOT CAUGHT BY A SPANISH NOBLE MAKING LOVE TO 12 POET HIS WIFE,

IF YOU'D LEFT THE SPANISH WOMAN ALONE AND NOT 99 POET FOUGHT THAT DUEL.

SPANK

AFRAID YOUR MAMA WOULD SPANK YOU IF SHE FOUND OUT$433 DYNAMO

BE JAYSUS, I'LL TAKE YOU OVER MY KNEE AND SPANK 73 MISBEG YOUR TAIL.

SPANKED

YOUNG MAN, I'VE NEVER SPANKED YOU YET, BUT THAT 264 AHWILD DON'T MEAN THAT I NEVER WILL/

OH, JOHN, YOU'RE SUCH A CHILD AT TIMES YOU OUGHT 529 DAYS TO BE SPANKED.

SPANKER — 1502

SPANKER
THE BOOM OF THE SPANKER EXTENDING OUT ABOVE THE 102 ELECTR DECK TO THE RIGHT.

SPANKIN'
AND DRIVE IN A CARRIAGE WID A NAYGUR COACHMAN 173 POET BEHIND SPANKIN' THOROUGHBREDS,

SPANKING
HE GOD, YOU'LL HAVE TO GIVE THAT DAMNED CAT OF 57 MISBEG YOURS A SPANKING FOR BRINGING IT
(THINKING HYSTERICALLY) (ISPANKING/... 193 STRANG
(CONTEMPTUOUSLY) AND GIVE YOU A SPANKING/ 193 STRANG

SPANKS
THE SON SPANKS THE FATHER/...)) 193 STRANG

SPARE
NAT MILLER IS IN HIS LATE FIFTIES, A TALL, DARK, 188 AHWILD SPARE MAN,
YOU NEEDN'T WORRY ABOUT THAT SPARE CABIN, UNCLE 104 BEYOND DICK,
I'D SPARE HER, FOR THE PRESENT, AT LEAST, 540 DAYS
HE IS A TALL MAN IN HIS EARLY FORTIES, WITH A 28 ELECTR SPARE, WIRY FRAME,
HE IS TALL, SPARE, BIG-BONED MAN OF FIFTY, 46 ELECTR
(BROWN NODS) IT'S TOO COLD, TOO SPARE, TOO LIKE A306 GGBROW TOMB, IF YOU'LL PARDON ME,
I WOKE UP AND HEARD HER MOVING AROUND IN THE SPARE 38 JOURNE ROOM.
(HESITANTLY AGAIN,) IT WAS HER BEING IN THE SPARE 38 JOURNE ROOM THAT SCARED ME.
YOU WENT IN THE SPARE ROOM FOR THE REST OF THE 47 JOURNE NIGHT,
FOR HEAVEN'S SAKE, HAVEN'T I OFTEN USED THE SPARE 47 JOURNE ROOM AS MY BEDROOM5
SHE WAS LYING DOWN IN THE SPARE ROOM WITH HER EYES 53 JOURNE WIDE OPEN.
IN THE SPARE ROOMS 57 JOURNE
SPARE THEM WHO ARE SO FULL OF LIFE AND JOY/ 317 LAZARU
IT IS CAESAR'S COMMAND THAT THEY SPARE NONE OF 317 LAZARU YOUR FOLLOWERS.
YOU ARE TRYING TO SPARE YOUR PEOPLE/ 319 LAZARU
YOUR FATHER NEVER HAD TIME TO SPARE OTHERS' 34 MANSNS FEELINGS.
HIS SPARE FRAME HAS PUT ON TEN POUNDS OR SO, 43 MANSNS
I COULDN'T SPARE THE TIME, FOR ONE THING, 47 MANSNS
IN YOUR SPARE TIME, WHEN I AM AWAY, 92 MANSNS
(KNEELING--PITIABLY) MERCY! SPARE US/ 393 MARCOM
AND I'LL HAVE TO GET THE SPARE ROOM READY. 72 STRANG

SPARED
THE BOY HAD PRAYED WITH PERFECT FAITH THAT HIS 510 DAYS FATHER'S LIFE MIGHT BE SPARED.
BUT HE BEGAN TO MAKE A CONDITION NOW--IF HIS 511 DAYS MOTHER WERE SPARED TO HIM/
(HE SINKS TO HIS KNEES) PRAY THAT ELSA'S LIFE MAY 559 DAYS BE SPARED TO YOU/
WELL, I SUPPOSE I COULD TELL HER, IF YOU WANT TO 87 MANSNS BE SPARED.

SPARELY
A LONG, LOW-CEILINGED, SPARELY FURNISHED CHAMBER, 273 LAZARU WITH WHITE WALLS

SPARING
BUT ALL THE SAME, THAT'S NOT YOUR REAL REASON FOR 33 ELECTR SPARING ME/

SPARK
(WITH A SPARK OF ASSERTIVENESS) 114 BEYOND
I'LL HAVE NO YOUNG SPARK SEDUCING MY DAUGHTER-- 438 DYNAMO
(WITH A FAINT SPARK OF HER OLD DEFIANCE) 134 MISBEG

SPARKLING
IT IS A CLEAR, BRIGHT NIGHT, THE SKY SPARKLING 281 LAZARU WITH STARS.

SPARKS
WHOSE LIPOSE LIPS ARE FIREWORKS, WHOSE EYES ARE 228 AHWILD RED-HOT SPARKS--
DREAMS LIKE SPARKS SOARING UP TO DIE IN THE COLD 27 STRANG DARK...

SPARS
A FOREST OF MASTS, SPARS, SAILS OF WOVEN BAMBOO 400 MARCOM LATHS,

SPARSELY
BOTH ARE SPARSELY FURNISHED WITH THE BARE 421 DYNAMO NECESSITIES.

SPASM
(A SPASM OF PAIN CONTRACTS HIS PALE FEATURES. 483 CARDIF
(HIS FACE TWITCHES AND HIS BODY WRITHES IN A FINAL489 CARDIF SPASM,
JONES CRIES OUT IN A FIERCE, EXHAUSTED SPASM OF 202 EJONES ANGUISHED PLEADING.)
(OION RECOVERS FROM HIS SPASM WITH A START 297 GGBROW
(A SPASM OF PAIN CROSSES HIS FACE.) 76 JOURNE
AND A SPASM OF PAIN COMES OVER HER FACE) 395 MARCOM
(A SPASM OF PAIN COVERS HER FACE--THEN WITH HATRED416 MARCOM AND DISDAIN)
(HIS FACE IS CONVULSED BY A SPASM OF PAIN 51 POET
(HIS FACE IS AGAIN CONVULSED BY A SPASM OF PAIN-- 55 POET PLEADINGLY.)

SPASMODIC
NOR HIS GHASTLY, SPASMODIC LAUGHTER) 286 LAZARU

SPASMODICALLY
HIS SHOULDERS CONTINUE TO HEAVE SPASMODICALLY BUT 532 INZONE HE MAKES NO FURTHER SOUND.

SPAT
YOU AND CALEB AIN'T HAD A SPAT, HAVE YOU, WITH 506 DIFRNT YOUR WEDDIN' ONLY TWO DAYS OFF?
YOU AND CALEB MUST HAVE HAD AN AWFUL SPAT/ 506 DIFRNT
AS THOUGH THAT OPPONENT WITHIN HAD SPAT AN 102 MANSNS EXTINGUISHING POISON OF DISDAIN--

SPATS
THE MEN ARE IN PRINCE ALBERTS, HIGH HATS, SPATS, 236 HA APE CANES, ETC.

SPATTED
A FAT, HIGH-HATTED, SPATTED GENTLEMAN RUNS OUT 239 HA APE FROM THE SIDE STREET.

SPATTERING
THERE IS A SPATTERING SMASH 249 HA APE
ON LIKE THE DREARY TEARS OF A TROLLOP SPATTERING 152 JOURNE IN A PUDDLE OF STALE BEER ON A

SPAWN
SPAWN O' SATAN/ 578 ROPE
SPAWN O' THE PIT/ 579 ROPE
SPAWN O' THE PIT/ 581 ROPE

SPEAK
SHE DON'T NEVER SPEAK TO ME NO MORE--JEST LOOKS AT538 'ILE ME 'S IF SHE DIDN'T KNOW ME.
(IMPATIENTLY) SPEAK YOUR SAY, MR. SLOCUM. 539 'ILE
WHO'S TO SPEAK FUR YE? 543 'ILE
SPEAK UP/ 543 'ILE
THEN SPEAK YOUR SAY AND BE QUICK ABOUT IT. 544 'ILE
I'VE BEEN MEANING TO SPEAK TO YOU ABOUT THOSE 192 AHWILD AWFUL BOOKS RICHARD IS READING.
AT THE TABLE'S NO PLACE TO SPEAK OF-- 230 AHWILD
DARN IT, SPEAK OF THE DEVIL, HERE HE COMES. 256 AHWILD
I'VE GOT A GOOD NOTION TO GO RIGHT HOME AND NEVER 278 AHWILD SPEAK TO YOU AGAIN/
(SHAKES CHRIS BY THE HAND) SPEAK OF THE DEVIL. 6 ANNA
AY GAT SPEAK WITH LARRY. 10 ANNA
(THEN BEFORE HE CAN SPEAK, SHE SHUFFLES HURRIEDLY 19 ANNA PAST HIM INTO THE BAR,
THE ONLY WOMEN YOU'D MEET IN THE PORTS OF THE 37 ANNA WORLD WHO'D BE WILLING TO SPEAK
WELL, DON'T YOU NEVER THINK IT NEITHER IF YOU WANT 42 ANNA ME EVER TO SPEAK TO YOU
THEN SHE BEGINS, FIGHTING TO CONTROL HER EMOTION 56 ANNA AND SPEAK CALMLY)
OH, I'M A GREAT COWARD SURELY, TO BE COMING BACK 70 ANNA TO SPEAK WITH YOU AT ALL.
FINALLY ANDREW GUES ON, AWKWARDLY, ATTEMPTING TO 83 BEYOND SPEAK CASUALLY)
WHY DIDN'T YOU WANT TO SPEAK OF ITS 88 BEYOND
SPEAK ABOUT YOUR TRIP--UNTIL AFTER YOU'D GONE. 88 BEYOND
YOU DARE TO--YOU DARE TO SPEAK LIKE THAT TO ME! 108 BEYOND
YOU SPEAK A WORD TO THE BUSUN, COCKY. 482 CARDIF
(THEY ALL TURN AND LOOK UP AT HIM SURPRISED TO 462 CARIBE HEAR HIM SPEAK.)
LETTER UPON LETTER--EACH WITH A SOAP BOX INCLOSED,501 DAYS SO SPEAK.
(WITH A SHUDDER) FOR GOD'S SAKE, DON'T SPEAK 509 DAYS ABOUT--
(RELIEVED) WAAL--IT WA'N'T NOTHIN' T' SPEAK ON. 231 DESIRE
(EMMA SEEMS ABOUT TO SPEAK BUT STOPS HELPLESSLY 513 DIFRNT AFTER ONE GLANCE AT HER FATHER.)
WAITING FOR HER TO SPEAK OR LOOK UP, 514 DIFRNT
I WANT TO SPEAK TO HER AND FIND OUT HOW I STAND 527 DIFRNT BEFORE HE SEES ME.
I WANT TO SPEAK TO CALEB. 547 DIFRNT
DON'T YOU EVER DARE SPEAK TO ME AGAIN/ 451 DYNAMO
AIN'T YOU GWINE--LOOK UP--CAN'T YOU SPEAK TO ME! 192 EJONES
HER LIPS MOVE AS IF SHE WERE GOING TO SPEAK, BUT 27 ELECTR SHE FIGHTS BACK THE WORDS.
THEY USED TO SPEAK THEN. 53 ELECTR
AND SPEAK WITH A SIMULATION OF OUTRAGED FEELING.) 63 ELECTR
I WANT TO SPEAK TO ORIN A MOMENT. 76 ELECTR
VINNIE, I--I MUST SPEAK WITH YOU A MOMENT--NOW 77 ELECTR ORIN IS HERE.
ANSWER ME WHEN I SPEAK TO YOU/ 78 ELECTR
CHRISTINE BEGINS TO SPEAK IN A LOW VOICE, COOLLY 91 ELECTR DEFIANT, ALMOST TRIUMPHANT)
HER LIPS OPEN AS IF TO SPEAK BUT SHE CLOSES THEM 92 ELECTR AGAIN.
WHY WON'T YOU SPEAK TO ME? 122 ELECTR
WHY DON'T YOU SPEAK TO HIM? 144 ELECTR
(THEN CHECKING HIMSELF ABRUPTLY AS HE IS ABOUT TO 161 ELECTR SPEAK--DULLY)
HE SAID HE'D NEVER SPEAK TO MOTHER OR ME AGAIN. 173 ELECTR
HAS A TERRIBLE STRUGGLE WITH HIMSELF, THEN WHILE 285 GGBROW SHE CONTINUES TO SPEAK,
I HEAR HIM SPEAK/ 322 GGBROW
(CUNNINGLY) I KNOW ENOUGH NOT TO SPEAK OUTA MY 248 HA APE TOIN.
HICKEY GLANCES AT WILLIE WHO, BEFORE HE CAN SPEAK,686 ICEMAN JUMPS FROM HIS CHAIR.)
WELL--HE IS ABOUT TO SPEAK, BUT HESITATES AND 515 INZONE FINISHES LAMELY)
CAN'T YOU SPEAK OUT! 38 JOURNE
(TRYING TO SPEAK NATURALLY,) 82 JOURNE
WE ARE WAITING FOR HIM TO SPEAK. 277 LAZARU
(IMPRESSIVELY) HE DID SPEAK ONCE. 277 LAZARU
SPEAK TO ME/ 283 LAZARU
(GRUFFLY) YOU MUST NOT SPEAK OF HIM/ 284 LAZARU
I DARE NOT SPEAK BEFORE HE QUESTIONS ME. 327 LAZARU
BUT IT WAS CAESAR'S COMMAND I SPEAK TO LAZARUS 332 LAZARU ALONE.
(WITH A COMPELLING DIGNITY) LET HIM SPEAK. 332 LAZARU
I KNOW IT IS FOLLY TO SPEAK--BUT-- 354 LAZARU
HE WOULD SPEAK/ 365 LAZARU
(CALLS TO THE SOLDIERS) LET HIM SPEAK/ 365 LAZARU
LET LAZARUS SPEAK/ 365 LAZARU
SPEAK/ 367 LAZARU
DON'T SPEAK/ 17 MANSNS
BESIDES, THIS IS HARDLY THE TIME TO SPEAK OF-- 37 MANSNS
I MIGHT COMPLAIN THAT YOU USED TO SPEAK OF OUR 77 MANSNS HOME AND OUR CHILDREN, WHILE NOW
SIMON, WITHOUT LOOKING AT HER, BEGINS TO SPEAK 103 MANSNS AGAIN.
SHE DID NOT SPEAK AGAIN, ALTHOUGH HE KNEW SHE 111 MANSNS REMAINED THERE,
NOT UNTIL I GIVE YOU PERMISSION TO SPEAK. 115 MANSNS
(THEY BOTH SPEAK TO EACH OTHER SIMULTANEOUSLY.. 123 MANSNS
IT IS DESPICABLE OF YOU TO SPEAK LIKE THAT 178 MANSNS

SPEAKS

SPEAK (CONT'D.)
DON'T SPEAK LIKE THAT--IT IS MAD YOU ARE/ 186 MANSNS
SPEAK TO ME, DARLING/ 190 MANSNS
IT SEEMED THAT AT ANY MOMENT SHE MUST AWAKE AND 352 MARCOM
SPEAK/
YOU SPEAK TO HIM, MARK. 362 MARCOM
(AIRILY) MY DEAR FRIEND, DON'T SPEAK OF BUSINESS.365 MARCOM
(INTERPOSING EAGERLY) IF I MIGHT SPEAK TO THE BOY380 MARCOM
IN PRIVATE A MINUTE--
AND SINCE THEN, ON HIS RETURNS, TO SPEAK WITH 387 MARCOM
YOU--A PRINCESS/
(HERE JUST AS MARCO IS HEARD STARTING TO SPEAK, 389 MARCOM
SPEAK TO MY HEART/ 437 MARCOM
THE HOUSE IS NOT, TO SPEAK MILDLY, A FINE EXAMPLE 1 MISBEG
OF NEW ENGLAND ARCHITECTURE.
SURE HE COULDN'T SPEAK FAIRER THAN THAT. 43 MISBEG
(HE GOES ON GRIMLY BEFORE HARDER CAN SPEAK) 61 MISBEG
AND SAYING I'D NEVER SPEAK TO HIM AGAIN. 79 MISBEG
I OUGHTN'T TO SPEAK TO YOU, IF I HAD ANY PRIDE. 102 MISBEG
I SPEAK ILL OF THE DEAD. 129 MISBEG
(HE PAUSES--STARTS TO SPEAK--PAUSES AGAIN.) 146 MISBEG
THERE'LL BE A SPEAK OPEN, AND SOME DRUNK LAUGHING.152 MISBEG
DIDN'T I TELL YOU TO SPEAK LOW AND NOT WAKE HIM/ 161 MISBEG
TO GET ME TO--(AS HE STARTS TO SPEAK) SHUT UP/ 162 MISBEG
(HE LOOKS MISERABLE, STARTS TO SPEAK, THINKS 164 MISBEG
BETTER OF IT.
YOU SAID NONE OF THE GENTRY WOULD SPEAK TO AULD 12 POET
MELODY,
SHE CAN SPEAK AS FINE AS ANY LADY IN THE LAND IF 41 POET
SHE WANTS.
I'D BE SO INSULTED I'D NEVER SPEAK TO HIM AGAIN. 64 POET
AND WHEN I DID SPEAK IT WAS TO SAY I HAD TO COME 65 POET
AND HELP YOU.
SHE STILL REFUSES TO NOTICE HIM AND HE IS FORCED 89 POET
TO SPEAK.
I WISH TO SPEAK TO MY DAUGHTER. 104 POET
YOU'D BETTER THINK WELL BEFORE YOU SPEAK, FATHER. 105 POET
SO HURT AND FULL OF HATRED HER LIPS TREMBLE AND 107 POET
SHE CANNOT SPEAK.
BUT SHE DOESN'T SPEAK. 137 POET
COME HERE, ANNIE, TILL I SPEAK TO YOU. 584 ROPE
SPEAK OF THE DIVIL AN' HERE HE IS/ 590 ROPE
HE WANTED TO SPEAK TO ME JUST BEFORE HE DIED... 4 STRANG
THIS TIME I DO SPEAK FOR HER SAKE. 21 STRANG
THE PRESIDENT WILL SPEAK AT THE FUNERAL... 23 STRANG
THEN JUST AS EACH OF THE MEN IS ABOUT TO SPEAK, 39 STRANG
WHY DOES HE SPEAK SO RESENTFULLY OF GORDON'S 39 STRANG
MEMORY?...
THEN, UNDER THE CIRCUMSTANCES, HAVING WEIGHED THE 46 STRANG
PROS AND CONS, SO TO SPEAK,
WHY DON'T YOU SPEAK PLAINLY. 59 STRANG
WITH NO ONE TO SPEAK TO EXCEPT SAM'S BUSINESS 143 STRANG
FRIENDS AND THEIR DEADLY WIVES.
I SPEAK AS YOUR FRIEND/ 178 STRANG
(STERNLY) FOR THE SAKE OF YOUR FUTURE HAPPINESS 178 STRANG
AND MY SON'S I'VE GOT TO SPEAK/
(BEAMING ALL OVER) YOU SPEAK SWEDISH$ 502 VOYAGE
THEY SPEAK, OSTENSIBLY TO THE OTHER, 452 WELDED
HE WAITS FOR HER TO SPEAK, NOT KNOWING WHAT TO 462 WELDED
THINK.
(THEN CALMING HERSELF AND TRYING TO SPEAK MATTER- 464 WELDED
OF-FACTLY)
THEIR LIPS MOVE AS IF THEY WERE TRYING TO SPEAK. 480 WELDED
SHE SEEMS ABOUT TO (IMPLORE HIM NOT TO SPEAK.) 484 WELDED
SPEAKEASIES
INFESTING CORNERS, DOORWAYS, CHEAP RESTAURANTS, 9 HUGHIE
THE BARS OF MINOR SPEAKEASIES,
SPEAKEASY
IT ISN'T DRUNKEN LAUGHTER IN A SPEAKEASY YOU WANT 152 MISBEG
TO HEAR AT ALL,
SPEAKIN'
YOU KNOW I'M SPEAKIN' TRUTH--THAT'S WHY YOU'RE 106 BEYOND
AFRAID TO ARGY/
WAAL--IN A MANNER O' SPEAKIN'--THAT'S THE PROMISE.204 DESIRE
AN' SCOTTY'LL TELL YOU IF I AIN'T SPEAKIN' TRUTH. 520 INZONE
=SPEAKIN' IN GENERAL, I 'AVE TRIED 'EM ALL, 161 JOURNE
(LOWERING HIS VOICE.) SPEAKIN' AV NORA, YOU NIVIR 13 POET
MENTIONED HER LAST NIGHT,
AND SPEAKIN' AV THE PIGS AND HIS FATHER ONE 158 POET
MINUTE,
BEGORKA, IF THAT WASN'T THE MAD MAJOR'S GHOST 169 POET
SPEAKIN'/
SPEAKIN' AV THE DEPARTED, MAY HIS SOUL ROAST IN 173 POET
HELL,
I AIN'T SPEAKIN' ON'Y FUR MESELF. 494 VOYAGE
WAS SPEAKIN' ENGLISH B'FORE I WAS OLD ENOUGH TO 502 VOYAGE
LEARN.
I JEST 'ATES TO 'EAR ANYONE SPEAKIN' ABAIT DYIN'. 506 VOYAGE
SPEAKING
(SPEAKING ALOUD TO HIMSELF--DERISIVELY) 550 'ILE
(SWALLOWING HARD--IN A HOARSE WHISPER, AS IF HE 551 'ILE
HAD DIFFICULTY IN SPEAKING)
(HIS FATHER'S VOICE IS HEARD SPEAKING TO HIS 186 AHWILD
MOTHER.
YOU KNOW, SPEAKING OF SWIMMING, 229 AHWILD
CHRIS SEEMS ON THE VERGE OF SPEAKING, HESITATES, 10 ANNA
(WHO HAS WATCHED HIM KEENLY WHILE HE HAS BEEN 21 ANNA
SPEAKING--
(DISMISSING THE SUBJECT) SPEAKING OF BEING SICK, 22 ANNA
I BEEN THERE MYSELF--
(AS IF SHE WERE SPEAKING TO A CHILD) 99 BEYOND
(CURIOUSLY) DIDN'T I HEAR YOU SPEAKING ABOUT ANDY117 BEYOND
A WHILE AGO$
YOU'RE SPEAKING OF--RUTH$ 134 BEYOND
ROB SHUT ME UP WITH ALMOST THE SAME WORDS WHEN I 139 BEYOND
TRIED SPEAKING TO HIM ABOUT IT.
(SPEAKING WITH AN EFFORT) I WON'T WAKE HER. 145 BEYOND
(SPEAKING WITH TREMENDOUS DIFFICULTY) 489 CARDIF

SPEAKING (CONT'D.)
(A PAUSE--RESTLESSLY) SPEAKING O' MILK, WONDER 218 DESIRE
HOW EBEN'S MANAGIN'$
(HE STAMPS OUT, RIGHT, WHILE HE IS SPEAKING. 505 DIFRNT
(HE RISES TO HIS FEET AS HE IS SPEAKING THIS 518 DIFRNT
LAST.)
(WHILE HE IS SPEAKING HE GOES OUT AND DISAPPEARS 548 DIFRNT
AFTER HIS MOTHER.
(AS SHE FINISHES SPEAKING, 446 DYNAMO
SAY, HERE'S ONE ON ME, ADA--SPEAKING OF PRAYING, 470 DYNAMO
'WHILE SHE HAS BEEN SPEAKING SHE HAS COME TOWARD 16 ELECTR
LAVINIA
AND I'M USED TO STRAIGHT SPEAKING. 22 ELECTR
(SPEAKING TO VINNIE AS THEY ENTER--HARSHLY) 120 ELECTR
SHE IS SPEAKING NOW THROUGH YOU/ 166 ELECTR
(WITH EXCITED EAGERNESS NOW, SPEAKING TO THE DEAD)166 ELECTR
(WHILE HE HAS BEEN SPEAKING, THE MOON HAS PASSED 267 GGBROW
GRADUALLY BEHIND A BLACK CLOUD.
SPEAKING OF MY CANNED MUSIC, OUR MR. BROWN HATES 285 GGBROW
THAT OLD BOX.
(AS HE IS SPEAKING, A WELL-DRESSED IMPORTANT STOUT305 GGBROW
MAN ENTERS THE DRAFTING ROOM.
(WHILE HE HAS BEEN SPEAKING THERE HAS BEEN A NOISE314 GGBROW
FROM THE STAIRS.
SPEAKING OF MARRIAGE, THAT WAS THE BIG REASON I 14 HUGHIE
DUCKED.
(WHILE HE IS SPEAKING WILLIE OBAN HAS OPENED HIS 594 ICEMAN
EYES.
(ABRUPTLY TO PARRITT) SPEAKING OF WHISKEY, SIR, 595 ICEMAN
REMINDS ME--
(WHILE HE IS SPEAKING, THE NEGRO, JOE, COMES IN 636 ICEMAN
FROM THE HALLWAY.
(WHILE HE IS SPEAKING, HICKEY COMES IN THE DOORWAY638 ICEMAN
AT REAR.
REMEMBER, LIEUTENANT, YOU ARE SPEAKING OF MY 651 ICEMAN
SISTER/
(WHILE HE IS SPEAKING THE FACES OF THE GANG HAVE 662 ICEMAN
LIGHTED UP VINDICTIVELY,
(AS HE IS SPEAKING HICKEY APPEARS SILENTLY IN THE 703 ICEMAN
DOORWAY AT REAR.
I REMEMBER I HEARD MYSELF SPEAKING TO HER, 716 ICEMAN
IT IS AS IF THEY WERE WAITING UNTIL SHE GOT 75 JOURNE
UPSTAIRS BEFORE SPEAKING.)
SPEAKING OF ACTING, MA'AM, HOW IS IT YOU NEVER 102 JOURNE
WENT ON THE STAGE$
SHE WERE SPEAKING IMPERSONALLY OF PEOPLE SEEN FROM113 JOURNE
A DISTANCE.)
AND SPEAKING WITH A STRANGE UNEARTHLY CALM 279 LAZARU
(AS HE FINISHES SPEAKING ALL THE SOUND OF MUSIC 331 LAZARU
AND VOICES FROM THE HOUSE CEASES
(HE HAS WALKED TOWARD THE THRONE WHILE HE IS 339 LAZARU
SPEAKING.
(HIS VOICE SPEAKING LOVINGLY, WITH A SURPASSING 367 LAZARU
CLEARNESS AND EXALTATION)
(HAS BEEN SPEAKING. 368 LAZARU
(BUT EVEN AS HE IS SPEAKING THE DOOR IS SLOWLY 27 MANSNS
OPENED OUTWARDS AND DEBORAH
AND HER WAY OF SPEAKING COPIES DEBORAH, 75 MANSNS
SPEAKING OF BUSINESS, TELL ME ABOUT THE COMPANY. 76 MANSNS
SPEAKING OF BUSINESS, 100 MANSNS
HE HEARD THE VOICE OF THE ENCHANTRESS SPEAKING 111 MANSNS
FROM THE OTHER SIDE,
(AS SHE IS SPEAKING THE MOON COMES FROM BEHIND A 162 MANSNS
CLOUD
YOU ARE SPEAKING OF MY MISTRESS. 178 MANSNS
(WHILE THEY HAVE BEEN SPEAKING, UNNOTICED BY THEM,352 MARCOM
IT HAS GROWN DARK.
(THEN SPEAKING) MAKE A MENTAL NOTE OF THAT. 365 MARCOM
(JUST AS HE FINISHES SPEAKING, KUKACHIN ENTERS 389 MARCOM
FROM THE LEFT.
I DON'T KNOW ANYTHING ABOUT BRAVELY SPEAKING. 403 MARCOM
SPEAKING WITH A PITYING SCORN.) 432 MARCOM
SPEAKING TO THE DEAD GIRL SOFTLY AS HE DOES SO-- 437 MARCOM
WITH A TREMBLING SMILE)
(BY THE TIME HE FINISHES SPEAKING, 128 POET
(AS IF THIS WERE THE FIRST TIME SHE WAS REALLY 140 POET
CONSCIOUS OF SARA SPEAKING.
(AS HE FINISHES SPEAKING LUKE APPEARS IN THE 587 ROPE
DOORWAY.
(BUT SPEAKING OF SAM'S BIRTH, YOU REALLY MUST 50 STRANG
MEET HIS MOTHER SOMETIME.
WHO IS SPEAKING TO ME... 62 STRANG
(SPEAKING MECHANICALLY IN A DULL VOICE) 63 STRANG
(SPEAKING GENTLY) I WANT YOU TO BE HAPPY, SAM. 71 STRANG
GENTLY) BUT, MADAME, I MUST CONFESS THE NED YOU 88 STRANG
ARE SPEAKING OF IS I.
(SPEAKING WITH GENTLE REPROACH) 167 STRANG
(SPEAKING SADLY) I'VE LOST MY SON, NED/ 167 STRANG
(IN THE TONE A MOTHER TAKES IN SPEAKING TO HER 169 STRANG
HUSBAND ABOUT THEIR BOY)
(SPEAKING TO HELL, VID ULSTER/ 498 VOYAGE
(CAPE NODS WITHOUT SPEAKING, JOHN GOES TO THE 451 WELDED
DOOR, ELEANOR ACCOMPANYING HIM)
SPEAKS
THE FIST IS GRADUALLY LOWERED AND KEENEY SPEAKS 539 'ILE
SLOWLY)
BACK TOWARD THE SITTING-ROOM WHEN SHE SPEAKS TO 215 AHWILD
HIM PITYINGLY)
HE WAVES HIS HAND AIMLESSLY AND SPEAKS WITH A 224 AHWILD
SILLY GRAVITY.)
HE STRAIGHTENS ALERTLY AND SPEAKS IN A VOICE THAT,252 AHWILD
IN SPITE OF HIS EFFORT,
SID WITHOUT OPENING HIS EYES, SPEAKS TO HIM 271 AHWILD
DROWSILY.)
(HE SIZES RICHARD UP SEARCHINGLY--THEN SUDDENLY 294 AHWILD
SPEAKS SHARPLY)
HE SPEAKS SHYLY.) 297 AHWILD

SPEAKS

SPEAKS (CONT'D.)
(THEN HE SIGHS AND SPEAKS WITH A GENTLE NOSTALGIC 298 AHWILD MELANCHOLY)
SHE SPEAKS IN A LOUD, MANNISH VOICE, 7 ANNA
SHE SPEAKS HURRIEDLY IN A LOW VOICE) 19 ANNA
(AFTER A PAUSE SHE SPEAKS MUSINGLY) 27 ANNA
SHE SPEAKS ALOUD TO HERSELF IN A TENSE, TREMBLING 67 ANNA VOICE)
SPEAKS WITH SOMBER PREMONITION AS ANNA RE-ENTERS 78 ANNA FROM THE LEFT)
AFTER A PAUSE HE SPEAKS WITH HAPPY HOPEFULNESS) 92 BEYOND
HE SPEAKS IN A LOW VOICE, FULL OF FEELING) 109 BEYOND
SHE SPEAKS IN AN UNCERTAIN VOICE, WITHOUT 112 BEYOND ASSERTIVENESS.
(AS HE GOES OUT HE SPEAKS BACK OVER HIS SHOULDER) 125 BEYOND
WHEN SHE SPEAKS HER VOICE IS WITHOUT TIMBRE, LOW 144 BEYOND AND MONOTONOUS.
THEN SPEAKS IN A LOW VOICE) 148 BEYOND
HIS VOICE IS MOURNFUL AS HE SPEAKS) 150 BEYOND
THEN HE GLANCES DOWN AT HIS BROTHER AND SPEAKS 168 BEYOND BROKENLY
THE CAPTAIN SPEAKS IN A LOW VOICE TO THE MATE) 485 CARDIF
HE SEES AND HEARS ONLY JOHN, EVEN WHEN LOVING 496 DAYS SPEAKS.
AFTER THE DOOR CLOSES BEHIND HIM JOHN SPEAKS 498 DAYS TENSELY)
THEN HE SPEAKS CASUALLY.) 505 DAYS
ELSA SPEAKS TO HER) 515 DAYS
(FINALLY SPEAKS QUIETLY) JACK, EVER SINCE WE CAME543 DAYS UPSTAIRS,
(JEERINGLY) THE ROMANTIC IDEALIST AGAIN SPEAKS/ 545 DAYS
SHE SPEAKS WITHOUT OPENING HER EYES, HARDLY ABOVE 554 DAYS A WHISPER,
(BENDS OVER JOHN'S CHAIR AND SPEAKS IN A LOW 554 DAYS CAUTIONING VOICE)
HE SPEAKS TO HIM IN A LOW VOICE) 556 DAYS
(HIS EYES FIXED ON JOHN'S FACE, SPEAKS IN A COLD 557 DAYS IMPLACABLE TONE)
THE NURSE GETS UP AND HE SPEAKS TO HER IN A 558 DAYS WHISPER,
SPEAKS AS IF IN ANSWER TO FATHER BAIRD'S PRAYER) 558 DAYS
IT'S THE HATRED YOU ONCE GAVE YOUR SOUL TO WHICH 559 DAYS SPEAKS, NOT YOU.
SPEAKS SOBBINGLY IN A STRANGE HUMBLE TONE OF 565 DAYS BROKEN REPROACH)
HE SPEAKS TIMIDLY AND HESITATINGLY, AS A MUCH 422 DYNAMO YOUNGER BOY MIGHT.
(GLANCES AT HIM AND SPEAKS IN A GENTLE TONE THAT 423 DYNAMO CARRIES A CHALLENGING QUALITY)
(SHE SPEAKS IN A MEEK, PERSUASIVE TONE) 423 DYNAMO
(HE TOSSES THE BOOK ON THE TABLE AND SPEAKS TO HIS429 DYNAMO WIFE)
(AS ADA BEGINS TO READ, HE SPEAKS TO HIS WIFE) 431 DYNAMO
(AS SHE SPEAKS REUBEN RUNS IN FROM THE RIGHT. 451 DYNAMO
MRS. FIFE SPEAKS TO ADA.) 459 DYNAMO
(HE KISSES THEM HUNGRILY AS HE SPEAKS-- 460 DYNAMO
(HE SPEAKS WITH MOCKING GENIALITY) HELLO/ 463 DYNAMO
(HE SPEAKS TO HIS FATHER IN A DEFENSIVE, ACCUSING 464 DYNAMO TONE)
SHE SPEAKS TO HIS RETREATING FIGURE WITH A STRANGE 42 ELECTR SINISTER AIR OF ELATION)
THEN CHRISTINE SPEAKS IN A DRY MOCKING TONE.) 45 ELECTR
WHEN HE SPEAKS, HIS DEEP VOICE HAS A HOLLOW 46 ELECTR REPRESSED QUALITY.
THEN LAVINIA SPEAKS.) 49 ELECTR
AND SHE SPEAKS WITH STRIDENT DENUNCIATION) 64 ELECTR
WHEN SHE SPEAKS IT IS JERKILY, WITH A STRANGE, 74 ELECTR VAGUE, PREOCCUPIED AIR.
SHE SPEAKS TO ORIN AND HER VOICE IS TENSELY QUIET 78 ELECTR AND NORMAL)
FINALLY LAVINIA SPEAKS TO THE CORPSE IN A GRIM 115 ELECTR BITTER TONE)
LAVINIA SPEAKS AGAIN IN CURT COMMANDING TONE THAT 122 ELECTR RECALLS HER FATHER)
(FINALLY SPEAKS STERNLY) HE PAID THE JUST PENALTY122 ELECTR FOR HIS CRIME.
LAVINIA WATCHES HIM UNEASILY AND SPEAKS SHARPLY) 144 ELECTR
ORIN SPEAKS CURTLY, HIS EYES FIXED ON LAVINIA) 164 ELECTR
HOLD OF HIS TORTURED IMAGINATION AND SPEAKS 166 ELECTR FASCINATEDLY TO HIMSELF)
SHE HOLDS THEM OUT TO SETH AND SPEAKS IN A 170 ELECTR STRANGE, EMPTY VOICE.)
SHE SPEAKS COLDLY AND ANGRILY) 266 GGBROW
SHE SPEAKS STRANGELY IN A 287 GGBROW
HE SPEAKS SUAVELY) 318 GGBROW
(COMES JUST INTO SIGHT AT LEFT AND SPEAKS FRONT 323 GGBROW WITHOUT LOOKING AT THEM--
ERIE USUALLY SPEAKS IN A LOW, GUARDED TONE, 9 HUGHIE
ROCKY SPEAKS TO LARRY OUT OF THE SIDE OF HIS 585 ICEMAN MOUTH)
IN A HALF-AWAKE ALCOHOLIC DAZE AND SPEAKS.) 592 ICEMAN
AND SPEAKS WITH A MOCKING SUAVITY.) 594 ICEMAN
(HE SPEAKS) YOU SEE, LARRYS 597 ICEMAN
SPEAKS ALOUD TO HIMSELF.) 603 ICEMAN
THE OLD GRANDSTAND FOOLOSOPHER SPEAKS/ 623 ICEMAN
AS THE LAUGHTER DIES HE SPEAKS IN HIS GIGGLING, 627 ICEMAN WHEEDLING MANNER.
HE SPEAKS WITH A DROWSY, AFFECTIONATELY 628 ICEMAN ENCOURAGING SMILE.
(SPEAKS UP SHAMEFACEDLY) LISTEN, BOYS, I'S SORRY.637 ICEMAN
HE SPEAKS MORE ALOUD TO HIMSELF THAN TO THEM) 638 ICEMAN
PARRITT LEANS TOWARD HIM AND SPEAKS INGRATIATINGLY649 ICEMAN IN A LOW SECRETIVE TONE.)
(HE SPEAKS IN HIS EAR IN CONFIDENTIAL WARNING) 655 ICEMAN
WHO SPEAKS WITH MUZZY, SELF-PITYING MELANCHOLY OUT656 ICEMAN OF A SENTIMENTAL DREAM.
(SPEAKS UP FROM HIS OWN PREOCCUPATION--STRANGELY) 668 ICEMAN

SPEAKS (CONT'D.)
HE LEANS OVER AND SPEAKS IN A LOW CONFIDENTIAL 677 ICEMAN TONE)
HOPE SPEAKS TO HIM IN A FLAT, DEAD VOICE) 691 ICEMAN
CORA SPEAKS WITH A TIRED WONDER AT HERSELF RATHER 700 ICEMAN THAN RESENTMENT TOWARD HIM)
AS HE SPEAKS, THERE IS A START FROM ALL THE CROWD,703 ICEMAN A SHRINKING AWAY FROM HIM.)
HE SPEAKS WITH A STRAINED ATTEMPT AT HIS OLD 704 ICEMAN AFFECTIONATE JOLLYING MANNER)
HE SPEAKS WITH A GROPING EAGERNESS) 717 ICEMAN
HE SPEAKS SIMPLY AND GRATEFULLY) 720 ICEMAN
(AT THE TABLE BY THE WINDOW HUGO SPEAKS TO LARRY 723 ICEMAN AGAIN.)
(HE LOWERS HIS VOICE AND SPEAKS SLOWLY) 514 INZONE
(THEN SHE SPEAKS WITH A GIRLISH GRAVITY.) 28 JOURNE
JAMIE SPEAKS WITH A COMPLETE CHANGE OF TONE.) 39 JOURNE
HE SPEAKS SLOWLY WITH A SUPERSTITIOUS DREAD.) 39 JOURNE
THEN SHE SPEAKS JEERINGLY.) 49 JOURNE
(AS SHE SPEAKS, CATHLEEN ENTERS FROM THE BACK 62 JOURNE PARLOR.)
WHEN SHE SPEAKS AGAIN, HER FACE HAS CLEARED AND IS 75 JOURNE CALM,
TYRONE SPEAKS, AT FIRST WITH A WARM, RELIEVED 126 JOURNE WELCOME.)
OR OF THE CLOCK, OF WHATEVER FLIES, OR SIGHS, OR 132 JOURNE ROCKS, OR SINGS, OR SPEAKS,
WHEN HE SPEAKS IT IS AS IF HE WERE DELIBERATELY 152 JOURNE GIVING WAY TO DRUNKENNESS AND
(THEN MARY SPEAKS, AND THEY FREEZE INTO SILENCE 171 JOURNE AGAIN, STARING AT HER.
AND SHE SPEAKS ALOUD TO HERSELF, NOT TO THEM.) 171 JOURNE
BUT BEFORE THEY CAN DRINK MARY SPEAKS AND THEY 175 JOURNE SLOWLY LOWER THEIR DRINKS TO THE
(SMILES GENTLY AND SPEAKS AS IF TO A GROUP OF 279 LAZARU INQUISITIVE CHILDREN)
(SPEAKS AMID A PROFOUND SILENCE. 289 LAZARU
FINALLY LAZARUS SPEAKS IN A VOICE OF INFINITE 291 LAZARU DISDAIN)
LAZARUS SPEAKS COMMANDINGLY) 318 LAZARU
CALIGULA SPEAKS GRUFFLY TO MIRIAM WITH A SNEER) 330 LAZARU
(SHE SPEAKS WITH MORE AND MORE VOLUPTUOUS 342 LAZARU SATISFACTION)
SHE SPEAKS TAUNTINGLY TO TIBERIUS) 343 LAZARU
SPEAKS TO HIMSELF WITH A MOCKING AFFECTION AS IF 348 LAZARU TO AN AMUSING CHILD)
HAVING GROWN CALMER NOW, CALIGULA SPEAKS AGAIN-- 358 LAZARU MOURNFUL AND BEWILDERED.)
HE SPEAKS QUIETLY, IN A DEEP VOICE WITH A SLIGHT 5 MANSNS DRAWL.
(SPEAKS QUIETLY IN A POLITE, CAREFULLY CONSIDERED 18 MANSNS AND ARTICULATED ENGLISH.)
HE SPEAKS RAPIDLY AND INCISIVELY. 69 MANSNS
(THEN AS JOEL GOES TOWARD THE DOOR, HE SPEAKS IN A 71 MANSNS CONCILIATING TONE.)
SHE SPEAKS WITH A CRUEL EAGERNESS.) 114 MANSNS
FORCING A CASUAL TONE, SHE SPEAKS TO HIM.) 121 MANSNS
(SPEAKS--FORCING A CASUAL TONE.) 122 MANSNS
DEBORAH SPEAKS WITH A STRANGE GENTLENESS.) 123 MANSNS
(SPEAKS TO SIMON WITH AN AMUSED, TEASING SMILE.) 127 MANSNS
DEBORAH SPEAKS QUICKLY AND LIGHTLY.) 136 MANSNS
(SHE OPENS THE DOOR AT RIGHT, STICKS HER HEAD IN 147 MANSNS AND SPEAKS TO JOEL.
HE SPEAKS WITH HURRIED ACQUIESCENCE.) 176 MANSNS
(HUMORING HER--BOBS HER AN AWKWARD SERVANT-GIRL 192 MANSNS CURTSY AND SPEAKS HUMBLY.)
KUBLA SPEAKS TO THE PRIESTS IN A VOICE OF COMMAND434 MARCOM
FINALLY HE SPEAKS TENDERLY TO HER WITH A SAD 435 MARCOM SMILE)
(BOWS SUBMISSIVELY--SPEAKS) YET WE MUST BOW HUMBLY436 MARCOM BEFORE THE OMNIPOTENT.
HE SPEAKS WITH A SURPRISING SAD GENTLENESS) 17 MISBEG
(WATCHES THE CRACK UNDER JOSIE'S DOOR AND SPEAKS 97 MISBEG HALF-ALOUD TO HIMSELF.
(SHE POURS OUT DRINKS AS SHE SPEAKS, A HALF 115 MISBEG TUMBLERFUL FOR HIM.
HE SPEAKS IN A TONE OF RANDOM CURIOSITY) 129 MISBEG
HE SPEAKS THICKLY AS IF HE WAS SUDDENLY VERY 137 MISBEG DRUNK)
(SPEAKS IN A TIRED, EMPTY TONE. 143 MISBEG
SHE HUGS HIM MORE TIGHTLY AND SPEAKS SOFTLY, 152 MISBEG STARING INTO THE MOONLIGHT)
SHE LOOKS DOWN AT HIM AGAIN AND SPEAKS SOOTHINGLY 153 MISBEG AS SHE WOULD TO A CHILD)
(SPEAKS IN A LOW GRIM TONE) STOP HIDING, FATHER. 157 MISBEG
SHE SPEAKS BITTERLY) 158 MISBEG
MEANWHILE HE SPEAKS WITH CARESSING COURTESY.) 69 POET
SHE SNATCHES HER HAND FROM HIS AND SPEAKS WITH 72 POET WITHERING CONTEMPT.)
SHE SPEAKS RAPIDLY IN A REMOTE, DETACHED WAY, 81 POET
(VAGUELY SURPRISED--SPEAKS RAPIDLY AGAIN.) 82 POET
SHE SPEAKS IN A LOW, CONFIDENTIAL TONE HERSELF, 84 POET SMILING NATURALLY.)
(HE STOPS--WHEN HE SPEAKS AGAIN IT IS BITTERLY.) 99 POET
HE SPEAKS QUIETLY.) 107 POET
(HE SPEAKS QUIETLY, BUT AS HE GOES ON 112 POET
THEN SHE CONTROLS HERSELF AND SPEAKS WITH QUIET, 115 POET BITING SARCASM.)
HE SPEAKS PROUDLY.) 116 POET
MEANWHILE, AS SOON AS HE THINKS SHE HAS GONE, 118 POET GADSBY SPEAKS.)
CREGAN SPEAKS, HIS ONLY THOUGHT TO GET HIM AWAY 128 POET FROM SARA.)
(FOLLOWING HIM, SPEAKS OVER HIS SHOULDER TO SARA.1129 POET
HER MOOD CHANGES TO RESENTMENT AND SHE SPEAKS AS 137 POET IF SARA HAD SPOKEN.)
SUDDENLY SPEAKS IN A JEERING MUMBLE TO HIMSELF.) 157 POET

SPEAKS (CONT'D.)
(SUDDENLY SPEAKS, WITHOUT LOOKING UP, IN THE 166 POET BROADEST BROGUE,
HE SPEAKS WITHOUT BROGUE, NOT TO THEM BUT ALOUD TO169 POET HIMSELF.)
(HE STARTS TO SOB BUT WRENCHES HIMSELF OUT OF IT 169 POET AND SPEAKS IN BROAD,
(SHE LEANS TOWARD HIM AND SPEAKS WITH TAUNTING 171 POET VINDICTIVENESS,
HE SPEAKS SLOWLY, WITH DIFFICULTY KEEPING HIS 171 POET WORDS IN BROGUE.)
(HE MUMBLES TO HIMSELF FOR A MOMENT--THEN SPEAKS 579 ROPE CLEARLY)
SWEENEY SPEAKS TO HIS WIFE IN A LOW TONE) 583 ROPE
SWEENEY SPEAKS SUDDENLY IN A STRANGE, AWED VOICE) 590 ROPE
HE SPEAKS WITH A CAREFUL EASE AS ONE WHO LISTENS 4 STRANG TO HIS OWN CONVERSATION,
SHE SPEAKS DIRECTLY TO HER FATHER IN A VOICE 13 STRANG TENSELY COLD AND CALM)
SHE STARES AT MARSDEN BLANKLY AND SPEAKS IN QUEER 26 STRANG FLAT TONES)
(HE SUDDENLY SPEAKS TO EVANS WITH A REALLY SAVAGE 75 STRANG SATISFACTION)
AND SPEAKS AS THOUGH SHE WERE HIDING A HURT 118 STRANG REPROACH BENEATH A JOKING TONE)
(CERTAIN OF HERSELF NOW, SHE COMES TO HIM AND 126 STRANG SPEAKS WITH CONFIDENT PLEASURE)
SSSHH--LISTEN--SOMEONE--(SHE SPEAKS IN AN 449 WELDED UNNATURAL, MECHANICAL TONE,
SHE GLANCES QUICKLY AT HIS FACE, THEN SPEAKS WITH 451 WELDED A KIND OF DULL REMORSE)
SHE SPEAKS WITH INTENSE, COLD HATRED) 460 WELDED
SHE TURNS AND SPEAKS TO SOMEONE WHO IS FOLLOWING 470 WELDED HER,
(THEN SHE SPEAKS SADLY BUT FIRMLY AS IF SHE HAD 486 WELDED COME TO A DECISION)
SHE SMILES AT HIM AND SPEAKS WITH A TENDER 487 WELDED WEARINESS)

SPEAR
HE STRIPS TO DISPLAY THAT SCAR ON HIS BACK HE GOT 593 ICEMAN FROM A NATIVE SPEAR
GIVE ME A SPEAR/ 369 LAZARU
(DASHES BACK AMONG THEM WAVING HIS BLOODY SPEAR 369 LAZARU AND RUSHING UP TO THE THRONE
(HE SNATCHES A SPEAR FROM A SOLDIER AND FIGHTS HIS369 LAZARU WAY DRUNKENLY TOWARD THE
(HE DISAPPEARS TOWARD THE FLAMES, HIS SPEAR HELD 369 LAZARU READY TO STAB.)
HE LUNGES WITH HIS SPEAR AT IMAGINARY FOES, 370 LAZARU JUMPING, DODGING FROM SIDE TO SIDE,
(SUDDENLY THROWING HIS SPEAR AWAY AND SINKING ON 371 LAZARU HIS KNEES,
ON THE RIGHT, AN OPEN PORTAL WITH A SENTRY PACING 358 MARCOM UP AND DOWN, SPEAR IN HAND,
ON HIS RIGHT A MONGOL WARRIOR IN FULL ARMOR WITH 377 MARCOM SHIELD AND SPEAR,

SPEARHEAD
IN A FORMATION LIKE A SPEARHEAD, 282 LAZARU
THE CHORUS OF OLD MEN IS AGAIN JOINED IN ITS 287 LAZARU SPEARHEAD FORMATION AT THE STAIRS,
IN THE SPEARHEAD FORMATION. 298 LAZARU

SPEARS
RAISING THEIR SPEARS ALOFT AND SALUTING LAZARUS 334 LAZARU

SPEC
AND THE ROAD IS HARD MACADAM WITH DIVIL A SPEC OF 44 MISBEG DUST,

SPECIAL
ANYTHING SPECIAL HAPPENED, ESSIE$ 234 AHWILD
I TOOK SPECIAL PAINS WITH IT, 239 AHWILD
AS IF IT WAS A SPECIAL NIGHT, 277 AHWILD
AND STOCKED UP WITH SOME SPECIAL GRUB ALL ON 103 BEYOND ROBERT'S ACCOUNT$
D'YOU THINK THIS SPECIAL DOCTOR'LL DO ROB ANY 152 BEYOND GOOD$
THEY ALWAYS HAD SOMETHIN' SPECIAL NICE COOKED FUR 468 CARIBE ME TO EAT,
A SPECIAL CURTAIN SHOWS THE HOUSE AS SEEN FROM THE 2 ELECTR STREET,
AND DID YOU HAVE ANY SPECIAL JOB IN THAT LINE YOU 248 HA APE WANTED TO PROPOSE TO US$
THEY'RE GLAD TO HAVE HIM, BUT IT'S THE SPECIAL 36 JOURNE STUFF THAT GETS HIM BY,
MY FATHER PAID FOR SPECIAL LESSONS, 104 JOURNE
THAT IS WHY I MUST ESCORT THIS JEW TO ROME--AS A 303 LAZARU SPECIAL HONOR/
(WITH A CRUEL SMILE) I HAVE THOUGHT OF A SPECIAL 345 LAZARU TEST FOR HIM, CAESAR,
IT WAS MY GRANDFATHER'S SPECIAL COMMAND, GIVEN TO 414 MARCOM YOU BY CHU-YIN, YOU TOLD ME,
I'LL HAVE A SPECIAL DINNER FOR YOU LIKE I'VE 38 POET ALWAYS HAD,
THE CAPT'IN SAYS AS 'E WANTS A MAN SPECIAL BAD-- 495 VOYAGE TER-NIGHT,

SPECIALIST
(AFTER A PAUSE) WELL, ANDY'S BRINGING A 145 BEYOND SPECIALIST WITH HIM WHEN HE COMES,
AM BRINGING SPECIALIST TO SEE ROB, 147 BEYOND
A SPECIALIST WILL TELL YOU IN A SECOND 147 BEYOND
YOU DON'T WANT TO BE ALL WORE OUT WHEN THE 151 BEYOND SPECIALIST COMES, DO YOU$
(BITTERLY,) AND WHAT COULD THE FINEST SPECIALIST 33 JOURNE IN AMERICA DO FOR EDMUND,
(MISERABLY DOGGED,) HE CALLED IN A SPECIALIST TO 118 JOURNE EXAMINE ME,
WHY SHOULDN'T I BELIEVE IT WHEN BOTH HARDY AND THE143 JOURNE SPECIALIST--$
HARDY AND THE SPECIALIST KNOW WHAT YOU'RE WORTH, 144 JOURNE

SPECIALIST (CONT'D.)
THERE WAS ANOTHER SANATORIUM THE SPECIALIST 149 JOURNE RECOMMENDED,
I'LL HAVE TO CALL IN A NERVE SPECIALIST... 12 STRANG
A WORD OF ADVICE AS TO THE BEST SPECIALIST, THE 76 STRANG VERY BEST,

SPECIALISTS
DANCING, BUT YOUR SPECIALISTS WERE AT TOTAL LOSS/ 100 STRANG

SPECIALLY
SPECIALLY WHEN IT'S BY A NICE HANDSOME KID LIKE 240 AHWILD YOU,
SPECIALLY NOW ARTER HIM BEIN' BORN, 254 DESIRE

SPECIALTY
WHAT IS HIS SPECIALTY$... 34 STRANG

SPECIE
STILL, IF WE HAD THAT TWO HUNDRED THOUSAND IN 49 MANSNS SPECIE NOW--

SPECIES
THAT SPECIES OF DEAD IS SO INVULNERABLY ALIVE/ 39 STRANG

SPECIFIC
MAY I ASK ON WHAT SPECIFIC ACTIONS OF HERS THIS 36 STRANG THEORY OF YOURS IS BASED$

SPECIFIES
WHICH SPECIFIES THAT YOU RELINQUISH ALL CLAIMS, OF122 POET WHATEVER NATURE,

SPECIMEN
YOU HAVEN'T FORGOTTEN WHAT A SICKLY SPECIMEN I WAS 89 BEYOND THEN, IN THOSE DAYS,

SPECK
YES, I LIED TO YOU--SEE--IT'S GONE--THE LAST 567 CROSS SPECK--
(EXULTANTLY) ARE YOU A SPECK OF DUST DANCED IN 308 LAZARU THE WINDS

SPECKED
A SMALL, DINGY ROOM, DIMLY LIGHTED BY TWO FLY- 236 AHWILD SPECKED GLOBES,
IN A FLY-SPECKED GILT CHANDELIER SUSPENDED FROM 236 AHWILD THE MIDDLE OF THE CEILING,
THE LIVING ROOM IS SMALL, LOW-CEILINGED, WITH 71 MISBEG FADED, FLY-SPECKED WALLPAPER,

SPECKS
*OUNCE AS SQUIRMING SPECKS WE CREPT FROM THE TIDES 324 LAZARU OF THE SEA,
I USED TO SEE THEIR BLOOD DANCE IN RED SPECKS 355 LAZARU BEFORE MY EYES

SPECS
SHE ALSO HAS ON HER SPECS, 249 AHWILD
HE HAS HIS READING SPECS ON AND IS RUNNING OVER 249 AHWILD ITEMS IN A NEWSPAPER,
ONLY THE GREENSHADED READING LAMP IS LIT AND BY 288 AHWILD ITS LIGHT MILLER, HIS SPECS ON,
MRS, MILLER LEANS FORWARD TO LOOK, PUSHING HER 292 AHWILD SPECS UP,)
HOPE COCKS ONE IRRITABLE EYE OVER HIS SPECS, 596 ICEMAN
(HE COCKS AN EYE OVER HIS SPECS AT MOSHER AND 610 ICEMAN GRINS WITH SATISFACTION)
(COCKS AN EYE OVER HIS SPECS AT THEM--WITH DROWSY 612 ICEMAN IRRITATION)

SPECTACLE
THE FEELINGS OF THE GOD-FEARING MANNON DEAD AT 145 ELECTR THAT SPECTACLE/
SPECTACLE OF MILDRED STANDING THERE IN HER WHITE 225 HA APE DRESS,
IN THE BOER WAR SPECTACLE AT THE ST, LOUIS FAIR 593 ICEMAN
A SWEET SPECTACLE FOR ME/ 167 JOURNE
LAUGHING WITH HER TO THINK OF THE PITIABLE 162 MANSNS SPECTACLE I MAKE WAITING IN VAIN/

SPECTACLES
(HE TAKES OFF HIS SPECTACLES AND PUTS THEM BACK IN292 AHWILD THEIR CASE AND STRAIGHTENS
HE IS LOUNGING AT EASE BEHIND THE BAR, A PAIR OF 3 ANNA SPECTACLES ON HIS NOSE,
(PICKS UP THE LETTER, ADJUSTING HIS SPECTACLES, 4 ANNA
HE WEARS SPECTACLES, 94 BEYOND
A HUMOROUS, GOOD-NATURED MOUTH, SMALL EYES BEHIND 496 DAYS HORN-RIMMED SPECTACLES,)
BEHIND HORN-RIMMED SPECTACLES, 8 HUGHIE
FROM BEHIND THICK-LENSED SPECTACLES, TINY HANDS 574 ICEMAN AND FEET,
HE WEARS FIVE-AND-TEN-CENT-STORE SPECTACLES WHICH 577 ICEMAN ARE SO OUT OF ALIGNMENT
(RAISES HIS HEAD AND PEERS AT ROCKY BLEARILY 579 ICEMAN THROUGH HIS THICK SPECTACLES--
(OPENS ONE EYE TO PEER OVER HIS SPECTACLES-- 581 ICEMAN DROWSILY)
SPECTACLES WITH A WELCOMING GIGGLE,) 618 ICEMAN
LOOKS UP THROUGH HIS THICK SPECTACLES AND GIGGLES 627 ICEMAN FOOLISHLY,)
(BLINKS AT HIM THROUGH HIS THICK SPECTACLES--WITH 634 ICEMAN GUTTURAL DENUNCIATION)
WHO LIFTS HIS HEAD FROM HIS ARMS AND BLINKS AT HIM691 ICEMAN THROUGH HIS THICK SPECTACLES,
HOPE BEANS OVER AND UNDER HIS CROOKED SPECTACLES 726 ICEMAN

SPECTATOR
THE STUDIED ALOOFNESS OF AN IRONICALLY AMUSED 68 POET SPECTATOR,
(IS NOW AN AMUSED SPECTATOR AGAIN-- 70 POET APOLOGETICALLY,)

SPECTATORS
THERE IS A CROWD OF CURIOUS SPECTATORS, 196 EJONES
WITH A SIGN,, *SPECTATORS MAY DISTINGUISH THE TRUE599 ICEMAN BARON BY HIS BLUE BEHIND,*
GROUPING IN A BIG SEMICIRCLE AS OF SPECTATORS IN A344 LAZARU THEATRE,

SPECULATING
I TOOK TO SPECULATING, 161 BEYOND

SPECULATION
I TRIED SPECULATION, 156 BEYOND

SPECULATION

SPECULATION (CONT'D.)
CONSERVATIVE MERCHANT LIKE HENRY KNOW OF SUCH WILD 32 MANSNS SPECULATIONS
(REALLY, IT'S HARDLY A DECENT TIME, IS IT, FOR 25 STRANG THAT KIND OF SPECULATION...
SPECULATIONS
BUT ALL THESE FANCIFUL SPECULATIONS ARE NONSENSE. 74 MANSNS
SPECULATIVE
HIS EYES IMPERSONALLY SPECULATIVE, 439 MARCOM
SPECULATIVELY
(THEN SPECULATIVELY) YOUTH NEEDS SO MUCH SLEEP 402 MARCOM AND OLD AGE SO LITTLE.
SPECULATOR
YOU'RE NOT A CUNNING REAL ESTATE SPECULATOR. 15 JOURNE

SPEECH
BUT HOW ABOUT THE FREEDOM OF SPEECH IN THE 194 AHWILD CONSTITUTION, THENS
WELL, RICHARD, I'VE ALWAYS FOUND I'VE HAD TO 195 AHWILD LISTEN TO AT LEAST ONE STUMP SPEECH
AS SID SWALLOWS HARD AND IS ABOUT TO BREAK INTO 257 AHWILD FURTHER SPEECH,
THERE IS AN AUTHORITATIVE NOTE IN HIS SPEECH AS 130 BEYOND THOUGH HE WERE ACCUSTOMED TO
(THERE IS A PERFECT STORM OF GROANS AND LAUGHTER 457 CARIBE AT THIS SPEECH.)
HER SPEECH IS SELF-ASSERTIVE AND CONSCIOUSLY 429 DYNAMO SLANGY.
AWKWARD IN MOVEMENT AND HESITATING IN SPEECH, 12 ELECTR OF FRENIZIED SELF-GLORIFICATION BY HIS SPEECH, DO 216 HA APE LIKEWISE.
(PADDY FROM THE START OF YANK'S SPEECH HAS BEEN 216 HA APE TAKING ONE GULP AFTER ANOTHER
AS FOR HER, DURING HIS SPEECH SHE HAS LISTENED, 225 HA APE PARALYZED WITH HORROR, TERROR,
IT'S FROM A SPEECH MADE IN THE SENATE BY A GUY 242 HA APE NAMED SENATOR QUEEN.
(THIS IS A LONG SPEECH FOR HIM 14 HUGHIE
I TOLD HER, "LISTEN, BABY, I GOT AN IMPEDIMENT IN 26 HUGHIE MY SPEECH.
HIS SPEECH IS EDUCATED, WITH THE GHOST OF A SCOTCH575 ICEMAN RHYTHM IN IT.
HE HAS THE SALESMAN'S MANNERISMS OF SPEECH, AN 619 ICEMAN EASY FLOW OF GLIB,
SPEECH/ 659 ICEMAN
SPEECH/ 659 ICEMAN
RAP THEIR SCHOONERS ON THE TABLE, CALL =SPEECH, 659 ICEMAN
THE EFFECT OF THIS SPEECH IS INSTANTANEOUS. 514 INZONE
BUT THE ACTOR SHOWS IN ALL HIS UNCONSCIOUS HABITS 13 JOURNE OF SPEECH.
A TRACE OF BLUR IN HIS SPEECH, HE DOES NOT SHOW 108 JOURNE IT.
HIS EYES ARE GLASSY, HIS FACE BLOATED, HIS SPEECH 154 JOURNE BLURRED,
(IT IS AS IF HE CAN NO LONGER CONTROL HIS SPEECH. 286 LAZARU
SHE HAS RID HER SPEECH OF BROGUE, EXCEPT IN 2 MANSNS MOMENTS OF EXTREME EMOTION.
HE IS GRAVELY SELF-IMPORTANT AND PRETENTIOUS IN 25 MANSNS MANNER AND SPEECH.
ALTHOUGH THE RHYTHM OF IRISH SPEECH STILL 75 MANSNS UNDERLIES IT.
AND BURSTS FORTH INTO A MEMORIZED SPEECH IN THE 431 MARCOM GRAND CHAMBER OF COMMERCE STYLE)
SMILE WITH INFINITE SILENCE UPON OUR SPEECH, 435 MARCOM
TO MAKE MATTERS EASIER FOR THEM HE IS DELIBERATE 56 MISBEG IN HIS SPEECH.
AND THERE IS A CERTAIN VAGUE QUALITY IN HIS MANNER100 MISBEG AND SPEECH.
BUT HER SPEECH HAS AT TIMES A SELF-CONSCIOUS, 16 POET STILTED QUALITY ABOUT IT.
(RESENTFULLY, BUT MORE CAREFUL OF HER SPEECH.) 23 POET
HE IS STIFFLY CORRECT IN DRESS AND MANNER, DRYLY 116 POET PURENTOUS IN SPEECH.
DESIRE FOR SPEECH HAD PARALYZED ALL POWER OF 594 ROPE ARTICULATION.

SPEECHES
DURING THE NEXT FEW SPEECHES HE MOVES SILENTLY TO 525 DAYS THE CORNER OF THE LONG TABLE
MAKIN' SPEECHES. 213 HA APE
DON'T LET ME BE A WET BLANKET, MAKING FOOL 621 ICEMAN SPEECHES ABOUT MYSELF.
(LAMELY) BEJEES, I'M NO GOOD AT SPEECHES. 659 ICEMAN

SPEECHLESS
THEY STAND SPEECHLESS AND BREATHLESS, PANTING LIKE239 DESIRE TWO ANIMALS.)
(SPEECHLESS WITH HORROR--CAN ONLY GASP) 155 ELECTR
I'M KNOCKED SPEECHLESS. 89 JOURNE
THE GUESTS STARE POP-EYED, OPEN-MOUTHED, 429 MARCOM SPEECHLESS FOR A SECOND.
THAT FOR A MOMENT SHE IS SPEECHLESS. 74 POET
(SHE STARES AT HIM FOR A MOMENT, SPEECHLESS WITH 98 POET ANGER--

SPEECHLESSLY
(GAPING AT HER SPEECHLESSLY FOR A MOMENT) 164 BEYOND
HE LEAPS TO HIS FEET, GLOWERING AT HER 225 DESIRE SPEECHLESSLY.)

SPEED
(C EFFORTS TO SPEED UP AND THE MUSIC SUFFERS IN 471 CARIBE THE PROCESS.)
RUNNING AT A SPEED OF ROTATION N, IS THEORETICALLY429 DYNAMO PROPORTIONAL TO D4 LN2...
DEY'RE SPEED, AIN'T DEYS 215 HA APE
SPEED, AIN'T ITS 217 HA APE
SPEED, DAT'S HER MIDDLE NAME/ 224 HA APE
SPEED, DAT'LL BE HER/ 232 HA APE
IT MOVES--SPEED--TWENTY-FIVE STORIES UP AND ME AT 238 HA APE DE TOP AND BOTTOM--MOVIN'/

SPEEDILY
BEWILDERED PAIN WHICH SPEEDILY TURNS TO RAGE AND 361 LAZARU REVENGEFUL HATRED)
BUT THE POLOS PROCEED SPEEDILY ON THEIR JOURNEY 364 MARCOM

SPELL
BUT, SO GREAT IS THE COMIC SPELL FOR HER EVEN IN 220 AHWILD HER BROTHER'S VOICE,
THE MYSTERY AND SPELL OF THE EAST WHICH LURES ME 85 BEYOND IN THE BOOKS I'VE READ,
THE MYSTERY AND SPELL, I HAVEN'T MET 'EM YET, 86 BEYOND
THAT FOOLIN' ON SHIPS IS ALL RIGHT FOR A SPELL, 115 BEYOND
ANYWAY, I WANT TO STAY TO HOME AND VISIT WITH YOU 137 BEYOND FOLKS A SPELL BEFORE I GO.
WE'RE PAYING FOR THE SPELL OF WARM WEATHER WE'VE 153 BEYOND BEEN HAVING.
IT WAS LAST SUMMER HE HAD A BAD SPELL FIRST, 154 BEYOND
I'M GOIN' OUT FUR A SPELL--UP THE ROAD. 210 DESIRE
(THEN RESIGNEDLY) WALL, LET'S GO HELP EBEN A 219 DESIRE SPELL AN' GIT WAKED UP.
NO. I'M WAITIN' IN HERE A SPELL. 220 DESIRE
(THIS BREAKS HER SPELL FOR HIM. 229 DESIRE
OH--UP THE ROAD A SPELL. 229 DESIRE
(TRYING TO BREAK FROM HER SPELL--CONFUSEDLY) 229 DESIRE
AFTER THAT IT WA'N'T SO LONESOME FUR A SPELL. 237 DESIRE
(WITH A DEEP SIGH) I'LL GO T' THE BARN AN' REST A253 DESIRE SPELL.
YE MUSTN'T--WAIT A SPELL--I WANT T' TELL YE.... 258 DESIRE
YE'D BEST LIE DOWN A SPELL. 263 DESIRE
I'LL STEP IN AGAIN FOR A SPELL AFORE SUPPER--THAT 498 DIFRNT IS, IF YOU WANT ME TO.
KIN I SET A SPELL? 514 DIFRNT
I'M GOING UP AND LIE DOWN FOR A SPELL. 518 DIFRNT
DU SET DOWN A SPELL, BENNY, 524 DIFRNT
HER BIG BODY RELAXED AS IF SHE HAD GIVEN HERSELF 486 DYNAMO UP COMPLETELY TO THE SPELL OF
I WOULD RATHER REST HERE FOR A SPELL. 47 ELECTR
THIS BREAKS THE SPELL FOR CHRISTINE 101 ELECTR
I'M GOING TO MAKE HER LET HIM VISIT US FOR A 159 ELECTR SPELL.
HUW D'YUH SPELL ITA 323 GGBROW
THE MEN ARE TAKING A BREATHING SPELL. 223 HA APE
OUTSIDE, THE SPELL OF ABNORMAL QUIET PRESSES 31 HUGHIE SUFFOCATINGLY UPON THE STREET,
(BREAKS THE SPELL) AW, HERE A CHURCH/ 639 ICEMAN
I'M SURE THE SPELL OF IT WE'VE HAD IS OVER NOW. 40 JOURNE
CASTING ON THE LISTENER AN ENTHRALLING SPELL. 280 LAZARU
HE FIGHTS THE SPELL BUT CANNOT CONTROL HIS JERKING286 LAZARU BODY
CALIGULA IS LISTENING SPELL-BOUND, HIS MOUTH OPEN,304 LAZARU A SPELL5
I GREW AFRAID THIS MAGICIAN HAD PUT YOU UNDER A 343 LAZARU SPELL.
A GREAT SPELL OF SILENCE SETTLES UPON ALL HIS 366 LAZARU HEARERS--
IT'S LIKE A SPELL THAT TRIES TO COME BETWEEN US. 82 MANSNS
BUT IT HELD HIM IN A SPELL AND HE COULD NEVER 111 MANSNS LEAVE IT.
(AS IF SUDDENLY EMERGING FROM A SPELL--WITH AN 127 MANSNS IMPULSIVE GRATEFUL RELIEF.)
WHEN YOU GET YOUR SORROWFUL SPELL ON. 106 MISBEG
IT WAS ONLY A SPELL OF CHILLS AND FEVER HE CAUGHT 73 POET FROM THE DAMP OF THE LAKE.
SQUAT HERE FOR A SPELL AND GIT YOUR WIND. 595 ROPE
(THIS BREAKS THE SPELL WHICH HAS CHAINED HER. 466 WELDED
(BREAKS THE SPELL OF HIS EXULTATION) 488 WELDED

SPELLBOUND
(SPELLBOUND, IN A WHISPER) YES. 90 BEYOND
THAT STARES AT HIM SPELLBOUND) 569 CROSS

SPELLED
BUT RUTH WAS SO SPELLED WITH ROBERT'S WILD POETRY 116 BEYOND NOTIONS.
SPELLED WITH A DOUBLE O, BY THE WAY-- 676 ICEMAN

SPELLS
HIS LIPS MOVING AS HE SPELLS OUT THE WORDS. 8 ANNA
ABOUT SPELLS AND THINGS WHEN YOU'RE ON THE SHIP. 86 BEYOND
SPELLS AND CHARMS TO 'ELP 'EM AGAINST YOUR SILVER 184 EJONES BULLET.
AND LET DEM PO' NIGGERS MAKE ALL DE FOOL SPELLS 185 EJONES DEY'SE A MIN' TO.
BEATIN' YER BLOODY DRUM AND CASTIN' YER SILLY 203 EJONES SPELLS/
YOU HAVEN'T HAD ONE OF THESE MORBID SPELLS SINCE 141 ELECTR WE LEFT THE ISLANDS.
BUT YOU CAN'T DO ANYTHING WITH HIM WHEN HE GETS 148 ELECTR HIS MORBID SPELLS.
I GET SPELLS. 305 GGBROW
(HE SPELLS IT OUT LABORIOUSLY B-E-R--THE NIXT IS 530 INZONE AN L, I THINK--I--AN' N.
DON'T GET IN ONE OF YOUR QUEER SPELLS, NOW. 120 MISBEG

SPEND
AY FORGAT AND AY SPEND ALL MONEY. 21 ANNA
SPEND AND BE A GOOD SPORT, THAT'S MY MOTTO. 522 DIFRNT
THAT'S AN AWFUL PILE TO SPEND, BENNY. 523 DIFRNT
THE GRAVEYARD'S FULL OF HANNONS AND THEY ALL SPEND130 ELECTR THEIR NIGHTS TO HIM HERE.
AND WHATEVER YOU'D LIKE, I CAN'T SPEND MY LIFE 652 ICEMAN SITTING HERE WITH YOU.
YOU'LL SOON SPEND HALF THE DAY PRIMPING BEFORE THE 27 JOURNE MIRROR.
YOUR FATHER WOULD NEVER SPEND THE MONEY TO MAKE IT 44 JOURNE RIGHT.
YOU'LL FIGURE IT WOULD BE A WASTE OF MONEY TO 80 JOURNE SPEND ANY MORE THAN YOU CAN HELP.
HE'D ONLY SPEND IT ON DRINK AND YOU KNOW WHAT A 82 JOURNE VILE, POISONOUS
SPEND MONEY TO MAKE THIS LOOK DECENT, WHILE YOU 141 JOURNE KEEP BUYING MORE PROPERTY,
LIKE A GENTLEMAN GUEST COME IN TO SPEND THE 82 MANSNS EVENING.

SPEND (CONT'D.)
FROM THEIR TALK, THEY MUST SPEND A GREAT DEAL OF 84 MANSNS
THEIR TIME IN HER GARDEN.
HEREAFTER, I SHALL SPEND MY EVENINGS THERE ALONE, 130 MANSNS
AND YOU MAY DO AS YOU PLEASE.
WE SPEND OUR LIVES SEARCHING FOR A MAGIC DOOR AND 180 MANSNS
A LOST KINGDOM OF PEACE--
I'LL GO DOWN TO THE INN AND SPEND MONEY AND GET 64 MISBEG
DRUNK AS MOSES/
WHAT I WANTS IS CASH---REGULAR COIN YUH KIN SPEND---599 ROPE
NOT DIRT.
ONE OF THOSE POOR DEVILS WHO SPEND THEIR LIVES 34 STRANG
(WITH A GRIN) IF I DRINK I YUST GET DRUNK AND 502 VOYAGE
SPEND ALL MONEY.
I SPEND ALL MONEY, I HAVE TO SHIP AWAY FOR ANOTHER506 VOYAGE
VOYAGE.

SPENDER
I NEVER SEEN SUCH A SPENDER. 237 AHWILD
AND THIS BUDDY OF MINE IS A SPORT AND A SPENDER. 523 DIFRNT

SPENDING
HOW ARE YOU SPENDING THE FESTIVE FOURTH, BOOLA- 190 AHWILD
BOOLAS
THE ARTIFICIALITIES THAT ENERGY HAD WON FOR ITSELF218 HA APE
IN THE SPENDING.)
HIS WIFE DEALT HIM FOUR BITS A DAY FOR SPENDING 21 HUGHIE
MONEY.
WELL, IT'S BETTER THAN SPENDING THE SUMMER IN A 44 JOURNE
NEW YORK HOTEL, ISN'T IT?
NO, THAT WOULD HAVE MEANT SPENDING SOME MONEY/ 141 JOURNE
AFTER SPENDING NINE YEARS AT THE COURT OF THE 356 MARCOM
GREAT KAAN

SPENDS
GOES RIGHT ON MAKIN' VIGE AFTER VIGE TO GRAB MORE 522 DIFRNT
AND NEVER SPENDS A NICKEL
I WANTS ACTION WHEN I SPENDS. 180 EJONES
WHEN HE SPENDS SO MUCH MONEY FOR EXTRA LESSONS. 171 JOURNE
AS DEBORAH'S CRYING GRADUALLY SPENDS ITSELF.) 167 MANSNS

SPENT
EVEN IF THERE WAS NOTHING ELSE HE SPENT HIS MONEY 213 AHWILD
ON.
CABIN, HIS BACK BOWED HIS HEAD IN HIS HANDS, IN AN 31 ANNA
ATTITUDE OF SPENT WEARINESS.)
(WITH SPENT WEARINESS) OH, WHAT'S THE USES 62 ANNA
YOU'VE SPENT EIGHT YEARS RUNNING AWAY FROM 161 BEYOND
YOURSELF.
HER MIND ALREADY SINKING BACK INTO THAT SPENT CALM169 BEYOND
(MEANINGLY) SEEMS LIKE HE'S SPENT MOST O' HIS 248 DESIRE
TIME IT' HUH SINCE YEW COME.
AIN'T HE SPENT EVERY DURN EVENIN' OF THE TIME HE'S533 DIFRNT
TO HOME BETWEEN TRIPS OVER
I'D LIKE TO SIT WHERE HE SPUN WHAT I HAVE SPENT. 282 GGBROW
ME ADVISING A SUCKER NOT TO BET WHEN I'VE SPENT A 22 HUGHIE
LOT OF MY LIFE
ONLY I SPENT THE DAY IN THE PARK. 723 ICEMAN
HE THINKS MONEY SPENT ON A HOME IS MONEY WASTED. 61 JOURNE
IF YOU'D SPENT MONEY FOR A DECENT DOCTOR WHEN SHE 140 JOURNE
WAS SO SICK AFTER I WAS BORN,
I'VE SPENT THOUSANDS UPON THOUSANDS IN CURES/ 141 JOURNE
(SUDDENLY SPENT AND MISERABLE.) 142 JOURNE
FOR A PRESENT, AND ON THE WAY HOME SHE SPENT IT 148 JOURNE
ALL ON FOOD.
WHERE HE SPENT HIS CHILDHOOD. 299 LAZARU
THEIR LIVES ARE SPENT IN HIDING. 309 LAZARU
THEIR LIVES ARE SPENT IN HIDING. 310 LAZARU
IT WOULD APPEAR I HAVE SPENT MY LIFE WITH A 32 MANSNS
STRANGER.
BUT THREE OF THE MORE ELDERLY MEN ARE TOO SPENT T0351 MARCOM
MOVE.)
THEY SPENT SO MUCH TIME CONFESSING THEIR SINS, 17 MISBEG
DIFFERENT FROM ALL THE OTHER NIGHTS YOU'D SPENT 171 MISBEG
WITH WOMEN.
HE AIN'T SPENT IT. 586 ROPE
DIVIL A PENNY HE'S SPENT. 586 ROPE
TO MYSELF, NOW THAT I'VE SPENT ONE NIGHT IN IT I 49 STRANG
KNOW THAT WHATEVER SPOOKS THERE
IT'S INCREDIBLE TO THINK SAM WAS BORN AND SPENT 49 STRANG
HIS CHILDHOOD HERE.

SPESHUL
AND YOUR PA AND JACK HAS BOUGHT NEW CLOTHES 511 DIFRNT
SPESHUL FOR IT,

SPESHULLY
MORE SPESHULLY HE CALLS TO MY MIND YOUR GRANDPAW'S 19 ELECTR
BROTHER, DAVID.

SPHERE
BY APPLYING MY NATURAL GOD-GIVEN TALENTS IN THEIR 160 JOURNE
PROPER SPHERE.
SHE MUST BE TAUGHT TO CONFINE HER ACTIVITIES TO 94 MANSNS
THEIR PROPER SPHERE--

SPHERES
CONES, CUNES, CUBES, CYLINDERS, SPHERES, PYRAMIDS, 25 MANSNS
ETC.

SPHERICAL
THE LEFT ONE PASSING BEHIND A SPHERICAL SHRUB AT 25 MANSNS
LEFT-FRONT TO THE HOUSE.

SPIC
CITIES AND SMALL TOWNS--NOT FLASHY BUT 619 ICEMAN
CONSPICUOUSLY SPIC AND SPAN.
YOU LOOK SPIC AND SPAN. 89 JOURNE

SPICES
PAINTED BY AN ARTIST WHO UWED FATHER FOR SPICES 357 MARCOM
AND COULDN'T PAY WITH MONEY.
IF SHE WEREN A MILLION YEN WORTH OF SILK OR SPICES,403 MARCOM
I WOULDN'T WORRY AN INSTANT,

SPICK
AND HUNT UP A WIFE SOMEWHERES FOR THAT SPICK 'N' 104 BEYOND
SPAN CABIN.
HE DRUV OFF IN THE BUGGY, ALL SPICK AN' SPAN, 209 DESIRE

SPICK (CONT'D.)
HE IS DRESSED IN FULL UNIFORM, LOOKING SPICK AND 410 MARCOM
SPAN AND SELF-CONSCIOUS.

SPIDERWEBS
THERE IS NOTHING IN THERE BUT DARK AND DUST AND 113 MANSNS
SPIDERWEBS--

SPIED
MAW SPIED ON HIM--'R SHE'D NEVER KNOWED. 213 DESIRE
'TWAS JUST THAT MOMENT I WOKE AND SPIED HIM. 519 INZONE

SPIEL
THE AUCTIONEER BEGINS HIS SILENT SPIEL. 197 EJONES
THERE'S A LONG SPIEL ABOUT 'ER. 242 HA APE
BUT I COULD HEAR HIM THROUGH THE WALL DOING HIS 681 ICEMAN
SPIEL TO SOMEONE ALL NIGHT LONG.

SPIES
DID YE NEVERR READ OF THE GERMAN SPIES 515 INZONE
AIN'T YOU READ IN THE PAPERS HOW ALL THEM GERMAN 521 INZONE
SPIES THEY BEEN CATCHIN' IN
THEY 'ANGS SPIES ASHORE. 524 INZONE
HOW D'YOU S'POSE SPIES GETS THEIR ORDERS AND SEND5529 INZONE
BACK WHAT THEY FINDS OUT IF
OUR SPIES REPORT THEIR MANY PETTY STATES ARE 421 MARCOM
ALWAYS QUARRELING.

SPIGGOTS
WITH SPIGGOTS AND A SMALL SHOW CASE OF BOTTLED 664 ICEMAN
GOODS.

SPIGODS
FROM WHICH THE LIQUOR IS DRAWN BY MEANS OF 3 ANNA
SPIGOTS.

SPIKE
GOT TO SPIKE HER GUNS WITH SAM/... 105 STRANG

SPILE YOUR CHANCES TO MAKE A MAN OUT O' YOURSELF. 102 BEYOND
OR THE MATE'LL BE DOWN ON OUR NECKS AN' SPILE THE 463 CARIBE
FUN.

SPILL
WANTA SPILL MY SUDS FOR ME? 9 ANNA
I'LL SPILL THE BEANS FOR BOTH OF YOU, IF YOU TRY 530 DIFRNT
TO GUM ME/
I'LL AGREE TO BEAT IT AND NOT SPILL THE BEANS FOR 545 DIFRNT
HIM WITH YOU.
DEY MIGHT SPILL DEIR GUTS, OR SOMETHIN'. 631 ICEMAN
BECAUSE I'M AFRAID BOOZE WOULD MAKE ME SPILL MY 658 ICEMAN
SECRETS, AS YOU THINK.
COME ALONG AND SPILL YOUR GUTS WHERE WE CAN GET IT717 ICEMAN
ON PAPER.
YET I'LL BET YOU'VE HEARD MAMA AND OLD GASPARD 163 JOURNE
SPILL SO MUCH BUNK ABOUT MY
SPILLING.
SPILLING THAT BUSINESS ABOUT PIPE DREAMS/ 626 ICEMAN

SPILT
WELL, NO USE SITTING HERE MOURNING OVER SPILT 234 AHWILD
MILK.
IT AIN'T ANY USE CRYING OVER SPILT MILK. 109 BEYOND
WITH THE IMPRINTS OF HOT DISHES AND SPILT FOOD. 144 BEYOND
THE SIGHS--THEN SPITS) WAAL--NO USE'N CRYIN' OVER218 DESIRE
SPILT MILK.

SPIN
SPIN DAT YARN, COCKY. 457 CARIBE
NARY A TOIL 'R SPIN 'R LICK O' WUK DO WE PUT IN/ 216 DESIRE
YUH'RE ON'Y DOLLS I WINDS UP TO SEE 'M SPIN. 238 HA APE

SPINACH
NO LIP OUT OF YOU, NEITHER, YOU DUTCH SPINACH/ 602 ICEMAN

SPINDLE
BETUNE YOU AND A GRAVE IN THE OCEAN BUT A SPINDLE-479 CARDIF
SHANKED,
(GLARES AT HARDER) WHERE'S YOUR MANNERS, YOU 57 MISBEG
SPINDLE-SHANKED JOCKEY$

SPINDLY
THE OIL SWITCHES, WITH THEIR SPINDLY STEEL LEGS, 483 DYNAMO
THEIR SQUARE,

SPINELESS
THE RESULT OF SOME SNIDE NEUTRALIZING OF LIFE 296 GGBROW
FORCES--A SPINELESS CACTUS--

SPINNING
STOP SPINNING YOUR NAPKIN RING/ 222 AHWILD
YOU HAVE MY HEAD SPINNING/ 49 MANSNS
OFF BALANCE AND SENDS HIM SPINNING DOWN THE STEPS 190 MANSNS
TO FALL HEAVILY AND LIE STILL

SPINS
(HE TURNS EAGERLY TOWARD LEFT BUT SUDDENLY HOGAN 60 MISBEG
GRABS HIS SHOULDER AND SPINS

SPIRAL
I THOUGHT OF A MILLION LIGHT YEARS TO A SPIRAL 41 STRANG
NEBULA--

SPIRES
IT'S ONE VIVID BLASPHEMY FROM SIDEWALK TO THE TIPS297 GGBROW
OF ITS SPIRES/

SPIRIT
HIS IRON SPIRIT WEAKENS AS HE LOCKS AT HER TEAR- 549 'ILE
STAINED FACE.)
THY SHARP SIGHS DIVIDE MY FLESH AND SPIRIT WITH 205 AHWILD
SOFT SOUND---
HIS SPIRIT STILL TOO EXALTED TO BE CONSCIOUS OF 292 AHWILD
HIS SURROUNDINGS.
THEY HAD SPIRIT IN THEM. 37 ANNA
(KINDLY BUT SKEPTICALLY) THAT'S THE RIGHT SPIRIT.102 BEYOND
ROBERT,
WHAT EVIL SPIRIT OF HATE POSSESSED ME TO MAKE ME--495 DAYS
HAVE YOU BEEN GREATLY TROUBLED IN SPIRIT BY 507 DAYS
ANYTHING LATELY$
IT WAS SOME EVIL SPIRIT THAT POSSESSED YOU/ 513 DAYS
BUT HIS EXPERIENCE HAD LEFT AN INDELIBLE SCAR ON 534 DAYS
HIS SPIRIT.
IF HE CONSTANTLY SENSED A MALIGNANT SPIRIT 535 DAYS
HIDING BEHIND LIFE,
A HIDDEN SPIRIT OF EVIL, TOOK POSSESSION OF HIM. 538 DAYS

SPIRIT

SPIRIT (CONT'D.)
TO BELIEVE IN THE POSSIBILITY OF NOBILITY OF 543 DAYS
SPIRIT IN OURSELVES/
SHE WILL BE BESIDE HIM IN SPIRIT IN THIS LIFE, 544 DAYS
WHERE THE SPIRIT DECAYS IN THE SINFUL SLOTH OF THE425 DYNAMO
FLESH...)
BUT EVEN WHEN HE WAS LITTLE I SENSED IN HIM HIS 426 DYNAMO
MOTHER'S REBELLIOUS SPIRIT...
AND HE THINKS IN TORTURED AGONY OF SPIRIT) 448 DYNAMO
I KNOW SHE CAME FROM THE SPIRIT OF THE GREAT 477 DYNAMO
MOTHER INTO WHICH SHE PASSED WHEN
ALIVE WITH THE MIGHTY SPIRIT OF HER ETERNAL LIFE/ 484 DYNAMO
MORE AND MORE THE SPIRIT OF TERROR GAINS 201 EJONES
POSSESSION OF HIM.
THE WHOLE SPIRIT AND MEANING OF THE DANCE HAS 201 EJONES
ENTERED INTO HIM.
HAS BECOME HIS SPIRIT. 201 EJONES
BUT THERE IS SECH A THING AS EVIL SPIRIT. 135 ELECTR
THERE WAS SOMETHING THERE MYSTERIOUS AND 147 ELECTR
BEAUTIFUL--A GOOD SPIRIT--OF LOVE--
SOMETHING ROSE UP IN ME--LIKE AN EVIL SPIRIT/ 155 ELECTR
BLESSED ARE THE POOR IN SPIRIT/ 273 GGBROW
BLESSED ARE THE POOR IN SPIRIT FOR THEY ARE BLIND/273 GGBROW
BLESSED ARE THE POOR IN SPIRIT, BROTHER/ 281 GGBROW
BLESSED ARE THE POOR IN SPIRIT/ 287 GGBROW
BLESSED ARE THE MEEK AND THE POOR IN SPIRIT/ 299 GGBROW
REGAINED THE SELF-CONFIDENT SPIRIT OF ITS YOUTH, 303 GGBROW
HER EYES SHINE WITH HAPPINESS.)
(BREEZILY, FEELING HIM OUT) THAT'S THE RIGHT 247 HA APE
SPIRIT.
(FOR A MOMENT IS SO HURT AND DEPRESSED HE HASN'T 27 HUGHIE
THE SPIRIT
ALAS, HIS WAS AN ADVENTUROUS SPIRIT THAT PINED IN 595 ICEMAN
CONFINEMENT.
THAT'S THE SPIRIT/ 623 ICEMAN
THAT'S THE SPIRIT/ 624 ICEMAN
THAT'S THE SPIRIT--DON'T LET ME BE A WET BLANKET--628 ICEMAN
THEY ARE TRYING TO ACT UP IN THE SPIRIT OF THE 629 ICEMAN
OCCASION
(A HOLIDAY SPIRIT OF GAY FESTIVITY HAS SEIZED THEM640 ICEMAN
ALL.
SCROUNGE/ THAT'S THE SPIRIT FOR HARRY'S BIRTHDAY/640 ICEMAN
(GRINS AT HIM) THAT'S THE SPIRIT, BROTHER-- 640 ICEMAN
COME ON, NOW, SHOW US A LITTLE OF THAT GOOD OLD 685 ICEMAN
BATTLE OF MODDER RIVER SPIRIT
UNTIL NOW THERE'S NO STRENGTH OF THE SPIRIT LEFT 78 JOURNE
IN HER
AS IF IN SPIRIT SHE WERE RELEASED TO BECOME AGAIN, 97 JOURNE
THE SPIRIT IS LOUSED/ 278 LAZARU
(AND BEGINS TO LAUGH FROM THE DEPTHS OF HIS 293 LAZARU
EXALTED SPIRIT.
AWAY WITH SUCH COWARDICE OF SPIRIT/ 324 LAZARU
SPIRIT. 337 LAZARU
(WITH MORE AND MORE OF A SPIRIT OF PERVERSE 342 LAZARU
CRUELTY)
A SPIRIT OF WOMAN MADE FLESH AND FLESH OF HER MADE 73 MANSNS
SPIRIT.
RUTHLESSLY DETERMINED TO DEVOUR AND LIVE AS THE 88 MANSNS
SPIRIT OF LIFE ITSELF/
WE--YOU AND I--IN PARTNERSHIP IN A NEW COMPANY OF 103 MANSNS
THE PURE SPIRIT,
THE SAME SWEET SAD MUSIC COMES FROM THE TREE AGAIN354 MARCOM
AS IF ITS SPIRIT WERE PLAYING
(GRINNING) THERE'S NO SPIRIT IN THE YOUNGSTERS 371 MARCOM
NOWADAYS I'LL BET HE WON'T.
THAT'S THE SPIRIT/ 411 MARCOM
IT MUST BE A PITIFUL LAND, POOR IN SPIRIT AND 421 MARCOM
MATERIAL WEALTH.
WILL SOBER HER SPIRIT AND SHE WILL SETTLE DOWN AS 424 MARCOM
A SENSIBLE WIFE SHOULD.
ONE IN IT HAD SPIRIT, GOD REST HER SOUL. 17 MISBEG
OCH, THERE'S NO SPIRIT IN YOU/ 51 MISBEG
LIKE A POOR SHEEP WITHOUT PRIDE OR SPIRIT-- 79 MISBEG
BE GOD, YOU'VE GOT THE PROUD, FIGHTING SPIRIT IN 96 MISBEG
YOU THAT NEVER SAYS DIE.
YET IN SPITE OF HER SLOVENLY APPEARANCE THERE IS A 20 POET
SPIRIT WHICH SHINES THROUGH
(WITH A FLARE OF SPIRIT.) I WON'T. 22 POET
AND SO I WILL REMAIN TO THE END, IN SPITE OF ALL 43 POET
FATE CAN DO TO CRUSH MY SPIRIT/
(WITH A DEPRECATING SMILE.) FAITH, I WAS FAR AWAY 58 POET
IN SPIRIT.
WOULD HAVE MORE BITTERLY DEPRESSED HIS SPIRIT. 82 POET
A SONG IN THE RIGHT SPIRIT, PIPER. 97 POET
(WITH BELLIGERENT SPIRIT.) AND SO HE HAS, I KNOW 139 POET
THAT/
SPIRIT SO BRAVE AND GENEROUS AND GAY/... 16 STRANG
HER EYES TRY TO ARMOR HER WOUNDED SPIRIT 26 STRANG
GORDON'S SPIRIT FOLLOWED ME FROM ROOM TO ROOM... 71 STRANG
YES--YES, NINA--YES--FOR YOUR HAPPINESS--IN THAT 89 STRANG
SPIRIT/
(LAUGHING) THAT'S THE SPIRIT/ 164 STRANG
YOU NEED ABOUT TEN, I THINK, TO GET YOU IN THE 164 STRANG
RIGHT SPIRIT TO SEE THE FINISH/
YOUR BODY AND SPIRIT, TOO, NINA/ 182 STRANG
GORDON'S SPIRIT/ 182 STRANG
(WITH ASSERTIVE LOYALTY) A RARE SPIRIT/ 183 STRANG
HASN'T OUR MARRIAGE KEPT THE SPIRIT OF THAT TIME--447 WELDED

SPIRITED
I FEEL LOW-SPIRITED ENOUGH. 131 JOURNE

SPIRITEDLY
(THEN SPIRITEDLY, WITH A PROUD TOSS OF HER HEAD.) 139 POET

SPIRITUAL
MARCUS' SPIRITUAL HUMP BEGINS TO DISGUST ME. 387 MARCOM

SPIRITLESS
IN A SPIRITLESS CHORUS. 653 ICEMAN
MY EARS NUMB WITH SPIRITLESS MESSAGES FROM THE 15 STRANG
DEAD...

SPIRITLESSLY
(SPIRITLESSLY) GOOD WORK. 691 ICEMAN
(SPIRITLESSLY) CLOSE THAT BIG CLAM OF YOURS, 692 ICEMAN
HICKEY.
(GRUMBLES SPIRITLESSLY) BEJEES, YOU MUST HAVE 693 ICEMAN
BEEN MONKEYING WITH THE BOOZE,

SPIRITS
(THEN WITH JOYOUS HIGH SPIRITS) 102 BEYOND
I'WILL PUT YEN IN GOOD SPIRITS. 461 CARIBE
OH, DON'T GIT IT IN YOUR HEADS I TAKE STOCK IN 135 ELECTR
SPIRITS TRESPASSIN' ROUND
I'M GLAD TO SEE YOU GETTING IN GOOD SPIRITS FOR 663 ICEMAN
HARRY'S PARTY.
WHEN YOU'RE IN LOW SPIRITS, OR HAVE A BAD COLD. 52 JOURNE
KEEP UP HIS SPIRITS, IF YOU CAN. 81 JOURNE
THEY'VE NO HIGH SPIRITS. 101 JOURNE
SHE WAS BURSTING WITH HEALTH AND HIGH SPIRITS AND 138 JOURNE
THE LOVE OF LOVING.
THESE PLAINS ARE HAUNTED BY EVIL SPIRITS. 349 MARCOM
HERE, THE NOISE OF THEM IN THE BAR KAPES UP MY 132 POET
SPIRITS, IN A WAY.
AND IN HEALTH AND SPIRITS SHE ISN'T MORE THAN 74 STRANG

SPIRITUAL
THERE'S A SPIRITUAL SIGNIFICANCE IN THAT PICTURE, 161 BEYOND
ANDY.
HE'D EVER WRITTEN BEFORE ABOUT ANY OF HIS GREAT 504 DAYS
SPIRITUAL DISCOVERIES.
A FEELING YOU WERE UNHAPPY, IN SOME GREAT 507 DAYS
SPIRITUAL DANGER.
ALL THIS WAS WHAT I HAD LONGED TO HEAR THE MAN I 524 DAYS
LOVED SAY ABOUT THE SPIRITUAL
THEY EXPLAIN AWAY THEIR SPIRITUAL COWARDICE 542 DAYS
DARK, SPIRITUAL, POETIC, PASSIONATELY 260 GGBROW
SUPERSENSITIVE,
HIS PALE FACE IS SINGULARLY PURE, SPIRITUAL AND 278 GGBROW
SAD.
YET LIGHTED FROM WITHIN BY A SPIRITUAL CALM AND 284 GGBROW
HUMAN KINDLINESS.
HIS OWN FACE IS GENTLER, MORE SPIRITUAL, 290 GGBROW
THE MOST EXULTANT HEIGHTS OF SPIRITUAL 320 LAZARU
AFFIRMATION.
BE DRIVEN TO SEEK SPIRITUAL SALVATION SOMEWHERE/ 363 MARCOM
SPIRITUALISTS'
WISH I COULD BELIEVE IN THE SPIRITUALISTS' BUNK. 151 MISBEG
SPIRITUALLY
UNTIL HE CAN BE EDUCATED TO OUTGROW THEM 8 MANSNS
SPIRITUALLY.
SO DELICATE AND FASTIDIOUS AND SPIRITUALLY 14 MANSNS
REMOTE--

SPIT
OH, GOD HELP ME, I'M A YELLOW COWARD FOR ALL MEN 70 ANNA
TO SPIT AT/
DEAD SPIT AN' IMAGE/ 211 DESIRE
DEAD SPIT 'N' IMAGE/ 217 DESIRE
EREN'S A CHIP O' YEW--SPIT 'N' IMAGE--HARD 'N' 222 DESIRE
BITTER'S A HICKORY TREE/
(BITTERLY) HE'S THE DEAD SPIT 'N' IMAGE O' YEW/ 231 DESIRE
DEAD SPIT 'N' IMAGE. 246 DESIRE
DEAD SPIT 'N' IMAGE O' YEW/ 252 DESIRE
HE WAS SO PURTY--DEAD SPIT 'N' IMAGE O' YEW. 261 DESIRE
IN MY THROAT LIKE POISONOUS VOMIT AND I LONG TO 192 ELECTR
SPIT IT OUT--AND CONFESS/
I WAS GOIN' TO SPIT IN HER PALE MUG, SEE/ 235 HA APE
WHEN YOU SPIT, IT BOUNCES/ 240 HA APE
DRIVIN' TROU--MOVIN'--IN DAT--TO MAKE HER--AND 244 HA APE
CAGE ME IN FOR HER TO SPIT ON/
TO HUMILIATE ME, AS IF SHE'D SPIT IN MY FACE/ 715 ICEMAN
HE MAKES ME WANT TO SPIT ON ALL I HAVE EVER 721 ICEMAN
DREAMED.
AND SPIT IN MY MIND, AND MY HEART, 102 MANSNS
SPIT CURSES ON ME TILL YE CHOKE. 582 ROPE
FUNNY WITH THE SPIT DRIBBLIN' OUTA HIS MOUTH LIKE 593 ROPE
HE WAS A MAD DOG.

SPITBALLS
THEY'D TURNED NAUGHTY SCHOOLBOYS AND WERE THROWING503 DAYS
SPITBALLS AT ALMIGHTY GOD AND
NU THROWIN' SPITBALLS IN MY SOUP OR THEM KIND OF 25 HUGHIE
GAGS.

SPITE
I GOT TO GIT IT IN SPITE OF ALL HELL, AND BY GOD, 543 'ILE
YOU'LL HAVE HIM SPOILED TO DEATH IN SPITE OF ME. 188 AHWILD
BUT YOU KNOW HOW MUCH I LIKE SID--IN SPITE OF 213 AHWILD
EVERYTHING.
IRRESPONSIBLE, NEVER MEANING TO HARM BUT HARMING 213 AHWILD
IN SPITE OF HIMSELF.
LILY AND MRS. MILLER LAUGH IN SPITE OF 231 AHWILD
THEMSELVES--THEN LOOK EMBARRASSED.
HE STRAIGHTENS ALERTLY AND SPEAKS IN A VOICE THAT,252 AHWILD
IN SPITE OF HIS EFFORT,
THAT'S JUST THE SORT OF DAMNED FOOL THING HE MIGHT267 AHWILD
DO IN SPITE THE MURIEL.
YOU FEEL, IN SPITE OF ALL HIS BOLD TALK OUT OF 268 AHWILD
BOOKS, THAT HE'S SO DAMNED
AND, IN SPITE OF YOUR DAMN FOOLISHNESS LAST NIGHT,294 AHWILD
SPITE OF ALL YOU USED TO WRITE ME ABOUT HATING IT. 21 ANNA
(THEN HALF AMUSED IN SPITE OF HERSELF) 31 ANNA
BUT MOVED AND PLEASED IN SPITE OF HERSELF--TAKES 34 ANNA
HIS HAND UNCERTAINLY)
(MOVED IN SPITE OF HERSELF AND TROUBLED BY THIS 38 ANNA
HALF-CONCEALED PROPOSAL--
(A BIT PLACATED, IN SPITE OF HIMSELF, BY BURKE'S 46 ANNA
EVIDENT SINCERITY--
SHE WILL IN SPITE OF YOU. 56 ANNA
IN SPITE OF THE DIVVIL/ 76 ANNA
I WAS LOVING YOU IN SPITE OF IT ALL AND WANTING TO 76 ANNA
BE WITH YOU, GOD FORGIVE ME.
(JOINING IN THE LAUGHTER IN SPITE OF HIMSELF) 86 BEYOND

SPITE

(CONT'D.)

YOU MEAN YOU'RE GOIN' IN SPITE OF--EVERYTHIN'S 106 BEYOND
IN SPITE OF ALL YOU AND ROBERT DID TO SOFTEN HIMS 116 BEYOND
YOU KNOW HOW HARD I'VE TRIED TO KEEP THINGS GOING 123 BEYOND
IN SPITE OF BAD LUCK--
(PICKING IT UP WITH EAGER CURIOSITY--AS IF IN 561 CROSS
SPITE OF HIMSELF)
(STARING AT HER FIXEDLY) SO I WILL STAY--IN SPITE565 CROSS
OF HELL/
(ELIOT LAUGHS AND JOHN CHUCKLES SHEEPISHLY IN 503 DAYS
SPITE OF HIMSELF.
IN SPITE OF OUR ARGUMENTS. 512 DAYS
HER AGE SHOWS, IN SPITE OF A HEAVY MAKE-UP. 515 DAYS
BECAUSE HE KNOWS, DAMN HIM, THAT IN SPITE OF ALL 520 DAYS
HE'S DONE TO KILL IT THERE'S
NOT TO DELIBERATELY DISFIGURE MYSELF OUT OF 521 DAYS
WOUNDED PRIDE AND SPITE.
AND IT SHOCKED JOHN TERRIBLY, POOR DEAR--IN SPITE 523 DAYS
OF ALL HIS OLD RADICAL IDEAS.
BUT, IN SPITE OF THAT, I SAY.. 542 DAYS
BUT, IN SPITE OF HIMSELF, 544 DAYS
FATHER BAIRD AND EVEN STILLWELL, IN SPITE OF 555 DAYS
HIMSELF,
(THEN ANGRILY) AND, BY GOD, IN SPITE OF HIS 557 DAYS
APPARENT GRIEF,
IN SPITE OF STILLWELL, SPRINGS UP TO A HALF- 563 DAYS
SITTING POSITION IN BED.
I'VE SWORN T' LIVE A HUNDRED AN' I'LL DO IT, IF 210 DESIRE
ON'Y T' SPITE YER SINFUL GREED/
IT'S JEST T' SPITE US--THE DAMNED OLD MULE/ 213 DESIRE
(THEY STARE INTO EACH OTHER'S EYES, HIS HELD BY 228 DESIRE
HERS IN SPITE OF
(IN SPITE OF HER OVERWHELMING DESIRE FOR HIM, 243 DESIRE
(HIS VOICE SHOWING EMOTION IN SPITE OF HIM) 260 DESIRE
HER FACE, IN SPITE OF ITS PLAIN FEATURES, GIVES AN494 DIFRNT
IMPRESSION OF PRETTINESS.
IN SPITE OF HER TWO HUNDRED AND MORE POUNDS SHE IS506 DIFRNT
SURPRISINGLY ACTIVE.
CALEB'S A MAN NO'TH TEN O' MOST AND, SPITE O' HIS 513 DIFRNT
BEIN' ON'Y A BOY YIT,
HE'S KIND AT BOTTOM, SPITE OF HIS ROUGH WAYS, AND 521 DIFRNT
HE'S BROUGHT YOU UP.
I'LL GO RIGHT THROUGH WITH WHAT I SAID I WOULD, IF545 DIFRNT
ONLY TO SPITE HIM/
AND, IN SPITE OF ITS FAT, IT HAS KEPT ITS GIRLISH 428 DYNAMO
NAIVETE AND FRESH COMPLEXION.
(THEN QUICKLY) I SUPPOSE YOU THINK I'M DOING IT 467 DYNAMO
TO SPITE YOU, BUT I'M NOT.
(MOVED IN SPITE OF HIMSELF, INSTINCTIVELY TAKES A 491 DYNAMO
STEP TOWARD HER--
(A TINY BIT AWED AND SHAKEN IN SPITE OF HIMSELF) 185 EJONES
VERY STRONG STILL IN SPITE OF HIS BEING MIDDLE- 197 EJONES
AGED.
LOUISA SMILES IN SPITE OF HERSELF. 7 ELECTR
BUT IN SPITE OF THESE DISSIMILARITIES, 10 ELECTR
I DON'T KNOW MUCH ABOUT HIM IN SPITE OF WHAT YOU 15 ELECTR
THINK.
(THEN AS IF THE CONVICTION WERE FORCING ITSELF ON 19 ELECTR
HER IN SPITE OF HERSELF)
IN SPITE OF MY BEGGING HIM NOT TO LEAVE ME ALONE. 31 ELECTR
I'M A FOOL TO LET YOU MAKE ME LOSE MY TEMPER--OVER 34 ELECTR
YOUR JEALOUS SPITE/
DON'T YOU REALIZE HE WOULD NEVER DIVORCE ME, OUT 38 ELECTR
OF SPITE
(THEN A TONE OF EAGERNESS BREAKING THROUGH IN 72 ELECTR
SPITE OF HERSELF)
IN SPITE OF HER FROZEN SELF-CONTROL, LAVINIA 122 ELECTR
RECOILS BEFORE THIS.
APPROACHES AS IF COMPELLED IN SPITE OF HERSELF 139 ELECTR
UNTIL SHE STANDS DIRECTLY UNDER
AND SHE APPROACHES AS IF COMPELLED IN SPITE OF 139 ELECTR
HERSELF
I'LL LIVE IN SPITE OF YOU/ 168 ELECTR
I WANT A LITTLE WHILE OF HAPPINESS--IN SPITE OF 176 ELECTR
ALL THE DEAD/
(THEN SUSPICIOUS IN SPITE OF HIMSELF) 176 ELECTR
SHE HAS GROWN MATURE AND MATERNAL, IN SPITE OF 270 GGBROW
YOUTH.
IN SPITE OF YOUR PROMISES. 271 GGBROW
(HER VOICE BREAKS A LITTLE IN SPITE OF HERSELF.) 276 GGBROW
IN SPITE OF HIMSELF, BROWN IS UNEASY. 295 GGBROW
IN SPITE OF HIMSELF, BROWN SQUIRMS AND ADOPTS A 297 GGBROW
PLACATING TONE)
THE MEN STARE AT HIM, STARTLED AND IMPRESSED IN 213 HA APE
SPITE OF THEMSELVES)
(WITH SPITE) YES, YOU ARE A NATURAL BORN GHOUL. 218 HA APE
OH, THEY DIDN'T WANT TO AT FIRST, IN SPITE OF MY 220 HA APE
SOCIAL SERVICE CREDENTIALS.
SHE SHIVERS WITH FRIGHT IN SPITE OF THE BLAZING 225 HA APE
HEAT.
(IN SPITE OF HIS STRUGGLES, THIS IS DONE WITH 250 HA APE
GUSTO AND ECLAT.
(MOVED IN SPITE OF HIMSELF) I REMEMBER WELL. 588 ICEMAN
(LARRY IS MOVED TO A PUZZLED PITY IN SPITE OF 590 ICEMAN
HIMSELF.
INTERESTED IN SPITE OF HIMSELF AND AT THE SAME 591 ICEMAN
TIME VAGUELY UNEASY.)
(LARRY STARES AT HIM, MOVED BY SYMPATHY AND PITY 592 ICEMAN
IN SPITE OF HIMSELF, DISTURBED.
SO IN SPITE OF HARRY'S THIRST AND HIS GENEROUS 594 ICEMAN
HEART, HE COMES OUT EVEN.
IN SPITE OF THE DIRTY DEAL SHE GAVE YOU. 680 ICEMAN
NOT ONLY THEN BUT ALWAYS AFTER, IN SPITE OF 712 ICEMAN
EVERYTHING I DID--(HE PAUSES--
HE WOULD HAVE GOT ME A JOB OUT OF PURE SPITE. 723 ICEMAN
HIS SKIN, IN SPITE OF BEING SUNBURNED A DEEP 20 JOURNE
BROWN, HAS A PARCHED SALLOWNESS.
(MOVED IN SPITE OF HIMSELF--HELPLESSLY.) 69 JOURNE

SPITEFUL

SPITE (CONT'D.)
EDMUND IS MOVED IN SPITE OF HIMSELF. 91 JOURNE
AND I LOVE YOU, DEAR, IN SPITE OF EVERYTHING. 112 JOURNE
I KNOW YOU STILL LOVE, ME, JAMES, IN SPITE OF 112 JOURNE
EVERYTHING.
IT'S AS IF, IN SPITE OF LOVING US, SHE HATED US/ 139 JOURNE
THAT'S WHAT YOU STILL BELIEVE IN YOUR HEART, IN 141 JOURNE
SPITE OF WHAT DOCTORS,
SHE HAD HER CHILDREN, TOO, AND I INSISTED, IN 142 JOURNE
SPITE OF THE EXPENSE.
I'M LIKE MAMA, I CAN'T HELP LIKING YOU, IN SPITE 143 JOURNE
OF EVERYTHING.
EVEN THE CENTURION STARES AT THE GROUND HUMBLY, IN291 LAZARU
SPITE OF HIMSELF.
THE ROMAN SOLDIERS IN SPITE OF THEIR EFFORTS ARE 304 LAZARU
PUSHED BACKWARD STEP BY STEP.)
(AS IF IN SPITE OF HIMSELF HE BOWS AWKWARDLY TO 327 LAZARU
LAZARUS)
SALUTING HIM AS IF IN SPITE OF THEMSELVES.) 334 LAZARU
FOR SERVING MY SPITE UPON MANKIND'S 339 LAZARU
(HIS VOICE TREMBLES IN SPITE OF HIMSELF) 346 LAZARU
YES, IN SPITE OF SORROW-- 347 LAZARU
HALF-LAUGHING IN SPITE OF HIMSELF, HALF-WEEPING 369 LAZARU
WITH RAGE)
IN SPITE OF IT, HER PREGNANCY, NOW SIX MONTHS 2 MANSNS
ALONG, IS APPARENT.
(SLOWLY--AS IF FORCING THE WORDS OUT IN SPITE OF 38 MANSNS
HERSELF.)
THEN GLOATING TRIUMPHANTLY BUT MOVED IN SPITE OF 169 MANSNS
HERSELF--
BUT CONSTANTLY DISTRACTED IN SPITE OF HIMSELF.) 350 MARCOM
(AMUSED IN SPITE OF HIMSELF) 362 MARCOM
TRIES TO STARE INSOLENTLY AT THE KING BUT, AWED IN366 MARCOM
SPITE OF HIMSELF,
(GRINNING IN SPITE OF HIMSELF) 381 MARCOM
(CANNOT CONTROL A LAUGH IN SPITE OF HIMSELF-- 389 MARCOM
HELPLESSLY)
THAT IN SPITE OF TYPHOONS, SHIPWRECKS, 411 MARCOM
PERPETRATED BY UNSCRUPULOUS JAPANESE TRADE-PIRATES422 MARCOM
WHO, IN SPITE OF HIS PROTESTS
HE SAID TELL THE GREAT KAAN THAT *IN SPITE OF 424 MARCOM
PERILS TOO NUMEROUS TO RELATE,
IN SPITE OF THAT, I THOUGHT I COULD RECOGNIZE 427 MARCOM
MAFFEO.
BUT YOU WERE TRUE IN SPITE OF THEM, WEREN'T YOUS 430 MARCOM
AND, IN SPITE OF HIMSELF, A SHADOW OF A SMILE-- 432 MARCOM
IN SPITE OF HIMSELF, CLING FOR A PASSING MOMENT TO439 MARCOM
THE PLAY JUST ENDED.
(MOVED IN SPITE OF HERSELF--BUT KEEPS HER BOLD, 103 MISBEG
PLAYFUL TONE)
(DEEPLY STIRRED, IN SPITE OF HERSELF--HER VOICE 129 MISBEG
TREMBLING)
(WATCHES HIM FOR A SECOND, FIGHTING THE LOVE THAT,141 MISBEG
IN SPITE OF HER,
HE IS DRIVEN TO GO ON IN SPITE OF HIMSELF) 145 MISBEG
IN SPITE OF HER STRENGTH, HOLDING HERSELF LIKE 157 MISBEG
THIS FOR HOURS.
IN SPITE OF HIMSELF, HE IS STARTLED--IN AN AWED, 158 MISBEG
ALMOST FRIGHTENED WHISPER)
YET IN SPITE OF HER SLOVENLY APPEARANCE THERE IS A 20 POET
SPIRIT WHICH SHINES THROUGH
BUT IN SPITE OF THIS, THERE IS SOMETHING 34 POET
FORMIDABLE AND IMPRESSIVE ABOUT HIM,
AND SO I WILL REMAIN TO THE END, IN SPITE OF ALL 43 POET
FATE CAN DO TO CRUSH MY SPIRIT/
(IN SPITE OF HIMSELF, THIS GETS UNDER HIS SKIN-- 45 POET
ANGRILY.)
FINALLY, IN SPITE OF HERSELF, SHE ASKS 58 POET
SHE IS IMPRESSED IN SPITE OF HERSELF 69 POET
SHE IS AGAIN CONFUSED AND, IN SPITE OF HERSELF, 70 POET
FRIGHTENED AND FASCINATED.
AND IN SPITE OF ITS OBVIOUSNESS, IT IS EFFECTIVE. 88 POET
IN SPITE OF HERSELF SHE IS SO STRUCK BY HIS 89 POET
APPEARANCE
HOW YOU CAN STILL LOVE FATHER AND BE PROUD OF IT, 150 POET
IN SPITE OF WHAT HE IS.
(IN SPITE OF HERSELF HER TEMPER HAS BEEN RISING. 155 POET
YOU GITTIN' RELIGION ALL OF A MOMENT JUST FOR 580 ROPE
SPITE ON ME 'CAUSE I'M LEFT--
HIS FACE, REPOSSESSING IN SPITE OF ITS TOO-SMALL, 6 STRANG
OVER-REFINED FEATURES,
(RUFFLED BUT AMUSED IN SPITE OF IT) 41 STRANG
IN SPITE OF THEIR BEING RICH FOR HEREABOUTS. 59 STRANG
IN SPITE OF ALL HE AND I FOUGHT AGAINST IT, 60 STRANG
(IRRITATED IN SPITE OF HERSELF) 69 STRANG
AND IT HASN'T IN SPITE OF WHAT YOU SAY. 102 STRANG
(SHOWING HIS JEALOUS RESENTMENT IN SPITE OF 102 STRANG
HIMSELF)
INTENTIONALLY TO SPITE ME/ 146 STRANG
(BURSTING OUT IN SPITE OF HERSELF--VIOLENTLY) 167 STRANG
HE'LL THINK I'M LYING FOR SPITE, THAT IT'S ONLY MY173 STRANG
CRAZY JEALOUSY/
(MOVED A LOT IN SPITE OF HERSELF) 506 VOYAGE
(HER FACE SHOWING A TRACE OF HURT IN SPITE OF 445 WELDED
HERSELF)
AS IF IN SPITE OF HIMSELF, WITHOUT A WORD,) 450 WELDED
FOR A MOMENT SHE SUBMITS, APPEARS EVEN TO RETURN 460 WELDED
HIS KISSES IN SPITE OF HERSELF.

SPITEFUL

SPITEFUL TRICK LIKE THAT--NO MATTER WHAT HE DID TO204 AHWILD
ME.
AND THEN SHE CALLS ME A FOOL REAL SPITEFUL AND 95 BEYOND
TACKS AWAY FROM ME QUICK.
THERE IS A TRACE IN HER EXPRESSION OF SOMETHING 116 BEYOND
HARD AND SPITEFUL.
ONLY REMEMBER, THE WORLD IS FULL OF SPITEFUL LIARS524 DAYS
WHO WOULD DO ANYTHING TO

SPITEFULLY

SPITEFULLY
(SPITEFULLY) WORK YOU'LL NEVER GET DONE BY 122 BEYOND
READING BOOKS ALL THE TIME.
(SPITEFULLY, WITH A GLANCE AT ANDREW'S LETTER ON 125 BEYOND
THE TABLE)

SPITS
HE SPITS 37 ANNA
(HE SPITS DISGUSTEDLY.) 480 CARDIF
(HE LEANS OVER THE SIDE OF HIS BUNK AND SPITS. 484 CARDIF
(HE SPITS CONTENTEDLY) SO I STOPS. 467 CARIBE
(HE SPITS LEISURELY) QUEER THING, LOVE, AIN'T ITS 467 CARIBE
HE SPITS ON THE GROUND WITH INTENSE DISGUST, TURNS203 DESIRE
AND GOES BACK INTO THE HOUSE.
(HE SIGHS--THEN SPITS) WAAL--NO USE'N CRYIN' OVER218 DESIRE
SPILT MILK.
(SPITS ALSO) AN' I SEE HER/ 222 DESIRE
(TURNS AWAY AND SPITS CONTEMPTUOUSLY) 222 DESIRE
HE SCOWLS BACK HIS THOUGHTS OF HER AND SPITS WITH 228 DESIRE
EXAGGERATED DISDAIN--
(HE SPITS WITH CONTEMPTUOUS DISGUST) 246 DESIRE
SETH STARES AT HER WORRIEDLY, SHAKES HIS HEAD AND 171 ELECTR
SPITS.
(HE SPITS OUT CONTEMPTUOUSLY) 649 ICEMAN
(HE SPITS ON HIS HANDS AGGRESSIVELY) 524 INZONE
AND SPITS ON THE GROUND INSULTINGLY. 283 LAZARU
(HE TAKES OFF HIS HELMET AND SPITS IT--THEN 301 LAZARU
WITH A GRIM SMILE)
(SHE SPITS IN HIS FACE AND LAUGHS HARSHLY) 361 LAZARU
(FINALLY SPITS WITH EXAGGERATED SCORN) 370 MARCOM
(HE SPITS DISGUSTEDLY) THE SCUM OF THE EARTH/ 17 MISBEG
(HE SPITS) IT'S EASY TO SEE YOU'VE A FINE COLLEGE 38 MISBEG
EDUCATION.
(HE SPITS CONTEMPTUOUSLY) WHAT A SWELL CHANCT. 593 ROPE

SPITTIN'
THERE, KITTY, DON'T GIT TO SPITTIN'. 498 DIFRNT

SPITTING
(SPITTING DISGUSTEDLY) FOG'S WORST ONE OF HER 26 ANNA
DIRTY TRICKS, PY YINGO/
WAY UP, BOTH OF THEM. (TO DRISCOLL) HE HAS BEEN 485 CARDIF
SPITTING BLOOD AGAINS
(SPITTING PLACIDLY) QUEER THINGS, MEM'RIES. 467 CARIBE
(SPITTING CALMLY) THERE'S LOVE FOR YOU. 470 CARIBE
(SPITTING TRANQUILLY) MORE MEM'RIES) 473 CARIBE
(SPITTING WITH DISGUST) HER--HERE--SLEEPIN' WITH 214 DESIRE
HIM--STEALIN' MY MAW'S FARM/
(SPITTING ON HIS HANDS--BELLIGERENTLY) 235 HA APE
(SPITTING DISGUSTEDLY) AW/ 519 INZONE
LIKE A VILLAGE IDIOT IN A COUNTRY STORE SPITTING 102 MANSNS
AT THE BELLY OF A STOVE--
AFTER SPITTING ON THE GROUND AT THEIR FEET WITH 370 MARCOM
ANGRY DISGUST.
(SPITTING--VEHEMENTLY) THAT'S CHILD'S TALK. 599 ROPE
(SPITTING DISGUSTEDLY) THERE'S A FUNNY BIRD OF A 498 VOYAGE
SAILURMAN FUR YE.

SPITTOONS
THE FLOOR, WITH IRON SPITTOONS PLACED HERE AND 573 ICEMAN
THERE, IS COVERED WITH SAWDUST.

SPLASH
IS HEARD REPLYING AND THEN A GREAT SPLASH AND A 407 MARCOM
LONG RATTLING OF CHAINS.
I SEEN IT SPLASH/ 589 ROPE

SPLATTERED
BUT IN THIS WAR I'VE SEEN TOO MANY WHITE WALLS 54 ELECTR
SPLATTERED WITH BLOOD

SPLEEN
I THINK PROBABLY HER SPLEEN IS OUT OF ORDER. 420 MARCOM
HER HIGHNESS'S SPLEEN BEING SLUGGISH AFTER THE 425 MARCOM
LONG CONFINEMENT ON SHIPBOARD."

SPLENDID
WHY, YOU'VE GOT A SPLENDID VOICE/ 257 AHWILD
YOU'VE NO IDEA, ROB, WHAT A SPLENDID PLACE 133 BEYOND
ARGENTINE IS.
(ENCOURAGINGLY) THAT'S SPLENDID. 530 DAYS
I THANK MR. ANTHONY FOR THIS SPLENDID OPPORTUNITY 261 GGBROW
TO CREATE MYSELF--
SPLENDID/ 316 GGBROW
BUT THAT SOUNDS SPLENDID/. 8 STRANG
HE IS A SPLENDID CHAP, CLEAN AND BOYISH, WITH REAL 46 STRANG
STUFF IN HIM, TOO.

SPLENDIDLY
YOU'VE DONE SPLENDIDLY. I'M PROUD OF YOU. 89 JOURNE

SPLENDOUR
MINIONS OF SPLENDOUR SHRINKING FROM DISTRESS/ 101 POET

SPLINTERED
THE BULWARKS OF THE JUNK ARE BATTERED AND 407 MARCOM
SPLINTERED.

SPLINTERING
A MOMENT LATER THERE IS THE SOUND OF SPLINTERING 114 ELECTR
WOOD

SPLIT
IN ALL MY TIME I TRIED NEVER TO SPLIT 11 ANNA
HER RACKET'S ENOUGH TO SPLIT A BUDY'S EARS. 117 BEYOND
I'LL SPLIT THE SKULL AV THE FIRST MAN AV YE STARTS458 CARIBE
TO FOIGHT.
I FEEL LIKE LAFFIN' TILL I'D SPLIT UP THE MIDDLE. 220 DESIRE
BUT CLARK PICKED UP AN AX AND SPLIT HIS SKULL/ 440 DYNAMO
WE SPLIT DAT UP AND SMASH TROU--TWENTY-FIVE KNOTS 217 HA APE
A HOUR/
HE'S BOUND BY HIS RELIGION TO SPLIT FIFTY-FIFTY 584 ICEMAN
WID YOU.
SO I CAN MAKE SOME MONEY AND NOT JUST SPLIT EVEN. 659 ICEMAN
WELL, IF YOU SPLIT THE MONEY I GAVE YOU WITH HIM, 129 JOURNE
LIKE A FOOL--
SO THAT HE LIVES SPLIT INTO OPPOSITES AND DIVIDED 49 MANSNS
AGAINST HIMSELF/
SIT DOWN BEFORE YOU SPLIT IN PIECES ON THE FLOOR 81 MISBEG

SPLITS
MAYBE HE HITS ME WID A WHIP AND I SPLITS HIS HEAD 181 EJONES
WID A SHOVEL AND RUNS AWAY AND

SPLITS (CONT'D.)
GIMME MY SHOVEL 'TIL I SPLITS HIS DAMN HEAD/ 195 EJONES

SPLITTIN'
AND ALL HANDS SPLITTIN' THEIR SIDES/ 503 DIFRNT

SPLITTING
AND SPLITTING THEIR SIDES/ 223 AHWILD
DURING DINNER I BEGAN TO GET A HEADACHE AND IT'S 540 DAYS
SPLITTING NOW.
HOLDING HIS HEAD IN HIS HANDS AS IF HE HAD A 680 ICEMAN
SPLITTING HEADACHE.)
GIVES A HARSH CACKLE WHICH CRACKS THROUGH THE 308 LAZARU
OTHER LAUGHTER WITH A SPLITTING
HE'LL SEE THE WHOLE OF BROADWAY SPLITTING THEIR 96 MISBEG
SIDES LAUGHING AT HIM--
I TOLD YOU I HAVE A SPLITTING HEADACHE/ 161 STRANG
IT BEGAN WITH THE SPLITTING OF A CELL A HUNDRED 448 WELDED
MILLION YEARS AGO INTO YOU AND

SPLOTCHED
AND THEY ARE NOW SO SPLOTCHED, PEELED, 573 ICEMAN

SPLOTCHES
FLAKED WITH STREAKS AND SPLOTCHES OF DIM LEMON. 1 MISBEG

SPLOTCHY
ALTHOUGH THE RESULT IS ONLY TO HEIGHTEN THEIR 629 ICEMAN
SPLOTCHY LEPROUS LOOK.

SPLUTTERING
(SPLUTTERING WITH RAGE) YOU VAS CRAZY FOOL, AY 48 ANNA
TAL YOU/
THE RUSSIAN COMES TO IN A FLASH, SPLUTTERING. 500 VOYAGE

SPOIL
ONLY DON'T SPOIL IT ALL NOW. 26 ANNA
BECAUSE I DIDN'T WANT TO SPOIL THIS LAST NIGHT 88 BEYOND
YOU'RE HERE.
BUT THAT WOULD SPOIL JOHN'S STORY, DON'T YOU 550 DAYS
THINKS
WHOM THEY LIKE TO TEASE AND SPOIL. 611 ICEMAN
SHE USED TO SPOIL ME AND MADE A PET OF ME. 667 ICEMAN
DAT'S RIGHT, WAIT ON HER AND SPOIL HER, YUH POOR 677 ICEMAN
SAP/
THE WATER'LL GIT IN AND SPOIL IT. 524 INZONE
AT LAST SHE SAID SHE REFUSED TO TOUCH IT ANY MORE 115 JOURNE
OR SHE MIGHT SPOIL IT.
EVEN IF SHE DOES SPOIL THEM. 78 MANSNS
(FORCING A LIGHT TONE) DO YOU WANT TO SPOIL OUR 129 MISBEG
BEAUTIFUL MOONLIGHT NIGHTS
SPOIL THIS DANNY/ 172 MISBEG
GOING OUT TO REVENGE AN INSULT TO YOU, WOULD SPOIL171 POET
YOUR SCHEMES.
UNFORTUNATELY, THE TENDENCY TO SPOIL THEM IN THE 9 STRANG
UNIVERSITY IS A POOR TRAINING--
I SUPPOSE, AFRAID IT WOULD SPOIL HER FIGURE... 74 STRANG
YOU'RE LETTING THAT OLD ASS SPOIL GORDON, YOU 146 STRANG
FOOL, YOU/

SPOILED
YOU'LL HAVE HIM SPOILED TO DEATH IN SPITE OF ME. 188 AHWILD
YOU'RE STILL THE SPOILED CRYBABY THAT SHE CAN MAKE 98 ELECTR
A FOOL OF
AND THEN BEEFS BECAUSE THEY'RE SPOILED. 61 JOURNE
(SHE COMES TO HIM.) YOU WANT TO BE PETTED AND 91 JOURNE
SPOILED AND MADE A FUSS OVER.
HE SPOILED ME. HE WOULD DO ANYTHING I ASKED. 104 JOURNE
I'M AFRAID HE SPOILED ME DREADFULLY. 114 JOURNE
YOU'VE SPOILED THAT GIRL SO, I PITY HER HUSBAND IF114 JOURNE
SHE EVER MARRIES.
THEIR EXPRESSION IS SPOILED, PETULANT AND SELF- 299 LAZARU
OBSESSED, WEAK BUT DOMINEERING.
(WITH A BOYISH GRIN) YOU'VE SPOILED IT, NELLY. 444 WELDED

SPOILING
AND MAKING HIM VAIN AND SPOILING HIM/ 64 MANSNS
YES, SHE IS SPOILING THEM. 78 MANSNS

SPOILT
SURE, LIVING WITH YOU HAS SPOILT ME FOR ANY OTHER 177 MISBEG
MAN, ANYWAY.

SPOKE
(WITH A GRIM SMILE) HERE IT COMES, THE TROUBLE 543 'ILE
YOU SPOKE OF, MR. SLOCUM.
AND I AIN'T SPOKE A WORD WITH NO ONE SINCE DAY 15 ANNA
BEFORE YESTERDAY.
OH, YOU MEAN WHEN HE SPOKE OF THE MIRACLES 160 BEYOND
WE'VE NEVER SPOKE A WORD ABOUT IT SINCE THAT DAY. 165 BEYOND
LET'S HAVE THE FACTS YOU SPOKE OF. 558 CROSS
YOU SPOKE TO MR. ELIOT AS IF ELSA WERE ILL. 506 DAYS
YEH PAW'S SPOKE A LOT OT YEH--... 225 DESIRE
YE'VE BEEN LYIN' T' ME EVERY WORD YE SPOKE, DAY 256 DESIRE
AN' NIGHT, SINCE WE FUST--
BUT AS SOON AS HE KNEW HE'D GOT ME INTO TROUBLE HE430 DYNAMO
SPOKE RIGHT UP--.
I KNOW HIS NAME'S NEVER BEEN ALLOWED TO BE SPOKE 19 ELECTR
AMONG MANNONS
EVEN IF HE NEVER SPOKE, I WOULD FEEL WHAT WAS IN 40 ELECTR
HIS MIND AND SOME NIGHT,
WHAT MADE YOU JUMP WHEN I SPOKE? 58 ELECTR
ORIN KEEPS TEASING THAT I WAS FLIRTING WITH THAT 147 ELECTR
NATIVE HE SPOKE ABOUT,
(AS IF SHE HADN'T HEARD) HE SPOKE OF HOW WELL YOU272 GGBROW
USED TO DRAW.
I ONLY SPOKE AS I DID ON ACCOUNT OF MARGARET--HIS 289 GGBROW
WIFE--
I'M SORRY I SPOKE. 42 JOURNE
YES, I SPOKE TOO SOON. 82 JOURNE
UNTIL, TONIGHT, WHEN I SPOKE TO YOU OF HOME, I 345 LAZARU
FELT NEW BIRTH-PAINS AS YOUR
MY MOTHER SPOKE TO ME AND SPOKE TO ME AND EVEN 356 LAZARU
WEPT, THAT TALL WOMAN,
WHAT THE ARRANGEMENTS HE SPOKE OF ARE. 131 MANSNS
WHICH SPOKE OF OUR LORD AS THE PRINCE OF PEACE. 394 MARCOM
MY LIPS SPOKE WITHOUT ME SAYING A WORD. 415 MARCOM
(DULLY) BUT IT WAS MY NAME YOU SPOKE. 416 MARCOM

1511 SPORTS

SPOKE (CONT'D.)

EVEN IN THE DAYS BEFORE IVIR I'D SPOKE A WORD TO 130 POET HIM,

IT WAS SIMON SPOKE FIRST, AND ONCE HE STARTED, 144 POET CON SPOKE WID THE AIRS AV A LORD. 154 POET "TO HELL WITH THE FARM," I SPOKE BACK. 585 ROPE WHAT CAN I EXPECT WHEN THE FIRST WORD YOU EVER 14 STRANG SPOKE IN THIS WORLD WAS AN INSULT (THEN BENIGNANTLY) BUT FIRST WE SPOKE A WORD 47 STRANG ABOUT YOU, EVANS, HE SPOKE OF YOU. 118 STRANG

SPOKEN

YOU KEEP YOUR MOUTH SHUT TILL YOU'RE SPOKEN TO-- 264 AHWILD (GOING ON AS IF HE HAD NOT SPOKEN) 290 AHWILD (AS IF IT WERE JOHN WHO HAD SPOKEN) 496 DAYS SHE HASN'T SPOKEN A SINGLE WORD SINCE HER FATHER'S 72 ELECTR DEATH/

YOU'VE HARDLY SPOKEN A WORD SINCE YOU MET ME. 75 ELECTR (IMMEDIATELY RECOVERS HER POISE--TO ORIN, AS IF 77 ELECTR LAVINIA HADN'T SPOKEN)

HE'S HARDLY SPOKEN TO YOU/ 642 ICEMAN (GOES ON AS IF LARRY HADN'T SPOKEN) 647 ICEMAN (AS IF LARRY HAD NEVER SPOKEN--FALTERINGLY) 649 ICEMAN (AS THOUGH HE HADN'T SPOKEN.) 113 JOURNE I HAVEN'T SPOKEN OF SUCH MATTERS IN SO LONG-- 9 MANSNS IT WOULD TAKE ONLY A RUMOR--A WHISPER SPOKEN IN 142 MANSNS THE RIGHT EAR.

(WITH GENUINE APPRECIATION) THAT IS BRAVELY 403 MARCOM SPOKEN.

BECAUSE HE'S EDUCATED AND QUIET-SPOKEN AND HAS 27 MISBEG POLITENESS EVEN WHEN HE'S

KEEP YOUR PLACE AND BE SOFT-SPOKEN TO YOUR 63 MISBEG BETTERS/

(AS IF SHE HADN'T SPOKEN) SO HE'LL KEEP AWAY FROM 90 MISBEG TEMPTATION BECAUSE HE CAN'T

(AS IF HE HADN'T SPOKEN) WHILE I'M ONLY A BIG, 118 MISBEG ROUGH, UGLY COP OF A WOMAN.

(AS IF SHE HADN'T SPOKEN) THERE'S ALWAYS THE 119 MISBEG AFTERMATH THAT POISONS YOU.

(AS IF SHE HADN'T SPOKEN--WITH HOPELESS LONGING) 151 MISBEG (AS IF SHE HADN'T SPOKEN.) SO, 113 POET SURELY YOU COULD NOT HAVE SPOKEN SERIOUSLY WHEN 122 POET YOU TALKED OF MARRIAGE.

HER MOOD CHANGES TO RESENTMENT AND SHE SPEAKS AS 137 POET IF SARA HAD SPOKEN.)

THE HAS SPOKEN WITH PERSUASIVE FEELING. 37 STRANG

SPONGE

COLLEGES TURN OUT LAZY LOAFERS TO SPONGE ON THEIR 260 GGBROW POOR OLD FATHERS/

AND SPONGE ON ME FOR THE REST OF YOUR LIFE/ 32 JOURNE OR WAS IT DAN ROCHE OR PADDY O'DOWD, OR SOME OTHER 48 POET DRUNKEN SPONGE--

INSTEAD OF BEING A SPONGE. 174 POET

SPONGER

HIS MANNER IS OILY AND FAWNING, THAT OF A BORN 52 POET SPONGER AND PARASITE.

SPONGERS

HE TURNS TO GIVE ORDERS TO THE SPONGERS IN THE 57 POET BAR.)

A GREAT DAY FOR THE SPONGERS AND A BAD DAY FOR 58 POET THIS INN/

SPONGES

OR LOANED MONEY TO SPONGES I KNEW WOULD NEVER PAY 146 JOURNE IT BACK--

AND THE BARROOM SPONGES AND RACETRACK TOUTS AND 30 MISBEG GAMBLERS ARE THROUGH WITH HIM

SPONGIN'

WITHOUT A NICKEL IN MY JEANS AND JUST SPONGIN' ON 523 DIFRNT HIM.

SPONGING

IT MAKES ME FEEL I'M SOME USE IN THIS HOUSE 212 AHWILD INSTEAD OF JUST SPONGING--

SPONGING/ 212 AHWILD

I DON'T LIKE SPONGING. 10 POET

SPOOFIN'

(TRYING TO FORCE A LAUGH) I WAS ON'Y SPOOFIN' 181 EJONES YER.

SPOOKS

WE LOVE THE SOUND OF BUT WHOSE MEANING WE PASS ON 42 STRANG TO SPOOKS TO LIVE BY/

TO MYSELF, NOW THAT I'VE SPENT ONE NIGHT IN IT I 49 STRANG KNOW THAT WHATEVER SPOOKS THERE

SEEING SPOOKS, THAT'S PRETTY FAR GONE, ISN'T ITS 466 WELDED

SPOOKY

IT IS A TRIFLE SPOOKY. 557 CROSS

SPOON

THEN SUDDENLY COMICALLY ANGRY, PUTTING THE SPOON 224 AHWILD DOWN WITH A BANG)

SPOON, IS THIS ANY WAY TO TREAT A PALS 224 AHWILD (HE PICKS UP HIS SPOON AND BEGINS TO EAT, 224 AHWILD HE ADDRESSES THE SPOON PLAINTIVELY) 224 AHWILD COME UP TONIGHT AND WE'LL SPOON IN THE MOONLIGHT 54 MISBEG

SPOONING

HER AND CALEB IS WORSER AT SPOONIN' THAN WHAT WE 506 DIFRNT ARE.

SPOONING

AT THE THOUGHT OF THESE TWO ANCIENTS SPOONING.) 192 AHWILD DON'T LET ME CATCH YOU AND AUNT LILY SPOONING ON A192 AHWILD BEACH TONIGHT--

NECKING, PETTING--WHATEVER YOU CALL IT--SPOONING 36 STRANG IN GENERAL--

(SPOONING/... 36 STRANG

SPOONS

DOWN WITH SPOONS/ 224 AHWILD JUST THINK OF WASTE EFFORT EATING SOUP WITH 225 AHWILD SPOONS--

(THEN DARKLY TO HIMSELF) NO MORE SPOONS FOR ME/ 225 AHWILD

SPOONS (CONT'D.)

TAKE OUT THEIR CUPS AND SPOONS, AND SIT DOWN 514 INZONE TOGETHER ON THE BENCHES.

KNIVES AND FORKS AND SPOONS RATTLE AGAINST PLATES.431 MARCOM KNIVES, SPOONS, SALTCELLAR, ETC. 96 POET

SPORT

SAY, YOU'RE A GOOD SPORT. 218 AHWILD NOT THE ATHLETIC BUT THE HELL-RAISING SPORT TYPE. 218 AHWILD (REALLY HURT, FORCES A FEEBLE SMILE TO HIS LIPS 230 AHWILD AND PRETENDS TO BE A GOOD SPORT

(WITH A MOCKING CHUCKLE) HE'S A HOT SPORT, CAN'T 237 AHWILD YOU TELL ITS

DIDN'T I SAY YOU WERE A SPORTS 238 AHWILD COME ON, OLD SPORT/ 262 AHWILD (WITH A GRIN) A SPORT, CHRIS IS. 7 ANNA BE A GAME SPORT AND DRINK TO THAT/ 78 ANNA YOU'RE A REGULAR, UP-TO-DATE SPORT--THE ONLY LIVE 520 DIFRNT ONE IN THIS DEAD DUMP.

YOU'RE A SPORT YOURSELF. 522 DIFRNT SPEND AND BE A GOOD SPORT, THAT'S MY MOTTO. 522 DIFRNT AND THIS BUDDY OF MINE, IS A SPORT AND A SPENDER. 523 DIFRNT AW, COME ON, BE A SPORT-- 546 DIFRNT CAN'T YOU TAKE IT LIKE A SPORTS 546 DIFRNT HE'S A REAL SPORT. 258 GGBROW SHE'S A GAME SPORT, BUT IT'S PRETTY DAMN TOUGH ON 277 GGBROW HER/

HE'S SUCH A GOOD SPORT AND BILLY AND HE WERE SUCH 277 GGBROW PALS ONCE.

SU BE A GOOD SPORT/ 304 GGBROW WHY, HE'S A REGULAR SPORT WHEN HE GETS STARTED/* 310 GGBROW WANTED WIND UP LIKE A SPORT *STEAD OF CROAKIN' 253 HA APE SLOW IN DERES

IN MANNER, HE IS CONSCIOUSLY A BROADWAY SPORT AND 9 HUGHIE A WISE GUY--

(BITINGLY.) SORRY IF I'M KEEPING YOU UP, SPORT. 15 HUGHIE IT USED TO HAND ME A LAUGH TO HEAR OLD HUGHIE 16 HUGHIE CRACKIN' LIKE A SPORT.

THEN I'D SAY, *OKAY, ARNOLD, I'M A GOOD SPORT, 32 HUGHIE I'LL GIVE YOU A BREAK.

I'D TELL HIM I BOUGHT ONE OF THOSE MERCEDES SPORT 32 HUGHIE ROADSTERS

WHERE THEY'D NEVER LOOK FOR A WOBBLY, PRETENDING 1588 ICEMAN WAS A SPORT.

HE RAN A COLORED GAMBLING HOUSE THEN AND WAS A 594 ICEMAN HELL OF A SPORT, SO THEY SAY.

JEES, HICKEY, IF YOU AIN'T A SPORT/ 640 ICEMAN HERE'S TO THE OLD GOVERNOR, THE BEST SPORT AND THE659 ICEMAN KINDEST.

I'D GET A LOT OF SPORT OUT OF SELLING MY LINE OF 661 ICEMAN SALVATION

AND MOP UP A COUPLE OF BEERS, THINKING I WAS A 709 ICEMAN HELL-ON-WHEELS SPORT.

(WITH A PAINFUL EFFORT TO BE A GOOD SPORT.) 22 JOURNE HE BEGAN DISSIPATING AND PLAYING THE BROADWAY 33 JOURNE SPORT TO IMITATE YOU.

COUNTRY GENTLEMAN, MILDLY INTERESTED IN SADDLE 55 MISBEG HORSES AND SPORT MODELS OF

HIS CLOTHES ARE THOSE OF A CHEAP SPORT. 52 POET I'M LEARNM' YOUR KID TO BE A SPORT, TIGHT-589 ROPE WAD.

(JOVIALLY) HELLO, OLD SPORT/ 594 ROPE COME ON AND SHAKE HANDS LIKE A GOOD SPORT. 595 ROPE AW RIGHT, OLD SPORT. 596 ROPE WELL, OLD SPORT, HERE GOES NOTHIN'. 596 ROPE SHE'S A SPORT, AW RIGHT/ 599 ROPE BRIGHT THINGS YUH CHUCKED IN THE OCEAN--AND YUH 601 ROPE KIN BE A REAL SPORT.

JACK, THE DEAD GAME SPORT... 6 STRANG FOR THE BOY, FOR ALL HIS GOOD LOOKS AND PROWESS IN 9 STRANG SPORT AND HIS COURSES.

SHE IS DRESSED IN SMART SPORT CLOTHES. 13 STRANG I WAS ALWAYS ONE OF THE FIRST TO GET BOUNCED OFF 29 STRANG THE SQUAD IN ANY SPORT.

(CONSOLINGLY) WELL, THE SPORT HERO USUALLY 30 STRANG DOESN'T STAR AFTER COLLEGE.

SHE'S ACTED LIKE A GOOD SPORT... 92 STRANG IT'S GREAT SPORT/ 121 STRANG SHE IS DRESSED IN A BRIGHT-COLORED SPORT COSTUME. 159 STRANG A GOOD SPORT WHO IS POPULAR WITH HER OWN SEX AS 159 STRANG WELL AS SOUGHT AFTER BY MEN.

NINA'S CERTAINLY BECOME THE PRIZE BUM SPORT/... 160 STRANG WE'LL MAKE A SPORT OUT OF YOU YET/ 164 STRANG COME LIKE A SPORT/ 507 VOYAGE

SPORTIN'

HE AIN'T GOT NO SPORTIN' BLOOD. 36 HUGHIE

SPORTING

GROOVE, HE IS BOYISH AND LIKABLE, OF AN EVEN, 184 STRANG MODEST, SPORTING DISPOSITION.

(BROKENLY) THAT'S DAMN FINE, DARRELL--DAMN FINE 194 STRANG AND SPORTING OF YOU/

SPORTS

(WITH AN EXCITED LAUGH) GOOD SPORTS, I'D CALL 28 ANNA 'EM.

BUT I REMEMBER ENOUGH ABOUT 'EM TO KNOW THEY WAS 522 DIFRNT GOOD SPORTS.

I DON'T KNOW ABOUT WICKED, BUT THEY'RE DARNED GOOD526 DIFRNT SPORTS.

WELL, IF YOU SIMPLY GOT TO BE A REGULAR DEVIL LIKE279 GGBROW ALL THE OTHER VISITING SPORTS

HE LOOKS AS THOUGH HE BELONGED IN A POOL ROOM 585 ICEMAN PATRONIZED BY WOULD-BE SPORTS.

DIS WAS A FIRST-CLASS HANGOUT FOR SPORTS IN DEM 601 ICEMAN DAYS.

THEY WERE SPORTS. 710 ICEMAN YOU ALWAYS DIVIDE WITH EACH OTHER, DON'T YOUS 94 JOURNE LIKE GOOD SPORTS.

THE CROWD HE WENT WITH WERE MOSTLY FELLOWS WHO 29 STRANG WERE GOOD AT SPORTS--

SPORTY

SPORTY
(RATHER PRIMLY) THEY WAS TOO SPORTY FOR THEIR 522 DIFRNT GOOD.
WEARING A LIGHT SUIT THAT HAD ONCE BEEN FLASHILY 575 ICEMAN SPORTY
HIS CLOTHES AND SHOES ARE NEW, COMPARATIVELY 585 ICEMAN EXPENSIVE, SPURTY IN STYLE.

SPOT
AND STANDS AS IF FIXED TO THE SPOT BY SOME 540 *ILE NAMELESS DREAD.
STORM AND FOG TO THE WAN SPOT IN THE WORLD WHERE 39 ANNA YOU WAS/
I'D HAVE TAKEN IT ON THE SPOT, ONLY I COULDN'T 133 BEYOND LEAVE UNCLE DICK IN THE LURCH.
STARING TOWARD THE SPOT ON SHORE WHERE THE SINGING456 CARIBE SEEMS TO COME FROM.)
AND I'SE GOT ALL DE MONEY IN SIGHT, I RESIGNS ON 180 EJONES DE SPOT AND BEATS IT QUICK.
HE POINTS TO THE SPOT WHERE JONES ENTERED THE 202 EJONES FOREST.
THE TOM-TOM SEEMS ON THE VERY SPOT, 202 EJONES SCATTERING SO THAT EACH ENTERS AT A DIFFERENT 203 EJONES SPOT.)
WHEN THEY REACH THE SPOT WHERE HIS MOTHER HAD SAT 138 ELECTR MOANING,
THE SAME SPOT ON THE SAME DOCK AS IN PROLOGUE 323 GGBROW THEY MAKE WIDE DETOURS TO AVOID THE SPOT 237 HA APE ONE SPOT OF CLEAR GRAY LIGHT FALLS ON THE FRONT OF251 HA APE ONE CAGE
BUT THIS TIME I'M ON A SPOT WHERE I GOT TO, IF I 18 HUGHIE AIN'T A SAP.
I'VE SEEN THE SAME LOOK ON GUYS' FACES WHEN THEY 30 HUGHIE KNEW THEY WAS ON THE SPOT,
I WAS SURE SURPRISED WHEN SHE GAVE ME THE TEN 608 ICEMAN SPOT.
I CAN SPOT IT IN OTHERS. 642 ICEMAN
BUT I THINK THIS IS THE SPOT WHERE I OWE IT TO YOU660 ICEMAN TO DO A LITTLE EXPLAINING AND
AT THE INDICATED SPOT IN THE LYRIC) 662 ICEMAN
ANY FOOL CAN SPOT THAT. 679 ICEMAN
HIS GREY HAIR IS THIN WITH A BALD SPOT LIKE A 13 JOURNE MONK'S TONSURE.
THERE IS INDICATION OF A BALD SPOT LIKE TYRONE'S. 19 JOURNE THIS ISN'T A DOLLAR. IT'S A TEN SPOT. 89 JOURNE
AS I LOOK BACK ON IT NOW, THAT NIGHT WAS THE HIGH 150 JOURNE SPOT IN MY CAREER.
HER WITHERED LIPS ARE ROUGED AND THERE IS A 161 MANSNS BEAUTY-SPOT ON EACH ROUGED CHEEK.
ROOTED TO THE SPOT. 177 MANSNS
I'D NEVER GIVE IT A THOUGHT IF I DIDN'T KNOW YOU 26 MISBEG HAD A SOFT SPOT IN YOUR HEART
HE HAS THINNING DARK HAIR, PARTED AND BRUSHED BACK 37 MISBEG TO COVER A BALD SPOT.
ON HIS BALD SPOT WITH THE END OF HER BROOM 73 MISBEG HANDLE.)
BY THE WAY, I LOCATED THE SPOT NEAR SEDAN WHERE 9 STRANG GORDON'S MACHINE FELL.
GORDON'S PROUD SPOT, FAIRNESS AND HONOR/... 10 STRANG
(TOUCHED ON A SORE SPOT--WITH A NASTY LAUGH-- 141 STRANG CUTTINGLY)
PERCEPTIBLE BALD SPOT ON TOP, 152 STRANG
(SHE POINTS TO THE SPOT WHERE THEY HAD STOOD 482 WELDED EMBRACED.)

SPOTLESS
INTO HER HOME, WHERE SHE KEPT EVERYTHING SO 713 ICEMAN SPOTLESS AND CLEAN.
EACH BUTTON IS SHINING AND THE CLOTH IS SPOTLESS. 88 POET

SPOTLESSLY
BUT EVERYTHING IN THIS HOME IS SPOTLESSLY CLEAN 421 DYNAMO AND IN ORDER,

SPOTS
HER FACE IS PINCHED AND DRAWN AND PALE, WITH 548 DAYS FLUSHED SPOTS OVER THE CHEEK BONES,
WHEN A LEOPARD COMPLAINS OF ITS SPOTS, IT MUST 220 HA APE SOUND RATHER GROTESQUE.
ONLY STAY IN THE JUNGLE WHERE YOUR SPOTS ARE 220 HA APE CAMOUFLAGE.
IT'LL MAKE SPOTS ON YOU--LIKE A LEOPARD. 227 HA APE
I SURE HIT THE HIGH SPOTS. 12 HUGHIE
LISTENING TO ME GABBIN' ABOUT HITTIN' THE HIGH 28 HUGHIE SPOTS.
RAPPING ON THE TABLE WITH HIS KNUCKLES AT THE 596 ICEMAN INDICATED SPOTS IN THE SONG...)
YOU SURE IS HITTIN' DE HIGH SPOTS, HICKEY. 640 ICEMAN
HE SPOTS HICKEY AND SLIDES INTO A CHAIR AT THE 708 ICEMAN LEFT OF THE DOORWAY.
YOU CAN'T CHANGE THE LEOPARD'S SPOTS. 31 JOURNE
YOU'VE JUST TOLD ME SOME HIGH SPOTS IN YOUR 153 JOURNE MEMORIES.
SPOTS. 1 MANSNS

SPOTTED
THE HIDEOUS SAFFRON-COLORED WALL-PAPER IS BLOTCHED236 AHWILD AND SPOTTED.
THE TABLE COVER IS SPOTTED AND ASKEW. 112 BEYOND
AT THE LEFT IS A BALD-SPOTTED CRIMSON PLUSH CHAIR.278 GGBROW
DEY SPOTTED ME AND GIMME DE BUM'S RUSH. 235 HA APE
HIS FACE IS SPOTTED WITH BLACK AND BLUE BRUISES. 239 HA APE
HE IS SLOVENLY DRESSED IN A DIRTY SHAPELESS 575 ICEMAN PATCHED SUIT, SPOTTED BY FOOD.
IT LAUGHS A HYENA LAUGHTER, SPOTTED, HOWLING ITS 289 LAZARU HUNGRY FEAR OF LIFE/
PASSING WITH WHITE BODIES SPOTTED BY THE LEPROUS 353 LAZARU FINGERS OF ONE'S LUSTS.
BUT I'D SPOTTED ONE PASSENGER WHO WAS USED TO 149 MISBEG DRUNKS AND COULD PRETEND TO LIKE

SPOTTING
SPOTTING WHAT THEIR PET PIPE DREAMS WERE, AND THEN711 ICEMAN KIDDING 'EM ALONG THAT LINE,

SPOTTY
IN THIS DIM, SPOTTY LIGHT THE ROOM IS FULL OF 139 ELECTR SHADOWS.

SPOUTED
WHILE HE SPOUTED BYRON TO PRETEND HIMSELF WAS A 176 POET LORD WID A TOUCH AV THE POET--

SPOUTIN'
(DISAPPROVINGLY) YUH'RE STILL SPOUTIN' THE ROTTEN595 ROPE OLD WORD O' GOD SAME'S EVER.

SPRAIN
I THOUGHT YOU WOULD SPRAIN YOUR WRIST/ 82 ELECTR

SPRANG
INTO THE DIVIL'S OWN STORM, AND SHE SPRANG WAN 36 ANNA HELL OF A LEAK UP FOR'ARD.
FROM WHICH IT SPRANG. 222 HA APE
AND SPRANG UP INTO THIS MIGHTY TREE TO TESTIFY 349 MARCOM FOREVER TO HIS MIRACULOUS POWERS
WHO SPRANG FROM THE FILTH OF A PEASANT HOVEL, WITH157 POET PIGS ON THE FLOOR--

SPRAWL
ONE OF THEM TORN FROM THE SPRAWL ON THE SIDEWALK 261 AHWILD HE HAD TAKEN,
THE SOLDIERS SPRAWL DOWN BESIDE THEM. 350 MARCOM

SPRAWLED
A HUGE FIREMAN SPRAWLED OUT ON THE RIGHT OF THE 456 CARIBE HATCH--
THE CHANTYMAN LIES SPRAWLED ON HIS BACK, SNORING 102 ELECTR IN A DRUNKEN SLUMBER.
DION IS SPRAWLED ON HIS BACK, FAST ASLEEP ON THE 278 GGBROW SOFA.
ON HIS RIGHT, IN A CHAIR FACING RIGHT, HUGO SITS 665 ICEMAN SPRAWLED FORWARD,
IN THE BAR SECTION, JOE IS SPRAWLED IN THE CHAIR 696 ICEMAN AT RIGHT OF TABLE, FACING LEFT.

SPRAWLING
(HE GIVES HIM ANOTHER PUSH THAT ALMOST SENDS HIM 247 AHWILD SPRAWLING.)
(GIVES HIM A PUSH AWAY THAT SENDS HIM SPRAWLING-- 265 DESIRE
(SAVAGELY--GIVING HIM A PUSH THAT SENDS HIM 237 HA APE SPRAWLING)
YANK LANDS SPRAWLING IN THE MIDDLE OF THE NARROW 250 HA APE COBBLED STREET.
(GIVING HIS FATHER ONE MORE SHAKE, WHICH SENDS HIM597 ROPE SPRAWLING ON THE FLOOR)

SPRAWLS
(HE LEAVES HER AND SPRAWLS IN THE CHAIR AT LEFT OF 96 ELECTR TABLE.
(HE SPRAWLS BACK ON HIS ELBOWS--CONFUSEDLY) 103 ELECTR
(SHE DUMPS HIM IN THE CHAIR WHERE HE SPRAWLS 81 MISBEG LIMPLY, HIS CHIN ON HIS CHEST.)
(HE SPRAWLS ON A CHAIR AT REAR OF THE TABLE AT 160 POET CENTER.)
MARY SPRAWLS FORWARD ON HER HANDS AND KNEES, 601 ROPE WHIMPERING.

SPRAY
I DISSOLVED IN THE SEA, BECAME WHITE SAILS AND 153 JOURNE FLYING SPRAY,

SPRAYED
THE WALLPAPER IS NOW A CREAM COLOR SPRAYED WITH 519 DIFRNT PINK FLOWERS.
HE WEARS A LIGHT BLUE UNIFORM COAT, SPRAYED WITH 175 EJONES BRASS BUTTONS,

SPREAD
WAAL--YE'VE THIRTY YEAR O' ME BURIED IN YE--SPREAD218 DESIRE OUT OVER YE--
THE HEAVY LIMBS SPREAD OUT TO A GREAT DISTANCE 347 MARCOM FROM THE TRUNK.
YOU'LL RUIN MY REPUTATION, IF YOU SPREAD THAT LIE 41 MISBEG ABOUT ME.

SPREADIN'
"R SPREADIN' MANURE. 208 DESIRE

SPREADING
QUIVERING LINE OF FLAME IS SPREADING SLOWLY 166 BEYOND

SPREADS
THEY UNHITCH THEIR WINGS, KATEY, AND SPREADS 'EM 95 BEYOND OUT ON A WAVE FOR A BED.
(HE SPREADS IT ON THE TABLE.) 561 CROSS
THE MAP OF THE ISLAND (HE SPREADS IT OUT ON THE 566 CROSS TABLE)
(HE BENDS DOWN AND SPREADS IT OUT IN THE LIGHT OF 573 CROSS THE LANTERN)
AS THE ACTION GOES ON, THE LIGHT IMPERCEPTIBLY 493 DAYS SPREADS UNTIL,
BEYOND THIS THE SURFACE OF THE RIVER SPREADS OUT, 199 EJONES THE INFECTION SPREADS TO THE CHORUS OF OLD MEN 293 LAZARU WHOSE SWAYING GRIEF FALLS INTO

SPREE
SHE THINKS THERE WEREN'T ANY GIRLS MIXED UP WITH 266 AHWILD RICHARD'S SPREE LAST NIGHT--
WE'LL HAVE A GOOD SPREE ON THAT TEN DOLLARS. 132 ELECTR

SPREER
THEN I MARRIED AN' HE TURNED OUT A DRUNKEN SPREER 226 DESIRE AN' SO HE HAD TO WUK FUR

SPRING
*YET AH, THAT SPRING SHOULD VANISH WITH THE ROSE/ 298 AHWILD WELL, SPRING ISN'T EVERYTHING IS IT, ESSIES 298 AHWILD
(HIS WHOLE BODY TENSE LIKE A SPRING--DULLY AND 59 ANNA GROPINGLY)
JUST AT THIS TIME, IN SPRING, WHEN EVERYTHING IS 88 BEYOND GETTING SO NICE.
IT IS AFTERNOON OF A CLOUDY DAY IN SPRING, 1932. 493 DAYS
A NEW DISCIPLINE FOR LIFE WILL SPRING INTO BEING, 542 DAYS A NEW WILL AND POWER TO LIVE,
I WAS FINISHIN' PLOWIN', IT WAS SPRING AN' MAY AN'209 DESIRE SUNSET, AN' GOLD IN THE WEST,
AN' NOW I'M RIDIN' OUT T' LEARN GOD'S MESSAGE T' 210 DESIRE ME IN THE SPRING.
IT'S SPRING AN' I'M FEELIN' DAMNED,= HE SAYS. 210 DESIRE

1513 SPRINGS

SPRING (CONT'D.)
"I'M RIDIN' OUT T' LEARN GOD'S MESSAGE T' ME IN 215 DESIRE THE SPRING LIKE THE PROPHETS
I WAS GROWIN' OLD IN THE SPRING. 221 DESIRE
THEN THIS SPRING THE CALL COME-- 238 DESIRE
(A NIGHT IN LATE SPRING THE FOLLOWING YEAR. 247 DESIRE
IT IS MID-AFTERNOON OF A FINE DAY IN LATE SPRING 493 DIFRNT OF THE YEAR 1890.
IT'S PURTY HEREABOUTS SOMETIMES--LIKE NOW, IN 515 DIFRNT SPRING--
IT IS LATE AFTERNOON OF A DAY IN THE EARLY SPRING 519 DIFRNT OF THE YEAR 1920.
IT WAS THIRTY YEARS AGO THIS SPRING. 537 DIFRNT
(SMILING) WALL, EVEN THAT DON'T MAKE YOU OUT NO 538 DIFRNT SPRING CHICKEN, EMMER.
DO YOU REMEMBER OUR FIRST SPRING HERE? 425 DYNAMO
I REMEMBER THAT IT'S SPRING--AND I'VE JUST 425 DYNAMO REMEMBERED THAT FIFE HAS A DAUGHTER/
BECAUSE HE HAPPENS TO BE A MINISTER'S SON-- 425 DYNAMO ESPECIALLY WHEN IT'S SPRING/
(HE BREATHES IN THE SPRING) (IGEE, THOSE LILACS 425 DYNAMO SMELL SWEET...
((WHAT'S POP GOING TO SPRING)... 439 DYNAMO
JONES LOOKS UP, STARTS TO SPRING TO HIS FEET, 200 EJONES REACHES A HALF-KNEELING.
THE THREE PLAYS TAKE PLACE IN EITHER SPRING OR 5 ELECTR SUMMER OF THE YEARS 1865-1866.)
IT IS AS IF HE WERE GOING TO SPRING AT THE FIGURE 36 ELECTR IN THE PAINTING.
PURITAN MAIDENS SHOULDN'T PEER TOO INQUISITIVELY 45 ELECTR INTO SPRING/
SO HE'S THE BEAU YOU'RE WAITING FOR IN THE SPRING 46 ELECTR MOONLIGHT/
BENEATH THE LIPS OF SPRING/ 267 GGBROW
RESEMBLING A BLURRED IMPRESSION OF A FALLOW FIELD 278 GGBROW IN EARLY SPRING.
SCENE--CYBEL'S PARLOR--ABOUT SUNSET IN SPRING 284 GGBROW SEVEN YEARS LATER.
SPRING BEARING THE INTOLERABLE CHALICE OF LIFE 322 GGBROW AGAIN/
SPRING AGAIN--LIFE AGAIN/ 322 GGBROW
ALWAYS SPRING COMES AGAIN BEARING LIFE/ 322 GGBROW
HE WHIRLS DEFENSIVELY WITH A SNARLING, MURDEROUS 225 HA APE GROWL, CROUCHING TO SPRING.
WITH A SPRING HE WRAPS HIS HUGE ARMS AROUND YANK 254 HA APE IN A MURDEROUS HUG.
THEY SEEM ABOUT TO CURSE HIM, TO SPRING AT HIM. 685 ICEMAN
THEIR ATTITUDES GROW TENSE AS IF THEY ARE ABOUT T0523 INZONE SPRING.
THEN IN THE SPRING SOMETHING HAPPENED TO ME. 176 JOURNE
SPRING LAUGHS FROM THE EARTH/ 280 LAZARU
(AS ONE, THEY SPRING TO THEIR FEET AND GO TO HIM, 175 MANSNS SEPARATING.
(THE TWO WOMEN SPRING TO THEIR FEET. 176 MANSNS
THE CAPTAIN AND CORPORALS SPRING UP ON THE WAGON) 354 MARCOM
IN THE SPRING WE SANG OF LOVE AND LAUGHED WITH 384 MARCOM YOUTH BUT NOW WE ARE PARTED BY
OUR PRINCESS WAS YOUNG AS SPRING, SHE WAS 436 MARCOM BEAUTIFUL AS A BIRD OR FLOWER.
CRUEL WHEN SPRING IS SMITTEN BY WINTER, WHEN BIRDS436 MARCOM ARE STRUCK DEAD IN FULL SONG.
HE DOESN'T DRINK MUCH EXCEPT WHEN HE ATTENDS HIS 55 MISBEG CLASS REUNION EVERY SPRING--
AND COME BACK NORTH WITH THEM IN THE SPRING, AND 143 MISBEG BE AT THE TRACK EVERY DAY.
IT IS BETWEEN SIX AND HALF-PAST IN THE EVENING OF 577 ROPE A DAY IN EARLY SPRING.
ABOUT NINE O'CLOCK IN THE MORNING OF A DAY IN LATE 48 STRANG SPRING OF THE FOLLOWING YEAR.
LIKE BRIDES JUST TRIPPING OUT OF CHURCH WITH THE 49 STRANG BRIDEGROOM, SPRING, BY THE ARM.
THE SADNESS OF SPRING.... 99 STRANG
WE'LL PICK FLOWERS TOGETHER IN THE AGING 200 STRANG AFTERNOONS OF SPRING AND SUMMER,

SPRINGIN'
CRYIN' OVER HER PICTURE AND DEN SPRINGIN' IT ON 580 ICEMAN YUH ALL OF A SUDDEN

SPRINGING
(SUDDENLY SPRINGING TO HIS FEET AND SMASHING HIS 9 ANNA FIST ON THE TABLE IN A RAGE)
(HALF SPRINGING TO HIS FEET--HIS FISTS CLENCHED) 57 ANNA
(SPRINGING TO HIS FEET AGAIN AND PACING UP AND 156 BEYOND DOWN)
(SPRINGING TO HIS FEET. 166 BEYOND
SUDDENLY AWARE OF HIS HATRED, HE HURLS HER AWAY 239 DESIRE FROM HIM, SPRINGING TO HIS FEET.
(SPRINGING TO HER FEET--SHOCKED BUT PLEASED) 533 DIFRNT
(SPRINGING TO HER FEET) OH/ 540 DIFRNT
(SPRINGING TO HER FEET--FURIOUSLY) 27 ELECTR
(SPRINGING UP--WITH WEAK INDIGNATION) 30 ELECTR
(SPRINGING UP) EZRA/ 60 ELECTR
(SPRINGING TO HIS FEET) FOR GOD'S SAKE, WHY 110 ELECTR DIDN'T YOU--
(RESENTFULLY--CLAPPING ON HIS MASK AGAIN AND 273 GGBROW SPRINGING TO HIS FEET--DERISIVELY)
(SPRINGING TO HIS FEET, HIS FACE CONVULSED WITH 298 GGBROW STRANGE AGONY)
(SPRINGING TO HIS FEET AND GLARING AT THEM 227 HA APE BELLIGERENTLY)
(SUDDENLY SPRINGING TO HIS FEET AND STARING ABOUT 342 LAZARU
(SPRINGING TO HER FEET.) I WILL GO/ 4 MANSNS
(SPRINGING TO HER FEET--BEWILDEREDLY) 58 STRANG
(SPRINGING TO HER FEET AND FINDING HER VOICE--WITH179 STRANG DESPAIRING ACCUSATION)
(SPRINGING TO ACTION, SMASHES IVAN'S DERBY OVER 500 VOYAGE HIS EARS)
(SPRINGING FROM HER CHAIR--EXCITEDLY) 454 WELDED

SPRINGING (CONT'D.)
(SPRINGING TO HER FEET) YOUR EGOTISM IS MAKING A 457 WELDED FOOL OF YOU/

SPRINGS
BURKE SPRINGS TO HIS FEET QUICKLY IN TIME TO MEET 49 ANNA THE ATTACK.
AND SWINGING IT HIGH OVER HIS SHOULDER, SPRINGS 60 ANNA TOWARD HER.
SHE SPRINGS TO HER FEET AND WALKS ABOUT THE CABIN 67 ANNA DISTRACTEDLY.
(HE SPRINGS TO HIS FEET AND INSTINCTIVELY GOES TO 125 BEYOND THE WINDOW
RUTH SPRINGS TO HER FEET AND COMES QUICKLY TO THE 150 BEYOND TABLE, LEFT.
ANDREW SPRINGS OUT OF HIS CHAIR.) 157 BEYOND
(HE SPRINGS FROM HIS CHAIR AND WALKS TO THE 163 BEYOND STOVE.)
RUTH GIVES A CRY OF HORROR AND SPRINGS TO HER 168 BEYOND FEET, SHUDDERING.
COCKY RISES TO HIS FEET, HIS FACE LIVID WITH RAGE,472 CARIBE AND SPRINGS AT PADDY.
HIGGINS SPRINGS TO THE COMPANIONWAY. 572 CROSS
(SHE SPRINGS TO HER FEET--DISTRACTEDLY) 549 DAYS
IN SPITE OF STILLWELL, SPRINGS UP TO A HALF- 563 DAYS SITTING POSITION IN BED.
HE SPRINGS TO HIS FEET SHAKING ALL OVER) 233 DESIRE
HE FREES HIMSELF FROM HER VIOLENTLY AND SPRINGS T0243 DESIRE HIS FEET.
(HE SPRINGS TOWARD THE PORCH BUT CABOT IS QUICKER 255 DESIRE AND GETS IN BETWEEN.)
(UNABLE TO ENDURE THIS, SPRINGS TO HIS FEET IN A 261 DESIRE FURY, THREATENING HER,
AND SPRINGS TO HER FEET--WITH WILD RAGE AND 264 DESIRE HATRED)
(SPRINGS TO HER FEET NERVOUSLY) 525 DIFRNT
(SPRINGS FROM HIS CHAIR IN EXTREME AGITATION AND 466 DYNAMO GRABBING HIS FATHER BY BOTH
(HE SPRINGS FROM HIS CHAIR AND LEANING ACROSS THE 466 DYNAMO TABLE,
(HE SPRINGS TO HIS FEET, 487 DYNAMO
(HE SPRINGS UP THE STAIRS TO HER, SHOUTING 488 DYNAMO FIERCELY) HARLOT/
WHEN SHE DOES SMITHERS SPRINGS FORWARD AND GRABS 174 EJONES HER FIRMLY BY THE SHOULDER.
THE OLD WOMAN SPRINGS TO HER FEET AND RUNS OUT OF 175 EJONES THE DOORWAY, REAR.
WITH ARMS UPRAISED AS IF HIS SHOVEL WERE A CLUB IN194 EJONES HIS HANDS HE SPRINGS
(THE WITCH DOCTOR SPRINGS TO THE RIVER BANK. 201 EJONES
THE WITCH DOCTOR SPRINGS BEHIND THE SACRED TREE 202 EJONES AND DISAPPEARS.
BUT AT HIS TOUCH SHE PULLS AWAY AND SPRINGS TO HER 24 ELECTR FEET.)
SPRINGS TO HIS FEET THREATENINGLY) 24 ELECTR
(PULLS HER HAND AWAY FROM HIM AND SPRINGS TO HER 56 ELECTR FEET WILDLY)
(SPRINGS TO HER FEET) VINNIE/ 91 ELECTR
ORIN SPRINGS FORWARD AND STANDS OVER THE BODY, HIS114 ELECTR PISTOL AIMED DOWN AT IT.
SHE SPRINGS TO HER FEET AND STANDS GLARING AT HER 122 ELECTR DAUGHTER WITH A TERRIBLE LOOK
(SPRINGS TO HER FEET, 163 ELECTR
(THEN SUMMONING HER WILL, SPRINGS TO HER FEET 165 ELECTR WILDLY)
(SHE SPRINGS UP AS IF SHE WERE GOING TO RUN IN THE171 ELECTR HOUSE.
HE SPRINGS TOWARD HER WITH OUTSTRETCHED ARMS BUT 266 GGBROW SHE SHRINKS AWAY WITH A
(SPRINGS TO HIS FEET--ASSERTIVELY) 272 GGBROW
(SPRINGS UP FRANTICALLY) NO/ 292 GGBROW
HE SPRINGS LIGHTLY TO THE SIDE OF THE PETRIFIED 318 GGBROW DRAFTSMEN--IN A WHISPER.)
(HE PUTS ON THE MASK AND SPRINGS TO THE LEFT 320 GGBROW
(HE SPRINGS TO HIS FEET AND ADVANCES ON PADDY 215 HA APE THREATENINGLY--
(SEEING A FIGHT--WITH A ROAR OF JOY AS HE SPRINGS 239 HA APE TO HIS FEET)
(SPRINGS TO HIS FEET, HIS FACE HARDENED VICIOUSLY)671 ICEMAN
SPRINGS FROM BEHIND THE LUNCH COUNTER WITH THE 672 ICEMAN BREAD KNIFE IN HIS HAND)
(HE PUSHES BACK HIS CHAIR AND SPRINGS TO HIS FEET)680 ICEMAN
(SPRINGS TO HIS FEET--STAMMERS DEFENSIVELY) 694 ICEMAN
ALL OF A SUDDEN ROCKY SENSES THEY ARE DETECTIVES 708 ICEMAN AND SPRINGS UP TO FACE THEM.
SMITTY SPRINGS FORWARD FURIOUSLY, ALMOST ESCAPING 527 INZONE FROM THEIR GRASPS.
SHE SPRINGS TO HER FEET, AS IF SHE WANTED TO RUN 42 JOURNE AWAY FROM THE SOUND.
SPRINGS TO HIS FEET NERVOUSLY.) 53 JOURNE
(SHE SPRINGS TO HER FEET. 107 JOURNE
THEN IN A BURST OF RAGE HE SPRINGS FROM HIS 162 JOURNE CHAIR.)
SUDDENLY CALIGULA THROWS THE CUP FROM HIM AND 317 LAZARU SPRINGS TO HIS FEET)
HE SPRINGS NEAR LAZARUS AGAIN, IN A FIENDISH 319 LAZARU ECSTASY.
UPWARD, IT SPRINGS LIKE A LARK FROM A FIELD, AND 345 LAZARU SINGS/
AND GRASS FOR SHEEP SPRINGS UP ON THE HILLS OF 349 LAZARU EARTH/
(SHE STARES--THEN AS IF READING ADMISSION IN HIS 361 LAZARU EYES, SHE SPRINGS TO HER FEET)
(SUDDENLY SPRINGS ON TIBERIUS IN A FURY AND 368 LAZARU GRABBING HIM BY THE
(SHE STARTS AWAKE AND SPRINGS TO HER FEET.) 22 MANSNS
SARA SPRINGS TO HER FEET AND STANDS TENSELY 50 MANSNS DEFENSIVE.

SPRINGS

SPRINGS (CONT'D.)
(HE SPRINGS TO HIS FEET, INDICATING THE CHAIR ACROSS THE TABLE.) 75 MANSNS
(SPRINGS UP AND HUGS HER TO HIM--PASSIONATELY.) 83 MANSNS
(SUDDENLY, MOVED BY A STRANGE URGENCY, HE SPRINGS 111 MANSNS TO HIS FEET
(HE SNAPS HIS BOOK SHUT AND SPRINGS TO HIS FEET-- 130 MANSNS
(HE SPRINGS TO HIS FEET AND TURNS ON SIMON IN A 154 MANSNS FURY.)
(THEN, JUST AS DEBORAH IS TURNING THE KNOB, SHE 165 MANSNS SPRINGS TOWARD HER.)
THEN SPRINGS FROM THEIR ARMS TO HIS FEET, 176 MANSNS STAMMERING DISGRACEFULLY.)
THE CAPTAIN SPRINGS OFF THE WAGON) 350 MARCOM
(TURNS TO HIM AND SPRINGS TO HIS FEET-- 362 MARCOM IMPERIOUSLY)
(SHE SPRINGS TO HER FEET, TURNS AWAY FOR A MOMENT,390 MARCOM THEN TURNS BACK,
(HE SPRINGS SWIFTLY TO THE TOP DECK AND BELLOWS) 406 MARCOM
SPRINGS FORWARD AND WRESTING THE DAGGER FROM HER 415 MARCOM HAND, FLINGS IT OVER THE SIDE.
(HE SPRINGS TO HIS FEET--FUMBLES IN HIS POCKETS 107 MISBEG FOR CIGARETTES--
RESPONDS TO HIS APPEAL--THEN SHE SPRINGS UP AND 141 MISBEG RUNS TO HIM--
MY INFORMATION IS, SHE SPRINGS FROM GENERATIONS OF 49 POET WELL-BRED GENTLEFOLK.
(SHE SPRINGS TO HER FEET.) I'VE HAD ENOUGH OF 112 POET YOUR MAD DREAMS/
(HE SPRINGS TO HIS FEET.) BUT FIRST, YOU YANKEE 122 POET SCUM, I'LL DEAL WITH YOU/
(MELODY LAUGHS CRAZILY AND SPRINGS TO HIS FEET. 159 POET
(SPRINGS TO HER FEET.) FATHER/ 176 POET
(REVOLTED AND ANGRY, HALF-SPRINGS TO HIS FEET) 35 STRANG
LOCK HERE, DARRELL,
(HE SPRINGS TO HIS FEET AS IF THIS IDEA WERE A PIN 67 STRANG STUCK IN HIM--
(HE SEEMS ABOUT TO SOB--THEN ABRUPTLY SPRINGS TO 101 STRANG HIS FEET WILDLY)
(SPRINGS TO HIS FEET) RIGHT0/ 149 STRANG
(HE SPRINGS UP, HIS FACE DISTORTED, AND CLUTCHES 475 WELDED THE WOMAN FIERCELY IN HIS ARMS)

SPRINKLED
A SHORT STOUT WOMAN WITH FADING LIGHT-BROWN HAIR 187 AHWILD SPRINKLED WITH GRAY,

SPRINKLER
TOM FORGOTTEN THE SPRINKLER... 22 STRANG

SPRINT
AND BREAKS INTO A SWERVING SPRINT DOWN THE ROAD.) 262 DESIRE
LET'S SEE YUH SPRINT/ 224 HA APE

SPRINTER
LIKE A SPRINTER RELEASED BY THE STARTING SHOT.) 186 AHWILD

SPRINTING
(WILDLY EXCITED) GORDON'S SPRINTING, ISN'T HE5 180 STRANG

SPROCKET
ON SPROCKET WHEELS 399 MARCOM

SPROUT
WHEN YE KIN MAKE CORN SPROUT OUT O' STONES, GOD'S 236 DESIRE LIVIN' IN YEW/

SPROUTED
YOU'VE SPROUTED HORNS LIKE A BLOODY ANTELOPE/ 662 ICEMAN

SPROUTING
EARTH OF WHICH MYRIAD BRIGHT-GREEN BLADES OF FALL- 81 BEYOND SOWN RYE ARE SPROUTING.

SPRUCE
I OUGHT TO SPRUCE UP A LITTLE. 212 AHWILD
THERE IS ONE SPRUCE, AUTHORITATIVE INDIVIDUAL--THE196 EJONES AUCTIONEER.
A GENERAL SPRUCE-UP. 603 ICEMAN
(LEN'S LOOKS SPRUCE AND CLEAN-SHAVEN. 674 ICEMAN
HE, TOO, HAS MADE AN EFFORT TO SPRUCE UP HIS 675 ICEMAN APPEARANCE.
HE IS SPRUCE, DRESSED IMMACULATELY, HIS FACE A BIT 50 STRANG TIRED AND RESIGNED.

SPRUCED
UNTIL I'VE SPRUCED UP ON A BATH AND COCKTAILS. 517 DAYS
HE IS DRESSED IN HIS STORE SUIT, SPRUCED UP, 228 DESIRE

SPRUNG
THE TWO MEN HAVE SPRUNG TO THEIR FEET. 59 ANNA
(GETTING UP) YUH KNOW WHAT WE SAID YUH'D GET IF 457 CARIBE YUH SPRUNG ANY OF THAT LYIN'
FROM BEHIND THE TRUNK OF THE TREE, AS IF HE HAD 200 EJONES SPRUNG OUT OF IT.
FOR MELODY HAS SPRUNG TO HIS FEET, 52 POET
HE SEEMS TO HAVE SPRUNG FROM A LINE DISTINCT FROM 137 STRANG ANY OF THE PEOPLE WE HAVE

SPRY
FUR HE ADDS REAL SPRY AND VICIOUS.. 210 DESIRE
HE'S AS SPRY ON HIS STUMPY LEGS AS A YEARLING-- 10 MISBEG

SPRYEST
(WITH A WINK AT THE OTHERS) YE'RE THE SPRYEST 250 DESIRE SEVENTY-SIX EVER I SEES, EPHRAIM/

SPUDS
DIGGING SPUDS IN THE MUCK FROM DAWN TO DARK, I 38 ANNA SUPPOSE$
CAN YOR PICTURE A GUOD BARKEEP LIKE CHUCK DIGGIN' 614 ICEMAN SPUDS$

SPUME
WITH THE WATER FOAMING INTO SPUME UNDER ME, 153 JOURNE

SPUN
I'D LIKE TO SIT WHERE HE SPUN WHAT I HAVE SPENT. 282 GGBROW

SPUNK
I THOUGHT THEY WOULD GIVE HER THE SPUNK TO LEAD 207 AHWILD HER OWN LIFE, AND NOT BE--
I'D NEVER THINK SHE HAD THAT MUCH SPUNK. 273 AHWILD
(SNAPPILY) IT WOULDN'T IF YOU POSSESSED A BIT OF 117 BEYOND SPUNK.
I'D NEVER DREAM HE HAD THAT MUCH SPUNK. 13 MISBEG

SPUNKY
I WAS A SPUNKY KID. 230 AHWILD

SPUR
STRAIN WHERE JUDGEMENTS ON THE SPUR OF THE MOMENT 153 BEYOND ARE COMPELLED TO BE ACCURATE.
LOOK AT HIM FLING HIMSELF ON HIS NAG AND SPUR THE 64 MISBEG POOR BEAST/

SPURN
WHERE YOU AFRAID I'D SPURN YOUS 301 GGBROW

SPURS
HE IS DRESSED IN A WORN RIDING SUIT OF DIRTY WHITE174 EJONES DRILL, PUTTEES, SPURS,
PATENT LEATHER LACED BOOTS WITH BRASS SPURS, AND A175 EJONES BELT WITH A LONG-BARRELED,
(LOOKING DOWN AT HIS FEET, THE SPURS CATCH HIS 193 EJONES EYE)
AND TO HELL WID DESE HIGH-FANGLED SPURS. 193 EJONES
BREECHES, IMMACULATELY POLISHED ENGLISH RIDING 56 MISBEG BOOTS WITH SPURS,

SPURT
A GALLANT SPURT DID IT/ 175 STRANG
ONE SPURT MORE WILL DO IT/ 181 STRANG

SPURTIN'
WITH THE BLOOD SPURTIN' OUT OF HIS NECK. 488 CARDIF

SPURTING
THEY'RE BOTH SPURTING/ 181 STRANG

SPUTTER
HARDER IS SO FLABBERGASTED BY THIS MAD ACCUSATION 62 MISBEG HE CANNOT EVEN SPUTTER.

SPUTTERING
AS THOUGH A BOMB WERE CONCEALED IN THE ROOM WITH A120 MANSNS FUSE SLOWLY SPUTTERING
(MANAGES TO GET IN THREE SPUTTERING WORDS) 63 MISBEG

SPUTTERS
SCOTT SPUTTERS WITH ANNOYANCE) 103 BEYOND
SHE GAGS AND SPUTTERS. 113 MISBEG

SPY
AND SPY ON THE RICH AND EXCLUSIVE MANNONS. 7 ELECTR
TO SPY ON ME. 88 ELECTR
WELL, YOU DIRTY SPY, YOU ROTTEN AGENT PROVOCATOR, 249 HA APE
WHAT'D THEY WANT PUTTIN' A SPY ON THIS OLD TUB 522 INZONE FOR$
SPY$ 527 INZONE
I'M NO DIRTY SPY. 527 INZONE
SPY IN PARIS WAS WRITIN' LOVE LETTERS TO SOME 529 INZONE WOMAN SPY IN SWITZERLAND WHO SENT
SO YOU PRETENDED TO BE ASLEEP IN ORDER TO SPY ON 47 JOURNE ME/
SHE CAN'T SUSPECT I'VE COME TO SPY ON HER. 78 JOURNE
I USETER SPY ON HIM WHEN I WAS A KID--MAW USED TO 599 ROPE MAKE ME--
PERHAPS SHE THOUGHT HER FATHER HAD SENT ME TO SPY 25 STRANG ON HER....
(THINKING IN A PANIC) (SHE SNEAKED INTO MY SOUL 42 STRANG TO SPY/....)

SPYIN'
IF YOU WANTS TO TRY YOUR DIRTY SPYIN' TRICKS ON US525 INZONE
SPYIN' ON ME/ 578 ROPE
SPYIN' TO WATCH ME/ 578 ROPE
SPYIN' ON ME/ 579 ROPE
SPYIN' TO SEE---OR--- 579 ROPE

SPYING
SHE'LL TELL THE WHOLE TOWN I WAS SPYING/... 436 DYNAMO
KNOWING EVERYONE IS SPYING ON ME, AND NONE OF YOU 46 JOURNE BELIEVE IN ME, OR TRUST ME.
OF SPYING ON HER ALL THE TIME AND NOT TRUSTING 57 JOURNE HER.
ALL I'VE FELT WAS DISTRUST AND SPYING AND 69 JOURNE SUSPICION.

SQUABBLE
I CALL THAT CARRYING YOUR EVERLASTING SQUABBLE 76 ELECTR WITH MOTHER A BIT TOO FAR/

SQUABBLING
(SHARPLY) STOP YOUR SQUABBLING, BOTH OF YOU/ 50 ELECTR

SQUAD
LEN ENTERS FROM THE LEFT, FOLLOWED BY A SMALL 202 EJONES SQUAD OF HIS SOLDIERS,
A SQUAD OF POLICE WITH DRAWN REVOLVERS, LED BY A 321 GGBROW GRIZZLY, BRUTAL-FACED CAPTAIN,
AS THE FIGHT IS AT ITS HEIGHT A ROMAN CENTURION 291 LAZARU AND A SQUAD OF EIGHT SOLDIERS
(THE SQUAD OF ROMAN SOLDIERS LED BY THE CENTURION,306 LAZARU
A SQUAD OF THE GUARD IN THE SAME UNIFORMS AS THE 326 LAZARU CHORUS,
A SQUAD OF THE GUARD SURROUND THE DAIS, COMMANDED 337 LAZARU BY FLAVIUS.
I WAS ALWAYS ONE OF THE FIRST TO GET BOUNCED OFF 29 STRANG THE SQUAD IN ANY SPORT.
WERE A FIRING SQUAD WHOSE EYES WERE ALSO 45 STRANG BANDAGED--AND ONLY I COULD SEE/

SQUALID
A SQUALID, DINGY ROOM DIMLY LIGHTED 493 VOYAGE

SQUANDERED
SO I SQUANDERED TWO BUCKS OF YOUR DOUGH TO ESCORT 159 JOURNE HER UPSTAIRS.
BUT ALL MY MONEY IS SQUANDERED. 316 LAZARU

SQUAR'
SHE OWNS UP FA'R 'N' SQUAR' T' HER DOIN'S. 230 DESIRE
THAT'S FA'R AN' SQUAR'. HAIN'T IT& 249 DESIRE
I'LL GIT SQUAR' WITH THE OLD SKUNK--AN' YEW/ 257 DESIRE

SQUARE
A SMALL, SQUARE COMPARTMENT ABOUT EIGHT FEET HIGH 535 'ILE WITH A SKYLIGHT IN THE CENTER
THE TYPE OF FOOTBALL LINESMAN OF THAT PERIOD, WITH186 AHWILD A SQUARE STOLID FACE,
(SHE GIVES HIM A LETTER FOLDED MANY TIMES INTO A 273 AHWILD TINY SQUARE.
(HELPFULLY) SQUARE-HEAD NAME. 4 ANNA

SQEAMISH

SQUARE (CONT'D.)
A SQUARE-HEAD TRYIN' TO KID MARTHY OWEN AT THIS LATE DAY/ 11 ANNA
WELL, YUH TREATED ME SQUARE, YUHSELF. 11 ANNA
THERE AIN'T A SQUARE-HEAD WORKIN' ON A BOAT MAN 11 ANNA
ENOUGH TO GIT AWAY WITH THAT.
YUH'RE A SCREAM, SQUARE-HEAD--AN HONEST-TER-GAWD KNOCKOUT/ 11 ANNA
YOU'RE NOT THE OLD SQUARE-HEAD'S WOMAN, I SUPPOSE 32 ANNA
YOU'LL BE TELLING ME NEXT--
THE OLD SQUARE--THE OLD SWEDE, I MEANS 34 ANNA
IN THE REAR WALL, TWO SMALL SQUARE WINDOWS AND A 41 ANNA
DOOR OPENING OUT ON THE DECK.
IT'S SQUARE FOOL'S BLATHER YOU HAVE ABOUT THE SEA 47 ANNA
DONE THIS AND THE SEA DONE
I'VE HALF A MIND TO HIT YOU A GREAT CLOUT WILL PUT 49 ANNA
SENSE IN YOUR SQUARE HEAD.
MAN OF THEM IS WORTH ANY TEN STOCK-FISH-SWILLING 49 ANNA
SQUARE-HEADS
OWN UP LIKE A MAN WHEN YOU'RE BATE FAIR AND 52 ANNA
SQUARE.
I'M OWNING UP TO EVERYTHING FAIR AND SQUARE. 58 ANNA
AN ANDREW SIXTY-FIVE YEARS OLD WITH A SHORT, 94 BEYOND
SQUARE, WHITE BEARD.
TEN SQUARE MILES WHERE WE'VE GOT AN ACRE. 133 BEYOND
GOD STIFFEN YOU, YE SQUARE-HEADED SCUT/ 481 CARDIF
RAISED SQUARE OF THE NUMBER ONE HATCH, COVERED 455 CARIBE
WITH CANVAS.
PLAY US A DANCE, YE SQUARE-HEAD SWAB/ 470 CARIBE
A STRAIGHT NOSE AND A SQUARE JAW, A WIDE MOUTH 493 DAYS
THAT HAS AN INCONGRUOUS FEMININE
IN TWO LINES AND DANCE A SQUARE DANCE. 250 DESIRE
I'D OWN UP TO EVERYTHING FAIR AND SQUARE I'D EVER 500 DIFRNT
DONE.
NO, IT WOULDN'T BE ACTIN' SQUARE WITH YOU. 532 DIFRNT
HIS FACE IS SQUARE, RIBBED WITH WRINKLES, THE 422 DYNAMO
FOREHEAD LOW, THE NOSE HEAVY.
OUT OF THE SQUARE OF LIGHT FROM THE OPEN DOORWAY) 474 DYNAMO
THE OIL SWITCHES, WITH THEIR SPINDLY STEEL LEGS, 483 DYNAMO
THEIR SQUARE,
SQUARE-SHOULDERED, MILITARY BEARING. 10 ELECTR
WOODENLY ERECT AND SQUARE-SHOULDERED.) 27 ELECTR
SQUARE-SHOULDERED AND STIFF, WITHOUT A BACKWARD 35 ELECTR
GLANCE.
THE LEGS CLOSE TOGETHER, THE SHOULDERS SQUARE, THE 43 ELECTR
HEAD UPRIGHT,
LIKE A STATUE OF A DEAD MAN IN A TOWN SQUARE. 55 ELECTR
OR WITH A SELF-CONSCIOUS SQUARE-SHOULDERED 73 ELECTR
STIFFNESS
SITTING ON A CHAIR IN A PARK OR STRADDLING A HORSE 94 ELECTR
IN A TOWN SQUARE--
TURNS, RIGID AND SQUARE-SHOULDERED, AND WALKS 101 ELECTR
WOODENLY FROM THE ROOM.)
LAVINIA IS STIFFLY SQUARE-SHOULDERED, HER EYES 119 ELECTR
HARD, HER MOUTH GRIM AND SET.
STANDING SQUARE-SHOULDERED AND STIFF LIKE A GRIM 123 ELECTR
SENTINEL IN BLACK.)
HIS SHINY WRINKLED FACE IS OBLONG WITH A SQUARE 129 ELECTR
WHITE CHIN WHISKER.
HER MOVEMENTS HAVE LOST THEIR SQUARE-SHOULDERED 137 ELECTR
STIFFNESS.
(SHE STOPS ABRUPTLY AND STIFFENS INTO HER OLD, 178 ELECTR
SQUARE-SHOULDERED ATTITUDE.
AND THEN TURNS AND STANDS FOR A WHILE, STIFF AND 179 ELECTR
SQUARE-SHOULDERED.
TONIGHT ON THE FOR'ARD SQUARE. 208 HA APE
GITTIN' SEASICK, SQUARE-HEADS 209 HA APE
I'D BE SQUARE WITH HER, WOULDN'T I 231 HA APE
I'LL GIT SQUARE WIT HER/ 232 HA APE
BUT I'LL GIT SQUARE WIT HER YET, YOU WATCH. 235 HA APE
DAT'LL SQUARE TINGS. 249 HA APE
TREES SQUARE A DAY, AND CAULIFLOWERS IN DE FRONT 250 HA APE
YARD--EKAL RIGHTS--
(HE PAUSES.) MAYBE YOU THINK I AIN'T GIVING HER A 24 HUGHIE
SQUARE SHAKE.
CRINKLY LONG BLACK HAIR STREAKED WITH GRAY, A 574 ICEMAN
SQUARE FACE WITH A PUG NOSE,
HIS LEAN FIGURE IS STILL ERECT AND SQUARE- 576 ICEMAN
SHOULDERED.
THE SIXTH IS A SQUARE JEWELER'S WATCH BOX. 629 ICEMAN
I'D SQUARE ME WITH MYSELF/ 706 ICEMAN
DAMN FOOL SQUARE-HEAD/ 514 INZONE
SOMETHIN' SQUARE TIED UP IN A RUBBER BAG. 528 INZONE
WHEN I WAS ON THE SQUAREHEAD SQUARE RIGGER, BOUND 153 JOURNE
FOR BUENOS AIRES.
A SQUARE IN ATHENS ABOUT TEN O-CLOCK AT NIGHT. 298 LAZARU
AN EXCITED CROWD OF GREEKS OF BOTH SEXES IS 298 LAZARU
GATHERED IN THE SQUARE.
WHO NOW COME DANCING INTO THE SQUARE, 306 LAZARU
CALIGULA AND CRASSUS ARE LEFT IN THE EMPTY SQUARE.311 LAZARU
HE CARRIES A SMALL, SQUARE BAG. 347 MARCOM
HIS EMPIRE COVERS MILLIONS OF SQUARE MILES 359 MARCOM
THE KAAN'S BEEN SQUARE WITH ME. 381 MARCOM
EACH HAS AT LEAST ONE PANE MISSING, A SQUARE OF 1 MISBEG
CARDBOARD TAKING ITS PLACE.
I WOULD CHARGE A SQUARE OF NAPOLEON'S OLD GUARD 71 POET
SINGLEHANDED
LIKE THE CHARGE ON THE FRENCH SQUARE/ 157 POET
THAT WAS THE SQUARE THING. 11 STRANG
(THINKING) (THE SQUARE THING/... 11 STRANG
SHE IS TWENTY, TALL WITH BROAD SQUARE SHOULDERS, 12 STRANG
DOWN'T I ALWAYS GIVE YER YER SHARE, FAIR AN' 494 VOYAGE
SQUARE, AS MAN TO MANS
FOUR--THREE BRITISHERS AN' A SQUARE-'EAD. 494 VOYAGE
SQUARED
(HAVING THUS SQUARED MATTERS SHE TAKES UP HER 291 AHWILD
SEWING AGAIN.

SQUARED (CONT'D.)
COMES OUT AND AROUND THE CORNER OF THE HOUSE, HIS 269 DESIRE
SHOULDERS SQUARED,
A DOORWAY WITH SQUARED TRANSOM AND SIDELIGHTS 2 ELECTR
FLANKED BY INTERMEDIATE COLUMNS.
SHOULDERS SQUARED. 13 JOURNE
SQUAREHEAD
WHEN I WAS ON THE SQUAREHEAD SQUARE RIGGER, BOUND 153 JOURNE
FOR BUENOS AIRES.
SQUARELY
(LOOKING ROBERT SQUARELY IN THE EYES) 134 BEYOND
ITS BACK SQUARELY TO THE DOOR IN THE CORNER. 66 STRANG
SQUARER
BUILT ON A SQUARER, SIMPLER MODEL, FLESHIER IN 203 DESIRE
BODY,
HE GRINS--THEN SQUARES HIS SHOULDERS AND AWAITS 245 DESIRE
HIS FATHER CONFIDENTLY.
(SHE SQUARES HER SHOULDERS, 168 ELECTR
THE SQUARES HIS SHOULDERS DEFIANTLY. 43 POET
I'LL NEVER FORGET THE BLAST OF DEATH FROM THE 99 POET
FRENCH SQUARES.
SQUARES HIS SHOULDERS, PULLS HIS COAT DOWN IN 22 STRANG
FRONT, SETS HIS TIE STRAIGHT,
SQUARING
THERE IS THE SAME SQUARING OF HIS SHOULDERS, 67 POET
ARROGANT LIFTING OF HIS HEAD,
SQUAT
HE IS A SHORT, SQUAT, BROAD-SHOULDERED MAN OF 5 ANNA
ABOUT FIFTY, WITH A ROUND,
(A SQUAT, UGLY LIVERPOOL IRISHMAN) 458 CARIBE
CATES IS SQUAT AND STOUT AND IS DRESSED IN 571 CROSS
DUNGAREE PANTS
HE IS A SQUAT, BOW-LEGGED, POWERFUL MAN, ALMOST A5513 DIFRNT
BROAD AS HE IS LONG--
WHO SQUAT DOWN ON THEIR HAUNCHES IN A SEMI- 203 EJONES
CIRCLE.)
HE IS A NEAPOLITAN-AMERICAN IN HIS LATE TWENTIES, 577 ICEMAN
SQUAT AND MUSCULAR.
(A SQUAT, SURLY-FACED SWEDE--GRUMPILY) 514 INZONE
A SQUAT, MUSCULAR MAN OF SIXTY, 299 LAZARU
(THE FOUR SQUAT TOGETHER IN A CIRCLE.) 306 MARCOM
ALL FOUR SQUAT AGAIN IN SILENCE.) 368 MARCOM
DAN ROCHE IS MIDDLE-AGED, SQUAT, BOWLEGGED, 51 POET
SQUAT HERE FOR A SPELL AND GIT YOUR WIND. 595 ROPE
SQUATS
HIS BIG HEAD SQUATS ON A NECK WHICH SEEMS PART OF 8 HUGHIE
HIS BEEFY SHOULDERS.
SIDE OF LAZARUS'S CHARIOT WHERE HE SQUATS ON HIS 308 LAZARU
HAMS AND,
ON THE STEP BELOW HER, CALIGULA SQUATS ON HIS 350 LAZARU
HAUNCHES, HIS ARMS ON HIS KNEES,
HE SLINKS NOISELESSLY UP THE STEPS OF THE DAIS AND357 LAZARU
SQUATS COWERINGLY AT
KUBAI SQUATS ON HIS THRONE, AGED AND SAD, 421 MARCOM
SQUATTED
SQUATTED AGAINST THE SIDE WALLS, 364 MARCOM
SQUATTED ON HIS HAUNCHES AT CENTER. 369 MARCOM
SQUATTING
HALF-SQUATTING POSITION AND 200 EJONES
(UNPERTURBABLY--SQUATTING DOWN HIMSELF) 203 EJONES
THE GIGANTIC ANIMAL HIMSELF IS SEEN SQUATTING ON 251 HA APE
HIS HAUNCHES ON A BENCH IN MUCH
THE FORMER SQUATTING ON HIS HAMS, MONKEY-WISE, AND311 LAZARU
BROODING SOMBERLY.)
CALIGULA IS SQUATTING ON HIS HAMS ON A SORT OF 313 LAZARU
THRONE-CHAIR OF IVORY AND GOLD.
THE FIRST SQUATTING ON THEIR HAMS LIKE SAVAGES (AS345 LAZARU
CALIGULA DOES)
THE MINSTREL, SQUATTING AT CENTER, IS THE ONLY ONE373 MARCOM
WHOSE BODY MOVES.
THE SQUATTING FIGURES OF THE PEOPLE ARE CLOTHED IN373 MARCOM
ROUGH ROBES.
IN THE FOREGROUND (THE PORT SIDE OF DECK) THE TWO407 MARCOM
ELDER POLOS ARE SQUATTING.
AS THE CURTAIN RISES MARY IS DISCOVERED SQUATTING 578 ROPE
CROSS-LEGGED ON THE FLOOR,
SQUAWKIN'
NO SQUAWKIN', SEE/ 254 HA APE
SQUEAK
BUT I WON'T BE DENYING 'TWAS A DAMN NARROW SQUEAK. 32 ANNA
SQUEAKED
AND THE PESKY OLD STAIRS SQUEAKED, AND MY HEART 281 AHWILD
WAS IN MY MOUTH,
SQUEAKY
TERRIFIED RATS, THEIR VOICES SQUEAKY NOW WITH 369 LAZARU
FRIGHT)
SQUEAL
SAYING HE'S BOUND BY HIS CONSCIENCE TO SQUEAL ON 431 DYNAMO
HIM/
I THOUGHT YOU LOVED ME BETTER'N ANYONE, AND YOU'D 449 DYNAMO
NEVER SQUEAL ON ME TO HIM/
(THEN SUDDENLY) LEAVE ME ALONE WITH HIM AND MAYBE321 GGBROW
I'LL GET HIM TO SQUEAL IT.
HE CAN GIVE YOU A RAFT OF PEASANT BRATS TO SQUEAL 114 POET
AND FIGHT
SQUEALED
HE WAS IN ON THE GRAFT, BUT MY OLD MAN NEVER 644 ICEMAN
SQUEALED ON HIM.
SQUEALIN'
SHUT UP, YE APE, AN' DON'T BE MAKIN' THAT 498 VOYAGE
SQUEALIN'.
SQUEALS
(HIS FATHER SQUEALS WITH TERROR AND TRIES TO 453 DYNAMO
BREAK AWAY FROM HIS HOLD.
SQUEAMISH
(LOOKING AROUND HIM WITH SQUEAMISH DISAPPROVAL) 74 STRANG

SQUEEZE

SQUEEZE
(WITH ANOTHER SQUEEZE--EMPHATICALLY) 494 DIFRNT
(THEN, AFTER A PAUSE, AS HE MAKES NO COMMENT EXCEPT494 DIFRNT
A CONCURRING SQUEEZE)
(PUTTING HIS ARM ABOUT HER WAIST AND GIVING HER A 506 DIFRNT
SQUEEZE--GRINNING)
THAT IT IS A DIFFICULT SQUEEZE TO PASS BETWEEN 573 ICEMAN
THEM.
SQUEEZED
ON THESE ARE SEATED, SQUEEZED IN TIGHT AGAINST ONE247 DESIRE
ANOTHER,
YOU'VE SQUEEZED 'EM DRY/ 178 EJONES
SQUEEZES
(IN HIS EXCITEMENT HE SQUEEZES HER HAND TIGHT.) 35 ANNA
(HE BENDS DOWN AND SQUEEZES HIS HUGE FORM THROUGH 45 ANNA
THE NARROW DOORWAY)
(DEEPLY MOVED--WITHOUT LOOKING AT ELSA, TAKES HER 524 DAYS
HAND AND SQUEEZES IT--HUSKILY)
THEN WITH A SUDDEN MOVEMENT HE SEIZES HER HANDS 232 DESIRE
AND SQUEEZES THEM.
(HE SQUEEZES HER AWKWARDLY--THEN STAMMERS) 146 ELECTR
HE SQUEEZES BETWEEN THE TABLES TO LARRY. 577 ICEMAN
THE SQUEEZES THROUGH THE TABLES AND DISAPPEARS, 586 ICEMAN
RIGHT-REAR, BEHIND THE CURTAIN.
SQUEEZIN'
BY MONEYLENDIN' AND SQUEEZIN' TENANTS AND EVERY 11 POET
MANNER OF TRICK.
SQUEEZING
SQUEEZING WITH DIFFICULTY BETWEEN THE CHINA CLOSET222 AHWILD
AND THE BACKS OF CHAIRS AT
(SQUEEZING HER) WALL, IT'S ABOUT TIME, AIN'T IT$ 496 DIFRNT
(SQUEEZING HIS HAND--WITH POSSESSIVE TENDERNESS) 270 GGBROW
(HE NODS) BUT YOU LOOK--(SQUEEZING HIS ARMS) 301 GGBROW
SQUELCHED
THAT SORT OF SQUELCHED ME. 520 DAYS
(A SILENCE AS IF HE HAD RESPECTABLY SQUELCHED 25 STRANG
HIMSELF--
SQUINT
YE'LL BE LUCKY IF ANY OF THIM LOOKS AT YE, YE 461 CARIBE
SQUINT-EYED RUNT.
SQUINTING
SLOWLY OPENS IT, AND, SQUINTING HIS EYES, 8 ANNA
COMMENCES TO READ LABORIOUSLY,
SQUINTS
(HE TAKES THE DRAWING FROM HER AND AT ONCE BECOMES275 GGBROW
INTERESTED AND SQUINTS AT IT
SQUIRE
(STARTLED FROM HIS THOUGHTS, BECOMES AT ONCE THE 101 POET
CONDESCENDING SQUIRE--
SQUIRM
YOU COULDN'T RESIST--WATCHING HIM SQUIRM/ 526 DAYS
WALTER IT WAS I, HIS OLD FRIEND--SO YOU CAN WATCH 527 DAYS
HIM SQUIRM SOME MORE/
THEY SQUIRM UPWARD TOWARD HIM IN TWISTED 190 EJONES
ATTITUDES.
SQUIRMING
(SQUIRMING AROUND ON HIS LAP) 241 AHWILD
SQUIRMING ABOUT UNCOMFORTABLY ON THE NARROW 275 AHWILD
GUNWALE.
(HE TICKLES THE LAUGHING, SQUIRMING MARY, 130 BEYOND
-UNGE AS SQUIRMING SPECKS WE CREPT FROM THE TIDES 324 LAZARU
OF THE SEA.
SQUIRMS
(HE SQUIRMS DISGUSTEDLY) THINK OF SOMETHING ELSE,276 AHWILD
CAN'T YOUS
(RICHARD SQUIRMS, HIS HEAD STILL LOWER) 294 AHWILD
(HE SQUIRMS AS IF HE HAD THE ITCH.) 219 DESIRE
A PAUSE--HER BODY SQUIRMS DESIROUSLY--SHE MURMURS 229 DESIRE
LANGUOROUSLY)
JONES SQUIRMS ON HIS BELLY NEARER AND NEARER, 201 EJONES
MOANING CONTINUALLY.)
JONES SQUIRMS TOWARD HIM. 201 EJONES
IN SPITE OF HIMSELF, BROWN SQUIRMS AND ADOPTS A 297 GGBROW
PLACATING TUNE)
(HE READS AMUSEDLY AS MARCO SQUIRMS). 360 MARCOW
SQUIRT
WELL, I'M GLAD THEY FIRED THAT YOUNG SQUIRT THEY 10 HUGHIE
TOOK ON WHEN HUGHIE GOT SICK.
SQUIRTER
NOT FROM NO HICK BEER-SQUIRTER LIKE YOU, SEE/ 248 AHWILD
SSHHH
(WARMINGLY) SSHHH/ 370 MARCOM
SSSH
SSSH/ 39 ANNA
(GUILE NG HIM CAREFULLY) SSSH/ 39 ANNA
SSSH/ 484 DYNAMO
(TRYING TO CALM HER) SSSH/ 284 LAZARU
SSSH/ 47 STRANG
SSSHH
(APPREHENSIVELY) SSSHH/ 536 *ILE
SSSHH/ 39 ANNA
SSSHH/ 478 CARDIF
SSSHHH/ 488 CARDIF
SSSHH/ 566 CROSS
SSSHH/ 567 CROSS
(SHUDDERING) SSSHH/ 571 CROSS
(PEREMPTORILY) SSSHH/ 203 EJONES
SSSHH/ 241 HA APE
SSSHH/ 243 HA APE
SSSHH/ 243 HA APE
SSSHHH/ 243 HA APE
(WARNINGLY) SSSHH/ 507 VOYAGE
STA*B*D
(IRRITABLY) BUT ALL THIS TALK AIN'T TELLIN' ME 103 BEYOND
WHAT I'M TO DO WITH THAT STA*B*D
ABOARD TO OCCUPY THAT STA*B*D CABINS 103 BEYOND
STAB
IT'S WORTH TAKIN' A STAB AT, DAMNED IF IT AIN'T. 545 DIFRNT

STAB
(CONT'D.)
AND AT THE FIRST GOOD CHANCE I GET STAB YOU IN THE166 JOURNE
BACK.
STAB. 304 LAZARU
AS IF HE EXPECTED SOMEONE TO STAB HIM IN THE BACK.311 LAZARU
(HE RAISES HIS HAND TO STAB LAZARUS IN THE BACK. 333 LAZARU
WHY UID YOU NOT STABS 334 LAZARU
STAB HIM/ 337 LAZARU
(HE DISAPPEARS TOWARD THE FLAMES, HIS SPEAR HELD 369 LAZARU
READY TO STAB.)
SURE, IF YOU'VE FOUND A SNAKE WHO CAN STAB YOU 78 MISBEG
WITH A KNIFE,
STABBED
YE STABBED HIM, AND BE DAMNED TO HIM, FOR THE 488 CARDIF
SKULKIN' SWINE HE WAS.
THAT STABBED ME IN THE FIELD BY TEWKSBURY. 168 JOURNE
THEY STABBED THEMSELVES, DANCING AS THOUGH IT WERE321 LAZARU
A FESTIVAL/
AS IF SOMETHING VITAL HAD BEEN STABBED IN HIM-- 51 POET
WITH A CRY OF TORTURED APPEAL.)
STABLE
SLIP ME DE INSIDE DOPE, DE INFORMATION RIGHT FROM 250 HA APE
DE STABLE--
(TURNS TO HIM) WHOSE STABLES 633 ICEMAN
HARRY'S PARTY AIN'T NO TIME TO BEAT UP YOUR 633 ICEMAN
STABLE.
HE BETTER LAY OFF ME AND MY STABLE/ 669 ICEMAN
TENDIN' BAR WHEN YUH GOT TWO GOOD HUSTLERS IN YOUR697 ICEMAN
STABLE/
YUH COULD EASY MAKE SOME GAL WHO'S A GOOD HUSTLER,702 ICEMAN
ANY START A STABLE.
WERE YOU BROUGHT UP IN A STABLES 57 MISBEG
IN THE WHOLE UNITED KINGDOM, WITH MY STABLE OF 49 POET
HUNTERS, AND--
BUT WE CAN GET A RIG AT THE LIVERY STABLE. 128 POET
HE WAS IN THE STABLE. 165 POET
HE ADVANCES INTO THE STABLE WITH A MOCKING SMILE 587 ROPE
ON HIS LIPS
STABLES
IN A GRAND MANSION LIKE A CASTLE, WITH SLOOS OF 21 MANSNS
SERVANTS, AND STABLES,
STABS
(HE STABS HIMSELF AND FALLS. 334 LAZARU
(HE STABS FLAVIUS WITH A SAVAGE CRY) 338 LAZARU
NUR A TREACHEROUS SNAKE IN THE GRASS WHO STABS YOU 78 MISBEG
IN THE BACK WITH A KNIFE--
STACCATO
STACCATO LAUGHTER OF WOMEN AND YOUTHS. 326 LAZARU
STACK
AND THE STACK OF DISHES RATTLES IN HIS TREMBLING 539 *ILE
HANDS.
BEGINS LADLING SOUP INTO THE STACK OF PLATES 223 AHWILD
BEFORE HER)
I WOULDN'T BELIEVE A THING HE SAID, IF HE SWORE ON 27 JOURNE
A STACK OF BIBLES/
IF HE SWORE ON A STACK OF BIBLES. 74 JOURNE
(SUDDENLY SLAPPING A STACK OF COINS INTO THE CHEST415 MARCOM
WITH A RESOUNDING CLANK)
STACKED
THE STEWARD HURRIES TO HIS STACKED-UP DISHES. 538 *ILE
A PILE OF WOOD IS STACKED UP CARELESSLY AGAINST 144 BEYOND
THE WALL BY THE STOVE.
A SMALL TABLE ON WHICH ARE STACKED HIS TEXTBOOKS, 421 DYNAMO
AND A CHAIR IN LEFT CORNER,
A SMALL PILE OF MANUSCRIPT IS STACKED BY HIS RIGHT149 ELECTR
HAND.
HE SITS DOWN, PICKS UP THE MORNING MAIL STACKED ON 69 MANSNS
HIS DESK,
IN THE REAR, TO THE LEFT, A STALL IN WHICH LUMBER 577 ROPE
IS STACKED UP.
STACKING
HE STOPS STACKING 535 *ILE
(HE BEGINS STACKING AND PACKING AGAIN.) 408 MARCOM
STACKS
MILLER STACKS UP AND THEN PUTS ON THE SIDEBOARD. 225 AHWILD
(PETER DOES SO, ARRANGING THEM IN STACKS OF FIVE, 219 DESIRE
A TABLE WITH PAPERS, STACKS OF PAMPHLETS, CHAIRS 245 HA APE
ABOUT IT, IS AT CENTER.
COINS AND PACKING STACKS OF THESE INTO A CHEST 407 MARCOM
THAT STANDS BETWEEN THEM.
STAFF
AND FOUND HER IN THE HAY WITH A STAFF OFFICER. 657 ICEMAN
THIS MORNING ABOUT A JOB ON HIS STAFF. 679 ICEMAN
THIS TREE WAS THE STAFF OF OUR FIRST FATHER, ADAM.349 MARCOM
THIS MUST BE THE HOLY TREE WHICH WAS ONCE THE 350 MARCOM
STAFF OF MAHOMET AND,
MULTITUDE OF YOUNG STAFF OFFICERS, ALL GORGEOUSLY 421 MARCOM
UNIFORMED AND ARMORED.
(HE TURNS TO HIS STAFF EXULTANTLY) 422 MARCOM
STAGE
CAN'T YOU SEE RICHARD'S ONLY A FOOL KID WHO'S JUST202 AHWILD
AT THE STAGE WHEN HE'S OUT TO
HE OUGHT TO BE ON THE STAGE/ 216 AHWILD
HE OUGHT TO BE ON THE STAGE. 223 AHWILD
THE STAGE IS DIVIDED INTO TWO SECTIONS, SHOWING A 3 ANNA
SMALL BACK ROOM IN THE RIGHT.
TWO-THIRDS OF THE WIDTH UP THE STAGE, 564 DAYS
EXTENDS ACROSS THE STAGE. 5 ELECTR
THE STREET ENTRANCE IS OFF-STAGE, LEFT. 7 HUGHIE
(INDIGNANTLY) A SWELL TIME TO STAGE YOUR FIRST 650 ICEMAN
BOUT, ON HARRY'S BIRTHDAY PARTY/
AT EXTREME LEFT-FRONT, ONE WITH FOUR CHAIRS, 664 ICEMAN
PARTLY ON AND PARTLY OFF STAGE.
WE ALL OUGHT TO GIT DRUNK AND STAGE A CELEBRATION 703 ICEMAN
THEY ARE ALL VERY DRUNK NOW, JUST A FEW DRINKS 727 ICEMAN
AHEAD OF THE PASSING-OUT STAGE.
TEMPERAMENTAL POSTURINGS OF THE STAGE STAR. 13 JOURNE
YOU FORCED ME ON THE STAGE. 32 JOURNE

STAGE (CONT'D.)
SPEAKING OF ACTING, MA'AM, HOW IS IT YOU NEVER 102 JOURNE
WENT ON THE STAGES
OR WITH ANYONE ON THE STAGE. 102 JOURNE
WOMEN USED TO WAIT AT THE STAGE DOOR JUST TO SEE 105 JOURNE
HIM COME OUT.
WHEN SHE GETS TO THE STAGE WHERE SHE GIVES THE OLD116 JOURNE
CRAZY EXCUSE ABOUT HER HANDS
I SHALL ARRANGE FOR PLACES IN THE STAGE. 38 MANSNS
SO I CAN RETURN ON THE FIRST STAGE TOMORROW. 51 MANSNS
WE ARRIVED ON THE STAGE ABOUT AN HOUR AGO 51 MANSNS
I SHALL GO TO THE CITY BY THE MORNING STAGE 60 MANSNS
I'M SENDING HIM TO THE CITY BY THE FIRST STAGE 62 MANSNS
I MUST TRANSPORT HER OVER THE FIRST STAGE BY DARK 351 MARCOM
TONIGHT/
(THE LIGHTS COME UP AGAIN ON THE BACK STAGE AS THE426 MARCOM
FORESTAGE IS FULLY REVEALED.
THE LIGHT GROWS DIMMER ON THE STAGE PROPER 426 MARCOM
OF ALL DISTURBING MEMORIES OF WHAT HAD HAPPENED ON439 MARCOM
THE STAGE.
EXCEPT ACTING ON THE STAGE WHILE HIS FATHER WAS 10 MISBEG
ALIVE TO GET HIM THE JOBS.
YOU SHOULD HAVE GONE ON THE STAGE. 25 MISBEG
AND DANCERS ON THE STAGE, TOO--WHEN HE COMES INTO 28 MISBEG
HIS ESTATE.
BUT THE STAGE LINE HAD BEEN DISCONTINUES 7 POET
WE'VE COME TO THE UGLY BITTER STAGE WHEN WE BLAME 144 STRANG
EACH OTHER/
STAGE A PARTY IN NEW YORK... 161 STRANG
HE IS IN THE LAST STAGE OF INTOXICATION, UNABLE TOSO3 VOYAGE
MOVE A MUSCLE.
(BITINGLY) YOU WERE ON THE STAGE SEVEN YEARS 457 WELDED
BEFORE I MET YOU.
STAGECOACH
IT HAD ONCE BEEN PROSPEROUS, A BREAKFAST STOP FOR 7 POET
THE STAGECOACH,
STAGED
DEY COULD PUT UP A BOUT OUGHTER BEEN STAGED AT DE 234 HA APE
GARDEN.
HE'D HAVE BEAT HER UP AND DEN GONE ON DE WOIST 636 ICEMAN
DRUNK HE'D EVER STAGED.
STAGGER
OF A TWO-WHEELED WAGON, STAGGER IN, STRAINING 350 MARCOM
FORWARD UNDER THE LASHES
(COCKY AND IVAN STAGGER TO THEIR FEET. 501 VOYAGE
STAGGERING
WHY, IT'S SIMPLY STAGGERING/ 225 AHWILD
STAGGERING BACK AGAINST THE CABIN WALL, WHERE HE 50 ANNA
REMAINS STANDING,
HE IS STAGGERING A BIT AND SHE IS LAUGHING 468 CARIBE
SHRILLY.)
(HE GETS WEARILY TO HIS FEET AND WALKS WITH BOWED 473 CARIBE
SHOULDERS, STAGGERING A BIT,
(GIVES HIM A FURIOUS PUSH WHICH SENDS HIM 264 DESIRE
STAGGERING BACK
(STAGGERING TO HIS FULL HEIGHT AND LOOKING UPWARD 299 GGBROW
DEFIANTLY)
(IS SWAYING AND STAGGERING, LIKE A MAN IN A 311 LAZARU
DRUNKEN STUPOR,
(HE GETS TO HIS FEET, STAGGERING A BIT, AND STEPS 138 MISBEG
DOWN TO THE GROUND.)
STAGGERS
SHE STAGGERS BACK AGAINST THE TABLE--THICKLY) 128 BEYOND
ROBERT STAGGERS WEAKLY IN FROM THE LEFT. 166 BEYOND
YANK STAGGERS OVER TOWARD SMITTY AND PEARL.) 469 CARIBE
HE STAGGERS OVER AND STANDS ON TOP OF THE HATCH, 470 CARIBE
HIS INSTRUMENT UNDER HIS ARM.)
(BROWN LETS GO OF HIM AND STAGGERS BACK TO HIS 299 GGBROW
CHAIR, PALE AND TREMBLING.)
BROWN STAGGERS BACK AND FALLS ON THE FLOOR BY THE 321 GGBROW
COUCH, MORTALLY WOUNDED.)
STAGGERS IN FROM THE LEFT.) 290 LAZARU
(SHE PULLS HIS ARMS AWAY SO VIOLENTLY THAT HE 137 MISBEG
STAGGERS BACK AND WOULD FALL DOWN
(HE SUDDENLY STAGGERS AS IF HE WERE VERY DRUNK, 182 STRANG
LEANING ON MARSDEN--
DARRELL STAGGERS BACK FROM THE FORCE OF THE BLOW, 193 STRANG
HOLDING HIS ARMS.)
STAGIN'
AND NOT BE RESPONSIBLE FOR ALL DE CRAZY STUNTS 669 ICEMAN
HE'S STAGIN' HERE.
STAGNATING
WE'LL GO WHERE PEOPLE LIVE INSTEAD OF STAGNATING, 149 BEYOND
AND START ALL OVER AGAIN.
STAGNATION
THERE IS AN ATMOSPHERE OF OPPRESSIVE STAGNATION IN696 ICEMAN
THE ROOM,
STAIN
THE CRIMSONS AND PURPLES IN THE WINDOWS WILL STAIN197 STRANG
OUR
STAINED
HIS IRON SPIRIT WEAKENS AS HE LOOKS AT HER TEAR- 549 'ILE
STAINED FACE.)
THREE TABLES WITH STAINED TOPS, FOUR CHAIRS AROUND236 AHWILD
EACH TABLE,
AND A SOFT, MUD-STAINED HAT PUSHED BACK ON HIS 82 BEYOND
HEAD.
A PRETTY BUT SICKLY AND ANEMIC-LOOKING CHILD WITH 116 BEYOND
A TEAR-STAINED FACE.
THE TOP OF THE COVERLESS TABLE IS STAINED 144 BEYOND
AND A SHREDDED WHITE SAILOR'S BLOUSE, STAINED WITH571 CROSS
IRON-RUST.
STAINED BY THE COLOR IN THE WINDOWS, FALLS ON THE 564 DAYS
WALL ON AND AROUND THE CROSS.
STAINED-GLASS WINDOWS. 564 DAYS
WHILE THIS IS HAPPENING THE LIGHT OF THE DAWN ON 566 DAYS
THE STAINED-GLASS WINDOWS

STAINED (CONT'D.)
THEIR CLOTHES, THEIR FACES, HANDS, BARE ARMS AND 204 DESIRE
THROATS ARE EARTH-STAINED.
HIS BODY IS STAINED ALL OVER A BRIGHT RED. 200 EJUNES
HE WEARS HIS EARTH-STAINED WORKING CLOTHES. 6 ELECTR
A BLOOD-STAINED BANDAGE IS WRAPPED AROUND HIS 240 HA APE
HEAD.)
ITS KNOT STAINED BY PERSPIRATION. 9 HUGHIE
STAINED AND DUSTY THAT THEIR COLOR CAN BEST BE 573 ICEMAN
DESCRIBED AS DIRTY.
THEIR TANNED BODIES AND MASKS DAUBED AND STAINED 298 LAZARU
WITH WINE LEES,
TRAVEL-STAINED AND WEARY. 423 MARCOM
HER FEET ARE BARE, THE SOLES EARTH-STAINED AND 3 MISBEG
TOUGH AS LEATHER.
(MIKE WEARS DIRTY OVERALLS, A SWEAT-STAINED BROWN 4 MISBEG
SHIRT.
SARA HAS LIFTED HER TEAR-STAINED FACE FROM HER 179 POET
HANDS AND IS STARING AT HIM
IN HIS TURN, DISHEVELED, DIRT-STAINED UNIFORM, 175 POET
IS STAINED AT THE CEILING LINE WITH DAMP BLOTCHES 48 STRANG
OF MILDEW.
UGLY WALLPAPER, DIRTY, STAINED, CRISS-CROSSED WITH470 WELDED
MATCH-STROKES.
STAINLESS
SHE WAS STAINLESS AND IMPERISHABLE. 282 GGBROW
STAIR
A BAMBOO STAIR LEADS UP TO THE HIGH POOP OF THE 400 MARCOM
JUNK FROM FRONT, LEFT.
ONE FOOT ON THE FIRST STAIR, LOOKING UP AT THE 466 WELDED
TOP.
STAIRS
(THERE IS THE NOISE OF SOMEONE COMING SLOWLY DOWN 538 'ILE
THE COMPANIONWAY STAIRS.
JUST AT THAT MOMENT THERE IS A CLATTER OF 550 'ILE
FOOTSTEPS ON THE STAIRS
LILY, YOU RUN UP THE BACK STAIRS AND GET YOUR 199 AHWILD
THINGS ON.
AND THEN I SNEAKED DOWN THE BACK STAIRS. 281 AHWILD
AND THE PESKY OLD STAIRS SQUEAKED, AND MY HEART 281 AHWILD
WAS IN MY MOUTH.
FARTHER BACK, THE STAIRS OF THE COMPANIONWAY. 555 CROSS
IN THE REAR, CENTER, A DOOR OPENING ON STAIRS 555 CROSS
WHICH LEAD TO THE LOWER HOUSE.
THEN I HEARD SOMEONE COME DOWN THE STAIRS AND GO 563 CROSS
OUT.
CAPTAIN BARTLETT TRAMPS DOWN THE STAIRS.) 567 CROSS
THEN COMES UP THE STAIRS.) 571 CROSS
AND JIMMY KANAKA RISE NOISELESSLY INTO THE ROOM 571 CROSS
FROM THE STAIRS.
(AS SHE GETS TO THE DOOR DOCTOR HIGGINS APPEARS, 572 CROSS
HURRYING UP THE STAIRS.)
(HE TURNS AND GOES, HIS BOOTS CLUMPING DOWN THE 238 DESIRE
STAIRS.
(WITH REAL SOLICITATION) AIR YE ABLE FUR THE 252 DESIRE
STAIRS
CAN BE HEARD BOUNDING UP THE STAIRS, 263 DESIRE
THE DOOR TO THE HALL AND THE STAIRS IS AT THE 421 DYNAMO
RIGHT, REAR.
AND THEN FROM THE STAIRS IN THE HALLWAY.) 445 DYNAMO
(SHE GOES UP THE STAIRS TO THE PLATFORM AND STANOS485 DYNAMO
DIRECTLY UNDER THE SWITCHES,
RUNS DOWN THE STAIRS TO THE LOWER OIL SWITCH 487 DYNAMO
GALLERY.
HE STARTS FOR THE STAIRS, 487 DYNAMO
AND DOWN THE STAIRS TO THE DYNAMO-ROOM FLOOR, 488 DYNAMO
(HE GLIDES STEALTHILY ACROSS TOWARD THE FOOT OF 488 DYNAMO
THE STAIRS.)
(REUBEN FIRES TWICE AND SHE JERKS BACK AND PITCHES488 DYNAMO
SIDEWAYS ON THE STAIRS.)
(HE SPRINGS UP THE STAIRS TO HER, SHOUTING 488 DYNAMO
FIERCELY) HARLOT/
THE STAIRS TO THE LOWER SWITCH GALLERY--SHE CALLS 488 DYNAMO
UNEASILY)
IN THE REAR WALL, CENTER, IS THE DOORWAY GIVING ON 79 ELECTR
THE MAIN HALL AND THE STAIRS.
AT LEFT IS THE CHART ROOM AND THE ENTRANCE TO THE 102 ELECTR
COMPANIONWAY STAIRS LEADING
TO THE COMPANIONWAY STAIRS AND CLOSES IT QUIETLY 109 ELECTR
BEHIND THEM.
THE COMPANIONWAY STAIRS LEAD DOWN TO THIS ALLEY 110 ELECTR
WAY.
THERE IS THE NOISE OF FOOTSTEPS CLIMBING THE 291 GGBROW
STAIRS IN THE HALLWAY.
THERE IS A SOUND OF HEAVY, HURRYING FOOTSTEPS ON 292 GGBROW
THE STAIRS.
(WHILE HE HAS BEEN SPEAKING THERE HAS BEEN A NOISE314 GGBROW
FROM THE STAIRS.
THE SOUND OF HIS FEET LEAPING DOWN THE STAIRS, 318 GGBROW
FIVE AT A TIME, CAN BE HEARD.
(HE HEARS A NOISE FROM THE STAIRS) 653 ICEMAN
IT WAS YOUR FAULT DE DAMNED BOX ALMOST FELL DOWN 676 ICEMAN
DE STAIRS.
YOU FOUND YOUR RHEUMATISM DIDN'T BOTHER YOU COMING684 ICEMAN
DOWN-STAIRS, DIDN'T YOUS
SHE HEARS EDMUND DESCENDING THE STAIRS IN THE 42 JOURNE
FRONT HALL
AND SEES EDMUND COMING DOWN THE STAIRS IN THE 88 JOURNE
HALL.)
AND IF SOMETIMES, ON THE STAIRS OF A PALACE, OR ON132 JOURNE
THE GREEN SIDE OF A DITCH,
AND TO THE LEFT OF DOOR A FLIGHT OF STAIRS GOES UP281 LAZARU
TO THE BALUSTRADED ROOF.
THE CHORUS OF OLD MEN IS AGAIN JOINED IN ITS 287 LAZARU
SPEARHEAD FORMATION AT THE STAIRS.
(HE WALKS DOWN THE NARROW STAIRS AND, MIRIAM 293 LAZARU
FOLLOWING HIM,

STAIRS

STAIRS (CONT'D.)
SEATED IN THE MIDDLE OF THE LOWER OF THE THREE 312 LAZARU
HIGH BROAD STAIRS THAT LEAD TO
CALIGULA RUSHES MADLY DOWN THE STAIRS 369 LAZARU
THE DOORWAY TO THE ENTRANCE HALL--AND THE STAIRS 43 MANSNS
TO THE SECOND FLOOR--
HE HEARS SARA COMING DOWN THE STAIRS IN THE HALL 44 MANSNS
AND AT ONCE REPRESSES HIS
WHEN SHE WAS STARTING TO DESCEND THE STEEP FRONT 179 MANSNS
STAIRS, IF--
AND I WILL FOLLOW HER TO THE TOP OF THE STAIRS--/ 181 MANSNS
AT THE FOOT OF THE STAIRS, CHU-YIN STANDS LIKE A 400 MARCOM
SENTINEL.
(THE THREE POLOS MAKE THEIR GRAND ENTRANCE FROM 428 MARCOM
THE STAIRS ON RIGHT.)
(THE MUSICIANS FORM A LINE, THREE ON EACH SIDE BY 428 MARCOM
THE STAIRS ON RIGHT)
OPENING ON A FLIGHT OF STAIRS TO THE FLOOR ABOVE. 7 POET
THEIR NINA'S VOICE CALLS DOWN THE STAIRS.) 123 STRANG
(COMES INTO VIEW IN THE HALL, OPPOSITE THE 123 STRANG
DOORWAY, AT THE FOOT OF THE STAIRS--
(DARKELL REMAINS STANDING LOOKING UP THE STAIRS IN124 STRANG
A SORT OF JOYOUS STUPOR.
(AS HE HEARS NINA COMING DOWN THE STAIRS) 125 STRANG
(RUSHING DOWN THE STAIRS--FRANTICALLY) 449 WELDED
CAPE IS OBLIVIOUS AND CONTINUES UP THE STAIRS. 449 WELDED
JUST NOW AT THE FOOT OF THE STAIRS--THE KNOCK ON 453 WELDED
THE DOOR WAS--LIBERATION.
STANDING AT THE HEAD OF THE STAIRS WAITING FOR 466 WELDED
ME--
THEN STOPS AS HE NOTICES THAT SHE ALSO HAS STOPPED466 WELDED
AT THE BOTTOM OF THE STAIRS.
(SHE ASCENDS THE STAIRS SLOWLY) 489 WELDED

STAIRWAY
AND THE STAIRWAY TO THE UPSTAIRS ROOMS. 236 AHWILD
NEAR EACH BULWARK THERE IS ALSO A SHORT STAIRWAY, 455 CARIBE
LIKE A SECTION OF FIRE ESCAPE,
AGAINST THE WALL ON THE RIGHT IS A STAIRWAY THAT 483 DYNAMO
EXTENDS BACKWARD HALF WAY UP
JUST INSIDE THE DOOR TO THE DYNAMO-ROOM ROOF AT 484 DYNAMO
THE TOP OF THE STAIRWAY.)
GIVING ON A HALLWAY AND THE MAIN STAIRWAY TO THE 7 POET
SECOND FLOOR.
IN THE REAR, A BALCONY WITH A STAIRWAY AT CENTER 443 WELDED
(WITH HIS ARMS AROUND HER HE LEADS HER TO THE 449 WELDED
STAIRWAY.
SMILES TO HERSELF AND WALKS BACK TO THE FOOT OF 487 WELDED
THE STAIRWAY.
(SHE REACHES THE TOP OF THE STAIRWAY AND STANDS 489 WELDED
THERE LOOKING DOWN AT HIM--

STAIRWELL
IS HEARD COMING DOWN THE STAIRWELL FROM THE FLOOR 43 MANSNS
ABOVE.

STAKE
BUT THERE WAS A STAKE OUT WHERE THE WHISTLING BUOY229 AHWILD
IS NOW, ABOUT A MILE OUT.
AND HE DARED ME TO RACE HIM OUT TO THE STAKE AND 230 AHWILD
BACK.
HE MIGHT BE WILLING TO STAKE ME TO A ROOM AND EATS 16 ANNA
TILL I GET RESTED UP.
THEN YOU THINK'S HE'LL STAKE ME TO THAT REST CURE 17 ANNA
I'M AFTER?
SO I'D STAKE HIM AT THE START TO HALF OF WHAT I 21 HUGHIE
GOT--IN CHICKEN FEED, I MEAN.
I'LL STAKE YOU, SEES 37 HUGHIE
IF YOU'RE BROKE, I'LL STAKE YOU TO BUCK ANY GAME 605 ICEMAN
YOU CHOOSE.
(DREAMILY) I'LL MAKE MY STAKE 605 ICEMAN
IT'S GOIN' TO DRINK IT DAT WAY AGAIN, TOO, SOON'S 1640 ICEMAN
MAKE MY STAKE/
I'LL GET DE MONEY FOR MY STAKE TODAY, SOMEHOW. 673 ICEMAN
SOMEWHERES/
SHE LAUGHED AND SAID, *HELLA, I'LL STAKE YOU, KID/ 710 ICEMAN
BOUND TO A HIGH STAKE AFTER HE HAD BEEN TORTURED, 363 LAZARU
(CALLING FROM OFF BESIDE THE STAKE) 364 LAZARU
AS THE SOLDIERS RAKE BACK THE FIRE FROM THE STAKE,366 LAZARU
HIGH UPON ITS STAKE/ THE FLAMES BELOW IT NOW 370 LAZARU
FLICKERING FITFULLY/
WILLING TO GAMBLE WITH THE HIGHEST POSSIBLE STAKE, 88 MANSNS
ALL SHE HAS.
WHERE MY ONLY CHILD'S HAPPINESS IS AT STAKE, I AM 120 POET
PREPARED TO MAKE EVERY POSSIBL

STAKED
I WAS STAKED TO THEM--AS A DISGUISE, SORT OF. 588 ICEMAN
HE'S ALWAYS STAKED ME WHEN HE HAD ANYTHING. 129 JOURNE

STAKES
KEEP THE CROSSING-STAKES BESIDE YOU, 155 JOURNE

STAKING
(GUILTILY) BUT HE'S BEEN VERY KIND AND GENEROUS 674 ICEMAN
STAKING ME.

STALE
OR LIKE THE DREARY TEARS OF A TRCLLOP SPATTERING 152 JOURNE
IN A PUDDLE OF STALE BEER ON A
BEEN GOING STALE EVER SINCE WE CAME BACK FROM THAT 67 STRANG
TRIP HOME.

STALK
ON SEEING HIS AUNT, HE GIVES HER A DARK LOOK AND 215 AHWILD
TURNS AND IS ABOUT TO STALK

STALKING
(AYAN STALKING MAJESTICALLY WITH AN INJURED MIEN) 423 MARCOM

STALKS
(HE STALKS OUT, SLAMMING THE DOOR BEHIND HIM.) 216 AHWILD
(DEEPLY OFFENDED, RICHARD DISDAINS TO REPLY BUT 216 AHWILD
STALKS WOUNDEDLY TO THE SCREEN
(SHE STALKS WITH STIFF DIGNITY TOWARD HER PLACE AT222 AHWILD
THE FOOT OF THE TABLE.
(HE STALKS OFF. 265 DESIRE
HIS FACE STONY, AND STALKS GRIMLY TOWARD THE BARN.269 DESIRE

STALKS (CONT'D.)
(HE TURNS AND STALKS STIFFLY WITH HURT DIGNITY 146 ELECTR
FROM THE ROOM.
(THE LADY STALKS BY WITHOUT A LOCK, WITHOUT A 237 HA APE
CHANGE OF PACE.
(STALKS BACK TO THE OTHERS-- 532 INZONE
AND STALKS OUT THE DOOR AT REAR. 60 MANSNS
(HE STALKS ON-- 370 MARCOM

STALL
OF COURSE, I'D STALL HIM OFF WHEN HE'D WANT TO 21 HUGHIE
SHOUT NIGHTS
I TELL YOU, PAL, I'D RATHER SLEEP IN THE SAME 21 HUGHIE
STALL WITH OLD MAN O' WAR
THE MARE, MOTHER, AND HASN'T HE SLEPT IN HER STALL162 POET
MANY A TIME
IN THE REAR, TO THE LEFT, A STALL IN WHICH LUMBER 577 ROPE
IS STACKED UP.

STALLIN'
(SWAGGERING ABOUT AGAIN) IF I WAS ONLY SURE HE 545 DIFRNT
WASN'T STALLIN'/

STALLING
I HAD TO DO A LOT OF LYING AND STALLING WHEN I GOT713 ICEMAN
HOME.
HE WAS STALLING. 30 JOURNE

STALLS
IN FRONT OF THE STALLS ON THE RIGHT STANDS A LONG,577 ROPE
ON THE RIGHT OF THE DOORWAY, THREE STALLS WITH 577 ROPE
MANGERS AND HAY-RICKS.

STAMMER
I WAS SO BASHFUL ALL I COULD DO WAS STAMMER AND 105 JOURNE
BLUSH LIKE A LITTLE FOOL.
(KNOWS HE IS TELLING THE TRUTH--SO RELIEVED SHE 132 MISBEG
CAN ONLY STAMMER STUPIDLY)
THAT THE CONTEMPT IS FORCED BACK AND SHE CAN ONLY 89 POET
STAMMER A BIT FOOLISHLY.)
HE CAN ONLY STAMMER HOARSELY.) 122 POET

STAMMERED
JUST STAMMERED. 154 JOURNE
AND HERE YOUR SIMON STAMMERED SO EMBARRASSEDLY I 110 POET
HAD TROUBLE MAKING HIM OUT--

STAMMERING
(STAMMERING) Y-Y-YES, SIR. 539 'ILE
(STAMMERING) ALL AV US--WAS IN A BIT AV A 472 CARIBE
HARNESS FOIGHT, SIR--AN' I DUNNO--
STAMMERING) 207 DESIRE
(STAMMERING BETWEEN FEAR AND RAGE--SHOUTING AFTER 530 DIFRNT
HER)
(PUSHING HER AWAY FROM--IN A STAMMERING PANIC) 482 DYNAMO
STAMMERING IS THE NATIVE ELOQUENCE OF US FOG 154 JOURNE
PEOPLE.
IN A DAZED AWAKENING CONFUSION, STAMMERING.) 130 MANSNS
(WITH A PITIFUL, STAMMERING, HYSTERICAL LAUGH.) 167 MANSNS
(SHE RUNS TO HER WILDLY AND GRABS HER ARM-- 169 MANSNS
STAMMERING WITH TERROR.)
THEN SPRINGS FROM THEIR ARMS TO HIS FEET, 176 MANSNS
STAMMERING DISTRACTEDLY.)
(STAMMERING) I MEAN, YOUR HONOR. 391 MARCOM
(STAMMERING) I HATE TO MAKE YOU UP BUT-- 93 STRANG
(STAMMERING) WELL--ALL RIGHT--LET'S SAY THAT PART103 STRANG
OF IT WAS ALL RIGHT THEN.
(NOT DARING TO BELIEVE WHAT HE HOPES--STAMMERING) 106 STRANG
(STAMMERING) NED TOLD YOU--WHAT'S 107 STRANG
(STAMMERING AND SWAYING) NO. 108 STRANG
(TRYING TO BE CALM BUT STAMMERING) 115 STRANG
(KISSES HER AWKWARDLY--STAMMERING) 130 STRANG
(THEN OVERCOME BY A RUSH OF BEWILDERED JOY-- 463 WELDED
STAMMERING)
(STAMMERING) WHAT--S 478 WELDED
(STAMMERING HYSTERICALLY) HOW'S 485 WELDED

STAMMERINGLY
(PICKING UP HER BAG--HALF-ALOUD--STAMMERINGLY) 24 ANNA
(ON THE VERGE OF HIS OUTBREAK--STAMMERINGLY) 59 ANNA
(STAMMERINGLY) YOUR HOLINESS-- 362 MARCOM
(STAMMERINGLY) MAYBE, NINA-- 63 STRANG
STAMMERINGLY) 99 STRANG
(STAMMERINGLY) NINA--I--I'VE COME BACK TO YOU--DOI30 STRANG
YOU--DO YOU STILL CARE--NINA'S
(STAMMERINGLY) NELLY--IT'S NO GOOD/ 480 WELDED

STAMMERS
(FLABBERGASTED--STAMMERS) YOU KNOW--/ 294 AHWILD
(STARTS VIOLENTLY--STAMMERS) 513 DAYS
(STAMMERS MISERABLY) SWEETHEART/ 530 DAYS
(STAMMERS CONFUSEDLY) NO--I--DON'T YOU SEE IT 538 DAYS
WASN'T HE'S
(STAMMERS CONFUSEDLY) BUT I--I DIDN'T MEAN-- 538 DAYS
FORGIVE ME.
(STAMMERS CONFUSEDLY) YES, YOU--YOU MUST BE 540 DAYS
CAREFUL DEAREST.
(STUNNED--STAMMERS) ELSA, I-- 549 DAYS
(STARTS BACK TO HIMSELF--STAMMERS WITH A CONFUSED 552 DAYS
AIR OF RELIEF)
(STAMMERS TORTUREDLY) I--I DON'T KNOW--I CAN'T 559 DAYS
THINK/
(STAMMERS) PLEASED TO MEET YOU. 436 DYNAMO
(STAMMERS) YOU BETTER NOT-- TALK LIKE THAT, OR---437 DYNAMO
YOU BETTER LOOK OUT/
(STAMMERS) I'LL TELL YOU, MOTHER--IF YOU PROMISE 446 DYNAMO
TO KEEP IT A SECRET--
UTTER THEM--FINALLY FINDING HIS VOICE, HE 451 DYNAMO
STAMMERS)
(STARING AT HIM, STAMMERS HIS NAME AGAIN 459 DYNAMO
HE STAMMERS) 466 DYNAMO
(STUNNED--STAMMERS IN GUILTY CONFUSION) 27 ELECTR
(WINCING AGAIN--STAMMERS HARSHLY) 31 ELECTR
SHE STAMMERS) 31 ELECTR
(STAMMERS) NO, NO, I--WHAT MAKES YOU SAY SUCH 55 ELECTR
THINGS/

STAMMERS (CONT'D.)
(STAMMERS LAMELY) I--I--REMEMBERED I FORGOT TO 57 ELECTR
SAY GOOD NIGHT, FATHER.
(THEN TRYING TO CALM HIMSELF STAMMERS) 61 ELECTR
(TREMBLING WITH GUILTY TERROR--STAMMERS.) 62 ELECTR
(STAMMERS) I TOLD HIM--ADAM WAS MY LOVER. 63 ELECTR
(EMBARRASSED--STAMMERS SHYLY) 72 ELECTR
(STAMMERS) GOD/ 99 ELECTR
(STAMMERS) WHY DO YOU LOOK AT ME--LIKE THATS 100 ELECTR
(FEELING HER GUILT, STAMMERS) 101 ELECTR
(STAMMERS) ORIN/ 120 ELECTR
STOPS AGAIN AND STAMMERS SHAKENLY) 123 ELECTR
(HE GRABS HER ARM AND STAMMERS DISTRACTEDLY) 124 ELECTR
(STAMMERS--POINTING) IT WAS HERE--SHE--THE LAST 138 ELECTR
TIME I SAW HER ALIVE--
(STAMMERS) VINNIE/ 143 ELECTR
(HE SQUEEZES HER AWKARDLY--THEN STAMMERS) 146 ELECTR
(STRANGELY SHAKEN AND TREMBLING--STAMMERS) 155 ELECTR
(MOVED--A PAUSE--STAMMERS) MIRACLES 265 GGBROW
HE STARES, BEWILDERED--STAMMERS) 288 GGBROW
HE STAMMERS GROPINGLY AMONG THE ECHOES OF ERIE'S 24 HUGHIE
LAST WORDS.)
HE STAMMERS DEFERENTIALLY.) 30 HUGHIE
(SHRINKS AWAY--STAMMERS) WHATS 592 ICEMAN
(STAMMERS) I--I'M TALKING TO HARRY. 657 ICEMAN
(THEN SUDDENLY HE IS EVEN MORE ASHAMED OF HIMSELF 663 ICEMAN
THAN THE OTHERS AND STAMMERS)
(SPRINGS TO HIS FEET--STAMMERS DEFENSIVELY) 694 ICEMAN
(STAMMERS, HIS EYES ON LARRY, WHOSE EYES IN TURN 694 ICEMAN
REMAIN FIXED ON HICKEY)
HE STAMMERS) 716 ICEMAN
BUT REACHES OUT FUMBLINGLY AND PATS LARRY'S ARM 721 ICEMAN
AND STAMMERS)
SHE STAMMERS.) 64 JOURNE
(A LOOK OF TERROR COMES INTO HER EYES AND SHE 68 JOURNE
STAMMERS.)
(SUDDENLY IS OVERCOME BY GUILTY CONFUSION-- 75 JOURNE
STAMMERS.)
(STAMMERS IN GUILTY CONFUSION FOR A SECOND.) 85 JOURNE
(STAMMERS PLEADINGLY.) PLEASE DON'T--TALK ABOUT 93 JOURNE
THINGS YOU DON'T UNDERSTAND/
HE STAMMERS MISERABLY.) 120 JOURNE
HE STAMMERS.) 145 JOURNE
(HIS MOUTH TWITCHING--FIGHTING AGAINST THE 286 LAZARU
COMPULSION IN HIM--STAMMERS)
HE STAMMERS AFTER THE SOLDIERS) 311 LAZARU
(HE STUTTERS AND STAMMERS WITH RAGE, HOPPING UP 359 LAZARU
AND DOWN GROTESQUELY.
(STAMMERS.) THAT'S A LIE/ 19 MANSNS
(STARING AT HIM WITH A FASCINATED DREAD-- 99 MANSNS
STAMMERS.)
GUILTILY STAMMERS TO HERSELF.) 103 MANSNS
(HE SWALLOWS AS IF HE WERE STRANGLING AND TEARS 143 MANSNS
HIS EYES FROM HERS--STAMMERS.)
(HE STAMMERS TO A HALT--HIS EYES FIXED ON HER IN 143 MANSNS
HELPLESS FASCINATION.
(STAMMERS CONFUSEDLY.) I--I THANK YOU-- 154 MANSNS
SHE STAMMERS.) 177 MANSNS
(STAMMERS IN CONFUSED HORROR.) 179 MANSNS
WITH HORRIFIED SUSPICION AND SHE GRABS HER BY THE 193 MANSNS
ARM AND STAMMERS.)
(STAMMERS) JIM-- (HASTILY FORCING HER PLAYFUL 118 MISBEG
TONE)
(HER FACE FULL OF REVULSION--STAMMERS) 149 MISBEG
HE STAMMERS DEFENSIVELY) 174 MISBEG
(STAMMERS) WAIT, JOSIE/ 174 MISBEG
SHE STAMMERS, WITH AN ATTEMPT AT LIGHTNESS.) 71 POET
(STAMMERS.) HE'S HERE, MRS. 73 POET
SHE STAMMERS.) 107 POET
(STAMMERS.) NO--NOT JAMIE-- (WILDLY.) OH, I 163 POET
CAN'T BEAR WAITING/
(SHE STAMMERS.) LISTEN/ 178 POET
(THE OLD MAN STUTTERS AND STAMMERS INCOHERENTLY AS594 ROPE
IF THE VERY INTENSITY OF HIS
EVANS STAMMERS IN CONFUSION, TRYING AT A 75 STRANG
NONCHALANT AIR)
(STOP--STAMMERS CONFUSEDLY) 94 STRANG
(LETTING HER WRISTS DROP--APPALLED--STAMMERS) 108 STRANG
(STAMMERS) YOU'RE NOT--GOING TO HAVE A CHILD-- 108 STRANG
(CRUSHED--STAMMERS) NO--I MEAN, YES--I WANT TO 133 STRANG
TELL YOU HOW DAMN GLAD I AM...
TREMBLING WITH RAGE, STAMMERS) 142 STRANG
(GROWING HARD--STAMMERS ANGRILY) 150 STRANG
CAPE STAMMERS IN A FIERCE WHISPER) 449 WELDED
HE STAMMERS) 465 WELDED
HE STAMMERS WILDLY) 475 WELDED
THEN MISERABLY HUMBLE, STAMMERS) 483 WELDED

STAMP
THE PEOPLE SEATED ALONG THE WALLS STAMP THEIR FEET250 DESIRE
THEN WITH A PRELIMINARY, SUMMONING STAMP OF HIS 200 EJONES
FOOT ON THE EARTH.
THERE IS A FOREIGN ATMOSPHERE ABOUT HIM, THE STAMP574 ICEMAN
OF AN ALIEN RADICAL.
THERE'S A FURRIN' STAMP ON UT BY THE LOOKS AV UT. 530 INZONE
THE STAMP OF HIS PROFESSION IS UNMISTAKABLY ON 13 JOURNE
HIM.
BROTHERS--LISTEN--WE MUST UNITE--IN ONE CAUSE-- 286 LAZARU
TU--STAMP OUT--THIS ABUMINATION/
THE STAMP OF AN EFFEMINATE CORRUPTION ON ALL THE 336 LAZARU
MALE,
OF ENDEAVORING TO STAMP OUT THEIR ANCIENT CULTURE/392 MARCOM
HER LITTLE FEET DANCED AWAY THE STAMP OF ARMIES. 437 MARCOM
THANK GOD, I STILL BEAR THE UNMISTAKABLE STAMP OF 43 POET
AN OFFICER AND A GENTLEMAN.
PLAYING A REEL AND THE STAMP OF DANCING FEET. 133 POET
AND THERE IS THE STAMP OF DANCING FEET. 182 POET

STAMPED
NUMERALS STAMPED ON IT, AND STARTS FILLING THE 187 AHWILD
PIPE.)
AND STAMPED UPON THE GLORIOUS CONSTITUTION OF 243 HA APE
THESE UNITED STATES/*
MCGLOIN HAS HIS OLD OCCUPATION OF POLICEMAN 576 ICEMAN
STAMPED ALL OVER HIM.
OF FINANCIAL PROSPERITY STILL STAMPED ON HIM FROM 150 MANSNS
LONG HABIT.
THE MAP OF IRELAND IS STAMPED ON HER FACE, 3 MISBEG

STAMPING
AND A STAMPING OF FEET. 567 CROSS
(EXCITEDLY, STAMPING HIS FOOT) 250 DESIRE
THE NOISE OF STAMPING FEET AND LAUGHING VOICES. 254 DESIRE
THE WITCH DOCTOR SWAYS, STAMPING WITH HIS FOOT, 201 EJONES
(A WHOLE CHORUS OF VOICES HAS TAKEN UP THIS 211 HA APE
REFRAIN, STAMPING ON THE FLOOR.
(HE DISAPPEARS THROUGH THE FRONT PARLOR AND CAN BE 78 JOURNE
HEARD STAMPING NOISILY
HA--HA--(TEARING HIS BEARD AND STAMPING WITH RAGE)282 LAZARU
THAT SHRANK BACK, STAMPING ON ITS OWN TOES. 30 MANSNS
AND THE DULL STAMPING OF FEET, A DOUBLE FILE OF 350 MARCOM
THIRTY MEN OF DIFFERENT AGES.
DRISCOLL, FOLLOWED BY A HEAVY STAMPING OF FEET.) 501 VOYAGE

STAMPS
PLOWED 'EM UNDER IN THE GROUND--(HE STAMPS 204 DESIRE
REBELLIOUSLY) --ROTTIN'--
(STAMPS HIS FOOT ON THE EARTH AND ADDRESSES IT 218 DESIRE
DESPERATELY)
(STAMPS A FOOT ON THE GROUND) 254 DESIRE
(HE STAMPS OUT, RIGHT, WHILE HE IS SPEAKING. 505 UIFRNT
(SUDDENLY WITH A FRIGHTENED GASP HE FLINGS THE 189 EJONES
MATCH ON THE GROUND AND STAMPS ON
(SHE STAMPS HER FOOT.) DO YOU HEAR, EDMUND/ 90 JOURNE
THE LATTER FIERCELY CRUMPLES IT UP AND THROWS IT 361 MARCOM
ON THE FLOOR AND STAMPS ON IT.)
(HERE HE STAMPS HIS FOOT. 391 MARCOM
(TURNS THE KNOB AND STAMPS IN) 73 MISBEG
(AS THE CHILD HESITATES, SHE STAMPS HER FOOT 588 ROPE
FURIOUSLY)
THE OLD MAN STAMPS HIS FOUT AND GESTICULATES 596 ROPE
WILDLY.

STANCHION
(HOLDING ON TO A STANCHION AND LEANING FAR OUT AT 101 STRANG
THE IMMINENT RISK OF FALLING

STANDARD
GETTING SID THE JOB ON THE WATERBURY STANDARD. 212 AHWILD
THE STANDARD OIL MILLIONAIRE, AND WON A GLORIOUS 23 JOURNE
VICTORY.
HE BEGAN BY SHOUTING THAT HE WAS NO SLAVE STANDARD 24 JOURNE
OIL COULD TRAMPLE ON.
AND HE'D BE DAMNED IF HE'D STAND FOR A STANDARD 25 JOURNE
OIL THEIR TRESPASSING.
I TOLD SHAUGHNESSY HE SHOULD HAVE REMINDED HARKER 25 JOURNE
THAT A STANDARD OIL
LIKE OUR BEAUTIFUL NEIGHBOR, HARDER, THE STANDARD 32 MISBEG
OIL THIEF, OLD YEARS AGO.
STANDARD OIL'S SAPPIEST CHILD, WHOM I KNOW YOU 47 MISBEG
BOTH LOVE SO DEARLY.
STANDARD OIL MONEY THAT WAS STOLEN 62 MISBEG
NONE OF YOUR DAMNED STANDARD OIL EXCUSES, OR BE 62 MISBEG
JAYSUS, I'LL BREAK YOU IN HALF/
AND I'LL BE DAMNED IF I'LL STAND FOR A STANDARD 63 MISBEG
OIL MAN TRESPASSING/
SURE, IT ISN'T REASONABLE FOR A STANDARD OIL MAN 63 MISBEG
TO HATE HOGS.
TO HELL WITH ENGLAND, AND GOD DAMN STANDARD OIL/ 72 MISBEG
STANDARDS.
I SUPPOSE IT WOULD BE DOWNRIGHT SNOBBERY TO HOLD 48 POET
TO OLD-WORLD STANDARDS.
APPARENTLY, HIS FATHER IS A GENTLEMAN--THAT IS, BY 48 POET
YANKEE STANDARDS.

STANDIN'
(TURNING AND SEEING HIM) DON'T BE STANDIN' THERE 543 'ILE
LIKE A GAWK, HARPOONER.
(GRUMBLINGLY) WHAT YUH TRYIN' TO DO, DUTCHY--KEEP 7 ANNA
ME STANDIN' OUT HERE ALL DAYS
STANDIN' ON THE BEACH HOWLIN' AND SCREAMIN', 503 DFRNT
WAS MEMBER IN GOOD STANDIN' O' DE BAPTIST CHURCHS 185 EJONES
YOU'LL FIND YER BLOODY 'AIR STANDIN' ON ENDEFORE185 EJONES
(REMEMBER MORNIN'
(DISGUSTEDLY) IMAGINE HIM STANDIN' FOR DAT STUFF/614 ICEMAN
HE WAS STANDIN' DERE. 617 ICEMAN
YOU'RE TALKIN' MORE THAN A PAIR AV AULD WOMEN 518 INZONE
WOULD BE STANDIN' IN THE ROAD,
HE WAS STANDIN' IN THE MIDDLE OF THE FO'C'STLE 518 INZUNE
THERE
HE WAS STANDIN' RIGHT THERE--(POINTING AGAIN) IN 519 INZUNE
HIS STOCKIN' FEET--
HE'S STANDIN' UP. 525 INZUNE
BUT WHEN YOU'RE STANDIN' OVER THE STOVE ALL DAY, 43 POET
YOU CAN'T HELP--
HE WAS STANDIN' THERE SHAKIN' HIS STICK AT ME, 592 ROPE

STANDING
(SUDDENLY SHE IS AWARE OF THE SCREEN DOOR STANDING187 AHWILD
HALF OPEN.)
NO USE STANDING HERE LIKE GAWKS. 217 AHWILD
(NORAH, STILL STANDING WITH THE SOUP TUREEN HELD 222 AHWILD
OUT STIFFLY IN FRONT OF HER,
(WHO IS STILL STANDING--WITH DRUNKEN GRAVITY) 226 AHWILD
RICHARD REMAINS STANDING, SUNK IN BITTER, GLOOMY 234 AHWILD
BUT MY DOGS WERE GIVING OUT STANDING AT THAT BAR. 244 AHWILD
(LILY AND MILDRED AND ARTHUR ARE STANDING ABOUT 262 AHWILD
AWKWARDLY WITH AMID,
AND IMAGINE ME STANDING THERE, AND FEELING SORRY 270 AHWILD
FOR YOU, LIKE A FOOL--
RICHARD REMAINS STANDING BY THE DOOR, STARING OUT 296 AHWILD
AT THE MOON.
ANNA IS DISCOVERED STANDING NEAR THE COIL OF ROPE 25 ANNA

STANDING

STANDING (CONT'D.)
STAGGERING BACK AGAINST THE CABIN WALL, WHERE HE 50 ANNA REMAINS STANDING.
(WHO HAS BEEN STANDING IN A STUPOR--SUDDENLY 61 ANNA GRASPING BURKE BY THE ARM--
HE REMAINS STANDING BY THE DOOR, HIS ARMS FOLDED, 99 BEYOND (COMES FORWARD FROM WHERE HE HAS BEEN STANDING BY 104 BEYOND THE DOOR, REAR, BROODING.
ANDREW REMAINS STANDING MOTIONLESS, HIS FACE PALE 108 BEYOND AND SET.)
(AS RUTH COMES FROM WHERE SHE HAS BEEN STANDING BY125 BEYOND THE DOORWAY
(THEY ARE BOTH STANDING. 127 BEYOND
I CAN SEE THE LIKENESS TO ROB STANDING OUT ALL 140 BEYOND OVER HER, CAN'T YOU?
SHE REMAINS STANDING THERE FOR A MINUTE. 166 BEYOND (LUCY HAS REMAINED STANDING BY THE LEFT CORNER OF 525 DAYS THE SOFA IN A STIFF,
LOVING MOVES SILENTLY OVER UNTIL HE IS STANDING 526 DAYS JUST BEHIND JOHN BUT A STEP
HE IS NOW STANDING BEHIND THE RIGHT END OF SOFA, 526 DAYS LUCY BEHIND THE LEFT END.
LOVING REMAINS STANDING AT RIGHT, REAR, OF JOHN.) 528 DAYS LOVING MOVES UNTIL HE IS STANDING DIRECTLY BEHIND 528 DAYS HIM.
LOVING REMAINS STANDING BEHIND HIM, 530 DAYS HE FINDS HE HAS WALKED IN A CIRCLE AND IS STANDING544 DAYS BEFORE THE OLD CHURCH.
LOVING REMAINS WHERE HE IS, STANDING MOTIONLESSLY 547 DAYS BY THE BOOKCASE.)
AND REMAINS STANDING BY THE BOOKCASE AT LEFT OF 547 DAYS DOORWAY.)
FATHER BAIRD IS STANDING BY THE MIDDLE OF THE BED,553 DAYS AT REAR.
AT REAR OF STILLWELL ON HIS RIGHT, A TRAINED NURSE553 DAYS IS STANDING.
WHO IS STANDING AT HIS RIGHT. 553 DAYS
REMAINS STANDING WITH HIS ARMS STRETCHED UP TO THE366 DAYS CROSS.
IS STANDING NEAR THE REAR DOOR WHERE THERE IS A 247 DESIRE SMALL KEG OF WHISKY
EBEN IS STANDING BY THE GATE LOOKING UP AT THE 253 DESIRE SKY.
SHE REMAINS STANDING WHERE SHE IS, LOOKING AFTER 259 DESIRE HIM--
HE IS STANDING BY THE VICTROLA ON WHICH A JAZZ 519 DIFRNT BAND IS PLAYING.
(STANDING IN FRONT OF HIM--FIDGETING) 526 DIFRNT
YOU GIVE ME THE FIDGETS STANDING THAT WAY/ 535 DIFRNT
HARRIET IS REVEALED STANDING OUTSIDE.) 547 DIFRNT
(STANDING UP AND LOOKING AT THE DOOR) 436 DYNAMO
I WOKE UP AND SAW HER STANDING BESIDE MY BED-- 477 DYNAMO
REUBEN AND ADA ARE DISCOVERED BY THE DIM LIGHT OF 483 DYNAMO THIS UPPER GALLERY STANDING.
(REMAINS BELOW--THINKING CONFUSEDLY) 485 DYNAMO
ADA IS STANDING BEFORE HIM, DIRECTLY BENEATH THE 486 DYNAMO SWITCHES AS BEFORE.
AND IS STANDING THERE WATCHING THEM) 18 ELECTR
LAVINIA IS DISCOVERED STANDING BY THE TABLE. 28 ELECTR
STANDING ABOVE AND A LITTLE TO THE RIGHT OF 45 ELECTR LAVINIA.
HIS MOVEMENTS ARE EXACT AND WOODEN AND HE HAS A 46 ELECTR MANNERISM OF STANDING AND
ARE STANDING TALKING IN LOW TONES) 69 ELECTR
WELL, WE AREN'T DOING ANYONE ANY GOOD STANDING 70 ELECTR HERE.
SHE ENTERS BUT REMAINS STANDING JUST INSIDE THE 82 ELECTR DOORWAY
ORIN IS STANDING BY THE HEAD OF THE BIER, AT THE 93 ELECTR REAR OF IT.
(BRANT, STANDING BY THE RAIL LOOKING AFTER HIM, 107 ELECTR
STANDING SQUARE-SHOULDERED AND STIFF LIKE A GRIM 123 ELECTR SENTINEL IN BLACK.)
A GROUP OF FIVE MEN IS STANDING ON THE DRIVE BY 129 ELECTR THE BENCH AT LEFT, FRONT.
AND GOES TO HAZEL WHO HAS BEEN STANDING 164 ELECTR BEWILDEREDLY.
(THEY START OFF, LEAVING BILLY STANDING THERE.) 259 GGBROW
HE KEEPS STANDING RESPECTFULLY IN BACK OF HER. 262 GGBROW
(SHE LOOKS UP AND SEES THE MASKED OIUN STANDING BY285 GGBROW THE PIANO--CALMLY)
STANDING ON YOUR GRAVE IN THE GARDEN/ 320 GGBROW
(STANDING UP AND GLARING AT LONG) 212 HA APE
SPECTACLE OF MILDRED STANDING THERE IN HER WHITE 225 HA APE DRESS.
AND THERE SHE WAS STANDING BEHIND US. 229 HA APE
(THE NIGHT CLERK FEELS THAT HE HAS BEEN STANDING A 13 HUGHIE LONG TIME AND HIS FEET ARE
AND SHE WAS SICK OF STANDING ON HER DOGS ALL DAY, 23 HUGHIE
AND IS STANDING IN THE HALL BEYOND IT FACING 611 ICEMAN RIGHT.
I'D BEEN STANDING ON THE CORNER SOME TIME BEFORE 622 ICEMAN CORA AND CHUCK CAME ALONG.
I'LL BET HE'S STANDING ON A STREET CORNER IN HELL 628 ICEMAN RIGHT NOW.
(STANDING BACK FROM THE PIANO TO REGARD THE FLOWER629 ICEMAN EFFECT)
EVEN JOE MOTT IS STANDING UP TO LOOK AT THE WINE 640 ICEMAN WITH AN ADMIRING GRIN.
ROCKY IS STANDING BEHIND HIS CHAIR, REGARDING HIM 696 ICEMAN WITH DULL HOSTILITY.
THE LATTER IS STANDING AT LEFT OF TABLE. 97 JOURNE
AS THE CURTAIN RISES, SHE IS STANDING BY THE 98 JOURNE SCREEN DOOR LOOKING OUT.
HELL, YOU CAN BEAT THAT STANDING ON YOUR HEAD. 164 JOURNE
BUT LAZARUS REMAINS STANDING. 278 LAZARU
YOU ARE STRANGE--STANDING THERE-- 278 LAZARU

STANDING (CONT'D.)
NOW EVERY ONE OF THESE IS STANDING UP, STRETCHING 318 LAZARU OUT HIS ARMS TOWARD LAZARUS.
STANDING LIKE THE MUMMIES OF LEGIONARIES AT 326 LAZARU ATTENTION.
THE LATTER STANDING LIKE A VICTIM) 333 LAZARU
MIRIAM REMAINS STANDING AT THE FOOT. 340 LAZARU
(STANDING-- 348 LAZARU
SO HE REMAINED FOR THE REST OF HIS LIFE STANDING 111 MANSNS BEFORE THE DOOR.
IS STANDING IN A GONDOLA BENEATH A BARRED WINDOW 355 MARCOM OF THE HOUSE.
WHO ARE STANDING AT CENTER. 364 MARCOM
YOUR LONG-STANDING HIGH REGARD FOR ME/ 393 MARCOM
UNTIL A SMALL MULTITUDE IS GATHERED STANDING IN 405 MARCOM SILENCE STARING UP AT THE POOP.
I'M AFRAID YOU'RE GOING TO CATCH COLD STANDING 406 MARCOM BAREHEADED IN THE NIGHT AIR.
WHO ARE STANDING STOLIDLY, AWAITING ORDERS) 406 MARCOM
YOU MAY BELIEVE IT OR NUT BUT LIKE A FLASH SHE WAS416 MARCOM STANDING THERE IN YOUR PLACE
I SHALL NOT LEAVE ONE TEMPLE STANDING 425 MARCOM
AND NOW THE THREE, STANDING BESIDE A BIG EMPTY 429 MARCOM SPACE
PAUSES, STANDING BESIDE THE BODY, STARING DOWN AT 438 MARCOM HER.
BE GOD, LOOK AT YOU STANDING THERE WITH THE CLUB/ 15 MISBEG
BUT WHEN IT COMES TO STANDING BY AND SEEING MY 62 MISBEG POOR PIGS MURTHERED ONE BY ONE--/
EVEN A CRYING JAG WOULD LOOK BETTER THAN JUST 148 MISBEG STANDING THERE.
SARA REMAINS STANDING BY THE SIDE OF THE CENTER 180 POET TABLE, HER SHOULDERS BOWED,
AND REMAINS STANDING BY THE DOORWAY IN STUBBORN 588 ROPE SILENCE.)
THE PICKS UP A COUPLE AND GOES TO WHERE SHE IS 590 ROPE STANDING.
(STANDING JUST INSIDE THE DOOR, HIS TALL, 4 STRANG
(STANDING NEAR HER, CONCEALING HIS CHAGRIN) 13 STRANG
DARRELL MOVES BACK AND TO ONE SIDE UNTIL HE IS 39 STRANG STANDING IN RELATIVELY THE SAME
I SEEMED TO FEEL GORDON STANDING AGAINST A WALL 45 STRANG WITH EYES BANDAGED AND THESE MEN
AND IS STANDING THERE WHEN DARRELL ENTERS, 76 STRANG FOLLOWED BY EVANS.
DARRELL REMAINS STANDING NEAR THE TABLE LOOKING 78 STRANG AFTER THEM.
STANDING BEHIND HER--TENDERLY) 83 STRANG
(DARRELL REMAINS STANDING LOOKING UP THE STAIRS IN124 STRANG A SORT OF JOYOUS STUPOR.
DARRELL REMAINS STANDING.) 127 STRANG
NINA REMAINS STANDING, DOMINATING THEM, 133 STRANG
(WHAT'S DAD STANDING UP FOR HIM TO HER FORS...)) 155 STRANG
MADELINE ARNOLD IS STANDING BY HIS SIDE. 158 STRANG
(TO DARRELL, WHO HAS GOTTEN UP BUT IS STILL 164 STRANG STANDING BY HIS CHAIR)
DARRELL REMAINS STANDING AND SEEMS TO BE A LITTLE 165 STRANG UNEASY.
(WHO IS STANDING NEXT TO NED, WHIRLS ON HIM IN A 181 STRANG FURIOUS PASSION)
(SHE REMAINS STANDING ON THE RAIL, LEANING OUT 182 STRANG DANGEROUSLY.
(STANDING ABOVE THEM--THINKING EXULTANTLY) 183 STRANG
(STILL STANDING ON THE RAIL, STARING AFTER 183 STRANG GORDON'S SHELL)
MADELINE STANDING BEHIND HIM, HER ARM ABOUT HIS 184 STRANG SHOULDERS.
(TURNING TO DARRELL, WHO IS STANDING WITH A SAD 195 STRANG RESIGNED EXPRESSION--
PLANE ASCEND FROM THE WATER, STANDING SIDE BY 198 STRANG SIDE.
STANDING AT THE HEAD OF THE STAIRS WAITING FOR 466 WELDED ME--
JUST AS HE WAS STANDING WHEN YOU KNOCKED AT OUR 466 WELDED DOOR, REMEMBER!
ELEANOR IS STANDING BY THE TABLE, LEANING HER BACK480 WELDED AGAINST IT, FACING THE DOOR.
OR RUN FORWARD AND GREET CAPE, WHO IS STANDING IN 480 WELDED THE DOORWAY.

STANDPOINT
THAT IS, IT IS BEAUTIFUL FROM THE STANDPOINT OF 67 POET THE ARTIST WITH AN EYE FOR BONE
FROM A STANDPOINT OF CONDUCT AND CHARACTER, IS 114 POET MICKEY MALOY, MY BARTENDER,

STAR
MY STAR-EYED MAVOURNEEN-- 226 AHWILD
OUR VERY OWN STAR. 93 BEYOND
(HE BENDS DOWN AND KISSES HER TENDERLY) OUR STAR/ 93 BEYOND
THE FIRST STAR. 93 BEYOND
THAT'S A STAR, AN' SOMEWHAT'S THEY'S HIM, AN' 211 DESIRE
HERE'S ME, AN' THAR'S MIN UP THE
SHE'S LIKE T'NIGHT, SHE'S SOFT 'N' WA'M, HER EYES 211 DESIRE KIN WINK LIKE A STAR,
STAR-GAZIN' IN DAYLIGHT! 245 DESIRE
WHY, YOU POOR FISH, THAT MURDER STORY IS IN 451 DYNAMO TODAY'S STAR--
THERE ISN'T A STAR. 151 ELECTR
(SOMBERLY) DARKNESS WITHOUT A STAR TO GUIDE US/ 151 ELECTR
YOU ARE MY EVENING STAR AND ALL MY PLEIADES/ 267 GGBROW
GOD HAS BECOME DISGUSTED AND MOVED AWAY TO SOME 319 GGBROW FAR ECSTATIC STAR
WE'LL PUT UP ONE LAST STAR BOUT DAT'LL KNOCK 'EM 253 HA APE OFFEN DEIR SEATS/
HERE'S DE STAR BOARDERS. 651 ICEMAN
TEMPERAMENTAL POSTURINGS OF THE STAGE STAR. 13 JOURNE
ASK OF THE WIND, OR OF THE WAVE, OR OF THE STAR, 132 JOURNE OR OF THE BIRD.

STARE

STAR (CONT'D.)
AND THE WIND, WAVE, STAR, BIRD, CLOCK, WILL ANSWER132 JOURNE
YOU.
GIVES THEM A THROBBING STAR-LIKE EFFECT. 281 LAZARU
A NEW STAR HAS APPEARED/ 289 LAZARU
LET YOUR HEART CLIMB ON LAUGHTER TO A STAR/ 360 LAZARU
I APPRECIATE THAT A NAPOLEON OF AFFAIRS MUST 99 MANSNS
BELIEVE IMPLICITLY IN HIS OWN STAR.
HE HAS THE MANNER AND APPEARANCE OF A SUCCESSFUL 390 MARCOM
MOVIE STAR AT A MASQUERADE
SMILE WITH INFINITE REMOTENESS UPON OUR SORROW, 435 MARCOM
SMILE AS A STAR SMILES/
(CONSOLINGLY) WELL, THE SPORT HERO USUALLY 30 STRANG
DOESN'T STAR AFTER COLLEGE.
AND BE A BIGGER STAR THAN GORDON EVER WAS, IF 120 STRANG
THAT'S POSSIBLE.

STAR*B*D
OFF THE STAR*B*D QUARTER 'BOUT FIVE MILES AWAY-- 551 'ILE
BIG ONES/

STARCHED
IN THE LEFT WALL IS ONE WINDOW WITH STARCHED WHITE 48 STRANG
CURTAINS LOOKING OUT ON A

STARE
RICHARD CONTINUES TO STARE AT THE LETTER FOR A 208 AHWILD
MOMENT--
(GIVES HER HUSBAND AN ACCUSING STARE) 252 AHWILD
(TURNS TO STARE AT HIM APPREHENSIVELY) 293 AHWILD
ANNA SUDDENLY BECOMES CONSCIOUS OF THIS APPRAISING 15 ANNA
STARE--RESENTFULLY)
(THE TWO STARE AT HIM. 78 ANNA
(MUSINGLY) SO I USED TO STARE OUT OVER THE FIELDS 89 BEYOND
TO THE HILLS, OUT THERE--
ROBERT AND THE CAPTAIN STARE AFTER THEM WITH 108 BEYOND
HORRIFIED EYES.
(RUTH KEEPS HER EYES FIXED ON HER LAP IN A TRANCE-158 BEYOND
LIKE STARE.)
ALL THE MEN TURN AND STARE AT HIM.) 478 CARDIF
STARE FRIGHTFULLY WIDE AT NOTHING. 571 CROSS
AND THIS MOCKING SCORN IS REPEATED IN THE 494 DAYS
EXPRESSION OF THE EYES WHICH STARE
LOVING REMAINS IN HIS CHAIR, HIS EYES FIXED BEFORE500 DAYS
HIM IN A HOSTILE STARE.
(STARTLED, TURNS TO STARE AT JOHN. 501 DAYS
FACING FRONT, HIS EYES FIXED IN THE SAME COLD 525 DAYS
STARE.
ELSA AND FATHER BAIRD START AND STARE AT JOHN 535 DAYS
UNEASILY.
(UNEASILY) WHY DO YOU STARE LIKE THATS 544 DAYS
STARE FROM BLACK HOLLOWS WITH A FROZEN ANGUISH AT 553 DAYS
ELSA'S FACE.
(HIS EYES FIXED ON JOHN'S FACE IN THE SAME STARE--558 DAYS
AS IF WITH THE ONE IMPULSE, STARE DUMBLY UP AT THE204 DESIRE
SKY, LEANING ON THEIR HOES.
(THEY STARE AT HIM. 205 DESIRE
(THEY TURN, STARTLED, AND STARE AT HIM. 205 DESIRE
THEY STARE AT HIM WITH INDIFFERENT CURIOSITY.) 207 DESIRE
THEY STARE AT HIM IN SURPRISE.) 208 DESIRE
THEY STARE AT HIM.) 214 DESIRE
THE TWO STARE AFTER HIM SUSPICIOUSLY. 215 DESIRE
(HE GOES OUT DOOR IN REAR, THEY STARE AFTER HIM 217 DESIRE
INDIFFERENTLY.)
THEY STARE UP AT THE SKY WITH A NUMBED 218 DESIRE
APPRECIATION.)
THEIR STARE HAVING A STRAINING, INGROWING QUALITY.221 DESIRE
SHE RETURNS THEIR STARE OF COLD APPRAISING 222 DESIRE
CONTEMPT WITH INTEREST--SLOWLY)
(THEY STARE AGAIN, EBEN OBSCURELY MOVED, 225 DESIRE
PHYSICALLY ATTRACTED TO HER--
THEY STARE AT EACH OTHER) 225 DESIRE
(THEY STARE INTO EACH OTHER'S EYES, HIS HELD BY 228 DESIRE
HERS IN SPITE OF
WHY D'YE STARE SO? 234 DESIRE
EBEN AND ABBIE STARE AT EACH OTHER THROUGH THE 239 DESIRE
WALL.
THEY STARE STRAIGHT AHEAD. 267 DESIRE
THEY STARE STRAIGHT AHEAD. 267 DESIRE
WINDOWS ON THE RIGHT SO SHE CAN STARE OUT AT THE 428 DYNAMO
SKY.
THE THREE STARE ABOUT THEM GAWKILY, AWED AND 8 ELECTR
UNCOMFORTABLE.
FOR A MOMENT, MOTHER AND DAUGHTER STARE INTO EACH 15 ELECTR
OTHER'S EYES.
(CONTINUES TO STARE AT HER SUSPICIOUSLY--GRIMLY) 35 ELECTR
(TURNING TO STARE AT HIM--SLOWLY) 39 ELECTR
(THEY BOTH STARE AT HIM, LAVINIA IN SURPRISE, 48 ELECTR
CHRISTINE IN UNEASY WONDER.
ALL THESE PEOPLE COMING TU STAND AROUND AND STARE 72 ELECTR
AT THE DEAD--AND AT ME.
FOR A MOMENT MOTHER AND DAUGHTER STARE INTO EACH 77 ELECTR
OTHER'S EYES.
WHY DO YOU KEEP FOLLOWING ME EVERYWHERE--AND STARE 77 ELECTR
AT ME LIKE THATS
DON'T STARE LIKE THAT/ 77 ELECTR
CHRISTINE CONTINUES TO STARE BLANKLY IN FRONT OF 122 ELECTR
HER.
THE EYES OF THE MANNON PORTRAITS STARE WITH A GRIM139 ELECTR
FORBIDDINGNESS.
YOU WATCHED HIM STARE AT YOUR BODY THROUGH YOUR 154 ELECTR
CLOTHES, STRIPPING YOU NAKED/
WITH THEIR FROZEN STARE =LOOKING OVER THE HEAD OF 157 ELECTR
LIFE,
REFLECT THE SUN IN A SMOULDERING STARE, AS OF 169 ELECTR
BROODING REVENGEFUL EYES.
THEY BOTH STARE AT DION, WHO, WITH A STUDIED 260 GGBROW
CARELESSNESS,
(THEY BOTH STARE AT HIM.) 260 GGBROW
THEY BOTH START AND STARE AT HIM.) 261 GGBROW
THEY STARE AFTER HIM--THEN SLOWLY FOLLOW. 262 GGBROW

STARE (CONT'D.)
THE TWO MASKS STARE AT EACH OTHER. 279 GGBROW
THEY STARE AT EACH OTHER. 280 GGBROW
(THEY STARE AT HER) I FORGOT TO TELL HIM 303 GGBROW
SOMETHING IMPORTANT THIS MORNING AND
(THEY STARE AT HER. 303 GGBROW
THE PEOPLE IN THE TWO ROOMS STARE. 318 GGBROW
THE MEN STARE AT HIM, STARTLED AND IMPRESSED IN 213 HA APE
SPITE OF THEMSELVES)
(THEY STARE AT EACH OTHER-A PAUSE-THEN YANK GOES 252 HA APE
ON SLOWLY AND BITTERLY)
(HIS GLASSY EYES STARE THROUGH ERIE'S FACE. 30 HUGHIE
(WILLIE OPENS HIS EYES TO STARE AROUND HIM WITH A 581 ICEMAN
BEWILDERED HORROR.)
(THEY STARE AT HIM IN AMAZED INCREDULITY.) 620 ICEMAN
(THEY ALL STARE, HOPING IT'S A GAG, 620 ICEMAN
(CONTINUING TO STARE--PUZZLEDLY) 624 ICEMAN
THEY STARE AT HIM WITH PUZZLED UNEASY 625 ICEMAN
FASCINATION.)
THEY ALL STARE AT HIM, THEIR FACES AGAIN PUZZLED, 628 ICEMAN
RESENTFUL AND UNEASY.)
(BUT THEY ONLY STARE AT HIM WITH HARD SNEERING 633 ICEMAN
EYES.)
HE PAUSES, AND FOR A SECOND THEY STARE AT HIM 639 ICEMAN
(THEY STARE AT HIM WITH STUNNED, BEWILDERED HURT. 660 ICEMAN
THEY STARE AT HIM, BITTER, UNEASY AND FASCINATED. 661 ICEMAN
THEY STARE AT HIM FASCINATEDLY. 661 ICEMAN
EXCEPT LARRY WHO CONTINUES TO STARE AT HIM.) 663 ICEMAN
THEY STARE AT HIM IN BEWILDERED, INCREDULOUS 664 ICEMAN
CONFUSION.)
THEY PAUSE TO STARE AT HIM, 672 ICEMAN
THEY STARE AT HICKEY. 695 ICEMAN
ALL THE GROUP AT THE TABLES BY HIM START AND STARE?17 ICEMAN
AT HIM
ALL SIT BOLT UPRIGHT ON THEIR BENCHES AND STARE AT>14 INZONE
DAVIS.)
THERE IS A PAUSE DURING WHICH THEY ALL STARE 517 INZONE
GLOOMILY AT THE FLOOR.)
THE OTHERS STARE AT HIM, HOLDING THEIR BREATHS. 520 INZONE
(THEY STARE AT HER WITH A GROWING DREAD.) 41 JOURNE
HIS EYES FALL TO STARE AT THE FLOOR, 58 JOURNE
(STUNG, JAMIE HAS TURNED TO STARE AT HER WITH 80 JOURNE
ACCUSING ANTAGONISM.
(TENSELY.) WHY DO YOU STARE LIKE THATS 63 JOURNE
(THEY STARE AT HER. 67 JOURNE
SHE FEELS THEM AND TURNS SHARPLY WITHOUT MEETING 68 JOURNE
HIS STARE.)
(TURNS TO STARE AT HIM CALMLY.) 75 JOURNE
(HIS TWO SONS STARE AT HIM CONTEMPTUOUSLY. 77 JOURNE
(SHE RISES FROM THE ARM OF HIS CHAIR AND GOES TO 94 JOURNE
STARE OUT THE WINDOWS AT RIGHT
THEY STOP IN THE DOORWAY TO STARE APPRAISINGLY AT 108 JOURNE
HER.
(THEY BOTH STARE AT THEIR CARDS UNSEEINGLY. 138 JOURNE
THEY STARE AT HER. 170 JOURNE
(THEY ALL STARE. 276 LAZARU
THE GUESTS STARE. 277 LAZARU
THE CROWDS OF MEN AND WOMEN ON EACH SIDE PUSH INTO278 LAZARU
THE ROOM TO STARE AT HIM.
THEY STARE AT HIM WITH ADMIRATION. 320 LAZARU
SHE STOPS TO STARE FOR A MOMENT WITH CRUEL 341 LAZARU
CONTEMPT AT MIRIAM.
TIBERIUS CONTINUES TO STARE INTO LAZARUS' EYES. 342 LAZARU
(DEBORAH RAISES HER EYES FOR A SECOND TO STARE AT 20 MANSNS
HER
(HE CLOSES HIS EYES, AND THEN OPENS THEM TO STARE 49 MANSNS
BEFORE HIM.)
THERE IS A PAUSE IN WHICH DEBORAH AND SARA STARE 52 MANSNS
AT EACH OTHER.
(THEY LAUGH AMUSEDLY TOGETHER--THEN STOP ABRUPTLY 61 MANSNS
AND STARE AT EACH OTHER.)
WHY, THERE'S NIGHTS AT HOME, WHEN YOU STARE 81 MANSNS
IS THAT WHEN YOU STARE AT US AS THOUGH YOU HATED 82 MANSNS
US$
SHE STOPS, MAKES HERSELF GO ON, FINALLY STOPS AND 103 MANSNS
TURNS TO STARE AT HIM.)
(THEY STOP ABRUPTLY AND STARE AT EACH OTHER-- 108 MANSNS
(HE TURNS TO STARE AT HER--FORCING A SMILE, 111 MANSNS
RESENTFULLY.)
HIS EYES CEASE READING AND STARE AT THE BOOK 119 MANSNS
PREOCCUPIEDLY.)
THE TWO WOMEN TURN TO STARE AT HIM, WITH A 119 MANSNS
STIRRING OF SUSPICION AND RESENTMENT.
(HE TURNS TO STARE AT HER WITH A VINDICTIVE 120 MANSNS
HOSTILITY.)
(SHE TURNS TO STARE AT HIM WITH A REVENGEFUL 121 MANSNS
HOSTILITY.
(SHE TURNS TO STARE AT HIM WITH VINDICTIVE 122 MANSNS
HOSTILITY.
GLOATING CRUELTY AND THEY STARE AT HIM WITH HATE. 126 MANSNS
WHY DO YOU STARE LIKE THATS 127 MANSNS
(HE STARTS AND TURNS TO STARE AT THEM 127 MANSNS
BEWILDEREDLY.)
(SHE AND DEBORAH SUDDENLY TURN AND STARE AT EACH 129 MANSNS
OTHER WITH DEFIANT,
HE TURNS TO STARE FROM ONE TO THE OTHER FOR A 129 MANSNS
MOMENT
THEY STARE AT SIMON DEFIANTLY AND APPREHENSIVELY. 130 MANSNS
FOR GOD'S SAKE, WHY DO YOU STARE LIKE THATS 130 MANSNS
THEY STARE AT THE DOOR. 131 MANSNS
(THERE IS A PAUSE DURING WHICH THEY BOTH STARE 136 MANSNS
STRAIGHT BEFORE THEM.
AS SARA CONTINUES TO STARE WITH FASCINATED, DREAMY148 MANSNS
LONGING AT THE PLAN.)
(HE TURNS TO STARE AT HER IN SURPRISED CONFUSION. 151 MANSNS
PLEASE DON'T STARE LIKE THAT/ 157 MANSNS
ABRUPTLY FRIGHTENED, SHE TURNS AWAY TO STARE ABOUT163 MANSNS
THE GARDEN UNEASILY.)

STARE

STARE (CONT'D.)
(THEY STARE AT HIM.) 175 MANSNS
(TURNS HIS HEAD TO STARE AT SARA WITHOUT 186 MANSNS
RECOGNITION.
(SHE BEGINS TO CHAFE HIS WRISTS AND TURNS TO STARE190 MANSNS
AT THE SUMMER-HOUSE--
HE AND THE LATTER STARE AT EACH OTHER, THEN BOW 347 MARCOM
PERFUNCTORILY.
(THEY ALL STARE AND BEGIN TO GROW WORRIED.) 349 MARCOM
THE OTHERS STARE AT IT, DUMBFOUNDED AND AWED. 351 MARCOM
THE MEN STARE FASCINATEDLY.) 352 MARCOM
STARE AT HIM. 366 MARCOM
TRIES TO STARE INSOLENTLY AT THE KING BUT, AWED IN366 MARCOM
SPITE OF HIMSELF,
(THEY STARE SILENTLY. 366 MARCOM
THEY STARE AT THE SNAKE-CHARMER, THE TWO OLDER MEN369 MARCOM
CYNICALLY.
MARCO IS DISCONCERTED AT THE KAAN'S STEADY 391 MARCOM
IMPERSONAL STARE.
(KUBLAI AND CHIN-YIN STARE AT HIM IN PETRIFIED 394 MARCOM
INCREDULITY.
(AS PEOPLE BEGIN TO COME IN AND STARE AT THE POOP 403 MARCOM
OF THE SHIP)
WHO STARE ABOUT WITH AWE AND ENVY AND ARE GREATLY 427 MARCOM
IMPRESSED BY THE GOLD PLATE.)
THE GUESTS STARE POP-EYED, OPEN-MOUTHED, 429 MARCOM
SPEECHLESS FOR A SECOND.
RAISE THEIR HEADS AND STARE BEFORE THEM IN 434 MARCOM
SILENCE.
AND STARE AT NOTHING AS IF HE WAS MOURNING OVER 33 MISBEG
SOME GHOST INSIDE HIM, AND--
(STARES GUILTILY AND TURNS TO STARE INTO HER 104 MISBEG
FACE--SUSPICIOUSLY)
TYRONE CONTINUES TO STARE AT NOTHING, BUT BECOMES 107 MISBEG
RESTLESS.
HE BECOMES AWARE OF THIS FOR THE FIRST TIME AND 151 MISBEG
TURNS SLOWLY TO STARE AT HER.)
(HER EYES LEAVE HIS FACE TO STARE UP AT THE SKY. 153 MISBEG
HIS EYES FIX ON JOSIE'S FACE IN A LONG, PROBING 157 MISBEG
STARE.)
HE AND SARA STARE AT EACH OTHER. 33 POET
HIS BLOODSHOT GRAY EYES HAVE AN INSULTING COLD 34 POET
STARE WHICH ANTICIPATES INSULT.
BUT TURNS TO STARE AT HIM WORRIEDLY AGAIN. 35 POET
THEY STARE AT HIM AND HE STARES SIGHTLESSLY AT THE153 POET
TABLE TOP.
(THEY STARE AT HIM. 166 POET
HIS EYES FIX ON HER IN A THREATENING STARE. 171 POET
(AS THE CHILD CONTINUES TO STARE AT HIM SILENTLY 583 ROPE
WITH EYES STUPID FROM FEAR.
THE MAN AND WOMAN STARE AT HIM IN PETRIFIED 587 ROPE
AMAZEMENT.)
HIS EYES STARE IDLY AT HIS DRIFTING THOUGHTS) 4 STRANG
THE CHIN ALMOST TOUCHING HIS CHEST, HIS EYES STARE 24 STRANG
SADLY AT NOTHING.)
WITH A DEFENSIVE STARE OF DISILLUSIONMENT. 26 STRANG
THE TWO MEN STARE AT EACH OTHER FOR A MOMENT, 34 STRANG
DARKELL WITH A FRANK PROBING,
SHE LOOKS FROM ONE TO THE OTHER WITH A QUEER, 39 STRANG
QUICK, INQUISITIVE STARE.
THE TWO MEN HAVE RISEN AND STARE AT HER ANXIOUSLY. 39 STRANG
I SUPPOSE YOU CAN'T HELP YOUR DIAGNOSING STARE. 79 STRANG
FOR A MOMENT THEY STARE INTO EACH OTHER'S EYES-- 84 STRANG
(TURNS AROUND TO STARE AT HER--THINKING) 177 STRANG
BUT DURING THE FOLLOWING SCENE THEY STARE STRAIGHT452 WELDED
AHEAD AND REMAIN MOTIONLESS.
I THOUGHT--(THEY STARE AT EACH OTHER--A PAUSE.) 480 WELDED
HE TURNS TO STARE AT HER.) 483 WELDED
(THEY STARE INTO EACH OTHER'S EYES. 487 WELDED
STARED
FOR DAYS AFTER, HE SAT AND STARED AT NOTHING. 26 ELECTR
HE STARED AT ME WITH AN IDIOTIC LOOK AS IF HE'D 95 ELECTR
SAT ON A TACK--
STARED THE FLOWERS OUT OF COUNTENANCE FOR HALF AN 11 MANSNS
HOUR, AND THEN--FLED/
(HAS STARED AT HER AT FIRST SUSPICIOUSLY-- 169 MANSNS
STARES
AND STARES AT THE ICE TO THE NO'THE'ARD. 536 *ILE
SHE STARES UP AT HIM WITH A STUPID EXPRESSION, A 551 *ILE
VAGUE SMILE ON HER LIPS.
MILDRED STARES AT HIM IN PUZZLED WONDERMENT. 195 AHWILD
(STARES AT HIM FOR A MOMENT, AS IF HE COULDN'T 207 AHWILD
COMPREHEND--
(STARES AFTER HIM WORRIEDLY--THEN SIGHS 209 AHWILD
PHILOSOPHICALLY)
(SHE STARES BEFORE HER BITTERLY. 243 AHWILD
(HE STARES AT BELLE GLOOMILY AND MUTTERS 245 AHWILD
TRAGICALLY)
RICHARD STARES AFTER HER OFFENDEDLY.) 245 AHWILD
(STARES AT ARTHUR WITH ILL-CONCEALED ASTONISHMENT,254 AHWILD
THEN GRINS)
MRS. MILLER STARES BEFORE HER, HER EXPRESSION 257 AHWILD
BECOMING MORE AND MORE DOLEFUL.
(HE SIGHS AND STARES AROUND HIM AT THE NIGHT) 277 AHWILD
(THEN, AS HE ONLY STARES BEFORE HIM BROODINGLY, 285 AHWILD
WHERE THE LIGHT IS DIMMEST, AND SITS DOWN ON THE 293 AHWILD
SOFA, AND STARES BEFORE HIM.
(STARES AT HIM WONDERINGLY FOR A MOMENT, 297 AHWILD
MILLER STARES AFTER HIM--THEN SAYS HUSKILY) 297 AHWILD
CHRIS STARES AT THE LETTER FOR A MOMENT-- 8 ANNA
WHO STARES AT HIM WITH A TWINKLE OF MALICIOUS 9 ANNA
HUMOR IN HER EYES)
MARTHA STARES AT HIM KEENLY. 11 ANNA
THE TWO WOMEN SIZE EACH OTHER UP WITH FRANK 14 ANNA
STARES.
STARES AT HER FOR A SECOND ANXIOUSLY--PATTING HER 24 ANNA
HAND)

STARES (CONT'D.)
SHE TURNS HER BACK ON THE PROCEEDINGS AND STARES 30 ANNA
OUT INTO THE FOG.
HE STARES AT THE PAPER FOR A WHILE, THEN PUTS IT 44 ANNA
ON TABLE.
SHE STARES BEFORE HER DESPONDENTLY, HER CHIN IN 63 ANNA
HER HANDS.
(ANNA STARES AT HIM. 65 ANNA
CHRIS STARES AT HIS BEER ABSENT-MINDEDLY. 77 ANNA
(HE GETS UP AND GOES BACK AND, OPENING THE DOOR, 78 ANNA
STARES OUT INTO THE DARKNESS.)
(AFTER A PAUSE, DURING WHICH HE STARES FIXEDLY AT 86 BEYOND
ROBERT'S AVERTED FACE)
RUBERT STARES AFTER HIM FOR A MOMENT.. 86 BEYOND
(ROBERT STARES AT HER IN STUPID ASTONISHMENT. 91 BEYOND
ANDREW STARES AT THE FLOOR.) 95 BEYOND
(SHE STARES DOWN AT THE KNITTING IN HER LAP--AFTER 96 BEYOND
A PAUSE)
RUTH STARES AT HIM IN ANNOYANCE.) 122 BEYOND
AND STARES OUT AT THE HORIZON.) 125 BEYOND
(RUBERT STARES AT HER IN AMAZEMENT. 126 BEYOND
(ROBERT STARES AT ROBERT IN HURT STUPEFACTION. 135 BEYOND
HER CHIN RESTING ON HER HANDS AS SHE STARES OUT 140 BEYOND
SEAWARD.)
ROBERT STARES AT HER WITH A GRIM, SOMBER 142 BEYOND
EXPRESSION.
(RUTH STARES AT THE STOVE IN SILENCE. 147 BEYOND
SHE STARES AT THE STOVE. 149 BEYOND
SHE SITS DOWN IN HER CHAIR AND STARES AT THE 151 BEYOND
STOVE--DULLY)
(STARES AT HER FOR A MOMENT, HIS RAGE EBBING AWAY,168 BEYOND
(STARES AT HIS WATCH FOR A MOMENT OR SO.. 484 CARDIF
(HE STARES STRAIGHT IN FRONT OF HIM WITH EYES 489 CARDIF
STARTING FROM THEIR SOCKETS)
SMITTY STARES BEFORE HIM AND DOES NOT SEEM TO KNOW470 CARIBE
THERE IS ANYONE ON DECK BUT
(HIS SISTER STARES AT HIM WITH DREAD FOREBODING. 565 CROSS
(WAIT STARES AT HIM SPELLBOUND) 569 CROSS
THEN STOPS ABRUPTLY AND STARES BEFORE HIM. 494 DAYS
LOVING STARES BEFORE HIM WITH A COLD, ANGRY 503 DAYS
DISDAIN.)
(STARES AT HIM, TAKEN ABACK--THEN QUIETLY) 506 DAYS
(STARES AT HIM FASCINATEDLY) 508 DAYS
THEN HE COMES SLOWLY BACK AND SITS DOWN IN HIS 513 DAYS
CHAIR AND STARES BEFORE HIM.
(STARES AT HER RESENTFULLY FOR A SECOND, THEN 519 DAYS
TURNS AWAY,
(STARES AT HER WITH A STRANGE PANIC) 520 DAYS
(STARES AT JOHN WITH FRIGHTENED BEWILDERMENT) 527 DAYS
SITS DOWN ON IT AND STARES BEFORE HIM WITH HUNTED 528 DAYS
EYES.
(HE STARES BEFORE HIM WITH A FASCINATED DREAD, 535 DAYS
(FATHER BAIRD STARTS AND STARES AT HIM WITH A 536 DAYS
SHOCKED EXPRESSION.)
(STARES AT JOHN AS IF HE HAD BECOME A STRANGER-- 538 DAYS
(STARES BEFORE HER, NOT SEEMING TO HAVE HEARD THIS539 DAYS
LAST--HER
LOVING'S MASKED FACE STARES AT JOHN, HIS EYES COLD541 DAYS
AND STILL.
(HE STARES FIXEDLY AT JOHN NOW AND ADDS SLOWLY) 544 DAYS
(FATHER BAIRD STARES AT HIM BUT KEEPS SILENT. 545 DAYS
FATHER BAIRD STARES AT HER SEARCHINGLY, HIS FACE 548 DAYS
SAD AND PITYING.)
(JOHN STARES AT HIM UNCERTAINLY FOR A MOMENT--THEN556 DAYS
OBEDIENTLY LIES DOWN)
HE STOPS AT THE FOOT OF THE CHAISE-LONGUE AND 558 DAYS
STARES DOWN AT THE SLEEPING JOHN.
(HE STARES AROUND HIM AT THE AIR, 558 DAYS
LOVING STARES OVER HIS HEAD WITH COLD, STILL 561 DAYS
EYES.
HE STARES BEFORE HIM WITH OBSESSED EYES) 562 DAYS
THEN COMES QUIETLY UP BESIDE HIM AND STARES 566 DAYS
SEARCHINGLY INTO HIS FACE.
(STARES AT HIM--GENTLY) IT'S ALL RIGHT NOW, JACK.567 DAYS
THEN HE PUTS HIS HANDS ON HIS HIPS AND STARES UP 203 DESIRE
AT THE SKY.
(HIS EYES FALL AND HE STARES ABOUT HIM FROWNINGLY.203 DESIRE
(STARES AT THEM INDIFFERENTLY FOR A SECOND, THEN 205 DESIRE
DRAWLS)
EBEN STARES FROM ONE TO THE OTHER WITH SURPRISE.) 216 DESIRE
EBEN STOPS BY THE GATE AND STARES AROUND HIM WITH 217 DESIRE
GLOWING, POSSESSIVE EYES.
EBEN STARES AT THEM AND THEY AT HIM.) 220 DESIRE
(HE STARES AT HER PENETRATINGLY. 221 DESIRE
SHE STARES BACK. 221 DESIRE
(SHE STARES AT THEM AND THEY AT HER.) 222 DESIRE
(HE STARES INTO HER EYES, TERRIBLY CONFUSED AND 227 DESIRE
TORN.
SHE STARES AT HIM MYSTIFIED. 231 DESIRE
HE STARES UP AT THE SKY) 231 DESIRE
(A PAUSE--HE STARES AT HER DESIROUSLY--HIS EYES 232 DESIRE
GROW AVID--
SHE STARES BEFORE HER WITH HARD ANGRY EYES.) 232 DESIRE
(STARES AT HER--AFTER A DEAD PAUSE) 233 DESIRE
(STARES AT HER--THEN A TERRIBLE EXPRESSION OF RAGE233 DESIRE
COMES OVER HIS FACE--
(TURNS AND STARES AT HER EAGERLY) 234 DESIRE
(HE STARES HOPELESSLY AT THE FLOOR.) 236 DESIRE
EBEN STOPS AND STARES. 236 DESIRE
HE STARES AT HER FOR A MOMENT--THEN HARSHLY) 238 DESIRE
ABBIE IS CONSCIOUS OF HIS MOVEMENT AND STARES AT 239 DESIRE
THE WALL.
(STARES AFTER HER FOR A WHILE, WALKING TOWARD THE 241 DESIRE
DOOR.
(STARES AT HIM SUSPICIOUSLY, TRYING TO MAKE HIM 254 DESIRE
OUT--A PAUSE--
(STARTLED, STARES AT HIM WITH HATRED FOR A 254 DESIRE
MOMENT--THEN DULLY)

STARES

STARES (CONT'D.)
HE STARES AT HER A BIT FRIGHTENEDLY) 260 DESRE
(STARES AT HER--BEWILDEREDLY) 263 DESRE
(GABOT STARES AT HER A SECOND, THEN BOLTS OUT THE 263 DESRE
REAR DOOR.
(HE GOES OUT--COMES AROUND TO THE GATE--STARES UP 265 DESRE
AT THE SKY.
EBEN STARES AT HIM DUMBLY) 265 DESRE
(STARES AT THEN, HIS FACE HARD. 267 DESRE
HE STARES--FEELS--STARES AGAIN. 268 DESRE
(HE COMES FORWARD--STARES AT EBEN WITH A TRACE OF 269 DESRE
GRUDGING ADMIRATION)
HE STARES BEFORE HIM RIGIDLY. 494 DIFRNT
EMMA STARES STONILY BEFORE HER AS IF SHE DIDN'T 507 DIFRNT
HEAR.)
(EMMA STARES STUBBORNLY BEFORE HER. 510 DIFRNT
SHE STARES AT HER SON WITH RESENTFUL ANNOYANCE.) 528 DIFRNT
SHE STARES STRAIGHT BEFORE HER, HER MOUTH SET 538 DIFRNT
THINLY.
(SHE STARES AT HIM BEWILDEREDLY. 544 DIFRNT
HE STARES BEFORE HIM WITH THE RESENTFUL AIR OF ONE422 DYNAMO
BROODING OVER A WRONG DONE
JUMPS TO HIS FEET AND STARES DOWN TOWARD THE ROOM 424 DYNAMO
I ALL THE TIME HE IS TALKING, HE STARES AT 436 DYNAMO
REUBEN'S FLUSTERED FACE.
(AS REUBEN STARES AT HIM BEWILDEREDLY) 436 DYNAMO
(REUBEN STARES AT HIM IN OPEN-MOUTHED AMAZEMENT.) 438 DYNAMO
(STARES AT FIFE WITH HORROR) 440 DYNAMO
(STARES AT HER IN ASTONISHMENT) 443 DYNAMO
(HER FATHER STARES AT HER PUZZLEDLY. 443 DYNAMO
(LIGHT, COMPLETELY STUNNED, STARES AT HER BLANKLY.445 DYNAMO
(SHE PUSHES HIM AWAY, BUT, HOLDING HIS SHOULDERS, 446 DYNAMO
STARES DOWN INTO HIS FACE)
(STOPS SHORT AND STARES AT FIFE WITH A RAGE THAT 450 DYNAMO
CHOKES HIM
ADA STARES BEFORE HER, THINKING RESENTFULLY) 455 DYNAMO
TABLE BUT LETS IT DROP AGAIN AND STARES BEFORE 455 DYNAMO
HIM.)
(SHE STARES AT HIM, FRIGHTENED AND FASCINATED, AND461 DYNAMO
SHAKES HER HEAD)
(STARES AT HIM WITH A STUNNED LOOK) 463 DYNAMO
AND STARES AT HIS SON'S FACE WITH STUPEFIED 463 DYNAMO
BEWILDERMENT)
(HE STARES AT HIS FATHER--UNEASILY) 464 DYNAMO
SHOULDERS, STARES HUNGRILY IN HIS FACE) 466 DYNAMO
REUBEN STARES BEFORE HIM, THINKING EXCITEDLY) 466 DYNAMO
(SUDDENLY MOVES AWAY FROM HER AND STARES AROUND 469 DYNAMO
HIM NERVOUSLY--
(HE STARES AT IT RAPTLY NOW) 474 DYNAMO
MRS. FIFE STARES AFTER HIM MOONINGLY. 478 DYNAMO
(STARES DOWN AT HER BODY FOR A MOMENT AND LETS THE488 DYNAMO
GUN FALL FROM HIS HANDS AND
(HE LIFTS HIS HEAD AND STARES AT THE FOREST. 188 EJONES
(HE STARES AT THE PLAIN BEHIND HIM APPREHENSIVELY,189 EJONES
HIS HAND ON HIS REVOLVER)
HE STARES UP AT THE TOPS OF THE TREES, 189 EJONES
(HE STARES FASCINATEDLY AT THE OTHER 192 EJONES
FOR HE STRAIGHTENS UP AND STARES ABOUT HIM 200 EJONES
HORRIFIEDLY--
HE STARES INTO THEM FASCINATEDLY. 201 EJONES
(LAVINIA STARES AT HIM. 11 ELECTR
CHRISTINE STARES AT HER COOLLY, 16 ELECTR
(LAVINIA STARES AT HER BUT REMAINS SILENT. 17 ELECTR
SHE STARES STRAIGHT AHEAD, HER FACE FROZEN, HER 18 ELECTR
EYES HARD.
(AT SOMETHING IN HER TONE HE STARES AT HER 21 ELECTR
SUSPICIOUSLY,
AND STARES AT HIM WITH SUCH A PASSION OF HATRED 27 ELECTR
THAT HE IS SILENCED.
SHE TURNS SLOWLY TO HER FATHER'S PORTRAIT AND FOR 28 ELECTR
A MOMENT STARES AT IT FIXEDLY.
(CHRISTINE STARES AT HER, OVERWHELMED BY THIS 30 ELECTR
ONSLAUGHT.
(STARES AT HER DAUGHTER--A PAUSE--THEN SHE LAUGHS 33 ELECTR
DRYLY)
(STARES AT HER WITH COLD SUSPICION.) 34 ELECTR
(BUT LAVINIA STARES BACK COLDLY INTO HER EYES 34 ELECTR
LAVINIA STARES AT HER. 34 ELECTR
SHE STARES AT HIM WITH HATRED AND ADDRESSES HIM 35 ELECTR
VINDICTIVELY.
(STARES AT HIM--AGITATEDLY) NO/ 36 ELECTR
(STARES AT HER) WHAT DO YOU MEANS 38 ELECTR
HE STARES AT IT WITH A STRANGE STUPID DREAD. 40 ELECTR
SHE STARES BACK INTO THEM, AS IF FASCINATED. 42 ELECTR
(STARES AT HER--THEN UNDERSTANDINGLY) 44 ELECTR
HE CONTINUES TO STAND LOOKING AT HER, WHILE SHE 44 ELECTR
STARES IN FRONT OF HER.)
(HE STEPS BACK AND STARES AT HER-- 47 ELECTR
MANNON LOOKS AT HIS WIFE WHO STARES BEFORE HER. 51 ELECTR
HE STARES AT HER, FASCINATED AND STIRRED.) 52 ELECTR
CHRISTINE STARES AT HIS BACK WITH HATRED. 53 ELECTR
(OPENS HER EYES AND STARES AT HIM WITH A STRANGE 54 ELECTR
TERROR)
(HE STARES AT HER--THEN ASKS PLEADINGLY) 55 ELECTR
(GRABS HER BY THE SHOULDERS AND STARES INTO HER 56 ELECTR
FACE)
CHRISTINE STARES AT HIM FASCINATEDLY-- 62 ELECTR
YOU--(SHE STOPS AND STARES AT HER MOTHER WITH A 63 ELECTR
HORRIFIED SUSPICION--
IMMEDIATELY SHE SNATCHES IT UP AND STARES AT IT, 64 ELECTR
(EVERYONE STARES AT HER, SHOCKED AND IRRITATED.) 69 ELECTR
BUT LAVINIA SIMPLY STARES AT HER, FROZEN AND 77 ELECTR
SILENT.
CHRISTINE STARES AFTER HER, HER STRENGTH SEEMS TO 78 ELECTR
LEAVE HER.
HE SITS DOWN IN THE CHAIR AT LEFT OF TABLE AND 84 ELECTR
STARES BEFORE HIM BITTERLY.

STARES (CONT'D.)
HE RELEASES HER HAND AND STARES AT HER, MORBIDLY 86 ELECTR
SUSPICIOUS)
LAVINIA STARES AT HER MOTHER A MOMENT--THEN ABOUT- 91 ELECTR
FACES STIFFLY TO FOLLOW HIM.)
CHRISTINE STARES AFTER HER-- 92 ELECTR
HE STARES AT HIS FATHER'S MASK-LIKE FACE 93 ELECTR
HE PAUSES AND STARES OVER HIS FATHER'S BODY 95 ELECTR
FASCINATEDLY AT NOTHING.)
(STARES AFTER HER WILDLY, THEN HER EYES FASTEN 101 ELECTR
AGAIN ON THE DEAD MAN'S FACE.
SHE STARTS BACK WITH A STIFLED SCREAM AND STARES 101 ELECTR
AT IT WITH GUILTY FEAR.)
HE COMES TO THE RAIL AND STARES EXPECTANTLY UP THE104 ELECTR
WHARF, OFF LEFT.
(STARES UP, STARTLED IN HIS TURN AND MOMENTARILY 104 ELECTR
SOBERED--HASTILY)
(STARES FASCINATEDLY AT BRANT'S STILL FACE) 114 ELECTR
HE STILL REMAINS STOOPING OVER THE BODY AND STARES115 ELECTR
INTO BRANT'S FACE.
SHE STARES BEFORE HER, WRINGING HER HANDS AND 121 ELECTR
MOANING.
(NOT HEEDING HER, STARES INTO HIS MOTHER'S FACE. 122 ELECTR
(THEN AS HE STARES, DUMBFOUNDED AND WONDERING, 124 ELECTR
(HE JERKS HIS HEAD AROUND AND STARES AT THE HOUSE 138 ELECTR
SHE STARES AT HIM WITH A STRANGE EAGER 143 ELECTR
POSSESSIVENESS.
STARES AT HIM FRIGHTENEDLY, HE SMILES AN UGLY 146 ELECTR
TAUNTING SMILE)
LAVINIA STARES AT ORIN WITH EYES FULL OF DREAD.) 148 ELECTR
THEN HE PUTS THE SHEET DOWN AND STARES UP AT THE 149 ELECTR
PORTRAIT.
(HE STARES AT HER FIXEDLY FOR A MOMENT--THEN 155 ELECTR
SATISFIED)
ORIN STARES AT HER DAZEDLY-- 156 ELECTR
(HE SLUMPS DOWN HEAVILY IN HIS FATHER'S CHAIR AND 156 ELECTR
STARES AT THE FLOOR.
(STARES AT HIM--SLOWLY) DO YOU REALLY WANT TO 159 ELECTR
MARRY HER--HOW--
(STARES INTO HER EYES, BENDING HIS HEAD UNTIL HIS 164 ELECTR
FACE IS CLOSE TO HERS--
HE STARES AT HER AND SLOWLY A DISTORTED 164 ELECTR
(HE STARES AT HER WITH THE LOST STRICKEN 166 ELECTR
EXPRESSION FOR A MOMENT MORE--
(HE STOPS ABRUPTLY AND STARES BEFORE HIM, AS IF 166 ELECTR
THIS IDEA WERE SUDDENLY TAKING
PETER STARES AFTER HIM PUZZLEDLY.) 167 ELECTR
(SHE STARES BEFORE HER AS IF SHE HAD NOT HEARD 170 ELECTR
HIM.
AND STARES BACK INTO THE SUN-GLARE WITH 170 ELECTR
UNBLINKING, FROZEN, DEFIANT EYES.)
LAVINIA'S EYES ARE HARD AND DEFIANT AS SHE STARES 171 ELECTR
BACK.
(SHE STOPS SHORT AND STARES AT LAVINIA. 171 ELECTR
SETH STARES AT HER WORRIEDLY, SHAKES HIS HEAD AND 171 ELECTR
SPITS.
(STARES STRAIGHT BEFORE HER. 172 ELECTR
(STARES AT HER FRIGHTENEDLY, NOT KNOWING WHAT TO 174 ELECTR
DO--
STARES AT HER WITH A STRICKEN LOOK OF HORRIFIED 177 ELECTR
REPULSION--
(HE STARES AT HER, STUNNED AND STUPID) 177 ELECTR
AND HIS MASK STARES WITH A FROZEN MOCKERY BEFORE 261 GGBROW
HIM.
(SHE STARES UP AT THE SKY) THE MOONLIGHT WAS 261 GGBROW
WARM, THEN.
DION STIFFENS AND HIS MASK STARES STRAIGHT AHEAD. 265 GGBROW
HE STARES AT THE SKY RAPTLY) 266 GGBROW
+ (HE STARES BEFORE HIM IN A SORT OF TRANCE, 269 GGBROW
AND GOES TO THE WINDOW AND STARES OUT.) 273 GGBROW
STARES AT HER BEWILDEREDLY) 278 GGBROW
(SHE STARES DOWN AT HIS MASK, HER FACE GROWING 279 GGBROW
HARD.
HE STARES, BEWILDERED--STAMMERS) 288 GGBROW
SHE STARES AHEAD UNMOVED AS IF SHE HADN'T HEARD. 289 GGBROW
HE RAISES THE MASK IN HIS HANDS AND STARES AT IT 291 GGBROW
WITH A PITYING TENDERNESS.
(HE DRINKS AND STARES MALEVOLENTLY. 295 GGBROW
AND STARES AT BROWN WITH TERRIBLE HATRED. 297 GGBROW
(HE STARES AT DION'S REAL FACE CONTEMPTUOUSLY) 299 GGBROW
(SHE SITS IN THE CHAIR WHERE DION HAD SAT AND 300 GGBROW
STARES STRAIGHT BEFORE HER.
(SHE STARES WONDERINGLY AT HIM AND HE AT HER. 301 GGBROW
HE STARES AT IT WITH BITTER, CYNICAL AMUSEMENT.) 305 GGBROW
AND STARES WITHOUT MOVING INTO THE EYES OF DION'S 307 GGBROW
MASK.
HE STARES AHEAD, THEN SHAKES OFF HIS THOUGHTS AND 312 GGBROW
CONCENTRATES ON HIS WORK--
AND STARES FROM ONE TO THE OTHER FOR A SECOND IN 320 GGBROW
CONFUSION.
AND STARES UP AT THE MOON WITH A WISTFUL, RESIGNED323 GGBROW
SWEETNESS)
CAGE AND, LEANING OVER THE RAILING, STARES IN AT 252 HA APE
ITS OCCUPANT,
WHO STARES BACK AT HIM, SILENT AND MOTIONLESS. 252 HA APE
HE SIMPLY DROOPS AND STARES ACQUIESCENTLY AT 7 HUGHIE
NOTHING.
(HE STARES AT THE LOBBY FLOOR. 19 HUGHIE
HE STARES AT THE FLOOR, TWIRLING HIS ROOM KEY--TO 27 HUGHIE
HIMSELF.)
(HE AGAIN STARES AT THE NIGHT CLERK APPEALINGLY, 29 HUGHIE
FORGETTING PAST REBUFFS.
HE STARES IN FRONT OF HIM. 574 ICEMAN
(STARES AT HIM--UNDERSTANDINGLY) SURE. I GET IT.584 ICEMAN
(STARES CALCULATINGLY AT PARRITT AND THEN LOOKS 586 ICEMAN
AWAY--
(STARES AT HIM CURIOUSLY) WHAT'S YOUR PIPE DREAM,587 ICEMAN
LARRY$

STARES

STARES (CONT'D.)

(STARES AT HIM, PUZZLED AND REPELLED--SHARPLY) 590 ICEMAN
(HE LOOKS AWAY. LARRY STARES AT HIM PUZZLEDLY, 591 ICEMAN
(STARES AT HIM) AND WERE YOUS 592 ICEMAN
(LARRY STARES AT HIM, MOVED BY SYMPATHY AND PITY 592 ICEMAN
IN SPITE OF HIMSELF, DISTURBED.
(STARES AT HIM ALMOST FRIGHTENEDLY-- 593 ICEMAN
(HIS VOICE FADES OUT AS HE STARES IN FRONT OF HIM.603 ICEMAN
PARRITT STARES AT HIM SNEERINGLY. 616 ICEMAN
HOPE STARES AT HICKEY) 625 ICEMAN
(PEARL STARES AT HIM, HER FACE GROWING HARD AND 633 ICEMAN
BITTER.
(STARES AT A BOTTLE GREEDILY, TEMPTED FOR A 645 ICEMAN
MOMENT--THEN BITTERLY)
(HOPE STARES AT HIM CONFUSEDLY. 656 ICEMAN
(JIMMY STARES AT HIM STRICKENLY. 657 ICEMAN
HE STARES AHEAD, DEEP IN HARRIED THOUGHT. 665 ICEMAN
AND DON'T GIVE ME NO ARGUMENT/ (HE STARES AT ROCKY671 ICEMAN
TRUCULENTLY.
(PARRITT STARES INTO HIS EYES GUILTILY FOR A 679 ICEMAN
SECOND.
AND STARES AT HOPE WITH GROWING UNEASINESS) 691 ICEMAN
(HOPE STARES DULLY AT THE TABLE TOP. 694 ICEMAN
(LARRY STARES AT HIM WITH GROWING HORROR AND 694 ICEMAN
SHRINKS BACK ALONG THE BAR AWAY
(JOE STARES AT HIM WITH SODDEN PERPLEXITY--THEN 700 ICEMAN
CLOSES HIS EYES.
HIS HEAD HAS SUNK FORWARD, AND HE STARES AT THE 701 ICEMAN
TABLE TOP.
(STARES AT HIM STUPIDLY--THEN PUSHES HIS CHAIR 703 ICEMAN
BACK AND GETS UP, GRUMBLING)
HE STARES BEFORE HIM, HIS HAND FALLING BACK-- 714 ICEMAN
QUIETLY)
HICKEY STARES AT THEM WITH STUPID INCOMPREHENSION.717 ICEMAN
(STARES AFTER PARRITT STUPIDLY) 721 ICEMAN
(STARES AT LARRY. 721 ICEMAN
IN HIS CHAIR BY THE WINDOW, LARRY STARES IN FRONT 728 ICEMAN
OF HIM.
(STARES AT HIM PUZZLEDLY, THEN QUOTES 32 JOURNE
MECHANICALLY.)
(STARES AT HIS FATHER, IGNORING HIS EXPLANATION.) 34 JOURNE
(STARES AT HIM--THEN LOOKS AWAY--AFTER A PAUSE.) 36 JOURNE
(SHE STIFFENS AND STARES AT HIM WITH A FRIGHTENED 41 JOURNE
DEFIANCE.
(SHE STARES AT HER HANDS WITH FASCINATED 41 JOURNE
REPULSION.)
(STARES AT HIM DEFIANTLY NOW.) 86 JOURNE
(HE STARES AT HER HOPELESSLY.) 87 JOURNE
(TYRONE STARES AT HER AND SIGHS HELPLESSLY. 88 JOURNE
AND STARES OUT WITH HER BACK TO THE FRONT PARLOR. 89 JOURNE
THEN HE STARES AT HIS FATHER'S FACE WITH UNEASY 90 JOURNE
SUSPICION.)
SHE STARES ABOUT THE ROOM WITH FRIGHTENED, 95 JOURNE
(CATHLEEN STARES AT HER, STUPIDLY PUZZLED. 100 JOURNE
(SHE GOES TO THE PORCH DOOR AND STARES OUT.) 102 JOURNE
(THEN HASTILY, AS CATHLEEN STARES IN STUPID 103 JOURNE
AMAZEMENT.)
NEVER HAVING A HOME-- (SHE STARES AT HER HANDS 104 JOURNE
WITH FASCINATED DISGUST.)
(SHE BRINGS HER HANDS FROM BEHIND HER BACK AND 104 JOURNE
DELIBERATELY STARES AT THEM--
HER FACE HARDENS AND SHE STARES AT HER HUSBAND 110 JOURNE
WITH ACCUSING HOSTILITY.)
(HE STARES AT HIS WATCH WITHOUT SEEING IT. 113 JOURNE
(TYRONE STARES AT HER AND SHAKES HIS HEAD 122 JOURNE
HELPLESSLY.
(HIS FACE GROWS HARD AND HE STARES AT HIS FATHER 140 JOURNE
WITH BITTER ACCUSATION.)
HIS FATHER STARES AT HIM FRIGHTENEDLY.) 146 JOURNE
HIS HEAD BOWS AND HE STARES DULLY AT THE CARDS ON 146 JOURNE
THE TABLE--VAGUELY.)
(MOVED, STARES AT HIS FATHER WITH UNDERSTANDING-- 151 JOURNE
SLOWLY.)
(THEN AS HIS FATHER STARES AT HIM, HE ADDS 152 JOURNE
QUICKLY.)
(STARES AT HIM-- 154 JOURNE
(STARTS AND STARES AT HIS BROTHER FOR A SECOND 161 JOURNE
WITH BITTER HOSTILITY--THICKLY.)
(HE STARES AT HIS BROTHER ACCUSINGLY.) 163 JOURNE
EDMUND STARES, IMPRESSED AND UNEASY. 165 JOURNE
HE STARES AT HIS BROTHER WITH BLEARY AFFECTION-- 165 JOURNE
(HE STARES AT EDMUND WITH INCREASING ENMITY.) 166 JOURNE
(SHE STARES BEFORE HER IN A SAD DREAM. 176 JOURNE
HE STARES DOWN AT THE MOB PITYINGLY, HIS FACE 289 LAZARU
CALM.)
(HE STARES UP AT THE STARS, RAPT IN CONTEMPLATION.290 LAZARU
EVEN THE CENTURION STARES AT THE GROUND HUMBLY, IN291 LAZARU
SPITE OF HIMSELF.
EVEN CRASSUS STARTS OFF AT THE ONCOMERS. 304 LAZARU
AND STARES UP INTO HIS FACE IN THE ATTITUDE OF A 308 LAZARU
CHAINED MONKEY.)
HE STARES OPEN-MOUTHED AT LAZARUS. 308 LAZARU
HE STARES BLINKINGLY AND INQUISITIVELY AT LAZARUS.313 LAZARU
THEN AT MIRIAM.
HE STARES AT LAZARUS WITH A SOMBER INTENTNESS. 314 LAZARU
(HE STARES AFTER THEM COMPASSIONATELY.) 323 LAZARU
(HE APPROACHES THE CROSS AND STARES AT IT MOODILY)327 LAZARU
(STARES AT LAZARUS--THEN OVER HIS SHOULDER AT 332 LAZARU
CALIGULA
CALIGULA TURNS AND STARES TOWARD HIM, 339 LAZARU
TIBERIUS STARES FOR A WHILE WITH SOMBER INTENSITY 340 LAZARU
AT LAZARUS)
TIBERIUS STARES INTO HIS EYES. 341 LAZARU
SHE STARES AT HIM DEFIANTLY. 342 LAZARU
(SHE STARES AT LAZARUS, HER WORDS CHALLENGING 343 LAZARU
HIM.)
(STARES AT HIM--DEEPLY MOVED) 354 LAZARU

STARES (CONT'D.)

(STOPS SHORT AND STARES AT LAZARUS, CONFUSED AND 357 LAZARU
STUTTERING)
(HE SUDDENLY LIFTS THE FACE OF CALIGULA AND STARES359 LAZARU
INTO HIS EYES)
(SHE STARES UP INTO HIS EYES DOUBTINGLY, RAISING 361 LAZARU
HER FACE TOWARD HIS)
(SHE STARES--THEN AS IF READING ADMISSION IN HIS 361 LAZARU
EYES, SHE SPRINGS TO HER FEET)
POMPEIA ALSO STARES AT LAZARUS. 363 LAZARU
HE STARES TOWARD THE FLAMES STUPIDLY--THEN SCREAMS368 LAZARU
DESPAIRINGLY ABOVE THE CHANT)
(THEN AS HE STARES AT HER IN PETRIFIED AMAZEMENT, 14 MANSNS
SIMON STARES AT HER FOR A MOMENT, DEEPLY MOVED, 18 MANSNS
AND SHE STARES BEFORE HER UNSEEINGLY.) 22 MANSNS
GADSBY STARES AROUND HIM, LOOKING FOR SOMEONE. 26 MANSNS
(STARES AT HIM--A SUDDEN TRANSFORMATION COMES OVER 31 MANSNS
HER.
(STARES AT HIM WONDERINGLY--SLOWLY.) 34 MANSNS
(HE STARES AROUND HIM WITH DISLIKE.) 36 MANSNS
FINISHED, HE LOWERS THE PAPER TO HIS LAP AND 44 MANSNS
STARES OVER IT.
(STARES AT HER--SMILINGLY.) YOU OBJECTED TO THATS 45 MANSNS
(STARES AFTER HER--JEERINGLY.) 57 MANSNS
(SIMON STARES AT HER IN RESENTFUL SURPRISE.) 58 MANSNS
(JOEL STARES AT HIM. IS ABOUT TO SAY SOMETHING 60 MANSNS
MORE, THEN BOWS STIFFLY.
(STARES AT HER.) IT IS NO LIE THAT YOU HAVE 61 MANSNS
CHANGED--INCREDIBLY.
(SUDDENLY HE STARES AT HIS MOTHER--SNEERINGLY.) 65 MANSNS
AS JOEL STARES IN COLD SURPRISE WITHOUT MAKING ANY 71 MANSNS
MOVE, HE BURSTS OUT ANGRILY.)
(STARES AT HIM--DEFIANTLY, AS I HAVE, YES. 79 MANSNS
(THEN, AS SHE STARES AT HIM UNEASILY--ABRUPTLY 92 MANSNS
BUSINESS-LIKE.)
(JOEL STARES AT HIM--THEN GOES OUT.) 95 MANSNS
AND SHE STARES AT THE DOOR IN THE WALL WITH DREAD. 95 MANSNS
(DEBORAH STARTS AND STARES AT HIM UNEASILY.) 98 MANSNS
(STARES AT HIM STRICKENLY--PLEADINGLY.) 98 MANSNS
(SHE SUDDENLY TURNS AND STARES AT HIM WITH 102 MANSNS
HATRED.)
(STIFFENS. STARES AT HER WITH HATRED FOR A 104 MANSNS
SECOND--THEN COLDLY, IN A CURT TONE.)
(STARES AT HER WITH A CURIOUS, OBJECTIVELY 114 MANSNS
APPRAISING LOOK--
(PULLING AWAY, STARES AT HIM WITH A PUZZLED 115 MANSNS
FRIGHTENED DREAD.)
DEBORAH HAS A BOOK IN HER HANDS, BUT SHE STARES 117 MANSNS
OVER IT.
(HE STARES AT HER WITH VINDICTIVE HOSTILITY.) 121 MANSNS
HE STARES AT THE PAGE.) 125 MANSNS
BUT HER NATURE HAS CHANGED--SHE STARES AT ME WITH 126 MANSNS
HATE--
(THEY HAVE COME TO SIMON WHO STARES AS IF HE DID 128 MANSNS
NOT NOTICE THEIR APPROACH.
HE SITS IN HIS CHAIR AND STARES AT HIS BOOK 130 MANSNS
AGAIN.)
(STARES AT HER SUSPICIOUSLY.) 134 MANSNS
HE STARES UP AND DOWN THE CURVES OF HER BODY WITH 140 MANSNS
A SLY DESIRE.)
SHE STARES IN THE MIRROR AT HERSELF ADMIRINGLY.) 143 MANSNS
(SHE STARES AROUND HER FRIGHTENEDLY.) 144 MANSNS
AND STARES INTO HIS FACE--FRIGHTENEDLY.) 145 MANSNS
(STARES AT HIM--FRIGHTENED AND RESENTFUL.) 145 MANSNS
(HE STARES AROUND HIM, THINKING AND FROWNING, 145 MANSNS
(STARES AT HER BACK-- 148 MANSNS
(STARES AT HIM WITH DREAD--BUT WITH A FASCINATED 160 MANSNS
EAGERNESS TOO.
SHE STOPS AND STARES AT IT FASCINATEDLY-- 162 MANSNS
DEBORAH STARES AT HER, FULLY AWAKE NOW. 165 MANSNS
(ABRUPTLY STRAIGHTENS UP AND STARES AT HER--WITH A168 MANSNS
MOCKING SMILE.)
SIMON TURNS AND STARES AT HIS MOTHER.) 177 MANSNS
(STARES AT IT WITH DREAD AND LONGING HERSELF-- 182 MANSNS
FORCING A BELITTLING TONE.)
(HE STARES OBSESSEDLY AT THE DOOR AGAIN.) 183 MANSNS
(STARES AT HER, UNABLE TO BELIEVE HER EARS.) 188 MANSNS
(STARTS AND STARES AT HER--IN AN AWED WHISPER.) 192 MANSNS
(SHE STARES AT DEBORAH AND SUDDENLY HER FACE IS 193 MANSNS
CONVULSED
(STARES AFTER HER--MISERABLY.) 194 MANSNS
HE STARES AT THEM AND LAUGHS COARSELY WITH RELIEF)350 MARCOM
(STARES AT HIS UNCLE--THEN MUTTERS FASCINATEDLY) 359 MARCOM
BUT STOPS AND STARES IMPUDENTLY AT THE LOVERS-- 370 MARCOM
NICOLO STARES AT HIS SON BITTERLY, MAFFED WITH 374 MARCOM
CONTEMPTUOUS PITY.
(MARCO STOPS OPEN-MOUTHED AND STARES FROM ONE TO 374 MARCOM
THE OTHER.)
KUKACHIN STARES AT HIM WITH BOUNDLESS ADMIRATION. 390 MARCOM
HOPING TO CATCH HIS EYE.
(KUBLAI STARES AT THIS EFFRONTERY 392 MARCOM
(THEN AS MARCO STARES AT HER UNCERTAINLY, 410 MARCOM
HE STARES AT HER, DUMBFOUNDED AND BEWILDERED.) 415 MARCOM
(THEN AS SHE STARES AT THE MINIATURE--PROUDLY) 416 MARCOM
(THE PRINCESS TAKES IT MECHANICALLY AND STARES AT 416 MARCOM
IT IN A STUPOR
(SHE SEEMS NOT TO HEAR OR TO SEE THEM BUT STARES 417 MARCOM
AHEAD STONILY.
KUBLAI STARES BLEAKLY AHEAD OF HIM.) 424 MARCOM
KUBLAI TAKES IT EAGERLY FROM HIS HAND AND STARES 426 MARCOM
FIXEDLY INTO IT.)
(SHE STARES AT HIM) YOU'D LIKE BEING TIED TO 8 MISBEG
MONEY, I KNOW THAT.
(STARES AT HER INCREDULOUSLY) 13 MISBEG
(STARES AT HIM) YOU OLD DIVVLE, YOU'VE ALWAYS A 26 MISBEG
TRICK HIDDEN BEHIND YOUR TRICKS.
(SURPRISED, STARES AT HIM) WHAT ABOUT THE FARMS 31 MISBEG

1525 STARING

STARES (CONT'D.)
(SHE STARES OFF--HER FACE SOFTENS AND GROWS PITYING) 35 MISBEG
(STARES AT HIM STARTLEDLY--THEN RESENTFULLY) 42 MISBEG
(STARES AT HER AGAIN) WHY ALL THE INTEREST LATELY 42 MISBEG
IN THE LADIES OF THE
(HE STARES AT THE DUMBFOUNDED HARDER WITH DROLL AMAZEMENT. 58 MISBEG
(STARES AT HER IN SURPRISE) WHY SO SERIOUS AND INDIGNANT, JOSIE? 67 MISBEG
(AGAIN STARES AT HIM) KNOW WHAT, FATHER& 77 MISBEG
(IN THE ACT OF TURNING DOWN THE LAMP, STOPS AND STARES AT HIM. 77 MISBEG
HOGAN STARES AFTER HER. 97 MISBEG
(STARES AT HER CURIOUSLY) YOU'VE GOT TOO DAMN MUCH PRIDE, JOSIE. 102 MISBEG
HE STARES VAGUELY AT NOTHING. 102 MISBEG
AND STARES DOWN AT HIS FACE WITH A PASSIONATE, 103 MISBEG
POSSESSIVE TENDERNESS.
FOR A SECOND SHE STARES AT HIM, 106 MISBEG
(HE STARES AT HER WITH A DELIBERATE SENSUALIST'S 114 MISBEG
LOOK THAT UNDRESSES HER)
HE PULLS HER HEAD DOWN AND STARES INTO HER EYES) 119 MISBEG
(STARES AT HER--THEN SHRUGS HIS SHOULDERS) 121 MISBEG
(STARES AT HIM, TOO STARTLED AND BEWILDERED TO BE 121 MISBEG
ANGRY.
(STILL HOLDING THE BURNING MATCH, STARES AT HER INI31 MISBEG
SURPRISE)
(STARES AT HER WITH A HURT AND SAD EXPRESSION-- 138 MISBEG
DULLY)
(STARES INTO THE MOONLIGHT--HAUNTEDLY) 145 MISBEG
(HE OPENS HIS EYES AND STARES INTO THE MOONLIGHT 147 MISBEG
AND NOW HE STARES TORTUREDLY THROUGH THE MOONLIGHT149 MISBEG
INTO THE DRAWING ROOM.)
SHE STARES AT HIS FACE) 165 MISBEG
HE STARES, DRAWING A DEEP BREATH. 172 MISBEG
(STARES AT HER, FIGHTING WITH HIMSELF. 174 MISBEG
THEN HE SINKS BACK IN HIS CHAIR AND STARES AT THE 37 POET
TABLE.
(STARES AT HER--AGAIN HE IS MOVED--QUIETLY.) 41 POET
HE STARES INTO HIS EYES IN THE GLASS AND RECITES 43 POET
FROM BYRON'S *CHILDE HAROLD.
(SHE STARES AT HIM SCORNFULLY. 46 POET
(SHE STARES AT HIM COLDLY. 47 POET
(STARES AT HIM AS IF SHE COULD NOT BELIEVE HER 50 POET
EARS.)
SHE STARES AT HIM AND A LOOK ALMOST OF FEAR COMES 51 POET
INTO HER EYES.
AND STARES AT THE BREAKFAST WITH A PITIFUL 56 POET
HELPLESSNESS.
HIS SHOULDERS SAG AND HE STARES AT THE TABLE TOP, 57 POET
WHEN SHE DOES, SHE STARES INCREDULOUSLY. 67 POET
AND STARES INTO HER EYES ARDENTLY.) 71 POET
(STARES AT HER, UNABLE TO DECIDE WHAT IS BEHIND 82 POET
ALL THIS
SHE STARES AT HIM FASCINATEDLY--THEN BLURTS OUT 89 POET
WITH IMPULSIVE ADMIRATION.)
HE STARES AT THE FRAGMENTS IN HIS HANDS WITH 92 POET
STUPID SURPRISE.
RILEY STARES AT HIM BEWILDEREDLY. 97 POET
(SHE STARES AT HIM FOR A MOMENT, SPEECHLESS WITH 98 POET
ANGER--
THEN STARES MOODILY BEFORE HIM. 100 POET
SHE STARES AT HER FATHER WITH ANGRY DISGUST.) 104 POET
(SHE STARES AT HIM IN DISMAY. 107 POET
(HE TAKES HIS HAND AWAY AND STARES AT HER HANDS-- 107 POET
WITH DISGUST, COMMANDINGLY.)
(STARES AT HIM FASCINATEDLY, ON THE EDGE OF 112 POET
HELPLESS, HYSTERICAL LAUGHTER.)
HE STARES AT GADSBY, THEN GOES ON IN A MORE 119 POET
FRIENDLY TONE.)
(GADSBY STARES AT HIM. 120 POET
SARA STARES BEFORE HER, THE LOOK OF DEFIANT 129 POET
DESPERATION HARDENING ON HER FACE.
(STARES AT HER--WONDERINGLY.) 141 POET
HE STARES AT HIS WIFE AND DAUGHTER AS IF HE DID 152 POET
NOT RECOGNIZE THEM.)
THEY STARE AT HIM AND HE STARES SIGHTLESSLY AT THEI53 POET
TABLE TOP.
(STARES AT HIM STARTLED AND WONDERING. 157 POET
(SARA STARES AT HIM IN STUNNED AMAZEMENT.) 165 POET
THEN SHE STARES AT HIM SUSPICIOUSLY, HER FACE 167 POET
HARDENING.)
(SHE STARES AT HIM, SICK AND DESPERATE. 176 POET
(STARES AT HER MOTHER. 181 POET
(STARES AT HER--MOVED.) YOU'RE A STRANGE, NOBLE 182 POET
WOMAN, MOTHER.
THEN HE PULLS OUT HIS WATCH MECHANICALLY AND 25 STRANG
STARES AT IT.
SHE STARES AT MARSDEN BLANKLY AND SPEAKS IN QUEER 26 STRANG
FLAT TONES)
(HE LAUGHS HARSHLY--THEN SUDDENLY SEES A MAN 28 STRANG
OUTSIDE THE DOORWAY AND STARES--
(STARES AT HIM, MORE ANNOYED, HER EYES HARDENING, 70 STRANG
THINKING)
(SHE SETTLES BACK AND STARES DREAMILY BEFORE HER-- 91 STRANG
A PAUSE)
(STARES INTENSELY BEFORE HIM. 99 STRANG
(THEN AS EVANS JUST STARES AT HIM DUMBLY IN A 106 STRANG
BLISSFUL SATISFACTION,
(STARES AFTER HIM DUMBLY IN THE SAME STATE OF 107 STRANG
HAPPY STUPEFACTION--MUMBLES)
SHE STARES OUT OVER HIS HEAD. 109 STRANG
MARSDEN STARES AT HIM.) 124 STRANG
AND STARES OUT) 148 STRANG
(SENSING HER THOUGHTS, SITS UP IN HER LAP AND 156 STRANG
STARES INTO HER FACE,

STARES (CONT'D.)
NINA LETS GO OF HER WRIST AND STARES AFTER THEM INI78 STRANG
A SORT OF STUNNED STUPOR)
(STARES INTO HER FACE WITH GREAT PITY NOW) 180 STRANG
STARES AT HER WITH STUNNED EYES) 180 STRANG
(STARES DOWN AT HIM STUPIDLY--THEN THINKING 182 STRANG
STRANGELY)
(STARES DOWN AT EVANS--SLOWLY, AS IF TRYING TO 182 STRANG
BRING HER MIND BACK TO HIM)
HE STARES ACCUSINGLY AT THEM AS THEY COME SLOWLY 189 STRANG
TOWARD HIM IN SILENCE.
(STARTLED, STARES AT HER--SHOCKED AND HORRIFIED-- 195 STRANG
SHE LETS THE LETTER FALL ON HER LAP AND STARES 443 WELDED
STRAIGHT BEFORE HER.
(CAPE STARES AT HER WITH A HOT GLANCE OF SCORN. 450 WELDED
(HE STARES UP AT HER WONDERINGLY. 452 WELDED
(HE TURNS HIS HEAD) AND STARES AT HER 453 WELDED
CHALLENGINGLY.)
(SHE STARES INTO HIS EYES AND SEEMS TO READ SOME 459 WELDED
CONFIRMATION OF HER STATEMENT)
(CAPE STARES AT HER ANOTHER SECOND-- 460 WELDED
(STARES DUMBLY INTO HER EYES FOR A LONG MOMENT-- 460 WELDED
HOARSELY, IN AGONY)
SUDDENLY HE STARES AS THE SOUND OF A MOTOR COMES 462 WELDED
FROM THE DRIVEWAY.
(HE STARES TOWARD HER, THEN STOPS--IN A LOW, 463 WELDED
UNCERTAIN VOICE)
HE STARES DOWN AT HER FACE, HIS OWN GROWING 465 WELDED
BEWILDERED AND AFRAID,
AND BRINGING HER OWN CLOSE TO IT STARES INTO HIS 466 WELDED
EYES.
(HE STARES AT HER WITH UNNATURAL INTENSITY) 473 WELDED
SHE STARES AT HIM AND MUTTERS RESENTFULLY) 473 WELDED
(STARES FROM THE BILL TO HIM, FLUSHING BENEATH HER474 WELDED
ROUGE)
(GETS UP AND TAKES HER FACE BETWEEN HIS HANDS AND 477 WELDED
STARES INTO HER EYES--
(STARES AT HER--AN EXPRESSION COMES AS IF HE WERE 477 WELDED
SEEING HER FOR THE FIRST TIME.
(STARTLED, TURNS AND STARES AT HER AVERTED FACE-- 483 WELDED
(TURNS AND STARES AT HER--A PAUSE--THEN HE ASKS 484 WELDED
WONDERINGLY, EAGERLY)
(CAPE STARES AT HER UNCERTAINLY, THEN SITS DOWN IN485 WELDED
HIS CHAIR AGAIN.)
(SHE STARES HIM IN THE EYES DEFIANTLY, 485 WELDED
TRIUMPHANTLY.)

STARIN'
HE'S ALWAYS STARIN' AT THE ICE. 536 'ILE
THAR'S TWO MEN LOAFIN' AT THE GATE AN' STARIN' AT 222 DESIRE
ME
AND SAKES, WHAT YOU STARIN' AT SO& 536 DIFRNT
HAVIN' TO STAND FUR 'EM CUMIN' AND STARIN' AT 252 HA APE
YUH--DE WHITE-FACED.
OUT ON THE HATCH STARIN' AT THE MOON LIKE A MON 518 INZONE
HALF-DAFT.

STARING
(SHE STANDS THERE STARING STRAIGHT BEFORE HER AS 941 'ILE
IF IN A DAZE.
SHE IS NOT LOOKING AT HIM BUT STARING DULLY IN 547 'ILE
FRONT OF HER.
BUT STARING AT THE LETTER WITH A SORT OF 208 AHWILD
FASCINATED DREAD.
(HE TURNS TO PASS BEHIND LILY, THEN STOPS, STARING232 AHWILD
DOWN AT HER)
(STARING BEFORE HER--SIGHS WORRIEDLY) 250 AHWILD
(STARING AT HIM AS IF SHE COULDN'T BELIEVE HER 261 AHWILD
EYES)
(STARING AFTER THEM--STILL AGHAST) 262 AHWILD
WHO HAS GONE TO THE WINDOW AT RIGHT AND IS STARING263 AHWILD
OUT FROWNINGLY.
(HE STANDS STARING AT THE MOON WITH A RAPT FACE. 277 AHWILD
AND THEY BOTH SIT IN A RAPT TRANCE, STARING AT THE287 AHWILD
MOON.
(STARING AT HIM WORRIEDLY) HELLO, RICHARD. 292 AHWILD
RICHARD REMAINS STANDING BY THE DOOR, STARING OUT 296 AHWILD
AT THE MOON.
(STARING AT HER IN AMAZEMENT--SLOWLY) 14 ANNA
(SHE PUFFS, STARING AT THE TABLE TOP. 15 ANNA
(WHO HAS BEEN STARING DOWN AT HER FACE ADMIRINGLY, 20 ANNA
NOT HEARING WHAT SHE SAYS--
SHE IS STARING OUT INTO THE FOG ASTERN WITH AN 25 ANNA
EXPRESSION OF WONDER.
STARING INTO HIS FACE ANXIOUSLY FOR SOME SIGN OF 33 ANNA
LIFE.)
(CHRIS COMES OUT OF THE CABIN AND STANDS STARING 38 ANNA
BLINKINGLY ASTERN.
STARING AT IT STUPIDLY FOR A SECOND, THEN 41 ANNA
AIMLESSLY PUTTING IT DOWN AGAIN.
SHE IS NOT READING BUT STARING STRAIGHT IN FRONT 41 ANNA
OF HER.
STARING INTO HIS EYES. 52 ANNA
CHRIS STANDS IN A STUPOR, STARING AT THE FLOOR.) 61 ANNA
ANNA SITS AT THE TABLE, STARING STRAIGHT IN FRONT 63 ANNA
OF HER.)
(SUDDENLY HOLDING HER AWAY FROM HIM AND STARING 76 ANNA
INTO HER EYES AS IF TO PROBE
STARING AT THE CARPET, PREOCCUPIED AND FROWNING. 94 BEYOND
WITH AN UNEASY SIDE GLANCE AT JAMES MAYO WHO IS 104 BEYOND
STARING AT HIS ELDER SON AS IF
STARING OUT TOWARD THE HORIZON SEAWARD. 129 BEYOND
(STARING AT HIS BROTHER--SLOWLY) 132 BEYOND
(STARING AT HIM INTENSELY) ARE YOU TELLING ME THEI38 BEYOND
TRUTH, ANDY MAYO?
(STANDS STARING AT HER FOR A MOMENT--THEN WALKS 140 BEYOND
AWAY SAYING IN A HURT TONE)
(STARING AT THE STOVE) YOU BETTER COME NEAR THE 145 BEYOND
FIRE WHERE IT'S WARM.

STARING

STARING (CONT'D.)
(THE TWO WOMEN REMAIN SILENT FOR A TIME STARING 152 BEYOND
DEJECTEDLY AT THE STOVE.)
HE SIGHS HEAVILY, STARING MOURNFULLY IN FRONT OF 154 BEYOND
HIM.
(UCKY SEES DRISCOLL AND STANDS STARING AT HIM 490 CARDIF
WITH OPEN MOUTH.
STARING TOWARD THE SPOT ON SHORE WHERE THE SINGING456 CAHIBE
SEEMS TO COME FROM.)
STARING OFF INTO VACANCY.) 466 CAHIBE
(HEN SITS STARING BEFORE HIM, 470 CAHIBE
RESTING HIS ELBOW, HIS CHIN ON HIS HAND, STARING 562 CROSS
SOMBERLY BEFORE HIM.
(STARING AT HER FIXEDLY) SO I WILL STAY--IN SPITE565 CROSS
OF HELL!
(STARING AT HER--IN A HARD VOICE) 563 DAYS
(STARING AT JOHN, WHOSE FACE IS AVERTED) 509 DAYS
(RECOVERED NOW--STARING AT HIM--QUIETLY) 512 DAYS
STARING DOWN AT HIM WITH COLD, SCORNFUL EYES. 530 DAYS
BUT SHE IS STARING STRAIGHT BEFORE HER WITH A 539 DAYS
STILL, SET FACE.
(STARING BEFORE HER STRANGELY--REPEATS 540 DAYS
FASCINATEDLY)
SHE IS STILL STARING BEFORE HER WITH THE SAME 541 DAYS
STRANGE FASCINATED DREAD.
(STRANGELY, STARING BEFORE HIM, 544 DAYS
LOVING STANDS BY HIS HEAD, STARING DOWN AT HIS 556 DAYS
FACE.
FATHER BAIRD REMAINS FOR A MOMENT STARING SADLY AT557 DAYS
THE FLOOR.
HER STARING EYES ON THE DOORWAY TO THE STUDY.) 563 DAYS
(HE WAITS, STARING AT THE CROSS WITH ANGUISHED 565 DAYS
EYES, HIS ARMS OUTSTRETCHED.
STARING UP AT THE SKY.) 211 DESIRE
(STARING AROUND THE FARM, HIS COMPRESSED FACE 218 DESIRE
TIGHTENED.
AND STANDS STARING AT HIM WITH HATE.) 227 DESIRE
SHE ROCKS LISTLESSLY, ENERVATED BY THE HEAT, 228 DESIRE
STARING IN FRONT OF HER WITH BORED.
ABBIE STANDS FOR A SECOND STARING AT HIM, HER EYES239 DESIRE
BURNING WITH DESIRE.
(STARING AT HER--HORRIBLY CONFUSED--DULLY) 240 DESIRE
HE STANDS STARING AT HER, HIS ARMS HANGING 241 DESIRE
DISJOINTEDLY FROM HIS SHOULDERS.
(HE SUDDENLY STOPS, STARING STUPIDLY BEFORE HIM.) 242 DESIRE
CABOT WALKS SLOWLY UP FROM THE LEFT, STARING UP AT245 DESIRE
THE SKY WITH A VAGUE FACE.)
SHE IS OBLIVIOUS, STARING AT THE DOOR. 249 DESIRE
STARING AT THE DOOR AS IF SHE WERE ALONE IN A 250 DESIRE
SILENT ROOM.)
STARING AT THE SKY BLINKINGLY. 252 DESIRE
(STARING AT HER WITH ANGUISHED, BEWILDERED EYES) 257 DESIRE
(STARING AT HIM--UNEASILY) WHAT'D HE MEAN ABOUT 500 DIFRNT
JIM BENSON, CALEB?
EMMA STANDS FOR A WHILE, STARING STONILY BEFORE 514 DIFRNT
HER.
(STARING AT HIM WITH STERN CONDEMNATION) 529 DIFRNT
(ONCE INSIDE THE DOOR, HE STANDS STARING ABOUT THE535 DIFRNT
ROOM, FROWNING.
(STARING AT HER SHARPLY--AFTER A PAUSE) 539 DIFRNT
(STARING AT HER WITH STUNNED EYES-- IN A HOARSE 542 DIFRNT
WHISPER)
STARING BEFORE HER WITH WAXY EYES. 548 DIFRNT
(TURNS AWAY AND LEANS OUT THE WINDOW STARING INTO 425 DYNAMO
THE NIGHT)
WHEN I TOLD YOU I'D CAUGHT HIM STARING AT ME, 432 DYNAMO
HE HOLDS THE OPEN BIBLE BUT HE IS STARING MODDILY 435 DYNAMO
OVER IT.
(PRETENDING TO BE SUNK IN THOUGHT HAS BEEN STARING439 DYNAMO
CALCULATINGLY AT REUBEN--
(STARING AFTER HIM WITH THE SAME LOOK OF 449 DYNAMO
DEFIANCE--CALLS JEERINGLY)
HE ADVANCES THREATENINGLY ON HIS FATHER WHO IS 451 DYNAMO
STARING AT ADA STUPIDLY.
(STARING AT HIM, STAMMERS HIS NAME AGAIN 459 DYNAMO
(STARING AT HIM HELPLESSLY) YES--NO--I DON'T 460 DYNAMO
THING--
(IS STARING AT HIM WITH EYES THAT SEARCH HIS FACE 460 DYNAMO
APPREHENSIVELY) RUBE?
HE STANDS THERE STARING AT THE DYNAMO AND 473 DYNAMO
LISTENING TO IT.)
AND STARING AT THE DYNAMOS AND HUMMING LIKE A 479 DYNAMO
HALF-WIT?
(WHIRLS AROUND AND STANDS STARING AT HER WITH 481 DYNAMO
STRANGE FIXITY FOR A MOMENT,
SHRINKING CLOSE TO REUBEN, WHO IS STARING AT ALL 484 DYNAMO
THIS
SHE IS STARING DREAMILY AT THE FRONT DYNAMO, 486 DYNAMO
HUMMING TO HERSELF.
(STARING TOWARD THE OTHER, 192 EJONES
JONES, WHO HAS BEEN STARING UP AT THE SKY, 194 EJONES
STARING DOWN AT THE SHOES IN HIS HANDS AS IF 196 EJONES
RELUCTANT TO THROW THEM AWAY.
AND STAND STARING AT THE HOUSE. 7 ELECTR
MINNIE IS OBLIVIOUS, STILL STARING AT THE HOUSE.) 7 ELECTR
(SEEING SHE IS PAYING NO ATTENTION TO HIM BUT IS 7 ELECTR
STARING WITH OPEN-MOUTHED AWE
WHO IS STARING AT HER WITH A FACE GROWN GRIM AND 17 ELECTR
HARD)
THEN RODS SLOWLY, STARING FIXEDLY AT HER MOTHER) 17 ELECTR
(STARING AT HER WITH A QUESTIONING DREAD--FORCING 18 ELECTR
A SCORNFUL SMILE)
(SHE IS SILENT, STARING BEFORE HER WITH HARD EYES, 22 ELECTR
RIGIDLY UPRIGHT.
TO FOLLOW SETH'S ADVICE--STARING AT HIM WITH 24 ELECTR
DELIBERATELY INSULTING SCORN)
(STARTLED AGAIN--STARING AT HER UNEASILY) 24 ELECTR
(STARING AT LAVINIA WITH HATRED) 31 ELECTR

STARING (CONT'D.)
SHE IS STARING AT THE PORTRAIT.) 37 ELECTR
(SHE HAS BEEN STARING BEFORE HER--NOW SHE SUDDENLY 40 ELECTR
TURNS ON BRANT--SLOWLY)
HE AND CHRISTINE START FRIGHTENEDLY AND STAND 42 ELECTR
STARING AT EACH OTHER.
SHE IS STARING, STRAIGHT BEFORE HER. 43 ELECTR
(IN A LOW VOICE, AS IF TO HERSELF, STARING AT THE 44 ELECTR
HOUSE)
AS IF AT ATTENTION, STARING AT HIS HOUSE, HIS WIFE 46 ELECTR
AND DAUGHTER.
(STARING AT HIM) YOU DON'T LOOK WELL. 49 ELECTR
LAVINIA STANDS STARING BEFORE HER-- 56 ELECTR
SHE STANDS STARING FASCINATEDLY UP AT THE WINDOW, 57 ELECTR
(SUDDENLY STARING AT HAZEL, AS IF STRUCK BY AN 72 ELECTR
IDEA)
(STARING AT HER-- 73 ELECTR
(HE STANDS STARING AT THE HOUSE) 74 ELECTR
(STARING AT HER BEWILDEREDLY) 76 ELECTR
(THEY ALMOST ROUGHLY, PUSHING HER BACK AND STARING 76 ELECTR
AT HER)
LAVINIA REMAINS BY THE FOOT OF THE STEPS, STARING 77 ELECTR
AFTER THEM.
(LAVINIA KEEPS HER BODY RIGID, HER EYES STARING 78 ELECTR
INTO HER MOTHER'S.
(STARING AT HER--IN A QUEER TONE OF GRATITUDE) 81 ELECTR
(THEN STARING AT HER SUSPICIOUSLY AGAIN) 82 ELECTR
(STARING AT HIM--IN A WHISPER) 84 ELECTR
(THEN SEIZING HER BY THE SHOULDERS AND STARING 89 ELECTR
INTO HER EYES--
(HAS BEEN STARING OVER HIS HEAD, LISTENING 90 ELECTR
FASCINATEDLY,
(IS NOT LOOKING DOWN AT HIS FATHER BUT IS 93 ELECTR
STARING STRAIGHT BEFORE HIM,
(THEY WAIT, STARING AT THE DOOR. 99 ELECTR
(THEN STARING AT HIS MOTHER STRANGELY) 101 ELECTR
(HE HUGS HER TO HIM, STARING OVER HER HEAD WITH 111 ELECTR
SAG BLANK EYES.)
(NOT HEEDING HER, STILL STARING AT BRANT-- 115 ELECTR
STRANGELY)
(ORIN STARTS AND GETS TO HIS FEET, STARING AT HER 122 ELECTR
CONFUSEDLY,
SHE WALKS TO THE CLUMP OF LILACS AND STANDS THERE 137 ELECTR
STARING AT THE HOUSE.)
AND PUSHES BACK A SHUTTER AND STANDS STARING OUT. 143 ELECTR
(HAS TURNED BACK AND IS STARING FASCINATEDLY AT 143 ELECTR
HER.
(HE TAKES HER HAND AUTOMATICALLY, STARING AT HER 143 ELECTR
STUPIDLY.)
(STARING AT HER AGAIN, DRINKING HER IN) 143 ELECTR
ALL THOSE HANDSOME MEN STARING AT YOU AND YOUR 154 ELECTR
STRANGE BEAUTIFUL HAIR?
(STARING AT HER WILDLY) WHAT DID SHE TELL? 161 ELECTR
(STARING AT HIM WITH FASCINATED HORROR) 165 ELECTR
(WHO HAS RAISED HER HEAD AND HAS BEEN STARING AT 166 ELECTR
HIM WITH DREAD
IT IS DEEPLY LINED, HAGGARD WITH SLEEPLESSNESS AND170 ELECTR
STARING,
HAZEL STANDS STARING AT HER. 173 ELECTR
(STARING AT HIM SEARCHINGLY--UNEASILY) 175 ELECTR
STARING INTO THE SUNLIGHT WITH FROZEN EYES. 179 ELECTR
ORIN IS SITTING BEHIND THE TABLE, STARING BEFORE 269 GGBROW
HIM.
(WHO HAS BEEN STARING AT HIM WITH TERROR, RAISING 292 GGBROW
HER MASK TO WARD OFF HIS FACE)
STARING FROM THE WOMAN ON THE BENCH TO THEIR 293 GGBROW
FATHER ACCUSINGLY.)
(THEY STOP, STARING AT HIM FIXEDLY, 293 GGBROW
(TRIUMPHANTLY, STARING INTO HIS EYES) 298 GGBROW
ITS EMPTY EYES STARING FRONT. 306 GGBROW
(SHE LOOKS AT BROWN, WHO IS STARING AT HER. 311 GGBROW
STARING DOWN ON THE PLAIN WITH FASCINATED LOATHING.314 GGBROW
SOLICITOUS EXPRESSION--PLEASANTLY TO THE STARING 314 GGBROW
DRAFTSMAN)
THEY ARE ALL STARING AT HIM WITH PETRIFIED 318 GGBROW
BEWILDERMENT.
(STARING AT HER--FASCINATED--WITH GREAT PEACE AS 320 GGBROW
IF HER PRESENCE COMFORTED HIM)
(SHE STANDS LIKE AN IDOL OF EARTH, HER EYES 323 GGBROW
STARING OUT OVER THE WORLD.)
(SUDDENLY HE BECOMES CONSCIOUS OF ALL THE OTHER 225 HA APE
MEN STARING AT SOMETHING.
THE OTHERS, MOST OF THEM SMOKING PIPES, ARE 226 HA APE
STARING AT YANK HALF-APPREHENSIVELY,
(STARING AT THE SIDE-- 233 HA APE
(WHO HAS BEEN STARING AT SOMETHING INSIDE--WITH 236 HA APE
QUEER EXCITEMENT)
(HE STOPS ABRUPTLY, STARING PROBINGLY AT THE 35 HUGHIE
CLERK.
(HE HESITATES, STARING AT LARRY WITH A STRANGE 587 ICEMAN
APPEAL.)
THEY ARE STARING AT HIM, UNEASY AND BEGINNING TO 621 ICEMAN
FEEL DEFENSIVE.
(HE IS STARING AHEAD OF HIM NOW 622 ICEMAN
WHAT ARE YOU STARING AT? 624 ICEMAN
(STARING AT HICKEY FROWNINGLY--MORE ALOUD TO 625 ICEMAN
HIMSELF THAN TO THEM)
HE IS STARING BEFORE HIM IN FROWNING, DISTURBED 629 ICEMAN
MEDITATION.
WHO IS STARING AT HIM GUILTILY NOW.) 637 ICEMAN
(IS STARING BEFORE HIM BROODINGLY. 638 ICEMAN
(HAS BEEN STARING INTO HIS EYES WITH A FASCINATED 641 ICEMAN
WONDERING DREAD)
(LARRY AGAIN IS STARING AT HIM FASCINATEDLY, 642 ICEMAN
LARRY IS RIGID ON HIS CHAIR, STARING BEFORE HIM. 646 ICEMAN
STARING IN FRONT OF THEM. 651 ICEMAN
THEY ARE AGAIN STARING AT HIM WITH BAFFLED 663 ICEMAN
UNEASINESS.

STARING

STARING (CONT'D.)
HE IS STARING IN FRONT OF HIM IN A TENSE, STRAINED665 ICEMAN IMMOBILITY.
STARING OVER THE SWINGING DOORS INTO THE STREET.) 677 ICEMAN
BEJESÉ, WHAT ARE ALL YOU BUMS HANGING AROUND 684 ICEMAN
STARING AT ME FOR!
STARING INWARD AT HIMSELF WITH CONTEMPT AND 689 ICEMAN HATRED.
HE WILL NOT LOOK AT PARRITT, WHO KEEPS STARING AT 696 ICEMAN HIM
(LOOKING AT SMITTY, WHO IS STARING AT THE DOORWAY 515 INZONE IN A DREAM.
(FOR A MOMENT HE SITS STARING IN FRONT OF HIM. 523 INZONE
WHY ARE YOU STARING, JAMES 20 JOURNE
(SUDDENLY SHE IS SELF-CONSCIOUSLY AWARE THAT THEY 41 JOURNE ARE BOTH STARING FIXEDLY AT
(EDMUND, WHO HAS BEEN STARING FRIGHTENEDLY BEFORE 53 JOURNE HIM, FORGETTING HIS BOOK,
(HE CATCHES EDMUND STARING AT HIM.) 55 JOURNE
(SHARPLY.) PLEASE STOP STARING/ 68 JOURNE
TYRONE LIGHTS A CIGAR AND GOES TO THE SCREEN DOOR, 71 JOURNE STARING OUT.
(SHE PAUSES, STARING BEFORE HER WITH UNNATURALLY 105 JOURNE BRIGHT, DREAMY EYES,
THEN SHE SETTLES BACK IN RELAXED DREAMINESS, 106 JOURNE STARING FIXEDLY AT NOTHING.
(EDMUND DRINKS BUT TYRONE REMAINS STARING AT THE 111 JOURNE GLASS IN HIS HAND.
LOOKING FOR SYMPATHY, BUT EDMUND IS STARING AT THE115 JOURNE FLOOR.)
(SHE STOPS, STARING BEFORE HER. 115 JOURNE
(HE GETS UP FROM HIS CHAIR AND STANDS STARING 120 JOURNE CONDEMNINGLY AT HER--BITTERLY.)
SHE KEEPS STARING OUT THE WINDOW UNTIL 121 JOURNE
(STARING BEFORE HIM.) THE FOG WAS WHERE I WANTED 131 JOURNE TO BE.
(HE SEES HIS FATHER STARING AT HIM WITH MINGLED 131 JOURNE WORRY AND IRRITATED DISAPPROVAL.
(STARING THROUGH THE FRONT PARLOR--WITH RELIEF.) 139 JOURNE
(THEN RESENTFULLY.) WHAT THE HELL ARE YOU STARING168 JOURNE AT?
STARING THROUGH THE FRONT PARLOR INTO THE HALL. 169 JOURNE
(THEN MARY SPEAKS, AND THEY FREEZE INTO SILENCE 171 JOURNE AGAIN, STARING AT HER.
(STARING DREAMILY BEFORE HER. 175 JOURNE
JUST NOW HE IS STARING STRAIGHT BEFORE HIM 274 LAZARU
THE PEOPLE REMAIN WITH GOBLETS UPLIFTED, STARING 279 LAZARU AT HIM.
ALL THESE PEOPLE ARE STARING FASCINATEDLY AT THE 282 LAZARU HOUSE, LISTENING ENTRANCED.
(HE TURNS HIS EYES FROM THEM, STARING STRAIGHT 291 LAZARU BEFORE HIM.
HE STANDS STARING BEFORE HIM STRANGELY. 303 LAZARU
CALIGULA HAS WHIRLED AROUND AND STANDS STARING, 333 LAZARU
THE LATTER STEPS BACK FROM HIM, STARING OPEN- 333 LAZARU MOUTHED, FASCINATED.
STARING AT THE DOORWAY IN THE REAR WITH 337 LAZARU SUPERSTITIOUS DREAD.
(WHO HAS BEEN STARING IN A BEWILDERED STUPOR FROM 339 LAZARU TIBERIUS,
STARING AT HIS FACE NOW THAT THE ROOM IS FLOODED 340 LAZARU
STARING AT LAZARUS WONDERINGLY) 340 LAZARU
(THEN SHE LAUGHS--A LOW, CRUEL LAUGH--STARING AT 342 LAZARU MIRIAM)
(SUDDENLY SPRINGING TO HIS FEET AND STARING ABOUT 342 LAZARU
POMPEIA STEPS NEARER TO LAZARUS, STARING AT HIM 347 LAZARU MOCKINGLY.
HE IS STARING STRAIGHT BEFORE HIM. 350 LAZARU
(STARING UP AT LAZARUS' FACE, 355 LAZARU
HE STANDS STARING AROUND HIM IN A PANIC OF FEAR 357 LAZARU THAT HE HAS BEEN OVERHEARD.
(STARING UP AT HIM IN PATHETIC CONFUSION) 359 LAZARU
(HE BEGINS TO LAUGH TRIUMPHANTLY, STARING DEEP 360 LAZARU INTO CALIGULA'S EYES)
THE DAIS AS IN THE PREVIOUS SCENE, STARING AT 362 LAZARU LAZARUS, LAUGHING CRUELLY.
GROUP AGAIN, STARING AFTER HIM, AND A WHISPER OF 363 LAZARU STRANGE, BEWILDERED
(RISING TO HER FEET LIKE ONE IN A TRANCE, STARING 366 LAZARU TOWARD LAZARUS)
IT IS THE SOUL, STARING INTO THE MIRROR OF ITSELF, 12 MANSNS
(STARING AT GADSBY-- 28 MANSNS
(HE HAS BEEN STARING AT DEBORAH, 30 MANSNS
(STARING AROUND HIM IN TURN--AS IF FIGHTING 37 MANSNS AGAINST AN INFLUENCE.)
(THEN HALTINGLY, AS IF THE INFLUENCE TOOK HOLD ON 37 MANSNS HIM, STARING AT HER.)
DEBORAH IS STARING BEFORE HER. 38 MANSNS
HE COMES TO THE TABLE AND STANDS STARING DOWN AT 43 MANSNS IT PREOCCUPIEDLY.
(HE SITS STARING BEFORE HIM, FROWNINGLY 75 MANSNS CONCENTRATED.
IT'S LIKE A STRANGER STARING AT ME. 80 MANSNS
STARING AT HIM WITH A FASCINATED DREAD-- 99 MANSNS STAMMERS.)
(STARING BEFORE HIM, TENSE AND CONCENTRATED.) 101 MANSNS
(STARING BEFORE HIM.) YES, MOTHER, 106 MANSNS
(HE BEGINS TO TELL THE STORY, STARING BEFORE HIM 110 MANSNS AS IF HE VISUALIZED IT.)
I FEEL SOMETHING IS STARING OVER MY SHOULDER--IT'S119 MANSNS STRANGE HERE
AFFECTIONATE AND CONTENTED, STARING DEFIANTLY AT 124 MANSNS SIMON.)
GRIPPING THE ARMS OF HIS CHAIR, STARING BEFORE HIM126 MANSNS FRIGHTENEDLY.
BUT THEY REMAIN STARING AS ONE AT HIM, THEIR EYES 131 MANSNS HARD AND UNFORGIVING.)

STARING (CONT'D.)
(STARING AT HER FASCINATEDLY--BLURTS OUT IN 153 MANSNS ANGUISH.)
(HE IS STARING BEFORE HIM WITH A FASCINATED 157 MANSNS YEARNING.)
(STARING AT HIM--IN A PANIC OF DREAD.) 159 MANSNS
THE GREAT DARK EYES STARING FROM BLACK HOLES. 161 MANSNS
HE STANDS STARING AT THEM. 171 MANSNS
(STARTS--STARING AT HIM UNEASILY.) 173 MANSNS
(STARING AT HIM--CANNOT CONTROL A SHUDDER.) 174 MANSNS
AS ONE, ON THE OTHER BENCH, STARING AT HIM, 175 MANSNS EXHAUSTED AND WITHOUT FEELING.)
STARING AT HIM WITH A FASCINATED UNEASINESS. 177 MANSNS
(STARING AT THE DOOR FASCINATEDLY.) 185 MANSNS
(TURNS HIS HEAD A LITTLE FROM STARING INSIDE THE 187 MANSNS SUMMER-HOUSE--
STARING INTO THE DARKNESS INSIDE. 187 MANSNS
STARING INTO THE DARKNESS INSIDE THE SUMMER-HOUSE.188 MANSNS
ONLY THEIR EYES MOVE, STARING FIXEDLY BUT 364 MARCOM
INDIFFERENTLY AT THE PULOS.
STARING AT HIM FROM A GREAT DISTANCE WITH 366 MARCOM INDIFFERENT CALM.
(THE MOTIONLESS STARING FIGURES ARE ALL INDIANS. 369 MARCOM
AND STARING ABOUT WITH AN APPRAISING CONTEMPT) 373 MARCOM
(SHE LAUGHS, WAVING THE POEM IN HER UPRAISED HAND,375 MARCOM STARING MOCKINGLY)
ALL THE PEOPLE IN THE ROOM ARE STARING AT HIM. 378 MARCOM
(STARING AT HIM FOR A LONG MOMENT WITH APPALLED 379 MARCOM APPRECIATION--ECSTATICALLY)
MARCO BOWS TO HER THE MORE GRATEFULLY AS KUBLAI 395 MARCOM AND CHU-YIN ARE STARING AT HIM
(WHO HAS BEEN STARING AT THEM WITH WEARY 399 MARCOM AMUSEMENT)
UNTIL A SMALL MULTITUDE IS GATHERED STANDING IN 405 MARCOM SILENCE STARING UP AT THE POOP.
(STARING AT THE PICTURE) 416 MARCOM
AND IS STARING SOMBERLY BEFORE HIM) 423 MARCOM
(STARING FIXEDLY) I SHALL OBSERVE 426 MARCOM DISPASSIONATELY.
(THEN AFTER STARING AT KUKACHIN FOR A SECOND, 437 MARCOM BITTERLY)
PAUSES, STANDING BESIDE THE BODY, STARING DOWN AT 438 MARCOM HER.
(STARING AT HIM RESENTFULLY) 23 MISBEG
TYRONE IS STARING AT HER. 41 MISBEG
(HE TURNS TO JOSIE, WHO IS STARING AT HARDER, MUCH 57 MISBEG TO HIS DISCOMFITURE.
(SHE COMES TO TYRONE, WHO STANDS STARING AFTER 101 MISBEG HOGAN WITH A PUZZLED LOOK.)
(STARING AT HER CURIOUSLY AGAIN) 102 MISBEG
HE SITS HUNCHED UP ON THE STEP, STARING AT 106 MISBEG NOTHING.
HE KEEPS STARING AT HER WITH A PUZZLED FROWN.) 113 MISBEG
(STARING AT NOTHING--VAGUELY) 119 MISBEG
(TYRONE IS STARING AT HER, A STRANGE BITTER 121 MISBEG DISGUST IN HIS EYES.
(SHE IS STARING AT HIM NOW WITH A LOOK OF 137 MISBEG FRIGHTENED HORROR.
(SLOWLY, STARING BEFORE HIM) 138 MISBEG
(HE PAUSES, STARING INTO THE MOONLIGHT WITH VACANT143 MISBEG EYES.)
STARING INTO THE MOONLIGHT.) 148 MISBEG
SHE HUGS HIM MORE TIGHTLY AND SPEAKS SOFTLY, 152 MISBEG STARING INTO THE MOONLIGHT)
HE FEELS JOSIE STARING AT HIM 173 MISBEG
WHO IS STARING AT THE FLOOR DEJECTEDLY AND HASN'T 27 POET BEEN LISTENING.
FOR GOD'S SAKE, STOP YOUR STARING/ 35 POET
(HE STANDS STARING IN THE MIRROR AND DOES NOT HEAR 67 POET THE LATCH OF THE STREET DOOR
(WHO HAS BEEN STARING AT HIM WITH SCORN UNTIL HE 91 POET SAYS THIS LAST--
SHE NOTICES HIM STARING AT HER AND GIVES HIM A 118 POET RESENTFUL, SUSPICIOUS GLANCE.
SHE IS STARING AT MELODY APPREHENSIVELY NOW.) 125 POET
(BUT HE IS STARING SIGHTLESSLY AT THE TABLE TOP 156 POET
STARING AT THE OPEN DOOR. 163 POET
SHE COMES BACK TO THE CENTER TABLE, STARING AT 165 POET MELODY.
(HE PAUSES, STARING AT HER-- 174 POET
SARA HAS LIFTED HER TEAR-STAINED FACE FROM HER 175 POET HANDS AND IS STARING AT HIM
HER HEAD HANGING, STARING AT THE FLOOR.) 180 POET
SHE IS STARING FIXEDLY AT A RAG DOLL WHICH SHE HAS578 ROPE
PROPPED UP AGAINST
(HE STANDS STARING UP AT THE ROPE AND TAPS IT 579 ROPE TESTINGLY SEVERAL TIMES WITH HIS
(STANDS STARING AT HIS FATHER, WHO IS STILL MAKING596 ROPE GESTURES FOR HIM TO JUMP.
(STARING AT HIM WONDERINGLY) 10 STRANG
(STARING AFTER HER--DULLY) ((THAT ISN'T NINA...)) 28 STRANG
(INDIGNANTLY)
(WHO HAS BEEN STARING AT HIM INQUISITIVELY) 30 STRANG
SEEMED STARING OUT OF HIS EYES WITH A BURNING 45 STRANG PAIN AND I WOKE UP CRYING.
(STARING OUT OVER HIS HEAD--WITH LOVING PITY, 70 STRANG THINKING)
STARING AT HER BOWED HEAD AS SHE REPEATS 89 STRANG SUBMISSIVELY)
(HE SUDDENLY TURNS TO EVANS WHO HAS BEEN STARING 106 STRANG AT HIM, PUZZLEDLY--
(SHE REMAINS IN A SITTING POSITION, STARING 108 STRANG BLANKLY BEFORE HER.
(STARING AT EVANS WONDERINGLY) 113 STRANG
CHARLIE'S STARING AT ME...)) 116 STRANG
SHE HESITATES JUST INSIDE THE DOOR, STARING INTO 125 STRANG DARRELL'S EYES.
(STARING AT HER WILDLY) SAM'S BABY$ 130 STRANG

STARING

STARING (CONTD.)
THEY SIT STARING BEFORE THEM IN SILENCE. 133 STRANG
(STARING AT HIM WITH REPULSION--WITH COOL DISDAIN)163 STRANG
(AFTER STARING AT HIM FOR A MOMENT--WALKING AWAY 174 STRANG
FROM HIM--
(WHO HAS BEEN STARING AT THEM WITH A FOOLISH GRIN)174 STRANG
(STARING BEFORE HER AS IF SHE WERE IN A TRANCE-- 179 STRANG
SIMPLY, LIKE A YOUNG GIRL)
(STARING AT HIM) NO, OLD MAN, WHAT'S THE 181 STRANG
TROUBLES
(TOUCHING DARRELL WHO HAS STOOD STARING STRAIGHT 182 STRANG
BEFORE HIM WITH A BITTER
(STILL STANDING ON THE RAIL, STARING AFTER 183 STRANG
GORDON'S SHELL)
(PROFESSIONALLY, STARING AT HER COLDLY) 183 STRANG
SHE TAKES THE NOSE AUTOMATICALLY, STARING AT HIM 188 STRANG
UNCOMPREHENDINGLY.)
STARING AT ME WITH SUCH COLD ENMITY... 190 STRANG
(STARING AT GORDON'S BACK RESENTFULLY) 191 STRANG
(STARING AT HIM STUPIDLY--THINKING) 194 STRANG
THEY HAVE BOTH BEEN STARING AT HIM STUPIDLY) 195 STRANG
(AS SHE REMAINS OBLIVIOUS, STARING AFTER THE 199 STRANG
PLANE--THINKING FATALISTICALLY)
(THEY SIT CLOSE, SHE STARING DREAMILY BEFORE HER, 446 WELDED
HE WATCHING HER FACE.)
SHE REMAINS THERE FOR A MOMENT STARING AT THE 451 WELDED
CLOSED DOOR,
STARING STRAIGHT BEFORE HER. 452 WELDED
EYES, STARING BACK WITH RESENTFUL ACCUSATION. 454 WELDED
(STARING AT HER) OH--I SEE--YOU MEAN, WHAT DID I 473 WELDED
COME HERE FOR)
(AGAIN STARING AT HER WITH STRANGE INTENSITY-- 473 WELDED
SUDDENLY WITH A QUEER LAUGH)
(STARING AT HER INTENTLY--SUDDENLY DEEPLY MOVED) 475 WELDED
POOR WOMAN!
STARING INTO EACH OTHER'S EYES WITH AN 480 WELDED
APPREHENSIVE QUESTIONING.
(FOR A TIME THEY BOTH SIT STARING BLEAKLY BEFORE 486 WELDED
THEM.
SHE DOES NOT TURN BUT REMAINS STARING AT THE DOOR 487 WELDED
IN FRONT OF HER.

STARK
BE GOD, THIS BUGHOUSE WILL DRIVE ME STARK, RAVING 605 ICEMAN
LUCKY YET!
IS IT STARK MAD YOU'VE GONE, SO YOU CAN'T TELL ANY 51 POET
MORE WHAT'S DEAD AND A LIE.

STARRED
BECAME MOONLIGHT AND THE SHIP AND THE HIGH DIM- 153 JOURNE
STARRED SKY/

STARS
HE CAN'T BE OUT DREAMIN' AT THE STARS HIS LAST 96 BEYOND
NIGHT.
COUNTIN' THE STARS TO SEE IF THEY ALL COME OUT 99 BEYOND
ARIGHT AND PROPER.
I WISH THE STARS WAS OUT, AND THE MOON, TOO. 489 CARDIF
BY WHAT DRIVES THE STARS THROUGH SPACE/ 461 DYNAMO
A SULTRY, HAZY SKY WITH FEW STARS VISIBLE. 468 DYNAMO
AND THINK OF THE STARS/ 477 DYNAMO
I CAN SEE THE STARS/ 286 GGROW
WHEN THE SKY'D BE BLAZING AND WINKING WID STARS. 214 HA APE
ALL DAT CRAZY TRIPE ABOUT STARS AND MOONS,-- 215 HA APE
THE QUOTES,--"THE FAULT, DEAR BRUTUS, IS NOT IN 162 JOURNE
OUR STARS, BUT IN OURSELVES
IT IS A CLEAR, BRIGHT NIGHT, THE SKY SPARKLING 281 LAZARU
WITH STARS.
THEY WILL BEGIN TO WORSHIP IN FILTHY IDOLATRY THE 283 LAZARU
SUN AND STARS AND MAN'S BODY--
LET ALL STARS BE FOR YOU HENCEFORTH SYMBOLS OF 289 LAZARU
SAVIORS--
TO THE STARS/ 289 LAZARU
(HE STARES UP AT THE STARS, RAPT IN CONTEMPLATION,290 LAZARU
ARMS OUTSTRETCHED TOWARD THE STARS, THEIR HEADS 290 LAZARU
THROWN BACK.)
THEN HE LOOKS, UP TO THE STARS AND, AS IF ANSWERING293 LAZARU
A QUESTION,
THEN YOU MAY LOVE THE STARS AS EQUALS/ 309 LAZARU
ARE THE STARS TOO PURE FOR YOUR SICK PASSIONS/ 310 LAZARU
MILLIONS OF LAUGHING STARS THERE ARE AROUND ME/ 348 LAZARU
NEW STARS ARE BORN OF DUST 348 LAZARU
A BUBBLE OF FROTH BLOWN FROM THE LIPS OF THE DYING353 LAZARU
TOWARD THE STARS/
LET HIM BLAZE TO THE STARS/ 367 LAZARU
STARS AND DUST/ 367 LAZARU
WE LOVE MEN FLAMING TOWARD THE STARS/ 367 LAZARU
WE LOVE MEN FLAMING TOWARD THE STARS/ 367 LAZARU
WE ARE STARS/ 368 LAZARU
ONCE WHEN HE LOOKED AT SUNRISE, ANOTHER TIME AT 397 MARCOM
SUNSET, ANOTHER AT THE STARS.

START
IT'S BETTER TO CRUSH SUCH THINGS AT THE START THANS43 'ILE
LET THEM MAKE HEADWAY.
THE MEN PULL OUT SHEATH-KNIVES AND START A RUSH, 544 'ILE
BUT STOP
(SHE COMES TO HERSELF WITH A START) 547 'ILE
FURTHERMORE, I'LL START A CAMPAIGN TO 203 AHWILD
WELL, WE'RE ABOUT READY TO START AT LAST, THANK 208 AHWILD
GOODNESS/
START EATING, EVERYBODY. 223 AHWILD
YOU'LL START NO TROUBLE IN HERE/ 247 AHWILD
SHE SMILES ON SEEING HER UNCLE, THEN GIVES A START272 AHWILD
ON SEEING RICHARD.)
THIS BRINGS HIM BACK TO EARTH WITH A START) 277 AHWILD
(HE COMES TO HIMSELF WITH A START. 293 AHWILD
THEY DRINK DOWN HALF THE CONTENTS AND START TO 4 ANNA
TALK TOGETHER HURRIEDLY IN LOW.
CHRIS GIVES A START--HURRIEDLY) 7 ANNA
DON'T START NOTHIN' YOU CAN'T FINISH/ 11 ANNA
(MISERABLY) AY DON'T START NUTTING, MARTHY. 11 ANNA

START (CONTD.)
(WITH A START--LOOKING AT HER INTENTLY) 14 ANNA
THAT WAS THE START. 16 ANNA
AND GIVING ME THE WRONG START. 18 ANNA
(WITH A START--MAKING A GESTURE WITH HER HAND AS 25 ANNA
IF TO IMPOSE SILENCE.
SHE GIVES A START WHEN SHE SEES BURKE SO NEAR HER, 31 ANNA
I WOULDN'T START NO TROUBLE WITH HIM IF I WAS YOU. 43 ANNA
BOTH MEN START. 50 ANNA
(HE SEES HER BAG AND GIVES A START) 64 ANNA
(WITH A START) WHAT YOU GOT IN YOUR POCKET, FOR 66 ANNA
PETE'S SAKE-
WITH A START, CONFUSEDLY) 72 ANNA
BUT I'LL BET BY THE TIME YOU GET THERE YOU'LL HAVE 73 ANNA
FORGOT ALL ABOUT ME AND START
(ROBERT TURNS WITH A START. 82 BEYOND
I'D STAY RIGHT HERE AND START IN PLOWING. 84 BEYOND
AND SOMEHOW AFTER A TIME I'D FORGET ANY PAIN I WAS 89 BEYOND
IN, AND START DREAMING.
(SHE TAKES HIS HAND, AND THEY START TO GO OFF 93 BEYOND
LEFT.
THEN I'M GOING TO START LEARNING RIGHT AWAY, AND 102 BEYOND
YOU'LL TEACH ME, WON'T YOU$
AND HAVE TO START IN WITH THINGS IN SUCH A TOPSY- 118 BEYOND
TURVY,
TO GET A START AT SOMETHING IN B. A. 132 BEYOND
YOU NEED THAT FOR YOUR START IN BUENOS AIRES. 134 BEYOND
(HE AND THE CAPTAIN START DOWN TO THE LEFT. 142 BEYOND
WE'LL GO WHERE PEOPLE LIVE INSTEAD OF STAGNATING, 149 BEYOND
AND START ALL OVER AGAIN.
I'LL BORROW THE MONEY FROM HIM TO GIVE US A GOOD 149 BEYOND
START IN THE CITY.
(EXCITEDLY) WE'LL MAKE A NEW START, RUTH--JUST 150 BEYOND
YOU AND I.
(COMING OUT OF HER SLEEP WITH A START) 151 BEYOND
AND I DON'T NEED BUT A SHOESTRING TO START WITH. 157 BEYOND
IT'S A FREE BEGINNING--THE START OF MY VOYAGE/ 168 BEYOND
START 'ER, DRISC. (ETC.) 499 CARIBE
(AS THEY START OFF LEFT) HO, YOU AIN'T 'ARF A 461 CARIBE
FOX, DRISC.
TWO OF THE MEN START DANCING TOGETHER, 471 CARIBE
INTENTIONALLY BUMPING INTO THE OTHERS.
THAT'LL TEACH YOU TO SMUGGLE RUM ON A SHIP AND 473 CARIBE
START A RIOT.
(GIVES A START--THEN BITTERLY)
AS IF HE WANTED TO START WRITING.) 498 DAYS
(CONTROLLING A START) TELLING YOU WHATS 498 DAYS
I'D BETTER GO UP AND START GETTING DRESSED. 529 DAYS
BUT BEFORE I START, THERE'S ONE THING I WANT TO 530 DAYS
IMPRESS ON YOU BOTH AGAIN. 533 DAYS
ELSA AND FATHER BAIRD START AND STARE AT JOHN 535 DAYS
UNEASILY.
(WITH A START) OH. 539 DAYS
ALL THEY WANT IS TO START THE MERRY-GO-ROUND OF 542 DAYS
BLIND GREED ALL OVER AGAIN.
(WITH AN INVOLUNTARY START) AH/ 547 DAYS
YE BETTER START THE FIRE, EBEN. 214 DESIRE
(GRINS AT HIM) WE'RE AIMIN' T' START BEIN' LILIES216 DESIRE
O' THE FIELD.
(THEY BOTH START BACK AROUND THE CORNER OF THE 219 DESIRE
HOUSE.
EBEN SITS UP WITH A START, LISTENING. 239 DESIRE
UPSTAIRS, CABOT IS STILL ASLEEP BUT AWAKENS WITH A262 DESIRE
START.
(THEY START.) 268 DESIRE
(EMBARRASSEDLY) WAAL--WE'D BEST START. 269 DESIRE
SO'S I CAN START HIS SUPPER. 505 DIFRNT
I'D LIKE TO SEE HIM START SOMETHING/ 544 DIFRNT
(COMING OUT OF HER DREAM WITH A START) 431 DYNAMO
GIVES A START AS A FLASH OF LIGHTNING FLICKERS 431 DYNAMO
OVER THE SKY)
WHY, IT WAS YOU SAID TO START UP AN ACQUAINTANCE 432 DYNAMO
WITH HIM,
I'LL HAVE TO START IN MAKING HIM THINK I'M THE 436 DYNAMO
DEVIL HIMSELF/...I)
BUT BEFORE WE START THAT, LET ME ASK YOU, 436 DYNAMO
HE GIVES A START AND HALF RISES FROM HIS CHAIR, 437 DYNAMO
(AS HE GIVES A START--SHARPLY) 446 DYNAMO
AND STOP LOOKING AT HIM OR HE'D START BREAKING 456 DYNAMO
PLATES.
(HIS FATHER GIVES A FRIGHTENED START, AS IF 463 DYNAMO
DODGING A BLOW.
THEN SOMETHING HAS TO WAKE YOU UP--AND START YOU 469 DYNAMO
THINKING AGAIN.
(TURNS ON HER WITH AN IRRITATED START) OH, YOU 479 DYNAMO
DID, DID YOU$
YOU GAVE ME A START, SEEING YOU ALL OF A SUDDEN. 481 DYNAMO
(THEN WITH A START, HE PUSHES HER AWAY FROM HIM 484 DYNAMO
ROUGHLY)
YES, YOU SHO' GIVE ME A START. 177 EJONES
WELL, BLIMEY, I GIVE YER A START, DIDN'T I$ 177 EJONES
IT TAKES DEM NIGGERS FROM NOW TO DARK TO GIT UP DE186 EJONES
NERVE TO START SOMETHIN'.
BY DAT TIME, I'SE GUT A HEAD START DEY NEVER KOTCH186 EJONES
UP.
JONES BECOMES CONSCIOUS OF IT--WITH A START, 192 EJONES
LOOKING BACK OVER HIS SHOULDER)
AND AT THAT SIGNAL ALL THE CONVICTS START TO WORK 194 EJONES
ON THE ROAD.
WILL ANY GENTLEMAN START THE BIDDINGS 197 EJONES
(THEY ARE ABOUT TO START WHEN THE FRONT DOOR OF 10 ELECTR
THE HOUSE IS OPENED AND LAVINIA
LAVINIA CANNOT REPRESS A START, 21 ELECTR
(CONCEALING A START--COOLLY) 32 ELECTR
I WAS AFRAID THAT MIGHT START HER THINKING. 36 ELECTR
HE AND CHRISTINE START FRIGHTENEDLY AND STAND 42 ELECTR
STARING AT EACH OTHER.
(CONTROLLING A START) DON'T BE STUPID, PLEASE/ 46 ELECTR

START

START (CONT'D.)
(WITH A START OF REPULSION, SHRINKING FROM HIS 52 ELECTR
HAND.)
(WITH A START--STRANGELY) ISLANDS/ 89 ELECTR
(IMMEDIATELY SENSES HER PRESENCE--CONTROLLING A 91 ELECTR
START, HARSHLY)
SO SHUT UP BEFORE YOU START/ 96 ELECTR
IT WOULD START SUSPICION-- 111 ELECTR
(THEY START FOR THE DOOR) WE'LL GO BY THE MAIN 113 ELECTR
DECK.
SO LET'S START RIGHT IN. 136 ELECTR
WE OUGHT TO START A FIRE. 137 ELECTR
SO MUCH DEPENDS UN HOW YOU START IN, NOW WE'RE 141 ELECTR
HOME.
I WANT YOU TO START AGAIN--BY FACING ALL YOUR 142 ELECTR
GHOSTS RIGHT NOW/
WE MIGHT AS WELL START MAKING OURSELVES USEFUL. 142 ELECTR
(SHE GIVES A START-- 147 ELECTR
LAVINIA APPEARS IN THE DOORWAY AND GIVES A START 161 ELECTR
(HAZEL GIVES A START 162 ELECTR
(CONCEALING A START OF FEAR--CHANGING TO A FORCED 172 ELECTR
REPROACHFUL TONE)
(SHE IS BROUGHT BACK TO HERSELF WITH A START BY 177 ELECTR
THIS NAME ESCAPING HER--
(THEY START OFF, LEAVING BILLY STANDING THERE.) 259 GGBROW
(WITH A START--RESENTFULLY) WHY MUST SHE LIE$ 261 GGBROW
(THEY BOTH START AND STARE AT HIM.) 261 GGBROW
(GIVES A START--IMMEDIATELY DEFENSIVELY MOCKING) 265 GGBROW
YOU MUSTN'T WORRY--YOU MUST START YOUR BEAUTIFUL 272 GGBROW
PAINTING AGAIN--
(THEN WITH A START HE OPENS HIS EYES AND, HALF 278 GGBROW
SITTING UP,
LET'S START/ 283 GGBROW
HE NEEDN'T START BOSSING LIKE A HUSBAND OR I'LL-- 285 GGBROW
(DION RECOVERS FROM HIS SPASM WITH A START 297 GGBROW
(WITH A SIGH) I THINK YOU'D BETTER START ON 301 GGBROW
BEFORE--RIGHT NOW--
(WITH A START, SHARPLY) WHAT MAKES YOU SAY THAT$ 311 GGBROW
(PADDY FROM THE START OF YANK'S SPEECH HAS BEEN 216 HA APE
TAKING ONE GULP AFTER ANOTHER
I START SOMEP'N AND DE WOILD MOVES/ 216 HA APE
I'M DE START/ 216 HA APE
ARE WE ALL READY TO START$ 221 HA APE
SO I'D STAKE HIM AT THE START TO HALF OF WHAT I 21 HUGHIE
GOT--IN CHICKEN FEED, I MEAN.
=NIL= I TOLD HIM, =IF YOU'RE GOING TO START 22 HUGHIE
PLAYIN' SUCKER
SHE'LL START BREAKING UP THE FURNITURE WITH YOU/= 22 HUGHIE
BELIEVE ME, PAL, I CAN STOP GUY$ THAT START 26 HUGHIE
TELLING ME THEIR FAMILY TROUBLES/
HAS IT A GOOD START$ 27 HUGHIE
THERE'D ALWAYS BE SOMETHING LEFT TO START IT GOING 33 HUGHIE
AGAIN.
WANT TO GIVE THESE DICE THE ONCE-OVER BEFORE WE 38 HUGHIE
START$
I'M WARNING YOU, AT THE START, SO THERE'LL BE NO 591 ICEMAN
MISUNDERSTANDING.
I'D SAVED MY DOUGH SO I COULD START MY OWN 600 ICEMAN
GAMBLIN' HOUSE.
BEJEES, YOU'LL PAY UP TOMORROW, OR I'LL START A 605 ICEMAN
HARRY HOPE REVOLUTION/
AND YOU AND HER NO-GOOD BROTHER START TO LAUGH/ 606 ICEMAN
AND YOUR CASE IS JUST THE OPPORTUNITY I NEED TO 607 ICEMAN
START.
DEN I TOINED HIM 'ROUND AND GIVE HIM A PUSH TO 617 ICEMAN
START HIM.
START THE SERVICE/ 620 ICEMAN
(THEY START AND GULP DOWN THEIR WHISKIES AND POUR 625 ICEMAN
ANOTHER.
(THEY START TO FLY AT EACH OTHER, BUT CHUCK AND 632 ICEMAN
ROCKY GRAB THEM FROM BEHIND.)
AND DON'T START BEEFIN' ABOUT CRICKETS ON DE FARM 632 ICEMAN
DRIVIN' US NUTS.
NOW DON'T START NUTTIN'/ 633 ICEMAN
(MARGIE AND PEARL START TAKING THEM FROM HIS ARMS 638 ICEMAN
AND PUTTING THEM ON THE TABLE.
YOU'RE NOT SO GOOD WHEN YOU START PLAYING SHERLOCK638 ICEMAN
HOLMES.
AND YOU START PLAYING HARRY'S FAVORITE TUNE, CORA.644 ICEMAN
THAT I MEANT YOU TO GUESS RIGHT FROM THE START. 648 ICEMAN
JUST START--/ 653 ICEMAN
LET'S START THE PARTY ROLLING/ 657 ICEMAN
WHICH THEY START SHOVING IN FRONT OF EACH MEMBER 658 ICEMAN
OF THE PARTY.)
I WAS NEVER ONE TO START TROUBLE. 660 ICEMAN
IT WAS JINXED FROM DE START, 665 ICEMAN
WHEN HE CAN START THE BOER WAR RAGING AGAIN/ 677 ICEMAN
WHO'LL START THE BALL ROLLING$ 685 ICEMAN
YUH COULD EASY MAKE SOME GAL WHO'S A GOOD HUSTLER,702 ICEMAN
AN' START A STABLE.
AS HE SPEAKS, THERE IS A START FROM ALL THE CROWD,703 ICEMAN
A SHRINKING AWAY FROM HIM.)
ONLY I'VE GOT TO START BACK AT THE BEGINNING OR 709 ICEMAN
YOU WON'T UNDERSTAND.
SO AS SOON AS I GOT ENOUGH SAVED TO START US OFF, 711 ICEMAN
WELL, IT'S ALL THERE, AT THE START, EVERYTHING 712 ICEMAN
THAT HAPPENED AFTERWARDS.
AND NOW I'D HAVE TO START SWEARING AGAIN THIS WAS 713 ICEMAN
THE LAST TIME.
(HE STOPS WITH A HORRIFIED START, AS IF SHOCKED 716 ICEMAN
OUT OF A NIGHTMARE,
ALL THE GROUP AT THE TABLES BY HIM START AND STARE717 ICEMAN
AT HIM
LOOKING AS IF HE'D LIKE TO FORGET HIS PRISONER AND718 ICEMAN
START CLEANING OUT THE PLACE.
(AS THEY START WALKING TOWARD REAR--INSISTENTLY) 719 ICEMAN
LOOK AT ME PRETENDING TO START FOR A WALK JUST TO 721 ICEMAN
KEEP HIM QUIET.

START (CONT'D.)
NOW DON'T START GRABBING AT THE PARTY, HARRY. 726 ICEMAN
JACK SLAPS HIM ROUGHLY ON THE SHOULDER AND HE 516 INZONE
COMES TO WITH A START)
THE MEN START TO THEIR FEET IN WILD-EYED TERROR 523 INZONE
(THEY START IN SEARCHING SMITTY, 526 INZONE
(THEY ALL START AS IF AWAKENING FROM A BAD DREAM 532 INZONE
AND GRATEFULLY CRAWL INTO THEIR
NOW DON'T START IN ON POOR JAMIE, DEAR. 18 JOURNE
HE'D BETTER START SOON, THEN. 18 JOURNE
(HASTILY,) BUT HE'S CERTAINLY MADE A DAMNED GOOD 36 JOURNE
START.
HE'S MADE A START. 36 JOURNE
WILLING TO START AT THE BOTTOM, 36 JOURNE
DON'T START JUMPING DOWN MY THROAT/ 37 JOURNE
THE WAY TO START WORK IS TO START WORK. 41 JOURNE
IT WAS WRONG FROM THE START. 44 JOURNE
NOW DON'T START IMAGINING THINGS, MAMA. 66 JOURNE
OR SHE MIGHT START HAVING MOST OF HER MEALS ALONE 56 JOURNE
UPSTAIRS.
DON'T START A BATTLE WITH ME. 98 JOURNE
WHEN YOU START AGAIN YOU NEVER KNOW EXACTLY HOW 107 JOURNE
MUCH YOU NEED.
IF YOU'RE GOING TO START THAT STUFF, I'LL BEAT IT.129 JOURNE
THEN THEY BOTH START, 138 JOURNE
WHY DIDN'T YOU SEND HER TO A CURE THEN, AT THE 141 JOURNE
START,
(WITH DRUNKEN PEEVISHNESS,) DON'T START YOUR 147 JOURNE
DAMNED ATHEIST MORBIDNESS AGAIN/
BUT IT WAS A GREAT BOX OFFICE SUCCESS FROM THE 150 JOURNE
START--
(EDMUND LOOKS UP WITH A START.) 167 JOURNE
DO YOU WANT TO START A ROW THAT WILL BRING MAMA 169 JOURNE
DOWNS
LAZARUS AND MIRIAM START TO FOLLOW.) 294 LAZARU
(AS THE SOLDIERS START TO MARCH AWAY BEHIND 322 LAZARU
CRASSUS,
(WITH A START BACKWARD--WITH FRIGHTENED AWE) 329 LAZARU
REST ON LAZARUS HE GIVES A START OF GENUINE 332 LAZARU
ASTONISHMENT.)
(JUMPING UP WITH A SHUDDERING START) 341 LAZARU
IF IT ISN'T JUST LIKE YOU TO START DREAMING A NEW 47 MANSNS
DREAM
AH NOW, DARLING, DON'T START THAT BLACK 49 MANSNS
LONELINESS--
WHEN WE WERE MARRIED WE GOT OUR START. 55 MANSNS
AND WE CAN START AGAIN AND LEARN TO BECOME 61 MANSNS
FRIENDS.
I'VE ALWAYS FELT GRATEFUL TO HER FOR GIVING US OUR 62 MANSNS
START IN LIFE.
AND A CHANCE TO MAKE A NEW START IN LIFE AS A GOOD 63 MANSNS
GRANDMOTHER.
(THEY START BACK, IGNORING SIMON, WHO HAS LISTENED 66 MANSNS
FROWNINGLY,
YOU WILL START YOUR WORK HERE TOMORROW MORNING. 92 MANSNS
THE TWO START RESENTFULLY. 108 MANSNS
(THEY START TO GO OFF, LEFT. 114 MANSNS
I'M TO START TOMORROW-- 132 MANSNS
I KNOW ONLY TOO WELL HOW TEMPTED YOU ARE TO 157 MANSNS
WHISPER AND START THE RUMOR OF THE
TO START US CLAWING AND TEARING AT EACH OTHER'S 170 MANSNS
HEARTS
IF YOU ARE GOING TO START HARPING ON THAT CHILDISH180 MANSNS
NONSENSE--
NOW, DEAR, YOU MUSTN'T START HARPING ON THAT 182 MANSNS
FANTASTIC CHILDISH NONSENSE AGAIN/
THAT REMINDS ME, BEFORE I START THE WHISPER, 191 MANSNS
I'LL BE ON THE RIGHT SIDE OF HIM FROM THE START, 356 MARCOM
THAT WILL DO US CREDIT AND START HAVING CHILDREN, 361 MARCOM
BLESS THE LORD/
WE COULD START RIGHT AWAY. 362 MARCOM
WE COULD START NOW--WITH SUCH FAVORABLE WEATHER-- 362 MARCOM
WHEN DO WE START$ 363 MARCOM
THIS IS OUR CHANCE TO MAKE A START. 372 MARCOM
THAT WILL DO US CREDIT AND START HAVING CHILDREN, 375 MARCOM
BLESS THE LORD/
(CONFUSEDLY) WE HAD TWO MONKS TO START WITH--BUT 376 MARCOM
THEY LEFT US AND WENT BACK.
I CAN START YOU UPON ANY CAREER YOU WISH, 380 MARCOM
(MANFULLY) I WANT TO START AT THE BOTTOM/ 382 MARCOM
(KUNACHIN GIVES A VIOLENT START WHICH HE DOES NOT 389 MARCOM
NOTICE
HE GIVES THE BABY ONE YEN TO START A SAVINGS 389 MARCOM
ACCOUNT AND ENCOURAGE ITS THRIFT.
THE PRINCESS AWAKES WITH A START.) 402 MARCOM
TO START IN ON RIDDLES JUST AT THE LAST MOMENT/ 406 MARCOM
DON'T START GETTING MORBID/ 412 MARCOM
(WITH A START, COMES TO HIMSELF AND BACKS AWAY 415 MARCOM
FROM THE PRINCESS IN TERROR)
A&D, AS THE MUSICIANS, OBEYING THIS SIGNAL, START 429 MARCOM
UP A GREAT BLARE,
(A FEW HUNGRY GUESTS START TO EAT. 431 MARCOM
(IMPATIENTLY) DON'T START PREACHING, LIKE YOU 8 MISBEG
LOVE TO, OR YOU'LL NEVER GO.
NOW DON'T START RAGING AGAIN, FATHER. 13 MISBEG
SO DON'T YOU START PREACHING TOO. 19 MISBEG
AND WE'D START DRINKING AND TELLING STORIES, AND 26 MISBEG
SINGING SONGS,
(THEY START TO GO IN THE FRONT DOOR, HOGAN IN THE 65 MISBEG
LEAD.)
I'LL GIVE YOU A WELCOME, IF YOU START CUTTING UP/ 72 MISBEG
LET'S START-- 95 MISBEG
THEN GET THE HELL OUT OF THAT CHAIR AND LET'S 96 MISBEG
START IT/
YOU START THE FIGHT. 99 MISBEG
ESPECIALLY WHEN HE'S NUTTY WITH GRIEF TO START 145 MISBEG
WITH.

START

START (CONT'D.)		
THIS IS THE ONLY WAY HE CAN START TELLING THE	146	MISBEG
STORY)		
CHRIST, IN A MINUTE YOU'LL START SINGING +MOTHER	148	MISBEG
MACKEE+/*		
I DON'T WANT YOU AROUND TO START SOME NEW SCHEME. 164		MISBEG
AND IT'S TIME FOR ME TO START WORK, NOT GO TO BED.172		MISBEG
HE HAD EDUCATION ABOVE MOST YANKS, AND HE HAD	27	POET
MONEY ENOUGH TO START HIM,		
AND START A LOT OF EVIL-MINDED GOSSIP.	110	POET
I'LL START HER ON HER WAY BY MAKING HER A WEDDING 173		POET
PRESENT AV THE MAJOR'S PLACE		
HALFS, AND YUH KI+ START THE ROTTEN FARM GOIN'	600	ROPE
AGEN		
I MUST START WORK TOMORROW...	5	STRANG
I'LL KNOW HOW TO START IN LIVING MY OWN LIFE	18	STRANG
AGAIN/		
(GIVES A START, AWAKENING FROM HIS DREAM)	31	STRANG
(AS HE GIVES A WINCING START)	44	STRANG
(SHE GIVES A START AND INSTINCTIVELY COVERS THE	50	STRANG
LETTER WITH HER HAND.)		
(WITH A GUILTY START--PROTESTINGLY)	54	STRANG
(IGOT TO START IN TO TELL HER...	57	STRANG
(GUSH), I OUGHT TO TRY AND GET A NEW START ON THIS 68		STRANG
BEFORE IT'S TIME...)		
IT'S ONLY WHEN I START THINKING, I BEGIN TO	91	STRANG
DOUBT....)		
(WITH A START--SHARPLY) WHYS	94	STRANG
I'M GOING TO START IN TRAINING HIM AS SOON AS HE'S120		STRANG
OLD ENOUGH--		
START HIS OWN FIRM I'M GOING TO FURNISH THE	128	STRANG
CAPITAL		
HE'S +0 SOONER HERE THAN I START...	134	STRANG
(PULLING OUT HIS WATCH) SOON BE TIME FOR THE	160	STRANG
START.		
THEY OUGHT TO BE LINED UP AT THE START ANY MINUTE 161		STRANG
NUN.		
TIME FOR THE START.	163	STRANG
YOU MUSTN'T START FEELING BITTER TOWARD HER.	185	STRANG
I'LL HAVE TO START AT THE BOTTOM BUT I'LL GET TO	189	STRANG
THE TOP IN A HURRY.		
(OLSON COMES TO HIMSELF WITH A START AND SHUTS THESO4		VOYAGE
DOOR.)		
(WITH A GUILTY START) I--I'M TIRED OUT.	450	WELDED
BETTER START ON YOUR PART--ONLY DON'T YOU OVERDO	451	WELDED
IT, TOO.		
(WITH A START--EVIDENTLY ANSWERING SOME TRAIN OF	471	WELDED
THOUGHT IN		
(SHE GETS UP TO START UNDRESSING.	474	WELDED
(WITH AN INVOLUNTARY START) UH/	482	WELDED
(TURNS AWAY WITH A START OF PAIN)	484	WELDED
STARTED		
WE'VE GRUB ENOUGH HARDLY TO LAST OUT THE VOYAGE	537	'ILE
BACK IF WE STARTED NOW.		
HOW LONG WOULD IT TAKE US TO REACH HUME--IF WE	548	'ILE
STARTED NOWS		
BURSTING WITH BOTTLED-UP ENERGY AND A LONGING TO	186	AHWILD
GET STARTED ON THE FOURTH,		
THEY'RE WHAT STARTED THE RUMPUS.	204	AHWILD
WE OUGHT TO GET STARTED SOON--IF WE'RE EVER GOING 206		AHWILD
TO MAKE THAT PICNIC.		
LET'S GET STARTED.	209	AHWILD
SO I SAID ALL RIGHT AND WE STARTED OUT.	230	AHWILD
I'D ADVISE YOU TO GET HIM STARTED FOR SOME OTHER	247	AHWILD
GIN MILL		
AND CAN'T GET STARTED RIGHT.	268	AHWILD
IF YOU'D LET ME FINISH WHAT I STARTED TO SAY/	290	AHWILD
IT WAS ONE OF THE SONS--THE YOUNGEST--STARTED ME--	18	ANNA
WHEN I WAS SIXTEEN.		
THE YOUNGEST SON--PAUL--THAT STARTED ME WRONG.	57	ANNA
LET ME FINISH NOW THAT I'VE STARTED.	139	BEYOND
THAT WAS WHAT I'D STARTED TO TELL.	164	BEYOND
(THEN HURRIEDLY) BUT, FOR PETE'S SAKE, LET'S NOT 497		DAYS
GET STARTED ON RELIGION.		
I DIDN'T MEAN--GO ON WITH WHAT YOU STARTED TO TELLS07		DAYS
ME--		
I--IT'S HARD GETTING STARTED.	534	DAYS
I'LL BET, AND IF THEM FOOLS HADN'T STARTED THIS	509	DIFNT
STORY GOING,		
BUT THEN IT STARTED TO COME IN AGAIN BLACK AS	537	DIFNT
BLACK ALL OF A SUDDEN,		
AND A WHOLE LOT OF ME WAS DEAD AND A NEW LOT	460	DYNAMO
STARTED LIVING.		
BEFORE I THOUGHT I STARTED TO DO A PRAYER ACT--	470	DYNAMO
THAT MEANS THE BLEEDIN' CEREMONY 'AS STARTED.	184	EJONES
STARTED ONE UF THE FUST WESTERN OCEAN PACKET	7	ELECTR
LINES.		
WERE LITTLE AND STARTED PLAYING TOGETHER--YOU AND	14	ELECTR
ORIN AND HAZEL AND I.		
(AS IF HE HAD DETERMINED, ONCE STARTED,	53	ELECTR
DO YOU MEAN TO TELL ME THERE'S ACTUALLY BEEN	76	ELECTR
GOSSIP STARTED ABOUT HERS		
GRANT HIMSELF STARTED IT--	94	ELECTR
A MONTH AFTER VINNIE AND ORIN SAILED STARTED IT.	135	ELECTR
WE'VE ONLY JUST STARTED TO OPEN THE PLACE UP.	143	ELECTR
IT HAS STARTED ALREADY--HIS BEING MADE UNHAPPY	173	ELECTR
THROUGH YOU/		
YOU'VE KEPT UP THE HARD DRINKING AND GAMBLING YOU 271		GGBROW
STARTED THE LAST YEAR ABROAD.		
(TRYING TO GET OLON STARTED)	282	GGBROW
WHY, HE'S A REGULAR SPORT WHEN HE GETS STARTED/*	310	GGBROW
IT'S BECAUSE I'VE STARTED TO LAUGH/	315	GGBROW
GRANDFATHER STARTED AS A PUDDLER.	220	HA APE
DE MOVE DE MERKER WHEN I GITS STARTED.	235	HA APE
I STARTED TO TELL DE JUDGE AND ALL HE SAYS WAS...	241	HA APE
HIS FUNERAL WAS WHAT STARTED ME OFF ON A BAT.	11	HUGHIE
I'D STARTED TO BE A HORSE PLAYER IN ERIE, THOUGH	15	HUGHIE
I'D NEVER SEEN A TRACK.		

STARTED

STARTED (CONT'D.)		
AND THEY STARTED TALKING, AND THE POOR BOOB NEVER	23	HUGHIE
STOOD A CHANCE.		
AFTER DINNER I STARTED TELLIN' 'EM A STORY	25	HUGHIE
AW, FER CHRIS' SAKE, DON'T GET DAT BUGHOUSE BUM	579	ICEMAN
STARTED/		
BEJEES, JIMMY'S STARTED THEM OFF SMOKING THE SAME 605		ICEMAN
HOP.		
ONCE HE STARTED.	613	ICEMAN
WHEN HE SAID THIS HE STARTED CRYING.	627	ICEMAN
HE'S STARTED A MOVEMENT THAT'LL BLOW UP THE WORLD/634		ICEMAN
WHAT STARTED DE SCRAPS	650	ICEMAN
WE KNOW YOU LIKE TO BELIEVE THAT WAS WHAT STARTED 657		ICEMAN
YOU ON THE BOOZE		
I DON'T KNOW WHY, BUT IT STARTED ME THINKING ABOUT666		ICEMAN
MUTHER--		
(HAS STOPPED CUTTING WHEN THE QUARREL STARTED--	672	ICEMAN
EXPOSTULATING)		
LET'S GET STARTED BEFORE HE COMES DOWN.	682	ICEMAN
HELL, THE SOONER I GET STARTED--	687	ICEMAN
IT'S TIME WE GOT STARTED.	687	ICEMAN
(EGGING HIMSELF ON) I'LL TAKE A GOOD LONG WALK	687	ICEMAN
NOW I'VE STARTED.		
STARTED OFF ON YOUR PERIODICAL, AIN'T YUHS	697	ICEMAN
BECAUSE YOU'D STARTED HITTIN' DE BOOZE.	698	ICEMAN
THE CLAMOR OF BANGING GLASSES DIES OUT AS ABRUPTLY716		ICEMAN
AS IT STARTED.		
THIS ONE WAS WRITTEN A YEAR BEFORE THE WAR STARTED531		INZONE
ANYWAY.		
WHAT STARTED US ON THISS	33	JOURNE
I DID PUT EDMUND WISE TO THINGS, BUT NOT UNTIL I	34	JOURNE
SAW HE'D STARTED TO RAISE HELL.		
THEY'VE STARTED CLIPPING THE HEDGE.	43	JOURNE
SHE'S JUST STARTED.	78	JOURNE
(TRYING AGAIN TO GET HIS APPEAL STARTED.)	92	JOURNE
YOU-- YOU'RE ONLY JUST STARTED. YOU CAN STILL	92	JOURNE
STOP.		
SHE MUST HAVE STARTED DOWN AND THEN TURNED BACK.	139	JOURNE
SHE ALWAYS STARTED AGAIN.	141	JOURNE
NO ONE IS PROUDER YOU'VE STARTED TO MAKE GOOD.	164	JOURNE
AND IT WAS YOUR BEING BORN THAT STARTED MAMA ON	166	JOURNE
DOPE.		
YOU STARTED SLEEPING IN YOUR OWN ROOM AWAY FROM	80	MANSNS
ME--		
IF YOU KNEW HOW UNHAPPY AND UGLY I'VE FELT SINCE	87	MANSNS
YOU STARTED SLEEPING ALONE--		
BUT SINCE HE STARTED PLAYING NAPOLEON TO SHOW OFF 142		MANSNS
HIS GENIUS TO YOU,		
A RUMOR STARTED AMONG THE MANY DEFEATED ENEMIES	156	MANSNS
WE SAW THAT SO CLEARLY WHEN HE FIRST STARTED TO	170	MANSNS
GOAD US		
WHO HAS STARTED VIOLENTLY AT THE MENTION OF	386	MARCOM
MARCO'S NAME--WORRIEDLY) IMPOSSIBLE/		
AND THEN HE STARTED TO PREACH ABOUT MY SINS--AND	17	MISBEG
YOURS.		
HE WENT TO THE INN AND STARTED DRINKING WHISKEY.	82	MISBEG
HE STARTED TALKING ABOUT YOU, AS IF YOU WAS ON HIS 87		MISBEG
MIND, WORRYING HIM--		
BE GOD, I THOUGHT YOU'D STARTED PLAYING VIRGIN	94	MISBEG
WITH ME		
I BORROWED SOME MONEY ON MY SHARE OF THE ESTATE,	143	MISBEG
AND STARTED GOING TO TRACKS.		
YOU'VE GOT ME STARTED.	146	MISBEG
(LOWERING HER VOICE.) SHE STARTED TALKING THE	79	POET
SECOND SHE GOT IN THE DOOR.		
THAN ANY NIGHT SINCE THIS SHEREEN STARTED/	134	POET
IT WAS SIMON SPOKE FIRST, AND ONCE HE STARTED,	144	POET
THEN HE STARTED TO SHUT THE DOOR.	155	POET
I MUST FINISH WHAT I STARTED TO SAY, FATHER.	14	STRANG
CONSIDERING HE'S JUST STARTED IN THE ADVERTISING	38	STRANG
GAME--		
AND HERE AND THERE HAS STARTED TO PEEL BACK WHERE	48	STRANG
THE STRIPS JOIN.		
I'VE ONLY JUST STARTED.	54	STRANG
OR HAD A HEADACHE, OR BUMPED HIS HEAD, OR STARTED	60	STRANG
CRYING.		
YOU STARTED OFF SO WELL...	67	STRANG
ONLY WAY TO GET HIM STARTED DOING ANYTHING.....)	77	STRANG
UH, I HAVEN'T EVEN STARTED YET.	121	STRANG
THE HAS STARTED TO GO TO HER.	126	STRANG
I WANTED TO PUT UP ALL THE MONEY TO BACK SAM WHEN 146		STRANG
HE STARTED.		
HE CAN'T GET STARTED ON ANYTHING UNLESS HE'S	155	STRANG
PUSHED.		
WHAT I STARTED TO SAY WAS,	170	STRANG
HE STARTED THROWING STONES INTO HIM AS IF HE WERE 171		STRANG
DRINKING AGAINST TIME.		
YES, AND WE OUGHT TO GET STARTED SOON.	188	STRANG
STARTEDLY		
(STARTEDLY) SSSSH/ I HEAR IT AGAIN.	357	MARCOM
STARTER		
HE'S ALWAYS LAPPED UP A GOOD STARTER ON HIS WAY	618	ICEMAN
HERE.		
(BOLDLY AGAIN) BUT HERE'S FOR A STARTER.	103	MISBEG
STARTIN'		
I COULD SEE IT STARTIN' TODAY.	542	'ILE
DIVIL TAKE ME IF I'M NOT STARTIN' TO BLUBBER LOIKE480		CARDIF
AN AULD WOMAN.		
IF YE'RE STARTIN' T' HOOF IT T' CALIFORNI-A	214	DESIRE
HE'S STARTIN' THE FIRE.	215	DESIRE
SUN'S STARTIN' WITH US FUR THE GOLDEN WEST.	218	DESIRE
AN' WE'RE STARTIN' OUT FUR THE GOLD FIELDS O'	223	DESIRE
CALIFORNI-A/		
I WONDER IF OEYTS'S STARTIN' AFTER ME+	188	EJONES
JEES, HARRY'S STARTIN' ACROSS DE STREET/	689	ICEMAN
STARTING		
LIKE A SPRINTER RELEASED BY THE STARTING SHOT.)	186	AHWILD
(STARTING UP HIS CHAIR AGAIN--ANGRILY)	243	AHWILD

STARTING

STARTING (CONT'D.)
MILDRED KEEPS STARTING TO RUN OVER POPULAR TUNES 259 AHWILD
BOOCASE AT REAR, CENTER, AND IS STARTING TO PUT 260 AHWILD
THEM ON)
STARTING RIGHT IN KIDDING AFTER WHAT YOU BEEN 31 ANNA
THROUGH.
(TEARS OF RAGE STARTING TO HIS EYES--HOARSELY) 107 BEYOND
(STARTING TO HIS FEET AND STRETCHING HIS ARMS 108 BEYOND
ACROSS THE TABLE TOWARD MAYO)
(HE STARES STRAIGHT IN FRONT OF HIM WITH EYES 489 CARDIF
STARTING FROM THEIR SOCKETS)
(JUST AS DRISCOLL IS CLEARING HIS THROAT PREPATORY460 CARIBE
TO STARTING THE NEXT VERSE)
(HIS EYES STARTING FROM HIS HEAD) 567 CROSS
(STARTING TO HIS FEET) I HEAR/ 571 CROSS
(STARTING AFTER HIM) JACK/ 563 DAYS
(THEY ARE STARTING OFF DOWN LEFT, REAR, 219 DESIRE
STARTING EYES SHOW THE AMOUNT OF «LIKKER» HE HAS 248 DESIRE
CONSUMED.)
(STARTING) ABBIE/ 252 DESIRE
(STARTING FOR THE DOOR IN REAR) 542 DIFRNT
(FROM THE FIRE HOUSE COMES THE SOUND OF A VICTROLA426 DYNAMO
STARTING A JAZZ RECORD.)
HE WALKS UP BY THE LILACS STARTING THE NEXT LINE 43 ELECTR
--OH, SHENANDOAH---
(HALF STARTING TO HER FEET IMPULSIVELY-- 48 ELECTR
BEING BORN WAS STARTING TO DIE. 54 ELECTR
(SHE IS STARTING TO HER FEET WHEN HER EYES FALL ON 64 ELECTR
THE LITTLE BOX ON THE RUG.
LAVINIA MUST HAVE BEEN STARTING TO GO ALONE. 69 ELECTR
(STARTING TO GO) AYE--AYE, SIR. 107 ELECTR
I WAS WITH HAZEL, IN THE KITCHEN, STARTING A 143 ELECTR
FIRE--
(STARTING TO GO, TRYING TO KEEP THE ENVELOPE 163 ELECTR
HIDDEN.
(RAISES HIS HEAD AS IF STARTING TO REMOVE THE 287 GGBROW
MASK)
(SUDDENLY STARTING AS IF AWAKENING FROM A DREAM, 240 HA APE
AND A BOTTLE FOR EACH TABLE, STARTING WITH LARRY'S619 ICEMAN
TABLE.
HERE'S THE REVOLUTION STARTING ON ALL SIDES OF YOU634 ICEMAN
AND YOU'RE SLEEPING THROUGH
HARRY'S STARTING DOWN WITH JIMMY. 653 ICEMAN
HE'S STARTING TO GET FOXY NOW AND THINKS HE'LL 717 ICEMAN
PLEAD INSANITY.
IF YOU'RE STARTING THAT STUFF AGAIN, I'LL BEAT IT. 26 JOURNE
(STARTING TO LAUGH) LAUGH/ 369 LAZARU
YOU'D THINK THIS WAS SOME INTRICATE INTRIGUE YOU 94 MANSNS
WERE STARTING.
(ABRUPTLY OVERCOME BY A PANIC OF DREAD, STARTING 102 MANSNS
TO HER FEET.)
YOU WERE STARTING TO REMEMBER A FAIRY TALE. 110 MANSNS
WHEN SHE WAS STARTING TO DESCEND THE STEEP FRONT 179 MANSNS
STAIRS, IF--
A SNAKE IS STARTING TO CRAWL FROM THE BASKET IN 369 MARCOM
FRONT OF HIM.
(STARTING TO HER FEET--DESPERATELY) 385 MARCOM
(HERE JUST AS MARCO IS HEARD STARTING TO SPEAK, 389 MARCOM
(ANGRILY--STARTING FOR THE FRONT DOOR) 73 MISBEG
(THEN ABRUPTLY, STARTING FOR THE SCREEN DOOR AT 97 MISBEG
LEFT)
STARTING TO PACE UP AND DOWN.) 124 POET
STARTING WITH A BURST OF CONFIDENCE EACH TIME, 70 STRANG
THEN....)
A MOMENT LATER HIS MOTOR IS HEARD STARTING--DIES 107 STRANG
AWAY.)
BUT I WAS STARTING TO SAY HOW SAM HAD MISSED YOU, 127 STRANG
DARRELL.
AND STARTING THE STATION AT ANTIGU... 139 STRANG
(STARTING TO GET UP--WORRIEDLY) 507 VOYAGE
WE'RE NOT «STARTING SOMETHING» NOW, ARE WE--AFTER 447 WELDED
OUR PROMISES
(HE FORCES A SMILE) YOU SEE, I'M ALREADY STARTING467 WELOED
TO NURSE ALONG
(STARTING--WITH WILD SCORN) DO YOU THINK I--/ 473 WELDED
(STARTING UP FROM HIS CHAIR AND TRYING TO TAKE HER485 WELDED
IN HIS ARMS--EXULTANTLY)

STARTLED
MRS. KEENEY APPEARS IN THE DOORWAY IN REAR AND 544 'ILE
LOOKS ON WITH STARTLED EYES.
HE LOOKS A BIT STARTLED STILL. 193 AHWILD
(RICHARD IS STARTLED AND SHOCKED BY THIS CURSE AND238 AHWILD
LOOKS DOWN AT THE TABLE)
(STARTLED--SHEEPISHLY) AW, DON'T GO DRAGGING THAT272 AHWILD
UP, UNCLE SID.
(STARTLED--IN APPREHENSIVE CONFUSION) 10 ANNA
(CHRIS GIVES A STARTLED EXCLAMATION) 29 ANNA
ANNA JUMPS TO HER FEET WITH A STARTLED EXCLAMATION 63 ANNA
AND LOOKS TOWARD THE DOOR
(STARTLED) WHAT--THEN YOU'RE GOING--HONESTS 72 ANNA
(THEY BREAK AWAY FROM EACH OTHER WITH STARTLED 77 ANNA
EXCLAMATIONS.)
(STARTLED) HELLO, RUTH/ 87 BEYOND
(WITH A STARTLED CRY WHEN HIS BROTHER APPEARS 101 BEYOND
BEFORE HIM SO SUDDENLY)
(RUTH IS STARTLED. 119 BEYOND
(A BIT STARTLED--GAZING AROUND HIM IN 556 CROSS
EMBARRASSMENT)
(STARTLED, TURNS TO STARE AT JOHN. 501 DAYS
(STARTLED) IS 507 DAYS
(STARTLED--FRIGHTENEDLY) DON'T/ 522 DAYS
(STARTLED--SMACKS HIS LIPS) I AIR HUNGRY/ 205 DESIRE
(THEY TURN, STARTLED, AND STARE AT HIM. 205 DESIRE
(STARTLED, STARES AT HIM WITH HATRED FOR A 254 DESIRE
MOMENT--THEN DULLY)
(THEY SEPARATE WITH STARTLED EXCLAMATIONS. 498 DIFRNT
(STARTLED) (GUILTY$... 446 DYNAMO

STARTLEDLY

STARTLED (CONT'D.)
MRS. FIFE TURNS AND GIVES A STARTLED EXCLAMATION 457 DYNAMO
AS SHE RECOGNIZES HIM.
(STARTLED--LOOKS AT HER WITH GROWING INTEREST) 458 DYNAMO
(STARTLED OUT OF HIS THOUGHTS, AT FIRST FROWNS, 468 DYNAMO
HE HAS STARTLED AND TERRIFIED JENNINGS BY THE 487 DYNAMO
THROAT
THERE IS A STARTLED CRY FROM MRS. FIFE AS SHE RUNS489 DYNAMO
TO THE BODY.
(STARTLED TO ALERTNESS, BUT PRESERVING THE SAME 182 EJONES
CARELESS TUNE)
(STARTLED, GLANCES AT HIM UNEASILY) 15 ELECTR
(STARTLED--AGITATEDLY) FATHER$ 19 ELECTR
(STARTLED AGAIN--STARING AT HER UNEASILY) 24 ELECTR
D (STARTLED) ABOUT ADAMS 35 ELECTR
THEY SEPARATE, STARTLED.) 56 ELECTR
STARTLED BY CHRISTINE'S COLLAPSE, 64 ELECTR
(STARES UP, STARTLED IN HIS TURN AND MOMENTARILY 104 ELECTR
SOBERED--HASTILY)
(NOTICING CYREL AND BROWN--STARTLED) 321 GGBROW
THE MEN STARE AT HIM, STARTLED AND IMPRESSED IN 213 HA APE
SPITE OF THEMSELVES)
(SUDDENLY HE LOOKS STARTLED. 714 ICEMAN
(ALL ARE STARTLED AND LOOK AT HIM WONDERINGLY.) 514 INZONE
(STARTLED BY HIS FALL, TERRIFIED. 311 LAZARU
HE STEPS BACK WITH A STARTLED EXCLAMATION. 327 LAZARU
HE GIVES A STARTLED GASP AND SHRINKS BACK, 340 LAZARU
CALLING)
(STARTLED AND REPELLED.) MOTHER/ 13 MANSNS
AS HE SEES HER FACE, GADSBY CANNOT RESTRAIN A 27 MANSNS
STARTLED EXCLAMATION.
HE IS STARTLED BY A HUBBUB FROM THE FLOOR ABOVE, 43 MANSNS
(STARTLED AND REPELLED.) SIMON/ 80 MANSNS
(STARTLED--RESENTFUL AND UNEASY.) 104 MANSNS
(STARTLED.) THEN I DO NOT CARE TO HEAR-- 110 MANSNS
(STARTLED AND UNABLE TO CONCEAL AN UPRUSH OF 132 MANSNS
JEALOUS HATE.)
(STARTLED AND BEWILDERED AS IF ONLY HALF AWAKENED 144 MANSNS
FROM A DREAM--
(THEY BOTH WHIRL ON HIM WITH STARTLED GASPS OF 172 MANSNS
TERROR
THEY GIVE A STARTLED EXCLAMATION AT WHAT THEY 350 MARCOM
SEE.)
BY ALL THE DEMONS, YOU STARTLED ME/ 350 MARCOM
WITH STARTLED SURPRISE, DRAWING HIS SWORD) 350 MARCOM
(STARTLED BY A NOISE FROM WITHIN) 357 MARCOM
SHE LOOKS STARTLED AND CONFUSED, STIRRED AND AT 51 MISBEG
THE SAME TIME FRIGHTENED.
(STARES AT HIM, TOO STARTLED AND BEWILDERED TO BE 121 MISBEG
ANGRY.
(STARTLED--VINDICTIVELY) SO HE ADMITTED IT, DID 135 MISBEG
HE$
IN SPITE OF HIMSELF, HE IS STARTLED--IN AN AWED, 158 MISBEG
ALMOST FRIGHTENED WHISPER)
FOR A MOMENT HIS FACE HAS AN ABSURDLY STARTLED, 68 POET
STUPID LOOK.
SHE IS STARTLED AND CAUGHT OFF GUARD. 69 POET
(STARTLED, REPEATS STUPIDLY.) 92 POET
(STARTLED FROM HIS THOUGHTS, BECOMES AT ONCE THE 101 POET
CONDESCENDING SQUIRE--
(ABRUPTLY COMES OUT OF HER PREOCCUPATION, STARTLED148 POET
AND UNEASY.)
(STARES AT HIM, STARTLED AND WONDERING. 157 POET
SHE IS STARTLED AND REPELLED BY HIS BROGUE. 166 POET
BENTLEY IS STARTLED.. 578 ROPE
(THEY ARE BOTH STARTLED BY THE HEAVY FOOTSTEPS OF 587 ROPE
SOMEONE APPROACHING OUTSIDE.
(STARTLED) OH, COME NOW/ 10 STRANG
(STARTLED) YES. 11 STRANG
I WAS AS STARTLED AS IF A MUMMY HAD DONE IT/ 41 STRANG
(AS EVANS LOOKS PUZZLED AND STARTLED HE ADDS WITH 47 STRANG
AN IRONICAL
(STARTLED--FORCING A SMILE, QUICKLY) 57 STRANG
(STARTLED--UNABLE TO HIDE A TRACE OF 82 STRANG
DISAPPOINTMENT)
(STARTLED, LOOKS UP AT HIM IN AMAZEMENT) 99 STRANG
(STARTLED--THINKING FRIGHTENEDLY AND CONFUSEDLY) 115 STRANG
(STARTLED, HER OWN VOICE STRAINING TO BE CASUAL) 145 STRANG
(STARTLED AND AFRAID SHE MAY HAVE GUESSED 146 STRANG
SOMETHING HE DOESN'T ACKNOWLEDGE TO
(STARTLED, BUT IMMEDIATELY FORCING A SMILE) 151 STRANG
(STARTLED--WITH NERVOUS IRRITATION) 161 STRANG
(STARTLED OUT OF HIS TRANCE--BEWILDEREDLY) 164 STRANG
(STARTLED, STARES AT HER--SHOCKED AND HORRIFIED-- 195 STRANG
(WITH A STARTLED MOVEMENT) NO--I--I'M--IA PAUSE. 462 WELDED
(STARTLED--THEN WITH BITTER MOCKERY) 474 WELDED
(STARTLED--WITH A FORCED LAUGH) 476 WELDED
(STARTLED, TURNS AND STARES AT HER AVERTED FACE-- 483 WELDED

STARTLEDLY
(SUDDENLY--STARTLEDLY) BUT WHERE'S RICHARDS 192 AHWILD
(STARTLEDLY) DESTROYED HIS HAPPINESS 536 DAYS
(STARTLEDLY) WHO'S THARS 212 DESIRE
(TURNS TO HER STARTLEDLY) DAMN IT, DON'T SNEAK 94 ELECTR
AROUND LIKE THAT/
BRANT LEAPS BACK FROM THE RAIL STARTLEDLY. 104 ELECTR
I WANT TO BE THE ONE-- (HE SEES HIS MOTHER-- 120 ELECTR
STARTLEDLY)
AT THE SIGHT OF LAVINIA HE STOPS STARTLEDLY, 143 ELECTR
(OPENS HER EYES AND LOOKS AT HIM STARTLEDLY) 175 ELECTR
(PARRITT TURNS STARTLEDLY AS HUGO PEERS MUZZILY 592 ICEMAN
WITHOUT RECOGNITION AT HIM.
AT ONCE THE LAUGHTER STOPS ABRUPTLY AND THEY TURN 628 ICEMAN
TO HIM STARTLEDLY.)
THEY ALL JUMP STARTLEDLY AND LOOK AT HIM WITH 634 ICEMAN
UNANIMOUS HOSTILITY.
(HE STOPS STARTLEDLY. 635 ICEMAN
WITH RISING VOLUME) WELL/ WELL// WELL/// (THEY 638 ICEMAN
ALL JUMP STARTLEDLY.

STARTLEDLY

STARTLEDLY (CONT'D.)
(HUGO BLINKS AT HIM STARTLEDLY, THEN LOOKS AWAY.) 640 ICEMAN
(THEY GAZE AT HIM STARTLEDLY. 663 ICEMAN
(HE STOPS, STARTLEDLY, A SUPERSTITIOUS AWE COMING 680 ICEMAN
INTO HIS FACE)
(HE PAUSES STARTLEDLY, SURPRISED AT HIMSELF--THEN 726 ICEMAN
WITH A
THEN THE TELEPHONE IN THE FRONT HALL RINGS AND ALL 73 JOURNE
OF THEM STIFFEN STARTLEDLY.)
THEN THEY BOTH JUMP STARTLEDLY AS THERE IS A NOISE154 JOURNE
FROM OUTSIDE THE HOUSE.
(HE JUMPS STARTLEDLY IN HIS CHAIR.) 75 MANSNS
(STARTLEDLY) CHU-YIN? 402 MARCOM
(STARES AT HIM STARTLEDLY--THEN RESENTFULLY) 42 MISBEG
SHE STOPS ABRUPTLY O4 THE FIRST STEP--STARTLEDLY 98 MISBEG
SHE TAKES A QUICK GLANCE AT HIS FACE--STARTLEDLY) 112 MISBEG
SHE LOOKS AT MARSDEN FOR A MOMENT STARTLEDLY AS IF 40 STRANG
SHE COULDN'T RECOGNIZE HIM.)
(STARTLEDLY) (WHAT'S THAT-- 81 STRANG
THEY JUMP STARTLEDLY AND TURN AROUND. 188 STRANG
NINA AND DARRELL JUMP STARTLEDLY AND GO TO THE 198 STRANG
NEAR OF THE TERRACE TO WATCH THE

STARTLES
THIS STARTLES YANK TO A REACTION. 226 HA APE
THIS INTERRUPTION STARTLES THEM. 672 ICEMAN
THIS REVELATION OF AN UNSEEN AUDIENCE STARTLES 58 MISBEG
HARDER.
THE UNEXPECTED VISION OF MELODY IN HIS UNIFORM 116 POET
STARTLES HIM

STARTLING
AND NATIVE RUM HAS PAINTED HIS POINTED NOSE TO A 174 EJONES
STARTLING RED.
ONE IS AT ONCE STRUCK BY THE STARTLING LIKENESS 28 ELECTR
BETWEEN HIM AND ADAM BRANT.
ONE IS AT ONCE STRUCK BY HIS STARTLING FAMILY 73 ELECTR
RESEMBLANCE TO EZRA MANNON AND
HIS MASK-LIKE FACE IS A STARTLING REPRODUCTION OF 93 ELECTR
THE FACE IN THE PORTRAIT ABOVE.
LOOK UP WITH A STARTLING CLARITY AGAINST THE SKY. 326 LAZARU
BUT THERE IS A STARTLING CHANGE IN HIS MANNER, 140 MANSNS
WHICH NOW SEEMS WEAK, INSECURE,
AND ARE MADE MORE STARTLING BY THE PALLOR OF HER 68 POET
COMPLEXION.
A STARTLING, COLORFUL, ROMANTIC FIGURE, 88 POET
THERE IS A STARTLING CHANGE IN EVANS. 111 STRANG
WHERE I SAW HIM HE WAS WITH A STARTLING LOOKING 119 STRANG
FEMALE--
SHE WAS CERTAINLY STARTLING LOOKING. 127 STRANG

STARTLINGLY
SUDDENLY AND STARTLINGLY ONE SEES IN HER FACE THE 28 JOURNE
GIRL SHE HAD ONCE BEEN.
SOUNDING STARTLINGLY INCONGRUOUS FROM HIM) 338 LAZARU
JUMPS STARTLINGLY IN TONE FROM A CARESSING 54 STRANG
GENTLENESS TO A BLUNTED FLAT
LOOKING STARTLINGLY MODERN AND DISTURBING AGAINST 66 STRANG
THE BACKGROUND OF CLASSICS IN

STARTS
THE MATE STARTS FOR THE DOORWAY.) 540 'ILE
(HE STARTS FOR THE DOOR) I GOT TO GIT ON DECK-- 550 'ILE
SHE SITS DOWN AND STARTS TO PLAY WILDLY AN OLD 551 'ILE
HYMN.
(SHE LAUGHS WILDLY AND HE STARTS BACK FROM HER IN 551 'ILE
ALARM)
NUMERALS STAMPED ON IT, AND STARTS FILLING THE 187 AHWILD
PIPE.)
(HE STARTS STIFFLY FOR THE DOOR.) 203 AHWILD
(HE PICKS THEM UP AND STARTS TO READ.) 204 AHWILD
(SHE STARTS FOR THE PANTRY.) 211 AHWILD
HE STARTS. 217 AHWILD
(HE STARTS OUT AND IS JUST ABOUT TO CLOSE THE DOOR219 AHWILD
WHEN HE THINKS OF SOMETHING)
(HE STARTS DRINKING THE SOUP. 224 AHWILD
AND EVERYONE STARTS IN PULLING THE CRACKED SHELLS 228 AHWILD
APART.)
(HE STARTS TO SING THE OLD ARMY HYMN) 233 AHWILD
(STARTS AUTOMATICALLY FOR THE DOOR TO THE BAR-- 241 AHWILD
(SHE STARTS FOR THE DOOR.) 241 AHWILD
HE STARTS AND STRUGGLES. 241 AHWILD
(REGARDS HER BITTERLY--THEN STARTS TO HIS FEET 246 AHWILD
BELLICOSELY--TO THE SALESMAN)
AND STARTS AROUND KISSING THEM ALL GOOD NIGHT.) 252 AHWILD
AND SHE STARTS AN ACCOMPANIMENT. 257 AHWILD
MILLER STARTS, THEN CLAPS HIS HANDS 257 AHWILD
ENTHUSIASTICALLY AND CALLS)
AS HE FINISHES, MILLER AGAIN STARTS AND APPLAUDS) 258 AHWILD
AND SHE STARTS ANOTHER ACCOMPANIMENT.) 258 AHWILD
MRS. MILLER GIVES A CRY AND STARTS TO GO TO HIM, 262 AHWILD
BUT SID STEPS IN HER WAY.)
(HE STARTS FOR THE FRONT PARLOR) 269 AHWILD
(HE STARTS FOR THE BACK PARLOR) 274 AHWILD
(HE STARTS TO PUT THE NOTE BACK IN HIS POCKET, 275 AHWILD
THEN STOPS AND KISSES IT--)
(HE STARTS TO STROLL AROUND WITH EXAGGERATED 277 AHWILD
CARELESSNESS,
AND STARTS RUNNING TOWARDS THE PATH. 285 AHWILD
MRS. MILLER STARTS FOR THE HALL WITH HIS HAT.) 293 AHWILD
(CHRIS STARTS FOR THE ENTRANCE TO THE BACK ROOM.) 19 ANNA
AS SOON AS THE DOOR CLOSES, ANNA STARTS TO HER 24 ANNA
FEET.)
(STARTS TO HIS FEET WITH FIERCE PROTEST) 29 ANNA
HE CLEARS HIS THROAT AND STARTS TO SING TO HIMSELF 41 ANNA
IN A LOW, DOLEFUL VOICE--)
CHRIS STARTS, MAKES A MOVE AS IF TO GET UP AND GO 45 ANNA
TO THE DOOR.
ANNA LOOKS AFTER HIM WILDLY, STARTS TO RUN AFTER 61 ANNA
HIM.
(ANNA STARTS, HER FACE GROWS HARD. 68 ANNA

STARTS

STARTS (CONT'D.)
(STARTS SLOWLY FOR THE DOOR--HESITATES--THEN AFTER 71 ANNA
A PAUSE)
(HE STARTS FOR THE DOOR--THEN STOPS TO TURN ON HER 73 ANNA
FURIOUSLY)
THEN RUTH TAKES HIS HAND AGAIN AND STARTS TO LEAD 93 BEYOND
HIM AWAY)
AND STARTS TO WHEEL THE INVALID'S CHAIR TOWARD THE118 BEYOND
SCREEN DOOR)
THEN SHE STARTS FOR THE KITCHEN BUT STANDS FOR A 121 BEYOND
MOMENT THINKING.
(HE STARTS IN PLAYING AGAIN. 481 CARDIF
(HE STARTS FOR THE DOORWAY.) 484 CARDIF
I'LL SPLIT THE SKULL AV THE FIRST MAN AV YE STARTS458 CARIBE
TO FOIGHT.
(PAUL STARTS PLAYING.. 471 CARIBE
(HE STARTS TO DESCEND.) 562 CROSS
(NAT PEERS THROUGH THE PORTHOLE AND STARTS BACK, 569 CROSS
(HE STARTS TO ASCEND.) 572 CROSS
(STARTS--WITH A SHUDDER) DAMN YOU! 494 DAYS
(HE STARTS FOR THE DOOR--THEN TURNS BACK) 497 DAYS
(STARTS VIOLENTLY--STAMMERS) 513 DAYS
(SHE STARTS TO BREAK DOWN, BUT FIGHTS THIS BACK 520 DAYS
AND BURSTS OUT VINDICTIVELY,
(SHE GIVES A BITTER LITTLE LAUGH AND STARTS TO GO 524 DAYS
AROUND THE LEFT OF SOFA--
(HE STARTS. 528 DAYS
(FATHER BAIRD STARTS AND STARES AT HIM WITH A 536 DAYS
SHOCKED EXPRESSION.)
(HE PAUSES FOR A SECOND, NERVING HIMSELF TO GO IN.537 DAYS
THEN STARTS AGAIN)
(STARTS--THEN TENSELY) YOU WANT ME TO PUT MYSELF 539 DAYS
IN THE WIFE'S PLACES
FATHER BAIRD STARTS AND LISTENS. 545 DAYS
JOHN STARTS TO PACE UP AND DOWN WITH NERVOUS 545 DAYS
RESTLESSNESS--THEN STOPS ABRUPTLY)
(HE STARTS TO TAKE HER IN HIS ARMS. 547 DAYS
(SHE STARTS AS IF TO RUN FROM THE ROOM.) 550 DAYS
JOHN STARTS TOWARD HER.) 551 DAYS
(STARTS BACK TO HIMSELF--STAMMERS WITH A CONFUSED 552 DAYS
AIR OF RELIEF)
(STARTS TO RESIST FEEBLY) LET ME GO! 555 DAYS
(STARTS TO HIS FEET--IN ANGUISH) 555 DAYS
(STARTS HALF-AWAKE--MUTTERS) 557 DAYS
(WITH A TORTURED CRY THAT STARTS HIM AWAKE) 558 DAYS
IN THE STUDY. FATHER BAIRD STARTS TO PACE BACK AND558 DAYS
FORTH, FROWNING.
(STARTS UP FROM HIS HALF-KNEELING POSITION, UNDER 559 DAYS
THE INFLUENCE OF THIS MEMORY)
I--HE STARTS FOR THE BEDROOM DOOR) 560 DAYS
(A SHUDDER RUNS OVER HIM AND HE STARTS AS IF 562 DAYS
AWAKENING FROM SLEEP)
(HE STARTS TO GO OUT.) 214 DESIRE
HE SCOWLS, STRIDES OFF THE PORCH TO THE PATH AND 228 DESIRE
STARTS TO WALK PAST HER
(HE STARTS TO WALK AWAY.) 229 DESIRE
(HE LAUGHS AND AGAIN STARTS TO WALK AWAY.) 230 DESIRE
SHE STARTS VIOLENTLY, LOOKS AT HIM, SEES HE IS NOT236 DESIRE
WATCHING HER.
(HE STARTS TO FIDDLE =LADY OF THE LAKE= FOUR YOUNG250 DESIRE
FELLOWS AND FOUR GIRLS FORM
(HE STARTS =POP, GOES 250 DESIRE
(STARTS TO DANCE, WHICH HE DOES VERY WELL AND WITH251 DESIRE
TREMENDOUS VIGOR.
(HE STARTS TO FIDDLE =TURKEY IN THE STRAW.= 253 DESIRE
(STARTS FOR THE DOOR.) 265 DESIRE
(HE STARTS TO RISE.) 517 DIFRNT
(SHE STARTS FOR THE DOOR AT RIGHT.) 527 DIFRNT
(AT SOME NOISE HE HEARS FROM WITHOUT, HE STARTS 534 DIFRNT
FRIGHTENEDLY)
(HE STARTS FOR THE DOOR ON THE RIGHT.) 534 DIFRNT
(EMMA STARTS) HARRIET LETS HER TONGUE RUN AWAY 539 DIFRNT
WITH HER AND SAYS DUMB FOOL
BUT WHEN HE STARTS IN HIS SNEAKIN' THIEVERY WITH 541 DIFRNT
YOU, EMMER,
HE STARTS GUILTILY AND HASTILY MAKES A REASSURING 424 DYNAMO
DECLARATION OF FAITH)
(STARTS FROM HIS DREAM BY THE WINDOW UPSTAIRS) 426 DYNAMO
(SHE STARTS OUT OF THE SHADOW OF THE LILACS AS IF 434 DYNAMO
TO CROSS THE STREET
(STARTS TO THRUST THE PAPER ON HER) 434 DYNAMO
(HE STARTS TO BREAK DOWN MISERABLY.) 449 DYNAMO
(STARTS AFTER HIM, CALLING FRIGHTENEDLY) REUBEN/ 451 DYNAMO
DON'T/ REUBEN/
AND STARTS WALKING OFF LEFT--WITH BITTER DEFIANCE1453 DYNAMO
(STARTS FOR HIS FATHER THREATENINGLY, HIS FISTS 465 DYNAMO
CLENCHED)
HE STARTS TO WALK HESITATINGLY OFF RIGHT-- 478 DYNAMO
(THEN AS SHE STARTS TO GO BACK THE WAY THEY HAVE 482 DYNAMO
COME,
HE STARTS FOR THE STAIRS, 487 DYNAMO
(HE STARTS FOR THE DOOR IN REAR.) 182 EJONES
IT STARTS AT A RATE EXACTLY CORRESPONDING TO 184 EJONES
NORMAL PULSE BEAT--
(JONES STARTS AT THE SOUND. 184 EJONES
GETTING THEIR COURAGE WORKED UP B'FORE THEY STARTS184 EJONES
AFTER YOU.
(HE STARTS FOR THE FOREST--HESITATES BEFORE THE 190 EJONES
PLUNGE--
(HE STARTS TO WHISTLE BUT CHECKS HIMSELF ABRUPTLY)191 EJONES
JONES STARTS, LOOKS UP, SEES THE FIGURES, 199 EJONES
STARTS WITH THE OTHERS. 199 EJONES
JONES LOOKS UP, STARTS TO SPRING TO HIS FEET, 200 EJONES
REACHES A HALF-KNEELING,
THEN HE STARTS BACKWARD SLOWLY, HIS ARMS REMAINING201 EJONES
OUT.
AND IF EZRA'S WIFE STARTS TO RUN YOU OFF FUR 8 ELECTR
TRESPASSIN',

STARTS

STARTS (CONT'D.)
(HE STARTS FOR THE STEPS--
(AGAIN STARTS--THEN SLOWLY AS IF ADMITTING A 10 ELECTR
SECRET UNDERSTANDING BETWEEN THEM)
(STARTS) OVER TO HAZEL AND PETER'S HOUSE. 11 ELECTR
(SHE STARTS AS IF TO GO INTO THE HOUSE.) 11 ELECTR
(STARTS AGAIN BUT KEEPS HER TONE COLD AND 12 ELECTR
COLLECTED) 12 ELECTR
(HE STARTS TO GO--LOOKS DOWN THE DRIVE AT LEFT) 20 ELECTR
HE STARTS ON SEEING LAVINIA 20 ELECTR
(THEN AS HE STARTS BACK IN CONFUSION, SHE SEIZES 24 ELECTR
THIS OPPORTUNITY
I DON'T WANT TO HEAR--(SHE STARTS TO GO TOWARD THE 25 ELECTR
HOUSE.)
(CHRISTINE STARTS. 29 ELECTR
(STARTS, LOOKS AT THE PORTRAIT AND QUICKLY DROPS 29 ELECTR
HER EYES.
(STARTS AS IF TO RETORT DEFIANTLY--THEN SAYS 45 ELECTR
CALMLY)
(GLANCES DOWN THE DRIVE, LEFT FRONT--THEN STARTS 46 ELECTR
TO HER FEET EXCITEDLY)
THEN STARTS PACING SELF-CONSCIOUSLY UP AND DOWN AT 51 ELECTR
THE RIGHT OF STEPS.)
(STARTS VIOLENTLY--IN A STRAINED VOICE) 58 ELECTR
THEN STARTS WITH TERROR AS SHE HEARS A NOISE FROM 62 ELECTR
THE HALL AND FRANTICALLY
CHRISTINE STARTS AND IMMEDIATELY BY AN EFFORT OF 78 ELECTR
WILL REGAINS CONTROL OVER
(SHE TURNS HER BACK AND STARTS TO GO INTO THE 83 ELECTR
HALL.)
(STARTS TO MAKE A BITTER RETORT, GLANCES AT PETER 83 ELECTR
AND HAZEL,
(STARTS UP FROM HIS CHAIR AND MAKES AN AUTOMATIC 83 ELECTR
MOTION AS IF TO SALUTE--
(LAVINIA STARTS AND HER EYES LIGHT UP WITH A CRUEL 92 ELECTR
HATRED.
SHE STARTS BACK WITH A STIFLED SCREAM AND STARES 101 ELECTR
AT IT WITH GUILTY FEAR.)
(BRANT STARTS AT THIS. 106 ELECTR
(BRANT STARTS GUILTILY. 106 ELECTR
MUTTERS A CURSE AND STARTS PACING UP AND DOWN THE 107 ELECTR
DECK)
(HE STARTS TO PACE UP AND DOWN AGAIN DISTRACTEDLY.121 ELECTR
ORIN TURNS FROM HER AND STARTS TO PACE UP AND DOWN121 ELECTR
BY THE STEPS.
HE STARTS TO PACE UP AND DOWN AGAIN--WITH SAVAGE 121 ELECTR
RESENTMENT)
(HER MOTHER STARTS. 122 ELECTR
(ORIN STARTS AND GETS TO HIS FEET, STARING AT HER 122 ELECTR
CONFUSEDLY,
LAVINIA GIVES A SHUDDERING GASP, TURNS BACK TO THE123 ELECTR
STEPS. STARTS TO GO UP THEM,
(SHE STARTS TO WORK. 142 ELECTR
(AS SHE STARTS AND 145 ELECTR
ORIN STARTS AS IF HE'D BEEN STRUCK. 148 ELECTR
(STARTS BACK AS IF HE'D BEEN STRUCK, 166 ELECTR
SHE STARTS TO RUN AFTER HIM, STOPS HER SELF, 167 ELECTR
(SHE STARTS TO GO BUT STOPS BY THE CLUMP OF 174 ELECTR
LILACS--PITYINGLY)
(WATCHES HIM GO--THEN WITH A LITTLE DESPERATE CRY 178 ELECTR
STARTS AFTER HIM)
DION STARTS BACK. 266 GGBROW
DION STARTS AND CLAPS THE MOCKING MASK ON HIS FACE269 GGBROW
AGAIN.
(HE LAUGHS WITH A SORT OF DIABOLICAL, IRONICAL 273 GGBROW
GLEE NOW, AND STARTS TO GO OUT.)
THE SAME SENTIMENTAL TUNE STARTS. 280 GGBROW
(SHE STARTS TO GO--THEN, AS IF REMINDED OF 280 GGBROW
SOMETHING--TO DION)
(HE STARTS TO GO OFF RIGHT. 287 GGBROW
(SUDDENLY STARTS AND CALLS WITH DEEP GRIEF) 287 GGBROW
WHICH STARTS UP ITS OLD SENTIMENTAL TUNE. 288 GGBROW
(SHE STARTS, JAMS OFF THE MUSIC AND REACHES FOR 288 GGBROW
HER MASK BUT HAS NO TIME TO PUT
(HE SLOWLY STARTS TO PUT THE MASK ON. 299 GGBROW
HE STARTS GUILTILY, LAYING THE MASK ON THE TABLE. 299 GGBROW
WHEN HE SEES MARGARET, HE STARTS BACK 303 GGBROW
APPREHENSIVELY.)
AT THIS SOUND, BROWN STARTS. 314 GGBROW
(A VOICE STARTS BAWLING A SONG.) 209 HA APE
(BLINKING ABOUT HIM, STARTS TO HIS FEET 210 HA APE
RESENTFULLY, SWAYING,
(HE STARTS TO SING IN A THIN, NASAL, DOLEFUL 210 HA APE
TONE.)
SHE STARTS, TURNS PALER, HER POSE IS CRUMBLING, 225 HA APE
WITH A GROWL HE STARTS TO GET UP AND STORM THE 250 HA APE
CLOSED DOOR.
(HE STARTS TOWARD THE ELEVATOR.) 35 HUGHIE
JEES, AIN'T DE OLD BASTARD A RIOT WHEN HE STARTS 578 ICEMAN
OAT BULL
(STARTS) DON'T BE A DAMNED FOOL/ 589 ICEMAN
AND STARTS BACK FOR THE ENTRANCE TO THE BACK ROOM.596 ICEMAN
(ROCKY STARTS FOR WILLIE.) 597 ICEMAN
THEN STARTS WITH WELL-ACTED SURPRISE) 606 ICEMAN
(STARTS AND LISTENS) SOMEONE'S COMING NOW. 610 ICEMAN
(HE STARTS TO GET UP BUT RELAXES AGAIN. 625 ICEMAN
(STARTS MOVING TOWARD HER THREATENINGLY) 632 ICEMAN
(STARTS) AH/ 648 ICEMAN
(AGAIN STARTS UP) I WON'T LISTEN/ 648 ICEMAN
WHO STARTS PLAYING AND SINGING IN A WHISKEY 653 ICEMAN
SOPRANO
(HE STARTS TO TURN AWAY. 656 ICEMAN
(LARRY STARTS AND FOR A SECOND LOOKS 657 ICEMAN
SUPERSTITIOUSLY FRIGHTENED.
HE STARTS HIS TOAST. 658 ICEMAN
(HE STARTS TO SIT DOWN.) 661 ICEMAN
(ROCKY STARTS AWAKE.) 667 ICEMAN
(STARTS--SCOWLING DEFENSIVELY) 677 ICEMAN

STARTS (CONT'D.)
(LOSES HIS CONTROL AND STARTS FOR HIM) 677 ICEMAN
(HE STARTS FOR THE STREET DOOR.) 677 ICEMAN
(JUMPS UP AND STARTS TO FOLLOW HIM--DESPERATELY) 680 ICEMAN
(MOSHER STARTS TO FLARE UP--THEN IGNORES HIM. 681 ICEMAN
MCGLOIN STARTS INTO THE BACK-ROOM SECTION.) 681 ICEMAN
MCGLOIN JUMPS UP FROM HIS CHAIR AND STARTS MOVING 685 ICEMAN
TOWARD THE DOOR.
(HE STARTS TO PUT HIS HEAD ON HIS ARMS BUT STOPS 691 ICEMAN
(STARTS-- IN A LOW WARNING VOICE) 698 ICEMAN
AS ROCKY ENTERS THE BACK ROOM AND STARTS OVER 700 ICEMAN
TOWARD LARRY'S TABLE.)
PARRITT BREAKS AND STARTS PLEADING) 701 ICEMAN
(STARTS FRIGHTENEDLY) EXECUTIONS 701 ICEMAN
(HE STARTS HIS STORY, HIS TONE AGAIN BECOMING 709 ICEMAN
MUSINGLY REMINISCENT)
EACH STARTS THE CHORUS OF HIS OR HER CHOICE. 727 ICEMAN
(HE STARTS THE CHORUS OF --SHE'S THE SUNSHINE OF 727 ICEMAN
PARADISE ALLEY.
GIVE A SHOUT IF HE STARTS THIS WAY. 518 INZONE
AN' THEN HE CRAWLS INTO HIS BUNK AN' SHUTS HIS 520 INZONE
EYES AN' STARTS IN SNORIN'.
(JACK STARTS TOWARD SMITTY'S BUNK. 520 INZONE
ALL WE KNOW IS HE SHIPS ON HERE IN LONDON 'BOUT A 522 INZONE
YEAR B'FORE THE WAR STARTS.
BUT THIS DIVIL'S TRICKERY IN THE DARRK--(HE STARTS524 INZONE
FOR SMITTY'S BUNK)
CLUTCHING HIS KNEE IN BOTH HANDS, STARTS HOPPING 526 INZONE
AROUND THE FORECASTLE,
(DRISCOLL TAKES THE DRIPPING BOX FROM THE WATER 527 INZONE
AND STARTS TO FIT IN THE KEY.
(HE STARTS TO GET UP.) 529 INZONE
I COULDN'T HELP REMEMBERING THAT WHEN SHE STARTS 38 JOURNE
SLEEPING ALONE IN THERE,
(WITHOUT TURNING--DRYLY.) YOU MEAN ONCE HE STARTS 65 JOURNE
LISTENING.
CAPTAIN TURNER STOPPED TO TALK AND ONCE HE STARTS 65 JOURNE
GABBING YOU CAN'T GET AWAY
(STARTS AND AT ONCE THE QUALITY OF UNNATURAL 67 JOURNE
DETACHMENT SETTLES ON HER FACE
AS THEY ENTER THE BACK PARLOR, STARTS TO FOLLOW 68 JOURNE
THEM.
(AS SHE STARTS THROUGH THE DOORWAY--PLEADING AND 75 JOURNE
REBUKING.)
(HE STARTS FOR THE FRONT-PARLOR DOORWAY.) 81 JOURNE
(AS TYRONE STARTS TO PROTEST.) 87 JOURNE
(STARTS AUTOMATICALLY ON A CUSTOMARY LECTURE.) 89 JOURNE
(HE STARTS TO PASS HIM.) 89 JOURNE
(STARTS TO BLURT OUT THE APPEAL HE NOW FEELS IS 92 JOURNE
QUITE HOPELESS.)
(SHE POURS OUT A BIG DRINK AND STARTS FOR THE BACK106 JOURNE
PARLOR WITH IT.)
SHE STARTS GUILTILY.) 107 JOURNE
STARTS TO SAY SOMETHING BUT STOPS.) 112 JOURNE
(STARTS GUILTILY WHEN SHE SEES TYRONE--WITH 122 JOURNE
DIGNITY.)
(STARTS TO WALK AWAY--BLANKLY.) 123 JOURNE
HE RETRIEVES THEM WITH DIFFICULTY, AND STARTS TO 125 JOURNE
SHUFFLE AGAIN.
(HE STARTS TO GET UP.) 128 JOURNE
(HE STARTS TO GET UP.) 129 JOURNE
(HE STARTS AND LOOKS GUILTILY.) 135 JOURNE
(HE STARTS AND FOR A SECOND LOOKS MISERABLE AND 135 JOURNE
FRIGHTENED.
THEN HE STARTS AS HE HEARS A SOUND FROM UPSTAIRS--136 JOURNE
WITH DREAD.)
(AS TYRONE STARTS TO DENY.) DON'T LIE ABOUT IT/ 145 JOURNE
TYRONE STARTS TO PROTEST, THEN GIVES IT UP. 152 JOURNE
(STARTS AND STARES AT HIS BROTHER FOR A SECOND 161 JOURNE
WITH BITTER HOSTILITY--THICKLY.)
A WALL SWITCH. AND A MOMENT LATER SOMEONE STARTS 169 JOURNE
PLAYING THE PIANO IN THERE--
TYRONE STARTS TO WIDE-AWARENESS AND SOBER DREAD, 170 JOURNE
(SHE STARTS TO MOVE AROUND TO BACK OF JAMIE'S 173 JOURNE
CHAIR.)
(THE SEVENTH GUEST OF SCENE ONE--STARTS TO 286 LAZARU
HARANGUE THE CROWD.
THE MUSIC STARTS ONCE MORE WITH A TRIUMPHANT CLASH306 LAZARU
OF CYMBALS,
(HE STARTS TO LOP OFF THE FLOWERS FROM THEIR STEMS311 LAZARU
WITH A SAVAGE INTENTNESS)
HA-HA--(HE STARTS TO LAUGH HARSHLY-- 324 LAZARU
(SHE STARTS TO GO TO HIM.) 332 LAZARU
AS HE STARTS TO ASCEND THESE, 334 LAZARU
(SHE STARTS. 342 LAZARU
(HE SUDDENLY STARTS TO HIS FEET--WITH HARSH 356 LAZARU
ARROGANCE AND PRIDE, THREATENINGLY)
(HE WALKS DOWN AND STARTS TO GO OFF, RIGHT--THEN 356 LAZARU
TURNS AND ADDRESSES LAZARUS
SHE STARTS AND DARTS BACK TO THE DOOR, 2 MANSNS
DEBORAH STARTS QUICKLY AND OPENS HER EYES 4 MANSNS
(SHE STARTS DAZEDLY. 13 MANSNS
I--I FEEL A LITTLE FAINT--I-- (SHE STARTS FOR THE 19 MANSNS
BENCH.)
(SHE STARTS AWAKE AND SPRINGS TO HER FEET.) 22 MANSNS
(HE STARTS TO GO WITH JOEL--THEN STOPS, AFTER A 38 MANSNS
GLANCE AT DEBORAH.)
STARTS TO OPEN THE OTHER, HESITATES, THEN 44 MANSNS
DETERMINEDLY OPENS IT.
(HE STARTS FOR THE STUDY DOOR AT THE LEFT, JOEL 52 MANSNS
FOLLOWING.)
I COULDN'T BEAR-- (SHE STARTS TO SOB.) 83 MANSNS
(STARTS--HER FIRST INSTINCTIVE REACTION 97 MANSNS
(DEBORAH STARTS AND STARES AT HIM UNEASILY.) 98 MANSNS
(SHE STARTS FOR THE PATH OFF LEFT. 102 MANSNS
(STARTS TO HER FEET IN A PANIC OF DREAD AND GRABS 111 MANSNS
HIS OTHER ARM.)

STARTS

STARTS (CONT'D.)

HE STARTS FORWARD IN HIS CHAIR AS IF HE WERE ABOUT126 MANSNS
TO FLY
(HE STARTS AND TURNS TO STARE AT THEM 127 MANSNS
BEWILDEREDLY.)
SIMON STARTS AND STIFFENS IN HIS CHAIR.) 129 MANSNS
(INSTINCTIVELY SHE STARTS TO PULL HER HAND AWAY.) 134 MANSNS
(STARTS TOWARD HER.) BELOVED/ 150 MANSNS
THE STARTS FOR THE DOOR. 158 MANSNS
(DEBORAH STARTS AND HALF-AWAKENS WITH A BEWILDERED165 MANSNS
CRY.
(STARTS--STARING AT HIM UNEASILY.) 173 MANSNS
(SHE STARTS OFF THE PATH AT LEFT, THEN HESITATES.)177 MANSNS
(SHE STARTS TO WALK AWAY.) 189 MANSNS
SHE STARTS--THEN INDIFFERENTLY.) WHO IS THAT 192 MANSNS
LYING AT YOUR FEET YOUR LOVERS
(STARTS AND STARES AT HER--IN AN AWED WHISPER.) 192 MANSNS
STARTS TO HIDE IT IN HIS JACKET, STOPS, MUTTERS 363 MARCOM
WITH BRAVE SELF-CONTEMPT)
THE THROWS THE POEM DOWN AGAIN, STARTS TO GO, 363 MARCOM
HESITATES, SUDDENLY TURNS BACK,
MARCO STARTS AS IF TO RUN AFTER HER ANGRILY. 375 MARCOM
(THE MESSENGER BOWS, STARTS BACK, THE POLOS 376 MARCOM
FOLLOWING HIM, MAFFEO CALLING)
CHU-YIN STARTS--THEN SMILES. 402 MARCOM
AND STARTS TO GO OUT SLOWLY WITH THE OTHERS IN THE439 MARCOM
AUDIENCE.
EXCEPT ONE THING--(AS SHE STARTS TO SHUT HIM UP-- 31 MISBEG
SHARPLY)
(SHE STARTS TO GO OFF TOWARD REAR-RIGHT.) 35 MISBEG
(SHE STARTS OFF AGAIN.) 36 MISBEG
(STARTS TO STAND UP) HELLO, JOSIE. 40 MISBEG
JOSIE STARTS--THEN FROWNS IRRITABLY) 72 MISBEG
(HE STARTS--SWERVES LEFT-- 80 MISBEG
THE STARTS OFF DOWN THE ROAD, LEFT-FRONT, WITH A 101 MISBEG
LAST WORD OVER HIS SHOULDER)
(STARTS GUILTILY AND TURNS TO STARE INTO HER 104 MISBEG
FACE--SUSPICIOUSLY)
(SHE STARTS TO GO INTO HER BEDROOM. 106 MISBEG
AND STARTS PACING BACK AND FORTH A FEW STEPS, 111 MISBEG
(STARTS--QUICKLY) I'M NOT. 116 MISBEG
(STARTS--SHARPLY) TRAINS 127 MISBEG
(HE STARTS AWAY.) 141 MISBEG
(HE PAUSES--STARTS TO SPEAK--PAUSES AGAIN.) 146 MISBEG
(HE STARTS TO GET UP.) 152 MISBEG
(HE STARTS TO DEFEND HIMSELF BUT THE LOOK ON HER 159 MISBEG
FACE MAKES HIM THINK BETTER OF
TO GET ME TO--(AS HE STARTS TO SPEAK) SHUT UP/ 162 MISBEG
(HE LOOKS MISERABLE, STARTS TO SPEAK, THINKS 164 MISBEG
BETTER OF IT.
MALOY STARTS TO GO IN THE BAR, AS IF HE TOO WANTED 15 POET
TO AVOID SARA.
(STARTS.) AH. 18 POET
(SHE STARTS TO GO TO THE DOOR AT RIGHT 35 POET
(HE STARTS LOOKING OVER THE PAPER AGAIN--SCOWLS AT 37 POET
SOMETHING--
HE STARTS AND TURNS QUICKLY AWAY FROM THE MIRROR. 44 POET
(HE STARTS TO ARRANGE HIS PIPES.) 54 POET
SHE STARTS TO SAY SOMETHING BITTER--STOPS-- 58 POET
(HE STARTS GUILTILY, ASHAMED OF BEING CAUGHT IN 58 POET
SUCH A WEAK MOOD.)
SHE STARTS TO GO OUT JUST AS HER MOTHER APPEARS IN 59 POET
THE DOORWAY.
(NORA STARTS TO TELL HER THE TRUTH--THEN THINKS 80 POET
BETTER OF IT.
(STARTS, AS IF AWAKENING--WITH A PLEASANT SMILE.) 84 POET
(DEBORAH STARTS FOR THE DOOR AT REAR, 85 POET
(SHE PUTS HER HANDS ON THE TABLE AND STARTS TO 107 POET
RISE.)
HE STARTS HIS FAMILIAR INCANTATION QUOTES FROM 116 POET
BYRON.)
MELODY STARTS GUILTILY AND STEPS QUICKLY AWAY FROM116 POET
THE MIRROR.
(SARA STARTS TO SAY SOMETHING BITTER 130 POET
NURA STARTS.) 130 POET
SHE STARTS FOR THE BAR WITH A SOB.) 130 POET
(STARTS--THEN INDIGNANTLY.) TO BED, IS IT! 131 POET
SHE STARTS AS THE DOOR FROM THE BAR IS OPENED. 133 POET
(STARTS AN EXASPERATED RETORT.) 135 POET
(SHE STARTS TO SOB. 137 POET
(SHE STARTS FOR THE STREET DOOR--GETS HALFWAY TO 139 POET
IT AND STOPS.)
(SHE STARTS AFTER HIM AND GRABS HIS ARM. 159 POET
(HE STARTS TO SOB BUT WRENCHES HIMSELF OUT OF IT 169 POET
AND SPEAKS IN BROAD
(STARTS TO RISE.) I'LL GET YOU-- 175 POET
HE STARTS TOWARD THE BAR DOOR.) 176 POET
(STARTS TOWARD HIM--BESEECHINGLY.) 177 POET
(HE STARTS TO TURN THE KNOB.) 178 POET
(IN THE BAR, RILEY STARTS PLAYING A REEL ON HIS 182 POET
PIPES
(MARY STARTS TO CRY SOFTLY, BUT COMES TO LUKE AND 589 ROPE
HANDS HIM THE DOLLAR.)
(SHE STARTS TOWARDS THE DOORWAY. 590 ROPE
(HALF STARTS TO HIS FEET--HORRIFIED) 596 ROPE
SOONER WE STARTS THE SOONER WE'RE RICH. 600 ROPE
(SHE GRABS HIM BY THE HAND AND STARTS TO PULL HIM 21 STRANG
AWAY.)
AND STARTS TO TAKE A BRISK TURN ABOUT THE ROOM. 22 STRANG
HE JUMPS TO HIS FEET AND STARTS TO GO TO DOOR-- 26 STRANG
(THEN HESITATES CONFUSEDLY)
MARSDEN STARTS, HIS FACE SUDDENLY ANGRY AND 26 STRANG
DEJECTED)
(HE STARTS, WITH A SOLEMN EARNESTNESS) MR. 31 STRANG
MARSDEN, I--THERE'S
(AS MARSDEN STARTS GUILTILY AND GLANCES AT HIM IN 37 STRANG
CONFUSION--WITH A LAUGH)

STARTS (CONT'D.)

(STARTS TOWARD THE DOOR) THINK I'LL GO OUT AND 42 STRANG
STRETCH MY LEGS.
(HE STARTS, FLINGING OFF HIS THOUGHT-- 55 STRANG
(HE STARTS TO GO TOWARD DOOR--THEN TURNS--FUSSILY) 74 STRANG
(HE STARTS FOR THE DOOR--THEN STRUCK BY A SUDDEN 76 STRANG
THOUGHT, STOPS)
(THEN SUDDENLY STARTS HER STORY IN A DULL 82 STRANG
MONOTONOUS TONE RECALLING THAT OF
(HE STARTS, LOOKS UP AT HER 88 STRANG
(HE STARTS FOR THE DOOR IN REAR.) 94 STRANG
HE STARTS TOWARD HER IMPULSIVELY) 95 STRANG
(STARTS TO HER FEET AUTOMATICALLY) 118 STRANG
(DARRELL STARTS, COMES INTO THE ROOM, PLAINLY 124 STRANG
GETTING A GRIP ON HIMSELF.
(STARTS AS IF OUT OF A DREAM--ANXIOUSLY) 170 STRANG
(HE ALMOST STARTS TO BLUBBER--ANGRILY) 175 STRANG
(HE STARTS TO GET UP. 501 VOYAGE
SHE HEARS IT, STARTS, SEEMS SUDDENLY BROUGHT BACK 449 WELDED
TO HERSELF.
THERE SHE SUDDENLY STARTS AS IF AWAKENING-- 464 WELDED
FRIGHTENEDLY.)
(HE STARTS FOR THE DOOR.) 469 WELDED
(HE STARTS AND NODS STUPIDLY. 471 WELDED
(HE STARTS, PASSES A TREMBLING HAND THROUGH HIS 471 WELDED
HAIR BEWILDEREDLY
(HE STARTS TO HIS FEET) THEN HATE WILL LET ME 474 WELDED
ALONE.

STARVATION
(INDIGNANTLY) IT'S A STARVATION SHIP. 480 CARDIF
FLEET OF MALAY CANOES PICKED THEM UP, AND FROM 559 CROSS
THIRST AND STARVATION
OF SICKNESS AND STARVATION AND I FOUND OUT THAT 26 ELECTR
WHEN SHE'D BEEN LAID UP,
AND SCREAM IN SILENCE AND BEAT ON THE WALLS UNTIL 40 MANSNS
YOU DIE OF STARVATION.

STARVE
STARVE MEN AND DRIVE ME MAD TO DO IT. 547 'ILE
AN' YER SON ALONG WITH YE--T' STARVE AN' DIE/ 257 DESIRE
AND WHAT IT FELT LIKE TO BE BROKE, AND STARVE, 145 JOURNE
(ECHOING HIS TUNE) OUR CHILDREN WILL STARVE/ 287 LAZARU
OUR CHILDREN WILL STARVE/ 287 LAZARU
I'D RATHER STARVE IN THE GUTTER LIKE A DOG/ 154 MANSNS
(THEN RESENTFULLY) YOU THINK I'D STARVE AT IT, 42 MISBEG
DON'T YOU.
YOU MEAN, MAKE MOTHER SLAVE TO KEEP HER FOR YOU, 49 POET
EVEN IF SHE HAS TO STARVE/
AND BY GOD, I'LL KEEP HER IF I HAVE TO STARVE 49 POET
MYSELF SO SHE MAY EAT.
AND WORK OUR HANDS TO THE BONE, OR STARVE ITSELF, 146 POET
STEAL OR STARVE/...)) 11 STRANG

STARVED
(ILL THE LAST MAN OF US IS STARVED TO DEATH OR 537 'ILE
FROZEN.
AND THE HANDS HALF STARVED WITH THE FOOD RUNNIN' 537 'ILE
LOW, ROTTEN AS IT IS,
YOU MUST BE STARVED. 47 ELECTR
AND I STARVED MY MOTHER'S STRENGTH TO DEATH UNTIL 356 LAZARU
SHE DIED.
THEY 'ARF STARVED THE 'ANDS ON THE LARST TRIP 495 VOYAGE

STARVIN'
ONE OF THESE 'ERE WOULD BUY SCOFF FOR A STARVIN' 235 HA APE
FAMILY FOR A YEAR/
I' HELL WIT DE STARVIN' FAMILY/ 235 HA APE
AFTER ME BUMMIN' AND STARVIN' ROUND THE ROTTEN 998 ROPE
EARTH,

STARVING
THE WAGE SLAVE GROUND UNDER THE HEEL OF THE 194 AHWILD
CAPITALIST CLASS, STARVING,
HE KNEW MY FATHER AND MOTHER WERE STARVING/ 25 ELECTR
AND AT LAST WE DIE AND THE STARVING SCAVENGER HOGS180 MANSNS
OF LIFE DEVOUR OUR CARRION/
A WEAK LAZY BACK AND THE APPETITE OF A DROVE OF 35 MISBEG
STARVING PIGS/
LAND THAT'S WATERED WITH THE TEARS OF STARVING 62 MISBEG
WIDOWS AND ORPHANS--
I'M STARVING. 67 MISBEG
TO A STARVING MAN...)) 134 STRANG

STATE
(APPEARS FROM THE FRONT PARLOR IN A GREAT STATE OF196 AHWILD
FLUSHED ANNOYANCE)
AND YOU, SID, IF YOU WERE IN ANY RESPONSIBLE 231 AHWILD
STATE,
IN THE STATE OF MIND HE WAS IN--PICK UP SOME TART,267 AHWILD
HE IS IN A GREAT STATE OF ANXIOUS EXPECTANCY, 275 AHWILD
JUST NOW SHE IS IN A GREAT THRILLED STATE OF TIMI0277 AHWILD
ADVENTUROUSNESS.
AND HE IS IN A FRIGHTENED STATE OF CONTRITION.) 284 AHWILD
BEST-PAYIN' FARMS IN THE STATE, TOO, AFORE HE GITS 97 BEYOND
THROUGH
AND TURN THIS FARM INTO THE CRACKIEST PLACE IN THE138 BEYOND
WHOLE STATE.
IN NOT LETTIN' ANDY KNOW THE STATE THIN'S WERE IN,152 BEYOND
LOOK AT THE STATE OF THIS ROOM/ 153 BEYOND
(IN A STATE OF MAD EXULTATION STRIDES TOWARD HIS 568 CROSS
SON)
HAD SUPPLANTED HIM WITH THE SLAVE-OWNING STATE-- 503 DAYS
HE IS TREMBLING ALL OVER, IN A STRANGE STATE OF 243 DESIRE
TERROR.
IN A STATE OF EXTREME HILARIOUS EXCITEMENT 247 DESIRE
INCREASED BY THE AMOUNT HE HAS DRUNK,
HE COMES UP FROM THE BARN IN A GREAT STATE OF 267 DESIRE
EXCITEMENT
IN AN EXTREME STATE OF AGITATION) 434 DYNAMO
(ALARMED BY THE STATE HE IS IN, PUTS HER ARMS 445 DYNAMO
AROUND
IN SUCH A STATE$ 446 DYNAMO

STATE

STATE (CONT'D.)
(COMES OUT OF THE STATE OF HUMILIATED STUPEFACTION452 DYNAMO
INTO WHICH THE KNOWLEDGE OF
SHE IS IN A STATE OF TENSE, EXULTANT EXCITEMENT. 42 ELECTR
SHE IS OBVIOUSLY IN A TERRIBLE STATE OF STRAINED 71 ELECTR
NERVES.
ESPECIALLY NOW IN THE MORBID, CRAZY STATE OF GRIEF 72 ELECTR
SHE'S IN/
SHE'S WORKED HERSELF INTO SUCH A STATE OF GRIEF 80 ELECTR
GOD KNOWS WHAT SHE MIGHT DO, IN HER STATE/ 88 ELECTR
SHE IS IN A STATE BORDERING ON COLLAPSE. 100 ELECTR
SHE IS IN A FRIGHTFUL STATE OF TENSION, UNABLE TO 117 ELECTR
KEEP STILL.
ORIN IS IN A STATE OF MORBID EXCITEMENT. 119 ELECTR
SHE IS IN A TERRIFIC STATE OF TENSION. 157 ELECTR
HE'S A DARNED FOOL TO MONKEY WITH A PISTOL--IN HIS167 ELECTR
STATE.
KINDLY STATE YOUR DISHONORABLE INTENTIONS, IF ANY/279 GGBROW
HE IS IN A WILD STATE. 294 GGBROW
IT WILL MAKE BROWN THE MOST EMINENT ARCHITECT IN 297 GGBROW
THIS STATE OF GOD'S COUNTRY.
DION IS HARD AT WORK ON HIS DESIGN FOR THE NEW 304 GGBROW
STATE CAPITOL.
ESPECIALLY NOT THE STATE. 591 ICEMAN
HE IS IN A PITIABLE STATE, HIS FACE PASTY, 644 ICEMAN
AND HIS NERVES IN A SHOCKING STATE OF SHAKES.) 674 ICEMAN
THAT'S WHY YOU'RE SENDING ME TO A STATE FARM-- 143 JOURNE
(IN GUILTY CONFUSION.) WHAT STATE FARMS 143 JOURNE
YOU KNOW DAMNED WELL HILLTOWN SANATORIUM IS A 144 JOURNE
STATE INSTITUTION/
THE STATE HAS THE MONEY TO MAKE A BETTER PLACE 144 JOURNE
THAN ANY PRIVATE SANATORIUM.
WHAT IF IT IS RUN BY THE STATE? 144 JOURNE
YOU CAN'T DENY IT'S THE TRUTH ABOUT THE STATE 144 JOURNE
FARM, CAN YOU?
I WON'T GO TO ANY DAMNED STATE FARM JUST TO SAVE 145 JOURNE
YOU
IF I TOOK THIS STATE FARM SANATORIUM FOR A GOOD 148 JOURNE
BARGAIN,
PROBABLY GIVE YOU A CASE TO TAKE WITH YOU TO THE 157 JOURNE
STATE FARM FOR PAUPER PATIENTS.
I'LL BET THIS STATE FARM STUFF IS POLITICAL GRAFT 164 JOURNE
GAME.
(IN A QUEER STATE OF MINGLED EXALTATION AND FEAR--319 LAZARU
HE IS IN A STATE OF QUEER CONFLICTING EMOTION, 326 LAZARU
BETWEEN YOU AND THE CHILDREN, THINGS WOULD SOON BE346 LAZARU
IN A FINE STATE/
YOU MUST ALLOW FOR YOUR PRESENT STATE OF MIND-- 74 MANSNS
BUT BEFORE I STATE THEM, 153 MANSNS
HE IS IN A STATE OF TERRIFIC TENSION, 171 MANSNS
DEAD QUEENS IN THE WEST USUALLY LIE IN STATE. 351 MARCOM
THE TWO DEFENDERS OF THE STATE. 364 MARCOM
DRESSED IN HIS HEAVY GOLD ROBES OF STATE. 377 MARCOM
HIS HONOR, MARCO POLO, MAYOR OF YANG-CHAU, SEEMS 386 MARCOM
ABOUT TO VISIT YOU IN STATE/
(IN A QUEER HYSTERICAL STATE WHERE SHE DELIGHTS IN413 MARCOM
SELF-HUMILIATION)
WHAT IF YOUR HUSBAND, GHAZAN KHAN, SHOULD FIND YOU413 MARCOM
IN SUCH A STATE?
BUT I DON'T HESITATE TO STATE THAT ALL THIS 431 MARCOM
ACTIVITY IS RELATIVELY UNIMPORTANT
THE GRAND GENTLEMAN MUST HAVE HIS THOROUGHBRED TO 22 POET
RIDE OUT IN STATE/
HE LEANS AGAINST THE WALL, IN AN EXTRAORDINARY 594 ROPE
STATE OF EXCITEMENT,
BUT IN THE PRESENT STATE OF HER MIND THE REAL AND 11 STRANG
THE UNREAL BECOME CONFUSED--
THE STATE OF HERS-- 12 STRANG
DISORGANIZED STATE THAN EVER, 26 STRANG
THE DINING ROOM OF THE EVANS' HOMESTEAD IN 48 STRANG
NORTHERN NEW YORK STATE--
SAID NINA'D GOTTEN INTO A BAD STATE AGAIN... 78 STRANG
STATE OF NERVOUS PANIC AND GUILTY CONSCIENCE. 92 STRANG
I KNOW IT'S AN IMPOSITION--BUT--I'VE BEEN IN SUCH 98 STRANG
A TERRIBLE STATE SINCE MOTHER--
(HE IS IN A STATE OF STRANGE ELATION BY THIS TIME)105 STRANG
(STARES AFTER HIM DUMBLY IN THE SAME STATE OF 107 STRANG
HAPPY STUPEFACTION--MUMBLES)
BUT I WAS IN A MORBID STATE... 112 STRANG
(THINKING IN A QUEER STATE OF JEALOUS CONFUSION) 116 STRANG
AND THIS IS HEIGHTENED BY THE FEVERISH STATE OF 125 STRANG
MIND SHE IS IN--
HE IS IN A TERRIFIC STATE OF CONFLICTING EMOTIONS,149 STRANG
(SHE'S GOTTEN INTO A FINE NEUROTIC STATE... 161 STRANG
THAT IN THE STATE OF MIND I HAD BEEN IN THEY HAD 459 WELDED
NO SIGNIFICANCE
(IN A TERRIBLE STATE, SOBBING WITH RAGE AND 460 WELDED
ANGUISH)
(IN A STUPID STATE OF BEWILDERMENT, 473 WELDED

STATELINESS
WITH AN ATMOSPHERE OF UNCOMFORTABLE, STILTED 79 ELECTR
STATELINESS.

STATELY
*BUILD THEE MORE STATELY MANSIONS, O MY SOUL, AS 148 MANSNS
THE SWIFT SEASONS ROLL/
HE MOVES IN STATELY FASHION TO THE THRONE 390 MARCOM
ON A GRAND ESTATE AV STATELY WOODLAND AND SOFT 173 POET
GREEN MEADOWS AND A LAKE.

STATEMENT
(HER MIND IS FILLED WITH PREMONITIONS BY THE FIRST137 BEYOND
PART OF HIS STATEMENT)
(THE COCKNEY SEEMS ABOUT TO CHALLENGE THIS LAST 176 EJONES
STATEMENT WITH THE FACTS BUT
SINCE HAZEL'S TEASING STATEMENT, 14 ELECTR
(MANAGING TO CONVEY HIS ENTIRE DISBELIEF OF THIS 18 ELECTR
STATEMENT IN ONE WORD)
AND CHARLIE CAN CORROBORATE MY STATEMENT, 16 STRANG

STATUE

STATEMENT (CONT'D.)
I'LL BE DAMNED IF I'LL LISTEN TO SUCH A RIDICULOUS 35 STRANG
STATEMENT/
(SHE STARES INTO HIS EYES AND SEEMS TO READ SOME 459 WELDED
CONFIRMATION OF HER STATEMENT
AS IF SHE WERE IMPERSONALLY IMPELLED TO MAKE THE 484 WELDED
STATEMENT)

STATEMENTS
MAKE NO STATEMENTS WHATEVER WITHOUT FIRST 679 ICEMAN
CONSULTING YOUR ATTORNEY.
I HAVE HAD THEM TAKE THE STATEMENTS OF MANY 343 LAZARU
WITNESSES.

STATEROOM
IN THE REAR WALL, AT RIGHT, IS A DOOR LEADING INTO109 ELECTR
THE CAPTAIN'S STATEROOM.
ORIN CAN BE HEARD IN THE STATEROOM PRYING OPEN 114 ELECTR
BRANT'S DESK.
SMASH OPEN EVERYTHING IN HIS STATEROOM. 114 ELECTR
THAT IS STUCK IN HIS BELT UNDER HIS CLKAD AND GOES114 ELECTR
INTO THE STATEROOM.
I'LL SINK THESE OVERBOARD FROM THE DOCK, ALONG 115 ELECTR
WITH WHAT WAS IN HIS STATEROOM.
(ORIN COMES IN FROM THE STATEROOM AND OVERHEARS 115 ELECTR
THE LAST OF HER PRAYER.)

STATES
SHE'LL BE LIVING HERE IN THE STATES, AND HER 47 ANNA
MARRIED TO ME.
HE IS DRESSED IN THE KHAKI UNIFORM OF A PRIVATE IN519 DIFRNT
THE UNITED STATES ARMY.
*COUNT OF THE STORY ABOUT YOUR BREAKIN' JAIL BACK 177 EJONES
IN THE STATES.
IT AIN'T 'EALTHY FOR A BLACK TO KILL A WHITE MAN 180 EJONES
IN THE STATES.
YOU TOLD THE BLACKS 'ERE ABOUT KILLIN' WHITE MEN 180 EJONES
IN THE STATES.
NOT BACK TO THE BLOODY STATES, I'LL LAY MY OATH. 180 EJONES
AND STAMPED UPON THE GLORIOUS CONSTITUTION OF 243 HA APE
THESE UNITED STATES/*
THIS OTHER JEW, THE REPORT STATES, 343 LAZARU
HAS PRESIDENT JACKSON'S FEUD WITH THE BANK OF THE 29 MANSNS
UNITED STATES
HE STATES HE HAD A LETTER FROM YOU MAKING AN 140 MANSNS
APPOINTMENT WITH SIMON.
OF A SENATOR FROM THE SOUTH OF THE UNITED STATES 390 MARCOM
OF AMERICA
OUR SPIES REPORT THEIR MANY PETTY STATES ARE 421 MARCOM
ALWAYS QUARRELING.

STATESMAN
THE LIPS OF AN ABLE SOLDIER-STATESMAN OF RIGID 337 LAZARU
PROBITY.

STATING
(SIMPLY STATING A FACT) YES. 203 EJONES

STATION
THEN I GAVE UP HOPE WHEN YOU DIDN'T SHOW UP AND I 71 ANNA
WENT TO THE RAILROAD STATION.
BUT--IN THE STATION--I COULDN'T GO. 71 ANNA
I WANT TO GET TO THE POLICE STATION BEFORE THE 449 DYNAMO
RAIN.
((HE WENT/...POLICE STATION/...THAT'LL FINISH ME 450 DYNAMO
WITH ADA/...))
I'LL GO TO THE PULICE STATION AND TELL 'EM THERE'S104 ELECTR
A ROBBER HERE--
YOU'LL GET OFF AT THE STATION, YOU BOOB, 250 HA APE
I'D RUN YOU IN BUT IT'S TOO LONG A WALK TO THE 251 HA APE
STATION.
YOU CAN CHANGE TO YOUR SUNDAY SUIT IN THE CAN AT 5 MISBEG
THE STATION OR IN THE TRAIN.
DIDN'T GIVE A DAMN ABOUT STATION. 24 MISBEG
YOU MEAN HE'D THINK HE WAS MARRYING BENEATH HIS 24 MISBEG
STATION?
IT ADDRESSES A PERSON OF INFERIOR STATION.) 34 POET
THERE IS SUCH A DIFFERENCE IN STATION. 122 POET
BUT THEY KNOCKED US SENSELESS AND RODE US TO THE 159 POET
STATION AND LOCKED US UP.
BUT ENJOY LIFE IN MY PROPER STATION AS AULD NICK 169 POET
MELODY'S SON.
BUT I'LL BE CONTENT TO STAY MESELF IN THE PROPER 170 POET
STATION I WAS BORN TO,
AND STARTING THE STATION AT ANTIGUA... 139 STRANG
I REALLY AM INTERESTED, OR I'D NEVER KEEP 140 STRANG
FINANCING THE STATION.
IT USED TO BE DRINK AND WOMEN, NOW IT'S TO THE 143 STRANG
STATION.
BUT OUR STATION IS A *HUGE SUCCESS,* AS SAM WOULD 165 STRANG
SAY.
(COLDLY) IT'S NOT LEFT TO YOU BUT TO THE STATION.192 STRANG
A HALF-MILLION FOR YOUR STATION TO BE USED IN 192 STRANG
BIOLOGICAL RESEARCH WORK.

STATIONED
THE FURNITURE IS STATIONED ABOUT WITH EXACT 79 ELECTR
PRECISION.

STATUE
THERE HE IS--LIKE A STATUE OF LOVE'S YOUNG DREAM. 298 AHWILD
IS LIKE THAT OF AN EGYPTIAN STATUE. 43 ELECTR
LIKE A STATUE OF A DEAD MAN IN A TOWN SQUARE, 55 ELECTR
HIM, BUT GRIMLY REMOTE AND AUSTERE IN DEATH, LIKE 93 ELECTR
THE CARVED FACE OF A STATUE.
YOU WERE ALWAYS LIKE A STATUE OF AN EMINENT DEAD 94 ELECTR
MAN--
HIS MOVEMENTS AND ATTITUDES HAVE THE STATUE-LIKE 137 ELECTR
QUALITY
THE MASK IS THE PURE PALLOR OF MARBLE, THE 274 LAZARU
EXPRESSION THAT OF A STATUE OF WOMAN.
HIS FACE RECALLS THAT OF A STATUE OF A DIVINITY OF274 LAZARU
ANCIENT GREECE
HIS FIGURE APPEARS IN ITS IMMOBILITY TO BE THE 313 LAZARU
STATUE OF THE GOD OF THE TEMPLE.

STATUE

STATUE (CONT'D.)
BUT AT THE SAME TIME RETAINING THE ALOOF SERENITY 350 LAZARU OF THE STATUE OF A GOD.
SO THAT'S WHAT THEY BELIEVE ABOUT THAT STONE 372 MARCOM STATUE, IS IT$
YOU'RE COLD COMFORT, SITTING SILENT LIKE A STATUE,140 POET AND ME MAKING TALK TO MYSELF.

STATUE'S
HER FACE IS WHITE AND CLEAR AS A STATUE'S. 434 MARCOM

STATUES
(THE TWO BROTHERS CONGEAL INTO TWO STIFF, GRIM- 221 DESIRE VISAGED STATUES.
LIKE THE OLD STONE STATUES OF GODS PEOPLE PRAYED 474 DYNAMO TO...
SITTING IN STIFF, POSED ATTITUDES THAT SUGGEST THE 46 ELECTR STATUES OF MILITARY HEROES.
WHERE HE MISTOOK ONE OF THE FEMALE STATUES FOR A 374 MARCOM REAL WOMAN AND--

STATUTE
I CROSSED IT OFF AND I WROTE ON THE STATUTE BOOKS 392 MARCOM
IT WAS SECTION ONE OF A BLANKET STATUTE 392 MARCOM

STAVE
(QUICKLY INTERPOSING, TRYING TO STAVE OFF THE 229 AHWILD STORY)

STAVES
ARMED WITH STAVES, KEEP BACK THE CROWD 298 LAZARU
DEALING OUT BLOWS WITH THEIR STAVES AT EVERYONE IN304 LAZARU REACH.
STAVES ARE ENOUGH. 304 LAZARU

STAY
STAY BY THE STOVE WHERE YE BELONG AND YE'LL FIND 536 'ILE NO NEED OF CHATTERIN'.
YOU'D BEST STAY BELOW TODAY. 540 'ILE
AND YOU BETTER STAY TO HOME WHERE YOU'VE GOT ALL 546 'ILE YOUR WOMAN'S COMFORTS.=
(THEN TO HIS FATHER) I THOUGHT I'D JUST STAY 194 AHWILD HOME PA--THIS MORNING, ANYWAY.
(TURNING TO THE OTHERS) MAYBE I BETTER STAY HOME 209 AHWILD WITH HIM, IF HE'S SICK.
YES, I'LL STAY, TOO. 209 AHWILD
I SHOULD THINK I COULD STAY UP TILL DICK-- 252 AHWILD
AW, MA, CAN'T I STAY UP A LITTLE LUNGERS 252 AHWILD
THE IDEA OF HIM DARING TO STAY OUT LIKE THIS/ 253 AHWILD
I'D LIKE YOU TO STAY, SID--FOR A WHILE, ANYWAY. 264 AHWILD
I MADE HIM STAY IN BED 264 AHWILD
I'VE A GOOD MIND TO SEND YOU STRAIGHT BACK TO BED 270 AHWILD AND MAKE YOU STAY THERE/
YOU STAY HERE, RICHARD, YOU HEAR$ 271 AHWILD
(CAN'T RESIST THIS) WELL, ALL RIGHT--ONLY I CAN'T280 AHWILD STAY ONLY A FEW MINUTES.
(PLEADINGLY) AW, YOU CAN STAY A LITTLE WHILE, 280 AHWILD CAN'T YOU$
IF YOU CAN STAY AWAY FROM 'EM, ALL THE BETTER--BUT295 AHWILD IF--WHY--HMM--
THEN YOU'LL GO TO YALE AND YOU'LL STAY THERE TILL 296 AHWILD YOU GRADUATE.
DON'T YOU STAY UP TILL ALL HOURS NOW. 297 AHWILD
SHE STAY ON DEM COUSINS' FARM 'TIL TWO YEAR AGO. 10 ANNA
AY WANT FOR HER STAY WITH ME. 10 ANNA
SHE'LL LIKELY WANT TO STAY ASHORE ANYWAY. 10 ANNA
YOU STAY WITH ME, PY GOLLY/ 22 ANNA
YOU STAY WITH ME. 22 ANNA
IT AIN'T GOOD FOK YOU STAY OUT HERE IN FOG, AY 25 ANNA TANK.
I WANT TO STAY OUT HERE--AND THINK ABOUT THINGS. 26 ANNA
WHY DIDN'T THAT GUY STAY WHERE HE BELONG$$ 29 ANNA
(GUILTILY) AY TOUGHT IT WAS BETTER ANNA STAY 47 ANNA AWAY.
YOU STAY RIGHT HERE, ANNA, YOU HEAR/ 55 ANNA
YOU STAY DERE, ANNA/ 56 ANNA
NO, YOU STAY HERE/ 62 ANNA
(PASSIONATELY) OH, I'D A RIGHT TO STAY AWAY FROM 76 ANNA YOU--BUT I COULDN'T/
I'D STAY RIGHT HERE AND START IN PLOWING. 84 BEYOND
THEN YOU MIGHT AS WELL STAY HERE, 85 BEYOND
IT'S HARD TO STAY--AND EQUALLY HARD TO GO, 87 BEYOND SOMETIMES.
HE WON'T MIND WHEN HE KNOWS IT'S FOR YOUR 92 BEYOND HAPPINESS TO STAY.
YOU DON'T MEAN TO TELL ME YOU'RE GOING TO LET HIM 102 BEYOND STAY, DO YOU, JAMES$
BUT YOU CAN'T EXPECT ME TO STAY AROUND HERE 109 BEYOND
AND COULDN'T IF I WAS TO STAY. 110 BEYOND
SO YOU'RE NOT GOING TO STAY ON THE FARMS 133 BEYOND
ANYWAY, I WANT TO STAY TO HOME AND VISIT WITH YOU 137 BEYOND FOLKS A SPELL BEFORE I GO.
AND PRAYING YOU WAS COMING HOME TO STAY, 138 BEYOND
OF COURSE I'LL STAY FOR DINNER IF I MISSED EVERY 142 BEYOND DAMNED SHIP IN THE WORLD.
GO TO BED AND STAY THERE--THAT'S HIS ONLY 145 BEYOND PRESCRIPTION.
YOU WANT TO STAY HERE. 149 BEYOND
YOU WROTE ROB YOU WAS COMING BACK TO STAY THIS 156 BEYOND TIME.
I WON'T STAY HERE ALONE WITH EVERYONE SNORIN'. 482 CARDIF
BUT I'M SCARED TO STAY HERE WITH ALL OF THEM 484 CARDIF SLEEPIN' AND SNORIN'.
YES, SURR, BUT IT DIDN'T STAY DOWN. 485 CARDIF
(MUSINGLY) IT MUST BE GREAT TO STAY ON DRY LAND 486 CARDIF ALL OF YOUR LIFE AND HAVE A
(STARING AT HER FIXEDLY) SO I WILL STAY--IN SPITE565 CROSS OF HELL/
I'VE GOT TO STAY HERE. 565 CROSS
AND HE WOULD LET ME STAY, RENT-FREE, AS CARETAKER.565 CROSS
NO, AS A FAVOR, STAY AROUND UNTIL THE ICE IS 500 DAYS BROKEN.
I ONLY WISH I COULD HAVE YOU STAY WITH US, BUT 506 DAYS THERE'S NO ROOM.

STAY (CONT'D.)
WELL--BUT I CAN'T STAY MORE THAN A SECOND. 526 DAYS
I THOUGHT YOU PROMISED ME IF I LET YOU STAY IN 555 DAYS HERE YOU'D KEEP QUIET.
YOU'LL STAY OUT OF HER ROOM--- 556 DAYS
(THEN IRRITABLY) WALL, LET HIM STAY. 234 DESIRE
I KIN HEAR HIS VOICE WARNIN' ME AGEN T' BE HARD 268 DESIRE AN' STAY ON MY FARM.
PROMISE ME, CALEB, THAT YOU'LL ALWAYS STAY 495 DIFRNT DIFF'RENT FROM THEM--
AND YOU'VE GOT TO STAY DIFF'RENT. 495 DIFRNT
THEN YOU WON'T PROMISE ME TO STAY DIFF'RENT FOR MY496 DIFRNT SAKE$
I'LL STAY SINGLE. 512 DIFRNT
AND O' COURSE I WANT TO STAY FRIENDS WITH YOU, 517 DIFRNT EMMER.
I WANT US TO STAY FRIENDS. 517 DIFRNT
I'LL STAY SINGLE. 517 DIFRNT
I AIN'T GOIN' TO STAY SINGLE. 518 DIFRNT
AND I DON'T WANT YOU TO THINK IT'S NEEDFUL FOR YOU518 DIFRNT TO STAY SINGLE 'CAUSE I--
(HE STANDS IN THE MIDDLE OF THE ROOM HESITATING 530 DIFRNT WHETHER TO RUN AWAY OR STAY,
YOU CAN STAY HERE WITH ME. 532 DIFRNT
YOU CAN STAY WITH ME--AND LET 'EM GOSSIP ALL 532 DIFRNT THEY'VE A MIND TO/
WHEN I BROKE MY ENGAGEMENT I SAID I WANTED TO STAY533 DIFRNT FRIENDS LIKE WE'D BEEN
THEN I KIN STAY/ 534 DIFRNT
YOU'LL STAY RIGHT HERE/ 534 DIFRNT
I'LL STAY AT BILL GRAINGER'S TONIGHT AND GET THE 534 DIFRNT MORNING TRAIN.
I'VE TOLD HIM HE CAN STAY HERE WITH ME TONIGHT. 542 DIFRNT
YOU ASKED ME TO STAY AND I'LL STICK. 546 DIFRNT
SURE I'LL STAY HERE WITH YOU/ 546 DIFRNT
DO YOU EXPECT A BOY OF HIS AGE TO STAY IN LIKE A 425 DYNAMO POOR STICK-IN-THE-MUD JUST
BUT I'M NOT GOING TO STAY OUT IN THE STORM...) 444 DYNAMO
BECAUSE I CAN'T STAY ON HERE WITHOUT A JOB. 461 DYNAMO
I'LL STAY FOR A COUPLE OF DAYS. 467 DYNAMO
(TURNING TO MRS. FIFE) YOU STAY HERE/ I'LL BE 481 DYNAMO BACK.
PETER CAN STAY A WHILE IF YOU WANT HIM TO. 13 ELECTR
I'VE GOT TO STAY HOME. 14 ELECTR
I TOLD HIM HE COULD--AND STAY TO SUPPER WITH US. 17 ELECTR
I'M GOING TO STAY WITH YOU/ 51 ELECTR
(TENSELY) I COULDN'T STAY IN. 71 ELECTR
DOCTOR BLAKE NUDGES BORDEN AND MOTIONS HIM TO STAY 71 ELECTR BEHIND.
STAY WITH ME A LITTLE WHILE, WON'T YOU$ 83 ELECTR
I CAN ONLY STAY A LITTLE WHILE, ADAM--WE'VE GOT TO109 ELECTR
THEY WENT TO BLACKRIDGE TO STAY OVERNIGHT AT THE 118 ELECTR BRADFORDS'.
(THEN GETTING UP) IF I'M GOING TO STAY ALL NIGHT 119 ELECTR
I CAN'T STAY STILL. 119 ELECTR
WE TOOK THE TRAIN THERE BUT WE DECIDED TO STAY 120 ELECTR RIGHT ON
AND A GALLON OF LICKER YOU DASN'T STAY THERE TILL 131 ELECTR MORNISS AT TEN O'CLOCK.
AN' YOU'RE TO STAY IN THE DARK AND NOT EVEN STRIKE131 ELECTR A MATCH.
HE AIN'T ANXIOUS TO STAY IN THAR LONG, I NOTICE. 133 ELECTR
I WOULDN'T STAY IN THERE FOR A MILLION. 134 ELECTR
SO I BET HIM HE DASN'T STAY IN THERE-- 135 ELECTR
ALL I KNOW IS I WOULDN'T STAY IN THERE ALL NIGHT 135 ELECTR
IF YOU WAS TO GIVE ME THE DURN.
WE HAD INTENDED TO STAY IN NEW YORK TONIGHT 143 ELECTR
YOU COME OVER TOMORROW AND STAY WITH US. 161 ELECTR
HAZEL HAS INVITED ME OVER TO THEIR HOUSE TO STAY 162 ELECTR FOR A WHILE--AND I'M GOING.
HE LEFT HOME AND WENT TO THE HOTEL TO STAY. 173 ELECTR
AT LEAST DION USED TO HAVE THE DECENCY TO STAY 313 GGBROW AWAY FROM THE OFFICE--
ONLY STAY IN THE JUNGLE WHERE YOUR SPOTS ARE 220 HA APE CAMOUFLAGE.
BE A SAP AND STAY HEALTHY. 11 HUGHIE
I'VE GOT TO STAY UNDER COVER, LARRY, LIKE I TOLD 587 ICEMAN YOU LAST NIGHT.
LET ME STAY HERE/ 598 ICEMAN
YOU'LL STAY WITH ME AT THE OLD PLACE AS LONG AS 605 ICEMAN YOU LIKE.
DON'T LET HICKEY PUT NO IDEAS IN YOUR NUTS IF YOU 631 ICEMAN WANTA STAY HEALTHY/
DE FUNNY TING IS, YUH CAN'T STAY SORE AT DE BUM 638 ICEMAN WHEN HE'S AROUND.
WAS SIT HERE AND STAY DRUNK. 645 ICEMAN
THEY'D RATHER STAY HIDING UP THERE, KIDDING EACH 653 ICEMAN OTHER ALONG.
I KNEW WHEN I CAME HERE I WOULDN'T BE ABLE TO STAY661 ICEMAN WITH YOU LONG.
LET HIM STAY. 666 ICEMAN
YUH'D LIKE ME TO STAY PARALYZED ALL DE TIME, SO'S 671 ICEMAN I'D BE LIKE YOU, A LOUSY PIMP/
=YEAH,= SHE'D SAY, =AND HUW LONG WILL YUH STAY 671 ICEMAN SOBER NOW$
STAY WHERE YUH BELONG, YUH DOITY NIGGER/ 672 ICEMAN
I DON'T STAY WHERE I'S NOT WANTED. 673 ICEMAN
LIKE A DRINK OF NICKEL ROTGUT THAT WON'T STAY 680 ICEMAN DOWN/
IF THERE WAS A MAD DOG OUTSIDE I'D GO AND SHAKE 688 ICEMAN HANDS WITH IT RATHER THAN STAY
STAY PASSED OUT, THAT'S THE RIGHT DOPE. 691 ICEMAN
I TRIED TO WISE DE REST OF DEM UP TO STAY CLEAR OF698 ICEMAN HIM.
AW RIGHT, STAY A BUM/ 702 ICEMAN
AND I'D STAY UP ALONE BECAUSE I COULDN'T SLEEP AND715 ICEMAN I DIDN'T WANT TO DISTURB HER,

STAY

(CONT'D.)

WHY DID THE BOYS STAY IN THE DINING ROOM, I 15 JOURNE WONDERS
ARE THEY GOING TO STAY IN THE DINING ROOM ALL DAYS 18 JOURNE
BUT I CAN'T STAY WITH YOU ANY LONGER, EVEN TO HEAR 29 JOURNE COMPLIMENTS.
SURE, WOULDN'T I RATHER RIDE IN A FINE AUTOMOBILE 102 JOURNE THAN STAY HERE AND LISTEN TO
(BROKENLY.) I---I CAN'T STAY HERE. 121 JOURNE
NO, STAY WHERE YOU ARE. LET IT BURN. 128 JOURNE
I HOPE TO GOD HE MISSES THE LAST CAR AND HAS TO 133 JOURNE STAY UPTOWN/
BECAUSE YOU'VE NEVER GIVEN HER ANYTHING THAT WOULD141 JOURNE HELP HER WANT TO STAY OFF IT,
YOU'VE HAD EVERYTHING---NURSES, SCHOOLS, COLLEGE, 146 JOURNE THOUGH YOU DIDN'T STAY THERE.
WE'D BETTER LET HIM STAY WHERE HE IS AND SLEEP IT 167 JOURNE OFF.
I CAN'T STAY UP ALL NIGHT LIKE I USED TO. 169 JOURNE
I BEGGED THEM TO STAY---WITH TEARS IN MY EYES/ 286 LAZARU
BUT WHEN MEN ARE KILLED I KNOW THEY STAY DEAD/ 303 LAZARU
STAY IN YOUR DREAMS AND LEAVE ME AND MINE ALONE. 21 MANSNS
YOU MUST STAY WITH US. 51 MANSNS
I SHOULD STAY AT THE HOTEL IN ANY CASE. 51 MANSNS
AND YOU STAY AWAY FROM HER GARDEN, TOO. 86 MANSNS
*AND REMEMBER THAT AS LONG AS YOU STAY WHERE YOU 111 MANSNS ARE
PLEASE STAY/ 169 MANSNS
WE MUST STAY HERE TOGETHER, TRUSTING EACH OTHER, 170 MANSNS
IF YOU CHOOSE TO STAY OUT HERE ALONE IN THE 177 MANSNS DARKNESS--
YOU WILL STAY HERE ALONE UNTIL YOU DO WHAT YOU 183 MANSNS MUST DO TO ESCAPE.
(SHE FORCES A SMILE) IT MAKES NO DIFFERENCE 386 MARCOM WHETHER I STAY OR GO,
STAY GABBING UNTIL FATHER CAME AND BEAT YOU TO A 10 MISBEG JELLY, BUT I WON'T.
DO YOU THINK HE'LL STAY ALL DAY WITH THE PIGS, YOU 10 MISBEG GABBING FOOLS
I WISH TO HELL I COULD STAY HERE/ 39 MISBEG
HE CAN HARDLY STAY IN THE SADDLE FOR LAUGHING/ 64 MISBEG
I'LL STAY HERE IN THIS CHAIR, AND YOU GO TO YOUR 76 MISBEG ROOM AND LET ME BE.
THEN YOU CAN SNEAK IN THE INN YOURSELF AND PICK 96 MISBEG THE WITNESSES TO STAY UP WITH
I'LL GET A ROOM AND TWO BOTTLES AND STAY DRUNK AS 100 MISBEG LONG AS I PLEASE/
BELIEVE ME, KID, WHEN I POISON THEM, THEY STAY 140 MISBEG POISONED/
I FOUND I COULDN'T STAY ALONE IN THE DRAWING ROOM.149 MISBEG
(TO HOGAN) GO IN THE HOUSE AND STAY THERE TILL 164 MISBEG HE'S GONE.
I WAS GLAD OF THE EXCUSE TO STAY AWAKE AND ENJOY 168 MISBEG THE BEAUTY OF THE MOON.
I CAN'T STAY ENTERTAINING YOU. 172 MISBEG
SHE DIDN'T WANT TEA AT ALL, BUT ONLY AN EXCUSE TO 18 POET STAY.
IF YOU THINK I'M GOING TO STAY HERE AND LISTEN 104 POET TO--
YES. YOU'D BETTER STAY HERE. 132 POET
I'D RATHER STAY ALONE. 137 POET
I HOPE HE'LL SLEEP, BUT I'M FEARED HE'LL STAY UP 137 POET DRINKIN',
ALL THE SAME, I WON'T STAY HERE THE RIST OF THE 138 POET NIGHT
(ROUGHLY.) STAY HERE, UNLESS YOU'RE A FOOL, SARA.160 POET
BUT I'LL BE CONTENT TO STAY MESELF IN THE PROPER 170 POET STATION I WAS BORN TO,
HE'S BEATEN AT LAST AND HE WANTS TO STAY BEATEN. 180 POET
AN' THE AULD LOON'LL STAY IN THE HOUSE, WHERE HE 583 ROPE BELONGS, THEN, MAYBE.
AND YOU STAY HERE, D'YOU HEAR, YE BRAT, TILL WE 601 ROPE CALL YE--OR I'LL SKIN YE ALIVE.
(SHARPLY) SHE MUST STAY AWAY UNTIL SHE GETS WELL. 21 STRANG
I'LL STAY WITH SAM. 63 STRANG
YOU'LL STAY RIGHT DOWNSTAIRS AND BRING THEM IN 72 STRANG HERE AND COVER UP MY ABSENCE.
CHARLIE WON'T STAY LONG IF NED IS HERE. 73 STRANG
YOU'LL STAY, OF COURSE, NEDS 104 STRANG
(THINKING) (THE MUST STAY... 105 STRANG
(WITH CERTAINTY) HE'LL STAY. 105 STRANG
I CAN'T STAY TO LUNCH. 106 STRANG
HE COULDN'T STAY. 107 STRANG
I ONLY INTENDED TO STAY A YEAR, AND IT'S OVER THAT126 STRANG SINCE--
YOU THINK I'LL STAY---TO BE YOUR LOVER---WATCHING 132 STRANG SAM WITH MY WIFE AND MY CHILD--
(IRRITATEDLY) (WHY DOES HE STAY SO LONG... 139 STRANG
IT'S ALWAYS SO WONDERFUL WHEN YOU FIRST COME BACK,143 STRANG BUT YOU ALWAYS STAY TOO LONG--
(THEN SERIOUSLY) AND WILL YOU PROMISE TO STAY 145 STRANG AWAY TWO YEARS--
(THINKING DULLY) (I MUSTN'T STAY TO LUNCH... 149 STRANG
(THINKING) (I'LL YELL THE TRUTH INTO YOUR EARS 152 STRANG IF I STAY A SECOND LONGER......
I'LL YELL OUT THE WHOLE BUSINESS IF I STAY/...) 152 STRANG
CAN'T STAY. 152 STRANG
(PLACATINGLY) I THOUGHT SOMEONE'D BETTER STAY 171 STRANG HERE
HE DIDN'T HAVE GUTS ENOUGH TO STAY AWAY FOR GOOD/ 186 STRANG
(ION, I WISH NED WOULD GO AWAY AND STAY AWAY 194 STRANG FOREVER....
THEY COULD NOT STAY WITH US, THEY COULD NOT GIVE 199 STRANG US HAPPINESS/
STAY HERE AND AVE A TALK WIV ME. 501 VOYAGE
YE'D BEST STAY HERE, ME TIMPERANCE LADY'S MAN. 504 VOYAGE
I CAN'T STAY A SECOND. 450 WELDED
(ALMOST FRIGHTENEDLY) DO STAY. 451 WELDED

STAYS

STAY (CONT'D.)
(SMILING TENSELY) WOULD I STILL BE WELCOME IF I'D463 WELDED COME--TO STAYS
I'D RATHER STAY UP AND SIT WITH YOU. 464 WELDED
(AFTER A PAUSE--EARNESTLY) THEN STAY HERE. 467 WELDED
(INSINUATINGLY) GOIN' TO STAY ALL NIGHTS 472 WELDED
I AST YOU, D'YOU WANTA STAY ALL NIGHTS 472 WELDED
YOU'D HAVE BEEN A FOOL TO STAY. 482 WELDED

STAYED
AFTER THAT, I HATED 'EM SO I'D KILLED 'EM ALL IF 18 ANNA I'D STAYED.
AND I'D HATE THE FARM IF I STAYED, HATE IT FOR 110 BEYOND BRINGIN' THINGS BACK.
JUST STAYED INDOORS AND TOOK TO READING BOOKS 155 BEYOND AGAIN.
THEN ROB MUST HAVE KNOWN EVERY MOMENT I STAYED 164 BEYOND HERE/
THAT'S WHY I STAYED ABOARD ALL THE TIME WHEN THE 515 DIFRNT BOYS WAS ASHORE.
AND TO THINK I STAYED MY HAND--/ 452 DYNAMO
MAYBE I'D GET SOME MESSAGE FROM HER IF I STAYED 467 DYNAMO HERES...))
IF I'D STAYED THE SAME POOR BOOB I USED TO BE YOU 470 DYNAMO MIGHT HAVE DIED AN OLD MAID.
WHY HAVE YOU STAYED AWAY FROM ME SO LONG, RUBES 485 DYNAMO
I KNOW HE HAS BEEN---AND YOU'VE STAYED AT HIS 29 ELECTR HOUSE--
(THEN WITH BITTER LONGING) IF I COULD ONLY HAVE 73 ELECTR STAYED AS I WAS THEN/
WOULD IT HELP YOU IF I STAYED WITH YOU TONIGHT-- 1119 ELECTR MEAN IF THEY DON'T COMES
YOU--YOU STAYED ALL THIS TIME--AT THE BRADFORDS'S 120 ELECTR
IF YOU'D STAYED THERE MUCH LONGER--THE CHUCKLES 141 ELECTR DISAGREEABLY)
IF WE'D STAYED ANOTHER MONTH, 145 ELECTR
HOW YOU STAYED AT HOME AND IDOLIZED THE CHILDREN/ 281 GGBROW
I SHOULDA STAYED ON A DRUNK. 17 HUGHIE
JEES, CORA, IF ALL DE GUYS YOU'VE STAYED WID WAS 632 ICEMAN SIDE BY SIDE,
IF YUH PUT ALL DE GUYS SHE'S STAYED WID SIDE BY 698 ICEMAN SIDE, DEY'D REACH TO CHICAGO.
ALTHOUGH IT MAKES ME FEEL LONELIER THAN IF I 85 JOURNE STAYED HERE.
I THINK IT WOULD BE MUCH BETTER FOR YOU IF YOU 92 JOURNE STAYED HOME THIS AFTERNOON AND
AND MY OLDER SISTER SEWED AND MY TWO YOUNGER 148 JOURNE STAYED AT HOME TO KEEP THE HOUSE.
AND I STAYED WITH HER TO PROVE IT, AND THAT 160 JOURNE CHEERED HER UP,
GLAD I STAYED WITH HER. CHRISTIAN ACT. 161 JOURNE
BUT MY MOTHER STAYED BY ME, AGRIPPINA WAS KEPT 356 LAZARU AWAY,
AND I'D STAYED AT HOME SO LONG I'D FORGOTTEN--BUT 88 MANSNS
I DON'T KNOW WHAT I MEAN--
I'D HAVE STAYED UP ANYWAY A BEAUTIFUL NIGHT LIKE 79 MISBEG THIS TO ENJOY THE MOONLIGHT,
BUT I'M FORGETTING HE STAYED AWAY BECAUSE HE WAS 92 MISBEG AFRAID HE'D BE TEMPTED.
AND I KNOW I WOULD HAVE STAYED ON. 146 MISBEG
I GOT DRUNK AND STAYED DRUNK. 147 MISBEG
I COULDN'T HAVE STAYED BUT A MINUTE IN ANY EVENT. 73 STRANG
I'VE STAYED TOO LONG UP HERE... 190 STRANG
YOU THOUGHT I'D STAYED HERE ALL THE TIMES 482 WELDED

STAYIN'
TELL HIM THAT YANK IS BAD TOOK AND I'LL BE STAYIN'482 CARDIF WID HIM A WHILE YET.
NU GOOD A-STAYIN' HERE NOW. 213 DESIRE
I'M MISSIN' A HULL LOT BY STAYIN' TO HOME. 510 DIFRNT
'STEAD OF STAYIN' TO HOME WITH HER. 531 DIFRNT
GUNBOAT IS STAYIN'. 183 EJONES
YOU STAYIN' THERE, TOOS 506 VOYAGE

STAYING
AND THIS EVENING I'M STAYING AT THE RANDS' FOR 191 AHWILD DINNER.
AND A LOT OF CRAZY STUFF ABOUT STAYING AWAY FROM 18 ANNA THE SEA--
BUT GIVING MY PAY DAY INTO HER HAND AND STAYING AT 38 ANNA HOME WITH HER AS MEEK AS A
YES, RUTH'LL BE STAYING TOO. 86 BEYOND
BUT NOW ROB'S STAYING ON HERE, THERE ISN'T ANY 105 BEYOND REASON FOR ME NOT TO GO.
THEY'RE DEVILS FOR STAYING UNDER WATER, YOU KNOW--560 CROSS
AND THEY FOUND--IN TWO CHESTS--
IT ISN'T GOOD FOR YOU STAYING IN THIS STUFFY ROOM 150 ELECTR IN THIS WEATHER.
YOU'RE CERTAINLY NOT STAYING HERE-- 280 GGBROW
WITHOUT YOUR STAYING AWAY AND WORRYING US TO 291 GGBROW DEATH/
IT'S STAYING SOBER AND WORKING THAT CUTS MEN OFF 626 ICEMAN IN THEIR PRIME.
I SHOULD HAVE INSISTED ON STAYING WITH EUGENE AND 88 JOURNE NOT HAVE LET YOU PERSUADE ME
BUT IF HE'S STAYING IN THE CITY, 137 POET
AND YET, BY STAYING HOME AND RESTING AND FINDING 16 STRANG HEALTHY OUTDOOR RECREATION
I GATHERED HE WAS STAYING OVER INDEFINITELY. 118 STRANG
THERE WAS NO POSSIBLE REASON FOR HER STAYING WITH 129 STRANG SAM, WHEN SHE LOVED DARRELL,

STAYS
WHAT GOOD IS GITTIN' MONEY IF YOU STAYS BACK IN 180 EJONES DIS RAGGEDY COUNTRYS
ONE OF US ALWAYS STAYS AROUND TO KEEP YOU COMPANY, 46 JOURNE
I HEARD YOU, AND AS FAR AS I'M CONCERNED IT STAYS 127 JOURNE ON.
MOTIONLESS, AND CHU-YIN WHO STAYS AT THE LEFT HAND437 MARCOM OF KUBLAI.
SHE NEVER GOES OUT AT ALL BUT STAYS HOME 31 POET

STAYS

STAYS (CONT'D.)
YOU'RE TO TAKE YOUR GRANDFATHER BACK TO THE 583 ROPE
HOUSE--AN' SEE TO IT HE STAYS THERE.

STEAD
A CANE-BOTTOMED AFFAIR WITH FANCY CUSHIONS SERVES 519 DIFRNT
IN ITS STEAD.
AS YOU LEARN, I WILL LET YOU ACT IN MY STEAD NOW 92 MANSNS
AND THEN

STEADIER
(HE POURS OUT ANOTHER BIG DRINK AND THIS TIME HIS 37 POET
HAND IS STEADIER.
HE IS STEADIER ON HIS FEET THAN LUKE. 600 ROPE

STEADILY
(LOOKING HIM IN THE EYES STEADILY) 53 ANNA
(LOOKING INTO HIS EYES STEADILY) 75 ANNA
SINGING AND LAUGHTER BECOMES STEADILY LOUDER. 304 LAZARU
WHICH STEADILY PUSHES THEM BACK INTO THE STREET. 304 LAZARU
THE BLARING OF MARCO'S BAND GROWS STEADILY 388 MARCOM
NEARER.)
ONE GROWS STEADILY CLOSER TO COMPLETE LIFE'S 402 MARCOM
THE CROWD OF PEOPLE HAS BEEN STEADILY AUGMENTED BY405 MARCOM
NEW ARRIVALS.
(THE ROAR OF THE ENGINE GROWS STEADILY NEARER NOW)198 STRANG

STEADY
(GRABBING HIS ARM) STEADY, NAT/ 261 AHWILD
AND AY BET YOU SOME DAY SHE MARRY GOOD, STEADY 13 ANNA
LAND FALLAR HERE IN EAST,
KEEPING HOLD OF THE PORT BULWARK WITH HIS RIGHT 30 ANNA
HAND TO STEADY HIMSELF.
BUT AY LIKE FOR YOU MARRY STEADY FALLAR GOT GOOD 43 ANNA
YOB ON LAND.
STEADY THERE, JIM/ 106 BEYOND
THINGS'VE BEEN GOIN' DOWN HILL STEADY. 114 BEYOND
(HE BREAKS DOWN LAMELY BEFORE YANK'S STEADY GAZE) 485 CARDIF
(FROM THE DISTANT HILLS COMES THE FAINT, STEADY 184 EJONES
THUMP OF A TOM-TOM,
DRIVING HER ON STEADY THROUGH THE NIGHTS AND THE 214 HA APE
DAYS/
HE BECAME A STEADY CHAMPAGNE DRINKER, THE WORST 137 JOURNE
KIND.
AT THE OPENING OF THE SCENE THERE IS HEARD THE 313 LAZARU
STEADY TRAMP OF DEPARTING TROOPS.
MARCO IS DISCONCERTED AT THE KAAN'S STEADY 391 MARCOM
IMPERSONAL STARE.
AND STEADY HIS NERVES. DURING THE FOLLOWING 37 MISBEG
DIALOGUE,
YOU'RE STEADY ON YOUR PINS, AIN'T YOU, YOU 96 MISBEG
SCHEMING OLD THIEF,
HE IS AS STEADY ON HIS FEET AS IF HE WERE 124 MISBEG
COMPLETELY SOBER.)
BUT IF YOU INSIST--(HE POURS A DRINK--A SMALL 46 POET
ONE--HIS HAND QUITE STEADY NOW.)

STEAL
THEY'RE LOOKING TO STEAL THE MONEY FROM YOU ONLY. 37 ANNA
AND THE OLD COMFORTING PEACE AND SECURITY AND JOY 545 DAYS
STEAL BACK INTO HIS HEART.
DIDN'T HE STEAL IT FROM HER$ 208 DESIRE
HE MARRIED HER T' STEAL 'EM. 242 DESIRE
WAAL, I'M A-GOIN' T' STEAL A WINK O' SLEEP. 245 DESIRE
WHAR'D YE STEAL THE LIKKER$ 246 DESIRE
'TWAS YER MAW'S FOLKS AIMED T' STEAL MY FARM FROM 254 DESIRE
ME.
IT'S HIM--YEW HAVIN' HIM--A-PURPOSE T' STEAL-- 257 DESIRE
THAT'S CHANGED EVERYTHIN'/
HE'LL STEAL THE FARM FUR YE/ 258 DESIRE
IF I COULD PROVE T' YE I WA'N'T SCHEMIN' T' STEAL 258 DESIRE
FROM YE--
GITTIN' ME T' LOVE YE--LYIN' YEW LOVED ME--JEST T'258 DESIRE
GIT A SON T' STEAL/
(DISTRACTEDLY) HE WON'T STEAL/ 258 DESIRE
STEAL THE LAST THIN' YE'D LEFT ME--MY PART O' 262 DESIRE
HIM--NO, THE HULL O' HIM--
NOT THE LIES YE JEST TOLD--BUT 'CAUSE YE WANTED T'262 DESIRE
STEAL AGE$--
PITY YE DIDN'T KNOW WHAR THIS WAS HIDDEN SO'S YE 268 DESIRE
COULD STEAL....
I KIN SEE HIS HAND USIN' EBEN T' STEAL T' KEEP ME 268 DESIRE
FROM WEAKNESS.
SO--YE DID STEAL IT/ 268 DESIRE
ME NO STEAL. 174 EJONES
I KNOWS YOU'SE SCARED TO STEAL FROM ME. 180 EJONES
YOU'VE ALWAYS SCHEMED TO STEAL MY PLACE/ 33 ELECTR
I WANTED YOU EVERY POSSIBLE MOMENT ME COULD STEAL/ 37 ELECTR
YOU STEAL EVEN FATHER'S LOVE FROM ME AGAIN/ 57 ELECTR
HE'D LIKE TO STEAL IT AS HE STEALS MY IDEAS-- 287 GGBROW
COMPLACENTLY-RIGHTEOUSLY.
(FORCING A SOUR GRIN) STEAL GERMS$ 296 GGBROW
WHY HAS HE TRIED TO STEAL CYBEL, AS HE ONCE TRIED 298 GGBROW
TO STEAL MARGARET$
MR. BROWN DOESN'T HAVE TO STEAL, DOES HE$ 300 GGBROW
HE'D STEAL ANYTHING IN REACH THAT WASN'T NAILED 25 HUGHIE
DOWN--WELL, I DIDN'T GET FAR.
YOU'D STEAL THE PENNIES OFF YOUR DEAD MOTHER'S 582 ICEMAN
EYES/
I WAS A FARMER BEFORE THE WAR YEN PLOODY LIMEY 676 ICEMAN
THIEVES STEAL MY COUNTRY.
IF I'VE A DROP TAKEN, I DIDN'T STEAL IT. 123 JOURNE
YOU WANT TO STEAL YOUR MOTHER AWAY, TO LEAVE ME 284 LAZARU
LONELY IN MY OLD AGE/
OR IN A DITCH WITH HIM, AND STEAL PRATIES FROM THE 20 MANSNS
FARMERS TO FEED HIM.
IT WAS NO PART OF THE BARGAIN THAT SHE SHOULD 85 MANSNS
STEAL YOUR CHILDREN.
SHE WOULD SEEM TO STEAL ALL IDENTITY FROM YOU-- 105 MANSNS
UNTIL THERE WAS BUT ONE WOMAN--
WAS A GREEDY INTERLOPER PLOTTING TO STEAL YOU FROM109 MANSNS
YOUR DREAMS/

STEAL (CONT'D.)
WHERE SHE CAN NEVER COME BACK TO STEAL WHAT'S 159 MANSNS
MINE--
THEN I'LL HAVE TO STEAL IT, AND THAT'S A WORSE 355 MARCOM
SIN.
HE'LL HAVE TIME TO STEAL A NAP BEFORE THEY OPEN 374 MARCOM
THE GATE.
YOU'D THINK I WAS ADVISING YOU TO STEAL-- 381 MARCOM
WHEN I FEEL SOMEONE'S TRYING TO STEAL WHAT'S 411 MARCOM
RIGHTFULLY MINE, FOR INSTANCE.
YOU'LL MAKE A NICE ONE, WHO'LL NEVER STEAL FROM 5 MISBEG
THE TILL, OR DRINK,
HOW MUCH DID YOU STEAL, JOSIE$ 15 MISBEG
WHO'D HAVE MONEY COMING TO HIM I COULD STEAL. 21 MISBEG
STEAL OR STARVE/....) 11 STRANG
TO STEAL MY WORK/.....)) 192 STRANG
NOW IN DEATH HE REACHES OUT TO STEAL PRESTON/... 192 STRANG

STEALIN'
(SPITTING WITH DISGUST) HER--HERE--SLEEPIN' WITH 214 DESIRE
HIM--STEALIN' MY MAW'S FARM/
SHE DON'T GO SNEAKIN' AN' STEALIN'--WHAT'S MINE. 230 DESIRE
HATE YE FUR STEALIN' HER PLACE--HERE IN HER HUM-- 242 DESIRE
YE'VE BEEN ON'Y PLAYIN' YER SNEAKIN', STEALIN' 257 DESIRE
GAME ALL ALONG--
THEY'RE STEALIN' THE CHICKENS, MUST BE. 547 DIFRNT
WHAT'D ANY GUY GO STEALIN' THIS EARLY--(AS HARRIET548 DIFRNT
TURNS AWAY ANGRILY--
BEEN STEALIN' A BIT, I S'POSE. 174 EJONES
DEREL'S LITTLE STEALIN' LIKE YOU DOES, AND DERE'S 178 EJONES
BIG STEALIN' LIKE I DOES.
FOR DE LITTLE STEALIN' DEY GITS YOU IN JAIL SOON 178 EJONES
OR LATE.
REPEATS ONE WORD OF IT, I ENDS YO' STEALIN' ON DIS181 EJONES
YEARTH MIGHTY DAMN QUICK/
THAT'S AGREED--AN' IT'S LIKE STEALIN' TEN DOLLARS 131 ELECTR
OFF YOU.

STEALING
OR STEALING FROM HIS FRIENDS, 48 ANNA
(THEN STEALING A GLANCE UP AT HIS FATHER'S FACE) 449 DYNAMO
FOR DE BIG STEALING DEY MAKE YOU EMPEROR. 178 EJONES
LITTLE BY LITTLE IT GREW LIKE MOTHER'S SOUL--AS IF141 ELECTR
YOU WERE STEALING HERS--
WHERE THE ONLY GRAFT HE'LL GET WILL BE STEALING 718 ICEMAN
TIN CANS FROM THE GOATS.
OF YOUR STEALING HER CHILDREN. 104 MANSNS
IT'S NO BETTER THAN STEALING, AND YOU HELP HIM. 8 MISBEG
YOU'D SWEAR ON A BIBLE WHILE YOU WERE STEALING IT/162 MISBEG

STEALS
HIS ARM STEALS ABOUT HER AS IF HE WERE NOT AWARE 90 BEYOND
OF THE ACTION)
THEY STEALS 'ORSES FIRST THING. 182 EJONES
I STEALS ALL I COULD GRAB. 196 EJONES
HE'D LIKE TO STEAL IT AS HE STEALS MY IDEAS-- 287 GGBROW
COMPLACENTLY--RIGHTEOUSLY.
(HALF TO HERSELF) YOUR FATHER CLAIMS HE STEALS 300 GGBROW
HIS IDEAS.

STEALTHILY
NEARER, AND STEALTHILY LIFTS A COUPLE AND CRABS 217 AHWILD
THEM INTO HIS MOUTH.
(WITH A QUICK LOOK TOWARD THE BAR, SHE STEALTHILY 239 AHWILD
PULLS UP HER DRESS--
SLINKS STEALTHILY AROUND THE REAR CORNER 427 DYNAMO
(PEERS STEALTHILY AROUND THE CORNER OF THE HEDGE 434 DYNAMO
DOWN THE STREET--
(HE WALKS TO THE HEDGE AND THEN, STEALTHILY, 462 DYNAMO
(HE GLIDES STEALTHILY ACROSS TOWARD THE FOOT OF 488 DYNAMO
THE STAIRS.
AS SHE SLIPS SLOWLY AND STEALTHILY FROM THE BED. 58 ELECTR
MOVES STEALTHILY OUT FROM THE DARKNESS BETWEEN THE107 ELECTR
SHIP AND THE WAREHOUSE, LEFT.
THEN ORIN AND LAVINIA COME IN STEALTHILY ALONG THE109 ELECTR
DECK FROM THE LEFT.
HE SLIDES HIS HAND BACK STEALTHILY OVER HIS 522 INZONE
MATTRESS AND HIS FINGERS MOVE,
SHE COMES STEALTHILY TO THE EDGE OF THE WOODS AT 2 MANSNS
LEFT-FRONT,
HE APPROACHES THE CORNER OF THE HOUSE STEALTHILY 157 MISBEG
ON TIPTOES.

STEAM
CAPTAIN KEENEY'S CABIN ON BOARD THE STEAM WHALING 535 *1LE
SHIP *ATLANTIC QUEEN*--
I--I LET OFF STEAM WHEN I SHOULDN'T. 83 ELECTR
SADLY) AYE, BUT IT AIN'T FUR LONG, STEAM IS 105 ELECTR
COMIN' IN, THE SEA IS FULL.
I'M STEAM AND OIL FOR DE ENGINES, 216 HA APE
I'M STEEL AND STEAM AND SMOKE AND DE REST OF IT/ 238 HA APE

STEAMER
SEE STEAMER PASS. 23 ANNA
DEIR STEAMER GAT WRECKED. 30 ANNA
AY SIGN ON STEAMER SAIL TOMORROW. 65 ANNA
SHE'S BRITISH STEAMER CALLED *LONDONDERRY*. 67 ANNA
*DO YOU THINK HE'D CONSIDER A BERTH AS SECOND ON A141 BEYOND
STEAMER, CAPTAIN$*
*JUST LANDED FROM STEAMER. 146 BEYOND
THE DAY BEFORE THE STEAMER SAILED 156 BEYOND
THE SEAMAN'S FORECASTLE OF THE BRITISH TRAMP 477 CARDIF
STEAMER *GLENCAIRN*ON A FOGGY NIGHT
(THE CAPTAIN AND THE SECOND MATE OF THE STEAMER 484 CARDIF
ENTER THE FORECASTLE.
A FORWARD SECTION OF THE MAIN DECK OF THE BRITISH 455 CARIBE
TRAMP STEAMER *GLENCAIRN*,
YES--UNTIL STEAMER SAIL FOR STOCKHOLM--IN TWO DAY.506 VOYAGE

STEAMER'S
THE BLAST OF THE STEAMER'S WHISTLE CAN BE HEARD 477 CARDIF
ABOVE ALL THE OTHER SOUNDS.
THE STEAMER'S WHISTLE SOUNDS PARTICULARLY LOUD IN 481 CARDIF
THE SILENCE.)

STEAMERS

AND NOW WHAT YOU GAT ON STEAMERS$ 49 ANNA
THE WHISTLES OF STEAMERS IN THE HARBOR CAN BE 63 ANNA
HEARD.
I'M SMOKE AND EXPRESS TRAINS AND STEAMERS AND 216 HA APE
FACTORY WHISTLES.
ALL DE FACTORIES, STEAMERS, BUILDINGS, JAILS-- 248 HA APE

STEAMERS'
COMES THE SOUND OF STEAMERS' WHISTLES AND THE 41 ANNA
PUFFING SNORT OF THE DONKEY
FROM THE HARBOR COMES THE MUFFLED, MOURNFUL WAIL 78 ANNA
OF STEAMERS' WHISTLES.)

STEAMING
CARRYING A LARGE STEAMING COFFEE-POT IN HIS HAND. 513 INZONE

STEAMSHIP
AY GAT DEM FALLARS IN STEAMSHIP OFFICE TO PAY YOU 66 ANNA
ALL MONEY COMING TO ME

STEATHILY
LAVINIA REACHES OUT STEATHILY AND SNATCHES UP THE 101 ELECTR
BOX.

STEEL
THE HEAVY STEEL BITS FOR MAKING FAST THE TOW 25 ANNA
LINES, ETC.
HE WAS SO ROMANTIC LOOKING WITH THOSE STEEL 430 DYNAMO
CLIMBING THINGS ON HIS LEGS...
CRISS-CROSSED STEEL BODIES--THE CONTAINERS INSIDE 483 DYNAMO
LOOKING LIKE BELLIES--
STEEL WORK, INSULATORS, BUSSES, SWITCHES, ETC. 483 DYNAMO
STRETCHING UPWARD TO THE ROOF.
THE OIL SWITCHES, WITH THEIR SPINDLY STEEL LEGS, 483 DYNAMO
THEIR SQUARE,
A STEEL LADDER RUNS UP ITS SIDE ON THE RIGHT TO A 486 DYNAMO
PLATFORM AROUND THE EXCITER.
THEN HIS BODY CRUMPLES TO THE STEEL PLATFORM 488 DYNAMO
MRS. FIFE POUNDS THE STEEL BODY OF THE GENERATOR 489 DYNAMO
IN A FIT OF CHILDISH ANGER)
TIERS OF NARROW, STEEL BUNKS, THREE DEEP, ON ALL 207 HA APE
SIDES.
CROSS EACH OTHER LIKE THE STEEL FRAME-WORK OF A 207 HA APE
CAGE.
IMPRISONED BY WHITE STEEL. 207 HA APE
CAGED IN BY STEEL FROM A SIGHT OF THE SKY LIKE 214 HA APE
BLOODY APES IN THE ZOO!
STEEL, DAT STANDS FOR DE WHOLE TING/ 216 HA APE
(AS HE SAYS THIS HE POUNDS WITH HIS FIST AGAINST 216 HA APE
THE STEEL BUNKS.
AND I'M STEEL--STEEL--STEEL/ 216 HA APE
I'M DE MUSCELS IN STEEL, DE PUNCH BEHIND IT/ 216 HA APE
AND I'M WHAT MAKES IRON INTO STEEL/ 216 HA APE
VIBRATING THROUGH THE STEEL WALLS AS IF SOME 217 HA APE
ENORMOUS BRAZEN GONG WERE IMBEDDED
BUT NONE OF THE ENERGY, NONE OF THE STRENGTH OF 219 HA APE
THE STEEL THAT MADE IT.
GRANDFATHER'S BLAST FURNACES, FLAMING TO THE SKY, 219 HA APE
MELTING STEEL,
SO I HAD TO TELL THEM THAT MY FATHER, THE 220 HA APE
PRESIDENT OF NAZARETH STEEL,
HE PLAYED WITH BOILING STEEL. 221 HA APE
THE GRATING, TEETH-GRITTING GRIND OF STEEL AGAINST223 HA APE
STEEL, OF CRUNCHING COAL.
IT HITS THE STEEL BULKHEAD WITH A CLANG AND FALLS 226 HA APE
CLATTERING ON THE STEEL FLOOR.
'E MAKES ARF THE BLOODY STEEL IN THE WORLO/ 228 HA APE
STEEL, DAT'S ME/ 238 HA APE
I'M STEEL AND STEAM AND SMOKE AND DE REST OF IT/ 238 HA APE
SEE DE STEEL WORKS 238 HA APE
THROUGH THE HEAVY STEEL BARS OF THE CELL AT THE 239 HA APE
EXTREME FRONT
STEEL, EH$ 240 HA APE
REACHES OUT AND SHAKES THE BARS--ALOUD TO HIMSELF, 240 HA APE
WONDERINGLY) STEEL.
THAT'S THE PRESIDENT OF THE STEEL TRUST, I BET. 242 HA APE
STEEL/ 244 HA APE
AS THE STREAM OF WATER HITS THE STEEL OF YANK'S 245 HA APE
CELL.)
DE STEEL TRUST AND ALL DAT MAKES IT GO. 248 HA APE
BLOW IT OFFEN DE OITH--STEEL--ALL DE CAGES-- 248 HA APE
I MEAN BLOW UP DE FACTORY, DE WOIKS, WHERE HE 249 HA APE
MAKES DE STEEL.
PRESIDENT OF THE STEEL TRUST, YOU MEANS 249 HA APE
TO BLOW UP DE STEEL, KNOCK ALL DE STEEL IN DE 249 HA APE
WOILD UP TO DE MOON.
NOW I AIN'T STEEL, AND DE WOILD OWNS ME. 250 HA APE
STEEL WAS ME, AND I OWNED DE WOILD. 250 HA APE
I WAS LOOKIN' AT DE SKYSCRAPERS--STEEL-- 252 HA APE
AND DEY WAS STEEL, TOO. 252 HA APE
KNOCK 'EM DOWN AND KEEP BUSTIN' 'EM TILL DEY 253 HA APE
CROAKS YUH WIT A GAT--WIT STEEL/
THERE'S TOO MUCH STONE AND STEEL. 27 HUGHIE
THERE'S TOO MUCH STONE AND STEEL. 27 HUGHIE
THERE'S TOO MUCH STEEL AND STONE. 33 HUGHIE
CHARRED BONES IN A CAGE OF TWISTED STEEL... 5 STRANG

STEELE'S
THERE'S A DRESS IN STEELE'S I'VE HAD MY EYE ON. 432 DYNAMO

STEELING
STEELING HERSELF FOR AN ORDEAL. 525 DAYS

STEELS
AND STEELS HIMSELF FOR WHAT IS COMING.) 293 AHWILD

STEELY
ALL THE BITTER HURT AND STEELY RESOLVE TO IGNORE 258 AHWILD
AND PUNISH HIM VANISH IN A
(IN A STEELY VOICE) I'VE BEEN THE BRAINS/ 297 GGBROW

STEEP
*WITH HEART AT REST I CLIMBED THE CITADEL'S STEEP 133 JOURNE
HEIGHT,
WHEN SHE WAS STARTING TO DESCEND THE STEEP FRONT 179 MANSNS
STAIRS, IF--

STEEPED
THE ROADSIDE, HOWEVER, IS STILL STEEPED IN THE 166 BEYOND
GRAYNESS OF THE DAWN,

STEER
I'LL THANK YOU TO STEER A CLEAR COURSE O' THAT. 542 'ILE
STEER CLEAR O' GALS OR THEY'LL SKIN YOUR HIDE OFF 106 ELECTR
AN' USE IT FUR A CARPET/
I'M GOING TO STEER CLEAR OF HIM. 625 ICEMAN

STEERAGE
I NEED NOT MUCH MONEY BECAUSE I AM NOT ASHAMED TO 676 ICEMAN
TRAVEL STEERAGE.

STEERED
WE STEERED DEM TO A REAL HOTEL. 612 ICEMAN
SO I STEERED HIM INTO A SIDE STREET WHERE IT WAS 617 ICEMAN
DARK
AND WHO STEERED YOU ON TO READING POETRY FIRSTS 164 JOURNE
ONE REASON I'VE STEERED CLEAR SINCE... 78 STRANG

STEERER
AN OLD GRAFTING FLATFOOT AND A CIRCUS BUNCO 602 ICEMAN
STEERER/

STEERIN'
I'VE NEVER BEEN A DAMN FOUL LIKE MOST, IF THAT'S 103 BEYOND
WHAT YOU'RE STEERIN' AT.
AND HIM STEERIN' THE BOAT. 482 CARDIF

STEERS
(HE TRIES TO KISS HER, BUT SHE WARDS HIM OFF AND 81 MISBEG
STEERS HIM BACK TO THE CHAIR.)
(HE STEERS THE WHIMPERING, HYSTERICAL BENTLEY TO 597 ROPE
THE DOORWAY)

STEINS
I DRINKS DAT OLD BUBBLY WATER IN STEINS/ 640 ICEMAN

STEM
NEARLY EVERY GUY I KNOW ON THE BIG STEM--AND I 14 HUGHIE
KNOW MOST OF 'EM--
HE'D ASK, =WHAT'S NEW ALONG THE BIG STEM= 16 HUGHIE

STEMS
(HE STARTS TO LOP OFF THE FLOWERS FROM THEIR STEMS311 LAZARU
WITH A SAVAGE INTENTNESS)

STENCH
A STENCH/ TEN THOUSAND OF THEM/ 132 BEYOND
ROBERT YOU FOUND IN THE EAST WAS A STENCHS 132 BEYOND
STENCH OF HUMAN LIFE/... 99 STRANG

STENDHAL
STENDHAL, PHILOSOPHICAL AND SOCIOLOGICAL WORKS BY 11 JOURNE
SCHOPENHAUER, NIETZSCHE, MARX,

STEP
WATCH YOUR STEP, KID. 219 AHWILD
(HIS FACE GROWN STERN AND ANGRY, TAKES A 261 AHWILD
THREATENING STEP TOWARD HIM)
(DRIFTING BACK ANOTHER STEP) 285 AHWILD
(SCORNFULLY, BUT DRIFTING BACK A STEP IN HIS 285 AHWILD
DIRECTION)
(HE MOVES A STEP TOWARD HER.) 69 ANNA
(HE TAKES A STEP TOWARD CHRIS THREATENINGLY.) 77 ANNA
I SUPPOSE IT'S NATURAL TO BE CROSS WHEN YOU'RE NOT 87 BEYOND
ABLE EVER TO WALK A STEP.
A HELP I'D BE TO YOU AND ME NOT ABLE TO MOVE A 151 BEYOND
STEP/
I'LL NOT MOVE A STEP OUT AV HERE-- 482 CARDIF
NAT SHRINKS BACKWARD A STEP) 568 CROSS
(MAKING A STEP TOWARD THEM) SEE/ 572 CROSS
LOVING MOVES SILENTLY OVER UNTIL HE IS STANDING 526 DAYS
JUST BEHIND JOHN BUT A STEP
(TAKES A STEP TOWARD THE DOOR) 562 DAYS
I DON'T WANT NEVER T' STEP INSIDE THE DOOR AGEN 219 DESIRE
AFTER HE'S BACK.
HE TAKES A STEP TOWARD HER, COMPELLED AGAINST HIS 229 DESIRE
WILL)
I'LL STEP IN AGAIN FOR A SPELL AFORE SUPPER--THAT 498 DIFRNT
IS, IF YOU WANT ME TO.
I'LL GO WITH YOU A STEP. 511 DIFRNT
(HE TAKES A THREATENING STEP FORWARD.) 468 DYNAMO
(THEN HARSHLY, TAKING A THREATENING STEP FORWARD) 463 DYNAMO
HE TAKES A THREATENING STEP TOWARD HER-- 481 DYNAMO
(MOVED IN SPITE OF HIMSELF, INSTINCTIVELY TAKES A 481 DYNAMO
STEP TOWARD HER--
THEN SHE BEGINS TO GLIDE NOISELESSLY, A STEP AT A 173 EJONES
TIME,
(HE TAKES A STEP FORWARD, THEN STOPS--WORRIEDLY) 191 EJONES
HE SHUTS NOISELESSLY WITH A QUEER PRANCING STEP 200 EJONES
(CHRISTINE SITS ON THE TOP STEP AT CENTER,. 47 ELECTR
HE SITS ON THE MIDDLE STEP AT RIGHT,. 47 ELECTR
ON THE LOWEST STEP AT LEFT. 48 ELECTR
I--ISHE TURNS AS IF TO RUN INTO THE ROOM, TAKES A 64 ELECTR
TOTTERING STEP--
(HE TAKES A STEP BUT LURCHES INTO THE SHADOW AND 104 ELECTR
LEANS AGAINST THE WAREHOUSE)
SINKS DOWN ON THE LOWEST STEP AND BEGINS TO MOAN 121 ELECTR
TO HERSELF.
LEARN TO KEEP STEP/ 267 GGBROW
I KNOW YUH GOT TO WATCH YOUR STEP WIT A STRANGER. 248 HA APE
STEP OUT AND SHAKE HANDS. 254 HA APE
LADIES AND GENTS, STEP FORWARD AND TAKE A SLANT AT254 HA APE
DE ONE AND ONLY--
(STUNG) YOU BROADS BETTER WATCH YOUR STEP OR-- 630 ICEMAN
BUT I KNOW WHAT'S GONNA HAPPEN IF HE DON'T WATCH 636 ICEMAN
HIS STEP.
(HE TAKES A THREATENING STEP TOWARD JOE. 637 ICEMAN
I'D BE ASHAMED TO HAVE THEM STEP IN THE DOOR. 64 JOURNE
(HE TAKES A THREATENING STEP TOWARD HIM. 64 JOURNE
THE LATTER MOVES BACK A STEP DEFENSIVELY, HIS FACE168 JOURNE
GROWING HARD.)
YOU'LL ONLY STEP ON IT AND TEAR IT AND GET IT 172 JOURNE
DIRTY DRAGGING IT ON THE FLOOR.
STEP BACK AMONG YOUR KIND/ 284 LAZARU
STEP BACK/ 300 LAZARU
THE ROMAN SOLDIERS IN SPITE OF THEIR EFFORTS ARE 304 LAZARU
PUSHED BACKWARD STEP BY STEP.)

STEP 1540

STEP (CONT'D.)
CLIMB TO THE STEP BELOW CRASSUS, FORMING BEHIND 320 LAZARU
HIM.
POMPEIA LIES FACE DOWN ON THE FIRST STEP AND BEATS349 LAZARU
IT WITH HER FIST.
ON THE TOP STEP, POMPEIA SITS, FACING RIGHT, HER 350 LAZARU
HANDS CLASPED ABOUT ONE KNEE.
THE OTHER LEG STRETCHED DOWN TO THE LOWER STEP. 350 LAZARU
ON THE STEP BELOW HER, CALIGULA SQUATS ON HIS 350 LAZARU
HAUNCHES, HIS ARMS ON HIS KNEES.
THE TEMPTATION TO ESCAPE---OPEN THE DOOR---STEP 28 MANSNS
BOLDLY ACROSS THE THRESHOLD.
(SHE SITS ON THE STEP OF THE SUMMER-HOUSE. 31 MANSNS
AFTER ALL, THIS IS AN INEVITABLE STEP IN THE 97 MANSNS
CORRUPTION OF YOUR CHARACTER
THE NEXT STEP MUST BE TO ACQUIRE MY OWN RANK. 100 MANSNS
BUT IT IS OBVIOUSLY THE LOGICAL FINAL STEP AT THAT101 MANSNS
END.
(MOVED AND FASCINATED, TAKES A STEP TOWARD HIM--- 103 MANSNS
TENDERLY.)
(SHRINKING BACK TO THE TOP STEP---DISTRACTEDLY.) 166 MANSNS
(SHE TAKES A STEP TOWARDS LEFT, STIFFLY, AS IF BY 177 MANSNS
A DETERMINED EFFORT OF WILL.
(SHE LEADS HIM A STEP TOWARDS THE DOOR-- 183 MANSNS
(WITH FORCED EAGERNESS, MOUNTS THE FIRST STEP.) 185 MANSNS
WHERE I CAN HEAR SOME MUSIC THAT I CAN KEEP STEP 403 MARCOM
TO.
(SHE SITS ON THE TOP STEP---BANTERINGLY) 40 MISBEG
SHE STOPS ABRUPTLY ON THE FIRST STEP---STARTLEDLY) 98 MISBEG
SHE SITS ON THE TOP STEP AND PULLS HIM DOWN ON THE102 MISBEG
STEP BENEATH HER.
HE SITS HUNCHED UP ON THE STEP, STARING AT 106 MISBEG
NOTHING.
SHE SITS ON THE TOP STEP, PULLING HIM DOWN BESIDE 115 MISBEG
HER BUT ON THE ONE BELOW.
YOU BETTER WATCH YOUR STEP. 124 MISBEG
IF YOU WON'T WATCH YOUR STEP, I'VE GOT TO. 126 MISBEG
THE TOP STEP AND PULLS HIM DOWN ON THE STEP BELOW 142 MISBEG
HER)
(HE TAKES A THREATENING STEP TOWARD HIM.) 53 POET
TAKING A STEP BACK AS THOUGH HE HAD BEEN SLAPPED 72 POET
IN THE FACE.
(SHE TAKES ONE STEP TOWARD HIM---THEN HER 164 POET
EXPRESSION BEGINS TO HARDEN.)
I KNOW HE'D ADVISE THAT TO GIVE YOU A FIRST STEP 171 POET
UP, DARLING.
(TO PAT) I'LL STEP OUTSIDE A SECOND AND GIVE YOU 589 ROPE
TWO A CHANCE
(SHE SHRINKS BACK A STEP) YOU CHUCK IT WHEN I SAY589 ROPE
THREE.
YOU OUGHT TO CONSIDER THIS STEP WITH GREAT CARE 15 STRANG
(SHE TAKES A WAVERING STEP TOWARD THE DOOR. 108 STRANG
YOU DON'T GET THAT FROM ME---HE HAS TAKEN A 150 STRANG
THREATENING STEP FORWARD.
I'VE GOT TO STEP AROUND AND SEE A FELLOW WHO LIVES152 STRANG
NEAR---BIOLOGIST.
(FURIOUSLY, TAKING A THREATENING STEP TOWARD HIM) 193 STRANG
(HE TAKES A STEP FORWARD AND SUDDENLY COLLAPSES 508 VOYAGE
OVER A CHAIR.
HER EYES MOVE IN THAT DIRECTION, SHE TAKES ANOTHER449 WELDED
JERKY STEP.
(THEN AS SHE TAKES A SLOW, MECHANICAL STEP TOWARD 449 WELDED
THE DOOR---WITH TENSE PLEADING)

STEPMAW'S
A GOOD STEPMAW'S SCURSE. 207 DESIRE

STEPPED
I GOT YOUR NUMBER THE MINUTE YOU STEPPED IN THE 15 ANNA
DOOR.
(HE HAS STEPPED ON TIPTOE INTO THE ROOM AND NOW 462 DYNAMO
SUDDENLY
BUT THAT OLD SHIVER OF DREAD TOOK ME THE MINUTE 54 STRANG
SHE STEPPED IN THE DOOR/...

STEPPIN'
I'M WORE OUT WITH YOU STEPPIN' ON MY TOES, YOU 471 CARIBE
CLUMSY MICK.
GUSH A'MIGHTY, LOOK AT JOHNNY COCK HIGH-STEPPIN'/ 250 DESIRE

STEPPING
(STEPPING FORWARD WITH AN AIR OF BRAVADO) I BE. 543 'ILE
(COLDLY---STEPPING BACK FROM HIM) 31 ANNA
(STEPPING BACK FROM HER---AGHAST) 263 DESIRE
(STEPPING AWAY WITH AN EXPRESSION OF REPULSION) 527 DIFRNT
(STEPPING BACK FROM HER IN HORROR) 542 DIFRNT
(STEPPING FORWARD INTO THE MOONLIGHT) 47 ELECTR
(STEPPING AWAY FROM YANK) VERY INTERESTING. 249 HA APE
(STEPPING BETWEEN THEM---SHARPLY) 332 LAZARU
YOU'RE STEPPING ON---(SHE KICKS IT AWAY FROM HER. 410 MARCOM

STEPS
MRS. MILLER GIVES A CRY AND STARTS TO GO TO HIM, 262 AHWILD
BUT SHE STEPS IN HER WAY.)
(MURIEL STEPS OUT A LITTLE AND LOOKS UP AND DOWN 280 AHWILD
FEARFULLY.
SHE STEPS INTO THE ROOM, THE REVOLVER IN HER RIGHT 69 ANNA
HAND BY HER SIDE.)
(HE STEPS OVER THE DITCH TO THE ROAD WHILE HE IS 86 BEYOND
TALKING.)
(HE KISSES HER PASSIONATELY AND STEPS TO THE 92 BEYOND
GROUND.
SHE OPENS THE DOOR AND STEPS INSIDE THE ROOM. 166 BEYOND
THE ENGLISHMAN STEPS SOFTLY OVER TO DRISCOLL. 483 CARDIF
(HE DOES A FEW JIG STEPS ON THE DECK.) 460 CARIBE
(HE GOES DOWN THE STEPS AND FOLLOWS HER INTO THE 466 CARIBE
FORECASTLE.
ASCENDS THE REMAINING STEPS AND ENTERS. 555 CROSS
HE ASCENDS IT A FEW STEPS 562 CROSS
(BARTLETT COMES DOWN THE STEPS OF THE 570 CROSS
COMPANIONWAY.
(SHE WARDS HIM OFF AND STEPS PAST HIM INTO THE 548 DAYS
STUDY.

STEPS (CONT'D.)
YEH WAS IT PUT ALL THE STEPS WE'VE WALKED ON THIS 208 DESIRE
FARM END TO END
THEY LISTEN TO HIS STEPS RECEDING.) 215 DESIRE
IS IRRITATED BY THE LAUGHTER AND STEPS FORWARD, 249 DESIRE
GLARING ABOUT HIM.
SLOW STEPS SOUND FROM THE PATH IN FRONT OF THE 514 DIFRNT
HOUSE.
(STEPS BACK FROM HER---ACCUSINGLY) 450 DYNAMO
(HE TAKES A FEW STEPS TOWARD THE WINDOW, THEN 452 DYNAMO
STOPS, THINKING BITTERLY)
(HE STEPS BACK, FROWNING) WAIT TILL LATER, ADA. 468 DYNAMO
STEPS INSIDE AND, AS SHE SEES REUBEN, 479 DYNAMO
(THEY GO DOWN THE FIRST FLIGHT OF STEPS. 484 DYNAMO
THEN, MAKING UP HIS MIND, HE STEPS QUICKLY ON 174 EJONES
TIPTOE INTO THE ROOM.
(HE STEPS JUST TO THE REAR OF THE TRIANGULAR 191 EJONES
CLEARING
BEFORE THE DOORWAY A FLIGHT OF FOUR STEPS LEADS 2 ELECTR
FROM THE GROUND TO THE PORTICO.
THE PORTICO AT THE TOP OF THE STEPS. 8 ELECTR
BUT AT ONCE SHE SHRUGS HER SHOULDERS WITH DISDAIN 9 ELECTR
AND COMES DOWN THE STEPS AND
(HE STARTS FOR THE STEPS--- 10 ELECTR
COMES OUT TO THE TOP OF THE STEPS WHERE HER MOTHER 10 ELECTR
HAD STOOD.
(SHE MOVES A FEW STEPS TOWARD THE HOUSE---THEN 17 ELECTR
TURNS AGAIN---
(MOVING TO THE STEPS) I AM GOING IN AND REST A 18 ELECTR
WHILE.
(SHE WALKS UP THE STEPS.) 18 ELECTR
(SHE TURNS HER BACK ON HIM AND WALKS TO THE STEPS 27 ELECTR
(SHE TURNS AT THE TOP OF THE STEPS AT THIS 27 ELECTR
LAVINIA IS SITTING ON THE TOP OF THE STEPS TO THE 43 ELECTR
PORTICO.
THEN SUDDENLY SEES LAVINIA ON THE STEPS AND STOPS 44 ELECTR
(UNABASHED, A BIT SHEEPISH.
SHE CLOSES THE DOOR AND COMES INTO THE MOONLIGHT 44 ELECTR
AT THE EDGE OF THE STEPS. 45 ELECTR
(SHE WALKS UP THE STEPS AGAIN.) 45 ELECTR
(HE MEETS HER AT THE FOOT OF THE STEPS AND KISSES 47 ELECTR
HER WITH A CHILL DIGNITY---
(HAS SLOWLY DESCENDED THE STEPS, HER EYES FIXED ON 47 ELECTR
HIM---TENSELY)
WOULDN'T YOU LIKE TO SIT HERE ON THE STEPS FOR A 47 ELECTR
WHILE?
(HE STEPS BACK AND STARES AT HER--- 47 ELECTR
(HE TURNS AND PACES UP AND DOWN TO THE RIGHT OF 49 ELECTR
STEPS.
(SHE GOES UP THE STEPS PAST HER MOTHER WITHOUT A 51 ELECTR
LOOK.
(HE SITS AWKWARDLY TWO STEPS BELOW HER, ON HER 51 ELECTR
LEFT.
THEN STARTS PACING SELF-CONSCIOUSLY UP AND DOWN AT 51 ELECTR
THE RIGHT OF STEPS.)
(HE ASCENDS TWO STEPS, HIS FACE TOWARD THE DOOR. 56 ELECTR
THEN WALKS STIFFLY DOWN THE STEPS AND STANDS 57 ELECTR
AGAIN.
AND THEN THEY TURN TO THE STEPS AND THE DOOR IS 67 ELECTR
CLOSED.
A FUNERAL WREATH IS FIXED TO THE COLUMN AT THE 67 ELECTR
RIGHT OF STEPS.
THEY COME DOWN THE STEPS TO THE DRIVE. 68 ELECTR
THERE THEY STOP TO WAIT FOR THE MEN WHO STAND AT 68 ELECTR
THE FOOT OF THE STEPS WHILE
(THEN GLANCING TOWARD THE MEN WHO HAVE MOVED A 69 ELECTR
LITTLE AWAY FROM THE STEPS AND
CHRISTINE MANNON COMES OUT AND STANDS AT THE HEAD 71 ELECTR
OF THE STEPS A MOMENT.
HAZEL NILES COMES OUT OF THE HOUSE TO THE HEAD OF 71 ELECTR
THE STEPS.
(SHE RUNS DOWN THE STEPS AND FLINGS HER ARMS 76 ELECTR
AROUND HIM.)
LAVINIA REMAINS BY THE FOOT OF THE STEPS, STARING 77 ELECTR
AFTER THEM.
SHE LEADS HIM UP THE STEPS) 77 ELECTR
(WHO HAS COME TO THE FOOT OF THE STEPS---HARSHLY) 77 ELECTR
CLOSING IT BEHIND HER, AND WALKS TO THE HEAD OF 77 ELECTR
THE STEPS.
SHE HURRIES UP THE STEPS AND OPENS THE DOOR. 78 ELECTR
CHRISTINE GIVES WAY TO FURY AND RUSHES DOWN THE 78 ELECTR
STEPS AND GRABS HER BY THE ARM
CHRISTINE LETS GO AND STEPS AWAY FROM HER. 78 ELECTR
AND WALKS WITH JERKY STEPS FROM THE ROOM LIKE SOME 92 ELECTR
TRAGIC MECHANICAL DOLL.
(HE FORCES HIMSELF TO OPEN THE DOOR AND STEPS 100 ELECTR
ASIDE.
(ORIN STEPS THROUGH THE DOOR 114 ELECTR
THEN STOPS AT THE TOP OF THE STEPS AND FACES 119 ELECTR
AROUND.
KNEELING ON THE STEPS BESIDE HER---DESPERATELY 121 ELECTR
PLEADING NOW)
ORIN TURNS FROM HER AND STARTS TO PACE UP AND DOWN121 ELECTR
BY THE STEPS.
LAVINIA, STANDS AT THE LEFT OF THE STEPS, RIGID AND21 ELECTR
ERECT, HER FACE MASK-LIKE.)
(HE WALKS MECHANICALLY UP THE STEPS---GAZING UP AT 122 ELECTR
THE HOUSE---STRANGELY)
LAVINIA GIVES A SHUDDERING GASP, TURNS BACK TO THE123 ELECTR
STEPS, STARTS TO GO UP THEM.
CHRISTINE SHRINKS BACKWARD UP THE STEPS UNTIL SHE 123 ELECTR
STANDS AT THE TOP
AND DOWN THE PORTICO STEPS, HIS FACE CHALKY WHITE 134 ELECTR
AND HIS EYES POPPING.)
(SHE WALKS UP THE STEPS TO THE PORTICO. 137 ELECTR
(SHE TAKES HIS ARM AND LEADS HIM TO THE STEPS. 138 ELECTR

STEPS

STEPS (CONT'D.)
SHE GETS HIM UP THE STEPS AND THEY PASS INTO THE 138 ELECTR
HOUSE.)
(HE STEPS BACK IN THE ROOM AS PETER APPEARS IN THE167 ELECTR
DOORWAY.)
I SEED YOU SETTIN' OUT HERE ON THE STEPS WHEN I 170 ELECTR
GOT UP AT FIVE THIS MORNIN'--
(SHE GOES AND SITS AT THE TOP OF THE STEPS, BOLT 170 ELECTR
UPRIGHT.
THEN STANDS HER GROUND ON THE TOP OF THE STEPS, 171 ELECTR
HER VOICE HARDENING)
AND WALKS TO THE FOOT OF THE STEPS. 171 ELECTR
(HE GOES PAST HER UP THE STEPS AND INTO THE HOUSE.179 ELECTR
(HE STEPS BACK CRUSHED, WITH HEAD BOWED. 263 GGBROW
(STEPS ARE HEARD FROM THE RIGHT. 265 GGBROW
YOU WAS CAMPING ON MY STEPS, SOUND ASLEEP. 278 GGBROW
THEN STEPS BACK) 293 GGBROW
WE MUST TAKE STEPS AT ONCE TO RUN ANTHONY TO 319 GGBROW
EARTH.
BUT FORCES HERSELF TO LEAVE THE ENGINEERS AND TAKE225 HA APE
A FEW STEPS NEARER THE MEN.
DOWN A MILE OF LADDERS AND STEPS TO BE HAVIN' A 228 HA APE
LOOK AT US.
(HE PRETENDS TO NOTICE WETJDEN FOR THE FIRST TIME 677 ICEMAN
AND STEPS AWAY FROM THE DOOR--
(COMES A FEW STEPS INSIDE THE BAR--WITH A STRAINED682 ICEMAN
BRIGHT GIGGLE)
HE STEPS SOFTLY OVER TO SMITTY AND CUTS THE ROPES 532 INZONE
ABOUT HIS ARMS AND ANKLES WITH
DISAPPEARS DOWN A FLIGHT OF STEPS LEADING TO THE 41 JOURNE
GROUND.
SHE WAITS RIGIDLY UNTIL HE DISAPPEARS DOWN THE 42 JOURNE
STEPS.
THEN HE GOES OUT ON THE PORCH AND DISAPPEARS DOWN 49 JOURNE
THE STEPS.
THERE'S YOUR FATHER COMING UP THE STEPS NOW. 64 JOURNE
AS IF SOMEONE HAD STUMBLED AND FALLEN ON THE FRONT154 JOURNE
STEPS.
THE FRONT STEPS TRIED TO TRAMPLE ON ME. 155 JOURNE
STEPS LEAD UP TO THIS DOOR, 281 LAZARU
WHOSE POINT IS PLACED AT THE FOOT OF THE STEPS 282 LAZARU
LEADING TO THE TERRACE.
LEAVING ONE NEUTRAL FIGURE BEFORE THE STEPS. 283 LAZARU
MOVING MECHANICALLY IN JERKY STEPS TO THE MUSIC 287 LAZARU
THE APEX AT THE CENTER OF THE STEPS AS BEFORE. 291 LAZARU
(STEPS BACK FROM HIM WITH AN UNEASY SHUDDER) 301 LAZARU
WHO HAD TAKEN LAZARUS PRISONER, MARCH IN WITH 306 LAZARU
DANCERS-STEPS.
WITHIN THE PORTICO ON ROWS OF CHAIRS PLACED ON A 312 LAZARU
SERIES OF WIDE STEPS WHICH ARE
A SLAVE WITH AN AMPHORA OF WINE CROUCHES ON THE 313 LAZARU
STEPS BY HIS CHAIR.
ASCENDS THE STEPS UNTIL HE STANDS A LITTLE BELOW 320 LAZARU
LAZARUS.
BELOW THE STEPS TO THE TERRACE, IN A LINE FACING 326 LAZARU
FRONT.
HE STEPS BACK WITH A STARTLED EXCLAMATION. 327 LAZARU
(WALKS UP THE STEPS TO THE CROSS AND, STRETCHING 329 LAZARU
TO HIS FULL HEIGHT,
THE LATTER STEPS BACK FROM HIM, STARING OPEN- 333 LAZARU
MOUTHED, FASCINATED.
AT THE STEPS BEFORE THE DOOR OF THE PALACE. 334 LAZARU
(LAZARUS HAS ASCENDED THE STEPS. 335 LAZARU
ON THE SIDE STEPS OF THE DAIS, FOUR ON RIGHT, 336 LAZARU
THREE ON LEFT.
(HE CLUMPS HEAVILY DOWN THE STEPS OF THE DAIS) 338 LAZARU
(HE LEAPS TO THE DAIS AND UP ITS STEPS IN A 338 LAZARU
FRENZY)
(THEN, AS THE BODY OF FLAVIUS FALLS HEAVILY AND 338 LAZARU
ROLLS DOWN THE STEPS AT RIGHT,
HIS SWORD CLATTERING DOWN THE STEPS TO THE FLOOR.1339 LAZARU
LAZARUS STEPS UP BESIDE TIBERIUS. 339 LAZARU
(HE MOUNTS THE STEPS OF THE DAIS AND SITS ON THE 340 LAZARU
COUCH AT LEFT OF TABLE--
(SHE LAUGHS SOFTLY AND STEPS FORWARD.) 342 LAZARU
(HE STEPS DOWN FROM THE DAIS TO MIRIAM'S SIDE AND 345 LAZARU
GENTLY HE LETS HER BODY SINK UNTIL IT RESTS
AGAINST THE STEPS OF THE DAIS.
POMPEIA STEPS NEARER TO LAZARUS, STARING AT HIM 347 LAZARU
MOCKINGLY.
POMPEIA RUNS TO THE FEET OF TIBERIUS AND CROUCHES 348 LAZARU
DOWN ON THE STEPS BELOW HIM.
CALIGULA, HIS HAND CLUTCHING HIS HEAD, POUNDS IT 349 LAZARU
AGAINST THE EDGE OF THE STEPS..
HE SLINKS NOISELESSLY UP THE STEPS OF THE DAIS AND357 LAZARU
SQUATS COWERINGLY AT
WILDLY--THEN STEPS DOWN FROM THE DAIS AND GOES OFF362 LAZARU
RIGHT, CRYING DISTRACTEDLY)
(SHE MOVES TO THE TOP OF THE STEPS LEADING TO THE 366 LAZARU
ARENA.)
(DESCENDING THE STEPS LIKE A SLEEP-WALKER) 366 LAZARU
SIMON'S MOTHER, STEPS INTO THE CLEARING FROM THE 2 MANSNS
PATH.
AND BEYOND THE WALL THE STEPS OF LIFE GROWIN' 19 MANSNS
FAINTER DOWN THE STREET.
THREE STEPS LEAD UP TO THE DOOR. 25 MANSNS
(HE GOES TO THE FOOT OF THE STEPS.) 27 MANSNS
IN HIS LETTERS HENRY SUGGESTS CERTAIN STEPS SHOULD 32 MANSNS
BE TAKEN WHICH,
(INDIFFERENTLY.) THEN YOU HAVE ONLY TO TAKE THE 32 MANSNS
STEPS, NICHOLAS.
(SHE ADVANCES UP THE STEPS--WITH A FINAL PUSH.) 40 MANSNS
DEBORAH IS SITTING ON THE STEPS LEADING UP TO THE 95 MANSNS
SUMMER-HOUSE DOOR,
AND GOES AND OPENS THE DOOR, THEN SITS DOWN BY THE 96 MANSNS
STEPS AGAIN.
HE SEES THE VOLUME OF BYRON ON THE STEPS. 106 MANSNS

STEPSON

STEPS (CONT'D.)
MOVES BACK DOWN THE STEPS OBEDIENTLY LIKE A COWED 111 MANSNS
BOY.
AND GOES PAST HER UP THE STEPS TO THE DOOR.) 111 MANSNS
TURNS TOWARDS THE DOOR AND SLOWLY BEGINS TO ASCEND164 MANSNS
THE STEPS.)
(SHRINKING BACK TO THE FOOT OF THE STEPS-- 166 MANSNS
GUILTILY.)
OFF BALANCE AND SENDS HIM SPINNING DOWN THE STEPS 190 MANSNS
TO FALL HEAVILY AND LIE STILL
SHE NOW STANDS ON THE TOP OF THE STEPS. 191 MANSNS
(COMING DOWN THE STEPS-- 192 MANSNS
(DEBORAH TURNS FROM HER TO ASCEND THE STEPS. 193 MANSNS
(ASCENDING THE STEPS, LOOKS BACK. 193 MANSNS
IT RISES IN THREE TIERS, THREE STEPS TO A TIER. 377 MARCOM
HE DISMOUNTS, AIDED BY THE STEPS OF YOUR IMPERIAL 388 MARCOM
PALACE!
AS HE STEPS ON, HE TAKES OFF HIS GILDED, 390 MARCOM
HE STEPS FORWARD AND OFFERS THIS TO THE PRINCESS, 391 MARCOM
WITH A BOYISH GRIN)
(SUDDENLY STEPS FORWARD--FLUSHED BUT PROUDLY) 397 MARCOM
THERE IS A DOOR WITH A FLIGHT OF THREE UNPAINTED 1 MISBEG
STEPS LEADING TO THE GROUND.
A FLIGHT OF STEPS LEADS TO THE FRONT DOOR. 1 MISBEG
FROM THESE STEPS THERE IS A FOOTPATH GOING AROUND 1 MISBEG
AN OLD PEAR TREE.
THE DOOR OF JOSIE'S BEDROOM OPENS AND SHE COMES 3 MISBEG
OUT ON THE STEPS.
(SHE GOES BACK TOWARD THE STEPS AS HER BROTHER, 3 MISBEG
MIKE,
SHE COMES DOWN THE STEPS AND GOES LEFT TO THE 3 MISBEG
CORNER OF THE HOUSE AND PEERS
HE GOES UP THE STEPS INTO HER ROOM 5 MISBEG
WITH THE BROOM HANDLE PROPPED AGAINST THE STEPS 11 MISBEG
NEAR HER RIGHT HAND.
(SHE SITS ON THE STEPS) 11 MISBEG
(HE MOVES TOWARD THE STEPS.) 13 MISBEG
(LAUGHS AND SITS ON THE STEPS, PUTTING THE CLUB 15 MISBEG
AWAY)
(RISES FROM THE STEPS WITH THE BROOM HANDLE IN HER 15 MISBEG
RIGHT HAND)
(SITS DOWN ON THE STEPS--WITH A CHANGE OF MANNER) 39 MISBEG
(SHE SITS ON THE STEPS, HE ON THE BOULDER) 55 MISBEG
(HE GOES UP THE STEPS) LET'S EAT, FOR THE LOVE OF 67 MISBEG
GOD.
(SHE TUGS AT HIS HAND AND HE FOLLOWS HER UP THE 68 MISBEG
STEPS.
JOSIE IS SITTING ON THE STEPS BEFORE THE FRONT 71 MISBEG
DOOR.
(PUSHES PAST HER DOWN THE STEPS--PEERING OFF LEFT-- 98 MISBEG
FRONT--
COME ON NOW AND WE'LL SIT ON MY BEDROOM STEPS AND 102 MISBEG
BE ROMANTIC IN THE MOONLIGHT,
AND STARTS PACING BACK AND FORTH A FEW STEPS, 111 MISBEG
(HE RELIEVES HER OF THE PITCHER AND TUMBLERS AS 111 MISBEG
SHE COMES DOWN THE STEPS.)
(SHE TAKES HIS ARM AND LEADS HIM TO HER BEDROOM 115 MISBEG
STEPS.
THE STEPS IF SHE DIDN'T GRAB HIS ARM IN TIME. 137 MISBEG
(HE STEPS UP BESIDE HER AND PUTS HIS ARM AROUND 137 MISBEG
HER
(HE GETS TO HIS FEET, STAGGERING A BIT, AND STEPS 138 MISBEG
DOWN TO THE GROUND.)
HE PEEKS AROUND THE CORNER, AND TAKES IN THE TWO 157 MISBEG
ON THE STEPS.
JOSIE SITS IN THE SAME POSITION ON THE STEPS, AS 157 MISBEG
IF SHE HAD NOT MOVED,
AND MEEKLY TIPTOES PAST HER UP THE STEPS AND GOES 164 MISBEG
IN.
HOGAN COMES OUT OF HER ROOM AND STANDS ON TOP OF 174 MISBEG
THE STEPS.
(SHE TURNS AS IF TO GO UP THE STEPS INTO THE 174 MISBEG
HOUSE.)
AT LEFT FRONT, TWO STEPS LEAD UP TO A CLOSED DOOR 7 POET
HE DESCENDS THE STEPS AND BOWS--PLEASANTLY. 33 POET
AND CORNELIUS MELODY APPEARS IN THE DOORWAY ABOVE 33 POET
THE TWO STEPS.
(SHE GOES TO THE DOOR AT RIGHT, AND STEPS ASIDE TO 75 POET
LET DEBORAH PRECEDE HER.)
MELODY STARTS GUILTILY AND STEPS QUICKLY AWAY FROM116 POET
THE MIRROR.
(STEPS BETWEEN THEM.) CON! 128 POET
(SHE TAKES A FEW MORE STEPS TOWARD THE DOOR--STOPS139 POET
AGAIN--SHE MUTTERS BEATENLY.)
(HE RENEWS HIS CHANT.) THEY HUNT OUR STEPS THAT W579 ROPE
CANNOT GO IN OUR STREETS.
(HE GIVES IT TO THE OLD MAN AS THEY COME TO THE 584 ROPE
DOORWAY AND QUICKLY STEPS BACK
(THERE IS THE NOISE OF STEPS FROM THE HALL AND 33 STRANG
DOCTOR EDMUND DARRELL ENTERS.
(AT THE SOUND OF STEPS FROM THE KITCHEN 56 STRANG
(SHE STEPS BETWEEN THEM PROTECTINGLY) 133 STRANG
(STEPS UP SUDDENLY BESIDE THEM--SHARPLY AND 178 STRANG
STERNLY COMMANDING)
(STEPS QUICKLY TO HER SIDE) I'M SORRY, NINA, BUT 179 STRANG
I WARNED YOU NOT TO MUDDLE.
(HE STEPS FORWARD AND SLAPS DARRELL ACROSS THE 193 STRANG
FACE VICIOUSLY.
(JOHN STEPS INTO THE ROOM. 450 WELDED
AT LAST HE COMES TO HIMSELF WITH A SHUDDER AND 460 WELDED
STEPS AWAY FROM HER.
HE STEPS PAST HER BACK INTO THE ROOM, 465 WELDED
CAPE STOPS TWO STEPS BELOW HER--IN A LOW, 489 WELDED
WONDERING TONE)

STEPSON
(THEN AFFECTIONATELY.) AND GORDON IS--WELL--SORT 179 STRANG
OF MY STEPSON, ISN'T HE&

STEREOTYPED

STEREOTYPED
WITH THE INTOLERABLE LIFELESS REALISTIC DETAIL OF 269 GGBROW
THE STEREOTYPED PAINTINGS

STERILE
STERILE...)) 67 STRANG

STERN
ON THE LEFT (THE STERN OF THE SHIP) 535 *ILE
(COMES TOWARD THE STEWARD--WITH A STERN LOOK ON 539 *ILE
HIS FACE.
(HIS FACE GROWN STERN AND ANGRY, TAKES A 261 AHWILD
THREATENING STEP TOWARD HIM)
TURNS AND FIXES HIS YOUNGEST SON WITH A STERN 264 AHWILD
FORBIDDING EYE)
AND THEN HE'D LEARN THAT YOU COULD BE TERRIBLE 265 AHWILD
STERN
NEAR THE STERN. 275 AHWILD
THE STERN SECTION IS IN MOONLIGHT. 275 AHWILD
(SHE LETS HIM LEAD HER TOWARD THE STERN OF THE 280 AHWILD
BOAT.)
(HE HELPS HER IN AND SHE SETTLES HERSELF IN THE 280 AHWILD
STERN SEAT OF THE BOAT.
SITTING DEJECTEDLY IN THE STERN OF THE BOAT, 285 AHWILD
APATHETIC FIGURE OF INJURED GRIEF)
THE STERN OF THE DEEPLY-LADEN BARGE. 25 ANNA
ANNA WALKS BACK TOWARD THE EXTREME STERN 30 ANNA
FOUR DAYS WE WAS IN IT WITH GREEN SEAS RAKING OVER 36 ANNA
HER FROM BOW TO STERN.
TOWARD THE STERN. 41 ANNA
BUT HIS FACE IS MORE STERN AND FORMIDABLE, 567 CROSS
(A STERN NOTE COMES INTO HIS VOICE) 506 DAYS
NOT A STERN, SELF-RIGHTEOUS BEING WHO CONDEMNED 510 DAYS
SINNERS TO TORMENT.
HIS EYES ON THE FLOOR, HIS EXPRESSION SAD AND A 541 DAYS
BIT STERN.
STERN-LOOKING PEOPLE IN UNCOMFORTABLE POSES ARE 493 DIFRNT
HUNG ON THE WALLS.
(STARING AT HIM WITH STERN CONDEMNATION) 529 DIFRNT
HAVE I BEEN TOO STERN?... 426 DYNAMO
HIS FACE IS HANDSOME IN A STERN, ALOOF FASHION. 28 ELECTR
HIS MOTHER WAS STERN WITH HIM, WHILE MARIE, 44 ELECTR
(DRAWING HIMSELF UP WITH A STERN PRIDE AND DIGNITY 55 ELECTR
(THE STERN SECTION OF A CLIPPER SHIP MOORED 102 ELECTR
ALONGSIDE A WHARF IN EAST BOSTON.
THE PART AFT OF THE MIZZENMAST IS VISIBLE WITH THE102 ELECTR
CURVE OF THE STERN AT RIGHT.
LAVINIA TURNS AND, STIFFLY ERECT, HER FACE STERN 125 ELECTR
AND MASK-LIKE,
(FRIGHTENED BUT MANAGING TO BE STERN) 148 ELECTR
HIS FACE IS STERN AND DISGUSTED BUT AT THE SAME 167 JOURNE
TIME PITYING.
HIS EYES ARE ACCUSING AND STERN. 291 LAZARU
THE LIPS ARE THIN AND STERN AND SELF-CONTAINED-- 337 LAZARU
THE KAAN IS LOOKING AT THE TWO BROTHERS WITH A 378 MARCOM
STERN AIR.
THE KAAN LOOKS FROM HER TO HIM AND HIS FACE GROWS 390 MARCOM
STERN.
AT THE LEFT, STERN TO, IS AN ENORMOUS JUNK, THE 399 MARCOM
FLAGSHIP.
THE PORTSIDE RAIL IS IN THE REAR, THE CURVE OF THE158 STRANG
STERN AT LEFT.
(WITH A SUDDEN CHANGE IN MANNER THAT IS ALMOST 445 WELDED
STERN)

STERNLY
(STERNLY) WOMAN, YOU AIN'T ADOIN' RIGHT 550 *ILE
(STERNLY) YOU KNOW THE AGREEMENT--RUM--NO MONEY. 473 CARIBE
(STERNLY) JACK/ 508 DAYS
HE STERNLY SCORNED MY OFFER. 523 DAYS
(STERNLY) JACK/ 545 DAYS
(STERNLY) YOU WOULD BE MORE HONEST WITH YOURSELF 547 DAYS
IF YOU SAID A SELF-DAMNED FOOL
(STERNLY--MORE TO BREAK HER MOOD THAN BECAUSE HE 550 DAYS
(STERNLY) DO YOU DARE SAY THAT--NOW? 559 DAYS
(STERNLY) THE KIND OF WOMEN I'VE SEEN IN CITIES 536 DIFRNT
WEARIN' IT--
(STERNLY TO REUBEN) I TRUST YOU MEAN HONORABLY BY438 DYNAMO
HER, YOUNG FELLOW.
THE PRISON GUARD POINTS STERNLY AT JONES WITH HIS 194 EJONES
WHIP.
(STERNLY) IT WAS HIS DUTY AS A MANNON TO GO/ 32 ELECTR
(STERNLY) ORIN/ 94 ELECTR
(THEN STERNLY) WHAT MADE YOU SAY SUCH THINGS JUST 94 ELECTR
THEN?
(FINALLY SPEAKS STERNLY) HE PAID THE JUST PENALTY122 ELECTR
FOR HIS CRIME.
(MORE STERNLY) WHO MURDERED FATHER? 142 ELECTR
(SHE ASKS STERNLY) 142 ELECTR
(STERNLY) BE SILENT/ 277 LAZARU
(STERNLY) BEHAVE YOURSELF, MARK/ 360 MARCOM
(STERNLY) SILENCE/ 380 MARCOM
FINALLY KUBLAI ADDRESSES HER STERNLY) 387 MARCOM
(STERNLY) NEO/ 142 STRANG
(STERNLY) I SWORE I'D NEVER AGAIN MEDDLE WITH 169 STRANG
HUMAN LIVES, NINA/
(THEN STERNLY) BUT I WILL NOT MEDDLE IN YOUR LIFE 170 STRANG
AGAIN/
(STERNLY) FOR THE SAKE OF YOUR FUTURE HAPPINESS 178 STRANG
AND MY SON'S I'VE GOT TO SPEAK/
(STERNLY--GRABBING HER BY THE WRIST) 178 STRANG
(STEPS UP SUDDENLY BESIDE THEM--SHARPLY AND 178 STRANG
STERNLY COMMANDING)
(STERNLY) IN HIS CONDITION, MR. EVANS MUST HAVE 183 STRANG
ABSOLUTE QUIET
(THEN STERNLY IN HER TURN, AS IF SWEARING A PLEDGE183 STRANG
TO HERSELF)

STERNNESS
BUT THERE WAS A STERNNESS IN HIS EYES, TOO, AN 507 DAYS
ACCUSATION AGAINST ME--
THEN QUIETLY, AN UNDERCURRENT OF STERNNESS IN HIS 538 DAYS
VOICE)

STERNNESS (CONT'D.)
(WITH A STRANGE STERNNESS, SEARCHES HIS FACE) 280 GGBROW
(SIMPLY, WITH A TRACE OF A SAD STERNNESS) 294 LAZARU
(SHE PAUSES--THEN WITH A STRANGE AUSTERE 64 STRANG
STERNNESS)

STERTOROUSLY
(HE FALLS BACK IN A COMA, BREATHING STERTOROUSLY. 62 ELECTR

STETIT
=STETIT UNUS IN ARCEM ERECTUS CAPITIS VICTORQUE AD 23 STRANG
SIDERA MITTIT STUEREOS OCULOS

STEW
STEW, STEW/ 480 CARDIF
WHO DE HELL YUH LAUGHIN' AT, YUH HALF-DEAD OLD 634 ICEMAN
STEW BUMS
LIKE A COUPLA STEW BUMS AND WASTIN' DEMSELVES. 702 ICEMAN
A STEW BUM IS A STEW BUM AND YUH CAN'T CHANGE HIM.703 ICEMAN
THERE'S STEW ON THE STOVE, YOU BAD-TEMPERED RUNT. 35 MISBEG
(ANGRILY) I'LL GO IN THE HOUSE, BUT ONLY TO SEE 36 MISBEG
THE STEW AIN'T BUNNED.
IT TURNS MY STOMACH WITH ITS STINK OF ONIONS AND 42 POET
STEW/

STEW'LL
A GOOD BEEF STEW'LL FIX YOU. 13 ANNA

STEWARD
THEN THE STEWARD ENTERS AND COMMENCES TO CLEAR THE535 *ILE
TABLE OF THE FEW DISHES WHICH
THE STEWARD HURRIES TO HIS STACKED-UP DISHES. 538 *ILE
THE NEXT DISH YOU BREAK, MR. STEWARD, YOU TAKE A 539 *ILE
BATH IN THE BERING SEA
THE STEWARD IS VISIBLY FRIGHTENED 539 *ILE
IT IS NIGH ON TWO BELLS, MR. STEWARD, AND THIS 539 *ILE
TRUCK NOT CLEARED YET.
(COMES TOWARD THE STEWARD--WITH A STERN LOOK ON 539 *ILE
HIS FACE.
KEENEY DRAWS BACK HIS FIST AND THE STEWARD SHRINKS539 *ILE
AWAY.
PICK UP THAT DISH, MR. STEWARD/ 539 *ILE
THE BOFSUN, THE SHIP'S CARPENTER, THE MESSROOM 455 CARIBE
STEWARD, AND THE DONKEYMAN--
I ARSKED A DECK STEWARD 'O SHE WAS AND 'E TOLD ME.228 HA APE
THE BLEEDIN' STEWARD AS WAITS ON 'EM, 'E TOLD ME 228 HA APE
ABOUT 'ER.

STEWED
I GUESS I'M MORE STEWED THAN I THOUGHT--IN THE 122 MISBEG
CENTER OF THE OLD BEAN, AT LEAST.
(SHRUGS HIS SHOULDERS) WELL, HE'S STEWED TO THE 131 MISBEG
EARS.

STHRIPPED
'TWAS HERE I WAS STHRIPPED AV ME LAST SHILLIN' 496 VOYAGE
WHIN I WAS ASLAPE.

STHRONG
YOU LOOK AS STHRONG AS AN OX. 482 CARDIF

STICK
NO, HE'S GOT TO BE PUNISHED, IF ONLY TO MAKE THE 289 AHWILD
LESSON STICK IN HIS MIND.
(MANNFULLY) THAT'S MY WORD, AND I'LL STICK TO IT/ 56 ANNA
AFTHER HIM TRYIN' TO STICK YOU IN THE BACK, AND 488 CARDIF
YOU NOT SUSPECTIN'.
WITH A CHARRED STICK, AND MY FATHER HAD CARE OF 560 CROSS
IT.
YE'LL NEED SOMETHIN' THAT'LL STICK T' YER RIBS. 214 DESIRE
IF WE WANT A BORN DONKEY YE'D KNOW YE'LL NEVER 254 DESIRE
OWN STICK NOR STONE ON IT.
(LAUGHING) LEAVE IT TO MEN FOLKS TO STICK UP FOR 499 DIFRNT
EACH OTHER, RIGHT OR WRONG.
YOU ASKED ME TO STAY AND I'LL STICK. 546 DIFRNT
DO YOU EXPECT A BOY OF HIS AGE TO STAY IN LIKE A 425 DYNAMO
POOR STICK-IN-THE-MUD JUST
ON THE END OF A STICK. 173 EJONES
IN THE OTHER A CHARM STICK WITH A BUNCH OF WHITE 200 EJONES
COCKATOO FEATHERS TIED TO THE
SAID FATHER WAS NO GOOD ON AN OFFENSIVE BUT HE'D 94 ELECTR
TRUST HIM TO STICK IN THE MUD
OLD STICK--SHORT FOR STICK-IN-THE-MUD. 94 ELECTR
I KNOW I USED TO BE AN AWFUL OLD STICK, BUT-- 143 ELECTR
THAT YOU'RE ONLY AN OLD STICK-IN-THE-MUD/ 260 GGBROW
DRAW AND HIT ME ON THE HEAD WITH A STICK AND 295 GGBROW
KICKED OUT MY PICTURE
IT'LL STICK TO YOU. 227 HA APE
THE BAR BENDS LIKE A LICORICE STICK UNDER HIS 244 HA APE
TREMENDOUS STRENGTH.
I'LL STICK, GET ME? 247 HA APE
YUH'LL STICK TO DE FINISH/ 253 HA APE
HOPE YOU STICK AROUND. 10 HUGHIE
I'D LIKE TO SEE SOME OF THEM HERE STICK THAT. 593 ICEMAN
YOU BETTER STICK TO THE PART OF OLD CEMETERY, THE 639 ICEMAN
BARKER FOR THE BIG SLEEP--
IF I HAS TO BORROW A GUN AND STICK UP SOME WHITE 673 ICEMAN
MAN, I GETS IT.
HE'D BORROWED DE GAT TO STICK UP SOMEONE, AND DEN 699 ICEMAN
DIDN'T HAVE DE GUTS.
I'LL STICK TO BROADWAY, AND A ROOM WITH A BATH, 35 JOURNE
WHY DIDN'T YOU STICK AROUND? 57 JOURNE
AND THEN YOU WENT TO THE CLUB TO MEET MCGUIRE AND 144 JOURNE
LET HIM STICK YOU
(UNEASILY) NO, STICK TO YOUR OWN TRADE, SIMON, 48 MANSNS
WHATEVER YOU DO.
WISPS OF HAY STICK TO HIS CLOTHES AND HIS FACE IS 157 MISBEG
SWOLLEN AND SLEEPY,
AND WHAT CHANCE WILL THIS AULD STICK AV A YANKEE 130 POET
HAVE AGAINST HIM?
STICK, TALKING TO HIMSELF AS HE DOES SO) 579 ROPE
(COMES OVER TO HER FATHER BUT WARILY KEEPS OUT OF 579 ROPE
RANGE OF HIS STICK)
(WITH A QUICK MOVEMENT HE HITS HER VICIOUSLY OVER 581 ROPE
THE ARM WITH HIS STICK.
(POINTING TO THE ROPE WITH HIS STICK) 582 ROPE

STICK (CONT'D.)
BENTLEY WAVES HIS STICK FRANTICALLY IN THE AIR, 583 ROPE
AND GROANS WITH RAGE.)
STANDS SHAKING HIS STICK AT SWEENEY AND HIS WIFE) 584 ROPE
HE WAS STANDIN' THERE SHAKIN' HIS STICK AT ME, 592 ROPE
I SEE HE AIN'T LOST THE OLD STICK. 594 ROPE
(BENTLEY POINTS WITH HIS STICK TO THE ROPE. 596 ROPE
STICK TO HIM... 71 STRANG
I'VE GOT TO STICK TO SAM/ 84 STRANG
SHE'LL STICK TO HIM/... 106 STRANG
DRISCOLL HAS UNBUTTONED HIS STIFF COLLAR AND ITS 496 VOYAGE
ENDS STICK OUT SIDEWAYS.

STICKIN'
I'M TELLIN' YUH I'M SICK OF STICKIN' WITH YUH, AND 11 ANNA
I'M LEAVING YUH FLAT, SEE$
DE BLACK HAND, DEY'RE A LOT OF YELLOW BACK- 248 HA APE
STICKIN' GINEES.
(NODS--THEN THOUGHTFULLY) WHY AIN'T HE OUT DERE 584 ICEMAN
STICKIN' BY HER$

STICKING
I'M A DIVIL FOR STICKING IT OUT WHEN THEM THAT'S 36 ANNA
WEAR GIVE UP.
WITH NICKEL PIPES STICKING OUT OF THE HOOD/ 32 HUGHIE
WITH HIS BIG TOES STICKING OUT OF THE UPPERS. 577 ICEMAN
STICKING TO THE OLD GRANDSTAND, EH$ 643 ICEMAN
WAGGING THEM AT THEIR EARS, STICKING OUT THEIR 366 LAZARU
TONGUES, SLAPPING THEIR BEHINDS,
LOOK AT THE HAY STICKING TO ME. 159 MISBEG
I'M STICKING... 71 STRANG

STICKLER
I'M A STICKLER FOR THESE LITTLE LITERARY 22 STRANG
CONVENTIONS, YOU KNOW/

STICKS
(TO SCOTT) DICK, YOU WOULDN'T BELIEVE HOW THEM 97 BEYOND
BOYS OF MINE STICKS TOGETHER.
STICKS HIS FOOT OUT AND THE WAVERING COUPLE 471 CARIBE
STUMBLE OVER IT
EBEN STICKS HIS HEAD OUT OF THE DINING-ROOM 205 DESIRE
WINDOW, LISTENING.)
AND ABBIE STICKS HER HEAD OUT. 224 DESIRE
EBEN STICKS HIS HEAD OUT OF HIS BEDROOM WINDOW. 228 DESIRE
ABBIE STICKS HER HEAD OUT. 244 DESIRE
AND FIFE STICKS HIS HEAD OUT OF HIS SITTING ROOM 445 DYNAMO
WINDOW
(STICKS HER HEAD OUT OF THEIR SITTING ROOM WINDOW 467 DYNAMO
AS HE PASSES THE LILAC HEDGE.
THE COAL DUST STICKS LIKE BLACK MAKE-UP, GIVING 226 HA APE
THEM A QUEER,
THE BLACK SMUDGE OF COAL DUST STILL STICKS LIKE 233 HA APE
MAKE-UP.
BORN AND RAISED IN THE STICKS, WASN'T YOU$ 13 HUGHIE
HAILS FROM THE STICKS. 14 HUGHIE
I BET YOU NEVER SEEN ONE, EXCEPT BACK AT THE OLD 22 HUGHIE
FAIR GROUNDS IN THE STICKS.
WHICH ONLY THE DRUNKEST YOKEL FROM THE STICKS 571 ICEMAN
AND WHATEVER STICKS TO THE CEILING IS MY SHARE/ 582 ICEMAN
BOOBS FROM DE STICKS. 612 ICEMAN
HE WAS A PREACHER IN THE STICKS OF INDIANA, LIKE 622 ICEMAN
I'VE TOLD YOU.
(SHE OPENS THE DOOR AT RIGHT, STICKS HER HEAD IN 147 MANSNS
AND SPEAKS TO JOEL.
MUST REMEMBER THE OLD ADAGE--STICKS AND STONES-- 155 MANSNS
AND POVERTY--BREAK--
(SHE STICKS OUT HER TONGUE. 413 MARCOM
THEY'RE ALL STICKS LIKE YOU. 8 MISBEG
AND JAMIE CREGAN STICKS HIS HEAD IN CAUTIOUSLY TO 151 POET
PEER AROUND THE ROOM.
HEAVY JAW, WHICH STICKS OUT PUGNACIOUSLY. 582 ROPE
(SHE STICKS OUT HER TONGUE AT HIM AND MAKES A FACE 52 STRANG
OF SUPERIOR SCORN)

STIFF
(AFTER A FURTIVE GLANCE AT THE STIFF AND SILENT 190 AHWILD
LILY--
(SHE STALKS WITH STIFF DIGNITY TOWARD HER PLACE AT222 AHWILD
THE FOOT OF THE TABLE.
(WITH STIFF MEEKNESS) VERY WELL, NAT. 223 AHWILD
ONLY LILY REMAINS STIFF AND SILENT.) 225 AHWILD
(ARTHUR GOES OUT WITH A STIFF, WOUNDED DIGNITY.) 264 AHWILD
(ANGRILY) WHERE'S MY LAGER AN' ALE, YUH BIG 8 ANNA
STIFF$
WHITE CURTAINS, CLEAN AND STIFF, ARE AT THE 41 ANNA
WINDOWS.
(LUCY HAS REMAINED STANDING BY THE LEFT CORNER OF 525 DAYS
THE SOFA, IN A STIFF,
(THE TWO BROTHERS CONGEAL INTO TWO STIFF, GRIM- 221 DESIRE
VISAGED STATUES.
WITHOUT SEEMING TO SEE THE TWO STIFF FIGURES AT 221 DESIRE
THE GATE)
ON THE LEFT, FORWARD, A STIFF PLUSH-COVERED CHAIR.493 DIFRNT
STIFF, WHITE CURTAINS ARE AT ALL THE WINDOWS. 494 DIFRNT
AND IS UNCOMFORTABLY SELF-CONSCIOUS AND STIFF 494 DIFRNT
THEREIN.
EMMA SITS STRAIGHT AND STIFF IN HER CHAIR FOR A 548 DIFRNT
WHILE,
HE'LL BE SCARED STIFF/... 432 DYNAMO
THERE IS SOMETHING STIFF, RIGID, UNREAL, 196 EJONES
MARIONETTISH ABOUT THEIR MOVEMENTS.
HER MOVEMENTS ARE STIFF AND SHE CARRIES HERSELF 10 ELECTR
WITH A WOODEN,
THE STUDY IS A LARGE ROOM WITH A STIFF, AUSTERE 28 ELECTR
ATMOSPHERE.
SQUARE-SHOULDERED AND STIFF, WITHOUT A BACKWARD 35 ELECTR
GLANCE.
HE STOPS SHORT IN THE SHADOW FOR A SECOND AND 46 ELECTR
STANDS, ERECT AND STIFF,
SITTING IN STIFF, POSED ATTITUDES THAT SUGGEST THE 46 ELECTR
STATUES OF MILITARY HEROES.

STIFF (CONT'D.)
(TERRIBLY WOUNDED, WITHDRAWN INTO HIS STIFF 56 ELECTR
SOLDIER ARMOR--
BUT IS IMMEDIATELY STIFF AND FROZEN AGAIN. 91 ELECTR
HEAVY GALES AROUND CAPE STIFF/ 104 ELECTR
STANDING SQUARE-SHOULDERED AND STIFF LIKE A GRIM 123 ELECTR
SENTINEL IN BLACK.)
HAZEL LOOKS SELF-CONSCIOUS AND STIFF. 161 ELECTR
AND THEN TURNS AND STANDS FOR A WHILE, STIFF AND 179 ELECTR
SQUARE-SHOULDERED,
BUT YUH'RE A STIFF, SEE$ 212 HA APE
FIRST CABIN STIFF. 242 HA APE
YUH'RE DE ON'Y ONE IN DE WOILD DAT DOES, YUH LUCKY253 HA APE
STIFF/
AND WEARS A SUNDAY-BEST BLUE SUIT WITH A HIGH 670 ICEMAN
STIFF COLLAR.
SCARED STIFF OF AUTOMOBILES. 688 ICEMAN
JAMIE AND I WOULD BE BORED STIFF. 44 JOURNE
HE HAS CHANGED TO A READY-MADE BLUE SERGE SUIT, 89 JOURNE
HIGH STIFF COLLAR AND TIE,
THAT WILL KNOCK YOU STIFF. 156 JOURNE
A FORGETFUL, STIFF-FINGERED GROPING, 170 JOURNE
THE FINGERS HAVE GOTTEN SO STIFF-- 171 JOURNE
HIS BODY HAS BECOME LESS ANGULAR AND STIFF. 288 LAZARU
(AWKWARDLY STIFF AND FORMAL.) 106 MANSNS
HER BODY STIFF FROM SITTING LONG IN THE SAME 71 MISBEG
POSITION.
YOU'RE STIFF AND CRAMPED, AND NO WONDER. 166 MISBEG
(HE DOES SO WITH DIFFICULTY, STILL IN A SLEEPY 166 MISBEG
DAZE, HIS BODY STIFF AND CRAMPED.
(SILENCED--WITH STIFF POLITENESS.) 85 POET
DRISCOLL HAS UNBUTTONED HIS STIFF COLLAR AND ITS 496 VOYAGE
ENDS STICK OUT SIDEWAYS.
PY YINGO, I PITY POOR FALLERS MAKE DAT TRIP ROUND 507 VOYAGE
CAPE STIFF DIS TIME YEAR.

STIFFEN
GOD STIFFEN IT/ 33 ANNA
(ANGRILY FOR A SECOND) GOD STIFFEN YOU/ 46 ANNA
GOD STIFFEN YOU/ 49 ANNA
GOD STIFFEN YOU/ 59 ANNA
(EXPLOSIVELY) GOD STIFFEN IT/ 77 ANNA
GOD STIFFEN YOU, YE SQUARE-HEADED SCUT/ 481 CARDIF
THEY STOP SHORT AND STIFFEN ALL IN A ROW, 293 GGBROW
DRUNK AS A LORD, GOD STIFFEN YOU/ 208 HA APE
(VINDICTIVELY) GOD STIFFEN HIM/ 223 HA APE
GOD STIFFEN US, ARE WE NEVER GOIN' TO TURN IN FUR 332 INZONE
A WINK AV SLEEP$
THEN THE TELEPHONE IN THE FRONT HALL RINGS AND ALL 73 JOURNE
OF THEM STIFFEN STARTLEDLY.)
HOGAN AND JOSIE STIFFEN, AND THEIR EYES BEGIN TO 47 MISBEG
GLITTER.
(WITH SUDDEN FURY) GOD STIFFEN YE, 496 VOYAGE

STIFFENED
RAW-BONED AND STOOP-SHOULDERED, HIS JOINTS 6 ELECTR
STIFFENED BY RHEUMATISM,

STIFFENING
(STIFFENING) OH/ 284 AHWILD
(STIFFENING IN HIS CHAIR--WITH ANGRY RESENTMENT) 503 DAYS
(STIFFENING DEFENSIVELY) WHAT IS WHAT$ 517 DAYS
(THEN STIFFENING) NAM--WHAT D'YE WANT$ 268 DESIRE
(STIFFENING--CURTLY) I DON'T KNOW WHAT YOU'RE 11 ELECTR
TALKING ABOUT.
(STIFFENING--BRUSQUELY) I DON'T KNOW ANYTHING 14 ELECTR
ABOUT LOVE/.
STIFFENING IN HER CHAIR--DEFIANTLY) 175 ELECTR
(HE STOPS, STIFFENING INTO HOSTILITY AS WETJOEN 675 ICEMAN
ENTERS FROM THE HALL.
(STIFFENING.) I THINK NOT ANY MORE EAGER THAN I 132 MANSNS
WAS--(SHE CHECKS HERSELF.
(STIFFENING--COLDLY.) I AM NOT REMAINING HERE. 177 MANSNS

STIFFENS
(THEY ALL LAUGH EXCEPT LILY, WHO BITES HER LIP AND190 AHWILD
STIFFENS.)
(ARTHUR STIFFENS DIGNIFIEDLY.) 190 AHWILD
(WITH A CONCENTRATED EFFORT THAT STIFFENS HIS BODY264 DESIRE
INTO A RIGID LINE
(SHE STOPS ABRUPTLY AND STIFFENS INTO HER OLD, 178 ELECTR
SQUARE-SHOULDERED ATTITUDE.
DION STIFFENS AND HIS MASK STARES STRAIGHT AHEAD. 265 GGBROW
(HE STIFFENS DEFENSIVELY) WHAT ARE YOU GIVING ME 593 ICEMAN
THE HARD LOOK FOR$
(JOE STIFFENS AND HIS EYES NARROW. 598 ICEMAN
HOPE STIFFENS RESENTFULLY FOR A SECOND. 622 ICEMAN
(AS JIMMY STIFFENS WITH A PATHETIC ATTEMPT AT 623 ICEMAN
DIGNITY--PLACATINGLY)
(SHE STIFFENS AND STARES AT HIM WITH A FRIGHTENED 41 JOURNE
DEFIANCE.
(STIFFENS DEFENSIVELY-- 101 JOURNE
(STIFFENS INTO SCORNFUL, DEFENSIVE STUBBORNNESS.) 118 JOURNE
(STIFFENS, AVOIDING HIS EYES AND FORCING A LAUGH.) 13 MANSNS
(STIFFENS, HER FACE BECOMES AS HARD AND COLD AS 33 MANSNS
JOEL'S.)
(STIFFENS, STARES AT HER WITH HATRED FOR A 104 MANSNS
SECOND--THEN COLDLY, IN A CURT TONE.)
SIMON STARTS AND STIFFENS IN HIS CHAIR.) 129 MANSNS
THEN STIFFENS REGALLY AND RETURNS HIS GAZE 387 MARCOM
UNFLINCHINGLY.
(JOSIE STIFFENS AS IF SHE'D BEEN INSULTED. 88 MISBEG
(STIFFENS) EXCUSE FOR WHAT, YOU OLD-- 97 MISBEG
(JOSIE STIFFENS AND HER FACE HARDENS. 126 MISBEG
(STIFFENS--HER FACE HARDENING) 130 MISBEG
SHE STIFFENS INTO HOSTILITY AND HER MOUTH SETS IN 33 POET
SCORN.
(STIFFENS--HAUGHTILY.) 40 POET
(STIFFENS) WARN ME ABOUT WHAT, MRS. HARFORD$ 84 POET
(STIFFENS ARROGANTLY.) I AM NOT, SIR. 117 POET
(STIFFENS DEFENSIVELY.) I MADE HER GO TO BED. 135 POET

STIFFENS

STIFFENS (CONT'D.)
IT PENETRATES MELODY'S STUPOR AND HE STIFFENS 166 POET
RIGIDLY ON HIS CHAIR,
(MELODY STIFFENS FOR A SECOND, BUT THAT IS ALL. 167 POET
(HIS BODY STIFFENS ON HIS CHAIR AND THE COARSE 171 POET
LEER VANISHES FROM HIS FACE.

STIFFLY
(HE STARTS STIFFLY FOR THE DOOR.) 203 AHWILD
(STIFFLY) WELL, I HOPE HE FINDS A WOMAN WHO'S 213 AHWILD
WILLING--
(STIFFLY) I CAN'T LOVE A MAN WHO DRINKS. 213 AHWILD
(SHE SITS DOWN STIFFLY AT THE FOOT OF THE TABLE.) 222 AHWILD
(NORAH, STILL STANDING WITH THE SOUP TUREEN HELD 222 AHWILD
OUT STIFFLY IN FRONT OF HER,
(HER EYES ON HER PLATE--STIFFLY) 224 AHWILD
(STIFFLY) WHAT MAKES YOU THINK SO$ 467 CARIBE
GO--PLEASE--(HIGGINS BOWS STIFFLY AND GOES OUT. 573 CRUSS
STIFFLY BESIDE HER ON THE EDGE OF THE SOFA. 241 DESIRE
(STIFFLY) A BODY'S AS OLD AS THEY FEELS--AND I 538 DIFRNT
FEEL RIGHT YOUNG.
(STIFFLY) HER 'N' ME AIN'T SUCH GOOD FRIENDS NO 539 DIFRNT
MORE, IF YOU MUST KNOW.
(STIFFLY) THERE'S NOTHING WORRYING ME. 12 ELECTR
TURNS STIFFLY AND GOES INTO THE HOUSE AND CLOSES 27 ELECTR
THE DOOR BEHIND HER.)
SEATED STIFFLY IN AN ARMCHAIR, HIS HANDS ON THE 28 ELECTR
ARMS,
HER THIN FIGURE, SEATED STIFFLY UPRIGHT, ARMS 43 ELECTR
AGAINST HER SIDES,
(GOING STIFFLY TO MEET HER) TRAIN WAS LATE. 47 ELECTR
THEN WALKS STIFFLY DOWN THE STEPS AND STANDS 57 ELECTR
AGAIN.
LAVINIA STARES AT HER MOTHER A MOMENT--THEN ABOUT- 91 ELECTR
FACES STIFFLY TO FOLLOW HIM.)
STIFFLY ERECT LIKE A SENTINEL AT ATTENTION. 93 ELECTR
THEN SUDDENLY TURNS BACK AND STANDS STIFFLY 115 ELECTR
UPRIGHT AND GRIM BESIDE THE BODY AND
LAVINIA IS STIFFLY SQUARE-SHOULDERED, HER EYES 119 ELECTR
HARD, HER MOUTH GRIM AND SET.
LAVINIA TURNS AND, STIFFLY ERECT, HER FACE STERN 125 ELECTR
AND MASK-LIKE,
(HE TURNS AND STALKS STIFFLY WITH HURT DIGNITY 146 ELECTR
FROM THE ROOM.
AND MARCHES STIFFLY FROM THE ROOM.) 168 ELECTR
HER ARMS HELD STIFFLY TO HER SIDES, HER LEGS AND 170 ELECTR
FEET PRESSED TOGETHER.
(JERKS UP STIFFLY WITH A LOOK OF ALARM) 171 ELECTR
(A BIT STIFFLY) YES, HE CERTAINLY DID. 275 GGBROW
MARGARET SAYS STIFFLY) 303 GGBROW
(INTERRUPTING HIM--STIFFLY) I CERTAINLY CAN'T 303 GGBROW
UNDERSTAND--
(SHE SITS ON THE CHAIR STIFFLY. 304 GGBROW
(TAKEN ABACK--A BIT STIFFLY) 314 GGBROW
THEIR HEADS HELD STIFFLY UP, LOOKING NEITHER TO 236 HA APE
RIGHT NOR LEFT.
(A BIT STIFFLY) I DON'T, NO. 578 ICEMAN
(STIFFLY) DE OLD IRISH BUNK, HUH$ 635 ICEMAN
(STIFFLY) VERY WELL. 651 ICEMAN
(HE COMES FROM BEHIND THE COUNTER AND GOES TO THE 673 ICEMAN
BAR--ADDRESSING ROCKY STIFFLY)
(HE WALKS STIFFLY TO THE STREET DOOR--THEN TURNS 673 ICEMAN
FOR A PARTING SHOT--BOASTFULLY)
(STIFFLY) NO, I--I'M THROUGH WITH THAT STUFF. 674 ICEMAN
(STIFFLY) I SAID I WAS, DIDN'T I$ 674 ICEMAN
(STIFFLY) NO. 677 ICEMAN
THEY ARE LIKE WAX FIGURES, SET STIFFLY ON THEIR 696 ICEMAN
CHAIRS,
THEIR FEET MOVING, THEIR BODIES SWAYING TO THE 282 LAZARU
MUSIC'S BEAT, STIFFLY.
(GETS TO HIS FEET--STIFFLY TO SIMON.) 60 MANSNS
(JOEL STARES AT HIM, IS ABOUT TO SAY SOMETHING 60 MANSNS
MORE, THEN BOWS STIFFLY.
HE COMES BACK AND SITS DOWN STIFFLY IN THE CHAIR,) 71 MANSNS
(STIFFLY.) YES, IT IS VERY RESTFUL HERE--. 106 MANSNS
(SHE TAKES A STEP TOWARDS LEFT, STIFFLY, AS IF BY 177 MANSNS
A DETERMINED EFFORT OF WILL,
(STIFFLY) I'M GOING. 6 MISBEG
(WALKS TOWARD HOGAN--STIFFLY) 56 MISBEG
(ASHAMED BUT DEFIANT--STIFFLY) 121 MISBEG
(STIFFLY.) MERELY A DISTANT COUSIN. 59 POET
(STIFFLY.) 100 POET
HE RISES TO HIS FEET, A BIT STIFFLY AND CAREFULLY,103 POET
AND BOWS.
(HE GETS UP AND BOWS STIFFLY.) 115 POET
HE IS STIFFLY CORRECT IN DRESS AND MANNER, DRYLY 116 POET
PORTENTOUS IN SPEECH,
HE BOWS A BIT STIFFLY, AND GADSBY FINDS HIMSELF 117 POET
RETURNING THE BOW.)
(STIFFLY) BARELY. 30 STRANG
SHE STRAIGHTENS UP IN HER CHAIR STIFFLY.) 56 STRANG
(STIFFLY) I'M NO LONGER A DOCTOR 172 STRANG
(REPELLED BY THIS IDEA--STIFFLY) 190 STRANG

STIFFNESS
OR WITH A SELF-CONSCIOUS SQUARE-SHOULDERED 73 ELECTR
STIFFNESS.
HER MOVEMENTS HAVE LOST THEIR SQUARE-SHOULDERED 137 ELECTR
STIFFNESS.
(WITH EMBARRASSED STIFFNESS.) 74 POET

STIFFS
NO STIFFS NEED APPLY. 212 HA APE
SHE WAS ALL IN WHITE-LIKE DEY WRAP AROUND STIFFS. 230 HA APE
WHERE'S ALL DE WHITE-COLLAR STIFFS YUH SAID WAS 234 HA APE
HERE--AND DE SKOITS--HER KINDS
YUH LOOK LIKE STIFFS LAID OUT FOR DE BONEYARD/ 238 HA APE
(GLANCING AROUND) JEES, POIL, IT'S DE MORGUE WID 611 ICEMAN
ALL DE STIFFS ON DECK.
BUT HERE YOU ARE, ACTING LIKE A LOT OF STIFFS 704 ICEMAN
CHEATING THE UNDERTAKER/

STIFLE
WHICH HARD USAGE HAS FAILED TO STIFLE, A SENSE OF 7 ANNA
HUMOR MOCKING,
(THEN WEEPING HYSTERICALLY AND TRYING TO STIFLE 439 DYNAMO
IT)
OUR SOBS STIFLE US, OUR TEARS WET THE GROUND, 436 MARCOM
(BEFORE SHE CAN STIFLE HER IMMEDIATE REACTION OF 69 STRANG
CONTEMPT AND DISLIKE)

STIFLED
LETS OUT A STIFLED GIGGLE. 229 AHWILD
WITH A STIFLED CRY SHE RUNS TOWARD THEM.) 255 DESIRE
(IN A STIFLED VOICE) LOOK OUT, EZRA/ 60 ELECTR
SHE STARTS BACK WITH A STIFLED SCREAM AND STARES 101 ELECTR
AT IT WITH GUILTY FEAR.)
AND SHRINKS BACK WITH A STIFLED GASP OF FEAR. 107 ELECTR
(WITH A STIFLED CRY) ORIN/ 167 ELECTR
IN A STIFLED VOICE BETWEEN HER CLENCHED TEETH) 172 ELECTR
(IN A STIFLED TONE) GOD DAMN YOU/ 701 ICEMAN
(IN A STIFLED VOICE.) WHAT'S THAT SHE'S CARRYING,172 JOURNE
EDMUNDS
(HE BEGINS TO LAUGH AGAIN BUT HE CHOKES ON A 169 POET
STIFLED SOB.
HIS KNEES AND BEGINS TO SOB--STIFLED TORN SOUNDS.) 43 STRANG

STIFLEDLY
(STIFLEDLY) LET'S GO HOME. 301 GGBROW

STIFLES
HER MOUTH TWITCHES AND DRAWS DOWN AT THE CORNERS 174 ELECTR
AS SHE STIFLES A SOB.
MIRIAM STIFLES A SCREAM. 333 LAZARU
ROCHE STIFLES A MALICIOUS GUFFAW.) 103 POET
(SHE STIFLES AN HYSTERICAL LAUGH) 108 STRANG
(SHE STIFLES ANOTHER LAUGH--THEN ON THE VERGE OF 108 STRANG
FAINTING, WEAKLY)

STIFLING
AND PUSHES BACK HER HAIR FROM HER FLUSHED FACE AS 526 DIFRNT
IF IT WERE STIFLING HER)
ONE OF THE MOST STIFLING DAYS I'VE EVER KNOWN. 43 MISBEG
I WOULDN'T CALL IT A DAMNED BIT STIFLING. 44 MISBEG

STILLED
AND NOW EVEN THE GREAT PALACE BELL IS STILLED-- 435 MARCOM
HALF MOCKINGLY BUT ASSERTIVELY)

STILLNESS
THERE IS A PAUSE OF DEAD STILLNESS. 252 HA APE
THERE IS A TENSE STILLNESS IN THE ROOM. 663 ICEMAN
AND AN AWED AND FRIGHTENED STILLNESS PREVAILS, FOR278 LAZARU
LAZARUS IS A STRANGE
IT WAS THE STILLNESS THAT FOLLOWS A SHRIEK OF 174 MANSNS
TERROR, WAITING TO BECOME AWARE--

STILLWELL'S
(HIS EYES ARE ON STILLWELL'S FACE, DESPERATELY 554 DAYS
TRYING TO READ SOME ANSWER THERE.

STILTED
EMBARRASSED AND SELF-CONSCIOUS AND HIS EXPRESSIONS 295 AHWILD
MORE STILTED.
IN FORCED STILTED TONES) 225 DESIRE
WITH AN ATMOSPHERE OF UNCOMFORTABLE, STILTED 79 ELECTR
STATELINESS.
BUT HER SPEECH HAS AT TIMES A SELF-CONSCIOUS, 16 POET
STILTED QUALITY ABOUT IT,

STILTEDLY
THE ATMOSPHERE IS AS STILTEDLY GRAVE 263 AHWILD
(TAKES HER HAND, SMILING IN RETURN--A BIT 50 MANSNS
STILTEDLY.)

STIMULANT
I MUST HAVE A STIMULANT-- 45 MISBEG

STIMULATION
WHICH IS IMPERVIOUS TO STIMULATION. 696 ICEMAN

STING
YOUR HAND IS A COOL MUD POULTICE ON THE STING OF 279 GGBROW
THOUGHT/
FLANNEL-MOUTH, GOLD-BRICK MERCHANT STING YOU WITH 80 JOURNE
ANOTHER PIECE OF BUM PROPERTY/
WHINE, STING, SUCK ONE'S BLOOD... 52 STRANG

STINGER
SHE DOES IT NOW AS IF SHE WISHED SHE WAS A 456 DYNAMO
MOSQUITO WITH A STINGER...

STINGINESS
YOUR STINGINESS IS TO BLAME-- 140 JOURNE
AND I KNOW WHO IS/ YOU ARE/ YOUR DAMNED 140 JOURNE
STINGINESS/
AND MISER STINGINESS. 580 ROPE

STINGS
SHE HAD YELLOW HAIR--THE KIND THAT BURNS AND 283 AHWILD
STINGS YOU/

STINGY
AND DON'T BE STINGY, BABY. 14 ANNA
HE'S A DAMN STINGY, UGLY OLD CUSS, IF YOU WANT MY 521 DIFRNT
DUPE ON HIM.
GOL DURN HIM, HE'S GITTIN' STINGY IN HIS OLD AGE. 130 ELECTR
WELL, USE MY DOUGH, DEN, IF YUH'RE SO STINGY. 682 ICEMAN
THERE'S NO SENSE LETTING YOUR FEAR OF THE 117 JOURNE
POORHOUSE MAKE YOU TOO STINGY.
(INSINUATINGLY) IS HE AS STINGY WITH HIS COIN AS 592 ROPE
HE USED TO BE$

STINK
AND LA PLATA--PHEW, THE STINK OF THE HIDES/ 487 CARDIF
WHAT'S THE MATTER IF THE TRUTH IS THAT THEIR 578 ICEMAN
FAVORING BREEZE HAS THE STINK OF
IT TURNS MY STOMACH WITH ITS STINK OF ONIONS AND 42 POET
STEW/

STINKIN'
AND DAMN THIS STINKIN' WHALIN' SHIP OF HIS, AND 536 'ILE
DAMN ME FOR A FOOL
ON A STINKIN' WHALIN' SHIP TO THE ARCTIC SEAS TO 537 'ILE
BE LOCKED IN BY THE ROTTEN ICE
THE STINKIN' OLD HYPUCRITE/ 216 DESIRE
ANYBODY THAT WANTS THIS STINKIN' OLD ROCK-PILE OF 221 DESIRE
A FARM KIN HEV IT.

STINKIN' (CONT'D.)
YE'LL NEVER LIVE T' SEE THE DAY WHEN EVEN A 230 DESIRE
STINKIN' WEED ON ITILL BELONG T' YEY
YE'RE NOTHIN' BUT A STINKIN' PASSEL O' LIES/ 256 DESIRE
THE OLD SKUNK'D JEST BE STINKIN' MEAN ENUF TO TAKE260 DESIRE
IT OUT ON THAT BABY.
(SERIOUSLY) IT'S A BLEEDIN' QUEER PLACE, THAT 185 EJONES
STINKIN' FOREST.
IF 'E LOST 'IS BLOODY WAY IN THESE STINKIN' WOODS 203 EJONES
'ED LIKELY TURN IN A CIRCLE
'E SAYS THIS 'ERE STINKIN' SHIP IS OUR 'OME. 211 HA APE
YUH LOUSY, STINKIN', YELLOW MUT OF A CATHOLIC- 225 HA APE
MOLDERIN' BASTARD/
BUT HE'S DEAD NOW, AND HIS LAST BIT AV LYIN' PRIDE168 POET
IS MURTHERED AND STINKIN'.
YOU'RE AS STINKIN' MEAN AS EVER. 589 ROPE
I'LL FIX YOUR HASH, YOU STINKIN' OLD MURDERER/ 596 ROPE

STINKING
SCUT STINKING OF PIGS AND DUNGS 48 ANNA
WHEN IT IS THEIR COURAGE TO POSSESS THEIR OWN 542 DAYS
SOULS WHICH IS DEAD--AND STINKING/
PUTTING ON AIRS, THE STINKING NIGGER/ 175 EJONES
(NAUSEATED--TURNS ON HIM) YOU STINKING ROTTEN 649 ICEMAN
LIAR/
STINKING BIT OF WITHERED OLD FLESH WHICH IS MY 689 ICEMAN
BEAUTIFUL LITTLE LIFE/
YOU STINKING OLD MISER-- 145 JOURNE
YOU CAN SHOW YOURSELF UP BEFORE THE WHOLE TOWN AS 145 JOURNE
SUCH A STINKING OLD TIGHTWAD/
DON'T CALL ME A STINKING MISER, 146 JOURNE
A STINKING OLD MISER. 146 JOURNE
YOU'RE STINKING NOW. 156 JOURNE
AND STINKING WITH LIES AND GREED AND TREACHERY/ 102 POET

STINKO
STINKO, DE BOT' OF 'EM. 612 ICEMAN
WE FIGGERED DEY WAS TOO STINKO TO BOTHER US MUCH 612 ICEMAN
AND WE COULD COP A GOOD SLEEP
LET'S GET STINKO, POIL. 640 ICEMAN
DEY PINCHED A COUPLA BOTTLES AND BRUNG DEM UP DEIR669 ICEMAN
ROOM AND GOT STINKO.
SO DEY PUT ON DEIR LIDS AND BEAT IT, DE BOT' OF 670 ICEMAN
DEM STINKO.
(POURING A DRINK) I'M GOIN' TO GET STINKO, SEE/ 690 ICEMAN
STINKO, AND HE PULLED A GAT AND SAID HE'D PLUG 699 ICEMAN
HICKEY FOR INSULTIN' HIM.
AND IS HE STINKO/ 725 ICEMAN
STINKO IS RIGHT. 725 ICEMAN
I'VE NEVER SEEN HIM THAT STINKO BEFORE. 101 MISBEG

STINKS
YOUR REPUTATION STINKS SO. 31 JOURNE

STINT
DON'T STINT YOURSELF. 53 MISBEG

STIR
I HAIN'T A-GOING TO STIR OUTA BED TILL BREAKFAST'S215 DESIRE
READY.
(ALL THE OCCUPANTS OF THE ROOM STIR ON THEIR 581 ICEMAN
CHAIRS
(THE DRUNKS AT THE TABLES STIR. 596 ICEMAN
(THERE IS A FAINT STIR FROM ALL THE CROWD, 701 ICEMAN
THEY STIR AND PUSH ABOUT RESTLESSLY WITH AN EAGER 298 LAZARU
CURIOSITY AND IMPATIENCE.
THERE IS A NEW STIR FROM THE CROWD WHO AGAIN PUSH 303 LAZARU
FORWARD.)

STIRNER
ENGELS, KROPOTKIN, MAX STIRNER, PLAYS BY IBSEN, 11 JOURNE
SHAW, STRINDBERG,

STIRRED
ROBERT SEEMED STIRRED UP ABOUT SOMETHING.. 98 BEYOND
HE STARES AT HER, FASCINATED AND STIRRED.) 52 ELECTR
(THEN AS IF THE WORDS STIRRED SOMETHING WITHIN HIM165 ELECTR
(GLANCES AT HIM--FOR A MOMENT HE IS STIRRED TO 702 ICEMAN
SARDONIC PITY)
SHE BREAKS AWAY, STIRRED AND HAPPY, BUT MODESTLY 83 MANSNS
EMBARRASSED--
HE LOOKS AT THEM, FASCINATED AND STIRRED, AND 366 MARCOM
MURMURS ENVIOUSLY)
SHE LOOKS STARTLED AND CONFUSED, STIRRED AND AT 51 MISBEG
THE SAME TIME FRIGHTENED.
(DEEPLY STIRRED, IN SPITE OF HERSELF--HER VOICE 129 MISBEG
TREMBLING)

STIRRIN'
DON'T YOU GO STIRRIN' IT UP AGAIN. 513 DIFRNT

STIRRING
(STIRRING A BIT--MUTTERINGLY) 33 ANNA
HAS LOOKED BACK AT HER WITH A STIRRING OF FOOLISH 52 ANNA
HOPE IN HIS EYES)
(STIRRING UNEASILY--MECHANICALLY) 524 DAYS
HER LARGE EYES DREAMY WITH THE REFLECTED STIRRING 278 GGBROW
OF PROFOUND INSTINCTS.
I WILL FEEL YOU STIRRING IN YOUR SLEEP, FOREVER 323 GGBROW
UNDER MY HEART/
I FEEL YOU STIRRING IN YOUR SLEEP, FOREVER UNDER 323 GGBROW
MY HEART.
HE MAKES A SLIGHT MOVEMENT, A STIRRING IN HIS 277 LAZARU
VISION.
OF THE WINE OF LIFE STIRRING FOREVER IN THE SAP 307 LAZARU
AND BLOOD AND LOAM OF THINGS.
BLOOD-STIRRING CALL TO THAT ULTIMATE ATTAINMENT IN318 LAZARU
WHICH ALL PREPOSSESSION WITH
ALREADY AT THE MERE PROSPECT OF ESCAPE, I FEEL A 40 MANSNS
REBIRTH STIRRING IN ME/
THE TWO WOMEN TURN TO STARE AT HIM, WITH A 119 MANSNS
STIRRING OF SUSPICION AND RESENTMENT.

STIRRUP
A STIRRUP CUP, AND WE'LL BE OFF. 128 POET

STIRS
(STIRS UNCOMFORTABLY) HMM/ 265 AHWILD

STIRS (CONT'D.)
ALL THE WINDOWS ARE OPEN, BUT NO BREEZE STIRS THE 112 BEYOND
SOILED WHITE CURTAINS.
(YANK GROANS AND STIRS UNEASILY, OPENING HIS EYES.482 CARDIF
THEN ELSA STIRS RESTLESSLY AND MOANS. 554 DAYS
(SHE STIRS AS IF TO GO INTO THE HOUSE) 457 DYNAMO
FOR HE STIRS, GRUNTS, 102 ELECTR
(STIRS, SIGHS AND MURMURS DREAMFULLY) 278 GGBROW
(DRUNK STIRS UNEASILY) TO BE MERELY A SUCCESSFUL 296 GGBROW
FREAK,
THEN STIRS HIMSELF, PUTS HIS HAND ON DION'S 299 GGBROW
BREAST.)
(HE STIRS UNEASILY. 309 GGBROW
HE STIRS ON HIS CHAIR, TRYING TO WAKE UP, 628 ICEMAN
EVERYONE IN THE GROUP STIRS WITH AWAKENING DREAD 705 ICEMAN
AND THEY ALL BEGIN TO GROW
TYRUNE STIRS IN HIS CHAIR. 176 JOURNE
SIMON STIRS UNEASILY AND HIS EYES CEASE TO FOLLOW 125 MANSNS
THE LINES.
(SIMON GROANS AND STIRS AND LOOKS UP AT HER. 194 MANSNS
(TYRUNE STIRS IN HIS SLEEP AND MOANS, 161 MISBEG

STITCHES
LISTEN TO JIM STILL IN STITCHES. 65 MISBEG

STOCK
TAWDRY FINERY OF PEASANT STOCK TURNED PROSTITUTE. 14 ANNA
MAN OF THEM IS WORTH ANY TEN STOCK-FISH-SWILLING 49 ANNA
SQUARE-HEADS
I AIN'T NEVER TOOK MUCH STOCK IN THE TRUCK THEM 486 CARDIF
SKYPILOTS PREACH.
I DON'T TAKE NO STOCK IN SECH SLOP/ 214 DESIRE
(PROUDLY.) HAIN'T WE RAISED 'EM T' BE FUST-RATE, 218 DESIRE
NUMBER ONE PRIZE STOCK$
AN' BURN YER BARN AN' KILL THE STOCK/ 223 DESIRE
MCBBE--MEBBE THEY'VE PIZENED THE STOCK--R' 225 DESIRE
SOMETHIN'/
I'VE TURNED THE COWS AN' OTHER STOCK LOOSE/ 267 DESIRE
WAAL, I GOT T' ROUND UP THE STOCK. 269 DESIRE
SHE RESEMBLES SOME PASSE STOCK ACTRESS OF FIFTY 520 DIFRNT
MADE UP FOR A HEROINE OF TWENTY.
TO LET HIM MAKE YOU A LAUGHING STOCK/ 38 ELECTR
OH, DON'T GIT IT IN YOUR HEADS I TAKE STOCK IN 135 ELECTR
SPIRITS TRESPASSIN' ROUND
THE YOUNGER LOOKING AS IF THE VITALITY OF HER 218 HA APE
STOCK HAD BEEN SAPPED BEFORE SHE
ALL THAT WAS BURNT OUT IN OUR STOCK BEFORE I WAS 219 HA APE
BORN.
AFTER ALL, I'M FROM OLD AMERICAN PIONEER STOCK. 649 ICEMAN
I HOPE YOU'LL LAY IN A GOOD STOCK AHEAD SO WE'LL 86 JOURNE
NEVER HAVE ANOTHER NIGHT LIKE
LEADING PART OF HIS IN A WEEK, AS YOU USED TO DO 136 JOURNE
IN STOCK IN THE OLD DAYS.
IF WE'D ONLY THE THOUSAND WE'D STOCK THE FARM GOOD587 ROPE
SAME'S WE DO WITH STOCK, TO GIVE THE MAN I LOVED A 63 STRANG
HEALTHY CHILD.

STOCK'D
WAAL--THE STOCK'D GOT T' BE WATERED. 208 DESIRE

STOCKED
AND STOCKED UP WITH SOME SPECIAL GRUB ALL ON 103 BEYOND
ROBERT'S ACCOUNT$

STOCKHOLDER
AS A STOCKHOLDER, IT IS MY RIGHT-- 70 MANSNS

STOCKHOLM
I GO HOME FROM HERE TO STOCKHOLM. 502 VOYAGE
ARE YE GOIN' UP TO--TO STOCKHOLM B'FORE YER SHIPS 502 VOYAGE
AWAY AGEN$
I WUS BORN IN STOCKHOLM. 502 VOYAGE
I WAS BORN THERE TOO--IN STOCKHOLM. 502 VOYAGE
AIN'T YER GOT SOME GEL BACK IN STOCKHOLMS 503 VOYAGE
BUT AIN'T STOCKHOLM A CITY SAME'S LONDON$ 503 VOYAGE
ON FARM YUST A LITTLE WAY FROM STOCKHOLM. 503 VOYAGE
YES--UNTIL STEAMER SAIL FOR STOCKHOLM--IN TWO DAY.506 VOYAGE

STOCKIN'
HE WAS STANDIN' RIGHT THERE--(POINTING AGAIN) IN 519 INZONE
HIS STOCKIN' FEET--

STOCKING
AND TAKES A PACKAGE OF CHEAP CIGARETTES FROM HER 239 AHWILD
STOCKING)
SHE PUTS THE FIVE RICHARD HAD GIVEN HER IN HER 243 AHWILD
STOCKING AND PICKS UP HER GLASS)
(DIGS INTO HER STOCKING AND GIVES HIM A DOLLAR) 243 AHWILD
AND HERE'S ONE OLD STOCKING--AND THERE'S THE OTHER121 BEYOND
OLD STOCKING.
AND ALL ARE IN THEIR STOCKING FEET. 477 CARDIF
(SHE HIKES HER SKIRT UP AND REACHES INSIDE THE TOP683 ICEMAN
OF HER STOCKING)
FORECASTLE FULLY DRESSED, BUT IN HIS STOCKING 513 INZONE
FEET,

STOCKINGS
(MECHANICALLY) COME AND LET ME TAKE OFF YOUR 118 BEYOND
SHOES AND STOCKINGS, MARY.
HE COMES FORWARD AND PICKS UP THE SHOES AND 121 BEYOND
STOCKINGS WHICH HE SHOVES CARELESSLY
(TAKING OFF HER SHOES AND STOCKINGS) 121 BEYOND
DOES YOUR MOTHER TAKE OFF YOUR SHOES AND STOCKINGS121 BEYOND
BEFORE YOUR NAP$
BUT THE LOWER PART OF HER SKIRT AND HER STOCKINGS 548 DAYS
AND SHOES ARE SOAKING WET.
SO ARE THE HIGH-HEELED PUMPS AND CLOCKED SILK 920 DIFRNT
STOCKINGS.
(GLANCING AT HER SHOES, STOCKINGS, AND DRESS) 537 DIFRNT
(THEY BOTH PULL UP THEIR SKIRTS TO GET THE MONEY 613 ICEMAN
FROM THEIR STOCKINGS.
AN AFRICAN SLAVE, DRESSED IN PINK LIVERY WITH 391 MARCOM
GREEN HAT AND SHOES AND STOCKINGS
FIVE FEET ELEVEN IN HER STOCKINGS AND WEIGHS 3 MISBEG
AROUND ONE HUNDRED AND EIGHTY.
BLACK STOCKINGS AND SHOES. 71 MISBEG

STOCKINGS

STOCKINGS (CONT'D.)
(WITH HEAVY SARCASM) IN YOUR BEST SHOES AND 79 MISBEG STOCKINGSS

STOCKS
AND IT'S SAFER THAN THE STOCKS AND BONDS OF WALL 16 JOURNE STREET SWINDLERS.

STOCKY
THE BARTENDER, A STOCKY YOUNG IRISHMAN WITH A 236 AHWILD FOXILY CUNNING,
HER BROTHER, THE CAPTAIN, IS SHORT AND STOCKY, 94 BEYOND THE UPPER PART OF HIS STOCKY FIGURE OUTLINED 455 CARIBE AGAINST THE SKY.
HE IS A HULKING, STOCKY-BUILT YOUNG FELLOW OF 25. 498 DIFRNT JOE MUTT IS A NEGRO, ABOUT FIFTY YEARS OLD, BROWN-574 ICEMAN SKINNED, STOCKY,
HE IS A STOCKY, MUSCULAR, SANDY-HAIRED 581 ROPE OLSON, A STOCKY, MIDDLE-AGED SWEDE WITH ROUND, 496 VOYAGE CHILDISH BLUE EYES.

STOICAL
(REASSURINGLY STOICAL NOW) YOU NEEDN'T WORRY, MA.271 AHWILD

STOICALLY
(TRYING WITH AGONY TO TAKE THIS STOICALLY-- 483 WELDED MUMBLING STUPIDLY)

STOIN
SAY, YOUSE, YUH LOOK LIKE DE STOIN OF A FERRYBOAT.238 HA APE

STOKEHOLD
I'M THINKING IF IT'S A STOKEHOLD OF A PROPER 38 ANNA LINER,

STOKEHOLE
AND IT'S GOD'S TRUTH--THERE'D BEEN MUTINY ITSELF 36 ANNA IN THE STOKEHOLE.
ANGRILY) IS IT CASTING INSULTS AT THE MEN IN THE 49 ANNA STOKEHOLE YE ARE, YE OLD APES
AN IRISHMAN AND A MAN OF THE STOKEHOLE-- 49 ANNA PUT ONE OF 'EM DOWN HERE FOR ONE WATCH IN DE 212 HA APE STOKEHOLE, WHAT'D HAPPENS
BREAKING OUR BACKS AND HEARTS IN THE HELL OF THE 214 HA APE STOKEHOLE--
HELL IN DE STOKEHOLES 215 HA APE PERMISSION TO VISIT THE STOKEHOLES 220 HA APE FOR THE STOKEHOLE. 220 HA APE NO, I MEAN THE STOKEHOLE. 221 HA APE FINE STOKEHOLE. 222 HA APE SURE WHAT ELSE BUT LOVE FOR US POOR BASTES IN THE 228 HA APE STOKEHOLE WOULD BE BRINGING A
IT PUT THE TOUCH OF HOME, SWATE HOME IN THE 230 HA APE STOKEHOLE.
DEN I SHIPPED IN DE STOKEHOLE. 234 HA APE MORE'N OUR TOLE BLOODY STOKEHOLE MAKES IN TEN 235 HA APE VOYAGES SWEATIN' IN 'ELL!
SHE WAS DOLLED UP ALL IN WHITE--IN DE STOKEHOLE. 241 HA APE

STOKEHOLES
IN THE STOKEHOLES OF SHIPS SINCE I WAS A LAD ONLY. 35 ANNA

STOKER
HE'S A STOKER. 43 ANNA FIREMAN--STOKER ON DE LINERS. 246 HA APE

STOKIN'
(DULLY) I WAS A FIREMAN--STOKIN' ON DE LINERS. 240 HA APE

STOLE
I FEEL--MEBBE SHE--BUT--I CAN'T FIGGER OUT--WHY-- 243 DESIRE WHEN YE'VE STOLE HER PLACE--
I'LL GIT RICH INAR AN' COME BACK AN' FIGHT HIM FUR257 DESIRE THE FARM HE STOLE--
BEIN' DRUNK ON NATIVE RUM THEY'D STOLE, 503 DIFRNT HOW YOU STOLE THE MONEY OUT OF THE BUREAU DRAWER--528 DIFRNT IT'S WHAT HIS FATHER STOLE FROM YOURS. 39 ELECTR YOU STOLE ALL LOVE FROM ME WHEN I WAS BORN/ 57 ELECTR SMASHED EVERYTHING AND STOLE TWO HUNDRED DOLLARS 105 ELECTR OFF HER SKIPPER.
DID YOU ASK HER WHY SHE STOLE MOTHER'S COLORS/ 144 ELECTR AND CONFESS THAT I STOLE YOUR PLACE OUT OF LOVE 307 GGBROW FOR HER,
STOLE HIS PAPERS MOST LIKELY--WHEN HE DON'T KNOW 522 INZONE HOW TO BOX THE COMPASS, HARDLY.
AND GIVE ME BACK THE FAITH YOU STOLE FROM ME, OR 1182 MANSNS WILL CHOOSE HER/
GIVE ME BACK WHAT YOU STOLE/ 375 MARCOM I STOLE THE MONEY FOR. 11 MISBEG YOU STOLE MY FINE SATCHEL FOR THAT LUMP/ 14 MISBEG AND STOLE MY MONEY TO GIVE TO THAT LOUSY ALTAR 15 MISBEG BOY, I'LL--
HE STOLE IT FROM A WAREHOUSE ON FAKED PERMITS. 115 MISBEG I THINK THE BOYS IS RIGHT WHEN THEY SAY HE STOLE 170 POET THE UNIFORM
STOLE YOUR MONEY AND RAN OFF AND LEFT YOU 581 ROPE AN' WHERE D'YOUSE SUPPOSE LUKE GOT THE HUNDRED 586 ROPE DOLLARS HE STOLES

STOLEN
HE'S STOLEN MY BRAIN/ 567 CROSS IT'S YOU WHO HAVE STOLEN ALL LOVE FROM ME SINCE 33 ELECTR THE TIME I WAS BORN/
IT WILL BE STOLEN IF I KEEP IT HERE/ 160 ELECTR BECAUSE IT'S PART OF THE CREATIVE LIFE BROWN'S 296 GGBROW STOLEN FROM ME/
NO MATTER HOW MUCH MONEY IT HAD STOLEN FROM THE 24 JOURNE POOR.
WHO HAS STOLEN YOUR PLACE IN BED/ 80 MANSNS (THEN VIRTUOUSLY) BUT I DON'T LIKE TAKING STOLEN 7 MISBEG MONEY.
(SEETHING) YOU'VE STOLEN MY SATCHEL TO GIVE HIM, 13 MISBEG I SUPPOSE,
STANDARD OIL MONEY THAT WAS STOLEN 62 MISBEG I LEFT D'DOND TO TEND BAR AND I'LL WAGER HE HAS 135 POET THREE DRINKS STOLEN ALREADY.
TOLD YOU TO YOUR FACE HE'D STOLEN AND WAS LEAVIN'.581 ROPE IF ONLY TO GET SOMETHING BACK FROM SAM OF ALL HE'S193 STRANG STOLEN FROM ME/...))

STOLID
THE TYPE OF FOOTBALL LINESMAN OF THAT PERIOD, WITH186 AHWILD A SQUARE STOLID FACE.
THERE IS A LOT OF STOLID, EARTHY PEASANT IN HIM, 13 JOURNE MIXED
HIS GLARING STOLID WITH THE DIGNITY OF ONE 439 MARCOM YET SHE IS NOT UGLY--RATHER PRETTY FOR HER BOVINE,471 WELDED STOLID TYPE--

STOLIDLY
(STOLIDLY) YOU'VE BEEN COUGHING AN AWFUL LOT 147 BEYOND LATELY.
WHO ARE STANDING STOLIDLY, AWAITING ORDERS) 406 MARCOM SHE LOOKS AT HIM STOLIDLY. 472 WELDED SHE SUBMITS STOLIDLY. 475 WELDED

STOMACH
WID NUTHIN' BUT WIND ON YO' STOMACH, O' COURSE YOU188 EJONES FEELS JIGGEDY.
IT'S A COWARD'S GAME I HAVE NO STOMACH FOR/ 37 ELECTR SO EARLY IN THE MORNING ON AN EMPTY STOMACH/ 606 ICEMAN RUINING MY STOMACH WITH ROTGUT. 652 ICEMAN ONE DRINK ON TOP OF YOUR HANGOVER AND AN EMPTY 686 ICEMAN STOMACH AND YOU'LL BE GREYEYED.
WHICH HAS A SOLDIERLY QUALITY OF HEAD UP, CHEST 13 JOURNE OUT, STOMACH IN,
AND IF HE HAD A NIGHTMARE WHEN HE WAS LITTLE, OR A110 JOURNE STOMACH-ACHE,
(DRYLY) YOUR STOMACH MUST BE OUT OF ORDER. 316 LAZARU SHE HAS A STRONGER STOMACH. 51 MISBEG AND ME WITH THE SIDES OF MY STOMACH KNOCKING 176 MISBEG TOGETHER.
TO TELL THE TRUTH, MY STOMACH IS OUT OF SORTS. 36 POET IT TURNS MY STOMACH WITH ITS STINK OF ONIONS AND 42 POET STEW/
HAVE THIS IN YOUR STOMACH FIRST/ 55 POET THEY TURN MY STOMACH/ 107 POET (ALMOST NAIVELY) MY MOTHER HAS A PAIN IN HER 77 STRANG STOMACH.
A GROSS BULK OF A MAN WITH AN ENORMOUS STOMACH. 493 VOYAGE

STOMACH'S
(DESPERATELY) I--I DON'T FEEL SO WELL--MY 208 AHWILD STOMACH'S SICK.

STOMACHIN'
TO BE STOMACHIN' THE SKUFF ON THIS RUSTY LIME- 480 CARDIF JUICER.

STOMACK'S
DOWN'T YER KNOW AS THEM BLOKES 'AS TWO STOMACKS 456 CARIBE LIKE A BLEEDIN' CAMELS

STONE
CRYING FOR BREAD FOR HIS CHILDREN AND ALL HE GETS 194 AHWILD IS A STONE/
AH SURE, MISTER SID, IT'S YOU THAT HAVE KISSED THE226 AHWILD BLARNEY STONE,
BY THE LINES OF STONE WALLS AND ROUGH SNAKE 81 BEYOND FENCES.
THE WALLS ARE OLD GRAY STONE. 564 DAYS THE SOUTH END OF THE HOUSE FACES FRONT TO A STONE 202 DESIRE WALL
HIM 'N' YM 'N' YEW 'N' ME 'N' THEN EBEN--MAKIN' 204 DESIRE STONE WALLS FOR HIM TO FENCE US
STONES ATOP O' STONES--MAKIN' STONE WALLS--YEAR 204 DESIRE ATOP O' YEAR--
(BREAKING IN HARSHLY) AN' MAKIN' WALLS--STONE 208 DESIRE ATOP OF STONE
AN' HE HAULS UP BY THE STONE WALL A JIFFY. 209 DESIRE ONTO A STONE WALL T' WALL IN YER HEART/ 209 DESIRE WE BEEN SLAVES T' STONE WALLS HERE. 218 DESIRE THE STONE WALLS AIR CRUMBLIN' AN' TUMBLIN'/ 221 DESIRE (HE PICKS A STONE FROM THE ROAD. 224 DESIRE YE KIN READ THE YEARS OF MY LIFE IN THEM WALLS, 237 DESIRE EVERY DAY A HEFTED STONE,
NARY A STONE. 237 DESIRE IF YE WAN'T A BORN DONKEY YE'D KNOW YE'LL NEVER 254 DESIRE OWN STICK NUR STONE ON IT.
CABOT GETS ONE HAND ON HIS THROAT AND PRESSES HIM 255 DESIRE BACK ACROSS THE STONE WALL.
I GOT T' BE--LIKE A STONE--A ROCK O' JEDGMENT/ 264 DESIRE WHO AM I TO CAST THE FIRST STONE AT REUBEN IF HE 435 DYNAMO DESIRES A WOMANS....
LIKE THE OLD STONE STATUES OF GODS PEOPLE PRAYED 474 DYNAMO TO.
(HE SEES THE FIRST WHITE STONE AND CRAWLS TO IT 188 EJONES WITH SATISFACTION)
(HE SCRAMBLES TO THE NEXT STONE AND TURNS IT OVER)188 EJONES DERE'S NUTHER STONE. 188 EJONES WHITE STONE, WHITE STONE, WHERE IS YOUS 188 EJONES (HE TURNS OVER THE STONE AND FEELS IN UNDER IT--IN188 EJONES A TONE OF DISMAY)
(WHILE HE IS TALKING HE SCRAMBLES FROM ONE STONE 189 EJONES TO ANOTHER,
HE LOOKS AROUND AT THE TREE, THE ROUGH STONE 200 EJONES ALTAR,
WITH THE WALL OF THE HOUSE PROPER WHICH IS OF GRAY 2 ELECTR CUT STONE.
SHIMMERING IN A LUMINOUS MIST ON THE WHITE PORTICO 5 ELECTR AND THE GRAY STONE WALL.
FIXED ON THE SOMBER STONE HOUSE. 43 ELECTR SETH HAS A STONE JUG IN HIS HAND. 129 ELECTR THE COLUMNS CAST BLACK BARS OF SHADOW ON THE GRAY 169 ELECTR STONE WALL BEHIND THEM.
HE GLARES INTO HER EYES, TURNED TO STONE. 225 HA APE THERE'S TOO MUCH STONE AND STEEL. 27 HUGHIE THERE'S TOO MUCH STONE AND STEEL. 27 HUGHIE THERE'S TOO MUCH STEEL AND STONE. 33 HUGHIE STONE COLD SOBER AND DEAD TO THE WORLD/ 626 ICEMAN YOU LOOK IN THEIR FACES AND TURN TO STONE. 131 JOURNE I WAS STONE COLD SOBER. 147 JOURNE I HELPED TO PAY AWAY THE STONE SO I WAS RIGHT 277 LAZARU BESIDE HIM.

STONE

(CONT'D.)
(CHANTING EXULTANTLY) THE STONE IS TAKEN AWAY/ 278 LAZARU
AT THE LEFT-REAR IS A STONE CHIMNEY. 1 MANSNS
TWO SMALL STONE BENCHES FACE RIGHT-FRONT AND LEFT- 25 MANSNS
FRONT.
GADSBY AND JOEL ON THE STONE BENCHES BY THE POOL, 31 MANSNS
(HE SITS ON THE STONE BENCH ON HER LEFT.) 96 MANSNS
(SHE SITS ON THE STONE BENCH AT RIGHT-REAR OF THE 163 MANSNS
POOL, CLOSING HER EYES.
BY THE STONE BENCH AT LEFT OF POOL. 190 MANSNS
SO THAT'S WHAT THEY BELIEVE ABOUT THAT STONE 372 MARCOM
STATUE, IS IT!
BUT SHE SEEMS TURNED TO STONE. 417 MARCOM
OVER DITCHES AND STREAMS AND STONE WALLS AND 102 POET
SEE THE PHILOSOPHER'S STONE...* 34 STRANG
THE TERRACE IS PAVED WITH ROUGH STONE. 184 STRANG
GORDON EVANS IS SITTING ON THE STONE BENCH, HIS 184 STRANG
CHIN PROPPED ON HIS HANDS,
THERE IS A STONE BENCH AT CENTER, A RECLINER AT 184 STRANG
RIGHT.

STONES

(HE TAKES FROM HIS POCKET A HEAVY BRACELET THICKLY561 CROSS
STUDDED WITH STONES AND
(WITH SARDONIC BITTERNESS) HERE--IT'S STONES ATOP204 DESIRE
OF THE GROUND--
STONES ATOP O' STONES--MAKIN' STONE WALLS--YEAR 204 DESIRE
ATOP O' YEAR--
(THEY BOTH THROW, THE STONES HITTING THE PARLOR 224 DESIRE
WINDOW WITH A CRASH OF GLASS.
WAAL--THIS PLACE WAS NOTHIN' BUT FIELDS O' STONES.236 DESIRE
WHEN YE KIN MAKE CORN SPROUT OUT O' STONES, GOD'S 236 DESIRE
LIVIN' IN YEW/
BUILD MY CHURCH ON A ROCK--OUT O' STONES AN' I'LL 237 DESIRE
BE IN THEM/
GOD'S IN THE STONES/ 237 DESIRE
I GOT WEAK--DESPAIRFUL--THEY WAS SO MANY STONES. 237 DESIRE
(HE SIGHS HEAVILY--A PAUSE) STONES. 237 DESIRE
EMMER CAN'T THROW STONES. 506 DIFRNT
THE FOREGROUND IS SANDY LEVEL GROUND DOTTED BY A 187 EJONES
FEW STONES AND CLUMPS OF
HOW COME ALL DESE WHITE STONES COME HEAH WHEN I 189 EJONES
ONLY REMEMBERS ONES
BUT HOW COME ALL DESE WHITE STONESS 189 EJONES
SEEMS LIKE I KNOW DAT TREE--AN' DEM STONES--AN ' 200 EJONES
DE RIVER.
IN BEDS THAT AIN'T GOT COBBLE STONES IN DE 612 ICEMAN
MATTRESS LIKE DE ONES IN DIS DUMP.
STONES/ 304 LAZARU
KNIVES, CLUBS, DAGGERS, STONES, BARE FISTS.) 305 LAZARU
THE MORTAR BETWEEN THE STONES OF THE CHIMNEY HAS 1 MANSNS
CRUMBLED AND FALLEN OUT IN
MUST REMEMBER THE OLD ADAGE--STICKS AND STONES-- 155 MANSNS
AND POVERTY--BREAK--
WHO USED IT TO TAP WATER OUT OF STONES AND FINALLY349 MARCOM
PLANTED IT.
LET POUR FROM THEM A PERFECT STREAM OF PRECIOUS 429 MARCOM
STONES
AND CHUCK SOME STONES IN THE OCEAN SAME'S WE 589 ROPE
USETER, REMEMBERS
A HEAP OF STONES, A MUD IMAGE, A DRAWING ON A 41 STRANG
WALL, A BIRD, A FISH, A SNAKE,

STONILY

(STONILY) YES. 72 ANNA
EMMA STARES STONILY BEFORE HER AS IF SHE DIDN'T 507 DIFRNT
HEAR.)
EMMA STANDS FOR A WHILE, STARING STONILY BEFORE 514 DIFRNT
HER.
(SHE SEEMS NOT TO HEAR OR TO SEE THEM BUT STARES 417 MARCOM
AHEAD STONILY.

STONY

(THEN AFTER A PAUSE--IN A VOICE OF DEAD, STONY 71 ANNA
CALM)
HER PALE, DEEPLY-LINED FACE HAS THE STONY LACK OF 144 BEYOND
EXPRESSION OF ONE TO WHOM
AND HARDENS HIS FACE INTO A STONY MASK--THROUGH 264 DESIRE
HIS TEETH TO HIMSELF)
HIS FACE STONY, AND STALKS GRIMLY TOWARD THE BARN.269 DESIRE
(HE LAUGHS LOUDLY--THEN NOTICING HIS SISTER'S 503 DIFRNT
STONY EXPRESSION.
THE EXPRESSION OF HIS FACE IS FIXED AND STONY, HIS200 EJONES
EYES HAVE AN OBSESSED GLARE,
CONCEALED INTO A STONY EMOTIONLESS EXPRESSION. 170 ELECTR
WAS BUYING DRINKS AND DAN AND BENNY WERE STONY. 676 ICEMAN

STOOD

DAVE, I'VE STOOD ALL I CAN STAND FROM YOU/ 203 AHWILD
AND HOW WELL--YOU'VE STOOD IT/ 227 AHWILD
YOU OUGHT TO HAVE KNOWN HE STOOD RIGHT OVER ME AND286 AHWILD
TOLD ME EACH WORD TO WRITE.
I'VE STOOD ENOUGH FROM YOU. 73 ANNA
(WITH A COMPLACENT GRIN) SAY, YOU CERTAINLY STOOD544 DIFRNT
UP FOR ME ALL RIGHT.
(HE WALKS SLOWLY OVER TO WHERE HE HAD STOOD WITH 444 DYNAMO
ADA--DULLY)
IT IS AS IF THE FOREST HAD STOOD ASIDE MOMENTARILY192 EJONES
TO LET THE ROAD PASS THROUGH
COMES OUT TO THE TOP OF THE STEPS WHERE HER MOTHER 10 ELECTR
HAD STOOD.
I SAW YOUR FACE WHEN YOU CAME BACK AND STOOD WITH 154 ELECTR
HIM IN FRONT OF OUR HUT/
TAKES HIS PLACE AT THE RAIL, WHERE YOUNG BROWN HAD260 GGBROW
STOOD.
I'VE ALWAYS STOOD UP FOR HIM WHATEVER HE'S DONE-- 289 GGBROW
SO YOU CAN BE PERFECTLY FRANK.
I REALLY DON'T BELIEVE I COULD EVER HAVE STOOD IF 292 GGBROW
IT WEREN'T FOR THE BOYS/
I'VE STOOD ENOUGH/ 298 GGBROW
AND THEY STARTED TALKING, AND THE POOR BOOB NEVER 23 HUGHIE
STOOD A CHANCE.
I'VE ALWAYS STOOD UP FOR HIM 593 ICEMAN
(TO ROCKY--DEFIANTLY) I'S STOOD TELLIN' PEOPLE 637 ICEMAN

STOOD

(CONT'D.)
I'VE STOOD IT LONG ENOUGH/ 687 ICEMAN
THAT NO WOMAN COULD HAVE STOOD ALL SHE STOOD AND 714 ICEMAN
STILL LOVED ME SO MUCH--
I REMEMBER I STOOD BY THE BED AND SUDDENLY I HAD 716 ICEMAN
TO LAUGH.
(COMES FORWARD FROM WHERE HE HAS STOOD IN THE BAR 719 ICEMAN
ENTRANCE--HOPEFULLY)
WHO HAS STOOD TENSELY WITH HIS EYES SHUT AS IF HE 530 INZONE
WERE UNDERGOING TORTURE DURING
IT HAS ALWAYS STOOD BETWEEN ME AND--
SHE STOOD IT FOR A WHILE. 102 JOURNE
AND SWINE SHALL ROOT WHERE THEY TEMPLE STOOD/ 160 JOURNE
* ---I STOOD 292 LAZARU
ALL MY LIFE SINCE THEN I HAVE STOOD OUTSIDE THAT 107 MANSNS
DOOR IN MY MIND. 182 MANSNS
I STOOD LOOKING DOWN 147 MISREG
I STOOD AMONG THEM, BUT NOT OF THEM....* 43 POET
BUT I STOOD THERE, DUMB AS A CALF, 65 POET
I STOOD AMONG THEM, BUT NOT OF THEM...* 67 POET
THEY COULDN'T DEEM ME ONE AV SUCH--I STOOD AMONG 177 POET
THIN, BUT NOT AV THIN....*
HE STOOD THERE WITH THE NOOSE OF THE ROPE ALMOST 590 ROPE
TOUCHIN' HIS HEAD.
(TOUCHING DARRELL WHO HAS STOOD STARING STRAIGHT 182 STRANG
BEFORE HIM WITH A BITTER
(IMPULSIVELY) THAT TIME YOU STOOD HERE AND CALLED470 WELDED
TO ME FOR HELP--
(SHE POINTS TO THE SPOT WHERE THEY HAD STOOD 482 WELDED
EMBRACED.)

STOOL

(A FAT SWEDE WHO IS SITTING ON A CAMP STOOL IN 457 CARIBE
FRONT OF HIS DOOR TALKING WITH
HE IS SITTING ON A CAMP STOOL IN FRONT OF HIS 458 CARIBE
DOOR, RIGHT FRONT)
THE DONKEYMAN QUIETLY SMOKING ON HIS STOOL,. 472 CARIBE
WITH A STOOL IN FRONT OF IT. 493 DIFRNT
CYBEL IS SEATED ON THE STOOL IN FRONT OF THE 278 GGBROW
PIANO.
SYMPATHETICALLY AS SHE COMES BACK AND SITS DOWN ON279 GGBROW
HER STOOL)
DION'S DRAFTING TABLE WITH A HIGH STOOL IN FRONT 290 GGBROW
IS AT CENTER.
DION IS SITTING ON THE STOOL IN BACK OF THE TABLE,290 GGBROW
ANOTHER STOOL IS TO THE LEFT OF IT. 290 GGBROW
THE SECRETARY IS PERCHED ON THE STOOL MAKING 245 HA APE
ENTRIES IN A LARGE LEDGER.
A DESK AND HIGH STOOL ARE IN ONE CORNER. 245 HA APE
(TURNING AROUND ON HIS STOOL) 246 HA APE
BEHIND THE DESK ARE A TELEPHONE SWITCHBOARD AND 7 HUGHIE
THE OPERATOR'S STOOL.
THE NIGHT CLERK SITS ON THE STOOL, FACING FRONT, 7 HUGHIE
HIS BACK TO THE SWITCHBOARD.
BOURGEOIS STOOL PIGEONS/ 579 ICEMAN
BUT I'D SWEAR THERE COULDN'T BE A YELLOW STOOL 588 ICEMAN
PIGEON AMONG THEM.
GOTTAMNED STOOL PIGEON/ 592 ICEMAN
I OUGHT TO HAVE REMEMBERED WHEN YOU'RE SOUSED YOU 592 ICEMAN
CALL EVERYONE A STOOL PIGEON.
AN OLD UPRIGHT PIANO AND STOOL HAVE BEEN MOVED IN 628 ICEMAN
SLUMPS DOWN ON THE PIANO STOOL.) 637 ICEMAN
JOE GETS OFF THE STOOL SULLENLY TO LET HER SIT 644 ICEMAN
DOWN.)
FARTHER BACK AGAINST THE WALL IS A HIGH DESK WITH 69 MANSNS
A TALL STOOL IN FRONT OF IT.
SARA IS DISCOVERED SEATED ON THE HIGH STOOL BEFORE139 MANSNS
HER DESK.
(SHE JUMPS FROM HER STOOL.) WHY DOESN'T HE COME! 144 MANSNS
SIMON GETS OFF HIS STOOL AND COMES TO SARA.) 155 MANSNS
MARCO IS SITTING ON A STOOL IN THE FOREGROUND, 358 MARCOM
FARTHER FRONT AT RIGHT, THERE IS A HIGH 7 POET
SCHOOLMASTER'S DESK WITH A STOOL.

STOOLS

ARE SITTING ON STOOLS BEHIND WHAT WAS FORMERLY 302 GGBROW
DION'S TABLE.

STOOP

A LITTLE STOOP SHOULDERED, MORE THAN A LITTLE 188 AHWILD
BALD,
HIS SHOULDERS HAVE A WEARY STOOP AS IF WORN DOWN 556 CROSS
THEIR SHOULDERS STOOP A BIT FROM YEARS OF FARM 204 DESIRE
WORK.
BUT STOOP-SHOULDERED FROM TOIL. 221 DESIRE
HER SHOULDERS STOOP, AND HER FIGURE IS FLABBY AND 528 DIFRNT
UGLY.
SMITHERS IS A TALL, STOOP-SHOULDERED MAN ABOUT 173 EJONES
FORTY.
RAW-BONED AND STOOP-SHOULDERED, HIS JOINTS 6 ELECTR
STIFFENED BY RHEUMATISM,
JOEL HARFORD IS TWENTY-NINE, TALL AND THIN, WITH A 25 MANSNS
SLIGHT STOOP IN HIS CARRIAGE.
THE STOOP IN HIS SHOULDERS IS MORE PRONOUNCED, 70 MANSNS
DOES HE IMAGINE THE CHURCH WOULD STOOP TO SUCH 359 MARCOM
BICKERINGS
SURE, HE'D NEVER STOUP TO THINK OF ME. 138 POET
HE IS A TALL, LEAN, STOOP-SHOULDERED OLD MAN OF 978 ROPE
SIXTY-FIVE.
THE STOOP TO HIS SHOULDERS OF A MAN WEAK 4 STRANG
MUSCULARLY.
THE STOOP OF HIS TALL FIGURE IS ACCENTUATED, HIS 159 STRANG
HAIR HAS GROWN WHITISH.
HE IS A MAN OF ABOUT FIFTY, TALL, LOOSE-LIMBED, A 450 WELDED
BIT STOOP-SHOULDERED,

STOOPED

HIS SHOULDERS ARC STOOPED AS IF UNDER TOO GREAT A 119 BEYOND
BURDEN.
STOOPED FIGURE LEANING BACK AGAINST THE BOOKS-- 4 STRANG
EXCEPT THAT HIS HAIR IS GRAYER AND HIS TALL FIGURE146 STRANG
MORE STOOPED.

STOOPING

STOOPING
HE STILL REMAINS STOOPING OVER THE BODY AND STARES115 ELECTR
INTO BRANT'S FACE.
THIS ACCENTUATES THE NATURAL STOOPING POSTURE 207 HA APE
WHICH SHOVELING COAL AND THE

STOOPS
HE STOOPS DOWN AND PICKS IT UP AND SMELLS OF IT.) 473 CARIBE
MARCU STOOPS ON HIS KNEES 418 MARCOM
HIS TALL, THIN BODY STOOPS AS IF A PART OF ITS 73 STRANG
SUSTAINING WILL HAD BEEN REMOVED.
THE STOOPS AND PICKS UP ONE SHEET OF PAPER. 76 STRANG
THE STOOPS DOWN AND FUMBLES IN HER BOSOM AND PULLS508 VOYAGE
OUT THE BANKNOTE.

STOOPSHOULDERED
TWO DRAFTSMEN, A MIDDLE-AGED AND A YOUNG MAN, BOTH302 GGBROW
STOOPSHOULDERED.

STOP
THE MEN PULL OUT SHEATH-KNIVES AND START A RUSH. 544 'ILE
BUT STOP
NOW, YOU WOMEN STOP PICKING ON SID. 190 AHWILD
STOP YOUR EVERLASTING TEASING, YOU TWO. 191 AHWILD
NEVER ENOUGH TO STOP DRINKING FOR. 213 AHWILD
DON'T STOP TO WASH UP OR ANYTHING. 221 AHWILD
STOP SPINNING YOUR NAPKIN RING/ 222 AHWILD
HURRY UP AND FINISH YOUR SOUP, AND STOP TALKING 225 AHWILD
NONSENSE/
(TURNING ON SID FURIOUSLY) WILL YOU PLEASE SIT 226 AHWILD
DOWN AND STOP MAKING A FOOL OF
SOMEONE OUGHT TO STOP ME. 231 AHWILD
BUT I'LL TELL HIM HE'S GOT TO STOP THIS DAMN 234 AHWILD
NONSENSE.
YOU STOP THAT TALK/ 235 AHWILD
IF YOU DON'T STOP TALKING FOURTH OF JULY--/ 251 AHWILD
STOP TRYING TO BE SO DARN FUNNY ALL THE TIME/ 255 AHWILD
I WISH YOU'D STOP JUMPING TO CONCLUSIONS/ 263 AHWILD
STOP WORRYING. 269 AHWILD
(SCORNFULLY) IS IT THE LIKE OF YOURSELF WILL STOP 45 ANNA
ME, ARE YOU THINKING$
YES, AY STOP IT IF IT COME TO VORST. 45 ANNA
AND NO OLD FOOL THE LIKE OF YOU WILL STOP US WHEN 49 ANNA
I'VE MADE UP MY MIND.
(WILDLY) STOP, YOU CRAZY FOOL/ 60 ANNA
(HIS FACE CRIMSON--TENSELY) STOP, PA/ 106 BEYOND
STOP/ ARE YOU MAD$ 108 BEYOND
IT'S ABOUT TIME YOU PUT A STOP TO HIS NONSENSE. 113 BEYOND
(IRRITABLY) WILL YOU STOP HARPING ON THAT, MA$ 117 BEYOND
DO STOP YOUR NAGGING AT ME, MA/ 117 BEYOND
(ANGRILY) STOP THAT KIND OF TALK, DO YOU HEAR$ 126 BEYOND
YOU FINDIN' FAULT--
(IN A VOICE OF COMMAND THAT FORCES OBEDIENCE) 128 BEYOND
STOP/
AND DIDN'T HE TRY TO STOP YOU FROM GOING$ 137 BEYOND
(RESENTFULLY) RUB'S TOO GOOD A CHUM TO TRY AND 137 BEYOND
STOP ME
FOR GOD'S SAKE, ANDY--WON'T YOU PLEASE STOP 139 BEYOND
TALKING/
YOU TELL THAT MOTHER OF YOURS SHE'S GOT TO STOP 148 BEYOND
SAYING
IT'S GOT TO STOP, I TELL YOU/ 148 BEYOND
STOP THAT COUGHING FOR GOODNESS' SAKE/ 149 BEYOND
STOP YOUR CROAKIN'/ 479 CARDIF
IT'S A GRAND IDEA AND WE'LL BE DOIN' UT SURE IF 487 CARDIF
YOU'LL STOP YOUR CRAZY NOTIONS--
I WISH THEY'D STOP THAT SONG. 459 CARIBE
DOCTOR TOLD ME I'D GOT TO STOP OR DIE. 467 CARIBE
DRINKING TO STOP THINKING. 468 CARIBE
STOP/ 565 CROSS
(IN TERROR) STOP/ 565 CROSS
DAMN YOU, STOP MAKING ME THINK--- 495 DAYS
(THEN WILDLY) OH, JOHN, STOP TALKING/ 550 DAYS
STOP THAT MOCKERY/ 551 DAYS
STOP YOUR DAMNED NONSENSE/ 555 DAYS
BUT THAT'S GOT TO STOP, DO YOU HEAR ME$ 556 DAYS
(TERRIFIED) STOP/ 560 DAYS
STOP TALKING DAMNED NONSENSE/ 560 DAYS
THEN THEY STOP SHORT.) 216 DESIRE
(THEY ARISE BRISKLY AND GO OUT REAR--APPEAR AROUND218 DESIRE
HOUSE AND STOP BY THE GATE.
(HE AND PETER STOP THEIR DANCE, HOLDING THEIR 223 DESIRE
SIDES.
I TRIED FUR T' STOP HIM. 233 DESIRE
HAW, WHAR WAS YE, WHY DIDN'T YE STOP HER$ 261 DESIRE
STOP IT. 506 DIFRNT
THAT'LL STOP 'EM, DAMN 'EM, AND MAKE 'EM LEAVE ME 534 DIFRNT
ALONE.
YOU DIDN'T STOP ABOUT BELIEVIN' THE FOOL STORIES 539 DIFRNT
THEY GOSSIPED ABOUT ME THAT
(SHE TRIES TO THROW HER ARMS ABOUT HIM TO STOP HIS543 DIFRNT
GOING.
STOP/ 547 DIFRNT
(SHAKING HER) STOP--NOW, EMMER/ 547 DIFRNT
I'VE GOT TO STOP HER/...)) 434 DYNAMO
((I'VE GOT TO STOP/.... 439 DYNAMO
IF YOU DON'T STOP YOUR BLASPHEMING, I'LL--I MEAN, 442 DYNAMO
IT'D SERVE YOU RIGHT IF I--
IF HE'D CRY I'D STOP HUTCHINS... 448 DYNAMO
AND STOP LOOKING AT HIM OR HE'D START BREAKING 456 DYNAMO
PLATES.
((I WISH HE'D STOP CRYING....)) 464 DYNAMO
STOP OR I'LL SHOUT/ 175 EJONES
BUT I HAS--AND ME MAKIN' LAWS TO STOP IT AT DE 177 EJONES
SAME TIME/
AND DAT BLACK TRASH DON'T DARE STOP HIM--NOT YIT, 186 EJONES
LEASTWAYS.
AT A SIGNAL FROM THE GUARD THEY STOP 194 EJONES
AND STOP DAT DRUM SOUNDING IN MY EARS/ 196 EJONES
BUT HE DIDN'T STOP THERE. 8 ELECTR
STOP LYING, I TELL YOU/ 30 ELECTR

STOP (CONT'D.)
STOP TELLING ME SUCH THINGS/ 31 ELECTR
STOP SAYING THAT/ 31 ELECTR
AND IF HE TRIES TO STOP ME--/ 38 ELECTR
WE'D STOP AT THE SOUTH PACIFIC ISLANDS I'VE TOLD 39 ELECTR
YOU ABOUT.
STOP IT/ 41 ELECTR
(SEEING THE MAN'S FIGURE STOP IN THE SHADOW--CALLS 46 ELECTR
EXCITEDLY)
(COMES TO A STOP IN HIS PACING DIRECTLY BEFORE HER 49 ELECTR
AND LOOKS INTO HER EYES--
(SHARPLY) STOP YOUR SQUABBLING, BOTH OF YOU/ 50 ELECTR
FOR GOD'S SAKE, STOP TALKING. 56 ELECTR
YOU TELL ME TO STOP TALKING--BY GOD, THAT'S FUNNY/ 56 ELECTR
AND SOMETIMES IT GETS OUT BEFORE I CAN STOP IT. 59 ELECTR
STOP TALKING LIKE THAT/ 60 ELECTR
STOP NAGGING AT ME WITH YOUR CRAZY SUSPICIONS/ 60 ELECTR
THERE, THEY STOP TO WAIT FOR THE MEN WHO STAND AT 68 ELECTR
THE FOOT OF THE STEPS WHILE
(THEY STOP TALKING SELF-CONSCIOUSLY AS ORIN AND 80 ELECTR
CHRISTINE ENTER FROM THE REAR.
AFTER THAT, MAYBE THEY'D STOP WAVING HANDKERCHIEFS 82 ELECTR
AND GABBING ABOUT HEROES/
THAT THERE ISN'T ANYTHING YOUR SISTER WILL STOP 85 ELECTR
AT--
BUT I'M GOING TO STOP YOUR DAMNED--BUT I'M A FOOL 97 ELECTR
TO PAY ANY ATTENTION TO YOU/
(WILDLY) STOP/ 98 ELECTR
(HARSHLY) STOP THAT DAMNED DIRGE/ 107 ELECTR
WHY DID YOU STOP ME$ 113 ELECTR
ORIN, FOR GOD'S SAKE, WILL YOU STOP TALKING CRAZY 116 ELECTR
AND COME ALONG$
THEY STOP IN SURPRISE ON SEEING SETH AND HIS 134 ELECTR
FRIENDS.
SEEMED TO ME ABNER'S BRAGGIN' GAVE ME A GOOD 135 ELECTR
CHANCE TO STOP IT
I WAS AIMIN' TO STOP THE DURNED GABBIN' THAT'S 135 ELECTR
BEEN GOIN' ROUND TOWN
DON'T STOP THERE, ORIN/ 137 ELECTR
(ANGRILY COMMANDING) STOP IT, DO YOU HEAR ME/ 140 ELECTR
(ANGRILY) STOP TALKING LIKE A FOOL/ 145 ELECTR
YOU'LL DAMN SOON STOP YOUR TRICKS WHEN YOU KNOW 152 ELECTR
WHAT I'VE BEEN WRITING/
WILL YOU STOP/ 152 ELECTR
(FURIOUSLY) STOP TALKING ABOUT HER/ 153 ELECTR
(CHOKINGLY) STOP IT/ 154 ELECTR
STOP TORTURING ME OR I--/ 155 ELECTR
STOP HARPING ON THAT/ 155 ELECTR
STOP MAKING ME HAVE THEM/ 156 ELECTR
STOP HAVING SUCH THOUGHTS/ 156 ELECTR
DURN IT, I HOPED SHE'D STOP THAT UNCE THE FUNERAL 170 ELECTR
WAS OVER.
WAS THERE ANYTHING IN WHAT ORIN WROTE THAT WOULD 176 ELECTR
STOP US FROM--
AND STOP AT MRS. YOUNG'S AND ASK THE CHILDREN TO 273 GGBROW
HURRY RIGHT HOME$
WILL YOU STOP AT THE BUTCHERS' AND HAVE THEM SEND 273 GGBROW
TWO POUNDS OF PORK CHOPS$
(CALMLY) STOP ACTING. 279 GGBROW
BUT PLEASE DON'T STOP STROKING MY ACHING BROW. 279 GGBROW
STOP HIDING. 285 GGBROW
WHEN I STOP TO THINK OF ALL YOU'VE MADE ME GO 292 GGBROW
THROUGH--
(THEY STOP, STARING AT HIM FIXEDLY, 293 GGBROW
THEY STOP SHORT AND STIFFEN ALL IN A ROW, 293 GGBROW
(HUSKILY) STOP, FOR GOD'S SAKE/ 299 GGBROW
WHEN THEY SEE MARGARET, THEY STOP IN SURPRISE.) 316 GGBROW
DE NOISE AND SMOKE AND ALL DE ENGINES MOVIN' DE 216 HA APE
WOULD, DEY STOP.
STOP HIM/ 232 HA APE
THEY DO NOT STOP, BUT DISAPPEAR IN THE DARK 239 HA APE
BACKGROUND AS IF THEY RAN ON,
STOP THERE/ 239 HA APE
THEY STOP NOT BEFORE MURDER TO GAIN THEIR ENDS, 243 HA APE
YUH CAN'T GRAB IT, AND YUH CAN'T STOP IT. 250 HA APE
LONG EXPERIENCE WITH GUESTS WHO STOP AT HIS DESK 11 HUGHIE
IN THE SMALL HOURS TO TALK
BEGINNING TO ACHE AND HE WISHES 492 WOULD STOP 13 HUGHIE
TALKING AND GO TO BED SO HE CAN
AND I'D STOP TO KID HIM ALONG AND TELL HIM THE 23 HUGHIE
TALE OF WHAT I'D HIM THAT DAY.
HE NEVER DARED STOP BEING A NIGHT CLERK, EVEN IF 24 HUGHIE
HE COULD.
BELIEVE ME, PAL, I CAN STOP GUYS THAT START 26 HUGHIE
TELLING ME THEIR FAMILY TROUBLES/
YES, IF IS A GODDAMNED RACKET WHEN YOU STOP TO 33 HUGHIE
THINK, ISN'T IT, 492$
YOU'VE NEVER LET ANYTHING STOP YOU FROM--- (HE 591 ICEMAN
CHECKS HIMSELF--
JUST STOP LYING ABOUT YOURSELF AND KIDDING 622 ICEMAN
YOURSELF ABOUT TOMORROWS.
YUH DON'T HAVE TO STOP JUST BECAUSE HE KIDDED YUH/656 ICEMAN
AS IF HE HATED HIMSELF FOR EVERY WORK HE SAID, AND660 ICEMAN
YET COULDN'T STOP)
BUT YOU'RE GETTING THE WRONG IDEA ABOUT POOR 663 ICEMAN
EVELYN, AND I'VE GOT TO STOP THAT.
AND DEN HE WENT ON TALKIN' AND TALKIN' LIKE HE 665 ICEMAN
COULDN'T STOP/
YUH CAN'T STOP HIM. 665 ICEMAN
THE ONLY WAY TO STOP IS TO STOP. 674 ICEMAN
WELL, I SAY ME STOP AT DE FOIST REG'LAR DUMP 682 ICEMAN
JUST STOP LYING TO YOURSELF-- 689 ICEMAN
GOD DAMN YOU, STOP SHOVING YOUR ROTTEN SOUL IN MY 706 ICEMAN
LAP/
YUH CAN'T STOP DE BASTARD TALKIN'. 708 ICEMAN
BUT THEY COULDN'T STOP EVELYN. 710 ICEMAN
NO, SIR, YOU COULDN'T STOP EVELYN. 710 ICEMAN

1549 — STOP / STOPPED

STOP (CONT'D.)
BECAUSE NOTHING BUT DEATH COULD STOP MY LOVING YOU. 711 ICEMAN
AND THEY STOP SINGING TO ROAR WITH LAUGHTER. 727 ICEMAN
STOP FAKING, PAPA. 25 JOURNE
(EAGERLY.) YES, THAT'S RIGHT, SHE DID STOP TO LISTEN OUTSIDE HIS ROOM. 38 JOURNE
STOP IT, MAMA. 46 JOURNE
STOP IT, MAMA/ 47 JOURNE
STOP SUSPECTING ME/ PLEASE, DEAR/ YOU HURT ME/ 47 JOURNE
(GRABS HER SHOULDER.) MAMA/ STOP IT/ 48 JOURNE
CAN'T YOU STOP TALKING LIKE THAT/ 49 JOURNE
(SHE CHUCKLES.) I'LL WAGER MISTER JAMIE WOULDN'T MISS THE TIME TO STOP WORK AND 52 JOURNE
STOP SNEERING AT YOUR FATHER/ 60 JOURNE
STOP THIS AT ONCE, DO YOU HEAR MES 64 JOURNE
STOP TALKING. 67 JOURNE
HE WOULDN'T STOP AFTER HE WAS STRICKEN. 67 JOURNE
(SHARPLY.) PLEASE STOP STARING/ 68 JOURNE
FOR GOD'S SAKE, STOP TALKING. 74 JOURNE
SHE CAN STILL STOP. 79 JOURNE
STOP WHATS WHAT ARE YOU TALKING ABOUTS 85 JOURNE
WON'T YOU STOP NOWS 85 JOURNE
IT WAS EASY FOR HIM TO STOP THE PAIN. 87 JOURNE
YOU-- YOU'RE ONLY JUST STARTED. YOU CAN STILL STOP. 92 JOURNE
I HAVE TO TAKE IT BECAUSE THERE IS NO OTHER THAT 103 JOURNE
CAN STOP THE PAIN--
THEY STOP IN THE DOORWAY TO STARE APPRAISINGLY AT 108 JOURNE
HER.
(MISERABLY.) STOP TALKING, MAMA. 109 JOURNE
(MISERABLY.) OH, STOP TALKING CRAZY, CAN'T YOU, MAMA/ 119 JOURNE
STOP TRYING TO BLAME HIM. 119 JOURNE
(PLACATINGLY.) ALL RIGHT, ALL RIGHT, I'LL STOP. 129 JOURNE
WILL YOU STOP REPEATING YOUR MOTHER'S CRAZY ACCUSATIONS. 142 JOURNE
STOP COUGHING, LAD. 145 JOURNE
STOP IT, JAMIE/ 163 JOURNE
I THOUGHT HE'D NEVER STOP TALKING. 167 JOURNE
JAMIE, FOR THE LOVE OF GOD, STOP IT/ 171 JOURNE
AND STOP RECITING THAT DAMNED MORBID POETRY. 175 JOURNE
THEN SUDDENLY THEY STOP, THE MUSIC DIES OUT, STOP/ 278 LAZARU
STOP IT, YOU FOOLS/ 282 LAZARU
HA-HA--STOP IT, CURSE YOU/ 282 LAZARU
(CONCERNEDLY) STOP. 311 LAZARU
HE WOULD STOP HER/ 342 LAZARU
INVOLUNTARILY ONE OF LAZARUS' HANDS HALF-REACHES 346 LAZARU
OUT AS IF TO STOP HER.)
STOP HIS LAUGHTER/ 346 LAZARU
THEY STOP AS THEY COME TO THE POOL. 366 LAZARU
(LAUGHINGLY.) STOP/ 26 MANSNS
(THEY LAUGH MUSEDLY TOGETHER--THEN STOP ABRUPTLY 49 MANSNS
AND STARE AT EACH OTHER.) 61 MANSNS
I WOULD PUT A STOP TO HER GREEDY SCHEMING, 72 MANSNS
STOP TEASING NOW AND TELL ME. 89 MANSNS
(THEY STOP ABRUPTLY AND STARE AT EACH OTHER-- 108 MANSNS
BUT I CAN'T STOP HIM. 142 MANSNS
AND I KNOW SHE'D STOP AT NOTHING NOW TO GET YOU AWAY WITH HER/ 149 MANSNS
I MUST STOP THINKING-- STOP/ 163 MANSNS
IF YOU'LL SWEAR TO STOP YOUR MAD SCHEMES, I'LL MAKE PEACE WITH YOU. 165 MANSNS
WHY CAN'T YOU STOPS 167 MANSNS
STOP/ 174 MANSNS
AS THEY REACH THE MIDDLE OF THE SHADE THEY STOP. 180 MANSNS
MESSER POLO, HIS IMPERIAL MAJESTY COMMANDS THAT YOU STOP TALKING. 350 MARCOM
AFTER ALL, WHEN YOU STOP TO THINK, WHO WAS IT FIRST TOLD THEM GOLD WAS MONEYS 389 MARCOM
I GUESS I'LL HAVE TO STOP OVERWORKING OR I'LL SUFFER A NERVOUS BREAKDOWN. 394 MARCOM
STOP/ 415 MARCOM
LET US STOP PLAYING/ 425 MARCOM
AND STOP YOUR SHAMELESS WAYS WITH MEN. 438 MARCOM
WILL YOU STOP YOUR LYING/ 8 MISBEG
JUST A SLAP BECAUSE SHE TOLD ME TO STOP SINGING, IT WAS AFTER DAYLIGHT. 12 MISBEG
BE GOD, THAT USED TO STOP HIM IN HIS TRACKS. 18 MISBEG
IT DIDN'T STOP HIM FROM SAYING 25 MISBEG
(SUDDENLY FURIOUS) STOP YOUR LYING/ 25 MISBEG
THE GREAT MR. HARDER INTENDS TO STOP HERE 29 MISBEG
GO GET THE BOTTLE AND ONE SMALL GLASS, OR HE'LL NEVER STOP NAGGING ME. 48 MISBEG
(EXASPERATEDLY) WILL YOU STOP YOUR WHISKEY DROOLING AND TALK PLAINS 52 MISBEG
AND STOP YOUR WHISKEY GABBLE ABOUT JIM. 75 MISBEG
WILL YOU STOP BLATHERING LIKE AN OLD WOMAN AND TELL ME PLAINLY WHAT HE'S DONE/ 79 MISBEG
COULDN'T YOU DO ANYTHING TO STOP IT, YOU OLD LOONS 85 MISBEG 83 MISBEG
(FURIOUSLY) STOP SAYING IT/ 88 MISBEG
YOU'LL NEVER DO IT UNLESS YOU'RE MORE SOCIABLE AND 93 MISBEG
STOP LOOKING AT HIM.
STOP LAUGHING/ 95 MISBEG
STOP IT, YOU DAMNED OLD FOOL, AND GET OUT OF HERE/101 MISBEG
(DULLY) I BETTER BEAT IT BACK TO THE INN AND GO 122 MISBEG
TO BED AND STOP BOTHERING YOU,
ONLY STOP TALKING/ 138 MISBEG
COME HERE TO ME, YOU GREAT FOOL, AND STOP YOUR SILLY BLATHER. 141 MISBEG
I DIDN'T WANT TO STOP IT/ 150 MISBEG
I COULDN'T STOP IT SINGING. 150 MISBEG
HIS SOBS BEGIN TO STOP EXHAUSTEDLY. 153 MISBEG
(SPEAKS IN A LOW GRIM TONE) STOP HIDING, FATHER. 157 MISBEG
I TOLD YOU TO STOP LYING, FATHER. 160 MISBEG
(UNEASILY) STOP TALKING SO QUEER. 160 MISBEG

STOP (CONT'D.)
WILL YOU STOP/ 161 MISBEG
(TORMENTEDLY) WILL YOU STOP TALKING AS IF YOU'D GONE MAD IN THE NIGHT/ 161 MISBEG
NOTHING CAN STOP YOU, CAN ITS 169 MISBEG
THE ONLY ONE LEFT TO BRING THE TWO OF YOU TO STOP YOUR DAMNED PRETENDING, 175 MISBEG
IT HAD ONCE BEEN PROSPEROUS, A BREAKFAST STOP FOR THE STAGECOACH, 7 POET
BY TELLING HIM A NEW COACH LINE WAS GOING TO STOP HERE. 26 POET
(SHE PAUSES.) DID YOU NOTICE A CARRIAGE STOP HERE 31 POET
THIS MORNING, MOTHERS
FOR GOD'S SAKE, STOP YOUR STARING/ 35 POET
IF SHE CAN REMEMBER SHE'S A GENTLEWOMAN AND STOP ACTING LIKE A BUGTROTTING 63 POET
FOR THE LOVE OF GOD, STOP-- 74 POET
SHE TALKED ON AND ON AS IF SHE COULDN'T STOP-- 87 POET
AH, WILL YOU STOP TELLING ME YOUR MAD DREAMS/ 91 POET
LET YOU STOP NOW, FATHER/ 114 POET
DON'T LET ME FORGET TO STOP AT THE BARN FOR MY WHIP. 128 POET
(DULLY.) I COULDN'T STOP HIM. 130 POET
(DISTRACTEDLY.) WILL YOU STOP/ 149 POET
YOU KNOW I TRIED TO STOP-- 150 POET
FOR THE LOVE AV GOD, STOP HIM, JAMIE/ 162 POET
(DRUNKENLY BELLIGERENT.) BE CHRIST, I'LL STOP HIM162 PUCT
FOR YOU, NORA.
STOP/ 166 POET
(DISTRACTEDLY.) STOP IT, I'M SAYIN'/ 165 POET
STOP IT/ 169 POET
(TO MELODY, FURIOUSLY.) FATHER, WILL YOU STOP THIS MAD GAME YOU'RE PLAYING--S 170 POET
(GOADED BEYOND BEARING.) I'LL MAKE YOU STOP YOUR 171 POET
DIRTY BROGUE
FOR THE LOVE OF GOD, STOP--LET ME GO--/ 178 POET
(NERVOUSLY) STOP THAT MAD CACKLIN', FOR THE LOVE 382 ROPE
OF HEAVEN/
GET ON NOW AN' STOP YOUR CURSIN'. 584 ROPE
((FOR GOD'S SAKE, STOP ACTING/... 28 STRANG
BUT, STOP TO THINK, YOU'RE JUST THE ONE WHO COULDN'T KNOW WHAT I MEAN. 40 STRANG
YOU OUGHT TO STOP TALKING. 42 STRANG
(IT MUST STOP SUCH THOUGHTS.... 69 STRANG
THEN I DECIDED TO STOP AND RENEW OUR ACQUAINTANCE. 76 STRANG
((STOP WHINING/... 92 STRANG
I MUST STOP THINKING/... 100 STRANG
BUT IT'S GOT TO STOP/ 103 STRANG
(MORE DESPERATELY) (I GOT TO STOP THIS/... 105 STRANG
THAT'LL STOP HER/... 106 STRANG
STOP IT/... 116 STRANG
STOP THESE THOUGHTS/... 117 STRANG
(MOVING UNEASILY) ((STOP IT/... 149 STRANG
(EXASPERATEDLY) FOR HEAVEN'S SAKE, STOP SWEARING 162 STRANG
SO MUCH/
STOP LAUGHING/ 194 STRANG
(ROUGHLY) STOP YER GRIZZLIN'/ 494 VOYAGE
PLEASE STOP, DEAR. 455 WELDED
(IRRITABLY) THEN LET'S STOP ARGUING, FOR HEAVEN'S456 WELDED
SAKE/
LET'S STOP. 456 WELDED
WHY DID YOU STOPS 466 WELDED
THEY BOTH STOP THERE FOR A MOMENT INSTINCTIVELY 469 WELDED
STOP THINKING, DAMN YOU/ 472 WELDED
STOP/ 475 WELDED
STOP/ 475 WELDED
THEIR HANDS CLASP AND THEY AGAIN STOP, SEARCHING EACH OTHER'S EYES. 480 WELDED

STOPGAP
DO YOU THINK DION WOULD CONSIDER IT--AS A TEMPORARY STOPGAP-- 277 GGBROW

STOPPED
THAT'S WHAT STOPPED ME (THEN WITH A BITTER CHANGE OF TONE) 282 AHWILD
(STOPPED FOR A MOMENT--THEN QUICKLY) 283 AHWILD
IT'S THE BARGE IDEA HAS ME STOPPED. 23 ANNA
I'M DARN GLAD I STOPPED AT HIGH SCHOOL, OR MAYBE I'D BEEN CRAZY TOO. 82 BEYOND
PUT YOURSELF IN MY PLACE, AND REMEMBER I HAVEN'T STOPPED LOVING HER, 110 BEYOND
EVEN THOUGH I'D STOPPED CARING FOR HIM AND OUR MARRIAGE HAD ALWAYS BEEN UNHAPPY, 520 DAYS
I THOUGHT HE WAS DRUNK--"R I'D STOPPED HIM GOIN'. 210 DESIRE
HE STOPPED BREATHIN'. 261 DESIRE
(ANOTHER PAUSE) I STOPPED TO HOME ON THE WAY BACKS14 DIFRNT
FROM THE STORE.
SHE WAS GETTIN' CRAZY WHEN YOUR CALLIN' STOPPED HER. 529 DIFRNT
SHE'D NEVER STOPPED LOVING HIM. 26 ELECTR
IF YOU STOPPED THINKING OF YOUR REVENGE FOR A MOMENT AND THOUGHT OF ME/ 38 ELECTR
THEN IS STOPPED BY SOME STRANGENESS HE FEELS ABOUT 53 ELECTR
HER STILL FACE.)
SHE WAS STOPPED MOANING, THE HORROR IN HER EYES IS122 ELECTR
DYING INTO BLANKNESS/
(SURPRISED) YOU STOPPED AT THE ISLANDS$ 144 ELECTR
WE STOPPED A MONTH. 145 ELECTR
(THE TWO DRAFTSMEN IN THE NEXT ROOM HAVE STOPPED WORK AND ARE LISTENING.) 313 GGBROW
WHILE THE OTHER MEN HAVE TURNED FULL AROUND AND STOPPED DUMBFOUNDED BY THE 225 HA APE
IT STOPPED SUDDEN AND SHE WAS JERKED INTO HIM, AND 23 HUGHIE
HE PUT HIS ARMS AROUND HER.
HUGHIE'S WIFE BUT IN AND STOPPED ME COLD. 25 HUGHIE
THAT ISN'T WHAT'S GOT HIM STOPPED. IT'S WHAT'S BEHIND THAT. AND IT'S A WOMAN. 643 ICEMAN
HE YELLS AT CORA WHO HAS STOPPED SINGING 654 ICEMAN

STOPPED

STOPPED (CONT'D.)
(HAS STOPPED CUTTING WHEN THE QUARREL STARTED-- 672 ICEMAN
EXPOSTULATING)
AW, HE'S STOPPED. 688 ICEMAN
SHE'D HAVE THOUGHT I'D STOPPED LOVING HER. 706 ICEMAN
SHE'D HAVE THOUGHT I'D STOPPED LOVING HER. 714 ICEMAN
SHE STOPPED IN THE HALL TO LISTEN, AS IF SHE 38 JOURNE
WANTED TO MAKE SURE I WAS.
CAPTAIN TURNER STOPPED TO TALK AND ONCE HE STARTS 65 JOURNE
GABBING YOU CAN'T GET AWAY
(EDMUND HAS STOPPED COUGHING. HE LOOKS SICK AND 146 JOURNE
WEAK.
I'D STOPPED TO THINK TOO LONG. 147 JOURNE
(EXCITEDLY--INTERRUPTING) MY HEART STOPPED/ 277 LAZARU
THEY HAVE STOPPED RECEDING. 40 MANSNS
ISN'T IT ABOUT TIME YOU STOPPED BEING SO CHILDISH, 7H MANSNS
AND FORGAVE--
(HAS STOPPED SEWING--THINKING.) 119 MANSNS
(HAS STOPPED READING--THINKING.) 120 MANSNS
YOU STOPPED ME FROM OPENING THE DOOR. 169 MANSNS
YOU MUST HAVE STOPPED AT THE INN FOR AN EYE- 41 MISBEG
OPENER--OR TEN OF THEM.
YOU STOPPED ME, DIDN'T YOU# 138 MISBEG
THERE WAS A GRAND CARRIAGE WITH A NIGGER COACHMAN 17 POET
STOPPED AT THE CORNER
FATHER FLYNN STOPPED ME ON THE ROAD YESTERDAY AND 26 POET
TOLD ME
BUT THEY TOLD ME AFTER I NEVER STOPPED GABBIN' 161 POET
ONE AV THE YANKEE GINTRY HAS STOPPED TO BE SEDUCED172 POET
BY MY SLUT AV A DAUGHTER/
HIS MUTHER NEVER STOPPED BABYING HIM. 157 STRANG
(HARSHLY) I'VE STOPPED MEDDLING IN SAM'S LIFE, I 173 STRANG
TELL YOU/
THEN STOPS AS HE NOTICES THAT SHE ALSO HAS STOPPED466 WELDED
AT THE BOTTOM OF THE STAIRS,

STOPPIN'
WHO'S STOPPIN' YUH$ 637 ICEMAN
WHAT LE HELL'S HE STOPPIN' FORS 689 ICEMAN

STOPPING
STOPPING EACH TIME TO SURVEY THE RESULT 249 AHWILD
CRITICALLY, BITING HER TONGUE,
(STOPPING ABRUPTLY) I WAS FORGETTING. 39 ANNA
THEN STOPPING TO PEER ABSENT-MINDEDLY OUT OF THE 41 ANNA
WINDOW.
(STOPPING ABRUPTLY AND LOWERING HIS VOICE 157 BEYOND
CAUTIOUSLY)
(STOPPING AND LOOKING ABOUT HIM) 167 BEYOND
(STOPPING EMMA AS SHE GOES TOWARD THE DOOR AS IF 527 DIFRNT
TO ANSWER HARRIET'S HAIL)
(HE STAGGERS ABOUT THE ROOM--FINALLY STOPPING 545 DIFRNT
BESIDE HER.
(THEN STOPPING--INDIFFERENTLY) 175 EJONES
(STOPPING, SUDDENLY, BEWILDEREDLY) 192 EJONES
AND THAT'S THE THANKS I GET FOR STOPPING YOU/ 105 MANSNS
(STOPPING FOR A MOMENT TO FRESHEN HIS MEMORY) 424 MARCOM
A CAR IS HEARD APPROACHING, STOPPING AT THE CURB 26 STRANG
BEYOND THE GARDEN.
IT'S STOPPING. 94 STRANG
(STOPPING HERSELF--THINKING FRIGHTENEDLY) 167 STRANG

STORE
I'M TAKING THE ADVERTISEMENT FOR MY STORE OUT OF 203 AHWILD
YOUR PAPER--
ENCOURAGE OUTSIDE CAPITAL TO OPEN A DRY-GOODS 204 AHWILD
STORE IN OPPOSITION TO YOU THAT
HE IS DRESSED IN HIS STORE SUIT, SPRUCED UP, 228 DESIRE
I GOT TO GO DOWN TO THE STORE AND GIT SOME THINGS 498 DIFRNT
FOR HARRIET AFORE I FORGETS
(ANOTHER PAUSE) I STOPPED TO HOME ON THE WAY BACKS14 DIFRNT
FROM THE STORE.
I HEARD THEM SAYING TO THE STORE THAT YOU'D BEEN 525 DIFRNT
UP CALLIN' ON THAT FILLY SMALL
SMALL IS A WIRY OLD MAN OF SIXTY-FIVE, A CLERK IN 129 ELECTR
A HARDWARE STORE.
FATE IS IN STORE FOR US, VINNIE--BUT I HAVEN'T 153 ELECTR
DARED PREDICT THAT--NOT YET--
SHE BELONGED IN DE WINDOW OF A TOY STORE, OR ON DE241 HA APE
TOP OF A GARBAGE CAN, SEE/
AFTER GRAMMAR SCHOOL, MY OLD MAN PUT ME TO WORK IN 14 HUGHIE
HIS STORE.
SHE WAS A SALES GIRL IN SOME PUNK DEPARTMENT 23 HUGHIE
STORE.
HE WEARS FIVE-AND-TEN-CENT-STORE SPECTACLES WHICH 577 ICEMAN
ARE SO OUT OF ALIGNMENT
HE HAS BADLY FITTING STORE TEETH, 577 ICEMAN
THIS NIGHT HAS OPENED MY EYES TO A GREAT CAREER IN160 JOURNE
STORE FOR ME. MY BOY/
LIKE A VILLAGE IDIOT IN A COUNTRY STORE SPITTING 102 MANSNS
AT THE BELLY OF A STOVE--
CLOSELY RESEMBLES THE FRONT OF A PRETENTIOUS 428 MARCOM
DELICATESSEN STORE.
WILL YOU KEEP AN EYE ON THE BAR WHILE I RUN TO THE 20 POET
STORE FOR A BIT AV 'BACCY$
I'LL TAKE A WALK TO THE STORE AND HAVE A TALK WITH 28 POET
NEILAN.
I'LL GO TO THE STORE AND GET SOMETHING TASTY. 39 POET
NOW SURE0N'LL HAVE TO GO DOWN TO THE STORE. 72 STRANG
I DON'T WANT TO HURRY YOU BUT NINA WANTS SOME 78 STRANG
THINGS AT THE STORE BEFORE IT

STOREKEEPER
FRESH FROM THE HUMILIATION OF CAJOLING THE 57 POET
STUREKEEPER TO EXTEND MORE CREDIT,

STORES
(HE TURNS AND SEES THE WINDOW DISPLAY IN THE TWO 235 HA APE
STORES FOR THE FIRST TIME)
AND YOU WILL WANT YOUR OWN STORES HERE IN THE CITY100 MANSNS
TO SELL YOUR GOODS.
OF THIS END, THE STORES ARE THE LAST POSSIBLE 157 MANSNS
LINK--

STORES (CONT'D.)
YOU STILL HAVE TO HAVE STORES TO RETAIL YOUR 157 MANSNS
COTTON GOODS--

STORIES
I RANG IN A JOKE IN ONE OF MY STORIES THAT TICKLED188 AHWILD
THE FOLKS THERE PINK.
AND WE'LL HAVE TO LISTEN TO ALL THOSE OLD STORIES 212 AHWILD
OF HIS
TELLIN' STORIES LIKE IT OUT O' THEIR EXPERIENCES. 502 DIFRNT
I KNOW FROM WHAT I CAN GUESS FROM HIS OWN STORIES 512 DIFRNT
PA NEVER WAS NO SAINT.
THAT MEANS UNCLE CALEB HAS COME AND SHE'S TOLD HIM527 DIFRNT
HER STORIES
YOU DIDN'T STOP ABOUT RELIEVIN' THE FOOL STORIES 539 DIFRNT
THEY GOSSIPED ABOUT ME THAT
(HASTILY) I HAVEN'T HEARD ANY STORIES-- 276 GGBROM
BUT I SUPPOSE THE GOSSIPS ARE TELLING THE SAME 276 GGBROM
SILLY STORIES ABOUT HIM THEY
IT MOVES--SPEED--TWENTY-FIVE STORIES UP AND ME AT 238 HA APE
OF TOP AND BOTTOM--MOVIN'/
I THOUGHT IT WAS UP TO ME TO PUT OUT SOMETHING, 25 HUGHIE
AND KIDS LIKE ANIMAL STORIES.
THEY WAS STORIES OF BIG GAMES AND KILLINGS 29 HUGHIE
YEAH, HUGHIE LAPPED UP MY STORIES LIKE THEY WAS 29 HUGHIE
DUCK SOUP.
YOU USED TO TAKE ME ON YOUR KNEE AND TELL ME 508 ICEMAN
STORIES
ALWAYS GOT A MILLION FUNNY STORIES. 610 ICEMAN
WHEN YOU'D READ ME FAIRY STORIES.. 12 MANSNS
AND WE'D START DRINKING AND TELLING STORIES, AND 26 MISBEG
SINGING SONGS.

STORK
FOR--AND CAN GUESS A STORK DIDN'T BRING HER DOWN 202 AHWILD
YOUR CHIMNEY/
YOU KNOW FANNY THE BARMAID AT THE RED STORK IN 489 CARDIF
CARDIFF$
MAYBE THE STORK BROUGHT HIM, BAD LUCK TO IT FOR A 59 MISBEG
DIRTY BIRD.
THEN A STORK BECAME THE ONLY CONCEIVABLE 75 STRANG
EXPLANATION/

STORM
INTO THE DIVIL'S OWN STORM, AND SHE SPRANG WAN 36 ANNA
HELL OF A LEAK UP FOR'ARD.
BUT TEN DAYS BACK WE MET UP WITH ANOTHER STORM THE 36 ANNA
LIKE OF THE FIRST.
STORM AND FOG TO THE WAN SPOT IN THE WORLD WHERE 39 ANNA
YOU WAS
IN THE REST OF YOUR YOUTH DO THE LIKE OF WHAT I 48 ANNA
DONE IN THE STORM AND AFTER.
(HASTILY--SEEING THE GATHERING STORM) 105 BEYOND
(THERE IS A PERFECT STORM OF GROANS AND LAUGHTER 497 CARIBE
AT THIS SPEECH.)
THAT WAS TWO WEEKS AFTER THE STORM, 598 CROSS
I BELIEVE THAT A STORM MUST BE COMING THIS WAY. 424 DYNAMO
A FAINT FLASH OF LIGHTNING FROM THE DISTANT STORM 424 DYNAMO
FLICKERS THROUGH HIS WINDOW.
BUT I'M NOT GOING TO STAY OUT IN THE STORM...) 444 DYNAMO
AFTER THAT STORM WAS OVER I'D CHANGED, BELIEVE ME/460 DYNAMO
THAT'S WHERE I WAS ALL DURING THE STORM THAT NIGHT460 DYNAMO
AFTER I LEFT HERE.
EVERY STORM THE WATER'D BEGIN TO DRIP DOWN AND 466 DYNAMC
MUTHER'D PUT THE WASH
UNTIL NOW HE IS INTERRUPTED BY A STORM OF 212 HA APE
CATCALLS, HISSES, BOOS,
(A PERFECT STORM OF HISSES, CATCALLS, BOOS, AND 243 HA APE
HARD LAUGHTER.)
WITH A GROWL HE STARTS TO GET UP AND STORM THE 250 HA APE
CLOSED DOOR.
AND THEN A STORM OF EXCITED TALK BREAKS LOOSE.) 523 INZONE
TAKING HIM TO ROME HAD BEEN THRICE BLOWN BACK BY A300 LAZARU
STORM.
I WILL NOT STORM. 39 MANSNS
OH, I EXPECT YOU TO STORM AT ME FOR PLEADING HER 39 MANSNS
CASE--

STORMILY
(BREAKING OUT STORMILY) I DON'T/ 91 BEYOND

STORMS
WINDYAMMER, AY VAS THROUGH HUNDRED STORMS VORSE'N 49 ANNA
DAT/
(GRINNING) NO MORE SEA, NO MORE BUM GRUB, NO MORE503 VOYAGE
STORMS--YUST NICE WORK.

STORMY
*SHE'S FAR ACROSS THE STORMY WATER WAY-AY, I'M 124 ELECTR
BOUND AWAY--

STORY
I GUESS I WAS DREAMING ABOUT THE OLD VIKINGS IN 546 'ILE
THE STORY-BOOKS AND I THOUGHT
(QUICKLY) INTERPOSING, TRYING TO STAVE OFF THE 229 AHWILD
STORY)
BUT IT'S A GOOD TRUE STORY FOR KIDS BECAUSE IT 230 AHWILD
ILLUSTRATES THE DANGER OF BEING
OF COURSE IT'S A GOOD STORY--AND YOU TELL IT 231 AHWILD
WHENEVER YOU'VE A MIND TO.
IT'S TOO LONG A STORY--AND LET THE DEAD PAST BURY 281 AHWILD
IT'S DEAD.
WASN'T THE WHOLE STORY OF IT AND MY PICTURE ITSELF 48 ANNA
I'M GOING TO TELL YOU A FUNNY STORY, SO PAY 56 ANNA
ATTENTION.
HE IS TELLING A STORY. 478 CARDIF
(HE GETS UP SMILING) AND THANK YOU FOR THE 562 CROSS
INTERESTING STORY.
AND I'LL MAKE YOU FACE IT IN THE END OF YOUR 499 DAYS
STORY--
BUT TO GET BACK TO MY STORY.. 503 DAYS
IT IS--A LOVE STORY. 505 DAYS
THEN, JUDGING FROM YOUR LETTERS, IT OUGHT TO BE A 505 DAYS
LOVE STORY.
IT'S REALLY THE STORY OF A MAN I ONCE KNEW. 509 DAYS

STORY (CONT'D.)
(UNDER LOVING'S COMPULSION, HE PICKS UP THE THREAD509 DAYS
OF THE STORY)
ON WITH HER STORY) 522 DAYS
BUT YOU TELL YOUR STORY JUST THE SAME. 530 DAYS
IT'S THE STORY OF A MAN I ONCE KNEW. 533 DAYS
BUT THIS PART IS ALL THE STORY OF THE MAN YOU 536 DAYS
KNEW, ISN'T ITS
I'M AFRAID YOU WILL FIND THIS PART OF HIS STORY 536 DAYS
HARD TO BELIEVE, ELSA.
BUT GO ON WITH YOUR STORY, JACK. 538 DAYS
THE QUESTION DOESN'T COME UP IN MY STORY, AS 539 DAYS
YOU'LL SEE, BUT--
AND TELL HIM THE REST OF YOUR STORY THERE. 540 DAYS
THE END OF YOUR STORY. 543 DAYS
GO ON WITH YOUR STORY. 544 DAYS
BUT IT'S ONLY A STORY. 545 DAYS
BUT THAT'S ENOUGH ABOUT THE DAMNED STORY. 545 DAYS
BUT THERE IS STILL ANOTHER END OF MY STORY--THE 545 DAYS
ONE SENSIBLE HAPPY END/
ONLY A STORY, JACKS 545 DAYS
I NEVER SHOULD HAVE TOLD HER THE STORY/ 547 DAYS
AND THEY WERE THE SAME AS THOSE IN YOUR STORY. 549 DAYS
BUT SO IS YOUR STORY ABOUT THE NOVEL A LIE. 549 DAYS
BUT THAT WOULD SPOIL JOHN'S STORY, DON'T YOU 550 DAYS
THINK.
DIDN'T MY STORY EXPLAINS 550 DAYS
SHE SEEMS TO HAVE TAKEN HER END IN YOUR STORY VERY551 DAYS
SERIOUSLY.
THAT MY PROPHECY IS COMING TRUE--HER END IN MY 554 DAYS
STORY.
HIDING BEHIND THE END OF MY STORY/ 555 DAYS
HER END IN YOUR STORY IS COMING TRUE. 558 DAYS
(IGNORING THIS) THERE IS A FATE IN THAT STORY, 560 DAYS
JACK--
THE TRUTH YOU HAVE YOURSELF REVEALED IN YOUR STORY560 DAYS
(THEN TERRIFIED AGAIN) WHAT MADE YOU SAY, A FATE 560 DAYS
IN MY STORY--THE WILL OF GODS
DO YOU THINK YOU CAN CHOOSE YOUR STUPID END IN 561 DAYS
YOUR STORY NOW,
A FATE IN MY STORY--THE WILL OF GOD/ 561 DAYS
A FATE IN MY STORY, UNCLE SAID--THE WILL OF GOD/ 562 DAYS
THE END WALL FACING US HAS TWO WINDOWS IN ITS 202 DESIRE
UPPER STORY.
OUT OF THER STORY BOOKS YOU'RE ALWAYS READIN', 499 DIFRNT
AIN'T HES
IS IT THAT STORY ABOUT CALEB AND THAT HEATHEN 508 DIFRNT
BROWN WOMAN YOU'RE TALKING ABOUTS
I'LL BET, AND IF THEM FOOLS HADN'T STARTED THIS 509 DIFRNT
STORY GOING,
STORY-BOOK NOTIONS, THAT'S THE TROUBLE WITH YOU, 510 DIFRNT
EMBER.
HE TOLD ME SOME FOOL STORY 'BOUT YOU FALLIN' OUT 513 DIFRNT
WITH CALEB.
SHE SAYS JACK'D TOLD YOU THAT STORY THEY'RE ALL 514 DIFRNT
TELLIN' AS A JOKE ON ME.
(WHO HAS FINISHED READING THE STORY) 431 DYNAMO
SO THE DAMNED IDIOT BLATHERS THE WHOLE STORY 431 DYNAMO
BREAKS OFF WITH THE GIRL AND GOES TO THE POLICE 431 DYNAMO
WITH THE STORY.
THIS STORY IN THE PAPER/ 431 DYNAMO
WHEREVER DID YOU GET HOLD OF THIS STORYS 447 DYNAMO
(WHILE HE HAS BEEN TELLING THIS STORY, 447 DYNAMO
WHY, YOU POOR FISH, THAT MURDER STORY IS IN 451 DYNAMO
TODAY'S STAR--
POP SIMPLY COPIED THAT STORY-- 451 DYNAMO
I WAS JUST TELLING YOUR OLD MAN IT WAS ONLY A 451 DYNAMO
MURDER STORY OUT OF THE PAPER
IS MUCH WIDER THAN THE RIGHT SECTION BUT IS A 473 DYNAMO
STORY LESS IN HEIGHT.
THE SWITCHBOARD ROOM ON THE RIGHT--ONE STORY UP-- 486 DYNAMO
ARE OF CONCRETE.
ONE STORY UP IN THE OTHER SECTION OF THE BUILDING.486 DYNAMO
*COUNT OF THE STORY ABOUT YOUR BREAKIN' JAIL BACK 177 EJONES
IN THE STATES.
(THEN WITH EASY LAUGH) YOU MEAN *COUNT OF DAT 180 EJONES
STORY 'BOUT ME BREAKIN' JAIL
IT'S A STORY I TELLS YOU BOYS YOU KNOWS I'SE DE 181 EJONES
KIND OF MAN DAT IF YOU EVAN
OH, HE DID TELL ME THE STORY OF HIS LIFE TO MAKE 15 ELECTR
HIMSELF OUT ROMANTIC.
I SUPPOSE CLIPPERS ARE TOO OLD A STORY TO THE 23 ELECTR
DAUGHTER OF A SHIPBUILDER.
(THEN GOING ON BITTERLY WITH HIS STORY) 26 ELECTR
YOU CAN MAKE UP SOME STORY ABOUT A SICK DOG ON 40 ELECTR
YOUR SHIP.
SHE IS JUST FINISHING HER STORY OF THE MURDER AND 110 ELECTR
THE EVENTS FOLLOWING IT.
(HE THRUSTS THE NEWSPAPER INTO HER HANDS, POINTING121 ELECTR
TO THE STORY)
AN' WHEN I GIT THROUGH TELLIN' MY STORY OF IT 135 ELECTR
ROUND TOWN TOMORROW
YES, TELL US YOUR SAD STORY. 240 HA APE
THE GUEST'S STORY OF HIS LIFE. 14 HUGHIE
TELLIN' SAPS A STORY TO MAKE 'EM BET/ 22 HUGHIE
AFTER DINNER I STARTED TELLIN' 'EM A STORY 25 HUGHIE
THE BIGGER THE STORY THE HARDER HE'D FALL. 28 HUGHIE
I SEE HE WANTS A BIG STORY TO CHEER HIM, 30 HUGHIE
I READ A STORY ABOUT HIM. 32 HUGHIE
THE STORY SAID HE WOULDN'T BOTHER PLAYING IN A 32 HUGHIE
POKER GAME
I HEAR A STORY HE'LL BE SO FULL OF HOP, 37 HUGHIE
IS A NARROW FIVE-STORY STRUCTURE OF THE TENEMENT 571 ICEMAN
TYPE.
YOU'VE TOLD THAT STORY TEN MILLION TIMES AND IF I 601 ICEMAN
HAVE TO HEAR IT AGAIN,
WE'VE ALL HEARD THAT STORY ABOUT HOW YOU CAME BACK657 ICEMAN
TO CAPE TOWN

STORY (CONT'D.)
(GOING ON WITH HIS STORY) DEY SAYS, *WE'RE TAKIN'670 ICEMAN
A HOLIDAY.
WHEN YOU KNOW THE STORY OF ME AND EVELYN, 704 ICEMAN
(TOO ABSORBED IN HIS STORY NOW TO NOTICE THIS-- 709 ICEMAN
(HE STARTS HIS STORY, HIS TONE AGAIN BECOMING 709 ICEMAN
MUSINGLY REMINISCENT)
(HE CHUCKLES) BUT THAT'S AHEAD OF MY STORY. 710 ICEMAN
IT WAS THE SAME OLD STORY, OVER AND OVER, FOR 713 ICEMAN
YEARS AND YEARS.
BEJEESS, YOU KNOW THE OLD STORY, 718 ICEMAN
(BY THIS TIME EVERYONE, JACK INCLUDED, IS 519 INZONE
LISTENING BREATHLESSLY TO HIS STORY)
STORY, FAIRLY BURSTING TO BREAK IN WITH HIS OWN 519 INZONE
REVELATIONS.)
(SURPRISED AND A BIT NETTLED TO HAVE TO SHARE HIS 519 INZONE
STORY WITH ANYONE)
THIS IS THE KID'S STORY. 22 JOURNE
(TACTFULLY. GO ON WITH YOUR STORY, EDMUND. 23 JOURNE
I'VE HEARD PAPA TELL THAT MACHINE SHOP STORY TEN 117 JOURNE
THOUSAND TIMES.
GO ON WITH YOUR STORY/ 277 LAZARU
THE HOUSE IS LOW, OF ONE STORY ONLY, ITS WALLS 281 LAZARU
WHITE.
THE STORY IS, THIS LAZARUS WAS DEAD FOUR DAYS 316 LAZARU
MY MIRROR TELLS ME A CRUELER STORY. 5 MANSNS
HIS EYES FIX ON ONE STORY. 44 MANSNS
MORE LIKE A CHARACTER IN YOUR STORY THAN A FLESH- 109 MANSNS
AND-BLOOD MOTHER.
OH, NOT IN YOUR STORY. 110 MANSNS
(HE BEGINS TO TELL THE STORY, STARING BEFORE HIM 110 MANSNS
AS IF HE VISUALIZED IT.)
I AM SURE I NEVER--I REMEMBER THE STORY AS AN 111 MAVSNS
IRONICALLY HUMOROUS TALE.
BUT I WAS VERY IMPRESSIONABLE THEN AND YOUR STORY 111 MANSNS
WAS VERY REAL TO ME.
AN OLD FAIRY STORY I MADE UP IN AN IDLE MOMENT TO 183 MANSNS
MAKE YOU LAUGH/
THE KINGDOM OF PEACE AND HAPPINESS IN YOUR STORY 183 MANSNS
IS LOVE.
WE ARE BACK HERE IN YOUR GARDEN ON THE DAY YOU 184 MANSNS
TOLD ME THAT STORY.
(HE GOES ON TELLING THE REST OF THE STORY WITH 366 MARCOM
MUCH EXAGGERATED JEWISH PANTOMIME
AS MAFFEO ENDS HIS STORY.) 367 MARCOM
UNTIL THE LOUD LAUGHTER AT THE END OF MAFFEO'S 370 MARCOM
STORY.
AS MAFFEO TELLS THE STORY, 370 MARCOM
AS HE RETURNS TO THE GROUP AT CENTER, MAFFEO HAS 371 MARCOM
JUST FINISHED HIS STORY.
I'LL HAVE TO GIVE MARCO SOME LESSONS IN HOW TO 374 MARCOM
TELL A SHORT STORY.
THIS IS THE FUNNIEST STORY YOU'VE EVER HEARD/ 374 MARCOM
TO MAKE MATTERS WORSE, A ONE-STORY, 1 MISBEG
LISTEN, AND I'LL TELL YOU A LITTLE STORY, JOSIE. 143 MISBEG
THIS IS THE ONLY WAY HE CAN START TELLING THE 146 MISBEG
STORY?
(HE PAUSES) HOPE I DIDN'T TELL YOU THE SAD STORY 170 MISBEG
OF MY LIFE
(HE TAKES UP THE STORY AGAIN.) 198 POET
AS IF JAMIE HAD JUST MADE SOME CLIMACTIC POINT IN 177 POET
HIS STORY.
(THEN SUDDENLY STARTS HER STORY IN A DULL 82 STRANG
MONOTONOUS TONE RECALLING THAT OF
(SARCASTICALLY) IF I AM TO BELIEVE YOUR STORY, 456 WELDED
YOU DIDN'T THINK SO.
(AFTER A PAUSE, TAKING UP HER STORY MATTER-OF- 483 WELDED
FACTLY)

STOUT
A SHORT STOUT WOMAN WITH FADING LIGHT-BROWN HAIR 187 AHWILD
SPRINKLED WITH GRAY.
HE IS A STOUT, JOWLY-FACED MAN IN HIS LATE 244 AHWILD
THIRTIES.
CATES IS SQUAT AND STOUT AND IS DRESSED IN 571 CROSS
DUNGAREE PANTS
HE IS ABOUT FORTY, STOUT, WITH A PREMATURELY BALD 496 DAYS
HEAD, A ROUND FACE.
HER STOUT FIGURE IS STILL FIRM AND ACTIVE, 422 DYNAMO
HIS WIFE IS TALL AND STOUT, WEIGHING WELL OVER TWO428 DYNAMO
HUNDRED.
STOUT AND UNCTUOUS, SNOBBISH AND INGRATIATING, 67 ELECTR
CONSCIOUS OF GODLINESS,
A STOUT, SELF-IMPORTANT OLD MAN WITH A STUBBORN 68 ELECTR
OPINIONATED EXPRESSION.
PROVINCIAL BUSINESS MAN, STOUT AND HEARTY IN HIS 257 GGBROW
EVENING DRESS.
(AS HE IS SPEAKING, A WELL-DRESSED IMPORTANT STOUT305 GGBROW
MAN ENTERS THE DRAFTING ROOM.
ERIE IS AROUND MEDIUM HEIGHT BUT APPEARS SHORTER 8 HUGHIE
BECAUSE HE IS STOUT
HE IS ABOUT FIFTY, A LITTLE UNDER MEDIUM HEIGHT, 610 ICEMAN
WITH A STOUT, ROLY-POLY FIGURE.
THE MOTHER IS TALL AND STOUT, OVER SIXTY-FIVE, A 275 LAZARU
GENTLE, SIMPLE WOMAN,
BUT HE IS TALL AND STOUT WITH A ROUND, JOVIAL FACE358 MARCOM
AND SMALL, CUNNING EYES.
SHE HAS GROWN INTO A STOUT MIDDLE AGE 427 MARCOM
GADSBY IS IN HIS LATE FORTIES, SHORT, STOUT, WITH 116 POET
A BIG, BALD HEAD, ROUND,
HE HAS GROWN STOUT. 137 STRANG
HE HAS GROWN VERY STOUT. 159 STRANG
KATE IS STOUT AND DARK.) 499 VOYAGE

STOUTER
HE IS DRESSED IN AN EXPENSIVE BUSINESS SUIT AND 153 BEYOND
APPEARS STOUTER)
HIS WIFE, LOUISA, IS TALLER AND STOUTER THAN HE 6 ELECTR
AND ABOUT THE SAME AGE.
CYBEL HAS GROWN STOUTER AND MORE VOLUPTUOUS, 284 GGBROW

STOUTER   1552

STOUTER (CONT'D.)
SHE HAS GROWN STOUTER, HAS MORE OF THE DEEP   320 GGBROW
OBJECTIVE CALM OF AN IDOL.)
IS AN INCH TALLER AND WEIGHS LESS, BUT APPEARS   19 JOURNE
SHORTER AND STOUTER
SHE HAS GROWN STOUTER, HER FACE HAS FILLED OUT.   90 STRANG
HE IS STOUTER, THE HAGGARD LOOK OF WORRY AND SELF-   111 STRANG
CONSCIOUS INFERIORITY HAS GONE
EVANS HAS GROWN STOUTER, HIS FACE IS HEAVY NOW,   151 STRANG

STOUTEST
(SHE IS THE OLDEST, STOUTEST, AND HOMELIEST OF THE464 CARIBE
FOUR--GRINNING BACK AT THEM)

STOUTISH
ABBIE TURNS TO HER LEFT TO A BIG STOUTISH MIDDLE- 248 DESIRE
AGED MAN WHOSE FLUSHED FACE AND

STOUTLY
(STOUTLY) YES, THANK GOD, THOUGH I'VE NOT SEEN A 37 ANNA
SIGHT OF IT IN FIFTEEN YEARS.
(STOUTLY) YOU DID, AND IF THERE WASN'T SO MANY   174 POET
AV THIM--

STOVE
IN THE CENTER OF THE ROOM, A STOVE.   535 *ILE
HIS TEETH ARE CHATTERING WITH THE COLD AND HE   536 *ILE
HURRIES TO THE STOVE.
STAY BY THE STOVE WHERE YE BELONG AND YE'LL FIND   536 *ILE
NO NEED OF CHATTERIN'.
THE CHIMNEY OF THE CABIN STOVE RISES A FEW FEET   25 ANNA
ABOVE THE ROOF.
FARTHER FORWARD A DOUBLE-HEATER STOVE WITH COAL   93 BEYOND
SCUTTLE, ETC.
A PILE OF WOOD IS STACKED UP CARELESSLY AGAINST   144 BEYOND
THE WALL BY THE STOVE.
AT THE RISE OF THE CURTAIN RUTH IS DISCOVERED   144 BEYOND
SITTING BY THE STOVE,
A BROWN COATING OF RUST COVERS THE UNBLACKED   144 BEYOND
STOVE.
HER MOTHER IS ASLEEP IN HER WHEEL CHAIR BESIDE THE145 BEYOND
STOVE TOWARD THE REAR.
(STARING AT THE STOVE) YOU BETTER COME NEAR THE   145 BEYOND
FIRE WHERE IT'S WARM.
(RUTH STARES AT THE STOVE IN SILENCE.   147 BEYOND
SHE STARES AT THE STOVE.   149 BEYOND
SHE SITS DOWN IN HER CHAIR AND STARES AT THE   151 BEYOND
STOVE--DULLY)
(SHE COMES BACK TO THE STOVE)   152 BEYOND
(SHE GETS WEARILY FROM THE CHAIR AND PUTS A FEW   152 BEYOND
PIECES OF WOOD IN THE STOVE)
(THE TWO WOMEN REMAIN SILENT FOR A TIME STARING   152 BEYOND
DEJECTEDLY AT THE STOVE.)
THEN SHE SHUTS THE DOOR AND RETURNS TO HER CHAIR   154 BEYOND
BY THE STOVE.
HE SPRINGS FROM HIS CHAIR AND WALKS TO THE   163 BEYOND
STOVE.)
EBEN TAKES BOILED POTATOES AND BACON FROM THE   206 DESIRE
STOVE AND PUTS THEM ON THE TABLE.
SHE STILL COMES BACK--STANDS BY THE STOVE THAR IN 209 DESIRE
THE EVENIN'--
COMES BACK AND PULLS UP A STRIP OF FLOORING IN   219 DESIRE
UNDER STOVE.
HE LOOKS FROM IT TO THE STOVE.   220 DESIRE
HE SITS DOWN AT THE TABLE, FACES THE STOVE AND   220 DESIRE
PULLS OUT THE PAPER.
THE STOVE HAS BEEN TAKEN DOWN TO GIVE MORE ROOM TO247 DESIRE
THE DANCERS.
HE SAYS IN WHALER'-- AND MY BOAT IS STOVE/   543 DIFRNT
=A DEAD WHALE OR A STOVE BOAT/=   543 DIFRNT
SHE COULDA BIT A PIECE OUT OF A STOVE LID, AFTER   608 ICEMAN
SHE FOUND IT OUT.
WHERE YOU ROASTED IN SUMMER, AND THERE WAS NO   148 JOURNE
STOVE IN WINTER,
LIKE A VILLAGE IDIOT IN A COUNTRY STORE SPITTING   102 MANSNS
AT THE BELLY OF A STOVE--
THERE'S STEW ON THE STOVE, YOU BAD-TEMPERED RUNT. 35 MISBEG
BUT WHEN YOU'RE STANDIN' OVER THE STOVE ALL DAY,   43 POET
YOU CAN'T HELP--
WE'LL JUST SHOVE THIS INTO THE STOVE TILL IT'S   600 ROPE
RED-HOT

STOW
STOW THAT PISTOL/   104 ELECTR
STOW YOUR DAMNED JAW/   105 ELECTR
(IMPATIENTLY) STOW IT/   495 VOYAGE

STOWAWAY
(WITH PRIDE) FROM STOWAWAY TO EMPEROR IN TWO   177 CJONES
YEARS/

STRADDLING
SITTING ON A CHAIR IN A PARK OR STRADDLING A HORSE 94 ELECTR
IN A TOWN SQUARE--

STRAGGLES
HER BLACK HAIR, STREAKED WITH GRAY, STRAGGLES IN   20 POET
UNTIDY WISPS ABOUT HER FACE.

STRAGGLING
A STRAGGLING LINE OF PILED ROCKS, TOO LOW TO BE   81 BEYOND
CALLED A WALL,
(A WIZENED RUNT OF A MAN WITH A STRAGGLING GRAY   456 CARIBE
MUSTACHE--
CUCKY, A WIZENED RUNT OF A MAN WITH A STRAGGLING   496 VOYAGE
GRAY MUSTACHE.

STRAGGLY
STRAGGLY WISPS FROM THE PILE OF RANK HAY FALL   601 ROPE
SILENTLY TO THE FLOOR

STRAIGHT
(SHE STANDS THERE STARING STRAIGHT BEFORE HER AS   541 *ILE
IF IN A DAZE.
(SHE GOES DIFFIDENTLY TO THE STRAIGHT-BACKED CHAIR88 AHWILD
BEFORE THE DESK AT RIGHT.
THE ONLY THING I CAN DO IS PUT IT UP TO HIM   206 AHWILD
STRAIGHT.

STRAIGHT (CONT'D.)
AND I'VE GOT TO WARN THAT YOUNG IMP TO KEEP HIS   214 AHWILD
FACE STRAIGHT.
AND DIDN'T THINK YOU'RE GIVING ME THE STRAIGHT   219 AHWILD
GOODS ABOUT HAVING BEEN AROUND
I TELL YOU STRAIGHT, I WOULDN'T ASK YOU TO COME IF219 AHWILD
I WASN'T IN A HOLE--
SIT UP STRAIGHT IN YOUR CHAIR/   222 AHWILD
DAMN IT, I'VE GOT TO HAVE A STRAIGHT TALK WITH   267 AHWILD
HIM--
HE'S SO TICKLED TO GET OUT OF IT FOR A WHILE HE   269 AHWILD
CAN'T SEE STRAIGHT/
I'VE A GOOD MIND TO SEND YOU STRAIGHT BACK TO BED 270 AHWILD
AND MAKE YOU STAY THERE/
YOU'D BETTER TELL HER STRAIGHT TO GET OUT/   10 ANNA
WELL, I'LL TELL YOU STRAIGHT, KIDDO, THAT MARTHY   15 ANNA
OWEN NEVER--
SHE IS NOT READING BUT STARING STRAIGHT IN FRONT   41 ANNA
OF HER.
I'D HAVE JUMPED AT THE CHANCE, I TELL YOU THAT   44 ANNA
STRAIGHT.
THEN HE GOES TO THE TABLE, SETS THE CLOTH STRAIGHT 44 ANNA
MECHANICALLY,
NIGHT IN THE FOG, AND AFTERWARDS SEEING THAT YOU   59 ANNA
HAS STRAIGHT GOODS STUCK ON ME,
IT'S THE STRAIGHT GOODS, HONEST&   60 ANNA
ANNA SITS AT THE TABLE, STARING STRAIGHT IN FRONT   63 ANNA
OF HER.)
(HE WALKS STRAIGHT FOR HER.)   69 ANNA
IN THE CORNER, A STRAIGHT-BACKED CHAIR,   93 BEYOND
AND ONE STRAIGHT-BACKED, ARE PLACED ABOUT THE   93 BEYOND
TABLE.
ANDREW IS TILTED BACK ON THE STRAIGHT-BACKED CHAIR 94 BEYOND
TO THE LEFT,
ANDREW STANDS RIGIDLY LOOKING STRAIGHT IN FRONT OF108 BEYOND
HIM.
YOU'VE GOT IT ALL STRAIGHT NOW, HAVEN'T YOU, ROBS 135 BEYOND
AND PLUMPS STRAIGHT DOWN TO THE BOTTOM.   479 CARDIF
THE STARES STRAIGHT IN FRONT OF HIM WITH EYES   489 CARDIF
STARTING FROM THEIR SOCKETS)
STRAIGHT FROM THE OLD BARBARY COAST IN FRISCO/   470 CARIBE
IN FRONT OF THE BENCH, A LONG TABLE WITH TWO   555 CROSS
STRAIGHT-BACKED CHAIRS,
A STRAIGHT NOSE AND A SQUARE JAW, A WIDE MOUTH   493 DAYS
THAT HAS AN INCONGRUOUS FEMININE
BUT HE IS LOOKING STRAIGHT AHEAD AND THEY TURN   535 DAYS
AWAY AGAIN.)
BUT SHE IS STARING STRAIGHT BEFORE HER WITH A   539 DAYS
STILL SET FACE.
HE'S HEADED STRAIGHT FOR A COMPLETE COLLAPSE.   556 DAYS
HIS EYES FIXED STRAIGHT BEFORE HIM.   563 DAYS
THEY BOTH REMAIN RIGID, LOOKING STRAIGHT AHEAD   241 DESIRE
WITH EYES FULL OF FEAR.)
HE KEEPS HIS EYES STRAIGHT AHEAD.)   260 DESIRE
THEY STARE STRAIGHT AHEAD.   267 DESIRE
THEY STARE STRAIGHT AHEAD.   267 DESIRE
SHE STARES STRAIGHT BEFORE HER, HER MOUTH SET   538 DIFRNT
THINLY.
I'LL GET HER TO PUT IT UP TO HIM STRAIGHT.   545 DIFRNT
EMMA SITS STRAIGHT AND STIFF IN HER CHAIR FOR A   548 DIFRNT
WHILE.
(THEN) IT'S STRAIGHT GOODS...   464 DYNAMO
THESE SWITCHES EXTEND IN A STRAIGHT ROW BACKWARD   483 DYNAMO
DOWN THE MIDDLE OF THE GALLERY.
HER BLACK EYEBROWS MEET IN A PRONOUNCED STRAIGHT   9 ELECTR
LINE ABOVE HER STRONG NOSE.
THE BLACK EYEBROWS MEETING IN A STRAIGHT LINE   10 ELECTR
ABOVE HER NOSE.
SHE STARES STRAIGHT AHEAD, HER FACE FROZEN, HER   18 ELECTR
EYES HARD.
FRAMED BY COAL-BLACK STRAIGHT HAIR WHICH HE WEARS   21 ELECTR
NOTICEABLY LONG,
BUT SHE IS LOOKING STRAIGHT BEFORE HER)   21 ELECTR
AND I'M USED TO STRAIGHT SPEAKING.   22 ELECTR
SHE IS STARING STRAIGHT BEFORE HER.   43 ELECTR
THICK STRAIGHT BLACK HAIR, LIGHT HAZEL EYES.   73 ELECTR
IT IS AN INTERIOR COMPOSED OF STRAIGHT SEVERE   79 ELECTR
LINES WITH HEAVY DETAIL.
HE IS NOT LOOKING DOWN AT HIS FATHER BUT IS   93 ELECTR
STARING STRAIGHT BEFORE HIM,
HE'LL COME STRAIGHT IN HERE.   114 ELECTR
EVERYTHING THAT'S STRAIGHT AND STRONG/   167 ELECTR
(STARES STRAIGHT BEFORE HER.   172 ELECTR
DION STIFFENS AND HIS MASK STARES STRAIGHT AHEAD.   265 GGBROW
(SHE SITS IN THE CHAIR WHERE DION HAD SAT AND   300 GGBROW
STARES STRAIGHT BEFORE HER.
THE STRAIGHT BACKS AND FULL CHESTS OF THEM/   213 HA APE
STRAIGHT AS STRING/   228 HA APE
IS ALL DAT STRAIGHT GOODS&   228 HA APE
(BEWILDEREDLY) IS DAT STRAIGHT GOODS--MONKEY FUR&236 HA APE
(BITTERLY) IT'S STRAIGHT ENUF.   236 HA APE
COME OUT WITH THAT STRAIGHT.   246 HA APE
HE IS TALL, RAW-BONED, WITH COARSE STRAIGHT WHITE 574 ICEMAN
HAIR,
YOU HAVE TO WEAR BLINDERS LIKE A HORSE AND SEE   590 ICEMAN
ONLY STRAIGHT IN FRONT OF YOU.
(LEANS OVER THE BAR AND STOPS LEWIS WITH A   677 ICEMAN
STRAIGHT-ARM SWIPE ON THE CHEST)
I WANT A STRAIGHT ANSWER/   693 ICEMAN
(SUDDENLY RAISES HIS HEAD FROM HIS ARMS AND,   694 ICEMAN
LOOKING STRAIGHT IN FRONT OF HIM,
I TOLD HER STRAIGHT, +YOU BETTER FORGET ME,   710 ICEMAN
EVELYN, FOR YOUR OWN SAKE.
STRAIGHT TO THE GARDEN'S CAGE AT THE LONDON ZOO,   723 ICEMAN
HER NOSE IS LONG AND STRAIGHT, HER MOUTH WIDE WITH 12 JOURNE
FULL, SENSITIVE LIPS.
SUNBLEACHED TO RED AT THE ENDS, BRUSHED STRAIGHT   20 JOURNE
BACK FROM IT.

1553 STRAINED

STRAIGHT (CONT'D.)
(SHE STOPS, LOOKING STRAIGHT AT HIM NOW, 49 JOURNE
JUST NOW HE IS STARING STRAIGHT BEFORE HIM 274 LAZARU
(HE TURNS HIS EYES FROM THEM, STARING STRAIGHT 291 LAZARU
BEFORE HIM.
THEY ALSO WEAR WIRE WIGS BUT OF STRAIGHT HAIR CUT 336 LAZARU
IN SHORT BOYISH MODE,
HE IS STARING STRAIGHT BEFORE HIM, 350 LAZARU
HER NOSE IS STRAIGHT AND FINELY MODELED. 1 MANSNS
A LONG YANKEE FACE, WITH INDIAN RESEMBLANCES, 4 MANSNS
SWARTHY, WITH A BIG STRAIGHT NOSE,
WHAT HENKY RECOMMENDED IS A STRAIGHT BUSINESS 34 MANSNS
DEAL.
(THERE IS A PAUSE DURING WHICH THEY BOTH STARE 136 MANSNS
STRAIGHT BEFORE THEM.
HER NOSE IS THIN AND STRAIGHT. 15 POET
THEN I COME OUT WITH IT STRAIGHT AND ASKED HIM 585 ROPE
ABOUT THE WILL--
SQUARES HIS SHOULDERS, PULLS HIS COAT DOWN IN 22 STRANG
FRONT, SETS HIS TIE STRAIGHT,
(WITH SATISFACTION) (EYES, I'VE GOT IT STRAIGHT 112 STRANG
NOW....)
(COMES STRAIGHT TO NINA) HELLO, NINA CARA NINA/ 146 STRANG
(TOUCHING DARRELL WHO HAS STOOD STARING STRAIGHT 182 STRANG
BEFORE HIM WITH A BITTER
THE MASS OF HER DARK BROWN HAIR IS COMBED STRAIGHT443 WELDED
BACK.
SHE LETS THE LETTER FALL ON HER LAP AND STARES 443 WELDED
STRAIGHT BEFORE HER,
BUT DURING THE FOLLOWING SCENE THEY STARE STRAIGHT452 WELDED
AHEAD AND REMAIN MOTIONLESS.
STARING STRAIGHT BEFORE HER. 452 WELDED
UNTIL THEY ARE STRETCHED OUT STRAIGHT TO RIGHT AND489 WELDED
LEFT, FORMING A CROSS.
STRAIGHTBACKED
OF THE UGLY TABLE WITH ITS SET OF STRAIGHTBACKED 48 STRANG
CHAIRS
STRAIGHTEN
(SHE APPEALS TO THE COMPANY WHO STRAIGHTEN UP ON 344 LAZARU
THEIR COUCHES WITH INTEREST.)
STRAIGHTENED
IT'S HIGH TIME I STRAIGHTENED OUT AND GOT DOWN TO 600 ICEMAN
BUSINESS AGAIN.
I'LL BE STRAIGHTENED OUT AND ON THE WAGON IN A DAY607 ICEMAN
OR TWO.
I'D JUST MADE UP MY MIND THAT AS SOON AS I COULD 623 ICEMAN
GET STRAIGHTENED OUT--
(HE HAS DROPPED THE BOOK IN HIS LAP AND 126 MANSNS
STRAIGHTENED HIMSELF TENSELY.
THEN YOU'LL --"T AS MUCH AS I DO TO GET HER 35 STRANG
STRAIGHTENED OUT.
STRAIGHTENING
(STRAIGHTENING AND THROWING OUT HIS CHEST--WITH A 39 ANNA
BOLD LAUGH)
(STRAIGHTENING UP AND LOOKING ABOUT AS IF HE WERE 57 ANNA
SEEKING A WAY TO ESCAPE--
THEN SUDDENLY STRAIGHTENING UP AND KICKING AS HIGH251 DESIRE
AS HE CAN WITH BOTH LEGS.
(FEELING HIS NEARNESS--STRAIGHTENING HIMSELF WITH 339 LAZARU
A CERTAIN DIGNITY)
(LOOKING UP AND STRAIGHTENING HIS CRAMPED BACK-- 408 MARCOM
WITH A RELIEVED SIGH)
LOOK AT THE BLUFF HE PUTS UP, STRAIGHTENING 35 MISBEG
HIMSELF AND GRINNING.
STRAIGHTENS
(KEENEY STRAIGHTENS HIMSELF LIKE A MAN COMING OUT 550 *ILE
OF A TRANCE.
HE STRAIGHTENS ALERTLY AND SPEAKS IN A VOICE THAT,252 AHWILD
IN SPITE OF HIS EFFORT,
(HE TAKES OFF HIS SPECTACLES AND PUTS THEM BACK IN292 AHWILD
THEIR CASE AND STRAIGHTENS
(SHE STRAIGHTENS UP--INDIGNANTLY) 115 BEYOND
THEN STRAIGHTENS OUT RIGIDLY.) 489 CARDIF
(HE BECOMES AWARE HE IS WANDERING, STRAIGHTENS 264 DESIRE
AGAIN.
THEN STRAIGHTENS HIMSELF AND TURNS TO MRS. FIFE) 478 DYNAMO
INSTANTLY JONES STRAIGHTENS UP. 194 EJONES
FOR HE STRAIGHTENS UP AND STARES ABOUT HIM 200 EJONES
HORRIFIEDLY--
STRAIGHTENS UP IN A SITTING POSITION IN LAVINIA'S 63 ELECTR
ARMS.
STRAIGHTENS UP WITH A THREATENING MOVEMENT. 112 ELECTR
ORIN STRAIGHTENS WOODENLY TO A SOLDIERLY 145 ELECTR
ATTENTION.
(HE HURRIEDLY STRAIGHTENS UP THE TABLE AND GRABS A149 ELECTR
BOOK AT RANDOM FROM THE
SHE BENDS DOWN AND KISSES HIM GENTLY--SHE 322 GGBROW
STRAIGHTENS UP AND LOOKS INTO SPACE--
(ABRUPTLY STRAIGHTENS UP AND STARES AT HER--WITH A168 MANSNS
MOCKING SMILE.)
TYRONE ROUSES HIMSELF AND STRAIGHTENS UP. 103 MISBEG
(MELODY STRAIGHTENS UP WITH A JERK, 72 POET
(HIS VOICE GROWS HUSKY AND UNCERTAIN--HE CONTROLS 24 STRANG
IT--STRAIGHTENS HIMSELF)
SHE STRAIGHTENS UP IN HER CHAIR STIFFLY.) 56 STRANG
(STRAIGHTENS UP AND TAKES IT, HIS EYES GRATEFUL 78 STRANG
NOW--HUMBLY)
STRAIGHTFORWARD
STRAIGHTFORWARD, GUILELESS AND GOOD-NATURED. 12 ELECTR
STRAIN
YOU'LL ONLY STRAIN YOURSELF. 211 AHWILD
STRAIN WHERE JUDGMENTS ON THE SPUR OF THE MOMENT 153 BEYOND
ARE COMPELLED TO BE ACCURATE.
FINALLY THE STRAIN WAS TOO MUCH. 156 BEYOND
AND THEN HE HAS TO GO AND GIVE HIMSELF AWAY WITH A501 DAYS
STRAIN OF HIS OLD HOLD
HIS FACE ALSO BEARS OBVIOUS TRACES OF SLEEPLESS 553 DAYS
STRAIN.

STRAIN (CONT'D.)
A FAINT STRAIN OF THEIR RETREATING VOICES IS 226 DESIRE
HEARD....
DOOR WHICH MUFFLES THE NOISE OF THE DYNAMO TO A 476 DYNAMO
MINOR STRAIN.
MAKING THE HEART STRAIN WITH THE DESIRE TO BEAT 486 DYNAMO
THE GROUPS STRAIN FORWARD ATTENTIVELY. 197 EJONES
YOU CAN'T REALIZE WHAT A STRAIN I'VE BEEN UNDER-- 52 ELECTR
(BEGINNING TO SNAP UNDER THE STRAIN--JUMPS TO HER 60 ELECTR
FEET AGAIN)
(THE STRAIN SNAPS FOR HIM AND HE LAUGHS WITH 101 ELECTR
SAVAGE IRONY)
THE STRAIN OF ORIN'S CONDUCT HAS TOLD ON HER. 146 ELECTR
CLEAN MANNON STRAIN/ 170 ELECTR
HIS EYES, HIS ARMS, HIS WHOLE BODY STRAIN UPWARD, 319 GGBROW
THAT OF THE BEGUILING NEVER-DO-WELL, WITH A STRAIN 19 JOURNE
OF THE SENTIMENTALLY POETIC.
AS IF THE STRAIN OF SITTING THROUGH LUNCH WITH 71 JOURNE
THEM HAD BEEN TOO MUCH FOR HER.
THE STRAIN IS OBVIOUS IN HIS CASUALNESS AS HE 74 JOURNE
ADDRESSES EDMUND.)
STRAIN OF MUSIC RECEDING INTO THE SILENCE OVER 324 LAZARU
STILL WATERS.)
ALL THIS CHILD-BEARING--IT MUST BE A STRAIN ON 7 MANSNS
SARA.
THE MENTAL STRAIN OF A MAN WHO HAS BEEN WORKING 43 MANSNS
TOO HARD
IT HAS BEEN A STRAIN GETTING THIS AFFAIR OF THE 71 MANSNS
RAILROAD SETTLED.
THIS RAILROAD DEAL HAS BEEN A STRAIN. 79 MANSNS
I KNOW YOU'VE JUST BEEN UNDER A SEVERE STRAIN. 156 MANSNS
I WOULDN'T STRAIN MY BRAINS ANY MORE, IF I WAS 9 MISBEG
YOU.
WALK BACK TO THE INN, THEN, AND GIVE IT A GOOD 46 MISBEG
STRAIN.
ONE BIG DRINK, AT LEAST, WHENEVER I STRAIN MY 46 MISBEG
HEART WALKING IN THE HOT SUN.
THERE IS A GROWING STRAIN BEHIND HER FREE-AND-EASY172 MISBEG
MANNER)
HIS EXPRESSION LOSES SOME OF ITS NERVOUS STRAIN. 36 POET
STRAIN OF WAITING AND HOPING SHE'D GET PREGNANT.... 68 STRANG
ONE GETS NO IMPRESSION OF NEUROTIC STRAIN FROM HER 90 STRANG
NOW.
THERE IS BENEATH THIS A SENSE OF GREAT MENTAL 137 STRANG
STRAIN.
STRAIN HIMSELF WHEN HE SMASHED IT, 144 STRANG
STRAINED
THEN CALLS IN A TONE OF STRAINED HEARTINESS.) 200 AHWILD
(CALLS BACK IN A VOICE WHOSE BREEZINESS RINGS A 515 DAYS
BIT STRAINED)
STRAINED ATTITUDE, THE EXPRESSION ON HER FACE THAT525 DAYS
OF ONE CAUGHT IN A CORNER.
JOHN IS TALKING IN A STRAINED TONE, MONOTONOUSLY, 541 DAYS
INSISTENTLY.
WAITS IN AN ATTITUDE OF STRAINED FIXITY. 239 DESIRE
SEVERAL ENLARGED PHOTOS OF STRAINED, 493 DIFRNT
(IN A STRAINED VOICE) WELL, AIN'T YOU GOING TO 502 DIFRNT
TELL ME?
FINALLY SHE SITS DOWN HELPLESSLY AND REMAINS FIXED514 DIFRNT
IN A STRAINED ATTITUDE.
(HE WAITS, HIS BODY STRAINED WITH SUSPENSE, 480 DYNAMO
(HE STANDS IN A STRAINED ATTITUDE OF ATTENTION, 494 DYNAMO
AND STRAINED IN A CHEERY EFFORT TO OVERCOME ITS 191 EJONES
OWN TREMORS.)
(HE FORCES A STRAINED SMILE) 53 ELECTR
(STARTS VIOLENTLY--IN A STRAINED VOICE) 58 ELECTR
SHE IS OBVIOUSLY IN A TERRIBLE STATE OF STRAINED 71 ELECTR
NERVES.
(PUTTING AN ARM AROUND HER--IN A STRAINED TONE) 72 ELECTR
(HER VOICE TENSE AND STRAINED) 83 ELECTR
(HER VOICE COMES THROUGH THE DOOR, FRIGHTENED AND 99 ELECTR
STRAINED)
(IN A STRAINED VOICE) IT'S THE SAME THING--WHAT 146 ELECTR
THE WAR DID TO HIM--
HIS REAL FACE HAS AGED GREATLY, GROWN MORE 269 GGBROW
STRAINED AND TORTURED,
WITH AN ABSURD STRAINED ATTENTION WITHOUT 600 ICEMAN
COMPREHENDING A WORD)
HE IS STARING IN FRONT OF HIM IN A TENSE, STRAINED665 ICEMAN
IMMOBILITY.
(TURNING TO LARRY WITH A STRAINED LAUGH) 679 ICEMAN
(PLEADING IN A STRAINED, DESPERATE TONE) 680 ICEMAN
(CLIMBS A FEW STEPS INSIDE THE BAR--WITH A STRAINED682 ICEMAN
BRIGHT GIGGLE)
HE SPEAKS WITH A STRAINED ATTEMPT AT HIS OLD 704 ICEMAN
AFFECTIONATE JOLLYING MANNER)
THEY STAND THAT WAY FOR A STRAINED MOMENT, 523 INZONE
THEN WITH A STRAINED CASUALNESS, AS HIS FATHER 136 JOURNE
POURS A DRINK.)
EDMUND SUDDENLY CANNOT HOLD BACK A BURST OF 151 JOURNE
STRAINED, IRONICAL LAUGHTER.
THE SOUND OF MUSIC IN A STRAINED THEME OF THAT 326 LAZARU
JOYLESS ABANDON WHICH IS VICE IS
(IN A STRAINED VOICE SHAKEN BY APPREHENSION AND 337 LAZARU
AWE)
THE BATTLE FOR THIS BANK HAS STRAINED YOUR 157 MANSNS
RESOURCES TO THE BREAKING POINT.
(A STRAINED PAUSE. 368 MARCOM
WHEN I NOTICED A RATHER STRAINED EXPRESSION BUT 425 MARCOM
THIS I TOOK TO BE FEVER DUE TO
IT IS STRAINED, NERVE-RACKED, HECTIC, 13 STRANG
(HE TYPES A SENTENCE OR TWO, A STRAINED FROWN OF 68 STRANG
CONCENTRATION ON HIS FACE.
(HIS VOICE SOUNDS FROM THE HALL WITH A STRAINED 145 STRANG
CASUALNESS)
(WITH STRAINED KINDLINESS) OLD WHATS 150 STRANG
THEN HER VOICE IN A STRAINED, HYSTERICAL PITCH-----462 WELDED
JOHN, I-------

STRAINED

STRAINED (CONT'D.)		
HER FACE STRAINED AND FRIGHTENED.	466 WELDED
HER WHOLE ATTITUDE STRAINED, EXPECTANT BUT	480 WELDED
FRIGHTENED.		
STRAINEDLY		
(SMILING STRAINEDLY) YES.	152 STRANG
STRAINGELY		
(STRAINGELY) THE SAME TRAIN/	72 ELECTR
STRAINING		
STRAINING HIS EYES TOWARD THE HORIZON)	167 BEYOND
THEIR STARE HAVING A STRAINING, INGROWING QUALITY.221 DESIRE		
(STRAINING HIS EYES) I KIN SEE 'EM--BUT I CAN'T 222 DESIRE		
MAKE OUT...		
AND RUNS FULL TILT INTO THE BENDING, STRAINING	239 HA APE
YANK.		
(THE GORILLA IS STRAINING AT HIS BARS, GROWLING. 254 HA APE		
BUT STRAINING OUR EARS LISTENING FOR THE SLIGHTEST152 JOURNE		
SOUND.		
STRAINING FORWARD AND DOWNWARD AS IF TO OVERWHELM 347 LAZARU		
THE TWO FIGURES		
HIS ARMS STRAINING UPWARD TO THE SKY, A TENDER,	371 LAZARU
HOLDING ITS BREATH AND STRAINING ITS EARS.	117 MANSNS
OF A TWO-WHEELED WAGON, STAGGER IN, STRAINING	350 MARCOM
FORWARD UNDER THE LASHES		
(STRAINING UP TOWARD HIM--WITH INTENSE LONGING--	97 STRANG
TRAINING)		
(STARTLED, HER OWN VOICE STRAINING TO BE CASUAL)	145 STRANG
(STRAINING HER IN HIS ARMS AND KISSING HER	444 WELDED
PASSIONATELY)		
(STRAINING HER TO HIM WITH FIERCE PASSION)	448 WELDED
(STRAINING HER TO HIM--WITH AWKWARD PASSION)	465 WELDED
(STRAINING PASSIONATELY FOR EXPRESSION)	488 WELDED
STRAINS		
STRAINS ITS TWISTED BRANCHES HEAVENWARDS, BLACK	81 BEYOND
AGAINST THE PALLOR OF DISTANCE.		
NAT STRAINS FORWARD IN HIS CHAIR.	570 CROSS
ABBIE STRAINS HER ARMS TOWARD HIM WITH FIERCE	243 DESIRE
PLEADING)		
AND STRAINS HER EARS.)	437 DYNAMO
(AGAIN THERE IS A MUFFLED GROAN FROM SMITTY AS HE 529 INZONE		
STRAINS AT HIS BONDS.)		
HER EYES OPEN AND SHE STRAINS FORWARD, SEIZED BY A 49 JOURNE		
FIT OF NERVOUS PANIC.		
BOTH SOLDIERS AND CROWD ARE INSPIRED TO BATTLE BY 304 LAZARU		
THESE STRAINS		
(THE STRAINS OF A DISTANT BAND CAN BE HEARD.)	386 MARCOM
HER LIPS PART, HER WHOLE BEING STRAINS OUT TO HIM.414 MARCOM		
MUSICAL FLOW OF WORDS, AS SHE STRAINS TO GRASP THE 84 POET		
IMPLICATION FOR HER.		
STRAITJACKET		
LIKE A STRAITJACKET/	193 EJONES
AND CALL DE OTHERS--AND A STRAITJACKET/	245 HA APE
STRANDS		
THEIR HAIR IS MATTED, INTERTWINED WITH SLIMY	571 CROSS
STRANDS OF SEAWEED.		
STRANGE		
THEY'D MAKE ANYONE LOOK STRANGE.	546 'ILE
YOUR EYES LOOK SO STRANGE-LIKE.	546 'ILE
(WORRIED BY HER STRANGE TONE AND THE FAR-AWAY LOOKS547 'ILE		
IN HER EYES)		
(CAUSTICALLY) HE READ HIS SCHOOL BOOKS, TOO,	192 AHWILD
STRANGE AS THAT MAY SEEM TO YOU.		
(HE IS SILENT, STUDYING HIS SOUP PLATE, AS IF IT	224 AHWILD
WERE SOME STRANGE ENIGMA.		
WITH THE GRAVITY OF A MAN CONFESSING HIS STRANGE	227 AHWILD
PECULIARITIES)		
SHE HAD STRANGE LOOKING EYES.	283 AHWILD
(WITH A TRACE OF STRANGE EXULTATION)	25 ANNA
THEN SHRINKS BACK FROM HIM WITH A STRANGE, BROKEN	38 ANNA
LAUGH)		
WHEN HE MAKES OUT ANNA IN SUCH INTIMATE PROXIMITY	38 ANNA
TO THIS STRANGE SAILOR.		
(A STRANGE TERROR SEEMS SUDDENLY TO SEIZE HER.	68 ANNA
HE ACTS SO STRANGE.	97 BEYOND
IT SOUNDS STRANGE TO HEAR YOU, ANDY, THAT I ALWAYS105 BEYOND		
THOUGHT HAD GOOD SENSE.		
YOU'RE A STRANGE COMBINATION, ANDY.	132 BEYOND
HIS VOICE IS SO STRANGE THAT RUTH TURNS TO LOOK AT149 BEYOND		
HIM IN ALARM)		
WHAT'LL THIS STRANGE DOCTOR THINK OF US!	153 BEYOND
PEARL LOOKS AT HIM CURIOUSLY, PUZZLED BY HIS	469 CARIBE
STRANGE ACTIONS.		
YOU'RE SO STRANGE.	566 CROSS
THERE IS AN EQUALLY STRANGE DISSIMILARITY.	493 DAYS
BUT AS HE GOES ON A STRANGE DEFIANT NOTE OF	495 DAYS
EXULTANCE COMES INTO HIS VOICE)		
HERE I'VE BEEN FEELING STRANGE.	501 DAYS
A STRANGE FEELING OF FEAR TOOK POSSESSION OF ME--	507 DAYS
(SMILING WITH A STRANGE WRYNESS)	516 DAYS
(STARES AT HER WITH A STRANGE PANIC)	520 DAYS
AND THEN CAME THE STRANGE PART OF IT.	522 DAYS
STRANGE, ISN'T IT. WHAT DIFFICULT PROBLEMS YOUR	528 DAYS
LITTLE DABBLE IN FICTION HAS		
ENTERTAINING A STRANGE PRIEST-UNCLE FOR THE FIRST 530 DAYS		
TIME.		
AND A STRANGE FASCINATION IT HAD FOR HIM.	535 DAYS
EYES FULL OF A STRANGE, HORRIFIED FASCINATION--	540 DAYS
SHE IS STILL STARING BEFORE HER WITH THE SAME	541 DAYS
STRANGE FASCINATED DREAD.		
LOVING, HIS EYES REMAINING FIXED ON ELSA WITH THE 550 DAYS		
SAME STRANGE LOOK.		
A STRANGE CASE.	557 DAYS
SPEAKS SOBBINGLY IN A STRANGE HUMBLE TONE OF	565 DAYS
BROKEN REPROACH)		
HIS EYES HAVE TAKEN ON A STRANGE, INCONGRUOUS	230 DESIRE
DREAMY QUALITY.		
(AFTER A PAUSE--WITH A STRANGE PASSION)	232 DESIRE
(TURNING TO HER WITH STRANGE PASSION)	238 DESIRE

STRANGE

STRANGE (CONT'D.)		
HE IS TREMBLING ALL OVER, IN A STRANGE STATE OF	243 DESIRE
TERROR.		
(WITH A STRANGE LOOK) MAW'S GONE BACK T' HER	245 DESIRE
GRAVE.		
(THEN WITH STRANGE INTENSITY)	259 DESIRE
(HE LAPSES INTO CRUSHED SILENCE--THEN WITH A	264 DESIRE
STRANGE EMOTION)		
(HE GOES TO THE DOOR--THEN TURNS--IN A VOICE FULL 265 DESIRE		
OF STRANGE EMOTION)		
(THEN IN A STRANGE WHISPER) WAIT, CALEB, I'M	549 DIFRNT
GOING DOWN TO THE BARN.		
(DUMBFOUNDED, NOT KNOWING WHAT TO MAKE OF THIS	447 DYNAMO
STRANGE TALE--		
IN A STRANGE VOICE)	469 DYNAMO
(WHIRLS AROUND AND STANDS STARING AT HER WITH	481 DYNAMO
STRANGE FIXITY FOR A MOMENT.		
= (HE SUDDENLY CHECKS HIMSELF AND FORCES A	481 DYNAMO
STRANGE, SHAMEFACED LAUGH)		
A STRANGE LOOK OF APPREHENSION CREEPS INTO HIS	184 EJONES
FACE FOR A MOMENT AS HE LISTENS.		
HE MOVES WITH A STRANGE DELIBERATION LIKE A SLEEP-200 EJONES		
WALKER OR ONE IN A TRANCE.		
THAT IN REPOSE GIVES ONE THE STRANGE IMPRESSION OF	6 ELECTR
A LIFE-LIKE MASK.		
ONE IS STRUCK AT ONCE BY THE STRANGE IMPRESSION IT	9 ELECTR
GIVES IN REPOSE OF BEING NOT		
ABOVE ALL, ONE IS STRUCK BY THE SAME STRANGE,	10 ELECTR
AND AN EXPRESSION OF STRANGE VINDICTIVE TRIUMPH	11 ELECTR
COMES INTO HER FACE.)		
THAT MUST BE WHY I'VE HAD THE STRANGE FEELING I'VE	19 ELECTR
KNOWN HIM BEFORE--		
FEELING SOMETHING STRANGE IN HER ATTITUDE BUT NOT	21 ELECTR
ABLE TO MAKE HER OUT--		
YOU'LL THINK IT STRANGE WHEN I TELL YOU.	22 ELECTR
IT IS COLD AND EMOTIONLESS AND HAS THE SAME	28 ELECTR
STRANGE SEMBLANCE OF A LIFELIKE MASK		
(THEN SUDDENLY--WITH A STRANGE JEALOUS BITTERNESS)	31 ELECTR
HE STARES AT IT WITH A STRANGE STUPID DREAD.	40 ELECTR
HE'S A STRANGE, HIDDEN MAN.	40 ELECTR
SHE SPEAKS TO HIS RETREATING FIGURE WITH A STRANGE	42 ELECTR
SINISTER AIR OF ELATION)		
IT'S ALL SO STRANGE/	44 ELECTR
YOU LOOK MORE BEAUTIFUL THAN EVER--AND STRANGE TO	52 ELECTR
ME.		
ONLY YOUR HAIR IS THE SAME--YOUR STRANGE BEAUTIFUL	52 ELECTR
HAIR I ALWAYS--		
(OPENS HER EYES AND STARES AT HIM WITH A STRANGE	54 ELECTR
TERROR)		
IS MY VOICE SO STRANGE TO YOU!	58 ELECTR
(THEN AFTER A PAUSE) I FEEL STRANGE, CHRISTINE.	59 ELECTR
(THEN IN A STRANGE FLAT TONE)	63 ELECTR
THE HOUSE HAS THE SAME STRANGE EERIE APPEARANCE,	67 ELECTR
WHEN HE SPEAKS IT IS JERKILY, WITH A STRANGE,	74 ELECTR
VAGUE, PREOCCUPIED AIR.		
(THEN IN AN AWED TONE) BUT THE HOUSE LOOKS	74 ELECTR
STRANGE.		
(WITH STRANGE EAGERNESS) YES/	85 ELECTR
SHE'S ALWAYS BEEN A MOODY AND STRANGE GIRL, YOU	86 ELECTR
KNOW THAT.		
SHE SEEMED STRANGE.	86 ELECTR
A STRANGE NOTING, WASN'T ITS	90 ELECTR
AND ADDRESSES IT WITH A STRANGE FRIENDLY MOCKERY)	93 ELECTR
(SHE ADDRESSES THE DEAD MAN DIRECTLY IN A STRANGE 101 ELECTR		
TONE OF DEFIANT SCORN)		
I FEEL SO STRANGE--SO SAD--AS IF I'D NEVER SEE YOU112 ELECTR		
AGAIN/		
IT'S STRANGE.	112 ELECTR
THAT IS STRANGE--WHEN YOU HAVE THE MEMORY OF	120 ELECTR
FATHER FOR COMPANY/		
(THEN WITH A STRANGE, SEARCHING GLANCE AT HER)	140 ELECTR
(WITH A STRANGE MALICIOUS AIR)	141 ELECTR
BUT NOW YOU'VE SUDDENLY BECOME STRANGE AGAIN.	141 ELECTR
(WITH A STRANGE SHY EAGERNESS)	141 ELECTR
SHE STARES AT HIM WITH A STRANGE EAGER	143 ELECTR
POSSESSIVENESS.		
(IN A SUDDEN STRANGE TONE OF JEERING MALICE)	144 ELECTR
BUT IT WILL PROVE A STRANGE REASON, I'M CERTAIN OF144 ELECTR		
THAT, WHEN I DO DISCOVER IT/		
(WITH A STRANGE SMILE) I WAS DEAD THEN.	144 ELECTR
HE COMES FORWARD, HIS EYES FIXED WITH A STRANGE	144 ELECTR
PREOCCUPATION.		
SO MANY STRANGE HIDDEN THINGS OUT OF THE MANNON	153 ELECTR
PAST COMBINE IN YOU/		
ALL THOSE HANDSOME MEN STARING AT YOU AND YOUR	154 ELECTR
STRANGE BEAUTIFUL HAIR/		
SHE HOLDS THEM OUT TO SETH AND SPEAKS IN A	170 ELECTR
STRANGE, EMPTY VOICE.)		
(WITH A STRANGE CRUEL SMILE OF GLOATING OVER THE	178 ELECTR
YEARS OF SELF-TORTURE)		
(HE KISSES HIS MOTHER, WHO RUNS WITH A STRANGE	261 GGBROW
HUMILITY AS IF SHE WERE A SERVANT		
(WITH A STRANGE STERNNESS, SEARCHES HIS FACE)	280 GGBROW
(WITH A STRANGE SMILE) LET'S SAY, NEVER ANYTHING	280 GGBROW
LESS/		
I REMEMBER A SWEET, STRANGE GIRL, WITH	282 GGBROW
AFFECTIONATE, BEWILDERED EYES		
(IN HER STRANGE VOICE) CYBEL'S GONE OUT TO DIG IN288 GGBROW		
THE EARTH AND PRAY.		
(SPRINGING TO HIS FEET, HIS FACE CONVULSED WITH	298 GGBROW
STRANGE AGONY)		
(WITH STRANGE GLIBNESS NOW) NO.	300 GGBROW
YOU WERE ALWAYS SO STRANGE AND ALOOF AND ALONE.	309 GGBROW
YOU'RE BEING HURRIED AND STRANGE AGAIN.	311 GGBROW
(HESITATINGLY) WELL--IT'S REALLY TOO SILLY--HE	311 GGBROW
SUDDENLY GOT AWFULLY STRANGE.		
GIVING HER A STRANGE ASPECT OF LONELY, DETACHED,	323 GGBROW
SMALL FEMININITY.		

STRANGE

STRANGE (CONT'D.)
(THEN, WITH STRANGE FINALITY) 323 GGBROW
WITH A STRANGE, AWKWARD, SWINGING RHYTHM. 223 HA APE
(HE HESITATES, STAKING AT LARRY WITH A STRANGE 587 ICEMAN
APPEAL.)
(WITH A STRANGE SMILE) I DON'T REMEMBER IT THAT 590 ICEMAN
WAY.
IT'S STRANGE THE QUEER WAY HE SEEMED TO RECOGNIZE 638 ICEMAN
HIM.
(GUILTILY BUT WITH A STRANGE UNDERTONE OF 646 ICEMAN
SATISFACTION)
IN A STRANGE, ARROGANTLY DISDAINFUL TONE, AS IF HE658 ICEMAN
WERE REBUKING A BUTLER)
(WITH A STRANGE UNDERCURRENT OF 666 ICEMAN
(WITH A STRANGE PATHETIC WISTFULNESS) 667 ICEMAN
(AGAIN HE HAS A STRANGE AIR OF EXONERATING HIMSELF680 ICEMAN
FROM GUILT
WITH A STRANGE, SLY, CALCULATING LOOK-- 702 ICEMAN
INGRATIATINGLY)
(HE ADDS WITH A STRANGE IMPRESSIVE SIMPLICITY) 706 ICEMAN
(HE BEGINS EAGERLY IN A STRANGE RUNNING NARRATIVE 707 ICEMAN
MANNER)
(A TOUCH OF STRANGE BITTERNESS COMES TO HIS 710 ICEMAN
VOICE FOR A MOMENT)
IN A LOW VOICE IN WHICH THERE IS A STRANGE 716 ICEMAN
EXHAUSTED RELIEF)
(WITH A STRANGE MAD EARNESTNESS) 718 ICEMAN
(LEANS TOWARD HIM--IN A STRANGE LOW INSISTENT 719 ICEMAN
VOICE)
YOU HAD A STRANGE WAY OF SHOWING YOUR 17 JOURNE
RESTLESSNESS.
(AGAIN WITH THE STRANGE OBSTINATE SET TO HER 29 JOURNE
FACE.)
SUDDENLY A STRANGE UNDERCURRENT OF REVENGEFULNESS 47 JOURNE
COMES INTO HER VOICE.)
(WITH A QUICK, STRANGE, CALCULATING, ALMOST SLY 49 JOURNE
GLANCE AT HIM.)
JAMIE GIVE HIM A STRANGE, ALMOST CONTEMPTUOUS 59 JOURNE
GLANCE.
(THEN WITH A STRANGE, ABRUPT CHANGE TO A DETACHED, 61 JOURNE
IMPERSONAL TONE.)
REGAINS THE QUALITY OF STRANGE DETACHMENT-- 64 JOURNE
CALMLY.)
(ABRUPTLY HER TONE AND MANNER CHANGE TO THE 64 JOURNE
STRANGE DETACHMENT SHE HAS SHOWN
(SHE PATS EDMUND'S CHEEK PLAYFULLY, THE STRANGE 68 JOURNE
DETACHMENT AGAIN IN HER MANNER.
(THEN SLIPPING AWAY INTO HER STRANGE DETACHMENT-- 69 JOURNE
QUITE CASUALLY.)
HER EXPRESSION SHOWS MORE OF THAT STRANGE 71 JOURNE
ALOOFNESS
BUT THERE IS THE STRANGE QUALITY OF DETACHMENT IN 72 JOURNE
IT.)
(WITH A STRANGE DERISIVE SMILE.) 75 JOURNE
(HER STRANGE, STUBBORN DEFENSE COMES BACK 85 JOURNE
INSTANTLY.)
(WITH STRANGE OBJECTIVE CALM.) 87 JOURNE
(SHE PAUSES--THEN LOWERING HER VOICE TO A STRANGE 93 JOURNE
TONE OF WHISPERED CONFIDENCE.)
THE STRANGE DETACHMENT IN HER MANNER HAS 97 JOURNE
INTENSIFIED.
BUT IN A STRANGE WAY THE REACTION HAS A MECHANICALI01 JOURNE
QUALITY.
(SHE GIVES A STRANGE LITTLE LAUGH.) 104 JOURNE
(SHE PAUSES--THEN ADDS WITH A STRANGE, SAD 110 JOURNE
DETACHMENT.)
THE STRANGE DETACHMENT COMES OVER HER MANNER AGAIN112 JOURNE
AS IF
(SHE SMILES AT TYRONE WITH A STRANGE, INCONGRUOUS 114 JOURNE
COQUETRY.)
YOUR FATHER IS A STRANGE MAN, EDMUND. 117 JOURNE
(HIS CRYING OVER--DROPS HIS HANDS FROM HIS FACE-- 163 JOURNE
WITH A STRANGE BITTERNESS.)
TAKES HIS HAND AGAIN AND BEGINS TO TALK THICKLY 165 JOURNE
BUT WITH A STRANGE,
(GIVES EDMUND A STRANGE LOOK OF MINGLED PITY AND 174 JOURNE
JEALOUS GLOATING.)
THAT STRANGE LIGHT SEEMS TO COME FROM WITHIN HIM/ 275 LAZARU
YOU ARE STRANGE--STANDING THERE-- 278 LAZARU
AND AN AWED AND FRIGHTENED STILLNESS PREVAILS, FOR278 LAZARU
LAZARUS IS A STRANGE,
AND SPEAKING WITH A STRANGE UNEARTHLY CALM 279 LAZARU
THEN, OF A SUDDEN, A STRANGE GAY LAUGHTER TREMBLED309 LAZARU
FROM HIS HEART
THE MOODS OF TIBERIUS ARE STRANGE, TO SAY THE 315 LAZARU
LEAST.
(HE CRIES WITH A STRANGE PITIFULNESS AND 319 LAZARU
BESEECHING)
I ADMIRE YOUR STRANGE MAGICIAN, CALIGULA. 341 LAZARU
(AGAIN OVERCOME--STUTTERING WITH STRANGE TERROR) 359 LAZARU
GROUP AGAIN, STARING AFTER HIM, AND A WHISPER OF 363 LAZARU
STRANGE, BEWILDERED,
(HIS VOICE COMES, RECOGNIZABLY THE VOICE OF 365 LAZARU
LAZARUS, YET WITH A STRANGE, FRESH,
(IN A STRANGE FRENZY NOW) HEAR ME, THOU DAEMON OF365 LAZARU
LAUGHTER!
STRANGE WILD MEASURES OF LIBERATED JOY. 368 LAZARU
(SHE ENDS ON A NOTE OF STRANGE, PASSIONATE 13 MANSNS
EXULTANCE.)
(WITH A STRANGE FRIGHTENED URGENCY.) 37 MANSNS
(FOR A MOMENT SHE LOOKS INTO SARA'S EYES WITH A 51 MANSNS
STRANGE,
DEBORAH AGAIN WITH THE STRANGE EARNEST, ALMOST 52 MANSNS
PLEADING LOOK.
(WITH A STRANGE DERISIVE SATISFACTION.) 54 MANSNS
IT IS STRANGE TO THINK OF YOU TWO AS FRIENDS. 62 MANSNS
(GAILY--BUT WITH A STRANGE UNDERCURRENT.) 67 MANSNS
(WITH A STRANGE EAGERNESS-TEASINGLY.) 79 MANSNS

STRANGE (CONT'D.)
THAT IS STRANGE. 82 MANSNS
(WITH A STRANGE HAPPY SATISFIED AIR.) 87 MANSNS
(WITH A STRANGE GLOATING AIR.) 91 MANSNS
(HE SITS DOWN AT HIS DESK--WITH A STRANGE SMILE OF 94 MANSNS
ANTICIPATION.
YOU ARE STILL SUCH A STRANGE, GREEDY BOY, DO YOU 99 MANSNS
KNOW IT?
YOU KNOW THERE IS NOTHING STRANGE ABOUT HER BEING 104 MANSNS
JEALOUS
(WITH A STRANGE CHALLENGING LOOK.) 111 MANSNS
(SUDDENLY, MOVED BY A STRANGE URGENCY, HE SPRINGS 111 MANSNS
TO HIS FEET
(WITH A STRANGE BITTERNESS.) 111 MANSNS
I FEEL SOMETHING IS STARING OVER MY SHOULDER--IT'S119 MANSNS
STRANGE HERE
THAT'S STRANGE. 121 MANSNS
THAT IS STRANGE. I WAS THINKING OF HER, TOO. 122 MANSNS
DEBORAH SPEAKS WITH A STRANGE GENTLENESS.) 123 MANSNS
I STILL FEEL HATRED LIKE A LIVING PRESENCE IN THIS125 MANSNS
ROOM--STRANGE--DRAWING CLOSE--
TU REAPPEAR AS ONE WOMAN--A WOMAN RECALLING MOTHER125 MANSNS
BUT A STRANGE WOMAN--
(HE GIVES A STRANGE CHUCKLE OF SATISFACTION, AND 129 MANSNS
CLOSES HIS EYES.)
THERE IS, HOWEVER, A STRANGE EXPRESSION OF PEACE 144 MANSNS
AND RELAXATION ON HIS FACE AS
(A STRANGE, CALCULATING GLOATING COMES INTO HIS 149 MANSNS
FACE.)
(WITH A STRANGE TENSE EXCITEMENT.) 156 MANSNS
IT MAKES YOU LOOK SO--STRANGE AND CRAZED--YOU 157 MANSNS
FRIGHTEN ME/
(IN A BURST OF STRANGE DEADLY HATRED.) 160 MANSNS
I AM AFRAID ALONE IN THIS GARDEN AT NIGHT--IT 163 MANSNS
BECOMES STRANGE--
(WITH STRANGE SCORN.) YOU ARE A FOOL/ 180 MANSNS
HIS FACE HAS A STRANGE, MAD, TRANCE-LIKE LOOK. 186 MANSNS
(WITH STRANGE REPRESSED FURY.) 189 MANSNS
(FLINGS HIS HAND AWAY--WITH A STRANGE BOASTFUL 190 MANSNS
ARROGANCE.)
(FEARFULLY) IT HAS A STRANGE LOOK/ 349 MARCOM
TO LOOK AT THIS STRANGE LIFE. 366 MARCOM
STRUCK HIM AS, STRANGE) 370 MARCOM
HE IS STRANGE, PERHAPS, TO PEOPLE WHO DO NOT 387 MARCOM
UNDERSTAND HIM.
THAT WAS UNWISE, FOR THUS HE HAS REMAINED A 388 MARCOM
STRANGER.
(THEN SUDDENLY IN A STRANGE VOICE) 393 MARCOM
SOMETHING STRANGE AND DIFFERENT-- 397 MARCOM
AND THE BLUE WATER ALONE UNDER A STRANGE SKY AMID 405 MARCOM
ALIEN FLOWERS AND FACES.
(GIVES HER A STRANGE, EMBARRASSED GLANCE AND THEN 18 MISBEG
LOOKS AWAY.
WITHOUT ANY REASON YOU CAN SEE, HE'LL SUDDENLY 33 MISBEG
TURN STRANGE, AND LOOK SAD,
WHAT A STRANGE THING/ 50 MISBEG
I AGREE, BUT FOR SOME STRANGE REASON HARDER 51 MISBEG
DOESN'T LOOK FORWARD TO THE TASTE OF
(GIVES HER A STRANGE SURPRISED LOOK--MOCKINGLY) 51 MISBEG
THEN ADDS WITH STRANGE, WONDERING SINCERITY) 103 MISBEG
(WITH STRANGE RELIEF) OH. 104 MISBEG
(IN A STRANGE TONE THAT IS ALMOST THREATENING) 114 MISBEG
(TYRONE IS STARING AT HER, A STRANGE BITTER 121 MISBEG
DISGUST IN HIS EYES.
WITH THE SAME STRANGE AIR OF ACTING UNCONSCIOUSLY)122 MISBEG
(HE PAUSES--THEN BURSTS OUT IN A STRANGE 126 MISBEG
THREATENING TONE)
(AGAIN WITH A STRANGE, SIMPLE GRATITUDE) 133 MISBEG
(SHE BEGINS TO SOB WITH A STRANGE FORLORN SHAME 136 MISBEG
AND HUMILIATION)
(A STRANGE CHANGE HAS COME OVER HIS FACE. 137 MISBEG
(IN A STRANGE WARNING TONE) YOU'D BETTER LOOK 144 MISBEG
OUT, JOSIE.
(WITH STRANGE TRIUMPHANT HARSHNESS) 146 MISBEG
WITH A STRANGE HORRIBLE SATISFACTION IN HIS TONE) 150 MISBEG
YOU'RE A STRANGE WOMAN, MOTHER. 25 POET
(WITH A STRANGE SUPERIOR SCORN.) 25 POET
SHE'S VERY STRANGE IN HER WAYS. 31 POET
(WITH A STRANGE, SCORNFUL VANITY.) 61 POET
I FEEL SHE'S STRANGE AND QUEER BEHIND HER LADY'S 80 POET
AIRS.
(THEN TALKING RAPIDLY AGAIN IN HER STRANGE 86 POET
DETACHED WAY.)
SARA WITH A STRANGE LOOK OF SATISFIED PRIDE.) 124 POET
(SUDDENLY WITH A FLASH OF HER STRANGE, FIERCE 131 POET
PRIDE IN THE POWER OF LOVE.)
(A STRANGE, TENDERLY AMUSED SMILE ON HER LIPS-- 139 POET
TEASINGLY.)
(STANDS TENSELY--BURSTS OUT WITH A STRANGE 162 POET
TRIUMPHANT PRIDE.)
ROUGHLY BUT WITH A STRANGE REAL TENDERNESS.) AND 174 POET
I LOVE YOU.
WITH A STRANGE, ANGUISHED LOOK OF DESPERATION. 175 POET
(STARES AT HER--MOVED.) YOU'RE A STRANGE, NOBLE 182 POET
WOMAN, MOTHER.
SWEENEY SPEAKS SUDDENLY IN A STRANGE, AWED VOICE) 590 ROPE
(AGAIN WITH THE STRANGE INTENSITY) 18 STRANG
(WITH A STRANGE SMILE) BUT SOME DAY I'LL READ IT 21 STRANG
ALL IN ONE OF YOUR BOOKS.
(IN A STRANGE MOCKING IRONIC TONE) 39 STRANG
(THEN WITH A STRANGE TWISTED SMILE) 39 STRANG
(IN STRANGE AGONY) (SHE'S HARD/... 40 STRANG
SHE GIVES A STRANGE LITTLE LAUGH) 43 STRANG
(WITH A STRANGE, PASSIONATE EAGERNESS) 43 STRANG
(IN A STRANGE, FAR-AWAY TONE, LOOKING UP NOT AT 44 STRANG
HIM BUT AT THE CEILING)
NOTHING REMAINS OF THE STRANGE FASCINATION OF HER 48 STRANG
FACE EXCEPT HER UNCHANGEABLY

STRANGE

Text	Line	Source
STRANGE (CONT'D.)		
IT'S AMAZING HOW LITTLE SHE IS LIKE HIM A STRANGE	50	STRANG
WOMAN		
SLEEPING IN A STRANGE BED, I SUPPOSE.	51	STRANG
(SHE PAUSES--THEN WITH A STRANGE AUSTERE	64	STRANG
STERNNESS)		
SHE'S A STRANGE GIRL...	78	STRANG
(WITH A STRANGE HAPPY INTENSITY)	82	STRANG
(THEN WITH A STRANGE MONOTONOUS INSISTENCE)	84	STRANG
(THINKING--IN A STRANGE SUPERSTITIOUS PANIC)	98	STRANG
(IN A STRANGE DAZED VOICE--	104	STRANG
(HE IS IN A STATE OF STRANGE ELATION BY THIS TIME)	105	STRANG
(CLAPPING HIM ON THE BACK--WITH A STRANGE	106	STRANG
JOVIALITY)		
(IN A STRANGE RAGE, THREATENINGLY)	120	STRANG
(FROM UPSTAIRS, HER VOICE STRANGE AND EXCITED)	123	STRANG
(WITH THE SAME STRANGE DRIVING INSISTENCE)	128	STRANG
(THINKING WITH A STRANGE CALCULATION)	129	STRANG
(WITH A STRANGE, SELF-ASSURED SMILE AT HIM)	131	STRANG
(THEN IN A STRANGE HALF-WHISPER)	133	STRANG
(WITH A STRANGE TRIUMPHANT CALM)	133	STRANG
(WITH A STRANGE GAIETY) SIT DOWN, ALL OF YOU/	133	STRANG
(SUDDENLY WITH A STRANGE UNNATURAL ELATION--	133	STRANG
(THEN IN A STRANGE OBJECTIVE TONE--THINKING)	134	STRANG
SHE HAS STRANGE DEVIOUS INTUITIONS THAT TAP THE	135	STRANG
HIDDEN CURRENTS OF LIFE...		
(THINKING WITH A STRANGE TORTURED SHAME)	145	STRANG
STRANGE EYES THAT WILL NEVER GROW OLD...	165	STRANG
STRANGE INTERLUDE IN WHICH WE CALL ON PAST AND	165	STRANG
FUTURE		
(WITH A SUDDEN STRANGE VIOLENCE)	169	STRANG
SHE HAS THE SAME STRANGE INFLUENCE OVER ME...	169	STRANG
(THINKING WITH A STRANGE SHUDDER OF MINGLED	169	STRANG
ATTRACTION AND FEAR AS SHE TOUCHES		
(WITH STRANGE QUIET) I THINK I STILL LOVE YOU A	170	STRANG
LITTLE, NED.		
(GETS UP AND BENDS OVER HER PATERNALLY, STROKING	180	STRANG
HER HAIR WITH A STRANGE,		
(FACING HIM--WITH A STRANGE FRIENDLINESS SLAPS HIM)	181	STRANG
ON THE BACK)		
(GETTING UP--THINKING WITH A STRANGE, WILD	181	STRANG
PASSION)		
(THINKING WITH A STRANGE ECSTASY)	197	STRANG
(LOOKING AT MARSDEN WITH A STRANGE YEARNING)	197	STRANG
(WITH A STRANGE SMILE) STRANGE INTERLUDE!	199	STRANG
YES, OUR LIVES ARE MERELY STRANGE DARK INTERLUDES	199	STRANG
STRANGE--THAT JOHN SHOULD POP IN ON US SUDDENLY	454	WELDED
LIKE THAT.		
(RESENTFULLY) I DON'T SEE ANYTHING STRANGE ABOUT	454	WELDED
IT.		
(AGAIN STARING AT HER WITH STRANGE INTENSITY--	473	WELDED
SUDDENLY WITH A QUEER LAUGH)		
YOU,--YOU'RE THE LAST DEPTH--(WITH A STRANGE, WILD)	473	WELDED
EXULTANCE, LEAPS TO HIS FEET)		
THEY INSTINCTIVELY REACH OUT THEIR HANDS IN A	480	WELDED
STRANGE CONFLICTING GESTURE OF A		
(SHE OPENS THE DOOR AND TURNS TO CAPE WITH A	487	WELDED
STRANGE SMILE)		
(RANGELY		
THEN QUICKLY FROM HIS FATHER TO HIS MOTHER AND	297	AHWILD
BACK AGAIN, STRANGELY.		
(STARING BEFORE HER STRANGELY--REPEATS	540	DAYS
FASCINATEDLY)		
(STRANGELY) HE KNOWS SHE KNOWS OF HIS SIN NOW.	544	DAYS
(STRANGELY, STARING BEFORE HIM,	544	DAYS
(STRANGELY CONFUSED IN HIS TURN--HURRIEDLY)	545	DAYS
(STRANGELY SERIOUS AND BITTERLY MOCKING AT THE	550	DAYS
SAME TIME)		
(STILL IN HIS ECSTATIC MYSTIC VISION--STRANGELY)	566	DAYS
(STRANGELY) I'D LIKE T' OWN MY PLACE UP THAR.	231	DESIRE
GETS SLOWLY TO HIS FEET--STRANGELY)	268	DESIRE
IN ATTITUDES STRANGELY ALOOF AND DEVOUT.)	269	DESIRE
(HE BREAKS OFF--THEN STRANGELY)	458	DYNAMO
(THEN STRANGELY) BUT MAYBE YOU COULD, AT THAT--IF	470	DYNAMO
YOU KNEW HOW/		
(STRANGELY) NOT LATELY--NOT SINCE I GAVE UP	478	DYNAMO
SEEING ADA.		
(STRANGELY) IT WAS SHE WHO MADE YOU COME.	481	DYNAMO
(STRANGELY) YOU'RE BEGINNING TO SEE, ADA/ IT IS	484	DYNAMO
ALIVE/		
(HE HOLDS IT IN HIS HAND, LOOKING AT IT	179	EJONES
ADMIRINGLY, AS IF STRANGELY FASCINATED.)		
ACCENTUATES STRANGELY THE RESEMBLANCE BETWEEN	45	ELECTR
THEIR FACES AND AT THE SAME TIME		
(THEN STRANGELY) HE USED TO BE MY BABY, YOU	72	ELECTR
KNOW--BEFORE HE LEFT ME.		
STRANGELY) YOU ARE GENUINELY GOOD AND PURE OF	73	ELECTR
HEART, AREN'T YOU$		
(STRANGELY) EVERYTHING IS CHANGED--IN SOME QUEER	81	ELECTR
WAY--		
(WITH A START--STRANGELY) ISLANDS/	89	ELECTR
IT SIMPLY STRUCK ME HE LOOKS SO STRANGELY	94	ELECTR
FAMILIAR--		
(THEN STARING AT HIS MOTHER STRANGELY)	101	ELECTR
(THEN STRANGELY, AS IF TO HIMSELF)	112	ELECTR
(NOT HEEDING HER, STILL STARING AT BRANT--	115	ELECTR
STRANGELY)		
(HE WALKS MECHANICALLY UP THE STEPS--GAZING UP AT	122	ELECTR
THE HOUSE--STRANGELY)		
I CAN'T GET OVER SETH ACTING SO STRANGELY.	136	ELECTR
(STRANGELY) I'VE JUST BEEN IN THE STUDY.	139	ELECTR
DON'T YOU KNOW HOW TERRIBLY YOU FRIGHTEN ME WHEN	140	ELECTR
YOU ACT SO STRANGELY$		
(STRANGELY SHAKEN AND TREMBLING--STAMMERS)	155	ELECTR
(STRANGELY) DON'T CRY.	156	ELECTR
(WITHOUT OPENING HER EYES--STRANGELY, AS IF TO	174	ELECTR
HERSELF)		
(WITHOUT OPENING HER EYES--STRANGELY)	174	ELECTR

STRANGELY (CONT'D.)

Text	Line	Source
SHE SPEAKS STRANGELY IN A	287	GGBROW
(LOOKS AT HIM FIXEDLY FOR A MOMENT--THEN	295	GGBROW
STRANGELY)		
(SPEAKS UP FROM HIS OWN PREOCCUPATION--STRANGELY)	668	ICEMAN
(STRANGELY, AS IF TALKING ALOUD TO HERSELF.)	41	JOURNE
(STRANGELY.) THAT'S WHAT MAKES IT SO HARD--FOR	48	JOURNE
ALL OF US.		
(STRANGELY.)	60	JOURNE
(SHE ADDS STRANGELY,	67	JOURNE
(SHE SMILES STRANGELY.) BUT IT CAN'T TONIGHT.	99	JOURNE
(TURNS ON HIM--WITH A STRANGELY TRIUMPHANT,	117	JOURNE
TAUNTING SMILE.)		
HE STANDS STARING BEFORE HIM STRANGELY.	303	LAZARU
(INCLINING HIS HEAD TO MARCELLUS--STRANGELY)	332	LAZARU
(STRANGELY) MY MOTHER WAS THE WIFE OF CAESAR.	352	LAZARU
SUDDENLY SHE SAYS, STRANGELY.)	17	MANSNS
(HE SMILES STRANGELY.) THAT MAY BE THE CHANGE IN	72	MANSNS
ACTIVITY I NEED.		
(STRANGELY.) WHO KNOWS$	86	MANSNS
(STRANGELY NOW--AS IF HE WERE TALKING ALOUD TO	91	MANSNS
HIMSELF.)		
(LOOKS AFTER HER AND SMILES STRANGELY--	94	MANSNS
IRONICALLY.)		
(STRANGELY, TENDERLY SYMPATHETIC.)	102	MANSNS
(WITH A VINDICTIVE SMILE--STRANGELY.)	133	MANSNS
(THEN STRANGELY) ONLY SOMETIMES IT DOESN'T.	131	MISBEG
THE TWO MAKE A STRANGELY TRAGIC PICTURE IN THE WAN	157	MISBEG
DAWN LIGHT--		
(STRANGELY) WHY WOULDN'T HE$	158	MISBEG
(SHE ADDS STRANGELY) NOT UNTIL THE DAWN HAS	158	MISBEG
BEAUTY IN IT.		
(SHE SMILES STRANGELY) EXCEPT A GREAT MIRACLE	159	MISBEG
THEY'D NEVER BELIEVE.		
YES, I DID FIND MY WALK ALONE IN THE WOODS A	86	POET
STRANGELY OVERPOWERING EXPERIENCE.		
(SHE SMILES STRANGELY.) MAYBE I DESERVED THE SLAP	181	POET
FOR INTERFERING.		
(SLOWLY AND STRANGELY) I'M NOT SICK.	18	STRANG
(STRANGELY) YOU COULDN'T SLEEP$	57	STRANG
(THINKING STRANGELY)	62	STRANG
(AS FROM A DISTANCE--STRANGELY)	64	STRANG
(STRANGELY) THEN IT'D BE EASY FOR YOU.	64	STRANG
(THINKING STRANGELY) ((THAT LOOK IN HIS EYES...	84	STRANG
(CONFUSEDLY, STRANGELY AND PURPOSEFULLY)	85	STRANG
(THINKING STRANGELY) ((LITTLE BOY/...	109	STRANG
(SHE SMILES STRANGELY)	112	STRANG
(THINKING STRANGELY) ((NOT TO BE AFRAID OF ONE'S	121	STRANG
SHADOW/...		
(MORE AND MORE STRANGELY TRIUMPHANT)	135	STRANG
(STRANGELY FORLORN) I DON'T KNOW WHAT YOU MEAN,	169	STRANG
NED.		
(STRANGELY) WE'RE ALWAYS DESIRING DEATH FOR	170	STRANG
OURSELVES OR OTHERS, AREN'T WE--		
(STRANGELY) WE WERE TALKING ABOUT SAM, WEREN'T	170	STRANG
WE$		
(STRANGELY) THERE ARE SO MANY CURIOUS REASONS WE	170	STRANG
DARE NOT THINK ABOUT FOR		
(STRANGELY) I KNOW/	170	STRANG
(STRANGELY) I AM THE OLD NINA/	171	STRANG
(THINKING STRANGELY--STRUGGLING WITH HIMSELF)	172	STRANG
(HE GRIPS HER HAND, STRANGELY MOVED.)	179	STRANG
(AS BEFORE--AFFECTIONATELY AND STRANGELY)	180	STRANG
(STARES DOWN AT HIM STUPIDLY--THEN THINKING	182	STRANG
STRANGELY)		
(HE SMILES STRANGELY.	188	STRANG
BESIDE HER--STRANGELY)	197	STRANG
(LOOKING UP AT THE SKY--STRANGELY)	199	STRANG
(LOOKS AT HIM, STRANGELY IMPRESSED--A PAUSE--	493	WELDED
SLOWLY)		

STRANGENESS

Text	Line	Source
THE GARISH STRANGENESS OF EVERYTHING EVIDENTLY	535	DIFRNT
INTERESTS AND PUZZLES HIM.		
AND A FEELING OF STRANGENESS AND AWE--TOUCHING HER	52	ELECTR
HAIR WITH AN AWKWARD CARESS)		
THEN IS STOPPED BY SOME STRANGENESS HE FEELS ABOUT	53	ELECTR
HER STILL FACE.)		
(EDMUND IS MADE APPREHENSIVE BY HER STRANGENESS.	61	JOURNE
THEN GOES ON WITH AN INCREASING BROODING	73	MANSNS
STRANGENESS.)		

STRANGER

Text	Line	Source
STRANGER IN THIS BURG--	15	ANNA
YOU'RE LIKE--A STRANGER.	21	ANNA
HELLO, STRANGER.	515	DAYS
IT WAS ANOTHER MAN, A STRANGER WHOSE EYES WERE	522	DAYS
HATEFUL AND FRIGHTENING.		
(STARES AT JOHN AS IF HE HAD BECOME A STRANGER--	538	DAYS
I'D FEEL THE SAME AT ANY STRANGER COMIN' T' TAKE	225	DESIRE
MY MAN'S PLACE.		
YOU AIN'T A STRANGER THAT'S GOT TO BE INVITED, ARE	535	DIFRNT
YOU$		
THE SAME FAMILIAR STRANGER I'VE NEVER KNOWN.	94	ELECTR
BUT SOME STRANGER WITH THE SAME BEAUTIFUL HAIR--	165	ELECTR
FOLLOWING THEM, AS IF HE WERE A STRANGER, WALKING	259	GGBROW
ALONE, IS THEIR SON, DION.		
KEEP THYSELF AS A PILGRIM AND A STRANGER UPON	290	GGBROW
EARTH.		
I KNOW YUH GOT TO WATCH YOUR STEP WIT A STRANGER.	248	HA APE
QUESTIONS OF A STRANGER, FOR THAT'S ALL YOU ARE TO	591	ICEMAN
ME.		
YES, GENEROUS STRANGER--I TRUST YOU'RE GENEROUS--	595	ICEMAN
A STRANGER IN OUR MIDST.	623	ICEMAN
APOLOGIZING AS TO A STRANGER)	677	ICEMAN
IT'S HARD FOR A STRANGER TO TELL, BUT AFTER	83	JOURNE
THIRTY-FIVE YEARS OF MARRIAGE--		
AS IT IS, I WILL ALWAYS BE A STRANGER WHO NEVER	153	JOURNE
FEELS AT HOME.		
HE IS LIKE A STRANGER FROM A FAR LAND.	276	LAZARU

STRANGER (CONT'D.)
IT WOULD APPEAR I HAVE SPENT MY LIFE WITH A 32 MANSNS
STRANGER.
IT'S LIKE A STRANGER STARING AT ME. 80 MANSNS
THIS FAMILIAR STRANGER TO WHOM WITH A TRUSTFUL 92 MANSNS
SMILE
TO WHOM I WAS A STRANGER. 147 MISBEG
PRACTICALLY A STRANGER. 147 MISBEG
BUT WENT AROUND TELLIN' EVERY STRANGER ALL MY 161 POET
SECRETS.
HE HAS BECOME THAT STRANGER, ANOTHER WOMAN'S 190 STRANG
LOVER....)
THE STRANGER IN YOU. 455 WELDED

STRANGERS
EVEN WHERE THEY'RE STRANGERS LIKE THAT PARRITT 642 ICEMAN
KID.
MY LOVE HAS FOLLOWED YOU OVER LONG ROADS AMONG 345 LAZARU
STRANGERS
I'D GET MORE COMFORT FROM STRANGERS. 76 MISBEG
OF THOUGHTS THAT ARE STRANGERS... 139 STRANG

STRANGEST
I HAD THE STRANGEST FEELING. 51 STRANG
HE HAS THE STRANGEST INFLUENCE OVER GORDON/... 172 STRANG

STRANGLE
(CLUTCHING AT HIS THROAT AS THOUGH TO STRANGLE 565 CROSS
SOMETHING WITHIN HIM--HOARSELY)

STRANGLED
(WITH A STRANGLED CRY OF JOY) 128 BEYOND
(AS THEY ENTER--A QUEER STRANGLED EMOTION IN HIS 221 DESIRE
OR CRACKING VOICE)
(INCOHERENTLY, STRANGLED BY HIS PASSION) 458 WELDED
(AS IF TO HERSELF--IN A STRANGLED VOICE) 460 WELDED
(IN A STRANGLED VOICE) GOOD-BY. 487 WELDED

STRANGLING
HIS HANDS OUTSTRETCHED AS IF HE WERE ALREADY 487 DYNAMO
STRANGLING HER--THEN STOPS)
(HE SWALLOWS AS IF HE WERE STRANGLING AND TEARS 143 MANSNS
HIS EYES FROM HERS--STAMMERS.)

STRAP
UNDER HIS ARM HE CARRIES SIX BOOKS, BOUND TOGETHER457 DYNAMO
WITH A STRAP.)
IF IT TOOK HER LAST CENT AND HER LAST STRAP/ 26 ELECTR

STRAPPED
HE HAS A PACK STRAPPED ON HIS BACK. 347 MARCOM
A MERCHANT, CARRYING IN EACH HAND A STRAPPED BOX 347 MARCOM

STRAPPING
THERE'S TOO MANY STRAPPING GREAT LADS ON THE SEA 33 ANNA
WOULD GIVE THEIR HEART'S BLOOD
SOME OF YOU BIG STRAPPING BOYS SIT BACK OF US ON 464 CARIBE
THE HATCH THERE SO'S THEN
HE IS A TALL, STRAPPING YOUNG FELLOW ABOUT TWENTY-587 ROPE
FIVE WITH A COARSE-FEATURED,
YOU OUGHT TO HAVE MARRIED A BIG STRAPPING, 70 STRANG
MOTHERLY--

STRATEGEMS
A GAME OF SECRET, CUNNING STRATEGEMS, 91 MANSNS

STRATEGY
(IGNORING HIM) GOOD STRATEGY, NO DOUBT, 677 ICEMAN
THE EXPERIENCED STRATEGY OF THE HOGANS IN VERBAL 56 MISBEG
BATTLE IS TO TAKE THE OFFENSIVE

STRATUM
BUT IN A DIFFERENT STRATUM OF SOCIETY, 67 ELECTR

STRAW
(HE PUTS THE STRAW HAT ON THE SEAT AMIDSHIPS AND 275 AHWILD
PULLS THE FOLDED LETTER OUT OF
KICKING AT THE SAND RESTLESSLY, TWIRLING HIS STRAW275 AHWILD
HAT.
HE CARRIES HIS STRAW HAT DANGLING IN HIS HAND, 292 AHWILD
QUITE UNAWARE OF ITS EXISTENCE.)
AND WEARS A BROAD-BRIMMED HAT OF COARSE STRAW 123 BEYOND
PUSHED BACK ON HIS HEAD)
(HE STARTS TO FIDDLE +TURKEY IN THE STRAW.+ 253 DESIRE
WANTING TO SWAP FOR TERBACKER AND OTHER TRADIN' 502 DIFRNT
STUFF WITH STRAW MATS AND
HE HAS ON A STRAW HAT WITH A VIVID BAND, 615 ICEMAN
HE HAS HIS STRAW HAT WITH THE GAUDY BAND IN HIS 670 ICEMAN
HAND
(RESENTFULLY PUTS HIS STRAW HAT ON HIS HEAD AT A 670 ICEMAN
DEFIANT TILT)
HE HAS LOST HIS STRAW HAT, HIS TIE IS AWRY, AND 697 ICEMAN
HIS BLUE SUIT IS DIRTY.
THAT WOULD HAVE BEEN THE LAST STRAW FOR HER. 705 ICEMAN
BUT BEARING EDMUND WAS THE LAST STRAW. 87 JOURNE
BUT THERE'S A STRAW THAT BREAKS THE CAMEL'S BACK. 127 JOURNE
ON HIS HEAD IS AN OLD WIDE-BRIMMED HAT OF COARSE 11 MISBEG
STRAW
HER STRAW-BLOND HAIR, FRAMING HER SUNBURNED FACE, 12 STRANG
IS BOBBED.
THEN SUDDENLY CLUTCHING AT A STRAW, TURNS 55 STRANG
HOPEFULLY TO HIS MOTHER)

STRAWBERRY
WE'RE GOING TO HAVE A PICNIC LUNCH ON STRAWBERRY 191 AHWILD
ISLAND.

STRAWS
FROZEN IN THE MIDST OF THEIR GAME OF JACK-STRAWS, 366 MARCOM
ARE LOOKING AT HIM.

STRAY
A RED BANDANA HANDKERCHIEF COVERING ALL BUT A FEW 173 EJONES
STRAY WISPS OF WHITE HAIR.

STRAYED
LIKE A COUPLE O' STRAYED HOGS. 222 DESIRE
THERE IS A LACK OF SELF-CONFIDENCE, A LOST AND 29 STRANG
STRAYED APPEALING AIR ABOUT HIM/

STRAYS
(HE STRAYS OVER TO THE WINDOW AND LOOKS OUT 94 STRANG
LISTLESSLY)

STREAKED
IS STREAKED WITH INTERLACING PURPLE VEINS. 7 ANNA

STREAKED (CONT'D.)
NOW STREAKED WITH GRAY, HER MUDDIED SHOES RUN DOWN144 BEYOND
AT THE HEEL.
HIS HAIR IS THE SAME--DARK, STREAKED WITH GRAY. 493 DAYS
CRINKLY LONG BLACK HAIR STREAKED WITH GRAY, A 574 ICEMAN
SQUARE FACE WITH A PUG NOSE,
HER BLACK HAIR, STREAKED WITH GRAY, STRAGGLES IN 20 POET
UNTIDY WISPS ABOUT HER FACE.
HIS HAIR IS STREAKED WITH GRAY. 137 STRANG

STREAKS
STREAKS OF SWEAT HAVE SMUDGED THE LAYER OF DUST ON119 BEYOND
HIS CHEEKS.
DEY GOT STREAKS A MILE WIDE. 224 HA APE
WITH STREAKS OF SENTIMENTAL MELANCHOLY 14 JOURNE
FLAKED WITH STREAKS AND SPLOTCHES OF DIM LEMON. 1 MISBEG
THE FIRST FAINT STREAKS UF COLOR, HERALDING THE 157 MISBEG
SUNRISE,

STREAM
AS THE STREAM OF WATER HITS THE STEEL OF YANK'S 245 HA APE
CELL.)
A STREAM OF WORDS THAT ISSUES CASUALLY, 71 JOURNE
A WIDE DOOR IS FLUNG OPEN AND A STREAM OF REDDISH 331 LAZARU
LIGHT COMES OUT AGAINST WHICH
LET POUR FROM THEM A PERFECT STREAM OF PRECIOUS 429 MARCOM
STONES
DARK INTERMINGLING CURRENTS THAT BECOME THE ONE 135 STRANG
STREAM OF DESIRE...

STREAMING
HE WIPES HIS FOREHEAD STREAMING WITH SWEAT. 252 DESIRE
THE TEARS STREAMING DOWN HER FACE AS HE LOOKS AT 413 MARCOM
IT.)

STREAMS
BRIGHT SUNLIGHT STREAMS THROUGH THE WINDOWS ON THE493 DIFRNT
LEFT,
OVER DITCHES AND STREAMS AND STONE WALLS AND 102 POET

STREET
OR I'LL CALL SULLIVAN FROM THE CORNER AND HAVE YOU248 AHWILD
RUN IN FOR STREET-WALKING/
IN THE REAR, A FAMILY ENTRANCE OPENING ON A SIDE 3 ANNA
STREET.
ON THE LEFT, FORWARD, OF THE BARROOM, A LARGE, 3 ANNA
WINDOW LOOKING OUT ON THE STREET.
SCENE---JOHNNY-THE-PRIEST'S+ SALOON NEAR SOUTH 3 ANNA
STREET, NEW YORK CITY.
TWO LONGSHOREMEN ENTER FROM THE STREET, WEARING 3 ANNA
THEIR WORKING
(AS JOHNNY GOES TOWARD THE STREET DOOR, 5 ANNA
(HE GOES TO THE STREET DOOR.) 7 ANNA
(CHRIS GOES THROUGH THE BAR AND CUT THE STREET 13 ANNA
DOOR.)
(SHE IS INTERRUPTED BY THE OPENING AND SHUTTING OF 19 ANNA
THE STREET DOOR IN THE BAR
AS I WAS A-ROAMIN' DOWN PARADISE STREET-- 459 CARIBE
(HE SINGS) AS I WAS A *ROAMIN' DOWN PARADISE 459 CARIBE
STREET--
AS I WAS A-ROAMIN' DOWN PARADISE STREET--GIVE US 460 CARIBE
SOME TIME TO BLOW THE MAN DOWN/
AND OF THE ELM TREES THAT LINE THE STREET CAN BE 493 DIFRNT
SEEN.
THROUGH THE SMALL LAWN WHICH SEPARATES THE HOUSE 493 DIFRNT
FROM THE STREET.
I GOT TO GO UP STREET NOW MORE'N EVER. 501 DIFRNT
HE HAD TO GO UP STREET. 501 DIFRNT
HE'S GONE UP STREET. 505 DIFRNT
HE HAS CHANGED TO A DARK SUIT, IS READY FOR + UP 507 DIFRNT
STREET.+
GO ON UP STREET IF YOU WANT TO JOKE. 511 DIFRNT
COME ON UP STREET, ALF. 511 DIFRNT
SO I GUESS I BETTER BEAT IT UP STREET. 524 DIFRNT
HE'S GONE UP STREET. 542 DIFRNT
HE LEFT A WHILE BACK--SAID HE WAS GOIN' UP 547 DIFRNT
STREET--I THINK.
THESE HOUSES STAND SIDE BY SIDE, FACING FRONT, ON -0 DYNAMO
THE STREET.
THAT SCOUNDREL CALLED SOMETHING AT ME ON THE 425 DYNAMO
STREET TODAY--
I GAVE HIM A STRONG HINT ON THE STREET TODAY THAT 432 DYNAMO
UPSET HIM.
(SHE STARTS OUT OF THE SHADOW OF THE LILACS AS IF 434 DYNAMO
TO GO DOWN THE STREET
(PEERS STEALTHILY AROUND THE CORNER OF THE HEDGE 434 DYNAMO
DOWN THE STREET--
FOR SHE'S NO BETTER THAN A STREET WALKER/ 450 DYNAMO
FROM THE STREET. 2 ELECTR
A SPECIAL CURTAIN SHOWS THE HOUSE AS SEEN FROM THE 2 ELECTR
STREET.
IN THE FOREGROUND, ALONG THE STREET, IS A LINE OF 2 ELECTR
LOCUST AND ELM TREES.
BETWEEN THE HOUSE AND THE STREET IS A LAWN. 2 ELECTR
FROM THE TWO ENTRANCES ON THE STREET. 5 ELECTR
I HAPPENED TO RUN INTO CAPTAIN BRANT ON THE STREET 17 ELECTR
IN NEW YORK.
I COULD INSULT HIM ON THE STREET BEFORE EVERYONE 38 ELECTR
AND MAKE HIM FIGHT ME/
(FROM THE STREET, AWAY OFF RIGHT FRONT, 123 ELECTR
I MET BILLY BROWN ON THE STREET. 271 GGBROW
(MEEKLY) ARE YOU GOING UP STREET, DION$ 273 GGBROW
(WORRIEDLY) I HOPE THEY'LL WATCH OUT, CROSSING 274 GGBROW
THE STREET.
THAT I'D LIKE TO RUN OUT NAKED INTO THE STREET AND286 GGBROW
LOVE THE WHOLE MOB TO DEATH
STREET-LIGHTED VIEW OF BLACK HOUSES ACROSS THE 290 GGBROW
WAY.
(THEN FURIOUSLY) I'LL THROW HER BACK ON THE 298 GGBROW
STREET!
A KNOCKING COMES ON THE STREET DOOR. 299 GGBROW
FOR IT'S DARK DOWN HERE AND ME OLD MAN'S IN WALL 230 HA APE
STREET MAKING MONEY/

STREET

STREET (CONT'D.)

AND SUNSHINE ON THE STREET ITSELF. 233 HA APE
UP THE SIDE STREET YANK AND LONG COME SWAGGERING. 233 HA APE
A GENERAL ATMOSPHERE OF CLEAN, WELL-TIDIED, WIDE 233 HA APE
STREET.
(POINTING TO A SKYSCRAPER ACROSS THE STREET 238 HA APE
(HE BENDS DOWN AND GRIPS AT THE STREET CURBING AS 238 HA APE
IF TO PLUCK IT OUT AND HURL
A FAT, HIGH-HATTED, SPATTED GENTLEMAN RUNS OUT 239 HA APE
FROM THE SIDE STREET.
YANK COMES DOWN THE STREET OUTSIDE. 245 HA APE
AND THE STREET OUTSIDE. 245 HA APE
MOONLIGHT ON THE NARROW STREET, BUILDINGS MASSED 245 HA APE
IN BLACK SHADOW.
(WHO HAS COME UP THE STREET IN TIME TO HEAR THIS 250 HA APE
LAST--WITH GRIM HUMOR)
YANK LANDS SPRAWLING IN THE MIDDLE OF THE NARROW 250 HA APE
COBBLED STREET.
THE STREET ENTRANCE IS OFF-STAGE, LEFT. 7 HUGHIE
ON A WEST SIDE STREET IN MIDTOWN NEW YORK. 7 HUGHIE
HE CAN TELL TIME BY SOUNDS IN THE STREET. 8 HUGHIE
FOOTSTEPS ECHO IN THE DESERTED LOBBY AS SOMEONE 8 HUGHIE
COMES IN FROM THE STREET.
SIT DOWN AGAIN AND LISTEN TO THE NOISES IN THE 13 HUGHIE
STREET AND THINK ABOUT NOTHING.
(HIS MIND ESCAPES TO THE STREET AGAIN 18 HUGHIE
THE CLERK'S MIND REMAINS IN THE STREET TO GREET 19 HUGHIE
THE NOISE OF A FAR-OFF EL TRAIN.
OUTSIDE, THE SPELL OF ABNORMAL QUIET PRESSES 31 HUGHIE
SUFFOCATINGLY UPON THE STREET,
THE GRAY SUBDUED LIGHT OF EARLY MORNING IN A 574 ICEMAN
NARROW STREET.
LIGHT COMES FROM THE STREET WINDOWS OFF RIGHT, 574 ICEMAN
FROM THE MARKET PEOPLE ACROSS THE STREET AND THE 594 ICEMAN
WATERFRONT WORKERS.
DANCING THE CAN CAN AT HIGH NOON ON BRATTLE 595 ICEMAN
STREET.
I MET DICK TRUMBULL ON THE STREET A YEAR OR TWO 604 ICEMAN
AGO.
I'LL TIE A DISSPOSSESS BOMB TO YOUR TAILS THAT'LL 606 ICEMAN
BLOW YOU OUT IN THE STREET/
COMES FROM THE STREET WINDOWS, OFF RIGHT. 610 ICEMAN
THE TWO GIRLS, NEITHER MUCH OVER TWENTY, ARE 611 ICEMAN
TYPICAL DOLLAR STREET WALKERS,
SO I STEERED HIM INTO A SIDE STREET WHERE IT WAS 617 ICEMAN
DARK
ALONG THE GOLDEN STREET/ 622 ICEMAN
HE PRACTICED ON STREET CORNERS UNDER A TORCHLIGHT.626 ICEMAN
I'LL BET HE'S STANDING ON A STREET CORNER IN HELL 628 ICEMAN
RIGHT NOW.
THERE IS SUNLIGHT IN THE STREET OUTSIDE, 664 ICEMAN
WITH THE SWINGING DOORS TO THE STREET BETWEEN 664 ICEMAN
THEM.
JEES, IF I WASN'T DRESSED UP, I'D GO OUT AND MOP 673 ICEMAN
UP DE STREET WID HIM/
(HE WALKS STIFFLY TO THE STREET DOOR--THEN TURNS 673 ICEMAN
FOR A PARTING SHOT--BOASTFULLY)
(HE PASSES ALONG THE FRONT OF BAR TO LOOK OUT IN 674 ICEMAN
THE STREET)
(THE SWINGING DOORS ARE PUSHED OPEN AND WILLIE 674 ICEMAN
OBAN ENTERS FROM THE STREET.
STARING OVER THE SWINGING DOORS INTO THE STREET.) 677 ICEMAN
(HE STARTS FOR THE STREET DOOR.) 677 ICEMAN
HE SAUNTERS TO THE BAR BETWEEN LARRY AND THE 681 ICEMAN
STREET ENTRANCE.)
THE STREET DOOR IS HEARD SLAMMING BEHIND THEM.) 683 ICEMAN
LOOKING AS IF YOU WERE SCARED THE STREET OUTSIDE 685 ICEMAN
WOULD BITE YOU/
THOUGHT YOU'D BE WILLING TO HELP ME ACROSS THE 687 ICEMAN
STREET, KNOWING I'M HALF BLIND.
HE PUSHES THE DOOR OPEN AND STRIDES BLINDLY OUT 688 ICEMAN
INTO THE STREET
JEES, DEY AIN'T MORE'N TWO AN HOUR COMES DOWN DIS 688 ICEMAN
STREET, DE OLD BOOB/
RIGHT IN DE MIDDLE OF DE STREET/ 689 ICEMAN
JEES, HARRY'S STARTIN' ACRUS DE STREET/ 689 ICEMAN
SEEN HIM SITTIN' ON DE DOCK ON WEST STREET, 699 ICEMAN
LOOKIN' AT DE WATER AND CRYIN'/
THEN FROM THE HALL COMES THE SLAM OF THE STREET 719 ICEMAN
DOOR.
AFTER ALL, HE WAS THE ONE WHO ADVISED ME TO BUY 15 JOURNE
THAT PLACE ON CHESTNUT STREET
AND IT'S SAFER THAN THE STOCKS AND BONDS OF WALL 16 JOURNE
STREET SWINDLERS.
FROM THE LINE OF THE STREET THAT RUNS FROM LEFT TO298 LAZARU
RIGHT, FRONT,
WHICH STEADILY PUSHES THEM BACK INTO THE STREET. 304 LAZARU
LOOKS ACROSS A STREET ON A LOWER LEVEL 312 LAZARU
STREET BEFORE LAZARUS TO THE GATE BEYOND. 313 LAZARU
THE RETURNING LEGIONS BURST THROUGH AND GATHER IN 320 LAZARU
A DENSE MOB IN THE STREET
AND BEYOND THE WALL THE STEPS OF LIFE GROWIN' 19 MANSNS
FAINTER DOWN THE STREET,
OPENING ON THE STREET. 25 MANSNS
LOOKING OUT ON THE FRONT GARDEN AND THE STREET. 43 MANSNS
IN THE LEFT WALL ARE TWO WINDOWS LOOKING OUT ON 69 MANSNS
THE STREET.
YES, AS YOU'D BE TO AN ACQUAINTANCE IN THE STREET/ 78 MANSNS
AS IF I WAS SOME LOW STREET GIRL WHO CAME THAT 88 MANSNS
NIGHT TO SELL HERSELF.
FARTHER FORWARD, A HIGH WINDOW LOOKING OUT ON THE 117 MANSNS
STREET, THEN A CHAIR.
TREATING HIS WIFE AS IF SHE WAS A WHORE HE'D PICK 121 MANSNS
UP ON THE STREET
AND ACTING AS IF I WAS A STREET WHORE-- 133 MANSNS
I DO NOT SEE WHY YOU SHOULD LAUGH--LIKE A COMMON 143 MANSNS
STREET WOMAN.

STREET (CONT'D.)

IN FRONT OF THE SUMMER-HOUSE AND THE DOOR TO THE 161 MANSNS
STREET IN THE WALL AT RIGHT.
AND LOOKS OUT IN THE STREET--THEN CLOSES IT 162 MANSNS
AGAIN--DULLY.)
NO COMMON MAN ON THE STREET WOULD TURN TO LOOK AT,166 MANSNS
THAT DOOR LEADS TO THE STREET. 186 MANSNS
HAVE YOU PLAYED AND THROWN INTO THE STREET TO BE 417 MARCOM
DEVOURED BY DOGS$
GAMBLERS WHO WOULD LIKE TO BE MISTAKEN FOR WALL 37 MISBEG
STREET BROKERS.
BETWEEN THE MIDDLE TWO IS THE STREET DOOR. 7 POET
THE STREET DOOR AT REAR IS FLUNG OPEN AND DAN 51 POET
ROCHE, PADDY O'DOWD,
(SHE TURNS HER BACK ON HIM AND GOES OUT THE STREET 55 POET
DOOR AT REAR.)
THE STREET DOOR IS OPENED AND SARA ENTERS. 57 POET
FOR A MOMENT, BLINDED BY THE SUDDEN CHANGE FROM 67 POET
THE BRIGHT GLARE OF THE STREET,
(HE STANDS STARING IN THE MIRROR AND DOES NOT HEAR 67 POET
THE LATCH OF THE STREET DOOR
YOU WILL FIND IT COMFORTABLE HERE, AWAY FROM THE 69 POET
GLARE OF THE STREET.
RECEDE ALONG THE STREET BEYOND THE HIGH WALL. 86 POET
SHE WALKS PAST SARA INTO THE STREET, TURNS LEFT, 86 POET
AND,
(THERE IS A KNOCK ON THE STREET DOOR BUT HE DOES 116 POET
NOT HEAR IT.
TO SEE THE WAY THEY'RE KICKING HIS BUTT DOWN THE 124 POET
STREET)
I'LL DRAG HIM OUT OF HIS HOUSE AND LASH HIM DOWN 125 POET
THE STREET FOR ALL HIS
THE STREET DOOR IS FLUNG OPEN AND O'DOWD AND ROCHE129 POET
PILE IN.
(SHE STARTS FOR THE STREET DOOR--GETS HALFWAY TO 139 POET
IT AND STOPS.)
HERE I'D GONE TO HIS ROOM WITH MY MIND MADE UP TO 144 POET
BE AS BOLD AS ANY STREET WOMAN
SHE HAS HEARD THE CLICK OF THE LATCH ON THE STREET151 POET
DOOR AT REAR.)
CREGAN THEN DISAPPEARS, LEAVING THE STREET DOOR 152 POET
HALF OPEN.)
THEY GRABBED US BEFORE WE KNEW IT AND DRAGGED US 157 POET
INTO THE STREET.
LAWN BETWEEN THE HOUSE AND THE QUIET RESIDENTIAL 3 STRANG
STREET.
RUN ALONG UP THE STREET AND GET THIS FILLED. 34 STRANG
IN THE REAR, A DOOR LEADING TO THE STREET. 493 VOYAGE
(THERE IS THE NOISE OF LOUD BOISTEROUS SINGING 496 VOYAGE
FROM THE STREET)
(HE OPENS THE STREET DOOR AND LOOKS OUT) 496 VOYAGE
(THE DOOR TO THE STREET IS OPENED AND NICK ENTERS,506 VOYAGE
JUST LITTLE WAY BACK FROM STREET HERE. 506 VOYAGE
ON THE WINDOW SHADE FROM SOME STREET LAMP. 470 WELDED

STREETS

ONE WALK DOWN ONE OF THEIR FILTHY NARROW STREETS 132 BEYOND
WITH THE TROPIC SUN BEATING ON
THE STREETS ARE FULL OF LAZARUSES. 315 GGBROW
BUILT IN THE DECADE 1900-10 ON THE SIDE STREETS OF 7 HUGHIE
THE GREAT WHITE WAY SECTOR.
NOT IF DE STREETS WAS BLOCKED WID SAILORS/ 669 ICEMAN
BEJEES, IT AIN'T SAFE TO WALK IN THE STREETS/ 690 ICEMAN
THE SUN WAS BROILING AND THE STREETS FULL OF 721 ICEMAN
AUTOMOBILES.
WHICH KNOWS THAT THOUGH ONE WERE TO CRY IT IN THE 354 LAZARU
STREETS TO MULTITUDES,
I SEE--A CITY WHOSE STREETS ARE CANALS--IT IS 426 MARCOM
EVENING--A HOUSE.
THE NOISE, THE LIGHTS OF THE STREETS, RECALL HIM 439 MARCOM
AT ONCE TO HIMSELF.
(HE RENEWS HIS CHANT) -THEY HUNT OUR STEPS THAT WE579 ROPE
CANNOT GO IN OUR STREETS.-
(A PAUSE) I REMEMBER STREETS--LIGHTS--DEAD FACES--472 WELDED
THEN YOU--YOUR FACE

STREETWALKING

TO SAVE MY GRANDMOTHER FROM STREETWALKING. 34 HUGHIE

STRENGTH

HE IS ABOUT THIRTY, IN THE FULL POWER OF HIS 30 ANNA
HEAVY-MUSCLED, IMMENSE STRENGTH.
AND ONLY FOR ME, I'M TELLING YOU, AND THE GREAT 32 ANNA
STRENGTH AND RIGHTS.
BUT, GLORY BE, IT'S A POWER OF STRENGTH IS IN THEM 33 ANNA
TWO FINE ARMS OF YOURS.
(PROUDLY) AND IF 'TWASN'T FOR ME AND MY GREAT 36 ANNA
STRENGTH, I'M TELLING YOU--
STRENGTH AND GUTS OF A MAN WAS IN ME$ 48 ANNA
AS IF HE WERE ONLY COLLECTING HIS STRENGTH TO RUSH 50 ANNA
AT HIM AGAIN.)
AS IF HER FINGERS HAD NO STRENGTH TO HOLD IT-- 69 ANNA
HYSTERICALLY)
(SIMPLY) FOR I'VE A POWER OF STRENGTH IN ME TO 74 ANNA
LEAD MEN THE WAY I WANT.
HER SMALL, REGULAR FEATURES ARE MARKED BY A 87 BEYOND
CERTAIN STRENGTH--
HIS VOICE RINGS WITH HOPEFUL STRENGTH AND ENERGY) 142 BEYOND
I'M GETTING BACK ALL MY STRENGTH. 150 BEYOND
HIS FALSE STRENGTH OF A MOMENT HAS EVAPORATED 151 BEYOND
RUB/ DON'T TALK. YOU'RE WASTING YOUR STRENGTH. 167 BEYOND
(HE SUDDENLY RAISES HIMSELF WITH HIS LAST 168 BEYOND
REMAINING STRENGTH AND POINTS TO THE
THAT'S NO WAY TO GET BACK YOUR STRENGTH. 532 DAYS
GIVE OUR STRENGTH. 204 DESIRE
THERE IS STRENGTH AND OBSTINACY IN HER JAW, A HARD221 DESIRE
DETERMINATION IN HER EYES.
YET THERE IS A WEAKNESS IN IT, A PETTY PRIDE IN 221 DESIRE
ITS OWN NARROW STRENGTH.
HER EYES TAKE HIM IN PENETRATINGLY WITH A 225 DESIRE
CALCULATING APPRAISAL OF HIS STRENGTH

STRENGTH

STRENGTH (CONT'D.)
THEY HAIN'T GOIN' T BE MUCH STRENGTH LEFT FUR 250 DESIRE
MOWIN' IN THE CORN LOT T'MORROW.
YE GOT THE DEVIL'S STRENGTH IN YE. 251 DESIRE
THE OLD MAN'S CONCENTRATED STRENGTH IS TOO MUCH 255 DESIRE
FOR EBEN.
SIXTY YEARS OLD BUT STILL IN THE PRIME OF HEALTH 513 DIFRNT
AND STRENGTH.
IT SUGGESTS, RATHER, AN INERT STRENGTH. 428 DYNAMO
AS IF SOME HIDDEN STRENGTH IN HIM HAD SUDDENLY 448 DYNAMO
BEEN TAPPED)
(HIS STRENGTH FAILING HIM--IN A FALTERING TONE 463 DYNAMO
HARDLY ABOVE A WHISPER)
I HAVEN'T THE STRENGTH TO RESIST EVIL. 466 DYNAMO
(THEN PROUDLY) AND I FOUND THE STRENGTH TO DO IT.478 DYNAMO
AN UNDERLYING STRENGTH OF WILL. 175 EJONES
WHAT'S MY STRENGTH GONNA COME FROM IF I DOESN'TS 189 EJONES
(HER STRENGTH GONE--SWAYING WEAKLY) 63 ELECTR
CHRISTINE STARES AFTER HER, HER STRENGTH SEEMS TO 78 ELECTR
LEAVE HER.
HAVING YOU AGAIN IS JUST THE MEDICINE I NEED TO 80 ELECTR
GIVE ME STRENGTH--
(HER EYES ON HIS FACE--AS IF SHE WERE WILLING HER 138 ELECTR
STRENGTH INTO HIM)
AND WEAKLY BECAUSE THE STRENGTH SHE HAS WILLED 142 ELECTR
INTO HIM HAS LEFT HER EXHAUSTED)
WHY MUST I BE SO ASHAMED OF MY STRENGTH, SO PROUD 264 GGBROW
OF MY WEAKNESS$
YOU'VE GIVEN MY WEAKNESS STRENGTH TO LIVE. 285 GGBROW
(SADLY) YOU'VE GIVEN ME STRENGTH TO DIE. 286 GGBROW
NOW I AM DRINKING YOUR STRENGTH, DION-- 307 GGBROW
HE SEEKS TO GAIN STRENGTH AND IS ABLE TO FORCE A 307 GGBROW
SAD LAUGH)
STRENGTH TO LOVE IN THIS WORLD AND DIE AND SLEEP 307 GGBROW
AND BECOME FERTILE EARTH,
YOUR WEAKNESS THE STRENGTH OF MY FLOWERS, 307 GGBROW
GIVE ME THE STRENGTH TO DESTROY THIS/ 314 GGBROW
AS HE GAINS STRENGTH, MOCKINGLY) 320 GGBROW
THEY RESPECT HIS SUPERIOR STRENGTH--THE GRUDGING 208 HA APE
RESPECT OF FEAR.
BUT NONE OF THE ENERGY, NONE OF THE STRENGTH OF 219 HA APE
THE STEEL THAT MADE IT.
THE BAR BENDS LIKE A LICORICE STICK UNDER HIS 244 HA APE
TREMENDOUS STRENGTH.
HE SUMMONS UP STRENGTH FOR A WITHERING CRACK.) 27 HUGHIE
HIS ONCE GREAT MUSCULAR STRENGTH HAS BEEN 575 ICEMAN
DEBAUCHED INTO FLACCID TALLOW.
AND HIS BEARING HAS A FORCED SWAGGER OF CONSCIOUS 675 ICEMAN
PHYSICAL STRENGTH.
I HAVE THE GREAT STRENGTH TO DO WORK OF TEN 676 ICEMAN
ORDINARY MENS.
(SMITHY STRUGGLES WITH ALL OF HIS STRENGTH 526 INZONE
HE NEEDS TO EAT TO KEEP UP HIS STRENGTH. 16 JOURNE
HAVE THE STRENGTH TO KEEP ON WHATS 70 JOURNE
WHY COULDN'T YOU HAVE THE STRENGTH TO KEEP ON$ 70 JOURNE
UNTIL NOW THERE'S NO STRENGTH OF THE SPIRIT LEFT 78 JOURNE
IN HER
YOU MUST LEARN TO HUSBAND YOUR STRENGTH. 91 JOURNE
AND COLLECT STRENGTH TO LEAN FORWARD. 305 LAZARU
REFINED IN THEM BY NOBILITY OF BLOOD BUT AT THE 312 LAZARU
SAME TIME WITH STRENGTH
BROAD AND CORPULENT BUT OF GREAT MUSCULAR STRENGTH337 LAZARU
STILL DESPITE HIS AGE.
AND I STARVED MY MOTHER'S STRENGTH TO DEATH UNTIL 356 LAZARU
SHE DIED.
O IMMORTAL GODS, GIVE THY BROTHER STRENGTH/ 369 LAZARU
HE IS TALL AND LOOSE-JOINTED WITH A WIRY STRENGTH 4 MANSNS
OF LIMB.
YOU'VE THE WISH FOR LIFE BUT YOU HAVEN'T THE 19 MANSNS
STRENGTH EXCEPT TO RUN AND HIDE
EXCEPT I LOVE YOU NOW WITH ALL OF ME AND ALL MY 88 MANSNS
STRENGTH.
(THINKING--REGRETFULLY.) I HAVE GROWN TO LEAN 120 MANSNS
UPON HER HEALTH AND STRENGTH--
BECAUSE HER STRENGTH AND HEALTH AND ACCEPTANCE OF 122 MANSNS
LIFE GAVE ME
HAVEN'T I ALWAYS SAID YOU'VE THE STRENGTH AND THE 158 MANSNS
POWER
DIDN'T HAVE THE STRENGTH TO WANT THEM BUT RAN AND 167 MANSNS
HID IN HER GARDEN.
THE STRENGTH HIS EVIL JEALOUS GREED HAS CORRUPTED 170 MANSNS
AND DESTROYED.
UNTIL WE GET BACK OUR OLD STRENGTH-- 170 MANSNS
HE KNOWS SHE'LL NEVER HAVE STRENGTH TO CLAIM HER 171 MANSNS
BODY OR SOUL HER OWN AGAIN/
WE COULD HAVE THE STRENGTH NOW AS WE ARE UNITED 171 MANSNS
AGAIN AS ONE WOMAN.
(WITH EXTRAORDINARY STRENGTH SHE GIVES HIM A PUSH 190 MANSNS
IN THE CHEST THAT DRIVES HIM
I MUST PRAY TO GOD FOR STRENGTH--FOR GUIDANCE/ 362 MARCOM
GREAT STRENGTH YOU HAD, AND GREAT PRIDE, HE SAID-- 88 MISBEG
AND GREAT GOODNESS, NO LESS/
IN SPITE OF HER STRENGTH, HOLDING HERSELF LIKE 157 MISBEG
THIS FOR HOURS.
IT HAS A BULL-LIKE, IMPERVIOUS STRENGTH, A TOUGH 33 POET
PEASANT VITALITY.
(FEELING HERSELF BORNE DOWN WEAKLY BY THE SHEER 71 POET
FORCE OF HIS PHYSICAL STRENGTH,
PLEASE, DOCTOR, YOU MUST GIVE HER STRENGTH TO DO 87 STRANG
THIS RIGHT THING
NOW SHE FEELS YOUR STRENGTH. 87 STRANG
STRENGTH ABOUT HER EXPRESSION, A RUTHLESS SELF-- 90 STRANG
CONFIDENCE IN HER EYES.
AND HE BEGAN TALKING BACK TO HIM ALL THE TIME AND 153 STRANG
SORT OF GAVE HIM HIS STRENGTH
IT IS A STRONG FACE BUT OF A STRENGTH WHOLLY 184 STRANG
MATERIAL IN QUALITY.
I STILL HAVE THE STRENGTH TO--/ 453 WELDED

STRENGTH (CONT'D.)
I HAVE TO REBEL WITH ALL MY STRENGTH--SEIZE ANY 453 WELDED
PRETEXT/

STRENGTHENED

THIS DEFENSE IS STRENGTHENED BY A NATURAL TENDENCY 6 STRANG
TOWARD A PRIM PROVINCIALISM

STRESS

BUT THERE ARE TIMES OF STRESS AND FLIGHT WHEN ONE 543 DAYS
HIDES IN ANY OLD EMPTY BARREL/

STRESSED

TO ONE OF OVER-STRESSED MORAL INDIGNATION.) 97 MANSNS

STRESSES

STRESSES THE RHYTHMIC FLOW OF THE DANCE.) 285 LAZARU

STRETCH

IT'S A STRETCH FOR ME, I'M GETTING SO FAT. 211 AHWILD
ITS SMALL STRETCH OF LAWN DIVIDED BY THE DIRT PATH112 BEYOND
LEADING TO THE DOOR FROM THE
THEY STRETCH THEIR ARMS OUT IN EVERY DIRECTION 296 LAZARU
SUPPLICATINGLY.)
THE POLOS RISE AND STRETCH SLEEPILY.) 376 MARCOM
(STARTS TOWARD THE DOOR) THINK I'LL GO OUT AND 42 STRANG
STRETCH MY LEGS.

STRETCHED

ONE OF HIS ARMS IS STRETCHED LIMPLY OVER THE SIDE 477 CARDIF
OF THE BUNK.
WHICH LIES STRETCHED OUT ON THE DECK BETWEEN THEM.472 CARIBE
JOHN RISES FROM HIS KNEES AND STANDS WITH ARMS 566 DAYS
STRETCHED UP AND OUT.
REMAINS STANDING WITH HIS ARMS STRETCHED UP TO THE566 DAYS
CROSS.
HIS ARMS STRETCHED OUT TO IT SUPPLICATINGLY.) 479 DYNAMO
DOOR, THE HAND WITH THE POISON STRETCHED OUT 64 ELECTR
BEHIND HER--WEAKLY)
THEIR ARMS STRETCHED OUT AS IF DEMANDING LAZARUS 288 LAZARU
FOR A SACRIFICIAL VICTIM.
THE OTHER LEG STRETCHED DOWN TO THE LOWER STEP. 350 LAZARU
THE DRY SKIN IS STRETCHED TIGHTLY OVER THE BONES 27 MANSNS
FOR THE DAY GUETH AWAY, FOR THE SHADOWS OF THE 579 ROPE
EVENING ARE STRETCHED OUT.+
(LEANING FORWARD TOWARD GORDON WITH HER ARMS 157 STRANG
STRETCHED OUT ENTREATINGLY BUT
UNTIL THEY ARE STRETCHED OUT STRAIGHT TO RIGHT AND489 WELDED
LEFT, FORMING A CROSS.

STRETCHER

DEY'D CARRY HIM OFF ON A STRETCHER. 212 HA APE

STRETCHES

(SHE STRETCHES AWKWARDLY OVER THE TABLE TO REACH 210 AHWILD
THE CHANDELIER THAT IS
(SHE STRETCHES OUT HER HANDS TO WARM THEM) 152 BEYOND
(ROBERT SMILES GRATEFULLY AND STRETCHES OUT HIS 162 BEYOND
HAND.
EBEN STRETCHES HIS ARMS UP TO THE SKY-- 211 DESIRE
REBELLIOUSLY.)
UNCONSCIOUSLY HE STRETCHES OUT HIS ARMS FOR HER 236 DESIRE
AND SHE HALF RISES.
HE STRETCHES UP HIS HANDS IN A TORTURED GESTURE) 239 DESIRE
(SHE STRETCHES OUT HER ARMS FOR HIM.) 244 DESIRE
HE STRETCHES OUT HIS ARMS AND CALLS TO SOME GOD 201 EJONES
WITHIN ITS DEPTHS.
(SHE STRETCHES OUT HER ARMS TO THE MOON) 263 GGBROW
(HE STRETCHES OUT HIS ARMS TO THE SKY) 286 GGBROW
(HE STRETCHES OUT HIS ARMS TO THE SKY--THEN 289 LAZARU
SUDDENLY POINTS)
(STRETCHES OUT HER HANDS TO CALIGULA IMPLORINGLY) 317 LAZARU
(HE STRETCHES HIS ARMS OUT TO HER BESEECHINGLY-- 438 MARCOM
STRETCHES HIS LEGS AS IF THEY HAD BECOME CRAMPED 439 MARCOM
BY TOO LONG AN EVENING.
CLUTCHING THE SUPPORTING ARM SHE STRETCHES OUT.) 80 MISBEG
(SHE STRETCHES AND RUBS HER NUMBED ARMS, GROANING 166 MISBEG
COMICALLY)
(SHE GETS TO HER FEET AND STRETCHES. 172 MISBEG
(HE STRETCHES OUT HIS HAND AWKWARDLY) 28 STRANG
STRETCHES ACROSS HIS CHECKED WAISTCOAT. 493 VOYAGE
THEN STRETCHES OUT HER ARMS WITH A PASSIONATE, 489 WELDED
TENDER GESTURE)

STRETCHIN'

AN' STRETCHIN' FIT TO KILL HISSELF'S IF HE'D BEEN 521 INZONE
DEAD ASLEEP.

STRETCHING

(STARTING TO HIS FEET AND STRETCHING HIS ARMS 108 BEYOND
ACROSS THE TABLE TOWARD MAYO)
STRETCHING A HAND OUT THE MAIL TO SUPPORT 151 BEYOND
HIMSELF.
AND OTHER EQUIPMENT STRETCHING UP THROUGH THE ROOF473 DYNAMO
TO THE OUTGOING FEEDERS.
STEEL WORK, INSULATORS, BUSSES, SWITCHES, ETC. 483 DYNAMO
STRETCHING UPWARD TO THE ROOF.
THEIR SIX CUPPED ARMS STRETCHING UPWARD. 483 DYNAMO
WITH YOUR ARMS LIKE HER ARMS, STRETCHING OUT FOR 484 DYNAMO
ME/
FISH--STRETCHING OUT TO SUCK ME IN-- 484 DYNAMO
STRETCHING HER ARMS UP IN THE SAME POSITION AS THE485 DYNAMO
SWITCH ARMS.)
STRETCHING OUT HIS ARMS TO THE EXCITER-HEAD 488 DYNAMO
HER SAILS STRETCHING ALOFT ALL SILVER AND WHITE, 214 HA APE
NOT A SOUND ON THE DECK,
ALL THE REST OF THE MEN TUMBLE OUT OF THEIR BUNKS,514 INZONE
STRETCHING AND GAPING.
(STRETCHING OUT THEIR ARMS IN THE DIRECTION FROM 302 LAZARU
WHICH LAZARUS IS EXPECTED--
STRETCHING OUT HIS HAND) 308 LAZARU
(HE TURNS, THROWING BACK HIS HEAD AND STRETCHING 318 LAZARU
UP HIS ARMS.
NOW EVERY ONE UP THESE IS STANDING UP, STRETCHING 318 LAZARU
OUT HIS ARMS TOWARD LAZARUS,
(WALKS UP THE STEPS TO THE CROSS AND, STRETCHING 329 LAZARU
TO HIS FULL HEIGHT,

STRETCHING

STRETCHING (CONT'D.)
THE OLD MAN TOTTERS OVER TO HIM, STRETCHING OUT A 595 ROPE
TREMBLING HAND.
HE LOOKS DOWN PASSIONATELY, STRETCHING OUT HIS 449 WELDED
ARMS, HIS EYES GLOWING)

STREWING
STREWING IT OVER THE FLOOR. 664 ICEMAN

STRICKEN
A STRICKEN LOOK COMES OVER SID'S FACE. 257 AHWILD
AS FOR SID, HE IS MOVED TO HIS REMORSEFUL, GUILT- 257 AHWILD
STRICKEN DEPTHS.
(HIS EYES SEEMED TO TAKE IN THE POVERTY-STRICKEN 155 BEYOND
APPEARANCE
(HE FLASHES IT ON HER TERROR-STRICKEN FACE, THEN 572 CROSS
QUICKLY AROUND THE ROOM.
YES, I FELT STRICKEN WITH GUILT, TOO-- 507 DAYS
ELSA'S FACE IS PALE AND SET, HER EYES HAVE A 537 DAYS
BEWILDERED, STRICKEN LOOK.
(WITH A GREAT PRETENSE OF GUILT-STRICKEN PROTEST) 440 DYNAMO
AND RUNS PANIC-STRICKEN OFF RIGHT, DRAGGING HIS 453 DYNAMO
MOANING WIFE BY THE ARM.
HIS WHOLE FACE IS A MASK OF STRICKEN LONELINESS. 455 DYNAMO
BUT HER FACE IS TORN BY A LOOK OF STRICKEN 28 ELECTR
ANGUISH.
WRINGING HER HANDS TOGETHER IN STRICKEN ANGUISH. 121 ELECTR
HIS FACE WEARS A DAZED EXPRESSION AND HIS EYES 139 ELECTR
HAVE A WILD, STRICKEN LOOK.
THE TORTURED MAD LOOK ON HIS FACE CHANGING TO A 166 ELECTR
STRICKEN TERRIFIED EXPRESSION)
(HE STARES AT HER WITH THE LOST STRICKEN 166 ELECTR
EXPRESSION FOR A MOMENT MORE--
STARES AT HER WITH A STRICKEN LOOK OF HORRIFIED 177 ELECTR
REPULSION--
STRICKEN LOOK AND TURNS AWAY AND SLUMPS INTO THE 655 ICEMAN
CHAIR ON MOSHER'S RIGHT.)
PANIC-STRICKEN RUN. 689 ICEMAN
(THEN HER EYES MEET HIS STRICKEN, ACCUSING LOOK. 64 JOURNE
HE WOULDN'T STOP AFTER HE WAS STRICKEN. 67 JOURNE
HIS PEOPLE WERE THE MOST IGNORANT KIND OF POVERTY-111 JOURNE
STRICKEN IRISH.
EDMUND'S FACE LOOKS STRICKEN AND SICK. 162 JOURNE
BREAKS INTO LAMENTING GRIEF AGAIN, GUILT-STRICKEN 295 LAZARU
BECAUSE OF ITS LAUGHTER.)
(THE CHORUSED WORD BEATS DOWN ALL SOUND INTO A 305 LAZARU
STRICKEN SILENCE.
(THEN GRIEF-STRICKEN) LAZARUS/ 371 LAZARU
WHEN I'M SO RICH AND YOU SO POVERTY-STRICKEN. 55 MANSNS
FATHER BECAME PANIC-STRICKEN 66 MANSNS
AND AT THE SAME TIME BAFFLED AND PANIC-STRICKEN.) 171 MANSNS
HER AIR IS GRIEF-STRICKEN. 384 MARCOM
(THE TERROR-STRICKEN COURIER SCRAMBLES OUT LIKE A 425 MARCOM
FLASH.
(LOOKS STRICKEN AND BEWILDERED--HER VOICE 89 MISBEG
TREMBLING)
(HIS SNEER CHANGES TO A LOOK OF STRICKEN GUILT AND111 MISBEG
GRIEF)
SHE LOOKS WEARY AND STRICKEN AND SAD. 153 MISBEG
AS IF YOU WERE SOME POVERTY-STRICKEN PEASANT'S 50 POET
DAUGHTER$
(HORROR-STRICKEN, LUNGES FROM HER CHAIR AND GRABS 172 POET
HIS ARM.)
AND THAT'S OBVIOUSLY BECAUSE I AM STRICKEN WITH A 85 STRANG
RECURRENCE OF AN OLD DESIRE...
(BEWILDERED AND TERROR-STRICKEN, TRYING FEEBLY TO 107 STRANG
PUSH HIM AWAY--THINKING)
(SUDDENLY OVERCOME BY A WAVE OF CONSCIENCE-- 156 STRANG
STRICKEN REMORSE AND PITY)
(THEN STRICKEN WITH GUILT) (POOR DEAR JANE/... 164 STRANG
(CANNOT BELIEVE HER EARS--SUDDENLY PANIC-STRICKEN)178 STRANG

STRICKENLY
(THEN CONSCIENCE-STRICKENLY) 441 DYNAMO
(HAS WINCED WHEN REUBEN WAS HIT--CONSCIENCE-- 448 DYNAMO
STRICKENLY)
(JIMMY STARES AT HIM STRICKENLY. 657 ICEMAN
(STRICKENLY.) PLEASE, DEAR. 45 JOURNE
(THEN GRIEF-STRICKENLY.) FOR THE LOVE OF GOD, 69 JOURNE
(STRICKENLY.) EXCUSES$ 69 JOURNE
(STRICKENLY.) EDMUND/ 141 JOURNE
(STARES AT HIM STRICKENLY--PLEADINGLY.) 98 MANSNS
(STRICKENLY.) YOU MEAN THEY ARE TO BE TAKEN FROM 104 MANSNS
ME$
STRICKENLY, IN A GUILTY WHISPER.) 144 MANSNS
(SHRINKS AS IF SHE'D BEEN STRUCK--STRICKENLY.) 186 MANSNS
(STRICKENLY) UGH, DON'T, FATHER/ 89 MISBEG
(STRICKENLY) JIM/ 137 MISBEG
(STRICKENLY) NO/ 173 MISBEG
(STRICKENLY.) DON'T, FATHER/ 158 POET
(THEN THINKING CONSCIENCE-STRICKENLY) 62 STRANG

STRICT
(WITH A SMILE) OH, I HAVEN'T NO STRICT RELIGIOUS 495 DIFRNT
NOTIONS ABOUT IT.
I AIN'T STRICT IN JUDGING 'EM AND YOU KNOW IT. 512 DIFRNT
(AFTER A PAUSE) YOU GOT QUEER, STRICT NOTIONS, 516 DIFRNT
EMMA.
HE'S SET IN HIS WAYS AND BELIEVES IN BEING STRICT 522 DIFRNT
WITH YOU--
TOO STRICT, I'VE TOLD HIM. 522 DIFRNT
I AIN'T AS STRICT AS I SEEM--ABOUT HEARIN' THINGS.526 DIFRNT
THAT THE ARMY AND STRICT DISCIPLINE'D MAYBE MAKE A540 DIFRNT
MAN OF HIM.
THEY'RE STRICT ABOUT TRESPASSIN'. 7 ELECTR
SHE WAS VERY STRICT WITH ME. 26 ELECTR
UH, I REALIZE MR. BROWN HAS GIVEN STRICT ORDERS 303 GGBROW
DION IS NOT TO BE DISTURBED.
HE SAYS, EMMA WAS BROUGHT UP STRICT. 26 HUGHIE
HE GIVE ME STRICT ORDERS NOT TO LET WILLIE HANG UP582 ICEMAN
NO MORE DRINKS, NO MATTER--
STRICT METHODISTS, TOO. 710 ICEMAN

STRICT (CONT'D.)
SHE WAS VERY PIOUS AND STRICT. 114 JOURNE
SHE TOOK SUCH STRICT CARE OF HER OWN, SHE WALKED 100 STRANG
MILES EVERY DAY.

STRICTLY
WELL, I WASN'T BROUGHT UP THAT STRICTLY AND, 23 ELECTR
SHOULD OR SHOULDN'T, AT ANY RATE,
I'LL TELL YOU A SECRET, JOSIAH--STRICTLY BETWEEN 71 ELECTR
YOU AND ME.
STRICTLY BUSINESS, LIKE DEY WAS FIGHTERS AND I WAS580 ICEMAN
DEAR MANAGER, SEE$
(HE BREAKS OFF, THICKLY.) NOT STRICTLY ACCURATE. 159 JOURNE
NATURALLY YOU COULD EXPECT NO MERCY IN A STRICTLY 59 MANSNS
BUSINESS DEAL, MOTHER.
BUT THE DOCTORS HAVE STRICTLY FORBIDDEN IT. 45 MISBEG
NO, I ASKED HIM TO KEEP WHAT I SAID STRICTLY 11 STRANG
CONFIDENTIAL.
WITH A CHANGE TO A STRICTLY PROFESSIONAL MANNER) 183 STRANG

STRIDENT
STRIDENT DEFIANCE) 58 ANNA
(WITH STRIDENT INTENSITY) YOU WOULD UNDERSTAND 30 ELECTR
(HER VOICE GROWN STRIDENT) DID YOU THINK YOU 61 ELECTR
COULD MAKE ME WEAK--
AND SHE SPEAKS WITH STRIDENT DENUNCIATION) 64 ELECTR
(GLARES AT HER AS IF THIS WERE THE LAST INSULT-- 123 ELECTR
WITH STRIDENT MOCKERY)
(HER VOICE STRIDENT, AS IF HER WILL WERE SNAPPING)151 ELECTR
(IN THE STRIDENT TONES OF A CIRCUS BARKER) 254 HA APE
THE FEMALE VOICES ARE HARSH, STRIDENT, MANNISH-- 336 LAZARU
(SHE BURSTS INTO STRIDENT LAUGHTER) 347 LAZARU
(THINKING WITH A STRIDENT ACCUSATION) 11 STRANG

STRIDENTLY
(INFURIATED BY HIS ACTION--STRIDENTLY) 58 ANNA
(STRIDENTLY) WHY SHOULDN'T IS 177 ELECTR
(STRIDENTLY) GANGWAY FOR TWO GOOD WHORES/ 725 ICEMAN
FALSELY, STRIDENTLY.) 362 LAZARU
(A BIT STRIDENTLY) LIVING LIKE THAT WITH THAT FEAR 60 STRANG
NEARLY DROVE ME CRAZY, TOO--

STRIDES
(KEENEY TURNS HIS BACK ON HIS WIFE AND STRIDES TO 552 'ILE
THE DOORWAY.
(HE STRIDES OFF IN AN INDIGNANT FURY OF MISERY 209 AHWILD
THROUGH THE FRONT PARLOR.)
(HE STRIDES ANGRILY AWAY THROUGH THE BACK PARLOR.)235 AHWILD
(BUT HE TURNS WITHOUT ANOTHER WORD AND STRIDES OUT 61 ANNA
OF THE DOORWAY.
(HE SHARES OVER HIS MUTTERED THREAT AND STRIDES 108 BEYOND
TOWARD THE DOOR REAR, RIGHT.)
(IN A STATE OF MAD EXULTATION STRIDES TOWARD HIS 568 CROSS
SON
(HE STRIDES TO THE COMPANIONWAY, FOLLOWED BY NAT. 569 CROSS
(HE STRIDES OFF DOWN THE ROAD TO THE LEFT.) 212 DESIRE
HE SCOWLS, STRIDES OFF THE PORCH TO THE PATH AND 228 DESIRE
STARTS TO WALK PAST HER
(HE TURNS AND STRIDES OFF UP THE ROAD. 230 DESIRE
HE STRIDES UP AND SLAPS EBEN ON THE BACK. 253 DESIRE
AND STRIDES INTO THE HOUSE AND THEN INTO THE 267 DESIRE
KITCHEN.
(CABOT TURNS AND STRIDES PAST THE MEN-- 269 DESIRE
(HE STRIDES AWAY FROM HER, STOPS, AND TURNS BACK--543 DIFRNT
SAVAGELY)
(HE TURNS AND STRIDES TOWARD THE DOOR.) 166 ELECTR
THE FATHER STRIDES TO THE CENTER BENCH AND SITS 260 GGBROW
DOWN.
(HE STRIDES OUT THE DOOR IN REAR. 217 HA APE
HE PUSHES THE DOOR OPEN AND STRIDES BLINDLY OUT 688 ICEMAN
INTO THE STREET
(THEN SUDDENLY PUTTING ON A BRAVE FRONT, HE 333 LAZARU
STRIDES UP BEHIND LAZARUS)
(HE TURNS AND STRIDES OFF INTO THE DARKNESS AT 357 LAZARU
RIGHT.)
(HE STRIDES TOWARD HER.) 5 MANSNS
(HE STRIDES TO THE STUDY DOOR AND OPENS IT--THEN 130 MANSNS
TURNS AND MURMURS.)
HE STRIDES INTO THE BAR. 129 POET
JUMPS UP TO MEET HIM AS HE STRIDES TOWARD HER.) 444 WELDED
(HE STRIDES TOWARD THE DOORWAY-- 466 WELDED
(HE STRIDES OVER TO HER.) 473 WELDED

STRIKE
(HYSTERICALLY) DON'T YOU STRIKE HIM, NAT/ 261 AHWILD
I CAN HEAR THE TOWN HALL STRIKE, IT'S SO STILL 275 AHWILD
TONIGHT...
FROM THE DISTANCE THE TOWN HALL CLOCK BEGINS TO 277 AHWILD
STRIKE.
BURKE DOES NOT STRIKE OR MISTREAT HIM IN ANY WAY, 49 ANNA
AND MAY GAWD STRIKE ME DEAD THIS MINUTE AND MY 73 ANNA
MOTHER, TOO, IF SHE WAS ALIVE,
AND MAY THE BLACKEST CURSE OF GOD STRIKE YOU IF 75 ANNA
YOU'RE LYING.
AND MAY THE BLACKEST CURSE OF OF GOD STRIKE ME IF 75 ANNA
I'M LYING/
(A SUDDEN UNEASINESS SEEMS TO STRIKE HIM) 96 BEYOND
(INDIGNANTLY) GAWD STRIKE ME DEAD IF IT AIN'T 478 CARDIF
TRUE, EVERY BLEEDIN' WORD OF IT.
THAT MY HERO'S SILLY IDEA THAT HE WAS POSSESSED BY538 DAYS
A DEMON MUST STRIKE YOU AS AN
I'M A-GOIN' IN THE MORNIN'--OR MAY GOD STRIKE ME 258 DESIRE
IT HELL/
LORD GOD UF HOSTS, WHY DOST THOU NOT STRIKE 423 DYNAMO
HIM...
WHO DEFIES THEE PUBLICLY TO STRIKE HIM DEAD$... 423 DYNAMO
GOD MAY STRIKE HIM/... 438 DYNAMO
IF THERE IS HIS GOD LET HIM STRIKE ME DEAD THIS 453 DYNAMO
SECOND/
(HASTILY) NO, GAWD STRIKE ME/ 180 EJONES
MAKES A THREATENING MOVE AS IF TO STRIKE HER 34 ELECTR
DAUGHTER'S FACE)
I HEARD THE CLOCK STRIKE. 59 ELECTR

STRIKE (CONT'D.)
THE SOUND OF THE SINGING SEEMS TO STRIKE A 102 ELECTR
RESPONSIVE CHORD IN HIS BRAIN.
AN' YOU'RE TO STAY IN THE DARK AND NOT EVEN STRIKE131 ELECTR
A MATCH.
THEN YOU CAN STRIKE THEM FOR A BIGGER SALARY THAN 604 ICEMAN
YOU GOT BEFORE, DO YOU SEE*
WE'RE GOIN' ON STRIKE AND YUH CAN LIKE IT OR LUMP 669 ICEMAN
IT/*
(HE SHAKES HIS HEAD) WHORES GOIN' ON STRIKE/ CAN 670 ICEMAN
YUH TIE DATS
GOD STRIKE ME PINK/ 526 INZONE
AND STRIKE DOWN EVERYONE IN THEIR WAY.) 291 LAZARU
STRIKE/ 304 LAZARU
STRIKE/ 305 LAZARU
WHY COULD YOU NOT STRIKE$ 334 LAZARU
STRIKE HIM DOWN/ 337 LAZARU
STRIKE/ 339 LAZARU
THE RODS AND SCOURGES ARE UPLIFTED OVER HIS BACK 348 LAZARU
TO STRIKE.
BUT STRIKE WHILE THE IRON IS HOT, YOU NINNY/ 380 MARCOM
DIDN'T I TELL YOU TO STRIKE UP WHEN I SET FOOT ON 406 MARCOM
THE DECK$
WOULD YOU STRIKE MY POOR INFIRM OLD FATHER, YOU 61 MISBEG
COWARD, YOU/
IF ONLY GOD WOULD STRIKE THEM DEAD/... 129 STRANG
GAWD STRIKE 'M BLIND/ 497 VOYAGE
STRIKES
(THE IRONY OF IT STRIKES HER SENSE OF HUMOR AND 17 ANNA
SHE LAUGHS HOARSELY.)
AND I'LL PROMISE TO BE HERE WHEN THE CLOCK 123 BEYOND
STRIKES--
(AS A CLOCK IN THE KITCHEN STRIKES SIX) SIX 152 BEYOND
O'CLOCK.
(THEN THE FACT OF HIS FATHER'S CHANGED APPEARANCE 463 DYNAMO
STRIKES HIM FOR THE FIRST
AS HER HAND STRIKES THE FLOOR THE FINGERS RELAX 64 ELECTR
IT STRIKES WHEN IT HAS A MIND TO. 70 ELECTR
THE JEST STRIKES HIM AS BEING UNFEELING-- 132 ELECTR
THE ORCHESTRA AT THE CASINO STRIKES UP A WALTZ) 259 GGBROW
HE STRIKES ME AS THE ONLY BLOODY SENSIBLE MEDICO 1627 ICEMAN
EVER HEARD OF.
WHAT STRIKES ONE IMMEDIATELY IS HER EXTREME 12 JOURNE
NERVOUSNESS.
(SUDDENLY PUSHES FORWARD IMPUDENTLY AND STRIKES A 321 LAZARU
GRANDIOSE ATTITUDE)
STANDS ON IT AND STRIKES A GRANDIOSE POSE) 369 LAZARU
ACCEPT, IF IT STRIKES YOU AS A PROFITABLE 58 MANSNS
OPPORTUNITY.
MARCO STRIKES A GOOD LISTENING ATTITUDE SO HE WILL431 MARCOM
BE SURE NOT TO MISS A WORD
(JOSIE'S RIGHT ARM STRIKES WITH SURPRISING 4 MISBEG
SWIFTNESS AND HER BIG HAND LANDS ON
(HE STRIKES A MATCH ON THE SEAT OF HIS OVERALLS 16 MISBEG
AND LIGHTS HIS PIPE)
STRIKES A MATCH WHICH LIGHTS UP HIS FACE. 107 MISBEG
(HIS EYES FASTEN ON THE DATE AND SUDDENLY HE 38 POET
STRIKES THE TABLE WITH HIS FIST.)
BUT SOMETHING UNUSUAL IN HIS ATTITUDE STRIKES HER 58 POET
(HE STRIKES A POSE WHICH IS A VULGAR BURLESQUE OF 176 POET
HIS OLD BEFORE-THE-MIRROR ONE
STRIKES$
AT LAST THOU STRIKEST/...!) 447 DYNAMO
(THREE BELLS ARE HEARD STRIKING.) 458 CARIBE
HE BEARS A STRIKING RESEMBLANCE TO HIS SON, 567 CROSS
STRIKING HIM DEAD IN FIVE MINUTES, WHY WAS IT 424 DYNAMO
NOTHING HAPPENED$.
IN STRIKING CONTRAST TO THE WHITE COLUMNS OF THE 5 ELECTR
PORTICO.
(CHRISTINE MANNON IS A TALL STRIKING-LOOKING WOMAN 8 ELECTR
OF FORTY
HIS FACE IN THE CANDLELIGHT BEARS A STRIKING 93 ELECTR
RESEMBLANCE TO THAT OF THE PORTRAIT
SHE NOW BEARS A STRIKING RESEMBLANCE TO HER MOTHER137 ELECTR
IN EVERY RESPECT.
IT MUST ONCE HAVE BEEN EXTREMELY PRETTY, AND IS 12 JOURNE
STILL STRIKING.
HANDS IN EVERY TENSE ATTITUDE OF STRIKING, 291 LAZARU
CLUTCHING, TEARING ARE SEEN UPRAISED.
AT FIRST, HE POSES TO HIMSELF, STRIKING AN 57 POET
ATTITUDE--
HER FACE IS STRIKING, HANDSOME RATHER THAN PRETTY, 12 STRANG
THE BONE STRUCTURE PROMINENT.
SHE IS PRETTIER IN A CONVENTIONAL WAY AND LESS 48 STRANG
STRIKING AND UNUSUAL.
STRIKINGLY
ITS LARGE EYES OF A DEEP BLUE SET OFF STRIKINGLY 87 BEYOND
BY THE SUN-BRONZED COMPLEXION.
IS STRIKINGLY BROUGHT OUT. 91 ELECTR
IN THE LIGHTED ROOM, THE CHANGE IN HER IS 139 ELECTR
STRIKINGLY APPARENT.
HER BODY HAS GROWN STRIKINGLY VOLUPTUOUS AND 139 MANSNS
PROVOCATIVELY FEMALE.
SHE REMAINS STRIKINGLY HANDSOME AND HER PHYSICAL 26 STRANG
APPEAL IS ENHANCED BY HER
STRINDBERG
ENGELS, KROPOTKIN, MAX STIRNER, PLAYS BY IBSEN, 11 JOURNE
SHAW, STRINDBERG,
STRING
AND I'D RATHER HAVE SOME FLESH ON MY BONES THAN BE291 AHWILD
BUILT LIKE A STRING BEAN AND
HE IS LIKE A MONKEY ON A STRING. 251 DESIRE
HE CARRIES A STRING OF COD HEADS.) 498 DIFRNT
DIS BABY PLAYS OUT HIS STRING TO DE END AND WHEN 184 EJONES
HE QUITS,
HIS TAIL IS A PIECE OF STRING THAT WAS LEFT WHEN 268 GGBROW
HE BROKE LOOSE FROM JEHOVAH AND

STRING (CONT'D.)
STRAIGHT AS STRING/ 228 HA APE
I'LL SHOW HER IF SHE TINKS SHE--SHE GRINDS DE 231 HA APE
ORGAN AND I'M ON DE STRING, HUH$
HE OPENS IT AND TAKES OUT A SMALL PACKET OF 528 INZONE
LETTERS ALSO TIED UP WITH STRING.
AND UNTIES THE STRING WHICH IS WOUND TIGHTLY 528 INZONE
AROUND THE TOP.
(TAUNTINGLY) I WILL BET A STRING OF PEARLS 342 LAZARU
AGAINST YOUR BODY FOR A NIGHT THAT
STRINGIN'
THEY BEEN STRINGIN' YE/ 212 DESIRE
STRINGS
AND KEEPS TIED TO HER FATHER'S APRON STRINGS/ 216 AHWILD
IT WOULD BE BAD FOR HIM TO GET TIED TO YOUR APRON 49 ELECTR
STRINGS AGAIN.
(APRON STRINGS... 51 STRANG
HE WAS SO TIED TO HER APRON STRINGS...)) 99 STRANG
STRIP
(SCENE--A STRIP OF BEACH ALONG THE HARBOR. 275 AHWILD
DISTANT STRIP OF CORAL BEACH, WHITE IN THE 455 CARIBE
MOONLIGHT.
COMES BACK AND PULLS UP A STRIP OF FLOORING IN 219 DESIRE
UNDER STOVE.
YOU WILL HAVE TO STRIP LIFE NAKED, AND FACE IT. 91 MANSNS
AND STRIP YOURSELF NAKED AND ACCEPT YOURSELF AS 91 MANSNS
YOU ARE
STRIP OFF THEIR UPPER CLOTHES, UNTIE THE DEAD MEN,353 MARCOM
THIS ROOM IS AT THE FRONT PART OF HIS HOUSE WITH 3 STRANG
WINDOWS OPENING ON THE STRIP OF
AN' I'LL STRIP TO ANY MAN IN THE CITY AV LONDON 498 VOYAGE
WON'T DHRINK TO THAT TOAST.
STRIPE
HIS PANTS ARE BRIGHT RED WITH A LIGHT BLUE STRIPE 175 EJONES
DOWN THE SIDE.
STRIPED
WEARS A CHEAP BLUE SUIT, A STRIPED COTTON SHIRT 45 ANNA
WITH A BLACK TIE.
STRIPED COTTON SHIRT OPEN AT THE NECK. 513 DIFRNT
THEY ARE DRESSED IN STRIPED CONVICT SUITS, THEIR 194 EJONES
HEADS ARE SHAVEN,
STRIPES
WITH A BRIGHT-COLORED BAND IN STRIPES AROUND HIS 275 AHWILD
FINGER.)
STRIPPED
HE IS STRIPPED TO THE WAIST, HAS ON NOTHING BUT A 30 ANNA
PAIR OF DIRTY DUNGAREE PANTS.
REVEALING HIMSELF STRIPPED TO THE WAIST) 193 EJONES
STRIPPED NAKED EXCEPT FOR A WHITE CLOTH AROUND HIS319 GGBROW
LOINS, IS BROWN.
SOME WEAR SINGLETS, BUT THE MAJORITY ARE STRIPPED 207 HA APE
TO THE WAIST.
A LINE OF MEN, STRIPPED TO THE WAIST, IS BEFORE 222 HA APE
THE FURNACE DOORS.
HE IS STRIPPED TO THE WAIST, HIS COAT, SHIRT, 576 ICEMAN
UNDERSHIRT,
STRIPPED TO THE WAIST, 350 MARCOM
'TIS LUCKY HE'S SOBER OR SHE'D HAVE HIM STRIPPED 508 VOYAGE
TO HIS LAST HA'PENNY.
STRIPPING
YOU WATCHED HIM STARE AT YOUR BODY THROUGH YOUR 154 ELECTR
CLOTHES, STRIPPING YOU NAKED/
STRIPS
THEY ARE SEPARATED BY NARROW STRIPS OF LAWN, -0 DYNAMO
STRIPS OF MATTING, DYED SCARLET, 173 EJONES
HE STRIPS TO DISPLAY THAT SCAR ON HIS BACK HE GOT 593 ICEMAN
FROM A NATIVE SPEAR
THE MOSS STUFFING BETWEEN THE LOGS HANGS HERE AND 1 MANSNS
THERE IN STRIPS.
AND HERE AND THERE HAS STARTED TO PEEL BACK WHERE 48 STRANG
THE STRIPS JOIN.
SHE STRIPS OFF A NOTE FURTIVELY AND SHOVES IT INTO508 VOYAGE
HER BOSOM.
STRIVE
STRIVE AFTER WHAT YOUR HEART DESIRES/ 400 MARCOM
STRIVEN
IN HER FIGHT TO REGAIN CONTROL OF HER NERVES SHE 26 STRANG
HAS OVER-STRIVEN AFTER THE COOL
STRIVING
STRIVING TO RAISE THEMSELVES ON END, FAILING AND 189 EJONES
SINKING PRONE AGAIN.
MAN'S FEEBLE STRIVING TO UNDERSTAND HIMSELF, 150 ELECTR
(STRIVING TO CONCEAL HER EAGERNESS AND RELIEF-- 277 GGBROW
JUDICIALLY)
(VERY FRIGHTENED, BUT STRIVING TO PUT UP A BRAVE 349 MARCOM
FRONT)
STRIVING WITH ALL HIS MIGHT TO COMPOSE A POEM TO 358 MARCOM
DONATA.
(STRIVING PITIFULLY TO AROUSE HIS JEALOUSY) 414 MARCOM
STRIVING WITH ALL HER WILL TO KISS HIM ON THE 466 WELDED
LIPS.
SWALLOWING HARD SEVERAL TIMES AS IF HE WERE 472 WELDED
STRIVING TO GET CONTROL OF HIS
STROKE
THE SHOCK TO MY SYSTEM BROUGHT ON A STROKE WHICH, 627 ICEMAN
AS A DOCTOR,
I KNOW. THE FAMOUS ONE STROKE OF GOOD LUCK. 15 JOURNE
CUTS OFF ALL THE REMAINING WITH ONE STROKE) 312 LAZARU
IT'S A STROKE OF FORTUNE HE IS HERE. 38 POET
IT IS MORE AS IF A SUDDEN SHOCK OR STROKE HAD 152 POET
SHATTERED HIS COORDINATION
(TRYING A BOLD CLOSING STROKE--JOKINGLY) 122 STRANG
STROKE/ 182 STRANG
STROKE/ 182 STRANG
STROKE/ 182 STRANG
ONLY A BAD STROKE. 183 STRANG
STROKED
GREAT RACE YOU STROKED LAST JUNE-- 194 STRANG

STROKES

STROKES
(HE STROKES HER HAIR. 386 MARCOM
HOLY JOSEPH, HE'D HAVE HAD THREE PARALYTIC 123 MISBEG
STROKES/
(SHE STROKES HIS HAIR) WE HAVE THE WHOLE NIGHT-- 452 WELDED
UGLY WALLPAPER, DIRTY, STAINED, CRISS-CROSSED WITH470 WELDED
MATCH-STROKES.

STROKING
(HE PRESSES HER TO HIM, STROKING HER HAIR 92 BEYOND
TENDERLY.
(BENDING DOWN AND STROKING HER HAIR-- 142 BEYOND
(WITH TENDER OBSTANCY--STROKING HER HAIR) 150 BEYOND
(STRUKING HER HAIR) PUSS, PUSS, PUSS/ 498 DIFRNT
(AGAIN WITH TENDERNESS, STROKING HIS HAIR-- 90 ELECTR
SMILING)
BUT PLEASE DON'T STOP STRUKING MY ACHING BROW. 279 GGBROW
(TENDERLY, STROKING HIS HAIR MATERNALLY) 285 GGBROW
ABOUT THE TIME HE WAS STROKING THE CREW AND THE 153 STRANG
FELLOW WHO WAS NUMBER SEVEN
(GETS UP AND BENDS OVER HER PATERNALLY, STROKING 180 STRANG
HER HAIR WITH A STRANGE,

STROLL
(HE STARTS TO STROLL AROUND WITH EXAGGERATED 277 AHWILD
CARELESSNESS.
WHAT THE HELL'S TO BE SCARED OF, JUST TAKING A 687 ICEMAN
STROLL AROUND MY OWN YARDS
A NICE LITTLE STROLL FOR THE PIGS. THAT'S ALL. 49 MISBEG
STROLL THROUGH TO WALLOW HAPPILY ALONG THE SHORES 50 MISBEG
OF THE ICE POND.
THE RESULT OF THOSE BREAKS IN THE FENCE IS THAT 50 MISBEG
YOUR PIGS STROLL--
ARE YOU GOING FOR A MORNING STROLLS 44 POET
WHAT DO YOU SAY TO A LITTLE STROLL DOWN TO THE 122 STRANG
SHORE AND BACKS

STROLLED
SO I STROLLED ABOUT AND FINALLY CAME TO ROOST IN 723 ICEMAN
THE PARK.

STROLLING
(STROLLING A LITTLE TOWARD HER BUT NOT TOO FAR-- 278 AHWILD
CARELESSLY)

STROLLS
WATCHING HER MOTHER AS SHE STROLLS THROUGH THE 10 ELECTR
GARDEN TO THE GREENHOUSE.
LIKE THE BEAT OF YOUR HEART, AS HE STROLLS AWAY 19 MANSNS
FORGETTING YOU.
(HE STROLLS OVER TO THE WINDOW WHISTLING WITH AN 55 STRANG
EXAGGERATEDLY CASUAL AIR.

STRONG
THEM ARE MIGHTY STRONG WORDS. 194 AHWILD
I ONLY HOPE GETTING YOUR EXTRA STRONG ONE RIGHT 195 AHWILD
AFTER BREAKFAST WILL LET ME OFF
HONEST, I'M AWFULLY STRONG FOR YOU/ 240 AHWILD
HONEST, I'M SO STRONG FOR YOU I CAN HARDLY WAIT TO241 AHWILD
GET YOU UPSTAIRS/
AY BET YOU SHE'S FINE, GOOD, STRONG GEL, POOTY 12 ANNA
LIKE HELL/
AND GOOD GROB FOR MAKE YOU STRONG, HEALTHY GEL. 23 ANNA
IT AIN'T STRONG, NEITHER. 23 ANNA
GEE, YOU'RE SOME STRONG, ALL RIGHT. 35 ANNA
BUT HE WAS BIG AND STRONG--(POINTING TO BURKE) 57 ANNA
LIKE YOU/
(WHO APPEARS TO BE FIGHTING SOME STRONG INWARD 86 BEYOND
EMOTION--IMPULSIVELY)
AND I'D PROMISE MYSELF THAT WHEN I GREW UP AND WAS 89 BEYOND
STRONG, I'D FOLLOW THAT ROAD,
(WITH A HAPPY LAUGH) MY, BUT YOU'RE STRONG/ 92 BEYOND
THERE'S THE BOY THAT WOULD MAKE A GOOD, STRONG 97 BEYOND
SEAFARIN' MAN--
HE USED TO BE SO FINE-LOOKING AND STRONG. 115 BEYOND
(CLASPING JOHN'S HAND IN A STRONG GRIP) 500 DAYS
(ADMIRINGLY) YE'RE TOO BIG AN' TOO STRONG FUR 225 DESIRE
THAT,
HAIN'T THE SUN STRONG AN' HOTS 229 DESIRE
(WITH A CAOLING SMILE) YE'RE A STRONG MAN YET, 234 DESIRE
HAIN'T YES
THEY WA'N'T STRONG ENUF FUR THAT/ 236 DESIRE
TEN TIMES AS STRONG AN' FIFTY TIMES AS HARD AS 236 DESIRE
EBEN.
HARRIET'S BENNY, YOU WAS SO BIG AND STRONG AND 524 DIFRNT
HANDSOME.
HIS BODY IS STILL ERECT, STRONG AND VIGOROUS. 535 DIFRNT
(THERE IS A STRONG FLASH OF DISTANT LIGHTNING 427 DYNAMO
ONE SENSES A STRONG TRACE OF HER MOTHER'S 429 DYNAMO
SENTIMENTALITY.)
I GAVE HIM A STRONG HINT ON THE STREET TODAY THAT 432 DYNAMO
UPSET HIM.
(WITH SUDDEN STRONG REVULSION) (AND TO THINK 446 DYNAMO
(HOW STRONG HE'S GOTTEN/... 462 DYNAMO
VERY STRONG STILL IN SPITE OF HIS BEING MIDDLE- 197 EJONES
AGED.
HE GOTUM STRONG CHARM. 203 EJONES
I COOK UM MONEY, MAKE UM SILVER BULLET, MAKE UM 203 EJONES
STRONG CHARM, TOO.
HIM GUT STRONG CHARM. 203 EJONES
HAS A STRONG SUGGESTION OF RIBALD HUMOR. 6 ELECTR
HER BLACK EYEBROWS MEET IN A PRONOUNCED STRAIGHT 9 ELECTR
LINE ABOVE HER STRONG NOSE.
SHE HAS A STRONG CHIN AND A CAPABLE SMILING MOUTH. 12 ELECTR
CATCH HIM OFF GUARD SOMETIME AND PUT IT UP TO HIM 20 ELECTR
STRONG-- AS IF YOU KNOWED IT--
STRONG HANDS AND HIS DEEP VOICE.) 21 ELECTR
A MOUTH THAT CAN BE STRONG AND WEAK BY TURNS. 21 ELECTR
BUT I HAVE A STRONG SUSPICION IT WAS LOVE KILLED 71 ELECTR
EZRA/
I'VE HAD SUCH A STRONG FEELING AT TIMES THAT IT 161 ELECTR
WOULD RELIEVE YOUR MIND
EVERYTHING THAT'S STRAIGHT AND STRONG/ 167 ELECTR
CAN'T YOU BE STRONG, PETER$ 176 ELECTR

STRONG
(CONT'D.)
THE DEAD ARE TOO STRONG/ 177 ELECTR
HER FIGURE LITHE AND STRONG, 262 GGBROW
I AM STRONG/ 266 GGBROW
SHE IS A STRONG, CALM SENSUAL BLONDE GIRL OF 278 GGBROW
TWENTY OR SO,
BUT YOU'RE STRONG. 280 GGBROW
YOU'RE STRONG. 285 GGBROW
THREE STRONG SONS/ 292 GGBROW
SAY WHAT YOU LIKE, IT'S STRONG IF IT IS BAD/ 299 GGBROW
(PROUDLY) I'M GLAD TO HAVE THREE SUCH STRONG BOYS300 GGBROW
TO PROTECT ME.
WHY AM I NOT STRONG ENOUGH TO PERISH--OR BLIND 314 GGBROW
ENOUGH TO BE CONTENTS
THEY ARE ALL TALL, ATHLETIC, STRONG AND HANDSOME- 323 GGBROW
LOOKING.
CLIPPERS WID TALL MASTS TOUCHING THE SKY--FINE 213 HA APE
STRONG MEN IN THEM,
AND WIND OVER THE MILES OF SHINY GREEN OCEAN LIKE 214 HA APE
STRONG DRINK TO YOUR LUNGS.
GOTT, HE'S STRONG/ 232 HA APE
UN'Y A BUG IS STRONG ENOUGH FOR DAT/ 243 HA APE
A STRONG RESEMBLANCE TO THE TYPE ANARCHIST AS 574 ICEMAN
PORTRAYED, BOMB IN HAND,
HIS EYELIDS FLUTTER CONTINUALLY AS IF ANY LIGHT 577 ICEMAN
WERE TOO STRONG FOR HIS EYES.
I HAVE A STRONG HUNCH YOU'VE COME HERE EXPECTING 591 ICEMAN
SOMETHING OF ME.
I WAS SO TOUGH AND STRONG I GRAB AXLE OF OX WAGON 599 ICEMAN
MIT FULL LOAD
(A BIT HURT AT THIS) THAT'S GOING PRETTY STRONG, 609 ICEMAN
HARRY.
HIS EYES ARE CLEAR AND HE LOOKS HEALTHY AND STRONG615 ICEMAN
AS AN OX.)
HE'S GOT HIS REFORM WAVE GOIN' STRONG DIS MORNIN'/665 ICEMAN
NOT THAT HE ISN'T STRONG ENOUGH, BUT HE'D PERSPIRE 29 JOURNE
AND HE MIGHT CATCH MORE COLD.
YES, THIS TIME YOU CAN SEE HOW STRONG AND SURE OF 37 JOURNE
HERSELF SHE IS.
THERE WASN'T ONE OF US THAT DIDN'T HAVE LUNGS AS 79 JOURNE
STRONG AS AN OX.
HER BODY IS STRONG AND BEAUTIFUL. 337 LAZARU
HE IS STRONG. 341 LAZARU
HIS FACE IS STRONG AND PROUD 350 LAZARU
(THEN HE TURNS AWAY) MY MOTHER, LIVIA, THAT 355 LAZARU
STRONG WOMAN, GIVING BIRTH TO ME,
STRONG AS A GREAT MAN, AND I CONSENTED THAT MY 356 LAZARU
LOVE BE MURDERED.
I AM TOO STRONG/ 359 LAZARU
ONE GETS THE IMPRESSION OF A STRONG BODY, FULL- 2 MANSNS
BREASTED.
TOO LARGE AND STRONG FOR HER FACE, SHOWING BIG, 2 MANSNS
EVEN,
ITS BAD POINTS ARE THICK ANKLES, LARGE FEET, AND 2 MANSNS
BIG HANDS, BROAD AND STRONG,
HER HANDS ARE SMALL WITH THIN, STRONG, TAPERING 3 MANSNS
FINGERS, AND SHE HAS TINY FEET.
SOMEONE STRONG AND HEALTHY AND SANE, WHO DARES TO 3 MANSNS
LOVE AND LIVE LIFE GREEDILY
LIFE IS TOO STRONG FOR YOU/ 19 MANSNS
BUT IT'S NOT TOO STRONG FOR ME/ 19 MANSNS
I'M TOO STRONG FOR YOU/ 19 MANSNS
WE FOUND TWO LETTERS IN FATHER'S STRONG-BOX, 31 MANSNS
THE ONLY MORAL LAW HERE IS THE STRONG ARE 71 MANSNS
REWARDED, THE WEAK ARE PUNISHED.
IS STILL EXCEEDINGLY PRETTY, STRONG AND HEALTHY, 75 MANSNS
WITH THE SAME FIRM,
(DEFINITELY.) BUT SHE KNOWS I'M TOO STRONG-- 82 MANSNS
BUT REMEMBER SHE IS STRONG, TOO. 114 MANSNS
I CANNOT KEEP THEM SEPARATE--THEY ARE TOO STRONG 129 MANSNS
HERE IN THEIR HOME--
I AM GOOD BECAUSE I AM STRONG. 152 MANSNS
I WAS STRONG ENOUGH TO TAKE IT. 152 MANSNS
(SHE PICKS DEBORAH UP IN HER STRONG ARMS, AS IF 167 MANSNS
SHE WEIGHED NOTHING.
I'M STRONG ENOUGH FOR THE TWO OF US. 169 MANSNS
IF NEITHER IS STRONG ENOUGH TO DESTROY THE OTHER 172 MANSNS
BEFORE
THERE IS A STRONG GENERAL RESEMBLANCE BETWEEN BOTH358 MARCOM
OF THEM AND MARCO.
THE LEGATE, TEDALDO, A MAN OF SIXTY WITH A STRONG,358 MARCOM
INTELLIGENT FACE.
YOU STRONG MAN/ (SHE LAUGHS.) 375 MARCOM
YOU WILL BE BLESSED WITH STRONG SONS 385 MARCOM
THE WILL OF LIFE TO CONTINUE THE STRONG. 385 MARCOM
ISN'T IT TIME TO PROTECT YOUR SOVEREIGNTY BY 392 MARCOM
STRONG MEASURES$
(THEN PERSUASIVELY) THE WEST MAY NOT BE STRONG 422 MARCOM
BUT IT IS CRAFTY.
SHE HAS LONG SMOOTH ARMS, IMMENSELY STRONG, 3 MISBEG
ALTHOUGH NO MUSCLES SHOW.
SHE IS MORE POWERFUL THAN ANY BUT AN EXCEPTIONALLY 3 MISBEG
STRONG MAN.
STRONG AS A BULL, AND AS VICIOUS AND 15 MISBEG
DISRESPECTFUL.
MAYBE HE'D LIKE A FINE STRONG HANDSOME FIGURE OF A 28 MISBEG
WOMAN FOR A CHANGE.
SURE, YOU'RE STRONG ENOUGH TO REFORM HIM. 29 MISBEG
I LIKE THEM TALL AND STRONG AND VOLUPTUOUS, NOW, 43 MISBEG
WITH BEAUTIFUL BIG BREASTS.
I'VE A STRONG HEAD. 113 MISBEG
YOU'RE REAL AND HEALTHY AND CLEAN AND FINE AND 118 MISBEG
WARM AND STRONG AND KIND--
YOU HAVE A BEAUTIFUL STRONG BODY, TOO, JOSIE-- 119 MISBEG
IT'S STRONG AND KIND AND WARM--LIKE YOU. 130 MISBEG
HE WAS AS STRONG AS AN OX, AND ON A THOROUGHBRED 13 POET
HORSE, IN HIS UNIFORM,

STRONG

STRONG (CONT'D.)
HE'S STRONG AS A BULL STILL FOR ALL THE WHISKEY 15 POET
HE'S DRUNK.
HER FIGURE IS STRONG AND GRACEFUL, WITH FULL, FIRM 16 POET
BREASTS AND HIPS,
IN WHICH THERE IS A STRONG UNDERCURRENT OF 51 POET
ENTREATY.)
THEY WOULD SEE THAT YOU ARE STRONG AND AMBITIOUS 83 POET
THE QUALITY OF THE FORMIDABLY STRONG, 88 POET
A STRONG LILT OF BROGUE COMING INTO HIS VOICE.) 102 POET
IT'S TIED STRONG--STRONG AS DEATH--(HE CACKLES 579 ROPE
WITH SATISFACTION)
I'VE A HEAD FOR STRONG DRINK, AS YE KNOW, BUT HE 585 ROPE
HASN'T.
SLIM STRONG HIPS AND LONG BEAUTIFULLY DEVELOPED 12 STRANG
LEGS--
OH, LIPS ON MY LIPS, OH, STRONG ARMS AROUND ME, 16 STRANG
OH,
BUT STRONG ENOUGH FOR THIS LADYLIKE SOUL....) 36 STRANG
HEALTHY AND STRONG AND BEAUTIFUL... 51 STRANG
STRONG... 53 STRANG
SHE ALWAYS HAD STRONG PHYSICAL ATTRACTION FOR 78 STRANG
ME....
(THINKING) (STRONG HANDS LIKE GORDON'S... 79 STRANG
(THINKING CAUSTICALLY) (GORDON MYTH STRONG AS 80 STRANG
EVER...
SHE ALWAYS LOVED A STRONG, HEALTHY BODY. 100 STRANG
WELL, WHATEVER IT IS THAT HAS BOUND US TOGETHER, 139 STRANG
IT'S STRONG/...
((BUT YOU'RE GETTING TOO STRONG, SAM....)) 154 STRANG
NED WAS NEVER AS STRONG AS I WAS. 154 STRANG
HE'S SO STRONG AND HANDSOME(....)) 163 STRANG
(WITH HECTIC JOVIALITY) I HOPE IT'S STRONG 164 STRANG
POISON/
AND STRONG, WHOSE BLOOD IS BLOOD AND NOT A 177 STRANG
SOOTHING SYRUP/
IT IS A STRONG FACE BUT OF A STRENGTH WHOLLY 184 STRANG
MATERIAL IN QUALITY.
'TIS ONLY A BIT AV A WAY AN' WE'RE TWO STRONG MEN 504 VOYAGE
IF WE ARE DHRUNK.
SHE GROWS ERECT AND STRONG. 466 WELDED
I'M AS STRONG AS HE/ 466 WELDED
HER VOICE IS HEAVY AND SLOW WITH THE STRONG TRACE 470 WELDED
OF A FOREIGN INTONATION.
TOO WEAK FOR THE STRONG, TOO STRONG FOR THE WEAK. 476 WELDED
YOU'RE THE PERFECT DEATH--BUT I'M TOO STRONG, OR 476 WELDED
WEAK--
GO NOW BEFORE--BE STRONG/ 487 WELDED
(ALMOST FAUNTINGLY) THEN GO NOW--IF YOU'RE STRONG487 WELDED
ENOUGH.
(THEN DETERMINEDLY) BUT EVEN IF YOU 487 WELDED
MISUNDERSTAND, I MUST BE STRONG FOR YOU/

STRONGER
BILL--AS SOON AS SHE'S FEELING STRONGER. 504 DAYS
BUT JOHN IS THE STRONGER NOW AND, 564 DAYS
I'M GITTIN' STRONGER. 210 DESIRE
HE'S STRONGER--INSIDE--THAN BOTH O' YE PUT 210 DESIRE
TOGETHER/
WHY, YOU ACTUALLY FEEL STRONGER AND BETTER 301 GGBROW
ALREADY/
DEYIL HAVE TO MAKE DE CAGES STRONGER AFTER WE'RE 254 HA APE
TROU/
THERE ARE SOME WHO WOULD DESCRIBE THEM IN EVEN 152 MANSNS
STRONGER TERMS.
YOU ARE SO MUCH STRONGER/ 165 MANSNS
WE WOULD HAVE BEEN SO MUCH STRONGER/ 170 MANSNS
BUT THAT IS BECAUSE HE IS SO DIFFERENT FROM OTHER 387 MARCOM
MEN, SO MUCH STRONGER/
SHE HAS A STRONGER STOMACH. 51 MISBEG
AS IF IT WERE FORCED OUT OF HIM BY AN IMPULSE 104 STRANG
STRONGER THAN HIS WILL)
MUCH BIGGER AND STRONGER IN THE TWO MONTHS SINCE 147 STRANG
I'VE SEEN HIM.
(SIMPLY) SOMETHING STRONGER. 485 WELDED

STRONGER'N
YOU DON'T GAT IT IN HEAD AY'M SCARED OF HIM YUST 43 ANNA
'CAUSE HE VAS STRONGER'N AY
AN' I'LL HEV YE FUR IT YET 'CAUSE I'M STRONGER'N 240 DESIRE
YEW BE/

STRONGEST
BUT THERE HAVE BEEN TIMES WHEN I'VE HAD THE 557 DAYS
STRONGEST SENSE OF--
I WAS JEST TWENTY AN' THE STRONGEST AN' HARDEST YE236 DESIRE
EVER SEEN--
I'VE THE GRANDEST, STRONGEST LOVER THAT WAS EVER 158 MANSNS
OWNED BY A WOMAN/

STRONGLY
HE IS A TALL, STRONGLY-BUILT MAN DRESSED IN A 472 CARIBE
PLAIN BLUE UNIFORM.)
(THEN STRONGLY) WAAL--WHAT IF I DID NEED A HUMB 226 DESIRE
(MORE AND MORE STRONGLY AND ASSERTIVELY, 264 GGBROW
AS YOUR ATTORNEY, DEBORAH, I STRONGLY ADVISE YOU 36 MANSNS
TO CONSENT.
BUT NEVER SO STRONGLY BEFORE--THERE IS A FINALITY 74 MANSNS
IN THIS--
STRONGLY SUGGESTS ONE IN MOURNING. 24 STRANG
I'VE FELT IT TOO STRONGLY, EVER SINCE 185 STRANG
(STRONGLY) ALL MY LIFE I'VE WAITED TO BRING YOU 197 STRANG
PEACE.

STROVE
AND HOW THESE THINGS ARE, THOUGH YE STROVE TO 173 JOURNE
SHOW, SHE WOULD NOT KNOW."

STRUCK
IF THIS ISN'T THE DEADEST BURG I EVER STRUCK/ 238 AHWILD
(STRUCK BY THE WORD) YES, CLEAN. 36 ANNA
(THEN STRUCK BY SOME THOUGHT--LOOKS AT HIM WITH 42 ANNA
KEEN SUSPICION--

STRUGGLE

STRUCK (CONT'D.)
THE TWO, SUDDENLY STRUCK BY THE SAME PREMUNITION, 128 BEYOND
LISTEN TO IT BREATHLESSLY.
HE STRUCK ME AS A NICE OLD GUY. 499 DAYS
(FALLS TO HIS KNEES AS IF HE'D BEEN STRUCK--HIS 261 DESIRE
VOICE TREMBLING WITH HORROR)
(COWERING--AS IF HE HAD STRUCK HER) 546 DIFRNT
ONE IS STRUCK AT ONCE BY THE STRANGE IMPRESSION IT 9 ELECTR
GIVES IN REPOSE OF BEING NOT
ONE IS IMMEDIATELY STRUCK BY HER FACIAL 10 ELECTR
RESEMBLANCE TO HER MOTHER.
STRUCK BY SOMETHING IN HER MANNER. 10 ELECTR
ABOVE ALL, ONE IS STRUCK BY THE SAME STRANGE, 10 ELECTR
(STRUCK BY THIS) YES. 12 ELECTR
ONE IS STRUCK AT A GLANCE BY THE PECULIAR QUALITY 20 ELECTR
HIS FACE IN REPOSE HAS OF
IT WAS THE FIRST TIME HE'D EVER STRUCK HER. 26 ELECTR
ONE IS AT ONCE STRUCK BY THE STARTLING LIKENESS 28 ELECTR
BETWEEN HIM AND ADAM BRANT.
ONE IS IMMEDIATELY STRUCK BY THE RESEMBLANCE 36 ELECTR
BETWEEN HIS FACE
ONE IS IMMEDIATELY STRUCK BY THE MASK-LIKE LOOK OF 46 ELECTR
HIS FACE IN REPOSE.
(SUDDENLY STARING AT HAZEL, AS IF STRUCK BY AN 72 ELECTR
IDEA)
ONE IS AT ONCE STRUCK BY HIS STARTLING FAMILY 73 ELECTR
RESEMBLANCE TO EZRA MANNON AND
(THEN HE IS STRUCK BY WHAT SHE SAID ABOUT HIS 86 ELECTR
FATHER--WOUNDEDLY)
IT SIMPLY STRUCK ME HE LOOKS SO STRANGELY 94 ELECTR
FAMILIAR--
(STRUCK BY A SUDDEN IDEA--GRASPS HIS ARM) 100 ELECTR
ORIN STARTS AS IF HE'D BEEN STRUCK. 148 ELECTR
(STARTS BACK AS IF HE'D BEEN STRUCK, 166 ELECTR
(WINCING AS IF SHE HAD STRUCK HIM IN THE FACE, 177 ELECTR
(STRUCK BY AN IDEA, HE JUMPS TO HIS FEET) 299 GGBROW
AS THOUGH STRUCK BY A SUDDEN PARALYSIS OF THE 677 ICEMAN
WILL.
AS IF THIS SENTIMENT STRUCK A RESPONSIVE CHORD IN 701 ICEMAN
THEIR NUMBED MINDS.
(EDMUND JERKS AS IF HE'D BEEN STRUCK. 161 JOURNE
COWERING MOVEMENT AS THOUGH HE HAD STRUCK HER IN 14 MANSNS
THE FACE.)
(SHRINKS AS IF SHE'D BEEN STRUCK--STRICKENLY.) 186 MANSNS
WAS BURIED IN THE GRAVE OF ABU ABDALLAH WHERE IT 350 MARCOM
STRUCK HIM AS STRANGE)
AND STRUCK THEM DEAD AT MY FEET! 370 MARCOM
CRUEL WHEN SPRING IS SMITTEN BY WINTER, WHEN BIRDS436 MARCOM
ARE STRUCK DEAD IN FULL SONG.
NORA LOOKS AS IF HE HAD STRUCK HER.) 42 POET
IN SPITE OF HERSELF SHE IS SO STRUCK BY HIS 89 POET
APPEARANCE
(STRUCK BY THIS--EAGERLY) EXACTLY MY OPINION. 31 STRANG
(STRUCK BY HER TONE--LOOKS UP) 57 STRANG
(STRUCK--CONFUSEDLY) YES--THAT'S TRUE, ISN'T ITS 62 STRANG
(HE STARTS FOR THE DOOR--THEN STRUCK BY A SUDDEN 76 STRANG
THOUGHT, STOPS)
(WITH SAVAGE SATISFACTION) (THAT STRUCK 115 STRANG
HOME/....
DARRELL NEVER STRUCK ME AS A GALAHAD. 116 STRANG
(SUDDENLY STRUCK--THINKING) (IKNP, HE'S JEALOUS 146 STRANG
OF GORDON LIKING CHARLIE/....))
(STRUCK BY THIS--IMPERSONALLY INTERESTED) 166 STRANG
(STRUCK BY A SUDDEN THOUGHT) 476 WELDED

STRUCTURE
THE EXCITER SET ON THE MAIN STRUCTURE LIKE A HEAD 473 DYNAMO
WITH BLANK,
A ROUGH STRUCTURE OF BOULDERS, LIKE AN ALTAR, IS 199 EJONES
BY THE TREE.
IS A NARROW FIVE-STORY STRUCTURE OF THE TENEMENT 571 ICEMAN
TYPE,
BUT IS THIN AND PALE WITH THE BONE STRUCTURE 12 JOURNE
PROMINENT.
IN ITS GENERAL STRUCTURE AND PARTICULARLY IN ITS 274 LAZARU
QUALITY OF DETACHED SERENITY.
AS IF ADDITIONS HAD BEEN MADE AT DIFFERENT TIMES 139 MANSNS
TO AN ORIGINAL STRUCTURE
STRUCTURE AND UNUSUAL CHARACTER. 67 POET
HER FACE IS STRIKING, HANDSOME RATHER THAN PRETTY, 12 STRANG
THE BONE STRUCTURE PROMINENT,

STRUGGLE
HIS FACE BETRAYS THE TREMENDOUS STRUGGLE GOING ON 549 'ILE
WITHIN HIM.
THEN HESITATES, A GREAT STRUGGLE GOING ON IN HIS 241 AHWILD
MIND--
AFTER AN EMBARRASSED STRUGGLE THEY MANAGE TO KISS 20 ANNA
EACH OTHER.)
(AFTER AN INWARD STRUGGLE--TENSELY--FORCING OUT 74 ANNA
THE WORDS WITH DIFFICULTY)
HE SAW CLEARLY THAT THIS SITUATION WAS THE CLIMAX 538 DAYS
OF A LONG DEATH STRUGGLE
(AS THEY ENTER--DESPERATELY, AS IF HE WERE 564 DAYS
BECOMING EXHAUSTED BY THE STRUGGLE)
HIS FACE A STUDY OF THE STRUGGLE HE IS MAKING 247 DESIRE
THEY GRAPPLE IN WHAT BECOMES IMMEDIATELY A 255 DESIRE
MURDEROUS STRUGGLE.
BUT HIS EYES CANNOT CONCEAL AN INWARD STRUGGLE, 535 DIFRNT
DESPERATE STRUGGLE TO KILL THE SHRINKING BOY IN 457 DYNAMO
HIM.
HAS A TERRIBLE STRUGGLE WITH HIMSELF, THEN WHILE 285 GGBROW
SHE CONTINUES TO SPEAK,
THEN STOPS, FIGHTING SOME QUEER STRUGGLE WITHIN 215 HA APE
HIMSELF--
(THEY HAVE ALL PILED ON HIM AND, AFTER A FIERCE 232 HA APE
STRUGGLE,
BUT HE IS TOO FLABBERGASTED TO MAKE A STRUGGLE, 249 HA APE
ANYWAY.

STRUGGLE

STRUGGLE (CONT'D.)
FOR A MOMENT THE STRUGGLE WITH HIS GRIEF CAN BE SEEN IN HIS FACE. 293 LAZARU
IN A BEWILDERED, STUBBORN STRUGGLE TO CONTROL HIMSELF. 311 LAZARU
(HE FAINTS WITH THE VIOLENCE OF HIS STRUGGLE AND FALLS IN A LIMP HEAP.) 311 LAZARU
(HE SIGHS SADLY--THEN AFTER A STRUGGLE OVERCOMING 343 LAZARU HIMSELF--WITH EXULTANCE)
THAT HAS GIVEN UP THE STRUGGLE TO BE SEXUALLY ATTRACTIVE AND LOOK 189 STRANG
SHE DOES NOT STRUGGLE 460 WELDED
A QUEER STRUGGLE IS APPARENT IN HER FACE, HER WHOLE BODY. 469 WELDED
(AFTER A MOMENT'S DEFIANT STRUGGLE WITH HERSELF-- 469 WELDED FORLORNLY)
(BROKENLY) I--I DIDN'T MEAN--(THEN AFTER A STRUGGLE--WITH DESPERATE BITTERNESS) 487 WELDED

STRUGGLES
HE STARTS AND STRUGGLES. 241 AHWILD
(SEES THE DOLL UNDER THE TABLE AND STRUGGLES ON HER MOTHER'S LAP. 117 BEYOND
(SHE STRUGGLES TO HER FEET. 135 BEYOND
(SHE STRUGGLES BUT DRISCOLL HOLDS HER TIGHT.) 471 CARIBE
(HE STRUGGLES TOWARD THE COMPANIONWAY.) 572 CROSS
AND STRUGGLES TO A SITTING POSITION.) 256 DESIRE
KEEPING HIS LIPS ON HERS WHILE SHE STRUGGLES INSTINCTIVELY FOR A MOMENT. 459 DYNAMO
SHE STRUGGLES TO GET AWAY, FIERCELY BUT SILENTLY. 174 EJONES
(HE STRUGGLES TO A SITTING POSITION) 103 ELECTR
(AROUSED BY THE WORD TO FIERCE BUT FUTILE STRUGGLES) 250 HA APE
(IN SPITE OF HIS STRUGGLES, THIS IS DONE WITH GUSTO AND ECLAT. 250 HA APE
AT FIRST HE STRUGGLES FIERCELY, BUT SEEING THE USELESSNESS OF THIS, 525 INZONE
(SMITH STRUGGLES WITH ALL OF HIS STRENGTH 526 INZONE
(HE STRUGGLES DESPERATELY TO CONTROL HIMSELF.) 286 LAZARU
(HE STRUGGLES AGAIN.) 287 LAZARU
(STRUGGLES WITH HIMSELF--THEN CALLS) 364 LAZARU
(HE STRUGGLES THROUGH THE GATE. 376 MARCOM
(HE STRUGGLES FROM HIS CHAIR AND STANDS SWAYING 79 MISBEG
(STRUGGLES UP IN HIS CHAIR--ANGRILY) 81 MISBEG
STRUGGLES TO RELEASE HER HAND. 71 POET
(STRUGGLES WITH HERSELF, CONFUSED AND IMPOTENT, TRYING TO 465 WELDED

STRUGGLING
(HE HESITATES, STRUGGLING TO EXPRESS HIS MEANING) 547 'ILE
(STRUGGLING WITH HER LAUGHTER) 232 AHWILD
(STRUGGLING FIERCELY) LEGGO OF ME, YOU BIG MUTT/ 33 ANNA
(HOLDING THE STRUGGLING CHRIS AT ARM'S LENGTH-- 49 ANNA
(ANNA STANDS UP, HESITATING, STRUGGLING BETWEEN JOY AND FEAR. 68 ANNA
(STRUGGLING) DID I SAY I HADS 565 CROSS
(STRUGGLING TO HER FEET, RUNS TO THE DOOR, CALLING262 DESIRE AFTER HIM)
(STRUGGLING TO CONVEY HER MEANING) 495 DIFRNT
(STRUGGLING WITH A GUFFAW) OH, CUI/ 521 DIFRNT
(STRUGGLING AWAY FROM HIM) HEY, CUT IT OUT/ 433 DYNAMO
REUBEN'S FACE SHOWS THAT HE ALSO IS STRUGGLING WITH CONFLICTING EMOTIONS. 468 DYNAMO
(SEEING THE USELESSNESS OF STRUGGLING, GIVES WAY TO FRANTIC TERROR. 174 EJONES
(IN A FRENZY--STRUGGLING TO GET OUT OF BED) 61 ELECTR
(STRUGGLING WITH HIM) NO/ 113 ELECTR
(STRUGGLING) LET HIM COME/ 677 ICEMAN
STRUGGLING WITH HIMSELF. 165 JOURNE
STRUGGLING UP FROM HIS STUPOR. 168 JOURNE
THE SOUNDS OF BLOWS AS THEY MEET IN A PUSHING, 290 LAZARU WHIRLING, STRUGGLING MASS
(LOOKS DOWN UPON THE STRUGGLING MASS AND CRIES IN 291 LAZARU A RINGING VOICE)
(STRUGGLING TO FREE HERSELF.) 81 MANSNS
(STRUGGLING TO RESIST.) BUT I PROMISED HER-- 147 MANSNS
(STRUGGLING WITH HERSELF.) SHE KNOWS, EVEN IN HER164 MANSNS DREAMS/
(STRUGGLING WITH HERSELF.) NO/ 178 MANSNS
(STRUGGLING FUTILELY AS THEY RUSH HIM THROUGH THE 124 POET DOOR.)
(COOLLY, STRUGGLING TO KEEP CONTROL, IGNORING THESE REMARKS) 17 STRANG
(STRUGGLING WITH HIMSELF--GOES TO DOOR AND CALLS WITH AFFECTIONATE BLANDNESS) 22 STRANG
(STRUGGLING--SHAKENLY) NO, I THINK I'D BETTER-- (THINKING DESPERATELY) 104 STRANG
(STRUGGLING WITH HERSELF--THINKING PITIABLY) 116 STRANG
(THEN STRUGGLING WITH HIMSELF--REMORSEFULLY) 147 STRANG
(DOGGEDLY--STRUGGLING WITH HIMSELF) 169 STRANG
WEAKLY STRUGGLING TO SHAKE OFF HER HANDS, WITHOUT LOWERING THE GLASSES) 172 STRANG
(THINKING STRANGELY--STRUGGLING WITH HIMSELF) 172 STRANG
(STRUGGLING WEAKLY--THINKING) 173 STRANG
(THEN STRUGGLING WITH HIMSELF--WITH A DEFENSIVE SELF-MOCKERY) 187 STRANG
(STRUGGLING WITH HERSELF--HARSHLY) 477 WELDED
STRUGGLING WITH HIMSELF--DISJOINTEDLY) 482 WELDED

STRUGGLINGLY
(TERRIBLY CONFUSED--STRUGGLINGLY) 368 MARCOM

STRUMED
AS IF THE LEAVES WERE TINY HARPS STRUMMED BY THE 352 MARCOM MIND.

STRUNG
WHY, NOTHING, EXCEPT YOU'VE SEEMED A BIT HIGH-STRUNG THE PAST FEW DAYS. 16 JOURNE
MARY IS YOUNG AND PRETTY, NERVOUS AND HIGH-STRUNG.275 LAZARU
AND EFFICIENT POISE, BUT SHE IS REALLY IN A MORE HIGHLY STRUNG, 26 STRANG

STRUTS
HE STRUTS NOISELESSLY WITH A QUEER PRANCING STEP 200 EJONES

STRUTTING
DID YOU SEE YOUNG ANTHONY STRUTTING AROUND THE BALLROOM IN DIRTY FLANNEL PANTS$ 258 GGBROW

STUBBLE
A LANTERN JAW WITH A WEEK'S STUBBLE OF BEARD, 574 ICEMAN
AT RIGHT-REAR, THROUGH A FIELD OF HAY STUBBLE TO A 1 MISBEG PATCH OF WOODS.

STUBBORN
(WILDLY) BECAUSE IT'S A STUPID, STUBBORN REASON. 547 'ILE
(COLDLY) WELL, BE STUBBORN THEN FOR ALL I CARE. 32 ANNA
AN UNDERLYING, STUBBORN FIXITY OF PURPOSE 87 BEYOND
THOUGH HE WAS TOO STUBBORN EVER TO OWN UP TO IT. 116 BEYOND
BREAKING HIS HEART JUST ON ACCOUNT OF HIS STUBBORN116 BEYOND PRIDE.
SHE'S THAT STUBBORN AND SELF-WILLED. 118 BEYOND
MOONLIGHT, WINNOWED BY THE WIND WHICH MOANS IN THES55 CROSS STUBBORN ANGLES OF THE OLD
SHUCKS, EMMA, YOU'LL GIT ME TO LOSE PATIENCE WITH512 DIFRNT YOU IF YOU ACT THAT STUBBORN.
THE STUBBORN JAW WEAKENED BY A BIG INDECISIVE MOUTH. 422 DYNAMO
HIS JAW IS STUBBORN, HIS THICK HAIR CURLY AND REDDISH-BLOND. 422 DYNAMO
IT IS A THIN, SMALL MOUTH, DETERMINED AND STUBBORN.422 DYNAMO
A STOUT, SELF-IMPORTANT OLD MAN WITH A STUBBORN 68 ELECTR OPINIONATED EXPRESSION.
BUT THERE IS AN AIR OF STUBBORN RESOLUTION ABOUT 171 ELECTR HER AS SHE MAKES UP HER MIND
WHAT'S THE USE OF BEING STUBBORN, NOW WHEN IT'S ALL OVER AND DEADS 691 ICEMAN
IT HAS THE STUBBORN SET OF AN OBSESSED DETERMINATION. 703 ICEMAN
EVELYN WAS STUBBORN AS ALL HELL ONCE SHE'D MADE UP710 ICEMAN HER MIND.
EVELYN WAS STUBBORN AS HELL. 713 ICEMAN
BUT HE'S STUBBORN AS HELL, INSIDE AND WHAT HE DOES IS WHAT HE WANTS TO DO. 35 JOURNE
(WITH A STUBBORN, BITTERLY RESENTFUL LOOK.) 42 JOURNE
IN AN EXPRESSION OF BLANK, STUBBORN DENIAL.) 63 JOURNE
(HER FACE AGAIN SETS IN STUBBORN DEFIANCE.) 69 JOURNE
(HER FACE SETTING INTO THAT STUBBORN DENIAL AGAIN.) 70 JOURNE
(HER STRANGE, STUBBORN DEFENSE COMES BACK INSTANTLY. 85 JOURNE
(THEN, CATCHING HERSELF, WITH AN INSTANT CHANGE TO 88 JOURNE STUBBORN DENIAL.)
(WITH STUBBORN BLANKNESS.) WHAT ARE YOU TALKING ABOUTS 103 JOURNE
HER FACE SETS IN STUBBORN DEFENSIVENESS-- RESENTFULLY.) 108 JOURNE
(THEN WITH A BITTER, STUBBORN PERSISTENCE.) 119 JOURNE
IN A BEWILDERED, STUBBORN STRUGGLE TO CONTROL HIMSELF. 311 LAZARU
IT ISN'T LIKE YOU TO ACT SO GRUDGING AND STUBBORN-- 67 MANSNS
(HE DOES NOT SEEM TO HEAR.) STILL SO VAIN AND STUBBORNS 128 MANSNS
ITS STUBBORN CHARACTER BECOME REPELLENTLY SENSUAL,139 MANSNS RUTHLESSLY CRUEL AND GREEDY.
YOU WERE SUCH A STUBBORN GREEDY LITTLE BOY. 184 MANSNS
(MARCO STANDS PUZZLED, IRRITATED, LOOKING STUBBORN, FRIGHTENED AND FOOLISH. 397 MARCOM
COME ON, NOW, DON'T BE STUBBORN WITH ME. 54 MISBEG
COME NOW, DON'T BE STUBBORN. 134 POET
AND REMAINS STANDING BY THE DOORWAY IN STUBBORN SILENCE.) 588 ROPE
DEFIANT EYES. HER FACE SET IN AN EXPRESSION OF STUBBORN RESOLVE. 12 STRANG
BUT INCREASINGLY STUBBORN AND SELF-OPINIONATED. 159 STRANG

STUBBORNNESS
(BUT SHE SEES THE LOOK OF OBSESSED STUBBORNNESS ON HER FATHER'S FACE 66 ANNA

STUBBORNLY
(HIS JAW SET STUBBORNLY) IT AIN'T THAT, ANNIE. 547 'ILE
(LOOKING AT ANDREW OVER HIS WIFE'S SHOULDER-- STUBBORNLY) 107 BEYOND
(EMMA STARES STUBBORNLY BEFORE HER. 510 DIFRNT
(HER FACE HARDENING STUBBORNLY.) 116 JOURNE
(THEN STUBBORNLY.) BUT IT'S JUST A SUMMER COLD. 122 JOURNE
(STUBBORNLY.) SO HE WAS. 127 JOURNE
IT'S JUST THAT YOU STUBBORNLY REFUSED TO BELIEVE THAT. 110 MANSNS
(STUBBORNLY) THERE IS NO GOD BUT ALLAH/ 368 MARCOM
(STUBBORNLY.) IT'S NO LIE. 24 POET
(STANDS STUBBORNLY AND BEGINS TO INTONE) 584 ROPE
ON THE VERGE OF TEARS YET STUBBORNLY DETERMINED) 149 STRANG

STUBBORNNESS
HER MOUTH AND CHIN ARE HEAVY, FULL OF A SELF-WILLED STUBBORNNESS. 494 DIFRNT
I CAN'T FIGURE IT--UNLESS IT'S JUST YOUR DAMNED PIGHEADED STUBBORNNESS/ 704 ICEMAN
(STIFFENS INTO SCORNFUL, DEFENSIVE STUBBORNNESS.) 118 JOURNE

STUBBY
WITH THICK, STUBBY FINGERS. 2 MANSNS
BUT SHE HAS LARGE FEET AND BROAD, UGLY HANDS WITH STUBBY FINGERS. 16 POET
A TWO WEEKS' GROWTH OF STUBBY PATCHES OF BEARD COVERS HIS JAWS AND CHIN. 578 ROPE

STUCCO
THE FIFE HOUSE, A SMALL BROWNISH-TINTED MODERN STUCCO BUNGALOW TYPE. -0 DYNAMO

STUCK
STUCK IN IT LIKE A FLY IN MOLASSES/ 536 'ILE
I--IT JUST STUCK IN MY MEMORY SOMEHOW. 199 AHWILD

STUCK (CONT'D.)

AS ONE GETS STUCK ON A DECENT GIRL AT HIS AGE-- 205 AHWILD
(MORE WORRIEDLY) I THOUGHT HE WAS REALLY STUCK ON205 AHWILD HER--
BUT ALWAYS GETS STUCK AND TURNS TO ANOTHER.) 259 AHWILD
NIGHT IN THE FOG, AND AFTERWARDS SEEING THAT YOU 59 ANNA WAS STRAIGHT GOODS STUCK ON ME,
AND THAT WAS WHY I GOT STUCK ON YOU, TOO. 59 ANNA
TO COLLEGE HAD MADE YOU STUCK-UP, 91 BEYOND
A BALL OF UNUSED YARN, WITH NEEDLES STUCK THROUGH 113 BEYOND IT,
I COULDN'T BE CONTENT ANY MORE STUCK HERE LIKE A 138 BEYOND FLY IN MOLASSES.
I MADE MONEY HAND OVER FIST AS LONG AS I STUCK TO 156 BEYOND LEGITIMATE TRADING.
AND WE'VE STUCK TOGETHER EVER SINCE THROUGH GOOD 480 CARDIF LUCK AND BAD.
AND I'LL BET ANYTHING HE'S AS STUCK ON YOU AS HE 522 DIFRNT EVER WAS--THE OLD FOOL/
(ROUGHLY) WELL, HE'S STILL STUCK ON YOU, AIN'T 532 DIFRNT HE$
HE'S STUCK ON YOU AND YOU KNOW IT. 533 DIFRNT
YOU DIDN'T THINK I WAS REALLY STUCK ON YOU, DID 546 DIFRNT YOU$
IT'S STUDYING THIS STUFF GIVES THOSE STUCK-UP 429 DYNAMO ENGINEERS THEIR DIPLOMAS...
I NEVER STUCK TO ONE LONG, I WANTED TO KEEP MOVING461 DYNAMO AND SEE EVERYTHING--
PAGAN TEMPLE FRONT STUCK LIKE A MASK ON PURITAN 17 ELECTR GRAY UGLINESS/
IT STUCK IN MY MIND--CLEAN-SCRUBBED AND 54 ELECTR WHITEWASHED--A TEMPLE OF DEATH/
THAT IS SAT IS STUCK IN HIS BELT UNDER HIS CLOAK 114 ELECTR AND GOES INTO THE STATEROOM.
WITH COLORED RAGS AROUND THEIR MIDDLES AND FLOWERS145 ELECTR STUCK OVER THEIR EARS$
HE SAID YOU'D HAVE MADE A GOOD ARCHITECT, IF YOU'D271 GGBROW STUCK TO IT.
THEY WANT AN ORIGINAL TOUCH OF MODERN NOVELTY 275 GGBROW STUCK IN TO LIVEN IT UP
I STUCK IT TILL I WAS EIGHTEEN BEFORE I TOOK A 14 HUGHIE RUN-OUT POWDER.
I GOT STUCK ON A WHORE AND WANTED DOUGH TO BLOW IN663 ICEMAN ON HER AND HAVE A GOOD TIME/
SHE ALWAYS STUCK UP FOR ME. 710 ICEMAN
NOT A BIT STUCK-UP OR VAIN. 105 JOURNE
YOU SHOULD HAVE STUCK AROUND WITH ME, KID. 160 JOURNE
YOU SHOULD HAVE STUCK WITH ME, KID. 161 JOURNE
AND STUCK OUT YOUR BEAUTIFUL BREASTS YOU KNOW HE 82 MISBEG ADMIRES,
IS BUT A HOVEL STUCK IN A CABBAGE PATCH. 112 POET
SCREAMING LIKE A STUCK PIG/ 155 POET
WELL, THERE THEY WERE STUCK IN THE PROFESSOR'S 52 STRANG HOUSE...
(HE SPRINGS TO HIS FEET AS IF THIS IDEA WERE A PIN 67 STRANG STUCK IN HIM--

STUD

WHEN THE HORSES WON'T RUN FOR ME, THERE'S DRAW OR 15 HUGHIE STUD.
I'D TELL HIM I WIN TEN GRAND FROM THE BOOKIES, AND 32 HUGHIE TEN GRAND AT STUD,

STUDDED

(HE TAKES FROM HIS POCKET A HEAVY BRACELET THICKLY561 CROSS STUDDED WITH STONES AND
STUDDED WITH PIMPLES FROM INGROWING HAIRS. 8 HUGHIE

STUDENT

AND BESIDES, I'M NOT KEEN ON BEING A STUDENT, 83 BEYOND
I WAS A BRILLIANT STUDENT AT LAW SCHOOL, TOO. 595 ICEMAN
BUT I DID MAKE MYSELF A BRILLIANT STUDENT, 595 ICEMAN
AND HE KNOWS THAT I REALLY WAS A BRILLIANT LAW 644 ICEMAN STUDENT.
BOTH SAID I HAD MORE TALENT THAN ANY STUDENT THEY 104 JOURNE REMEMBERED.
BECAUSE HE WAS SO LIKABLE AND SUCH A BRILLIANT 110 JOURNE STUDENT.

STUDENTS

I'VE NEVER PRACTICED BUT I WAS ONE OF THE MOST 607 ICEMAN BRILLIANT STUDENTS IN LAW SCHOOL.
ALL THE STUDENTS WERE WISE AND I HAD THEM ROLLING 39 MISBEG IN THE AISLES AS I SHOWED
AS MARSDEN IS ONE OF HIS OLD STUDENTS, WHOM, IN 7 STRANG ADDITION,
ONLY STUDENTS HERE FOR HER... 22 STRANG

STUDIED

BUT YOU STUDIED TO BECOME AN OFFICER/ 132 BEYOND
WITH STUDIED CARELESSNESS, WHISTLING A TUNE, 187 EJONES
WITH A STUDIED CASUALNESS) 17 ELECTR
WITH TOUCHES OF STUDIED CARELESSNESS, 21 ELECTR
THEY BOTH STARE AT DION, WHO, WITH A STUDIED 260 GGBROW CARELESSNESS,
THESE HAVE THE QUALITY OF BELONGING TO A STUDIED 13 JOURNE TECHNIQUE.
I STUDIED SHAKESPEARE AS YOU'D STUDY THE BIBLE. 150 JOURNE
THE STUDIED ALOOFNESS OF AN IRONICALLY AMUSED 68 POET SPECTATOR.
AND EVER SINCE THEN I'VE STUDIED HER CASE. 35 STRANG
I HAVE STUDIED TO CURE THE BODY'S UNHAPPINESS... 86 STRANG

STUDIES

FATHER BAIRD LOOKS UP AND STUDIES JOHN'S FACE 543 DAYS SEARCHINGLY, HOPEFULLY.)
THE KAAN STUDIES HIS SULLEN BUT RELIEVED FACE WITH380 MARCOM AMUSEMENT)
GORDON WAS ALWAYS NEAR THE TOP IN HIS STUDIES, 121 STRANG WASN'T HE$

STUDIO

LEADING DOWN TO THE STUDIO FLOOR. 443 WELDED

STUDIOUS

IS THAT OF A RETIRING, STUDIOUS NATURE. 6 STRANG

STUDY

STUDIOUSLY

(HE TAKES OFF HIS SHOES, HIS EYES STUDIOUSLY 188 EJONES AVOIDING THE FOREST.

STUDY

"A STUDY FOR A MATE'S C'TIFICATE RIGHT OFF-- 96 BEYOND
ARE YOU GOING UP TO YOUR STUDY FOR A WHILE$ 530 DAYS
YOU JUST SEND UNCLE AND ME OFF TO MY STUDY. 533 DAYS
YOU CAN GO WITH YOUR UNCLE UP TO YOUR STUDY-- 540 DAYS
FATHER BAIRD GOES INTO THE HALL, TURNING LEFT TO 541 DAYS GO UPSTAIRS TO THE STUDY.
FOLLOWING FATHER BAIRD AND JOHN TO THE STUDY.) 541 DAYS
(SCENE--JOHN LOVING'S STUDY ON THE UPPER FLOOR OF 541 DAYS THE APARTMENT.
(SHE WARDS HIM OFF AND STEPS PAST HIM INTO THE 548 DAYS STUDY.
BUT THIS SCENE ALSO REVEALS THE INTERIOR OF ELSA'S553 DAYS BEDROOM AT LEFT OF STUDY.)
THE STUDY IS SHOWN AS IN PRECEDING SCENE, 553 DAYS
(THEY LEAD JOHN TO THE DOOR TO THE STUDY AT RIGHT.555 DAYS
LOVING, COME INTO YOUR STUDY. 555 DAYS
THEY LEAD JOHN TO THE CHAISE-LONGUE AT RIGHT, 555 DAYS FRONT, OF STUDY.
IN THE STUDY, FATHER BAIRD STARTS TO PACE BACK AND558 DAYS FORTH, FROWNING,
TURNING BACK INTO THE STUDY BUT LEAVING THE 561 DAYS COMMUNICATING DOOR AJAR,
(HE GOES THROUGH THE DOOR TO THE STUDY, MOVING 563 DAYS LIKE ONE IN A TRANCE,
(FATHER BAIRD HAS COME IN FROM THE STUDY AND IS 563 DAYS APPROACHING THE BED.
(JOHN GOES OUT THE DOOR IN REAR OF STUDY AND 563 DAYS (SCENE IS FORCED OUT BEFORE HIM.)
HER STARING EYES ON THE DOORWAY TO THE STUDY.) 563 DAYS
HIS FACE A STUDY OF THE STRUGGLE HE IS MAKING, 247 DESIRE
I'VE GOT TO STUDY MY ALGEBRA. 443 DYNAMO
(SCENE--IN THE HOUSE--EZRA MANNON'S STUDY. 28 ELECTR
THE STUDY IS A LARGE ROOM WITH A STIFF, AUSTERE 28 ELECTR ATMOSPHERE.
HE IS EXACTLY LIKE THE PORTRAIT IN HIS STUDY, 46 ELECTR WHICH WE HAVE SEEN IN ACT TWO,
HIS FACE LOOKS EXACTLY LIKE EZRA'S IN THE PAINTING 79 ELECTR IN THE STUDY,
LIKE THE STUDY, BUT MUCH LARGER, 79 ELECTR
(SCENE--THE SAME AS ACT TWO OF "HOMECOMING"--EZRA 93 ELECTR MANNON'S STUDY.
THEN ORIN'S HORRIFIED CRY COMES FROM THE 123 ELECTR STUDY AS HE FINDS HIS MOTHER'S B
WHERE EZRA MANNON'S STUDY IS. 123 ELECTR
(STRANGELY) I'VE JUST BEEN IN THE STUDY. 139 ELECTR
(SCENE--SAME AS ACT THREE OF "THE HUNTED"--EZRA 149 ELECTR MANNON'S STUDY--
LAVINIA ENTERS FROM THE HALL IN THE REAR, HAVING 157 ELECTR JUST COME FROM THE STUDY.
(HE RUSHES OUT AND CAN BE HEARD GOING ACROSS THE 160 ELECTR HALL TO THE STUDY.
(TURNING TO ORIN--SHARPLY) I THOUGHT YOU WERE IN 162 ELECTR THE STUDY.
I'M JUST GOING IN THE STUDY TO CLEAN MY PISTOL. 167 ELECTR
(THERE IS A MUFFLED SHOT FROM THE STUDY ACROSS THE167 ELECTR HALL.)
THERE IS NO ANSWER BUT THE SOUND OF THE STUDY 167 ELECTR DOOR BEING SHUT.
AFTER HE'S THROUGH COLLEGE, BILLY MUST STUDY FOR A258 GGBROW PROFESSION OF SOME SORT,
GOING TO HAVE HIM STUDY ARCHITECTURE AFTERWARDS, 260 GGBROW TOO, SO'S HE CAN HELP EXPAND
HE WOULD HAVE SENT ME TO EUROPE TO STUDY AFTER I 104 JOURNE GRADUATED FROM THE CONVENT.
I STUDIED SHAKESPEARE AS YOU'D STUDY THE BIBLE. 150 JOURNE
IN THE MIDDLE OF THE LEFT WALL IS A CLOSED DOOR 43 MANSNS LEADING INTO SIMON'S STUDY.
BUT WHAT A WAY FOR ME--AND YOU IN YOUR STUDY 44 MANSNS TRYING TO WRITE/
THERE I WAS AT NIGHT IN MY STUDY TRYING TO 46 MANSNS CONVINCE MYSELF OF THE POSSIBILITY OF
BUT YOU WOULD SEND ME INTO MY STUDY TO WORK ON IT 46 MANSNS LIKE A REGULAR SLAVE-DRIVER/
A FRANK STUDY OF THE TRUE NATURE OF MAN AS HE 47 MANSNS REALLY IS AND NOT AS HE PRETENDS
(HE TURNS AND OPENS THE STUDY DOOR AND BOWS CURTLY 52 MANSNS TO JOEL TO PRECEDE HIM.
I SUGGEST SIMON TAKE YOU TO HIS STUDY. 52 MANSNS
(HE STARTS FOR THE STUDY DOOR AT THE LEFT, JOEL 52 MANSNS FOLLOWING.)
(SHE STOPS ABRUPTLY AND SITS DOWN AGAIN AS THE 57 MANSNS DOOR FROM THE STUDY IS OPENED AND
IN THE MIDDLE OF THE REAR WALL IS THE DOOR TO 117 MANSNS SIMON'S STUDY.
I'M GOING TO MY STUDY. 130 MANSNS
(HE STRIDES TO THE STUDY DOOR AND OPENS IT--THEN 130 MANSNS PAUSES AND MURMURS.)
HE TURNS QUICKLY, GOES INTO HIS STUDY, AND LOCKS 131 MANSNS THE DOOR.
(UNEASILY.) AND THEY'RE STILL HAPPENING--EVEN IF 136 MANSNS HE IS LOCKED IN HIS STUDY.
I HEARD YOU FROM MY STUDY QUARRELING OUT HERE, 174 MANSNS
YOU COULD NOT POSSIBLY HAVE HEARD US IN YOUR 174 MANSNS STUDY.
(WITH A QUIET SMILE) I SHALL STUDY THIS 379 MARCOM APOTHEOSIS WITH UNWEARIED INTEREST,
DID THEIR POPE MEAN THAT A FOOL IS A WISER STUDY 381 MARCOM FOR A RULER OF FOOLS.
KUBLAI SITS IN A SOMBER STUDY, FROWNING AND BITING388 MARCOM HIS LIPS.
AND HIS SOUL MAY BE BORN AND THAT WILL MAKE A VERY388 MARCOM INTERESTING STUDY--
THE SAME AS SCENE ONE, PROFESSOR LEEDS' STUDY. 24 STRANG

STUDY

STUDY (CONT'D.)
(CONFUSED--HUSKILY) IN HERE--I'M IN THE STUDY, NINA. 26 STRANG
THE PROFESSOR'S STUDY AGAIN. 66 STRANG
(I BET THE OLD MAN TURNS OVER IN HIS GRAVE AT MY 67 STRANG
WAITING AIDS IN HIS STUDY...
((WHAT A MESS THEY'VE MADE OF THIS STUDY... 74 STRANG
I'D LIKE A CHANCE TO STUDY HIM MORE CLOSELY....)) 76 STRANG
AS WAS THE PROFESSOR'S STUDY IN THE LAST ACT. 90 STRANG
STUDY/... 105 STRANG
(VERY HURRIEDLY) YES--GOING TO STUDY OVER THERE 106 STRANG
FOR A YEAR OR SO.
HE'S GOING OVER FOR A YEAR OR SO TO STUDY. 107 STRANG
I DIDN'T STUDY/ 130 STRANG
(PERFUNCTORILY) BIOLOGY MUST BE AN INTERESTING 147 STRANG
STUDY.
ON THE WALL, A FRAMED PORTRAIT STUDY OF ELEANOR. 462 WELDED
(WITH A WRY SMILE) STUDY YOUR PART. 469 WELDED

STUDYING
HE IS SILENT, STUDYING HIS SOUP PLATE, AS IF IT 224 AHWILD
WERE SOME STRANGE ENIGMA.
HER EYES STUDYING CABOT CRAFTILY.) 234 DESIRE
(AFTER A PAUSE IN WHICH SHE ROCKS BACK AND FORTH 511 DIFRNT
STUDYING HER DAUGHTER'S FACE--
ALL THE EVENINGS I THOUGHT HE WAS HERE STUDYING...427 DYNAMO
IT'S STUDYING THIS STUFF GIVES THOSE STUCK-UP 429 DYNAMO
ENGINEERS THEIR DIPLOMAS...
I'M STUDYING A LOT OF SCIENCE. 458 DYNAMO
I'M CONSIDERING STUDYING LAW. 150 ELECTR
(MOCKINGLY) STUDYING THE LAW OF CRIME AND 150 ELECTR
PUNISHMENT, AS YOU SAW.
YOU SEE, I BEGAN STUDYING AMERICAN HISTORY. 648 ICEMAN
(STUDYING HIM KEENLY--AMUSED) 29 STRANG
ONLY FOR THE OBJECTIVE SATISFACTION OF STUDYING 33 STRANG
HIS OWN AND THEIR REACTIONS.

STUFF
THIS STUFF DOESN'T MEAN ANYTHING TO ME-- 202 AHWILD
THAT STUFF IS WARM--TOO DAMNED WARM, IF YOU ASK 205 AHWILD
ME/
GEE, THAT'S GOOD STUFF, ALL RIGHT. 243 AHWILD
THAT'S THE OLD STUFF, KID. 245 AHWILD
RICHARD HAD JUST COPIED STUFF OUT OF BOOKS, AND 292 AHWILD
KIDS WOULD BE KIDS AND SO ON.
STUFF I COULDN'T MAKE HEAD OR TAIL TO. 18 ANNA
AND A LOT OF CRAZY STUFF ABOUT STAYING AWAY FROM 18 ANNA
THE SEA--
BUT THOSE COUSINS WAS ALWAYS TALKING CROPS AND 27 ANNA
THAT STUFF.
I'M NEEDIN' THAT--AND 'TIS FINE STUFF. 31 ANNA
THE MEN I KNOW DON'T PULL THAT ROUGH STUFF WHEN 32 ANNA
LADIES ARE AROUND.
(WITH A RELIEVED SMILE) OH--THE OLD STUFF, EH$ 50 ANNA
SAY, WHERE DO YOU GET THAT STUFF$ 55 ANNA
(WITH AN EXASPERATED LAUGH) GEE, WON'T YOU EVER 65 ANNA
CAN THAT STUFF$
I SUPPOSE IT'S THAT YEAR IN COLLEGE GAVE YOU A 82 BEYOND
LIKING FOR THAT KIND OF STUFF.
'TIS FOINE RUM, THE RALE STUFF. 462 CARIBE
WHERE D'YOU GET THAT STUFF$ 465 CARIBE
WHY LIMIT THE STUFF OF DREAMS$ 560 CROSS
POINTING OUT TO SEA--MOCKING ME WITH STUFF LIKE 566 CROSS
THIS/
WANTIN' TO SWAP FOR TERBACCER AND OTHER TRADIN' 502 DIFRNT
STUFF WITH STRAW MATS AND
(WITH A GRIN) AND IF YOU FALL FOR THAT JAZZ 520 DIFRNT
STUFF,
BOASTFULLY) WHERE DID YOU GET THAT STUFF ABOUT 544 DIFRNT
ASKIN' HIM NOT TO HURT ME$
IF THEY MEAN THAT STUFF ABOUT KICKIN' ME OUT OF 546 DIFRNT
HOME--
IT'S STUDYING THIS STUFF GIVES THOSE STUCK-UP 429 DYNAMO
ENGINEERS THEIR DIPLOMAS...
HE CAN'T GET AWAY WITH THAT STUFF WITH ME/...)) 432 DYNAMO
(CONFUSED) AW, MOM, WHERE D'YOU GET THAT STUFF$ 432 DYNAMO
THE OLD STUFF/...)) 459 DYNAMO
AND THEN YOU WATCH ME CONVERT HER OVER FROM THAT 461 DYNAMO
OLD GOD STUFF OF HIS/
SURE, THAT'S THE STUFF/...)) 472 DYNAMO
THE OLD PRAYER STUFF/...)) 474 DYNAMO
ALL THIS STUFF SCARES ME. 484 DYNAMO
WHAT WAS THAT STUFF YOU WROTE ABOUT SOME CAPTAIN 76 ELECTR
BRANT COMING TO SEE MOTHER$
IF YOU THINK YOU'RE GOING TO TELL ME A LOT OF 96 ELECTR
CRAZY STUFF ABOUT MOTHER,
IT'S ONLY SOME STUFF SHE TAKES TO MAKE HER SLEEP/ 97 ELECTR
(JUBILANTLY) BILLY'S GOT THE STUFF IN HIM TO WIN,259 GGBROW
I THINK THE =RUBAIYAT'S= GREAT STUFF, DON'T YOU$ 262 GGBROW
WHERE D'YUH GET DAT BEER STUFF$ 209 HA APE
NIX ON DAT OLD SAILING SHIP STUFF/ 210 HA APE
YUH DON'T GET DE STUFF. 215 HA APE
DAT'S NEW STUFF/ 215 HA APE
DAT'S DE STUFF/ 217 HA APE
DAT'S DE STUFF/ 224 HA APE
(APPROVINGLY) THAT'S THE STUFF/ 224 HA APE
TINK I'M GOIN' TO LET HER GIT AWAY WIT DAT STUFF$ 231 HA APE
NOT DAT KIND OF STUFF-- 231 HA APE
I DON'T STAND FOR DAT STUFF FROM NOBODY. 231 HA APE
AW, CUT DE SOB STUFF/ 235 HA APE
(CYNICALLY) DE OLD STUFF, I BET. 241 HA APE
THERE'S YOUR APE STUFF AGAIN. 244 HA APE
YOU SEEM TO BE WISE TO A LOT OF STUFF NONE OF US 247 HA APE
KNOWS ABOUT.
GIMME DE STUFF, DE OLD BUTTER--AND WATCH ME DO DE 249 HA APE
REST/
SURE, IT WAS GREAT STUFF. 252 HA APE
NIX ON THE MR. SMITH STUFF, CHARLIE. 20 HUGHIE
HIS WIFE HAD DONE A LOT OF STUFF TO DOLL IT UP. 25 HUGHIE
JUST CHEAP STUFF TO MAKE IT COMFORTABLE. 25 HUGHIE

STUFF (CONT'D.)
THAT'S THE STUFF. 36 HUGHIE
HE'S GOIN' TO PULL DAT SLAVE-GIRL STUFF ON ME ONCE$79 ICEMAN
TOO OFTEN.
BUT DE FARM STUFF IS DE SAPPIEST PART. 614 ICEMAN
(DISGUSTEDLY) IMAGINE HIM STANDIN' FOR DAT STUFF/614 ICEMAN
AND I TELLS HER I'M OFF DE STUFF FOR LIFE. 616 ICEMAN
(THEY ALL SAY LAUGHINGLY, =SURE, HARRY,= =RIGHTO,=618 ICEMAN
=THAT'S THE STUFF,=
JUST BECAUSE I'M THROUGH WITH THE STUFF DON'T 620 ICEMAN
YOU'LL HAVE TO EXCUSE ME, BOYS AND GIRLS, BUT I'M 620 ICEMAN
OFF THE STUFF, FOR KEEPS.
OF COURSE, I WAS ONLY KIDDING CORA WITH THAT STUFF622 ICEMAN
ABOUT SAVING YOU.
(HE TURNS TO HICKEY) THAT'S THE STUFF, HICKEY. 623 ICEMAN
AW, I DON'T MIND DE BOITHDAY STUFF SO MUCH. 630 ICEMAN
(DOING THE SAME TO PEARL) NIX ON DE ROUGH STUFF, 632 ICEMAN
POLL.
AND THE WAITING FOR THE BIG SLEEP STUFF IS A PIPE 641 ICEMAN
DREAM.
I MEAN THE OLD REAL LOVE STUFF THAT CRUCIFIES YOU.643 ICEMAN
I REMEMBER HER PUTTING ON HER HIGH-AND-MIGHTY 647 ICEMAN
FREE-WOMAN STUFF,
THAT FAMILY-RESPECT STUFF IS ALL BOURGEOIS, 648 ICEMAN
PROPERTY-OWNING CRAP.
WELL, SIT DOWN, DE BOT' OF YUH, AND CUT OUT DE 650 ICEMAN
ROUGH STUFF.
APOLOGIZE FOR SOME OF THE ROUGH STUFF I'VE HAD TO 660 ICEMAN
PULL ON YOU.
(HEARTILY ENCOURAGING) THAT'S THE STUFF, HARRY/ 660 ICEMAN
AND HE GIVE WILLIE DE DOUGH TO BUY HIS STUFF BACK 665 ICEMAN
FROM SOLLY'S.
DE SAME OLD STUFF OVER AND OVER/ 671 ICEMAN
(STIFFLY) NO, I--I'M THROUGH WITH THAT STUFF. 674 ICEMAN
THAT'S THE STUFF, MAC. 685 ICEMAN
THAT'S THE STUFF, HICKEY/ 689 ICEMAN
YOU'RE RID OF ALL THAT NAGGING DREAM STUFF NOW. 690 ICEMAN
HE'S TRYING TO KID HIMSELF WITH THAT GRANDSTAND 700 ICEMAN
PHILOSOPHER STUFF/
SO FORGET DAT WHORE STUFF. 725 ICEMAN
WITH US LOADED DEEP WITH ALL KINDS O' DYNAMITE AND516 INZONE
STUFF THE LIKE O' THAT/
WHAT'S THE USE OF READIN' THAT STUFF EVEN IF-- 530 INZONE
IF YOU'RE STARTLING THAT STUFF AGAIN, I'LL BEAT IT. 26 JOURNE
I HEARD HIM PULL THAT TOUCH OF MALARIA STUFF, 29 JOURNE
AND KNEW HE'D LAUGH AT ME IF I TRIED THE GOOD 34 JOURNE
ADVICE, OLDER BROTHER STUFF.
WORKING HIS WAY ALL OVER THE MAP AS A SAILOR AND 35 JOURNE
ALL THAT STUFF.
THEY'RE GLAD TO HAVE HIM, BUT IT'S THE SPECIAL 36 JOURNE
STUFF THAT GETS HIM BY.
(SHRUGS HIS SHOULDERS.) THE SAME OLD STUFF. 40 JOURNE
NOR THE STUFF YOU READ AND CLAIM YOU ADMIRE. 76 JOURNE
(BITTERLY SCORNFUL.) LEAVE IT TO YOU TO HAVE SOME 86 JOURNE
OF THE STUFF HIDDEN.
THE DAMNED STUFF IS HALF WATER/ 116 JOURNE
IF YOU'RE GOING TO START THAT STUFF, I'LL BEAT IT.129 JOURNE
=WE ARE SUCH STUFF AS DREAMS ARE MADE ON,= 131 JOURNE
WE ARE SUCH STUFF AS MANURE IS MADE ON, SO LET'S 131 JOURNE
DRINK UP AND FORGET IT.
WHEN I REMEMBER ALL THE ROTTEN STUFF I'VE PULLED/ 145 JOURNE
CAN THE WISE STUFF, KID. 156 JOURNE
I'VE HEARD THAT GASPARD STUFF A MILLION TIMES. 158 JOURNE
(HE PAUSES.) AND THEN THIS STUFF OF YOU GETTING 163 JOURNE
CONSUMPTION.
I'LL BET THIS STATE FARM STUFF IS POLITICAL GRAFT 164 JOURNE
GAME.
HELL, I USED TO WRITE BETTER STUFF FOR THE LIT 164 JOURNE
MAGAZINE IN COLLEGE/
NOT DRUNKEN BULL, BUT =IN VINO VERITAS= STUFF. 165 JOURNE
BUT I DIDN'T MEAN TO TELL YOU THAT LAST STUFF--GO 166 JOURNE
THAT FAR BACK.
I'LL BE WAITING TO WELCOME YOU WITH THAT =MY OLD 166 JOURNE
PAL= STUFF.
STUFF AND NONSENSE/ 38 MANSNS
I WORK LIKE A SLAVE ALL DAY TO STUFF YOUR 130 MANSNS
INSATIABLE MAWS
IT WASN'T BAD STUFF EITHER, CONSIDERING I'D HAD NO399 MARCOM
PRACTICE.
STUFF HIM WITH FOOD AND GOLD AND SEND HIM HOME. 419 MARCOM
(A BIT SHAMEFACEDLY) FORGET THAT STUFF, JOSIE. 104 MISBEG
OH, TO HELL WITH THE ROUGH STUFF, JOSIE/ 106 MISBEG
(IRRITABLY) NIX ON THE RAW STUFF, JOSIE. 114 MISBEG
DON'T LET ME PULL THAT STUFF. 119 MISBEG
I SUPPOSE THAT DOES SOUND LIKE MOANING-AT-THE-BAR 123 MISBEG
STUFF.
FOR CHIRST SAKE, QUIT THE SMUT STUFF, CAN'T YOU/ 127 MISBEG
HOW ABOUT YOUR NOT TALKING THE OLD SMUT STUFF TO 127 MISBEG
ME$
I'M A FOOL TO LET THIS STUFF ABOUT PHIL GET UNDER 133 MISBEG
MY SKIN, BUT--
SAME OLD STUFF. 165 MISBEG
CUT OUT THE ROUGH STUFF, KID. 166 MISBEG
NONE OF MY USUAL MORNING-AFTER STUFF-- 171 MISBEG
WHY DO I HAVE TO PULL THAT LOUSY STUFF$ 172 MISBEG
RISE OF CURTAIN, ACT-FOUR STUFF. 172 MISBEG
EXCEPT I'VE PULLED SOME PRETTY ROTTEN STUFF WHEN 1173 MISBEG
WAS DRAWING A BLANK.
IT'S REAL STUFF. 591 ROPE
SAY, GIVE US A REST ON THAT STUFF, WILL YUH$ 595 ROPE
(INDIGNANTLY) HE USED TO HIDE STUFF FROM THE OLD 599 ROPE
LADY.
AND I'M CONVINCED HE'S GOT THE RIGHT STUFF IN HIM 38 STRANG
TO SUCCEED.
HE IS A SPLENDID CHAP, CLEAN AND BOYISH, WITH REAL 46 STRANG
STUFF IN HIM, TOO.
THAT MY STUFF WAS EXACTLY WHAT THEY WANTED, 54 STRANG
ALL THE STUFF BEEN USED ALREADY... 67 STRANG

1567 STUNNED

STUFF (CONT'D.)
COLE ALWAYS USED TO SAY I HAD THE STUFF, AND NED 68 STRANG
CERTAINLY THOUGHT SO....)
WAS I WRONG IN THINKING HE HAD STUFF IN HIM$... 78 STRANG
YOU'VE GOT THE STUFF IN YOU/ 106 STRANG
(TURNING TO DARRELL) AND THAT ISN'T FATHER STUFF 162 STRANG
EITHER, NED/

STUFF'S
THIS WAR ZONE STUFF'S GOT YER GOAT, DRISC-- 517 INZONE

STUFFED
HE IS DRESSED IN A HEAVY BLUE JACKET AND BLUE 539 'ILE
PANTS STUFFED INTO HIS SEA-BOOTS.
I DON'T WANT HIM TO GET THE IDEA HE'S GOT A 289 AHWILD
STUFFED SHIRT
HE WEARS CORDUROY TROUSERS STUFFED DOWN INTO HIGH 556 CROSS
LACED BOOTS.)
I SUPPOSE YOUR FATHER HAS STUFFED YOU WITH HIS 25 ELECTR
LIES ABOUT MY MOTHER/
I'D JUDGE YOU TO BE A PLUTOCRAT, YOUR POCKETS 596 ICEMAN
STUFFED WITH ILL-GOTTEN GAINS.
HOW MANY TIMES I WISH TO PINCH YOU TO DISCOVER IF 33 MANSNS
YOU'RE STUFFED/
HE'S A STUFFED MORAL ATTITUDE/ 60 MANSNS
UNTIL HE BECOMES HIS OWN IDEAL FIGURE, AN IDOL OF 418 MARCOM
STUFFED SELF-SATISFACTION/
THE TWO ELDER POLOS, CARRYING THEIR CHEST, THEIR 420 MARCOM
POCKETS STUFFED,
BUT YOUR HEAD WAS STUFFED WITH MUSH AND LOVE, AND 83 MISBEG
YOU WOULDN'T--

STUFFIN'
IT AIN'T SO DEEP BUT WHAT I KIN WHALE THE STUFFIN'133 ELECTR
OUT O' YOU
IF YUH OPENED YOUR YAP, I'D KNOCK DE STUFFIN' OUTA671 ICEMAN
YUH/=

STUFFING
THE MOSS STUFFING BETWEEN THE LOGS HANGS HERE AND 1 MANSNS
THERE IN STRIPS.

STUFFS
(HE STUFFS THE LOCKET BACK--STOPS BEFORE THE 366 MARCOM
THRONE--
THE CLOTHES OF THE RULER AND HIS COURT ARE OF RICH373 MARCOM
SILK STUFFS,
HE CUTS THE PLUG AND STUFFS HIS PIPE--WITHOUT 15 MISBEG
RANCOR)
WHICH HE STUFFS INTO HIS POCKET WITH A GRUNT OF 508 VOYAGE
SATISFACTION.

STUFFY
IT ISN'T GOOD FOR YOU STAYING IN THIS STUFFY ROOM 150 ELECTR
IN THIS WEATHER.
THE OLD PLACE WAS TOO STUFFY. 274 GGBROW

STUMBLE
STICKS HIS FOOT OUT AND THE WAVERING COUPLE 471 CARIBE
STUMBLE OVER IT
AND THEN THE DOOR WOULD OPEN AND IN I'D STUMBLE-- 713 ICEMAN
LOOKING LIKE WHAT I'VE SAID--
AND YOU STUMBLE ON TOWARD NOWHERE, FOR NO GOOD 153 JOURNE
REASON/
(HE CONTINUES TO STUMBLE TOWARD LEFT) 311 LAZARU

STUMBLED
AS IF SOMEONE HAD STUMBLED AND FALLEN ON THE FRONT154 JOURNE
STEPS.
IF SOMEONE STUMBLED AND FELL AGAINST HER 179 MANSNS

STUMBLES
HE STUMBLES AWAY FROM HER, AND SHE COMMENCES 551 'ILE
SOFTLY TO PLAY THE ORGAN AGAIN.)
(THEN SHE LETS HER BAG DROP, STUMBLES OVER TO HER 24 ANNA
CHAIR AGAIN,
MAT BURKE STUMBLES IN AROUND THE PORT SIDE OF THE 30 ANNA
CABIN.
HE STUMBLES INTO THE DITCH AND LIES THERE FOR A 166 BEYOND
MOMENT.
(STUMBLES WEAKLY FROM BENEATH THE CROSS) 565 DAYS
(HE STUMBLES OUT THE DOOR--IN A SHORT WHILE 264 DESIRE
RETURNS TO THE KITCHEN--
EBEN STUMBLES OVER AND THROWS HIMSELF ON HIS KNEES266 DESIRE
BESIDE HER SOBBING BROKENLY.)
AND IT CRASHES OPEN AND HE STUMBLES OVER IT AND 451 DYNAMO
DISAPPEARS IN THE HALL.)
(HE STUMBLES HASTILY AROUND THE TABLE TO THE DAZED466 DYNAMO
REUBEN AND WITH A PITIFUL
THE OLD MAN TURNS AND STUMBLES BACK TO HIS CHAIR. 466 DYNAMO
JONES STUMBLES IN FROM THE FOREST ON THE RIGHT. 192 EJONES
(HE TURNS AND STUMBLES BLINDLY FROM THE ROOM. 101 ELECTR
AND STUMBLES TO THE BAR AT LARRY'S RIGHT.) 690 ICEMAN
TIBERIUS, HIS EYES FIXED ON CALIGULA, STUMBLES 339 LAZARU
AGAINST THE BODY OF FLAVIUS.
SHE MEANS IT TO BE ONLY A SLAP, BUT HIS HEAD JERKS 4 MISBEG
BACK AND HE STUMBLES.
(STUMBLES TO HER FEET--TIMIDLY.) 34 POET
RILEY STUMBLES VAGUELY AFTER THEM. 104 POET

STUMBLING
BUT WE CAN BOTH JUSTLY LAY SOME OF THE BLAME FOR 161 BEYOND
OUR STUMBLING ON GOD.
STUMBLING AND CRAWLING THROUGH THE UNDERGROWTH. 198 EJONES
(STUMBLING AROUND THE BAR TO THE DOOR ON LEFT-- 495 VOYAGE
SOBBING)

STUMP
WELL, RICHARD, I'VE ALWAYS FOUND I'VE HAD TO 195 AHWILD
LISTEN TO AT LEAST ONE STUMP SPEECH
IN THE CENTER IS A BIG DEAD STUMP WORN BY TIME 195 EJONES
HE SLINKS CAUTIOUSLY TO THE STUMP IN THE CENTER 195 EJONES
(SITS DOWN ON THE STUMP AGAIN) 196 EJONES
THEY ARE PLACED TO THE LEFT OF THE STUMP, BESIDE 197 EJONES
JONES.)
SCREAMS AND LEAPS MADLY TO THE TOP OF THE STUMP 197 EJONES
MOTIONING FOR HIM TO STAND ON THE STUMP--THE 197 EJONES
AUCTION BLOCK.

STUMP (CONT'D.)
THE AUCTIONEER HOLDS UP HIS HAND, TAKING HIS PLACE197 EJONES
AT THE STUMP.
THE STUMP. 197 EJONES

STUMPED
BE CHRIST, YOU HAVE ME STUMPED. 80 MISBEG

STUMPY
AND HIS STUMPY LEGS TERMINATING IN LARGE FLAT 5 ANNA
FEET.
ON A STUMPY RUNT OF A MAN LIKE THE OLD SWEDE. 33 ANNA
GLORY BE TO GOD, IT'S BOLD TALK YOU HAVE FOR A 47 ANNA
STUMPY RUNT OF A MAN/
HE'S AS SPRY ON HIS STUMPY LEGS AS A YEARLING-- 10 MISBEG
A BARREL-LIKE TRUNK, STUMPY LEGS, AND BIG FEET. 11 MISBEG

STUNG
(DRAWS BACK HIS HAND AS IF HE HAD BEEN STUNG-- 217 AHWILD
(FOR MURIEL HAS BITTEN HIS HAND AND IT HURTS, AND 284 AHWILD
STUNG BY THE PAIN,
(STUNG, RISING UNSTEADILY TO HIS FEET 32 ANNA
(STUNG-- 49 ANNA
(STUNG) EXACTLY, JOHN. 526 DAYS
(SHE IS STUNG AND FLUSHES ANGRILY. 226 DESIRE
(STUNG--TURNS ON HER FURIOUSLY) 228 DESIRE
(STUNG--FIERCELY) 230 DESIRE
(STUNG) YE LIE/ 254 DESIRE
(STUNG BUT PRETENDING INDIFFERENCE--WITH A WINK) 176 EJONES
(STUNG BEYOND BEARING-- 34 ELECTR
(STUNG, GRABBING HER BY THE SHOULDERS--FIERCELY) 41 ELECTR
(STUNG) THAT'S ENOUGH FROM YOU/ 98 ELECTR
(STUNG, HARSHLY) THE DAMN FOOL HE KNOWS BETTER'N 260 GGBROW
ANYONE IF I HADN'T HELD HIM
(STUNG) NO. 289 GGBROW
(STUNG--ANGRILY) BOSH/ 296 GGBROW
(STUNG--BY THE NAME, GETS UP--HARSHLY) 310 GGBROW
(STUNG--WITH A GROWL OF RAGE) 230 HA APE
(GRINNING) STUNG HER FOR TWO DOLLARS AND A HALF, 609 ICEMAN
WASN'T IT, ED?
(STUNG) WHAT THE DEVIL ARE YOU HINTING AT, 623 ICEMAN
ANYWAYS?
(STUNG) YOU BROADS BETTER WATCH YOUR STEP OR-- 630 ICEMAN
(STUNG) SAY, LISTEN, YOUSE/ 634 ICEMAN
(STUNG--PULLS BACK A FIST THREATENINGLY) 653 ICEMAN
(STUNG) YOU'D LIE, THEN? 666 ICEMAN
(STUNG--TURNS ON HIM VICIOUSLY) 668 ICEMAN
(STUNG INTO RECOVERING ALL HIS OLD FUMING 718 ICEMAN
TRUCULENCE)
(STUNG.) THAT'S ENOUGH/ 30 JOURNE
(STUNG.) THAT'S A LIE/ 34 JOURNE
(STUNG INTO SNEERING JEALOUSY.) 35 JOURNE
(STUNG.) I DON'T PULL THAT/ 38 JOURNE
(STUNG, JAMIE HAS TURNED TO STARE AT HER WITH 60 JOURNE
ACCUSING ANTAGONISM.
(STUNG FOR A MOMENT--THEN SHRUGGING HIS SHOULDERS, 76 JOURNE
DRYLY.)
(STUNG.) I'LL SEND HIM WHEREVER HARDY THINKS 79 JOURNE
BEST/
(STUNG.) SO I'M TO BLAME BECAUSE THAT LAZY HULK 111 JOURNE
(STUNG--ANGRILY.) BE QUIET/ 140 JOURNE
(STUNG, TURNS ON HIM IN A RAGE.) 169 JOURNE
(STUNG) BE STILL/ 343 LAZARU
(STUNG TO FURY, A FLASH OF BITTER HATRED IN HER 14 MANSNS
EYES.
(STUNG--HER INWARD ANGER BEGINNING TO SHOW, AND 18 MANSNS
WITH IT HER BROGUE,
(BOUNDING TO HIS FEET AS IF A WASP HAD STUNG HIM) 348 MARCOM
(SHE DRAWS HER HAND FROM HIS AS IF SHE HAD BEEN 412 MARCOM
STUNG.)
(STUNG) SHUT UP/ 79 MISBEG
(STUNG) SHUT UP/ 99 MISBEG
(STUNG) LISTEN TO ME, JIM/ 127 MISBEG
(STUNG INTO DEFIANT ANGER.) YES, I'VE THE MARE/ 49 POET
(STUNG TO FURY, GLARES AT HER WITH HATRED. 114 POET
(STUNG.) COWARD, IS UT? 126 POET
(THINKING--STUNG) (HE'S THINKING OF THOSE MEN IN115 STRANG
THE HOSPITAL...
(STUNG--MOCKINGLY) IT WAS YOU WHO TAUGHT ME THE 132 STRANG
SCIENTIFIC APPROACH, DOCTOR/
(STUNG YET AMUSED BY THE OTHER'S TONE--IRONICALLY)147 STRANG
(STUNG--BITINGLY) IT'S AN UNNATURAL PASSION 457 WELDED
CERTAINLY--IN YOUR CASE.
(STUNG--BITINGLY) DON'T ACT MORAL INDIGNATION/ 458 WELDED
(STUNG--IN A PASSION AGAIN AT ONCE) 458 WELDED

STUNNED
AND TURN TO HER IN A STUNNED AMAZEMENT. 56 ANNA
BUT HE IS TOO STUNNED AND BEWILDERED YET TO FIND A 58 ANNA
VENT FOR IT.
(STUNNED) RUTH/ 164 BEYOND
(STUNNED--STAMMERS) ELSA, I-- 549 DAYS
(NO LONGER DOUBTING--STUNNED) 213 DESIRE
(STUNNED--DULLY) HE TOLD YEW.../ 257 DESIRE
COMES TO ABBIE, THE STUNNED EXPRESSION STILL ON 264 DESIRE
HIS FACE--HOARSELY)
NOTING EVERY DETAIL WITH A NUMB, STUNNED 536 DIFRNT
ASTONISHMENT.)
(STARING AT HER WITH STUNNED EYES-- IN A HOARSE 542 DIFRNT
WHISPER)
(LIGHT, COMPLETELY STUNNED, STARES AT HER BLANKLY.445 DYNAMO
(STARES AT HIM WITH A STUNNED LOOK) 463 DYNAMO
(STUNNED) WHAT'S THAT& 24 ELECTR
(STUNNED--STAMMERS IN GUILTY CONFUSION) 27 ELECTR
(STUNNED) I DON'T BELIEVE IT/ 87 ELECTR
(HE STARES AT HER, STUNNED AND STUPID) 177 ELECTR
MARGARET REMAINS, STUNNED WITH HORROR. 318 GGBROW
(THEY STARE AT HIM WITH STUNNED, BEWILDERED HURT. 660 ICEMAN
(A GASP COMES FROM THE STUNNED COMPANY. 663 ICEMAN
THE NAZARENES STAND PARALYZED AND STUNNED. 290 LAZARU
STUNNED ME, EVEN/ 14 MANSNS

STUNNED

STUNNED (CONT'D.)
(STUNNED) WHY, I'VE GOT A LETTER OF INTRODUCTION 348 MARCOM TO HER
YOU'RE STUNNED, I CAN SEE THAT. 394 MARCOM
I SEE YOU ARE STUNNED AGAIN. 395 MARCOM
(SHE PINS THE BLAZING DIAMOND FIGURE ON THE BREAST419 MARCOM OF THE STUNNED MARCO)
(STUNNED.) GONE$ 91 POET
(STUNNED--WEAKLY.) GOD FORGIVE YOU! 108 POET
(SARA STARES AT HIM IN STUNNED AMAZEMENT.) 165 POET
(WHO HAS LISTENED WITH AMAZED HORROR--PROFOUNDLY 83 STRANG SHOCKED AND STUNNED)
HIS EYES HAVE A DAZED LOOK AS IF HE WERE STILL TOO 98 STRANG STUNNED TO COMPREHEND CLEARLY
NINA LETS GO OF HER WRIST AND STARES AFTER THEM IN178 STRANG A SORT OF STUNNED STUPOR)
STARES AT HER WITH STUNNED EYES) 180 STRANG

STUNNING
THE BACKGROUND BACKDROP IS BRILLIANT, STUNNING 284 GGBROW WALLPAPER,
THIS COSTUME IS A QUEER JUMBLE OF STUNNING EFFECTS390 MARCOM THAT RECALL THE PARADE

STUNS
THIS CLASH OF SOUNDS STUNS ONE'S EARS WITH ITS 223 HA APE RENDING DISSONANCE.

STUNT
(CYNICALLY AMUSED) AFRAID IT WILL STUNT MY 240 AHWILD GROWTHS
(WITH A TICKLED CHUCKLE) GOSH, THAT'D BE THE REAL545 DIFRNT STUNT AW RIGHT, AW RIGHT.
BEJEES, IS THAT A NEW STUNT, DRINKING YOUR CHASER 620 ICEMAN FIRSTS
BEJEES, THAT'S A FINE STUNT, TO GO TO SLEEP ON US/625 ICEMAN
ALL I'M TINKIN' IS, FLOWERS IS DAT LOUSE HICKEY'S 630 ICEMAN STUNT.
THAT WAS A SILLY STUNT FOR A FREE ANARCHIST WOMAN,646 ICEMAN WASN'T IT,
BUT GOD ALMIGHTY, THIS LAST STUNT OF YOURS IS TOO 145 JOURNE MUCH/

STUNTED
STUNTED BUSHES COWERING CLOSE AGAINST THE EARTH T0187 EJONES ESCAPE THE BUFFETING OF THE

STUNTS
AND NOT BE RESPONSIBLE FOR ALL DE CRAZY STUNTS 669 ICEMAN HE'S STAGIN' HERE.
WHAT HAD I TO DO WITH ALL THE CRAZY STUNTS HE'S 35 JOURNE PULLED IN THE LAST FEW YEARS--

STUPEFACTION
ANDREW STARES AT ROBERT IN HURT STUPEFACTION. 135 BEYOND
WITH HORRIFIED STUPEFACTION) 437 DYNAMO
SHOCKED LOOK OF STUPEFACTION. 438 DYNAMO
(COMES OUT OF THE STATE OF HUMILIATED STUPEFACTION452 DYNAMO INTO WHICH THE KNOWLEDGE OF
(STARES AFTER HIM DUMBLY IN THE SAME STATE OF 107 STRANG HAPPY STUPEFACTION--MUMBLES)

STUPEFIED
(LOOKING AT THE STUPEFIED CHRIS CURIOUSLY) 19 ANNA
AND STARES AT HIS SON'S FACE WITH STUPEFIED 463 DYNAMO BEWILDERMENT)
(STUPEFIED) THAT MEANS PRESTON/ 192 STRANG

STUPENDOUS
(WITH A STUPENDOUS SIGH) OH, GLORY BE TO GOD, I'M 75 ANNA AFTER BELIEVING YOU NOW/

STUPID
(WILDLY) BECAUSE IT'S A STUPID, STUBBORN REASON. 547 *ILE
I USED TO THINK HOMEPORT WAS A STUPID, MONOTONOUS 548 *ILE PLACE.
SHE STARES UP AT HIM WITH A STUPID EXPRESSION, A 551 *ILE VAGUE SMILE ON HER LIPS.
THE FOURTH OF JULY IS A STUPID FARCE/ 194 AHWILD
(ANGRILY) HE'S A DUMB FOOL--A STUPID DUMB FOOL, 213 AHWILD THAT'S WHAT HE IS/
I DO WISH YOU WOULDN'T ENCOURAGE THAT STUPID GIRL 223 AHWILD BY TALKING TO HER,
STUPID FACE AND A CYNICALLY WISE GRIN, STANDS JUST236 AHWILD INSIDE THE BAR ENTRANCE,
LIFE IS ALL A STUPID FARCE/ 271 AHWILD
IT WAS YOUR FAULT FOR BEING SO STUPID/ 286 AHWILD
BUT I THOUGHT YOU HAD NO USE FOR HER, THOUGHT SHE 290 AHWILD WAS STUPID.
YOU SURE WERE--NOT ONLY A FOOL BUT A DOWNRIGHT, 294 AHWILD STUPID, DISGUSTING FOOL/
NO NICE GIRL WANTS TO GIVE HER LOVE TO A STUPID 294 AHWILD DRUNK/
HE GOES TO THE DOOR, SILENT AND STUPID--THEN 62 ANNA TURNS)
IF I'M NOT THE STUPID BODY/ 87 BEYOND
YOU STUPID THING/ 91 BEYOND
(THE EXPRESSION OF STUPID BEWILDERMENT GIVING WAY 91 BEYOND TO ONE OF OVERWHELMING JOY.
(ROBERT STARES AT HER IN STUPID ASTONISHMENT. 91 BEYOND
(COLORING) BECAUSE I'M TOO STUPID TO UNDERSTAND 122 BEYOND THEM,
WITH A HEAVY, STUPID FACE AND SHIFTY, CUNNING 123 BEYOND EYES.
THE STUPID DAMN FOOL/ 125 BEYOND
AND THE STUPID WAY YOU DO THINGS/ 126 BEYOND
AND ALWAYS READING YOUR STUPID BOOKS INSTEAD OF 127 BEYOND WORKING.
YOU CAN'T KNOW HOW AWFUL AND STUPID IT IS-- 136 BEYOND
IT'S OUTRAGEOUS. IT'S STUPID/ YOU DON'T LOVE ME/165 BEYOND
HE IS A DARK BURLY FELLOW WITH A ROUND STUPID 483 CARDIF FACE.
(THE STUPID-FACED SEAMAN, WHO COMES IN AFTER 483 CARDIF SMITTY,
YOU'D BETTER BE PREPARED FOR ANY STUPID FOLLY. 498 DAYS
(HURRIEDLY) IF YOU KNEW ALL THE STUPID 516 DAYS ENGAGEMENTS THAT PILE UP--

STUPID (CONT'D.)
THE STUPID LIVES WE LEAD--AND, OF COURSE, THE 517 DAYS USUAL FINANCIAL WORRIES.
WHAT A STUPID FOOL/ 520 DAYS
ALL THAT SAVED ME FROM DOING SOMETHING STUPID WAS 521 DAYS THE FAITH I HAD THAT SOMEWHERE
PLEASE FORGET THE STUPID ROT I'VE SAID. 524 DAYS
AT THEIR STUPID COWARDICE. 542 DAYS
NATURALLY, HE COULD NEVER BE SO STUPID AS TO CURSE545 DAYS WHAT HE KNEW DIDN'T EXIST/
SNEERING TO HERSELF ABOUT MY STUPID FAITH IN YOU. 549 DAYS
AND I SEE THROUGH YOUR STUPID TRICK--TO USE THE 559 DAYS FEAR OF DEATH TO--
IN A MOMENT OF STUPID MADNESS/ 560 DAYS
DO YOU THINK YOU CAN CHOOSE YOUR STUPID END IN 561 DAYS YOUR STORY NOW.
YOU'RE CARRYING--THAT STUPID/ 498 DIFRNT
YOU'RE TOO DUMB STUPID AND BAD YOURSELF TO EVER 505 DIFRNT KNOW WHAT I'M THINKING.
(WITH QUEER, STUPID INSISTENCE) 527 DIFRNT
HUTCHINS, YOU'RE GETTING JUST TOO STUPID/ 426 DYNAMO
YOU MAY CALL ME AS STUPID AS YOU LIKE 426 DYNAMO
THIS DUNCE-- THIS STUPID DOLT--NOW I SHALL BE THE 452 DYNAMO BUTT OF ALL THEIR SNEERS/
EAGER-LISTENER TYPE, WITH A SMALL ROUND FACE, 6 ELECTR ROUND STUPID EYES,
(SNATCHING HER HAND BACK) DON'T BE STUPID, 14 ELECTR PETER/.
BUT--DON'T BE STUPID, SETH-- 20 ELECTR
(THEN WITH A CONFUSED, STUPID PERSISTENCE 24 ELECTR
WHAT PUT SUCH A STUPID IDEA IN YOUR HEADS 36 ELECTR
HE STARES AT IT WITH A STRANGE STUPID DREAD. 40 ELECTR
(CONTROLLING A START) DON'T BE STUPID, PLEASE/ 46 ELECTR
AND ALL ON ACCOUNT OF A STUPID LETTER VINNIE HAD 51 ELECTR NO BUSINESS TO WRITE.
TO ACCUSE ME OF FLIRTING WITH A STUPID SHIP 51 ELECTR CAPTAIN/
IF YOU ARE GOING TO SAY STUPID THINGS, I'LL GO IN 59 ELECTR MY OWN ROOM.
A STUPID SHIP CAPTAIN I HAPPENED TO MEET AT YOUR 87 ELECTR GRANDFATHER'S
I THOUGHT WHAT A JOKE IT WOULD BE ON THE STUPID 95 ELECTR GENERALS LIKE FATHER IF EVERYONE
OH, ORIN, HOW CAN YOU BE SO STUPID$ 96 ELECTR
NOW YOU'RE BEING STUPID AGAIN/ 150 ELECTR
WILL YOU NEVER LOSE YOUR STUPID GUILTY CONSCIENCE/152 ELECTR
(HE STARES AT HER, STUNNED AND STUPID) 177 ELECTR
DEFENSIVE FACE, OBSTINATE TO THE POINT OF STUPID 259 GGBROW WEAKNESS.
HE'S JUST A STUPID OLD FOOL/ 312 GGBROW
HE'S TOO STUPID. 249 HA APE
LAUGH LIKE FOOLS, LEEDLE STUPID PEOPLES/ 627 ICEMAN
BUT BE OF GOOD CHEER, LEEDLE STUPID PEOPLES/ 635 ICEMAN
AND THAT STUPID BOUNDER OF A BOER. 675 ICEMAN
AND TIRED OF WATCHING THE STUPID GREED OF THE 689 ICEMAN HUMAN CIRCUS,
(WITH HIS SILLY GIGGLE) HELLO, HARRY, STUPID 691 ICEMAN PROLETARIAN MONKEY-FACE/
(WITH GUTTURAL RAGE) GOTTAMNED STUPID PROLETARIAN095 ICEMAN SLAVES/
IT WAS ALL A STUPID LIE--MY NONSENSE ABOUT 707 ICEMAN TOMORROW.
HE COMPLAINS WITH A STUPID, NAGGING INSISTENCE) 711 ICEMAN
HICKEY STARES AT THEM WITH STUPID INCOMPREHENSION.717 ICEMAN
STUPID FOOL/ 721 ICEMAN
GOTTAMNED STUPID BOURGEOIS/ 724 ICEMAN
STUPID BOURGEOIS MONKEYS/ 727 ICEMAN
DO YOU THINK I'M--(CHOKINGLY) YOU STUPID CURS/ 527 INZONE
IT IS STUPID OF JAMIE. 44 JOURNE
SOMEONE BESIDES THE SERVANTS--THAT STUPID 46 JOURNE CATHLEEN/
IT'S STUPID. 47 JOURNE
SO EVERY YEAR I HAVE STUPID, LAZY GREENHORNS TO 61 JOURNE DEAL WITH.
OH, I KNOW JAMIE WAS ONLY SEVEN, BUT HE WAS NEVER 87 JOURNE STUPID.
HER STUPID, GOOD-HUMORED FACE WEARS A PLEASED AND 97 JOURNE FLATTERED SIMPER.
(THEN HASTILY, AS CATHLEEN STARES IN STUPID 103 JOURNE AMAZEMENT.)
MADE WHORES FASCINATING VAMPIRES INSTEAD OF POOR, 165 JOURNE STUPID,
ACCORDING TO YOUR STUPID LIES, HE RAISED HIM FROM 283 LAZARU THE DEAD/
YES TO THE STUPID AS TO THE WISE/ 343 LAZARU
BUT HOW STUPID/ 3 MANSNS
WE MUST PROTECT MAN FROM HIS STUPID POSSESSIVE 8 MANSNS INSTINCTS
AND RID THE WORLD OF THIS STUPID RACE OF MEN AND 9 MANSNS WASH THE EARTH CLEAN/
BUT LET'S FORGET MY STUPID JOKE 14 MANSNS
I THINK I CAN PROMISE I'LL SOON WIN BACK FOR YOU 57 MANSNS ALL HIS STUPID FOLLY HAS LOST.
WHAT A STUPID THING TO SAY, MOTHER/ 62 MANSNS
YOU CAN HAVE THE STUPID EFFRONTERY TO CRITICIZE MY 70 MANSNS LEADERSHIP
A LIE THAT I WOULD BE STUPID TO PERMIT TO GET IN 71 MANSNS MY WAY, OR IN MY COMPANY'S WAY.
DON'T BE STUPID. 78 MANSNS
THE STUPID VULGAR FOOL/ 114 MANSNS
(THINKING.) THIS IS STUPID/ 119 MANSNS
WE'VE UNDERSTOOD EACH OTHER AND WHAT MIGHT HAVE 124 MANSNS DEVELOPED INTO A STUPID QUARREL
YOU ARE EVEN MORE STUPID THAN I THOUGHT. 168 MANSNS
HOW COULD WE BE SO BLIND AND STUPID/ 170 MANSNS
WHAT IS EVIL IS THE STUPID THEORY THAT MAN IS 172 MANSNS NATURALLY WHAT WE CALL VIRTUOUS

STUPID (CONT'D.)
OF THE STUPID INSANE IMPULSION OF MAN'S PETTY 179 MANSNS
VANITY
POETRY'S ALL STUPID, ANYWAY. 361 MARCOM
THEY PRAY TO HIM ALSO AND DO MANY OTHER STUPID 374 MARCOM
THINGS.
WELL, THEN, IF YOU WILL CONFESS THAT YOUR SOUL IS 380 MARCOM
A STUPID INVENTION OF YOUR
LIFE IS SO STUPID. IT IS SO MYSTERIOUS/ 399 MARCOM
SHE WILL BE MIDDLE-AGED--FAT--AND STUPID/ 416 MARCOM
ONE MUST HAVE STUPID WRITINGS THAT MEN CAN 423 MARCOM
UNDERSTAND.
IN ORDER TO LIVE EVEN WISDOM MUST BE STUPID/ 423 MARCOM
THEN THE STUPID MAN BECOMES THE PERFECT 426 MARCOM
INCARNATION OF OMNIPOTENCE.
OH, HE WAS FULL OF STUPID GAB, AS USUAL. 20 MISBEG
AND THE MEN THAT WANT ME ARE NO BETTER THAN STUPID 28 MISBEG
BULLS.
NATURALLY LETHARGIC, A BIT STUPID. 56 MISBEG
AND NOW LOOK AT YOU, THE STUPID OBJECT YOU ARE, 81 MISBEG
MUMBLING AND DROOLING/
BE GOD, YOU OUGHT TO SEE WHAT A STUPID SHEEP THAT 88 MISBEG
MAKES HIM.
I'M SORRY I WAS SO STUPID AND DIDN'T SEE-- 141 MISBEG
(HASTILY.) OH, AIN'T I STUPID NOT TO REMEMBER. 38 POET
FOR A MOMENT HIS FACE HAS AN ABSURDLY STARTLED, 68 POET
STUPID LOOK.
HE STARES AT THE FRAGMENTS IN HIS HANDS WITH 92 POET
STUPID SURPRISE.
(AS THE CHILD CONTINUES TO STARE AT HIM SILENTLY 583 ROPE
WITH EYES STUPID FROM FEAR.
TO HIS WIFE) IT'S SOFT-MINDED SHE IS, LIKE I'VE 583 ROPE
ALWAYS TOLD YOU, AN' STUPID.
US COUNTRY FOLKS IS STUPID IN MOST WAYS. 593 ROPE
OH, STUPID KID/.... 6 STRANG
I KNEW IT WAS A STUPID, MORBID BUSINESS, THAT I 45 STRANG
WAS MORE MAIMED THAN THEY WERE.
YET I KEPT ON, FROM ONE TO ONE, LIKE A STUPID, 45 STRANG
(WITH A SORT OF DULL, STUPID WONDERMENT) 62 STRANG
AND STUPID, FOR THEN NO ONE COULD BE THE HAPPIER 86 STRANG
FOR HER ACT/
IT MAY BE STUPID BUT I'VE GOT A GUILTY CONSCIENCE/103 STRANG
(SHARPLY) DON'T BE STUPID/. 114 STRANG
(FRIGHTENED--ANGRILY) DON'T BE STUPID, NED/ 144 STRANG
WHAT DO I CARE ABOUT THIS STUPID RACES... 162 STRANG
AS A STUPID MISTAKE... 166 STRANG
WHY, SHE'S HARDLY EVEN PRETTY AND SHE'S DEADLY 168 STRANG
STUPID.
THOSE STUPID PEOPLE WITH THEIR SOCIAL CONDOLENCES 190 STRANG
WERE KILLING ME.
(BUT I'D LIKE TO JOLT HIS STUPID SELF- 191 STRANG
COMPLACENCY...
A SLOVENLY BARMAID WITH A STUPID FACE SODDEN WITH 493 VOYAGE
DRINK IS MOPPING OFF THE BAR.
(WITH A STUPID GRIN) KATE. 499 VOYAGE
DON'T BE STUPID/ 455 WELDED
HER FACE, ROUGED, POWDERED, PENCILED, IS BROAD AND471 WELDED
STUPID.
(IN A STUPID STATE OF BEWILDERMENT, 473 WELDED

STUPIDER
BE CHRIST, YOU'RE STUPIDER THAN I THOUGHT YOU, IF 168 POET
YOU CAN'T SEE THAT.

STUPIDITY
BLIND STUPIDITY OF LIFE THAT IT MUST LIVE 561 DAYS
BUT THE OPPOSITES OF THE SAME STUPIDITY WHICH IS 649 ICEMAN
RULER AND KING OF LIFE.
AMIABLE, IGNORANT, CLUMSY, AND POSSESSED BY A 51 JOURNE
DENSE, WELL-MEANING STUPIDITY.
AND ALL THE HYPOCRITICAL VALUES WE SET ON THE 79 MANSNS
RELATIONSHIP ARE MERE STUPIDITY.
WHAT GOOD ARE WISE WRITINGS TO FIGHT STUPIDITYS 423 MARCOM
CAN YOU CONFESS YOURSELF WEAKER THAN HIS 425 MARCOM
STUPIDITYS
(WITH DOGGED STUPIDITY) I DON'T/ 98 STRANG

STUPIDLY
STARING AT IT STUPIDLY FOR A SECOND, THEN 41 ANNA
AIMLESSLY PUTTING IT DOWN AGAIN.
STUPIDLY) 61 ANNA
(CHRIS TURNS STUPIDLY AND GOES OUT. 62 ANNA
HE MUTTERS STUPIDLY) 63 ANNA
(STUPIDLY) I DIDN'T SEE IT. 472 CARIBE
(STUPIDLY--AS IF HYPNOTIZED) AH-EH. 227 DESIRE
(HE SUDDENLY STOPS, STARING STUPIDLY BEFORE HIM.) 242 DESIRE
(NODDING STUPIDLY) AY-EH. 265 DESIRE
HE ADVANCES THREATENINGLY ON HIS FATHER WHO IS 451 DYNAMO
STARING AT ADA STUPIDLY.
(STANDS LOOKING AT HIM STUPIDLY. 464 DYNAMO
(STUPIDLY) YOU DIDN'T GO--TO BLACKRIDGES 120 ELECTR
(HE TAKES HER HAND AUTOMATICALLY, STARING AT HER 143 ELECTR
STUPIDLY.)
AS STUPIDLY GREEDY FOR POWER AS THE WORST 588 ICEMAN
CAPITALIST THEY ATTACK.
(STARES AT HIM STUPIDLY--THEN PUSHES HIS CHAIR 703 ICEMAN
BACK AND GETS UP, GRUMBLING)
(STARES AFTER PARRITT STUPIDLY) 721 ICEMAN
(REITERATES STUPIDLY) WHAT'S MATTER, LARRYS 724 ICEMAN
(STUPIDLY) I DON'T HEAR BELL RING. 516 INZONE
(CATHLEEN STARES AT HER, STUPIDLY PUZZLED. 100 JOURNE
(THEN, STUPIDLY PUZZLED.) GOOD EXCUSES 101 JOURNE
(SHE PAUSES--THEN STUPIDLY.) 102 JOURNE
(STUPIDLY PUZZLED.) YOU'VE TAKEN SOME OF THE 104 JOURNE
MEDICINES
HE STARES TOWARD THE FLAMES STUPIDLY--THEN SCREAMS368 LAZARU
DESPAIRINGLY ABOVE THE CHANT)
(KNOWS HE IS TELLING THE TRUTH--SO RELIEVED SHE 132 MISBEG
CAN ONLY STAMMER STUPIDLY)
(STARTLED, REPEATS STUPIDLY.) 92 POET
(NUMB WITH FRIGHT--MUMBLES STUPIDLY.) 163 POET

STUPIDLY (CONT'D.)
(MUTTERS STUPIDLY.) NOT JAMIES 163 POET
HER FACE IS STUPIDLY EXPRESSIONLESS. 578 ROPE
(STUPIDLY) WHOS 584 ROPE
(NODDING HIS HEAD SEVERAL TIMES--STUPIDLY) 27 STRANG
(MARSDEN NODS STUPIDLY) I'LL TAKE NED UP. 28 STRANG
(STUPIDLY) SOMEONE--AT THE DOOR. 97 STRANG
(STUPIDLY) LEFTS 107 STRANG
(STARES DOWN AT HIM STUPIDLY--THEN THINKING 182 STRANG
STRANGELY)
(DOING SO MECHANICALLY--STUPIDLY) 194 STRANG
(STARING AT HIM STUPIDLY--THINKING) 194 STRANG
(THEY HAVE BOTH BEEN STARING AT HIM STUPIDLY) 195 STRANG
(HE STARTS AND NODS STUPIDLY. 471 WELDED
(HE GLANCES UP AT HER STUPIDLY BUT DOESN'T ANSWER.472 WELDED
A BIT BEWILDEREDLY, BREAKING AWAY FROM HIM WITH A 480 WELDED
LITTLE SHIVER--STUPIDLY)
(TRYING WITH AGONY TO TAKE THIS STOICALLY-- 483 WELDED
MUMBLING STUPIDLY)

STUPOR
CHRIS SEEMS IN A STUPOR OF DESPAIR, HIS HOUSE OF 58 ANNA
CARDS FALLEN ABOUT HIM.
(WHO HAS BEEN STANDING IN A STUPOR--SUDDENLY 61 ANNA
GRASPING BURKE BY THE ARM--
CHRIS STANDS IN A STUPOR, STARING AT THE FLOOR.) 61 ANNA
JONES GETS TO HIS FEET IN A HYPNOTIZED STUPOR. 194 EJONES
OH, I KNOW YOU THOUGHT I WAS IN A STUPOR OF 153 ELECTR
GRIEF--BUT I WASN'T BLIND/
BROWN REMAINS IN A STUPOR FOR A MOMENT-- 299 GGBROW
(HE GLARES SCORNFULLY AT YANK, WHO IS SUNK IN AN 250 HA APE
OBLIVIOUS STUPOR)
CARRYING OUT MECHANICALLY THE MOTIONS OF GETTING 696 ICEMAN
DRUNK BUT SUNK IN A NUMB STUPOR
SUNK IN THE SAME STUPOR AS THE OTHER OCCUPANTS OF 701 ICEMAN
THE ROOM.
STRUGGLING UP FROM HIS STUPOR. 168 JOURNE
(TRYING TO SHAKE OFF HIS HOPELESS STUPOR.) 174 JOURNE
(IS SWAYING AND STAGGERING, LIKE A MAN IN A 311 LAZARU
DRUNKEN STUPOR.
(WHO HAS BEEN STANDING IN A BEWILDERED STUPOR FROM 339 LAZARU
TIBERIUS.
IN A PETRIFIED, BEWILDERED STUPOR. 339 LAZARU
(THE PRINCESS TAKES IT MECHANICALLY AND STARES AT 416 MARCOM
IT IN A STUPOR
AND LEFT HIM IN A STUPOR. 152 POET
HE APPEARS COMPLETELY POSSESSED BY A PARALYZING 164 POET
STUPOR.)
IT PENETRATES MELODY'S STUPOR AND HE STIFFENS 166 POET
RIGIDLY ON HIS CHAIR.
(DARRELL REMAINS STANDING LOOKING UP THE STAIRS IN124 STRANG
A SORT OF JOYOUS STUPOR.
NINA LETS GO OF HER WRIST AND STARES AFTER THEM IN178 STRANG
A SORT OF STUNNED STUPOR)
(HE SLUMPS DOWN ON THE CHAIR AGAIN, SUNK IN A 473 WELDED
SOMBER STUPOR.

STURDILY
(STURDILY) YOU DON'T KNOW THAT FOR SURE, EMMER. 517 DIFRNT
HE IS STURDILY BUILT, BUT SEEMS ALMOST PUNY 3 MISBEG

STURDY
LOOK AT THE MUSCLES IN HIS ARMS AND HIS STURDY 197 EJONES
LEGS.
IT IS HOME-MADE, HEAVILY CONSTRUCTED, AND IS STILL 1 MANSNS
STURDY.
MALOY IS TWENTY-SIX, WITH A STURDY PHYSIQUE AND AN 8 POET
AMIABLE, CUNNING FACE.

STUTTER
HE'D STUTTER LIKE HE WAS PARALYZED. 16 HUGHIE
OH, NELLY, NELLY, I WANT TO SAY SO MUCH WHAT I 488 WELDED
FEEL BUT I CAN ONLY STUTTER LIKE

STUTTERING
(STOPS SHORT AND STARES AT LAZARUS, CONFUSED AND 357 LAZARU
STUTTERING)
(AGAIN OVERCOME--STUTTERING WITH STRANGE TERROR) 359 LAZARU

STUTTERINGLY
STUTTERINGLY.) 197 EJONES

STUTTERS
(SHE STUTTERS INCOHERENTLY, OVERCOME BY RAGE.) 127 BEYOND
(SO AMAZED AT THEIR EFFRONTERY THAT HE STUTTERS IN223 DESIRE
CONFUSION)
HE STUTTERS) 192 EJONES
(HE STUTTERS AND STAMMERS WITH RAGE, HOPPING UP 359 LAZARU
AND DOWN GROTESQUELY.
(THE OLD MAN STUTTERS AND STAMMERS INCOHERENTLY AS594 ROPE
IF THE VERY INTENSITY OF HIS

STY
A COOP/ A PEN/ A STY/ A KENNEL/ 240 HA APE
ITS FULFILLED DESIRE A SNORING IN A STY IN THE MUD330 LAZARU
AMONG SWINE.
LET US LEAVE THIS VILE STY OF LUST AND HATRED AND 185 MANSNS
THE WISH TO MURDER/
CONTENTMENT IS A WARM STY FOR THE EATERS AND 400 MARCOM
SLEEPERS/
GRUNTIN' LOIKE A PIG IN A STY. 500 VOYAGE

STYLE
HE IS DRESSED IN PREP SCHOOL REFLECTION OF THE 193 AHWILD
COLLEGE STYLE OF ARTHUR.)
TOO YOUTHFUL AND EXTREME IN STYLE. 516 DAYS
SHE IS DRESSED SOBERLY AND NEATLY IN HER BLACK 494 DIFRNT
SUNDAY BEST, STYLE OF THE PERIOD.
YOU'LL BUMP YOURSELF ORF IN STYLE, WON'T YERS 184 EJONES
GAWD BLIMEY, BUT YER DIED IN THE 'EIGHT O' STYLE, 204 EJONES
ANYHOW/
FAMILY IN THE MEAGER STYLE TO WHICH THEY'LL HAVE 271 GGBROW
TO BECOME ACCUSTOMEDS
HIS CLOTHES AND SHOES ARE NEW, COMPARATIVELY 585 ICEMAN
EXPENSIVE, SPORTY IN STYLE.
(QUOTES ALOUD TO HIMSELF IN A GUTTURAL DECLAMATORY592 ICEMAN
STYLE)

STYLE 1570

STYLE (CONT'D.)
DRESSED IN SIMILAR STYLE, 615 ICEMAN
HE WANT THIS TO COME OFF IN STYLE, 644 ICEMAN
HE STOPS SINGING TO DENOUNCE THEM IN HIS MOST 727 ICEMAN
FIERY STYLE)
WITH DISCRIMINATING TASTE AND STYLE NOW, AND 75 MANSNS
EXPENSIVELY,
HIS CLOTHES IN THE STYLE OF THE ITALIAN MERCHANT 347 MARCOM
CLASS
AND BURSTS FORTH INTO A MEMORIZED SPEECH IN THE 431 MARCOM
GRAND CHAMBER OF COMMERCE STYLE)
THIS GET-UP SUGGESTS THAT HE FOLLOWS A STYLE SET 37 MISBEG
BY WELL-GROOMED BROADWAY
FINELY TAILORED CLOTHES OF THE STYLE WORN BY 34 POET
ENGLISH ARISTOCRACY
AS LONG AS YOU AND YOUR FINE THOROUGHBRED MARE CAN 59 POET
LIVE IN STYLE/

STYLES
WITH AN IMMENSE MANSION, A CONGLOMERATE OF VARIOUS139 MANSNS
STYLES OF ARCHITECTURE,

STYLISH
I LIKE TO THE QUICK BETTER MYSELF---MORE STYLISH. 272 AHWILD
SHE IS DRESSED IN STYLISH, EXPENSIVE CLOTHES AND A270 GGBROW
FUR COAT,

SU'TIN'
DEM NIGGERS HEAH DAT FO' SU'TIN'/ 190 EJONES

SUAVELY
(SUAVELY) GOSSIP/ 306 GGBROW
HE SPEAKS SUAVELY) 318 GGBROW

SUAVES)
(PUTTING ON HIS SUAVEST MANNER, 176 EJONES

SUAVITY
AND SPEAKS WITH A MOCKING SUAVITY.) 594 ICEMAN

SUB
IT WOULD'A BEEN CLEAR'S A LIGHTHOUSE TO ANY SUB 521 INZONE
THAT WAS WATCHIN'--

SUBCONSCIOUSLY
HAVE MIRRORED HIS DESCRIPTION AS THOUGH, 126 MANSNS
SUBCONSCIOUSLY,
(SARDONICALLY) PERHAPS HE REALIZES SUBCONSCIOUSLY143 STRANG
THAT I AM HIS FATHER,

SUBDUE
THEY APPEAR TO PROTECT AND AT THE SAME TIME 202 DESIRE
SUBDUE.

SUBDUED
(THERE IS THE SOUND OF SUBDUED SOBBING FROM THE 543 'ILE
DOOR IN THE REAR,
MILDRED AND TOMMY ARE SUBDUED, COVERTLY WATCHING 263 AHWILD
THEIR FATHER.
(IN A SUBDUED VOICE) THEN ALL THE OTHERS WAS 36 ANNA
DROWNEDS
(SUBDUED--HIS FACE MELANCHOLY) 77 ANNA
THERE IS THE SUBDUED BABBLE OF VOICES FROM THE 466 CARIBE
CROWD INSIDE BUT THE MOURNFUL
(SUBDUED) PLEASE, MISTER-- 473 CARIBE
THE GRAY SUBDUED LIGHT OF EARLY MORNING IN A 574 ICEMAN
NARROW STREET.
A FRESH BOY'S VOICE IS HEARD SINGING A LOVE SONG 355 MARCOM
IN A SUBDUED TONE.

SUBJECT
CHANGES THE SUBJECT ABRUPTLY BY TURNING TO ARTHUR1190 AHWILD
(SHE CHANGES THE SUBJECT ABRUPTLY) 212 AHWILD
(SHE TURNS AWAY, WIPING A TEAR FURTIVELY--THEN 214 AHWILD
ABRUPTLY CHANGING THE SUBJECT)
(TRYING TO SWITCH THE SUBJECT) 229 AHWILD
(CHANGING THE SUBJECT) SO YOU'RE FAITHFUL TO YOUR243 AHWILD
ONE LOVE, EH?
(DISMISSING THE SUBJECT) SPEAKING OF BEING SICK, 22 ANNA
I BEEN THERE MYSELF--
(CHANGING THE SUBJECT ABRUPTLY) 37 ANNA
(FROWNING) SEEMS TO ME THIS AIN'T NO SUBJECT TO 105 BEYOND
JOKE OVER--NOT FOR ANDY.
(DISMISSING THE SUBJECT) BUT WE'VE AGREED NOT TO 160 BEYOND
TALK OF IT.
(CHANGES THE SUBJECT TACTFULLY) 497 DAYS
I STILL FEEL THE SAME ON THAT SUBJECT. 497 DAYS
(HE DISMISSES THE SUBJECT BY LOOKING DOWN AT HIS 498 DAYS
PAD.
BUT DON'T YOU THINK I'M ABOUT EXHAUSTED AS A 504 DAYS
SUBJECT, UNCLE?
(QUICKLY--CHANGING THE SUBJECT) 506 DAYS
(THEN CHANGING THE SUBJECT ABRUPTLY) 516 DAYS
(AGAIN CHANGING THE SUBJECT) 516 DAYS
SHE AGAIN HURRIEDLY CHANGES THE SUBJECT) 516 DAYS
THAT I SUPPOSE I'M HIPPED ON THE SUBJECT. 524 DAYS
I TOLD YOU THAT WAS ONE SUBJECT WE'D AGREE ON/ 532 DAYS
I'VE LISTENED PATIENTLY WHILE YOU'VE DISCUSSED 543 DAYS
EVERY SUBJECT UNDER THE SUN
PRETENDING TO DISMISS THE SUBJECT) 523 DIFRNT
(HE LOOKS ABOUT HIM, SEEKING A NEUTRAL SUBJECT FOR524 DIFRNT
CONVERSATION.)
BEGINS TO READ IN A DETERMINED EFFORT TO GET HIS 426 DYNAMO
MIND OFF THE SUBJECT.)
(CHANGING THE SUBJECT ABRUPTLY) 178 EJONES
HE SNATCHES AT A CHANCE TO CHANGE THE SUBJECT-- 188 EJONES
SOLICITOUSLY)
SCANDAL BEING FOR HIM MERELY THE SUBJECT MOST 6 ELECTR
POPULAR WITH HIS AUDIENCE.
(THEN ABRUPTLY CHANGING THE SUBJECT) 8 ELECTR
SHE ABRUPTLY CHANGES THE SUBJECT) 16 ELECTR
(AS IF ANXIOUS TO CHANGE THE SUBJECT, LOOKING AT 17 ELECTR
THE FLOWERS SHE CARRIES)
HE CHANGES THE SUBJECT UNEASILY) 38 ELECTR
LET'S CHANGE THE SUBJECT/ 49 ELECTR
(ABRUPTLY CHANGING THE SUBJECT) 59 ELECTR
(ABRUPTLY CHANGING THE SUBJECT) 75 ELECTR
(CHANGING THE SUBJECT CALCULATINGLY) 106 ELECTR
I--(THEN EMBARRASSEDLY CHANGING THE SUBJECT) 144 ELECTR

SUBJECT (CONT'D.)
(THEN CHANGING THE SUBJECT ABRUPTLY) 145 ELECTR
(THEN, WISHING TO LEAVE ON A PLEASANT CHANGE OF 305 GGBROW
SUBJECT--FORCING A SMILE)
(CHANGING THE SUBJECT) BELIEVE ME, THEY'VE 310 GGBROW
NOTICED THE CHANGE IN YOU/
I SWITCHED THE SUBJECT ON HUGHIE, SEE, ON PURPOSE. 26 HUGHIE
(HE CHANGES THE SUBJECT--EARNESTLY.) 33 HUGHIE
(HE CHANGES THE SUBJECT ABRUPT) 587 ICEMAN
(THEN RESENTING BEING MOVED, CHANGES THE SUBJECT) 588 ICEMAN
PARRITT CHANGES THE SUBJECT) 590 ICEMAN
(HE CHANGES THE SUBJECT ABRUPTLY) 590 ICEMAN
THEN LOOKS AWAY AND GRASPS EAGERLY THIS CHANCE TO 593 ICEMAN
CHANGE THE SUBJECT.
IT SEEMED RATHER POINTLESS TO DISCUSS MY OTHER 601 ICEMAN
SUBJECT.
(WARNING TO HIS SUBJECT, SHAKES HIS HEAD SADLY) 627 ICEMAN
WELL, THIS FORCES MY HAND, I GUESS, YOUR BRINGING 663 ICEMAN
UP THE SUBJECT OF EVELYN.
(AS IF THAT FINISHED THE SUBJECT, HE COMES FORWARD694 ICEMAN
TO HOPE AND SITS BESIDE HIM,
(AS IF SHE WANTED TO DISMISS THE SUBJECT BUT 16 JOURNE
CAN'T.)
(TO THE BOYS, CHANGING THE SUBJECT.) 22 JOURNE
I'M NOT INTERESTED IN THE SUBJECT. NEITHER ARE 33 JOURNE
YOU.
(CHANGING THE SUBJECT--FORCING A SMILE.) 41 JOURNE
(SHE CATCHES JAMIE GIVING HER A BITTER GLANCE AND 60 JOURNE
CHANGES THE SUBJECT.)
(UNEASY NOW--CHANGING THE SUBJECT.) 66 JOURNE
(CHANGING THE SUBJECT.) ARE WE GOING TO HAVE THIS111 JOURNE
DRINK, OR AREN'T WE$
(THEN AS EDMUND IS STILL GRINNING, HE CHANGES THE 128 JOURNE
SUBJECT.)
GOD KNOWS, I DON'T LIKE THE SUBJECT EITHER. 129 JOURNE
(WITH DEFENSIVE DRYNESS.) PERHAPS IT WOULD BE 135 JOURNE
WISE TO CHANGE THE SUBJECT.
PERHAPS IT WOULD BE TACTFUL OF ME TO CHANGE THE 135 JOURNE
SUBJECT.
TYRONE CHANGES THE SUBJECT.) 143 JOURNE
(CHANGING THE SUBJECT.) HOW ABOUT OUR GAMES 149 JOURNE
(CHANGING THE SUBJECT.) WHAT DID YOU DO UPTOWN 158 JOURNE
TONIGHT$
BUT LET US CHANGE THE SUBJECT. 316 LAZARU
AND DON'T THINK I DON'T SEE HOW YOU'VE CHANGED THE 83 MANSNS
SUBJECT TO HER
I FORBID YOU EVER TO MENTION THIS SUBJECT AGAIN. 113 MANSNS
(ABRUPTLY CHANGING THE SUBJECT.) 134 MANSNS
(ABRUPTLY CHANGING THE SUBJECT.) 147 MANSNS
(THEN ABRUPTLY CHANGING THE SUBJECT) 348 MARCOM
(TIMOROUSLY-- ANXIOUS TO CHANGE THE SUBJECT) 351 MARCOM
WOULD BE SUBJECT TO A FINE/ 392 MARCOM
(HURRYING ON TO ANOTHER SUBJECT--BOISTEROUSLY) 393 MARCOM
(THEN CHANGING THE SUBJECT ABRUPTLY) 411 MARCOM
THAT WHICH IS SUBJECT TO DEATH SHOULD NOT DIE. 434 MARCOM
BUT DON'T TRY TO CHANGE THE SUBJECT AND FILL ME 14 MISBEG
WITH BLARNEY.
(SHE GETS TO HER FEET, ABRUPTLY CHANGING THE 35 MISBEG
SUBJECT)
(SHE CHANGES THE SUBJECT ABRUPTLY) 124 MISBEG
(ABRUPTLY CHANGING THE SUBJECT) 133 MISBEG
(ABRUPTLY CHANGING THE SUBJECT) 172 MISBEG
(SHE CHANGES THE SUBJECT ABRUPTLY--CLOSING 27 POET
MICKEY'S BAR BOOK.)
(CHANGING THE SUBJECT.) WELL, 30 POET
(CHANGING THE SUBJECT.) I CAN SEE THE HARFORD LAD 30 POET
IS FALLING IN LOVE WITH YOU.
(ANXIOUS TO BRING HIM BACK TO THE SUBJECT) 599 ROPE
BUT I THINK WE'D BETTER LET THE SUBJECT DROP, 33 STRANG
DON'T YOUS
(A BIT SHAMEFACEDLY--CHANGING THE SUBJECT HASTILY) 38 STRANG
(THEN CHANGING THE SUBJECT) 55 STRANG
LIFE AND SHE'S MORBIDLY JEALOUS OF YOU AND SUBJECT179 STRANG
TO QUEER DELUSIONS/
(CHANGING THE SUBJECT OF HIS THOUGHTS ABRUPTLY) 189 STRANG
SUBJECT'S
AND NOW THAT THE SUBJECT'S COME UP OF ITS OWN 295 AHWILD
ACCORD, IT'S A GOOD TIME--

SUBJECTS
IF HE'D ONLY CHOOSE SOME OTHER SUBJECTS BESIDES 288 AHWILD
LOOSE WOMEN.
I CAN THINK OF MORE INTERESTING SUBJECTS. 15 ELECTR
(AS IF THEY WERE SUBJECTS MOVED BY HYPNOTIC 282 LAZARU
SUGGESTION--
WHY, DO NOT MY FAITHFUL SUBJECTS DRAW 354 LAZARU
(HE TURNS AS IF ADDRESSING AN AMPHITHEATRE FULL OF370 LAZARU
HIS SUBJECTS)
HE RULES OVER MILLIONS OF SUBJECTS, 359 MARCOM

SUBMARINES
I DON'T THINK THERE'S MUCH DANGER OF MEETING ANY 514 INZONE
OF THEIR SUBMARINES,
IT IS NOT THE SUBMARINES ONLY WE'VE TO FEAR, I'M 515 INZONE
THINKIN'/
(FRETFULLY) I HOPE BRITISH NAVY BLOW 'EM TO HELL,515 INZONE
THOSE SUBMARINES, BY DAMN/
'E AINT ARE A SLY ONE WIV 'IS TALK OF SUBMARINES,523 INZONE
GAWD BLIND 'IM/

SUBMARINES
D'YE NO KEN THE DANGER O' SHOWIN' A LICHT WI' A 514 INZONE
PACK O' SUBMARINES LYIN' ABOOT

SUBMISSION
(AT LAST INSULTED BEYOND ALL PRUDENT SUBMISSION.) 154 MANSNS
(RUBLAI'S HEAD BENDS IN SUBMISSION, 401 MARCOM
(BOWING HIS HEAD IN SUBMISSION--FATALISTICALLY) 434 MARCOM

SUBMISSIVE
ALTHOUGH NOW IT HAS LOST ALL ITS BITTERNESS AND 249 AHWILD
BECOME SUBMISSIVE AND RESIGNED

SUBMISSIVE (CONT*D.)
BEATS THOSE IN THE ROOM INTO AN ABJECT SUBMISSIVE 349 LAZARU
PANIC.
SUBMISSIVELY
(THEN AS THE TAOIST, SUBMISSIVELY) 434 MARCOM
(THEN AS THE OTHERS, SUBMISSIVELY) 434 MARCOM
(SUBMISSIVELY) DEATH IS. 435 MARCOM
(BOWS SUBMISSIVELY--SPEAKS) YET WE MUST BOW HUMBLY436 MARCOM
BEFORE THE OMNIPOTENT.
HIS SHOULDERS ARE COLLAPSED SUBMISSIVELY. 67 STRANG
HIS EYES DOWN--SHE BENDS HER HEAD MEEKLY AND 88 STRANG
SUBMISSIVELY--SOFTLY)
STARING AT HER BOWED HEAD AS SHE REPEATS 89 STRANG
SUBMISSIVELY)
(SUBMISSIVELY--BUT WITH A LOOK OF BITTER SCORN AT 157 STRANG
HIM)
SUBMISSIVENESS
HE APPEARS TO LISTEN WITH AGREEABLE SUBMISSIVENESS 11 HUGHIE
AND BE IMPRESSED.
SUBMIT
THEY SUBMIT SHRINKINGLY. 108 JOURNE
SUBMITS
AT FIRST, HE SUBMITS DUMBLY. 239 DESIRE
FOR A MOMENT SHE SUBMITS, APPEARS EVEN TO RETURN 460 WELDED
HIS KISSES IN SPITE OF HERSELF.
SHE SUBMITS STOLIDLY. 475 WELDED
SUBMITTING
(SUBMITTING TO HIS KISS--WORRIEDLY) 150 BEYOND
SUBS
THEM*S THE KIND THE SUBS IS LAYIN* FOR. 517 INZONE
IT*S A GOOD LIGHT NIGHT FOR THE SUBS IF THERE*S 523 INZONE
ANY ABOUT.
SUBSERVIENTLY
HE MUMBLES SUBSERVIENTLY.) 194 EJONES
SUBSIDE
(HE STANDS AGAINST THE WAREHOUSE, WAITING FOR THE 104 ELECTR
SWAYING WORLD TO SUBSIDE.
THEY SUBSIDE, AND ROCKY AND CHUCK LET GO OF THEM. 677 ICEMAN
WHICH SUBSIDE INTO THE FORMER HUM OF EXPECTANCY.) 301 LAZARU
SUBSIDES
RICHARD SUBSIDES INTO SCOWLING GLOOM. 243 AHWILD
(RICHARD SUBSIDES, MUTTERING TO HIMSELF) 244 AHWILD
(HE SUBSIDES MEEKLY. 141 ELECTR
(HE SUBSIDES MEEKLY AGAIN. 145 ELECTR
(HE SUBSIDES MEEKLY ON HIS CHAIR, HIS HAND PRESSED287 GGBROW
TO HIS HEART.)
(THE UPROAR SUBSIDES. 211 HA APE
(THE NOISE SUBSIDES.) 243 HA APE
(BUT HE CAN*T GET A RISE OUT OF THEM AND HE 598 ICEMAN
SUBSIDES INTO A FUMING MUMBLE.
(FOR THE MOMENT THIS ARGUMENT SUBSIDES.) 630 ICEMAN
PARRITT INSTANTLY SUBSIDES AND BECOMES SELF- 650 ICEMAN
CONSCIOUS AND DEFENSIVE.
AND CHUCK SUBSIDES INTO COMPLAINING GLOOM) 671 ICEMAN
(MOSHER SUBSIDES. 682 ICEMAN
(PARRITT SUBSIDES, HIDING HIS FACE IN HIS HANDS 706 ICEMAN
AND SHUDDERING.)
AND THE UPROAR SUBSIDES OBEDIENTLY. 44 MANSNS
(SUBSIDES, BUT HIS FACE LOOKS SORROWFUL AND OLD-- 176 MISBEG
DULLY)
(AS MARY*S GRIEF SUBSIDES A TRIFLE, HER VOICE IS 26 STRANG
HEARD, FLAT AND TONELESS)
SUBSIDING
(SUBSIDING AS IF REALIZING THE USELESSNESS OF THIS537 *ILE
OUTBURST--SHAKING HIS HEAD--
(SUBSIDING AT LAST) HAH, HAH, HE*S A CASE, IF 233 AHWILD
EVER THERE WAS ONE/
(SUBSIDING GRUMPILY) THIS IS A FREE COUNTRY, 134 ELECTR
AIN*T IT.
SUBSTANCE
A PASSING BACK INTO HER SUBSTANCE, BLOOD OF HER 43 STRANG
BLOOD AGAIN, PEACE OF HER PEACE/
SUBSTANTIAL
FIRST COME THE GUESTS, MALE AND FEMALE, A CROWD OF427 MARCOM
GOOD SUBSTANTIAL BOURGEOIS,
SUBSTITUTE
AND I MUST SAY, AS A LOVE SUBSTITUTE OR EVEN A 520 DAYS
PLEASURABLE DIVERSION,
HAS MY FOUR SONS TO SUBSTITUTE FOR ME, AND THE 73 MANSNS
WIFE HAVING THEM,
(SMILING) YES, PERHAPS UNCONSCIOUSLY PRESTON IS A166 STRANG
COMPENSATING SUBSTITUTE.
I WAS NEVER MORE TO YOU THAN A SUBSTITUTE FOR YOUR174 STRANG
DEAD LOVER/
SUBSTITUTES
SINCE THEN WE HAVE BOTH BEEN CONDEMNED TO AN 183 MANSNS
INSATIABLE GREED FOR SUBSTITUTES--
SUBTLE
(THEN WITH SUBTLE FLATTERY) THEY*RE ALL WELL 207 AHWILD
ENOUGH, IN THEIR WAY,
SHE IS DRESSED WITH A CAREFUL, SUBTLE EXTRA TOUCH 308 GGBROW
TO ATTRACT THE EYE.
THE MURDER WAS SUBTLE AND CRUEL-- 355 LAZARU
THAT SUBTLE AND CRAFTY WOMAN/ 356 LAZARU
SHE IMAGINES SHE HAS BEEN VERY SUBTLE, THAT I HAVE 72 MANSNS
NOT SEEN.
HAVE SEEMED, THROUGH THE SUBTLE POWER OF MOTHER*S 73 MANSNS
FANTASTIC WILL,
(SMILING.) MOTHER HAS ALWAYS HAD A SUBTLE TALENT 77 MANSNS
FOR CONTRIVING IT SO THAT
WE HAVE BUILT UP A SECRET LIFE OF SUBTLE 148 STRANG
SYMPATHIES AND CONFIDENCES...
SUBTLY
ALTHOUGH AT TIMES ONE OR ANOTHER MAY SUBTLY SENSE 496 DAYS
HIS PRESENCE.
AND PARTICULARLY THE PROFESSOR HIMSELF--SUBTLY 7 STRANG
EMBARRASSED.

SUBTRACTION
SUBTRACTION IS MY FORTE. 602 ICEMAN
SUBTRACTS
DEATH SUBTRACTS ANTHONY AND I SELL OUT--BILLY 272 GGBROW
GRADUATES--
SUBURB
IN A SEASHORE SUBURB NEAR NEW YORK. 90 STRANG
SUBWAY
MET HER ON A SUBWAY TRAIN. 23 HUGHIE
SUCCEED
(WITH A GRIM SMILE) SHE DIDN*T SUCCEED, AS YOU 26 ELECTR
NOTICE/
NEVER WANTED YOU SUCCEED AND MAKE ME LOOK EVEN 165 JOURNE
WORSE BY COMPARISON.
I*M SURE YOU*LL SUCCEED. 357 MARCOM
I*VE GOT TO SUCCEED AND--(SUDDENLY BLURTS OUT) 380 MARCOM
WHAT CAN YOU PAY ME/
AND I*M CONVINCED HE*S GOT THE RIGHT STUFF IN HIM 38 STRANG
TO SUCCEED.
OH, HE*LL SUCCEED ALL RIGHT... 113 STRANG
SUCCEEDED
YOU CAN*T DENY THAT WITHOUT HELP I*VE SUCCEEDED 148 BEYOND
IN--
(BITTERLY) HAS SHE SUCCEEDED IN CONVINCING YOU 96 ELECTR
I*M OUT OF MY MIND/
HAS HE NOT ALWAYS SUCCEEDED WHERE OTHERS FAILED/ 387 MARCOM
SUCCEEDING
THEN SARA*S VOICE TRYING TO QUIET THEM AND, FOR 43 MANSNS
THE MOMENT, SUCCEEDING.
OH, IT CAN*T HELP SUCCEEDING... 177 STRANG
SUCCEEDS
KICKS AGAIN AT THE BUCKET BUT ONLY SUCCEEDS IN 526 INZONE
HITTING COCKY ON THE SHIN.
FINALLY HE SUCCEEDS, AND TAKES A DEEP INHALE, 111 MISBEG
SUCCESS
ANDY*S MADE A BIG SUCCESS OF HIMSELF--THE KIND HE 147 BEYOND
WANTED.
MUSINGLY) WHEN YOU PROPOSED, I THOUGHT YOUR 259 GGBROW
FUTURE PROMISED SUCCESS--MY FUTURE--
HE TELLS EVERYBODY THE SUCCESS IS ALL DUE TO HIS 260 GGBROW
ENERGY--
SO HERE*S WISHING YOU ALL THE SUCCESS AND 263 GGBROW
HAPPINESS IN THE WORLD, MARGARET--
HE*S BOUND HEAVEN-BENT FOR SUCCESS. 272 GGBROW
I*VE DESIGNED EVEN HIS SUCCESS--DRUNK AND LAUGHING297 GGBROW
AT HIM--
LAST SCENE--THE SELF-ASSURED SUCCESS. 303 GGBROW
THAT THIS EMBITTERED FAILURE ANTHONY IS HURLING IN317 GGBROW
THE TEETH OF OUR SUCCESS--
THAT ALL A GUY HAD TO DO WAS COME TO THE BIG TOWN 23 HUGHIE
AND OLD MAN SUCCESS WOULD BE
AS HISTOR HISTORY PROVES, TO BE A WORLDLY SUCCESS 590 ICEMAN
AT ANY THING, ESPECIALLY REVOL
WITH THE AIR OF A HOST WHOSE PARTY IS A HUGE 726 ICEMAN
SUCCESS, AND RAMBLES ON HAPPILY)
I*LL NEVER BE A SUCCESS IN THE GRANDSTAND--OR 726 ICEMAN
ANYWHERE ELSE/
EDMUND TRIES TO COPY THIS DEFENSE BUT WITHOUT 71 JOURNE
SUCCESS.
A GREAT MONEY SUCCESS--IT RUINED ME WITH ITS 149 JOURNE
PROMISE OF AN EASY FORTUNE.
THAT GOD-DAMNED PLAY I BOUGHT FOR A SONG AND MADE 149 JOURNE
SUCH A GREAT SUCCESS IN--
BUT IT WAS A GREAT BOX OFFICE SUCCESS FROM THE 150 JOURNE
START--
GRAB OPPORTUNITY BY THE FORELOCK. KEY TO MY 156 JOURNE
SUCCESS.
I SHALL ATTAIN THE PINNACLE OF SUCCESS/ 160 JOURNE
(MOCKINGLY.) THE SECRET OF MY SUCCESS/ 165 JOURNE
I*D LIKE TO SEE YOU BECOME THE GREATEST SUCCESS IN165 JOURNE
THE WORLD.
JUDGING FROM YOUR LETTERS, YOU MUST BE MAKING A 14 MANSNS
GREAT SUCCESS OF IT.
ONE WOULD THINK YOU WERE ASHAMED OF YOUR SUCCESS. 15 MANSNS
THE DANGER IS THAT YOUR DISCONTENT WILL GROW AND 17 MANSNS
GROW WITH YOUR SUCCESS UNTIL--
I WANT TO BE PROUD OF WHAT YOU ARE, OF THE GREAT 61 MANSNS
SUCCESS I SEE BEFORE YOU.
FOR MATERIAL SUCCESS. 61 MANSNS
THE REACTION OF EMPTINESS AFTER SUCCESS--YOU*VE 74 MANSNS
ALWAYS FELT IT--
I OWE HER ALL MY SUCCESS. 88 MANSNS
HE HAS THE LOOK OF SUCCESS, 150 MANSNS
YOU WERE BORN WITH SUCCESS IN YOUR POCKET/ 363 MARCOM
TRAINING FOR SUCCESS, ETC. 66 STRANG
WHEN I GET BACK I*LL EXPECT TO HEAR YOU*RE ON THE 106 STRANG
HIGHROAD TO SUCCESS/
A LITTLE SUCCESS.... 113 STRANG
BOUND FOR SUCCESS SAM IS. 128 STRANG
(MY EXPERIMENT WITH THE GUINEA PIGS HAS BEEN A 134 STRANG
SUCCESS...
THE GOOD SAMUEL IS AN A ONE SUCCESS. 141 STRANG
HIS TYPE LOGICALLY DEVELOPED BY TEN YEARS OF 159 STRANG
CONTINUED SUCCESS AND ACCUMULATING
BUT OUR STATION IS A *HUGE SUCCESS,* AS SAM WOULD 165 STRANG
SAY.
HE HAS BEEN TOO THOROUGHLY TRAINED TO PROGRESS 184 STRANG
ALONG A CERTAIN GROOVE TO SUCCESS
SUCCESS TO YER BLOOMIN* FARM AN* MAY YER LIVE LONG507 VOYAGE
AN* *APPY ON IT.
THE PLAY WAS SUCH A MARVELOUS SUCCESS/ 447 WELDED
SUCCESSFUL
THE FATHER IS FIFTY OR MORE, THE TYPE OF BUSTLING,257 GGBROW
GENIAL, SUCCESSFUL,
SUCCESSFUL SERIOUS ONE, THE GREAT GOD MR. BROWN, 282 GGBROW
INSTEAD/
SUCCESSFUL PROVINCIAL AMERICAN OF FORTY. 288 GGBROW
(BROWN STIRS UNEASILY) TO BE MERELY A SUCCESSFUL 296 GGBROW
FREAK,

SUCCESSFUL

SUCCESSFUL (CONT'D.)
(THE SUCCESSFUL ARCHITECT NOW--URBANELY) 306 GGROW
ONCE IN A WHILE ONE OF THEM MAKES A SUCCESSFUL 593 ICEMAN
TOUCH SOMEWHERE.
HIS CLOTHES ARE THOSE OF A SUCCESSFUL DRUMMER 619 ICEMAN
WHOSE TERRITORY CONSISTS OF MINOR
SOME DAY WHEN YOU'RE ALL WELL, AND I SEE YOU 93 JOURNE
HEALTHY AND HAPPY AND SUCCESSFUL,
I WOULD HAVE BEEN MUCH MORE SUCCESSFUL AS A SEA 153 JOURNE
GULL OR A FISH.
YOU ARE GETTING YOUR FATHER'S SUCCESSFUL-MERCHANT 6 MANSNS
LOOK.
YES, HAVEN'T I ALWAYS SAID JOEL IS GOD'S MOST 61 MANSNS
SUCCESSFUL EFFORT IN TAXIDERMY/
YOU WILL BE SUCCESSFUL. 91 MANSNS
IS NOT TOO SUCCESSFUL--BUT EACH IS LYING AND 123 MANSNS
ACTING, OF COURSE--
HE HAS THE MANNER AND APPEARANCE OF A SUCCESSFUL 390 MARCOM
MOVIE STAR AT A MASQUERADE.
THE SUCCESSFUL SEDUCER OF OLD. 70 POET
(THEN GLOOMILY) (MY RUNNING AWAY WAS ABOUT AS 112 STRANG
SUCCESSFUL AS HIS...
YOU MUST ADMIT YOU WERE ANYTHING BUT SUCCESSFUL/ 457 WELDED
AND WE'LL ALL THREE BE ENORMOUSLY SUCCESSFUL/ 469 WELDED
SUCCESSFULLY
NO MAN CAN RUN A CIRCUS SUCCESSFULLY WHO BELIEVES 681 ICEMAN
GUYS CHEW COFFEE BEANS BECAUSE
IF THEY CAN BE SUCCESSFULLY NEGOTIATED, MAY SAVE 32 MANSNS
THE FIRM.
THEN YOU CAN GO ON--SUCCESSFULLY--WITH A CLEAR 91 MANSNS
VISION--WITHOUT FALSE SCRUPLE--
IS LAUNCHED SUCCESSFULLY. 94 MANSNS
YOU MUST ADMIT I GOT RID OF HER VERY SUCCESSFULLY.177 MANSNS
I ENDED IT WITH AN EXPERIMENT WHICH RESULTED SO 140 STRANG
SUCCESSFULLY THAT ANY FURTHER
SUCK
FISH--STRETCHING OUT TO SUCK ME IN-- 484 DYNAMO
WHINE, STING, SUCK ONE'S BLOOD... 52 STRANG
SUCKER
YES, EVERYONE KNOWS YOU'RE AN OLD SUCKER, NAT, TOO204 AHWILD
DECENT FOR YOUR OWN GOOD.
DON'T BE A SUCKER, KID/ 243 AHWILD
HAVE IT YOUR OWN WAY AND BE A SUCKER/ 243 AHWILD
LOVE IS HELL ON A POOR SUCKER. 272 AHWILD
I'M NO SUCKER, NO MATTER WHAT YOU THINK/ 289 AHWILD
YE OLD BLOOD SUCKER/ 223 DESIRE
LIFE CAN COST TOO MUCH EVEN FOR A SUCKER TO AFFORD286 GGBROW
IT--LIKE EVERYTHING ELSE.
I'M A SUCKER FOR BLONDES. 12 HUGHIE
I'M NO SUCKER. 12 HUGHIE
CLOSEST I EVER COME TO BEING PLAYED FOR A SUCKER. 14 HUGHIE
HE WAS JUST A SUCKER. 18 HUGHIE
BECAUSE HE WAS A SUCKER, SEE-- 20 HUGHIE
«NIX,» I TOLD HIM, «IF YOU'RE GOING TO START 22 HUGHIE
PLAYIN' SUCKER
ME ADVISING A SUCKER NOT TO BET WHEN I'VE SPENT A 22 HUGHIE
LOT OF MY LIFE
BUT I SOON SEE HE WAS CRYIN' FOR MORE, AND WHEN A 28 HUGHIE
SUCKER CRIES FOR MORE,
(HE ADDS SADLY.) AND SO HE WAS, AT THAT--EVEN IF 31 HUGHIE
HE WAS A SUCKER.
AFFECTIONATE WINK WITH WHICH A WISE GUY REGALES A 38 HUGHIE
SUCKER.)
NO ONE EVER PLAYED HARRY HOPE FOR A SUCKER/ 582 ICEMAN
IT'S DE SUCKER GAME YOU AND HUGO CALL DE MOVEMENT.584 ICEMAN
I ALWAYS GAVE A SUCKER SOME CHANCE. 609 ICEMAN
AND A TON OF GOOD ADVICE ABOUT WHAT A SUCKER HE IS651 ICEMAN
TO STAND FOR US.
D'YOU THINK I'M A SUCKERS 654 ICEMAN
I'M SICK OF BEING PLAYED FOR A SUCKER/ 660 ICEMAN
HICKEY AIN'T MADE NO SUCKER OUTA YOU, HUH$ 676 ICEMAN
I'VE PLAYED SUCKER FOR DAT CRUMMY BLONDE LONG 697 ICEMAN
ENOUGH.
I WANNA COLLECT DE DOUGH I WOULDN'T TAKE DIS 699 ICEMAN
MORNIN', LIKE A SUCKER.
SO DON'T BE A SUCKER, SEE$ 702 ICEMAN
SHE WAS A SUCKER FOR A PIPE DREAM. 710 ICEMAN
AND PLAYING SUCKER FOR EVERY CON MAN WITH A GOLD 141 JOURNE
MINE, OR A SILVER MINE.
TRUST AND BE A SUCKER. 66 MISBEG
JUST BECAUSE THAT BROADWAY SUCKER THINKS YOU'RE 94 MISBEG
ONE,
BE GOD, YOU'LL MAKE HIM THE PRIZE SUCKER OF THE 95 MISBEG
WORLD/
SUCKER'S
MADE FUN OF WORK AS SUCKER'S GAME. 165 JOURNE
SUCKERS
WHEN, NO MATTER HOW MUCH HE'D WIN ON A RUN OF LUCK 20 HUGHIE
LIKE SUCKERS HAVE SOMETIMES,
MAKING SUCKERS OF THE DAMNED. 628 ICEMAN
DAT LOUSE HICKEY'S CUTTINLY MADE A PRIZE COUPLA 670 ICEMAN
SUCKERS OUTA YOUSE.
LOT OF LOUD-MOUTHED FAKERS, WHO WERE CHEATING 701 ICEMAN
SUCKERS WITH A PHONY PIPE DREAM.
UNY SUCKERS WOIK. 702 ICEMAN
LISTENING TO MY OLD MAN WHOOPING UP HELL FIRE AND 709 ICEMAN
SCARING THOSE HOOSIER SUCKERS
WE'RE ALL FALL GUYS AND SUCKERS AND WE CAN'T BEAT 76 JOURNE
THE GAME/
WHERE EVERYONE LANDS IN THE END, EVEN IF MOST OF 161 JOURNE
THE SUCKERS WON'T ADMIT IT.
SUCKERS'
HE'D READ SOMEWHERE--IN THE SUCKERS' ALMANAC, I 23 HUGHIE
GUESS--
SUDDEN
(IN A SUDDEN RAGE, SHAKING HIS FIST AT THE 536 'ILE
SKYLIGHT)
(IN SUDDEN TERROR) ANSWER ME/ 551 'ILE

SUDDEN

SUDDEN (CONT'D.)
(THEN WITH SUDDEN EXCITEMENT) 277 AHWILD
(THEN HAS A SUDDEN THOUGHT) BUT I'VE DONE ALL 292 AHWILD
THIS TALKING ABOUT MURIEL AND
(WITH SUDDEN PASSION) MEN, I HATE 'EM--ALL OF 16 ANNA
'EM/
(THEN WITH SUDDEN INTEREST) SAY, DO YOU HANG 16 ANNA
AROUND THIS DUMP MUCHS
(WITH SUDDEN MELANCHOLY) IT'S A HARD AND LONESOME 37 ANNA
LIFE, THE SEA IS.
(WITH SUDDEN CHANGE OF TONE--PERSUASIVELY) 43 ANNA
(GLANCING AT HIM WITH SUDDEN ALARM) 43 ANNA
WITH A SUDDEN HUSH OF ANGER, DRAWING BACK HIS 49 ANNA
FIST)
(THEN WITH A SUDDEN JOYOUS DEFIANCE) 51 ANNA
(DESPERATELY) BUT WHAT'S COME OVER YOU SO SUDDENN 53 ANNA
(WITH A SUDDEN WEARINESS IN HER VOICE) 58 ANNA
COMING AT ME SO SUDDEN AND ME THINKING I WAS 69 ANNA
ALONE.
(THEN WITH SUDDEN WILD GRIEF) 69 ANNA
HIS FACE LIGHTS UP WITH A SUDDEN HAPPY THOUGHT. 76 ANNA
(WITH SUDDEN FIERCE QUESTIONING) 76 ANNA
WELL, IF YOU GET TO BE A MILLIONAIRE ALL OF A 85 BEYOND
SUDDEN,
(WITH SUDDEN INTENSITY) OH, ROB, WHY DO YOU WANT 88 BEYOND
TO GOS
(OVERCOME BY A SUDDEN FEAR) YOU WON'T GO AWAY ON 91 BEYOND
THE TRIP,
(A SUDDEN UNEASINESS SEEMS TO STRIKE HIM) 96 BEYOND
WHATEVER GOT INTO HER OF A SUDDEN$ 100 BEYOND
UPSETTIN' ALL YOUR PLANS SO SUDDEN/ 100 BEYOND
(IN A MORE KINDLY TONE) WHAT'S COME OVER YOU SO 105 BEYOND
SUDDEN, ANDY$
(WITH SUDDEN ANGUISH) OH, ANDY, YOU CAN'T GO/ 137 BEYOND
(AFTER A PAUSE--A SUDDEN SUSPICION FORMING IN HER 138 BEYOND
MIND)
RUTH TURNS AND GRABS HER UP IN HER ARMS WITH A 140 BEYOND
SUDDEN FIERCE TENDERNESS.
(WITH A SUDDEN EXASPERATION) 148 BEYOND
(WITH SUDDEN EXASPERATION) OH, I WISH YOU'D NEVER152 BEYOND
MARRIED THAT MAN/
(A SUDDEN, HORRIBLE SUSPICION ENTERING HIS MIND) 155 BEYOND
(APPALLED BY A SUDDEN THOUGHT) 158 BEYOND
(WITH SUDDEN FIERCENESS) HOW COULD I HELP ITS 164 BEYOND
HE'S DEAD. (WITH A SUDDEN BURST OF FURY) 168 BEYOND
THIS IS FOLLOWED BY A SUDDEN SILENCE 456 CARIBBE
(WITH A SUDDEN HARSHNESS) DIDN'T I TELL YOU HE'S 557 CROSS
MADS
(WITH SUDDEN TERROR) IT WASN'T--FATHERS 563 CROSS
(WITH SUDDEN MEANING--DELIBERATELY) 565 CROSS
NO, I DON'T--(THEN IN A SUDDEN FRENZY) YES/ 567 CROSS
BUT I DID WONDER A LITTLE AT YOUR SUDDEN COMPLETE 516 DAYS
IGNORING OF OUR EXISTENCE.
(THEN WITH SUDDEN VINDICTIVE ANGER) 215 DESIRE
A SUDDEN HORRIBLE THOUGHT SEEMS TO ENTER CABOT'S 225 DESIRE
HEAD)
(AGITATEDLY) WHAT'S ALL THIS SUDDEN LIKIN' YE'VE 232 DESIRE
TUK TO EBEN$
THEN WITH A SUDDEN MOVEMENT HE SEIZES HER HANDS 232 DESIRE
AND SQUEEZES THEM,
(THEN WITH A SUDDEN FORCED REASSURANCE) 234 DESIRE
I KNOWED SUDDEN I LOVED YE YET, AN' ALLUS WOULD 266 DESIRE
LOVE YE/
(WITH A SUDDEN GUFFAW) OH, HELL, YES/ 499 DIFRNT
OR ARE YOU GONE CRAZY ALL OF A SUDDEN$ 504 DIFRNT
BUT THEN IT STARTED TO COME IN AGAIN BLACK AS 537 DIFRNT
BLACK ALL OF A SUDDEN.
(UNHEEDING--WITH A SUDDEN OMINOUS CALM) 543 DIFRNT
(WITH SUDDEN FURY) DAMN HIS HIDE/ 546 DIFRNT
(AFTER A TENSE PAUSE--WITH A SUDDEN OUTBURST OF 549 DIFRNT
WILD GRIEF)
(THEN WITH A SUDDEN AIR OF HAVING DECIDED 549 DIFRNT
SOMETHING IRREVOCABLY)
WHY HAS REUBEN TAKEN A SUDDEN NOTION TO GOING OUT 425 DYNAMO
IN THE EVENING LATELY$
(SHE HAS COME TO THE BED--WITH SUDDEN FEAR) 427 DYNAMO
A SUDDEN THRILL OF DESIRE OVERCOMES HIS TIMIDITY) 433 DYNAMO
(WITH A SUDDEN CHANGE TO SEVERITY) 436 DYNAMO
(WITH SUDDEN STRONG REVULSION) (IANO TO THINK 446 DYNAMO
I FELT A SUDDEN HUNCH I HAD TO COME... 457 DYNAMO
(THEN WITH A SUDDEN BURST OF THREATENING 460 DYNAMO
ASSERTIVENESS)
(THEN WITH SUDDEN EAGERNESS) 461 DYNAMO
(WITH A SUDDEN RENEWAL OF HIS UNNATURAL 477 DYNAMO
EXCITEMENT, BREAKS AWAY FROM HER)
(THEN THINKING WITH SUDDEN FEAR AND DOUBT) 478 DYNAMO
YOU GAVE ME A START, SEEING YOU ALL OF A SUDDEN. 481 DYNAMO
(THIS PUTS A SUDDEN IDEA INTO HIS HEAD--THINKING 481 DYNAMO
EXCITEDLY.)
THEN WITH A SUDDEN HUNGRY PASSION) 482 DYNAMO
(IN A SUDDEN FIT OF ANGER FLINGS THE BELL 182 EJONES
CLATTERING INTO A CORNER)
(WITH SUDDEN FORCED DEFIANCE--IN AN ANGRY TONE) 189 EJONES
THEN WITH SUDDEN ANGER.) 193 EJONES
(WITH A SUDDEN TERROR) LAWD GOD, DON'T LET ME SEE193 EJONES
NO MORE O' DEM HANTS/
(WITH A SUDDEN FLURRY OF JEALOUSY) 34 ELECTR
WHERE DID SHE DISAPPEAR TO ALL OF A SUDDEN$ 68 ELECTR
AND IT'S A POOR TIME, WHEN THIS HOUSEHOLD IS 70 ELECTR
AFFLICTED BY SUDDEN DEATH, TO BE--
WHAT'S MADE YOU TAKE SUCH A FANCY TO HAZEL ALL OF 84 ELECTR
A SUDDEN
(STRUCK BY A SUDDEN IDEA--GRASPS HIS ARM) 100 ELECTR
EZRA DYIN' SUDDEN HIS FIRST NIGHT TO HUM--THAT WAS133 ELECTR
DURNED QUEER.
(WITH SUDDEN HARSHNESS) FORGETS 140 ELECTR
(UNHEEDING--WITH A SUDDEN TURN TO BITTER RESENTFUL140 ELECTR
DEFIANCE)

SUDDEN (CONT'D.)
(IN A SUDDEN STRANGE TONE OF JEERING MALICE) 144 ELECTR
(WITH SUDDEN INTENSITY) NO/ 148 ELECTR
(WITH A SUDDEN FLARE OF DELIBERATELY EVIL TAUNTING)155 ELECTR
(THEN WITH SUDDEN ANGER AS HE SEES THE GROWING 165 ELECTR
HORRIFIED REPULSION ON HER FACE)
A MANNON HAS COME TO MEAN SUDDEN DEATH TO 'EM. 170 ELECTR
(WITH A SUDDEN SHIVER) THE NIGHTS ARE SO MUCH 259 GGBROW
COLDER THAN THEY USED TO BE/
THEN WITH A SUDDEN GESTURE HE CLAPS HIS 266 GGBROW
(THEN, IN A SUDDEN EXCITABLE PASSION) 281 GGBROW
HE GRABS UP THE MASK IN A SUDDEN PANIC AND, AS A 291 GGBROW
KNOCK COMES ON THE DOOR,
(WITH SUDDEN WILDNESS--TORTUREDLY, SINKING ON HIS 292 GGBROW
KNEES BESIDE HER)
THERE IS A SUDDEN LOUD THUMPING ON THE FRONT DOOR 294 GGBROW
AND THE RINGING OF THE BELL.
(THEN WITH SUDDEN FRENZIED DEFIANCE) 298 GGBROW
FUNNY HIS FIRING HIM ALL OF A SUDDEN LIKE THAT. 302 GGBROW
(WITH SUDDEN DESPERATION) MARGARET, I'VE GOT TO 305 GGBROW
TELL YOU/
THEN, IN A SUDDEN PANIC OF DREAD, 307 GGBROW
(THEN WITH A SUDDEN MOVEMENT HE FLOURISHES THE 315 GGBROW
DESIGN BEFORE HER)
(WITH A SUDDEN GOATISH CAPER) 317 GGBROW
(THEN WITH A SUDDEN COMPLETE CHANGE OF TONE-- 317 GGBROW
ANGRILY)
THIS DRIVES YANK INTO A SUDDEN FURY. 225 HA APE
(THEY ARE SILENT, PUZZLED BY HIS SUDDEN RESENTMENT)227 HA APE
(WITH SUDDEN ANGRY DISGUST) AW, HELL/ 234 HA APE
(THEN WITH SUDDEN RAGE, RATTLING HIS CELL BARS) 240 HA APE
(THEN, WITH SUDDEN PASSIONATE DESPAIR) 254 HA APE
SIMPLE GUY LIKE HUGHIE WILL ALL OF A SUDDEN GET 21 HUGHIE
SOMETHING RIGHT.
IT STOPPED SUDDEN AND SHE WAS JERKED INTO HIM, AND 23 HUGHIE
HE PUT HIS ARMS AROUND HER,
CRYIN' OVER HER PICTURE AND DEN SPRINGIN' IT ON 580 ICEMAN
YUH ALL OF A SUDDEN
(HE YAWNS AGAIN) GOD, I'M SLEEPY ALL OF A SUDDEN.625 ICEMAN
PARRITT ASKS HIM WITH A SUDDEN TAUNT IN HIS VOICE)646 ICEMAN
AS THOUGH STRUCK BY A SUDDEN PARALYSIS OF THE 677 ICEMAN
WILL.
(THEN IN A SUDDEN FURY, HIS VOICE TREMBLING WITH 688 ICEMAN
HATRED)
ALL OF A SUDDEN ROCKY SENSES THEY ARE DETECTIVES 708 ICEMAN
AND SPRINGS UP TO FACE THEM,
(WITH SUDDEN SAVAGERY) CALLS THEYSELVES 'UMAN 517 INZONE
BEIN'S, TOO/
(WITH SUDDEN TENSENESS). 17 JOURNE
(WITH SUDDEN NERVOUS EXASPERATION.) 26 JOURNE
WHY ARE YOU SO SUSPICIOUS ALL OF A SUDDEN& 45 JOURNE
AND, FOR PETE'S SAKE, MAMA, WHY JUMP ON JAMIE ALL 61 JOURNE
OF A SUDDEN&
BUT WHY ALL OF A SUDDEN--& 90 JOURNE
(WITH SUDDEN, BIG-BROTHERLY SOLICITUDE, GRABBING 156 JOURNE
THE BOTTLE.)
THEN A SUDDEN SWELLING CHORUS OF FORLORN 295 LAZARU
BEWILDERMENT,
(WITH THE SUDDEN GRANDIOSE POSTURING OF A BAD 301 LAZARU
ACTOR)
(WITH SUDDEN PASSIONATE INTENSITY BUT ONLY HALF 303 LAZARU
ALOUD AS IF TO HIMSELF)
THEN, OF A SUDDEN, A STRANGE GAY LAUGHTER TREMBLED309 LAZARU
FROM HIS HEART
(IN A SUDDEN OUTBURST AS IF HE WERE DRUNK WITH 321 LAZARU
EXCITEMENT,
(THEN WITH A SUDDEN EXASPERATION) 329 LAZARU
(THERE IS THE SUDDEN BLARING OF A TRUMPET FROM 331 LAZARU
WITHIN THE PALACE.
WAS IT NOT BECAUSE OF A SUDDEN YOU LOVED HIM AND 334 LAZARU
COULD NOT&
(THEN WITH SUDDEN HARSHNESS) 361 LAZARU
(WITH SUDDEN EXCITEMENT) 364 LAZARU
(IN A SUDDEN PANICKY FLURRY--FEVERISHLY) 367 LAZARU
(STARES AT HIM--A SUDDEN TRANSFORMATION COMES OVER 31 MANSNS
HER.
(WITH SUDDEN DISMAY.) THEN YOU DECIDED IT ALL-- 62 MANSNS
WITHOUT WAITING TO ASK ME/
I DO NOT POSSESS THE ENTIRE CONFIDENCE IN THIS 67 MANSNS
SUDDEN FRIENDSHIP
(HE CHECKS HIMSELF WITH A SUDDEN WARY GLANCE AT 73 MANSNS
JOEL.)
SOMETIMES AT NIGHT WHEN YOU SIT IN THE PARLOR WITH 80 MANSNS
US, ALL OF A SUDDEN,
(WITH A SUDDEN FIERCE PASSION SHE GRABS HIS HEAD 80 MANSNS
AND TURNS HIS FACE UP TO HERS.)
(WITH A SUDDEN UNDERLYING HOSTILITY.) 131 MANSNS
(WITH SUDDEN REVULSION, PUSHES BACK FROM HIM.) 145 MANSNS
(HE SMILES AT HER WITH A SUDDEN AWKWARD 183 MANSNS
TENDERNESS.)
(WITH SUDDEN CUNNING MOTION, HE SNATCHES IT FROM 360 MARCOM
MARCO'S HAND.
(THEN WITH A SUDDEN WHIMSICALITY) 363 MARCOM
(GENUINELY OVERCOME BY A SUDDEN SHAME) 371 MARCOM
THERE IS A SUDDEN DEAD SILENCE. 377 MARCOM
(WITH SUDDEN FURY) YOU'RE A HEATHEN LIAR/ 380 MARCOM
(HE TURNS WITH A SUDDEN FIERCENESS ON THE BAND 406 MARCOM
(WITH SUDDEN FEAR) SO SOON& 411 MARCOM
(LOOKS AT HIM WITH A SUDDEN DAWNING OF HOPE-- 411 MARCOM
GENTLY)
(WITH A SUDDEN CHANGE--SOFTLY) 412 MARCOM
(THEN WITH A SUDDEN INSPIRATION) 422 MARCOM
(WITH SUDDEN REVULSION) FOR GOD'S SAKE, CUT OUT 42 MISBEG
THAT KIND OF TALK, JOSIE/
(WITH SUDDEN RAGE) GOD'S CURSE ON HIM, 83 MISBEG
YOU'RE FULL OF SLY ADVICE ALL OF A SUDDEN, AIN'T 93 MISBEG
YOU&
MUST HAVE GOT HIM ALL OF A SUDDEN. 101 MISBEG

SUDDENLY

SUDDEN (CONT'D.)
SURE, YOU'RE FULL OF FINE COMPLIMENTS ALL OF A 118 MISBEG
SUDDEN,
(THEN WITH SUDDEN ANGUISHED LONGING) 153 MISBEG
(A SUDDEN REVULSION OF FEELING CONVULSES HIS FACE. 42 POET
GLORY BE, BUT YOU'VE CHANGED ALL OF A SUDDEN. 64 POET
FOR A MOMENT, BLINDED BY THE SUDDEN CHANGE FROM 67 POET
THE BRIGHT GLARE OF THE STREET,
(WITH A SUDDEN REVERSAL OF FEELING--ALMOST 77 POET
VINDICTIVELY.)
SHE WARNED HIM A SUDDEN WEDDING WOULD LOOK 110 POET
DAMNABLY SUSPICIOUS
IT IS OBVIOUS THAT WERE THERE A SUDDEN WEDDING 110 POET
WITHOUT A SUITABLE PERIOD OF
IT IS MORE AS IF A SUDDEN SHOCK OR STROKE HAD 152 POET
SHATTERED HIS COORDINATION
HE MIGHT COME TO ALL AV A SUDDEN AND GIVE YOU A 160 POET
HELL AV A THRASHIN'.
(THERE IS A SUDDEN LULL IN THE NOISE FROM THE BAR,180 POET
AT A SUDDEN NOISE FROM OUTSIDE SHE JUMPS TO HER 578 ROPE
FEET, PEEKS OUT,
THEM AS BAD AS HIM COMES TO A SUDDEN END. 581 ROPE
MARY PULLS AT HIS HAND IN A SUDDEN FIT OF IMPISH 584 ROPE
GLEE, AND LAUGHS SHRILLY)
(WITH SUDDEN DECISION) YOU'D BEST LAVE HIM TO ME 590 ROPE
TO WATCH OUT FOR.
(WITH SUDDEN LUGUBRIOUSNESS) 598 ROPE
(WITH SUDDEN FURY) I'LL FIX HIS HASH/ 598 ROPE
THIS IS RATHER A SUDDEN DECISION, ISN'T IT& 15 STRANG
(WITH A SUDDEN INTENSITY IN HER TONE) 18 STRANG
(TURNING TO MARSDEN--WITH A SUDDEN GIRLISHNESS) 21 STRANG
(THEN WITH SUDDEN BITTERNESS) 25 STRANG
(THEN IN A SUDDEN FLURRY) (SHALL I TELL HIM&... 31 STRANG
(THINKING WITH SUDDEN AGONY) 44 STRANG
(WITH SUDDEN JEALOUS SUSPICION) 50 STRANG
AND THEN ALL OF A SUDDEN SHE BECAME CONTENTED... 52 STRANG
(WITH SUDDEN TENDERNESS--GATHERING NINA UP IN HER 65 STRANG
ARMS, BROKENLY)
(WITH SUDDEN RELIEVED EXCITEMENT) 68 STRANG
(HE STARTS FOR THE DOOR--THEN STRUCK BY A SUDDEN 76 STRANG
THOUGHT, STOPS)
(WITH A SUDDEN CHANGE OF MOOD SHE LAUGHS GAILY AND 80 STRANG
NATURALLY)
(WITH SUDDEN ALARM) (BUT AM I&... 91 STRANG
(THEN WITH SUDDEN TERROR) (AND IF SHE SAYS 92 STRANG
YES&...
(IN A SUDDEN PANIC--THINKING) 101 STRANG
(THEN WITH SUDDEN ANGUISH) (OH, AFTERNOONS... 110 STRANG
(WITH SUDDEN RESISTANCE PULLS AWAY--DETERMINEDLY) 122 STRANG
(TAKING HIM IN HER ARMS--WITH SUDDEN ALARM) 131 STRANG
(THEN WITH SUDDEN SCORNFUL REVULSION) 149 STRANG
(THEN WITH SUDDEN ALARM) (HE'S FORGOTTEN GORDON 166 STRANG
FOR THIS PRESTO&....)
(WITH A SUDDEN STRANGE VIOLENCE) 169 STRANG
(WITH SUDDEN FIERCE INTENSITY) 172 STRANG
(WITH SUDDEN FURY) GOD STIFFEN YE. 496 VOYAGE
(WITH A SUDDEN CHANGE IN MANNER THAT IS ALMOST 445 WELDED
STERN)
BUT NOW THEY'RE AS ALIVE AS YOU ARE--(WITH A 445 WELDED
SUDDEN GRIN----
(WITH SUDDEN PASSION) IT'S WRONG, NELLY. 446 WELDED
(WITH SUDDEN FURIOUS ANGER) GOD, WHAT I FEEL OF 448 WELDED
THE TRUTH OF THIS--THE BEAUTY/
(HE FORCES A GRIN--THEN ABRUPTLY CHANGING AGAIN, 448 WELDED
WITH A SUDDEN FIERCE PLEADING)
(WITH A SUDDEN QUEER, EXULTANT PRIDE) 469 WELDED
(WITH A SUDDEN BURST OF WILD LAUGHTER) 472 WELDED
(STRUCK BY A SUDDEN THOUGHT) 476 WELDED
(--(WITH A SUDDEN TWISTED GRIN) 483 WELDED
IT IS AS IF NOW BY A SUDDEN FLASH FROM WITHIN THEY487 WELDED
RECOGNIZED THEMSELVES,
(THEN WITH A SUDDEN TEARFUL GAIETY) 489 WELDED

SUDDENLY
THEN SUDDENLY BURSTS FORTH) 546 'ILE
(SHE SUDDENLY COVERS HER FACE WITH HER HANDS AND 548 'ILE
COMMENCES TO SOB.)
(SUDDENLY THROWING HER ARMS AROUND HIS NECK AND 548 'ILE
CLINGING TO HIM)
(HIS VOICE SUDDENLY GRIM WITH DETERMINATION) 550 'ILE
(HIS FACE SUDDENLY GROWN HARD WITH DETERMINATION) 552 'ILE
(RICHARD FOR A SECOND, LOOKS SUDDENLY GUILTY AND 196 AHWILD
CRUSHED.
(SUDDENLY--SOLEMNLY AUTHORITATIVE) 197 AHWILD
(SUDDENLY--WITH A SAD PATHOS, QUOTES AWKWARDLY AND)198 AHWILD
SHYLY)
(HAS BEEN READING THE SLIPS, A BROAD GRIN ON HIS 205 AHWILD
FACE--SUDDENLY HE WHISTLES)
(SUDDENLY PUTS BOTH HANDS ON HIS SHOULDERS-- 206 AHWILD
QUIETLY)
(SUDDENLY SHE COMES DIRECTLY TO THE POINT) 213 AHWILD
RAISED AS THEY COME IN AND FOR A MOMENT AFTER, 221 AHWILD
THEN SUDDENLY CAUTIOUSLY LOWERED.
(THEN SUDDENLY) WELL, ALL RIGHT THEN/ 224 AHWILD
THEN SUDDENLY HE GRINS MISTILY AND NODS WITH 224 AHWILD
SATISFACTION)
THEN SUDDENLY COMICALLY ANGRY, PUTTING THE SPOON 224 AHWILD
DOWN WITH A BANG)
SUDDENLY ALL HAPPINESS AGAIN) 225 AHWILD
EVEN LILY SUDDENLY LETS OUT AN HYSTERICAL GIGGLE 226 AHWILD
AND IS FURIOUS WITH HERSELF FOR
(IS ABOUT TO TAKE HIS FIRST BITE--STOPS SUDDENLY 227 AHWILD
AND ASKS HIS WIFE)
(RICHARD SUDDENLY BURSTS OUT LAUGHING AGAIN.) 228 AHWILD
WHEN SUDDENLY I HEARD A SORT OF GASP FROM BEHIND 230 AHWILD
ME--LIKE THIS--"HELP."
THEN SUDDENLY I THOUGHT OF THE PILE. 230 AHWILD
(THEN SUDDENLY IN THE TONES OF A SIDE-SHOW BARKER)231 AHWILD
MILLER GUFFAWS--THEN SUDDENLY GROWS SHOCKED.) 231 AHWILD

SUDDENLY

SUDDENLY (CONT'D.)
(SUDDENLY IN A HOARSE WHISPER TO HIS MOTHER, 231 AHWILD
PARLOR--THEN SUDDENLY TURNS AND SAYS WITH A BOW) 232 AHWILD
(SUDDENLY GETS UP FROM HER CHAIR AND STANDS 233 AHWILD
RIGIDLY, HER FACE WORKING--JERKILY)
(THEN SUDDENLY) DO YOU KNOW WHAT I THINK? 235 AHWILD
(SUDDENLY RECITES SENTIMENTALLY) 244 AHWILD
(SUDDENLY WITH DIRE EMPHASIS) 246 AHWILD
(SUDDENLY SENTIMENTAL) POOR KID. 247 AHWILD
THEN TURNS SUDDENLY, THE DISCOVERY OF ANOTHER 253 AHWILD
EXCUSE LIGHTING UP HIS FACE.)
(THEN SUDDENLY, LOOKING THROUGH THE FRONT PARLOR 256 AHWILD
GRUMPILY)
(AFTER SWALLOWING HARD, SUDDENLY BLURTS OUT) 257 AHWILD
(SUDDENLY TURNS TOWARD LILY--HIS VOICE CHOKED WITH258 AHWILD
TEARS--
(HER FACE SUDDENLY SAD AND TIRED AGAIN-- 259 AHWILD
(SUDDENLY) WHAT TIME IS IT NOW, NAT& 259 AHWILD
(SUDDENLY HE LISTENS AND SAYS) 260 AHWILD
(THEN SUDDENLY HIS WHOLE EXPRESSION CHANGES, HIS 261 AHWILD
PALLOR TAKES ON A GREENISH,
(THEN SUDDENLY HE LAUGHS) NO USE TALKING, YOU 268 AHWILD
CERTAINLY TAKE THE CAKE!
(THEN SUDDENLY) MY GOODNESS, I WONDER WHAT TIME 271 AHWILD
IT'S GETTING TO BE.
(THEN SUDDENLY FEELING THIS ENTHUSIASM BEFORE 273 AHWILD
MILDRED IS ENTIRELY THE WRONG NOTE
(SHE SUDDENLY JUMPS TO HER FEET IN A TEARFUL FURY)284 AHWILD
(THEN SUDDENLY DEFIANT) AND WHAT IF I DID KISS 286 AHWILD
HER ONCE OR TWICE&
MILLER SIZES HIM UP KEENLY--THEN SUDDENLY SMILES 293 AHWILD
AND ASKS WITH QUIET MOCKERY)
(HE SIZES RICHARD UP SEARCHINGLY--THEN SUDDENLY 294 AHWILD
SPEAKS SHARPLY)
(SUDDENLY HE CAN GO NO FARTHER AND WINDS UP 295 AHWILD
HELPLESSLY)
BUT THEN SUDDENLY HIS FACE IS TRANSFIGURED 297 AHWILD
THEN SUDDENLY POUNDS HIS FIST ON THE TABLE WITH 8 ANNA
HAPPY EXCITEMENT)
CHRIS SUDDENLY BECOMES DESPERATELY ILL AT EASE. 9 ANNA
(SUDDENLY GROWING SOMBER--IN A LOW TONE) 9 ANNA
(SUDDENLY SPRINGING TO HIS FEET AND SMASHING HIS 9 ANNA
FIST ON THE TABLE IN A RAGE)
SO--YUH'RE--(SHE SUDDENLY BURSTS OUT INTO HOARSE, 14 ANNA
IRONICAL LAUGHTER)
ANNA SUDDENLY BECOMES CONSCIOUS OF THIS APPRAISING 15 ANNA
STARE--RESENTFULLY)
(PROMPTLY) I'LL TAKE A--(THEN SUDDENLY REMINDED-- 23 ANNA
CONFUSEDLY)
HE SUDDENLY CHANGES HIS TONE TO ONE OF BOISTEROUS 33 ANNA
JOVIALITY)
(TURNS SUDDENLY AND SHAKES HIS FIST OUT AT THE 40 ANNA
SEA--WITH BITTER HATRED)
(SHE BREAKS OFF SUDDENLY) 44 ANNA
(SUDDENLY SEEMING TO COME TO A BOLD DECISION--WITH 50 ANNA
A DEFIANT GRIN AT CHRIS)
(SUDDENLY GETTING AN IDEA AND POINTING AT CHRIS-- 54 ANNA
EXASPERATEDLY)
(WHO HAS BEEN STANDING IN A STUPOR--SUDDENLY 61 ANNA
GRASPING BURKE BY THE ARM--
(HIS FACE SUDDENLY CONVULSED WITH GRIEF AND RAGE) 68 ANNA
(A STRANGE TERROR SEEMS SUDDENLY TO SEIZE HER. 68 ANNA
(SUDDENLY BENDING DOWN TO HER AND GRASPING HER ARM 70 ANNA
INTENSELY)
(IT SUDDENLY COMES TO HER THAT THIS IS THE SAME 72 ANNA
SHIP HER FATHER IS SAILING ON)
(SUDDENLY SEEMS TO HAVE A SOLUTION. 74 ANNA
(SUDDENLY HOLDING HER AWAY FROM HIM AND STARING 76 ANNA
INTO HER EYES AS IF TO PROBE
(HE TURNS AWAY, SUDDENLY RELEASING ROBERT'S HAND) 86 BEYOND
(HE BREAKS OFF SUDDENLY WITH A LAUGH) 90 BEYOND
(SUDDENLY REALIZING THAT HIS ARM IS AROUND HER, 90 BEYOND
(SHE SUDDENLY THROWS HER ARMS ABOUT HIS NECK AND 91 BEYOND
HIDES HER HEAD ON HIS SHOULDER)
ROBERT SUDDENLY STOPS AND TURNS AS THOUGH FOR A 93 BEYOND
LAST LOOK
(SUDDENLY TURNING TO THEM) THERE'S ONE THING NONE 96 BEYOND
OF YOU
I HADN'T INTENDED TELLING HER ANYTHING BUT-- 100 BEYOND
SUDDENLY--I FELT I MUST.
(WITH A STARTLED CRY WHEN HIS BROTHER APPEARS 101 BEYOND
BEFORE HIM SO SUDDENLY)
HE THOUGHT HE HAD SUDDENLY GONE MAD) 104 BEYOND
(SUDDENLY OVERCOME WITH ANGER AND GRIEF.. 107 BEYOND
THE TWIN, SUDDENLY STRUCK BY THE SAME PREMONITION, 128 BEYOND
LISTEN TO IT BREATHLESSLY,
(IN A VOICE WHICH IS SUDDENLY RINGING WITH THE 167 BEYOND
HAPPINESS OF HOPE)
(HE SUDDENLY RAISES HIMSELF WITH HIS LAST 168 BEYOND
REMAINING STRENGTH AND POINTS TO THE
(HE SUDDENLY LAUGHS WILDLY AND PUT HIS ARM AROUND 469 CARIBE
HER WAIST AND PRESSES HER TO
(LOOKS AT HIM AND SUDDENLY UNDERSTANDS THAT WHAT 566 CROSS
SHE DREADS HAS COME TO PASS--
THE SOUND OF THE WIND AND SEA SUDDENLY CEASES AND 570 CROSS
THERE IS A HEAVY SILENCE.
(SUDDENLY) HARK/ 570 CROSS
(SUDDENLY--IN ALARM) COME UP/ 572 CROSS
(HIS TONE SUDDENLY COLD AND HOSTILE) 497 DAYS
(THEN SUDDENLY) THERE'S SOMETHING I WANT TO TELL 506 DAYS
YOU, JACK.
THEN, AS I PRAYED, SUDDENLY AS IF BY SOME WILL 507 DAYS
OUTSIDE ME,
(HIS VOICE SUDDENLY CHANGES TO HARD BITTERNESS) 510 DAYS
(HIS VOICE SUDDENLY TAKES ON A TONE OF BITTER 511 DAYS
HATRED)
«ONCE, LONG AGO--- (THEN, SUDDENLY WITH REPENTANT 517 DAYS
SHAMEFACEDNESS)

SUDDENLY (CONT'D.)
SUDDENLY, I DON'T KNOW HOW TO EXPLAIN IT, YOU'LL 522 DAYS
THINK I'M CRAZY,
(SUDDENLY--HIS FACE FULL OF THE BITTEREST, 531 DAYS
TORTURED SELF-LOATHING--
THEN, SUDDENLY, AS IF IN REPLY, LOVING GIVES A 535 DAYS
LITTLE MOCKING LAUGH,
AT THE THOUGHT OF HIS WIFE, SUDDENLY IT WAS AS IF 538 DAYS
SOMETHING OUTSIDE HIM,
THEN SUDDENLY HE BURSTS OUT) 547 DAYS
AS IF HE SUDDENLY SENSED A PRESENCE THERE THE 551 DAYS
PRIEST IS PRAYING TO.
I FORGOT THAT YOU WERE--(THEN SUDDENLY HECTIC 551 DAYS
AGAIN)
THEN SUDDENLY FORCES CONTROL ON HERSELF AND GETS 551 DAYS
SHAKILY TO HER FEET)
SUDDENLY OVERCOME BY A WAVE OF DROWSINESS HE TRIES555 DAYS
IN VAIN TO FIGHT BACK)
(SUDDENLY HE SEEMS TO SEE FATHER BAIRD FOR THE 558 DAYS
FIRST TIME--WITH A CRY OF APPEAL-
(THEN SUDDENLY--WITH EAGERNESS) 559 DAYS
(SUDDENLY MOANS FRIGHTENEDLY) 561 DAYS
(HE SUDDENLY GETS TO HIS FEET AS IF IMPELLED BY 562 DAYS
SOME FORCE OUTSIDE HIM.
ELSA SUDDENLY COMES OUT OF THE HALF-COMA SHE IS IN563 DAYS
WITH A CRY OF TERROR AND,
THE OUTER DOORS BEYOND THE ARCHED DOORWAY ARE 564 DAYS
SUDDENLY PUSHED OPEN WITH A CRASH
THEN STOPS SUDDENLY, AND LOOKING UP AT THE CROSS 565 DAYS
AGAIN,
(HIS EYES FIXED ON THE FACE OF THE CRUCIFIED 565 DAYS
SUDDENLY LIGHTING UP AS IF HE NOW
(SUDDENLY) EIGHTEEN YEAR AGO. 204 DESIRE
(SUDDENLY TURNS TO EBEN) LOOKY HERE/ 206 DESIRE
(SUDDENLY EXPLODING) WHY DIDN'T YE NEVER STAND 208 DESIRE
BETWEEN HIM 'N' MY MAW WHEN HE
(SUDDENLY) MEBBE YE'LL TRY T' MAKE HER YOUR'N, 214 DESIRE
TOO&
(HE SUDDENLY THROWS HIS HEAD BACK BOLDLY AND 217 DESIRE
GLARES WITH HARD,
(SUDDENLY) HE NEVER WAS MUCH O' A HAND AT 217 DESIRE
MILKIN', EBEN WASN'T.
(SUDDENLY ROARING WITH RAGE) 223 DESIRE
SUDDENLY HE BECOMES CONSCIOUS OF HER PRESENCE AND 225 DESIRE
LOOKS UP.
(SUDDENLY) MEBBE THE LORD'LL GIVE US A SON. 234 DESIRE
(SUDDENLY RAISES HIS HEAD AND LOOKS AT HER-- 236 DESIRE
SCORNFULLY)
(THEN SUDDENLY) BUT I GIVE IN T' WEAKNESS ONCE. 237 DESIRE
SUDDENLY AWARE OF HIS HATRED, HE HURLS HER AWAY 239 DESIRE
FROM HIM, SPRINGING TO HIS FEET.
(HE SUDDENLY STOPS, STARING STUPIDLY BEFORE HIM,) 242 DESIRE
SUDDENLY, AS IN THE BEDROOM, 243 DESIRE
THEN SUDDENLY WILD PASSION OVERCOMES HER. 243 DESIRE
(HIS FACE SUDDENLY LIGHTING UP WITH A FIERCE, 243 DESIRE
TRIUMPHANT GRIN)
(SUDDENLY HOLDING OUT HIS HAND--SOBERLY) 246 DESIRE
(SUDDENLY JOVIAL AGAIN) GOOD FUR THE COWS/ 246 DESIRE
(SUDDENLY TURNING TO A YOUNG GIRL ON HER RIGHT) 247 DESIRE
(SUDDENLY GRIM) I GOT A LOT IN ME--A HELL OF A 249 DESIRE
LOT--FOLKS DON'T KNOW ON.
(THEN SUDDENLY, UNABLE TO RESTRAIN HIMSELF ANY 250 DESIRE
LONGER,
THEN SUDDENLY STRAIGHTENING UP AND KICKING AS HIGH251 DESIRE
AS HE CAN WITH BOTH LEGS.
(EBEN SUDDENLY LAUGHS, ONE SHORT SARDONIC BARK.. 254 DESIRE
SUDDENLY LAUGHS WILDLY AND BROKENLY) 255 DESIRE
(SUDDENLY TRIUMPHANT WHEN HE SEES HOW SHAKEN EBEN 255 DESIRE
IS)
(HE SUDDENLY BREAKS DOWN, SOBBING WEAKLY.) 256 DESIRE
SUDDENLY, SHE BREAKS DOWN AND SOBS, 259 DESIRE
(HIS MOOD SUDDENLY CHANGING TO HORROR, SHRINKS 261 DESIRE
AWAY FROM HER)
SUDDENLY BREAKING OFF PASSIONATELY) 262 DESIRE
(SUDDENLY RAGING) HA? 262 DESIRE
(SUDDENLY LIFTS HER HEAD AND TURNS ON HIM--WILDLY)263 DESIRE
SUDDENLY CABOT TURNS--GRIMLY THREATENING) 265 DESIRE
(HE SUDDENLY CUTS A MAD CAPER) 268 DESIRE
(SUDDENLY CALLS) I LIED THIS MORNIN', JIM. 269 DESIRE
(GROWING SUDDENLY VERY EMBARRASSED AS IF SOME 497 DIFRNT
MEMORY OCCURRED TO HIM)
(SUDDENLY NOTICING THE EXPRESSION OF MISERY ON 506 DIFRNT
EMMA'S FACE--ASTONISHED)
SUDDENLY HE BLURTS OUT DESPAIRINGLY) 518 DIFRNT
(THEN SUDDENLY, WAGGING AN ADMONISHING FINGER AT 525 DIFRNT
HIM
SUDDENLY HIS FACE LIGHTS UP WITH A CRUEL GRIN 531 DIFRNT
(INSPIRED BY ALARM AND DESIRE FOR REVENGE SUDDENLY534 DIFRNT
BLURTS OUT)
(THEN SUDDENLY REALIZING THE CAUSE OF HIS 535 DIFRNT
DISCOMFITURE, SHE SMILES PITYINGLY,
(SUDDENLY BURSTING INTO HYSTERICAL TEARS) 537 DIFRNT
THEN, AS IF SUDDENLY AFRAID OF WHAT HER ANSWER 538 DIFRNT
WILL BE, HE BREAKS OUT QUICKLY)
(SUDDENLY ALERT--SHARPLY) SH/ 547 DIFRNT
(SUDDENLY HORRIFIED AT HIMSELF) 423 DYNAMO
THAT SUDDENLY REVEALS REUBEN IN HIS HIDING PLACE 427 DYNAMO
BY THE HEDGE.
(SUDDENLY--WITH A PLACID CERTAINTY) 432 DYNAMO
(SHE SUDDENLY RAISES HERSELF ON TIPTOE AND KISSES 433 DYNAMO
HIM--WITH A LITTLE LAUGH)
ATTENTION BEFORE AND SUDDENLY HE HAS AN 434 DYNAMO
INSPIRATION AND GRINS ELATEDLY)
(HE SUDDENLY JUMPS UP AND MUMBLES TO FIFE) 442 DYNAMO
(SUDDENLY JUMPING TO HER FEET AND PEERING UP 444 DYNAMO
THROUGH THE LEAVES AT MRS. FIFE)
AS IF SOME HIDDEN STRENGTH IN HIM HAD SUDDENLY 448 DYNAMO
BEEN TAPPED)

SUDDENLY

SUDDENLY (CONT*D.)
(HE SUDDENLY IS REMINDED OF SOMETHING--THINKING 450 DYNAMO
WILDLY)
(SUDDENLY FLARES UP INTO A TEMPER) 451 DYNAMO
(SUDDENLY SHE LEANS OVER AND KISSES HER MOTHER 456 DYNAMO
AFFECTIONATELY)
(THEN AS SUDDENLY CHANGING TO A PASSIONATE TONE OF460 DYNAMO
DESIRE)
(HE HAS STEPPED ON TIPTOE INTO THE ROOM AND NOW 462 DYNAMO
SUDDENLY)
(SUDDENLY WITH A PLEASED GRIN) 463 DYNAMO
(LIGHT AVERTS HIS EYES AND SUDDENLY HIDES HIS FACE465 DYNAMO
IN HIS HANDS.)
(THEN SUDDENLY) SAY, I THINK I'LL GO AND VISIT 467 DYNAMO
MOTHER'S GRAVE.
(SUDDENLY MOVES AWAY FROM HER AND STARES AROUND 469 DYNAMO
HIM NERVOUSLY--
AND THEN SUDDENLY IT HIT ME THAT THERE WAS NOTHING470 DYNAMO
TO PRAY TO.
(HE SIGHS WITH LONGING, HIS BODY SUDDENLY GONE 477 DYNAMO
LIMP AND WEARY.)
(SUDDENLY CRIES OUT WITH A NOTE OF DESPAIR) 479 DYNAMO
MOTHER?
(HIS TENSE, SUPPLICATING ATTUTUDE SUDDENLY 480 DYNAMO
RELAXING DEJECTEDLY)
* (HE SUDDENLY CHECKS HIMSELF AND FORCES A 481 DYNAMO
STRANGE, SHAMEFACED LAUGH)
(THEN SUDDENLY GRABBING HER BY THE ARM) 482 DYNAMO
(HE SUDDENLY BENDS HIS FACE TO HER FACE, 484 DYNAMO
(SUDDENLY) 175 EJONES
(SUDDENLY RELAXING) SHO* YOU HAS--AND YOU BETTER 181 EJONES
BE.
HE CONTROLS HIMSELF AND SUDDENLY BURSTS INTO A LOW182 EJONES
(CHUCKLING LAUGH)
(SUDDENLY WITH A FRIGHTENED GASP HE FLINGS THE 189 EJONES
MATCH ON THE GROUND AND STAMPS ON
(STOPPING, SUDDENLY, BEWILDEREDLY) 192 EJONES
SUDDENLY THE GUARD APPROACHES HIM ANGRILY, 194 EJONES
THREATENly.
UNMINDFUL OF THEIR NOISELESS APPROACH, SUDDENLY 194 EJONES
LOOKS DOWN AND SEES THEM.
JONES SUDDENLY BECOMES AWARE THAT HIS HANDS ARE 195 EJONES
EMPTY.
(SUDDENLY HE THROWS HIMSELF ON HIS KNEES 196 EJONES
(SUDDENLY CONVULSED WITH RAGING HATRED AND FEAR) 197 EJONES
BORNE ON A FRESHENING BREEZE, HAS SUDDENLY BECOME 11 ELECTR
LOUDER.
CHRISTINE WHY DID YOU SUDDENLY TAKE THAT NOTIONS 29 ELECTR
(THEN SUDDENLY--WITH A STRANGE JEALOUS BITTERNESS) 31 ELECTR
(SUDDENLY BECOMING RIGID AND COLD AGAIN--SLOWLY) 32 ELECTR
(SHE HAS BEEN STARING BEFORE HER--NOW SHE SUDDENLY 40 ELECTR
TURNS ON BRANT--SLOWLY)
IF HE DIED SUDDENLY NOW, NO ONE WOULD THINK IT WAS 40 ELECTR
ANYTHING BUT HEART FAILURE.
BUT--IF HE DIES SUDDENLY, WON'T VINNIE--- 40 ELECTR
THEN WHAT MAKES YOU SUDDENLY SO SCRUPULOUS ABOUT 41 ELECTR
HIS DEATH?
THEN, AS IF AN IDEA HAD SUDDENLY COME TO HER, 42 ELECTR
THEN SUDDENLY SEES LAVINIA ON THE STEPS AND STOPS 44 ELECTR
ABRUPTLY, A BIT SHEEPISH.
HE SUDDENLY LEANS OVER TOWARD HER AND, LOWERING 44 ELECTR
HIS VOICE, ASKS SOBERLY)
(WHO HAS BEEN WATCHING HIM JEALOUSLY--SUDDENLY 49 ELECTR
PULLING HIM BY THE ARM--
(SUDDENLY JUMPING TO HIS FEET--BRUSQUELY) 49 ELECTR
(THEN SUDDENLY CATCHING CHRISTINE'S SCORNFUL 51 ELECTR
GLANCE
SUDDENLY COMES AND LEANS OVER HER AWKWARDLY, AS IF 53 ELECTR
TO KISS HER.
(SUDDENLY UNEASY AGAIN) DON'T KEEP YOUR EYES SHUT 53 ELECTR
LIKE THAT!
(SUDDENLY HE REACHES OVER AND TAKES HER HAND) 55 ELECTR
THEN HANNON'S VOICE COMES SUDDENLY FROM THE BED, 58 ELECTR
DULL AND LIFELESS.)
(THEN, AS IF ALL THE BITTERNESS AND HURT IN HIM 60 ELECTR
HAD SUDDENLY BURST ITS DAM)
(THEN HER VOICE CHANGES, AS IF SHE HAD SUDDENLY 61 ELECTR
RESOLVED ON A COURSE OF ACTION.
(SUDDENLY HE FALLS BACK, GROANING, DOUBLED UP ON 61 ELECTR
HIS LEFT SIDE.
THEN SUDDENLY A WILD LOOK OF TERROR COMES OVER HIS 62 ELECTR
FACE.
THEN HER KNEES SUDDENLY BUCKLE UNDER HER AND SHE 64 ELECTR
FALLS IN A DEAD FAINT AT THE
(SUDDENLY STARING AT HAZEL, AS IF STRUCK BY AN 72 ELECTR
IDEA)
THEN THE DOOR IS SUDDENLY OPENED AGAIN AND 77 ELECTR
CHRISTINE COMES OUT.
I SUDDENLY FEEL AS IF I WERE GOING TO FAINT, SO I 80 ELECTR
RUSHED OUT IN THE FRESH AIR.
(THEN SUDDENLY) DO YOU STILL SING, HAZEL? 83 ELECTR
ON BOTH SIDES SUDDENLY SAW THE JOKE WAR WAS ON 95 ELECTR
THEM AND LAUGHED AND SHOOK HANDS/
SUDDENLY SHE APPEALS TO HIM DISTRACTEDLY) 101 ELECTR
(HE LURCHES OUT INTO THE MOONLIGHT--SUDDENLY 104 ELECTR
PUGNACIOUS)
THE CHANTYMAN SUDDENLY BEGINS TO SING THE CHANTY 106 ELECTR
«HANGING JOHNNY» WITH
HE SUDDENLY LOOKS AROUND UNEASILY) 108 ELECTR
(THEN SUDDENLY, WITH A LITTLE SHUDDER) 112 ELECTR
SUDDENLY SHE GLANCES FRIGHTENEDLY AT THE CLOCK) 112 ELECTR
THEN SUDDENLY TURNS BACK AND STANDS STIFFLY 115 ELECTR
UPRIGHT AND GRIM BESIDE THE BODY AND
LAVINIA SUDDENLY MAKES A MO TION, AS IF TO HOLD 123 ELECTR
HER BACK.
(HE SUDDENLY BREAKS DOWN AND WEEPS IN HYSTERICAL 124 ELECTR
ANGUISH.
(SUDDENLY LOOKING OFF DOWN LEFT) 134 ELECTR

SUDDENLY (CONT*D.)
SHE SUDDENLY ADDRESSES THEM IN A HARSH RESENTFUL 139 ELECTR
VOICE.)
BUT NOW YOU'VE SUDDENLY BECOME STRANGE AGAIN. 141 ELECTR
SHE SEEMS SUDDENLY WEAK AND FRIGHTENED.) 146 ELECTR
(SUDDENLY FILLED WITH GRATEFUL LOVE FOR HIM, 147 ELECTR
AND THAT'S WHY YOU SUDDENLY DISCARDED MOURNING IN 153 ELECTR
FRISCO AND BOUGHT NEW CLOTHES--
(THEN SUDDENLY HE BREAKS DOWN AND BECOMES WEAK AND155 ELECTR
PITIFUL)
(THEN SUDDENLY HER HORROR TURNING INTO A VIOLENT 156 ELECTR
RAGE--
SUDDENLY HE SAYS HARSHLY AGAIN) 156 ELECTR
(SUDDENLY WITH A LITTLE SHIVER) 158 ELECTR
(SUDDENLY TAKING HER HAND--EXCITEDLY) 160 ELECTR
(SUDDENLY GETS BETWEEN HER AND THE DOOR--WITH 163 ELECTR
ANGRY ACCUSATION)
(HE STOPS ABRUPTLY AND STARES BEFORE HIM, AS IF 166 ELECTR
THIS IDEA WERE SUDDENLY TAKING
(SUDDENLY SHE BURSTS OUT) IT'S A LIE ABOUT ORIN 171 ELECTR
KILLING HIMSELF BY ACCIDENT!
SHE AND MOTHER SUDDENLY GOT A LOT OF CRAZY NOTIONS175 ELECTR
IN THEIR HEADS.
(THEN SUDDENLY THROWING HER ARMS AROUND HIM) 176 ELECTR
(THEN SUDDENLY SEIZING ON THIS AS A WAY OUT--WITH 177 ELECTR
CALCULATED COARSENESS)
(THEN SUDDENLY WITH A HOPELESS, DEAD FINALITY) 177 ELECTR
(SUDDENLY CALLS BACK OVER HER SHOULDER) 259 GGBROW
(SUDDENLY--PLEADING) YOU SIMPLY MUST SEND HIM TO 260 GGBROW
COLLEGE?
(SUDDENLY TURNS ON DION FURIOUSLY) 261 GGBROW
(HE SUDDENLY CUTS A GROTESQUE CAPER, LIKE A 262 GGBROW
HARLEQUIN AND DARTS OFF,
THEN HE SUDDENLY CLAPS HIS MASK OVER HIS FACE 265 GGBROW
AGAIN WITH A GESTURE OF DESPAIR
(HE SUDDENLY TEARS OFF HIS MASK--IN A PASSIONATE 268 GGBROW
AGONY)
(SUDDENLY REACHES OUT AND TAKES UP A COPY OF THE 269 GGBROW
NEW TESTAMENT
(HE SUDDENLY TAKES HER HAND AND KISSES IT 271 GGBROW
GRATEFULLY)
SUDDENLY) 275 GGBROW
(SUDDENLY HOLDING OUT HIS HAND TO HER. 280 GGBROW
(SUDDENLY SHAKING HIM) WHAT IN HELL HAS COME OVER281 GGBROW
YOU, ANYWAY?
(AT THE MENTION OF BROWN, DION TREMBLES AS IF 285 GGBROW
SUDDENLY POSSESSED,
(THEN SUDDENLY WITH A LOOK OF HORROR) 286 GGBROW
(SUDDENLY STARTS AND CALLS WITH DEEP GRIEF) 287 GGBROW
(SUDDENLY TAKES ONE OF HER HANDS AND KISSES IT-- 289 GGBROW
INSINUATINGLY)
I HAD LOVED AND TRUSTED HIM AND SUDDENLY THE GOOD 295 GGBROW
GOD WAS DISPROVED IN HIS
THEN SUDDENLY BECOMES DEADLY CALM 297 GGBROW
(HE SUDDENLY CANNOT HELP KISSING THE MASK) 308 GGBROW
(HESITATINGLY) WELL--IT'S REALLY TOO SILLY--HE 311 GGBROW
SUDDENLY GOT AWFULLY STRANGE.
(THEN SUDDENLY, HYSTERICALLY ANGRY AND TERRIFIED) 319 GGBROW
(THEN SUDDENLY) LEAVE ME ALONE WITH HIM AND MAYBE321 GGBROW
I'LL GET HIM TO SQUEAL IT.
(SUDDENLY--WITH ECSTASY) I KNOW/ 322 GGBROW
SUDDENLY CRIES OUT IN A VOICE FULL OF OLD SORROW) 213 HA APE
(HE SUDDENLY BURSTS FORTH VEHEMENTLY, GROWING MORE215 HA APE
AND MORE EXCITED
(SUDDENLY HE BECOMES CONSCIOUS OF ALL THE OTHER 225 HA APE
MEN STARING AT SOMETHING
(SUDDENLY STARTING AS IF AWAKENING FROM A DREAM, 240 HA APE
SUDDENLY YANK JUMPS TO HIS FEET WITH A FURIOUS 244 HA APE
GROAN AS IF SOME APPALLING
(CHECKING HIMSELF AS SUDDENLY) 254 HA APE
(SOMETHING, THE TONE OF MOCKERY, PERHAPS, SUDDENLY254 HA APE
ENRAGES THE ANIMAL.
AND THE CLERK'S MIND IS NOW SUDDENLY IMPERVIOUS 32 HUGHIE
(HE SUDDENLY ROUSES HIMSELF AND THERE IS SOMETHING 34 HUGHIE
SUDDENLY HIS FACE LIGHTS UP WITH A SAVING 35 HUGHIE
REVELATION.
(SUDDENLY YELLS IN HIS NIGHTMARE) 581 ICEMAN
(SUDDENLY HIS EYES OPEN WIDE) 583 ICEMAN
THEN IRRITABLY AS IF SUDDENLY PROVOKED AT HIMSELF 590 ICEMAN
FOR TALKING SO MUCH)
HUGO SUDDENLY RAISES HIS HEAD FROM HIS ARMS 592 ICEMAN
AS IF HE SUDDENLY WERE AFRAID OF HIS OWN 593 ICEMAN
THOUGHTS--FORCING A SMILE)
(SUDDENLY TURNS AND BEAMS ON HOPE) 601 ICEMAN
(SUDDENLY HE CATCHES HOPE'S EYES FIXED ON HIM 607 ICEMAN
CONDEMNINGLY.
(FROWNINGLY PUZZLED AGAIN) BUT I DON'T SEE-- 624 ICEMAN
(SUDDENLY BREEZILY GOOD-NATURED)
HIS TONE SUDDENLY CHANGES TO ONE OF GUTTURAL 627 ICEMAN
SOAPBOX DENUNCIATION
(SUDDENLY SHE IS MOLLIFIED AND SMILES) 635 ICEMAN
(SUDDENLY GIVES A LAUGH--IN HIS COMICALLY INTENSE,644 ICEMAN
CRAZY TONE)
SUDDENLY THERE IS A NOISE OF ANGRY, CURSING VOICES650 ICEMAN
AND A SCUFFLE FROM THE HALL.
HUGO IS THE LAST, SUDDENLY COMING TO AND 653 ICEMAN
SCRAMBLING TO HIS FEET.
HOPE SUDDENLY BECOMES ALMOST TEARFULLY 656 ICEMAN
SENTIMENTAL)
(THEN SUDDENLY HE IS EVEN MORE ASHAMED OF HIMSELF 663 ICEMAN
THAN THE OTHERS AND STAMMERS)
(SUDDENLY WITH DESPERATE URGENCY) 667 ICEMAN
(SUDDENLY ROCKY'S EYES WIDEN) 668 ICEMAN
THEIR FIGHTING FURY SUDDENLY DIES OUT AND THEY 672 ICEMAN
APPEAR DEFLATED AND SHEEPISH.)
(SUDDENLY RAISES HIS HEAD FROM HIS ARMS AND, 694 ICEMAN
LOOKING STRAIGHT IN FRONT OF HIM,
(SUDDENLY HIS FACE HARDENS WITH HATRED) 698 ICEMAN

SUDDENLY

SUDDENLY (CONT*D.)
(SUDDENLY LUNGES TO HIS FEET DAZEDLY--MUMBLES IN 699 ICEMAN HUMBLED APOLOGY)
(HE SUDDENLY LOOKS CONFUSED--HALTINGLY) 703 ICEMAN
(SUDDENLY BURSTS OUT) I'VE GOT TO TELL YOU! 708 ICEMAN
(SUDDENLY HE LOOKS STARTLED. 714 ICEMAN
I REMEMBER I STOOD BY THE BED AND SUDDENLY I HAD 716 ICEMAN TO LAUGH.
(SUDDENLY GIVES UP AND RELAXES LIMPLY IN THE 716 ICEMAN CHAIR--
(THEN SUDDENLY HE LOOKS AT HICKEY 717 ICEMAN
HE SEEMS SUDDENLY AT PEACE WITH HIMSELF. 720 ICEMAN
(HE STANDS ON THE BENCH AND LOOKS AROUND--SUDDENLY514 INZONE EXPLODING)
(SUDDENLY JUMPING TO HIS FEET--NERVOUSLY) 514 INZONE
(HIS VOICE IS SUDDENLY MOVED BY DEEP FEELING.) 17 JOURNE
SUDDENLY AND STARTLINGLY ONE SEES IN HER FACE THE 28 JOURNE GIRL SHE HAD ONCE BEEN.
SUDDENLY JAMIE BECOMES REALLY MOVED.) 35 JOURNE
(HE IS SUDDENLY SHAMEFACED.) 35 JOURNE
IT IS AS IF SUDDENLY A DEEP BOND OF COMMON FEELING 36 JOURNE EXISTED BETWEEN THEM IN WHICH
(SUDDENLY HE FROWNS AT JAMIE SUSPICIOUSLY.) 37 JOURNE
(SUDDENLY SHE IS SELF-CONSCIOUSLY AWARE THAT THEY 41 JOURNE ARE BOTH STARING FIXEDLY AT
I DON'T UNDERSTAND WHY YOU SHOULD SUDDENLY SAY 45 JOURNE SUCH THINGS.
SUDDENLY A STRANGE UNDERCURRENT OF REVENGEFULNESS 47 JOURNE COMES INTO HER VOICE.)
BUT SUDDENLY SHE GROWS TERRIBLY TENSE AGAIN. 49 JOURNE
(SUDDENLY PRIMLY VIRTUOUS.) I'D NEVER SUGGEST A 52 JOURNE MAN OR A WOMAN TOUCH DRINK.
HE SUDDENLY LOOKS A TIRED, BITTERLY SAD OLD MAN. 67 JOURNE
(SUDDENLY IS OVERCOME BY GUILTY CUNFUSION-- 75 JOURNE STAMMERS.)
(HE SUDDENLY HUGS HER TO HIM--BROKENLY.) 85 JOURNE
(SUDDENLY TURNS TO THEM IN A CONFUSED PANIC OF 90 JOURNE FRIGHTENED ANGER.)
(SHE SUDDENLY THRUSTS HER HANDS BEHIND HER BACK.) 104 JOURNE
SHE SUDDENLY LOSES ALL THE GIRLISH QUALITY 107 JOURNE
(SUDDENLY HER WHOLE MANNER CHANGES. 108 JOURNE
SUDDENLY IT IS TOO MUCH FOR HER AND SHE BREAKS OUT)22 JOURNE AND SOBS.)
(SUDDENLY HE REMEMBERS EDMUND'S ILLNESS AND 128 JOURNE INSTANTLY BECOMES GUILTY AND
(SUDDENLY SPENT AND MISERABLE.) 142 JOURNE
(HE SUDDENLY SMILES-- 142 JOURNE
EDMUND SUDDENLY CANNOT HOLD BACK A BURST OF 151 JOURNE STRAINED, IRONICAL LAUGHTER.
THEN SUDDENLY THE TUNE WENT FALSE, THE DANCERS 159 JOURNE WEARIED OF THE WALTZ..."
THEN SUDDENLY HE LOOKS UP, HIS FACE HARD, AND 161 JOURNE QUOTES JEERINGLY.)
BATTLE, BUT SUDDENLY HE SEEMS TO SOBER UP TO A 162 JOURNE SHOCKED REALIZATION OF WHAT HE
(SUDDENLY POINTS A FINGER AT HIM AND RECITES WITH 168 JOURNE DRAMATIC EMPHASIS.)
SUDDENLY ALL FIVE BULBS OF THE CHANDELIER IN THE 169 JOURNE FRONT PARLOR ARE TURNED ON FROM
HE HAS SUDDENLY SOBERED UP, TOO--DULLY.) 173 JOURNE
SUDDENLY LAZARUS SAID *YES* AS IF HE WERE 277 LAZARU ANSWERING A QUESTION IN JESUS' EYES.
THEN SUDDENLY THEY STOP, THE MUSIC DIES OUT, 278 LAZARU
(SUDDENLY IN A DEEP VOICE--WITH A WONDERFUL 278 LAZARU EXULTANT ACCEPTANCE IN IT)
(SUDDENLY AGAIN--NOW IN A VOICE OF LOVING 279 LAZARU EXALTATION)
(SUDDENLY BLURTS OUT THE QUESTION WHICH IS IN THE 279 LAZARU MINDS OF ALL)
(SUDDENLY LAUGHING SOFTLY OUT OF HIS VISION, AS IF279 LAZARU TO HIMSELF,
THEN THE MUSIC SUDDENLY STOPS AND THE CHANT OF 282 LAZARU YOUTHFUL VOICES IS HEARD..)
SUDDENLY APPEARS ON THE ROOF OF THE HOUSE. 288 LAZARU
(HE STRETCHES OUT HIS ARMS TO THE SKY--THEN 289 LAZARU SUDDENLY POINTS)
(SUDDENLY--WITH DEEP GRIEF) AND JESUS WHO WAS THE292 LAZARU SON
(SUDDENLY POINTING TO HIS FOLLOWERS WHO ARE 294 LAZARU DANCING AND LAUGHING OBLIVIOUSLY--
WITHOUT KNOWING IT SUDDENLY WERE LIFTED. 300 LAZARU
(SUDDENLY WITH A DISTORTED WARPED SMILE) 300 LAZARU
(SUDDENLY BECOMING TERRIBLY UNEASY AT SOME 303 LAZARU THOUGHT)
CALIGULA SUDDENLY DROPS HIS SWORD AND COVERING HIS308 LAZARU FACE WITH HIS HANDS WEEPS
THE CROWD NOW ALL JOIN IN WITH HIM, CALIGULA 308 LAZARU SUDDENLY UNCOVERS HIS FACE,
SUDDENLY CALIGULA THROWS THE CUP FROM HIM AND 317 LAZARU SPRINGS TO HIS FEET)
ARE SUDDENLY HEARD FROM BEYOND THE WALL BEGINNING 319 LAZARU TO LAUGH THEIR HOARSE,
(SUDDENLY PUSHES FORWARD IMPUDENTLY AND STRIKES A 321 LAZARU GRANDIOSE ATTITUDE)
THEN SUDDENLY, TERRIFIED, SLINKS AWAY AND SIDLES 324 LAZARU OFF AT RIGHT.)
(SUDDENLY LAUGHS SOFTLY) WHY DO YOU DELIGHT IN 331 LAZARU BELIEVING EVIL OF YOURSELF,
(THEN SUDDENLY PUTTING ON A BRAVE FRONT, HE 333 LAZARU STRIDES UP BEHIND LAZARUS)
SUDDENLY HIS LAUGHTER IS RELEASED) 334 LAZARU
(THEN SUDDENLY KNEELS AND BENDS OVER IT 334 LAZARU IMPLORINGLY)
(SUDDENLY--EAGERLY) YES/ 334 LAZARU
SUDDENLY HIS LAUGHTER CRACKS, CHANGES, 338 LAZARU
(AS HE SUDDENLY SEES THE SHINING FIGURE OF LAZARUS338 LAZARU
TIBERIUS SUDDENLY WHIRLS AROUND AS IF HE FELT A 340 LAZARU DAGGER AT HIS BACK.)

SUDDENLY (CONT*D.)
(TIBERIUS BROODS--THEN SUDDENLY) 341 LAZARU
(THEN SUDDENLY) BUT WHAT IS THE JEWESS TO ME* 342 LAZARU
(SUDDENLY SPRINGING TO HIS FEET AND STARING ABOUT 342 LAZARU
(HE SUDDENLY SLAPS LAZARUS VICIOUSLY ACROSS THE 348 LAZARU FACE)
(SHE DREAMS, HER EYES AGAIN FIXED ON LAZARUS--THEN351 LAZARU SUDDENLY TURNING TO CALIGULA)
(SUDDENLY--TURNING TO LAZARUS NOW) 351 LAZARU
(HE SUDDENLY STARTS TO HIS FEET--WITH HARSH 356 LAZARU ARROGANCE AND PRIDE, THREATENINGLY)
(HIS LAUGHTER SUDDENLY BREAKS OFF INTO A WHIMPER 357 LAZARU AND
(HE SUDDENLY LIFTS THE FACE OF CALIGULA AND STARES359 LAZARU INTO HIS EYES)
(SUDDENLY, IN A QUIET BUT COMPELLING VOICE) 359 LAZARU
(BURSTING SUDDENLY INTO CHOKING, JOYFUL LAUGHTER--360 LAZARU LIKE A VISIONARY.)
(SUDDENLY RISING TO HIS FEET HE CALLS IMPLORINGLY)364 LAZARU
SUDDENLY THE FLAMES WAVER, DIE DOWN. 367 LAZARU
(SUDDENLY SPRINGS ON TIBERIUS IN A FURY AND 368 LAZARU GRABBING HIM BY THE
SUDDENLY THE SILENCE SEEMS TO CRUSH DOWN UPON HIM.370 LAZARU
(THEN SUDDENLY, WITH A RETURN TO GROTESQUENESS-- 371 LAZARU HARSHLY)
(SUDDENLY THROWING HIS SPEAR AWAY AND SINKING ON 371 LAZARU HIS KNEES,
BUT A TIME COMES WHEN, SUDDENLY, 11 MANSNS
(SUDDENLY SEEMS TO LOOSE HERSELF--ARROGANTLY.) 13 MANSNS
SUDDENLY SHE SAYS, STRANGELY.) 17 MANSNS
(SUDDENLY OVERCOME BY CONTRITION.) 17 MANSNS
SUDDENLY A LITTLE SHUDDER RUNS OVER HER. 27 MANSNS
(SUDDENLY, ANGRY AT HERSELF.) 39 MANSNS
(SUDDENLY SHE IS CONSCIOUS OF THE EXPRESSION ON 40 MANSNS GADSBY'S FACE
(SHE LAUGHS--THEN SUDDENLY SHAMEFACED.) 44 MANSNS
(THEN SUDDENLY SUSPICIOUS.) WAIT/ 55 MANSNS
(SHE STOPS ABRUPTLY, HER EXPRESSION SUDDENLY 57 MANSNS BITTERLY RESENTFUL.)
THEN SUDDENLY CHUCKLES, WITH A CHANGE OF MANNER 60 MANSNS TOWARD DEBORAH.)
I DO NOT SEE WHY YOU SHOULD SUDDENLY TAKE 61 MANSNS
(SUDDENLY FRIGHTENED AND HURT.) 64 MANSNS
(SUDDENLY HE STARES AT HIS MOTHER--SNEERINGLY.) 65 MANSNS
SLEEP WITH IT, DREAM OF IT--AND THEN SUDDENLY ONE 72 MANSNS DAY IT IS ACCOMPLISHED--
(SHE KISSES HIM--THEN SUDDENLY EMBARRASSED AND 88 MANSNS SHY, PUSHES BACK FROM HIM.)
THEN SUDDENLY LIFTS IT AND BURSTS OUT.) 90 MANSNS
(SHE KISSES HIM SUDDENLY WITH PASSIONATE 90 MANSNS GRATITUDE.)
(HE SUDDENLY FROWNS RESENTFULLY. 94 MANSNS
SUDDENLY SHE STOPS, AND LISTENS TO SOMETHING 95 MANSNS BEYOND THE WALL AT RIGHT.
(SUDDENLY HE TURNS ON HER--HARSHLY ACCUSING.) 99 MANSNS
(SHE SUDDENLY TURNS AND STARES AT HIM WITH 102 MANSNS HATRED.)
(SUDDENLY, MOVED BY A STRANGE URGENCY, HE SPRINGS 111 MANSNS TO HIS FEET
(SUDDENLY CALM AND RELIEVED AND A BIT GUILTY.) 113 MANSNS
HER VOICE SUDDENLY TAKES ON A RESENTFUL COMMANDING114 MANSNS TONE..
(CONQUERING HER FEAR AND SUDDENLY GLOATING, TAKES 115 MANSNS HIS ARM--EAGERLY.)
(AS IF SUDDENLY EMERGING FROM A SPELL--WITH AN 127 MANSNS IMPULSIVE GRATEFUL RELIEF.)
(SHE AND DEBORAH SUDDENLY TURN AND STARE AT EACH 129 MANSNS OTHER WITH DEFIANT,
(SUDDENLY LOOKS UP, BUT AVOIDS THEIR EYES.) 130 MANSNS
SUDDENLY HE HAS THE BEATEN QUALITY OF ONE BEGGING 131 MANSNS FOR PITY.
(SUDDENLY EXPLODES, SLAMMING HER RULE ON THE 140 MANSNS DESK.)
THEN SUDDENLY TEARS HER EYES FROM THE MIRROR 144 MANSNS
(SHE SUDDENLY SHIVERS WITH REPULSION AND TEARS HER144 MANSNS EYES FROM THE MIRROR
I SUDDENLY REMEMBERED SOMETHING I HAD NEVER 145 MANSNS REMEMBERED BEFORE.
(SUDDENLY BURSTS OUT-- 154 MANSNS
(SHE SUDDENLY BREAKS--WITH A SOB.) 155 MANSNS
(SUDDENLY RESENTFUL AND ANGRY HERSELF.) 159 MANSNS
(SHE SUDDENLY STOPS AND LISTENS, TENSELY--EAGERLY.162 MANSNS
(SHE SUDDENLY STOPS AND PRESSES HER HANDS TO HER 163 MANSNS HEAD TORTUREDLY.)
(HE SUDDENLY BREAKS AND SINKS ON THE BENCH AT LEFT174 MANSNS OF POOL.
SUDDENLY THEIR FACES, AS ONE FACE, ARE CONVULSED 175 MANSNS BY PITYING,
(AS THEY ARE ABOUT TO SIT, HE SUDDENLY EXCLAIMS.) 176 MANSNS
(SUDDENLY TAUNTING.) AH, 180 MANSNS
I HAVE NEVER FORGOTTEN THE ANGUISHED SENSE OF 184 MANSNS BEING SUDDENLY BETRAYED.
(SUDDENLY IN A PANIC.) BUT HURRY, MOTHER/ 185 MANSNS
THEN SUDDENLY--SHARPLY AND SUSPICIOUSLY.) 192 MANSNS
(SHE STARES AT DEBORAH AND SUDDENLY HER FACE IS 193 MANSNS CONVULSED
SUDDENLY THEY HEAR A NOISE FROM THE LEFT. 349 MARCOM
(SUDDENLY, POINTING OFF LEFT) 349 MARCOM
(SUDDENLY, POINTING TO THE TREE) 349 MARCOM
(SUDDENLY LAMENTING) BUT ALLAH AFFLICTED ME/ 351 MARCOM
(THEN SUDDENLY--CONSOLED) WELL, IT*S A NEW 359 MARCOM WORLD'S RECORD, ANYWAY.
ARE YOU SUDDENLY POSSESSED BY A DEVIL-- 360 MARCOM
(HE THROWS THE POEM DOWN AGAIN, STARTS TO GO, 363 MARCOM HESITATES, SUDDENLY TURNS BACK.
(SUDDENLY FREEING HIMSELF-FRIGHTENEDLY) 368 MARCOM
(SUDDENLY) MANY WONDERS HAVE COME TO PASS IN 368 MARCOM THESE REGIONS.

SUDDENLY

SUDDENLY (CONT'D.)
(SUDDENLY THE CALL TO PRAYER SOUNDS FROM MUEZZINS 369 MARCOM
IN THE MINARETS OF THE MOSQUE.
TEN-- (MARCO SUDDENLY KISSES HER.) 371 MARCOM
(SUDDENLY) THE BUDDHA TAUGHT THAT ONE'S LOVING-- 372 MARCOM
KINDNESS SHOULD EMBRACE ALL
(SUDDENLY) I SAW TWO OF THEM WITH A BOWL OF 372 MARCOM
RICE--
(SUDDENLY GETS TO HIS FEET AND FACES HER-- 374 MARCOM
DISGUSTEDLY)
SUDDENLY A SHOUT RISES FROM THE LIPS OF ALL THE 375 MARCOM
TARTARS.
THANK YOU, SIR--I MEAN, YOUR LORDSHIP--YOUR--(THEN378 MARCOM
SUDDENLY) BEFORE I FORGET--
(SUDDENLY TO MARCO) HAVE YOU AN IMMORTAL SOUL$ 379 MARCOM
(SUDDENLY--WITH A CONFIDENTIAL AIR) 379 MARCOM
I'VE GOT TO SUCCEED, AND--(SUDDENLY BLURTS OUT) 380 MARCOM
WHAT CAN YOU PAY ME
(HE SUDDENLY LOOKS AT MAFFEO WITH A CRAFTY WINK) 381 MARCOM
(THEN SUDDENLY FORCING A SMILE) 385 MARCOM
(THEN SUDDENLY IN A STRANGE VOICE) 393 MARCOM
(CONQUERED-- SUDDENLY OVERPOWERED BY A GREAT 393 MARCOM
SMILE)
(SUDDENLY STEPS FORWARD--FLUSHED BUT PROUDLY) 397 MARCOM
HE SUDDENLY BAWLS TO SOMEONE IN THE SHIP) 403 MARCOM
(SUDDENLY WITH A SLY SMILE TO HIMSELF) 404 MARCOM
(HE SUDDENLY BREAKS INTO A GRIN AGAIN) 406 MARCOM
(WORRIEDLY, SUDDENLY REACHES OUT TO TAKE HER HAND)412 MARCOM
(SUDDENLY WILDLY BITTER) I WILL ASSUREDLY/ 412 MARCOM
(SUDDENLY SLAPPING A STACK OF COINS INTO THE CHEST415 MARCOM
WITH A RESOUNDING CLANK)
(THEN SUDDENLY FORCING A SMILE) 419 MARCOM
(SUDDENLY RUNS UP TO THE UPPER DECK AND STANDS 420 MARCOM
OUTLINED AGAINST THE SKY,
(THEN SUDDENLY RAGING) OUT OF MY SIGHT, DOG, 425 MARCOM
BEFORE I HAVE YOU IMPALED/
(THEN SUDDENLY--TO THE CHAMBERLAIN) 426 MARCOM
(SUDDENLY WITH A GREAT GASP) 428 MARCOM
(SUDDENLY WITH HIS HAIL-FELLOW-WELL-MET JOVIALITY)429 MARCOM
(SUDDENLY HIS EYES TWINKLE AND HE GRINS 15 MISBEG
ADMIRINGLY)
(SUDDENLY FURIOUS) STOP YOUR LYING/ 29 MISBEG
WITHOUT ANY REASON YOU CAN SEE, HE'LL SUDDENLY 33 MISBEG
TURN STRANGE AND LOOK SAD.
(AS SHE TURNS TO GO--SUDDENLY BELLICOSE) 35 MISBEG
(SHE GLANCES AT TYRONE PROVOKINGLY--THEN SUDDENLY 54 MISBEG
WORRIED AND PROTECTIVE)
SWITCHING SUDDENLY FROM JARRING SHOUTS TO LOW, 56 MISBEG
CONFIDENTIAL VITUPERATION.
(HE TURNS EAGERLY TOWARD LEFT BUT SUDDENLY HOGAN 60 MISBEG
GRABS HIS SHOULDER AND SPINS
THIS FARM HAS SUDDENLY BECOME A GOLD MINE. 65 MISBEG
(SUDDENLY--WITH SARDONIC AMUSEMENT) 65 MISBEG
(SUDDENLY IN A BURST OF HUMILIATED ANGER, 71 MISBEG
(HOGAN SUDDENLY BEGINS TO CHUCKLE) 87 MISBEG
(BUT WHEN SHE GETS TO THE DOOR, SHE APPEARS 97 MISBEG
SUDDENLY HESITANT AND TIMID--
(SUDDENLY, BEGINS TO TALK MECHANICALLY) 102 MISBEG
(SUDDENLY, WITH INTENSE HATRED) 107 MISBEG
(THEN AS SUDDENLY HE LETS HER GO) 114 MISBEG
SUDDENLY HE BREAKS AWAY--IN A TONE OF GUILTY 119 MISBEG
IRRITATION)
SUDDENLY HE SLAPS AT HER HAND, KNOCKING THE GLASS 121 MISBEG
TO THE GROUND.)
SUDDENLY HE BLURTS OUT WITH GUILTY LOATHING) 122 MISBEG
HE LOOKS UP SUDDENLY INTO HER EYES--WARNINGLY) 126 MISBEG
(SUDDENLY SHE KISSES HIM WITH FIERCE PASSION) 136 MISBEG
HE SPEAKS THICKLY AS IF HE WAS SUDDENLY VERY 137 MISBEG
DRUNK)
AND ONE DAY SHE SUDDENLY BECAME ILL. 147 MISBEG
(SUDDENLY SHE PUSHES HIM AWAY FROM HER AND SHAKES 166 MISBEG
HIM ROUGHLY)
AND I SUDDENLY HAD A CRAZY NOTION I'D COME UP HERE167 MISBEG
AND SLEEP WITH MY HEAD ON
YOU MEAN YOU--(SUDDENLY) WAIT A MINUTE. 167 MISBEG
AND THEN SUDDENLY, FOR NO REASON, ALL THE FUN WENT170 MISBEG
OUT OF IT.
(THIS CLICKS IN HIS MIND AND SUDDENLY HE REMEMBERS)173 MISBEG
EVERYTHING AND JOSIE SEES
(SUDDENLY HER EXULTANT EXPRESSION CRUMBLES AND SHE 26 POET
BREAKS DOWN.)
(HIS EYES FASTEN ON THE DATE AND SUDDENLY HE 38 POET
STRIKES THE TABLE WITH HIS FIST.)
(SUDDENLY SHE SMILES CONFIDENTLY.) 65 POET
A FASCINATED FEAR SUDDENLY SEIZES HER. 69 POET
(SUDDENLY HE IS ABLE TO BECOME THE POLISHED 74 POET
GENTLEMAN AGAIN--
SUDDENLY SHE BLURTS OUT IMPULSIVELY.) 85 POET
POSSESSIVE NATURE CAN BE--WHEN SUDDENLY ONE IS 86 POET
ATTACKED BY IT.
LO AND BEHOLD, SUDDENLY MY LADY ACTS AS IF I HAD 90 POET
INSULTED HER.
(THEN HIS FACE SUDDENLY LIGHTS UP WITH PATHETIC 92 POET
EAGERNESS
HE SUDDENLY FEELS HER PRESENCE AND TURNS HIS HEAD.103 POET
SO I DO NOT SEE-- (SUDDENLY AN IDEA COMES TO HIM. 119 POET
(SUDDENLY WITH A FLASH OF HER STRANGE, FIERCE 131 POET
PRIDE IN THE POWER OF LOVE.)
SHE STANDS LOOKING AT HER MOTHER, AND SUDDENLY SHE136 POET
BECOMES SHY AND UNCERTAIN--
(SHE RISES SUDDENLY FROM HER CHAIR--WITH BRAVE 139 POET
DEFIANCE.)
(SHE LAUGHS--THEN SUDDENLY LOOKS GUILTY.) 150 POET
SUDDENLY SPEAKS IN A JEERING MUMBLE TO HIMSELF.) 157 POET
(SUDDENLY SHE IS OVERCOME BY A BITTER, TORTURED 162 POET
REVULSION OF FEELING.)
(SUDDENLY SPEAKS, WITHOUT LOOKING UP, IN THE 166 POET
BROADEST BROGUE.

SUDDENLY (CONT'D.)
SUDDENLY HIS FACE LOSES THE COARSE, LEERING, 169 POET
THEN SUDDENLY KISSES HER ON THE LIPS. 174 POET
AS IF HE SAW HIS LAST HOPE OF ESCAPE SUDDENLY CUT 178 POET
OFF.)
(SHE PAUSES--HER TIRED, WORN FACE BECOMES SUDDENLY181 POET
SHY AND TENDER.)
SWEENEY SPEAKS SUDDENLY IN A STRANGE, AWED VOICE) 590 ROPE
WHAT THE HELL--(HE IS SUDDENLY CONVULSED WITH 592 ROPE
LAUGHTER AND SLAPS HIS THIGHS)
(SUDDENLY FINDING HIS VOICE--CHANTS) 594 ROPE
(SUDDENLY) SO I WAS KIDDIN'.. 598 ROPE
(SUDDENLY RAGING) I'LL PAY HIM BACK AN RIGHT/ 600 ROPE
(HIS FACE SUDDENLY FULL OF AN INTENSE PAIN AND 6 STRANG
DISGUST)
(SUDDENLY BLURTING OUT RESENTFULLY) 8 STRANG
(THEN RATHER IRONICALLY) AND SO GORDON TOLD NINA 11 STRANG
HE'D SUDDENLY REALIZED IT
(THEN SUDDENLY IN A SWEET, GENUINELY 14 STRANG
AFFECTIONATE SMILE)
HOW UNFAIR TO ME SUDDENLY DECIDED IT WOULD BE/ 20 STRANG
I KNOW NOW WHY GORDON SUDDENLY DROPPED ALL IDEA OF 20 STRANG
MARRIAGE BEFORE HE LEFT.
MARSDEN STARTS, HIS FACE SUDDENLY ANGRY AND 26 STRANG
DEJECTED)
((POOR OLD PROFESSOR/....)) (THEN SUDDENLY JEERING 28 STRANG
AT HIMSELF)
(TEARS COME TO HIS EYES SUDDENLY 28 STRANG
SUDDENLY ASKING A NECESSARY QUESTION IN HER 28 STRANG
NURSE'S COOL, EFFICIENT TONES)
(HE LAUGHS HARSHLY--THEN SUDDENLY SEES A MAN 28 STRANG
OUTSIDE THE DOORWAY AND STARES--
(HE SUDDENLY BLURTS OUT) YOU'VE KNOWN NINA--MISS 29 STRANG
LEEDS--
(SUDDENLY, DRYLY 38 STRANG
(SUDDENLY REMINDED OF THE DEAD MAN--IN PENITENTLY 39 STRANG
SAD TONES)
IT'S BECAUSE I'VE SUDDENLY SEEN THE LIES IN THE 40 STRANG
SOUNDS CALLED WORDS.
(SUDDENLY, WITH PITY YET WITH SCORN) 42 STRANG
(SUDDENLY JUMPING TO HER FEET AND GOING TO HIM-- 43 STRANG
(THEN SUDDENLY IN A MATTER-OF-FACT TONE THAT IS 46 STRANG
MOCKINGLY LIKE HER FATHER'S)
(THEN SUDDENLY SENSING MARSDEN'S CURIOSITY-- 51 STRANG
PERFUNCTORILY)
THEN SUDDENLY CLUTCHING AT A STRAW, TURNS 55 STRANG
HOPEFULLY TO HIS MOTHER)
(SUDDENLY BREAKING OUT--FRENZIEDLY) 60 STRANG
(THEN SUDDENLY SNAPPING AND BURSTING OUT IN A 63 STRANG
DESPAIRING CRY)
(THEN SUDDENLY IN GUILTY AGONY) 64 STRANG
(SUDDENLY FEELING HER PRESENCE, JERKS HIMSELF TO 69 STRANG
HIS FEET--
(HE SUDDENLY SPEAKS TO EVANS WITH A REALLY SAVAGE 75 STRANG
SATISFACTION)
(THEN SUDDENLY) I'VE JUST THOUGHT--SAM SAID HE 82 STRANG
HAPPENED TO RUN INTO YOU.
(THEN SUDDENLY STARTS HER STORY IN A DULL 82 STRANG
MONOTONOUS TONE RECALLING THAT OF
(HER VOICE SUDDENLY BECOMING FLAT AND LIFELESS) 83 STRANG
(SUDDENLY FALLING ON HIS KNEES AND TAKING HER HAND 89 STRANG
IN BOTH OF HIS AND KISSING IT
HE SUDDENLY APPEARED AGAIN... 91 STRANG
(SUDDENLY WITH CALM CONFIDENCE) 91 STRANG
(SUDDENLY TAKING HER IN HIS ARMS AND KISSING HER 97 STRANG
FRANTICALLY)
(THE SUDDENLY BURSTS INTO A FLOOD OF GARRULITY) 100 STRANG
(SUDDENLY WITH AN INSULTING, UGLY SNEER, RAISING 101 STRANG
HIS VOICE)
(THE SUDDENLY TURNS TO EVANS WHO HAS BEEN STARING 106 STRANG
AT HIM, PUZZLEDLY--
(THEN SUDDENLY BREAKING FROM HIM--WILDLY) 107 STRANG
(HE SUDDENLY FALLS ON HIS KNEES) 107 STRANG
(SUDDENLY TURNS TO EVANS--SAVAGELY) 108 STRANG
(SUDDENLY RAGING) (THEIR HONOR/... 129 STRANG
I SUDDENLY FEEL AFRAID OF HIM/...)) 129 STRANG
(SUDDENLY TAKING HER IN HIS ARMS AND KISSING HER 130 STRANG
AGAIN AND AGAIN--PASSIONATELY)
(THEN SUDDENLY RESISTING AND PUSHING HIM AWAY) 130 STRANG
(SUDDENLY WITH A STRANGE UNNATURAL ELATION-- 133 STRANG
(SUDDENLY TURNING ON HIM) WHEN ARE YOU GOING BACK140 STRANG
TO THE WEST INDIES, NED$
(SUDDENLY JUMPS UP AND CONFRONTS DARRELL, HIS 142 STRANG
FISTS CLENCHED,
(THEN SUDDENLY FORLORNLY TENDER) 144 STRANG
(SUDDENLY MOVING AWAY FROM DARRELL, LOOKING AROUND145 STRANG
HER UNEASILY)
(SUDDENLY STRUCK--THINKING) ((WHY, HE'S JEALOUS 146 STRANG
OF GORDON LIKING CHARLIE/...))
(THEN SUDDENLY MISERABLY SELF-CONTEMPTUOUS) 148 STRANG
(SUDDENLY) I'VE GOT A JOB FOR YOU, CHARLIE--MAKE 149 STRANG
THE SALAD DRESSING FOR LUNCH.
(SUDDENLY) WHY WAS I NAMED GORDONS 153 STRANG
(SUDDENLY OVERCOME BY A WAVE OF CONSCIENCE- 156 STRANG
STRICKEN REMORSE AND PITY)
(SUDDENLY EXPLODING, POUNDS HIS FIST ON THE RAIL) 163 STRANG
(SUDDENLY APPEARS IN THE DOOR FROM THE CABIN, HER 167 STRANG
FACE FLUSHED WITH EXCITEMENT)
(SHE SUDDENLY GETS UP AND GOES TO HIM AND TAKES 169 STRANG
ONE OF HIS HANDS IN BOTH OF
(THEN SUDDENLY WITH A GRIN) YOU OUGHT TO SEE 171 STRANG
CHARLIE/
((HOW I HATE HER/....)) (THEN SUDDENLY WITH A 176 STRANG
DEADLY CALCULATION--THINKING)
(CANNOT BELIEVE HER EARS--SUDDENLY PANIC-STRICKEN)178 STRANG
(STEPS UP SUDDENLY BESIDE THEM--SHARPLY AND 178 STRANG
STERNLY COMMANDING)

SUDDENLY

SUDDENLY (CONT'D.)
THEN SUDDENLY HORRIFIED AT WHAT HE IS DOING BUT 181 STRANG
STILL ANGRY,
(HE SUDDENLY) STAGGERS AS IF HE WERE VERY DRUNK, 182 STRANG
LEANING ON MARSDEN--
(SUDDENLY WITH A CRY OF PAIN, SINKS ON HER KNEES 182 STRANG
BESIDE THE BODY)
(HIS VOICE SUDDENLY BREAKING WITH A SINCERE HUMAN 183 STRANG
GRIEF)
(THEN SUDDENLY) WHERE'S MOTHER--STILL IN THE 188 STRANG
HOUSE$
(SUDDENLY, HAVING GOT BACK HIS CONTROL, TURNS TO 191 STRANG
THEN--COLDLY)
(HIS FACE SUDDENLY FLUSHING WITH ANGER) 192 STRANG
(SUDDENLY BREAKING DOWN--CHOKINGLY) 193 STRANG
THEN SUDDENLY HE BLURTS OUT INDIGNANTLY) 195 STRANG
(IVAN BLUBBERS SOME INCOHERENT PROTEST--THEN 498 VOYAGE
SUDDENLY FALLS ASLEEP.)
(SUDDENLY GETTING TO HIS FEET IN A BEFUDDLED 498 VOYAGE
MANNER)
(HE ROARS WITH CHILDISH LAUGHTER, THEN SUDDENLY 506 VOYAGE
BECOMES SERIOUS)
(HE SUDDENLY SEES THAT OLSON IS NOT THERE, AND 508 VOYAGE
TURNS TO JOE)
(HE TAKES A STEP FORWARD AND SUDDENLY COLLAPSES 508 VOYAGE
OVER A CHAIR,
BUT SHE SUDDENLY BECOMES AWARE OF SOME PRESENCE IN444 WELDED
THE ROOM
(SUDDENLY PUSHING HIM AT ARMS' LENGTH--WITH A 444 WELDED
HAPPY LAUGH)
(SUDDENLY KISSING HIM) OH, I'M SO HAPPY YOU'RE 445 WELDED
BACK.
(HE SUDDENLY PULLS HER HEAD DOWN AND KISSES HER 446 WELDED
IMPULSIVELY)
SHE HEARS IT, STARTS, SEEMS SUDDENLY BROUGHT BACK 449 WELDED
TO HERSELF.
(SUDDENLY EXPLODES IN FURIOUS PROTEST) 451 WELDED
IT'S SO BEAUTIFUL--AND THEN--SUDDENLY I'M BEING 453 WELDED
CRUSHED.
STRANGE--THAT JOHN SHOULD POP IN ON US SUDDENLY 454 WELDED
LIKE THAT.
(THEN SUDDENLY SHE MAKES UP HER MIND AND COMES TO 455 WELDED
HIM)
(SUDDENLY) WHY DO YOU ACT SO JEALOUS--OF THOSE 456 WELDED
OTHERS$
(THEN SUDDENLY WITH ANGUISHED REMORSE) 458 WELDED
HER FACE SEEMS SUDDENLY TO CONGEAL. 459 WELDED
(SHE SUDDENLY PUSHES HIM AWAY AND GLARES AT HIM AT460 WELDED
ARMS' LENGTH.
SUDDENLY HE STARES AS THE SOUND OF A MOTOR COMES 462 WELDED
FROM THE DRIVEWAY.
THERE SHE SUDDENLY STARTS AS IF AWAKENING-- 464 WELDED
FRIGHTENEDLY.)
JOHN SUDDENLY GROWS AWARE OF THIS. 465 WELDED
THEN SHE WAVERS AND SUDDENLY BOLTS BACK INTO THE 466 WELDED
ROOM, GROPINGLY.
(SHE SHUDDERS--THEN SUDDENLY BURSTS OUT WILDLY) 467 WELDED
(SUDDENLY GRASPING HIS ARM) WAIT. 469 WELDED
(AGAIN STARING AT HER WITH STRANGE INTENSITY-- 473 WELDED
SUDDENLY WITH A QUEER LAUGH)
(THEN SUDDENLY REMINDED OF SOMETHING SHE REGARDS 474 WELDED
HIM CALCULATINGLY--
(STARING AT HER INTENTLY--SUDDENLY DEEPLY MOVED) 475 WELDED
POOR WOMAN
(SHE SUDDENLY GIVES HIM A FURIOUS PUSH 477 WELDED
(SUDDENLY TURNS AND ADDRESSES HIM DIRECTLY IN A 481 WELDED
SAD, SYMPATHETIC TONE)
SUDDENLY SHE LAUGHS WITH A SAD SELF-MOCKERY) 482 WELDED
SUDDENLY HIS FACE GROWS CONVULSED. 484 WELDED
(HE TURNS SUDDENLY--HOPEFULLY) 484 WELDED
SUDDENLY HE TURNS TO HER--DESPERATELY) 486 WELDED
SUDDENLY HE CAN STAND IT NO LONGER, 487 WELDED
(THEN SUDDENLY REMORSEFUL, CATCHING HER HAND AND 487 WELDED
COVERING IT WITH KISSES)
(SUDDENLY GLARING AT HER SUSPICIOUSLY) 487 WELDED
SUDDENNESS
(HIS VOICE WITH SURPRISING SUDDENNESS TAKES ON A 545 DAYS
SAVAGE VINDICTIVE QUALITY)
(HIS MOOD SWITCHING WITH DRUNKEN SUDDENNESS) 249 DESIRE
SUDDIN
FOR IF HE SEEN HIM SUDDIN IT'S LIKELY THE LITTLE 590 ROPE
WITS HE HAS LEFT WOULD LEAVE
SUDDINT
WHIN ALL AV A SUDDINT WE HEARD A GREAT SLITHERIN' 481 CARDIF
CRASH.
SUDS
WANTA SPILL MY SUDS FOR ME$ 9 ANNA
(SHOUTS FROM NEXT ROOM) DON'T I GET THAT BUCKET 10 ANNA
O' SUDS, DUTCHY$
SUE
I'LL SUE YOU FOR LIBEL. 204 AHWILD
HE TOLD HARKER HE WAS HIRING A LAWYER TO SUE HIM 24 JOURNE
FOR DAMAGES.
(FURIOUSLY) AND YOU'LL PAY IT, OR I'LL SUE YOU, 63 MISBEG
SO HELP ME CHRIST/
THAT WE'LL SUE HIM FOR OUTRAGING YOUR VIRTUE$ 95 MISBEG
SUED
WOULD SEEM TO SMILE THE LESS, OF ALL THAT 101 POET
FLATTERED--FOLLOWED--SOUGHT, AND SUED.
SUEY
SHE WOKE UP CHUCK AND DRAGGED HIM OUTA DE HAY TO 613 ICEMAN
GO TO A CHOP SUEY JOINT.
SUEZ
=SHIP ME SOMEWHERE EAST OF SUEZ-=* 599 ICEMAN
SUFFER
LET HER SUFFER, FOR A CHANGE. 277 AHWILD
HAVING TO SUFFER ALL THE TIME BECAUSE YOU'VE NEVER127 BEYOND
BEEN MAN ENOUGH

SUFFER

SUFFER (CONT'D.)
YOU'LL HAVE TO SUFFER TO WIN BACK--(HIS VOICE 162 BEYOND
GROWS WEAKER AND HE SIGHS WEARILY)
ME COOKIN' COOKIN'--DOIN' HER WORK--THAT MADE ME 209 DESIRE
KNOW HER, SUFFER HER SUFFERIN'--
AN' I'D SUFFER MUSS LEAVIN' YE, GOIN' WEST, 267 DESIRE
THINKIN' O' YE DAY AN' NIGHT,
I DON'T WANT YEW T' SUFFER/ 267 DESIRE
YOU AND I, WHO ARE INNOCENT, WOULD SUFFER A WORSE 97 ELECTR
PUNISHMENT THAN THE GUILTY--
BUT I'D RATHER SUFFER THAT THAN LET THE MURDER OF 97 ELECTR
OUR FATHER GO UNPUNISHED/
=SUFFER THESE LITTLE ONES/= 270 GGBROW
LET MARGARET SUFFER/ 319 GGBROW
LET THE WHOLE WORLD SUFFER AS I AM SUFFERING/ 319 GGBROW
AND GET HER RID OF ME SO I COULDN'T MAKE HER 705 ICEMAN
SUFFER ANY MORE,
GOD, CAN YOU PICTURE ALL I MADE HER SUFFER, AND 713 ICEMAN
ALL THE GUILT SHE MADE ME FEEL,
THAT I SUFFER FROM RHEUMATISM IN MY HANDS 116 JOURNE
I WANT TO SEE HIM SUFFER, TO HEAR HIS LAUGHTER 342 LAZARU
CHOKE IN HIS THROAT WITH PAIN/
HE SEEMED NOT TO SUFFER BUT TO BE IMPATIENT AND 30 MANSNS
EXASPERATED--
FORMS OF LIFE, THAT ONE'S COMPASSION SHOULD SUFFER372 MARCOM
WITH THE SUFFERING,
THERE'D BE THE DEVIL TO PAY IF YOU SHOULD SUFFER A412 MARCOM
RELAPSE OF THAT FEVER
I GUESS I'LL HAVE TO STOP OVERWORKING OR I'LL 415 MARCOM
SUFFER A NERVOUS BREAKDOWN.
SUFFERS 146 MISBEG
CHRIST, I OUGHT TO SUFFER/ 146 MISBEG
(PITYINGLY) MAYBE YOU'D BETTER NOT--IF IT WILL 146 MISBEG
MAKE YOU SUFFER.
AND DIVIL A CARE HOW YOU GOT IT, OR WHO YOU ROBBED163 MISBEG
OR MADE SUFFER/
MAKE HER SUFFER WHAT I WAS MADE TO SUFFER/... 58 STRANG
SHE'S GOT TO SUFFER, TOO/... 59 STRANG
HOW HE MADE ME SUFFER/...... 112 STRANG
POOR NED, I'VE MADE HIM SUFFER A GREAT DEAL.../) 138 STRANG
OF HOW HE'S MADE US SUFFER/ 173 STRANG
(THINKING BITTERLY) (EVEN IN DEATH SAM MAKES 192 STRANG
PEOPLE SUFFER...))
I CAN'T BEAR TO WATCH HIM SUFFER ANYMORE/... 194 STRANG
I LIED TO MAKE YOU SUFFER MORE THAN YOU WERE 483 WELDED
MAKING ME SUFFER.
(A PAUSE--GENTLY) YOU MUST NOT SUFFER TOO MUCH. 486 WELDED
SUFFERED
IF YOU KNEW HOW I'VE SUFFERED--/ 279 AHWILD
AND THAT WOULD'VE BEEN WORSE, FOR RUTH WOULD'VE 110 BEYOND
SUFFERED THEN.
REMEMBER, ANDY, RUTH HAS SUFFERED DOUBLE HER 162 BEYOND
SHARE.
AND YET HE NEVER SAID OR SHOWED--GOD, HOW HE MUST 164 BEYOND
HAVE SUFFERED/
RUTH HAS SUFFERED--REMEMBER, ANDY--ONLY THROUGH 168 BEYOND
SACRIFICE--
I COULDN'T HELP IT--AND HE KNEW HOW I'D SUFFERED, 168 BEYOND
TOO.
O BROTHER WHO LIVED AND LOVED AND SUFFERED AND 565 DAYS
DIED WITH US,
YOU POOR DARLING, HOW YOU MUST HAVE SUFFERED/ 76 ELECTR
FOR ALL THE INJUSTICE YOU SUFFERED AT YOUR 86 ELECTR
FATHER'S HANDS.
IN THE ARMY, WE USED TO SAY WE SUFFERED MORE 119 POET
CASUALTIES
I LONGED FOR YOU--AND SUFFERED/ 130 STRANG
ONLY THE OTHER MALE, NED, SEEMS TO HAVE SUFFERED 134 STRANG
DETERIORATION.))
WE'VE SUFFERED ALL OUR LIVES FOR HIS SAKE/ 173 STRANG
OH, NINA--POOR LITTLE NINA--MY NINA--HOW YOU MUST 180 STRANG
HAVE SUFFERED/
IF HE ONLY KNEW WHAT SHE'S SUFFERED FOR HIS 191 STRANG
SAKE/...
NEO HAS SUFFERED TOO MUCH/...)) 192 STRANG
SUFFERIN'
ME COOKIN'--DOIN HER WORK--THAT MADE ME KNOW HER, 209 DESIRE
SUFFER HER SUFFERIN'--
SUFFERING
AND HE IS NOW SUFFERING FROM A BAD CASE OF 256 AHWILD
HANGOVER--
AS IF THE TWO DAYS JUST PAST HAD BEEN ONES OF 63 ANNA
SUFFERING AND SLEEPLESS NIGHTS.
SUFFERING FROM THE AFTEREFFECTS OF HIS DRUNK. 63 ANNA
(COMPASSIONATELY) YES, YOU ALWAYS WERE--AND YOU 89 BEYOND
SUFFERING SO MUCH, TOO/
TO THINK THAT I SHOULD BE THE CAUSE OF YOUR 110 BEYOND
SUFFERING.
ALL OUR SUFFERING HAS BEEN A TEST THROUGH WHICH WE150 BEYOND
HAD TO PASS.
OTHERWISE OUR SUFFERING WOULD BE MEANINGLESS--AND 150 BEYOND
THAT IS UNTHINKABLE.
ONLY THROUGH CONTACT WITH SUFFERING, ANDY, WILL 162 BEYOND
YOU--AWAKEN.
YOU'VE GOT A CHANCE NOW TO UNDO SOME OF ALL THE 165 BEYOND
SUFFERING YOU'VE BROUGHT ON ROB.
FOR ALL THE RUIN AND SUFFERING YOU HAD BROUGHT ON 466 DYNAMO
HER--AND ON ME/
I KNOW YOU'RE SUFFERING, VINNIE-- 174 ELECTR
YOU'RE SUFFERING/ 175 ELECTR
(WITH A SUFFERING BEWILDERMENT) 264 GGBROW
SUFFERING FACE. 272 GGBROW
IS THE MASK OF THE BRAVE FACE SHE PUTS ON BEFORE 291 GGBROW
THE WORLD TO HIDE HER SUFFERING
(HE TEARS OFF HIS MASK AND REVEALS A SUFFERING 305 GGBROW
FACE THAT IS RAVAGED AND HAGGARD.
LET THE WHOLE WORLD SUFFER AS I AM SUFFERING/ 319 GGBROW
LIKE WHEN YOU'RE SICK AND SUFFERING LIKE HELL 625 ICEMAN

SUFFERING (CONT'D.)
(HER FACE IS DRAWN IN AN EXPRESSION OF INTENSE SUFFERING BY THE MEMORY. 74 JOURNE
CALM BUT FURROWED DEEP WITH THE MARKS OF FORMER 274 LAZARU
SUFFERING
HAS LONG AGO BECOME NAIVELY INSENSITIVE TO ANY 299 LAZARU
HUMAN SUFFERING BUT ITS OWN.
FORGIVE ME YOUR SUFFERING/ 329 LAZARU
FORMS OF LIFE, THAT ONE'S COMPASSION SHOULD SUFFER372 MARCOM
WITH THE SUFFERING.
IT IS THE FACE OF A WOMAN WHO HAS KNOWN REAL 407 MARCOM
SORROW AND SUFFERING.
(HIS FACE HAS BECOME SAD WITH A MEMORY OF THE 4 STRANG
BEWILDERED SUFFERING
TO MAKE HER INSENSITIVE TO SUFFERING, 26 STRANG
(THINKING MISERABLY) (NOW SHE KNOWS MY 63 STRANG
SUFFERING...
I KNOW WHAT YOU'RE SUFFERING. 64 STRANG
THE TRACES OF FORMER SUFFERING ARE MARKED ON HER 111 STRANG
FACE.
TO MAKE ME JEALOUS, THAT MY SUFFERING PLEASES YOU,455 WELDED
SUFFERINGLY
(THINKING SUFFERINGLY) (WHY DOES HE KEEP ON 195 STRANG
CALLING ME DARRELL...
SUFFERS
IC EFFORTS TO SPEED UP AND THE MUSIC SUFFERS IN 471 CARIBE
THE PROCESS.)
THEY HAVEN'T KILLED IT--THAT LONELY LIFE OF ONE'S 477 WELDED
OWN WHICH SUFFERS IN SOLITUDE.
SUFFICIENT
BEFORE THE COMPANY CAN BE FREE AND INDEPENDENT AND 93 MANSNS
SELF-SUFFICIENT.
TO MAKE THE COMPANY ENTIRELY SELF-SUFFICIENT. 101 MANSNS
THAT IS QUITE SUFFICIENT TO CONVERT A TARTAR 363 MARCOM
BARBARIAN/
SUFFICIENTLY
BUT SUFFICIENTLY EMPHATIC TO FORM A DISTURBING 189 AHWILD
PUNCTUATION TO THE CONVERSATION.)
I THINK OUR FRIEND IS NOW SUFFICIENTLY FEARFUL AND150 MANSNS
HUMILIATED.
SUFFOCATES
HIS BREATH IN THE SAME AIR SUFFOCATES ME/ 357 LAZARU
SUFFOCATING
IT'S SUFFOCATING/ 151 ELECTR
(AS IF HE WERE SUFFOCATING, HE PULLS THE MASK FROM272 GGBROW
HIS RESIGNED, PALE,
WHILE MOTHER AND I WERE SWEATING AND SUFFOCATING 106 POET
IN THE HEAT OF THE KITCHEN
SUFFOCATINGLY
OUTSIDE, THE SPELL OF ABNORMAL QUIET PRESSES 31 HUGHIE
SUFFOCATINGLY UPON THE STREET.
SUFFUSED
THE SKY ABOVE THE ROOF IS SUFFUSED WITH DEEP 203 DESIRE
COLORS,
SUFFUSED, EERIE GLOW. 190 EJONES
SUFFUSES
AN EXPRESSION OF OVERWHELMING JOY SUFFUSES HIS 595 ROPE
WORN FEATURES.)
SUGAR
'CAUSE I RUN WIDE OPEN FOK YEARS AND PAYS MY SUGAR601 ICEMAN
ON DE DOT.
MAN ALIVE, FROM WHAT THE BOYS TELL ME, THERE'S 653 ICEMAN
SUGAR GALORE THESE DAYS.
HE MISTOOK RAT POISON FOK FLOUR, OR SUGAR, OR 147 JOURNE
SOMETHING.
SUGGEST
SITTING IN STIFF, POSED ATTITUDES THAT SUGGEST THE 46 ELECTR
STATUES OF MILITARY HEROES.
(HARSHLY) WILL MRS. ANTHONY HELPFULLY SUGGEST 271 GGBROW
WHAT$
(SUDDENLY PRIMLY VIRTUOUS.) I'D NEVER SUGGEST A 52 JOURNE
MAN OR A WOMAN TOUCH DRINK,
BUT NOW YOU SUGGEST IT-- 52 JOURNE
I SUGGEST SIMON TAKE YOU TO HIS STUDY. 52 MANSNS
SO HENRY HARFORD DOES ME THE HONOR--TO SUGGEST 122 POET
THAT, DOES HE$
HE CAN SUGGEST A GOOD OBSTETRICIAN... 50 STRANG
WHY IN THE DEVIL DID I EVER SUGGEST IT TO HER$... 74 STRANG
IT GIVES HER THE COURAGE TO ASK YOU, DOCTOR, TO 87 STRANG
SUGGEST THE FATHER.
SUGGESTED
EXACTLY WHAT WE SUGGESTED/ 317 GGBROW
I SAID, OF COURSE, I WOULD DO ANYTHING SHE 176 JOURNE
SUGGESTED.
YOUR POSITION IS--ER--PRECARIOUS, UNLESS--WHAT 33 MANSNS
HENRY SUGGESTED IS THIS$...
ONE FURTHER THING HENRY SUGGESTED, 35 MANSNS
(CARELESSLY.) WHY, ALL I UNDERSTAND ABOUT IT IS 55 MANSNS
THAT MY HUSBAND SUGGESTED THAT
THAT FATHER SUGGESTED SHE OFFER ME. 65 MANSNS
HE SAID HE SUGGESTED THE IDEA TO HARDER-- 48 MISBEG
AND SHE ONLY SUGGESTED HE WAIT A YEAR, SHE DIDN'T 144 POET
MAKE HIM PROMISE.
HAVE YOU SUGGESTED THIS MATCH TO NINA$ 38 STRANG
SUGGESTING
DID I ACTUALLY HEAR YOU SUGGESTING WORK ON THE 40 JOURNE
FRONT HEDGE, JAMIE$
IS HE SUGGESTING ME$... 87 STRANG
SUGGESTION
NOW, I'VE GOT A BETTER SUGGESTION THAN THAT. 191 AHWILD
THERE IS NO SUGGESTION OF PRIMNESS ABOUT THE 94 BEYOND
WHOLE.
THERE IS EVEN A SUGGESTION OF RUTHLESS CUNNING 153 BEYOND
ABOUT THEM.
THEIR FLESH IN THE GREEN LIGHT HAS THE SUGGESTION 571 CROSS
OF DECOMPOSITION.
SINISTER PURPOSE BEHIND MY SUGGESTION. 495 DAYS

SUGGESTION (CONT'D.)
THERE IS AN ABSURD SUGGESTION OF ROUGE ON HER 520 DIFRNT
TIGHT CHEEKS AND THIN LIPS.
HAS A STRONG SUGGESTION OF RIBALD HUMOR. 6 ELECTR
THERE IS STILL A SUGGESTION OF OLD AUTHORITY 575 ICEMAN
LURKING IN HIM
(AS IF THEY WERE SUBJECTS MOVED BY HYPNOTIC 282 LAZARU
SUGGESTION--
HENRY'S SUGGESTION IS THAT YOU AND JOEL APPROACH 34 MANSNS
SIMON--
BUT THERE IS ALSO A SUGGESTION OF PAUNCH. 69 MANSNS
WITH A SUGGESTION OF WEARINESS AND RESIGNATION NOW 70 MANSNS
I WILL BE HAPPY TO CONSIDER ANY SUGGESTION YOU-- 106 MANSNS
ON THE MERITS OF MIKE'S SUGGESTION. 23 MISBEG
GIVING THE WINDOWS A SUGGESTION OF LIFELESS CLOSED 24 STRANG
EYES AND MAKING THE ROOM SEEM
PALLOR AND THE MYSTERIOUS SUGGESTION ABOUT HER OF 26 STRANG
HIDDEN EXPERIENCE.
BUT I MADE THE SUGGESTION BEFORE SHE HAD THAT 74 STRANG
ABORTION PERFORMED/...
ANY SUGGESTION YOU CAN MAKE, CHARLIE, WILL BE 122 STRANG
GRATEFULLY RECEIVED.
SUGGESTIONS
HAVE YOU ANY SUGGESTIONS$ 275 GGBROW
CHARLIE'S COMING TO BRING HIS SUGGESTIONS ON MY 72 STRANG
OUTLINE FOR GORDON'S BIOGRAPHY.
I JUST DROPPED IN TO BRING BACK HER OUTLINE WITH 73 STRANG
THE SUGGESTIONS I'VE MADE.
TORN BY TWO CONFLICTING SUGGESTIONS. 449 WELDED
SUGGESTS
IT SUGGESTS, RATHER, AN INERT STRENGTH. 428 DYNAMO
IN OUTLINE, HIS FACE SUGGESTS A ROMAN CONSUL ON AN294 GGBROW
OLD COIN.
WHICH SUGGESTS THE LAST MARCH OF THE CONDEMNED. 683 ICEMAN
IN HIS LETTERS HENRY SUGGESTS CERTAIN STEPS SHOULD 32 MANSNS
BE TAKEN WHICH,
THIS GET-UP SUGGESTS THAT HE FOLLOWS A STYLE SET 37 MISBEG
BY WELL-GROOMED BROADWAY
TAKE HIS MILK TO OUR YANKEE GUEST, AS YOUR MOTHER 60 POET
SUGGESTS.
MR. HARFORD SUGGESTS IT WOULD BE ADVISABLE THAT 122 POET
YOU GO WEST--TO OHIO, SAY.
STRONGLY SUGGESTS ONE IN MOURNING. 24 STRANG
SUICIDE
BUT SUICIDE IS THE ACT OF A COWARD. 282 AHWILD
COMMIT SUICIDE$, HUH$ 12 ANNA
MAYBE I'VE COMMITTED SUICIDE/ 115 ELECTR
I'VE ALWAYS FELT IT, EVEN BEFORE THE GENERAL'S 136 ELECTR
DEATH AND HER SUICIDE.
AND ON TOP OF THAT FATHER'S DEATH--AND THE SHOCK 146 ELECTR
OF MOTHER'S SUICIDE.
YOU WANT TO DRIVE ME TO SUICIDE AS I DROVE MOTHER/166 ELECTR
YOU KNOW SHE'D NEVER COMMIT SUICIDE. 668 ICEMAN
D'YUH MEAN YUH TINK SHE COMMITTED SUICIDE, 'COUNT 668 ICEMAN
OF HIS CHEATIN' OR SOMETHIN$
JEEZ, IF SHE COMMITTED SUICIDE, YUH GOT TO FEEL 669 ICEMAN
SORRY FOR HICKEY, HUH$
I DIDN'T SAY POOR EVELYN COMMITTED SUICIDE. 693 ICEMAN
(REVENGEFULLY) YOU DROVE YOUR POOR WIFE TO 693 ICEMAN
SUICIDE$
HE'S THE BALMY KIND WHAT COMMITS SUICIDE. 524 INZONE
PARTICULARLY THE TIME I TRIED TO COMMIT SUICIDE AT147 JOURNE
JIMMIE THE PRIEST'S.
THAT I WILL OUTRAGE YOUR SENSE OF PROPRIETY BY 29 MANSNS
SUICIDE.
SUICIDES
COMMIT MORE MURDERS AND SUICIDES THAN-- 77 STRANG
SUING
THERE WAS THE SCANDAL OF THAT WOMAN WHO HAD BEEN 86 JOURNE
YOUR MISTRESS, SUING YOU.
SUIT
HE IS DRESSED IN WHAT HAD ONCE BEEN A VERY NATTY 188 AHWILD
LOUD LIGHT SUIT BUT IS NOW A
MRS. MILLER, AFTER A HELPLESS GLANCE AT HIM, 227 AHWILD
FOLLOWS SUIT.
HE IS DRESSED IN A WRINKLED, ILL-FITTING DARK SUIT 5 ANNA
OF SHORE CLOTHES,
WEARS A CHEAP BLUE SUIT, A STRIPED COTTON SHIRT 45 ANNA
WITH A BLACK TIE.
AN I B'LIEVE IN LETTIN' YOUNG FOLKS RUN THEIR 98 BEYOND
AFFAIRS TO SUIT THEMSELVES.
YOU CAN'T ORDER THE TIDES ON THE SEAS TO SUIT YOU,102 BEYOND
AND THE SOONER I'M IN THE GRAVE AND OUT O' THEIR 113 BEYOND
WAY THE BETTER IT'D SUIT THEM.
THAT OUGHT TO SUIT YOU. 145 BEYOND
HE IS DRESSED IN AN EXPENSIVE BUSINESS SUIT AND 153 BEYOND
APPEARS STOUTER)
HE IS DRESSED IN A DARK SUIT, WHITE SHIRT AND 493 DAYS
COLLAR, A DARK TIE.
(HE FOLLOWS SUIT. 217 DESIRE
HE IS DRESSED IN HIS DISMAL BLACK SUNDAY SUIT. 221 DESIRE
HE IS DRESSED IN HIS STORE SUIT, SPRUCED UP. 228 DESIRE
HE HAS CHANGED TO A DARK SUIT, IS READY FOR * UP 507 DIFRNT
STREET.
HE IS DRESSED IN AN OLD BAGGY SUIT MUCH THE WORSE 513 DIFRNT
FOR WEAR.
AND WEARS THE COAT OF HIS OLD SUIT. 457 DYNAMO
HE IS DRESSED IN A WORN RIDING SUIT OF DIRTY WHITE174 EJONES
DRILL, PUTTEES, SPURS.
HE HAS GROWN DREADFULLY THIN AND HIS BLACK SUIT 138 ELECTR
HANGS LOOSELY ON HIS BODY.
TOO FAR AWAY TO SUIT ME/ 175 ELECTR
THE FATHER WEARS AN ILL-FITTING BLACK SUIT, LIKE A259 GGBROW
MOURNER.
(LIKE AN IDOL) SUIT YOURSELF. 286 GGBROW
(WITH A QUEER LOOK) WHY, DION, THAT ISN'T YOUR 316 GGBROW
SUIT.

SUIT

SUIT (CONT'D.)

HE WEARS AN ILL-FITTING BLUE SERGE SUIT, WHITE SHIRT AND COLLAR, A BLUE TIE. 8 HUGHIE

THE SUIT IS OLD AND SHINES AT THE ELBOWS AS IF IT HAD BEEN WAXED AND POLISHED. 8 HUGHIE

HE WEARS A LIGHT GREY SUIT CUT IN THE EXTREME, TIGHT-WAISTED, BROADWAY MODE. 9 HUGHIE

WEARING A LIGHT SUIT THAT HAD ONCE BEEN FLASHILY SPORTY 575 ICEMAN

HE IS SLOVENLY DRESSED IN A DIRTY SHAPELESS PATCHED SUIT, SPOTTED BY FOOD. 575 ICEMAN

HE IS DRESSED IN AN OLD COAT FROM ONE SUIT AND PANTS FROM ANOTHER. 577 ICEMAN

SOLD HIS SUIT AND SHOES AT SOLLY'S TWO DAYS AGO. 581 ICEMAN

I MUST HAVE THIS SUIT CLEANED AND PRESSED. 600 ICEMAN

A LOUD SUIT, TIE AND SHIRT, AND YELLOW SHOES. 615 ICEMAN

AND WEARS A SUNDAY-BEST BLUE SUIT WITH A HIGH STIFF COLLAR. 670 ICEMAN

HE IS SHAVED AND WEARS AN EXPENSIVE, WELL-CUT SUIT, GOOD SHOES AND CLEAN LINEN. 674 ICEMAN

HIS ANCIENT TWEED SUIT HAS BEEN BRUSHED AND HIS FRAYED LINEN IS CLEAN. 674 ICEMAN

HOPE IS DRESSED IN AN OLD BLACK SUNDAY SUIT, BLACK683 ICEMAN TIE, SHOES, SOCKS.

HE HAS LOST HIS STRAW HAT, HIS TIE IS AWRY, AND HIS BLUE SUIT IS DIRTY. 697 ICEMAN

(HE DRINKS AND THEY FOLLOW SUIT.) 719 ICEMAN

HE WEARS A THREADBARE, READY-MADE, GREY SACK SUIT 13 JOURNE AND SHINELESS BLACK SHOES.

HE IS DRESSED IN AN OLD SACK SUIT, NOT AS SHABBY AS TYRONE'S. 19 JOURNE

IN THAT FILTHY OLD SUIT I'VE TRIED TO MAKE HIM THROW AWAY. 43 JOURNE

HE HAS CHANGED TO A READY-MADE BLUE SERGE SUIT, HIGH STIFF COLLAR AND TIE. 89 JOURNE

TYRONE LIFTS HIS GLASS AND HIS SONS FOLLOW SUIT MECHANICALLY. 175 JOURNE

(THINKING.) I'M NOT A THOUGHT HE MOVES AROUND IN 122 MANSNS HIS MIND TO SUIT HIS PLEASURE--

YOU CAN CHANGE TO YOUR SUNDAY SUIT IN THE CAN AT THE STATION OR IN THE TRAIN. 5 MISBEG

IT'D SUIT YOU. 5 MISBEG

HE IS DRESSED IN AN EXPENSIVE DARK-BROWN SUIT, 37 MISBEG

THAT'D SUIT ME. 93 MISBEG

I'LL SOON BE LIVELY ENOUGH TO SUIT YOU. 167 POET

BUT IF HE SHOULD BRING SUITS... 12 STRANG

HE IS DRESSED CAREFULLY IN AN ENGLISH MADE SUIT OF 24 STRANG BLUE SERGE SO DARK AS TO SEEM

I'LL PICK OUT A WIFE FOR YOU--GUARANTEED TO SUIT/.114 STRANG

HE IS DRESSED IN A SHABBY SUIT, WHICH MUST HAVE 493 VOYAGE ONCE BEEN CHEAPLY FLASHY.

SUITABLE

A SUITABLE SENTIMENTAL HUSH FALLS ON THE ROOM.) 603 ICEMAN

WHERE ELSE COULD I FIND SUITABLE FEMININE COMPANIONSHIPS AND LOVE. 158 JOURNE

IT WOULD BE A GREAT PRIDE TO HER, I'M SURE, TO KNOW YOU FOUND HER SUITABLE/ 49 POET

IT IS OBVIOUS THAT WERE THERE A SUDDEN WEDDING WITHOUT A SUITABLE PERIOD OF 110 POET

MINE WOULDN'T BE SUITABLE FOR US. 198 STRANG

SUITABLY

AND SUITABLY REWARDING, ANYONE WHO SHOULD MURDER 180 MANSNS US.

SUITCASE

A SUITCASE STANDS IN THE MIDDLE OF THE FLOOR. 63 ANNA

HE TAKES OUT A SMALL BUNCH OF KEYS AND UNLOCKS THES13 INZONE SUITCASE.

REASSURED, HE LEANS DOWN AND CAUTIOUSLY PULLS OUT 513 INZONE A SUITCASE

SHOVES THE SUITCASE BACK UNDER THE BUNK, CLIMBS 513 INZONE INTO HIS BUNK AGAIN.

SMITTY OPENS THE SUITCASE AND TAKES OUT A SMALL 513 INZONE BLACK TIN BOX.

HE HAS A SUITCASE, HAT, AND OVERCOAT WHICH HE SETS444 WELDED INSIDE ON THE FLOOR.

SUITCASES

IN UNDER THE BUNKS A GLIMPSE CAN BE HAD OF SEA- 477 CARDIF CHESTS, SUITCASES, SEA-BOOTS, ETC

SUITE

AND WHILE I'M SIGNING UP FOR THE BRIDAL SUITE 23 HUGHIE

SUITED

A CASSOCK WOULD SEEM MORE SUITED TO HIM THAN THE APRON HE WEARS. 3 ANNA

SURE IT'S A SWEET NAME IS SUITED TO YOU. 39 ANNA

LIVING SUITED HIM... 190 STRANG

SUITORS

AS ELDERLY SUITORS FOR MY BODY, ROUES IN THEIR BORED, WITHERED HEARTS. 29 MANSNS

SUITS

(WITH A HARD LAUGH) THAT SUITS ME DOWN TO THE GROUND. 14 ANNA

(OFFENDED) THE BACK OF MY HAND TO YOU THEN, IF THAT SUITS YOU BETTER. 52 ANNA

JUST WHEN IT SUITS ME TO HAVE IT. 95 BEYOND

THAT SUITS ME. 125 BEYOND

THEY ARE DRESSED IN DIRTY PATCHED SUITS OF DUNGAREE, FLANNEL SHIRTS. 477 CARDIF

THE MAJORITY ARE DRESSED IN PATCHED SUITS OF DUNGAREE. 455 CARIBE

(HE SUITS THE ACTION TO THE WORD AND ROARS WITH MEANINGLESS LAUGHTER.) 470 CARIBE

SUITS ME. 213 DESIRE

SUITS ME. 219 DESIRE

THAT SUITS YE, DON'T IT, ESSIE, NOW YE GOT REUB AFORE YE 250 DESIRE

AND WHATEVER YOU THINK IS BEST, SUITS ME. 516 DIFRNT

THEY ARE DRESSED IN STRIPED CONVICT SUITS, THEIR HEADS ARE SHAVEN. 194 EJONES

SUITS (CONT'D.)

IT SUITS YOUR TEMPERAMENT. 17 ELECTR

WHATEVER SUITS YOU. 464 WELDED

SULK

DON'T SULK. 320 GGBROW

SULKILY

(SULKILY) I WASN'T ASLEEP. 269 AHWILD

(SULKILY) I DON'T CARE. 270 AHWILD

(AS THE OTHERS SMILE--SULKILY) 104 BEYOND

(SULKILY) I DON'T CARE. 107 BEYOND

(AT A NOISE OF FOOTSTEPS FROM THE HALL--SULKILY) 303 GGBROW

(A BIT SHAMEFACED--SULKILY) WHO WANTS TO$ 632 ICEMAN

(SULKILY) I APOLOGIZE, CAPTAIN LEWIS--BECAUSE HARRY IS MY GOOT FRIEND. 651 ICEMAN

SULKING

(TURNING BACK TO THE SULKING MARY) 601 ROPE

SULKY

A BIT SULKY AND IMPATIENT WITH HER) 279 AHWILD

(LIKE A SULKY CHILD) I'M TOO TIRED. 320 GGBROW

TOWARD THE LEFT END OF THE TABLE, WHERE, LIKE TWO 650 ICEMAN SULKY BOYS.

AS WE WOULD BE AT THE MISCHIEF OF A BAD SULKY BOY.126 MANSNS

SULLEN

HIS MANNER IS SULLEN AND ANGRY. 535 *ILE

(THE MEN STAND HUDDLED TOGETHER IN A SULLEN SILENCE. 544 *ILE

BENNY GOES TO OPEN IT, HIS EXPRESSION TURNING 528 DIFRNT SURLY AND SULLEN.

TRUCULENT SWAGGER AND HIS GOOD-NATURED FACE IS SET636 ICEMAN IN SULLEN SUSPICION.)

HIS MANNER IS SULLEN, HIS FACE SET IN GLOOM. 664 ICEMAN

HIS MANNER IS GROUCHY AND SULLEN. 697 ICEMAN

THE KAAN STUDIES HIS SULLEN BUT RELIEVED FACE WITH380 MARCOM AMUSEMENT)

HE HAS A COMMON IRISH FACE, ITS EXPRESSION SULLEN, 4 MISBEG OR SLYLY CUNNING,

SULLENLY

(SULLENLY) NUTTING. 43 ANNA

(SULLENLY) POOTY GOOT--IF IT AIN'T FOR SOME FALLS. 45 ANNA

(SULLENLY) I DO THE BEST I KNOW HOW. 123 BEYOND

(SULLENLY) BLARSTED FAT-'EADS/ 478 CARDIF

(SULLENLY) I CAN'T WRITE ME NAME. 465 CARIBE

BENNY SLOUCHES TO THE DOOR--SULLENLY) 547 DIFRNT

(THE WOMAN KEEPS SULLENLY SILENT. 174 EJONES

(SULLENLY) NO. 114 ELECTR

(SULLENLY) FORGET NOTHIN'/ 227 HA APE

(SULLENLY) DAT'S MY BUSINESS. 637 ICEMAN

JOE GETS OFF THE STOOL SULLENLY TO LET HER SIT DOWN. 644 ICEMAN

THEIR FACES ARE SULLENLY ANGRY, THEIR CLOTHES DISARRANGED FROM THE TUSSLE.) 650 ICEMAN

(JOE SULLENLY GOES BACK BEHIND THE COUNTER AND SLAPS THE KNIFE ON TOP OF IT. 672 ICEMAN

JOE POURS A BRIMFUL DRINK--SULLENLY) 673 ICEMAN

(SULLENLY) SURE, ANYTING YUH SAY, BABY. 682 ICEMAN

(SULLENLY) MY WHEEL... 516 INZONE

(MARCO REMAINS SULLENLY APART, SHAMEFACED AND ANGRY, HIS FISTS CLENCHED. 360 MARCOM

(WALKS SULLENLY OFF TO LEFT. 370 MARCOM

(OUT OF HER REACH--SULLENLY) 5 MISBEG

(SULLENLY--BUT CAREFUL TO KEEP HIS VOICE LOW.) 100 POET

(GLARING AT MARSDEN, SULLENLY) 127 STRANG

(SULLENLY) I DON'T CARE/ 142 STRANG

SULLENNESS

HE FORGETS HIS SULLENNESS AND BECOMES HIS OLD SELF644 ICEMAN AGAIN.)

SULLIVAN

OR I'LL CALL SULLIVAN FROM THE CORNER AND HAVE YOU248 AHWILD RUN IN FOR STREET-WALKING/

AND BIG TIM SULLIVAN, FLANKED BY FRAMED LITHOGRAPHS OF JOHN L. SULLIVAN 664 ICEMAN

SULTRY

THE NOON ENERVATION OF THE SULTRY, SCORCHING DAY 112 BEYOND

A SULTRY, HAZY SKY WITH FEW STARS VISIBLE. 468 DYNAMO

OUTSIDE THE DAY IS STILL FINE BUT INCREASINGLY SULTRY. 51 JOURNE

SUM

AN' WHATO YEW GIT THAT SUM O' MONEY, ANYWAYS$ 213 DESIRE

MR. HARFORD IS PREPARED TO PAY YOU THE SUM OF THREE THOUSAND DOLLARS-- 122 POET

SUMMED

(SCORNFULLY) THAT'S ABOUT THE WAY HE SUMMED UP .126 BEYOND HIS IMPRESSIONS OF THE EAST.

SUMMER

IN THE DISTANCE, THE ORCHESTRA OF A SUMMER HOTEL CAN BE HEARD. 275 AHWILD

SUN-BAKED DAY IN MID-SUMMER, THREE YEARS LATER. 112 BEYOND

IT WAS LAST SUMMER HE HAD A BAD SPELL FIRST, 154 BEYOND

AS IF IT HAD BEEN ALLOWED TO REMAIN FALLOW THE PRECEDING SUMMER. 166 BEYOND

SHE IS BEAUTIFUL WITH THAT INDIAN SUMMER RENEWAL OF PHYSICAL CHARM WHICH COMES 514 DAYS

IT IS SUNSET OF A DAY AT THE BEGINNING OF SUMMER IN THE YEAR 1850. 203 DESIRE

I MUSTN'T FORGET TO MAKE RAMSAY CHANGE TO HIS SUMMER UNDERWEAR THIS WEEK... 429 DYNAMO

THE THREE PLAYS TAKE PLACE IN EITHER SPRING OR SUMMER OF THE YEARS 1865-1866.) 5 ELECTR

ON THE EVENING OF A CLEAR DAY IN SUMMER A YEAR LATER. 129 ELECTR

SUMMER AND FALL AND DEATH AND PEACE AGAIN/ 322 GGBROW

IT IS BETWEEN 3 AND 4 A. M. OF A DAY IN THE SUMMER OF 1928. 7 HUGHIE

ON AN EARLY MORNING IN SUMMER, 1912. 573 ICEMAN

IT IS AROUND THE MIDDLE OF THE MORNING OF HOPE'S BIRTHDAY, A HOT SUMMER DAY. 664 ICEMAN

SUMMER (CONT'D.)
(SCENE LIVING ROOM OF JAMES TYRONE'S SUMMER HOME ON A MORNING IN AUGUST, 1912. 11 JOURNE
OF COURSE, THERE'S NOTHING TAKES AWAY YOUR APPETITE LIKE A BAD SUMMER COLD. 16 JOURNE
A SUMMER COLD MAKES ANYONE IRRITABLE. 26 JOURNE
WITH THAT SUMMER COLD TALK. 29 JOURNE
WHO PREY ON THE RICH SUMMER PEOPLE-- 31 JOURNE
IT'S NOT ANCIENT HISTORY THAT YOU HAVE TO COME HOME EVERY SUMMER TO LIVE ON ME. 32 JOURNE
AND I'VE HAD TO COME HERE EVERY SUMMER. 44 JOURNE
WELL, IT'S BETTER THAN SPENDING THE SUMMER IN A NEW YORK HOTEL, ISN'T IT$ 44 JOURNE
AND YOUR FATHER WON'T EVEN PAY THE WAGES THE BEST SUMMER HELP ASK. 61 JOURNE
AND NOT MERELY SUMMER PLACES. 61 JOURNE
YOU DON'T HAVE TO KEEP HOUSE WITH SUMMER SERVANTS WHO DON'T CARE 61 JOURNE
THE SUMMER WILL SOON BE OVER, THANK GOODNESS. 72 JOURNE
(THEN STUBBORNLY.) BUT IT'S JUST A SUMMER COLD. 122 JOURNE
NO HOME EXCEPT THIS SUMER DUMP IN A PLACE SHE HATES AND YOU'VE REFUSED EVEN TO 141 JOURNE
WHERE YOU ROASTED IN SUMMER, AND THERE WAS NO STOVE IN WINTER, 148 JOURNE
MAMA/ IT ISN'T A SUMMER COLD/ I'VE GOT CONSUMPTION/ 174 JOURNE
SUMMER LAUGHS IN THE AIR/ 280 LAZARU
YOUR PATHETIC SUMMER-HOUSE A TEMPLE OF LOVE THE KING HAS BUILT 3 MANSNS
IN THE SIDE OF THE SUMMER-HOUSE FACING FRONT IS A NARROW ARCHED DOOR. 25 MANSNS
AT CENTER IS AN OCTAGONAL SUMMER-HOUSE. 25 MANSNS
AT LEFT AND RIGHT OF THE SUMMER-HOUSE ARE SHRUBS, 25 MANSNS
(DRYLY, INDICATING THE SUMMER-HOUSE.) 26 MANSNS
(TURNS TO THE SUMMER-HOUSE AND CALLS.) 27 MANSNS
(SHE SITS ON THE STEP OF THE SUMMER-HOUSE, 31 MANSNS
IT IS LATE SUMMER, 1840. 69 MANSNS
IT ALL DEPENDS--DO YOU KNOW IF SHE EVER GOES IN THE SUMMER-HOUSE NOW$ 86 MANSNS
IN THAT SUMMER-HOUSE OF HERS FOR FEAR SHE'D NEVER COME OUT AGAIN. 86 MANSNS
AND IVY-COVERED WALLS OF THE SUMMER-HOUSE. 95 MANSNS
THE CORNER OF THE HARFORD GARDEN WITH THE OCTAGONAL CHINESE SUMMER-HOUSE. 95 MANSNS
DEBORAH IS SITTING ON THE STEPS LEADING UP TO THE SUMMER-HOUSE DOOR, 95 MANSNS
THE WATER IN THE SMALL OVAL POOL BEFORE THE SUMMER-HOUSE 95 MANSNS
I WOULD SIT LOCKED IN THE SUMMER-HOUSE HERE-- 102 MANSNS
TO GO IN THE SUMMER-HOUSE BUT YOU$ 109 MANSNS
YOU WOULD BE SITTING THERE BEFORE THE SUMMER-HOUSE, 109 MANSNS
THERE IS A CONNECTION WITH THE SUMMER-HOUSE. 110 MANSNS
WITH THE DOOR THERE TO YOUR FORBIDDEN SUMMER-HOUSE. 111 MANSNS
IT IS EARLY MORNING IN MID-SUMMER OF THE FOLLOWING139 MANSNS YEAR, 1841.
AND MOTHER SHOULD PUT IT OVER THE MAGIC DOOR TO HER SUMMER-HOUSE. 148 MANSNS
WITH HER IDIOTIC SUPERSTITIOUS TERROR OF THE HAUNTED SUMMER-HOUSE/ 159 MANSNS
IN FRONT OF THE SUMMER-HOUSE AND THE DOOR TO THE STREET IN THE WALL AT RIGHT. 161 MANSNS
THE CORNER OF DEBORAH'S GARDEN WITH THE SUMMER-HOUSE. 161 MANSNS
AND SHINES CLEARLY ON THE SUMMER-HOUSE DOOR. 162 MANSNS
(THE MOON AGAIN COMES FROM BEHIND A CLOUD AND SHINES ON THE SUMMER-HOUSE. 163 MANSNS
(HER EYES FASTEN ON THE SUMMER-HOUSE DOOR AGAIN. 163 MANSNS
(HIS EYES FASTEN ON THE SUMMER-HOUSE DOOR WITH A FASCINATED LONGING.) 182 MANSNS
WHEN SHE SEES THEM BOTH STILL OUTSIDE THE SUMMER-HOUSE, 185 MANSNS
(TURNS HIS HEAD A LITTLE FROM STARING INSIDE THE SUMMER-HOUSE-- 187 MANSNS
STARING INTO THE DARKNESS INSIDE THE SUMMER-HOUSE.188 MANSNS
(SHE BEGINS TO CHAFE HIS WRISTS AND TURNS TO STARE190 MANSNS AT THE SUMMER-HOUSE--
THE DOOR OF THE SUMMER-HOUSE HAS SLOWLY OPENED AND191 MANSNS DEBORAH HAS APPEARED.
(SHE GOES INTO THE SUMMER-HOUSE AND CLOSES THE DOOR BEHIND HER.) 194 MANSNS
THE LITTLE THRONE ROOM IN THE BAMBOO SUMMER PALACE384 MARCOM OF THE KAAN AT XANADU.
HOT SUMMER... 4 STRANG
SHE HAS PLAYED A LOT OF GOLF AND TENNIS THIS SUMMER, 8 STRANG
SHE LOVED BATHING AND BOATING IN THE SUMMER EVEN AFTER SHE WAS SIXTY, 100 STRANG
HER SKIN STILL RETAINS A TRACE OF SUMMER TAN 137 STRANG
WE'LL PICK FLOWERS TOGETHER IN THE AGING AFTERNOONS OF SPRING AND SUMMER, 200 STRANG
NO SUMMER FOOLS ABOUT. 456 WELDED
SUMMER'S
IT'S A FINE SUMMER'S DAY 685 ICEMAN
PIG IN NEXT SUMMER'S ICE WATER. 51 MISBEG
SUMMERHOUSE
THE LAST CHRYSANTHEMUM WITHERS BESIDE THE DESERTED384 MARCOM SUMMERHOUSE.
SUMMERNIGHT
TOO YOUNG ART THOU TO WASTE THIS SUMMERNIGHT--= 276 AHWILD
SUMMERS
COLLEGE, I KEPT HIM AWAY AT SCHOOL IN WINTER AND CAMP IN SUMMERS AND I WENT TO 60 STRANG
SUMMITS
THEIR SUMMITS CROWNED WITH THICK GROVES OF PALM TREES. 173 EJONES

SUMMON
BEFORE I SUMMON THE POLICE/ 186 MANSNS
WHY DID YOU SUMMON HIM$ 389 MARCOM
I WILL SUMMON A SERVANT TO INQUIRE YOUR PLEASURE. 117 POET
SUMMONED
IT WAS THE VOICE OF SOME CHRISTIAN DEVIL YOU SUMMONED/ 353 MARCOM
SUMMONING
(THEN SUMMONING HER COURAGE--MORE RESOLUTELY) 63 ANNA
(THEN SUMMONING HIS MANHOOD) 441 DYNAMO
THEN WITH A PRELIMINARY, SUMMONING STAMP OF HIS FOOT ON THE EARTH, 200 EJONES
(THEN SUMMONING HER WILL, SPRINGS TO HER FEET WILDLY) 165 ELECTR
(SIGHS--THEN SUMMONING HIS ACTOR'S HEARTINESS.) 123 JOURNE
HIS LAUGHTER RISES WITH MORE AND MORE SUMMONING POWER. 333 LAZARU
SUMMONINGLY
(OBLIVIOUS TO HIM--SUMMONINGLY) 227 DESIRE
SUMMONS
AS IF IN RESPONSE TO HIS SUMMONS THE BEATING OF THE TOM-TOM GROWS TO A FIERCE, 200 EJONES
HE SUMMONS UP STRENGTH FOR A WITHERING CRACK.) 27 HUGHIE
(WITH A BESEECHING SUMMONS) LAZARUS, COME FORTH/ 277 LAZARU
(HIS LAUGHTER BURSTS FORTH NOW IN ITS HIGHEST PITCH OF ECSTATIC SUMMONS TO THE 368 LAZARU
= AS IF IT WERE AN INCANTATION BY WHICH HE SUMMONS 43 POET PRIDE TO JUSTIFY HIS LIFE TO

SUN
BEST WAIT FOR A DAY WHEN THE SUN SHINES. 540 'ILE
(DESPERATELY) BUT THE SUN NEVER SHINES IN THIS TERRIBLE PLACE. 540 'ILE
AND WHEN IT GOES AND WE GIT SOME SUN ANNIE'LL PERK542 'ILE UP.
A CHUBBY, SUN BURNT BOY OF ELEVEN WITH DARK EYES, 186 AHWILD
HASN'T SUN--PERFECT RIGHT TO SET$ 224 AHWILD
YUST WATER ALL ROUND, AND SUN AND FRESH AIR, 23 ANNA
(SCORNFULLY) NO, AND I WASN'T HEARING HER SAY THE 53 ANNA SUN IS SHINING EITHER.
HUSKY, SUN-BRONZED, HANDSOME IN A LARGE-FEATURED, MANLY FASHION. 82 BEYOND
ITS LARGE EYES OF A DEEP BLUE SET OFF STRIKINGLY BY THE SUN-BRONZED COMPLEXION. 87 BEYOND
FIND OUT WHERE THE SUN WAS HIDING HIMSELF. 90 BEYOND
IN THE SUN LIKE A SLAVE WITHOUT GETTING A WORD OF 107 BEYOND THANKS FOR IT.
SUN-BAKED DAY IN MID-SUMMER, THREE YEARS LATER. 112 BEYOND
HIS FACE BURNED BY THE SUN AND UNSHAVEN FOR DAYS. 119 BEYOND
DETECTED THROUGH THE BLEACHED, SUN-SCORCHED GRASS.129 BEYOND
ONE WALK DOWN ONE OF THEIR FILTHY NARROW STREETS 132 BEYOND WITH THE TROPIC SUN BEATING ON
THE SUN HURTS HER EYES, THAT'S ALL. 142 BEYOND
I'M GOING TO SEE THE SUN RISE. 150 BEYOND
NO SUN YET. IT ISN'T TIME. 151 BEYOND
WHERE HE CAN SEE THE SUN RISE, AND COLLAPSES WEAKLY. 166 BEYOND
THE SUN COMES SO SLOWLY. 167 BEYOND
IN A DITCH BY THE OPEN ROAD--WATCHING THE SUN RISE. 167 BEYOND
THE SUN/ 168 BEYOND
I'VE LISTENED PATIENTLY WHILE YOU'VE DISCUSSED EVERY SUBJECT UNDER THE SUN 543 DAYS
AS IF THE SUN HAD RISEN. 566 DAYS
HIS OLD SNAKE'S EYES WAS GLITTERIN' IN THE SUN LIKE HE'D BEEN DRINKIN' A JUGFUL 209 DESIRE
HAIN'T THE SUN STRONG AN' HOT$ 229 DESIRE
I'M GOIN' T' LEAVE THE SHUTTERS OPEN AND LET IN THE SUN 'N' AIR. 245 DESIRE
GOLD SUN--FIELDS O' GOLD IN THE WEST/ 262 DESIRE
LOOKS 'S IF THE SUN WAS FUL RIZ A'MOST. 263 DESIRE
WITH A GREAT, RED, WEATHER-BEATEN FACE SEAMED BY SUN WRINKLES. 513 DIFRNT
BASKING CONTENTEDLY IN THE SUN. 454 DYNAMO
I KNOW WHY DOGS LOVE TO LIE IN THE SUN... 454 DYNAMO
(THE SUN IS HOT... 454 DYNAMO
(BLINKING PLACIDLY IN THE SUN) 456 DYNAMO
DAT WHY I MAKE HAY WHEN DE SUN SHINE. 180 EJONES
BRILIN' SUN. 187 EJONES
IT IS SHORTLY BEFORE SUNSET AND THE SOFT LIGHT OF 5 ELECTR THE DECLINING SUN SHINES.
THE CLOUDS LIKE DOWN ON THE MOUNTAIN TOPS, THE SUN 24 ELECTR DROWSING IN YOUR BLOOD,
OUTSIDE THE SUN IS BEGINNING TO SET 28 ELECTR
I'VE SEEN TOO MANY ROTTING IN THE SUN TO MAKE GRASS GREENER/ 60 ELECTR
I LOVE EVERYTHING THAT GROWS SIMPLY--UP TOWARD THE167 ELECTR SUN--
REFLECT THE SUN IN A SMOULDERING STARE, AS OF BROODING REVENGEFUL EYES. 169 ELECTR
AND STARES BACK INTO THE SUN-GLARE WITH UNBLINKING, FROZEN, DEFIANT EYES.) 170 ELECTR
I'LL CLOSE IT UP AND LEAVE IT IN THE SUN AND RAIN 171 ELECTR TO DIE.
(SOMBERLY) WHEN PAN WAS FORBIDDEN THE LIGHT AND WARMTH OF THE SUN HE GREW 297 GGBROW
THE SUN WILL BE RISING AGAIN. 322 GGBROW
AND WE'D SEE THE MOUNTAINS OF SOUTH AMERICY WID THE RED FIRE OF THE SETTING SUN 214 HA APE
SUN WARMING THE BLOOD OF YOU, 214 HA APE
WID DIMLY A SIGHT OF SUN OR A BREATH OF CLEAN AIR-- 214 HA APE
A WARM SUN ON THE CLEAN DECKS. 214 HA APE
THAT A GREAT WAVE WID SUN IN THE HEART OF IT MAY SWEEP ME OVER THE SIDE SOMETIME 215 HA APE
BUT IT'S HOT ENOUGH IN THE SUN-- 221 HA APE
DE SUN WAS WARM, DEY WASN'T NO CLOUDS, AND DERE WAS A BREEZE BLOWIN'. 252 HA APE
SURE, I SEEN DE SUN COME UP. 252 HA APE

SUN 1582

SUN (CONT'D.)

UNITED BENEATH THE FLAG ON WHICH THE SUN NEVER 599 ICEMAN SETS.

THE SUN WAS BROILING AND THE STREETS FULL OF 721 ICEMAN AUTOMOBILES.

THE HOT SUN WILL SWEAT SOME OF THAT BOOZE FAT OFF 41 JOURNE YOUR MIDDLE.

WITH A FAINT HAZINESS IN THE AIR WHICH SOFTENS THE 51 JOURNE GLARE OF THE SUN.

GET A LITTLE SUN AND FRESH AIR. 84 JOURNE BUT THAT'S JUST FROM GOING OUT IN THE SUN. 91 JOURNE BECAME THE SUN, THE HOT SAND, GREEN SEAWEED 153 JOURNE ANCHORED TO A ROCK,

BENEATH THE HOT SUN/ 276 LAZARU THEY WILL BEGIN TO WORSHIP IN FILTHY IDOLATRY THE 283 LAZARU SUN AND STARS AND MAN'S BODY--

THEY TEND HIS FLOCKS AND LAUGH TOWARD THE SUN/ 287 LAZARU NOW WE RE-ENTER THE SUN/ 324 LAZARU ONCE AS QUIVERING FLECKS OF RHYTHM WE BEAT DOWN 324 LAZARU FROM THE SUN.

IN THE SUN AND THERE WOULD BE ECHOING LAUGHTER 330 LAZARU FROM THE SKY AND UP FROM THE

OF CLOSE WALLS OF EARTH BAKED IN THE SUN. 346 LAZARU SARA MUST BE WONDERING WHAT IS KEEPING ME, NOW THE102 MANSNS SUN IS SETTING.

CONTRASTING WITH THE BLINDING GLARE OF THE NOON 347 MARCOM SUN

(WITH RELIEF) PHOO! (THEN BREAKING THE ICE) THE 348 MARCOM SUN WOULD COOK YOU/

*YOU ARE LOVELY AS THE GOLD IN THE SUN. 360 MARCOM THE BLINDING GLARE OF THE SETTING SUN FLOODS IN 376 MARCOM FROM BEYOND.

YOU ARE LOVELY AS THE GOLD IN THE SUN. 399 MARCOM FIRE WAS THE SUN/ 408 MARCOM FIRE WAS THE SUN/ 408 MARCOM FIRE WAS THE SUN/ 408 MARCOM WHERE THERE IS NEITHER SUN NOR WIND NOR JOY NOR 409 MARCOM SORROW/

A CLOUD HIDES THE SUN. 417 MARCOM THE SUN SHINES AGAIN. 417 MARCOM OLD MEN SHOULDN'T RUN AROUND RAGING IN THE NOON 12 MISBEG SUN.

I NEED HARD WORK IN THE SUN TO CLEAR IT. 35 MISBEG ONE BIG DRINK, AT LEAST, WHENEVER I STRAIN MY 46 MISBEG HEART WALKING IN THE HOT SUN.

THERE'S A LOT OF THINGS HE'LL HAVE TO EXPLAIN WHEN134 MISBEG HE COMES AT SUN--

BUT I'LL HAVE TO MAKE YOU LEAVE BEFORE SUN-RISE. 137 MISBEG THE DRIVE IN THE HOT SUN AND THE WALK THROUGH THE 19 POET WOODS FOR NOTHING.

RATHER HANDSOME FACE BRONZED BY THE SUN. 587 ROPE TURN ON THE SUN INTO THE SHADOWS OF LIES-- 176 STRANG HIS SUN-BRONZED FACE IS EXTREMELY HANDSOME. 184 STRANG MY LIFE IS COOL GREEN SHADE WHEREIN COMES NO 107 STRANG SCORCHING ZENITH SUN OF PASSION AND

SUN'LL

BUT THE SUN'LL COME--SOON. 151 BEYOND

SUN'S

THE SUN'S HOT TODAY/ 119 BEYOND HORIZON WHERE THE EDGE OF THE SUN'S DISC IS RISING168 BEYOND FROM THE RIM OF THE HILLS)

(GAZING UP AT THE SKY) SUN'S DOWNIN' PURTY. 205 DESIRE SUN'S STARTIN' WITH US FUR THE GOLDEN WEST. 218 DESIRE SUN'S A-RIZIN'. 269 DESIRE (THEN EMBARRASSED--IRRITABLY) GOSH, THIS SUN'S 456 DYNAMO HOT/

THE WINDOWS OF THE LOWER FLOOR REFLECT THE SUN'S 5 ELECTR RAYS IN A RESENTFUL GLARE.

SUNBLEACHED

SUNBLEACHED TO RED AT THE ENDS, BRUSHED STRAIGHT 20 JOURNE BACK FROM IT.

SUNBONNET

SHE WEARS A FADED GINGHAM DRESS AND A TORN 579 ROPE SUNBONNET.)

SUNBURN

DARRELL'S DEEP SUNBURN OF THE TROPICS HAS FADED, 190 STRANG

SUNBURNED

HIS HEAVY FACE IS SUNBURNED, HANDSOME IN A COARSE,498 DIFRNT GOOD-NATURED ANIMAL FASHION.

HIS FAIR SKIN IS SUNBURNED A REDDISH, FRECKLED 19 JOURNE TAN.

HIS SKIN, IN SPITE OF BEING SUNBURNED A DEEP 20 JOURNE BROWN, HAS A PARCHED SALLOWNESS.

HER SKIN, IN CONTRAST TO THE MASK, IS SUNBURNED 274 LAZARU AND EARTH-

BLACK HAIR AS COARSE AS A HORSE'S MANE, FRECKLED, 3 MISBEG SUNBURNED FAIR SKIN,

ARMS AND FACE ARE SUNBURNED AND FRECKLED. 11 MISBEG HER STRAW-BLOND HAIR, FRAMING HER SUNBURNED FACE, 12 STRANG IS BOBBED.

SUNBURNT

WAY, SUNBURNT AND HEALTHY, BEGINNING TO TAKE ON 56 MISBEG FAT, HE IS SIMPLY IMMATURE.

SUNDA

YOU KNOW THE *SUNDA* SAILS AROUND THE HORN FUR 83 BEYOND YOKOHAMA FIRST.

(PROTESTINGLY) AND THE *SUNDA* AIN'T AN OLD 96 BEYOND SHIP--LEASTWAYS, NOT VERY OLD--

SO YOU'RE NOT ACUMIN' ON THE *SUNDA* WITH ME$ 102 BEYOND HE SAYS HE CAN'T CALCULATE EXACTLY ON ACCOUNT O' 115 BEYOND THE *SUNDA* BEING A SAIL BOAT.

HE WENT DOWN TO THE PORT TO SEE TO THINGS ON THE 135 BEYOND *SUNDA.*

SAME AS LISTENIN' TO THE ORGAN OUTSIDE O' CHURCH 466 CARIBE OF A SUNDAY.

HE IS DRESSED IN HIS DISMAL BLACK SUNDAY SUIT. 221 DESIRE A HOT SUNDAY AFTERNOON TWO MONTHS LATER. 228 DESIRE

SUNDAY (CONT'D.)

HE, ALSO, IS GOT UP IN BLACK SUNDAY BEST 494 DIFRNT SHE IS DRESSED SOBERLY AND NEATLY IN HER BLACK 494 DIFRNT SUNDAY BEST, STYLE OF THE PERIOD.

CALEB'S A SUNDAY GO-TO-MEETIN' SAINT, AIN'T HES 499 DIFRNT AMOS AMES, CARPENTER BY TRADE BUT NOW TAKING A 6 ELECTR HOLIDAY AND DRESSED IN HIS SUNDAY

AND I'LL WATER YOUR GRAVE EVERY SUNDAY AFTER 132 ELECTR CHURCH.

A CORNER OF FIFTH AVENUE IN THE FIFTIES ON A FINE 233 HA APE SUNDAY MORNING.

ALWAYS GOT TOO BIG A HEAD ON SUNDAY MORNIN', DAT 234 HA APE WAS DEM.

THE GUARD GIVE ME THE SUNDAY TIMES. 242 HA APE (SHE LOOKS AROUND) JEES, DE MORGUE ON A RAINY 615 ICEMAN SUNDAY NIGHT/

AND WEARS A SUNDAY-BEST BLUE SUIT WITH A HIGH 670 ICEMAN STIFF COLLAR.

HOPE IS DRESSED IN AN OLD BLACK SUNDAY SUIT, BLACK683 ICEMAN TIE, SHOES, SOCKS.

IT WAS A FINE SUNDAY MORNING. 688 ICEMAN LAST EASTER SUNDAY WHEN FATHER AND UNCLE READ A 394 MARCOM PRAYER

YOU CAN CHANGE TO YOUR SUNDAY SUIT IN THE CAN AT 5 MISBEG THE STATION OR IN THE TRAIN.

I WOULDN'T PUT IT PAST HIM TO DROP IT IN THE 16 MISBEG COLLECTION PLATE NEXT SUNDAY.

SHE HAS CHANGED TO HER SUNDAY BEST, A CHEAP DARK- 71 MISBEG BLUE DRESS.

YOU'VE CHANGED TO YOUR SUNDAY BEST A LOT LATELY. 28 POET (SHE KISSES HER.) I'LL CHANGE TO MY SUNDAY DRESS 28 POET SHE HAS CHANGED TO HER SUNDAY DRESS, 44 POET AFTER NOT BEIN' AT SUNDAY MEETIN' YOURSELF FOR 580 ROPE MORE'N TWENTY YEARS/

SUNDAYS

YOU WON'T MEET HAIR LIKE YOURS AND HERS AGAIN IN A 22 ELECTR MONTH OF SUNDAYS.

LIQUOR IN THE BACK ROOM OF THE BAR AFTER CLOSING 571 ICEMAN HOURS AND ON SUNDAYS,

SUNDOWN'S

SUNDOWN'S AT SIX-THUTY OR DERE-ABOUTS. 183 EJONES

SUNDRY

I TOLD PHIL THE GLAD TIDINGS A BOUGHT DRINKS FOR131 MISBEG ALL AND SUNDRY.

SUNG

WHAT WAS THE SONG THEY SUNGS 268 DESIRE SHE'D HAVE SUNG HYMNS OF JOY ! ANY OF US HAD 454 DYNAMO DIED/

* SUNG BY A CHANTYMAN WITH THE CREW COMING IN ON 102 ELECTR THE CHORUS.

I'LL GIVE HIM A TASTE OF HOW *SHENANDOAH* OUGHT T'103 ELECTR BE SUNG/

WHEN THE HEART FAILS, BE SUNG ASLEEP. 385 MARCOM AND EVERYWHERE WHERE SONGS ARE SUNG THEY SHALL BE 418 MARCOM IN PRAISE OF YOUR BEAUTY/

SUNK

RICHARD REMAINS STANDING, SUNK IN BITTER, GLOOMY 234 AHWILD MRS. MILLER WHO HAS AGAIN SUNK INTO WORRIED 256 AHWILD BROODING.

(AS CHRIS REMAINS SUNK IN GLOOMY REFLECTION) 9 ANNA HIS SHOULDERS BOWED, HIS HEAD SUNK FORWARD 67 ANNA DEJECTEDLY.

AND I HAVING IT TIED ROUND MY NECK WHEN MY LAST 75 ANNA SHIP SUNK.

HIS CHIN SUNK FORWARD ON HIS CHEST, 94 BEYOND ABBIE HAS SUNK BACK LIFELESSLY INTO HER FORMER 264 DESIRE POSITION.

(PRETENDING TO BE SUNK IN THOUGHT HAS BEEN STARING439 DYNAMO CALCULATINGLY AT REUBEN--

SHE'D SUNK HER LAST SHRED OF PRIDE AND WRITTEN TO 26 ELECTR YOUR FATHER ASKING FOR A LOAN.

(HIS VOICE HAS SUNK LOWER AND LOWER, AS IF HE WERE 95 ELECTR TALKING TO HIMSELF.

ALL IS SUNK BUT HONOR, AS THE FELLER SAYS. 104 ELECTR (HE GLARES SCORNFULLY AT YANK, WHO IS SUNK IN AN 250 HA APE OBLIVIOUS STUPOR)

AND THEIR SHIPS ARE LONG SINCE LOOTED AND SCUTTLED578 ICEMAN AND SUNK ON THE BOTTOMS

(BUT THEY ARE ALL SUNK IN THEIR OWN APPREHENSIONS 683 ICEMAN AND IGNORE HER.

CARRYING OUT MECHANICALLY THE MOTIONS OF GETTING 696 ICEMAN DRUNK BUT SUNK IN A NUMB STUPOR

HIS HEAD HAS SUNK FORWARD, AND HE STARES AT THE 701 ICEMAN TABLE TOP

SUNK IN THE SAME STUPOR AS THE OTHER OCCUPANTS OF 701 ICEMAN THE ROOM.

IMAGINE ME SUNK TO THE FAT GIRL IN A HICK TOWN 161 JOURNE HOOKER SHOP/

I SUPPOSE IT'S BECAUSE I FEEL SO DAMNED SUNK. 162 JOURNE HER BLACK EYES ARE SUNK IN DEEP HOLLOWS BENEATH 27 MANSNS THEIR HEAVY BROWS

SUNK TOO MUCH CAPITAL IN NEW SHIPS-- 32 MANSNS DO YOU THINK I HAVE SUNK TO YOUR LEVEL$ 154 MANSNS (SUNK IN DRUNKEN DEFEATIST AGAIN) 83 MISBEG BY THE IMMORTAL, I MAY HAVE SUNK TO KEEPING AN INN 37 POET (IS NOT LISTENING--SUNK IN BITTER BROODING.) 41 POET SHE IS SUNK IN MEMORIES OF OLD FEARS AND HER 131 POET PRESENT WORRY ABOUT THE DUEL.

HIS TALL, THIN BODY SAGS WEARILY IN THE CHAIR, HIS 24 STRANG HEAD IS SUNK FORWARD,

(HE SLUMPS DOWN ON THE CHAIR AGAIN, SUNK IN A 473 WELDED SOMBER STUPOR.

SUNKEN

HIS UNSHAVEN CHEEKS ARE SUNKEN AND SALLOW. 553 DAYS HIS EYES ARE DEEPLY SUNKEN. 476 DYNAMO HIS EYES APPEAR FEVERISH AND HIS CHEEKS ARE 20 JOURNE SUNKEN.

SUNKEN (CONT'D.)
EXCEPT THAT HIS SUNKEN CHEEKS ARE FLUSHED AND HIS 108 JOURNE
EYES LOOK BRIGHT AND FEVERISH.
HER FOREHEAD IS HIGH AND A TRIFLE BULGING, WITH 2 MANSNS
SUNKEN TEMPLES.
HIS COUNTENANCE IS PALE AND HAGGARD, HIS EYES DEEP144 MANSNS
SUNKEN.
HIS MOUTH IS SUNKEN IN, TOOTHLESS. 52 POET
HIS MOUTH IS A SUNKEN LINE DRAWN IN UNDER HIS 578 ROPE
LARGE, BEAK-LIKE NOSE.

SUNLIGHT
THE ROOM IS FAIRLY LARGE, HOMELY LOOKING AND 185 AHWILD
CHEERFUL IN THE MORNING SUNLIGHT.
HIS FACE, LIGHTED UP BY THE SHAFT OF SUNLIGHT FROM220 DESIRE
THE WINDOW.
BRIGHT SUNLIGHT STREAMS THROUGH THE WINDOWS ON THE493 DIFRNT
LEFT.
IT IS LATE AFTERNOON BUT THE SUNLIGHT STILL BLAZES173 EJONES
YELLOWLY BEYOND THE PORTICO
SOFT GOLDEN SUNLIGHT SHIMMERS IN A LUMINOUS MIST 169 ELECTR
ON THE GREEK TEMPLE PORTICO.
(SHE LEANS BACK IN THE SUNLIGHT AND CLOSES HER 171 ELECTR
EYES.
I'LL HAVE THE SHUTTERS NAILED CLOSED SO NO 178 ELECTR
SUNLIGHT CAN EVER GET IN.
STARING INTO THE SUNLIGHT WITH FROZEN EYES. 179 ELECTR
THERE IS SUNLIGHT IN THE STREET OUTSIDE. 664 ICEMAN
NO SUNLIGHT COMES INTO THE ROOM NOW THROUGH THE 51 JOURNE
WINDOWS AT RIGHT.
THE TOMB IS FULL OF SUNLIGHT/ 360 LAZARU
THE CLEARING IS PARTLY IN SUNLIGHT, PARTLY 1 MANSNS
SHADOWED BY THE WOODS.
LATE AFTERNOON SUNLIGHT FROM BEYOND THE WALL AT 95 MANSNS
RIGHT FALLS ON THE POINTED ROOF
THAT OUR SILK-MAKERS MAY PRESERVE THEIR SHARE OF 422 MARCOM
THE ETERNAL SUNLIGHT/
SUNLIGHT SHINES IN THROUGH THE WINDOWS AT REAR. 8 POET
COVERED SIDE PORCH, SO THAT NO SUNLIGHT EVER GETS 48 STRANG
TO THIS ROOM AND THE LIGHT
CONTRASTED WITH THE SOFT GOLDEN HAZE OF LATE 158 STRANG
AFTERNOON SUNLIGHT

SUNLIT
IT IS A BEAUTIFUL SUNLIT MORNING IN LATE JUNE. 384 MARCOM

SUNNY
IT IS AFTERNOON OF A SUNNY DAY ABOUT A WEEK LATER. 41 ANNA
IT IS A LARGE, SUNNY ROOM, THE FURNITURE EXPENSIVEL137 STRANG
BUT EXTREMELY SIMPLE.

SUNRISE
IT MUST BE NEAR SUNRISE, ISN'T IT& 162 BEYOND
THE SKY IS BEGINNING TO GROW FLUSHED WITH SUNRISE.217 DESIRE
THE SKY IS BRILLIANT WITH THE SUNRISE. 262 DESIRE
EBEN STOPS THERE AND POINTS TO THE SUNRISE SKY) 269 DESIRE
ONCE WHEN HE LOOKED AT SUNRISE, ANOTHER TIME AT 397 MARCOM
SUNSET, ANOTHER AT THE STARS.
YOU SAIL AT SUNRISES 403 MARCOM
AND SUNRISE OF THE FOLLOWING DAY. 1 MISBEG
YOUR PART IN IT IS TO COME AT SUNRISE WITH 92 MISBEG
WITNESSES AND CATCH US IN--
I COME AT SUNRISE WITH MY WITNESSES, AND YOU'VE 94 MISBEG
FORGOT TO LOCK YOUR DOOR.
THE FIRST FAINT STREAKS OF COLOR, HERALDING THE 157 MISBEG
SUNRISE.
DON'T THINK I WOKE YOU JUST TO ADMIRE THE SUNRISE.172 MISBEG
WITH ALL THE COLORS OF AN EXCEPTIONALLY BEAUTIFUL 172 MISBEG
SUNRISE.
(WATCHING THE SUNRISE--MECHANICALLY) 172 MISBEG
ARE YOU GOING TO MOON AT THE SUNRISE FOREVER, 176 MISBEG

SUNS
ALL DAY CRAZY TRIPE ABOUT SUNS AND WINDS, FRESH 215 HA APE
AIR AND DE REST OF IT--

SUNSET
I NEVER REMEMBER SEEING--MORE BEAUTIFUL SUNSET. 224 AHWILD
AND THE SKY ABOVE THEM GLOWS WITH THE CRIMSON 81 BEYOND
FLUSH OF THE SUNSET.
HE IS READING A BOOK BY THE FADING SUNSET LIGHT. 82 BEYOND
AT THE HILLS AND THE DYING SUNSET FLUSH.) 93 BEYOND
IT IS SUNSET OF A DAY AT THE BEGINNING OF SUMMER 203 DESIRE
IN THE YEAR 1850.
(STILL UNDER THE INFLUENCE OF SUNSET--VAGUELY) 204 DESIRE
I WAS FINISHIN' PLOWIN', IT WAS SPRING AN' MAY AN'209 DESIRE
SUNSET, AN' GOLD IN THE WEST.
IT IS A LITTLE AFTER SUNSET AND THE EQUIPMENT ON 476 DYNAMO
THE ROOF IS OUTLINED BLACKLY
IT IS SHORTLY BEFORE SUNSET AND THE SOFT LIGHT OF 5 ELECTR
THE DECLINING SUN SHINES
IT IS SHORTLY AFTER SUNSET BUT THE AFTERGLOW IN 129 ELECTR
THE SKY
SCENE--CYBEL'S PARLOR--ABOUT SUNSET IN SPRING 284 GGBROW
SEVEN YEARS LATER.
A DISSOLVING TOUCH OF SUNSET STILL LINGERS ON THE 275 LAZARU
HORIZON.
IT IS LATE AFTERNOON, JUST BEFORE SUNSET. 373 MARCOM
ONCE WHEN HE LOOKED AT SUNRISE, ANOTHER TIME AT 397 MARCOM
SUNSET, ANOTHER AT THE STARS.
ARE FAINTLY TINGED WITH GOLD BY THE FIRST GLOW OF 577 ROPE
SUNSET.
THEY LIE THERE IN A GLITTERING PILE, SHIMMERING IN602 ROPE
THE FAINT SUNSET GLOW--
IT MUST BE IN THE HOUR BEFORE SUNSET WHEN THE 198 STRANG
EARTH DREAMS IN AFTERTHOUGHTS AND

SUNSETS
I GOT TO KNOW ALL THE DIFFERENT KINDS OF SUNSETS 90 BEYOND
BY HEART.
AND ALL THOSE SUNSETS TOOK PLACE OVER THERE--(HE 90 BEYOND
POINTS) BEYOND THE HORIZON.

SUNSHINE
SUNSHINE ON THE DECK IN A GREAT FLOOD, THE FRESH 218 HA APE
SEA WIND BLOWING ACROSS IT.

SUNSHINE (CONT'D.)
AND SUNSHINE ON THE STREET ITSELF. 233 HA APE
A FLOOD OF MELLOW, TEMPERED SUNSHINE. 233 HA APE
SHE BEGINS GROPINGLY TO PICK OUT =THE SUNSHINE OF 644 ICEMAN
PARADISE ALLEY=)
=SHE IS THE SUNSHINE OF PARADISE ALLEY.= 645 ICEMAN
=SHE'S THE SUNSHINE OF PARADISE ALLEY.= 653 ICEMAN
(HE STARTS THE CHORUS OF =SHE'S THE SUNSHINE OF 727 ICEMAN
PARADISE ALLEY.
SUNSHINE COMES THROUGH THE WINDOWS AT RIGHT. 12 JOURNE
(HASTILY.) I MEAN, TAKE ADVANTAGE OF THE SUNSHINE 41 JOURNE
BEFORE THE FOG COMES BACK.
IT WOULD BE MUCH BETTER FOR YOU TO GO OUT IN THE 49 JOURNE
FRESH AIR AND SUNSHINE.
SUNSHINE, COOLED AND DIMMED IN THE SHADE OF TREES, 3 STRANG

SUNSTROKE
BEJEES, I COULD FEEL MYSELF GETTING SUNSTROKE, AND721 ICEMAN
AN AUTOMOBILE DAMN
I WON'T WALK OUT IN THIS HEAT AND GET SUNSTROKE. 53 JOURNE
YOU'LL GET SUNSTROKE. 12 MISBEG
TO HELL WITH SUNSTROKE/ 12 MISBEG

SUNUP
IT'S NIGH SUNUP. 212 DESIRE

SUPER-SENSITIVE
MORBIDLY R8IDLY SUPER-SENSITIVE ALREADY, 45 STRANG

SUP
TAKE A SMALL SUP AN' PASS UT TO THE NIXT. 462 CARIBE
TAKE A SUP AN' FORGIT IT. 593 ROPE

SUPER
MORBIDLY SUPER-SENSITIVE ALREADY, 45 STRANG

SUPERCILIOUS
FEIGNED CYNICAL AMUSEMENT OR A PRETENDED 337 LAZARU
SUPERCILIOUS INDIFFERENCE.
BUT ASSUMES A SUPERCILIOUS, INSECURE AIR 56 MISBEG

SUPERCILIOUSLY
(UNIMPRESSED--SUPERCILIOUSLY) 219 HA APE

SUPERFLUOUSLY
HOW SUPERFLUOUUS/ 317 GGBROW
MEDDLING WITH HUMAN LIVES WOULD HAVE BEEN 140 STRANG
SUPERFLUOUSLY/

SUPERINTENDENT
MAY HE ROAST IN HELL AND HIS LIMEY SUPERINTENDENT 32 MISBEG
WITH HIM.
THAT ENGLISH SCUM OF A SUPERINTENDENT/ 48 MISBEG
AND BEING TORMENTED ALWAYS BY THE COMPLAINTS OF 51 MISBEG
HIS LIMEY SUPERINTENDENT.

SUPERIOR
(WITH SUPERIOR DIGNITY) THAT'S MY BUSINESS. 187 AHWILD
(SCORNFULLY SUPERIOR) THAT SILLY SKIRT PARTY/ 194 AHWILD
(SUPERIOR) NO. 195 AHWILD
WHICH HE IMMEDIATELY TRIES TO COVER UP WITH A 207 AHWILD
SUPERIOR CARELESSNESS)
(HE GIVES HIS SISTER A SUPERIOR SCORNFUL GLANCE) 274 AHWILD
OH, DON'T BE SO SUPERIOR AND SCORNFUL, ELSA. 519 DAYS
HIS FACE IS RIGIDLY COMPOSED, BUT HIS SUPERIOR 280 GGBROW
DISGUST FOR DION CAN BE SEEN.
THEY RESPECT HIS SUPERIOR STRENGTH--THE GRUDGING 208 HA APE
RESPECT OF FEAR.
IN THE CYNICAL LEER OF ONE WHO POSSESSES SUPERIOR, 9 HUGHIE
INSIDE INFORMATION.
WITHOUT MALICE, FEELING SUPERIOR TO NO ONE, A 576 ICEMAN
SINNER AMONG SINNERS.
BUT HE LIES THERE, KIDDING HIMSELF HE IS SUPERIOR 134 JOURNE
(IGNORING THIS.) BUT WHO AM I TO FEEL SUPERIORS 135 JOURNE
(ABRUPTLY HIS TONE BECOMES SCORNFULLY SUPERIOR.) 146 JOURNE
ROUSSEAU WAS SIMPLY HIDING FROM HIMSELF IN A 47 MANSNS
SUPERIOR, IDEALISTIC DREAM--
FOR A BEAUTIFUL LADY WHO HAS ALWAYS AFFECTED A 101 MANSNS
SUPERIOR DISDAIN
(WITH A STRANGE SUPERIOR SCORN.) 25 POET
(LUKE SMILES A SUPERIOR (KNOWING SMILE) HE HAS 592 ROPE
ONLY THE FARM,
AS A SUPERIOR WITH CONDESCENDING DISDAIN, PITY, 3 STRANG
AND EVEN AMUSEMENT.
SUPERIOR MANNER OF THE CLASSROOM TOWARD THE WORLD 6 STRANG
AT LARGE.
(CONTINUING IN HIS PROFESSOR'S SUPERIOR MANNER) 15 STRANG
(REPELLED--WITH A SUPERIOR SNEER) 19 STRANG
(SHE STICKS OUT HER TONGUE AT HIM AND MAKES A FACE 52 STRANG
OF SUPERIOR SCORN)
A SCIENTIFIC MIND SUPERIOR TO THE MORAL SCRUPLES 88 STRANG
SHE ALWAYS THOUGHT HER HAD A SUPERIOR MIND. 88 STRANG
AREN'T YOU THE SUPERIOR BACHELOR. 114 STRANG
(BUT WHY AM I SO SUPERIORS... 123 STRANG
(THINKING--GOOD-NATUREDLY SUPERIOR) 152 STRANG
(IN A TONE OF SUPERIOR MANLY UNDERSTANDING, 157 STRANG
AND MAKES THEM FEEL SUPERIOR BECAUSE THEY'RE 190 STRANG
LIVING.
BECAUSE I RESENT YOUR SUPERIOR ATTITUDE 456 WELDED

SUPERIORITY)
(WITH THE CONQUEROR'S CONSCIOUS SUPERIORITY) 193 AHWILD
PRETTY FACE MARRED BY A SELF-CONSCIOUS EXPRESSION 217 HA APE
OF DISDAINFUL SUPERIORITY. 222 DESIRE
HE USUALLY HAS THE SELF-CONFIDENT ATTITUDE OF 56 MISBEG
ACKNOWLEDGED SUPERIORITY.
IT'S THE ONE POINT OF SUPERIORITY YOU CAN LAY 36 POET
CLAIM TO, ISN'T IT&
(WITH A TINGE OF SATISFIED SUPERIORITY) 191 STRANG

SUPERIORLY
(HE GRINS SUPERIORLY) DIDN'T YOU HEAR HIM THIS 254 AHWILD
MORNING SHOWING OFF BAWLING OUT

SUPERNATURAL
WITHOUT IT LOOKING LIKE THE FIRST SUPERNATURAL 297 GGBROW
BANK/
IS IT A CHARM BY WHICH YOU INVOKE A SUPERNATURAL 354 LAZARU
FORCES

SUPERNATURAL

SUPERNATURAL (CONT'D.)
(A SOUND OF TENDER LAUGHTER, OF AN INTOXICATING, 352 MARCOM SUPERNATURAL GAIETY.

SUPERS
I'D LEFT A GOOD JOB AS A MACHINIST TO TAKE SUPERS*150 JOURNE PARTS

SUPERSENSITIVE
DARK, SPIRITUAL, POETIC, PASSIONATELY 260 GGBROW SUPERSENSITIVE,

SUPERSENSITIVENESS
HIS UNUSUAL FACE IS A HARROWED BATTLEFIELD OF 443 WELDED SUPERSENSITIVENESS,
PERHAPS IT'S ALL MY SUPERSENSITIVENESS--(PATTING 456 WELDED HER HAND AND FORCING A SMILE)

SUPERSTITION
(SNEERINGLY) OLD SUPERSTITION, BORN OF FEAR/ 508 DAYS
AND IMMEDIATELY BEGAN BUILDING A NEW SUPERSTITION 535 DAYS OF LOVE AROUND HER.
THAT COWARDLY SOMETHING IN HIM HE DESPISES AS 544 DAYS SUPERSTITION SEDUCES HIS REASON
HOW CAN YOU BELIEVE SUCH CHILDISH SUPERSTITION/ 545 DAYS
THERE'S TRUTH IN THE OLD SUPERSTITION THAT YOU'D 657 ICEMAN BETTER LOOK OUT WHAT YOU CALL
(HE READS) -FROM THE EAST, LAND OF THE FALSE GODS328 LAZARU AND SUPERSTITION,

SUPERSTITIONS
AND HE HAD DENIED ALL HIS OLD SUPERSTITIONS/ 534 DAYS
ALL THE SUPERSTITIONS OF HIS CHILDHOOD, 544 DAYS

SUPERSTITIOUS
BURKE BANISHES HIS SUPERSTITIOUS PREMONITIONS WITH 78 ANNA A DEFIANT JERK OF HIS HEAD,
YOU POOR, DAMNED SUPERSTITIOUS FOOL/ 495 DAYS
STILL SUPERSTITIOUS 495 DAYS
OH, HE WAS A REMARKABLY SUPERSTITIOUS YOUNG FOOL/ 510 DAYS
IT DROVE THE YOUNG IDIOT INTO A PANIC OF 511 DAYS SUPERSTITIOUS REMORSE.
INCREDIBLE SUPERSTITIOUS EXCUSE TO LIE OUT OF HIS 538 DAYS RESPONSIBILITY.
BUT WHAT SUPERSTITIOUS NONSENSE YOU MAKE ME 562 DAYS REMEMBER.
(CLUTCHES THE ARMS OF HIS CHAIR IN SUPERSTITIOUS 441 DYNAMO TERROR.
(THERE IS A GREAT FLASH OF LIGHTNING AND HE STANDS444 DYNAMO PARALYZED WITH SUPERSTITIOUS
GIVES A GASP OF SUPERSTITIOUS FRIGHT.) 452 DYNAMO
I MAY BE A FOOL BUT I'M BEGINNING TO FEEL 174 ELECTR SUPERSTITIOUS ABOUT IT MYSELF.
(ALOUD TO HIMSELF WITH A SUPERSTITIOUS SHRINKING) 663 ICEMAN
(HE STOPS, STARTLEDLY, A SUPERSTITIOUS AWE COMING 680 ICEMAN INTO HIS FACE)
HE SPEAKS SLOWLY WITH A SUPERSTITIOUS DREAD,) 39 JOURNE
STARING AT THE DOORWAY IN THE REAR WITH 337 LAZARU SUPERSTITIOUS DREAD.
(WITH SUPERSTITIOUS DREAD) WHAT DOST THOU MEAN, 344 LAZARU DAEMONS
A SHUDDERING MURMUR OF SUPERSTITIOUS FEAR COMES 348 LAZARU FROM THEM AS THEY SHRINK BACK
THE TRUTH IS I HAVE BECOME SUPERSTITIOUS-- 113 MANSNS
WITH HER IDIOTIC SUPERSTITIOUS TERROR OF THE 139 MANSNS HAUNTED SUMMER-HOUSE/
(SCORNFULLY) YOU ARE A PAIR OF SUPERSTITIOUS 349 MARCOM SHEEP/
THE OTHERS VISIBLY TREMBLING WITH SUPERSTITIOUS 352 MARCOM HORROR.)
(THINKING--IN A STRANGE SUPERSTITIOUS PANIC) 98 STRANG

SUPERSTITIOUSLY
(AWED BY HIS MANNER--SUPERSTITIOUSLY) 75 ANNA
(LARRY STARTS AND FOR A SECOND LOOKS 657 ICEMAN SUPERSTITIOUSLY FRIGHTENED.
(BEHIND THE LUNCH COUNTER--BROODING 673 ICEMAN SUPERSTITIOUSLY)
(THEN SUPERSTITIOUSLY LOOKING UP AT THE SKY WITH 301 LAZARU CRINGING FOREBODING)
(HE HANDS HIM THE LETTER BUT THE CAPTAIN BACKS 351 MARCOM AWAY SUPERSTITIOUSLY).
DEFIANT DARING, SHUDDERS SUPERSTITIOUSLY AND 367 MARCOM SHRINKS AWAY.
(HE SHRINKS SUPERSTITIOUSLY--THEN ANGRILY, 161 POET REACHING FOR THE DECANTER.)

SUPERVISING
MRS. MILLER IS SUPERVISING AND HELPING THE SECOND 210 AHWILD GIRL, NORAH,

SUPERVISION
A LITTLE PERSONAL SUPERVISION IS IN ORDER. 525 DAYS
YOUR SUPERVISION IS MENTIONED BUT I SUPPOSE IF YOU192 STRANG WON'T CARRY ON,

SUPPER
YOU CAN SEE HIM WHEN YOU COME HOME FOR SUPPER, 268 AHWILD CAN'T YOUS
DARNED WELL I TOLD YOU I'M NOT COMING HOME TO 269 AHWILD SUPPER TONIGHT.
I'VE GOT TO WASH UP SOME AS LONG AS RUTH'S MA IS 86 BEYOND COMING OVER FOR SUPPER.
RUTH URGES) WE'LL BE LATE FOR SUPPER, ROB. 93 BEYOND
DID YOU NOTICE, JAMES, HOW QUEER EVERYONE WAS AT 98 BEYOND SUPPER.
AND KIDS TO PLAY WITH AT NIGHT AFTER SUPPER WHEN 486 CARDIF YOUR WORK WAS DONE.
I'LL STEP IN AGAIN FOR A SPELL AFORE SUPPER--THAT 498 DIFRNT IS, IF YOU WANT ME TO.
SO'S I CAN START HIS SUPPER. 505 DIFRNT
I GOT TO SEE IF CALEB'S GOT BACK WITH THEM SUPPER 511 DIFRNT THINGS.
YOU BETTER GET HOME TO SUPPER. 479 DYNAMO
I TOLD HIM HE COULD--AND STAY TO SUPPER WITH US. 17 ELECTR
YOU ATE A GOOD SUPPER TONIGHT--FOR YOU. 151 ELECTR
JOEL WILL REMEMBER ONE NIGHT AT SUPPER WHEN I 29 MANSNS ACTUALLY ASKED MY HUSBAND.

SUPPER (CONT'D.)
IT'S GETTING NEAR SUPPER TIME, THAT'S ALL-- 114 MANSNS
JUST NOW I THINK WE HAD BETTER GO IN TO SUPPER. 115 MANSNS
HOURS SINCE SUPPER EVEN--THE CHILDREN WATCHING, 162 MANSNS THEIR PRYING EYES SNEERING--
THEN AFTER SUPPER OUT HERE AGAIN--WAITING AGAIN-- 162 MANSNS WHY DO I
IT'S GITTIN' NEAR SUPPER-TIME AND YOU GOT TO TAKE 579 ROPE YOUR MEDICINE B'FORE IT.
HERE I AM ARGYIN' WITH YOUR LUNATIC NOTIONS AND 581 ROPE THE SUPPER NOT READY.
HAVE YE NO SUPPER AT ALL MADE, YE LAZY SLUTS 582 ROPE
I'LL COME AND GIT YOUR SUPPER IN A MINUTE. 584 ROPE
DO WE GET ANY SUPPERS 591 ROPE
(WHININGLY) YOU GOT TO SEE TO HIM, PAT, IF YOU 594 ROPE WANT ANY SUPPER.
WE'LL BE GOIN' TO SUPPER SOON. 598 ROPE
T'HELL WITH SUPPER. 601 ROPE

SUPPER'S
SUPPER'S READY. 205 DESIRE
WAAL--SUPPER'S GITTIN' COLD. 205 DESIRE
MAW SAYS SUPPER'S READY. 600 ROPE

SUPPLANTED
HAD SUPPLANTED HIM WITH THE SLAVE-OWNING STATE-- 503 DAYS

SUPPLICATING
(SUPPLICATING TERROR) 543 DIFRNT
(HIS TENSE, SUPPLICATING ATTITUDE SUDDENLY 480 DYNAMO RELAXING DEJECTEDLY)
HIS FACE AVERTED FROM HERS--IN A VOICE THAT IS 485 DYNAMO ALMOST SUPPLICATING)
AN AGONIZED MOAN OF SUPPLICATING LAUGHTER COMES 349 LAZARU FROM THEM ALL.)

SUPPLICATINGLY
(SUPPLICATINGLY) DAVID/ 550 'ILE
(SUPPLICATINGLY) AND YOU TANK--MAYBE--YOU FORGIVE 65 ANNA ME SOMETINE
(SUPPLICATINGLY) AND YOU'LL COME WITH US, NAT-- 564 CROSS AND FATHER, TOO--AND THEN--
HIS ARMS STRETCHED OUT TO IT SUPPLICATINGLY,) 479 DYNAMO
AND SINKS TO THE GROUND, EMBRACING HIS KNEES 174 EJONES SUPPLICATINGLY)
THEY STRETCH THEIR ARMS OUT IN EVERY DIRECTION 296 LAZARU SUPPLICATINGLY.)
SUPPLICATINGLY) 302 LAZARU
(BENDING DOWN--SUPPLICATINGLY) 347 LAZARU
HIS FACE TOWARD LAZARUS, SUPPLICATINGLY) 371 LAZARU

SUPPLICATION
AND RAISES HIS HANDS UP TO THE FIGURE OF CHRIST INS64 DAYS SUPPLICATION)
(CLASPING HIS HANDS ABOVE IN SUPPLICATION) 264 GGBROW
AS THEY PRAY SILENTLY IN THEIR AGONIZED 319 GGBROW SUPPLICATION.

SUPPLICATIONS
SEEM LIKE QUEER HINDU IDOLS TORTURED INTO 483 DYNAMO SCIENTIFIC SUPPLICATIONS.

SUPPORT
(ENCOURAGED BY THIS SUPPORT) 544 'ILE
LEANING WEAKLY AGAINST IT FOR SUPPORT. 145 BEYOND
STRETCHING A HAND OUT TO THE WALL TO SUPPORT 151 BEYOND HIMSELF.
A NICE THIN' FOR ME TO HAVE TO SUPPORT HIM OUT OF 152 BEYOND WHAT I'D SAVED
CATCHING AT THE TABLE FOR SUPPORT--TERRIFIEDLY) 92 ELECTR
LEANING AGAINST A COLUMN FOR SUPPORT) 119 ELECTR
THEN JEERINGLY) SO MY WIFE THINKS IT BEHOOVES ME 271 GGBROW TO SETTLE DOWN AND SUPPORT MY
HIS HAND ON EACH SIDE OF HIS HEAD FOR SUPPORT. 575 ICEMAN
I HELP TO SUPPORT IT. I'M TAXED TO DEATH-- 144 JOURNE
AND EARNED JUST ENOUGH TO SUPPORT MYSELF, AND KEPT 16 MANSNS MY DREAMS.
WHOSE GREED CAN BE USED TO BRING IN MONEY TO 73 MANSNS SUPPORT WOMAN/
TO SUPPORT YOUR FAMILY EXCEPT IN A SHAMEFUL 153 MANSNS POVERTY.
AND BUILD HIS OWN CABIN, AND DO ALL THE WORK, AND 29 POET SUPPORT HIMSELF SIMPLY,
AS HE REACHES THE TABLE AND LEANS ONE HAND ON IT 578 ROPE FOR SUPPORT.
D'YOU NOT REMEMBER THE LETTER SHE WROTE TELLIN' 586 ROPE HIM HE COULD SUPPORT LUKE ON THE
AND HOW WILL YOU SUPPORT YOURSELF, IF I MAY ASKS 17 STRANG
(THEY SUPPORT OLSON TO THE DOOR.) 508 VOYAGE
SHE SWAYS IRRESOLUTELY TOWARD HIM, AGAIN REACHING 449 WELDED TO THE BANNISTER FOR SUPPORT.
ONLY PUTTING OUT HER HAND ON THE FLOOR TO SUPPORT 460 WELDED HERSELF.)
TO THE SIDE OF THE DOORWAY FOR SUPPORT--DULLY) 465 WELDED

SUPPORTED
WITH HIS CHIN SUPPORTED IN HIS HAND) 456 CARIBE
HE SANK DOWN AND DOWN AND MY MOTHER WORKED AND 25 ELECTR SUPPORTED HIM.
HE IS ASLEEP, HIS NODDING HEAD SUPPORTED BY HIS 575 ICEMAN LEFT HAND.

SUPPORTIN'
I'VE BEEN PAYIN' THE INT'RIST AN' SUPPORTIN' 592 ROPE HIMSELF AN' HIS DOCTOR BILLS BY THE

SUPPORTING
HE IS SUPPORTING THE LIMP FORM OF A MAN DRESSED IN 30 ANNA DUNGAREES,
JOHNSON COMES ALONG THE DECK TO PORT, SUPPORTING 31 ANNA THE FOURTH MAN,
SUPPORTING HERSELF BY THE TABLE, GASPING FOR 128 BEYOND BREATH.
(HURRYING TO HIS SIDE AND SUPPORTING HIM) 151 BEYOND
HE COMES AND SITS DOWN ON HIS CHAIR AGAIN, 162 BEYOND SUPPORTING HIS HEAD ON HIS HANDS.
THE LINES OF BUNKS, THE UPRIGHTS SUPPORTING THEM, 207 HA APE
CLUTCHING THE SUPPORTING ARM SHE STRETCHES OUT.) 80 MISBEG

SUPPOSE

SUPPORTING (CONT'D.)
HE IS HALF LEADING, HALF SUPPORTING MELODY. 152 POET
SUPPORTING HIS HEAD WITH THE OTHER HAND. 595 ROPE
SUPPORTING THE INERT FORM OF IVAN BETWEEN THEM. 503 VOYAGE

SUPPORTS
AND SUPPORTS HIS HEAD WHILE HE DRINKS IN GREAT 486 CARDIF
GULPS.)
SHE LEANS AGAINST HIM WEAKLY AND HE SUPPORTS HER 107 ELECTR
WITH HIS ARM AROUND HER)
(SAGS WEAKLY AND SUPPORTS HERSELF AGAINST THE 167 ELECTR
TABLE--
(RUSHES TO HER, SUPPORTS HER TO SOFA AT RIGHT) 108 STRANG

SUPPOSE
(SMILING) OFF TO THE RANDS'S, I SUPPOSE. 191 AHWILD
I SUPPOSE DICK IS DEEP IN NICK CARTER OR OLD CAP 193 AHWILD
COLLIER.
AND THEN THERE WAS KIPLING--BUT I SUPPOSE HE'S NOT198 AHWILD
SO BAD.
(SHE SIGHS) BUT I SUPPOSE WITH THAT DARNED SACHEM212 AHWILD
CLUB PICNIC IT'S MORE LIKELY
I SUPPOSE YOU THINK I OUGHT TO BE HEARTBROKEN 216 AHWILD
ABOUT MURIEL--
HE GOT THAT OUT OF ONE OF THOSE BOOKS, I SUPPOSE. 216 AHWILD
GETTING HUNGRY, I SUPPOSE$ 216 AHWILD
BUT I SUPPOSE WE REALLY SHOULDN'T. 233 AHWILD
I SUPPOSE SHE'S RIGHT. 234 AHWILD
(BRISTLING) I'M NOT GOOD ENOUGH TO TALK ABOUT 243 AHWILD
HER, I SUPPOSE$
I SUPPOSE HE SNEAKED OFF TO WATCH THE FIREWORKS. 254 AHWILD
(BITTINGLY) I SUPPOSE THAT WAS BEFORE EATING 265 AHWILD
LOBSTER SHELLS
I SUPPOSE YOU'LL HAVE HIM OUT WITH YOU PAINTING 269 AHWILD
THE TOWN RED THE NEXT THING/
I SUPPOSE THAT'S MORE OF THOSE DARNED BOOKS-- 271 AHWILD
AND I SUPPOSE YOU JUST SAT AND LET YOURSELF BE 285 AHWILD
KISSED/
(THEN AFTER A PAUSE) AND I SUPPOSE YOU'LL TELL ME285 AHWILD
YOU DIDN'T FALL IN LOVE WITH
ARTHUR'S OUT WITH ELSIE RAND, I SUPPOSE$ 292 AHWILD
BUT HE'LL GET OVER THAT, I SUPPOSE. 292 AHWILD
NAT, DO YOU SUPPOSE HE'S BEEN--S 293 AHWILD
I SUPPOSE I WOULDN'T. 294 AHWILD
BUT, HELLY, I SUPPOSE YOU BOYS TALK ALL THIS OVER 295 AHWILD
AMONG YOURSELVES
I SUPPOSE TONIGHT YOU NEEDN'T. 298 AHWILD
YOU'RE NOT THE OLD SQUARE-HEAD'S WOMAN, I SUPPOSE 32 ANNA
YOU'LL BE TELLING ME NEAT--
DIGGING SPUDS IN THE MUCK FROM DAWN TO DARK, I 38 ANNA
SUPPOSE$
D'YOU SUPPOSE I AIN'T BEEN THINKING TOO$ 64 ANNA
BEAT ME UP OR KILL ME, I SUPPOSE. 64 ANNA
PLENTY OF DAMES THERE, I SUPPOSE$ 73 ANNA
AND I SUPPOSE 'TIS THE SAME LIES YOU TOLD THEM ALL 73 ANNA
BEFORE THAT YOU TOLD TO ME$
I SUPPOSE IT'S THAT YEAR IN COLLEGE GAVE YOU A 82 BEYOND
LIKING FOR THAT KIND OF STUFF.
YES, I SUPPOSE IT IS. 84 BEYOND
SUPPOSE I TOLD YOU THAT WAS THE ONE AND ONLY 85 BEYOND
REASON FOR MY GOINGS
I SUPPOSE I SHOULDN'T COMPLAIN THIS WAY. 87 BEYOND
I SUPPOSE IT'S NATURAL TO BE CROSS WHEN YOU'RE NOT 87 BEYOND
ABLE EVER TO WALK A STEP.
THAT'S WHY I'M GOING NOW, I SUPPOSE. 90 BEYOND
I SUPPOSE YOU'RE RIGHT, KATEY. 101 BEYOND
WHAT D'YOU SUPPOSE MY OFFICERS IS GOIN' TO THINK 103 BEYOND
WHEN THERE'S NO ONE COMES
I SUPPOSE IT'D BE HARD FOR YOU TO EXPLAIN ANYONE$107 BEYOND
DOES HE SUPPOSE YOU'RE RUNNIN' A HOTEL--WITH NO 113 BEYOND
ONE TO HELP WITH THINGS$*
I SUPPOSE IT DOES SEEM SMALL TO YOU NOW. 133 BEYOND
(INDIFFERENTLY) YES, I SUPPOSE HE HAS. 136 BEYOND
(WITH FIERCE SCORN) I SUPPOSE YOU'RE SO USED TO 155 BEYOND
THE IDEA
WHY DO YOU SUPPOSE HE WANTED US TO PROMISE WE'D-- 163 BEYOND
BUT SUPPOSE YOU COULDN'T PUT THEM OUT OF YOUR 467 CARIBE
MINDS
SUPPOSE THEY HAUNTED YOU WHEN YOU WERE AWAKE AND 467 CARIBE
WHEN YOU WERE ASLEEP--
I SUPPOSE THIS IS ALL MEANT TO BE LIKE A SHIP'S 556 CROSS
CABINS
THE TREASURE, I SUPPOSE, IS WHERE-- 561 CROSS
(THEN GETTING UP) WELL, I SUPPOSE I BETTER GET 497 CROSS
BACK TO MY OFFICE.
WELL, I SUPPOSE BECAUSE, NOT HAVING SEEN YOU, 505 DAYS
I'M ONLY ASKING YOU TO SUPPOSE. 522 DAYS
(SHE FORCES A LAUGH) I SUPPOSE ALL THIS SOUNDS 522 DAYS
TOO PREPOSTEROUS.
BUT SUPPOSE JOHN WERE UNFAITHFUL TO YOU-- 522 DAYS
THAT I SUPPOSE I'M HIPPED ON THE SUBJECT. 524 DAYS
WHY DO YOU SUPPOSE I EVER DID IT, EXCEPT FOR HIS 526 DAYS
BENEFIT--IF YOU WANT THE TRUTH$
(WITH A SIGH) I SUPPOSE PA AND MA TURNED OVER IN 535 DIFRNT
THEIR GRAVES.
I SUPPOSE I DO. 538 DIFRNT
YOU DON'T SUPPOSE I'D BE SAYIN' IT IF IT WASN'T 540 DIFRNT
SO$
CAN'T THEM THINGS HAPPEN JUST AS WELL AS ANY 542 DIFRNT
OTHER-- WHAT D' YOU SUPPOSE--
AND WHAT DO YOU SUPPOSE THAT YOUNG SKUNK DOES$ 431 DYNAMO
I SUPPOSE YOU WANT TO RUN OVER AND WARN YOUR FINE 450 DYNAMO
FRIENDS/
I SUPPOSE I'LL HAVE TO DIE SOMETIME... 454 DYNAMO
I SUPPOSE THAT'S WHY HE ACTED THE WAY HE DID TO 456 DYNAMO
RUBE/
(THEN QUICKLY) I SUPPOSE YOU THINK I'M DOING IT 467 DYNAMO
TO SPITE YOU, BUT I'M NOT.
D'YOU SUPPOSE I EVER WAS A FISH, RAMSAY$ 479 DYNAMO

SUPPOSE (CONT'D.)
I SUPPOSE YOU'LL SAY AS THAT SWANK ABOUT THE 178 EJONES
SILVER BULLET AIN'T LUCK--
YOU HAVE HEARD THE NEWS, I SUPPOSE$ 17 ELECTR
WELL, I SUPPOSE THAT'S THE USUAL WAY OF IT. 22 ELECTR
I SUPPOSE CLIPPERS ARE TOO OLD A STORY TO THE 23 ELECTR
DAUGHTER OF A SHIPBUILDER.
BUT I SUPPOSE IT WOULD BE FOOLISH TO EXPECT 24 ELECTR
ANYTHING BUT CHEAP ROMANTIC LIES
I SUPPOSE YOUR FATHER HAS STUFFED YOU WITH HIS 25 ELECTR
LIES ABOUT MY MOTHER/
AND I SUPPOSE YOU BOAST THAT NOW YOU'VE DUNE SO, 27 ELECTR
DON'T YOU$
I SUPPOSE ANNIE TOLD YOU I'D BEEN TO VISIT HAZEL 29 ELECTR
AND PETER WHILE YOU WERE AWAY.
I SUPPOSE YOU'LL HARDLY LET YOUR FATHER GET IN THE 32 ELECTR
DOOR BEFORE YOU TELL HIM/
AND I SUPPOSE KNOWING WHO HE WAS GAVE YOU ALL THE 32 ELECTR
MORE *SATISFACTION*--
SUPPOSE I REFUSE/ 33 ELECTR
I SUPPOSE YOU THINK YOU'LL BE FREE TO MARRY ADAM 64 ELECTR
NOW/
I SUPPOSE I'D COME TO EXPECT HE WOULD LIVE 74 ELECTR
FOREVER.
OH, YOU DID--YOU FOUND--AND I SUPPOSE YOU CONNECT 77 ELECTR
THAT--
AND AS FOR HER GOING TO THE POLICE--DO YOU SUPPOSE 88 ELECTR
I WOULDN'T PREVENT THAT--
I SUPPOSE YOU'VE BEEN TELLING HIM YOUR VILE LIES, 100 ELECTR
YOU--
I SUPPOSE IT'S THE ONLY WAY OUT FOR US NOW. 111 ELECTR
I SUPPOSE IT WAS--BUT-- (SHE STOPS AND SIGHS--THEN137 ELECTR
WORRIEDLY)
I SUPPOSE CONGRATULATIONS ARE IN ORDER. 148 ELECTR
WELL, AS I'VE PRACTICALLY FINISHED IT--I SUPPOSE 1152 ELECTR
MIGHT AS WELL TELL YOU.
(BITTERLY) DO YOU SUPPOSE FOR A MOMENT SHE'LL 161 ELECTR
EVER LET ME GO$
I SUPPOSE--WE CAN'T EXPECT YOU TOMORROW--NOW. 164 ELECTR
AND I SUPPOSE YOU THINK THAT'S ALL IT MEANS, 164 ELECTR
(WITH A SIGH) WELL, I SUPPOSE WE'VE BEEN 259 GGBROW
COMFORTABLE.
I SUPPOSE THEY'LL BE ALL RIGHT OVER THERE, DON'T 270 GGBROW
YOU$
BUT I SUPPOSE THE GOSSIPS ARE TELLING THE SAME 276 GGBROW
SILLY STORIES ABOUT HIM THEY
BUT, DAMN IT, I SUPPOSE YOU'RE TOO MUCH OF A 281 GGBROW
ROTTEN CYNIC TO BELIEVE I MEAN WHAT
(FORCING A TIRED SMILE) I SUPPOSE SO, DION. 291 GGBROW
(WITH TIRED SOLICITUDE) I SUPPOSE YOU HAVEN'T 291 GGBROW
EATEN A THING, AS USUAL.
I SUPPOSE HE'S OFF DROWNING HIS SORROW/ 302 GGBROW
WELL, I SUPPOSE--SEARCH ME. 304 GGBROW
(AGAIN AFFECTED AND BORED) YES, I SUPPOSE I DO. 219 HA APE
WELL, I SUPPOSE MARRIAGE AIN'T SUCH A BUM RACKET, 12 HUGHIE
IF YOU'RE MADE FOR IT.
YOU WON THE MONEY GAMBLING, I SUPPOSE-- 34 HUGHIE
I SUPPOSE WHOEVER IT WAS MADE A BARGAIN WITH THE 588 ICEMAN
BURNS MEN
I SUPPOSE YOU DON'T REMEMBER A DAMNED THING ABOUT 588 ICEMAN
IT.
SO I SUPPOSE THEY DIDN'T THINK OF ME UNTIL 588 ICEMAN
AFTERWARD.
(FORCING A CASUAL TONE) I DON'T SUPPOSE YOU'VE 591 ICEMAN
HAD MUCH CHANCE
HELL, WHY D'YOU SUPPOSE I'M HERE EXCEPT TO HAVE A 621 ICEMAN
PARTY.
I SUPPOSE IT'D TICKLE YOU IF ME AND MARGIE DID 633 ICEMAN
WHAT DAT LOUSE, HICKEY,
(EXCITEDLY) D'YUH SUPPOSE DAT HE DID CATCH HIS 636 ICEMAN
WIFE CHEATIN'S
DO YOU SUPPOSE I'D DELIBERATELY SET OUT TO GET 642 ICEMAN
UNDER EVERYONE'S SKIN
I SUPPOSE, BECAUSE I WAS ONLY A KID, 646 ICEMAN
I SUPPOSE WHAT SHE REALLY MEANT WAS, COME BACK TO 647 ICEMAN
HER.
I SUPPOSE SHE MIGHT AS WELL BE. 667 ICEMAN
I SUPPOSE$ 668 ICEMAN
(TAUNTINGLY) YES, I SUPPOSE YOU'D LIKE THAT, 668 ICEMAN
WOULDN'T YOU$
HE CAN'T HELP HIS INSULTING MANNER, I SUPPOSE. 674 ICEMAN
BUT IT MIGHT AS WELL BE TODAY, I SUPPOSE. 684 ICEMAN
AND NOW IT'S MY TURN, I SUPPOSE$ 688 ICEMAN
(WITH FORCED JEERING) I SUPPOSE YOU THINK I OUGHT701 ICEMAN
TO DIE BECAUSE I SOLD OUT A
I SUPPOSE YOU THINK I'M A LIAR, 714 ICEMAN
DO YOU SUPPOSE I GIVE A DAMN ABOUT LIFE NOW$ 719 ICEMAN
I SUPPOSE YOU THINK I OUGHT TO HAVE MADE THOSE 720 ICEMAN
DICKS TAKE ME AWAY WITH HICKEY.
(LOWERING HIS VOICE) AN' THEN WHAT D'YOU SUPPOSE 519 INZONE
HE DID$
IT'S A SECRET CONFAB THEY DON'T WANT ME TO HEAR, I 15 JOURNE
SUPPOSE.
I SUPPOSE HE WANTS HIS RENT LOWERED. 22 JOURNE
I SUPPOSE YOU'RE REGRETTING YOU WEREN'T THERE 26 JOURNE
DON'T YOU SUPPOSE I'M AS GLAD OF THAT AS YOU ARE/ 39 JOURNE
I SUPPOSE BECAUSE IT'S THE ONLY HOME WE'VE HAD, 44 JOURNE
JUST BECAUSE I FEEL ROTTEN AND BLUE, I SUPPOSE. 45 JOURNE
JAMIE WAS PRETENDING TO BE ASLEEP, TOO, I'M SURE, 47 JOURNE
AND I SUPPOSE YOUR FATHER--
BUT I SUPPOSE YOU'RE REMEMBERING I'VE PROMISED 48 JOURNE
BEFORE ON MY WORD OF HONOR.
BUTTER WOULDN'T MELT IN YOUR MOUTH, I SUPPOSE. 52 JOURNE
BUT I SUPPOSE LIFE HAS MADE HIM LIKE THAT, AND HE 61 JOURNE
CAN'T HELP IT.
I SUPPOSE YOU DID, MARY. 69 JOURNE
YES, I SUPPOSE YOU CAN'T HELP SUSPECTING THAT. 93 JOURNE

SUPPOSE 1586

SUPPOSE (CONT'D.)
I SUPPOSE YOU'LL DIVIDE THAT TEN DOLLARS YOUR 94 JOURNE
FATHER GAVE YOU WITH JAMIE.
WELL, I SUPPOSE I SWORE AT TIMES, TOO, AND I DON'T 99 JOURNE
LIKE TO ADMIT IT.
HE STILL HAS SOME MONEY LEFT, I SUPPOSE, AND IT'S 122 JOURNE
BURNING A HOLE IN HIS POCKET.
ANOTHER ATHEIST, I SUPPOSE. 134 JOURNE
AMONG THE SOUSES IN THE HOTEL BAR, I SUPPOSE/ 140 JOURNE
I SUPPOSE IT'S BECAUSE I FEEL SO DAMNED SUNK. 162 JOURNE
(HIS VOICE FLUTTERS.) I SUPPOSE I CAN'T FORGIVE 162 JOURNE
HER--YET.
(DULLY.) HER WEDDING GOWN, I SUPPOSE. 172 JOURNE
I SUPPOSE I, TOO, HAVE MY PRICE--IF THEY WERE ONLY301 LAZARU
CLEVER ENOUGH TO DISCOVER IT/
THIS PLACE REMINDED ME, I SUPPOSE. 8 MANSNS
MY LIFE, I SUPPOSE YOU MIGHT CALL IT, SINCE I HAVE 28 MANSNS
NEVER LIVED EXCEPT IN MIND.
YES, I SUPPOSE IT IS MY DUTY TO SEE IT ONLY IN 37 MANSNS
THAT LIGHT.
BUT I SUPPOSE YOU STILL DREAM YOU'RE THE KING OF 53 MANSNS
FRANCE'S SWEETHEART/
YOUR BODY FELT SWINDLED AND IT MADE YOU 80 MANSNS
SUSPICIOUS, I SUPPOSE.
WELL, I SUPPOSE I COULD TELL HER, IF YOU WANT TO 87 MANSNS
BE SPARED.
THAT, I SUPPOSE, CONSTITUTES THE HUMOROUS IRONY 111 MANSNS
YOU REMEMBERED$
(FORCING A LAUGH.) I SUPPOSE I AM TOO OLD A DOG 152 MANSNS
TO LEARN NEW TRICKS
YES, I SUPPOSE, ENTIRELY SELFISH--NO TIME TO 155 MANSNS
REMEMBER SELF.
BUT SUPPOSE THEY DON'T CHOOSE TO LET HIM CHOOSE$ 173 MANSNS
SUPPOSE I WAS 174 MANSNS
DO YOU SUPPOSE ALMIGHTY GOD WOULD ALLOW INFIDELS 365 MARCOM
TO CUT UP NOAH'S ARK INTO
I SUPPOSE THEY'RE ENGAGED--LIKE DONATA AND ME. 366 MARCOM
(UNCERTAINLY) NO, I SUPPOSE NOT. 381 MARCOM
THERE ALWAYS HAVE BEEN WARS AND THERE ALWAYS WILL 394 MARCOM
BE, I SUPPOSE.
(INQUISITIVELY) I SUPPOSE YOU FEEL YOUR HEAVY 403 MARCOM
RESPONSIBILITY
I'VE HAD MY FUN AND I SUPPOSE IT'S ABOUT TIME I 404 MARCOM
SETTLED DOWN.
OR I SUPPOSE I'D BETTER SAY MAJESTY NOW THAT WE'VE410 MARCOM
REACHED PERSIA--
I SUPPOSE YOU ARE RELIEVED TO GET ME HERE ALIVE 413 MARCOM
AND DELIVER ME--LIKE A COW/
(WITH A CUNNING LEER) NOT EVEN JIM TYRONE, I 8 MISBEG
SUPPOSE$
(SARCASTICALLY) I SUPPOSE YOU'VE NEVER THOUGHT OF 9 MISBEG
THAT$
(SEETHING) YOU'VE STOLEN MY SATCHEL TO GIVE HIM, 13 MISBEG
I SUPPOSE.
(SCORNFULLY) I'M TO PRETEND I'M A PURE VIRGIN, I 34 MISBEG
SUPPOSE$
FOR I SUPPOSE YOU'LL HAVE THE FOXINESS TO ASK HIM 36 MISBEG
TO HAVE A BITE TO EAT TO KEEP
(FORCING A SCORNFUL SMILE) I'M SHOCKING YOU, I 42 MISBEG
SUPPOSE$
YOU'VE GONE ON THE WATER-WAGON, I SUPPOSE$ 45 MISBEG
HOW D'YOU SUPPOSE HE GOT HERE$ 59 MISBEG
AH, WELL, I SUPPOSE THE TEMPTATION WAS TOO GREAT. 86 MISBEG
I SUPPOSE IT'S BECAUSE I HAVE A PICTURE OF THEM INIT7 MISBEG
MY MIND
I SUPPOSE THAT DOES SOUND LIKE MOANING-AT-THE-BAR 123 MISBEG
STUFF.
I SUPPOSE BECAUSE IT SEEMS CRAZY FOR YOU TO HOLD 130 MISBEG
MY BIG UGLY PAW SO TENDERLY.
WHAT THE HELL ELSE DO YOU SUPPOSE I CAME FOR$ 137 MISBEG
I SUPPOSE I HAD SOME MAD IDEA SHE COULD MAKE ME 149 MISBEG
FORGET--
I SUPPOSE I BORED THE HELL OUT OF YOU WITH A LOT 169 MISBEG
OF DRUNKEN DRIVEL.
(BITTERLY.) I SUPPOSE YOU'RE BOUND TO SUSPECT-- 32 POET
(IN A LIGHT TONE.) FAITH, I SUPPOSE I MUST HAVE 44 POET
LOOKED A VAIN PEACOCK.
I SUPPOSE IT WOULD BE DOWNRIGHT SNOBBERY TO HOLD 48 POET
TO OLD-WORLD STANDARDS.
I SUPPOSE I MAY EXPECT THE YOUNG MAN TO REQUEST AN 49 POET
INTERVIEW WITH ME
I SUPPOSE IT'S A FREE DRINK YOU'RE AFTER. 54 POET
I SUPPOSE YOU'VE GIVEN ORDERS TO POOR MOTHER TO 59 POET
COOK A GRAND FEAST FOR YOU.
I SUPPOSE SHE THINKS SHE'S SUCH A GREAT LADY 77 POET
I SUPPOSE SOMEONE AROUND HERE THAT HATES FATHER-- 78 POET
AND WHO DOESN'T$
I SUPPOSE SHE DID IT TO FIND OUT BY WATCHING HIM 108 POET
HOW FAR--
I SUPPOSE IT WOULD NEVER OCCUR TO YOU THAT 112 POET
AN' WHERE D'YOU SUPPOSE LUKE GOT THE HUNDRED 586 ROPE
DOLLARS HE STOLE$
D'YOU SUPPOSE THAT HARLOT RAN OFF WITH IT$ 586 ROPE
I SUPPOSE YOU FOUND EVERYTHING COMPLETELY CHANGED 7 STRANG
SINCE BEFORE THE WAR.
(THEN JEALOUSLY) I'LL SUPPOSE EVERY SINGLE DAMNED 25 STRANG
INMATE HAS FALLEN IN LOVE WITH
SUPPOSE I OUGHT TO SAY SOMETHING ABOUT HIS BOOKS, 29 STRANG
SUPPOSE I'LL LOSE OUT WITH NINA, TOO...!) 30 STRANG
WANTS TO EVADE ALL RESPONSIBILITY FOR HER, I 37 STRANG
SUPPOSE...
AND I SUPPOSE THAT'S THE LOGICAL CONCLUSION TO THE 40 STRANG
WHOLE EVASIVE MESS, ISN'T IT$
STILL I SUPPOSE IT'S JUST FRIENDLY... 51 STRANG
SLEEPING IN A STRANGE BED, I SUPPOSE. 51 STRANG
DISCUSS NINA'S PREGNANCY, I SUPPOSE... 53 STRANG
I SUPPOSE I OUGHT TO GO UP AND SAY HELLO TO AUNT 55 STRANG
BESSIE.

SUPPOSE (CONT'D.)
VAGUELY) WELL, I SUPPOSE YOU'VE GOT TO BE CAREFUL 73 STRANG
OF EVERY LITTLE THING WHEN
I SUPPOSE, AFRAID IT WOULD SPOIL HER FIGURE... 74 STRANG
I SUPPOSE YOU CAN'T HELP YOUR DIAGNOSING STARE. 79 STRANG
I SUPPOSE I WILL. 81 STRANG
THEN WHAT DO YOU SUPPOSE WOULD BE HIS FINISH$ 84 STRANG
BUT I SUPPOSE HE'S STILL TOO BROKEN UP OVER HIS 94 STRANG
MOTHER'S DEATH TO WRITE.
AND I SUPPOSE THERE ARE LITTLE MARSDENS-- 117 STRANG
I SUPPOSE NINA'S BEEN BOASTING ABOUT THAT 134 STRANG
ALREADY...
SUPPOSE IT'S THE EXCITEMENT OF NED TURNING UP... 134 STRANG
DO YOU SUPPOSE HE--$ 146 STRANG
I SUPPOSE I SHOULD SAY MAN NOW HE'S IN HIS 166 STRANG
THIRTIES.
BUT HE DON'T COUNT, I SUPPOSE/ 166 STRANG
UH--I SUPPOSE YOU WANTED TO MAKE SURE SO YOU COULD172 STRANG
HOPE HE'D GO INSANE$
AND MINE, TOO, I SUPPOSE. 186 STRANG
I SUPPOSE IT WAS DAMNED HARD ON HIM. 186 STRANG
OH, I SUPPOSE I'M UNFAIR. 186 STRANG
(THEN WITH A BITTER LAUGH) I SUPPOSE THEY'LL BE 186 STRANG
GETTING MARRIED NOW/
I SUPPOSE IT WAS THAT DISCOVERY THAT LED TO THEIR 188 STRANG
GENERAL USE AT FUNERALS--
I SUPPOSE IT WAS FINDING OUT SHE LOVED DARRELL... 189 STRANG
I SUPPOSE HE LEFT IT TO ME... 191 STRANG
YOUR SUPERVISION IS MENTIONED BUT I SUPPOSE IF YOU192 STRANG
WON'T CARRY ON.
(SADLY SMILING) YOU, CHARLIE, I SUPPOSE. 197 STRANG
I DON'T SUPPOSE WE'LL EVER SEE YOU AGAIN, NED. 197 STRANG
I SUPPOSE I CAN GUESS--MY GOING TO THE DOORS-- 451 WELDED
I SUPPOSE YOU THINK THAT WITHOUT YOUR WORK I-- 457 WELDED
(WITH A SNEER OF RAGE) AND I SUPPOSE YOU WERE$ 457 WELDED
I SUPPOSE YOU'VE KNOWN IT. 476 WELDED
(TAKEN ABACK, TURNING AWAY) NO, I SUPPOSE-- 485 WELDED
SUPPOSED
IT'S BAD ENOUGH FOR BOYS BUT FOR A YOUNG GIRL 250 AHWILD
SUPPOSED TO HAVE MANNERS--
A SHORT TIME IS SUPPOSED TO ELAPSE BETWEEN SCENES 486 DYNAMO
TWO AND THREE.)
SEVERAL MINUTES ARE SUPPOSED TO ELAPSE. 109 ELECTR
(THEN WITH A GRIN) AN' YOU'RE SUPPOSED TO GO IN 131 ELECTR
SOBER.
I SUPPOSED HE'D WRITTEN YOU. 115 STRANG
I SUPPOSED HE'S NO BETTER THAN THE REST OF YOU. 116 STRANG
I SUPPOSED THE THOUGHT OF A WIFE TAKING YOU AWAY 143 STRANG
FROM ME WOULD BE TOO MUCH--
YES--OF COURSE--I SUPPOSED-- 483 WELDED
SUPPOSES
HE BEGINS TALKING TO ABBIE WHOM HE SUPPOSES BESIDE263 DESIRE
HIM.)
SUPPOSING
SUPPOSING IT COMES BEFORE$ 195 AHWILD
WELL, SUPPOSING I TAKE HER$ 234 AHWILD
SUPPOSING I WAS TO TELL YOU THAT IT'S JUST BEAUTY 85 BEYOND
THAT'S CALLING ME,
(SUPPOSING ANY ONE SHOULD SEE ME... 435 DYNAMO
(I SUPPOSING ANYONE SAW ME... 474 DYNAMO
(BUT SUPPOSING THE MIRACLE DOESN'T HAPPEN 478 DYNAMO
TONIGHT$...
SUPPOSING THEY DON'T$ 175 ELECTR
SUPPOSING SOMEONE CAME IN/ 83 MANSNS
SUPPOSE I GO OFF OPENLY WITH ADAM/ 33 ELECTR
SUPPRESS
EVEN LILY CANNOT SUPPRESS A SMILE.) 192 AHWILD
HIS FACE TENSE WITH THE EFFORT TO SUPPRESS HIS 58 ANNA
GRIEF AND RAGE.)
SUPPRESSED
CONVERSATION WITH AIR OF SUPPRESSED EXCITEMENT.458 CARBBE
(THEN WITH SUPPRESSED EXCITEMENT) 563 DAYS
(A SUPPRESSED LAUGH.) 249 DESIRE
(SUPPRESSED LAUGHTER. 250 DESIRE
(A SUPPRESSED LAUGH. 252 DESIRE
AND CLOSED IT AFTER HIM SILENTLY, SHAKING WITH 318 GGBROW
SUPPRESSED LAUGHTER.
(WITH SUPPRESSED EXCITEMENT) 518 INZONE
(HIS VOICE TREMBLING WITH SUPPRESSED FURY.) 170 JOURNE
(A SUPPRESSED LAUGH FROM THOSE AROUND HIM.) 276 LAZARU
SHE TURNS HER BACK FOR A MOMENT, SHAKING WITH 61 MISBEG
SUPPRESSED LAUGHTER.
(WITH SUPPRESSED FURY) YOU'RE A--/ 82 MISBEG
HIS VOICE TREMBLING A LITTLE WITH SUPPRESSED 123 STRANG
EMOTION)
(WITH AN EXTRAVAGANT SUPPRESSED EXULTANCE) 135 STRANG
SUPPRESSES
(BUT MELODY SUPPRESSES ANY ANGRY REACTION. 103 POET
SUPPRESSING
(TARTLY, BUT EVIDENTLY SUPPRESSING HER USUAL SMILE198 AHWILD
WHERE HE IS CONCERNED)
(SUPPRESSING ANNOYANCE, CALLS OUT WITH FORCED GOOD294 GGBROW
NATURE)
ALTHOUGH SHE IS NOW MORE CAPABLE OF SUPPRESSING 26 STRANG
AND CONCEALING IT.
(THEN SUPPRESSING AN OUTBREAK OF HYSTERICAL 135 STRANG
TRIUMPHANT LAUGHTER ONLY BY A
SUPPRESSED
THEN IN A VOICE THAT BETRAYS A DEEP UNDERCURRENT 47 ELECTR
OF SUPPRESSED FEELING)
SUPREMACY
IT DOES NOT DO TO HOLD ONE'S ENEMY IN THE BATTLE 98 MANSNS
FOR SUPREMACY IN TOO MUCH
WHOSE SILK INDUSTRY IS BEGINNING TO THREATEN THE 422 MARCOM
SUPREMACY OF OUR OWN.

SUPREME

SUPREME PONTIFF EMPEROR OF ROME GOD AMONG GODS 316 LAZARU
HAIL/
AND WENT OUT AS A BEGGAR ON THE ROADS TO SEEK THE 372 MARCOM
SUPREME ENLIGHTENMENT

SUREST

(EMPHATICALLY) SUREST THING YOU KNOW. 17 ANNA

SURF

AN INSISTENT MONOTONE OF THUNDERING SURF, MUFFLED 555 CROSS
AND FAR-OFF,
AND ALWAYS THE SURF ON THE BARRIER REEF 24 ELECTR
THE SURF ON THE BARRIER REEF SINGING A CROON IN 112 ELECTR
YOUR EARS LIKE A LULLABY/
THE TRADE WIND IN THE COCO PALMS--THE SURF ON THE 147 ELECTR
REEF--

SURFACE

ITS GLASSY SURFACE SET OFF BY THREE SMALL, GARISH-519 DIFRNT
COLORED RUGS,
BEYOND THIS THE SURFACE OF THE RIVER SPREADS OUT, 199 EJONES
THE MOONLIT SURFACE OF THE RIVER BEYOND AND PASSES200 EJONES
HIS HAND OVER HIS HEAD
SHE IS OBVIOUSLY CONCEALING BENEATH A SURFACE CALM150 ELECTR
BY THE SOUND OF THAT SURFACE CAR. 25 HUGHIE
(WITH A RESENTMENT THAT HAS A QUALITY OF BEING 61 JOURNE
AUTOMATIC AND ON THE SURFACE.
THERE IS PEACE DEEP IN THE SEA BUT THE SURFACE IS 409 MARCOM
SORROW.
HIS NOVELS JUST WELL-WRITTEN SURFACE... 34 STRANG
I WOULD BE BUSY--SURFACE LIFE--NO MORE DEPTHS, 46 STRANG
PLEASE GOD/
BEST EFFORTS AND BRING HIS LATENT ABILITY TO THE 46 STRANG
SURFACE.
YES, IT WOULD BE A CAREER FOR ME TO BRING A CAREER 46 STRANG
TO HIS SURFACE.
ON THE SURFACE, THAT'S INSANE... 135 STRANG
WITH THE OLD SURFACE RITUAL OF COVETING OUR 170 STRANG
NEIGHBOR'S ASS)

SURFACES

THE WALLS ARE PLAIN PLASTERED SURFACES TINTED A 28 ELECTR
DULL GRAY
THE WALLS ARE PLAIN PLASTERED SURFACES, LIGHT GRAY 79 ELECTR
WITH A WHITE TRIM.

SURGE

A SURGE OF LOVE AND DESIRE OVERCOMES HIS TIMIDITY 143 ELECTR
AND HE BURSTS OUT)

SURGEON

HIS FATHER NOTED PHILADELPHIA SURGEON... 125 STRANG

SURGING

IN A FLASH A WHOLESALE FIGHT HAS BROKEN OUT AND 472 CARIBE
THE DECK IS A SURGING CROWD OF

SURLILY

(SURLILY) IN THE SITTING-ROOM. 220 AHWILD
(SURLILY) AW, SHUT UP, MID. 228 AHWILD
(LOOKING UP AND DOWN THE AVENUE--SURLILY) 234 HA APE
(SURLILY) I WOULD LIKE TO, I PROMISE YOU/ 301 LAZARU
(SURLILY.) I HAVE. 16 POET

SURLY

(THEN WITH SURLY DIGNITY) I DON'T FEEL LIKE 256 AHWILD
SINGING TONIGHT, PA.
BENNY GOES TO OPEN IT, HIS EXPRESSION TURNING 528 DIFRNT
SURLY AND SULLEN.
(A SQUAT, SURLY-FACED SWEDE--GRUMPILY) 514 INZONE
AND ARE SURLY AND QUICK-TEMPERED WITH THE GREEKS. 298 LAZARU
A SURLY EXPRESSION ON HIS FACE. 594 ROPE
THE SURLY EXPRESSION DISAPPEARS FROM LUKE'S FACE, 594 ROPE
SURLY AND CONTEMPTUOUS... 6 STRANG

SURMISE

AND YOU RETURN HIS LOVE, I SURMISE. 47 POET
SURMISE WHATEVER YOU PLEASE. 47 POET

SURMISED

I HAD SURMISED IT, SIR. 332 LAZARU

SURMOUNTED

SURMOUNTED BY A SHINY BALD SCALP FRINGED WITH 578 ROPE
SCANTY WISPS OF WHITE HAIR.

SURPASSETH

HER BLINDNESS SURPASSETH ALL UNDERSTANDING/ 271 GGBROW

SURPASSING

(HIS VOICE SPEAKING LOVINGLY, WITH A SURPASSING 367 LAZARU
CLEARNESS AND EXALTATION)

SURPRISE

KEENEY HEARS HIS WIFE'S HYSTERICAL WEEPING AND 545 *ILE
TURNS AROUND IN SURPRISE--
(THEN WITH A GRIN) YOU SURPRISE ME AT TIMES WITH 291 AHWILD
YOUR DEEP WISDOM.
(WITH PLEASED SURPRISE AS SHE SEES BURKE, 50 ANNA
(TURNING TO HER QUICKLY, IN SURPRISE--SLOWLY) 88 BEYOND
AND SURPRISE US--HIM AND THE CAPTAIN. 117 BEYOND
(IN SURPRISE) NO, OF COURSE NOT. 137 BEYOND
FROM NOW ON I'LL PICK UP SO QUICK I'LL SURPRISE 145 BEYOND
YOU--
(IN SURPRISE) WARNED ME4 556 CROSS
(WITH AMUSED SURPRISE) WHATS 496 DAYS
OH, I THOUGHT I'D SURPRISE YOU. 505 DAYS
(THEY SHAKE HANDS) A PLEASANT SURPRISE. 525 DAYS
IT MUST HAVE BEEN A SURPRISE FOR YOU. 528 DAYS
BUT AS HE FEELS HER PULSE HIS EXPRESSION CHANGES 563 DAYS
TO ONE OF EXCITED SURPRISE.)
(THEY LOOK AT HIM IN SURPRISE) 207 DESIRE
THEY STARE AT HIM IN SURPRISE.) 208 DESIRE
EBEN STARES FROM ONE TO THE OTHER WITH SURPRISE.) 216 DESIRE
(ABBIE APPEARS IN THE DOORWAY UPSTAIRS AND STANDS 252 DESIRE
LOOKING IN SURPRISE AND
HE LOOKS TOWARD THE WINDOW AND GIVES A SNORT OF 262 DESIRE
SURPRISE AND IRRITATION--
(TO HIS SURPRISE, TURNS ON HIM ANGRILY) 442 DYNAMO
YOU HIDE BEHIND THOSE BUSHES AND WE'LL SURPRISE 459 DYNAMO
HER/
(WITH A TEASING SMILE) ADA, I'VE GOT A BIG 459 DYNAMO
SURPRISE FOR YOU.

SURPRISE (CONT'D.)

ABOUT HIM WITH NUMBED SURPRISE WHEN HE SEES THE 193 EJONES
ROAD.
WERE YOU HOPING IT WOULD BE A CRUSHING SURPRISE TO 32 ELECTR
ME?
(THEY BOTH STARE AT HIM, LAVINIA IN SURPRISE, 48 ELECTR
CHRISTINE IN UNEASY WONDER.
THEY STOP IN SURPRISE ON SEEING SETH AND HIS 134 ELECTR
FRIENDS.
WE'LL FIND HAZEL AND PETER AND SURPRISE THEM-- 138 ELECTR
PETER HAS DIFFICULTY IN HIDING HIS PAINED SURPRISE144 ELECTR
AT ORIN'S SICKLY APPEARANCE.)
(WITH DAZED SURPRISE) WHAT/ 271 GGBROW
(THIS IN SURPRISE--THEN WITH EAGER PLEASURE) 274 GGBROW
THIS IS A PLEASANT SURPRISE, MARGARET. 274 GGBROW
THIS IS A PLEASANT SURPRISE/ 303 GGBROW
WHEN THEY SEE MARGARET, THEY STOP IN SURPRISE.) 316 GGBROW
(THEY SHAKE THEIR HEADS IN SOLEMN SURPRISE) 317 GGBROW
OH, YOU CAN'T SURPRISE ME THAT WAY. 37 HUGHIE
THEN STARTS WITH WELL-ACTED SURPRISE) 606 ICEMAN
(REGARDS HIM WITH SURPRISE AT FIRST, THEN WITH A 623 ICEMAN
PUZZLED INTEREST)
WHY, ME AND THE TAXI MAN MADE ENOUGH NOISE GETTING638 ICEMAN
MY BIG SURPRISE IN THE HALL.
YOU AND ROCKY GO IN THE HALL AND GET THE BIG 639 ICEMAN
SURPRISE.
BRING ON THE BIG SURPRISE/ 657 ICEMAN
(GRIMLY) IT WOULDN'T SURPRISE ME. 668 ICEMAN
(AS CHUCK LOOKS AT HIM WITH DULL SURPRISE HE 698 ICEMAN
LOWERS HIS VOICE TO A WHISPER)
FROM ONE TO THE OTHER OF THE MEN IN SURPRISE. 523 INZONE
(WITH GENUINE SURPRISE--TURNING TO HER) 327 LAZARU
OH, I MAY SURPRISE MYSELF, I THINK. 40 MANSNS
THIS IS A SURPRISE, MOTHER. 51 MANSNS
(SIMON STARES AT HER IN RESENTFUL SURPRISE.) 58 MANSNS
AS JOEL STARES IN COLD SURPRISE WITHOUT MAKING ANY 71 MANSNS
MOVE, HE BURSTS OUT ANGRILY.)
HER EXPRESSION CHANGES TO ONE OF ALARMED SURPRISE 95 MANSNS
(FEIGNING SURPRISE.) THAT I HAD ASKED HER4 96 MANSNS
(TURNS TO HER IN SURPRISE.) BUT I THOUGHT YOU SAW101 MANSNS
THAT, MOTHER.
(HE EXAMINES THE VOLUME--WITH PLEASED BOYISH 107 MANSNS
SURPRISE.)
WITH STARTLED SURPRISE, DRAWING HIS SWORD) 350 MARCOM
(IN SURPRISE) OF COURSE/ 379 MARCOM
IT'S NOTHING TO THE BIG SURPRISE I'VE GOT IN 393 MARCOM
RESERVE FOR YOU.
HIS APPEARANCE EXCITES GENERAL COMMENT AND 439 MARCOM
SURPRISE
(STARES AT HER IN SURPRISE) WHY SO SERIOUS AND 67 MISBEG
INDIGNANT, JOSIE?
(THEN HE LOOKS AT HER IN DRUNKEN SURPRISE-- 88 MISBEG
THICKLY)
TYRONE REGARDS HIM WITH VAGUE SURPRISE.) 101 MISBEG
(STILL HOLDING THE BURNING MATCH, STARES AT HER IN131 MISBEG
SURPRISE)
(AWAKE NOW, BLINKING HIS EYES--WITH DAZED 166 MISBEG
SURPRISE)
WHAT A PLEASANT SURPRISE THIS WILL BE FOR SIMON. 75 POET
HE STARES AT THE FRAGMENTS IN HIS HANDS WITH 92 POET
STUPID SURPRISE.
AN' HE LOOKS AT ME IN SURPRISE, *WHAT MONEYS* 585 ROPE
A SURPRISE, TOO/. 7 STRANG
(LOOKING AT HIM WITH AMUSED SURPRISE) 8 STRANG
(WITH SIMPLE SURPRISE) NED$ 45 STRANG
(LOOKING AFTER HIM WITH ANGER MIXED WITH ALARMED 75 STRANG
SUSPICION AND SURPRISE)
(THEN AS THEY BOTH LOOK AT HIM IN SURPRISE HE 99 STRANG
REALIZES WHAT HE HAS SAID--
SHE WAS SAYING IT TO SURPRISE YOU WITH AT HER OWN 106 STRANG
PROPER TIME--
THIS IS A WONDERFUL SURPRISE/ 126 STRANG
(HE WALKS UP DEFIANTLY AND CONFRONTS DARRELL WHO 150 STRANG
TURNS TO HIM IN SURPRISE)
I THOUGHT I WOULD YUST GIVE HER SURPRISE. 506 VOYAGE
(JOYOUSLY) THIS IS A SURPRISE/ 444 WELDED
AT THE TOP, CAPE TURNS IN SURPRISE AT NOT FINDING 449 WELDED
HER.
(AS SHE SEES WHO IT IS--IN A RELIEVED TONE OF 450 WELDED
SURPRISE)
(WITH AN ASSUMED SURPRISE BUT WITH A GUILTY AIR, 451 WELDED

SURPRISED

(WITH SURPRISED EXCITEMENT) WELL, IF YOU DON'T 272 AHWILD
SOLEMNLY SWEAR YOU WON'T--
(HE LOOKS AT HIS HAT AS IF HE WERE SURPRISED AT 293 AHWILD
ITS EXISTENCE.
(SURPRISED) YOU'VE NOT SEEN HER IN FIFTEEN YEARS$ 9 ANNA
(SURPRISED AND PLEASED BY HIS EAGERNESS--WITH A 22 ANNA
SMILE)
(SURPRISED) WORK ON LAND, IS IT$ 37 ANNA
(SURPRISED) WHY, YES. 77 ANNA
(SURPRISED) NO, HE DIDN'T MENTION YOU, I CAN 138 BEYOND
REMEMBER.
(SURPRISED AND HORRIFIED) WHY, DAMN IT, THIS IS 155 BEYOND
FRIGHTFUL/
(SURPRISED) HAVE YOU REALLY, HONESTLY REACHED 161 BEYOND
THAT CONCLUSION$
(THEY ALL TURN AND LOOK UP AT HIM SURPRISED TO 462 CARIBE
HEAR HIM SPEAK.)
(SURPRISED) HELLO/ 473 CARIBE
(GIVES JOHN A SURPRISED GLANCE) 497 DAYS
(GIVES JOHN A SURPRISED, DISAPPROVING GLANCE) 499 DAYS
ELIOT ALSO LOOKS AT HIM, SURPRISED AND 501 DAYS
DISAPPROVING OF THIS TAUNT.
(SURPRISED) WHAR AIR YE GOIN'$ 238 DESIRE
SURPRISED) 263 DESIRE
(SURPRISED) BETTER'N YOUR PA$ 495 DIFRNT
(SURPRISED) DID YOU KNOW ABOUT IT BEFORE JACK-- 508 DIFRNT

SURPRISED

SURPRISED (CONT'D.)
(TOO EXCITED TO BE SURPRISED) 548 DIFRNT
(SURPRISED--SIZING HER UP PUZZLEDLY) 24 ELECTR
I DON'T WONDER YOU'RE SURPRISED/ 32 ELECTR
AND I WASN'T SURPRISED NEITHER. 70 ELECTR
(SURPRISED) WHY, NO. 118 ELECTR
(SURPRISED) YOU STOPPED AT THE ISLANDS$ 144 ELECTR
(SURPRISED) THE ONE TIME I RAN INTO HIM, I 275 GGBROW
THOUGHT HE TOLD ME
(SURPRISED) GOOD-BY. 323 GGBROW
(SURPRISED BUT ADMIRINGLY) YUH MEAN TC SAY YUH 248 HA APE
ALWAYS RUN WIDE OPEN--LIKE DIS$
(WITH A SURPRISED, REFLECTIVE AIR.) 21 HUGHIE
DON'T BE SURPRISED. 37 HUGHIE
(SURPRISED AND RESENTFUL) HE DID, DID HE$ 583 ICEMAN
MY RELATIONS VILL SO SURPRISED BE. 605 ICEMAN
I WAS SURE SURPRISED WHEN SHE GAVE ME THE TEN 608 ICEMAN
SPOT.
(THEN, AS HE SEES THEY ARE SURPRISED AT HIS 636 ICEMAN
VEHEMENCE, HE ADDS HASTILY)
I WOULDN'T BE SURPRISED. 643 ICEMAN
(HE PAUSES STARTLEDLY, SURPRISED AT HIMSELF--THEN 726 ICEMAN
WITH A
(SURPRISED AND A BIT NETTLED TO HAVE TO SHARE HIS 519 INZONE
STORY WITH ANYONE)
(SURPRISED-- 332 LAZARU
BUT I DON'T KNOW WHY I SHOULD BE SURPRISED. 97 MANSNS
(HE TURNS TO STARE AT HER IN SURPRISED CONFUSION. 151 MANSNS
NO ONE IS SURPRISED EXCEPT THE TWO POLOS WHO GET 368 MARCOM
UP TO GAPE AT HIM
(SURPRISED, STARES AT HIM) WHAT ABOUT THE FARM$ 31 MISBEG
(GIVES HER A STRANGE SURPRISED LOOK--MOCKINGLY) 51 MISBEG
(VAGUELY SURPRISED BY HER TONE) 106 MISBEG
(SURPRISED) HELLO/ 112 MISBEG
(GLANCES UP AT HER, SURPRISED--THEN SHRUGS HIS 136 MISBEG
SHOULDERS)
(HE DRINKS--THEN LOOKS PLEASANTLY SURPRISED) 173 MISBEG
(VAGUELY SURPRISED--SPEAKS RAPIDLY AGAIN.) 82 POET
(CREGAN IS SURPRISED AND PLEASED BY THE WARMTH OF 92 POET
HIS WELCOME.
MELODY, IN HIS TURN, IS SURPRISED. 116 POET
HE WAS SURPRISED TO HEAR ME TALKIN' OF MONEY. 585 ROPE
(SURPRISED) OVER SIXTY-FIVE, ISN'T SHE$ 74 STRANG
(SURPRISED) YOU'RE SAILING$ 106 STRANG
(SURPRISED) YOUR UNCLE NED$ 154 STRANG
(SURPRISED) UH, COME NOW, NINA, AREN'T YOU BEING 155 STRANG
A LITTLE HARD ON NED$
(SURPRISED AND ASHAMED) I'LL LEAVE IT HERE, THEN.474 WELDED
SURPRISING
(HIS VOICE WITH SURPRISING SUDDENNESS TAKES ON A 545 DAYS
SAVAGE VINDICTIVE QUALITY)
(WITH SURPRISING VINDICTIVENESS) 284 LAZARU
(JOSIE'S RIGHT ARM STRIKES WITH SURPRISING 4 MISBEG
SWIFTNESS AND HER BIG HAND LANDS ON
HE SPEAKS WITH A SURPRISING SAD GENTLENESS) 17 MISBEG
HER VOICE TREMBLES WITH SURPRISING MEEKNESS) 121 MISBEG
SURPRISINGLY
IN FACT, HE LOOKS SURPRISINGLY HEALTHY. 269 AHWILD
IN SPITE OF HER TWO HUNDRED AND MORE POUNDS SHE IS506 DIFRNT
SURPRISINGLY ACTIVE.
(HE BEGINS TO SING IN A SURPRISINGLY GOOD TENOR 103 ELECTR
VOICE.
SHE NOW HAS THE LOOK OF A SURPRISINGLY YOUTHFUL 95 MANSNS
GRANDMOTHER.
MARK IS SURPRISINGLY QUICK AT FIGURES. 360 MARCOM
SURRENDER
HE SEES CLEARLY BY THE LIGHT OF REASON THE 545 DAYS
DEGRADATION OF HIS PITIABLE SURRENDER
WHEN I SURRENDER ALL TO THEE--WHEN I HAVE FORGIVEN565 DAYS
THEE--
YOU AIN'T GOIN' TO GIT AMOS DRUNK TONIGHT, 7 ELECTR
SURRENDER OR NO SURRENDER/.
THE FIRST TIME WAS CELEBRATIN' LEE'S SURRENDER 44 ELECTR
I CAME HOME TO SURRENDER TO YOU--WHAT'S INSIDE ME. 95 ELECTR
HE HAD TO SURRENDER/ 677 ICEMAN
YOU DO NOT SURRENDER TO HER INFLUENCE AGAIN. 114 MANSNS
AND SHE IS GOOD NOW, NOT EVIL--SHE LOVES ME--AND 129 MANSNS
SO I CAN SURRENDER AND BE HERS-
SO YOU WON'T SURRENDER, EH$ 395 MARCOM
WE DIE BUT WE NEVER SURRENDER/ 395 MARCOM
SURRENDERED
(SCORNFULLY) SO HE WEAKLY SURRENDERED-- 535 DAYS
SURRENDERING
(FAINTLY, AT LAST SURRENDERING. 566 DAYS
WHAT DO YOU THINK OF THE NEWS OF LEE SURRENDERING, 21 ELECTR
CAPTAINS
AND SURRENDERING HIMSELF LIKE A COMMANDER AGAINST 55 ELECTR
HOPELESS ODDS)
SURREPTITIOUS
(THEN WARNINGLY, MAKING A SURREPTITIOUS SIGNAL AS 45 ELECTR
HE SEES THE FRONT DOOR OPENING
SURREPTITIOUSLY
(GLANCES AT HER UNEASILY, PEEKS SURREPTITIOUSLY AT255 AHWILD
HIS WATCH--
(THE TWO ELDER ARE SURREPTITIOUSLY SNATCHING AT 419 MARCOM
THE COINS
(HAS BEEN LOOKING AT MARSDEN SURREPTITIOUSLY OVER 113 STRANG
HIS PAPER)
SURROUND
WHICH SURROUND THE HOUSE, A HEAVILY WOODED RIDGE 2 ELECTR
IN THE BACKGROUND.
(THEY SURROUND HIM, THROW OVER HIS SHOULDERS AND 307 LAZARU
HEAD THE FINELY DRESSED HIDE OF
A SQUAD OF THE GUARD SURROUND THE DAIS, COMMANDED 337 LAZARU
BY FLAVIUS.)
SURROUNDED
(SMILING) THEN, FROM ALL REPORTS, WE SEEM TO BE 292 AHWILD
COMPLETELY SURROUNDED BY LOVE/

SURROUNDED (CONT'D.)
HE GOT SURROUNDED AT POAKDEBERG/ 677 ICEMAN
SURROUNDING
THE AURA OF LIGHTS SURROUNDING HIS BODY SEEMING TO312 LAZARU
GLOW MORE BRIGHTLY THAN EVER.
SURROUNDING--THREATENING--ME-- 125 MANSNS
SURROUNDINGS
HIS SPIRIT STILL TOO EXALTED TO BE CONSCIOUS OF 292 AHWILD
HIS SURROUNDINGS.
FORGETFUL FOR A MOMENT OF HIS SURROUNDINGS AND 192 EJONES
REALLY BELIEVING IT IS A LIVING
HE SEEMS OBLIVIOUS TO HIS SURROUNDINGS. 95 POET
PUZZLED GLANCE AS IF HE WERE AWARE OF HIS 471 WELDED
SURROUNDINGS FOR THE FIRST TIME.)
SURROUNDS
ON THE EDGE OF A NARROW BRICK-PAVED WALK WHICH 25 MANSNS
SURROUNDS A LITTLE OVAL POOL.
SURVEY
STOPPING EACH TIME TO SURVEY THE RESULT 249 AHWILD
CRITICALLY, BITING HER TONGUE.
AND SURVEY HER INSOLENTLY FROM HEAD TO TOE. 68 POET
SURVEYING
(SURVEYING HIM, ANGER COMING INTO HER EYES) 241 AHWILD
(SURVEYING RICHARD CONTEMPTUOUSLY) 246 AHWILD
(SURVEYING MILDRED'S HANDIWORK--SMILING) 250 AHWILD
(SURVEYING HIM JEERINGLY) WHY HAIN'T YE BEEN IN 254 DESIRE
T' DANCES
SURVEYS
(HE COMES NEARER THE TABLE AND SURVEYS IT. 217 AHWILD
(SURVEYS HIM APPRECIATIVELY) 218 AHWILD
(FINALLY SURVEYS THE TWO WORDS SHE HAS BEEN 249 AHWILD
WRITING AND IS SATISFIED WITH THEM)
(SURVEYS HIM OVER HIS GLASSES, NOT WITH 253 AHWILD
ENTHUSIASM--SHORTLY)
(AS CHUCK COMES FROM BEHIND THE BAR, ROCKY SURVEYS670 ICEMAN
HIM DERISIVELY)
(SURVEYS HIM DELIBERATELY, HIS LITTLE PIG EYES 56 MISBEG
GLEAMING WITH MALICE)
SHE SURVEYS HIM RESENTFULLY) 96 MISBEG
AND SURVEYS HIMSELF.) 43 POET
SURVIVAL
WITH THE OLD PATHETIC LIE OF SURVIVAL AFTER DEATH.544 DAYS
SURVIVE
BUT SOON WERE FORCED TO DETERIORATE IN ORDER TO 7 HUGHIE
SURVIVE.
MUST SURVIVE IN MY PETTINESS FOREVER/= 324 LAZARU
SURVIVED
HAVE SURVIVED THE RENOVATION AND SERVE TO 519 DIFRNT
EMPHASIZE IT ALL THE MORE BY CONTRAST.
SURVIVES
UNTIL ONLY ONE OF YOU SURVIVES/ 130 MANSNS
SO--IT STILL SURVIVES IN YOU. 477 WELDED
SUSANNAH
TO THE OLD TUNE OF =OH, SUSANNAH/= 224 DESIRE
SUSPECT
AND SOCIALISM, TOO, I SUSPECT, FROM SOME DIRE 193 AHWILD
DECLARATIONS HE'S MADE.
NAT, I SUSPECT--PLOT/ 227 AHWILD
(MOCKINGLY) I HOPE YOU DON'T SUSPECT SOME HIDDEN.495 DAYS
AND YOU'D BE THE LAST ONE HE'D EVER SUSPECT. 526 DAYS
THEY ALWAYS SUSPECT THE SEA. 23 ELECTR
THERE'LL BE NO REASON FOR HER TO SUSPECT. 40 ELECTR
(DULLY) BUT HOW CAN YOU DO IT--SO NO ONE WILL 40 ELECTR
SUSPECT$
(TAKEN ABACK) WHAT MAKES YOU THINK I SUSPECT YOU$ 51 ELECTR
NOW PLEASE TELL ME JUST WHAT IT IS YOU SUSPECT ME 51 ELECTR
OF$
WHO'D EVER SUSPECT--IT'S QUEER. 69 ELECTR
BUT DON'T YOU SEE HOW INSANE--TO SUSPECT--WHEN 77 ELECTR
DOCTOR BLAKE KNOWS HE DIED OF--/
(IN A QUICK WHISPER) DON'T LET HER KNOW YOU 100 ELECTR
SUSPECT HER.
SHE'D SUSPECT YOU WEREN'T GOING TO YOUR FATHER'S 108 ELECTR
NOW--
WE GOT IT IN BOSTON TO SEE WHOM THE POLICE WOULD 121 ELECTR
SUSPECT.
YOU SWEAR YOU'LL NEVER SUSPECT ME--OF ANYTHING$ 175 ELECTR
ARE YOU BEGINNING TO SUSPECT ME$ 175 ELECTR
SHE SAID SHE WOULDN'T GIVE A DAMN WHAT I DID 591 ICEMAN
EXCEPT SHE'D BEGUN TO SUSPECT I WAS
BECAUSE THEN I WON'T SUSPECT WHATEVER HE DID ABOUT643 ICEMAN
THE GREAT CAUSE.
IT MAKES ME FEEL YOU SUSPECT I MUST HAVE HATED 705 ICEMAN
YOU.
(PERSUASIVELY.) YOU'RE ALL WRONG TO SUSPECT 56 JOURNE
ANYTHING.
SHE CAN'T SUSPECT I'VE COME TO SPY ON HER. 78 JOURNE
YOU SUSPECT RIGHT NOW I'M THINKING TO MYSELF THAT 163 JOURNE
PAPA IS OLD AND CAN'T LAST
THE FOOLS OF ROMANS WILL NEVER SUSPECT HIM/ 300 LAZARU
(THEN WITH GRIM HUMOR) DEATH IN BED I SUSPECT, 303 LAZARU
THERE'S NOTHING TO SUSPECT/ 77 MANSNS
IT'S MEAN AND WRONG OF ME TO SUSPECT HER. 83 MANSNS
AND NO ONE WOULD EVER SUSPECT ANYTHING BUT NATURAL179 MANSNS
ILLNESS
(DRYLY) I SUSPECT SO. 402 MARCOM
BECAUSE IT'S SO ANCIENT NO ONE WOULD SUSPECT YOU'D 23 MISBEG
TRY IT.
I DON'T SUSPECT HIM. 34 MISBEG
YES, DON'T LET HIM SUSPECT IT, OR YOU WOULDN'T 99 MISBEG
FOOL HIM.
SO HE CAN'T SUSPECT YOU TOLD ME. 99 MISBEG
(BITTERLY.) I SUPPOSE YOU'RE BOUND TO SUSPECT-- 32 POET
ONE WOULD NEVER SUSPECT THAT SHE IS THE MIDDLE- 67 POET
AGED MOTHER OF TWO GROWN SONS.
SO HER HUSBAND WON'T SUSPECT SHE CAME HERE. 79 POET
BUT I SUSPECT THE WAR FOR INDEPENDENCE WAS MERELY 82 POET

SUSPECT (CONT'D.)

I SUSPECT YOU ARE STILL HOLDING AGAINST ME MY UNFORTUNATE BLUNDER — 90 POET

SHE WOULD BE BOUND TO SUSPECT THAT YOU MIGHT BE HIS MISTRESS. — 109 POET

DO YOU KNOW WHAT I'M INCLINED TO SUSPECT, DOCTOR$ — 38 STRANG
I SUSPECT SHE IS TERRIBLY LONELY ALL BY HERSELF IN — 50 STRANG THIS BIG HOUSE.

FOR FEAR HE MIGHT GET TO SUSPECT SOMETHING. — 61 STRANG
WHEN I REMEMBERED GORDON AND LOOKED AT HIS FATHER — 75 STRANG I HAD EITHER TO SUSPECT A

HE'LL NEVER SUSPECT ANYTHING/... — 75 STRANG
SO I SUSPECT... — 76 STRANG
WHAT DO YOU SUSPECT IS WRONG WITH THE PATIENT NOW, — 79 STRANG DOCTOR$

DOES HE SUSPECT$...) — 115 STRANG
DOES HE SUSPECT ABOUT THE BABY TOO$... — 117 STRANG
NEVER LET HIM SUSPECT ABOUT LITTLE GORDON....) — 119 STRANG
THE HAPPINESS I HAVE GIVEN HIM HAS MADE HIM TOO — 132 STRANG SURE OF HIMSELF EVER TO SUSPECT

OH, I DON'T MEAN I SUSPECT YOU--NOW-- — 458 WELDED
(WITH THE SAME WRY SMILE) WHILE I BEGIN TO — 469 WELDED SUSPECT THAT IN A WAY I'M LUCKY--

I WANT TO TELL YOU THAT TONIGHT--JOHN AND I-- — 484 WELDED NOTHING YOU MAY EVER SUSPECT--

SUSPECTED

YES, IT IS TRUE, IF YOU MUST KNOW, AND YOU'D NEVER227 AHWILD HAVE SUSPECTED IT,

AND SHE SUSPECTED MY GROWING DOUBTS AS TIME WENT — 561 CROSS ON.

I'VE SUSPECTED AT TIMES THAT UNDERNEATH HE WANTS--557 DAYS
IT'S ONLY SINCE YOU SUSPECTED WHO I WAS/ — 25 ELECTR
BUT I'VE SUSPECTED LATELY THAT WASN'T THE REAL REASON-- — 29 ELECTR

I'VE SUSPECTED SOMETHING--LATELY-- — 29 ELECTR
I'D NEVER HAVE SUSPECTED SHE HAD THAT MUCH FEELING 68 ELECTR IN HER.

AND YET YOU QUESTION ME AS IF YOU SUSPECTED ME, — 88 ELECTR TOO/

I NEVER REALLY SUSPECTED, OR I'D HAVE KILLED HIM--155 ELECTR AND YOU, TOO/

ORIN SUSPECTED I'D LUSTED WITH HIM/ — 177 ELECTR
YUH'D TINK HE SUSPECTED ME AND CHUCK — 631 ICEMAN
YUH'D TINK HE SUSPECTED CHUCK WASN'T GOIN' TO LAY 631 ICEMAN OFF PERIODICALS--

JAMIE SUSPECTED YOU'D CRY POORHOUSE TO HARDY AND — 144 JOURNE HE WORMED THE TRUTH OUT OF HIM.

ALWAYS SUSPECTED OF HOPING FOR THE WORST. — 163 JOURNE
HITHERTO MAN HAS ALWAYS SUSPECTED HIS LIFE, — 352 LAZARU
AS I HAVE SUSPECTED. — 115 MANSNS
I SUSPECTED A FLAW BUT YOU ARE PERFECT. — 380 MARCOM
I HAVE SUSPECTED HER LOVE FOR HIM FOR A LONG TIME.388 MARCOM
BUT ADMIRAL POLO SUSPECTED MY DEPARTURE — 424 MARCOM
I'VE OFTEN SUSPECTED YOU SNEAK OUT OF BED IN THE — 23 MISBEG NIGHT TO PICK YOUR OWN POCKETS.

BUT I NEVER SUSPECTED YOU WERE A WISE WOMAN TOO, — 149 POET
HE SUSPECTED BEFORE...) — 124 STRANG
(SITTING DOWN BESIDE HER) I SUSPECTED AS MUCH. — 197 STRANG

SUSPECTIN'

AFTER HIM TRYIN' TO STICK YOU IN THE BACK, AND — 488 CARDIF YOU NOT SUSPECTIN'.

SUSPECTING

STOP SUSPECTING ME/ PLEASE, DEAR/ YOU HURT ME/ — 47 JOURNE
YOU'RE AS BAD AS JAMIE, SUSPECTING EVERYONE/ — 85 JOURNE
YES, I SUPPOSE YOU CAN'T HELP SUSPECTING THAT. — 93 JOURNE
(RESENTFULLY) I WON'T HAVE YOU SUSPECTING JIM — 34 MISBEG WITHOUT ANY CAUSE, D'YOU HEAR ME/

AND YOU TRUSTING HIM LIKE A POOR SHEEP, AND NEVER — 99 MISBEG SUSPECTING--

SUSPECTS

VINNIE SUSPECTS ME OF HAVING POISONED YOUR FATHER/ 88 ELECTR
BUT SUSPECTS SHE'S BEING INSULTED/ — 134 JOURNE
YOU DO NOT KNOW HOW BITTERLY SARA SUSPECTS ME. — 39 MANSNS
BUT NINA SUSPECTS NOW THAT YOU--$ — 11 STRANG
HE SUSPECTS MY REVULSION... — 69 STRANG
I-- I DIDN'T KNOW--YOU SEEMED SO COLD--DAMN — 130 STRANG MARSDEN--HE SUSPECTS, DOESN'T HE$

HE SUSPECTS WHAT I KNOW--THAT I'VE ACTED LIKE A — 142 STRANG COWARD AND WEAKLING TOWARD HIM/

SUSPEND

ALL I ASK IS FOR YOU TO SUSPEND JUDGMENT AND GIVE 642 ICEMAN IT A CHANCE.

SUSPENDED

FROM THE MIDDLE OF THE CEILING A HANGING LAMP IS — 535 *ILE SUSPENDED.

SUSPENDED FROM THE MIDDLE OF THE CEILING AND — 210 AHWILD MANAGES TO TURN ONE LIGHT ON--

IN A FLY-SPECKED GILT CHANDELIER SUSPENDED FROM — 236 AHWILD THE MIDDLE OF THE CEILING.

SUSPENDED IN THE SKYLIGHT IS A SHIP'S COMPASS. — 109 ELECTR
THERE IS A SUSPENDED, WAITING SILENCE. — 711 ICEMAN
SHE WAS LEFT SUSPENDED. — 35 STRANG
THERE IS A CUMBERSOME HANGING LAMP SUSPENDED FROM — 48 STRANG CHAINS OVER THE EXACT CENTER

SUSPENDED IN THE MOVEMENT OF THE TIDE, I FEEL LIFE 92 STRANG MOVE IN ME.

SUSPENDED IN ME... — 92 STRANG

SUSPENDERS

A FAT-BELLIED FINALITY, AS DIGNIFIED AS THE — 313 GGBROW SUSPENDERS OF AN ASSEMBLYMAN/

SUSPENSE

(WHO HAS BEEN FIDGITING RESTLESSLY--UNABLE TO BEAR264 AHWILD THE SUSPENSE A MOMENT LONGER)

IN SUSPENSE BETWEEN SUSPICION AND HOPE) — 431 DYNAMO
(HE WAITS, HIS BODY STRAINED WITH SUSPENSE, — 480 DYNAMO
YOU'RE KEEPING US ALL IN SUSPENSE. — 624 ICEMAN
TO MAKE AN END OF SUSPENSE AND GAIN FORGETFULNESS 156 MANSNS AND PEACE AT ANY COST--

SUSPICION

(REGARDING HER BROTHER WITH SMILING SUSPICION) — 189 AHWILD
(HE STOPS, FEELING HIS WIFE'S EYES FIXED ON HIM, — 291 AHWILD WITH INDIGNANT SUSPICION.)

(WITH FRIGHTENED SUSPICION NOW) — 293 AHWILD
(THEN STRUCK BY SOME THOUGHT--LOOKS AT HIM WITH — 42 ANNA KEEN SUSPICION--

(WITH A DARK GLANCE OF SUSPICION AT HER) — 76 ANNA
THEY'RE LIABLE AS NOT TO SUSPICION IT WAS A WOMAN 103 BEYOND
I'D PLANNED TO SHIP ALONG,
(AFTER A PAUSE--A SUDDEN SUSPICION FORMING IN HER 138 BEYOND MIND)

(A SUDDEN, HORRIBLE SUSPICION ENTERING HIS MIND) — 155 BEYOND
SUSPICION WHICH MIGHT BE AROUSED BY WHAT HAS GONE 494 DAYS BEFORE.

THE OLE CRITTER'S LIABLE T' SUSPICION AN' COME — 245 DESIRE SNEAKIN' UP.

I'D NEVER SUSPICION SECH WEAKNESS FROM A BOY LIKE 249 DESIRE YEW.

CABOT PEERS AT HIM WITH RENEWED SUSPICION) — 254 DESIRE
AN' THEY'LL ALL B'LIEVE ME, FUR THEY SUSPICION — 267 DESIRE EVERYTHIN' WE'VE DONE.

IN SUSPENSE BETWEEN SUSPICION AND HOPE) — 431 DYNAMO
(HAS GLANCED AT HER WITH SUSPICION) — 432 DYNAMO
THAT'S NOT FIRST GIVE ME A SUSPICION OF WOT WAS — 182 EJONES UP.

FROM SOME SUSPICION THAT SHE KNOWS IS IN HIS MIND) 18 ELECTR
(STARES AT HER WITH COLD SUSPICION.) — 34 ELECTR
AND THE SOONER I DO IT THE LESS SUSPICION — 41 ELECTR THERE'LL BE/

YOU--(SHE STOPS AND STARES AT HER MOTHER WITH A — 63 ELECTR HORRIFIED SUSPICION--

THE LOOK OF SUSPICION CHANGING TO A DREADFUL, — 64 ELECTR HORRIFIED CERTAINTY.

BUT I HAVE A STRONG SUSPICION IT WAS LOVE KILLED — 71 ELECTR EZRA/

(MELTING, ALL HIS SUSPICION FORGOTTEN) — 76 ELECTR
SURELY YOU CAN'T STILL HAVE THAT INSANE — 77 ELECTR SUSPICION--THAT I--

ORIN GIVES HIS MOTHER A SIDELONG GLANCE OF UNEASY — 83 ELECTR SUSPICION.

(THE LOOK OF SUSPICION AGAIN COMES TO ORIN'S EYES. 84 ELECTR
(THICKLY, TRYING TO FIGHT BACK HIS JEALOUS — 98 ELECTR SUSPICION)

(IN A TONE OF AWAKENING SUSPICION) — 98 ELECTR
IT WOULD START SUSPICION-- — 111 ELECTR
SO THERE'LL BE NO SUSPICION ABOUT US. — 113 ELECTR
NOW AFTER IT'S ALL PAST AND FORGOTTEN--WHEN THERE 152 ELECTR ISN'T THE SLIGHTEST SUSPICION--

SO THERE WILL BE NO SUSPICION ON YOU/ — 155 ELECTR
(TURNS ON HIM WITH FUMING SUSPICION) — 605 ICEMAN
TRUCULENT SWAGGER AND HIS GOOD-NATURED FACE IS SE636 ICEMAN IN SULLEN SUSPICION.)

(LOOKS AT HIM WITH FRIGHTENED SUSPICION) — 656 ICEMAN
DO YOU KNOW, LARRY, I ONCE HAD A SNEAKING — 667 ICEMAN SUSPICION THAT MAYBE

BUT A SUSPICION GREW AFTERWARDS INTO A CONVICTION 677 ICEMAN AMONG THE BOERS

IF YOU'D KNOWN HER AT ALL, YOU'D NEVER GET SUCH A 693 ICEMAN CRAZY SUSPICION.

THEY PUSH HIS ARMS AWAY, REGARDING HIM WITH AMAZED725 ICEMAN SUSPICION.)

A PUZZLED EXPRESSION COMES OVER HIS FACE, FOLLOWED$13 INZONE BY ONE OF SUSPICION.

HE IS SEEMINGLY UNAWARE OF THE DARK GLANCES OF — 522 INZONE SUSPICION

LIVING IN THIS ATMOSPHERE OF CONSTANT SUSPICION, — 46 JOURNE
(HE GIVES HER AN INSTINCTIVE LOOK OF SUSPICION-- — 49 JOURNE
ALL I'VE FELT WAS DISTRUST AND SPYING AND — 69 JOURNE SUSPICION.

THEN HE STARES AT HIS FATHER'S FACE WITH UNEASY — 90 JOURNE SUSPICION.)

TYRONE SCOWLS AND LOOKS AT HIS WIFE WITH SHARP — 116 JOURNE SUSPICION--ROUGHLY.)

WEAKNESS OF THOUGHT, OR WATCHING ONE ANOTHER WITH289 LAZARU SUSPICION/

GLARE OUT WITH A SHIFTY FEVERISH SUSPICION AT — 299 LAZARU EVERYONE.

A NOBLE LOVE ABOVE SUSPICION AND DISTRUST/ — 352 LAZARU
BUT I'VE HAD A DARK SUSPICION FOR SOME TIME. — 46 MANSNS
(GLANCING FROM ONE TO THE OTHER--WITH A TRACE OF — 61 MANSNS SUSPICION.)

(SHE GIVES HIM A LOOK OF FRIGHTENED SUSPICION.) — 80 MANSNS
I BITTERLY RESENT YOUR INTRUDING HERE AND — 98 MANSNS ATTEMPTING TO CREATE SUSPICION

THE TWO WOMEN TURN TO STARE AT HIM, WITH A — 119 MANSNS STIRRING OF SUSPICION AND RESENTMENT.

I HAVE A SUSPICION, SARA, — 131 MANSNS
I HAVE THE SAME SUSPICION MYSELF, DEBORAH. — 131 MANSNS
HOW CAN I HAVE SUCH A MAD SUSPICION$ — 163 MANSNS
(SHE PAUSES--THEN WITH INCREASING BITTERNESS AND — 163 MANSNS SUSPICION.)

SECURITY OR FAITH OR LOVE BUT ONLY DANGER AND — 184 MANSNS SUSPICION AND DEVOURING GREED/

WITH HORRIFIED SUSPICION AND SHE GRABS HER BY THE 193 MANSNS ARM AND STAMMERS.)

MY HIDEOUS SUSPICION IS THAT GOD IS ONLY AN — 426 MARCOM INFINITE, INSANE ENERGY

(WITH SHARP SUSPICION) I COULD, — 14 MISBEG
WHICH OUGHT TO INSPIRE GRATITUDE IN YOU AND NOT — 109 POET SUSPICION.

(WITH SUDDEN JEALOUS SUSPICION) — 50 STRANG
(LOOKING AFTER HIM WITH ANGER MIXED WITH ALARMED — 75 STRANG SUSPICION AND SURPRISE)

GOT RID OF EVEN THAT SLIGHT SUSPICION... — 78 STRANG
MARSDEN FOLLOWS HIM, GLARING AT HIS BACK WITH — 124 STRANG ENMITY AND SUSPICION.

CHANCE TO AVERT SUSPICION... — 125 STRANG

SUSPICION

SUSPICION (CONT'D.)
(WITH SUDDEN DESPAIRING SUSPICION) 129 STRANG

SUSPICIONED
LIKE I SUSPICIONED AT FUST--T' SWALLER IT ALL--AN'255 DESIRE
ME, TOO.../
ANY MEBBE I SUSPICIONED IT ALL ALONG. 264 DESIRE
I MUST'VE SUSPICIONED--SOMETHIN'. 264 DESIRE
BUT HE NEVER SUSPICIONED NOTHING. 20 HUGHIE

SUSPICIONS
WHEN I SLEEPS, DEY SNEAKS A SLEEP, TOO, AND I 181 EJONES
PRETENDS I NEVER SUSPICIONS IT.
STOP NAGGING AT ME WITH YOUR CRAZY SUSPICIONS/ 60 ELECTR
(THEN QUICKLY) BUT I WAS GOING TO GIVE YOU AN 87 ELECTR
EXAMPLE OF HER INSANE SUSPICIONS
THAT HIS SUSPICIONS ARE JUSTIFIED. 58 JOURNE
BUT IF HIS SUSPICIONS ARE AROUSED HER TENDERNESS 58 JOURNE
MAKES HIM RENOUNCE THEM AND HE
AND SEEMED SUCH A DEVOUT GIRL THAT HE FORGOT HIS 39 MISBEG
SUSPICIONS.
BE GOD, I HAD MY SUSPICIONS, AT LEAST, 83 MISBEG

SUSPICIOUS
(EVASIVE AND SUSPICIOUS) WHY$ 44 ANNA
BUT PUZZLED AND SUSPICIOUS) 46 ANNA
(STILL SUSPICIOUS OF HIM) WELL, I'LL TAKE CARE OF 67 ANNA
THIS FOR A WHILE,
AND I WAS STILL YOUR SUSPICIOUS GUARDIAN. 505 DAYS
(FORCING A SMILE) IS THAT THE SUSPICIOUS GUARDIAN506 DAYS
LOOKS
BUT THIS FELLOW WHO WAS ENGAGED TO HER GOT 440 DYNAMO
SUSPICIOUS AND ONE NIGHT HE SNEAKED
IN MANNER HE IS SHREWD, SUSPICIOUS, EVASIVE. 175 EJONES
DON'T YOU KNOW I MADE HIM FLIRT WITH YOU, SO YOU 34 ELECTR
WOULDN'T BE SUSPICIOUS
ONLY ENOUGH SO THEY'D BE SUSPICIOUS AND WATCH YOU 35 ELECTR
TOO.
(NOW JEALOUS AND SUSPICIOUS OF HIS DAUGHTER) 50 ELECTR
BENEATH THE SEARCHING SUSPICIOUS GLANCE MANNION NOW 50 ELECTR
DIRECTS AT HER.)
NO--IT WAS YOUR FAULT--YOU MADE HIM SUSPICIOUS-- 63 ELECTR
HE RELEASES HER HAND AND STARES AT HER, MORBIDLY 86 ELECTR
SUSPICIOUS)
DEEP IN SUSPICIOUS BROODING. 93 ELECTR
HE LOOKS AROUND HIM QUICKLY WITH AN UNEASY 104 ELECTR
SUSPICIOUS AIR.
THEY LOOK SUSPICIOUS AND AFRAID OF LIFE NOW/ 175 ELECTR
(THEN SUSPICIOUS IN SPITE OF HIMSELF) 176 ELECTR
(MADE MORE UNEASY AND SUSPICIOUS BY THIS) 176 ELECTR
(THEN MADE A BIT RESENTFUL BY THE SUSPICIOUS 247 HA APE
GLANCES FROM ALL SIDES)
(ALERT AND SUSPICIOUS BUT WITH AN EASY LAUGH) 247 HA APE
(LARRY GIVES HIM AN UNEASY SUSPICIOUS GLANCE, THEN596 ICEMAN
LOOKS AWAY.
(LARRY GIVES HIM A SUSPICIOUS GLANCE, THEN LOOKS 625 ICEMAN
HASTILY AWAY.)
HAS REVERTED TO UNEASY, SUSPICIOUS DEFENSIVENESS.1059 ICEMAN
(INSTANTLY SUSPICIOUS AND ANGRY) 671 ICEMAN
WHO GIVES HIM A SCOWLING, SUSPICIOUS GLANCE AND 674 ICEMAN
THEN IGNORES HIM.
(FLASHES HIM A SUSPICIOUS GLANCE. 722 ICEMAN
I CAN'T HELP BEING SUSPICIOUS. ANY MORE THAN YOU 37 JOURNE
CAN.
SHE GIVES A QUICK, SUSPICIOUS GLANCE FROM ONE TO 39 JOURNE
THE OTHER.
WHY ARE YOU SO SUSPICIOUS ALL OF A SUDDEN$ 45 JOURNE
I GUESS I'M A DAMNED SUSPICIOUS LOUSE. 58 JOURNE
YOU'RE WELCOME TO COME UP AND WATCH ME IF YOU'RE 75 JOURNE
SO SUSPICIOUS.
SARA SUSPICIOUS, PUZZLED.) 53 MANSNS
(THEN SUDDENLY SUSPICIOUS.) WAIT/ 55 MANSNS
YOUR BODY FELT SWINDLED AND IT MADE YOU 80 MANSNS
SUSPICIOUS, I SUPPOSE.
UNTIL NOTHING IS WHAT IT SEEMS TO BE, AND WE ALL 82 MANSNS
GET SUSPICIOUS OF EACH OTHER.
WHY, WHAT A MEAN SUSPICIOUS THOUGHT--ABOUT YOUR 109 MANSNS
POOR DEVOTED MOTHER, DEAR/
EACH SNEAKS A SUSPICIOUS, PROBING GLANCE AT THE 136 MANSNS
OTHER.
BUT THAT'S IN THE CITY WHERE HE'S SUSPICIOUS. 21 MISBEG
DON'T BE SO SUSPICIOUS. 26 MISBEG
HE WAS A BIT SUSPICIOUS AT FIRST, BUT DUTCH 39 MISBEG
MAISIE--HER PROFESSIONAL NAME--
I'M BECOMING SUSPICIOUS. 66 MISBEG
I CAN'T SNEAK AWAY OR HE'D BE SUSPICIOUS. 99 MISBEG
IF YOU'RE SUSPICIOUS I'M TRYING TO GET YOU 116 MISBEG
SOUSED--WELL, HERE GOES.
SARA FOLLOWS HER, HER EXPRESSION CONFUSED, 85 POET
SUSPICIOUS.
SHE WARNED HIM A SUDDEN WEDDING WOULD LOOK 110 POET
DAMNABLY SUSPICIOUS.
SHE NOTICES HIM STARING AT HER AND GIVES HIM A 118 POET
RESENTFUL, SUSPICIOUS GLANCE.
FIRST LIVED TOGETHER--JEALOUS AND SUSPICIOUS OF 456 WELDED
EVERYTHING AND EVERYBODY/

SUSPICIOUSLY
(SHE SEARCHES HIS FACE SUSPICIOUSLY, 35 ANNA
(SUSPICIOUSLY) FIX WHAT UP$ 64 ANNA
LOOKING AT HIM SUSPICIOUSLY) 66 ANNA
(A PAUSE. THEY LOOK AT HIM SUSPICIOUSLY, AND HE 213 DESIRE
AT THEM)
(THEY LOOK SUSPICIOUSLY AT THE PAPER. 213 DESIRE
(SUSPICIOUSLY) WHAR WAS YE ALL NIGHT$ 214 DESIRE
THE TWO STARE AFTER HIM SUSPICIOUSLY. 215 DESIRE
(SUSPICIOUSLY) WHAT'S COME OVER YE$ 246 DESIRE
(STARES AT HIM SUSPICIOUSLY, TRYING TO MAKE HIM 254 DESIRE
OUT--A PAUSE--
AND SEVERAL BOOKS THAT LOOK SUSPICIOUSLY LIKE 493 DIFRNT
CHEAP NOVELS.

SUSPICIOUSLY (CONT'D.)
(SUSPICIOUSLY) CALEB DIDN'T SEEM WILLING TO TELL 501 DIFRNT
ME MUCH ABOUT THEIR TOUCHING.
(SUSPICIOUSLY) WHY SHOULD I NEED YOU NOW ANY 539 DIFRNT
MORE'N ANY OTHER TIMES
(SUSPICIOUSLY) WHAT IS IT$ 547 DIFRNT
HE SEES THE WOMAN AND STOPS TO WATCH HER 174 EJONES
SUSPICIOUSLY.
(SUSPICIOUSLY) WHY DON'T I$ 180 EJONES
(HE LOOKS AROUND HIM SUSPICIOUSLY) 193 EJONES
(AT SOMETHING IN HER TONE HE STARES AT HER 21 ELECTR
SUSPICIOUSLY.
(STILL SUSPICIOUSLY--WITH A TOUCH OF SCORN) 34 ELECTR
(CONTINUES TO STARE AT HER SUSPICIOUSLY--GRIMLY) 35 ELECTR
(SUSPICIOUSLY) IF WHAT$ 35 ELECTR
(AFTER A PAUSE)--SUSPICIOUSLY) 45 ELECTR
(THEN SUSPICIOUSLY) WHAT ARE YOU BEING SO 76 ELECTR
MYSTERIOUS ABOUT$
ORIN GLANCES AT HIS MOTHER SUSPICIOUSLY AND DRAWS 77 ELECTR
AWAY FROM HER.)
ORIN IS QUESTIONING HER SUSPICIOUSLY.) 80 ELECTR
(THEN STARING AT HER SUSPICIOUSLY AGAIN) 82 ELECTR
SUSPICIOUSLY) 96 ELECTR
(LOOKS FROM HER TO PETER SUSPICIOUSLY) 146 ELECTR
(GLANCES AT HIM SUSPICIOUSLY, BUT FORCES A CASUAL 150 ELECTR
AIR)
AND SITS ON THE SOFA AT RIGHT, ADOPTING A 161 ELECTR
SUSPICIOUSLY CARELESS ATTITUDE.
AWARE THAT LAVINIA IS WATCHING HER SUSPICIOUSLY-- 163 ELECTR
DEFIANTLY TO ORIN)
(THEN AS SHE DOESN'T ANSWER--MORE SUSPICIOUSLY) 177 ELECTR
(THEN SUSPICIOUSLY) IS IT--WHAT ORIN WROTE$ 177 ELECTR
HIS DROOP-LIDDED EYES SUSPICIOUSLY WARY OF 9 HUGHIE
NONEXISTENT EAVESDROPPERS.
HE TAKES IT, GLANCES AT IT SUSPICIOUSLY, 700 ICEMAN
GLANCING AROUND HIM SUSPICIOUSLY. 513 INZONE
(HE AND SCOTTY LOOK AT SMITTY SUSPICIOUSLY-- 514 INZONE
HARSHLY)
(SUSPICIOUSLY) WHAT D'YUH MEANS 516 INZONE
(SUDDENLY HE FROWNS AT JAMIE SUSPICIOUSLY.) 37 JOURNE
OF WATCHING SUSPICIOUSLY EACH CARD I LED TO MYSELF102 MANSNS
FROM ACROSS THE TABLE--
(STARES AT HER SUSPICIOUSLY.) 134 MANSNS
(SUSPICIOUSLY AGAIN--SNEERING AT HERSELF.) 163 MANSNS
(HAS STARED AT HER AT FIRST SUSPICIOUSLY-- 169 MANSNS
THEN SUDDENLY--SHARPLY AND SUSPICIOUSLY.) 192 MANSNS
(SHE REGARDS HIM SUSPICIOUSLY, BUT HIS FACE IS 22 MISBEG
BLANK.
(STARES GUILTILY AND TURNS TO STARE INTO HER 104 MISBEG
FACE--SUSPICIOUSLY)
(EYES HIM SUSPICIOUSLY--THEN SITS DOWN.) 46 POET
THEN SHE STARES AT HIM SUSPICIOUSLY, HER FACE 167 POET
HARDENING.)
(COMES INTO THE BARN (PEERING AROUND HIM 578 ROPE
SUSPICIOUSLY.
(AGITATED--THINKING SUSPICIOUSLY) 31 STRANG
(SUSPICIOUSLY) NO DOUBT. 31 STRANG
(THINKING SUSPICIOUSLY) (SHE DOESN'T WANT HER 36 STRANG
BACK...
(THINKING SUSPICIOUSLY) (IS THIS DOCTOR HER 38 STRANG
LOVER$...
(SUSPICIOUSLY--DRYLY NON-COMMITTAL) 38 STRANG
SUSPICIOUS) NEAT... 76 STRANG
THINKING SUSPICIOUSLY--MORBIDLY AGITATED) 99 STRANG
(THINKING SUSPICIOUSLY) (I LOOK OUT/... 103 STRANG
(THINKING SUSPICIOUSLY) (DOES HE ACTUALLY 122 STRANG
IMAGINE I...
THEY WATCH HIM SUSPICIOUSLY) 129 STRANG
(THINKING SUSPICIOUSLY) (WHAT A QUEER 188 STRANG
CREATURE/...
(SUDDENLY GLARING AT HER SUSPICIOUSLY) 487 WELDED

SUSTAINING
HIS TALL, THIN BODY STOOPS AS IF A PART OF ITS 73 STRANG
SUSTAINING WILL HAD BEEN REMOVED.

SUTINLY
AN' I SUTINLY HOPES YOU AIN'T BLISTERIN' NONE. 188 EJONES

SVALLOW
AND DAT OLE DAVIL, SEA, SOONER, LATER SHE SVALLOW 28 ANNA
DEM UP.

SVEAR
AY SVEAR TO GOD, AY NEVER TANK DAT/ 42 ANNA
AY SVEAR/ 47 ANNA

SVEDEN
IN SVEDEN FIVE YEAR OLD. 9 ANNA
SHE GAT TIRED VAIT ALL TIME SVEDEN FOR ME VEN AY 9 ANNA
DON'T NEVER COME.
AY DUN'T KNOW, ANNA, VHY AY NEVER COME HOME SVEDEN 21 ANNA
IN OLD YEAR.
GO SOUTH AMERICA, GO AUSTRALIA, GO ABOARD SHIP 21 ANNA
SAIL FOR SVEDEN.
AY NEVER COME HOME ONLY FEW TIMES VEN YOU VAS KIT 21 ANNA
IN SVEDEN.
ALL MEN IN OUR VILLAGE ON COAST, SVEDEN, GO TO 27 ANNA
SEA.

SVEDISH
YOU KNOW DAT SVEDISH WORDS 24 ANNA

SVEET
HE'S SAILING BACK TO HOME, SVEET HOME/ 676 ICEMAN

SVINE
IRISH SVINE, YOU/ 49 ANNA
THAT BOURGEOIS SVINE, HICKEY/ 634 ICEMAN
CAPITALIST SVINE/ 727 ICEMAN

SWAB
PLAY US A DANCE, YE SQUARE-HEAD SWAB/ 470 CARIBE
LOOK HERE, YE MURDHERIN' SWAB. 525 INZONE
D'YOU HEAR THE LADY TALKIN' TO YE, YE ROOSHUN 500 VOYAGE
SWAB$
IRISH WHISKEY, YE SWAB. 503 VOYAGE

SWABS

SWABS
(TURNS TO HER) A TERRIBLE END FOR THE LIKE OF 36 ANNA
THEM SWABS DOES LIVE ON LAND,
SHRIVELED SWABS DOES BE WORKING IN CITIES 48 ANNA

SWAG
ONE OF THE KINGS OF OUR REPUBLIC BY DIVINE RIGHT 47 MISBEG
OF INHERITED SWAG.

SWAGGER
TO THE ROAD WITH A GRAND SWAGGER OF IGNORING HER 228 DESIRE
EXISTENCE.
(WITH A SWAGGER AND A COLD SMILE ON HIS LIPS HE 459 DYNAMO
WALKS THROUGH THE GAP JUST AS
(WITH A GRIN AND A SWAGGER) I'M A CHIP OFFEN DE 234 HA APE
OLD BLOCK, GET ME?
TRUCULENT SWAGGER AND HIS GOOD-NATURED FACE IS SET636 ICEMAN
IN SULLEN SUSPICION.)
AND HIS BEARING HAS A FORCED SWAGGER OF CONSCIOUS 675 ICEMAN
PHYSICAL STRENGTH.
(HE WALKS TO THE DOOR WITH A CARELESS SWAGGER AND 721 ICEMAN
DISAPPEARS IN THE HALL.

SWAGGERING
(SWAGGERING ABOUT AGAIN) IF I WAS ONLY SURE HE 545 DIFRNT
WASN'T STALLIN'/
HE TURNS AND LOOKS AT HER FOR A MOMENT--THEN WITH 457 DYNAMO
A SWAGGERING IMPUDENCE.)
UP THE SIDE STREET YANK AND LONG COME SWAGGERING. 233 HA APE
THEY HESITATE AND STAND TOGETHER AT THE CORNER, 233 HA APE
SWAGGERING.

SWAGGERS
(HE SWAGGERS ABOUT THE ROOM--FINALLY STOPPING 545 DIFRNT
BESIDE HER.
(HE SWAGGERS AWAY AND DELIBERATELY LURCHES INTO A 237 HA APE
TOP-HATTED GENTLEMAN.
(HE SWAGGERS OUT THROUGH THE SWINGING DOORS.) 673 ICEMAN

SWAIN
I MUST SAY YOU TREAT YOUR ONE DEVOTED SWAIN PRETTY 16 ELECTR
RUDELY.

SMALLER
LET'S TAKE A SMALLER. 217 DESIRE
YE'RE AIMIN' T' SMALLER UP EVERYTHIN' AN' MAKE IT 229 DESIRE
YOUNG.
(RESENTFULLY) I KNOWED WELL IT WAS ON'Y PART O' 240 DESIRE
YER PLAN T' SMALLER EVERYTHIN'/
LIKE I SUSPICIONED AT FUST--T' SMALLER IT ALL--AN'*255 DESIRE
ME, TOO.../
'AVE WE GOT TER SMALLER 'ER HINSULTS LIKE DOGS$ 228 HA APE

SWALLEYED
MY BELLY FEELS LOIKE I'D SWALLEYED A DOZEN RIVETS 480 CARDIF
AT THE THOUGHT AV UT/

SWALLOW
(TAKES A SWALLOW OF WATER-- 62 ELECTR
(BUT HE PUTS THE JUG TO HIS LIPS AND TAKES AN 131 ELECTR
ENORMOUS SWALLOW.)
(HE TAKES A LONG SWALLOW FROM HIS BOTTLE. 213 HA APE
HE CAN'T BREATHE AND SWALLOW COAL DUST, BUT I KIN,215 HA APE
SEES
(HE TAKES A LARGE SWALLOW. 593 ROPE
HE PICKS UP THE BOTTLE AND TAKES A LONG SWALLOW. 597 ROPE
NICK TAKES A SWALLOW OF HIS BEER 497 VOYAGE

SWALLOWED
YOU'VE SWALLOWED THE ANCHOR. 48 ANNA
IS SWALLOWED AT ONE GULP LIKE A WHINING GNAT BY 358 LAZARU
THE CRETIN'S SILENCE OF

SWALLOWING
(SWALLOWING HARD--IN A HOARSE WHISPER, AS IF HE 551 'ILE
HAD DIFFICULTY IN SPEAKING)
(AFTER SWALLOWING HARD, SUDDENLY BLURTS OUT) 257 AHWILD
(SWALLOWING HARD, LOOKS QUICKLY FROM ONE TO THE 99 BEYOND
OTHER OF THEM--
(SWALLOWING HARD--CHOKINGLY) 568 CROSS
SHE'D HATE ME FOR SWALLOWING MY PRIDE AFTER HE'S 68 STRANG
NEVER BEEN TO SEE US...
SWALLOWING HARD SEVERAL TIMES AS IF HE WERE 472 WELDED
STRIVING TO GET CONTROL OF HIS

SWALLOWS
AS SID SWALLOWS HARD AND IS ABOUT TO BREAK INTO 257 AHWILD
FURTHER SPEECH,
AND SWALLOWS AS IF AN ACRID TASTE HAD COME INTO 297 AHWILD
HIS MOUTH--
HE SWALLOWS PAINFULLY SEVERAL TIMES--FORCES A WEAK268 DESIRE
SMILE AT LAST)
(HE GIVES HER HAND A FINAL SHAKE--SWALLOWS HARD-- 264 GGBROW
THEN MANFULLY)
GULPS DOWN THE WHISKEY IN BIG SWALLOWS.) 582 ICEMAN
(THE SWALLOWS AS IF HE WERE STRANGLING AND TEARS 143 MANSNS
HIS EYES FROM HERS--STAMMERS.)
(SHE SWALLOWS HARD, CATCHING HER BREATH) 18 STRANG
(THE SWALLOWS HARD AS IF HE WERE CHOKING BACK A 92 STRANG
SOB--THEN SAVAGELY)
HE SWALLOWS HALF HIS GLASS OF GINGER BEER AND 507 VOYAGE
MAKES A WRY FACE.)

SWAM
WE SWAM AND SWAM AND WERE PRETTY EVENLY MATCHED. 230 AHWILD
WHEN SAINT PATRICK DROVE THE SNAKES OUT OF IRELAND718 ICEMAN
THEY SWAM TO NEW YORK AND
WAS IT NOT YOU WHO SWAM TO ME AS I WAS DROWNINGS 411 MARCOM

SWAMPED
FLASH, SWAMPED BY A PITYING LOVE FOR HIM. 258 AHWILD

SWANK
I SUPPOSE YOU'LL SAY AS THAT SWANK ABOUT THE 178 EJONES
SILVER BULLET AIN'T LUCK--
BLIMEY, WASN'T THAT SWANK FOR YER--AND PLAIN, FAT-178 EJONES
'EADED LUCK$

SWAP
BUT YE KIN RIDE ON A BOAT IF YE'LL SWAP. 214 DESIRE
WANTIN' TO SWAP FOR TERBACCER AND OTHER TRADIN' 502 DIFRNT
STUFF WITH STRAW MATS AND

SWAPPED
LITTLE CRITTER--YE MUST'VE SWAPPED YER SOUL T' 262 DESIRE
HELL/
(EMOTIONLESSLY) I SWAPPED IT T' SIM AN' PETER FUR268 DESIRE
THEIR SHARE O' THE FARM--

SWAPPING
JOKING AND LAUGHING AND SINGING AND SWAPPING LIES.715 ICEMAN

SWAR
I SWAR IT/ 235 DESIRE

SWARTHY
HE HAS A BIG AQUILINE NOSE, BUSHY EYEBROWS, 21 ELECTR
SWARTHY COMPLEXION, HAZEL EYES.
THE SAME AQUILINE NOSE, HEAVY EYEBROWS, SWARTHY 73 ELECTR
COMPLEXION.
BUT HIS BODY IS THIN AND HIS SWARTHY COMPLEXION 73 ELECTR
SALLOW.
HIS HAGGARD SWARTHY FACE IS SET IN A BLANK 138 ELECTR
LIFELESS EXPRESSION.)
WITH A FLAT, SWARTHY FACE AND BEADY EYES. 577 ICEMAN
WITH A FAT, AMIABLE, SWARTHY FACE. 615 ICEMAN
A LONG YANKEE FACE, WITH INDIAN RESEMBLANCES, 4 MANSNS
SWARTHY, WITH A BIG STRAIGHT NOSE.
HER OLIVE COMPLEXION HAS TURNED A DISPLEASING 27 MANSNS
SWARTHY COLOR.

SWATE
THAT'D BE A SWATE MATCH, SURELY/ 48 ANNA
TWO SWATE LITTLE SLIPS AV THINGS, NEAR AS WHITE AS462 CARIBE
YOU AN' ME ARE, FOR THAT
IT PUT THE TOUCH OF HOME, SWATE HOME IN THE 230 HA APE
STOKEHOLE.

SWAY
THEIR BODIES SWAY LIMPLY, NERVELESSLY, 571 CROSS
THE FIGURES SWAY UP AFTER HIM.) 572 CROSS
THEN THEYEN THEY BEGIN TO SWAY SLOWLY FORWARD 199 EJONES
TOWARD EACH OTHER AND BACK AGAIN I
THEIR FEET MOVE, THEIR BODIES SWAY, 286 LAZARU
AND BY THE CHORUS WHO SWAY RHYTHMICALLY 436 MARCOM

SWAYING
HER BODY SWAYING A LITTLE FROM SIDE TO SIDE TO THE552 'ILE
RHYTHM OF THE HYMN.
SWAYING A LITTLE, BLINKING HIS EYES IN THE LIGHT. 260 AHWILD
(THEN WITH A TRACE OF SYMPATHY, AS SHE NOTICES HIM 32 ANNA
SWAYING FROM WEAKNESS)
AT THE FOOT OF IT HORNE PUTS A SWAYING HAND ON HIS572 CROSS
SHOULDER
HE STANDS SWAYING TOWARD HER HELPLESSLY.) 240 DESIRE
(SHE STOPS AT THE DOOR WEAKLY, SWAYING, ABOUT TO 262 DESIRE
FALL)
(HE BEGINS TO HUM, SWAYING HIS BODY-- 474 DYNAMO
SWAYING BACK AND FORTH. 199 EJONES
(HER STRENGTH GONE--SWAYING WEAKLY) 63 ELECTR
(HE STANDS AGAINST THE WAREHOUSE, WAITING FOR THE 104 ELECTR
SWAYING WORLD TO SUBSIDE.
(BLINKING ABOUT HIM, STARTS TO HIS FEET 210 HA APE
RESENTFULLY, SWAYING,
SWAYING IN THE TIDE. 593 JOURNE
(SWAYING AND BLINKING IN THE DOORWAY--IN A LOUD 154 JOURNE
VOICE.)
THEIR FEET MOVING, THEIR BODIES SWAYING TO THE 282 LAZARU
MUSIC'S BEAT, STIFFLY,
THE INFECTION SPREADS TO THE CHORUS OF OLD MEN 293 LAZARU
WHOSE SWAYING GRIEF FALLS INTO
HIS BODY SWAYING AND TWITCHING. 304 LAZARU
(IS SWAYING AND STAGGERING, LIKE A MAN IN A 311 LAZARU
DRUNKEN STUPOR.
MIRIAM IS KNEELING IN HER BLACK ROBES, SWAYING 313 LAZARU
BACKWARD AND FORWARD.
(SWAYING, LOOKING AT THE PEACH IN HER HAND. 347 LAZARU
SWAYING ITS HEAD TO THE THIN, SHRILL WHINE OF A 369 MARCOM
GOURD.
(HE STRUGGLES FROM HIS CHAIR AND STANDS SWAYING 79 MISBEG
(STAMMERING AND SWAYING) NO-- 108 STRANG
MARSDEN APPEARS SWAYING IN THE CABIN DOORWAY 174 STRANG
YELLING = GORDON=/
(TURNS ROUND, SWAYING A BIT, AND PEERS AT HIM 496 VOYAGE
ACROSS THE BAR)
SHE STANDS SWAYING, HOLDING ON TO THE BANNISTER AS449 WELDED
IF IN A DAZE.
(SHE STANDS SWAYING, REACHING OUT HER HAND 465 WELDED

SWAYINGLY
(HE MAKES HIS WAY SWAYINGLY TO THE OPENING IN THE 699 ICEMAN
CURTAIN AT REAR AND TACKS DOWN

SWAYS
(HE SWAYS WEAKLY.) 151 BEYOND
(SHE SWAYS WEAKLY. 551 DAYS
(HE SWAYS DIZZILY ON HIS FEET, PASSING HIS HAND 478 DYNAMO
OVER HIS EYES--
HE BEATS TIME WITH HIS HANDS AND SWAYS HIS BODY TO201 EJONES
AND FRO FROM THE WAIST.
THE WITCH DOCTOR SWAYS, STAMPING WITH HIS FOUT, 201 EJONES
(HE SWAYS FORWARD TO THE TABLE, RECITING KIPLING.)155 JOURNE
(SHE SWAYS WEAKLY AS THOUGH SHE WERE ABOUT TO 19 MANSNS
FAINT--EXHAUSTEDLY.
HE SWAYS DIZZILY, CLUTCHING HIS HEAD--THEN GOES 159 POET
TOWARD THE DOOR AT LEFT FRONT.)
(HE SWAYS TO HIS FEET, THE CHISEL IN HIS HAND) 600 ROPE
SHE SWAYS IRRESOLUTELY TOWARD HIM, AGAIN REACHING 449 WELDED
TO THE BANNISTER FOR SUPPORT.

SWEAR
LILY, I SWEAR TO YOU IF ANY MAN OFFERS ME A DRINK,190 AHWILD
I'LL KILL HIM--
YOU SHOULDN'T SWEAR-- 195 AHWILD
(WITH SURPRISED EXCITEMENT) WELL, IF YOU DON'T 272 AHWILD
SOLEMNLY SWEAR YOU WON'T--
I SWEAR/ 279 AHWILD
YOU'VE GOT TO SWEAR TO ME-- 279 AHWILD
YOU MUSN'T SWEAR/ 281 AHWILD
I SWEAR, MURIEL. 286 AHWILD

SWEAR

SWEAR (CONT'D.)
IF YOU'LL SWEAR TO ME YOU DIDN'T THINK OF LOVING 286 AHWILD
THAT--
AY SWEAR DAT YEN YOUR MO'DER DIE. 21 ANNA
YOU VAS GATTING LARN TO SWEAR. 42 ANNA
WOULD YOU BE WILLING TO SWEAR AN OATH, NOW-- 74 ANNA
WILL YOU SWEAR ON THIS$ 75 ANNA
BUT IT'S THE TRUTH AND I AIN'T SCARED TO SWEAR. 75 ANNA
(EAGERLY) SURE, I'LL SWEAR, MAT--ON ANYTHING/ 75 ANNA
WELL--WHAT DO YOU WANT ME TO SWEAR$ 75 ANNA
I SWEAR IT BY GOD/ 75 ANNA
I SWEAR IT. 75 ANNA
SWEAR I'M THE ONLY MAN IN THE WORLD IVIR YOU FELT 75 ANNA
LOVE FOR.
(VERY EARNESTLY) AND I'M WARNING YOU NOW, IF 75 ANNA
YOU'D SWEAR AN OATH ON THIS,
BE CAREFUL WHAT YOU'D SWEAR, I'M SAYING. 75 ANNA
(FORCIBLY) I SWEAR IT/ 75 ANNA
DIDN'T YOU HEAR ME SWEAR$ 76 ANNA
I SWEAR I WOULDN'T HAVE, ANDY/ 110 BEYOND
I SWEAR TO YOU I'D HAVE NEVER SAID A WORD TO RUTH.110 BEYOND
(STILL UNCONVINCED) ARE YOU SURE--WILL YOU 138 BEYOND
SWEAR--
I'LL TAKE CARE OF HER, I SWEAR TO YOU, ROB/ 168 BEYOND
I CAN SWEAR TO THAT. 534 DAYS
(SUFFLY) I DO WISH YOU WOULDN'T SWEAR SO AWFUL 494 DIFRNT
MUCH, CALEB.
YES, I'D SWEAR. 500 DIFRNT
(PLEADINGLY) YOU'D SWEAR THAT, CALEB$ 500 DIFRNT
JIM COULDN'T SWEAR HE DID NEITHER. 505 DIFRNT
NOBODY KIN SWEAR THAT FOR SARTIN. 509 DIFRNT
I DON'T ASK YOU TO SWEAR ON THE BIBLE-- 439 DYNAMO
OH, I DIDN'T MEAN TO SWEAR,--- 439 DYNAMO
WHEN I DIDN'T SWEAR ON THE BIBLES...) 442 DYNAMO
YES, I'LL SWEAR ON THE BIBLE I WON'T TELL HIM. 447 DYNAMO
YOU'LL SWEAR IT ON THE BIBLE$ 447 DYNAMO
(MECHANICALLY) YOU SWEAR TO HER$ 485 DYNAMO
(IN THE SAME TUNE) YES, I SWEAR. 485 DYNAMO
IF I'VE DONE ANYTHING TO OFFEND YOU, I SWEAR IT 22 ELECTR
WASN'T MEANT.
I SWEAR BEFORE GOD IT IS ONLY YOU I-- 27 ELECTR
BY GOD, I SWEAR IT/ 37 ELECTR
YOU SWEAR YOU WON'T--NO MATTER WHAT YOU MUST DO$ 37 ELECTR
I SWEAR TO YOU/ 88 ELECTR
I SWEAR TO YOU--/ 89 ELECTR
I SWEAR BY OUR DEAD FATHER I AM TELLING YOU THE 97 ELECTR
TRUTH/
YOU SWEAR YOU'LL NEVER SUSPECT ME--OF ANYTHINGS 175 ELECTR
BUT I'D ST I'D SWEAR THERE COULDN'T BE A YELLOW 588 ICEMAN
STOOL PIGEON AMONG THEM.
VE SWEAR IT, HARRY/ 602 ICEMAN
I SWEAR I'D NEVER ACT LIKE I HAVE 661 ICEMAN
SHE HAS A BLONDE, I THINK, BUT I COULDN'T SWEAR TO7O7 ICEMAN
IT.
AND I SWEAR I NEVER MEANT YOU TO GO THERE IF YOU 148 JOURNE
DIDN'T WANT TO.
MANY WHO HAVE SEEN HIM SWEAR HE IS DIONYSUS, RE- 300 LAZARU
ARISEN FROM HADES/
I SWEAR YOU SHALL NOT LAUGH AT DEATH WHEN I AM 324 LAZARU
DEATH/
I COULD SWEAR HE SMILES--WITH HIS LAST BREATH/ 329 LAZARU
AND I SWEAR TO YOU I WILL TRY. 39 MANSNS
(HE LIFTS HER FACE TO HIS.) I SWEAR--/ 83 MANSNS
UNTIL I SWEAR TO YOU I FELT I COULD BY JUST ONE 102 MANSNS
TINY FURTHER WISH,
LET US SWEAR THAT AGAIN, SARA/ 135 MANSNS
AND I SWEAR/ 135 MANSNS
I SWEAR I WON'T/ 135 MANSNS
BY THE ETERNAL, AS MY FATHER USED TO SWEAR, 143 MANSNS
I SWEAR TO YOU/ 158 MANSNS
OH, SWEAR TO ME AGAIN YOU WOULD NOT DECEIVE ME-- 164 MANSNS
IF YOU'LL SWEAR TO STOP YOUR MAD SCHEMES, I'LL 167 MANSNS
MAKE PEACE WITH YOU.
I SWEAR BY ALMIGHTY GOD I'LL MURDER YOU IF YOU TRY168 MANSNS
THAT.
AND I SWEAR BY GOD I'LL COME BACK AND MARRY YOU, 357 MARCOM
(SOLEMNLY) YES, I SWEAR TO, MARK. 357 MARCOM
MY FATHER AND UNCLE CAN SWEAR-- 396 MARCOM
HE'LL KEEP ACTING NATURAL ENOUGH, AND YOU'D SWEAR 33 MISBEG
HE WASN'T BAD AT ALL.
YOU'D SWEAR ON A BIBLE WHILE YOU WERE STEALING IT/162 MISBEG
I SWEAR BY ALL THE SAINTS-- 162 MISBEG
IT'S HARD TO TELL BUT SHE'S TOO YOUNG FOR HIS 18 POET
MOTHER, I'D SWEAR.
THIS WILL HAVE A GOOD END FOR SAM, I SWEAR TO 96 STRANG
THAT/---
I SWEAR TO YOU/. 119 STRANG
(LAUGHING HYSTERICALLY) YES--I SWEAR I SAW HIM-- 466 WELDED
(DESPERATELY) I SWEAR TO YOU--/ 485 WELDED
SWEARIN'
THE CAPTAIN'LL HAVE YOU OUT ON DECK CURSIN' AND 485 CARDIF
SWEARIN' LUKE A TROOPER
AND HIM SWEARIN', DE BIG LIAR, HE'LL NEVER GO ON 614 ICEMAN
NO MORE PERIODICALS/
SWEARING
OH THE MISSUS'LL BE SWEARING IT WAS ME AT THEM/ 217 AHWILD
HEAR YOU SWEARING A LIE/ 75 ANNA
TO BE SWEARING AN OATH ON A CATHOLIC CROSS AND YOU 76 ANNA
WAN OF THE OTHERS.
AND INSIDE I KEPT SWEARING TO MYSELF THAT I'D SHOW521 DAYS
WALTER--
IS IT TRUE WHAT BILLY TOLD ME--ABOUT YOUR SWEARING301 GGBROW
OFF FOREVER$
AND NOW I'D HAVE TO START SWEARING AGAIN THIS WAS 713 ICEMAN
THE LAST TIME.
I KEPT SWEARING TO HER EVERY NIGHT THAT THIS TIME 715 ICEMAN
I REALLY WOULDN'T,
GROANING AND SWEARING.) 526 INZONE

SWEARING (CONT'D.)
(EXASPERATEDLY) FOR HEAVEN'S SAKE, STOP SWEARING 162 STRANG
SO MUCH/
(THEN STERNLY IN HER TURN, AS IF SWEARING A PLEDGE183 STRANG
TO HERSELF)
SWEARS
HE SWEARS HE'S NEVER KNOWN A HEDDA IN HIS LIFE. 266 AHWILD
HE SWEARS DEFENSIVELY) 111 MISBEG
SWEAT
STREAKS OF SWEAT HAVE SMUDGED THE LAYER OF DUST ONL19 BEYOND
HIS CHEEKS.
'VE 'ARNED HERE BY OUR SWEAT. 205 DESIRE
BLOOD AN' BONE AN' SWEAT--ROTTED AWAY--FERTILIZIN'218 DESIRE
YE--RICHIN' YER SOUL--
MINE, WHAT I'D MADE OUT O' NOTHIN' WITH MY OWN 232 DESIRE
SWEAT N' BLOOD/
HE WIPES HIS FOREHEAD STREAMING WITH SWEAT. 252 DESIRE
RIVULETS OF SOOTY SWEAT HAVE TRACED MAPS ON THEIR 224 HA APE
BACKS.
WE ROAST THEM IN THEIR OWN SWEAT-- 229 HA APE
WELL, WE PAYS FOR IT WIV OUR BLOODY SWEAT, IF YER 234 HA APE
WANTS TO KNOW/
WELL, DO ME GOOD TO SWEAT THE BOOZE OUT OF ME. 687 ICEMAN
THE HOT SUN WILL SWEAT SOME OF THAT BOOZE FAT OFF 41 JOURNE
YOUR MIDDLE.
HE IS WIPING SWEAT FROM HIS FOREHEAD WITH A 53 JOURNE
HANDKERCHIEF.
(MIKE WEARS DIRTY OVERALLS, A SWEAT-STAINED BROWN 4 MISBEG
SHIRT.
SWEATED
I HAD SWEATED OUT OF THEM THAT YOU'D WANT TO KNOW 391 MARCOM
HUH, I DID IT--SO HERE I AM.
AFTER I SWEATED BLOOD TO PULL YOU THROUGH ONCE 412 MARCOM
ALREADY/
SWEATER
HE IS AN OLD, GRIZZLED MAN DRESSED IN DUNGAREE 535 'ILE
PANTS, A SWEATER,
HE IS DRESSED IN SWEATER, FUR CAP, ETC. 536 'ILE
HE WEARS A SWEATER AND LINEN KNICKERS, COLLEGIATE 53 STRANG
TO THE LAST DEGREE.
NINA IS IN THE CHAIR AT CENTER, KNITTING A TINY 111 STRANG
SWEATER.
SWEATERS
ALL ARE DRESSED ALIKE--SWEATERS, SEA-BOOTS, ETC. 543 'ILE
SWEATIN'
HENKE I'M SWEATIN' BLOOD IN THE ARMY AFTER RISKIN' 523 DIFRNT
MY LIFE IN FRANCE
MANY'S A TIME I'VE SEED A SKIPPER AN' MATES 105 ELECTR
SWEATIN' BLOOD TO BEAT WORK OUT OF A
SWEATIN', BURNIN' UP, EATIN' COAL DUST/ 212 HA APE
MORE'N OUR 'OLE BLOODY STOKEHOLE MAKES IN TEN 235 HA APE
VOYAGES SWEATIN' IN 'ELL/
SWEATING
TELL ME, AND DON'T KEEP ME SWEATING BLOOD. 54 ANNA
I'M SICK OF DIGGING IN THE DIRT AND SWEATING 107 BEYOND
A BUDDHIST, A KASHMIRI TRAVELING MERCHANT COMES 347 MARCOM
IN, PUFFING AND SWEATING,
(THE FILES OF BLEEDING AND SWEATING MEN COLLAPSE 350 MARCOM
IN PANTING, GROANING HEAPS.
WHILE MOTHER AND I WERE SWEATING AND SUFFOCATING 106 POET
IN THE HEAT OF THE KITCHEN
SWEATY
MY HANDS VAS SWEATY/ 676 ICEMAN
SWEDE
THE DECKHAND, JOHNSON, A YOUNG BLOND SWEDE, 30 ANNA
FOLLOWS HIM.
ON A STUMPY RUNT OF A MAN LIKE THE OLD SWEDE. 33 ANNA
THE OLD SQUARE--THE OLD SWEDE, I MEANS 34 ANNA
THE OLD SWEDE IS LIKE A CHILD IN HIS HANDS. 49 ANNA
HE GIVES CHRIS A PUSH WITH THE FLAT OF HIS HAND 50 ANNA
WHICH SENDS THE OLD SWEDE
(A SWEDE WITH A DROOPING BLOND MUSTACHE--WITH 478 CARDIF
PONDEROUS SARCASM)
(A FAT SWEDE WHO IS SITTING ON A CAMP STOOL IN 457 CARIBE
FRONT OF HIS DOOR TALKING WITH
(A SQUAT, SUNK-FACED SWEDE--GRUMPILY) 514 INZONE
OLSON, A STOCKY, MIDDLE-AGED SWEDE WITH ROUND, 496 VOYAGE
CHILDISH BLUE EYES.
SWEDEN
(ASTONISHED) YOU WUS BORN IN SWEDEN$ 502 VOYAGE
THEN IT MUST BE SWEDEN. 502 VOYAGE
SWEDISH
(SHRINKS AWAY FROM HIM, HALF FRIGHTENED) WHAT'S 20 ANNA
THATS SWEDISH$
(A SWEDISH FIREMAN--FROM THE REAR OF THE HATCH) 457 CARIBE
(BEAMING ALL OVER) YOU SPEAK SWEDISH$ 502 VOYAGE
SOW I NEVER KNEW SWEDISH. 502 VOYAGE
SWEENEY
TELL IT TO SWEENEY/ 237 HA APE
SWEENEY'S
(STILL LOOKING AT SWEENEY'S HAND) 591 ROPE
SWEEP
THAT A GREAT WAVE WID SUN IN THE HEART OF IT MAY 215 HA APE
SWEEP ME OVER THE SIDE SOMETIME
TIME YOU BEGUN TO SWEEP UP IN DE BAR. 583 ICEMAN
THEY PUSH FORWARD AGGRESSIVELY AND ALMOST SWEEP 300 LAZARU
THE SOLDIERS FROM THEIR FEET.)
THE CROWDS CHEER AND SWEEP IN.) 361 MARCOM
SWEEPIN'
THE WHITE WINGS GOT SOME JOB SWEEPIN' DIS UP. 234 HA APE
SWEEPING
(SHE MAKES A SWEEPING GESTURE SEAWARD) 27 ANNA
THE SOUND OF WIND AND RAIN SWEEPING DOWN ON THE 454 DYNAMO
TOWN FORM THE HILLS IS HEARD.)
(SHE MAKES A SWEEPING GESTURE TOWARD THE HILLS IN 175 EJONES
THE DISTANCE.)
(HE MAKES HIM A SWEEPING, MOCKING BOW.) 282 GGBROW

1593

SWELTERING

SWEEPING (CONT'D.)
(WITH A GESTURE OF SWEEPING THE JEWELERS INTO 235 HA APE OBLIVION)
WITH SWEEPING GESTURES AND FEROCIOUS CAPERS) 370 LAZARU
I WAS SWEEPING AND NORA WAS SCRUBBING THE KITCHEN. 17 POET
(SHE MAKES A SWEEPING BOW.) 66 POET

SWEEPS
SWEEPS EVERYTHING OFF THE TABLE ONTO THE FLOOR. 548 DIFRNT
AS THE CURTAIN RISES, HE FINISHES A GAME AND 125 JOURNE
SWEEPS THE CARDS TOGETHER.

SWEET
WHO BUT A MAN THAT'S HAD WOULD TAKE HIS WOMAN--AND537 'ILE
AS SWEET A WOMAN AS EVER WAS--
SHE IS A SLIGHT, SWEET-FACED LITTLE WOMAN DRESSED 539 'ILE
IN BLACK.
=IN THE SWEET BYE AND BYE WE WILL MEET ON THAT 233 AHWILD
BEAUTIFUL SHORE.=
HAVE A SWEET. 239 AHWILD
THAT YOUTH'S SWEET-SCENTED MANUSCRIPT SHOULD 298 AHWILD
CLOSE/
(TAKING A PACKAGE OF SWEET CAPORAL CIGARETTES FROM 15 ANNA
HER BAG)
SURE IT'S A SWEET NAME IS SUITED TO YOU. 39 ANNA
A SWEET, WHOLESOME COUPLE THEY'D MAKE. 98 BEYOND
OUT, TOOTY SWEET/ 526 DIFRNT
(HE BREATHES IN THE SPRING) (GEE, THOSE LILACS 425 DYNAMO
SMELL SWEET...
(THINKING JEERINGLY) (HOME, SWEET HOME/... 457 DYNAMO
I DIDN'T--AND IT HASN'T THE LESS SWEET FOR THAT/ 23 ELECTR
YOU'RE THE SAME, HAZEL--SWEET AND GOOD. 81 ELECTR
I USED TO HEAR YOU SINGING AT THE QUEEREST TIMES-- 83 ELECTR
SO SWEET AND CLEAR AND PURE/
THAT EVERYTHING ABOUT LOVE COULD BE SWEET AND 154 ELECTR
NATURAL.
FROM THE CASINO COMES THE SOUND OF THE SCHOOL 257 GGBROW
QUARTET RENDERING =SWEET ADELINE=
BUT WITH A SWEET AND GENTLE FACE THAT HAD ONCE 259 GGBROW
BEEN BEAUTIFUL.
I REMEMBER A SWEET, STRANGE GIRL, WITH 282 GGBROW
AFFECTIONATE, BEWILDERED EYES
HER OWN FACE IS STILL SWEET AND PRETTY BUT LINED, 291 GGBROW
AND MAKE OF OUR SWEET AND LOVELY CIVILIZATION A 244 HA APE
SHAMBLES.
AS VESPASIAN REMARKED, THE SMELL OF ALL WHISKEY IS596 ICEMAN
SWEET.
AIN'T DAT A SWEET PICTURE/ 614 ICEMAN
EVEN WHEN I HAD TWO QUARTS OF ROTGUT UNDER MY BELT661 ICEMAN
AND JOKED AND SANG =SWEET
DEN SHE'D YELL, =DAT'S A SWEET WAY TO TALK TO DE 671 ICEMAN
GOIL YUH'RE GOIN' TO MARRY.=
AND LET ME STILL CLUTCH GREEDILY TO MY YELLOW 689 ICEMAN
HEART THAT SWEET TREASURE,
WON'T I LOOK SWEET WID A WIFE DAT 698 ICEMAN
WHY DON'T YOU LAUGH AND SING =SWEET ADELINE=S 705 ICEMAN
THE ONLY PLACE I LIKED WAS THE POOL ROOMS, WHERE I709 ICEMAN
COULD SMOKE SWEET CAPORALS.
I'D HAVE TO PROMISE, SHE WAS SO SWEET AND GOOD, 710 ICEMAN
THOUGH I KNEW DARNED WELL--
I GOT ALL WORKED UP, SHE WAS SO PRETTY AND SWEET 710 ICEMAN
AND GOOD.
SURELY THE KISSES OF HER BOUGHT RED MOUTH WERE 134 JOURNE
SWEET.
A FINE, BRAVE, SWEET WOMAN. 148 JOURNE
A SWEET SPECTACLE FOR ME/ 167 JOURNE
(WITH A SWEET SMILE OF AFFECTIONATE TRUST.) 171 JOURNE
SHE IS SO SWEET AND GOOD. A SAINT ON EARTH. I 175 JOURNE
LOVE HER DEARLY.
WHAT A MELLOW, SWEET FRUIT/ 347 LAZARU
WE'RE NOT GOING TO EAT YOU, DARLING, IF YOU ARE 129 MANSNS
THAT SWEET.
FROM THE BRANCHES OF THE TREE COMES A SOUND OF 352 MARCOM
SWEET SAD MUSIC
THE SAME SWEET SAD MUSIC COMES FROM THE TREE AGAIN354 MARCOM
AS IF ITS SPIRIT WERE PLAYING
A SWEET WOMAN. 18 MISBEG
I EXPECT YOU TO BE VERY SWEET TO ME. 67 MISBEG
(HURT AND MOURNFUL) A SWEET DAUGHTER 73 MISBEG
AND A SWEET WELCOME HOME IN THE DEAD OF NIGHT. 73 MISBEG
AND YOU GAVE HIM A SWEET SMILE, AND ROLLED YOUR 82 MISBEG
BIG BEAUTIFUL COW'S EYES AT HIM.
YOU'RE A SWEET, KIND WOMAN, NORA--TOO KIND. 42 POET
THAT'S SWEET OF YOU, PATCH. 54 POET
WITH HER SWEET, FRIENDLY SMILE.) 73 POET
(A SWEET SMILE OF PLEASED COQUETRY LIGHTS UP HER 136 POET
DRAWN FACE.)
(MOCKING BITTERLY) (=NOTHING HALF SO SWEET IN 6 STRANG
LIFE AS LOVE'S YOUNG DREAM,
(THEN SUDDENLY EXPANDING IN A SWEET, GENUINELY 14 STRANG
AFFECTIONATE SMILE)
AND YET AS SOON AS HE SAW HER HE WAS SWEET ENOUGH. 50 STRANG
YET A SWEET LOVING-KINDNESS, 53 STRANG
SHE'S SO PRETTY AND SWEET/ 56 STRANG
NO, POOR DEAR MOTHER WAS SO SWEET, SHE NEVER HATED 99 STRANG
ANYONE...
(CONFIDENTLY) AND YOU CAN BET YOUR SWEET LIFE I 121 STRANG
WILL MAKE IT/
HE WAS SO WONDERFUL AND SWEET TO ME. 184 STRANG

SWEETBREADS
WE HAD SWEETBREADS ON TOAST. 254 AHWILD
I NEVER COULD SEE ANYTHING TO SWEETBREADS. 255 AHWILD

SWEETER
OH, RUTH, OUR LOVE IS SWEETER THEN ANY DISTANT 92 BEYOND
DREAM/
A SWEETER WOMAN NEVER DREW BREATH. 603 ICEMAN
MIND YOU, I'M NOT SAYING ANYTHING AGAINST POOR 14 POET
NORA. A SWEETER WOMAN NEVER LIVE
(HE RECITES.) =BUT SWEETER STILL THAN THIS, THAN 47 POET
THESE, THAN ALL,

SWEETEST
I THINK YOU'RE ONE OF THE SWEETEST KIDS I'VE EVER 238 AHWILD
MET--
THINKING OF ALL THE WRONG I'D DONE TO THE SWEETEST714 ICEMAN
WOMAN IN THE WORLD
THEY'RE THE SWEETEST HANDS IN THE WORLD. 41 JOURNE
ETERNAL DEBT OF GRATITUDE, WHO IS THE SWEETEST, 98 MANSNS
KINDEST, MUST GENEROUS-HEARTED--
SURE, I'VE ALWAYS KNOWN YOU'RE THE SWEETEST WOMAN 149 POET
IN THE WORLD, MOTHER.

SWEETHEART
I LOVE YOU, TOO--SWEETHEART/ 287 AHWILD
(STAMMERS MISERABLY) SWEETHEART/ 530 DAYS
SWEETHEART/ 551 DAYS
HE KISSES THE MASK FIRST--THEN KISSES HER FACE, 292 GGBROW
MURMURING, =AND YOU, SWEETHEART/
AND YOU'RE NOT DEAD SWEETHEART/ 323 GGBROW
NO DEAREST OR SWEETHEART TO THIS MAN. 531 INZONE
BUT I SUPPOSE YOU STILL DREAM YOU'RE THE KING OF 53 MANSNS
FRANCE'S SWEETHEART/
OF COURSE I HAVEN'T, SWEETHEART/ 83 MANSNS
SWEETHEART/ 89 MANSNS
YOUR BODY IS BEAUTIFUL, SWEETHEART/ 91 MANSNS
SWEETHEART/ 145 MANSNS
AN OLD SWEETHEART OF MINE. 54 MISBEG
YOU CAN TAKE YOUR BAD TEMPER OUT ON YOUR 101 MISBEG
SWEETHEART HERE.
WHO THE HELL ARE YOU, SWEETHEARTS 165 MISBEG
HE'S NEVER HAD A SWEETHEART. 19 POET
(GRINNING.) THEN MAYBE SHE'S AN OLD SWEETHEART 19 POET
(JEERINGLY.) SURE, HE'S ONLY GONE TO PAY A CALL 161 POET
ON HIS SWEETHEART,
SWEETHEART/ 187 STRANG
SWEETHEART/ 444 WELDED

SWEETHEARTS,
HELLO DERE, SWEETHEARTS/ 725 ICEMAN
YOU'VE HAD TOO MANY SWEETHEARTS. 20 MISBEG
WITH ALL THE SWEETHEARTS YOU'VE HAD, YOU MUST HAVE 28 MISBEG
A CATCHING WAY WITH MEN.

SWEETNESS
SOFT AND FULL OF SWEETNESS. 187 AHWILD
AND STARES UP AT THE MOON WITH A WISTFUL, RESIGNED323 GGBROW
SWEETNESS)
IT WAS WRITTEN ALL OVER HER FACE, SWEETNESS AND 714 ICEMAN
LOVE AND PITY AND FORGIVENESS.
(IN A VOICE OF UNEARTHLY SWEETNESS) 348 LAZARU
AND MAKES HER LOVABLE, A SIMPLE SWEETNESS AND 20 POET
CHARM,
WITH A DEEPER SWEETNESS/...) 43 STRANG

SWELL
(HE CALLS ENCOURAGEMENT) THAT'S SWELL DOPE, YOUNG245 AHWILD
FELLER.
IF THAT AIN'T A SWELL JOB TO FIND YOUR LONG LOST 17 ANNA
OLD MAN WORKING AT/
OH, I'M A SWELL LITTLE PICKER, AM RIGHT. 520 DIFRNT
I GOT A SWELL CHANCE TELLIN' THAT TO UNCLE CALEB. 523 DIFRNT
BUT I COULD HAVE A SWELL TIME EVEN IN THIS DUMP 523 DIFRNT
GEE, YOU'VE HAD THIS OLD PLACE FIXED UP SWELL 524 DIFRNT
SINCE I WAS TO HOME LAST.
AND IT SURE LOOKS SWELL--NOTHING CHEAP ABOUT IT. 525 DIFRNT
(FLATTERINGLY) AW, YOU LOOK SWELL. 527 DIFRNT
AND YOU CAN SEE WHAT A SWELL CHANCE YOU'VE GOT OF 533 DIFRNT
TALKIN' HIM OVER NOW.
HE'D HAVE A SWELL CHANCE/ 544 DIFRNT
ONCE IN DE WOODS IN DE NIGHT, DEY GOT A SWELL 183 EJONES
CHANCE O' FINDIN' DIS BABY/
SWELL CHANCE OF FOOLIN' YOU/ 582 ICEMAN
THAT'S A SWELL NEW HAT, BESS, LOOKS VERY 609 ICEMAN
BECOMING--SIX DOLLARS.
(INDIGNANTLY) A SWELL TIME TO STAGE YOUR FIRST 650 ICEMAN
BOUT, ON HARRY'S BIRTHDAY PARTY/
(AMUSEDLY) ALWAYS A HIGH-TONED SWELL AT HEART, 658 ICEMAN
EH, HUGO/
ONLY A LAZY GROUND SWELL AND A SLOW DROWSY ROLL OF153 JOURNE
THE SHIP.
ON THE DEEP GROUND SWELL OF THE GUARD'S LAUGHTER. 337 LAZARU
(BEGINNING TO SWELL OUT A BIT MATTER-OF-FACTLY) 363 MARCOM
SWELL CHANCE/ 68 MISBEG
(HE SPITS CONTEMPTUOUSLY) WHAT A SWELL CHANCT. 593 ROPE

SWELLED
THE REAL NAME OF WHICH IS SWELLED HEAD/ 302 GGBROW
JUST BECAUSE WE ACT VICE TO HIM, HE GETS A SWELLED637 ICEMAN
NUT/
YOU'VE BEEN GETTING A SWELLED HEAD LATELY. ABOUT 163 JOURNE
NOTHING/

SWELLING
A CONFUSED, INCHOATE UPROAR SWELLING INTO A SORT 207 HA APE
OF UNITY, A MEANING---
(HE EXTENDS HIS RIGHT ARM, SWELLING OUT THE GREAT 231 HA APE
MUSCLES)
SWELLING OUT HIS CHEST AND POUNDING ON IT WITH HIS252 HA APE
FIST.
SWELLING UP AND DOWN LIKE THE SOUND OF AN ORGAN 289 LAZARU
FROM A DISTANT CHURCH)
THEN A SUDDEN SWELLING CHORUS OF FORLORN 295 LAZARU
BEWILDERMENT
HE HAS A CUT OVER HIS LEFT EYE, A BLUE SWELLING ON152 POET
HIS LEFT CHEEKBONE,

SWELLS
RHYTHMICALLY AS IF TO THE PULSE OF LONG SWELLS OF 572 CROSS
THE DEEP SEA.)
(HE SWELLS WITH PRIDE.) THAT WAS SOME DISPLAY, 31 HUGHIE

SWELTERING
IF YOU THINK IT'S FUN SWELTERING IN THAT OVEN OF A122 BEYOND
KITCHEN

SWEPT

SWEPT
THE FLOOR HAS BEEN SWEPT CLEAN OF SAWDUST AND 628 ICEMAN SCRUBBED,
(CALIGULA AND CRASSUS ARE SWEPT TO ONE SIDE, LEFT,306 LAZARU
IN THE TYPHOON WHEN A WAVE SWEPT ME FROM THE DECK,411 MARCOM

SWERVE
THEY DRINK AND THEN SWERVE OVER TO OLSON'S TABLE.)504 VOYAGE

SWERVES
(HE STARTS--SWERVES LEFT-- 80 MISBEG

SWERVING
AND BREAKS INTO A SWERVING SPRINT DOWN THE ROAD.) 262 DESIRE

SWIFT
WELL, I RAN INTO A COUPLE OF SWIFT BABIES FROM NEW218 AHWILD
HAVEN THIS AFTER,
I MEAN REAL SWIFT ONES THAT THERE'S SOMETHING 219 AHWILD
DOING WITH,
(THE PRIEST GIVES A SWIFT, REPROACHFUL LOOK AT 510 DAYS
JOHN, SEEMS ABOUT TO PROTEST,
«SWIFT BE THINE APPROACHING FLIGHT/ 286 GGBROW
BUT WITH A SWIFT IMPULSIVE MOVEMENT SHE REACHES 82 JOURNE
OUT AND CLASPS HIS ARM,)
SWIFT THY DELIVERANCE/ 302 LAZARU
SWIFT THY DELIVERANCE/ 302 LAZARU
«BUILD THEE MORE STATELY MANSIONS, O MY SOUL, AS 148 MANSNS
THE SWIFT SEASONS ROLL/
MAFFEO RECOGNIZES THEM IMMEDIATELY--IN A SWIFT 365 MARCOM
ASIDE TO HIS BROTHER,)

SWIFTLY
THEN GIROS UP HIS COURAGE AND TEARS IT OPEN AND 208 AHWILD
BEGINS TO READ SWIFTLY,
A PIGEON-HOLE AND RETREATS SWIFTLY TO HER CHAIR 119 BEYOND
WITH IT,
SWIFTLY RISES TO A BRILLIANT INTENSITY OF CRIMSON 566 DAYS
AND GREEN AND GOLD,
BACKS SWIFTLY TOWARD THE DOOR IN REAR AND GOES 259 DESIRE
OUT,
(GATHERS THEM UP SWIFTLY AND THROWS THEM AGAIN,) 38 HUGHIE
SHE GOES SWIFTLY AWAY TO THE WINDOWS AT LEFT 89 JOURNE
THE DANCERS CAN BE SEEN WHIRLING SWIFTLY BY THE 281 LAZARU
WINDOWS,
SWIFTLY FROM LAZARUS, REMAINING HUDDLED ONE 348 LAZARU
AGAINST THE OTHER,
(SHE LAUGHS SOFTLY AND PASSES SWIFTLY ACROSS THE 367 LAZARU
ARENA TOWARD LAZARUS,)
THE WAGON IS PULLED SWIFTLY AWAY, 354 MARCOM
(THE SPRINGS SWIFTLY TO THE TOP DECK AND BELLOWS) 406 MARCOM
THEN SHE MOVES SWIFTLY TO THE RIGHT OF THE HOUSE 3 MISBEG
AND LOOKS BACK,)
HE SLINKS SWIFTLY AROUND THE CORNER 10 MISBEG
(SMILING AT HIM SWIFTLY AND MECHANICALLY) 41 STRANG
(THEIR EYES FOLLOW THE PLANE AS IT COMES SWIFTLY 198 STRANG
NEARER AND PASSES DIRECTLY OVER
(SHE BENDS DOWN SWIFTLY AND KISSES HIS HEAD, TURNS487 WELDED
AWAY QUICKLY)

SWIFTNESS
(JOSIE'S RIGHT ARM STRIKES WITH SURPRISING 4 MISBEG
SWIFTNESS AND HER BIG HAND LANDS ON

SWIG
HEY A SWIG, 251 DESIRE
TAKE A GOOD SWIG, 131 ELECTR
(HE TAKES A SWIG JUST AS SETH COMES OUT OF THE 133 ELECTR
HOUSE,
A HALF PINT OF THAT DYNAMITE IN ONE SWIG WILL FIX 583 ICEMAN
HIM FOR A WHILE--
(HE TAKES AN ENORMOUS SWIG FROM THE BOTTLE,) 53 MISBEG

SWILL
BLOODY SWILL/ 480 CARDIF
THAN GETTING ALL FOUR FEET IN A TROUGH OF 543 DAYS
SWILL/(HE LAUGHS SARDONICALLY)
AND GOTTEN SWILL FOR GRUB, AN' I KNOW HE DIDN'T 106 ELECTR
HAVE NO HEART IN HIM/
SWILL MY LICKER SO'S YOU KIN SKIN ME OUT O' MY 130 ELECTR
BET,
THERE'S PRETTY GIRLS IN CARTHAGE AND WINE TO SWILL314 LAZARU
IN CARTHAGE,

SWILLED
YE'VE SWILLED MY LIKKER AN' GUZZLED MY VITTLES 249 DESIRE
LIKE HOGS, HAIN'T YES

SWILLING
MAN OF THEM IS WURTH ANY TEN STOCK-FISH-SWILLING 49 ANNA
SQUARE-HEAUS

SWIM
SWIM FARS 228 AHWILD
THERE'S NO WIND HARDLY AND SHE KIN SWIM LIKE A 503 DIFRNT
FISH
SU THEY TELLS HER THE CAPTAIN HAD SENT FOR HER AND503 DIFRNT
SHE WAS TO SWIM RIGHT OUT AND
IT'S LIKE TRYING TO SWIM IN GLUE/ 434 DYNAMO

SWIMMER
WELL, YOU OUGHT TO BE A GOOD SWIMMER, IF YOU TAKE 228 AHWILD
AFTER ME,
A FINE ATHLETIC GIRL OF THE SWIMMER, TENNIS 12 STRANG
PLAYER, GOLFER TYPE,

SWIMMERS
VENETIANS MAKE THE BEST SWIMMERS IN THE WORLD, 411 MARCOM
WATCHING THE BURNING, FROZEN NAKED SWIMMERS DROWN 14 STRANG
AT LAST....)

SWIMMIN'
SHE KEEPS SWIMMIN' ROUND AND YELLIN' FOR CALEB, 503 DIFRNT
HE MUST BE SWIMMIN' IN DE NORTH RIVER YET/ 617 ICEMAN

SWIMMING
WELL, AS I WAS SAYING, RED AND I WENT SWIMMING 229 AHWILD
THAT DAY,
NUTHING--GO ON WITH YOUR SWIMMING--DON'T MIND ME, 229 AHWILD
YOU KNOW, SPEAKING OF SWIMMING, 229 AHWILD
WENT IN SWIMMING THERE AND I SAVED HIS LIFE, 229 AHWILD
AND SEVERAL OTHER TIMES IN MY LIFE, WHEN I WAS 153 JOURNE
SWIMMING FAR OUT,

SWIMS
AND WHEN THEY UPS ANCHORS, SHE DIVES IN THE WATER 503 DIFRNT
AND SWIMS OUT AFTER 'EM,
THE CRAZY CUSS GIVES UP AND SWIMS BACK TO HOME, 503 DIFRNT
HOWLIN' ALL THE TIME,

SWIN
AND POEMS BY SWIN SOMETHING-- 198 AHWILD

SWINBURNE
«POEMS AND BALLADS» BY SWINBURNE, MA, 198 AHWILD
(THEN FALLING BACK ON SWINBURNE--BUT WITH 287 AHWILD
PASSIONATE SINCERITY)
POETRY BY SWINBURNE, ROSSETTI, WILDE, ERNEST 11 JOURNE
DOWSON, KIPLING, ETC,
THIS DOWSON, AND THIS BAUDELAIRE, AND SWINBURNE 135 JOURNE
AND OSCAR WILDE,
I'LL BET YOU RECITED KIPLING AND SWINBURNE AND 160 JOURNE
DOWSON AND GAVE HER
SWINBURNE, FOR EXAMPLES 164 JOURNE
(HE RECITES AGAIN FROM THE SWINBURNE POEM,) 174 JOURNE

SWINBURNE'S
SWINBURNE'S COPY, 205 AHWILD
AND THAT SWINBURNE'S GOT A FINE SWING TO HIS 288 AHWILD
POETRY--
(HE RECITES FROM SWINBURNE'S «A LEAVE-TAKING» AND 173 JOURNE
DOES IT WELL,

SWINDLE
WON'T BE THE PUBLIC SWINDLE I CAN PROVE YOURS IS/ 204 AHWILD
OR ANY KIND OF GET-RICH-QUICK SWINDLE/ 141 JOURNE
JUST BECAUSE I DON'T WANT DOCTORS TO THINK I'M A 146 JOURNE
MILLIONAIRE THEY CAN SWINDLE,
ATTORNEY OR NO ATTORNEY, I COULD EASILY SWINDLE 60 MANSNS
YOU OUT OF IT, IF I LIKED,
HE WAS, AND DIDN'T YOU SWINDLE HIM, AND MAKE ME 24 MISBEG
HELP YOU AT ITS
IF I HAD NOT BEEN A CREDULOUS GULL AND LET THE 40 POET
THIEVING YANKEES SWINDLE ME
AND FOR LYIN' TRICKS TO SWINDLE THE BLOODY FOOLS 170 POET
OF GINTRY,

SWINDLED
YOU WERE SWINDLED AGAIN AS YOU ALWAYS ARE, 84 JOURNE
I SHOULD HAVE SWINDLED HER INTO GIVING HERSELF BY 74 MANSNS
PROMISING MARRIAGE--
YOUR BODY FELT SWINDLED AND IT MADE YOU 80 MANSNS
SUSPICIOUS, I SUPPOSE,
YOU PRIDE YOURSELF YOU HAVE CUNNINGLY SWINDLED 141 MANSNS
HIM,
(HE LAUGHS GRATINGLY,) BUT IT'S YOU WHO HAVE BEEN142 MANSNS
SWINDLED/
HE'S BOUND TO BE SWINDLED OUT OF IT, ANYWAY, 30 MISBEG
AND AFTER THE WAY THE YANKS SWINDLED HIM WHEN HE 26 POET
CAME HERE,
THE LAND OUR GREAT GENTLEMAN WAS SWINDLED INTO 30 POET
BUYING
THE LAND THE YANKEES SWINDLED HIM INTO BUYIN' FOR 173 POET
HIS AMERICAN ESTATE,
SWINDLED BY GOD OUT OF JOY/... 187 STRANG

SWINDLER
ARE YOU WILLING TO BECOME A CONSCIOUS THIEF AND 154 MANSNS
SWINDLER$
SWINDLER'S
FEELING MY SWINDLER'S VICTORIOUS GLOATING DIE INTO102 MANSNS
BOREDOM AND DISCONTENT--

SWINDLERS
AND IT'S SAFER THAN THE STOCKS AND BONDS OF WALL 16 JOURNE
STREET SWINDLERS,

SWINDLES
THERE'S A CRUEL SKINFLINT OF A LANDLORD WHO 63 MISBEG
SWINDLES ME OUT OF MY LAST DROP OF

SWINDLING
BECAUSE ALWAYS TOO LAZY TO CARRY CROOKEDNESS 576 ICEMAN
BEYOND PETTY SWINDLING,
YOU HAVE LET HIM BEAT YOU DOWN LIKE A SWINDLING 59 MANSNS
HORSE-TRADER/
LIKE PLAIN SWINDLING AND THEFT, 154 MANSNS
THE PAPER IS FULL OF THE LATEST SWINDLING LIES 37 POET
YOU MAY TELL THE SWINDLING TRADER, HARFORD, 123 POET

SWINE
FIT ONLY FOR SWINE IS WOT I SAY, 480 CARDIF
YE STABBED HIM, AND BE DAMNED TO HIM, FOR THE 488 CARDIF
SKULKIN' SWINE HE WAS/
LOOK AT THE DIRTY SWINE/ 465 CARIBE
YOU SWINE/ 470 CARIBE
YOU GOD-DAMNED ROTTEN SWINE/ 531 DAYS
WITCH DOCTORS, OR WHATEVER THE 'ELL YER CALLS THE 185 EJONES
SWINE,
I AM A ROTTEN SWINE TO--DAMN VINNIE/ 93 ELECTR
HOW ELSE COULD YOU EVER HAVE IMAGINED YOU LOVED 121 ELECTR
THAT LOW SWINE/
JENNINGS--THE FIRST---HE'S A ROTTEN SWINE-- 208 HA APE
THEM LAZY, BLOATED SWINE WHAT TRAVELS FIRST CABIN$212 HA APE
TELL 'IM 'E'S A BLOODY SWINE/ 224 HA APE
'ERE THEY COME, THE BLEEDIN' SWINE, 236 HA APE
CAPITALIST SWINE/ 579 ICEMAN
AND THE LAST WAS THE BREED OF SWINE CALLED MEN IN 590 ICEMAN
GENERAL,
(IN A BURST OF FUTILE FURY) YOU DIRTY SWINE/ 686 ICEMAN
(SHOUTING) WHAT IS UT, YE SWINES 526 INZONE
AND SWINE SHALL ROOT WHERE THY TEMPLE STOOD/ 292 LAZARU
ITS FULFILLED DESIRE A SNORING IN A STY IN THE MUD930 LAZARU
AMONG SWINE,
O MY GOOD PEOPLE, MY FAITHFUL SCUM, MY BROTHER 370 LAZARU
SWINE,
THERE IS NO SOUL EVEN IN YOUR LOVE, WHICH IS NO 416 MARCOM
BETTER THAN A MATING OF SWINE/
HE'S A MEAN AULD SWINE, 598 ROPE
IT MAKES ME FEEL--LIKE A SWINE/ 95 STRANG
ARISE AND SHINE, YE OHRUNKEN SWINE/ 500 VOYAGE
(LOOKING AT JOE ANGRILY) BEEN 'ITTIN' 'ER AGEN, 508 VOYAGE
'AVE YER, YER COWARDLY SWINE/

SWINE (CONT'D.)
I'LL «LAY ME DOWN AMONG THE SWINE.» 474 WELDED

SWINEPOT
THE BLOODY SWINEPOT/ 431 DYNAMO

SWING
AND THAT SWINBURNE'S GOT A FINE SWING TO HIS 288 AHWILD
POETRY--
SWING YOUR PARTNER T' THE RIGHT/ 250 DESIRE
SWING YOUR PARTNER TO THE LEFT/ 250 DESIRE
YE'D OUGHT T' BE BOTH HUNG ON THE SAME LIMB AN' 267 DESIRE
LEFT THAR T' SWING IN THE BREEZE
THEY SWING THEIR PICKS, THEY SHOVEL, BUT NOT A 194 EJONES
SOUND COMES FROM THEIR LABOR.
(HE LETS DRIVE A TERRIFIC SWING, 239 HA APE
THEY CARRY SILVER CENSERS WHICH THEY SWING IN 433 MARCOM
UNISON TOWARD THE CORPSE OF
LOOSE A ROUND-HOUSE SWING THAT MISSES TYRONE BY A 101 MISBEG
COUPLE OF FEET,
AND THAT'S WHY HE TOOK A SWING AT MES 133 MISBEG
I WANTER SWING. 600 ROPE
(WHINING) I WANTER SWING. 600 ROPE
AND LAUNCHES HERSELF FOR A SWING. 601 ROPE

SWINGING
AT LEFT, FRONT, IS THE SWINGING DOOR LEADING TO 236 AHWILD
THE BAR.
WATCHING THEM OVER THE SWINGING DOOR. 237 AHWILD
BARTENDER AND THE SALESMAN APPEAR JUST INSIDE THE 244 AHWILD
SWINGING DOOR.
AND MARCHES HIM IGNOMINIOUSLY TOWARD THE SWINGING 247 AHWILD
DOOR.)
AND A MOMENT LATER THE OUTER DOORS ARE HEARD 247 AHWILD
SWINGING BACK AND FORTH.)
BEYOND IT, THE MAIN ENTRANCE--A DOUBLE SWINGING 3 ANNA
DOOR.
AND SWINGING IT HIGH OVER HIS SHOULDER, SPRINGS 60 ANNA
TOWARD HER.
(SWINGING HER UP ABOVE HIS HEAD--LOVINGLY) 119 BEYOND
SWINGING AS ON A PIVOT FROM THE COAL WHICH LIES IN223 HA APE
HEAPS ON THE FLOOR BEHIND TO
WITH A STRANGE, AWKWARD, SWINGING RHYTHM. 223 HA APE
WITH THE SWINGING DOORS TO THE STREET BETWEEN 664 ICEMAN
THEM.
(HE STAGGERS OUT THROUGH THE SWINGING DOORS.) 673 ICEMAN
(THE SWINGING DOORS ARE PUSHED OPEN AND WILLIE 674 ICEMAN
OBAN ENTERS FROM THE STREET.
STARING OVER THE SWINGING DOORS INTO THE STREET.) 677 ICEMAN
BUT LEWIS, HIS HAND ABOUT TO PUSH THE SWINGING 677 ICEMAN
DOORS OPEN, HESITATES.
(HE PUSHES THE SWINGING DOORS OPEN AND MAKES A 685 ICEMAN
BRAVE EXIT.
(HE PUTS A RELUCTANT HAND ON THE SWINGING DOOR) 687 ICEMAN
HE COMES LURCHING BLINDLY THROUGH THE SWINGING 689 ICEMAN
DOORS

SWINGS
(SWINGS HIS FEET OVER THE SIDE OF HIS BUNK, STOPS 481 CARDIF
PLAYING HIS ACCORDION.
(THE DOOR SWINGS WIDE OPEN, REVEALING SUE 562 CROSS
BARTLETT.
HE HAS A LARGE BELL IN HIS HAND AND THIS HE SWINGS203 DESIRE
MECHANICALLY.
(HE GRABS THE CHAIR BY ITS BACK AND SWINGS IT OVER596 ROPE
HIS

SWINISH
THE MOST SWINISH AND CONTEMPTIBLE OF MEN/ 354 LAZARU

SWIPE
AND SHE GIVES MILLER A NASTY SWIPE ON THE SIDE OF 226 AHWILD
THE HEAD
(LEANS OVER THE BAR AND STOPS LEWIS WITH A 677 ICEMAN
STRAIGHT-ARM SWIPE ON THE CHEST)
IT'S GOING TO BE THE SADDEST MEMORY OF MY LIFE I 21 MISBEG
DIDN'T GET ONE LAST SWIPE AT
I WAS GOING TO TAKE A SWIPE AT JIM, TOO, BUT I 85 MISBEG
COULDN'T DO IT.
WHEN IT WAS ALL OVER, I GOT UP AND TOOK A SWIPE AT 85 MISBEG
SIMPSON, BUT I MISSED HIM.
BE JAYSUS, THAT REMINDS ME I OWE YOU A SWIPE ON 100 MISBEG
THE JAW FOR SOMETHING.

SWIPED
ONE WAS WHERE I SWIPED THE HUNDRED. 599 ROPE

SWIRL
(THEY SWIRL TO THEIR PLACES BEHIND THE LONG TABLE.431 MARCOM

SWIRLS
HOW THE BLACK SMOKE SWIRLS BACK AGAINST THE SKY/ 218 HA APE

SWISHING
BUT THE LAPPING OF RIPPLES AGAINST THE PILES AND 257 GGBROW
THEIR SWISHING ON THE BEACH--

SWITCH
(TRYING TO SWITCH THE SUBJECT) 229 AHWILD
(SHE PUTS HER HAND ON THE READING-LAMP SWITCH) 298 AHWILD
(SHE GOES TO THE DOOR AND PUTS HER HAND ON THE 430 DYNAMO
SWITCH)
IN THE SWITCH GALLERIES, BY A DIM LIGHT, 473 DYNAMO
THERE IS A DIM LIGHT ABOVE IN THE SWITCH GALLERIES476 DYNAMO
AS IN THE PREVIOUS SCENE.
THE INTERIORS OF THE UPPER AND LOWER SWITCH 483 DYNAMO
GALLERIES ARE REVEALED.
STRETCHING HER ARMS UP IN THE SAME POSITION AS THE485 DYNAMO
SWITCH ARMS.)
HE NOW WALKS DELIBERATELY BACK THROUGH THE DOOR TO487 DYNAMO
THE OIL SWITCH GALLERY.
RUNS DOWN THE STAIRS TO THE LOWER OIL SWITCH 487 DYNAMO
GALLERY.
THE STAIRS TO THE LOWER SWITCH GALLERY--SHE CALLS 488 DYNAMO
UNEASILY)
A WALL SWITCH, AND A MOMENT LATER SOMEONE STARTS 169 JOURNE
PLAYING THE PIANO IN THERE--

SWITCHBOARD
IT IS OF DOUBLE WIDTH AND EXTENDS OVER THE 483 DYNAMO
SWITCHBOARD ROOM ALSO.
THE SWITCHBOARD ROOM ON THE RIGHT--ONE STORY UP-- 486 DYNAMO
ARE OF CONCRETE.
THE SWITCHBOARD ROOM IS A SMALL COMPARTMENT TO THE486 DYNAMO
RIGHT OF THE DYNAMO ROOM.
IN IT ARE THE SWITCHBOARD AND A COUPLE OF CHAIRS. 486 DYNAMO
THE INTERIORS OF THE DYNAMO AND SWITCHBOARD ROOMS 486 DYNAMO
ARE NOW ALSO REVEALED.
(HE DASHES OVER INTO THE SWITCHBOARD ROOM 487 DYNAMO
I SEE SWITCHBOARD ROOM.... 487 DYNAMO
(HE TURNS AND RUNS HEADLONG THROUGH THE 488 DYNAMO
SWITCHBOARD ROOM.
BEHIND THE DESK ARE A TELEPHONE SWITCHBOARD AND 7 HUGHIE
THE OPERATOR'S STOOL.
THE NIGHT CLERK SITS ON THE STOOL, FACING FRONT, 7 HUGHIE
HIS BACK TO THE SWITCHBOARD.

SWITCHED
I SWITCHED THE SUBJECT ON HUGHIE, SEE, ON PURPOSE. 26 HUGHIE

SWITCHES
(HE FOLLOWS MILDRED INTO THE FRONT PARLOR, WHERE 256 AHWILD
HE SWITCHES ON THE LIGHTS.)
(AS THE RECORD STOPS--SWITCHES OFF THE MACHINE) 520 DIFRNT
OF THE DISCONNECTING SWITCHES, DOUBLE BUSSES, 473 DYNAMO
BELOW THE DISCONNECTING SWITCHES IS A RAISED 483 DYNAMO
PLATFORM.
THESE SWITCHES EXTEND IN A STRAIGHT ROW BACKWARD 483 DYNAMO
DOWN THE MIDDLE OF THE GALLERY.
THE LOWER GALLERY OF THE OIL SWITCHES IS 483 DYNAMO
THE UPPER GALLERY CONTAINS THE DISCONNECTING 483 DYNAMO
SWITCHES AND THE DOUBLE BUSSES.
STEEL WORK, INSULATORS, BUSSES, SWITCHES, ETC. 483 DYNAMO
STRETCHING UPWARD TO THE ROOF.
THE OIL SWITCHES, WITH THEIR SPINDLY STEEL LEGS, 483 DYNAMO
THEIR SQUARE,
WHEN ALL THESE SWITCHES AND BUSSES AND WIRES 484 DYNAMO
SEEMED LIKE THE ARMS OF A DEVIL
(PLEADINGLY--POINTING TO THE PLATFORM BENEATH THE 484 DYNAMO
DISCONNECTING SWITCHES)
(SHE GOES UP THE STAIRS TO THE PLATFORM AND STANDS485 DYNAMO
DIRECTLY UNDER THE SWITCHES.
ADA IS STANDING BEFORE HIM, DIRECTLY BENEATH THE 486 DYNAMO
SWITCHES AS BEFORE.
BENEATH THE DISCONNECTING SWITCHES. 486 DYNAMO
(HE GRABS DION BY THE ARM AND SWITCHES OFF THE 283 GGBROW
LIGHT.)
HE SWITCHES ON THE READING LAMP ON THE TABLE. 306 GGBROW
(HE PRESSES A BUTTON AT REAR WHICH SWITCHES OFF 610 ICEMAN
THE LIGHTS.
(HE ABRUPTLY SWITCHES FROM THIS ELOQUENCE TO A 62 MISBEG
MATTER-OF-FACT TONE)

SWITCHING
HIS MOOD SWITCHING WITH DRUNKEN SUDDENNESS) 249 DESIRE
(SWITCHING SUDDENLY FROM JARRING SHOUTS TO LOW, 56 MISBEG
CONFIDENTIAL VITUPERATION.
(SWITCHING TO FIERCENESS AND GRABBING HIS LAPEL 63 MISBEG
AGAIN)

SWITZERLAND
SPY IN PARIS WAS WRITIN' LOVE LETTERS TO SOME 529 INZONE
WOMAN SPY IN SWITZERLAND WHO SENT

SWIVEL
AT CENTER, A FINE MAHOGANY DESK WITH A SWIVEL 274 GGBROW
CHAIR IN BACK OF IT.

SWOLLEN
SWOLLEN-KNUCKLED, SENSITIVE FINGERS DROOPING IN 107 JOURNE
COMPLETE CALM.
THE KNUCKLES ARE ALL SWOLLEN. THEY'RE SO UGLY. 171 JOURNE
WISPS OF HAY STICK TO HIS CLOTHES AND HIS FACE IS 157 MISBEG
SWOLLEN AND SLEEPY.
HIS FACE IS BATTERED, NOSE RED AND SWOLLEN, LIPS 151 POET
CUT AND PUFFED.
BOTH HIS HANDS ARE SWOLLEN, WITH SKINNED KNUCKLES.152 POET
AS ARE CREGAN'S.
APPEARS VULGAR AND COMMON, WITH A LOOSE, LEERING 167 POET
GRIN ON HIS SWOLLEN LIPS.)

SWOON
I KISS YOUR RUBY LIPS AND YOU SWOON, 360 MARCOM

SWOONING
(HALF SWOONING) MARCO/ 430 MARCOM
(ALMOST SWOONING IN HIS ARMS) 449 WELDED

SWOONS
BEATIFIC VISION SWOONS ON THE EMPTY POOLS OF THE 32 HUGHIE
NIGHT CLERK'S EYES.

SWORD
THE COWARD DOES IT WITH A KISS, THE BRAVE MAN WITH245 AHWILD
A SWORD/=
I SHORTENED MY SWORD AND LET HIM HAVE THE POINT 95 ELECTR
UNDER THE EAR.
(WITH THE SAME SMILE) THE SWORD, MY OLD HYENA/ 301 LAZARU
LET US HAVE OUR SWORD 304 LAZARU
DRAWING HIS SWORD AND FLOURISHING IT DRUNKENLY-- 305 LAZARU
HIS EYES GLAZED)
(DRAWING HIS OWN SWORD IN A FRENZY) 305 LAZARU
CALIGULA SUDDENLY DROPS HIS SWORD AND COVERING HIS308 LAZARU
FACE WITH HIS HANDS WEEPS
(SWORD IN HAND HE WHIRLS TO CONFRONT LAZARUS, 308 LAZARU
(THE SWORD HAS FALLEN TO HIS SIDE. 308 LAZARU
HOPS TO HIS FEET AND SNATCHES UP HIS SWORD 311 LAZARU
DEFENSIVELY.
DANCING A HOPPING GROTESQUE SWORD DANCE BEHIND 319 LAZARU
HIM, CHANTING AS HE DOES SO.
THEN CALIGULA BREAKS INTO A CRY OF FEAR AND A SOB,320 LAZARU
AND, CASTING HIS SWORD ASIDE,
CALIGULA WALKS BEHIND, HIS DRAWN SWORD IN HIS 326 LAZARU
HAND.
CALIGULA STANDS WITH UPRAISED SWORD BY THE CHAIR 338 LAZARU
OF CAESAR.

SWORD

SWORD (CONT'D.)
FLOURISHING HIS SWORD AND COMES RUNNING INTO THE 338 LAZARU
ROOM, SHOUTING)
(HE POINTS TO THE BODY OF FLAVIUS WITH HIS SWORD) 338 LAZARU
HIS SWORD CLATTERING DOWN THE STEPS TO THE FLOOR.1339 LAZARU
WITH STARTLED SURPRISE, DRAWING HIS SWORD) 350 MARCOM
(HE DRAWS HIS SWORD) COVER HER FACE, ACCURSED 353 MARCOM
SORCERER/
(HE GRIPS HIS SWORD) 353 MARCOM
LEANING ON HIS SWORD. 358 MARCOM
(HE MAKES A SIGN TO A SOLDIER WHO FLOURISHES HIS 380 MARCOM
SWORD.)
WAS IT NOT YOUR BRAVE SWORD THAT WARDED OFF THEIR 411 MARCOM
CURVED KNIVES FROM MY BREAST
THERE'S NO ANGEL WITH A FLAMING SWORD THERE NOW, 469 WELDED
IS THERE?

SWORDS
WAVING THEIR SILLY SWORDS, SO AFRAID THEY COULDN'T677 ICEMAN
SHOW OFF HOW BRAVE THEY WAS/
CONCEALED SWORDS AND KNIVES ARE BROUGHT OUT BY 290 LAZARU
BOTH SIDES.)
THEY SOON FIND IT NECESSARY TO USE THEIR SWORDS, 291 LAZARU
KNIVES AND SWORDS FLASH ABOVE THE HEADS OF THE 291 LAZARU
MASS.
ORDER THEM TO USE THEIR SWORDS, CNEIUS. 300 LAZARU
 304 LAZARU
(HIS SOLDIERS RAISE THEIR SWORDS. 305 LAZARU
(TO THE SOLDIERS) DRAW YOUR SWORDS/ 305 LAZARU
I AM AFRAID OF THEIR POISON AND THEIR SWORDS AND 309 LAZARU
THEY TORE OUR SWORDS AWAY FROM US, LAUGHING, AND 321 LAZARU
WE LAUGHED WITH THEM/
WE LEFT OUR SWORDS WITH THEM/ 321 LAZARU
MEN STILL NEED THEIR SWORDS TO SLASH AT GHOSTS IN 328 LAZARU
THE DARK.
THEY ONLY REMEMBERED--TO GO OUT AND PICK UP THEIR 328 LAZARU
SWORDS/
SOLDIERS WITH DRAWN SWORDS LEAP FORWARD AND SEIZE 379 MARCOM
HIM, TRUSSING HIM UP.
(WITH A GREAT FIERCE SHOUT AND A CLANKING OF 422 MARCOM
SWORDS) DEATH/

SWORDSMEN
I USED TO BE ONE OF THE CRACK SWORDSMEN OF 412 MARCOM
VENICE--

SWORE
AT LEAST, THAT'S WHAT HE SWORE TO ME LAST NIGHT. 190 AHWILD
I SWORE, DIDN'T I? 76 ANNA
I SWORE I WASN'T GOING TO 87 BEYOND
AND HE SWORE HE'D FORECLOSE IMMEDIATELY UNLESS-- 563 CROSS
COME BACK AS I SWORE SHE MUST/ 568 CROSS
THE MARY ALLEN LOADED WITH GOLD AS I SWORE SHE 569 CROSS
WOULD BE--CARRYIN' HER LOWERS--
NOT A REEF IN 'EM--MAKIN' PORT, BOY, AS I SWORE 569 CROSS
SHE MUST--
THEY'RE BACK ON EARTH AGAIN AS I SWORE THEY'D COME570 CROSS
BACK.
(PLEADINGLY) REMEMBER YOU SWORE ON THE BIBLE 447 DYNAMO
YOU'D NEVER TELL/
THAT I SWORE ON MY MOTHER'S BODY I'D REVENGE HER 27 ELECTR
DEATH ON HIM.
YOU SWORE TO ME YOU WERE ALL OVER THEM, OR I'D 141 ELECTR
NEVER HAVE AGREED TO COME HOME.
I SWORE I'D HAVE NO MORE DRINKS ON HICKEY, IF I 680 ICEMAN
DIED OF DROUGHT/
SWORE I'D NEVER GO OUT AGAIN. 688 ICEMAN
I WOULDN'T BELIEVE A THING HE SAID, IF HE SWORE ON 27 JOURNE
A STACK OF BIBLES/
IF HE SWORE ON A STACK OF BIBLES. 74 JOURNE
I SWORE AFTER EUGENE DIED I WOULD NEVER HAVE 87 JOURNE
ANOTHER BABY.
I TELL YOU I SWORE TO MYSELF YEARS AGO 36 MANSNS
I SWORE TO HER I WOULD NEVER INTERFERE. 103 MANSNS
HE SWORE TO ME ON HIS HONOR, LYING IN MY ARMS/ 166 MANSNS
SIMON SWORE HE'D NEVER COME TO YOU AGAIN. 167 MANSNS
WE SWORE TO EACH OTHER THAT WE WOULD CONSTANTLY 170 MANSNS
BEAR IN MIND IT WAS HE, NOT US.
HE'D SWORE HE'D NEVER HAVE CHILDREN, 59 STRANG
I SWORE TO LIVE COOLLY... 85 STRANG
(STERNLY) I SWORE I'D NEVER AGAIN MEDDLE WITH 169 STRANG
HUMAN LIVES, NINA/
WE SWORE TO HAVE A TRUE SACRAMENT--OR NOTHING/ 448 WELDED

SWORN
(PROTESTS HALF-HEARTEDLY) BUT HE'S ALWAYS SWORN 213 AHWILD
HE GOT RAKED INTO THAT PARTY
(LYING BOLDLY) I DID WANT TO--ONLY I--(THEN HE 242 AHWILD
ADDS SOLEMNLY) I'VE SWORN OFF.
(KISSES HIM) WHAT DID YOU MEAN A MINUTE AGO WHEN 243 AHWILD
YOU SAID YOU'D SWORN OFF?
I'VE SWORN T' LIVE A HUNDRED AN' I'LL DO IT, IF 210 DESIRE
ONY T' SPITE YER SINFUL GREED/
(AS EMMA MAKES NO REPLY) JACK SAYS AS YOU'VE 508 DIFRNT
SWORN YOU WAS BREAKIN' WITH CALEB.
AFTER HE'D SWORN HIS WORD OF HONOR-- 451 DYNAMO
IT WASN'T THAT KIND OF REVENGE I HAD SWORN ON MY 110 ELECTR
MOTHER'S BODY/
HE SAID HE'D SWORN OFF TONIGHT--FOREVER--FOR YOUR 300 GGBROW
SAKE--AND THE KIDS/
SURE. I'D HAVE SWORN THAT, TOO, LARRY. 588 ICEMAN
AND I'D SWORN IT WOULD NEVER HAPPEN AGAIN. 713 ICEMAN
FUNNY. I COULD HAVE SWORN I HAD THE KEY. 6 MANSNS
I WOULD HAVE SWORN HE WOULD BE THE LAST MAN ON 31 MANSNS
EARTH
(AFTER A PAUSE--WEARILY) WE'VE SWORN TO SO MUCH. 485 WELDED

SWUM
WAAL, THAT FOOL BROWN GAL B'LIEVED 'EM AND SHE 503 DIFRNT
SWUM RIGHT OFF, TICKLED TO DEATH.
(A PAUSE) THAT NIGHT WHEN SHE SWUM OUT AND GOT 515 DIFRNT
ABOARD WHEN I WAS ALONE.

SWUNG
THE DOOR ON THE LEFT IS SWUNG OPEN AND LARRY 4 ANNA
ENTERS.

SYDNEY
SYDNEY, BUENOS AIRES-- 132 BEYOND

SYDNEY'S
YES, SYDNEY'S A GOOD TOWN. 132 BEYOND

SYMBOL
THE SYMBOL OF HATE AND DERISION/ 564 DAYS
IT'S A SYMBOL OF HIS LIFE--A LAMP BURNING OUT IN A150 ELECTR
ROOM OF WAITING SHADOWS/
AS IF THEY WERE THE VISIBLE SYMBOL OF HER GOD) 157 ELECTR
THAT THEIR PASSING MAY BE A SYMBOL TO THE WORLD 318 LAZARU
THAT THERE IS NO DEATH/
AND TO PROVE MY ESCAPE--AS A SYMBOL--WATCH AND 40 MANSNS
BEAR WITNESS, NICHOLAS/
THE HEAD OF A BRONZE DRAGON, OUR ANCIENT SYMBOL OF389 MARCOM
YANG.
I WILL THIS AS A SYMBOL OF RELEASE--OF THE END OF 472 WELDED
ALL THINGS/

SYMBOLIC
A SYMBOLIC OPPORTUNITY FOR HIM. 82 POET

SYMBOLICAL
SYMBOLICAL OF THE PEACE WE HAVE FOUND. 197 STRANG

SYMBOLISM
BUT DIONYSUS IN HIS MIDDLE PERIOD, MORE 307 LAZARU
COMPREHENSIVE IN HIS SYMBOLISM.

SYMBOLS
LET ALL STARS BE FOR YOU HENCEFORTH SYMBOLS OF 289 LAZARU
SAVIORS--

SYMMETRICAL
THE SERVANTS ARRANGE THESE ON THE TABLE, IN 428 MARCOM
SYMMETRICAL GROUPS.

SYMONS'
THE SYMONS' TRANSLATION OF BAUDELAIRE'S PROSE 132 JOURNE
POEM.)
(HE RECITES THE SYMONS' TRANSLATION OF 133 JOURNE
BAUDELAIRE'S «EPILOGUE.»

SYMPATHETIC
I'LL NEED THEM TO GIVE SYMPATHETIC TREATMENT TO 558 CROSS
HIS CASE
(WITH A CHEERING, SYMPATHETIC AIR) 71 ELECTR
(SYMPATHETIC AND AT THE SAME TIME EXASPERATED) 159 ELECTR
(ABRUPTLY HE BECOMES SINCERELY SYMPATHETIC AND 684 ICEMAN
EARNEST)
(ALL THE GROUP AROUND HIM ARE SAD AND SYMPATHETIC,719 ICEMAN
TOO.
YOU WERE ALWAYS SUCH A SYMPATHETIC AUDIENCE. 9 MANSNS
(STRANGELY, TENDERLY SYMPATHETIC.) 102 MANSNS
YET FULL OF A SYMPATHETIC HUMANITY. 377 MARCOM
(IMMEDIATELY SYMPATHETIC, GETS UP AND GOES TO HIM 98 STRANG
IMPULSIVELY)
A DRIVING FORCE WHICH CAN BE SYMPATHETIC AND CRUEL443 WELDED
AT THE SAME TIME.
(SUDDENLY TURNS AND ADDRESSES HIM DIRECTLY IN A 481 WELDED
SAD, SYMPATHETIC TONE)

SYMPATHETICALLY
(SYMPATHETICALLY) I KNOW. 200 AHWILD
(PUTS HER AROUND HIM SYMPATHETICALLY) 215 AHWILD
(SYMPATHETICALLY) OF COURSE, SID. 257 AHWILD
(SHE SIGHS SYMPATHETICALLY) POOR LILY/ 291 AHWILD
(NODDING HER HEAD SYMPATHETICALLY) 14 ANNA
(SHE HAS BEEN LISTENING SYMPATHETICALLY) 18 ANNA
(COMING TO HER, ALMOST SYMPATHETICALLY) 263 DESIRE
HARRIET TURNS IN THE DOORWAY--SYMPATHETICALLY) 511 DIFRNT
SYMPATHETICALLY AS SHE COMES BACK AND SITS DOWN ON279 GGBROW
HER STOOL)
YANK GRINS SYMPATHETICALLY) 252 HA APE
(SYMPATHETICALLY NOW) NO, IT WOULDN'T BE. 587 ICEMAN
(SYMPATHETICALLY) YUH LOOK SICK, WILLIE. 674 ICEMAN
(SYMPATHETICALLY) HELL/ 530 INZONE
(SYMPATHETICALLY) HOT AS HELL/ 347 MARCOM
IT HAS GOT TO BE DONE SYMPATHETICALLY OR I WON'T 113 STRANG
BE ABLE TO WORK...
(SYMPATHETICALLY) IT ISN'T FOR YOU--NOR FOR 192 STRANG
PRESTON.

SYMPATHIES
WE HAVE BUILT UP A SECRET LIFE OF SUBTLE 148 STRANG
SYMPATHIES AND CONFIDENCES...

SYMPATHIZE
OH, I SEE, YES, I SYMPATHIZE WITH HER, TOO-- 404 MARCOM
INQUISITIVE FRIENDLINESS, ALWAYS WILLING TO 4 STRANG
LISTEN, EAGER TO SYMPATHIZE.
WHY DO I SYMPATHIZE...!) 39 STRANG

SYMPATHIZED
YOU WOULD APPRECIATE IT, IF YOU HAD SEEN HOW I 549 DAYS
SYMPATHIZED WITH HER.

SYMPATHIZING
WHY, JUST NOW HE PATS ME ON THE SHOULDER, LIKE HE 646 ICEMAN
WAS SYMPATHIZING WITH ME.

SYMPATHY
(IMMEDIATELY ALL SYMPATHY-- 208 AHWILD
BY A SMILE OF SHY UNDERSTANDING AND SYMPATHY. 297 AHWILD
(THEN WITH A TRACE OF SYMPATHY, AS SHE NOTICES HIM 32 ANNA
SWAYING FROM WEAKNESS)
(LOOKS AT HIM WITH A CERTAIN SYMPATHY) 63 ANNA
(HE PAUSES, THEN CONTINUES IN A TONE OF TENDER 147 BEYOND
SYMPATHY)
THE MAN FELT A GREAT SYMPATHY FOR HER-- 537 DAYS
(FIGHTING AGAINST HIS GROWING ATTRACTION AND 226 DESIRE
SYMPATHY--HARSHLY)
(THEN WITH DEEP SYMPATHY) IT'S DURNED HARD ON YOU, 11 ELECTR
VINNIE.
AND A GREAT SYMPATHY AND TENDERNESS) 292 GGBROW
BUT WITH A DEEP UNDERCURRENT OF SYMPATHY) 252 HA APE
(LARRY STARES AT HIM, MOVED BY SYMPATHY AND PITY 592 ICEMAN
IN SPITE OF HIMSELF, DISTURBED.
THEY HAVE MY FULL AND ENTIRE SYMPATHY. 621 ICEMAN

SYMPATHY (CONT'D.)
HICKEY PATS HIM ON THE BACK AGAIN--WITH SINCERE 657 ICEMAN
SYMPATHY)
JOE'S, =ALL I GOT WAS SYMPATHY=. 727 ICEMAN
(HIS SON LOOKS AT HIM, FOR THE FIRST TIME WITH AN 36 JOURNE
UNDERSTANDING SYMPATHY.
(SHE RAISES HER HANDS AND REGARDS THEM WITH 103 JOURNE
MELANCHOLY SYMPATHY.
LOOKING FOR SYMPATHY, BUT EDMUND IS STARING AT THE115 JOURNE
FLOOR.)
(HE LAUGHS--THEN SOBERLY, WITH GENUINE SYMPATHY.) 135 JOURNE
THAT ONE'S SYMPATHY SHOULD UNDERSTAND ALL THINGS, 372 MARCOM
MY OWN DAUGHTER HAS NO FEELINGS OR SYMPATHY. 74 MISBEG
(GENTLY AND WITH DEEP SYMPATHY) 64 STRANG

SYMPTOMS
FROM THE SYMPTOMS MRS. MANNON DESCRIBED FROM HIS 70 ELECTR
LETTER TO HER
I RECOGNIZE THE SYMPTOMS. 643 ICEMAN
HE DOES NOT APPEAR TO BE DRUNK--THAT IS, HE SHOWS 100 MISBEG
NONE OF THE USUAL SYMPTOMS.
WATCHING SYMPTOMS... 79 STRANG
I'D WATCH HIM AND READ SYMPTOMS OF INSANITY INTO 139 STRANG
EVERY MOVE HE MADE...

SYRIAN
EGYPTIAN, SYRIAN, CAPPADOCIAN, LYDIAN, PHRYGIAN, 306 LAZARU
CILICIAN, PARTHIAN.

SYRINGAS
BY THE LEFT CORNER OF THE HOUSE IS A BIG CLUMP OF 2 ELECTR
LILACS AND SYRINGAS.
BY THE EDGE OF THE DRIVE, LEFT FRONT, IS A THICK 5 ELECTR
CLUMP OF LILACS AND SYRINGAS.

SYRUP
AND STRONG, WHOSE BLOOD IS BLOOD AND NOT A 177 STRANG
SOOTHING SYRUP/=

SYSTEM
STILL I FIGURE IT'S BETTER TO GET IT OUT OF MY 139 BEYOND
SYSTEM
I THOUGHT YOU'D GOT THAT OUT OF YOUR SYSTEM LONG 496 DAYS
AGO WHEN YOU GOT ENGAGED TO
THE SHOCK TO MY SYSTEM BROUGHT ON A STROKE WHICH, 627 ICEMAN
AS A DOCTOR,
MY SYSTEM, AND NOT BE LOUSY BARFLIES, NO GOOD TO 702 ICEMAN
DEMSELVES OR NOBODY ELSE.
I KNOW YOUR SYSTEM/ 140 JOURNE
I SIMPLY REVERSED THE OLD SYSTEM. 392 MARCOM
CONFIDENT THAT WITH THE SYSTEM I'VE INSTITUTED 393 MARCOM
EVERYTHING WILL GO ON
UNDER YOUR PRESENT SYSTEM, WITH BATTERING RAMS, '394 MARCOM
I PLAYED MY SYSTEM, BUT I FOUND I DIDN'T CARE IF 1143 MISBEG
WON OR LOST.
SO THE BIG DREAM WAS THAT SOME DAY I'D HAVE ENOUGH143 MISBEG
' DOUGH TO PLAY A CAGEY SYSTEM
IT'LL DO HER GOOD TO TALK THIS OUT OF HER 42 STRANG
SYSTEM...
BUT PERHAPS SHE CAN WRITE HIM OUT OF HER 81 STRANG
SYSTEM....))

T*
MY MONTH'S UP TODAY AND I WANT WHAT'S OWIN' T* ME.124 BEYOND
(IMPUDENTLY) DON' MAKE NO DIFF'RENCE T* ME 124 BEYOND
WHETHER THERE BE OR NOT.
I'LL GIVE HIM A TASTE OF HOW =SHENANDOAH= OUGHT T*103 ELECTR
BE SUNG/
I'VE SAILED ON MANNON HOOKERS AN' BEEN WORKED T* 106 ELECTR
DEATH
T* HELL WIT DE STARVIN' FAMILY/ 235 HA APE
T* HELL WIT YOUSE/ 237 HA APE
T* HELL WIT IT/ 253 HA APE

T'AIN'T
T'AIN'T OUR'N, NO SIRREE/ 221 DESIRE
T'AIN'T HUMAN T* BE AS BAD AS THAT BE/ 257 DESIRE
(HARSHLY) T'AIN'T NO USE LYIN' NO MORE. 258 DESIRE
BUT T'AIN'T THE FARM SO MUCH--NOT NO MORE--IT'S 258 DESIRE
YEW FOOLIN' ME--

T'AINT
(DECISIVELY) BUT T'AINT THAT. 208 DESIRE

T'ANKS
T'ANKS. 14 ANNA

T'BE
HER EYES WEEPIN' AN' BLOODY WITH SMOKE AN' CINDERS209 DESIRE
SAME'S THEY USED T'BE.

T'BEEN
SALVATION ARMY, THAT'S WHAT YOU'D OUGHT T'BEEN 602 DESIRE
GENERAL IN/

T'GETHER
AN* IF YE DENY IT, I'LL SAY WE PLANNED IT 267 ICEMAN
T'GETHER--
AN* THE CABOTS'LL FIND SOLUMON'S MINES T'GETHER/ 268 DESIRE
(WITH A MEANING WINK) *E AN* FREDA WENT AHT 508 DESIRE
T'GETHER 'BOUT FIVE MINUTES PAST.

T'HELL
(WITH A FIERCE EXULTATION) T'HELL WITH EBEN/ 249 VOYAGE
(GASPINGLY) T'HELL--WITH YE/ 256 DESIRE
T'HELL WIT HOME/ 211 HA APE
T'HELL WITH SUPPER. 601 HA APE

T'HELP
WHO'LL YE GIT T'HELP YE UN THE FARM IN HIS PLACE--255 ROPE

T'INK
(WITH A CYNICAL GRIN) CAN'T YOUSE SEE I'M TRYIN' 210 DESIRE
TO T'INK$
WANTER KNOW WHAT I T'INK$ 212 HA APE

T'NIGHT
THEY HAIN'T GOIN' T* BE MUCH STRENGTH LEFT FUR 250 DESIRE
HOWIN' IN THE CORN LOT T'MORROW.

T'MORROW
SHE'S LIKE T'NIGHT, SHE'S SOFT 'N' WA'M, HER EYES 211 DESIRE
KIN WINK LIKE A STAR,

T'OTHER
THEY'S WHALE T'OTHER SIDE O' THIS FLOE AND WE'RE 550 'ILE
GOING TO GIT 'EM.
CALIFORNI-A'S T'OTHER SIDE O' EARTH, A'MOST. 205 DESIRE
T'OTHER WAY. 500 DIFRNT

T'OUSAND
MONKEY FUR--TWO T'OUSAND BUCKS/ 236 HA APE

T'PAY
WAS SLAVIN' HER TO HER GRAVE--T'PAY HER BACK FUR 208 DESIRE
THE KINDNESS SHE DONE T* YEW$

T'ROWS
I T'ROWS DOWN A FIFTY-DOLLAR BILL LIKE IT WAS 601 ICEMAN
TRASH PAPER AND SAYS,

T'S
THAT'LL GIVE ME D. T'S. ANYWAY/ 601 ICEMAN

T'US
TWO-THIRDS BELONGS T'US. 208 DESIRE

T'VE
YE NEEDN'T T'VE FRET, ABBIE, I WA'N'T AIMIN' T* 256 DESIRE
KILL HIM.

T'WAS
WALLER SAID T'WAS NO USE. 586 ROPE
FOR T'WAS ALWAYS A PAYIN' PLACE IN THE AULD DAYS. 507 ROPE

T'WUK
WAAL--LET'S GIT T'WUK. 216 DESIRE

TABLE
IN FRONT OF THE BENCH, A TABLE. 535 'ILE
THEN THE STEWARD ENTERS AND COMMENCES TO CLEAR THE535 'ILE
TABLE OF THE FEW DISHES WHICH
THERE IS A NOISE FROM THE DOORWAY ON THE RIGHT AND536 'ILE
HE DARTS BACK TO THE TABLE.
FIVE CHAIRS ARE GROUPED ABOUT THE TABLE--THREE 185 AHWILD
ROCKERS AT LEFT, RIGHT.
AT CENTER IS A BIG, ROUND TABLE WITH A GREEN- 185 AHWILD
SHADED READING LAMP,
AND SLOUCHES BACK INTO THE ARMCHAIR AT LEFT REAR 187 AHWILD
OF TABLE.
HE GOES TO THE TABLE, LIGHTS HIS PIPE AND PICKS UP187 AHWILD
THE LOCAL MORNING PAPER,
(HE SINKS IN ROCKER AT RIGHT OF TABLE) 188 AHWILD
(SHE PICKS UP A MAGAZINE FROM THE TABLE AND BEGINS188 AHWILD
TO ROCK, FANNING HERSELF.)
(HE POINTS TO THE ROCKING CHAIR AT THE RIGHT OF 193 AHWILD
TABLE NEAR HIS.)
(RICHARD OBEDIENTLY TAKES THE CHAIR AT RIGHT OF 194 AHWILD
TABLE, OPPOSITE HIS FATHER)
(SITTING DOWN IN THE CHAIR AT THE RIGHT OF TABLE--201 AHWILD
ACIDLY)
HE PUSHES THE SLIPS OF PAPER ACROSS THE TABLE 202 AHWILD
(CONTEMPTUOUSLY)
HERE'S A LETTER FROM MURIEL FOR YOUR SON (PUTS IT 203 AHWILD
ON THE TABLE) IT MAKES CLEAR,
(HIS FISTS CLENCHED, LEANS ACROSS THE TABLE) 203 AHWILD
(NOTICES THE SLIPS OF PAPER ON THE TABLE) 204 AHWILD
POINTS TO THE SLIPS OF PAPER ON THE TABLE) 207 AHWILD
(HE TAKES THE LETTER FROM THE TABLE) 207 AHWILD
THE TABLE, WITH A CHAIR AT EACH END, LEFT AND 210 AHWILD
RIGHT.
(SHE STRETCHES AWKWARDLY OVER THE TABLE TO REACH 210 AHWILD
THE CHANDELIER THAT IS
IN THE SETTING OF THE TABLE. 210 AHWILD
ESPECIALLY NOW WHEN ALL THE LEAVES OF THE TABLE 210 AHWILD
ARE IN.
SHE JARS HEAVILY AGAINST THE TABLE.) 211 AHWILD
WELL, SHE'S GOT THE TABLE ALL WRONG. 211 AHWILD
(BEGINNING TO HELP WITH THE TABLE) 212 AHWILD
(HE COMES NEARER THE TABLE AND SURVEYS IT, 217 AHWILD
DINNER'S COMING RIGHT ON THE TABLE. 221 AHWILD
AT RIGHT OF THOSE AT REAR OF TABLE FACING FRONT. 221 AHWILD
LILY SITS IN THE ONE OF THOSE AT LEFT, BY THE HEAD221 AHWILD
OF THE TABLE,
THE REAR OF THE TABLE.) 222 AHWILD
(SHE STARES WITH STIFF DIGNITY TOWARD HER PLACE AT222 AHWILD
THE FOOT OF THE TABLE,
(SHE BRINGS THE SOUP AROUND THE HEARD OF THE 222 AHWILD
TABLE, PASSING MILLER.)
(SHE SITS DOWN STIFFLY AT THE FOOT OF THE TABLE.) 222 AHWILD
HE OUGHT TO BE AT THIS TABLE EATING SOMETHING TO 223 AHWILD
SOBER HIM UP.
TAKE YOUR ELBOWS OFF THE TABLE/ 223 AHWILD
(COMING TO HIS PLACE AT THE HEAD OF THE TABLE, 223 AHWILD
(ADDRESSING THE TABLE NOW. 227 AHWILD
ONE MORE SOUND OUT OF YOU, YOUNG MAN AND YOU'LL 229 AHWILD
LEAVE THE TABLE/
(THERE IS A BURST OF LAUGHTER FROM AROUND THE 230 AHWILD
TABLE.
RICHARD AND BELLE ARE DISCOVERED SITTING AT THE 236 AHWILD
TABLE AT CENTER,
THREE TABLES WITH STAINED TOPS, FOUR CHAIRS AROUND236 AHWILD
EACH TABLE.
A BRASS CUSPIDOR IS ON THE FLOOR BY EACH TABLE. 236 AHWILD
AT THE MIDDLE OF TABLE, REAR, FACING FRONT. 236 AHWILD
(RICHARD IS STARTLED AND SHOCKED BY THIS CURSE AND238 AHWILD
LOOKS DOWN AT THE TABLE)
(COMING TO THE TABLE--WITH A WINK AT BELLE) 238 AHWILD
(SETTING THEM ON THE TABLE) HERE'S YOUR PLEASURE.242 AHWILD
(PASSES BY HER TO THE TABLE AT RIGHT--GRINNING 244 AHWILD
GENIALLY)
I'M GOING OVER AND SIT AT HIS TABLE FOR A WHILE, 244 AHWILD
SEE.
(HE MOVES TOWARD THEIR TABLE.) 246 AHWILD
MRS. MILLER SITS BY THE TABLE AT RIGHT, FRONT. 249 AHWILD
MILLER IS SITTING IN HIS FAVORITE ROCKING CHAIR AT249 AHWILD
LEFT OF TABLE, FRONT.
LILY IS SITTING IN THE ARMCHAIR BY THE TABLE AT 249 AHWILD
REAR, FACING RIGHT.
(SHE PASSES THE TABLE TO SHOW HER AUNT 250 AHWILD
LILY.

TABLE

TABLE (CONT'D.)
(HE SITS DOWN IN THE ARMCHAIR AT LEFT OF TABLE, 254 AHWILD
REAR)
I WOULDN'T HAVE THE PESKY THINGS ON MY TABLE/ 255 AHWILD
OF TABLE AND IMMEDIATELY YAWNS) 264 AHWILD
(COMES AND SITS IN HER FATHER'S CHAIR AT RIGHT, 272 AHWILD
FRONT OF TABLE)
HIS WIFE IN THE ROCKER AT RIGHT, FRONT, OF TABLE. 288 AHWILD
SEVERAL BOOKS ARE PILED ON THE TABLE BY HIS ELBOW.288 AHWILD
(CHUCKLES AT SOMETHING HE READS--THEN CLOSES THE 288 AHWILD
BOOK AND PUTS IN ON THE TABLE.
MILLER IS SITTING IN HIS ROCKER AT LEFT, FRONT, OF288 AHWILD
TABLE.
AT THE HEAD OF THE TABLE. 289 AHWILD
(SHE COMES BACK TO THE TABLE AND HE FOLLOWS HER, 293 AHWILD
STILL HALF IN A DREAM.
(SHE COMES FORWARD AND SITS AT THE TABLE IN THE 7 ANNA
RIGHT CORNER, FRONT.)
THEN SUDDENLY POUNDS HIS FIST ON THE TABLE WITH 8 ANNA
HAPPY EXCITEMENT)
LARRY BRINGS IN THE DRINKS AND SETS THEM ON THE 8 ANNA
TABLE.
(SUDDENLY SPRINGING TO HIS FEET AND SMASHING HIS 9 ANNA
FIST ON THE TABLE IN A RAGE)
(HE TAKES HER DRINK IN TO MARTHY AND SITS DOWN AT 10 ANNA
THE TABLE.
DON'T BE BREAKIN' THE TABLE, YOU OLD GOAT/ 13 ANNA
(HE SMASHES HIS FIST ON THE TABLE WITH A BANG.) 13 ANNA
SHE COMES AND SINKS WEARILY IN A CHAIR BY THE 14 ANNA
TABLE, LEFT FRONT.)
(SHE SHUFFLES OVER TO ANNA'S TABLE AND SITS DOWN 15 ANNA
OPPOSITE HER.
(SHE PUFFS, STARING AT THE TABLE TOP. 15 ANNA
CHRIS COMES IN AND SETS THE DRINKS DOWN ON THE 24 ANNA
TABLE--
ANNA IS SEATED IN THE ROCKING-CHAIR BY THE TABLE, 41 ANNA
WITH A NEWSPAPER IN HER HANDS.
A TABLE WITH TWO CANE-BOTTOMED CHAIRS STANDS IN 41 ANNA
THE CENTER OF THE CABIN.
A DILAPIDATED WICKER ROCKER, PAINTED BROWN, IS 41 ANNA
ALSO BY THE TABLE.
THEN HE GOES TO THE TABLE, SETS THE CLOTH STRAIGHT 44 ANNA
MECHANICALLY.
HE STARES AT THE PAPER FOR A WHILE, THEN PUTS IT 44 ANNA
ON TABLE.
(HE SITS DOWN OPPOSITE CHRIS AT THE TABLE AND 45 ANNA
LEANS OVER TOWARD HIM)
(BANGING THE TABLE WITH HIS FIST--FURIOUSLY) 47 ANNA
(POUNDING THE TABLE) THE SEA'S THE ONLY LIFE FOR 48 ANNA
A MAN WITH GUTS IN HIM ISN'T
(HE SITS DOWN AT THE LEFT OF TABLE.) 51 ANNA
(ADVANCING TOWARD THE TABLE--PROTESTING TO BURKE) 51 ANNA
(SHE STANDS AT THE TABLE REAR. 56 ANNA
THROWING HERSELF INTO THE CHAIR AND HIDING HER 59 ANNA
FACE IN HER HANDS ON THE TABLE
AND POUNDING ON THE TABLE WITH HER HANDS) 61 ANNA
THE CABIN IS LIGHTED BY A SMALL LAMP ON THE TABLE. 63 ANNA
ANNA SITS AT THE TABLE, STARING STRAIGHT IN FRONT 63 ANNA
OF HER.)
(HE SITS IN A CHAIR BY THE TABLE, SETTING DOWN THE 63 ANNA
CAN OF BEER.
THIS FAILS TO DISTRACT HER, AND FLINGING THE 67 ANNA
MAGAZINE BACK ON THE TABLE,
(SHE PUTS IT IN THE DRAWER OF TABLE AND CLOSES THE 67 ANNA
DRAWER.)
(ANNA TAKES A MAGAZINE FROM THE TABLE. 67 ANNA
SHE RUSHES TO THE TABLE, 68 ANNA
HEARING NO SOUND, HE CLOSES THE DOOR BEHIND HIM 68 ANNA
AND COMES FORWARD TO THE TABLE.
IN THE CENTER OF THE TABLE, A LARGE OIL READING 93 BEYOND
LAMP.
AN OAK DINING-ROOM TABLE WITH A RED COVER, 93 BEYOND
AND ONE STRAIGHT-BACKED, ARE PLACED ABOUT THE 93 BEYOND
TABLE.
HIS HANDS ON THE TABLE IN FRONT OF HIM. 94 BEYOND
(HE SLAPS THE TABLE WITH THE PALMS OF HIS HANDS 94 BEYOND
AND LAUGHS LOUDLY.
JAMES MAYO SITS IN FRONT OF THE TABLE. 94 BEYOND
(SLAPPING THE TABLE) HO/ 95 BEYOND
(HE POUNDS ON THE TABLE, ATTEMPTING TO COVER UP 103 BEYOND
THIS CONFESSION OF WEAKNESS.)
(HE POUNDS THE TABLE WITH HIS FISTS IN 103 BEYOND
EXASPERATION.)
(STARTING TO HIS FEET AND STRETCHING HIS ARMS 108 BEYOND
ACROSS THE TABLE TOWARD MAYO)
A CHILD'S DOLL, WITH ONE ARM GONE, LIES UNDER THE 112 BEYOND
TABLE.
THE TABLE COVER IS SPOTTED AND ASKEW. 112 BEYOND
MRS. ATKINS TO THE RIGHT OF THE TABLE, MRS. 112 BEYOND
MAYO'S FACE HAS LOST ALL CHARACTER.
A PLACE IS SET AT THE END OF THE TABLE, LEFT, FOR 112 BEYOND
SOMEONE'S DINNER.
LIES ON THE TABLE BEFORE MRS. MAYO.) 113 BEYOND
(WITH A DISAPPROVING GLANCE AT THE PLACE SET ON 113 BEYOND
THE TABLE)
SHE SITS IN THE ROCKER IN FRONT OF THE TABLE AND 116 BEYOND
SIGHS WEARILY.
RUTH GLANCES AT THE PLACE SET ON THE TABLE) 117 BEYOND
(MARY SITS DOWN ON THE FLOOR BEFORE THE TABLE 117 BEYOND
(SEES THE DOLL UNDER THE TABLE AND STRUGGLES ON 117 BEYOND
HER MOTHER'S LAP.
(SITTING DOWN IN THE CHAIR ON THE LEFT OF TABLE 119 BEYOND
AND CUDDLING MARY ON HIS LAP)
RUTH COMES OUT OF THE KITCHEN AND GETS THE PLATE 121 BEYOND
FROM THE TABLE.
ROBERT CONTINUES TO READ, OBLIVIOUS TO THE FOOD ON121 BEYOND
THE TABLE.)
UNDER THE TABLE. 121 BEYOND

TABLE (CONT'D.)
(SPITEFULLY, WITH A GLANCE AT ANDREW'S LETTER ON 125 BEYOND
THE TABLE)
SUPPORTING HERSELF BY THE TABLE, GASPING FOR 128 BEYOND
BREATH.
SHE STAGGERS BACK AGAINST THE TABLE--THICKLY) 128 BEYOND
THE TOP OF THE COVERLESS TABLE IS STAINED 144 BEYOND
STANDS ON THE TABLE, PRESENTS AN APPEARANCE OF 144 BEYOND
DECAY, OF DISSOLUTION.
(HE WALKS WEAKLY TO A ROCKER BY THE SIDE OF THE 145 BEYOND
TABLE
RUTH SPRINGS TO HER FEET AND COMES QUICKLY TO THE 150 BEYOND
TABLE, LEFT,
(HE THROWS OFF HIS CAP AND HEAVY OVERCOAT ON THE 153 BEYOND
TABLE,
WHICH SHE SETS ON THE TABLE BESIDE THE OTHER. 153 BEYOND
HE COMES FORWARD AND SINKS DOWN IN THE ROCKER ON 154 BEYOND
THE RIGHT OF TABLE,
ANDREW POUNDS ON THE TABLE WITH HIS FIST) 155 BEYOND
IN FRONT OF THE BENCH, A LONG TABLE WITH TWO 555 CROSS
STRAIGHT-BACKED CHAIRS.
A SKYLIGHT EXTENDING FROM OPPOSITE THE DOOR TO 555 CROSS
ABOVE THE LEFT EDGE OF THE TABLE.
AND RESTS LIKE TIRED DUST IN CIRCULAR PATCHES UPON555 CROSS
THE FLOOR AND TABLE.
(HE SITS DOWN IN THE CHAIR TO THE LEFT OF THE 556 CROSS
TABLE)
(WALKING SLOWLY TOWARD THE TABLE) 556 CROSS
(SITTING GINGERLY ON THE CHAIR IN FRONT OF TABLE) 557 CROSS
(HE SPREADS IT ON THE TABLE.) 561 CROSS
THROWS IT ON THE TABLE NEAR THE LANTERN.) 561 CROSS
THEN HE GOES OVER TO THE TABLE, TURNING THE 562 CROSS
LANTERN VERY LOW, AND SITS DOWN.
(COMES TO THE TABLE) I WAS READING. 563 CROSS
THE MAP OF THE ISLAND (HE SPREADS IT OUT ON THE 566 CROSS
TABLE)
(HE TURNS FROM HER AND GOES BACK TO HIS SEAT BY 570 CROSS
THE TABLE.
A THIRD CHAIR IS AT RIGHT OF TABLE. 493 DAYS
THIS LIGHT IS CONCENTRATED AROUND THE TWO FIGURES 493 DAYS
SEATED AT THE TABLE.
LOVING SITS IN THE ARMCHAIR AT REAR OF TABLE. 493 DAYS
AT REAR OF TABLE, AN ARMCHAIR, FACING FRONT, 493 DAYS
BEFORE IT, A CHAIR, ITS BACK TO THE WINDOW, AND A 493 DAYS
TABLE.
(HE SITS DOWN IN THE CHAIR AT RIGHT OF TABLE WHERE505 DAYS
FATHER BAIRD HAD SAT,
(THE TELEPHONE ON THE TABLE RINGS. 513 DAYS
IN FRONT OF THIS WINDOW IS A TABLE WITH A LAMP, 514 DAYS
AT RIGHT OF CHAIR, A SMALL TABLE WITH A LAMP, 514 DAYS
AT RIGHT OF TABLE, IN THE CENTER OF THE ROOM, A 514 DAYS
SOFA.
DURING THE NEXT FEW SPEECHES HE MOVES SILENTLY TO 525 DAYS
THE CORNER OF THE LONG TABLE
IN THE CHAIR BY THE END OF THE TABLE BEFORE THE 532 DAYS
WINDOW.
IN FRONT OF TABLE A SIMILAR CHAIR. 541 DAYS
A LONG TABLE WITH A LAMP IS AT CENTER, FRONT. 541 DAYS
LOVING IN THE CHAIR AT LEFT OF TABLE. 541 DAYS
AT LEFT OF TABLE IS A CHAIR. 541 DAYS
THE PRIEST IS SITTING ON THE CHAISE-LONGUE, JOHN 541 DAYS
IN THE CHAIR AT FRONT OF TABLE,
(SINKS DOWN IN THE CHAIR BY THE TABLE AND WAITS 547 DAYS
TENSELY--
LOVING HAS COME UP AND STANDS BY THE RIGHT END OF 548 DAYS
TABLE, AT RIGHT, REAR,
(SHE SITS IN THE CHAIR IN FRONT OF TABLE. 548 DAYS
AT REAR OF THIS DOOR, IN THE MIDDLE OF THE WALL, 553 DAYS
IS A DRESSING TABLE.
LOVING KEEPS PACE WITH THEM, PASSING TO REAR OF 555 DAYS
TABLE.)
PASSING IN FRONT OF THE TABLE. 555 DAYS
LOVING HAS COME AROUND BEHIND THE TABLE AND SLIPS 560 DAYS
IN AFTER HIM.
TABLE, FRONT, COMES QUICKLY TO THE DOORWAY. 560 DAYS
GOES BACK AS FAR AS THE TABLE. 561 DAYS
FATHER BAIRD LOOKS UP AS THEY PASS THE TABLE.) 563 DAYS
A PINE TABLE IS AT CENTER, A COOKSTOVE IN THE 206 DESIRE
RIGHT REAR CORNER.
EBEN TAKES BOILED POTATOES AND BACON FROM THE 206 DESIRE
STOVE AND PUTS THEM ON THE TABLE.
FOUR ROUGH WOODEN CHAIRS, A TALLOW CANDLE ON THE 206 DESIRE
TABLE.
AN' ON THE TABLE/ 215 DESIRE
(AS THEY GO BACK TO THE TABLE) 216 DESIRE
SHOWS THE INTERIOR OF THE KITCHEN WITH A LIGHTED 216 DESIRE
CANDLE ON TABLE.
(PUTTING HIS MUDDY BOOTS UP ON THE TABLE, TILTING 217 DESIRE
BACK HIS CHAIR.
(THEY DRINK--PUFF RESOLUTELY--SIGH--TAKE THEIR 217 DESIRE
FEET DOWN FROM THE TABLE.)
TAKES OUT A CANVAS BAG AND PUTS IT ON TABLE, 219 DESIRE
HE SITS DOWN AT THE TABLE, FACES THE STOVE AND 220 DESIRE
PULLS OUT THE PAPER.
(SHE LOOKS AT THE TABLE, PROUDLY) 227 DESIRE
IN THE KITCHEN, BY THE LIGHT OF A TALLOW CANDLE ON259 DESIRE
THE TABLE, EBEN IS SITTING.
IN THE KITCHEN, ABBIE SITS AT THE TABLE, HER BODY 262 DESIRE
LIMP AND EXHAUSTED,
NEAR THE TABLE, THREE PLUSH-COVERED CHAIRS, TWO OF493 DIFRNT
WHICH ARE ROCKERS.
ON THE TABLE, A LARGE CHINA LAMP, A BULKY BIBLE 493 DIFRNT
WITH A BRASS CLASP,
IN THE CENTER OF THE ROOM THERE IS A CLUMSY, 493 DIFRNT
MARBLE-TOPPED TABLE.
(HE INDICATES THE NOVELS ON THE TABLE.) 496 DIFRNT
SHE SITS IN ONE OF THE ROCKERS BY THE TABLE, HER 501 DIFRNT
FACE GREATLY TROUBLED.

TABLE

(CONT'D.)
(SHE COMES BACK BY THE TABLE, FIGHTING TO CONCEAL 501 DIFRNT
HER AGITATION.
THEN POINTS TO A CHAIR ON THE OTHER SIDE OF THE 507 DIFRNT
TABLE)
ONLY THE OLD BIBLE, WHICH STILL PRESERVES ITS 519 DIFRNT
PLACE OF HONOR ON THE TABLE,
THE TABLE AT CENTER IS OF VARNISHED OAK. 519 DIFRNT
SHE IS SEATED IN A ROCKER BY THE TABLE. 519 DIFRNT
PLACED WITH PRECISION IN FRONT OF THE TWO DOORS 519 DIFRNT
AND UNDER THE TABLE.
(SHE SITS IN A ROCKER BY THE TABLE.) 531 DIFRNT
(SHE PLUMPS HERSELF INTO A ROCKER BY THE TABLE-- 535 DIFRNT
THE TABLE SOBBING HYSTERICALLY. 544 DIFRNT
SWEEPS EVERYTHING OFF THE TABLE ONTO THE FLOOR. 548 DIFRNT
THERE IS A LIGHTED KEROSENE LAMP ON THE TABLE. 421 DYNAMO
HIS WIFE'S ROCKER IS AT THE RIGHT OF THE TABLE. 421 DYNAMO
ON THE TABLE AT CENTER ARE A CHEAP OIL READING 421 DYNAMO
LAMP, A BIBLE,
IN THE SITTING ROOM BELOW THERE IS A TABLE AT 421 DYNAMO
CENTER, FRONT.
A SMALL TABLE ON WHICH ARE STACKED HIS TEXTBOOKS, 421 DYNAMO
AND A CHAIR IN LEFT CORNER,
(HE SITS DOWN BY THE TABLE AND, PICKING UP HIS 426 DYNAMO
BIBLE,
THERE IS A TABLE AT CENTER, FRONT, IN THE SITTING 428 DYNAMO
ROOM,
THERE IS A DRESSING TABLE WITH A BIG MIRROR 428 DYNAMO
AGAINST THE REAR WALL, RIGHT,
RAMSAY FIFE IS SEATED AT THE LEFT OF THE TABLE, 428 DYNAMO
(HE TOSSES THE BOOK ON THE TABLE AND SPEAKS TO HIS429 DYNAMO
WIFE)
(HE SEES THE NEWSPAPER ON THE TABLE AND REACHES 430 DYNAMO
FOR IT,
HE FORCES HIM TO SIT IN THE CHAIR ACROSS THE TABLE436 DYNAMO
FROM HIM.
(WITH A GREAT PRETENSE OF INDIFFERENCE SHE GETS A 443 DYNAMO
BOOK FROM THE TABLE AND SITS
TABLE BUT LETS IT DROP AGAIN AND STARES BEFORE 455 DYNAMO
HIM.)
(HE BREAKS DOWN, SOBBING, AND BURIES HIS HEAD IN 456 DYNAMO
HIS ARMS ON THE TABLE)
LIGHT IS STILL SITTING, HIS FACE HIDDEN IN HIS 462 DYNAMO
ARMS ON THE TABLE,
HE TURNS AND SLUMPS INTO THE CHAIR AT THE FAR SIDE464 DYNAMO
OF THE TABLE)
(HE STUMBLES HASTILY AROUND THE TABLE TO THE DAZED466 DYNAMO
REUBEN AND WITH A PITIFUL
(HE SPRINGS FROM HIS CHAIR AND LEANING ACROSS THE 466 DYNAMO
TABLE,
LAVINIA IS DISCOVERED STANDING BY THE TABLE. 28 ELECTR
A LARGE TABLE WITH AN ARMCHAIR ON EITHER SIDE, 28 ELECTR
RIGHT AND LEFT,
LAVINIA GOES BACK TO HER FATHER'S CHAIR AT LEFT OF 29 ELECTR
TABLE.)
FINALLY, AS IF MAKING UP HER MIND IRREVOCABLY, SHE 35 ELECTR
COMES TO THE TABLE,
COMES AND SITS IN MANNON'S CHAIR ON THE LEFT OF 36 ELECTR
TABLE.
HE BRINGS THE CHAIR AT RIGHT OF TABLE CLOSE TO 37 ELECTR
HERS.)
AT LEFT, FRONT, IS A TABLE WITH A LAMP ON IT AND A 58 ELECTR
CHAIR BESIDE IT.
SHE TIPTOES TO THE TABLE, LEFT FRONT, 58 ELECTR
CHRISTINE HASTILY SITS DOWN IN THE CHAIR BY THE 59 ELECTR
TABLE.
SNATCHES UP THE BOX FROM THE TABLE AND HOLDS IT 62 ELECTR
BEHIND HER BACK,
HER FINGERS RELEASE THE BOX ON THE TABLE TOP AND 62 ELECTR
SHE BRINGS HER HAND IN FRONT OF
(SHE SHRINKS BACK TO THE TABLE, THE HAND WITH THE 62 ELECTR
BOX HELD OUT BEHIND HER,
AT THE LEFT CENTER OF THE ROOM, FRONT, IS A TABLE 79 ELECTR
WITH TWO CHAIRS.
ARE A WALL TABLE AND CHAIR AND A WRITING DESK AND 79 ELECTR
CHAIR.
CHRISTINE GOES AROUND THE TABLE TO THE CHAIR 81 ELECTR
OPPOSITE ORIN AND SITS DOWN.)
IN THE CHAIR AT RIGHT OF TABLE. 81 ELECTR
HE SITS DOWN IN THE CHAIR AT LEFT OF TABLE AND 84 ELECTR
STARES BEFORE HIM BITTERLY.
(COMING FORWARD AND SITTING ACROSS THE TABLE FROM 84 ELECTR
HIM--
CATCHING AT THE TABLE FOR SUPPORT--TERRIFIEDLY) 92 ELECTR
THERE IS A LAMP ON THIS TABLE. 93 ELECTR
THE TABLE AND CHAIRS WHICH HAD BEEN AT CENTER HAVE 93 ELECTR
BEEN MOVED TO THE LEFT.
(SHE SINKS IN THE CHAIR AT RIGHT OF TABLE.) 93 ELECTR
(HE LEAVES HER AND SPRAWLS IN THE CHAIR AT LEFT OF 96 ELECTR
TABLE.
THE OTHER TWO AT THE TABLE ENDS, LEFT AND RIGHT. 109 ELECTR
ON THE TABLE IS A BOTTLE OF WHISKEY, HALF FULL, 109 ELECTR
BENEATH IT IS A PINE TABLE WITH THREE CHAIRS, ONE 109 ELECTR
AT REAR,
AT THE RIGHT END OF THE TABLE. 110 ELECTR
IN THE CABIN, BRANT IS SEATED AT THE RIGHT OF 110 ELECTR
TABLE,
(ORIN PUTS HIS REVOLVER ON THE TABLE AND TAKES A 114 ELECTR
CHISEL.
BRANT PITCHES FORWARD TO THE FLOOR BY THE TABLE, 114 ELECTR
ROLLS OVER,
AND PUT THE LANTERN ON THE TABLE AT FRONT. 139 ELECTR
ORIN IS SITTING IN HIS FATHER'S CHAIR AT LEFT OF 149 ELECTR
TABLE,
BOOKCASE AND LAYS IT OPEN ON THE TABLE AS IF HE 149 ELECTR
HAD BEEN READING.
(HE HURRIEDLY STRAIGHTENS UP THE TABLE AND GRABS A149 ELECTR
BOOK AT RANDOM FROM THE

TABLE (CONT'D.)
(SHE COMES OVER TO THE TABLE) 150 ELECTR
(HE SLUMPS DOWN IN HIS CHAIR AT LEFT OF TABLE) 151 ELECTR
ORIN UNLOCKS THE TABLE DRAWER, PULLS OUT HIS 156 ELECTR
MANUSCRIPT, AND TAKES UP HIS PEN.)
SHE COMES TO THE TABLE AND TURNS UP THE LAMP. 157 ELECTR
THE LAMP ON THE TABLE IS LIGHTED BUT TURNED LOW. 157 ELECTR
AND PRETENDS TO BE GLANCING THROUGH A BOOK ON THE 157 ELECTR
TABLE.
MECHANICALLY SHE HIDES THE SEALED ENVELOPE IN A 167 ELECTR
DRAWER OF THE TABLE AND
(SAGS WEAKLY AND SUPPORTS HERSELF AGAINST THE 167 ELECTR
TABLE--
WHICH IS ON THE TABLE AND, PUTTING A FINGER IN AT 269 GGBROW
RANDOM,
AN ARMCHAIR AT LEFT, A TABLE WITH A CHAIR IN BACK 269 GGBROW
OF IT AT CENTER,
DION IS SITTING BEHIND THE TABLE, STARING BEFORE 269 GGBROW
HIM.
WHICH IS ON THE TABLE BEFORE HIM. 290 GGBROW
DION'S DRAFTING TABLE WITH A HIGH STOOL IN FRONT 290 GGBROW
IS AT CENTER.
DION IS SITTING ON THE STOOL IN BACK OF THE TABLE,290 GGBROW
THE READING LAMP ON THE TABLE IS THE ONLY LIGHT. 294 GGBROW
(THEN ADVANCING TO THE TABLE WITH A SORT 294 GGBROW
THE HEAVY TABLE AT CENTER IS EXPENSIVE. 294 GGBROW
HE STARTS GUILTILY, LAYING THE MASK ON THE TABLE. 299 GGBROW
ARE SITTING ON STOOLS BEHIND WHAT WAS FORMERLY 302 GGBROW
DION'S TABLE.
(THEY BEND OVER THEIR TABLE. 302 GGBROW
HE SWITCHES ON THE READING LAMP ON THE TABLE. 306 GGBROW
BROWN TAKES OFF HIS OWN MASK AND LAYS IT ON THE 306 GGBROW
TABLE BEFORE DION'S.
WHICH HE PUTS ON THE TABLE AND PINS HIS PLAN UPON,310 GGBROW
GOES AND TAKES A ROLLED-UP PLAN FROM THE TABLE 310 GGBROW
DRAWER--DULLY)
THE TWO DRAFTSMEN ARE BENT OVER THEIR TABLE, 313 GGBROW
WORKING.
THE MASK OF DION STANDS ON THE TABLE BENEATH THE 319 GGBROW
LIGHT, FACING FRONT.
ON HIS KNEES BESIDE THE TABLE, FACING FRONT, 319 GGBROW
WHEN DEY GOT TROUGH DERE WASN'T A CHAIR OR TABLE 234 HA APE
WIT A LEG UNDER IT.
ARE GROUPED ABOUT THE TABLE. 245 HA APE
A TABLE WITH PAPERS, STACKS OF PAMPHLETS, CHAIRS 245 HA APE
ABOUT IT, IS AT CENTER.
THERE'S LITERATURE ON THE TABLE. 247 HA APE
EVER REGARDED AS ANYTHING BUT A NOISOME TABLE 571 ICEMAN
DECORATION,
BY PUTTING A PROPERTY SANDWICH IN THE MIDDLE OF 571 ICEMAN
EACH TABLE,
A TABLE, SIMILARLY PLACED AT REAR OF FRONT TABLES 573 ICEMAN
TWO AND THREE,
IS A TABLE OF THE SECOND ROW WITH FIVE CHAIRS. 573 ICEMAN
A FOURTH CHAIR IS AT RIGHT OF TABLE, FACING LEFT. 574 ICEMAN
ALL FOUR CHAIRS AT THE MIDDLE TABLE, FRONT, ARE 574 ICEMAN
OCCUPIED.
AT FRONT IS A TABLE WITH FOUR CHAIRS. 574 ICEMAN
AT RIGHT OF TABLE, OPPOSITE JOE, IS CECIL LEWIS-- 574 ICEMAN
--THE CAPTAIN---.
JOE MOTT SITS AT LEFT-FRONT OF THE TABLE, FACING 574 ICEMAN
FRONT.
HUGO IN A CHAIR FACING RIGHT, LARRY AT REAR OF 574 ICEMAN
TABLE FACING FRONT,
IN THE BACK ROOM, LARRY SLADE AND HUGO KALMAR ARE 574 ICEMAN
AT THE TABLE AT LEFT-FRONT,
HE IS ASLEEP NOW, BENT FORWARD IN HIS CHAIR, HIS 574 ICEMAN
ARMS FOLDED ON THE TABLE,
AT CENTER OF THE TABLE, REAR, JAMES CAMERON 574 ICEMAN
HE IS HUNCHED FORWARD, BOTH ELBOWS ON THE TABLE, 575 ICEMAN
AT THE TABLE AT RIGHT, FRONT, HARRY HOPE, THE 576 ICEMAN
PROPRIETOR, SITS IN THE MIDDLE.
COLLAR AND TIE CRUSHED UP INTO A PILLOW ON THE 576 ICEMAN
TABLE IN FRONT OF HIM,
HIS HEAD ON HIS LEFT ARM OUTSTRETCHED ALONG THE 577 ICEMAN
TABLE EDGE.
IN A CHAIR FACING RIGHT AT THE TABLE IN THE SECOND577 ICEMAN
LINE,
ROCKY TAKES THE BOTTLE AND PUTS IT ON THE TABLE 578 ICEMAN
WHERE WILLIE OBAN IS)
HIS HEAD SINKS TO THE TABLE AGAIN AND HE IS AT 579 ICEMAN
ONCE FAST ASLEEP.)
(LARRY POURS A DRINK FROM THE BOTTLE ON WILLIE'S 580 ICEMAN
TABLE AND GULPS IT DOWN.
(BEHIND HIM, IN THE CHAIR AT LEFT OF THE MIDDLE 583 ICEMAN
TABLE,
(INDICATES THE CHAIR ON THE RIGHT OF TABLE) 585 ICEMAN
HE COMES FORWARD AND SITS AT THE TABLE AND SLUMPS 586 ICEMAN
BACK,
THE SAME APPLIES TO HARRY HIMSELF AND HIS TWO 594 ICEMAN
CRONIES AT THE FAR TABLE.
RAPPING ON THE TABLE WITH HIS KNUCKLES AT THE 596 ICEMAN
INDICATED SPOTS IN THE SONG...)
LEWIS IS GAZING ACROSS THE TABLE AT JOE MOTT, 598 ICEMAN
GOOD GOD! HAVE I BEEN DRINKING AT THE SAME TABLE 598 ICEMAN
WITH A BLOODY KAFFIR?
MEANWHILE, AT THE MIDDLE TABLE, 598 ICEMAN
(HE REACHES ON THE TABLE AS IF HE EXPECTED A GLASS606 ICEMAN
TO BE THERE--
AND I'LL SHOW YOU THE PRETTIEST (RAP, RAP, RAP ON 607 ICEMAN
TABLE) THAT EVER YOU DID SEE.
(AS SHE AND PEARL COME TO THE TABLE AT RIGHT, 611 ICEMAN
FRONT, FOLLOWED BY ROCKY)
(MARGIE AND PEARL SIT AT LEFT, AND REAR, OF TABLE,612 ICEMAN
ROCKY AT RIGHT OF IT.
(COMES BACK TO THE TABLE--DISGUSTEDLY) 614 ICEMAN
AT LARRY'S TABLE, PARRITT IS GLARING RESENTFULLY 615 ICEMAN
TOWARD THE GIRLS.)

TABLE

TABLE (CONT'D.)

CHUCK TAKES AN EMPTY CHAIR FROM HOPE'S TABLE AND 615 ICEMAN PUTS IT BY HERS AND SITS DOWN.

MOVES TO THE MIDDLE TABLE TO SHAKE HANDS WITH 619 ICEMAN LEWIS, JOE MOTT,

AT THE FRONT OF THE TABLE IN THE SECOND ROW WHICH 619 ICEMAN IS HALF BETWEEN HOPE'S TABLE

AND A BOTTLE FOR EACH TABLE, STARTING WITH LARRY'S619 ICEMAN TABLE.

(COMING TO HICKEY'S TABLE, PUTS A BOTTLE OF 620 ICEMAN WHISKEY, A GLASS AND A CHASER ON IT--

(AS ROCKY PUTS DRINK ON HIS TABLE) 620 ICEMAN

AND HE POUNDS THE TABLE WITH A SMALL FIST) 627 ICEMAN

WHO HAD PASSED INTO HIS CUSTOMARY COMA AGAIN, HEAD627 ICEMAN ON TABLE,

AT RIGHT, FRONT, IS A TABLE WITHOUT CHAIRS. 628 ICEMAN

LONG TABLE WITH AN UNEVEN LINE OF CHAIRS BEHIND 628 ICEMAN IT, AND CHAIRS AT EACH END.

THIS IMPROVISED BANQUET TABLE IS COVERED WITH OLD 628 ICEMAN TABLE CLOTHS.

NEAR THE MIDDLE OF THE ROW OF CHAIRS BEHIND THE 629 ICEMAN TABLE, LARRY SITS, FACING FRONT,

BY THE SEPARATE TABLE AT RIGHT, FRONT, 629 ICEMAN

IN THE MIDDLE OF THE SEPARATE TABLE AT RIGHT, 629 ICEMAN FRONT,

SEVERAL PACKAGES, TIED WITH RIBBON, ARE ALSO ON 629 ICEMAN THE TABLE.

ARMS ON TABLE, HEAD ON ARMS, A FULL WHISKEY GLASS 629 ICEMAN BY HIS HEAD.

CHUCK SITS IN A CHAIR AT THE FOOT ((LEFT)) OF THE629 ICEMAN BANQUET TABLE.

POUNDING THE TABLE WITH HIS GLASS) 634 ICEMAN

(HAS TAKEN A GLASS FROM THE TABLE 637 ICEMAN

(MARGIE AND PEARL START TAKING THEM FROM HIS ARMS 638 ICEMAN AND PUTTING THEM ON THE TABLE.

(HE LOOKS OVER THE TABLE WHERE THE CAKE IS) 643 ICEMAN

AND MOVES AWAY TO TAKE A CHAIR IN BACK OF THE LEFT645 ICEMAN END OF THE TABLE.

(PARRITT SLINKS TO A CHAIR AT THE LEFT END OF THE 650 ICEMAN TABLE,

TOWARD THE LEFT END OF THE TABLE, WHERE, LIKE TWO 650 ICEMAN SULKY BOYS,

AT THE TABLE, LARRY, PARRITT, WILLIE, WETJOEN AND 651 ICEMAN LEWIS SIT MOTIONLESS,

(HE LETS ROCKY PUSH HIM IN A CHAIR, AT THE RIGHT 653 ICEMAN END OF THE TABLE, REAR.)

EVERYBODY AT THE TABLE STANDS UP MECHANICALLY. 653 ICEMAN

AND TURNS HIM TO FACE THE TABLE WITH THE CAKE AND 655 ICEMAN PRESENTS)

GOVERNOR, YOU SIT AT THE HEAD OF THE TABLE HERE. 657 ICEMAN

(HE MAKES HARRY SIT DOWN ON THE CHAIR AT THE END 657 ICEMAN OF THE TABLE, RIGHT.

HICKEY BUSTLES DOWN TO THE LEFT END OF TABLE) 657 ICEMAN

NEAR THE MIDDLE OF THE TABLE. 658 ICEMAN

(RAPPING ON THE TABLE FOR ORDER WHEN THERE IS 658 ICEMAN NOTHING BUT A DEAD SILENCE)

BUT HICKEY IS NOW LOOKING UP THE TABLE AT HOPE. 658 ICEMAN

THEN SETS IT BACK ON THE TABLE WITH A GRIMACE OF 658 ICEMAN DISTASTE--

(HE POUNDS HIS SCHOONER ON THE TABLE) 659 ICEMAN

RAP THEIR SCHOONERS ON THE TABLE, CALL "SPEECH, 659 ICEMAN

THEN DROPS HIS EYES AND LOOKS FURTIVELY AROUND TE 660 ICEMAN TABLE.

RAPPING WITH KNUCKLES ON GLASSES ON THE TABLE 662 ICEMAN

THERE IS A TABLE AT LEFT, FRONT, OF BARROOM 664 ICEMAN PROPER, WITH FOUR CHAIRS.

AT LEFT OF THE BARROOM TABLE, ANOTHER WITH FIVE 664 ICEMAN CHAIRS AT LEFT-REAR OF IT,

THE BANQUET TABLE OF ACT TWO HAS BEEN BROKEN UP, 664 ICEMAN

HE COMES FORWARD AND DROPS WEARILY IN THE CHAIR AT665 ICEMAN RIGHT OF LARRY'S TABLE,

ARMS AND HEAD ON THE TABLE AS USUAL, A WHISKEY 665 ICEMAN GLASS BESIDE HIS LIMP HAND.

AT THE BARROOM TABLE, FRONT, LARRY SITS IN A 665 ICEMAN CHAIR, FACING RIGHT-FRONT,

AT REAR OF THE FRONT TABLE AT LEFT OF THEM, IN A 665 ICEMAN CHAIR FACING LEFT,

SHOVE HIM BACK TO HIS OWN TABLE, ROCKY. 668 ICEMAN

(GETS UP--TO LARRY) IF YOU THINK MOVING TO 669 ICEMAN ANOTHER TABLE WILL GET RID OF ME/

AT THIS MOMENT LARRY POUNDS ON THE TABLE WITH HIS 672 ICEMAN FIST

HUGO, WHO HAS AWAKENED AND RAISED HIS HEAD WHEN 672 ICEMAN LARRY POUNDED ON THE TABLE,

(HE GOES BACK AND SITS AT THE LEFT OF THE SECOND 674 ICEMAN TABLE, FACING PARRITT.

(IS REGARDING PARRITT ACROSS THE TABLE FROM HIM 677 ICEMAN WITH AN EAGER, CALCULATING EYE.

HE PUTS HIS ELBOWS ON THE TABLE. 680 ICEMAN

HE GOES TO THE TABLE WHERE HE HAD BEEN BEFORE, 680 ICEMAN

MCGLOIN GOES TO THE FIRST TABLE BEYOND HIM AND 681 ICEMAN SITS WITH HIS BACK TO THE BAR)

AND HE SETS THE BOTTLE ON THE TABLE WITH A JAR 691 ICEMAN THAT ROUSES HUGO,

AND SETTLES INTO THE CHAIR AT THE NEXT TABLE WHICH692 ICEMAN FACES LEFT.

POUNDS ON THE TABLE FRIGHTENEDLY WITH HIS SMALL 694 ICEMAN FISTS)

HOPE STARES DULLY AT THE TABLE TOP. 694 ICEMAN

WITH ITS SINGLE TABLE AT RIGHT OF CURTAIN, FRONT. 695 ICEMAN

BUT THIS TABLE NOW HAS ONLY ONE CHAIR, 695 ICEMAN

BUT THE TABLE WHICH WAS AT CENTER, FRONT, 695 ICEMAN

FINALLY, AT RIGHT OF TABLE IS JIMMY TOMORROW. 696 ICEMAN

AT RIGHT OF TABLE, AN EMPTY CHAIR, FACING LEFT. 696 ICEMAN

AT RIGHT, REAR, OF HIM, ALSO AT THIS TABLE, 696 ICEMAN GENERAL WETJOEN SITS FACING FRONT.

AT RIGHT, REAR, OF WETJOEN, BUT BESIDE THE LAST 696 ICEMAN TABLE OF THE GROUP, SITS WILLIE.

TABLE (CONT'D.)

IN THE BAR SECTION, JOE IS SPRAWLED IN THE CHAIR 696 ICEMAN AT RIGHT OF TABLE, FACING LEFT.

THE ONE CHAIR BY THE TABLE AT RIGHT, REAR, OF THEM696 ICEMAN IS VACANT.

THE TABLE AT RIGHT, REAR, OF IT IN THE SECOND ROW,696 ICEMAN

ON WILLIE'S LEFT, AT REAR OF TABLE, IS HOPE. 696 ICEMAN

AROUND THE REAR OF THIS TABLE ARE FOUR EMPTY 696 ICEMAN CHAIRS.

BEFORE THE MIDDLE TABLE OF HIS GROUP, 696 ICEMAN

AT THE FIRST TABLE AT RIGHT OF CENTER, CORA SITS 696 ICEMAN AT LEFT, FRONT, OF IT,

AND THE LAST TABLE AT RIGHT IN THE FRONT ROW, 696 ICEMAN

TWO BOTTLES OF WHISKEY ARE ON EACH TABLE, WHISKEY 696 ICEMAN AND CHASER GLASSES,

IN BACK OF THIS TABLE ARE THREE EMPTY CHAIRS. 696 ICEMAN

ON HOPE'S LEFT, AT RIGHT, REAR, OF TABLE, IS 696 ICEMAN MOSHER.

LARRY, HUGO AND PARRITT ARE AT THE TABLE AT LEFT, 696 ICEMAN FRONT.

HE FEELS HIS WAY AROUND IT TO THE TABLE AT ITS 699 ICEMAN

TO THE MIDDLE TABLE OF THE THREE AT RIGHT, FRONT. 699 ICEMAN

AS ROCKY ENTERS THE BACK ROOM AND STARTS OVER 700 ICEMAN TOWARD LARRY'S TABLE.)

HIS HEAD HAS SUNK FORWARD, AND HE STARES AT THE 701 ICEMAN TABLE TOP,

LARRY'S HANDS ON THE TABLE HAVE CLINCHED INTO 701 ICEMAN FISTS.

OF LARRY'S TABLE AND SITS IN THE ONE CHAIR THERE, 704 ICEMAN FACING FRONT.

IN THE BAR HE COMES FORWARD AND SLUMPS IN A CHAIR 704 ICEMAN AT THE TABLE, FACING FRONT,)

(COMES TO THE TABLE AT RIGHT, REAR, 704 ICEMAN

(BURSTS OUT, POUNDING HIS GLASS ON THE TABLE) 707 ICEMAN

THEN ROCKY, AT THE TABLE IN THE BAR, 708 ICEMAN

(TRIES TO WARD THIS OFF BY POUNDING WITH HIS GLASS715 ICEMAN ON THE TABLE--

THE TABLE WHERE HIS COMPANION, LIEB, IS SITTING. 716 ICEMAN

ROCKY NOTICES HIS LEAVING AND GETS UP FROM THE 716 ICEMAN TABLE IN THE REAR AND GOES BACK

LARRY'S TABLE.) 719 ICEMAN

AT THE TABLE BY THE WINDOW LARRY'S HANDS GRIP THE 722 ICEMAN EDGE OF THE TABLE.

(AT THE TABLE BY THE WINDOW HUGO SPEAKS TO LARRY 723 ICEMAN AGAIN.)

AT THE TABLE BY THE WINDOW LARRY HAS UNCONSCIOUSLY724 ICEMAN SHUT HIS EYES AS HE LISTENS.

HE CHANGES AGAIN, GIGGLING GOOD-NATUREDLY, AND 724 ICEMAN SITS AT REAR OF THE MIDDLE TABLE)

(HE SHRINKS QUICKLY PAST THE TABLE WHERE HICKEY 724 ICEMAN HAD SAT TO THE REAR OF THE GROUP

HE GETS UP HASTILY AND MOVES AWAY FROM THE TABLE, 724 ICEMAN

WHILE HUGO JUMPS TO HIS FEET AND, POUNDING ON THE 727 ICEMAN TABLE WITH HIS FIST,

(THEY POUND THEIR GLASSES ON THE TABLE, ROARING 728 ICEMAN WITH LAUGHTER,

A SMALL WICKER TABLE AND AN ORDINARY OAK DESK ARE 11 JOURNE

THREE OF THEM WICKER ARMCHAIRS, THE FOURTH--AT 12 JOURNE RIGHT FRONT OF TABLE--

AROUND THE TABLE WITHIN READING-LIGHT RANGE ARE 12 JOURNE FOUR CHAIRS.

AT CENTER IS A ROUND TABLE WITH A GREEN SHADED 12 JOURNE READING LAMP,

(SHE COMES FORWARD TO STAND BY THE RIGHT OF 14 JOURNE TABLE.)

(SHE LAUGHS AND SITS IN THE WICKER ARMCHAIR AT 14 JOURNE RIGHT REAR OF TABLE.

CATHLEEN MUST BE WAITING TO CLEAR THE TABLE. 15 JOURNE

FROM A BOX ON THE TABLE AND CUTS OFF THE END WITH 15 JOURNE A LITTLE CLIPPER.

HER HANDS APPEAR ON THE TABLE TOP, MOVING 15 JOURNE RESTLESSLY.

HE LIGHTS HIS CIGAR AND SITS DOWN IN THE ROCKER AT 15 JOURNE RIGHT OF TABLE,

HER FINGERS PLAY NERVOUSLY ON THE TABLE TOP.) 16 JOURNE

SHE GOES BACK TO THE TABLE.) 18 JOURNE

COME IN THE LIVING ROOM AND GIVE CATHLEEN A CHANCE 18 JOURNE TO CLEAR THE TABLE.

(HE SLUMPS DOWN IN THE CHAIR AT LEFT OF TABLE NEXT 21 JOURNE TO HIS BROTHER.

HER HANDS ROVING OVER THE TABLE TOP, AIMLESSLY 42 JOURNE MOVING OBJECTS AROUND.

SHE SINKS DOWN IN ONE OF THE WICKER ARMCHAIRS AT 49 JOURNE REAR OF TABLE.

SHE PUTS THE TRAY ON THE TABLE. 51 JOURNE

EDMUND SITS IN THE ARMCHAIR AT LEFT OF TABLE, 51 JOURNE READING A BOOK.

(HE SITS ACROSS THE TABLE FROM EDMUND--IRRITABLY.) 54 JOURNE

THE POURS WATER IN THE GLASS AND SETS IT ON THE 54 JOURNE TABLE BY EDMUND.)

(HE LEANS OVER THE TABLE TO GIVE HIS BROTHER'S ARM 57 JOURNE AN AFFECTIONATE GRASP.)

HER HANDS PLAY RESTLESSLY OVER THE TABLE TOP. 62 JOURNE

HE COMES TO THE TABLE WITH A QUICK MEASURING LOOK 65 JOURNE AT THE BOTTLE OF WHISKEY.

(HER EYES BECOME FIXED ON THE WHISKEY GLASS ON THE 67 JOURNE TABLE BESIDE HIM--SHARPLY.)

THE TRAY WITH THE BOTTLE OF WHISKEY HAS BEEN 71 JOURNE REMOVED FROM THE TABLE.

AS SHE TALKS, SHE COMES TO THE LEFT OF THE TABLE 71 JOURNE AND STANDS, FACING FRONT,

EDMUND SITS IN A CHAIR BY THE TABLE, 71 JOURNE

THE OTHER PLAYING OVER THE TABLE TOP. 71 JOURNE

MARY'S FINGERS PLAY MORE RAPIDLY ON THE TABLE TOP. 73 JOURNE

SHE COMES AND STANDS BY THE TABLE, ONE HAND 95 JOURNE DRUMMING ON IT,

TABLE

(CONT'D.)
THE LATTER IS STANDING AT LEFT OF TABLE. 97 JOURNE
AND PITCHER OF ICE WATER IS ON THE TABLE, 97 JOURNE
(SHE LAUGHS, COMING TO THE TABLE.) 99 JOURNE
(SHE PUTS HER GLASS ON THE TABLE AND MAKES A 99 JOURNE
MOVEMENT TOWARD THE BACK PARLOR.)
(SHE SITS IN THE ROCKER AT RIGHT OF TABLE.) 99 JOURNE
(SHE SITS IN THE ARMCHAIR AT RIGHT REAR OF TABLE. 103 JOURNE
I'M NOT HUNGRY BUT I'LL SIT AT THE TABLE AND WE'LL106 JOURNE
GET IT OVER WITH.
(SHE SITS AT LEFT REAR OF TABLE, EDMUND AT LEFT OF108 JOURNE
TABLE.
IN THE LIVING ROOM ONLY THE READING LAMP ON THE 125 JOURNE
TABLE IS LIGHTED.
TYRONE IS SEATED AT THE TABLE. 125 JOURNE
THERE IS A FRESH FULL BOTTLE ON THE TABLE, 125 JOURNE
HIS HEAD BOWS AND HE STARES DULLY AT THE CARDS ON 146 JOURNE
THE TABLE--VAGUELY.)
HONKY-TONK TABLE TOP. 152 JOURNE
(HE SWAYS FORWARD TO THE TABLE, RECITING KIPLING.)155 JOURNE
TYRONE COMES TO THE TABLE AND SITS DOWN. 169 JOURNE
(DROPS HIS HAND FROM HIS FACE, HIS EYES ON THE 173 JOURNE
TABLE TOP.
TABLE, FORGETTING THEM.) 175 JOURNE
ON A RAISED PLATFORM AT THE MIDDLE OF THE ONE 274 LAZARU
TABLE PLACED LENGTHWISE
A TABLE IN FRONT OF IT. 335 LAZARU
ON THIS TABLE, AND ON ALL THE TABLES FOR HIS 335 LAZARU
GUESTS.
(HE PUTS OUT THE LAMP ON HIS TABLE HIMSELF. 338 LAZARU
(HE MOUNTS THE STEPS OF THE DAIS AND SITS ON THE 340 LAZARU
COUCH AT LEFT OF TABLE--
POMPEIA LEANS OVER AND TAKES A PEACH FROM THE BOWL342 LAZARU
OF FRUIT ON CAESAR'S TABLE
TIBERIUS GROVELS HALF UNDER THE TABLE, HIS HANDS 349 LAZARU
COVERING HIS EARS,
LAUGHING, HE ASCENDS THE DAIS AND PLACES HER ON 349 LAZARU
THE TABLE AS ON A BIER.
ALL THE LAMPS ARE OUT EXCEPT THE ONE ON THE TABLE 350 LAZARU
ON THE DAIS WHICH,
ON THE OTHER SIDE OF THE TABLE, AT THE END OF THE 350 LAZARU
COUCH,
HALF-KNEELING BENEATH THE TABLE ON WHICH MIRIAM 358 LAZARU
LIES,
HE COMES TO THE TABLE AND STANDS STARING DOWN AT 43 MANSNS
IT PREOCCUPIEDLY.
AT FRONT, TO THE LEFT OF CENTER, IS A TABLE WITH A 43 MANSNS
LAMP AND THREE CHAIRS.
HE PICKS UP TWO FOLDED NEWSPAPERS FROM THE TABLE, 44 MANSNS
PUTS ONE PAPER ASIDE,
SIMON SITS IN THE CHAIR AT LEFT-FRONT OF TABLE, 44 MANSNS
SIMON SITS IN HIS OLD PLACE AT LEFT-FRONT OF 50 MANSNS
TABLE.
JOEL TAKES THE CHAIR AT REAR OF TABLE.) 51 MANSNS
(HE SITS AT THE TABLE--JOEL BEHIND IT--CURTLY.) 59 MANSNS
AS THE CURTAIN RISES, SIMON ENTERS AT REAR AND 69 MANSNS
COMES TO HIS TABLE,
AND MAKE AN INSTANT DECISION, SETTING IT ON THE 70 MANSNS
TABLE AT HIS RIGHT.
(HE SPRINGS TO HIS FEET, INDICATING THE CHAIR 75 MANSNS
ACROSS THE TABLE.)
WITH GROWING AMUSEMENT, SHE TIPTOES FORWARD UNTIL 75 MANSNS
SHE STANDS BY HIS TABLE.)
(SHE GETS UP AND COMES AROUND THE TABLE TO HIM.) 79 MANSNS
THE ADVERSARY ACROSS THE TABLE IN WHOSE EYES ONE 92 MANSNS
CAN READ
OF WATCHING SUSPICIOUSLY EACH CARD I LED TO MYSELF102 MANSNS
FROM ACROSS THE TABLE--
TOWARD FRONT, AT LEFT, IS AN OVAL TABLE WITH 117 MANSNS
ANOTHER LAMP.
SIMON ACROSS THE TABLE FROM HER IN THE CHAIR AT 117 MANSNS
REAR-RIGHT OF IT,
AND, FARTHER BACK, A TABLE. 117 MANSNS
AGAINST THE RIGHT WALL, TOWARD REAR, ANOTHER 117 MANSNS
TABLE.
AS THE CURTAIN RISES, SARA IS SITTING IN THE CHAIR117 MANSNS
AT LEFT-FRONT OF THE TABLE,
ANOTHER CHAIR IS AT LEFT-FRONT OF THIS TABLE, 117 MANSNS
FACING DIRECTLY FRONT.
A CHAIR IS BY RIGHT-REAR OF THIS TABLE, FACING 117 MANSNS
RIGHT-FRONT.
AT EXTREME LEFT-FRONT A SMALL TABLE AGAINST THE 117 MANSNS
WALL.
AT LEFT-REAR OF THE FIREPLACE IS A LONG SOFA WITH 117 MANSNS
A SMALL TABLE AND READING-LAMP
(SARA GOES AROUND THE TABLE AND PASSES BEHIND 123 MANSNS
SIMON, IGNORING HIM.
(SARA GOES SLOWLY TOWARD HER OLD CHAIR AT LEFT- 136 MANSNS
FRONT OF TABLE.
WHY, EVERY PLATE ON HIS TABLE IS SOLID GOLD/ 363 MARCOM
AT THE CENTER OF THE FORESTAGE IS A GREAT BANQUET 426 MARCOM
TABLE
WITH THE TRAINED EYE FOR DISPLAY OF WINDOW- 428 MARCOM
DRESSERS, UNTIL THE TABLE,
THE SERVANTS ARRANGE THESE ON THE TABLE, IN 428 MARCOM
SYMMETRICAL GROUPS,
WHICH HAS BEEN PURPOSELY LEFT AT THE VERY CENTER 429 MARCOM
OF THE TABLE AT THE FRONT.
(THEY SWIRL TO THEIR PLACES BEHIND THE LONG TABLE.431 MARCOM
THERE IS A TABLE AT CENTER, A DISREPUTABLE OLD 71 MISBEG
MORRIS CHAIR BESIDE IT,
AND LIGHTS A KEROSENE LAMP ON THE TABLE. 71 MISBEG
(PUTS HER CLUB ON THE TABLE--GRIMLY) 74 MISBEG
SIMPSON CAME AND SAT AT THE TABLE WITH US-- 85 MISBEG
JOSIE STOPS BY THE TABLE IN THE LIVING ROOM TO 111 MISBEG
TURN DOWN THE LAMP
WE'LL USE THE BOULDER FOR A TABLE AND I'LL BE 112 MISBEG
BARKEEP.

TABLE (CONT'D.)
I REMEMBER NOW I WAS SITTING ALONE AT A TABLE IN 167 MISBEG
THE INN.
(HE SITS AT RIGHT OF TABLE.) 8 POET
MICKEY MALOY SITS AT THE TABLE AT LEFT FRONT, 8 POET
FACING RIGHT.
(SHE LOWERS HERSELF PAINFULLY ON THE NEAREST CHAIR 21 POET
AT THE REAR OF THE TABLE AT
AND HE SETS THE GLASS BACK ON THE TABLE WITH A 35 POET
BANG.
FROM THE CARAFE ON THE TABLE. 35 POET
AND GOES TO THE TABLE AT CENTER FRONT, AND SITS IN 35 POET
THE CHAIR SHE HAD OCCUPIED.
THEN HE SINKS BACK IN HIS CHAIR AND STARES AT THE 37 POET
TABLE.
(HIS EYES FASTEN ON THE DATE AND SUDDENLY HE 38 POET
STRIKES THE TABLE WITH HIS FIST.)
BUT I'LL NOT SINK TO DINING AT THE SAME TABLE. 39 POET
(HE POINTS TO THE TABLE AT LEFT FRONT.) 39 POET
(UNCONSCIOUSLY HE REACHES OUT FOR THE DECANTER ON 45 POET
THE TABLE--
(HE HOLDS OUT A CHAIR FOR HER AT REAR OF THE TABLE 46 POET
AT CENTER.)
SHE ARRANGES HIS BREAKFAST ON THE TABLE AT FRONT 55 POET
CENTER, BUSTLING GARRULOUSLY.)
NORA SLUMPS ON A CHAIR AT THE REAR OF THE TABLE 56 POET
HE SITS AT REAR OF THE TABLE AT LEFT FRONT. 57 POET
HIS SHOULDERS SAG AND HE STARES AT THE TABLE TOP, 57 POET
AND I'LL HAVE THE HONOR OF WAITING ON TABLE. 59 POET
(HE DRAWS OUT A CHAIR AT REAR OF THE LARGER TABLE 68 POET
IN THE FOREGROUND--
(HE PUTS HIS HAND OVER ONE OF HER HANDS ON THE 71 POET
TABLE
(SHE SITS AT THE END OF CENTER TABLE RIGHT AND 76 POET
RELAXES WEARILY.
SARA SITS AT REAR OF THE CENTER TABLE AND WAITS, 81 POET
SARA CLOSES THE DOOR AND COMES BACK SLOWLY TO THE 87 POET
HEAD OF THE TABLE AT CENTER.
HE COMES SLOWLY AROUND THE TABLE AT LEFT FRONT, 89 POET
UNTIL HE STANDS AT THE END OF THE CENTER TABLE 89 POET
FACING HER.
(HE SITS AT RIGHT OF TABLE AT LEFT FRONT AS MELODY 92 POET
SITS AT REAR.)
THE DECANTER AND MELODY'S GLASS ARE ALREADY ON THE 92 POET
TABLE.)
MELODY STANDS GRIPPING THE BACK OF THE CHAIR AT 92 POET
THE FOOT OF THE TABLE
AN EMPTY AND A HALF-EMPTY BOTTLE OF PORT ARE ON 95 POET
THE TABLE BEFORE MELODY AND
RILEY, O'DOWD, AND ROCHE SIT AT THE TABLE AT LEFT 95 POET
FRONT.
THE THREE AT THE TABLE HAVE A DECANTER OF WHISKEY. 95 POET
WITH ROCHE ACROSS THE TABLE FROM HIM, HIS BACK TO 95 POET
MELODY.
MELODY SITS AT THE HEAD OF THIS TABLE. 95 POET
IT IS AROUND EIGHT THAT EVENING AND THERE ARE 95 POET
CANDLES ON THE CENTER TABLE.
THE OTHER CHAIRS AT THIS TABLE ARE UNOCCUPIED. 95 POET
IN A PLAN OF BATTLE ON THE TABLE BEFORE HIM. 96 POET
(ROCHE AND O'DOWD ROAR AFTER HIM, BEATING TIME ON 96 POET
THE TABLE WITH THEIR GLASSES--
(HOLDS HIS PLATE ON THE TABLE WITH ONE HAND SO SHE 97 POET
CANNOT TAKE IT.
I HAVE TRIED TO TEACH THE WAITRESS NOT TO SNATCH 98 POET
PLATES FROM THE TABLE
(MELODY, EXCITED NOW, BEATS TIME ON THE TABLE WITH102 POET
HIS GLASS ALONG WITH CREGAN.
AND IT'S THE LAST TIME YOU'LL EVER TAKE 104 POET
SATISFACTION IN HAVING ME WAIT ON TABLE
DRAWS OUT HIS CHAIR AT THE HEAD OF THE CENTER 104 POET
TABLE FOR HER--POLITELY.)
SHE SITS DOWN AND HE SITS AT REAR OF TABLE, 105 POET
(INSTINCTIVELY JERKS HER HANDS BACK UNDER THE 107 POET
TABLE GUILTILY.
KEEP YOUR THICK WRISTS AND UGLY, PEASANT PAWS OFF 107 POET
THE TABLE IN MY PRESENCE.
(SHE PUTS HER HANDS ON THE TABLE AND STARTS TO 107 POET
RISE.)
IT WAS MY DUTY AS YOUR FATHER TO DEMAND HE LAY HIS108 POET
CARDS ON THE TABLE.
(LETTING GO, HE BANGS HIS FIST ON THE TABLE.) 115 POET
FORGETTING TO CLEAR THE FEW REMAINING DISHES ON 115 POET
THE CENTER TABLE.
(GADSBY COMES FORWARD AND TAKES THE CHAIR AT THE 117 POET
HEAD OF THE CENTER TABLE,
(HE SITS DOWN ON THE CHAIR ON GADSBY'S LEFT, AT 119 POET
REAR OF TABLE--
(HIS PENT-UP RAGE BURSTS OUT--SMASHING HIS FIST ON122 POET
THE TABLE.)
NORA SITS AT THE FOOT OF THE TABLE AT CENTER. 133 POET
THE ROOM IS IN DARKNESS EXCEPT FOR ONE CANDLE ON 133 POET
THE TABLE, CENTER.
(PUTTING THE DECANTER AND GLASS ON THE TABLE.) 133 POET
(TAKES A SIP, THEN PUTS THE GLASS ON THE TABLE AND134 POET
PUSHES IT AWAY LISTLESSLY.)
(SARA SITS DOWN ON HER LEFT AT REAR OF TABLE. 137 POET
HE WALKS DAZEDLY TO HIS CHAIR AT THE HEAD OF THE 152 POET
CENTER TABLE.
NORA STANDS CLOSE BY HIS SIDE, BEHIND THE TABLE, 153 POET
ON HIS RIGHT.
THEY STARE AT HIM AND HE STARES SIGHTLESSLY AT THE153 POET
TABLE TOP.
(BUT HE IS STARING SIGHTLESSLY AT THE TABLE TOP 156 POET
(SITTING DOWN AT REAR OF THE SMALL TABLE AT LEFT 160 POET
FRONT--ANGRILY.)
(HE SPRAWLS ON A CHAIR AT REAR OF THE TABLE AT 160 POET
CENTER.)

TABLE 1602

TABLE (CONT'D.)
(SHE RETREATS QUICKLY INTO THE ROOM AND BACKS 163 POET
AROUND THE TABLE AT LEFT FRONT
(DUMPS MELODY DOWN ON THE NEAREST CHAIR AT LEFT UF164 POET
THE SMALL TABLE--
(HE SHUDDERS AND PUTS THE PISTOL ON THE TABLE 165 POET
SHAKENLY.)
SHE COMES BACK TO THE CENTER TABLE, STARING AT 165 POET
MELODY.
BUT HIS EYES REMAIN FIXED ON THE TABLE TOP.) 166 POET
NORA SINKS ON THE CHAIR AT REAR OF THE TABLE. 166 POET
(SHE REACHES OUT AND TOUCHES ONE OF HIS HANDS ON 167 POET
THE TABLE TOP WITH A FURTIVE
HIS RIGHT HAND GROPING ALONG THE TABLE TOP UNTIL 172 POET
IT CLUTCHES THE DUELING PISTOL.
AND LETS THE PISTOL SLIDE FROM HIS FINGERS ON THE 172 POET
TABLE.
(SHE SINKS DOWN ON HER CHAIR AT REAR OF THE CENTER172 POET
TABLE
BUT IT KNOCKS HER OFF BALANCE BACK TO THE END OF 179 POET
THE TABLE AT CENTER.)
SARA REMAINS STANDING BY THE SIDE OF THE CENTER 180 POET
TABLE, HER SHOULDERS BOWED.
ROUGHLY CONSTRUCTED CARPENTER'S TABLE, EVIDENTLY 577 ROPE
HOME-MADE.
A KEG CONTAINING NAILS AND OTHER TOOLS OF THE 577 ROPE
CARPENTRY TRADE ARE ON THE TABLE.
SHE RUNS TO THE CARPENTER'S TABLE AND CRAWLS UNDER578 ROPE
IT.
AS HE REACHES THE TABLE AND LEANS ONE HAND ON IT 578 ROPE
FOR SUPPORT.
(HE SITS DOWN ON THE BENCH TO THE LEFT OF TABLE) 584 ROPE
(SHE SITS DOWN ON THE BENCH IN FRONT OF TABLE. 584 ROPE
(HE BROODS FOR A MOMENT IN SILENCE--THEN HITS THE 585 ROPE
TABLE FURIOUSLY WITH HIS FIST)
(THEY SHAKE HANDS AND SIT DOWN BY THE TABLE, 591 ROPE
(AFTER TAKING A DRINK HIMSELF, PUTS BOTTLE ON 591 ROPE
TABLE)
(HE GUIDES THE OLD MAN TO THE BENCH AT LEFT OF 595 ROPE
TABLE)
(HE HANDS THE BOTTLE TO SWEENEY, WHO DRINKS AND 595 ROPE
PUTS IT BACK ON THE TABLE.)
(BANGING THE TABLE WITH HIS FISTS) 598 ROPE
(BANGING THE TABLE) I SAID I'D GIT EVEN AND I 598 ROPE
WILL GIT EVEN--
(HE PICKS UP THE CHISEL FROM THE TABLE) 600 ROPE
THERE IS A FAIR-SIZED TABLE, A HEAVY ARMCHAIR, A 3 STRANG
ROCKER,
THE TABLE, WITH THE PROFESSOR'S ARMCHAIR AT ITS 3 STRANG
LEFT.
(HE SITS IN HIS CHAIR ON THE LEFT OF THE TABLE 7 STRANG
WHILE MARSDEN SITS IN THE
EVERYTHING ON THE TABLE, PAPERS, PENCILS, PENS, 24 STRANG
ETC.
THE READING LAMP ON THE TABLE IS LIT. 24 STRANG
THERE'S HIS TABLE... 27 STRANG
GOES TO THE TABLE AND TAKING A PRESCRIPTION PAD 33 STRANG
FROM HIS POCKET,
MARSDEN UNCONSCIOUSLY TAKES THE PROFESSOR'S PLACE 34 STRANG
BEHIND THE TABLE.
MARSDEN SITS BY THE TABLE. 41 STRANG
NINA IS SEATED AT THE FOOT OF THE TABLE, HER BACK 48 STRANG
TO THE WINDOW.
UF THE UGLY TABLE WITH ITS SET OF STRAIGHTBACKED 48 STRANG
CHAIRS
THE TABLE HAS BECOME NEUROTIC. 66 STRANG
THE TABLE, ALTHOUGH IT IS THE SAME, IS NO LONGER 66 STRANG
THE PROFESSOR'S TABLE.
THE ROCKING CHAIR IS NO LONGER AT CENTER BUT HAS 66 STRANG
BEEN PULLED NEARER THE TABLE.
ON THE FLOOR BESIDE THE TABLE ARE AN OVERFLOWING 66 STRANG
WASTEPAPER BASKET,
THE REST OF THE TABLE IS LITTERED WITH AN INK 66 STRANG
BOTTLE, PENS, PENCILS, ERASERS,
AND PUTS IT BACK CAREFULLY ON THE TABLE.) 76 STRANG
GOES OVER AND STANDS BY THE TABLE) 76 STRANG
TO PLACE IT AS CAREFULLY ON THE TABLE) 77 STRANG
DARRELL REMAINS STANDING NEAR THE TABLE LOOKING 78 STRANG
AFTER THEM.
(HE MOVES AROUND THE TABLE EXAMINING ITS DISORDER 78 STRANG
CRITICALLY.
THERE IS A MORRIS CHAIR AND A ROUND GOLDEN OAK 90 STRANG
TABLE AT LEFT OF CENTER.
(HE SINKS DOWN IN THE CHAIR BY THE TABLE AT LEFT. 97 STRANG
EVANS IS SITTING BY THE TABLE AT LEFT, 111 STRANG
MARSDEN TAKES EVANS' CHAIR BY THE TABLE. 124 STRANG
EVANS IN HIS OLD PLACE BY THE TABLE, MARSDEN AT 133 STRANG
CENTER,
(SHE RAPS WITH BOTH KNUCKLES IN A FIERCE TATTOO ON135 STRANG
THE TABLE)
TWO CHAIRS ARE BY THE TABLE AT LEFT. 137 STRANG
THERE IS A SMALLER TABLE AT CENTER, AND A CHAISE 137 STRANG
LONGUE.
DARRELL IS SITTING BY THE TABLE AT LEFT, WATCHING 137 STRANG
NINA.
NINA IS SITTING BY THE TABLE AT CENTER, DARRELL IN1S8 STRANG
THE CHAIR FARTHEST LEFT.
A WICKER TABLE WITH ANOTHER CHAIR IS AT CENTER. 158 STRANG
A WICKER TABLE AND ARMCHAIR AT LEFT. 184 STRANG
HE TURNS AWAY AND WALKS TO THE TABLE. 190 STRANG
THEN HE BECKONS TO JOE, WHO COMES OVER TO THE 495 VOYAGE
TABLE AND SITS DOWN)
THE SEAMEN COME TO THE TABLE, FRONT.) 496 VOYAGE
NICK SLINKS INTO THE ROOM AFTER THEM AND SITS DOWN496 VOYAGE
AT A TABLE IN REAR.
(BELLOWING, AND POINTING TO NICK AS JOE BRINGS THE497 VOYAGE
DRINKS TO THE TABLE)
AND NEARLY UPSETTING THE TABLE) 498 VOYAGE

TABLE (CONT'D.)
(THE WOMEN COME FORWARD TO THE TABLE, WEARING 499 VOYAGE
THEIR BEST SET SMILES.)
(HE TAKES OUT A ROLL OF NOTES FROM HIS INSIDE 500 VOYAGE
POCKET AND LAYS ONE ON THE TABLE.
(SMILING--PUTS HER HAND OVER HIS ON THE TABLE) 501 VOYAGE
NICK FOLLOWS THEM AND SITS DOWN AT THE TABLE IN 503 VOYAGE
REAR.)
THEY DRINK AND THEN SWERVE OVER TO OLSON'S TABLE.1504 VOYAGE
(HE LAYS A COIN ON THE TABLE.) 505 VOYAGE
(LEADING HIM BACK TO THE TABLE--COUGHING) 505 VOYAGE
(JOE BRINGS OLSON'S DRINK TO THE TABLE AND SETS IT505 VOYAGE
BEFORE HIM.)
(JOE GOES BACK OF THE BAR, MAKING A SIGN TO NICK 505 VOYAGE
TO GO TO THEIR TABLE.
(HE POURS OUT HER DRINK AND BRINGS IT TO THE 505 VOYAGE
TABLE)
THEY SIT AT THE TABLE NEAREST TO THE DOOR. 506 VOYAGE
(COMING HASTILY OVER TO THE TABLE, 507 VOYAGE
AND LAYS A HANDFUL OF CHANGE ON THE TABLE.) 508 VOYAGE
SHE PICKS UP A LETTER FROM THE TABLE, WHICH SHE 443 WELDED
OPENS AND READS.
(SHE TAKES THE BOX FROM THE TABLE AND HOLDS IT OUT450 WELDED
TO HIM.)
FINALLY, MAKING AN EFFORT OF WILL, SHE WALKS BACK 451 WELDED
TO THE TABLE.
ELEANOR IS STANDING BY THE TABLE, LEANING HER BACK480 WELDED
AGAINST IT, FACING THE DOOR.

TABLE'S
AT THE TABLE'S NO PLACE TO SPEAK OF-- 230 AHWILD

TABLECLOTH
OF A COLD PORK PUDDING AGAINST A BACKGROUND OF 218 HA APE
LINOLEUM TABLECLOTH IN THE
(HE MARKS THE TABLECLOTH.) THAT WERE PUSHING BACK 99 POET
THE GUARDS.

TABLECLOTHS
ALL THESE TABLES ARE SET WITH WHITE TABLECLOTHS, 7 POET
ETC.

TABLES
THREE TABLES WITH STAINED TOPS, FOUR CHAIRS AROUND236 AHWILD
EACH TABLE.
IN THE BACK ROOM ARE FOUR ROUND WOODEN TABLES WITH 3 ANNA
FIVE CHAIRS GROUPED ABOUT
THE BACK ROOM IS CRAMMED WITH ROUND TABLES AND 573 ICEMAN
CHAIRS PLACED SO CLOSE TOGETHER
A TABLE, SIMILARLY PLACED AT REAR OF FRONT TABLES 573 ICEMAN
TWO AND THREE,
THE THIRD ROW OF TABLES, FOUR CHAIRS TO ONE AND 573 ICEMAN
SIX TO THE OTHER.
THERE ARE THREE ROWS OF TABLES, FROM FRONT TO 573 ICEMAN
BACK.
AT REAR OF, AND HALF BETWEEN, FRONT TABLES ONE AND573 ICEMAN
TWO
BETWEEN THE FIRST TWO TABLES, SITS WILLIE OBAN, 577 ICEMAN
HE SQUEEZES BETWEEN THE TABLES TO LARRY. 577 ICEMAN
(HE SQUEEZES THROUGH THE TABLES AND DISAPPEARS, 586 ICEMAN
RIGHT-REAR, BEHIND THE CURTAIN.
(THE DRUNKS AT THE TABLES STIR. 596 ICEMAN
THAT ROCKY IS TOO DAMNED FAST CLEANING TABLES. 606 ICEMAN
THE OTHER TABLES AND CHAIRS THAT HAD BEEN IN THE 628 ICEMAN
ROOM HAVE BEEN MOVED OUT.
AT CENTER, FRONT, FOUR OF THE CIRCULAR TABLES ARE 628 ICEMAN
PUSHED TOGETHER TO FORM ONE
AND THE TABLES ARE AGAIN IN THE CROWDED 664 ICEMAN
ARRANGEMENT OF ACT ONE.
THE TABLES IN THE BACK ROOM HAVE A NEW 695 ICEMAN
ARRANGEMENT.
THE TWO TABLES ON EITHER SIDE OF THE DOOR AT REAR 695 ICEMAN
ARE UNCHANGED.
ALL THE GROUP AT THE TABLES BY HIM START AND STARE717 ICEMAN
AT HIM
(THE CROWD AT THE GROUPED TABLES ARE GRASPING AT 717 ICEMAN
HOPE NOW.
TO THE LEFT OF CENTER SEVERAL LONG TABLES PLACED 273 LAZARU
LENGTHWISE TO THE WIDTH OF THE
BEFORE THESE COUCHES, A SERIES OF NARROW TABLES IS335 LAZARU
SET.
ON THIS TABLE, AND ON ALL THE TABLES FOR HIS 335 LAZARU
GUESTS,
(THEY NOW STAND UP AND COMING FROM BEHIND THEIR 344 LAZARU
TABLES.
IT WOULD SERVE HIM RIGHT IF WE TURNED THE TABLES 171 MANSNS
ON HIM, SARA.
AT LEFT AND RIGHT, REAR, ARE TWO MORE TABLES, 7 POET
ALL THESE TABLES ARE SET WITH WHITE TABLECLOTHS, 7 POET
ETC.
IN THE FOREGROUND ARE TWO TABLES. 7 POET
FINISH GETTIN' DRUNK IN THE BAR AND LAVE ME CLEAR 103 POET
THE TABLES!
POUNDING OF GLASSES ON BAR AND TABLES, 180 POET
AT ONE OF THE TABLES, FRONT, A ROUND-SHOULDERED 493 VOYAGE
YOUNG FELLOW IS SITTING.
ON THE RIGHT, TABLES WITH CHAIRS AROUND THEM. 493 VOYAGE

TABOOS
BUT I'M NOT HIS FATHER OSTENSIBLY, THERE ARE NO 143 STRANG
TABOOS,

TACK
(GLANCES AT HIM--THEN RESOLVES ON A NEW TACK-- 238 AHWILD
PATTING HIS HAND)
(THEN AT SOMETHING IN HER FACE HE HURRIEDLY GOES 23 ELECTR
OFF ON ANOTHER TACK)
HE STARED AT ME WITH AN IDIOTIC LOOK AS IF HE'D 95 ELECTR
SAT ON A TACK--
THEN VENTURES ON ANOTHER TACK, MATTER-OF-FACTLY) 277 GGBROW
(HE'S ON THE WRONG TACK WITH HIS PROFESSOR'S 15 STRANG
MANNER...
YOU JUMPED OFF MY LAP AS THOUGH YOU'D SAT ON A 157 STRANG
TACK/

TACKED
THE BACKDROP FOR BOTH ROOMS IS OF PLAIN WALL WITH 302 GGBROW
A FEW TACKED-UP DESIGNS AND
AND TACKED ON THE RIGHT WALL BESIDE HER DESK IS A 139 MANSNS
LARGE ARCHITECT'S DRAWING
ONE-ROOM ADDITION HAS BEEN TACKED ON AT RIGHT. 1 MISBEG

TACKING
ALTHOUGH TACKING BACK AND FORTH IN THESE 126 BEYOND
BLISTERING SEAS IS A ROTTEN JOB TOO/=

TACKLE
WE HADN'T DARED TACKLE BEFORE. 95 ELECTR

TACKLING
AND I'D NEVER THINK IT WAS IN YOU TO COME TACKLING 50 ANNA
ME ALONE.

TACKS
(SHARPLY) LET'S GET DOWN TO BRASS TACKS. 201 AHWILD
AND THEN SHE CALLS ME A FOOL REAL SPITEFUL AND 95 BEYOND
TACKS AWAY FROM ME QUICK.
(IMPATIENTLY) COME, MR. BARTLETT, LET'S GET DOWN 558 CROSS
TO BRASS TACKS.
WELL, HERE GOES--THE BRASS TACKS. 559 CROSS
(HE MAKES HIS WAY SWAYINGLY TO THE OPENING IN THE 699 ICEMAN
CURTAIN AT REAR AND TACKS DOWN

TACT
HE--ER--EVIDENTLY RELIED ON YOUR TACT AND 35 MANSNS
DIPLOMACY, DEBORAH, TO CONVINCE HER.

TACTFUL
PERHAPS IT WOULD BE TACTFUL OF ME TO CHANGE THE 135 JOURNE
SUBJECT.

TACTFULLY
(AS SHE SEES MILLER ABOUT TO EXPLODE--INTERPOSES 229 AHWILD
TACTFULLY)
(TACTFULLY) I THINK I'LL GO FOR A WALK, TOO. 264 AHWILD
AND TACTFULLY REFRAINS FROM ALL QUESTIONS.) 296 AHWILD
(CHANGES THE SUBJECT TACTFULLY) 497 DAYS
(TACTFULLY) I WON'T DISTURB YOU ANY FURTHER. 290 GGBROW
(TACTFULLY.) GO ON WITH YOUR STORY, EDMUND. 23 JOURNE

TACTLESS
IT WAS A TACTLESS QUESTION. 127 STRANG

TACTLESSLY
(BREAKS IN TACTLESSLY) MAYBE IT IS FATE. 69 ELECTR

TAG
FROM EACH PIECE HANGS AN ENORMOUS TAG FROM WHICH A233 HA APE
DOLLAR SIGN AND NUMERALS IN

TAGGED
SHE HAD ME TAGGED FOR A BUM, AND SEEIN' ME MADE 26 HUGHIE
HER SURE SHE WAS RIGHT.

TAGS
AND HIS SHIFTY ONCE-OVER GLANCES NEVER MISS THE 9 HUGHIE
PRICE TAGS HE DETECTS ON

TAGUS
HERE'S THE RIVER TAGUS. 96 POET

TAIL
OR TAIL OF, ONLY IT WASN'T A PLAY. 197 AHWILD
SOMETIMES I CAN'T MAKE HEAD OR TAIL OF HIM. 209 AHWILD
WITH A GOOD BOOT IN THE TAIL TO HELP HIM/ 248 AHWILD
STUFF I COULDN'T MAKE HEAD OR TAIL TO. 18 ANNA
OH, GOD HELP ME, I CAN'T MAKE HEAD OR TAIL TO IT 53 ANNA
AT ALL/
I COULDN'T MAKE HEAD OR TAIL TO THEM. 146 BEYOND
SHE'D HAIR LONG'S A HOSS' TAIL--AN' YALLER LIKE 204 DESIRE
GOLD/.
ITS BUSHY TAIL HANGING DOWN IN FRONT. 200 EJONES
THEY'RE NOT EASY TO MAKE HEAD OR TAIL OF. 68 ELECTR
BY CHRIST, I'LL GO BACK AN' GIVE HER A SEABOOT IN 104 ELECTR
HER FAT TAIL
HIS TAIL IS A PIECE OF STRING THAT WAS LEFT WHEN 268 GGBROW
HE BROKE LOOSE FROM JEHOVAH AND
AND LITTLE ME AT THE TAIL-END OF IT ALL. 219 HA APE
TELL HIM TO SALT DE TAIL OF DAT EAGLE/ 242 HA APE
GIVE THEM A BOOT IN THE TAIL FOR ME. 8 MISBEG
AND KNOCKED ONE OF THEM TAIL OVER TIN CUP AGAINST 14 MISBEG
THE PIEPEN.
BE JAYSUS, I'LL TAKE YOU OVER MY KNEE AND SPANK 73 MISBEG
YOUR TAIL.
IF I KNOCK YOU TAIL OVER TINCUP OUT OF THAT CHAIR/ 79 MISBEG
I CAN'T PUT HEAD NOR TAIL TO IT. 595 ROPE
AND I'D FORGET MY LONGING FOR FREEDOM, I'D COME 139 STRANG
WAGGING MY TAIL...

TAILED
A MAN CAN'T TAKE DE POT ON A BOB-TAILED FLUSH ALL 182 EJONES
DE TIME.

TAILORED
HE IS DRESSED WITH A FASTIDIOUS PROPRIETY IN WELL- 25 MANSNS
TAILORED MOURNING BLACK.
HE IS DRESSED IN A BEAUTIFULLY TAILORED ENGLISH 56 MISBEG
TWEED COAT AND WHIPCORD RIDING
FINELY TAILORED CLOTHES OF THE STYLE WORN BY 34 POET
ENGLISH ARISTOCRACY
HE IS EXPENSIVELY TAILORED.) 152 STRANG
HE IS DRESSED IN HIS ALL BLACK, METICULOUS, 187 STRANG
PERFECTLY TAILORED MOURNING COSTUME.

TAILORING
OF DISTINCTLY ENGLISH TAILORING. 4 STRANG

TAILS
I'LL TIE A DISPOSSESS BOMB TO YOUR TAILS THAT'LL 606 ICEMAN
BLOW YOU OUT IN THE STREET/
ONE BY ONE, LOOKIN' LIKE POOCHES WID DEIR TAILS 699 ICEMAN
BETWEEN DEIR LEGS.
NO, GUINEA PIGS HAVE NO TAILS... 139 STRANG

TAINT
THERE IS A TAINT OF BLOOD IN THE AIR THAT POISONS 329 LAZARU
THE BREATH OF THE SEA.

TAKEN
THAT THEY CANNOT BE TAKEN OFF WITH SHOES ON.) 187 AHWILD
(MILLER HAS TAKEN THE SLIPS AND IS READING THEM 202 AHWILD
FROWNINGLY.
WHEN YOU'VE A DROP TAKEN/ 226 AHWILD

TAKEN (CONT'D.)
I'VE TAKEN DOWN THE DISTANCE EVERY TIME YOU'VE 230 AHWILD
SAVED REDD'S LIFE FOR THIRTY YEARS
(HE HAS TAKEN HIS COLLAR AND TIE FROM WHERE THEY 260 AHWILD
HANG FROM ONE CORNER OF THE
ONE OF THEM TORN FROM THE SPRAWL ON THE SIDEWALK 261 AHWILD
HE HAD TAKEN.
DO YOU WANT HIM TO BE TAKEN DOWN SICK$ 268 AHWILD
(TAKEN DOWN--DISGUSTEDLY) NO, I DON'T/ 271 AHWILD
(A BIT TAKEN ABACK) NO. 296 AHWILD
IT MAKES ME FEEL CLEAN--OUT HERE--'S IF I'D TAKEN 26 ANNA
A BATH.
ROBERT IS SO MUCH TAKEN UP WITH WHAT HE IS GOING 99 BEYOND
TO SAY
IT WAS GOD'S WILL THAT HE SHOULD BE TAKEN. 114 BEYOND
I'D HAVE TAKEN IT ON THE SPOT, ONLY I COULDN'T 133 BEYOND
LEAVE UNCLE DICK IN THE LURCH.
I'VE TAKEN A HOLIDAY IN HONOR OF YOUR ARRIVAL. 136 BEYOND
FIGHTS, WE'VE HAD, GOD HELP US, BUT 'TWAS ONLY 480 CARDIF
WHEN WE'D A BIT AV DRINK TAKEN.
THEY SAY FOR HIS OWN GOOD HE MUST BE TAKEN AWAY. 564 CROSS
(IN A HARD VOICE) UNLESS WE HAVE--FATHER--TAKEN 564 CROSS
AWAY.
(WHO HAS TAKEN A CHAIR BY HER BROTHER--IN A 570 CROSS
WARNING WHISPER)
(STARES AT HIM, TAKEN ABACK--THEN QUIETLY) 506 DAYS
THEN HIS MOTHER, WORN OUT BY NURSING HIS FATHER 511 DAYS
AND BY HER GRIEF, WAS TAKEN ILL.
MY PLOT, UP TO THE LAST PART, WHICH IS WHOLLY 533 DAYS
IMAGINARY, IS TAKEN FROM LIFE.
(TAKEN ABACK, GIVES JOHN A WONDERING LOOK--THEN 534 DAYS
APOLOGETICALLY)
(HIS VOICE HAS TAKEN ON A NOTE OF INTENSE 544 DAYS
LUNGING.)
YOU'VE TAKEN A CHILL. 548 DAYS
SHE HAS TAKEN OFF HER COAT AND HAT DOWNSTAIRS, 548 DAYS
YOU'VE TAKEN A BAD CHILL. 550 DAYS
SHE SEEMS TO HAVE TAKEN HER END IN YOUR STORY VERY551 DAYS
SERIOUSLY.
HIS EYES HAVE TAKEN ON A STRANGE, INCONGRUOUS 230 DESIRE
DREAMY QUALITY.
ON ACCOUNT OF THE HEAT HE HAS TAKEN OFF EVERYTHING235 DESIRE
BUT HIS UNDERSHIRT AND PANTS.
THE STOVE HAS BEEN TAKEN DOWN TO GIVE MORE ROOM TO247 DESIRE
THE DANCERS.
(TAKEN ABACK--FROWNING) SO ALL THE TOWN KNOWS 502 DIFRNT
ABOUT IT?
THE TURN THE CONVERSATION HAS TAKEN SEEMS TO HAVE 526 DIFRNT
AROUSED A HECTIC.
WHY HAS REUBEN TAKEN A SUDDEN NOTION TO GOING OUT 425 DYNAMO
IN THE EVENING LATELY$
THEN FALLS BY SLOW GRADATIONS OF TONE INTO SILENCE199 EJONES
AND IS TAKEN UP AGAIN.
AND IS TAKEN UP AGAIN IN A NOTE OF SAVAGE HOPE. 201 EJONES
YES, I MIGHT HAVE SEEN YOU DIDN'T APPEAR MUCH 23 ELECTR
TAKEN
HE'D TAKEN TO DRINK. 25 ELECTR
(TAKEN ABACK) WHAT MAKES YOU THINK I SUSPECT YOU$ 51 ELECTR
FATHER HAS TAKEN A FANCY TO HIM FOR SOME REASON. 52 ELECTR
YOU DON'T THINK YOU ARE GOING TO BE--TAKEN ILL, DO 60 ELECTR
YOU$
WHAT A TRAGEDY TO BE TAKEN HIS FIRST NIGHT HOME 69 ELECTR
(THEN AS ORIN LOOKS TAKEN ABACK) 85 ELECTR
BILLY WOULD LIKE TO THINK ME TAKEN IN FLAGRANTE 280 GGBROW
DELICTO, EH$
AND DISILLUSIONMENT, AND WHICH SHE HAS JUST TAKEN 291 GGBROW
OFF.
(TAKEN ABACK--A BIT STIFFLY) 314 GGBROW
(A WHOLE CHORUS OF VOICES HAS TAKEN UP THIS 211 HA APE
REFRAIN, STAMPING ON THE FLOOR,
IS TAKEN ABACK BY THE COMMONPLACENESS OF THE ROOM 246 HA APE
AND THE MEN IN IT.
(HE HAS TAKEN TWO ONE-DOLLAR BILLS AND SOME CHANGE 37 HUGHIE
FROM HIS POCKET.
THAT YOU'D TAKEN THE PLACE OF MY OLD MAN. 588 ICEMAN
WE SHOULD HAVE TAKEN YOU TO THE LONDON ZOO 599 ICEMAN
BUT WHEN SHE WAS TAKEN, I TOLD THEM, »NO, BOYS, I 603 ICEMAN
CAN'T DO IT.
WHY, I'D ONLY TAKEN ONE SIP OF IT. 606 ICEMAN
ONLY EIGHTY YEARS OLD WHEN HE WAS TAKEN. 627 ICEMAN
HE'S TAKEN ON DE PARTY LIKE IT WAS HIS BOITHDAY. 630 ICEMAN
(HAS TAKEN A GLASS FROM THE TABLE 637 ICEMAN
WANT THE COPS TO CLOSE THE JOINT AND GET MY 654 ICEMAN
LICENSE TAKEN AWAY$
=I AIN'T NEVER TAKEN YOU DOUGH 'CEPT WHEN I WAS 671 ICEMAN
DRUNK AND NOT WORKIN'/=
(BEAMING AT HIM) NO OFFENSE TAKEN, YOU TANNED 723 ICEMAN
LIMEY/
WHOA. IF THE BRITISH GOVERNMENT HAD TAKEN MY 723 ICEMAN
ADVICE,
AND SEVERAL OTHERS HAD BEEN TAKEN DOWN WITH 24 JOURNE
CHOLERA
HE HAS TAKEN OFF COLLAR AND TIE AND CARRIES THEM 53 JOURNE
IN HIS HAND.
TAKEN IN MODERATION AS AN APPETIZER, IS THE BEST 65 JOURNE
OF TONICS.
(STUPIDLY PUZZLED.) YOU'VE TAKEN SOME OF THE 104 JOURNE
MEDICINES
IF I DIDN'T KNOW BETTER, I'D THINK YOU'D A DROP 104 JOURNE
TAKEN.
I MUST GO UPSTAIRS. I HAVEN'T TAKEN ENOUGH. 107 JOURNE
(WITH ANGRY DISGUST.) I HOPE TO GOD YOU HAVEN'T 116 JOURNE
TAKEN TO DRINK ON TOP OF--
I HAVEN'T TAKEN ENOUGH. 121 JOURNE
IF I'VE A DROP TAKEN, I DIDN'T STEAL IT. 123 JOURNE
HE HAS TAKEN OFF HIS COAT AND HAS ON AN OLD BROWN 125 JOURNE
DRESSING GOWN.

TAKEN

TAKEN (CONT'D.)
I'VE ALWAYS FEARED IT WOULD CHANGE AND EVERYTHING 146 JOURNE
I HAD WOULD BE TAKEN AWAY.
TAKEN YOUR MIND OFF YOUR TROUBLES. 161 JOURNE
EVEN HIS DEFENSIVE DRUNKENNESS TAKEN FROM HIM, 172 JOURNE
LEAVING HIM SICK AND SOBER.
(CHANTING EXULTANTLY) THE STONE IS TAKEN AWAY/ 278 LAZARU
THIS IS TAKEN UP BY THE CROWD-- UNPLEASANT, 300 LAZARU
RESENTFUL LAUGHTER.
WHO HAD TAKEN LAZARUS PRISONER, MARCH IN WITH 306 LAZARU
DANCERS-STEPS.
(HER VOICE TREMBLING) EVEN IF GOD HAS TAKEN OUR 347 LAZARU
LITTLE ONES--
YOUR REBUKE IS WELL TAKEN, NICHOLAS. 31 MANSNS
THEY CAN BE TAKEN ONLY WITH YOUR CONSENT, 32 MANSNS
IN HIS LETTERS HENRY SUGGESTS CERTAIN STEPS SHOULD 32 MANSNS
BE TAKEN WHICH,
IT IS AS THOUGH SHE HAD SLOWLY TAKEN POSSESSION OF 73 MANSNS
SARA
HER MANNER HAS TAKEN ON A LOT OF DEBORAH'S WELL- 75 MANSNS
BRED, SELF-ASSURED POISE,
(STRICKENLY.) YOU MEAN THEY ARE TO BE TAKEN FROM 104 MANSNS
ME?
REGRETFULLY.) HE'S A FOOL TO THINK SHE COULD EVER120 MANSNS
HAVE TAKEN MY CHILDREN--
ITS OWN INDIFFERENCE--BECAUSE SHE NO LONGER WANTS 126 MANSNS
ME--HAS TAKEN ALL SHE NEEDED--
I WOULD MAKE HIM PAY FOR ME UNTIL I HAD TAKEN 133 MANSNS
EVERYTHING HE POSSESSED
WE'VE TAKEN HIS BANE FROM HIM. 140 MANSNS
AH, HE'S TAKEN TO PAYING YOUR OLD MOTHER A MORNING140 MANSNS
VISIT
(HER FACE HAS TAKEN ON A SOFT, DREAMY, ECSTATIC 162 MANSNS
LOOK--EXULTANTLY.)
IF YOU THINK I CAN BE TAKEN IN BY SUCH AN OBVIOUS 176 MANSNS
SHAM--
IT WAS MY BIRTHDAY AND I'D TAKEN A DROP TOO MUCH--348 MARCOM
A VERY UNUSUAL THING FOR ME.
SHE IS BEING TAKEN HOME TO CATHAY FOR BURIAL-- 351 MARCOM
COMES FROM HER LIPS AND IS TAKEN UP IN CHORUS IN 352 MARCOM
THE BRANCHES OF THE TREE
(TAKEN ABACK FOR A MOMENT--THEN CRAFTILY) 353 MARCOM
HE SEEMS TO HAVE TAKEN A FANCY TO MARK. 362 MARCOM
MY FATHER AND UNCLE HAVE TAKEN ME INTO THE FIRM. 382 MARCOM
(SOMEWHAT TAKEN ABACK, PUZZLEDLY) 382 MARCOM
I CAN TELL YOU EACH THING THAT HAPPENED TONIGHT AS 81 MISBEG
CLEAR AS IF I'D NOT TAKEN A
(DEFENSIVELY.) YOU MEAN HE'D A DROP TOO MUCH 21 POET
TAKEN LAST NIGHT?
I SHOULD NOT HAVE TAKEN OFFENSE. 70 POET
(DEBORAH IS SO TAKEN ABACK BY HIS EFFRONTERY 74 POET
I AM SURE MRS. HARFORD IS WAITING TO BE TAKEN TO 74 POET
HER SON.
TU LET YOURSELF BE TAKEN IN BY SUCH AN OBVIOUS BIT106 POET
OF CLEVER ACTING.
(WITH ENTHUSIASM.) THERE'LL BE MORE MONEY TAKEN 134 POET
OVER THE BAR
NO MATTER WHAT HE'S TAKEN/ 137 POET
AND HE MUST HAVE TAKEN A ROOM IN THE CITY SO HE'LL137 POET
BE NEAR THE GROUND.
HE'S NOT TAKEN A DROP SINCE WE LEFT HERE. 153 POET
THANK YOU KINDLY BUT I'VE ALREADY TAKEN YOUR WISE 171 POET
ADVICE, FATHER.
I'D HAVE TAKEN YOUR HAND AWHILE BACK, AN' GLAD TO,591 ROPE
BUT FOR HER BEIN' WITH US.
FIRST AND FOREMOST, THERE IS YOUR HEALTH TO BE 16 STRANG
TAKEN INTO CONSIDERATION.
(BEGINNING TO BE TAKEN BY HIS LIKABLE BOYISH 28 STRANG
QUALITY)
(TAKEN ABACK) WHY--ER--NOTHING, SIR. 32 STRANG
I'VE TAKEN CARE OF HER. 59 STRANG
I'VE TAKEN CARE OF HER SO MANY YEARS, LIVED HER 62 STRANG
LIFE FOR HER WITH MY LIFE,
(HE HAS TAKEN SOME PAPERS OUT OF HIS POCKET AND 73 STRANG
HANDS THEM TO EVANS)
HE'S ALWAYS TAKEN A FRIENDLY INTEREST... 113 STRANG
(TAKEN ABACK--CONFUSEDLY) ON--ALL RIGHT, NINA. 126 STRANG
YOU DON'T GET THAT FROM ME--(HE HAS TAKEN A 150 STRANG
THREATENING STEP FORWARD.
THAT MIGHT PAY ME BACK A LITTLE FOR ALL HE'S TAKEN173 STRANG
FROM ME/....)
NOT SINCE YOUR FATHER WAS TAKEN SICK, SHE HASN'T, 185 STRANG
DEAR.
DO I HEAR MY NAME TAKEN IN VAIN? 197 STRANG
AND HAS TAKEN THE ROLL OF MONEY FROM HIS INSIDE 508 VOYAGE
POCKET
(TAKEN ABACK, TURNING AWAY) NO, I SUPPOSE-- 485 WELDED

TAKIN'
I AIN'T TAKIN' NO CHANCES. 464 CARIBE
IF THAT'S WHAT HIS COMIN'S DONE T' ME--KILLIN' 258 DESIRE
YEWR LOVE--TAKIN' YEW AWAY--
YOU'LL MAKE UP WITH HIM, AND I S'POSE I'M A FOOL 510 DIFRNT
TO BE TAKIN' IT SO SERIOUS.
IT'S WORTH TAKIN' A STAB AT, DAMNED IF IT AIN'T. 545 DIFRNT
WHAT'RE YOU TAKIN' IT SO DAMNED SERIOUS FOR-- ME 546 DIFRNT
ASKIN' YOU TO MARRY ME, I MEANS
I'VE 'EARD MYSELF YOU 'AD TURNED YER COAT AN' WAS 185 EJONES
TAKIN' UP WITH THEIR BLASTED
(THEN CURIOUSLY) AIN'T YER TAKIN' NO LUGGAGE WITH186 EJONES
YER?
TAKIN' ALL DE WOIST PUNCHES FROM BOT' OF 'EM. 253 HA APE
I WAS WISE I WAS TAKIN' A CHANCE. 35 HUGHIE
I KNOW YOU CAN'T AFFORD TAKIN' NO CHANCES. 37 HUGHIE
DE BUYS WASN'T TAKIN' YUH SERIOUS. 637 ICEMAN
(GOING ON WITH HIS STORY) DEY SAYS, "WE'RE TAKIN'670 ICEMAN
A HOLIDAY."
WELL, YUH'RE TAKIN' OVER NOW, GET ME, NO MATTER 697 ICEMAN
HOW PLASTERED YUH ARE/

TAKIN' (CONT'D.)
DEY'D LIKE TAKIN' CARE OF YUH. 702 ICEMAN
THEY'D ONLY BE TAKIN' ALL THE CREDIT AND MAKIN' 528 INZONE
HEROES OF THEMSELVES.
WE'D BEST BE TAKIN' THIS TO THE SKIPPER, D'YOU 528 INZONE
THINK, MAYBE?
FAIX, YOU'RE TAKIN' IT AISY. 9 POET
(INDIGNANTLY.) YOU'RE TAKIN' IT COOL ENOUGH, 154 POET
ALWAYS TAKIN' SIDES WITH THE RICH YANKS AGAINST 157 POET
THE POOR IRISH/
AN' HIM TAKIN' LEAVE OF HIS SENSES ALTOGETHER. 587 ROPE
AN' WHAT'LL YE BE TAKIN' FOR YOUR THIRST? 499 VOYAGE
NO, OLLIE, WE'LL BE TAKIN' THIS LAD HOME TO HIS 504 VOYAGE
BED.

TAKING
(WITH DIGNITY) I AND BERT TURNER ARE TAKING ELSIE191 AHWILD
AND ETHEL HAND CANOEING.
(THEY ALL LAUGH NOW, TAKING THIS AS A CUE.) 195 AHWILD
LILY IS SHOCKED BUT, TAKING HER CUE FROM THEM, 195 AHWILD
SMILES.
(WITHOUT TAKING OFFENSE--IN SAME FLAT, BRITTLE 201 AHWILD
VOICE)
I'M TAKING THE ADVERTISEMENT FOR MY STORE OUT OF 203 AHWILD
YOUR PAPER--
(EMBARRASSEDLY) YES, I THOUGHT--IF SID'S TAKING 212 AHWILD
ME TO THE FIREWORKS--
HIS TAKING UP WITH BAD WOMEN. 213 AHWILD
(TAKING ONE) SURE? 239 AHWILD
(DISCOMFITED--TAKING HIS ARM FROM AROUND HER-- 279 AHWILD
(TAKING HER HAND AND TUGGING AT IT GENTLY) 280 AHWILD
YOU'RE ACTUALLY TAKING THIS MURIEL CRUSH OF 291 AHWILD
RICHARD'S SERIOUSLY, DO YOU?
(QUICKLY--TAKING IT) OH, DEN IT COMES FROM MY 8 ANNA
DAUGHTER, ANNA.
TAKING IN HIS EMBARRASSMENT WITH A MALICIOUS 11 ANNA
TWINKLE OF AMUSEMENT IN HER EYE.
(LIGHTING ONE AND TAKING A DEEP INHALE) 15 ANNA
TAKING IN EVERY DETAIL OF HER FACE. 15 ANNA
(TAKING A PACKAGE OF SWEET CAPORAL CIGARETTES FROM 15 ANNA
HER BAG)
TAKING CARE OF OTHER PEOPLE'S KIDS, 18 ANNA
WHAT IS IT YOU DO WHEN YOU'RE NOT TAKING A TRIP 35 ANNA
WITH THE OLD MANS
(TAKING ONE OF HIS ARMS OVER HER SHOULDER) 39 ANNA
WHERE'S THE HARM IN HIS TAKING ME AROUND? 42 ANNA
(MOCKINGLY) THAT'S WHAT YOUR TAKING ME TO SEA HAS 43 ANNA
DONE FOR ME.
SHE'S TAKING MY ORDERS FROM THIS OUT NOT YOURS. 56 ANNA
TAKING CARE OF OTHER PEOPLE'S KIDS-- 58 ANNA
AND YOU TAKING UP WITH THIS ONE AND THAT ONE ALL 73 ANNA
THE YEARS OF YOUR LIFE?
I'LL HAVE TO BE TAKING YOUR NAKED WORD FOR IT AND 76 ANNA
HAVE YOU ANYWAY, I'M THINKING--
WHEN YOU'RE TAKING OUR ROBBIE AWAY FROM US, IN THE 95 BEYOND
MIDDLE OF THE NIGHT,
YOU SHOULDN'T BE TAKING IT SO HARD, 'S FAR AS I 96 BEYOND
KIN SEE.
(TAKING HIS HAND) THANKS, ANDY, IT'S FINE OF YOU 101 BEYOND
TO--
(TAKING OFF HER SHOES AND STOCKINGS) 121 BEYOND
(ABSENT-MINDEDLY, WITHOUT TAKING HIS EYES FROM THE122 BEYOND
BOOK)
(TAKING HIS HAND AND DANCING HAPPILY BESIDE HIM) 136 BEYOND
(HER VOICE VAGUELY FRIGHTENED, TAKING HER FATHER'S142 BEYOND
HAND)
HOW CAN YOU OF ALL PEOPLE THINK OF TAKING MONEY 148 BEYOND
FROM HIM?
(TAKING A THERMOMETER FROM HIS POCKET AND PUTTING 484 CARDIF
IT INTO YANK'S MOUTH)
(TAKING OUT HIS WATCH AND FEELING YANK'S PULSE) 484 CARDIF
(THE BOTTLE PASSES FROM HAND TO HAND, EACH MAN 462 CARIBE
TAKING A SIP
THAT FOOLED HIM BY TAKING MY ARM AND THEN THROWING564 CROSS
ME ASHORE--
(TAKING THE HINT) WELL, I'LL MOVE ALONG. 498 DAYS
FATHER BAIRD SAYS QUIETLY, WITHOUT ANY SIGN OF 501 DAYS
TAKING OFFENSE)
TAKING CARE OF JOHN. 516 DAYS
(LAUGHING--GIVES HER A HUG) YOU'RE NOT TAKING ME 516 DAYS
SERIOUSLY, ARE YOU?
LOVING TAKING UP A POSITION DIRECTLY BEHIND HIM 555 DAYS
(TAKING ONE ARM AND SIGNALING FATHER BAIRD TO TAKE555 DAYS
THE OTHER--
(HER VOICE TAKING POSSESSION) 222 DESIRE
(SHE LAUGHS A LOW HUMID LAUGH WITHOUT TAKING HER 229 DESIRE
EYES FROM HIM
(REACHING OUT AND TAKING HIS HAND) 233 DESIRE
(TAKING ONE OF HIS HANDS IN HERS AND PATTING IT) 242 DESIRE
(TAKING HIS ARM) YOU COME WITH ME. 514 DIFRNT
(WITH A GREAT PRETENCE OF GRIEF, TAKING ONE OF HER531 DIFRNT
HANDS IN HIS)
TAKING DOWN ALL THE CURTAINS WITH QUICK MECHANICAL548 DIFRNT
MOVEMENTS.
WHERE IS SHE TAKING HIMS... 434 DYNAMO
(TAKING HIS HAND-- IN A BULLYING TONE) 434 DYNAMO
HIS EYES FIXED FOR A MILE ON HIS HOME, TAKING IN 457 DYNAMO
EVERY DETAIL.
(THEN HARSHLY, TAKING A THREATENING STEP FORWARD) 463 DYNAMO
(TAKING HER HAND--INSISTENTLY) COME WITH ME/ 482 DYNAMO
THE AUCTIONEER HOLDS UP HIS HAND, TAKING HIS PLACE197 EJONES
AT THE STUMP.
AMOS AMES, CARPENTER BY TRADE BUT NOW TAKING A 6 ELECTR
HOLIDAY AND DRESSED IN HIS SUNDAY
WHO WAS TAKING CARE OF FATHER'S LITTLE SISTER WHO 19 ELECTR
DIED.
(COMING AND TAKING HER HAND WHICH SHE FORCES 21 ELECTR
HERSELF TO HOLD OUT TO HIM)
HE'S TAKING MEDICINE. 40 ELECTR

TAKING (CONT'D.)
IF IT WAS A QUESTION OF SOME WOMAN TAKING YOU FROM 41 ELECTR
ME,
(TAKING HIS ARM) COME INSIDE WITH ME AND I'LL GET 47 ELECTR
YOU SOMETHING TO EAT.
(SHE MOVES UP, PAST HER DAUGHTER, TAKING MANNON'S 56 ELECTR
HAND.
(REACHING OUT AND TAKING HIS HAND) 85 ELECTR
(THEN HE ASKS TENDERLY, TAKING HER HAND) 89 ELECTR
(SOOTHINGLY, COMING TO HIM AND TAKING HIS ARM) 96 ELECTR
(TAKING HIS HANDS OFF HER SHOULDERS AND RISING) 99 ELECTR
AND HE WAS TAKING VINNIE WITH HIM 108 ELECTR
(THEN TAKING HIM IN WITH A SMILING APPRECIATIVE 143 ELECTR
POSSESSIVENESS)
(SUDDENLY TAKING HER HAND--EXCITEDLY) 160 ELECTR
(HE STOPS ABRUPTLY AND STARES BEFORE HIM, AS IF 166 ELECTR
THIS IDEA WERE SUDDENLY TAKING
(TAKING IT--VAGUELY) OHS 275 GGBROW
(TAKING OFF HER MASK-- 279 GGBROW
(TAKING OFF HIS MASK--SLOWLY) 282 GGBROW
(WITHOUT TAKING OFFENSE) CUT IT/ 285 GGBROW
(TAKING OFF HIS MASK, 285 GGBROW
(TAKING OFF HER MASK, GLADLY.) 301 GGBROW
(HARDLY TAKING IT--RESERVEDLY) 303 GGBROW
BROWN SITS DOWN AT HIS DESK, TAKING OFF THE MASK 305 GGBROW
AGAIN.
(TAKING HER TONE--EXULTANTLY) 322 GGBROW
(TAKING A GRIMY NOTEBOOK AND AN INCH-LONG PENCIL 323 GGBROW
FROM HIS POCKET)
(TAKING A GULP FROM HIS BOTTLE--GOOD-NATUREDLY) 211 HA APE
(PADDY FROM THE START OF YANK'S SPEECH HAS BEEN 216 HA APE
TAKING ONE GULP AFTER ANOTHER
THE MEN ARE TAKING A BREATHING SPELL. 223 HA APE
(TAKING A DEEP BREATH) DIS AIN'T SO BAD AT DAT, 234 HA APE
HUHS
(TAKING THE KEY, GIVES THE CLERK THE ONCE-OVER. 10 HUGHIE
*WITH A PRETTY NURSE TAKING CARE OF HIM= 26 HUGHIE
TAKING CARE OF YOU AND SHOOTING AWAY YOUR SNAKES, 610 ICEMAN
(TAKING ON A SALESMAN'S PERSUASIVENESS) 622 ICEMAN
(MARGIE AND PEARL START TAKING THEM FROM HIS ARMS 638 ICEMAN
AND PUTTING THEM ON THE TABLE.
(THEN WITH A SIMPLE EARNESTNESS, TAKING A CHAIR BY641 ICEMAN
LARRY.
WE'VE HEARD HARRY PULL THAT BLUFF ABOUT TAKING A 652 ICEMAN
WALK EVERY BIRTHDAY
WE'VE HEARD HIS BULL ABOUT TAKING A WALK AROUND 660 ICEMAN
THE WARD FOR YEARS,
WHAT THE HELL'S TO BE SCARED OF, JUST TAKING A 687 ICEMAN
STROLL AROUND MY OWN YARD$
YOU KNOW HOW IT IS WHEN YOU KEEP TAKING CHANCES. 712 ICEMAN
TAKING IN THE PARTY AND THE CHANGED ATMOSPHERE.) 725 ICEMAN
(TAKING A SMALL BUNCH OF KEYS FROM SMITTY'S 526 INZONE
POCKET)
(TAKING THEM) WE'LL SOON BE KNOWIN'. 527 INZONE
(TAKING UP THE BOTTOM LETTER) 531 INZONE
JAMIE RISES FROM HIS CHAIR AND, TAKING OFF HIS 41 JOURNE
COAT, GOES TO THE DOOR.
(WORRIEDLY, TAKING HIS ARM.) 42 JOURNE
THEY BOWED TO YOUR FATHER AND HE BOWED BACK AS IF 43 JOURNE
HE WERE TAKING A CURTAIN CALL.
AND YOU WON'T WORRY YOURSELF SICK, AND YOU'LL KEEP 48 JOURNE
ON TAKING CARE OF YOURSELF--
SHE'S BEEN TAKING A NAP. 52 JOURNE
THEN SHE WASN'T TAKING A NAP$ 57 JOURNE
(TAKING HIS HAND.) COME AND SIT DOWN. 91 JOURNE
I FORGOT I'M TAKING A DRIVE. 94 JOURNE
(HE RECITES FROM SWINBURNE'S *A LEAVE-TAKING* AND 173 JOURNE
DOES IT WELL.
(HE RECITES FROM *A LEAVE-TAKING* AGAIN WITH 173 JOURNE
INCREASED BITTERNESS.)
TAKING HIM TO ROME HAD BEEN THRICE BLOWN BACK BY A300 LAZARU
STORM.
(SUSPICIOUSLY LAUGHS WEAKLY WITHOUT TAKING OFFENSE.) 315 LAZARU
(TAKING IT UP IN A TONE BETWEEN CHANTING AND THEIR318 LAZARU
OLD SOLEMN INTONING)
(AS IF TAKING AN OATH WITH ONE VOICE) 323 LAZARU
AND, TAKING TIBERIUS' HAND IN HER OTHER, SHE 342 LAZARU
KISSES IT AND CALLS INSISTENTLY)
TAKING HER HEAD IN BOTH HIS HANDS, HE KISSES HER 345 LAZARU
ON THE LIPS.)
TAKING THE PEACH AND MAKING A HUMBLE COURTESY 346 LAZARU
BEFORE HER)
AS IF HE WERE TAKING AN OATH TO LIFE ON HER HEART,349 LAZARU
LOOKS UPWARD AND LAUGHS,
AND PLEASURE IN TAKING VENGEANCE ON MYSELF. 356 LAZARU
(TAKING HIS TONE--MOCKINGLY) 366 LAZARU
TO ANNOUNCE THAT WE ARE TAKING OVER FATHER'S 62 MANSNS
COMPANY.
PERHAPS SARA WOULD EVEN INSIST ON TAKING MOTHER 72 MANSNS
WITH US/
AS SARA WAS IN TAKING YOU. 75 MANSNS
TO KEEP ANYONE FROM TAKING WHAT SHE REGARDED AS 88 MANSNS
HERS.
WELL, MOTHER WON'T APPROVE OF MY TAKING YOU AWAY, 91 MANSNS
AS WELL AS THE CHILDREN.
UNTIL FINALLY YOU WILL FIND YOURSELF CAPABLE OF 92 MANSNS
TAKING MY PLACE.
(BREAKS IN AND TAKES IT UP, TAKING ON HER TONE.) 107 MANSNS
TAKING HER HAND FROM HIS ARM. 115 MANSNS
(THINKING.) YOU'D THINK TAKING THE CHILDREN AWAY 118 MANSNS
MEANT NOTHING TO HER--
UNTIL HE FINALLY TRICKS ME INTO UNLOCKING THE 163 MANSNS
DOOR, TAKING HIS HAND--
(HIS TERROR GOING AND RAGE TAKING ITS PLACE, LEAPS352 MARCOM
TO HIS FEET)
UNCLE SAYS TAKING CHANCES--NECESSARY CHANCES, OF 356 MARCOM
COURSE--

TAKING (CONT'D.)
(TAKING UP THE READING FROM HIS BOOK IN THE SAME 370 MARCOM
TONE)
(TAKING HIS HAND AND KISSING IT) 385 MARCOM
(TAKING IT--FLUSHING WITH PLEASURE) 391 MARCOM
(BRISKLY--TAKING OPERATIONS IN HAND) 403 MARCOM
YOU ARE TAKING ADVANTAGE OF THIS BEING THE LAST 414 MARCOM
DAY TO SHIRK YOUR DUTY/
EACH HAS AT LEAST ONE PANE MISSING, A SQUARE OF 1 MISBEG
CARDBOARD TAKING ITS PLACE.
(THEN VIRTUOUSLY) BUT I DON'T LIKE TAKING STOLEN 7 MISBEG
MONEY.
(TURNS ON HIM ANGRILY) ARE YOU TAKING MIKE'S 22 MISBEG
SCHEME SERIOUSLY, YOU OLD GOATS
IF YOU THINK JIM HASN'T BEEN TAKING IN YOUR FINE 29 MISBEG
POINTS, YOU'RE A FOOL.
(WHO HAS BEEN TAKING EVERYTHING IN WITHOUT SEEMING 42 MISBEG
TO)
HOGAN, FOR TAKING IT EASY ON SUCH A BLAZING HOT 43 MISBEG
DAY,
ARE YOU TAKING IT AS AN INSULT$ 88 MISBEG
TAKING HIS SIDE AGAINST YOUR POOR OLD FATHER, ARE 101 MISBEG
YOU$
YOU'LL BE TAKING A TRAIN BACK TO YOUR DEAR OLD 130 MISBEG
BROADWAY TOMORROW NIGHT,
(INSTINCTIVELY SHE DRAWS AWAY, TAKING HER ARMS 149 MISBEG
FROM AROUND HIM.)
WHEN YOU WAS UPSTAIRS AT THE BACK TAKING HIM HIS 17 POET
BREAKFAST,
TAKING A STEP BACK AS THOUGH HE HAD BEEN SLAPPED 72 POET
IN THE FACE.
I CANNOT IMAGINE YOU TAKING THAT SERIOUSLY. 85 POET
(TAKING IT--WITH A LOOK OF DISGUST AT HIS HALF- 589 ROPE
SISTER)
(AFTER TAKING A DRINK HIMSELF, PUTS BOTTLE ON 591 ROPE
TABLE)
(TAKING IT AS A JOKE--WITH A LOUD GUFFAW) 596 ROPE
HE'S ALWAYS TRYING TO BULLY HER INTO TAKING BETTER 31 STRANG
CARE OF HERSELF.
GOES TO THE TABLE AND TAKING A PRESCRIPTION PAD 33 STRANG
FROM HIS POCKET,
AND IN HIS CAR WE WERE TAKING THIS DEFERRED 50 STRANG
HONEYMOON,
AND CALL HER TO ACCOUNT FOR HOW SHE'S TAKING CARE 56 STRANG
OF YOU/
(THEN TAKING A SIP OF COFFEE, AND TRYING TO BE 57 STRANG
PLEASANTLY CASUAL)
I WAS GLAD TAKING CARE OF THEM TWO KEPT ME SO BUSY 60 STRANG
(TEASINGLY) BUT I HEARD YOU WERE *TAKING AN 80 STRANG
OPPORTUNITY* TO GO IN FOR
(WITH A SMILE) WELL, YOU'RE THE TAKING KIND FOR 80 STRANG
WHOM OPPORTUNITIES ARE MADE/
(SARCASTICALLY) THEN YOU DON'T BELIEVE IN TAKING 81 STRANG
YOUR OWN MEDICINES
(TAKING HIS OTHER HAND AND SLOWLY PULLING HIM 87 STRANG
AROUND TO FACE HER.
(SUDDENLY FALLING ON HIS KNEES AND TAKING HER HAND 89 STRANG
IN BOTH OF HIS AND KISSING IT
(SUDDENLY TAKING HER IN HIS ARMS AND KISSING HER 97 STRANG
FRANTICALLY)
(TAKING HIS ARM AND HUSTLING HIM GENIALLY TOWARD 122 STRANG
THE DOOR)
HIS EYES WANDER ABOUT THE ROOM, GREEDILY TAKING IT124 STRANG
IN.)
HIS VOICE TAKING ON A PLEADING UNCERTAIN QUALITY) 126 STRANG
(SUDDENLY TAKING HER IN HIS ARMS AND KISSING HER 130 STRANG
AGAIN AND AGAIN--PASSIONATELY)
(TAKING HIM IN HER ARMS--WITH SUDDEN ALARM) 131 STRANG
TO KILL HAPPINESS IS A WORSE MURDER THAN TAKING 133 STRANG
LIFE/.
IT WAS I WHO SHAMED HIM INTO TAKING UP BIOLOGY 139 STRANG
I SUPPOSED THE THOUGHT OF A WIFE TAKING YOU AWAY 143 STRANG
FROM ME WOULD BE TOO MUCH--
(TAKING HIS HAND AWAY, SHARPLY) 160 STRANG
(RECOVERING HIS GOOD NATURE--WITH A GRIN, TAKING 164 STRANG
HIS ARM)
AND WHY AM I TAKING THIS YOUNG GORDON'S PARTS.... 168 STRANG
(EXASPERATEDLY, TAKING DOWN HIS GLASSES) 177 STRANG
I OUGHT TO HAVE INSISTED ON HIS TAKING BETTER CARE185 STRANG
OF HIMSELF.
(FURIOUSLY, TAKING A THREATENING STEP TOWARD HIM) 193 STRANG
(TURNS TO NED, GRATEFULLY TAKING HIS HAND AND 196 STRANG
PRESSING IT)
(TAKING A SMALL BOTTLE FROM BEHIND THE BAR) 495 VOYAGE
(VAGUELY TAKING OFF HIS DERBY HAT AND PUTTING IT 497 VOYAGE
ON AGAIN--PLAINTIVELY)
(HESITATINGLY) WE'VE BEEN TAKING EACH OTHER TOO 446 WELDED
MUCH FOR GRANTED.
(TAKING ONE) THANKS, NELLY. 450 WELDED
(AFTER A PAUSE, TAKING UP HER STORY MATTER-OF- 483 WELDED
FACTLY)
(AFTER A PAUSE, LOOKING BEFORE HIM--ASSERTIVELY, 485 WELDED
AS IF TAKING A PLEDGE)

TAL

IT'S SHORT LETTER, DON'T TAL ME MUCH MORE'N DAT. 8 ANNA
YOU TAL ME LIE FOR TAL MARTHY, LARRY, SO'S SHE GAT 10 ANNA
OFF BARGE QUICK.
(JOVIALLY) SHE'S GOOD GEL, AY TAL YOU/ 12 ANNA
AY TAL YOU ALL ABOUT EVERYTANG--AND YOU TAL ME ALL 22 ANNA
TANGS HAPPEN TO YOU.
ANNA, AY LIKE SEE YOU LIKE HELL, AY TAL YOU/ 22 ANNA
AY TAL YOU, ANNA, VE CALABRATE, YES-- 23 ANNA
IT'S ROTTEN, AY TAL YOU, FOR GO TO SEA. 28 ANNA
YOUR MO'DER SHE TAL YOU SAME TANG IF SHE VAS 28 ANNA
ALIVE.
(THREATENINGLY) YOU HURRY, AY TAL YOU/ 39 ANNA
(FORCIBLY) DAT VAS MILLION TIMES VORSE, AY TAL 43 ANNA
YOU/

TAL 1606

TAL (CONT'D.)
OH, AY TAL HIM SAME TANG. 43 ANNA
(DESPONDENTLY) ALL RIGHT, AY TAL HIM. 44 ANNA
SHE TAL ME YUST BEFORE SHE GO OUT SHE NEVER MARRY 46 ANNA
FALLAR LIKE YOU.
(SPUTTERING WITH RAGE) YOU VAS CRAZY FOOL, AY 48 ANNA
TAL YOU/
(SCORNFULLY) YES, YOU VAS HELL OF FALLAR, HEAR 48 ANNA
YOU TAL IT/
YOU TAL HIM YOU DON'T VANT FOR HEAR HIM TALK, 51 ANNA
ANNA.
HE TAL THE SAME TANG TO GEL EVERY PORT HE GO/ 51 ANNA
AY TAL YOU SHE DON'T/ 55 ANNA
IF DAT IRISH FALLAR DON'T NEVER COME, YOU DON'T 62 ANNA
NEVER TAL ME DEM TANGS,
YOU DON'T NEVER GAT TO DO--DAT VAY--NO MORE, AY 64 ANNA
TAL YOU.
YANK TAL HIM, PY GOLLY/ 224 HA APE

TALAVERA
(PROUDLY,) I GOT THIS CUT FROM A SABER AT 10 POET
TALAVERA, BAD LUCK TO IT/
HE SERVED UNDER ME AT TALAVERA, AS YOU KNOW. 38 POET
THE ANNIVERSARY OF TALAVERA/ 38 POET
HE, AT LEAST, KNOWS TALAVERA IS NOT THE NAME OF A 57 POET
NEW BRAND OF WHISKEY.
IT'S THE ANNIVERSARY OF TALAVERA, IS ITS 58 POET
FOR IT IS THE ANNIVERSARY OF THE BATTLE OF 71 POET
TALAVERA.
BY THE ETERNAL, I'LL WAGER SHE BELIEVED WHAT I 76 POET
TOLD HER OF TALAVERA
FOR SHAME, YOU DOG, NOT TO REMEMBER TALAVERA. 93 POET
(EXCITEDLY.) TALAVERA, IS ITS 93 POET
AND HERE, TALAVERA. 96 POET
TALAVERA WAS A DEVILISH THIRSTY DAY, IF YOU'LL 98 POET
REMEMBER.
IT IS THE ANNIVERSARY OF THE BATTLE OF TALAVERA, 119 POET
SIR, AND--
LIKE THE GLORIOUS FIELD OF TALAVERA/ 157 POET
HE CAN HAUNT ITS GRAVE IF HE LIKES, AND BOAST TO 169 POET
THE LONELY NIGHT AV TALAVERA
(ROUGHLY.) TO HELL WID TALAVERA/ 176 POET
HE'LL LAUGH AND SING AND HELP YOU CELEBRATE 176 POET
TALAVERA--
THE TRUTH--TALAVERA--THE DUKE PRAISING YOUR 178 POET
BRAVERY--AN OFFICER IN HIS ARMY--
(HER VOICE TREMBLES.) MAY THE HERO OF TALAVERA 182 POET
REST IN PEACE/

TALE
INTO HIS EYES OF ONE ABOUT TO EMBARK ON AN OFT- 229 AHWILD
TOLD TALE OF CHILDHOOD ADVENTURE)
(JOKINGLY) THAT'S A FINE FAIRY TALE TO BE 8 ANNA
TELLIN'--YOUR DAUGHTER/
WORRAL, IF WE CAN RELIEVE YOUR OWN TALE AV UT. 463 CARIBE
I GET THE SAME TALE OF WOE FROM EVERY ONE IN OUR 501 DAYS
PART OF THE COUNTRY.
YOUR COMPLACENT ASSUMPTION THAT LIKE THE PRODIGAL 507 DAYS
OF HIS FAIRY TALE, I--
JACK WINDS UP HIS TALE.) 510 DIFRNT
(DUMBFOUNDED, NOT KNOWING WHAT TO MAKE OF THIS 447 DYNAMO
STRANGE TALE--
(IN A PASSION OF EAGERNESS TO GET THE GUILTY TALE 447 DYNAMO
OFF HIS CONSCIENCE)
WHO TOLD YER THAT FAIRY TALES 177 EJONES
WHAT TALE YOU GOING TO GIVE HER WHEN YOU LOSE ITS 22 HUGHIE
ERIE TAKES UP HIS TALE.) 22 HUGHIE
AND I'D STOP TO KID HIM ALONG AND TELL HIM THE 23 HUGHIE
TALE OF WHAT I'D WIN THAT DAY.
BY GOD, IF HE WAS, I'D TELL HIM A TALE THAT'D MAKE 28 HUGHIE
HIS EYES POP/
MADE UP THE FAIRY TALE ABOUT THE EXILED PRINCE AND 75 MANSNS
THE MAGIC DOOR--
WHEN I WAS STILL AT THE FAIRY-TALE AGE, 109 MANSNS
YOU WERE STARTING TO REMEMBER A FAIRY TALE. 110 MANSNS
I AM SURE I NEVER--I REMEMBER THE STORY AS AN 111 MANSNS
IRONICALLY HUMOROUS TALE.
A HAPPY ENDING TO THAT TALE. 111 MANSNS
THE DOOR OF THE TALE BECAME IDENTIFIED IN MY MIND 111 MANSNS
AND BEGGING HER TO TELL ME A FAIRY TALE/ 121 MANSNS
AN EVIL GODMOTHER CONJURED TO LIFE FROM THE PAGES 161 MANSNS
OF A FAIRY TALE.
OR, OBSESSED BY A FAIRY TALE, 180 MANSNS
BUT TO CONNECT THE DOOR AND THAT SILLY TALE WITH 183 MANSNS
THE ACTUAL WOODEN DOOR--
SO I HAD TO DO SOMETHING TO WARN YOU, AND I 184 MANSNS
THOUGHT A FAIRY TALE--
GOD HELP YOU, IT MUST BE A WONDERFUL THING TO LIVE 50 POET
IN A FAIRY TALE

TALENT
YOU'VE A FINE TALENT FOR THAT, IF FOR NOTHING 26 JOURNE
ELSE.
YOU HAD THE TALENT TO BECOME A FINE ACTOR/ YOU 33 JOURNE
HAVE IT STILL.
BOTH SAID I HAD MORE TALENT THAN ANY STUDENT THEY 104 JOURNE
REMEMBERED.
I'D LOST THE GREAT TALENT I ONCE HAD THROUGH YEARS150 JOURNE
OF EASY REPETITION,
AT LEAST OLD AGE HAS NOT IMPAIRED YOUR TALENT FOR 57 MANSNS
ACTING, DEBORAH/
(SMILING.) MOTHER HAS ALWAYS HAD A SUBTLE TALENT 77 MANSNS
FOR CONTRIVING IT SO THAT
YOU HAVE THE NATURAL TALENT. 91 MANSNS
HAS THE TALENT BUT DOESN'T DARE... 34 STRANG
I'VE GIVEN MY TALENT TO MAKING FOOLS FEEL PLEASED 120 STRANG
WITH THEMSELVES IN ORDER THAT

TALENTED
(WITH WILD MUCKERY) ASK HIM IF HE CAN'T FIND AN 273 GGBRDW
OPENING FOR A TALENTED YOUNG
THE MOST TALENTED OF ITS YOUNG MERCHANTS. 15 MANSNS

TALENTS
BY APPLYING MY NATURAL GOD-GIVEN TALENTS IN THEIR 160 JOURNE
PROPER SPHERE,
WITH MY UNDREAMED-OF TALENTS AS A GOOD WOMAN/ 40 MANSNS

TALES
SO DON'T MOCK ME WITH FAIRY TALES ABOUT ARIZONA, 160 BEYOND
OR ANY SUCH ROT AS THAT.
DAMNED OLD FOOL WITH HIS BEDTIME TALES FOR SECOND 513 DAYS
CHILDHOOD
THAT IS, IF HE'S BEEN TELLIN' TALES. 501 DIFRNT
HE WON'T TELL NO MORE TALES, I RECKON. 514 DIFRNT
MA'LL TELL HIM ALL HER TALES, AND HE'LL BE SORE AT523 DIFRNT
ME RIGHT OFF.
AND I GIVE HIM PLENTY OF GAMBLING TALES. 28 HUGHIE
I SURE TOOK HIM AROUND WITH ME IN TALES AND SHOWED 29 HUGHIE
HIM ONE HELL OF A TIME.
THE TALES ABOUT GAMBLING WASN'T. 29 HUGHIE
AS I WAS SAYING, YOU MUST TAKE HER TALES OF THE 138 JOURNE
PAST WITH A GRAIN OF SALT.
WHY DO I TELL YOU THESE OLD TALES$ 356 LAZARU
AND YOU WOULD READ TALES ALOUD TO ME, HERE. 109 MANSNS
FAIRY TALES, INDEED/ 111 MANSNS
I KNOW YOU'D NEVER CARRY TALES TO HIM. 17 POET
AND NOT FRIGHTEN YOU WITH FAIRY TALES ABOUT HELL. 27 POET
HAVE BEEN LONG-WINDED FAIRY TALES FOR GROWN-UPS-- 176 STRANG

TALK
DID YE HEAR ANY TALK IN THE FO'C'S'TLES 537 'ILE
SHE TALKS TO HIM--WHEN SHE DOES TALK--RIGHT 538 'ILE
ENOUGH.
YE'VE BEEN BELOW HERE GOSSIPIN' OLD WOMAN'S TALK 539 'ILE
WITH THAT BOY.
ME AND MR. SLOCUM HAS BUSINESS TO TALK ABOUT-- 541 'ILE
SHIP'S BUSINESS.
KITCHEN AGAIN, AND HEAR A WOMAN'S VOICE TALKING TO547 'ILE
ME AND BE ABLE TO TALK TO
WELL, I THOUGHT WE'D JUST SIT AROUND AND REST AND 191 AHWILD
TALK.
ALL THIS LYING TALK ABOUT LIBERTY--WHEN THERE IS 194 AHWILD
NO LIBERTY/
NAT, YOU'VE GOT TO TALK TO DAVE. 199 AHWILD
HE KNOWS IT WAS ALL TALK. 204 AHWILD
I'VE GOT SOMETHING ELSE TO TALK TO YOU ABOUT 206 AHWILD
BESIDES FIRECRACKERS.
WE WON'T TALK ANY MORE ABOUT IT. 207 AHWILD
DON'T TALK ABOUT HER/ 211 AHWILD
WHAT NONSENSE YOU TALK/ 212 AHWILD
BUT DON'T TALK TO ME ABOUT MARRYING HIM--BECAUSE 1213 AHWILD
NEVER COULD.
(A LITTLE SHOCKED) YOU MUSN'T TALK THAT WAY. 215 AHWILD
YOU STOP THAT TALK/ 235 AHWILD
YOU KEEP THAT DAMN FOOL TALK TO YOURSELF, YOU HEAR235 AHWILD
ME--
THAT'S THE TALK I LIKE TO HEAR. 239 AHWILD
(SHARPLY) NIX ON THAT LINE OF TALK/ 243 AHWILD
(BRISTLING) I'M NOT GOOD ENOUGH TO TALK ABOUT 243 AHWILD
HER, I SUPPOSE$
HEY, I DON'T STAND FOR THAT KIND OF TALK-- 248 AHWILD
DON'T TALK THAT HORRIBLE SLANG. 250 AHWILD
THE WAY YOU TALK AT TIMES, 251 AHWILD
DAMN IT, I'VE GOT TO HAVE A STRAIGHT TALK WITH 267 AHWILD
HIM--
YOU FEEL, IN SPITE OF ALL HIS BOLD TALK OUT OF 268 AHWILD
BOOKS THAT HE'S SO DAMNED
YOU TALK AS IF YOU WEREN'T SORRY FOR WHAT YOU DID 270 AHWILD
LAST NIGHT/
BUT YOU'RE A SILLY GABBLER YOURSELF WHEN YOU TALK 271 AHWILD
THAT WAY/
DON'T FORGET YOUR FATHER'S BEEN WAITING TO TALK TO293 AHWILD
YOU/
BUT, HELL, I SUPPOSE YOU BOYS TALK ALL THIS OVER 295 AHWILD
AMONG YOURSELVES
IT'S ABOUT TIME YOU AND I HAD A SERIOUS TALK 295 AHWILD
ABOUT--HMMM--
THAT'S THE TALK/ 296 AHWILD
BY GOD, I'M PROUD OF YOU WHEN YOU TALK LIKE THAT/ 296 AHWILD
DON'T TALK THAT WAY. 298 AHWILD
THEY DRINK DOWN HALF THE CONTENTS AND START TO 4 ANNA
TALK TOGETHER HURRIEDLY IN LOW
AY TALK TO YOHNNY. 7 ANNA
YOU TALK SAME AS THEY ALL DO. 20 ANNA
(HURT--HUMBLY) AIN'T NO HARM FOR YOUR FADER TALK 20 ANNA
DAT VAY, ANNA.
IT SOUNDS GOOD TO HEAR SOMEONE--TALK TO ME THAT 22 ANNA
WAY.
AND DON'T YOU TALK NO MORE ABOUT GATTING YOB. 22 ANNA
LET'S TALK OF SOMETHING ELSE. 26 ANNA
(GLANCING AT HER MOODILY) DAT'S FOOLISH TALK, 26 ANNA
ANNA.
YOU SEE HER MORE, YOU DON'T TALK DAT VAY. 26 ANNA
FUNNY I DON'T KNOW NOTHING ABOUT SEA TALK-- 27 ANNA
(IMPRESSED BY HIS TONE) YOU TALK--NUTTY TONIGHT 29 ANNA
YOURSELF.
BUT NEVER MIND THAT FIGHT TALK. 32 ANNA
(WITH A HALF LAUGH) WELL--(SHE SITS DOWN) BUT WE 35 ANNA
WON'T TALK ABOUT ME, SEE$
BUT LET'S NOT TALK ABOUT ME. 35 ANNA
IS IT I'VE GIVEN YOU OFFENSE WITH MY TALK OF THE 37 ANNA
LIKE OF THEM
NEVER MIND THAT TALK. 39 ANNA
(WITH RISING IRRITATION) SOME DAY YOU'RE GOING TO 43 ANNA
GET ME SO MAD WITH THAT TALK,
AY DON'T TALK NO MORE DEN, ANNA. 44 ANNA
SO LET YOU NOT BE MAKING TALK TO ME ABOUT LEAVING 47 ANNA
HER.
GLORY BE TO GOD, IT'S BOLD TALK YOU HAVE FOR A 47 ANNA
STUMPY RUNT OF A MAN/
YOU TAL HIM YOU DON'T VANT FOR HEAR HIM TALK, 51 ANNA
ANNA.

TALK

TALK (CONT'D.)
(DISTRACTEDLY) SO, FOR GAWD'S SAKE, LET'S TALK OF 54 ANNA SOMETHING ELSE.
WE'VE HAD ENOUGH OF TALK/ 55 ANNA
SIT DOWN AND THEN LET ME TALK FOR A MINUTE. 56 ANNA
'TIS QUARE, ROUGH TALK, THAT--FOR A DACENT GIRL 57 ANNA THE LIKE OF YOU/
LET ME TALK FOR A CHANGE/ 57 ANNA
(IN AGONY) DON'T TALK DAT VAY, ANNA/ 58 ANNA
WE'LL TALK ABOUT IT LATER, SEES 66 ANNA
WE TALK AGAIN BEFORE AY GO, YES$ 67 ANNA
(IN THE SAME HARD VOICE) WELL, CAN'T YOU TALKS 69 ANNA
(BEWILDEREDLY) AND ME TO LISTEN TO THAT TALK FROM 70 ANNA A WOMAN LIKE YOU AND BE
DON'T TORMENT WITH THAT TALK/ 72 ANNA
I'M A FOOL TO BE WASTING TALK ON YOU AND YOU 73 ANNA HARDENED IN BADNESS.
(HAPPILY--TO HER FATHER) THAT'S THE WAY TO TALK/ 77 ANNA
HE STOPS TO TALK TO ROBERT, LEANING ON THE HOE HE 82 BEYOND CARRIES.)
BUT I GUESS YOU'RE RIGHT NOT TO TALK ABOUT IT. 86 BEYOND
(WITH A SIGH) I OUGHTN'T TO TALK THAT WAY 88 BEYOND
(INDIGNANTLY) HOW CAN YOU TALK THAT WAY, DICK 95 BEYOND SCOTT,
(ON THE VERGE OF TEARS) IT'S ALL RIGHT FOR YOU TO 96 BEYOND TALK.
(AS HE BEGINS TO TALK ANDREW ENTERS QUIETLY FROM 99 BEYOND THE REAR,
YOU TALK AS IF I WASN'T CONCERNED NOHOW IN THIS 103 BEYOND HERE BUSINESS.
TO SORTA TALK TO AND SHOW THINGS TO, AND TEACH, 103 BEYOND KINDA.
(IRRITABLY) BUT ALL THIS TALK AIN'T TELLIN' ME 103 BEYOND WHAT I'M TO DO WITH THAT STA'B'D
LET ME TALK, KATEY. 105 BEYOND
YOU TALK LIKE THAT 'BOUT THIS FARM--THE MAYO 108 BEYOND FARM--WHERE YOU WAS BORN--
YOU MUSTN'T TALK THAT WAY, SARAH. 113 BEYOND
LET'S TALK OF SOMETHING PLEASANT. 117 BEYOND
(ANGRILY) STOP THAT KIND OF TALK, DO YOU HEARS 126 BEYOND YOU FINDIN' FAULT--
A FINE ONE TO TALK ABOUT ANYONE ELSE-- 126 BEYOND
POETRY TALK THAT YOU LEARNED OUT OF BOOKS/ 127 BEYOND
LET'S TALK ABOUT SOMETHING INTERESTING. 131 BEYOND
(SOBERLY) THERE'S SOMETHING I WANT TO TALK ABOUT,133 BEYOND ROB--THE FARM.
BUT FOR GOD'S SAKE, LET'S NOT TALK ABOUT IT/ 135 BEYOND
(MISUNDERSTANDING) I KNOW I OUGHTN'T TO TALK 139 BEYOND ABOUT SUCH FOOLISHNESS TO YOU.
I DON'T WANT TO TALK/ 140 BEYOND
(WEARILY) YOU OUGHTN'T TO TALK ABOUT HIM NOW WHEN152 BEYOND HE'S SICK IN HIS BED.
DON'T TALK SO LOUD. 152 BEYOND
I WANT TO TALK TO YOU, AND I'M GOING TO. 159 BEYOND
(WITH A SHUDDER) DON'T TALK THAT WAY, FOR GOD'S 159 BEYOND SAKE/
(DISMISSING THE SUBJECT) BUT WE'VE AGREED NOT TO 160 BEYOND TALK OF IT.
YOU'VE ASKED ME NOT TO TALK--AND I WON'T AFTER 160 BEYOND I'VE MADE MY POSITION CLEAR.
WE CAN TALK LATER ON. 162 BEYOND
EVEN IF HE DID TALK THEM WAY UP IN THE AIR, LIKE 163 BEYOND HE ALWAYS SEES THINGS.
ROB: DON'T TALK. YOU'RE WASTING YOUR STRENGTH. 167 BEYOND
(GRUMBLINGLY) I DON'T TAKE NO BACK-TALK FROM THAT462 CARIBE DECK-SCRUBBIN' SHRIMP.
YOU AIN'T GOING TO TALK SO MUCH, YOU HEARS 463 CARIBE
DON'T TALK SO LOUD OR YOU DON'T GET ANY--YOU NOR 464 CARIBE NO MAN.
THEY TALK OF A COMPLAINT. 564 CROSS
YOU CAN TALK/ 564 CROSS
YOU COULDN'T TALK THIS WAY IF YOU WERE YOURSELF. 566 CROSS
YOU TALK AS IF-- 567 CROSS
AND YOU TALK OF COURAGE AND HONOR/ 498 DAYS
YOU TALK AS IF I WERE AFRAID OF SOMETHING. 503 DAYS
(TURNS TO HIM SHAMEFACEDLY) DON'T TALK THAT WAY, 505 DAYS UNCLE.
(QUIETLY) WOULD YOU TALK THAT WAY IF ELSA SHOULD 509 DAYS DIE$
(WITH A TWISTED SMILE) I THOUGHT WE WEREN'T GOING517 DAYS TO TALK ABOUT MY TROUBLES/
(REPELLED) DON'T TALK IN THAT DISGUSTING WAY. 519 DAYS
DON'T TALK LIKE THAT/ 520 DAYS
I HEARD A LITTLE TALK ABOUT THAT ONCE, TOO/ 523 DAYS
BUT LET'S NOT TALK ABOUT WALTER. 528 DAYS
LET'S TALK OF SOMETHING ELSE. 530 DAYS
(UNEASILY) OH, YOU MUSTN'T TALK THAT WAY, JOHN. 534 DAYS
I DON'T WANT TO TALK ANY MORE ABOUT IT/ 545 DAYS
WHAT'S THE GOOD OF TALKS 550 DAYS
I WANT TO TALK WITH YOU ABOUT YOUR WIFE'S 555 DAYS CONDITION.
(FORCING AN EASY TONE) WHAT'S ALL THIS TALKS 556 DAYS
WELL, TALK WON'T HELP HER, THAT'S SURE. 557 DAYS
AN' TALK O' TURNIN' ME OUT IN THE ROAD. 233 DESIRE
THAT'S WHY EBEN KEEPS A-TALKIN' HIS FOOL TALK O' 237 DESIRE THIS BEIN' HIS MAW'S FARM.
(BITTERLY) I KIN TALK T' THE COWS. 238 DESIRE
(THREATENINGLY) YE CAN'T TALK THAT WAY T' ME/ 240 DESIRE
(THEN TENDERLY REBUKING) YE OUGHTN'T T' TALK O' 245 DESIRE SAD THIN'S--THIS MORNIN'.
(THEN FROWNING) BUT DON'T LET'S TALK ABOUT THAT 497 DIFRNT SORT O' RUCTIONS.
YOU OUGHT TO HAVE A TALK WITH JIM BENSON, EMMER. 500 DIFRNT
MET HIM THIS AFTERNOON AND ME AND HIM HAD A LONG 501 DIFRNT TALK.
I WANT TO TALK WITH YOU 'BOUT SOMETHIN'. 514 DIFRNT
THAT'S ALL TALK, BENNY. 521 DIFRNT
YOU NEEDN'T BE SCARED--TO TALK OPEN WITH ME. 526 DIFRNT

TALK (CONT'D.)
BURIED AND IF WE HAND HER A LINE OF TALK MAYBE 526 DIFRNT SHE'LL DRAG OUT THE OLD BOTTLE."
HE'S WAITIN' TO TALK TO YOU. 528 DIFRNT
AND GET HIM TO TALK TO HER. 530 DIFRNT
WHY, I ONLY SAT DOWN FOR A MINUTE TO GIVE YOU A 531 DIFRNT CHANCE TO TALK TO HER.
I CAN TALK TO YOUR UNCLE CALEB. 532 DIFRNT
(HASTILY) LAND SAKES, DON'T LET'S TALK OF THAT. 537 DIFRNT
(OUTRAGED) YOU CAN TALK THAT WAY ABOUT HIM 541 DIFRNT
SAY, I THINK I'LL GO OVER AND TALK TO MA AFTER A 545 DIFRNT WHILE.
YOU BETTER LET ME TALK TO HIM FIRST. 426 DYNAMO
BENEATH HER FLIP TALK, HOWEVER, 429 DYNAMO
I DARE YOU TO BRING HIM IN TONIGHT, AND LET ME 432 DYNAMO TALK TO HIM AND YOU LISTEN.
I WANT A DAMNED SERIOUS TALK WITH YOU, YOUNG MAN/ 436 DYNAMO
(STAMMERS) YOU BETTER NOT-- TALK LIKE THAT, OR---437 DYNAMO YOU BETTER LOOK OUT/
DON'T YOU DARE TALK LIKE THAT/ 442 DYNAMO
HOW DARE YOU TALK SO DISRESPECTFULLY--/ 449 DYNAMO
I'VE TOLD YOU A MILLION TIMES HOW DUMB THAT TALK 455 DYNAMO IS AND YET YOU KEEP ON HARPING--
TO HAVE A TALK WITH MOTHER, ANYWAY... 457 DYNAMO
I DON'T WANT TO SEE HIM BUT I WANT TO HAVE A TALK 461 DYNAMO WITH MOTHER.
I'LL TALK TO HIM RIGHT NOW...!! 462 DYNAMO
WELL, I'M NOT HERE TO TALK TO YOU, EITHER. 463 DYNAMO
DON'T YOU WANT TO TALK TO ME$ 463 DYNAMO
(AFTER A PAUSE--DULLY) DID SHE EVER TALK ABOUT 465 DYNAMO ME$
(IRRITATEDLY) CUT OUT THAT TALK OF BEING SCARED/ 469 DYNAMO
TALK SENSE, ADA/ 470 DYNAMO
MAKE HIM TALK TURKEY AND SAY WHEN IS HE PLANNING 479 DYNAMO TO MARRY ADA/
BUT IF YOU'VE GOT TO TALK TO HIM, 479 DYNAMO
(IN A PASSION) I'LL HAVE A TALK WITH THAT LAD 479 DYNAMO
PLEASE DON'T TALK LIKE THAT--WHEN YOU KNOW HOW I 484 DYNAMO LOVE YOU/
TALK POLITE, WHITE MAN/ 176 EJONES
TALK POLITE, YOU HEAH ME/ 176 EJONES
LISTENING TO DE WHITE QUALITY TALK, IT'S DAT SAME 178 EJONES FACT,
AND TEACH SOME OF DEM ENGLISH BEFO' I KIN TALK TO 179 EJONES 'EMS
DAT'S ALL TALK. 180 EJONES
TALK PLAIN. 181 EJONES
AN' ALL DAT OLE WOMAN'S TALKS 185 EJONES
BUT I AIN'T GOT DE TIME TO WASTE ON NO MORE FOOL 185 EJONES TALK WID YOU.
DON'T TALK/ 193 EJONES
(THEN TRYING TO TALK HIMSELF INTO CONFIDENCE) 193 EJONES
THEY TALK IN LOW VOICES.) 8 ELECTR
(THEN AGITATEDLY) BUT I DON'T WANT TO TALK ANY 15 ELECTR MORE ABOUT IT.
(HARSHLY) I'VE GOT TO HAVE A TALK WITH YOU, 18 ELECTR MOTHER--BEFORE LONG/
BUT WHAT IS IT YOU WANT TO TALK ABOUTS 18 ELECTR
THERE WAS TALK THEY'D GONE OUT WEST, 19 ELECTR
MAYBE I BORED YOU WITH MY TALK OF CLIPPER SHIPS 23 ELECTR AND MY LOVE FOR THEM$
I'M GOING IN TO TALK TO HER NOW. 27 ELECTR
BELAY, I TOLD YOU, WITH THAT KIND OF TALK/ 27 ELECTR
I TOLD YOU I HAD TO TALK TO YOU. 29 ELECTR
HE SAID HE HAD TO TALK TO ME ABOUT YOU. 30 ELECTR
WHAT A FRAUD YOU ARE, WITH YOUR TALK OF YOUR 33 ELECTR FATHER AND YOUR DUTY/
YOUR SILLY TALK ABOUT RESEMBLANCES--DON'T SIT 37 ELECTR THERE.
(PASSIONATELY) DON'T TALK LIKE THAT/ 39 ELECTR
THE ONLY TALK HAS BEEN THAT HE CAME TO COURT 52 ELECTR VINNIE/
THEY MADE ME TALK--BECAUSE THEY ANSWERED. 53 ELECTR
I CAN TALK BETTER. 53 ELECTR
IT HAS ALWAYS BEEN HARD FOR ME TO TALK--ABOUT 53 ELECTR FEELINGS.
(HER EYES CLOSED--TENSELY) DON'T TALK, EZRA. 53 ELECTR
GOD, I WANT TO TALK TO YOU, CHRISTINE/ 53 ELECTR
WHAT HAS THIS TALK OF DEATH TO DO WITH ME$ 54 ELECTR
(WITH DREAD) I DON'T WANT TO TALK/ 59 ELECTR
I WISH YOU WOULDN'T TALK LIKE THAT, EZRA. 59 ELECTR
WE'D BETTER LIGHT THE LIGHT AND TALK A WHILE. 59 ELECTR
(TENSELY) I DON'T WANT TO TALK OF THE PAST/ 59 ELECTR
WHEN I TALK TO HER SHE WON'T ANSWER ME. 72 ELECTR
PETER IS ALL RIGHT BUT--I WANT TO TALK TO YOU 74 ELECTR ALONE.
BUT THERE'S NO TIME TO TALK NOW. 76 ELECTR
(TENSELY) I WISH YOU WOULDN'T TALK OF DEATH/ 83 ELECTR
WE'LL TALK OF SOMETHING ELSE. 89 ELECTR
FOR GOD'S SAKE, DON'T TALK LIKE THAT/ 89 ELECTR
I'VE GOT TO TALK TO YOU--AND I DON'T WANT TO BE 94 ELECTR INTERRUPTED.
I'VE GOT TO TALK TO YOU/ 95 ELECTR
DIDN'T YOU THINK IT WOULD BE BETTER TO POSTPONE 96 ELECTR OUR TALK UNTIL--
BY GOD, YOU MUST BE CRAZY EVEN TO TALK OF--/ 96 ELECTR
I WON'T TALK TO A CRAZY WOMAN/ 97 ELECTR
DON'T TALK OF THAT FOR A MOMENT/ 108 ELECTR
AND HOW COULD I KNOW HE WOULD TALK TO ME THE WAY 110 ELECTR HE DID$
DON'T TALK LIKE THAT/ 112 ELECTR
(GRUFFLY) LET'S NOT TALK OF HER ANY MORE. 112 ELECTR
(WITH A SHUDDER) PLEASE DON'T TALK ABOUT--HE IS 117 ELECTR BURIED/
HOW DARE YOU TALK--/ 120 ELECTR
I HEARD SOME SILLY TALK BUT DIDN'T PAY ANY 135 ELECTR ATTENTION--

TALK 1608

TALK (CONT'D.)
(SHARPLY) YOU PROMISED YOU WEREN'T GOING TO TALK 141 ELECTR
ANY MORE MORBID NONSENSE.
(THEN HE TURNS AWAY AGAIN IN CONFUSION AND TAKES 143 ELECTR
REFUGE IN A BURST OF TALK)
OH, I KNOW IT MUST SOUND FUNNY HEARING ME TALK 146 ELECTR
LIKE THAT.
YOU WEREN'T TO TALK NONSENSE, REMEMBER/ 146 ELECTR
AND SETTLE OUT IN THE COUNTRY AWAY FROM FOLKS AND 147 ELECTR
THEIR EVIL TALK.
(PLEADING DISTRACTEDLY) DON'T TALK ABOUT IT/ 155 ELECTR
(GETTING UP) IF YOU'RE GOING TO TALK LIKE THAT--/158 ELECTR
I'LL TALK TO HER. 158 ELECTR
DON'T TALK LIKE THAT/ 160 ELECTR
LET HER TALK ALL SHE LIKES, HAZEL. 162 ELECTR
HOW DARE YOU TALK THAT WAY TO ME/ 163 ELECTR
NOT UNDERSTANDING WHAT IS BEHIND THEIR TALK BUT 164 ELECTR
SENSING SOMETHING SINISTER,
WHAT TERRIBLE THING HAVE YOU BEEN THINKING 165 ELECTR
LATELY--BEHIND ALL YOUR CRAZY TALK$
I WOULD TALK TOO MUCH/ 165 ELECTR
DURING THE LATTER PART OF HIS TALK-- 166 ELECTR
AND BEGINS TO TALK VOLUBLY TO DROWN OUT THOUGHT) 167 ELECTR
I DIDN'T COME TO TALK ABOUT ORIN. 172 ELECTR
HE FOUGHT WITH MOTHER LAST NIGHT WHEN SHE TRIED TO173 ELECTR
TALK TO HIM--
I NEVER HEARD YOU TALK THAT WAY BEFORE, PETER-- 175 ELECTR
BITTER/
I WANT TO HAVE A SERIOUS TALK WITH YOU, YOUNG MAN/271 GGBROW
WHY DON'T YOU HAVE A TALK WITH HIM$ 272 GGBROW
I'M SURE WHEN I TALK TO HIM--HE'S COMING HOME TO 277 GGBROW
DINNER--
I WON'T LISTEN TO YOU TALK THAT WAY ABOUT 281 GGBROW
MARGARET/
BUT I KNOW I SHOULDN'T TALK THIS WAY, OLD MAN/ 281 GGBROW
LET'S TALK. 289 GGBROW
THEY TALK AS THEY WORK. 302 GGBROW
FINALLY, HE BEGINS TO TALK TO IT IN A BITTER, 307 GGBROW
MOCKING TONE.
TALK IS CHEAP, LONG. 213 HA APE
IN A FLASH ALL IS HILARIOUS AMIABILITY AGAIN, BACK213 HA APE
SLAPPING, LOUD TALK, ETC.)
WHAT DE HELL--SAY, LEMME TALK/ 215 HA APE
SAY, LISTEN TO ME--WAIT A MOMENT--I GOTTER TALK, 215 HA APE
SEE.
IT WOULD BE RUDE TO TALK ABOUT ANYTHING TO YOU. 220 HA APE
LET'S JUST TALK. 220 HA APE
I TOUGHT I WAS IN A CAGE AT DE ZOO-BUT DE APES 240 HA APE
DON'T TALK, DO DEYS
THEN YANK BEGINS TO TALK IN A FRIENDLY 252 HA APE
CONFIDENTIAL TONE, HALF MOCKINGLY,
IT BEATS IT WHEN YOU TRY TO TINK IT OR TALK IT-- 253 HA APE
IT'S WAY DOWN-DEEP--BEHIND--
YUH CAN'T TALK NEIDER. 253 HA APE
LONG EXPERIENCE WITH GUESTS WHO STOP AT HIS DESK 11 HUGHIE
IN THE SMALL HOURS TO TALK
I SAYS, *HOLD ON, YOU TALK *S IF ANARCHISTS AND 584 ICEMAN
SOCIALISTS WAS DE SAME.*
THAT'S A HELL OF A WAY FOR YOU TO TALK, AFTER WHAT590 ICEMAN
HAPPENED TO HER/
BOOZE IS THE ONLY THING YOU EVER TALK ABOUT/ 601 ICEMAN
(SADLY) TRUE.
YOU DUMB BROADS CUT THE LOUD TALK. 612 ICEMAN
DEY GIVE YUH AN EARFUL EVERY TIME YUH TALK TO 'EM/614 ICEMAN
AN' DEN HER PRETENDIN'--BUT IT GIVES ME A PAIN TO 614 ICEMAN
TALK ABOUT IT.
(WHO HAS BEEN THE LEAST IMPRESSED BY HICKEY'S TALK626 ICEMAN
AND IS THE FIRST TO RECOVER
YUH CAN'T TALK LIKE DAT TO ME, YUH FAT DAGO 632 ICEMAN
HOOKER/
(INJUREDLY) NOW, LISTEN, THAT'S NO WAY TO TALK TO641 ICEMAN
AN OLD PAL.
BUT I'VE GOT TO TALK TO YOU. 648 ICEMAN
WE COULD TALK EVERYTHING OVER THERE. 648 ICEMAN
THERE'S NOTHING TO TALK OVER/ 648 ICEMAN
OR I'LL TALK TO HICKEY. 648 ICEMAN
WHAT HAPPENED TO ME AND KEEP YOUR DOOR LOCKED SO 666 ICEMAN
I CAN'T TALK TO YOU.
DEN SHE'D YELL, *DAT'S A SWEET WAY TO TALK TO DE 671 ICEMAN
GOIL YUH'RE GOIN' TO MARRY.*
I TALK FOOLISHNESS. 672 ICEMAN
I'D LIKE TO HAVE A TALK WITH YOU. 677 ICEMAN
IF I'M TO TAKE YOUR CASE, WE OUGHT TO HAVE A TALK 681 ICEMAN
BEFORE WE LEAVE.
(CONTEMPTUOUSLY) WE'LL HAVE NO TALK. 681 ICEMAN
ALL THAT TALK OF HIS ABOUT TOMORROW, FOR EXAMPLE. 723 ICEMAN
(CORA BEGINS TO TALK IN THE GROUP AT RIGHT.) 723 ICEMAN
HE IS LEANING ACROSS IN FRONT OF WETJOEN TO TALK 724 ICEMAN
TO ED MOSHER ON HOPE'S LEFT.)
AN' LOOK HERE, AIN'T YOU NOTICED HE DON'T TALK 521 INZONE
NATURAL$
HE DON'T TALK EXACTLY LIKE A TOFF, DOES HE, COCKY$522 INZONE
AN' HE DON'T TALK IT LIKE US, THAT'S CERTAIN. 522 INZONE
AND THEN A STORM OF EXCITED TALK BREAKS LOOSE.) 523 INZONE
'E AIN'T ARF A SLY ONE WIV 'IS TALK OF SUBMARINES,523 INZONE
GAWD BLIND 'IM/
TALK AISY NOW IF YE KNOW WHAT'S BEST FOR YOU. 526 INZONE
(WITH A GROWL) NIX ON THE ROUGH TALK, SEE/ 527 INZONE
WE'LL HAVE NO TALK OF REDUCING. 14 JOURNE
WITH THAT SUMMER COLD TALK. 29 JOURNE
YOU TALK AS IF YOU THOUGHT-- 34 JOURNE
YOU USED TO TALK ABOUT WANTING TO BECOME A 36 JOURNE
NEWSPAPER MAN BUT YOU WERE NEVER
GOD, PAPA, THIS OUGHT TO BE ONE THING WE CAN TALK 37 JOURNE
OVER FRANKLY WITHOUT A BATTLE.
(THEN DULLY.) I KNOW IT'S USELESS TO TALK. 45 JOURNE
OR EVEN AN AFTERNOON, SOME WOMAN FRIEND I COULD 46 JOURNE
TALK TO--

TALK (CONT'D.)
THAT'S THE WAY YOU TALK WHEN-- 47 JOURNE
THERE'S ABSOLUTELY NO REASON TO TALK AS IF YOU 48 JOURNE
EXPECTED SOMETHING DREADFUL/
I HOPE HE DOESN'T FORGET LUNCH LISTENING TO 54 JOURNE
HIMSELF TALK.
CAPTAIN TURNER STOPPED TO TALK AND ONCE HE STARTS 65 JOURNE
GABBING YOU CAN'T GET AWAY
I'LL DROP IN MYSELF AND HAVE A TALK WITH YOU 73 JOURNE
BEFORE THAT.
(ANGRILY.) CUT OUT THAT KIND OF TALK/ 76 JOURNE
I'M GOING TO TALK TO HER. 78 JOURNE
(SHRUGS HIS SHOULDERS.) YOU CAN'T TALK TO HER 78 JOURNE
NOW.
(THEN DULLY RESIGNED.) BUT WHAT'S THE GOOD OF 78 JOURNE
TALK$
BE CAREFUL WITH YOUR TALK. 88 JOURNE
DON'T TALK. 92 JOURNE
(STAMMERS PLEADINGLY.) PLEASE DON'T--TALK ABOUT 93 JOURNE
THINGS YOU DON'T UNDERSTAND/
ABRUPTLY.) BUT LET'S NOT TALK OF OLD THINGS THAT 102 JOURNE
COULDN'T BE HELPED.
WHERE THERE ARE PEOPLE YOU CAN TALK AND JOKE WITH.108 JOURNE
I WAS SO LONESOME I KEPT CATHLEEN WITH ME JUST TO 112 JOURNE
HAVE SOMEONE TO TALK TO.
BUT I'M A FOOL TO TALK REASON TO YOU. 117 JOURNE
ALL THIS TALK ABOUT LOVING ME-- 120 JOURNE
(HURRIEDLY.) BUT LET'S NOT TALK ABOUT IT. 132 JOURNE
HOW DARE YOU TALK OF SOMETHING YOU KNOW NOTHING 140 JOURNE
ABOUT/
(THEN IN A RAGE.) HOW DARE YOU TALK TO YOUR 141 JOURNE
FATHER LIKE THAT,
WITH NO ONE SHE COULD TALK TO, 141 JOURNE
THERE WAS ALWAYS THE MEMBERS OF MY COMPANY TO TALK142 JOURNE
TO, IF SHE'D WANTED.
DON'T YOU KNOW HARDY WILL TALK AND THE WHOLE 145 JOURNE
DAMNED DOWN WILL KNOW/
YOU TALK OF WORK/ 148 JOURNE
ALL I WANTED WAS A LITTLE HEART-TO-HEART TALK 160 JOURNE
MAY NOT GET ANOTHER CHANCE TO TALK. 165 JOURNE
TAKES HIS HAND AGAIN AND BEGINS TO TALK THICKLY 165 JOURNE
BUT WITH A STRANGE,
I HEARD THE LAST PART OF HIS TALK. 167 JOURNE
I HAD A TALK WITH MOTHER ELIZABETH. 175 JOURNE
I COULD COME BACK TO SEE HER AND WE WOULD TALK IT 176 JOURNE
OVER AGAIN.
(MATTER-OF-FACTLY) KILL HIM BEFORE CAESAR CAN 303 LAZARU
TALK TO HIM.
THE SENATORS BEGIN TO TALK TO EACH OTHER IN LOW 314 LAZARU
VOICES.)
TALK TO HIM/ 329 LAZARU
TO TALK LIKE A GARRULOUS OLD WOMAN, 346 LAZARU
TALK TO THEMSELVES, FOR THEY HAVE REACHED THAT 354 LAZARU
HOPELESS WISDOM OF EXPERIENCE
(HE LAUGHS BITTERLY) AND SO I TALK ALOUD, 355 LAZARU
LAZARUS/
I TALK TO MY LONELINESS/ 355 LAZARU
YOU TALK AS THOUGH I WERE A SLAVE. 7 MANSNS
(MOCKINGLY.) YOU TO TALK OF HONOR WHEN IN YOUR 19 MANSNS
DREAM$ WHAT ARE YOU
(ABRUPTLY.) I BEG YOUR PARDON, MRS. HARFORD, FOR 21 MANSNS
BORING YOU WITH TALK OF MY FAT
WHY SHOULD YOU TALK OF BEING ODDS 37 MANSNS
I TALK AS IF I WERE PLANNING TO PRETEND AND PLAY A 39 MANSNS
PART/
AND NOW, LET US NOT TALK OF BUSINESS ANY MORE-- 56 MANSNS
FROM THEIR TALK, THEY MUST SPEND A GREAT DEAL OF 84 MANSNS
THEIR TIME IN HER GARDEN.
AH, DON'T TALK OF IT THAT WAY-- 88 MANSNS
THAT'S A NICE WAY TO TALK TO A DECENT WIFE/ 90 MANSNS
I DON'T KNOW WHAT YOU MEAN BY THAT QUEER TALK OF 92 MANSNS
MARKED CARDS AND LOADED DICE.
(PULLING AWAY.) I WISH YOU WOULDN'T TALK AS IF 93 MANSNS
LOVE--
IT GAVE ME A CHANCE TO TALK OVER WITH HER A NEW 97 MANSNS
ARRANGEMENT AT THE OFFICE.
AND ALL DURING THE FOLLOWING SCENE TALK IN 125 MANSNS
WHISPERS, THEIR EYES FIXED ON SIMON.)
THAT'S THE WAY I LIKE YOU TO TALK--ABOUT LIFE AND 150 MANSNS
LOVE--NOT ABOUT DEATH--
THE REAL REASON I CAME HERE WAS TO HAVE A SENSIBLE167 MANSNS
TALK WITH YOU.
FOR HEAVEN'S SAKE, LET'S NOT TALK BUSINESS/ 366 MARCOM
I WOULD SAY, RATHER THAT EVER SINCE YOU WERE OLD 385 MARCOM
ENOUGH TO TALK,
YOU TALK LIKE THE LADIES IN POEMS WHO HAVE 385 MARCOM
LOST THEIR LOVERS/
(WARNINGLY) HIS HONOR WISHES TO TALK BUSINESS. 391 MARCOM
YOU SHOULDN'T TALK THAT WAY. 412 MARCOM
THAT'S NICE TALK FOR A WOMAN. 8 MISBEG
ANYWAY, TALK ALL YOU PLEASE TO PUT ME OFF, I'LL 9 MISBEG
BET MY LAST PENNY YOU'VE COOKED
I LIKE HIM, IF THAT'S WHAT YOU MEAN, BUT IT'S ONLY 27 MISBEG
TO TALK TO.
I'VE NOTICED WHEN YOU TALK ROUGH AND BRAZEN LIKE 34 MISBEG
YOU DO TO TOUGH MEN,
I'LL TALK AS I PLEASE, AND IF HE DON'T LIKE IT HE 34 MISBEG
CAN LUMP IT/
(WITH SUDDEN REVULSION) FOR GOD'S SAKE, CUT OUT 42 MISBEG
THAT KIND OF TALK, JOSIE/
DON'T TALK NONSENSE TO SNEAK OUT OF TREATING JIM. 52 MISBEG
HE'S SAID HE ISN'T HERE. ANYWAY, SO WE WON'T TALK 59 MISBEG
TO HIM BEHIND HIS BACK.
(APPEARS DRUNKER, HIS HEAD WAGGING, HIS VOICE 74 MISBEG
THICK, HIS TALK RAMBLING)
(EXASPERATEDLY) WILL YOU STOP YOUR WHISKEY 75 MISBEG
DROOLING AND TALK PLAINS

TALK (CONT'D.)
I NEVER HEARD YOU TALK THAT WAY BEFORE, NO MATTER 77 MISBEG
HOW DRUNK YOU WERE.
TO TALK TO MESELF SO I'LL KNOW SOMEONE WITH BRAINS 80 MISBEG
IS LISTENING.
SO YOU'D ACT BOLD FOR A CHANGE INSTEAD OF GIVING 93 MISBEG
HIM BRAZEN TALK HE'S TIRED OF
THAT'S THE TALK/ 94 MISBEG
(SUDDENLY, BEGINS TO TALK MECHANICALLY) 102 MISBEG
(TENSELY) YOU'RE A FINE ONE TO TALK OF PROMISES/ 106 MISBEG
OCH, DON'T TALK LIKE THAT. 112 MISBEG
THAT'S THE TALK. 115 MISBEG
DRUNK OR NOT, DON'T YOU TALK THAT WAY TO ME OR-- 127 MISBEG
I HATE YOU WHEN YOU TALK LIKE THAT. 129 MISBEG
(SHE HUGS HIM PROTECTIVELY) DON'T TALK LIKE THAT/144 MISBEG
TALK LOW, NOW. 157 MISBEG
IT WAS HIS TALK OF THE BEAUTY HE SAW IN YOU THAT 175 MISBEG
MADE ME HOPE--
IT'S ONLY BY ACCIDENT I HEARD TALK OF 9 POET
DIDN'T HE SEND YOU TO SCHOOL SO YOU COULD TALK 23 POET
LIKE A GENTLEMAN'S DAUGHTER$
DON'T TALK AS IF YOU HATED HIM. 24 POET
YOU'RE A FINE ONE TO TALK TO, MOTHER. 27 POET
I'LL TAKE A WALK TO THE STORE AND HAVE A TALK WITH 28 POET
NEILAN.
(ADMIRINGLY.) MUSHA, BUT YOU'VE BOASTFUL TALK/ 31 POET
DON'T TALK SO BOULD. 32 POET
THERE'S A POWER AV TALK ABOUT THE TWO AV YOU 32 POET
ALREADY.
HOW DARE YOU TALK TO ME LIKE A COMMON, IGNORANT-- 45 POET
YOU'RE MY DAUGHTER, DAMN YOU.
(AFTER A PAUSE--TIMIDLY.) ALL THE SAME, YOU 62 POET
SHOULDN'T TALK TO SARA
AH, HOW CAN I TALK SUCH CRAZINESS/ 77 POET
(A PAUSE. HE BEGINS TO TALK IN AN ARROGANTLY 90 POET
AMUSED TONE.)
I WAS ABOUT TO TELL YOU OF THE TALK I HAD THIS 107 POET
AFTERNOON WITH YOUNG HARFORD.
NOT WISHING TO EMBARRASS HIM FURTHER WITH TALK OF 111 POET
MONEY.
WILL YOU TELL ME PLAINLY WHAT YOU MEAN BY YOUR 121 POET
TALK OF SETTLEMENTS
YOU TALK LIKE A SCHEMING PEASANT/ 126 POET
(GRINS.) THAT'S THE TALK. 135 POET
NONE OF YOUR TALK AGAINST SARA, NOW/ 135 POET
(BITTERLY.) ARRAH, DON'T TALK LIKE A LOON/ 138 POET
YOU'RE COLD COMFORT, SITTING SILENT LIKE A STATUE,140 POET
AND ME MAKING TALK TO MYSELF.
YOU'VE HAD A TALK WITH THE LADS 142 POET
BUT WE DIDN'T TALK OF IT MUCH. 145 POET
(FRIGHTENEDLY.) I'VE NEVER HEARD HIM TALK LIKE 160 POET
THAT IN ALL THE YEARS--
I'LL TALK OF OUR FIGHT IN THE CITY ONLY, BECAUSE 165 POET
IT'S ALL I WANT TO REMEMBER.
IT'S QUARE, SURELY, FOR THE TWO AV YE TO OBJECT 168 POET
WHEN I TALK IN ME NATURAL
(TURNS TO HER--GRINNINGLY.) THAT'S THE TALK, 174 POET
DARLIN!/
AND NOT TALK LIKE YOU WAS ASHAMED OF ME, YOUR 176 POET
FATHER.
COURTIN' THAT HARLOT THAT WAS THE TALK O' THE 580 ROPE
WHOLE TOWN/
YOU'VE BEEN DRINKIN' IN TOWN OR YOU WOULDN'T TALK 583 ROPE
THAT WAY.
EASY GOES WITH THAT TALK/ 588 ROPE
(WITH A GRIN) THAT'S THE TALK, KID. 589 ROPE
(THREATENINGLY) AND THEN I'M GOINTER COME AND 589 ROPE
TALK TURKEY TO YOU, SEE$
(SPITTING--VEHEMENTLY) THAT'S CHILD'S TALK. 599 ROPE
(TRYING TO CONTROL HIS IRRITATION AND TALK IN AN 9 STRANG
OBJECTIVE TONE)
(THINKING--TERRIFIED) ((I MUST TALK HER OUT OF 15 STRANG
IF...
IT'S EASY TO TALK... 33 STRANG
SHE'LL BE DOWN ANY MINUTE, AND I'VE GOT A LOT TO 35 STRANG
TALK OVER WITH YOU.
(JEERINGLY) OH, LET ME TALK, CHARLIE/ 41 STRANG
I WANT TO TALK TO YOU, CHARLIE. 42 STRANG
IT'LL DO HER GOOD TO TALK THIS OUT OF HER 42 STRANG
SYSTEM...
SAM SAID YOU WANTED TO TALK TO ME. 57 STRANG
THE REST IS JUST TALK/ 64 STRANG
(THE BELL RINGS AGAIN) ((I MUST GIVE NED A GOOD 73 STRANG
CHANCE TO TALK TO HER...))
FOR PETE'S SAKE, HAVE A GOOD HEART-TO-HEART TALK 78 STRANG
WITH HER, NED/
WHY DOES SHE TALK SO MUCH ABOUT BEING HAPPY$... 84 STRANG
THIS TALK OF HAPPINESS SEEMS TO ME EXTRANEOUS...)) 86 STRANG
I HAD A TALK OVER THE PHONE WITH APPLEBY 95 STRANG
YESTERDAY
I MUST TALK/... 100 STRANG
(MEANINGLY) AND WE WANT TO HAVE A LONG TALK WITH 105 STRANG
YOU AFTER LUNCH, SAM--
AFTER LUNCH, TALK... 105 STRANG
(VAGUELY MAKING TALK) I GOT CHARLIE TO LIE DOWN. 105 STRANG
WHAT DID NINA MEAN, YOU WANT A LONG TALK WITH ME$ 105 STRANG
I MUST TALK TO HIM ABOUT OUR BABY....)) 128 STRANG
AND YOU TWO PROBABLY HAVE A LOT TO TALK OVER. 129 STRANG
HOW DARE YOU TALK LIKE THAT TO YOUR UNCLE NED/ 142 STRANG
I HATE YOU WHEN YOU TALK THAT WAY/ 144 STRANG
WHAT'S ALL THIS TALK ABOUT FIGHTINGS 154 STRANG
I WANT TO TALK TO HIM. 164 STRANG
AND WHY SHOULDN'T I HAVE A TALK WITH GORDONS... 169 STRANG
WE CAN TALK TOGETHER OF THE OLD DAYS... 191 STRANG
BUT SAM DIDN'T EVEN KNOW PRESTON--EXCEPT FROM 192 STRANG
HEARING ME TALK ABOUT HIM/
OW, DOWNT TALK, DISC/ 498 VOYAGE
STAY 'ERE AN' AVE A TALK WIV ME. 501 VOYAGE

TALK (CONT'D.)
IT SOUND NICE TO HEAR THE OLD TALK YUST ONCE IN A 502 VOYAGE
TIME.
AN' ME 'AVIN SECH A NICE TALK, 'N ALL. 504 VOYAGE
(TO MAKE TALK) WHERE'S YER MATES POPPED ORF TER$ 505 VOYAGE
OW, DON'T TALK LIKE THAT/ 506 VOYAGE
YOU DON'T KNOW HOW MUCH IT MEANS TO HAVE YOU TALK 445 WELDED
LIKE THAT/
LET'S TALK OF SOMETHING ELSE. 456 WELDED
(LOOKING UP AT HIM QUEERLY) SAY, YOU TALK NUTTY. 473 WELDED
I DON'T LIKE YOUR LINE OF TALK. 473 WELDED

TALKATIVE
ONE GETS OLD, ONE BECOMES TALKATIVE, ONE WISHES TO354 LAZARU

TALKATIVENESS
(THEN WITH ALCOHOLIC TALKATIVENESS.) 153 JOURNE

TALKED
HE'S TALKED TO ME 'BOUT YOU LOTS O' TIMES. 19 ANNA
IN TALKING THE SAME OLD BULL YOU TALKED TO ME TO 73 ANNA
THE FIRST ONE YOU MEET.
HE'S BEEN DREAMING OVER THIS TRIP EVER SINCE IT 96 BEYOND
WAS FIRST TALKED ABOUT.
YOU OUGHTN'T TO HAVE TALKED TO HIM THAT WAY, ANDY,108 BEYOND
'BOUT THE DAMN FARM.
I'VE TALKED TO ROBERT THOUSANDS OF TIMES 113 BEYOND
I WAS AFRAID. HE TALKED SO CRAZY. I COULDN'T 151 BEYOND
QUIET HIM.
HE TALKED AS IF WE WERE MERELY HIS TENANTS, CURSE 563 CROSS
HIM/
HE CAME YESTERDAY AND TALKED WITH ME. 563 CROSS
AIN'T I TALKED HIM OVER WITH YOU AND ASKED YOUR 540 DIFRNT
ADVICE ABOUT HIM
WE'VE HARDLY TALKED AT ALL/ 49 ELECTR
(HE HAS TALKED WITH INCREASING BITTERNESS. 75 ELECTR
WAIT UNTIL YOU'VE TALKED TO ME/ 76 ELECTR
HE GOT FRIENDLY AND TALKED. 23 HUGHIE
YOU TALKED TO HIM WHEN YOU WENT UPTOWN YESTERDAY, 30 JOURNE
DIDN'T YOU$
YES. I HAVE TALKED WITH SARA 59 MANSNS
BECAUSE I WAS SURE OF YOUR CONSENT AND I KNEW 62 MANSNS
MOTHER HAD TALKED TO YOU.
I TALKED RECENTLY WITH A POET WHO HAD FLED FROM 386 MARCOM
THERE IN HORROR.
SHE HAS ONLY TALKED TO HIM ONCE OR TWICE EVERY TWO388 MARCOM
YEARS OR SO/
HE REMEMBERED WELL ENOUGH, FOR HE TALKED ABOUT 89 MISBEG
IT--
AND THAT DRIVEL HE TALKED ABOUT OWING ME ONE--WHAT132 MISBEG
GOT INTO HIS HEAD, I WONDER.
GENTLY MAYBE IF YOU TALKED ABOUT YOUR GRIEF FOR 144 MISBEG
HER, IT WOULD HELP YOU.
THE ONE THING YOU TALKED A LOT ABOUT WAS THAT YOU 170 MISBEG
WANTED THE NIGHT WITH ME TO BE
YOU TALKED ABOUT HOW YOU'D WATCHED TOO MANY DAWNS 171 MISBEG
COME CREEPING GRAVELY OVER
SHE TALKED ON AND ON AS IF SHE COULDN'T STOP-- 87 POET
HAND, BUT HE MUST UNDERSTAND THAT I COULD NOT 110 POET
COMMIT MYSELF UNTIL I HAD TALKED
SURELY YOU COULD NOT HAVE SPOKEN SERIOUSLY WHEN 122 POET
YOU TALKED OF MARRIAGE.
(LOST IN HER HAPPINESS.) AND THEN WE PUT OUT THE 147 POET
LIGHT AND TALKED ABOUT HOW
IT'S THE SAME CRAZY BLATHER HE'S TALKED EVERY ONCE158 POET
IN A WHILE
OH, WIFE, WHY DID YOU DIE, YOU WOULD HAVE TALKED 15 STRANG
TO HER.
SHE TALKED SO BRAZENLY ABOUT GIVING HERSELF... 25 STRANG
YOU SEE, NINA'S TALKED A LOT ABOUT YOU. 32 STRANG
WE'VE TALKED ABOUT OUR CHILD WISELY, 91 STRANG
DISPASSIONATELY....
IT'S TIME I TALKED TO NED... 128 STRANG

TALKER
HE WAS A NICE ENOUGH MAN, GOOD COMPANY AND A GOOD 137 JOURNE
TALKER.

TALKIN'
WE WAS JUST TALKIN' ABOUT YOU. 6 ANNA
THAT'S THE TALKIN'/ 11 ANNA
I'VE HEARD OLD CHRIS TALKIN' ABOUT YOUR BEIN' A 18 ANNA
NURSE GIRL OUT THERE.
(IRRITABLY) WHAT IS THIS FOOLISHNESS YOU'RE 100 BEYOND
TALKIN' OF$
TALKIN' CRAZY LIKE THAT. 105 BEYOND
(IN A HUSHED WHISPER) WE'D BEST NOT BE TALKIN' SO478 CARDIF
TALKIN' ABAHT SHIPWRECKS IN THIS 'ERE BLOOMIN' 482 CARDIF
FOG.
FOR THE LOVE AV THE SAINTS DON'T BE TALKIN' LOIKE 483 CARDIF
THAT/
(WITH A GROAN) LAD, LAD, DON'T BE TALKIN'. 486 CARDIF
WHAT WAS WE TALKIN' OF A MINUTE AGO$ 487 CARDIF
FOR THE LOVE AV GOD DON'T BE TALKIN' LOIKE THAT/ 489 CARDIF
SURE, IT'S NOT YOU SHOULD BE TALKIN', 463 CARIBE
(ANGRILY) TO HELL WID THIS TALKIN'. 465 CARIBE
YE WAS TALKIN' A'MIGHTY LOUD. 231 DESIRE
THAT'S WHY EBEN KEEPS A-TALKIN' HIS FOOL TALK O' 237 DESIRE
THIS BEIN' HIS MAW'S FARM.
I WANT TO GIVE THAT JIM BENSON A TALKIN' TO HE 501 DIFRNT
WON'T FORGIT IN A HURRY--
YOU GIVE HIM A GOOD TALKIN'-TO AND HE WON'T DO IT 511 DIFRNT
AGAIN.
BUT WHAT'S THE GOOD OF TALKIN'$ 523 DIFRNT
(DISGUSTEDLY) NOW YOU'RE TALKIN' TIGHT LIKE HIM. 523 DIFRNT
AND YOU CAN SEE WHAT A SWELL CHANCE YOU'VE GOT OF 533 DIFRNT
TALKIN' HIM OVER NOW.
(FRIGHTENEDLY) WHAT--WHAT'RE YOU TALKIN' ABOUT, 545 DIFRNT
BENNYS
DRINKIN' RUM AND TALKIN' BIG DOWN IN DE TOWN. 176 EJONES
AIN'T A MAN'S TALKIN' BIG WHAT MAKES HIM BIG--LONG179 EJONES
AS HE MAKES FOLKS BELIEVE ITS

TALKIN'

TALKIN' (CONT'D.)
BUT I AIN'T TALKIN' WILD JUST DE SAME. 179 EJONES
WHAT IS I TALKIN' ABOUTS 184 EJONES
YOU AIN'T TALKIN' TO ME. 185 EJONES
WE AIN'T TALKIN' 'BOUT HER. 8 ELECTR
BEEN TALKIN' OF GHOSTS. 133 ELECTR
THAT'S TALKIN', VINNIE/ 171 ELECTR
YER BEEN ACTIN' AN' TALKIN' 'S IF IT WAS ALL A 235 HA APE
BLEEDIN' PERSONAL MATTER
WHO IS THAT DOOR TALKIN'S 240 HA APE
(SERIOUS AND JOKING) DAT'S DE TALKIN'/ 242 HA APE
BUT I KIN MAKE A BLUFF AT TALKIN' AND TINKIN'-- 253 HA APE
A'MOST GIT AWAY WIT IT--A'MOST/
YOU BETTER CALL ME ERIC, TOO, PAL, OR I WON'T KNOW 14 HUGHIE
WHEN YOU'RE TALKIN' TO ME.
THERE'S ALWAYS BUCKS TO PICK UP FOR LITTLE ERRANDS 15 HUGHIE
I AIN'T TALKIN' ABOUT.
(HASTILY.) ANYWAY, THIS TIME I'M TALKIN' ABOUT, 23 HUGHIE
WHAT THE HELL YOU TALKIN' ABOUTS 33 HUGHIE
WHO D'YOU TINK YOU'RE TALKIN' TOS 633 ICEMAN
TALKIN' FIGHT, HUHS 637 ICEMAN
AND DEN HE WENT ON TALKIN' AND TALKIN' LIKE HE 665 ICEMAN
COULDN'T STOP/
BUT IF DE BASTARD KEEPS ON TALKIN'-- 703 ICEMAN
YUH CAN'T STOP DE BASTARD TALKIN'. 708 ICEMAN
(IRRITABLY) FOR THE LOVE AV HIVIN, DON'T BE 517 INZONE
TALKIN' ABOUT UT.
YOU'RE TALKIN' MORE THAN A PAIR AV AULD WOMEN 518 INZONE
WOULD BE STANDIN' IN THE ROAD,
WHAT'RE YUH TALKIN' ABOUTS 521 INZONE
THEN LISTEN TO ME--AN' UT'S DRISCOLL TALKIN'-- 524 INZONE
THERE'S NO TALKIN' TO YOU 16 POET
(PROTESTS MISERABLY.) IT WAS THE DRINK TALKIN', 24 POET
NOT HIM.
THAT'S THE TALKIN'. 134 POET
(DRUNKENLY.) AH, DON'T BE TALKIN'/ 161 POET
SOBBIN' AND BEGGIN' HER FORGIVENESS AND TALKIN' OF161 POET
DISHONOR AND DEATH--
D'YOU KNOW WHO'S TALKIN'S 581 ROPE
IT'S NO USE TALKIN' TO HIM, PAT. 583 ROPE
HE WAS SURPRISED TO HEAR ME TALKIN' OF MONEY. 585 ROPE
DON'T BE TALKIN' SO MUCH. 601 ROPE
NOW YOU'RE TALKIN'. 499 VOYAGE
D'YOU HEAR THE LADY TALKIN' TO YE, YE ROOSHUN 500 VOYAGE
SWABS

TALKING
KITCHEN AGAIN, AND HEAR A WOMAN'S VOICE TALKING TO547 *ILE
ME AND BE ABLE TO TALK TO
OH, I HEARD YOU TALKING WITH THE SECOND MATE. 547 *ILE
NO USE TALKING TO HIM, LILY. 190 AHWILD
YOU'VE GOT TO GIVE HIM A GOOD TALKING TO--(SHE 192 AHWILD
GETS UP FROM HER CHAIR)
YOU OUGHT TO GET A PUNCH IN THE NOSE FOR TALKING 195 AHWILD
THAT WAY ON THE FOURTH/
(SOLEMNLY) SON, IF I DIDN'T KNOW IT WAS YOU 195 AHWILD
TALKING,
I'LL TELL YOU, IF HE WON'T--AND YOU GIVE HIM A 196 AHWILD
GOOD TALKING TO.
OH, IT'S NO GOOD TALKING, ESSIE. 213 AHWILD
NO IT'S NO GOOD IN YOUR TALKING, ESSIE. 213 AHWILD
I DO WISH YOU WOULDN'T ENCOURAGE THAT STUPID GIRL 223 AHWILD
BY TALKING TO HER.
HURRY UP AND FINISH YOUR SOUP, AND STOP TALKING 225 AHWILD
NONSENSE/
(AS IF HE WERE TALKING TO HIS PLATE) 229 AHWILD
THAT'S TALKING/ 238 AHWILD
IF YOU DON'T STOP TALKING FOURTH OF JULY--/ 251 AHWILD
AND DID YOU HEAR HIM TALKING ABOUT SOME HEDDAS 262 AHWILD
(THEN SUDDENLY HE LAUGHS) NO USE TALKING, YOU 268 AHWILD
CERTAINLY TAKE THE CAKE/
(AS SHE IS TALKING, RICHARD APPEARS IN THE DOORWAY269 AHWILD
FROM THE SITTING-ROOM.
IT WAS ONLY MY DESPAIR TALKING. 271 AHWILD
NOW YOU'RE TALKING SENSE/ 271 AHWILD
WHO WAS TALKING ABOUT YOUS 291 AHWILD
(THEN HAS A SUDDEN THOUGHT) BUT I'VE DONE ALL 292 AHWILD
THIS TALKING ABOUT MURIEL AND
I KNOW THAT SOUNDS HARD AND UNFEELING, BUT WE'RE 295 AHWILD
TALKING FACTS AND--
BUT THOSE COUSINS WAS ALWAYS TALKING CROPS AND 27 ANNA
THAT STUFF.
(TALKING ALOUD TO HIMSELF) ROW, YE DIVIL/ 31 ANNA
I'M CLUMSY IN MY WITS WHEN IT COMES TO TALKING 37 ANNA
PROPER WITH A GIRL THE LIKE OF
WHO D'YOU THINK YOU'RE TALKING TO--A SLAVES 39 ANNA
BUT YOU KEEP ON TALKING JUST THE SAME. 43 ANNA
(EARNESTLY) LET US BE TALKING IT OUT NOW AS MAN 46 ANNA
TO MAN.
VE VAS TALKING ABOUT SHIPS AND FALLARS ON SEA. 50 ANNA
LISTEN HERE, I'M TALKING TO YOU NOW/ 57 ANNA
BUT WHAT'S THE USE OF TALKINGS 66 ANNA
IN TALKING THE SAME OLD BULL YOU TALKED TO ME TO 73 ANNA
THE FIRST ONE YOU MEET.
WHAT'S THE USE OF ME TALKINGS 74 ANNA
(HE STEPS OVER THE DITCH TO THE ROAD WHILE HE IS 86 BEYOND
TALKING.)
IT'S NO USE TALKING TO YOU, YOU CHUMP/ 86 BEYOND
HE DID WHEN HE WAS TALKING TO ME THIS EVENING. 96 BEYOND
A FINE ONE YOU ARE TO BE TALKING ABOUT LOVE, 103 BEYOND
DICK--
(AFTER A SLIGHT PAUSE) IT'S NO USE TALKING ANY 105 BEYOND
MORE ABOUT IT.
YOU'LL BE SORRY FOR TALKING LIKE THAT. 127 BEYOND
I KNOW MY TALKING ABOUT BUSINESS MAKES YOU WANT TO133 BEYOND
CHOKE ME, DOESN'T ITS
(INDIGNANTLY) WHAT'RE YOU TALKING ABOUTS 138 BEYOND
FOR GOD'S SAKE, ANDY--WON'T YOU PLEASE STOP 139 BEYOND
TALKING/

TALKING (CONT'D.)
(FROWNING--IRRITABLY) WHAT AM I TALKING ABOUTS 147 BEYOND
(SHRUGGING HIS SHOULDERS) WHAT'S THE USE OF 148 BEYOND
TALKING TO YOUS
HE'S JUST BEEN TALKING TO ME OUT HERE. 151 BEYOND
(DULLY) HE WAS TALKING--WILD--LIKE HE USED TO-- 163 BEYOND
I'D GOT TO THE END OF BEARING THINGS--WITHOUT 164 BEYOND
TALKING.
FIVE MEN ARE SITTING ON THE BENCHES TALKING. 477 CARDTI
(A FAT SWEDE WHO IS SITTING ON A CAMP STOOL IN 457 CARIBE
FRONT OF HIS DOOR TALKING WITH
(THE SOUND OF WOMEN'S VOICES CAN BE HEARD TALKING 461 CARIBE
AND LAUGHING.)
AS IF SHE WERE TALKING ALOUD TO HERSELF) 540 DAYS
JOHN IS TALKING IN A STRAINED TONE, MONOTONOUSLY, 541 DAYS
INSISTENTLY.
IT IS AS IF HE WERE DETERMINEDLY TALKING TO KEEP 542 DAYS
HIMSELF FROM THINKING.
I LISTEN TO PEOPLE TALKING ABOUT THIS UNIVERSAL 542 DAYS
BREAKDOWN WE ARE IN AND I MARVEL
(THEN WILDLY) OH, JOHN, STOP TALKING/ 550 DAYS
I SEEM TO BE TALKING NONSENSE. 551 DAYS
STOP TALKING DAMNED NONSENSE/ 560 DAYS
HE BEGINS TALKING TO ABBIE WHOM HE SUPPOSES BESIDE263 DESIRE
HIM.)
TALKING AND LAUGHING DURING THE FOLLOWING SCENE.) 507 DIFRNT
IS IT THAT STORY ABOUT CALEB AND THAT HEATHEN 508 DIFRNT
BROWN WOMAN YOU'RE TALKING ABOUTS
JACK AND ROGERS PASS OUT. TALKING AND LAUGHING. 511 DIFRNT
I'LL GIVE CALEB A TALKING-TO BEFORE HE COMES OVER.511 DIFRNT
(ALL THE TIME HE IS TALKING, HE STARES AT 436 DYNAMO
REUBEN'S FLUSTERED FACE.
HE'S ACTUALLY IN THERE TALKING TO THAT ATHEIST/...437 DYNAMO
(TURNS AND GLARES AT HER) I'M GLAD YOU'RE TALKING450 DYNAMO
LIKE THAT/
(WATCHING FROM HIS WINDOW) (HE'S TALKING TO 451 DYNAMO
FIFE/...
SOMETIMES I'D GO IN A PLANT AND GET TALKING TO THE461 DYNAMO
GUYS JUST TO HANG AROUND.
BUT WHAT'S THE USE OF TALKING ABOUT ITS 470 DYNAMO
I CAN'T GET USED TO YOU TALKING LIKE THAT. 470 DYNAMO
HE IS TALKING WITH UNNATURAL EXCITEMENT AS THEY 476 DYNAMO
COME IN.
I WAS TALKING TO REUBEN. 479 DYNAMO
(WHILE HE IS TALKING HE SCRAMBLES FROM ONE STONE 189 EJONES
TO ANOTHER.
(HE STOPS TALKING TO LISTEN) 191 EJONES
(STIFFENING--CURTLY) I DON'T KNOW WHAT YOU'RE 11 ELECTR
TALKING ABOUT.
I DON'T KNOW WHAT YOU'RE TALKING ABOUT/ 27 ELECTR
I'M TALKING TO YOU AS A WOMAN NOW, NOT AS MOTHER 31 ELECTR
TO DAUGHTER/
WHILE THEY ARE DOING THIS HE KEEPS ON TALKING IN 48 ELECTR
HIS ABRUPT SENTENCES.
THAT IS, HE KEPT TALKING TO «MOTHER.» 49 ELECTR
(WITHOUT OPENING HER EYES) WHY ARE YOU TALKING OF 54 ELECTR
DEATH/
(TENSELY) I DON'T KNOW WHAT YOU'RE TALKING ABOUT. 54 ELECTR
YOU TELL ME TO STOP TALKING--BY GOD, THAT'S FUNNY/ 56 ELECTR
FOR GOD'S SAKE, STOP TALKING. 56 ELECTR
STOP TALKING LIKE THAT/ 60 ELECTR
I DON'T KNOW WHAT--YOU'RE TALKING BOUT. 63 ELECTR
HE KEPT TALKING OF LOVE AND DEATH--HE FORCED ME TO 63 ELECTR
TELL HIM/
OVERHEARD HER MOTHER TALKING TO LAVINIA IN THE 69 ELECTR
HALL.
ARE STANDING TALKING IN LOW TONES) 69 ELECTR
(THE THREE MEN JOIN THE WOMEN BY THE BENCH, BORDEN 69 ELECTR
TALKING AS THEY COME)
BUT WHAT NONSENSE I'M TALKING/ 73 ELECTR
BUT WHAT THE DEVIL ARE ME TALKING ABOUT ME FORS 75 ELECTR
(THEN ANGRILY) WHAT THE HELL ARE YOU TALKING 76 ELECTR
ABOUT, ANYWAYS
(THEY STOP TALKING SELF-CONSCIOUSLY AS ORIN AND 80 ELECTR
CHRISTINE ENTER FROM THE REAR.
YOU'RE TALKING AS IF HE WERE--ALIVE/ 81 ELECTR
I MEANT TO LOOK AT HIM THE FIRST THING--BUT I GOT 83 ELECTR
TALKING--I'LL GO IN RIGHT NOW.
(HIS VOICE HAS SUNK LOWER AND LOWER, AS IF HE WERE 95 ELECTR
TALKING TO HIMSELF.
WE'RE FOOLS TO BE TALKING OUT HERE. 109 ELECTR
HE KEPT TALKING OF DEATH/ 110 ELECTR
(AS IF TALKING TO HIMSELF) THIS IS LIKE MY DREAM.115 ELECTR
ORIN, FOR GOD'S SAKE, WILL YOU STOP TALKING CRAZY 116 ELECTR
AND COME ALONGS
YOU LET ME DO THE TALKING/ 120 ELECTR
(DULLY NOW) YOU'VE KEPT TALKING ABOUT THEM ALL 140 ELECTR
THE VOYAGE HOME.
(UNEASILY) NOW DON'T BEGIN TALKING NONSENSE 141 ELECTR
AGAIN, PLEASE/
(WITH A TRACE OF CONFUSION) I DON'T KNOW WHAT 141 ELECTR
YOU'RE TALKING ABOUT.
(ANGRILY) STOP TALKING LIKE A FOOL/ 145 ELECTR
(FURIOUSLY) STOP TALKING ABOUT HER/ 153 ELECTR
WHICH HE GIVES TO HAZEL, TALKING BREATHLESSLY, 160 ELECTR
WITH NERVOUS JERKS OF HIS HEAD.
WHAT ARE YOU TALKING ABOUT, VINNIES 176 ELECTR
YOU'RE TALKING CRAZY/ 177 ELECTR
I'M GOING TO GIVE DION A GOOD TALKING-TO ONE OF 278 GGBROW
THESE DAYS/
DEEP FAR-OFF VOICE--AND YET LIKE A MOTHER TALKING 288 GGBROW
TO HER LITTLE SON)
WHAT ARE YOU TALKING ABOUTS 289 GGBROW
IT SOUNDS TO ME LIKE BACCHUS, ALIAS THE DEMON RUM,297 GGBROW
DOING THE TALKING.
(WITH A SHEEPISH GRIN) I'LL BET FATHER SAID THAT 300 GGBROW
WHEN HE WAS JUST TALKING.
(HE GOES OFF LEFT, BUT CAN BE HEARD TALKING) 308 GGBROW

TALKING (CONT'D.)
(IN SAME TONE) I CAN ALMOST HEAR HIM TALKING. 318 GGBROW
YERRA, WHAT'S THE USE OF TALKINGS 214 HA APE
I DON'T KNOW WHAT YOU'RE TALKING ABOUT. 220 HA APE
TALKING IN TUNELESS, SIMPERING VOICES. 236 HA APE
OH, HELL! WHAT'S THE USE OF TALKINGS 250 HA APE
BEGINNING TO ACHE AND HE WISHES 492 WOULD STOP 13 HUGHIE
TALKING AND GO TO BED SO HE CAN
AND THEY STARTED TALKING, AND THE POOR BOOB NEVER 23 HUGHIE
STOOD A CHANCE.
WHAT'S HE BEEN TALKING ABOUTS 30 HUGHIE
ERIE BEGINS TALKING AGAIN BUT THIS TIME IT IS 30 HUGHIE
OBVIOUSLY ALOUD TO HIMSELF.
AND HE WON'T GO TO BED, HE'S STILL TALKING, AND 30 HUGHIE
THERE IS NO ESCAPE.)
=WHAT'S HE BEEN TALKING ABOUTS 31 HUGHIE
WHEEDLING PLAYFULNESS, AS THOUGH HE WERE TALKING 579 ICEMAN
TO A CHILD)
THEN IRRITABLY AS IF SUDDENLY PROVOKED AT HIMSELF 590 ICEMAN
FOR TALKING SO MUCH)
WE WAS TALKING ABOUT POOR OLD BESSIE, 606 ICEMAN
TALKING MUSH ABOUT HER, TOO/ 606 ICEMAN
(SCATHINGLY) YOU TALKING OF YOUR DEAR SISTER/ 608 ICEMAN
AS IF HE WERE TALKING ALOUD TO HIMSELF AS MUCH AS 622 ICEMAN
TO THEM.
ANY TIME YOU THINK I'M TALKING OUT OF TURN, JUST 624 ICEMAN
TELL ME TO GO CHASE MYSELF/
(UNEASY AGAIN) WHAT ARE YOU TALKING ABOUTS 624 ICEMAN
(WHILE HE IS TALKING, THEY 626 ICEMAN
(STAMMERS) I---I'M TALKING TO HARRY. 657 ICEMAN
YOU'RE RIGHT, ROCKY, I'M TALKING TOO MUCH. 659 ICEMAN
(ABRUPTLY) BUT I WAS TALKING ABOUT HOW SHE MUST 667 ICEMAN
FEEL NOW ABOUT ME.
THIS GABBY YOUNG PUNK WAS TALKING MY EAR OFF, 668 ICEMAN
THAT'S ALL.
CONTINUAL TALKING, BUT HIS BUSTLING ENERGY APPEARS684 ICEMAN
NERVOUSLY INTENSIFIED.
LIKE SLEEPERS TALKING OUT OF A DULLY IRRITATING 701 ICEMAN
DREAM, THE HELL WITH IT/
HE'LL KEEP ON TALKING. 703 ICEMAN
(BUT LARRY DOESN'T HEAR, AND JOE BEGINS TALKING INT23 ICEMAN
THE GROUP AT RIGHT.)
WHAT ARE YOU TALKING ABOUTS 527 INZONE
YOU CAN'T HEAR ME TALKING TO MYSELF, THAT'S ALL. 32 JOURNE
(STRANGELY, AS IF TALKING ALOUD TO HERSELF.) 41 JOURNE
AND ABOUT THE OLD MAN, WHAT'S THE USE OF TALKINGS 44 JOURNE
CAN'T YOU STOP TALKING LIKE THAT/ 49 JOURNE
THE OLD MAN WAS TALKING TO OLD CAPTAIN TURNER. 54 JOURNE
BUT HE KEPT ON TALKING TO THAT MAN, TELLING HIM OF 62 JOURNE
THE TIME WHEN---
I DON'T KNOW WHAT YOU'RE TALKING ABOUT. 63 JOURNE
NOW YOU'RE TALKING IN RIDDLES LIKE JAMIE. 64 JOURNE
AS IF SHE WERE NOW TALKING ALOUD TO HERSELF RATHER 67 JOURNE
THAN TO TYRONE.)
STOP TALKING. 67 JOURNE
I DON'T KNOW WHAT YOU'RE TALKING ABOUT. 70 JOURNE
SHE IS TALKING AS SHE ENTERS--- 71 JOURNE
FOR GOD'S SAKE, STOP TALKING. 76 JOURNE
YOU DON'T KNOW WHAT YOU'RE TALKING ABOUT. 77 JOURNE
STOP WHATS WHAT ARE YOU TALKING ABOUTS 85 JOURNE
WITH HER MERELY AS AN EXCUSE TO KEEP TALKING.) 98 JOURNE
(WITH STUBBORN BLANKNESS.) WHAT ARE YOU TALKING 103 JOURNE
ABOUTS
(MISERABLY.) STOP TALKING, MAMA. 109 JOURNE
(MISERABLY.) OH, STOP TALKING CRAZY, CAN'T YOU, 119 JOURNE
MAMA/
I DON'T KNOW WHAT YOU'RE TALKING ABOUT, JAMES. 123 JOURNE
NOW YOU'RE TALKING/ 129 JOURNE
I'M TALKING SENSE. 131 JOURNE
WE'RE TALKING ABOUT MAMA/ 140 JOURNE
WHICH SHE NEVER MAKES UNLESS IT'S THE POISON 142 JOURNE
TALKING.
DON'T KNOW WHAT MADE ME---BOOZE TALKING--- YOU KNOW 162 JOURNE
ME, KID.
I THOUGHT HE'D NEVER STOP TALKING. 167 JOURNE
WATCHING LAZARUS WITH FRIGHTENED AWE, TALKING 273 LAZARU
HESITANTLY IN LOW WHISPERS.
TALKING DOWN TO HER FACE--WITH A TENDER SMILE) 362 LAZARU
WHAT ARE YOU TALKING ABOUTS 61 MANSNS
BUT OUR TALKING HERE HAD WAKENED JONATHAN AND I 61 MANSNS
HAD TO GET HIM BACK TO SLEEP.
SIMON WAS TALKING OVER THIS BUSINESS---FOR THE LAST 62 MANSNS
TIME, I HOPE.
AND MORE AND MORE IT SEEMS HE IS TALKING TO 72 MANSNS
(STRANGELY NOW---AS IF HE WERE TALKING ALOUD TO 91 MANSNS
HIMSELF.)
(ANGRILY.) YOU ARE TALKING NONSENSE/ 105 MANSNS
DO YOU KNOW, THIS MORNING, TALKING WITH MOTHER, 145 MANSNS
(WHILE SHE IS TALKING, UNNOTICED BY THEM BOTH, 171 MANSNS
SIMON APPEARS BEHIND THEM.
I DON'T KNOW WHAT YOU'RE TALKING ABOUT, MOTHER. 173 MANSNS
AND YOU AND SARA BEGIN TALKING AS IF YOU, 173 MANSNS
PERSONALLY,
WHO ARE YOU TALKING TO, MOTHERS 187 MANSNS
WHO IS TALKINGS 191 MANSNS
MESSER POLO, HIS IMPERIAL MAJESTY COMMANDS THAT 389 MARCOM
YOU STOP TALKING.
HE SMILES. HE IS TALKING LOUDLY SO EVERYONE CAN 389 MARCOM
OVERHEAR.
MARCO IS TALKING. 394 MARCOM
I'M BY NATURE A SILENT MAN, AND I LET MY ACTIONS 404 MARCOM
DO THE TALKING.
YOU'RE TALKING AS IF YOU WERE DELIRIOUS/ 413 MARCOM
AND I WAS TALKING TO HER, NOT TO YOU AT ALL/ 416 MARCOM
IT WASN'T YOU I WAS SEEING AND TALKING TO, NOT A 416 MARCOM
PRINCESS AT ALL.
MARCO TALKING EARNESTLY TO THE OBLIVIOUS GHAZAN 419 MARCOM

TALKING (CONT'D.)
BUT IT'S NO GOOD TALKING NOW---NO GOOD AT ALL---NO 83 MISBEG
GOOD.
HE STARTED TALKING ABOUT YOU, AS IF YOU WAS ON HIS 87 MISBEG
MIND, WORRYING HIM---
WE'VE DONE ENOUGH TALKING. 95 MISBEG
MAYBE YOU KNOW WHAT YOU'RE TALKING ABOUT--- 120 MISBEG
(UNEASILY) WHAT ARE YOU TALKING ABOUTS 122 MISBEG
THE BROOKLYN BOYS ARE TALKING AGAIN. 122 MISBEG
YOU SEE, SHE WAS ONE OF THE SMUTTIEST TALKING PIGS127 MISBEG
I'VE EVER LISTENED TO.
WHAT ARE YOU TALKING ABOUTS 127 MISBEG
HOW ABOUT YOUR NUT TALKING THE OLD SMUT STUFF TO 127 MISBEG
MES
(ABRUPTLY) WHAT WERE WE TALKING ABOUT BEFORES 128 MISBEG
(GOES ON WITHOUT REAL INTEREST, TALKING TO KEEP 132 MISBEG
FROM THINKING)
HE MUTTERS VAGUELY, AS IF TALKING TO HIMSELF) 138 MISBEG
ONLY STOP TALKING/ 138 MISBEG
(UNEASILY) STOP TALKING SO QUEER. 160 MISBEG
(TORMENTEDLY) WILL YOU STOP TALKING AS IF YOU'D 161 MISBEG
GONE MAD IN THE NIGHT/
I'LL DO THE TALKING NOW. 162 MISBEG
BUT WHAT'S THE GOOD OF TALKINGS 164 MISBEG
I DON'T KNOW WHAT YOU'RE TALKING ABOUT. 174 MISBEG
NOW YOU'RE TALKING. 177 MISBEG
TALKING OVER OLD TIMES WITH JAMIE CREGAN. 42 POET
BUT YOU UNDERSTAND, IT WAS THE LIQUOR TALKING, IF 42 POET
I SAID ANYTHING TO WOUND YOU.
THEY ALL HAVE HANGOVERS, AND ROCHE IS TALKING 51 POET
BOISTEROUSLY.
(LOWERING HER VOICE.) SHE STARTED TALKING THE 79 POET
SECOND SHE GOT IN THE DOOR
(THEN TALKING RAPIDLY AGAIN IN HER STRANGE 86 POET
DETACHED WAY.)
I DIDN'T MEAN--THE WHISKEY TALKING---AS YOU SAID. 107 POET
AS YOUR MOTHER KNOWS, IT'S THE LIQUOR TALKING, 115 POET
NOT---
I DO NOT KNOW WHAT YOU ARE TALKING ABOUT, SIR, 120 POET
(WHILE SHE IS TALKING THE DOOR FROM THE BAR OPENS 123 POET
AND ROCHE, O'DOWD,
HE'S ONLY TALKING. 125 POET
ONLY TALKING, AN IS 125 POET
OH, IT'S LIKE TALKING TO CRAZY MEN/ 126 POET
YOU'VE A QUEER WAY OF TALKING. 141 POET
BUT I'M TALKING GREAT NONSENSE. 150 POET
STICK. TALKING TO HIMSELF AS HE DOES SO) 579 ROPE
TALKING TO HER.) 587 ROPE
(THE PROFESSOR OF DEAD LANGUAGES IS TALKING 15 STRANG
AGAIN.
(THINKING) ((TALKING/... 16 STRANG
IT'S NO USE TALKING, FATHER. 16 STRANG
(BLUNTLY) AND THAT'S WHY I'VE DONE ALL THIS 37 STRANG
TALKING.
WHAT SHE IS SAYING INTERESTS HIM AND HE FEELS 40 STRANG
TALKING IT OUT WILL DO HER GOOD.
YOU OUGHT TO STOP TALKING. 42 STRANG
(THINKING FRIGHTENEDLY) ((WHO IS TALKING...) 87 STRANG
(THINKING--WORRIEDLY) ((WHAT'S CHARLIE TALKING 128 STRANG
ABOUTS...
((HE'S TALKING ABOUT ME... 141 STRANG
AND HE BEGAN TALKING BACK TO HIM ALL THE TIME AND 153 STRANG
SORT OF GAVE HIM HIS STRENGTH
(COMES IN FROM THE REAR WHILE THEY ARE TALKING. 154 STRANG
YOU'LL HAVE TO GIVE GORDON A GOOD TALKING TO, NED.169 STRANG
(STRANGELY) WE WERE TALKING ABOUT SAM, WEREN'T 170 STRANG
WES
(FRIGHTENEDLY) YOU'RE TALKING LIKE THE OLD NINA 170 STRANG
NOW---WHEN I FIRST LOVED YOU.
BUT HERE I AM TALKING WHILE MY LAST CHAPTERS ARE 177 STRANG
IN THE MAKING---
(THINKING UNEASILY) ((THEY'RE TALKING ABOUT ME...196 STRANG
SHE IS ALTERNATELY LOOKING AT JOE AND FEVERISHLY 506 VOYAGE
TRYING TO KEEP OLSON TALKING.
NOW YOU'RE TALKING SENSE. 465 WELDED
YOU'RE TALKING ROT/ 486 WELDED

TALKS
SHE TALKS TO HIM--WHEN SHE DOES TALK--RIGHT 538 'ILE
ENOUGH.
MCCOMBER TALKS ON.) 202 AHWILD
MRS. ATKINS KNITS NERVOUSLY AS SHE TALKS. 113 BEYOND
(VERY MUCH RUFFLED) THAT'S LIKE THEY TALKS... 125 BEYOND
HIS FACE IS FLUSHED AND HE TALKS RATHER WILDLY) 467 CARLBE
THEY WATCH THE PAPER BURN WITH FASCINATED EYES AS 567 CROSS
HE TALKS)
SHOP, I TALKS LARGE WHEN I AIN'T GOT NOTHIN' TO 179 EJONES
BACK IT UP.
HE TALKS IN A DRAWLING WHEEZY CACKLE. 129 ELECTR
IN THE MEANTIME SMALL TALKS TO SETH.) 131 ELECTR
(AS HE TALKS, MARGOT PEARL 651 ICEMAN
(AS HE TALKS HE HAS BEEN MOVING TOWARD THE DOOR. 687 ICEMAN
HE TALKS IT TOO DAMN 521 INZONE
GUS HE TALKS ITS 521 INZONE
AN' TALKS ENGLISH AS GOOD AS ANYONES 521 INZONE
AS SHE TALKS, SHE GLANCES EVERYWHERE EXCEPT AT ANY 66 JOURNE
OF THEIR FACES.)
AS SHE TALKS, SHE COMES TO THE LEFT OF THE TABLE 71 JOURNE
AND STANDS, FACING FRONT.
SHE TALKS TO CATHLEEN WITH A CONFIDING 97 JOURNE
FAMILIARITY.
(TALKS MORE FAMILIARLY THAN USUAL BUT NEVER WITH 98 JOURNE
INTENTIONAL IMPERTINENCE
SHE TALKS EXCITEDLY.) 108 JOURNE
SHE TALKS ON AS IF UNAWARE OF THEIR SILENCE.) 109 JOURNE
THE SHYLY EAGER, TRUSTING SMILE IS ON HER LIPS AS 175 JOURNE
SHE TALKS ALOUD TO HERSELF.)
HE TALKS TO LAZARUS HALF OVER HIS SHOULDER. 350 LAZARU
THE OLD LECHER TALKS TO HIMSELF. 355 LAZARU

TALKS

TALKS (CONT'D.)

HE TALKS TO HIMSELF LIKE A MAN IN SECOND CHILDHOOD. 357 LAZARU

ON AND TALKS LIKE A BROADWAY CROOK HIMSELF, 33 MISBEG
HE'S THE WAY I TOLD YOU ABOUT THIS MORNING, WHEN 82 MISBEG
HE TALKS LIKE A BROADWAY CROOK,
I HAVE ENJOYED MY TALKS WITH 47 POET
SHE TALKS IN A HIGH-PITCHED, SING-SONG WHINE. 579 ROPE
AND SHE TALKS INTERMINABLY, CHARLIE--INTENTIONAL 8 STRANG
NONSENSE, ONE WOULD SAY/.
I KNOW THAT FROM THE WAY SHE TALKS ABOUT YOU. 36 STRANG

TALKY

ASSERTIVE AND TALKY. 373 MARCOM

TALL

MILDRED IS FIFTEEN, TALL AND SLENDER, WITH BIG, 186 AHWILD
IRREGULAR FEATURES.
HE IS TALL, HEAVY, BARREL-CHESTED AND MUSCULAR, 186 AHWILD
LILY MILLER, HER SISTER-IN-LAW, IS FORTY-TWO, 187 AHWILD
TALL, DARK AND THIN.
NAT MILLER IS IN HIS LATE FIFTIES, A TALL, DARK, 188 AHWILD
SPARE MAN,
HE IS TALL, BLOND, DRESSED IN EXTREME COLLEGIATE 218 AHWILD
CUT.)
SHE IS A TALL, BLOND, FULLY-DEVELOPED GIRL OF 13 ANNA
TWENTY, HANDSOME AFTER A LARGE,
HE IS A TALL, SLENDER YOUNG MAN OF TWENTY-THREE. 81 BEYOND
HE IS A TALL, STRONGLY-BUILT MAN DRESSED IN A 472 CARIBE
PLAIN BLUE UNIFORM.)
NAT BARTLETT IS VERY TALL, GAUNT, AND LOOSE- 556 CROSS
FRAMED.
SHE IS A TALL, SLENDER WOMAN OF TWENTY-FIVE, 562 CROSS
JIMMY IS A TALL, SINEWY, BRONZED YOUNG KANAKA. 571 CROSS
STILLWELL IS IN HIS EARLY FIFTIES, TALL, WITH A 553 DAYS
SHARP,
THEY ARE TALL MEN, MUCH OLDER THAN THEIR HALF- 203 DESIRE
BROTHER--
HE IS TWENTY-FIVE, TALL AND SINEWY. 203 DESIRE
CABOT IS SEVENTY-FIVE, TALL AND GAUNT, WITH GREAT,221 DESIRE
WIRY, CONCENTRATED POWER,
CALEB WILLIAMS IS TALL AND POWERFULLY BUILT, ABOUT494 DIFRNT
THIRTY.
CALEB'S SISTER IS A TALL, DARK GIRL OF TWENTY. 505 DIFRNT
AND A ROW OF TALL MAPLES IN THE BACKGROUND BEHIND -0 DYNAMO
THE YARDS AND THE TWO HOUSES.
HE IS SEVENTEEN, TALL AND THIN. 422 DYNAMO
HIS WIFE IS TALL AND STOUT, WEIGHING WELL OVER TW0428 DYNAMO
HUNDRED
SMITHERS IS A TALL, STOOP-SHOULDERED MAN ABOUT 173 EJONES
FORTY.
HE IS A TALL, POWERFULLY-BUILT, FULL-BLOODED NEGRO175 EJONES
OF MIDDLE AGE.
TALL TREES WHOSE TOPS ARE LOST TO VIEW. 195 EJONES
THE PROPERTY IS ENCLOSED BY A WHITE PICKET FENCE 2 ELECTR
AND A TALL HEDGE.
A WHITE WOODEN PORTICO WITH SIX TALL COLUMNS 2 ELECTR
CONTRASTS
BEHIND THE DRIVEWAY THE WHITE GRECIAN TEMPLE 5 ELECTR
PORTICO WITH ITS SIX TALL COLUMNS
IS AN OLD MAN OF SEVENTY-FIVE WITH WHITE HAIR AND 6 ELECTR
BEARD, TALL,
(CHRISTINE MANNON IS A TALL STRIKING-LOOKING WOMAN 8 ELECTR
OF FORTY
TALL, LIKE HER MOTHER, HER BODY IS THIN, FLAT- 10 ELECTR
BREASTED AND ANGULAR,
IN FIGURE HE IS TALL, BROAD-SHOULDERED AND 21 ELECTR
POWERFUL.
(URTY) --TALL, WHITE CLIPPERS,= YOU CALLED THEM. 23 ELECTR
HE IS A TALL MAN IN HIS EARLY FORTIES, WITH A 28 ELECTR
SPARE, WIRY FRAME.
HE IS TALL, SPARE, BIG-BONED MAN OF FIFTY, 46 ELECTR
BILLY BROWN IS A HANDSOME, TALL AND ATHLETIC BOY 257 GGBROW
OF NEARLY EIGHTEEN.
THE FATHER IS A TALL LEAN MAN OF FIFTY-FIVE UR 259 GGBROW
SIXTY WITH A GRIM,
SEEMING TO GROW TALL AND PROUD--THEN WITH A LAUGH 308 GGBROW
OF BOLD SELF-ASSURANCE)
THEY ARE ALL TALL, ATHLETIC, STRONG AND HANDSOME- 323 GGBROW
LOOKING.
CLIPPERS WHO TALL MASTS TOUCHING THE SKY--FINE 213 HA APE
STRONG MEN IN THEM,
TALL, THIN, WITH A SCRAWNY NECK AND JUTTING ADAM'S 8 HUGHIE
APPLE.
HE IS TALL, RAW-BONED, WITH COARSE STRAIGHT WHITE 574 ICEMAN
HAIR,
HE IS EIGHTEEN, TALL AND BROAD-SHOULDERED BUT 585 ICEMAN
THIN, GANGLING AND AWKWARD.
IN APPEARANCE LAZARUS IS TALL AND POWERFUL, ABOUT 274 LAZARU
FIFTY YEARS OF AGE.
THE MOTHER IS TALL AND STOUT, OVER SIXTY-FIVE, A 275 LAZARU
GENTLE, SIMPLE WOMAN.
THE TALL FIGURE OF LAZARUS, DRESSED IN A WHITE 288 LAZARU
ROBE,
AN OLD MAN OF SEVENTY-SIX, TALL, 337 LAZARU
MY MOTHER SPOKE TO ME AND SPOKE TO ME AND EVEN 356 LAZARU
WEPT, THAT TALL WOMAN,
SHE IS SMALL, NOT OVER FIVE FEET TALL, 2 MANSNS
HE IS TALL AND LOOSE-JOINTED WITH A WIRY STRENGTH 4 MANSNS
OF LIMB.
JOEL HARFORD IS TWENTY-NINE, TALL AND THIN, WITH A 25 MANSNS
SLIGHT STOOP IN HIS CARRIAGE.
FARTHER BACK AGAINST THE WALL IS A HIGH DESK WITH 69 MANSNS
A TALL STOOL IN FRONT OF IT.
AT LEFT OF THIS DOOR, A TALL CABINET STANDS 69 MANSNS
AGAINST THE WALL.
HE IS A TALL, FULL-CHESTED MAN IN HIS SIXTIES, 150 MANSNS
WITH A FINE-LOOKING ROMAN FACE,
BUT HE IS TALL AND STOUT WITH A ROUND, JOVIAL FACE358 MARCOM
AND SMALL, CUNNING EYES.

TALL (CONT'D.)

A TALL MAJOR-DOMO 426 MARCOM
I LIKE THEM TALL AND STRONG AND VOLUPTUOUS, NOW, 43 MISBEG
WITH BEAUTIFUL BIG BREASTS.
AS OBVIOUSLY IRISH AS MALOY, HE IS MIDDLE-AGED, 8 POET
TALL, WITH A LANTERN-JAWED FACE.
(CORNELIUS MELODY IS FORTY-FIVE, TALL, BROAD- 33 POET
SHOULDERED, DEEP-CHESTED,
SHE IS SMALL, A LITTLE OVER FIVE FEET TALL, WITH A 67 POET
FRAGILE, YOUTHFUL FIGURE.
HE IS A TALL, LEAN, STOOP-SHOULDERED OLD MAN OF 578 ROPE
SIXTY-FIVE.
HE IS A TALL, STRAPPING YOUNG FELLOW ABOUT TWENTY-587 ROPE
FIVE WITH A COARSE-FEATURED,
HE IS A TALL THIN MAN OF THIRTY-FIVE, METICULOUSLY 3 STRANG
WELL-DRESSED IN TWEEDS
(STANDING JUST INSIDE THE DOOR, HIS TALL, 4 STRANG
SHE IS TWENTY, TALL WITH BROAD SQUARE SHOULDERS, 12 STRANG
HIS TALL, THIN BODY SAGS WEARILY IN THE CHAIR, HIS 24 STRANG
HEAD IS SUNK FORWARD,
HIS TALL, THIN BODY STOOPS AS IF A PART OF ITS 73 STRANG
SUSTAINING WILL HAD BEEN REMOVED.
EXCEPT THAT HIS HAIR IS GRAYER AND HIS TALL FIGURE146 STRANG
MORE STOOPED.
HER SKIN IS DEEPLY TANNED, HER FIGURE TALL AND 159 STRANG
ATHLETIC.
THE STOOP OF HIS TALL FIGURE IS ACCENTUATED, HIS 159 STRANG
HAIR HAS GROWN WHITISH.
GORDON IS OVER SIX FEET TALL WITH THE FIGURE OF A 184 STRANG
TRAINED ATHLETE.
DRISCOLL IS A TALL, POWERFUL IRISHMAN,. 496 VOYAGE
MICHAEL IS THIRTY-FIVE, TALL AND DARK. 443 WELDED
HER FIGURE IS TALL, 443 WELDED
HE IS A MAN OF ABOUT FIFTY, TALL, LOOSE-LIMBED, A 450 WELDED
BIT STOOP-SHOULDERED,

TALLER

I'M TALLER. 211 AHWILD
HIS WIFE, LOUISA, IS TALLER AND STOUTER THAN HE 6 ELECTR
AND ABOUT THE SAME AGE.
HE SEEMS TALLER AND SLENDERER BECAUSE OF HIS 13 JOURNE
BEARING.
A COUPLE OF INCHES TALLER, THIN AND WIRY. 19 JOURNE
IS AN INCH TALLER AND WEIGHS LESS, BUT APPEARS 19 JOURNE
SHORTER AND STOUTER

TALLOW

FOUR ROUGH WOODEN CHAIRS, A TALLOW CANDLE ON THE 206 DESIRE
TABLE.
BOTH ROOMS ARE LIGHTED DIMLY AND FLICKERINGLY BY 235 DESIRE
TALLOW CANDLES.)
THE TWO BEDROOMS ARE DIMLY LIGHTED BY A TALLOW 247 DESIRE
CANDLE IN EACH.
IN THE KITCHEN, BY THE LIGHT OF A TALLOW CANDLE ON259 DESIRE
THE TABLE, EBEN IS SITTING.
HIS ONCE GREAT MUSCULAR STRENGTH HAS BEEN 575 ICEMAN
DEBAUCHED INTO FLACCID TALLOW.

TALONS

THEY RAISE CLENCHED FISTS OR HANDS DISTENDED INTO 287 LAZARU
THREATENING TALONS.

TAMED

THERE, NATURE IS TAMED, CONSTRAINED TO OBEY AND 86 POET
ADORN.

TAMMANYITE

HOPE BEING A FORMER MINOR TAMMANYITE AND STILL 571 ICEMAN
POSSESSING FRIENDS,

TAMN

(TURNING TO HIM) SHUD UP, YOU TAMN FOOL, PADDY/ 458 CARIBE
TAMN BLACK TIEF/ 462 CARIBE
TAMN FOOL/ 212 HA APE

TAMNED

DOT GOT-TAMNED LIAR, HICKEY. 635 ICEMAN
(BEAMING AT HIM) NO OFFENSE TAKEN, YOU TAMNED 723 ICEMAN
LIMEY/

TAMPERING

WHO'S BEEN TAMPERING WITH MY WHISKEYS 116 JOURNE

TAN

HIS SHOES ARE TAN AND WHITE, HIS SOCKS WHITE SILK, 9 HUGHIE
HIS POINTED TAN BUTTONED SHOES. 575 ICEMAN
HIS FAIR SKIN IS SUNBURNED A REDDISH, FRECKLED 19 JOURNE
TAN.
HER SKIN STILL RETAINS A TRACE OF SUMMER TAN 137 STRANG

TANG

(EAGERLY) SURE TANG. 12 ANNA
YOUR MOTHER SHE TAL YOU SAME TANG IF SHE VAS 28 ANNA
ALIVE.
UH, AY TAL HIM SAME TANG. 43 ANNA
DEN YOU DO RIGHT TANG, EH$ 46 ANNA
HE TAL THE SAME TANG TO GEL EVERY PORT HE GO/ 51 ANNA
(COMMANDINGLY) YOU DON'T DO ONE TANG HE SAY, 55 ANNA
ANNA/
(EAGERLY) YOU SAY RIGHT TANG, ANNA, PY GOLLY/ 65 ANNA
AY TANK DAT'S BEST TANG FOR YOU. 65 ANNA

TANGLED

YOU DO BEAT ALL FOR GETTIN' FOLKS' MINDS ALL 100 BEYOND
TANGLED UP, ROBERT.
BY THE BURDEN OF HIS MASSIVE HEAD WITH ITS HEAVY 556 CROSS
SHOCK OF TANGLED BLACK HAIR.
BEFORE I FELL IN LOVE WITH GORDON SHAW AND ALL 191 STRANG
THIS TANGLED MESS OF LOVE AND

TANGS

AY TAL YOU ALL ABOUT EVERYTANG--AND YOU TAL ME ALL 22 ANNA
TANGS HAPPEN TO YOU.
YOU SEE MANY TANGS YOU DON'T SEE BEFORE. 23 ANNA
IT'S DAT DAMN SAILOR FALLAR LEARN YOU BAD TANGS. 43 ANNA
YOU TANK AY LIKE HEAR DEM TANGSS 61 ANNA
IF DAT IRISH FALLAR DON'T NEVER COME, YOU DON'T 62 ANNA
NEVER TAL ME DEM TANGS.
ALL BAD TANGS DAT HAPPEN TO YOU. 65 ANNA

TANK

BY GOLLY, AY TANK AY'M TOO DRUNK FOR READ DIS 8 ANNA
LETTER FROM ANNA.
AY TANK AY SAT DOWN FOR A MINUTE. 8 ANNA
YUST TANK, ANNA SAY SHE'S COMIN' HERE RIGHT AVAY/ 8 ANNA
AY TANK IT'S BETTER DEM COUSINS KEEP ANNA. 9 ANNA
AY TANK IT'S BETTER ANNA LIVE ON FARM, DEN SHE 9 ANNA
DON'T KNOW DAT OLE DAVIL, SEA,
(SERIOUSLY) AY DON'T TANK DAT. 11 ANNA
'CAUSE AY TANK AY'M NO GOOD FOR HER. 12 ANNA
(HIS FACE BEAMING) WHAT YOU TANK SHE LOOK LIKE, 12 ANNA
MARTHY$
VEN AY TANK AGAIN, IT'S TOO LATE. 21 ANNA
(SLOWLY) AY TANK, AFTER YOUR MO'DER DIE, VEN AY 21 ANNA
VAS AVAY ON VOYAGE,
AY DON'T TANK DEY GOT MUCH FANCY DRINK FOR YOUNG 23 ANNA
GEL IN DIS PLACE, ANNA.
(DULLY) YES, AY TANK. 23 ANNA
IT'S GOOD FOR YOU, AY TANK--LITTLE BIT--FOR GIVE 23 ANNA
YOU APPETITE.
WHAT YOU TANK YOU LIKE FOR DRINK, EH$ 23 ANNA
DON'T YOU TANK SHE VAS POOTY GEL, LARRY$ 24 ANNA
IT AIN'T GOOD FOR YOU STAY OUT HERE IN FOG, AY 25 ANNA
TANK.
VELL, FOG LIFT IN MORNING, AY TANK. 26 ANNA
AY TANK AY'M DAM FOOL FOR BRING YOU ON VOYAGE, 29 ANNA
ANNA.
DEY COME UP BY BOW, AY TANK. 29 ANNA
DAT AIN'T NICE FOR YOUNG GEL, YOU TANK$ 42 ANNA
YOU HAVE GOOD TIME HERE, AY TANK. 42 ANNA
AY SVEAR TO GOD, AY NEVER TANK DAT/ 42 ANNA
(SNORTS SCORNFULLY) PY YIMINY, YOU GO CRAZY, AY 44 ANNA
TANK/
(HIS FACE DARKENING) MAYBE YOU TANK YOU LOVE HIM, 44 ANNA
DEN$
MAYBE--YOU TANK YOU MARRY HIM$ 44 ANNA
AND NOW VEN SHE COME ON FIRST TRIP--YOU TANK AY 46 ANNA
VANT HER LEAVE ME (LONE AGAIN$
YOU TANK AY LAT HER LIFE BE MADE SORRY BY YOU LIKE 47 ANNA
HER MO'DER'S VAS BY ME/
(DARKLY) YOU SEE IF AY'M MAN--MAYBE QUICKER'N YOU 48 ANNA
TANK.
YOU VAS GOING OUT OF HEAD, AY TANK, ANNA. 57 ANNA
AY TANK AY GO ASHORE, TOO. 61 ANNA
(BREAKING DOWN--WEEPING) AY TANK YOU VASN'T DAT 61 ANNA
KIND OF GEL, ANNA.
AY TANK MAYBE IT'S BETTER ANNA MARRY YOU NOW. 61 ANNA
YOU TANK AY LIKE HEAR DEM TANGS$ 61 ANNA
AY'M SICK FROM TANK TOO MUCH ABOUT YOU, ABOUT ME. 64 ANNA
AY TANK DAT'S BEST TANG FOR YOU. 65 ANNA
(SUPPLICATINGLY) AND YOU TANK--MAYBE--YOU FORGIVE 65 ANNA
ME SOMETIMES
AY ONLY BRING YOU BAD LUCK, AY TANK. 65 ANNA
YES, AY TANK IF DAT OLE DAVIL GAT ME BACK SHE 66 ANNA
LEAVE YOU ALONE DEN.
AND AY TANK NOW IT AIN'T NO USE FIGHT WITH SEA. 66 ANNA
GIVE ME FEVER, AY TANK. 66 ANNA
(THEN AFTER A PAUSE) PY GOLLY, AY TANK AY GO LIE 67 ANNA
DOWN.
AY TANK DEN IT'S ALL FAULT OF DAT IRISH FALLAR. 67 ANNA
I TANK SO. 503 VOYAGE
I TANK I GO SEE IF DEY ARE IN BOARDING HOUSE ALL 505 VOYAGE
RIGHT.
I TANK I SHOULD GO AFTER DEM. 505 VOYAGE
I DON' TANK SO. 505 VOYAGE
I DON'T SEE MY MOTHER OR MY BROTHER IN--LET ME 506 VOYAGE
TANK--
I TANK I GO ROUND TO BOARDING HOUSE. 507 VOYAGE
I TANK SOMETING GO WRONG WITH DRISC AND COCKY. 507 VOYAGE

TANKING
AY'VE BEEN TANKING, AND AY GUESS IT VAS ALL MY 65 ANNA
FAULT--

TANKS
(REACHING OUT) TANKS. 244 HA APE
WHO ARE ALL THESE TANKS$ 593 ICEMAN
I'LL TELL HIM WHAT HE CAN DO WITH HIMSELF, HIS 132 MISBEG
BANK-ROLL, AND TIN OIL TANKS.

TANNED
HIS SKIN IS TANNED AND WEATHER-BEATEN. 457 DYNAMO
THE TROPICS HAVE TANNED HIS NATURALLY PASTY FACE 174 EJONES
WITH ITS SMALL
THEIR TANNED BODIES AND MASKS DAUBED AND STAINED 298 LAZARU
WITH WINE LEES,
AND HE'D HAVE DRAGGED AULD HARFORD FROM HIS BURROW156 POET
AND TANNED HIS YANKEE HIDE
HIS SKIN IS TANNED ALMOST BLACK BY HIS YEARS IN 159 STRANG
THE TROPICS.
HER SKIN IS DEEPLY TANNED, HER FIGURE TALL AND 159 STRANG
ATHLETIC,

TANTALIZING
(WITH A TANTALIZING SNEER) SHE'S PURTIER'N YEW 230 DESIRE
BE/

TANTALIZINGLY
AT THIS GESTURE, ABBIE LAUGHS TANTALIZINGLY, 228 DESIRE
HERE THE ADORNMENTS OF EXTREME WEALTH ARE 233 HA APE
TANTALIZINGLY DISPLAYED.
SHE LAUGHS TANTALIZINGLY.) 146 MANSNS
(SHE KISSES HIM TANTALIZINGLY.) 146 MANSNS
(HE PAUSES TANTALIZINGLY) 47 MISBEG

TANTRUM
(HE TURNS FROM HER IN A TANTRUM) TO HELL WITH 479 DYNAMO
YOU/
SHE'S IN A TANTRUM OVER YOUR BEING LATE AGAIN, AND 66 JOURNE
I DON'T BLAME HER.
WHO SMILES AT HIM AFFECTIONATELY AS AT A CHILD IN 359 LAZARU
A TANTRUM.)

TANTRUMS
HE HAS THE FACE OF AN OLD FAMILY HORSE, PRONE TO 576 ICEMAN
TANTRUMS,

TAO
(TO THE PRIESTS OF TAO) PRIEST OF TAO, 434 MARCOM

TAOIST
THE FOREMOST TWO, A CONFUCIAN AND A TAOIST, 433 MARCOM
(THEN AS THE TAOIST, SUBMISSIVELY) 434 MARCOM

TAOISTS
TO ARGUE WITH HIS BUDDHISTS AND TAOISTS AND 359 MARCOM
CONFUCIANS

TAP
AUTOMATICALLY HE BEGINS TO TAP ONE FOOT IN TIME, 259 AHWILD
WHO USED IT TO TAP WATER OUT OF STONES AND FINALLY349 MANCOM
PLANTED IT.
IT WAS ONLY A LOVE TAP TO WAKEN YOUR WITS, SO 5 MISBEG
YOU'LL USE THEM.
WHEN HE'S NOTHING BUT A DRUNKEN BUM WHO NEVER DONE 10 MISBEG
A TAP OF WORK IN HIS LIFE,
SHE HAS STRANGE DEVIOUS INTUITIONS THAT TAP THE 135 STRANG
HIDDEN CURRENTS OF LIFE...

TAPERING
TAPERING OFF. 10 HUGHIE
I'M TAPERING OFF. 644 ICEMAN
I'M TAPERING OFF, AND IN THE MORNING I'LL BE FRESH652 ICEMAN
AS A DAISY.
THEY WERE ONCE BEAUTIFUL HANDS, WITH LONG, 12 JOURNE
TAPERING FINGERS,
HER HANDS ARE SMALL WITH THIN, STRONG, TAPERING 3 MANSNS
FINGERS, AND SHE HAS TINY FEET.
SHE HAS TINY, HIGH-ARCHED FEET AND THIN, TAPERING 68 POET
HANDS.

TAPERS
ORNAMENTS, TAPERS, HAVE BEEN NAILED ON THE TRUNK 347 MARCOM
OR TIED TO THE BRANCHES.

TAPEWORM
YOU'VE GOT A TAPEWORM, THAT'S WHAT I THINK. 220 AHWILD

TAPPED
AS IF SOME HIDDEN STRENGTH IN HIM HAD SUDDENLY 448 DYNAMO
BEEN TAPPED)
AND TAPPED AND TAPPED ENOUGH TO WAKE THE DEAD 597 ICEMAN
THE TIME HE WAS TAPPED FOR AN EXCLUSIVE SENIOR 55 MISBEG
SOCIETY
(WHAT) A FOUNT OF MEANINGLESS ENERGY HE'S 122 STRANG
TAPPED/...

TAPPEE
WELL, WHAT'S ON THE TAPPEE FOR ALL OF YOU TODAYS 189 AHWILD

TAPROOM
THE TAPROOM OF THE TAVERN IN ITS PROSPEROUS DAYS, 7 POET

TAPS
(FINALLY TAPS HIM GENTLY ON THE SHOULDER) 966 DAYS
(HE TAPS HER BUNDLE WITH HIS RIDING WHIP 174 EJONES
SIGNIFICANTLY.)
ROCKY LOOKS AT CHUCK AND TAPS HIS HEAD 674 ICEMAN
DISGUSTEDLY.
(TAPS LEWIS ON THE SHOULDER--SERVILELY APOLOGETIC)700 ICEMAN
(TAPS HICKEY ON THE SHOULDER) 717 ICEMAN
(HE STANDS STARING UP AT THE ROPE AND TAPS IT 579 ROPE
TESTINGLY SEVERAL TIMES WITH HIS
(HE TAPS MADELINE ON THE SHOULDER AND DRAWS HER 178 STRANG

TAR
ITS WALLS AND SLOPING ROOF ARE COVERED WITH TAR 1 MISBEG
PAPER, FADED TO DARK GRAY.

TARNATION
(AFTER A PAUSE) WHAR IN TARNATION D'YE S'POSE HE 209 DESIRE
WENT, SIM$

TART
A TYPICAL COLLEGE «TART» OF THE PERIOD, AND OF THE236 AHWILD
CHEAPER VARIETY,
AND MAKES THIS TART A ROMANTIC EVIL VAMPIRE IN HIS241 AHWILD
EYES.
SAID SHE LOOKED LIKE A TART. 267 AHWILD
IN THE STATE OF MIND HE WAS IN--PICK UP SOME TART.267 AHWILD
HOW ABOUT THAT TART YOU WENT TO BED WITH AT THE 294 AHWILD
PLEASANT BEACH HOUSE$
I GAVE THEM A TART. 284 GGBROW
YUH SKINNY TART/ 230 HA APE
(FURIOUSLY) DE LOUSY TART/ 235 HA APE
I SEE YUH, YUH WHITE-FACED TART, YUH/ 239 HA APE
SO YUH'RE WHAT SHE SEEN WHEN SHE LOOKED AT ME, DE 252 HA APE
WHITE-FACED TART/
SHE MAY BE A TART, BUT-- 614 ICEMAN
(CONSIDERATELY) SURE, DAT'S ALL I MEANT, A TART. 616 ICEMAN
WHEN IT WAS GETTING MIXED UP WITH A TART 615 ICEMAN
BEFORE I'LL TROW IT IN HER FACE SHE WAS A TART. 616 ICEMAN
AND CHUCK AIN'T NEVER GOIN' TO TROW IT IN MY FACE 631 ICEMAN
DAT I WAS A TART, NEIDER.
I MAY BE A TART, BUT I AIN'T A CHEAP OLD WHORE 632 ICEMAN
LIKE YOU/
HEY, YOU DUMB TART, QUIT BANGING THAT BOX/ 654 ICEMAN
ONE REGULAR GUY AND ONE ALL-RIGHT TART GONE TO 683 ICEMAN
HELL/
ANY TART. 712 ICEMAN
I PICKED UP A NAIL FOR SOME TART IN ALTOONA. 713 ICEMAN
IT WAS THE TART THE DETECTIVE AGENCY GOT AFTER ME 719 ICEMAN
WHO PUT IT IN MY MIND.
HIDING IN A BROADWAY HOTEL ROOM WITH SOME FAT 134 JOURNE
TART--HE LIKES THEM FAT--
I MADE A BET WITH ANOTHER SENIOR I COULD GET A 38 MISBEG
TART FROM THE HAYMARKET TO VISIT
IF I WAS A DAINTY, PRETTY TART HE'D BE PROUD I'D 92 MISBEG
RAISE A RUMPUS ABOUT HIM.
FOR GOD'S SAKE, YOU'RE NOT A TART. 127 MISBEG
DIRTY WINDOWPANES, WITH SOME TART SNORING BESIDE 171 MISBEG
YOU--

TARTAR
THAT OF A BEAUTIFUL TARTAR PRINCESS OF TWENTY- 351 MARCOM
THREE.
THAT IS QUITE SUFFICIENT TO CONVERT A TARTAR 363 MARCOM
BARBARIAN/

TARTAR

TARTAR (CONT'D.)
FROM THE DARKNESS COMES THE SOUND OF A SMALL 373 MARCOM
TARTAR KETTLE-DRUM, ITS BEATS
(THE PROSTITUTE ENTERS DRESSED NOW AS A TARTAR. 374 MARCOM
THE TWO TARTAR MERCHANTS ENTER AND THERE IS THE 374 MARCOM
SAME PANTOMIME OF GREETING
THE TWO TARTAR MERCHANTS FALL ASLEEP. 374 MARCOM
MUSIC FROM FULL CHINESE AND TARTAR BANDS CRASHES 377 MARCOM
UP TO A TREMENDOUS BLARING
LOOSE TARTAR TRAVELING DRESS AND LOOK QUITE 429 MARCOM
SHABBY.

TARTARS
SUDDENLY A SHOUT RISES FROM THE LIPS OF ALL THE 375 MARCOM
TARTARS.
(THE TARTARS SIT UP. 376 MARCOM
THEY LOOKED LIKE GREASY TARTARS TO ME. 427 MARCOM
TARTARS CONQUERING ON DRIED MARES' MILK... 67 STRANG

TARTLY
(TARTLY, BUT EVIDENTLY SUPPRESSING HER USUAL SMILE198 AHWILD
WHERE HE IS CONCERNED)
(TARTLY--GIVING HER SON A REBUKING LOOK) 216 AHWILD
(THEN RECOVERING HERSELF--TARTLY) 222 AHWILD
(TARTLY) YOU'RE A HAWK, AIN'T YOUS 464 CARIBE
SHE ADDS TARTLY, HER CONFIDENCE RESTORED AND HER 433 DYNAMO
TEMPER A BIT RUFFLED)
(TARTLY) I CAN'T ABIDE THAT WOMAN/ 68 ELECTR
(TARTLY) REALLY, BILLY, I BELIEVE YOU ARE DRUNK/ 315 GGBROW

TARTS
TARTS, DAT'S WHAT, DE WHOLE BUNCH OF 'EM. 211 HA APE
DEY'SE ALL TARTS, GET ME$ 211 HA APE
TARTS/ 238 HA APE
SKINNY TARTS AND DE BOOBS WHAT MARRY 'EM--MAKIN' 252 HA APE
TARTS CAN'T HANG ON TO DOUGH. 580 ICEMAN
OUR TARTS, MARGIE AND POLL, DEY'RE JUST A SIDE 980 ICEMAN
LINE TO PICK UP SOME EXTRA DOUGH.
SHE HAWLED ME OUT BECAUSE I WAS GOING AROUND WITH 591 ICEMAN
TARTS.
NEVER THOUGHT I'D SEE THE DAY WHEN HARRY HOPE'S 610 ICEMAN
WOULD HAVE TARTS ROOMING IN IT.
WE'RE TARTS, BUT DAT'S ALL. 613 ICEMAN
AND EVELYN ALWAYS KNEW ABOUT THE TARTS I'D BEEN 712 ICEMAN
WITH
AND SHE COULDN'T AFFORD TO RUN A HOME FOR FAT 159 JOURNE
TARTS.
SURE, ALL THE PRETTY LITTLE TARTS ON BROADWAY, NEW 21 MISBEG
YORK.
AND BY THE TIME THE PRETTY LITTLE TARTS, 30 MISBEG
WHAT'S THE MATTER WITH THE TARTS IN TOWN, THEY LET 41 MISBEG
YOU DO IT$
I'LL BET NONE OF HIS TARTS O4 BROADWAY EVER GOT A 95 MISBEG
THOUSANDTH PART OF THAT OUT OF
THEN YOU'LL HAVE ALL THE PRETTY LITTLE TARTS TO 106 MISBEG
COMFORT YOU
DON'T ALL THE PRETTY LITTLE BROADWAY TARTS GET 116 MISBEG
SOUSED WITH YUUS
(STILL BITTER) THAT'S WHO, AND NONE OF YOUR 166 MISBEG
DAMNED TARTS/
NO KINDER AT HEART THAN DOLLAR TARTS/....) 40 STRANG

TASK
I HATE TO GO BEFORE MY TASK IS COMPLETED, ED HE 627 ICEMAN
SOBBED.
HAVING ACCOMPLISHED A TASK--A VICTOR, MORE OR 388 MARCOM
LESS, ACTING THE HERO.
AN IMPOSSIBLE TASK, YOU OBJECT$ 394 MARCOM
HE RELIED ON ME TO PROVE EQUAL TO THE TASK 411 MARCOM
IT WAS AN IMPOSSIBLE TASK. 114 POET

TASTE
ALWAYS TASTE LIKE SOAP TO ME. 255 AHWILD
AND SWALLOWS AS IF AN ACRID TASTE HAD COME INTO 297 AHWILD
HIS MOUTH--
PY GULLY, LARRY, DAT GRUB TASTE GOOD. 19 ANNA
'TISN'T MUCH BUT TWILL SERVE TO TAKE THE BLACK 462 CARIBE
TASTE OUT AV YOUR MOUTHS
TOO FURRIN LOOKIN' FOR MY TASTE. 9 ELECTR
GIVE THEM A TASTE OF MURDER/ 82 ELECTR
I'LL GIVE HIM A TASTE OF HOW *SHENANDOAH* OUGHT T'103 ELECTR
BE SUNG/
HE'LL KNOW BY THE TASTE. 101 JOURNE
WHERE THE HELL DO YOU GET YOUR TASTE IN 134 JOURNE
LITERATURE$
(THICKLY.) WHERE YOU GET YOUR TASTE IN AUTHORS-- 135 JOURNE
THAT DAMNED LIBRARY OF YOURS/
TASTE FIRST OF WHAT HE EATS--EVEN WERE I THE ONE 331 LAZARU
TO GIVE IT TO HIM/
SHE IS DRESSED WITH EXTREME CARE AND GOOD TASTE, 3 MANSNS
ENTIRELY IN WHITE.)
FURNISHED WITHOUT NOTICEABLE GOOD OR BAD TASTE, 43 MANSNS
WITH DISCRIMINATING TASTE AND STYLE NOW, AND 75 MANSNS
EXPENSIVELY.
THE GUESTS GAZE, SMELL, TASTE.) 429 MARCOM
A TASTE OF THAT CLUB YOU'VE GOT, WHEN HE CAME HOME 29 MISBEG
TO YOU PARALYZED.
I AGREE, BUT FOR SOME STRANGE REASON HARDER 51 MISBEG
DOESN'T LOOK FORWARD TO THE TASTE OF
YOU'VE HAD A GOOD TASTE OF BELIEVING HIS WORD, 78 MISBEG
(HE DRINKS HIS WHISKEY AS IF TO WASH A BAD TASTE 129 MISBEG
FROM HIS MOUTH--
TAKE ANOTHER TASTE. 10 POET
IT GAVE HIS PRIDE THE TASTE FOR REVENGE AND AFTER 12 POET
THAT HE WAS ALWAYS LOOKIN' FOR
HAVE ANOTHER TASTE. 15 POET
I'VE NO TASTE FOR ANYTHING. 134 POET
WELL--MAYBE--A TASTE, ONLY. 134 POET
I CAME IN TO SEE HOW YOU WAS, AND BRING YOU A 134 POET
TASTE TO PUT HEART IN YOU.
A TASTE OF WHISKEY WOULD BRING HIM BACK, IF HE'D 153 POET
ONLY TAKE IT, BUT HE WON'T.
I'VE NUT HAD A TASTE FOR HOURS. 175 POET

TASTE (CONT'D.)
WILL YE HAVE A TASTE$ 591 ROPE
AS A RESULT OF THE RURAL TASTE FOR GRANDEUR IN THE 48 STRANG
EIGHTIES.
A ROOM THAT IS A TRIBUTE TO NINA'S GOOD TASTE. 137 STRANG

TASTED
THE BEST SHORE DINNER YOU EVER TASTED AND I DON'T 190 AHWILD
WANT YOU COMING HOME--
I DO NOT EAT NOR DRINK UNTIL YOU HAVE TASTED 301 LAZARU
FIRST.
THE BEST CHICKEN MEDICINE I'VE EVER TASTED. 53 MISBEG

TASTELESS
HUGGING IT, CRAMMING IT DOWN THEIR TASTELESS 113 STRANG
GULLETS/....

TASTELESSNESS
FURNISHED WITH SCRUPULOUS MEDIUM-PRICED 185 AHWILD
TASTELESSNESS OF THE PERIOD.

TASTES
YOU'VE GOT EXTRAVAGANT TASTES, I'M SORRY TO SEE. 245 AHWILD

TASTING
AS IF IT WERE SOME NASTY-TASTING MEDICINE. 237 AHWILD

TASTY
I'LL GO TO THE STORE AND GET SOMETHING TASTY. 39 POET

TAT
(CHILDISHLY PLEASED--GRATEFULLY GIVING TIT FOR 291 AHWILD
TAT)

TATTERED
HIS SKINNY BODY IS CLOTHED IN RAGS AND THERE IS 52 POET
NOTHING UNDER HIS TATTERED COAT

TATTERS
HIS PANTS ARE IN TATTERS. 195 EJONES

TATTLED
EVER SINCE THEM FOOLS ON THE SLOCUM TATTLED 568 CROSS

TATTOO
(SHE RAPS WITH BOTH KNUCKLES IN A FIERCE TATTOO ON135 STRANG
THE TABLE)

TAUGHT
FOR HOW COULD I FORGET THE PRE--PRECEPTS TAUGHT ME232 AHWILD
AT MOTHER'S DYING KNEE.
HE TAUGHT ME TO WAIT AND HOPE WITH HIM--WAIT AND 866 CROSS
HOPE--DAY AFTER DAY.
HE TAUGHT HIMSELF TO TAKE A RATIONALISTIC 534 DAYS
ATTITUDE.
THEY TAUGHT ME TO CALL YOU = AUNT= WHEN I WAS A 521 DIFRNT
KID.
I THOUGHT I'D TAUGHT YOU NEVER TO CRY. 47 ELECTR
HE TAUGHT IT TO ME, YOU MIGHT SAY/ 75 ELECTR
I'D SHOW YOU THEN I HADN'T BEEN TAUGHT TO KILL FOR 89 ELECTR
NOTHING/
WHAT'S THE PRAYER YOU TAUGHT ME--OUR FATHER--$ 322 GGBROW
TAUGHT AT OUR FATHER'S KNEE, SEALED, SIGNED, 243 HA APE
YOU'VE TAUGHT ME THAT LESSON ONLY TOO WELL. 31 JOURNE
THAT LOAFER TAUGHT THEM THAT/ 287 LAZARU
THEY MUST BE A TAUGHT TO LAUGH AGAIN/= 310 LAZARU
WHO TAUGHT THE TREASON THAT FEAR AND DEATH WERE 370 LAZARU
DEAD$
SHE MUST BE TAUGHT TO CONFINE HER ACTIVITIES TO 94 MANSNS
THEIR PROPER SPHERE--
HE HAS TAUGHT US THAT WHATEVER IS IN ONESELF IS 172 MANSNS
GOOD.
(SUDDENLY) THE BUDDHA TAUGHT THAT ONE'S LOVING-- 372 MARCOM
KINDNESS SHOULD EMBRACE ALL
OH, CHU-YIN, MY BEST FRIEND, WAS THE PRAYER I 437 MARCOM
TAUGHT THEM HIS WISDOM.
IT'S TIME I TAUGHT YOU A LESSON. 73 MISBEG
I'M GLAD YOU'VE BEEN TAUGHT A LESSON/ 158 POET
(THEN VINDICTIVELY.) BUT I'VE TAUGHT HER ONE, 158 POET
TOO.
(STUNG--MOCKINGLY) IT WAS YOU WHO TAUGHT ME THE 132 STRANG
SCIENTIFIC APPROACH, DOCTOR/
EACH PERFORMANCE OF YOURS HAS TAUGHT ME SOMETHING.445 WELDED

TAUNT
ELIOT ALSO LOOKS AT HIM, SURPRISED AND 501 DAYS
DISAPPROVING OF THIS TAUNT.
(A SNEERING TAUNT IN HIS VOICE) 509 DAYS
(FLINGING IT AT HIM LIKE A SAVAGE TAUNT) 544 DIFRNT
(HE IMMEDIATELY FEELS ASHAMED OF THIS TAUNT AND 626 ICEMAN
ADDS APOLOGETICALLY)
PARRITT ASKS HIM WITH A SUDDEN TAUNT IN HIS VOICE1646 ICEMAN
(SEEMINGLY UNMOVED BY THIS TAUNT--CALMLY.) 106 POET
AN ABSURD TAUNT, WHEN YOU REALLY HAVE SUCH PRETTY 107 POET
HANDS AND FEET, MY DEAR.
AS IF SHE WANTED TO TAUNT ME/.... 8 STRANG
(THINKING BITTERLY) (IA TAUNT... 14 STRANG

TAUNTING
(CALCULATEDLY TAUNTING) SAY, HONEST, ARE THINGS 238 AHWILD
THAT SLOW UP AT HARVARDS
AS HE PASSES HER, GIVES A SNEERING, TAUNTING 228 DESIRE
CHUCKLE.)
(WITH TAUNTING SCORN) HE DOESN'T LOVE YOU/ 32 ELECTR
AND BECOMES DELIBERATELY TAUNTING) 61 ELECTR
STARES AT HIM FRIGHTENEDLY, HE SMILES AN UGLY 146 ELECTR
TAUNTING SMILE)
(WITH A SUDDEN FLARE OF DELIBERATELY EVIL TAUNTING155 ELECTR
(MORE AND MORE WITH A DELIBERATE, PROVOCATIVE 662 ICEMAN
TAUNTING)
BUT HICKEY HAS REMAINED UNMOVED BY ALL THIS 662 ICEMAN
TAUNTING.
(TURNS ON HIM--WITH A STRANGELY TRIUMPHANT, 117 JOURNE
TAUNTING SMILE.)
(AGAIN TAUNTING BRUTALLY) YOU MAY BE IN HIS PLACE328 LAZARU
SOON/
LOOKING AT LAZARUS WITH TAUNTING CRUELTY) 345 LAZARU
WITH A FORCED, TAUNTING MOCKERY) 366 LAZARU
(CARELESSLY TAUNTING.) BUT IF YOU CARE TO DROP IN103 MANSNS
HERE ONCE IN A WHILE
(LAUGHINGLY, WITH AN UNDERCURRENT OF TAUNTING 111 MANSNS
SATISFACTION.)

TAUNTING (CONT'D.)
MADE MORE EFFECTIVE BY A PROVOCATIVE HINT OF 114 MANSNS
TAUNTING BEHIND IT.)
(SLOWLY, HARDLY ABOVE A WHISPER, BUT WITH A 131 MANSNS
TAUNTING.
(ABRUPTLY HIS TONE BECOMES SLYLY TAUNTING.) 131 MANSNS
(SUDDENLY TAUNTING.) AH, 180 MANSNS
(A ROAR OF COARSE TAUNTING LAUGHTER FROM THE MEN. 368 MARCOM
(ANGERED--WITH TAUNTING BROGUE.) 48 POET
(SHE LEANS TOWARD HIM AND SPEAKS WITH TAUNTING 171 POET
VINDICTIVENESS.
LUST WITH A LOATHSOME JEER TAUNTING MY SENSITIVE 100 STRANG
TIMIDITIES/....

TAUNTINGLY
(TAUNTINGLY) DON'T YE LIKE THE IRISH, YE OLD 49 ANNA
BARONS
HE THROWS THE KNIFE INTO A FAR CORNER OF THE 49 ANNA
ROOM--TAUNTINGLY.
(TAUNTINGLY) SOUR GRAPES, AREN'T THEY, DICKS 103 BEYOND
(AS ABBIE DISAPPEARS IN HOUSE--WINKS AT PETER AND 222 DESIRE
SAYS TAUNTINGLY)
(TAUNTINGLY) WOULDN'T YE LIKE US TO SEND YE BACK 223 DESIRE
SOME SINFUL GOLD.
(TAUNTINGLY) MEBBE--BUT SHE'S BETTER'N YEW. 230 DESIRE
(THEN TAUNTINGLY) WHEN I KISSED YE BACK, MEBBE I 239 DESIRE
THOUGHT 'TWAS SOMEONE ELSE.
(TAUNTINGLY) MEBBE/ 240 DESIRE
(TAUNTINGLY) AN OLD MAID/ 512 DIFRNT
(AS SHE HESITATES-- TAUNTINGLY) 432 DYNAMO
(AS HE STILL HOLDS BACK--TAUNTINGLY) 433 DYNAMO
(GRABBING HER BY THE ARM--TAUNTINGLY) 25 ELECTR
(TAUNTINGLY) IF5 34 ELECTR
(MORE TAUNTINGLY) BUT PERHAPS YOUR LOVE HAS BEEN 41 ELECTR
ONLY A LIE YOU TOLD ME--
(SHE LAUGHS WITH BITTER MOCKERY--THEN TAUNTINGLY) 45 ELECTR
CHRISTINE SMILES TAUNTINGLY) 91 ELECTR
(SHE LAUGHS TAUNTINGLY. 92 ELECTR
(THEN TO HER HUSBAND-TAUNTINGLY) 260 GGBROW
(TAUNTINGLY) I'VE BEEN CELEBRATING 295 GGBROW
(RATHER TAUNTINGLY) GO EASY. 296 GGBROW
(A BIT TAUNTINGLY) THEN YOU--THE I IN YOU-- 307 GGBROW
(MORE TAUNTINGLY) SHE WILL HAVE CHILDREN BY ME/ 307 GGBROW
(TAUNTINGLY) SURE, I WILL. 634 ICEMAN
(A VICTORIOUS GLEAM IN HER EYE--TAUNTINGLY) 634 ICEMAN
(HE GRINS TAUNTINGLY) YOU SHOULD HAVE REMEMBERED 657 ICEMAN
(TAUNTINGLY) YES, I SUPPOSE YOU'D LIKE THAT, 668 ICEMAN
WOULDN'T YOU5
(TAUNTINGLY) UND I CAN GO HOME TO MY COUNTRY/ 677 ICEMAN
(THE PRIEST GOES ON TAUNTINGLY) 283 LAZARU
(TAUNTINGLY) NOW THEIR JAIL-BIRD IS A KING, NO 284 LAZARU
LESS/
(TAUNTINGLY) THE LEGIONS DID SLAY THEM/ 328 LAZARU
(TAUNTINGLY) I WILL BET A STRING OF PEARLS 342 LAZARU
AGAINST YOUR BODY FOR A NIGHT THAT
SHE SPEAKS TAUNTINGLY TO TIBERIUS) 343 LAZARU
(TAUNTINGLY) HA-HA-HA-HA/ 362 LAZARU
(ALMOST TAUNTINGLY.) WE KNOW YOU DIDN'T. 78 MANSNS
(TAUNTINGLY.) MADE HIMS 166 MANSNS
(TAUNTINGLY) YES, LUKE/ 580 ROPE
(ALMOST TAUNTINGLY) THEN GO NOW--IF YOU'RE STRONG87 WELDED
ENOUGH.

TAUNTS
AS HE FINISHES, A CHORUS OF SNEERING TAUNTS 662 ICEMAN
BEGINS.
YOUR LAUGHTER TAUNTS ME/ 358 LAZARU
AFRAID OF HIS TAUNTS... 6 STRANG

TAUT
HER LIPS ARE BLOODLESS, DRAWN TAUT IN A GRIM LINE.170 ELECTR
THE CLERK'S FACE IS TAUT WITH VACANCY. 29 HUGHIE
HER CHEEK BONES STAND OUT, HER MOUTH IS TAUT IN 26 STRANG
HARD LINES OF A CYNICAL SCORN.
HER FACE IS THIN, HER CHEEKS TAUT, HER MOUTH DRAWN158 STRANG
WITH FORCED SMILING.

TAUTENED
LARRY'S FACE HAS TAUTENED, BUT HE PRETENDS HE 701 ICEMAN
DOESN'T HEAR.

TAVERN
=JACK, OH, JACK, WAS A SAILOR LAD AND HE CAME TO A596 ICEMAN
TAVERN FOR GIN.
(SCENE THE DINING ROOM OF MELODY'S TAVERN, IN A 7 POET
VILLAGE A FEW MILES FROM BOSTON.
THE TAPROOM OF THE TAVERN IN ITS PROSPEROUS DAYS, 7 POET
THE TAVERN IS OVER A HUNDRED YEARS OLD. 7 POET
AND FOR SOME YEARS NOW THE TAVERN HAS FALLEN UPON 7 POET
NEGLECTED DAYS.
I SAID YOU WAS OUT FOR A WALK, AND THE TAVERN 18 POET
WASN'T OPEN YET, ANYWAY.
IF I COULD RECONCILE MUSELF TO BEING THE 70 POET
PROPRIETOR OF A TAWDRY TAVERN,
I CAME HERE TO SEEK A PRIVATE INTERVIEW WITH THE 117 POET
PROPRIETOR OF THIS TAVERN.

TAWDRY
DRESSED WITH TAWDRY FLASHINESS. 236 AHWILD
TAWDRY FINERY OF PEASANT STOCK TURNED PROSTITUTE. 14 ANNA
A BACKGROUND IN TAWDRY DISHARMONY WITH THE CLEAR 233 HA APE
LIGHT
DRESSED IN THE USUAL TAWDRY GET-UP. 611 ICEMAN
IF I COULD RECONCILE MUSELF TO BEING THE 70 POET
PROPRIETOR OF A TAWDRY TAVERN,

TAX
DON'T TAX YOUR MEMORY TRYING TO RECALL THOSE 254 AHWILD
ANCIENT DAYS OF YOUR YOUTH.
AND LET EVERYONE CONTRIBUTE ONE ONE-HUNDREDTH PER 237 HA APE
CENT OF THEIR INCOME TAX.
THERE IS A NEW IMPORT TAX AND TRADE IS VERY 348 MARCOM
UNSETTLED.
MY TAX SCHEME, YOUR MAJESTY, 392 MARCOM
AND I REPEALED THE TAX ON LUXURIES. 392 MARCOM

TAX (CONT'D.)
FUR ONE THING I FOUND THEY HAD A HIGH TAX ON 392 MARCOM
EXCESS PROFITS.
THE TAX WASN'T DEMOCRATIC ENOUGH TO MAKE IT PAY/ 392 MAKCOM

TAXED
I HELP TO SUPPORT IT. I'M TAXED TO DEATH-- 144 JOURNE

TAXES
DEBTS TO THIS ONE AND THAT, TAXES, INTEREST 148 BEYOND
UNPAID/
LOOK AT THE TAXES YOU'VE PUT ON 'EM/ 178 EJONES
ABOUT TAXES AND MORTGAGES. 80 JOURNE
WELL, I WAS SENDING IN TO YOUR TREASURY THE TAXES 391 MARCOM
OF YANG-CHAU.
A LAW THAT TAXES EVERY NECESSITY IN LIFE, 392 MARCOM

TAXI
(HIS MIND DARTS BACK FROM A CRUISING TAXI AND 21 HUGHIE
BLINKS BEWILDEREDLY IN THE LIGHT..
WHY, ME AND THE TAXI MAN MADE ENOUGH NOISE GETTING638 ICEMAN
MY BIG SURPRISE IN THE HALL
JUST WANTED TO REMIND YOU TO CALL FOR A TAXI IN 22 STRANG
GOOD TIME.

TAXIDERMY
YESS, HAVEN'T I ALWAYS SAID JOEL IS GUD'S MOST 61 MANSNS
SUCCESSFUL EFFORT IN TAXIDERMY/

TAY
AND RUT-TEN PO-TAY-TOES/ 481 CARDIF

TCHEE
TCHEE-TCHEE, TCHEE-TCHEE, TCHEE-TCHEE, TCHEE- 6 ANNA
TCHEE.=
TCHEE-TCHEE, TCHEE-TCHEE, TCHEE-TCHEE, TCHEE- 12 ANNA
TCHEE.=

TE
THEN DROPS HIS EYES AND LOOKS FURTIVELY AROUND TE 660 ICEMAN
TABLE.

TEA
TEA-PARTY.= I SAYS TO YOU, 546 *ILE
YOU DON'T GET ANY DESSERT OR TEA AFTER LOBSTER, 228 AHWILD
YOU KNOW.
BRINGING HIS PLATE HEAPED WITH FOOD, AND A CUP OF 121 BEYOND
TEA.
AND THE DISH-WATHER THEY DISGUISE WID THE NAME AV 480 CARDIF
TEA/
U' SHUAY TEA-KETTLES, THE OLD DAYS IS DYIN', AND 105 ELECTR
WHERE'LL YOU AN' ME BE THEN5
SHE KEPT LOOKING AROUND, AND SAID SHE'D LIKE A CUP 18 POET
OF TEA.
SHE DIDN'T WANT TEA AT ALL, BUT ONLY AN EXCUSE TO 18 POET
STAY.
CARRYING A TRAY WITH TOAST, EGGS, BACON, AND TEA. 55 POET
IT'S TIME FOR TEA... 21 STRANG
MOTHER IS WAITING TEA...)) 21 STRANG

TEACH
I'M HOPING BEFORE YOU LEAVE NEW HAVEN THEY'LL FIND192 AHWILD
TIME TO TEACH YOU
AND THEN THERE ARE ALL THE BOYS AND GIRLS I TEACH 214 AHWILD
EVERY YEAR.
THEN I'M GOING TO START LEARNING RIGHT AWAY, AND 102 BEYOND
YOU'LL TEACH ME, WON'T YOUS
TO SORTA TALK TO AND SHOW THINGS TO, AND TEACH, 103 BEYOND
KINDA,
THAT'LL TEACH YOU TO SMUGGLE RUM ON A SHIP AND 473 CARIBE
START A RIOT.
WE NEED A NEW LEADER WHO WILL TEACH US THAT IDEAL,543 DAYS
(GIGGLING) I WILL--IF YOU'LL TEACH ME. 521 DIFRNT
AND DENNY'S GOIN' TO TEACH ME. 537 DIFRNT
SOME WAY THAT SHE'D TEACH YOU TO KNOW HER...) 676 DYNAMO
AND TEACH SOME OF DEM ENGLISH BEFO' I KIN TALK TO 179 EJONES
'EM5
ALWAYS TRYING TO TEACH ME MANNERS/ 144 ELECTR
AND WE'LL HAVE CHILDREN AND LOVE THEM AND TEACH 147 ELECTR
THEM TO LOVE LIFE
THAT'LL TEACH HER THE VALUE OF A DOLLAR/ 260 GGBROW
LITTLE BY LITTLE I'LL TEACH HER TO KNOW ME, 307 GGBROW
DID THE SOCIOLOGY YOU TOOK AT COLLEGE TEACH YOU 218 HA APE
THAT--
YOU TEACH YOURSELF NEVER TO FORGET A NAME OR A 624 ICEMAN
FACE.
THAT'LL TEACH YOU TO BE MISNAMIM' A MAN, YE SNEAK.527 INZONE
I'LL GIVE YOU A THRASHING THAT'LL TEACH YOU--/ 128 JOURNE
(CONTEMPTUOUSLY) WELL, MAYBE HE CAN TEACH YOU TO 303 LAZARU
LAUGH AT FEAR.
I HAVE HEARD YOU TEACH THAT FOLLY. 340 LAZARU
BUT THIS IS A MORAL LESSON TO TEACH YOU 429 MAKCOM
HE'LL TEACH YOU THE TRADE. 5 MISBEG
OH, THAT'LL TEACH HIM TO DOUBLE-CROSS HIS FRIENDS/ 95 MISBEG
(LAUGHING AGAIN) AND HERE'S WHAT'LL BE THE 95 MISBEG
GREATEST JOKE TO TEACH HIM A LESSON.
I'LL TEACH HIM WHO'S THE JUKER/ 99 MISBEG
THAT'LL TEACH YOU TO POUR OUT BATHS INSTEAD OF 113 MISBEG
DRINKS.
THE DAMNED OLD SCHEMER, I'LL TEACH HIM TO-- 134 MISBEG
HE'LL TEACH YOU TO KEEP YOUR PLACE, AND GOD HELP 17 POET
YOU.
I HAVE TRIED TO TEACH THE WAITRESS NOT TO SNATCH 98 POET
PLATES FROM THE TABLE.
FAITH, I'LL GIVE YOU A BOX ON THE EAR THAT'LL TEACH176 POET
YOU RESPECT,
THAT'LL TEACH YOU, ME PROUD SARA/ 179 POET
I HOPE I'LL TEACH YOU NOT TO BE SO COCKSURE IN 82 STRANG
FUTURE.
I'LL TEACH HER/...)) 147 STRANG
TEACH ME TO BE RESIGNED TO BE AN ATOM/...)) 199 STRANG

TEACHER
SHE CONFORMS OUTWARDLY TO THE CONVENTIONAL TYPE OF187 AHWILD
OLD-MAID SCHOOL TEACHER.
RATHER PRIM-LOOKING WOMAN OF FIFTY-FIVE WHO HAD 94 BEYOND
ONCE BEEN A SCHOOL TEACHER.
TEACHER SAYS ABOUT HER VOICE, 531 INZONE

TEACHER

TEACHER (CONT'D.)
MOTHER ELIZABETH AND MY MUSIC TEACHER 103 JOURNE
THEN IF THERE IS NO DEATH, O TEACHER, TELL ME WHY 308 LAZARU
I LOVE TO KILLS

TEACHERS
ALL HIS TEACHERS TOLD US WHAT A FINE BRAIN HE HAD.110 JOURNE
OR TEACHERS OF LAUGHTER IF THEY WISH TO LAUGH 329 LAZARU
LUNGS/

TEACHES
JESUS TEACHES TO BE KIND. 285 LAZARU
(HYSTERICALLY) HE TEACHES TO GIVE UP ALL AND 285 LAZARU
FOLLOW HIM/
AND HE TEACHES PEOPLE TO LAUGH AT DEATH. 302 LAZARU

TEACHIN'
THEY'RE TEACHIN' ME. 246 DESIRE

TEACHING
NOT ABLE TO GO BACK TEACHING SCHOOL ON ACCOUNT OF 545 *ILE
BEING DAVE KEENEY'S WIFE.
YOU NEED REST AFTER TEACHING A PACK OF WILD 212 AHWILD
INDIANS OF KIDS ALL YEAR.
FOR TEACHING THAT WE SHOULD HAVE A NOBLER AIM FOR 543 DAYS
OUR LIVES
AND I'VE BEEN TEACHING MARY HOW TO TAKE CARE OF 17 STRANG
YOU.

TEACHINGS
BUT WHERE ARE THE HUNDRED WISE MEN OF THE SACRED 378 MARCOM
TEACHINGS OF LAO-TSEU AND

TEAKITTLE
BEFORE THE AULD TEAKITTLE SANK. 481 CARDIF

TEAM
TO TIGER INN AND HE'S FULLBACK ON THE FOOTBALL 283 AHWILD
TEAM--

TEAM'D
THE TEAM'D RUN AWAY, I'LL BET. 82 BEYOND

TEAR
HIS IRON SPIRIT WEAKENS AS HE LOOKS AT HER TEAR- 549 *ILE
STAINED FACE.)
(SHE TURNS AWAY, WIPING A TEAR FURTIVELY--THEN 214 AHWILD
ABRUPTLY CHANGING THE SUBJECT)
A PRETTY BUT SICKLY AND ANEMIC-LOOKING CHILD WITH 116 BEYOND
A TEAR-STAINED FACE.
(HE BLINKS BACK ONE TEAR, WIPING HIS SLEEVE ACROSS264 DESIRE
HIS NOSE.)
PURR, SCRATCH, TEAR, KILL, GORGE YOURSELF AND BE 220 HA APE
HAPPY--
THEY WOULD TEAR DOWN SOCIETY, PUT THE LOWEST SCUM 244 HA APE
IN THE SEATS OF THE MIGHTY.
HER HOUND FACE SHOWING MORE OF THE WEAR AND TEAR 615 ICEMAN
OF HER TRADE THAN THEIRS.
YOU'LL ONLY STEP ON IT AND TEAR IT AND GET IT 172 JOURNE
DIRTY DRAGGING IT ON THE FLOOR.
AND ALL THE WORLD IS BITTER AS A TEAR. 173 JOURNE
SHE WILL TEAR YOU TO PIECES AND DEVOUR YOU." 111 MANSNS
TEAR THIS HOUSE APART, DEVOUR EACH OTHER, IF YOU 130 MANSNS
MUST!
WE WOULD TEAR DOWN THEIR CHRISTIAN IDOLS AND SET 422 MARCOM
UP THE IMAGE OF THE BUDDHA?
WHEN YOU'D COME HOME DRUNK AND WANT TO TEAR DOWN 18 MISBEG
THE HOUSE FOR THE FUN OF IT.
I REMEMBERED THE LAST TWO LINES OF A LOUSY TEAR- 150 MISBEG
JERKER SONG I'D HEARD WHEN I WAS
SARA HAS LIFTED HER TEAR-STAINED FACE FROM HER 175 POET
HANDS AND IS STARING AT HIM
YE'D NEVER SHED A TEAR THE RIST AV YOUR LOIFE. 498 VOYAGE
AND WE'LL TORTURE AND TEAR, AND CLUTCH FOR EACH 480 WELDED
OTHER'S SOULS/

TEARFUL
(LIFTS A TEARFUL, HUMBLY GRATEFUL, PATHETIC FACE 259 AHWILD
TO HER--
SHE HAS EVIDENTLY HAD NO REST YET FROM A 263 AHWILD
SLEEPLESS, TEARFUL NIGHT.
(SHE SUDDENLY JUMPS TO HER FEET IN A TEARFUL FURY)284 AHWILD
(THEN WITH A SUDDEN TEARFUL GAIETY) 489 WELDED

TEARFULLY
(ALMOST TEARFULLY) GEE, I HATE TO GO HOME AND 277 AHWILD
CATCH HELL.
(ALMOST TEARFULLY) BUT YOU OUGHT TO HAVE KNOWN PA283 AHWILD
MADE ME--
(THEN TEARFULLY) AND THERE I WAS RIGHT AT THAT 284 AHWILD
TIME LYING IN BED NOT ABLE TO
(TEARFULLY) NO? NO, NO, DADA, NO? 129 BEYOND
(HOPE SUDDENLY BECOMES ALMOST TEARFULLY 650 ICEMAN
SENTIMENTAL)
(TEARFULLY INDIGNANT) AIN'T YUH GOIN' TO WISH US 683 ICEMAN
HAPPINESS
(TEARFULLY) AND ME, DARLINGS 284 LAZARU
(CRIES TEARFULLY) FORGIVE ME, LAZARUS/ 334 LAZARU

TEARIN'
WE'LL BE KICKIN' UP AN' TEARIN' AWAY DOWN THE 221 DESIRE
ROAD/

TEARING
(HE CHOKES, HIS FACE CONVULSED WITH AGONY, HIS 489 CARDIF
HANDS TEARING AT HIS SHIRT-FRONT.
TEARING THE SHADE.) 224 DESIRE
THE FRONT DOOR IS FLUNG OPEN AND SMALL COMES 134 ELECTR
TEARING OUT
HA--HA--TEARING HIS BEARD AND STAMPING WITH RAGE)282 LAZARU
TEARING THEIR HAIR SOME EVEN BEATING THEIR HEADS 290 LAZARU
ON THE GROUND
HANDS IN EVERY TENSE ATTITUDE OF STRIKING, 291 LAZARU
CLUTCHING, TEARING ARE SEEN UPRAISED.
TO START US CLAWING AND TEARING AT EACH OTHER'S 170 MANSNS
HEARTS
THAT YOU WOULD GO ON WITH YOUR HORRIBLE DUEL, 174 MANSNS
CLAWING AND TEARING EACH OTHER,
CLAWING AND TEARING AT EACH OTHER LIKE TWO DRUNKEN174 MANSNS
DRABS.
RENT IN TWAIN BY YOUR TEARING GREEDY CLAWS! 174 MANSNS

TEARING (CONT'D.)
TEARING HIS HAIR IN A PERFECT FRENZY OF BALKED 359 MARCOM
INSPIRATION.
TEARING YOUR HEART WITH DIRTY FINGER NAILS/... 40 STRANG

TEARS
AS IF HE WERE ABOUT TO BREAK INTO TEARS. 208 AHWILD
THEN GIRDS UP HIS COURAGE AND TEARS IT OPEN AND 208 AHWILD
BEGINS TO READ SWIFTLY.
(WIPING THE TEARS FROM HER EYES--DEFIANTLY) 227 AHWILD
(DESOLATELY, ALMOST ON THE VERGE OF TEARS) 251 AHWILD
(SUDDENLY TURNS TOWARD LILY--HIS VOICE CHOKED WITH258 AHWILD
TEARS--
(SHE BURSTS INTO TEARS.) 260 AHWILD
(ON THE VERGE OF HUMILIATED TEARS) 278 AHWILD
(GOES OVER AND PATS HER ON THE SHOULDER, THE TEARS 62 ANNA
RUNNING DOWN HIS FACE)
(ON THE POINT OF TEARS) I COULDN'T BEAR IT/ 74 ANNA
(ON THE VERGE OF TEARS) IT'S ALL RIGHT FOR YOU TO 96 BEYOND
TALK.
ANDREW SOOTHES HIS MOTHER WHO IS ON THE VERGE OF 106 BEYOND
TEARS.)
(TEARS OF RAGE STARTING TO HIS EYES--HOARSELY) 107 BEYOND
DOLEFUL EXPRESSION OF BEING CONSTANTLY ON THE 112 BEYOND
VERGE OF COMFORTLESS TEARS.
(WIPING TEARS FROM HER EYES WITH HER HANDKERCHIEF1114 BEYOND
(ON THE VERGE OF TEARS OR WEAKNESS) 148 BEYOND
(ON THE VERGE OF TEARS AT HER INABILITY TO KEEP 471 CARIBE
THEM IN THE FORECASTLE OR MAKE
A GUST OF AIR TEARS DOWN INTO THE ROOM. 567 CROSS
AND WHEN IT RAINS THEIR TEARS TRICKLE DOWN 202 DESIRE
MONOTONOUSLY AND ROT ON THE SHINGLES.
IN A VAIN EFFORT TO CONCEAL TRACES OF HER TEARS. 505 DIFRNT
(SUDDENLY BURSTING INTO HYSTERICAL TEARS) 537 DIFRNT
(TEARS OF MORTIFICATION AND GENUINE HURT COME TO 442 DYNAMO
HER EYES--
(FORCES BACK HER TEARS AND JUMPS UP) 443 DYNAMO
(LIGHT FINALLY TEARS HIS COAT FROM REUBEN'S GRIP 453 DYNAMO
TEARS OUT A DRAWER AND GETS THE REVOLVER 487 DYNAMO
(HE TEARS OFF HIS COAT AND FLINGS IT AWAY FROM 193 EJUNES
HIM.
TEARS OFF A SLIP OF PAPER AND WRITES TWO WORDS ON 35 ELECTR
IT.
(AWKWARDLY MOVED) TEARS ARE QUEER TOKENS OF 47 ELECTR
HAPPINESS/
(SHE BURSTS INTO TEARS AND HIDES HER FACE AGAINST 47 ELECTR
HIS SHOULDER.)
(OBEDIENTLY FORCING BACK HER TEARS. 47 ELECTR
(SHE TEARS HERSELF FROM HIS ARMS. 112 ELECTR
(HYSTERICAL TEARS COME TO HER EYES. 119 ELECTR
(TEARS HER HAND AWAY--VIOLENTLY) 124 ELECTR
(SHE TEARS HER EYES FROM THEIRS AND, TURNING AWAY,139 ELECTR
(HER VOICE TREMBLES AND SHE SEEMS ABOUT TO BURST 159 ELECTR
INTO TEARS)
(HE SUDDENLY TEARS OFF HIS MASK--IN A PASSIONATE 268 GGBROW
AGONY)
UNTIL AT LAST THROUGH TWO TEARS I WATCHED HER DIE 282 GGBROW
(HE TEARS THE MASK FROM HIS FACE. 292 GGBROW
(HE TEARS OFF HIS MASK AND REVEALS A SUFFERING 305 GGBROW
FACE THAT IS RAVAGED AND HAGGARD AND
(HE TEARS THE PLAN INTO FOUR PIECES. 317 GGBROW
THE LAUGHTER OF HEAVEN SOWS EARTH WITH A RAIN OF 322 GGBROW
TEARS.
(TEARS COME TO HIS EYES. 599 ICEMAN
(SHE PUTS HER ARM AROUND PEARL--ON THE VERGE OF 654 ICEMAN
TEARS HERSELF)
SHE SEEMS TO HAVE FORGOTTEN THE TEARS WHICH ARE 91 JOURNE
STILL IN HER EYES.)
(HIS FACE WORKS AND HE BLINKS BACK TEARS--WITH 112 JOURNE
QUIET INTENSITY.)
(HIS VOICE TREMBLES, HIS EYES BEGIN TO FILL WITH 118 JOURNE
TEARS.)
NOT FOR VAIN TEARS I WENT UP AT THAT HOUR. 133 JOURNE
(HE WIPES TEARS FROM HIS EYES.) 148 JOURNE
I CAN REMEMBER HER HUGGING AND KISSING US AND 148 JOURNE
SAYING WITH TEARS OF JOY RUNNING
OR LIKE THE DREAMY TEARS OF A TROLLOP SPATTERING 152 JOURNE
IN A PUDDLE OF STALE BEER ON A
SOBER. NOT THE MAUDLIN TEARS OF DRUNKENNESS.) 162 JOURNE
(BLINKING BACK TEARS HIMSELF.) 162 JOURNE
I BEGGED THEM TO STAY--WITH TEARS IN MY EYES/ 286 LAZARU
(BUT AT THIS MOMENT A NAZARENE YOUTH, EXHAUSTED BY290 LAZARU
GRIEF AND TEARS,
(ALMOST IN TEARS, BUT IF HE KNOWS A CHARM AGAINST303 LAZARU
DEATH
WITH ANGRY BOYISH RESENTFULNESS THAT IS CLOSE TO 332 LAZARU
TEARS)
TEARS MAY BECOME A WOMAN WHILE SHE'S YOUNG. 5 MANSNS
(HE SWALLOWS AS IF HE WERE STRANGLING AND TEARS 143 MANSNS
HIS EYES FROM HERS--STAMMERS.)
THEN SUDDENLY TEARS HER EYES FROM THE MIRROR 144 MANSNS
(SHE SUDDENLY SHIVERS WITH REPULSION AND TEARS HER144 MANSNS
EYES FROM THE MIRROR
SIMON TEARS HIS EYES FROM SARA.) 150 MANSNS
WILD HYSTERICAL TEARS. 161 MANSNS
(TAKES IT AND CALMLY TEARS IT UP) 353 MARCOM
MY HEART IS BITTER AND TEARS BLUR MY EYES. 384 MARCOM
(TURNS TO HIM--ON THE VERGE OF TEARS-- 387 MARCOM
REBELLIOUSLY)
TEARS COME TO HIS EYES. 389 MARCOM
I FEEL THERE ARE TEARS IN YOUR EYES. 401 MARCOM
THE TEARS STREAMING DOWN HER FACE AS HE LOOKS AT 413 MARCOM
IT.)
(BROKENLY) MY EYES FILLED WITH TEARS. 426 MARCOM
OUR SOBS STIFLE US, OUR TEARS WET THE GROUND, 436 MARCOM
(HE WEEPS, HIS TEARS FALLING ON HER CALM WHITE 439 MARCOM
FACE.)
(HER VOICE HAS SOFTENED, AND SHE BLINKS BACK 7 MISBEG
TEARS.

TEARS (CONT'D.)
(GRABS IT AND TEARS IT FROM HIS HAND WITH ONE 61 MISBEG
POWERFUL TWIST--FIERCELY)
LAND THAT'S WATERED WITH THE TEARS OF STARVING 62 MISBEG
WIDOWS AND ORPHANS--
SHE TEARS OFF THE FLOWER PINNED TO HER BOSOM AND 71 MISBEG
THROWS IT IN THE CORNER)
(ON THE VERGE OF ANGRY TEARS) 74 MISBEG
(TENSELY, ON THE VERGE OF TEARS) 84 MISBEG
(SHE ENDS UP ON THE VERGE OF BITTER HUMILIATED 96 MISBEG
TEARS.)
(BEWILDEREDLY--ON THE VERGE OF TEARS.) 37 POET
(INSTANTLY ON THE VERGE OF GRATEFUL TEARS.) 39 POET
SARA HIDES HER FACE ON HER SHOULDER, ON THE VERGE 65 POET
OF TEARS.)
AND THERE ARE TEARS OF HUMILIATED PRIDE IN HER 123 POET
EYES.)
TEARS WELL FROM HER EYES.) 137 POET
WEEP GREAT TEARS AND APPEAL TO HIS HONOR TO MARRY 171 POET
YOU AND SAVE YOURS.
(MARY'S TEARS IMMEDIATELY CEASE. 589 ROPE
(ON THE VERGE OF DRUNKEN TEARS) 598 ROPE
(HIS FACE TWITCHES AS IF HE WERE ON THE VERGE OF 10 STRANG
TEARS--HE THINKS DESPERATELY)
NO MORE GORDON, GORDON, GORDON. LOVE AND PRAISE 22 STRANG
AND TEARS, ALL FOR GORDON/...
(TEARS COME TO HIS EYES SUDDENLY 28 STRANG
(TEARS IT OFF--HANDS IT TO EVANS) 33 STRANG
THEN TEARS THE SHEET OUT OF THE MACHINE WITH AN 67 STRANG
EXCLAMATION OF DISGUST.
HE TEARS HIMSELF AWAY FROM HER. 97 STRANG
(HE TURNS AWAY, HIS FACE IS SCREWED UP IN HIS 133 STRANG
EFFORT TO HOLD BACK HIS TEARS.
ON THE VERGE OF TEARS YET STUBBORNLY DETERMINED) 149 STRANG
TEARS THE RIGGING OFF AND THROWS THE DISMANTLED 150 STRANG
HULL AT DARNELL'S FEET)
(HIS LIPS TREMBLE, TEARS COME TO HIS EYES) 162 STRANG
THERE AREN'T MANY TEARS LEFT... 190 STRANG
ON THE VERGE OF TEARS HERSELF) 475 WELDED
(BURSTING INTO TEARS) BECAUSE I LOVE YOU/ 485 WELDED

TEASE
HE'D TEASE AN OLD WOMAN TO GET MONEY OUT OF HER, 528 DIFRNT
AND HER ALONE IN THE WORLD.
WHOM THEY LIKE TO TEASE AND SPOIL. 611 ICEMAN
DON'T TEASE HER NOW/ 427 MARCOM
SHE ONLY PUTS ON THE BROGUE TO TEASE YOU. 41 POET
YOU'RE A GREAT TEASE, SARA. 45 POET

TEASIN'
JEST JOKIN' AN' TEASIN'.... 233 DESIRE

TEASING
STOP YOUR EVERLASTING TEASING, YOU TWO. 191 AHWILD
(THEN WITH A TEASING SMILE AT RICHARD) 220 AHWILD
I'D GIVE YOU A GOOD PIECE OF MY MIND FOR TEASING 231 AHWILD
NAT LIKE THAT.
AND THEN ALL OF US TEASING HIM AND HURTING HIS 265 AHWILD
FEELINGS ALL DAY--
(TEASING LOVINGLY) EMMER DON'T KNOW YOU LIKE I 513 DIFRNT
(PLEASED BUT AMUSED--TEASING HER AS HE WOULD A BIG429 DYNAMO
CHILD)
(WITH A TEASING SMILE) ADA, I'VE GOT A BIG 459 DYNAMO
SURPRISE FOR YOU.
(WITH A TEASING GLANCE AT HER BROTHER) 13 ELECTR
SINCE HAZEL'S TEASING STATEMENT, 14 ELECTR
(SHE LAUGHS THEN WITH A TEASING AIR) 87 ELECTR
(IMPRESSED BUT FORCING A TEASING TONE) 135 ELECTR
OF COURSE, HE KNOWS YOU'RE ONLY TEASING ME--BUT 145 ELECTR
YOU SHOULDN'T GO ON LIKE THAT.
ORIN KEEPS TEASING THAT I WAS FLIRTING WITH THAT 147 ELECTR
NATIVE HE SPOKE ABOUT.
(WITH A TEASING LAUGH) I'M AFRAID WE'RE 148 ELECTR
INTERRUPTING, ORIN.
(IGNORES THIS--RECOGNIZING HIM NOW, BURSTS INTO 592 ICEMAN
HIS CHILDISH TEASING GIGGLE)
AS IF HE WERE PLAYFULLY TEASING CHILDREN) 627 ICEMAN
(SMILES NOW WITH TEASING AFFECTION.) 15 JOURNE
I'VE BEEN TEASING YOUR FATHER ABOUT HIS SNORING. 20 JOURNE
ARE YOU POURING COALS OF FIRE ON MY HEAD FOR 29 JOURNE
TEASING YOU ABOUT SNORING
(HASTILY.) I'M ONLY TEASING, DEAR. 42 JOURNE
(IN A FORCED TEASING TONE.) GOOD HEAVENS, HOW 59 JOURNE
DOWN IN THE MOUTH YOU LOOK.
(TEASING INDIFFERENTLY.) OH, I'M SURE YOU'LL HOLD 83 JOURNE
IT WELL.
I'VE ALWAYS HAD SUCH FUN TEASING HIM ABOUT IT. 99 JOURNE
(SHE GIVES A TEASING, GIRLISH LAUGH.) 99 JOURNE
(WITH A FEEBLE ATTEMPT AT TEASING.) 115 JOURNE
TEASING TONE BUT WITH AN INCREASING UNDERCURRENT 120 JOURNE
OF RESENTMENT.)
NOW HE GRINS, TEASING AFFECTIONATELY.) 128 JOURNE
(HE GRINS WITH AFFECTIONATE TEASING.) 132 JOURNE
TEASING THEM, SIFTING INTO THE CROWD, THEIR CHORUS306 LAZARU
IN A HALF CIRCLE.
FORGIVE MY TEASING. 39 MANSNS
AND SHE BURSTS INTO NATURAL TEASING LAUGHTER.) 40 MANSNS
STOP TEASING NOW AND TELL ME. 89 MANSNS
(WITH A SOFT TEASING LAUGH.) 99 MANSNS
(SHE PATS HIS HAIR--WITH A TEASING LAUGH.) 106 MANSNS
(WITH A TEASING LAUGH, RUFFLING HIS HAIR 106 MANSNS
PLAYFULLY.)
(SPEAKS TO SIMON WITH AN AMUSED, TEASING SMILE.) 127 MANSNS
TAKE A POSSESSIVE GRATIFICATION IN TEASING A YOUNG128 MANSNS
BASHFUL SON.
(WITH A CHANGE TO A LOVER'S PLAYFUL TEASING--PATS 160 MANSNS
HER CHEEK.)
(THEN RESUMING HIS TONE OF TENDER TEASING) 385 MARCOM
(THEN CONTROLLING HIMSELF--FORCING AN AMUSED 401 MARCOM
TEASING TONE)

TEASING (CONT'D.)
(HALF SMILING AND HALF WEEPING AT HIS TEASING) 402 MARCOM
DON'T BE TEASING. 16 MISBEG
(WITH A TEASING SMILE WHICH IS HALF SAD) 19 MISBEG
I WAS TEASING YOU. 106 MISBEG
(REVERTING TO A TEASING TONE) 135 MISBEG
(FORCES A TEASING SMILE AND A LITTLE OF HER OLD 175 MISBEG
MANNER)
(TURNS TO HIM, FORCING A TEASING SMILE) 177 MISBEG
(FORCING HER TEASING MANNER AGAIN) 177 MISBEG
LEAVE SIMON OUT OF YOUR TEASING. 17 POET
(PLACATINGLY.) CAN'T YOU TAKE A BIT OF TEASING, 17 POET
SARA
(WITH A TEASING SMILE.) I'M THINKIN' IT ISN'T ON 28 POET
NEILAN ALONE
(GAILY TEASING.) I HAD IT WITH ME, MOTHER, 143 POET
(SHE PAUSES--THEN TEASING LOVINGLY.) 149 POET
(TRYING TO ROUSE HER--IN A TEASING TONE.) 182 POET
THEN SOOTHINGLY WITH A TEASING INCONGRUOUS GAIETY) 44 STRANG
(SWINGING BUT FORCING A TEASING AIR) 114 STRANG
(SADLY TEASING) IF YOU'VE WAITED THAT LONG, 197 STRANG
CHARLIE,

TEASINGLY
(TEASINGLY) BET I KNOW, JUST THE SAME/ 187 AHWILD
(TEASINGLY) I CAN TELL YOU, IF HE WON'T. 190 AHWILD
(TEASINGLY) DID YOU KISS ELSIE GOOD NIGHTS 255 AHWILD
(SMILING TEASINGLY) I CAN SEE WHERE YOU'RE 288 AHWILD
BECOMING CORRUPTED BY THOSE BOOKS.
(THEN SMILING TEASINGLY) WELL, IF YOU LOVE ME SO 529 DAYS
MUCH, PROVE IT BY TELLING ME.
(THEN TEASINGLY) BUT DO YOU KNOW WHAT I THINK IS 533 DAYS
BEHIND ALL THIS SOLICITUDE OF
ROGERS SAYS TEASINGLY) 510 DIFRNT
(COMES AND PUTS AN ARM AROUND HIS SHOULDER-- 431 DYNAMO
TEASINGLY)
(TEASINGLY) BUT YOU HAVEN'T SAID YET YOU'RE GLAD 143 ELECTR
TO SEE ME/
(TEASINGLY) NOW, I'M BEGINNING TO GET JEALOUS, 147 ELECTR
TOO.
(WITH A WINK AT MARGIE--TEASINGLY) 612 ICEMAN
(TEASINGLY) JEES, WHAT'S THE DIFFERENCE--S 613 ICEMAN
(TEASINGLY) MY, HARRY/ SUCH LANGUAGE/ 615 ICEMAN
(SHE LAUGHS TEASINGLY--THEN PATS LARRY ON THE 635 ICEMAN
SHOULDER AFFECTIONATELY)
(TEASINGLY.) OH YOU/ 14 JOURNE
(TEASINGLY.) YES, IT'S TERRIBLE THE WAY WE ALL 18 JOURNE
PICK ON YOU, ISN'T ITS
(TURNING TO EDMUND BUT AVOIDING HIS EYES-- 25 JOURNE
TEASINGLY AFFECTIONATE.)
(SHE PATS HIS HAND--TEASINGLY.) 110 JOURNE
(HE SMILES TEASINGLY AND SIGHS.) 136 JOURNE
(TEASINGLY.) OH, YOU WERE ALWAYS YOUR OWN 13 MANSNS
AUDIENCE, TOO.
DEBORAH'S REMAINS TEASINGLY MOCKING.) 69 MANSNS
(WITH A STRANGE EAGERNESS--TEASINGLY.) 79 MANSNS
TEASINGLY.) 80 MANSNS
(SHE LAUGHS SOFTLY--TEASINGLY.) 99 MANSNS
(SHE SMILES TEASINGLY.) 103 MANSNS
(SHE LAUGHS TEASINGLY.) 127 MANSNS
(PLAINLY ENJOYING THIS, MOVES HER BODY 141 MANSNS
SEDUCTIVELY--TEASINGLY.)
SHE LAUGHS TEASINGLY. 143 MANSNS
TEASINGLY.) NOW, JOEL DARLIN', YOU SHOULDN'T LOOK143 MANSNS
AT ME LIKE THAT.
(TEASINGLY) YOUR SON AND YOUR MONEY ARE SOON 365 MARCOM
PARTED, BROTHER.
(GRINNING TEASINGLY) YOU'RE TOO YOUNG. 371 MARCOM
(TEASINGLY) WHAT DESPAIR? 385 MARCOM
(SMILING AT HIM AS AT A BOY--TEASINGLY) 399 MARCOM
(TEASINGLY) IF IT'S WHATS 124 MISBEG
(HE TURNS TO SMILE AT HER TEASINGLY) 124 MISBEG
(TEASINGLY) YOU AND YOUR LOVERS, MESSALINA--WHEN 134 MISBEG
YOU'VE NEVER--
(TEASINGLY.) AND WHAT DID YOU DO$ 65 POET
(A STRANGE, TENDERLY AMUSED SMILE ON HER LIPS-- 139 POET
TEASINGLY.)
(TEASINGLY.) I'M HIS NURSE, AREN'T I$ 142 POET
(SHE LAUGHS TEASINGLY) DEAR OLD CHARLIE/ 21 STRANG
(TEASINGLY) HELLO/ 51 STRANG
(STANDS STILL AND LOOKS AT HIM TEASINGLY) 51 STRANG
(TEASINGLY) I OUGHT TO CUT YOU DEAD AFTER THE 79 STRANG
SHAMEFUL WAY YOU'VE IGNORED US/
(TEASINGLY) BUT I HEARD YOU WERE +TAKING AN 80 STRANG
OPPORTUNITY TO GO IN FOR
(TEASINGLY) BY THE WAY, IF IT ISN'T TOO RUDE TO 81 STRANG
INQUIRE, AREN'T YOU GETTING
(TEASINGLY) POOH/ 114 STRANG
(TEASINGLY) WELL, IF I'M RESPONSIBLE, CHARLIE, 114 STRANG
TEASINGLY THERE'S NO DANGER OF YOUR EVER MAKING 114 STRANG
A LOVE MATCH, IS THERE.
(TEASINGLY) WHAT DO YOU KNOW ABOUT BEAUSS 153 STRANG
(SNUGGLING GORDON'S HEAD AGAINST HERS--LAUGHING 156 STRANG
TEASINGLY)
(TEASINGLY) BUT YOU'RE SUCH A RELENTLESS 447 WELDED
IDEALIST.

TEASPOONFUL
YOUR REMEDY WAS TO GIVE HIM A TEASPOONFUL OF 111 JOURNE
WHISKEY TO QUIET HIM.
I CAN REMEMBER THAT TEASPOONFUL OF BOOZE EVERY 111 JOURNE
TIME I WOKE UP WITH A NIGHTMARE.

TECH
(DULLY) DON'T--TECH ME. 252 DESIRE
DON'T YE TECH ME/ 261 DESIRE
DON'T YE DARE TECH ME/ 264 DESIRE
AND THEN, SPEAK AS POETS GO, WE DIDN'T TECH AT ONE497 DIFRNT
THE LAST YEAR--

TECHED

TECHED
ISLANDS THEY TECHED. 508 DIFRNT
I'VE TECHED THAR FOR WATER MORE'N ONCE MYSELF. 513 DIFRNT
TECHNICAL
GLANCING THROUGH THE PAGES OF A TECHNICAL BOOK ON 428 DYNAMO
HYDRO-ELECTRIC ENGINEERING.
TECHNICALITY
THIS FOOD TECHNICALITY IS IGNORED AS IRRELEVANT. 571 ICEMAN
TECHNIQUE
ABOUT THEMSELVES HAS GIVEN HIM A FOOLPROOF 11 HUGHIE
TECHNIQUE OF SELF-DEFENSE.
BEFORE HE PERFECTED HIS TECHNIQUE OF NOT 14 HUGHIE
LISTENING--
THESE HAVE THE QUALITY OF BELONGING TO A STUDIED 13 JOURNE
TECHNIQUE.
TEET'
I'LL DRIVE YER TEET' DOWN YER TROAT/ 225 HA APE
TEETERIN'
IF SHE HAIN'T, SHE'S TEETERIN' ON THE EDGE. 210 DESIRE
TEETH
HIS TEETH ARE CHATTERING WITH THE COLD AND HE 536 *ILE
HURRIES TO THE STOVE.
(TRYING TO CONTROL HIS CHATTERING TEETH-- 536 *ILE
DERISIVELY)
I TOLD HIM IN HIS TEETH I LOVED YOU. 51 ANNA
TEETH AN A LIAR IF HE HAD THE MISFORTUNE TO TAKE A461 CARDIF
BITE AT ONE/
(SHE IS SHAKEN AGAIN BY A WAVE OF UNCONTROLLABLE 550 DAYS
CHILL. HER TEETH CHATTER.
THEY'RE TREMBLIN' AN' LONGIN' T' KISS ME, AN' YER 240 DESIRE
TEETH T' BITE/
AND HARDENS HIS FACE INTO A STONY MASK--THROUGH 264 DESIRE
HIS TEETH TO HIMSELF)
(BETWEEN HIS CLENCHED TEETH) 542 DIFRNT
BUCK TEETH AND BIG FEET, HER MANNER DEFENSIVELY 67 ELECTR
SHARP AND ASSERTIVE.
HE'S SHYIN' AT THE FURNITURE COVERS AN' HIS TEETH 133 ELECTR
ARE CLICKIN' A'READY.
IN A STIFLED VOICE BETWEEN HER CLENCHED TEETH) 172 ELECTR
THAT THIS EMBITTERED FAILURE ANTHONY IS HURLING IN317 GGBROW
THE TEETH OF OUR SUCCESS--
THE GRATING, TEETH-GRITTING GRIND OF STEEL AGAINST223 HA APE
STEEL, OF CRUNCHING COAL.
HIS LIPS DRAWN BACK OVER HIS TEETH, HIS SMALL EYES225 HA APE
GLEAMING FEROCIOUSLY.
HIS BIG UNEVEN TEETH ARE IN BAD CONDITION. 8 HUGHIE
IN A SHADE OF BLUE THAT SETS TEETH ON EDGE, AND A 9 HUGHIE
GAY RED AND BLUE FOULARD TIE.
BUCK TEETH IN A SMALL RABBIT MOUTH. 575 ICEMAN
WAITING FOR ANY EXCUSE TO SHY AND PRETEND TO TAKE 576 ICEMAN
THE BIT IN ITS TEETH.
HE HAS BADLY FITTING STORE TEETH. 577 ICEMAN
(HIS TEETH CHATTERING) I MUST KILL HIM/ 308 LAZARU
HIS TEETH CAN BE HEARD CHATTERING TOGETHER IN 358 LAZARU
NERVOUS FEAR.
WHITE TEETH WHEN SHE SMILES. 2 MANSNS
TO CLEANSE HIS TEETH, AND THEN THROWING IT AWAY, 349 MARCOM
IT TOOK ROOT.
(GRITTING HIS TEETH) ALL RIGHT. 362 MARCOM
(BETWEEN HIS TEETH) WHAT A DOLT/ 368 MARCOM
AND HER SMILE, REVEALING EVEN WHITE TEETH, GIVES 3 MISBEG
IT CHARM.
WITH BEAUTIFUL EYES AND HAIR AND TEETH AND A 29 MISBEG
SMILE.
THE MOUTH, WITH FULL LIPS AND EVEN, WHITE TEETH, 67 POET
IS TOO LARGE FOR HER FACE.
--IT'S MORTGAGED TO THE TEETH. 585 ROPE
BY A LONG RELIANCE ON CLENCHED TEETH. 53 STRANG
SHE MUTTERS FIERCELY BETWEEN HER CLENCHED TEETH) 466 WELDED
TEETOTAL
THAT DON'T MEAN I'M A TEETOTAL GROUCH AND CAN'T BE621 ICEMAN
IN THE PARTY.
HICKEY MAY BE A LOUSY, INTERFERING PEST, NOW HE'S 652 ICEMAN
GONE TEETOTAL ON US.
TO PROVE I'M NOT TEETOTAL 658 ICEMAN
TEETOTALER
I WOULDN'T GIVE A TRAUNEEN FOR A TEETOTALER. 101 JOURNE
TEETOTALISM
I'VE WATCHED MANY CASES OF ALMOST FATAL 626 ICEMAN
TEETOTALISM.
TEETOTALLER
YOU'RE SUCH A VIRTUOUS TEETOTALLER-- 93 MISBEG
TELEGRAM
(AFTER A PAUSE, OPENING THE OTHER TELEGRAM) 147 BEYOND
YOU SENT THAT TELEGRAM TO ME COLLECT. 155 BEYOND
WE'VE JUST HAD A TELEGRAM. 136 ELECTR
TELEGRAMS
(AFTER A PAUSE) HAVE YOU GOT HIS TWO TELEGRAMS 146 BEYOND
WITH YOUS
TELEGRAPH
AND WE COULDN'T AFFORD TO TELEGRAPH. 155 BEYOND
I'M THINKIN HE WOULDN'T USE THE TELEGRAPH OR 437 DYNAMO
TELEPHONE OR RADIO FOR THEY'RE
THE TELEGRAPH FELLER SAYS LEE IS A GONER SURE THIS 11 ELECTR
TIME/.
TELEPHONE
TELEPHONE) 500 DAYS
(THE TELEPHONE ON THE TABLE RINGS. 513 DAYS
(THE TELEPHONE IN THE HALL RINGS AND MARGARET GOES519 DAYS
TOWARD THE DOOR IN REAR TO
I'M THINKIN HE WOULDN'T USE THE TELEGRAPH OR 437 DYNAMO
TELEPHONE OR RADIO FOR THEY'RE
THE TELEPHONE RINGS. 274 GGBROW
BEHIND THE DESK ARE A TELEPHONE SWITCHBOARD AND 7 HUGHIE
THE OPERATOR'S STOOL.
THEN THE TELEPHONE IN THE FRONT HALL RINGS AND ALL 73 JOURNE
OF THEM STIFFEN STARTLEDLY.)
(QUICKLY.) YOU CAN TELEPHONE AND SAY YOU DON'T 92 JOURNE
FEEL WELL ENOUGH.

TELEPHONE (CONT'D.)
SAY IT A THIRD TIME AND I'LL SEND MY DAUGHTER TO 59 MISBEG
TELEPHONE THE ASYLUM.
TELL
I GOT TO GIT THE ILE, I TELL YOU 542 *ILE
TELL 'EM TO COME. 543 *ILE
(FURIOUSLY) TELL 'EM TO GO TO--(CHECKS HIMSELF 543 *ILE
AND CONTINUES GRIMLY)
US, AND YOU CAN TELL THE REST THE SAME. 545 *ILE
TELL ME/ 549 *ILE
I GOT TO GIT THE ILE, I TELL YE. 550 *ILE
WANT ME TO TELL YOU HER INITIALS? E.R./ 187 AHWILD
(TEASINGLY) I CAN TELL YOU, IF HE WON'T. 190 AHWILD
YOU TELL ME THIS MINUTE WHERE YOU'VE HIDDEN THOSE 196 AHWILD
BOOKS/
I'LL TELL YOU, IF HE WON'T--AND YOU GIVE HIM A 196 AHWILD
GOOD TALKING TO.
TO HEAR HIM TELL IT, MAYBE/ 197 AHWILD
WELL, I CAN'T TELL YOU BEFORE LILY AND MILDRED. 198 AHWILD
SHE NEVER CAN ANSWER THE FRONT DOOR RIGHT UNLESS 1199 AHWILD
TELL HER EACH TIME.
BUT TELL HIM TO GO TO HELL, ANYWAY. 200 AHWILD
I'M JUST GOING TO CALL YOUR BLUFF AND TELL YOU 203 AHWILD
THAT.
AND IT WON'T GO IN AGAIN, I TELL YOU. 203 AHWILD
I TELL YOU YOU SCARED THE PANTS OFF HIM. 204 AHWILD
SID COULDN'T TELL US. 208 AHWILD
HE'S BEEN EATING BLUEFISH FOR YEARS--ONLY I TELL 214 AHWILD
HIM EACH TIME IT'S WEAKFISH.
OR I'LL HAVE TO TELL ON YOU TO PROTECT ME GOOD 217 AHWILD
NAME/
TELL ART I WANT TO SEE HIM A SECOND-- 218 AHWILD
I MIGHT TELL YOU, IF YOU CAN KEEP YOUR FACE SHUT. 218 AHWILD
I TELL YOU STRAIGHT, I WOULDN'T ASK YOU TO COME IF219 AHWILD
I WASN'T IN A HOLE--
HOW OFTEN HAVE I GOT TO TELL YOUS 222 AHWILD
OF COURSE IT'S A GOOD STORY--AND YOU TELL IT 231 AHWILD
WHENEVER YOU'VE A MIND TO.
BUT TELL HIM HE'S GOT TO STOP THIS DAMN 234 AHWILD
NONSENSE.
(WITH A MOCKING CHUCKLE) HE'S A HOT SPORT, CAN'T 237 AHWILD
YOU TELL ITS
KEEP AN EYE OUT FOR THAT BARTENDER, KID, AND TELL 239 AHWILD
ME IF YOU SEE HIM COMING.
TELL ME. 241 AHWILD
GO OUT AND TELL THE BARTENDER YOU WANT A ROOM. 241 AHWILD
TELL ME ANOTHER/ 242 AHWILD
YOU'RE ONLY LIKE A LOT OF PEOPLE WHO MEAN WELL, TO243 AHWILD
MEAN THEN TELL IT.
YES, AND I TELL YOU I'M THE POPE--BUT YOU DON'T 247 AHWILD
HAVE TO BELIEVE ME.
THAT'S WHAT WE'VE BEEN TRYING TO TELL YOUR MOTHER.254 AHWILD
I CAN'T TELL YOU-- 259 AHWILD
(ACCUSINGLY) YOU DON'T MEAN TO TELL ME YOU'RE 263 AHWILD
GOING BACK WITHOUT SEEING HIMS
WHY IS EVERYONE SCARED TO TELL MES 264 AHWILD
SHALL I GO UP NOW AND TELL HIM TO GET DRESSED, YOU266 AHWILD
WANT TO SEE HIM,S
AND I CAN TELL YOU IT RELIEVED MY MIND MORE'N 266 AHWILD
ANYTHING.
IF ALL GOES TO SHOW YOU NEVER CAN TELL BY 269 AHWILD
APPEARANCES--
I'M NEVER GOING TO BE SUCH A FOOL AGAIN, I TELL 272 AHWILD
YOU.
THEN YOU CAN TELL PA AND MA WHERE I'VE GONE-- 274 AHWILD
TELL ME, DICK/ 281 AHWILD
BEGIN AT THE BEGINNING AND TELL ME/ 281 AHWILD
(THEN WITH REAL FEELING) ONLY IT ISN'T PAST, I 281 AHWILD
CAN TELL YOU/
YOU TELL ME WHAT YOU DID/ 282 AHWILD
TELL THAT TO THE MARINES/ 285 AHWILD
(THEN AFTER A PAUSE) AND I SUPPOSE YOU'LL TELL ME285 AHWILD
YOU DIDN'T FALL IN LOVE WITH
AND I'M GOING TO TELL HIM HE CAN'T GO TO YALE, 289 AHWILD
SEEING HE'S SO UNDEPENDABLE.
I SAID ID TELL HIM THAT NOW--BLUFF-- 290 AHWILD
THEN MILLER ASKS INCREDULOUSLY.) YOU DON'T MEAN 291 AHWILD
TO TELL ME
A MAN NEVER CAN TELL WHAT HE'S LETTING HIMSELF IN 291 AHWILD
FOR--
I CAN'T TELL THAT, PA. 294 AHWILD
TELL HER TO GET THE HELL OUT OF IT. 10 ANNA
YOU'D BETTER TELL HER STRAIGHT TO GET OUT/ 10 ANNA
LEMME TELL YUH, DUTCHY, 11 ANNA
WELL, I'LL TELL YOU STRAIGHT, KIDDO, THAT MARTHY 15 ANNA
OWEN NEVER--
SAY, WHAT'S HE LIKE, TELL ME, HONESTS 17 ANNA
I WANTA TELL YUH SOMETHIN'. 19 ANNA
TELL ME. 22 ANNA
IT SOUNDS GOOD TO HEAR YOU TELL IT. 23 ANNA
(FROWNING PERPLEXEDLY) I DON'T KNOW HOW TO TELL 28 ANNA
YOU YUST WHAT I MEAN.
BUT TELL ME, ISN'T THIS A BARGE I'M ON--OR ISN'T 31 ANNA
ITS
YOU TELL ME ABOUT YOURSELF AND ABOUT THE WRECK. 35 ANNA
TELL ME ABOUT THE WRECK, LIKE YOU PROMISED ME YOU 35 ANNA
WOULD.
(FLATTERED) I'LL TELL YOU, SURELY. 35 ANNA
WELL, I'LL TELL YOU. 35 ANNA
YOU'RE IKISH, OF COURSE I CAN TELL THAT. 37 ANNA
BUT YOU WAS GOING TO TELL ME ABOUT YOURSELF. 37 ANNA
I'M GOING TO TURN LOOSE ON YOU AND TELL YOU-- 43 ANNA
I'D HAVE JUMPED AT THE CHANCE, I TELL YOU THAT 44 ANNA
STRAIGHT.
TELL HIM WHERE I AM, WILL YOUS 44 ANNA
(SHE TURNS TO BURKE) YOU TELL ME, MAT, SINCE HE 51 ANNA
DON'T WANT TO.
TELL ME WHAT IT'S ALL ABOUT. 51 ANNA

1619 TELL

TELL (CONT'D.)
TELL ME, AND DON'T KEEP ME SWEATING BLOOD. 54 ANNA
(RESOLUTELY) I CAN'T TELL YOU--AND I WON'T. 54 ANNA
FOR THE LOVE OF GOD, TELL ME THEN, 54 ANNA
WELL, LEMME TELL YOU--(SHE GLANCES AT BURKE AND 54 ANNA
STOPS ABRUPTLY)
I WASN'T GOING TO TELL YOU, BUT YOU FORCED ME INTO 56 ANNA
IT.
CAN TELL ME WHAT TO DO/ 56 ANNA
I'M GOING TO TELL YOU SOMETHING--AND THEN I'M 56 ANNA
GOING TO BEAT IT.
I'M GOING TO TELL YOU A FUNNY STORY, SO PAY 56 ANNA
ATTENTION.
FIRST THING IS, I WANT TO TELL YOU TWO GUYS 56 ANNA
SOMETHING.
I WAS CAGED IN, I TELL YOU--YUST LIKE IN YAIL-- 58 ANNA
WILL YOU BELIEVE IT IF I TELL 59 ANNA
AND NOW, GIVE ME A BAWLING OUT AND BEAT IT, LIKE I 59 ANNA
CAN TELL YOU'RE GOING TO.
I S'POSE IF I TRIED TO TELL YOU I WASN'T--THAT-- 59 ANNA
AND I WAS ASHAMED TO TELL YOU THE TRUTH-- 59 ANNA
(WILDLY) LOOK OUT, I TELL YOU/ 69 ANNA
TELL ME IT'S A LIE, I'M SAYING/ 70 ANNA
TELL ME 'TWAS A LIE, ANNA, 71 ANNA
(SAVAGELY) I HATED 'EM, I TELL YOU/ 73 ANNA
THAT'S WHAT I BEEN TRYING TO TELL YOU ALL ALONG/ 74 ANNA
SUPPOSING I WAS TO TELL YOU THAT IT'S JUST BEAUTY 85 BEYOND
THAT'S CALLING ME,
THEN YOU MUST TELL ME THAT, TOO. 90 BEYOND
YOU TELL THINGS SO BEAUTIFULLY/ 90 BEYOND
I WASN'T GOING TO TELL YOU, BUT I FEEL I HAVE TO. 91 BEYOND
WE'LL GO AND TELL THEM AT ONCE. 92 BEYOND
YOU'LL TELL THEM YOU CAN'T GO ON ACCOUNT OF ME, 92 BEYOND
WON'T YOU$
PLEASE TELL ME YOU WON'T GO/ 92 BEYOND
TELL THEM YOU'VE DECIDED NOT TO. 92 BEYOND
CAPTAIN, SHE SAYS, *WOULD YOU BE SO KIND AS TO 94 BEYOND
TELL ME
NO NEED TO TELL ME THAT. 98 BEYOND
YES, THERE IS SOMETHING--SOMETHING I MUST TELL 99 BEYOND
YOU--ALL OF YOU.
YOU DON'T MEAN TO TELL ME YOU'RE GOING TO LET HIM 102 BEYOND
STAY, DO YOU, JAMES$
(DISGRUNTEDLY) IT'S HARD TO TELL WHO'S JOKIN' AND104 BEYOND
WHO'S NOT IN THIS HOUSE.
(FACING HIS FATHER) I AGREE WITH YOU, PA, AND I 105 BEYOND
TELL YOU AGAIN,
AND TELL A BARE-FACED LIE/ 106 BEYOND
TELL ME THE TRUTH/ 110 BEYOND
I'VE GOT TO, I TELL YOU. 110 BEYOND
BUT I FORGOT, SHE SAID NOT TO TELL YOU-- 114 BEYOND
(WEARILY) YOU CAN TELL ME IF YOU WANT TO. 115 BEYOND
AND ANYTHING ELSE YOU TELL ME TO. 123 BEYOND
TELL ME ABOUT YOUR TRIP. 131 BEYOND
IT WAS ALL-WOOL-AND-A-YARD-WIDE-HELL, I'LL TELL 132 BEYOND
YOU.
AND I'LL TELL YOU, ROB, 132 BEYOND
AND I'LL TELL RUTH, TOO, IF I CAN GET UP THE 135 BEYOND
NERVE.
(SLOWLY) PERHAPS--FOR HER SAKE--YOU'D BETTER NOT 135 BEYOND
TELL HER.
I TELL YOU, I FEEL RIPE FOR BIGGER THINGS THAN 138 BEYOND
SETTLING DOWN HERE.
WHAT DID ROB TELL YOU--ABOUT ME$ 138 BEYOND
(WRINGING HER HANDS) OH, I WISH I COULD TELL IF 138 BEYOND
YOU'RE LYING OR NOT/
(EARNESTLY) I TELL YOU, RUTH, 138 BEYOND
*TELL HIM I'LL HOLD THE BERTH OPEN FOR HIM UNTIL 141 BEYOND
LATE THIS AFTERNOON,* HE SAYS.
WALK DOWN WITH ME TO THE HOUSE AND YOU CAN TELL ME142 BEYOND
MORE
A SPECIALIST WILL TELL YOU IN A SECOND 147 BEYOND
(DULLY) MAKES NO DIFFERENCE. I HAD TO TELL ANDY 147 BEYOND
SOMETHING, DIDN'T I$
IT'S GOT TO STOP, I TELL YOU/ 148 BEYOND
YOU TELL THAT MOTHER OF YOURS SHE'S GOT TO STOP 148 BEYOND
SAYING
I CAN TELL HIM SO'S ROB'LL NEVER KNOW. 152 BEYOND
TELL ME THE TRUTH. 155 BEYOND
TELL ME/ 155 BEYOND
(DULLY) THERE'S NOTHING MUCH TO TELL. 155 BEYOND
HE COULDN'T TELL--AND LEFT ONE AFTER ANOTHER. 155 BEYOND
I AM SORRY I HAVE TO TELL YOU THIS. 158 BEYOND
TELL ME ABOUT YOURSELF, ANDY. 160 BEYOND
TELL ME. 161 BEYOND
(SHE SIGHS WEARILY) IT CAN'T DO NO HARM TO TELL 164 BEYOND
YOU NOW--
THAT WAS WHAT I'D STARTED TO TELL. 164 BEYOND
TELL HIM YOU ONLY SAID SO BECAUSE YOU WERE MAD 165 BEYOND
TELL HIM SOMETHING, ANYTHING, THAT'LL BRING HIM 165 BEYOND
PEACE/
TELL HIM YOU NEVER LOVED ME--IT WAS ALL A MISTAKE.165 BEYOND
DON'T I TELL YOU/ 167 BEYOND
TELL HIM THAT YANK IS BAD TOOK AND I'LL BE STAYIN'482 CARDIF
WID HIM A WHILE YET.
I'M DYIN', I TELL YUH. 482 CARDIF
DIDN'T I TELL YOU YOU WASN'T HALF AS SICK AS YOU 485 CARDIF
THOUGHT YOU WAS$
I HEARD WHAT HE SAID, AND IF I DIDN'T I C'D TELL 485 CARDIF
BY THE WAY I FEEL.
'TWAS A RARE TREAT TO 'EAR 'IM TELL WHAT 'APPENED 457 CARIBE
TO 'IM AMONG 'EM.
(SARCASTICALLY) THAT'S RIGHT--TELL THE OLD MAN 458 CARIBE
ABOUT UT, AN' THE MATE, TOO.
DID YOU TELL 'EM THEY GOTTER SIGN FOR WHAT THEY 464 CARIBE
GITS--AND HOW TO SIGN$
AH CAN TELL A GENELMAN FAHS AH CAN SEE 'IM. 469 CARIBE

TELL (CONT'D.)
(WITH A SUDDEN HARSHNESS) DIDN'T I TELL YOU HE'S 557 CROSS
MAD$
DOES HE TELL$ 557 CROSS
RELY ON ME NOT TO TELL HIM, THEN. 558 CROSS
TELL ME. 563 CROSS
I SAW, I TELL YOU. 570 CROSS
I TELL YOU AGAIN WHAT I HAVE ALWAYS TOLD YOU... 495 DAYS
GOOD GOD, DON'T TELL ME THE LITERARY BUG IS BITING496 DAYS
YOU AGAIN$
TELL ME ABOUT THIS NOVEL OF YOURS, JOHN. 497 DAYS
(CONFUSED) WELL, TO TELL THE TRUTH, I HAVEN'T 497 DAYS
GIVEN IT A THOUGHT IN YEARS, BUT--
OH, I KNEW THERE WAS SOMETHING I'D FORGOTTEN TO 497 DAYS
TELL YOU.
NOTHING TO TELL YET. 497 DAYS
AND BETTER GET THE END OF YOUR NOVEL DECIDED UPON,498 DAYS
SO YOU CAN TELL YOUR PLOT--
IT WAS IMPORTANT, SHE SAID TO TELL YOU. 498 DAYS
TELL HIM TO GET OUT/ 499 DAYS
YOU NEEDN'T TELL ME, FATHER. 502 DAYS
(HE SMILES) TO TELL YOU THE TRUTH, 505 DAYS
(THEN SUDDENLY) THERE'S SOMETHING I WANT TO TELL 506 DAYS
YOU, JACK.
I DIDN'T MEAN--GO ON WITH WHAT YOU STARTED TO TELL507 DAYS
ME.
YOU'LL SEE IN WHAT I'M GOING TO TELL YOU. 507 DAYS
WHEN WILL YOU TELL ME$ 509 DAYS
WHEN WILL YOU TELL ME THE REST OF IT$ 512 DAYS
I WANT TO TELL YOU AGAIN, UNCLE, HOW GRAND IT IS 512 DAYS
TO HAVE YOU HERE--
TELL HER I'M OUT. 513 DAYS
TELL HER TO COME RIGHT UP. 515 DAYS
BUT TELL ME ALL YOUR NEWS. 516 DAYS
OR DID YOU JUST TELL THEM TO SAY THAT$ 516 DAYS
TELL ME. 517 DAYS
DO YOU MEAN TO TELL ME YOU'RE AS MUCH IN LOVE WITH517 DAYS
HIM NOW AS WHEN YOU MARRIED
I INTENDED TO TELL FATHER I WAS THROUGH AS 519 DAYS
WALTER'S WIFE.
I'VE GOT TO TELL YOU JUST HOW IT CAME TO HAPPEN-- 521 DAYS
SO YOU'LL SEE.
BUT I WAS IN HELL, I CAN TELL YOU, 521 DAYS
WHY DID I HAVE TO TELL YOU, I WONDER$ 522 DAYS
AND EVEN IF I WERE ROTTEN ENOUGH TO COME RIGHT OUT526 DAYS
AND TELL HER,
I'LL HAVE TO TELL HER MYSELF 527 DAYS
AND WALTER WILL HAVE TO TELL THAT TO EVERY ONE, 527 DAYS
TOO--TO LIVE UP TO HIS POSE/
YOU HAD BETTER MAKE UP YOUR MIND NOW TO TELL THE 528 DAYS
REST OF YOUR NOVEL TONIGHT--
TELL ME, HAVE YOU BEEN DOING ANYTHING MORE ON THE 530 DAYS
REST OF YOUR IDEA FOR A NOVEL$
GOD, I CAN'T TELL YOU/ 530 DAYS
BUT YOU TELL YOUR STORY JUST THE SAME. 530 DAYS
HE WANTED TO TELL HIS WIFE AND BEG FOR 539 DAYS
FORGIVENESS--
AND TELL HIM THE REST OF YOUR STORY THERE. 540 DAYS
(GETS UP--WORRIEDLY) BUT WHY DIDN'T YOU TELL ME$ 540 DAYS
THAT'S WHY I FEEL IT'S IMPORTANT YOU TELL IT--NOW.543 DAYS
SHALL I TELL YOU WHERE I WENT, AND WHY$ 548 DAYS
OH, SHE DIDN'T TELL ME IT WAS YOU. 549 DAYS
FOR GOD'S SAKE, JOHN, DON'T LIE TO ME ANY MORE OR 549 DAYS
I--I KNOW, I TELL YOU/
MY DEAR CHILD, I CAN'T TELL YOU HOW DEEPLY-- 550 DAYS
FOR THE LOVE OF GOD, DON'T TELL ME YOU TOOK HIS 550 DAYS
MORBID NONSENSE SERIOUSLY.
I TELL YOU THERE IS NOTHIN--NOTHING/ 552 DAYS
FOR GOD'S SAKE, TELL ME YOU KNOW SHE ISN'T GOING 556 DAYS

TELL ME THAT AND I'LL DO ANYTHING YOU ASK/ 556 DAYS
I TELL YOU THAT'S ENDED/ 562 DAYS
TELL HIM HE MUSTN'T WORRY. 563 DAYS
(SARDONICALLY) I TELL THAT T' PAW--WHEN HE COMES/208 DESIRE
AN' PAW KIN TELL YEW SOMETHIN' TOO/ 210 DESIRE
HOW COULD YE TELL THAT FAR$ 219 DESIRE
AN' I TELL YE I KIN FEEL 'EM A-COMIN', TOO/ 219 DESIRE
(THEN QUIETLY) I'LL TELL EBEN. 222 DESIRE
YE BETTER NOT TELL HIM IT'S YEW HOUSE. 222 DESIRE
I KIN TELL THAT BY LOOKIN' AT YE. 226 DESIRE
(MALICIOUSLY) I'LL TELL HIM YE SAID THAT/ 226 DESIRE
TRYIN' T' TELL YERSELF I HAIN'T PURTY T'YE. 229 DESIRE
(VENGEFULLY) JUST LET ME TELL YE A THING OR TWO 233 DESIRE
'BOUT EBEN/
(VEHEMENTLY) I'D DO ANYTHIN' YE AXED, I TELL YE/ 235 DESIRE
(VICIOUSLY) I DON'T TAKE T'YE, I TELL YE/ 239 DESIRE
TELL ME ABOUT YER MAW, EBEN. 242 DESIRE
I'LL TELL THE OLD MAN I HAIN'T FEELIN' PERT. 245 DESIRE
(RAISING HIS VOICE) BET I KIN TELL YE, ABBIE, 248 DESIRE
WHAT EBEN'S DOIN'/
WAAL, WHILE THEY'S LIFE THEY'S ALLUS HOPE. I'VE 250 DESIRE
HEERD TELL.
I CAN'T TELL NONE. 252 DESIRE
IT'S HIS'N, I TELL YE--HIS'N ARTER I DIE-- 254 DESIRE
(WITH FIERCE DETERMINATION) I'M A-GOIN', I TELL 257 DESIRE
YE/
I'LL TELL HIM THE TRUTH 'BOUT THE SON HE'S SO 257 DESIRE
PROUD O'/
YE MUSTN'T--WAIT A SPELL--I WANT T' TELL YE.... 258 DESIRE
(VIOLENTLY) I HATE YE, I TELL YE/ 258 DESIRE
I BEEN A-THINKIN'--AN' I HAIN'T GOIN' T' TELL PAW 260 DESIRE
NOTHIN'.
WHY DIDN'T YE TELL ME$ 260 DESIRE
I'LL TELL HIM EVERYTHIN'/ 262 DESIRE
I KILLED HIM, I TELL YE/ 263 DESIRE
YE'D BETTER TELL ME *PA./ 264 DESIRE
DID YE TELL THE SHERIFF$ 265 DESIRE

TELL

TELL (CONT'D.)
(DEFENSIVELY) THEY'S MORE TO IT NOR YEW KNOW, 265 DESIRE
MAKES HIM TELL.
AN' IT'S MY MURDER, TOO, I'LL TELL THE SHERIFF-- 266 DESIRE
DON'T TELL ME, FOR INSTANCE, YOU THINK I'M 495 DIFRNT
BETTER'N YOUR PA OR JACK--
AIN'T NOTHIN' TO TELL. THAT'S WHY. 497 DIFRNT
NOTHING YOU'D BE ASHAMED TO TELL MES 500 DIFRNT
(SUSPICIOUSLY) CALEB DIDN'T SEEM WILLING TO TELL 501 DIFRNT
ME MUCH ABOUT THEIR TOUCHING
ON'T I DIDN'T TELL YE, MIND. 502 DIFRNT
THEN I'LL TELL YOU WHAT JIM TOLD ME. 502 DIFRNT
(IN A STRAINED VOICE) WELL, AIN'T YOU GOING TO 502 DIFRNT
TELL MES
YOU TELL HIM WHAT I SAID. 504 DIFRNT
(OFFENDED) HELL, YOU'RE A NICE ONE TO TELL A 504 DIFRNT
JOKE TO/
I BEEN THINKING THINGS OVER, TELL HIM--AND I TAKE 504 DIFRNT
BACK MY PROMISE--
I WANT YOU TO TELL HIM-- 504 DIFRNT
I WANT YOU TO TELL HIM I'VE CHANGED MY MIND AND I 504 DIFRNT
AIN'T GOING TO MARRY HIM.
I'M GOIN' TO TELL MA AND SIC HER ONTO YOU. 505 DIFRNT
I'VE MADE UP MY MIND. I TELL YOU THAT RIGHT HERE 507 DIFRNT
AND NOW.
COME ON IN HERE. TELL I TELL YOU. 507 DIFRNT
(AFTER A PAUSE) JACK WAS A DUMB FOOL TO TELL YOU 508 DIFRNT
'BOUT THEM GOIN'S-ON AT THEM
I ASKED JACK TO TELL HIM WHEN HE COMES BACK. 508 DIFRNT
THEN I'LL TELL HIM MYSELF. 508 DIFRNT
YOU CAN'T TELL ME YOU'VE GOT OVER ALL LIKIN' FOR 511 DIFRNT
HIM
HE WON'T TELL NO MORE TALES, I RECKON. 514 DIFRNT
SHE COULDN'T UNDERSTAND ENOUGH ENGLISH FOR ME TO 515 DIFRNT
TELL HER HOW I FELT--
SOME JAZZ, I'LL TELL THE WORLD/ 520 DIFRNT
AND HOW OFTEN HAVE I GOT TO TELL YOU NOT TO CALL 521 DIFRNT
ME AUNT EMMERS
MA'LL TELL HIM ALL HER TALES, AND HE'LL BE SORE AT523 DIFRNT
ME RIGHT OFF.
DIDN'T YOU TELL ME YOU ENLISTED AGAIN 'CAUSE YOU 523 DIFRNT
WERE SICK UP THIS SMALL PLACE
BUT YOU CAN TELL HOW GOOD I THINK YOU ARE FROM ME 524 DIFRNT
BEEN OVER HERE SO MUCH--
TELL ME/ 526 DIFRNT
(EAGERLY) TELL ME/ 526 DIFRNT
TELL ME ALL ABOUT 'EM. 526 DIFRNT
ASK ME NO QUESTIONS AND I'LL TELL YOU NO LIES. 527 DIFRNT
BUT WON'T YOU TELL MES 527 DIFRNT
AND I'M GOIN' TO TELL EMMA ABOUT YOU 529 DIFRNT
TELL HIM/ 530 DIFRNT
AND I KIN SEE IT'S COME TO THE P'INT WHERE I GOT 530 DIFRNT
TO TELL YOUR UNCLE CALEB EVERY
AND IF MY WORD DON'T HAVE NO INFLUENCE, I'LL TELL 530 DIFRNT
YOUR UNCLE CALEB EVERYTHING.
THAT'S WHAT MA COME OVER TO TELL ME-- 531 DIFRNT
BUT EVERY TIME HE'D EVEN HINT AT BEIN' ENGAGED 533 DIFRNT
AGAIN I'D ALWAYS TELL HIM WE WAS
THINGS'D BE DIFF'RENT AND I'D TELL 'EM ALL TO GO 534 DIFRNT
TO HELL.
YOU COME TELL ME WHEN HE'S GONE. 534 DIFRNT
(JUBILANTLY) TELL HIM. 534 DIFRNT
WHY, YOU DON'T MEAN TO TELL ME YOU DON'T LIKE IT 535 DIFRNT
NEITHER, CALEB$
(EVASIVELY) I AIN'T ENOUGH USED TO IT YET--TO 536 DIFRNT
TELL.
I GOT DAMNED GOOD CAUSE, I TELL YE/ 541 DIFRNT
TELL ME YOU WON'T HURT HIM/ 543 DIFRNT
TELL ME WHAT YOUR DOPE IS. 546 DIFRNT
JUST SO YOU'D TELL HIM AND GET HIS GOAT RIGHT. 546 DIFRNT
WHAT D'YOU TELL HER I WAS HERE FOR, YOU OLD FOOLS 547 DIFRNT
(HIS VOICE BOOMING) AND I TELL YOU, AMELIA, IT IS424 DYNAMO
GOD'S WILL/
TELL ME, HAS REUBEN BEEN HAVING ANYTHING TO DO 425 DYNAMO
WITH THAT CURSED PACK NEXT DOORS
I'VE GOT TO GET UP MY NERVE AND TELL HER THAT I 425 DYNAMO
LOVE HER...))
((GONE TO BED$...SO EARLY$...WAS HE SICK AND 427 DYNAMO
DIDN'T TELL ME$...))
HE'S HONOR BOUND TO TELL HIS FUTURE SON-IN-LAW THE431 DYNAMO
SECRET OF HIS PAST.
UH, JUST WAIT TILL I TELL HER WHAT I THINK OF 434 DYNAMO
HER(...))
SHE'LL TELL THE WHOLE TOWN I WAS SPYING/... 436 DYNAMO
(WITH A LEER) AND HOW DOES GOD CALL YOU, TELL ME$437 DYNAMO
SHE'LL TELL HOW I WAS CRYING(...)) 439 DYNAMO
FOR WHAT I WAS COMING TO TELL YOU WAS THAT I WAS 440 DYNAMO
CLARK/
((BUT I WON'T TELL THEM/...EVER/... 441 DYNAMO
((HE WAS THREATENING POP ALREADY HE'D TELL ON 442 DYNAMO
HIM/...
HE WOULDN'T WANT ME TO TELL ON HER FATHER...)) 442 DYNAMO
YOU NEEDN'T BE AFRAID I'LL TELL-- BUT YOU OUGHT TO442 DYNAMO
GO AND TELL YOURSELF/
I WON'T TELL THE POLICE, YOU NEEDN'T WORRY. 442 DYNAMO
I WISH I COULD TELL HER... 446 DYNAMO
YOU CAN ALWAYS TELL MOTHER EVERYTHING. 446 DYNAMO
DO YOU MEAN TO SAY YOU REFUSE TO TELL YOUR OWN 446 DYNAMO
MOTHER,
TELL MOTHER/ 446 DYNAMO
(STAMMERS) I'LL TELL YOU, MOTHER--IF YOU PROMISE 446 DYNAMO
TO KEEP IT A SECRET--
I CAN'T TELL ANYONE/ 446 DYNAMO
JUST BETWEEN ME AND YOU--AND NEVER TELL FATHER. 446 DYNAMO
HE HAD A GOOD REASON TO TELL ME/ 447 DYNAMO
(PLEASINGLY) REMEMBER YOU SWORE ON THE BIBLE 447 DYNAMO
YOU'D NEVER TELL/

TELL (CONT'D.)
I ASKED HIM IF I COULD MARRY ADA AND HE THOUGHT HE447 DYNAMO
WAS HONOR BOUND TO TELL ME/
YES, I'LL SWEAR ON THE BIBLE I WON'T TELL HIM. 447 DYNAMO
YOU LED ME ON TO TELL/ 449 DYNAMO
DID YOU TELL--$ 451 DYNAMO
DIDN'T I TELL YOU/ 453 DYNAMO
I'LL TELL HER YOU'RE HERE. 457 DYNAMO
(WITH A COLD SMILE) WELL, NEVER MIND WHAT--BUT 458 DYNAMO
YOU CAN TELL HER I'VE CHANGED.
YOU CAN TELL HER I'VE READ UP ON LOVE IN BIOLOGY, 458 DYNAMO
AND I KNOW WHAT IT IS NOW,
YOU CAN TELL HIM I'VE JOINED HIS CHURCH. 458 DYNAMO
TELL YOUR OLD MAN I'D SURE 461 DYNAMO
TELL HER I'M SORRY FOR ACTING SO ROUGH TO HER THAT464 DYNAMO
NIGHT(...)
((HAVE I GOT TO TELL HIMS... 466 DYNAMO
MUST I TELL THIS$...)) 466 DYNAMO
TELL ME AND MAYBE I CAN HELP YOU FORGET IT. 469 DYNAMO
TELL HER TO FORGIVE ME, AND TO HELP ME FIND YOUR 474 DYNAMO
TRUTH/
THERE MUST BE SOMETHING IN HER SONG THAT'D TELL 474 DYNAMO
YOU IF YOU HAD EARS TO HEAR/...
DID I TELL YOU THAT OUR BLOOD PLASM IS THE SAME 477 DYNAMO
RIGHT NOW
SHE DIED TO TELL ME SHE HAD AT LAST FOUND ME 478 DYNAMO
WORTHY OF HER LOVE.
CAN'T YOU TELL MES 480 DYNAMO
DON'T PRESS AGAINST ME, I TELL YOU/ 484 DYNAMO
WHAT CAN I DO TO GET YOU TO FORGIVE ME$...TELL 487 DYNAMO
ME/...YES/...
BUT TELL ME WHAT'S UP. 174 EJONES
(WITH GREAT CURIOSITY) TELL 'IMS 174 EJONES
(COWERINGLY) I TELL, MISTER. 174 EJONES
NO TELL HIM/ 174 EJONES
NO TELL HIM, MISTER/ 174 EJONES
WHAT NEWS YOU GOT TO TELL MES 176 EJONES
I'LL TELL YER THAT BIT O' NEWS I WAS GOIN' TO. 181 EJONES
CAN'T TELL NOTHIN' FROM DER TRESS/ 189 EJONES
DON'T DE BAPTIS' PARSON TELL YOU DAT MANY TIMES 193 EJONES
YOU FELL HER I GOT PERMISSION FROM VINNIE TO SHOW 8 ELECTR
YOU ROUND.
I'LL TELL YOU LATER. 9 ELECTR
TELL MINNIE ABOUT OLD ABE MANNON'S BROTHER DAVID 9 ELECTR
MARRYIN' THAT FRENCH CANUCK
I'LL TELL YOU LATER, VINNIE. 12 ELECTR
OH, HE DID TELL ME THE STORY OF HIS LIFE TO MAKE 15 ELECTR
HIMSELF OUT ROMANTIC.
I BELIEVE ANYTHING YOU TELL ME TO BELIEVE. 19 ELECTR
WHY DID YOU HAVE TO TELL MES 20 ELECTR
I AIN'T NEVER HEARD TELL OF IT BEFORE. 20 ELECTR
YOU'LL THINK IT STRANGE WHEN I TELL YOU. 22 ELECTR
DID MOTHER TELL YOU YOU COULD KISS MES 23 ELECTR
WHY DO YOU TELL ME THIS$ 26 ELECTR
I'D TELL HIM WHAT I TELL YOU NOW-- 27 ELECTR
STOP LYING. I TELL YOU/ 30 ELECTR
I SUPPOSE YOU'LL HARDLY LET YOUR FATHER GET IN THE 32 ELECTR
DOOR BEFORE YOU TELL HIM/
(CUTTINGLY) WILL YOU KINDLY COME TO THE POINT AND 32 ELECTR
TELL ME WHAT YOU INTEND
I WON'T TELL HIM, PROVIDED YOU GIVE UP BRANT AND 32 ELECTR
NEVER SEE HIM AGAIN--
YOU CAN TELL HIM WHAT YOU'VE GOT TO DO-- 35 ELECTR
AND TELL HIM IF HE EVER DARES COME HERE AGAIN--/ 35 ELECTR
NO, NO, I TELL YOU/ 36 ELECTR
I'LL TELL HIM MYSELF. 38 ELECTR
HE'VE SO MUCH TO TELL YOU. 49 ELECTR
(GRUFFLY) IF IT WAS SERIOUS, I'D TELL YOU, SO 49 ELECTR
YOU'D BE PREPARED.
(DEFIANTLY TO HER MOTHER) HOW CAN YOU TELL HIM HE 49 ELECTR
LOOKS TIREDS
NOW PLEASE TELL ME JUST WHAT IT IS YOU SUSPECT ME 51 ELECTR
OF$
IT WAS YOUR DUTY TO TELL HIM FLATLY HE WASN'T 52 ELECTR
WANTED/
BUT I WAS JEALOUS A MITE, TO TELL YOU THE TRUTH. 53 ELECTR
YOU TELL ME TO STOP TALKING--BY GOD, THAT'S FUNNY/ 56 ELECTR
IT'S MY DUTY TO TELL HIM ABOUT HER/ 57 ELECTR
HE KEPT TALKING OF LOVE AND DEATH--HE FORCED ME TO 63 ELECTR
TELL HIM/
TELL ME/ 63 ELECTR
TELL ME WHAT TO DO/ 64 ELECTR
I'LL TELL YOU A SECRET, JOSIAH--STRICTLY BETWEEN 71 ELECTR
YOU AND ME.
I'VE GOT TO TELL YOU SOMETHING TOO/ 76 ELECTR
DO YOU MEAN TO TELL ME THERE'S ACTUALLY BEEN 76 ELECTR
GOSSIP STARTED ABOUT HERS
DON'T BELIEVE THE LIES SHE'LL TELL YOU/ 76 ELECTR
TELL ME/ 78 ELECTR
ME/ 78 ELECTR
TO TELL ORIN YOUR LIES AND GET HIM TO GO TO THE 78 ELECTR
POLICE/
ME AND HE REALIZED SHE'D TELL ANY LIE SHE COULD 85 ELECTR
TO--
I TELL YOU, ORIN, YOU CAN'T REALIZE HOW SHE'S 86 ELECTR
CHANGED WHILE YOU'VE BEEN AWAY/
I'LL TELL YOU THE TRUTH, MOTHER/ 86 ELECTR
THERE'S NOTHING TO TELL--EXCEPT IN VINNIE'S MORBID 86 ELECTR
REVENGEFUL MIND/
DID SHE TELL FATHER THATS 88 ELECTR
I WANT TO TELL YOU SOMETHING. 89 ELECTR
WELL, YOU CAN GO AHEAD NOW AND TELL ORIN ANYTHING 91 ELECTR
YOU WISH/
DON'T TELL HIM ABOUT ADAM/ 92 ELECTR
I'LL TELL YOU THE JOKE 94 ELECTR
IF YOU THINK YOU'RE GOING TO TELL ME A LOT OF 96 ELECTR
CRAZY STUFF ABOUT MOTHER,
TELL ME THAT ISN'T TRUE, AT LEAST/ 98 ELECTR

TELL

TELL (CONT'D.)
I TELL YOU SHE WENT TO HIS ROOM/ 99 ELECTR
TELL ME YOU'RE LYING OR--/ 99 ELECTR
DID SHE TELL YOU WHAT SHE'S GOING TO DO, ORINS 100 ELECTR
DIDN'T I TELL YOU/ 100 ELECTR
I'LL GO TO THE POLICE STATION AND TELL 'EM THERE'S104 ELECTR
A RUBBER HERE--
I HER'D TELL ROBBERS BROKE IN THE 104 ELECTR
AN' YOU'RE THE KINO TO CRACK SAIL ON, I KIN TELL 106 ELECTR
BY YOUR CUT.
TELL ME YOU LOVE ME/ 108 ELECTR
TELL ME WE'RE GOING TO BE HAPPY/ 112 ELECTR
OH, ADAM, TELL ME YOU DON'T REGRET/ 112 ELECTR
WE'D HAVE BEEN ARRESTED--AND THEN I'D HAVE TO TELL113 ELECTR
THE TRUTH TO SAVE US.
(GRIMLY) YOU NEEDN'T TELL ME WHAT TO DO. 114 ELECTR
I CAN'T TELL YOU HOW GRATEFUL I'D BE/ 119 ELECTR
I'LL HAVE TO RUN HOME AND TELL MOTHER, SO SHE 119 ELECTR
WON'T WORRY.
TELL ME-- 120 ELECTR
TELL ME--/ 120 ELECTR
TELL HIM MOTHER HAS KILLED HERSELF IN A FIT OF 124 ELECTR
INSANE GRIEF OVER FATHER'S DEATH.
WILL YOU REMEMBER TO TELL HIM THATS 125 ELECTR
I'LL TELL HIM, VINNIE--ANYTHING YOU SAY. 125 ELECTR
(INCREDULOUSLY) YOU AREN'T GOING TO TELL ME YOU 135 ELECTR
THINK THE HOUSE IS HAUNTED TOO.
AN' NOW I'VE GOT THAT OFF MY CHEST, TELL ME ABOUT 136 ELECTR
'EM.
TELL ME/ 138 ELECTR
TELL ME YOU KNOW THERE ARE NONE, ORIN/ 138 ELECTR
TELL ME/ 142 ELECTR
PLEASE TELL HAZEL WHAT I'VE TOLD YOU. 148 ELECTR
I WANT TO TELL YOU WHAT'S WRONG WITH ORIN--SO YOU 148 ELECTR
AND HAZEL CAN HELP ME.
ALL RIGHT, IF YOU WON'T TELL ME. 150 ELECTR
TELL ME WHAT YOU'VE WRITTEN/ 152 ELECTR
WELL, AS I'VE PRACTICALLY FINISHED IT--I SUPPOSE I152 ELECTR
MIGHT AS WELL TELL YOU.
(AGHAST) DO YOU MEAN TO TELL ME YOU'VE ACTUALLY 153 ELECTR
WRITTEN--
FOR GOD'S SAKE, TELL ME YOU'RE LYING, VINNIE/ 155 ELECTR
I CAN'T TELL YOU. 160 ELECTR
BUT, YOU SILLY BOY, VINNIE TOLD PETER HERSELF WHAT161 ELECTR
IT IS AND TOLD HIM TO TELL
AND THEN YOU COULD HIDE ME AND WHEN SHE CAME FOR 161 ELECTR
ME TELL HER I WASN'T THERE.
IF YOU COULD TELL ME WHAT IT IS. 161 ELECTR
SO IN CASE I DID TELL YOU--OH, SHE'S CUNNING/ 161 ELECTR
I DON'T TELL LIES, ORIN/ 161 ELECTR
(STARING AT HER WILDLY) WHAT DID SHE TELLS 161 ELECTR
TELL HER TO GIVE IT TO ME/ 164 ELECTR
WHY DIDN'T YOU TELL ME TO GET IN THE HOUSE AND LIE170 ELECTR
DOWN/
TELL HER TO SET THEM AROUND INSIDE. 170 ELECTR
AND I DID, I TELL YOU/ 177 ELECTR
AND TELL HANNAH TO THROW OUT ALL THE FLOWERS. 179 ELECTR
BECAUSE I WANTED TO TELL YOU SOMETHING. 262 GGBROW
I'LL TELL DION YOU'RE HERE. 264 GGBROW
(FORCING A GRIN) YOU CAN TELL HER I'LL SEE THAT 266 GGBROW
YOU BEHAVE/
TELL ME/ 267 GGBROW
IF YOU'D HEARD HER DEFEND YOU, LIE ABOUT YOU, TELL281 GGBROW
ME HOW HARD YOU WERE WORKING.
TELL ME--I'VE ALWAYS BEEN CURIOUS-- 289 GGBROW
CYBEL SAID TO TELL YOU SHE'D BE BACK NEXT WEEK, 289 GGBROW
MR. BROWN.
TELL YOUR MOTHER SHE'LL GET WORD FROM MR. BROWN'S 293 GGBROW
HOUSE.
TELL HIM IT'S THE DEVIL COME TO CONCLUDE A 294 GGBROW
BARGAIN.
(THEY STARE AT HER) I FORGOT TO TELL HIM 303 GGBROW
SOMETHING IMPORTANT THIS MORNING AND
SO IF YOU'LL TELL HIM I'M HERE--(THEY DON'T MOVE. 303 GGBROW
(WITH SUDDEN DESPERATION) MARGARET, I'VE GOT TO 305 GGBROW
TELL YOU/
PEOPLE TELL ME YOU HAD AN ASSISTANT, ANTHONY, 306 GGBROW
COME AND HEAR HER TELL ME HOW SHE LOVES YOU/ 308 GGBROW
COME WITH ME AND TELL HER AGAIN I LOVE HER/ 308 GGBROW
I TELL YOU I'LL MURDER THIS GOD-DAMNED DISGUSTING 311 GGBROW
GREAT GOD BROWN WHO STANDS
MAYBE I SHOULDN'T TELL YOU THIS. 311 GGBROW
TELL ME--ISN'T HE DRINKING HARD$ 316 GGBROW
I'LL TELL HIM YOU'RE HERE. 317 GGBROW
TELL ME OR I'LL FIX YUH/ 321 GGBROW
SO I HAD TO TELL THEM THAT MY FATHER, THE 220 HA APE
PRESIDENT OF NAZARETH STEEL,
TELL 'IM 'E'S A BLOODY SWINE/ 224 HA APE
I TELL YER WE GOT A CASE. 228 HA APE
(PHILOSOPHICALLY) I WOULD TAKE A WISE MAN TO TELL228 HA APE
ONE FROM THE OTHER.
I'LL TELL HER WHERE TO GIT OFF/ 232 HA APE
TELL IT TO SWEENEY/ 237 HA APE
YES. TELL US YOUR SAD STORY. 240 HA APE
I STARTED TO TELL DE JUDGE AND ALL HE SAYS WAS.. 241 HA APE
SURE, I'LL TELL YOUSE. 241 HA APE
TELL HIM TO SALT DE TAIL OF DAT EAGLE/ 242 HA APE
AND TELL HER DE HAIRY APE DONE IT. 249 HA APE
AND TELL HIM THAT ALL HE'LL EVER GET ON US, OR 249 HA APE
EVER HAS GOT,
YOU CAN GO BACK AND TELL WHATEVER SKUNK IS PAYING 249 HA APE
YOU BLOOD-MONEY FOR BETRAYING
TELL ME WHERE HIS WOIKS IS, HOW TO GIT THERE, ALL 249 HA APE
DE DOPE.
HE CAN TELL TIME BY SOUNDS IN THE STREET. 8 HUGHIE
COULDN'T TELL HIM NOTHING. 10 HUGHIE
THEN I'D TELL HIM HOW I'D DONE. 16 HUGHIE
AND I'D TELL HIM THE LATEST OFF THE GRAPEVINE. 16 HUGHIE

TELL (CONT'D.)
I'D TELL HIM, -JUST LET THAT WIFE OF YOURS KNOW 16 HUGHIE
YOU'RE CHEATIN'.
WHAT I ALWAYS TELL JESS WHEN SHE NAGS ME TO WORRY 19 HUGHIE
ABOUT SOMETHING--
I TELL YOU, PAL, I'D RATHER SLEEP IN THE SAME 21 HUGHIE
STALL WITH OLD MAN O' WAR
AND I'D STOP TO KID HIM ALONG AND TELL HIM THE 23 HUGHIE
TALE OF WHAT I'D WIN THAT DAY.
HE CAN TELL 24 HUGHIE
HE'LL TELL YOU YOU HAD ENOUGH ALREADY. 27 HUGHIE
WHY DIDN'T YOU TELL ME YOU WAS DEEF, BUDDY$ 27 HUGHIE
BY GOD, IF HE WAS, I'D TELL HIM A TALE THAT'D MAKE 28 HUGHIE
HIS EYES POP/
I COULD TELL BY HUGHIE'S FACE BEFORE HE WENT TO 30 HUGHIE
THE HOSPITAL, HE WAS THROUGH.
I'D TELL HIM I BOUGHT ONE OF THOSE MERCEDES SPORT 32 HUGHIE
ROADSTERS
I'D TELL HIM I LAY THREE BABES FROM THE FOLLIES-- 32 HUGHIE
TWO BLONDES AND ONE BRUNETTE/
I'D TELL HIM I WIN TEN GRAND FROM THE BOOKIES, AND 32 HUGHIE
TEN GRAND AT STUD.
TELL DEM COME TAKE JOE'S BODY AWAY, 'CAUSE HE'S 586 ICEMAN
SURE ENUF DEAD.
YOU DIDN'T TELL ME ANYTHING. 587 ICEMAN
YOU USED TO TAKE ME ON YOUR KNEE AND TELL ME 588 ICEMAN
STORIES
(IN A LOWERED VOICE BUT EAGERLY, AS IF HE WANTED 588 ICEMAN
THIS CHANCE TO TELL ABOUT IT)
SHE DIDN'T TELL ME, BUT SHE'D KEPT ALL YOUR 589 ICEMAN
LETTERS.
I ASKED HER NOT TO TELL ANYONE. 593 ICEMAN
TELL ME SOME MORE ABOUT THIS DUMP. 593 ICEMAN
I DIDN'T TELL YOU TO BEAT UP THE POOR GUY. 598 ICEMAN
HOW MUCH ROOM RENT DO YOU OWE ME, TELL ME THATS 602 ICEMAN
AND MAYBE TELL 'EM I'LL LET 'EM DEAL ME A HAND IN 604 ICEMAN
THEIR GAME AGAIN.
JA, CECIL. I KNOW HOW BEAUTIFUL IT MUST BE, FROM 605 ICEMAN
ALL YOU TELL ME MANY TIMES.
THE BOYS TELL ME THERE'S FINE PICKINGS THESE DAYS,607 ICEMAN
SHE USED TO TELL ME, -I DON'T KNOW WHAT YOU CAN 608 ICEMAN
SEE IN THAT WORTHLESS, DRUNKEN,
OR, YOU NEVER CAN TELL, 608 ICEMAN
AND HE SAYS, -TELL DE GANG I'LL BE ALONG IN A 617 ICEMAN
MINUTE.
-LADY,- HE SAYS, -CAN YUH KINDLY TELL ME DE 617 ICEMAN
NEAREST WAY
TELL HIM WE'RE WAITIN' TO BE SAVED/ 618 ICEMAN
TELL US ABOUT YOURSELF. 619 ICEMAN
THIS DUMB BROAD WAS TRYIN' TO TELL US YOU'D 619 ICEMAN
CHANGED, BUT YOU AIN'T A DAMNED BIT.
NO, I FORGOT TO TELL ROCKY-- 620 ICEMAN
IT WAS GOING ON TWELVE WHEN I WENT IN THE BEDROOM 622 ICEMAN
TO TELL EVELYN I WAS LEAVING.
NO, DON'T TELL ME, JIMMY. 623 ICEMAN
ANY TIME YOU THINK I'M TALKING OUT OF TURN, JUST 624 ICEMAN
TELL ME TO GO CHASE MYSELF/
I CAN TELL YOU'RE HAVING TROUBLE WITH YOURSELF 624 ICEMAN
TELL US MORE ABOUT HOW YOU'RE GOING TO SAVE US. 624 ICEMAN
BUT I DON'T NEED NO HICKEY TO TELL ME, 626 ICEMAN
GUILLOTINING OFF HIS CHEST, TELL ME MORE ABOUT 627 ICEMAN
YOUR DOCTOR FRIEND, ED.
ON'T HE DON'T REALLY TELL YUH. 631 ICEMAN
WHY DON'T YUH TELL DEM TO LAY OFF ME$ 636 ICEMAN
AFRAID IF HE GOT DRUNK, HE'D TELL-- 638 ICEMAN
BUT I HAVE A FEELING HE'S DYING TO TELL US, INSIDE638 ICEMAN
HIM, AND YET HE'S AFRAID.
TELL ME ABOUT HIM. 642 ICEMAN
THAT'S ANOTHER LIE YOU TELL YOURSELF, LARRY, 643 ICEMAN
I'VE GOT TO TELL YOU, LARRY/ 648 ICEMAN
MAN ALIVE, FROM WHAT THE BOYS TELL ME, THERE'S 653 ICEMAN
SUGAR GALORE THESE DAYS,
ONLY TELL HIM TO LAY OFF ME. 653 ICEMAN
(GRUMPILY) TELL HIM TO LAY OFF ME. 653 ICEMAN
AMUSEDLY) YES, WE'VE ALL HEARD YOU TELL US YOU 656 ICEMAN
THOUGHT THE WORLD OF HER.
I DIDN'T WANT TO TELL YOU YET. 663 ICEMAN
HELL, I DON'T HAVE TO TELL YOU--YOU ALL KNOW WHAT 663 ICEMAN
I WAS LIKE.
I'M SORRY TO TELL YOU MY DEARLY BELOVED WIFE IS 663 ICEMAN
AND SHE'D ALWAYS TELL ME THE TRUTH. 667 ICEMAN
ANYONE IN THE COAST GROUD COULD TELL YOU 667 ICEMAN
JEES, IF SHE'D DONE DAT, HE WOULDN'T TELL US HE 668 ICEMAN
WAS GLAD ABOUT IT, WOULD HE$
AND GO UP TO TELL DEM TO CAN DE NOISE. 669 ICEMAN
WHEN HE SAYS HE'S GLAD SHE CROAKED, AND YUH CAN 669 ICEMAN
TELL HE MEANS ITS
DIDN'T I TELL YOU HE'D BROUGHT DEATH WITH HIM$ 672 ICEMAN
DOT LONGSHOREMAN BOSS, DAN, HE TELL ME ANY TIME I 676 ICEMAN
LIKE, HE TAKE ME ON.
FLATFOOT MICK TRYING TO TELL ME WHERE I GOT OFF/ 681 ICEMAN
THEN YOU'LL TELL YOURSELF YOU WOULDN'T STAND A 686 ICEMAN
CHANCE IF YOU WENT UP SOUSED TO
LARRY VILL TELL YOU I HAF NEVER BEEN SO CRAZY 691 ICEMAN
TRUNK.
I TELL YOU I KNOW FROM MY OWN EXPERIENCE/ 692 ICEMAN
TELL US THAT/ 693 ICEMAN
THEN SLOWLY) NO, I'M SORRY TO HAVE TO TELL YOU MY694 ICEMAN
POOR WIFE WAS KILLED.
I'M GOIN' TO TELL HARRY I'M QUITTIN'. 697 ICEMAN
IF YOU OBJECTS TO MY SITTIN' HERE, CAPTAIN, JUST 700 ICEMAN
TELL ME AND I PULLS MY FREIGHT.
ANYBODY COULD TELL YOU I SHOULD FEEL HONORED A 700 ICEMAN
BLOODY KAFFIR WOULD LOWER HIMSELF
I REMEMBER I HAD SOMETING ON MY MIND TO TELL YUH. 701 ICEMAN
I'M CERTAIN IF I TELL YOU ABOUT IT FROM THE 707 ICEMAN
BEGINNING,

TELL

TELL (CONT'D.)

I DON'T NEED TO TELL ANYONE. 707 ICEMAN
(SUDDENLY BURSTS OUT) I'VE GOT TO TELL YOU/ 708 ICEMAN
I'D TELL HER ALL MY FAULTS, HOW I LIKED MY BOOZE 711 ICEMAN
EVERY ONCE IN A WHILE,
IN EACH LETTER I'D TELL HER HOW I MISSED HER, BUT 711 ICEMAN
I'D KEEP WARNING HER, TOO.
I'D TELL HER, IT'S THE LAST TIME. 712 ICEMAN
SOMEONE I COULD TELL A DIRTY JOKE TO AND SHE'D 712 ICEMAN
LAUGH.
BUT I COULD TELL SHE THOUGHT IT WAS DIRTY, NOT 712 ICEMAN
FUNNY.
I WAS GOING TO TELL HER IT WAS THE END. 715 ICEMAN
YOU'VE GOT A CRUST TRYING TO TELL US ABOUT HICKEY/718 ICEMAN
HE MAKES ME TELL LIES ABOUT MYSELF. 721 ICEMAN
"TELL ME, NANA, IS THAT BOER GENERAL, THE ONE WITH723 ICEMAN
THE BLUE BEHINDS$
THE BOYS TELL ME THE RUBES ARE WASTING ALL THEIR 724 ICEMAN
MONEY BUYING FOOD
(THEY MAKE DERISIVE NOISES AND TELL HIM TO SIT 724 ICEMAN
DOWN.
I TELL YOU DIS ROTTEN COFFEE GIVE ME BELLY-ACHE/ 515 INZONE
I'LL TELL YOU IN A MINIT. 517 INZONE
I'VE GOT SOMETHING I WANT TO TELL THE BOYS 518 INZONE
AND I'VE SOMETHIN' MYSELF TO TELL ABOUT HIS 518 INZONE
LORDSHIP.
(TO THE OTHERS) THEN SCOTTY KIN TELL YOU IF I'M 519 INZONE
LYIN' OR NOT.
AN' SCOTTY'LL TELL YOU IF I AIN'T SPEAKIN' TRUTH. 520 INZONE
HOW'D IT COME TO GET OPEN, TELL ME THATS 521 INZONE
WILL YOU TELL US TO OUR FACESS 526 INZONE
MAYBE IT'S DYNAMITE--OR SOMETHIN'--YOU CAN'T NEVER528 INZONE
TELL.
YOU CAN'T NEVER TELL. 529 INZONE
WHAT'D I TELL YOUS 530 INZONE
(MEANINGLY) WHAT'D I TELL YOUS 530 INZONE
YOU WERE SNORING SO HARD I COULDN'T TELL WHICH WAS 17 JOURNE
THE FOGHORN/
I CAN'T TELL YOU THE DEEP HAPPINESS IT GIVES ME, 17 JOURNE
DARLING.
(GRINA.) I MEANT TO TELL YOU LAST NIGHT, PAPA, 22 JOURNE
AND FORGOT IT.
A COLD/ ANYONE CAN TELL THAT/ 27 JOURNE
YOU DARE TELL ME WHAT I CAN AFFORDS 31 JOURNE
WHATEVER BULL THEY HAND YOU, THEY TELL ME HE'S A 36 JOURNE
PRETTY BUM REPORTER.
BUT I NEEDN'T TELL YOU, JAMIE. 36 JOURNE
(TENSELY.) BUT GO ON AND TELL ME-- 37 JOURNE
THERE'S NOTHING TO TELL. 37 JOURNE
NOTHING, I TELL YOU. 38 JOURNE
TELL ME THE TRUTH. 45 JOURNE
I INSIST YOU TELL ME WHY YOU ACT SO DIFFERENTLY 46 JOURNE
THIS MORNING--
YOU DIDN'T TELL ME-- 56 JOURNE
MAMA DIDN'T TELL HER SHE WOULDN'T BE DOWN TO 56 JOURNE
LUNCH.
BUT I WAS WISE TEN YEARS OR MORE BEFORE WE HAD TO 57 JOURNE
TELL YOU.
AND NOW YOU TELL ME SHE GOT YOU TO LEAVE HER ALONE 57 JOURNE
UPSTAIRS ALL MORNING.
I'VE TOLD CATHLEEN TIME AND AGAIN SHE MUST GO 60 JOURNE
WHEREVER HE IS AND TELL HIM.
TELL BRIDGET I'M SORRY BUT SHE'LL HAVE TO WAIT A 62 JOURNE
FEW MINUTES UNTIL MISTER TYRONE
I MUST TELL BRIDGET. 64 JOURNE
IT'S DIFFICULT TO TELL FROM HER COOKING 72 JOURNE
BUT PLEASE DON'T TRY TO TELL ME. 74 JOURNE
WHY SHOULDN'T I TELL HARDY THE TRUTHS 80 JOURNE
IT'S HARD FOR A STRANGER TO TELL, BUT AFTER 83 JOURNE
THIRTY-FIVE YEARS OF MARRIAGE--
AND I NEVER KNOW WHERE TO TELL SMYTHE TO GO. 85 JOURNE
(CYNICALLY.) DID DOC HARDY TELL YOU I WAS GOING TO 90 JOURNE
DIES
HE'LL ONLY TELL YOU SOME LIE. 92 JOURNE
AND TELL YOUR FATHER. 95 JOURNE
I'LL TELL HER I KEPT YOU WITH ME. 100 JOURNE
I CAN TELL THE MASTER IS WORRIED ABOUT HIM. 100 JOURNE
BY THE TIME HE COMES HOME HE'LL BE TOO DRUNK TO 101 JOURNE
TELL THE DIFFERENCE.
TELL BRIDGET I WON'T WAIT. 106 JOURNE
SHE'D GRUMBLE, "YOU NEVER TELL ME, NEVER MIND WHAT114 JOURNE
IT COSTS.
BUT IT WAS IMPORTANT TO ME, I CAN TELL YOU/ 114 JOURNE
YOU'D NEVER TELL HER, NEVER MIND THE COST. 115 JOURNE
ANY FOOL COULD TELL-- MARY, ANSWER ME/ 116 JOURNE
I'VE HEARD PAPA TELL THAT MACHINE SHOP STORY TEN 117 JOURNE
THOUSAND TIMES.
(IGNORING THIS.) DON'T TELL ME ABOUT HARDY/ 118 JOURNE
I'M GOING TO TELL YOU WHETHER YOU WANT TO HEAR OR 119 JOURNE
NOT.
AND YOU WON'T EVEN LISTEN WHEN I TRY TO TELL YOU 120 JOURNE
HOW SICK--
YOU'D TELL ME NEXT YOU WERE GOING TO DIE-- 120 JOURNE
I CAN TELL WHEN YOU'RE ACTING/ 122 JOURNE
THEN IT DOESN'T TAKE A SOOTHSAYER TO TELL HE'S 129 JOURNE
PROBABLY IN THE WHOREHOUSE.
THE DOCTORS DID TELL ME IT'S A GOOD PLACE. 148 JOURNE
I COULDN'T TOUCH WHAT I TRIED TO TELL YOU JUST 154 JOURNE
NOW.
DID YOU TELL GASPARD I GOT IT OUT OF DOC HARDY 158 JOURNE
SO GOT TO TELL YOU NOW. 165 JOURNE
OR MIGHT NOT BE DRUNK ENOUGH TO TELL YOU TRUTH. 165 JOURNE
BUT I DIDN'T MEAN TO TELL YOU THAT LAST STUFF--GO 166 JOURNE
THAT FAR BACK.
THINK OF ME AS DEAD--TELL PEOPLE, "I HAD A 166 JOURNE
BROTHER, BUT HE'S DEAD."
SHE'LL TELL ME IT ISN'T FAIR TO MY FATHER 171 JOURNE

TELL (CONT'D.)

AND TELL ME TO PRAY TO THE BLESSED VIRGIN, AND 171 JOURNE
THEY'LL BE WELL AGAIN IN NO TIME.
I TELL YOU I WAS NEVER HERE IN THIS HOUSE WHEN LAZARUS 276 LAZARU
DIED/
THAT DAY I RETURNED DID I NOT TELL YOU YOUR FEAR 289 LAZARU
WAS NO MORES
SONS OF GOD WHO APPEARED ON WORLDS LIKE OURS TO 289 LAZARU
TELL THE SAVING TRUTH TO EARS
THEN IF THERE IS NO DEATH, O TEACHER, TELL ME WHY 308 LAZARU
I LOVE TO KILLS
BUT I TELL YOU TO LAUGH IN THE MIRROR, THAT SEEING309 LAZARU
YOUR LIFE GAY.
(THEN WITH AN IRONIC SMILE) BUT YOU NEED NOT TELL327 LAZARU
TIBERIUS THAT, GOOD FLAVIUS.
TELL ME/ 331 LAZARU
CAESAR WISHED ME TO BID YOU WELCOME, TO TELL YOU 333 LAZARU
HOW MUCH REGARD HE HAS FOR YOU.
TELL ME YOU LIE, MARCELLUS/ 334 LAZARU
TELL ME, HOW COULD THAT BES 342 LAZARU
TO TELL ME YOU UNDERSTAND AND LAUGH WITH ME AT 346 LAZARU
LASTS
(LAZARUS DOES NOT REPLY) IF THOU DOST NOT TELL 350 LAZARU
ME, I MUST ALWAYS DOUBT THERE.
WHY DO I TELL YOU THESE OLD TALESS 356 LAZARU
AND YET--HE MUST KNOW SOMETHING--AND IF HE WOULD--364 LAZARU
EVEN NOW HE COULD TELL--
HE TOLD THE SERVANT TO TELL ME HE WOULD COME. 4 MANSNS
TELL ME, SIMON, DO YOU EVER THINK NOW OF THE BOOK 8 MANSNS
YOU WERE SO EAGER TO WRITES
YOU WOULD BE HORRIBLY SHOCKED IF I SHOULD TELL YOU 13 MANSNS
THE NATURE OF THE PART I PLAY
SO TELL ME-- 13 MANSNS
BUT BEFORE THAT I WANT TO TELL YOU HOW SORRY I WAS 19 MANSNS
WHEN SIMON LAUGHED.
I TELL YOU, BEFORE YOU CALLED, I SAW THAT DOOR, 29 MANSNS
I TELL YOU I AM STILL TEMPTED-- 30 MANSNS
I TELL YOU I SWORE TO MYSELF YEARS AGO 36 MANSNS
NO, THAT IS WHY I CAN SAFELY TELL YOU ALL MY 39 MANSNS
SECRETS, NICHOLAS.
(ABRUPTLY.) BUT ALL I WANTED TO TELL YOU WAS MY 47 MANSNS
FINAL DECISION ABOUT THE BOOK.
I TELL YOU, SARA, THE MORE I THINK OF IT, THE MORE 48 MANSNS
OPPORTUNITIES I FORESEE.
YOU CAN EXPLAIN YOUR MISSION THERE, AND LEAVE ME 52 MANSNS
TO TELL SARA.
YOU CAN TELL ME THAT. 55 MANSNS
AND I NEED NOT TELL YOU HOW DELIGHTED I WOULD BE. 56 MANSNS
I TELL YOU, SARA, THIS IS EXACTLY THE CHANCE FOR 63 MANSNS
EXPANSION WE WERE HOPING FOR.
SO GO ON NOW AND TELL ME, DARLING. 64 MANSNS
SPEAKING OF BUSINESS, TELL ME ABOUT THE COMPANY. 76 MANSNS
AND DON'T TELL ME MOTHER MINDS MY INDIFFERENCE. 79 MANSNS
DON'T TELL ME YOU'RE JEALOUS OF THE CHILDREN--WITH 79 MANSNS
MES
TELL ME--/ 80 MANSNS
TELL ME YOU HAVEN'T, SIMON/ 83 MANSNS
AND DIDN'T SHE TELL ME HERSELF SHE'D GOT TO THE 86 MANSNS
POINT WHERE SHE DIDN'T DARE GO
BUT WHO WILL TELL HERS 86 MANSNS
WELL, I SUPPOSE I COULD TELL HER, IF YOU WANT TO 87 MANSNS
BE SPARED.
DO YOU MEAN TO TELL ME A VIRTUOUS WIFE AND MOTHER 89 MANSNS
TOO/
TELL ME PLAINLY WHAT YOUR PLAN IS. 89 MANSNS
STOP TEASING NOW AND TELL ME. 89 MANSNS
I'M NOT ANXIOUS TO TELL HER--WELL, IT'LL DO HER 93 MANSNS
GOOD/
MOTHER WILL BE CURIOUS ABOUT YOUR VISIT HERE BUT 93 MANSNS
DON'T TELL HER ANYTHING.
TELL THEM TO COME IN. 94 MANSNS
(SMILINGLY.) YOU WILL UNDERSTAND WHY WHEN I TELL 97 MANSNS
YOU THE ONE PERSON WHO
DON'T TELL ME YOU ARE JEALOUS OF YOUR CHILDREN, 100 MANSNS
TOO/
(HE BEGINS TO TELL THE STORY, STARING BEFORE HIM 110 MANSNS
AS IF HE VISUALIZED IT.)
I CAN'T WAIT TO TELL HER YOU ARE GOING TO BE WITH 115 MANSNS
ME EACH EVENING.
AND BEGGING HER TO TELL ME A FAIRY TALE/ 121 MANSNS
DO TELL US WHAT YOU DREAMED. 127 MANSNS
THEN I THINK WE CAN NOW SAFELY TELL EACH OTHER 131 MANSNS
HE WISHED TO TELL YOU AND MADE ME PROMISE I 131 MANSNS
WOULDN'T.
TELL ME YOUR SECRET, DAUGHTER. 132 MANSNS
AND I'LL UNDERSTAND WHEN YOU TELL ME-- 132 MANSNS
BUT NOW TELL ME WHAT HE MADE YOU AGREE TO. 134 MANSNS
TELL ME ABOUT THE CHILDREN WHEN THEY WERE WITH 135 MANSNS
YOU, LIKE YOU ALWAYS DO.
TELL YOU, AS WOMAN TO WOMAN, 135 MANSNS
TELL ME YOU LOVE ME. 145 MANSNS
YOU CAN TELL JOEL TO HAVE HIM SENT IN. 147 MANSNS
I AM PLEASED TO TELL YOU THAT IS THE REASON. 153 MANSNS
WHY DO I LIE AND TELL MYSELF IT IS I WHO HAVE LED 163 MANSNS
SIMON BACK INTO THE PAST,
AND I'VE MORE TO TELL YOU. 166 MANSNS
YOU CAME HERE TO TELL ME--SO YOU COULD GLOAT/ 166 MANSNS
FOOL, IF I DIDN'T TELL YOU HE'D COME HOME WITH ME 166 MANSNS
AND FORGOTTEN ALL ABOUT YOU.
I HEARD YOU. I TELL YOU. 174 MANSNS
I TELL YOU I KNOW. 185 MANSNS
SARA--WAIT--FORGIVE--I WANT TO SAY--MY GRATITUDE--189 MANSNS
WANT TO TELL YOU--
TO TELL ALL OUR ENEMIES AND COMBINE WITH THEM TO 191 MANSNS
POUNCE DOWN AND RUIN US/
BUT--TELL ME THIS, ARE YOU HAPPY NOW, MY LADYS 193 MANSNS
FOR THE LOVE OF GOD, DEBORAH, TELL ME YOU'RE NOT 193 MANSNS
JUST PRETENDING NOW--

TELL

TELL (CONT'D.)
AT LEAST SO THEY INSTRUCTED ME TO TELL PEOPLE TO 348 MARCOM
GET THEM TO BUY.
(SOFTLY) GO ON AND TELL ME, MARK. 355 MARCOM
TELL THE GREAT KAAN HE MUST HAVE BEEN IMPOSED UPON363 MARCOM
BY YOUR PATRIOTIC LIES.
WOULD YOU TELL ME HOW OLD YOU ARE$ 366 MARCOM
(WITH A WINK) I'LL TELL YOU A GOOD ONE 366 MARCOM
I'LL HAVE TO GIVE MARCO SOME LESSONS IN HOW TO 374 MARCOM
TELL A SHORT STORY.
YOU SHALL TELL ME ABOUT YOUR SOUL 380 MARCOM
TELL ME, WHAT SHALL I DO WITH HIM$ 382 MARCOM
TELL ME, CAN YOU HAVE FALLEN IN LOVE$ 386 MARCOM
(HESITATINGLY) BUT, TO TELL THE TRUTH, I WANT TO 393 MARCOM
RESIGN ANYHOW.
WELL, I'LL TELL YOU THE SECRET. 393 MARCOM
WHAT WILL YOUR POPE SAY WHEN YOU TELL HIM I'M 396 MARCOM
STILL UNCONVERTED
(WITH FORCED GAIETY) AND TELL YOUR POPE YOUR 397 MARCOM
EXAMPLE HAS DONE MUCH
I'LL TELL YOU A GOOD JOKE ON ME, YOUR HIGHNESS. 399 MARCOM
TELL ME--ALL YOU CAN TELL--PARTICULARLY WHAT HIS 401 MARCOM
IMMORTAL SOUL IS LIKE/
YOU CAN TELL HIM THAT I'VE ALWAYS DONE MY DUTY BY 403 MARCOM
HIM
WELL, YOU TELL HIM I'LL SEE TO IT SHE KEEPS IN 404 MARCOM
GOOD CONDITION.
DIDN'T I TELL YOU TO STRIKE UP WHEN I SET FOOT ON 406 MARCOM
THE DECK$
AND TELL THE KAAN--ANYTHING HE WANTS--WRITE ME-- 407 MARCOM
JUST VENICE--
I WILL TELL THEM BOTH OF YOUR HEROIC CRUELTY IN 412 MARCOM
SAVING ME FROM DEATH/
YOUR FIRST LETTER TO THE GREAT KAAN, AND ALSO TELL412 MARCOM
YOUR HUSBAND$
AND TELL CHU-YIN I LOVE HIM TOO.* 424 MARCOM
HE SAID TELL THE GREAT KAAN THAT *IN SPITE OF 424 MARCOM
PERILS TOO NUMEROUS TO RELATE,
I CAN TELL WITHOUT BITING IT. 427 MARCOM
I CAN'T TELL. 428 MARCOM
I TELL YOU I WOULDN'T HAVE MARRIED THE PRETTIEST 430 MARCOM
GIRL IN CATHAY/
DIDN'T I TELL YOU HALF-PAST ELEVEN$ 4 MISBEG
AND WHO'LL TELL CUSTOMERS THEY'VE HAD ENOUGH AND 5 MISBEG
BETTER GO HOME JUST WHEN
TELL YOUR CONSCIENCE IT'S A BIT OF THE WAGES HE'S 7 MISBEG
NEVER GIVEN YOU.
DON'T TELL ME/ 9 MISBEG
I'LL TELL THE TRUTH THEN. 14 MISBEG
TO TELL THE TRUTH, I NEVER LIKED HIM. 16 MISBEG
BUT TO TELL THE TRUTH, I'M WELL SATISFIED YOU'RE 20 MISBEG
WHAT YOU ARE.
(BEGINNING TO BOIL) I TELL YOU, JOSIE, 21 MISBEG
YOU NEVER CAN TELL WHAT HE MIGHTN'T DO HERE IN THE 21 MISBEG
COUNTRY, WHERE HE'S INNOCENT.
I NEVER CAN TELL TO THIS DAY WHEN YOU PUT THAT 23 MISBEG
DEAD MUG ON YOU.
(DRYLY) YES, THAT'S WHAT HE'D TELL ME, 25 MISBEG
YOU'D TELL HIM YOU'D VACATE THE PREMISES 25 MISBEG
AND GAPE AT HIM AND TELL HIM HE WAS THE HANDSOMEST 25 MISBEG
MAN IN THE WORLD.
SO NO ONE CAN TELL AT TIMES WHAT YOU'RE AFTER. 26 MISBEG
DON'T TELL ME YOU COULDN'T LEARN TO LOVE THE 30 MISBEG
ESTATE HE'LL COME INTO.
I CAN TELL. 32 MISBEG
IT CAME THROUGH A REAL-ESTATE MAN WHO WOULDN'T 32 MISBEG
TELL WHO HIS CLIENT WAS.
HE SAID HE TOLD THE AGENT TO TELL WHOEVER IT WAS 32 MISBEG
THE PLACE WASN'T FOR SALE.
BAD LUCK TO YOU, CAN'T YOU TELL US WHO$ 47 MISBEG
IN FACT, HE ASKED ME TO TELL YOU HE HOPES YOU KILL 48 MISBEG
HIM.
I TELL YOU A SMALL GLASS AND YOU GIVE HIM A 53 MISBEG
BUCKET/
AND YOU CAN TELL ME YOUR THOUGHTS. 54 MISBEG
(TO HARDER, JEERINGLY) COME, TELL US THE TRUTH, 58 MISBEG
ME HONEY.
TELL ME NOW. IF IT ISN'T A SECRET, 63 MISBEG
THAT CAN'T BELIEVE A MAN WOULD TELL HER A LIE/ 80 MISBEG
I CAN TELL YOU EACH THING THAT HAPPENED TONIGHT AS 81 MISBEG
CLEAR AS IF I'D NOT TAKEN A
HE HAD ONE OF HIS QUEER FITS WHEN YOU CAN'T TELL. 82 MISBEG
(FURIOUSLY) YOU'LL TELL THAT LIE ABOUT MY LOVE 83 MISBEG
ONCE TOO OFTEN/
WILL YOU STOP BLATHERING LIKE AN OLD WOMAN AND 83 MISBEG
TELL ME PLAINLY WHAT HE'S DONE/
FAITH, YOU DON'T HAVE TO TELL ME. 88 MISBEG
(ANGRILY) DIDN'T YOU TELL ME TO GET HOLD OF MY 93 MISBEG
WITS$
A FATHER TO TELL HIS DAUGHTER HOW TO-- 94 MISBEG
DO I HAVE TO TELL YOU HIS WEAKNESS AGAIN$ 95 MISBEG
AND HE'LL GIVE ANYTHING TO KEEP US QUIET, I TELL 96 MISBEG
YOU.
MAYBE I'LL TELL YOU--LATER, WHEN I'M-- THAT'LL 122 MISBEG
CURE YOU--FOR ALL TIME/
(QUIETLY) HE DIDN'T TELL ME. 131 MISBEG
I TOLD SIMPSON TO TELL HARDER I DID. 132 MISBEG
I'LL TELL HIM WHAT HE CAN DO WITH HIMSELF, HIS 132 MISBEG
BANK-ROLL AND TEN OIL TANKS.
LISTEN, AND I'LL TELL YOU A LITTLE STORY, JOSIE. 143 MISBEG
(UNEASILY) WHY DID YOU TELL ME THIS$ 144 MISBEG
(PUZZLED) YOU SAID YOU'D TELL ME ABOUT THE BLONDE145 MISBEG
ON THE TRAIN.
(HE PAUSES--DULLY) NO, I CAN'T TELL YOU, JOSIE. 145 MISBEG
AFTER ALL, I SAID I'D TELL YOU LATER, DIDN'T I$ 145 MISBEG
IF I COULD TELL HER IT WAS BECAUSE I MISSED HER SO$158 MISBEG
MUCH

TELL (CONT'D.)
FOR THE LOVE OF GOD, CAN'T YOU TELL ME WHAT 160 MISBEG
HAPPENED TO YOU$
DIDN'T I TELL YOU TO SPEAK LOW AND NOT WAKE HIM/ 161 MISBEG
I CALLED YOU HERE TO TELL YOU I'VE SEEN THROUGH 162 MISBEG
ALL THE LIES YOU TOLD LAST NIGHT
DON'T TELL ME YOU DIDN'T COUNT ON THAT, AND YOU 164 MISBEG
SUCH A CLEVER SCHEMER/
YOU CAN TELL. 169 MISBEG
(HE PAUSES) HOPE I DIDN'T TELL YOU THE SAD STORY 170 MISBEG
OF MY LIFE
(HIS FACE CLEARING.) TELL ME WHAT I SAID AND I'LL 11 POET
TELL YOU IF IT WAS LIES.
(LOWERING HIS VOICE.) TELL ME, HAS HE DONE ANY 13 POET
RAMPAGIN' WID WOMEN HERE$
MAYBE, IF YOU'D COME DOWN FROM YOUR HIGH HORSE, I 17 POET
COULD TELL YOU SOME NEWS.
OR I'LL TELL MY FATHER OF YOUR IMPUDENCE. 17 POET
IT'S HARD TO TELL, BUT SHE'S TOO YOUNG FOR HIS 18 POET
MOTHER, I'D SWEAR.
WHY WOULD I TELL HER, WHEN SHE NEVER MENTIONED 19 POET
HIM$
(ANGRILY.) YOU CAN'T MUCH LONGER, I TELL YOU/ 24 POET
YOU OUGHT TO TELL THE GOOD FATHER WE AREN'T THE 27 POET
IGNORANT SHANTY SCUM
IT'S EASY TO TELL YOUNG MASTER HARFORD HAS A TOUCH 30 POET
AV THE POET IN HIM--
I CAN TELL SHE'S HAD GREAT INFLUENCE OVER HIM. 31 POET
TO TELL THE TRUTH, MY STOMACH IS OUT OF SORTS. 36 POET
WHY DON'T YOU TELL ME TO EXAMINE MY OWN CONDUCT$ 41 POET
I WAS ABOUT TO TELL YOU HOW EXCEEDINGLY CHARMING 45 POET
AND PRETTY YOU LOOK, MY DEAR.
IS IT STARK MAD YOU'VE GONE, SO YOU CAN'T TELL ANY 51 POET
MORE WHAT'S DEAD AND A LIE,
UNLESS YE TELL HIM. 55 POET
YOU NEEDN'T TELL ME. 58 POET
I TELL YOU SHE MISTOOK MY MEANING, AND NOW YOU-- 61 POET
TO HEAR YOU TELL IT, YOU'D THINK IT WAS YOU WHO 61 POET
SEDUCED ME/
WOULDN'T SHE TELL SIMON THAT ANYWAY, 79 POET
(NORA STARTS TO TELL HER THE TRUTH--THEN THINKS 80 POET
BETTER OF IT.
AND IT'LL BE HARD TO TELL WHAT SHE'S REALLY UP TO. 80 POET
BUT YOU CAN'T TELL-- 87 POET
TELL HIM I'M TOO BUSY. 88 POET
(HASTILY.) BUT WHAT I WANT TO TELL YOU IS I AM 90 POET
SORRY IT HAPPENED, SARA,
AND I THINK YOU WILL FIND WHAT I HAVE TO TELL YOU 105 POET
OF GREAT INTEREST.
I WAS ABOUT TO TELL YOU OF THE TALK I HAD THIS 107 POET
AFTERNOON WITH YOUNG HARFORD.
ARRAH, DON'T TELL ME SHE'S MADE A FOOL OF YOU 109 POET
AGAIN/
TELL ME THIS/ 110 POET
BUT I MUST TELL YOU MY TIME IS SHORT. 119 POET
WILL YOU TELL ME PLAINLY WHAT YOU MEAN BY YOUR 121 POET
TALK OF SETTLEMENT$
YOU MAY TELL THE SWINDLING TRADER, HARFORD, 123 POET
(SHE APPEALS TO CREGAN.) TELL HIM I'M TELLING THE126 POET
TRUTH, JAMIE.
DON'T TELL ME NOT TO WORRY. 137 POET
TELL US WHAT HAPPENED, JAMIE. 154 POET
TELL HIM, HE SAYS, *IF HE KNOWS WHAT'S GOOD FOR 155 POET
HIM HE'LL SEE ME.
KAPE YOUR MOUTH SHUT, AND LAVE ME TELL IT, AND 155 POET
YOU'LL SEE IF HE LET THEM/
IT'LL BE JAMIE COMING TO TELL US-- 163 POET
AND DON'T BE AFRAID, SARA, THAT I'LL TELL THE BOYS165 POET
A WORD AV THIS.
DIDN'T I TELL YOU THERE WAS A GREAT JOKE IN ITS 169 POET
(GRINNING AGAIN.) I'VE MEANT TO TELL YOU OFTEN, 174 POET
AND DON'T REMEMBER WHAT THE MAJOR USED TO TELL 174 POET
YOU.
MAKIN' ME TELL MAD LIES TO EXCUSE HIS DIVILMENTS. 175 POET
BE GOD, I'VE A BIT OF NEWS TO TELL THE BOYS 178 POET
I'LL EVEN TELL SIMON--THAT AFTER HIS FATHER'S 178 POET
INSULT TO YOU--
BUT I TELL YOU AGEN THAT LUKE OF YOURS AIN'T 581 ROPE
COMIN' BACK.
WHAT DID HE TELL YOU$ 585 ROPE
I COULD TELL BY HIS FACE. 585 ROPE
HE'S A CUTE ONE, AW, HE'D BE ASKIN' A FEE TO TELL 585 ROPE
YOU YOUR NAME,
NOT BURYIN' IT LIKE YOUR MISER FOLKS'D TELL YOU. 589 ROPE
(GETTING UP) I'LL TELL HIM A LITTLE AT A TIME 590 ROPE
TELL HE KNOWS.
AND TELL THE OLD MAN I'M HERE AND I'LL SEE HIM IN 591 ROPE
A WHILE.
WHAT DID I TELL YOU$ 596 ROPE
BUT I'LL TELL YUH SOMETHING YOU CAN PUT IN YOUR 598 ROPE
PIPE AND SMOKE.
YOU JUST WATCH ME. I TELL YUH/ 598 ROPE
THEN YOU 'N' ME *ULL MAKE HIM TELL/ 600 ROPE
I KNOW A TRICK OR TWO ABOUT MAKIN' PEOPLE TELL 600 ROPE
WHAT THEY DON'T WANTER.
HE'LL TELL THEN--ANYTHING WE WANTS HIM TO TELL. 600 ROPE
WE'LL GIT EVEN ON HIM, YOU 'N' ME--AND HE'LL TELL 600 ROPE
WHERE ITS HID.
(ARGUING WITH HIMSELF) (I$HALL I TELL HIM$.... 8 STRANG
(I'VE GOT TO TELL HIM... 10 STRANG
BUT I GATHER HE DIDN'T TELL HER IT WAS YOUR 11 STRANG
SCALPEL ORIGINALLY$
(WONDERINGLY) YOU DON'T MEAN TO TELL ME SHE HAS 11 STRANG
ACCUSED YOU OF ALL THIS$
AND I MUSTN'T TELL HIM.... 17 STRANG
I MUSTN'T LET GO OR I'LL TELL HIM EVERYTHING... 17 STRANG
(SEVERELY) YOU SERIOUSLY MEAN TO TELL ME YOU, IN 17 STRANG
YOUR CONDITION,

TELL

TELL (CONT'D.)
(WITH ASPERITY) BUT I TELL YOU IT'S QUITE IMPOSSIBLE/ 17 STRANG
(THINKING DESPERATELY) (I'M BEGINNING TO TELL HIM/... 18 STRANG
(THINKING GLUMLY) (WON'T TELL HIM I TRIED FOR FLYING SERVICE... 30 STRANG
(THEN IN A SUDDEN FLURRY) (SHALL I TELL HIM... 31 STRANG
SOMETHING I OUGHT TO TELL YOU, I THINK. 32 STRANG
YOU WANT TO TELL ME YOU'RE IN LOVE WITH NINA$ 32 STRANG
WHILE INNUMERABLE PLAIN ONES TELL HIM DREAMS ABOUT 34 STRANG
SNAKES./
(THINKING) (HOW MUCH NEED I TELL HIM... 35 STRANG
CAN'T TELL HIM THE RAW TRUTH ABOUT HER PROMISCUITY.. 35 STRANG
I WISH HE WOULDN'T TELL ME/...)) 35 STRANG
I'VE WANTED TO RUN HOME AND 'FESS UP, TELL HOW BAD 44 STRANG
I'VE BEEN, AND BE PUNISHED/
YOU WILL, WON'T YOU--OR TELL ME HOW TO PUNISH MYSELF$ 44 STRANG
TELL NO ONE... 49 STRANG
(KISSES HER--JOYOUSLY) I'LL TELL HER THAT. 49 STRANG
(GOT TO START IN TO TELL HER... 57 STRANG
(A BIT VIOLENTLY) I TELL YOU IT'D BE A CRIME--A 58 STRANG
CRIME WORSE THAN MURDER/
(TELL HER/... 58 STRANG
HE DIDN'T TELL ME UNTIL AFTER WE WERE MARRIED. 59 STRANG
AND NOW YOU TELL ME I'VE GOT TO TELL MY-- 61 STRANG
WHY DIDN'T YOU TELL HIM HE MUST NEVER MARRY/ 61 STRANG
BUT I CAN'T TELL YOU NOT TO LEAVE HIM, NOT IF YOU 62 STRANG
DON'T LOVE HIM.
WOULDN'T TELL ME... 67 STRANG
YOU CAN'T TELL THAT/...)) 68 STRANG
FORGOT TO TELL NINA... 68 STRANG
I CAN'T TELL HIM IT'S WITH PITY... 69 STRANG
HE COULDN'T TELL WHAT TRAIN. 72 STRANG
(THEN CONFUSEDLY) SAY, I FORGOT TO TELL YOU NED'S 72 STRANG
COMING OUT TONIGHT.
(EXCITEDLY) WHY DIDN'T YOU TELL ME BEFORE, YOU 72 STRANG
BIG BOOBY/
COME UP AND TELL ME IF IT'S NED--AND GET RID OF 73 STRANG
CHARLIE$
DID I TELL YOU I ONCE LOOKED UP GORDON'S FAMILY IN 75 STRANG
BEACHAMPTON$
WHY DIDN'T YOU TELL ME IF I WAS INTERRUPTING--YOUR 75 STRANG
WRITING/
I'LL GO UP AND TELL NINA YOU'RE HERE, NED. 76 STRANG
HOPE SHE'LL TELL 78 STRANG
SHE'S GOING TO TELL..)) 81 STRANG
TELL ME. 82 STRANG
WHY DON'T YOU BEGIN AT THE BEGINNING AND TELL ME 82 STRANG
ALL ABOUT IT$
TELL HER YOU'VE DECIDED... 92 STRANG
(TELL HER/... 92 STRANG
GOSH, NED, I CAN'T TELL YOU HOW GRATEFUL I AM/ 95 STRANG
WHY DOESN'T SHE TELL HIM SHE'S PREGNANT$... 96 STRANG
I TELL YOU I DON'T/ 97 STRANG
I'LL TELL HIM/... 100 STRANG
SHE MEANT, TELL HIM... 105 STRANG
AND AFTER LUNCH WE'LL TELL SAM...)) 105 STRANG
TELL HER THAT, SAM/ 106 STRANG
SO I'M GOING TO TELL YOU ALTHOUGH NINA'LL BE FURIOUS WITH ME. 106 STRANG
BOTH UP YOU, TELL HER/ 106 STRANG
TELL HIM ABOUT BABY/... 106 STRANG
AND TELL NINA I'LL EXPECT TO FIND YOU BOTH HAPPY 106 STRANG
IN YOUR CHILD--
DIDN'T HE TELL YOU HE WAS SAILING FOR EUROPE$ 107 STRANG
I'LL TELL SAM HE WAS LYING/... 108 STRANG
HE SAID TO TELL YOU THAT. 109 STRANG
I TELL YOU, THE MOMENT NED TOLD ME, SOMETHING HAPPENED TO ME/ 109 STRANG
I CAN'T TELL HIM WITHOUT NED TO HELP ME/... 109 STRANG
DID I TELL YOU I RAN INTO DOCTOR DARRELL IN 115 STRANG
MUNICH$
(MORE CALMLY NOW) WHY ON EARTH DIDN'T YOU TELL US115 STRANG
BEFORE, CHARLIE$
WHAT A FOOL I WAS EVER TO TELL HIM/...)) 115 STRANG
WHY DID HE TELL ME$...)) 116 STRANG
(MOCKINGLY) DO TELL US ABOUT ALL YOUR VARIOUS 117 STRANG
MISTRESSES IN FOREIGN PARTS.
NINA WANTED TO TELL SAM... 124 STRANG
NOW I'LL TELL HIM MYSELF/...)) 124 STRANG
CAN'T TELL IF SHE LOVES/...)) 126 STRANG
DO TELL US/ 127 STRANG
MAKES IT EASIER TO TELL HIM THE TRUTH... 128 STRANG
I'LL TELL SAM THE TRUTH NO MATTER WHAT/...) 129 STRANG
I CAN TELL SAM--AND I WILL--RIGHT NOW--BY GOD I 132 STRANG
WILL/
HE WANTS TO TELL YOU SOMETHING, SAM. 133 STRANG
(CRUSHED--STAMMERS) NO--I MEAN, YES--I WANT TO 133 STRANG
TELL YOU HOW DAMN GLAD I AM...
(I CAN'T TELL HIM/... 133 STRANG
TELL HIM THAT IF I DIDN'T THINK HE'D LAUGH AT ME 134 STRANG
GIVING HIM ADVICE...
AND TELL HIM TO GET OUT AND NEVER COME BACK/... 138 STRANG
I'LL TELL DAD/ 142 STRANG
YOU'D BETTER TELL HIM YOU KISSED ME GOOD-BY TO GET146 STRANG
RID OF ME/
WITHOUT MY HAVING TO TELL HIM...)) 147 STRANG
(INTENSELY) THERE ARE THINGS WE DON'T TELL, YOU 151 STRANG
AND I/
YOU DON'T HAVE TO TELL ME/ 151 STRANG
AND SOMETIME I'M GOING TO TELL HIM I SAW YOU-- 151 STRANG
I WASN'T GOING TO TELL DAD ANYWAY, HONEST I 151 STRANG
WASN'T/
IF I WAS TO TELL DAD ON YOU/ 151 STRANG

TELL (CONT'D.)
THERE ARE THINGS A MAN OF HONOR DOESN'T TELL 151 STRANG
ANYONE--
(DREAMILY) TELL ME ABOUT HIM AGAIN, WILL YOU, 153 STRANG
DAD--
COME OVER HERE AND TELL ME ABOUT YOUR BIRTHDAY. 153 STRANG
OH, MOTHER GOD, GRANT MY PRAYER THAT SOME DAY WE 156 STRANG
MAY TELL OUR SON THE TRUTH AND
(OUR MOTHER GOD, GRANT THAT I MAY SOME DAY TELL 158 STRANG
THIS FOOL THE TRUTH/...))
SHE'LL TELL ME SOMETIME... 164 STRANG
TELL ME YOUR SECRET. 165 STRANG
(THEN FORCING A SMILE) SO TELL ME WHAT FOUNTAIN 165 STRANG
OF YOUTH YOU'VE FOUND.
AGE IS BEGINNING TO TELL ON NINA'S FACE... 168 STRANG
I'LL TELL HIM GORDON ISN'T HIS CHILD/... 171 STRANG
AND THREATEN TO TELL GORDON TOO, UNLESS/... 171 STRANG
THEN IT'S TIME TO TELL HIM THE 172 STRANG
NED MUST TELL HIM TOD/... 172 STRANG
ENOUGH TO MAKE HIM TELL SAM/...)) 172 STRANG
YOU'VE GOT TO TELL HIM/ 173 STRANG
TELL SAM THE TRUTH$... 173 STRANG
OBSESSED, BUT SAM WON'T BELIEVE ME IF I'M THE 173 STRANG
ONLY ONE TO TELL HIM/
(HARSHLY) I'VE STOPPED MEDDLING IN SAM'S LIFE, I 173 STRANG
TELL YOU/
BY GOD, I'D LIKE TO TELL HIM, AT THAT/...)) 173 STRANG
YOU'VE GOT TO TELL HIM TOO, NED/ 173 STRANG
HE'LL NEVER TELL SAM NOW... 174 STRANG
YOU MUST TELL HIM, NED/ 174 STRANG
(THINKING DULLY) (SHE'LL TELL SAM... 175 STRANG
I'LL TELL SAM/ 175 STRANG
I'VE WANTED ALL MY LIFE TO TELL HER/...) 175 STRANG
SAM SAID TO TELL YOU GORDON WAS ON EVEN TERMS WITH175 STRANG
THE LEADERS/
(WHY NOT TELL HER$... 176 STRANG
(I CAN TELL HER... 177 STRANG
I CAN PRETEND I'M FORCED TO TELL HER... 177 STRANG
YOU CAN'T TELL A DAMN THING--WHICH IS WHICH OR 177 STRANG
WHO'S AHEAD--
COULDN'T YOU TELL ME LATER, MRS. EVANS--AFTER THE 178 STRANG
RACE$
(NOT HEEDING--IMPRESSIVELY) THERE'S SOMETHING I 178 STRANG
MUST TELL YOU.
TO TELL YOU THAT MRS. EVANS ISN'T HERSELF. 178 STRANG
TELL YOU TO A LIVING SOUL--ABOVE ALL NOT TO 178 STRANG
GORDON/
CAN YOU TELL WHICH IS WHICH, MADELINE$ 179 STRANG
I WAS GOING TO TELL MADELINE THAT SO SHE WOULDN'T 179 STRANG
MARRY GORDON.
I FORGIVE EVEN YOUR TRYING TO TELL MADELINE--YOU 180 STRANG
WANTED TO KEEP GORDON--
I WILL NEVER TELL HIM ANYTHING THAT MIGHT DISTURB 183 STRANG
HIS PEACE/
I'LL TELL YOU, MADELINE/ 185 STRANG
SHALL I TELL HER YOU WANT TO SEE HER$ 188 STRANG
HE'D BETTER CHANGE HIS TUNE OR I'LL CERTAINLY BE 191 STRANG
TEMPTED TO TELL HIM...
I'LL TELL HIM/... 193 STRANG
I'VE GOT TO TELL YOU SOMETHING-- 195 STRANG
DID YOU STILL WANT TO TELL GORDON SOMETHING, NED$ 196 STRANG
IT'S SARPAS$ NINE ANY TIME AS SOME ONE WAS A 495 VOYAGE
COMIN' IN, TELL YOU.
I'LL GO AH' AN' TELL 'EM. 496 VOYAGE
(GRUMBLINGLY) I TELL YOU--DOT IS RI-IGHT. 500 VOYAGE
(INDIGNANTLY) I TELL YOU--DOT'S SOMETHING I DON' 500 VOYAGE
LI-IKE/
TELL ME SOMETHIN' ABAHT YESELF. 502 VOYAGE
I WRITE TO HER FROM BONOS ERES BUT I DON'T TELL 506 VOYAGE
HER I COME HOME.
TELL DRISC--I GO HOME. 508 VOYAGE
TELL ME ALL ABOUT IT. 444 WELDED
(A PAUSE--THEN SCORNFULLY) DON'T TELL ME YOU'RE 448 WELDED
BECOMING JEALOUS OF JOHN AGAIN$
HE DOES, I TELL YOU/ 459 WELDED
TELL ME WHAT HAPPENED BETWEEN YOU AND MICHAEL/ 467 WELDED
I HAD TO TELL THAT LIE/ 468 WELDED
DON'T DO THAT, I TELL YOU/ 477 WELDED
YES, I WISH TO TELL YOU THE TRUTH. 482 WELDED
HAVEN'T YOU SOMETHING YOU WANT TO TELL$ 482 WELDED
I'VE CHANGED, I TELL YOU/ 483 WELDED
THEN I MAY AS WELL TELL YOU I--(HE CHECKS HIMSELF 484 WELDED
AND TURNS AWAY.)
I ONLY TELL YOU THIS FOR MY OWN SATISFACTION. 484 WELDED
I WANT TO TELL YOU THAT TONIGHT--JOHN AND I-- 484 WELDED
NOTHING YOU MAY EVER SUSPECT--
SHALL I TELL YOU WHAT HAPPENED TO ME$ 484 WELDED
TELL ME THAT. 484 WELDED
EVERYTHING IS CHANGED, I TELL YOU/ 485 WELDED
(DESPERATELY) I TELL YOU I--/ 485 WELDED

TELL
HE PACKA DA WALLOP, I TELLA YOU/ 209 HA APE
AND YOU THINK YOU'RE TELLIN' ME SOMETHIN' NEW, 539 'ILE
MR. SLOCUM$
(ICILY) YOU'RE TELLIN' ME NOTHIN' I DON'T KNOW. 544 'ILE
(JOKINGLY) THAT'S A FINE FAIRY TALE TO BE 8 ANNA
TELLIN'--YOUR DAUGHTER/
I'M TELLIN' YUH I'M SICK OF STICKIN' WITH YUH, AND 11 ANNA
I'M LEAVING YUH FLAT, SEES
(IRRITABLY) BUT ALL THIS TALK AIN'T TELLIN' ME 103 BEYOND
WHAT I'M TO DO WITH THAT STRAN'D
IF THIS FOG KEEPS UP, I'M TELLIN' YE, WE'LL NO BE 481 CARDIF
IN CARDIFF FOR A WEEK OR MORE.
(APPEALING TO THE OTHERS) AM I TELLIN' HIM A LIE$482 CARDIF
WHAT ARE YE TELLIN' ME$ 243 DESIRE
SHE'S TELLIN' YE T' LOVE ME. 243 DESIRE
SHE'S TELLIN' YE T' LOVE ME, EBEN/ 243 DESIRE

TELLING

TELLIN' (CONT'D.)
(SOBERLY--A BIT DISTURBED) I WAS TELLIN' EMMER 499 DIFRNT
NOT TO TAKE ME THAT HIGH.
THAT IS, IF HE'S BEEN TELLIN' TALES. 501 DIFRNT
HE WAS TELLIN' ME ALL 'BOUT THEIR VIGE. 501 DIFRNT
THE BOYS HAS BEEN TELLIN' THE HULL TOWN. 502 DIFRNT
TELLIN' STORIES LIKE IT OUT O' THEIR EXPERIENCES. 502 DIFRNT
IS IT--'COUNT OF THAT JOKE ABOUT CALEB I WAS 504 DIFRNT
TELLIN' YOU?
WAAL, EMMER, WHAT'S THIS FOOLISHNESS JACK'S BEEN 507 DIFRNT
TELLIN' ABOUT--
AN' ALL 'COUNT O' THAT JOKE THEY'RE TELLIN' 513 DIFRNT
HERE'S EMMER TELLIN' YOU THE TRUTH AFTER YOU HAIR-513 DIFRNT
PULLIN' ME ALL THESE YEARS
SHE SAYS JACK'D TOLD YOU THAT STORY THEY'RE ALL 514 DIFRNT
TELLIN' AS A JOKE ON ME.
BUT THAT AIN'T NO GOOD REASON FOR TELLIN' IT. 515 DIFRNT
I GOT A SWELL CHANCE TELLIN' THAT TO UNCLE CALEB. 523 DIFRNT
IT AIN'T COUNT O' NOTHIN' HARRIET'S BEEN TELLIN' 539 DIFRNT
YOU, IS IT?
OH, NOTHIN' WORTH TELLIN'. 539 DIFRNT
(ICILY FORMAL) WOULD YOU MIND TELLIN' HIM I WANT 547 DIFRNT
TO SEE HIM?
AN' WHEN I GIT THROUGH TELLIN' MY STORY OF IT 135 ELECTR
ROUND TOWN TOMORROW
AN' I'M ONLY TELLIN' YOU FUR ONE REASON-- 136 ELECTR
WE'RE WAITIN' TO HEAR WHAT THEY LANDED YOU FOR--OR241 HA APE
AIN'T YUH TELLIN'S
TELLIN' SAPS A STORY TO MAKE 'EM BET/ 22 HUGHIE
AFTER DINNER I STARTED TELLIN' 'EM A STORY 25 HUGHIE
I BEEN TELLIN' MYSELF, THIS GUY AIN'T LIKE OLD 36 HUGHIE
HUGHIE.
YEAH, CHUCK, IT'S LIKE I'M TELLIN' DESE BROADS 630 ICEMAN
ABOUT DE CAKE.
HE'S BUTTIN' IN ALL OVER DE PLACE, TELLIN' 631 ICEMAN
EVERYBODY WHERE DEY GET OFF.
(TO ROCKY--DEFIANTLY) I'S STOOD TELLIN' PEOPLE 637 ICEMAN
WHEN HE FORGETS DE BUGHOUSE PREACHIN', AND QUITS 638 ICEMAN
TELLIN' YUH WHERE YUH GET OFF.
BUT HIS TELLIN' ABOUT HIS WIFE CROAKIN' PUT DE K. 665 ICEMAN
O. ON IT.
HE'LL BE TELLIN' ALL ABOUT IT SOON. 708 ICEMAN
RIGHT AS RAIN, I'M TELLIN' YE/ 519 INZONE
AN' THIN THERE'S A LOT AV BLARNEY TELLIN' HIM HOW 530 INZONE
MUCH SHE MISSES HIM
BUT WENT AROUND TELLIN' EVERY STRANGER ALL MY 161 POET
SECRETS.
DID YOU HEAR HIM TELLIN' ME HE LOVED ME, SARA$ 181 POET
KELLAR OF THE BANK TELLIN' ME ONCE. 586 ROPE
D'YOU NOT REMEMBER THE LETTER SHE WROTE TELLIN' 586 ROPE
HIM HE COULD SUPPORT LUKE ON THE
"TIS NOT HIM'D BE TELLIN'. 600 ROPE

TELLING
WELL, I DON'T MIND TELLING YOU I GOT MIGHTY 230 AHWILD
SCARED.
I KEPT TELLING YOU ALL DAY I WAS IN DELICATE 232 AHWILD
CONDITION AND YET YOU KEPT FORCING
NAT MILLER, YOU'RE TELLING ME A FIB, SO'S NOT TO 250 AHWILD
WORRY ME.
RAND WAS TELLING ME HE LIKED NOTHING BETTER THAN 255 AHWILD
TO HEAR YOU SING--
WELL, I'D THOUGHT OF TELLING YOU YOU COULDN'T GO 296 AHWILD
TO YALE--
I WAS TELLING HER I'D RATHER YOU GAVE ME A JOB ON 296 AHWILD
THE PAPER BECAUSE THEN SHE AND
AND ONLY FOR ME, I'M TELLING YOU, AND THE GREAT 32 ANNA
STRENGTH AND RIGHTS.
YOU'RE NOT THE OLD SQUARE-HEAD'S WOMAN, I SUPPOSE 32 ANNA
YOU'LL BE TELLING ME NEXT--
(EARNESTLY) 'TIS NO LIE I'M TELLING YOU ABOUT THE 34 ANNA
WOMEN.
AND YOU'LL BE TELLING ME A BIT OF YOURSELF, 35 ANNA
LET YOU SIT DOWN, NOW, MISS, AND I'LL BE TELLING 35 ANNA
YOU A BIT OF MYSELF.
(PROUDLY) AND IF 'TWASN'T FOR ME AND MY GREAT 36 ANNA
STRENGTH, I'M TELLING YOU--
BUT FOR THE LIKE OF US DOES BE ROAMING THE SEAS, A 36 ANNA
GOOD END, I'M TELLING YOU--
HE WASN'T TELLING NO LIE. 37 ANNA
I'M TELLING YOU THERE'S THE WILL OF GOD IN IT THAT 39 ANNA
BROUGHT ME SAFE THROUGH THE
AND I'M TELLING YOU SHE'LL NOT. 46 ANNA
I'LL SEE MYSELF AND ANNA MARRIED THIS DAY, I'M 47 ANNA
TELLING YOU.
'TIS YOUR OWN MAD NOTIONS I'M AFTER TELLING. 48 ANNA
'TIS THAT YOU'RE NEEDING IN YOUR FAMILY, I'M 49 ANNA
TELLING YOU--
HE'S NOT AFTER TELLING YOU THE WHOLE OF IT. 50 ANNA
'TIS MAD YOU ARE, I'M TELLING YOU/ 53 ANNA
DO YOU HEAR WHAT I'M TELLING YOUS 56 ANNA
I'M SHIPPING AWAY OUT OF THIS, I'M TELLING YOU/ 61 ANNA
THAT AIN'T TELLING ME WHY YOU GOT ITS 67 ANNA
SHE'S GONE OUT OF THIS LONG AGO, I'M TELLING YOU, 68 ANNA
I'LL NOT FORGET 'TIL MY DYING DAY, I'M TELLING 71 ANNA
YOU,
IF I AIN'T TELLING YOU THE HONEST TRUTH/ 73 ANNA
(SLOWLY) IF 'TIS TRUTH YOU'RE AFTER TELLING, I'D 74 ANNA
HAVE A RIGHT, MAYBE,
AND I'M TELLING YOU THERE'S GREAT POWER IN IT, 75 ANNA
I'M TELLING YOU/ 77 ANNA
(CHARMED BY HIS LOW, MUSICAL VOICE TELLING THE 89 BEYOND
DREAMS OF HIS CHILDHOOD)
TELLING ME TO LOOK OUT AND BE QUIET. 89 BEYOND
YOU MUSTN'T MIND MY TELLING YOU THIS, RUTH. 91 BEYOND
I WAS JUST TELLING YOUR FATHER WHEN YOU CAME IN-- 100 BEYOND
I HADN'T INTENDED TELLING HER ANYTHING BUT-- 100 BEYOND
SUDDENLY--I FELT I MUST.
IT WOULDN'T BE ANY USE TELLING US THAT NOW. 101 BEYOND

TELLING (CONT'D.)
BUT I'VE KEPT ON TELLING MYSELF THAT I MUST BE 127 BEYOND
WRONG--LIKE A FOOL/
I'M TELLING YOU THE TRUTH WHEN I SAY I'D FORGOTTEN134 BEYOND
LONG AGO.
I'VE JUST BEEN TELLING HIM ALL ABOUT IT. 137 BEYOND
(STARING AT HIM INTENSELY) ARE YOU TELLING ME THE138 BEYOND
TRUTH, ANDY MAYOS
HE IS TELLING A STORY. 478 CARDIF
WHAT'S THE USE OF TELLING--WHEN THEY BELIEVE--WHENS64 CROSS
THEY'RE AFRAIDS
AND, FOR HEAVEN'S SAKE, DON'T GO TELLING ELSA I'M 513 DAYS
UNHAPPY.
WALTER HAS BEEN TELLING PEOPLE. 526 DAYS
(THEN BITTERLY) AND HOW LONG DO YOU THINK YOU'LL 527 DAYS
BE ABLE TO RESIST TELLING
(THEN SMILING TEASINGLY) WELL, IF YOU LOVE ME SO 529 DAYS
MUCH, PROVE IT BY TELLING ME.
(CONTROLLING A START) TELLING YOU WHAT& 529 DAYS
TO GET OUT OF TELLING US THE REST OF HIS NOVEL, 533 DAYS
TELLING ME I OWE IT TO MYSELF TO PASS FOR 429 DYNAMO
ENGINEER'S PAPERS.
(WHILE HE HAS BEEN TELLING THIS STORY, 447 DYNAMO
HE'S TELLING/---))
I WAS JUST TELLING YOUR OLD MAN IT WAS ONLY A 451 DYNAMO
MURDER STORY OUT OF THE PAPER 451 DYNAMO
THE CONSCIOUSNESS OF THE EVIL OF THE LIE HE IS 466 DYNAMO
TELLING
BUT I'VE GOT TO FINISH TELLING YOU ALL I'VE COME 477 DYNAMO
TO KNOW ABOUT HER--
I HEARD YOU TELLING HIM---I LOVE YOU, ADAM.---AND 30 ELECTR
KISSING HIM/
STOP TELLING ME SUCH THINGS/ 31 ELECTR
AND NOT GIVE VINNIE THE SATISFACTION OF TELLING 36 ELECTR
HIM.
(THEN TURNING AWAY AGAIN) YOU REMEMBER MY TELLING 39 ELECTR
YOU HE HAD WRITTEN
YOU MURDERED HIM JUST THE SAME--BY TELLING HIM/ 64 ELECTR
I SWEAR BY OUR DEAD FATHER I AM TELLING YOU THE 97 ELECTR
TRUTH/
I HEARD HER TELLING HIM, "I LOVE YOU, ADAM." 99 ELECTR
I SUPPOSE YOU'VE BEEN TELLING HIM YOUR VILE LIES, 100 ELECTR
YOU--
YOU'RE TELLING ME IT WAS. 101 ELECTR
ORIN WAS TELLING ME OF AN ISLAND-- 112 ELECTR
DO YOU REMEMBER ME TELLING YOU HOW THE FACES OF 115 ELECTR
THE MEN I KILLED CAME BACK AND
YOU--YOU'RE JUST TELLING ME THAT--TO PUNISH ME, 120 ELECTR
AREN'T YOUS
AND I WAS JUST TELLING HER HOW WELL SHE LOOKED IN 144 ELECTR
COLOR.
HE KEEPS TELLING ME/ 152 ELECTR
BUT I SUPPOSE THE GOSSIPS ARE TELLING THE SAME 276 GGROW
SILLY STORIES ABOUT HIM THEY
HE'S FALLEN IN LOVE, I'M TELLING YOU. 227 HA APE
BUT I'M TELLING YOU IT'S LOVE THAT'S IN IT. 228 HA APE
'TWAS TOUCHING, I'M TELLING YOU/ 230 HA APE
SHE'S HAD HER BELLY-FULL, I'M TELLING YOU. 232 HA APE
BELIEVE ME, PAL, I CAN STOP GUYS THAT START 26 HUGHIE
TELLING ME THEIR FAMILY TROUBLES/
492 WON'T GO TO BED AND INSISTS UN TELLING ME 26 HUGHIE
JOKES.
WHAT'S HE BEEN TELLING ME& 31 HUGHIE
WOULD YOU MIND TELLING ME IF IT'S REALLY TRUE WHEN 35 HUGHIE
ARNOLD ROTHSTEIN PLAYS POKER,
AIN'T I TELLING HIM THE TRUTH, COMRADE HUGOS 579 ICEMAN
TELLING PEOPLE YOU THROW THE MONEY UP IN THE AIR 582 ICEMAN
I'M TELLING YOU THIS SO YOU'LL KNOW WHY IF DON 584 ICEMAN
ACTS A BIT QUEER.
(IRRITABLY) I'M TELLING YOU I DON'T KNOW ANYTHING584 ICEMAN
AND I DON'T WANT TO KNOW.
(HE PAUSES--SERIOUSLY) BUT I'M TELLING YOU SOME 607 ICEMAN
DAY BEFORE LONG
TELLING THEM THERE'S NOTHING LIKE SNAKE OIL FUR A 628 ICEMAN
BAD BURN.
THEY'LL BE TOO BUSY TELLING HARRY WHAT A DRUNKEN 651 ICEMAN
CROOK I AM
I'M TELLING YOU, ED, IT'S SERIOUS THIS TIME. 651 ICEMAN
GOD HELP US POOR BUMS IF YOU'D EVER GET TO TELLING658 ICEMAN
US WHERE TO GET OFF/
THEY WERE ALWAYS TELLING JOKES. 710 ICEMAN
AND THEN TELLING HERSELF EVEN IF IT WAS TRUE, HE 712 ICEMAN
COULDN'T HELP IT,
I KEEP TELLING HIM THAT BUT HE SAYS HE SIMPLY HAS 16 JOURNE
NO APPETITE.
(HEARTILY,) JUST WHAT I'VE BEEN TELLING HER, 20 JOURNE
JAMIE.
SHE BEGINS TELLING ME ABOUT HER RELATIVES 29 JOURNE
BUT I SEEM TO BE ALWAYS PICKING ON YOU, TELLING 58 JOURNE
YOU DON'T DO THIS
BUT HE KEPT UN TALKING TO THAT MAN, TELLING HIM OF 62 JOURNE
THE TIME WHEN--
BECAUSE YOU WROTE TELLING ME YOU MISSED ME AND 87 JOURNE
WERE SO LONELY,
DO YOU KNOW WHAT I WAS TELLING HER, DEARS 112 JOURNE
(DRYLY.) THANKS FOR TELLING ME YOUR GREAT SECRET.155 JOURNE
THEN, SOON AS I GOT IN THE DOOR, MAMIE BEGAN 159 JOURNE
TELLING ME ALL HER TROUBLES.
AT THE LAST JUDGMENT, YOU'LL BE AROUND TELLING 165 JOURNE
EVERYONE IT'S IN THE BAG.
MY SAYING WHAT I'M TELLING YOU NOW PROVES IT. 166 JOURNE
AND IT ISN'T TELLING ME WHY YOU'RE HERE OR WHAT 53 MANSNS
YOU WANT OF ME.
WHAT HAS THIS GOT TO DO WITH THE BUSINESS HIS 55 MANSNS
BROTHER IS TELLING SIMONS
(SMILING.) I'M ALL THE TIME TELLING HIM HOW PROUD 64 MANSNS
I AM,

TELLING

TELLING (CONT'D.)
LAUGHING AND TELLING EACH OTHER ABOUT THE 120 MANSNS CHILDREN--
HE SAID I WAS STILL SO BEAUTIFUL TO HIM AND I KNEW133 MANSNS HE WAS TELLING THE TRUTH.
HE'LL NEVER COME HERE AGAIN. I'M TELLING YOU/ 166 MANSNS THE GOES ON TELLING THE REST OF THE STORY WITH 366 MARCOM MUCH EXAGGERATED JEWISH PANTOMIME
I CAN SEE WHERE I'LL HAVE TO BE TELLING HER WHAT 406 MARCOM TO DO EVERY SECOND.
I DON'T MIND TELLING YOU, DONATA, I'M WORTH OVER 430 MARCOM TWO MILLIONS/
AND WE'D START DRINKING AND TELLING STORIES, AND 26 MISBEG SINGING SONGS,
I WAS TELLING YOU I COULD SEE THE MERIT IN YOUR 26 MISBEG MARRYING HIM.
THERE'S NO USE TELLING THE TRUTH TO A BAD-TEMPERED 80 MISBEG WOMAN IN LOVE.
WELL, I KNOW MY FATHER'S VIRTUES WITHOUT YOU 124 MISBEG TELLING ME.
AND DON'T BE TELLING ME OF YOUR OLD FLAMES, ON 129 MISBEG TRAINS OR NOT.
(KNOWS HE IS TELLING THE TRUTH--SO RELIEVED SHE 132 MISBEG CAN ONLY STAMMER STUPIDLY)
WHY, I REMEMBER TELLING HIM TONIGHT I'D EVEN 133 MISBEG WRITTEN MY BROTHER.
THIS IS THE ONLY WAY HE CAN START TELLING THE 146 MISBEG STORY)
BUT I KNOW ALL ABOUT IT WITHOUT YOU TELLING ME. 13 POET
WELL, THANK YOU FOR TELLING ME, 14 POET
BY TELLING HIM A NEW COACH LINE WAS GOING TO STOP 26 POET HERE.
I'VE JUST BEEN TELLING HIM I BEGGED ANOTHER 60 POET MONTH'S CREDIT FROM NEILAN.
IT'S BECAUSE SIMON'S FATHER GOT A LETTER TELLING 78 POET HIM ABOUT US.
AH, WILL YOU STOP TELLING ME YOUR MAD DREAMS/ 91 POET (SHE APPEALS TO CREGAN.) TELL HIM I'M TELLING THE126 POET TRUTH, JAMIE.
I KNOW IT'S NO USE TELLING YOU THERE WON'T BE ANY 140 POET DUEL, MOTHER.
THEN I WAS CRYING AND TELLING HIM HOW AFRAID I'D 144 POET BEEN HIS MOTHER HATED ME.
(SHARPLY.) WHIST, I'M TELLING YOU/ 151 POET
ALWAYS TELLING YOU HOW BENEFICIAL THE TRAINING AT 24 STRANG THE HOSPITAL WOULD BE FOR HER
NEWSY, LOVELESS SCRIPTS, TELLING NOTHING WHATEVER 25 STRANG ABOUT HERSELF...
AND THAT'S WHY I'M TELLING YOU/ 60 STRANG
WHAT REASON COULD I GIVE, WITHOUT TELLING HIM 61 STRANG EVERYTHING$
SHE KNOWS THAT I LOVE HER WITHOUT MY TELLING... 148 STRANG
WHAT'S THE USE OF MY TELLING YOU$ 154 STRANG
SO YOU SEE I'D BE TELLING SAM A LIE IF I BOASTED 174 STRANG THAT I--AND I'M A MAN OF HONOR/

TELLS
HE TELLS THE TRUTH ABOUT REAL LOVE/ 198 AHWILD
IS THAT WHAT HE TELLS PEOPLE/ 18 ANNA
AND THEN THEY TELLS THE FISH TO WHISTLE TO 'EM 95 BEYOND WHEN IT'S TIME TO TURN OUT.
(DULLY) HE NEVER TELLS HER. 539 DAYS
SO THEY TELLS HER THE CAPTAIN HAD SENT FOR HER AND903 DIFRNT SHE WAS TO SWIM RIGHT OUT AND
AND I TELLS YOU, AFTER A YEAR OR MORE ABOARD SHIP,514 DIFRNT
WHEN HE TELLS HIM THE LIES ABOUT US-- 533 DIFRNT
(JUDICIALLY) YOU HEAR WHAT I TELLS YOU, SMITHERS.178 EJONES
I HAS DE SILVER BULLET MOULDED AND I TELLS 'EM 179 EJONES WHEN DE TIME COMES I KILLS MYSELF
I TELLS 'EM DAT'S CAUSE I'M DE ON'Y MAN IN DE 179 EJONES WUHLD BIG ENUFF TO GIT ME.
WELL, I TELLS YOU, SMITHERS, MAYBE I DOES KILL ONE180 EJONES WHITE MAN BACK.
IT'S A STORY I TELLS YOU SO'S YOU KNOWS I'SE DE 181 EJONES KIND OF MAN DAT IF YOU EVAH
I TELLS YOU I'SE SAFE'S 'F I WAS IN NEW YORK CITY.186 EJONES
HE TELLS EVERYBODY THE SUCCESS IS ALL DUE TO HIS 260 GGBROW ENERGY--
(QUICKLY) HE ALWAYS TELLS PEOPLE THAT. 276 GGBROW
THEY'LL KNEEL AND WORSHIP THE IRONIC SILENUS WHO 297 GGBROW TELLS THEM THE BEST GOOD IS
(FRIGHTENEDLY) KEEP YER BLOOMIN' MOUTH SHUT, I 237 HA APE TELLS YER.
»NOT A DAMNED DRINK DE HOUSE,» HE TELLS ME, 578 ICEMAN
TO GIVE HIM THE KUSH TO A CURE, BUT DE LAWYER 581 ICEMAN TELLS HARRY WI%
FOLKS IN DE KNOW TELLS ME, SEE DE MAN AT DE TOP, 600 ICEMAN DEN YOU NEVER HAS TROUBLE.
»JEES, BABY,» I TELLS HER, »WHY SHOULD IS 616 ICEMAN
AND I TELLS HIM, HOW DO I KNOW YUH'RE OFF OF 616 ICEMAN PERIODICALS FUR LIFES
AND I TELLS HER I'M OFF DE STUFF FOR LIFE. 616 ICEMAN
SO I TELLS HER AT DE FERRY, »KIDDO, YUH CAN GO TO 697 ICEMAN JOISEY, OR TO HELL,
OF THE LETTER THEY SEES ON'Y THE WORDS WHAT TELLS 529 INZONE THEM WHAT THEY WANTS TO KNOW.
HE TELLS THEM THERE IS NO DEATH AT ALL/ 302 LAZARU
SURELY YOUR GOOD SENSE TELLS YOU-- 370 LAZARU
MY MEMORY TELLS ME A CRUELER STORY. 5 MANSNS
BUT EVERYONE TELLS US 76 MANSNS
WHEN HE TELLS HER HE IS COMING TO MY GARDEN EVERY 118 MANSNS EVENING--
AS MAFFEO TELLS THE STORY, 370 MARCOM
HE TELLS HIM-- 389 MARCOM
HE TELLS HER IT WAS THE PRIESTS TRICKED HIM INTO 14 POET MARRYING HER.
(MUCKINGLY.) IS THAT WHAT HE TELLS YOU, AND YOU 19 POET BELIEVE HIM$
THEY PROMISED FAITHFUL THEY'D COME, I TELLS YER. 495 VOYAGE

TEMERITY
(THEN ALARMED AT HIS OWN TEMERITY--HASTILY) 411 MARCOM

TEMPER
(MAKING A TREMENDOUS EFFORT TO CONTROL HIS TEMPER)202 AHWILD
YOU NEEDN'T LOSE YOUR TEMPER. 203 AHWILD
(LOSING HIS TEMPER--HARSHLY) 235 AHWILD
GEE, FORGIVE ME FOR LOSING MY TEMPER AND BAWLING 242 AHWILD YOU OUT. WILL YOU$
KEEP YOUR TEMPER/ 261 AHWILD
DON'T GO LOSING YOUR TEMPER AGAIN. 265 AHWILD
AND THEN YOU LOST YOUR TEMPER AND WERE SO SHARP 265 AHWILD WITH HIM RIGHT AFTER DINNER.
(WORRIEDLY) NOW YOU KEEP YOUR TEMPER, NAT, 266 AHWILD REMEMBER/
(DEFENSIVELY AGGRESSIVE) NOW DON'T LOSE YOUR 268 AHWILD TEMPER AT ME, NAT MILLER/
(WITH A CHUCKLE) BAD TEMPER, NOTHING. 269 AHWILD
GOOD GRACIOUS, DICK, YOU DO ACT SILLY, FLYING INTO103 BEYOND A TEMPER OVER NOTHING.
(LOSING HIS TEMPER--BITTERLY) 107 BEYOND
(FLYING INTO A PETTY TEMPER) 146 BEYOND
SHE ADDS TARTLY, HER CONFIDENCE RESTORED AND HER 433 DYNAMO TEMPER A BIT RUFFLED)
(SUDDENLY FLARES UP INTO A TEMPER) 451 DYNAMO
(IMMEDIATELY FLYING INTO A TEMPER) 454 DYNAMO
MY, BUT HE'S IN A BREAKFAST TEMPER, THOUGH. 456 DYNAMO
I'M A FOOL TO LET YOU MAKE ME LOSE MY TEMPER--OVER 34 ELECTR YOUR JEALOUS SPITE/
I MUSTN'T LOSE MY TEMPER/ 61 ELECTR
KEEP YER BLOOMIN' TEMPER. 236 HA APE
(GRINS GENIALLY) YES, DEAR OLD BESS HAD A QUICK 608 ICEMAN TEMPER.
I LOST MY TEMPER/ 660 ICEMAN
(FOR THE FIRST TIME LOSES HIS TEMPER) 692 ICEMAN
NOW, JAMES, DON'T LOSE YOUR TEMPER. 26 JOURNE
(LOSING HIS TEMPER.) YOU OUGHT TO BE KICKED OUT 76 JOURNE IN THE GUTTER/
IF SHE DON'T GET SOMETHING TO QUIET HER TEMPER, 106 JOURNE
YOU SHOULDN'T GOAD ME INTO LOSING MY TEMPER. 128 JOURNE
(TRYING TO CONTROL HIS TEMPER.) 140 JOURNE
I'LL ONLY LOSE MY TEMPER. 154 JOURNE
(TYRONE TURNS AWAY, TRYING TO CONTROL HIS TEMPER.1168 JOURNE
I ASK YOUR PARDON FOR LOSING MY TEMPER, MRS. 19 MANSNS HARFORD.
FOR ALTHOUGH FLIGHTY IN TEMPER AND OF A PASSIONATE424 MARCOM DISPOSITION,
I'VE BEEN HOLDING MY TEMPER, BECAUSE WE'RE SAYING 9 MISBEG GOOD-BYE.
TO HELL WITH YOUR TEMPER, YOU OVERGROWN COW/ 12 MISBEG
OR MAYBE I'LL LOSE MY TEMPER, TOO. 12 MISBEG
(HIS TEMPER RISING AGAIN) AND I KNOW DAMNED WELL 13 MISBEG HE HADN'T
DON'T FLY IN A TEMPER. 29 MISBEG
(BEGINNING TO LOSE HIS TEMPER) 58 MISBEG
YOU CAN TAKE YOUR BAD TEMPER OUT ON YOUR 101 MISBEG SWEETHEART HERE.
(CONTROLLING HIS TEMPER.) I AM NOT HUNGRY, NORA. 36 POET
SHE GOADS ME INTO LOSING MY TEMPER, AND I SAY 61 POET THINGS--
(SHE WAITS DEFIANTLY, AS IF EXPECTING HIM TO LOSE 105 POET HIS TEMPER AND CURSE HER.
(IN SPITE OF HERSELF HER TEMPER HAS BEEN RISING. 155 POET
I'LL ONLY LOSE MY TEMPER IF YOU 454 WELDED
THEN WHY LOSE YOUR TEMPERS 456 WELDED
(LOSING HER TEMPER COMPLETELY) 497 WELDED

TEMPERAMENT
IT SUITS YOUR TEMPERAMENT. 17 ELECTR
(WITH A SNEER) ARTISTIC TEMPERAMENT, MAYBE-- 302 GGBROW

TEMPERAMENTAL
OR BECAUSE HE POSES AS ARTISTIC AND 289 GGBROW TEMPERAMENTAL--OR BECAUSE HE'S SO WILD--
TEMPERAMENTAL POSTURINGS OF THE STAGE STAR. 13 JOURNE

TEMPERAMENTALLY
TEMPERAMENTALLY TIMID, HIS DEFENSE IS AN 6 STRANG ASSUMPTION OF HIS COMPLACENT,

TEMPERANCE
I'M NOT GOING TO READ YOU ANY TEMPERANCE LECTURE. 294 AHWILD
YOU DON'T THINK I'D COME AROUND HERE PEDDLING SOME620 ICEMAN BRAND OF TEMPERANCE BUNK
GLAD TO SEE BROTHER HICKEY HASN'T CORRUPTED YOU TO681 ICEMAN TEMPERANCE.
WHILE YOU GIVE THEM A LECTURE ON TEMPERANCE. 5 MISBEG
THEY WAS TOO BUSY PREACHING TEMPERANCE TO HAVE 17 MISBEG TIME FOR A DRINK.

TEMPERED
MY GOODNESS, I NEVER SAW YOU SO SAVAGE-TEMPERED/ 268 AHWILD
I NEVER SAW NAT SO BAD-TEMPERED. 269 AHWILD
BUT GOOD-TEMPERED. 7 ANNA
HIGH-TEMPERED GIRLS (THEN HE ADDS HALF-BOLDLY) 37 ANNA THE LIKE OF YOURSELF.
MINE WERE TEMPERED IN HELL/ 316 GGBROW
A FLOOD OF MELLOW, TEMPERED SUNSHINE. 233 HA APE
AND ARE SURLY AND QUICK-TEMPERED WITH THE GREEKS. 298 LAZARU
(WITH PROVOKING CALM) DON'T BE CALLING ME NAMES, 12 MISBEG YOU BAD-TEMPERED OLD HORNET.
THERE'S STEW ON THE STOVE, YOU BAD-TEMPERED RUNT. 35 MISBEG
THERE'S NO USE TELLING THE TRUTH TO A BAD-TEMPERED 80 MISBEG WOMAN IN LOVE.
OCH, DON'T BE THREATENING ME, YOU BAD-TEMPERED OLD177 MISBEG TICK.
HIS EYES ARE FULL OF A QUICK-TEMPERED 137 STRANG SENSITIVENESS.

TEMPERS
GINNIES GOT AWFUL TEMPERS. 613 ICEMAN

TEMPEST
'CEPTIN' WHEN THAT DURN TEMPEST BLOWED US SOUTH 497 DIFRNT WHERE THE TEMPEST BLOWED 'EM. 501 DIFRNT
(SHE BURSTS INTO A TEMPEST OF SOBS.) 494 VOYAGE

TEMPLAR
UNIFORMS OF OUR MODERN KNIGHTS TEMPLAR, OF 390 MARCOM
COLUMBUS, OF PYTHIAS,

TEMPLE
DON'T YOU REALIZE WE'RE IN HER TEMPLE NOW/ 484 DYNAMO
IT IS A LARGE BUILDING OF THE GREEK TEMPLE TYPE 2 ELECTR
THAT WAS THE VOGUE
BEHIND THE DRIVEWAY THE WHITE GRECIAN TEMPLE 5 ELECTR
PORTICO WITH ITS SIX TALL COLUMNS
THE TEMPLE PORTICO IS LIKE AN INCONGRUOUS WHITE 5 ELECTR
MASK
AS A TEMPLE FOR HIS HATRED. 17 ELECTR
PAGAN TEMPLE FRONT STUCK LIKE A MASK ON PURITAN 17 ELECTR
GRAY UGLINESS/
THE PURE WHITE TEMPLE FRONT SEEMS MORE THAN EVER 43 ELECTR
LIKE AN INCONGRUOUS MASK
IT STUCK IN MY MIND--CLEAN-SCRUBBED AND 54 ELECTR
WHITEWASHED--A TEMPLE OF DEATH/
STILL BATHES THE WHITE TEMPLE PORTICO IN A CRIMSON129 ELECTR
LIGHT.
SOFT GOLDEN SUNLIGHT SHIMMERS IN A LUMINOUS MIST 169 ELECTR
ON THE GREEK TEMPLE PORTICO.
WHICH GRANDFATHER BUILT AS A TEMPLE OF HATE AND 171 ELECTR
DEATH/
MAY YOU DESIGN THE TEMPLE OF MAN'S SOUL/ 299 GGBROW
WE CAN DEVOTE THE PROCEEDS TO REHABILITATING THE 237 HA APE
VEIL OF THE TEMPLE.
AND YOU CAN'T BUILD A MARBLE TEMPLE OUT OF A 590 ICEMAN
MIXTURE OF MUD AND MANURE,
AND SWINE SHALL ROOT WHERE THY TEMPLE STOOD/ 292 LAZARU
IS THE FACADE OF A TEMPLE. 298 LAZARU
IN THE FOREGROUND IS THE PORTICO OF A TEMPLE 312 LAZARU
BETWEEN WHOSE MASSIVE COLUMNS ONE
HIS FIGURE APPEARS IN ITS IMMOBILITY TO BE THE 313 LAZARU
STATUE OF THE GOD OF THE TEMPLE,
AND MAKE THE PILLARS OF THE TEMPLE DANCE.) 321 LAZARU
WE WILL BUILD YOU A TEMPLE, LAZARUS, AND MAKE YOU 322 LAZARU
A GOD/
YOUR PATHETIC SUMMER-HOUSE A TEMPLE OF LOVE THE 3 MANSNS
KING HAS BUILT
AS I LEAD HIM INTO THE LITTLE TEMPLE OF LOVE HE 4 MANSNS
BUILT FOR ME--
AS IF IT WERE SOME SECRET TEMPLE OF WHICH YOU WERE109 MANSNS
HIGH PRIESTESS/
LET EACH NEW TEMPLE, NOBLER THAN THE LAST, 148 MANSNS
IN OUR TEMPLE OF LOVE WHERE THERE IS ONLY BEAUTY 164 MANSNS
AND FORGETFULNESS/
THE BACKGROUND FOR THE RULER'S THRONE IS NOW A 369 MARCOM
BUDDHIST TEMPLE
THE CLAMOR OF THE TEMPLE BELLS SLOWLY DIES OUT IN 372 MARCOM
THE DISTANCE.)
(THE TEMPLE BELLS BEGIN TO RING IN CHORUS. 372 MARCOM
IT SEEMS AN IRISHMAN GOT DRUNK IN TANGUT AND 374 MARCOM
WANDERED INTO A TEMPLE
I SHALL NOT LEAVE ONE TEMPLE STANDING 425 MARCOM
HE CAME HOME AND LIVED IN A LITTLE TEMPLE OF 83 POET
LIBERTY HE HAD BUILT
FROM A BIG RAW BRUISE ON HIS FOREHEAD, NEAR THE 152 POET
TEMPLE,

TEMPLES
EXCEPT FOR A FRINGE OF HAIR AROUND HIS TEMPLES AND618 ICEMAN
THE BACK OF HIS HEAD.
HIS HOLLOW TEMPLES AND HIS BULBOUS, SENSUAL NOSE. 299 LAZARU
HIS FISTS PRESSED TO HIS TEMPLES. 350 LAZARU
(POUNDING HIS TEMPLES WITH HIS FISTS--TORTURED) 352 LAZARU
HER FOREHEAD IS HIGH AND A TRIFLE BULGING, WITH 2 MANSNS
SUNKEN TEMPLES.
(SHE PRESSES BOTH HANDS TO HER TEMPLES.) 30 MANSNS
THERE ARE PATCHES OF GREY OVER HIS TEMPLES. 69 MANSNS

TEMPO
DECLAIMING IN A QUEER CAMP MEETING PREACHER'S 232 DESIRE
TEMPO)
THE WEASEL,= INCREASING THE TEMPO WITH EVERY VERSE251 DESIRE
UNTIL AT THE END HE IS
BUT THERE IS ORDER IN IT, RHYTHM, A MECHANICAL 223 HA APE
REGULATED RECURRENCE, A TEMPO.

TEMPORARILY
(FURIOUSLY--AS IF HE FELT HIMSELF TEMPORARILY 562 DAYS
BEATEN)
MY OPINION IS THE POOR SAP IS TEMPORARILY BUGHOUSE626 ICEMAN
FROM OVERWORK.
AS A MATTER OF FACT, ROCKY, I ONLY WISH A POST 676 ICEMAN
TEMPORARILY.
I AM TEMPORARILY HARD PRESSED. 50 POET

TEMPORARY
DO YOU THINK DION WOULD CONSIDER IT--AS A 277 GGBROW
TEMPORARY STOPGAP--
TEMPORARY, OF COURSE, BUT I CANNOT DENY I AM 120 POET
PINCHED AT THE MOMENT--

TEMPT
(THEN HE SMILES) YOU COULDN'T TEMPT HIM, NO WAYS. 97 BEYOND
MURDERER AN' THIEF I'M NOT, YE STILL TEMPT ME/ 262 DESIRE
WE DON'T WANT TO TEMPT HIM INTO SIN. 620 ICEMAN
THEY TEMPT HIM, AND HE'S LONELY, HE HASN'T GOT ME.712 ICEMAN
IT'S ONLY HIS BODY.
TO TEMPT MEN'S GREED INTO ENSLAVING ONE ANOTHER. 8 MANSNS
DO YOU THINK YOU CAN TEMPT ME NOW WHEN I AM AN 36 MANSNS
UGLY,
WELL, BY THE ETERNAL, I'LL SMASH IT SO THERE'LL BE191 MANSNS
NOTHING LEFT TO TEMPT ME/
I HAVE LITTLE LEFT TO TEMPT YOU. 119 POET
AND TEMPT HIM BECAUSE I KNEW HIS HONOR WOULD MAKE 144 POET
HIM MARRY ME RIGHT AWAY IF--

TEMPTATION
BETTER PUT HER IN INSTITUTION WHERE SHE'LL BE 232 AHWILD
REMOVED FROM TEMPTATION/
(JEERINGLY) AND NOW WE COME TO THE GREAT 544 DAYS
TEMPTATION

TEMPTATION (CONT'D.)
IT'S THE GREAT TEMPTATION... 485 DYNAMO
I NEVER COULD LEARN TO HANDLE TEMPTATION. 712 ICEMAN
IT WAS TOO GREAT A TEMPTATION. 150 JOURNE
THE TEMPTATION TO ESCAPE--OPEN THE DOOR--STEP 28 MANSNS
BOLDLY ACROSS THE THRESHOLD,
BORROWED TOO FREELY, AND THEN YIELDED TO THE 32 MANSNS
TEMPTATION
FOR THEN YOU GROW CONFUSED AND THE TEMPTATION 156 MANSNS
SEIZES YOU TO HURL YOURSELF--
AH, WELL, I SUPPOSE THE TEMPTATION WAS TOO GREAT. 86 MISBEG
(AS IF SHE HADN'T SPOKEN) SO HE'LL KEEP AWAY FROM 90 MISBEG
TEMPTATION BECAUSE HE CAN'T
IT WAS A GREAT TEMPTATION, WHEN I SAW NO ONE IN 9 POET
THE BAR,
MY UNIFORM SO INVITINGLY THAT I COULD NOT RESIST 89 POET
THE TEMPTATION TO PUT IT ON
THE GREAT TEMPTATION, ISN'T ITS 476 WELDED

TEMPTATIONS
CERTAIN NATURAL FEELINGS AND TEMPTATIONS--THAT'LL 295 AHWILD
WANT TO BE GRATIFIED--

TEMPTED
(TEMPTED AND TORTURED, IN A LONGING WHISPER) 165 ELECTR
(STARES AT A BOTTLE GREEDILY, TEMPTED FOR A 645 ICEMAN
MOMENT--THEN BITTERLY)
GOOD GOD, YOU WONDER I WAS TEMPTED TO OPEN THAT 30 MANSNS
DOOR AND ESCAPE/
I TELL YOU I AM STILL TEMPTED-- 30 MANSNS
I FEEL TEMPTED TO LIVE IN LIFE AGAIN--AND I AM 38 MANSNS
AFRAID/
I HATE MYSELF FOR HAVING PERMITTED MY MIND TO BE 124 MANSNS
TEMPTED--
I KNOW ONLY TOO WELL HOW TEMPTED YOU ARE TO 157 MANSNS
WHISPER AND START THE RUMOR OF THE
IF HE EVER WAS TEMPTED TO WANT ME, HE'D BE ASHAMED 92 MISBEG
OF IT.
BUT I'M FORGETTING HE STAYED AWAY BECAUSE HE WAS 92 MISBEG
AFRAID HE'D BE TEMPTED.
HE WON'T BE TEMPTED AT ALL. 93 MISBEG
HE'D BETTER CHANGE HIS TUNE OR I'LL CERTAINLY BE 191 STRANG
TEMPTED TO TELL HIM...

TEMPTS
IT'S ONLY A SMALL MILL AND THAT'S WHAT TEMPTS 146 POET
SIMON.

TEN
AROUND FIVE-TEN IN HEIGHT BUT LOOKING MUCH SHORTER538 *ILE
YOU BEEN WITH ME NIGH ON TEN YEAR AND I'VE LEARNED542 *ILE
YE WHALIN'.
BUT IS ENTIRELY BALD, AND LOOKS TEN YEARS OLDER. 201 AHWILD
THE HELL OF SKUNKS LIKE MCCOMBER IS THAT AFTER 204 AHWILD
BEING WITH THEM TEN MINUTES YOU
HE'S UP AT THE RANDS'--WON'T BE HOME BEFORE TEN, 218 AHWILD
ANYWAY.
YOU CAN GET BACK BY HALF-PAST TEN OR ELEVEN, 219 AHWILD
THOUGH. ALL RIGHT.
I GET TEN DOLLARS FROM EVERYONE ELSE. 241 AHWILD
*AND THEN--AT TEN O'CLOCK--ELIOT LOVBURG WILL 246 AHWILD
COME--
ONLY A LITTLE PAST TEN. 250 AHWILD
PRETENDING TO BE ASLEEP BY TEN O'CLOCK. 280 AHWILD
SCENE--TEN DAYS LATER. 25 ANNA
IT IS TEN O'CLOCK AT NIGHT. 25 ANNA
HALF PAST TEN. 27 ANNA
BUT TEN DAYS BACK WE MET UP WITH ANOTHER STORM THE 36 ANNA
LIKE OF THE FIRST,
WAN OE THEM IS WORTH ANY TEN STOCK-FISH-SWILLING 49 ANNA
SQUARE-HEADS
WITH YOUR OWN BRUTHER WHO'S TEN TIMES THE MAN YOU 126 BEYOND
EVER WAS OR EVER WILL BE/
A STENCH/ TEN THOUSAND OF THEM/ 132 BEYOND
TEN SQUARE MILES WHERE WE'VE GOT AN ACRE. 133 BEYOND
I COUNTED TEN MILLION SHEEP IF I COUNTED ONE. 147 BEYOND
I'VE SAVED TEN THOUSAND FROM THE WRECKAGE, MAYBE 157 BEYOND
TWENTY.
*APPENED TEN YEAR AGO COME CHRISTMAS. 478 CARDIF
ABOUT TEN MINUTES TO EIGHT IN THE EVENING.) 478 CARDIF
AND ROT-TEN PO-TAY-TOES/ 481 CARDIF
I'M WUTH TEN O' YE YIT, OLD'S I BE/ 227 DESIRE
(THEN MOODILY) BUT AFTER THREE SCORE AND TEN THE 232 DESIRE
LORD WARNS YE T' PREPARE.
TEN TIMES AS STRONG AN' FIFTY TIMES AS HARD AS 236 DESIRE
EBEN.
TEN EYES FUR AN EYE, THAT WAS MY MOTTER/ 251 DESIRE
CALEB'S A MAN WO'TH TEN O' MOST AND, SPITE O' HIS 513 DIFNT
BEIN' ONY A BOY YIT,
WHEN DAT MURDERIN' NIGGER OLE LEM HIRED TO KILL ME178 EJONES
TAKES AIM TEN FEET AWAY AND
(REMINISCENTLY) IF DEY'S ONE THING I LEARNS IN 178 EJONES
TEN YEARS ON DE PULLMAN CA'S
YOU AIN'T NEVER LEARNED ARY WORD ER IT, SMITHERS, 179 EJONES
IN DE TEN YEARS YOU BEEN HEAH,
IS A LARGE PORTRAIT OF EZRA MANNON HIMSELF, 28 ELECTR
PAINTED TEN YEARS PREVIOUSLY.
HIS WIFE, ABOUT TEN YEARS HIS JUNIOR, 67 ELECTR
THE SHIP IS UNLOADED AND HER BLACK SIDE RISES NINE102 ELECTR
ON TEN FEET
TEN DOLLARS IN THIS POCKET--{HE PULLS THE POCKET 103 ELECTR
INSIDE OUT--
AND A GALLON OF LICKER YOU DASN'T STAY THERE TILL 131 ELECTR
MOONRISE AT TEN O'CLOCK.
THAT'S AGREED--AN' IT'S LIKE STEALIN' TEN DOLLARS 131 ELECTR
OFF YOU.
I'M LETTIN' YOU IN THE MANNON HOUSE AND I'M 131 ELECTR
BETTIN' YOU TEN DOLLARS
WE'LL HAVE A GOOD SPREE ON THAT TEN DOLLARS. 132 ELECTR
ALL I'M WONDERIN' IS, HAS HE GOT TEN DOLLARS$. 133 ELECTR
IT IS TEN IN THE MORNING OF A DAY ABOUT A MONTH 302 GGBROW
LATER.

TEN

TEN (CONT'D.)
WID TEN DOCTURS AND NURSES FEEDIN' HER SALTS TO 232 HA APE
CLEAN THE FEAR OUT OF HER.
MORE'N OUR 'OLE BLOODY STOKEHOLE MAKES IN TEN 235 HA APE
VOYAGES SWEATIN' IN 'ELL/
EIGHT OR TEN MEN, LONGSHOREMEN, IRON WORKERS, AND 245 HA APE
THE LIKE.
YEAH, I'D'A LAID TEN TO ONE ON IT. 12 HUGHIE
MUST HAVE BEEN TEN YEARS AGO--YES, EDDIE, THE 12 HUGHIE
OLDEST, IS ELEVEN NOW--
BUT I'LL LAY TEN TO ONE YOU'RE FORTY-THREE OR 13 HUGHIE
MAYBE FORTY-FOUR.
I'D BE WORTH TEN MILLION DOLLARS. 20 HUGHIE
THERE'S TEN OF THEM BORN EVERY MINUTE. 20 HUGHIE
THIS OLD TURTLE NEVER WINS A RACE, BUT HE WAS AS 25 HUGHIE
FOXY AS TEN GUYS.
MAYBE IT SOUNDED LIKE TEN, BUT IT WAS TWO, AND 26 HUGHIE
THAT'S ALL YOU GET.
SHE GIVES ME AN ARGUMENT I PROMISED HER TEN BUCKS. 26 HUGHIE
I'D TELL HIM I WIN TEN GRAND FROM THE BOOKIES, AND 32 HUGHIE
TEN GRAND AT STUD,
AND TEN GRAND IN A CRAP GAME/ 32 HUGHIE
HE WEARS FIVE-AND-TEN-CENT-STORE SPECTACLES WHICH 577 ICEMAN
ARE SO OUT OF ALIGNMENT
BUT DE SOCIALIST, SOMETIMES, HE'S GOT A JOB, AND 584 ICEMAN
IF HE GETS TEN BUCKS,
HE HAD THE GUTS TO SERVE TEN YEARS IN THE CAN IN 593 ICEMAN
HIS OWN COUNTRY
(GRINS) GOTTY TO DINK, TEN BETTER LIMEY OFFICERS,599 ICEMAN
AT LEAST.
YOU'VE TOLD THAT STORY TEN MILLION TIMES AND IF I 601 ICEMAN
HAVE TO HEAR IT AGAIN,
TEN. 608 ICEMAN
CHANGE A TEN-DOLLAR BILL FOR HERS 608 ICEMAN
TEN, TWENTY, THIRTY, FORTY, FIFTY, SIXTY, SEVENTY,608 ICEMAN
EIGHTY, NINETY, A DOLLAR.
I WAS SURE SURPRISED WHEN SHE GAVE ME THE TEN 608 ICEMAN
SPOT.
TEN, TWENTY--THOSE ARE PRETTY SHOES YOU GOT ON, 609 ICEMAN
BESS--
TEN, TWENTY, THIRTY--WHAT'S ON AT THE CHURCH 609 ICEMAN
TONIGHT, BESS?
TEN, TWENTY, THIRTY, FIFTY, SEVENTY, EIGHTY, 609 ICEMAN
NINETY--
(HE PULLS A BIG ROLL FROM HIS POCKET AND PEELS OFF621 ICEMAN
A TEN-DOLLAR BILL.
EACH FOR TEN YEARS. 630 ICEMAN
HE ROTTED TEN YEARS IN PRISON FOR HIS FAITH/ 641 ICEMAN
EACH FOR TEN YEARS, EH8 656 ICEMAN
I CAN LICK TEN OF YOUSE WID ONE MIT/ 671 ICEMAN
I HAVE THE GREAT STRENGTH TO DO WORK OF TEN 676 ICEMAN
ORDINARY MENS.
HAVE TEN DRINKS, BEJEES/ 724 ICEMAN
GIVE ME TEN DRINKS, HARRY. 724 ICEMAN
HAVE TEN DRINKS, BEJEES/ 725 ICEMAN
IT IS ABOUT TEN MINUTES OF TWELVE ON A NIGHT IN 513 INZONE
THE FALL OF THE YEAR 1915.
ENGLAND HAS BEEN LIVIN' THERE FOR TEN, OFTEN AS 521 INZONE
NOT TWENTY YEARS.
JAMES TYRONE IS SIXTY-FIVE BUT LOOKS TEN YEARS 13 JOURNE
YOUNGER.
TEN FOGHORNS COULDN'T DISTURB YOU. 17 JOURNE
EDMUND IS TEN YEARS YOUNGER THAN HIS BROTHER, 19 JOURNE
AND TEN FOGHORNS COULDN'T WAKE YOU. 20 JOURNE
YOU'D THINK YOU WERE THE ONE TEN YEARS OLDER. 21 JOURNE
BUT I WAS WISE TEN YEARS OR MORE BEFORE WE HAD TO 57 JOURNE
TELL YOU.
THIS ISN'T A DOLLAR. IT'S A TEN SPOT. 89 JOURNE
I SUPPOSE YOU'LL DIVIDE THAT TEN DOLLARS YOUR 94 JOURNE
FATHER GAVE YOU WITH JAMIE.
HE NEVER WENT TO SCHOOL AFTER HE WAS TEN. 111 JOURNE
YOUR FATHER HAD TO GO TO WORK IN A MACHINE SHOP 117 JOURNE
WHEN HE WAS ONLY TEN YEARS OLD.
I'VE HEARD PAPA TELL THAT MACHINE SHOP STORY TEN 117 JOURNE
THOUSAND TIMES.
WHEN I WAS TEN MY FATHER DESERTED MY MOTHER AND 147 JOURNE
WENT BACK TO IRELAND TO DIE.
BECAUSE I WAS THE MAN OF THE FAMILY. AT TEN YEARS148 JOURNE
OLD/
IT'S ONLY SEVEN DOLLARS A WEEK BUT YOU GET TEN 149 JOURNE
TIMES THAT VALUE.
HE SEEMS TEN YEARS YOUNGER, AT THE PRIME OF FORTY.288 LAZARU
TEN DEAD AND MORTALLY WOUNDED LIE ON THE GROUND, 291 LAZARU
A SQUARE IN ATHENS ABOUT TEN O-CLOCK AT NIGHT. 298 LAZARU
THE CABIN IS TEN FEET BY FIFTEEN, 1 MANSNS
HIS SPARE FRAME HAS PUT ON TEN POUNDS OR SO, 43 MANSNS
TEN SOLDI IN SILVER. 365 MARCOM
YOU NEED ONLY ME NOW TO MAKE YOU INTO A REAL MAN--371 MARCOM
FOR TEN PIECES OF GOLD.
I KISSED YOU BEFORE HE SAID TEN WHAT. 371 MARCOM
TEN--(MARCO SUDDENLY KISSES HER.) 371 MARCOM
READY TO SAIL FOR PERSIA WITHIN TEN DAYS. 388 MARCOM
THIS IS MONEY, LEGALLY VALUED AT TEN YEN'S WORTH 393 MARCOM
OF ANYTHING YOU WISH TO BUY,
IT'S WURTH TEN YEN. 393 MARCOM
SEE TEN YEN WRITTEN ON IT, DON'T YOU8 393 MARCOM
THINK OF GETTING TEN YEN FOR THIS PIECE OF PAPER. 394 MARCOM
VALUING EACH LIFE CONSERVATIVELY AT TEN YEN, 394 MARCOM
WOULD COST YOU THE LIVES OF TEN THOUSAND MEN, 394 MARCOM
OF FLESH WHICH WILL NOT HAVE SHRIEKED THROUGH TEN 425 MARCOM
DAYS' TORTURE BEFORE IT DIED/
YOU MUST HAVE STOPPED AT THE INN FOR AN EYE- 41 MISBEG
OPENER--OR TEN OF THEM.
TEN OF THEM, FATHER. 62 MISBEG
AND TEN MORE DIED OF CHOLERA AFTER DRINKING THE 63 MISBEG
DIRTY WATER IN IT.
THERE'S NEVER A PROMISE OF GOD OR MAN GOES NORTH 66 MISBEG
OF TEN THOUSAND BUCKS.

TEN (CONT'D.)
(OVERWHELMED) TEN THOUSAND/ 84 MISBEG
TEN THOUSAND, CASH. 84 MISBEG
WE'LL MAKE HIM SIGN A PAPER HE OWES ME TEN 95 MISBEG
THOUSAND DOLLARS THE MINUTE THE
DON'T I LOOK TEN THOUSAND DOLLARS' WORTH TO ANY 98 MISBEG
DRINKS
TEN GRAND/ 132 MISBEG
HE OUGHT TO KNOW I WOULDN'T DOUBLE-CROSS YOU AND 133 MISBEG
HIM FOR TEN MILLION/
I DRANK ENOUGH TO KNOCK OUT TEN MEN. 145 MISBEG
AND I WAS MORE MELANCHOLY THAN TEN HAMLETS. 170 MISBEG
SHE LEFT TEN MINUTES AGO, OR MORE. 91 POET
YOU WAS WORTH ANY TEN MEN IN THE ARMY THAT DAY/ 93 POET
BY GOD, I'LL FACE HIM AT TEN PACES OR ACROSS A 124 POET
HANDKERCHIEF/
I COULD BEAR TEN OF IT. 138 POET
SHE IS A SKINNY, OVERGROWN GIRL OF TEN, WITH THIN,578 ROPE
(TEEN AFTER NINE.--- 25 STRANG
SHE MUST BE AT LEAST TEN YEARS OLDER THAN YOU, 114 STRANG
LARGE AND MATRONLY AND PLACID,
LATE AFTERNOON IN LATE JUNE, TEN YEARS LATER-- 158 STRANG
HIS TYPE LOGICALLY DEVELOPED BY TEN YEARS OF 159 STRANG
CONTINUED SUCCESS AND ACCUMULATING
YOU NEED ABOUT TEN, I THINK, TO GET YOU IN THE 164 STRANG
RIGHT SPIRIT TO SEE THE FINISH/
SAM SAID TEN AND THEN TOOK THE BOTTLE AWAY WHEN 175 STRANG
I'D HAD ONLY FIVE/
MUST BE MORE THAN TEN YEAR. 506 VOYAGE
TEN THOUSAND YEARS--ABOUT--ISN'T ITS OR TWENTYS 474 WELDED

TENANT
BUT SHAUGHNESSY, THE TENANT ON THAT FARM OF YOURS. 22 JOURNE
HARKER WILL THINK YOU'RE NO GENTLEMAN FOR 23 JOURNE
HARBORING A TENANT WHO ISN'T HUMBLE IN
THE PLAY TAKES PLACE IN CONNECTICUT AT THE HOME OF 1 MISBEG
TENANT FARMER, PHIL HOGAN,
KNOWING THEY'D NEVER FIND ANOTHER TENANT. 31 MISBEG

TENANTS
HE TALKED AS IF WE WERE MERELY HIS TENANTS, CURSE 563 CROSS
HIM/
WE'RE ONLY TENANTS AND WE COULD BE THROWN OUT ON 31 MISBEG
OUR NECKS ANY TIME,
BY MUNKEYSHININ' AND SQUEEZIN' TENANTS AND EVERY 11 POET
MANNER OF TRICK.

TEND
I'LL HAVE TO GO DOWN AND TEND TO THE SHIP WHEN HE 135 BEYOND
COMES.
LET EBEN TEND TO THIN'S IF HE'S A MIND T', 215 DESIRE
THEY TEND HIS FLOCKS AND LAUGH TOWARD THE SUN/ 287 LAZARU
HE'D DO HIS PART AND TEND THE BAR HIMSELF. 23 POET
(INDIGNANTLY.) HIM, A GENTLEMAN, TEND BAR/ 24 POET
I LEFT O'DOWD TO TEND BAR AND I'LL WAGER HE HAS 135 POET
THREE DRINKS STOLEN ALREADY.
I'LL FIRE MICKEY AND TEND THE BAR MYSELF, LIKE MY 174 POET
FATHER'S SON OUGHT TO.
WAS GLAD ENOUGH TO GET ME BACK HOME AGEN, AND PAT 581 ROPE
WITH ME, TO TEND THE PLACE,
YOU MUST TEND HIM NIGHT AND DAY/ 183 STRANG
WE'D TEND OUR FLAME ON AN ALTAR, NOT IN A KITCHEN 448 WELDED
RANGE/

TENDED
HE'S ALWAYS TENDED TO US. 145 BEYOND
HE *TENDED* TO PA AND MA AND--(HIS VOICE BREAKS) 145 BEYOND
AND TO--MARY.
OF EVERYTHING BEING METICULOUSLY TENDED AND 95 MANSNS
TRIMMED.
WAS IT NOT YOU WHO TENDED ME NIGHT AND DAY, 412 MARCOM
HER TRAINING HAS ALSO TENDED TO COARSEN HER FIBER 26 STRANG
A TRIFLE,

TENDENCY
DUE TO HER RESTRAINING A TENDENCY TO LAPSE INTO 16 POET
BROGUE.
THIS DEFENSE IS STRENGTHENED BY A NATURAL TENDENCY 6 STRANG
TOWARD A PRIM PROVINCIALISM
UNFORTUNATELY, THE TENDENCY TO SPOIL THEM IN THE 9 STRANG
UNIVERSITY IS A POOR TRAINING--

TENDER
(HER VOICE SINKS TO A TREMULOUS, TENDER WHISPER AS139 BEYOND
SHE FINISHES.)
(HE PAUSES, THEN CONTINUES IN A TONE OF TENDER 147 BEYOND
SYMPATHY)
(AFTER A PAUSE--WITH A TENDER SMILE) 148 BEYOND
(WITH TENDER OBSTANCY--STROKING HER HAIR) 150 BEYOND
ARE YOU TRYING THE BOSSY TENDER HUSBAND ON ME, 548 DAYS
JOHNS
SHE IS TENDER) 243 DESIRE
SHE LOOKS AT EBEN WITH TENDER, LANGOUROUS EYES AND244 DESIRE
CALLS SOFTLY.)
YET HIS EYES ARE EXPRESSIVELY TENDER AND 494 DIFNT
PROTECTING WHEN HE GLANCES DOWN AT HER
SHE IS BENDING OVER HIM IN A TENDER ATTITUDE, ONE 486 DYNAMO
HAND REACHING DOWN.
HE'S GENTLE AND TENDER, HE'S EVERYTHING YOU'VE 61 ELECTR
NEVER BEEN.
(WITH A TENDER SMILE) WE HAD A SECRET LITTLE 85 ELECTR
WORLD OF OUR OWN IN THE OLD DAYS,
(WITH A TENDER GRIN) YOU'RE MY ONLY GIRL/ 90 ELECTR
(THEN CONQUERING HER HORROR--RESOLUTELY TENDER AND160 ELECTR
SOOTHING)
AND A RAPT, TENDER, GIRLISH SMILE.) 105 JOURNE
THE MOUTH OF MIRIAM IS SENSITIVE AND SAD, TENDER 274 LAZARU
WITH AN EAGER,
LISTENS TO HIS LAUGHTER WITH A TENDER SMILE OF 280 LAZARU
BEING HAPPY IN HIS HAPPINESS--
MIRIAM IS BESIDE HIM, DRESSED IN BLACK, SMILING 307 LAZARU
THE SAME SAD TENDER SMILE.
TALKING DOWN TO HER FACE--WITH A TENDER SMILE) 362 LAZARU
THE LAUGHTER OF GOD IS MORE PROFOUNDLY TENDER/ 362 LAZARU

TENDER

TENDER (CONT'D.)
LAUGHTER IS TENDER/ 363 LAZARU
TENDER LAUGHTER COMES FROM THEM.) 363 LAZARU
HIS ARMS STRAINING UPWARD TO THE SKY, A TENDER, 371 LAZARU
(A SOUND OF TENDER LAUGHTER, OF AN INTOXICATING, 352 MARCOM
SUPERNATURAL GAIETY.
(THEN RESUMING HIS TONE OF TENDER TEASING) 385 MARCOM
THERE IS PASSION IN HER KISS BUT IT IS A TENDER, 141 MISBEG
PROTECTIVE MATERNAL PASSION.
(IN A TENDER CROONING TONE LIKE A LULLABY) 153 MISBEG
(HER FACE SAD, TENDER AND PITYING--GENTLY) 177 MISBEG
(WITH A TENDER SMILE.) OH, HE ISN'T LIKE HIS 29 POET
KIND, OR LIKE ANYONE ELSE AT ALL.
(SHE PAUSES--HER TIRED, WORN FACE BECOMES SUDDENLY181 POET
SHY AND TENDER.)
(AT ONCE FORGETTING HER OWN EXHAUSTION, IS ALL 182 POET
TENDER, LOVING HELP AND COMFORT.)
TENDER, LOVING... 16 STRANG
MUST HAVE ONCE BEEN OF A ROMANTIC, TENDER, 53 STRANG
CLINGING-VINE BEAUTY.
(THEN SUDDENLY FORLORNLY TENDER) 144 STRANG
(THINKING WITH A SORT OF TENDER, LOVING SCORN FOR 186 STRANG
HIS BOYISH NAIVETE)
(THINKING RESENTFULLY) (WHAT A TENDER TONE SHE 192 STRANG
TAKES TOWARD HIM/...
HE WILL BE TENDER... 197 STRANG
(WITH A TENDER SMILE) OH--SOMETIMES. 444 WELDED
YOU'RE SURE YOU DIDN'T FORCE IT--(WITH A TENDER 445 WELDED
SMILE AT HIM)
(WITH A TENDER SMILE--MUSINGLY) 446 WELDED
(WITH A TENDER SMILE) OF THE FIRST TIME WE MET-- 446 WELDED
AT REHEARSAL, REMEMBERS
SHE SMILES AT HIM AND SPEAKS WITH A TENDER 487 WELDED
WEARINESS)
(WITH A LOW TENDER CRY AS IF SHE WERE AWAKENING T0488 WELDED
MATERNITY)
THEN STRETCHES OUT HER ARMS WITH A PASSIONATE, 489 WELDED
TENDER GESTURE)

TENDERING
I SHALL DO THE LADY THE HONOR OF TENDERING HER MY 90 POET
HUMBLE APOLOGIES

TENDERLY
EVEN KISSES HIM TENDERLY AND IMPULSIVELY ON HIS 258 AHWILD
BALD HEAD
(TENDERLY PLAYFUL) I WASN'T LOOKING FOR ANDY, 87 BEYOND
SMARTY. IF THAT'S WHAT YOU MEAN.
HE PRESSES HER CLOSE TO HIM--SLOWLY AND TENDERLY) 91 BEYOND
(HE PRESSES HER TO HIM, STROKING HER HAIR 92 BEYOND
TENDERLY.
(HE BENDS DOWN AND KISSES HER TENDERLY) OUR STAR/ 93 BEYOND
(SMOOTHING MARY'S HAIR--TENDERLY) 121 BEYOND
FINALLY ROBERT TURNS TO HER TENDERLY) 129 BEYOND
(TENDERLY) STILL LOVE ME DO YOU? 529 DAYS
(THEN TO ELSA IN A TENDERLY CHIDING TONE) 532 DAYS
(THEN FORCING A TENDERLY BULLYING TONE) 548 DAYS
(THEN TENDERLY REBUKING) YE OUGHTN'T T' TALK O' 245 DESIRE
SAD THIN'S--THIS MORNIN'.
(TENDERLY) EBEN. 256 DESIRE
(CARESSING HIS HAIR--TENDERLY) 266 DESIRE
(KISSING HER--TENDERLY) YE CAN'T HE'P YERSELF. 267 DESIRE
(TENDERLY AND SOOTHINGLY) WHY DID YOU SAY A 485 DYNAMO
MINUTE AGO, IF I LOVED YOUS
(TOUCHING THE BANDAGE ON HIS HEAD--TENDERLY) 76 ELECTR
(IMMEDIATELY ASHAMED OF HIMSELF--TENDERLY, PUTTING 80 ELECTR
HIS ARM AROUND HER)
(TENDERLY SOOTHING HER) TURN ME AGAINST YOUS 88 ELECTR
THEN HE ASKS TENDERLY, TAKING HER HAND) 89 ELECTR
(TENDERLY JOKING) HELLO, WOMAN/ 268 GGBROW
(TENDERLY) YOU CRAZY CHILD? 268 GGBROW
(SHE REACHES OUT AND TAKES HIS HAND--TENDERLY) 272 GGBROW
(TENDERLY, STROKING HIS HAIR MATERNALLY) 285 GGBROW
(HE SIGHS TENDERLY) DEAR OLD BESS. 609 ICEMAN
(KISSES HIM--TENDERLY.) ALL YOU NEED IS YOUR 43 JOURNE
MOTHER TO NURSE YOU.
HER MANNER BECOMES TENDERLY SOLICITOUS. 72 JOURNE
(TENDERLY.) NO. 112 JOURNE
AND BEGINS TO LAUGH LOW AND TENDERLY. 318 LAZARU
(HE LAUGHS AGAIN, HIS LAUGHTER DYING LINGERINGLY 324 LAZARU
AND TENDERLY ON HIS LIPS LIKE A
(PUTS HIS ARM AROUND HER AND RAISES HER TO HER 325 LAZARU
FEET--TENDERLY)
(HE KISSES HER FOREHEAD TENDERLY.) 329 LAZARU
(COMING TO HER--TENDERLY) I WILL NOT LEAVE YOU/ 329 LAZARU
GENTLY PUSHES THE LION'S HAIR OUT OF ITS EYES-- 329 LAZARU
TENDERLY)
(TENDERLY) ONLY A LITTLE LONGER/ 330 LAZARU
(LAUGHING SOFTLY AND TENDERLY. 362 LAZARU
I WALK WITH THE KING IN THE GARDENS--HE WHISPERS 4 MANSNS
TENDERLY..
(SHE GRASPS HIS HAND AND PRESSES IT--TENDERLY 45 MANSNS
POSSESSIVE.)
(SHE KISSES HIM--TENDERLY.) GOODBYE, MY DARLING/ 93 MANSNS
(STRANGELY, TENDERLY SYMPATHETIC.) 102 MANSNS
(MOVED AND FASCINATED, TAKES A STEP TOWARD HIM-- 103 MANSNS
TENDERLY.)
(SHE TAKES HIS ARM--TENDERLY.) 114 MANSNS
(PATS HER HAND--TENDERLY PERSUASIVE, BUT HIS EYES 184 MANSNS
FIXED ON THE DOOR.)
(COLDLY AND TENDERLY) YOU MUSTN'T, MARK. 355 MARCOM
(TENDERLY) YOU SILLY BOY/ 355 MARCOM
KUBLAI LOOKS DOWN AT HER TENDERLY.) 384 MARCOM
AFTER A PAUSE DURING WHICH HE LOOKS AT HER 386 MARCOM
THOUGHTFULLY--TENDERLY)
(THEN AFTER A PAUSE--TENDERLY) 386 MARCOM
CHU-YIN CONTINUES TENDERLY) 401 MARCOM
(THEN TENDERLY) FAREWELL, LITTLE FLOWER/ LIVE. 401 MARCOM
FINALLY HE SPEAKS TENDERLY TO HER WITH A SAD 435 MARCOM
SMILE)

TENDERNESS

TENDERLY (CONT'D.)
I SUPPOSE BECAUSE IT SEEMS CRAZY FOR YOU TO HOLD 130 MISBEG
MY BIG UGLY PAW SO TENDERLY.
(SHE WHISPERS TENDERLY) COME. 137 MISBEG
(HUGGING HIM TENDERLY) OF COURSE I'LL UNDERSTAND,145 MISBEG
JIM, DARLING.
(TENDERLY.) I KNOW, ACUSHLA. 23 POET
(PUTS HER ARMS AROUND HER MOTHER--TENDERLY.) 28 POET
(SHE LAUGHS TENDERLY.) 32 POET
(SHE LAUGHS TENDERLY.) AND THEN YOU'D HAVE 64 POET
LAUGHED TO SEE HIM.
(TENDERLY SOLICITOUS NOW, PUTS AN ARM AROUND HER.)131 POET
(A STRANGE, TENDERLY AMUSED SMILE ON HER LIPS-- 139 POET
TEASINGLY.)
(SHE LAUGHS TENDERLY.) OH, IT WAS THE CUTEST 143 POET
THING I'VE EVER DONE, MOTHER.
(SHE SMILES TENDERLY.) 145 POET
AND HUGS HIM TENDERLY.) 164 POET
(SHE COMES OVER AND HUGS HER--THEN SHE SMILES 182 POET
TENDERLY.)
(HE KISSES HER HAIR AGAIN TENDERLY AND SMILES AT 44 STRANG
HIMSELF--
(REACHING OUT HER HAND TENDERLY, TRYING TO TOUCH 58 STRANG
NINA)
(TENDERLY--BUT HAVING TO FORCE HERSELF TO SAY IT) 71 STRANG
STANDING BEHIND HER--TENDERLY) 83 STRANG
(SMILING TENDERLY--THINKING) 102 STRANG
(THINKING TENDERLY) (LET HIS PRIDE PUT ALL THE 102 STRANG
BLAME ON ME/...
(TENDERLY) NED TOLD ME--THE SECRET--AND I'M SO 107 STRANG
HAPPY, DEAR/
(TENDERLY) THAT WE'RE GOING TO HAVE A CHILD, 107 STRANG
DEAR.
(IMMEDIATELY ON THE CREST AGAIN--TENDERLY) 109 STRANG
(TENDERLY AND BOYISHLY) AND I'M GOING TO MAKE YOU109 STRANG
HAPPY FROM NOW ON, NINA..
(LOOKING OVER AT HER--TENDERLY REPROACHFUL) 116 STRANG
TENDERLY IN A SORT OF PLEADING) 145 STRANG
GOES TO HER AND PUTS HIS HAND ON HER HEAD-- 145 STRANG
TENDERLY)
(TENDERLY, SMOOTHING HIS HAIR) 184 STRANG
(PUSHING HIM AWAY--TENDERLY) 195 STRANG
(LIFTING HER HAND TO HIS LIPS--TENDERLY) 196 STRANG
(THEN TENDERLY) IT HAS BEEN A LONG DAY. 200 STRANG
HE KISSES HER TENDERLY.) 444 WELDED
(TENDERLY) HAPPY? 444 WELDED
(SHE SMILES TENDERLY) AND THEN WE FIGHT/ 448 WELDED
(TENDERLY) I'LL ALWAYS BELIEVE FATE SHOULD HAVE 469 WELDED
LET ME LOVE YOU, INSTEAD..
(RAMBLING TENDERLY) MICHAEL--I--I WAS AFRAID-- 480 WELDED
TENDERNESS
(WITH ROUGH TENDERNESS) WELL, ANNIES 540 'ILE
(PUTTING AN ARM AROUND HER SHOULDER--WITH GRUFF 545 'ILE
TENDERNESS)
THEN OVERCOME BY A WAVE OF FIERCE TENDERNESS) 20 ANNA
RUTH TURNS AND GRABS HER UP IN HER ARMS WITH A 140 BEYOND
SUDDEN FIERCE TENDERNESS.
WHO IS INFINITE TENDERNESS AND PITY/ 559 DAYS
BUT THERE IS A TRACE OF TENDERNESS, OF INTERESTED 251 DESIRE
DISCOVERY.
(WITH ROUGH TENDERNESS) OH, HELL, EMMER, 496 DIFRNT
GETS UP AND PATS HER ON THE SHOULDER--WITH ROUGH 537 DIFRNT
TENDERNESS)
HIM, HER IMMEDIATE REACTION ONE OF MATERNAL 446 DYNAMO
TENDERNESS.
(PATTING HER HAIR--WITH GRUFF TENDERNESS) 51 ELECTR
(HE SMILES WITH A DREAMY TENDERNESS) 90 ELECTR
(AGAIN WITH TENDERNESS, STROKING HIS HAIR-- 90 ELECTR
SMILING)
AS HE STOPS, AN AGONIZING TENDERNESS FOR HIM WELLS 90 ELECTR
UP IN HER--
(THEN IMMEDIATELY REPENTANT HE KISSES HER--WITH 108 ELECTR
ROUGH TENDERNESS)
(ROUSING HIMSELF GUILTILY--PATS HER HAND--WITH 111 ELECTR
GRUFF TENDERNESS)
(HE PATS HER HAND WITH AWKWARD TENDERNESS. 174 ELECTR
(SQUEEZING HIS HAND--WITH POSSESSIVE TENDERNESS) 270 GGBROW
HE RAISES THE MASK IN HIS HANDS AND STARES AT IT 291 GGBROW
WITH A PITYING TENDERNESS.
AND A GREAT SYMPATHY AND TENDERNESS) 292 GGBROW
TRIUMPHANT TENDERNESS MINGLED WITH HER GRIEF) 323 GGBROW
(WITH AN AWKWARD, UNEASY TENDERNESS.) 41 JOURNE
PROTECTIVE TENDERNESS.) 48 JOURNE
BUT IF HIS SUSPICIONS ARE AROUSED HER TENDERNESS 58 JOURNE
MAKES HIM RENOUNCE THEM AND HE
HE PATS HER SHOULDER WITH AN AWKWARD TENDERNESS.) 91 JOURNE
(SMILES WITH DETACHED TENDERNESS AT EDMUND.) 110 JOURNE
THEN JESUS SMILED SADLY BUT WITH TENDERNESS, 277 LAZARU
A SMILE THAT HAS LOST ITS OLD PASSIONATE 75 MANSNS
TENDERNESS.
(HER EXPRESSION SOFTENS TO A CONDESCENDING 126 MANSNS
MATERNAL TENDERNESS.)
BOTH THEIR EXPRESSIONS CHANGE TO A TRIUMPHANT 137 MANSNS
POSSESSIVE TENDERNESS.)
(HE SMILES AT HER WITH A SUDDEN AWKWARD 183 MANSNS
TENDERNESS.)
(WITH A FIERCE, PASSIONATE, POSSESSIVE 194 MANSNS
TENDERNESS.)
WITH A BEAUTIFUL TENDERNESS OF GRIEF) 438 MARCOM
AND STARES DOWN AT HIS FACE WITH A PASSIONATE, 103 MISBEG
POSSESSIVE TENDERNESS.
(SHE KISSES HIM AGAIN--WITH PASSIONATE TENDERNESS)137 MISBEG
WITH FIERCE, POSSESSIVE, MATERNAL TENDERNESS) 141 MISBEG
(BENDS OVER HIM WITH A BROODING MATERNAL 152 MISBEG
TENDERNESS)
HER FACE SOFTENS WITH A MATERNAL TENDERNESS-- 165 MISBEG
SADLY)
GUILTY TENDERNESS. 37 POET

TENDERNESS

TENDERNESS (CONT'D.)
TENDERNESS--PLEADINGLY.)   167 POET
ROUGHLY BUT WITH A STRANGE REAL TENDERNESS.) AND 174 POET
    I LOVE YOU.
(WITH SUDDEN TENDERNESS--GATHERING NINA UP IN HER 65 STRANG
    ARMS, BROKENLY)
(WITH DEEP TENDERNESS) GOOD NIGHT, DARLING.   136 STRANG
(WATCHING HIM--BROODING WITH LOVING TENDERNESS--   138 STRANG
    SAULY)
(LOOKS UP AT HIM WITH DEEP TENDERNESS AND   145 STRANG
    ADMIRATION)
(WITH REMORSEFUL TENDERNESS)   145 STRANG
OF ALARM, TENDERNESS, PERPLEXITY, PASSIONATE HOPE.462 WELDED
(WITH DEEP, PASSIONATE TENDERNESS)   489 WELDED
TENDIN'
TENDIN' BAR WHEN YUH GOT TWO GOOD HUSTLERS IN YOUR697 ICEMAN
    STABLE/
TENEMENT
IS A NARROW FIVE-STORY STRUCTURE OF THE TENEMENT   571 ICEMAN
    TYPE.
TENFOLD
ALL HER FORMER UNEASINESS COMES BACK ON MRS.   253 AHWILD
    MILLER TENFOLD.
HIS OWN EMBARASSMENT MADE TENFOLD PAINFUL BY HIS   295 AHWILD
    FATHER'S)
TENNIS
SHE HAS PLAYED A LOT OF GOLF AND TENNIS THIS   8 STRANG
    SUMMER.
A FINE ATHLETIC GIRL OF THE SWIMMER, TENNIS   12 STRANG
    PLAYER, GOLFER TYPE.
TENOR
(HE BEGINS TO SING IN A SURPRISINGLY GOOD TENOR   103 ELECTR
    VOICE.
A VERY DRUNKEN SENTIMENTAL TENOR BEGINS TO SING)..211 HA APE
THROWS BACK HIS HEAD, AND SINGS IN A FALSETTO   619 ICEMAN
    TENOR)
AS IF THEIR MINDS HAD PARTLY SENSED THE TENOR OF   119 MANSNS
    HIS THOUGHT,
HIS VOICE THE QUAVERING GHOST OF A TENOR BUT STILL 96 POET
    TRUE--
TENSE
HER EYES ARE FIXED ON HER BOOK, HER BODY TENSE AND257 AHWILD
    RIGID.)
HIS FACE TENSE WITH THE EFFORT TO SUPPRESS HIS   58 ANNA
    GRIEF AND RAGE.)
(HIS WHOLE BODY TENSE LIKE A SPRING--DULLY AND   59 ANNA
    GROPINGLY)
SHE SPEAKS ALOUD TO HERSELF IN A TENSE, TREMBLING   67 ANNA
    VOICE)
(HIS FACE TENSE AND DRAWN COMES FORWARD AND HOLDS 101 BEYOND
    OUT HIS HAND, FORCING A SMILE)
WHERE SHE REMAINS WATCHING ROBERT IN A TENSE,   150 BEYOND
    EXPECTANT ATTITUDE.
AT PRESENT, HOWEVER, HIS EXPRESSION IS ONE OF   153 BEYOND
    TENSE ANXIETY.
JOHN'S CORDIAL SMILE VANISHES AND HIS FACE TAKES   526 DAYS
    ON A TENSE, HARRIED LOOK.
JOHN'S EXPRESSION CHANGES AND BECOMES TENSE AND   530 DAYS
    HUNTED AGAIN.
WITH THE TENSE EFFORT SHE IS MAKING NOT TO GIVE   537 DAYS
    HERSELF AWAY.)
HIS FACE TENSE, FEELING DESPERATELY THAT HE IS   558 DAYS
    FACING INEVITABLE TRAGEDY,
(IN A LOW, TENSE VOICE--AS IF HE WERE THINKING   561 DAYS
    ALOUD)
(AFTER A LONG, TENSE PAUSE--DULLY)   515 DIFRNT
(AFTER A TENSE PAUSE--WITH A SUDDEN OUTBURST OF   549 DIFRNT
    WILD GRIEF)
(HIS TENSE, SUPPLICATING ATTUTUDE SUDDENLY   480 DYNAMO
    RELAXING DEJECTEDLY)
AND SITS DOWN IN A TENSE POSITION, READY FOR   195 EJUNES
    INSTANT FLIGHT.
WHOLE TENSE ATTITUDES IS CLEARLY REVEALED THE   16 ELECTR
    BITTER ANTAGONISM BETWEEN THEM.
THEN SHE TURNS AND STANDS IN TENSE CALCULATING   35 ELECTR
    THOUGHT.
SHE IS IN A STATE OF TENSE, EXULTANT EXCITEMENT.   42 ELECTR
(WITH A TENSE INTAKE OF BREATH)   49 ELECTR
AND REGAINS HER TENSE CONTROL OF HERSELF.)   71 ELECTR
BUT THE EXPRESSION OF HIS MOUTH GIVES AN   73 ELECTR
    IMPRESSION OF TENSE OVERSENSITIVENESS
(HER VOICE TENSE AND STRAINED)   83 ELECTR
HER EYES FULL OF TENSE CALCULATING FEAR.)   84 ELECTR
HIS ATTITUDE IS TENSE AND NERVOUS AND HE KEEPS ONE104 ELECTR
    HAND IN HIS COAT POCKET.
(IN TENSE DESPERATION) I WISH ORIN AND VINNIE   119 ELECTR
    WOULD COME/
(HER EYES CAUGHT BY SOMETHING DOWN THE DRIVE--IN A119 ELECTR
    TENSE WHISPER)
A TENSE VOICE)   151 ELECTR
(ALOUD TO HIMSELF--IN HIS COMICALLY TENSE, CRAZY   605 ICEMAN
    WHISPER)
(LETS OUT A TENSE BREATH) AW RIGHT, HICKEY.   640 ICEMAN
THERE IS A TENSE STILLNESS IN THE ROOM.   663 ICEMAN
HE IS STARING IN FRONT OF HIM IN A TENSE, STRAINED665 ICEMAN
    IMMOBILITY.
(THERE IS A SECOND'S TENSE SILENCE.)   693 ICEMAN
TENSE ON THEIR CHAIRS.)   705 ICEMAN
THEN A TENSE INDRAWN BREATH LIKE A GASP FROM THE   706 ICEMAN
    CROWD.
THEIR ATTITUDES GROW TENSE AS IF THEY ARE ABOUT TO523 INZONE
    SPRING.
NOW YOU CAN FEEL HER GROWING TENSE AND FRIGHTENED   37 JOURNE
    UNDERNEATH.
THERE IS A TENSE PAUSE.   49 JOURNE
BUT SUDDENLY SHE GROWS TERRIBLY TENSE AGAIN.   49 JOURNE
(THEY GROW TENSE WITH A HOPEFUL, FEARFUL   58 JOURNE
    EXPECTANCY.

TENSE (CONT'D.)
(ROUGHLY, TO HIDE HIS TENSE NERVES.)   68 JOURNE
THERE IS A TENSE SILENCE.   162 JOURNE
HANDS IN EVERY TENSE ATTITUDE OF STRIKING,   291 LAZARU
    CLUTCHING, TEARING ARE SEEN UPRAISED.
(WITH AN UNDERCURRENT OF TENSE EAGERNESS.)   37 MANSNS
BUT ONE SENSES AN INNER TENSE EXCITEMENT, A VITAL   50 MANSNS
    EAGER MENTAL ALIVENESS.
HIS EXPRESSION IS THAT OF ONE HABITUALLY TENSE.   69 MANSNS
FOR A MOMENT THERE IS A TENSE SILENCE.   95 MANSNS
(STARING BEFORE HIM, TENSE AND CONCENTRATED.)   101 MANSNS
FOR A MOMENT AFTER THE CURTAIN RISES THERE IS AN   117 MANSNS
    ATMOSPHERE OF TENSE QUIET
HOW TENSE THE QUIET IS IN THIS HOUSE TONIGHT--   120 MANSNS
(THINKING--WITH A TENSE DREAD.)   125 MANSNS
(WITH A STRANGE TENSE EXCITEMENT.)   156 MANSNS
HER FACE GROWS TENSE AS SHE CONCENTRATES HER WILL.163 MANSNS
(HIS TENSE QUIET BEGINNING TO SNAP.)   172 MANSNS
(WITH A TENSE CASUALNESS.) YOU ARE MISTAKEN,   172 MANSNS
    MOTHER.
(GOES ON IN THE SAME TONE OF TENSE QUIET.)   179 MANSNS
(HE HAS REMAINED TENSE AND MOTIONLESS,   188 MANSNS
HE LOOKS FOR A MOMENT CRITICALLY, THEN HE GROWS   414 MARCOM
    TENSE.
ONE SENSES A TENSE EXPECTANCY OF SOME SIGN FROM   433 MARCOM
    THE THRONE.
JIM. DON'T--(FORCING A TENSE LITTLE LAUGH)   129 MISBEG
(TEASE) SO YOU ACCEPTED&   132 MISBEG
(THEN AS SHE TAKES A SLOW, MECHANICAL STEP TOWARD 449 WELDED
    THE DOOR--WITH TENSE PLEADING)
FOR A LONG, TENSE MOMENT THEY REMAIN FIXED,   480 WELDED
PUTS HER HAND ON THE KNOB--THEN STOPS AS TENSE AS 487 WELDED
    HE.
TENSED
HIS BODY TENSED DEFENSIVELY.)   500 DAYS
TENSELY
(SHE SITS DOWN AGAIN AND BENDS OVER HER BOOK   256 AHWILD
    TENSELY.
(AFTER AN INWARD STRUGGLE--TENSELY--FORCING OUT   74 ANNA
    THE WORDS WITH DIFFICULTY)
(HE PULLS ROBERT'S HAND FROM HIS SIDE AND GRIPS IT 86 BEYOND
    TENSELY.)
(HIS FACE CRIMSON--TENSELY) STOP, PA/   106 BEYOND
(TENSELY) YES.   498 DAYS
AFTER THE DOOR CLOSES BEHIND HIM JOHN SPEAKS   498 DAYS
    TENSELY)
(TENSELY) YES.   528 DAYS
(AFTER A SECOND'S PAUSE--TENSELY)   539 DAYS
(STARTS--THEN TENSELY) YOU WANT ME TO PUT MYSELF   539 DAYS
    IN THE WIFE'S PLACE&
(GRASPS AT THIS--TENSELY) YES, I'M AFRAID IT HAS   540 DAYS
    BEEN TOO EXCITING--
(SINKS DOWN IN THE CHAIR BY THE TABLE AND WAITS   547 DAYS
    TENSELY--
(TENSELY) I'M SORRY, FATHER.   548 DAYS
(TENSELY) DON'T/   550 DAYS
(TENSELY) THIS AIN'T A JOKE, JACK--WHAT I MEAN.   504 DIFRNT
(HIS FISTS CLENCHING-- TENSELY)   542 DIFRNT
(THEN HER COLD DISCIPLINED MASK BREAKING FOR A   12 ELECTR
    MOMENT--TENSELY)
WHY I'VE FELT--(THEN TENSELY AS IF SHE WERE ABOUT   19 ELECTR
    TO BREAK DOWN)
(HAS SLOWLY DESCENDED THE STEPS, HER EYES FIXED ON 47 ELECTR
    HIM---TENSELY)
(THEN SINKING BACK--TENSELY)   48 ELECTR
(HER EYES CLOSED--TENSELY) DON'T TALK, EZRA.   53 ELECTR
(TENSELY) I DON'T KNOW WHAT YOU'RE TALKING ABOUT.   54 ELECTR
(TENSELY) I DON'T WANT TO TALK OF THE PAST/   59 ELECTR
ASKING TENSELY AS SHE DOES SO.)   62 ELECTR
(TENSELY) I COULDN'T STAY IN.   71 ELECTR
(TENSELY) AS IF I HADN'T TRIED/   72 ELECTR
SHE SPEAKS TO ORIN AND HER VOICE IS TENSELY QUIET   78 ELECTR
    AND NORMAL)
(TENSELY) I WISH YOU WOULDN'T TALK OF DEATH/   83 ELECTR
HE IS LISTENING TENSELY.   110 ELECTR
(TENSELY--SHAKING HIM BY THE ARM)   116 ELECTR
(TENSELY) WHAT HAVE YOU WRITTEN&   152 ELECTR
(TRYING TO KEEP CALM--TENSELY)   153 ELECTR
(TENSELY) YES.   164 ELECTR
(TENSELY) BY GOD, I HATE TO BELIEVE IT OF ANY OF   588 ICEMAN
    THE CROWD.
(TENSELY) NO, THANKS.   644 ICEMAN
(TENSELY) I'VE WARNED YOU--   645 ICEMAN
(TENSELY) LEAVE WHAT'S DEAD IN ITS GRAVE.   646 ICEMAN
WHO HAS STOOD TENSELY WITH HIS EYES SHUT AS IF HE   530 INZONE
    WERE UNDERGOING TORTURE DURING
(TENSELY.) BUT GO ON AND TELL ME--   37 JOURNE
(TENSELY.) WELL, WHAT WAS IT&   38 JOURNE
(TENSELY.) WHY DO YOU STARE LIKE THAT&   63 JOURNE
(PLEADS TENSELY.) FOR CHRIST'S SAKE, PAPA, FORGET!152 JOURNE
    IT/
EDMUND SITS TENSELY.   169 JOURNE
SARA SPRINGS TO HER FEET AND STANDS TENSELY   50 MANSNS
    DEFENSIVE.
(TENSELY.) I HAD ONCE REACHED A POINT WHERE I HAD1O2 MANSNS
    GROWN SO LUST.
(HE HAS DROPPED THE BOOK IN HIS LAP AND   126 MANSNS
    STRAIGHTENED HIMSELF TENSELY.
(TENSELY.) I AM MAKING MYSELF UNDERSTAND.   133 MANSNS
(SHE SUDDENLY STOPS AND LISTENS, TENSELY--EAGERLY.162 MANSNS
(DEBORAH IS STILL NOW AND LISTENING TENSELY, BUT   167 MANSNS
    SHE DOES NOT RAISE HER HEAD.)
(TENSELY--MAKING A FUTILE MOVEMENT TO RISE.)   178 MANSNS
(TENSELY.) OH, IF YOU KNEW HOW DESPERATELY I LONG178 MANSNS
    TO ESCAPE HER
(TENSELY.) I KNOW VERY WELL IT IS A WOODEN DOOR--183 MANSNS
(TENSELY, ON THE VERGE OF TEARS)   84 MISBEG

TENSELY (CONT'D.)
(TENSELY) FOR THE LOVE OF GOD, DON'T HARP ON HIS 93 MISBEG
LIES.
(TENSELY) WELL, I CAN/ 96 MISBEG
(TENSELY) YOU'RE A FINE ONE TO TALK OF PROMISES/ 106 MISBEG
(TENSELY--SICKENED BY HIS HYPOCRISY) 123 MISBEG
(TENSELY) DON'T, JIM. 129 MISBEG
(TENSELY) OCH, FOR THE LOVE OF GOD--/ 130 MISBEG
(TENSELY) HOW WOULD I KNOW, IF YOU DON'T$ 132 MISBEG
(TENSELY) NO. 136 MISBEG
(THROWS HER ARMS AROUND HIM AND PULLS HIM BACK-- 152 MISBEG
TENSELY)
(TENSELY) THIS ONE ISN'T GRAY, JIM. 165 MISBEG
(TENSELY) I DO, AND I'M HAPPY YOU FEEL THAT WAY, 171 MISBEG
JIM.
SHE WATCHES HIM TENSELY. 172 MISBEG
(TENSELY.) WHAT TRICK DO YOU MEAN$ 60 POET
(TENSELY.) BE QUIET/ 75 POET
(HE PAUSES, AS IF HE EXPECTS HER TO BE FURIOUS, 108 POET
BUT SHE REMAINS TENSELY SILENT.
(TENSELY.) OH, WOULD SHE/ 109 POET
(TENSELY.) OH, SHE'S CLEVER, ALL RIGHT/ 110 POET
(TENSELY.) I WON'T LET HIM DESTROY MY LIFE WITH 131 POET
HIS MADNESS.
(STANDS TENSELY--BURSTS OUT WITH A STRANGE 162 POET
TRIUMPHANT PRIDE.)
(THIS IS BECOMING UNBEARABLE FOR HER--TENSELY.) 168 POET
(TENSELY.) FATHER/ 169 POET
SHE SPEAKS DIRECTLY TO HER FATHER IN A VOICE 13 STRANG
TENSELY COLD AND CALM)
(TENSELY, CLUTCHING HER BY THE ARM) 451 WELDED
(TENSELY) SO YOU BELIEVE--THAT GUTTER GOSSIP$ 458 WELDED
(VERY PALE--TENSELY) WHAT RELATIONSHIP$ 458 WELDED
SMILING TENSELY) WOULD I STILL BE WELCOME IF I'D463 WELDED
COME--TO STAY$
(TENSELY, HOPING AGAIN NOW--PLEADINGLY) 467 WELDED
TENSENESS
INSTANTLY HIS BODY SHIFTS TO A FIGHTING TENSENESS) 36 ELECTR
(WITH SUDDEN TENSENESS). 17 JOURNE
TENSION
(THEN AS IF SEEKING RELIEF FROM THE TENSION IN A 20 ANNA
VOLUBLE CHATTER)
SHE IS IN A FRIGHTFUL STATE OF TENSION, UNABLE TO 117 ELECTR
KEEP STILL.
(THIS BREAKS THE TENSION, AND THE OLD MEN GIVE WAY)134 ELECTR
TO AN HYSTERICAL, BOISTEROUS.
SHE IS IN A TERRIFIC STATE OF TENSION. 157 ELECTR
(TRYING NOT TO LISTEN, HAS LISTENED WITH 680 ICEMAN
INCREASING TENSION)
WHILE AT THE SAME TIME PERVERSELY EXCITED AND 326 LAZARU
ELATED BY HIS OWN MORBID TENSION.
(GRADUALLY HER TENSION RELAXES, HER EYES BECOME 21 MANSNS
DREAMY.
A QUALITY OF NERVOUS TENSION, 43 MANSNS
AS IF SOME LONG PATIENT TENSION HAD SNAPPED-- AS IF 74 MANSNS
I NO LONGER HAD THE POWER TO
(THEN HER TENSION SNAPPING SHE BURSTS INTO SOBS 144 MANSNS
HE IS IN A STATE OF TERRIFIC TENSION, 171 MANSNS
A TERRIBLE TENSION OF WILL ALONE MAINTAINING SELF- 13 STRANG
POSSESSION.
HER MOVEMENTS ARE THOSE OF EXTREME NERVOUS 69 STRANG
TENSION.)
NERVOUS TENSION PRONOUNCED... 79 STRANG
A PASSIONATE TENSION, A SELF-PROTECTING, ARROGANT 444 WELDED
DEFIANCE OF LIFE AND HIS OWN
TENT
THE GRANDEST CROWD OF REGULAR GUYS EVER GATHERED 609 ICEMAN
UNDER ONE TENT/
AND THE RUBBER COVER FOR THE TYPEWRITER LIKE A 66 STRANG
COLLAPSED TENT.
TENTERHOOKS
AND SHE IS OBVIOUSLY ON TENTERHOOKS OF NERVOUS 249 AHWILD
UNEASINESS.
WHICH HAS HIM ON TENTERHOOKS. 41 ANNA
TENTH
FORCED HIM TO SELL FOR ONE-TENTH ITS WORTH, YOU 25 ELECTR
MEAN/
YOU KNOW YOU BOAST YOU CAN DRESS IN ONE-TENTH THE 82 JOURNE
TIME IT TAKES THE BOYS.
TER
(GRINS AND SINGS) *DUNNO WHAT TER CALL'IM BUT HE'S189 AHWILD
MIGHTY LIKE A ROSE-VELT.*
YUH'RE A SCREAM, SQUARE-HEAD--AN HONEST-TER-GAWD 11 ANNA
KNOCKOUT/
(AFTER A PAUSE) I PROMISED THE CAPT'N FAITHFUL 495 VOYAGE
I'D GET 'EM ONE. AND TER-NIGHT.
THE CAPT'N SAYS AS 'E WANTS A MAN SPECIAL BAD-- 495 VOYAGE
TER-NIGHT.
THEY SAILS AT DAY-BREAK TER-MORRER. 495 VOYAGE
(TO MAKE TALK) WHERE'S YER MATES POPPED ORF TER$ 505 VOYAGE
TERBACCER
WANTIN' TO SWAP FOR TERBACCER AND OTHER TRADIN' 502 DIFRNT
STUFF WITH STRAW MATS AND
TERM
WITH THE OPENING OF THE NEW TERM ONLY A FEW WEEKS 12 STRANG
OFF/...
NEW TERM... 22 STRANG
TREMBLING
(HIS VOICE IS LOWERED TO A TREMBLING WHISPER) 147 BEYOND
TERMINATING
AND HIS STUMPY LEGS TERMINATING IN LARGE FLAT 5 ANNA
FEET.
TERMINATION
THE TERMINATION OF OUR TRIP, PARTICULARLY ON THE 425 MARCOM
LAST DAY.
TERMORRER
AND TERMORRER MORNIN', KID, I'LL GIVE YUH A WHOLE 601 ROPE
HANDFUL OF THEM SHINY,

TERRIBLE

TERMORRER (CONT'D.)
TERMORRER. 601 ROPE
TERMORUM
YOU'LL FIND YER BLOODY 'AIR STANDIN' ON END BEFORE185 EJONES
TERMORROW MORNIN'.
TERMS
ARE YOU, TOO, THINKING IN TERMS OF TIME, OLD FOOL 360 LAZARU
SO SOON TO RE-ENTER INFINITY$
AS THOUGH HE HAD AN IMPORTANT APPOINTMENT WITH GOD 30 MANSNS
TO DISCUSS TERMS.
NOT VERY EASY TERMS FOR THEM TO ACCEPT, BUT THEY 76 MANSNS
HAD NO CHOICE.
MIGHT REORGANIZE YOUR BANKRUPTCY--IF I MAY PUT IT 103 MANSNS
IN TERMS YOU UNDERSTAND.
THERE ARE SOME WHO WOULD DESCRIBE THEM IN EVEN 152 MANSNS
STRONGER TERMS.
(NOTHING LEFT BUT TO ACCEPT HER TERMS... 134 STRANG
SAM SAID TO TELL YOU GORDON WAS ON EVEN TERMS WITH175 STRANG
THE LEADERS/
AGE'S TERMS 187 STRANG
TERNIGHT
TERNIGHT WHEN IT'S PITCH BLACK IN THE FOREST. 185 EJONES
JUST WAIT TILL HE'S ASLEEP AND I'LL SHOW YUH-- 394 ROPE
TERNIGHT.
TERRACE
BETWEEN THIS AND THE HOUSE IS A SMALL RAISED 281 LAZARU
TERRACE.
WHOSE POINT IS PLACED AT THE FOOT OF THE STEPS 282 LAZARU
LEADING TO THE TERRACE.
LAUGHING, THE FOLLOWERS DANCE TO IT IN WEAVING 285 LAZARU
PATTERNS ON THE TERRACE.
THEY POUR IN A LAUGHING ROUT FROM THE DOORWAY ONTO285 LAZARU
THE TERRACE.
THEY HUDDLE INTO GROUPS ON THE ROOF AND ON THE 295 LAZARU
TERRACE.
THE NEAR FOREGROUND IS A MARBLE TERRACE 326 LAZARU
BELOW THE STEPS TO THE TERRACE, IN A LINE FACING 326 LAZARU
FRONT.
THE TERRACE IS PAVED WITH ROUGH STONE. 184 STRANG
A TERRACE ON THE EVANS' ESTATE ON LONG ISLAND. 184 STRANG
IN THE REAR, THE TERRACE OVERLOOKS A SMALL HARBOR 184 STRANG
WITH THE OCEAN BEYOND.
NINA AND DARRELL JUMP STARTLEDLY AND GO TO THE 198 STRANG
REAR OF THE TERRACE TO WATCH THE
TERRFIED
(STARTLED BY HIS FALL, TERRFIED, 311 LAZARU
TERRIBLE
(DESPERATELY) BUT THE SUN NEVER SHINES IN THIS 540 'ILE
TERRIBLE PLACE.
AND THIS TERRIBLE SHIP, AND THIS PRISON OF A ROOM,545 'ILE
AND THE ICE ALL AROUND.
IF I DON'T GET AWAY FROM HERE, OUT OF THIS 546 'ILE
TERRIBLE SHIP, I'LL GO MAD/
WHY, NAT, I DON'T SEE HOW YOU--IT LOOKED TERRIBLE 198 AHWILD
BLASPHEMOUS--PARTS I READ.
(DOLEFULLY) YES--BUT IT'S SAD--TERRIBLE SAD. 257 AHWILD
OH, IT'S TOO TERRIBLE/ 262 AHWILD
AND THEN HE'D LEARN THAT YOU COULD BE TERRIBLE 265 AHWILD
STERN
(GIVING IN TO HER WORRY) I WISH YOU WOULDN'T SAY 271 AHWILD
THOSE TERRIBLE THINGS--
WHY, THAT'S A TERRIBLE PLACE/ 282 AHWILD
THAT WAS A TERRIBLE TIME, GOD HELP US. 36 ANNA
(TURNS TO HER) A TERRIBLE END FOR THE LIKE OF 36 ANNA
THEM SWABS DOES LIVE ON LAND.
(WITH A SHUDDER) WHAT A TERRIBLE END/ 36 ANNA
A TERRIBLE, FEARFUL OATH 74 ANNA
APPALLED BY SOME TERRIBLE DOUBT.) 76 ANNA
WE'RE GLAD YOU AIN'T GOIN', YOUR MA AND I, FOR 101 BEYOND
WE'D HAVE MISSED YOU TERRIBLE.
SHE'S MISSED YOU TERRIBLE. WE ALL HAVE. 136 BEYOND
(AFTER A PAUSE) YES, THESE YEARS HAVE BEEN 147 BEYOND
TERRIBLE FOR BOTH OF US.
HE LOOKS--(HE SHUDDERS) TERRIBLE/ 155 BEYOND
MARY'S DYING BROKE HIM UP TERRIBLE-- 155 BEYOND
EXCLAIMING IN A TERRIBLE VOICE) 566 CROSS
I KNOW YOU HAVE THE MOST VIVID RECOLLECTION OF HIS494 DAYS
TERRIBLE SIN.
HE IMAGINED HER SICKNESS WAS A TERRIBLE WARNING TO511 DAYS
HIM.
(SNEERINGLY) YOUR TERRIBLE SIN BEGINS TO CLOSE IN513 DAYS
ON YOU, EH$
(STARES AT HER--THEN A TERRIBLE EXPRESSION OF RAGE233 DESIRE
COMES OVER HIS FACE--
(WITH TERRIBLE GLOATING) AN' THAT'S WHAT'S 255 DESIRE
HAPPENED, HAIN'T IT$
IT AIN'T EVEN THAT I THINK YOU'VE DONE NOTHING 516 DIFRNT
TERRIBLE WRONG.
AND GETS PRICKLY HEAT AND THEN HE'S TERRIBLE 429 DYNAMO
CROSS...)
OH, THIS IS TERRIBLE/... 436 DYNAMO
SHE LOOKS TERRIBLE... 448 DYNAMO
A TERRIBLE LIE/ 466 DYNAMO
(A TERRIBLE LOOK OF MURDER COMES ON HIS FACE. 487 DYNAMO
HIS EYES ARE FIXED ON HER IN A TERRIBLE ACCUSING 62 ELECTR
GLARE.
SHE LOOKS TERRIBLE, DOESN'T SHE$ 68 ELECTR
SHE IS OBVIOUSLY IN A TERRIBLE STATE OF STRAINED 71 ELECTR
NERVES.
WHAT A TERRIBLE HOMECOMING THIS IS FOR HIM/ 80 ELECTR
SHE GOT SO SHE'D SAY THE MOST TERRIBLE THINGS 86 ELECTR
ABOUT EVERYONE.
SHE SPRINGS TO HER FEET AND STANDS GLARING AT HER 122 ELECTR
DAUGHTER WITH A TERRIBLE LOOK.
OR SOMETHING TERRIBLE WILL HAPPEN/ 161 ELECTR
WHAT TERRIBLE THING HAVE YOU BEEN THINKING 165 ELECTR
LATELY--BEHIND ALL YOUR CRAZY TALK$

TERRIBLE

TERRIBLE (CONT'D.)
(SHE CONTROLS HERSELF WITH A TERRIBLE EFFORT OF WILL. 167 ELECTR
BUT I KNOW TERRIBLE THINGS MUST HAVE HAPPENED-- 172 ELECTR
THERE IS NO TERRIBLE THING/ 172 ELECTR
THAT YOU'LL ONLY DRAG HIM INTO THIS TERRIBLE 172 ELECTR
THING--WHATEVER IT IS--
SHE WAS TERRIBLE OLD-FASHIONED. 261 GGBROW
(WITH TERRIBLE DESPAIR) PRIDE/ 272 GGBROW
HAS A TERRIBLE STRUGGLE WITH HIMSELF, THEN WHILE 289 GGBROW
SHE CONTINUES TO SPEAK,
(THEN HE CLAPS ON HIS MASK WITH A TERRIBLE EFFORT 288 GGBROW
OF WILL--MOCKINGLY)
HIS CLOTHES ARE DISHEVELED, HIS MASKED FACE HAS A 294 GGBROW
TERRIBLE DEATHLIKE INTENSITY,
AND STARES AT BROWN WITH TERRIBLE HATRED. 297 GGBROW
(WITH A TERRIBLE COMPOSURE) NO/ 298 GGBROW
YOUR FACE--IS TERRIBLE. 305 GGBROW
CAN'T YOU SEE THIS IS AN INSULT--A TERRIBLE, 317 GGBROW
BLASPHEMOUS INSULT/
HE IS IMPOSING A TERRIBLE DISCIPLINE ON HIMSELF TO318 GGBROW
AVOID DANCING AND LAUGHING.
(HE HAS THE TERRIBLE GROTESQUE AIR, IN CONFESSING 667 ICEMAN
HIS SORDID BASENESS,
(TEASINGLY.) YES, IT'S TERRIBLE THE WAY WE ALL 18 JOURNE
PICK ON YOU. ISN'T IT$
(SHOCKED BUT GIGGLING.) HEAVENS, WHAT A TERRIBLE 25 JOURNE
TONGUE THAT MAN HAS/
AND IT WOULD BE TERRIBLE-- 45 JOURNE
SHE'D A TERRIBLE HEADACHE, SHE SAID. 53 JOURNE
I KNEW SOMETHING TERRIBLE WOULD HAPPEN. 88 JOURNE
IT WAS A TERRIBLE ORDEAL. I REMEMBER, HEARING YOU 136 JOURNE
MURDER THE LINES.
IT'S TERRIBLE, HOW ABSENT-MINDED I'VE BECOME. 171 JOURNE
MAJESTIC FIGURE WHOSE UNDERSTANDING SMILE SEEMS 278 LAZARU
TERRIBLE AND ENIGMATIC TO THEM.)
THIS IS TOO GLORIOUS A VICTORY FOR YOU, TOO 289 LAZARU
TERRIBLE A LONELINESS/
BREAKS OUT INTO A TERRIBLE HYSTERICAL GIGGLE) 312 LAZARU
HIS VOICE RINGING MORE AND MORE WITH A TERRIBLE 349 LAZARU
UNBEARABLE POWER AND BEAUTY THAT
AND SO THE WORMS OF THEIR LITTLE FEARS EAT THEM 352 LAZARU
AND GROW FAT AND TERRIBLE AND
OR I SHALL LOSE PATIENCE WITH YOU--AND--(WITH A 354 LAZARU
GRIM SMILE) I CAN BE TERRIBLE/
AND A HOPE AT MY AGE DEMANDS A TERRIBLE EXPIATION 356 LAZARU
ON ITS SLAVE/
WELL, OUT WITH THE TERRIBLE SECRET, MOTHER. 13 MANSNS
BECOMES SO TERRIBLE THAT I WOULD DO ANYTHING, GIVE 28 MANSNS
ANYTHING TO ESCAPE/
(WITH A TERRIBLE INTENSITY.) 102 MANSNS
HAUNTED BY TERRIBLE GHOSTS AND RULED OVER BY A 111 MANSNS
HIDEOUS OLD WITCH.
IT'S A TERRIBLE THING HE CAN HATE HIS OWN MOTHER 122 MANSNS
SO/
DO YOU NOT KNOW THERE IS A TERRIBLE PUNISHMENT FOR192 MANSNS
TRESPASSING IN MY DOMAINS
(SHEEPISHLY) YOU MEAN IT WAS A TERRIBLE INSULT 415 MARCOM
WHEN I CALLED YOU--BY YOUR NAME$
I'M AFRAID YOU WERE BORN TO BE A TERRIBLE WANTON 20 MISBEG
WOMAN.
IT'S A TERRIBLE THING TO BREAK THE HABIT OF YEARS. 41 MISBEG
YOU'RE A TERRIBLE BLARNEYING LIAR, JIM, BUT THANK 43 MISBEG
YOU JUST THE SAME.
(SMILING) TERRIBLE. 44 MISBEG
IF IT'S THAT, GOD PITY YOU, YOU'RE A TERRIBLE 124 MISBEG
FOOL.
THEY'VE BEEN FIGHTIN' TERRIBLE. 152 POET
HE WAS A TERRIBLE LIAR, AS I REMEMBER HIM. 170 POET
BUT IT'S TERRIBLE TO BE SO ALONE IN THIS... 8 STRANG
BECAUSE OF THE TERRIBLE CHANGE IN HER ATTITUDE 10 STRANG
TOWARD ME.
BEFORE SOME TERRIBLE ENIGMA, 12 STRANG
A TERRIBLE TENSION OF WILL ALONE MAINTAINING SELF- 13 STRANG
POSSESSION.
WITH WHAT TERRIBLE RECOGNITION/... 15 STRANG
(THINKING FRIGHTENEDLY) (HOW TERRIBLE SHE IS/... 40 STRANG
IT'S TOO TERRIBLE FOR YOU--SAM'S OWN MOTHER--HOW 58 STRANG
WOULD YOU HAVE FELT IF SOMEONE--
(WITH TERRIBLE IRONIC BITTERNESS) 61 STRANG
I KNOW IT'S AN IMPOSITION--BUT--I'VE BEEN IN SUCH 98 STRANG
A TERRIBLE STATE SINCE MOTHER--
(BROKENLY) YOU DON'T KNOW, NINA--HOW TERRIBLE-- 98 STRANG
IT'S TERRIBLE/
TYPICAL TERRIBLE CHILD OF THE AGE... 122 STRANG
I ALWAYS GET A TERRIBLE FEELING AFTER HE'S BEEN 139 STRANG
BACK A WHILE
AND THEN THERE'LL BE THE SAME OLD TERRIBLE SCENE 143 STRANG
OF HATE AND YOU'LL RUN AWAY--
(IN A TERRIBLE STATE, SOBBING WITH RAGE AND 460 WELDED
ANGUISH)

TERRIBLY
(TERRIBLY FLUSTERED) SURE, I'VE HEARD THAT OLD 237 AHWILD
PARODY LOTS OF TIMES.
HE HAS HAD A HARD DAY AND IS TERRIBLY SLEEPY BUT 249 AHWILD
WILL NOT ACKNOWLEDGE IT.
HE SHOWS NO AFTER EFFECTS EXCEPT THAT HE IS 263 AHWILD
TERRIBLY SLEEPY.
(FRIGHTENED--IMMEDIATELY BECOMES TERRIBLY 278 AHWILD
SINCERE--GRABBING HER HAND)
(MADE TERRIBLY CURIOUS BY HIS OMINOUS TONE) 281 AHWILD
HIGH-TONED APPEARANCE AWE HIM TERRIBLY. 20 ANNA
HER FACE IS PALE, LOOKS TERRIBLY TIRED AND WORN, 63 ANNA
(TERRIBLY SHAKEN--FAINTLY) I CAN'T, MAT. 71 ANNA
MY EXAMINATION REVEALED THAT BOTH OF HIS LUNGS ARE158 BEYOND
TERRIBLY AFFECTED.
I AM AFRAID YOU WILL BE TERRIBLY SHOCKED-- 509 DAYS

TERRIBLY (CONT'D.)
AND IT SHOCKED JOHN TERRIBLY, POOR DEAR--IN SPITE 523 DAYS
OF ALL HIS OLD RADICAL IDEAS.
JUST BECAUSE YOU'VE PAMPERED ME SO TERRIBLY THE 529 DAYS
PAST FEW YEARS/
AND I DIDN'T APPEAR SO TERRIBLY UNHAPPY THEN, DID 529 DAYS
I$
(HE STARES INTO HER EYES, TERRIBLY CONFUSED AND 227 DESIRE
TORN.
BOTH BECOME TERRIBLY NERVOUS, UNEASY. 239 DESIRE
HE IS TERRIBLY EXCITED AND BADLY FRIGHTENED.) 548 DIFRNT
(TERRIBLY SHAKEN) YOU'RE A LIAR/ 463 DYNAMO
(THEN SOLICITOUSLY) YOU MUST BE TERRIBLY TIRED. 67 ELECTR
(TERRIBLY WOUNDED, WITHDRAWN INTO HIS STIFF 56 ELECTR
SOLDIER ARMOR--
WASN'T THE LONG TRAIN TRIP TERRIBLY HARD ON YOU, 81 ELECTR
DEAR$
I WAS FEELING SO TERRIBLY SAD--AND NERVOUS HERE. 117 ELECTR
IT MUST BE TERRIBLY LONELY FOR YOU. 117 ELECTR
YOU'RE ONLY TERRIBLY WORN OUT. 118 ELECTR
SHE SAID YOU WERE TERRIBLY FRIGHTENED AT BEING 120 ELECTR
ALONE HERE.
DON'T YOU KNOW HOW TERRIBLY YOU FRIGHTEN ME WHEN 140 ELECTR
YOU ACT SO STRANGELY$
I'M TERRIBLY NERVOUS TONIGHT. 151 ELECTR
AND TERRIBLY FRIGHTENED. 164 ELECTR
YOU LOOK TERRIBLY WORN OUT. 174 ELECTR
HE'S SO TERRIBLY LOYAL, AND HE'S ALWAYS LIKED 277 GGBROW
BILLY BROWN SO MUCH/
THE MASK IS NOW TERRIBLY RAVAGED. 285 GGBROW
TERRIBLY/ 310 GGBROW
BUT SUDDENLY SHE GROWS TERRIBLY TENSE AGAIN. 49 JOURNE
HE'D BE SO TERRIBLY HURT. 62 JOURNE
MARY IS TERRIBLY NERVOUS AGAIN. 71 JOURNE
SHE'S BEEN TERRIBLY FRIGHTENED ABOUT YOUR ILLNESS,139 JOURNE
FOR ALL HER PRETENDING.
(LOOKING AROUND HER. SOMETHING I MISS TERRIBLY. 173 JOURNE
(SUDDENLY BECOMING TERRIBLY UNEASY AT SOME 303 LAZARU
THOUGHT)
(HE GIVES A HARSH LAUGH) TIBERIUS MUST BE 328 LAZARU
TERRIBLY AFRAID OF YOU.
NEEDING MY LOVE SO TERRIBLY/ 134 MANSNS
HE HAS CHANGED GREATLY. GROWN TERRIBLY THIN, 144 MANSNS
HER SMALL, GIRLISH FIGURE HAS GROWN SO TERRIBLY 161 MANSNS
EMACIATED THAT SHE GIVES
ON WHY DOES SHE FORCE ME TO HATE HER SO TERRIBLYS 162 MANSNS
(TERRIBLY CONFUSED--STRUGGLINGLY) 368 MARCOM
SHE IS TERRIBLY ALARMED. 389 MARCOM
HE MUST BE TERRIBLY RICH--IF IT'S REALLY HIM. 427 MARCOM
HE'S TERRIBLY ASHAMED OF HIS SINFUL INCLINATIONS 32 POET
(GOES ON, UNHEEDINGLY.) SIMON WAS TERRIBLY ANGRY 145 POET
AT HIS FATHER FOR THAT.
IT HAS UPSET ME TERRIBLY/... 45 STRANG
I SUSPECT SHE IS TERRIBLY LONELY ALL BY HERSELF IN 50 STRANG
THIS BIG HOUSE.
BUT THERE'S NOTHING TO BE TERRIBLY SORRY ABOUT/ 69 STRANG
I'M TERRIBLY SORRY/ 69 STRANG
NOTHING SERIOUS BUT IT ANNOYS HER TERRIBLY. 73 STRANG
SHE'S TERRIBLY WORRIED. 77 STRANG
I MUST BE TERRIBLY CAREFUL OF CHARLIE/....) 118 STRANG
WE'VE MISSED YOU TERRIBLY. 126 STRANG
AND I'VE MISSED YOU--TERRIBLY/ 127 STRANG
HE'D BE TERRIBLY HURT IF YOU DIDN'T. 145 STRANG
(THINKING--TERRIBLY TORN) (WHY DO I LIKE HIM 151 STRANG
NOW$...
IT'S TERRIBLY FAINT BUT--NAVY AND WASHINGTON ARE 168 STRANG
LEADING--GORDON'S THIRD/
I'M TERRIBLY ANXIOUS TO HEAR WHAT YOU'VE DONE. 445 WELDED

TERRIFIC
HE WENT THROUGH A TERRIFIC INNER CONFLICT. 534 DAYS
SHE IS IN A TERRIFIC STATE OF TENSION. 157 ELECTR
THEN FROM THESE FIERY ROUND HOLES IN THE BLACK A 223 HA APE
FLOOD OF TERRIFIC LIGHT AND
BY THE TERRIFIC IMPACT OF THIS UNKNOWN, ABYSMAL 225 HA APE
BRUTALITY, NAKED AND SHAMELESS.
(HE LETS DRIVE A TERRIFIC SWING. 239 HA APE
TREE--(A TERRIFIC CHORUS OF BARKING AND YAPPING.) 243 HA APE
TERRIFIC FLASHES OF LIGHTNING AND CRASHES OF 318 LAZARU
THUNDER SEEM A RESPONSIVE
HE IS IN A STATE OF TERRIFIC TENSION, 171 MANSNS
HE IS IN A TERRIFIC STATE OF CONFLICTING EMOTIONS,149 STRANG

TERRIFIED
MRS. KEENEY LOOKS AT THE MATE WITH TERRIFIED 550 *ILE
EYES.)
(TERRIFIED) WHAT D'YOU MANE$ 53 ANNA
(WHEELING ABOUT WITH A TERRIFIED GASP) 69 ANNA
(TERRIFIED) YANK/ 484 CARDIF
(WITH A TERRIFIED GLANCE AT THE ROOF ABOVE) 566 CROSS
(TERRIFIED--APPEALINGLY) NAT/ 567 CROSS
(TERRIFIED) WHY$ 555 DAYS
(TERRIFIED) STOP/ 560 DAYS
(THEN TERRIFIED AGAIN) WHAT MADE YOU SAY, A FATE 560 DAYS
IN MY STORY--THE WILL OF GODS
(TERRIFIED) YE WON'T--LEAVE ME$ 257 DESIRE
(IMMEDIATELY TERRIFIED) I CAN'T, ADA/ 433 DYNAMO
HE HAS STARTLED AND TERRIFIED JENNINGS BY THE 487 DYNAMO
THROAT
IN A TERRIFIED WHISPER) 488 DYNAMO
(TERRIFIED) THINK I'D PEACH ON YERS 181 EJONES
IN A TERRIFIED GASP) 192 EJONES
(HE JERKS OUT HIS REVOLVER IN A FRENZY OF 192 EJONES
TERRIFIED RAGE)
JONES BELLOWS WITH BAFFLED, TERRIFIED RAGE, 195 EJONES
(HAS CALMED HERSELF, BUT HER EYES ARE STILL 89 ELECTR
TERRIFIED AND HER VOICE TREMBLES)
HER VOICE BECOMES TERRIFIED) 100 ELECTR
I'M SO TERRIFIED OF VINNIE/ 111 ELECTR
I'M TERRIFIED AT EVERY SOUND. 119 ELECTR

1633

TERRIFIED — TESTAMENT

TERRIFIED (CONT'D.)
(SHE STOPS ABRUPTLY, TERRIFIED BY HER OWN WORDS.) 156 ELECTR
THE TORTURED MAD LOOK ON HIS FACE CHANGING TO A 166 ELECTR
STRICKEN TERRIFIED EXPRESSION)
(RUSHING INTO THE NEXT ROOM, SHOUTS IN TERRIFIED 318 GGBROW
TUNES)
(THEN SUDDENLY, HYSTERICALLY ANGRY AND TERRIFIED) 319 GGBROW
I KNOW IT'S STILL HARD FOR YOU NOT TO BE TERRIFIED706 ICEMAN
BY DEATH.
MARY'S FACE IS TERRIFIED AND HER HANDS FLUTTER 73 JOURNE
DISTRACTEDLY.
THEN I BECAME TERRIFIED. 113 JOURNE
SHE TREMBLES AND HER EXPRESSION BECOMES TERRIFIED.174 JOURNE
(HIS LIPS TREMBLE, HIS EYES ARE TERRIFIED, 303 LAZARU
TERRIFIED AS CALIGULA BY THE FACES HE MAKES/ 309 LAZARU
HE WAS TERRIFIED BY THE MULTITUDE OF LAUGHING 316 LAZARU
IDIOTS
THEN SUDDENLY, TERRIFIED, SLINKS AWAY AND SIDLES 324 LAZARU
OFF AT RIGHT.)
(WITH A TERRIFIED CRY) LAZARUS/ 332 LAZARU
HER TERRIFIED EYES ON MIRIAM. 348 LAZARU
(TERRIFIED) NO, CAESAR/ 365 LAZARU
TERRIFIED RATS, THEIR VOICES SQUEAKY NOW WITH 369 LAZARU
FRIGHT)
MY POOR HEART WAS TERRIFIED YOU HAD FORGOTTEN I 164 MANSNS
WAS WAITING.
(TERRIFIED) BUT, YOUR HOLINESS, WE DARE NOT 363 MARCOM
REPEAT--HE'D HAVE US KILLED/
(MIKE GRABS THE SATCHEL, TERRIFIED. 10 MISBEG
IF HE'LL FALL ASLEEP, THAT'S THE BEST THING-- 159 POET
(ABRUPTLY SHE IS TERRIFIED.)
SARA IS TERRIFIED BUT SHE STANDS UNFLINCHINGLY.) 172 POET
SHE SHRINKS AWAY, LOOKING AT HIM WITH TERRIFIED 583 ROPE
EYES)
(SWEENEY RUSHES OVER AND PICKS THE TERRIFIED OLD 597 ROPE
MAN UP)
(THINKING--TERRIFIED) ((GOINGS.... 15 STRANG
(THINKING--TERRIFIED) (I MUST TALK HER OUT OF 15 STRANG
IT/...
(THINKING WITH TERRIFIED FOREBODING) 58 STRANG
SHE'S TERRIFIED BY THE IDEA OF CANCER. 77 STRANG
BUT EVERY DAY I GREW MORE TERRIFIED.... 91 STRANG
(IMMEDIATELY TERRIFIED AND BEATEN--THINKING) 93 STRANG
(TERRIFIED) (DOES SHE STILL LOVE ME$... 125 STRANG

TERRIFIEDLY
(THEN BESEECHING TERRIFIEDLY) 196 EJONES
CATCHING AT THE TABLE FOR SUPPORT--TERRIFIEDLY) 92 ELECTR
BUT IMMEDIATELY THROWS HERSELF IN THEM AGAIN-- 112 ELECTR
TERRIFIEDLY)
(TERRIFIEDLY) TO--BOSTON--S 120 ELECTR
(AS HE REACHES THEM--TERRIFIEDLY) 134 ELECTR

TERRITORY
THIS COUNTRY, WITH ITS IMMENSE TERRITORY CANNOT 40 POET
DEPEND

TERROR
(IN SUDDEN TERROR) ANSWER ME/ 551 'ILE
(WITH MOCK TERROR--SCREAMS IN FALSETTO) 246 AHWILD
(A STRANGE TERROR SEEMS SUDDENLY TO SEIZE HER. 68 ANNA
ROBERT LOOKS AT RUTH WHO SHRINKS AWAY FROM HIM IN 160 BEYOND
TERROR.
IT CREAKS SLIGHTLY AND NAT JUMPS TO HIS FEET--IN A562 CROSS
THICK VOICE OF TERROR)
(WITH SUDDEN TERROR) IT WASN'T--FATHERS 563 CROSS
(IN TERROR) STOP/ 565 CROSS
(HE FLASHES IT ON HER TERROR-STRICKEN FACE, THEN 572 CROSS
QUICKLY AROUND THE ROOM.
THEN A LOOK OF TERROR COMES INTO HIS FACE AND HE 531 DAYS
SHUDDERS.)
HE WAS SEIZED BY FITS OF TERROR, 534 DAYS
TO THEM, THAT IS TERROR. 542 DAYS
JOHN'S EYES ARE FIXED ON ELSA'S FACE WITH A 561 DAYS
GROWING TERROR.
ELSA SUDDENLY COMES OUT OF THE HALF-COMA SHE IS IN563 DAYS
WITH A CRY OF TERROR AND,
HE IS TREMBLING ALL OVER, IN A STRANGE STATE OF 243 DESIRE
TERROR.
HER FACE FULL OF TERROR YET WITH AN UNDERCURRENT 259 DESIRE
OF DESPERATE TRIUMPH.
SUPPLICATING TERROR) 543 DIFRNT
(CLUTCHES THE ARMS OF HIS CHAIR IN SUPERSTITIOUS 441 DYNAMO
TERROR,
TERROR) 444 DYNAMO
(HIS FATHER SQUEALS WITH TERROR AND TRIES TO 453 DYNAMO
BREAK AWAY FROM HIS HOLD.
(SEEING THE USELESSNESS OF STRUGGLING, GIVES WAY 174 EJONES
TO FRANTIC TERROR.
JONES LOOKS DOWN, LEAPS BACKWARD WITH A YELL OF 190 EJONES
TERROR,
(WITH A SUDDEN TERROR) LAWD GOD, DON'T LET ME SEE193 EJONES
NO MORE O' DEM HA'NTS/
OVER HIS FACE ABJECT TERROR GIVE WAY TO 197 EJONES
MYSTIFICATION, TO GRADUAL REALIZATION--
A SHUDDER OF TERROR SHAKES HIS WHOLE BODY AS THE 199 EJONES
WAIL RISES UP ABOUT HIM AGAIN.
MORE AND MORE THE SPIRIT OF TERROR GAINS 201 EJONES
POSSESSION OF HIM.
(OPENS HER EYES AND STARES AT HIM WITH A STRANGE 54 ELECTR
TERROR)
THEN SUDDENLY A WILD LOOK OF TERROR COMES OVER HIS 62 ELECTR
FACE.
(TREMBLING WITH GUILTY TERROR--STAMMERS.) 62 ELECTR
THEN STARTS WITH TERROR AS SHE HEARS A NOISE FROM 62 ELECTR
THE HALL AND FRANTICALLY
BUT SHE IS SO CRAZY I KNOW SHE THINKS--(THEN, WITH 88 ELECTR
REAL TERROR, CLINGING TO HIM)
(FULL OF NEW TERROR NOW--FOR BRANT'S LIFE-- 89 ELECTR
DISTRACTEDLY)

TERROR (CONT'D.)
SEIZED BY AN HYSTERICAL TERROR, BY SOME FEAR SHE 92 ELECTR
HAS KEPT HIDDEN)
SHE STOPS IN TERROR AND, HER EYES STILL FIXED ON 101 ELECTR
HIS FACE,
(WITH A CRY OF TERROR) OH--OH/ 120 ELECTR
(HE IS INTERRUPTED BY A MUFFLED YELL OF TERROR 134 ELECTR
FROM THE HOUSE.
(IN A LOW VOICE) YES, THAT IS WHAT I LIVE IN 152 ELECTR
TERROR OF--
(WHO HAS BEEN STARING AT HIM WITH TERROR, RAISING 292 GGBROW
HER MASK TO WARD OFF HIS FACE)
AS FOR HER, DURING HIS SPEECH SHE HAS LISTENED, 225 HA APE
PARALYZED WITH HORROR, TERROR,
(DISSOLVES INTO PITIABLE TERROR) 597 ICEMAN
(GLARES AT HIM IN ANGRY TERROR) 706 ICEMAN
THE MEN START TO THEIR FEET IN WILD-EYED TERROR 523 INZONE
(A LOOK OF TERROR COMES INTO HER EYES AND SHE 68 JOURNE
STAMMERS.)
(WITH DULL, RESIGNED TERROR NOW) 296 LAZARU
(WITH AN HYSTERICAL CRY OF DEFIANT TERROR) 308 LAZARU
SEEMING TO BE FILLED WITH A NERVOUS DREAD AND 326 LAZARU
TERROR OF EVERYTHING ABOUT HIM,
(MIRIAM GIVES A CRY OF TERROR.) 328 LAZARU
IF FLEEING IN TERROR FROM THE LAUGHTER WHICH NOW 334 LAZARU
BEATS AT THE WALLS.)
JUMPS TO HIS FEET IN A PANIC OF TERROR, AND RUNS 335 LAZARU
TOWARD TH PALACE DOOR, CALLING)
QUAKING WITH TERROR NOW AS IF THIS LAUGH WAS MEANT339 LAZARU
FOR HIM, DROPS TO HIS KNEES.
HE IS LAUGHING WITH THE AGONY AND TERROR OF DEATH.349 LAZARU
(AGAIN OVERCOME--STUTTERING WITH STRANGE TERROR) 359 LAZARU
(IN TERROR) NO, CAESAR/ 366 LAZARU
IT WAS ONE TERROR TOO MANY, TO HAVE BEEN LAUGHING 370 LAZARU
YOUR LAUGHTER IN THE NIGHT,
(HE IS GROVELING IN A PAROXYSM OF TERROR, 371 LAZARU
OR THE WICKED WITCH, AND I'D BE ALL GOOSE-FLESH 12 MANSNS
WITH TERROR
WITH HER IDIOTIC SUPERSTITIOUS TERROR OF THE 159 MANSNS
HAUNTED SUMMER-HOUSE/
(SHE RUNS TO HER WILDLY AND GRABS HER ARM-- 169 MANSNS
STAMMERING IN TERROR.)
(THEY BOTH WHIRL ON HIM WITH STARTLED GASPS OF 172 MANSNS
TERROR
IT WAS THE STILLNESS THAT FOLLOWS A SHRIEK OF 174 MANSNS
TERROR, WAITING TO BECOME AWARE--
(HIS TERROR GOING AND RAGE TAKING ITS PLACE, LEAPS352 MARCOM
TO HIS FEET)
(WITH A START, COMES TO HIMSELF AND BACKS AWAY 415 MARCOM
FROM THE PRINCESS IN TERROR)
(THE TERROR-STRICKEN COURIER SCRAMBLES OUT LIKE A 425 MARCOM
FLASH.
(THEY STAND PARALYZED BY TERROR, CLINGING TO EACH 163 POET
OTHER.
THE OLD MAN COWERS ON THE BENCH IN ABJECT TERROR.)597 ROPE
(WITH APPREHENSIVE TERROR) (GUTTER-- 35 STRANG
(WITH A GUILTY TERROR) ((IN MORE WAYS THAN ONE, I 67 STRANG
GUESS....))
(BENDING DOWN FOR ANOTHER SHEET, HIS VOICE 77 STRANG
TREMBLING WITH TERROR)
(THEN WITH SUDDEN TERROR) ((AND IF SHE SAYS 92 STRANG
YES....
(IN TERROR) ((WHAT THOUGHTS/... 100 STRANG
(BEWILDERED AND TERROR-STRICKEN, TRYING FEEBLY TO 107 STRANG
PUSH HIM AWAY--THINKING)
(THINKING IN TERROR) 171 STRANG

TERRORIST
A DANGEROUS TERRORIST, HUGO/ 596 ICEMAN

TERRITORY
HIS CLOTHES ARE THOSE OF A SUCCESSFUL DRUMMER 619 ICEMAN
WHOSE TERRITORY CONSISTS OF MINOR

TEST
ALL OUR SUFFERING HAS BEEN A TEST THROUGH WHICH WE150 BEYOND
HAD TO PASS
BITING ONE OR TWO TO TEST THEM.) 219 DESIRE
SHE WANTS ME TO--AS A FINAL TEST--TO PROVE I'M 485 DYNAMO
PURIFIED--
ARE YOU GOING TO PROVE, THE FIRST TIME YOUR LOVE 41 ELECTR
IS PUT TO A REAL TEST,
THIS IS THE TEST/ 138 ELECTR
IT WILL BE FUN TO PUT IT TO THE TEST. 220 HA APE
IF HE'S GOT THE GUTS TO GO THROUGH WITH THE TEST, 686 ICEMAN
THEN CERTAINLY YOU--
YOU'VE FACED THE TEST AND COME THROUGH. 690 ICEMAN
UNTIL I'D MADE IT A REAL FINAL TEST TO MYSELF--AND715 ICEMAN
TO HER.
AS IF THIS DRINK WERE A CRUCIAL TEST, 719 ICEMAN
THEN I WOULDN'T MIND PUTTING MYSELF TO A TEST BY 175 JOURNE
GOING HOME AFTER I GRADUATED,
THIS IS THEIR TEST. 294 LAZARU
YOU ARE SMALL AND WEAK LIKE OTHER MEN WHEN THE 319 LAZARU
TEST COMES/
(WITH A CRUEL SMILE) I HAVE THOUGHT OF A SPECIAL 345 LAZARU
TEST FOR HIM, CAESAR.
HE FELT SHE WAS LYING TO TEST HIS COURAGE. 111 MANSNS
THIS WILL TEST YOUR NERVE, MARK/ 362 MARCOM
BUT WAIT--A TEST/ 379 MARCOM
IT IS A TEST OF MYSELF I WANT TO MAKE AS A PENALTY426 MARCOM
FOR MY WEAKNESS A MOMENT AGO.
HE SHOULD TEST HIS LOVE AND YOURS BY LETTING A 109 POET
DECENT INTERVAL OF TIME ELAPSE
TEST OF MANHOOD... 6 STRANG

TESTAMENT
HE TOSSES THE TESTAMENT ASIDE CONTEMPTUOUSLY) 269 GGBROW
(SUDDENLY REACHES OUT AND TAKES UP A COPY OF THE 269 GGBROW
NEW TESTAMENT
MY HEART, NOT BROWN--(MOCKINGLY) MY LAST WILL AND299 GGBROW
TESTAMENT/

TESTAMENT (CONT'D.)

TESTAMENT (CONT'D.)
((IT'S IN EVERY HEADLINE OF THIS DAILY NEWER 123 STRANG
TESTAMENT...
TESTED
NOR TILL WE'VE TESTED IT'S GOOD MONEY/ 215 DESIRE
(HARSHLY) UNTIL I HAVE TESTED HIM WITH HIS OWN 351 LAZARU
LIFE/
TESTIFY
WE'LL TESTIFY YOU WAS CRAZY/ 719 ICEMAN
AND SPRANG UP INTO THIS MIGHTY TREE TO TESTIFY 349 MARCOM
FOREVER TO HIS MIRACULOUS POWERS
TESTILY
(HIS INTEREST DIVERTED BY THIS EXCUSE TO BEEF-- 726 ICEMAN
TESTILY)
(HIS VANITY PIQUED--TESTILY.) 17 JOURNE
(SEEING HER PREOCCUPATION NOW--DEEPLY HURT-- 54 STRANG
TESTILY)
TESTIMONIAL
LIKE A CURED CRIPPLE'S TESTIMONIAL OFFERING IN A 566 DAYS
SHRINE.)
TESTING
(EXULTANTLY--BUT AS IF TESTING HER, WARNINGLY) 488 WELDED
TESTINGLY
HE STANDS STAKING UP AT THE ROPE AND TAPS IT 579 ROPE
TESTINGLY SEVERAL TIMES WITH HIS
THEY TOUCH EACH OTHER TESTINGLY 480 WELDED
TESTY
HE ATTEMPTS TO HIDE HIS DEFENSELESSNESS BEHIND A 576 ICEMAN
TESTY TRUCULENT MANNER,
THEY HE UNDERSTANDS--WITH HIS NATURAL TESTY 722 ICEMAN
MANNER)
TETHER
(DESPERATELY--AT THE END OF HER TETHER) 173 ELECTR
TEWKSBURY
THAT STABBED ME IN THE FIELD BY TEWKSBURY. 168 JOUANE
TEXAS
YUH COULD WALK ON 'EM FROM HERE TO TEXAS/ 632 ICEMAN
RESTRICTING THE MIGRATION OF NON-NORDIC BIRDS INTO390 MARCOM
TEXAS,
TEXT
OPENS AND READS ALOUD THE TEXT AT WHICH IT POINTS)269 GGBROW
TEXTBOOKS
A SMALL TABLE ON WHICH ARE STACKED HIS TEXTBOOKS, 421 DYNAMO
AND A CHAIR IN LEFT CORNER,
TEXTILE
IN A TEXTILE-MILL TOWN ABOUT FORTY MILES FROM THE 43 MANSNS
CITY.
TH
PEARL SLAPS HIM ACROSS THE SIDE OF TH 471 CARIBE
JUMPS TO HIS FEET IN A PANIC OF TERROR, AND RUNS 335 LAZARU
TOWARD TH PALACE DOOR, CALLING)
THA'
THA' RIGHTS 470 CARIBE
THACKERAY
THEN, THE MOST MODERN PROBABLY BEING THACKERAY. 3 STRANG
THANK
I'LL THANK YOU TO STEER A CLEAR COURSE O' THAT. 542 'ILE
(FLUSTERED AND GRATEFUL) I--I'D LIKE TO, SID 191 AHWILD
THANK YOU.
WELL, WE'RE ABOUT READY TO START AT LAST, THANK 208 AHWILD
GOODNESS/
(GRATEFULLY) THANK YOU, LILY. 211 AHWILD
(RESPECT IN HIS VOICE) THANK YOU, SIR. 239 AHWILD
OH, THANK GOD, THANK GOD/ 260 AHWILD
(STOUTLY) YES, THANK GOD, THOUGH I'VE NOT SEEN A 37 ANNA
SIGHT OF IT IN FIFTEEN YEARS.
(MUCH MOVED) THANK YOU, PA. 101 BEYOND
BUT, THANK THE LORD, 114 BEYOND
AND THANK YOU FOR NOT INTERFERING. 117 BEYOND
IT'S BETTER NOW, DEAR, THANK YOU. 129 BEYOND
(GAILY) BUT THANK THE LORD, ALL THOSE DAYS ARE 136 BEYOND
OVER NOW.
(PROUDLY) AND I'VE MANAGED TO KEEP THINGS GOING, 148 BEYOND
THANK GOD.
THANK GOD I CAME BACK BEFORE IT WAS TOO LATE. 156 BEYOND
(WITH AN AFFECTIONATE SMILE) FINE/ THANK YOU/ 160 BEYOND
THANK YE, SORA. 486 CARDIF
THANK YOU FOR THE COMPLIMENT.. 469 CARIBE
(HE GETS UP SMILING) AND THANK YOU FOR THE 562 CROSS
INTERESTING STORY.
THANK YOU, JACK. 501 DAYS
AND, THANK HEAVEN, IT WAS LONG AGO. 506 DAYS
AND I THANK GOD HE IS/ 522 DAYS
THANK YOU, LUCY. 524 DAYS
I'VE GOT ENOUGH ON MY OWN, THANK YOU. 527 DAYS
THANK YOU, FATHER. 532 DAYS
NO, DEAR, THANK YOU. 533 DAYS
THANK GOD/ 544 DAYS
THANK GOD/ 545 DAYS
THANK YEW FOR THE RIDE. 220 DESIRE
THANK YEW. 220 DESIRE
THANK YEW. 242 DESIRE
(LOVINGLY) THANK YOU, CALEB. 496 DIFRNT
THANK YE, EMMER. 513 DIFRNT
I WANT TO SAY GOOD-BY AND THANK YOU FOR ALL YOU'VE531 DIFRNT
DONE.
HE DOESN'T CARE ANYTHING ABOUT GIRLS YET, THANK 423 DYNAMO
GOODNESS/,))
THANK YOU, THANKS. 436 DYNAMO
(LORD GOD OF RIGHTEOUS VENGEANCE, I THANK 447 DYNAMO
THEE/...
THANK YOU. 21 ELECTR
YOU CAN THANK VINNIE, EZRA/ 35 ELECTR
(SHE KISSES HIM) BUT IT'S ALL OVER NOW, THANK 76 ELECTR
GOD.
AT LEAST HAZEL HASN'T CHANGED, THANK GOD/ 81 ELECTR
THANK YE, SIR. 106 ELECTR
OH, THANK GOD/ 113 ELECTR

THANK (CONT'D.)

NO, YOU'RE THE SAME, THANK GOODNESS/ 143 ELECTR
THANK YOU, PETER. 146 ELECTR
THANK YOU FOR YOUR ANXIETY ABOUT MY HEALTH/ 151 ELECTR
AS THE LAST MALE MANNON--THANK GOD FOR THAT, EH/ 152 ELECTR
NO, THANK YOU, SETH. 170 ELECTR
THANK GOD/ 171 ELECTR
I THANK MR. ANTHONY FOR THIS SPLENDID OPPORTUNITY 261 GGBROW
TO CREATE MYSELF--
THANK YOU/ 290 GGBROW
THANK YOU/ 290 GGBROW
(WEARILY REPROVING) THANK GOODNESS I'VE FOUND 291 GGBROW
YOU/
THANK YOU, MOTHER. 322 GGBROW
THANK YOU FOR HAPPINESS/ 323 GGBROW
WELL, THANK GOODNESS, IT'S ABOUT TIME FOR THEM TO 220 HA APE
COME FOR US.
(GRATEFULLY.) THANK YOU, ERIE. 36 HUGHIE
I HAVEN'T ANY LEFT, THANK GOD. 587 ICEMAN
AND I'LL THANK YOU TO KEEP YOUR LIFE TO YOURSELF. 591 ICEMAN
THEY WOULDN'T THANK YOU FOR IT. 594 ICEMAN
THANK YOU, HARRY, OLD CHUM. 601 ICEMAN
I'LL THANK YOU TO KEEP YOUR HANDS OFF ME/ 684 ICEMAN
YOU'LL THANK ME WHEN IT'S ALL OVER. 686 ICEMAN
(FRIGHTENEDLY) NO, THANK YOU. 691 ICEMAN
(TIPSILY) WELL, I THANK GAWD NOW 723 ICEMAN
(WITH HEARTY SATISFACTION.) BUT THANK GOD, 14 JOURNE
THANK HEAVENS, THE FOG IS GONE. 17 JOURNE
THE SUMMER WILL SOON BE OVER, THANK GOODNESS. 72 JOURNE
THANK YOU. 89 JOURNE
GOSH, THANK YOU, PAPA. 90 JOURNE
IT WILL SOON BE NIGHT, THANK GOODNESS. 102 JOURNE
(WITH RELIEF.) THANK YOU, MA'AM. 106 JOURNE
THANK GOD. 139 JOURNE
(IN A LOW VOICE.) THANK GOD HE'S ASLEEP. 167 JOURNE
THANK YOU. YOU ARE VERY KIND. 172 JOURNE
I THANK YOU, PRETTY LADY. 346 LAZARU
(SINKS DOWN ON THE BENCH.) THANK YOU. 19 MANSNS
EXCEPT I THANK GOD I FREED MYSELF IN TIME, AND 47 MANSNS
THEN ME/ YOU.
THANK YOU FOR THE WARNING. 52 MANSNS
OH, THANK YOU, SARA. 55 MANSNS
NO, THANK YOU, MRS. 55 MANSNS
(ALMOST ANGRILY.) I CAN TAKE CARE OF MY CHILDREN, 76 MANSNS
THANK YOU--
THANK YOU, MOTHER. 100 MANSNS
(PATTING SARA'S HAND.) THANK GOODNESS, 124 MANSNS
THANK YOU, MOTHER. 132 MANSNS
AND THANK YOU FOR YOUR KINDNESS. 143 MANSNS
THANK YOU. 151 MANSNS
I-- I DON'T KNOW HOW TO THANK YOU--I APOLOGIZE FOR 153 MANSNS
HAVING MISJUDGED YOU--
(STAMMERS CONFUSEDLY.) I--I THANK YOU-- 154 MANSNS
I ACCEPT THE POSITION, MADAM--AND THANK YOU 155 MANSNS
AGAIN--FOR YOUR--CHARITY/
THANK YOU, MADAM, FOR REMINDING ME OF MY DUTY. 155 MANSNS
AH, THANK GOD, YOU CAN CRY. 167 MANSNS
HE'D THANK ME FOR IT/ 168 MANSNS
THANK YOU, MOTHER. 176 MANSNS
THANK YOU FOR YOUR GREAT KINDNESS, MY LADY. 193 MANSNS
WHY, THANK YOU, GOOD WOMAN. 193 MANSNS
THANK YOU, BROTHER. 378 MARCOM
THANK YOU, SIR-- I MEAN, YOUR LORDSHIP--YOUR--(THEN378 MARCOM
SUDDENLY) BEFORE I FORGET--
THANK YOU, YOUR MAJESTY. 383 MARCOM
OH, THANK YOU SO MUCH, MARCO POLO/ 391 MARCOM
I THANK YOU/ 393 MARCOM
THANK YOU FOR REMINDING ME. 403 MARCOM
(QUICKLY) THANK YOU, PRINCESS. 412 MARCOM
I WOULD I HAD THE GIFT OF ORATORY TO THANK YOU 431 MARCOM
FITTINGLY, BUT I AM A SIMPLE MAN.
AH, THANK GOD. 3 MISBEG
THANK YOU, JOSIE. 7 MISBEG
I DON'T WANT A DECENT MAN, THANK YOU. 8 MISBEG
I DON'T KNOW IF I SHOULD THANK GOD FOR BEING LIKE 17 MISBEG
YOU.
THANK GOD, YOU'RE LIKE ME AND YOUR MOTHER. 17 MISBEG
NO, THANK YOU/ 29 MISBEG
(PLEASED, BUT JEERING) THANK YOU KINDLY FOR YOUR 29 MISBEG
COMPLIMENTS.
YOU'RE A TERRIBLE BLARNEYING LIAR, JIM, BUT THANK 43 MISBEG
YOU JUST THE SAME.
WELL, THANK GOD FOR SMALL FAVORS. 77 MISBEG
AH, THANK GOD, THAT SOUNDS NATURAL/ 94 MISBEG
WELL, THANK GOD. 101 MISBEG
THANK GOD/ 111 MISBEG
THANK YOU KINDLY. 121 MISBEG
(STILL MEEK) NO, THANK YOU. 122 MISBEG
YOU OUGHT TO THANK ME FOR LETTING YOU SEE-- 138 MISBEG
THANK GOD, IT'S BEAUTIFUL. 164 MISBEG
THANK GOD FOR THAT. 173 MISBEG
(WITH HUMBLE GRATITUDE) THANK GOD FOR THAT, 175 MISBEG
DARLING.
THANK YOU KINDLY. 9 POET
WELL, THANK YOU FOR TELLING ME, 14 POET
THANK YOU. 16 POET
THANK YOU, NORA. 20 POET
THANK YOU. 34 POET
THANK GOD, I STILL BEAR THE UNMISTAKABLE STAMP OF 43 POET
AN OFFICER AND A GENTLEMAN.
THANK GOD FOR YOU, LORD BYRON-- 44 POET
OH, THANK YE, YER HONOR. 45 POET
I'LL THANK YOU NOT TO INTERFERE. 51 POET
THANK YE, YER HONOR. 54 POET
AH, THANK GOD FOR THAT. 60 POET
(TAKES THE MILK.) THANK YOU, MOTHER. 60 POET
THANK YOU. 69 POET
THANK YOU FOR REMINDING ME OF MY DUTY TO SARA. 76 POET

1635 — THAT'D

THANK (CONT'D.)
THANK GOD, IF HE'S PUTTING ON HIS UNIFORM, HE'LL 80 POET
BE HOURS BEFORE THE MIRROR.
THANK YOU, MRS. HARFORD. 81 POET
NOTHING. THANK YOU. 86 POET
THANK GOD, I STILL HAVE WINE IN MY CELLAR FIT FOR 98 POET
A GENTLEMAN.
ALL THE SAME, I THANK YOU FOR YOUR TOAST. 101 POET
(WITH BITTER ANGER.) THANK GOD IT'S OVER, 104 POET
THANK GOD FOR THAT, AT LEAST/ 111 POET
CONSENT OR NOT, I WANT TO THANK YOU FOR YOUR KIND 115 POET
FATHERLY ADVICE
THANK YOU, BUT I WANT NOTHING, SIR. 117 POET
BUT I THANK YOU FOR THE THOUGHT. 134 POET
THANK GOD. 140 POET
I'LL THANK YOU TO MIND YOUR OWN BUSINESS, JAMIE 160 POET
CREGAN.
OH, THANK GOD/ 164 POET
THANK YOU KINDLY BUT I'VE ALREADY TAKEN YOUR WISE 171 POET
ADVICE, FATHER.
NOW IT'S DEAD--THANK GOD--AND I'LL MAKE A BETTER 180 POET
WIFE FOR SIMON.
HE'S GONE. THANK GOD/ 584 ROPE
THANK GOD HE'S OFF DOWN TO THE HOUSE, 597 ROPE
THANK GOD, CHARLIE'S LIKE ONE OF THE FAMILY... 12 STRANG
(VERY SLEEPILY) THANK YOU, FATHER. 46 STRANG
THANKS--I-- I REALLY DON'T KNOW HOW TO THANK-- 47 STRANG
(WITH A FORCED SMILE) NO, THANK YOU. 52 STRANG
THANK HEAVENS, 72 STRANG
THANK YOU. 74 STRANG
GOOD NIGHT, DOCTOR--AND THANK YOU. 78 STRANG
THANK YOU. 78 STRANG
NO, I'VE ENOUGH GUILT IN MY MEMORY NOW, THANK YOU/ 84 STRANG
(WITH A CRY OF TRIUMPH) THANK GOD/ 97 STRANG
((THANK GOD FOR MARSDEN.... 99 STRANG
QUITE ALL RIGHT NOW. THANK YOU. 99 STRANG
((OH, GOD, I THANK YOU/)) (NINA COMES ON FROM THE107 STRANG
KITCHEN.
THANK YOU--NEO. 107 STRANG
I AM BEGINNING TO FORGET, THANK GOD/....)) 112 STRANG
(THINKING--PROUDLY) ((THANK GOD FOR SAMMY/... 116 STRANG
THANK YOU. 136 STRANG
AND YOU OUGHT TO THANK GOD HE DOESN'T/ 141 STRANG
NO, THANK YOU, NINA/... 141 STRANG
THANK GOD, I AM ONLY A MOTHER NOW/... 149 STRANG
(EAGERLY) THANK YOU. 159 STRANG
((THANK GOD, I CAN WATCH HER OBJECTIVELY AGAIN... 161 STRANG
THANK GOD MY SLAVERY IS OVER/... 161 STRANG
NO MORE, THANK GOD/...)) 163 STRANG
THANK GOD/... 174 STRANG
(GRATEFULLY) THANK YOU. 179 STRANG
THANK YOU, UNCLE CHARLIE/ 188 STRANG
THANK YOU FOR THAT/ 196 STRANG
HOW CAN I EVER THANK YOUS 196 STRANG
THANK YOU, FATHER--HAVE I BEEN WICKED$ 200 STRANG
(SHAKING HIS HEAD) NOTING DIS TIME, THANK YOU. 498 VOYAGE
YOU OUGHT TO THANK ME FOR BREATHING LIFE INTO 459 WELDED
THEM/
THANKED
WELL, GOD BE THANKED, YOU WEREN'T DREAMING OF ANY 90 MANSNS
OTHER/
OH, HE THANKED ME KINDLY. 17 MISBEG
AND PHIL THANKED ME. 133 MISBEG
BUT THAT I'VE SAVED, GOD BE THANKED. 22 POET
IT IS THAT I SHED MY BLOOD FOR A COUNTRY THAT 40 POET
THANKED ME WITH DISGRACE.
GOD BE THANKED/ 142 POET
THANKFUL
I'LL BE THANKFUL TO YOU, HONEST. 60 ANNA
THAT, AT LEAST, IS CERTAIN--A CERTAINTY WE SHOULD 508 DAYS
BE THANKFUL FOR.
I BE THANKFUL T' YE. 207 DESIRE
WALL, I'M THANKFUL FUR HIM SAVIN' ME THE TROUBLE. 265 DESIRE
THERE'S THAT MUCH TO BE THANKFUL FOR, ANYWAY....)) 55 STRANG
THANKFULNESS
WITH WHAT HUMBLE GRATITUDE WOULD I GIVE 38 MANSNS
THANKFULNESS TO GOD
THANKIN'
UGH, DON'T BE THANKIN' US, MA'AM. 73 POET
THANKING
LET YOU END ME WITH A SHOT AND I'LL BE THANKING 69 ANNA
YOU.
I WAS THANKING GOD--FOR OUR BABY/ 109 STRANG
THANKLESS
=TO HAVE A THANKLESS CHILD.= 89 JOURNE
THANKS
ALL RIGHT, DICK, THANKS--ONLY HURTS A LITTLE. 206 AHWILD
HERE I AM, THANKS TO YOUR AND NAT'S KINDNESS, WITH214 AHWILD
THE BEST HOME IN THE WORLD.
OH, FINE PA. THANKS. 228 AHWILD
GEE--OH, THANKS-- 242 AHWILD
THANKS, AGAIN/ 242 AHWILD
THANKS, KID. 242 AHWILD
HERE'S HOW--AND THANKS AGAIN. 243 AHWILD
THANKS, LILY. 259 AHWILD
THANKS. 22 ANNA
(WITH A HARD LAUGH) THANKS. 66 ANNA
(HER LIPS TREMBLING PITIFULLY) THANKS/ 70 ANNA
AND I'LL BE SAYING PRAYERS OF THANKS ON MY TWO 71 ANNA
KNEES TO THE ALMIGHTY GOD/
(TAKING HIS HAND) THANKS, ANDY, IT'S FINE OF YOU 101 BEYOND
TO--
THANKS, UNCLE DICK. 102 BEYOND
IN THE SUN LIKE A SLAVE WITHOUT GETTING A WORD OF 107 BEYOND
THANKS FOR IT.
AND NO THANKS TO THAT OLD FOOL OF A COUNTRY QUACK,145 BEYOND
EITHER.
OH, FINE, THANKS. 516 DAYS

THANKS (CONT'D.)
(DRYLY) THANKS, LIAR/ 517 DAYS
(FIERCELY) AN' FUR THANKS HE KILLED HER/ 207 DESIRE
(FURIOUSLY) SO THAT'S THE THANKS I GIT FUR 233 DESIRE
MARRYIN' YE--
THANK YOU, THANKS. 436 DYNAMO
(GRATEFULLY) RIGHTO--AND THANKS TER YER. 186 EJUNES
NO, THANKS/ 47 ELECTR
THANKS FOR MEETING ME. 84 ELECTR
I'VE HAD A THOROUGH TRAINING AT THIS GAME--THANKS 114 ELECTR
TO YOU AND FATHER.
I OWE HIM A VOTE OF THANKS/ 147 ELECTR
THANKS BE TO BROWN FOR REMINDING ME. 295 GGBROW
THANKS FOR THIS ONE LAST FAVOR, DION/ 320 GGBROW
(THROWING IT IN DRAWER) THANKS. 247 HA APE
AND, THANKS TO WHISKEY, HE'S THE ONLY ONE DOESN'T 579 ICEMAN
KNOW IT.
(AVIDLY) THANKS. 582 ICEMAN
(HUSKILY) THANKS, HARRY. 598 ICEMAN
I SAID, =YES, I DO SEE, DICK, AND MANY THANKS FOR 604 ICEMAN
THE TIP.=
(SHOVES THE KEY IN HIS POCKET) THANKS, ROCKY. 620 ICEMAN
WHEN, THANKS TO MY MIRACULOUS CURE, 628 ICEMAN
(TENSELY) NO, THANKS. 644 ICEMAN
ALL I CAN SAY IS THANKS TO EVERYBODY AGAIN FOR 659 ICEMAN
REMEMBERING ME ON MY BIRTHDAY.
BEJEEES, THANKS, ALL OF YOU. 659 ICEMAN
WHEN ALL DE THANKS WE GET IS HE LOOKS DOWN ON US. 669 ICEMAN
NO, THANKS. 674 ICEMAN
THOUGH CAN'T SAY I SLEPT MUCH, THANKS TO THAT 675 ICEMAN
INTERFERING ASS, HICKEY.
GOOD-BYE, HARRY, AND THANKS FOR ALL YOUR KINDNESS.686 ICEMAN
THANKS, LARRY. 720 ICEMAN
JESUS, LARRY, THANKS. 721 ICEMAN
THE ONLY THANKS IS TO HAVE YOU SNEER AT ME FOR A 32 JOURNE
DIRTY MISER,
NO, THANKS/ 35 JOURNE
GRAND. THANKS, MAMA. 43 JOURNE
THANKS FOR HANDING ME A GOOD EXCUSE. 52 JOURNE
YOU, WHO, THANKS TO HIM, HAVE NEVER HAD TO WORK 60 JOURNE
HARD IN YOUR LIFE/
THANKS. 146 JOURNE
(DRYLY.) THANKS FOR TELLING ME YOUR GREAT SECRET.155 JOURNE
(MISERABLY.) THANKS, KID. 162 JOURNE
AND A FINER BARGAIN THAN I WOULD HAVE DREAMED 63 MANSNS
POSSIBLE, THANKS TO MOTHER.
AND THAT'S THE THANKS I GET FOR STOPPING YOU/ 165 MANSNS
SMILING YOUR THANKS AS I PROMISE YOU A LARGE 360 MARCOM
FORTUNE IF YOU WILL BE TRUE,
AND LOOK AT THE CROWD WE'VE DRAWN, THANKS TO MY 405 MARCOM
BAND/
YOU DIDN'T GET MUCH THANKS FROM MIKE, I'LL WAGER. 17 MISBEG
FOR YOUR HELP.
THANKS, JOSIE. 103 MISBEG
(SIMPLY) THANKS, JOSIE. 105 MISBEG
NOT NOW, THANKS. 116 MISBEG
THANKS. 122 MISBEG
(SIMPLY) THANKS, JOSIE. 129 MISBEG
THANKS, JOSIE. 133 MISBEG
(SIMPLY) THANKS, JOSIE. 141 MISBEG
THANKS, JOSIE. 152 MISBEG
THANKS, JOSIE. 167 MISBEG
SHALL THANKS TO HIM/ 159 POET
THANKS. 598 ROPE
THANKS/ 33 STRANG
THANKS--I--- I REALLY DON'T KNOW HOW TO THANK-- 47 STRANG
UNTIL HE'D EXPLAINED IT WAS THANKS TO HIS KINDNESS 50 STRANG
FOR THEY WON'T BE ALONE, THANKS TO ME.... 129 STRANG
THE THANKS I GET FOR SAVING SAM AT THE SACRIFICE 171 STRANG
OF MY OWN HAPPINESS/...
THANKS. 450 WELDED
(TAKING ONE) THANKS, NELLY. 450 WELDED
THANKS FOR THAT AFTERTHOUGHT--BUT DO YOU EXPECT ME457 WELDED
TO BELIEVE IT.
NO--THANKS. 475 WELDED
THANKSGIVIN'
HE'S DOWN T' THE CHURCH OFFERIN' UP PRAYERS O' 248 DESIRE
THANKSGIVIN'.
THANKSGIVING
WELL, I REMEMBER ONE THANKSGIVING, OR MAYBE IT WAS 148 JOURNE
CHRISTMAS,
THASH
THASH MORE LIKE IT. 155 JOURNE
THAT'D
THAT'D BE THE TIME IT'D TAKE HIM TO WALK FROM THE 260 AHWILD
BEACH
THAT'D BORE ME MORE THAN IT WOULD YOU. 294 AHWILD
THAT'D BE A SWATE MATCH, SURELY/ 48 ANNA
AND DRINKING OCEANS OF BOOZE THAT'D MAKE ME 70 ANNA
FORGET.
THAT'D GIVE ME A CHANCE-- 141 BEYOND
AND SEA-BISCUIT THAT'D BREAK THE 480 CARDIF
THERE AIN'T MUCH IN ALL THAT THAT'D MAKE YUH SORRY486 CARDIF
TO LOSE IT, DRIS/
WHY, I WAS THAT ANXIOUS TO BRING BACK YOUR PA'S 497 DIFRNT
SHIP WITH A FINE VIGE THAT'D
(EAGERLY) SAY, THAT'D BE GREAT/ 526 DIFRNT
(WITH A TICKLED CHUCKLE) GOSH, THAT'D BE THE REAL545 DIFRNT
STUNT AW RIGHT, AW RIGHT.
THERE MUST BE SOMETHING IN HER SONG THAT'D TELL 474 DYNAMO
YOU IF YOU HAD EARS TO HEAR/...
THAT'D MAKE IT RIGHT. 20 ELECTR
LIKE I WAS BRINGING YOU ALL A NEW BRAND OF DOPE 286 GGBROW
THAT'D MAKE YOU FORGET
THAT'D KNOCK YOUR EYE OUT/ 16 HUGHIE
BY GOD, IF HE WAS, I'D TELL HIM A TALE THAT'D MAKE 28 HUGHIE
HIS EYES POP/
I'D ALWAYS KNOW I'D MAKE A WIN THAT'D FIX IT. 35 HUGHIE

THAT'D

THAT'D (CONT'D.)
MY BIRTHDAY, TOMORROW, THAT'D BE THE RIGHT TIME T0804 ICEMAN
TURN OVER A NEW LEAF.
AND THROW OVERBOARD THE DAMNED LYING PIPE DREAM 621 ICEMAN
THAT'D BEEN MAKING ME MISERABLE,
THAT'D BE CRAZY. 78 MANSNS
THAT'D SUIT ME. 93 MISBEG
FAITH, IF IT CAME TO SEDUCING, IT'D BE ME THAT'D 32 POET
HAVE TO DO IT.
UP THE PRIEST TO HEAR MY CONFESSION AND GIVE ME 138 POET
GOD'S FORGIVENESS THAT'D BRING
YOUR FATHER'D BE SATISFIED WITH HARFORD'S APOLOGY 140 POET
AND THAT'D END IT.
IF THAT'D HAPPEN... 55 STRANG
(IF THAT'D ONLY HAPPEN/... 55 STRANG
THAT'D SET HER FREE... 93 STRANG
THAT'RE
HE'S A TIGHT--WAD AND I HATE FOLKS THAT'RE TIGHT 522 DIFRNT
WITH THEIR COIN.
THAT'SALL
AND THAT'SALL THE GOOD IT DOES/ 188 AHWILD
THATCH
PATCH RILEY IS AN OLD MAN WITH A THATCH OF DIRTY 52 POET
WHITE HAIR.
THAWING
(THAWING OUT, IN HIS TOTAL MISUNDERSTANDING OF THEL19 POET
SITUATION.)
THEATER
AND I HAVE NO INFLUENCE EXCEPT IN THE THEATER. 32 JOURNE
(IGNORES THIS.) I'VE NEVER FELT AT HOME IN THE 102 JOURNE
THEATER.
BEFORE I MET MR. TYRONE I HARDLY KNEW THERE WAS 102 JOURNE
SUCH A THING AS A THEATER.
I TOLD MYSELF IT MUST BE SOME BUSINESS CONNECTED 113 JOURNE
WITH THE THEATER.
I KNEW SO LITTLE ABOUT THE THEATER. 113 JOURNE
IN 1874 WHEN EDWIN BOOTH CAME TO THE THEATER IN 150 JOURNE
CHICAGO WHERE I WAS LEADING MAN,
BECAUSE I LOVED THE THEATER. 150 JOURNE
I WAS ON MY WAY HOME FROM THE THEATER AND I 450 WELDED
THOUGHT I'D DROP IN FOR A SECOND.
(MOCKINGLY) AND AFTER THE THEATER, TOO/ 454 WELDED
THEATER
GROUPING IN A BIG SEMICIRCLE AS OF SPECTATORS IN A344 LAZARU
THEATRE,
THE LIGHTS COME UP BRILLIANTLY IN THE THEATRE. 439 MARCOM
THEATRICAL
WHILE THEY WATCH THE DISCONCERTING EFFECT OF THIS 58 MISBEG
THEATRICAL MIRTH ON HARDER.)
THEE
THOU DRAVEST LOVE FROM THEE, WHO DRAVEST ME.* 508 DAYS
DEAR JESUS, GRANT ME THE GRACE TO BRING JACK BACK 558 DAYS
TO THEE/
I DEFY THEE/ 565 DAYS
I HATE THEE/ 565 DAYS
I HAVE COME BACK TO THEE/ 565 DAYS
I CAN FORGIVE MYSELF--THROUGH THEE/ 565 DAYS
I CURSE THEE/ 565 DAYS
WHEN I SURRENDER ALL TO THEE--WHEN I HAVE FORGIVEN565 DAYS
THEE.
*QUICKLY MUST THOU BE GONE FROM HENCE, SEE THEN 290 GGBROW
HOW MATTERS STAND WITH THEE.
NOR DOST THOU KNOW WHAT SHALL BEFALL THEE AFTER 290 GGBROW
DEATH.
AND I WILL BELIEVE IN THEE/ 314 GGBROW
SHUT THEE FROM HEAVEN WITH A DOME MORE VAST, TILL 148 MANSNS
THOU AT LENGTH ART FREE,
*BUILD THEE MORE STATELY MANSIONS, O MY SOUL, AS 148 MANSNS
THE SWIFT SEASONS ROLL/
* BEHOLD, EVERY ONE THAT USETH PROVERBS SHALL USE 579 ROPE
THIS PROVERB AGAINST THEE,
(CHANTS) *POUR OUT THY FURY UPON THE HEATHEN THAT582 ROPE
KNOW THEE NOT,
THEFT
LIKE PLAIN SWINDLING AND THEFT. 154 MANSNS
THEH
(INSTINCTIVELY CROSSES HIMSELF--THEH SCORNFULLY) 582 ROPE
THEIF
AND HE'D BE DAMNED IF HE'D STAND FOR A STANDARD 25 JOURNE
OIL THEIF TRESPASSING.
THEIRS
DAMN THAT SONG OF THEIRS (HE TAKES ANOTHER BIG 466 CARIBE
DRINK)
(SHE TEARS HER EYES FROM THEIRS AND, TURNING AWAY,139 ELECTR
(ACIDLY) THEY'D HAVE GUNS IN THEIRS. 609 ICEMAN
HER ROUND FACE SHOWING MORE OF THE WEAR AND TEAR 615 ICEMAN
OF HER TRADE THAN THEIRS,
THEIRS. 311 LAZARU
WITH THE PLAIN BETWEEN OUR LINES AND THEIRS. 96 POET
THEM'S
THEM'S MY COWS/ 217 DESIRE
THEME
THE SOUND OF MUSIC IN A STRAINED THEME OF THAT 326 LAZARU
JOYLESS ABANDON WHICH IS VICE IS
THEMSELVES
WHEN THEY FIND THEMSELVES CONFRONTED BY THE 544 'ILE
REVOLVERS OF KEENEY AND THE MATE.)
LILY AND MRS. MILLER LAUGH IN SPITE OF 231 AHWILD
THEMSELVES--THEN LOOK EMBARRASSED.
(AS THEY RANGE THEMSELVES AT THE BAR) 4 ANNA
AN I B'LIEVE IN LETTIN' YOUNG FOLKS RUN THEIR 98 BEYOND
AFFAIRS TO SUIT THEMSELVES..
THERE IS A PAUSE, DURING WHICH BOTH FIGHT TO 489 CARDIF
CONTROL THEMSELVES)
(THEY ALL SET THEMSELVES TO WAIT) 458 CARIBE
LIGHTING PIPES, CIGARETTES, AND MAKING THEMSELVES 459 CARIBE
COMFORTABLE.
THAT THEY MIGHT BE SAVED FROM THEMSELVES. 510 DAYS

THEMSELVES (CONT'D.)
IT IS SO OBVIOUS THAT THEY DELIBERATELY CHEAT 542 DAYS
THEMSELVES
(HIS EYES FASTEN THEMSELVES ON THE CROSS AND HE 564 DAYS
GIVES A CRY OF HOPE)
PERSONAL REMARKS TO THE DANCERS THEMSELVES. 250 DESIRE
STRIVING TO RAISE THEMSELVES ON END, FAILING AND 189 EJONES
SINKING PRONE AGAIN.
THEY GROUP THEMSELVES ABOUT 196 EJONES
HE POINTS TO JONES, APPEALS TO THE PLANTERS TO SEE197 EJONES
FOR THEMSELVES.
UNISON AS IF THEY WERE LAZILY LETTING THEMSELVES 199 EJONES
FOLLOW THE LONG ROLL OF A SHIP
WHEN IT COMES TO FACING THE TRUTH ABOUT 25 ELECTR
THEMSELVES
IT TAKES THE MANNONS TO PUNISH THEMSELVES FOR 178 ELECTR
BEING BORN!
UH, NO, GIRLS ONLY ALLOW THEMSELVES TO LOOK AT 265 GGBROW
WHAT IS SEEN/
THEY'VE GOT TO ABSOLVE THEMSELVES BY FINDING A 320 GGBROW
GUILTY ONE/
THE MEN THEMSELVES SHOULD RESEMBLE THOSE PICTURES 207 HA APE
IN WHICH THE APPEARANCE OF
THE MEN STARE AT HIM, STARTLED AND IMPRESSED IN 213 HA APE
SPITE OF THEMSELVES)
CALLING THEMSELVES THE INDUSTRIAL WORKERS OF THE 242 HA APE
WORLD.
THROW THEMSELVES ON YANK AND BEFORE HE KNOWS IT 249 HA APE
ABOUT THEMSELVES HAS GIVEN HIM A FOOLPROOF 11 HUGHIE
TECHNIQUE OF SELF-DEFENSE.
I SAW MEN DIDN'T WANT TO BE SAVED FROM THEMSELVES,579 ICEMAN
THE MATERIAL THE IDEAL FREE SOCIETY MUST BE 590 ICEMAN
CONSTRUCTED FROM IS MEN THEMSELVES
AND FEEL AT PEACE WITH THEMSELVES, WHY THE HELL 621 ICEMAN
SHOULDN'T THEYS
CHATTING EXCITEDLY AMONG THEMSELVES AND TO CHUCK 640 ICEMAN
AND ROCKY IN THE BAR.)
GRAB THE LAST TWO THEMSELVES AND SIT DOWN IN THE 658 ICEMAN
TWO VACANT CHAIRS REMAINING
AS IF ALL AT ONCE THEY SAW A CHANCE TO REVENGE 662 ICEMAN
THEMSELVES.
THEY LOOK AWAY FROM HIM, SHOCKED AND MISERABLY 663 ICEMAN
ASHAMED OF THEMSELVES,
PRETENDING YOU BELIEVED WHAT THEY WANTED TO 711 ICEMAN
BELIEVE ABOUT THEMSELVES.
THEY'D ONLY BE TAKIN' ALL THE CREDIT AND MAKIN' 528 INZONE
HEROES OF THEMSELVES.
PLAINLY HOLDING THEMSELVES IN FOR FEAR OF WHAT THE280 LAZARU
NEXT ONE WILL THINK.)
THEMSELVES. 295 LAZARU
THE PEOPLE IN THE CROWD ARE HOLDING THEMSELVES IN 298 LAZARU
RESTRAINT WITH DIFFICULTY.
THEY HAVE ALREADY CONVINCED THEMSELVES THIS 302 LAZARU
LAZARUS IS A REINCARNATION OF
THEN PROSTRATE THEMSELVES) 307 LAZARU
THEY STABBED THEMSELVES, DANCING AS THOUGH IT WERE321 LAZARU
A FESTIVAL
YOU MADE THEM THINK YOUR FOLLOWERS KILLED 328 LAZARU
THEMSELVES.
SALUTING HIM AS IF IN SPITE OF THEMSELVES.) 334 LAZARU
THREW THEMSELVES ON HIM AND BEGGED FOR HIS LOVE. 341 LAZARU
TALK TO THEMSELVES, FOR THEY HAVE REACHED THAT 354 LAZARU
HOPELESS WISDOM OF EXPERIENCE
POUR IN FROM EACH SIDE OF THE ROOM AND DANCE 362 LAZARU
FORWARD TO GROUP THEMSELVES AROUND
EVEN TO THEMSELVES. 91 MANSNS
WHICH IN THEMSELVES ARE PERFECTLY LOGICAL-- 179 MANSNS
(THEY PROSTRATE THEMSELVES, THEIR FACES TO THE 350 MARCOM
GROUND.
ALL EXCEPT THE POLOS PROSTRATE THEMSELVES BEFORE 372 MARCOM
THE BUDDHA.)
(THEN THEY ALL PROSTRATE THEMSELVES ON THE GROUND 376 MARCOM
AS HE CHANTS)
THEY PROSTRATE THEMSELVES AT THE FOOT OF THE 390 MARCOM
THRONE.
WITH ONE MOVEMENT THEY PROSTRATE THEMSELVES AS THE405 MARCOM
PRINCESS COMES FROM THE CABIN
DRAGGING THEIR BOX BETWEEN THEM AND PROSTRATE 417 MARCOM
THEMSELVES AT HER FEET)
WITH ONE MOTION THE WOMEN THROW THEMSELVES 433 MARCOM
PROSTRATE ON THE FLOOR.
BUT AT THE SAME TIME ARE ABLE TO PULL THEMSELVES 72 MISBEG
TOGETHER WHEN THEY WISH AND BE
(HE TURNS AROUND AND HIS EYES FIX THEMSELVES ON 592 ROPE
THE ROPE)
HE WON'T WANT NO MORE PEOPLE TO HANG THEMSELVES 600 ROPE
WHEN I GIT THROUGH WITH HIM.
NOT EVEN THEMSELVES/....)) 6 STRANG
GIVING THEMSELVES AWAY... 6 STRANG
THEY WERE IMPORTANT TO THEMSELVES, IF I REMEMBER 45 STRANG
RIGHTLY.
I'VE GIVEN MY TALENT TO MAKING FOOLS FEEL PLEASED 120 STRANG
WITH THEMSELVES IN ORDER THAT
DON'T YOU LIKE BOATS FOR THEMSELVES 150 STRANG
WHAT IDIOTS WOMEN MAKE OF THEMSELVES ABOUT THESE 168 STRANG
GORDONS/...
THE PEOPLE HAVE TO YELL AND SCREAM TO MAKE 181 STRANG
THEMSELVES HEARD.)
AND EVEN IF IT WERE TRUE, YOU'D FIND IT WAS THEY 456 WELDED
WHO OFFERED THEMSELVES/
IT IS AS IF NOW BY A SUDDEN FLASH FROM WITHIN THEY487 WELDED
RECOGNIZED THEMSELVES.
THENCE
GALLERY, AND FROM THENCE UP TO THE DOOR FROM THE 483 DYNAMO
ROOF OF THE DYNAMO ROOM.
AND THENCE BACK THROUGH A SCRAGGLY ORCHARD OF 1 MISBEG
APPLE TREES TO THE BARN.

THEORETICALLY
RUNNING AT A SPEED OF ROTATION N, IS THEORETICALLY429 DYNAMO
PROPORTIONAL TO D4 LN2*...

THEORIES
THE DEVIL TAKE THEIR THEORIES/... 429 DYNAMO

THEORY
IT'S ME WHO FIXES IT WITHOUT ANY THEORY/.....) 429 DYNAMO
WHAT IS EVIL IS THE STUPID THEORY THAT MAN IS 172 MANSNS
NATURALLY WHAT WE CALL VIRTUOUS
MAY I ASK ON WHAT SPECIFIC ACTIONS OF HERS THIS 36 STRANG
THEORY OF YOURS IS BASED$

THERE'D
IF THERE'D BEEN ONE OF HEDDA GABLER'S PISTOLS 281 AHWILD
AND IT'S GOD'S TRUTH--THERE'D BEEN MUTINY ITSELF 36 ANNA
IN THE STOKEHOLE.
LIKE THERE'D BE ON LAND. 38 ANNA
THERE'D BE BOUND TO BE SUCH A SCENE WITH THEM ALL 92 BEYOND
TOGETHER.
THE HEAT IN THERE'D KILL YOU. 117 BEYOND
A NICE MESS THERE'D BE THEN/ 122 BEYOND
IF IT WERE, I SAY, THERE'D BE HALF FOR YOU FOR 566 CROSS
YOUR WEDDING PORTION.
THERE'D ALWAYS BE SOMETHING LEFT.= 27 HUGHIE
THERE'D ALWAYS BE SOMETHING LEFT TO START IT GOING 33 HUGHIE
AGAIN.
THERE'D BE THE DEVIL TO PAY IF YOU SHOULD SUFFER A412 MARCOM
RELAPSE OF THAT FEVER
WITHOUT IT THERE'D BE NO POPULATION. 28 MISBEG
(PERSUASIVELY) THERE'D BE NO HARM TRYING IT, 28 MISBEG
ANYWAY.
BUT THERE'D BE MONEY IN IT, AND WHEN HE'D FINISHED164 MISBEG
KILLING HIMSELF,
THERE'D NEVER BE SAME FUN OR EXCITEMENT. 177 MISBEG
THERE'VE
(FROWNING) THERE'VE BEEN LOTS OF TIMES LATELY 133 BEYOND
THAT

THEREBY
HIS PARENTS BORE HIM ON EARTH AS IF THEY WERE 296 GGBROW
THEREBY ENTERING HIM IN A BABY
THEREBY WILL BE BORN YOUR NEW GREATNESS/ 309 LAZARU
BLADDER AND THINKS THEREBY HE IS EVIL, THE ENEMY 359 LAZARU
OF GOD/

THEREFORE
=THEREFORE PUT MONEY IN THY PURSE.= 165 JOURNE
(HE LAUGHS GRIMLY) THEREFORE I HATE THEM. 340 LAZARU
THEREFORE THERE IS NO GOD/= 352 LAZARU
=WE ARE SICK,= THEY SAY, =THEREFORE THERE IS NO 352 LAZARU
GOD IN US.
THEREFORE THE OLD--LIKE CHILDREN-- 354 LAZARU
THEREFORE YOU'D SIMPLY ADURE IT. 49 STRANG

THEREIN
AND IS UNCOMFORTABLY SELF-CONSCIOUS AND STIFF 494 DIFRNT
THEREIN.
EVERYONE ADMITS THEREIN TIBERIUS IS BY RIGHT THEIR354 LAZARU
CAESAR/

THERESA
SISTER THERESA WILL GIVE ME A DREADFUL SCOLDING. 171 JOURNE

THERMOMETER
(TAKING A THERMOMETER FROM HIS POCKET AND PUTTING 484 CARDIF
IT INTO YANK'S MOUTH)
THEN TAKES THE THERMOMETER FROM YANK'S MOUTH AND 485 CARDIF
GOES TO THE LAMP TO READ IT.

THEY'RE
THEY'RE UPSTATE COUNTRY FOLKS--FRUIT GROWERS AND 38 STRANG
FARMERS, WELL OFF, I BELIEVE.
THEY'RE ONLY WORDS, REMEMBER/ 41 STRANG
THEY'RE COMING IN... 53 STRANG
THEY'RE ANXIOUS TO KEEP HIM... 113 STRANG
THEY'RE OFF/ 167 STRANG
THAT IS, THEY'RE ENGAGED. 168 STRANG
THEY'RE THE ONES TO FEAR, HE SAID--NAVY 171 STRANG
ESPECIALLY.
THEY'RE COMING/ 175 STRANG
BUT THEY'RE GETTING CLOSER. 178 STRANG
THEY'RE BOTH SPURTING/ 181 STRANG
THEY'RE PRETTY. 188 STRANG
AND MAKES THEM FEEL SUPERIOR BECAUSE THEY'RE 190 STRANG
LIVING.
PERHAPS I'M MORBID BUT I ALWAYS HAVE THE FEELING 190 STRANG
THAT THEY'RE SECRETLY GLAD
(THINKING UNEASILY) (ITHEY'RE TALKING ABOUT ME...196 STRANG
THEY'RE ALL DEAD. 199 STRANG

THEY'S
WHERE THEY'S ONLY THE ICE TO SEE. 537 'ILE
THEY'S CLEAR WATER 'S FAR 'S YOU CAN SEE. 537 'ILE
BEST NOT HAVE HER ON DECK IF THEY'S GOIN' TO BE 541 'ILE
ANY TROUBLE.
AND THEY'S PLENTY O' WATER. 541 'ILE
AND TROUBLE THEY'S GOING TO BE. 541 'ILE
THEY'S ENOUGH TO LAST A LONG TIME YIT, IF THEY'RE 541 'ILE
CAREFUL WITH IT.
AND THEY'S WHALE HERE, PLENTY OF 'EM. 543 'ILE
THEY'S WHALE T'OTHER SIDE O' THIS FLOE AND WE'RE 550 'ILE
GOING TO GIT 'EM.
THEY'S TROUBLE ENOUGH IN THE WORLD WITHOUT MAKIN' 508 DIFRNT
MORE.

THICK
HIS THICK HAIR IS LONG AND GRAY. 538 'ILE
AND THE QUIET SO THICK YOU'RE AFRAID TO HEAR YOUR 538 'ILE
OWN VOICE.
SMALL BLUE EYES AND THICK SANDY HAIR. 186 AHWILD
THAT WOMAN--SHE'S THAT THICK. 199 AHWILD
SHE'S THAT THICK, YOU HONESTLY WOULDN'T BELIEVE IT211 AHWILD
POSSIBLE.
I'LL FIX YOU FOR THIS, YOU THICK MICK, IF I HAVE 248 AHWILD
TO GO TO JAIL FOR IT.
HIS LARGE MOUTH, OVERHUNG BY A THICK, DROOPING, 5 ANNA
YELLOW MUSTACHE,

THICK (CONT'D.)
A THICK NECK IS JAMMED LIKE A POST INTO THE HEAVY 5 ANNA
TRUNK OF HIS BODY.
HER THICK, GRAY HAIR IS PILED ANYHOW IN A GREASY 7 ANNA
MOP ON TOP OF HER ROUND HEAD.
HER JOWLY, MOTTLED FACE, WITH ITS THICK RED NOSE, 7 ANNA
A LANTERN SET UP ON AN IMMENSE COIL OF THICK 25 ANNA
HAWSER SHEDS A DULL,
IT'D TAKE MORE THAN A BIT OF A BLOW TO CRACK MY 33 ANNA
THICK SKULL.
YOU DAMN THICK HEAD/ 73 ANNA
FINALLY HE IS UNABLE TO BEAR THE THICK SILENCE A 95 BEYOND
MINUTE LONGER, AND BLURTS OUT)
THEY'VE BEEN THICK AS THIEVES ALL THEIR LIVES, 98 BEYOND
(FROM THE ALLEYWAY) GAWD BLIMEY, THE FOG'S THICK 482 CARDIF
AS SOUP.
IT CREAKS SLIGHTLY AND NAT JUMPS TO HIS FEET--IN A562 CROSS
THICK VOICE OF TERROR)
WITH THICK WHITE HAIR, RUDDY COMPLEXION. 500 DAYS
THEY CLUMP HEAVILY ALONG IN THEIR CLUMSY THICK- 204 DESIRE
SOLED BOOTS CAKED WITH EARTH.
THEY'S NOTHIN' IN THAT THICK SKULL O' YOUR'N BUT 254 DESIRE
NOISE--LIKE A EMPTY KEG IT BE/
SHE HAS LIGHT BROWN HAIR, THICK AND HEAVY. 494 DIFRNT
HIS SANDY HAIR IS THICK AND DISHEVELED. 513 DIFRNT
HIS JAW IS STUBBORN, HIS THICK HAIR CURLY AND 422 DYNAMO
REDDISH-BLOND.
THEIR SUMMITS CROWNED WITH THICK GROVES OF PALM 173 EJONES
TREES.
I STANDS HIM ON HIS THICK HEAD MORE'N ONCE BEFO' 183 EJONES
DIS.
BY THE EDGE OF THE DRIVE, LEFT FRONT, IS A THICK 5 ELECTR
CLUMP OF LILACS AND SYRINGAS,
WHICH BRINGS OUT THE PECULIAR COLOR OF HER THICK 9 ELECTR
CURLY HAIR.
(HER VOICE BECOMES THICK, AS IF SHE WERE DROWSY 63 ELECTR
AND FIGHTING OFF SLEEP.
THICK STRAIGHT BLACK HAIR, LIGHT HAZEL EYES. 73 ELECTR
THERE WAS A THICK MIST 95 ELECTR
(THICK WITH RAGE) I'LL SHOW YUH WHO'S A APE, YUH 241 HA APE
BUM/
FROM BEHIND THICK-LENSED SPECTACLES, TINY HANDS 574 ICEMAN
AND FEET.
THE NOSE IS THIN AND HIS LIPS ARE NOT NOTICEABLY 575 ICEMAN
THICK.
THE SLEEVES OF HIS COLLARLESS SHIRT ARE ROLLED UP 577 ICEMAN
ON HIS THICK, POWERFUL ARMS
(RAISES HIS HEAD AND PEERS AT ROCKY BLEARILY 579 ICEMAN
THROUGH HIS THICK SPECTACLES--
CHUCK IS A TOUGH, THICK-NECKED, BARREL-CHESTED 615 ICEMAN
ITALIAN-AMERICAN,
EVEN HUGO COMES OUT OF HIS COMA TO RAISE HIS HEAD 618 ICEMAN
AND BLINK THROUGH HIS THICK
LOOKS UP THROUGH HIS THICK SPECTACLES AND GIGGLES 627 ICEMAN
FOOLISHLY.)
(BLINKS AT HIM THROUGH HIS THICK SPECTACLES--WITH 634 ICEMAN
GUTTURAL DENUNCIATION)
WHO LIFTS HIS HEAD FROM HIS ARMS AND BLINKS AT HIM691 ICEMAN
THROUGH HIS THICK SPECTACLES.
WHEN THAT THICK-HEAD GOES 'N' LEAVES 'EM OPENS 514 INZONE
A THICK SILENCE SETTLES OVER THE FORECASTLE. 522 INZONE
I'LL HAVE TO CONFESS IT'S A BIT TOO THICK FOR ME 525 INZONE
TO ENJOY.
HER HIGH FOREHEAD IS FRAMED BY THICK, PURE WHITE 12 JOURNE
HAIR.
A COLLAR-LESS SHIRT WITH A THICK WHITE 13 JOURNE
HANDKERCHIEF
HOW THICK THE FOG IS. 102 JOURNE
(HIS VOICE THICK.) WHO'S THATS 125 JOURNE
(VAGUELY--HIS VOICE THICK.) IT'S MADNESS, YES. 134 JOURNE
THEIR VOICES SOUND THICK AND HARSH AND ANIMAL-LIKE287 LAZARU
WITH ANGER AS THEY MUTTER AND
AND CHANT IN A THICK VOICE) 305 LAZARU
THE NIGHT IS THICK AND OPPRESSIVE. 312 LAZARU
THICK WALLS SEEM WAITING TO FALL, 330 LAZARU
HIS WORDS ARE A THICK GARBLE I COULD NOT HEAR. 357 LAZARU
WITH THICK, STUBBY FINGERS. 2 MANSNS
HER MOUTH, ON THE OTHER HAND, HAS A TOUCH OF 2 MANSNS
COARSE SENSUALITY ABOUT ITS THICK,
ITS BAD POINTS ARE THICK ANKLES, LARGE FEET, AND 2 MANSNS
BIG HANDS, BROAD AND STRONG,
A WIDE SENSITIVE MOUTH, A FINE FOREHEAD, LARGE 4 MANSNS
EARS, THICK BROWN HAIR,
HOWEVER, I WOULD STILL BE NAUSEATED BY THEIR THICK 9 MANSNS
ANKLES.
WITH ITS LONG UPPER LIP AND SMALL NOSE, THICK 3 MISBEG
BLACK EYEBROWS,
HE HAS A THICK NECK, LUMPY, SLOPING SHOULDERS, 11 MISBEG
(APPEARS DRUNKER, HIS HEAD WAGGING, HIS VOICE 74 MISBEG
THICK, HIS TALK RAMBLING)
PALE, HOLLOW-CHEEKED, FRAMED BY THICK, CURLY IRON- 34 POET
GRAY HAIR.
FRAMED BY THICK, WAVY, RED-BROWN HAIR. 67 POET
KEEP YOUR THICK WRISTS AND UGLY, PEASANT PAWS OFF 107 POET
THE TABLE IN MY PRESENCE,
TOTTER FEEBLY UNDER HIM AS HE SHUFFLES SLOWLY 578 ROPE
ALONG BY THE AID OF A THICK CANE.
SHORT LEGS AND THICK ANKLES... 6 STRANG
HIS THICK HAIR IS IRON-GRAY. 159 STRANG
THE THICK FINGERS OF HIS BIG HANDS ARE LOADED WITH493 VOYAGE
CHEAP RINGS.

THICKENED
ONCE FINELY MODELED, NOW GROSS AND THICKENED, THE 337 LAZARU
FOREHEAD LOWERING AND GRIM.

THICKHEADS
HE MUTTERS DISGUSTEDLY) THICKHEADS/ 366 MARCOM

THICKLY
SHE STAGGERS BACK AGAINST THE TABLE--THICKLY) 128 BEYOND

THICKLY 1638

THICKLY (CONT'D.)
HE TAKES FROM HIS POCKET A HEAVY BRACELET THICKLY561 CRUSS
STUDDED WITH STONES AND
(THICKLY, TRYING TO FIGHT BACK HIS JEALOUS 98 ELECTR
SUSPICION)
(THICKLY HUMOROUS.) I WOULDN'T WORRY ABOUT THE 133 JOURNE
VIRTUE PART OF IT,
(THICKLY.) WHERE YOU GET YOUR TASTE IN AUTHORS-- 135 JOURNE
THAT DAMNED LIBRARY OF YOURS/
(SHRUGS HIS SHOULDERS-- THICKLY.) 158 JOURNE
(HE BREAKS OFF, THICKLY.) NOT STRICTLY ACCURATE. 159 JOURNE
(STARTS AND STARES AT HIS BROTHER FOR A SECOND 161 JOURNE
WITH BITTER HOSTILITY--THICKLY.)
(THICKLY.) I'LL HAVE A DRINK. 164 JOURNE
TAKES HIS HAND AGAIN AND BEGINS TO TALK THICKLY 165 JOURNE
BUT WITH A STRANGE,
(THICKLY.) ALL RIGHT, KID. 169 JOURNE
HE SAYS THICKLY) 314 LAZARU
(THICKLY) SHE IS DEAD, AND I DO NOT HEAR YOU 347 LAZARU
LAUGH/
(THICKLY) NO MATTER. 75 MISBEG
(THICKLY) LET IT BURN TO THE GROUND. 76 MISBEG
(THICKLY) HE'S ONE AND A PRIZE ONE, BUT I DON'T 78 MISBEG
MEAN HIM.
(HIS HEAD NODDING, HIS EYES BLINKING--THICKLY) 83 MISBEG
(THEN HE LOOKS AT HER IN DRUNKEN SURPRISE-- 88 MISBEG
THICKLY)
HE SPEAKS THICKLY AS IF HE WAS SUDDENLY VERY 137 MISBEG
DRUNK)
(THICKLY) THE DAMNED SON-OF-A-GUN/ 597 ROPE

THIEF
MISTER DICK, YOU THIEF, LAVE THEM OLIVES ALONE, 217 AHWILD
(GROWLING) DIRTY THIEF/ 462 CARIBE
D'LIEVE A LYIN' THIEF/ 258 DESIRE
MURDERER AN' THIEF 'R NOT, YE STILL TEMPT ME/ 262 DESIRE
PUT A SNEAK IN ONE AND IT GIVES HIM THE COURAGE TO541 DIFRNT
BE A THIEF/
THINK I'M A BLEEDIN' THIEF, YOU WOULD. 179 EJONES
COME DOWN OUT O' THAT AND I'LL SHOW YE WHO'S A 105 ELECTR
THIEF/
A NATURAL BORN CROOK, THE GODDAMNEDEST THIEF, 25 HUGHIE
I'M NOT USED TO BEING TREATED LIKE A THIEF. 103 JOURNE
A FINE LORD WHOM OUR HIGH PRIESTS HAVE HAD 284 LAZARU
ARRESTED LIKE A THIEF/
THIEF/ 361 LAZARU
ARE YOU WILLING TO BECOME A CONSCIOUS THIEF AND 154 MANSNS
SWINDLER$
LET WHO WILL CRY THIEF/ 155 MANSNS
YOU THIEF/ 185 MANSNS
(FURIOUSLY) YOU THIEF, YOU/ 14 MISBEG
LIKE OUR BEAUTIFUL NEIGHBOR, HARDER, THE STANDARD 32 MISBEG
OIL THIEF, OLD YEARS AGO.
YOU'RE STEADY ON YOUR PINS, AIN'T YOU, YOU 96 MISBEG
SCHEMING OLD THIEF,
THAT THIEF OF A LAWYER WILL WARN HIM-- 128 POET
MAD AS YOU ARE, FOR THINKIN' THAT THIEF OF A SON 582 ROPE
OF YOURS WOULD
NO--EXCEPT WAIT AN' PRAY THAT YOUNG THIEF IS DEAD 586 ROPE
AN' WON'T COME BACK.
A THIEF LIKE HIM AIN'T COME BACK FOR NO GOOD. 590 ROPE
(FURIOUSLY) FLINGIN' AWAY DOLLARS, THE DIRTY 590 ROPE
THIEF, AN' US WITHOUT--
AN' THE THIEF COULD TAKE THE FARM FROM US TOMORROW590 ROPE
IF HIMSELF TURNED A LUNATIC.
I HATED HIM AS ONE HATES A THIEF ONE MAY NOT 20 STRANG
ACCUSE NOR PUNISH.

THIEFS
HE KNOWS DAMN WELL THERE AIN'T NO THIEFS IN THIS 520 INZONE
FUC*S*ILE, DUN'T HES

THIERS'
THIERS' HISTORY OF THE CONSULATE AND EMPIRE, 11 JOURNE
SMOLLETT'S HISTORY OF ENGLAND,

THIEVERY
BUT WHEN HE STARTS IN HIS SNEAKIN' THIEVERY WITH 541 DIFRNT
YOU, EMMER,
WHAT SNEAKIN' THIEVERY WITH ME$ 541 DIFRNT

THIEVES
THEY'VE BEEN THICK AS THIEVES ALL THEIR LIVES, 98 BEYOND
AND THERE HAVE BEEN A LOT OF WATERFRONT THIEVES 104 ELECTR
AROUND HERE LATELY.
WE MUST MAKE IT LOOK AS IF THIEVES KILLED HIM. 114 ELECTR
REMEMBER/
THAT HE WAS KILLED BY WATERFRONT THIEVES. 121 ELECTR
I VAS A FARMER BEFORE THE WAR VEN PLODDY LIMEY 676 ICEMAN
THIEVES STEAL MY COUNTRY.
THE DAMNED THIEVES OF THE LAW DID THEIR WORST TO 118 POET
ME MANY YEARS AGO IN IRELAND.

THIEVIN'
BUT A THIEVIN' SHEBEEN KEEPER WHO GOT RICH 11 POET
BUT THE BLOOD OF THIEVIN' AULD NEU MELODY WHO KEPT138 POET
A DIRTY SHEBEENS

THIEVING
IF I HAD NOT BEE4 A CREDULOUS GULL AND LET THE 40 POET
THIEVING YANKEES SWINDLE ME
CURSING LIKE A DRUNKEN, FOUL-MOUTHED SON OF A 157 POET
THIEVING SHEBEEN KEEPER

THIGH
DRISCOLL LAUGHS AND SLAPS HIS THIGH) 464 CARIBE
(THIS TICKLES HIS HUMOR AND HE SLAPS HIS THIGH AND245 DESIRE
LAUGHS)
(SLAPPING HIS THIGH AND GUFFAWING) 204 EJONES
(SLAPPING HIS THIGH--ANGRILY) 522 INZONE
(HE BURSTS INTO AN EXTRAVAGANT ROAR OF LAUGHTER, 58 MISBEG
SLAPPING HIS THIGH.
(HE SLAPS HIS THIGH) O JAYSUS, THIS IS A GREAT 64 MISBEG
DAY FOR THE POOR AND OPPRESSED/
(HE SLAPS HIS THIGH ENTHUSIASTICALLY) 95 MISBEG

THIGHS
(THEY LAUGH UPROARIOUSLY, SLAPPING THEIR THIGHS.) 223 DESIRE
HER WAIST WIDE BUT SLENDER BY CONTRAST WITH HER 3 MISBEG
HIPS AND THIGHS.
WHAT THE HELL--(HE IS SUDDENLY CONVULSED WITH 592 ROPE
LAUGHTER AND SLAPS HIS THIGHS)

THIM
GOD'S CURSE ON THE TWO AV THIM/ 480 CARDIF
SHE SAID SHE CUD SNAKE UT ON BOARD IN THE BOTTOMS 458 CARIBE
AV THIM BASKETS AV FRUIT
TIS THIM RIGHT ENOUGH. 460 CARIBE
YE'LL BE LUCKY IF ANY OF THIM LOOKS AT YE, YE 461 CARIBE
SQUINT-EYED RUNT.
THERE'S FOIVE AV THIM SHE TOOK ABOARD-- 462 CARIBE
LOOK AT YANK, HUD YE, WID HIS ARRM AROUND THE 463 CARIBE
MIDDLE AV WAN AV THIM.

THIM'LL
THE RIST OF THIM'LL BE COMIN' FOR'ARD WHIN SHE 463 CARIBE
COMES.

THIN
AND A TIGHTLY CLENCHED, THIN-LIPPED MOUTH. 538 'ILE
LILY MILLER, HER SISTER-IN-LAW, IS FORTY-TWO, 187 AHWILD
TALL, DARK AND THIN.
HE IS OF MEDIUM HEIGHT, NEITHER FAT NOR THIN. 193 AHWILD
HE IS A THIN, DRIED-UP LITTLE MAN WITH A HEAD TOO 200 AHWILD
LARGE FOR HIS BODY PERCHED ON
WITH HIS PALE, THIN, CLEAN-SHAVEN FACE, MILD BLUE 3 ANNA
EYES AND WHITE HAIR.
SHE IS A THIN, PALE-FACED, UNINTELLIGENT-LOOKING 112 BEYOND
WOMAN OF ABOUT FORTY-EIGHT,
THE SKY TO THE EAST IS ALREADY ALIGHT WITH BRIGHT 166 BEYOND
COLOR AND A THIN,
SIDE AND WRITHES ON THE THIN MATTRESS OF HIS BUNK.484 CARDIF
SHAKE A LEG AN' COME ABOARD THIN. 461 CARIBE
GIT OUT AV THE WAY THIN, YE BIG HULK, AN' GIVE US 470 CARIBE
SOME
GOD BLARST YOU FOR HAVIN' SUCH BIG FEET, THIN, 471 CARIBE
A WIDE THIN-LIPPED MOUTH SHADOWED BY AN UNKEMPT 556 CROSS
BRISTLE OF MUSTACHE.
HE HAS BLACK HAIR, MUSTACHE, A THIN CURLY TRACE OF203 DESIRE
BEARD.
SHE IS VERY PALE, HER FACE IS THIN AND DRAWN, 247 DESIRE
ALTHOUGH HER BODY IS SLIGHT AND THIN, THERE IS A 494 DIFRNT
QUICK,
THERE IS AN ABSURD SUGGESTION OF ROUGE ON HER 520 DIFRNT
TIGHT CHEEKS AND THIN LIPS.
HER HAIR IS GRAY, HER FACE THIN, LINED AND 528 DIFRNT
CAREWORN,
IT IS A THIN SMALL MOUTH, DETERMINED AND STUBBORN.422 DYNAMO
HE IS SEVENTEEN, TALL AND THIN. 422 DYNAMO
HIS THIN MOUTH IS FULL OF THE MALICIOUS HUMOR OF 428 DYNAMO
THE PRACTICAL JOKER.
HE HAS GROWN VERY THIN, HIS DUNGAREES SAG ABOUT 476 DYNAMO
HIS ANGULAR FRAME.
HE IS MIDDLE AGED, THIN BROWN IN COLOR, 191 EJONES
IT IS THIN AND AGED, THE WRATH OF WHAT MUST ONCE 6 ELECTR
HAVE BEEN A GOOD BARITONE.
THE UPPER A THIN BOW, SHADOWED BY A LINE OF HAIR. 9 ELECTR
BUT ON HER THIN BODY IT LOOKS TOO LARGE AND 10 ELECTR
HEAVY.)
TALL, LIKE HER MOTHER, HER BODY IS THIN, FLAT- 10 ELECTR
BREASTED AND ANGULAR,
HER THIN FIGURE, SEATED STIFFLY UPRIGHT, ARMS 43 ELECTR
AGAINST HER SIDES,
THE SOUND OF SETH'S THIN, AGED BARITONE MOURNFULLY 43 ELECTR
SINGING.
BUT HIS BODY IS THIN AND HIS SWARTHY COMPLEXION 73 ELECTR
SALLOW.
HER EYES GROW BLEAK AND HER MOUTH TIGHTENS TO A 91 ELECTR
THIN LINE.
HE IS A THIN, WIRY MAN OF SIXTY-FIVE OR SO, WITH A102 ELECTR
TOUSLED MOP OF BLACK HAIR,
SETH'S THIN WRATH OF A BARITONE IS RAISED IN HIS 123 ELECTR
FAVORITE MOURNFUL *SHENANDOAH*,
HER BODY, FORMERLY SO THIN AND UNDEVELOPED, HAS 137 ELECTR
FILLED OUT.
HE HAS GROWN DREADFULLY THIN AND HIS BLACK SUIT 138 ELECTR
HANGS LOOSELY ON HIS BODY.
HER BODY, DRESSED IN DEEP MOURNING, AGAIN APPEARS 170 ELECTR
FLAT-CHESTED AND THIN.
THE MOTHER IS A THIN FRAIL FADED WOMAN, 259 GGBROW
(HE STARTS TO SING IN A THIN, NASAL, DOLEFUL 210 HA APE
TONE.)
A THIN, SHRILL NOTES FROM SOMEWHERE OVER-HEAD IN 223 HA APE
THE DARKNESS.
TALL, THIN, WITH A SCRAWNY NECK AND JUTTING ADAM'S 8 HUGHIE
APPLE.
THE NOSE IS THIN AND HIS LIPS ARE NOT NOTICEABLY 575 ICEMAN
THICK.
SO THIN THE DESCRIPTION *BAG OF BONES* WAS MADE 576 ICEMAN
FOR HIM.
HE IS IN HIS LATE THIRTIES, OF AVERAGE HEIGHT, 577 ICEMAN
THIN.
HE IS EIGHTEEN, TALL AND BROAD-SHOULDERED BUT 585 ICEMAN
THIN, GANGLING AND AWKWARD.
CORA IS A THIN PEROXIDE BLONDE, A FEW YEARS OLDER 615 ICEMAN
THAN PEARL AND MARGIE,
(BOLDLY) HERE GOES, THIN/ 528 INZONE
AN' THIN THERE'S A LOT AV BLARNEY TELLIN' HIM HOW 530 INZONE
MUCH SHE MISSES HIM
BUT IS THIN AND PALE WITH THE BONE STRUCTURE 12 JOURNE
PROMINENT.
HIS GREY HAIR IS THIN WITH A BALD SPOT LIKE A 13 JOURNE
MONK'S TONSURE.
A COUPLE OF INCHES TALLER, THIN AND WIRY. 19 JOURNE
ALL THE SAME, YOU'VE GROWN MUCH TOO THIN. 42 JOURNE
THE FATHER IS A SMALL, THIN, FEEBLE OLD MAN OF 275 LAZARU
OVER EIGHTY, MEEK AND PIOUS.
THE LIPS ARE THIN AND STERN AND SELF-CONTAINED-- 337 LAZARU

1639 THINGS

THIN (CONT'D.)
HIS WHOLE BODY IS NOW RELAXED, AT REST, A DREAMY 342 LAZARU
SMILE SOFTENS HIS THIN.
HER HANDS ARE SMALL WITH THIN, STRONG, TAPERING 3 MANSNS
FINGERS, AND SHE HAS TINY FEET.
JOEL HARFORD IS TWENTY-NINE, TALL AND THIN, WITH A 25 MANSNS
SLIGHT STOOP IN HIS CARRIAGE.
HE HAS CHANGED GREATLY, GROWN TERRIBLY THIN. 144 MANSNS
MARCO'S FATHER, NICOLO, IS A SMALL THIN MIDDLE- 358 MARCOM
AGED MAN,
SWAYING ITS HEAD TO THE THIN, SHRILL WHINE OF A 369 MARCOM
GOURD.
ALL OF THEM AGED, WITH BENT BODIES, THEIR THIN, 433 MARCOM
HER NOSE IS THIN AND STRAIGHT. 15 POET
PADDY O'DOWD IS THIN, ROUND-SHOULDERED, FLAT- 51 POET
CHESTED, WITH A PIMPLY COMPLEXION.
THE NOSE IS DELICATE AND THIN, A TRIFLE AQUILINE. 67 POET
SHE HAS TINY, HIGH-ARCHED FEET AND THIN, TAPERING 68 POET
HANDS.
HIS THIN LEGS, TWISTED BY RHEUMATISM, 578 ROPE
SHE IS A SKINNY, OVERGROWN GIRL OF TEN, WITH THIN,578 ROPE
SHE IS A THIN, SLOVENLY, WORN-OUT-LOOKING WOMAN OF579 ROPE
ABOUT FORTY WITH A DRAWN.
HE IS A TALL THIN MAN OF THIRTY-FIVE, METICULOUSLY 3 STRANG
WELL-DRESSED IN TWEEDS
HIS THIN LIPS IRONICAL AND A BIT SAD. 4 STRANG
HER THIN BODY AND PALE LOST FACE... 8 STRANG
HIS TALL, THIN BODY SAGS WEARILY IN THE CHAIR, HIS 24 STRANG
HEAD IS SUNK FORWARD,
ITS MOUTH INTO THE THIN LINE AROUND A LOCKED DOOR, 53 STRANG
SHE HAS GROWN THIN AGAIN, HER FACE IS PALE AND 68 STRANG
DRAWN,
HIS TALL, THIN BODY STOOPS AS IF A PART OF ITS 73 STRANG
SUSTAINING WILL HAD BEEN REMOVED.
DARRELL IS PALE, THIN, NERVOUS, UNHEALTHY LOOKING.124 STRANG
HER FACE IS THIN, HER CHEEKS TAUT, HER MOUTH DRAWN158 STRANG
WITH FORCED SMILING.

THIN'
I NEVER HEARD OF SUCH A THIN'. 117 BEYOND
A NICE THIN' FOR ME TO HAVE TO SUPPORT HIM OUT OF 152 BEYOND
WHAT I'D SAVED
(A PAUSE) BUT YE CAN'T HITCH YER MIND T' ONE 237 DESIRE
THIN' DAY AN' NIGHT.
DID YE THINK I WAS IN LOVE WITH YE--A WEAK THIN' 240 DESIRE
LIKE YEWS
MEBBE I KIN TAKE BACK ONE THIN' GOD DOES/ 259 DESIRE
STEAL THE LAST THIN' YE'D LEFT ME--MY PART O' 262 DESIRE
HIM--NO, THE HULL O' HIM--
THIN' NO MATTER HOW IT BREAKS HIM UP, 530 DIFRNT
A DURN QUEER THIN' FUR A SODGER TO KILL HIMSELF 170 ELECTR
CLEANIN' HIS GUN.

THIN'S
(WITH BITTER SCORN) SO--YOU WANT TO GO OUT INTO 106 BEYOND
THE WORLD AND SEE THIN'S$
YOU LIE WHEN YOU SAY YOU WANT TO GO 'WAY--AND SEE 106 BEYOND
THIN'S/
THE WAY THIN'S ARE NOW/ 117 BEYOND
IN NOT LETTIN' ANDY KNOW THE STATE THIN'S WERE IN.152 BEYOND
I'LL SAY THE THIN'S I DIDN'T SAY THEN T' HIM/ 209 DESIRE
LET EBEN TEND TO THIN'S IF HE'S A MIND T'. 215 DESIRE
MY FEET FEEL ITCHIN' T' WALK AN' WALK--AN' JUMP 220 DESIRE
HIGH OVER THIN'S--AN'....
YE KIN FEEL IT BURNIN' INTO THE EARTH--NATURE-- 229 DESIRE
MAKIN' THIN'S GROW--
YE'RE GITTIN' THIN'S ALL MIXED. 236 DESIRE
WHAR I'D MADE THIN'S GROW OUT O' NOTHIN'-- 237 DESIRE
YE'D ONY TO PLOW AN' SOW AN' THEN SET AN' SMOKE 237 DESIRE
YER PIPE AN' WATCH THIN'S GROW.
THEY'S THIN'S POKIN' ABOUT IN THE DARK--IN THE 238 DESIRE
CORNERS.
(THEN TENDERLY REBUKING) YE OUGHTN'T T' TALK O' 245 DESIRE
SAD THIN'S--THIS MORNIN'.
IT DON'T DO TO MONKEY WITH THEM THIN'S. 132 ELECTR

THINE
THINE EYES BLIND ME, THY TRESSES BURN ME, 205 AHWILD
«SWIFT BE THINE APPROACHING FLIGHT/ 286 GGBROW
UNTIL IN THE END THEY DO IT TO AVENGE THEE, FOR 343 LAZARU
THINE HONOR AND GLORY/
LEAVING THINE OUTGROWN SHELL-- 148 MANSNS
«THE PUNISHMENT OF THINE INIQUITY IS ACCOMPLISHED,579 ROPE
O DAUGHTER OF ZION..
HE WILL VISIT THINE INIQUITY, O DAUGHTER OF EDOM,.579 ROPE
(LOUDLY) «HE WILL VISIT THINE INIQUITY-- 580 ROPE

THING'LL
A WHACK ON THE EAR'S THE ONLY THING'LL LEARN 'EM. 470 CARIBE

THING'S
AND WHEN A THING'S DIED, TIME CAN'T MAKE NO 517 DIFRNT
DIFF'RENCE.
THIS THING'S GOT ME SO BALLED UP I DON'T KNOW HOW 546 DIFRNT
I STAND.
DARN THING'S GOTTEN SO RUSTY. 167 ELECTR

THINGS
DID YE EVER HEAR OF A MAN WHO WASN'T CRAZY DO THE 537 'ILE
THINGS HE DOES$
I'M AFEARED THERE'LL BE TROUBLE WITH THE HANDS 539 'ILE
FROM THE LOOK O' THINGS.
(SLOWLY) THEY WANTS TO GIT BACK TO THEIR FOLKS 542 'ILE
AN' THINGS, I S'POSE.
(INDIGNANTLY) THAT AIN'T FAIR, SIR, TO SAY SUCH 542 'ILE
THINGS.
IT'S BETTER TO CRUSH SUCH THINGS AT THE START THAN543 'ILE
LET THEM MAKE HEADWAY.
AND THINGS WAS DULL-LIKE. 546 'ILE
THERE'S FINE THINGS IN IT, SEEMS TO ME--TRUE 198 AHWILD
THINGS.
SOME OF THE THINGS I SIMPLY COULDN'T READ, THEY 198 AHWILD
WERE SO INDECENT--ALL ABOUT--

THINGS (CONT'D.)
LILY, YOU RUN UP THE BACK STAIRS AND GET YOUR 199 AHWILD
THINGS ON.
I THOUGHT, MAYBE, READING THOSE THINGS--THEY'RE 207 AHWILD
BEAUTIFUL, AREN'T THEY, PA$
NO, TWO THINGS--THINGS I'VE TOLD YOU OVER AND 211 AHWILD
OVER, BUT YOU ALWAYS FORGET.
GOOD GRACIOUS, IF I'M NOT FORGETTING ONE OF THE 214 AHWILD
MOST IMPORTANT THINGS/
YOU KNOW, SOMETHING HAPPENS AND THINGS LIKE THAT 215 AHWILD
COME UP
THINGS LIKE WHAT COME UP$ 215 AHWILD
CYNICAL THINGS. 216 AHWILD
THINGS OUT OF THOSE INDECENT BOOKS/ 216 AHWILD
YOU SHOULDN'T NOTICE SUCH THINGS--AT YOUR AGE/ 220 AHWILD
NEVER KNEW LILY TO COME OUT WITH THINGS THAT WAY 234 AHWILD
BEFORE.
(CALCULATEDLY TAUNTING) SAY, HONEST, ARE THINGS 238 AHWILD
THAT SLOW UP AT HARVARD$
I WOULDN'T HAVE THE PESKY THINGS ON MY TABLE/ 255 AHWILD
DON'T GET TO IMAGINING THINGS, NOW/ 260 AHWILD
NOW, NOW, YOU MUSN'T GET TO IMAGINING SUCH THINGS/262 AHWILD
I'VE A WHOLE PILE OF THINGS THAT HAVE GOT TO BE 263 AHWILD
DONE TODAY.
WHEN HE DID SUCH AWFUL THINGS. 265 AHWILD
ABOUT WOMEN AND ALL THOSE THINGS. 267 AHWILD
(GIVING IN TO HER WORRY) I WISH YOU WOULDN'T SAY 271 AHWILD
THOSE TERRIBLE THINGS--
STILL, I CAN'T LET HIM DO SUCH THINGS AND GO SCOT-289 AHWILD
FREE.
WHEN YOU'RE ONLY A KID YOURSELF AND WANT TO GO OUT 18 ANNA
AND SEE THINGS.
WELL, HE'S GOT QUEER NOTIONS ON SOME THINGS. 18 ANNA
(HER VOICE RISING ANGRILY) SAY, WHAT'RE YOU 26 ANNA
TRYING TO DO--MAKE THINGS ROTTEN$
I WANT TO STAY OUT HERE--AND THINK ABOUT THINGS. 26 ANNA
I FEEL AS IF I WAS--OUT OF THINGS ALTOGETHER. 26 ANNA
I TAKE CARE OF KIDS FOR PEOPLE AND LEARN THEM 35 ANNA
THINGS.
HE PRETENDS TO BE ENGAGED IN SETTING THINGS SHIP- 41 ANNA
SHAPE.
A LOT OF THINGS THAT'LL OPEN YOUR EYES. 43 ANNA
THEN PROMISE ME YOU'LL CUT OUT SAYING NASTY THINGS 44 ANNA
ABOUT MAT BURKE EVERY CHANCE
SEEING ALL THINGS, AND NOT GIVING A DAMN FOR 48 ANNA
SAVING UP MONEY.
WHERE DO YOU COME IN BUTTING IN AND MAKING THINGS 54 ANNA
WORSES
MAYBE THINGS WOULD BE DIFFERENT/ 58 ANNA
AND BEING ON THE SEA HAD CHANGED ME AND MADE ME 59 ANNA
FEEL DIFFERENT ABOUT THINGS,
WE'RE POOR NUTS, AND THINGS HAPPEN, AND WE YUST 65 ANNA
GET MIXED IN WRONG, THAT'S ALL.
BUT AS A PLACE TO WORK AND GROW THINGS, YOU HATE 84 BEYOND
IT.
I GUESS I REALIZE THAT YOU'VE GOT YOUR OWN ANGLE 84 BEYOND
OF LOOKING AT THINGS.
WE CAN'T HELP THOSE THINGS, ROB. 86 BEYOND
ABOUT SPELLS AND THINGS WHEN YOU'RE ON THE SHIP. 86 BEYOND
OH, ROB, I DO WISH SHE'D TRY TO MAKE THE BEST OF 87 BEYOND
THINGS THAT CAN'T BE HELPED.
YOU TELL THINGS SO BEAUTIFULLY/ 90 BEYOND
SONGS THAT TOLD OF ALL THE WONDERFUL THINGS THEY 90 BEYOND
HAD
WE'LL BE SO HAPPY HERE TOGETHER WHERE IT'S NATURAL 92 BEYOND
AND WE KNOW THINGS.
WHEN HE SAID I COULD FIND ALL THE THINGS I WAS 92 BEYOND
SEEKING FOR HERE.
AIN'T THAT A WOMAN'S WAY O' SEEIN' THINGS FOR YOU$ 95 BEYOND
SHE NEEDS A MAN, A FIRST-CLASS FARMER, TO TAKE 98 BEYOND
HOLD O' THINGS..
WELL, MAYBE A WOMAN'S EYES IS SHARPER IN SUCH 98 BEYOND
THINGS, BUT--
WHY, THINGS BEIN' AS THEY BE, ROBERT'S FREE TO DO 102 BEYOND
AS HE'S A MIND TO.
TO SORTA TALK TO AND SHOW THINGS TO, AND TEACH, 103 BEYOND
KINDA.
'N' NEW SHEETS'N'BLANKETS 'N' THINGS. 103 BEYOND
I FEEL I OUGHTN'T TO MISS THIS CHANCE TO GO OUT 106 BEYOND
INTO THE WORLD AND SEE THINGS.
AND I'D HATE THE FARM IF I STAYED, HATE IT FOR 110 BEYOND
BRINGIN' THINGS BACK.
AND TOLD HIM HOW THINGS OUGHT TO BE DONE. 113 BEYOND
(DULLY) ROBBIE'S ALWAYS LATE FOR THINGS. 113 BEYOND
DOES HE SUPPOSE YOU'RE RUNNIN' A HOTEL--WITH NO 113 BEYOND
ONE TO HELP WITH THINGS$$
AND YOU CAN'T DENY THAT THINGS HAVE BEEN GOIN' 114 BEYOND
FROM BAD TO WORSE
THINGS MIGHT BE WORSE. 114 BEYOND
AND IT'S MY DUTY NOT TO LET SUCH THINGS GO ON 115 BEYOND
BEHIND YOUR BACK.
MAYBE ROBBIE'LL MANAGE TILL ANDY GETS BACK AND 115 BEYOND
SEES TO THINGS.
AND HAVE TO START IN WITH THINGS IN SUCH A TOPSY- 118 BEYOND
TURVY.
(SIGHING) I S'POSE IT ISN'T ROB'S FAULT THINGS GO118 BEYOND
WRONG WITH HIM.
THINGS AREN'T AS THEY MIGHT BE. 118 BEYOND
WE'LL SHOW MAMA WE KNOW HOW TO DO THOSE THINGS, 121 BEYOND
WUN'T WE$
(IN EXASPERATION) WHY DO YOU GOAD ME INTO SAYING 122 BEYOND
THINGS I DON'T MEAN$
TO KEEP THINGS WARM FOR YOU, YOU'RE MISTAKEN. 122 BEYOND
AND I'VE GOT TO PULL THINGS THROUGH SOMEHOW. 123 BEYOND
YOU KNOW HOW HARD I'VE TRIED TO KEEP THINGS GOING 123 BEYOND
IN SPITE OF BAD LUCK.
SAY A WORD OF ENCOURAGEMENT ONCE IN A WHILE WHEN 123 BEYOND
THINGS GO WRONG,

THINGS

THINGS (CONT'D.)

WHY DON'T YOU TAKE THINGS INTO CONSIDERATION 123 BEYOND
«HOW'RE THINGS UP TO THE MAYO PLACE»-- 124 BEYOND
GAD, THE THINGS HE'S SEEN AND EXPERIENCED/ 125 BEYOND
BUT HIS ATTITUDE TOWARD THINGS IS-- 126 BEYOND
AND THE STUPID WAY YOU DO THINGS/ 126 BEYOND
TO WORK AND DO THINGS LIKE OTHER PEOPLE. 127 BEYOND
HE'LL ATTEND TO THINGS LIKE THEY SHOULD BE. 127 BEYOND
WELL, THERE WAS SO MUCH DIRTY WORK GETTING THINGS 131 BEYOND
SHIP-SHAPE AGAIN I MUST HAVE
THINGS DON'T SEEM TO BE-- 131 BEYOND
I WALKED OVER IT THIS MORNING WITH RUTH--AND SHE 133 BEYOND
TOLD ME ABOUT THINGS--
IT'S A NEW COUNTRY WHERE BIG THINGS ARE OPENING 133 BEYOND
UP--
(AFTER A PAUSE) IT'S TOO BAD PA COULDN'T HAVE 134 BEYOND
LIVED TO SEE THINGS THROUGH.
IT DON'T SOUND WELL FOR ME, GETTING OVER THINGS SO134 BEYOND
EASY.
HE WENT DOWN TO THE PORT TO SEE TO THINGS ON THE 135 BEYOND
«SUNDA.»
HE NEVER TAKES ANY INTEREST IN THINGS. 136 BEYOND
(WITH A FROWN) THINGS ARE RUN DOWN, THAT'S A 136 BEYOND
FACT/
WHY DO YOU WANT TO HIRE A MAN TO OVERSEE THINGS? 137 BEYOND
TO SETTLE DOWN ON THE FARM AND SEE TO THINGS. 138 BEYOND
WHEN I GET A MAN TO DIRECT THINGS THE FARM'LL BE 138 BEYOND
SAFE ENOUGH.
I TELL YOU, I FEEL RIPE FOR BIGGER THINGS THAN 138 BEYOND
SETTLING DOWN HERE.
IT'LL HELP CLEAR THINGS UP. 139 BEYOND
(PROUDLY) AND I'VE MANAGED TO KEEP THINGS GOING. 148 BEYOND
THANK GOD.
(AS HE HELPS THE DOCTOR WITH HIS THINGS) 154 BEYOND
THINGS KEPT GETTING WORSE, THAT'S ALL--AND ROB 155 BEYOND
DIDN'T SEEM TO CARE.
THEN, BEFORE THINGS BROKE, I LEFT--I WAS SO 156 BEYOND
CONFIDENT I COULDN'T BE WRONG.
IT'S TOO BAD--THINGS SEEM TO GO WRONG SO. 157 BEYOND
IN THE MEANTIME I'LL MAKE THINGS FLY AROUND HERE. 157 BEYOND
THE THINGS HE SAID TO ME HAD TRUTH IN THEM-- 163 BEYOND
EVEN IF HE DID TALK THEM WAY UP IN THE AIR, LIKE 163 BEYOND
HE ALWAYS SEES THINGS.
I'D GOT TO THE END OF BEARING THINGS--WITHOUT 164 BEYOND
TALKING.
I--YOU--WE'VE BOTH MADE A MESS OF THINGS/ 168 BEYOND
DON'T BE THINKIN' SUCH THINGS/ 482 CARDIF
SUCH THINGS ARE NOT FOR THE LOIKES AV US. 487 CARDIF
THE FEVER UT IS, THAT MAKES YOU SEE SUCH THINGS. 488 CARDIF
IT MAKES YOU THINK OF--WELL--THINGS YOU OUGHT TO 459 CARIBE
FURGET.
TWO SKATE LITTLE SLIPS AV THINGS, NEAR AS WHITE AS462 CARIBE
YOU AN' ME ARE, FOR THAT
NOT THAT I AIN'T HAD MY SHARE OF THINGS GOIN' 467 CARIBE
WRONG.
(SPITTING PLACIDLY) QUEER THINGS, MEM'RIES. 467 CARIBE
(GRINLY) THE THINGS HE WANTS TO SEE CAN'T BE MADE557 CROSS
OUT IN DAYLIGHT--
YOU DIDN'T DRAG ME UP HERE TO MAKE THINGS MORE 558 CROSS
OBSCURE, DID YOU?
I TOOK HIM UP HERE TO SEE HOW THINGS WERE--TO ASK 563 CROSS
HIM ABOUT FATHER.
WHAT COULD BE MORE HORRIBLE THAN THINGS AS THEY 563 CROSS
ARE?
IT IS DANGEROUS--TO CALL THINGS. 495 DAYS
AS SHE HELPS HER OFF WITH HER THINGS. ELSA CALLS515 DAYS
I'VE BEEN ACCUSED OF SO MANY ROTTEN THINGS I NEVER524 DAYS
DID
I'LL GET YOUR THINGS. 528 DAYS
YOU MUSTN'T SAY THINGS LIKE THAT. 529 DAYS
I MEAN THERE'S THINGS THAT'S ALL RIGHT FOR THEM TO495 DIFRNT
DO THAT WOULDN'T BE FOR YOU--
I MEAN I JUST LOOK AT THINGS DIFF'RENT FROM WHAT 496 DIFRNT
THEY DO--
GETTING MARRIED, FOR EXAMPLE, AND OTHER THINGS. 496 DIFRNT
TOO.
FUNNY THINGS THAT'S BEEN DONE WHEN THEY WAS AWAY. 497 DIFRNT
I HATE TO THINK OF SUCH THINGS--EVEN JOKING. 497 DIFRNT
I GOT TO GO DOWN TO THE STORE AND GIT SOME THINGS 498 DIFRNT
FOR HARRIET AFORE I FORGETS
I BEEN THINKING THINGS OVER, TELL HIM--AND I TAKE 504 DIFRNT
BACK MY PROMISE--
AND HERE I BE WAITIN' IN THE KITCHEN FOR HIM TO 505 DIFRNT
BRING BACK THE THINGS
AIN'T NO GOOD REPEATIN' SECH THINGS. 508 DIFRNT
HER AND ME JUST LOOKS AT THINGS DIFF'RENT, THAT'S 510 DIFRNT
ALL.
DON'T YOU TWO GIT TO FIGHTIN'--TO MAKE THINGS 510 DIFRNT
WORSE.
I GOT TO SEE IF CALEB'S GOT BACK WITH THEM SUPPER 511 DIFRNT
THINGS.
THEN SORT O' THINGS OUGHT TO BE KEPT AMONG MEN. 515 DIFRNT
(FORCING A SMILE) I GUESS THERE'S WORSE THINGS 517 DIFRNT
THAN BEING AN OLD MAID.
THINGS BEING WHAT THEY BE AND ME BEING WHAT I AM--517 DIFRNT
I WON'T MARRY NO MAN.
I AIN'T AS STRICT AS I SEEM--ABOUT HEARIN' THINGS.526 DIFRNT
FOLKS WOULD BE SAYIN' ALL SORTS OF BAD THINGS IN 532 DIFRNT
NO TIME.
IT DIDN'T FIT IN WITH THEM NEW THINGS. 535 DIFRNT
YOU'RE GOT UP IN THEM THINGS LIKE A YOUNG GIRL 537 DIFRNT
GOIN' TO A DANCE.
THINGS SHE DON'T REALLY MEAN. 539 DIFRNT
HOW DARE YOU SAY SUCH THINGS$ 541 DIFRNT
CAN'T THEM THINGS HAPPEN JUST AS WELL AS ANY 542 DIFRNT
OTHER-- WHAT DO YOU SUPPOSE--
HE WAS SO ROMANTIC LOOKING WITH THOSE STEEL 430 DYNAMO
CLIMBING THINGS ON HIS LEGS...

THINGS (CONT'D.)

HE CAN ANSWER ALL YOUR ARGUMENTS EASY-- WITH 436 DYNAMO
THINGS RIGHT OUT OF THE BIBLE/
RAMSAY SAYS AWFUL MEAN THINGS SOMETIMES... 439 DYNAMO
DO YOU EXPECT ME TO BELIEVE FIFE'S SUCH AN IDIOT 447 DYNAMO
AS TO CONFESS SUCH THINGS TO
THE DYING SEE THINGS BEYOND... 466 DYNAMO
THERE'S SOME THINGS I'D LIKE TO GET OFF MY CHEST--467 DYNAMO
EVEN IF SHE CAN'T HEAR ME.
I WANT TO FACE THINGS. 469 DYNAMO
IT MAKES YOU FEEL THINGS... 473 DYNAMO
HOW ALL THINGS END UP IN HER/ 477 DYNAMO
U DYNAMO, WHO GIVES LIFE TO THINGS, HEAR MY 480 DYNAMO
PRAYER/
YOU JUS' GET SEEIN' DEM THINGS 'CAUSE YO' BELLY'S 193 EJONES
EMPTY AND YOU'S SICK WID
YOU FOOL NIGGER, DEY AIN'T NO SUCH THINGS/ 193 EJONES
DESE WOODS IS SHO' FULL O' DE QUEEREST THINGS AT 193 EJONES
NIGHT.
I WANTED TO BE ALONE--TO THINK OVER THINGS. 16 ELECTR
WHAT THINGS, IF I MAY ASK$. 16 ELECTR
YOU ALWAYS MAKE SUCH A MYSTERY OF THINGS, VINNIE. 18 ELECTR
I WAS ONLY LEADING YOU ON TO FIND OUT THINGS/ 25 ELECTR
STOP TELLING ME SUCH THINGS/ 31 ELECTR
I JUST LED HIM ON--TO FIND OUT THINGS/ 34 ELECTR
HE DID ONE OF THE BRAVEST THINGS I'VE SEEN IN THE 48 ELECTR
WAR.
I'VE GOT TO EXPLAIN SOME THINGS--INSIDE ME--TO MY 53 ELECTR
WIFE--TRY TO ANYWAY/
IT WAS SEEING DEATH ALL THE TIME IN THIS WAY GOT 53 ELECTR
ME TO THINKING THESE THINGS.
KEEPS ME HIDING THE THINGS I'D LIKE TO SHOW. 55 ELECTR
SOMETHING QUEER IN ME KEEPS ME MUM ABOUT THE 55 ELECTR
THINGS I'D LIKE MOST TO SAY--
(STAMMERS) NO, NO, I--WHAT MAKES YOU SAY SUCH 55 ELECTR
THINGS?
I DIDN'T MEAN TO SAY THOSE THINGS. 59 ELECTR
IF YOU ARE GOING TO SAY STUPID THINGS, I'LL GO IN 59 ELECTR
MY OWN ROOM.
HE GOT THINGS DONE. 69 ELECTR
GIVE ME A CHANCE TO GET USED TO THINGS/ 75 ELECTR
TO BEAR THINGS. 80 ELECTR
AND TRY NOT TO THINK ABOUT THINGS. 84 ELECTR
THAT SHE WILL EVEN ACCUSE ME OF THE VILEST, MOST 85 ELECTR
HORRIBLE THINGS/
YOU SIMPLY WOULDN'T BELIEVE IT, IF I TOLD YOU SOME 86 ELECTR
OF THE THINGS.
SHE GOT SO SHE'D SAY THE MOST TERRIBLE THINGS 86 ELECTR
ABOUT EVERYONE.
HE BOASTED THAT YOU HAD DONE ONE OF THE BRAVEST 94 ELECTR
THINGS HE'D SEEN IN THE WAR/
(THEN STERNLY) WHAT MADE YOU SAY SUCH THINGS JUST 94 ELECTR
THEN?
ONE OF THE BRAVEST THINGS HE'D SEEN/ 94 ELECTR
MY GOD, HOW CAN YOU THINK SUCH THINGS OF MOTHERS 96 ELECTR
(GRIMLY) I WAS GOING TO GIVE THEM A FIGHT FOR 108 ELECTR
IT--IF THINGS WENT WRONG.
SO MANY THINGS HAVE HAPPENED I COULDN'T FORESEE--1109 ELECTR
CAME TO WARN YOU--
BUT SOMETHING MADE THINGS HAPPEN/ 110 ELECTR
HOW ELSE COULD YOU EVER HAVE SAID THE THINGS-- 121 ELECTR
DON'T WANT YOU RUNNIN' INTO FURNITURE AN' BREAKIN'131 ELECTR
THINGS.
BEN USED TO HEAR THINGS CLAWIN' AT THE WALLS AN' 132 ELECTR
WINDERS
YOU KNOW HOW THEM THINGS GROW. 135 ELECTR
WHAT WOULD VINNIE SAY IF SHE KNEW YOU DID SUCH 135 ELECTR
THINGS/.
AN' I'VE FELT IT, GOIN' IN THERE DAYTIMES TO SEE 135 ELECTR
TO THINGS--
WHAT WE NEED MOST IS TO GET BACK TO SIMPLE NORMAL 140 ELECTR
THINGS AND BEGIN A NEW LIFE.
THINGS WERE ALWAYS REMINDING ME OF YOU--THE SHIP 146 ELECTR
AND THE SEA--
HE WAS JEALOUS AND MAD AND SAID THINGS HE WAS 148 ELECTR
SORRY FOR AFTER
SO MANY STRANGE HIDDEN THINGS OUT OF THE MANNON 153 ELECTR
PAST COMBINE IN YOU/
(BREAKING) HOW CAN YOU SAY SUCH DREADFUL THINGS 153 ELECTR
TO ME, AFTER ALL I--
BUT I KNOW TERRIBLE THINGS MUST HAVE HAPPENED-- 172 ELECTR
ANY MORE THAN I CAN PROVE A LOT OF THINGS ORIN 172 ELECTR
HINTED AT/
(AVOIDING HER EYES) SOME THINGS WOULD MAKE ANYONE175 ELECTR
BITTER/
WHO CULTIVATES A NAIVELY INNOCENT AND BRAVELY 274 GGBRON
HOPEFUL ATTITUDE TOWARD THINGS AND
THINGS HAVE COME MY WAY WITHOUT MY DOING MUCH 275 GGBRON
ABOUT IT.
HE DOESN'T WANT ANYONE EVEN TO LOOK AT HIS THINGS,276 GGBRON
IMAGINE/
WHAT BEAUTIFUL THINGS YOU WERE PAINTING. 281 GGBRON
IT'S JUST ONE OF A LOT OF THINGS YOU DO TO KEEP 285 GGBRON
LIFE LIVING.
(MOCKING) AREN'T WOMEN LOYAL--TO THEIR VANITY AND287 GGBRON
THEIR OTHER THINGS//
THAT'S THE TROUBLE WITH KNOWING THINGS. 11 HUGHIE
A GUY GETS CARELESS AND GABS ABOUT THINGS HE KNOWS 11 HUGHIE
AND WHEN HE COMES TO ME'S
BUT THEY SAY MOST OF THE THINGS WE WORRY ABOUT 18 HUGHIE
NEVER HAPPEN.
HE SAYS, «THEY'RE THE MOST BEAUTIFUL THINGS IN THE 21 HUGHIE
WORLD, I THINK.»
SO MANY GUESTS HAVE CALLED HIM SO MANY THINGS. 24 HUGHIE
LEAST YOU COULD DO--KEEP THINGS QUIET-- THE FALLS 582 ICEMAN
ASLEEP)
TOO INTERESTED IN OUTSIDE THINGS AND LOSING 592 ICEMAN
INTEREST IN THE MOVEMENT.

1641 THINK'S

THINGS (CONT'D.)
(DREAMING ALOUD AGAIN) GET MY THINGS FROM THE 604 ICEMAN
LAUNDRY.
(FLATTERINGLY) HARRY, YOU SURE SAY THE FUNNIEST 606 ICEMAN
THINGS/
THEY'RE THE THINGS THAT REALLY POISON AND RUIN A 622 ICEMAN
GUY'S LIFE
THE THINGS I'VE IMAGINED/ 644 ICEMAN
ALL THINGS ARE THE SAME MEANINGLESS JOKE TO ME, 649 ICEMAN
BEEN THINKING THINGS OVER. 675 ICEMAN
MAKES THINGS LOOK BLACK. 687 ICEMAN
SHE WAS ALWAYS ON YOUR NECK, MAKING YOU HAVE 688 ICEMAN
AMBITION AND GO OUT AND DO THINGS,
I HEAR MYSELF SAY CRAZY THINGS. 691 ICEMAN
I SAY CRAZY THINGS/ 695 ICEMAN
WE DON'T WANT TO KNOW THINGS THAT WILL MAKE US 706 ICEMAN
HELP SEND YOU TO THE CHAIR/
MADE UP MY MIND THE ONLY WAY I CAN CLEAR THINGS UP707 ICEMAN
FOR YOU,
IT PUTS THINGS IN MY MIND-- 709 ICEMAN
AND I KNEW I COULD KID PEOPLE AND SELL THINGS. 710 ICEMAN
EVEN WHEN I'D ADMIT THINGS AND ASK HER 710 ICEMAN
FORGIVENESS,
AND ONCE YOU'RE HAPPY YOU WON'T WANT TO DO ANY OF 711 ICEMAN
THE BAD THINGS YOU'VE DONE ANY
I'D GET SEEING THINGS IN THE WALL PAPER. 712 ICEMAN
ABOUT HOW TRAVELING MEN GET THINGS FROM DRINKING 713 ICEMAN
CUPS ON TRAINS.
IF YOU'D SEEN ALL THE DAMNED-FOOL THINGS HE MADE 718 ICEMAN
US DO/
I'VE NEVER BEEN ANY GOOD AT DECIDING THINGS. 719 ICEMAN
BEJEEES, IT DOES QUEER THINGS TO YOU, 721 ICEMAN
HOW BIG'D YOU THINK THEM--(HE HESITATES) --THINGS 520 INZONE
HAS TO BE--
AN' THERE'S A LOT O' THINGS A SAILOR'LL SEE IN THE522 INZONE
PORTS HE PUTS IN
IT AIN'T BY LETTERS AND SUCH THINGS,$ 529 INZONE
LOVIN' BLARNEY, AN' HER SINGIN' IS DOIN', AND 531 INZONE
THE GREAT THINGS THE DUTCH
YOU ALWAYS IMAGINE THINGS/ 27 JOURNE
I DID PUT EDMUND WISE TO THINGS, BUT NOT UNTIL I 34 JOURNE
SAW HE'D STARTED TO RAISE HELL.
I DON'T UNDERSTAND WHY YOU SHOULD SUDDENLY SAY 45 JOURNE
SUCH THINGS.
NOW DON'T START IMAGINING THINGS, MAMA, 46 JOURNE
AND ONCE THEY'RE DONE THEY MAKE YOU DO OTHER 61 JOURNE
THINGS UNTIL AT LAST EVERYTHING
NONE OF US CAN HELP THE THINGS LIFE HAS DONE TO 61 JOURNE
US.
YOU KNOW I DON'T LIKE THE DAMNED THINGS. 84 JOURNE
THE THINGS LIFE HAS DONE TO US WE CANNOT EXCUSE OR 85 JOURNE
EXPLAIN.
OR HELP THINGS THAT CANNOT BE HELPED-- 85 JOURNE
OH, I KNOW IT'S FOOLISH TO IMAGINE DREADFUL THINGS 88 JOURNE
WHEN THERE'S NO REASON FOR
DON'T SAY HORRIBLE THINGS. 91 JOURNE
(STAMMERS PLEADINGLY.) PLEASE DON'T--TALK ABOUT 93 JOURNE
THINGS YOU DON'T UNDERSTAND/
ABRUPTLY.) BUT LET'S NOT TALK OF OLD THINGS THAT 102 JOURNE
COULDN'T BE HELPED.
IT HAS MADE ME FORGIVE SO MANY OTHER THINGS. 106 JOURNE
MEN DON'T NOTICE SUCH THINGS. 114 JOURNE
YOU SAY SUCH MEAN, BITTER THINGS WHEN YOU'VE DRUNK123 JOURNE
TOO MUCH.
I'VE PUT UP WITH A LOT FROM YOU BECAUSE FROM THE 127 JOURNE
MAD THINGS YOU'VE DONE AT TIMES
OR FOR THAT MATTER, IF YOU INSIST ON JUDGING 142 JOURNE
THINGS BY WHAT SHE SAYS WHEN SHE'S
LIKE THE VEIL OF THINGS AS THEY SEEM DRAWN BACK BY153 JOURNE
AN UNSEEN HAND.
TOO MANY DAMNED THINGS HAVE HAPPENED TODAY. 157 JOURNE
FAMILIAR THINGS SHE ACCEPTS AUTOMATICALLY AS 170 JOURNE
NATURALLY BELONGING THERE BUT WHICH
AND SHE HAS THINGS IN HER MEDICINE CHEST THAT'LL 171 JOURNE
CURE ANYTHING.
THERE IS NO HELP, FOR ALL THESE THINGS ARE SO, 173 JOURNE
AND HOW THESE THINGS ARE, THOUGH YE STROVE TO 173 JOURNE
SHOW, SHE WOULD NOT KNOW.*
OF THE WINE OF LIFE STIRRING FOREVER IN THE SAP 307 LAZARU
AND BLOOD AND LOAM OF THINGS.
BETWEEN YOU AND THE CHILDREN, THINGS WOULD SOON BE346 LAZARU
IN A FINE STATE/
BUT THE THINGS YOU SAID-- 19 MANSNS
I CAME OUT OF THE CABIN BECAUSE THERE'S A LOT OF 19 MANSNS
THINGS I WANT TO SAY TO YOU.
I WILL HAVE TOO MANY IMPORTANT THINGS ON MY MIND 67 MANSNS
WE'VE ALLOWED THINGS TO GET IN A CONFUSED MUDDLE 85 MANSNS
AT HOME.
I WON'T LET YOU SAY SUCH WICKED THINGS. 86 MANSNS
I BEGIN TO SEE A LOT OF THINGS I'VE BEEN BLIND TO. 86 MANSNS
YOU NOW HAVE THE COURAGE TO FACE SOME OF THE 101 MANSNS
THINGS THAT HAVE REALITY.
I KNOW I HAVE, BUT--A LOT OF THINGS HAVE HAPPENED 136 MANSNS
SINCE THEN TO DISTURB MY MIND.
FIDDLES AROUND UNNECESSARILY GATHERING UP HER 137 MANSNS
SEWING THINGS.
YOU MUST FAITHFULLY DO THINGS WHICH MAY APPEAR TO 154 MANSNS
YOUR OLD CONCEPTIONS OF HONOR
I AM SAYING THESE THINGS BECAUSE, IN ORDER TO 154 MANSNS
AVOID ALL FUTURE MISUNDERSTANDING,
FOR GOD'S SAKE, HOW CAN YOU SAY SUCH THINGS TO 182 MANSNS
YOUR MOTHER
IT'S INSANE OF YOU TO MAKE ME CONFESS SUCH 184 MANSNS
HORRIBLE THINGS/
THAT ONE'S SYMPATHY SHOULD UNDERSTAND ALL THINGS, 372 MARCOM
ALL PERSONS AND THINGS OF EQUAL IMPORTANCE. 372 MARCOM
THEY PRAY TO HIM ALSO AND DO MANY OTHER STUPID 374 MARCOM
THINGS.

THINGS (CONT'D.)
I'VE BEEN SO USED TO BEING OUT, OVERCOMING 398 MARCOM
OBSTACLES, GETTING THINGS DONE,
THRILL OR A GOOD LAUGH AND GET YOUR MIND OFF 399 MARCOM
SERIOUS THINGS
LITTLE DAUGHTER, ALL RARE THINGS ARE SECRET WHICH 400 MARCOM
CANNOT BE REVEALED TO ANYONE.
HE'S DONE A LOT OF MAD THINGS, WHEN HE WAS THAT 34 MISBEG
WAY, HE WAS SORRY FOR AFTER.
FENCES ARE QUEER THINGS. 50 MISBEG
FUNNY THINGS THAT FLAY THE HIDE OFF THEM, OR PLAY 83 MISBEG
CRUEL JOKES ON THEM.
BUT ALL THE SAME THERE'S THINGS BESIDES YOUR 89 MISBEG
BEAUTIFUL SOUL HE FEELS DRAWN TO.
THERE'S A LOT OF THINGS HE'LL HAVE TO EXPLAIN WHEN134 MISBEG
HE COMES AT SUN--
I WANTED TO CLEAN THINGS UP, THAT'S ALL--FOR 136 MISBEG
PHIL'S SAKE AS WELL AS YOURS.
I WAS SEEING THINGS. 138 MISBEG
I THOUGHT THEY WERE THE MOST BEAUTIFUL THINGS IN 143 MISBEG
THE WORLD.
THINGS A MAN CAN DO WHEN HE'S CRAZY DRUNK, AND 145 MISBEG
DRAWS A BLANK--
SHE HAD ONLY ME TO ATTEND TO THINGS FOR HER AND 146 MISBEG
TAKE CARE OF HER.
BUT THERE ARE THINGS I CAN NEVER FORGET-- 147 MISBEG
WOULDN'T HAVE TO FACE THE ROTTEN THINGS YOU'RE 171 MISBEG
AFRAID YOU SAID AND DID THE NIGHT
AND THERE ARE FEW THINGS IN IT THAT DO NOT CALL 40 POET
FOR BITTER REGRET.
(THEN IRRITABLY.) BUT WHY DO I DISCUSS SUCH 41 POET
THINGS WITH YOU\
SHE GOADS ME INTO LOSING MY TEMPER, AND I SAY 61 POET
THINGS--
IT'S ONE OF THE THINGS I'VE HELD AGAINST MY 84 POET
FATHER.
(CONSOLINGLY.) AH WELL, THAT'S THE BAD LUCK OF 99 POET
THINGS.
(THEN QUIETLY.) THERE ARE THINGS I SAID WHICH I 115 POET
REGRET--EVEN NOW.
AH, THEN YOU WERE EXPECTING--THAT MAKES THINGS 119 POET
EASIER.
WE HAD BETTER THINGS TO DISCUSS. 145 POET
AND SAID HE MEANT ALL THE BOLD THINGS HE'D WRITTEN147 POET
IN THE POEMS I'D SEEN.
BACK AFTER FIVE YEARS OF BUMMIN' ROUND THE ROTTEN 588 ROPE
OLD EARTH IN SHIPS AND THINGS.
TO GIT ALL THE DIRTY THINGS YUH'RE THINKIN' ABOUT 589 ROPE
ME OFF YOUR CHEST.
WE'VE NO CHANCE TO LEARN THE THINGS A TRAVELIN' 593 ROPE
LAD LIKE YUH'D BE KNOWIN'.
AND WORKIN' MYSELF TO DEATH ON SHIPS AND THINGS-- 598 ROPE
BRIGHT THINGS YUH CHUCKED IN THE OCEAN--AND YUH 601 ROPE
KIN BE A REAL SPORT.
YOU SEE, I'M TRYING TO SEE THINGS THROUGH CLEARLY 9 STRANG
AND UNSENTIMENTALLY.
TODAY I'VE MADE UP MY MIND TO FACE THINGS. 20 STRANG
THERE ARE WORSE THINGS THAN BEING A TRAINED 22 STRANG
NURSE....
THE BEAUTIFUL THINGS WE HAVE TO KEEP DIARIES TO 25 STRANG
REMEMBER/....))
WITH YOU THE LIES HAVE BECOME THE ONLY TRUTHFUL 40 STRANG
THINGS.
NO, I DON'T THINK ANY OF THOSE THINGS, MRS. EVANS. 57 STRANG
SUCH LITTLE THINGS AT THE BACK OF BIG THINGS/ 60 STRANG
STILL, THERE ARE SOME THINGS A HUSBAND HAS A RIGHT 67 STRANG
TO KNOW--
LIFE IS SO FULL OF A NUMBER OF THINGS/= 74 STRANG
I DON'T WANT TO HURRY YOU BUT NINA WANTS SOME 78 STRANG
THINGS AT THE STORE BEFORE IT
BANAL NEWNESS OFF THE ROOM WITH SOME OF HER OWN 90 STRANG
THINGS FROM HER OLD HOME BUT THE
ALL THINGS ARE EACH OTHER'S.... 91 STRANG
OF ALL THINGS I DON'T WANT TO FALL IN LOVE WITH 91 STRANG
YOU/=
I HAVEN'T TIME, I'VE GOT A MILLION THINGS TO DO. 106 STRANG
HOW QUEERLY THINGS WORK OUT/... 112 STRANG
HOW THINGS WERE GOING WITH YOU WHEN I SAW YOU IN 127 STRANG
MUNICH.
THERE ARE THINGS ONE MAY NOT SAY.... 133 STRANG
THERE ARE THINGS ONE MAY NOT DO AND LIVE WITH 133 STRANG
ONESELF AFTERWARDS....
(INTENSELY) THERE ARE THINGS WE DON'T TELL, YOU 151 STRANG
AND I/
THERE ARE THINGS A MAN OF HONOR DOESN'T TELL 151 STRANG
ANYONE--
EVEN THOUGH HE DOES DO WEAK THINGS SOMETIMES. 160 STRANG
THINGS HAVE GONE PRETTY FAR.... 163 STRANG
I CAN'T THINK OF THESE THINGS AS REAL ANY MORE.... 165 STRANG
THINKING THINGS/ 170 STRANG
FROM THINGS SHE WROTE ME BEFORE SHE DIED, 172 STRANG
(THEN ASHAMED) (HOW CAN I THINK SUCH THINGS.... 183 STRANG
THERE ARE MANY THINGS STILL TO BE DONE THIS 187 STRANG
EVENING...
THERE ARE SOME THINGS I FEEL I OUGHT TO SAY TO 188 STRANG
HER--AND DARRELL.
THERE ARE CERTAIN THINGS CONNECTED WITH DAD'S WILL191 STRANG
I THOUGHT I OUGHT TO--
I WILL THIS AS A SYMBOL OF RELEASE--OF THE END OF 472 WELDED
ALL THINGS/

THINGS'D
THINGS'D BE DIFF'RENT AND I'D TELL 'EM ALL TO GO 534 DIFRNT
TO HELL.

THINGS'VE
THINGS'VE BEEN GOIN' DOWN HILL STEADY. 114 BEYOND

THINK'S
THEN YOU THINK'S HE'LL STAKE ME TO THAT REST CURE 17 ANNA
I'M AFTER$

THINK'S 1642

THINK'S (CONT'D.)
(THEN WORRIEDLY) SAY, ED, WHAT THE HELL YOU 610 ICEMAN
THINK'S HAPPENED TO HICKEY$

THINKER
I CAN REMEMBER WHEN I COULDN'T PICK UP AN 497 DAYS
ADVANCED-THINKER ORGAN WITHOUT RUNNING
HE IS SEATED FORWARD ON A BENCH IN THE EXACT 226 HA APE
ATTITUDE OF RODIN'S =THE THINKER.=
YANK SITS DOWN AGAIN IN THE SAME ATTITUDE OF =THE 227 HA APE
THINKER.=
CROUCHED ON THE EDGE OF HIS COT IN THE ATTITUDE OF239 HA APE
RODIN'S =THE THINKER.=
IN THE ATTITUDE OF RODIN'S =THE THINKER.= 244 HA APE
IN AS NEAR TO THE ATTITUDE OF RODIN'S =THE 250 HA APE
THINKER=
THE SAME ATTITUDE AS RODIN'S =THE THINKER.= 251 HA APE
I'LL GET ANYTHING IT WAS SOME QUICK-THINKER WHO'D 394 MARCOM
JUST DISCOVERED A GOLD MINE/
(WITH AN AIR OF AN INDEPENDENT THINKER) 404 MARCOM
AND WHO WANTS A GREAT THINKER AROUND THE HOUSE$ 416 MARCOM
THE FOREHEAD OF A THINKER, THE EYES OF A DREAMER, 443 WELDED

THINKIN
I'M THINKIN HE WOULDN'T USE THE TELEGRAPH OR 437 DYNAMO
TELEPHONE OR RADIO FOR THEY'RE

THINKIN'
I WARN'T THINKIN' OF MYSELF, SIR--'BOUT TURNIN' 542 'ILE
HOME, I MEAN.
THINKIN' IT MIGHT BE SOOTHIN' TO YE TO BE PLAYIN' 546 'ILE
IT TIMES WHEN THEY WAS CALMS
(IMPATIENTLY) IT AIN'T THE MONEY I'M THINKIN' OF.547 'ILE
THAT'LL BE IN MINNESOTA, I'M THINKIN'. 5 ANNA
SHE'LL NOT LIKE THAT, I'M THINKIN'. 10 ANNA
I WAS THINKIN' OF SOMETHIN' ELSE. 14 ANNA
GUESS THEY WAS ALL THINKIN' ABOUT TOMORROW, SAME 98 BEYOND
AS US.
WHY, I WAS THINKIN'-- 100 BEYOND
YE WERE NEVERR IN NEW GUINEA IN YOURR LIFE, I'M 478 CARDIF
THINKIN'.
DON'T BE THINKIN' SUCH THINGS/ 482 CARDIF
I WAS JUST THINKIN' IT AINT AS BAD AS PEOPLE 486 CARDIF
THINK--DYIN'.
BUT WHAT'S THE USE AV THINKIN' AV UTS 487 CARDIF
(HASTILY) DON'T BE THINKIN' AV THAT NOW. 488 CARDIF
THINKIN' IT FOR THE PAST THREE YEARS, YE BIN-- 568 CROSS
BIN THINKIN' ME MAD, DID YE$ 568 CROSS
THINKIN' ALLUS HE'LL DIE SOON. 208 DESIRE
JEST WHAT I WAS A-THINKIN'. 213 DESIRE
THEN I GOT A-THINKIN' O' WHAT YE'D SAID O' HIM AN'214 DESIRE
HER AN' I SAYS,
(A PAUSE) I WAS THINKIN' O' HIM. 216 DESIRE
AN' I WAS MAD AT THINKIN'--YE'D LEAVE HIM THE 233 DESIRE
FARM.
I BEEN THINKIN' O' IT ALL ALONG. 234 DESIRE
DON'T GIT RILED THINKIN' O' HIM. 242 DESIRE
AN' LOOK WHAR HE BE FUR THINKIN' HIS PAW WAS EASY/256 DESIRE
I BEEN A-THINKIN'--AN' I HAIN'T GOIN' T' TELL PAW 260 DESIRE
NOTHIN'.
I GOT TO THINKIN' O' YEW. 266 DESIRE
I GOT TO THINKIN' HUW I'D LOVED YE. 266 DESIRE
AN' I'D SUFFER WUSS LEAVIN' YE, GOIN' WEST, 267 DESIRE
THINKIN' O' YE DAY AN' NIGHT,
I WAS THINKIN' O' HOW YOU MIGHT FEEL--EVEN DOWN 515 DIFRNT
THERE.
NOW WHEN THE THIRTY YEARS ARE PAST--I WAS THINKIN'538 DIFRNT
THAT MAYBE--
ON'Y--I WAS THINKIN' ALL THIS LAST VIGE--THAT 538 DIFRNT
MAYBE--
SAY, I BEEN THINKIN' IT OVER AND I GUESS I'LL CALL$545 DIFRNT
HIS BLUFF.
I WAS ONLY THINKIN' O' THE BLOODY LIES 180 EJONES
WAS YOU THINKIN' I'SE AIMIN' TO HOLD DOWN DIS JOB 180 EJONES
FOR LIFE$
YOU AIN'T THINKIN' THAT WOULD BE 'M, I 'OPES 203 EJONES
(THEN IMPRESSIVELY) IT'S ABOUT HER BABY I'VE BEEN 20 ELECTR
THINKIN', VINNIE.
JEE$, I GET DE EARACHE JUST THINKIN' OF IT/ 669 ICEMAN
IT IS NO THE SUBMARINES ONLY WE'VE TO FEAR, I'M 515 INZONE
THINKIN'.
I MASHA THINKI' O' MINES EITHER. 515 INZONE
I'M A SICK KID THINKIN' AND JUMPIN' AT IVRY BIT AV 517 INZONE
A NOISE.)
THEN WE'LL BE MAKIN' UT OURS, I'M THINKIN'. 526 INZONE
THIS'LL BE UT, I'M THINKIN'. 527 INZONE
(WITH A TEASING SMILE.) I'M THINKIN' IT ISN'T ON 28 POET
NEILAN ALUNE
I-- I WAS ONLY THINKIN' YOU'D FEEL BETTER IF YOU'D 35 POET
A BIT AV FOOD IN YOU.
MAD AS YOU ARE, FOR THINKIN' THAT THIEF OF A SON 582 ROPE
OF YOURS WOULD
TO GIT ALL THE DIRTY THINGS YUH'RE THINKIN' ABOUT 589 ROPE
ME OFF YOUR CHEST.
YOUR MOTHER GOT RID OF IT ALL I'M THINKIN'. 592 ROPE
DON'T BE THINKIN' ABOUT IT. 598 ROPE
HOW KIN I HELP THINKIN'--AND HIM MY OWN FATHER$ 598 ROPE
(WITH A WINK) I WAS THINKIN' AS ONE OF 'EM FROM 496 VOYAGE
=THE GLENCARRIN= DO--
WE'LL ALL BE HAVIN' A DHRINK, I'M THINKIN'. 497 VOYAGE
UT'S DEAD HE IS, I'M THINKIN', FOR HE'S AS LIMP AS503 VOYAGE
A BLARSTED CORPSE.

THINKING
(THINKING TO HUMOR HER) 'TIS NO FIT PLACE FOR A 548 'ILE
WOMAN, THAT'S SURE.
I WASN'T THINKING ONLY OF $10. 190 AHWILD
ALWAYS THINKING OF BEING AFRAID. 207 AHWILD
I WASN'T EVEN THINKING ABOUT HER. 215 AHWILD
I WAS THINKING ABOUT LIFE. 215 AHWILD
AND I DATED THEM UP FOR TONIGHT, THINKING I COULD 218 AHWILD
CATCH ART.

THINKING (CONT'D.)
I DON'T WANT THEM THINKING I'M TRAVELLING AROUND 219 AHWILD
WITH ANY HIGH-SCHOOL KID.
I WAS THINKING OF SOMETHING ELSE. 237 AHWILD
(THINKING ALOUD) MUST BE NEARLY NINE.... 275 AHWILD
GOSH, TIME PASSES--WHEN YOU'RE THINKING. 278 AHWILD
BUT I GOT TO THINKING ABOUT LIFE. 278 AHWILD
(THINKING IT WELL TO RUB IN THIS ASPECT-- 294 AHWILD
DISGUSTEDLY)
AND I WAS THINKING MAYBE, SEEING HE AIN'T NEVER 16 ANNA
DONE A THING FOR ME IN MY LIFE,
LET YOU NOT BE THINKING I'M THE LIKE OF THEM THREE 32 ANNA
WEAK SCUTS COME IN THE BOAT
BUT I DO BE THINKING IVER SINCE THE FIRST LOOK MY 33 ANNA
EYES TUUK AT YOU,
(PASSIONATELY) I'M THINKING I'D RATHER BE FRIENDS 34 ANNA
WITH YOU THAN HAVE MY WISH
I'M A HARD, ROUGH MAN AND I'M NOT FIT, I'M 34 ANNA
THINKING,
FOR I'M THINKING A FINE GIRL THE LIKE OF YOU AIN'T 35 ANNA
LIVING ALWAYS ON THIS TUB.
(INTERESTEDLY) I'M THINKING YOU HAVE A BIT OF IT 36 ANNA
IN YOUR BLOOD, TOO.
I'M THINKING IF IT'S A STOKEHOLD OF A PROPER 38 ANNA
LINER,
AND I'M THINKING THAT MAYBE THEN I'D HAVE THE LUCK 38 ANNA
TO FIND A FINE DACENT GIRL--
(WITH A MOURNFUL LAUGH) WELL, I BEEN THINKING I 44 ANNA
WAS MYSELF THE LAST FEW DAYS.
(SCORNFULLY) IS IT THE LIKE OF YOURSELF WILL STOP 45 ANNA
ME, ARE YOU THINKING$
BUT FIRST I'M THINKING I'LL TAKE THIS CHANCE WHEN 45 ANNA
WE'RE ALONE TO HAVE A WORD
(HEARTILY) LET YOU NOT BE THINKING I HAVE NO 46 ANNA
HEART AT ALL.
BE SAYING TO HER, AND I'M THINKING IT'S A POOR 47 ANNA
WEAK THING YOU ARE,
I'M THINKING. 47 ANNA
I'M THINKING 'TIS OUT OF YOUR WITS YOU'VE GOT WITH 48 ANNA
FRIGHT OF THE SEA.
I BEEN THINKING AND THINKING--I DIDN'T WANT TO, 51 ANNA
MAT, I'LL OWN UP TO THAT--
I BEEN THINKING IT OVER AND THINKING IT OVER DAY 54 ANNA
AND NIGHT ALL WEEK.
I'M THINKING YOU'RE THE LIKE OF THEM WOMEN CAN'T 55 ANNA
MAKE UP THEIR MIND TILL THEY'RE
YOU DON'T SAY NOTHING--EITHER OF YOU--BUT I KNOW 58 ANNA
WHAT YOU'RE THINKING.
HAD GOT ME TO THINKING FOR THE FIRST TIME, 59 ANNA
AND ME THINKING THOUGHTS ABOUT YOU, AND HAVING 60 ANNA
GREAT LOVE FOR YOU,
(FURIOUSLY) THOUGH I DO BE THINKING I'D HAVE A 60 ANNA
GOOD RIGHT
D'YOU SUPPOSE I AIN'T BEEN THINKING TOO$ 64 ANNA
THERE'S NO ONE HERE, I'M THINKING, AND 'TIS A 68 ANNA
GREAT FOOL I AM TO BE COMING.
OR IS IT THINKING I'D BE FRIGHTENED BY THAT OLD 69 ANNA
TIN WHISTLES
COMING AT ME SO SUDDEN AND ME THINKING I WAS 69 ANNA
ALONE,
WOULDN'T BE SEEING OR THINKING MORE OF YOU. 70 ANNA
I'M RAVING LIKE A REAL LUNATIC, I'M THINKING. 70 ANNA
'TIL I DO BE THINKING A MADHOUSE IS THE PROPER 70 ANNA
PLACE FOR ME.
THINKING MAYBE YOU'D THINK OVER ALL I'D SAID--AND 71 ANNA
MAYBE--
I'D BEEN WAITING HERE ALL ALONE FOR TWO DAYS, 71 ANNA
THINKING MAYBE YOU'D COME BACK--
BUT I GOT TO THINKING ABOUT YOU--AND I COULDN'T 71 ANNA
TAKE THE TRAIN--I COULDN'T/
I'M THINKING YOU WERE, SURELY. 73 ANNA
THINKING THAT ABOUT ME/ 74 ANNA
AND WOMEN, TOO, MAYBE, AND I'M THINKING I'D CHANGE 74 ANNA
YOU TO A NEW WOMAN ENTIRELY,
AND I'M THINKING 'TWASN'T YOUR FAULT, MAYBE, 74 ANNA
I'LL HAVE TO BE TAKING YOUR NAKED WORD FOR IT AND 76 ANNA
HAVE YOU ANYWAY, I'M THINKING--
(KISSING HER) AND I WAS THINKING--(WITH A LAUGH) 91 BEYOND
WHAT FOOLS WE'VE BOTH BEEN/
NEVER MIND WHAT YOU WERE THINKING, JAMES. 100 BEYOND
NOT AFTER ALL THE PLANS I'D MADE TO HAPPEN ON THIS110 BEYOND
PLACE THINKING--
(HIS VOICE BREAKS) THINKING SHE CARED FOR ME. 110 BEYOND
THEN SHE STARTS FOR THE KITCHEN BUT STANDS FOR A 121 BEYOND
MOMENT THINKING.
I'M ONLY SAYING WHAT I'VE BEEN THINKING FOR YEARS.127 BEYOND
WHAT ARE YOU THINKING OF$ 128 BEYOND
I REMEMBER THINKING ABOUT YOU AT THE WORST OF IT, 132 BEYOND
AND SAYING TO MYSELF...
I'M CERTAIN NOW I NEVER WAS IN LOVE--I WAS GETTING134 BEYOND
FUN OUT OF THINKING I WAS--
THINKING OF WHAT YOU TWO MIGHT THINK. 134 BEYOND
AND NOT BE WORRIED THINKING ONE OF US MIGHT HAVE 139 BEYOND
THE WRONG NOTION.
I GAVE UP TRYING FINALLY AND JUST LAID THERE IN 147 BEYOND
THE DARK THINKING.
I WAS THINKING ABOUT YOU, RUTH-- 147 BEYOND
HE MIGHT BE THINKING OF-- 163 BEYOND
EVERYBODY KNEW IT--AND FOR THREE YEARS I'D BEEN 164 BEYOND
THINKING--
DRINKING TO STOP THINKING. 468 CARIBE
(WITH A TWISTED GRIN) THINKING AND--THE INDICATE$468 CARIBE
THE BOTTLE IN HIS HAND)
AND I WAS THINKING, TOO, 495 DAYS
(DEFENSIVELY) I DON'T KNOW WHAT YOU'RE THINKING 499 DAYS
ABOUT.
(WITHOUT LOOKING AT HIM) THINKING OF IT--TO PASS 505 DAYS
THE TIME.

THINKING

THINKING (CONT'D.)

I AM THINKING THAT SUCH LOVE NEEDS THE HOPE AND 508 DAYS
PROMISE OF ETERNITY TO FULFILL
I KEPT THINKING OF MR. LOVING'S UNCLE. 515 DAYS
I'M THINKING OF WHAT IT WOULD DO TO HER. 527 DAYS
IT IS AS IF HE WERE DETERMINEDLY TALKING TO KEEP 542 DAYS
HIMSELF FROM THINKING.
(IN A LOW, TENSE VOICE--AS IF HE WERE THINKING 561 DAYS
ALOUD)
BUT LOTS AND LOTS OF THE OTHERS DOES THE SAME 497 DIFRNT
THING WITHOUT THINKING NOTHING
(LAUGHING) I WASN'T THINKING OF WHALES, SILLY/ 497 DIFRNT
I BEEN THINKING THINGS OVER, TELL HIM--AND I TAKE 504 DIFRNT
BACK MY PROMISE--
YOU'RE TOO DUMB STUPID AND BAD YOURSELF TO EVER 505 DIFRNT
KNOW WHAT I'M THINKING.
WHAT AM I THINKING OF$ 535 DIFRNT
IT ONLY GETS ME THINKING HOW OLD I AM. 537 DIFRNT
THAT LIGHTNING HAD NOTHING TO DO WITH WHAT I WAS 524 DYNAMO
THINKING...)
(SITS THINKING GLOOMILY) (NEVER LIED TO HER... 426 DYNAMO
(THINKING GLOOMILY) (I MUST BE HONEST WITH 435 DYNAMO
MYSELF...
HE'S AFRAID, I'M THINKING... 436 DYNAMO
I'M THINKING YOUR JEHOVAH MIGHT AIM A THUNDERBOLT 437 DYNAMO
AT ME
YOU OUGHT TO SEE HIM IN HIS TRUE COLORS SO YOU'D 443 DYNAMO
NOT BE THINKING TOO MUCH ABOUT
(THINKING WITH A FIERCE, REVENGEFUL JOY) 447 DYNAMO
(THEN THINKING WITH GUILTY SHAME) 447 DYNAMO
(EXPECTING THE NEXT BLOW, THINKING WITH A GRIM 448 DYNAMO
ELATION)
(HE SUDDENLY IS REMINDED OF SOMETHING--THINKING 450 DYNAMO
WILDLY)
(HE TAKES A FEW STEPS TOWARD THE WINDOW, THEN 452 DYNAMO
STOPS, THINKING BITTERLY)
(THINKING WITH A SLEEPY CONTENT) 454 DYNAMO
I WAS THINKING OF POOR MRS. LIGHT-- 454 DYNAMO
THEN WHY ARE YOU ALL THE TIME THINKING ABOUT 455 DYNAMO
HIM...
ADA STARES BEFORE HER, THINKING RESENTFULLY) 455 DYNAMO
(THINKING DULLY) (ANOTHER DAY...EMPTY... 455 DYNAMO
(THINKING JEERINGLY) (HOME, SWEET HOME/... 457 DYNAMO
(THINKING GROPINGLY) (IT'S REUBEN... 463 DYNAMO
(THINKING MORE CLEARLY NOW--AN UNSTRUNG FURY 463 DYNAMO
RISING WITHIN HIM)
WHEN I READ THEM I REALIZED THAT AMELIA HAD BEEN 465 DYNAMO
THINKING OF YOU ALL THE TIME.
REUBEN STARES BEFORE HIM, THINKING EXCITEDLY) 466 DYNAMO
(THEN AN IDEA COMES TO HIM--THINKING) 467 DYNAMO
THEN CHECKS HIMSELF, THINKING REMORSEFULLY) 468 DYNAMO
THEN SOMETHING HAS TO WAKE YOU UP--AND START YOU 469 DYNAMO
THINKING AGAIN.
WHAT IS IT YOU'RE THINKING ABOUT$ 469 DYNAMO
AND I WANT TO KEEP ON THINKING... 472 DYNAMO
(THINKING EXASPERATEDLY) (THAT DAMNED RUBE/... 478 DYNAMO
(THEN THINKING WITH SUDDEN FEAR AND DOUBT) 478 DYNAMO
AYE, A JELLYFISH, I'M THINKING$ 479 DYNAMO
(THINKING WITH UNNATURAL EXCITEMENT) 480 DYNAMO
(THIS PUTS A SUDDEN IDEA INTO HIS HEAD--THINKING 481 DYNAMO
EXCITEDLY.)
(THINKING FRIGHTENEDLY) (FOR GOD'S SAKE, WHAT'S 482 DYNAMO
COME OVER HIM...
(REMAINS STANDING BELOW--THINKING CONFUSEDLY) 485 DYNAMO
(THINKING TORTUREDLY) (MOTHER/... 487 DYNAMO
(THEN THINKING WITH AN ANGUISHED APPEAL) 488 DYNAMO
(THEN THINKING HE HAS AT LAST HIT ON THE CAUSE 23 ELECTR
I WAS ONLY THINKING--OF YOUR BLESSED ISLES. 24 ELECTR
I WAS THINKING OF HIM/ 32 ELECTR
I KNOW YOU'RE THINKING ALREADY HOW YOU CAN FOOL ME 34 ELECTR
I WAS AFRAID THAT MIGHT START HER THINKING. 36 ELECTR
(SLOWLY) I WAS THINKING--PERHAPS WE HAD BETTER GO 37 ELECTR
TO THE SITTING-ROOM.
IF YOU STOPPED THINKING OF YOUR REVENGE FOR A 38 ELECTR
MOMENT AND THOUGHT OF ME/
SOMETHING I'VE BEEN THINKING OF EVER SINCE I 40 ELECTR
REALIZED HE MIGHT SOON COME HOME.
IT WAS SEEING DEATH ALL THE TIME IN THIS WAY GOT 53 ELECTR
ME TO THINKING THESE THINGS.
THAT'S ALWAYS BEEN THE MANNONS' WAY OF THINKING. 54 ELECTR
I'VE BEEN THINKING OF WHAT WE COULD DO TO GET BACK 55 ELECTR
TO EACH OTHER.
ABLE ONLY TO KEEP MY MIND FROM THINKING OF WHAT 55 ELECTR
I'D LOST/
I'VE BEEN LYING HERE THINKING. 58 ELECTR
I TORE MY INSIDES OUT FOR YOU--THINKING YOU'D 61 ELECTR
UNDERSTAND/
OH, I KNOW WHAT YOU'RE THINKING/ 75 ELECTR
WHAT ARE YOU THINKING$ 77 ELECTR
WHEN ALL SHE IS THINKING OF RIGHT NOW IS HOW SHE 98 ELECTR
CAN USE YOU
I'VE BEEN THINKING OF YOU ALL THE WAY HOME AND 143 ELECTR
WONDERING--
THAT'S ALL I'M THINKING ABOUT, DEAR. 151 ELECTR
WERE YOU THINKING OF THAT WHEN WE WERE THERE$ 154 ELECTR
WHAT TERRIBLE THING HAVE YOU BEEN THINKING 165 ELECTR
LATELY--BEHIND ALL YOUR CRAZY TALK$
(EAGERLY AND PLACATINGLY) JUST WHAT I'VE BEEN 258 GGBROW
THINKING, MY DEAR.
BITTERLY) THINKING ONE WAS CREATING BEFORE ONE 271 GGBROW
DISCOVERED ONE COULDN'T/
FOR THE DAY THAT WAS, WAS ENOUGH, FOR WE WAS FREE 213 HA APE
MEN--AND I'M THINKING 'TIS
FEEDING THE BLOODY FURNACE--FEEDING OUR LIVES 214 HA APE
ALONG WID THE COAL, I'M THINKING--
I'LL BE SITTIN' HERE AT ME EASE, AND DRINKING, AND217 HA APE
THINKING,
SHE'LL BE IN BED NOW, I'M THINKING, 232 HA APE

THINKING (CONT'D.)

HE IS NOT THINKING. 7 HUGHIE
HE IS THINKING... 17 HUGHIE
RESIGNED COMES NEARER, AS IF EACH WAS GIVIN' THE 24 HUGHIE
OTHER A BREAK BY THINKING.
I WAS THINKING, I'D RATHER BE SHOT. 25 HUGHIE
YOU'RE TOO BUSY THINKING UP WAYS TO CHEAT ME, 582 ICEMAN
(LOOKING AWAY) OH, I KNOW YOU'RE THINKING, THIS 587 ICEMAN
GUY HAS A HELL OF A NERVE.
THINKING EVERY GUY YOU SEE MIGHT BE A DICK. 587 ICEMAN
GUSH, THINKING OF THE OLD TICKET WAGON BRINGS 609 ICEMAN
THOSE DAYS BACK.
I'VE BEEN THINKING ABOUT YOU EVER SINCE I LEFT THE621 ICEMAN
HOUSE--
THINKING ABOUT ALL OF YOU. 622 ICEMAN
CONSIDERING IT'S A HELL OF A WAYS, AND I SAT IN 622 ICEMAN
THE PARK FOR A WHILE THINKING.
THINKING TO YOURSELVES, THE OLD, LYING, PIPE- 660 ICEMAN
DREAMING FAKER,
I DON'T KNOW WHY, BUT IT STARTED ME THINKING ABOUT666 ICEMAN
MOTHER--
BEEN THINKING THINGS OVER. 675 ICEMAN
CAN'T HELP THINKING THE LAST TIME I WENT OUT WAS 688 ICEMAN
TO BESSIE'S FUNERAL.
I GUESS HE GOT LOOKING AT THE FIRE ESCAPE AND 700 ICEMAN
THINKING HOW HANDY IT WAS,
THINKING OF WHAT HE MUST HAVE DONE HAS GOT ME SO I701 ICEMAN
DON'T KNOW ANY MORE WHAT I
HE'S BEEN THINKING OF ME, TOO, ROCKY. 701 ICEMAN
AND MOP UP A COUPLE OF BEERS, THINKING I WAS A 709 ICEMAN
HELL-ON-WHEELS SPORT.
THINKING OF ALL THE WRONG I'D DONE TO THE SWEETEST714 ICEMAN
WOMAN IN THE WORLD
I'D GET THINKING HOW PEACEFUL IT WAS HERE, SITTING715 ICEMAN
AROUND WITH THE OLD GANG,
I WAS ONLY THINKING HOW WELL YOU LOOK. 20 JOURNE
HIS QUIETNESS FOOLS PEOPLE INTO THINKING THEY CAN 35 JOURNE
DO WHAT THEY LIKE WITH HIM.
I COULDN'T SLEEP BECAUSE I WAS THINKING ABOUT YOU. 47 JOURNE
I WAS THINKING OF THAT LITTLE THING. 54 JOURNE
I KNOW THE GAME BACKWARDS AND I'VE BEEN THINKING 57 JOURNE
ALL MORNING OF THE WAY SHE
I KNOW YOU CAN'T HELP THINKING IT'S A HOME. 75 JOURNE
YOU SUSPECT RIGHT NOW I'M THINKING TO MYSELF THAT 163 JOURNE
PAPA IS OLD AND CAN'T LAST
ARE YOU, TOO, THINKING IN TERMS OF TIME, OLD FOOL 360 LAZARU
SO SOON TO RE-ENTER INFINITY$
(DERISIVELY.) AH, YOU ARE THINKING OF THE SIMON 3 MANSNS
THAT WAS, YOUR SIMON--
BUT I WAS THINKING MOST OF YOUR GRANDCHILDREN-- 39 MANSNS
I AM THINKING OF FATHER'S COMPANY, NOT OF YOU-- 71 MANSNS
(THINKING.) THEY DO NOT SIT TOGETHER ON THE SOFA 118 MANSNS
AS HAS BEEN THEIR WONT--
(REASSURING HERSELF--THINKING.) 118 MANSNS
(THINKING.) YOU'D THINK TAKING THE CHILDREN AWAY 118 MANSNS
MEANT NOTHING TO HER--
(THINKING.) IN THE GARDEN, AT THE END, I WAS SO 118 MANSNS
SURE OF HIM--BUT--
(THINKING.) SHE IS ONLY PRETENDING TO WORK ON HER118 MANSNS
NEEDLE-POINT--
(THINKING.) THIS IS STUPID/ 119 MANSNS
(THINKING--FROWNING.) I CONTROL THE GAME NOW AND 119 MANSNS
CAN HAVE IT PLAYED AS I WISH--
(HAS STOPPED SEWING--THINKING.) 119 MANSNS
(THINKING.) HE ISN'T READING--JUST PRETENDING 119 MANSNS
TO--SMILING TO HIMSELF--SLY--
(THINKING.) WHAT IS HE THINKING, I WONDERS 119 MANSNS
(THINKING.) I KNOW THAT SMILE--WHEN HE'S MANAGED 119 MANSNS
A FOXY DEAL FOR THE COMPANY--
(THINKING-- 120 MANSNS
(THINKING--REGRETFULLY.) I HAVE GROWN TO LEAN 120 MANSNS
UPON HER HEALTH AND STRENGTH--
HE SITTING ALONE, THINKING OUT SCHEMES FOR HIS 120 MANSNS
COMPANY--NOT BOTHERING US--
(HAS STOPPED READING--THINKING.) 120 MANSNS
WE WOULD LAUGH TOGETHER, THINKING OF THE 120 MANSNS
CHILDREN--
(THINKING.) WHAT THE DEVIL POSSESSED ME TO ASK 120 MANSNS
SARA TO COME TO THE OFFICE$
(THINKING--UNEASILY.) PERHAPS I SHOULD HAVE 120 MANSNS
WAITED.
(THINKING--RESENTFULLY.) BY THAT LIE I'VE PUT 121 MANSNS
MOTHER BACK IN MY MIND--
I WAS THINKING OF MOTHER, AS IT HAPPENS. 121 MANSNS
(THINKING.) 121 MANSNS
(THINKING.) HIS PROPOSAL TO VISIT ME EACH 121 MANSNS
EVENING--
(THINKING--RESENTFULLY.) HE LIED--HE SAID THAT TO121 MANSNS
HURT HER--
I WAS THINKING OF SARA. 122 MANSNS
THAT IS STRANGE. I WAS THINKING OF HER, TOO. 122 MANSNS
SHE CAN'T READ--SHE'S THINKING HOW SHE'LL MISS THE122 MANSNS
CHILDREN--ALONE ALL DAY--
(THINKING.) SHE HAD BEGUN TO LOOK UPON ME AS A 122 MANSNS
SECOND MOTHER--
(THINKING.) I'M NOT A THOUGHT HE MOVES AROUND IN 122 MANSNS
HIS MIND TO SUIT HIS PLEASURE--
(THINKING--RESENTFULLY.) POOR WOMAN/ 122 MANSNS
(THINKING--WITH CONTEMPTUOUS RELIEF.) 123 MANSNS
(THINKING.) IF SHE'D SIT WITH ME HERE AS ON OTHER123 MANSNS
NIGHTS--
(THINKING--WITH A TENSE DREAD.) 125 MANSNS
HE GOES ON THINKING WITH INCREASING DREAD.) 126 MANSNS
(THINKING--WITH A MINGLING OF FASCINATED DREAD AND129 MANSNS
AN ANGUISHED YEARNING.)
WHAT ARE YOU THINKING, DAUGHTER$ 136 MANSNS
(THINKING.) THEN MY DARLING WILL HAVE ONLY ME/ 137 MANSNS

THINKING

(CONT'D.)
(THINKING.) THEN MY BELOVED SON WILL HAVE NO ONE 137 MANSNS
BUT ME/
(HE STARES AROUND HIM, THINKING AND FROWNING, 145 MANSNS
OF COURSE YOU ARE RIGHT IN THINKING THERE IS 156 MANSNS
CONSTANT DANGER--
I MUST STOP THINKING-- 163 MANSNS
AS IF I DID NOT ONCE THINK EXACTLY AS YOU HAVE 181 MANSNS
BEEN THINKING.
I HATE IDLENESS WHERE THERE'S NOTHING TO OCCUPY 398 MARCOM
YOUR MIND BUT THINKING.
(WITH A FORCED LAUGH, THINKING SHE IS JOKING) 411 MARCOM
AND ALL THE TWENTY-ODD YEARS I KEPT THINKING OF 430 MARCOM
YOU.
THE NEXT MOMENT I WAS ON THE FLOOR THINKING A MULE 18 MISBEG
HAD KICKED ME.
I'LL KEEP THINKING IT OVER, AND YOU DO THE SAME. 30 MISBEG
WELL, AND ME THINKING ALL ALONG IT WAS YOUR 45 MISBEG
HEAD.
(KIDDINGLY) JUST WHAT I'VE BEEN THINKING FOR SOME 54 MISBEG
TIME, JOSIE.
THINKING IT'S THE CUTEST JOKE IN THE WORLD, THE 83 MISBEG
FOOLS HE'S MADE OF US.
BUT I WAS THINKING HOW DO I KNOW WHAT I WOULDN'T 86 MISBEG
DO FOR FIVE THOUSAND CASH.
THINKING YOU'RE A VIRGINS 92 MISBEG
THEN IT'S MIKE'S SECOND SCHEME YOU'RE THINKING 92 MISBEG
ABOUT!
IT'S THE ESTATE MONEY YOU'RE THINKING OF, ISN'T 94 MISBEG
IT.
THINKING YOU DON'T KNOW WHAT HE'S DONE TO US THIS 98 MISBEG
NIGHT.
YOU'D BE APOLOGIZING TO ME, NOT THINKING OF HIM. 101 MISBEG
(GOES ON WITHOUT REAL INTEREST, TALKING TO KEEP 132 MISBEG
FROM THINKING)
FORGIVE MY SELFISHNESS, THINKING ONLY OF MYSELF. 142 MISBEG
I'M NOT THINKING OF THAT, AND WELL YOU KNOW IT. 159 MISBEG
THINKING YOU'D USE ME TO GET YOUR DIRTY GREASY 162 MISBEG
PAWS ON THE MONEY HE'LL HAVE/
I WAS THINKING AFTER 175 MISBEG
(WITH A CHUCKLE.) YOU KEPT THINKING ABOUT HIS 11 POET
INSULTS AFTER HE'D GONE OUT.
(THINKING THIS OVER FOR A MOMENT.) 14 POET
BUT--WELL, THERE'S NO USE THINKING OF IT NOW-- 19 POET
I KNOW WHAT YOU'RE THINKING/ 36 POET
LOWERING HER VOICE UNCONSCIOUSLY AS IF SHE WERE 81 POET
THINKING ALOUD TO HERSELF.)
SHE STANDS THINKING, HER EXPRESSION PUZZLED, 87 POET
APPREHENSIVE, AND RESENTFUL.
HE'D BEEN THINKING AND HE'D AN OFFER FROM AN OLD 146 POET
COLLEGE FRIEND WHO'D INHERITED
MERCIFUL GOD, WHAT AM I THINKING! 162 POET
THINKING OF MOTHER... 6 STRANG
SHE SAID SHE WANTED TO FINISH THINKING SOMETHING 7 STRANG
OUT--
(HE SIGHS--THINKING WITH A TRACE OF GUILTY ALARM) 7 STRANG
(THINKING FRIGHTENEDLY) 8 STRANG
(THINKING PITYINGLY) (WANDERING FROM ROOM TO 8 STRANG
ROOM--
(THINKING) ((THE MORNING NEWS OF GORDON'S DEATH 8 STRANG
CAME...
(THINKING, OBLIVIOUS TO THIS REMARK) 8 STRANG
(WATCHING HIM--THINKING WITH A CONDESCENDING 9 STRANG
AFFECTION)
(THINKING RESENTFULLY) 9 STRANG
(THINKING CYNICALLY) ((A SHREWD MOVE/... 10 STRANG
(THINKING IRONICALLY) ((TRUSTED TO HIS HONOR 11 STRANG
AGAIN...
(THINKING WITH A STRIDENT ACCUSATION) 11 STRANG
(THINKING) ((THE SQUARE THING/... 11 STRANG
(THINKING CYNICALLY) ((AS ALWAYS IN ALL MINDS... 11 STRANG
(THINKING WORRIEDLY) ((I HOPE SHE WON'T MAKE A 12 STRANG
SCENE...
(THINKING SELF-MOCKINGLY BUT A BIT WORRIED ABOUT 12 STRANG
HIMSELF)
(THINKING DISTRACTEDLY) (WHAT DOES SHE MEANS... 13 STRANG
(THINKING DISTRACTEDLY) ((THAT LOOK IN HER 13 STRANG
EYES/...
(THINKING WEARILY) ((WHAT HAS CHARLIE DONE8... 13 STRANG
(TROUBLED--THINKING) ((SHE HAS CHANGED... 13 STRANG
(THINKING) ((WHAT IS SHE THINKING8... 14 STRANG
THINKING OF ME, SCRIBBLING IN PRESS BUREAU... 14 STRANG
(THINKING BITTERLY) ((A TAUNT... 14 STRANG
(THINKING TORTUREDLY) ((COLD LIPS... 14 STRANG
(THINKING WEARILY) ((THE FATHERS LAUGH AT LITTLE 14 STRANG
DAUGHTER NINA...
(THINKING WITH WEARY SCORN) 15 STRANG
(THINKING--TERRIFIED) ((GOING8... 15 STRANG
(THINKING--TERRIFIED) ((I MUST TALK HER OUT OF 15 STRANG
IT/...
(LOOKING AT NINA--THINKING WITH ALARM) 15 STRANG
(THINKING WITH WEARY RELIEF) 15 STRANG
(THINKING WITH ALARM) ((WHAT'S THIS8... 15 STRANG
(THINKING ANGRILY) ((HER EYES... 16 STRANG
(THINKING TORTUREDLY) ((GORDON DARLING, 16 STRANG
(THINKING) ((TALKING/... 16 STRANG
YOUR DEGREE BEFORE YOU ATTEMPT--(THINKING 17 STRANG
DESPERATELY) ((NO USE/...
THINKING OF GORDON... 17 STRANG
(THINKING DESPERATELY) ((I MUST KEEP CALM... 17 STRANG
(THINKING FURIOUSLY) ((GORDON'S FRIEND... 17 STRANG
(THINKING WITH INDIGNANT REVULSION) 17 STRANG
(THINKING DESPERATELY) ((I'M BEGINNING TO TELL 18 STRANG
HIM/...
(THINKING SAVAGELY) ((I HOPE GORDON IS IN 18 STRANG
HELL/...))
(THINKING) ((GIVE HERSELF8... 18 STRANG
(THINKING--FURIOUSLY) ((WHAT AN ANIMAL/... 19 STRANG

THINKING (CONT'D.)
(THINKING WITH NERVOUS REPULSION) 20 STRANG
(THINKING IN AGONY) ((GOD DAMN IN HELL... 21 STRANG
(THINKING TIMIDLY) ((IN SHORT, 21 STRANG
(THINKING) ((NINA HAS CHANGED... 21 STRANG
(SHE PAUSES AND LOOKS ABOUT THE ROOM--THINKING 27 STRANG
CONFUSEDLY)
(THINKING WOUNDEDLY) ((I HOPED SHE WOULD THROW 27 STRANG
HERSELF IN MY ARMS...
(THINKING BITTERLY) 30 STRANG
(THINKING CYNICALLY) ((THIS GORDON WORSHIPPER 30 STRANG
MUST BE THE APPLE OF NINA'S
(THINKING GLUMLY) ((WON'T TELL HIM I TRIED FOR 30 STRANG
FLYING SERVICE...
(AGITATED--THINKING SUSPICIOUSLY) 31 STRANG
(THINKING) 31 STRANG
(THINKING) ((HE CERTAINLY SEEMS ALL FOR ME... 31 STRANG
((IN A SORT OF PANIC--THINKING) 32 STRANG
(THINKING--AT FIRST WITH A GRUDGING APPRECIATION 33 STRANG
AND ENVY)
(THINKING SNEERINGLY) ((AMUSING, THESE YOUNG 33 STRANG
DOCTORS8...
(THINKING) ((HOW MUCH NEED I TELL HIM8... 35 STRANG
(THINKING SUSPICIOUSLY) ((HE DOESN'T WANT HER 36 STRANG
BACK.
(THINKING) ((WHAT DOES HE MEANS... 36 STRANG
(THINKING--THINKING) 36 STRANG
(THINKING) ((WHAT DOES HE MEANS... 36 STRANG
(IRONICALLY--THINKING) 36 STRANG
(HE MAKES A SILLY GESTURE TOWARD THE DOOR-- 37 STRANG
THINKING CONFUSEDLY)
(THINKING IN AGONY) ((FRIGHTENED8... 37 STRANG
(THINKING SUSPICIOUSLY) ((IS THIS DOCTOR HER 38 STRANG
LOVER8...
(THINKING CYNICALLY) ((NOT TO MENTION THE LIVING 39 STRANG
WHO HAVE HAD HER)...
(THINKING BAFFLEDELY) ((WRONG AGAIN/... 39 STRANG
(THINKING FRIGHTENEDLY) ((HOW TERRIBLE SHE IS/... 40 STRANG
(THINKING TREMBLINGLY) ((HERE.... 42 STRANG
(THINKING--IN A PANIC) ((I DON'T WANT TO BE ALONE 42 STRANG
WITH HER/...
(ANSWERING HIS LOOK--THINKING) 42 STRANG
(THINKING IN A PANIC) ((SHE SNEAKED INTO MY SOUL 42 STRANG
TO SPY/...))
(THINKING INTENSELY) ((IF I LOVE HER/... 44 STRANG
(THINKING WITH WILD AGONY) ((DEAR OLD CHARLIE/... 44 STRANG
(THINKING WITH SUDDEN AGONY) 44 STRANG
(THINKING WITH BITTER CONFUSION) 45 STRANG
(THINKING IN AGONY) ((BUT WHY8... 45 STRANG
(LOOKING UP FROM THE LETTER, THINKING 49 STRANG
EMBARRASSEDLY)
(THINKING AMUSEDLY) ((IF HE KNEW WHAT I'D JUST 50 STRANG
WRITTEN...
(THINKING GLUMLY) ((I THOUGHT SHE'D FORGOTTEN 51 STRANG
HIM...
(THINKING WITH A TRACE OF PITYING CONTEMPT) 51 STRANG
(THINKING WORRIEDLY) ((SLIPPING BACK INTO THAT 51 STRANG
MORBID TONE...
(SHE DISAPPEARS INTO THE KITCHEN--THINKING WITH 52 STRANG
BITTER PAIN)
THAT'S JUST WHAT I WAS THINKING ABOUT-- 54 STRANG
(THINKING APPREHENSIVELY) ((I DO HOPE I'M 54 STRANG
WRONG/...
(THINKING WITH INTENSE LONGING) 55 STRANG
(THINKING WITH GRIM RELIEF) ((HE DON'T KNOW... 55 STRANG
(THINKING APPREHENSIVELY) 56 STRANG
(THINKING FRIGHTENEDLY) ((WHAT IS BEHIND WHAT 57 STRANG
SHE'S SAYING8...
(THINKING IN AN AGONY OF APPREHENSION) 57 STRANG
(THINKING) ((HOW HER FACE CHANGES8/... 57 STRANG
(THINKING FIERCELY--EVEN WITH SATISFACTION) 58 STRANG
(THINKING FIERCELY) ((NOW'S MY CHANCE/...)) 58 STRANG
((TONELESSLY)
(THINKING WITH TERRIFIED FOREBODING) 58 STRANG
(THINKING) ((I KNOW WHAT SHE'S DOING NOW... 59 STRANG
(WHO HAS BEEN LISTENING DISTRACTEDLY--THINKING) 59 STRANG
THINKING ANY MINUTE THE CURSE MIGHT GET HIM, EVERY 60 STRANG
TIME HE WAS SICK,
(THINKING STRANGELY) 62 STRANG
(THEN THINKING CONSCIENCE-STRICKENLY) 62 STRANG
(THINKING MISERABLY) ((NOW SHE KNOWS MY 63 STRANG
SUFFERING...
(THINKING LONGINGLY) 64 STRANG
(THINKING TORMENTEDLY) 67 STRANG
(STARING OUT OVER HIS HEAD--WITH LOVING PITY, 70 STRANG
THINKING)
(STARES AT HIM, MORE ANNOYED, HER EYES HARDENING, 70 STRANG
THINKING)
(THINKING SADLY) ((I PROMISED HER... 71 STRANG
(THINKING FRIGHTENEDLY) ((THAT DULL PAIN SHE 73 STRANG
COMPLAINS OF...
(THINKING VINDICTIVELY) ((SERVE HER RIGHT, THE 73 STRANG
OLD SCANDAL-MONGER,
(ANNOYED IN HIS TURN--THINKING) 74 STRANG
TO HAVE SUCH THOUGHTS WHEN MOTHER IS SICK AND I 75 STRANG
OUGHT TO BE THINKING ONLY OF
(WATCHING HIM--THINKING) ((NEAT, 76 STRANG
(THINKING RESENTFULLY) ((WHAT A BOOR/... 76 STRANG
THINKING GRIMLY) 77 STRANG
THINKING ABOUT MARSDEN) 78 STRANG
WAS I WRONG IN THINKING HE HAD STUFF IN HIM8... 78 STRANG
(THINKING ADMIRINGLY) ((WONDERFUL-LOOKING AS 79 STRANG
EVER...
(THINKING) ((STRONG HANDS LIKE GORDON'S... 79 STRANG
WHEN WHAT I WAS REALLY THINKING WAS WHAT FINE EYES 80 STRANG
YOU HAD,
(THINKING CAUSTICALLY) ((GORDON MYTH STRONG AS 80 STRANG
EVER...
(THINKING WITH A CERTAIN SATISFACTION) 80 STRANG
(AFTER A QUICK, KEEN GLANCE, THINKING) 81 STRANG

THINKING

THINKING (CONT'D.)
(CAUSTICALLY THINKING) 81 STRANG
(THINKING DISAPPOINTEDLY AND ASHAMED OF HIMSELF FOR BEING DISAPPOINTED) 82 STRANG
(THINKING WITH THE SAME EAGERNESS TO BELIEVE SOMETHING HE HOPES) 82 STRANG
(THINKING IN A REAL PANIC OF HORROR-- 83 STRANG
(INSTANTLY REPELLED--THINKING WITH SCORNFUL JEALOUSY) 83 STRANG
(BEWILDEREDLY THINKING) ((THAT LOOK IN HER EYES.... 84 STRANG
(THINKING CONFUSEDLY) ((WHAT DO I HAVE TO DO)... 84 STRANG
(THINKING STRANGELY) ((THAT LOOK IN HIS EYES... 84 STRANG
(THINKING) ((I HAVE A FRIEND WHO HAS A WIFE... 85 STRANG
(THINKING) ((LET ME SEE... 85 STRANG
WHAT DAMNED ROT I'M THINKING/...)) 85 STRANG
BUT THIS NEEDS A LOT OF THINKING OVER. 85 STRANG
(THINKING AS BEFORE) ((THIS DOCTOR IS NOTHING TO ME BUT A HEALTHY MALE... 85 STRANG
(WORRIEDLY THINKING) ((HAVE I EVER BEEN HAPPY)... 86 STRANG
(THINKING DETERMINEDLY) ((I MUST HAVE MY BABY/...)) ((TIMIDLY-- 86 STRANG
(ANXIOUSLY THINKING) ((AM I RIGHT TO ADVISE THIS)... 86 STRANG
(THINKING GUILTILY AND INSTINCTIVELY MOVING AWAY FROM HER) 87 STRANG
(THINKING FRIGHTENEDLY) ((WHO IS TALKING)... 87 STRANG
(THINKING FRIGHTENEDLY) ((WHOSE HAND IS THIS)... 87 STRANG
(THINKING) ((DOES HE)... 88 STRANG
(THINKING FRIGHTENEDLY) ((WHAT'S THAT SHE SAID)... 88 STRANG
(THINKING FRIGHTENEDLY) ((DID SHE SAY NED)... 88 STRANG
(RAISING HER HEAD--THINKING--PROUDLY TRIUMPHANT) 89 STRANG
(THINKING--FIERCELY TRIUMPHANT) 89 STRANG
IT'S ONLY WHEN I START THINKING, I BEGIN TO DOUBT...)) 91 STRANG
(THINKING AS IF SHE FOUND IT HARD TO CONCENTRATE ON HIM, 93 STRANG
(THINKING IN AGONY) ((WHAT'S SHE THINKING)... 93 STRANG
(IMMEDIATELY TERRIFIED AND BEATEN--THINKING) 93 STRANG
(THINKING DESPONDENTLY) ((LATELY, SHE JUMPS ON ME 96 STRANG
EVERY CHANCE SHE GETS...
(THINKING GUILTILY) ((ONE MINUTE I FEEL ASHAMED OF HIM MAKING SUCH A FOOL OF 94 STRANG
(THINKING BITTERLY) ((SOMETIMES I ALMOST HATE HER/... 96 STRANG
(THINKING EXULTANTLY AT FIRST) 96 STRANG
(THINKING FRIGHTENEDLY) ((WHY DOESN'T HE TAKE ME IN HIS ARMS)... 96 STRANG
(THINKING PASSIONATELY, LOOKING AT HIM) 96 STRANG
(TURNS AWAY FROM HER--THINKING BITTERLY) 96 STRANG
THINKING TORTUREDLY) 97 STRANG
(FIGHTING HIMSELF--THINKING) 97 STRANG
(STRAINING UP TOWARD HIM--WITH INTENSE LONGING-- THINKING) 97 STRANG
((WHAT IS HE THINKING)... 97 STRANG
(THINKING WITH HELPLESS ANNOYANCE) 98 STRANG
(THINKING--IN A STRANGE SUPERSTITIOUS PANIC) 98 STRANG
THINKING SUSPICIOUSLY--MORBIDLY AGITATED) 99 STRANG
(THINKING--ANSWERING HER LOOK--DEFIANTLY) 99 STRANG
NINA LOOKS ACROSS HIM AT DARRELL--TRIUMPHANTLY-- THINKING) 99 STRANG
HE RAISES HIS HEAD AND HALF-PUSHES HER AWAY-- RESENTFULLY, THINKING) 99 STRANG
(HAS GOTTEN UP FROM HIS CHAIR--WITH RELIEF-- THINKING) 99 STRANG
I MUST STOP THINKING/... 100 STRANG
(IN A SUDDEN PANIC--THINKING) 101 STRANG
(SMILING TENDERLY--THINKING) 102 STRANG
THINKING UNEASILY) 102 STRANG
THINKING) 102 STRANG
(THINKING TENDERLY) ((LET HIS PRIDE PUT ALL THE BLAME ON ME/... 102 STRANG
(THINKING) ((HE IS JEALOUS OF GORDON/... 102 STRANG
(THINKING SUSPICIOUSLY) ((LOOK OUT/... 103 STRANG
THAT HIS THINKING OUR CHILD WAS HIS WOULD DO HIM ANY GOOD) 104 STRANG
(THINKING FASCINATEDLY) ((I SEE MY HAPPINESS IN HER EYES... 104 STRANG
(STRUGGLING--SHAKENLY) NO, I THINK I'D BETTER-- (THINKING DESPERATELY) 104 STRANG
(THINKING MISERABLY) 104 STRANG
(THINKING) ((HE MUST STAY... 105 STRANG
THINKING AS HE GOES) 106 STRANG
(BEWILDERED AND TERROR-STRICKEN, TRYING FEEBLY TO 107 STRANG
PUSH HIM AWAY--THINKING)
(THINKING DISJOINTEDLY) ((WHY DID I DOUBT MYSELF... 107 STRANG
(THINKING FRENZIEDLY) ((I WON'T BEAR IT/... 108 STRANG
(THINKING IN ANGUISH) ((NED DOESN'T LOVE ME/... 108 STRANG
(THINKING JUBILANTLY) 108 STRANG
THINKING IN ANGUISH) 108 STRANG
(THINKING IN ANGUISH) ((I CAN'T SAY THAT TO HIM/... 109 STRANG
(THINKING STRANGELY) ((LITTLE BOY/... 109 STRANG
(THINKING) ((SHE'S NEVER CALLED ME SAMMY BEFORE... 109 STRANG
THINKING AS IF SHE WERE REPEATING THE WORDS OF SOME INNER VOICE OF LIFE) 109 STRANG
(THINKING) ((I WONDER IF THERE'S A DRAFT IN THE BABY'S ROOM)... 111 STRANG
(THINKING) ((WHAT A CHANGE/.... 112 STRANG
(THINKING ANGRILY) ((SHE PICKS SOMEONE BEYOND THEI14 STRANG
AGE/....
THINKING SAVAGELY) 114 STRANG
(WINCING--THINKING) ((SHE CAN'T BELIEVE ANY WOMAN114 STRANG
COULD POSSIBLY LOVE ME/....))

THINKING (CONT'D.)
(THINKING--STUNG) ((HE'S THINKING OF THOSE MEN IN115 STRANG
THE HOSPITAL...
(STARTLED--THINKING FRIGHTENEDLY AND CONFUSEDLY) 115 STRANG
(STRUGGLING WITH HERSELF--THINKING PITIABLY) 116 STRANG
(LOOKING AT EVANS--CONTEMPTUOUSLY THINKING) 116 STRANG
(THINKING IN A QUEER STATE OF JEALOUS CONFUSION) 116 STRANG
(THINKING PROUDLY) ((I'M PROUD OF THAT... 116 STRANG
(THINKING--JEALOUSLY) ((THEN SHE DID LOVE HIM/... 116 STRANG
(THINKING--PROUDLY) ((THANK GOD FOR SAMMY/... 116 STRANG
(FRIGHTENEDLY--THINKING) ((WHAT DOES HE MEAN)... 117 STRANG
(THINKING--TORMENTEDLY) ((THE THOUGHT OF THAT WOMAN/... 117 STRANG
(SCORNFULLY ASHAMED OF HIMSELF--THINKING) 117 STRANG
(THINKING) ((HE HAS FORGOTTEN ME... 118 STRANG
(THINKING--LONGINGLY) ((COME BACK)... 118 STRANG
(SHE GLANCES AT MARSDEN, THINKING CALCULATINGLY. 118 STRANG
(JOYFULLY--THINKING) ((NED ASKED ABOUT MY BABY/.... 118 STRANG
(THINKING SHAMEFACEDLY) ((WHY HAVE I BEEN TRYING 118 STRANG
TO HURT HER)...
(THINKING--CRUELLY) ((PAH/.... 119 STRANG
(THINKING EXCITEDLY) ((I ALMOST CONFESSED I LOVED119 STRANG
HER/....
(THINKING) ((IT'S TRUE, TOD/... 119 STRANG
(WITH A SORT OF PITY--THINKING) 120 STRANG
(THINKING STRANGELY) ((NOT TO BE AFRAID OF ONE'S 121 STRANG
SHADOW/...
(THINKING--SATISFIED) 122 STRANG
(THINKING SUSPICIOUSLY) ((DOES HE ACTUALLY 122 STRANG
IMAGINE I...
(THINKING--CAUTIOUSLY) 124 STRANG
(THINKING DISJOINTEDLY) ((HERE AGAIN/... 124 STRANG
(THINKING) ((HE HAS TWO BROTHERS... 125 STRANG
THINKING A FIERCE QUESTION) 125 STRANG
(HEARING HER COMING--IN A PANIC--THINKING) 125 STRANG
(THINKING-- 125 STRANG
(THINKING WITH TRIUMPHANT HAPPINESS) 126 STRANG
(THINKING--MORE AND MORE AT SEA) 126 STRANG
(WHO IS WATCHING THEM KEENLY--THINKING) 126 STRANG
(THINKING IN A PANIC) ((THAT TONE/... 126 STRANG
(THINKING TRIUMPHANTLY--WITH A CERTAIN CRUELTY) 126 STRANG
(THINKING WITH ALARM NOW) ((SHE'S CHANGED/... 126 STRANG
(WINCING--THINKING) ((THAT HURTS... 127 STRANG
(THINKING--TRIUMPHANTLY MOCKING) 127 STRANG
OH, I DON'T REMEMBER--((THINKING APPREHENSIVELY WITH A BITTER RESENTMENT) 127 STRANG
YES (THINKING) 128 STRANG
(PUZZLED AND IRRITATED--THINKING CONFUSEDLY) 128 STRANG
(THINKING) 128 STRANG
(THINKING--WORRIEDLY) ((WHAT'S CHARLIE TALKING ABOUT)... 128 STRANG
(THINKING--WITH A SAD BITTER IRONY) 128 STRANG
(SMILINGLY GETS TO HIS FEET--THINKING) 129 STRANG
(THINKING WITH A STRANGE CALCULATION) 129 STRANG
(THINKING--WITH HORRIFIED CONFUSION) 129 STRANG
WHAT IS HE THINKING).... 129 STRANG
(THINKING ABJECTLY) ((I COULDN'T... 133 STRANG
THINKING MISERABLY) 133 STRANG
(GLANCING FURTIVELY OVER HIS SHOULDER AT NINA-- BROODINGLY THINKING) 134 STRANG
(THEN IN A STRANGE OBJECTIVE TONE--THINKING) 134 STRANG
(THINKING AS HE PLAYS--RESENTFULLY) 138 STRANG
OUR LOVE HAS BECOME THE INTIMATE THINKING TOGETHER139 STRANG
(WATCHING NINA--SADLY) ((ALWAYS THINKING OF HER 139 STRANG
SON)...
(THINKING--WITH AN APATHETIC BITTERNESS) 139 STRANG
WE SIT TOGETHER IN SILENCE, THINKING... 139 STRANG
((WHAT IS SHE THINKING)... 139 STRANG
(STOPS PLAYING TO LISTEN--THINKING) 140 STRANG
(SADLY--THINKING) ((TO ROT AWAY IN PEACE... 140 STRANG
(THINKING RESENTFULLY) ((HE'S ALWAYS MAKING FUN 141 STRANG
OF MY FATHER)...
(THINKING) ((HE'S TALKING ABOUT ME... 141 STRANG
(THINKING CYNICALLY) ((SHE EXPECTS ME TO LOVE THE141 STRANG
CHILD SHE DELIBERATELY TOOK
(THINKING CONTEMPTUOUSLY) ((BOY OF HIS)... 141 STRANG
(THINKING ANGRILY) 142 STRANG
(THINKING REMORSEFULLY) ((IS THIS MY FAULT)... 142 STRANG
(THINKING VINDICTIVELY) 142 STRANG
(THINKING BITTERLY) ((SAM'S/... 143 STRANG
(THINKING WITH A STRANGE TORTURED SHAME) 145 STRANG
(SUDDENLY STRUCK--THINKING) ((WHY, HE'S JEALOUS 146 STRANG
OF GORDON LIKING CHARLIE/...))
(THINKING TRIUMPHANTLY) ((HE'S TRYING TO INSULT 147 STRANG
ME...
(THINKING WITH SCORNFUL PITY) 147 STRANG
(THINKING IRRITABLY) ((NED'S GETTING HATEFUL AGAIN/... 147 STRANG
(THINKING RESENTFULLY) ((IS SHE TRYING TO HUMILIATE ME BEFORE HIM)... 147 STRANG
(CONFUSEDLY) YES--DECIDEDLY--BUT HARDLY IN MY 148 STRANG
LINE--(THINKING IN ANGUISH--
(THINKING IN ANGUISH) ((DAMNED COWARD AND WEAKLING/)) 148 STRANG
(LOOKING AT HIM--PITYING--THINKING) 148 STRANG
(PASSIONATELY--THINKING) ((MY LOVE IS FINER THAN 148 STRANG
ANY SHE HAS KNOWN/...
(THINKING DULLY) ((I MUSTN'T STAY TO LUNCH... 149 STRANG
(THINKING WITH ANGRY ANGUISH) 150 STRANG
(IMMEDIATELY REALIZING WHAT IS COMING--THINKING WITH SOMBER ANGUISH) 150 STRANG
(THINKING--TERRIFIED TURN) ((WHY DO I LIKE HIM NOW)... 151 STRANG
(THINKING--GOOD-NATUREDLY SUPERIOR) 152 STRANG
(THINKING CONFUSEDLY) ((WHY DID I CALL HIM THAT 152 STRANG
WHEN I SAID I NEVER WOULD).

THINKING

THINKING (CONT'D.)
(THINKING) (I'LL YELL THE TRUTH INTO YOUR EARS 152 STRANG
IF I STAY A SECOND LONGER...
(THINKING) (I HOPE HE NEVER COMES BACK/... 152 STRANG
(WRITING--THINKING) (IT HURTS NOW/... 152 STRANG
(THINKING KEENLY) (THAT'S WHY DARRELL HATES ME 153 STRANG
BEING CALLED GORDON...
SHE COMES FORWARD SLOWLY--THINKING RESENTFULLY) 154 STRANG
(THINKING CONTEMPTUOUSLY) (NED IS WEAK...) 154 STRANG
(THEN APPREHENSIVELY)
(THINKING FRIGHTENEDLY) (WHY DOES HE ASK 154 STRANG
THAT...)
(THINKING PITYINGLY) (YOU POOR BOOBY/... 154 STRANG
(THINKING) (SHE MUST HAVE LOVED GORDON BETTER'N 154 STRANG
DAD EVEN/...))
(THEN CAUTIOUSLY THINKING) (SHE'S CHEATING... 155 STRANG
(MOVING A LITTLE NEARER--SEARCHING HER FACE-- 155 STRANG
THINKING)
(MOVING AWAY FROM HIS FATHER AGAIN--RESENTFULLY-- 155 STRANG
THINKING)
(THINKING TRIUMPHANTLY) (THAT'S RIGHT, SAM... 155 STRANG
(THINKING--OVERJOYED) (THEN/... 155 STRANG
THINKING) 156 STRANG
(TRIUMPHANTLY THINKING) (THAT MAKES UP FOR HIS 156 STRANG
KISS/...
(SHE'S THINKING ABOUT THAT DARRELL NOW/... 156 STRANG
(THINKING FRIGHTENEDLY) 157 STRANG
(THINKING WITH A LOOK OF INTENSE HATRED) 157 STRANG
(WITHOUT LOWERING THE GLASSES FROM HER EYES-- 160 STRANG
THINKING GOOD-NATUREDLY)
(THINKING WITH INTENSE BITTERNESS) 160 STRANG
(THINKING--BITTERLY) 160 STRANG
(LOOKING BACK AT NINA RESENTFULLY--THINKING) 160 STRANG
(THINKING IRRITABLY) (NINA IN THE DUMPS/... 161 STRANG
(EXAMINING NINA CRITICALLY--THINKING) 161 STRANG
(KEENLY OBSERVANT--THINKING) 161 STRANG
(THINKING INTENSELY) (YOU VULGAR BOOR/... 161 STRANG
(VAGUELY IRRITATED--THINKING) 162 STRANG
(THINKING INDIFFERENTLY) (NED STILL FEELS 162 STRANG
JEALOUS...
(THINKING) (HE'S RIGHT... 162 STRANG
(THINKING--IMMEDIATELY) (OH, I DON'T MEAN 163 STRANG
THAT...
(INTENSELY--THINKING) (IF HE'D ONLY DIE/...) 163 STRANG
(RESTRAINING HIS ANGER WITH DIFFICULTY--THINKING) 163 STRANG
(THINKING INDIGNANTLY) 163 STRANG
(THINKING KEENLY) (THERE'S A DEATH WISH... 163 STRANG
(THINKING) (SHHH... 163 STRANG
(THEN AFTER A LOOK IN HER EYES--THINKING) 164 STRANG
(THINKING RESENTFULLY) (SHE TAKES A FINE DO-- 164 STRANG
THIS-LITTLE-GIRL TONE TOWARD
(THINKING CAUTIOUSLY) (I MUST KEEP VERY COOL AND165 STRANG
SENSIBLE OR HE WON'T HELP
(THINKING SADLY) (MY OLD LOVER... 165 STRANG
(THINKING WITH MELANCHOLY INTEREST) 165 STRANG
THINKING CAUTIOUSLY) 165 STRANG
(THINKING DESPERATELY) (I MUST MAKE HIM REMEMBER166 STRANG
GORDON IS HIS CHILD OR I CAN
(THINKING WITH BITTER SORROW) 166 STRANG
(THEN CONTROLLING HERSELF--THINKING CYNICALLY) 166 STRANG
(THINKING KEENLY) (HELLO/... 167 STRANG
(THINKING RESENTFULLY) (HE'S SNEERING AT HIS OWN167 STRANG
SON/...)
(THINKING WITH SATISFACTION) 167 STRANG
(STOPPING HERSELF--THINKING FRIGHTENEDLY) 167 STRANG
(THINKING CYNICALLY) (OH, SO YOU'LL COMPROMISE 168 STRANG
ON HIS SLEEPING WITH HER...
(THINKING WITH A SNEER) (#GORDON'S THIRD/# 168 STRANG
(IN CONFUSION--THINKING BITTERLY) 168 STRANG
THINKING) 169 STRANG
(THINKING WITH A STRANGE SHUDDER OF MINGLED 169 STRANG
ATTRACTION AND FEAR AS SHE TOUCHES
(STILL MORE DISTURBED--THINKING) 169 STRANG
(AUDIBLY) THINKING DOESN'T MATTER A DAMN/ 170 STRANG
THINKING THINGS/ 170 STRANG
(THINKING BITTERLY) (MADELINE'S GORDON/... 171 STRANG
(THINKING IN TERROR) 171 STRANG
(LOOKING UP THE RIVER--WITH VINDICTIVE 171 STRANG
BITTERNESS--THINKING)
(THINKING STRANGELY--STRUGGLING WITH HIMSELF) 172 STRANG
(THINKING--ALARMED) (WHAT IS SHE AFTER NOW--WHAT172 STRANG
DOES SHE WANT ME FOR$...)
(THINKING INTENSELY) (OH, I MUST MAKE HIM LOVE 172 STRANG
ME AGAIN...
(THINKING) (I'D LIKE TO SEE HIS FACE WHEN I TOLD173 STRANG
HIM HIS FAMOUS OARSMAN ISN'T
(THINKING--WEAKLY) (YES, IF IT HADN'T BEEN FOR 173 STRANG
SAM I WOULD HAVE BEEN HAPPY/...
(STRUGGLING WEAKLY--THINKING) 173 STRANG
(WITH DESPERATE RANCOR--THINKING) 173 STRANG
(THINKING) (AHA... 173 STRANG
(HE RAISES HIS GLASSES AND LOOKS UP THE RIVER-- 174 STRANG
THINKING EXULTANTLY)
(THINKING--DAZEDLY STILL, BUT IN A TUNE OF RELIEF)174 STRANG
THINKING WITH A DULL FATALISM) 174 STRANG
(THINKING DULLY) (SHE'LL TELL SAM... 175 STRANG
(THINKING FRIGHTENEDLY) (THE DEVIL/... 175 STRANG
(HOW I HATE HER/...) (THEN SUDDENLY WITH A 176 STRANG
DEADLY CALCULATION--THINKING)
(WITH BITTER HATRED--THINKING) 176 STRANG
(TURNS AROUND TO STARE AT HER--THINKING) 177 STRANG
(WITH A SMILE OF CRUEL TRIUMPH--THINKING) 177 STRANG
(THINKING) (WHY IS SHE CALLING MADELINE'S... 177 STRANG
(WHO HAS COME CLOSER--RESENTFULLY THINKING) 178 STRANG
(MOVES FROM THE RAIL TOWARD THEM--THINKING KEENLY)178 STRANG
(THINKING) (DAMN THAT DARRELL/... 179 STRANG
(GETTING UP--THINKING WITH A STRANGE, WILD 181 STRANG
PASSION)

THINKING (CONT'D.)
(STARES DOWN AT HIM STUPIDLY--THEN THINKING 182 STRANG
STRANGELY)
(STANDING ABOVE THEM--THINKING EXULTANTLY) 183 STRANG
(LOOKING DOWN AT HIM--THINKING YEARNINGLY) 183 STRANG
(THINKING) 185 STRANG
(THINKING WITH A SORT OF TENDER, LOVING SCORN FOR 186 STRANG
HIS BOYISH NAIVETE)
(THINKING IN AMAZEMENT, BUT NOT WITHOUT A QUEER 186 STRANG
SATISFACTION)
(SCANDALIZED AS AN OLD MAID--THINKING) 187 STRANG
(LOOKING AT THEM--GAILY MUCKING--THINKING) 187 STRANG
(THINKING WITH SNEERING PITY) 188 STRANG
(THINKING SUSPICIOUSLY) (WHAT A QUEER 188 STRANG
CREATURE/...
THINKING) 189 STRANG
THINKING RESENTFULLY) 189 STRANG
(THINKING RESIGNEDLY) 190 STRANG
(THINKING SADLY, LOOKING AT HIS BACK) 190 STRANG
(ALSO AFTER A QUICK KEEN GLANCE AT GORDON'S FACE--190 STRANG
THINKING)
THINKING BITTERLY) 190 STRANG
(GLANCING AT GORDON SEARCHINGLY--THINKING SADLY) 190 STRANG
(THINKING RESENTFULLY) (WHAT A TENDER TONE SHE 192 STRANG
TAKES TOWARD HIM/...
(THINKING TORTUREDLY) (BUT IT'S FOR SCIENCE/... 192 STRANG
(IN ANGUISH--THINKING) (HOW CAN GORDON INSULT 192 STRANG
POOR NED LIKE THAT/...
(THINKING BITTERLY) (EVEN IN DEATH SAM MAKES 192 STRANG
PEOPLE SUFFER...))
(THINKING FURIOUSLY) (IT'S WORSE... 192 STRANG
(THINKING HYSTERICALLY) (SPANKING/... 193 STRANG
(THINKING VINDICTIVELY) (I HOPE HE KNOWS THE 193 STRANG
TRUTH, FOR IF HE DOESN'T, BY GOD,
(THINKING--AT FIRST FRIGHTENEDLY) 193 STRANG
(STARING AT HIM STUPIDLY--THINKING) 194 STRANG
(LAUGHING HYSTERICALLY--THINKING) 194 STRANG
(THINKING IN DESPERATE HYSTERICAL ANGUISH) 194 STRANG
(THINKING SUFFERINGLY) (WHY DOES HE KEEP ON 195 STRANG
CALLING ME DARRELL...
(THINKING TORTUREDLY) (OH, HE MUSTN'T/... 195 STRANG
I'D KILL MYSELF IF I EVER EVEN CAUGHT MYSELF 196 STRANG
THINKING.../))
THINKING TROUBLEDLY) 196 STRANG
(THINKING UNEASILY) (THEY'RE TALKING ABOUT ME...196 STRANG
(THINKING WITH A STRANGE ECSTASY) 197 STRANG
(AS SHE REMAINS OBLIVIOUS, STARING AFTER THE 199 STRANG
PLANE--THINKING FATALISTICALLY)
(REACTING AUTOMATICALLY AND WINCING WITH PAIN-- 200 STRANG
THINKING MECHANICALLY)
(AFTER A PAUSE) WHAT ARE YOU THINKING$ 446 WELDED
I WAS THINKING OF HOW MISTAKENLY I'D PICTURED YOU 446 WELDED
BEFORE THAT.
BUT SHOWING BY THEIR TONE IT IS A THINKING ALOUD 452 WELDED
TO ONESELF,
STOP THINKING, DAMN YOU/ 472 WELDED

THINKS
ALL HE THINKS ON IS GITTIN' THE ILE-- 537 'ILE
(EXCITEDLY) WHAT IS IT HE THINKS HE'S GOIN' TO 537 'ILE
DO$
AND EVERYONE THINKS OF HER AS AN ATTRACTIVE GIRL. 186 AHWILD
(HE STARTS OUT AND IS JUST ABOUT TO CLOSE THE DOOR219 AHWILD
WHEN HE THINKS OF SOMETHING)
SHE THINKS THERE WEREN'T ANY GIRLS MIXED UP WITH 266 AHWILD
RICHARD'S SPREE LAST NIGHT--
SHE SAYS SHE THINKS SHE CAN DO IT. 273 AHWILD
YOU BETTER DO WHAT YOUR PA THINKS BEST--AND I'D 287 AHWILD
LIKE YOU TO BE AT YALE.
(SNIFFS, BUT THINKS IT BETTER TO LET THIS PASS) 290 AHWILD
HE THINKS THE WORLD OF YOU, HONEST HE DOES. 19 ANNA
THEN THINKS BETTER OF IT AND SITS STILL. 45 ANNA
FOR THE BEST OPPORTUNITY IN THE WORLD OF THE KIND 88 BEYOND
PA THINKS OF.
THINKS SHE KNOWS BETTER THAN AN OLD, SICK BODY 113 BEYOND
LIKE ME.
THAT WAS OVER A MONTH AGO, AND ROBBIE THINKS 115 BEYOND
THEY'RE OVERDUE NOW.
SHE IMMEDIATELY THINKS BETTER OF THIS AND SITS 119 BEYOND
WITH THE LETTER IN HER HANDS
WHEN I THINKS O' YOU WANTIN' TO GET BACK DOWN 141 BEYOND
SOUTH TO THE PLATE AGEN.
THINKS I WANTS THE OLE CAPTAIN TO PUT ME OFF THE 464 CARIBE
SHIP, DO YOU$
HE THINKS THAT HE MAY SET FIRE TO THE HOUSE--DO 564 CROSS
ANYTHING---
THINKS I AT THIS JUNCTURE, WELL, 503 DAYS
THINKS BETTER OF IT, AND DROPS HIS EYES.) 510 DAYS
LIKE EBEN THINKS$ 215 DESIRE
(THINKS A MOMENT--THEN RELUCTANTLY) 232 DESIRE
SOME THINKS ONE THING AND SOME ANOTHER. 503 DIFRNT
GOODNESS SAKES, EMMER, ALL THE MEN THINKS THAT-- 509 DIFRNT
HE THINKS IT GIVES HIM THE PRIVILEGE TO BE A 540 DIFRNT
BULLY.
HE THINKS HE'S FOUND A GOOD SHIELD TO COVER UP HIS541 DIFRNT
NATURAL-BORN LAZINESS--
(AS SHE THINKS SHE SEES A RELENTING SOFTNESS COME 543 DIFRNT
INTO HIS FACE AS HE LOOKS DOWN
(THINKS SCORNFULLY) (HE IS ALWAYS SO SURE OF 423 DYNAMO
WHAT GOD WILLS/
MRS. LIGHT THINKS WORRIEDLY) 427 DYNAMO
AND HE THINKS IN TORTURED AGONY OF SPIRIT) 448 DYNAMO
HE THINKS REVERENTIALLY) 475 DYNAMO
I'LL SEE THAT'S WHAT HE THINKS. 41 ELECTR
BUT SHE IS SO CRAZY I KNOW SHE THINKS--(THEN, WITH 88 ELECTR
REAL TERROR, CLINGING TO HIM)
ALL HE THINKS OF IS DEATH/ 92 ELECTR
THINKS FOR A SECOND IT IS HER MOTHER'S GHOST AND 143 ELECTR
GIVES AN EXCLAMATION OF DREAD.

1647 THIRTIES

THINKS (CONT'D.)
THEN JEERINGLY) SO MY WIFE THINKS IT BEHOOVES ME 271 GGBROW
TO SETTLE DOWN AND SUPPORT MY
BUT HE THINKS THE CASE LOOKS SHABBY AND HE WANTS 285 GGBROW
IT JUNKED.
THINKS HE MAY HAVE GOTTEN IN THE WRONG PLACE, 246 HA APE
ERIE THINKS HE IS IMPRESSED.) 12 HUGHIE
OH, I SEE WHAT HE THINKS/ 634 ICEMAN
HE THINKS I AM FINISH. IT IS TOO LATE, 634 ICEMAN
HE THINKS LIES EVEN WORSE, DAT I-- 634 ICEMAN
AND YET HE THINKS THE MOVEMENT IS JUST A CRAZY 647 ICEMAN
PIPE DREAM...
IT MUST KILL HER WHEN SHE THINKS OF ME-- 667 ICEMAN
THIS DAMNED FOOL THINKS COPS ARE AFTER ME/ 679 ICEMAN
(BURSTS OUT WITH HIS TRUE REACTION BEFORE HE 679 ICEMAN
THINKS TO IGNORE HIM)
SO HE THINKS I OUGHT TO TAKE A HOP OFF THE FIRE 701 ICEMAN
ESCAPE/
HE'S STARTING TO GET FOXY NOW AND THINKS HE'LL 717 ICEMAN
PLEAD INSANITY.
(WITH APPRECIATION, BEFORE HE THINKS.) 24 JOURNE
(ADMIRINGLY BEFORE HE THINKS.) 25 JOURNE
DOCTOR HARDY THINKS IT MIGHT BE A BIT OF MALARIAL 27 JOURNE
FEVER
(SLOWLY.) HE THINKS IT'S CONSUMPTION, DOESN'T HE, 30 JOURNE
PAPA.
THAT ISN'T WHAT HE THINKS ANY MORE. 30 JOURNE
HE'S RIGHT NOT TO GIVE A DAMN WHAT ANYONE THINKS. 43 JOURNE
HE'S CERTAINLY A FOOL TO CARE WHAT ANYONE THINKS. 59 JOURNE
HE THINKS MONEY SPENT ON A HOME IS MONEY WASTED. 61 JOURNE
(STUNG.) I'LL SEND HIM WHEREVER HARDY THINKS 79 JOURNE
BEST/
SHE THINKS I ALWAYS BELIEVE THE WORST, BUT THIS 162 JOURNE
TIME I BELIEVED THE BEST.
BLADDER AND THINKS THEREBY HE IS EVIL, THE ENEMY 359 LAZARU
OF GOD/
(ANSWERS BEFORE HE THINKS.) YES. 6 MANSNS
LIFE--OR THINKS ONE WANTS. 77 MANSNS
IF ANY WOMAN THINKS SHE CAN TAKE YOU FROM ME, 81 MANSNS
SHE THINKS.) 136 MANSNS
KEEPING HER BACK TURNED TO DEBORAH, WHILE SHE 137 MANSNS
THINKS.)
IT WAS ONLY WHAT EVERY WOMAN THINKS AT TIMES IN 144 MANSNS
HER HEART--
(PLUNGING IN CONFIDENTLY ON WHAT HE THINKS IS A 392 MARCOM
SURE POINT OF ATTACK)
IF HER HUSBAND THINKS AT THE END OF THE VOYAGE 404 MARCOM
THAT MY WORK DESERVES A BONUS--
MAYBE HE THINKS IF HE CAUGHT YOU WITH JIM AND HAD 9 MISBEG
WITNESSES TO PROVE IT,
HE'LL GO BACK TO THE BROADWAY HE THINKS IS HEAVEN, 30 MISBEG
LOOK AT HIM WHEN HE THINKS NO ONE IS WATCHING, 35 MISBEG
WITH HIS EYES ON THE GROUND.
AND HE THINKS THE BEST WAY TO GET RID OF YOU WOULD 66 MISBEG
BE TO BECOME YOUR LANDLORD.
HE THINKS YOU'RE A POOR INNOCENT VIRGIN/ 88 MISBEG
HE THINKS IT'S ALL BOASTING AND PRETENDING YOU'VE 88 MISBEG
DONE ABOUT BEING A SLUT.
(THEN ANGRILY) SO HE THINKS ALL HE HAS TO DO IS 90 MISBEG
CROOK A FINGER AND I'LL FALL FOR
JUST BECAUSE THAT BROADWAY SUCKER THINKS YOU'RE 94 MISBEG
ONE.
WHEN HE THINKS A LOT OF OTHER GUYS MADE IT. 135 MISBEG
(HE LOOKS MISERABLE, STARTS TO SPEAK, THINKS 164 MISBEG
BETTER OF IT,
DAUGHTER AND THEN YOU'D LAUGH TO SEE CON, IF HE 13 POET
THINKS SHE'S GENTRY.
(SHE ADDS BEFORE SHE THINKS.) 30 POET
SIMON DOESN'T CARE WHAT HIS FATHER THINKS. 31 POET
I SUPPOSE SHE THINKS SHE'S SUCH A GREAT LADY 77 POET
(NORA STARTS TO TELL HER THE TRUTH--THEN THINKS 80 POET
BETTER OF IT.
(BEFORE HE THINKS.) BUT I TOLD YOUR MOTHER TO 91 POET
KEEP HER HERE UNTIL--
MEANWHILE, AS SOON AS HE THINKS SHE HAS GONE, 118 POET
GADSBY SPEAKS.)
THAT SHOWS YOU WHAT GOD THINKS OF YOUR CURSES--AN'583 ROPE
HIM DEAF TO YOU/
AN' HE THINKS YOU'LL BE COMIN' HOME TO HANG 592 ROPE
YOURSELF.
(HE SNICKERS) SO YUH THINKS THE OLD MAN'S FLAT 593 ROPE
BROKE, DO YUH/
HIS FACE NOW FULL OF SELFISH RELIEF AS HE THINKS) 7 STRANG
(HE THINKS RESENTFULLY) 7 STRANG
(HIS FACE TWITCHES AS IF HE WERE ON THE VERGE OF 10 STRANG
TEARS--HE THINKS DESPERATELY)
MOTHER THINKS SHE'S BEHAVED QUITE INEXCUSABLY...) 25 STRANG
HE THINKS SHE'LL MARRY ME IN THE END... 31 STRANG
I KNOW HOW MUCH SHE THINKS OF YOU. 32 STRANG
(THE THINKS HE MEANS THAT... 33 STRANG
SHE THINKS WITH RESIGNED FINALITY) 71 STRANG
(LOOKING AFTER HER--THINKS) (SHE SEEMS BETTER 73 STRANG
TONIGHT...
HE'S UNHAPPY NOW BECAUSE HE THINKS HE ISN'T ABLE 84 STRANG
TO GIVE ME A CHILD.
SHE THINKS NEO... 88 STRANG
SAM THINKS I'M FINEST FELLOW IN WORLD... 105 STRANG
HE THINKS HE HAS PALMED ME OFF ON SAM FOREVER/... 108 STRANG
IN FACT, I'M SO CONFIDENT HE IS THAT AS SOON AS HE128 STRANG
THINKS THE TIME IS RIPE TO
POOR CHARLIE, HE ONLY THINKS HE OUGHT TO DESIRE 149 STRANG
ME/...
HE THINKS I'M AN OLD WOMAN/ 175 STRANG
SHE THINKS GORDON IS SAM'S SON.)) 176 STRANG
(WELL, WHAT DOES IT MATTER WHAT HE THINKS OF 193 STRANG
ME...

THINLY
SHE STARES STRAIGHT BEFORE HER, HER MOUTH SET 538 DIFRNT
THINLY.
(WITH AN OBVIOUSLY FAKE AIR OF CONTRITION THINLY 184 MANSNS
MASKING A CRUEL SATISFACTION.)
(INDIGNANT AT MELODY'S INSULTS TO HIS PROFESSION--119 POET
WITH A THIN, VEILED SNEER.)

THINNER
MUCH THINNER THAN HE SHOULD BE, 20 JOURNE
HIS FACE HAS BECOME THINNER, MORE HEAVILY LINED 69 MANSNS
AND GAUNT AND ANGULAR.
SHE APPEARS OLDER THAN IN THE PREVIOUS SCENE, HER 26 STRANG
FACE IS PALE AND MUCH THINNER.
HE SEEMS MUCH THINNER, HIS FACE DRAWN AND SALLOW. 67 STRANG
YOU LOOK THINNER. 132 STRANG

THINNING
SO IS HIS THINNING BROWN HAIR, POWDERED WITH 8 HUGHIE
DANDRUFF.
HE HAS MOUSE-COLORED THINNING HAIR, A LITTLE 575 ICEMAN
BULBOUS NOSE,
HIS HAIR IS THINNING AND ALREADY 19 JOURNE
HIS HEAD IS ROUND WITH THINNING SANDY HAIR. 11 MISBEG
HE HAS THINNING DARK HAIR, PARTED AND BRUSHED BACK 37 MISBEG
TO COVER A BALD SPOT.

THIRD
A THIRD CHAIR IS AT RIGHT OF TABLE, 493 DAYS
(SNEERINGLY) AS FOR THE THIRD PART, 494 DAYS
THE THIRD HAS THE APPEARANCE OF A PROSPEROUS 79 ELECTR
SHIPOWNER OF COLONIAL DAYS.
AND NOW IS ANYTHING A PAYING GUEST WANTS IT TO BE, 7 HUGHIE
A THIRD CLASS DUMP,
THE THIRD ROW OF TABLES, FOUR CHAIRS TO ONE AND 573 ICEMAN
SIX TO THE OTHER.
THREE LADIES OF THE PAVEMENT THAT ROOM ON THE 594 ICEMAN
THIRD FLOOR.
A THIRD BACK BY THE REAR WALL WITH FIVE CHAIRS, 664 ICEMAN
AND FINALLY,
(ANGRILY) *COS DRISC HEARD THE FIRST SEND THE 515 INZONE
THIRD BELOW TO WAKE THE SKIPPER
EVEN IN THIS HICK BURG HE'S RATED THIRD CLASS/ 30 JOURNE
THIRD-RATERS. 131 JOURNE
(HE TURNS OUT THE THIRD BULB, SO ONLY THE READING 151 JOURNE
LAMP IS ON.
(THE THIRD GUEST OF SCENE ONE RUSHES IN 290 LAZARU
BREATHLESSLY, SHOUTING)
THE SECOND RANK CROUCHING OVER THEM, THE THIRD 345 LAZARU
LEANING OVER THE SECOND.
SAY IT A THIRD TIME AND I'LL SEND MY DAUGHTER TO 59 MISBEG
TELEPHONE THE ASYLUM.
DURING MY CAREER AS A THIRD-RATE HAM. 128 MISBEG
THE THIRD DRINK BEGINS TO WORK AND HIS FACE 43 POET
BECOMES ARROGANTLY SELF-ASSURED.
THEN THE THIRD MAN PUNCHED CON AND I GAVE HIM A 156 POET
KICK WHERE IT'D DO HIM LEAST
AND IF A THIRD PARTY SHOULD KNOW A LITTLE 86 STRANG
HAPPINESS...
IT'S TERRIBLY FAINT BUT--NAVY AND WASHINGTON ARE 168 STRANG
LEADING--GORDON'S THIRD/
(THINKING WITH A SNEER) (I=GORDON'S THIRD/= 168 STRANG
LAST I GOT, GORDON THIRD, NAVY AND WASHINGTON 171 STRANG
LEADING.

THIRD'LL
AND THE THIRD'LL BE WHEN YOUR PAW GITS HOME/ 44 ELECTR

THIRDS
TWO-THIRDS OF THE WIDTH OF THE STAGE, 564 DAYS
TWO-THIRDS BELONGS THUS. 208 DESIRE
AS THE DOOR IS TWO-THIRDS OPEN. 27 MANSNS

THIRST
ADARIN' MAD WID THE THIRST, 482 CARDIF
FLEET OF MALAY CANOES PICKED THEM UP, MAD FROM 559 CROSS
THIRST AND STARVATION.
THEY BEGAN TO GO MAD--HUNGER, THIRST, AND THE 560 CROSS
REST--AND THEY BEGAN TO FORGET.
SO IN SPITE OF HARRY'S THIRST AND HIS GENEROUS 594 ICEMAN
HEART, HE COMES OUT EVEN.
I KNOW DAMNED WELL HE HAS NO APPETITE THIS EARLY 36 MISBEG
IN THE DAY, BUT ONLY A THIRST.
IF YOU NEED A DRINK YOU'LL HAVE TO BUY IT FROM HIM 46 MISBEG
OR DIE OF THIRST.
I'M DYIN' AV THIRST. 175 POET
AN' WHAT'LL YE BE TAKIN' FOR YOUR THIRSTS 499 VOYAGE
(TO JOE) GIVE US A DHRINK, FOR I'M PERISHING WID 503 VOYAGE
THE THIRST.
I'M NOT THIRSTY. 238 AHWILD
GEE, I'M THIRSTY. 23 ANNA
(SKEPTICALLY) BROKES YOU HAVEN'T THE THIRSTY 595 ICEMAN
LOOK OF THE IMPECUNIOUS.
(IN THE SAME FALSE VOICE) OUR GUESTS LOOK 429 MARCOM
THIRSTY.
WELL, NO ONE CAN SAY OF ME THAT I TURNED AWAY 54 POET
ANYONE I KNEW THIRSTY
THERE IS A CHORUS OF EAGER, THIRSTY WELCOME FROM 63 POET
INSIDE.
TALAVERA WAS A DEVILISH THIRSTY DAY, IF YOU'LL 98 POET
REMEMBER.
DON'T BE WISHIN' HIM HARM, FOR IT'S THIRSTY WE'D 100 POET
BE WITHOUT HIM.

THIRTEEN
THE ELDEST IS ABOUT FOURTEEN, THE TWO OTHERS 293 GGBROW
THIRTEEN AND TWELVE.

THIRTEENTH
OF THE THIRTEENTH CENTURY ARE TRAVEL-WORN. 347 MARCOM
FOR HE IS DRESSED AS A VENETIAN MERCHANT OF THE 439 MARCOM
LATER THIRTEENTH CENTURY.

THIRTIES
HE IS A STOUT, JOWLY-FACED MAN IN HIS LATE 244 AHWILD
THIRTIES.
THE NURSE IS A PLUMP WOMAN IN HER LATE THIRTIES. 554 DAYS

THIRTIES

THIRTIES (CONT'D.)
HE IS IN HIS LATE THIRTIES, OF AVERAGE HEIGHT, 577 ICEMAN
THIN.
(HARDER IS IN HIS LATE THIRTIES BUT LOOKS YOUNGER 55 MISBEG
BECAUSE HIS FACE IS UNMARKED
I SUPPOSE I SHOULD SAY MAN NOW HE'S IN HIS 166 STRANG
THIRTIES.

THIRTY
HE IS A MAN OF THIRTY OR SO.) 539 *ILE
IT'S NEVER BEEN SO BAD BEFORE IN THE THIRTY YEAR 1543 *ILE
BEEN ACOMIN* HERE.
MAKING GOOD MONEY IN WATERBURY, TOO--THIRTY-FIVE A213 AHWILD
WEEK.
I'VE TAKEN DOWN THE DISTANCE EVERY TIME YOU'VE 230 AHWILD
SAVED RED'S LIFE FOR THIRTY YEARS
THE JUDGE GIVE ALL US GIRLS THIRTY DAYS. 16 ANNA
HE IS ABOUT THIRTY, IN THE FULL POWER OF HIS 30 ANNA
HEAVY-MUSCLED, IMMENSE STRENGTH.
HE APPEARS MUCH OLDER THAN HIS THIRTY YEARS. 556 CROSS
HE IS A SLIGHT, MEDIUM-SIZED PROFESSIONAL-LOOKING 556 CROSS
MAN OF ABOUT THIRTY-FIVE.
DINNER IS AT SEVEN-THIRTY. 512 DAYS
SHE IS THIRTY-FIVE BUT LOOKS MUCH YOUNGER. 514 DAYS
SIMEON IS THIRTY-NINE AND PETER THIRTY-SEVEN-- 203 DESIRE
HE HAIN'T NEVER BEEN OFF THIS FARM 'CEPTIN' T' THE205 DESIRE
VILLAGE IN THIRTY YEAR OR
GOT HIMSELF HITCHED TO A FEMALE 'BOUT THIRTY- 212 DESIRE
FIVE--AN' PURTY, THEY SAYS...
WAAL--YE'VE THIRTY YEAR O' ME BURIED IN YE--SPREAD218 DESIRE
OUT OVER YE--
TWENTY-DOLLAR PIECES--THIRTY ON 'EM. 219 DESIRE
ABBIE IS THIRTY-FIVE, BUXOM, FULL OF VITALITY. 221 DESIRE
SEVENTY-SIX AN' HIM NOT THIRTY YIT-- 256 DESIRE
CALEB WILLIAMS IS TALL AND POWERFULLY BUILT, ABOUT494 DIFRNT
THIRTY.
THIRTY YEARS IF IT'S NEEDFUL/ 518 DIFRNT
IN THIRTY YEARS WE'LL BOTH BE DEAD AND GONE, 518 DIFRNT
PROBABLY.
(SCENE--THIRTY YEARS AFTER--THE SCENE IS THE SAME 519 DIFRNT
BUT NOT THE SAME.
THE THIRTY YEARS HAVE TRANSFORMED EMMA INTO A 519 DIFRNT
WITHERED,
(COYLY) I HAVEN'T GIVEN HIM THE SLIGHTEST REASON 533 DIFRNT
TO HOPE IN THIRTY YEARS.
HERE WITH YOU--FOR THE LAST THIRTY YEARS$ 533 DIFRNT
IN APPEARANCE, HE HAS CHANGED BUT LITTLE IN THE 535 DIFRNT
THIRTY YEARS SAVE THAT HIS HAIR
IT WAS THIRTY YEARS AGO THIS SPRING. 537 DIFRNT
NOW WHEN THE THIRTY YEARS ARE PAST--I WAS THINKIN'538 DIFRNT
THAT MAYBE--
THIRTY O' THE BEST YEARS OF A MAN'S LIFE OUGHT TO 538 DIFRNT
BE PROOF ENOUGH
I SAID I'D WAIT THIRTY YEARS--IF NEED BE. 538 DIFRNT
THIRTY YEARS--THAT'S A HELL OF A LONG TIME TO 538 DIFRNT
WAIT, EMMERE.
D'YOU REMEMBER WHAT HAPPENED THIRTY YEARS BACK$ 538 DIFRNT
I WON'T-- NOT EVEN IF YOU HAVE WAITED THIRTY 543 DIFRNT
YEARS.
THIRTY O' THE BEST YEARS OF MY LIFE FLUNG FOR A 943 DIFRNT
YELLER DOG LIKE HIM TO FEED ON.
JENNINGS, THE OPERATOR ON DUTY, A MAN OF THIRTY OR486 DYNAMO
SO, IS SEATED AT THE DESK.
THIS CURTAIN REVEALS THE EXTENSIVE GROUNDS--ABOUT 2 ELECTR
THIRTY ACRES--
THIRTY-SIX, I THINK. 20 ELECTR
ALTHOUGH HE IS ONLY TWENTY, HE LOOKS THIRTY. 74 ELECTR
WHY, HE LEFT HOME AT EIGHT-THIRTY/ 303 GGBROW
HE IS A HUSKY, FINE-LOOKING MAN OF THIRTY-FIVE OR 220 HA APE
SO.
AT THE END OF THIRTY YEARS' DEVOTION TO THE CAUSE,590 ICEMAN
THAT I WAS NEVER MADE FOR IT.
TEN, TWENTY, THIRTY, FORTY, FIFTY, SIXTY, SEVENTY,608 ICEMAN
EIGHTY, NINETY, A DOLLAR.
TEN, TWENTY, THIRTY--WHAT'S ON AT THE CHURCH 609 ICEMAN
TONIGHT, BESS$
TEN, TWENTY, THIRTY, FIFTY, SEVENTY, EIGHTY, 609 ICEMAN
NINETY--
TWENTY, THIRTY, FORTY, FIFTY, SIXTY--YOU'RE 609 ICEMAN
COUNTING WITH ME, BESS, AREN'T YOUS
HE'S NEARLY THIRTY-FOUR. 18 JOURNE
JAMIE, THE ELDER, IS THIRTY-THREE. 19 JOURNE
WILL YOU LISTEN TO YOUR FATHER, JAMIE--AFTER 29 JOURNE
THIRTY-FIVE YEARS OF MARRIAGE/
IT'S HARD FOR A STRANGER TO TELL, BUT AFTER 83 JOURNE
THIRTY-FIVE YEARS OF MARRIAGE--
I'VE LOVED HIM DEARLY FOR THIRTY-SIX YEARS. 101 JOURNE
THIRTY-SIX YEARS AGO, BUT I CAN SEE IT AS CLEARLY 105 JOURNE
AS IF IT WERE TONIGHT/
AND IN ALL THOSE THIRTY-SIX YEARS, 105 JOURNE
THIRTY-FIVE TO FORTY THOUSAND DOLLARS NET PROFIT A150 JOURNE
SEASON
AT FROM THIRTY-FIVE TO FORTY THOUSAND NET PROFIT ALSO JOURNE
SEASON/
MIRIAM IS A SLENDER, DELICATE WOMAN OF THIRTY- 274 LAZARU
FIVE, DRESSED IN DEEP BLACK.
LAZARUS NOW LOOKS LESS THAN THIRTY-FIVE. 307 LAZARU
THIRTY YEARS$ YEARS OF DISCIPLINE AND I--HALT, 311 LAZARU
TRAITOR/
THE SENATORS ARE DIVIDED INTO TWO GROUPS ON EACH 312 LAZARU
SIDE, THIRTY IN EACH.
HE SEEMS NO MORE THAN THIRTY. 317 LAZARU
HE IS A MAN OF ABOUT THIRTY-FIVE, 332 LAZARU
HIS LARGE-FEATURED YANKEE FACE LOOKS HIS THIRTY- 43 MANSNS
ONE YEARS.
AND LOOKS OLDER THAN THE THIRTY-FIVE HE IS. 69 MANSNS
AND THE DULL STAMPING OF FEET, A DOUBLE FILE OF 350 MARCOM
THIRTY MEN OF DIFFERENT AGES,
AROUND THIRTY, I'D SAY. 18 POET

THIRTY (CONT'D.)
DEBORAH IS FORTY-ONE, BUT LOOKS TO BE NO MORE THAN 67 POET
THIRTY.
HE IS A TALL THIN MAN OF THIRTY-FIVE, METICULOUSLY 3 STRANG
WELL-DRESSED IN TWEEDS
(LOOKS AT HIS WATCH) (FIVE-THIRTY JUST... 23 STRANG
NOT UNTIL AFTER I'M THIRTY-FIVE, AT LEAST/ 81 STRANG
NINA IS THIRTY-FIVE, IN THE FULL BLOOM OF HER 137 STRANG
WOMANHOOD.
I'M THIRTY-FIVE... 138 STRANG
SHE IS A WOMAN OF THIRTY. 443 WELDED
MICHAEL IS THIRTY-FIVE, TALL AND DARK. 443 WELDED

THIS'D
*THIS'D CURE ROB OF THEM IDEAS OF HIS ABOUT THE 132 BEYOND
BEAUTIFUL SEA.

THIS'LL
THIS'LL WARM HIM FOR YOU. 239 AHWILD
THIS'LL DO FOR ME AN' SCUTTY TO TIE HIM. 525 INZONE
THIS'LL BE UT, I'M THINKIN'. 527 INZONE

THISTLE
RATHER BE GRATEFUL IF A THISTLE CAN BRING FORTH 360 MARCOM
FIGS.

THISTLES
THE MILKWEED AND THE THISTLES IS IN THRIVING 40 MISBEG
CONDITION.

THOMAS
READING ALOUD FROM THE *IMITATION OF CHRIST* BY 290 GGBROW
THOMAS A KEMPIS TO HIS MASK.

THOMPSON'S
DO YOU KNOW FRANCIS THOMPSON'S POEM--THE HOUND OF 508 DAYS
HEAVENS

THORGHT
THORGHT YER WEREN'T 'ARF A FOX, DIDN'T YER$ 526 INZONE
ON'Y YOUR MATE THERE WAS ARSKIN' FUR GELS AN' I 499 VOYAGE
THORGHT AS 'OW YER'D LIKE 'EM TO

THORN
(UBLIVIOUS) (BUT, LORD, THOU KNOWEST WHAT A 423 DYNAMO
THORN IN THE FLESH THAT ATHEIST,

THOROUGH
I'VE HAD A THOROUGH TRAINING AT THIS GAME--THANKS 114 ELECTR
TO YOU AND FATHER.
A THOROUGH KNOWLEDGE OF THE LAW CLOSE AT HAND IN 595 ICEMAN
THE HOUSE
BUT I WENT UP THERE ONCE AND MADE A THOROUGH 172 STRANG
INVESTIGATION OF HIS FAMILY.

THOROUGHBRED
HE WAS AS STRONG AS AN OX, AND ON A THOROUGHBRED 13 POET
HORSE, IN HIS UNIFORM,
THE GRAND GENTLEMAN MUST HAVE HIS THOROUGHBRED TO 22 POET
RIDE OUT IN STATE/
BUT HE CAN AFFORD TO KEEP A THOROUGHBRED MARE 23 POET
BECAUSE YOU MADE MOTHER PAY THE FEED BILL FOR YOUR 44 POET
FINE THOROUGHBRED MARE/
(BITTERLY.) WELL, YOU'VE A BEAUTIFUL THOROUGHBRED 49 POET
MARE NOW, AT LEAST--
AS LONG AS YOU AND YOUR FINE THOROUGHBRED MARE CAN 59 POET
LIVE IN STYLE/
IN THE APPEARANCE OF A THOROUGHBRED HORSE. 69 POET
WHEN YOU WENT RIDING ON YOUR THOROUGHBRED 106 POET
THOROUGHBRED MARE
AND HIS GAB ABOUT HIS BEAUTIFUL THOROUGHBRED MARE 161 POET
IS MADDER STILL.
PRANCING AROUND DRUNK ON HIS BEAUTIFUL 168 POET
THOROUGHBRED MARE--

THOROUGHBREDS
AND DRIVE IN A CARRIAGE WID A NAYGUR COACHMAN 173 POET
BEHIND SPANKIN' THOROUGHBREDS.

THOROUGHLY
(THOROUGHLY EXASPERATED) IS IT NO SHAME YOU HAVE 73 ANNA
AT ALL$
(THOROUGHLY CONVINCED AT LAST) 523 INZONE
(THOROUGHLY SORTED FACTS, TO PROVE HOW THOROUGHLY I WAS 29 MANSNS
RESIGNED TO REALITY,
CHEST THUNDERS WITH EGOTISM AND IS TOO HARD FOR 43 STRANG
TIRED HEADS AND THOROUGHLY
HE HAS BEEN TOO THOROUGHLY TRAINED TO PROGRESS 184 STRANG
ALONG A CERTAIN GROOVE TO SUCCESS

THOT
WHOT'S THOT$ 461 CARIBE
(GRUFFLY) GIMME THOT/ 465 CARIBE

THOU
(HE QUOTES RHETORICALLY) *OH THOU, 198 AHWILD
AND THOU BESIDE ME SINGING IN THE WILDERNESS--- 199 AHWILD
TOO YOUNG ART THOU TO WASTE THIS SUMMERNIGHT--- 276 AHWILD
*AH, FONDEST, BLINDEST, WEAKEST, I AM HE WHOM THOU508 DAYS
SEEKEST
THOU DRAVEST LOVE FROM THEE, WHO DRAVEST ME.* 508 DAYS
THOU WILT NOT--DO THAT TO ME AGAIN--WILT THOU$ 552 DAYS
THOU WILT NOT--TAKE LOVE FROM ME AGAIN-- 552 DAYS
MAKE HIM SEE THAT THOU, ALONE, HAST THE WORDS OF 558 DAYS
ETERNAL LIFE.
THOU HAS HEARD ME AT LAST/ 565 DAYS
O SUN OF MAN, I AM THOU AND THOU ART I/ 565 DAYS
WHY HAST THOU FORSAKEN ME$ 565 DAYS
THE LOVE THAT THOU ONCE TOOK FROM ME/ 565 DAYS
WHO KNOWETH THE TORTURED HEARTS OF MEN, CANST THOU565 DAYS
NOT FORGIVE--NOW--
THOU CANST NOT CONQUER ME/ 565 DAYS
THOU HAST ALWAYS LOVED ME/ 565 DAYS
THOU HAST NOT FORSAKEN ME/ 565 DAYS
THOU HAS CONQUERED, LORD. 566 DAYS
THOU ART THE WAY--THE TRUTH-- 566 DAYS
THOU ART--THE END. 566 DAYS
LORD GOD OF HUSTS, WHY DOST THOU NOT STRIKE 423 DYNAMO
HIM$...
IF THOU DIDST, I WOULD PROCLAIM THE AWFUL WARNING 423 DYNAMO
OF IT ALL OVER AMERICA/...

THOU

THOU (CONT'D.)
(OBLIVIOUS) (BUT, LORD, THOU KNOWEST WHAT A 423 DYNAMO
THORN IN THE FLESH THAT ATHEIST,
AT LAST THOU STRIKES/.../)
(HE CHANTS FLIPPANTLY) I LOVE, THOU LOVEST, HE 447 DYNAMO 265 GGBROW
LOVES, SHE LOVES/
LEAD ON, ALMIGHTY BROWN, THOU KINDLY LIGHT/ 284 GGBROW
=QUICKLY, MUST THOU BE GONE FROM HENCE, SEE THEN 290 GGBROW
HOW MATTERS STAND WITH THEE.
NOR DOST THOU KNOW WHAT SHALL BEFALL THEE AFTER 290 GGBROW
DEATH.
DO NOW, BELOVED, DO NOW ALL THOU CANST 290 GGBROW
BECAUSE THOU KNOWST NOT WHEN THOU SHALT DIE. 290 GGBROW
LEARN NOW TO DIE TO THE WORLD THAT THOU MAYST 290 GGBROW
BEGIN TO LIVE WITH CHRIST/
BECAUSE THOU HAST NOT HERE A LASTING ABODE. 291 GGBROW
BLESSED ART THOU AMONG WOMEN.= 107 JOURNE
THOU KNOWEST, O SATAN, PATRON OF MY PAIN, 133 JOURNE
WHETHER THOU SLEEP, WITH HEAVY VAPOURS FULL, 134 JOURNE
SODDEN WITH DAY, OR,
O DIVIDED HOUSE, THOU SHALT CRUMBLE TO DUST, 292 LAZARU
THOU HAST CONQUERED DEATH/ 310 LAZARU
THOU HAST SLAIN FEAR/ 320 LAZARU
THOU HAST SLAIN DEATH/ 320 LAZARU
THEN WHY DOST THOU LAUGH AGAINST CAESARS 339 LAZARU
THOU ART NOT COME TO CONTRIVE MY MURDERS 339 LAZARU
THOU CANST NOT MAKE ME FEAR DEATH, DAEMON/ 339 LAZARU
(AT FIRST FALTERINGLY) SO--THOU ART NOT EVIL$ 339 LAZARU
WHATEVER MAGIC THOU DIDST TO ME, DAEMON, I BESEECH343 LAZARU
THEE UNDO IT/
COULDST THOU BUT HEAR, JESUS/ 343 LAZARU
(WITH SUPERSTITIOUS DREAD) WHAT DOST THOU MEAN, 344 LAZARU
DAEMONS
(LAZARUS DOES NOT REPLY) IF THOU DOST NOT TELL 350 LAZARU
ME, I MUST ALWAYS DOUBT THEE,
WHO LAUGHS NOW, LAZARUS--THOU OR CAESARS 364 LAZARU
(IN A STRANGE FRENZY NOW) HEAR ME, THOU DAEMON OF365 LAZARU
LAUGHTER/
SHUT THEE FROM HEAVEN WITH A DOME MORE VAST, TILL MANSNS
THOU AT LENGTH ART FREE,
WHAT HAVE I DONE THAT, THOU SHOULDST TORTURE ME$ 413 MARCOM
= THOU WAS NOT BORN FOR DEATH, 103 MISBEG
=O LORD, THOU HAST SEEN MY WRONG.. 584 ROPE
JUDGE THOU MY CAUSE. 584 ROPE
THOU HAST SEEN ALL THEIR VENGEANCE AND ALL THEIR 584 ROPE
IMAGINATIONS AGAINST ME--=

THOUGH

(THEN ENTHUSIASTICALLY) SAY, ISN'T IT A GREAT 196 AHWILD
BOOK, THOUGH--
THOUGH I CAN'T SEE WHY HIS MOTHER FAILED IN HER 202 AHWILD
DUTY.
I'M AFRAID I'VE GOT TO AGREE WITH HIM, THOUGH, 207 AHWILD
THOUGH AFTER HE'S THROUGH WITH HIS BETTING ON 213 AHWILD
HORSE RACES, AND DICE.
YOU CAN GET BACK BY HALF-PAST TEN OR ELEVEN, 219 AHWILD
THOUGH, ALL RIGHT.
THOUGHT I'D BE RUSTY, NOT HAVING BEEN IN ALL THESE 228 AHWILD
YEARS.
THOUGH, AS I'VE SAID, HE WAS BIGGER AND OLDER THAN230 AHWILD
ME, BUT FINALLY I DREW AHEAD.
CAN'T I, THOUGH/ 274 AHWILD
THAT'S HATCHED A DUCK--THOUGH LORD KNOWS I 292 AHWILD
WOULDN'T IN HER SHOES/
LONG TIME AGO, THOUGH. 5 ANNA
SAY, THOUGH--IF YOU'RE LONELY--IT'S FUNNY--WHY 22 ANNA
AIN'T YOU EVER MARRIED AGAINS
(RUEFULLY) THOUGH IT'S A GREAT JACKASS I AM TO BE 34 ANNA
MISTAKING YOU.
(STOUTLY) YES, THANK GOD, THOUGH I'VE NOT SEEN A 37 ANNA
SIGHT OF IT IN FIFTEEN YEARS.
(FURIOUSLY) THOUGH I DO BE THINKING I'D HAVE A 60 ANNA
GOOD RIGHT
THOUGH 'TIS WELL YOU KNOW I'D HAVE A RIGHT TO COME 68 ANNA
BACK AND MURDER YOU.
THOUGH HE'S BEEN TRYING NOT TO SHOW IT. 83 BEYOND
HER FACE, THOUGH INCLINED TO ROUNDNESS, IS 87 BEYOND
UNDENIABLY PRETTY.
AS THOUGH HE WERE THROWING OFF SOME DISTURBING 93 BEYOND
THOUGHT--WITH A LAUGH)
ROBERT SUDDENLY STOPS AND TURNS AS THOUGH FOR A 93 BEYOND
LAST LOOK.
PUTS HER HANDS ON HIS SHOULDERS AS THOUGH TO TRY 107 BEYOND
TO PUSH HIM BACK IN THE CHAIR
THOUGH HE WAS TOO STUBBORN EVER TO OWN UP TO IT. 116 BEYOND
THERE IS AN AUTHORITATIVE NOTE IN HIS SPEECH AS 130 BEYOND
THOUGH HE WERE ACCUSTOMED TO
(CLUTCHING AT HIS THROAT AS THOUGH TO STRANGLE 565 CROSS
SOMETHING WITHIN HIM--HOARSELY)
EVEN THOUGH I'D STOPPED CARING FOR HIM AND OUR 520 DAYS
MARRIAGE HAD ALWAYS BEEN UNHAPPY,
AN' THEN IT'S STILL MINE--EVEN THOUGH I BE SIX 234 DESIRE
FOOT UNDER.
IN THE MOONLIGHT--THOUGH IT WAS WARM--AND I WANTED515 DIFRNT
TO WRAP A BLANKET ROUND HER.
REUBEN LOOKS UP AND GIVES A WILD LAUGH AS THOUGH 452 DYNAMO
THE THUNDER ELATED HIM.
MY, BUT HE'S IN A BREAKFAST TEMPER, THOUGH. 456 DYNAMO
YOU CAN'T BEAR THAT THOUGH, EVEN AT THE PRICE OF 33 ELECTR
MY DISGRACE, CAN YOUS
OH, DOESN'T IT, THOUGH$ 85 ELECTR
BUT SAY, HASN'T SHE CHANGED, THOUGH$ 144 ELECTR
I'M JEALOUS OF YOUR WIFE, EVEN THOUGH I KNOW YOU 286 GGBROW
DO LOVE HER.
COME TO NOW, THOUGH. 10 HUGHIE
I'D STARTED TO BE A HORSE PLAYER IN ERIE, THOUGH 15 HUGHIE
I'D NEVER SEEN A TRACK.
(HIS TRAIN OF THOUGH INTERRUPTED--IRRITABLY.) 34 HUGHIE

THOUGH

THOUGH (CONT'D.)
WHEEDLING PLAYFULNESS, AS THOUGH HE WERE TALKING 579 ICEMAN
TO A CHILD)
HE LOOKS AS THOUGH HE BELONGED IN A POOL ROOM 585 ICEMAN
PATRONIZED BY WOULD-BE SPORTS.
AND HOPE ANSWERS WITH IDENTICAL PANTOMIME, AS 608 ICEMAN
THOUGH TO SAY, =POOR DOPES.=
I KNOW YOU'RE RIGHT, THOUGH, BECAUSE I ASKED HER. 667 ICEMAN
THOUGH CAN'T SAY I SLEPT MUCH, THANKS TO THAT 675 ICEMAN
INTERFERING ASS, HICKEY.
AS THOUGH STRUCK BY A SUDDEN PARALYSIS OF THE 677 ICEMAN
WILL.
TOO DAMNED HOT FOR A WALK, THOUGH, IF YOU ASK ME. 687 ICEMAN
EVEN THOUGH I KNOW SHE WISHES NOW I WAS DEAD/ 709 ICEMAN
I'D HAVE TO PROMISE, SHE WAS SO SWEET AND GOOD, 710 ICEMAN
THOUGH I KNEW DARNED WELL--
I FELT AS THOUGH A TON OF GUILT WAS LIFTED OFF MY 716 ICEMAN
MIND.
EVEN THOUGH MR. TYRONE HAS MADE ME GO WITH HIM ON 102 JOURNE
ALL HIS TOURS,
(AS THOUGH HE HADN'T SPOKEN.) 113 JOURNE
YOU'VE GOT BRAINS IN THAT HEAD OF YOURS, THOUGH 128 JOURNE
YOU DO YOUR BEST TO DENY THEM.
YOU'VE HAD EVERYTHING--NURSES, SCHOOLS, COLLEGE, 146 JOURNE
THOUGH YOU DIDN'T STAY THERE.
I CRIED, TOO, THOUGH I TRIED HARD NOT TO, 148 JOURNE
AND HOW, THESE THINGS ARE, THOUGH YE STROVE TO 173 JOURNE
SHOW, SHE WOULD NOT KNOW.=
NAY, AND THOUGH ALL MEN SEEING HAD PITY ON ME, SHE174 JOURNE
WOULD NOT SEE.=
BUT WE, WE ARE HENCE, WE ARE GONE, AS THOUGH WE 174 JOURNE
HAD NOT BEEN THERE.
AND THOUGH I WAS HALF-DEAD WITH FRIGHT I FOUND 277 LAZARU
MYSELF LAUGHING, TOO/
AS THOUGH HIS LIFE, SO LONG REPRESSED IN HIM BY 309 LAZARU
FEAR,
THEY STABBED THEMSELVES, DANCING AS THOUGH IT WERE321 LAZARU
A FESTIVAL/
THOUGH YOU WERE CAESAR THIS MINUTE I WOULD LAUGH 322 LAZARU
AT YOU/
WHOM HE THOUGH HE HAD KILLED, TO THE BODY OF 339 LAZARU
FLAVIUS--
AND THOUGH I BURST WITH PRIDE, I CANNOT LAUGH WITH352 LAZARU
JOY/
WHICH KNOWS THAT THOUGH ONE WERE TO CRY IT IN THE 354 LAZARU
STREETS TO MULTITUDES,
YOU HARP ON AGE AS THOUGH I WERE A WITHERED OLD 3 MANSNS
HAG/
YOU TALK AS THOUGH I WERE A SLAVE. 7 MANSNS
I AM AFRAID, THOUGH YOU MIGHT LISTEN KINDLY, YOU 10 MANSNS
COULD NOT HEAR ME, SIMON.
THIS IS REAL LIFE, EVEN THOUGH IT BE PAST. 13 MANSNS
COWERING MOVEMENT AS THOUGH HE HAD STRUCK HER IN 14 MANSNS
THE FACE.)
THOUGH AFTER ALL I'VE HEARD, I KNOW NOW I WAS A 18 MANSNS
FOOL TO BE AFRAID OF YOU.
(SHE SWAYS WEARILY AS THOUGH SHE WERE ABOUT TO 19 MANSNS
FAINT--EXHAUSTEDLY.)
HER BACK IS TO THE DOOR AS THOUGH SHE HAD GROPED 27 MANSNS
BACKWARDS IN THE DARKNESS,
AS THOUGH HE HAD AN IMPORTANT APPOINTMENT WITH GOD 30 MANSNS
TO DISCUSS TERMS
(SCOLDING HIM AS THOUGH HE WERE A SMALL BOY.) 49 MANSNS
IT IS AS THOUGH SHE HAD SLOWLY TAKEN POSSESSION OF 73 MANSNS
SARA
BUT IT'S AS THOUGH THE MINUTE YOU CAME HOME I FELT 82 MANSNS
EVERYTHING BEGIN TO CHANGE
IS THAT WHEN YOU STARE AT US AS THOUGH YOU HATED 82 MANSNS
US$
AS THOUGH YOU WERE AN UNDERSTUDY LEARNING TO PLAY 92 MANSNS
MY PART.
AS THOUGH SARA AND I WERE ENGAGED IN SOME 98 MANSNS
FANTASTIC DUEL.
AS THOUGH THAT OPPONENT WITHIN HAD SPAT AN 102 MANSNS
EXTINGUISHING POISON OF DISDAIN--
EVEN THOUGH I HAD MARKED THEM ALL-- 102 MANSNS
UM, EVEN, AS THOUGH IT WERE MON. 107 MANSNS
THEN, AS THOUGH THE MEANING OF THE SILENCE WERE 118 MANSNS
BECOMING AUDIBLE,
AS THOUGH A BOMB WERE CONCEALED IN THE ROOM WITH A120 MANSNS
FUSE SLOWLY SPUTTERING
HAVE MIRRORED HIS DESCRIPTION AS THOUGH, 126 MANSNS
SUBCONSCIOUSLY,
AND FURTIVE, AS THOUGH HE WERE THROWN OFF BALANCE 140 MANSNS
BY SOME EMOTION
(FRIGHTENEDLY.) YOU SOUND AS THOUGH YOU'D LIKE-- 142 MANSNS
YOU WOULDN'T----/
AS THOUGH NOT QUITE REALIZING YET WHERE HE IS OR 145 MANSNS
HOW HE GOT THERE.)
UNQUESTIONINGLY, AS THOUGH YOU WERE THE MEANEST 153 MANSNS
WORKER IN MY MILLS.
IN ASTONISHMENT AS THOUGH THIS EVIDENCE OF A 370 MARCOM
HUMANITY COMMON WITH HIS
EVEN THOUGH YOU WISH YOUR OWN UNHAPPINESS, 398 MARCOM
STILL, EVEN THOUGH THEY CANNOT BE HOUSE-BROKEN, 402 MARCOM
I WILL COMPEL HIM TO LOVE ME, EVEN THOUGH I NEVER 414 MARCOM
LOVE HIM/
AGAIN YOUR WISH IS MY WILL, EVEN THOUGH I WILL NOT419 MARCOM
LIVE UNTIL I SEE YOU AGAIN/
THOUGH IT'D BE HARD TO FIND A DECENT MAN WHO'D 8 MISBEG
HAVE YOU NOW.
THOUGH I SHOULDN'T SAY IT, BECAUSE IF YOU WAS THE 20 MISBEG
DECENT KIND,
WOULD YOU, THOUGH/ 73 MISBEG
HE AS MUCH AS TULD ME HIS REASON, THOUGH HE 89 MISBEG
WOULDN'T COME OUT WITH IT PLAIN.
I KEEP HOPING IT'S A LIE, EVEN THOUGH I KNOW I'M A123 MISBEG
DAMNED FOOL.

THOUGH

THOUGH (CONT'D.)
AS THOUGH WHAT HE TOLD CONCERNED SOME MAN HE HAD 146 MISBEG
KNOWN,
(LAUGHING.) HAVEN'T I, THOUGH/ 33 POET
THOUGH IT IS DIFFICULT AT TIMES FOR MY PRIDE TO 48 POET
REMEMBER
TAKING A STEP BACK AS THOUGH HE HAD BEEN SLAPPED 72 POET
IN THE FACE.
EVEN THOUGH IT WOULD HAVE FURTHERED YOUR 91 POET
INTERESTS.
THOUGH I'D TRIED HARD TO LEAVE IT BEHIND. 143 POET
WORKING FOR HIS FATHER HE HAS THE ABILITY FOR 146 POET
TRADE, THOUGH HE HATES IT.
THOUGH WHY I DID, I DON'T KNOW. 180 POET
(THOUGH HE IS MOST LIBERAL--EVEN RADICAL--IN HIS 7 STRANG
TOLERANT UNDERSTANDING
AS THOUGH I'D LOOKED INTO THE EYES OF A 25 STRANG
PROSTITUTE...
LIKABLE QUALITY THOUGH...)) 29 STRANG
IT WAS JUST AS THOUGH HE'D FORGOTTEN HE HAD A 50 STRANG
MOTHER.
WILDLY, MAKES A MOTION AS THOUGH TO TAKE HER IN 89 STRANG
HIS ARMS.
AS THOUGH NOW IT DEFINITELY BELONGED TO THE TYPE 111 STRANG
OF PERSON IT WAS BUILT FOR.
AND SPEAKS AS THOUGH SHE WERE HIDING A HURT 118 STRANG
REPROACH BENEATH A JOKING TONE)
ISN'T THIS KID OF MINE A WHOPPER FOR HIS AGE, 152 STRANG
THOUGH/
YOU JUMPED OFF MY LAP AS THOUGH YOU'D SAT ON A 157 STRANG
TACK/
EVEN THOUGH HE DOES DO WEAK THINGS SOMETIMES. 160 STRANG
HE LOOKS AS THOUGH HIS BLOOD PRESSURE MIGHT BE 170 STRANG
HIGHER THAN IT OUGHT TO BE.
THOUGHT
I THOUGHT MAYBE--I'D GO ON DECK, DAVID, TO GET A 540 *ILE
BREATH OF FRESH AIR.
(THE THOUGHT OF THIS DRIVES HIM INTO A FRENZY, 542 *ILE
I GUESS I WAS DREAMING ABOUT THE OLD VIKINGS IN 546 *ILE
THE STORY-BOOKS AND I THOUGHT
(PLEASED) I THOUGHT IT WAS PRETTY FAIR MYSELF. 188 AHWILD
WELL, I THOUGHT WE'D JUST SIT AROUND AND REST AND 191 AHWILD
TALK.
AT THE THOUGHT OF THESE TWO ANCIENTS SPOONING.) 192 AHWILD
I THOUGHT HE CAME IN WITH US FROM BREAKFAST. 192 AHWILD
(THEN TO HIS FATHER) I THOUGHT I'D JUST STAY 194 AHWILD
HOME, PA--THIS MORNING, ANYWAY.
(THEN APPALLED BY ANOTHER THOUGHT) 199 AHWILD
I THOUGHT YOU'D GET AROUND TO THAT, SO I BROUGHT 201 AHWILD
SOME OF THE PROOFS WITH ME.
(MORE WORRIEDLY) I THOUGHT HE WAS REALLY STUCK ON205 AHWILD
HER--
I THOUGHT THEY WOULD GIVE HER THE SPUNK TO LEAD 207 AHWILD
HER OWN LIFE, AND NOT BE--
I THOUGHT, MAYBE, READING THOSE THINGS--THEY'RE 207 AHWILD
BEAUTIFUL, AREN'T THEY, PA5
(EMBARRASSEDLY) YES, I THOUGHT--IF SID'S TAKING 212 AHWILD
ME TO THE FIREWORKS--
(IRRITABLY) DAMN, I THOUGHT HE'D BE HERE FOR 218 AHWILD
DINNER.
(IMPRESSED) HELL, YOU KNOW MORE THAN I THOUGHT. 219 AHWILD
I THOUGHT YOU WERE THE ORIGINAL OF THE HEART BOWED228 AHWILD
DOWN TODAY.
THEN SUDDENLY I THOUGHT OF THE PILE. 230 AHWILD
I THOUGHT SHE 'D GOT COMPLETELY OVER HER 234 AHWILD
FOOLISHNESS ABOUT HER LONG AGO.
AND THE GUILTY THOUGHT OF MURIEL, 241 AHWILD
WE THOUGHT IT WAS RICHARD. 254 AHWILD
I THOUGHT YOU'D ONLY SIT ON ME. 255 AHWILD
TO PUNISH HIM--AND I THOUGHT HE OUGHT TO, ANYWAY, 265 AHWILD
AFTER BEING SO SICK.
I THOUGHT YOU WEREN'T GOING TO GIVE HIM ANY 265 AHWILD
DINNER--TO PUNISH HIM.
(GUILTILY) WELL--IN HIS WEAKENED CONDITION--I 265 AHWILD
THOUGHT IT BEST--
I CAN'T KIND OF FEEL THAT IT'S ALL AS BAD AS I 266 AHWILD
THOUGHT IT WAS.
HE THOUGHT IT WAS A GOOD JOKE TO GET HIM SOUSED. 267 AHWILD
I THOUGHT YOU WERE ASLEEP/ 269 AHWILD
I NEVER THOUGHT YOU HAD SUCH NERVE/ 274 AHWILD
I THOUGHT EVERYTHING WAS DEAD AND PAST BETWEEN US.278 AHWILD
I THOUGHT YOU'D BE WAITING RIGHT HERE AT THE END 278 AHWILD
OF THE PATH.
THAT'S WHY I THOUGHT IT WOULD BE THE BEST PLACE. 280 AHWILD
I THOUGHT YOUR LOVE FOR ME WAS DEAD. 281 AHWILD
I THOUGHT YOU'D NEVER LOVED ME, THAT YOU'D ONLY 281 AHWILD
BEEN CRUELLY MOCKING ME--
AND I THOUGHT, WHAT DIFFERENCE DOES IT MAKE WHAT 1282 AHWILD
DO NOW5
BUT I THOUGHT, SHE'S DEAD TO ME NOW AND WHY 282 AHWILD
SHOULDN'T I THROW IT AWAY5
I THOUGHT, WHEN I'M DEAD, SHE'LL BE SORRY SHE 282 AHWILD
RUINED MY LIFE/
AND, ANYWAY, I THOUGHT TO MYSELF, SHE ISN'T WORTH 282 AHWILD
IT.
YOU THOUGHT I WHAT5 290 AHWILD
BUT I THOUGHT YOU-- 290 AHWILD
BUT I THOUGHT YOU HAD NO USE FOR HER, THOUGHT SHE 290 AHWILD
WAS STUPID.
(THEN HAS A SUDDEN THOUGHT) BUT I'VE DONE ALL 292 AHWILD
THIS TALKING ABOUT MURIEL AND
NO MATTER HOW BAD I THOUGHT SHE HAD TREATED ME-- 294 AHWILD
WELL, I'D THOUGHT OF TELLING YOU YOU COULDN'T GO 296 AHWILD
TO YALE--
MURIEL THOUGHT YOU'D WANT ME TO. 296 AHWILD
(AS IF HE HADN'T THOUGHT OF THAT BEFORE, STOPS) 298 AHWILD
(AND, I THOUGHT I'D NEVER GET HERE/ 14 ANNA
I THOUGHT HE MUST BE NUTTY. 18 ANNA

THOUGHT (CONT'D.)
WELL, WHEN I MADE UP MY MIND TO COME TO SEE YOU, I 22 ANNA
THOUGHT YOU WAS A YANITOR--
I NEVER THOUGHT LIVING ON SHIPS WAS SO DIFFERENT 26 ANNA
FROM LAND.
I THOUGHT YOU WAS SOME MERMAID OUT OF THE SEA COME 31 ANNA
TO TORMENT ME.
(WITH A LAUGH) I THOUGHT YOU'D SAY THAT. 38 ANNA
I THOUGHT YOU WAS SAYING-- 38 ANNA
(ANGRILY AGAIN) IF I EVER DREAMT YOU THOUGHT, 42 ANNA
(THEN STRUCK BY SOME THOUGHT--LOOKS AT HIM WITH 42 ANNA
KEEN SUSPICION--
I SAID I WAS SURE--I TOLD HIM I THOUGHT YOU HAVE A 51 ANNA
BIT OF LOVE FOR ME TOO.
(THEN JEERINGLY) I THOUGHT YOU'D BEATEN IT FOR 63 ANNA
GOOD
(WITH A SHUDDER) SAY, YOU'RE CRAZIER THAN I 67 ANNA
THOUGHT.
HIS FACE LIGHTS UP WITH A SUDDEN HAPPY THOUGHT. 76 ANNA
AS SOON AS SHE IS GONE BURKE RELAPSES INTO AN 77 ANNA
ATTITUDE OF GLOOMY THOUGHT.
THEN I THOUGHT OF LEAVING YOU. 91 BEYOND
I WAS TOO PROUD TO LET YOU SEE I CARED BECAUSE I 91 BEYOND
THOUGHT THE YEAR YOU HAD AWAY
AND THE PAIN OF THAT THOUGHT REVEALED TO ME IN A 91 BEYOND
FLASH--
AND YOU THOUGHT YOURSELF TOO EDUCATED TO WASTE ANY 91 BEYOND
TIME ON ME.
AS THOUGH HE WERE THROWING OFF SOME DISTURBING 93 BEYOND
THOUGHT--WITH A LAUGH)
(AVOIDING HER EYES) I THOUGHT MAYBE ROBERT WANTED 97 BEYOND
TO TONIGHT.
(PURSUING HER TRAIN OF THOUGHT) 98 BEYOND
AND I THOUGHT SHE LOVED--SOMEONE ELSE. 100 BEYOND
(HE WIPES HIS PERSPIRING BROW IN ANGUISH AT THIS 103 BEYOND
THOUGHT)
HE THOUGHT HE HAD SUDDENLY GONE MAD) 104 BEYOND
IT SOUNDS STRANGE TO HEAR YOU, ANDY, THAT I ALWAYS105 BEYOND
THOUGHT HAD GOOD SENSE,
I NEVER THOUGHT I'D LIVE TO SEE THE DAY WHEN A SON106 BEYOND
O' MINE'D LOOK ME IN THE FACE
I NEVER LOVED HER, AND THE THOUGHT OF SUCH A THING107 BEYOND
NEVER ENTERED MY HEAD.
I'VE OFTEN THOUGHT SINCE IT MIGHT HAVE BEEN BETTER116 BEYOND
THE OTHER WAY.
I THOUGHT WE WERE BOUND DOWN FOR DAVY JONES, SURE.131 BEYOND
WHY, I THOUGHT I TOLD YOU EVERYTHING IN MY 131 BEYOND
LETTERS.
WHY WE'VE ALL THOUGHT--WE'VE ALL BEEN HOPING 137 BEYOND
THAN EVER I THOUGHT IT WAS IN THE OLD DAYS. 138 BEYOND
PASSIN' BY THE HOME I THOUGHT I'D DROP IN 141 BEYOND
(LOOKING AT HIM WITH FRIGHTENED EYES AS IF SHE 150 BEYOND
THOUGHT HE HAD GONE MAD)
I SAW WHAT I THOUGHT WAS A CHANCE TO BECOME A 156 BEYOND
MILLIONAIRE AGAIN.
IF HE'S GROWN SO TOUCHY HE'D NEVER ACCEPT A CENT 157 BEYOND
IF HE THOUGHT I WAS HARD UP.+
(APPALLED BY A SUDDEN THOUGHT) 158 BEYOND
AND THEN I THOUGHT THAT WHEN MARY CAME IT'D BE 163 BEYOND
DIFFERENT, AND I'D LOVE HIM.+
GOOD GOD, BUT I NEVER THOUGHT--(HE STOPS, 164 BEYOND
SHUDDERING AT HIS REMEMBRANCE)
SO I THOUGHT I'D TRY TO END AS I MIGHT HAVE--IF 167 BEYOND
I'D HAD THE COURAGE--ALONE--
I THOUGHT I'D GIVEN YOU THE SLIP. 167 BEYOND
MY BELLY FEELS LUKE I'D SWALLLEYED A DOZEN RIVETS 480 CARDIF
AT THE THOUGHT AV UT.
(SLOWLY) I THOUGHT I WAS GOIN' THEN. 483 CARDIF
THE PAIN AIN'T SO BAD NOW, BUT I THOUGHT IT HAD ME484 CARDIF
THEN.
DIDN'T I TELL YOU YOU WASN'T HALF AS SICK AS YOU 485 CARDIF
THOUGHT YOU WAS5
I NEVER TOLD YUH THIS, 'CAUSE I THOUGHT YOU'D 487 CARDIF
LAUGH AT ME.
I THOUGHT THEIR BREATHS SMELLED DAMN QUEER. 473 CARIBE
I DIDN'T KNOW--I THOUGHT YOU WERE IN YOUR ROOM. 563 CROSS
THE WISH IS FATHER TO THAT THOUGHT, EH5 494 DAYS
WHY, NOTHING--EXCEPT I THOUGHT YOU'D AGREED THAT 494 DAYS
THE FURTHER
I THOUGHT YOU'D GOT THAT OUT OF YOUR SYSTEM LONG 496 DAYS
AGO WHEN YOU GOT ENGAGED TO
(CONFUSED) WELL, TO TELL THE TRUTH, I HAVEN'T 497 DAYS
GIVEN IT A THOUGHT IN YEARS. BUT--
WELL, I THOUGHT I MIGHT AS WELL DO SOMETHING WITH 497 DAYS
ALL THIS LEISURE.
I THOUGHT I BETTER BREAK THE NEWS IN PERSON. 499 DAYS
HE WAS PARTICULARLY DELIGHTED WHEN HE THOUGHT 502 DAYS
THEY'D ABOLISHED LOVE AND
OH, I THOUGHT I'D SURPRISE YOU. 505 DAYS
ON HIS KNEES, WHEN EVERY ONE THOUGHT HE WAS 511 DAYS
PRAYING/
I ONLY THOUGHT I MIGHT BE ABLE TO HELP. 517 DAYS
(WITH A TWISTED SMILE) I THOUGHT WE WEREN'T GOING517 DAYS
TO TALK ABOUT MY TROUBLES/
HIS HAPPINESS FILLED ME WITH RAGE--THE THOUGHT 521 DAYS
THAT HE MADE OTHERS HAPPY.
WHEN I FIRST MET HIM I THOUGHT I WAS THROUGH WITH 523 DAYS
MARRIAGE FOR GOOD.
I THOUGHT I HEARD A FAMILIAR VOICE WHEN I CAME IN.525 DAYS
I THOUGHT, AS I'D TOLD UNCLE TO COME EARLY, I 525 DAYS
BETTER--
DO YOU IMAGINE I EVER THOUGHT IT WAS ANYTHING BUT 526 DAYS
REVENGE ON YOUR PART5
YES, I--I'VE GOT MOST OF IT THOUGHT OUT. 530 DAYS
(MOCKINGLY) OR THOUGHT I KNEW. 533 DAYS
BUT THIS TIME HE THOUGHT IT WOULD HELP HIM TO 537 DAYS
ESCAPE HIMSELF FOR A WHILE.

THOUGHT

THOUGHT (CONT'D.)
HE THOUGHT OF HIS WIFE--(HE FORCES A LAUGH) BUT, 537 DAYS
AS I'VE
AND, AS IF SHE GUESSED HIS THOUGHT, SHE CAME TO 537 DAYS
HIM.
PURELY AS AN OBSERVER, HE THOUGHT--THE POOR IDIOT/537 DAYS
AT THE THOUGHT OF HIS WIFE, SUDDENLY IT WAS AS IF 538 DAYS
SOMETHING OUTSIDE HIM,
THAT'S WHAT I THOUGHT YOU'D SAY. 539 DAYS
I WENT OUT BECAUSE I THOUGHT I'D LIKE TO DROP IN 549 DAYS
ON ONE OF LUCY'S PARTIES.
I THOUGHT YOU PROMISED ME IF I LET YOU STAY IN 555 DAYS
HERE YOU'D KEEP QUIET.
I THOUGHT HE WAS DRUNK--'R I'D STOPPED HIM GOIN'. 210 DESIRE
AND EVERY TIME I THOUGHT OF HOME I WISHED IT 224 DESIRE
WASN'T ME/
A SUDDEN HORRIBLE THOUGHT SEEMS TO ENTER CABOT'S 225 DESIRE
HEAD)
HAIN'T YE NEVER THOUGHT O' THAT AFORES 234 DESIRE
WHEN I THOUGHT O' THAT I DIDN'T FEEL LONESOME. 237 DESIRE
(THEN TAUNTINGLY) WHEN I KISSED YE BACK, MEBBE I 239 DESIRE
THOUGHT T'WAS SOMEONE ELSE.
I THOUGHT YE MIGHTN'T. 240 DESIRE
I THOUGHT YE MIGHT HAVE TIME T' RUN AWAY--WITH 266 DESIRE
ME--AN'...
S'CUSE ME, EMMER, IT JUMPED OUT O' MY MOUTH AFORE 494 DIFRNT
I THOUGHT.
SHE THOUGHT ON'Y THE SKIPPER WAS GOOD ENOUGH FOR 503 DIFRNT
HER, I RECKON.
(PROUDLY) YES, I AM DIFF'RENT--AND THAT'S JUST 508 DIFRNT
WHAT I THOUGHT CALEB WAS, TOO--
ME, I THOUGHT IT WAS A GOOD JOKE ON CALEB. 508 DIFRNT
HE WASN'T MARRIED THEN AND I S'POSE HE THOUGHT HE 509 DIFRNT
WAS FREE TO DO AS HE'D A MIND
BUT D'YOU S'POSE HE'S EVER GIVE HER ANOTHER 509 DIFRNT
THOUGHT?
HAD DONE THIS I'D THOUGHT IT WAS A JOKE, TOO. 512 DIFRNT
I LOVED--WHAT I THOUGHT HE WAS-- 512 DIFRNT
CALEB ALWAYS SEEMED DIFF'RENT--AND I THOUGHT HE 512 DIFRNT
WAS.
'CAUSE YOU THOUGHT IT WA'N'T. 513 DIFRNT
AND WHEN WE GROWED UP AND GOT ENGAGED I THOUGHT 516 DIFRNT
THAT MORE AND MORE.
THEN I THOUGHT WHEN THE WAR COME, AND HE WAS 540 DIFRNT
DRAFTED INTO IT,
THE THOUGHT OF THAT GIRL OF HIS NEVER ENTERED MY 426 DYNAMO
HEAD UNTIL A MOMENT AGO--
(THIS THOUGHT DRIVES HIM FRANTIC-- 426 DYNAMO
ALL THE EVENINGS I THOUGHT HE WAS HERE STUDYING...427 DYNAMO
PRETENDING TO BE SUNK IN THOUGHT HAS BEEN STARING439 DYNAMO
CALCULATINGLY AT REUBEN--
(I) THOUGHT I'D WALK AROUND AND THINK UP SOME 444 DYNAMO
LIE...
THEN ALL I CAN SAY IS THAT MY BOY I THOUGHT I 446 DYNAMO
COULD TRUST HAS TURNED INTO A LIAR
I ASKED HIM IF I COULD MARRY ADA AND HE THOUGHT HE447 DYNAMO
WAS HONOR BOUND TO TELL ME/
I THOUGHT YOU LOVED ME BETTER'N ANYONE, AND YOU'D 449 DYNAMO
NEVER SQUEAL ON ME TO HIM/
(TRIUMPHANTLY) YOU THOUGHT YOU HAD HIM CAUGHT IN 451 DYNAMO
YOUR SNARES, DID YOU&
HE'D BE MEAN AT FIRST TO ANY MAN HE THOUGHT YOU 456 DYNAMO
CARED FOR--
WHY, I THOUGHT-- DIDN'T THEY SEND FOR YOUS 461 DYNAMO
I WAS JUST PASSING THIS WAY AND THOUGHT I'D DROP 463 DYNAMO
IN TO SAY HELLO TO MOTHER.
I NEVER GAVE HER MY ADDRESS BECAUSE I THOUGHT 465 DYNAMO
SHE'D ONLY WRITE BAWLING ME OUT.
BEFORE I THOUGHT, I STARTED TO DO A PRAYER ACT-- 470 DYNAMO
AND I THOUGHT YOU WAS NICE AND LOVED US/ 489 DYNAMO
THEN YER AIN'T SO FOXY AS I THOUGHT YER WAS. 176 EJONES
(SMILING AT HIS SECRET THOUGHT) 178 EJONES
(IMMEDIATELY IN ANSWER TO HIS PRAYER COMES THE 202 EJONES
THOUGHT OF THE ONE BULLET LEFT)
(THEN AFTER A SECOND'S THOUGHT--WONDERINGLY) 203 EJONES
THAT'S WHERE I THOUGHT YOU'D GONE, MEBBE. 11 ELECTR
I MAY ONLY BE FLATTERING MYSELF, BUT I THOUGHT YOU 23 ELECTR
LIKED ME.
YOU DON'T GIVE ONE THOUGHT TO FATHER--WHO IS SO 30 ELECTR
GOOD--WHO TRUSTED YOU/
THEN SHE TURNS AND STANDS IN TENSE CALCULATING 35 ELECTR
THOUGHT.
I THOUGHT, BY GOD, I'LL TAKE HER FROM HIM AND 36 ELECTR
THAT'LL BE PART OF MY REVENGE/
IF YOU STOPPED THINKING OF YOUR REVENGE FOR A 38 ELECTR
MOMENT AND THOUGHT OF ME/
(PASSIONATELY) HAVE YOU THOUGHT OF THIS SIDE OF 41 ELECTR
HIS HOMECOMING--
I THOUGHT I'D TAUGHT YOU NEVER TO CRY. 47 ELECTR
I BELIEVE HE EVEN THOUGHT MOTHER WAS FLIRTING WITH 50 ELECTR
HIM.
I THOUGHT YOU OUGHT TO WARN MOTHER SHE WAS FOOLISH 50 ELECTR
TO ALLOW HIM TO COME HERE.
THAT DIDN'T APPEAR WORTH A THOUGHT ONE WAY OR 54 ELECTR
ANOTHER.
I THOUGHT ABOUT MY LIFE--LYING AWAKE NIGHTS--AND 54 ELECTR
ABOUT YOUR LIFE.
(EMBARRASSED--IRRITABLY) THOUGHT YOU'D GONE TO 56 ELECTR
BED, YOUNG LADY/
I THOUGHT I'D WALK A LITTLE. 56 ELECTR
I THOUGHT YOU WERE ASLEEP. 58 ELECTR
I HAD A HORRIBLE DREAM--I THOUGHT I HEARD FATHER 62 ELECTR
CALLING ME--
I THOUGHT IT WOULD NEVER END, 74 ELECTR
I THOUGHT SHE'D SURELY BE WAITING FOR ME. 74 ELECTR
I NEVER THOUGHT HIS HEART WAS WEAK. 74 ELECTR
MY HEAD GOT ACHING TILL I THOUGHT IT WOULD 82 ELECTR
EXPLODE.

THOUGHT (CONT'D.)
I THOUGHT YOU WOULD SPRAIN YOUR WRIST/ 82 ELECTR
BUT I NEVER THOUGHT HE WENT AS FAR AS TO--HATE ME. 86 ELECTR
VINNIE THOUGHT HE WAS COMING TO COURT HER. 87 ELECTR
IF I THOUGHT THAT DANCED--/ 89 ELECTR
I THOUGHT WHAT A JOKE IT WOULD BE ON THE STUPID 95 ELECTR
GENERALS LIKE FATHER IF EVERYONE
WHEN ALL SHE'S THOUGHT OF IS THIS LOW LOVER OF 98 ELECTR
HERS--/
HE THOUGHT THE WAR HAD MADE A MAN OF YOU/ 98 ELECTR
I HATE THE THOUGHT OF IT/ 101 ELECTR
BECAUSE HE THOUGHT A CHANGE WOULD BRING HER BACK 108 ELECTR
TO HER SENSES.
WE CAN'T GET CARGO AS SOON AS THE OWNER THOUGHT. 111 ELECTR
(SHE THROWS OFF THIS THOUGHT--HARSHLY) 115 ELECTR
AND AFTERWARDS I THOUGHT IT WOULD BE A GOOD 118 ELECTR
OPPORTUNITY FOR ME TO GO TO NEW YORK
BUT I THOUGHT WHEN VINNIE AND ORIN CAME BACK SHE 136 ELECTR
WOULD BE ALL RIGHT.
I THOUGHT YOU'D FORGOTTEN LONG AGO-- 140 ELECTR
I--I THOUGHT YOU WERE--/ 143 ELECTR
I'VE THOUGHT OF YOU SO MUCH/ 146 ELECTR
WHEN YOU KNOW ALL SHE WANTED WAS TO LEAVE YOU 152 ELECTR
WITHOUT A THOUGHT AND MARRY THAT--
I THOUGHT IF I COULD SEE IT CLEARLY IN THE PAST I 153 ELECTR
MIGHT BE ABLE TO FORETELL WHAT
I NEVER GAVE HIM A THOUGHT/ 153 ELECTR
ON. I KNOW YOU THOUGHT I WAS IN A STUPOR OF 153 ELECTR
GRIEF--BUT I WASN'T BLIND/
HAVEN'T YOU THOUGHT THAT, ORIN? 161 ELECTR
(TURNING TO ORIN--SHARPLY) I THOUGHT YOU WERE IN 162 ELECTR
THE STUDY.
(MORE AND MORE HYPNOTIZED BY THIS TRAIN OF 166 ELECTR
THOUGHT)
AND BEGINS TO TALK VOLUBLY TO DROWN OUT THOUGHT) 167 ELECTR
MUSINGLY) WHEN YOU PROPOSED, I THOUGHT YOUR 259 GGBROW
FUTURE PROMISED SUCCESS--MY FUTURE--
(ALREADY PREOCCUPIED WITH ANOTHER THOUGHT--COMES 270 GGBROW
AND SITS IN CHAIR ON LEFT)
(SURPRISED) THE ONE TIME I RAN INTO HIM, I 275 GGBROW
THOUGHT HE TOLD ME
(DIFFIDENTLY) I THOUGHT HE MIGHT BE SENSITIVE 277 GGBROW
ABOUT WORKING FOR--
YOUR HAND IS A COOL MUD POULTICE ON THE STING OF 279 GGBROW
THOUGHT/
HE WANTED WHAT HE THOUGHT WAS MY LOVE OF THE 287 GGBROW
FLESH/
I--I BEG YOUR PARDON--I THOUGHT-- 288 GGBROW
I THOUGHT YOU CAUGHT THEM. 296 GGBROW
HOW MANY MILLION TIMES BROWN HAS THOUGHT HOW MUCH 298 GGBROW
BETTER FOR HER IT WOULD HAVE
FOR A MOMENT, I THOUGHT IT WAS DION, YOUR VOICE 304 GGBROW
SOUNDED SO MUCH.
I'VE NEVER THOUGHT OF BILLY BROWN EXCEPT AS A 312 GGBROW
FRIEND, AND LATELY NOT EVEN THAT/
THOUGHT HAD CRASHED ON HIM--BEWILDEREDLY) 244 HA APE
(HE LAUGHS.) YOU'DA THOUGHT HUGBIE WOULDA GOT 20 HUGHIE
WISE SOMETHING WAS OUT OF ORDER
I THOUGHT IT WAS UP TO ME TO PUT OUT SOMETHING, 25 HUGHIE
AND KIDS LIKE ANIMAL STORIES.
HE THOUGHT GAMBLING WAS ROMANTIC. 28 HUGHIE
HE THOUGHT GANGSTERS WAS ROMANTIC. 28 HUGHIE
THOUGHT I MIGHT AS WELL SEE IF YOU WERE AROUND. 585 ICEMAN
I THOUGHT YOU'D BE ASLEEP. 985 ICEMAN
I'D NEVER HAVE THOUGHT SHE WAS A WOMAN WHO'D KEEP 589 ICEMAN
LETTERS.
BUT I'LL BET MOTHER HAS ALWAYS THOUGHT IT WAS ON 590 ICEMAN
HER ACCOUNT.
YOU THOUGHT I WAS GOING TO HIT HIM& 593 ICEMAN
I THOUGHT EVERYONE IN THE WORLD-- 595 ICEMAN
I HAD A CRAZY THOUGHT IN MY HEAD. 605 ICEMAN
NEVER THOUGHT I'D SEE THE DAY WHEN HARRY HOPE'S 610 ICEMAN
WOULD HAVE TARTS ROOMING IN IT.
HE THOUGHT HE WAS IN LUCK. 612 ICEMAN
(CHUCKLES) BEJEES, HE'S THOUGHT UP A NEW GAG/ 617 ICEMAN
I THOUGHT TO MYSELF, 639 ICEMAN
I THOUGHT YOU WERE IN THE GRANDSTAND. 641 ICEMAN
HARRY'LL CERTAINLY BE TOUCHED BY YOUR THOUGHT OF 643 ICEMAN
HIM.
(HE SHUDDERS) I THOUGHT I'D GO CRAZY. 644 ICEMAN
I OPENED UP BECAUSE I THOUGHT IT MUST BE YOU, 645 ICEMAN
I THOUGHT YOU WERE MY FRIEND/ 645 ICEMAN
AND YOU THOUGHT A WOMAN YOU LOVED WAS A PIECE OF 647 ICEMAN
PRIVATE PROPERTY YOU OWNED.
BUT I NEVER THOUGHT MOTHER WOULD BE CAUGHT. 649 ICEMAN
AND YOU KNOW WHAT THAT BITCH AND ALL HER FAMILY 651 ICEMAN
THOUGHT OF ME.
JEES, HARRY, I NEVER THOUGHT YOU'D SAY THAT--LIKE 654 ICEMAN
YUH MEANT IT.
AMUSEDLY) YES, WE'VE ALL HEARD YOU TELL US YOU 656 ICEMAN
THOUGHT THE WORLD OF HER,
HE STARES AHEAD, DEEP IN HARRIED THOUGHT. 665 ICEMAN
IT DIDN'T DO DEM NO GOOD IF DEY THOUGHT DEY'D 665 ICEMAN
SHAKE HIM.
BUT I NEVER THOUGHT THE COPS WOULD GET HER/ 667 ICEMAN
(GOING BACK TO HIS TRAIN OF THOUGHT) 669 ICEMAN
YES, HARRY, I CERTAINLY THOUGHT THEY'D HAVE HAD 684 ICEMAN
THE GUTS TO BE GONE
THOUGHT YOU'D BE WILLING TO HELP ME ACROSS THE 687 ICEMAN
STREET, KNOWING I'M HALF BLIND.
(DISGUSTEDLY) JEES, HARRY, I THOUGHT YUH HAD SOME 690 ICEMAN
GUTS/
BE GOD, I THOUGHT YOU WERE A GONER/ 690 ICEMAN
SCHWARTZ THOUGHT HE WAS DRUNK AND I LET HIM TINK 699 ICEMAN
IT.
I THOUGHT YOU WERE DELIBERATELY HOLDING BACK, 704 ICEMAN
WHILE I WAS AROUND.
SHE'D HAVE THOUGHT I'D STOPPED LOVING HER. 706 ICEMAN

THOUGHT

THOUGHT (CONT'D.)
(GOES ON OBLIVIOUSLY) SOMETIMES I'D TRY SOME JOKF712 ICEMAN
I THOUGHT WAS A CINKER ON
BUT I COULD TELL SHE THOUGHT IT WAS DIRTY, NOT 712 ICEMAN
FUNNY.
I GOT SO I THOUGHT OF IT ALL THE TIME, 714 ICEMAN
SHE'D HAVE THOUGHT I'D STOPPED LOVING HER. 714 ICEMAN
I THOUGHT, GOD, IF SHE'D ONLY NEVER WAKE UP, SHE'D715 ICEMAN
NEVER KNOW.
AS IF THEY CAUGHT HIS THOUGHT, 717 ICEMAN
THAT I WAS CRAZY AFTERWARDS WHEN I LAUGHED TO 720 ICEMAN
MYSELF AND THOUGHT,
I THOUGHT YOU WAS A GUNER. 722 ICEMAN
WHO IS DEEP IN THOUGHT AND IS NOT LISTENING TO THES15 INZONE
CONVERSATION.)
I THOUGHT I ATE A LOT, 14 JOURNE
SHAUGHNESSY ALMOST WEPT BECAUSE HE HADN'T THOUGHT 25 JOURNE
OF THAT ONE, BUT
YOU TALK AS IF YOU THOUGHT-- 34 JOURNE
MULTIPLYINGLY.) I KNOW YOU MAY HAVE THOUGHT IT WAS 35 JOURNE
FOR THE BEST, JAMIE.
I THOUGHT THAT WAS A DAMNED FOOL IDEA, AND I TOLD 35 JOURNE
HIM SO.
I THOUGHT I'D NEVER GET AWAY. 41 JOURNE
(BITTERLY.) BUT I SEE WHAT YOU THOUGHT. 47 JOURNE
WELL, I HADN'T THOUGHT OF THAT-- 52 JOURNE
THAT'S WHAT WE THOUGHT THE OTHER TIMES. 57 JOURNE
ACTED LAST NIGHT WHEN SHE THOUGHT WE WERE ASLEEP. 57 JOURNE
I THOUGHT LUNCH WAS READY. 66 JOURNE
HE THOUGHT, LIKE YOU, THAT WHISKEY IS A GOOD 67 JOURNE
TONIC/
I THOUGHT I'D BETTER LIE DOWN THIS MORNING. 68 JOURNE
I THOUGHT YOU DID. 76 JOURNE
(DULLY.) IT'S WHAT YOU THOUGHT. 79 JOURNE
I NEVER THOUGHT A CHILD OF MINE-- IT DOESN'T COME 79 JOURNE
FROM MY SIDE OF THE FAMILY.
PLACE, BECAUSE YOU THOUGHT THAT WOULD MAKE ME 88 JOURNE
FORGET HIS DEATH.
(BITTERLY.) I THOUGHT HE WAS AN OLD IDIOT. 94 JOURNE
I THOUGHT THAT UGLY MONKEY, SMYTHE, WOULD DRIVE US 98 JOURNE
IN A DITCH OR AGAINST A TREE.
WHO WOULD HAVE THOUGHT JAMIE WOULD GROW UP TO 110 JOURNE
DISGRACE US.
I THOUGHT TO MYSELF, 115 JOURNE
I'VE THOUGHT YOU WEREN'T QUITE RIGHT IN YOUR HEAD.127 JOURNE
I THOUGHT YOU'D GONE BACK UPTOWN TO MEET HIM. 129 JOURNE
WRITING IT TO A DUMB BARMAID, WHO THOUGHT HE WAS A135 JOURNE
POOR CRAZY SOUSE.
I THOUGHT SHE'D NEVER GOT OVER HER SICKNESS, 141 JOURNE
THAT'S ALL.
I WONDER WHAT THEY THOUGHT OF YOU WHEN THEY HEARD 144 JOURNE
YOU MOANING POORHOUSE AND
LIGHTS--HIS MIND GOING BACK TO ITS LINE OF 151 JOURNE
THOUGHT.)
EXCEPT MAMIE BURNS THOUGHT I'D GONE BUGHOUSE. 160 JOURNE
I THOUGHT HE'D NEVER STOP TALKING. 167 JOURNE
(GRUMBLINGLY.) I THOUGHT WE WERE INVITED HERE TO 276 LAZARU
EAT--
WEARINESS OF THOUGHT, OR WATCHING ONE ANOTHER WITH289 LAZARU
SUSPICION
(SUDDENLY BECOMING TERRIBLY UNEASY AT SOME 303 LAZARU
THOUGHT)
HE THOUGHT, 309 LAZARU
WHAT GOOD IS WINE IF IT CANNOT KILL THOUGHTS 317 LAZARU
(WITH A CRUEL SMILE) I HAVE THOUGHT OF A SPECIAL 345 LAZARU
TEST FOR HIM, CAESAR.
THE SMOKE POURED FROM THE WINDOWS' THE NEIGHBORS 346 LAZARU
THOUGHT THE HOUSE WAS BURNING/
AND I THOUGHT YOU MIGHT BE A DAEMON. 348 LAZARU
I THOUGHT YOU MIGHT HAVE A MAGIC CURE-- 348 LAZARU
(GENTLY) I KNOW THAT AGE AND TIME ARE BUT 354 LAZARU
TIMIDITIES OF THOUGHT.
ONCE OR TWICE I THOUGHT IT FALTERED-- THE DRAWS IN357 LAZARU
HIS BREATH WITH AN AVID GASP--
I THOUGHT YOU WANTED TO SEE ME ALONE. 7 MANSNS
FOR A MOMENT I THOUGHT YOU WERE SERIOUS-- 14 MANSNS
I THOUGHT IT WOULD MAKE YOU LAUGH. 15 MANSNS
MY THOUGHT WAS FANCIFUL--THAT PERHAPS THUS YOU 15 MANSNS
CONTINUED TO HIDE FROM YOURSELF.
BUT I NEVER THOUGHT YOU'D BOAST OF IT/ 18 MANSNS
IF I THOUGHT IT MEANT HIS HAPPINESS, I'D LIVE HERE 20 MANSNS
IN THIS HUT,
(WITH A FAINT SMILE.) I THOUGHT YOU WERE A FOOL. 20 MANSNS
HE THOUGHT, AS THEY WOULD HAVE TO SELL THEIR 35 MANSNS
PRESENT HOME AND COME TO THE CITY,
(BITTERLY.) UNLESS SHE THOUGHT I WOULDN'T LET YOU 45 MANSNS
GO WITHOUT ME.
THE WAY HE DREADS THE THOUGHT OF LIVING IN THE 66 MANSNS
SAME HOUSE WITH ME/
UNLESS YOU'VE HAD THE THOUGHT YOURSELF-- 80 MANSNS
IF I THOUGHT YOU WANTED ANOTHER WOMAN--/ 80 MANSNS
(FURIOUS AT THE THOUGHT, SHE GRABS HIS SHOULDERS 81 MANSNS
AND SHAKES HIM FIERCELY.)
I THOUGHT THE CHILDREN-- 81 MANSNS
I THOUGHT THAT YOU BOTH LIVED IN A PERFECT UNITY 82 MANSNS
OF INTERESTS AND DESIRES NOW.
AND I THOUGHT YOU'D FORGOTTEN--FORGIVE ME, 85 MANSNS
DARLING.
I THOUGHT I SHOULD PAY THEM THE COURTESY 94 MANSNS
AND PITYING SARA FOR WHAT I MISTAKENLY THOUGHT WAS100 MANSNS
HER BLIND TRUSTFULNESS,
(TURNS TO HER IN SURPRISE.) BUT I THOUGHT YOU SAW101 MANSNS
THAT, MOTHER.
I THOUGHT THIS LOOKED FAMILIAR. 107 MANSNS
I THOUGHT SHE SOUNDED A LITTLE UNEASY. 108 MANSNS
WHY, WHAT A MEAN SUSPICIOUS THOUGHT--ABOUT YOUR 109 MANSNS
POOR DEVOTED MOTHER, DEAR/

THOUGHT (CONT'D.)
ONE WOULD HAVE THOUGHT YOU WERE AFRAID THAT EVEN 109 MANSNS
YOUR OWN CHILD
AND THERE'S SOMETHING MORE BEHIND IT-- I THOUGHT 118 MANSNS
THEY'D NEVER COME IN--
AH, I'M A FOOL TO WASTE A THOUGHT ON HER-- 118 MANSNS
AS IF THEIR MINDS HAD PARTLY SENSED THE TENOR OF 119 MANSNS
HIS THOUGHT--
I THOUGHT YOU-- 121 MANSNS
I THOUGHT YOU-- 122 MANSNS
(THINKING.) I'M NOT A THOUGHT HE MOVES AROUND IN 122 MANSNS
HIS MIND TO SUIT HIS PLEASURE--
I THOUGHT--I BEG YOUR PARDON--I MUST HAVE DOZED 130 MANSNS
OFF AGAIN--
I THOUGHT, CONSIDERING HIS POSITION, I HAD BETTER 140 MANSNS
ANNOUNCE HIM MYSELF.
AND WITH NO THOUGHT IN HIS HEART OR BRAIN BUT THE 148 MANSNS
GREAT NEED TO LOVE ME/
I AM SURE IN YOUR DREAMS YOU HAVE ALREADY THOUGHT 148 MANSNS
OF MORE.
I THOUGHT THAT WAS THE CHEAPEST WAY TO TAKE 152 MANSNS
POSSESSION OF YOUR BANK.
YOU ARE EVEN MORE STUPID THAN I THOUGHT. 168 MANSNS
THE FEELING OF LIVING LIFE SO DEEPLY SURE OF 171 MANSNS
ITSELF, NOT NEEDING THOUGHT,
HE IS MUCH NEARER THE END THAN I HAD THOUGHT. 173 MANSNS
SO I CANNOT SEE WHY THE THOUGHT SHOULD MAKE YOU 181 MANSNS
SHUDDER NOW.
SO I HAD TO DO SOMETHING TO WARN YOU, AND I 184 MANSNS
THOUGHT A FAIRY TALE--
(SHE PAUSES GUILTILY.) GOD FORGIVE ME, I'M HAPPY 191 MANSNS
AT THE MERE THOUGHT OF IT,
HIS HOLINESS THOUGHT YOU MUST HAVE A SENSE OF 379 MARCOM
HUMOR.
(THEN HASTILY) WHY, WE--WE'VE ALREADY THOUGHT OF 381 MARCOM
THAT--
AND NOW I WANT TO SHOW ANOTHER LITTLE AID TO 394 MARCOM
GOVERNMENT THAT I THOUGHT OUT.
IT'S SO SIMPLE--AND YET, WHO EVER THOUGHT OF IT 394 MARCOM
BEFORE ME?
I THOUGHT TO MYSELF, WELL, IT'S FUNNY, 394 MARCOM
(CONFIDENTIALLY) STILL I THOUGHT THE BAND WAS A 403 MARCOM
GOOD IDEA--
I HAVEN'T EVER THOUGHT OF LOVING ANYONE ELSE. 404 MARCOM
THAN TO PASS ETERNITY IN AVOIDING THOUGHT. 426 MARCOM
IN SPITE OF THAT, I THOUGHT I COULD RECOGNIZE 427 MARCOM
MAPPED.
(SARCASTICALLY) I SUPPOSE YOU'VE NEVER THOUGHT OF 9 MISBEG
THATS
IT'S THE THOUGHT OF THAT PIOUS LUMP HAVING MY 16 MISBEG
MONEY THAT MADDENS ME.
SO THE ONLY HOPE, HE THOUGHT, WAS FOR ME TO CATCH 21 MISBEG
SOME INDECENT MAN.
I ONLY THOUGHT YOU WANTED MY OPINION. 22 MISBEG
AS IF HE HADN'T A THOUGHT BEYOND ENJOYING HIS 22 MISBEG
PIPE.)
(MILDLY) I THOUGHT YOU WANTED MY HONEST OPINION 23 MISBEG
I'D NEVER GIVE IT A THOUGHT IF I DIDN'T KNOW YOU 26 MISBEG
HAD A SOFT SPUT IN YOUR HEART
I THOUGHT YOU NEVER GOT UP TILL AFTERNOON. 41 MISBEG
SURE I THOUGHT I WAS DOING MY DUTY AS HOSTESS 42 MISBEG
MAKING HIM FEEL AT HOME.
(EVADES THE CHALLENGE) I NEVER THOUGHT I'D SEE 74 MISBEG
THE DAY WHEN A DAUGHTER OF MINE
THOUGHT SOMETHING MUST BE QUEER, YOU COMING HOME 75 MISBEG
BEFORE THE INN CLOSED,
BUT THEN I THOUGHT MAYBE FUR ONCE YOU'D DRUNK ALL 75 MISBEG
YOU COULD HOLD.
I ONLY THOUGHT YOU'D LIKE TO KNOW YOU'D HAD THAT 90 MISBEG
MUCH REVENGE.
HE GULD I THOUGHT YOU'D STARTED PLAYING VIRGIN 94 MISBEG
WITH ME
I THOUGHT YOU WANTED TO MAKE HIM PAY FOR HIS BLACK 94 MISBEG
TREACHERY AGAINST US,
I NEVER THOUGHT-- 98 MISBEG
(AS IF HE HADN'T LISTENED) I THOUGHT YOU'D HAVE 103 MISBEG
GIVEN ME UP AND GONE TO BED.
AS IF IN A CELL OF HIS OWN THOUGHT. 111 MISBEG
I THOUGHT WHEN I LEFT YOU REALLY WERE DYING UN ME.112 MISBEG
I THOUGHT YOU NEVER TOUCHED IT. 113 MISBEG
I GUESS IT'S MORE STEWED THAN I THOUGHT--IN THE 122 MISBEG
CENTER OF THE OLD BEAN, AT LEAST.
(FORCING A LAUGH) I'VE JUST HAD A THOUGHT. 123 MISBEG
FOR A MOMENT I THOUGHT YOU WERE THAT BLONDE PIG-- 138 MISBEG
FUR THIS ONE NIGHT, BECAUSE I THOUGHT YOU LOVED 141 MISBEG
ME.
I THOUGHT THEY WERE THE MOST BEAUTIFUL THINGS IN 143 MISBEG
THE WORLD.
I THOUGHT--(ABRUPTLY HIS EXPRESSION BECOMES 151 MISBEG
SNEERING AND CYNICAL--HARSHLY)
I THOUGHT THERE WAS STILL HOPE. 161 MISBEG
SURE, WHY WOULDN'T ME, YOU THOUGHT. 164 MISBEG
I'M NOT A PIG THAT HAS NO UTHER THOUGHT BUT 174 MISBEG
EATING/
AND IF I GAVE A THOUGHT TO HIS MONEY AT ALL, THAT 175 MISBEG
WAS THE LEAST OF IT.
HE'S DONE A POWER AV BOASTIN' ABOUT HIS DUELS, BUT 12 POET
I THOUGHT HE WAS LYIN'.
IT'S WHEN YOU DUN'T GIVE A THOUGHT FOR ALL THE 25 POET
IF'S AND WANT-TO'S IN THE WORLD/
HE HAS NO THOUGHT-- 32 POET
I AM AFRAID I MAY HAVE--THE THOUGHT OF OLD TIMES-- 42 POET
I BECOME BITTER.
AS IF YOU THOUGHT SHE'D BE UP TO ANYTHING TO CATCH 62 POET
YOUNG HARFORD.
I HAD THOUGHT HIS IMPLACABLY HONEST DISCOVERY 81 POET
THAN I THOUGHT SHE POSSESSED. 109 POET
HE MUST HAVE THOUGHT YOU'D GONE OUT OF YOUR MIND/ 111 POET

THOUGHTS

THOUGHT (CONT'D.)
WHOSE ONLY THOUGHT IS MONEY AND WHO HAS 113 POET
SHAMELESSLY THROWN HERSELF AT A YOUNG
WHEN I CALLED, I THOUGHT IT WAS ONE OF THE DAMNED 117 POET
RIFFRAFF
HE HAD NOT THOUGHT THE INTRUDER WOULD BE A 117 POET
GENTLEMAN.
THAT IS WHAT I THOUGHT YOU WERE EXPECTING WHEN YOU122 POET
MENTIONED A SETTLEMENT.
CREGAN SPEAKS, HIS ONLY THOUGHT TO GET HIM AWAY 128 POET
FROM SARA.)
BUT I THANK YOU FOR THE THOUGHT. 134 POET
(RESENTFULLY.) IT'S A WONDER SHE WOULDN'T HAVE 135 POET
MORE THOUGHT FOR YOU
THERE'S NO HEART OR THOUGHT FOR HIMSELF IN DIVIL A137 POET
ONE AV THIM.
JUST AT THE THOUGHT HE'D EVER FIGHT A DUEL. 140 POET
AND IT'S CRAZY TO GIVE IT A THOUGHT. 140 POET
WHEN I THOUGHT THERE WAS DANGER THEY'D BE RUINED 143 POET
FOREVER8
BUT I WAS SO DRUNK WITH LOVE, I'D LOST ALL THOUGHT149 POET
OR CARE ABOUT MARRIAGE.
BE CHRIST, YOU'RE STUPIDER THAN I THOUGHT YOU, IF 168 POET
YOU CAN'T SEE THAT.
I THOUGHT HE MIGHT BE IN THE BUG-HOUSE BY THIS 592 ROPE
TIME.
(TO PAT) AN' I THOUGHT HE WAS ONLY KIDDIN'. 596 ROPE
I THOUGHT YOU'D BE KILLIN' HIM THAT TIME WITH THE 597 ROPE
CHAIR.
BUT I THOUGHT HE WAS TRYIN' TO KID ME, TOO. 598 ROPE
I THOUGHT 'TWAS JOKIN' YE WAS. 598 ROPE
BUT I HONESTLY THOUGHT THAT WENCH WOULD FEEL 6 STRANG
HUMILIATED IF I...
AND SHE ACTS TOWARD ME EXACTLY AS IF SHE THOUGHT I 11 STRANG
HAD DELIBERATELY DESTROYED
I'VE THOUGHT IT ALL OUT AND DECIDED THAT I SIMPLY 14 STRANG
THAT SIX MONTHS AGO THE DOCTORS THOUGHT IT MIGHT 16 STRANG
BE YEARS BEFORE--
SO YOU SEE, FATHER, I'VE THOUGHT OF EVERYTHING 17 STRANG
PERHAPS SHE THOUGHT HER FATHER HAD SENT ME TO SPY 25 STRANG
ON HER...
DETERMINEDLY PUTS AN END TO HIS TRAIN OF THOUGHT 25 STRANG
I THOUGHT SHE'D BE ALONE/...) 26 STRANG
I THOUGHT THERE MIGHT BE A CHANCE. 27 STRANG
FLATLY) I DIDN'T WANT HIM TO SEE WHAT HE WOULD 27 STRANG
HAVE THOUGHT WAS ME.
NED THOUGHT I BETTER COME ALONG, TOO--MIGHT BE OF 30 STRANG
SOME USE.
I JUST THOUGHT YOU OUGHT TO KNOW. 32 STRANG
WHAT A VILE THOUGHT/... 33 STRANG
I THOUGHT OF A MILLION LIGHT YEARS TO A SPIRAL 41 STRANG
NEBULA--
(THINKING GLUMLY) (I THOUGHT SHE'D FORGOTTEN 51 STRANG
HIM...
AND HE THOUGHT I HAD THE MAKINGS OF A REAL FIND. 54 STRANG
(HE STARTS, FLINGING OFF HIS THOUGHT-- 55 STRANG
(DEJECTEDLY) OH-- I THOUGHT PERHAPS-- 55 STRANG
I THOUGHT I WAS PLAIN, BUT I'LL BE PLAINER. 59 STRANG
MAYBE I ALMOST HAVE--LATELY--BUT ONLY WHEN I 61 STRANG
THOUGHT OF HIS BABY/
AND I THOUGHT SAM WAS SO NORMAL--SO HEALTHY AND 61 STRANG
SANE--NOT LIKE ME/
AND I THOUGHT YOU'D LOVE HIM LIKE I DID HIS 61 STRANG
FATHER,
I THOUGHT HE'D GIVE ME SUCH HEALTHY, 61 STRANG
I THOUGHT YOU WERE A REAL FIND, BUT YOUR WORK'S 67 STRANG
FALLEN OFF TO NOTHING...))
COLE ALWAYS USED TO SAY I HAD THE STUFF, AND NED 68 STRANG
CERTAINLY THOUGHT SO....))
I THOUGHT YOU WERE LYING DOWN. 69 STRANG
AND YET I'VE GIVEN MYSELF TO MEN BEFORE WITHOUT A 72 STRANG
THOUGHT
I THOUGHT SHE WANTED A CHILD... 74 STRANG
(HE STARTS FOR THE DOOR--THEN STRUCK BY A SUDDEN 76 STRANG
THOUGHT, STOPS)
((AND I THOUGHT HE WAS SO INGROWN HE DIDN'T CARE A 77 STRANG
DAMN ABOUT ANYONE/...
(THEN SUDDENLY) I'VE JUST THOUGHT--SAM SAID HE 82 STRANG
HAPPENED TO RUN INTO YOU.
((ALL WRONG, WHAT I THOUGHT... 82 STRANG
YOU THOUGHT HE'D BE AN IDEAL HUSBAND FOR ME/ 83 STRANG
I'VE THOUGHT AND THOUGHT ABOUT IT. 84 STRANG
WHAT IS IT PRECISELY THAT SAM'S WIFE HAS THOUGHT 85 STRANG
SO MUCH OF DOING8
WIFE SHE CAN'T BEAR THE THOUGHT NOW OF GIVING 88 STRANG
HERSELF TO ANY MAN SHE COULD
SHE ALWAYS THOUGHT NED HAD A SUPERIOR MIND. 88 STRANG
I THOUGHT WE'D GET SOME WORD FROM CHARLIE THIS 94 STRANG
MORNING SAYING IF HE WAS COMING
HE WAS SO HANDSOME AND GRACEFUL, SHE ALWAYS 100 STRANG
THOUGHT.
I HAVEN'T BEEN ABLE TO BE AS IMPERSONAL AS I 102 STRANG
THOUGHT I COULD BE.
WHY, I WAS ONLY PICKING OUT A TYPE I THOUGHT WOULD114 STRANG
BE GOOD FOR YOU, CHARLIE--
HE'S SO PROUD OF BEING THOUGHT A DON JUAN/... 117 STRANG
(THINKING--TORMENTEDLY) ((THE THOUGHT OF THAT 117 STRANG
WOMAN...
AND I THOUGHT YOU WERE ABSOLUTELY TRUE TO ME, 119 STRANG
CHARLIE/.
WHY HAVE I NEVER THOUGHT OF THAT8... 129 STRANG
I THOUGHT OF SAM/ 130 STRANG
I THOUGHT OF MYSELF AND MY CAREER/ 130 STRANG
GOD, HOW I'VE THOUGHT OF THEM--LYING AWAKE-- 130 STRANG
I THOUGHT I HEARD THE BABY. 133 STRANG
I SUPPOSED THE THOUGHT OF A WIFE TAKING YOU AWAY 143 STRANG
FROM ME WOULD BE TOO MUCH--
IT WAS A BEAUTIFUL LITTLE BOAT, I THOUGHT. 150 STRANG

THOUGHT (CONT'D.)
I THOUGHT ONCE HER CHANGE OF LIFE WAS OVER 160 STRANG
I WISH I THOUGHT THAT. 163 STRANG
I THOUGHT IT WOULD MEAN PEACE. 165 STRANG
I THOUGHT HE WAS ONLY FLIRTING WITH HER-- 168 STRANG
(BUT SHE CANNOT BEAR THIS THOUGHT--VINDICTIVELY) 168 STRANG
(PLACATINGLY) I THOUGHT SOMEONE'D BETTER STAY 171 STRANG
HERE
I SIMPLY THOUGHT YOU MEANT-- 186 STRANG
I WOULD HAVE THOUGHT BITTERLY, «THE GORDONS HAVE 187 STRANG
ALL THE LUCK/»
THERE ARE CERTAIN THINGS CONNECTED WITH DAD'S WILL191 STRANG
I THOUGHT I OUGHT TO--
SO GRATEFULLY AND FORGIVINGLY, I THOUGHT... 191 STRANG
I AM SAD BUT THERE'S COMFORT IN THE THOUGHT 191 STRANG
(COLDLY SNEERING) I THOUGHT IT MUST BE A JOKE 192 STRANG
MYSELF--BUT DAD INSISTED.
I THOUGHT SHE TOLD HIM...!) 194 STRANG
I'VE NEVER THOUGHT THAT/... 196 STRANG
I WAS ON MY WAY HOME FROM THE THEATER AND I 450 WELDED
THOUGHT I'D DROP IN FOR A SECOND.
I THOUGHT NELLY'D PROBABLY HAVE HEARD FROM YOU. 450 WELDED
IT'S ONLY THAT I'VE THOUGHT I'VE FELT YOU DRAWING 456 WELDED
AWAY--/
WHAT ELSE COULD I HAVE THOUGHTS 458 WELDED
BUT I THOUGHT YOU'D UNDERSTAND--THAT I'D BEEN 458 WELDED
SEARCHING FOR SOMETHING--
IT MAKES ME LOWER THAN YOU THOUGHT, BUT YOU'RE 459 WELDED
GLAD TO KNOW IT JUST THE SAME/
WHEN HE FIRST ENGAGED ME--I'D HEARD THE GOSSIP--I 459 WELDED
THOUGHT HE EXPECTED--
I THOUGHT YOU UNDERSTOOD. 459 WELDED
I MAY HAVE THOUGHT YOU ONCE LOVED-- 459 WELDED
(THEN FOLLOWING HER OWN LINE OF THOUGHT, SHE 467 WELDED
I TRIED TO FIRE THEM--THOUGHT I HAD--BUT WHEN YOU 467 WELDED
CAME TONIGHT--
(WITH A START--EVIDENTLY ANSWERING SOME TRAIN OF 471 WELDED
THOUGHT IN
GAWD, I THOUGHT YOU'D GET US BOTH PINCHED. 471 WELDED
I THOUGHT OF THAT--BUT IT'S EVASION. 472 WELDED
(STRUCK BY A SUDDEN THOUGHT) 476 WELDED
(HE SHAKES HIS HEAD AS IF TO DRIVE SOME THOUGHT 476 WELDED
FROM HIS MIND
I THOUGHT--(THEY STARE AT EACH OTHER--A PAUSE.) 480 WELDED
YOU THOUGHT I'D STAYED HERE ALL THE TIMES 482 WELDED
AND I HAD THOUGHT OF HER ONLY AS REVENGE--THE 485 WELDED
LOWEST OF THE LOW/

THOUGHTFUL
(SHE BECOMES VERY THOUGHTFUL, HER FACE GROWING 234 DESIRE
SHREWD.
(HIS TONE FORCED) WELL, IT WAS THOUGHTFUL OF HIM.656 ICEMAN
BEJEES, THAT'S THOUGHTFUL OF YOU. 656 ICEMAN
SHE HAS A FINE THOUGHTFUL FOREHEAD. 1 MANSNS
YOU ARE SO THOUGHTFUL AND GOOD. 170 MANSNS
EXCEPT THAT HIS EXPRESSION IS GRAVER AND MORE 76 STRANG
THOUGHTFUL.

THOUGHTFULLY
(HE PAUSES THOUGHTFULLY, CONSIDERING THIS-- 224 AHWILD
(THEN AFTER A PAUSE, THOUGHTFULLY) 291 AHWILD
(THOUGHTFULLY) SAILORS NEVER DO GO HOME HARDLY, 37 ANNA
DO THEY8
(THOUGHTFULLY--BEGINNING TO SEE THIS SIDE OF THE 101 BEYOND
ARGUMENT)
(THOUGHTFULLY) YES, I GUESS I WILL. 141 BEYOND
(THOUGHTFULLY) I'VE BEEN WONDERING WHAT THE GREAT161 BEYOND
CHANGE WAS IN YOU.
(AFTER A PAUSE--THOUGHTFULLY) 219 DESIRE
(HE CLICKS THE DICE IN HIS HAND--THOUGHTFULLY.) 36 HUGHIE
(NODS--THEN THOUGHTFULLY) WHY AIN'T HE OUT DERE 584 ICEMAN
STICKIN' BY HER8
HE GOES ON THOUGHTFULLY) 663 ICEMAN
AFTER A PAUSE DURING WHICH HE LOOKS AT HER 386 MARCOM
THOUGHTFULLY--TENDERLY)

THOUGHTS
DURING WHICH SHE SEEMS TO BE ENDEAVORING TO 940 'ILE
COLLECT HER THOUGHTS)
(DAZEDLY--TRYING TO COLLECT HIS THOUGHTS) 950 'ILE
THOUGHTS. 239 AHWILD
ALMOST DESECRATING THOUGHTS) 276 AHWILD
(HAS BEEN BUSY WITH HER OWN THOUGHTS DURING THIS 289 AHWILD
LAST--
SHE LOOKS UNHAPPY, TROUBLED, FROWNINGLY 41 ANNA
CONCENTRATED ON HER THOUGHTS.
AND ME THINKING THOUGHTS ABOUT YOU, AND HAVING 60 ANNA
GREAT LOVE FOR YOU.
TORMENTED WITH THOUGHTS OF MAT BURKE AND THE GREAT 61 ANNA
WRONG YOU'VE DONE HIM/
TRYING DESPERATELY TO BANISH HER THOUGHTS BY 67 ANNA
LOOKING AT THE PICTURES.
AND ME TORMENTED WITH THOUGHTS. 71 ANNA
(MOODILY PREOCCUPIED WITH HIS OWN THOUGHTS-- 78 ANNA
(IMMERSED IN HIS OWN THOUGHTS--ENTHUSIASTICALLY) 125 BEYOND
(TOO OCCUPIED WITH HIS OWN THOUGHTS TO HEAR HER-- 125 BEYOND
VINDICTIVELY)
(BURIED IN HIS OWN THOUGHTS--BITTERLY) 126 BEYOND
WHEN I'M HAVIN' THE SAME THOUGHTS MYSELF, TOIME 487 CARDIF
AFTHER TOIME.
I FEEL--(THEN, AS IF DESPERATELY TRYING TO SHAKE 495 DAYS
OFF HIS THOUGHTS)
A PENNY FOR YOUR THOUGHTS, JOHN. 528 DAYS
(SHUDDERING--CLUTCHES HIS HEAD IN BOTH HANDS AS IF551 DAYS
TO CRUSH OUT HIS THOUGHTS)
HE SCOWLS BACK HIS THOUGHTS OF HER AND SPITS WITH 228 DESIRE
EXAGGERATED DISDAIN--
THEN, EVIDENTLY UNABLE TO KEEP SILENT ABOUT HIS 236 DESIRE
THOUGHTS,
(GOING ON WITH HIS OWN THOUGHTS) 260 DESIRE

THOUGHTS

THOUGHTS (CONT'D.)
(TOO ABSORBED IN HER OWN THOUGHTS TO LISTEN TO 260 DESIRE HIM--PLEADINGLY)
(PREOCCUPIED WITH HIS OWN THOUGHTS--GOING TO THE 501 DIFRNT DOOR IN REAR)
THOUGHTS ON FINDING SOME WAY TO MAKE GOOD HIS 531 DIFRNT BLUFF.
HIS WIFE IS PRETENDING TO READ, BUT HER THOUGHTS 422 DYNAMO ARE ACTIVELY ELSEWHERE.
(A MURDERER'S THOUGHTS/ 423 DYNAMO
(HE LOOKS AROUND UNEASILY, AFRAID OF WHERE HIS 424 DYNAMO THOUGHTS ARE LEADING HIM.
(HIS THOUGHTS WHIRLING IN HIS HEAD) 448 DYNAMO
I PREOCCUPIED WITH HER OWN THOUGHTS) 458 DYNAMO
(STARTLED OUT OF HIS THOUGHTS, AT FIRST FROWNS, 468 DYNAMO
HIS THOUGHTS SEIZING ON THIS COINCIDENCE) 481 DYNAMO
AS IF HE DIDN'T KNOW WHERE TO HIDE, HIS THOUGHTS 487 DYNAMO HOUNDED BY REMORSE)
(THEN SHAKING HIMSELF LIKE A WET DOG TO GET RID OF1B8 EJUNES THESE DEPRESSING THOUGHTS)
HIS SILENCE ALWAYS CREEPS INTO MY THOUGHTS. 40 ELECTR
SHE'LL BE COMING BACK--AND YOU'RE NOT GOOD AT 42 ELECTR HIDING YOUR THOUGHTS.
CHRIST, I WON'T HAVE SUCH THOUGHTS/ 93 ELECTR
LISTENING TO MY GLOOMY THOUGHTS/ 118 ELECTR
STOP HAVING SUCH THOUGHTS/ 156 ELECTR
(TORTUREDLY--BEGINS TO PACE UP AND DOWN, MUTTERING157 ELECTR HER THOUGHTS ALOUD)
OH, GOD, DON'T LET ME HAVE SUCH THOUGHTS/ 157 ELECTR
HE STARES AHEAD, THEN SHAKES OFF HIS THOUGHTS AND 312 GGBROW CONCENTRATES ON HIS WORK--
(CONTINUING THE TREND OF HIS THOUGHTS AS IF HE HAD229 HA APE NEVER BEEN INTERRUPTED--
(UNHEEDING--GROPING IN HIS THOUGHTS) 241 HA APE
AS IF HE SUDDENLY WERE AFRAID OF HIS OWN 593 ICEMAN THOUGHTS--FORCING A SMILE)
(PREOCCUPIED WITH HIS OWN THOUGHTS) EHS SURE. 600 ICEMAN
THAT THEIR THOUGHTS ARE NOT ON WHAT SHE IS SAYING 71 JOURNE ANY MORE THAN HER OWN ARE.
(FOLLOWING HER OWN THOUGHTS) 351 LAZARU
I HAVE ONLY TO BE PATIENT. KEEP MY MIND OFF BITTER 4 MANSNS THOUGHTS.
MOTHERS SHOULD NEVER HAVE SUCH THOUGHTS, SHOULD 12 MANSNS THEYS
WHAT RUBBISH THOUGHTS FOR A MAN OF MY YEARS AND 37 MANSNS PROFESSION/
THOUGHTS AND LOOKS BACK TOWARD THE DOORWAY AT REAR 44 MANSNS SMILINGLY.
I WILL NOT HAVE YOU PUT SUCH THOUGHTS IN MY MIND 98 MANSNS ABOUT A WOMAN TO WHOM I OWE AN
---IN A SHROUD OF THOUGHTS WHICH WERE NOT THEIR 108 MANSNS THOUGHTS.---
THEIR THOUGHTS ARE HEARD.) 118 MANSNS
I WAS PREOCCUPIED WITH MY THOUGHTS. 121 MANSNS
I OUGHT TO HAVE KNOWN YOU GUESSED MY THOUGHTS. 123 MANSNS
AS HIS THOUGHTS HAVE PROGRESSED THE EXPRESSIONS ON126 MANSNS THE TWO WOMEN'S FACES
I CAN STILL FEEL HIS THOUGHTS REACHING OUT-- 136 MANSNS
AND WHAT IF I WAS HAVING THOUGHTS ABOUT JOEL& 144 MANSNS
ME, TO HAVE SUCH THOUGHTS/ 144 MANSNS
I--I WAS TRYING TO CONCENTRATE MY THOUGHTS ON THE 172 MANSNS FINAL SOLUTION OF THE PROBLEM.
MY THOUGHTS IN THIS AUTUMN ARE LONELY AND SAD, 384 MARCOM
A TRIFLE PUZZLED, AND NOT A LITTLE IRRITATED AS 439 MARCOM HIS THOUGHTS.
(CONTROLLING HER ANGER) YOU'RE FULL OF BRIGHT 9 MISBEG THOUGHTS.
AND YOU CAN TELL ME YOUR THOUGHTS. 54 MISBEG
I COULDN'T SLEEP WITH MY THOUGHTS TORMENTED THE 76 MISBEG WAY THEY ARE.
HER THOUGHTS ARE ON THE RECEDING FIGURE OF TYRONE 176 MISBEG AGAIN.
AND FEEL ONE WITH NATURE, AND THINK GREAT THOUGHTS 29 POET ABOUT WHAT LIFE MEANS.
WHAT DO I CARE WHAT YOU SAY WHEN THE BLACK 42 POET THOUGHTS ARE ON YOU
(STARTLED FROM HIS THOUGHTS, BECOMES AT ONCE THE 101 POET CONDESCENDING SQUIRE--
TO DRIVE OUT BLACK THOUGHTS AND RHEUMATISM, 134 POET
(PREOCCUPIED WITH HER OWN THOUGHTS.) 181 POET
HIS EYES STARE IDLY AT HIS DRIFTING THOUGHTS) 4 STRANG
THEN HE SHAKES HIS HEAD, FLINGING OFF HIS 5 STRANG THOUGHTS.
(HER VOICE BECOMING A BIT UNCANNY, HER THOUGHTS 18 STRANG BREAKING THROUGH)
THOSE DON'T SOUND LIKE YOUR THOUGHTS. 19 STRANG
(HIS THOUGHTS AT EBB, WITHOUT EMPHASIS, SLUGGISH 24 STRANG AND MELANCHOLY)
DAMNED THOUGHTS/... 31 STRANG
SO MANY MANY WORDS HAVE JAMMED UP INTO THOUGHTS IN 41 STRANG MY POOR HEAD/
THOUGHTS/... 52 STRANG
I HAVEN'T HAD SUCH THOUGHTS... 52 STRANG
FORCING HIS THOUGHTS INTO OTHER CHANNELS) 67 STRANG
(I MUST STOP SUCH THOUGHTS... 69 STRANG
TO HAVE SUCH THOUGHTS WHEN MOTHER IS SICK AND I 75 STRANG OUGHT TO BE THINKING ONLY OF
SO EACH TIME HER THOUGHTS COME TO THE MAN SHE MUST 88 STRANG SELECT THEY ARE AFRAID TO GO
(IN TERROR) (WHAT THOUGHTS/... 100 STRANG
HIS THOUGHTS BITTER AND DESPERATE LIKE A CORNERED 105 STRANG FUGITIVE'S.)
STOP THESE THOUGHTS/... 117 STRANG
WHAT INANE THOUGHTS/...)) 123 STRANG
(WHAT UNGRATEFUL THOUGHTS ON MY SON'S 138 STRANG BIRTHDAY/...
OF THOUGHTS THAT ARE STRANGERS... 139 STRANG
THOUGHTS THAT NEVER KNOW THE OTHER'S THOUGHTS... 139 STRANG

THOUGHTS (CONT'D.)
TIME TO GO WHEN THOSE THOUGHTS COME... 149 STRANG
(SENSING HER THOUGHTS, SITS UP IN HER LAP AND 156 STRANG STARES INTO HER FACE.
(HE READ MY THOUGHTS/... 157 STRANG
(THEN WITH A SHUDDER AT HIS THOUGHTS) 183 STRANG
(CHANGING THE SUBJECT OF HIS THOUGHTS ABRUPTLY) 189 STRANG
YOU DEVIL, YOU, YOU READ THOUGHTS INTO MY MIND/ 460 WELDED
(SHE IS GOING DOWN, PREOCCUPIED WITH HER OWN 467 WELDED THOUGHTS.
THOUGHTS KEEP ALIVE. 474 WELDED

THOUSAND
WE'VE BEEN OVER THIS A THOUSAND TIMES BEFORE, AND 212 AHWILD STILL YOU GO ON/
WE'VE BEEN OVER THIS A THOUSAND TIMES BEFORE AND 213 AHWILD I'LL ALWAYS FEEL THE SAME AS
IN EVERY THOUSAND YEARS--BUT, DEARIE ME, HOW HE 231 AHWILD DOES ENJOY IT/
(KISSING HIM) I'LL GIVE YOU A THOUSAND, IF YOU 242 AHWILD WANT 'EM.
YES, SIR, I'VE HEARD HIM SAY THAT VERY THING A 272 AHWILD THOUSAND TIMES. MUST BE.
THAT'LL PROTECT HIM MORE THAN A THOUSAND 289 AHWILD LECTURES--
INADIE AND I WILL ASK YOUR PARDON A THOUSAND 34 ANNA TIMES--AND ON MY KNEES, IF YE LIKE.
A STENCH/ TEN THOUSAND OF THEM/ 132 BEYOND
(AFTER A PAUSE) I'VE GOT OVER A THOUSAND SAVED, 134 BEYOND AND YOU CAN HAVE THAT.
(EASILY) SIX THOUSAND MILES MORE OR LESS. 137 BEYOND
AND YET IT'S A CHANCE IN A THOUSAND-- 141 BEYOND
I'VE SAVED TEN THOUSAND FROM THE WRECKAGE, MAYBE 157 BEYOND TWENTY.
SMITH SAID HE WOULD GIVE TWO THOUSAND CASH IF I 565 CROSS WOULD SELL THE PLACE TO HIM--
(SCORNFULLY) TWO THOUSAND/ 565 CROSS
THE GUILT WHICH TORTURES HIM A THOUSAND-FOLD NOW 544 DAYS SHE IS DEAD.
BUT MOTHER MEANS A THOUSAND TIMES MORE TO ME THAN 98 ELECTR HE EVER DID/
WE ARE WHERE CENTURIES ONLY COUNT AS SECONDS AND 323 GGBROW AFTER A THOUSAND LIVES OUR EYES
PUT ABOUT A THOUSAND GUYS' NAMES IN A HAT--ALL SHE 15 HUGHIE COULD REMEMBER--
AH, BE DAMNED/ HAVEN'T I HEARD THEIR VISIONS A 608 ICEMAN THOUSAND TIMES$
I DON'T CARE WHERE HE IS, EXCEPT I WISH IT WAS A 636 ICEMAN THOUSAND MILES AWAY/
GOD, HOW MANY THOUSAND TIMES--/ 33 JOURNE
BUT YOU'VE HEARD ME SAY THIS A THOUSAND TIMES. 61 JOURNE
I'VE HEARD PAPA TELL THAT MACHINE SHOP STORY TEN 117 JOURNE THOUSAND TIMES.
THIRTY-FIVE TO FORTY THOUSAND DOLLARS NET PROFIT A150 JOURNE SEASON
AT FROM THIRTY-FIVE TO FORTY THOUSAND NET PROFIT A150 JOURNE SEASON/
IT WON'T TAKE LONG FOR US TO GET THE HUNDRED 48 MANSNS THOUSAND WE HAVE SET AS OUR GOAL.
WE'VE GOT FIFTY THOUSAND DOLLARS, THE MOST OF IT 48 MANSNS IN GOLD ENGLISH GUINEAS.
STILL, IF WE HAD THAT TWO HUNDRED THOUSAND IN 49 MANSNS SPECIE NOW--
FATHER WOULD RATHER HAVE FACED RUIN A THOUSAND 59 MANSNS TIMES--
IT CONTAINS ONE THOUSAND ARABIAN LIES, WITH ONE 348 MARCOM OVER FOR GOOD MEASURE.
(DRYLY) FIVE HUNDRED THOUSAND NAMES ARE SIGNED TO392 MARCOM IT.
FROM THE INHABITANTS OF YANG-CHAU ENUMERATING OVER392 MARCOM THREE THOUSAND CASES
WOULD COST YOU THE LIVES OF TEN THOUSAND MEN. 394 MARCOM
THIS AMOUNT TO ONE HUNDRED THOUSAND YEN. 394 MARCOM
IT'S NINE HUNDRED THOUSAND NOW IN OUR MONEY, ISN'T408 MARCOM IT&
CALL IT FOUR THOUSAND YOU OWE ME. 63 MISBEG
TWENTY PIGS AT TWO HUNDRED, THAT'S FOUR THOUSAND. 63 MISBEG
AND A THOUSAND TO CURE THE SICK AND COVER FUNERAL 63 MISBEG EXPENSES FOR THE DEAD.
THERE'S NEVER A PROMISE OF GOD OR MAN GOES NORTH 66 MISBEG OF TEN THOUSAND BUCKS.
HARDER OFFERS TO GIVE HIM FIVE THOUSAND CASH AS A 84 MISBEG LOAN AGAINST THE ESTATE THE
(OVERWHELMED) TEN THOUSAND/ 84 MISBEG
TEN THOUSAND, CASH. 84 MISBEG
OUT, THAT HE'D EVER MISS A DATE WITH FIVE THOUSAND 85 MISBEG DOLLARS.
BUT I WAS THINKING HOW DO I KNOW WHAT I WOULDN'T 86 MISBEG DO FOR FIVE THOUSAND CASH.
WE'LL MAKE HIM SIGN A PAPER HE OWES ME TEN 95 MISBEG THOUSAND DOLLARS THE MINUTE THE
DON'T I LOOK TEN THOUSAND DOLLARS' WORTH TO ANY 98 MISBEG DRUNK&
I AM NO LONGER THE MASTER OF MELODY CASTLE AND AN 48 POET ESTATE OF THREE THOUSAND ACRES
MR. HARFORD IS PREPARED TO PAY YOU THE SUM OF 122 POET THREE THOUSAND DOLLARS--
YOU'LL HAVE A THOUSAND YEARS IN HELL, I WOULDN'T 149 POET CARE/
BUT THE THOUSAND DOLLARS PAW GOT FOR THE MORTGAGE 585 ROPE JUST BEFORE THAT WOMAN RAN
IF WE'D ON'Y THE THOUSAND ME TO STOCK THE FARM GOOD587 ROPE
I'VE TOLD MYSELF THIS A THOUSAND TIMES 84 STRANG
BUT I'LL NEED A HUNDRED THOUSAND--AND WHERE WILL I121 STRANG GET IT&
AND A HUNDRED THOUSAND, NO LESS/... 122 STRANG
NEVER MIND THE HUNDRED THOUSAND. 122 STRANG
I CAN'T STAND HEARING THOSE SAME REPROACHES I'VE 143 STRANG HEARD A THOUSAND TIMES BEFORE/

THOUSAND (CONT'D.)
IT'S A THOUSAND TO ONE AGAINST IT AT THIS LATE 172 STRANG
DAY.
TEN THOUSAND YEARS--ABOUT--ISN'T ITS OR TWENTY$ 474 WELDED
THOUSANDS
I'VE TALKED TO ROBERT THOUSANDS OF TIMES 113 BEYOND
I'VE GOT USED TO THE FEEL OF CAMPS WITH THOUSANDS 53 ELECTR
OF MEN AROUND ME AT NIGHT--
I'VE SPENT THOUSANDS UPON THOUSANDS IN CURES/ 141 JOURNE
THERE ARE THOUSANDS OF THEM OUTSIDE THE WALL. 316 LAZARU
ACCOMPANIMENT FROM THE HEAVENS TO THIS LAUGHTER UF318 LAZARU
THOUSANDS WHICH THROBS IN
OF THE THOUSANDS OF BELLS IN THE CITY, BIG AND 432 MARCOM
LITTLE, NEAR AND FAR.
THOUSANDTH
WELL, IT WON'T BE THE FIRST TIME, WILL IT-- OR THE 69 JOURNE
THOUSANDTHS
I'LL BET NONE OF HIS TARTS ON BROADWAY EVER GOT A 95 MISBEG
THOUSANDTH PART OF THAT OUT OF
THRAITOR
AN' NOW WHAT'S TO BE DONE WID THAT BLACK-HEARTED 524 INZONE
THRAITORS
THRASHIN'
HE MIGHT COME TO ALL AV A SUDDEN AND GIVE YOU A 160 POET
HELL AV A THRASHIN'.
THRASHING
I'LL GIVE YOU A THRASHING THAT'LL TEACH YOU--/ 128 JOURNE
THREAD
(UNDER LOVING'S COMPULSION, HE PICKS UP THE THREAD509 DAYS
OF THE STORY)
THREADBARE
THREADBARE TRAILS, LEADING TO THE KITCHEN AND 144 BEYOND
OUTER DOORS.
HE IS DRESSED IN THREADBARE BLACK CLOTHES 574 ICEMAN
LIKE HUGO, HE WEARS THREADBARE BLACK, AND 575 ICEMAN
EVERYTHING ABOUT HIM IS CLEAN.
HE WEARS A THREADBARE, READY-MADE, GREY SACK SUIT 13 JOURNE
AND SHINELESS BLACK SHOES.
HE HAS ON A THREADBARE BROWN OVERCOAT BUT WEARS NO578 ROPE
HAT.)
THREAT
I CAN FEEL THE THREAT IN THE AIR. 549 'ILE
(A BIT SHAKEN BY THIS THREAT--BUT IN THE SAME FLAT204 AHWILD
TONE)
(WORRIEDLY IMPRESSED BY THIS THREAT--BUT 271 AHWILD
PRETENDING SCORN)
(HE SHAKES OVER HIS MUTTERED THREAT AND STRIDES 108 BEYOND
TOWARD THE DOOR REAR, RIGHT.)
(THIS IN A TONE OF COLD THREAT.) 238 DESIRE
(A VEILED THREAT IN HER TONE) 238 DESIRE
UNCONSCIOUSLY REPEATING THE EXACT THREAT 156 ELECTR
TO THE THREAT OF NIGHT AND SILENCE AS IT PURSUES 32 HUGHIE
AN IDEAL OF FAME AND GLORY
(SMILINGLY, BUT WITH A THREAT UNDERNEATH.) 92 MANSNS
(HE CHECKS HIMSELF, HIS EYES GLEAMING WITH A WILD 159 MANSNS
THREAT.)
SO WHAT THREAT--I CAN'T THINK OF ANY HE WOULDN'T 96 MISBEG
LAUGH AT.
(DOESN'T BELIEVE THIS THREAT BUT IS FRIGHTENED BY 17 POET
THE POSSIBILITY.)
PERHAPS YOU THINK I CANNOT CARRY OUT THAT THREAT. 53 POET
(SHE SEARCHES HIS FACE, UNEASY NOW, FEELING A 105 POET
THREAT HIDDEN BEHIND HIS COLD.
(DESPERATELY, AS A LAST, FRANTIC THREAT.) 129 POET
(WITH A THREAT IN HIS VOICE) 588 ROPE
I DON'T DOUBT--YOU KEPT YOUR THREAT. 484 WELDED
THREATEN
DID SHE THREATEN TO GO TO THE POLICES 100 ELECTR
AND HE NEVER PAYS THAT TILL I THREATEN TO EVICT 23 JOURNE
HIM.
I CAN'T THREATEN HER, OR SHE'D THREATEN SHE'D 71 JOURNE
LEAVE.
THESE SKIES THREATEN. 329 LAZARU
VILE JEW, DO YOU DARE THREATEN ME WITH DEATH/ 341 LAZARU
WHOSE SILK INDUSTRY IS BEGINNING TO THREATEN THE 422 MARCOM
SUPREMACY OF OUR OWN.
WOULD BE SUCH A COWARD AS TO THREATEN HER OLD 74 MISBEG
FATHER
AND I RAISE THE ROOF AND THREATEN HIM IF HE DON'T 94 MISBEG
MARRY YOU--
JUST WHAT DO YOU WANT ME TO THREATEN HIM WITH WHEN 95 MISBEG
I CATCH YOUS
AND THREATEN TO TELL GORDON TOO, UNLESS/... 171 STRANG
THREATENED
OR TO REMEMBER THE THREATENED PUNISHMENT. 292 AHWILD
SO I THREATENED HIM I MIGHT GIVE YOU BOTH AN 530 DAYS
OUTLINE OF THE REST TONIGHT.
AS IF THE MUSIC HELD SOME MEANING THAT THREATENED 9 ELECTR
HER.
I MADE SUCH A PUBLIC NUISANCE OF MYSELF THAT THE 149 MISBEG
CONDUCTOR THREATENED IF I
AND AT FATHER TOO WHEN I TOLD HOW HE THREATENED 145 POET
HE'D KILL ME.
THREATENIN'
WHO THE HELL ARE YOU TO BE THREATENIN' THE LIFE OF104 ELECTR
AN HONEST CHANTYMANS
THREATENING
(MAKES A THREATENING MOVE--BEN SHRINKS AWAY) 536 'ILE
I CAN HEAR THE SILENCE THREATENING ME-- 549 'ILE
(HE MAKES A THREATENING MOVEMENT.) 203 AHWILD
(HIS FACE GROWN STERN AND ANGRY, TAKES A 261 AHWILD
THREATENING STEP TOWARD HIM)
(UNABLE TO ENDURE THIS, SPRINGS TO HIS FEET IN A 261 DESIRE
FURY, THREATENING HER.
SUDDENLY CABOT TURNS--GRIMLY THREATENING) 265 DESIRE
(THE WAS THREATENING POP ALREADY HE'D TELL ON 442 DYNAMO
HIM/...

THREATENING (CONT'D.)
OF BEING A CONDEMNED SINNER ALONE IN THE 444 DYNAMO
THREATENING NIGHT)
(HE TAKES A THREATENING STEP FORWARD.) 448 DYNAMO
(THEN WITH A SUDDEN BURST OF THREATENING 460 DYNAMO
ASSERTIVENESS)
(THEN HARSHLY, TAKING A THREATENING STEP FORWARD) 463 DYNAMO
HE TAKES A THREATENING STEP TOWARD HER-- 481 DYNAMO
SHE GOES ON WITH A THREATENING UNDERCURRENT IN HER 17 ELECTR
VOICE)
(THEN HER MANNER BECOMING THREATENING) 33 ELECTR
LAVINIA'S MANNER BECOMES THREATENING AGAIN) 34 ELECTR
MAKES A THREATENING MOVE AS IF TO STRIKE HER 34 ELECTR
DAUGHTER'S FACE)
STRAIGHTENS UP WITH A THREATENING MOVEMENT. 112 ELECTR
(WITH A CHANGE TO A HARSH THREATENING TONE) 156 ELECTR
BUT A RARE AND THREATENING PAUSE OF SILENCE HAS 29 HUGHIE
FALLEN ON THE CITY.
(HE TAKES A THREATENING STEP TOWARD JOE, 637 ICEMAN
(HIS TONE IS THREATENING. 703 ICEMAN
(HE TAKES A THREATENING STEP TOWARD HIM. 64 JOURNE
(WITH THREATENING ANGER.) LISTEN TO ME/ 127 JOURNE
(HE TAKES A THREATENING STEP TOWARD HIM. 64 JOURNE
THEY RAISE CLENCHED FISTS OR HANDS DISTENDED INTO 287 LAZARU
THREATENING TALONS.
SOMBERLY CONTEMPTUOUS AND THREATENING) 353 LAZARU
SAYING YOU LOVE-- IN A FRENZY, HE JUMPS TO HIS 359 LAZARU
FEET THREATENING LAZARUS)
DRAWING HERSELF UP WITH FIERCE, THREATENING 14 MANSNS
ARROGANCE.)
SURROUNDING--THREATENING--ME-- 125 MANSNS
THREATENING SCORN IN HER TONE.) 131 MANSNS
SOMBER AND THREATENING--AND SOMETHING IN MY NATURE163 MANSNS
RESPONDS--
AND THERE IS A WILD LOOK IN HIS EYES CALCULATING 171 MANSNS
AND THREATENING
DO YOU WANT TO CREATE A PUBLIC SCANDAL, CURSING 174 MANSNS
AND THREATENING EACH OTHERS
(MAKES A THREATENING MOVE TOWARD HIM) 10 MISBEG
DON'T BE THREATENING ME. 15 MISBEG
(IN A STRANGE TONE THAT IS ALMOST THREATENING) 114 MISBEG
(HE PAUSES--THEN BURSTS OUT IN A STRANGE 126 MISBEG
THREATENING TONE)
OCH, DON'T BE THREATENING ME, YOU BAD-TEMPERED OLD177 MISBEG
TICK.
(HE TAKES A THREATENING STEP TOWARD HIM.) 53 POET
AND WAS WARNING AND THREATENING ME. 87 POET
(ARROGANTLY THREATENING.) ARE YOU PRESUMING TO 99 POET
QUESTION MY CONDUCT
(SHE MAKES A THREATENING MOVE TOWARD HIM, 115 POET
(BEWILDERED FOR A SECOND--THEN IN A THREATENING 120 POET
TONE.)
(ADDRESSING HIM--IN HIS QUIET, THREATENING TONE 123 POET
NOW.)
(HE MAKES A THREATENING MOVE TOWARD HER.) 128 POET
HIS EYES FIX ON HER IN A THREATENING STARE. 171 POET
(THREATENING HER GOOD-HUMOREDLY.) 176 POET
(HIS VOICE RISES TO A THREATENING ROAR) 597 ROPE
YOU DON'T GET THAT FROM ME--(HE HAS TAKEN A 150 STRANG
THREATENING STEP FORWARD.
(FURIOUSLY, TAKING A THREATENING STEP TOWARD HIM) 193 STRANG
HE WENT AWAY THREATENING, BOASTING HE'D-- 465 WELDED
THREATENINGLY
(HE RECITES THREATENINGLY) +THE DAYS GROW HOT, O 195 AHWILD
BABYLON/
(THREATENINGLY) I'LL GIVE YOU A GOOD PUNCH IN THE246 AHWILD
SNOOT, THAT'S WHAT/
(THREATENINGLY) YOU HURRY, AY TAL YOU/ 39 ANNA
(THREATENINGLY) YELL--YOU SEE/ 47 ANNA
(RAISING HIS FIST THREATENINGLY) 70 ANNA
(FURIOUSLY, AS IF THIS WERE THE LAST INSULT-- 73 ANNA
ADVANCING ON HIM THREATENINGLY)
(HE TAKES A STEP TOWARD CHRIS THREATENINGLY.) 77 ANNA
(HE CLENCHES HIS FIST ABOVE HIS HEAD AND ADVANCES 108 BEYOND
THREATENINGLY ON ANDREW)
(SHAKING HIS FINGER THREATENINGLY AT HIM) 227 DESIRE
(THREATENINGLY) YE CAN'T TALK THAT WAY T' ME/ 240 DESIRE
(THREATENINGLY) GIT OUT AFORE I MURDER YE/ 240 DESIRE
(HE RAISES HIS CLENCHED FISTS THREATENINGLY.) 255 DESIRE
(THREATENINGLY) AND IF HE'S TOO TIGHT, 545 DIFNT
HE ADVANCES THREATENINGLY ON HIS FATHER WHO IS 451 DYNAMO
STARING AT ADA STUPIDLY.
(STARTS FOR HIS FATHER THREATENINGLY, HIS FISTS 465 DYNAMO
CLENCHED)
SMITHERS RAISES HIS WHIP THREATENINGLY) 174 EJONES
SPRINGS TO HIS FEET THREATENINGLY) 24 ELECTR
(SHE CANNOT RESTRAIN HER RAGE--THREATENINGLY) 35 ELECTR
(THREATENINGLY) NOW IF YOU DON'T, I'LL GO TO THE 96 ELECTR
POLICE/
(THREATENINGLY) YOU DARE SAY THAT ABOUT MOTHER/ 99 ELECTR
THEN LEANS OVER THE RAIL AGAIN AND CALLS 104 ELECTR
THREATENINGLY.)
(THREATENINGLY) SO THAT'S IT/ 148 ELECTR
TURNS AROUND THREATENINGLY----IN A TONE OF 209 HA APE
CONTEMPTUOUS AUTHORITY)
(THEY CROWD AROUND LONG THREATENINGLY.) 213 HA APE
(HE SPRINGS TO HIS FEET AND ADVANCES ON PADDY 215 HA APE
THREATENINGLY.
(THREATENINGLY) SAY/ 230 HA APE
(THREATENINGLY) BUT YOU'VE BROKE THE CAMEL'S BACK 602 ICEMAN
THIS TIME, BEJEES/
(STARTS MOVING TOWARD HER THREATENINGLY) 632 ICEMAN
(THREATENINGLY) THE HELL YOU WON'T/ 650 ICEMAN
(STUNG--PULLS BACK A FIST THREATENINGLY) 653 ICEMAN
(THREATENINGLY) BEJEES, IF YOU SAY I DIDN'T-- 656 ICEMAN
(TO PARRITT, THREATENINGLY) YUH HEARD LARRYS 669 ICEMAN
(ROCKY TURNS ON HIM THREATENINGLY. 683 ICEMAN
(THREATENINGLY, GRADUALLY RISING TO HATRED) 288 LAZARU
THE NAZARENES LEAP TO THEIR FEET THREATENINGLY. 290 LAZARU

THREATENINGLY

THREATENINGLY (CONT'D.)
(THEN THREATENINGLY) YOU SHALL BE GIVEN FULL 340 LAZARU
OPPORTUNITY TO PROVE IT/
(THREATENINGLY) AND I WARN YOU TO ANSWER DIRECTLY353 LAZARU
IN PLAIN WORDS--
(HE SUDDENLY STARTS TO HIS FEET--WITH HARSH 356 LAZARU
ARROGANCE AND PRIDE, THREATENINGLY)
(THREATENINGLY) GIVE IT TO ME, YOU, OR I'LL MAKE 375 MARCUM
TROUBLE/
(THREATENINGLY) GIVE ME WHAT WAS WRAPPED UP IN 375 MARCUM
THAT, D'YOU HEAR/
(HE RISES FROM THE BOULDER THREATENINGLY) 15 MISBEG
(THREATENINGLY) WE'VE HAD ENOUGH OF THAT. 59 MISBEG
IS HEARD CALLING BACK THREATENINGLY.) 64 MISBEG
(THREATENINGLY) IF YOU'RE GOING TO YOUR ROOM, 80 MISBEG
YOU'D BETTER GO QUICK/
HE HALF RISES FROM HIS CHAIR THREATENINGLY.) 51 POET
(LEANS FORWARD THREATENINGLY.) 121 POET
(HE ADVANCES TOWARD BENTLEY THREATENINGLY.) 582 ROPE
(THREATENINGLY) AND THEN I'M GUNTER COME AND 589 ROPE
TALK TURKEY TO YOU. SEES
(IN A STRANGE RAGE, THREATENINGLY) 120 STRANG
(SHRINKING BACK FROM HER--THREATENINGLY) 132 STRANG
(THREATENINGLY) GUV US WHAT YER TOOK/ 508 VOYAGE
(SHE RAISES HER FIST THREATENINGLY OVER HIS HEAD.)477 WELDED
THREATENINGLY) 484 WELDED
THREATENINGLY
SUDDENLY THE GUARD APPROACHES HIM ANGRILY, 194 EJONES
THREATENINGLY.
THREATENS
(HE READS) = THERE IS A MENACE EXISTING IN THIS 242 HA APE
COUNTRY TODAY WHICH THREATENS
THREATS
(NEITHER OF THE TWO IS IMPRESSED EITHER BY HIS 598 ICEMAN
INSULTS OR HIS THREATS.
(FORCING HER USUAL REACTION TO HIS THREATS) 177 MISBEG
THRESHOLD
PERHAPS YOU ARE ON THE THRESHOLD OF THAT TIME NOW.508 DAYS
THE TEMPTATION TO ESCAPE--OPEN THE DOOR--STEP 28 MANSNS
BOLDLY ACROSS THE THRESHOLD.
AND THE MOMENT YOU CROSS THE THRESHOLD 111 MANSNS
BUT JUST AS HE WAS ABOUT TO OPEN IT AND CROSS THE 111 MANSNS
THRESHOLD.
SHE TURNS AND STOPS ON THE THRESHOLD, CONFRONTING 190 MANSNS
THE DARKNESS--
THREW
AN' SHE SAID SHE THREW YOU OVER 'CAUSE YOU WAS 467 CARIBE
DRUNK.
AN' YOU SAID YOU WAS DRUNK 'CAUSE SHE THREW YOU 467 CARIBE
OVER.
AND REALIZED HE WAS IN LOVE WITH HER, IT THREW HIMS35 DAYS
INTO A PANIC OF FEAR.
WHEN SHE THREW HERSELF INTO HIS ARMS, HE WAS 537 DAYS
REPELLED.
THEY LOCKED HIM IN THE CAN AND THREW AWAY THE KEY.595 ICEMAN
IN--SOMETHING THEY THREW OUT OF THE D. T. WARD IN 713 ICEMAN
BELLEVUE
THREW THEMSELVES ON HIM AND BEGGED FOR HIS LOVE. 341 LAZARU
I THREW ALL I'VE DONE IN THE FIREPLACE AND BURNED 46 MANSNS
IT.
I MADE A VOW OF PERPETUAL BACHELORHOOD WHEN YOU 114 STRANG
THREW ME OVER IN SAM'S FAVOR/.
THRICE
BLESSED, THRICE BLESSED ARE THE MEEK/. 292 GGBROW
TAKING HIM TO ROME HAD BEEN THRICE BLOWN BACK BY A300 LAZARU
STORM.
THRICK
(GLOWERING AT THEM) WHAT DIVIL'S THRICK ARE YE UP499 VOYAGE
TO NOW, THE TWO AV YES
THRICKS
COME NONE AV YOUR DOG'S THRICKS ON ME THIS TRIP OR496 VOYAGE
I'LL--
THRIFT
HE GIVES THE BABY ONE YEN TO START A SAVINGS 389 MARCOM
ACCOUNT AND ENCOURAGE ITS THRIFT.
THRILL
CAN'T YOU FEEL THE THRILL OF IT, TOO-- 150 BEYOND
A SUDDEN THRILL OF DESIRE OVERCOMES HIS TIMIDITY) 433 DYNAMO
THAT OUGHT TO GIVE ME A NEW THRILL, AUNT. 220 HA APE
THRILL OR A GOOD LAUGH AND GET YOUR MIND OFF 399 MARCOM
SERIOUS THINGS
(WITH A THRILL OF LOVE) MARCO/ 412 MARCOM
THRILLED
BUT AT THE SAME TIME THRILLED AND PROUD OF 236 AHWILD
MINGLING WITH THE PACE THAT KILLS.
JUST NOW SHE IS IN A GREAT THRILLED STATE OF TIMID277 AHWILD
ADVENTUROUSNESS.
THE THREE GIRLS GATHER AROUND HICKEY, FULL OF 639 ICEMAN
THRILLED CURIOSITY.)
WITH THE THRILLED APPRECIATION INSPIRED BY A FREAK368 MARCOM
IN A SIDESHOW.
(THRILLED) THAT IS BEAUTIFUL/ 399 MARCOM
HIS MOTHER, CONFIDENT OF THRILLED ADULATION) 54 STRANG
THRILLING
THAT SOUNDS THRILLING. 222 HA APE
(HIS VOICE THRILLING WITH EXULTANCE) 366 LAZARU
(HIS VOICE THRILLING FOR THIS SECOND WITH 415 MARCOM
OBLIVIOUS PASSION)
(AFTER A PAUSE--HIS VOICE THRILLING WITH 418 MARCOM
ADMIRATION)
THRILLS
AFTER EXHAUSTING THE MORBID THRILLS OF SOCIAL 219 HA APE
SERVICE WORK ON NEW YORK'S EAST
THRIVE
IT THRIVE AND BREED AND BECOME MULTITUDES AND EAT 297 GGBROW
UNTIL BROWN IS CONSUMED/
THRIVED
YOU'VE EATEN BLUEFISH FOR YEARS AND THRIVED ON IT 227 AHWILD

THRIVING
THE MILKWEED AND THE THISTLES IS IN THRIVING 40 MISBEG
CONDITION.
THROAT
(IGNORING HER--CLEARING HIS THROAT IMPORTANTLY) 256 AHWILD
CHRIS CLEARS HIS THROAT) 11 ANNA
HE CLEARS HIS THROAT AND STARTS TO SING TO HIMSELF 41 ANNA
IN A LOW, DOLEFUL VOICE...=
(UNSHAKEN--PLEASANTLY) THAT'S A LIE IN YOUR 46 ANNA
THROAT, DIVIL MEND YOU/
(CLEARING HIS THROAT) 104 BEYOND
(SITTING DOWN AND CLEARING HIS THROAT--IN A 157 BEYOND
PERFUNCTORY, IMPERSONAL VOICE)
A RATTLING NOISE THROBS FROM HIS THROAT. 168 BEYOND
HIS BREATH IS CHUKIN' IN HIS THROAT LOIKE WATHER 479 CARDIF
GURGLIN' IN A POIPE.
(JUST AS DRISCOLL IS CLEARING HIS THROAT PREPATORY460 CARIBE
TO STARTING THE NEXT VERSE)
(CLUTCHING AT HIS THROAT AS THOUGH TO STRANGLE 565 CROSS
SOMETHING WITHIN HIM--HOARSELY)
(SHE TUGS AT THE HAND ON EBEN'S THROAT) 255 DESIRE
CABOT GETS ONE HAND ON HIS THROAT AND PRESSES HIM 255 DESIRE
BACK ACROSS THE STONE WALL.
HIS TWITCHING FINGERS SEEMING TO REACH OUT FOR HER261 DESIRE
THROAT)
WITH A DIRTY COLORED HANDKERCHIEF KNOTTED ABOUT 457 DYNAMO
HIS THROAT.
ON YOU WHEN YOU'VE HAD IT CRAMMED DOWN YOUR THROAT470 DYNAMO
FROM THE TIME YOU WERE BORN/
HE HAS STARTLED AND TERRIFIED JENNINGS BY THE 487 DYNAMO
THROAT
HE CLEARS HIS THROAT AS IF ABOUT TO SAY 51 ELECTR
SOMETHING--
IN MY THROAT LIKE POISONOUS VOMIT AND I LONG TO 152 ELECTR
SPIT IT OUT--AND CONFESS/
WITH A HOARSE CRY OF FURY GRABS HER BY THE THROAT1155 ELECTR
(HE LEAPS ON DION AND GRABS HIM BY THE THROAT.) 298 GGBROW
(HE REACHES OUT HIS HANDS AS IF TO TAKE THE MASK 307 GGBROW
BY THE THROAT.
(AS IF IMPELLED, HE CLEARS HIS THROAT AND 318 GGBROW
ADDRESSES THE MASK IMPORTANTLY)
HE POURS A BRIMFUL DRINK AND TOSSES IT DOWN HIS 586 ICEMAN
THROAT.
SHE--HIS THROAT AND EYES FILL UP. 603 ICEMAN
SITTING WITH A PARCHED THROAT WAITING FOR HARRY 607 ICEMAN
HOPE TO BUY A DRINK.
KNOTTED LOOSELY AROUND HIS THROAT. 13 JOURNE
DON'T START JUMPING DOWN MY THROAT/ 37 JOURNE
IT'S BAD FOR YOUR THROAT. 58 JOURNE
YOU DON'T WANT TO GET A SURE THROAT ON TOP OF YOUR 58 JOURNE
COLD.
HER HANDS FLUTTERING OVER THE BOSOM OF HER DRESS, 89 JOURNE
UP TO HER THROAT AND HAIR.
HIS DRESSING GOWN WET WITH FOG, THE COLLAR TURNED 167 JOURNE
UP AROUND HIS THROAT.
I WANT TO SEE HIM SUFFER, TO HEAR HIS LAUGHTER 342 LAZARU
CHOKE IN HIS THROAT WITH PAIN/
THROAT CHOKES HIM, FORCING HIM BACK ON THE 369 LAZARU
THRONE--SCREAMING)
CLEARING HIS THROAT IMPORTANTLY.) 30 MANSNS
HE CLEARS HIS THROAT, THE CROWD STANDS PETRIFIED, 389 MARCOM
(HERE HE CLEARS HIS THROAT WITH AN IMPORTANT COUGH431 MARCOM
AS I WAS SAYING, MY THROAT IS PARCHED AFTER THE 44 MISBEG
LONG DUSTY WALK I TOOK JUST FOR
IT PARCHES THE MEMBRANCES IN YOUR THROAT. 44 MISBEG
I CAN'T HAVE THEM, FOR MY THROAT ISN'T PARCHED AT 44 MISBEG
ALL.
POUR THE WHOLE BOTTLE DOWN YOUR THROAT, IF YOU 138 MISBEG
LIKE/
(BLOWS HIS NOSE, WIPES HIS EYES, SIGHS, CLEARS HIS 22 STRANG
THROAT.
LIKE A BRUTAL, HAIRY HAND, RAW AND RED, AT MY 99 STRANG
THROAT.
(CLEARING HIS THROAT UNEASILY) 196 STRANG
THEN, WITH A SNARL OF FURY LIKE AN ANIMAL'S HE 460 WELDED
SEIZES HER ABOUT THE THROAT WITH
THROAT'S
MY THROAT'S BURNIN' UP. 486 CARDIF
MY THROAT'S LIKE A FURNACE. 489 CARDIF
THROATED
IN A GREAT, FULL-THROATED PAEAN AS THE LAUGHTER OF280 LAZARU
LAZARUS RISES HIGHER AND
THROATS
THROATS LIKE A PAIR OF DOGS, AND I MARRIED WITH 46 ANNA
ANNAS
THEIR CLOTHES, THEIR FACES, HANDS, BARE ARMS AND 204 DESIRE
THROATS ARE EARTH-STAINED.
(THE CHORUSED WORD HAS A BRAZEN METALLIC QUALITY 210 HA APE
AS IF THEIR THROATS WERE
METALLIC QUALITY AS IF THEIR THROATS WERE 227 HA APE
PHONOGRAPH HORNS.
(THE WORD HAS A BRAZEN, METALLIC QUALITY AS IF 227 HA APE
THEIR THROATS WERE
AS IF THEIR THROATS WERE PHONOGRAPH HORNS. 229 HA APE
AS IF THEIR THROATS WERE PHONOGRAPH HORNS. 229 HA APE
AS IF THEIR THROATS WERE PHONOGRAPH HORNS. 229 HA APE
I DON'T WANT TO CRAM IT DOWN YOUR THROATS. 707 ICEMAN
LAZARUS' LAUGHTER IS ECHOED FROM THE THROATS OF 306 LAZARU
THE MULTITUDE OF HIS FOLLOWERS
DO YOU IMAGINE I'D PREFER TO HAVE YOU AT EACH 78 MANSNS
OTHER'S THROATS$
IT'D MEAN YOU AND HIMSELF WOULD BE AT EACH OTHER'S 22 POET
THROATS FROM DAWN TO DARK.
THROATY
PENETRATED DOMINATINGLY BY THE HARSH, THROATY, 473 DYNAMO
METALLIC PURR OF THE DYNAMO.
THE DYNAMO'S THROATY METALLIC PURR RISES SLOWLY IN489 DYNAMO
VOLUME

1657

THROB

THROUGH

THROB
THEN SILENCE BROKEN ONLY BY THE FAR-OFF QUICKENED 190 EJONES
THROB OF THE TOM-TOM.
ALL THIS IN SILENCE SAVE FOR THE OMINOUS THROB OF 197 EJONES
THE TOM-TOM.
CONTROLLED BY THE THROB OF THE TOM-TOM IN THE 199 EJONES
DISTANCE, TO A LONG,
WHIMPERING WITH FEAR AS THE THROB OF THE TOM-TOM 202 EJONES
FILLS THE SILENCE ABOUT HIM

THROBBING
(THE THROBBING WHINE OF A MOTOR SOUNDS FROM THE 153 BEYOND
DISTANCE OUTSIDE.)
FLIGHT AND THE THROBBING OF THE TOM-TOM, STILL FAR195 EJONES
DISTANT.
THE FIRES AT NIGHT AND THE DRUM THROBBING IN MY 147 ELECTR
HEART--
THE BLOODY ENGINES POUNDING AND THROBBING AND 214 HA APE
SHAKING--
THE MONOTONOUS THROBBING BEAT OF THE ENGINES. 223 HA APE
GIVES THEM A THROBBING STAR-LIKE EFFECT. 281 LAZARU

THROBS
A RATTLING NOISE THROBS FROM HIS THROAT. 168 BEYOND
EXULTANT BOOM WHOSE THROBS SEEM TO FILL THE AIR 200 EJONES
WITH VIBRATING RHYTHM.
(THE ROOM ROCKS, THE AIR OUTSIDE THROBS 281 LAZARU
ACCOMPANIMENT FROM THE HEAVENS TO THIS LAUGHTER OF318 LAZARU
THOUSANDS WHICH THROBS IN

THRONE
LEAD FROM THE FOOT OF THE THRONE TO THE TWO 173 EJONES
ENTRANCES.
THIS IS VERY APPARENTLY THE EMPEROR'S THRONE. 173 EJONES
(HE SITS DOWN ON HIS THRONE WITH EASY DIGNITY) 176 EJONES
(HE REACHES BELOW THE THRONE AND PULLS OUT A BIG, 182 EJONES
COMMON DINNER BELL WHICH IS PAINTED THE SAME VIVID182 EJONES
SCARLET AS THE THRONE.
(HE REACHES IN UNDER THE THRONE AND PULLS OUT AN 185 EJONES
EXPENSIVE PANAMA HAT
CALIGULA IS SQUATTING ON HIS HAMS ON A SORT OF 313 LAZARU
THRONE-CHAIR OF IVORY AND GOLD.
I WILL LAUGH WITH THE PRIDE OF A BEGGAR SET UPON 328 LAZARU
THE THRONE OF MAN?
COME DOWN FROM MY THRONE, CALIGULA. 339 LAZARU
(HE HAS WALKED TOWARD THE THRONE WHILE HE IS 339 LAZARU
SPEAKING.
IN FRONT OF THE THRONE IS A MARBLE RAILING 363 LAZARU
TIBERIUS SITS ON THE THRONE. 363 LAZARU
CAESAR'S THRONE IS ON THE LEFT AT THE EXTREME 363 LAZARU
FRONT, FACING RIGHT.
HYPOCRITICAL TYPE, GROUPED ON EACH SIDE OF THE 363 LAZARU
THRONE OF CAESAR ON A LOWER TIER.
WHO SIT ON THE BANKED TIERS OF MARBLE BEHIND AND 363 LAZARU
TO THE REAR OF THE THRONE.
(DASHES BACK AMONG THEM WAVING HIS BLOODY SPEAR 369 LAZARU
AND RUSHING UP TO THE THRONE
THROAT CHOKES HIM, FORCING HIM BACK ON THE 369 LAZARU
THRONE--SCREAMING)
"MY THRONE IT IS YOUR HEART, BELOVED, AND MY FAIR 4 MANSNS
KINGDOM YOUR BEAUTY."
I PREFER TO BE THE SECRET POWER BEHIND THE 13 MANSNS
THRONE.
"MY THRONE IT IS YOUR HEART, BELOVED, AND MY FAIR 22 MANSNS
KINGDOM YOUR BEAUTY"--
STAND IN ATTITUDES OF PATIENT SERVILITY BEFORE THE358 MARCOM
THRONE.
IS SEATED ON A SORT OF THRONE PLACED AGAINST THE 358 MARCOM
REAR WALL.
FORMING A SORT OF SEMI-CIRCLE WITH THE THRONE AT 364 MARCOM
CENTER.
BEFORE THE MOSQUE IS A THRONE ON WHICH SITS A 364 MARCOM
MAHOMETAN RULER.
(HE STUFFS THE LOCKET BACK--STOPS BEFORE THE 366 MARCOM
THRONE--
LOOKING DIRECTLY ABOVE AND IN BACK OF THE RULER'S 369 MARCOM
THRONE IS AN IMMENSE BUDDHA.
THE BACKGROUND FOR THE RULER'S THRONE IS NOW A 369 MARCOM
BUDDHIST TEMPLE
(HE IGNORES THE THRONE. 371 MARCOM
IN THE BACK OF THE THRONE AND ABOVE IT IS A SMALL 373 MARCOM
IDOL MADE OF FELT AND CLOTH.
IMMEDIATELY BEFORE THE GATE IS A RUDE THRONE ON 373 MARCOM
WHICH SITS A MONGOL RULER WITH
ON THE MAIN FLOOR, GROUPED CLOSE TO THE THRONE 377 MARCOM
AREA.
THE SCENE IS REVEALED AS THE GRAND THRONE ROOM IN 377 MARCOM
THE PALACE OF KUBLAI.
ON THE LEVEL OF THE THRONE BELOW KUBLAI ARE.. 377 MARCOM
IS THE THRONE OF THE GREAT KAAN. 377 MARCOM
WALK TO THE FOOT OF THE THRONE AND KNEEL BEFORE 378 MARCOM
THE KAAN.
(MARCO TURNS RATHER FRIGHTENEDLY AND COMES TO THE 382 MARCOM
THRONE AND KNEELS)
THE KAAN RECLINES COMFORTABLY ON HIS CUSHIONED 384 MARCOM
BAMBOO THRONE.
THE LITTLE THRONE ROOM IN THE BAMBOO SUMMER PALACE384 MARCOM
OF THE KAAN AT XANADU.
HE MOVES IN STATELY FASHION TO THE THRONE 390 MARCOM
(SHE BOWS AND RETIRES BACKWARD TO THE LEFT SIDE OF390 MARCOM
THE THRONE.
THEY PROSTRATE THEMSELVES AT THE FOOT OF THE 390 MARCOM
THRONE.
ON A SILVER THRONE AT CENTER KUKACHIN IS SITTING 407 MARCOM
THE GRAND THRONE ROOM IN THE IMPERIAL PALACE AT 421 MARCOM
CAMBALUC.
KUBLAI SQUATS ON HIS THRONE, AGED AND SAD, 421 MARCOM
HE SINKS INTO A HEAP BEFORE THE THRONE. 423 MARCOM
(HE SINKS DEJECTEDLY ON HIS THRONE AGAIN. 425 MARCOM
THE KAAN ON HIS THRONE AND CHU-YIN ARE SEEN DIMLY,426 MARCOM
BEHIND AND ABOVE.

THRONE (CONT'D.)
KUBLAI SITS AT THE TOP OF HIS THRONE, CROSS-LEGGED432 MARCOM
IN THE POSTURE OF AN IDOL.
(WHO FROM THE HEIGHT OF HIS GOLDEN THRONE, CRYSTAL432 MARCOM
IN HAND,
GRAND THRONE ROOM IN THE IMPERIAL PALACE AT 432 MARCOM
CAMBALUC, ABOUT TWO YEARS LATER.
ONE SENSES A TENSE EXPECTANCY OF SOME SIGN FROM 433 MARCOM
THE THRONE.
(AFTER A PAUSE, GETS UP AND, DESCENDING FROM HIS 437 MARCOM
THRONE,

THRONG
(HIS FAMILY AND THE GUESTS IN THE ROOM NOW THRONG 278 LAZARU
ABOUT LAZARUS TO EMBRACE HIM.

THROUGH
AND THE LIGHT WHICH COMES THROUGH THE SKYLIGHT IS 535 *ILE
SICKLY AND FAINT.
AYE, I COULD HEAR HER THROUGH THE DOOR A WHILE 538 *ILC
BACK.
SHE LIFTS UP ONE OF THE CURTAINS AND LOOKS THROUGH540 *ILE
A PORTHOLE.
THEN GET HER READY AND WE'LL DRIVE HER THROUGH. 550 *ILE
THERE'S A CLEAR PASSAGE THROUGH THE FLOE, AND 550 *ILE
CLEAR WATER BEYOND.
(A MOMENT LATER THE MATE'S FACE APPEARS THROUGH 551 *ILE
THE SKYLIGHT.
THE MATE'S FACE APPEARS AGAIN THROUGH THE 552 *ILE
SKYLIGHT.)
(BUT TOMMY IS ALREADY THROUGH THE SCREEN DOOR, 186 AHWILD
WHICH HE LEAVES OPEN BEHIND HIM.)
(GRINNING THROUGH HIS ANNOYANCE) 189 AHWILD
(SHE BUSTLES OFF, REAR RIGHT, THROUGH THE FRONT 192 AHWILD
PARLOR.)
(SHE AND LILY HURRY OUT THROUGH THE BACK PARLOR.) 199 AHWILD
MILLER GLANCES THROUGH THE FRONT PARLOR TOWARD THE200 AHWILD
FRONT DOOR.
(HE DISAPPEARS THROUGH THE BACK-PARLOR DOOR, 200 AHWILD
LAUGHING.)
(HE TAKES RICHARD'S ARM AND THEY ALSO DISAPPEAR 200 AHWILD
THROUGH THE BACK PARLOR DOOR.
I'M NOT THROUGH WITH YOU, YET. 200 AHWILD
WHEN I GET THROUGH, 204 AHWILD
WHEN YOU READ THROUGH THAT LITERATURE YOU WISHED 207 AHWILD
ON HIS INNOCENT DAUGHTERS
(HE MOVES AWKWARDLY AND SELF-CONSCIOUSLY OFF 208 AHWILD
THROUGH THE FRONT PARLOR.
(HE STRIDES OFF IN AN INDIGNANT FURY OF MISERY 209 AHWILD
THROUGH THE FRONT PARLOR.)
(HE AND THE TWO WOMEN MOVE OFF THROUGH THE FRONT 210 AHWILD
PARLOR.
THOUGH AFTER HE'S THROUGH WITH HIS BETTING ON 213 AHWILD
HORSE RACES, AND DICE,
MILLER BUSTLES OUT THROUGH THE BACK PARLOR. 214 AHWILD
(SMILING) HE SAYS HE'S THROUGH WITH MURIEL NOW. 216 AHWILD
SHE'S THROUGH WITH HIM, HE MEANS/ 216 AHWILD
(AS HE IS FINISHING, HIS MOTHER COMES BACK THROUGH216 AHWILD
THE BACK PARLOR.)
(THEY GO OUT THROUGH THE BACK PARLOR. 217 AHWILD
(MILDRED RUNS IN THROUGH THE BACK PARLOR. 220 AHWILD
LILY APPEARS THROUGH THE BACK PARLOR, NERVOUS AND 220 AHWILD
APPREHENSIVE.
(HE RUSHES OUT THROUGH THE BACK PARLOR, CALLING) 220 AHWILD
PASS YOUR PLATES AS SOON AS YOU'RE THROUGH, 228 AHWILD
EVERYBODY.
(HE TURNS AND MARCHES SOLEMNLY OUT THROUGH THE 233 AHWILD
BACK PARLOR, SINGING)
(MILDRED AND TOMMY GO OUT THROUGH THE SCREEN DOOR.234 AHWILD
(HE STRIDES ANGRILY AWAY THROUGH THE BACK PARLOR.1235 AHWILD
(HE RUSHES HIM THROUGH THE SCREEN DOOR 247 AHWILD
(A MOMENT LATER ARTHUR ENTERS THROUGH THE FRONT 253 AHWILD
PARLOR, WHISTLING SOFTLY.
AND SID, HE'D SLEEP THROUGH AN EARTHQUAKE. 256 AHWILD
(THEN SUDDENLY, LOOKING THROUGH THE FRONT PARLOR 256 AHWILD
GRUMPILY
IN THE MIDST OF THIS, SID ENTERS THROUGH THE FRONT256 AHWILD
PARLOR.
(HIS ARM AROUND RICHARD-LEADING HIM OFF THROUGH 262 AHWILD
THE FRONT PARLOR)
ARE DISCOVERED COMING IN THROUGH THE BACK PARLOR 263 AHWILD
FROM DINNER IN THE DINING-ROOM.
(MILDRED TAKES TOMMY'S HAND AND LEADS HIM OUT 264 AHWILD
THROUGH THE FRONT PARLOR.
(SHE GOES OUT THROUGH THE FRONT PARLOR. 264 AHWILD
(SHE GOES OUT THROUGH THE FRONT PARLOR.) 266 AHWILD
I'M THROUGH WITH IT/ 271 AHWILD
(HE DISAPPEARS THROUGH THE BACK PARLOR. 274 AHWILD
(EXCITEDLY) DICK, YOU HAVE NO IDEA WHAT I WENT 280 AHWILD
THROUGH TO GET HERE TONIGHT/
I WAS SO SCARED, AND THEN I SNEAKED OUT THROUGH 281 AHWILD
THE BACK YARD,
AND YOU DON'T REALIZE WHAT I'VE BEEN THROUGH FOR 281 AHWILD
YOU--AND WHAT I'M IN FOR--
SO I SAID TO MYSELF, I'M THROUGH WITH WOMEN. 282 AHWILD
MOONLIGHT SHINES THROUGH THE SCREEN DOOR AT RIGHT.280 AHWILD
NEAR.
SHE DISAPPEARS THROUGH THE FRONT PARLOR. 293 AHWILD
IN THROUGH THE SCREEN DOOR, WALKING TOGETHER 298 AHWILD
TOWARD THE FRONT PARLOR
(READS THROUGH THE LETTER HURRIEDLY) 9 ANNA
(CHRIS GOES THROUGH THE BAR AND OUT THE STREET 13 ANNA
DOOR.)
(THE "ANDY" COMES AGAIN THROUGH THE WALL OF FOG, 29 ANNA
SOUNDING MUCH NEARER THIS TIME.
STARTING RIGHT IN KIDDING AFTER WHAT YOU BEEN 31 ANNA
THROUGH.
I'M TELLING YOU THERE'S THE WILL OF GOD IN IT THAT 39 ANNA
BROUGHT ME SAFE THROUGH THE
(AS SHE GUIDES HIM THROUGH THE CABIN DOOR) 39 ANNA

THROUGH

THROUGH (CONT'D.)
(HE BENDS DOWN AND SQUEEZES HIS HUGE FORM THROUGH 45 ANNA THE NARROW DOORWAY)
WINDYAMMER, MY VAS THROUGH HUNDRED STORMS VORSE'N 49 ANNA DAT/
'S IF ALL I'D BEEN THROUGH WASN'T ME AND DIDN'T 59 ANNA COUNT AND WAS YUST LIKE IT NEVER
PLAIN EVIDENCE OF THE FIGHTING HE HAS BEEN THROUGH 68 ANNA ON HIS BOAT.
YOU'RE A HARD THROUGH AND THROUGH. 84 BEYOND
BEST-PAYIN' FARMS IN THE STATE, TOO, AFORE HE GITS 97 BEYOND THROUGH/
I'M THROUGH, THROUGH FOR GOOD AND ALL. 107 BEYOND
THOUGH IT THE YARD CAN BE SEEN. 112 BEYOND
THROUGH THE OPEN DOOR TO THE KITCHEN COMES THE 112 BEYOND CLATTER OF DISHES BEING WASHED.
A BALL OF UNUSED YARN, WITH NEEDLES STUCK THROUGH 113 BEYOND IT.
THROUGH THE WILL OF GOD. 113 BEYOND
SAID HE DIDN'T KNOW HOW HE'D PULL THROUGH 'TIL 115 BEYOND HARVEST WITHOUT IT,
AND I'VE GOT TO PULL THINGS THROUGH SOMEHOW. 123 BEYOND
HUMDRUM FARM LIFE, AFTER ALL HE'S BEEN THROUGH. 125 BEYOND
DETECTED THROUGH THE BLEACHED, SUN-SCORCHED GRASS.129 BEYOND
I'D RATHER GO THROUGH A TYPHOON AGAIN THAN WRITE A131 BEYOND LETTER.
(WITH EAGER INTEREST) THEN YOU WERE THROUGH A 131 BEYOND TYPHOONS
(AFTER A PAUSE) IT'S TOO BAD PA COULDN'T HAVE 134 BEYOND LIVED TO SEE THINGS THROUGH.
I'M THROUGH WITH THE SEA FOR GOOD AS A JOB. 137 BEYOND
ALL OUR SUFFERING HAS BEEN A TEST THROUGH WHICH WE150 BEYOND HAD TO PASS.
(EXULTINGLY) AND WE DID PASS THROUGH IT/ 150 BEYOND
LIFE OWES US SOME HAPPINESS AFTER WHAT WE'VE BEEN 150 BEYOND THROUGH.
BUT-- I CAN'T GET IT THROUGH MY HEAD. 155 BEYOND
ONLY THROUGH CONTACT WITH SUFFERING, ANDY, WILL 162 BEYOND YOU--AWAKEN.
RUTH HAS SUFFERED--REMEMBER, ANDY--ONLY THROUGH 168 BEYOND SACRIFICE--
AND WE'VE STUCK TOGETHER IVER SINCE THROUGH GOOD 480 CARDIF LUCK AND BAD.
WE'LL PULL YOU THROUGH ALL RIGHT--AND--HM--WELL-- 485 CARDIF CUMING, ROBINSONS
I BEEN THROUGH IT MANY'S THE TIME. 468 CARIBE
HOUSE, CREEPS WEARILY IN THROUGH THE PORTHOLES 555 CROSS
AND YOU KNOW YOUR WAY THROUGH THE HOUSE. 558 CROSS
(NAT PEERS THROUGH THE PORTHOLE AND STARTS BACK, 569 CROSS
CLEAR MOONLIGHT FLOODS THROUGH THE PORTHOLES. 572 CROSS
THROUGH JACK'S LETTERS. 500 DAYS
WE'VE BEEN THROUGH THE SAME FRIGHTFUL TRIALS. 502 DAYS
WELL, YOU CAN APPRECIATE THEN WHAT I WENT THROUGH,502 DAYS
AND HE WAS RUNNING THROUGH GREEK PHILOSOPHY 503 DAYS
BUT THE NEXT I KNEW, HE WAS THROUGH WITH THE EAST.503 DAYS
I INTENDED TO TELL FATHER I WAS THROUGH AS 519 DAYS WALTER'S WIFE.
(LOOKS UP IN AMAZEMENT) YOU WENT THROUGH THATS 521 DAYS
HE SEEMED TO LOOK THROUGH ME AT SOME ONE ELSE. 522 DAYS
WHEN I FIRST MET HIM I THOUGHT I WAS THROUGH WITH 523 DAYS MARRIAGE FOR GOOD.
(SHE DISAPPEARS THROUGH THE DINING-ROOM DOOR. 526 DAYS
TO SAVE HER THE HUMILIATION OF HEARING IT THROUGH 527 DAYS DIRTY GOSSIP?
SHE GOES OUT THROUGH THE DINING-ROOM DOOR.) 532 DAYS
NO, YOU ONLY WENT THROUGH THE MOTIONS. 532 DAYS
HE WENT THROUGH A TERRIFIC INNER CONFLICT. 534 DAYS
REMEMBER, ALL THIS TIME HE SAW THROUGH HER. 537 DAYS
I KNOW YOU CAN IMAGINE THE HELL HE WENT THROUGH 538 DAYS FROM THE MOMENT HE CAME TO
IF HE CAN ONLY BELIEVE AGAIN IN HIS OLD GOD OF 544 DAYS LOVE, AND SEEK HER THROUGH HIM.
(A CHILL RUNS THROUGH HER BODY.) 548 DAYS
(COMES THROUGH THE DOORWAY AT REAR--SHARPLY) 550 DAYS
ON THE DOOR THROUGH WHICH ELSA HAS JUST 551 DAYS DISAPPEARED.
FATHER BAIRD OPENS THE DOOR AND THEY PASS THROUGH,555 DAYS LOVING SLIPPING AFTER THEM.
I'VE SEEN MANY WORSE CASES WHERE THE PATIENT 557 DAYS PULLED THROUGH.
AND I SEE THROUGH YOUR STUPID TRICK--TO USE THE 559 DAYS FEAR OF DEATH TO--
THROUGH THE SECRET LONGING OF YOUR OWN HEART FOR 560 DAYS FAITH/
(HE GOES THROUGH THE DOOR TO THE STUDY, MOVING 563 DAYS LIKE ONE IN A TRANCE.
I CAN FORGIVE MYSELF--THROUGH THEE/ 565 DAYS
(FATHER BAIRD COMES IN HURRIEDLY THROUGH THE 566 DAYS ARCHED DOORWAY.
(IN HER MOST SEDUCTIVE TONES WHICH SHE USES ALL 225 DESIRE THROUGH THIS SCENE)
THEIR NOT GLANCES SEEM TO MEET THROUGH THE WALL. 236 DESIRE
EDEN AND ABBIE STARE AT EACH OTHER THROUGH THE 239 DESIRE WALL.
AND HARDENS HIS FACE INTO A STONY MASK--THROUGH 264 DESIRE HIS TEETH TO HIMSELF)
HE LUNCHES THROUGH THE GATE. 265 DESIRE
I CUT ACROSS THE FIELDS AN' THROUGH THE WOODS. 266 DESIRE
THROUGH THE WINDOW AND THE SCREEN DOOR IN THE REAR493 DIFRNT
THE FRESH GREEN OF THE LAWN
THROUGH THE SMALL LAWN WHICH SEPARATES THE HOUSE 493 DIFRNT FROM THE STREET.
BRIGHT SUNLIGHT STREAMS THROUGH THE WINDOWS ON THE493 DIFRNT LEFT.
PEERING THROUGH THE SCREEN AND CATCHING SIGHT OF 505 DIFRNT EMMA, HARRIET CALLS)
HE WHISTLES, GOES THROUGH THE MOTIONS OF DANCING 519 DIFRNT TO THE MUSIC.

THROUGH (CONT'D.)
OH, YOU'RE LOW, YOU'RE LOW ALL THROUGH LIKE YOUR 528 DIFRNT PA WAS--AND SINCE YOU
THEY ONLY GOT THROUGH WITH THE WORK TWO WEEKS AGO.535 DIFRNT
BENNY SNEAKS THROUGH THE DOOR ON RIGHT, HESITATES 544 DIFRNT FOR A WHILE.
I'LL GO RIGHT THROUGH WITH WHAT I SAID I WOULD, IF545 DIFRNT ONLY TO SPITE HIM/
THAN GO THROUGH THE POVERTY AND HUMILIATION I'VE 423 DYNAMO HAD TO FACE/...
A FAINT FLASH OF LIGHTNING FROM THE DISTANT STORM 424 DYNAMO FLICKERS THROUGH HIS WINDOW.
HE STANDS BY THIS, WAITING NERVOUSLY, PEERING 427 DYNAMO THROUGH THE GAP AT THE FIRE HOUSE.
GLANCING THROUGH THE PAGES OF A TECHNICAL BOOK ON 428 DYNAMO HYDRO-ELECTRIC ENGINEERING.
(COMES THROUGH THE HEDGE TO HER SHEEPISHLY) 433 DYNAMO
(SUDDENLY JUMPING TO HER FEET AND PEERING UP 444 DYNAMO THROUGH THE LEAVES AT MRS. FIFE)
THEN I'M THROUGH WITH YOU/ 450 DYNAMO
I'M THROUGH WITH THE LOT OF YOU/ 453 DYNAMO
(WITH A SWAGGER AND A COLD SMILE ON HIS LIPS HE 459 DYNAMO WALKS THROUGH THE GAP JUST AS
BY WHAT DRIVES THE STARS THROUGH SPACE/ 461 DYNAMO
AND CAN BE SEEN GOING THROUGH THE DOOR IN REAR.) 473 DYNAMO
AND OTHER EQUIPMENT STRETCHING UP THROUGH THE ROOF473 DYNAMO TO THE OUTGOING FEEDERS
THROUGH THE WINDOW AND THE OPEN DOOR OF THE DYNAMO473 DYNAMO ROOM,
THROUGH THE UPPER WINDOW OF THE RIGHT SECTION OF 473 DYNAMO THE BUILDING.
THE DYNAMO CAN BE PARTLY SEEN THROUGH THE WINDOW. 476 DYNAMO
DRIVING THROUGH SPACE, ROUND AND ROUND, JUST LIKE 477 DYNAMO THE ELECTRONS IN THE ATOM/
BUT I'LL MAKE THE OLD FOOL GET DOWN ON HIS KNEES 481 DYNAMO TO HER YET BEFORE I'M THROUGH
AND PULLS HER THROUGH THE DOOR FROM THE ROOF TO 483 DYNAMO THE GALLERIES.)
THE NEAREST DYNAMO, WHICH WE HAVE SEEN PREVIOUSLY 486 DYNAMO THROUGH THE DOORWAY,
ITS HYPNOTIC, METALLIC PURR WHICH FLOWS 486 DYNAMO INSISTENTLY THROUGH THE EARS.
HE NOW WALKS DELIBERATELY BACK THROUGH THE DOOR TO487 DYNAMO THE OIL SWITCH GALLERY.
THROUGH THE DOOR AT LEFT OF THE GALLERY. 487 DYNAMO
(HE TURNS AND RUNS HEADLONG THROUGH THE 488 DYNAMO SWITCHBOARD ROOM.
I CRACKS DE WHIP AND DEY JUMPS THROUGH. 179 EJONES
YOU'LL 'AVE TO CUT THROUGH THE BIG FOREST-- 183 EJONES
I COULD GO THROUGH ON DEM TRAILS WID MY EYES SHUT.183 EJONES
YOU'D 'AVE TO 'USTLE TO GET THROUGH THAT FOREST IN183 EJONES TWELVE HOURS.
ITS BEAMS, DRIFTING THROUGH THE CANOPY OF LEAVES, 190 EJONES MAKE A BARELY PERCEPTIBLE.
IT IS AS IF THE FOREST HAD STOOD ASIDE MOMENTARILY192 EJONES TO LET THE ROAD PASS THROUGH
(AS IF THERE WERE A SHOVEL IN HIS HANDS HE GOES 194 EJONES THROUGH WEARY,
JONES FORCES HIS WAY IN THROUGH THE FOREST ON THE 195 EJONES LEFT.
THROUGH. 198 EJONES
STUMBLING AND CRAWLING THROUGH THE UNDERGROWTH. 198 EJONES
(THEY CROWD TO THE REAR OF THE BENCH BY THE LILAC 8 ELECTR CLUMP AND PEER THROUGH THE
WATCHING HER MOTHER AS SHE STROLLS THROUGH THE 10 ELECTR GARDEN TO THE GREENHOUSE.
EXCEPT FOR WHAT MOONLIGHT FILTERS FEEBLY THROUGH 58 ELECTR THE SHUTTERS.
(SHE HURRIES THROUGH THE DOORWAY INTO HER ROOM 61 ELECTR
AFTER PASSING UNHARMED THROUGH THE WHOLE WAR/ 69 ELECTR
(THEN A TONE OF EAGERNESS BREAKING THROUGH IN 72 ELECTR SPITE OF HERSELF)
(SHE TAKES HIS HAND AND LEADS HIM THROUGH THE DOOR 77 ELECTR AND CLOSES IT BEHIND THEM.
I SOON SAW THROUGH HIS LITTLE SCHEME AND HE'LL 87 ELECTR NEVER CALL HERE AGAIN.
IF YOU KNEW ALL THE HELL I'VE BEEN THROUGH/ 87 ELECTR
IT REALLY BEGAN THE NIGHT BEFORE WHEN I SNEAKED 95 ELECTR THROUGH THEIR LINES.
WOULD BE DRAGGED THROUGH THE HORROR OF A MURDER 97 ELECTR TRIAL/
(HER VOICE COMES THROUGH THE DOOR, FRIGHTENED AND 99 ELECTR STRAINED)
AND YOU'RE SO BLIND YOU CAN'T SEE THROUGH HER/ 99 ELECTR
(HE GUIDES HER WITH HIS ARM AROUND HER THROUGH THE109 ELECTR DOOR
I THINK IT'S THROUGH WITH ME NOW, ANYWAY/ 112 ELECTR
(URIN STEPS THROUGH THE DOOR 114 ELECTR
(PUTTING IT IN HIS POCKET) WE'VE GOT TO GO 115 ELECTR THROUGH HIS POCKETS
THEN SHE LETS IT SLIP THROUGH HER FINGERS, 121 ELECTR
AN' I SEED EZRA'S GHOST DRESSED LIKE A JUDGE 134 ELECTR COMIN' THROUGH THE WALLS--
AN' WHEN I GIT THROUGH TELLIN' MY STORY OF IT 135 ELECTR ROUND TOWN TOMORROW
I SEE A LIGHT THROUGH THE SHUTTERS OF THE SITTING-138 ELECTR ROOM.
REMEMBER ALL I'VE GONE THROUGH ON YOUR ACCOUNT. 141 ELECTR
I WOULDN'T LIVE THROUGH THOSE HORRIBLE DAYS AGAIN 141 ELECTR FOR ANYTHING ON EARTH.
SO I'M AFRAID YOU CAN'T HOPE TO GET RID OF ME 151 ELECTR THROUGH HAZEL.
YOU WATCHED HIM STARE AT YOUR BODY THROUGH YOUR 154 ELECTR CLOTHES, STRIPPING YOU NAKED/
AND PRETENDS TO BE GLANCING THROUGH A BOOK ON THE 157 ELECTR TABLE.
SHE IS SPEAKING NOW THROUGH YOU/ 166 ELECTR
BUT I'M THROUGH WITH YOU FOREVER NOW, DO YOU HEAR5168 ELECTR

1659 THROUGH

THROUGH (CONT'D.)

IT HAS STARTED ALREADY--HIS BEING MADE UNHAPPY 173 ELECTR THROUGH YOU/

THEY WILL AFTER WE ARE MARRIED--OR I'M THROUGH 175 ELECTR WITH THEM/

AFTER HE'S THROUGH COLLEGE, BILLY MUST STUDY FOR A258 GGBROW PROFESSION OF SOME SORT,

AND I'D LOVE TO RUN MY FINGERS THROUGH HIS HAIR-- 263 GGBROW AND I LOVE HIM/

AND PEACE SINKS DEEP THROUGH THE SEA/ 264 GGBROW

UNTIL AT LAST THROUGH TWO TEARS I WATCHED HER DIE 282 GGBROW

WHEN I STOP TO THINK OF ALL YOU'VE MADE ME GO 292 GGBROW THROUGH

I'VE FULFILLED HER WILL AND IF SHE'S THROUGH WITH 296 GGBROW ME NOW IT'S ONLY BECAUSE I WAS

A SHUDDER PASSES THROUGH BOTH OF THEM. 301 GGBROW

HE CAN BE HEARD FEELING HIS WAY IN THROUGH THE 306 GGBROW DARK.

(CHILLINGLY) THEN IF DION IS THROUGH, WHY CAN'T 1315 GGBROW SEE HIM?

(WITH A QUICK PRANCING MOVEMENT, HE HAS OPENED THE318 GGBROW DOOR, GONE THROUGH,

THEN YOU'D SEE HER DRIVING THROUGH THE GRAY NIGHT,214 HA APE

DRIVING HER ON STEADY THROUGH THE NIGHTS AND THE 214 HA APE DAYS/

THROUGH WHICH YANK'S VOICE CAN BE HEARD BELLOWING)216 HA APE

VIBRATING THROUGH THE STEEL WALLS AS IF SOME 217 HA APE ENORMOUS BRAZEN GONG WERE IMBEDDED

FILE THROUGH THE DOOR SILENTLY CLOSE UPON EACH 217 HA APE OTHER'S HEELS IN WHAT IS VERY

HIGH OVERHEAD ONE HANGING ELECTRIC BULB SHEDS JUST222 HA APE ENOUGH LIGHT THROUGH THE

HE BLINKS UPWARD THROUGH THE MURK TRYING TO FIND 225 HA APE THE OWNER OF THE WHISTLE,

YUH COULD SEE DE BONES THROUGH 'EM. 231 HA APE

WE MUST IMPRESS OUR DEMANDS THROUGH PEACEFUL 236 HA APE MEANS--

THROUGH THE HEAVY STEEL BARS OF THE CELL AT THE 239 HA APE EXTREME FRONT

NOTHING EXCITING HAS HAPPENED IN ANY NIGHT I'VE 24 HUGHIE EVER LIVED THROUGH/=

BEFORE SHE'S THROUGH, I WON'T HAVE A FRIEND LEFT.= 26 HUGHIE

I SHOULD USE HIM TO HELP ME LIVE THROUGH THE 30 HUGHIE NIGHT.

(HIS GLASSY EYES STARE THROUGH ERIE'S FACE. 30 HUGHIE

I COULD TELL BY HUGHIE'S FACE BEFORE HE WENT TO 30 HUGHIE THE HOSPITAL. HE WAS THROUGH.

TWO WINDOWS, SO GLAZED WITH GRIME ONE CANNOT SEE 573 ICEMAN THROUGH THEM,

HE HAS NO SOCKS, AND HIS BARE FEET SHOW THROUGH 577 ICEMAN HOLES IN THE SOLES.

COMES FROM THE BAR THROUGH THE CURTAIN AND STANDS 577 ICEMAN LOOKING OVER THE BACK ROOM.

IF I'VE BEEN THROUGH WITH THE MOVEMENT LONG SINCE,579 ICEMAN IT'S BEEN THROUGH WITH HIM.

(RAISES HIS HEAD AND PEERS AT ROCKY BLEARILY 579 ICEMAN THROUGH HIS THICK SPECTACLES--

I'M THROUGH WITH THE MOVEMENT LONG SINCE. 579 ICEMAN

NOW HE'S THROUGH. 581 ICEMAN

I'M THROUGH WITH IT/ 581 ICEMAN

(HE SQUEEZES THROUGH THE TABLES AND DISAPPEARS, 586 ICEMAN RIGHT-REAR, BEHIND THE CURTAIN.

(HASTILY) WHY, ALL I'VE BEEN THROUGH. 587 ICEMAN

IF I AM THROUGH LONG SINCE WITH ANY CONNECTION 588 ICEMAN WITH THEM.

I FOUND OUT THROUGH MOTHER. 589 ICEMAN

YOU'RE THROUGH/ 592 ICEMAN

I'M THROUGH.= 603 ICEMAN

I WENT THROUGH MY FATHER'S PAPERS BEFORE THE 607 ICEMAN

THAT SHOWS EVEN THROUGH THEIR BLOBBY MAKE-UP. 611 ICEMAN

YOU'RE THROUGH WITH LIFE. 616 ICEMAN

EVEN HUGO COMES OUT OF HIS COMA TO RAISE HIS HEAD 618 ICEMAN AND BLINK THROUGH HIS THICK

JUST BECAUSE I'M THROUGH WITH THE STUFF DON'T 620 ICEMAN

LOOKS UP THROUGH HIS THICK SPECTACLES AND GIGGLES 627 ICEMAN FOOLISHLY.)

(BLINKS AT HIM THROUGH HIS THICK SPECTACLES--WITH 634 ICEMAN GUTTURAL DENUNCIATION)

HERE'S THE REVOLUTION STARTING ON ALL SIDES OF YOU634 ICEMAN AND YOU'RE SLEEPING THROUGH

(SHE BEGINS TO PLAY THROUGH THE CHORUS AGAIN. 645 ICEMAN

I'M THROUGH/ 649 ICEMAN

WAIT TILL HICKEY GETS THROUGH WITH YOU/ 650 ICEMAN

CORA, AT THE PIANO, KEEPS RUNNING THROUGH THE 651 ICEMAN TUNE, WITH SOFT PEDAL.

ANYWAY, I'VE PROMISED YOU YOU'LL COME THROUGH ALL 654 ICEMAN RIGHT, HAVEN'T I?

AND, FINALLY, HE HAD TO SEE THROUGH HIMSELF, TOO. 661 ICEMAN

BUT OLD HICKEY COULD NEVER BE SO DRUNK HE DIDN'T 661 ICEMAN HAVE TO SEE THROUGH PEOPLE.=

YOU CAN IMAGINE WHAT SHE WENT THROUGH. 663 ICEMAN

MY GETTING THROUGH WITH THE MOVEMENT. 667 ICEMAN

(HE STAGGERS OUT THROUGH THE SWINGING DOORS.) 673 ICEMAN

(STIFFLY) NO, I--I'M THROUGH WITH THAT STUFF. 674 ICEMAN

(HE GOES TO RIGHT OF DOOR BEHIND THE LUNCH COUNTER677 ICEMAN AND LOOKS THROUGH THE WINDOW.

AND YOU'RE THE GUY WHO KIDS HIMSELF HE'S THROUGH 679 ICEMAN WITH THE MOVEMENT/

BUT I COULD HEAR HIM THROUGH THE WALL DOING HIS 681 ICEMAN SPIEL TO SOMEONE ALL NIGHT LONG.

(HE PUSHES THE DOOR OPEN AND LUMBERS THROUGH IT 685 ICEMAN

BEEN THROUGH THE MILL. 685 ICEMAN

IF HE'S GOT THE GUTS TO GO THROUGH WITH THE TEST, 686 ICEMAN THEN CERTAINLY YOU--

HE'LL COME THROUGH ALL RIGHT. 686 ICEMAN

JIMMY TURNS AND DASHES THROUGH THE DOOR, 686 ICEMAN

FROM WHAT I'VE SEEN OF 'EM THROUGH THE WINDOW, 687 ICEMAN

THROUGH (CONT'D.)

(HE GOES TO THE END OF THE BAR TO LOOK THROUGH THE688 ICEMAN WINDOW--DISGUSTEDLY)

HE COMES LURCHING BLINDLY THROUGH THE SWINGING 689 ICEMAN DOORS

YOU'VE FACED THE TEST AND COME THROUGH. 690 ICEMAN

WHO LIFTS HIS HEAD FROM HIS ARMS AND BLINKS AT HIM691 ICEMAN THROUGH HIS THICK SPECTACLES.

I PROMISE YOU THEY'LL BOTH COME THROUGH ALL RIGHT.692 ICEMAN

I'VE BEEN THROUGH IT. 692 ICEMAN

IT WAS A BULLET THROUGH THE HEAD THAT KILLED 693 ICEMAN EVELYN.

I'M THROUGH WID DIS LOUSY JOB, ANYWAY/ 697 ICEMAN

(CHUCK COMES THROUGH THE CURTAIN AND LOOKS FOR 700 ICEMAN CORA

I'M THROUGH WITH WHORES. 702 ICEMAN

THE ONE POSSIBLE WAY TO MAKE UP TO HER FOR ALL I'D705 ICEMAN MADE HER GO THROUGH,

HE'S THROUGH, NOW. 719 ICEMAN

THROUGH. 531 INZONE

YOU GO THROUGH THE OTHERS, DRISC, AND SING OUT IF 531 INZONE YOU SEES ANYTHIN' QUEER.

SUNSHINE COMES THROUGH THE WINDOWS AT RIGHT. 12 JOURNE

(SHE DISAPPEARS THROUGH THE BACK PARLOR. 29 JOURNE

NO SUNLIGHT COMES INTO THE ROOM NOW THROUGH THE 51 JOURNE WINDOWS AT RIGHT.

(HE STOPS--LOOKING THROUGH THE FRONT PARLOR TOWARD 58 JOURNE THE HALL--

(CATHLEEN MUTTERS, "YES, MA'AM," AND GOES OFF 62 JOURNE THROUGH THE BACK PARLOR,

(TYRONE COMES IN THROUGH THE FRONT PARLOR. 64 JOURNE

(SHE GOES THROUGH THE BACK PARLOR. 64 JOURNE

(RETURNING THROUGH THE BACK PARLOR, CALLS.) 66 JOURNE

AS IF THE STRAIN OF SITTING THROUGH LUNCH WITH 71 JOURNE THEM HAD BEEN TOO MUCH FOR HER.

(AT ONCE, THROUGH AN ASSOCIATION OF IDEAS SHE 72 JOURNE TURNS TO EDMUND.

(HE GOES OUT THROUGH THE FRONT PARLOR.) 73 JOURNE

(SHE TURNS AND DISAPPEARS THROUGH THE BACK PARLOR. 75 JOURNE

(AS SHE STARTS THROUGH THE DOORWAY--PLEADING AND 75 JOURNE REBUKING.)

(HE DISAPPEARS THROUGH THE FRONT PARLOR AND CAN BE 78 JOURNE HEARD STAMPING NOISILY

(BEHIND HER JAMIE DISAPPEARS THROUGH THE FRONT 81 JOURNE PARLOR.)

(WITH AN UNEASY GLANCE THROUGH THE FRONT PARLOR,) 88 JOURNE

(HE HURRIES AWAY THROUGH THE FRONT PARLOR. 91 JOURNE

YOU WOULD THINK THEY'D BEEN THROUGH SOME HORRIBLE 104 JOURNE ACCIDENT/

(SHE DISAPPEARS THROUGH THE BACK PARLOR. 106 JOURNE

(THE LIGHT IN THE HALL IS TURNED ON AND SHINES 108 JOURNE THROUGH THE FRONT PARLOR TO FALL

(TYRONE COMES IN THROUGH THE FRONT PARLOR. 108 JOURNE

DURING THE TWO YEARS HE LIVED BEFORE I LET HIM DIE110 JOURNE THROUGH MY NEGLECT.

(HE GOES THROUGH THE BACK PARLOR.) 117 JOURNE

(HE HURRIES AWAY THROUGH THE FRONT PARLOR. 121 JOURNE

(SHE HEARS TYRONE RETURNING AND TURNS AS HE COMES 121 JOURNE IN, THROUGH THE BACK PARLOR.

(SHE MOVES OFF THROUGH THE FRONT PARLOR. 123 JOURNE

(SHE TURNS WITH HUFFY DIGNITY AND DISAPPEARS 123 JOURNE THROUGH THE BACK PARLOR.)

HE WALKS HEAVILY OFF THROUGH THE BACK PARLOR 125 JOURNE TOWARD THE DINING ROOM.)

SO THAT NOW NO LIGHT SHINES THROUGH THE FRONT 125 JOURNE PARLOR.

HE PEERS OVER HIS PINCE-NEZ THROUGH THE FRONT 125 JOURNE PARLOR.)

HE COMES IN THROUGH THE FRONT PARLOR. 126 JOURNE

(STARING THROUGH THE FRONT PARLOR--WITH RELIEF.) 139 JOURNE

A DIRTY BARN OF A PLACE WHERE RAIN DRIPPED THROUGH148 JOURNE THE ROOF.

WHERE THE ONLY LIGHT CAME THROUGH TWO SMALL FILTHY148 JOURNE WINDOWS.

I'D LOST THE GREAT TALENT I ONCE HAD THROUGH YEARS150 JOURNE OF EASY REPETITION.

EDMUND WATCHES WITH AMUSEMENT JAMIE'S WAVERING 154 JOURNE PROGRESS THROUGH THE FRONT

TYRONE COMES IN QUIETLY THROUGH THE SCREEN DOOR 167 JOURNE FROM THE PORCH.

AND HE BEGINS TO BREATHE HEAVILY THROUGH HIS 169 JOURNE MOUTH.

STARING THROUGH THE FRONT PARLOR INTO THE HALL. 169 JOURNE

(FOR A SECOND HE SEEMS TO HAVE BROKEN THROUGH TO 174 JOURNE HER.

IT IS AS IF THIS REACTION WERE TRANSMITTED THROUGH286 LAZARU THE CHORUS TO THE CROWD.)

AT THIS MOMENT THE VOICE OF LAZARUS COMES RINGING 305 LAZARU THROUGH THE AIR

GIVES A HARSH CACKLE WHICH CRACKS THROUGH THE 308 LAZARU OTHER LAUGHTER WITH A SPLITTING

AND A HIGH NOTE OF LAUGHTER SOARING THROUGH CHAOS 309 LAZARU FROM THE DEEP HEART OF GOD

WHOSE MASKS, HELMETS AND ARMORED SHOULDERS CAN BE 313 LAZARU SEEN AS THEY PASS THROUGH THE

BUT HOW CAN WE WITNESS AT NIGHT AND THROUGH A 315 LAZARU WALL?

THE RETURNING LEGIONS BURST THROUGH AND GATHER IN 320 LAZARU A DENSE MOB IN THE STREET

OF ONE WHO LEANS TO EVIL MORE THROUGH WEAKNESS 332 LAZARU THAN ANY INSTINCTIVE URGE.

OLIVE-COLORED WITH THE RED OF BLOOD SMOLDERING 336 LAZARU THROUGH WITH GREAT, DARK,

MONEY SLIPS THROUGH YOUR FINGERS. 346 LAZARU

HE RUNS OUT THROUGH THE ARCHED DOORWAY AT REAR.) 360 LAZARU

HE WALKS AROUND THE DAIS AND CARRIES THE BODY OUT 362 LAZARU THROUGH THE DOORWAY IN REAR.

FORMING AN AISLE THROUGH WHICH HE PASSES-- 363 LAZARU

THROUGH

THROUGH (CONT'D.)
THEN AFTER HE HAS GONE OUT THROUGH THE ARCH, THEY 363 LAZARU
CLOSE INTO A SEMICIRCULAR
(SHE PICKS HER WAY DAINTILY THROUGH THE GRASS 3 MANSNS
TOWARD THE BENCH.)
(THERE IS A SOUND FROM UP THE PATH AT LEFT-FRONT, 4 MANSNS
THROUGH THE WOODS.
FOR I CONSTANTLY SENSE IN THE SECONDS AND MINUTES 12 MANSNS
AND HOURS FLOWING THROUGH ME,
TO BECOME THE FAVORITE OF THE KING AND MAKE HIM, 13 MANSNS
THROUGH HIS PASSION FOR HER,
LIKE PUSHING OPEN A DOOR IN THE MIND AND THEN 28 MANSNS
PASSING THROUGH
I KNOW THAT BECAUSE THE REPORTS WERE MADE THROUGH 34 MANSNS
ME.
THE SOUND OF SCUFFLING COMING THROUGH THE CEILING, 43 MANSNS
I'M ONLY DOING IT BECAUSE IT WAS THROUGH THE MONEY 55 MANSNS
YOU LOANED US
AND AT ONCE BECOMES CONCENTRATED ON GOING THROUGH 69 MANSNS
IT,
IN ORDER TO MAKE OF MY WIFE A SECOND SELF THROUGH 73 MANSNS
WHICH SHE COULD LIVE AGAIN.
HAVE SEEPED, THROUGH THE SUBTLE POWER OF MOTHER'S 73 MANSNS
FANTASTIC WILL,
THROUGH THE EVIL MAGIC OF A BEAUTIFUL ENCHANTRESS,110 MANSNS
PASSING DOWN THROUGH GENERATIONS, 350 MARCOM
(WITH A QUICK MOVEMENT OF HIS OWN HAND, CAPTURES 355 MARCOM
HERS THROUGH THE BARS)
A HAND IS THRUST OUT TO HIM THROUGH THE BARS. 355 MARCOM
WE'RE NOW PASSING THROUGH KINGDOMS WHERE THEY 365 MARCOM
WORSHIP MAHOMET,
AND I'M THROUGH WITH YOU, ANYWAY. 375 MARCOM
A FILE OF SOLDIERS, ACCOMPANYING A RICHLY-DRESSED 376 MARCOM
COURT MESSENGER, COME THROUGH.
HE STRUGGLES THROUGH THE GATE. 376 MARCOM
(THEY PASS THROUGH THE GATE.) 376 MARCOM
I'VE BROUGHT YOU THROUGH IN GOOD SHAPE. 411 MARCOM
AFTER I SWEATED BLOOD TO PULL YOU THROUGH ONCE 412 MARCOM
ALREADY
A SOUND OF DANCE MUSIC AND LAUGHTER COMES THROUGH 421 MARCOM
THE CLOSED DOORS.)
OF FLESH WHICH WILL NOT HAVE SHRIEKED THROUGH TEN 425 MARCOM
DAYS' TORTURE BEFORE IT DIED?
I BEGIN TO SEE THROUGH THE WALLS--AH! 426 MARCOM
(A PROCESSION OF SERVANTS BEGINS TO FILE ONE BY 428 MARCOM
ONE THROUGH THE RANKS OF
AT RIGHT-REAR, THROUGH A FIELD OF HAY STUBBLE TO A 1 MISBEG
PATCH OF WOODS.
AND THENCE BACK THROUGH A SCRAGGLY ORCHARD OF 1 MISBEG
APPLE TREES TO THE BARN.
SURE, ALL I WANTED WAS TO GIVE HIM THE FUN OF 26 MISBEG
SEEING THROUGH THEM
HE ALWAYS SARA THROUGH YOUR TRICKS. 26 MISBEG
AND THE BARROOM SPONGES AND RACETRACK TOUTS AND 30 MISBEG
GAMBLERS ARE THROUGH WITH HIM
IT CAME THROUGH A REAL-ESTATE MAN WHO WOULDN'T 32 MISBEG
TELL WHO HIS CLIENT WAS.
(SHE GOES IN THROUGH HER BEDROOM, SLAMMING THE 36 MISBEG
DOOR BEHIND HER.
STROLL THROUGH TO WALLOW HAPPILY ALONG THE SHORES 50 MISBEG
OF THE ICE POND.
BEFORE I'M THROUGH WITH YOU. 63 MISBEG
OPEN THIS DOOR, I'M SAYING, BEFORE I DRIVE A FIST 73 MISBEG
THROUGH IT.
HOGAN'S MOURNFUL SONG DRIFTS BACK THROUGH THE 103 MISBEG
MOONLIGHT QUIET.--
AND ALL WE SEE NOW OF ITS LIGHTED INTERIOR IS 111 MISBEG
THROUGH THE TWO WINDOWS.
SHE GOES THROUGH HER BEDROOM AND APPEARS IN THE 111 MISBEG
OUTER DOORWAY.
(JOSIE CAN BE SEEN THROUGH THE WINDOWS, RETURNING 111 MISBEG
FROM THE KITCHEN.
YOU DON'T ASK HOW I SAW THROUGH YOUR BLUFF, JOSIE.135 MISBEG
BUT I WENT THROUGH THE NECESSARY MOTIONS AND NO 147 MISBEG
ONE GUESSED HOW DRUNK--
AND NOW HE STARES TORTURELY THROUGH THE MOONLIGHT149 MISBEG
INTO THE DRAWING ROOM.)
I CALLED YOU HERE TO TELL YOU I'VE SEEN THROUGH 162 MISBEG
ALL THE LIES YOU TOLD LAST NIGHT
(HE GOES IN THE HOUSE THROUGH HER ROOM. 177 MISBEG
SUNLIGHT SHINES IN THROUGH THE WINDOWS AT REAR. 8 POET
HE IS GLANCING THROUGH A NEWSPAPER. 8 POET
THE DRIVE IN THE HOT SUN AND THE WALK THROUGH THE 19 POET
WOODS FOR NOTHING.
YET IN SPITE OF HER SLOVENLY APPEARANCE THERE IS A 20 POET
SPIRIT WHICH SHINES THROUGH
HIS FATHER WILL PASS MUSTER, BUT IT'S THROUGH HIS 49 POET
MOTHER, I BELIEVE.
THERE'S ALWAYS ONE LAST TRICK TO GET HIM THROUGH 60 POET
HIS HONOR.
HE NEAR SANK THROUGH THE BED WITH SHAME AT HIS 64 POET
BOLDNESS.
AT THIS MOMENT SARA AND HER MOTHER ENTER THROUGH 72 POET
THE DOORWAY AT RIGHT.
AS IF SHE HADN'T THE BRAINS TO SEE THROUGH HIM. 80 POET
(SHE TURNS IN PANICKY FLIGHT AND DISAPPEARS 88 POET
THROUGH THE DOORWAY, RIGHT.
YOU WASN'T TOUCHED EXCEPT YOU'D A BULLET THROUGH 99 POET
YOUR COAT.
BY GOD, IT'S A MIRACLE ANY OF US CAME THROUGH/ 99 POET
WHAT WOULD I BE WAITIN' FOR BUT FOR YOU TO GET 103 POET
THROUGH WITH YOUR BLATHER
FENCES, THE FOX DOUBLING UP THE MOUNTAINSIDE 103 POET
THROUGH THE FURZE AND THE HEATHER--
I'LL PUT A BULLET THROUGH HIM, SC HELP ME, CHRIST/124 POET
(STRUGGLING FUTILELY AS THEY RUSH HIM THROUGH THE 124 POET
DOOR.)

THROUGH (CONT'D.)
BECAUSE IT WAS THROUGH HIM SHE FOUND THE LOVE IN 150 POET
HERSELF.
(MELODY FEELS HIS WAY GROPINGLY THROUGH THE DOOR 159 POET
AND DISAPPEARS.
GREGAN IS SHAKEN BY THE EXPERIENCE HE HAS JUST 164 POET
BEEN THROUGH
SEEN THROUGH THE OPEN DOORWAY, 577 ROPE
MARY DARTS FROM UNDERNEATH AND DASHES OUT THROUGH 578 ROPE
THE DOORWAY.
HE WON'T WANT NO MORE PEOPLE TO HANG THEMSELVES 600 ROPE
WHEN I GIT THROUGH WITH HIM.
NICK GOES THROUGH ALL THE OTHER POCKETS 508 VOYAGE
I KNEW I HAD FINALLY WON--THROUGH YOUR WORK/ 447 WELDED
SHE WALKS THROUGH THE DOORWAY.) 466 WELDED
(HE STARTS, PASSES A TREMBLING HAND THROUGH HIS 471 WELDED
HAIR BEWILDEREDLY
THROUGH SEPARATE WAYS LOVE HAS BROUGHT US BOTH TO 477 WELDED
THIS ROOM.
LIFE GUIDES ME BACK THROUGH THE HUNDRED MILLION 488 WELDED
YEARS TO YOU.
IT BECOMES IMPOSSIBLE THAT THEY SHOULD EVER DENY 488 WELDED
LIFE, THROUGH EACH OTHER.
THROUGHOUT
AND CONTINUES AT INTERVALS THROUGHOUT THE SCENE, 189 AHWILD
WHICH HE TRIES TO HOLD THROUGHOUT THE SCENE) 294 GGBROW
POMPEIA, WHOSE GAZE HAS REMAINED FIXED ON LAZARUS 398 LAZARU
THROUGHOUT,
EMPHASIZE AND INTENSIFY ELEANOR AND MICHAEL 443 WELDED
THROUGHOUT THE PLAY.
THROWING
(THEN THROWING OFF HIS MELANCHOLY, WITH A LOVING 298 AHWILD
SMILE AT HER)
THROW
AND THROW AWAY THE KEY. 194 AHWILD
AND ONCE OR TWICE, TO THROW THE DICE IS A 246 AHWILD
GENTLEMAN'S GAME.
BUT I THOUGHT, SHE'S DEAD TO ME NOW AND WHY 282 AHWILD
SHOULDN'T I THROW IT AWAY?
(PLACATINGLY) THROW IT OVERBOARD IF YOU WANT. 67 ANNA
DON'T LET ME FIND YOU HERE--IN THE MORNIN'--OR-- 108 BEYOND
OR--I'LL THROW YOU OUT/
DID YOU HEAR HIM THROW THE WORD PREACHING IN MY 501 DAYS
FACE, MR. ELIOT,
(THEY BOTH THROW, THE STONES HITTING THE PARLOR 224 DESIRE
WINDOW WITH A CRASH OF GLASS.
(HE TRIES TO THROW CABOT ASIDE. 255 DESIRE
APPEARS ABOUT TO THROW HERSELF ON HER KNEES BESIDE259 DESIRE
THE CRADLE.--
EMMEE CAN'T THROW STONES. 506 DIFRNT
(SHE TRIES TO THROW HER ARMS ABOUT HIM TO STOP HIS543 DIFRNT
GOING.
BUT HE CAN'T THROW ME OVER THIS WAY/...) 480 DYNAMO
STARING DOWN AT THE SHOES IN HIS HANDS AS IF 196 EJONES
RELUCTANT TO THROW THEM AWAY.
(THEN, AS IF SOME BURDEN OF DEPRESSION WERE ON HIM 53 ELECTR
THAT HE HAD TO THROW OFF,
AND TELL HANNAH TO THROW OUT ALL THE FLOWERS. 179 ELECTR
(THEN FURIOUSLY) I'LL THROW HER BACK ON THE 298 GGBROW
STREET/
SHE LEAPS UP AND RUNS BACK TO THROW HER ARMS 308 GGBROW
AROUND BROWN
THROW HIM OUT/? 213 HA APE
I WILL THROW THIS ONE INTO THE SEA WHEN I COME 221 HA APE
BACK.
I HAVE AN OLD COAT YOU MIGHT THROW OVER-- 221 HA APE
THEY USE THE SHOVELS TO THROW OPEN THE FURNACE 223 HA APE
DOORS.
THROW OPEN THEIR FURNACE DOORS WITH A DEAFENING 224 HA APE
CLANG.
THROW THEMSELVES ON YANK AND BEFORE HE KNOWS IT 249 HA APE
THROW HIM OUT, BOYS. 250 HA APE
BOY, IF THEY'D EVER LET ME THROW 'EM THAT WAY IN A 20 HUGHIE
REAL GAME.
TELLING PEOPLE YOU THROW THE MONEY UP IN THE AIR 582 ICEMAN
AND I CAN THROW HIM A LINE OF BULL THAT'LL KID HIM609 ICEMAN
I WON'T BE SO UNREASONABLE
AND THROW OVERBOARD THE DAMNED LYING PIPE DREAM 621 ICEMAN
THAT'D BEEN MAKING ME MISERABLE.
MAYBE I THROW A TWENTY-DOLLAR BILL ON DE BAR AND 673 ICEMAN
SAY, «DRINK IT UP.
(HE TRIES TO THROW THE DRINK IN HICKEY'S FACE, 686 ICEMAN
I'M A ROTTEN LOUSE TO THROW THAT IN YOUR FACE. 693 ICEMAN
I'LL GO UP AND THROW HIM OFF/ 726 ICEMAN
I'LL THROW UT OUT WAN AV THE PORTHOLES AN' BE DONE524 INZONE
WID UT.
IN THAT FILTHY OLD SUIT I'VE TRIED TO MAKE HIM 43 JOURNE
THROW AWAY.
I'M NO MILLIONAIRE, WHO CAN THROW MONEY AWAY/ 80 JOURNE
TU TRY AND THROW YOURSELF OFF THE DOCK/ 86 JOURNE
THAT TIME I RAN DOWN IN MY NIGHTDRESS TO THROW 118 JOURNE
MYSELF OFF THE DOCK.
THROW YOUR GAZE UPWARD/ 289 LAZARU
(THEY SURROUND HIM, THROW OVER HIS SHOULDERS AND 307 LAZARU
HEAD THE FINELY DRESSED HIDE OF
TRUTH AMONG YOUR ENEMIES--TO THROW OFF THE BURDEN 157 MANSNS
OF RESPONSIBILITY AND GUILT--
YOU MEAN, THROW HIM IN THE PIT--TO FIGHT IT OUT 171 MANSNS
WITH HIMSELF?
THROW OPEN THE DOORS/ MUSIC/ 423 MARCOM
THEY THROW IT AWAY LIKE DIRT. 429 MARCOM
WITH ONE MOTION, THE WOMEN THROW THEMSELVES 433 MARCOM
PROSTRATE ON THE FLOOR.
THE HORSE, WHEN YOU GOT THE CROWLEYS TO THROW IN 14 MISBEG
THE SATCHEL FOR GOOD MEASURES
PLEASE DON'T THROW ME TODAY, DARLIN', AND I'LL 58 MISBEG
GIVE YOU AN EXTRA BUCKET OF OATS.
PANTS AND THROW YOU IN AND LOCK THE DOOR ON YOU/ 74 MISBEG

THROW

THROW (CONT'D.)
(TO ROCHE AND O'DOWD.) THROW THIS THING OUT/ 123 POET
WATCH ME THROW IT. 589 ROPE
THROW THAT/ 589 ROPE
THAT'S ALL IT'S GOOD FOR--TO THROW AWAY.. 589 ROPE
CAN I THROW IT NOW? 589 ROPE
LEMME THROW 'NOTHER/ 590 ROPE
I DON' WANTER THROW ROCKS. 591 ROPE
THROW THEM. 591 ROPE
LEMMEE THROW 'NOTHER O' THEM. 591 ROPE
LEMME THROW 'NOTHER/ 591 ROPE
LEMME THROW 'NOTHER. 591 ROPE
I WANT COIN YUH KIN THROW AWAY-- 599 ROPE
(SHE TURNS AND RUNS OUT TO THROW THEM AS THE 602 ROPE
CURTAIN FALLS.)
(THINKING WOUNDEDLY) (I! HOPED SHE WOULD THROW 27 STRANG
HERSELF IN MY ARMS...
I'LL JUST CARRY NINA UPSTAIRS AND PUT HER ON HER 47 STRANG
BED AND THROW SOMETHING OVER
REALLY, MADAME, IF YOU CAN'T THROW OVERBOARD ALL 87 STRANG
SUCH IRRELEVANT MORAL IDEAS.
BY JOVE, I'LL HAVE TO THROW COLD WATER ON THAT 122 STRANG
FANCY....)
TO DRAG THAT RELATIONSHIP OUT OF THE PAST AND 458 WELDED
THROW IT IN MY FACE/

THROWBACK
HE SEES IT CLEARLY AS A THROWBACK TO BOYHOOD 544 DAYS
EXPERIENCES.

THROWED
IS THAT WHY YE THROWED ME OFF JEST NOWS 240 DESIRE
WHAT ELSE IS THERE FOR ME TO DO WHEN THEY'VE 532 DIFRNT
THROWED ME OUTS
AND SINCE YOU'VE THROWED HIM OUT OF HIS HOUSE IN 542 DESIRE
YOUR MAD JEALOUSNESS.
RIGHT AFTER THEY WAS THROWED OUT THEY MARRIED AND 19 ELECTR
WENT AWAY.

THROWIN'
DON'T BE THROWIN' COLD WATER, LAMPS. 460 CARIBE
THAT DURNED IDJUT, HANNAH, IS THROWIN' FITS AGIN. 158 ELECTR
NO THROWIN' SPITBALLS IN MY SOUP OR THEM KIND OF 25 HUGHIE
GAGS.

THROWING
(SUDDENLY THROWING HER ARMS AROUND HIS NECK AND 548 'ILE
CLINGING TO HIM)
THROWING 'EM OFF AGAIN JUST BEFORE THEY WENT OFF--206 AHWILD
HE WAS THROWING FIRECRACKERS AND CATCHING THEM ON 206 AHWILD
THE BACK OF HIS HAND AND
(STRAIGHTENING AND THROWING OUT HIS CHEST--WITH A 39 ANNA
BOLD LAUGH)
IT MUST HAVE BEEN SOME ARGUMENT WHEN YOU GOT TO 50 ANNA
THROWING CHAIRS.
THROWING HERSELF INTO THE CHAIR AND HIDING HER 59 ANNA
FACE IN HER HANDS ON THE TABLE
(THROWING THE CHAIR AWAY INTO A CORNER OF THE 60 ANNA
ROOM--HELPLESSLY)
AS THOUGH HE WERE THROWING OFF SOME DISTURBING 93 BEYOND
THOUGHT--WITH A LAUGH)
(THROWING HIMSELF BETWEEN FATHER AND BROTHER) 108 BEYOND
(RISING AND THROWING HER ARMS AROUND HIM-- 108 BEYOND
HYSTERICALLY)
(THROWING HIS HAT OVER ON THE SOFA--WITH A GREAT 119 BEYOND
SIGH OF EXHAUSTION)
(THROWING ASIDE HER DOLL, RUNS TO HIM WITH A HAPPY119 BEYOND
CRY)
(ANXIOUSLY) YOU DON'T MEAN YOU'RE THROWING UP 124 BEYOND
YOUR JOB HERE?
(THROWING HER AWAY FROM HIM. 128 BEYOND
(HE PUTS IT BACK IN HIS POCKET AND SHAKES HIS HEAD561 CROSS
AS IF THROWING OFF A BURDEN)
THAT FOILED HIM BY TAKING MY ARM AND THEN THROWING564 CROSS
ME ASHORE--
(RUSHING TO THE DOOR AND THROWING IT OPEN) 571 CROSS
THEY'D TURNED NAUGHTY SCHOOLBOYS AND WERE THROWING503 DAYS
SPITBALLS AT ALMIGHTY GOD AND
(THROWING HER ARMS AROUND HIM) 233 DESIRE
THEN, THROWING THE SHELLS ON THE FLOOR WITH AN 544 DIFRNT
IMPUDENT CARELESSNESS)
IMMOBILITY, TO FORM A BACKGROUND THROWING INTO 187 EJONES
RELIEF ITS BROODING.
HE IS THROWING A PAIR OF DICE ON THE GROUND BEFORE191 EJONES
HIM, PICKING THEM UP,
MECHANICAL GESTURES OF DIGGING UP DIRT, AND 194 EJONES
THROWING IT TO THE ROADSIDE.
THROWING THEIR LIGHT ABOVE ON THE PORTRAIT AND 93 ELECTR
BELOW ON THE DEAD MAN.
(THEN SUDDENLY THROWING HER ARMS AROUND HIM) 176 ELECTR
THROWING HER MASK AWAY FROM HIM ON NO LONGER 301 GGBROW
NEEDING IT)
THROWING HER KIMONO OVER HIS BARE BODY, DRAWING 322 GGBROW
HIS HEAD ON TO HER SHOULDER.)
(THROWING OFF HER RUGS AND GETTING TO HER FEET) 221 HA APE
(THROWING IT IN DRAWER) THANKS. 24 HA APE
FLAT, THROWING ASHES AND CIGAR BUTTS ON HER 606 ICEMAN
CARPET.
(HE TURNS, THROWING BACK HIS HEAD AND STRETCHING 318 LAZARU
UP HIS ARMS.
(SUDDENLY THROWING HIS SPEAR AWAY AND SINKING ON 371 LAZARU
HIS KNEES,
TO CLEANSE HIS TEETH, AND THEN THROWING IT AWAY, 349 MARCOM
IT TOOK ROOT.
(JUMPING UP, THROWING HIS PAPER ASIDE) 119 STRANG
CAN YOU IMAGINE HIM THROWING HIMSELF AWAY ON A 168 STRANG
LITTLE FOOL LIKE THAT?
HE STARTED THROWING SCOTCH INTO HIM AS IF HE WERE 171 STRANG
DRINKING AGAINST TIME.
(THEN DETERMINEDLY THROWING OFF THIS MOOD-- 447 WELDED
REPROACHFULLY FORCING A JOKING TONE)

THROWS

THROWING (CONT'D.)
HER BODY REACTS AS IF SHE WERE THROWING OFF A 449 WELDED
LOAD.)
WITH CHEST OUT AND HEAD THROWN BACK--RESENTFULLY) 32 ANNA
HE IS THROWN DOWN BACKWARD AND, IN FALLING, 33 ANNA
WHEN YOU CONSIDER THAT YOU'VE ALWAYS GOT A HOME 85 BEYOND
AND GRUB THROWN IN.
(FROWNING) IT'S A PIECE OF GOOD LUCK THROWN IN 141 BEYOND
YOUR WAY--AND--
MOMENT LATER THE DOOR IS THROWN OPEN 470 CARIBE
WITH A PIECE OF CLOTH THROWN OVER IT TO DIM ITS 553 DAYS
LIGHT.
EXCITED MOOD INTO WHICH THE NOTION OF A SON HAS 235 DESIRE
THROWN HIM.
THE JOKE HAS THROWN HIM--BURSTING INTO A FATUOUS 452 DYNAMO
RAGE--TO HIS WIFE)
(AGAIN THROWN OFF GUARD--FURIOUSLY) 27 ELECTR
(WITH LIGHT LEAPS HE VANISHES, HIS HEAD THROWN 318 GGBROW
BACK,
BESIDES, HIS HEAD IS THROWN BACK, 225 HA APE
AND SOUL THROWN IN/ 236 HA APE
HIS HEAD IS THROWN BACK, HIS BIG MOUTH OPEN. 576 ICEMAN
HE WAS CAUGHT RED-HANDED AND THROWN OFF THE FORCE.594 ICEMAN
IF I EVER SEEN YOU THROWN FIFTY CENTS ON THE BAR 601 ICEMAN
NO,
(HE IS THROWN TO THE FLOOR AND HELD THERE) 527 INZONE
YOU'VE THROWN YOUR SALARY AWAY EVERY WEEK ON 31 JOURNE
WHORES AND WHISKEY/
I MIGHT AS WELL HAVE THROWN THE MONEY OUT THE 84 JOURNE
WINDOW.
I WEPT WHEN HE WAS THROWN IN PRISON-- 105 JOURNE
ALTHOUGH ALL MY LIFE SINCE I HAD ANYTHING I'VE 146 JOURNE
THROWN MONEY OVER THE BAR TO BUY
ARMS UPSTRETCHED TOWARD THE STARS, THEIR HEADS 290 LAZARU
THROWN BACK.)
HE BENDS AND PICKS UP THE BODY OF MIRIAM IN HIS 349 LAZARU
ARMS AND, HIS HEAD THROWN BACK,
HER HEAD IS THROWN BACK AND SHE IS GAZING UP INTO 350 LAZARU
LAZARUS' FACE.
A WOMAN HAS THROWN HERSELF IN THE FLAMES, CAESAR/ 367 LAZARU
AND FURTIVE, AS THOUGH HE WERE THROWN OFF BALANCE 140 MANSNS
BY SOME EMOTION
LIKE TWO MAD FEMALE ANIMALS HE HAD THROWN IN A 171 MANSNS
PIT--
HAVE YOU FLAYED AND THROWN INTO THE STREET TO BE 417 MARCOM
DEVOURED BY DOGS.
(THE DOORS ARE THROWN OPEN. 423 MARCOM
THEIR HEADS ARE THROWN BACK, 433 MARCOM
WE'RE ONLY TENANTS AND WE COULD BE THROWN OUT ON 31 MISBEG
OUR NECKS ANY TIME.
WHOSE ONLY THOUGHT IS MONEY AND WHO HAS 113 POET
SHAMELESSLY THROWN HERSELF AT A YOUNG
YOU HAD HIM THROWN OUT UP HERE LIKE A TRAMP. 126 POET
AFTER THE LAST ONE IS THROWN SHE RUSHES BACK INTO 602 ROPE
THE BARN TO GET MORE.)
DARRELL SEEMS TO HAVE THROWN BACK-- 158 STRANG
HALF-MILLIONS AREN'T BEING THROWN AWAY FOR NOTHING192 STRANG
EVERY DAY.
(HER HEAD THROWN BACK, HER EYES SHUT--SLOWLY, 489 WELDED

THROWS
(SHE RUNS OVER TO HIM AND THROWS HER ARMS AROUND 546 'ILE
HIM, WEEPING.
(SHE THROWS HER ARMS AROUND HIM, WEEPING AGAINST 549 'ILE
HIS SHOULDER.
(HE GIVES HER CHAIR A PUSH THAT ALMOST THROWS HER 248 AHWILD
TO THE FLOOR)
HE EXCHANGES NODS WITH JOHNNY AND THROWS A LETTER 4 ANNA
ON THE BAR.)
(HE THROWS CHANGE ON THE BAR.) 6 ANNA
(HE THROWS CHANGE ON THE BAR.) 8 ANNA
AND THROWS IT OVER HER SHOULDERS) 44 ANNA
HE THROWS THE KNIFE INTO A FAR CORNER OF THE 49 ANNA
ROOM--TAUNTINGLY.
(HE THROWS HIMSELF AT BURKE, KNIFE IN HAND, 49 ANNA
KNOCKING HIS CHAIR OVER BACKWARDS.
HE THROWS HIMSELF INTO THE ROCKING-CHAIR-- 68 ANNA
DESPONDENTLY)
(SHE SUDDENLY THROWS HER ARMS ABOUT HIS NECK AND 91 BEYOND
HIDES HER HEAD ON HIS SHOULDER)
(RUSHES OVER AND THROWS HER ARMS ABOUT HIM) 100 BEYOND
(HE THROWS OFF HIS CAP AND HEAVY OVERCOAT ON THE 153 BEYOND
TABLE.
THE FULL MOON, HALFWAY UP THE SKY, THROWS A CLEAR 455 CARIBE
LIGHT ON THE DECK.
(HE DRINKS THE LAST DROP IN THE BOTTLE AND THROWS 473 CARIBE
IT BEHIND HIM ON THE HATCH.)
THROWS IT ON THE TABLE NEAR THE LANTERN.) 561 CROSS
JOHN THROWS HIMSELF ON HIS KNEES BEFORE IT 564 DAYS
(HE SUDDENLY THROWS HIS HEAD BACK BOLDLY AND 217 DESIRE
GLARES WITH HARD,
THEN WITH A LITTLE CRY SHE RUNS OVER AND THROWS 239 DESIRE
HER ARMS ABOUT HIS NECK,
(THROWS HIMSELF ON HIS KNEES BESIDE THE SOFA AND 244 DESIRE
GRABS HER IN HIS ARMS--
(SHE THROWS HIM A KISS. 245 DESIRE
(SHE THROWS HER ARMS AROUND HIM. 252 DESIRE
(THROWS HIS HEAD BACK AND LAUGHS COARSELY) 254 DESIRE
(SHE THROWS HERSELF ON HER KNEES BEFORE HIM, 257 DESIRE
WEEPING)
THROWS BACK THE COVERS AND BEGINS HURRIEDLY 263 DESIRE
PULLING ON HIS CLOTHES.
EBEN STUMBLES OVER AND THROWS HIMSELF ON HIS KNEES266 DESIRE
BESIDE HER SOBBING BROKENLY.)
EMMA BURSTS INTO SOBS AND THROWS HERSELF ON A 505 DIFRNT
CHAIR.
SHE TAKES THE CUSHIONS AND THROWS THEM ON. 548 DIFRNT

THROWS

THROWS (CONT'D.)
SHE THROWS THEM ON A PILE IN THE MIDDLE OF THE 548 DIFRNT FLOOR.
THROWS HIS ARMS AROUND HER) 445 DYNAMO
(HE THROWS THE BELT ON THE BED--TO HIS WIFE) 449 DYNAMO
(HE THROWS HIS ARMS OUT OVER THE EXCITER, HIS 488 DYNAMO HANDS GRASP THE CARBON BRUSHES.
HE THROWS HIMSELF ON THE GROUND, DOG-TIRED.) 187 EJONES
(SUDDENLY HE THROWS HIMSELF ON HIS KNEES 196 EJONES
AND THROWS HIMSELF DOWN AGAIN TO SHUT OUT THE 199 EJONES SIGHT.
SHE THROWS HER ARMS AROUND AND KISSES HIM 42 ELECTR PASSIONATELY)
(SHE RUNS TO HIM AND THROWS HER ARMS AROUND HIM 47 ELECTR AND KISSES HIM)
(HE THROWS HIMSELF ON HIS KNEES BESIDE HER AND 88 ELECTR PUTS HIS ARM AROUND HER)
SHE THROWS HER ARMS AROUND ORIN AS IF SEEKING 100 ELECTR PROTECTION FROM HIM)
BUT IMMEDIATELY THROWS HERSELF IN THEM AGAIN-- 112 ELECTR TERRIFIEDLY)
LAVINIA HAS BEEN DREADING THIS AND THROWS HERSELF 113 ELECTR IN HIS WAY, GRASPING HIS ARM.)
(SHE THROWS OFF THIS THOUGHT--HARSHLY) 115 ELECTR
LETS HERSELF GO AND THROWS HER ARMS AROUND HIM) 147 ELECTR
(SHE GOES TO THE WINDOW AND THROWS THE SHUTTERS 151 ELECTR OPEN AND LOOKS OUT)
TORN BY REMORSE, RUNS AFTER HIM AND THROWS HER 166 ELECTR ARMS AROUND HIM)
THEN THROWS HERSELF INTO PETER'S ARMS, 167 ELECTR
HE WALKS QUICKLY TO THE BENCH AT CENTER AND THROWS264 GGBROW HIMSELF ON IT,
(SHE THROWS HER ARMS AROUND HIM AND HIDES HER HEAD268 GGBROW ON HIS SHOULDER.)
(HE THROWS OPEN THE DOOR AND USHERS HER INTO HIS 304 GGBROW PRIVATE OFFICE.)
(THROWS HERSELF ON HER KNEES, TAKES THE MASK AND 321 GGBROW KISSES IT--HEARTBROKENLY)
(IS HEARD NOW--THROWS HIS HEAD BACK WITH A MOCKING216 HA APE BURST OF LAUGHTER)
THEN PICKS IT UP, THROWS IT IN THE CAGE, SHUTS THE254 HA APE DOOR.
HE THROWS THIS OPEN) 254 HA APE
(GATHERS THEM UP SWIFTLY AND THROWS THEM AGAIN.) 38 HUGHIE
(THROWS THE DICE.) FOUR'S MY POINT. 38 HUGHIE
THROWS BACK HIS HEAD, AND SINGS IN A FALSETTO 619 ICEMAN TENOR)
HE DELIBERATELY THROWS HIS WHISKEY GLASS ON THE 673 ICEMAN FLOOR AND SMASHES IT.) HEY!
THROWS A DIM LIGHT AROUND THE PLACE. 513 INZONE
(SHE GETS UP AND THROWS HER ARMS AROUND HIM 122 JOURNE
SUDDENLY CALIGULA THROWS THE CUP FROM HIM AND 317 LAZARU SPRINGS TO HIS FEET)
(THROWS OFF HIS MOOD.) OH, I'M NOT. 49 MANSNS
(THROWS OFF HER MOOD--SMILINGLY.) 57 MANSNS
(THEN, FORCING A LAUGH, SHE THROWS HERSELF IN HIS 145 MANSNS ARMS AGAIN.)
(SHE THROWS HER ARMS AROUND SARA AND BEGINS TO SOB169 MANSNS HYSTERICALLY.)
(THROWS HERSELF FORWARD AND FLINGS HER ARMS AROUND188 MANSNS DEBORAH'S LEGS--PLEADING.)
THE LATTER FIERCELY CRUMPLES IT UP AND THROWS IT 361 MARCOM ON THE FLOOR AND STAMPS ON IT.)
(HE THROWS THE POEM DOWN AGAIN, STARTS TO GO, 363 MARCOM HESITATES, SUDDENLY TURNS BACK,
(SHE THROWS IT AT HIS FEET. 375 MARCOM
HE THROWS OPEN THE WINDOW AND CALLS IN A LOUD, 389 MARCOM COMMANDING TONE)
SHE THROWS HERSELF AT KUBLAI'S FEET.) 389 MARCOM
(SHE THROWS HER HEAD BACK, HER ARMS OUTSTRETCHED. 414 MARCOM
SHE TAKES HANDFULS AND THROWS THEM OVER THE 419 MARCOM KNEELING FORMS OF THE POLOS,
(HE THROWS HIMSELF ON HIS FACE AT KUBLAI'S FEET) 425 MARCOM
SHE TEARS OFF THE FLOWER PINNED TO HER BOSOM AND 71 MISBEG THROWS IT IN THE CORNER)
(THROWS HER ARMS AROUND HIM AND PULLS HIM BACK-- 152 MISBEG TENSELY)
INSTINCTIVELY HE THROWS THE GLASS AWAY, 173 MISBEG
WHEN HE THROWS IT IN HER FACE HE HAD TO MARRY HER 13 POET BECAUSE--
HE THROWS HIS PAPER DOWN AND BURSTS OUT IN BITTER 36 POET ANGER.)
(SHE THROWS THE DOLLAR AWAY AND BENDS DOWN TO SEE 589 ROPE IT HIT THE WATER.)
SHE THROWS THEM ONE AFTER ANOTHER INTO THE OCEAN 602 ROPE AS FAST AS SHE CAN
(SHE THROWS HERSELF ON HER KNEES BESIDE HIM AND 43 STRANG HIDES HER FACE IN HER HANDS ON
CRUMPLES IT UP AND THROWS IT VIOLENTLY ON THE 67 STRANG FLOOR,
TEARS THE RIGGING OFF AND THROWS THE DISMANTLED 150 STRANG HULL AT DARRELL'S FEET)
DRISCOLL THROWS THE BEER LEFT IN HIS GLASS INTO 500 VOYAGE IVAN'S FACE.
(SHE TURNS AWAY FROM HIM AND THROWS HERSELF ON A 452 WELDED CHAIR.
(SHE THROWS HERSELF INTO HIS ARMS.) 465 WELDED
AWAY AND THROWS HERSELF ON THE COUCH IN A FIT OF 467 WELDED ABANDONED SOBBING.)

THRUST
(STARTS TO THRUST THE PAPER ON HER) 434 DYNAMO
A HAND IS THRUST OUT TO HIM THROUGH THE BARS. 355 MARCOM

THRUSTING
(BOILING OVER WITH INDIGNATION, THRUSTING THE 431 DYNAMO PAPER ON HER,

THRUSTS
(HE THRUSTS THE NEWSPAPER INTO HER HANDS, POINTING121 ELECTR TO THE STORY)

THRUSTS (CONT'D.)
(HE JERKS A BILL OUT OF HIS POCKET AND THRUSTS IT 134 ELECTR ON SETH)
HE THRUSTS HIS HEAD DOWN ON HIS ARMS 692 ICEMAN
(SHE SUDDENLY THRUSTS HER HANDS BEHIND HER BACK.) 104 JOURNE

THUD
(SHE SETS THE SOUP TUREEN DOWN WITH A THUD IN 222 AHWILD FRONT OF MRS. MILLER
THERE IS A LOUD THUD.) 66 ANNA
SOMETHING HURTLING DOWN, FOLLOWED BY A MUFFLED, 726 ICEMAN CRUNCHING THUD.
THE FORECASTLE WITH A DULL, HEAVY THUD. 523 INZONE
TO THE FLOOR WITH A MUFFLED, METALLIC THUD. 601 ROPE
(PUSHING HIM BACK ON HIS CHAIR WITH A THUD) 498 VOYAGE

THUG
HE WAS A GREAT BIG THUG BUT-- 283 AHWILD

THUMB
AND I'LL BE UNDER YOUR THUMB FOR THE REST OF MY 35 ELECTR LIFE/
DON'T LET HER BABY YOU THE WAY SHE USED TO AND GET 76 ELECTR YOU UNDER HER THUMB AGAIN.
AND EVEN IF SHE'S GOT YOU SO UNDER HER THUMB AGAIN 96 ELECTR THAT YOU DOUBT MY WORD,
HOP, YOU KIDNEY-FOOTED GANG OF THUMB-FINGERED 406 MARCOM INFIDELS/
ONLY THE MAJOR, DAMN HIM, HAD ME UNDER HIS PROUD 174 POET THUMB.
(HE JERKS HIS THUMB AT OLSON.) 497 VOYAGE
INDICATES THE MEN IN THE REAR WITH A JERK OF HIS 507 VOYAGE

THUMBING
A CHILDISH NOSE-THUMBING AT NOTHINGNESS 561 DAYS
GESTURES AND NOISES, THUMBING THEIR FINGERS TO 366 LAZARU THEIR NOSES.

THUMP
HITS HIS HEAD A HARD THUMP AGAINST THE BULWARK. 33 ANNA
(FROM THE DISTANT HILLS COMES THE FAINT, STEADY 184 EJONES THUMP OF A TOM-TOM,
THEN BACK AGAINST THE WAREHOUSE WITH A THUMP. 104 ELECTR
FOLLOWED BY A RESOUNDING THUMP AND A CHORUS OF 43 MANSNS LAUGHTER.
(SETTING DOWN THE BAGS WITH A THUMP 373 MARCOM

THUMPIN'
THIS WAS A BIG THUMPIN' NOISE NO RAT'D MAKE. 548 DIFRNT

THUMPING
THE TOM-TOM'LL BE THUMPING OUT THERE BLOOMIN' 175 EJONES SOON.
THERE IS A SUDDEN LOUD THUMPING ON THE FRONT DOOR 294 GGBROW AND THE RINGING OF THE BELL.

THUMPS
(SHE THUMPS DOWN THE DISH IN FRONT OF HIM WITH A 226 AHWILD SIGH OF RELIEF.)

THUNDER
NOW WHAT IN THUNDER DOES THAT DAMNED OLD-- 199 AHWILD
WE'LL WATCH THE DAWN COME UP LIKE THUNDER OUT OF 288 AHWILD CHINA/
YOU KIN GO TO THUNDER, JIM MAYO/ 104 BEYOND
WE HARBY 'BOLISHES SHET GATES, AN' OPEN GATES, AN'221 DESIRE ALL GATES, BY THUNDER/
WAAL, THEN, BY THUNDER, YE'LL GIT ME HARD AN' SEE 237 DESIRE HOW YE LIKE IT/
THUNDER 'N' LIGHTIN', ABBIE/ 263 DESIRE
THUNDER, I KNOW YOU AIN'T, EMMER. 497 DIFRNT
SHE'S MAD AS THUNDER AT YOU 'CAUSE I COME OVER 531 DIFRNT HERE SO MUCH
AND A LOW RUMBLE OF THUNDER. 421 DYNAMO
(THE CLAP OF THUNDER FROM THE PRECEDING FLASH 441 DYNAMO COMES WITH A GREAT RUMBLE.)
IN THIS DARKNESS THE CLAP OF THUNDER FROM THE 443 DYNAMO PRECEDING FLASH COMES.
THE THUNDER CLOUDS ARE GETTING NEARER THE MOON... 444 DYNAMO
(THERE IS A CRASH OF THUNDER. 445 DYNAMO
THE ROLL OF THE THUNDER FROM THE PRECEDING FLASH 446 DYNAMO COMES CRASHING AND RUMBLING.
(THEN HURRIEDLY, AS A CRASH OF THUNDER COMES) 449 DYNAMO
REUBEN LOOKS UP AND GIVES A WILD LAUGH AS THOUGH 452 DYNAMO THE THUNDER ELATED HIM.
(THERE IS A TREMENDOUS CRASH OF THUNDER, 452 DYNAMO
AND THUNDER RUMBLES AND CRASHES BUT THERE IS NO 312 LAZARU RAIN.
TERRIFIC FLASHES OF LIGHTNING AND CRASHES OF 318 LAZARU THUNDER SEEM A RESPONSIVE
WAR IS A WASTE OF MONEY WHICH EATS INTO THE 394 MARCOM PROFITS OF LIFE LIKE THUNDER/

THUNDERBOLT
I'M THINKING YOUR JEHOVAH MIGHT AIM A THUNDERBOLT 437 DYNAMO AT ME
A THUNDERBOLTS 422 MARCOM

THUNDERIN'
HER'S SO THUNDERIN' SOFT--LIKE HIS MAW. 231 DESIRE
THUNDERIN' MOSES, THAT'S THE FUST TIME EVER I 513 DIFRNT HEERED GOOD O' MYSELF BY LISTENIN'/
THUNDERIN' MOSES, WHAT THE HELL D'YOU WANT CALEB 513 DIFRNT TO BE--

THUNDERING
AN INSISTENT MONOTONE OF THUNDERING SURF, MUFFLED 555 CROSS AND FAR-OFF,
CHEST THUNDERS WITH EGOTISM AND IS TOO HARD FOR 43 STRANG TIRED HEADS AND THOROUGHLY

THURSDAY
YOU'D BETTER MEET ME HERE THURSDAY NIGHT. 111 ELECTR

THUS
(HAVING THUS SQUARED MATTERS SHE TAKES UP HER 291 AHWILD SEWING AGAIN.
WHILE HIS ATTENTION IS THUS OCCUPIED, 196 EJONES
THE SPACE THUS ENCLOSED IS LIKE THE DARK, NOISOME 198 EJONES HOLD OF SOME ANCIENT VESSEL.

THUS (CONT'D.)
THUS MAKING A BACK ROOM LEGALLY A HOTEL 571 ICEMAN
RESTAURANT.
(HE QUOTES FROM THUS SPAKE ZARATHUSTRA.) 78 JOURNE
THUS IN EACH CROWD-- 273 LAZARU
THUS SANG HIS LIFE TO LAZARUS WHILE HE LAY DEAD/ 310 LAZARU
MY THOUGHT WAS FANCIFUL--THAT PERHAPS THUS YOU 19 MANSNS
CONTINUED TO HIDE FROM YOURSELF.
THAT WAS UNWISE, FOR THUS HE HAS REMAINED A 388 MARCOM
STRANGE.
PRAY THUS/ 435 MARCOM
THUTY
THREE-THUTY. 182 EJONES
SUNDOWN'S AT SIX-THUTY OR DERE-ABOUTS. 183 EJONES
THWART
THAT HE MUST DO SOMETHING TO THWART IT AT ONCE. 558 DAYS
THY
'TIS COOL BENEATH THY WILLOW TREES/= 195 AHWILD
= THAT I COULD DRINK WITH THY VEINS AS WINE, AND 205 AHWILD
EAT THY BREASTS LIKE HONEY.
=MY LIFE IS BITTER WITH THY LOVE. 205 AHWILD
THINE EYES BLIND ME, THY TRESSES BURN ME, 205 AHWILD
THAT FROM FACE TO FEET THY BODY WERE ABOLISHED AND205 AHWILD
CONSUMED,
THY SHARP SIGHS DIVIDE MY FLESH AND SPIRIT WITH 205 AHWILD
SOFT SOUND--=
AND IN MY FLESH THY VERY FLESH ENTOMBED/= 205 AHWILD
LET ME BELIEVE IN THY LOVE AGAIN/ 565 DAYS
O LORD OF LOVE, FORGIVE THY POOR BLIND FOOL/ 566 DAYS
THE RESURRECTION AND THE LIFE, AND HE THAT 566 DAYS
BELIEVETH IN THY LOVE,
(WITH A SARDONIC CHUCKLE) HONOR THY FATHER/ 205 DESIRE
LORD GOD O' HOSTS, SMITE THE UNDUTIFUL SONS WITH 227 DESIRE
THY WUST CUSS/
I AM THY SHORN, BALD, NUDE SHEEP/ 283 GGBROW
=INTO THY HANDS, O LORD,= 286 GGBROW
KEEP THY HEART FREE AND RAISED UPWARDS TO GOD 291 GGBROW
FEAR THY NEIGHBOR AS THYSELF/ 294 GGBROW
MERCY ON THY POOR CLOD, THY CLOD OF UNHALLOWED 319 GGBROW
EARTH, THY CLAY,
LEAVE THY LOW-VAULTED PAST/ 148 MANSNS
HE WILL DISCOVER THY SINS.= 579 ROPE
(CHANTS) =POUR OUT THY FURY UPON THE HEATHEN THAT582 ROPE
KNOW THEE NOT,
AND UPON THE FAMILIES THAT CALL NOT ON THY NAME.= 582 ROPE
=GIVE THEM SORROW OF HEART, THY CURSE UNTO THEM. 584 ROPE
THYSELF
KEEP THYSELF AS A PILGRIM, AND A STRANGER UPON 290 GGBROW
FEAR THY NEIGHBOR AS THYSELF/ 294 GGBROW
TIA
I'D JUST ROLLED IN FROM TIA JUANA. 22 HUGHIE
TIARAS
FASHIONED IN ORNATE TIARAS, CROWNS, NECKLACES, 233 HA APE
COLLARS, ETC.
TIBBETTS
AND SHE WON'T SEE ANYONE BUT OLD DOCTOR 73 STRANG
TIBBETTS...
TIBOTS
TIBOTS 'N' HARRIS 'N' SIMMS AND THE REST--AND ALL542 'ILE
O' HOMEPORT MAKIN FUN O' ME$
TIBI
=FORTUNATE SENEX, ERGO TUA RURA MANEBUNT, ET TIBI 37 MISBEG
MAGNA SATIS,
TICK
DAT'S ME NOW--I DON'T TICK, SEES 250 HA APE
HEARING THE FOG DRIP FROM THE EAVES LIKE THE 152 JOURNE
UNEVEN TICK OF A RUNDOWN,
(THEN CONTEMPTUOUSLY) YOU'RE A DIRTY TICK AND 10 MISBEG
IT'D SERVE YOU RIGHT IF I LET YOU
SURE, EVERYONE SAYS YOU'RE A WICKED OLD TICK, AS 17 MISBEG
CROOKED AS A CORKSCREW,
AND THE DIRTY TICK ACCUSED YOU AND ME OF MAKING UP 21 MISBEG
A FOXY SCHEME TO TRAP JIM.
DON'T CALL HIM A TICK. 22 MISBEG
THE DIRTY TICK/ 22 MISBEG
AH, HERE YOU COME, DO YOU, AS FULL AS A TICK/ 72 MISBEG
YOU DIRTY LITTLE TICK/ 93 MISBEG
YOU WERE AS FULL AS A TICK. 168 MISBEG
OCH, DON'T BE THREATENING ME, YOU BAD-TEMPERED OLD177 MISBEG
TICK.
TICKET
(SHE TAKES THE TICKET FROM HER DRESS AND TRIES TO 71 ANNA
HOLD IT BEFORE HIS EYES)
I'D BOUGHT MY TICKET AND EVERYTHING. 71 ANNA
(IN THE SAME TONE) MY BAG'S PACKED AND I GOT MY 72 ANNA
TICKET.
SO THAT'S THE TICKET/ 175 EJONES
WHISKY, THAT'S THE TICKET/ 209 HA APE
WHO ONCE WORKED FOR A CIRCUS IN THE TICKET WAGON. 594 ICEMAN
THE FIRST RUBE THAT CAME TO MY WAGON FOR A TICKET 608 ICEMAN
GOSH, THINKING OF THE OLD TICKET WAGON BRINGS 609 ICEMAN
THOSE DAYS BACK.
THAT'S THE TICKET/ 686 ICEMAN
TICKLE
I SUPPOSE IT'D TICKLE YOU IF ME AND MARGIE DID 633 ICEMAN
WHAT DAT LOUSE, HICKEY,
TICKLED
I RANG IN A JOKE IN ONE OF MY STORIES THAT TICKLED188 AHWILD
THE FOLKS THERE PINK.
AS IF NAT AND I WEREN'T ONLY TOO TICKLED TO DEATH 212 AHWILD
TO HAVE YOU/
HE'S SO TICKLED TO GET OUT OF IT FOR A WHILE HE 269 AHWILD
CAN'T SEE STRAIGHT/
(THEN HASTILY) MUSTN'T LET HER KNOW I'M SO 277 AHWILD
TICKLED.
YOU KNOW DARNED WELL HOW TICKLED I AM TO HAVE YOU 505 DAYS
HERE.

TICKLED (CONT'D.)
WAAL, THAT FOOL BROWN GAL B'LIEVED 'EM AND SHE 503 DIFRNT
SWUM RIGHT OFF, TICKLED TO DEATH.
(WITH A TICKLED CHUCKLE) GOSH, THAT'D BE THE REAL545 DIFRNT
STUNT AW RIGHT, AW RIGHT.
(JOKINGLY) YOU NEEDN'T LOOK SO DARNED TICKLED 160 ELECTR
ABOUT IT/
I KNOW HE'D BE ONLY TOO TICKLED TO HELP HIM OUT. 277 GGBROW
HALF-AMUSED, AS IF THEY SAW A JOKE SOMEWHERE 226 HA APE
THAT TICKLED THEM.
HE WAS TICKLED PINK. 16 HUGHIE
BUT HUGHIE LOOKED SO TICKLED I COULDN'T WELSH ON 25 HUGHIE
HIM.
=SURE, HUGHIE,= I TOLD HIM, =I'LL BE TICKLED TO 25 HUGHIE
DEATH.=
(HE LAUGHS, IMMENSELY TICKLED.) 584 ICEMAN
AND WON'T ALL THE OLD GANG BE TICKLED TO DEATH 652 ICEMAN
WHEN I SHOW UP ON THE LOT/
I TOLD HIM YOU'D BE TICKLED TO DEATH OVER THE 25 JOURNE
GREAT IRISH VICTORY.
WELL, I'M NOT TICKLED TO DEATH. 25 JOURNE
SHE WASN'T SO TICKLED ABOUT IT--LATER ON. 126 MISBEG
SHE WAS TICKLED TO DEATH TO GET ME PIE-EYED. 126 MISBEG
AND YOU'RE BOTH OF YOU TICKLED TO DEATH TO SEE ME,588 ROPE
AIN'T YUH$
I S'POSE YUH'RE TICKLED TO PIECES TO SEE ME--LIKE 594 ROPE
HELL/
TICKLES
(HE PUSHES HER BACK ON THE SOFA AND TICKLES HER 194 AHWILD
WITH FREE HAND,
(HE TICKLES THE LAUGHING, SQUIRMING MARY, 130 BEYOND
(THIS TICKLES HIS HUMOR AND HE SLAPS HIS THIGH AND245 DESIRE
LAUGHS)
(THIS FANCY TICKLES HIM AND HE GIVES A CACKLING 609 ICEMAN
LAUGH.)
THAT TICKLES ME MORE THAN ANYTHING ELSE. 120 STRANG
TICKLIN'
HE SAYS, =QUIT TICKLIN' ME.= 617 ICEMAN
TICKLISH
(HE CHUCKLES GRIMLY) A TICKLISH DECISION FOR YOU,149 ELECTR
YOUR HONOR/
TICKS
AND HE WOUND UP BY BY SAYING THAT HE HAD TO PUT UP 24 JOURNE
WITH POISON IVY, TICKS,
I DON'T LIKE TICKS BUT I'LL SAY THIS FOR THEM, 22 MISBEG
WHISKEY, AND THERE'S POISON IVY, AND TICKS AND 63 MISBEG
POTATO BUGS,
TIDE
GOD A'MIGHTY, KATE, I CAN'T GIVE ORDERS TO THE 95 BEYOND
TIDE THAT IT'S GOT TO BE HIGH
AND A FRIENDLY BREWERY TO TIDE HIM OVER. 594 ICEMAN
SWAYING IN THE TIDE. 153 JOURNE
(SO OVERCOME BY A RISING TIDE OF SAVAGE, 122 POET
HUMILIATED FURY,
BREATHING IN THE TIDE I DREAM AND BREATHE BACK MY 91 STRANG
DREAM INTO THE TIDE...
I AM LIVING A DREAM WITHIN THE GREAT DREAM OF THE 91 STRANG
TIDE...
SUSPENDED IN THE MOVEMENT OF THE TIDE, I FEEL LIFE 92 STRANG
MOVE IN ME,
BREATHING IN THE TIDE I DREAM AND BREATHE MY DREAM110 STRANG
BACK INTO THE TIDE...
TIDES
YOU CAN'T ORDER THE TIDES ON THE SEAS TO SUIT YOU,102 BEYOND
THE MOON IS DROWNED IN THE TIDES OF MY HEART. 264 GGBROW
I WANT THE TIDES OF MY BLOOD TO LEAVE MY HEART AND264 GGBROW
FOLLOW HIM/
I WANT HIM TO SLEEP IN THE TIDES OF MY HEART/ 323 GGBROW
=ONCE AS SQUIRMING SPECKS WE CREPT FROM THE TIDES 324 LAZARU
OF THE SEA.
IN THE TOIL OF TIDES. 409 MARCOM
TIDIED
A GENERAL ATMOSPHERE OF CLEAN, WELL-TIDIED, WIDE 233 HA APE
STREET.
SHE HAS TIDIED UP AND ARRANGED HER HAIR. 40 MISBEG
TIDIES
FOUR CHAIRS, THREE ROCKERS WITH CROCHETED TIDIES 93 BEYOND
ON THEIR BACKS,
TIDINGS
(DULLY.) THAT DIDN'T SOUND LIKE GLAD TIDINGS. 73 JOURNE
I TOLD PHIL THE GLAD TIDINGS AND BOUGHT DRINKS FOR131 MISBEG
ALL AND SUNDRY.
TIDY
I GOT TO RUN UPSTAIRS AND TIDY MYSELF A LITTLE. 527 DIFRNT
WE CAN AT LEAST TIDY UP THE ROOMS A LITTLE AND GET136 ELECTR
THE FURNITURE COVERS OFF.
GO IN THE HOUSE NOW, AND WASH YOUR FACE, AND TIDY 36 MISBEG
YOUR DRESS,
I HAD A PEEK IN IT ONE DAY I WENT TO TIDY UP THE 32 POET
CABIN FOR HIM,
TIE
AW SAY, YOU FRESH KID, TIE THAT BULL OUTSIDE/ 195 AHWILD
HE HAS DISCARDED COLLAR AND TIE, COAT AND SHOES, 249 AHWILD
AND WEARS AN OLD, WORN,
(HE HAS TAKEN HIS COLLAR AND TIE FROM WHERE THEY 260 AHWILD
HANG FROM ONE CORNER OF THE
WEARS A CHEAP BLUE SUIT, A STRIPED COTTON SHIRT 45 ANNA
WITH A BLACK TIE,
AND A BLUE FLANNEL SHIRT WITH A BRIGHT COLORED 81 BEYOND
TIE.
HE IS DRESSED IN A DARK SUIT, WHITE SHIRT AND 493 DAYS
COLLAR, A DARK TIE,
HALF TIES THE TIE MECHANICALLY, PUTS ON COAT, 241 DESIRE
TAKES HIS HAT,
GIVING A TOUCH TO HIS SHIRT AND TIE, 145 ELECTR
LONG IS DRESSED IN SHORE CLOTHES, WEARS A BLACK 233 HA APE
WINDSOR TIE, CLOTH CAP.

TIE

(CONT'D.)
HE WEARS AN ILL-FITTING BLUE SERGE SUIT, WHITE 8 HUGHIE SHIRT AND COLLAR, A BLUE TIE.
IN A SHADE OF BLUE THAT SETS TEETH ON EDGE, AND A 9 HUGHIE GAY RED AND BLUE FOULARD TIE.
EVEN HIS FLOWING WINDSOR TIE IS NEATLY TIED. 574 ICEMAN
FADED PINK SHIRT AND BRIGHT TIE BELONG TO THE SAME575 ICEMAN VINTAGE.
COLLAR AND TIE CRUSHED UP INTO A PILLOW ON THE 576 ICEMAN TABLE IN FRONT OF HIM.
I'LL TIE A DISPOSSESS BOMB TO YOUR TAILS THAT'LL 606 ICEMAN BLOW YOU OUT IN THE STREET/
A LOUD SUIT, TIE AND SHIRT, AND YELLOW SHOES. 615 ICEMAN
CAN YUH TIE ITS 616 ICEMAN
(HE SHAKES HIS HEAD) WHORES GOIN' ON STRIKE/ CAN 670 ICEMAN YUH TIE DAT&
HOPE IS DRESSED IN AN OLD BLACK SUNDAY SUIT, BLACK683 ICEMAN TIE, SHOES, SOCKS.
HE HAS LOST HIS STRAW HAT, HIS TIE IS AWRY, AND 697 ICEMAN HIS BLUE SUIT IS DIRTY.
THIS'LL DO FUR ME AN' SCOTTY TO TIE HIM. 525 INZONE
HE FINALLY STANDS CALM, AND ALLOWS DAVIS AND 525 INZONE SCOTTY TO TIE UP HIS ARMS.)
STAND HIM UP, NOW, AND TIE HIS FEET, TOO, SO HE'LL528 INZONE NOT BE MOVIN'.
AND WEARS A COLLAR AND TIE. 19 JOURNE
HE WEARS A SHIRT, COLLAR AND TIE, NO COAT, OLD 20 JOURNE FLANNEL TROUSERS, BROWN SNEAKERS.
HE HAS TAKEN OFF COLLAR AND TIE AND CARRIES THEM 53 JOURNE IN HIS HAND.
(PUTTING ON HIS COLLAR AND TIE.) 54 JOURNE
HE HAS CHANGED TO A READY-MADE BLUE SERGE SUIT, 89 JOURNE HIGH STIFF COLLAR AND TIE.
MAKE UP YOUR MIND YOU'VE GOT TO TIE A CAN TO ME-- 166 JOURNE GET ME OUT OF YOUR LIFE--
(THEY LOWER THE SAIL, AND BEGIN TO TIE IT UP 408 MARCOM TRIMLY.)
SILK HANDKERCHIEF IN BREAST POCKET, A DARK TIE. 37 MISBEG
SQUARES HIS SHOULDERS, PULLS HIS COAT DOWN IN 22 STRANG FRONT, SETS HIS TIE STRAIGHT.
(MEANINGL) HE HAS NO TIE OVER HERE TC REMAIN 116 STRANG FAITHFUL TO, HAS HE&
WHAT IS THIS TIE OF OLD HAPPINESS BETWEEN OUR 172 STRANG FLESHS...))
HE HAS LOST HIS TIE. 496 VOYAGE

TIED
AND KEEPS TIED TO HER FATHER'S APRON STRINGS/ 216 AHWILD
I COULD LICK THE THREE OF THEM SITTING DOWN WITH 32 ANNA ONE HAND TIED BEHIND ME.
OR WOULD YOU HAVE HER TIED FOR LIFE TO THE LIKE OF 48 ANNA THEM SKINNY.
AND I HAVING IT TIED ROUND MY NECK WHEN MY LAST 75 ANNA SHIP SUNK.
SHE WEARS A GINGHAM DRESS WITH A SOILED APRON TIED116 BEYOND AROUND HER WAIST.)
GUSH, I NEVER SAW A FATHER SO TIED UP IN A KID AS 140 BEYOND ROB IS/
NAKED EXCEPT FOR THE FUR OF SOME SMALL ANIMAL TIED200 EJONES ABOUT HIS WAIST.
IN THE OTHER A CHARM STICK WITH A BUNCH OF WHITE 200 EJONES COCKATOO FEATHERS TIED TO THE
IT WOULD BE BAD FOR HIM TO GET TIED TO YOUR APRON 49 ELECTR STRINGS AGAIN.
AS LONG AS VINNIE'S TIED DOWN TO HIM WE CAN'T GET 159 ELECTR MARRIED.
EVEN HIS FLOWING WINDSOR TIE IS NEATLY TIED. 574 ICEMAN
SEVERAL PACKAGES, TIED WITH RIBBON, ARE ALSO ON 629 ICEMAN THE TABLE.
AND DON'T'LL BE TIED FOR LIFE TO A NO-GOOD SOAK, 671 ICEMAN
HE OPENS IT AND TAKES OUT A SMALL PACKET OF 528 INZONE LETTERS ALSO TIED UP WITH STRING.
SOMETHIN' SQUARE TIED UP IN A RUBBER BAG. 528 INZONE
ORNAMENTS, TAPERS, HAVE BEEN NAILED ON THE TRUNK 347 MARCOM OR TIED TO THE BRANCHES.
WITH A PINK RIBBON TIED AROUND ITS NECK. 391 MARCOM
WELL, FOLKS, ARE YOU ALL TONGUE-TIED& 429 MARCOM
(SHE STARES AT HIM) YOU'D LIKE BEING TIED TO 8 MISBEG MONEY, I KNOW THAT.
AND I WOULDN'T MARRY THE BEST MAN ON EARTH AND BE 8 MISBEG TIED DOWN TO HIM ALONE.
(SCORNFULLY) BETTER MYSELF BY BEING TIED DOWN 29 MISBEG
AND HER OLD CLOTHES ARE LIKE A BAG COVERING IT, 20 POET TIED AROUND THE MIDDLE.
IT'S TIED STRUNG--STRONG AS DEATH--(HE CACKLES 579 ROPE WITH SATISFACTION)
SO YOU MIGHT 'S WELL TAKE DOWN THAT UGLY ROPE 581 ROPE YOU'VE HAD TIED THERE SINCE HE RUN
A DIRTY GRAY BAG TIED TO THE END OF THE ROPE FALLS601 ROPE
BEING TIED TO A WIFE WHO'S TOO SICK TO BE A WIFE. 70 STRANG
HE WAS SO TIED TO HER APRON STRINGS...)) 99 STRANG
AND MY HANDS ARE TIED AS FAR AS SHARING THE ESTATE114 STRANG WITH HER IS CONCERNED.

TIEF
TAWN BLACK TIEF/ 462 CARIBE

TIER
RUNS BACK DOWN THE TIER, AND ABRUPTLY CEASES.) 240 HA APE
(HE SHAKES THE BARS OF HIS CELL DOOR TILL THE 244 HA APE WHOLE TIER TREMBLES.
HYPOCRITICAL TYPE, GROUPED ON EACH SIDE OF THE 363 LAZARU THRONE OF CAESAR ON A LOWER TIER.
IT RISES IN THREE TIERS, THREE STEPS TO A TIER. 377 MARCOM

TIERS
TIERS OF NARROW, STEEL BUNKS, THREE DEEP, ON ALL 207 HA APE SIDES.
AT RIGHT, THE USUAL NUMBERED TIERS OF MAILBOXES, 7 HUGHIE AND ABOVE THEM A CLOCK.
WHO SIT ON THE BANKED TIERS OF MARBLE BEHIND AND 363 LAZARU TO THE REAR OF THE THRONE.

TIERS (CONT'D.)
IT RISES IN THREE TIERS, THREE STEPS TO A TIER. 377 MARCOM

TIES
HALF TIES THE TIE MECHANICALLY, PUTS ON COAT, 241 DESIRE TAKES HIS HAT.
(JACK HANDS HIM ONE AND HE TIES IT TIGHTLY AROUND 528 INZONE SMITTY'S HEAD OVER THE WASTE)
(AIRILY) I DON'T KNOW WHAT TIES HE HAS OR HASN'T 116 STRANG GOT.

TIGER
TO TIGER INN AND HE'S FULLBACK ON THE FOOTBALL 283 AHWILD TEAM--

TIGHT
I LIKE TO BE HELD TIGHT, DON'T YOUS 240 AHWILD
HOLD ME TIGHT. 240 AHWILD
SLEEP TIGHT. 252 AHWILD
(IN HIS EXCITEMENT HE SQUEEZES HER HAND TIGHT.) 35 ANNA
(SHE STRUGGLES BUT DRISCOLL HOLDS HER TIGHT.) 471 CARIBE
ON THESE ARE SEATED, SQUEEZED IN TIGHT AGAINST ONE247 DESIRE ANOTHER.
THERE IS AN ABSURD SUGGESTION OF ROUGE ON HER 520 DIFRNT TIGHT CHEEKS AND THIN LIPS.
HE'S A TIGHT-WAD AND I HATE FOLKS THAT'RE TIGHT 522 DIFRNT WITH THEIR COIN.
(DISGUSTEDLY) NOW YOU'RE TALKIN' TIGHT LIKE HIM. 523 DIFRNT
HIS FOLKS AIN'T TIGHT-WADS LIKE MINE. 523 DIFRNT
(THREATENINGLY) AND IF HE'S TOO TIGHT, 545 DIFANT
(PLEASINGLY) PUT YOUR ARMS AROUND ME TIGHT AND 469 DYNAMO KISS ME AGAIN.
(TURNS TO HIM SHARPLY) YOU GO NOW AND CLOSE THE 179 ELECTR SHUTTERS AND NAIL THEM TIGHT.
HUG ME TIGHT, DARLIN'. 230 HA APE
HE WEARS A LIGHT GREY SUIT CUT IN THE EXTREME, 9 HUGHIE TIGHT-WAISTED, BROADWAY MODE.
MY OLD MAN WAS A TIGHT OLD BASTARD. 709 ICEMAN
THE BASQUE WAS BONED AND VERY TIGHT. 115 JOURNE
TIGHT LIPS, AND HER JAW IS A LITTLE TOO LONG AND 2 MANSNS HEAVY FOR THE REST OF HER FACE.
IT'S LIKE WALKING A TIGHT-ROPE OVER AN ABYSS-- 156 MANSNS
TIGHT-FITTING AND DRAWN IN AT THE WAIST, 37 MISBEG

TIGHT*WAD
I'M LEARNIN' YOUR KID TO BE A SPORT, TIGHT*WAD. 589 ROPE

TIGHTENED
(STARING AROUND THE FARM, HIS COMPRESSED FACE 218 DESIRE TIGHTENED,

TIGHTENING
(TIGHTENING HIS GRASP--ROUGHLY) EASY/ 174 EJONES

TIGHTENS
HER EYES GROW BLEAK AND HER MOUTH TIGHTENS TO A 91 ELECTR THIN LINE.
(LARRY'S FACE TIGHTENS BUT HE KEEPS SILENT. 646 ICEMAN

TIGHTER
(HOLDING HIM TIGHTER--VOLUBLY) 167 ELECTR
(UNCONSCIOUSLY HE GRIPS HER TIGHTER, ALMOST 451 WELDED SHAKING HER.)

TIGHTLY
AND A TIGHTLY CLENCHED, THIN-LIPPED MOUTH. 538 *ILE
THE ALMOST EMPTY BOTTLE TIGHTLY CLUTCHED IN ONE 470 CARIBE HAND.
(HE PRESSES HIS LIPS TIGHTLY TOGETHER AN EFFORT TO423 DYNAMO APPEAR IMPLACABLE THAT GIVES
SHE WEARS HER HAIR PULLED TIGHTLY BACK, AS IF TO 10 ELECTR CONCEAL ITS NATURAL CURLINESS,
AND UNTIES THE STRING WHICH IS WOUND TIGHTLY 528 INZONE AROUND THE TOP.
(JACK HANDS HIM ONE AND HE TIES IT TIGHTLY AROUND 528 INZONE SMITTY'S HEAD OVER THE WASTE)
ALTHOUGH SHE IS NOT TIGHTLY CORSETED, 12 JOURNE
THE DRY SKIN IS STRETCHED TIGHTLY OVER THE BONES 27 MANSNS
SHE HUGS HIM MORE TIGHTLY AND SPEAKS SOFTLY, 152 MISBEG STARING INTO THE MOONLIGHT)

TIGHTWAD
I'M NO TIGHTWAD. 239 AHWILD
DON'T WANT DE BOSS TO GET WISE WHEN HE'S GOT ONE 578 ICEMAN OF HIS TIGHTWAD BUNS ON.
BUT I DON'T WANT YOU TO THINK I'M A TIGHTWAD. 586 ICEMAN
A TIGHTWAD, 616 ICEMAN
(EYES HIM JEERINGLY) WHY, HELLO, TIGHTWAD KID. 650 ICEMAN
I KNOW WHAT'S EATIN' YOU, TIGHTWAD/ 682 ICEMAN
HELLO, TIGHTWAD. 700 ICEMAN
YOU CAN SHOW YOURSELF UP BEFORE THE WHOLE TOWN AS 145 JOURNE SUCH A STINKING OLD TIGHTWAD/
WHERE IS THE OLD TIGHTWAD& 155 JOURNE
HE LOVES TO PLAY TIGHTWAD, BUT THE PEOPLE HE LIKES123 MISBEG KNOW BETTER.
INSIDE, HE WAS A LOUSY TIGHTWAD BASTARD. 128 MISBEG

TIKE
I ON'Y TIKE A NIP 'O' BRANDY NOW AN' AGEN FUR MY 501 VOYAGE 'EALTH.
OW, TIKE SOMETHIN'. 505 VOYAGE
TIKE 'ER AHT OF 'ERE/ 508 VOYAGE
(THEY DO SO) TIKE 'IM TO THE *AMINDRA---YER KNOWS 508 VOYAGE THAT, DON'T YER&
'ERE, YOU TWO, TIKE 'IM IN UNDER THE ARMS LIKE 'E 508 VOYAGE WAS DRUNK.

YOU MIGHT AS WELL GO OUT IN THE KITCHEN AND WAIT 211 AHWILD TILL I RING.
(WHO HAS REMAINED DETACHED) KAPE HIM DOWN TIL 232 HA APE HE'S COOLED OFF.

TILES
THE FLOOR IS OF WHITE TILES. 173 EJONES

TILLY
AND BILL SAYS, * LET'S GO SEE TILLY SMALL.* 525 DIFRNT
I HEARD THEM SAYING TO THE STORE THAT YOU'D BEEN 525 DIFRNT UP CALLIN' ON THAT TILLY SMALL
AND SURE I'LL PROMISE NOT TO SEE TILLY NO MORE. 526 DIFRNT

1665 TIME

TILLY (CONT'D.)

(HE GETS TO HIS FEET) AND AS FOR AN OLD BUM LIKE 527 DIFRNT
TILLY--NOT ME/
WITH YOUR DRUNKEN CARRYIN'S-ON WITH THAT HARLOT, 528 DIFRNT
TILLY SMALL, NIGHT AFTER NIGHT.

TILT

AND RUNS FULL TILT INTO THE BENDING, STRAINING 239 HA APE
YANK,
(RESENTFULLY PUTS HIS STRAW HAT ON HIS HEAD AT A 670 ICEMAN
DEFIANT TILT)

TILTED

ANDREW IS TILTED BACK ON THE STRAIGHT-BACKED CHAIR 94 BEYOND
TO THE LEFT,

TILTING

(PUTTING HIS MUDDY BOOTS UP ON THE TABLE, TILTING 217 DESIRE
BACK HIS CHAIR,

TILTS

(HE TAKES THE BOTTLE WITH BOTH TWITCHING HANDS AND582 ICEMAN
TILTS IT TO HIS LIPS AND

TIM

AND BIG TIM SULLIVAN, FLANKED BY FRAMED 664 ICEMAN
LITHOGRAPHS OF JOHN L. SULLIVAN

TIMBER

IT IS PROPPED UP ABOUT TWO FEET ABOVE GROUND BY 1 MISBEG
LAYERS OF TIMBER BLOCKS.

TIMBRE

WHEN SHE SPEAKS HER VOICE IS WITHOUT TIMBRE, LOW 144 BEYOND
AND MONOTONOUS.

TIME

(MORE KINDLY) WHERE WAS IT YE'VE BEEN ALL O' THE 536 *ILE
TIME--THE FO'C'S'TLE5
KEEP US ALL HERE AFTER OUR TIME IS WORKED OUT 537 *ILE
WITH THE DAMNED ICE ALL THE TIME, 538 *ILE
I'VE FELT IT IN THE AIR THIS LONG TIME PAST. 539 *ILE
THEY'S ENOUGH TO LAST A LONG TIME YIT, IF THEY'RE 541 *ILE
CAREFUL WITH IT.
THE TIME HE SIGNED UP FOR IS DONE TODAY. 544 *ILE
AT RIGHT OF THIS DOORWAY, ANOTHER BOOKCASE, THIS 185 AHWILD
TIME A SMALL, OPEN ONE,
YOU OUGHT TO KNOW BETTER BY THIS TIME. 190 AHWILD
NO, NOT THIS TIME, ESSIE. 190 AHWILD
IT'S NOT MY IDEA OF HAVING A GOOD TIME IN 192 AHWILD
VACATION.
I'M HOPING BEFORE YOU LEAVE NEW HAVEN THEY'LL FIND192 AHWILD
TIME TO TEACH YOU
I'M GOING TO BEAT IT--JUST TIME TO CATCH THE 199 AHWILD
EIGHT-TWENTY TROLLEY.
SHE NEVER CAN ANSWER THE FRONT DOOR RIGHT UNLESS 1199 AHWILD
TELL HER EACH TIME.
JUST PICTURE OLD DAVE DIGESTING THAT FOR THE FIRST205 AHWILD
TIME/
(SEES THE SLIPS FOR THE FIRST TIME AND IS OVERCOME207 AHWILD
BY EMBARRASSMENT,
HAVING A CRANKY OLD MAID AROUND ALL THE TIME. 212 AHWILD
(AGITATEDLY) I DON'T THINK HE WILL--THIS TIME-- 212 AHWILD
NOT AFTER HIS PROMISE.
HE'S BEEN EATING BLUEFISH FOR YEARS--ONLY I TELL 214 AHWILD
HIM EACH TIME IT'S WEAKFISH.
(REALLY SHOCKED THIS TIME) I DON'T LIKE YOU WHEN 216 AHWILD
YOU SAY SUCH HORRIBLE,
AND HANG AROUND UNTIL IT'S 219 AHWILD
NOW I THINK OF IT, I'VE FELT UPSET AFTERWARDS 228 AHWILD
EVERY DAMNED TIME WE'VE HAD FISH/
HAVE A GOOD TIME AT THE BEACH, MILDRED. 228 AHWILD
(BY THIS TIME THE FAMILY ARE BEGINNING TO EXCHANGE229 AHWILD
AMUSED, GUILTY GLANCES.
I'VE TAKEN DOWN THE DISTANCE EVERY TIME YOU'VE 230 AHWILD
SAVED RED'S LIFE FOR THIRTY YEARS
BUT AT THE SAME TIME THRILLED AND PROUD OF 236 AHWILD
MINGLING WITH THE PACE THAT KILLS.
YOU'LL CATCH UP IN TIME/ 237 AHWILD
(KISSING HIM AGAIN) JUST THINK OF THE WONDERFUL 241 AHWILD
TIME EDITH AND YOUR FRIEND WINT
AND THIS TIME I'LL BLOW YOU JUST TO SHOW MY 242 AHWILD
APPRECIATION.
STOPPING EACH TIME TO SURVEY THE RESULT 249 AHWILD
CRITICALLY, BITING HER TONGUE,
AND EVERY TIME HE SENSES ANY OF THE FAMILY 249 AHWILD
GLANCING IN HIS DIRECTION,
(WITH ANOTHER SIGH) WHAT TIME IS IT NOW, NATS 250 AHWILD
WHAT TIME IS IT NOW, NATS 253 AHWILD
STOP TRYING TO BE SO DARN FUNNY ALL THE TIME/ 255 AHWILD
I WILL SOME OTHER TIME. 256 AHWILD
AUTOMATICALLY HE BEGINS TO TAP ONE FOOT IN TIME, 259 AHWILD
(SUDDENLY) WHAT TIME IS IT NOW, NATS 259 AHWILD
THAT'D BE THE TIME IT'D TAKE HIM TO WALK FROM THE 260 AHWILD
BEACH.
I WAS ONLY WISHING THIS HADN'T COME UP--JUST AT 264 AHWILD
THIS PARTICULAR TIME.
I DID ALL WITH WILBUR AND LAWRENCE AND 268 AHWILD
ARTHUR, WHEN IT CAME TIME--
(THEN SUDDENLY) MY GOODNESS, I WONDER WHAT TIME 271 AHWILD
IT'S GETTING TO BE.
THAT'S A FINE TIME TO THINK OF-/... 276 AHWILD
THAT'LL MAKE THE TIME PASS QUICKER. 276 AHWILD
WHERE WAS I THIS TIME LAST NIGHTS 276 AHWILD
I'LL HAVE TO MEMORIZE THE REST AND RECITE IT TO 277 AHWILD
MURIEL THE NEXT TIME.
AH, WHO EVER HEARD OF A WOMAN EVER BEING ON TIME. 277 AHWILD
I OUGHT TO KNOW ENOUGH ABOUT LIFE BY THIS TIME NOT277 AHWILD
TO EXPECT.
GOSH, TIME PASSES--WHEN YOU'RE THINKING. 278 AHWILD
THAT'S THE TIME PA AND MA COME UP TO BED, AS 280 AHWILD
REGULAR AS CLOCK WORK.
BUT YOU'LL HAVE OODLES OF TIME TO DO THAT. 280 AHWILD
HE WAS TOO DRUNK BY THAT TIME. 283 AHWILD
AND THIS TIME I MEAN IT/ 284 AHWILD

TIME (CONT'D.)

(THEN TEARFULLY) AND THERE I WAS RIGHT AT THAT 284 AHWILD
TIME LYING IN BED NOT ABLE TO
IT'S LOVE, NOT LIQUOR, THIS TIME. 293 AHWILD
THIS TIME, LOOKS GUILTY AND A BIT DEFIANT, 293 AHWILD
AND NOW THAT THE SUBJECT'S COME UP OF ITS OWN 295 AHWILD
ACCORD, IT'S A GOOD TIME--
IT'S ABOUT TIME YOU AND I HAD A SERIOUS TALK 295 AHWILD
ABOUT--HMMM--
FIRST TIME HE'S DONE THAT IN YEARS. 297 AHWILD
GIMME A SCOOP THIS TIME--LAGER AND PORTER. 4 ANNA
JUST ON TIME. 4 ANNA
LONG TIME AGO, THOUGH. 5 ANNA
LONG TIME AY VAIT FOR YOU. 6 ANNA
WHERE ARE YOU IN FROM THIS TIMES 7 ANNA
SOME OTHER TIME. 7 ANNA
VE MAKE SLOW VOYAGE--DIRTY VEDDER--YUST FOG, FOG, 7 ANNA
FOG, ALL BLOODY TIME/
(BEAMING) PY GOLLY, DAT'S GOOD NEWS ALL AT ONE 8 ANNA
TIME FOR OLE FALLAR/
AY NEVER GAT HOME ONLY FEW TIME DEM YEAR. 9 ANNA
SHE GAT TIRED VAIT ALL TIME SVEDEN FOR ME VEN AY 9 ANNA
DON'T NEVER COME.
IN ALL MY TIME I TRIED NEVER TO SPLIT 11 ANNA
BUT ALL TIME AY HOPE LIKE HELL SOME DAY SHE VANT 12 ANNA
FOR SEE ME AND DEN SHE COME.
AND AY GO VISIT DEM EVERY TIME AY GAT IN PORT 13 ANNA
NEAR/
YUH DON'T KNOW WHAT TIME YOUR KID'S LIABLE TO SHOW 13 ANNA
UP.
(AS IF SHE WERE GREETING HIM FOR THE FIRST TIME) 19 ANNA
(EARNESTLY) I KNOW OLD CHRIS WELL FOR A LONG 19 ANNA
TIME.
AH, AY VORK ON LAND LONG TIME AS YANITOR. 21 ANNA
YUST SHORT TIME AGO AY GOT DIS YOB CAUSE AY VAS 21 ANNA
SICK, NEED OPEN AIR.
AY DUN'T SEE YOU FOR LONG TIME, YOU DON'T FORGAT 22 ANNA
DAT.
DIS ONE TIME BECAUSE VE MEET AFTER MANY YEAR. 23 ANNA
SHE CALABRATE DIS ONE TIME WITH ME--AND SMALL BEER 24 ANNA
FOR ME.
(RECEIVING NO REPLY, HE CALLS AGAIN, THIS TIME 25 ANNA
WITH APPARENT APPREHENSION)
WHAT TIME IS THAT5 27 ANNA
HARD VORK ALL TIME. 28 ANNA
SURE--LIKE I'D BEEN LIVING A LONG, LONG TIME--OUT 28 ANNA
HERE IN THE FOG.
(THIS TIME SOUNDING NEARER BUT UP FORWARD TOWARD 29 ANNA
THE BOW)
(THE =AHOY= COMES AGAIN THROUGH THE WALL OF FOG, 29 ANNA
SOUNDING MUCH NEARER THIS TIME.
THAT WAS A TERRIBLE TIME, GOD HELP US. 36 ANNA
THIS IS THE FIRST TIME I'VE HAD A WORD WITH A 37 ANNA
RALE, DACENT WOMAN.
LONG TIME AY VAIT FOR YOU.= 41 ANNA
YOU GO ASHORE ALL TIME, EVERY DAY AND NIGHT VEEK 42 ANNA
WE'VE BEEN HERE.
YOU HAVE GOOD TIME HERE, AY TANK. 42 ANNA
AIN'T I GOT A RIGHT TO HAVE AS GOOD A TIME AS I 42 ANNA
CANS
HE MIGHT FORGET SOME TIME THAT YOU WAS OLD AND MY 43 ANNA
FATHER--
BUT DIVIL TAKE YOU, THERE'S A TIME COMES TO EVERY 46 ANNA
MAN, ON SEA OR LAND,
BURKE SPRINGS TO HIS FEET QUICKLY IN TIME TO MEET 49 ANNA
THE ATTACK.
'TWAS ONLY A BIT OF AN ARGUMENT WE WAS HAVING TO 50 ANNA
PASS THE TIME TILL YOU'D COME.
YOU AIN'T GOT TIME-- 51 ANNA
TIS A QUARE TIME TO JOKE WITH ME, AND DON'T BE 53 ANNA
DOING IT, FOR THE LOVE OF GOD.
(POINTING TO CHRIS) I'VE BEEN MEANING TO TURN IT 56 ANNA
LOOSE ON HIM EVERY TIME HE'D
WE'VE NO TIME TO BE WASTING. 56 ANNA
HAD GOT ME TO THINKING FOR THE FIRST TIME, 59 ANNA
SHE MAKE YOU FIGHT WITH ME ALL TIME/ 62 ANNA
A FINE THING--YOU LEAVING ME ALONE ON THIS BARGE 64 ANNA
ALL THAT TIME/
(NOTICING THE REVOLVER FOR THE FIRST TIME) 69 ANNA
(FIERCELY) AND EACH TIME I'D BE HITTING ONE A 70 ANNA
CLOUT IN THE MUG,
BUT I'LL BET BY THE TIME YOU GET THERE YOU'LL HAVE 73 ANNA
FORGOT ALL ABOUT ME AND START
(WITH A LAUGH) AND SAY, IT'S ABOUT TIME FOR YOU 77 ANNA
AND MAT TO KISS AND MAKE UP.
FOG, FOG, FOG, ALL BLOODY TIME. 78 ANNA
WHAT IS IT THIS TIME--POETRY, I'LL BET. 82 BEYOND
IMAGINE ME READING POETRY AND PLOWING AT THE SAME 82 BEYOND
TIME.
(MOODILY) THAT'S A LONG TIME. 83 BEYOND
JUST BECAUSE YOU SEE ME READING BOOKS ALL THE 83 BEYOND
TIME.
ALWAYS FIGHTING AND SEPARATED A LOT OF THE TIME, 83 BEYOND
JUST AT THIS TIME, IN SPRING, WHEN EVERYTHING IS 88 BEYOND
GETTING SO NICE.
AND SOMEHOW AFTER A TIME I'D FORGET ANY PAIN I WAS 89 BEYOND
IN, AND START DREAMING.
AND YOU THOUGHT YOURSELF TOO EDUCATED TO WASTE ANY 91 BEYOND
TIME ON ME.
THE NEXT TIME I HEARS ONE 94 BEYOND
AND THEN THEY TELLS THE FISH TO WHISTLE TO 'EM 95 BEYOND
WHEN IT'S TIME TO TURN OUT.
YOU MIGHT SAY, JUST TO GET ON THAT OLD BOAT OF 95 BEYOND
YOURS ON TIME/
AND BEEN A WIDDER WITH ONLY A DAUGHTER, AND LAID 98 BEYOND
UP ALL THE TIME TO BOOT, MRS.
WHAT HAVE YOU BEEN DOIN' ALL THIS TIME-- 99 BEYOND

TIME

	(CONT'D.)	
TIME		
WHY, ROBERT AIN'T GUT NO TIME FOR RUTH, 'CEPT AS A 99 BEYOND	
FRIEND/	
(REPROACHFULLY) YOU MIGHT'VE EVEN NOT WASTED TIME 99 BEYOND	
LOOKIN' FOR THAT ONE--	
SHE'LL LIKELY COME AROUND TO IT IN TIME.	99 BEYOND
SHE'D LOVED ALL THE TIME, BUT I HADN'T SEEN IT.	100 BEYOND
OR AT ANY FUTURE TIME, EITHER.	100 BEYOND
YOU AIN'T GOT MUCH TIME TO FIND HER, DICK.	104 BEYOND
PA'LL SEE HOW I FELT--AFTER A TIME.	110 BEYOND
«IT'S ABOUT TIME YOU PUT A STOP TO HIS NONSENSE.	113 BEYOND
WASTIN' TIME DOIN' EVERYTHING THE WRONG WAY--	113 BEYOND
MANY'S THE TIME I'VE SAID TO HER,	113 BEYOND
WE CAN GIVE PRAISE TO GOD THEN THAT HE'LL BE BACK 115 BEYOND	
IN THE NICK OF TIME.	
SEEMS AS IF SHE CRIES ALL THE TIME ON PURPOSE TO	116 BEYOND
SET A BODY'S NERVES ON EDGE.	
SHE GETS IT RIGHT FROM HER PA--BEIN' SICKLY ALL	116 BEYOND
THE TIME.	
I ARGUED AGAINST IT AT THE TIME.	116 BEYOND
(PULLING HER BACK) IT'S TIME FOR YOUR NAP.	117 BEYOND
IT'S A WONDER ROB WOULDN'T TRY TO GET TO MEALS ON 117 BEYOND	
TIME ONCE IN A WHILE.	
WHAT'S THE GOOD OF YOUR COMPLAINING ALL THE TIMES 118 BEYOND	
YOU KNOW IT'S TIME FOR HER NAP AND YOU'LL GET HER 119 BEYOND	
ALL WAKED UP.	
I SHOULD THINK YOU'D KNOW IT BY HEART BY THIS	120 BEYOND
TIME.	
(SPITEFULLY) WORK YOU'LL NEVER GET DONE BY	122 BEYOND
READING BOOKS ALL THE TIME.	
I MEAN TO BE HERE ON TIME.	122 BEYOND
I'LL HAVE A HARD TIME GETTING ANOTHER MAN AT SUCH 124 BEYOND	
SHORT NOTICE.	
HAVING TO SUFFER ALL THE TIME BECAUSE YOU'VE NEVER127 BEYOND	
BEEN MAN ENOUGH	
COOKING AND WASHING DISHES ALL THE TIME.	136 BEYOND
THE SAME REASON THAT MADE YOU GO LAST TIME THAT'S 139 BEYOND	
DRIVING YOU AWAY AGAIN.	
AFTER THE WAY I PLAYED THE DUMB FOOL ABOUT GOING	139 BEYOND
AWAY LAST TIME.	
I WANT YOU TO BELIEVE I PUT ALL THAT SILLY	139 BEYOND
NONSENSE BACK OF ME A LONG TIME AGO--	
AND BE UPSET ALL THE TIME I'M HERE ON MY FOOL	139 BEYOND
ACCOUNT.	
WHAT TIME IS IT NOW, I WONDER$	142 BEYOND
AND I WON'T COME BACK WITH EMPTY HANDS NEXT TIME. 142 BEYOND	
WILL THERE BE TIMES	142 BEYOND
YOU AIN'T GOT SO MUCH TIME, ANDY.	142 BEYOND
(MEANINGLY) IT MUST BE YOUR DINNER TIME NOW.	143 BEYOND
(WITH BITTER MOCKERY) FIVE YEARS/ IT'S A LONG	146 BEYOND
TIME.	
(HE CALCULATES) WHAT TIME IS IT NOWS ROUND SIX, 147 BEYOND	
MUST BE.	
NO SUN YET. IT ISN'T TIME.	151 BEYOND
(THE TWO WOMEN REMAIN SILENT FOR A TIME STARING	152 BEYOND
DEJECTEDLY AT THE STOVE.)	
OF THE ROOM FOR THE FIRST TIME)	155 BEYOND
AND ALL THIS TIME I'VE BEEN--WHY I'VE HAD	155 BEYOND
EVERYTHING/	
(WITHOUT EMOTION) A LETTER TAKES SOME TIME TO GET155 BEYOND	
WHERE YOU WERE--	
YOU WROTE ROB YOU WAS COMING BACK TO STAY THIS	156 BEYOND
TIME.	
(IN A LOUD TONE) THERE'S A TIME COMES--WHEN YOU	156 BEYOND
DON'T MIND ANY MORE--ANYTHING.	
AFTER RUTH PUT ME TO BED BEFORE YOU CAME, I SAW IT160 BEYOND	
CLEARLY FOR THE FIRST TIME.	
SOMETHING HAPPENED FIVE YEARS BACK, THE TIME YOU	163 BEYOND
CAME HOME FROM THE TRIP.	
ONLY THIS TIME IT SOUNDED--UNNATURAL, DON'T YOU	163 BEYOND
THINK$	
THEN--YOU LOVED ME--THAT TIME I CAME HOME$	164 BEYOND
(DOGGEDLY) I'D KNOWN YOUR REAL REASON FOR LEAVING164 BEYOND	
HOME THE FIRST TIME--	
WE MUST TRY TO HELP EACH OTHER--AND--IN TIME--	168 BEYOND
WE'LL COME TO KNOW WHAT'S RIGHT--	
THE OLD VOICES CALLING ME TO COME--(EXULTANTLY)	168 BEYOND
AND THIS TIME I'M GOING/	
HE STOPS FROM TIME TO TIME TO LISTEN TO THE	477 CARDIF
CONVERSATION.	
IF THIS HAD ONLY HAPPENED A WEEK LATER WE'D BE IN 485 CARDIF	
CARDIFF IN TIME TO--	
YOU AND HE HAVE BEEN SHIPMATES A LONG TIMES	485 CARDIF
REMEMBER THE TIME WE WAS THERE ON THE BEACH	487 CARDIF
AND THE TIME YOU WAS PINCHED BY THE COPS IN PORT	488 CARDIF
SAID$	
AND THE TIME WE WAS BOTH LOCKED UP IN SIDNEY FOR	488 CARDIF
FIGHTING.	
IT WAS IN NEW GUINEA, TIME I WAS SHIPWRECKED	457 CARIBE
THERE.	
PY YINGO, WE HAVE ONE HELL OF A TIME/	458 CARIBE
SHE'LL BE BRINGIN' SOME BLACK WOMEN WITH HER THIS 458 CARIBE	
TIME--	
AS I WAS A-ROAMIN' DOWN PARADISE STREET--GIVE US	460 CARIBE
SOME TIME TO BLOW THE MAN DOWN/	
GIVE US SOME TIME TO BLOW THE MAN DOWN/	460 CARIBE
GIVE US SOME TIME TO BLOW THE MAN DOWN/	460 CARIBE
GIVE US SOME TIME TO BLOW THE MAN DOWN/	460 CARIBE
I DONE MY SHARE O' DRINKIN' IN MY TIME.	467 CARIBE
I BEEN THROUGH IT MANY'S THE TIME.	468 CARIBE
THE MATE LOOKS UP AND SEES THE WOMEN ON THE HATCH 473 CARIBE	
FOR THE FIRST TIME.)	
SMITTY LISTENS TO IT INTENTLY FOR A TIME..	473 CARIBE
THE TIME IS AN EARLY HOUR OF A CLEAR WINDY NIGHT	555 CROSS
IN THE FALL OF THE YEAR 1900.	
AND HE SUSPECTED MY GROWING DOUBTS AS TIME WENT	561 CROSS
ON.	

TIME	(CONT'D.)	
(HIS VOICE SINGULARLY TUNELESS AND COLD BUT AT THE494 DAYS	
SAME TIME INSISTENT)	
YOUR HEAD'S MANHOOD UP TO THE TIME HE (A SNEER	494 DAYS
COMES INTO HIS VOICE)	
AT THE SAME TIME HIS FEATURES AUTOMATICALLY ASSUME495 DAYS	
THE MEANINGLESSLY AFFABLE	
WE HAVEN'T SEEN MUCH OF LUCY, EITHER, FOR A LONG	498 DAYS
TIME.	
THIS TIME ELIOT COMES IN IMMEDIATELY, WITHOUT	499 DAYS
WAITING FOR AN ANSWER.)	
(CONSTRAINED AND AT THE SAME TIME AFFECTIONATE)	500 DAYS
I HOPE YOU'RE HAVING A GOOD TIME, YOU TWO.	502 DAYS
AND HIS LETTERS FOR A TIME EXTOLED PASSIONLESS	503 DAYS
CONTEMPLATION SO PASSIONATELY	
(WITHOUT LOOKING AT HIM) THINKING OF IT--TO PASS 505 DAYS	
THE TIME.	
(HE SIGHS) IT HAS BEEN A LONG TIME--TOO LONG.	505 DAYS
AND I'VE HAD A GREAT LONGING FOR SOME TIME TO SEE 506 DAYS	
YOU AGAIN.	
THERE COMES A TIME IN EVERY MAN'S LIFE WHEN HE	508 DAYS
MUST HAVE HIS GOD FOR FRIEND.	
PERHAPS YOU ARE ON THE THRESHOLD OF THAT TIME NOW.508 DAYS	
IT WOULD GIVE ME A CHANCE TO GET YOUR AND ELSA'S 512 DAYS	
CRITICISMS AT THE SAME TIME.	
OH, SOME TIME WHILE YOU'RE HERE, MAYBE.	512 DAYS
WHAT TIME DOES JOHN USUALLY GET HOME$	516 DAYS
BUT HONESTLY, YOU'RE MISTAKEN THIS TIME.	517 DAYS
THE FIRST TIME I KNEW HE'D BEEN UNFAITHFUL I DID	519 DAYS
THE CORRECT THING	
I--HONESTLY, I HARDLY KNOW YOU THIS TIME, YOU'VE	519 DAYS
CHANGED SO.	
IF YOU ONLY COULD REALIZE HOW MUCH THAT MEANT TO	523 DAYS
ME--ESPECIALLY AT THAT TIME.	
BEEN A LONG TIME SINCE WE'VE HAD THIS PLEASURE.	525 DAYS
YOU'LL HAVE TO MEET HIM SOME TIME.	527 DAYS
WHILE THERE IS STILL TIME/	528 DAYS
ENTERTAINING A STRANGE PRIEST-UNCLE FOR THE FIRST 530 DAYS	
TIME.	
HE WAS HAPPY AGAIN FOR THE FIRST TIME SINCE HIS	535 DAYS
PARENTS' DEATH--	
IT WAS THE FIRST TIME.	536 DAYS
BUT THIS TIME HE THOUGHT IT WOULD HELP HIM TO	537 DAYS
ESCAPE HIMSELF FOR A WHILE.	
REMEMBER, ALL THIS TIME HE SAW THROUGH HER.	537 DAYS
BY WHINING THAT THE TIME FOR INDIVIDUALISM IS	542 DAYS
PAST.	
A MAN WHO WILL PROVE THAT MAN'S FLEETING LIFE IN	543 DAYS
TIME AND SPACE CAN BE NOBLE.	
AND ALL THE TIME I WAS LOVING YOU,	549 DAYS
WHEN ALL THAT TIME I LOVED YOU SO,	550 DAYS
(STRANGELY SERIOUS AND BITTERLY MOCKING AT THE	550 DAYS
SAME TIME)	
NOW, FOR ELSA'S SAKE--WHILE THERE IS STILL TIME.	558 DAYS
(FRIGHTENEDLY) STILL TIMES	558 DAYS
(SUDDENLY HE SEEMS TO SEE FATHER BAIRD FOR THE	558 DAYS
FIRST TIME--WITH A CRY OF APPEAL--	
I KNOW YOU COULDN'T BLASPHEME AT SUCH A TIME--NOT 559 DAYS	
YOUR TRUE SELF.	
HEAR ME WHILE THERE IS STILL TIME/	565 DAYS
THEY APPEAR TO PROTECT AND AT THE SAME TIME	202 DESIRE
SUBDUE.	
(MATTER-OF-FACTLY) WE NEVER HAD NO TIME T'	209 DESIRE
NEEDLE.	
BY THE TIME YE GIT THAR MEBBE YE'LL KISS HER	211 DESIRE
INSTEAD/	
I BEGIN T' BELLER LIKE A CALF AN' CUSS AT THE SAME214 DESIRE	
TIME, I WAS SO DURN MAD--	
AND EVERY TIME I THOUGHT OF HOME I WISHED IT	224 DESIRE
WASN'T ME/	
AMUSED BUT AT THE SAME TIME PIQUED AND IRRITATED. 228 DESIRE	
(WEAKLY) WHAT D'YE WANT T' WASTE TIME ON HER FUR$230 DESIRE	
I HAD NO TIME T' FOOL AWAY COUNTIN' 'EM.	237 DESIRE
(HE PAUSES) ALL THE TIME I KEPT GITTIN'	237 DESIRE
LONESOMER.	
YE WON'T HEV NONE LEFT FUR NEXT TIME.	244 DESIRE
(MEANINGLY) SEEMS LIKE HE'S SPENT MOST O' HIS	248 DESIRE
TIME T' HUM SINCE YEW COME.	
(THIS TIME APPEALING TO NOBODY IN PARTICULAR)	248 DESIRE
I THOUGHT YE MIGHT HAVE TIME T' RUN AWAY--WITH	266 DESIRE
ME--AN'--	
BEING SEA-FARING MEN, AWAY FROM THEIR WOMEN FOLKS 495 DIFRNT	
MOST OF THE TIME.	
WITH YOUR PA AND JACK CUSSIN' ABOUT THE HOUSE ALL 495 DIFRNT	
THE TIME.	
(SQUEEZING HER) WAAL, IT'S ABOUT TIME, AIN'T ITS 496 DIFRNT	
MY FUST VIGE AS SKIPPER, YOU DON'T S'POSE I HAD	497 DIFRNT
TIME FOR NO MONKEY-SHININ'.	
BUT YOU DID THINK OF ME AND MISS ME ALL THE TIME	498 DIFRNT
YOU WAS GONE, DIDN'T YOUS	
CAUGHT YE THAT TIME, BY GUM/	498 DIFRNT
PLAYING SILLY JOKES ALL THE TIME.	499 DIFRNT
MOST O' THE WHALIN' MEN HEREABOUT HAVE RUN UP	502 DIFRNT
AGAINST IT IN THEIR TIME.	
THE CRAZY CUSS GIVES UP AND SWIMS BACK TO HOME,	503 DIFRNT
HOWLIN' ALL THE TIME.	
NOT IN TWO DAYS, NOR NO TIME.	506 DIFRNT
THUNDERIN' MOSES, THAT'S THE FUST TIME EVER I	513 DIFRNT
HEERD GOOD O' MYSELF BY LISTENIN'/	
BUT IT'S PURTY THERE ALL THE TIME--	515 DIFRNT
(A PAUSE) I WISH YOU COULD SEE THEM ISLANDS,	515 DIFRNT
EMMER, AND BE THERE FOR A TIME.	
THAT'S WHY I STAYED ABOARD ALL THE TIME WHEN THE	515 DIFRNT
BOYS WAS ASHORE.	
AND WHEN A THING'S DIED, TIME CAN'T MAKE NO	517 DIFRNT
DIFF'RENCE.	
(SHAKING HER HEAD--SLOWLY) IT AIN'T A QUESTION OF517 DIFRNT	
TIME, CALEB.	

TIME

(CONT'D.)

AND AT THE SAME TIME IRRITATING AND DISGUSTING-- 520 DIFRNT
AND YOU ALMOST WAS MY AUNT-IN-LAW ONE TIME FROM 521 DIFRNT
WHAT I'VE HEARD.
UNCLE CALEB LIVIN' NEXT DOOR ALL THESE YEARS AND 522 DIFRNT
COMIN' TO CALL ALL THE TIME
AND HE'LL SHOW ME A GOOD TIME, AND IF I HAD A 523 DIFRNT
HUNDRED DOLLARS--
BUT I COULD HAVE A SWELL TIME EVEN IN THIS DUMP 523 DIFRNT
HE WON'T COME FOR A LONG TIME YET. 524 DIFRNT
I TOLD HER TO CUT THE ROUGH WORK AND BEHAVE--AND A525 DIFRNT
NICE TIME WAS HAD BY ALL.
GOOD-BY FOR GOOD THIS TIME. 531 DIFRNT
FOLKS WOULD BE SAYIN' ALL SORTS OF BAD THINGS IN 532 DIFRNT
NO TIME.
YOU KNOW HOW LITTLE TIME HE'S HAD TO HOME BETWEEN 533 DIFRNT
VYGES.
AIN'T HE SPENT EVERY DURN EVENIN' OF THE TIME HE'S533 DIFRNT
TO HOME BETWEEN TRIPS OVER
BUT EVERY TIME HE'D EVEN HINT AT BEIN' ENGAGED 533 DIFRNT
AGAIN I'D ALWAYS TELL HIM HE WAS
(HE BEGINS TO LOOK AT HER AS IF HE WERE SEEING HER536 DIFRNT
FOR THE FIRST TIME.
WAN'T YOUR HAIR TURNIN' GRAY LAST TIME I WAS TO 536 DIFRNT
HOME?
I WAS GETTIN' OLD BEFORE MY TIME. 536 DIFRNT
(QUICKLY) HELL, I DON'T MEAN THAT KIND O' TIME. 537 DIFRNT
D'YOU KNOW WHAT TIME THIS BE, EMMER& 537 DIFRNT
(AFTER A PAUSE) I KNOW YOU TOLD ME TIME AND AGAIN538 DIFRNT
NOT TO GO BACK TO THAT.
THIRTY YEARS--THAT'S A HELL OF A LONG TIME TO 538 DIFRNT
WAIT, EMMER--
I WANT YOU TO TAKE TIME TO THINK IT ALL OVER. 538 DIFRNT
YOU KNOW 'S WELL AS ME WHAT A HARD TIME SHE'S HAD.539 DIFRNT
(SUSPICIOUSLY) WHY SHOULD I NEED YOU NOW ANY 539 DIFRNT
MORE'N ANY OTHER TIMES
TIME.
BUT I'VE WATCHED HIM GROW UP FROM A BOY AND EVERY 540 DIFRNT
TIME I'VE COME TO HOME
IF HE'S WILLIN' TO DIG IN HIS JEANS FOR SOME REAL 545 DIFRNT
COIN--REAL DOUGH; THIS TIME/
IS NOT THE TIME RIPE TO SMITE THIS BLASPHEMER 423 DYNAMO
(IMPATIENTLY) DON'T YOU KNOW THAT MAN WELL ENOUGH425 DYNAMO
BY THIS TIME NOT TO PAY
IT'S A LONG TIME TO LIVE IN THIS AWFUL LITTLE 425 DYNAMO
HOUSE/
NO TIME ELAPSES BETWEEN SCENES ONE AND TWO. 427 DYNAMO
THE FIRST TIME HE EVER DID SUCH A THING/ 427 DYNAMO
(WITH A CHUCKLE) HIM ARGUING WITH ME AND AT THE 429 DYNAMO
SAME TIME ADMITTING + FIFE.
IT'S TIME I TOOK A HAND IN THIS... 432 DYNAMO
NO TIME ELAPSES BETWEEN SCENES TWO AND THREE.) 435 DYNAMO
(IADA'S A LONG TIME BRINGING HIM... 436 DYNAMO
(ALL THE TIME HE IS TALKING, HE STARES AT 436 DYNAMO
REUBEN'S FLUSTERED FACE.
BUT THIS TIME VERY DIMLY, AS IF THE MOON WERE 443 DYNAMO
BEHIND CLOUDS--
WHAT ON EARTH CAN AMELIA BE DOING WITH REUBEN ALL 443 DYNAMO
THIS TIMES...))
NO TIME ELAPSES BETWEEN SCENES THREE AND FOUR.) 443 DYNAMO
((IT COMES EVERY TIME/... 444 DYNAMO
(VINDICTIVELY) I PROMISE I WON'T STAND BETWEEN 445 DYNAMO
HIM AND PUNISHMENT THIS TIME/
NO, YOU NEEDN'T THINK I'M GOING TO GET YOU OFF 448 DYNAMO
THIS TIME/
THEN WHY ARE YOU ALL THE TIME THINKING ABOUT 455 DYNAMO
HIM&...
POOR RUBE/...WHAT'S HE BEEN DOING ALL THIS TIME, I455 DYNAMO
WONDERS...))
I'M SURE HE'S BEEN WISHING FOR A LONG TIME THAT 456 DYNAMO
LIGHT BOY'D COME HOME
I'VE GOT NO TIME FOR HER NOW. 457 DYNAMO
((SINGING ALL THE TIME ABOUT EVERYTHING IN THE 458 DYNAMO
WORLD...
THEY'RE SINGING ALL THE TIME ABOUT EVERYTHING IN 458 DYNAMO
THE WORLD/
TIME, AND HE BLURTS OUT IN A TONE THAT IS ALMOST 463 DYNAMO
KINDLY) SAY, YOU LOOK ALL IN.
SHE HOPED FOR A TIME YOU'D COME BACK BUT FINALLY 465 DYNAMO
SHE GAVE UP HOPING--
WHEN I READ THEM I REALIZED THAT AMELIA HAD BEEN 465 DYNAMO
THINKING OF YOU ALL THE TIME.
ON YOU WHEN YOU'VE HAD IT CRAMMED DOWN YOUR THROAT470 DYNAMO
FROM THE TIME YOU WERE BORN/
AT THE SAME TIME TRYING TO REASSURE HERSELF) 471 DYNAMO
NO TIME ELAPSES BETWEEN SCENES ONE AND TWO.) 483 DYNAMO
A SHORT TIME IS SUPPOSED TO ELAPSE BETWEEN SCENES 486 DYNAMO
TWO AND THREE.)
THEN SHE BEGINS TO GLIDE NOISELESSLY, A STEP AT A 173 EJONES
TIME.
*E'S CUNNIN' ENOUGH TO KNOW WHEN 'IS TIME 'S COME.175 EJONES
YOU DIDN'T LET ME IN ON YO' CROOKED WORK OUT O' NO177 EJONES
KIND FEELIN'S DAT TIME.
(WITH A GRIN) DE LONG GREEN, DAT'S ME EVERY TIME/177 EJONES
AND IT DIDN'T TAKE LONG FROM DAT TIME TO GIT DESE 177 EJONES
FOOL.
SO I HAS--AND ME MAKIN' LAWS TO STOP IT AT DE 177 EJONES
SAME TIME/
THE TIME OF THE REVOLUTION, WASN'T ITS 178 EJONES
AND IT WAS LUCK 'E DIDN'T 'IT YOU THAT TIME. 178 EJONES
I HAS DE SILVER BULLET MOULDED AND I TELLS 'EM 179 EJONES
WHEN DE TIME COMES I KILLS MYSELF
OH, LAWD, FROM DAT TIME ON I HAS DEM ALL EATIN' 179 EJONES
OUT OF MY HAND.
I KNOWS DIS EMPEROR'S TIME IS SHO'T. 180 EJONES
(WARNINGLY) MAYBE IT'S GETTIN' TIME FOR YOU TO 181 EJONES
RESIGN.
MAKING A BLUFF DEY WAS WUKIN' ALL DE TIME. 182 EJONES

(CONT'D.)

A MAN CAN'T TAKE DE POT ON A BOB-TAILED FLUSH ALL 182 EJONES
DE TIME.
I'LL BE 'CROSS DE PLAIN TO DE EDGE OF DE FOREST BY189 FJONFS
TIME DARK COMES.
I GOT PLENTY O' TIME TO MAKE IT EASY. 183 EJONES
(FIERCELY) AND DIS TIME I LEAVE HIM A DEAD NIGGER183 EJONES
FO' SHO'/
AN' OUTPLAY DE WHOLE LOT O' DEM ALL OVAH DE BOARD 184 EJONES
ANY TIME O' DE DAY ER NIGHT/
I'SE AFTER DE COIN, AN' I LAYS MY JESUS ON DE 185 EJONES
SHELF FOR DE TIME BEIN'.
BUT I AIN'T GOT DE TIME TO WASTE ON NO MORE FOOL 185 EJONES
TALK WID YOU.
BY DAT TIME, I'SE GOT A HEAD START DEY NEVER KOTCH186 EJONES
UP WID.
IN DE NICK O' TIME, TOO/ 187 EJONES
COME TIME TO EAT/ 188 EJONES
IT'S TIME YOU GIT A REST. 188 EJONES
ALL THE TIME MUTTERING REASSURINGLY) 188 EJONES
TIME YOU BEAT IT IN DE WOODS WIDOUT NO LONG WAITS.190 EJONES
TIME FO' ME TO MOVE. 191 EJONES
DON'T DE BAPTIST PARSON TELL YOU DAT MANY TIMES 193 EJONES
IN THE CENTER IS A BIG DEAD STUMP WORN BY TIME 195 EJONES
AT THE SAME TIME, A LOW MELANCHOLY MURMUR RISES 199 EJONES
AMONG THEM.
BUT THE NEXT TIME, HIS VOICE, AS IF UNDER SOME 199 EJONES
UNCANNY COMPULSION,
HIS BONE RATTLE CLICKING THE TIME. 201 EJONES
HE BEATS TIME WITH HIS HANDS AND SWAYS HIS BODY TO201 EJONES
AND FRO FROM THE WAIST.
FINALLY THE TIME OF THE PANTOMIME HALTS ON A HOWL 201 EJONES
OF DESPAIR,
WHO IS AT THE SAME TIME DEVOID OF EVIL INTENT, 6 ELECTR
THE TELEGRAPH FELLER SAYS LEE IS A GONER SURE THIS 11 ELECTR
TIME/.
IT'S TIME. 11 ELECTR
I AIN'T GOT TIME NOW ANYWAYS. 12 ELECTR
I'M NOT GIVING UP HOPE BUT WHAT YOU'LL CHANGE YOUR 14 ELECTR
MIND IN TIME.
I GUESS IT WAS THE LAST TIME HE WAS HERE. 15 ELECTR
EACH TIME I COME BACK AFTER BEING AWAY IT APPEARS 17 ELECTR
MORE LIKE A SEPULCHRE/.
*CERTIN' YOUR GRANDPAW LET OUT TO ME ONE TIME SH'D 19 ELECTR
HAD THE BABY--A BOY.
(HE LAUGHS AGAIN BUT LESS CERTAINLY THIS TIME, 23 ELECTR
IT WAS THE FIRST TIME HE'D EVER STRUCK HER. 26 ELECTR
ONE TIME WHEN WE WERE ALONE HE ASKED ME TO FORGIVE 26 ELECTR
HIM HITTING HER.
NO TIME HAS ELAPSED. 28 ELECTR
(DESPERATELY) IT WAS THE FIRST TIME I HAD EVER 30 ELECTR
BEEN THERE.
AND MOST OF THE TIME I WAS CARRYING HIM, 31 ELECTR
IT'S YOU WHO HAVE STOLEN ALL LOVE FROM ME SINCE 33 ELECTR
THE TIME I WAS BORN/
AND I WANT HIM OUT OF THE HOUSE BY THE TIME I GET 35 ELECTR
BACK. DO YOU HEAR&
(SEES THE PORTRAIT FOR THE FIRST TIME. 36 ELECTR
THE TIME FOR SKULKING AND LYING IS OVER--AND BY 37 ELECTR
GOD I'M GLAD OF IT--
AND I'M AFRAID OF TIME/ 39 ELECTR
SHE HURRIES ON SO AS NOT TO GIVE HIM TIME FOR 40 ELECTR
REFLECTION)
I'M SURE EVERYONE KNOWS ABOUT EZRA'S WEAK HEART BY 40 ELECTR
THIS TIME.
ARE YOU GOING TO PROVE, THE FIRST TIME YOUR LOVE 41 ELECTR
IS PUT TO A REAL TEST,
(DISAPPROVINGLY) THIS IS THE SECOND TIME THIS 44 ELECTR
WEEK I'VE CAUGHT YOU COMING HOME
THE FIRST TIME WAS CELEBRATIN' LEE'S SURRENDER 44 ELECTR
AND THIS TIME IS DROWNIN' MY SORROW FOR THE 44 ELECTR
PRESIDENT GITTIN' SHOT/
ACCENTUATES STRANGELY THE RESEMBLANCE BETWEEN 45 ELECTR
THEIR FACES AND AT THE SAME TIME
HE WAS OUT OF HIS HEAD FOR A LONG TIME. 49 ELECTR
IT WAS SEEING DEATH ALL THE TIME IN THIS WAY GOT 53 ELECTR
ME TO THINKING THESE THINGS.
TIME TO TURN IN. 56 ELECTR
NO TIME FOR A WALK, IF YOU ASK ME. 56 ELECTR
IT'S TIME WE WERE GETTING HOME. 69 ELECTR
AND IT'S A POOR TIME, WHEN THIS HOUSEHOLD IS 70 ELECTR
AFFLICTED BY SUDDEN DEATH, TO BE--
AND ANGINA IS NO RESPECTER OF TIME AND PLACE. 70 ELECTR
SHE'S A DAMNED HANDSOME WOMAN AND HE'D BEEN AWAY A 71 ELECTR
LONG TIME.
BUT THERE'S NO TIME TO TALK NOW. 76 ELECTR
(WORRIED AND PLEASED AT THE SAME TIME) 80 ELECTR
AND LATER ON ALL THE TIME I WAS OUT OF MY HEAD I 90 ELECTR
SEEMED REALLY TO BE THERE.
THE TIME OF THE OPENING OF THIS ACT PRECEDES BY A 93 ELECTR
FEW MOMENTS THAT OF THE END OF
MANY'S A TIME I'VE SEED A SKIPPER AN' MATES 105 ELECTR
SWEATIN' BLOOD TO BEAT WORK OUT OF A
(HARSHLY) IT'S NO TIME/ 108 ELECTR
(THEN, WITHOUT GIVING HER TIME TO ANSWER HIS 108 ELECTR
QUESTION,
LOOK AT THE TIME/ 112 ELECTR
THAT'S THE TIME FOR YOU-- 114 ELECTR
SO THIS TIME AT LAST YOU ARE WAITING TO MEET ME 120 ELECTR
WHEN I COME HOME/
YOU--YOU STAYED ALL THIS TIME--AT THE BRADFORDS'S 120 ELECTR
CAN'T MIND THEIR OWN BUSINESS IN THE LITTLE TIME 133 ELECTR
LEFT TO 'EM.
FIRST TIME I EVER HEARD YOU SAY YOU WERE AFRAID OF135 ELECTR
ANYTHING.
WE'VE GOT SO LITTLE TIME. 136 ELECTR
(STAMMERS--POINTING) IT WAS HERE--SHE--THE LAST 138 ELECTR
TIME I SAW HER ALIVE--

TIME 1668

(CONT'D.)

THE LAST TIME HE HAD SEEN HER ALIVE--ACT FIVE OF 138 ELECTR
--THE HUNTED--
(WITH AN APPREHENSIVE GLANCE AT PETER--PLEADING 146 ELECTR
AND AT THE SAME TIME WARNING)
HE RETURNS IT, AROUSED AND AT THE SAME TIME A 147 ELECTR
LITTLE SHOCKED BY HER BOLDNESS.
UH, I DIDN'T MEAN HE'S THE WAY HE IS TONIGHT MOST 148 ELECTR
OF THE TIME.
(THEN WITH A HARSH LAUGH) AND, AT THE SAME TIME, 151 ELECTR
A MILLION TIMES MORE VILE.
HE HAD MADE ME FEEL FOR THE FIRST TIME IN MY LIFE 154 ELECTR
NO TIME HAS ELAPSED SINCE THE PRECEDING ACT. 157 ELECTR
(SYMPATHETIC AND AT THE SAME TIME EXASPERATED) 159 ELECTR
BUT NOT CUNNING ENOUGH THIS TIME/ 161 ELECTR
BUT IN REALITY HE IS MERELY KILLING TIME, CHEWING 169 ELECTR
TOBACCO.
(FEELING GUILTY AND AT THE SAME TIME DEFIANT AND 172 ELECTR
SURE SHE IS RIGHT)
THE FIRST TIME HE EVER DID SUCH A THING/ 173 ELECTR
YOU'VE HAD AN AWFULLY HARD TIME OF IT, BUT NEVER 174 ELECTR
MIND, WE'LL BE MARRIED SOON.
AT THE SAME TIME LOOKING AT THE GROUND AROUND HIM 178 ELECTR
I KNOW THEY WILL SEE TO IT I LIVE FOR A LONG TIME/178 ELECTR
MY MOTHER USED TO BELIEVE THE FULL OF THE MOON WAS261 GGBROW
THE TIME TO SOW.
THAT ONE TIME HE KISSED ME--I CAN'T FORGET IT/ 262 GGBROW
MY END OF IT IS A SURE THING, AND HAS BEEN FOR A 263 GGBROW
LONG TIME.
TIME FOR SCHOOL/ 267 GGBROW
TIME TO EXIST/ 267 GGBROW
TIME TO GET UP/ 267 GGBROW
TIME TO LEARN/ 267 GGBROW
BUT AT THE SAME TIME, IN SOME QUEER WAY, MORE 269 GGBROW
SELFLESS AND ASCETIC.
FROM THE TIME I REALIZED IT WASN'T IN ME TO BE AN 271 GGBROW
ARTIST--EXCEPT IN LIVING--
(THIS TIME WITH FORCED CONVICTION) 271 GGBROW
BILLY WAS IN LOVE WITH MARGARET AT ONE TIME. 272 GGBROW
(SURPRISED) THE ONE TIME I RAN INTO HIM, I 275 GGBROW
THOUGHT HE TOLD ME
YOU SEE THE CHILDREN TAKE UP SUCH A LOT OF HIS 276 GGBROW
TIME.
SHE CHEWS GUM LIKE A SACRED COW FORGETTING TIME 278 GGBROW
WITH AN ETERNAL END.
AFTER ALL, I COULDN'T KEEP CHASING AFTER YOU AND 281 GGBROW
BE SNUBBED EVERY TIME.
THAT LAST TIME I LOOKED, HER PURITY HAD FORGOTTEN 282 GGBROW
ME.
PASS AWAY THE TIME, WHILE ONE IS WAITING--FOR 282 GGBROW
ONE'S NEXT INCARNATION.
WHEN THE TIME COMES, YOU'LL FIND IT'S EASY. 286 GGBROW
I'M AFRAID YOU'RE GOING AWAY A LONG LONG TIME. 288 GGBROW
(SHE STARTS, JAMS OFF THE MUSIC AND REACHES FOR 288 GGBROW
HER MASK BUT HAS NO TIME TO PUT
I'VE BEEN ON THE VERGE--OF A BREAKDOWN--FOR SOME 305 GGBROW
TIME.
BROWN HAS JUST TIME TO TURN HIS HEAD AND GET HIS 306 GGBROW
MASK ON.)
IT'S TIME HE WERE HOME. 308 GGBROW
AND ALL THE TIME I KNEW YOU WERE SO LONELY/ 309 GGBROW
IS GETTING A BIT QUEER AND IT'S TIME HE TOOK A 311 GGBROW
VACATION.
TIME TO BECOME RESPECTABLE AGAIN/ 314 GGBROW
HE WAS PROBABLY HITTING IT UP ON THE Q.T. ALL THE 314 GGBROW
TIME.
ALTHOUGH THE GOSSIPS ARE BEGINNING TO SAY I'M 315 GGBROW
SOUSED ALL THE TIME/
BUT IT MUST HAVE BEEN FUNNY FOR YOU WHEN YOU CAME 315 GGBROW
HERE THE LAST TIME--
SOUSED TO THE EARS ALL THE TIME/ 316 GGBROW
THE SOUND OF HIS FEET LEAPING DOWN THE STAIRS, 318 GGBROW
FIVE AT A TIME, CAN BE HEARD.
KNOWS HER LIFE PURPOSE WELL ACCOMPLISHED BUT IS AT323 GGBROW
THE SAME TIME A BIT EMPTY AND
(FOR THE FIRST TIME, SEEMING TO TAKE NOTICE OF THE 209 HA APE
UPROAR ABOUT HIM.
I GOT YUH DE FOIST TIME. 211 HA APE
ME TIME IS PAST DUE. 215 HA APE
TIME MELLOUS PIPES. 218 HA APE
WELL, THANK GOODNESS, IT'S ABOUT TIME FOR THEM TO 220 HA APE
COME FOR ME.
IT'S TIME. 220 HA APE
(HE TURNS AND SEES THE WINDOW DISPLAY IN THE TWO 235 HA APE
STORES FOR THE FIRST TIME)
DE PUNCH, DAT'S ME EVERY TIME, SEE? 236 HA APE
THAT'S THEM EVERY TIME/ 241 HA APE
WHAT WE NEED IS MEN WHO CAN HOLD THEIR JOBS---AND 247 HA APE
WORK FOR US AT THE SAME TIME.
(WHO HAS COME UP THE STREET IN TIME TO HEAR THIS 250 HA APE
LAST--WITH GRIM HUMOR)
ANY TIME HE CALLS. 250 HA APE
(THEN MATTER-OF-FACTLY) BUT I'VE NO TIME FOR 251 HA APE
KIDDING.
HOW D'YUH FEEL SITTIN' IN DAT PEN ALL DE TIME. 252 HA APE
HE CAN TELL TIME BY SOUNDS IN THE STREET. 8 HUGHIE
(THE NIGHT CLERK FEELS THAT HE HAS BEEN STANDING A 13 HUGHIE
LONG TIME AND HIS FEET ARE
I'VE MADE SOME KILLINGS IN MY TIME THE GANG STILL 15 HUGHIE
GAB ABOUT.
(HE PAUSES--BOASTFULLY.) SOME QUEENS I'VE BROUGHT 16 HUGHIE
HERE IN MY TIME, BROTHER--
BUT THE LAST TIME HE WAS ABLE TO FEEL DESPAIR WAS 17 HUGHIE
BACK AROUND WORLD WAR DAYS.
BUT THIS TIME I'M ON A SPOT WHERE I GOT TO, IF I 18 HUGHIE
AIN'T A SAP.
(HIS MIND ARRIVES JUST IN TIME TO CATCH THIS 19 HUGHIE
LAST--WITH A BRIGHT GRIMACE.)

(CONT'D.)

TIME IS THAT MUCH OLDER. 19 HUGHIE
AND IT TAKES IT SOME TIME TO GET BACK. 19 HUGHIE
Y'KNOW I HAD HUGHIE SIZED UP FOR A SAP THE FIRST 22 HUGHIE
TIME I SEE HIM.
(HASTILY.) ANYWAY, THIS TIME I'M TALKIN' ABOUT, 23 HUGHIE
THE TIME HE HAD ME OUT TO DINNER IN THEIR FLAT. 24 HUGHIE
THAT TIME HE TOOK ME HOME TO DINNER. 25 HUGHIE
IS IT A REAL GOOD ONE THIS TIMES 27 HUGHIE
THAT'S THE BEST I'VE HEARD IN A LONG TIME/ 27 HUGHIE
I SURE TOOK HIM AROUND WITH ME IN TALES AND SHOWED 29 HUGHIE
HIM ONE HELL OF A TIME.
THE SECOND TIME I WENT, THEY WOULDN'T LET ME SEE 30 HUGHIE
HIM.
THE FIRST TIME, HIS WIFE WAS THERE AND GIVE ME A 30 HUGHIE
DIRTY LOOK.
ERIE BEGINS TALKING AGAIN BUT THIS TIME IT IS 30 HUGHIE
OBVIOUSLY ALOUD TO HIMSELF.
(BUT THIS TIME IT IS ERIE WHO DOESN'T HEAR HIM. 32 HUGHIE
IT WAS UP TO ME TO GIVE HUGHIE A BIG-TIME SEND- 33 HUGHIE
OFF.
AFTER THAT, I COULDA MADE 'EM ONE AT A TIME OR ALL 36 HUGHIE
TOGETHER/
WHY, ONE TIME DOWN IN NEW ORLEANS I LIT A CIGAR 36 HUGHIE
WITH A C NOTE, JUST FOR A GAG.
Y'KNOW, IT'S TIME I QUIT CARRYIN' THE TORCH FOR 38 HUGHIE
HUGHIE.
THE WALLS AND CEILING ONCE WERE WHITE, BUT IT WAS 573 ICEMAN
A LONG TIME AGO.
AND AT THE SAME TIME OF A LIKABLE, AFFECTIONATE 575 ICEMAN
BOY WHO HAS NEVER GROWN UP.
BUT TIME AND WHISKEY HAVE MELTED IT DOWN INTO A 576 ICEMAN
GOOD-HUMORED.
HELL, GETTIN' RID ON DE ISLAND MOST OF DE TIME IF IT 580 ICEMAN
WASN'T FER ME.
DE OLD LADY'S OFF OF WILLIE FOR KEEPS DIS TIME ANDS81 ICEMAN
HE CAN GO TO HELL.
(LAZILY) NEVER MIND DE TIME. 583 ICEMAN
TIME YOU BEGUN TO SWEEP UP IN DE BAR. 583 ICEMAN
GETTIN' NEAR TIME TO OPEN UP. 583 ICEMAN
IF HICKEY AIN'T COME, IT'S TIME JOE GOES TO SLEEP 983 ICEMAN
AGAIN.
GUESS I'LL GET BACK IN DE BAR AND CATCH A COUPLA 586 ICEMAN
WINKS BEFORE OPENING-UP TIME.
IT WILL BE TIME ENOUGH TO DREAM OF SILK PURSES. 590 ICEMAN
INTERESTED IN SPITE OF HIMSELF AND AT THE SAME 591 ICEMAN
TIME VAGUELY UNEASY.)
BUT IT'S NO DAMNED JOKE RIGHT AT THIS TIME. 593 ICEMAN
THAT'S CAPTAIN LEWIS, A ONE-TIME HERO OF THE 593 ICEMAN
BRITISH ARMY.
BUT AT THE SAME TIME SHOWING HIS AFFECTION FOR 593 ICEMAN
THEM)
ALTHOUGH THAT WAS SOME TIME BEFORE 595 ICEMAN
IT'S HIGH TIME I STRAIGHTENED OUT AND GOT DOWN TO 600 ICEMAN
BUSINESS AGAIN.
YET THERE WAS A TIME WHEN MY CONVERSATION WAS MORE601 ICEMAN
COMPREHENSIVE.
BUT HE DON'T GIVE ME TO TIME TO ANSWER. 601 ICEMAN
(THREATENINGLY) BUT YOU'VE BROKE THE CAMEL'S BACK 602 ICEMAN
THIS TIME, BEJEES/
TIME I TOOK HOLD OF MYSELF. 603 ICEMAN
MY BIRTHDAY, TOMORROW, THAT'D BE THE RIGHT TIME TO604 ICEMAN
TURN OVER A NEW LEAF.
WELL, CONDITIONS MUST BE BETTER BY THIS TIME. 604 ICEMAN
(ACIDLY) ANY TIME YOU ONLY TAKE ONE SIP OF A 606 ICEMAN
DRINK.
I'LL BE FOUND INNOCENT THIS TIME AND REINSTATED. 607 ICEMAN
(HE CHUCKLES REMINISCENTLY) REMEMBER THE TIME SHE608 ICEMAN
SENT ME DOWN TO THE BAR TO
ABOUT SHARING THE PROFITS NEXT TIME. 609 ICEMAN
HICKEY'D NEVER TURN UP DIS TIME OF DE MORNIN'/ 610 ICEMAN
OPENIN' TIME, BOSS. 610 ICEMAN
IT'S ABOUT TIME DEY SHOWED. 610 ICEMAN
WANTA HAVE A GOOD TIME, KIDS 611 ICEMAN
DEY BEEN DREAMIN' IT FOR YEARS, EVERY TIME CHUCK 614 ICEMAN
GOES ON DE WAGON.
AND BUTT OF 'EM ARGUIN' ALL DE TIME. 614 ICEMAN
DEY GIVE YUH AN EARFUL EVERY TIME YUH TALK TO 'EM/614 ICEMAN
I SAYS, «HELLO, HANDSOME, WANTA HAVE A GOOD TIMES»616 ICEMAN
FIRST TIME I EVER HEARD YOU WORRY ABOUT SLEEP. 620 ICEMAN
ALL THE TIME I WAS WALKING OVER HERE-- 621 ICEMAN
I DIDN'T MAKE SUCH BAD TIME EITHER FOR A FAT GUY, 622 ICEMAN
I'D BEEN STANDING ON THE CORNER SOME TIME BEFORE 622 ICEMAN
CORA AND CHUCK CAME ALONG.
SURE, YOU'RE GOING TO--THIS TIME. 622 ICEMAN
ANY TIME YOU THINK I'M TALKING OUT OF TURN, JUST 624 ICEMAN
TELL ME TO GO CHASE MYSELF
FIRST TIME I'VE EVER BEEN EAST. 624 ICEMAN
GIVE HIM TIME, HARRY, AND HE'LL COME OUT OF IT. 626 ICEMAN
IT IS TIME I GOT MY JOB BACK--ALTHOUGH I HARDLY 626 ICEMAN
NEED HIM TO REMIND ME.
I DIDN'T EVEN HAVE TIME TO GET DRUNK. 627 ICEMAN
THE LAST TIME WE GOT PARALYZED TOGETHER HE TOLD 627 ICEMAN
ME--
THIS TIME IT PENETRATES HICKEY'S EXHAUSTED 628 ICEMAN
SLUMBER.
(FURIOUS AND AT THE SAME TIME BEWILDERED BY THEIR 633 ICEMAN
DEFIANCE)
HARRY'S PARTY AIN'T NO TIME TO BEAT UP YOUR 633 ICEMAN
STABLE.
I NOTICE HICKEY AIN'T PULLED DAT OLD ICEMAN GAG 636 ICEMAN
DIS TIME.
HERE I AM IN THE NICK OF TIME. 638 ICEMAN
THE EXPRESSION ON THEIR FACES FOR THE FIRST TIME) 640 ICEMAN
I'VE HAD A BELLYFUL OF IT IN MY TIME, AND IT'S ALL641 ICEMAN
WRONG.
BUT THIS TIME HIS HABITUAL PASS-OUT HAS A QUALITY 641 ICEMAN
OF HIDING.)

TIME

TIME (CONT'D.)
WELL, WELL, NOT MUCH TIME BEFORE TWELVE. 643 ICEMAN
(HE BEATS TIME WITH HIS FINGER AND SINGS IN A LOW 645 ICEMAN
VOICE)
FOR THE LOVE OF GOD, LEAVE ME IN PEACE THE LITTLE 649 ICEMAN
TIME THAT'S LEFT TO ME/
(INDIGNANTLY) A SWELL TIME TO STAGE YOUR FIRST 650 ICEMAN
BOUT, ON HARRY'S BOITHDAY PARTY/
I'M TELLING YOU, ED, IT'S SERIOUS THIS TIME. 651 ICEMAN
BUT IF YOU THINK MY LOVING RELATIVES WILL HAVE 651 ICEMAN
TIME TO DISCUSS YOU,
IT'S TIME I QUIT FOR A WHILE. 652 ICEMAN
I HAD A HARD TIME GETTING THEM TO MOVE/ 653 ICEMAN
NOT THIS TIME/ 655 ICEMAN
(THIS TIME HE DOES TURN AWAY.) 656 ICEMAN
YES, LARRY, I'M GOING TO DRINK WITH YOU THIS TIME.658 ICEMAN
(HE DRAINS THE REMAINDER OF HIS DRINK, BUT THIS 659 ICEMAN
TIME HE DRINKS ALONE.
BUT THIS TIME I HAD TO--FOR YOUR OWN GOOD/ 660 ICEMAN
NOT IN THE TIME AT MY DISPOSAL. 661 ICEMAN
WHY, IF I HAD ENOUGH TIME, 661 ICEMAN
AND I PROMISE YOU, BY THE TIME THIS DAY IS OVER, 661 ICEMAN
I'VE NOTICED HE HASN'T SHOWN HER PICTURE AROUND 662 ICEMAN
THIS TIME/
IT'S HARDLY AN APPROPRIATE TIME. 663 ICEMAN
(IRRITABLY) IF I AIN'T A SAP TO LET CHUCK KID ME 665 ICEMAN
INTO WORKIN' HIS TIME
I GOT STUCK ON A WHORE AND WANTED DOUGH TO BLOW IN667 ICEMAN
ON HER AND HAVE A GOOD TIME/
AND EVERY TIME DEY'D CRAWL MY FRAME WID DE SAME 669 ICEMAN
OLD ARGUMENT.
YUH'D LIKE ME TO STAY PARALYZED ALL DE TIME, SO'S 671 ICEMAN
I'D BE LIKE YOU, A LOUSY PIMP/
HE PROMISED ANY TIME I FELT AN ENERGETIC FIT HE'D 675 ICEMAN
GET ME A POST WITH THE CUNARD--
TIME I TURNED OVER A NEW LEAF, AND ALL THAT. 675 ICEMAN
DOT LONGSHOREMAN BOSS, DAN, HE TELL ME ANY TIME I 676 ICEMAN
LIKE, HE TAKE ME ON.
(HE PRETENDS TO NOTICE WETJOEN FOR THE FIRST TIME 677 ICEMAN
AND STEPS AWAY FROM THE DOOR--
WELL, TIME I WAS ON MY MERRY WAY TO SEE MY CHAP AT677 ICEMAN
THE CONSULATE.
BUT THAT MAY TAKE TIME. 679 ICEMAN
AND THIS TIME HE TAKES THE CHAIR AT REAR FACING 680 ICEMAN
DIRECTLY FRONT.
HICKEY JUST TOLD US, AIN'T IT TIME WE BEAT IT, IF 682 ICEMAN
WE'RE REALLY GOIN'.
BY THIS TIME. 684 ICEMAN
TIME I PUSHED OFF. 685 ICEMAN
IT'S TIME WE GOT STARTED. 687 ICEMAN
TWENTY YEARS IS A LONG TIME. 687 ICEMAN
WASN'T NONE OF THEM AROUND THE LAST TIME, TWENTY 687 ICEMAN
YEARS AGO.
I REMEMBER NOW CLEAR AS DAY THE LAST TIME BEFORE 688 ICEMAN
SHE--
CAN'T HELP THINKING THE LAST TIME I WENT OUT WAS 688 ICEMAN
TO BESSIE'S FUNERAL.
(RESENTFULLY) WELL, DIS IS DE TIME I DO TOUCH IT/690 ICEMAN
(FOR THE FIRST TIME LOSES HIS TEMPER) 692 ICEMAN
GIVE HIM TIME. 692 ICEMAN
WELL, WELL, YOU DID MANAGE TO GET A RISE OUT OF ME692 ICEMAN
THAT TIME.
IT'S TIME YOU BEGAN TO FEEL HAPPY-- 695 ICEMAN
I'M A SAP TO WASTE TIME ON YUH. 703 ICEMAN
I WAS HOPING BY THE TIME I GOT BACK YOU'D BE LIKE 704 ICEMAN
YOU OUGHT TO BE/
I SAW I COULDN'T DO IT BY KILLING MYSELF, LIKE I 705 ICEMAN
WANTED TO FOR A LONG TIME.
AND THERE'S DAMNED LITTLE TIME LEFT NOW. 705 ICEMAN
WE MAY HATE YOU FOR WHAT YOU'VE DONE HERE THIS 706 ICEMAN
TIME,
I KNEW EXACTLY WHAT I WANTED TO BE BY THAT TIME. 710 ICEMAN
AS IF I HAD NO RIGHT TO BE HAVING SUCH A GOOD TIME711 ICEMAN
AWAY FROM EVELYN.
I'D TELL HER, IT'S THE LAST TIME. 712 ICEMAN
YOU MAY BE LUCKY FOR A LONG TIME, BUT YOU GET 712 ICEMAN
NICKED IN THE END.
AND SHE'D SAY, "I KNOW IT'S THE LAST TIME, TEDDY. 712 ICEMAN
BUT AT THE SAME TIME SICK OF HOME. 712 ICEMAN
IT WAS ONLY A HARMLESS GOOD TIME TO ME. 712 ICEMAN
THE SAME WAY SHE FORGAVE ME EVERY TIME I'D TURN UP713 ICEMAN
AFTER A PERIODICAL DRUNK.
AND NOW I'D HAVE TO START SWEARING AGAIN THIS WAS 713 ICEMAN
THE LAST TIME.
HER EYES FOLLOWED ME ALL THE TIME. 714 ICEMAN
I GOT SO I THOUGHT OF IT ALL THE TIME. 714 ICEMAN
EVERY TIME I SAW MYSELF IN THE MIRROR. 714 ICEMAN
AND I KNEW IF I CAME THIS TIME, IT WAS THE FINISH.715 ICEMAN
AND AS THE TIME GOT NEARER TO WHEN I WAS DUE TO 715 ICEMAN
COME HERE FOR MY DRUNK AROUND
I KNOW YOU'LL CONQUER IT THIS TIME, AND WE'LL BE 715 ICEMAN
SO HAPPY, DEAR."
BUT ALL THE TIME I SAW HOW CRAZY AND ROTTEN OF ME 715 ICEMAN
THAT WAS,
I KEPT SWEARING TO HER EVERY NIGHT THAT THIS TIME 715 ICEMAN
I REALLY WOULDN'T,
ALL THE TIME I'VE BEEN HERE/ 717 ICEMAN
(BEGINS TO BRISTLE IN HIS OLD-TIME MANNER) 717 ICEMAN
IT WAS A WASTE OF TIME COMING HERE. 718 ICEMAN
(THIS TIME THERE IS AN EAGER LAUGH FROM THE GROUP.722 ICEMAN
ALL THE TIME THAT BAS--POOR OLD HICKEY WAS HERE, I722 ICEMAN
DIDN'T HAVE THE HEART--
THERE WAS NO GOOD TRYING TO EXPLAIN TO A CRAZY 724 ICEMAN
GUY, BUT IT AIN'T THE RIGHT TIME.
JEES, ROCKY, DID WE HAVE A BIG TIME AT CONEY/ 725 ICEMAN
NEXT TIME I SHIP ON WINDJAMMER BOSTON TO RIVER 515 INZONE
PLATE,
I READ IT IN THE PAPER MANY TIME. 515 INZONE

TIME (CONT'D.)
(BY THIS TIME EVERYONE, JACK INCLUDED, IS 519 INZONE
LISTENING BREATHLESSLY TO HIS STORY)
AIN'T HE GRUMBLANT ABOUT BEIN COLD ALL THE TIMES 521 INZONE
(SARCASTICALLY) OR A MINE THAT DIDN'T GO OFF-- 523 INZONE
THAT TIME--
HE LOOKS CURIOUSLY OVER AT SMITTY FROM TIME TO 531 INZONE
TIME.
ALL THE TIME I WAS AWAY IN BERLIN AND BLINDLY 532 INZONE
TRUSTED YOU.
THE SAME TIME. 15 JOURNE
YOU REALLY MUST NOT WATCH ME ALL THE TIME, JAMES. 17 JOURNE
(MALICIOUSLY.) I'LL BET THE NEXT TIME YOU SEE 23 JOURNE
HARKER AT THE CLUB AND GIVE HIM
AROUND LUNCH TIME. 33 JOURNE
YOU MADE HIM OLD BEFORE HIS TIME, 34 JOURNE
HIS HEALTH HAS BROKEN DOWN AND HE MAY BE AN 34 JOURNE
INVALID FOR A LONG TIME.
(HIS SON LOOKS AT HIM, FOR THE FIRST TIME WITH AN 36 JOURNE
UNDERSTANDING SYMPATHY.
(GRUDGINGLY AGAIN.) NOT THAT THEY'D EVER GET HIM 36 JOURNE
ANYWHERE ON THE BIG TIME.
IT COULDN'T HAVE COME AT A WORSE TIME FOR HIM. 36 JOURNE
YES, THIS TIME YOU CAN SEE HOW STRONG AND SURE OF 37 JOURNE
HERSELF SHE IS.
IT ISN'T THIS TIME/ 38 JOURNE
I REALLY OUGHT TO GO UPSTAIRS AND LIE DOWN UNTIL 49 JOURNE
LUNCH TIME AND TAKE A NAP.
IT'LL BE LUNCH TIME SOON. 51 JOURNE
(SHE CHUCKLES.) I'LL WAGER MISTER JAMIE WOULDN'T 52 JOURNE
MISS THE TIME TO STOP WORK AND
SHE'S ALWAYS ON TIME WITHOUT ANY CALLING. 52 JOURNE
IT'S TIME/ 53 JOURNE
OH, ABOUT THE TIME I CAME DOWN TO THE HEDGE, I 55 JOURNE
GUESS.
OF SPYING ON HER ALL THE TIME AND NOT TRUSTING 57 JOURNE
HER.
IT DOES THIS TIME/ 57 JOURNE
I'VE BEEN AS HAPPY AS HELL BECAUSE I'D REALLY 58 JOURNE
BEGUN TO BELIEVE THAT THIS TIME--
I'VE TOLD CATHLEEN TIME AND AGAIN SHE MUST GO 60 JOURNE
WHEREVER HE IS AND TELL HIM.
BUT HE KEPT ON TALKING TO THAT MAN, TELLING HIM OF 62 JOURNE
THE TIME WHEN--
WITH A FOND SOLICITUDE WHICH IS AT THE SAME TIME 67 JOURNE
REMOTE.)
WELL, IT WON'T BE THE FIRST TIME, WILL IT-- OR THE 69 JOURNE
THOUSANDTHS
YET AT THE SAME TIME, IN CONTRAST TO THIS, 71 JOURNE
(SHAKENLY.) YES, MARY, IT'S NO TIME-- 75 JOURNE
(BITTERLY.) ONLY I WISH SHE HADN'T LED ME TO HOPE 76 JOURNE
THIS TIME.
YOU SHOULDN'T TREAT HIM WITH SUCH CONTEMPT ALL THE 81 JOURNE
TIME.
YOU KNOW YOU BOAST YOU CAN DRESS IN ONE-TENTH THE 82 JOURNE
TIME IT TAKES THE BOYS.
(HASTILY.) I MEAN, YOU HAVE PLENTY OF TIME. 82 JOURNE
I WAS AFRAID ALL THE TIME I CARRIED EDMUND. 88 JOURNE
BY GOD, LOOK AT THE TIME/ 91 JOURNE
(EXCITEDLY.) IT'S SIMPLY A WASTE OF TIME AND 92 JOURNE
MONEY SEEING HIM.
I NEVER LIED ABOUT ANYTHING ONCE UPON A TIME. 93 JOURNE
AND AT THE SAME TIME I WILL LAUGH BECAUSE I WILL 94 JOURNE
BE SO SURE OF MYSELF.
(THEN, WORRIEDLY.) WHAT TIME IS IT, MA'AMS 99 JOURNE
BY THE TIME HE COMES HOME HE'LL BE TOO DRUNK TO 101 JOURNE
TELL THE DIFFERENCE.
FOR A TIME AFTER MY MARRIAGE I TRIED TO KEEP UP MY104 JOURNE
MUSIC.
AT THE SAME TIME HE WAS SIMPLE, AND KIND, AND 105 JOURNE
UNASSUMING,
I'M AFRAID JAMIE HAS BEEN LOST TO US FOR A LONG 109 JOURNE
TIME, DEAR.
I CAN REMEMBER THAT TEASPOONFUL OF BOOZE EVERY 111 JOURNE
TIME I WOKE UP WITH A NIGHTMARE.
WHEN IS DINNER, MAMA. IT MUST BE TIME. 113 JOURNE
(FORCES A CASUAL TONE.) ISN'T IT DINNER TIME, 115 JOURNE
DEARS
I USED TO HOPE I WOULD HAVE A DAUGHTER AND WHEN IT115 JOURNE
CAME TIME FOR HER TO MARRY--
I USED TO TAKE IT OUT FROM TIME TO TIME WHEN I WAS115 JOURNE
LONELY.
YOU'RE FOREVER SCOLDING ME FOR BEING LATE, BUT NOW115 JOURNE
I'M ON TIME FOR ONCE,
THAT TIME I RAN DOWN IN MY NIGHTDRESS TO THROW 118 JOURNE
MYSELF OFF THE DOCK.
AT THIS TIME OF NIGHT, BURNING UP MONEY/ 126 JOURNE
(IMPRESSED AND AT THE SAME TIME REVOLTED.) 131 JOURNE
BE DRUNKEN, IF YOU WOULD NOT BE MARTYRED SLAVES OF132 JOURNE
TIME.
IF YOU WOULD NOT FEEL THE HORRIBLE BURDEN OF TIME 132 JOURNE
WEIGHING ON YOUR SHOULDERS AND
SHE'LL BE NOTHING BUT A GHOST HAUNTING THE PAST BY137 JOURNE
THIS TIME.
BUT AFTER THAT HE MADE UP FOR LOST TIME. 137 JOURNE
AT LEAST, I KNOW SHE DID THIS TIME/ 139 JOURNE
AT THE SAME TIME CRYING GORGEOUS AND MAKING IT 140 JOURNE
PLAIN YOU WANTED A CHEAP ONE/
PARTICULARLY THE TIME I TRIED TO COMMIT SUICIDE AT147 JOURNE
JIMMIE THE PRIEST'S.
AND BY THE TIME I WOKE UP TO THE FACT I'D BECOME A149 JOURNE
SLAVE TO THE DAMNED THING AND
AND THE TIME CAME WHEN THAT MISTAKE RUINED MY 149 JOURNE
CAREER AS A FINE ACTOR.
AND FOR A TIME AFTER THAT I KEPT ON UPWARD WITH 150 JOURNE
AMBITION HIGH.
THEN ANOTHER TIME, ON THE AMERICAN LINE, 153 JOURNE
A CALM SEA, THAT TIME. 153 JOURNE

TIME

TIME (CONT'D.)
BY THE TIME I HIT MAMIE'S DUMP I FELT VERY SAD 159 JOURNE
HELL OF A GOOD TIME, AT THAT. 160 JOURNE
HELL OF A GOOD TIME. 161 JOURNE
BECAUSE THIS TIME MAMA HAD ME FOOLED. 162 JOURNE
SHE THINKS I ALWAYS BELIEVE THE WORST, BUT THIS 162 JOURNE
TIME I BELIEVED THE BEST.
NEVER FORGET THE FIRST TIME I GOT WISE. 163 JOURNE
HIS FACE IS STERN AND DISGUSTED BUT AT THE SAME 167 JOURNE
TIME PITYING.
IT'LL PASS THE TIME UNTIL SHE-- 169 JOURNE
AS IF AN AWKWARD SCHOOLGIRL WERE PRACTICING IT FOR170 JOURNE
THE FIRST TIME.
AND TELL ME TO PRAY TO THE BLESSED VIRGIN, AND 171 JOURNE
THEY'LL BE WELL AGAIN IN NO TIME.
ALL THE SAME, I DON'T THINK SHE WAS SO 175 JOURNE
UNDERSTANDING THIS TIME.
BUT I KNEW IT WAS SIMPLY A WASTE OF TIME. 176 JOURNE
I FELL IN LOVE WITH JAMES TYRONE AND WAS SO HAPPY 176 JOURNE
FOR A TIME.
IT IS SOME TIME AFTER THE MIRACLE AND JESUS HAS 275 LAZARU
GONE AWAY.)
IT WAS THE FIRST TIME I HAD SEEN HIM SMILE IN 276 LAZARU
YEARS.
JESUS LOOKED INTO HIS FACE FOR WHAT SEEMED A LONG 277 LAZARU
TIME AND
THEY RESENT THIS DUTY, WHICH HAS ALREADY KEPT THEM298 LAZARU
THERE FOR A LONG TIME,
AT THE SAME TIME THE DISTANT SOUND OF EXULTANT 304 LAZARU
MUSIC.
LAZARUS LOOKS AT THEM, SEEMING TO SEE EACH AND ALL307 LAZARU
AT THE SAME TIME,
REFINED IN THEM BY NOBILITY OF BLOOD BUT AT THE 312 LAZARU
SAME TIME WITH STRENGTH
IT IS TIME. 317 LAZARU
THEN SEVERAL AT A TIME, THEN MULTITUDES, JOIN IN 318 LAZARU
HIS LAUGHTER.
WHILE AT THE SAME TIME PERVERSELY EXCITED AND 326 LAZARU
ELATED BY HIS OWN MORBID TENSION.
CALIGULA AND MIRIAM SEE THE LION FOR THE FIRST 327 LAZARU
TIME.
ESCAPE NOW, YOU FOOL, WHILE THERE IS STILL TIME/ 329 LAZARU
YOU HEARD EVEN THE GALLEY SLAVES LAUGH AND CLANK 331 LAZARU
TIME WITH THEIR CHAINS/
WILL HE LAUGH WHEN HE HAS YOUR BODY BROKEN ONE 334 LAZARU
BONE AT A TIME WITH HAMMERS$
FOR PILATE CRUCIFIED HIM A SHORT TIME AFTER AND 343 LAZARU
IS IT TIME AT LAST$ 345 LAZARU
WHEN YOU LAID IT THE LAST TIME, WE ALL HAD TO RUN 346 LAZARU
FOR OUR LIVES, CHOKING,
IS IT TIME AT LAST$ 346 LAZARU
BUT AT THE SAME TIME RETAINING THE ALOOF SERENITY 350 LAZARU
OF THE STATUE OF A GOD.
NOW I KNOW LOVE FOR THE FIRST TIME IN MY LIFE/ 351 LAZARU
THAT BY THE TIME DEATH COMES THEY ARE TOO LIFELESS352 LAZARU
TO FEAR IT/
(GENTLY) I KNOW THAT AGE AND TIME ARE BUT 354 LAZARU
TIMIDITIES OF THOUGHT,
AND THERE IS SO LITTLE TIME LEFT--AND ONE IS 354 LAZARU
ALONE/
ARE YOU, TOO, THINKING IN TERMS OF TIME, OLD FOOL 360 LAZARU!
SO SOON TO RE-ENTER INFINITY$
REMAINS LOOKING INTO HIS EYES A LONG TIME, 361 LAZARU
SHRINKING BACK FROM HIM WITH
WHILE AWAY THE TIME--WITH ANY DREAM, NO MATTER HOW 4 MANSNS
ABSURD--
AND IT IS A POOR TIME TO BEGIN. 5 MANSNS
WE SHALL BE GOVERNED BY THE IGNORANT GREEDY MOB 8 MANSNS
FOR ALL FUTURE TIME.
BUT A TIME COMES WHEN, SUDDENLY, 11 MANSNS
NOTHING HAS HAPPENED, EXCEPT TIME AND CHANGE. 11 MANSNS
AND RETURN TO COMMON SENSE IN THE LITTLE TIME LEFT 14 MANSNS
US.
I SAID I HAD HAD NO TIME LATELY-- 16 MANSNS
I WILL FACE CHANGE AND UGLINESS, AND TIME AND 22 MANSNS
DEATH, AND MAKE MYSELF RESIGNED/
AND AT THE SAME TIME PATHETICALLY CONFUSED.) 26 MANSNS
YOU SHOULD SURELY BE EXPERIENCED IN FACING FACTS 29 MANSNS
BY THIS TIME.+
AND WE HAVE NO TIME TO LISTEN-- 30 MANSNS
YOUR FATHER NEVER HAD TIME TO SPARE OTHERS' 34 MANSNS
FEELINGS.
YOU ARE WASTING YOUR TIME, GENTLEMEN. 36 MANSNS
BESIDES, THIS IS HARDLY THE TIME TO SPEAK OF-- 37 MANSNS
(FORCING A SMILE--CONTEMPUOUS AND AT THE SAME 38 MANSNS
TIME AFFECTIONATE.)
YOU KNOW I'VE NEVER HAD A LETTER FROM HER SINCE I 45 MANSNS
SAW HER THAT TIME AT MY CABIN.
BUT I'VE HAD A DARK SUSPICION FOR SOME TIME. 46 MANSNS
AND YET ALL THE TIME SHE OWED EVERYTHING TO HIS 47 MANSNS
BUSINESS--
EXCEPT I THANK GOD I FREED MYSELF IN TIME, AND 47 MANSNS
THEN MET YOU.
I COULDN'T SPARE THE TIME, FOR ONE THING. 47 MANSNS
AND WHEN THE TIME COMES WE WILL BE IN A POSITION 48 MANSNS
IT IS A LONG TIME SINCE OUR MEETING AT THE CABIN. 53 MANSNS
THAT IS WHAT TIME DOES TO US ALL. 61 MANSNS
SIMON WAS TALKING OVER THIS BUSINESS--FOR THE LAST 62 MANSNS
TIME, I HOPE.
MANY A TIME I LOOKED IN AT YOU AND NEVER DISTURBED 63 MANSNS
YOU.
(SMILING.) I'M ALL THE TIME TELLING HIM HOW PROUD 64 MANSNS
I AM.
BUT I HAVE PROMISED MYSELF THAT AS SOON AS I HAD 72 MANSNS
TIME,
AND I BECOME EMPTY, BUT AT THE SAME TIME RESTLESS 72 MANSNS
AND AIMLESS,

TIME (CONT'D.)
BUT AT THE SAME TIME BY BECOMING SARA, LEAVE ME 73 MANSNS
LIFELESS,
ISN'T IT ABOUT TIME YOU STOPPED BEING SO CHILDISH, 78 MANSNS
AND FORGAVE--$
YOU HAVEN'T LOOKED WELL FOR A LONG TIME. 79 MANSNS
I THINK I BEGAN TO NOTICE IT AROUND THE TIME 80 MANSNS
I SHOULDN'T SAY FROM YOUR ACTIONS FOR A LONG 81 MANSNS
TIME--
A LONG TIME SINCE YOU'VE GIVEN ME THE CHANCE/ 83 MANSNS
IT'S A LONG TIME SINCE YOU'VE KISSED ME--LIKE 83 MANSNS
THAT, DARLING.
FROM THEIR TALK, THEY MUST SPEND A GREAT DEAL OF 84 MANSNS
THEIR TIME IN HER GARDEN.
SO WHEN THE TIME COMES THEY WILL BE CAPABLE OF 84 MANSNS
SERVING OUR COMPANY--
AND AT THE SAME TIME AMUSED AND CURIOUSLY 90 MANSNS
FASCINATED AND DELIGHTED.)
IN YOUR SPARE TIME, WHEN I AM AWAY, 92 MANSNS
(PITYINGLY, BUT AT THE SAME TIME SCORNFULLY.) 93 MANSNS
YOU MUST BE BECOMING RICHER AND MORE POWERFUL ALL 100 MANSNS
THE TIME.
THERE WAS ONCE UPON A TIME A YOUNG KING OF A HAPPY110 MANSNS
LAND WHO,
YET, AT THE SAME TIME, HE FELT SHE WAS NOT LYING, 111 MANSNS
AND HE WAS AFRAID.
REMEMBERING THE LAST TIME I WAS IN THERE--AND I 113 MANSNS
WAS AFRAID--
=IT'S TIME YOU CAME IN, DO YOU HEAR ME$+ 114 MANSNS
IT'S GETTING NEAR SUPPER TIME, THAT'S ALL.= 114 MANSNS
IN A VERY SHORT TIME HE WILL BEG US ON HIS KNEES 135 MANSNS
TO RESTORE THAT PEACE
AS IF HE'D WASTE HIS TIME IN HER CRAZY GARDEN 137 MANSNS
EVERY EVENING.
HE TRIES TO REPRESS, WHICH FASCINATES AND AT THE 140 MANSNS
SAME TIME HUMILIATES HIM.
YOU'RE WASTING MY TIME AND I'M SICK OF YOU/ 142 MANSNS
I WASN'T MORE THAN A YEAR OLD AT THE TIME. 145 MANSNS
HAVEN'T YOU LEARNED BY THIS TIME THAT MY GREATEST 146 MANSNS
HAPPINESS IS TO PROVE TO YOU--
WHAT DO YOU WANT ME TO PAY YOU THIS TIMES 146 MANSNS
JUST IN TIME FOR MY EVENING VISIT WITH MOTHER. 147 MANSNS
WELL, I'LL MAKE UP FOR LOST TIME. 147 MANSNS
I'LL HAVE TIME TO DISPOSE OF HIM BEFORE I CATCH MY148 MANSNS
TRAIN.
YES, I SUPPOSE, ENTIRELY SELFISH--NO TIME TO 155 MANSNS
REMEMBER SELF.
YET AT THE SAME TIME SHE IS A PREY TO A PASSIONATE161 MANSNS
ANGER
HOW MANY TIMES NOW HAVE I RUN TO OPEN THE DOOR, 162 MANSNS
HOPING EACH TIME--$
I PASSED THE TIME PLEASANTLY IN DREAMING-- 163 MANSNS
FIND SOME WAY TO PASS THE TIME-- 163 MANSNS
ONLY IN A SILLY FANCY--TO WHILE AWAY THE TIME-- 166 MANSNS
YOU REALIZE THAT ANY TIME I CHOOSE I CAN TAKE 168 MANSNS
SIMON AWAY WITH ME/
YOU OLD LUNATIC, YOU'LL SEE IF I HAVE ANY PITY ON 169 MANSNS
YOU THE NEXT TIME/
AND AT THE SAME TIME BAFFLED AND PANIC-STRICKEN.) 171 MANSNS
BUT GOD BE PRAISED I'M BACK IN TIME/ 185 MANSNS
LET US ESCAPE BACK INTO PEACE--WHILE THERE IS 185 MANSNS
STILL TIME/
YOU ARE JUST IN TIME--TO BID US FAREWELL/ 186 MANSNS
(CRUELLY SCORNFUL AND AT THE SAME TIME UNEASY.) 187 MANSNS
ALL THE TIME THE THREE SET UP MISERABLE SCREAMS OF353 MARCOM
PROTEST,
WILL YOU KEEP LOOKING AT THIS ALL THE TIME YOU'RE 357 MARCOM
AWAY AND NEVER WILL FORGET ME$
HE'LL HAVE TIME ENOUGH FOR THAT, BUT WITH US TIME 362 MARCOM
IS MONEY.
FOR A TIME THE CHURCH BELLS, WHICH HAVE NEVER 363 MARCOM
CEASED RINGING,
BETTER LUCK NEXT TIME. 368 MARCOM
THIS IS A GOOD TIME TO MOVE ON AGAIN. 369 MARCOM
MARCO IS LOOKING AT THE PEOPLE BUT THIS TIME HE 370 MARCOM
ASSUMES THE CASUAL,
AT THE SAME MOMENT TWO MERCHANTS, THIS TIME 370 MARCOM
BUDDHISTS, COME IN.
ONLY THIS TIME IT IS ALL DONE IN PANTOMIME 370 MARCOM
WE'LL HAVE TIME TO STEAL A NAP BEFORE THEY OPEN 374 MARCOM
THE GATE.
YOU'LL BE ABLE TO WHISPER TO US IN TIME TO TAKE 381 MARCOM
ADVANTAGE--
BUT EACH TIME YOU RETURN FROM A JOURNEY YOU MUST 382 MARCOM
RELATE TO ME ALL THE
AS A CHILD MIGHT, BUT AT THE SAME TIME THERE IS 382 MARCOM
SOMETHING WARPED, DEFORMED--
WHO BROUGHT HER HOME EACH TIME A HUMBLE, FOOLISH, 388 MARCOM
TOUCHING LITTLE GIFT$
I HAVE SUSPECTED HER LOVE FOR HIM FOR A LONG TIME.388 MARCOM
ISN'T IT TIME TO PROTECT YOUR SOVEREIGNTY BY 392 MARCOM
STRONG MEASURES$
(FLATTERED BUT AT THE SAME TIME NONPLUSSED) 393 MARCOM
WHEN YOU HAVE TIME, I WISH YOU'D LOOK THIS OVER. 395 MARCOM
YOU'RE UP AGAINST NEW METHODS THIS TIME, 395 MARCOM
ANOTHER AT THE MOON, AND EACH TIME HE SAID THAT 397 MARCOM
NATURE WAS WONDERFUL/
ONCE WHEN HE LOOKED AT SUNRISE, ANOTHER TIME AT 397 MARCOM
SUNSET, ANOTHER AT THE STARS,
UNTIL IT'S TIME TO GO TO BED. 399 MARCOM
A FOREMAN SITS WITH A DRUM AND GONG WITH WHICH HE 400 MARCOM
MARKS A PERFECT TIME FOR THE
FOR THE LAST TIME, FAREWELL, LITTLE FLOWER OF MY 401 MARCOM
LIFE/
AND I WON'T FAIL HIM THIS TIME. 403 MARCOM
AND LET PEOPLE KNOW SHE'S LEAVING AT THE SAME 403 MARCOM
TIME.

TIME

TIME	(CONT'D.)	

I'VE HAD MY FUN AND I SUPPOSE IT'S ABOUT TIME I 404 MARCOM
SETTLED DOWN.
YOU ARE AT SOME TIME EVERY DAY OF THE VOYAGE, 404 MARCOM
BUT, AS I'VE PROVED TO YOU PEOPLE IN CATHAY TIME 404 MARCOM
AND AGAIN,
THAT ONE AT A TIME IS TROUBLE ENOUGH. 405 MARCOM
TAKE A FOOL'S ADVICE AND DON'T THINK SO MUCH OR 406 MARCOM
YOU'LL GET OLD BEFORE YOUR TIME/
LIKE A RED EMBER FLARING UP FOR THE LAST TIME 413 MARCOM
AND MY BODY MAY RESIST DEATH FOR A LONG TIME YET. 423 MARCOM
BY THE TIME YOU RECEIVE THIS THEY WILL BE MARRIED 424 MARCOM
IN VENICE.
MARCO, THE TRUE RULER OF THE WORLD, WILL HAVE COME426 MARCOM
TO VENICE BY THIS TIME.
LATELY, TO WHILE AWAY TIME, I EXPERIMENTED WITH 426 MARCOM
THE CRYSTAL.
IMAGINE HER WAITING ALL THIS TIME/ 427 MARCOM
(SOFTLY) ANY TIME/ (THEY HUG.) 430 MARCOM
OH, MAYBE ONE OR TWO OR SU--BUT I DIDN'T HAVE TIME430 MARCOM
TO WASTE ON FEMALES.
MARCO BEGINS AGAIN BUT THIS TIME THE CLAMOR IS TOO432 MARCOM
GREAT, HIS WORDS ARE LOST,
IT IS TIME YOU WERE ASLEEP. 438 MARCOM
THEY WAS TOO BUSY PREACHING TEMPERANCE TO HAVE 17 MISBEG
TIME FOR A DRINK.
THEY SPENT SO MUCH TIME CONFESSING THEIR SINS, 17 MISBEG
AND BY THE TIME HE LEFT 26 MISBEG
AND BY THE TIME THE PRETTY LITTLE TARTS, 30 MISBEG
HASN'T HE TOLD US AND PROMISED YOU CAN BUY IT IN 31 MISBEG
EASY TIME PAYMENTS
WE'RE ONLY TENANTS AND WE COULD BE THROWN OUT ON 31 MISBEG
OUR NECKS ANY TIME.
WHEN IT'S DINNER TIME$ 35 MISBEG
WELL, I'LL BET THIS IS ONE TIME HE'S GOING TO 46 MISBEG
TREAT.
NOT THIS TIME. 47 MISBEG
BUT EACH TIME ON THE FOLLOWING NIGHT IT GETS 50 MISBEG
BROKEN DOWN AGAIN.
SHE LOOKS STARTLED AND CONFUSED, STIRRED AND AT 51 MISBEG
THE SAME TIME FRIGHTENED.
THEN IT'S TIME-- 52 MISBEG
(KIDDINGLY) JUST WHAT I'VE BEEN THINKING FOR SOME 54 MISBEG
TIME, JOSIE.
THE TIME HE WAS TAPPED FOR AN EXCLUSIVE SENIOR 55 MISBEG
SOCIETY
DON'T YOU KISS YOUR HORSE EACH TIME YOU MOUNT AND 58 MISBEG
BEG HIM,
SAY IT A THIRD TIME AND I'LL SEND MY DAUGHTER TO 59 MISBEG
TELEPHONE THE ASYLUM.
(NOTICES THE BOTTLE ON THE BOULDER FOR THE FIRST 60 MISBEG
TIME--
IT'S DINNER TIME. 65 MISBEG
(THEN QUICKLY) BUT I'VE NO TIME NOW TO LISTEN TO 68 MISBEG
YOUR KIDDING.
ON THE BUREAU IS AN ALARM CLOCK WHICH SHOWS THE 71 MISBEG
TIME TO BE FIVE PAST ELEVEN.
BUT AT THE SAME TIME ARE ABLE TO PULL THEMSELVES 72 MISBEG
TOGETHER WHEN THEY WISH AND BE
IT'S TIME I TAUGHT YOU A LESSON. 73 MISBEG
I WOULDN'T WASTE YOUR TIME MENTIONING IT, 77 MISBEG
IT'S THE FIRST TIME I EVER SAW YOU SO PARALYZED 81 MISBEG
YOU COULDN'T SHAKE THE WHISKEY
WE'VE NO TIME TO WASTE. 97 MISBEG
(DRYLY) JUST IN TIME FOR THE BIG BOUT. 100 MISBEG
AND THIS ACT FOLLOWS THE PRECEDING WITHOUT ANY 111 MISBEG
LAPSE OF TIME.
IT'S THE FIRST TIME I EVER HEARD YOU COMPLAIN A 113 MISBEG
DRINK WAS TOO BIG.
MAYBE I'LL TELL YOU--LATER, WHEN I'M-- THAT'LL 122 MISBEG
CURE YOU--FOR ALL TIME/
I DON'T REMEMBER WHICH TIME--OR ANYTHING MUCH-- 128 MISBEG
THE STEPS IF SHE DIDN'T GRAB HIS ARM IN TIME. 137 MISBEG
FROM THE TIME I WAS A KID, I LOVED RACE-HORSES. 143 MISBEG
AFTER THAT, I KEPT SO DRUNK I DID DRAW A BLANK 147 MISBEG
MOST OF THE TIME.
BUT ALL THE TIME I KEPT SAYING TO MYSELF, +YOU 148 MISBEG
LOUSY HAM/
TIME I GOT A MOVE ON. 151 MISBEG
HE BECOMES AWARE OF THIS FOR THE FIRST TIME AND 151 MISBEG
TURNS SLOWLY TO STARE AT HER.)
THIS TIME, YOU'VE TOLD ONE TOO MANY. 159 MISBEG
IT'S TIME. 164 MISBEG
IT'S TIME. 165 MISBEG
WHAT TIME IS IT$ 165 MISBEG
TONE WITH HIM, BUT ALL THE TIME WAITING TO SEE HOW166 MISBEG
MUCH HE WILL REMEMBER)
I REMEMBER I WAS HAVING A GRAND TIME AT THE INN, 170 MISBEG
CELEBRATING WITH PHIL.
AND IT'S TIME FOR ME TO START WORK, NOT GO TO BED.172 MISBEG
THERE'S NO TRADE THIS TIME O' DAY. 9 POET
BUT HE WAS ASHAMED OF HER IN HIS PRIDE AT THE SAME 14 POET
TIME
GIVES HER MOTHER AN IMPATIENT BUT AT THE SAME TIME 21 POET
WORRIED GLANCE.
HE HAS GREAT LOVE FOR YOU, EVEN IF YOU DO BE 23 POET
PROVOKIN' HIM ALL THE TIME.
YOU KEEP ON SLAVIN' FOR HIM WHEN IT'S THAT HAS 24 POET
MADE YOU OLD BEFORE YOUR TIME/
(HE POURS OUT ANOTHER BIG DRINK AND THIS TIME HIS 37 POET
HAND IS STEADIER.
I HAVE WANTED A QUIET CHAT WITH YOU FOR SOME TIME. 46 POET
BUT IT'LL BE THE LAST TIME. 59 POET
IT'S TIME FOR IT, AND I KNEW YOU'D BE GOING 60 POET
UPSTAIRS.
AND THE NEXT TIME I'LL KEEP MY WITS. 65 POET
BUT THIS TIME MELODY GIVES NO PARTING ORDERS 66 POET

TIME	(CONT'D.)	

FOR THE SECOND TIME IN ONE MORNING BEFORE THE 68 POET
MIRROR.
I AM MAJOR CORNELIUS MELODY, ONE TIME OF HIS 70 POET
MAJESTY'S SEVENTH DRAGOONS,
I HAVE ONLY TIME FOR A SHORT VISIT-- 74 POET
SHE DIDN'T WASTE MUCH TIME. 80 POET
THIS IS THE FIRST TIME I HAVE SEEN SIMON 81 POET
OF COURSE, IT IS SOME TIME SINCE HE HAS WRITTEN. 81 POET
AND AT THE SAME TIME HOPEFUL. 85 POET
THIS TIME I REALLY AM GOING. 86 POET
ANYTHING TO GIVE HER TIME. 87 POET
BUT LETTING ME KNOW ALL THE TIME SHE HAD A MEANING 87 POET
BEHIND IT,
AND GIVE HIM TIME TO GET OVER HIS RAGE. 87 POET
(ROURKE AND O'DOWD ROAR AFTER HIM, BEATING TIME ON 96 POET
THE TABLE WITH THEIR GLASSES--
(MELODY, EXCITED NOW, BEATS TIME ON THE TABLE WITH102 POET
HIS GLASS ALONG WITH CREGAN.
I HAVE NO TIME. 104 POET
AND IT'S THE LAST TIME YOU'LL EVER TAKE 104 POET
SATISFACTION IN HAVING ME WAIT ON TABLE
HE SHOULD TEST HIS LOVE AND YOURS BY LETTING A 109 POET
DECENT INTERVAL OF TIME ELAPSE
AND THERE WAS A TIME WHEN I POSSESSED WEALTH AND 112 POET
POSITION.
I WISHED TIME TO REFLECT ON A FURTHER ASPECT OF 112 POET
THIS PROPOSED MARRIAGE.
BUT THIS TIME, I WON'T GIVE YOU THE SATISFACTION--113 POET
ONE TIME OF HIS MAJESTY'S SEVENTH DRAGOONS, 117 POET
BUT I MUST TELL YOU MY TIME IS SHORT. 119 POET
THE DEVIL OF IT IS, THIS COMES AT A DIFFICULT TIME120 POET
FOR ME.
IT'S THE FIRST TIME IN MY LIFE I EVER HEARD ANYONE125 POET
SAY CON MELODY WAS A COWARD/
(BY THE TIME HE FINISHES SPEAKING, 128 POET
BUT I'LL NOT WORRY THIS TIME, AND LET YOU NOT, 130 POET
EITHER.
IT LOOKS GENTLE AND CALM AND AT THE SAME TIME 136 POET
DREAMILY HAPPY AND EXULTANT.
(AS IF THIS WERE THE FIRST TIME SHE WAS REALLY 140 POET
CONSCIOUS OF SARA SPEAKING.
(REBUKINGLY.) ALL THIS TIME--IN THE DEAD OF THE 142 POET
NIGHT/
JUST ENOUGH TO BE COMFORTABLE, AND HE'D HAVE TIME 146 POET
OVER TO WRITE HIS BOOK.
AND ALL THE TIME WE WERE KISSING EACH OTHER, WILD 147 POET
WITH HAPPINESS.
IF HE'D SAY TO ME, FOR EVERY TIME YOU KISS SIMON 149 POET
THE MARE, MOTHER, AND HASN'T HE SLEPT IN HER STALL162 POET
MANY A TIME
IT'S THE DAMNEDEST JOKE A MAN IVIR PLAYED ON 166 POET
HIMSELF SINCE TIME BEGAN.
IT'S GITTIN' NEAR SUPPER-TIME AND YOU GOT TO TAKE 579 ROPE
YOUR MEDICINE B'FORE IT.
(GETTING UP) I'LL TELL HIM A LITTLE AT A TIME 590 ROPE
TILL HE KNOWS.
I THOUGHT HE MIGHT BE IN THE BUG-HOUSE BY THIS 592 ROPE
TIME.
HE'S FOXY TO PRITIND HE'S LOONY, BUT HE'S HIS WITS592 ROPE
WITH HIM ALL THE TIME.
I'LL GIT EVERY CENT HE'S GOT THIS TIME. 593 ROPE
(HE SHAKES HIS HEAD DOUBTFULLY, AT THE SAME TIME 593 ROPE
FIXING LUKE WITH A KEEN GLANCE
'TWAS A LONG TIME PAST. 593 ROPE
ANY TIME. 594 ROPE
I THOUGHT YOU'D BE KILLIN' HIM THAT TIME WITH THE 597 ROPE
CHAIR.
THAT WAS A LONG TIME BACK. 599 ROPE
AND WHEN I GOES THIS TIME I AIN'T NEVER COMIN' 599 ROPE
BACK.
AND I SEEN HIM MANY A TIME AT HIS SNEAKIN'. 599 ROPE
I WANT TO SHOW THE GANG A REAL TIME, 599 ROPE
OF THE ADOLESCENT BOY HE HAD BEEN AT THE TIME OF 5 STRANG
HIS FATHER'S DEATH.
(THEN MATTER-OF-FACTLY) I WAS WASTING MY TIME, 7 STRANG
TOO.
AND FOR A TIME I ACTUALLY FELT RELEASED/..... 9 STRANG
BUT AT THE TIME-- 10 STRANG
THAT IS, OF COURSE I MEAN FOR THE TIME BEING, AND 15 STRANG
I REALLY THINK--
YES, I MUST SAY I CAN'T SEE YOU AS A PEACE-TIME 17 STRANG
FLORENCE NIGHTINGALE, NINA/
THIS TIME I DO SPEAK FOR HER SAKE. 21 STRANG
IT'S TIME FOR TEA.... 21 STRANG
JUST WANTED TO REMIND YOU TO CALL FOR A TAXI IN 22 STRANG
GOOD TIME.
AS IF HE WERE THIS TIME ACTUALLY ADDRESSING 25 STRANG
ANOTHER PERSON)
(IRRALLY, IT'S HARDLY A DECENT TIME, IS IT, FOR 25 STRANG
THAT KIND OF SPECULATION...
(WHAT TIME IS IT$....) 25 STRANG
YOU SEE YOU'VE BEEN DEAD FOR ME A LONG TIME.... 27 STRANG
NOT THAT I DON'T HOPE SHE'D COME TO LOVE ME IN 32 STRANG
TIME--
SHE OUGHT TO LOVE GORDON FOR A LONG TIME YET. 32 STRANG
I KNOW IT'S HARDLY THE PROPER TIME-- 32 STRANG
DAMN LITTLE TIME TO CONVINCE HIM.... 34 STRANG
TIME GIVE HAPPINESS TO VARIOUS FELLOW WAR-VICTIMS 35 STRANG
BY PRETENDING TO LOVE THEM.
(SHORTLY AND DRYLY) WE CAN'T WASTE TIME BEING 35 STRANG
SENTIMENTAL, MARSDEN/
PERHAPS I KNEW AT THE TIME BUT I'VE FORGOTTEN. 45 STRANG
AND IT'S TIME YOU WERE HAVING CHILDREN-- 46 STRANG
AND IT WILL BE TIME ENOUGH TO LET NED 49 STRANG
MAY ONCE HAVE BEEN HAVE PACKED UP THEIR 49 STRANG
MANIFESTATIONS A LONG TIME AGO AND
FIRST TIME IN A LONG WHILE....) 51 STRANG

TIME

TIME
(CONT'D.)

AND, AT THE SAME TIME, THE GRIMMEST... 53 STRANG
AND IT'S ONLY A QUESTION OF TIME WHEN--WHY, TO 54 STRANG
SHOW YOU, COLE--
AND RIGHT TO THE TIME THE PAINS COME ON. 58 STRANG
THINKING ANY MINUTE THE CURSE MIGHT GET HIM, EVERY 60 STRANG
TIME HE WAS SICK,
(IGOSH, I OUGHT TO TRY AND GET A NEW START ON THIS 68 STRANG
BEFORE IT'S TIME...)
STARTING WITH A BURST OF CONFIDENCE EACH TIME, 70 STRANG
THEN...)
FUN A TIME AFTER... 71 STRANG
THAT TIME I KISSED HER... 78 STRANG
I HAVEN'T MUCH TIME. 81 STRANG
I NEED YOUR ADVICE--YOUR SCIENTIFIC ADVICE THIS 84 STRANG
TIME, IF YOU PLEASE, DOCTOR.
THIS IS NO TIME FOR TIMIDITY/ 86 STRANG
SO EACH TIME HER THOUGHTS COME TO THE MAN SHE MUST 88 STRANG
SELECT THEY ARE AFRAID TO GO
SHE IS AGAIN THE PREGNANT WOMAN OF ACT THREE BUT 90 STRANG
THIS TIME THERE IS A TRIUMPHANT
IT'S ABOUT TIME FOR NED TO COME, ISN'T IT& 93 STRANG
I HADN'T SEEN HER IN SOME TIME, SO HER DEATH WAS 101 STRANG
NEVER VERY REAL TO ME.
AND THIS TIME NEVER COME BACK/...) 102 STRANG
(GENTLY AND CARESSINGLY) BUT THIS TIME I'M GOING 104 STRANG
TO THINK OF MY OWN HAPPINESS--
(HE IS IN A STATE OF STRANGE ELATION BY THIS TIME)105 STRANG
WHILE THERE'S TIME/... 105 STRANG
I HAVEN'T TIME, I'VE GOT A MILLION THINGS TO DO. 106 STRANG
SHE WAS SAVING IT TO SURPRISE YOU WITH AT HER OWN 106 STRANG
PROPER TIME--
THE LAST TIME I WAS HERE THE AIR WAS POISONED... 112 STRANG
(MALICIOUSLY) HE SEEMED IN FINE FEATHER--SAID HE 115 STRANG
WAS HAVING A GAY TIME.
(SOLICITOUSLY) ISN'T IT TIME TO NURSE HIM AGAIN& 118 STRANG
(HE GRINS--THEN SERIOUSLY) IT WAS ABOUT TIME I GOT121 STRANG
HOLD OF MYSELF.
TILL THE NEXT TIME/... 122 STRANG
IT'S TIME I TOOK A HAND IN THIS... 126 STRANG
WELL, SHE WAS MY MISTRESS--FOR A TIME--I WAS 127 STRANG
LONELY.
IT'S TIME I TALKED TO NED... 128 STRANG
IN FACT, I'M SO CONFIDENT HE IS THAT AS SOON AS HE128 STRANG
THINKS THE TIME IS RIPE TO
THE TIME FOR LYING IS PAST/ 130 STRANG
I TRIED NOT TO THIS TIME--BUT I HAD TO, NINA/ 131 STRANG
LET US DO THE PRESCRIBING THIS TIME/ 132 STRANG
THAT'S SETTLED FOR ALL TIME/... 133 STRANG
HAVEN'T NOTICED HER THAT WAY IN A LONG TIME... 134 STRANG
LAST TIME HE WAS GONE MORE'NA YEAR... 138 STRANG
RUNNING AWAY TO COME BACK EACH TIME MORE 139 STRANG
ABJECT/...
EACH TIME AFTER A FEW MONTHS MY LOVE CHANGES TO 140 STRANG
BITTERNESS...
OR I'LL SEND YOU AWAY, AND THEN AFTER A TIME I'LL 143 STRANG
CALL YOU BACK,
EVEN IF I CALL YOU BACK BEFORE THEN--AND WORK THIS145 STRANG
TIME, REALLY WORKS
NOT THIS TIME... 147 STRANG
LAST TIME I WAS HERE YOU WERE LEAVING FOR THE WEST147 STRANG
INDIES IN A WEEK BUT I SEE
YES, I'M GOING THIS WEEK AND I EXPECT TO BE GONE 147 STRANG
AT LEAST TWO YEARS THIS TIME--
TIME TO GO WHEN THOSE THOUGHTS COME... 149 STRANG
I'VE TOLD YOU TIME AND AGAIN. 153 STRANG
ABOUT THE TIME HE WAS STROKING THE CREW AND THE 153 STRANG
FELLOW WHO WAS NUMBER SEVEN
AND HE BEGAN TALKING BACK TO HIM ALL THE TIME AND 153 STRANG
SORT OF GAVE HIM HIS STRENGTH
HANGING AROUND ALL THE TIME. 155 STRANG
SHE IS DESPERATELY TRYING TO CONCEAL THE OBVIOUS 158 STRANG
INROADS OF TIME BY AN
(PULLING OUT HIS WATCH) SOON BE TIME FOR THE 160 STRANG
START.
OF COURSE, THE DAMNED RADIO HAS TO PICK OUT THIS 160 STRANG
TIME TO GO DEAD/
TIME FOR THE START. 163 STRANG
WHAT HOPE THAT WOULD HAVE GIVEN ME AT ONE TIME/...163 STRANG
IT'S TIME THESE GORDONS TOOK A GOOD LICKING FROM 167 STRANG
LIFE/...)
YOUR TIME FOR THAT IS OVER/ 170 STRANG
HE STARTED THROWING SCOTCH INTO HIM AS IF HE WERE 171 STRANG
DRINKING AGAINST TIME.
AND THIS TIME I WILL NOT LET MY GORDON GO FROM ME 171 STRANG
FOREVER/
I LOVED YOU HORRIBLY AT THAT TIME, NINA--HORRIBLY/172 STRANG
THAT TIME. SHE WAS JEALOUS BECAUSE SAM LOVED ME 172 STRANG
THEN IT'S TIME TO TELL HIM THE 172 STRANG
(INTENSELY) OH, IF I'D ONLY GONE AWAY WITH YOU 173 STRANG
THAT TIME
IT'S TIME HE GAVE US BACK OUR SON/ 173 STRANG
HIS MOTHER TOLD ME THAT TIME SO I WOULDN'T HAVE 179 STRANG
HIS BABY.
(HAS BEEN SHRIEKING AT THE SAME TIME) 182 STRANG
AT THE SAME TIME, ALTHOUGH ENTIRELY AN 184 STRANG
UNIMAGINATIVE CODE-BOUND GENTLEMAN OF HIS
REALLY GOOD-BYE FOREVER THIS TIME.... 190 STRANG
(I(KNEW THE TIME WOULD COME AT LAST WHEN I WOULD 197 STRANG
HEAR HER ASK THAT/...
THEY PROMISED FAITHFUL THEY'D 'APPEN IN TONIGHT'--494 VOYAGE
THEM AS WHOSE TIME WAS DONE.
THERE'S LOTS O' TIME YET. 495 VOYAGE
IT'S 'ARPAST NINE AN' TIME AS SOME ONE WAS A 495 VOYAGE
COMIN' IN. TELL 'EM.
(WITH A GOOD-NATURED GRIN) I BANE A GOOD BOY DIS 497 VOYAGE
NIGHT, FOR ONE TIME.
I WUS ON FARM LONG TIME WHEN I WUS KID. 498 VOYAGE

TIME
(CONT'D.)

(SHAKING HIS HEAD) OUTING DIS TIME, THANK YOU. 498 VOYAGE
(IVAN SEEMS TO SEE THE WOMEN FOR THE FIRST TIME 500 VOYAGE
AND GRINS FOOLISHLY.)
IT SOUND NICE TO HEAR THE OLD TALK YUST ONCE IN A 502 VOYAGE
TIME.
SIT DOWN AND REST FOR TIME, DRISC. 504 VOYAGE
WE'LL BE COMIN' BACK IN A SHORT TIME, SURELY. 504 VOYAGE
THERE AIN'T NO TIME TO BE DAWDLIN'. 505 VOYAGE
AND I MEAN ALL THE TIME TO GO BACK HOME AT END OF 506 VOYAGE
VOYAGE.
SO DIS TIME I SAY TO MYSELF.. 506 VOYAGE
AND I WANT TO GO HOME DIS TIME. 506 VOYAGE
I WRITE ONCE IN A WHILE AND SHE WRITE MANY TIME.. 506 VOYAGE
PY YINGO, I PITY POOR FALLARS MAKE DAT TRIP ROUND 507 VOYAGE
CAPE STIFF DIS TIME YEAR.
I SAIL ON HER ONCE LONG TIME AGO--THREE MASTS, 507 VOYAGE
FULL RIG, SKYS'L-YARDERS
ROTTEN GRUB AND DEY MAKE YOU WORK ALL TIME-- 507 VOYAGE
A DRIVING FORCE WHICH CAN BE SYMPATHETIC AND CRUEL443 WELDED
AT THE SAME TIME.
(WITH A TENDER SMILE) OF THE FIRST TIME WE MET-- 446 WELDED
AT REHEARSAL, REMEMBER&
HASN'T OUR MARRIAGE KEPT THE SPIRIT OF THAT TIME--447 WELDED
OH, MY OWN, MY OWN--TO THE END OF TIME/ 448 WELDED
THE KNOCK IS REPEATED, THIS TIME WITH AUTHORITY, 449 WELDED
ASSURANCE.
WHILE AT THE SAME TIME, YOU'RE JEALOUS OF ANY 453 WELDED
SEPARATENESS IN ME.
SHE SITS DOWN, THIS TIME FACING HIM, AND LOOKS AT 455 WELDED
HIM UNEASILY.)
ANY OLD TIME AT ALL, NELLY. 463 WELDED
MAKE THIS YOUR HOME--AND MAYBE--IN TIME-- 467 WELDED
(IMPULSIVELY) THAT TIME YOU STOOD HERE AND CALLED470 WELDED
TO ME FOR HELP--
PUZZLED GLANCE AS IF HE WERE AWARE OF HIS 471 WELDED
SURROUNDINGS FOR THE FIRST TIME.)
(SHE SIGHS AGAIN, THIS TIME WITH A SORT OF RESTFUL471 WELDED
CONTENT)
WHAT TIME IS IT& 472 WELDED
(STARES AT HER--AN EXPRESSION COMES AS IF HE WERE 477 WELDED
SEEING HER FOR THE FIRST TIME.
PROTECTIVE HARDING OFF AND AT THE SAME TIME A 480 WELDED
SEEKING POSSESSION.
YOU THOUGHT I'D STAYED HERE ALL THE TIME& 482 WELDED
(FOR A TIME THEY BOTH SIT STARING BLEAKLY BEFORE 486 WELDED
THEM.

TIME'LL
MAYBE THE TIME'LL COME WHEN YOU'LL BE WILLIN' TO 517 DIFRNT

TIME'S
WHAT TIME'S IT GETTING TO BE& 212 AHWILD
WHAT TIME'S IT GITTIN' TO BE, I WONDERS 191 EJONES
WHAT TIME'S IT, ROCKY& 583 ICEMAN

TIMELESS
(SHE KISSES HIM ON THE LIPS WITH A TIMELESS KISS.)323 GGBROW

TIMER
I'M AN OLD TIMER IN THIS FLEABAG. 10 HUGHIE

TIMERS
FROM WHAT DE OLD-TIMERS SAY, 581 ICEMAN

TIMES
THINKIN' IT MIGHT BE SOOTHIN' TO YE TO BE PLAYIN' 546 'ILE
IT TIMES WHEN THEY WAS CALMS
WE'VE BEEN OVER THIS A THOUSAND TIMES BEFORE, AND 212 AHWILD
STILL YOU GO ON/
WE'VE BEEN OVER THIS A THOUSAND TIMES BEFORE AND 213 AHWILD
I'LL ALWAYS FEEL THE SAME AS
WELL, I MUST SAY I'VE NEVER NOTICED YOU TO HANG 216 AHWILD
BACK AT MEAL TIMES (TO LILY)
SURE LOTS OF TIMES. 219 AHWILD
AND IF I DIDN'T, YOU'VE TOLD ME FOUR TIMES 222 AHWILD
ALREADY/
GUESS I HAVE TOLD THAT TOO MANY TIMES AND BORED 230 AHWILD
EVERYONE.
SURE, LOTS OF TIMES. 237 AHWILD
(TERRIBLY FLUSTERED) SURE, I'VE HEARD THAT OLD 237 AHWILD
PARODY LOTS OF TIMES.
LOTS OF TIMES. 241 AHWILD
THE WAY YOU TALK AT TIMES, 251 AHWILD
I'VE TRIED TO A COUPLE OF TIMES. 268 AHWILD
YES, SIR, I'VE HEARD HIM SAY THAT VERY THING A 272 AHWILD
THOUSAND TIMES, MUST BE.
(SHE GIVES HIM A LETTER FOLDED MANY TIMES INTO A 273 AHWILD
TINY SQUARE.
MURIEL'S A MILLION TIMES PRETTIER ANYWAY. 276 AHWILD
BUT I'VE TOLD YOU A MILLION TIMES THAT PA-- 286 AHWILD
(THEN WITH A GRIN) YOU SURPRISE ME AT TIMES WITH 291 AHWILD
YOUR DEEP WISDOM.
HOW MANY TIMES HAVE I TOLD YOU TO HANG UP YOUR HAT293 AHWILD
IN THE HALL WHEN YOU COME IN/
HE'S TALKED TO ME 'BOUT YOU LOTS O' TIMES. 19 ANNA
AY NEVER COME HOME ONLY FEW TIMES VEN YOU VAS KIT 21 ANNA
IN SWEDEN.
I'VE TOLD YOU A HUNDRED TIMES I HATED IT. 27 ANNA
IT ALL SEEMS LIKE I'D BEEN HERE BEFORE LOTS OF 28 ANNA
TIMES--ON BOATS--
INDADE AND I WILL ASK YOUR PARDON A THOUSAND 34 ANNA
TIMES--AND ON MY KNEES, IF YE LIKE.
IT'S GREAT POWER I HAVE IN MY HAND AND ARM, AND I 35 ANNA
DO BE FORGETTING IT AT TIMES.
(FORCIBLY) DAT VAS MILLION TIMES VORSE, AY TAL 43 ANNA
YOU/
(AFTER A SLIGHT PAUSE) AND OTHER TIMES MY EYES 89 BEYOND
WOULD FOLLOW THIS ROAD.
I LIKED TO BE ALL ALONE--THOSE TIMES. 90 BEYOND
I'VE TALKED TO ROBERT THOUSANDS OF TIMES 113 BEYOND
WITH YOUR OWN BROTHER WHO'S TEN TIMES THE MAN YOU 126 BEYOND
EVER WAS OR EVER WILL BE/

1673

TIMES

TIMES (CONT'D.)
SAY, IT SURE BRINGS BACK OLD TIMES TO BE UP HERE 131 BEYOND
WITH YOU
(FROWNING) THERE'VE BEEN LOTS OF TIMES LATELY 133 BEYOND
THAT
IT'LL BE LIKE OLD TIMES. 136 BEYOND
SEVERAL TIMES I'VE BEEN ALMOST A MILLIONAIRE--ON 156 BEYOND
PAPER--
I'VE SHIP'S BELL IS HEARD HEAVILY EIGHT TIMES. 482 CARDIF
D'YOU REMEMBER THE TIMES WE HAD IN BUENOS AIRES$ 487 CARDIF
OR TIMES HAS CHANGED SINCE I PUT IN HERE LAST. 458 CARIBE
(REGRETFULLY) THEM WAS GOOD TIMES, THOSE DAYS. 467 CARIBE
I'VE BEEN AFRAID MYSELF--AT TIMES. 564 CROSS
ALTHOUGH AT TIMES ONE OR ANOTHER MAY SUBTLY SENSE 496 DAYS
HIS PRESENCE.
DO YOU THINK I HAVEN'T IMAGINED HER DEATH MANY 509 DAYS
TIMES
I'VE PHONED YOU A DOZEN TIMES, BUT YOU WERE ALWAYS516 DAYS
OUT.
OH, JOHN, YOU'RE SUCH A CHILD AT TIMES YOU OUGHT 529 DAYS
TO BE SPANKED.
AT THESE TIMES HE WANTED ONLY TO DIE. 534 DAYS
SO GREAT WAS THE FORCE OF THIS OBSESSION AT TIMES 536 DAYS
BUT THERE ARE TIMES OF STRESS AND FLIGHT WHEN ONE 543 DAYS
HIDES IN ANY OLD EMPTY BARREL/
HE FEELS AT TIMES AN ABSURD IMPULSE TO PRAY. 544 DAYS
BUT THERE HAVE BEEN TIMES WHEN I'VE HAD THE 557 DAYS
STRONGEST SENSE OF--
I'VE SUSPECTED AT TIMES THAT UNDERNEATH HE WANTS--557 DAYS
TEN TIMES AS STRONG AN' FIFTY TIMES AS HARD AS 236 DESIRE
EBEN.
CAN'T YE SEE IT'S GOT T' BE THAT AN' MORE--MUCH 243 DESIRE
MORE--A HUNDRED TIMES MORE--
THEY KISS SEVERAL TIMES. 244 DESIRE
HE SWALLOWS PAINFULLY SEVERAL TIMES--FORCES A WEAK268 DESIRE
SMILE AT LAST/
JACK'S A DURN FOOL AT TIMES, EMMER-- 500 DIFRNT
MOST TIMES IT'S... 513 DIFRNT
OH, YOU NEEDN'T THINK WE'RE ALL SO BEHIND THE 521 DIFRNT
TIMES TO HOME HERE JUST BECAUSE
ESPECIALLY SINCE YOU'VE BEEN TO HOME THESE LAST 524 DIFRNT
FEW TIMES AND COME TO CALL SO
AND FEELIN' EVEN MORE IN BETWEEN TIMES WHEN I WAS 538 DIFRNT
TO HOME LIVIN' RIGHT NEXT DOOR
HIT A MILLION TIMES/... 448 DYNAMO
I'VE TOLD YOU A MILLION TIMES HOW DUMB THAT TALK 455 DYNAMO
IS AND YET YOU KEEP ON HARPING--
HAS SHE COME MANY TIMES, REUBEN$ 478 DYNAMO
YOU KNOW, ADA, THERE USED TO BE TIMES WHEN I WAS 484 DYNAMO
SCARED HERE TOO--
NO USE'N YOU RAKIN' UP OLE TIMES. 177 EJONES
I'SE PAID YOU BACK ALL YOU DONE FOR ME MANY TIMES.177 EJONES
SO MANY TIMES DAT I KNOWS IT HIGH AN' LOW LIKE A 183 EJONES
BOOK.
BORNE ON THE LIGHT PUFFS OF WIND THIS MUSIC IS AT 5 ELECTR
TIMES QUITE LOUD,
BUT HE'S ONLY BEEN HERE FOUR TIMES IN ALL, I 52 ELECTR
THINK.
HE LOOKS SO MUCH LIKE HIS FATHER AT TIMES--AND 73 ELECTR
LIKE--
I USED TO HEAR YOU SINGING AT THE QUEEREST TIMES-- 83 ELECTR
SO SWEET AND CLEAR AND PURE/
WHO TOOK IT INTO HIS SILLY HEAD TO CALL HERE A FEW 87 ELECTR
TIMES WITHOUT BEING ASKED.
BUT MOTHER MEANS A THOUSAND TIMES MORE TO ME THAN 98 ELECTR
HE EVER DID/
IT'S WORTH IT A MILLION TIMES/ 111 ELECTR
THERE'S TIMES WHEN A MAN'S A DARN FOOL NOT TO BE 135 ELECTR
SCARED.
(THEN WITH A HARSH LAUGH) AND, AT THE SAME TIME, 151 ELECTR
A MILLION TIMES MORE VILE.
HE SCARES ME AT TIMES--AND VINNIE--I'VE WATCHED 158 ELECTR
HER LOOKING AT YOU.
I'VE HAD SUCH A STRONG FEELING AT TIMES THAT IT 161 ELECTR
WOULD RELIEVE YOUR MIND
THERE ARE TIMES NOW WHEN YOU DON'T SEEM TO BE MY 165 ELECTR
SISTER, NOR MOTHER,
HOW MANY MILLION TIMES BROWN HAS THOUGHT HOW MUCH 298 GOBROW
BETTER FOR HER IT WOULD HAVE
BUT THAT HAS BEEN DONE SO MANY TIMES. 237 HA APE
THE GUARD GIVE ME THE SUNDAY TIMES. 242 HA APE
THE KIND OF SAP YOU'D TAKE TO THE CLEANERS A 20 HUGHIE
MILLION TIMES
THAT ONE EYE AT TIMES PEERS HALF OVER ONE GLASS 577 ICEMAN
I'VE SAID THE SAME THING TO HER LOTS OF TIMES TO 590 ICEMAN
KID HER.
HE NEVER WORRIES IN HARD TIMES BECAUSE THERE'S 594 ICEMAN
ALWAYS OLD FRIENDS FROM THE DAYS
WAS A POLICE LIEUTENANT BACK IN THE FLUSH TIMES OF594 ICEMAN
GRAFT WHEN EVERYTHING WENT.
YOU'VE TOLD THAT STORY TEN MILLION TIMES AND IF I 601 ICEMAN
HAVE TO HEAR IT AGAIN,
JA, CECIL, I KNOW HOW BEAUTIFUL IT MUST BE, FROM 605 ICEMAN
ALL YOU TELL ME MANY TIMES.
AH, BE DAMNED/ HAVEN'T I HEARD THEIR VISIONS A 608 ICEMAN
THOUSAND TIMES$
IT'S GIVEN ME TOO MANY GOOD TIMES. 621 ICEMAN
(DOUBTFULLY) BUT HICKEY WASN'T SICKING HIM ON 652 ICEMAN
THOSE TIMES.
(EXASPERATEDLY) BUT I'VE EXPLAINED THAT A MILLION704 ICEMAN
TIMES/
BUT WE REMEMBER THE OLD TIMES, TOO, 706 ICEMAN
AND TIMES NEVER WAS SO HARD. 724 ICEMAN
GOD, HOW MANY THOUSAND TIMES--/ 33 JOURNE
SHE'S A DIFFERENT WOMAN ENTIRELY FROM THE OTHER 37 JOURNE
TIMES.
THAT'S WHAT WE THOUGHT THE OTHER TIMES. 57 JOURNE
BUT YOU'VE HEARD ME SAY THIS A THOUSAND TIMES. 61 JOURNE

TIMID

TIMES (CONT'D.)
AND SHE DOES DO HER BEST AT TIMES. 71 JOURNE
IT'S TOO BAD THEY SEEM TO BE JUST THE TIMES YOU'RE 72 JOURNE
SURE TO BE LATE, JAMES.
THERE IS AT TIMES AN UNCANNY GAY, FREE 97 JOURNE
YOUTHFULNESS IN HER MANNER.
WELL, I SUPPOSE I SNORE AT TIMES, TOO, AND I DON'T 99 JOURNE
LIKE TO ADMIT IT.
HOW MANY TIMES I WAS TO WAIT IN UGLY HOTEL ROOMS. 113 JOURNE
I'VE HEARD PAPA TELL THAT MACHINE SHOP STORY TEN 117 JOURNE
THOUSAND TIMES.
IT'S PRETTY HARD TO TAKE AT TIMES, HAVING A DOPE 120 JOURNE
FIEND FOR A MOTHER/
I'VE PUT UP WITH A LOT FROM YOU BECAUSE FROM THE 127 JOURNE
BAD THINGS YOU'VE DONE AT TIMES
IT'S ONLY SEVEN DOLLARS A WEEK BUT YOU GET TEN 149 JOURNE
TIMES THAT VALUE.
AND SEVERAL OTHER TIMES IN MY LIFE, WHEN I WAS 153 JOURNE
SWIMMING FAR OUT,
I'VE HEARD THAT GASPARD STUFF A MILLION TIMES. 158 JOURNE
BELIEVED THAT MYSELF AT TIMES, BUT IT'S A FAKE. 165 JOURNE
THE TIMES ARE OUT OF ORDER. 316 LAZARU
THE TIMES ARE RIPE FOR SUCH A BOOK. 8 MANSNS
HOW MANY TIMES I WISH TO PINCH YOU TO DISCOVER IF 33 MANSNS
YOU'RE STUFFED/
THERE ARE TIMES WHEN I ALMOST RESPECT YOU, JOEL. 34 MANSNS
BUT I ADMIT I AM NO NAPOLEON, ALTHOUGH AT TIMES I 37 MANSNS
HAVE DREAMED--
AND YOU HAD THE BRAINS TO SEE THE HARD TIMES 48 MANSNS
COMING BEFORE ANYONE.
THE HARD TIMES WON'T TOUCH THAT. 48 MANSNS
FATHER WOULD RATHER HAVE FACED RUIN A THOUSAND 59 MANSNS
TIMES--
A VACATION WOULD BE IN ORDER AT SUCH TIMES. 72 MANSNS
I'VE FELT MYSELF AT TIMES--OH, ONLY ONCE IN A 82 MANSNS
WHILE--
BY GOD, THERE HAVE BEEN TIMES WHEN, 105 MANSNS
I HAVE FORGOTTEN HIM SEVERAL TIMES BEFORE IN MY 133 MANSNS
LIFE.
AS IF ADDITIONS HAD BEEN MADE AT DIFFERENT TIMES 139 MANSNS
TO AN ORIGINAL STRUCTURE
IT HAS ONLY WHAT EVERY WOMAN THINKS AT TIMES IN 144 MANSNS
HER HEART--
NEW TIMES, NEW CUSTOMS--AND METHODS. 152 MANSNS
HOW MANY TIMES NOW HAVE I RUN TO OPEN THE DOOR, 162 MANSNS
HOPING EACH TIME--$
THERE HAVE BEEN TIMES AT THE OFFICE WHEN I-- 172 MANSNS
THEY RELATE THAT IN OLD TIMES THREE KINGS FROM 368 MARCOM
THIS COUNTRY WENT TO WORSHIP A
HE SAVED MY LIFE THREE TIMES AT THE RISK OF HIS 424 MARCOM
OWN.
SO NO ONE CAN TELL AT TIMES WHAT YOU'RE AFTER. 26 MISBEG
SIMPSON SEZ HE'S HAD IT REPAIRED A DOZEN TIMES. 50 MISBEG
HOW MANY TIMES HAVE I MENDED THAT FENCE, JOSIE$ 62 MISBEG
IT WAS ONLY BECAUSE THERE'S TIMES YOU HAVE TO SING 75 MISBEG
TO KEEP FROM CRYING.
(QUICKLY) BUT I'VE BEEN TO THE COAST A LOT OF 128 MISBEG
TIMES.
BUT IT WOULD BE A MILLION TIMES WORSE AFTER-- 140 MISBEG
BUT HER SPEECH HAS AT TIMES A SELF-CONSCIOUS, 16 POET
STILTED QUALITY ABOUT IT.
I'VE TOLD YOU A HUNDRED TIMES TO SEE THE DOCTOR. 21 POET
THERE IS A CURSED DESTINY IN THESE DECADENT TIMES. 37 POET
IF THEY ARE RABBLE, THEY'RE FULL OF DROLL HUMOR AT 38 POET
TIMES.
I AM AFRAID I MAY HAVE--THE THOUGHT OF OLD TIMES-- 42 POET
I BECOME BITTER.
TALKING OVER OLD TIMES WITH JAMIE CREGAN. 42 POET
THOUGH IT IS DIFFICULT AT TIMES FOR MY PRIDE TO 48 POET
REMEMBER
BUT DOUBTLESS SIMON HAS TOLD YOU I AM A BIT 84 POET
ECCENTRIC AT TIMES.
(THEN MOURNFULLY.) IT'S LIKE THE AULD TIMES COME 130 POET
AGAIN.
(HE STANDS STARING UP AT THE ROPE AND TAPS IT 579 ROPE
TESTINGLY SEVERAL TIMES WITH HIS
AND YOU'RE NOT TOO FIRM IN THE HEAD YOURSELF AT 583 ROPE
TIMES, GOD HELP YOU/
THE TWO TIMES I'VE VISITED THE HOSPITAL SHE'S BEEN 25 STRANG
PLEASANT ENOUGH...
(NODDING HIS HEAD SEVERAL TIMES--STUPIDLY) 27 STRANG
YES, A GOOD MANY TIMES LATELY IN A HALF-JOKING 38 STRANG
WAY.
I AM--A HUNDRED TIMES MORE THAN I DESERVE/ 71 STRANG
I LOVED IT SO IT SEEMED AT TIMES THAT GORDON MUST 83 STRANG
BE ITS REAL FATHER.
I'VE TOLD MUSELF THIS A THOUSAND TIMES 84 STRANG
I CAN'T STAND HEARING THOSE SAME REPROACHES I'VE 143 STRANG
HEARD A THOUSAND TIMES BEFORE/
I BANE DRUNK MANY TIMES, MISS FREDA. 501 VOYAGE
IT SEEMS AT TIMES AS IF SOME JEALOUS DEMON OF THE 452 WELDED
COMMONPLACE WERE MOCKING US.
(UNHEEDING) AND WHAT MAKES ME HATE YOU AT THOSE 455 WELDED
TIMES IS THAT I KNOW YOU LIKE
AS FOR MY WORK, YOU'VE ACKNOWLEDGED A MILLION 457 WELDED
TIMES--
SWALLOWING HARD SEVERAL TIMES AS IF HE WERE 472 WELDED
STRIVING TO GET CONTROL OF HIS

TIMEY
NUT LIKE THEM SLOW, OLD-TIMEY TUNES. 520 DIFRNT
IT WAS SO GLOOMY AND OLD-TIMEY BEFORE, I JUST 535 DIFRNT
COULDN'T BEAR IT.
(OFFENDED) I AIN'T OLD-TIMEY AND OLD-MAIDY LIKE 1536 DIFRNT
WAS.

TIMID
HE LOOKS HORRIBLY TIMID, EMBARRASSED AND GUILTY, 236 AHWILD
JUST NOW SHE IS IN A GREAT THRILLED STATE OF TIMID277 AHWILD
ADVENTUROUSNESS.

TIMID

TIMID (CONT'D.)
(HE PUTS A TIMID ARM AROUND HER AWKWARDLY.) 279 AHWILD
(THERE IS A TIMID KNOCK ON THE DOOR IN REAR. 63 ANNA
IN CONTRAST TO HIS DIFFIDENT, TIMID ATTITUDE OF 457 DYNAMO
BEFORE,
(MECHANICALLY, REACTING INSTINCTIVELY FOR A MOMENT459 DYNAMO
AS THE TIMID BOY OF FORMERLY,
WITH A TIMID LOOK OF MINGLED HAPPINESS AND 468 DYNAMO
APPREHENSION.
BUT TIMID AND 67 ELECTR
(HE TURNS TO THE OBLIVIOUS LARRY--WITH A TIMID 721 ICEMAN
EAGERNESS)
BUT A TIMID LITTLE BOY HIDING FROM LIFE BEHIND MY 135 MANSNS
SKIRTS/
(BUT WHEN SHE GETS TO THE DOOR, SHE APPEARS 97 MISBEG
SUDDENLY HESITANT AND TIMID--
HE'S SO TIMID, HE HASN'T TOLD ME YET, BUT I'LL GET 30 POET
HIM TO SOON.
(PUTS A TIMID HAND ON HIS ARM.) 35 POET
TEMPERAMENTALLY TIMID, HIS DEFENSE IS AN 6 STRANG
ASSUMPTION OF HIS COMPLACENCY.
CHARLIE SITS BESIDE THE FIERCE RIVER, IMMACULATELY 13 STRANG
TIMID, COOL AND CLOTHED.
WHY HAVE YOU ALWAYS BEEN SO TIMID, CHARLIE$ 42 STRANG
(BEGINNING TO ADOPT A TIMID, DIFFIDENT, GUILTY 86 STRANG
TONE)
HAPPINESS HATES THE TIMID/ 86 STRANG
I'VE BEEN A TIMID BACHELOR OF ARTS, NOT AN 148 STRANG
ARTIST/...

TIMIDITIES
(GENTLY) I KNOW THAT AGE AND TIME ARE BUT 354 LAZARU
TIMIDITIES OF THOUGHT.
LUST WITH A LOATHSOME JEER TAUNTING MY SENSITIVE 100 STRANG
TIMIDITIES/...

TIMIDITY
TIMIDITY, DISGUST AT THE MONEY ELEMENT, SHOCKED 241 AHWILD
MODESTY,
A SUDDEN THRILL OF DESIRE OVERCOMES HIS TIMIDITY) 433 DYNAMO
A SURGE OF LOVE AND DESIRE OVERCOMES HIS TIMIDITY 143 ELECTR
AND HE BURSTS OUT)
THIS IS NO TIME FOR TIMIDITY/ 86 STRANG

TIMIDLY
(HESITATING TIMIDLY ON THE EDGE OF THE SHADOW) 278 AHWILD
(DUCKING HER HEAD AWAY--TIMIDLY) 279 AHWILD
(HE PUTS A HAND TO HER FOREHEAD TIMIDLY.) 540 DAYS
HE SPEAKS TIMIDLY AND HESITATINGLY, AS A MUCH 422 DYNAMO
YOUNGER BOY MIGHT.
(STUMBLES TO HER FEET--TIMIDLY.) 34 POET
(AFTER A PAUSE--TIMIDLY.) ALL THE SAME, YOU 62 POET
SHOULDN'T TALK TO SARA
(TIMIDLY.) DON'T BE CURSING HER AND TORMENTING 75 POET
YOURSELF.
(THINKING TIMIDLY) (EIN SHORT, 21 STRANG
(AS IF TO REASSURE HIMSELF--TIMIDLY) 40 STRANG
(TIMIDLY) I'M AFRAID OF--OF LIFE, NINA. 42 STRANG
(THINKING DETERMINEDLY) (IT MUST HAVE MY 86 STRANG
BABY/...) (TIMIDLY--
HE LOOKS AT HER EMBARRASSEDLY, THEN GOES ON 467 WELDED
GENTLY, TIMIDLY PERSUASIVE)

TIMMS
TIMMS IS THE BEST FARM HEREABOUTS. 124 BEYOND
WON'T THEY LAUGH AT YOU JUST THE SAME WHEN YOU'RE 124 BEYOND
WORKING FOR TIMMS$

TIMMS'
AN' I GOT A JOB UP TO TIMMS' PLACE. 124 BEYOND

TIMOROUSLY
(TIMOROUSLY-- ANXIOUS TO CHANGE THE SUBJECT) 351 MARCOM
SAM LOOKS TIMOROUSLY HAPPY, 53 STRANG

TIMOUROUSLY
(HE TREMBLES TIMOUROUSLY--APPEALING TO LAZARUS) 343 LAZARU

TEMPERANCE
WID THE EXCIPSHUN AV OUR TIMPERANCE FRIEND, GOD 500 VOYAGE
PITY HIM/
YE'D BEST STAY HERE, ME TIMPERANCE LADY'S MAN. 504 VOYAGE

TIN
A TIN PAIL FULL OF FOAMING BEER IS IN HIS HAND. 63 ANNA
OR IS IT THINKING I'D BE FRIGHTENED BY THAT OLD 69 ANNA
TIN WHISTLE$
INTO THE BEDROOM--REAPPEARS IMMEDIATELY WITH THE 77 ANNA
TIN CAN OF BEER IN HIS HAND--
ON THE FLOOR NEAR IT, A PAIL WITH A TIN DIPPER. 477 CARDIF
(HE GETS A TIN DIPPER FROM THE BUCKET AND BATHES 483 CARDIF
YANK'S FOREHEAD WITH THE WATER.
AND WHAT'S DAT TIN BOX O' GRUB I HID ALL WRAPPED 189 EJONES
UP IN OIL/
AND NOT CARRY YOURSELF LIKE A TIN SOLDIER 145 ELECTR
WHERE THE ONLY GRAFT HE'LL GET WILL BE STEALING 718 ICEMAN
TIN CANS FROM THE GOATS.
ON THE FLOOR NEAR THE DOORWAY IS A PAIL WITH A TIN513 INZONE
DIPPER.
SMITHY OPENS THE SUITCASE AND TAKES OUT A SMALL 513 INZONE
BLACK TIN BOX.
THEY ALL JUMP NERVOUSLY AS THE TIN CUP HITS THE 517 INZONE
FLOOR WITH A BANG.
AND KNOCKED ONE OF THEM TAIL OVER TIN CUP AGAINST 14 MISBEG
THE PIGPEN.
I'LL TELL HIM WHAT HE CAN DO WITH HIMSELF, HIS 132 MISBEG
BANK-ROLL, AND TIN OIL TANKS.

TINCUP
IF I KNOCK YOU TAIL OVER TINCUP OUT OF THAT CHAIR/ 79 MISBEG

TING
PY GUTT, YANK SAY RIGHT TING/ 213 HA APE
I MEAN DE TING DAT'S DE GUTS OF ALL DIS. 215 HA APE
SURE TING/ 215 HA APE
STEEL, DAT STANDS FOR DE WHOLE TING/ 216 HA APE
I'M DE TING IN COAL DAT MAKES IT BOIN,. 216 HA APE
I'M DE TING IN NOISE DAT MAKES YUH HEAR IT.. 216 HA APE
I'M DE TING IN GOLD DAT MAKES IT MONEY/ 216 HA APE

TING (CONT'D.)
BUT US GUYS, WE'RE IN DE MOVE, WE'RE AT DE BOTTOM,216 HA APE
DE WHOLE TING IS US/
(WITH GROWING ANGER) BUT ONE TING I'M WISE TO, AW231 HA APE
RIGHT/
(VEHEMENTLY) SURE TING I DO/ 234 HA APE
(DEFIANTLY) SURE TING/ 240 HA APE
SHE WAS LIKE SOME DEAD TING DE CAT BRUNG IN. 241 HA APE
(PLEASED) SURE TING. 580 ICEMAN
IF DERE'S ONE TING MOR'N ANUDDER I CARES NUTTIN' 584 ICEMAN
ABOUT,
BUT I SAYS, «SURE TING, HONEY BOY, I'LL BE ONLY 617 ICEMAN
TOO GLAD.»
JEES, ROCKY, DAT'S A FINE HELL OF A TING TO SAY 633 ICEMAN
(SMILING) SURE TING/ 635 ICEMAN
DE FUNNY TING IS, YUH CAN'T STAY SORE AT DE BUM 638 ICEMAN
WHEN HE'S AROUND.
DID YUH NOTICE HIM DRAG JIMMY OUT DE FOIST TING 665 ICEMAN
AND DE FOIST TING I KNOW YUH'LL HAVE ME OUT 671 ICEMAN
HUSTLIN' AGAIN, YOUR OWN WIFE/»
NOT A DAMNED TING. 697 ICEMAN
(EAGERLY) SURE TING, BABY. 723 ICEMAN
MY BROTHER HE WRITE SAME TING TOO. 506 VOYAGE

TING'S
DIS TING'S GOT MY GOAT RIGHT. 231 HA APE
DIS TING'S IN YOUR INSIDE, BUT IT AIN'T YOUR 250 HA APE
BELLY.

TINGE
SEA-SICK TINGE, HIS EYES SEEM TO BE TURNED INWARD 261 AHWILD
UNEASILY--
(PITYINGLY--WITH A TINGE OF SCORN IN HER VOICE) 49 ELECTR
HE WEARS A HALF-MASK OF CRIMSON, DARK WITH A 299 LAZARU
PURPLISH TINGE,
(WITH A TINGE OF SATISFIED SUPERIORITY) 191 STRANG

TINGED
QUIETLY, WITH A MOCKING IRONY TINGED WITH A 148 MANSNS
BITTER, TRAGIC SADNESS.)
HIS EXPRESSION TINGED WITH AN IRONIC HUMOR AND 377 MARCOM
BITTERNESS
ARE FAINTLY TINGED WITH GOLD BY THE FIRST GLOW OF 577 ROPE
SUNSET.
ONE FEELS A POWERFUL IMAGINATION TINGED WITH 443 WELDED
SOMBER SADNESS--

TINGS
DEY'S SOME TINGS I AIN'T GOT TO BE TOLE. 177 EJONES
(WITH NAIVE ADMIRATION) SAY, DEM TINGS IS PRETTY,235 HA APE
HUH$
DEY TURN TINGS ROUND, DO DEY$ 244 HA APE
SO DEY BLOW UP TINGS, DO DEY$ 244 HA APE
YUH WANTER BLOW TINGS UP, DON'T YUH$ 248 HA APE
DAT'LL FIX TINGS/ 249 HA APE
DAT'LL SQUARE TINGS. 249 HA APE
BUT DERE'S TINGS I DON'T TAKE FROM YOU NOR NOBODY,636 ICEMAN
SEE$

TINK
YUST TINK OF IT/ 478 CARDIF
THEY BURY SOMEBODY--PY CHIMINY CHRISTMAS, I TINK 456 CARIBE
SO FROM WAY IT SOUND.
HERE SHE COMES, I TINK. 460 CARIBE
ALL DE RICH GUYS DAT TINK DEY'RE SOMEP'N, THEY 216 HA APE
AIN'T NOTHIN'/
YES, TINK/ 227 HA APE
TINK, DAT'S WHAT I SAID/ 227 HA APE
CAN'T YOUSE SEE I'M TRYIN' TO TINK$ 227 HA APE
TINK I'M GOIN' TO LET HER GIT AWAY WIT DAT STUFF$ 231 HA APE
TINK I WANTER LET HER PUT SOMEP'N OVER ON ME$ 231 HA APE
(ENRAGED) YUH TINK I MADE HER SICK, TOO, DO YUH$ 232 HA APE
I'LL TINK OF A WAY/ 235 HA APE
SAY, WHO D'YUH TINK YUH'RE BUMPIN'$ 237 HA APE
TINK YUH OWN DE OITH$ 237 HA APE
YOUSE GUYS LIVE ON IT AND TINK YUH'RE SOMEP'N. 238 HA APE
«TOITY DAYS TO TINK IT OVER.» 241 HA APE
TINK IT OVER/ 241 HA APE
LEMME TINK. 246 HA APE
(BITTERLY) SO DEM BOIDS DON'T TINK I BELONG. 250 HA APE
NEIDER.
IT BEATS IT WHEN YOU TRY TO TINK IT OR TALK IT-- 253 HA APE
IT'S WAY DOWN--DEEP--BEHIND--
I AIN'T GOT NO PAST TO TINK IN, NOR NOTHIN' DAT'S 253 HA APE
COMIN', ON'Y WHAT'S NOW--
YOU CAN'T TINK, CAN YUH$ 253 HA APE
EVEN HIM DIDN'T TINK I BELONGED. 254 HA APE
JEES, YUH'D TINK HE MEANT IT/ 578 ICEMAN
HELL, YUH'D TINK I WUZ A PIMP OR SOMETHIN'. 580 ICEMAN
YUH'D NEVER TINK ALL DESE BUMS HAD A GOOD BED 580 ICEMAN
UPSTAIRS TO GO TO.
WELL, DON'T TINK I'M INTERESTED IN DIS PARRITT 584 ICEMAN
GUY.
PIANO/ WHAT D'YUH TINK DIS DUMP IS, A DUMP$ 597 ICEMAN
MAYBE YOU TINK WE WASN'T GLAD WHEN DE HOUSE DICK 612 ICEMAN
COME UP.
WAY HE GRABS, YUH'D TINK IT WAS HIM DONE DE WOIK. 613 ICEMAN
I TINK YUH'RE A COUPLA GOOD KIDS. 613 ICEMAN
AND WHAT D'YUH TINK HE SAID$ 616 ICEMAN
WHAT DE HELL YUH TINK I TINK I'M MARRYIN', A 616 ICEMAN
VOIGIN$
(SHE GIGGLES) AND WHAT D'YUH TINK HE DOES$ 617 ICEMAN
YUH'D TINK HE SUSPECTED ME AND CHUCK 631 ICEMAN
YUH'D TINK HE SUSPECTED CHUCK WASN'T GOIN' TO LAY 631 ICEMAN
OFF PERIODICALS--
AND IF YUH TINK WE'RE JUST KIDDIN' OURSELVES, 631 ICEMAN
WE'LL SHOW YUH/»
YUH'D TINK DEY WAS ELEPHANTS/ 632 ICEMAN
YUH MEAN YOU TINK I'M A WHORE, TOO, HUH$ 633 ICEMAN
WHO D'YUH TINK YUH'RE TALKIN' TO$ 633 ICEMAN
WHAT D'YUH TINK I AM$ 633 ICEMAN
YEAH, WHO D'YUH TINK YUH'RE KIDDIN', LARRY$ 666 ICEMAN

TINK

(CONT'D.)
D'YUH MEAN YUH TINK SHE COMMITTED SUICIDE, 'COUNT 668 ICEMAN
OF HIS CHEATIN' OR SOMETHINGS
YUH DON'T TINK IT'S JUST A GAG OF HIS& 668 ICEMAN
A GUY OUGHTA GIVE HIS BRIDE ANYTHING SHE WANTS ON 670 ICEMAN
DE WEDDIN' DAY, I SHOULD TINK/
WHAT'S SHE TINK DIS IS, DE WALDORF& 670 ICEMAN
DON'T TINK YUH CAN KID ME WID DAT WATER-WAGON 671 ICEMAN
BULL/
YUH TINK YUH'RE LEAVIN' HERE, HUH& 675 ICEMAN
BUT I'LL BET YOU TINK YUH'RE GOIN' OUT AND LAND A 676 ICEMAN
JOB, TOO.
YUH'D TINK HE WAS PARALYZED OR SOMETHIN'/ 689 ICEMAN
WHO D'YUH TINK YUH'RE KIDDIN'/ 690 ICEMAN
SCHWARTZ THOUGHT HE WAS DRUNK AND I LET HIM TINK 699 ICEMAN
IT.
YUH'D TINK HE WAS FAZED IF YUH'D SEEN HIM COME IN.699 ICEMAN
WHAT YUH TINK, PARRITT& 702 ICEMAN
ALL DE HUSTLERS TINK YUH'RE ACES. 702 ICEMAN
TINK I KNOW DE NAMES OF ALL DE GUYS--$ 708 ICEMAN
MINE, I TINK. 516 INZONE

TINK'S
WHO D'YUH TINK'S RUNNIN' DIS GAME, ME OR YOU& 224 HA APE
WHAT D'YUH TINK'S HAPPENED TO HIM& 636 ICEMAN

TINKER
BILL TINKER WAS WITH ME AND WE WAS BOTH WISHIN' WES25 DIFRNT
HAD A DRINK.
LIVING LIKE A TRAMP OR A TINKER, AND HIM A RICH 29 POET
GENTLEMAN'S SON.

TINKER'S
I DON'T GIVE A TINKER'S DAMN-- 643 ICEMAN
I DO NOT CARE A TINKER'S DAMN WHAT IT IS IN YOUR 60 MANNS
EYES.

TINKIN'
WHAT'S TINKIN' GOT TO DO WIT ITS 217 HA APE
(CONTEMPTUOUSLY) TINKIN' AND DREAMIN', WHAT'LL 217 HA APE
THAT GET YUH&
DAT'S WHAT YUH'RE TINKIN', HUH& 248 HA APE
AND I KEPT TINKIN'--AND DEN I BEAT IT UP HERE TO 252 HA APE
SEE WHAT YOUSE WAS LIKE.
TINKIN' IS HARD--{HE PASSES ONE HAND ACROSS HIS 253 HA APE
FOREHEAD WITH A PAINFUL GESTURE.
BUT I KIN MAKE A BLUFF AT TALKIN' AND TINKIN'-- 253 HA APE
A'MOST GIT AWAY WIT IT--A'MOST/
ALL I'M TINKIN' IS, FLOWERS IS DAT LOUSE HICKEY'S 630 ICEMAN
STUNT.
SHE SAYS, «YEAH, BUT AFTER A WEEK YUH'LL BE 671 ICEMAN
TINKIN' WHAT A SAP YOU WAS.
I GOT TINKIN', CHRIST. 697 ICEMAN
(IGNORING THIS) I GOT TINKIN', TOO, JEES, 698 ICEMAN

TINKING
I WAS TINKING HOW YOU WAS BOT' REG'LAR GUYS. 702 ICEMAN

TINKLING
FROM THE FRONT PARLOR COMES THE TINKLING OF A 256 AHWILD
PIANO
THE TINKLING OF MANY LITTLE BELLS AND YOUR VOICE. 330 LAZARU

TINKS
HE TINKS WE'RE LOAFIN'. 223 HA APE
I'LL SHOW HER IF SHE TINKS SHE--SHE GRINDS DE 231 HA APE
ORGAN AND I'M ON DE STRING, HUH&
SHE TINKS SHE KIN GET AWAY WITH MOIDER--BUT NOT 235 HA APE
WIT ME/
I TINKS, AIN'T TWO GUYS LIKE DEM SAPS TO BE 702 ICEMAN
HANGIN' ROUND
SO I TINKS, DEY'RE MY PALS AND I OUGHT TO WISE UP 702 ICEMAN
TWO GOOD GUYS LIKE DEM TO PLAY

TINNED
AND I GOT TINNED GRUB BURIED ON DE EDGE O' DE 186 EJONES
FOREST.

TINTED
THE FIFE HOUSE, A SMALL BROWNISH-TINTED MODERN -0 DYNAMO
STUCCO BUNGALOW TYPE,
THE WALLS ARE PLAIN PLASTERED SURFACES TINTED A 28 ELECTR
DULL GRAY
AGAINST THE BACKGROUND OF HORIZON CLOUDS STILL 602 ROPE
TINTED WITH BLURRED CRIMSON SHE

TINY
A BLUNT FORMLESS NOSE AND A TINY SLIT OF A MOUTH. 200 AHWILD
(SHE GIVES HIM A LETTER FOLDED MANY TIMES INTO A 273 AHWILD
TINY SQUARE.
(A TINY BIT AWED AND SHAKEN IN SPITE OF HIMSELF) 185 EJONES
A TINY GALE OF LOW MOCKING LAUGHTER LIKE A 190 EJONES
RUSTLING OF LEAVES.
FROM BEHIND THICK-LENSED SPECTACLES, TINY HANDS 574 ICEMAN
AND FEET.
IN TINY RUFFLES AROUND THE NECK AND SLEEVES, 115 JOURNE
AND HIS BODY ILLUMINED BY A SOFT RADIANCE AS OF 274 LAZARU
TINY PHOSPHORESCENT FLAMES.
HER HANDS ARE SMALL WITH THIN, STRONG, TAPERING 3 MANNS
FINGERS, AND SHE HAS TINY FEET.
UNTIL I SWEAR TO YOU I FELT I COULD BY JUST ONE 102 MANSNS
TINY FURTHER WISH.
I NATURALLY DESIRED ONE PLACE, NO MATTER HOW TINY,110 MANSNS
THAT WOULD BE MINE ALONE.
AS IF THE LEAVES WERE TINY HARPS STRUMMED BY THE 352 MARCOM
WIND.
SHE HAS TINY, HIGH-ARCHED FEET AND THIN, TAPERING 68 POET
HANDS.
HIS MOTHER IS A TINY WOMAN WITH A FRAIL FIGURE, 53 STRANG
HER HEAD AND FACE,
NINA IS IN THE CHAIR AT CENTER, KNITTING A TINY 111 STRANG
SWEATER.

TION
LAVINIA SUDDENLY MAKES A MO TION, AS IF TO HOLD 123 ELECTR
HER BACK.

TIP
(HE TIP TOES TO THE CRADLE AND PEERS DOWN-- 263 DESIRE
PROUDLY)

TIP

(CONT'D.)
HEY, FELLER, TAKE A TIP FROM ME. 242 HA APE
HIS FACE IS ROUND, HIS SNUB NOSE FLATTENED AT THE 8 HUGHIE
TIP.
TAKE MY TIP, PAL. 11 HUGHIE
TAKE MY TIP, PAL, AND DUN'T NEVER TRY TO BUY FROM 27 HUGHIE
A DOPE PEDDLER.
I SAID, «YES, I DO SEE, DICK, AND MANY THANKS FOR 604 ICEMAN
THE TIP.»
UNTIL, AS IT IS FINALLY LOST, HE IS ON TIP-TOES, 371 LAZARU
WHEN I DO GIVE YOU A TIP, WHAT DO I GET FROM POLU 381 MARCOM
BROTHERS&
BUT HERE'S ONE TIP. 34 MISBEG
I WON'T LEAVE THE LAMP LIT FOR YOU TO TIP OVER AND 76 MISBEG
BURN DOWN THE HOUSE.

TIPPED
AND SOMEONE INSIDE THE MOVEMENT MUST HAVE SOLD OUTS88 ICEMAN
AND TIPPED THEM OFF.

TIPS
(HE GIVES HER CHANGE AND SHE TIPS HIM A DIME, AND 243 AHWILD
HE GOES OUT.
IT'S ONE VIVID BLASPHEMY FROM SIDEWALK TO THE TIPS297 GGBROW
OF ITS SPIRES/
HE STOPS BEFORE THE TWO AND TIPS HIS CAP, VISIBLY 220 HA APE
EMBARRASSED AND ILL-AT-EASE.)

TIPSILY
(GRANULY--AND QUITE TIPSILY) 242 AHWILD
(BOLDLY DRAWS HIS CHAIR CLOSER AND PUTS AN ARM 242 AHWILD
AROUND HER--TIPSILY)
(TIPSILY) HE'S TOO--DAMN FRESH/ 247 AHWILD
(TIPSILY) WELL, NOW THAT OUR LITTLE ROBESPIERRE 627 ICEMAN
HAS GOT THE DAILY BIT OF
(A BIT TIPSILY) WHAT'S DAT, BOSS& 722 ICEMAN
(TIPSILY) WELL, I THANK GAWD NOW 723 ICEMAN
(GUILY.) YES, MARY, THE LESS YOU SAY NOW-- (THEN 109 JOURNE
TO EDMUND, A BIT TIPSILY.)
(CHUCKLES TIPSILY, LETTING HIMSELF GO NOW AND BE 158 JOURNE
DRUNK.)

TIPSINESS
FIGHTING IT OUT WITH THE GROWING TIPSINESS 241 AHWILD

TIPSY
(THEN WITH TIPSY GRAVITY) ONLY YOU OUGHTN'T TO 243 AHWILD
LEAD THIS KIND OF LIFE.
CATHLEEN BLINKS HER EYES TO FIGHT OFF DROWSINESS 104 JOURNE
AND A TIPSY FEELING.)
(FIGHTING TIPSY DROWSINESS--SENTIMENTALLY.) 106 JOURNE
(THE SOUNDS MAKE TIPSY AND LOOKS IT.) 130 JOURNE
HE IS HECTICALLY TIPSY. 174 STRANG

TIPTOE
(SHE SUDDENLY RAISES HERSELF ON TIPTOE AND KISSES 433 DYNAMO
HIM--WITH A LITTLE LAUGH)
(HE HAS STEPPED ON TIPTOE INTO THE ROOM AND NOW 462 DYNAMO
SUDDENLY
THEN, MAKING UP HIS MIND, HE STEPS QUICKLY ON 174 EJONES
TIPTOE INTO THE ROOM.
HE APPROACHES THE CORNER OF THE HOUSE STEALTHILY 157 MISBEG
ON TIPTOE.

TIPTOES
THEN TIPTOES OVER TO THE CLOSED DOORS IN REAR 536 'ILE
(TIPTOES OVER TO THE DOOR AND LISTENS) 538 'ILE
SHE HEARS THE VOICE FROM THE ROOM AND TIPTOES TO 121 BEYOND
THE DOOR TO LOOK IN.
(HE TIPTOES TO THE SIDE OF THE BUNK) 479 CARDIF
(HE CLOSES THE DOOR AND TIPTOES CAREFULLY TO THE 562 CRUSS
COMPANIONWAY.
IN THE ROOM ABOVE, EBEN GETS TO HIS FEET AND 251 DESIRE
TIPTOES OUT THE DOOR IN REAR.
SHE TIPTOES TO THE TABLE, LEFT FRONT, 58 ELECTR
(HE TIPTOES AWAY AS IF HE WERE AFRAID OF BEING 161 ELECTR
FOUND CLOSE TO HER
TIPTOES SOFTLY UP TO IT, LISTENS, IS IMPRESSED BY 245 HA APE
THE SILENCE
(AUTOMATICALLY, AS HIS MIND TIPTOES INTO THE NIGHT 20 HUGHIE
AGAIN.)
SCOTTY TIPTOES PAST SMITTY OUT INTO THE 532 INZONE
DARKNESS....
WITH GROWING AMUSEMENT, SHE TIPTOES FORWARD UNTIL 75 MANSNS
SHE STANDS BY HIS TABLE.)
AND MEEKLY TIPTOES PAST HER UP THE STEPS AND GOES 164 MISBEG
IN.

TIRADE
THEN HE INTERRUPTS THE CHANTYMAN'S TIRADE BY A 105 ELECTR
SHARP COMMAND.)
EDMUND HAS LOOKED AWAY FROM HIM, TRYING TO IGNORE 164 JOURNE
THIS TIRADE.)

TIRED
BUT BEHIND THE GLASSES HER GRAY EYES ARE GENTLE 187 AHWILD
AND TIRED.
I WAS GOING ALONG EASY, WITH LOTS IN RESERVE, NOT 230 AHWILD
A BIT TIRED.
(HER FACE SUDDENLY SAD AND TIRED AGAIN-- 259 AHWILD
(A TIRED, HARASSED, DEEPLY WORRIED LOOK ON HIS 262 AHWILD
FACE--SOOTHING HER)
I'M DEAD TIRED. 297 AHWILD
I'M CERTAIN GOD KNOWS I'M TOO DARNED TIRED. 298 AHWILD
SHE GAT TIRED VAIT ALL TIME SVEDEN FOR ME VEN AY 9 ANNA
DON'T NEVER COME.
YOU LOOK LITTLE TIRED, DAT'S ALL. 22 ANNA
TIRED TO DEATH. 22 ANNA
YOU LOOK TIRED, ANNA. 24 ANNA
AND I CAN LICK ALL HANDS ON THIS TUB, WAN BE WAN, 32 ANNA
TIRED AS I AM/
HER FACE IS PALE, LOOKS TERRIBLY TIRED AND WORN, 63 ANNA
I'M SICK AND TIRED OF THE WHOLE DAMN BUSINESS. 107 BEYOND
BUT I'M SICK AND TIRED OF IT--WHETHER YOU WANT TO 107 BEYOND
BELIEVE ME OR NOT--
HE OUGHT TO BE TIRED OF TRAVELIN' 115 BEYOND
AN EAGER EXPRESSION COMES OVER RUTH'S TIRED FACE. 118 BEYOND

TIRED

TIRED (CONT'D.)

MA'S TIRED. 147 BEYOND
AS HE PEEKS OUT HIS BODY SEEMS GRADUALLY TO SAG, 150 BEYOND
TO GROW LIMP AND TIRED.
YOU'RE TIRED OUT, ROB. 162 BEYOND
AND RESTS LIKE TIRED DUST IN CIRCULAR PATCHES UPGN555 CROSS
THE FLOOR AND TABLE.
WOULD YOU BRING HER TIRED SOUL BACK TO HIM AGAIN 565 CROSS
TO BE BRUISED AND WOUNDED$
TIRED OF PRETENDING TO MYSELF I HAVE TO GO ON FOR 519 DAYS
THE CHILDREN'S SAKES.
AND I'M TIRED OF PRETENDING I DON'T MIND, TIRED OF519 DAYS
REALLY MINDING UNDERNEATH.
WELL, DON'T LET YOURSELF GET TIRED NOW, YOU HEAR$ 533 DAYS
I THINK YOU'VE TIRED ELSA OUT WITH YOUR 540 DAYS
SENSATIONAL IMAGININGS, JACK.
HE'S VERY TIRED. 563 DAYS
SHE'D GOT TOO TIRED. 209 DESIRE
SHE'D GOT TOO USED T' BEIN' TOO TIRED. 209 DESIRE
LISTEN, ABBIE--IF YE EVER GIT TIRED O' EBEN, 248 DESIRE
REMEMBER ME/
WELL, I JUST GOT TIRED OF MOPIN' ALONE IN THIS 536 DIFRNT
HOUSE.
I'M TIRED. 470 DYNAMO
HE THROWS HIMSELF ON THE GROUND, DOG-TIRED.) 187 EJONES
LAWD/ I'SE TIRED/ 193 EJONES
(THEN SOLICITOUSLY) YOU MUST BE TERRIBLY TIRED. 47 ELECTR
BUT PROBABLY THAT'S BECAUSE YOU'RE SO TIRED. 49 ELECTR
(DEFIANTLY TO HER MOTHER) HOW CAN YOU TELL HIM HE 49 ELECTR
LOOKS TIRED$
YOU WILL ONLY MAKE YOURSELF MORE TIRED, KEEPING ON 51 ELECTR
YOUR FEET.
I'M TIRED, EZRA. 53 ELECTR
YOUR FATHER IS TIRED. 56 ELECTR
MARGARET SIGHS WITH A TIRED INCOMPREHENSION 273 GGBROW
(FORCING A TIRED SMILE) I SUPPOSE SO, OION. 291 GGBROW
(WITH TIRED SOLICITUDE) I SUPPOSE YOU HAVEN'T 291 GGBROW
EATEN A THING, AS USUAL.
(HE KISSES HER GENTLY) I'M TIRED. 309 GGBROW
(LIKE A SULKY CHILD) I'M TOO TIRED. 320 GGBROW
YOU'RE TIRED. 322 GGBROW
FLAT WHEELED AND TIRED. 25 HUGHIE
AN EXPRESSION OF TIRED TOLERANCE GIVING HIS FACE 574 ICEMAN
THE QUALITY
AND I'M DAMNED TIRED, AND IT CAN'T COME TOO SOON 578 ICEMAN
FOR ME.
HAVEN'T BEEN ABLE TO SLEEP LATELY AND I'M TIRED AS620 ICEMAN
HELL.
I'M A BIT TIRED AND SLEEPY BUT OTHERWISE I FEEL 621 ICEMAN
GREAT.
I'M OLD AND TIRED. 650 ICEMAN
I'S SICK AND TIRED OF MESSIN' ROUND WID WHITE MEN.673 ICEMAN
I'S TIRED OF LOAFIN' 'ROUND WID A LOT OF BUMS. 673 ICEMAN
AND TIRED OF WATCHING THE STUPID GREED OF THE 689 ICEMAN
HUMAN CIRCUS.
HUCKEY'S FACE IS SET IN AN EXPRESSION OF TIRED, 696 ICEMAN
CALLOUS TOUGHNESS.
CORA SPEAKS WITH A TIRED WONDER AT HERSELF RATHER 700 ICEMAN
THAN RESENTMENT TOWARD HIM)
SMITTY AGAIN TRIES TO BREAK LOOSE BUT HE IS TOO 527 INZONE
TIRED
EXCEPT I NATURALLY FEEL TIRED AND NERVOUS THIS 49 JOURNE
MORNING, AFTER SUCH A BAD NIGHT.
SHE WAS TIRED OUT. 56 JOURNE
HE SUDDENLY LOOKS A TIRED, BITTERLY SAD OLD MAN. 67 JOURNE
UH, I'M SO SICK AND TIRED OF PRETENDING THIS IS A 67 JOURNE
HOME/
DOWN HER TIRED FACE.. 148 JOURNE
(DROWSILY.) I'M DOG TIRED. 169 JOURNE
TOO POOR AND TIRED AND UGLY AND OLD TO CARE, TOO 361 LAZARU
SLAVISH--/
SIMON I AM TIRED. 49 MANSNS
HE SEEMED SO NERVOUS AND TIRED OUT AND DISTRACTED,132 MANSNS
(SHARPLY MATTER-OF-FACT.) I'VE EXPLAINED UNTIL 147 MANSNS
I'M TIRED
IT IS SHE WHO IS TIRED OF YOU. 178 MANSNS
HE SIGHS TIRED AND HURT.) 347 MARCOM
(AFTER A PAUSE) YOU ARE TIRED, PRINCESS. 401 MARCOM
CENTURIES WITHER INTO TIRED DUST. 417 MARCOM
THAT'S BECAUSE I SOON GET TIRED OF ANY MAN AND 20 MISBEG
GIVE HIM HIS WALKING PAPERS.
SO YOU'D ACT BOLD FOR A CHANGE INSTEAD OF GIVING 93 MISBEG
HIM BRAZEN TALK HE'S TIRED OF
(SPEAKS IN A TIRED, EMPTY TONE. 143 MISBEG
I KNOW YOU'LL UNDERSTAND THE REASON, AND NOT THINK172 MISBEG
I'M TIRED OF YOUR COMPANY.
(SHE SMILES.) IT HAS BEEN A MOST CONFUSING 86 POET
MORNING FOR A TIRED
AND TO POSSESS, AND ROAM ALONG, THE WORLD'S TIRED 101 POET
DENIZEN.
I'M DEAD TIRED, MOTHER. 131 POET
YOU'RE TIRED ENOUGH-- 160 POET
(HE GRINS.) AND I AIN'T TIRED A BIT. 175 POET
(SHE PAUSES--HER TIRED, WORN FACE BECOMES SUDDENLY181 POET
SHY AND TENDER.)
CHEST THUNDERS WITH EGOTISM AND IS TOO HARD FOR 43 STRANG
TIRED HEADS AND THOROUGHLY
HE IS SPRUCE, DRESSED IMMACULATELY, HIS FACE A BIT 50 STRANG
TIRED AND RESIGNED.
YOU LOOK SO TIRED. 99 STRANG
I'VE GOTTEN OVER-TIRED, I GUESS. 136 STRANG
HOW TIRED... 183 STRANG
(WITH A GUILTY START) I---I'M TIRED OUT. 450 WELDED
(WITH A TIRED SMILE) NO. 469 WELDED
GAWD, I'M TIRED/ 471 WELDED
ITS MOVEMENTS JUST NOW ARE THOSE OF A TIRED 471 WELDED
SCRUBWOMAN.

TIREDLY
HER BODY SAGS TIREDLY. 157 MISBEG

TIREDNESS
IT'S MAN OF YOUR KISSES I'M NEEDING TO TAKE THE 33 ANNA
TIREDNESS FROM ME BONES.
I'M HALF DEAD WITH TIREDNESS AND SLEEPINESS. 162 MISBEG
SHE WAS DROPPIN' WITH TIREDNESS AND DESTROYED WITH135 POET
WORRY.
YOU'RE DESTROYED WITH TIREDNESS, THAT'S ALL. 182 POET

TIRESOME
WELL, MISS MELODY, THIS IS TIRESOME OF ME TO STAND 84 POET
HERE GIVING YOU A DISCOURSE

TIRING
IT'S DAMNED TIRING, THIS WAITING FOR THE END. 615 ICEMAN
IT'S SUCH A TIRING TRIP UPTOWN IN THE DIRTY OLD 92 JOURNE
TROLLEY ON A HOT DAY LIKE THIS.

TIS
TIS ONLY ON THE SEA HE'S FREE, AND HIM ROVING THE 48 ANNA
FACE OF THE WORLD.
(THEN WITH AN AMUSED LAUGH) WELL, TIS A BOLD OLD 50 ANNA
MAN YOU ARE JUST THE SAME.
TIS A QUARE TIME TO JOKE WITH ME, AND DON'T BE 53 ANNA
DOING IT, FOR THE LOVE OF GOD.
TIS MAD YOU ARE, I'M TELLING YOU/ 53 ANNA
TIS THIM RIGHT ENOUGH. 460 CARIBE

TISSUE
I KEPT IT WRAPPED UP IN TISSUE PAPER IN MY TRUNK. 115 JOURNE

TISSUES
OR AN UNGUENT YOU RUB INTO THE SKIN TO REVITALIZE 354 LAZARU
THE OLD BONES AND TISSUES$

TIT
(CHILDISHLY PLEASED--GRATEFULLY GIVING TIT FOR 291 AHWILD
TAT)

TITLE
ONE WAS A BOOK OF HIS PLAYS AND THE OTHER HAD A 197 AHWILD
LUNG TITLE I COULDN'T MAKE HEAD
INSOFAR AS ONE IN TRADE CAN LAY CLAIM TO THE 48 POET
TITLE.
BUT I CAN'T EVEN REMEMBER A TITLE OF ONE...) 29 STRANG

TITLES
AND RUNS HIS EYES OVER THE TITLES OF BOOKS. 545 DAYS
THE TITLES OF THESE BOOKS FACE IN ALL DIRECTIONS, 66 STRANG

TITTER
(ANOTHER TITTER.) 248 DESIRE
(HER REMARK IS REPEATED DOWN THE LINE WITH MANY A 248 DESIRE
GUFFAW AND TITTER UNTIL IT
(THEY ALL TITTER EXPECTANTLY.) 248 DESIRE
(WITH A COQUETTISH TITTER) LAND SAKES, BENNY, 522 DIFRNT
(WITH A TITTER OF DELIGHT) D'YOU KNOW, BENNY, 533 DIFRNT
THE BELLES TITTER BEWITCHINGLY. 197 EJONES
(BORED) SOME NEW WIT OF TIBERIUS, NATURALLY-- 314 LAZARU
(WITH A MEANING TITTER) -- 315 LAZARU
(A TITTER OF LAUGHTER.)

TU'S
IT'S WHEN YOU DON'T GIVE A THOUGHT FOR ALL THE 25 POET
IF'S AND WANT-TO'S IN THE WORLD/

TOAD
(HURLING HIS CAP AT PAUL) FASTER, YE TOAD/ 471 CARIBE
(SCORNFULLY) ARE YE FRIGHTENED, YE TOADS 520 INZONE

TOAST
HE HAD SWEETBREADS ON TOAST. 254 AHWILD
GRINS UP AT HER, AND DRINKS TO HER TOAST.) 78 ANNA
HERE'S THE TOAST, LADIES AND GENTS/ 658 ICEMAN
BUT I WANT TO BE SOCIABLE AND PROPOSE A TOAST IN 658 ICEMAN
HONOR OF OUR OLD FRIEND, HARRY.
HE STARTS HIS TOAST. 658 ICEMAN
A TOAST, TOAST, NEIGHBORS/ 279 LAZARU
(ECHOING THEM) A TOAST/ 279 LAZARU
(IN A FORCED ECHO) A TOAST/ 279 LAZARU
CARRYING A TRAY WITH TOAST, EGGS, BACON, AND TEA. 55 POET
THE DIVIL WAS IN THE TOAST. 55 POET
(CORRECTING HIS TOAST WITH EMPHASIS.) 96 POET
I'LL TOAST HIM ON THAT. 100 POET
ALL THE SAME, I THANK YOU FOR YOUR TOAST. 101 POET
THEN MELODY'S VOICE IS PLAINLY HEARD IN THE 180 POET
SILENCE AS HE SHOUTS A TOAST..
A TOAST FOR YE... 497 VOYAGE
ANY I'LL STRIP TO ANY MAN IN THE CITY AV LONDON 498 VOYAGE
WON'T DHRINK TO THAT TOAST.
'ERE'S A TOFF TOAST FOR YER.. 501 VOYAGE
'ERE'S A TOAST FUR YER... 507 VOYAGE
(WITH FEIGNED INDIGNATION) DOWN'T YER LIKE MY 507 VOYAGE
TOAST$

TOASTS
(THEY ALL JOIN IN WITH THE USUAL HUMOROUS TOASTS.1620 ICEMAN
THERE'LL BE SOME DRINKING AND TOASTS FIRST, OF 643 ICEMAN

TOBACCO
THEIR SHARE O' THE FOUR HUNDRED BARREL WOULDN'T 542 'ILE
KEEP 'EM IN CHEWIN' TOBACCO.
(HE OSTENTATIOUSLY TAKES FROM HIS POCKET A TOBACCO187 AHWILD
POUCH WITH A BIG Y AND CLASS
AND THE AIR IS HEAVY WITH RANCID TOBACCO SMOKE. 477 CARDIF
DON'T YOU BOYS FORGET TO MARK DOWN CIGARETTES OR 465 CARIBE
TOBACCO OR FRUIT, REMEMBER/
BUT IN REALITY HE IS MERELY KILLING TIME, CHEWING 169 ELECTR
(DRISCOLL TAKES A BLACK RUBBER BAG RESEMBLING A 528 INZONE
LARGE TOBACCO POUCH FROM THE BOX
(TAKES A CLAY PIPE AND PLUG OF TOBACCO AND KNIFE 15 MISBEG
FROM HIS POCKET.
HE PULLS OUT TOBACCO AND A PAPER AND ROLLS A 593 ROPE
CIGARETTE AND LIGHTS IT.

TOBACCY
YE MUST WRITE DOWN TOBACCY OR FRUIT OR SOMETHIN' 463 CARIBE
THE LOIKE AV THAT.

TODAY
THEY SAID IF HE DON'T PUT BACK SOUTH FOR HOME 537 'ILE
TODAY THEY'RE GOIN' TO MUTINY.

1677 — TOGETHER

TODAY (CONT'D.)

THE TWO YEARS THEY SIGNED UP FOR IS UP TODAY. 539 'ILE
BEST NOT TODAY, ANNIE. 540 'ILE
(FROWNING) BEST NOT TODAY, ANNIE. 540 'ILE
YOU'D BEST STAY BELOW TODAY. 540 'ILE
AND THE TWO YEARS THEY SIGNED ON FUR IS UP TODAY. 541 'ILE
I COULD SEE IT STARTIN' TODAY. 542 'ILE
THE TIME WE SIGNED UP FOR IS DONE TODAY. 544 'ILE
WHERE ARE YOU GOING TODAY, ARTS 187 AHWILD
WELL, WHAT'S ON THE TAPPEE FOR ALL OF YOU TODAYS 189 AHWILD
OH, I KNOW HE'LL BE CAREFUL TODAY. WON'T YOU, SIUS190 AHWILD
WHAT WERE YOU PLANNING TO DO WITH YOURSELF TODAYS 196 AHWILD
THE GREATEST PLAYWRIGHT ALIVE TODAY/ 197 AHWILD
BUT WHAT MADE ME BREAK IT OFF IS AS CLEAR TO ME 213 AHWILD
TODAY AS IT WAS THEN.
(THEN LAUGHINGLY) WE DID HAVE THE DARNDEST FUN 223 AHWILD
TODAY/
I THOUGHT YOU WERE THE ORIGINAL OF THE HEART BOWED228 AHWILD
DOWN TODAY.
SHE WAS IN WADING TODAY. 230 AHWILD
=CAN'T GET AWAY TO MARRY YOU TODAY, MY WIFE WON'T 259 AHWILD
LET ME/=
I'VE A WHOLE PILE OF THINGS THAT HAVE GOT TO BE 263 AHWILD
DONE TODAY/
DON'T KNOW WHAT'S THE MATTER WITH ME TODAY. 264 AHWILD
YOU KNOW AS WELL AS I DO HE NEEDS ALL THE SLEEP HE268 AHWILD
CAN GET TODAY--
REMEMBER, YOU'RE NOT ALLOWED OUT TODAY--FOR A 271 AHWILD
PUNISHMENT.
THEN I CHANGED MY MIND AND DECIDED NOT TO GO 64 ANNA
TODAY.
I SIGNED ON TODAY AT NOON, DRUNK AS I WAS--AND 72 ANNA
SHE'S SAILING TOMORROW.
THE SUN'S HOT TODAY/ 119 BEYOND
MY MONTHS UP TODAY AND I WANT WHAT'S GWIN' T' ME.124 BEYOND
(GENTLY) NO, DEAR, NOT TODAY. 129 BEYOND
DADA DOESN'T FEEL LIKE PLAYING TODAY. 129 BEYOND
(RUEFULLY) SEEMS IF I PUT MY FOOT IN IT WHENEVER139 BEYOND
I OPEN MY MOUTH TODAY.
EVERYBODY HEREABOUTS SEEMS TO BE ON EDGE TODAY. 140 BEYOND
I COULDN'T WORK TODAY. 267 DESIRE
I'M QUITTIN' HERE TODAY/ 267 DESIRE
GEE, MA, YOU OUGHTA SEE HER TODAY. 529 DIFRNT
THAT SCOUNDREL CALLED SOMETHING AT ME ON THE 425 DYNAMO
STREET TODAY.
I GAVE HIM A STRONG HINT ON THE STREET TODAY THAT 432 DYNAMO
UPSET HIM.
DON'T YER NOTICE NOTHIN' FUNNY TODAYS 176 EJONES
AIN'T NOTICED ANY OF THE GUARDS OR SERVANTS ABOUT 181 EJONES
THE PLACE TODAY, I 'AVEN'T.
SOMETHING I'D MADE UP MY MIND TO ASK YOU TODAY. 14 ELECTR
HE SAID HE WAS COMING UP HERE TODAY TO TAKE OVER 17 ELECTR
HIS SHIP
YOU'RE PUZZLING TODAY, MISS LAVINIA. 22 ELECTR
MARRY ME TODAY, PETER/ 176 ELECTR
TODAY WAS A NARROW ESCAPE--FOR US/ 307 GGBROW
(CAREFULLY CASUAL) I HEAR YOU WERE IN TO SEE ME 310 GGBROW
TODAYS
THE ELDEST WAS SAYING TO ME TODAY.. 310 GGBROW
OH, SOMETHING THAT HAPPENED TODAY. 311 GGBROW
HE FINISHED IT TODAY. 316 GGBROW
THIS IS DADDY'S BEDTIME SECRET FOR TODAY.. 318 GGBROW
YOU SEEM TO BE GOING IN FOR SINCERITY TODAY. 219 HA APE
I BEEN READIN' ABOUT 'EM TODAY IN THE PAPER. 242 HA APE
(HE READS) = THERE IS A MENACE EXISTING IN THIS 242 HA APE
COUNTRY TODAY WHICH THREATENS
HERE TODAY, GONE TOMORROW, SO WHAT'S THE GOOD OF 18 HUGHIE
BEEFIN'S
DOWN TODAY AND UP TOMORROW. 37 HUGHIE
YES, IT'S TODAY AT LAST, JIMMY. 655 ICEMAN
AND I MEAN IT WHEN I SAY I HOPE TODAY WILL BE THE 659 ICEMAN
BIGGEST DAY IN YOUR LIFE.
YOU'LL BE IN A TUDAY WHERE THERE IS NO YESTERDAY 661 ICEMAN
OR TOMORROW TO WORRY YOU.
I'LL GOT DE MONEY FOR MY STAKE TODAY, SOMEHOW, 673 ICEMAN
SOMEWHERES/
BUT IT MIGHT AS WELL BE TODAY, I SUPPOSE. 684 ICEMAN
HE'S TO PHONE ME TODAY BEFORE EDMUND GOES TO HIM. 30 JOURNE
WELL, IF WE'RE GOING TO CUT THE FRONT HEDGE TODAY, 39 JOURNE
WE'D BETTER GO TO WORK.
BUT YOU FEEL BETTER TODAY, DON'T YOU$ 42 JOURNE
YOU MUSTN'T LET YOURSELF BE TOO DOWNHEARTED, LAD, 143 JOURNE
BY THE BAD NEWS YOU HAD TODAY.
TOO MANY DAMNED THINGS HAVE HAPPENED TODAY. 157 JOURNE
A LORD WHO IS IN THE COMMON PRISON AT JERUSALEM, 1284 LAZARU
HEARD TODAY/
WHO APPEARED TODAY WITH THAT CHARLATAN. 316 LAZARU
I WAS WONDERING IF YOU WOULD BRING HER WITH YOU 7 MANSNS
TODAY.
SHE IS GOING TO DISCOVER, BEGINNING TODAY, AND 73 MANSNS
SARA, TOO, THAT WHENEVER I WISH,
I CONCLUDED A DEAL TODAY WHICH ADDS A RAILROAD TO 100 MANSNS
THE COMPANY'S PROPERTIES.
BUT I AM FORGETTING I ARRANGED ALL THAT TODAY. 131 MANSNS
AND WHEN I THINK OF ALL HE'S DONE TODAY TO MAKE US134 MANSNS
HATE EACH OTHER--I
BUT I HAVE TO RUN DOWN TO THE MILLS TODAY. 146 MANSNS
THEN IT MUST BE THE AIR ITSELF SMELLS OF WHISKEY 45 MISBEG
TODAY.
PLEASE DON'T THROW ME TODAY, DARLIN', AND I'LL 58 MISBEG
GIVE YOU AN EXTRA BUCKET OF OATS.
ANYTHING GOES TODAY. 65 MISBEG
I'M LEAVING YOU TODAY, LIKE MY BROTHERS LEFT. 164 MISBEG
YOU'D LEAVE HIM TODAY, IF YOU HAD ANY PRIDE/ 25 POET
TODAY IS THE 27TH/ 38 POET
YOU'VE NEVER MISSED CELEBRATIN' IT AND YOU WON'T 38 POET
TODAY.
ABSTEMIOUS TODAY. 46 POET

TODAY (CONT'D.)

LOST IN MEMORIES OF A GLORIOUS BATTLE IN SPAIN, 58 POET
NINETEEN YEARS AGO TODAY.
TODAY OF ALL DAYS IT IS HARD TO FORGET, 71 POET
WHY DID SHE HAVE TO COME TODAYS 77 POET
I MUSTN'T LET HIM SEE--BUT I WON'T GO TO HIM AGAIN 88 POET
TODAY, MOTHER.
OUR IMPOTENT POSE OF TODAY TO BEAT THE LOUD DRUM 5 STRANG
ON FORNICATION/....
TODAY I'VE MADE UP MY MIND TO FACE THINGS. 20 STRANG
I WISH I HADN'T COME HERE TODAY/...)) 20 STRANG
HOW DO YOU FEEL TODAYS 97 STRANG
I CAME OUT TODAY TO SAY GOOD-BYE. 106 STRANG
HE MUST HAVE KNOWN IT TODAY WHEN HE SAID HE LOVED 108 STRANG
ME....)
TAKE TODAY, FOR INSTANCE. 144 STRANG
I'M NOT THE SLIGHTEST BIT INTERESTED IN THIS RACE 167 STRANG
TODAY, FOR EXAMPLE/
GORDON REALLY SHOULD GET BEATEN TODAY--FOR THE 175 STRANG
GOOD OF HIS SOUL, NINA.
WE OTHERS HAVE GOT TO BEAT HIM TDAY/ 175 STRANG
TODAY'S
WHY, YOU POOR FISH, THAT MURDER STORY IS IN 451 DYNAMO
TODAY'S STAR--

TOE

(HE STANDS NEAR THE PATH, LEFT, KICKING AT THE 140 BEYOND
GRASS WITH THE TOE OF HIS SHOE.
AND SURVEY HER INSOLENTLY FROM HEAD TO TOE. 68 POET

TOES

AND ROT-TEN PO-TAY-TOES/ 481 CARDIF
I'M MORE OUT WITH YOU STEPPIN' ON MY TOES, YOU 471 CARIBE
CLUMSY MICK.
(THE TIP TOES TO THE CRADLE AND PEERS DOWN-- 263 DESIRE
PROUDLY)
(HE LOOKS DOWN AT HIS FEET, WORKING HIS TOES 196 EJONES
INSIDE THE SHOES--WITH A GROAN)
WITH HIS BIG TOES STICKING OUT OF THE UPPERS. 577 ICEMAN
UNTIL, AS IT IS FINALLY LOST, HE IS ON TIP-TOES, 371 LAZARU
THAT SHRANK BACK, STAMPING ON ITS OWN TOES. 30 MANSNS

TOFF

NOT LIKE ANY TUFF AS I EVER MET UP WIV. 522 INZONE
HE DON'T TALK EXACTLY LIKE A TOFF, DOES HE, COCKYS522 INZONE
=ERE'S A TOFF TOAST FUR YER.. 501 VOYAGE

TOGA

(HE REACHES OUT AND PULLS BACK THE TOGA FROM HIS 339 LAZARU
FACE.
(HE DRAWS HIS TOGA OVER HIS FACE.) 339 LAZARU

TOGEDDER

ALL TOGEDDER NOW/ 224 HA APE
ALL TOGEDDER NOW--ONE--TWO-- 243 HA APE

TOGETHER

(THE MEN STAND HUDDLED TOGETHER IN A SULLEN 544 'ILE
SILENCE.
RUBBING HIS HANDS TOGETHER GENIALLY) 223 AHWILD
IT SEEMS AGES SINCE WE'VE BEEN TOGETHER/ 279 AHWILD
(HE KISSES HER TREMBLINGLY AND FOR A MOMENT THEIR 287 AHWILD
LIPS REMAIN TOGETHER.
(THEN RUBBING HIS HANDS TOGETHER--WITH A BOYISH 292 AHWILD
GRIN OF PLEASURE)
AND WINTER--IF YOU'RE TOGETHER. 298 AHWILD
IN THROUGH THE SCREEN DOOR, WALKING TOGETHER 298 AHWILD
TOWARD THE FRONT PARLOR
THEY DRINK DOWN HALF THE CONTENTS AND START TO 4 ANNA
TALK TOGETHER HURRIEDLY IN LOW
BEAUTIFUL LIFE TOGETHER TO THE END OF OUR DAYS/ 52 ANNA
(HE STANDS WRINGING HIS HANDS TOGETHER AND BEGINS 59 ANNA
TO WEEP.)
WHILE WE'VE ALWAYS BEEN TOGETHER--JUST THE TWO OF 83 BEYOND
US.
ANDY AND YOU AND I--WHY IT SEEMS AS IF WE'D ALWAYS 88 BEYOND
BEEN TOGETHER.
AND IT AND I WOULD FIND THE SEA TOGETHER. 89 BEYOND
(MYSTIFIED) BUT YOU AND ANDY WERE ALWAYS 91 BEYOND
TOGETHER/
WE'LL BE SO HAPPY HERE TOGETHER WHERE IT'S NATURAL 92 BEYOND
AND WE KNOW THINGS.
THERE'D BE BOUND TO BE SUCH A SCENE WITH THEM ALL 92 BEYOND
TOGETHER.
(TO SCOTT) DICK, YOU WOULDN'T BELIEVE HOW THEM 97 BEYOND
BUYS O' MINE STICKS TOGETHER.
I ALWAYS SORTER HOPED THEY'D HITCH UP TOGETHER 98 BEYOND
SOONER OR LATER.
THEY'RE ALWAYS TOGETHER. 98 BEYOND
JINED TOGETHER THEY'D MAKE A JIM-DANDY OF A PLACE, 98 BEYOND
AND WATCH YOU TWO TOGETHER, DAY AFTER DAY--AND ME 110 BEYOND
ALONE.
BUT RUTH AND ROBERT SEEM HAPPY ENOUGH TOGETHER. 116 BEYOND
WHY CAN'T WE PULL TOGETHER$ WE USED TO. 123 BEYOND
I WAS SORRY FOR IT BEFORE WE'D BEEN TOGETHER A 127 BEYOND
MONTH.
SO'S WE THREE CAN BE TOGETHER SAME'S YEARS AGO, 139 BEYOND
TO GREET THE DAWN OF A NEW LIFE TOGETHER. 150 BEYOND
AND YOU'VE LIVED TOGETHER FOR FIVE YEARS WITH THIS165 BEYOND
BETWEEN YOUS
AND WE'VE STUCK TOGETHER IVER SINCE THROUGH GOOD 480 CARDIF
LUCK AND BAD.
TWO OF THE MEN START DANCING TOGETHER, 471 CARIBE
INTENTIONALLY BUMPING INTO THE OTHERS.
WE'LL GO AWAY WITH IT TOGETHER. 572 CROSS
I PROPOSED QUITE FRANKLY THAT WE SHOULD SIMPLY 523 DAYS
LIVE TOGETHER AND EACH KEEP
THEY STAND TOGETHER FOR A MOMENT IN FRONT OF THE 204 DESIRE
HOUSE AND,
(TOGETHER) AYEH. 205 DESIRE
(TOGETHER) AY-EH. 205 DESIRE
(TOGETHER) IN CALIFORNI-A/ 205 DESIRE
THEIR BODIES BUMPING AND RUBBING TOGETHER AS THEY 206 DESIRE
HURRY CLUMSILY TO THEIR FOOD,

TOGETHER

TOGETHER (CONT'D.)
HE'S STRONGER--INSIDE--THAN BOTH O' YE PUT 210 DESIRE
TOGETHER/
HIS EYES ARE SMALL, CLOSE TOGETHER, AND EXTREMELY 221 DESIRE
NEARSIGHTED,
LEAPING UP AND CRACKING HIS HEELS TOGETHER, 251 DESIRE
THEY KISS--THEN BEND OVER THE CRADLE TOGETHER) 252 DESIRE
YOU'VE BOTH THE WHOLE PACK OF 'EM PUT TOGETHER. 496 DIFRNT
PLAYIN' TOGETHER. 507 DIFRNT
EVER SINCE YOU WAS CHILDREN YOU BEEN LIVIN' SIDE 512 DIFRNT
BY SIDE, GOIN' ROUND TOGETHER.
(HE PRESSES HIS LIPS TIGHTLY TOGETHER AN EFFORT TO423 DYNAMO
APPEAR IMPLACABLE THAT GIVES
UNDER HIS ARM HE CARRIES SIX BOOKS, BOUND TOGETHER457 DYNAMO
WITH A STRAP.)
ALL EXCHANGE COURTLY GREETINGS IN DUMB SHOW AND 196 EJONES
CHAT SILENTLY TOGETHER.
"LET'S A BETTER MAN THAN THE LOT O' YOU PUT 203 EJONES
TOGETHER.
WERE LITTLE AND STARTED PLAYING TOGETHER--YOU AND 14 ELECTR
URLIN AND HAZEL AND I.
THE LEGS CLOSE TOGETHER, THE SHOULDERS SQUARE, THE 43 ELECTR
HEAD UPRIGHT.
IT'S EVIDENTLY TRYING TO PULL HIMSELF TOGETHER. 44 ELECTR
I'VE A NOTION IF WE'D LEAVE THE CHILDREN AND GO 55 ELECTR
OFF ON A VOYAGE TOGETHER--TO THE
MRS. BURDEN AND MRS. HILLS WALK TOGETHER 68 ELECTR
OH, HOW HAPPY WE'LL BE TOGETHER, YOU AND I, 86 ELECTR
WILL YOU BELIEVE ME WHEN YOU FIND THEM TOGETHER5 99 ELECTR
WRINGING HER HANDS TOGETHER IN STRICKEN ANGUISH. 121 ELECTR
AND FIND PEACE TOGETHER? 165 ELECTR
HER ARMS HELD STIFFLY TO HER SIDES, HER LEGS AND 170 ELECTR
FEET PRESSED TOGETHER.
THEN SEES LAVINIA AND IMMEDIATELY MAKES AN EFFORT 174 ELECTR
TO PULL HIMSELF TOGETHER AND
SAY, LET'S YOU AND ME ROOM TOGETHER AT COLLEGE-- 266 GGBROW
TOGETHER, MY FRIEND/ 319 GGBROW
AND THE SEA JOINED ALL TOGETHER AND MADE IT ONE. 214 HA APE
THEY HESITATE AND STAND TOGETHER AT THE CORNER, 233 HA APE
SWAGGERING.
AFTER THAT, I COULDA MADE 'EM ONE AT A TIME OR ALL 36 HUGHIE
TOGETHER/
THE BACK ROOM IS CRAMMED WITH ROUND TABLES AND 573 ICEMAN
CHAIRS PLACED SO CLOSE TOGETHER
GET TOGETHER WITH THE BOYS. 604 ICEMAN
IT'S ALWAYS FAIR WEATHER, WHEN GOOD FELLOWS GET 619 ICEMAN
TOGETHER/
THE LAST TIME WE GOT PARALYZED TOGETHER HE TOLD 627 ICEMAN
ME--
AT CENTER, FRONT, FOUR OF THE CIRCULAR TABLES ARE 628 ICEMAN
PUSHED TOGETHER TO FORM ONE
(MOSHER AND MCGLOIN ENTER TOGETHER FROM THE HALL. 651 ICEMAN
(THEY ADVANCE, THEIR HEADS TOGETHER, 651 ICEMAN
BEHIND THIS, HE IS SICK AND FEEBLY HOLDING HIS 675 ICEMAN
BULGE-SODDEN BODY TOGETHER.)
WE WENT OUT TO CHURCH TOGETHER. 688 ICEMAN
BEJEES, WE'LL GO ON A GRAND OLD SOUSE TOGETHER/ 690 ICEMAN
ARE NOW ARMED SO CLOSELY TOGETHER THAT THEY FORM 696 ICEMAN
ONE GROUP.
TAKE OUT THEIR CUPS AND SPOONS, AND SIT DOWN 514 INZONE
TOGETHER ON THE BENCHES.
MARY TYRONE AND HER HUSBAND ENTER TOGETHER FROM 12 JOURNE
THE BACK PARLOR,
(THEIR SONS JAMES, JR., AND EDMUND ENTER TOGETHER 19 JOURNE
FROM THE BACK PARLOR.
AS THE CURTAIN RISES, HE FINISHES A GAME AND 125 JOURNE
SWEEPS THE CARDS TOGETHER.
OVER THE SKY AND SEA WHICH SLEPT TOGETHER. 153 JOURNE
SING ALL ONCE MORE TOGETHER. 174 JOURNE
THEY ALL LISTEN, HUDDLED TOGETHER LIKE SHEEP.) 290 LAZARU
(RATHER SHAMEFACEDLY PULLS HIMSELF TOGETHER--THEN 303 LAZARU
BROODINGLY)
HIS TEETH CAN BE HEARD CHATTERING TOGETHER IN 358 LAZARU
NERVOUS FEAR.
(BEWILDERED-- BUT WHY DON'T WE WALK TOGETHER AS 17 MANSNS
FAR AS THE ROADS
I HAVE KNOWN HENRY SINCE WE WERE BOYS TOGETHER. 31 MANSNS
(THEY LAUGH AMUSEDLY TOGETHER--THEN STOP ABRUPTLY 61 MANSNS
AND STARE AT EACH OTHER.)
HAVE TO LIVE TOGETHER IN THE SAME HOME DAY AFTER 67 MANSNS
DAY.
AS I WATCHED YOU TOGETHER IN THE HOUSE AT NIGHT, 105 MANSNS
AND THE PARTS WE MARKED TOGETHER, 107 MANSNS
(HE JOINS IN HERE AND THEY BOTH FINISH TOGETHER.) 108 MANSNS
AND WE WILL GO TOGETHER-- 113 MANSNS
LET US GO IN--TOGETHER. 114 MANSNS
(THINKING.) THEY DO NOT SIT TOGETHER ON THE SOFA 118 MANSNS
AS HAS BEEN THEIR WONT--
WE WOULD LAUGH TOGETHER, THINKING OF THE 120 MANSNS
CHILDREN--
SHE AND I WOULD BE SITTING TOGETHER ON THE SOFA, 120 MANSNS
THEY GROUP TOGETHER IN BACK OF HIM, 128 MANSNS
(THEY LAUGH SOFTLY TOGETHER.) 135 MANSNS
WE MUST STAY HERE TOGETHER, TRUSTING EACH OTHER, 170 MANSNS
OH GOD, THINK OF HOW SIMPLY CONTENTED WE COULD BE 171 MANSNS
ALONE TOGETHER.
ALL THEY HAVE TO DO IS TO WAIT TOGETHER AND STAND 173 MANSNS
APART.
(HE BEGINS TO SOB EXHAUSTEDLY--THE TWO WOMEN SIT 174 MANSNS
TOGETHER,
LET US SIT DOWN AND REST FOR A MOMENT TOGETHER 176 MANSNS
THEN.
WE WILL GO TOGETHER SO FAR AWAY FROM THE REALITY 181 MANSNS
THE POLOS GROUP TOGETHER IN THE FOREGROUND, 362 MAHCOM
HOLDING A WHISPERED CONFERENCE.
(THE FOUR SQUAT TOGETHER IN A CIRCLE.) 366 MARCOM
WELL, I AM SURE YOU WISH TO CELEBRATE THIS FAMILY 382 MARCOM
TRIUMPH TOGETHER,

TOGETHER (CONT'D.)
I GRIEVE FOR THE DAYS WHEN WE LINGERED TOGETHER IN384 MARCOM
THIS SAME GARDEN,
THEIR VOICES RISE TOGETHER IN A LONG, RHYTHMIC 433 MARCOM
WAIL OF MOURNING.
DID WE NOT ONCE PLAY SUCH GAMES TOGETHER, YOU AND 437 MARCOM
I5
TOGETHER TILL AFTER THE COWLEYS HAD HIM A DAY OR 14 MISBEG
TWO.
YOU AND ME HAVE NEVER BEEN BEAT WHEN WE PUT OUR 30 MISBEG
BRAINS TOGETHER.
I'D LIKE BOTH OF THEM TO CALL TOGETHER. 49 MISBEG
(THEY ALL LAUGH TOGETHER. 65 MISBEG
BUT AT THE SAME TIME ARE ABLE TO PULL THEMSELVES 72 MISBEG
TOGETHER WHEN THEY WISH AND BE
HAVING A DRINK TOGETHER/ 90 MISBEG
YOU SEEMED TO ENJOY IT THE WHILE WE WERE SITTING 168 MISBEG
HERE TOGETHER
AND ME WITH THE SIDES OF MY STOMACH KNOCKING 176 MISBEG
TOGETHERS
MICKEY CAN'T PUT TWO AND TWO TOGETHER WITHOUT 26 POET
MAKING FIVE.
BUT WILL BE CONTENT WITH LITTLE AND LIVE IN PEACE 29 POET
AND FREEDOM TOGETHER.
AND PATCH RILEY ATTEMPT TO PILE IN TOGETHER 51 POET
YOU CAN MATCH TONGUES TOGETHER. 114 POET
SOON WE'D GET MARRIED, AND HOW HAPPY WE'D BE THE 147 POET
REST OF OUR LIVES TOGETHER.
I REMEMBER YOU AND ME USED TO GIT ON FINE 588 ROPE
TOGETHER--LIKE HELL/
WHY DON'T YOU JUST GO ON BEING HAPPY TOGETHER, 57 STRANG
JUST YOU TWO5
WOULD BRING US ALONE TOGETHERS... 74 STRANG
HE SEES THEIR TWO HANDS TOGETHER BUT MISTAKES 104 STRANG
THEIR MEANING.)
I GATHERED THEY WERE LIVING TOGETHER. 115 STRANG
(HE COMES, PUTS HIS ARM ABOUT HER WAIST, KISSES 119 STRANG
HER AND THEY GO OUT TOGETHER.)
WHAT HAS BOUND US TOGETHER ALL THESE YEARS5... 138 STRANG
WE SIT TOGETHER IN SILENCE, THINKING.... 139 STRANG
OUR LOVE HAS BECOME THE INTIMATE THINKING TOGETHER139 STRANG
WELL, WHATEVER IT IS THAT HAS BOUND US TOGETHER, 139 STRANG
IT'S STRONG/...
(HE PUTS HIS ARM ABOUT HER WAIST AND THEY GO OUT 149 STRANG
TOGETHER LAUGHINGLY.
THEY ALL LAUGH HAPPILY TOGETHER.) 156 STRANG
WE CAN TALK TOGETHER OF THE OLD DAYS.... 191 STRANG
CLOSING OUR LIFE TOGETHER WITH THAT SMILE... 191 STRANG
WE'LL PICK FLOWERS TOGETHER IN THE AGING 200 STRANG
AFTERNOONS OF SPRING AND SUMMER,
TO BE IN LOVE WITH PEACE TOGETHER--TO LOVE EACH 200 STRANG
OTHER'S PEACE.
TO SLEEP WITH PEACE TOGETHER--/ 200 STRANG
THEY WHISPER TOGETHER EXCITEDLY.) 504 VOYAGE
WAS ONLY OUR PAST TOGETHER I WANTED TO REMEMBER. 447 WELDED
(SHE KISSES HIM) DO YOU REMEMBER--OUR FIRST NIGHT447 WELDED
TOGETHER5
YOU AND I--YEAR AFTER YEAR-TOGETHER--FORMS OF OUR 448 WELDED
BODIES MERGING INTO ONE FORM..
(AFTER A PAUSE--SOMBERLY) YOU MENTIONED OUR YEARS455 WELDED
TOGETHER AS PROOF--
FIRST LIVED TOGETHER--JEALOUS AND SUSPICIOUS OF 456 WELDED
EVERYTHING AND EVERYBODY/
OUR LIFE IS TO BEAR TOGETHER OUR BURDEN WHICH IS 488 WELDED
OUR GOAL--ON AND UP/
FOR A MOMENT AS THEIR HANDS TOUCH THEY FORM 489 WELDED
TOGETHER ONE CROSS.

TOGS
THAT'S WHY I DRESSED UP IN THESE TOGS. 135 BEYOND

TOID
YOUSE NEEDN'T PUT ME TROU DE TOID DEGREE. 247 HA APE

TOIL
NARY A TOIL 'R SPIN 'R LICK O' WUK DO WE PUT IN/ 216 DESIRE
BUT STOOP-SHOULDERED FROM TOIL. 221 DESIRE
IN THE TOIL OF TIDES. 409 MARCOM

TOILET
IS THE TOILET WITH A SIGN =THIS IS IT= ON THE 573 ICEMAN
DOOR.
(TRIES TO IGNORE THIS.) I HAVE TO GET TOOTH 86 JOURNE
POWDER AND TOILET SOAP AND COLD
ONE CANNOT MAKE A DECENT TOILET IN THAT DINGY HOLE 44 POET

TOILING
SLAVING AND TOILING AS USUAL, I SEE. 39 MISBEG

TOIME
TRYIN' TO LOOK AS WISE AS AN OWL ON A TREE, AND 479 CARDIF
ALL THE TOIME HE NOT
AND MANY'S THE TOIME I'D A BEEN ON THE BEACH OR 480 CARDIF
WORSE, BUT FOR HIM.
JUST ABOUT THIS TOIME UT WAS, TOO. 481 CARDIF
WHEA I'M HAVIN' THE SAME THOUGHTS MYSELF, TOIME 487 CARDIF
AFTHER TOIME.
THAT LAD'S NOT WASTIN' ANY TOIME. 463 CARIBE

TOIN
CALL DE TOIN ON HER/ 224 HA APE
TOIN OFF DAT WHISTLE/ 225 HA APE
TOIN DE HOSE ON. 245 HA APE
(CUNNINGLY) I KNOW ENOUGH NOT TO SPEAK OUTA MY 248 HA APE
TOIN.

TOINED
DEN I TOINED HIM 'ROUND AND GIVE HIM A PUSH TO 617 ICEMAN
START HIM.
DE MINUTE YOUR BACK IS TOINED, DEY'RE CHEATIN' MI0698 ICEMAN
DE ICEMAN OR SOMEONE.

TOITY
=TOITY DAYS TO TINK IT OVER.= 241 HA APE

TOKEN

IF HER HIGHNESS--MAJESTY--WILL ACCEPT A SMALL 391 MARCOM TOKEN OF MY ESTEEM--
TOKEN TO ME THAT--NEVER MIND. 172 MISBEG
TOKEN OF WHATS 172 MISBEG
I WAS HOPING YOU'D FEEL BEAUTY IN IT--BY WAY OF A 172 MISBEG TOKEN.
BUT I HAD THIS TOKEN ON MY CHEEK TO REMEMBER A 99 POET FRENCH SABER BY.

TOKENS

(AWKWARDLY MOVED) TEARS ARE QUEER TOKENS OF 47 ELECTR HAPPINESS/

TOL'

DEY TOL' ME YOU DONE DIED FROM DAT RAZOR CUT I 192 EJONES GIVES YOU.

TOLD

(RUSHING OUT TO SHUT IT) I'VE TOLD HIM AGAIN AND 188 AHWILD AGAIN--
YOU MIND WHAT YOUR PA TOLD YOU/ 189 AHWILD
AND HE TOLD HIM ABOUT-- 196 AHWILD
A FELLOW AT COLLEGE TOLD ME. 197 AHWILD
AND HE TOLD HER HE'D COMMITTED BIGAMY. 197 AHWILD
I TOLD HER TO BE CAREFUL-- 207 AHWILD
NO, TWO THINGS--THINGS I'VE TOLD YOU OVER AND 211 AHWILD OVER, BUT YOU ALWAYS FORGET.
(GUILTILY) WELL, I'VE NEVER TOLD YOU, 214 AHWILD
YOU REMEMBER WHAT I TOLD YOU ABOUT THAT FISH. 220 AHWILD
AND IF I DIDN'T, YOU'VE TOLD ME FOUR TIMES 222 AHWILD ALREADY/
INTO HIS EYES OF ONE ABOUT TO EMBARK ON AN OFT- 229 AHWILD TOLD TALE OF CHILDHOOD ADVENTURE)
GUESS I HAVE TOLD THAT TOO MANY TIMES AND BORED 230 AHWILD EVERYONE.
TOLD ME AT THE PICNIC AFTER HE'D GOT ENOUGH DUTCH 234 AHWILD COURAGE IN HIM.
THE BOY WHO'S UPSTAIRS WITH MY FRIEND TOLD ME, BUT247 AHWILD I DIDN'T PAY MUCH ATTENTION.
(GUILTILY) HE TOLD ME HE WAS OVER EIGHTEEN. 247 AHWILD
WHO WAS IT BUT YOU TOLD ME TO HAND HIM DYNAMITE IN248 AHWILD THAT FIZZ$
NOW, ESSIE, I JUST TOLD YOU A MINUTE AGO. 253 AHWILD
I TOLD YOU I DID, SID- AND I DO. 259 AHWILD
(QUICKLY) AT LEAST, SO I'VE BEEN TOLD. 267 AHWILD
DARNED WELL I TOLD YOU I'M NOT COMING HOME TO 269 AHWILD SUPPER TONIGHT.
IF I TOLD MURIEL THAT/ 273 AHWILD
SHE'D SAY ANYTHING YOU TOLD HER TO. 279 AHWILD
BUT I'VE TOLD YOU, PA-- 282 AHWILD
WHEN YOU'D TOLD ME IN THAT LETTER YOU'D NEVER SEE 283 AHWILD ME AGAINS
BUT I'VE TOLD YOU I DIDN'T MEAN--(THEN FALTERING 284 AHWILD BUT FASCINATED)
I TOLD HER I LOVED YOU AND NEVER COULD LOVE ANYONE285 AHWILD ELSE.
BUT I'VE TOLD YOU A MILLION TIMES THAT PA-- 286 AHWILD
YOU OUGHT TO HAVE KNOWN HE STOOD RIGHT OVER ME AND286 AHWILD TOLD ME EACH WORD TO WRITE.
I'VE TOLD YOU HOW SORRY HE WAS, AND HOW HE SAID 289 AHWILD HE'D NEVER TOUCH LIQUOR AGAIN.
MY, BUT I'M GLAD MILDRED TOLD ME WHERE RICHARD 289 AHWILD WENT OFF TO.
AND I TOLD YOU ABOUT GETTING THAT BUSINESS FROM 292 AHWILD LAWSON, DIDN'T I$
HOW MANY TIMES HAVE I TOLD YOU TO HANG UP YOUR HAT293 AHWILD IN THE HALL WHEN YOU COME IN/
IF THEY'VE TOLD YOU ABOUT HER DOWN THERE, THEY 294 AHWILD MUST HAVE TOLD YOU I DIDN'T/
HE'S GOT A DAUGHTER SOMEWHERES OUT WEST, I THINK 5 ANNA HE TOLD ME ONCE.
SHE TOLD ME IT WAS YOU. 20 ANNA
THAT DAME WAS HERE TOLD ME YOU WAS CAPTAIN OF A 21 ANNA COAL BARGE--
I'VE TOLD YOU A HUNDRED TIMES I HATED IT. 27 ANNA
I'M AFTER HEARING A LOT OF IT FROM YOU AND A LOT 47 ANNA MORE THAT ANNA'S TOLD ME YOU DO
YOU'D BE WISHING ANNA MARRIED TO A FAMER, SHE TOLD 48 ANNA ME.
I SAID I WAS SURE--I TOLD HIM I THOUGHT YOU HAVE A 51 ANNA BIT OF LOVE FUR ME TOO.
I TOLD HIM IN HIS TEETH I LOVED YOU. 51 ANNA
SO YOU TOLD HIM, THAT MATS 51 ANNA
WHO TOLD YOU I WAS$ 57 ANNA
AND IF I TOLD YOU THAT YUST GETTING OUT IN THIS 59 ANNA BARGE,
AND ME TORMENTED WITH THE WICKEDNESS YOU'D TOLD UF 69 ANNA YOURSELF,
(WITH PASSIONATE ENTREATY) ALL THE BADNESS YOU 70 ANNA TOLD ME TWO DAYS BACK,
AND I SUPPOSE 'TIS THE SAME LIES YOU TOLD THEM ALL 73 ANNA BEFORE THAT YOU TOLD TO ME$
I WAS A LAD ONLY, AND SHE TOLD ME TO KEEP IT BY ME 75 ANNA IF I'D BE WAKING OR SLEEPING
SUPPOSE I TOLD YOU THAT WAS THE ONE AND ONLY 85 BEYOND REASON FOR MY GOINGS
HE TOLD ME YOU WERE HERE. 87 BEYOND
BUT YOU HAVEN'T TOLD ME YOUR REASON FOR LEAVING 89 BEYOND YET$
I KNEW THE SEA WAS OVER BEYOND THOSE HILLS,--THE 89 BEYOND FOLKS HAD TOLD ME--
SONGS THAT TOLD OF ALL THE WONDERFUL THINGS THEY 90 BEYOND HAD
(FLUSHING) RUTH TOLD ME THIS EVENING THAT--SHE 100 BEYOND LOVED ME.
I TOLD HER I HADN'T BEEN CONSCIOUS OF MY LOVE 100 BEYOND UNTIL AFTER THE TRIP HAD BEEN
I DON'T SEE WHY RUTH PUTS UP WITH IT, AND I'VE 113 BEYOND TOLD HER SO.
AND TOLD HIM HOW THINGS OUGHT TO BE DONE. 113 BEYOND
DO YOU KNOW WHAT SHE TOLD ME LAST NIGHT$ 114 BEYOND

TOLD

(CONT'D.)
ROBERT TOLD HER HE'D HAVE TO MORTGAGE THE FARM-- 115 BEYOND
AIN'T THAT JUST WHAT I TOLD YOU$ 118 BEYOND
RUTH TOLD ME I'D PROBABLY FIND YOU UP TOP-SIDE 130 BEYOND HERE.
WHY, I THOUGHT I TOLD YOU EVERYTHING IN MY 131 BEYOND LETTERS.
AND IS WHAT YOU'VE TOLD ME ALL YOU REMEMBER ABOUT 132 BEYOND IT$
I WALKED OVER IT THIS MORNING WITH RUTH--AND SHE 133 BEYOND TOLD ME ABOUT THINGS--
AFTER WHAT I SHOWED YOU AND TOLD YOU 136 BEYOND
AND HE COULD SEE JUST AS SOON'S I TOLD HIM WHAT A 137 BEYOND GOOD CHANCE IT WAS.
(FIERCELY) YOU TOLD HIM--WHAT YOU'VE TOLD ME$ 139 BEYOND
I DIDN'T KNOW IF YOU'D WANT TO SHIP AWAY AGEN SO 141 BEYOND QUICK AN' I TOLD HIM SO.
YOU KNOW THE DOCTOR TOLD YOU NOT TO GET UP AND 145 BEYOND MOVE ROUND.
TILL I ANSWERED THAT AND TOLD HIM. 146 BEYOND
(CALLOUSLY) I ONLY WROTE WHAT DOCTOR SMITH TOLD 146 BEYOND ME.
(DULLY) I WANTED TO SEND YOU WORD ONCE, BUT HE 154 BEYOND ONLY GOT MAD WHEN I TOLD HIM.
I NEVER TOLD HIM. 155 BEYOND
GOOD HEAVENS, YOU HAVEN'T TOLD HIM THIS, HAVE YOU.158 BEYOND DOCTOR$
AND THEN TO MAKE SURE I LISTENED AT THE DOOR TO 160 BEYOND WHAT HE TOLD YOU.
AND I TOLD HIM ALL I'VE TOLD YOU. 164 BEYOND
YOU TOLD ROB--YOU LOVED ME$ 164 BEYOND
(WITH AN IRONICAL SMILE) THE DOCTOR TOLD ME TO GO167 BEYOND TO THE FAR-OFF PLACES--
HE TOLD YOU--TO REMEMBER. 168 BEYOND
GOD DAMN YOU, YOU NEVER TOLD HIM/ 168 BEYOND
I NEVER TOLD YOU THIS, 'CAUSE I THOUGHT YOU'D 487 CARDIF LAUGH AT ME.
DOCTOR TOLD ME I'D GOT TO STOP OR DIE. 467 CARIBE
I TOLD YOU HE HAD. 557 CROSS
BUT MY FATHER REALIZING, AS HE TOLD ME, WHAT WAS 560 CROSS HAPPENING TO THEM,
THEY WERE PICKED UP SOON AFTER, MAD AS HATTERS, AS560 CROSS I HAVE TOLD YOU.
AND IN THE PRESENCE OF THE OTHERS TOLD ME THE 560 CROSS DREAM.
(DESPAIRINGLY) BUT YOU TOLD HIM HOW FOOLISH THAT 564 CROSS WAS, DIDN'T YOU$
OLD SMITH TOLD ME I COULD LIVE HERE INDEFINITELY 565 CROSS WITHOUT PAYING--AS CARETAKER--
I TOLD HIM. 565 CROSS
I TELL YOU AGAIN WHAT I HAVE ALWAYS TOLD YOU... 495 DAYS
BUT YOU HAVEN'T TOLD ME YET HOW YOU HAPPENED TO 506 DAYS COME EAST.
I TOLD MYSELF IT WAS FOOLISH. 507 DAYS
AS I EXPLAINED TO ELSA, WHEN I TOLD HER ABOUT THE 509 DAYS FIRST PART,
BILL TOLD ME YOU'D CALLED. 513 DAYS
MR. LUVING PHONED ME HE TOLD HIM TO COME EARLY. 515 DAYS
MOTHER WAS THERE, AND I BROKE DOWN AND TOLD HER. 519 DAYS
(WITH A HARD LAUGH) I TOLD YOU I WAS IN HELL, 521 DAYS DIDN'T I$
I THOUGHT AS I'D TOLD UNCLE TO COME EARLY, I 525 DAYS BETTER--
YOU TOLD HIM$ 526 DAYS
(HESITATES--THEN DEFIANTLY) I TOLD HIM. 526 DAYS
WELL, I TOLD UNCLE THE FIRST PART AND HE WAS 530 DAYS CURIOUS, TOO.
I TOLD YOU THAT WAS ONE SUBJECT WE'D AGREE ON/ 532 DAYS
YOU FORGET I'M SIMPLY FOLLOWING WHAT THIS MAN TOLD534 DAYS ME.
I NEVER SHOULD HAVE TOLD HER THE STORY/ 547 DAYS
SHE TOLD YOU$ 549 DAYS
LUCY TOLD ME ALL ABOUT IT THIS AFTERNOON. 549 DAYS
SO IT WAS YOU WHO TOLD ON YOURSELF. 549 DAYS
BECAUSE I HAVE DECIDED YOU MUST BE TOLD THE TRUTH 559 DAYS
NOW, PREACHER FROM NEW DOVER, HE BRUNG THE NEWS-- 212 DESIRE TOLD IT T'OUR PREACHER
I BEEN WAITIN'--MAM TOLD ME. 213 DESIRE
AIR YE ANY THE WISER FUR ALL I'VE TOLD YE$ 238 DESIRE
SHE TOLD ME YE WAS SNEAKIN' 'ROUND TRYIN' T' MAKE 255 DESIRE LUVE T' HER
(STUNNED--DULLY) HE TOLD YEW.../ 257 DESIRE
IF I TOLD HIM, 260 DESIRE
I TOLD YE I'D DO IT/ 260 DESIRE
NUT THE LIES YE JEST TOLD--BUT 'CAUSE YE WANTED T'262 DESIRE STEAL AGEN--
IF YE'D LOVED ME, I'D NEVER TOLD NO SHERIFF ON YC 265 DESIRE NO MATTER WHAT YE DID,
I TOLD HIM. 266 DESIRE
(BROKENLY) BUT I TOLD THE SHERIFF. 266 DESIRE
YOU NEVER TOLD ME NOTHING ABOUT THAT, 497 DIFRNT
THEN I'LL TELL YOU WHAT JIM TOLD ME. 502 DIFRNT
WHAT YOU TOLD ONLY GOES TO PROVE I WAS WRONG ABOUT504 DIFRNT IT.
IF YOU WAS LIKE MOST FOLKS I'D TOLD IT TO YOU. 508 DIFRNT
AND PA TOLD ME THAT NIGHT. 508 DIFRNT
(RESENTFULLY) AND YOU NEVER TOLD ME/ 508 DIFRNT
I ALWAYS TOLD YE I WAS GOOD, AIN'T I--GOOD AS HELL513 DIFRNT I RE$
HE TOLD ME SOME FOOL STORY 'BOUT YOU FALLIN' OUT 513 DIFRNT WITH CALEB.
SHE SAYS JACK'D TOLD YOU THAT STORY THEY'RE ALL 514 DIFRNT TELLIN' AS A JOKE ON ME.
WAAL, I GUESS WHAT HE TOLD IS TRUE ENOUGH. 515 DIFRNT
HE ONLY TOLD ME THE TRUTH, DIDN'T HE$ 515 DIFRNT
YOU'LL REMEMBER WHAT I TOLD YE 'BOUT WAITIN', 518 DIFRNT EMMER$

TOLD 1680

TOLD (CONT'D.)
WHO TOLD YOU I GOT THEM JUST FOR YOUS 520 DIFRNT
TOO STRICT, I'VE TOLD HIM. 522 DIFRNT
I TOLD HER TO CUT THE ROUGH WORK AND BEHAVE--AND A525 DIFRNT
NICE TIME WAS HAD BY ALL.
THAT MEANS UNCLE CALEB HAS COME AND SHE'S TOLD HIM527 DIFRNT
HER STORIES
I TOLD HIM THE TRUTH, IF THAT'S WHAT YOU MEAN. 528 DIFRNT
FOLKS HAVE BEEN LYIN' TO HER ABOUT ME, LIKE I TOLD532 DIFRNT
YOU, AND SHE'S TOLD HIM.
(AFTER A PAUSE) I KNOW YOU TOLD ME TIME AND AGAIN538 DIFRNT
NOT TO GO BACK TO THAT.
(VEHEMENTLY) I AIN'T JUDGED HIM BY WHAT FOLKS 540 DIFRNT
HAVE TOLD ME.
I'VE TOLD HIM HE CAN STAY HERE WITH ME TONIGHT. 542 DIFRNT
I TOLD YOU I CARRIED HIM HOME. 549 DIFRNT
WHEN I TOLD YOU I'D CAUGHT HIM STARING AT ME, 432 DYNAMO
WELL, MAYBE I SHOULDN'T HAVE TOLD YOU, 441 DYNAMO
HE TOLD ME HIMSELF. 447 DYNAMO
I'VE JUST TOLD/... 447 DYNAMO
(BUT I'VE TOLD/... 447 DYNAMO
AND YOU CALLED ADA A HARLOT--AFTER I TOLD YOU I 450 DYNAMO
LOVED HER WITH ALL MY HEART/
POP TOLD YOU TO PROVE YOU WERE YELLOW/ 451 DYNAMO
OVERWHELMED BY THE CONVICTION THAT WHAT SHE HAS 451 DYNAMO
TOLD HIM IS TRUE.)
I'VE TOLD YOU A MILLION TIMES HOW DUMB THAT TALK 455 DYNAMO
IS AND YET YOU KEEP ON HARPING--
YOUR POP TOLD ME TO GET OUT OF THE ROOM 456 DYNAMO
OUGHT I TO HAVE TOLD HIM... 462 DYNAMO
AND TOLD ME ABOUT HOW WE ALL USED TO LIVE IN THE 479 DYNAMO
OCEAN ONCE.
WHO TOLD YER THAT FAIRY TALES 177 EJONES
YOU SAID YER'D GOT A CHARM SO'S NO LEAD BULLET'D 178 EJONES
KILL YEA. YOU TOLD 'EM.
YOU TOLD THE BLACKS 'ERE ABOUT KILLIN' WHITE MEN 180 EJONES
IN THE STATES.
THERE'S WHERE HANNAH SAID YOU'D TOLD HER YOU WAS 11 ELECTR
GOIN'.
I TOLD HIM HE COULD--AND STAY TO SUPPER WITH US. 17 ELECTR
YOUR MOTHER TOLD ME-- 21 ELECTR
YOUR MOTHER HAS TOLD ME HOW CLOSE YOU'VE ALWAYS 22 ELECTR
BEEN TO HIM.
YOU WERE INTERESTED WHEN I TOLD YOU OF THE ISLANDS 23 ELECTR
IN THE SOUTH SEAS WHERE I WAS
I'LL BET HE NEVER TOLD YOU YOUR GRANDFATHER, ABE 25 ELECTR
MANNON, AS WELL AS HIS BROTHER,
I TOLD YOU ONCE I DON'T WANT TO HEAR-- 26 ELECTR
BELAY, I TOLD YOU, WITH THAT KIND OF TALK/ 27 ELECTR
I SUPPOSE ANNIE TOLD YOU I'D BEEN TO VISIT HAZEL 29 ELECTR
AND PETER WHILE YOU WERE AWAY.
I TOLD YOU I HAD TO TALK TO YOU. 29 ELECTR
I TOLD YOU MYSELF I RAN INTO HIM BY ACCIDENT-- 30 ELECTR
TOLD MYSELF IT WASN'T HUMAN NOT TO LOVE MY OWN 31 ELECTR
CHILD, BORN OF MY BODY.
HE TOLD ME WHEN HE SAID HE LOVED ME. 32 ELECTR
I WANT TO KNOW RIGHT NOW WHETHER YOU'RE GOING TO 33 ELECTR
DO WHAT I TOLD YOU OR NOT/
BUT IF YOU TOLD YOUR FATHER, I'D HAVE TO GO AWAY 33 ELECTR
WITH ADAM.
AS YOU'D TOLD ME TO DO TO BLIND HER. 37 ELECTR
I WENT TO SEE OUR OLD FAMILY DOCTOR AND TOLD HIM 39 ELECTR
ABOUT EZRA'S LETTER.
WE'D STOP AT THE SOUTH PACIFIC ISLANDS I'VE TOLD 39 ELECTR
YOU ABOUT.
(MORE TAUNTINGLY) BUT PERHAPS YOUR LOVE HAS BEEN 41 ELECTR
ONLY A LIE YOU TOLD ME--
I TOLD YOU MY SECRET FEELINGS. 61 ELECTR
(AGHAST) YOU TOLD HIM THAT--WHEN YOU KNEW HIS 63 ELECTR
HEART--/
(STAMMERS) I TOLD HIM--ADAM WAS MY LOVER. 63 ELECTR
AND WHAT SHE TOLD ME 70 ELECTR
I'D OFTEN TOLD EZRA HE WAS ATTEMPTING MORE THAN 70 ELECTR
ONE MAN COULD HANDLE
(QUICKLY) FATHER TOLD YOU THAT, TOO$ 74 ELECTR
HE TOLD ME THE TROUBLE HE HAD WASN'T SERIOUS. 74 ELECTR
I TOLD YOU I CAN'T GET USED TO THE IDEA OF HIS 75 ELECTR
BEING DEAD.
YOU SIMPLY WOULDN'T BELIEVE IT, IF I TOLD YOU SOME 86 ELECTR
OF THE THINGS.
YOU HAVEN'T TOLD ME ABOUT THAT BRANT YET. 86 ELECTR
(THEN HURRYING ON) BUT I HAVEN'T TOLD YOU THE 87 ELECTR
WORST YET.
I TOLD YOU SHE'D GONE CRAZY/ 88 ELECTR
I HAVEN'T TOLD YOU THE MOST HORRIBLE THING OF ALL/ 88 ELECTR
I'VE ALREADY TOLD HIM--SO YOU MIGHT AS WELL SAVE 91 ELECTR
YOURSELF THE TROUBLE.
I TOLD HIM HOW YOU LIED ABOUT MY TRIPS TO NEW 91 ELECTR
YORK--FOR REVENGE/
EVEN WHEN WE WERE LITTLE YOU ALWAYS KNEW I TOLD 96 ELECTR
YOU THE TRUTH, DIDN'T YOU$
SHE TOLD ME ALL ABOUT THAT/ 97 ELECTR
SHE TOLD ME YOUR ROTTEN LIES--ABOUT HIM--ABOUT 98 ELECTR
FOLLOWING HER TO NEW YORK.
SO THAT'S WHAT SHE TOLD YOU/ 98 ELECTR
TOLD ME HOW FINE I COULD SING/ 104 ELECTR
HE TOLD HER-- 108 ELECTR
SO I TOLD HIM BY ALL MEANS TO GO. 109 ELECTR
WHEN HE WAS DYING HE POINTED AT ME AND TOLD HER I 110 ELECTR
WAS GUILTY/
AND MY ISLAND/ I TOLD HER ABOUT--WHICH WAS SHE AND 113 ELECTR
I--SHE WANTS TO GO THERE--
TO THE ISLAND I HAD TOLD YOU ABOUT--OUR ISLAND-- 121 ELECTR
THAT WAS YOU AND I/
YOU TOLD ME THAT IF YOU COULD COME HOME AND FACE 141 ELECTR
YOUR GHOSTS,
THE STRAIN OF ORIN'S CONDUCT HAS TOLD ON HER. 146 ELECTR
PLEASE TELL HAZEL WHAT I'VE TOLD YOU. 148 ELECTR

TOLD (CONT'D.)
BUT, YOU SILLY BOY, VINNIE TOLD PETER HERSELF WHAT161 ELECTR
IT IS AND TOLD HIM TO TELL 174 ELECTR
I'VE TOLD PETER ABOUT THAT, VINNIE. 175 ELECTR
SHE TOLD YOU$ 175 ELECTR
HE'S SENDING BILLY TO COLLEGE--MRS. BROWN JUST 260 GGBROW
TOLD ME--
HE PARTICULARLY TOLD ME TO ASK YOU TO DROP IN. 272 GGBROW
(SURPRISED) THE ONE TIME I RAN INTO HIM, I 275 GGBROW
THOUGHT HE TOLD ME
BUT I TOLD HIM THAT JUST BECAUSE HE'S BEEN KEEPING285 GGBROW
ME SO LONG,
YOU DON'T NEED TO BE TOLD THAT. 287 GGBROW
(SHE REMOVES HIS MASK) HAVEN'T I TOLD YOU TO TAKE 288 GGBROW
OFF YOUR MASK IN THE HOUSE$
IS IT TRUE WHAT BILLY TOLD ME--ABOUT YOUR SWEARING301 GGBROW
OFF FOREVER$
NO, NOT SINCE BROWN TOLD US HE'D CANNED HIM. 302 GGBROW
HASN'T HE TOLD YOU ALL THIS$ 304 GGBROW
(RELENTING) HE TOLD ME YOU'D AGREED TO ASK ME AND304 GGBROW
THE BOYS NOT TO COME HERE--
I SHOULD NEVER HAVE TOLD YOU-- BUT I NEVER 312 GGBROW
IMAGINED YOU'D TAKE IT SERIOUSLY.
(APPALLED) YOU DON'T MEAN TO SAY--MR. BROWN NEVER317 GGBROW
TOLD YOU$
I TOLD YOUR FATHER I WOULD NOT. 219 HA APE
HAD TOLD ME IT WOULD BE ALL RIGHT. 220 HA APE
I ASKED A DECK STEWARD 'D SHE WAS AND 'E TOLD ME.228 HA APE
THE BLEEDIN' STEWARD AS WAITS ON 'EM, 'E TOLD ME 228 HA APE
ABOUT 'ER.
HUGHIE TOLD ME HE DIDN'T HAVE NO RELATIONS LEFT-- 11 HUGHIE
THEN SHE TOLD HER MA, AND HER MA TOLD HER PA, 15 HUGHIE
CALL ME ERIE, LIKE I TOLD YOU. 20 HUGHIE
«NIRA,» I TOLD HIM, «IF YOU'RE GOING TO START 22 HUGHIE
PLAYIN' DE PONIES,
» HE TOLD ME. 22 HUGHIE
TOLD THE KIDS IT WAS BEDTIME AND HUSTLED 'EM OFF 25 HUGHIE
LIKE I WAS GIVING 'EM MEASLES.
«SURE, HUGHIE,» I TOLD HIM, «I'LL BE TICKLED TO 25 HUGHIE
DEATH.»
YOU CAN BET SHE TOLD HUGHIE NEVER INVITE ME AGAIN, 26 HUGHIE
AND HE NEVER DID.
I TOLD HER, «LISTEN, BABY, I GOT AN IMPEDIMENT IN 26 HUGHIE
MY SPEECH.
IT WAS LIKE DOPE TO ME, I TOLD HIM. 28 HUGHIE
I TOLD HIM I KNEW ALL THE BIG SHOTS. 28 HUGHIE
TOLD YOU TO USE YOUR JUDGMENT. 582 ICEMAN
BUT WHAT HE TOLD YOU$ 583 ICEMAN
I WOULDN'T KNOW HIM IF HE HADN'T TOLD ME WHO HE 583 ICEMAN
WAS.
I'VE GOT TO STAY UNDER COVER, LARRY, LIKE I TOLD 587 ICEMAN
YOU LAST NIGHT.
IF WE DID QUARREL, IT WAS BECAUSE I TOLD HER I'D 589 ICEMAN
BECOME CONVINCED
I TOLD HER, «YOU'VE ALWAYS ACTED THE FREE WOMAN, 591 ICEMAN
YOU'VE TOLD THAT STORY TEN MILLION TIMES AND IF I 601 ICEMAN
HAVE TO HEAR IT AGAIN,
BUT WHEN SHE WAS TAKEN, I TOLD THEM, «NO, BOYS, I 603 ICEMAN
CAN'T DO IT.
AND TOLD US ALL TO GIT DRESSED AND TAKE DE AIR/ 612 ICEMAN
WE TOLD DE GUYS WE'D WAIT FOR DEM 'ROUND DE 612 ICEMAN
CORNER.
AND SOME TOUGH GUY'D JUST TOLD HER BABIES WASN'T 614 ICEMAN
BAKING DOWN DE CHIMNEY BY A BOID
«JUST KEEP GOIN',» I TOLD HIM. 617 ICEMAN
HE WAS A PREACHER IN THE STICKS OF INDIANA, LIKE 622 ICEMAN
I'VE TOLD YOU.
IT'S THE DEADLIEST HABIT KNOWN TO SCIENCE, A GREAT626 ICEMAN
PHYSICIAN ONCE TOLD ME.
THE LAST TIME WE GOT PARALYZED TOGETHER HE TOLD 627 ICEMAN
ME--
I TOLD HIM DAT'S AW RIGHT FOR DE BUMS IN DIS DUMP.631 ICEMAN
I TOLD HIM, «I'M ON DE WAGON FOR KEEPS AND CORA 631 ICEMAN
KNOWS IT.»
I TOLD HIM--, SURE, I KNOW IT. 631 ICEMAN
YEAH, STILL PRETENDIN' HE'S DE ONE EXCEPTION, LIKE635 ICEMAN
HICKEY TOLD HIM.
I TOLD HIM, «I'LL TAKE A LOT FROM YOU, HICKEY, 636 ICEMAN
LIKE EVERYONE ELSE IN DIS DUMP,
I TOLD SCHWARTZ, DE COP, WE'S CLOSED FOR DE PARTY.637 ICEMAN
CUT IT OUT, I TOLD YUH/ 639 ICEMAN
I REMEMBER THAT YOU GOT MAD AND YOU TOLD HER, «I 647 ICEMAN
DON'T LIKE LIVING WITH A WHORE.
I'D NEVER LET MYSELF BELIEVE A WORD YOU TOLD ME. 650 ICEMAN
IF YOU TOLD US NOW WHAT IT WAS HAPPENED TO YOU 661 ICEMAN
ESPECIALLY SINCE HE TOLD US HIS WIFE WAS DEAD. 666 ICEMAN
I'LL ADMIT WHAT I TOLD YOU LAST NIGHT WAS A LIE-- 667 ICEMAN
YEAH, I TOLD HER, WHAT WOULD ME USE FOR SHERRY, 670 ICEMAN
I'VE TOLD YOU YOU CAN'T MAKE ME JUDGE YOU/ 680 ICEMAN
HICKEY JUST TOLD US. AIN'T IT TIME WE BEAT IT, IF 682 ICEMAN
WE'RE REALLY GOIN'$
LIKE HICKEY'S TOLD YOU$ 684 ICEMAN
I TOLD YOU IT WOULDN'T. 684 ICEMAN
I TOLD YOU YOU WEREN'T HALF AS SICK AS YOU 684 ICEMAN
PRETENDED.
AND YET, AS I'VE TOLD YOU OVER AND OVER, 685 ICEMAN
YOU KNOW WHAT I TOLD YOU ABOUT THE WRONG KIND OF 690 ICEMAN
PITY.
YOU'VE GOT TO BELIEVE WHAT I TOLD YOU/ 694 ICEMAN
SHE SAYS IT WAS HER TOLD YOU TO GO TO HELL, 698 ICEMAN
I TOLD HER STRAIGHT, «YOU BETTER FORGET ME, 710 ICEMAN
EVELYN, FOR YOUR OWN SAKE.
I TOLD MOLLIE ARLINGTON MY TROUBLE. 710 ICEMAN
THE QUACK I WENT TO GOT ALL MY DOUGH AND THEN TOLD713 ICEMAN
ME I WAS CURED
I TOLD YOUR MOTHER I KNEW DAMNED WELL IT WOULD BE 22 JOURNE
ONE ON ME,

TOLD

TOLD (CONT'D.)
AND HARKER'S FOREMAN TOLD HIM HE WAS SURE 23 JOURNE
SHAUGHNESSY HAD BROKEN THE FENCE ON
HE TOLD HARKER HE WAS HIRING A LAWYER TO SUE HIM 24 JOURNE
FOR DAMAGES.
HE TOLD ME HE NEVER GAVE HARKER A CHANCE TO OPEN 24 JOURNE
HIS MOUTH.
I TOLD SHAUGHNESSY HE SHOULD HAVE REMINDED HARKER 25 JOURNE
THAT A STANDARD OIL
I TOLD HIM YOU'D BE TICKLED TO DEATH OVER THE 25 JOURNE
GREAT IRISH VICTORY.
I HOPE YOU TOLD HIM I'D BE MAD AS HELL-- 25 JOURNE
I THOUGHT THAT WAS A DAMNED FOOL IDEA, AND I TOLD 35 JOURNE
HIM SO.
SHE TOLD ME HERSELF THE FOGHORN KEPT HER AWAKE ALL 38 JOURNE
NIGHT.
SHE TOLD ME ALL ABOUT HER SECOND COUSIN ON THE 41 JOURNE
POLICE FORCE IN ST. LOUIS.
BUT DOCTOR HARDY WAS RIGHT WHEN HE TOLD YOU TO CUT 55 JOURNE
OUT THE REDEYE.
I'VE TOLD CATHLEEN TIME AND AGAIN SHE MUST GO 60 JOURNE
WHEREVER HE IS AND TELL HIM.
HE'S TOLD US TO. 62 JOURNE
YOU KNOW DOCTOR HARDY TOLD YOU-- 94 JOURNE
I'VE TOLD HIM, YOU MUST THINK I'M HARD UP THAT I'D 99 JOURNE
NOTICE A MONKEY LIKE YOU.
SO DID HE, HE TOLD ME AFTERWARDS. 105 JOURNE
ALL HIS TEACHERS TOLD US WHAT A FINE BRAIN HE HAD.110 JOURNE
YOU TOLD ME NOT TO PAY ATTENTION. 111 JOURNE
I TOLD MYSELF IT MUST BE SOME BUSINESS CONNECTED 113 JOURNE
WITH THE THEATER.
MY FATHER TOLD ME TO BUY ANYTHING I WANTED AND 114 JOURNE
NEVER MIND WHAT IT COST.
HE TOLD THEM HE HAD A PREMONITION HE WOULD DIE 117 JOURNE
SOON.
JAMIE TOLD ME. 118 JOURNE
I TOLD HIM I HAD ONCE. 118 JOURNE
I TOLD HER THE MADAME SAID YOU WOULDN'T BE HOME. 125 JOURNE
(WITH SHARP IRRITATION.) I TOLD YOU TO TURN OUT 126 JOURNE
THAT LIGHT/
AS I'VE TOLD YOU BEFORE, YOU MUST TAKE HER 137 JOURNE
MEMORIES WITH A GRAIN OF SALT.
WHO REALLY KNOW SOMETHING ABOUT IT, HAVE TOLD YOU/141 JOURNE
I'LL BET YOU TOLD HER ALL SHE HAD TO DO WAS USE A 141 JOURNE
LITTLE WILL POWER/
ALL I TOLD THEM WAS I COULDN'T AFFORD ANY 144 JOURNE
MILLIONAIRE'S SANATORIUM
I'M SIMPLY REPEATING WHAT I WAS TOLD. 149 JOURNE
MAYBE I SHOULDN'T HAVE TOLD YOU. 151 JOURNE
I'M GLAD YOU'VE TOLD ME THIS, PAPA. 151 JOURNE
YOU'VE JUST TOLD ME SOME HIGH SPOTS IN YOUR 153 JOURNE
MEMORIES.
(RELUCTANTLY.) YES. I TOLD HIM I WOULDN'T GO 158 JOURNE
THERE.
TOLD ME YEARS AGO TO CUT OUT BOOZE OR I'D SOON BE 164 JOURNE
DEAD--AND HERE I AM.
SOMETHING I OUGHT TO HAVE TOLD YOU LONG AGO--FOR 165 JOURNE
YOUR OWN GOOD.
BUT I TOLD YOU HOW MUCH I'D HOPED-- 171 JOURNE
I TOLD HER I WANTED TO BE A NUN. 175 JOURNE
BUT MOTHER ELIZABETH TOLD ME I MUST BE MORE SURE 175 JOURNE
THAN THAT, EVEN.
I TOLD MOTHER I HAD HAD A TRUE VISION WHEN I WAS 175 JOURNE
PRAYING IN THE SHRINE OF OUR
FLAVIUS HAS TOLD CAESAR. 331 LAZARU
YOU HEARD WHAT THE OLD FOOL, TIBERIUS, TOLD THE 370 LAZARU
MOB.
HE TOLD THE SERVANT TO TELL ME HE WOULD COME. 4 MANSNS
(SHE SITS DOWN AGAIN.) YOU HAVEN'T TOLD ME A WORD 10 MANSNS
ABOUT YOURSELF YET.
I TOLD YOU IT IS MY WISH 58 MANSNS
AS I HAVE TOLD JOEL, I WILL ACCEPT FATHER'S 59 MANSNS
PROPOSAL ONLY ON ONE CONDITION.
I TOLD JOEL I DID NOT WANT EVEN THE ONE-HALF 65 MANSNS
INTEREST IN MOTHER'S HOME.
I TOLD YOU THERE COULD BE NO QUESTION OF 65 MANSNS
OBLIGATIONS.
SHE TOLD ME BEFORE SHE LEFT YOU HAD ASKED HER TO 96 MANSNS
COME THERE.
SARA HAS PROBABLY TOLD YOU OF HER VISIT TO MY 96 MANSNS
OFFICE THIS MORNING.
AND THE WISH IN HIS HEART TOLD HIM HIS QUEST WAS 111 MANSNS
ENDED.
BUT I'VE TOLD YOU YOU'LL HAVE THEM BACK. 134 MANSNS
I'VE TOLD YOU BEFORE I'M WILLING TO LET HER HAVE 147 MANSNS
THE CHILDREN FOR COMPANY AGAIN--
SHE HAS TOLD THEM TO BEWARE OF ME, I AM A LITTLE 162 MANSNS
CRAZY--
I'VE TOLD YOU THE TRUTH. 167 MANSNS
WE ARE BACK HERE IN YOUR GARDEN ON THE DAY YOU 184 MANSNS
TOLD ME THAT STORY.
(QUIETLY AND EXHAUSTEDLY.) I'VE TOLD YOU I'M 189 MANSNS
BEYOND SCHEMING.
(ROUND-EYED) A MAN TOLD ME THAT NOAH'S ARK IS 364 MARCOM
STILL SOMEWHERE AROUND HERE.
AN ARMENIAN DOILY-DEALER TOLD ME DOWN IN BAGDAD. 366 MARCOM
I'VE GOT A GOOD ONE AN IDOL-POLISHER TOLD ME IN 374 MARCOM
TIBET.
YOU ONCE TOLD ME A PRINCESS MUST NEVER WEEP. 386 MARCOM
AND ANOTHER, A MAN OF WIDE CULTURE, TOLD ME, 387 MARCOM
I TOLD YOU HE DOES NOT KNOW. 389 MARCOM
AFTER ALL, WHEN YOU STOP TO THINK, WHO WAS IT 394 MARCOM
FIRST TOLD THEM GOLD WAS MONEY$
IT WAS MY GRANDFATHER'S SPECIAL COMMAND, GIVEN TO 414 MARCOM
YOU BY CHU-YIN, YOU TOLD ME.
JUST A SLAP BECAUSE SHE TOLD ME TO STOP SINGING, 18 MISBEG
IT WAS AFTER DAYLIGHT.
BUT IT STILL WORKS NOW AND AGAIN, I'M TOLD, 22 MISBEG

TOLD (CONT'D.)
AND YOU'D GET A LETTER SAYING HIS AGENT TOLD HIM 24 MISBEG
YOU WERE A YEAR BEHIND IN THE
HASN'T HE TOLD US AND PROMISED YOU CAN BUY IT ON 31 MISBEG
EASY TIME PAYMENTS
HE SAID HE TOLD THE AGENT TO TELL WHOEVER IT WAS 32 MISBEG
THE PLACE WASN'T FOR SALE.
THE AGENT GOT AN OFFER LAST MONTH, JIM TOLD ME, 32 MISBEG
BIGGER THAN MINE.
I TOLD YOU NOT TO ANNOY THE GENTLEMAN WITH YOUR 42 MISBEG
ROUGH TONGUE.
(HE SMILES KIDDINGLY) ANYWAY, WHO TOLD YOU I FALL 43 MISBEG
FOR THE DAINTY DULLS$
I'M GLAD YOU TOLD ME. 45 MISBEG
TOLD HIM YOU'D BE OVERWHELMED WITH AWE IF HE 48 MISBEG
DEIGNED TO INTERVIEW YOU IN PERSON.
SIMPSON TOLD ME. 48 MISBEG
HE KNOWS YOU DID IT AND HE TOLD HIS MASTER SO. 50 MISBEG
YOU KNOW THAT OFFER I TOLD YOU ABOUT$ 65 MISBEG
YOU JUST TOLD YOUR UNWORTHY OLD MAN I WAS KIDDING. 67 MISBEG
HE'S THE WAY I TOLD YOU ABOUT THIS MORNING, WHEN 82 MISBEG
HE TALKS LIKE A BROADWAY CROOK,
HE AS MUCH AS TOLD ME HIS REASON, THOUGH HE 89 MISBEG
WOULDN'T COME OUT WITH IT PLAIN.
THAT'S THE TRUTH BEHIND THE LIES HE TOLD YOU OF 92 MISBEG
HIS CONSCIENCE AND HIS FEAR ME
I TOLD YOU THIS MORNING IF HE EVER BROKE HIS 92 MISBEG
PROMISE TO US I'D DO ANYTHING AND
I TOLD YOU I DIDN'T CARE HOW DIRTY A TRICK-- 92 MISBEG
I'VE TOLD YOU I'D DO ANYTHING NOW/ 93 MISBEG
I'LL LET HIM GO ON AS IF YOU HADN'T TOLD ME WHAT 99 MISBEG
HE'S DONE--
SO HE CAN'T SUSPECT YOU TOLD ME. 99 MISBEG
WHO TOLD YOU--$ 127 MISBEG
I TOLD PHIL THE GLAD TIDINGS AND BOUGHT DRINKS FOR131 MISBEG
ALL AND SUNDRY.
HE WAS SOBER WHEN I TOLD HIM. 131 MISBEG
A LITTLE BIRD TOLD ME. 131 MISBEG
I TOLD SIMPSON TO TELL HARDER I DID. 132 MISBEG
WHAT DO YOU THINK HE TOLD SIMPSON TO OFFER$ 132 MISBEG
I KNEW YOU'D NEVER--I TOLD HIM--(SHE KISSES HIM 133 MISBEG
AGAIN) OH, JIM, I LOVE YOU.
AS THOUGH WHAT HE TOLD CONCERNED SOME MAN HE HAD 146 MISBEG
KNOWN,
THAT'S WHY I TOLD YOU. 151 MISBEG
I SHOULDN'T HAVE TOLD YOU. 151 MISBEG
THIS TIME, YOU'VE TOLD ONE TOO MANY. 159 MISBEG
I'VE TOLD YOU ONCE. 160 MISBEG
I TOLD YOU TO STOP LYING, FATHER. 160 MISBEG
(SELF-MOCKINGLY) SURE, HASN'T HE TOLD ME I'M 161 MISBEG
BEAUTIFUL TO HIM AND HE LOVES ME--
I CALLED YOU HERE TO TELL YOU I'VE SEEN THROUGH 162 MISBEG
ALL THE LIES YOU TOLD LAST NIGHT
SO YOU TOLD ME LAST NIGHT. 10 POET
YOU'RE FORGETTING WHAT HIMSELF TOLD YOU LAST NIGHT 10 POET
AS HE WENT UP TO BED.
IF I WAS MAD AT CON, AND ME BLIND DRUNK, I MUST 11 POET
HAVE TOLD YOU A POWER OF LIES.
SO I TOLD HER, BUT SHE DIDN'T GO. 18 POET
I HOPE YOU TOLD HER I'M THE OWNER'S DAUGHTER, TOO. 18 POET
(WORRIED AGAIN.) MAYBE YOU OUGHT TO HAVE TOLD HER 19 POET
HE'S HERE SICK TO SAVE HER
I'VE TOLD YOU A HUNDRED TIMES TO SEE THE DOCTOR. 21 POET
YOU TOLD ME YOU HAD THE MONEY PUT ASIDE. 22 POET
I'VE TOLD YOU BEFORE HE WANTED TO GET AWAY FROM 29 POET
HIS FATHER'S BUSINESS.
HE'S SO TIMID, HE HASN'T TOLD ME YET, BUT I'LL GET 30 POET
HIM TO SOON.
SHE MUST BE A QUEER CREATURE, FROM ALL HE'S TOLD 31 POET
ME.
I TOLD YOU ONCE--/ 35 POET
I TOLD YOU NOT TO USE THIS ENTRANCE/ 54 POET
SURE, FROM ALL SHE'S TOLD ME, 62 POET
(GUESSES AT ONCE THIS MUST BE THE WOMAN MICKEY HAD 72 POET
TOLD HER ABOUT.
BY THE ETERNAL, I'LL WAGER SHE BELIEVED WHAT I 76 POET
TOLD HER OF TALAVERA
(UTTER UNEASILY.) ONLY, LIKE SIMON'S TOLD ME, 80 POET
AND HE HAS TOLD ME HOW FOND HE IS OF YOU. 81 POET
BUT DOUBTLESS SIMON HAS TOLD YOU I AM A BIT 84 POET
ECCENTRIC AT TIMES.
YOUR FATHER TOLD ME-- 87 POET
OH, NO, I'M SURE SHE TOLD HIM IF HE WAS SURE HE 87 POET
LOVED ME AND I MEANT HIS
(BEFORE HE THINKS.) BUT I TOLD YOUR MOTHER TO 91 POET
KEEP HER HERE UNTIL--
HE SAID HIS MOTHER HAD TOLD HIM THE SAME THING. 108 POET
I TOLD HIM HE MUST APPRECIATE, AS A GENTLEMAN, 108 POET
YES, AND HE SAID HE HAD TOLD HIS MOTHER, 109 POET
HE TOLD YOU THAT$ 109 POET
I TOLD HIM I AGREED WITH HIS MOTHER. 110 POET
(IGNORES THIS.) I TOLD HIM I APPRECIATED THE 110 POET
HONOR HE DID ME IN ASKING FOR YOUR
THERE WAS ANOTHER REASON WHY I TOLD YOUNG HARFORU 112 POET
I TOLD YOU WHEN YOU WERE DRUNK LIKE THIS-- 113 POET
I COULD HAVE TOLD YOU YOU WAS WASTIN' BREATH. 130 POET
SO I KISSED HIM AND TOLD HIM HE WAS TOO A POET, 145 POET
AND ALWAYS WOULD BE,
AND THEN SIMON TOLD ME HOW SCARED HE'D BEEN 145 POET
AND AT FATHER TOO WHEN I TOLD HIM HOW HE THREATENED 149 POET
HE'D KILL ME.
SO I KISSED HIM AND TOLD HIM HE WAS THE HANDSOMEST145 POET
IN THE WORLD, AND HE IS,
AND I TOLD HIM NEVER MIND, THAT IF WE HAD TO LIVE 146 POET
IN A HUT,
HAVEN'T YOU TOLD ME OF THE PRIDE IN YOUR LOVE$ 148 POET
IT'S ONLY WHAT I TOLD YOU TO EXPECT. 152 POET
BUT THEY TOLD ME AFTER I NEVER STOPPED GABBIN' 161 POET

TOLD

TOLD (CONT'D.)
THE YOUNG LAD WANTS TO MARRY HER AS SOON AS CAN 172 POET
BE, SHE TOLD ME,
YOU AIN'T FERGITTIN' WHAT THE DOCTOR TOLD YOU WHENS79 ROPE
HE WAS HERE LAST, BE YOUR
AND TOLD HIM TO HANG HIMSELF ON IT WHEN HE EVER 581 ROPE
CAME HOME AGEN.
TOLD YOU TO YOUR FACE HE'D STOLEN AND WAS LEAVIN'.581 ROPE
(TO HIS WIFE) IT'S SOFT-MINDED SHE IS, LIKE I'VE 583 ROPE
ALWAYS TOLD YOU, AN' STUPID..
BECAUSE THE AULD MAN WAS CRAZY AN' ON HIS LAST 585 ROPE
LEGS, I TOLD HIM,
AN' THE WHISKEY LOOSENED HIS TONGUE TILL HE'D TOLD585 ROPE
ALL HE KNEW.
HE TOLD YOU--ABOUT PAW'S WILLS 585 ROPE
HE TOLD IT, IF HE WASN'T YOUR FATHER. 587 ROPE
HE'LL NOT LAST LONG IN HIS SENSES, THE DOCTOR TOLD587 ROPE
ME.
SHE TOLD ME YOU WAS UP HERE. 588 ROPE
WHEN I TOLD HIM HE'D COME BACK THERE WAS NO 594 ROPE
HOLDIN' HIM.
(THEN RATHER IRONICALLY) AND SO GORDON TOLD NINA 11 STRANG
HE'D SUDDENLY REALIZED IT
DECIDEDLY, I TOLD HIM, IN JUSTICE TO NINA, 11 STRANG
YOU TOLD HIM IT'D BE UNFAIR, YOU PUT HIM ON HIS 20 STRANG
HONOR, DIDN'T YOUR
WAIT, HE TOLD GORDON/ 20 STRANG
IT'S ME--, I MEAN--MISS LEEDS TOLD ME TO COME IN 28 STRANG
HERE.
(I WISH SHE HADN'T TOLD ME THIS... 45 STRANG
(SHOULD I HAVE TOLD HIM?... 49 STRANG
WHY HAVEN'T I TOLD SAM?... 49 STRANG
CALLED ME INTO HIS OFFICE AND TOLD ME HE'D HAD HIS 54 STRANG
EYE ON ME.
I DON'T THINK SHE'S TOLD SAMMY BUT I GOT TO MAKE 54 STRANG
SURE....))
I TOLD HIM HIS FATHER WAS SICK. 60 STRANG
YOU TOLD ME YOU DID LOVE SAMMY/ 61 STRANG
YOUNG FOLKS DON'T NOWADAYS--UNTIL I'D SEEN YOU AND 61 STRANG
TOLD YOU EVERYTHING.
AFTER ALL I'VE TOLD YOU/ 62 STRANG
DOCTOR TOLD HER SHE MUSN'T, SHE SAID... 68 STRANG
HE WENT TO SEE YOU AND TOLD YOU HOW WORRIED HE WAS 82 STRANG
ABOUT ME AND ASKED YOU OUT TO
AND THEN SAM'S MOTHER TOLD ME I COULDN'T HAVE MY 83 STRANG
BABY.
I'VE TOLD MYSELF IT'S WHAT I OUGHT TO DO. 84 STRANG
I'VE TOLD MYSELF THIS A THOUSAND TIMES. 84 STRANG
(GOUTLY) I'VE BEEN CONSIDERING WHAT SAM'S WIFE 86 STRANG
TOLD ME AND HER REASONING IS
AT LAST YOU'VE TOLD ME/ 97 STRANG
HAVE YOU FORGOTTEN ALL HIS MOTHER TOLD YOUS 103 STRANG
I HAVEN'T TOLD ANYONE. 106 STRANG
WHEN SHE KNOWS I'VE TOLD HIM THAT, SHE'LL SEE IT'S106 STRANG
HOPELESS/...
(STAMMERING) NEU TOLD YOU--WHATS 107 STRANG
(TENDERLY) NED TOLD ME--THE SECRET--AND I'M SO 107 STRANG
HAPPY, DEAR/
HE TOLD YOU ME--ME--YOU, THE FATHER--$ 107 STRANG
I TELL YOU, THE MOMENT NED TOLD ME, SOMETHING 109 STRANG
HAPPENED TO ME/
WHY HASN'T HE TOLD ME BEFORE?... 115 STRANG
I TOLD HIM I HADN'T. 118 STRANG
YOU COULD HAVE TOLD HIM WHAT A WORLD-BEATER WE'VE 118 STRANG
GOT/
ONE OF THEIR PEOPLE WHO'S BECOME A GOOD PAL OF 121 STRANG
MINE TOLD ME THAT IN CONFIDENCE.
I'VE TOLD YOU TIME AND AGAIN. 153 STRANG
YOU TOLD ME ONCE HE WAS MOTHER'S BEAU--WHEN SHE 153 STRANG
WAS A GIRL.
YOU TOLD ME TO LIE TO YOUR SON AGAINST YOU... 156 STRANG
I TOLD YOU I HAVE A SPLITTING HEADACHE/ 161 STRANG
HE ONCE TOLD ME SHAW WAS AN OLD BEAU OF HIS 163 STRANG
MOTHER'S...
BUT THERE'S STILL SOME SECRET BETWEEN THEM SHE'S 164 STRANG
NEVER TOLD ME...
I WON'T MEDDLE AGAIN WITH HUMAN LIVES, I TOLD YOU/172 STRANG
SHE TOLD YOU THE TRUTH. 172 STRANG
(THINKING) (I'D LIKE TO SEE HIS FACE WHEN I TOLD173 STRANG
HIM HIS FAMOUS OARSMAN ISN'T
I TOLD YOU I'D NEVER MEDDLE AGAIN WITH HUMAN 174 STRANG
LIVES/
AS SAM'S MOTHER TOLD MES... 176 STRANG
HIS MOTHER TOLD ME THAT TIME SO I WOULDN'T HAVE 179 STRANG
HIS BABY.
IF HE HADN'T INTERFERED NINA WOULD HAVE TOLD... 179 STRANG
I'VE NEVER TOLD YOU, BUT I'VE ALWAYS FELT, EVER 185 STRANG
SINCE I WAS A LITTLE KID,
I DON'T BELIEVE DAD TOLD YOU ABOUT HIS WILL, DID 191 STRANG
HE, MOTHERS
I THOUGHT SHE TOLD HIM....) 194 STRANG
(I TOLD HIM HE HIT HIS FATHER... 194 STRANG
WHY, YOU'VE TOLD ME YOURSELF HE WAS IN LOVE WITH 455 WELDED
YOU FOR YEARS.
I TOLD YOU HOW LITTLE THESE MEN HAD MEANT TO ME, 459 WELDED
(FINALLY--IN A GENTLE TONE) NELLY, DON'T YOU 464 WELDED
THINK IT'D HELP IF YOU TOLD ME--
I TOLD HIM I'D BEEN YOUR MISTRESS WHILE HE WAS 468 WELDED
AWAY/

TOLE
YOU KNOW, MARTHY, AY'VE TOLE YOU AY DON'T SEE MY 9 ANNA
ANNA SINCE SHE VAS LITTLE GEL.
IT'S GAWD'S TROOF, WHAT I TOLE YER. 457 CARIBE
UEY'S SOME TINGS I AIN'T GOT TO BE TOLE. 177 EJONES
I TOLE YER YER'D LOSE 'IM, DIDN'T IS 203 EJONES
PAID CRF THIS ARTERNOON, THEY TOLE ME. 493 VOYAGE

TOLERANCE
ERIE GOES ON WITH GOOD-NATURED TOLERANCE.) 12 HUGHIE

1682

TOLERANCE (CONT'D.)
AN EXPRESSION OF TIRED TOLERANCE GIVING HIS FACE 574 ICEMAN
THE QUALITY
(WITH DISDAINFUL TOLERANCE, 54 POET
(WITH A POSSESSIVE SMILE OF TOLERANCE) 101 STRANG

TOLERANT
GLANCING AT THEM WITH A TOLERANT DISLIKE.) 206 DESIRE
THEY GRIN HANGOVER GRINS OF TOLERANT AFFECTION AT 598 ICEMAN
HIM AND WINK AT EACH OTHER.
TRIES TO BE CONTEMPTUOUSLY TOLERANT 60 MISBEG
(WITH TOLERANT GOOD-HUMOR) ON THE LEVEL I B'LIEVE 595 ROPE
THE OLD BOY'S GLAD TO SEE ME
(THOUGH HE IS MOST LIBERAL--EVEN RADICAL--IN HIS 7 STRANG
TOLERANT UNDERSTANDING

TOLERANTLY
AND IS TOLERANTLY LAX IN HIS DISCIPLINE.) 611 ICEMAN
(BORED BUT TOLERANTLY) WHAT CAN I DO EXCEPT 358 MARCOM
ADVISE YOU TO BE PATIENTS
SMILING TOLERANTLY.) 101 POET

TOLERATE
YE'RE ONLY LIVIN' HERE 'CAUSE I TOLERATE YE/ 230 DESIRE
I WILL NOT TOLERATE ANY MORE OF YOUR INTERFERENCE/130 MANSNS
I MAY TOLERATE THEIR PRESENCE OUT OF CHARITY, 39 POET
I WILL TOLERATE NO NIGGARDLY TRADER'S HAGGLING ON 112 POET
HIS PART.

TOLERATED
AN OUTCAST WITHOUT MEANING OR FUNCTION IN MY OWN 73 MANSNS
HOME BUT PLEASANTLY TOLERATED

TOLLING
THE DOLEFUL TOLLING OF BELLS, ON LONG POINT, 25 ANNA
(SCENE--SIX MONTHS LATER. THE TOLLING OF A CHURCH)358 MARCOM
BELL IS FIRST HEARD.

TOLLS
THE SHIP'S BELL TOLLS FOUR BELLS. 473 CARIBE

TOM-TOM
IT AIN'T THE DAMNED MONEY WHAT'S KEEPIN' ME UP IN 542 'ILE
THE NORTHERN SEAS, TOM.
(WITH SATISFACTION) I WARN'T MUCH AFEARED O' 542 'ILE
THAT, TOM.
WHEN TOM COMES FROM THIS VOYAGE YOU'LL BE MARRIED 564 CROSS
AND OUT OF THIS
THE TOM-TOM'LL BE THUMPING OUT THERE BLOOMIN' 175 EJONES
SOON.
(FROM THE DISTANT HILLS COMES THE FAINT, STEADY 184 EJONES
THUMP OF A TOM-TOM,
LISTENING TO THE FAR-OFF BUT INSISTENT BEAT OF THE186 EJONES
TOM-TOM.
HE SITS IN A WEARY ATTITUDE, LISTENING TO THE 188 EJONES
RHYTHMIC BEATING OF THE TOM-TCM)
THE RATE OF THE BEAT OF THE FAR-OFF TOM-TOM 189 EJONES
INCREASES PERCEPTIBLY AS HE DOES SO.
THEN SILENCE BROKEN ONLY BY THE FAR-OFF QUICKENED 190 EJONES
THROB OF THE TOM-TOM.
EXCEPT FOR THE BEATING OF THE TOM-TOM, 190 EJONES
(THE BEAT OF THE FAR-OFF TOM-TOM IS PERCEPTIBLY 192 EJONES
LOUDER AND MORE RAPID.
(AFTER A PAUSE, LISTENING TO THE INSISTENT BEAT OF193 EJONES
THE TOM-TOM IN THE DISTANCE)
FLIGHT AND THE THROBBING OF THE TOM-TOM, STILL FAR195 EJONES
DISTANT,
ALL THIS IN SILENCE SAVE FOR THE OMINOUS THROB OF 197 EJONES
THE TOM-TOM.
CRYING WITH FEAR--AND BY THE QUICKENED, EVER 198 EJONES
LOUDER BEAT OF THE TOM-TOM.)
CONTROLLED BY THE THROB OF THE TOM-TOM IN THE 199 EJONES
DISTANCE, TO A LONG,
THE TOM-TOM BEATS LOUDER, QUICKER, WITH A MORE 199 EJONES
INSISTENT, TRIUMPHANT PULSATION.)
AS IF IN RESPONSE TO HIS SUMMONS THE BEATING OF 200 EJONES
THE TOM-TOM GROWS TO A FIERCE,
CHAINED SLAVES, TO THE RHYTHMIC BEAT OF THE TOM- 200 EJONES
TOM.
FURIOUS EXULTATION, THE TOM-TOM BEATS MADLY. 202 EJONES
WHIMPERING WITH FEAR AS THE THROB OF THE TOM-TOM 202 EJONES
FILLS THE SILENCE ABOUT HIM.
THE TOM-TOM SEEMS ON THE VERY SPOT, 202 EJONES
THE BEATING OF THE TOM-TOM ABRUPTLY CEASES. 203 EJONES
TOM FORGOTTEN THE SPRINKLER... 22 STRANG

TOM-TOM'LL
THE TOM-TOM'LL BE THUMPING OUT THERE BLOOMIN' 175 EJONES
SOON.

TOMB
A GRIM, REPRESSED ROOM LIKE A TOMB IN WHICH THE 241 DESIRE
FAMILY HAS BEEN INTERRED ALIVE.
THIS PALACE OF 'IS IS LIKE A BLEEDIN' TOMB. 174 EJONES
I FELT OUR TOMB NEEDED A LITTLE BRIGHTENING. 17 ELECTR
(REPROACHFULLY) IT IS A TOMB--JUST NOW, ORIN. 74 ELECTR
LIKE A TOMB. 74 ELECTR
(BROWN NODS) IT'S TOO COLD, TOO SPARE, TOO LIKE A300 GGRBON
TOMB, IF YOU'LL PARDON ME.
FOR FOUR DAYS HE LAY IN THE TOMB/ 275 LAZARU
JUST AS HE APPEARED IN THE OPENING OF THE TOMB, 277 LAZARU
WRAPPED IN HIS SHROUD--
DO YOU NOT KNOW THIS LAZARUS DIED AND THEN BY HIS 343 LAZARU
MAGIC ROSE FROM HIS TOMBS
OUR TOMB NEAR OUR HOME, LAZARUS, IN WHICH YOU AND 346 LAZARU
MY CHILDREN WAIT FOR ME.
THE TOMB IS FULL OF SUNLIGHT/ 360 LAZARU
SLOWLY ARISES FROM THE PAST OF THE RACE OF MEN 360 LAZARU
THAT WAS HIS TOMB OF DEATH/
HIS WORDS ARISING FROM THE TOMB CF A SOUL IN PUFFS 16 STRANG
OF ASHES....)
AND HIS TOMB DESECRATED... 74 STRANG
IF OUR MARRIAGE SHOULD BE PURELY THE PLACING OF 148 STRANG
OUR ASHES IN THE SAME TOMB...
THE PLACE IS LIKE A BLEEDIN' TOMB. 493 VOYAGE

TOMMY

AND HAD TO GO TO TOMMY MOORE'S BOARDING HOUSE TO 487 CARDIF GET SHIPPED&

I'M GOING TO REFUSE TO PRINT YOUR DAMNED AD AFTER 203 AHWILD TOMORROW/

YOU'LL TAKE A GOOD DOSE OF SALTS TOMORROW MORNING 271 ANNA AND NO NONSENSE ABOUT IT/

SEE YOU TOMORROW. 5 ANNA

BUT I'M GOING FIRST THING TOMORROW, SO IT'LL BE 64 ANNA THE SAME IN THE END.

AY SIGN ON STEAMER SAIL TOMORROW. 65 ANNA

I SIGNED ON TODAY AT NOON, DRUNK AS I WAS--AND 72 ANNA SHE'S SAILING TOMORROW.

I'LL GO TO NEW YORK TOMORROW. 72 ANNA

WELL, THE TRIP YOU'RE LEAVING ON TOMORROW WILL 83 BEYOND KEEP YOU MOVING ALL RIGHT.

BECAUSE I'M GOING AWAY TOMORROWS 87 BEYOND

GUESS THEY WAS ALL THINKIN' ABOUT TOMORROW, SAME 98 BEYOND AS US.

I'M NOT GOING--I MEAN--I CAN'T GO TOMORROW WITH 100 BEYOND UNCLE DICK--

YOU GO--TOMORROW MORNIN'--AND BY GOD--DON'T COME 108 BEYOND BACK--DON'T DARE COME BACK--

YOU'LL GET YOUR MONEY TOMORROW WHEN I GET BACK 125 BEYOND FROM TOWN--NOT BEFORE/

STILL--DAMN IT ALL--TOMORROW MORNING IS SOON. 141 BEYOND

TOMORROW MORNIN'. 141 BEYOND

YOU'LL BE BETTER TOMORROW. 485 CARDIF

OR I'LL MAKE A COMPLAINT ASHORE TOMORROW AND HAVE 473 CARIBSE YOU LOCKED UP.

SAY, LET'S ME 'N' YOU GIT MARRIED, EMMER-- 534 DIFRNT TOMORROW, EH$

SAY YOU WILL--FIRST THING TOMORROW. 534 DIFRNT

AND HE'S ASKED ME TO MARRY HIM TOMORROW. 542 DIFRNT

FIRST THING TOMORROW. 542 DIFRNT

TOMORROW. 543 DIFRNT

YOU MEAN--IF HE'S WILLING TO BRIBE YOU WITH MONEY,545 DIFRNT YOU WON'T MARRY ME TOMORROWS

ONLY NOT TOMORROW, WE'D BETTER WAIT AND SEE-- 546 DIFRNT

DAWN TOMORROW I'LL BE OUT AT DE ODER SIDE AND ON 183 EJONES DE COAST WHAR DAT FRENCH

MY WOUND IS HEALED AND I'VE GOT ORDERS TO LEAVE 13 ELECTR TOMORROW

YOU SAIL TO BOSTON TOMORROW, TO WAIT FOR CARGOS 40 ELECTR

HE MIGHT ARRIVE TONIGHT--OR TOMORROW--OR THE NEXT 46 ELECTR DAY.

AND HAD A BIG PUBLIC FUNERAL TOMORROW. 69 ELECTR

AN' WHEN I GIT THROUGH TELLIN' MY STORY OF IT 135 ELECTR ROUND TOWN TOMORROW.

TOMORROW. 136 ELECTR

(DETERMINEDLY) BUT I'M GOING TO MAKE HIM PROMISE 159 ELECTR TO COME OVER TOMORROW.

YOU COME OVER TOMORROW AND STAY WITH US. 161 ELECTR

ORIN IS COMING TOMORROW. 162 ELECTR

WE'LL EXPECT YOU TOMORROW, AND HAVE YOUR ROOM 163 ELECTR READY.

I SUPPOSE--WE CAN'T EXPECT YOU TOMORROW--NOW. 164 ELECTR

SEE YOU TOMORROW/ 288 GGBROW

TOMORROW WE MAY BE WITH HIM IN PARADISE! 291 GGBROW

TOMORROW I'LL HAVE MOVED ON TO THE NEXT HELL/ 292 GGBROW

HERE TODAY, GONE TOMORROW, SO WHAT'S THE GOOD OF 18 HUGHIE BEEFIN'S

=LET THIS RIDE ON THE NOSE OF WHATEVER HORSE 22 HUGHIE YOU'RE BETTING ON TOMORROW,

DOWN TODAY AND UP TOMORROW. 37 HUGHIE

HIM YESTERDAY, ME OR YOU TOMORROW, AND WHO CARES, 38 HUGHIE AND WHAT'S THE DIFFERENCES

---JIMMY TOMORROW---SITS FACING FRONT. 574 ICEMAN

JAMES CAMERON---JIMMY TOMORROW--- 575 ICEMAN

IT'LL BE A GREAT DAY FOR THEM, TOMORROW--- 578 ICEMAN

BEGINNIN' TOMORROW,= HE SAYS. 578 ICEMAN

(GRINNING) I'LL BE GLAD TO PAY UP--TOMORROW. 578 ICEMAN

HE'S THE LEADER OF OUR TOMORROW MOVEMENT. 593 ICEMAN

HIS NICKNAME HERE IS JIMMY TOMORROW. 593 ICEMAN

JIMMY TOMORROW NODS, HIS EYES BLINKING. 598 ICEMAN

(JIMMY TOMORROW BLINKS BENIGNANTLY FROM ONE TO THE599 ICEMAN OTHER.

WORST IS BEST HERE, AND EAST IS WEST, AND TOMORROW600 ICEMAN IS YESTERDAY.

WITH A PATHETIC ATTEMPT AT A BRISK, NO-MORE- 600 ICEMAN NONSENSE AIR) TOMORROW, YES.

TOMORROW VIDDOUT FAIL/ 602 ICEMAN

YOU SHALL BE PAID TOMORROW. 602 ICEMAN

YOU PAY UP TOMORROW OR OUT YOU GO/ 602 ICEMAN

I MUST HAVE MY SHOES SOLED AND HEELED AND SHINED 603 ICEMAN FIRST THING TOMORROW MORNING.

THE TOMORROW MOVEMENT IS A SAD AND BEAUTIFUL 603 ICEMAN THING, TOO/

MY BIRTHDAY, TOMORROW, THAT'D BE THE RIGHT TIME TO604 ICEMAN TURN OVER A NEW LEAF.

ALL I HAVE TO DO IS GET FIXED UP WITH A DECENT 604 ICEMAN FRONT TOMORROW.

BEJAES, YOU'LL PAY UP TOMORROW, OR I'LL START A 605 ICEMAN HARRY HOPE REVOLUTION/

AND THE ONE WHERE JIMMY TOMORROW IS. 619 ICEMAN

(HE LOOKS AT JIMMY TOMORROW) 622 ICEMAN

I KNOW ALL ABOUT TOMORROW. 623 ICEMAN

AND NO TOMORROW ABOUT IT/ 623 ICEMAN

BUT HE'LL PROBABLY BE HIS NATURAL SELF AGAIN 625 ICEMAN TOMORROW--

SEEING I GOT IT ALL SET FOR MY BIRTHDAY TOMORROW. 626 ICEMAN

HE'S GOT HARRY AND JIMMY TOMORROW RUN RAGGED, 631 ICEMAN

YUH HEARD HER SAY =TOMORROW,= DIDN'T YUHS 632 ICEMAN

WE'RE GOIN' TO GET MARRIED TOMORROW. 632 ICEMAN

AND, ALONG WITH HARRY AND JIMMY TOMORROW, YOU'RE 643 ICEMAN THE ONE I WANT MOST TO HELP.

TOMORROW (CONT'D.)

BY TOMORROW MORNING I'LL BE ON THE WAGON. 644 ICEMAN TOMORROW/ 647 ICEMAN

IF HE GETS HIM TO TAKE THAT WALK TOMORROW. 651 ICEMAN

I'LL SEE THE BOSS TOMORROW. 652 ICEMAN

I'M CLEARING OUT TOMORROW MORNING ANYWAY. 652 ICEMAN

HARRY HOPE AND JIMMY TOMORROW APPEAR IN THE HALL 653 ICEMAN OUTSIDE THE DOOR.

TOMORROW MORNING. 655 ICEMAN

FOR A MOMENT THERE IS A PAUSE, BROKEN BY JIMMY 656 ICEMAN TOMORROW

YOU'LL BE IN A TODAY WHERE THERE IS NO YESTERDAY 661 ICEMAN OR TOMORROW TO WORRY YOU.

AND MAKES YOU HIDE BEHIND LOUSY PIPE DREAMS ABOUT 661 ICEMAN TOMORROW.

DID THIS GREAT REVELATION OF THE EVIL HABIT OF 662 ICEMAN DREAMING ABOUT TOMORROW

(DERISIVELY) NOW YUH CAN SELL DEM BACK TO HIM 674 ICEMAN AGAIN TOMORROW.

THEN HARRY HOPE ENTERS FROM THE HALL, FOLLOWED BY 683 ICEMAN JIMMY TOMORROW.

I MERELY MENTIONED I WOULD FEEL MORE FIT TOMORROW.684 ICEMAN

IT'S EXACTLY THOSE DAMNED TOMORROW DREAMS WHICH 685 ICEMAN KEEP YOU FROM MAKING PEACE WITH

(PLEADS ABJECTLY) TOMORROW/ 686 ICEMAN

I'LL BE IN GOOD SHAPE TOMORROW/ 686 ICEMAN

I WILL TOMORROW/ 686 ICEMAN

FINALLY, AT RIGHT OF TABLE, IS JIMMY TOMORROW. 696 ICEMAN

JIMMY TOMORROW WAS DE LAST. 699 ICEMAN

OR LIE TO YOURSELVES ABOUT REFORMING TOMORROWS 705 ICEMAN

CAN'T YOU SEE THERE IS NO TOMORROW NOW$ 705 ICEMAN

(HE APPEALS MECHANICALLY TO (JIMMY TOMORROW) 707 ICEMAN

IT WAS ALL A STUPID LIE--MY NONSENSE ABOUT 707 ICEMAN TOMORROW.

YOU COULDN'T SHAKE HER FAITH THAT IT HAD TO COME 713 ICEMAN TRUE--TOMORROW/

TOMORROW/ 721 ICEMAN

ALL THAT TALK OF HIS ABOUT TOMORROW, FOR EXAMPLE, 721 ICEMAN

I'LL KICK YOU OUT IN THE GUTTER TOMORROW, SO HELP 171 JOURNE ME GOD.

GIVE US YOUR ANSWER TOMORROW. 322 LAZARU

WHEN YOU AWAKE TOMORROW, TRY TO REMEMBER/ 323 LAZARU

BUT TOMORROW HE WILL JEER WHILE HYENAS GNAW AT 358 LAZARU YOUR SKULL AND LICK YOUR BRAIN.

WE WILL GO AND SEE SIMON TOMORROW. 38 MANSNS

SO I CAN RETURN ON THE FIRST STAGE TOMORROW. 51 MANSNS

YOU WILL START YOUR WORK HERE TOMORROW MORNING. 92 MANSNS

I'M TO START TOMORROW-- 132 MANSNS

IF YOU HAD TO PAY THE DEBTS ON THE PROPERTIES HE 142 MANSNS HAS MADE OVER TO YOU TOMORROW---

I'LL TAKE THEM THERE TOMORROW. 188 MANSNS

BE GOD, YOU'LL BELIEVE IT TOMORROW/ 84 MISBEG

HE'LL BE WITH TOMORROW NIGHT ON BROADWAY. 91 MISBEG

DON'T EXPECT ME HOME TONIGHT, MISS HOGAN, OR 101 MISBEG TOMORROW EITHER, MAYBE.

YOU'LL BE TAKING A TRAIN BACK TO YOUR DEAR OLD 130 MISBEG BROADWAY TOMORROW NIGHT.

TOMORROW NIGHTS 131 MISBEG

AND THEN WHEN HE COMES TOMORROW MORNING TO DRIVE 132 MISBEG ME TO THE EXECUTOR'S OFFICE.

IF SHE'D WAITED TILL TOMORROW, EVEN, I'D HAVE GOT 77 POET HIM TO ASK ME TO MARRY HIM.

I'LL BE FREE ON THE MOUNTAINSIDE WHILE YOU'LL LIE 102 POET LOW TOMORROW.=

=MAYBE I'M WRONG,= SAYS HE, =BUT I DOUBT THAT 102 POET YOU'LL BE AS GAY TOMORROW.

IF HE WASN'T SICK, I'D--BUT I'LL GET HIM OUT OF 127 POET HERE TOMORROW/

AND TOMORROW HE'LL BE HIMSELF AGAIN--MAYBE. 180 POET

AN' THE THIEF COULD TAKE THE FARM FROM US TOMORROW590 ROPE

IF HIMSELF TURNED A LUNATIC.

I MUST START WORK TOMORROW. . . 5 STRANG

TRY TOMORROW IN MY BEDROOM. . . 67 STRANG

AND I HOPE YOUR MOTHER IS FEELING BETTER TOMORROW. 75 STRANG

TAKE HER TO SEE HIM--TOMORROW/ 77 STRANG

I'LL TAKE HER TO SEE HIM TOMORROW. 78 STRANG

WE'D BETTER GET MARRIED TOMORROW. 197 STRANG

TOMORROWS

=YESTERDAY THIS DAY'S MADNESS DID PREPARE 261 AHWILD TOMORROW'S SILENCE, TRIUMPH,

JIMMY TOMORROW'S IS =A WEE DOCK AND DORIS=. 727 ICEMAN

TOMORROWS

THEY'VE ALL A TOUCHING CREDULITY CONCERNING 578 ICEMAN TOMORROWS.

WITH A FEW HARMLESS PIPE DREAMS ABOUT THEIR 587 ICEMAN YESTERDAYS AND TOMORROWS,

JUST STOP LYING ABOUT YOURSELF AND KIDDING 622 ICEMAN YOURSELF ABOUT TOMORROWS.

TON

A TON OF LEADS 66 ANNA

(CYNICALLY) YEAH, AND A TON OF HOP/ 578 ICEMAN

AND A TON OF GOOD ADVICE ABOUT WHAT A SUCKER HE IS651 ICEMAN TO STAND FOR US.

THEN I FELT AS IF A TON OF GUILT HAD BEEN LIFTED 693 ICEMAN OFF MY MIND.

I FELT AS THOUGH A TON OF GUILT WAS LIFTED OFF MY 716 ICEMAN MIND.

GOD, SHE WEIGHS A TON. 159 JOURNE

TONE

(THE SAME TONE OF AWE CREEPING INTO HIS VOICE) 536 *ILE

(A TONE OF COMMAND IN HIS VOICE) 540 *ILE

(MARKED BY HER STRANGE TONE AND THE FAR-AWAY LOOK547 *ILE IN HER EYES)

VOICES ARE HEARD IN A CONVERSATIONAL TONE FROM THE185 AHWILD DINING-ROOM BEYOND THE BACK

(BREAKS IN IN A FORCED JOKING TONE THAT CONCEALS A190 AHWILD DEEP EARNESTNESS)

TONE

TONE (CONT'D.)
THEN CALLS IN A TONE OF STRAINED HEARTINESS.) 200 AHWILD
(A BIT SHAKEN BY THIS THREAT--BUT IN THE SAME FLAT204 AHWILD TONE)
(ADOPTING A FORCED, INNOCENT TONE.) 206 AHWILD
(AS HE ENTERS--WARNINGLY, IN A LOW TONE) 218 AHWILD
(SITS DOWN BUT BENDS FORWARD TO CALL TO HIS WIFE 223 AHWILD IN A CONFIDENTIAL TONE)
A JOKE'S A JOKE, BUT--(HE ADDRESSES HIS WIFE IN A 227 AHWILD WOUNDED TONE)
(SENSING THE HURT IN HIS TONE, COMES TO HIS 230 AHWILD RESCUE)
(ADOPTING A JOKING TONE) I'M GOING TO BUY A CLOCK250 AHWILD FOR IN HERE.
(MADE TERRIBLY CURIOUS BY HIS OMINOUS TONE) 281 AHWILD
THAT'S WHAT STOPPED ME (THEN WITH A BITTER CHANGE 282 AHWILD OF TONE)
(SUDDENLY GROWING SOMBER--IN A LOW TONE) 9 ANNA
(IRRITATED BY THE OTHER'S TONE--SCORNFULLY) 15 ANNA
(THEN SEEING HER IRRITATION, HE HASTILY ADOPTS A 26 ANNA MORE CHEERFUL TONE)
(IMPRESSED BY HIS TONE) YOU TALK--NUTTY TONIGHT 29 ANNA YOURSELF.
(THEN MORE SERIOUSLY BUT STILL IN A BOASTFUL TONE, 31 ANNA
HE SUDDENLY CHANGES HIS TUNE TO ONE OF BOISTEROUS 33 ANNA JOVIALITY)
(THEN ATTEMPTING A SEVERE TONE AGAIN) 34 ANNA
(IN THE SAME TONE) WHY, SURE. 38 ANNA
(ALL HER EMOTIONS IMMEDIATELY TRANSFORMED INTO 39 ANNA RESENTMENT AT HIS BULLYING TONE)
(WITH SUDDEN CHANGE OF TONE--PERSUASIVELY) 43 ANNA
(AS HE SEES CHRIS--IN A JOVIAL TONE OF MOCKERY) 45 ANNA
(TO ANNA--ALSO IN AN AUTHORITATIVE TONE) 55 ANNA
SHE DRAWS AWAY FROM HIM, INSTINCTIVELY REPELLED BY 55 ANNA HIS TONE.
(HE GETS TO HIS FEET CONFIDENTLY, ASSUMING A 55 ANNA MASTERFUL TONE)
(THERE IS SOMETHING IN HER TONE THAT MAKES THEM 56 ANNA FORGET THEIR QUARREL
(TRYING TO KEEP UP HER HARD, BITTER TONE, 59 ANNA
(TRYING TO FALL INTO AN EASY, CARELESS TONE) 69 ANNA
(IN A COLD HARD TONE) WHAT ARE YOU DOING HERE$ 69 ANNA
(IN THE SAME TONE) MY BAG'S PACKED AND I GOT MY 72 ANNA TICKET.
(AS HE GOES OUT--IN A LOW TONE) 97 BEYOND
(HURRIEDLY--IN A TONE OF WARNING) 100 BEYOND
(HURT BY THE INSINUATION HE FEELS IN ANDREW'S 104 BEYOND TONE)
(HURT BY HIS BROTHER'S TONE) 104 BEYOND
(IN A MORE KINDLY TONE) WHAT'S COME OVER YOU SO 105 BEYOND SUDDEN, ANDY$
(NOT NOTICING THE SARCASM IN ROBERT'S TONE) 133 BEYOND
(EXCITEDLY--IN A RATHER BOASTFUL TONE) 138 BEYOND
(STANDS STARING AT HER FOR A MOMENT--THEN WALKS 140 BEYOND AWAY SAYING IN A HURT TONE)
(TURNING TO LOOK AT ANDREW--IN A TONE OF FIERCE 141 BEYOND RESENTMENT)
(HE PAUSES, THEN CONTINUES IN A TONE OF TENDER 147 BEYOND SYMPATHY)
(IN A LOUD TONE) THERE'S A TIME COMES--WHEN YOU 156 BEYOND DON'T MIND ANY MORE--ANYTHING.
(HE DROPS HIS MOCKING AND ADOPTS A CALM, 560 CROSS DELIBERATE TONE AGAIN)
(IN A CROONING, MONOTONOUS TONE) 571 CROSS
(FORCING A HUMOROUS TONE) WHAT, BESIDES THE 496 DAYS POORHOUSE, IS ON YOUR MIND, BILL$
(HIS TONE SUDDENLY COLD AND HOSTILE) 497 DAYS
(IN A JOKING TONE) BUT WHEN I HAVE, BILL, 497 DAYS
(THE HIDDEN SINISTER NOTE AGAIN CREEPING INTO HIS 498 DAYS COOLLY CASUAL TONE)
(THEN HE TURNS TO ELIOT--IN A JOKING TONE) 501 DAYS
(HE GOES ON TO ELIOT WITH A RENEWAL OF HIS 502 DAYS HUMOROUSLY COMPLAINING TONE)
(IN A BITTER, SNEERING TONE) 508 DAYS
(HIS VOICE SUDDENLY TAKES ON A TONE OF BITTER 511 DAYS HATRED)
IN A CASUAL TONE) AND THAT'S THE END OF PART ONE,511 DAYS AS I'VE OUTLINED IT.
(HE LISTENS--THEN ANXIETY CREEPING INTO HIS TONE) 513 DAYS
THEN STOPS ABRUPTLY AND CONTINUES IN HIS TONE OF 513 DAYS COLD, SINISTER INSISTENCE)
(WITH A RETURN OF HER FLIPPANT TONE) 520 DAYS
(QUICKLY, RAISING HIS VOICE TO A CONVERSATIONAL 527 DAYS TONE)
(WITH A FLIPPANT SNEER) HARDLY THE LOVER-LIKE 527 DAYS TONE. IS IT$
(THEN TO ELSA IN A TENDERLY CHIDING TONE) 532 DAYS
I NEED HER DEATH FOR MY END. (THEN IN A SINISTER,539 DAYS JEERING TONE)
HE FORCES A SMILE AND ADOPTS A JOKING TONE) 539 DAYS
(SLOWLY, IN HIS COLD TONE WITH ITS UNDERCURRENT OF540 DAYS SINISTER HIDDEN MEANING)
(AFTER A WORRIED GLANCE AT HER--AN UNDERCURRENT OF540 DAYS WARNING IN HIS QUIET TONE)
JOHN IS TALKING IN A STRAINED TONE, MONOTONOUSLY, 541 DAYS INSISTENTLY.
(THEN IN AN ABRUPT, ANGRY TONE) 545 DAYS
(FORCING A LIGHT TONE--AS SHE COMES FORWARD) 548 DAYS
(THEN FORCING A TENDERLY BULLYING TONE) 548 DAYS
(THEN WITH A HARD, MOCKING TONE) 548 DAYS
IN A TONE OF DESPAIRING BITTERNESS.) 554 DAYS
(IN A COLD, INEXORABLE TONE) 554 DAYS
(HASTILY, IN A FORCED TONE OF REASSURANCE) 555 DAYS
(FORCING AN EASY TONE) WHAT'S ALL THIS TALK$ 556 DAYS
(THEN IN A TONE OF EXASPERATED DEJECTION) 557 DAYS
(HIS EYES FIXED ON JOHN'S FACE, SPEAKS IN A COLD 557 DAYS IMPLACABLE TONE)

TONE (CONT'D.)
(IN THE SAME LOW TONE, BUT WITH A COLD, DRIVING 561 DAYS INTENSITY)
SPEAKS SOBBINGLY IN A STRANGE HUMBLE TONE OF 565 DAYS BROKEN REPROACH)
(IN SAME TONE) BACON$ BACON/ 206 DESIRE
(IN A QUIETING TONE) LISTEN, EPHRAIM. 233 DESIRE
(THIS IN A TONE OF COLD THREAT.) 238 DESIRE
(A VEILED THREAT IN HER TONE) 238 DESIRE
(COMING CLOSER TO HER--IN A LOW, CONFIDENTIAL 502 DIFRNT TONE, CHUCKLINGLY)
(IN A JOKING TONE--WITH A MEANING GLANCE AT EMMA) 510 DIFRNT
(IN A TONE OF FINALITY AS IF THIS SETTLED THE 512 DIFRNT MATTER)
(IN THE SAME COLD TONE) YES. 514 DIFRNT
(MADE HOPELESS AGAIN BY HER TONE--CLASPS HER HAND 518 DIFRNT MECHANICALLY--DULLY)
(IN A SNARLING TONE) I S'POSE YOU'VE BEEN GIVIN' 528 DIFRNT HIM AN EARFUL OF LIES ABOUT
(WORRIED BY THE FINALITY IN HER TONE--PLACATINGLY)529 DIFRNT
(TRYING A CONFIDENTIAL TONE) 529 DIFRNT
SHE TRIPS LIGHTLY TO THE DOOR AND OPENS IT-- 534 DIFRNT FORCING A LIGHT, CARELESS TONE)
FINALLY, HE VENTURES IN A GENTLE TONE) 537 DIFRNT
(ROUSING HERSELF--FORCING A CARELESS TONE) 538 DIFRNT
WITH A TRACE OF SOMETHING LIKE PITY SHOWING IN HIS546 DIFRNT TONE)
HE INSTINCTIVELY IMITATES HIS FATHER'S TONE, 422 DYNAMO
BOOMING SELF-PROTECTINGLY.
(GLANCES AT HIM AND SPEAKS IN A GENTLE TONE THAT 423 DYNAMO CARRIES A CHALLENGING QUALITY)
(SHE SPEAKS IN A MEEK, PERSUASIVE TONE) 423 DYNAMO
(TAKING HIS HAND-- IN A BULLYING TONE) 434 DYNAMO
(GLANCES AT HER IRRITABLY--THEN WITH A CALCULATING430 DYNAMO TONE TO REUBEN)
(MADE VISIBLY UNEASY BUT FORCING A MANLY TONE) 439 DYNAMO
(HARSHLY AND CONDEMNINGLY--IN HIS FATHER'S TONE) 440 DYNAMO
(CHANGING TO A TONE OF WHEEDLING AFFECTION) 446 DYNAMO
(MADE UNEASY BY SOMETHING IN HER TONE-- 447 DYNAMO INSISTENTLY)
(FRIGHTENED BY THE CHANGE IN HIM BUT ATTEMPTING A 449 DYNAMO BULLYING TONE)
FIFE CALLS TO LIGHT IN A MOCKING TONE) 450 DYNAMO
(IN A TONE IN WHICH THERE IS NOW A NOTE OF PANIC) 459 DYNAMO
(THEN AS SUDDENLY CHANGING TO A PASSIONATE TONE OF460 DYNAMO DESIRE)
TIME. AND HE BLURTS OUT IN A TONE THAT IS ALMOST 463 DYNAMO KINDLY) SAY, YOU LOOK ALL IN.
(HIS STRENGTH FAILING HIM---IN A FALTERING TONE 463 DYNAMO HARDLY ABOVE A WHISPER)
(GOING ON AS IF HE HADN'T HEARD--IN A TONE OF 463 DYNAMO MONOTONOUS GRIEF)
(FORCING A CASUAL TONE) WHAT DID SHE DIE OF$ 464 DYNAMO
(HE SPEAKS TO HIS FATHER IN A DEFENSIVE, ACCUSING 464 DYNAMO TONE)
(IN A LIGHTER TONE--MOCKINGLY) 467 DYNAMO
(TRYING TO FORCE A JOKING TONE) 469 DYNAMO
(A PAUSE--THEN HE GOES ON IN THE SAME FASCINATED 474 DYNAMO TONE)
THEN STOPS WHEN HE CAN'T CATCH THE RIGHT TONE. 474 DYNAMO
(THEN IN HER TONE OF CHILDISH MOONING) 479 DYNAMO
IN A QUEER, DETACHED TONE) 481 DYNAMO
(IN THE SAME TONE) YES, I SWEAR. 485 DYNAMO
(IN THE SAME TONE--SLIGHTLY BOASTFUL) 181 EJONES
(STARTLED TO ALERTNESS, BUT PRESERVING THE SAME 182 EJONES CARELESS TONE)
(IN THE SAME MOCKING TONE) 182 EJONES
IN A TONE OF AWE.) 188 EJONES
(HE GRUMBLES IN A LOUD TONE TO COVER UP A GROWING 188 EJONES UNEASINESS)
(HE TURNS OVER THE STONE AND FEELS IN UNDER IT--IN188 EJONES A TONE OF DISMAY)
(WITH SUDDEN FORCED DEFIANCE--IN AN ANGRY TONE) 189 EJONES
MAN THAT HE SEES--IN A TONE OF HAPPY RELIEF) 192 EJONES
THEN FALLS BY SLOW GRADATIONS OF TONE INTO SILENCE199 EJONES AND IS TAKEN UP AGAIN.
SMITHERS LEANS OVER HIS SHOULDER--IN A TONE OF 204 EJONES FRIGHTENED AWE)
(STARTS AGAIN BUT KEEPS HER TONE COLD AND 12 ELECTR COLLECTED)
(SHE FORCES A SMILE BUT HER TONE IS REALLY HURT.) 13 ELECTR
YOU WILL KINDLY NOT TAKE THAT TONE WITH ME, 18 ELECTR PLEASE$
(HE HAS KEPT HER HAND AND HE DROPS HIS VOICE TO A 21 ELECTR LOW LOVER-LIKE TONE.
(AT SOMETHING IN HER TONE HE STARES AT HER 21 ELECTR SUSPICIOUSLY.
(BROUGHT BACK WITH A SHOCK, ASTONISHED AT HER 22 ELECTR TONE)
(WATCHING HER CAREFULLY--KEEPING HIS CASUAL TONE) 22 ELECTR
(DROPPING HIS VOICE TO A REVERENT, HUSHED TONE. 22 ELECTR
(IN A DRY, BRITTLE TONE) I REMEMBER YOUR 23 ELECTR ADMIRATION FOR
HE COMES CLOSER TO HER, DROPPING HIS VOICE AGAIN 24 ELECTR TO HIS LOVE MAKING TONE)
(FURIOUS AT HER TONE) NO/ 27 ELECTR
(THEN ABRUPTLY CHANGING TONE) 39 ELECTR
THEN CHRISTINE SPEAKS IN A DRY MOCKING TONE.) 45 ELECTR
(FORCING A LIGHT TONE) COMPLIMENTS FROM ONE'S 47 ELECTR HUSBAND)
(CURTLY--A TRACE OF JEALOUSY IN HIS TONE) 48 ELECTR
(FORCING A GENTLE TONE) SIT DOWN, EZRA. 51 ELECTR
THEN EMBARRASSED BY THIS SHOW OF EMOTION, ADDS IN 52 ELECTR A GRUFF, JOKING TONE)
YOU NEEDN'T ADOPT THAT PITIFUL TONE/ 61 ELECTR
(THEN IN A STRANGE FLAT TONE) 63 ELECTR
(PUTTING AN ARM AROUND HER--IN A STRAINED TONE) 72 ELECTR

TONE

(CONT'D.)
(THEN A TONE OF EAGERNESS BREAKING THROUGH IN 72 ELECTR SPITE OF HERSELF)
(THEN IN AN AWED TONE) BUT THE HOUSE LOOKS 74 ELECTR STRANGE.
(A TRACE OF RESENTMENT HAS CREPT INTO HIS TONE) 74 ELECTR
THEN WITH BITTER, HURT DISAPPOINTMENT IN HIS TONE) 74 ELECTR
IN A TONE SHE VAINLY TRIES TO MAKE KINDLY AND 77 ELECTR PERSUASIVE)
FEAR CREEPS INTO CHRISTINE'S TONE) 77 ELECTR
(STARING AT HER--IN A QUEER TONE OF GRATITUDE) 81 ELECTR
(FROM THE DOORWAY--IN A BRUSQUE COMMANDING TONE 83 ELECTR LIKE HER FATHER'S)
IN HER GENTLE MOTHERLY TONE) 84 ELECTR
(THEN QUICKLY--WITH A BITTER, JOKING TONE) 95 ELECTR
(IN A TONE OF AWAKENING SUSPICION) 98 ELECTR
(SHE ADDRESSES THE DEAD MAN DIRECTLY IN A STRANGE 101 ELECTR TONE OF DEFIANT SCORN)
(NOTICING THE HURT IN HIS TONE--MISERABLY) 111 ELECTR
(LOOKS AROUND THE CABIN CALCULATINGLY-THEN IN A 114 ELECTR TONE OF COMMAND)
FINALLY LAVINIA SPEAKS TO THE CORPSE IN A GRIM 115 ELECTR BITTER TONE)
(THEN, AS IF TO HERSELF--IN A LOW DESPERATE TONE) 118 ELECTR
LAVINIA SPEAKS AGAIN IN CURT COMMANDING TONE THAT 122 ELECTR RECALLS HER FATHER)
(IMPRESSED BUT FORCING A TEASING TONE) 135 ELECTR
(THEN WITH A CHANGE OF TONE) 136 ELECTR
SHE HESITATES AND STANDS LOOKING AT THE HOUSE--IN 137 ELECTR A LOW TONE, ALMOST OF DREAD)
(TURNS BACK AND CALLS COAXINGLY IN THE TONE ONE 137 ELECTR WOULD USE TO A CHILD)
CONCEALING HER APPREHENSION UNDER A COAXINGLY 138 ELECTR MOTHERLY TONE)
(SHOCKED BACK TO AWARENESS BY HER TONE--PITIFULLY 140 ELECTR CONFUSED)
(HIS TONE BECOMING SLY, INSINUATING AND MOCKING. 144 ELECTR
(IN A SUDDEN STRANGE TONE OF JEERING MALICE) 144 ELECTR
SHE FORCES A SMILE AND A MOTHERLY TONE) 145 ELECTR
(THEN AFTER A QUICK LOOK AT HIM--IN A CONFIDING 148 ELECTR TONE)
(AS IF HE HADN'T HEARD--IN THE SAME SINISTER 154 ELECTR MOCKING TONE)
(WITH A CHANGE TO A HARSH THREATENING TONE) 156 ELECTR
(FRIGHTENED BY HIS TONE) WHAT DO YOU MEANS 160 ELECTR
(SHE GLANCES SHARPLY AT HAZEL--FORCING A JOKING 162 ELECTR TONE)
(UNEASINESS CREEPING INTO HER TONE) 162 ELECTR
HIS TONE INSTANTLY CHANGES TO ONE OF PASSIONATE 165 ELECTR PLEADING)
(CONCEALING A START OF FEAR--CHANGING TO A FORCED 172 ELECTR REPROACHFUL TONE)
THEN TURNS AWAY, SAYING IN A LOST, EMPTY TONE) 178 ELECTR
(LOOKING UPWARD AT THE MOON AND SINGING IN LOW 262 GGBROW TONE AS THEY ENTER)
(HE SITS DOWN ON THE BENCH AT RIGHT, FORCING A 265 GGBROW JOKING TONE)
(WITH MORE AND MORE MASTERY IN HIS TONE) 267 GGBROW
(FROWNS CONFUSEDLY--THEN FORCING A PLAYFUL TONE) 271 GGBROW
(WITHOUT LOOKING AT HIM--IN A COMFORTING, MOTHERLY273 GGBROW TONE)
(FORCING A GAY TONE) YES, INDEED/ 276 GGBROW
(TRYING A BULLYING TONE--ROUGHLY) 281 GGBROW
(IN THE SAME TONE) 285 GGBROW
(IN SAME TONE) AND I LOVE MARGARET/ 291 GGBROW
(IN A FRIENDLY TONE) I KNOW. 293 GGBROW
(IN THE SAME AWKWARD, SELF-CONSCIOUS TONE, ONE 293 GGBROW AFTER ANOTHER)
(MAINTAINING THE SAME INDULGENT, BIG-BROTHERLY 294 GGBROW TONE,
IN SPITE OF HIMSELF, BROWN SQUIRMS AND ADOPTS A 297 GGBROW PLACATING TONE)
(IN A TRANCELIKE TONE) =OUR FATHER WHO ART IN 299 GGBROW HEAVEN.=
FINALLY, HE BEGINS TO TALK TO IT IN A BITTER, 307 GGBROW MOCKING TONE.
(THEN WITH A SUDDEN COMPLETE CHANGE OF TONE-- 317 GGBROW ANGRILY)
(IN SAME TONE) I CAN ALMOST HEAR HIM TALKING. 318 GGBROW
(TAKING HER TONE--EXULTANTLY) 322 GGBROW
(FORCING A JOKING TONE) BUT YOU MUSTN'T WASTE 323 GGBROW JUNE ON AN OLD WOMAN LIKE ME/
TURNS AROUND THREATENINGLY---IN A TONE OF 209 HA APE CONTEMPTUOUS AUTHORITY)
(HE STARTS TO SING IN A THIN, NASAL, DOLEFUL 210 HA APE TONE..)
(IN A MORE PLACATED BUT STILL CONTEMPTUOUS TONE) 211 HA APE
(HIS TONE OF EXALTATION CEASES. 214 HA APE
(IN A PASSIONLESS TONE) I DETEST YOU, AUNT. 218 HA APE
(IN A MOCKING TONE) PURR, LITTLE LEOPARD. 220 HA APE
(IN THE SAME TONE) POSER/ 222 HA APE
(IN AN EXULTANT TONE OF COMMAND) 223 HA APE
(THE WHOLE CROWD OF MEN AND WOMEN CHORUS AFTER HER238 HA APE IN THE SAME TONE OF AFFECTED
(IN A VAGUE MOCKING TONE) SAY, WHERE DO I GO FROM251 HA APE HERE$
PITCHED IN A CONVERSATIONAL TONE CAN BE HEARD. 251 HA APE
THEN YANK BEGINS TO TALK IN A FRIENDLY 252 HA APE CONFIDENTIAL TONE, HALF MOCKINGLY,
(HE LAUGHS--THEN IN A SAVAGE TONE) 253 HA APE
(SOMETHING, THE TONE OF MOCKERY, PERHAPS, SUDDENLY254 HA APE ENRAGES THE ANIMAL.
YANK KEEPS HIS MOCKING TONE--HOLDS OUT HIS HAND) 254 HA APE
ERIE USUALLY SPEAKS IN A LOW, GUARDED TONE, 9 HUGHIE
HE APPEARS NOT UNFAVORABLY IMPRESSED BUT HIS TONE 10 HUGHIE STILL HOLDS RESENTMENT.)
(IN A TONE OF ONE WHO IS WEARILY RELIEVED 10 HUGHIE

TONE

(CONT'D.)
ERIE LEANS ON THE DESK--IN A DEJECTED, 17 HUGHIE CONFIDENTIAL TONE.)
(IN THE VAGUE TONE OF A CORPSE WHICH ADMITS IT 18 HUGHIE ONCE OVERHEARD A FAVORABLE RUMOR
(WITH AN ABRUPT CHANGE TO A BULLYING TONE) 579 ICEMAN
IN A GUTTURAL DECLAMATORY TONE) 579 ICEMAN
(FORCING A CASUAL TONE) I DON'T SUPPOSE YOU'VE 591 ICEMAN HAD MUCH CHANCE
(ABRUPTLY HIS TONE SHARPENS WITH RESENTFUL 591 ICEMAN WARNING)
(HE BREAKS INTO HIS WHEEDLING, BULLYING TONE) 592 ICEMAN
HUGO EXCLAIMS AUTOMATICALLY IN HIS TONE OF 592 ICEMAN DENUNCIATION)
(FORCING A TONE OF IRRITATION) 625 ICEMAN
(HIS TONE SUDDENLY CHANGES TO ONE OF GUTTURAL 627 ICEMAN SOAPBOX DENUNCIATION
(IGNORES THIS--TO LARRY, IN A LOW TONE OF HATRED) 634 ICEMAN
(A BITTER MOCKING CONTEMPT CREEPS INTO HIS TONE) 635 ICEMAN
(HIS TONE BECOMES AGGRESSIVE) 637 ICEMAN
(IN A LOW ANGRY TONE) WHAT A NOIVE/ 637 ICEMAN
(GIVES HUGO A PITYING GLANCE--IN A LOW TONE OF 641 ICEMAN ANGER)
(SUDDENLY GIVES A LAUGH--IN HIS COMICALLY INTENSE,644 ICEMAN CRAZY TONE)
(MASKING PITY BEHIND A SARDONIC TONE) 645 ICEMAN
PARRITT LEANS TOWARD HIM AND SPEAKS INGRATIATINGLY645 ICEMAN IN A LOW SECRETIVE TONE.)
(FORCING A CASUAL TONE) NOTHING, OLD CHAP. 650 ICEMAN
FORCING AN UNCONVINCING ATTEMPT AT HIS NATURAL 654 ICEMAN TONE)
(HIS TONE FORCED) WELL, IT WAS THOUGHTFUL OF HIM.656 ICEMAN
IN A STRANGE, ARROGANTLY DISDAINFUL TONE, AS IF HE658 ICEMAN WERE REBUKING A BUTLER)
(LOOKING AROUND AT THEM--IN A KINDLY, REASSURING 663 ICEMAN TONE)
(FORCING AN INDIFFERENT TONE) 666 ICEMAN
SOMETHING LIKE SATISFACTION IN HIS PITYING TONE) 667 ICEMAN
(ABRUPTLY IN A HAUGHTY FASTIDIOUS TONE) 672 ICEMAN
HE LEANS OVER AND SPEAKS IN A LOW CONFIDENTIAL 677 ICEMAN TONE)
LARRY HE HAD OCCUPIED BEFORE--IN A LOW, 680 ICEMAN INSINUATING, INTIMATE TONE)
(PLEADING IN A STRAINED, DESPERATE TONE) 680 ICEMAN
(GETS UP--IN A CALLOUS, BRUTAL TONE) 699 ICEMAN
(KEEPS HIS EYES ON LARRY--IN A JEERINGLY 700 ICEMAN CHALLENGING TONE)
PARRITT GOES ON, HIS TONE BECOMING MORE INSISTENT)701 ICEMAN
(IN A STIFLED TONE) GOD DAMN YOU/ 701 ICEMAN
(HIS TONE IS THREATENING 703 ICEMAN
GOES ON IN A TONE OF FOND, SENTIMENTAL 709 ICEMAN REMINISCENCE)
(HE STARTS HIS STORY, HIS TONE AGAIN BECOMING 709 ICEMAN MUSINGLY REMINISCENT)
(HE BURSTS OUT IN A TONE OF ANGUISH THAT HAS ANGER713 ICEMAN AND HATRED BENEATH IT)
(TO LARRY IN A LOW INSISTENT TONE) 714 ICEMAN
(AT THE TONE OF HIS VOICE, 717 ICEMAN
THEN LOOKS AROUND AT THE OTHERS, AND ASSUMES THE 722 ICEMAN OLD KIDDING TONE OF THE
HE TURNS TO THEM, TRYING HARD TO ASSUME A CARESS520 INZONE TONE)
(IN A CASUAL TONE WHICH TO THEM SOUNDS SINISTER) 523 INZONE
(TURNS SMILINGLY TO THEM, IN A MERRY TONE THAT IS 20 JOURNE A BIT FORCED.)
JAMIE SPEAKS WITH A COMPLETE CHANGE OF TONE.) 39 JOURNE
SHE ATTEMPTS A LIGHT, AMUSED TONE.) 43 JOURNE
(HE GOES TO THE SCREEN DOOR--FORCING A JOKING 49 JOURNE TONE.)
(KEEPING HER TONE.) WELL, THAT'S THE EFFECT IT 59 JOURNE ALWAYS HAS, ISN'T IT$
(IN A FORCED TEASING TONE.) GOOD HEAVENS, HOW 59 JOURNE DOWN IN THE MOUTH YOU LOOK,
HER EYES WAVER GUILTILY AND SHE ADDS IN A TONE 60 JOURNE WHICH BEGINS TO PLACATE.)
(THEN WITH A STRANGE, ABRUPT CHANGE TO A DETACHED, 61 JOURNE IMPERSONAL TONE.)
(ABRUPTLY HER TONE AND MANNER CHANGE TO THE 64 JOURNE STRANGE DETACHMENT SHE HAS SHOWN
(INSTANTLY CHANGING TO A DETACHED TONE.) 90 JOURNE
(SHE PAUSES--THEN LOWERING HER VOICE TO A STRANGE 93 JOURNE TONE OF WHISPERED CONFIDENCE.)
(HER TONE HAS BECOME MORE AND MORE FAR-OFF AND 103 JOURNE DREAMY.)
(SHE PAUSES--THEN BEGINS TO RECITE THE HAIL MARY 107 JOURNE IN A FLAT, EMPTY TONE.)
(IN A DETACHED REMINISCENT TONE.) 111 JOURNE
(IN A CHANGED TONE--REPENTANTLY.) 112 JOURNE
(FORCES A CASUAL TONE.) ISN'T IT DINNER TIME, 115 JOURNE DEAR$
(ABRUPTLY, IN A DETACHED, MATTER-OF-FACT TONE.) 117 JOURNE
TEASING TONE BUT WITH AN INCREASING UNDERCURRENT 120 JOURNE OF RESENTMENT.)
(COMES TO HIM--HER FACE IS COMPOSED IN PLASTER 123 JOURNE AGAIN AND HER TONE IS REMOTE.)
(ABRUPTLY HIS TONE BECOMES SCORNFULLY SUPERIOR.) 146 JOURNE
(HE PAUSES--THEN WITH MAUDLIN HUMOR, IN A HAM- 160 JOURNE ACTOR TONE.)
(IN A CRUEL, SNEERING TONE WITH HATRED IN IT.) 161 JOURNE
(ABRUPTLY HIS TONE CHANGES TO DISGUSTED 164 JOURNE CONTRITION.
(ECHOING HIS TONE) OUR CHILDREN WILL STARVE/ 287 LAZARU
(AT FIRST IN A TONE OF GREAT AWE--TO HIS SOLDIERS)293 LAZARU
(TAKING IT UP IN A TONE BETWEEN CHANTING AND THEIR318 LAZARU OLD SOLEMN INTONING)
(FORCING A LIGHT TONE) LAZARUS LAUGHED AND 327 LAZARU
(IN A TONE OF HUSHED GRIEF) I MAY NOT LAUGH 331 LAZARU EITHER.

TONE

TONE (CONT'D.)
(IN AN INGRATIATING TONE) GREETING, GAIUS. 332 LAZARU
(THEN IN A LOW TUNE TO HER) 343 LAZARU
(TAKING HIS TONE--MOCKINGLY) 366 LAZARU
(THEN IN A MORE CONVERSATIONAL TONE, PUTTING ASIDE370 LAZARU
HIS GRANDIOSE AIRS,
(CONTROLLING HERSELF--IN A FORCED REASONABLE 4 MANSNS
TONE.)
(RISING--IN A TONE OF ARROGANT PLEASURE.) 5 MANSNS
(EMBARRASSEDLY--FORCING A JOKING TONE.) 20 MANSNS
THEN SARA'S VOICE IS HEARD IN A COMMANDING TONE, 44 MANSNS
(THEN AS JOEL GOES TOWARD THE DOOR, HE SPEAKS IN A 71 MANSNS
CONCILIATING TONE.)
(ABRUPTLY, WITH A BUSINESS-LIKE TONE.) 85 MANSNS
(GLANCING AROUND THE GARDEN--WITH A TONE OF 99 MANSNS
NOSTALGIC YEARNING.)
(STIFFENS. STARES AT HER WITH HATRED FOR A 104 MANSNS
SECOND--THEN COLDLY, IN A CURT TONE.)
(BREAKS IN AND TAKES IT UP, TAKING ON HER TONE.) 107 MANSNS
CALLING, IN A TONE OF REPRESSED UNEASINESS.. 108 MANSNS
HER VOICE SUDDENLY TAKES ON A RESENTFUL COMMANDING114 MANSNS
TUNE..
IN A TONE OF WARNING ADVICE 114 MANSNS
(IN A LIKE CASUAL TONE.) IS 121 MANSNS
FORCING A CASUAL TONE, SHE SPEAKS TO HIM.) 121 MANSNS
(SPEAKS--FORCING A CASUAL TONE.) 122 MANSNS
(ECHOING HIS TONE.) NO.. 122 MANSNS
(ABRUPTLY HIS TONE BECOMES SLYLY TAUNTING.) 131 MANSNS
THREATENING SCORN IN HER TONE.) 131 MANSNS
(WITH A CHANGE OF TONE TO THAT OF THE DOTING 135 MANSNS
MOTHER.)
(FORCING A TOO-CARELESS TONE.) 140 MANSNS
(STOPS CRYING INSTANTLY AT THE TONE OF HIS VOICE, 145 MANSNS
HOLDS HIM BY THE SHOULDERS,
(FORCING A JOKING TONE.) FOR THE LOVE OF HEAVEN, 145 MANSNS
DON'T YOU KNOW WHO I AM&
(HUMILIATED, BUT FORCING A REASONABLE TONE.) 153 MANSNS
(ABRUPTLY, WITH A MATTER-OF-FACT TONE.) 158 MANSNS
(FORCING A DETERMINED, EXULTING TONE.) 164 MANSNS
(HER TONE BECOMES MORE AND MORE PERSUASIVE 167 MANSNS
(WITH AN ABRUPT CHANGE TO HIS MATTER-OF-FACT 173 MANSNS
TONE.)
(GOES ON IN THE SAME TONE OF TENSE QUIET.) 179 MANSNS
(STARES AT IT WITH DREAD AND LONGING HERSELF-- 182 MANSNS
FORCING A BELITTLING TONE.)
(IN A TONE OF HAUGHTY COMMAND.) 191 MANSNS
(HE LOOKS AT THE TREE--THEN IN AN AWED TONE) 350 MARCOM
A FRESH BOY'S VOICE IS HEARD SINGING A LOVE SONG 355 MARCOM
IN A SUBDUED TONE.
TEDALOO SMILES AND ADDRESSES HIM IN AN 359 MARCOM
AFFECTIONATE, HUMOROUS TONE)
HE LOOKS AROUND--THEN BEGINS IN A CAUTIOUS LOWERED366 MARCOM
TONE)
LOOKS FINALLY AT THE BUDDHA--IN A SMART-ALECK 370 MARCOM
TONE)
(TAKING UP THE READING FROM HIS BOOK IN THE SAME 370 MARCOM
TONE)
(TRYING TO CONCEAL HIS FEAR UNDER A QUAVERING, 380 MARCOM
JOKING TONE)
KUKACHIN RECITES IN A LOW TONE.. 384 MARCOM
(FORCING A CONSOLING TONE) COME, LITTLE FLOWER, 385 MARCOM
(THEN RESUMING HIS TONE OF TENDER TEASING) 385 MARCOM
HE THROWS OPEN THE WINDOW AND CALLS IN A LOUD, 389 MARCOM
COMMANDING TONE)
(HE ADDRESSES THE FORTRESS IN A MATTER-OF-FACT 395 MARCOM
TONE)
(FROM BELOW, RECITES IN A CALM, SOOTHING TONE) 401 MARCOM
(THEN CONTROLLING HIMSELF--FORCING AN AMUSED 401 MARCOM
TEASING TONE)
(TRYING TO RENEW HIS JOKING TONE) 401 MARCOM
(IN A HURT TONE) I DON'T SEE WHY YOU'RE TRYING TO419 MARCOM
INSULT ME--
(HER TONE BECOMES DERISIVELY AMUSED) 5 MISBEG
(SHE ADDS IN A HARD, SCORNFUL TONE) 21 MISBEG
(HE ABRUPTLY SWITCHES FROM THIS ELOQUENCE TO A 62 MISBEG
MATTER-OF-FACT TONE)
(WITH A QUICK CHANGE OF PACE TO A WHEEDLING 63 MISBEG
CONFIDENTIAL TONE)
(TRACE OF BITTERNESS BENEATH HIS AMUSED TONE) 66 MISBEG
HER TONE BECOMES PERSUASIVE) 77 MISBEG
(TRYING A LIGHT TONE) SURE, THERE'S A LOT OF 78 MISBEG
THOSE IN THE NEIGHBORHOOD.
(IN A BRAZEN TONE) SURE, THOSE IN MY TRADE HAVE TO 97 MISBEG
LOOK THEIR BEST?
(HURRIEDLY REGAINING HER PLAYFUL TONE) 103 MISBEG
(MOVED IN SPITE OF HERSELF--BUT KEEPS HER BOLD, 103 MISBEG
PLAYFUL TONE)
(FORCING A PLAYFUL TONE) FOR THE SIN OF WANTING 104 MISBEG
TO BE IN BED WITH ME.
SHE FORCES A LIGHT TONE) 105 MISBEG
(VAGUELY SURPRISED BY HER TONE) 106 MISBEG
HE GOES ON WITH AN ABRUPT CHANGE OF TONE) 114 MISBEG
(IN A STRANGE TONE THAT IS ALMOST THREATENING) 114 MISBEG
(IN A FORCED, KIDDING TONE) I HOPE IT WILL BE.. 117 MISBEG
(STAMMERS) JIM-- (HASTILY FORCING HER PLAYFUL 118 MISBEG
TONE)
SUDDENLY HE BREAKS AWAY--IN A TONE OF GUILTY 119 MISBEG
IRRITATION)
(SHE GIVES HIS SHOULDER A SHAKE--FORCING A LIGHT 120 MISBEG
TONE)
(IN A LIGHT TONE) BRING THE BOTTLE BACK SO IT'LL 124 MISBEG
BE HANDY
SHE FORCES A LIGHT TONE) 126 MISBEG
(HE PAUSES--THEN BURSTS OUT IN A STRANGE 126 MISBEG
THREATENING TONE)
(FORCING A LIGHT TONE) DO YOU WANT TO SPOIL OUR 129 MISBEG
BEAUTIFUL MOONLIGHT NIGHTS
HE SPEAKS IN A TONE OF RANDOM CURIOSITY) 129 MISBEG

TONE (CONT'D.)
(SHE JERKS HER HAND AWAY--THEN HASTILY FORCES A 130 MISBEG
JOKING TONE)
(HIS TONE BECOMES HURT AND BITTER) 133 MISBEG
(REVERTING TO A TEASING TONE) 135 MISBEG
(TURNING BACK--BITTER ACCUSATION IN HIS TONE NOW) 139 MISBEG
(WITH A PERVERSE, JEERING NOTE OF VINDICTIVE 140 MISBEG
BOASTFULNESS IN HIS TONE)
(FORCING A TREMBLING ECHO OF HER PLAYFUL TONE) 142 MISBEG
(SPEAKS IN A TIRED, EMPTY TONE, 143 MISBEG
(IN A STRANGE WARNING TONE) YOU'D BETTER LOOK 144 MISBEG
OUT, JOSIE.
(A DEEP CONFLICT SHOWS IN HIS EXPRESSION AND TONE.145 MISBEG
WITH A STRANGE HORRIBLE SATISFACTION IN HIS TONE) 150 MISBEG
SHE GOES IN A GENTLE, BULLYING TONE) 153 MISBEG
(IN A TENDER CROONING TONE LIKE A LULLABY) 153 MISBEG
SHE KEEPS HER VOICE LOW, BUT HER TONE IS 157 MISBEG
COMMANDING)
SHE GOES ON IN THE SAME TONE, WITHOUT LOOKING AT 157 MISBEG
HIM)
(SPEAKS IN A LOW GRIM TONE) STOP HIDING, FATHER. 157 MISBEG
(HE ATTEMPTS A JOKING TONE) IS IT YOU WHO'S THE 160 MISBEG
VIRGINS
TONE WITH HIM, BUT ALL THE TIME WAITING TO SEE HOW166 MISBEG
MUCH HE WILL REMEMBER)
(THEN AS SHE STILL DOESN'T HEAR, HE PUTS ON HIS 176 MISBEG
OLD, FUMING IRASCIBLE TONE)
(HER TONE CHANGES TO A SNEER.) 30 POET
(HIS TONE CONDESCENDS. 34 POET
(IN A LIGHT TONE.) FAITH, I SUPPOSE I MUST HAVE 44 POET
LOOKED A VAIN PEACOCK,
(KEEPING HIS TONE LIGHT.) FAITH, SARA, 45 POET
(TO ROCHE--AN IMPRESSIVE MENACE IN HIS TONE.) 53 POET
(WITHOUT TURNING TO HER--IN HIS CONDESCENDINGLY 55 POET
POLITE TONE.)
(HIS EYES AGAIN CATCH HERS AND HOLD THEM--HIS TONE 70 POET
INSINUATINGLY CARESSING.)
(HIS TONE MORE CARESSING.) 71 POET
(BLURTS OUT WITH NO APOLOGY IN HIS TONE BUT 72 POET
ANGRILY.
SARA GOES ON, CHANGING HER TONE.) 80 POET
SHE SPEAKS IN A LOW, CONFIDENTIAL TONE HERSELF, 84 POET
SMILING NATURALLY.)
(A PAUSE. HE BEGINS TO TALK IN AN ARROGANTLY 90 POET
AMUSED TONE.)
QUIET, GENTLEMANLY TONE. 105 POET
(HE ADDS IN A FORCED TONE, A TRACE OF MOCKERY IN 107 POET
IT.)
THERE IS AN INCREASING VINDICTIVENESS IN HIS 112 POET
TONE.)
HE UNBENDS, ALTHOUGH HIS TONE IS STILL A BIT CURT.117 POET
(DOES NOT LIKE HIS TONE--INSOLENTLY SARCASTIC.) 117 POET
HE STARES AT GADSBY, THEN GOES ON IN A MORE 119 POET
FRIENDLY TONE.)
(SCOWLS AT HIS TONE BUT, AS HE COMPLETELY 120 POET
MISUNDERSTANDS GADSBY'S MEANING,
(BEWILDERED FOR A SECOND--THEN IN A THREATENING 12' POET
TONE.)
(MISUNDERSTANDING HIM, REPLIES IN A TONE ALMOST 120 POET
OPENLY CONTEMPTUOUS.)
(IGNORING THE INSULTS, FORCES A PLACATING TONE.) 121 POET
(WATCHING HIM UNEASILY, ATTEMPTS A REASONABLE, 122 POET
PERSUASIVE TONE.)
(ADDRESSING HIM--IN HIS QUIET, THREATENING TONE 123 POET
NOW.)
(TRYING TO ROUSE HER--IN A TEASING TONE.) 182 POET
SHEEHY SPEAKS TO HIS WIFE IN A LOW TONE) 583 ROPE
(TRYING TO CONTROL HIS IRRITATION AND TALK IN AN 9 STRANG
OBJECTIVE TONE)
(IN HER COOL TONE) WHY, NOTHING. 13 STRANG
(FORCING A JOKING TONE) LITTLE YOU KNOW THE 14 STRANG
DEADLY RISKS I RAN, NINA/
(WITH A PERSUASIVE QUIZZING TONE) 17 STRANG
(WITH A SUDDEN INTENSITY IN HER TONE) 18 STRANG
WHY, EVEN THE MANNER IN WHICH YOU ADDRESS ME--THE 18 STRANG
TONE YOU TAKE--
(THEN VENTURING ON AN UNCERTAIN TONE OF 21 STRANG
PLEASANTRY)
(THEN FORCING A KINDLY TONE) 33 STRANG
HAVE TO TONE IT DOWN FOR HIM... 35 STRANG
(HARSHLY--BUT TRYING TO FORCE A JOKING TONE) 38 STRANG
(IN A STRANGE MOCKING IRONIC TONE) 39 STRANG
(HE FORCES A LAUGH--THEN IN A FRIENDLY 39 STRANG
CONFIDENTIAL TONE)
(IN A STRANGE, FAR-AWAY TUNE, LOOKING UP NOT AT 44 STRANG
HIM BUT AT THE CEILING)
(THEN SUDDENLY IN A MATTER-OF-FACT TONE THAT IS 46 STRANG
MOCKINGLY LIKE HER FATHER'S)
(IN THE TONE LIKE HER FATHER'S) 46 STRANG
(BLANDLY--IN THE TONE LIKE HER FATHER'S) 46 STRANG
(THINKING WORRIEDLY) (SLIPPING BACK INTO THAT 51 STRANG
MORBID TONE...
THAT JOKING TONE HIDES HER REAL CONTEMPT/.../) 52 STRANG
JUMPS STARTLINGLY IN TONE FROM A CARESSING 54 STRANG
GENTLENESS TO A BLUNTED FLAT
(STRUCK BY HER TONE--LOOKS UP) 57 STRANG
--BANK& OUT-- BEFORE THE CLASS, SHE FORCES A 69 STRANG
PLAYFUL TONE)
(CUTTING HIM WITH A CARELESS SNEERING TONE) 70 STRANG
(THEN SUDDENLY STARTS HER STORY IN A DULL 82 STRANG
MONOTONOUS TONE RECALLING THAT OF
(IN SAME TONE) KNOW WHATS 82 STRANG
(IN THE SAME INSISTENT TONE) 85 STRANG
(BEGINNING TO ADOPT A TIMID, DIFFIDENT, GUILTY 86 STRANG
TONE)
(IN SAME TONE) THE MAN SHOULD LIKE AND ADMIRE 88 STRANG
HER,

1687 TONGUES

TONE

(CONT'D.)

(IN SAME TONE) AND THE MAN SHOULD HAVE A MIND 88 STRANG THAT CAN TRULY UNDERSTAND--
IN A TONE OF CURT DISMISSAL) 95 STRANG
(FLUSHING GUILTILY--FORCING A CONFIDENT TONE) 95 STRANG
(THE WORDS AND THE TONE SHOCK HIS PRIDE TO LIFE. 99 STRANG
(APPREHENSIVELY, FORCING A TONE OF ANNOYED REBUKE)102 STRANG
(IN SAME TONE) NEG LIED TO YOU/ 108 STRANG
AND SPEAKS AS THOUGH SHE WERE HIDING A HURT 118 STRANG REPROACH BENEATH A JOKING TONE)
(VERY SERIOUSLY--IN A CONFIDENTIAL TONE) 121 STRANG
(LOOKING AT MARSDEN KEENLY BUT PUTTING ON A JOKING)21 STRANG TONE)
(THINKING IN A PANIC) ((THAT TONE/... 126 STRANG
(WINCING--IN A FORCED TONE) AND I'D TRUST SAM 127 STRANG WITH ANYTHING.
(THEN IN A STRANGE OBJECTIVE TONE--THINKING) 134 STRANG
(STUNG YET AMUSED BY THE OTHER'S TONE--IRONICALLY)147 STRANG
(IN A TONE OF SUPERIOR MANLY UNDERSTANDING, 157 STRANG
ADOPTING A PLAYFUL TONE) 157 STRANG
((THAT TONE IN HER VOICE/... 160 STRANG
(IN A JOKING TONE) OH, I GUESS SAM'S ALL RIGHT, 163 STRANG NINA.
(THINKING RESENTFULLY) ((SHE TAKES A FINE DO-- 164 STRANG THIS-LITTLE-GIRL TONE TOWARD
(IN THE TONE A MOTHER TAKES IN SPEAKING TO HER 169 STRANG HUSBAND ABOUT THEIR BOY)
(IN HER TONE) AND I STILL LOVE YOU A LITTLE, 170 STRANG NINA.
(THINKING--DAZEDLY STILL, BUT IN A TONE OF RELIEF)174 STRANG
(BUT RETURNING TO HIS BITTER TONE) 185 STRANG
(THEN COMING BACK TO HIS OLD TONE) 185 STRANG
(IN THE SAME TONE) NICE& 185 STRANG
(OUTRAGED BY SOMETHING IN HER TONE-- 186 STRANG
(PUTTING ON A TONE OF JOKING ANNOYANCE) 190 STRANG
(THINKING RESENTFULLY) ((WHAT A TENDER TONE SHE 192 STRANG TAKES TOWARD HIM/...
DON'T TAKE THAT TONE WITH ME OR I'LL FORGET YOUR 193 STRANG AGE--
(WITH AN IRONICAL SMILE--FORCING A JOKING TONE) 196 STRANG
(PATERNALLY--IN HER FATHER'S TONE) 199 STRANG
THEN ADDS IN A GRUDGING TONE) 501 VOYAGE
(THEN DETERMINEDLY THROWING OFF THIS MOOD-- 447 WELDED REPROACHFULLY FORCING A JOKING TONE)
SSSHH--LISTEN--SOMEONE-- (SHE SPEAKS IN AN 449 WELDED UNNATURAL, MECHANICAL TONE.
(WITH A RETURN TO HER NATURAL TONE--BUT 449 WELDED HYSTERICAL)
(AFTER A GLANCE AT HER HUSBAND--IN A FORCED TONE) 450 WELDED
(IN A FROZEN TONE) OH,--ALL RIGHT--ALL RIGHT. 450 WELDED
(AS SHE SEES WHO IT IS--IN A RELIEVED TONE OF 450 WELDED SURPRISE)
IN A FORCED TONE) 452 WELDED
BUT SHOWING BY THEIR TONE IT IS A THINKING ALOUD 452 WELDED TO ONESELF,
(AVERTING HIS EYES AND ADDRESSING HER DIRECTLY IN 454 WELDED A COLD, SARCASTIC TONE)
(FINALLY--IN A GENTLE TONE) NELLY, DON'T YOU 464 WELDED THINK IT'D HELP IF YOU TOLD ME--
(FORCING A LIGHT TONE) WELL, I'LL BE RESIGNED TO 467 WELDED WAIT AND HOPE THEN--
(AFTER A PAUSE--IN A CALMING, SERIOUS TONE) 467 WELDED
(IN A BLAND, ABSENT-MINDED TONE WHICH WOUNDS HIM) 467 WELDED
VOICE--FINALLY BLURTS OUT IN A TONE OF 472 WELDED DESPERATION)
(IN SAME TONE) IT'S GETTIN' LATE. 473 WELDED
(SUDDENLY TURNS AND ADDRESSES HIM DIRECTLY IN A 481 WELDED SAD, SYMPATHETIC TONE)
(IN THE SAME MECHANICAL TONE) 483 WELDED
(IN HER SAME TONE) YES/ 488 WELDED
CAPE STOPS TWO STEPS BELOW HER--IN A LOW, 489 WELDED WONDERING TONE)

TONED

HIS VOICE, WHEN NOT RAISED IN A HOLLOW BOOM, IS 5 ANNA TONED DOWN TO A SLY,
HIGH-TONED APPEARANCE AWE HIM TERRIBLY. 20 ANNA
AND DESIGN HAS BEEN TONED DOWN INTO A NEUTRAL 421 DYNAMO BLUR.
(AMUSEDLY) ALWAYS A HIGH-TONED SWELL AT HEART, 658 ICEMAN EH, HUGOS
THE BELLS, EXCEPT FOR ONE SLOW DEEP-TONED ONE IN 433 MARCOM THE PALACE ITSELF,
WITH HIS QUOTIN' LATIN AND HIS HIGH-TONED JESUIT 10 MISBEG COLLEGE EDUCATION,

TONELESS

(HIS VOICE SINGULARLY TONELESS AND COLD BUT AT THE494 DAYS SAME TIME INSISTENT)
TALKING IN TONELESS, SIMPERING VOICES. 236 HA APE
(AS MARY'S GRIEF SUBSIDES A TRIFLE, HER VOICE IS 26 STRANG HEARD, FLAT AND TONELESS)

TONELESSLY

(THINKING FIERCELY) ((NOW'S MY CHANCE/...)) 58 STRANG (TONELESSLY)

TONELESSNESS

(WITH AN EVEN MORE BLUNTED FLAT RELENTLESS 59 STRANG TONELESSNESS)

TONES

(A TRACE OF AWE IN HIS TONES--HE GLANCES UPWARD) 536 'ILE
(IN RELIEVED TONES--SEEING WHO IT IS) 536 'ILE
(THEN SUDDENLY IN THE TONES OF A SIDE-SHOW BARKER)231 AHWILD
(HE ADDRESSES RICHARD IN TONES OF EXAGGERATED 246 AHWILD MELODRAMA)
TONES. 4 ANNA
(SHE SOOTHES HIM IN DULL TONES) 149 BEYOND
(IN THE TOO-CASUAL TONES WHICH BETRAY AN INWARD 556 CROSS UNEASINESS)
(HE BREAKS OFF AND CONTINUES IN MATTER-OF-FACT 558 CROSS TONES)

TONES

(CONT'D.)

THEN IN POSSESSIVE TONES) 224 DESIRE
IN FORCED STILTED TONES) 225 DESIRE
(IN HER MOST SEDUCTIVE TONES WHICH SHE USES ALL 225 DESIRE THROUGH THIS SCENE)
ARE STANDING TALKING IN LOW TONES) 69 ELECTR
(HE GLANCES AT HIS MASK TRIUMPHANTLY--IN TONES OF 266 GGBROW DELIVERANCE)
(RUSHING INTO THE NEXT ROOM, SHOUTS IN TERRIFIED 318 GGBROW TONES)
(IN THE STRIDENT TONES OF A CIRCUS BARKER) 254 HA APE
(IN AWED TONES) MON, BUT IT'S CLEAR OUTSIDE THE 518 INZONE NIGHT/
(IN LOW TONES) WHERE'S SMITTY, SCOTTYS 518 INZONE
(IN ALARMED TONES) HUSH, MON/ 522 INZONE
(WITH INSISTENT CURIOSITY BUT IN LOW AWED TONES) 279 LAZARU
THEN FROM THE DARKNESS ARE THEIR VOICES HEARD IN 357 MARCOM HUSHED TONES)
IN SNEERING, CONVERSATIONAL TONES 25 STRANG
SHE STARES AT MARSDEN BLANKLY AND SPEAKS IN QUEER 26 STRANG FLAT TONES)
(IN SAME TONES) IT'S TOO BAD. 27 STRANG
SUDDENLY ASKING A NECESSARY QUESTION IN HER 28 STRANG NURSE'S COOL, EFFICIENT TONES)
(SUDDENLY REMINDED OF THE DEAD MAN--IN PENITENTLY 39 STRANG SAD TONES)
(STILL IN HER FATHER'S TONES--VERY PATERNALLY-- 46 STRANG LOOKING DOWN)
(SMILING KINDLY AT EVANS--STILL IN HER FATHER'S 47 STRANG TONES)
(HER FACE BECOMING DEFENSIVE--IN BLUNTED TONES, A 55 STRANG TRIFLE
(IN HER BLUNT FLAT TONES--WITH A MECHANICAL 57 STRANG RAPIDITY TO HER WORDS)
(THEN AS NINA SHRINKS AWAY FROM HER HAND--IN HER 58 STRANG BLUNTED TONES)

TONGUE

BUT YOU WAIT TILL HE COMES BACK TONIGHT/ 270 AHWILD

TONGUE STOPPING EACH TIME TO SURVEY THE RESULT 249 AHWILD CRITICALLY, BITING HER TONGUE,
BE SURE AND KEEP THIS IN UNDER YOUR TONGUE, NOT 484 CARDIF OVER IT.
DRUV OFF CLACKIN' HIS TONGUE AN' WAVIN' HIS WHIP. 209 DESIRE
HE JUST CAN'T KEEP HIS TONGUE FROM WAGGIN', THAT'S500 DIFRNF ALL'S THE MATTER WITH HIM.
(EMMA STARTS) HARRIET LETS HER TONGUE RUN AWAY 539 DIFRNF WITH HER AND SAYS DUMB FOOL
HE HAS A BITING TONGUE. 428 DYNAMO
KEEP YOUR TONGUE OUT OF THIS/ 438 DYNAMO
(WALKS TOWARD HIM) HOLD YOUR TONGUE/ 448 DYNAMO
OF A SIMILAR SCANDAL-BEARING TYPE, HER TONGUE IS 6 ELECTR SHARPENED BY MALICE.
SHE PUTS THE PELLET ON HIS TONGUE AND PRESSES THE 62 ELECTR GLASS OF WATER TO HIS LIPS)
I'D LIKE TO CUT MY DIRTY TONGUE OUT/ 663 ICEMAN
(SHOCKED BUT GIGGLING.) HEAVENS, WHAT A TERRIBLE 25 JOURNE TONGUE THAT MAN HAS/
WITH THOSE OTHER FIVE-DOLLARS-TO-LOOK-AT-YOUR-- 31 JOURNE TONGUE FELLOWS, NOT THEIR SKILL.
AND KEEP YOUR DIRTY TONGUE OFF IRELAND, 34 JOURNE
HOLD YOUR FOUL TONGUE AND YOUR ROTTEN BROADWAY 76 JOURNE LOAFER'S LINGO/
AND KEEP YOUR DIRTY TONGUE OFF IRELAND/ 80 JOURNE
TONGUE HE HAS WHEN HE'S DRUNK. 83 JOURNE
HOLD YOUR TONGUE/ 90 JOURNE
OR HE'LL POISON LIFE FOR YOU WITH HIS DAMNED 109 JOURNE SNEERING SERPENT'S TONGUE/
HE HAS A TONGUE LIKE AN ADDER WHEN HE'S DRUNK. 154 JOURNE
MY DIRTY TONGUE. LIKE TO CUT IT OUT. 162 JOURNE
HAVEN'T YOU A TONGUE IN YOUR HEAD& 168 MANSNS
WILL YOU LET ME SEE YOUR TONGUES 413 MARCOM
(SHE STICKS OUT HER TONGUE. 413 MARCOM
WELL, FOLKS, ARE YOU ALL TONGUE-TIED& 429 MARCOM
(QUIETLY) THEN KEEP YOUR TONGUE OFF HIM. 4 MISBEG
(SHE COMES TO HIM) DON'T MIND MY ROUGH TONGUE, 6 MISBEG
YOU'VE A TONGUE AS DIRTY AS THE OLD MAN'S. 8 MISBEG
HAVEN'T YOU A TONGUE IN YOUR HEAD, YOU GREAT SLUT 12 MISBEG YOU&
SO WATCH YOUR TONGUE. 34 MISBEG
I TOLD YOU NOT TO ANNOY THE GENTLEMAN WITH YOUR 42 MISBEG ROUGH TONGUE.
(SHOUTS) HOLD YOUR DIRTY TONGUE/ 59 MISBEG
(WITH A PLEASED SMILE.) I'M AFRAID YOU'VE BLARNEY 39 POET ON YOUR TONGUE THIS MORNING.
MUSHA, BUT IT'S YOU HAVE THE BLARNEYIN' TONGUE, 45 POET GOD FORGIVE YOU/
RUNNING HIS TONGUE OVER HIS DRY LIPS, SHE SAYS 54 POET ACIDLY, WITH NO TRACE OF BROGUE,)
(REBUKINGLY.) HIMSELF WENT IN THE BAR TO BE OUT 64 POET OF REACH OF YOUR TONGUE.
BUT WHEN HE FOUND HIS TONGUE, HE AGREED WITH ME 108 POET MOST HEARTILY.
SO YOU'VE FOUND YOUR TONGUE, HAVE YOU& 140 POET
TONGUE, AND YOURS, AND DON'T PUT ON AIRS LOIKE THE168 POET LATE LAMENTED AULD LIAR AND
HAUNT YOUR BRAZEN TONGUE/ 171 POET
WHAT A SNAKE'S TONGUE HE HAS IN HIM/ 584 ROPE
AN' THE WHISKEY LOOSENED HIS TONGUE TILL HE'D TOLD589 ROPE ALL HE KNEW.
SHE HAS THE DIVIL'S OWN TONGUE, AS YE KNOW, 591 ROPE
(SHE STICKS OUT HER TONGUE AT HIM AND MAKES A FACE 52 STRANG OF SUPERIOR SCORN)
SLIP OF THE TONGUE/ 181 STRANG

TONGUES

THEY WERE THERE IN ALL THEIR VULGARITY, THEIR 521 DAYS POISONOUS, ENVIOUS TONGUES

TONGUES

TONGUES (CONT'D.)
DE GANG IS EXPECTIN' YUH WID DEIR TONGUES HANGIN' 617 ICEMAN
OUT A YARD LONG...
WAGGING THEM AT THEIR EARS, STICKING OUT THEIR 366 LAZARU
TONGUES, SLAPPING THEIR BEHINDS,
YOU CAN MATCH TONGUES TOGETHER. 114 POET

TONIC
WELL, I HOPE WHITECHAPEL WILL PROVIDE THE NEEDED 219 HA APE
NERVE TONIC.
HE THOUGHT, LIKE YOU, THAT WHISKEY IS A GOOD 67 JOURNE
TONIC/

TONICS
TAKEN IN MODERATION AS AN APPETIZER, IS THE BEST 65 JOURNE
OF TONICS.

TONIGHT
WE'RE GOING TO HAVE DINNER IN THE EVENING TONIGHT,190 AHWILD
YOU KNOW--
WANT TO COME WITH ME TO THE FIREWORKS DISPLAY AT 191 AHWILD
THE BEACH TONIGHTS
DON'T LET ME CATCH YOU AND AUNT LILY SPOONING ON A192 AHWILD
BEACH TONIGHT--
DON'T PASS THE PLATES ON THE WRONG SIDE AT DINNER 211 AHWILD
TONIGHT.
WE'RE HAVING IT TONIGHT-- 214 AHWILD
AND I DATED THEM UP FOR TONIGHT, THINKING I COULD 218 AHWILD
CATCH ART.
(THEY GETTING AN IDEA) BUT SAY, HAVE YOU GOT 218 AHWILD
ANYTHING ON FOR TONIGHTS
I DIDN'T MEAN TO--I'M NOT FEELING MYSELF TONIGHT. 233 AHWILD
I'VE BEEN SINGING A LOT TONIGHT. 256 AHWILD
(THEN WITH SURLY DIGNITY) I DON'T FEEL LIKE 256 AHWILD
SINGING TONIGHT, PA.
WELL, WHY COULDN'T IT HAPPEN, WITH EVERYONE THAT 260 AHWILD
OWNS ONE OUT TONIGHT,
DARNED WELL I TOLD YOU I'M NOT COMING HOME TO 269 AHWILD
SUPPER TONIGHT.
AND SHE'S GOING TO TRY AND SNEAK OUT AND MEET ME 273 AHWILD
TONIGHT.
I'LL SEE HER TONIGHT IF IT'S THE LAST THING I EVER274 AHWILD
DO/
I CAN HEAR THE TOWN HALL STRIKE, IT'S SO STILL 275 AHWILD
TONIGHT...
GEE, I LOVE TONIGHT. 277 AHWILD
GEE, IT'S BEAUTIFUL TONIGHT. 277 AHWILD
TONIGHT, WILL YOUS 279 AHWILD
GOSH, YOU'RE PRETTY TONIGHT, MURIEL/ 279 AHWILD
(EXCITEDLY) DICK, YOU HAVE NO IDEA WHAT I WENT 280 AHWILD
THROUGH TO GET HERE TONIGHT/
AND I HAD SAND ENOUGH TO SNEAK OUT AND MEET YOU 286 AHWILD
TONIGHT, DIDN'T IS
NOTHING WOULD HAVE KEPT ME FROM SEEING YOU 287 AHWILD
TONIGHT--
JUST BECAUSE WE KNOW HE'S STILL ALL RIGHT TONIGHT 289 AHWILD
BETTER GET TO BED EARLY TONIGHT, SON, HADN'T YOUS 297 AHWILD
I SUPPOSE TONIGHT YOU NEEDN'T. 298 AHWILD
MIND IF I DON'T SAY MY PRAYERS TONIGHT, ESSIES 298 AHWILD
YOU ACT FUNNY TONIGHT, ANNA. 26 ANNA
I DO FEEL SORT OF--NUTTY, TONIGHT. 28 ANNA
(IMPRESSED BY HIS TONE) YOU TALK--NUTTY TONIGHT 29 ANNA
YOURSELF.
(AFTER A PAUSE) WHAT'S COME OVER ANDY TONIGHT, I 97 BEYOND
WONDERS
(AVOIDING HER EYES) I THOUGHT MAYBE ROBERT WANTED 97 BEYOND
TO TONIGHT.
BACK TONIGHT, ANDYS 97 BEYOND
FOR THE LOT AV US WHIN SHE CAME BACK ON BOARD 458 CARIBE
TONIGHT.
AND YOU'LL COME TO TAKE HIM AWAY TONIGHT--FOR 558 CROSS
SURES
YOU THINK IT'S BEST TO WAKE HIM TONIGHTS 562 CROSS
I'VE PUT THEM BEHIND ME TONIGHT--FOREVER/ 566 CROSS
(BROKENLY) HE'S BAD TONIGHT, NAT. 569 CROSS
YOU HAD BETTER MAKE UP YOUR MIND NOW TO TELL THE 528 DAYS
REST OF YOUR NOVEL TONIGHT--
SO I THREATENED HIM I MIGHT GIVE YOU BOTH AN 530 DAYS
OUTLINE OF THE REST TONIGHT.
(A BIT FRIGHTENEDLY) AIR YE AILIN' TONIGHT, 238 DESIRE
EPHRAIMS
THEY 'S ONE ROOM HAIN'T MINE YET, BUT IT'S A-GOIN'240 DESIRE
T' BE TONIGHT.
BENNY--I'D HEARD YOU WAS DUE TO HOME TONIGHT. 534 DIFRNT
I'LL STAY AT BILL GRAINGER'S TONIGHT AND GET THE 534 DIFRNT
MORNING TRAIN.
I'VE TOLD HIM HE CAN STAY HERE WITH ME TONIGHT. 542 DIFRNT
IT'S WARM TONIGHT... 429 DYNAMO
I DARE YOU TO BRING HIM IN TONIGHT, AND LET ME 432 DYNAMO
TALK TO HIM AND YOU LISTEN,
IT'S CERTAINLY GRAND TONIGHT, ISN'T ITS 433 DYNAMO
(THEN TORTUREDLY) (OH, GOD, WHY DID I EVER COME 441 DYNAMO
HERE TONIGHTS...)
LET'S TAKE A WALK TONIGHT. 460 DYNAMO
SEE YOU TONIGHT. 468 DYNAMO
(WITH HIS COLD SMILE) YOU MEAN FORGIVES US FOR 470 DYNAMO
WHAT WE DID TONIGHTS
I KNOW THE MIRACLE WILL HAPPEN TO ME TONIGHT 477 DYNAMO
(BUT SUPPOSING THE MIRACLE DOESN'T HAPPEN 478 DYNAMO
TONIGHTS...)
TONIGHT THE MIRACLE WILL HAPPEN/ 482 DYNAMO
THERE WON'T BE A SOBER MAN IN TOWN TONIGHT/. 7 ELECTR
YOU AIN'T GOIN' TO GIT AMUS DRUNK TONIGHT, 7 ELECTR
SURRENDER OR NO SURRENDER/.
TONIGHT AFTER THE CAPTAIN LEAVES YOU, IF YOU LIKE. 18 ELECTR
FATHER MIGHT ARRIVE TONIGHT. 44 ELECTR
HE MIGHT ARRIVE TONIGHT--OR TOMORROW--OR THE NEXT 46 ELECTR
DAY.
YOU THINK HE MIGHT COME TONIGHTS 46 ELECTR
WE HAD JUST GIVEN UP HOPE OF YOUR COMING TONIGHT. 47 ELECTR
I DIDN'T MEAN--I--I'M NERVOUS TONIGHT. 53 ELECTR

TONIGHT (CONT'D.)
I SHOULDN'T HAVE BOTHERED YOU WITH THAT 53 ELECTR
FOOLISHNESS ABOUT BRANT TONIGHT.
YOU WERE LYING TO ME TONIGHT AS YOU'VE ALWAYS 60 ELECTR
LIED/
IS THAT WHY YOU WERE SO WILLNG TO GIVE YOURSELF 60 ELECTR
TONIGHTS
I BEEN ROBBED ONCE TONIGHT/ 104 ELECTR
(THEN WITH AN EFFORT) I'LL WRITE CLARK AND DAWSON111 ELECTR
TONIGHT
WOULD IT HELP YOU IF I STAYED WITH YOU TONIGHT-- 1119 ELECTR
MEAN IF THEY DON'T COMES
(WITH EVIDENT RELUCTANCE) YOU WANT TO DO IT 136 ELECTR
TONIGHTS
WE HAD INTENDED TO STAY IN NEW YORK TONIGHT 143 ELECTR
OH, I DON'T MEAN HE'S THE WAY HE IS TONIGHT MOST 148 ELECTR
OF THE TIME/
I'M TERRIBLY NERVOUS TONIGHT. 151 ELECTR
YOU ATE A GOOD SUPPER TONIGHT--FOR YOU. 151 ELECTR
IT'S BLACK AS PITCH TONIGHT. 151 ELECTR
I WONDER IF DIDN-- I SAW HIM LOOKING AT ME AGAIN 263 GGBROW
TONIGHT--OH, I WONDER.../
HE SAID HE'D SWORN OFF TONIGHT--FOREVER--FOR YOUR 300 GGBROW
SAKE--AND THE KIDS/
(WITH A TRACE OF JEALOUSY) WHERE ARE YOUR OTHER 310 GGBROW
BIG BOYS TONIGHTS
DOESN'T BEE LOOK BEAUTIFUL TONIGHT, MOTHERS 323 GGBROW
TONIGHT-- 208 HA APE
TONIGHT ON THE FOR'ARD SQUARE. 208 HA APE
GOT ANYTHING ON FOR TONIGHTS 237 HA APE
AND GUV HE'S ON'Y GOT TILL TONIGHT TO MAKE IT. 580 ICEMAN
TEN, TWENTY, THIRTY--WHAT'S ON AT THE CHURCH 609 ICEMAN
TONIGHT, BESSS
HE'LL BE GOOD AND RIPE FOR MY BIRTHDAY PARTY 618 ICEMAN
TONIGHT AT TWELVE
SAME AS I'VE ALWAYS DONE, AND HELP CELEBRATE YOUR 621 ICEMAN
BIRTHDAY TONIGHTS
DON'T EXPECT US TO WORK TONIGHT, 'CAUSE WE WON'T, 669 ICEMAN
SEES
HE'LL BE BACK TONIGHT ASKIN' HARRY FOR HIS ROOM 674 ICEMAN
AND BUMMIN' ME FOR A CALL.
IT'D SOIVE YOU RIGHT IF I WOULDN'T GIVE DE KEYS 682 ICEMAN
BACK TO YUH TONIGHT.
BY TONIGHT THEY'LL ALL BE HERE AGAIN. 688 ICEMAN
I COULDN'T HELP FEELIN' SORRY FOR DE POOR BUMS 698 ICEMAN
WHEN DEY SHOWED UP TONIGHT,
YOU WILL BE DRUNK TONIGHT. 69 JOURNE
OH, WELL, I WON'T MIND IT TONIGHT. 82 JOURNE
NOT THAT I WOULD MIND ANYTHING HE SAID TONIGHT, 83 JOURNE
WHEN IT'S ONLY THE BEGINNING OF THE AFTERNOON, 86 JOURNE
WHAT WILL YOU BE TONIGHTS
I DON'T MIND IT TONIGHT. LAST NIGHT IT DROVE ME 98 JOURNE
CRAZY.
(SHE SMILES STRANGELY.) BUT IT CAN'T TONIGHT. 99 JOURNE
THIRTY-SIX YEARS AGO, BUT I CAN SEE IT AS CLEARLY 105 JOURNE
AS IF IT WERE TONIGHT/
LET'S NOT KID EACH OTHER, PAPA. NOT TONIGHT. 132 JOURNE
BUT TONIGHT I'M SO HEARTSICK I FEEL AT THE END OF 149 JOURNE
EVERYTHING.
WHAT'S THE MATTER WITH THE OLD MAN TONIGHTS 156 JOURNE
BUT TONIGHT DOESN'T COUNT. 157 JOURNE
(CHANGING THE SUBJECT.) WHAT DID YOU DO UPTOWN 158 JOURNE
TONIGHTS
UNTIL TONIGHT, WHEN I SPOKE TO YOU OF HOME, I 345 LAZARU
FELT NEW BIRTH-PAINS AS YOUR
ESCAPE TONIGHT TIBERIUS' MOOD IS TO PLAY 358 LAZARU
SENTIMENTAL
I COULDN'T GET INTERESTED IN IT TONIGHT, ANYWAY. 44 MANSNS
WE MUST OBTAIN SIMON'S DECISION TONIGHT, MOTHER, 51 MANSNS
TONIGHT--IT'S NOT THE HOME IT'S BEEN--NOT LIKE 120 MANSNS
HOME AT ALL--NO PEACE--
HOW TENSE THE QUIET IS IN THIS HOUSE TONIGHT-- 120 MANSNS
GOD KNOWS I COULD HARDLY BE UNAWARE OF IT TONIGHT/174 MANSNS
I MUST TRANSPORT HER OVER THE FIRST STAGE BY DARK 391 MARCOM
TONIGHT/
(WITH A SIGH) IT'S BEAUTIFUL TONIGHT. 356 MARCOM
SHALL I EXPECT YOU AGAIN TONIGHTS 374 MARCOM
TONIGHTS 411 MARCOM
THE MESSENGER SAID GHAZAN KHAN WOULD COME TO TAKE 411 MARCOM
YOU ASHORE TONIGHT.
IF YOU GOT HIM ALONE TONIGHT-- 28 MISBEG
COME UP TONIGHT AND WE'LL SPOON IN THE MOONLIGHT 54 MISBEG
(IN A HOARSE WHISPER) MEET ME TONIGHT, AS USUAL, 64 MISBEG
DOWN BY THE PIPPEN.
AND YOU, JOSIE, PLEASE REMEMBER WHEN I KEEP THAT 67 MISBEG
MOONLIGHT DATE TONIGHT
AS IF I HADN'T ENOUGH AFTER WHAT'S HAPPENED 74 MISBEG
TONIGHT.
I CAN TELL YOU EACH THING THAT HAPPENED TONIGHT AS 81 MISBEG
CLEAR AS IF I'D NOT TAKEN A
SAY YOU WON'T BE BACK TONIGHT. 99 MISBEG
DON'T EXPECT ME HOME TONIGHT, MISS HOGAN, OR 101 MISBEG
TOMORROW EITHER, MAYBE.
HOLY JOSEPH, YOU'RE FULL OF RIDDLES TONIGHT. 102 MISBEG
(BLURTS OUT BITTERLY) YES, YOU'VE PROVED THAT 103 MISBEG
TONIGHT, HAVEN'T YOUS
STILL, IT SEEMS TO BELONG TONIGHT--IN THE 104 MISBEG
MOONLIGHT--OR IN MY MIND--
LAY OFF THAT LINE, FOR TONIGHT AT LEAST. 105 MISBEG
(HE ADDS SLOWLY) I'D LIKE TONIGHT TO BE 105 MISBEG
DIFFERENT.
YOU PROMISED YOU'D CAN IT TONIGHT. 106 MISBEG
THE BOOZE AT THE INN DIDN'T WORK TONIGHT, 106 MISBEG
TO HAVE ME PRETEND I'M AN INNOCENT VIRGIN TONIGHT.114 MISBEG
THERE'S ONLY TONIGHT, AND THE MOON, AND 115 MISBEG
THAT'S ALL FOR TONIGHT. 115 MISBEG
WE'VE AGREED THERE IS ONLY TONIGHT-- 117 MISBEG
FOR TONIGHT ONLY, YOU MEANS 117 MISBEG

TONIGHT (CONT'D.)

HERE'S TO TONIGHT. 121 MISBEG
BUT IT SEEMS LIKE TONIGHT. 128 MISBEG
ALL RIGHT, I'LL TRY AND BELIEVE THAT--FOR TONIGHT.129 MISBEG
PHIL CERTAINLY HAS A PRIZE BUN ON TONIGHT. 132 MISBEG
WHY, I REMEMBER TELLING HIM TONIGHT I'D EVEN 133 MISBEG
WRITTEN MY BROTHER
HE WOULD NEVER ADMIT IT UNTIL TONIGHT. 135 MISBEG
I'LL HAVE HAD TONIGHT AND YOUR LOVE TO REMEMBER 137 MISBEG
FOR THE REST OF MY DAYS/
HAVEN'T YOU SAID YOURSELF THERE'S ONLY TONIGHTS 137 MISBEG
I COULDN'T BELIEVE THAT UNTIL TONIGHT--BUT NOW I 137 MISBEG
KNOW.
AND YOU PROMISED TONIGHT WOULD BE DIFFERENT. 139 MISBEG
I WAS A DAMNED FOOL TO COME TONIGHT. 139 MISBEG
SURE, IF THERE'S ONE THING I OWE YOU TONIGHT, 142 MISBEG
AFTER ALL MY LYING AND SCHEMING,
UNTIL I KNEW TONIGHT THE TRUTH OF WHAT YOU SAID 149 POET
THIS MORNING.
AND I'M GOING ON THE NINE-FORTY TONIGHT. 15 STRANG
HOW DID YOU HAPPEN TO COME OUT HERE TONIGHTS 30 STRANG
SHE'S GOT TO GET SOME SLEEP TONIGHT. 34 STRANG
NED'S COMING OUT TONIGHT... 68 STRANG
(THEN CONFUSEDLY) SAY, I FORGOT TO TELL YOU NED'S 72 STRANG
COMING OUT TONIGHT.
(LOOKING AFTER HER--THINKS) (SHE SEEMS BETTER 73 STRANG
TONIGHT....
(NO USE TRYING TO THINK OUT THAT PLOT TONIGHT... 129 STRANG
(YAWNING) BLIMEY IF BIZNESS AIN'T 'ARF SLOW 493 VOYAGE
TONIGHT.
DAT'S WHY I DON'T DRINK NOTING TONIGHT BUT DIS-- 506 VOYAGE
BELLY-WASH/
AFTER ALL WE'D BEEN TO EACH OTHER TONIGHT--/ 452 WELDED
IF YOU'D SEEN HIM TONIGHT, YOU WOULDN'T ENVY HIM. 465 WELDED
I TRIED TO FIRE THEM--THOUGHT I HAD--BUT WHEN YOU 467 WELDED
CAME TONIGHT--
AGAIN TONIGHT, WHEN YOU TRY TO GIVE YOURSELF TO ME468 WELDED
OUT OF HATE FOR HIM/
I WANT TO TELL YOU THAT TONIGHT--JOHN AND I-- 484 WELDED
NOTHING YOU MAY EVER SUSPECT--
(WITH A HARSH LAUGH) ARE YOU FORGETTING WE TRIED 486 WELDED
THAT ONCE TONIGHTS

TONIGHT'
THEY PROMISED FAITHFUL THEY'D 'APPEN IN TONIGHT'--494 VOYAGE
THEM AS WHOSE TIME WAS DONE.

TONK
HONKY-TONK TABLE TOP/ 152 JOURNE

TONS
WITH ME SHOVELING A MILLION TONS OF COAL 35 ANNA

TONSURE
HIS GREY HAIR IS THIN WITH A BALD SPOT LIKE A 13 JOURNE
MONK'S TONSURE.

TOOL
THE MIRACLE WAS DONE IN CONJUNCTION WITH ANOTHER 343 LAZARU
JEW ACTING AS THIS MAN'S TOOL.
AND BECAME THEIR TOOL AND ACCOMPLICE. 83 POET

TOOLS
A KEG CONTAINING NAILS AND OTHER TOOLS OF THE 577 ROPE
CARPENTRY TRADE ARE ON THE TABLE.

TOOT
(WITH FORCED CASUALNESS) YOU'VE BEEN ON THIS TOOT295 GGBROW
FOR A WEEK NOW.

TOOTH
(TRIES TO IGNORE THIS.) I HAVE TO GET TOOTH 86 JOURNE
POWDER AND TOILET SOAP AND COLD
DE QUOTES.) *HOW SHARPER THAN A SERPENT'S TOOTH 89 JOURNE
IT IS--*

TOOTHLESS
HIS MOUTH IS SUNKEN IN, TOOTHLESS. 52 POET

TOOTHPICK
SAVAGELY CHEWING A TOOTHPICK. 263 AHWILD

TOOTY
OUI, TOOTY SWEET/ 526 DIFRNT

TOP
HE IS SO NERVOUS FROM FRIGHT THAT HE KNOCKS OFF 538 *ILE
THE TOP ONE,
AND HE SMASHES HIS FIST DOWN ON THE MARBLE TOP OF 542 *ILE
THE SIDEBOARD)
PADDED SHOULDERS AND PANTS HALF-PEGGED AT THE TOP,187 AHWILD
THAT'S WHY HE CAME OUT TOP OF HIS CLASS. 192 AHWILD
AND ONE CAME AND HE WASN'T QUICK ENOUGH, AND IT 206 AHWILD
WENT OFF ALMOST ON TOP OF--
UGLY SIDEBOARD WITH THREE PIECES OF OLD SILVER ON 210 AHWILD
ITS TOP.
THE TOP OF THE BANK IS GRASSY AND THE TRAILING 275 AHWILD
BOUGHS OF WILLOW TREES EXTEND OUT
AND ON TOP OF THAT, TO TORTURE ME MORE, HE GAVE ME281 AHWILD
YOUR LETTER.
HER THICK, GRAY HAIR IS PILED ANYHOW IN A GREASY 7 ANNA
MOP ON TOP OF HER ROUND HEAD.
(SHE PUFFS, STARING AT THE TABLE TOP. 15 ANNA
AND DIVIL A SIGHT THERE WAS OF SHIP OR MEN ON TOP 36 ANNA
OF THE SEA.
A SNAKE-FENCE SIDLES FROM LEFT TO RIGHT ALONG THE 81 BEYOND
TOP OF THE BANK,
(PUTTING ONE HAND ON TOP OF ANDREW'S WITH A 83 BEYOND
GESTURE ALMOST OF SHYNESS)
(THE TOP OF A HILL ON THE FARM. 129 BEYOND
THE TOP OF THE HILL SLOPES DOWNWARD SLIGHTLY 129 BEYOND
TOWARD THE LEFT.
RUTH TOLD ME I'D PROBABLY FIND YOU UP TOP-SIDE 130 BEYOND
HERE.
AS IT WAS WE CAME OUT MINUS A MAIN TOP-MAST 131 BEYOND
(SHE JUMPS LIGHTLY TO THE TOP OF A ROCK AND SITS 136 BEYOND
DOWN)
THE TOP OF THE COVERLESS TABLE IS STAINED 144 BEYOND
THE FIRST ONE'S UN TOP. 146 BEYOND

TOP (CONT'D.)
THEN CRAWLS WITH A GREAT EFFORT TO THE TOP OF THE 166 BEYOND
BANK
SITTING ON THE TOP BUNK IN THE LEFT FOREGROUND, A 477 CARDIF
NORWEGIAN, PAUL.
LEADING UP TO THE FORECASTLE HEAD--THE TOP OF THE 455 CARIBE
FORECASTLE--
(THE GIRLS REACH DOWN IN THEIR BASKETS IN UNDER 465 CARIBE
THE FRUIT WHICH IS ON TOP AND
HERE'S YOUR HEALTH, OLD TOP/ 467 CARIBE
HE STAGGERS OVER AND STANDS ON TOP OF THE HATCH, 470 CARIBE
HIS INSTRUMENT UNDER HIS ARM.)
THE WOMEN SHRIEK AND TAKE REFUGE ON TOP OF THE 472 CARIBE
HATCH.
A ROOM ERECTED AS A LOOKOUT POST AT THE TOP OF HIS555 CROSS
HOUSE
THEIR BASES ABOVE THE LEVEL OF THE TOP OF THE 564 DAYS
DOORWAY, ARE TWO NARROW,
I'LL YELL 'EM AT THE TOP O' MY LUNGS. 209 DESIRE
I'LL GIT THE SHOTGUN AN' BLOW HIS SOFT BRAINS T' 233 DESIRE
THE TOP O' THEM ELUMS/
THE INTERIOR OF THE TWO BEDROOMS ON THE TOP FLOOR 235 DESIRE
IS SHOWN.
AN' I SAYS, I'LL BLOW HIS BRAINS T' THE TOP O' 255 DESIRE
THEM ELUMS--
THERE IS ONE SMALL WINDOW ON THE TOP FLOOR FRONT 427 DYNAMO
OF THE
AND THAT'S THE RIGHT PLACE FOR US TO LOVE--ON TOP 460 DYNAMO
OF THAT HILL--CLOSE TU
WE'LL WALK OUT TO THE TOP OF LONG HILL. 460 DYNAMO
THAT PART ON TOP IS LIKE A HEAD.... 474 DYNAMO
JUST INSIDE THE DOOR TO THE DYNAMO-ROOM ROOF AT 484 DYNAMO
THE TOP OF THE STAIRWAY.)
(IN A COWARDLY WHINE) NO 'ARM MEANT, OLD TOP. 176 EJONES
SCREAMS AND LEAPS MADLY TO THE TOP OF THE STUMP 197 EJONES
THEY'VE BEEN TOP DOG AROUND HERE FOR NEAR ON TWO 8 ELECTR
HUNDRED YEARS
THE PORTICO AT THE TOP OF THE STEPS. 8 ELECTR
COMES OUT TO THE TOP OF THE STEPS WHERE HER MOTHER 10 ELECTR
HAD STOOD.
IT WOULD BE TOO HORRIBLE--ON TOP OF--/ 20 ELECTR
(SHE TURNS AT THE TOP OF THE STEPS AT THIS 27 ELECTR
LAVINIA IS SITTING ON THE TOP OF THE STEPS TO THE 43 ELECTR
PORTICO.
(CHRISTINE SITS ON THE TOP STEP AT CENTER,. 47 ELECTR
HER FINGERS RELEASE THE BOX ON THE TABLE TOP AND 62 ELECTR
SHE BRINGS HER HAND IN FRONT OF
AND NOW, WITH THE SHOCK OF YOUR FATHER'S DEATH ON 86 ELECTR
TOP OF EVERYTHING,
THEN STOPS AT THE TOP OF THE STEPS AND FACES 119 ELECTR
AROUND.
CHRISTINE SHRINKS BACKWARD UP THE STEPS UNTIL SHE 123 ELECTR
STANDS AT THE TOP
AND ON TOP OF THAT FATHER'S DEATH--AND THE SHOCK 146 ELECTR
OF MOTHER'S SUICIDE,
(SHE GOES AND SITS AT THE TOP OF THE STEPS, BOLT 170 ELECTR
UPRIGHT.
THEN STANDS HER GROUND ON THE TOP OF THE STEPS, 171 ELECTR
HER VOICE HARDENING)
THERE IS A CHEAP ALARM CLOCK ON TOP OF THE PIANO. 278 GGBROW
THE CHEAP ALARM CLOCK IS STILL ON TOP OF IT. 284 GGBROW
THE SWAGGERS AWAY AND DELIBERATELY LURCHES INTO A 237 HA APE
TOP-HATTED GENTLEMAN.
IT MOVES--SPEED--TWENTY-FIVE STORIES UP AND ME AT 238 HA APE
DE TOP AND BOTTOM--MOVIN'/
SHE BELONGED IN DE WINDOW OF A TCY STORE, OR ON DE241 HA APE
TOP OF A GARBAGE CAN, SEE/
HOLDIN' ME DOWN WIT HIM AT DE TOP/ 244 HA APE
HIS SANDY HAIR IS FALLING OUT AND THE TOP OF HIS 8 HUGHIE
HEAD IS BALD.
AND AROUND THE TUP PRINTED IN FORGET-ME-NOTS WAS 31 HUGHIE
GOOD-BY, OLD PAL.
FOLKS IN DE KNOW TELLS ME, SEE DE MAN AT DE TOP, 600 ICEMAN
DEN YOU NEVER HAS TROUBLE,.
AND FEEL THE EFFECT OF THE DRINKS ON TOP OF HIS 626 ICEMAN
HANGOVER--GENIALLY)
THE VASE BEING A BIG SCHOONER GLASS FROM THE BAR, 629 ICEMAN
ON TOP OF THE PIANO.
AND YOU TWO HOOKERS, SCREAMING AT THE TOP OF YOUR 654 ICEMAN
LUNGS/
(JOE SULLENLY GOES BACK BEHIND THE COUNTER AND 672 ICEMAN
SLAPS THE KNIFE ON TOP OF IT.
(SHE HIKES HER SKIRT UP AND REACHES INSIDE THE TOPbB3 ICEMAN
OF HER STOCKING)
ONE DRINK ON TOP OF YOUR HANGOVER AND AN EMPTY 686 ICEMAN
STOMACH AND YOU'LL BE DREYEYED.
HOPE STARES DULLY AT THE TABLE TOP. 694 ICEMAN
HIS HEAD HAS SUNK FORWARD, AND HE STARES AT THE 701 ICEMAN
TABLE TOP,
WRATHFULLY, AT THE TOP OF HIS LUNGS) 526 INZONE
AND UNTIES THE STRING WHICH IS WOUND TIGHTLY 528 INZONE
AROUND THE TOP.
THEY HAD A PIECE O' PAPER WITH PIECES CUT OUT OF 529 INZONE
IT AN' WHEN THEY PUTS IT ON TOP
THERE'S NO ADDRESS ON THE TOP AV UT. 530 INZONE
HER HANDS APPEAR ON THE TABLE TOP, MOVING 15 JOURNE
RESTLESSLY.
HER FINGERS PLAY NERVOUSLY ON THE TABLE TOP.) 16 JOURNE
HER HANDS ROVING OVER THE TABLE TOP, AIMLESSLY 42 JOURNE
MOVING OBJECTS AROUND.
YOU DON'T WANT TO GET A SORE THROAT UN TOP OF YOUR 58 JOURNE
COLD.
HE MADE HIS WAY UP FROM IGNORANCE AND POVERTY TO 60 JOURNE
THE TOP OF HIS PROFESSION/
HER HANDS PLAY RESTLESSLY OVER THE TABLE TOP. 62 JOURNE
JAMIE FILLS A PIPE FROM A JAR ON TOP OF THE 71 JOURNE
BOOKCASE AT REAR.
THE OTHER PLAYING OVER THE TABLE TOP. 71 JOURNE

TOP 1690

TUP (CONT'D.)
MARY'S FINGERS PLAY MORE RAPIDLY ON THE TABLE TOP. 73 JOURNE
THE BAD NEWS COMING ON TOP OF WHAT'S HAPPENED TO 81 JOURNE
MAMA MAY HIT HIM HARD.
(WITH ANGRY DISGUST.) I HOPE TO GOD YOU HAVEN'T 116 JOURNE
TAKEN TO DRINK ON TOP OF--
HONKY-TONK TABLE TOP. 152 JOURNE
(DROPS HIS HAND FROM HIS FACE, HIS EYES ON THE 173 JOURNE
TABLE TOP.
FORCE INTO HIS RIGHT HAND THE MYSTIC ROD OF 307 LAZARU
DIONYSUS WITH A PINE CONE ON TOP,
A LAMP REFLECTING DOWNWARD HAS BEEN FIXED AT THE 326 LAZARU
TOP OF THE CROSS TO LIGHT UP AN
(SMILINGLY LAZARUS ASCENDS TO WHERE TIBERIUS 340 LAZARU
POINTS AT THE TOP OF THE DAIS.
ON THE TOP STEP, POMPEIA SITS, FACING RIGHT, HER 350 LAZARU
HANDS CLASPED ABOUT ONE KNEE,
HER CHIN RESTING ON HER HANDS ON TOP OF THE MARBLE363 LAZARU
RAIL.
(SHE MOVES TO THE TOP OF THE STEPS LEADING TO THE 366 LAZARU
ARENA.)
(SHRINKING BACK TO THE TOP STEP--DISTRACTEDLY.) 166 MANSNS
AND I WILL FOLLOW HER TO THE TOP OF THE STAIRS--/ 181 MANSNS
SHE NOW STANDS ON THE TOP OF THE STEPS. 191 MANSNS
ON TOP OF A MOUNTAIN. 364 MARCOM
ON GOLDEN CUSHIONS AT THE TOP KUBLAI SITS 377 MARCOM
ABOVE, ON TOP OF THE POOP. 400 MARCOM
(HE SPRINGS SWIFTLY TO THE TOP DECK AND BELLOWS) 406 MARCOM
KUBLAI SITS AT THE TOP OF HIS THRONE, CROSS-LEGGED432 MARCOM
IN THE POSTURE OF AN IDOL.
THE PRINCESS LIFT THE BIER OF KUKACHIN TO THE TOP 434 MARCOM
OF THE CATAFALQUE.
THERE IS A BIG BOULDER WITH A FLAT-TOP. 3 MISBEG
(SHE SITS ON THE TOP STEP--BANTERINGLY) 40 MISBEG
(HE SETS THE BOTTLE ON TOP OF THE BOULDER.) 54 MISBEG
WAILING AN OLD IRISH LAMENT AT THE TOP OF HIS 72 MISBEG
LUNGS.
(HIS ANGER EVAPORATES AND HE RUBS THE TOP OF HIS 73 MISBEG
HEAD
SHE SITS ON THE TOP STEP AND PULLS HIM DOWN ON THE102 MISBEG
STEP BENEATH HER.
SHE SITS ON THE TOP STEP, PULLING HIM DOWN BESIDE 115 MISBEG
HER BUT ON THE ONE BELOW.
THE TOP STEP AND PULLS HIM DOWN ON THE STEP BELOW 142 MISBEG
HER)
HUGAH COMES OUT OF HER ROOM AND STANDS ON TOP OF 174 MISBEG
THE STEPS.
(WITH AN ANSWERING GRIN.) TOP O' THE MORNIN'. 8 POET
TOP O' ME HEAD. 8 POET
EVERYWHERE THE SCUM RISES TO THE TOP. 37 POET
HIS SHOULDERS SAG AND HE STARES AT THE TABLE TOP, 57 POET
THEY STARE AT HIM AND HE STARES SIGHTLESSLY AT THE153 POET
TABLE TOP.
(BUT HE IS STAKING SIGHTLESSLY AT THE TABLE TOP 156 POET
BUT HIS EYES REMAIN FIXED ON THE TABLE TOP.) 166 POET
(SHE REACHES OUT AND TOUCHES ONE OF HIS HANDS ON 167 POET
THE TABLE TOP WITH A FURTIVE
HIS RIGHT HAND GROPING ALONG THE TABLE TOP UNTIL 172 POET
IT CLUTCHES THE DUELING PISTOL.
THE INTERIOR OF AN OLD BARN SITUATED ON TOP OF A 577 ROPE
HIGH HEADLAND OF THE SEACOAST.
NEAR THIS BIN, A CHOPPING-BLOCK WITH AN AX DRIVEN 577 ROPE
INTO THE TOP OF IT.
SHE CLIMBS AND STANDS ON THE TOP OF THE CHAIR 601 ROPE
THE TOP OF HIS HEAD BALD. 6 STRANG
SHE LIVES ON THE TOP FLOOR OF THIS HOUSE, HASN'T 59 STRANG
BEEN OUT OF HER ROOM IN YEARS.
THE ORIGINAL, ARE SLAPPED HELTER-SKELTER ON TOP OF 66 STRANG
EACH OTHER ON IT.
ON TOP OF ALL THE REST/... 83 STRANG
GORDON WAS ALWAYS NEAR THE TOP IN HIS STUDIES, 121 STRANG
WASN'T HE.
PERCEPTIBLE BALD SPOT ON TOP. 152 STRANG
HIS HEAD HAS GROWN QUITE BALD ON TOP. 159 STRANG
I'LL HAVE TO START AT THE BOTTOM BUT I'LL GET TO 189 STRANG
THE TOP IN A HURRY.
AT THE TOP, CAPE TURNS IN SURPRISE AT NOT FINDING 449 WELDED
HER.
ONE FOOT ON THE FIRST STAIR, LOOKING UP AT THE 466 WELDED
TOP.
(HE PUTS IT ON TOP OF THE WASHSTAND AND TURNS TO 474 WELDED
HER--EMBARRASSEDLY)
(SHE REACHES THE TOP OF THE STAIRWAY AND STANDS 489 WELDED
THERE LOOKING DOWN AT HIM--

TOPICS
I HATE TO BRING UP DISAGREEABLE TOPICS, BUT 89 JOURNE
THERE'S THE MATTER OF CARFARE.
WE DON'T SEEM ABLE TO AVOID UNPLEASANT TOPICS, DO 137 JOURNE
WE\

TOPMOST
(AT THE TOPMOST PITCH OF DESPERATE, 176 ELECTR

TOPPED
ON THE RIGHT, TO THE REAR, A MARBLE-TOPPED 535 'ILE
SIDEBOARD.
IN THE REAR, LEFT, A MARBLE-TOPPED SIDEBOARD WITH 555 CROSS
A SHIP'S LANTERN ON IT.
IN THE CENTER OF THE ROOM THERE IS A CLUMSY, 493 DIFRNT
MARBLE-TOPPED TABLE.

TOPS
THREE TABLES WITH STAINED TOPS, FOUR CHAIRS AROUND236 AHWILD
EACH TABLE,
FRINGED WITH COCU PALMS WHOSE TOPS RISE CLEAR OF 455 CARIBE
THE HORIZON.
HE STARES UP AT THE TOPS OF THE TREES, 189 EJONES
TALL TREES WHOSE TOPS ARE LOST TO VIEW. 195 EJONES
THE CLOUDS LIKE DOWN ON THE MOUNTAIN TOPS, THE SUN 24 ELECTR
DRAINING IN YOUR BLOOD.
SHADOWS OVER THE TOPS OF TREES/ 287 GGBROW

TOPS (CONT'D.)
PAINTING THEIR WHITE TOPS AND THE CLOUDS FLOATING 214 HA APE
BY THEM/
THAT TOPS THE WALL THAT ENCLOSES THE ARENA. 363 LAZARU

TOPSY
AND HAVE TO START IN WITH THINGS IN SUCH A TOPSY- 118 BEYOND
TURVY,
TURN ALMIGHTY GOD'S REVEALED PLAN FOR THE WORLD 244 HA APE
TOPSY-TURVY,

TORCH
AND I'M STILL CARRYING THE TORCH FOR HUGHIE. 18 HUGHIE
Y'KNOW, IT'S TIME I QUIT CARRYIN' THE TORCH FOR 38 HUGHIE
HUGHIE.

TORCHES
THE FLICKERING LIGHT OF TORCHES. 321 LAZARU
THERE IS THE BLARE OF A TRUMPET, THE REFLECTIONS 417 MARCOM
OF LATERNS AND TORCHES,

TORCHLIGHT
HE PRACTICED ON STREET CORNERS UNDER A TORCHLIGHT.626 ICEMAN

TURE
AND THEN AFTERWARDS TORE IT DOWN AND BUILT THIS 19 ELECTR
ONE
I TORE MY INSIDES OUT FOR YOU--THINKING YOU'D 61 ELECTR
UNDERSTAND/
NO, I'M FORGETTING I TORE IT UP--AFTERWARDS. 714 ICEMAN
THEY TORE OUR SWORDS AWAY FROM US, LAUGHING, AND 321 LAZARU
ME LAUGHED WITH THEM/
WE TORE EACH OTHER TO PIECES. 467 WELDED

TORMENT
I THOUGHT YOU WAS SOME MERMAID OUT OF THE SEA COME 31 ANNA
TO TORMENT ME.
DON'T TORMENT WITH THAT TALK/ 72 ANNA
NOT A STERN, SELF-RIGHTEOUS BEING WHO CONDEMNED 510 DAYS
SINNERS TO TORMENT,
WITHOUT A SINGLE DAMNED HOPE OR LYING DREAM LEFT 704 ICEMAN
TO TORMENT YOU/
SEIZE ON HIM, FURIES, TAKE HIM INTO TORMENT.= 168 JOURNE
SHE KEEPS HIM DREAMING IN HER GARDEN TO MAKE HIM 144 MANSNS
LATE ON PURPOSE TO TORMENT ME/
AREN'T YOU ASHAMED YOU HAVEN'T ENOUGH FEELING NOT 64 POET
TO TORMENT HIM.
DON'T TORMENT ME WITH YOUR SINFUL QUESTIONS/ 149 POET
PUTTIN' ON THE BROGUE TO TORMENT US. 167 POET
AND YOUR BABY, YOU'D BE BRINGING IT INTO TORMENT. 58 STRANG
HE DOUBLED THE TORMENT OF FEAR WE LIVED IN. 58 STRANG

TORMENTED
TORMENTED WITH THOUGHTS OF MAT BURKE AND THE GREAT 61 ANNA
WRONG YOU'VE DONE HIM/
AND ME TORMENTED WITH THE WICKEDNESS YOU'D TOLD OF 69 ANNA
YOURSELF.
AND ME TORMENTED WITH THOUGHTS. 71 ANNA
HE LOOKS HAGGARD AND TORMENTED. 174 ELECTR
AND BEING TORMENTED ALWAYS BY THE COMPLAINTS OF 51 MISBEG
HIS LIMY SUPERINTENDENT.
I COULDN'T SLEEP WITH MY THOUGHTS TORMENTED THE 76 MISBEG
WAY THEY ARE.
HE KNOWS WELL HOW TORMENTED I'D BE WAITING. 138 POET
(TORMENTED BY LOVE AND PITY AND REMORSE) 144 STRANG

TORMENTEDLY
(ARGUING TORMENTEDLY WITHIN SELF) 422 DYNAMO
(THEN ARGUING TORMENTEDLY WITH HIMSELF) 474 DYNAMO
(TORMENTEDLY.) NO/ 49 JOURNE
(TORMENTEDLY) DON'T, JIM. 135 MISBEG
(TORMENTEDLY) WILL YOU STOP TALKING AS IF YOU'D 161 MISBEG
GONE MAD IN THE NIGHT/
THINKING TORMENTEDLY) 67 STRANG
(THINKING--TORMENTEDLY) ((THE THOUGHT OF THAT 117 STRANG
WOMAN/....

TORMENTIN'
BUT DICKINSON WAS TORMENTIN' YOUR FATHER WITH HIS 22 POET
FEED BILL FOR THE MARE.
IT WAS A GREAT SORROW TORMENTIN' ME THAT THE DUEL 142 POET
WOULD COME BETWEEN YOU.

TORMENTING
HER FACE BETRAYING THE CONFLICT THAT IS TORMENTINGS14 DIFRNT
HER.
THEY ARE TORMENTING HIM. 366 LAZARU
TORMENTING HIM--AND WHO DOESN'TS 33 MISBEG
HIS CONSCIENCE WAS TORMENTING HIM. 89 MISBEG
(TIMIDLY.) DON'T BE CURSING HER AND TORMENTING 75 POET
YOURSELF.
EVEN NOW HE'S ALL HEAT AND ENERGY AND THE 196 STRANG
TORMENTING DRIVE OF NOON...

TORMINT
AND I HAVE THE BLACK TORMINT IN MY MIND THAT IT'S 138 POET
THE FAULT OF THE MORTAL SIN
AND I'M NOT PUTTIN' ON BROGUE TO TORMINT YOU, ME 168 POET
DARLIMT.
FAIX, IT WAS NIVIR SO CLEAR WHILE THE MAJOR LIVED 175 POET
TO TORMINT ME.
GOD REST HIS SOUL IN THE FLAMES AV TORMINT/ 177 POET

TORN
ONE OF THEM TORN FROM THE SPRAWL ON THE SIDEWALK 261 AHWILD
HE HAD TAKEN,
HIS CLOTHES TORN AND DIRTY, COVERED WITH SAWDUST 68 ANNA
AS IF HE HAD BEEN GROVELING ON
BUT STILL UNCERTAIN, TORN BETWEEN DOUBT AND THE 74 ANNA
DESIRE TO BELIEVE--HELPLESSLY)
AND A SINGLET TORN OPEN ACROSS HIS HAIRY CHEST. 571 CROSS
(HE STARES INTO HER EYES, TERRIBLY CONFUSED AND 227 DESIRE
TORN.
(TORN BETWEEN CURIOSITY AND A SENSE OF BEING ONE 507 DIFRNT
TOO MANY)
HIS UNIFORM IS RAGGED AND TORN. 192 EJONES
HIS PANTS HAVE BEEN SO TURN AWAY 198 EJONES
BUT HER FACE IS TORN BY A LOOK OF STRICKEN 28 ELECTR
ANGUISH.

TORN

TORN (CONT'D.)
TURN BY REMORSE, RUNS AFTER HIM AND THROWS HER 166 ELECTR
ARMS AROUND HIM)
HIS FACE IS TORN AND TRANSFIGURED BY JOY. 266 GGBROW
FINALLY A VOICE SEEMS TORN OUT OF HIM. 319 GGBROW
THE CLOTHES HE HAS TORN OFF IN HIS AGONY ARE 319 GGBROW
SCATTERED ON THE FLOOR.
(TORN BY THE CONFLICT--TORTUREDLY) HA-HA-HA-- 293 LAZARU
(TORN--ARGUING WITH HIS FEAR) 365 LAZARU
HIS ASPECT IS WILD, HIS HAIR DISHEVELED, HIS 368 LAZARU
CLOTHES TORN.
THE MAN HIMSELF IS IN DANGER OF BEING TORN APART 173 MANSNS
BETWEEN THEM--
VOTIVE OFFERINGS, PIECES OF CLOTH TORN FROM 347 MARCOM
CLOTHING, BANGLES, ARMLETS,
HIS SCARLET UNIFORM IS FILTHY AND TORN AND PULLED 152 POET
AWRY.
(MORE AND MORE HUMILIATED AND ANGRY AND TORN BY 157 POET
CONFLICTING EMOTIONS
IN HIS TORN, DISHEVELED, DIRT-STAINED UNIFORM, 175 POET
SHE WEARS A FADED GINGHAM DRESS AND A TORN 579 ROPE
SUNBONNET.)
TURN WITH THE AGONY OF LOVE AND BIRTH. 43 STRANG
HIS KNEES AND BEGINS TO SOB--STIFLED TORN SOUNDS.) 43 STRANG
(TORN BETWEEN HOPE AND FEAR) 97 STRANG
(THINKING--TERRIBLY TORN) ((WHY DO I LIKE HIM 151 STRANG
NOW?...
PASSIONATELY EMBITTERED AND TORN. 158 STRANG
TORN BY TWO CONFLICTING SUGGESTIONS. 449 WELDED
IN THE LEFT WALL, CENTER, A SMALL WINDOW WITH A 470 WELDED
TORN DARK SHADE PULLED DOWN.

TORPEDO
WHAT NEVER HIT NO MINE OR TORPEDO. 515 INZONE
IF A TORPEDO HITS THIS HOOKER WE'LL ALL BE IN HELL516 INZONE
FEET, AS YOU MIGHT SAY, IF WE GETS 'IT BE A 517 INZONE
TORPEDO OR MINE.

TORPEDOED
I ONLY PUT THAT BOX THERE SO I COULD GET IT QUICK 527 INZONE
IN CASE WE WERE TORPEDOED.

TORPEDOES
THE BANG OF FIRECRACKERS AND TORPEDOES BEGINS FROM189 AHWILD
THE REAR OF THE HOUSE, LEFT.

TORSO
OBLONG EYES ABOVE A GROSS, ROUNDED TORSO. 473 DYNAMO

TORTURE
AND ON TOP OF THAT, TO TORTURE ME MORE, HE GAVE ME281 AHWILD
YOUR LETTER.
TO TORTURE ME? 281 AHWILD
DID YOU HAVE TO TORTURE HIM$ 164 BEYOND
I WANTED TO TORTURE HER? 124 ELECTR
DON'T YOU SEE HOW YOU TORTURE ME$ 152 ELECTR
(WITH A STRANGE CRUEL SMILE OF GLOATING OVER THE 178 ELECTR
YEARS OF SELF-TORTURE)
HIS FACE IS THAT OF AN ASCETIC, A MARTYR, FURROWED284 GGBROW
BY PAIN AND SELF-TORTURE.
WHO HAS STOOD TENSELY WITH HIS EYES SHUT AS IF HE 530 INZONE
WERE UNDERGOING TORTURE DURING
I BEGIN TO KNOW THE TORTURE OF THE FEAR OF DEATH, 330 LAZARU
LAZARUS--
AND IN REVENGE AND SELF-TORTURE HIS LOVE HAS BEEN 352 LAZARU
FAITHLESS/
TORTURE HIM, CAESAR/ 362 LAZARU
TORTURE HIM, CAESAR, THE MAN WHO LAUGHS AT YOU/ 362 LAZARU
AND UNDER PENALTY OF TORTURE 351 MARCOM
WHAT HAVE I DONE THAT THOU SHOULDST TORTURE ME$ 413 MARCOM
OF FLESH WHICH WILL NOT HAVE SHRIEKED THROUGH TEN 425 MARCOM
DAYS' TORTURE BEFORE IT DIED/
DO NOT TORTURE YOURSELF/ 425 MARCOM
SHE LOVES TO TORTURE/...)) 40 STRANG
HOW CAN YOU TORTURE US LIKE THAT/ 144 STRANG
I'LL SEND YOU A COUPLE OF MILLION CELLS YOU CAN 170 STRANG
TORTURE WITHOUT HARMING
OUR GHOSTS WOULD TORTURE US TO DEATH/ 196 STRANG
YOU ONLY WANT TO TORTURE-- 460 WELDED
SHE CONFESSED/ SHE WAS PROUD OF HER HATE/ SHE 475 WELDED
WAS PROUD OF MY TORTURE.
AND WE'LL TORTURE AND TEAR, AND CLUTCH FOR EACH 488 WELDED
OTHER'S SOULS/

TORTURED
(SUDDENLY--HIS FACE FULL OF THE BITTEREST, 531 DAYS
TORTURED SELF-LOATHING--
HE WOULD FEEL A TORTURED LONGING TO PRAY AND BEG 534 DAYS
FOR FORGIVENESS.
(WITH A TORTURED CRY THAT STARTS HIM AWAKE) 558 DAYS
WHO KNOWETH THE TORTURED HEARTS OF MEN, CANST THOU565 DAYS
NOT FORGIVE--NOW--
HE STRETCHES UP HIS HANDS IN A TORTURED GESTURE) 239 DESIRE
WITH TORTURED PASSION) 257 DESIRE
(TORTURED BY FOREBODING-- 502 DIFRNT
(HIDING HER FACE IN HER HANDS-- WITH A TORTURED 545 DIFRNT
MOAN)
AND HE THINKS IN TORTURED AGONY OF SPIRIT) 448 DYNAMO
SEEM LIKE QUEER HINDOO IDOLS TORTURED INTO 483 DYNAMO
SCIENTIFIC SUPPLICATIONS.
WITH TORTURED LONGING) 90 ELECTR
(WITH TORTURED SELF-ACCUSATION) 124 ELECTR
(TEMPTED AND TORTURED, IN A LONGING WHISPER) 165 ELECTR
THE TORTURED MAD LOOK ON HIS FACE CHANGING TO A 166 ELECTR
STRICKEN TERRIFIED EXPRESSION)
HOLD OF HIS TORTURED IMAGINATION AND SPEAKS 166 ELECTR
FASCINATEDLY TO HIMSELF)
HIS REAL FACE HAS AGED GREATLY, GROWN MORE 269 GGBROW
STRAINED AND TORTURED.
(THEN WITH TORTURED BITTERNESS) 273 GGBROW
PEACE, POOR TORTURED ONE, BRAVE PITIFUL PRIDE OF 291 GGBROW
MAN,
A REAL DEMON, TORTURED INTO TORTURING OTHERS) 294 GGBROW

TOSS

TORTURED (CONT'D.)
HIS OWN FACE TORTURED AND DISTORTED BY THE DEMON 305 GGBROW
OF DION'S MASK)
(WITH A SHOW OF TORTURED DERISION) 311 GGBROW
HIS REAL FACE IS NOW SICK, GHASTLY, TORTURED, 314 GGBROW
HOLLOW-CHEEKED AND FEVERISH-EYED)
MAY THE CHAIR BRING HIM PEACE AT LAST, THE POOR 719 ICEMAN
TORTURED BASTARD/
(PLEADS DISTRACTEDLY) GO, FOR THE LOVE OF CHRIST,170 ICEMAN
YOU MAD TORTURED BASTARD,
(HE GIVES A HARD, TORTURED LAUGH.) 166 JOURNE
THE SELF-TORTURED, INTROSPECTIVE,. 273 LAZARU
(A SELF-TORTURED MAN--GLOOMILY) 276 LAZARU
MATURING AND OLD AGE ARE REPRESENTED IN THE TYPES 312 LAZARU
OF THE SELF-TORTURED,
(TORTURED WITH REMORSE) NO/ 334 LAZARU
IN EACH OF THE THREE TYPES OF THE INTROSPECTIVE, 336 LAZARU
SELF-TORTURED,.
MIRIAM'S BODY IS SEEN TO RISE IN A WRITHING 348 LAZARU
TORTURED LAST EFFORT.)
(POUNDING HIS TEMPLES WITH HIS FISTS--TORTURED) 352 LAZARU
IN BRIEF, I MARRIED THE WHORE, SHE TORTURED ME, MY356 LAZARU
MOTHER'S SCHEMING PROSPERED--
BUT I FEEL THAT WAS NOT ALL OF IT, THAT MY MOTHER 356 LAZARU
WISHED TO KEEP ME TORTURED
YOU SHALL BE TORTURED AS YOU HAVE TORTURED/ 361 LAZARU
HOW HE MUST HAVE TORTURED YOU/ 361 LAZARU
BOUND TO A HIGH STAKE AFTER HE HAD BEEN TORTURED, 363 LAZARU
THAT I WILL NOT ENDURE BEING THE TORTURED CAPTIVE 30 MANSNS
OF MY MIND MUCH LONGER--
(HE OPENS HIS EYES AND GIVES A TORTURED, SNEERING 148 MISBEG
LAUGH,
AS IF SOMETHING VITAL HAD BEEN STABBED IN HIM-- 51 POET
WITH A CRY OF TORTURED APPEAL.)
(SUDDENLY SHE IS OVERCOME BY A BITTER, TORTURED 162 POET
REVULSION OF FEELING.)
AND I KNEW TOO THAT I WAS TORTURING THESE TORTURED 45 STRANG
MEN,
(THINKING WITH A STRANGE TORTURED SHAME) 145 STRANG
(FORCING A TORTURED SMILE) NOT FOR ANYTHING IN 196 STRANG
THE WORLD/
(WITH TORTURED EXULTANCE) FLY UP TO HEAVEN, 198 STRANG
GORDON/
(WITH A LAST TORTURED PROTEST) 198 STRANG
THERE IS SOMETHING TORTURED ABOUT HIM-- 444 WELDED
HER WHOLE TORTURED FACE EXPRESSES AN ABYSMAL SELF-460 WELDED
LOATHING,
(HE SITS IN ANGUISH, IN A TORTURED RESTRAINT. 487 WELDED

TORTUREDLY
(TORTUREDLY) FOR GOD'S SAKE/ 531 DAYS
(STAMMERS TORTUREDLY) I--I DON'T KNOW--I CAN'T 559 DAYS
THINK/
(TORTUREDLY) NO/ 561 DAYS
(TORTUREDLY) DID YE GO T' SEE HER$ 240 DESIRE
(TORTUREDLY) I WISH HE NEVER WAS BORN/ 257 DESIRE
(THEN TORTUREDLY) ((OH, GOD, WHY DID I EVER COME 441 DYNAMO
HERE TONIGHT$...))
(THINKING TORTUREDLY) ((MOTHER,... 487 DYNAMO
(TORTUREDLY) YES. 99 ELECTR
WAITING FOR ME IN THERE, WHERE--(TORTUREDLY) BUT 140 ELECTR
SHE WASN'T/
(TORTUREDLY--BEGINS TO PACE UP AND DOWN, MUTTERING157 ELECTR
HER THOUGHTS ALOUD)
(WITH SUDDEN WELLNESS--TORTUREDLY, SINKING ON HIS 292 GGBROW
KNEES BESIDE HER)
(TORTUREDLY) YOU LIE/ 298 GGBROW
(AGAIN HE BENDS DOWN TO THE MASK AS IF LISTENING--307 GGBROW
TORTUREDLY)
(TORTUREDLY ARGUING TO HIMSELF IN A SHAKEN 726 ICEMAN
WHISPER)
(TORN BY THE CONFLICT--TORTUREDLY) HA-HA-HA-- 293 LAZARU
(SHE SUDDENLY STOPS AND PRESSES HER HANDS TO HER 163 MANSNS
HEAD TORTUREDLY.)
AND NOW HE STARES TORTUREDLY THROUGH THE MOONLIGHT149 MISBEG
INTO THE DRAWING ROOM.)
FOR A SECOND HE BREAKS--TORTUREDLY.) 115 POET
(HE GRINS TORTUREDLY) ((WHY?... 5 STRANG
(THINKING TORTUREDLY) ((COLD LIPS... 14 STRANG
(THINKING TORTUREDLY) ((GORDON DARLING, 16 STRANG
(TORTUREDLY) ((ASHES/... 16 STRANG
(TORTUREDLY) WHAT WILL HAPPENS 62 STRANG
THINKING TORTUREDLY) 97 STRANG
(TORTUREDLY--TRYING INCOHERENTLY TO FORCE OUT A 182 STRANG
LAST DEPARTING PROTEST)
(THINKING TORTUREDLY) ((BUT IT'S FOR SCIENCE/... 192 STRANG
(THINKING TORTUREDLY) ((OH, HE MUSTN'T/... 195 STRANG
(TORTUREDLY) WOUNDS/ WOUNDS/ 458 WELDED

TORTURES
THE GUILT WHICH TORTURES HIM A THOUSAND-FOLD NOW 544 DAYS
SHE IS DEAD.
HE TWISTS AND WRINGS AND TORTURES OUR LIVES WITH 73 ELECTR
OTHERS' LIVES UNTIL--

TORTURING
A TORTURING REMORSE FOR MURDERED HAPPINESS/ 561 DAYS
HE WAS TORTURING ME/ 110 ELECTR
STOP TORTURING ME OR I--/ 155 ELECTR
YOU'RE LIKE A DEVIL TORTURING ME/ 156 ELECTR
A REAL DEMON, TORTURED INTO TORTURING OTHERS) 294 GGBROW
THEY'RE TORTURING HIM/ 312 GGBROW
BEYOND ALL TORTURING DOUBT, 171 MANSNS
AND I KNEW TOO THAT I WAS TORTURING THESE TORTURED 45 STRANG
MEN,
WHEN I GAVE MYSELF WITH A MAD PLEASURE IN 71 STRANG
TORTURING MYSELF FOR HIS

TOSS
(GIGGLES--THEN WITH A COQUETTISH TOSS OF HER HEAD)191 AHWILD
(WITH AN ARCH TOSS OF HER HEAD) 251 AHWILD

TOSS

TOSS (CONT'D.)
(WITH A TOSS OF HER HEAD) I CAN PLAY AS WELL AS 256 AHWILD
ELSIE RAND, AT LEAST/
(SHE GIVES A LITTLE REBELLIOUS TOSS OF HER HEAD-- 175 JOURNE
WITH GIRLISH PIQUE.)
(WITH A PROUD TOSS OF HER HEAD--BOASTFULLY) 20 MISBEG
(WITH A DEFIANT TOSS OF HER HEAD) 34 MISBEG
(DEFIANT AGAIN, WITH AN ARROGANT TOSS OF HER 29 POET
HEAD.)
(WITH AN ARROGANT TOSS OF HER HEAD.) 27 POET
(IMPULSIVELY, WITH A PROUD TOSS OF HER HEAD.) 112 POET
(WITH A TOSS OF HER HEAD.) GET ALONG WITH YOU/ 136 POET
(THEN SPIRITEDLY, WITH A PROUD TOSS OF HER HEAD.) 139 POET

TOSSED
LIKE A PENNY OF CHARITY TOSSED TO A BEGGAR. 152 MANSNS

TOSSER
WAKE UP OUR DEMON BOMB-TOSSER, CHUCK. 658 ICEMAN

TOSSES
(HE TOSSES A COIN ON THE BAR.) 4 ANNA
(HE TOSSES IT DOWN) AHAH/ 31 ANNA
(HE TOSSES THE BOOK ON THE TABLE AND SPEAKS TO HIS429 DYNAMO
WIFE)
(REACHES IN HIS POCKET AND TOSSES HIM DOWN A 106 ELECTR
SILVER DOLLAR)
HE TOSSES THE TESTAMENT ASIDE CONTEMPTUOUSLY) 269 GGBROW
HE POURS A BRIMFUL DRINK AND TOSSES IT DOWN HIS 586 ICEMAN
THROAT.
(HE TOSSES IT TO ROCKY) I'D RATHER SLEEP IN THE 682 ICEMAN
GUTTER THAN PASS ANOTHER NIGHT
ROCKY TOSSES THE KEYS ON THE SHELF--DISGUSTEDLY) 682 ICEMAN
(HE TOSSES DOWN HIS DRINK WITH A LIFELESS, 694 ICEMAN
AUTOMATIC MOVEMENT--COMPLAININGLY)
(HE SITS IN THE CHAIR BY CHUCK AND POURS A DRINK 719 ICEMAN
AND TOSSES IT DOWN.
(SHE TOSSES HER HEAD--INDIGNANTLY.) 176 JOURNE
(HE TOSSES A HANDFUL OF GOLD TO THE SERVANTS AND 429 MARCOM
ANOTHER TO THE MUSICIANS.
(HE TOSSES DOWN HIS DRINK IN ONE GULP, OLSON SIPS 497 VOYAGE
HIS GINGER ALE.
(SHE TOSSES DOWN HER BRANDY. 507 VOYAGE

TOSSING
I DIDN'T WANT TO DISTURB YOU BY TOSSING AROUND. 59 ELECTR
TOSSING AND ROLLING AROUND. 715 ICEMAN
I HEAR HIM TOSSING ABOUT... 69 STRANG

TOTAL
HARDLY, JAMIE--BUT NOT A TOTAL RUIN YET, I HOPE. 93 POET
(THAWING OUT, IN HIS TOTAL MISUNDERSTANDING OF THE119 POET
SITUATION.)
DANCING, BUT YOUR SPECIALISTS WERE AT TOTAL LOSS/ 100 STRANG

TOTALLY
(TOTALLY UNPREPARED FOR THIS APPROACH-- 293 AHWILD
SHAMEFACEDLY MUTTERS)
IS TOTALLY AT VARIANCE WITH HER HEALTHY OUTDOOR 13 STRANG
PHYSIQUE.

TOTED
AND I SEE YOU'VE TOTED ONE OF THE OLD BOOKS ALONG 82 BEYOND
WITH YOU.

TOTTER
TUTTER FEEBLY UNDER HIM AS HE SHUFFLES SLOWLY 578 ROPE
ALONG BY THE AID OF A THICK CANE.

TOTTERING
BURKE, WEAK AND TOTTERING, IS CAUGHT OFF HIS 33 ANNA
GUARD.
I--(SHE TURNS AS IF TO RUN INTO THE ROOM, TAKES A 64 ELECTR
TOTTERING STEP--

TOTTERS
THE OLD MAN TOTTERS OVER TO HIM, STRETCHING OUT A 595 ROPE
TREMBLING HAND.

TOUCH
(A TOUCH OF RESENTMENT IN HIS VOICE) 540 'ILE
LIPS THAT TOUCH LIQUOR SHALL NEVER TOUCH YOURS/ 232 AHWILD
I'VE TOLD YOU HOW SORRY HE WAS, AND HOW HE SAID 289 AHWILD
HE'D NEVER TOUCH LIQUOR AGAIN.
(VIRTUOUSLY) YOU KNOW I NEVER TOUCH IT. 12 ANNA
THERE IS A TOUCH OF THE POET ABOUT HIM EXPRESSED 81 BEYOND
(WITH A TOUCH OF IMPATIENCE) 466 CARIBE
THIS HAIR FURNISHES THE ONLY TOUCH OF COLOR ABOUT 562 CROSS
HER.
DO YOU THINK I COULD TOUCH ITS 566 CROSS
DON'T TOUCH HIM, NAT/ 573 CROSS
(SHRINKS FROM HIS TOUCH) NO, NO, IT'S NOTHING. 540 DAYS
ADDRESSING THE CROSS NOT WITHOUT A FINAL TOUCH OF 566 DAYS
PRIDE IN HIS HUMILITY)
THEY HAIN'T MANY T' TOUCH YE, EPHRAIM--A SON AT 249 DESIRE
SEVENTY-SIX.
SHE SHRINKS FROM HIS TOUCH.) 252 DESIRE
SO THAT NOTHIN' HUMAN KIN NEVER TOUCH 'EM/ 268 DESIRE
HE PATS EMMA ON THE BACK WITH A PLAYFUL TOUCH THAT513 DFRNT
ALMOST JARS HER OFF HER FEET)
NO, I WON'T TOUCH HIM. 343 DFRNT
HER MOUTH HAS A TOUCH OF 428 DYNAMO
(THEN WITH A TOUCH OF SEVERITY) 431 DYNAMO
(FIERCELY) YOU'LL NEVER DARE TOUCH ME AGAIN, YOU 452 DYNAMO
OLD FOOL/
AND DIDN'T GET WHAT YOU WANTED AND WAS SO DAMNED 460 DYNAMO
SCARED TO TOUCH YOU.
(SHRINKING AWAY) DON'T TOUCH ME/ 487 DYNAMO
NEVER TOUCH HER FLESH AGAIN... 487 DYNAMO
ON'Y I AIN'T 'LOWIN' NARY BODY TO TOUCH DIS BABY. 180 EJONES
AND THERE IS NOT A TOUCH OF FEMININE ALLUREMENT TO 10 ELECTR
HER SEVERELY PLAIN GET-UP.
BUT AT HIS TOUCH SHE PULLS AWAY AND SPRINGS TO HER 24 ELECTR
FEET.)
(WITH COLD FURY) DON'T YOU TOUCH ME/ 24 ELECTR
(STILL SUSPICIOUSLY--WITH A TOUCH OF SCORN) 34 ELECTR
HAS THE DISHEVELED TOUCH OF THE FUGITIVE. 110 ELECTR
GIVING A TOUCH TO HIS SHIRT AND TIE. 145 ELECTR
MAKE THE CAPTAIN TOUCH THERE ON THE WAY BACK. 145 ELECTR

TOUCH (CONT'D.)
A SKIN, O GOD, THAT I MUST WEAR ARMOR IN ORDER TO 265 GGBROW
TOUCH OR TO BE TOUCHED$
SHE IS DRESSED AS IN SCENE ONE BUT WITH AN ADDED 274 GGBROW
TOUCH OF EFFECTIVE PRIMPING
THEY WANT AN ORIGINAL TOUCH OF MODERN NOVELTY 275 GGBROW
STUCK IN TO LIVEN IT UP
SHE IS DRESSED WITH A CAREFUL, SUBTLE EXTRA TOUCH 308 GGBROW
TO ATTRACT THE EYE.
THEN LEAPING TO HIS FEET HE PUTS OUT ONE HAND TO 319 GGBROW
TOUCH THE MASK LIKE A
I WOULD LIKE TO BE SINCERE, TO TOUCH LIFE 219 HA APE
SOMEWHERE
EYES, WHERE A HASTY DOUSING DOES NOT TOUCH, 226 HA APE
IT PUT THE TOUCH OF HOME, SWATE HOME IN THE 230 HA APE
STOKEHOLE.
(EAGERLY, WITH A TOUCH OF BRAVADO) 249 HA APE
FEEDIN' YOUR FACE--SINKERS AND COFFEE--DAT DON'T 250 HA APE
TOUCH IT.
(WITH A TOUCH OF BRAVADO.) AND I AIN'T DONE SO 15 HUGHIE
BAD, PAL.
IT'S FUNNY HOW MOTHER KEPT IN TOUCH WITH YOU SO LONG. 589 ICEMAN
ONCE IN A WHILE ONE OF THEM MAKES A SUCCESSFUL 593 ICEMAN
TOUCH SOMEWHERE.
THE LEWD PURITAN TOUCH, OBVIOUSLY, AND IT GROWS 597 ICEMAN
MORE MARKED AS WE GO ON.
I CAN GET BACK MY MAGIC TOUCH WITH CHANGE EASY, 609 ICEMAN
BE GOD, I FELT HE'D BROUGHT THE TOUCH OF DEATH ON 663 ICEMAN
HIM/
I FEEL THE COLD TOUCH OF IT ON HIM. 668 ICEMAN
BE GOD, YOU CAN'T SAY HICKEY HASN'T THE MIRACULOUS677 ICEMAN
TOUCH TO RAISE THE DEAD.
I KNOW YOU HARDLY EVER TOUCH IT. 690 ICEMAN
(RESENTFULLY) WELL, DIS IS DE TIME I DO TOUCH IT/690 ICEMAN
SO YUH WON'T TOUCH IT, HUH 702 ICEMAN
(A TOUCH OF STRANGE BITTERNESS COMES INTO HIS 710 ICEMAN
VOICE FOR A MOMENT)
I AIN'T GOIN' TO TOUCH IT. 520 INZONE
WHEN SHE IS MERRY, THERE IS A TOUCH OF IRISH LILT 13 JOURNE
IN IT.
I'LL BET THEY'RE COOKING UP SOME NEW SCHEME TO 15 JOURNE
TOUCH THE OLD MAN.
APPROPRIATE TOUCH. 25 JOURNE
ALL JAMIE MEANT WAS EDMUND MIGHT HAVE A TOUCH OF 27 JOURNE
SOMETHING ELSE, TOO.
I HEARD HIM PULL THAT TOUCH OF MALARIA STUFF. 29 JOURNE
(WITH A TOUCH OF PRIDE.) WHATEVER EDMUND'S DONE, 35 JOURNE
(SUDDENLY PRIMLY VIRTUOUS.) I'D NEVER SUGGEST A 52 JOURNE
MAN OR A WOMAN TOUCH DRINK.
NO ONE CAN FIND OR TOUCH YOU ANY MORE. 99 JOURNE
A TOUCH OF GRIPPE IS NOTHING. 101 JOURNE
BUT EVEN THEY CAN'T TOUCH ME NOW. 104 JOURNE
AT LAST SHE SAID SHE REFUSED TO TOUCH IT ANY MORE 115 JOURNE
OR SHE MIGHT SPOIL IT.
I COULDN'T TOUCH WHAT I TRIED TO TELL YOU JUST 154 JOURNE
NOW.
A BACKGROUND WHICH DOES NOT TOUCH HER 171 JOURNE
PREOCCUPATION.
YOU MUST NOT TRY TO TOUCH ME. 174 JOURNE
A DISSOLVING TOUCH OF SUNSET STILL LINGERS ON THE 275 LAZARU
HORIZON.
HER MOUTH, ON THE OTHER HAND, HAS A TOUCH OF 2 MANSNS
COARSE SENSUALITY ABOUT ITS THICK,
I WILL NOT LET IT TOUCH ME. 21 MANSNS
I WOULD TOUCH ANYTHING OF YOURS$ 21 MANSNS
IT'S THE TOUCH OF THE POET IN YOU/ 47 MANSNS
THE HARD TIMES WON'T TOUCH THAT. 48 MANSNS
WITH JUST THE CORRECT TOUCH OF QUIET RESIGNATION 50 MANSNS
IN HER BEARING
(AS IF THE TOUCH OF HIS HAND ALARMED HER--SHRINKS 103 MANSNS
BACK, TURNING AWAY FROM HIM--
(SHE SITS DOWN, CLOSE BESIDE HER, SO THEIR ARMS 123 MANSNS
TOUCH.)
UNTIL THEIR FACES TOUCH THE SIDE OF HIS HEAD. 128 MANSNS
THEIR OTHER ARMS GO AROUND HIM SO THAT THEIR HANDS128 MANSNS
TOUCH HIS CHEST.)
PULLING THEIR HANDS AWAY SO THEY NO LONGER TOUCH 129 MANSNS
ON HIS CHEST.
THAT LAST TOUCH FINISHED HIM, AND THAT WAS ALL 155 MANSNS
YOUR OWN.
HOW DARE YOU TOUCH ME/ 165 MANSNS
DO NOT DARE TO TOUCH ME/ 190 MANSNS
THE DREAMER WITH A TOUCH OF THE POET IN HIS SOUL, 191 MANSNS
AND THE HEART OF A BOY?
DO NOT PRESUME TO TOUCH ME/ 193 MANSNS
ALLAH FORBID I TOUCH WHAT BELONGS TO A CORPSE/ 351 MARCOM
I AM SURE IT WOULD TOUCH YOUR LADY'S HEART. 361 MARCOM
AND GIVE A TOUCH TO YOUR HAIR. 36 MISBEG
IF YOU DARE TOUCH THAT FENCE AGAIN, 64 MISBEG
(DULLY) DON'T WANT TO TOUCH ME NOW, EH$ 151 MISBEG
DON'T SAY-- DON'T WANT TO TOUCH YOU-- 151 MISBEG
HER MOUTH, ON THE OTHER HAND, HAS A TOUCH OF 15 POET
COARSENESS AND SENSUALITY
IT'S EASY TO TELL YOUNG MASTER HARFORD HAS A TOUCH 30 POET
AV THE POET IN HIM--
THERE IS A ROMANTIC TOUCH OF THE POET BEHIND HIS 48 POET
YANKEE PILLOW.
(HE TRIES TO TOUCH BRIMS WITH MELODY'S GLASS, 93 POET
IT WOULD BE BENEATH ME TO TOUCH SUCH VILE 123 POET
LICKSPITTLE.
FULL AV DACENCY, AND DREAMS, AND LOONEY, TOO, WID A171 POET
TOUCH AV THE POET IN HIM.
WHILE HE SPOUTED BYRON TO PRETEND HIMSELF WAS A 176 POET
LORD WID A TOUCH AV THE POET--
(GRASPING HIS ARM) DON'T TOUCH HIM, PAT. 582 ROPE
AN' MIND YOU DON'T TOUCH THE CHILD WITH IT OR I'LL584 ROPE
BEAT YOU TO A JELLY.

TOUCH

TOUCH (CONT'D.)

(SEVERELY) DON'T YUH DARE TOUCH THAT ROPE, D'YUH 600 ROPE HEARS

(WITH A TOUCH OF ASPERITY) YES, I SAID IT, AND I 10 STRANG GAVE HIM MY REASON.

(A TOUCH OF ASPERITY IN HIS VOICE) 16 STRANG

LITTLE NINA WAS NEVER ALLOWED TO TOUCH ANYTHING... 27 STRANG

(REACHING OUT HER HAND TENDERLY, TRYING TO TOUCH 58 STRANG NINA)

DON'T TOUCH ME/ 61 STRANG

THE LAST TOUGH/... 76 STRANG

I SHOULD HAVE KEPT IN TOUCH ON THAT ACCOUNT... 76 STRANG

(GOING FURTHER TOWARD HIM--SHE CAN NOW TOUCH HIM 87 STRANG WITH HER HAND)

TOUCH OF HER SKIN/... 97 STRANG

THE TOUCH OF HER SOFT SKIN/... 104 STRANG

IF I EVEN TOUCH HER...!) 104 STRANG

(WITH A TOUCH OF HER FATHER'S MANNER) 136 STRANG

SURELY NO ONE COULD EVER TOUCH SHAW IN ANYTHING/ 162 STRANG

OLD TOUCH OF HER FLESH... 169 STRANG

I WON'T TOUCH A LIFE THAT HAS MORE THAN ONE CELL/ 169 STRANG

TOUCH OF HER FLESH... 169 STRANG

I WISH SHE WOULDN'T TOUCH ME... 172 STRANG

SO NEAR THAT BY A SLIGHT MOVEMENT EACH COULD TOUCH452 WELDED THE OTHER,

THEY TOUCH EACH OTHER TESTINGLY 480 WELDED

FOR A MOMENT AS THEIR HANDS TOUCH THEY FORM 489 WELDED TOGETHER ONE CROSS.

TOUCHED

(TOUCHED--EMBARRASSED BY THIS UNFAMILIAR EMOTION) 22 ANNA

(TOUCHED BUT A BIT EMBARRASSED) 65 ANNA

GOD KNOWS WHERE, FOR THERE WAS NO SIGN ON THE 560 CROSS ISLAND THAT MAN HAD EVER TOUCHED

BUT THERE'S PLENTY OF DIVERSION GOING ON IN THE 497 DIFRNT PORTS YOU TOUCHED,

(SENTIMENTALLY TOUCHED--BEAMING ON HIM) 458 DYNAMO

(TOUCHED, COMING BACK TO HER) 83 ELECTR

A SKIN, O GOD, THAT I MUST WEAR ARMOR IN ORDER TO 265 GGBROW TOUCH OR TO BE TOUCHED!

IT HAS ALWAYS BEEN SUCH AGONY FOR ME TO BE 279 GGBROW TOUCHED/

(TOUCHED) I KNOW BILLY WAS ALWAYS DION ANTHONY'S 281 GGBROW FRIEND.

(BOASTINGLY) WE'D KILL ANYONE THAT TOUCHED YOU, 300 GGBROW WOULDN'T WE$

THE ELDER LIKE A GRAY LUMP OF DOUGH TOUCHED UP 218 HA APE WITH ROUGE,

YOU'VE TOUCHED EVERY DAMNED ONE OF THEM. 609 ICEMAN

HARRY'LL CERTAINLY BE TOUCHED BY YOUR THOUGHT OF 643 ICEMAN HIM.

HE HARDLY TOUCHED ANYTHING EXCEPT COFFEE. 16 JOURNE

YOU HARDLY TOUCHED A THING AT LUNCH. 72 JOURNE

I WAS GRATEFUL AND TOUCHED. 85 JOURNE

(TOUCHED, RETURNS HIS HUG.) YOU'RE WELCOME, LAD. 90 JOURNE

I HAVEN'T TOUCHED A PIANO IN SO MANY YEARS. 104 JOURNE

IT'S TRUE HE NEVER TOUCHED A DROP TILL HE WAS 137 JOURNE FORTY.

(TOUCHED AND GREEDY.) I THINK IT'S VERY GENEROUS 56 MANSNS OF YOU, MRS. HARFORD.

THE VETERAN IS TOUCHED. 389 MARCOM

I THOUGHT YOU NEVER TOUCHED IT. 113 MISBEG

HE SEEMED TOUCHED AND GRATEFUL. 134 MISBEG

YOU WASN'T TOUCHED EXCEPT YOU'D A BULLET THROUGH 99 POET YOUR COAT.

YOU CAN SEE NO ONE AIN'T TOUCHED YOUR OLD ROPE. 581 ROPE

FROM KNOWING SHE'S TOUCHED BOTTOM AND THERE'S NO 35 STRANG FARTHER TO GO/

THE BOOKS IN THE CASES HAVE NEVER BEEN TOUCHED, 66 STRANG

(TOUCHED) IT'S TOO LATE, NED. 82 STRANG

(TOUCHED ON A SORE SPOT--WITH A NASTY LAUGH-- 141 STRANG CUTTINGLY)

(THEN TOUCHED, SHE COMES TO HIM AND PUTS HER ARMS 475 WELDED AROUND HIS SHOULDERS.

TOUCHES

GREAT FATHER (SHE TOUCHES HER FOREHEAD TO THE 175 EJONES FLOOR WITH QUICK MECHANICAL JERK)

HE TOUCHES JONES ON THE SHOULDER PEREMPTORILY, 197 EJONES

THE WITCH DOCTOR PRANCES UP TO HIM, TOUCHES HIM 201 EJONES WITH HIS WAND.

WITH TOUCHES OF STUDIED CARELESSNESS, 21 ELECTR

(HE REACHES UP AND TOUCHES HER HAIR CARESSINGLY. 90 ELECTR

(HE TOUCHES HER HAIR CARESSINGLY. 165 ELECTR

(CORA GOES BACK TO GIVE THE SCHOONER OF FLOWERS A 629 ICEMAN FEW MORE TOUCHES.)

AS SOON AS YOUR HEAD TOUCHES THE PILLOW YOU'RE OFF 20 JOURNE

HE TOUCHES ONE HAND ON HER BREAST, 349 LAZARU

BUT WITH PATHETICALLY OBVIOUS TOUCHES OF 161 MANSNS CALCULATING

LEANS OUT AND TOUCHES IT WITH 366 MARCOM

THIS MARCO TOUCHES ME. 381 MARCOM

YOUR GENEROUS AND WHOLE-HEARTED WELCOME TOUCHES ME431 MARCOM PROFOUNDLY.

(SHE TOUCHES HIS GLASS WITH HERS.) 113 MISBEG

(TOUCHES HIS GLASS TO CREGAN'S--GRACIOUSLY 94 POET CONDESCENDING.)

THEN, KEEPING HER FACE TURNED AWAY FROM HER 131 POET MOTHER, TOUCHES HER SHOULDER.)

(SHE REACHES OUT AND TOUCHES ONE OF HIS HANDS ON 167 POET THE TABLE TOP WITH A FURTIVE

SHE TOUCHES MY HAND, HER EYES GET IN MINE, I LOSE 105 STRANG MY WILL...!)

(THINKING WITH A STRANGE SHUDDER OF MINGLED 169 STRANG ATTRACTION AND FEAR AS SHE TOUCHES

(HE TOUCHES MADELINE ON THE SHOULDER) 177 STRANG

(HE TOUCHES NINA'S ARM--IN A LOW VOICE) 182 STRANG

(SHE TOUCHES HER BREAST.) 470 WELDED

THEN INSTINCTIVELY I SEEK YOU--MY HAND TOUCHES 488 WELDED YOU/

TOUGHEST

TOUCHIN'

DON'T BE TOUCHIN' UT, JACK/ 520 INZONE

HE STOOD THERE WITH THE NOOSE OF THE ROPE ALMOST 590 ROPE TOUCHIN' HIS HEAD.

TOUCHING

ITS BOW ABOUT TOUCHING THE BANK, EVIDENTLY MADE 275 AHWILD FAST TO THE TRUNK OF A WILLOW.

(TOUCHING CHRIS' ARM PERSUASIVELY) 13 ANNA

(WHO HAS COME SO CLOSE THAT THE REVOLVER IS ALMOST 69 ANNA TOUCHING HIS CHEST)

SHE'D NEVER BELIEVE ME, SHE HAS SUCH A TOUCHING 526 DAYS FAITH IN YOU.

(WITHOUT TOUCHING HIM, MAKES A MOTION OF PUSHING 563 DAYS HIM ASIDE)

BUT ALWAYS WITHOUT TOUCHING HIM, ENDEAVORS TO KEEP564 DAYS FROM ENTERING THE CHURCH.

(SUSPICIOUSLY) CALEB DIDN'T SEEM WILLING TO TELL 501 DIFRNT ME MUCH ABOUT THEIR TOUCHING

LIKE A BEGINNER ON THE TYPEWRITER TOUCHING TWO NEWS48 DIFRNT LETTERS)

TOUCHING HIS HAIR,) 487 DYNAMO

FACING ONE ANOTHER WITH THEIR BACKS TOUCHING THE 199 EJONES FOREST WALLS

SO THAT'S WHY YOU COULDN'T STAND MY TOUCHING YOU 25 ELECTR JUST NOW, IS IT$

AND A FEELING OF STRANGENESS AND AWE--TOUCHING HER 52 ELECTR HAIR WITH AN AWKWARD CARESS)

(TOUCHING THE BANDAGE ON HIS HEAD--TENDERLY) 76 ELECTR

(AGAIN MOMENTARILY SOBERED--TOUCHING HIS FOREHEAD)104 ELECTR

IT SEEMED I WAS NEVER REALLY TOUCHING YOU. 309 GGBROW

CLIPPERS WID TALL MASTS TOUCHING THE SKY--FINE 213 HA APE STRONG MEN IN THEM.

WIDOUT TOUCHING A PORT, 214 HA APE

'TWAS TOUCHING, I'M TELLING YOU/ 230 HA APE

THEY'VE ALL A TOUCHING CREDULITY CONCERNING 578 ICEMAN TOMORROWS.

ISN'T A PIPE DREAM OF YESTERDAY A TOUCHING THINGS 603 ICEMAN

HE AVOIDS TOUCHING HER OR LOOKING AT HER. 71 JOURNE

ALMOST TOUCHING THE FILES IN ORDER TO SEE/ 148 JOURNE

TOUCHING THE LION WITH INTENTIONAL PROVOKING 328 LAZARU BRUTALITY)

(THEY BEND CLOSER TO EACH OTHER UNTIL THEIR HEADS 125 MANSNS ARE ABOUT TOUCHING,

WHO BROUGHT HER HOME EACH TIME A HUMBLE, FOOLISH, 388 MARCOM TOUCHING LITTLE GIFT/

THE CHIN ALMOST TOUCHING HIS CHEST, HIS EYES STARE 24 STRANG SADLY AT NOTHING.)

STILL HIS DEVOTION TO HER IS TOUCHING... 51 STRANG

IT'S EVEN RATHER TOUCHING. 82 STRANG

OUR URN SIDE BY SIDE AND TOUCHING ONE ANOTHER... 148 STRANG

(TOUCHING DARRELL WHO HAS STOOD STARING STRAIGHT 182 STRANG BEFORE HIM WITH A BITTER

TOUCHY

KNOWIN' HOW TOUCHY HE IS ABOUT IT. 108 BEYOND

I'M TOUCHY ABOUT NOTHING LATELY. 146 BEYOND

IF HE'S GROWN SO TOUCHY HE'D NEVER ACCEPT A CENT 157 BEYOND

IF HE THOUGHT I WAS HARD UP,

I KNOWED YOU WAS TOUCHY AND DIFFERENT FROM MOST. 508 DIFRNT

HER MANNER IS TOUCHY AND IRRITABLE AND SHE HAS 454 DYNAMO LOST HER FORMER AIR OF FLIPPANCY.

IN HOPE THE EFFECT IS APPARENT ONLY IN A 654 ICEMAN BRISTLING, TOUCHY, PUGNACIOUS ATTITUDE.

YOU MUSTN'T BE SO TOUCHY. 21 JOURNE

TOUGH

HE'D A BEEN A TOUGH OLD BIRD. 478 CARDIF

I'M SOUND 'N' TOUGH AS HICKORY/ 232 DESIRE

SHE'S A GAME SPORT, BUT IT'S PRETTY DAMN TOUGH ON 277 GGBROW HER.

IT'S PRETTY TOUGH ON HER. 289 GGBROW

A GANG OF BLOKES-A TOUGH GANG. 242 HA APE

I SEEN LOTS OF TOUGH NUTS DAT DE GANG CALLED 252 HA APE GORILLAS.

I'VE HAD TOUGH BREAKS TOO, BUT WHAT THE HELL, I 15 HUGHIE ALWAYS GET BY.

HIS FACE WOULD BE HARD AND TOUGH 575 ICEMAN

A TOUGH GUY BUT SENTIMENTAL, IN HIS WAY, AND GOOD-577 ICEMAN NATURED.

IT MUST BE A TOUGH LIFE. 594 ICEMAN

(UNCOMFORTABLY) TOUGH LUCK. 595 ICEMAN

I VAS SO TOUGH AND STRONG I GRAB AXLE OF OX WAGON 599 ICEMAN MIT FULL LOAD

ALL SIX OF US COLORED BOYS, WE WAS TOUGH AND I WAS599 ICEMAN DE TOUGHEST.

AND SOME TOUGH GUY'D JUST TOLD HER BABIES WASN'T 614 ICEMAN BRUNG DOWN DE CHIMNEY BY A BOID

CHUCK IS A TOUGH, THICK-NECKED, BARREL-CHESTED 615 ICEMAN ITALIAN-AMERICAN.

HE WALKS WITH A TOUGH, 636 ICEMAN

UH, I KNOW THE TRUTH IS TOUGH AT FIRST. 642 ICEMAN

IT'LL BE AS TOUGH FOR US AS IF SHE WASN'T GONE. 652 ICEMAN

OH, I KNOW IT'S TOUGH ON HIM RIGHT NOW, THE SAME 692 ICEMAN AS IT IS ON HARRY.

AND SAID HE WASN'T A GAMBLIN' MAN OR A TOUGH GUY 699 ICEMAN NO MORE.

HE IS A YOUNG AMERICAN WITH A TOUGH, GOOD-NATURED 515 INZONE FACE.

HER FEET ARE BARE, THE SOLES EARTH-STAINED AND 3 MISBEG TOUGH AS LEATHER.

BUT HE HAD A TOUGH HIDE AND DIDN'T HEED THEM. 12 POET

IT HAS A BULL-LIKE, IMPERVIOUS STRENGTH, A TOUGH 33 POET PEASANT VITALITY.

TOUGHEST

ALL SIX OF US COLORED BOYS, WE WAS TOUGH AND I WAS599 ICEMAN DE TOUGHEST.

WELL, I KNEW YOU'D BE THE TOUGHEST TO CONVINCE OF 643 ICEMAN ALL THE GANG, LARRY.

TOUGHNESS

TOUGHNESS
ROCKY'S FACE IS SET IN AN EXPRESSION OF TIRED, 696 ICEMAN
CALLOUS TOUGHNESS.

TOUGH
(GUILTILY) AY TOUGHT IT VAS BETTER ANNA STAY 47 ANNA
AWAY.
I TOUGHT SHE WAS A GHOST. 229 HA APE
I TOUGHT SHE WAS A GHOST, SEES 230 HA APE
AND DEN I SEEN YOUSE LOOKIN' AT SOMEP'N AND I 230 HA APE
TOUGHT HE'D SNEAKED DOWN TO COME
I TOUGHT I WAS IN A CAGE AT DE ZOO-BUT DE APES 240 HA APE
DON'T TALK, DO DEYS
I TOUGHT SHE WAS A GHOST. 241 HA APE
(MORE EASILY) I TOUGHT I'D BUMPED INTO DE WRONG 246 HA APE
DUMP.
I TOUGHT IT WAS LOCKED-- 247 HA APE
DAT'S WHAT SHE TOUGHT. 252 HA APE
I TOUGHT I WOULD YUST GIVE HER SURPRISE. 506 VOYAGE

TOUR
WHY DID I INVITE NINA AND SAM ON THIS TOUR... 52 STRANG

TOURAINE
LA TOURAINE. 208 HA APE

TOURS
EVEN THOUGH MR. TYRONE HAS MADE ME GO WITH HIM ON 102 JOURNE
ALL HIS TOURS.

TOUSAND
IF I DRINK ONE I WANT DRINK ONE TOUSAND. 505 VOYAGE

TOUSLED
THE FRINGE OF HAIR AROUND HIS BALDNESS TOUSLED AND256 AHWILD
TUFTY.
HE IS A THIN, WIRY MAN OF SIXTY-FIVE OR SO, WITH A102 ELECTR
TOUSLED MOP OF BLACK HAIR.

TOUTS
AND THE BARROOM SPONGES AND RACETRACK TOUTS AND 30 MISBEG
GAMBLERS ARE THROUGH WITH HIM

TOW
THE HEAVY STEEL BITS FOR MAKING FAST THE TOW 25 ANNA
LINES, ETC.

TOWARD
(WITH A FRIGHTENED GLANCE TOWARD THE DOOR ON 538 *ILE
RIGHT)
(COMES TOWARD THE STEWARD--WITH A STERN LOOK ON 539 *ILE
HIS FACE.
(EDGING UP TOWARD THE HARPOONER) 544 *ILE
(HE TURNS AWAY FROM HER SILENTLY AND WALKS TOWARD 550 *ILE
THE COMPANIONWAY.
(AS JOHNNY GOES TOWARD THE STREET DOOR, 5 ANNA
(WALKS AWAY FROM HER TOWARD THE CABIN--THEN COMES 26 ANNA
BACK)
(THIS TIME SOUNDING NEARER BUT UP FORWARD TOWARD 29 ANNA
THE BOW)
(HE PICKS UP A COIL OF ROPE AND HURRIES OFF TOWARD 30 ANNA
THE BOW.
ANNA WALKS BACK TOWARD THE EXTREME STERN 30 ANNA
(THEN BENDING FORWARD TOWARD HER WITH VERY INTENSE 34 ANNA
EARNESTNESS)
(HE COMES TOWARD THEM, RAGING, HIS FISTS CLENCHED) 39 ANNA
(WITH JUBILANT HAPPINESS--AS THEY PROCEED TOWARD 39 ANNA
THE CABIN)
TOWARD THE STERN. 41 ANNA
(HE SITS DOWN OPPOSITE CHRIS AT THE TABLE AND 45 ANNA
LEANS OVER TOWARD HIM)
(ADVANCING TOWARD THE TABLE--PROTESTING TO BURKE) 51 ANNA
SHE WALKS TO THE DOORWAY IN REAR--STANDS WITH HER 52 ANNA
BACK TOWARD THEM, LOOKING OUT.
AND SWINGING IT HIGH OVER HIS SHOULDER, SPRINGS 60 ANNA
TOWARD HER.
(HE TURNS TOWARD THE DOOR.) 61 ANNA
ANNA JUMPS TO HER FEET WITH A STARTLED EXCLAMATION 63 ANNA
AND LOOKS TOWARD THE DOOR
(HE MOVES A STEP TOWARD HER.) 69 ANNA
(HE TAKES A STEP TOWARD CHRIS THREATENINGLY.) 77 ANNA
AND CAN BE SEEN IN THE DISTANCE WINDING TOWARD THE 81 BEYOND
HORIZON LIKE A PALE RIBBON
AND TURNS HIS HEAD TOWARD THE HORIZON, GAZING OUT 82 BEYOND
OVER THE FIELDS AND HILLS.
WINDING OFF INTO THE DISTANCE, TOWARD THE HILLS, 89 BEYOND
AS IF IT, TOO,
(STARTING TO HIS FEET AND STRETCHING HIS ARMS 108 BEYOND
ACROSS THE TABLE TOWARD MAYO)
THE SHAKES OVER HIS MUTTERED THREAT AND STRIDES 108 BEYOND
TOWARD THE DOOR REAR, RIGHT.)
(BENDING OVER TOWARD HER--IN A LOW VOICE) 115 BEYOND
AND STARTS TO WHEEL THE INVALID'S CHAIR TOWARD THE118 BEYOND
SCREEN DOOR)
SHE GLANCES THE DOOR FURTIVELY--THEN GETS 118 BEYOND
UP AND GOES TO THE DESK.
BUT HIS ATTITUDE TOWARD THINGS IS-- 126 BEYOND
THE TOP OF THE HILL SLOPES DOWNWARD SLIGHTLY 129 BEYOND
TOWARD THE LEFT.
STARING OUT TOWARD THE HORIZON SEAWARD. 129 BEYOND
A BIG BOULDER STANDS IN THE CENTER TOWARD THE 129 BEYOND
REAR.
(SHE WALKS TOWARD THE ROCK AND ADDRESSES ROBERT 135 BEYOND
COLDLY)
HAS MOVED SO HER BACK IS TOWARD THEM, 140 BEYOND
MARY WALKS BACKWARD TOWARD ROBERT, HER WONDERING 142 BEYOND
EYES FIXED ON HER MOTHER.)
TOWARD THE END OF OCTOBER FIVE YEARS LATER. 144 BEYOND
HER MOTHER IS ASLEEP IN HER WHEEL CHAIR BESIDE THE145 BEYOND
STOVE TOWARD THE REAR.
(SHE GETS WEARILY TO HER FEET AND WALKS SLOWLY 166 BEYOND
TOWARD THE BEDROOM)
(GRABBING HIS HAT HE TAKES RUTH'S ARM AND SHOVES 166 BEYOND
HER TOWARD THE DOOR)
STRAINING HIS EYES TOWARD THE HORIZON) 167 BEYOND
WAVING A HAND TOWARD THE LAND) 456 CARIBE
STARING TOWARD THE SPOT ON SHORE WHERE THE SINGING456 CARIBE
SEEMS TO COME FROM.)

TOWARD (CONT'D.)
(NUDDING TOWARD THE SHORE) DON'T YUH KNOW THIS IS457 CARIBE
THE WEST INDIES,
(THEY ALL RUSH TO THE SIDE AND LOOK TOWARD THE 460 CARIBE
LAND.)
(WALKING TOWARD HIM--TRUCULENTLY) 461 CARIBE
YANK STAGGERS OVER TOWARD SMITTY AND PEARL.) 469 CARIBE
(WALKING SLOWLY TOWARD THE TABLE) 556 CROSS
(HE BENDS TOWARD THE DOCTOR--INTENSLY) 558 CROSS
(IN A STATE OF MAD EXULTATION STRIDES TOWARD HIS 568 CROSS
SON.
(MAKING A STEP TOWARD THEM) SEE/ 572 CROSS
(HE STRUGGLES OVER THE COMPANIONWAY.) 572 CROSS
LIKE TWO FRIENDLY OXEN TOWARD THEIR EVENING MEAL. 206 DESIRE
(THEY BOTH PLOD MECHANICALLY TOWARD THE DOOR 216 DESIRE
BEFORE THEY REALIZE.
(HE TURNS AND WALKS QUICKLY OFF LEFT, REAR, TOWARD217 DESIRE
THE BARN.
FOR THE BARN WHEN EBEN APPEARS FROM THERE HURRYING219 DESIRE
TOWARD THEM.
(LOOKING OFF TOWARD BARN) THAR HE BE--UNHITCHIN'.220 DESIRE
(IN A FURY NOW, RUSHING TOWARD THEM) 224 DESIRE
(HE ALMOST RUNS OFF DOWN TOWARD THE BARN. 225 DESIRE
HE TAKES A STEP TOWARD HER, COMPELLED AGAINST HIS 229 DESIRE
WILL)
THEN HIS ARMS DROP, HE SHAKES HIS HEAD AND PLODS 239 DESIRE
OFF TOWARD THE BARN.
HE STANDS SWAYING TOWARD HER HELPLESSLY.) 240 DESIRE
(STARES AFTER HER FOR A WHILE, WALKING TOWARD THE 241 DESIRE
DOOR.
(THEN GOES SLOWLY TOWARD THE DOOR IN REAR.) 241 DESIRE
ABBIE STRAINS HER ARMS TOWARD HIM WITH FIERCE 243 DESIRE
PLEADING)
(HE GOES OFF TOWARD THE BARN LAUGHING.) 246 DESIRE
(HE GOES TOWARD DOOR.) 247 DESIRE
OF MEANING NODS OF THE HEAD TOWARD CABOT WHO, 247 DESIRE
THEY CROWD BACK TOWARD THE WALLS, MUTTERING, 250 DESIRE
LOOKING AT HIM RESENTFULLY.)
TOWARD THE CRADLE AND STANDS THERE LOOKING DOWN AT251 DESIRE
THE BABY.
(HE GOES WEARILY TOWARD THE BARN.) 253 DESIRE
(HE SPRINGS TOWARD THE PORCH BUT CABOT IS QUICKER 255 DESIRE
AND GETS IN BETWEEN.)
WITH A STIFLED CRY SHE RUNS TOWARD THEM.) 255 DESIRE
BACKS SWIFTLY TOWARD THE DOOR IN REAR AND GOES 259 DESIRE
OUT.
HE LOOKS TOWARD THE WINDOW AND GIVES A SNORT OF 262 DESIRE
SURPRISE AND IRRITATION--
(HE GOES TOWARD THE BARN, LAUGHING HARSHLY. 265 DESIRE
HIS FACE STONY, AND STALKS GRIMLY TOWARD THE BARN.269 DESIRE
(LOOKING TOWARD THE DOOR APPREHENSIVELY) 522 DIFRNT
(STOPPING EMMA AS SHE GOES TOWARD THE DOOR AS IF 527 DIFRNT
TO ANSWER HARRIET'S HAIL)
(SHE MOVES LIKE A SLEEPWALKER TOWARD THE DOOR IN 549 DIFRNT
THE REAR AS THE CURTAIN FALLS.)
IN THE BEDROOM ABOVE, REUBEN'S EYES ARE TURNED 422 DYNAMO
TOWARD THE WINDOW.
JUMPS TO HIS FEET AND STARES DOWN TOWARD THE ROOM 424 DYNAMO
(HE GOES TO THE WINDOW AND LOOKS TOWARD THE FIFE 424 DYNAMO
HOME)
(SHE GOES TOWARD THE DOOR IN REAR, 426 DYNAMO
TOWARD THE LILAC HEDGE AND THE LIGHT HOME. 428 DYNAMO
(SHE WALKS TOWARD THE GAP IN THE HEDGE.) 433 DYNAMO
(HURRYING TOWARD THE DOOR AS IF IN FLIGHT) 442 DYNAMO
(HE WALKS TOWARD THE DOOR ON RIGHT.) 443 DYNAMO
(PUSHING HIM TOWARD THE CLOSET IN REAR) 445 DYNAMO
AND LOOKS TOWARD THE LIGHT HOME.) 445 DYNAMO
(WALKS TOWARD HIM) HOLD YOUR TONGUE/ 446 DYNAMO
(TURNING TOWARD THE DOOR) KEEP REUBEN HERE. 449 DYNAMO
(HE TAKES A FEW STEPS TOWARD THE WINDOW, THEN 452 DYNAMO
STOPS, THINKING BITTERLY)
(SHE LOOKS TOWARD THE LIGHT HOUSE--WITH DROWSY 454 DYNAMO
MELANCHOLY)
(WALKS TOWARD HER, THE SMILE FROZEN ON HIS LIPS, 459 DYNAMO
HIS EYES FIXED ON HERS)
(THEN PICKING UP HIS BOOKS AND TURNING TOWARD HIS 461 DYNAMO
HOME)
THEN TURNS BACK TOWARD HER OWN FRONT DOOR AND 470 DYNAMO
BEGINS TO CRY SOFTLY.
AND WALKS OFF RIGHT TOWARD THE FRONT DOOR OF HIS 470 DYNAMO
HOUSE.)
HE TAKES A THREATENING STEP TOWARD HER-- 481 DYNAMO
(MOVED IN SPITE OF HIMSELF, INSTINCTIVELY TAKES A 481 DYNAMO
STEP TOWARD HER--
THIS WALL THEN TURNS AND ASCENDS DIAGONALLY 483 DYNAMO
TOWARD THE LEFT TO THE UPPER
BENDING HER BACKWARD AND DOWN TOWARD THE FLOOR OF 485 DYNAMO
THE PLATFORM.
(HE GLIDES STEALTHILY ACROSS TOWARD THE FOOT OF 488 DYNAMO
THE STAIRS.)
TOWARD THE DOORWAY IN THE REAR. 173 EJONES
(SHE MAKES A SWEEPING GESTURE TOWARD THE HILLS IN 175 EJONES
THE DISTANCE.)
(AS JONES WALKS TOWARD THE DOOR IN REAR-- 186 EJONES
CAUTIONINGLY)
AND WINDING AWAY FROM IT AGAIN TOWARD THE RIGHT. 190 EJONES
THEY SQUIRM UPWARD TOWARD HIM IN TWISTED 190 EJONES
ATTITUDES.
(STARING TOWARD THE OTHER, 192 EJONES
THEN THEY BEGIN TO SWAY SLOWLY FOREWARD TOWARD 199 EJONES
EACH OTHER AND BACK AGAIN IN
JONES SQUIRMS TOWARD HIM. 201 EJONES
MOTIONS WITH HIDEOUS COMMAND TOWARD THE WAITING 201 EJONES
MONSTER.
WALKS OFF TOWARD THE FLOWER GARDEN, 9 ELECTR
(SHE GETS UP AND WALKS TOWARD RIGHT TO CONCEAL HER 15 ELECTR
AGITATION.

TOWARD (CONT'D.)

*WHILE SHE HAS BEEN SPEAKING SHE HAS COME TOWARD 16 ELECTR LAVINIA
(SHE MOVES A FEW STEPS TOWARD THE HOUSE--THEN 17 ELECTR TURNS AGAIN--
(SHE NODS SCORNFULLY TOWARD THE HOUSE) 17 ELECTR
CHRISTINE GLANCES AT HER FLOWERS AGAIN AND TURNS 17 ELECTR TOWARD THE HOUSE)
I DON'T WANT TO HEAR--(SHE STARTS TO GO TOWARD THE 25 ELECTR HOUSE.)
(SHE MOVES TOWARD THE DOOR TO WAIT FOR HIM. 35 ELECTR
(URGING HIM TOWARD THE DOOR) 42 ELECTR
HE SUDDENLY LEANS OVER TOWARD HER AND, LOWERING 44 ELECTR HIS VOICE, ASKS SOBERLY)
(LEANS TOWARD HER, HIS VOICE TREMBLING WITH DESIRE 52 ELECTR
(HE ASCENDS TWO STEPS, HIS FACE TOWARD THE DOOR. 56 ELECTR
(SHE EDGES AWAY FROM LAVINIA TOWARD HER BEDROOM 63 ELECTR TOWARD LEFT FRONT UNTIL THEY ARE BY THE BENCH. 68 ELECTR
(THEN GLANCING TOWARD THE MEN WHO HAVE MOVED A 69 ELECTR LITTLE AWAY FROM THE STEPS AND
(AS THEY ENTER LOOKS EAGERLY TOWARD THE HOUSE-- 74 ELECTR
BUT I CANNOT UNDERSTAND YOUR ATTITUDE TOWARD ME. 77 ELECTR
HIS FACE DRIFTED OUT OF THE MIST TOWARD MINE. 95 ELECTR
SO I BEGAN TO LAUGH AND WALKED TOWARD THEIR LINES 95 ELECTR WITH MY HAND OUT.
I MET A REB CRAWLING TOWARD OUR LINES. 95 ELECTR
(HE MOVES RELUCTANTLY TOWARD THE DOOR.) 100 ELECTR
(HE GOES TOWARD THE PORTICO, SMALL FOLLOWING HIM, 131 ELECTR AND IS IMMEDIATELY FRIGHTENED AND UNEASY AND 139 ELECTR HURRIES TOWARD THE DOOR, CALLING)
(SHE GOES TOWARD HIM, SMILING AS HER MOTHER MIGHT 143 ELECTR HAVE SMILED)
HAZEL MOVES TOWARD LAVINIA TO GREET HER, 148 ELECTR
(SHE TRIES AWKWARDLY TO SIDLE TOWARD THE DOOR.) 163 ELECTR
(HE TURNS AND STRIDES TOWARD THE DOOR.) 166 ELECTR
I LOVE EVERYTHING THAT GROWS SIMPLY--UP TOWARD THE167 ELECTR SUN--
(STOPS SINGING AND STANDS PEERING OFF LEFT TOWARD 169 ELECTR THE FLOWER GARDEN--
(WARNING TOWARD THE CLERK.) SAY, NOW I NOTICE, 11 HUGHIE YOU DON'T LOOK LIKE HUGHIE.
SAUNTERING LONGINGLY TOWARD THE DAWN'S RELEASE. 24 HUGHIE
(HE STARTS TOWARD THE ELEVATOR.) 35 HUGHIE
HIS ARMS DANGLING TOWARD THE FLOOR. 576 ICEMAN
HIS HEAD DROOPING JERKILY TOWARD ONE SHOULDER. 576 ICEMAN
(LEANS TOWARD HIM, A COMICAL INTENSITY IN HIS LOW 578 ICEMAN VOICE)
HE LEANS TOWARD THEM, DRUNK NOW FROM THE EFFECT OF594 ICEMAN THE HUGE DRINK HE TOOK,
(LEANS TOWARD HIM--CONFIDENTIALLY) 600 ICEMAN
(HE GOES BACK TOWARD THE DOOR AT LEFT OF THE BAR.1610 ICEMAN
AFFECTIONATE SISTERS TOWARD A BULLYING BROTHER 611 ICEMAN
THEIR ATTITUDE TOWARD ROCKY IS MUCH THAT OF TWO 611 ICEMAN MATERNAL,
HIS ATTITUDE TOWARD THEM IS THAT OF THE OWNER OF 611 ICEMAN TWO PERFORMING PETS
AT LARRY'S TABLE, PARRITT IS GLARING RESENTFULLY 615 ICEMAN TOWARD THE GIRLS.)
IT IS GETTING ON TOWARD MIDNIGHT OF THE SAME DAY. 628 ICEMAN
(STARTS MOVING TOWARD HER THREATENINGLY) 632 ICEMAN
(HE TAKES A THREATENING STEP TOWARD JOE, 637 ICEMAN
(LEANING TOWARD LARRY CONFIDENTIALLY--IN A LOW 644 ICEMAN SHAKEN VOICE)
PARRITT LEANS TOWARD HIM AND SPEAKS INGRATIATINGLY645 ICEMAN IN A LOW SECRETIVE TONE.)
TOWARD THE LEFT END OF THE TABLE, WHERE, LIKE TWO 650 ICEMAN SULKY BOYS,
(BENDING TOWARD HIM--IN A LOW, INGRATIATING, 666 ICEMAN APOLOGETIC VOICE)
(HE PUSHES A BOTTLE TOWARD HIM.) 674 ICEMAN
(AS ROCKY SHOVES A BOTTLE TOWARD HIM HE SHAKES HIS681 ICEMAN HEAD)
(MOSHER TURNS AROUND TOWARD HIM FURIOUSLY 682 ICEMAN
MCGLOIN JUMPS UP FROM HIS CHAIR AND STARTS MOVING 685 ICEMAN TOWARD THE DOOR.
(AS HE TALKS HE HAS BEEN MOVING TOWARD THE DOOR. 687 ICEMAN
HAS BEEN PUSHED TOWARD RIGHT SO THAT IT AND 695 ICEMAN
(ROCKY PUSHES THE BOTTLE TOWARD HIM APATHETICALLY)699 ICEMAN
AS ROCKY ENTERS THE BACK ROOM AND STARTS OVER 700 ICEMAN TOWARD LARRY'S TABLE.)
CORA SPEAKS WITH A TIRED WONDER AT HERSELF RATHER 700 ICEMAN THAN RESENTMENT TOWARD HIM)
(MOVING AWAY FROM HIM TOWARD RIGHT--SHARPLY) 703 ICEMAN
(AS THEY START WALKING TOWARD REAR--INSISTENTLY) 719 ICEMAN
(LEANS TOWARD HIM--IN A STRANGE LOW INSISTENT 719 ICEMAN VOICE)
(HE GETS TO HIS FEET AND TURNS TOWARD THE DOOR.) 721 ICEMAN
UNCONSCIOUSLY HIS HEAD IS INCLINED TOWARD THE 722 ICEMAN WINDOW AS HE LISTENS.)
ALL OF THE GROUP TURN TOWARD THE DOOR AS THE TWO 724 ICEMAN APPEAR.
(JACK STARTS TOWARD SMITTY'S BUNK. 520 INZONE
(HE REACHES TOWARD THE MATTRESS.) 524 INZONE
BENEATH THEM IS A WICKER COUCH WITH CUSHIONS, ITS 11 JOURNE HEAD TOWARD REAR.
(SHE IS SILENT ON THIS, KEEPING HER HEAD TURNED 15 JOURNE TOWARD THEIR VOICES.
(HE STOP--LOOKING THROUGH THE FRONT PARLOR TOWARD 58 JOURNE THE HALL--
(SHARPLY--LETTING HER RESENTMENT TOWARD HIM COME 60 JOURNE OUT.)
(HE TAKES A THREATENING STEP TOWARD HIM. 64 JOURNE
(HE MAKES A MOVE TOWARD THE FRONT-PARLOR DOORWAY, 82 JOURNE
(HE TURNS TOWARD THE FRONT PARLOR, ANXIOUS TO 83 JOURNE ESCAPE.)
HE TURNS AWAY TOWARD THE FRONT PARLOR 88 JOURNE
(SHE PUTS HER GLASS ON THE TABLE AND MAKES A 99 JOURNE MOVEMENT TOWARD THE BACK PARLOR.)

TOWARD (CONT'D.)

(SHE GOES TOWARD THE FRONT PARLOR-- 107 JOURNE
(SHE KISSES HIM MECHANICALLY AND TURNS TOWARD THE 123 JOURNE FRONT PARLOR.)
HE WALKS WEARILY OFF THROUGH THE BACK PARLOR 125 JOURNE TOWARD THE DINING ROOM.)
AND YOU STUMBLE ON TOWARD NOWHERE, FOR NO GOOD 153 JOURNE REASON!
(WITH THE SHY POLITENESS OF A WELL-BRED YOUNG GIRL172 JOURNE TOWARD AN ELDERLY GENTLEMAN
WILL TURN A LITTLE TOWARD US, SIGHING. 174 JOURNE
(JAMIE PUSHES THE BOTTLE TOWARD HIM. 175 JOURNE
THEIR ARMS OUTSTRETCHED TOWARD LAZARUS) 275 LAZARU
WINE IS POURED AND ALL RAISE THEIR GOBLETS TOWARD 278 LAZARU LAZARUS--
THEY TEND HIS FLOCKS AND LAUGH TOWARD THE SUN/ 287 LAZARU
TO TWIST THEIR BODIES TOWARD AND AWAY FROM EACH 288 LAZARU OTHER
(THEY CROWD TOWARD THE GATEWAY, 288 LAZARU
YOU LAUGHED--DISCORDANTLY, HOARSELY, BUT WITH A 289 LAZARU GROPING TOWARD JOY.
ARMS UPSTRETCHED TOWARD THE STARS, THEIR HEADS 290 LAZARU THROWN BACK.)
(HE TURNS TOWARD THE ROMANS AND LAUGHS SNEERINGLY,300 LAZARU
(HE CONTINUES TO STUMBLE TOWARD LEFT) 311 LAZARU
(HE HAS WALKED TOWARD LAZARUS.) 317 LAZARU
NOW EVERY ONE OF THESE IS STANDING UP, STRETCHING 318 LAZARU OUT HIS ARMS TOWARD LAZARUS,
POINTING TOWARD THE LION WITH A TREMBLING HAND.) 327 LAZARU
(HE ADVANCES TOWARD LAZARUS, SMILING, 332 LAZARU
MOVING SLOWLY ON TOWARD THE PALACE IN THE REAR. 333 LAZARU
(HE TURNS AWAY FROM HIM AND WALKS, LAUGHING, 333 LAZARU TOWARD THE ARCH IN REAR.
JUMPS TO HIS FEET IN A PANIC OF TERROR, AND RUNS 335 LAZARU TOWARD THE PALACE DOOR, CALLING)
(RAISES HIS HEAD UNEASILY, LOOKS BACK TOWARD THE 335 LAZARU PALACE,
CALIGULA TURNS AND STARES TOWARD HIM, 339 LAZARU
(HE HAS WALKED TOWARD THE THRONE WHILE HE IS 339 LAZARU SPEAKING.
(A PAUSE--THEN IN A LOW VOICE, BENDING DOWN TOWARD340 LAZARU LAZARUS)
MOVE FORWARD TOWARD THE DAIS.) 344 LAZARU
(SHE RAISES THE PEACH TOWARD HER MOUTH. 346 LAZARU
A BUBBLE OF FROTH BLOWN FROM THE LIPS OF THE DYING353 LAZARU TOWARD THE STARS/
(THEN CONFIDINGLY, LEANING OVER TOWARD LAZARUS) 354 LAZARU
(SHE STARES UP INTO HIS EYES DOUBTINGLY, RAISING 361 LAZARU HER FACE TOWARD HIS)
TURNED A LITTLE TOWARD FRONT. 363 LAZARU
(RISING TO HER FEET LIKE ONE IN A TRANCE, STARING 366 LAZARU TOWARD LAZARUS)
(SHE LAUGHS SOFTLY AND PASSES SWIFTLY ACROSS THE 367 LAZARU ARENA TOWARD LAZARUS.)
WE LOVE MEN FLAMING TOWARD THE STARS/ 367 LAZARU
WE LOVE MEN FLAMING TOWARD THE STARS/ 367 LAZARU
HE STARES TOWARD THE FLAMES STUPIDLY--THEN SCREAMS368 LAZARU DESPAIRINGLY ABOVE THE CHANT)
(HE SNATCHES A SPEAR FROM A SOLDIER AND FIGHTS HIS369 LAZARU WAY DRUNKENLY TOWARD THE
(HE DISAPPEARS TOWARD THE FLAMES, HIS SPEAR HELD 369 LAZARU READY TO STAB.
HIS FACE TOWARD LAZARUS, SUPPLICATINGLY) 371 LAZARU
(SHE PICKS HER WAY DAINTILY THROUGH THE GRASS 3 MANSNS TOWARD THE BENCH.)
(HE STRIDES TOWARD HER.) 5 MANSNS
TURNS AS IT TURNS UNTIL IT FACES TOWARD LEFT-- 27 MANSNS FRONT,
KEEPING HER FACE TURNED TOWARD SOMETHING FROM 27 MANSNS WHICH SHE RETREATS.
I UNDERSTAND HER FEELING TOWARD ME. 39 MANSNS
THOUGHTS AND LOOKS BACK TOWARD THE DOORWAY AT REAR 44 MANSNS SMILINGLY.
THEN SUDDENLY CHUCKLES, WITH A CHANGE OF MANNER 60 MANSNS TOWARD DEBORAH.)
SUCH AN ANTAGONISTIC ATTITUDE TOWARD ME. 61 MANSNS
MAYBE YOU DON'T KNOW OR YOU COULDN'T ACT SO 65 MANSNS UNFRIENDLY TOWARD HER,
(THEN AS JOEL GOES TOWARD THE DOOR, HE SPEAKS IN A 71 MANSNS CONCILIATING TONE.)
(HE TURNS TOWARD THE DOOR TO RIGHT.) 71 MANSNS
(MOVED AND FASCINATED, TAKES A STEP TOWARD HIM-- 103 MANSNS TENDERLY.)
AGAINST THE RIGHT WALL, TOWARD REAR, ANOTHER 117 MANSNS TABLE.
TOWARD FRONT, AT LEFT, IS AN OVAL TABLE WITH 117 MANSNS ANOTHER LAMP.
TOWARD--AND THE SILENCE WAITS--HANDS CLAPPED OVER 120 MANSNS ITS EARS--
(HE TURNS TOWARD THE DOOR AT LEFT, AVOIDING THEIR 130 MANSNS EYES.)
(SARA GOES SLOWLY TOWARD HER OLD CHAIR AT LEFT-- 136 MANSNS FRONT OF TABLE.
AND GOES BACK TOWARD THE SOFA. 137 MANSNS
(SHE TURNS BACK TOWARD THE DESK AT RIGHT-REAR. 148 MANSNS
(STARTS TOWARD HER.) BELOVED/ 150 MANSNS
(THEN, JUST AS DEBORAH IS TURNING THE KNOB, SHE 165 MANSNS SPRINGS TOWARD HER.)
(ANGRILY, TURNING TOWARD THE PATH OFF LEFT.) 169 MANSNS
IT BEGINS TO BE, TO DIRECT ITSELF TOWARD A 181 MANSNS CONSUMMATION,
TOWARD EVERY SECRET PRIVATE CORNER OF MY SOUL. 184 MANSNS
(HIS VOICE HAS DROPPED, HE POINTS TOWARD THE 351 MARCOM COFFIN.
(HE PULLS HER WILLING HAND DOWN TOWARD HIS LIPS.) 355 MARCOM
(AS A NOISE OF SHOUTING COMES TOWARD THEM) 361 MARCOM
(HE ADVANCES BOLDLY TOWARD THE ALTAR, 362 MARCOM

TOWARD

TOWARD (CONT'D.)
(THEY ALL BEND THEIR HEADS TOWARD HIM WITH EXPECTANT GRINS. 366 MARCOM
(HE MOVES TOWARD HER WITH A SIGH OF HALF-IMPATIENCE WITH HER WHIMS.) 414 MARCOM
TOWARD HERS, THEIR LIPS SEEM ABOUT TO MEET IN A KISS. 415 MARCOM
THEY RETIRE TOWARD THE LEFT. 419 MARCOM
(CONTINUING) *BUT I HAVE NEVER NOTED ANY UNNATURAL CHANGE IN THEM EXCEPT TOWARD 425 MARCOM
IMMEDIATELY THE WOMEN ALL TURN WITH ARMS OUTSTRETCHED TOWARD THE CATAFALQUE. 433 MARCOM
THEY CARRY SILVER CENSERS WHICH THEY SWING IN UNISON TOWARD THE CORPSE OF THE 433 MARCOM
(SHE GOES BACK TOWARD THE STEPS AS HER BROTHER, MIKE 3 MISBEG
AROUND IT TOWARD THE BARN. 3 MISBEG
(MAKES A THREATENING MOVE TOWARD HIM) 10 MISBEG
HE'S LOOKING TOWARD THE MEADOW. 10 MISBEG
(HE MOVES TOWARD THE STEPS.) 13 MISBEG
(HE PAUSES--THEN WITH GREAT SERIOUSNESS, TURNING TOWARD HER) 31 MISBEG
(SHE STARTS TO GO OFF TOWARD REAR-RIGHT.) 35 MISBEG
(WALKS TOWARD HOGAN--STIFFLY) 56 MISBEG
(HE TURNS EAGERLY TOWARD LEFT BUT SUDDENLY HOGAN GRABS HIS SHOULDER AND SPINS 60 MISBEG
(THEY TURN BACK TOWARD THE HOUSE. 64 MISBEG
(HE LEANS TOWARD HER AND WHISPERS) 88 MISBEG
(HE SHRUGS HIS SHOULDERS HOPELESSLY AND TURNS TOWARD THE ROAD.) 139 MISBEG
(HE TURNS TOWARD THE ROAD--BITTERLY) 140 MISBEG
(HE TURNS TOWARD THE ROAD.) 173 MISBEG
MALOY PUSHES THE DECANTER TOWARD HIM.) 10 POET
(HE PUSHES THE BOTTLE TOWARD CREGAN.) 15 POET
HER HABITUAL MANNER TOWARD HER IS ONE 21 POET
(COMING TOWARD HIM.) YOU LOOK PALE. 34 POET
(HE TAKES A THREATENING STEP TOWARD HIM.) 53 POET
SHE MOVES TOWARD THE DOOR AT RIGHT, DETERMINED TO IGNORE HIM. 57 POET
HE GLANCES TOWARD THE BAR AS IF HE LONGED TO RETURN THERE TO ESCAPE HER. 59 POET
(SHE NODS SCORNFULLY TOWARD HER FATHER.) 60 POET
SHE HURRIES TOWARD THEM QUICKLY. 72 POET
THEN, REMEMBERING MELODY'S ORDERS, GLANCES TOWARD THE DOOR AT LEFT FRONT. 80 POET
(MELODY HAS SHOVED THE DECANTER TOWARD HIM. 93 POET
AND HERE'S OUR CAVALRY BRIGADE IN A VALLEY TOWARD OUR LEFT; IF YOU'LL REMEMBER. 96 POET
(SHE MAKES A THREATENING MOVE TOWARD HIM, 115 POET
MELODY LEANS TOWARD HIM CONFIDENTIALLY.) 120 POET
(NORA TURNS OBEDIENTLY TOWARD THE DOOR AT RIGHT, BEGINNING TO CRY.) 125 POET
(HE MAKES A THREATENING MOVE TOWARD HER.) 128 POET
HE TURNS TOWARD THE BAR DOOR.) 129 POET
(SHE TAKES A FEW MORE STEPS TOWARD THE DOOR--STOPS139 POET
AGAIN--SHE MUTTERS BEATENly.)
SHE MAKES AN IMPULSIVE MOVE TOWARD HIM.) 157 POET
HE SWAYS DIZZILY, CLUTCHING HIS HEAD--THEN GOES TOWARD THE DOOR AT LEFT FRONT.) 159 POET
SARA AND ME WAS DEAD WITH FEAR-- (SHE GOES TOWARD 164 POET
THEM.) CON/
(SHE TAKES ONE STEP TOWARD HIM--THEN HER EXPRESSION BEGINS TO HARDEN.) 164 POET
(HE TURNS TOWARD THE BARROOM.) 165 POET
(SHE LEANS TOWARD HIM AND SPEAKS WITH TAUNTING VINDICTIVENESS. 171 POET
HE STARTS TOWARD THE BAR DOOR.) 176 POET
(STARTS TOWARD HIM--BESEECHINGLY.) 177 POET
(SHE NODS TOWARD THE BAR.) 181 POET
HE LOOKS TOWARD THE SEA AND HIS VOICE QUAVERS IN A579 ROPE
DOLEFUL CHANT)
(HE ADVANCES TOWARD BENTLEY THREATENINGLY.) 582 ROPE
(PUSHING HIM TOWARD THE DOOR. 584 ROPE
(GLANCING APPREHENSIVELY TOWARD THE DOOR--WITH A GREAT SIGH) 590 ROPE
(SWEENEY PUSHES THE BOTTLE TOWARD HIM. 592 ROPE
HE RAISES IT TOWARD THE ROPE) 592 ROPE
(PUSHING THE BOTTLE TOWARD HIM) 593 ROPE
(HE SLAPS LUKE ON THE SHOULDER AND PUSHES THE BOTTLE TOWARD HIM) 598 ROPE
AND JOE GIVES HIM A SIGNIFICANT WINK AND NODS TOWARD THE DOOR ON THE LEFT. 497 VOYAGE
(THEY LURCH TOWARD THE DOOR. 504 VOYAGE
GLANCING TOWARD ELEANOR, TRYING NOT TO MAKE THE SLIGHTEST NOISE. 444 WELDED
JUMPS UP TO MEET HIM AS HE STRIDES TOWARD HER.) 444 WELDED
(HE WALKS TOWARD HIS BAG-- 445 WELDED
(THEN AS SHE TAKES A SIGN, MECHANICAL STEP TOWARD 449 WELDED
THE DOOR--WITH TENSE PLEADING)
SHE SWAYS IRRESOLUTELY TOWARD HIM, AGAIN REACHING 449 WELDED
TO THE BANNISTER FOR SUPPORT.
JOHN HAS GOTTEN UP, GONE TOWARD THE DOOR IN THE REAR. 462 WELDED
A DOOR IS IN THE REAR, TOWARD RIGHT. 462 WELDED
(HE STARES TOWARD HER, THEN STOPS--IN A LOW, UNCERTAIN VOICE) 463 WELDED
(SHE MOVES TOWARD THE DOOR.) 465 WELDED
(HE STRIDES TOWARD THE DOORWAY-- 466 WELDED
(AFTER A PAUSE, WITH A GESTURE TOWARD THE DOOR AND469 WELDED
A WEARY, BEATEN SMILE)
(HE LAUGHS HARSHLY AND TURNS WITH A QUICK MOVEMENT476 WELDED
TOWARD THE DOOR)
THEY COME TOWARD EACH OTHER. 480 WELDED
HE LEAPS TO HIS FEET AND JUMPS TOWARD THE DOOR WITH A PLEADING CRY) 487 WELDED

TOWARDS
(HE BENDS HIS FACE TOWARDS HERS.) 279 AHWILD
AND STARTS RUNNING TOWARDS THE PATH. 285 AHWILD

TOWARDS (CONT'D.)
(THEN GOING TOWARDS DOOR) I'M A-GOIN' T' DANCE. 259 DESIRE
OF HER CHANGED ATTITUDE TOWARDS HIM--WITH A LAUGH.) 23 ELECTR
(THEY TURN TOWARDS THE DOOR AT REAR, LAUGHINGLY.) 67 MANSNS
(SHE IS MOVING TOWARDS THE BOOKKEEPER'S ROOM 144 MANSNS
TURNS TOWARDS THE DOOR AND SLOWLY BEGINS TO ASCEND164 MANSNS
THE STEPS.)
(SHE TAKES A STEP TOWARDS LEFT, STIFFLY, AS IF BY 177 MANSNS
A DETERMINED EFFORT OF WILL.
(SHE LEADS HIM A STEP TOWARDS THE DOOR-- 183 MANSNS
(SHE STARTS TOWARDS THE DOORWAY. 590 ROPE
(SHE HURRIES OVER TO HER, GLANCING EAGERLY OVER HER SHOULDER TOWARDS THE RIVER) 178 STRANG

TOWED
TUG COME AND VE GAT TOWED OUT ON VOYAGE-- 23 ANNA

TOWER
AND SAW THE CITY AS FROM A TOWER, HOSPITAL, BROTHEL, PRISON, AND SUCH HELLS. 133 JOURNE
THE WALLS TOWER MAJESTICALLY IN SHADOW, 432 MARCOM

TOWERING
THE MASTS WITH EVERY SAIL WHITE IN THE MOONLIGHT, 153 JOURNE
TOWERING HIGH ABOVE ME.
IN THE REAR THE TOWERING PILE OF THE CIRCULAR AMPHITHEATRE IS FAINTLY OUTLINED 363 LAZARU

TOWERS
LEADING TO THE TRANSMISSION TOWERS. 473 DYNAMO

TOWN
(SCENE--SITTING-ROOM OF THE MILLER HOME IN A LARGE185 AHWILD
SMALL-TOWN IN CONNECTICUT--
WATERBURY'S NIFTY OLD TOWN WITH THE LID OFF, WHEN 188 AHWILD
YOU GET TO KNOW THE ROPES.
I'LL GET OUT THE BUICK AND WE'LL DRIVE AROUND TOWN191 AHWILD
AND OUT TO THE LIGHTHOUSE AND
THERE WON'T BE A PERSON IN TOWN WILL BUY A DISHRAG204 AHWILD
IN YOUR PLACE/
HE ALWAYS WAS THE BEST NEWS-GETTER THIS TOWN EVER 234 AHWILD
HAD.
IF HE EVER FINDS OUT I SERVED HIS KID, HE'LL RUN ME OUT OF TOWN. 248 AHWILD
I RESENT THE IMPLICATION THAT I CORRESPOND WITH ALL THE TRAMPS AROUND THIS TOWN. 267 AHWILD
IF YOU HAVE ANY GUTS YOU WILL RUN THAT BASTARD OUT267 AHWILD
OF TOWN.*
I SUPPOSE YOU'LL HAVE HIM OUT WITH YOU PAINTING THE TOWN RED THE NEXT THING/ 269 AHWILD
I CAN HEAR THE TOWN HALL STRIKE, IT'S SO STILL TONIGHT... 275 AHWILD
FROM THE DISTANCE THE TOWN HALL CLOCK BEGINS TO STRIKE. 277 AHWILD
EVERY MAN OF YOUR MEANS IN TOWN IS SENDING HIS BOYS TO COLLEGE/ 289 AHWILD
CAPE TOWN. 67 ANNA
CAPE TOWN. 72 ANNA
CAPE TOWN. 72 ANNA
WHAT KIND OF A PLACE IS THIS CAPE TOWNS 73 ANNA
YOU'LL GET YOUR MONEY TOMORROW WHEN I GET BACK FROM TOWN--NOT BEFORE/ 125 BEYOND
YES, SYDNEY'S A GOOD TOWN. 132 BEYOND
NEVER GITTIN' OUTA SAILOR-TOWN, HARDLY, IN ANY PORT. 486 CARDIF
AND THAT FIGHT ON THE DOCK AT CAPE TOWN-- 488 CARDIF
SAILOR-TOWN DIVES, MADE MORE GROTESQUE BY THE FACT471 CARIBE
THAT ALL THE COUPLES ARE
THEY PASS BY ON THE ROAD AT NIGHTS COMING BACK TO 564 CROSS
THEIR FARMS FROM TOWN.
FOR ALL THE YOUNG FELLERS IN TOWN TO MAKE EYES AT.497 DIFRNT
THE BUYS HAS BEEN FELLIN' THE HULL TOWN. 502 DIFRNT
(TAKEN ABACK--FROWNING) SO ALL THE TOWN KNOWS ABOUT IT$ 502 DIFRNT
IF YOU'VE BEEN WIDE AWAKE TO ALL THAT'S HAPPENED IN THIS TOWN 509 DIFRNT
I LIKE YOU VERY, VERY MUCH, BENNY--BETTER THAN ANYONE IN THE TOWN-- 524 DIFRNT
AW, THESE SMALL TOWN BOOBS THINK YOU'RE RAISING HELL IF YOU'RE UP AFTER ELEVEN. 525 DIFRNT
OR ABOUT ANY DAME IN THIS TOWN, FOR THAT MATTER-- 526 DIFRNT
'CEPTIN YOU.
THESE SMALL TOWN SKIRTS DON'T HAND ME NOTHIN'. 526 DIFRNT
THE GIRLS IN TOWN HERE ARE JUST RANK AMATOORS. 527 DIFRNT
YOU KNOW THIS DUMP OF A TOWN, 532 DIFRNT
THEY'RE ALL DOWN ON ME ANYWAY BECAUSE I'M DIFF'RENT FROM SMALL-TOWN BOOBS LIKE 532 DIFRNT
YOU'RE THE BEST GUY IN THIS TOWN/ 534 DIFRNT
IF YOU MEAN THE NASTY LIES THE FOLKS IN THIS TOWN ARE MEAN ENOUGH TO GOSSIP 539 DIFRNT
WHY, HE'S BRAGGED ALL OVER TOWN ABOUT BEIN' ABLE TO BORROW ALL THE MONEY FROM 541 DIFRNT
(THE EXTERIOR OF THE HOMES OF THE LIGHTS AND THE FIFES IN A SMALL TOWN IN -0 DYNAMO
THEN I'LL BUY YOU THE BEST DRESS YOU CAN FIND IN THE TOWN/ 432 DYNAMO
ALL THE PIOUS FOLKS IN THIS TOWN THINK I'VE A BAD 434 DYNAMO
RECORD BEHIND ME--
SHE'LL TELL THE WHOLE TOWN I WAS SPYING/... 436 DYNAMO
YOU KNOW, DON'T YOU, THAT NO ONE KNOWS WHAT I DONE440 DYNAMO
BEFORE I CAME TO THIS TOWN.
TWENTY YEARS AGO THERE WAS A MAN BY THE NAME OF ANDREW CLARK LIVED IN THE TOWN 440 DYNAMO
THE SOUND OF WIND AND RAIN SWEEPING DOWN ON THE TOWN FORM THE HILLS IS HEARD.) 454 DYNAMO
ABOUT TWO MILES FROM THE TOWN. 473 DYNAMO
DRINKIN' RUM AND TALKIN' BIG DOWN IN DE TOWN. 176 EJONES
IN THE DISTANCE, FROM THE TOWN, A BAND IS HEARD PLAYING "JOHN BROWN'S BODY." 5 ELECTR
CHORUS REPRESENTING THE TOWN COME TO LOOK AND LISTEN 7 ELECTR
THERE WON'T BE A SOBER MAN IN TOWN TONIGHT/. 7 ELECTR

TOWN (CONT'D.)
YOU KNOW HOW FOLKS IN TOWN GOSSIP, FATHER. 50 ELECTR
YOU CAN ASK ANYONE IN TOWN. 52 ELECTR
AND WHY FOLKS IN TOWN LOOK ON ME AS SO ABLE/ 55 ELECTR
LIKE A STATUE OF A DEAD MAN IN A TOWN SQUARE. 55 ELECTR
THE TOWN AS A HUMAN BACKGROUND FOR THE DRAMA OF 67 ELECTR
THE MANNONS.
HILLS IS THE TYPE OF WELL-FED MINISTER OF A 67 ELECTR
PROSPEROUS SMALL-TOWN CONGREGATION--
WHOLE TOWN COULD HAVE PAID THEIR RESPECTS TO HIM, 69 ELECTR
HE WAS MAYOR OF THE TOWN AND A NATIONAL WAR HERO-- 69 ELECTR
BUT IT DOES SEEM AS IF EZRA SHOULD HAVE BEEN LAID 69 ELECTR
OUT IN THE TOWN HALL WHERE THE
THE TOWN WON'T FIND ANOTHER AS ABLE AS EZRA IN A 70 ELECTR
HURRY.
SITTING ON A CHAIR IN A PARK OR STRADDLING A HORSE 94 ELECTR
IN A TOWN SQUARE--
(GLOOMILY) BUT EVERYONE IN THE TOWN WOULD KNOW 111 ELECTR
YOU WERE GONE.
= A CHORUS OF TYPES REPRESENTING THE TOWN AS A 129 ELECTR
HUMAN BACKGROUND
ALL I SAY IS IF THEY HADN'T BEEN MANNONS WITH THE 133 ELECTR
TOWN LICKIN' THEIR BOOTS.
ALL I KNOW IS I WOULDN'T STAY IN THERE ALL NIGHT 135 ELECTR
IF YOU WAS TO GIVE ME THE TOWN.
AN' WHEN I GIT THROUGH TELLIN' MY STORY OF IT 135 ELECTR
ROUND TOWN TOMORROW
I WAS AIMIN' TO STOP THE DURNED GABBIN' THAT'S 135 ELECTR
BEEN GOIN' ROUND TOWN
I HATE THIS DAMNED TOWN NOW AND EVERYONE IN IT/ 175 ELECTR
IN THE HOMES SECTION OF THE TOWN-- 269 GGBROW
AND MAKE IT LOOK DIFFERENT FROM OTHER TOWN HALLS. 275 GGBROW
PERHAPS I CAN LOCATE HIM LATER AROUND TOWN 277 GGBROW
SOMEWHERE.
I'VE BEEN LOOKING ALL OVER TOWN FOR YOU. 280 GGBROW
I HAVEN'T SEEN DION AROUND TOWN SINCE THEN. 302 GGBROW
THEY CAN'T BELIEVE IN JOY IN THIS TOWN EXCEPT BY 315 GGBROW
THE BOTTLE.
BUT I'VE LIVED HERE IN THE BIG TOWN SO LONG I 14 HUGHIE
CONSIDER MYSELF A NEW YORKER NOW.
THAT ALL A GUY HAD TO DO WAS COME TO THE BIG TOWN 23 HUGHIE
AND OLD MAN SUCCESS WOULD BE
AND HAD A SHOT AT DIFFERENT JOBS IN THE OLD HOME 23 HUGHIE
TOWN BUT COULDN'T MAKE THE
THEN YOU CAN TAKE THE UNION CASTLE FROM 605 ICEMAN
SOUTHAMPTON TO CAPE TOWN.
WE'VE ALL HEARD THAT STORY ABOUT HOW YOU CAME BACK657 ICEMAN
TO CAPE TOWN
AND SO WAS THAT DAMNED HICK TOWN. 709 ICEMAN
WE HAD ONE HOOKER SHOP IN TOWN, AND, OF COURSE, I 709 ICEMAN
LIKED THAT TOO.
WELL, YOU KNOW WHAT A SMALL TOWN IS. 709 ICEMAN
THE TOWN WAS GETTING MORE LIKE A JAIL. 710 ICEMAN
THE HITCH WAS HOW TO GET THE RAILROAD FARE TO THE 710 ICEMAN
BIG TOWN.
THE NIGHT BEFORE I LEFT TOWN, I HAD A DATE WITH 710 ICEMAN
EVELYN.
SO I BEAT IT TO THE BIG TOWN. 711 ICEMAN
WHIN WE WAS IN CAPE TOWN SIVIN MONTHS AGO-- 531 INZONE
(SNEERING JEALOUSLY AGAIN.) A HICK TOWN RAG/ 36 JOURNE
I'VE ALWAYS HATED THIS TOWN AND EVERYONE IN IT. 44 JOURNE
SHE WEARS THE DRESS INTO WHICH SHE HAD CHANGED FOR 97 JOURNE
HER DRIVE TO TOWN, A SIMPLE,
I WAS SCARED OUT OF MY WITS RIDING BACK FROM TOWN. 98 JOURNE
YOU CAN SHOW YOURSELF UP BEFORE THE WHOLE TOWN AS.145 JOURNE
SUCH A STINKING OLD TIGHTWAD/
DON'T YOU KNOW HARDY WILL TALK AND THE WHOLE 145 JOURNE
DAMNED TOWN WILL KNOW/
IMAGINE ME SUNK TO THE FAT GIRL IN A HICK TOWN 161 JOURNE
HOOKER SHOP/
ABOUT A FEW POEMS IN A HICK TOWN NEWSPAPER/ 164 JOURNE
YOU LET HICK TOWN BOOBS FLATTER YOU WITH BUNK 164 JOURNE
ABOUT YOUR FUTURE--
YOU BOASTED THAT THE TOWN CONSIDERED YOU 15 MANSNS
IN A TEXTILE-MILL TOWN ABOUT FORTY MILES FROM THE 43 MANSNS
CITY.
WELL, YOU WOULDN'T KNOW THE OLD TOWN NOW. 393 MARCOM
WHAT'S THE MATTER WITH THE TARTS IN TOWN, THEY LET 41 MISBEG
YOU DO ITS
EXCEPT I'M EVEN MORE BORED IN THE SO-CALLED GOOD 105 MISBEG
HOTELS IN THIS HICK TOWN.
(HE MOVES) I'LL GRAB THE LAST TROLLEY FOR TOWN. 152 MISBEG
COURTIN' THAT HARLOT THAT WAS THE TALK O' THE 580 ROPE
WHOLE TOWN/
WHEN I LEFT FOR THE TOWN HE LOOKED TOO WEAK TO 582 ROPE
LIFT A FOOT.
YOU'VE BEEN DRINKIN' IN TOWN OR YOU WOULDN'T TALK 583 ROPE
THAT WAY.
THE LIBRARY OF PROFESSOR LEEDS' HOME IN A SMALL 3 STRANG
UNIVERSITY TOWN IN NEW ENGLAND.
THIS PLEASANT OLD TOWN AFTER THREE MONTHS... 5 STRANG
IN THIS TOWN DOZING... 5 STRANG
YOU DRIVE TO TOWN WITH HIM, GIVE ME A CHANCE TO 56 STRANG
GET TO KNOW MY DAUGHTER-IN-LAW.
HE CAME TO THE TOWN I LIVED IN, NO ONE THERE KNEW 59 STRANG
ABOUT THE EVANSES.
YOU'D BETTER GO AND SHAVE, HADN'T YOU, IF YOU'RE 95 STRANG
GOING TO TOWNS
I'LL BE OUT OF TOWN VISITING. 106 STRANG
THAT HE'D BE VISITING FRIENDS OUT OF TOWN UNTIL HE108 STRANG
SAILED.
HOW DID SHE KNOW I WAS BACK IN TOWNS... 161 STRANG
AN' I AIN'T SLINGIN' ME 'OOK ABAHT THE 'OLE 494 VOYAGE
BLEEDIN' TOWN FUR NOW MAN.

TOWN'S
HE BECAME ONE OF THE TOWN'S BEST CITIZENS, 431 DYNAMO
THIS TOWN'S REAL PROUD OF EZRA. 8 ELECTR
HE'S THE TOWN'S WORST OLD GOSSIP. 40 ELECTR

TRACE

TOWN'S (CONT'D.)
THEY WERE ONE OF THE TOWN'S BEST, RICH FOR THAT 710 ICEMAN
HICK BURG,
AND THIS TOWN'S NOT SO BAD. 44 JOURNE

TOWNS
ON THE OUTSKIRTS OF ONE OF THE SMALL NEW ENGLAND 2 ELECTR
SEAPORT TOWNS.
AND I GUESS EVERYBODY IN TOWNS KNOWS IT---THEY'RE 263 GGBROW
ALWAYS KIDDING ME--
CITIES AND SMALL TOWNS--NOT FLASHY BUT 619 ICEMAN
CONSPICUOUSLY SPIC AND SPAN.

TOWNSEND
I WISH TOWNSEND WOULDN'T GO FORCING HIS BOOKS ON 429 DYNAMO
ME

TOWNSFOLK
IN CHARACTER HE IS THE TOWNSFOLK TYPE OF GARRULOUS 6 ELECTR
GOSSIP-MONGER
THESE LAST THREE ARE TYPES OF TOWNSFOLK RATHER 6 ELECTR
THAN INDIVIDUALS, A
ARE, AS WERE THE AMES, OF ACT ONE OF =HOMECOMING,= 67 ELECTR
TYPES OF TOWNSFOLK,
ARE, AS WERE THE TOWNSFOLK OF THE FIRST ACTS OF 129 ELECTR
=HOMECOMING= AND =THE HUNTED,

TOY
AND I FELT LIKE A FORSAKEN TOY AND CRIED TO BE 282 GGBROW
BURIED WITH HER,
SHE BELONGED IN DE WINDOW OF A TOY STORE, OR ON DE241 HA APE
TOP OF A GARBAGE CAN, SEE/
OF A PERVERSELY MAGNIFIED CHILD'S TOY GARDEN, 161 MANSNS
DISTORTED AND ARTIFICIAL.

TOYS
AND THEY--'ER AND 'ER BLOODY CLARSS--BUYS 'EM FOR 235 HA APE
TOYS TO DANCE ON 'EM/
YOU'VE NEVER CARED ABOUT CHILDREN, EXCEPT AS TOYS 65 MANSNS
TO PLAY WITH--
GOOD GOD, I'LL BE PLAYING WITH TOYS NEXT, 121 MANSNS

TRACE
(A TRACE OF AWE IN HIS TONES--HE GLANCES UPWARD) 536 'ILE
(THEN A TRACE OF SHOCKED REPROOF SHOWING IN HIS 205 AHWILD
VOICE)
(WITH A TRACE OF GENUINE FEELING IN HER VOICE) 20 ANNA
WITH A TRACE OF SCORN IN HER VOICE) 21 ANNA
(WITH A TRACE OF STRANGE EXULTATION) 25 ANNA
(THEN WITH A TRACE OF SYMPATHY, AS SHE NOTICES HIM 32 ANNA
SWAYING FROM WEAKNESS)
NOT WITHOUT A TRACE OF HIS OWN ADMIRATION) 35 ANNA
(WITH A FAINT TRACE OF A SMILE) 42 ANNA
ANNA CONTINUES SLOWLY, A TRACE OF SADNESS IN HER 44 ANNA
VOICE)
A TRACE OF RESENTMENT IN HER VOICE) 55 ANNA
(WITH A TRACE OF DEFIANCE) WELL, THE POINT IS 100 BEYOND
THIS, PA...
THERE IS A TRACE IN HER EXPRESSION OF SOMETHING 116 BEYOND
HARD AND SPITEFUL.
(WITH A TRACE OF IRRITATION) RIGHTS 120 BEYOND
THE FAINT TRACE OF A PATH LEADING UPWARD TO IT 129 BEYOND
FROM THE LEFT FOREGROUND CAN BE
(WITH A TRACE OF SCORN) 132 BEYOND
(A TRACE OF APPEAL IN HIS VOICE) 135 BEYOND
(WITHOUT A TRACE OF FEELING) 146 BEYOND
(WITH A FAINT TRACE OF IRONY) 160 BEYOND
(SLOWLY--WITH A TRACE OF MELANCHOLY) 459 CARIBE
(WITH A TRACE OF CONDESCENSION) 557 DAYS
HE HAS BLACK HAIR, MUSTACHE, A THIN CURLY TRACE UF203 DESIRE
BEARD.
BUT THERE IS A TRACE OF TENDERNESS, OF INTERESTED 251 DESIRE
DISCOVERY,
(HE COMES FORWARD--STARES AT EBEN WITH A TRACE OF 269 DESIRE
GRUDGING ADMIRATION)
NOT WITHOUT A TRACE OF MALICE) 535 DIFRNT
(FROWNING--WITH A TRACE OF RESENTMENT) 539 DIFRNT
WITH A TRACE OF SOMETHING LIKE PITY SHOWING IN HIS546 DIFRNT
TONE)
SHE DOES ALL THIS WITHOUT A TRACE OF CHANGE IN HER548 DIFRNT
EXPRESSION--
ONE SENSES A STRONG TRACE OF HER MOTHER'S 429 DYNAMO
SENTIMENTALITY.)
(RAISES HERSELF TO HER FEET PLACIDLY, WITHOUT A 434 DYNAMO
TRACE OF RESENTMENT)
(CURTLY--A TRACE OF JEALOUSY IN HIS TONE) 48 ELECTR
(A TRACE OF RESENTMENT HAS CREPT INTO HIS TONE) 74 ELECTR
(WITH A TRACE OF CONFUSION) I DON'T KNOW WHAT 141 ELECTR
YOU'RE TALKING ABOUT.
(ANGRILY, BUT WITH A TRACE OF GUILTY CONFUSION) 153 ELECTR
I'VE TRIED TO TRACE TO ITS SECRET HIDING PLACE IN 153 ELECTR
THE MANNONS PAST
(THEN WITH A TRACE OF RESENTMENT) 295 GGBROW
(WITH A TRACE OF JEALOUSY) WHERE ARE YOUR OTHER 310 GGBROW
BIG BOYS TONIGHT$
(PROTESTING WITH A TRACE OF GENUINE EARNESTNESS) 219 HA APE
(HE CALLS TO HOPE WITH A FIRST TRACE OF UNDERLYING692 ICEMAN
UNEASINESS)
(SOURLY, BUT WITH A TRACE OF ADMIRATION.) 24 JOURNE
A TRACE OF BLUR IN HIS SPEECH, HE DOES NOT SHOW 108 JOURNE
IT.
(SIMPLY, WITH A TRACE OF A SAD STERNNESS) 294 LAZARU
WITH NO TRACE OF THEIR ANCIENT NOBILITY OR COURAGE315 LAZARU
REMAINING--THAT AND NO MORE/
(GLANCING FROM ONE TO THE OTHER--WITH A TRACE OF 61 MANSNS
SUSPICION.)
(WITH A TRACE OF VINDICTIVE SATISFACTION.) 79 MANSNS
(WITH A TRACE OF MOCKERY.) BUT WHAT IS HERS IS 96 MANSNS
YOURS.
(WITH A TRACE OF A BITING SMILE) 367 MARCOM
WITH A FAINT TRACE OF GRUDGING RESPECT) 13 MISBEG
(WITH A TRACE OF BITTERNESS) 20 MISBEG
(TRACE OF BITTERNESS BENEATH HIS AMUSED TONE) 66 MISBEG

TRACE

TRACE (CONT'D.)

IT WAS LIFE I WAS CURSING-- (WITH A TRACE OF HIS 176 MISBEG NATURAL MANNER)

RUNNING HIS TONGUE OVER HIS DRY LIPS, SHE SAYS 54 POET ACIDLY, WITH NO TRACE UF BROGUE.)

HOPELESSNESS AND DEFEAT BRINGING A TRACE OF REAL 57 POET TRAGEDY

WITH A TRACE OF GENUINE PITY IN HER VOICE.) 58 POET (HE ADDS IN A FORCED TONE, A TRACE OF MOCKERY IN 107 POET IT.)

THE FAINT TRACE OF WHAT WAS ONCE A ROAD LEADING TO577 ROPE THE BARN.

(HE SIGHS--THINKING WITH A TRACE OF GUILTY ALARM) 7 STRANG (THINKING WITH A TRACE OF PITYING CONTEMPT) 51 STRANG (STARTLED--UNABLE TO HIDE A TRACE OF 82 STRANG DISAPPOINTMENT)

(WITH A TRACE OF CONTEMPT) (IPOOR CHARLIE... 98 STRANG HER SKIN STILL RETAINS A TRACE OF SUMMER TAN 137 STRANG (WITH A TRACE OF A SNEER) 140 STRANG WITH A TRACE OF A PATRONIZING AIR) 147 STRANG (THEN GLANCING AT MARSDEN--WITH A TRACE OF A 162 STRANG SNEER)

(GOOD-NATUREDLY, WITH A TRACE OF PRIDE) 163 STRANG (WITH A TRACE OF MALICE--DRYLY) 168 STRANG (WITH A TRACE OF ANGER) 191 STRANG (HER FACE SHOWING A TRACE OF HURT IN SPITE OF 445 WELDED HERSELF)

(A PAUSE--THEN WITH A TRACE OF SCORNFUL 447 WELDED RESENTMENT)

SAYING KINDLY BUT WITH A FAINT TRACE OF 465 WELDED BITTERNESS)

HER VOICE IS HEAVY AND SLOW WITH THE STRONG TRACE 470 WELDED OF A FOREIGN INTONATION.

(AFTER A PAUSE--WITH A TRACE OF BITTER HUMOR) 482 WELDED

TRACED

WHATEVER OF RESEMBLANCE ROBERT HAS TO HIS PARENTS 94 BEYOND MAY BE TRACED TO HER.

RIVULETS OF SOOTY SWEAT HAVE TRACED MAPS ON THEIR 224 HA APE BACKS.

TRACES

THIS BEAUTY IS A TRIFLE DIMMED NOW BY TRACES OF 514 DAYS RECENT ILLNESS.

HIS FACE ALSO BEARS OBVIOUS TRACES OF SLEEPLESS 553 DAYS STRAIN.

IN A VAIN EFFORT TO CONCEAL TRACES OF HER TEARS. 505 DIFRNT BUT STILL WITH TRACES OF A DOLL-LIKE PRETTINESS. 615 ICEMAN (THEY TAKE HOLD OF HIS CHARIOT TRACES, 311 LAZARU THE TRACES OF FORMER SUFFERING ARE MARKED ON HER 111 STRANG FACE.

TRACING

THEY ARE TRACING PLANS. 302 GGBROW WITH ONLY THE FIRST TRACING OF WRINKLES ABOUT THE 2 MANSNS EYES AND MOUTH.

TRACK

I CAN'T KEEP TRACK OF THEM. 292 AHWILD I AM SIRED BY GOLD AND DAMNED BY IT, AS THEY SAY 219 HA APE AT THE RACE TRACK--

I'D STARTED TO BE A HORSE PLAYER IN ERIE, THOUGH 15 HUGHIE I'D NEVER SEEN A TRACK.

IT WAS JUST THE TRACK, AND THE CROWD, AND THE 21 HUGHIE HORSES GOT HIM.

YOU THINK I'M ON THE WRONG TRACK AND YOU'RE GLAD 1643 ICEMAN AM.

BUT WE'VE GONE OFF THE TRACK. 26 MISBEG AND COME BACK NORTH WITH THEM IN THE SPRING, AND 143 MISBEG BE AT THE TRACK EVERY DAY.

TRACKED

WE TRACKED ON 'N' ON. 237 DESIRE

TRACKER

ONE OF THE SOLDIERS, EVIDENTLY A TRACKER, IS 202 EJONES PEERING ABOUT KEENLY ON THE GROUND.

TRACKS

COULDN'T YOU REALIZE--WHY, I NEARLY DROPPED IN MY 155 BEYOND TRACKS WHEN I SAW HIM/

(WEARILY) HOW LONG I BEEN MAKIN TRACKS IN DESE 191 EJONES WOODS&

BUT AT THE FIRST SIGHT OF HIS FACE HE STOPS IN HIS308 LAZARU TRACKS, TREMBLING.

BE GOD, THAT USED TO STOP HIM IN HIS TRACKS. 25 MISBEG I BORROWED SOME MONEY ON MY SHARE OF THE ESTATE, 143 MISBEG AND STARTED GOING TO TRACKS.

TRACTABLE

MOREOVER,REOVER, OF A GOOD DISPOSITION, 197 EJONES INTELLIGENT AND TRACTABLE.

TRADE

SHE RELAPSES INTO THE FAMILIAR FORM AND FLASHES 23 ANNA ONE OF HER WINNING TRADE SMILES

AND IT'LL GIVE HIM A TRADE FOR THE REST OF HIS 96 BEYOND LIFE, IF HE WANTS TO TRAVEL.

WAAL, IS IT FAIR TRADES 213 DESIRE TAKE GUN'N IN TRADE DUR IT/ 223 DESIRE TRADE WIND. 187 EJONES AMOS AMES, CARPENTER BY TRADE BUT NOW TAKING A 6 ELECTR HOLIDAY AND DRESSED IN HIS SUNDAY

(BITTERLY) THAT'S HIS TRADE--BEING ROMANTIC/, 15 ELECTR THE WARM EARTH IN THE MOONLIGHT, THE TRADE WINDS 112 ELECTR RUSTLING THE COCO PALMS,

THE TRADE WIND IN THE COCO PALMS--THE SURF ON THE 147 ELECTR REEF--

(THEN MECHANICALLY FLASHING A TRADE SMILE AT 280 GGBROW BILLY)

OH, TO BE SCUDDING SOUTH AGAIN WID THE POWER OF 214 HA APE THE TRADE WIND

CATERING TO THE CATCH-AS-CATCH-CAN TRADE. 7 HUGHIE THIS PLACE HAS A FINE TRADE 594 ICEMAN HER ROUND FACE SHOWING MORE OF THE WEAR AND TEAR 615 ICEMAN OF HER TRADE THAN THEIRS,

TRADE (CONT'D.)

AND A BARGAINER SO EASY TO CHEAT IT HURT ONE'S 276 LAZARU CONSCIENCE TO TRADE WITH HIM/

*HOW IS TRADE THESE DAYS& 29 MANSNS IT'S A DIFFICULT PERIOD FOR TRADE THIS COUNTRY IS 47 MANSNS IN NOW.

AND WE CAN'T DISMISS THE SHIPPING TRADE AS 48 MANSNS SOMETHING THAT DOESN'T CONCERN US.

(UNEASILY.) NO, STICK TO YOUR OWN TRADE, SIMON, 48 MANSNS WHATEVER YOU DO.

YOU'RE BECOMING THE YOUNG NAPOLEON OF TRADE HERE 76 MANSNS IN THE CITY.

GO BACK AND PLY YOUR TRADE THERE. 186 MANSNS THERE IS A NEW IMPORT TAX AND TRADE IS VERY 348 MARCOM UNSETTLING

(SHAKING HIS HEAD) THIS UNCERTAINTY IS BAD FOR 359 MARCOM TRADE.

REMEMBER ANY CLIMATE IS HEALTHY WHERE TRADE IS 370 MARCOM BRISK.

(THEN BRISKLY) AND HAVE WE YOUR PERMISSION TO 398 MARCOM TRADE IN THE PORTS ALONG THE WAYS

PERPETRATED BY UNSCRUPULOUS JAPANESE TRADE-PIRATES422 MARCOM WHO, IN SPITE OF HIS PROTESTS

HE'LL TEACH YOU THE TRADE. 5 MISBEG DIDN'T I HELP YOU IN THE TRADE FOR 13 MISBEG (IN A BRAZEN TONE) SURE, THOSE IN MY TRADE HAVE TO 97 MISBEG LOOK THEIR BEST/

THERE'S NO TRADE THIS TIME O' DAY. 9 POET BECAUSE HE DIDN'T LIKE BEING IN TRADE, 29 POET BUT AT LEAST I'VE A CONSCIENCE IN MY TRADE, 37 POET INSOFAR AS ONE IN TRADE CAN LAY CLAIM TO THE 48 POET TITLE.

AND FINALLY WERE EVEN DRIVEN TO EMBRACE THE 83 POET PROFITS OF THE SLAVE TRADE--

HAD TO MAKE A LARGE, GREEDY FORTUNE OUT OF 83 POET PRIVATEERING AND THE NORTHWEST TRADE,

WORKING FOR HIS FATHER HE HAS THE ABILITY FOR 146 POET TRADE, THOUGH HE HATES IT.

A KEG CONTAINING NAILS AND OTHER TOOLS OF THE 577 ROPE CARPENTRY TRADE ARE ON THE TABLE.

WITH GOOD LUCK IN THE TRADE, MAYBE WE'LL HAVE 587 ROPE ENOUGH.

ON'Y A BIT NOW AN' AGEN WHEN THERE AIN'T NO 494 VOYAGE RECULAR TRADE.

(FORCING A TRADE SMILE--WITH AN ATTEMPT AT 471 WELDED LIGHTNESS)

(THEN AFRAID SHE MAY LOSE HIS TRADE BY THIS 473 WELDED REBUFF)

TRADER

AND BY THE COCKNEY TRADER SMITHERS. 202 EJONES YOU HAVE LET HIM BEAT YOU DOWN LIKE A SWINDLING 59 MANSNS HORSE-TRADER/

UNTIL I COULD HARDLY RECOGNIZE MY SON IN THE 97 MANSNS UNSCRUPULOUS GREEDY TRADER,

SOULLESS TRADER IN THE SLAVE MARKET OF LIFE YOU 178 MANSNS HAVE BECOME--/

(FROM THE LEFT A MAGIAN, A PERSIAN, DRESSED IN THE347 MARCOM FASHION OF A TRADER,

WHO IS HE BUT A MONEY-GRUBBING TRADERS 112 POET (YOU MAY TELL THE SWINDLING TRADER, HARFORD, 123 POET TRADER'S)

I HATE THAT SMUG, LUSTFUL, GREEDY TRADER'S SMILE 119 MANSNS OF HIS/

I WILL TOLERATE NO NIGGARDLY TRADER'S HAGGLING ON 112 POET HIS PART.

TRADERS

THE AMBITION TO BE A NAPOLEON AMONG TRADERS/ 74 MANSNS FOR GREEDY TRADERS LIKE MY FATHER AND ME. 101 MANSNS BUT YOU TRADERS ARE LIKE FLEAS, ONE FINDS YOU 350 MARCOM EVERYWHERE/

TRADES

YOU KNOW HOW MUCH THE *FLYING TRADES* MEANS TO 33 ELECTR HIM.

YOU CAN COME ON THE * FLYING TRADES.* 38 ELECTR AND CLARK AND DAWSON WOULD BE WILLING TO SELL THE 39 ELECTR *FLYING TRADES.*

THEN YOU MUST WAIT ON THE *FLYING TRADES* UNTIL 40 ELECTR YOU HEAR FROM ME

THE WORK ON THE *FLYING TRADES* IS ALL FINISHED, 40 ELECTR ISN'T IT&

THE *FLYING TRADES* WON'T BE SAILING FOR A MONTH 111 ELECTR OR MORE.

THEY'LL HAVE TO FIND ANOTHER SKIPPER FOR THE 111 ELECTR *FLYING TRADES.*

(HUSKILY) SO IT'S GOOD-BYE TO YOU, *FLYING 114 ELECTR TRADES*/

FULL MOON IN THE TRADES. 153 JOURNE EVEN IF IT IS A GREAT COMPANY THAT TRADES WITH THE 29 POET WHOLE WORLD IN ITS OWN SHIPS.

TRADIN'

WANTIN' TO SWAP FOR TERBACCER AND OTHER TRADIN' 502 DIFRNT STUFF WITH STRAW MATS AND

AIN'T I PERFECTED YOU AND WINKED AT ALL DE CROOKED177 EJONES TRADIN' YOU BEEN DOIN'

DOUGH YOU KNOW IT'S MONEY IN YO' POCKET TRADIN' 179 EJONES WID 'EM IF YOU DOES.

TRADING

I MADE MONEY HAND OVER FIST AS LONG AS I STUCK TO 156 BEYOND LEGITIMATE TRADING..

TRADITIONAL

TRADITIONAL EXPRESSION OF BEWILDERED, 433 MARCOM UNCOMPREHENDING GRIEF THAT IS LIKE A MASK.

TRAFFIC

THE CAR EDGES AWAY INTO THE TRAFFIC AND MARCO 439 MARCOM POLO.

TRAGEDIAN

(GAILY MOCKING) TRAGIC IS THE PLIGHT OF THE 309 LAZARU TRAGEDIAN WHOSE ONLY AUDIENCE IS

TRAGEDY

HE EXUDES TRAGEDY. 215 AHWILD
HIS FACE TENSE, FEELING DESPERATELY THAT HE IS 558 DAYS
FACING INEVITABLE TRAGEDY.
WHAT A TRAGEDY TO BE TAKEN HIS FIRST NIGHT HOME 69 ELECTR
(HE PAUSES--THEN SADLY) THAT IS YOUR TRAGEDY/ 289 LAZARU
BUT THIS IS WAR AND NOT A TRAGEDY. 395 MARCOM
HOPELESSNESS AND DEFEAT BRINGING A TRACE OF REAL 57 POET
TRAGEDY
AND GOD KNOWS I KNOW THE SORDID TRAGEDY OF SUCH A 113 POET
UNION.
IT'S MOTHER HAS HAD THE TRAGEDY/ 113 POET

TRAGIC

AS HE READS HIS FACE GROWS MORE AND MORE WOUNDED 208 AHWILD
AND TRAGIC.
(WITH A TRAGIC SNEER) LIFE/ 215 AHWILD
(THEN SOLEMNLY TRAGIC) IT'S ONLY THAT I'VE GOT A 239 AHWILD
WEIGHT ON MY MIND.
RICHARD SITS IN TRAGIC GLOOM. 271 AHWILD
(UNABLE TO RESIST FALLING INTO HIS TRAGIC LITERARY279 AHWILD
POSE FOR A MOMENT)
LIFE SEEMED LIKE A TRAGIC FARCE. 281 AHWILD
(WITH TRAGIC BITTERNESS) WHY SHOULDN'T I, 283 AHWILD
OH, THE WHOLE AFFAIR IS SO SENSELESS--AND TRAGIC. 109 BEYOND
IT'S TRAGIC. NO OTHER WORD--UNLESS THE WORD BE 501 DAYS
COMIC.
TRAGIC AND REVEALING TO ME. 533 DAYS
(WITH A TRAGIC SIGH) THERE'S NOT A LIVING SOUL 440 DYNAMO
KNOWS IT,
AND WALKS WITH JERKY STEPS FROM THE ROOM LIKE SOME 92 ELECTR
TRAGIC MECHANICAL DOLL.
HER FACE HAS BECOME A TRAGIC DEATH MASK. 122 ELECTR
EVEN GRATEFUL TO HER, I THINK, FOR GIVING ME SUCH 708 ICEMAN
A GOOD TRAGIC EXCUSE
YOU LOVE TO MAKE A SCENE OUT OF NOTHING SO YOU CAN120 JOURNE
BE DRAMATIC AND TRAGIC.
(GAILY MOCKING) TRAGIC IS THE PLIGHT OF THE 309 LAZARU
TRAGEDIAN WHOSE ONLY AUDIENCE IS
QUIETLY, WITH A MOCKING IRONY TINGED WITH A 148 MANSNS
BITTER, TRAGIC SADNESS.)
THE TWO MAKE A STRANGELY TRAGIC PICTURE IN THE WAN157 MISBEG
DAWN LIGHT--
A BYRONIC HERO, NOBLE, EMBITTERED, DISDAINFUL, 57 POET
DEFYING HIS TRAGIC FATE.
HE BECOMES A ROMANTIC, TRAGIC FIGURE, 70 POET
SUCH A MARRIAGE WOULD BE A TRAGIC MISALLIANCE FOR 113 POET
HIM--
ESPECIALLY AFTER THE SHOCK OF HIS TRAGIC DEATH. 9 STRANG
GOODNESS, SAM, HOW TRAGIC YOU CAN GET ABOUT 69 STRANG
NOTHING AT ALL/
WHAT A TRAGIC JOKE IT WAS ON BOTH OF US/... 72 STRANG
NO SORROW, NO TRAGIC MEMORIES... 113 STRANG
IT HAS THE TRAGIC EFFECT OF MAKING HER FACE SEEM 158 STRANG
OLDER

TRAGICALLY

(HE STARES AT BELLE GLOOMILY AND MUTTERS 245 AHWILD
TRAGICALLY)
(GLOWERING AT HER--TRAGICALLY) 246 AHWILD
HER FACE GROWING TRAGICALLY SAD. 257 AHWILD
(TRAGICALLY) WELL, AFTER YOUR OLD-- 281 AHWILD
WEARILY TO HIS FEET, HIS SHOULDERS BOWED, LOOKING 560 DAYS
TRAGICALLY OLD AND BEATEN--
HER EYES ARE TRAGICALLY SAD IN REPOSE AND HER 137 STRANG
EXPRESSION IS SET AND MASKLIKE.

TRAIL

SOMEWHERE OUT ON THE LONG TRAIL--THE TRAIL THAT IS288 AHWILD
ALWAYS NEW--
ALWAYS ON THE TRAIL OF TRUTH/ 535 DAYS
AND DE EMPEROR BETTER GIT HIS FEET SMOKIN' UP DE 182 EJONES
TRAIL.
AN' THESE BLACKS 'ERE CAN SNIFF AND FOLLOW A TRAIL183 EJONES
IN THE DARK LIKE 'HOUNDS.
WHEN I WAS FOLLOWIN' DE TRAIL ACROSS DE PLAIN IN 189 EJONES
BROAD DAYLIGHTS
THE HEAVY, PLODDING FOOTSTEPS OF SOMEONE 191 EJONES
APPROACHING ALONG THE TRAIL FROM THE
ALONG THE SAWDUST TRAIL TO SALVATION 661 ICEMAN

TRAILING

THE TOP OF THE BANK IS GRASSY AND THE TRAILING 275 AHWILD
BOUGHS OF WILLOW TREES EXTEND OUT
THEY BEND THEIR TRAILING BRANCHES DOWN OVER THE 202 DESIRE
ROOF.
OVER ONE ARM, CARRIED NEGLECTFULLY, TRAILING ON 170 JOURNE
THE FLOOR,
THE WEDDING GOWN TRAILING ON THE FLOOR. 171 JOURNE
AT THE RISING OF THE CURTAIN SOME TRAILING CLOUDS 577 ROPE
NEAR THE HORIZON,

TRAILS

THREADBARE TRAILS, LEADING TO THE KITCHEN AND 144 BEYOND
OUTER DOORS.
I COULD GO THROUGH ON DEM TRAILS WID MY EYES SHUT.183 EJONES
EVEN IF YOU KNEW ALL THE BLOOMIN' TRAILS LIKE A 183 EJONES
NATIVE.
(HIS VOICE TRAILS OFF. 169 JOURNE
I WANT-- (HIS VOICE TRAILS OFF INTO SILENCE.) 120 MISBEG

TRAIN

WHEN I'M DOING MY BEST TO TRAIN-- 223 AHWILD
NO--TRAVELING--DAY AND A HALF ON THE TRAIN. 14 ANNA
NOT SINCE THIS MORNING ON THE TRAIN. 15 ANNA
I WENT ASHORE TO GET A TRAIN FOR NEW YORK. 64 ANNA
BUT I GOT TO THINKING ABOUT YOU--AND I COULDN'T 71 ANNA
TAKE THE TRAIN--I COULDN'T/
(PURSUING HER T 'N OF THOUGHT) 98 BEYOND
EXCEPT TO CARRY SOME PLACE I CAN'T GET TO BY 132 BEYOND
TRAIN.
(HE READS) =LE. .: FOR HOME ON MIDNIGHT TRAIN. 147 BEYOND
HE DON'T GET IN FROM NEW BEDFORD TILL THE NIGHT 522 DIFRNT
TRAIN AND

TRAIN (CONT'D.)

I'LL STAY AT BILL GRAINGER'S TONIGHT AND GET THE 534 DIFRNT
MORNING TRAIN.
(THEN AFTER A PAUSE) BUT THE NIGHT TRAIN GOT IN 46 ELECTR
LONG AGO.
(GOING STIFFLY TO MEET HER) TRAIN WAS LATE. 47 ELECTR
WENT TO THE TRAIN WITH PETER NILES TO MEET ORIN. 68 ELECTR
SHE WAS INSISTING PETER SHOULD ESCORT HER TO MEET 69 ELECTR
THE TRAIN.
PETER AND VINNIE OUGHT TO BE BACK SOON, IF THE 72 ELECTR
TRAIN ISN'T LATE.
(STRANGELY) THE SAME TRAIN/ 72 ELECTR
WASN'T THE LONG TRAIN TRIP TERRIBLY HARD ON YOU, 81 ELECTR
DEARS
AND IN BOSTON WE WAITED UNTIL THE EVENING TRAIN 120 ELECTR
GOT IN.
WE TOOK THE TRAIN THERE BUT WE DECIDED TO STAY 120 ELECTR
RIGHT ON
WE MET THAT TRAIN. 120 ELECTR
(MORE AND MORE HYPNOTIZED BY THIS TRAIN OF 166 ELECTR
THOUGHT)
THE CLERK'S MIND REMAINS IN THE STREET TO GREET 19 HUGHIE
THE NOISE OF A FAR-OFF EL TRAIN.
MET HER ON A SUNDAY TRAIN. 23 HUGHIE
THERE WAS A BLONDE MOVIE DOLL ON THE TRAIN--AND I 23 HUGHIE
WAS LUCKY IN THEM DAYS.
(HIS TRAIN OF THOUGH INTERRUPTED--IRRITABLY.) 34 HUGHIE
AND DERE HE IS SITTIN' BEHIND A BIG DESK, LOOKIN' 600 ICEMAN
AS BIG AS A FREIGHT TRAIN.
(GOING BACK TO HIS TRAIN OF THOUGHT) 669 ICEMAN
SHE OUGHT TO BE A TRAIN ANNOUNCER. 54 JOURNE
I'LL HAVE TIME TO DISPOSE OF HIM BEFORE I CATCH MY148 MANSNS
TRAIN.
(HE GLANCES AT HIS WATCH.) AND NOW I'LL HAVE TO 158 MANSNS
GO AND CATCH MY TRAIN.
(HE LAUGHS AND KISSES HER.) I MUST CATCH MY 160 MANSNS
TRAIN.
ATTENDED BY A TRAIN OF NOBLES AND SLAVES WITH 417 MARCOM
LIGHTS.
YOU CAN CHANGE TO YOUR SUNDAY SUIT IN THE CAN AT 5 MISBEG
THE STATION OR IN THE TRAIN,
AND DON'T FORGET TO GET OFF THE TRAIN AT 7 MISBEG
BRIDGEPORT.
JIM CAN TAKE THE NEXT TRAIN TO NEW YORK. 84 MISBEG
THAT FAT BLONDE PIG ON THE TRAIN--I GOT HER DRUNK/122 MISBEG
NO TRAIN. 122 MISBEG
WHAT TRAINS 122 MISBEG
DO YOU MEAN THE BLONDE ON THE TRAINS 127 MISBEG
(STARTS--SHARPLY) TRAINS 127 MISBEG
YOU'LL BE TAKING A TRAIN BACK TO YOUR DEAR OLD 130 MISBEG
BROADWAY TOMORROW NIGHT.
(PUZZLED) YOU SAID YOU'D TELL ME ABOUT THE BLONDE145 MISBEG
ON THE TRAIN.
I HAD TO GO OUT AND WANDER UP AND DOWN THE TRAIN 149 MISBEG
LOOKING FOR COMPANY.
AND I'M THE WHORE ON THE TRAIN TO HIM NOW, NOT-- 166 MISBEG
NINE-FORTY, THE TRAIN... 23 STRANG
DETERMINEDLY PUTS AN END TO HIS TRAIN OF THOUGHT 25 STRANG
HE COULDN'T TELL WHAT TRAIN. 72 STRANG
THEY RUN TO THE RAIL AND TRAIN THEIR GLASSES UP 176 STRANG
THE RIVER.)
(WITH A START--EVIDENTLY ANSWERING SOME TRAIN OF 471 WELDED
THOUGHT IN

TRAINED

AT REAR OF STILLWELL ON HIS RIGHT, A TRAINED NURSE553 DAYS
IS STANDING.
YES, I TRAINED HIM AND HE'S VERY INGENIOUS. 306 GGBROW
BEJEES, YOU'VE EVEN BORROWED FISH FROM THE TRAINED609 ICEMAN
SEALS
HE HAS TRAINED TO DO A PROFITABLE ACT UNDER HIS 611 ICEMAN
MANAGEMENT.
PERFORMANCE AS A TRAINED SEAL. 168 JOURNE
CALIGULA IS A TRAINED APE, A HUMPED CRIPPLE/ 360 LAZARU
WE WANT THEM TRAINED TO LIVE WITH REALITY 84 MANSNS
WITH THE TRAINED EYE FOR DISPLAY OF WINDOW- 428 MARCOM
DRESSERS, UNTIL THE TABLE,
IT'S WELL TRAINED YOU'VE GOT THE POOR RETAINERS ON 54 POET
YOUR AMERICAN ESTATE
THERE ARE WORSE THINGS THAN BEING A TRAINED 22 STRANG
NURSE...
OF INTENSE PASSION WHICH HE HAS RIGIDLY TRAINED 33 STRANG
HIMSELF TO CONTROL AND SET FREE
HE HAS BEEN TOO THOROUGHLY TRAINED TO PROGRESS 184 STRANG
ALONG A CERTAIN GROOVE TO SUCCESS
GORDON IS OVER SIX FEET TALL WITH THE FIGURE OF A 184 STRANG
TRAINED ATHLETE.
BUT HE'S TRAINED ME TOO WELL IN HIS IDEAL. 469 WELDED

TRAININ'

DAT SOFT EMPEROR JOB AIN'T NO TRAININ' FO' A LONG 187 EJONES
HIKE OVAH DAT PLAIN IN DE

TRAINING

WHAT ARE YOU IN TRAINING FOR--WRITING CHECKS 251 AHWILD
IT WAS PART OF MY TRAINING AS A SOLDIER UNDER HIM. 75 ELECTR
I'VE HAD A THOROUGH TRAINING AT THIS GAME--THANKS 114 ELECTR
TO YOU AND FATHER.
DON'T FORGET I HAD MY FIRST BUSINESS TRAINING WITH 48 MANSNS
MY FATHER'S COMPANY.
UNFORTUNATELY, THE TENDENCY TO SPOIL THEM IN THE 9 STRANG
UNIVERSITY IS A POOR TRAINING--
I WILL FINISH MY TRAINING. 17 STRANG
I'VE ALREADY HAD SIX MONTHS' TRAINING FOR A NURSE. 17 STRANG
ALWAYS TELLING YOU HOW BENEFICIAL THE TRAINING AT 24 STRANG
THE HOSPITAL WOULD BE FOR HER
HER TRAINING HAS ALSO TENDED TO COARSEN HER FIBER 26 STRANG
A TRIFLE.
TRAINING FOR SUCCESS, ETC. 66 STRANG
(FORCING A SMILE) HOW ABOUT TRAINING HIS MINDS 120 STRANG

TRAINING

TRAINING (CONT'D.)

I'M GOING TO START IN TRAINING HIM AS SOON AS HE'S120 STRANG OLD ENOUGH--

TRAINS

I'M SMOKE AND EXPRESS TRAINS AND STEAMERS AND 216 HA APE FACTORY WHISTLES.

ONLY SO MANY EL TRAINS PASS IN ONE NIGHT, 19 HUGHIE

HE JUMPS UP, LOOKIN' AS BIG AS TWO FREIGHT TRAINS,601 ICEMAN

ABOUT HOW TRAVELING MEN GET THINGS FROM DRINKING 713 ICEMAN CUPS ON TRAINS.

YOUR SEASON WILL OPEN AGAIN AND WE CAN GO BACK TO 72 JOURNE SECOND-RATE HOTELS AND TRAINS.

WITH WEEK AFTER WEEK OF ONE-NIGHT STANDS, IN 87 JOURNE TRAINS WITHOUT PULLMANS,

ONE-NIGHT STANDS, CHEAP HOTELS, DIRTY TRAINS, 104 JOURNE LEAVING CHILDREN,

THE ONE-NIGHT STANDS AND FILTHY TRAINS AND CHEAP 109 JOURNE HOTELS,

AND DON'T BE TELLING ME OF YOUR OLD FLAMES, ON 129 MISBEG TRAINS OR NOT.

THE CHEERING FROM THE OBSERVATION TRAINS CAN BE 180 STRANG HEARD.)

TRAIT

UR RATHER, I INHERIT THE ACQUIRED TRAIT OF THE BY-219 HA APE PRODUCT, WEALTH.

THEY THINK IT IS A FAMILY TRAIT. 396 MARCOM

AND PROVE I HAD THAT ONE TRAIT AT LEAST IN COMMON/ 41 STRANG

TRAITOR

AND AIN'T HE TURNED TRAITOR--MOCKIN' AT ME AND 568 CROSS SAYIN' IT'S ALL A LIE--

YOU--YOU TRAITOR/ 163 ELECTR

YOU, LARRY RENEGADE/ TRAITOR/ I VILL HAVE YOU 634 ICEMAN SHOT/

I BEGAN TO FEEL I WAS A TRAITOR FOR HELPING A LOT 649 ICEMAN OF CRANKS

HE IS A TRAITOR TO JESUS/ 283 LAZARU

HALT, TRAITOR/ 311 LAZARU

THIRTY YEARS' YEARS OF DISCIPLINE AND I--HALT, 311 LAZARU TRAITOR/

YOU ARE A TRAITOR, LAZARUS/ 319 LAZARU

(FRENZIEDLY) SILENCE, IMPIOUS TRAITOR/ 322 LAZARU

DIE, TRAITOR/ 369 LAZARU

YOU TRAITOR/ 185 MANSNS

(SADLY) I NEVER KNEW YOU WERE SUCH A BLACK 25 MISBEG TRAITOR, AND YOU ONLY A CHILD.

TRAITORS

TOO LATE FOR TRAITORS, BOY, TOO LATE/ 569 CROSS

SO MAY ALL TRAITORS DIE/" 720 ICEMAN

TRAMP

WHY DIDN'T YOU PUT ME WISE, YOU LOUSY TRAMP YOU/ 248 AHWILD

SURE--AND ANOTHER TRAMP WITH HER. 19 ANNA

GO AND BE A TRAMP LIKE YOU'VE ALWAYS WANTED. 127 BEYOND

"SHE'S THE 'EL PASO, ' A BRAND NEW TRAMP," HE 141 BEYOND SAYS.

THE SEAMAN'S FORECASTLE OF THE BRITISH TRAMP 477 CARDIF STEAMER =GLENCAIRN=ON A FOGGY NIGHT

A FORWARD SECTION OF THE MAIN DECK OF THE BRITISH 455 CARIBE TRAMP STEAMER =GLENCAIRN=.

EVERY TRAMP I MADE GOT TO BE A FOLLIES' DOLL. 28 HUGHIE

I CAN'T LOOK LIKE A TRAMP WHEN I-- 600 ICEMAN

(KISSING HIM) AW, YUH BIG TRAMP/ 610 ICEMAN

(IGNORING THIS) ME AND DIS OVERGROWN TRAMP HAS 616 ICEMAN BEEN SCRAPPIN' ABOUT IT.

SHE SAYS, "IS DERE A LAW YUH CAN'T GO OUT AND BUY 670 ICEMAN DE MAKINGS, YUH BIG TRAMP?"

HERE, YUH BIG TRAMP/ 683 ICEMAN

AN OLD NO-GOOD DRUNKEN TRAMP, AS DUMB AS HE IS, 701 ICEMAN

THEY ALL SAID I WAS A NO-GOOD TRAMP. 709 ICEMAN

WHAT I'D WANT WAS SOME TRAMP I COULD BE MYSELF 712 ICEMAN WITH WITHOUT BEING ASHAMED--

YOU'RE NOT LIKE YOUR DAMNED TRAMP OF A BROTHER. 128 JOURNE

(HE QUOTES FROM KIPLING'S "SESTINA OF THE TRAMP- 161 JOURNE ROYAL."

SHE CALLED HIM THE MESSIAH--THAT COMMON BEGGAR, 284 LAZARU THAT TRAMP/

(THEY TRAMP, DANCING, OFF. 294 LAZARU

AT THE OPENING OF THE SCENE THERE IS HEARD THE 313 LAZARU STEADY TRAMP OF DEPARTING TROOPS.

THE LEGIONS TRAMP AWAY.) 323 LAZARU

LIVING LIKE A TRAMP OR A TINKER, AND HIM A RICH 29 POET GENTLEMAN'S SON.

YOU HAD HIM THROWN OUT OF HERE LIKE A TRAMP. 126 POET

TRAMP'S

IF DIS BIG TRAMP'S GOIN' TO MARRY ME, HE OUGHT TO 632 ICEMAN DO IT.

TRAMPING

COME TRAMPING UP AT THE DOUBLE-QUICK. 291 LAZARU

THERE (GREAT BASS CHORUS OF MARCHING TRAMPING 320 LAZARU LAUGHTER.)

HOW DARE YOU COME TRAMPING IN HERE IN THAT MANNER/ 53 POET

TRAMPLE

HE BEGAN BY SHOUTING THAT HE WAS NO SLAVE STANDARD 24 JOURNE OIL COULD TRAMPLE ON.

THE FRON STEPS TRIED TO TRAMPLE ON ME. 155 JOURNE

TRAMPLED

TRAMPLED BY THE FEET OF FRIEND AND FOE ALIKE. 291 LAZARU

TRAMPLING

UMM, JUST AS, AFTER A BANGING OF DOORS, CRASHING 321 GGBROW OF GLASS, TRAMPLING OF FEET.

TRAMPS

THEM LOUSY TRAMPS IS ALWAYS GETTING THIS DUMP IN 249 AHWILD DUTCH/

I RESENT THE IMPLICATION THAT I CORRESPOND WITH 267 AHWILD ALL THE TRAMPS AROUND THIS TOWN.

CAPTAIN BARTLETT TRAMPS DOWN THE STAIRS.) 567 CROSS

I USED TO INTRODUCE HIM TO THE TRAMPS I'D DRAG 16 HUGHIE HOME WITH ME.

WELL, HOW'D YOU TRAMPS DUS 612 ICEMAN

TRAMPS (CONT'D.)

NOR AN OLD MEN'S HOME FOR LOUSY ANARCHIST TRAMPS 660 ICEMAN THAT OUGHT TO BE IN JAIL/

THEY'RE JUST GOLD-DIGGING TRAMPS. 117 MISBEG

(I'VE SLEPT WITH DRUNKEN TRAMPS ON TOO MANY NIGHTS/121 MISBEG

(WITH REVULSION) GOD, DON'T MAKE ME THINK OF 171 MISBEG THOSE TRAMPS NOW/

TRANCE

(KEENEY STRAIGHTENS HIMSELF LIKE A MAN COMING OUT 550 'ILE OF A TRANCE.

AND THEY BOTH SIT IN A RAPT TRANCE, STARING AT THE287 AHWILD MOON.

HE WALKS LIKE ONE IN A TRANCE, HIS EYES SHINING 292 AHWILD WITH A DREAMY HAPPINESS,

(RUTH KEEPS HER EYES FIXED ON HER LAP IN A TRANCE-158 BEYOND LIKE STARE.)

(AS IF IN A TRANCE) THERE WAS SOMETHING HORNE 573 CROSS HANDED HIM.

(HE GOES THROUGH THE DOOR TO THE STUDY, MOVING 563 DAYS LIKE ONE IN A TRANCE,

HAS AN EXPRESSION OF TRANCE. 220 DESIRE

HE LOOKS AROUND HIM WITH THE RAPT EXPRESSION OF 482 DYNAMO ONE IN A TRANCE)

HE MOVES WITH A STRANGE DELIBERATION LIKE A SLEEP-200 EJONES WALKER OR ONE IN A TRANCE.

AND THE WAY HE ACTED--LIKE SOMEONE IN A TRANCE/ 136 ELECTR

* (HE STARES BEFORE HIM IN A SORT OF TRANCE, 269 GGBROW

(LISTENING AS IN A TRANCE TO THE MUSIC AND WHAT IS305 LAZARU GOING ON BEHIND HIM--

(RISING TO HER FEET LIKE ONE IN A TRANCE, STARING 366 LAZARU TOWARD LAZARUS)

DELIBERATELY HYPNOTIZING HERSELF INTO A TRANCE. 163 MANSNS

HIS FACE HAS A STRANGE, MAD, TRANCE-LIKE LOOK. 186 MANSNS

HER EYES HAVE A STILL, FIXED, SIGHTLESS, TRANCE- 191 MANSNS LIKE LOOK.

WALKS SLOWLY AND WOODENLY LIKE A MAN IN A TRANCE 98 STRANG INTO THE ROOM.

(STARTLED OUT OF HIS TRANCE--BEWILDEREDLY) 164 STRANG

(STARING BEFORE HER AS IF SHE WERE IN A TRANCE-- 179 STRANG SIMPLY, LIKE A YOUNG GIRL)

THEY SEEM IN A FORGETFUL, HAPPY TRANCE AT FINDING 480 WELDED EACH OTHER AGAIN.

TRANCELIKE

(IN A TRANCELIKE TONE) =OUR FATHER WHO ART IN 299 GGBROW HEAVEN.=

TRANQUILLY

(SPITTING TRANQUILLY) MORE MEM'RIES$ 473 CARIBE

TRANSATLANTIC

(THE FIREMEN'S FORECASTLE OF A TRANSATLANTIC LINER207 HA APE

TRANSCENDS

HIS FACE EXPRESSES SORROW AND A HAPPINESS THAT 350 LAZARU TRANSCENDS SORROW.

TRANSFERS

ROCKY TRANSFERS HIS ANGER TO HIM) 634 ICEMAN

TRANSFIGURED

(SHE TURNS ROUND TO THEM, HER FACE TRANSFIGURED 540 'ILE WITH JOY)

BUT THEN SUDDENLY HIS FACE IS TRANSFIGURED 297 AHWILD

HIS FACE IS TRANSFIGURED WITH THE ECSTASY OF A 570 CROSS DREAM COME TRUE.)

HIS FACE IS TORN AND TRANSFIGURED BY JOY. 266 GGBROW

AND OUT OF EARTH'S TRANSFIGURED BIRTH--PAIN THE 322 GGBROW LAUGHTER OF MAN RETURNS TO BLESS

TRANSFIGURING

(THE NIGHT CLERK DREAMS, A RAPT HERO WORSHIP 32 HUGHIE TRANSFIGURING HIS PIMPLY FACE.

TRANSFIXED

(HE WALKS QUICKLY INTO THE CLEAR SPACE--THEN 192 EJONES STANDS TRANSFIXED AS HE SEES JEFF--

(EACH PERSON STANDS TRANSFIXED, FROZEN IN THE LAST291 LAZARU MOVEMENT.)

HE STANDS THERE TRANSFIXED, DISORGANIZED, 450 WELDED TREMBLING ALL OVER.)

TRANSFORM

GOD HIMSELF CANNOT TRANSFORM A SOW'S EAR INTO A 114 POET SILK PURSE/

TRANSFORMATION

(WITH AN ABRUPT TRANSFORMATION INTO A DETACHED 120 JOURNE BULLYING MOTHERLINESS.)

(STARES AT HIM--A SUDDEN TRANSFORMATION COMES OVER 31 MANSNS HER.

TRANSFORMED

SHE LOOKS HEALTHY, TRANSFORMED, THE NATURAL COLOR 25 ANNA HAS COME BACK TO HER FACE.

(ALL HER EMOTIONS IMMEDIATELY TRANSFORMED INTO 39 ANNA RESENTMENT AT HIS BULLYING TONE)

THE THIRTY YEARS HAVE TRANSFORMED EMMA INTO A 519 DIFRNT WITHERED,

THIS MANNER IS AT ONCE TRANSFORMED. 720 ICEMAN

I HAVE TRANSFORMED WHAT WAS FATHER'S BANKRUPT 70 MANSNS BUSINESS.

YOU WOULD BE ASTOUNDED AT THE WAY SHE HAS 73 MANSNS TRANSFORMED HERSELF.

(HER PANIC IS TRANSFORMED INTO AN OUTRAGED FURY.) 111 MANSNS

(BUT INSTANTLY HIS PAIN IS TRANSFORMED INTO RAGE. 51 POET

HIS EMBARRASSMENT IS TRANSFORMED INTO RESENTFUL 116 POET ANGER.

(HIS FACE TRANSFORMED WITH HAPPINESS) 71 STRANG

TRANSLATED

TRANSLATED VERY FREELY INTO IRISH ENGLISH, 38 MISBEG SOMETHING LIKE THIS.

TRANSLATION

(HE QUOTES A TRANSLATION OF THE CLOSING COUPLET 591 ICEMAN SARDONICALLY)

THE SYMONS' TRANSLATION OF BAUDELAIRE'S PROSE 132 JOURNE POEM.)

(HE RECITES THE SYMONS' TRANSLATION OF 133 JOURNE BAUDELAIRE'S =EPILOGUE.=

TRANSMISSION
LEADING TO THE TRANSMISSION TOWERS. 473 DYNAMO
TRANSMITTED
IT IS AS IF THIS REACTION WERE TRANSMITTED THROUGH286 LAZARU
THE CHORUS TO THE CROWD.)
TRANSOM
A DOORWAY WITH SQUARED TRANSOM AND SIDELIGHTS 2 ELECTR
FLANKED BY INTERMEDIATE COLUMNS.
WITH ORIN BENDING DOWN BY THE TRANSOM, LISTENING.1110 ELECTR
(ON THE DECK ABOVE, ORIN, WHO HAS BENT CLOSER TO 112 ELECTR
THE TRANSOM,
TRANSPARENT
ON HER ENTRANCE HER FACE IS MASKED WITH AN EXACT 262 GGBROW
ALMOST TRANSPARENT REPRODUCTION
BELOW HIS MASK HIS OWN SKIN IS OF AN ANAEMIC 299 LAZARU
TRANSPARENT PALLOR.
TRANSPORT
I MUST TRANSPORT HER OVER THE FIRST STAGE BY DARK 351 MARCOM
TONIGHT/
IF YOU'D EATEN SOME OF THE FOOD THEY GAVE ME ON MY 14 STRANG
RENOVATED TRANSPORT.
TRANSPORTED
HIS EXPRESSION BECOMES TRANSPORTED WITH A GREAT 43 STRANG
HAPPINESS--
TRANSVAAL
ME, IN OLD DAYS IN TRANSVAAL. 599 ICEMAN
IN OLD DAYS IN TRANSVAAL, I LIFT LOADED OXCART BY 676 ICEMAN
THE AXLE/
TRAP
CLOSE THAT TRAP IF YUH DON'T WANT A DUCKIN' OVER 457 CARIBE
THE SIDE.
THAT HE FELT CAUGHT IN A TRAP, DESPERATE-- 536 DAYS
SHUT YOUR DAMNED TRAP/ 646 ICEMAN
AND BE DROWNED LIKE A RAT IN A TRAP IN THE 517 INZONE
BARGAIN. MAYBE--
AND THE DIRTY TICK ACCUSED YOU AND ME OF MAKING UP 21 MISBEG
A FOXY SCHEME TO TRAP JIM.
WITH YOU TWO SCHEMING PEASANTS LAYING SNARES TO 60 POET
TRAP HIM/
HER BODY IS A TRAP/... 105 STRANG
TRAPPED
EACH DAY IS A CAGE IN WHICH HE FINDS HIMSELF 203 DESIRE
TRAPPED BUT INWARDLY UNSUBDUED.
TRAPPIN'S
I GITS RID O' DEM FRIPPETY EMPEROR TRAPPIN'S AN' 1193 EJONES
TRAVELS LIGHTER.
TRAPS
SHOOTING OFF THEIR LOUD TRAPS ON SOAPBOXES 592 ICEMAN
TRASH
LOOKED TO ME LIKE CHEAP TRASH. 197 AHWILD
IT'S A SHAME TO FOOL DESE BLACK TRASH AROUND HEAH,183 EJONES
DEYRE SO EASY.
AIN'T COME TO DAT YIT AND I NEVER WILL--NOT WID 184 EJONES
TRASH NIGGERS LIKE DESE YERE.
AND DAT BLACK TRASH DON'T DARE STOP HIM--NOT YIT, 186 EJONES
LEASTWAYS.
I TROWS DOWN A FIFTY-DOLLAR BILL LIKE IT WAS 601 ICEMAN
TRASH PAPER AND SAYS,
I DON'T LOWER MYSELF DRINKIN' WID NO WHITE TRASH/=673 ICEMAN
TRAUNEEN
I WOULDN'T GIVE A TRAUNEEN FOR A TEETOTALER. 101 JOURNE
TRAVEL
AND IT'LL GIVE HIM A TRADE FOR THE REST OF HIS 96 BEYOND
LIFE, IF HE WANTS TO TRAVEL.
BUT DON'T WANT HIM TO TRAVEL ALL HIS LIFE. 96 BEYOND
I NEED NOT MUCH MONEY BECAUSE I AM NOT ASHAMED TO 676 ICEMAN
TRAVEL STEERAGE.
JEES, LOOK AT DE OLD BASTARD TRAVEL/ 689 ICEMAN
DEAREST MAN--(HIS EYES TRAVEL DOWN THE PAGE) 530 INZONE
ON HAVING A NURSE TO TRAVEL WITH HER. 142 JOURNE
OF THE THIRTEENTH CENTURY ARE TRAVEL-WORN. 347 MARCOM
I WANT TO TRAVEL AND SEE THE WORLD AND ALL THE 356 MARCOM
DIFFERENT PEOPLE.
ALL THE POLOS ARE WEARY AND THEIR CLOTHES SHABBY 373 MARCOM
AND TRAVEL-WORN.
TRAVEL-STAINED AND WEARY. 423 MARCOM
NORA WAS AS PRETTY A GIRL AS YOU'D FIND IN A 14 POET
YEAR'S TRAVEL.
TRAVELED
=I JUMPED ABOARD THE LIZA SHIP, AND TRAVELED ON 224 DESIRE
THE SEA.
LIKE IT WAS FUN IN THE OLD DAYS, WHEN I TRAVELED 661 ICEMAN
HOUSE TO HOUSE.
TRAVELIN'
HE OUGHT TO BE TIRED OF TRAVELIN' 115 BEYOND
TRAVELIN' ALL OVER THE WORLD AND NEVER SEEIN' NONE486 CARDIF
OF IT.
AND I COULDN'T SHOW MYSELF UP AS A CHEAP SKATE BY 523 DIFRNT
TRAVELIN' 'ROUND WITH HIM
THAT'S TRAVELIN'/ 36 HUGHIE
WE'VE NO CHANCE TO LEARN THE THINGS A TRAVELIN' 593 ROPE
LAD LIKE YOU'D BE KNOWIN'.
TRAVELING
NO--TRAVELING--DAY AND A HALF ON THE TRAIN. 14 ANNA
AND IF YOU'RE SET ON TRAVELING, 85 BEYOND
SICK OF TRAVELING. 23 HUGHIE
BUT YOU KNOW HOW IT IS, TRAVELING AROUND. 712 ICEMAN
ABOUT HOW TRAVELING MEN GET THINGS FROM DRINKING 713 ICEMAN
CUPS ON TRAINS.
EVEN TRAVELING WITH YOU SEASON AFTER SEASON, 87 JOURNE
A BUDDHIST, A KASHMIRI TRAVELING MERCHANT COMES 347 MARCOM
IN, PUFFING AND SWEATING.
AND TRAVELING THERE AND BACK'S 356 MARCOM
LOOSE TARTAR TRAVELING DRESS AND LOOK QUITE 429 MARCOM
SHABBY.
TRAVELLING
I DON'T WANT THEM THINKING I'M TRAVELLING AROUND 219 AHWILD
WITH ANY HIGH-SCHOOL KID.

TRAVELLING (CONT'D.)
IT HAS KEPT ME OUT IN THE OPEN AIR AND BEEN 140 STRANG
CONDUCIVE TO TRAVELLING AND
TRAVELS
THEN THEIR GAZE TRAVELS TO A POINT IN FRONT OF 551 DAYS
FATHER BAIRD.
I TRAVELS LIGHT WHEN I WANTS TO MOVE FAST. 186 EJONES
I GITS RID O' DEM FRIPPETY EMPEROR TRAPPIN'S AN' 1193 EJONES
TRAVELS LIGHTER.
THEN LAZY, BLOATED SWINE WHAT TRAVELS FIRST CABIN$212 HA APE
A SECOND CLASS TRAVELS AROUND, IS ALLOWED HIS 301 MARCOM
EXPENSES.
TRAY
LUCY AVOIDS HER EYES, NERVOUSLY FLIPPING HER 516 DAYS
CIGARETTE OVER THE ASH TRAY.
TRAY LADEN WITH SCHOONERS OF CHAMPAGNE 658 ICEMAN
SHE PUTS THE TRAY ON THE TABLE. 51 JOURNE
SHE CARRIES A TRAY ON WHICH IS A BOTTLE OF BONDED 51 JOURNE
BOURBON.
HE PUTS THE GLASS HASTILY ON THE TRAY AND SITS 53 JOURNE
DOWN AGAIN, OPENING HIS BOOK.
THE TRAY WITH THE BOTTLE OF WHISKEY HAS BEEN 71 JOURNE
REMOVED FROM THE TABLE.
THE TRAY WITH THE BOTTLE OF WHISKEY, GLASSES, 97 JOURNE
THE WHISKEY BOTTLE ON THE TRAY IS THREE-QUARTERS 125 JOURNE
EMPTY.
CARRYING A TRAY WITH TOAST, EGGS, BACON, AND TEA. 55 POET
(SARA GOES OUT RIGHT, CARRYING A TRAY LADEN WITH 99 POET
PLATES.)
TRAYS
IN FRONT OF SOFA, A LOW STAND WITH CIGARETTE BOX 514 DAYS
AND ASH TRAYS.
TREACH'ROUS
BAD CESS TO YE, YOU'RE THE TREACH'ROUS ONE/ 584 ROPE
TREACHEROUS
NOR A TREACHEROUS SNAKE IN THE GRASS WHO STABS YOU 78 MISBEG
IN THE BACK WITH A KNIFE--
SO I ONLY CALLED HIM A DIRTY LYING SKUNK OF A 86 MISBEG
TREACHEROUS BASTARD.
TREACHERY
REUBEN COULD NEVER BE GUILTY OF SO BASE A 426 DYNAMO
TREACHERY/.
IT WOULD BE TREACHERY TO GOD/...)) 435 DYNAMO
HONOR OR DISHONOR, FAITH OR TREACHERY ARE NOTHING 649 ICEMAN
TO ME
I THOUGHT YOU WANTED TO MAKE HIM PAY FOR HIS BLACK 94 MISBEG
TREACHERY AGAINST US.
AND STINKING WITH LIES AND GREED AND TREACHERY/ 102 POET
I MUST PAY FOR MY COWARDLY TREACHERY TO GORDON/ 18 STRANG
DARRELL'S LOVE MUST HAVE SEEMED LIKE TREACHERY... 112 STRANG
TREAD
THE SILENCE IS UNBROKEN EXCEPT FOR THE MEASURED 535 'ILE
TREAD OF SOMEONE WALKING UP AND
TREASON
WHO TAUGHT THE TREASON THAT FEAR AND DEATH WERE 370 LAZARU
DEAD/
TREASONABLE
OF CIRCULATING SUCH TREASONABLE OPINIONS AGAINST 392 MARCOM
ME.
TREASURE
(WITH AN ANSWERING SMILE) TREASURE, OF COURSE. 560 CROSS
BURY THE TREASURES 560 CROSS
TREASURE, TO BE SURE. 560 CROSS
A SAMPLE OF THE RICHEST OF THE TREASURE.. 561 CROSS
SET SAIL TO BRING BACK THE TREASURE. 561 CROSS
YOU BELIEVED IN THE TREASURE THEN$ 561 CROSS
THE TREASURE, I SUPPOSE, IS WHERE-- 561 CROSS
I'LL KNOW HOW TO HUMOR HIM WHEN HE RAVES ABOUT 562 CROSS
TREASURE.
AND A TREASURE THAT NEVER WAS. 563 CROSS
AND THE TREASURE-- 566 CROSS
(WITH A TWISTED SMILE) YOU FORGET I'M HEIR TO THE566 CROSS
TREASURE, TOO.
THE TREASURE IS OURS ONLY. 572 CROSS
=THE TREASURE IS BURIED WHERE THE CROSS IS MADE.= 573 CROSS
AND LET ME STILL CLUTCH GREEDILY TO MY YELLOW 689 ICEMAN
HEART THIS SWEET TREASURE,
IT MUST BE TREASURE/ 350 MARCOM
TREASURY
WELL, I WAS SENDING IN TO YOUR TREASURY THE TAXES 391 MARCOM
OF YANG-CHAU
TREAT
SHE CAN'T TREAT ME LIKE THAT/ 208 AHWILD
I'LL SHOW HER SHE CAN'T TREAT ME THE WAY SHE'S 220 AHWILD
DONE/
SPOON, IS THIS ANY WAY TO TREAT A PAL$ 224 AHWILD
WHY DON'T YOU EVER GIVE US FOLKS AT HOME HERE A 255 AHWILD
TREATS
IF WOMEN ARE TOO SURE OF YOU, THEY TREAT YOU LIKE 277 AHWILD
SLAVES.
AND THEY TREATED ME WORSE THAN THEY DARE TREAT A 18 ANNA
HIRED GIRL.
TREAT HER RIGHT, SEE$ 19 ANNA
(DISGUSTEDLY) GOD A'MIGHTY, KATE, YOU TREAT 99 BEYOND
ROBERT AS IF HE WAS ONE YEAR OLD/
BECAUSE I'M DYING IS NO REASON YOU SHOULD TREAT ME160 BEYOND
AS AN IMBECILE OR A COWARD.
'TWAS A RARE TREAT TO 'EAR 'IM TELL WHAT 'APPENED 457 CARIBE
TO 'IM AMONG 'EM.
I HOPE ELSA WILL FEEL I'M ONE OF THE FAMILY AND 533 DAYS
TREAT ME WITHOUT CEREMONY.
(WORRIEDLY, BUT TRYING TO PRETEND TO TREAT IT 550 DAYS
LIGHTLY, REASSURINGLY)
AT FIRST, CALEB TRIES TO TREAT HER GENTLE AND ARGY 503 DIFRNT
WITH HER TO GO BACK.
TREAT HIM FIRM BUT GENTLE AND YOU'LL SEE HE WON'T 511 DIFRNT
NEVER DO IT AGAIN IN A HURRY.

TREAT

TREAT (CONT'D.)
I MUST SAY YOU TREAT YOUR ONE DEVOTED SWAIN PRETTY 16 ELECTR
RUDELY.
I BET YOU I'D NEVER LET THEM TREAT ONE OF MINE 280 GGBROW
THAT WAY/
TREAT 'EM ROUGH, DAT'S ME. 211 HA APE
TREAT 'EM WIV THE PROPER CONTEMPT. 236 HA APE
HE'D SAY, *HELLO, ERIE, HUW'D THE BANGTAILS TREAT 15 HUGHIE
YOU*,
I TREAT DEM FINE. 580 ICEMAN
I'LL TREAT YOU WHITE. 605 ICEMAN
CAN'T TREAT YOU NO WHITER DAN DAT, CAN I$ 605 ICEMAN
AND I TREAT YOU GOILS RIGHT, DON'T I$ 613 ICEMAN
I GOT IT AS A TREAT FOR THE THREE OF YOU MORE THAN639 ICEMAN
ANYONE.
GEE, LARRY, THAT'S A HELL OF A WAY TO TREAT ME, 669 ICEMAN
WHEN I'VE TRUSTED YOU,
YOU SHOULDN'T TREAT HIM WITH SUCH CONTEMPT ALL THE 81 JOURNE
TIME.
BESIDES, I WANTED TO TREAT CATHLEEN BECAUSE I HAD 116 JOURNE
HER DRIVE UPTOWN WITH ME.
I'M WRONG TO TREAT YOU. YOU'VE HAD ENOUGH 129 JOURNE
ALREADY.
WELL, I'LL BET THIS IS ONE TIME HE'S GOING TO 46 MISBEG
TREAT.
HOW CAN YOU TREAT HIM THAT WAYS 95 STRANG

TREATED
AND SERVE HIM RIGHT AFTER THE MANNER HE'S TREATED 537 'ILE
THEM--
WHAT DOES HE CARE IF HE DIES, AFTER THE WAY SHE'S 235 AHWILD
TREATED HIM?
NO MATTER HOW BAD I THOUGHT SHE HAD TREATED ME-- 294 AHWILD
WELL, YUH TREATED ME SQUARE, YUHSELF. 11 ANNA
AND THEY TREATED ME WORSE THAN THEY DARE TREAT A 18 ANNA
HIRED GIRL.
YOU HAVEN'T ANY COMPLAINT TO MAKE ABOUT THE WAY 124 BEYOND
YOU'VE BEEN TREATED, HAVE YOUS
TREATED SIMILARLY TO THAT OF SCENE ONE 274 GGBROW
HARDY'S TREATED HIM WHENEVER HE WAS SICK UP HERE, 33 JOURNE
SINCE HE WAS KNEE HIGH.
I'M NOT USED TO BEING TREATED LIKE A THIEF. 103 JOURNE
YOU TREATED CATHLEEN AND BRIDGET, ISN'T THAT IT, 116 JOURNE
MAMAS
SAID ABOUT HOW HE'D TREATED ME/ 118 JOURNE
I'VE TREATED YOU ROTTENLY, IN MY WAY, MORE THAN 145 JOURNE
ONCE.
TWICE NOW YOU'VE TREATED MY LOVE WITH THE MOST 468 WELDED
HUMILIATING CONTEMPT--

TREATING
AND HOW IS THE WORLD TREATING YOU THIS AFTERNOON, 45 ANNA
ANNA'S FATHERS
HUW'RE THE BANGTAILS TREATING YOUS* 30 HUGHIE
IF IT WAS THE ICEMAN OF DEATH HIMSELF TREATING/ 680 ICEMAN
NOT BECAUSE OF THE ROTTEN WAY YOU'RE TREATING ME. 145 JOURNE
TREATING HIS WIFE AS IF SHE WAS A WHORE HE'D PICK 121 MANSNS
UP ON THE STREET
DON'T TALK NONSENSE TO SNEAK OUT OF TREATING JIM. 52 MISBEG
NOT WITH ALL THE DRINKS HIMSELF'S BEEN TREATING 16 POET
TO.

TREATISES
VOLUMES OF THE ENCYCLOPEDIA BRITANNICA MIXED UP 66 STRANG
WITH POPULAR TREATISES ON MIND

TREATMENT
I'LL NEED THEM TO GIVE SYMPATHETIC TREATMENT TO 558 CROSS
HIS CASE
BUT NOT THE TREATMENT I'D RECOMMEND FOR ANGINA. 71 ELECTR
THE TREATMENT OF THIS SCENE, OR OF ANY OTHER SCENE207 HA APE
IN THE PLAY,
WITH MODERN TREATMENT-- 34 JOURNE
I THINK YOUR TREATMENT HAS BEEN RATHER HARD TO 469 WELDED
TAKE, NELLY--

TREATS
AND WHEN I GET A LEAVE TO HOME, EVERYONE TREATS ME523 DIFRNT
LIKE A WET DOG.
HE TREATS YOU LIKE A CRIMINAL/ 74 JOURNE
I'VE SEEN THE WAY HE TREATS HER NOW. 14 POET
I DO HATE HIM FOR THE WAY HE TREATS YOU. 24 POET

TREE
DEN MY TREE BRO'DER OLDERN ME, DEY GO ON SHIPS. 27 ANNA
FROM THE CENTER OF THIS AN OLD, GNARLED APPLE 81 BEYOND
TREE, JUST BUDDING INTO LEAF,
PASSING BENEATH THE APPLE TREE. 81 BEYOND
YOU*KE AS MUCH A PRODUCT OF IT AS AN EAR OF CORN 84 BEYOND
IS, OR A TREE.
FURTHER RIGHT, A LARGE OAK TREE. 129 BEYOND
PROPPING HER DOLL UP AGAINST THE TREE, COMES OVER 129 BEYOND
AND CLAMBERS TO HIS SIDE.)
THE APPLE TREE IS LEAFLESS AND SEEMS DEAD. 166 BEYOND
TRYIN' TO LOOK AS WISE AS AN OWL ON A TREE, AND 479 CARDIF
ALL THE TOINE HE NOT
-DAMNED LIKE AN OLD BARE HICKORY TREE FIT ON'Y FUR210 DESIRE
BURNIN',* HE SAYS.
EBEN'S A CHIP O' YEW--SPIT 'N' IMAGE--HARD 'N' 222 DESIRE
BITTER'S A HICKORY TREE/
BUT IT OWNS YEH. TOO--AN' MAKES YE GROW BIGGER-- 229 DESIRE
LIKE A TREE--LIKE THEM ELUMS--
THIS HOUSE AN' EVERY EAR UP CORN AN' EVERY TREE 232 DESIRE
DOWN T' THE LAST BLADE O' HAY/
THE INTERLOCKED ROPES OF CREEPERS REACHING UPWARD 198 EJONES
TO ENTWINE THE TREE TRUNKS
A ROUGH STRUCTURE OF BOULDERS, LIKE AN ALTAR, IS 199 EJONES
BY THE TREE.
(THE FOOT OF A GIGANTIC TREE BY THE EDGE OF A 199 EJONES
GREAT RIVER.
HE LOOKS AROUND AT THE TREE, THE ROUGH STONE 200 EJONES
ALTAR,
FROM BEHIND THE TRUNK OF THE TREE, AS IF HE HAD 200 EJONES
SPRUNG OUT OF IT,

TREE (CONT'D.)
SEEMS LIKE I KNOW DAT TREE--AN' DEM STONES--AN' 200 EJONES
DE RIVER.
THE WITCH DOCTOR POINTS WITH HIS WAND TO THE 201 EJONES
SACRED TREE, TO THE RIVER BEYOND,
THE NEAREST TREE TRUNKS ARE DIMLY REVEALED 202 EJONES
THE WITCH DOCTOR SPRINGS BEHIND THE SACRED TREE 202 EJONES
AND DISAPPEARS.
THE GREEN OF THE LAWN AND SHRUBBERY, THE BLACK AND 5 ELECTR
GREEN OF THE PINE TREE.
A BIG PINE TREE IS ON THE LAWN AT THE EDGE OF THE 5 ELECTR
DRIVE BEFORE THE RIGHT CORNER
ONE--TWO--TREE--(HIS VOICE RISING EXULTANTLY IN 224 HA APE
THE JOY OF BATTLE)
TREE--(A TERRIFIC CHORUS OF BARKING AND YAPPING.) 243 HA APE
TREE SQUARE A DAY, AND CAULIFLOWERS IN DE FRONT 250 HA APE
YARD--EKAL RIGHTS--
VE VILL EAT BIRTHDAY CAKE AND TRINK CHAMPAGNE 658 ICEMAN
BENEATH THE VILLOW TREE/
'TIS COOL BENEATH THY WILLOW TREE/ 728 ICEMAN
I THOUGHT THAT UGLY MONKEY, SMYTHE, WOULD DRIVE US 98 JOURNE
IN A DITCH OR AGAINST A TREE.
AS ONE LEANS AGAINST A TREE, DEEP-ROOTED IN THE 120 MANSNS
COMMON EARTH--
(SCENE--A SACRED TREE ON A VAST PLAIN IN PERSIA 347 MARCOM
NEAR THE CONFINES OF INDIA.
THAT RESEMBLES A MODERN SAMPLE CASE, PLODS WEARILY347 MARCOM
TO THE FOOT OF THE TREE.
AND EVER SINCE THIS TREE HAS BEEN SACRED TO HIM/ 349 MARCOM
THIS TREE IS SACRED TO THE FOUNDER OF THE ONE TRUE349 MARCOM
RELIGION, ZOROASTER.
THIS TREE WAS THE STAFF OF OUR FIRST FATHER, ADAM.349 MARCOM
WHO BROUGHT A SHOOT OF THE TREE OF LIFE DOWN FROM 349 MARCOM
PARADISE AND PLANTED IT HERE?
I AM GOING TO OFFER A PRAYER FOR PROTECTION TO 349 MARCOM
THIS TREE SACRED TO BUDDHA.
AND SPRANG UP INTO THIS MIGHTY TREE TO TESTIFY 349 MARCOM
FOREVER TO HIS MIRACULOUS POWERS
(SUDDENLY, POINTING TO THE TREE) 349 MARCOM
AND GREW BY THE WILL OF ALLAH INTO THIS TREE. 350 MARCOM
(HE LOOKS AT THE TREE--THEN IN AN AWED TONE) 350 MARCOM
HE MAKES OBEISANCE AND PRAYS TO THE TREE AS DO 350 MARCOM
THE SOLDIERS.
THIS MUST BE THE HOLY TREE WHICH WAS ONCE THE 350 MARCOM
STAFF OF MAHOMET AND,
FROM THE BRANCHES OF THE TREE COMES A SOUND OF 352 MARCOM
SWEET SAD MUSIC
FINALLY HER LIPS PART AND HER EYES OPEN TO LOOK UP352 MARCOM
AT THE TREE.)
COMES FROM HER LIPS AND IS TAKEN UP IN CHORUS IN 352 MARCOM
THE BRANCHES OF THE TREE
THE SAME SWEET SAD MUSIC COMES FROM THE TREE AGAIN354 MARCOM
AS IF ITS SPIRIT WERE PLAYING
ON THE GROUND UNDER THE SACRED TREE THREE BODIES 354 MARCOM
LIE IN CRUMPLED HEAPS.
FROM THESE STEPS THERE IS A FOOTPATH GOING AROUND 1 MISBEG
AN OLD PEAR TREE,
SURE, YOU CAN CHARM A BIRD OUT OF A TREE WHEN YOU 28 POET
WANT TO.

TREEING
THE TREES ARE TREEING WITH ONE ANOTHER, AND YOU, 51 STRANG
IF I MISTAKE NOT,

TREES
'TIS COOL BENEATH THY WILLOW TREES/ 195 AHWILD
THE TOP OF THE BANK IS GRASSY AND THE TRAILING 275 AHWILD
BOUGHS OF WILLOW TREES EXTEND OUT
I LOVE THE SAND AND THE TREES, AND THE GRASS, AND 277 AHWILD
THE WATER AND THE SKY,
KEEPING IN THE DARK UNDER THE TREES, MY, BUT IT 281 AHWILD
WAS EXCITING/
LET'S GO OUT IN UNDER THE TREES IN BACK WHERE 118 BEYOND
THERE'S A BREATH OF FRESH AIR.
AND OF THE ELM TREES THAT LINE THE STREET CAN BE 493 DIFRNT
SEEN.
EVERYTHING IS DIFF'RENT DOWN THERE--THE WEATHER-- 515 DIFRNT
AND THE TREES AND WATER.
THEIR SUMMITS CROWNED WITH THICK GROVES OF PALM 173 EJONES
TREES.
WIDOUT NO JEALOUS NIGGER GUNNIN' AT ME FROM BEHIND179 EJONES
DE TREES.
(CARELESSLY) DEY'RE ALL OUT IN DE GARDEN SLEEPIN'181 EJONES
UNDER DE TREES.
TREES AND ME, WE'SE FRIENDS AND DAR'S A FULL MOON 185 EJONES
COMIN' BRING ME LIGHT.
TRUNKS OF THE NEAREST TREES BE MADE OUT, ENORMOUS 187 EJONES
PILLARS OF DEEPER BLACKNESS.
CAN'T TELL NOTHIN' FROM DEM TREES/ 189 EJONES
HE STARES UP AT THE TOPS OF THE TREES, 189 EJONES
AIN'T NOTHIN' DERE BUT DE TREES/ 190 EJONES
TALL TREES WHOSE TOPS ARE LOST TO VIEW. 195 EJONES
THE LIMBS OF THE TREES MEET OVER IT 198 EJONES
BY THE RIGHT CORNER OF THE HOUSE IS A GROVE OF 2 ELECTR
PINE TREES.
IN THE FOREGROUND, ALONG THE STREET, IS A LINE OF 2 ELECTR
LOCUST AND ELM TREES.
(MANNION PACES TO THE RIGHT AND STANDS LOOKING AT 53 ELECTR
THE TREES.
THE RIGHT HALF OF THE HOUSE IS IN THE BLACK SHADOW11T ELECTR
CAST BY THE PINE TREES BUT
I KNOW I'D HAVE FOUND HER SOME MOONLIGHT NIGHT 145 ELECTR
DANCING UNDER THE PALM TREES--
ONCE WE'RE MARRIED AND HAVE A HOME WITH A GARDEN 167 ELECTR
AND TREES/
SHADOWS OVER THE TOPS OF TREES/ 287 GGBROW
'TIS COOL BENEATH THY WILLOW TREES/ 592 ICEMAN
'TIS COOL BENEATH THY VILLUW TREES/ 627 ICEMAN
AND VE VILL EAT HOT DOGS AND TRINK FREE BEER 635 ICEMAN
BENEATH THE VILLOW TREES/

1703 TREMBLING

TREES (CONT'D.)
(WITH HIS SILLY GIGGLE) VE VILL TRINK VINE 640 ICEMAN
BENEATH THE WILLOW TREES/
YOU'D HAVE BEEN DRINKING OUR BLOOD BENEATH THOSE 658 ICEMAN
WILLOW TREES/
SOON YOU WILL EAT HOT DOGS BENEATH THE WILLOW 672 ICEMAN
TREES AND TRINK FREE VINE--
THERE AIN'T ANY COOL WILOW TREES--EXCEPT YOU GROW691 ICEMAN
YOUR OWN IN A BOTTLE.
ALWAYS THERE IS BLOOD BENEATH THE WILLOW TREES/ 695 ICEMAN
BENEATH THE WILLOW TREES/ 721 ICEMAN
TREES, BUT USUALLY THEY BEAR HUMAN FRUIT/ 327 LAZARU
OAK, PINE, BIRCH, AND MAPLE TREES. 1 MANSNS
AND THE TREES ALONG THE BRICK WALL AT REAR GLOW IN 95 MANSNS
DIFFERENT SHADES OF GREEN.
AND THENCE BACK THROUGH A SCRAGGLY ORCHARD OF 1 MISBEG
APPLE TREES TO THE BARN.
SUNSHINE, COOLED AND DIMMED IN THE SHADE OF TREES, 3 STRANG
DRIFTED AWAY OVER THE GRASS, WISPS OF MIST BETWEEN 49 STRANG
THE APPLE TREES.
AROUND IT ARE ACRES AND ACRES OF APPLE TREES IN 49 STRANG
FULL BLOOM.
THE TREES ARE TREEING WITH ONE ANOTHER, AND YOU, 51 STRANG
IF I MISTAKE NOT,
GREEN BUDS ON THE SLIM TREES... 99 STRANG

TRELLIS
AND THE CLIMBING ROSES ON THE TRELLIS TO THE SIDE 548 *ILE
OF THE HOUSE--THEY'RE BUDDING.

TREMBLE
I'M THE ONLY ONE IN THIS HOUSE SEEMS TO CARE--(HER251 AHWILD
LIPS TREMBLE.)
BEGINS TO TREMBLE ALL OVER. 488 DYNAMO
HER VOICE BEGINS TO TREMBLE.) 91 JOURNE
(HIS LIPS TREMBLE, HIS EYES ARE TERRIFIED, 303 LAZARU
(HE BEGINS TO TREMBLE ALL OVER AS IF IN A 359 LAZARU
SEIZURE--CHOKINGLY)
SO HURT AND FULL OF HATRED HER LIPS TREMBLE AND 107 POET
SHE CANNOT SPEAK.
(SHE BEGINS TO TREMBLE--IN A HORRIFIED WHISPER.) 163 POET
(BUT HIS VOICE BEGINS TO TREMBLE UNCERTAINLY AGAIN 93 STRANG
AS HE CALLS)
(HIS LIPS TREMBLE, TEARS COME TO HIS EYES) 162 STRANG

TREMBLED
THEN, OF A SUDDEN, A STRANGE GAY LAUGHTER TREMBLED309 LAZARU
FROM HIS HEART

TREMBLES
KEENEY'S VOICE TREMBLES) 551 *ILE
(HIS VOICE TREMBLES) AY'M GETTING OLE. 22 ANNA
(HE TREMBLES WITH VIOLENT PASSION. 149 BEYOND
AND NOW--(HIS VOICE TREMBLES AS HE FIGHTS TO 480 CARDIF
CONTROL HIS EMOTION)
HE TREMBLES ALL OVER WITH THE FERVOR OF HIS HOPES)1235 DESIRE
SHE TRIES TO KEEP HER VOICE INDIFFERENT BUT IT 30 ELECTR
TREMBLES A LITTLE.)
SHE TREMBLES WITH DREAD. 78 ELECTR
(HAS CALMED HERSELF, BUT HER EYES ARE STILL 89 ELECTR
TERRIFIED AND HER VOICE TREMBLES)
(HER VOICE TREMBLES AND SHE SEEMS ABOUT TO BURST 159 ELECTR
INTO TEARS)
(AT THE MENTION OF BROWN, DION TREMBLES AS IF 285 GGBROW
SUDDENLY POSSESSED.
(HE SHAKES THE BARS OF HIS CELL DOOR TILL THE 244 HA APE
WHOLE TIER TREMBLES.
IT FAIR GIVES ME THE TREMBLES SITTIN' STILL IN 520 INZONE
'ERE.
(HIS VOICE GROWS HUSKY AND TREMBLES A LITTLE.) 36 JOURNE
(HIS VOICE TREMBLES, HIS EYES BEGIN TO FILL WITH 118 JOURNE
TEARS.)
SHE TREMBLES AND HER EXPRESSION BECOMES TERRIFIED.174 JOURNE
(HE TREMBLES TIMOUROUSLY--APPEALING TO LAZARUS) 343 LAZARU
(HIS VOICE TREMBLES IN SPITE OF HIMSELF) 346 LAZARU
SIMON TREMBLES WITH HIS EFFORT TO CONTROL HIMSELF.176 MANSNS
YOU JEST, BUT YOUR VOICE TREMBLES. 380 MARCOM
(HER VOICE TREMBLES) SO THAT WAS HIS REASON-- 90 MISBEG
(JEERINGLY, BUT HER VOICE TREMBLES) 118 MISBEG
HER VOICE TREMBLES WITH SURPRISING MEEKNESS) 121 MISBEG
(HER VOICE TREMBLES--BUT SHE GOES ON DETERMINEDLY)142 MISBEG
HIS HAND TREMBLES SO VIOLENTLY THAT WHEN HE 35 POET
ATTEMPTS TO RAISE THE GLASS
(HER VOICE TREMBLES.) MAY THE HERO OF TALAVERA 182 POET
REST IN PEACE/
(HIS VOICE TREMBLES.) 10 STRANG
(TRIUMPHANTLY) (HOW HIS HAND TREMBLES/..... 118 STRANG
(HIS VOICE TREMBLES. 190 STRANG

TREMBLIN'
THEY'RE TREMBLIN' AN' LONGIN' T' KISS ME, AN' YER 240 DESIRE
TEETH T' BITE/

TREMBLING
HE STANDS AGHAST, TREMBLING WITH DREAD. 538 *ILE
AND THE STACK OF DISHES RATTLES IN HIS TREMBLING 539 *ILE
HANDS.
(THEN, HER LIPS TREMBLING) RICHARD'S ALWAYS 258 AHWILD
WHISTLING THAT.
RICHARD OPENS IT WITH A TREMBLING EAGERNESS AND 273 AHWILD
READS.
(DOWNING HER PORT AT A GULP LIKE A DRINK OF 24 ANNA
WHISKY--HER LIPS TREMBLING)
(DEEPLY MOVED AND TROUBLED--FORCING A TREMBLING 51 ANNA
LAUGH)
(HER VOICE TREMBLING) THAT KISS WAS FOR GOOD-BY, 53 ANNA
MAI.
HIS VOICE TREMBLING WITH PASSION) 60 ANNA
SHE SPEAKS ALOUD TO HERSELF IN A TENSE, TREMBLING 67 ANNA
VOICE)
(HER LIPS TREMBLING PITIFULLY) THANKS/ 70 ANNA
(HER LIPS TREMBLING) I WISH ROBBIE WEREN'T GOING. 96 BEYOND
(HER REPRESSED VOICE TREMBLING) 126 BEYOND

TREMBLING (CONT'D.)
(HE GOES TO THE DOOR AND GENTLY PUSHES THE 128 BEYOND
TREMBLING RUTH AWAY FROM IT.
(SHE AGAIN HIDES HER FACE IN HER HANDS, HER BOWED 139 BEYOND
SHOULDERS TREMBLING.)
(THEN SHE HURRIES BACK, TREMBLING WITH FRIGHT) 166 BEYOND
(POINTING TO THE BODY--TREMBLING WITH THE VIOLENCE168 BEYOND
OF HIS RAGE)
THEN COMES BACK AND PUTS A TREMBLING HAND ON 490 CARDIF
YANK'S CHEST
YOU MUSTN'T LET THIS--YOU'RE ALL EXCITED AND 570 CROSS
TREMBLING, NAT.
SAW THERE THE ANSWER TO HIS PRAYER--IN A VOICE 565 DAYS
TREMBLING WITH HOPE AND JOY)
HE IS TREMBLING ALL OVER, IN A STRANGE STATE OF 243 DESIRE
TERROR.
EBEN HIDES HIS HEAD IN HIS HANDS, TREMBLING ALL 261 DESIRE
OVER AS IF HE HAD THE AGUE.
(FALLS TO HIS KNEES AS IF HE'D BEEN STRUCK--HIS 261 DESIRE
VOICE TREMBLING WITH HORROR)
(HE LOOKS INTO HER EYES AND FORCES A TREMBLING 267 DESIRE
SMILE)
(HER VOICE TREMBLING) IT'S *COUNT OF SOMETHING I 504 DIFRNT
GOT IN MY OWN HEAD--
HE COWERS, TREMBLING--THEN CRIES LIKE A FRIGHTENED445 DYNAMO
LITTLE BOY) MOTHER/
(HE LIGHTS A MATCH WITH TREMBLING FINGERS 445 DYNAMO
(GESTURE PUTS A TREMBLING HAND ON HIS HEAD-- 466 DYNAMO
PLEADINGLY)
(PITIFULLY--HER VOICE TREMBLING) 469 DYNAMO
JONES STANDS TREMBLING--THEN WITH A CERTAIN 192 EJONES
REASSURANCE)
(TURNING AWAY--HER VOICE STILL TREMBLING) 34 ELECTR
(LEANS TOWARD HER, HIS VOICE TREMBLING WITH DESIRE 52 ELECTR
(TREMBLING WITH GUILTY TERROR--STAMMERS.) 62 ELECTR
LAVINIA IS TREMBLING BUT HER FACE REMAINS HARD AND 92 ELECTR
EMOTIONLESS.
(HER VOICE TREMBLING) BUT I'M AFRAID I'M NOT MUCH111 ELECTR
TO
(AS HE HESITATES, TREMBLING VIOLENTLY, SHE GRABS 142 ELECTR
HIS ARM FIERCELY)
(STRANGELY SHAKEN AND TREMBLING--STAMMERS) 155 ELECTR
(HANDS HIM THE ENVELOPE--IN A TREMBLING VOICE) 164 ELECTR
IN A FAINT, TREMBLING VOICE) 167 ELECTR
AFTER A PAUSE--IN A TREMBLING VOICE) 173 ELECTR
IN A TREMBLING, EXPIRING VOICE) 272 GGBROW
(BROWN LETS GO OF HIM AND STAGGERS BACK TO HIS 299 GGBROW
CHAIR, PALE AND TREMBLING.)
(HIS VOICE TREMBLING) THEN I HAVE MADE YOU 309 GGBROW
HAPPY--HAPPIER THAN EVER BEFORE--
A QUESTION IS TREMBLING ON HIS PARTED LIPS, 35 HUGHIE
(GROWS RIGID--HIS VOICE TREMBLING WITH REPRESSED 677 ICEMAN
ANGER)
(THEN IN A SUDDEN FURY, HIS VOICE TREMBLING WITH 688 ICEMAN
HATRED)
(MOPPING HIS BROW WITH A TREMBLING HAND) 523 INZONE
(HIS VOICE TREMBLING WITH RAGE. 527 INZONE
(HE CHOKES HUSKILY, HIS VOICE TREMBLING WITH RAGE,149 JOURNE
(HIS VOICE TREMBLING WITH SUPPRESSED FURY.) 170 JOURNE
BUT AT THE FIRST SIGHT OF HIS FACE HE STOPS IN HIS308 LAZARU
TRACKS, TREMBLING.
(TREMBLING, IN A QUEER AGITATION) 308 LAZARU
(THE SENATORS ARE NOW TREMBLING. 317 LAZARU
PULLING TOWARD THE LION WITH A TREMBLING HAND.) 327 LAZARU
(TREMBLING BUT WITH A PRETENSE OF CARELESSNESS) 340 LAZARU
(HER VOICE TREMBLING) EVEN IF GOD HAS TAKEN OUR 347 LAZARU
LITTLE ONES--
(HIS VOICE TREMBLING A BIT) FAREWELL, BODY OF 362 LAZARU
MIRIAM.
PULLING HER HAND FROM THE DOOR, AND STANDS DAZED 165 MANSNS
AND TREMBLING.
HE REACHES OUT AND TAKES ONE OF HER HANDS AND SHE 177 MANSNS
STOPS, TREMBLING.
(TREMBLING) SSST/ I HAVE A FOREBODING OF EVIL. 350 MARCOM
THE OTHERS VISIBLY TREMBLING WITH SUPERSTITIOUS 352 MARCOM
HORROR.)
(RISING--PALE AND TREMBLING) 361 MARCOM
(THE TWO ELDER POLOS ARE BOWED TO THE GROUND, 392 MARCOM
TREMBLING WITH APPREHENSION.
(HE GOES GRANDLY, PRECEDED HURRIEDLY BY THE 383 MARCOM
TREMBLING NICOLO AND MAFFEO.
SPEAKING TO THE DEAD GIRL SOFTLY AS HE DOES SO-- 437 MARCOM
WITH A TREMBLING SMILE)
HE DISAPPEARS ON LEFT, BUT A SECOND LATER HIS 64 MISBEG
VOICE, TREMBLING WITH ANGER,
(LOOKS STRICKEN AND BEWILDERED--HER VOICE 89 MISBEG
TREMBLING)
HIS HAND IS TREMBLING SO VIOLENTLY HE CANNOT LIGHT111 MISBEG
THE CIGARETTE.)
(DEEPLY STIRRED, IN SPITE OF HERSELF--HER VOICE 129 MISBEG
TREMBLING)
(SHE FORCES A TREMBLING SMILE--FAINTLY) 136 MISBEG
(FORCING A TREMBLING ECHO OF HER PLAYFUL TONE) 142 MISBEG
DESPITE HIS TREMBLING HAND HE MANAGES TO POUR A 37 POET
DRINK
ROUGHLY, HIS VOICE TREMBLING.) 164 POET
(BENTLEY PASSES HIS TREMBLING HAND ALL OVER LUKE, 595 ROPE
FEELING OF HIS ARMS.
THE OLD MAN TOTTERS OVER TO HIM, STRETCHING OUT A 595 ROPE
TREMBLING HAND.
HER VOICE TREMBLING WITH THE EFFORT TO KEEP IT IN 16 STRANG
CONTROL--ICILY)
SOOTHES HER WITH UNCERTAIN TREMBLING WORDS) 43 STRANG
(BENDS DOWN, PATS HER HEAD WITH TREMBLING HANDS, 43 STRANG
(BENDING DOWN FOR ANOTHER SHEET, HIS VOICE 77 STRANG
TREMBLING WITH TERROR)
(HE BENDS DOWN, TREMBLING ALL OVER, TO PICK UP 77 STRANG
ANOTHER PIECE OF PAPER.)

TREMBLING

TREMBLING (CONT'D.)
HIS VOICE TREMBLING A LITTLE WITH SUPPRESSED 123 STRANG
EMOTION)
(BAFFLEDLY--HIS LIPS TREMBLING) 142 STRANG
TREMBLING WITH RAGE, STAMMERS) 142 STRANG
THEN IN A TREMBLING VOICE OF DEEPLY WOUNDED 150 STRANG
AFFECTION)
(HIS VOICE TREMBLING) I DIDN'T REALLY REALIZE HE 184 STRANG
WAS GONE--
HE STANDS THERE TRANSFIXED, DISORGANIZED, 450 WELDED
TREMBLING ALL OVER.)
(TREMBLING ALL OVER WITH THE VIOLENCE OF HIS 458 WELDED
PASSION)
(TREMBLING WITH RAGE) I'LL NEVER FORGET YOU SAID 458 WELDED
THAT?
YOU'RE TREMBLING. 462 WELDED
(HE STARTS, PASSES A TREMBLING HAND THROUGH HIS 471 WELDED
HAIR BEWILDEREDLY
AND FORCES A TREMBLING, MOCKING SMILE) 476 WELDED
THEN, AS IF UNCONSCIOUSLY, FALTERINGLY, WITH 480 WELDED
TREMBLING SMILES,
TREMBLINGLY
(TREMBLINGLY) YES, SIR. 539 'ILE
(THEN TREMBLINGLY) YOU SAID--YOU'D LET ME-- 287 AHWILD
(HE KISSES HER TREMBLINGLY AND FOR A MOMENT THEIR 287 AHWILD
LIPS REMAIN TOGETHER.
(SHRINKING AWAY--TREMBLINGLY) 264 DESIRE
EMMA OARS TREMBLINGLY AT HER CHEEKS WITH A 534 DIFRNT
HANDKERCHIEF.
(TREMBLINGLY) OH, GORRY, I'SE SKEERED IN DIS 200 EJONES
PLACE/
(THEN TO THOSE ABOUT HIM--TREMBLINGLY) 362 MARCOM
(AFTER A PAUSE--TREMBLINGLY) 386 MARCOM
THEN, AFTER A MOMENT, HE PASSES HIS HAND OVER HER 438 MARCOM
FACE--TREMBLINGLY--
(SHE DOES SO TREMBLINGLY) LEAD HIM TO THE HOUSE. 584 ROPE
(THINKING TREMBLINGLY) (HERE... 42 STRANG
(TREMBLINGLY NOW-- 88 STRANG
(TREMBLINGLY) SAMMY/ 109 STRANG
(IN A RAGE--TREMBLINGLY) THEN--HERE'S WHAT--I 150 STRANG
THINK OF YOU/
TREMBLINGLY UNCERTAIN WHETHER TO RUN AND HIDE 480 WELDED
FROM,
TREMENDOUS
HIS FACE BETRAYS THE TREMENDOUS STRUGGLE GOING ON 549 'ILE
WITHIN HIM.
(MAKING A TREMENDOUS EFFORT TO CONTROL HIS TEMPER)202 AHWILD
(STARTS TO DANCE, WHICH HE DOES VERY WELL AND WITH251 DESIRE
TREMENDOUS VIGOR.
(THERE IS A TREMENDOUS CRASH OF THUNDER. 452 DYNAMO
ALL ARE HAIRY-CHESTED, WITH LONG ARMS OF 207 HA APE
TREMENDOUS POWER, AND LOW,
HE TAKES A TREMENDOUS GULP AT ONE OF THEM. 209 HA APE
THE BAR BENDS LIKE A LICORICE STICK UNDER HIS 244 HA APE
TREMENDOUS STRENGTH.
IT WOULD BE OF TREMENDOUS ADVANTAGE TO OUR MILLS-- 48 MANSNS
AND WHAT A TREMENDOUS BARGAIN I HAVE GOT/ 66 MANSNS
MUSIC FROM FULL CHINESE AND TARTAR BANDS CRASHES 377 MARCOM
UP TO A TREMENDOUS BLARING.
THE DESTRUCTION OF PROPERTY AND LOSS OF LIFE WOULD395 MARCOM
BE TREMENDOUS/
LET THERE BE FOOD IN TREMENDOUS AMOUNTS/ 418 MARCOM
HIS LIPS MOVE CONVULSIVELY AS HE MAKES A 596 ROPE
TREMENDOUS EFFORT TO UTTER WORDS.)
TREMENDOUS EFFORT! 135 STRANG
(MAKING A TREMENDOUS VISIBLE EFFORT HE KISSES HER 473 WELDED
ON THE LIPS.
TREMENS
I WAS ON THE VERGE OF DELIRIUM TREMENS/ 284 AHWILD
I RUNNED AWAY WHEN ME OLD LADY CROAKED WIT DE 234 HA APE
TREMENS.
I'D KNOW I HAD DELIRIUM TREMENS/ 601 ICEMAN
TREMOR
HER HANDS HAVE A NERVOUS TREMOR. 517 DAYS
THERE IS NO TREMOR IN THEM NOW.) 103 JOURNE
TREMORS
AND STRAINED IN A CHEERY EFFORT TO OVERCOME ITS 191 EJONES
OWN TREMORS.)
TREMULOUS
AND INSTEAD--(HER VOICE GROWS TREMULOUS) ALL I 545 'ILE
FIND IS ICE AND COLD--
(SHE LIFTS UP HER HEAD AND LOOKS INTO HIS EYES 91 BEYOND
WITH A TREMULOUS SMILE)
(HER VOICE SINKS TO A TREMULOUS, TENDER WHISPER AS139 BEYOND
SHE FINISHES.)
TREMULOUS WAIL OF DESPAIR THAT REACHES A CERTAIN 199 EJONES
PITCH, UNBEARABLY ACUTE,
TREMULOUSLY
(TREMULOUSLY--GRATEFUL FOR HIS SOLICITUDE) 406 MARCOM
TRENCHES
THE NEXT MORNING I WAS IN THE TRENCHES. 95 ELECTR
TREND
(CONTINUING THE TREND OF HIS THOUGHTS AS IF HE HAD229 HA APE
NEVER BEEN INTERRUPTED--
TRESPASS
(HE ADDRESSES SARA.) HOW DARE YOU TRESPASS HERES 186 MANSNS
TRESPASSERS
(BITTERLY) WE'RE TRESPASSERS 'ERE. 233 HA APE
TRESPASSIN'
THEY'RE STRICT ABOUT TRESPASSIN'. 7 ELECTR
AND IF EZRA'S WIFE STARTS TO RUN YOU OFF FUR 8 ELECTR
TRESPASSIN',
UH, DON'T GIT IT IN YOUR HEADS I TAKE STOCK IN 135 ELECTR
SPIRITS TRESPASSIN' ROUND
TRESPASSING
DOES IT GIVE THEM THE PRIVILEGE OF TRESPASSING. 16 ELECTR
AND HE'D BE DAMNED IF HE'D STAND FOR A STANDARD 25 JOURNE
OIL THEIR TRESPASSING.

TRESPASSING (CONT'D.)
DO YOU NOT KNOW THERE IS A TERRIBLE PUNISHMENT FOR192 MANSNS
TRESPASSING IN MY DOMAINS
AND I'LL BE DAMNED IF I'LL STAND FOR A STANDARD 63 MISBEG
OIL MAN TRESPASSING/
TRESSES
THINE EYES BLIND ME, THY TRESSES BURN ME, 205 AHWILD
TRIAL
OH, BELIEVE ME, I'LL SEE TO IT THAT COMES OUT IF 91 ELECTR
ANYTHING EVER GETS TO A TRIAL/
SUCH A PUBLIC DISGRACE AS A MURDER TRIAL WOULD BE/ 91 ELECTR
WOULD BE DRAGGED THROUGH THE HORROR OF A MURDER 97 ELECTR
TRIAL/
THEY'LL BE COMING UP FOR TRIAL SOON, AND THERE'S 584 ICEMAN
NO CHANCE FOR THEM.
(SHE SMILES MOCKINGLY) I KNOW WHAT A TRIAL IT'S 6 MISBEG
BEEN TO YOU, MIKE,
REGARD IT AS AN INTERLUDE, OF TRIAL AND 199 STRANG
PREPARATION, SAY,
TRIALS
WE'VE BEEN THROUGH THE SAME FRIGHTFUL TRIALS. 502 DAYS
AFTER ENDURING BITTER TRIALS, AND NUMBERLESS 111 MANSNS
DISAPPOINTMENTS,
TRIANGLE
THE FORWARD TRIANGLE CUT OFF BY THE ROAD IS A 81 BEYOND
SECTION OF A FIELD FROM THE DARK
THE SIDES OF WHICH ALMOST MEET AT THE FAR END TO 477 CARDIF
FORM A TRIANGLE.
CROUCHING ON HIS HAUNCHES AT THE REAR OF THE 191 EJONES
TRIANGLE.
USE ME TO ARRANGE A CONVENIENT TRIANGLE FOR 38 STRANG
HERS...))
TRIANGULAR
FENCING IN A SMALL TRIANGULAR CLEARING. 190 EJONES
(HE STEPS JUST TO THE REAR OF THE TRIANGULAR 191 EJONES
CLEARING
ONLY YOU MUST ADMIT THESE TRIANGULAR SCENES ARE, 96 STRANG
TO SAY THE LEAST, HUMILIATING.
TRIBE
THE HULL TRIBE CHASED ME. 251 DESIRE
THE DEVIL TAKE ALL YOUR TRIBE, SAY I. 118 POET
TRIBUNE
CAESAR IS CAESAR THE AUGUST ONE PRINCE OF THE 315 LAZARU
SENATE TRIBUNE OVER TRIBUNES
TRIBUNES
CAESAR IS CAESAR THE AUGUST ONE PRINCE OF THE 315 LAZARU
SENATE TRIBUNE OVER TRIBUNES
TRIBUTE
(HE STOPS TO PAY TRIBUTE OF A SIGH TO THE MEMORY 29 HUGHIE
OF BRAVE DAYS
I ASK, AS A FITTING TRIBUTE TO HIS CHARACTER, 418 MARCOM
A ROOM THAT IS A TRIBUTE TO NINA'S GOOD TASTE. 137 STRANG
TRICK
SPITEFUL TRICK LIKE THAT--NO MATTER WHAT HE DID TO204 AHWILD
ME
BECAUSE IT SEEMED SORT OF A SNEAKING TRICK, 214 AHWILD
OAT'S YOUR DIRTY TRICK, DAMN OLE DAVIL, YOU/ 40 ANNA
AY'M OLE BIRD MAYBE, BUT AY BET AY SHOW HIM TRICK 43 ANNA
OR TWO.
THAN A COWARDLY TRICK/ 495 DAYS
AND I SEE THROUGH YOUR STUPID TRICK--TO USE THE 559 DAYS
FEAR OF DEATH TO--
I SEE YER GAME NOW--THE SAME OLD SNEAKIN' TRICK-- 261 DESIRE
SAY, THAT WAS A DIRTY TRICK/ 465 DYNAMO
YES, YER TURNED THE BLEEDIN' TRICK, ALL RIGHT. 178 EJONES
IT'S A COWARD'S TRICK/ 41 ELECTR
IT WAS A DIRTY TRICK. 295 GGBROWN
A DIRTY TRICK ON MY CLASSMATES, INSPIRED BY 595 ICEMAN
REVENGE. I FEAR.
HELL OF A TRICK TO GO DEAD ON YOU LIKE THIS. 625 ICEMAN
WHO'D DO A DIRTY TRICK LIKE THAT? 521 IHCOME
IT'S A ROTTEN TRICK THE WAY HE KEEPS MEALS 61 JOURNE
WAITING.
(AMUSEDLY.) OH, WE'LL PLAY JAMIE'S TRICK ON HIM. 100 JOURNE
JAMIE'S BEEN AWAY AND HE WOULDN'T OVERDO HIS TRICK116 JOURNE
LIKE THIS, ANYWAY.
IT WAS ONLY BY SOME MAGICIAN'S TRICK 328 LAZARU
A TRICK? 340 LAZARU
AND I MUST ALWAYS DOUBT THAT IT WAS NOT SOME 351 LAZARU
TRICK--
THERE IS NO TRICK NOW, SARA. 53 MANSNS
AH, WHAT TRICK ARE YOU UP TO NOWS 53 MANSNS
IF YOU'RE NOT LYING TO PLAY ME SOME TRICK/ 54 MANSNS
TRICK SARA INTO BEING AN ACCESSORY IN THE MURDER 73 MANSNS
OF THAT OLD SELF
WELL, I WOULDN'T PUT IT PAST THE OLD MAN TO TRY 9 MISBEG
ANY TRICK.
AND SOMETIMES AN OLD TRICK IS BEST 22 MISBEG
TRICK LIKE THAT ON JIM/ 22 MISBEG
YOU LIKE JIM AND YOU'D NEVER PLAY A DIRTY TRICK ON 23 MISBEG
HIM,
I WOULDN'T CALL IT A DIRTY TRICK ON HIM TO GET YOU 24 MISBEG
FOR A WIFE.
(STARES AT HIM) YOU OLD DIVIL, YOU'VE ALWAYS A 26 MISBEG
TRICK HIDDEN BEHIND YOUR TRICKS,
THAT WAS THE REAL TRICK. 26 MISBEG
WHAT THE HELL D'YOU MEAN BY YOUR CONTEMPTIBLE 62 MISBEG
TRICK OF BREAKING DOWN YOUR FENCE
ANYWAY, I WANTED TO FIND OUT WHAT TRICK HE HAD UP 85 MISBEG
HIS SLEEVE.
I TOLD YOU I DIDN'T CARE HOW DIRTY A TRICK-- 92 MISBEG
AND DON'T WORRY I CAN'T DO MY PART OF THE TRICK. 94 MISBEG
BY MONEYLENDIN' AND SQUEEZIN' TENANTS AND EVERY 11 POET
MANNER OF TRICK.
(TENSELY.) WHAT TRICK DO YOU MEANS 60 POET
THERE'S ALWAYS ONE LAST TRICK TO GET HIM THROUGH 60 POET
HIS HONOR/
WHO DID A DIRTY TRICK LIKE THAT? 78 POET

1705

TRICK (CONT'D.)

TRICKS
DIDN'T I GUESS THAT WOULD BE HER TRICK/ 109 POET
OF COURSE, IF YOU TRICK HARFORD INTO GETTING YOU 109 POET
OF COURSE, IF YOU TRICK HARFORD INTO GETTING YOU 114 POET
WITH CHILD.
ON HOW TO TRICK SIMON. 115 POET
HE'S SET IN HIS PROUD, NOBLE WAYS, BUT SHE'LL FIND173 POET
THE RIGHT TRICK/
THAT'S WHAT'LL LEARN YUH A CUTE TRICK OR TWO. 593 ROPE
I KNOW A TRICK OR TWO ABOUT MAKIN' PEOPLE TELL 600 ROPE
WHAT THEY DON'T WANTER.
IT'S SOME TRICK.....)) 37 STRANG
NOW MARRYING SAM OUGHT TO DO THE TRICK. 37 STRANG
WHAT A DEVILISH, COWARDLY TRICK TO PLAY ON POOR 124 STRANG
UNSUSPECTING SAM/...))
IT WAS A ROTTEN, DIRTY TRICK/ 194 STRANG
(HASTILY) NO TRICK, SHIPMATE/ 499 VOYAGE

TRICKED
HE TELLS HER IT WAS THE PRIESTS TRICKED HIM INTO 14 POET
MARRYING HER.

TRICKERY
THERE'S SOME DIVIL'S TRICKERY IN IT. 76 ANNA
BUT THIS DIVIL'S TRICKERY IN THE DARKK--(HE STARTS524 INZONE
FOR SMITTY'S BUNK)

TRICKIN'
YE'RE A WHORE--A DAMN TRICKIN' WHORE/ 256 DESIRE
(BROKENLY) AY-EH--AN' YE WAS TRICKIN' ME/ 258 DESIRE

TRICKLE
AND WHEN IT RAINS THEIR TEARS TRICKLE DOWN 202 DESIRE
MONOTONOUSLY AND ROT ON THE SHINGLES.

TRICKLES
TRICKLES OF DRIED BLOOD RUN DOWN TO HIS JAW. 152 POET

TRICKS
AND SEE TO IT THEY DON'T TRY NONE OF THEIR 545 'ILE
SKULKIN' TRICKS.
DAT OLE DAVIL SEA MAKE DEM CRAZY FOOLS WITH HER 21 ANNA
DIRTY TRICKS.
(SPITTING DISGUSTEDLY) FOG'S VORST ONE OF HER 26 ANNA
DIRTY TRICKS, PY YINGO/
OR ANY OF THE BLACK TRICKS THAT A LANDLUBBER'D 48 ANNA
WASTE HIS LIFE ON.
IT'S HER DIRTY TRICKS/ 62 ANNA
AY DON'T KNOW--IT'S DAT FUNNY VAY OLE DAVIL SEA DO 78 ANNA
HER VORST DIRTY TRICKS, YES.
STILL UP ILL UP TO YOUR OLD TRICKS, YOU OLD 131 BEYOND
BEGGAR/
SHE KNOWS YER TRICKS--SHE'LL BE TOO MUCH FUR YE-- 255 DESIRE
SHE WANTS THE FARM HER'N--
OF ALL THE DIRTY TRICKS/ 431 DYNAMO
LET DEM TRY DEIR HEATHER TRICKS. 185 EJONES
YOU'LL DAMN SOON STOP YOUR TRICKS WHEN YOU KNOW 152 ELECTR
WHAT I'VE BEEN WRITING/
MORE CIRCUS CON TRICKS/ 608 ICEMAN
UP TO YOUR OLD TRICKS, EH$ 717 ICEMAN
IF HE PULLS ANY RUBBER-HOSE TRICKS, YOU LET ME 718 ICEMAN
KNOW/
IF YOU WANTS TO TRY YOUR DIRTY SPYIN' TRICKS ON US525 INZONE
I'M ON TO YOUR TRICKS. 65 JOURNE
NOW I TAKE HIM OUT UNDER THE SKY, WHERE I CAN 360 LAZARU
WATCH HIS MONKEY TRICKS.
(FORCING A LAUGH.) I SUPPOSE I AM TOO OLD A DOG 152 MANSNS
TO LEARN NEW TRICKS
UNTIL HE FINALLY TRICKS ME INTO UNLOCKING THE 163 MANSNS
DOOR, TAKING HIS HAND--
(STARES AT HIM) YOU OLD DIVIL, YOU'VE ALWAYS A 26 MISBEG
TRICK HIDDEN BEHIND YOUR TRICKS.
HE ALWAYS SAW THROUGH YOUR TRICKS. 26 MISBEG
THAT'LL SHOW HIM TWO CAN PLAY AT TRICKS/ 95 MISBEG
AND IF ALL OTHER TRICKS FAIL, 60 POET
I WANTED TO LEARN WHAT TRICKS SHE MIGHT BE UP TO, 79 POET
SO I'LL BE ABLE TO FIGHT THEM.
AND FOR LYIN' TRICKS TO SWINDLE THE BLOODY FOOLS 170 POET
OF GINTRY.
I SEEN YER A-PLAYIN' YER SNEAKIN' TRICKS, BUT YER 508 VOYAGE
CAN'T FOOL JOE.

TRIED
I'VE TRIED TO A COUPLE OF TIMES. 268 AHWILD
BUT I'M NOT SORRY I TRIED IT ONCE-- 271 AHWILD
IN ALL MY TIME I TRIED NEVER TO SPLIT 11 ANNA
I TRIED TO CUT IT OUT-- BUT-- 51 ANNA
I S'POSE IF I TRIED TO TELL YOU I WASN'T--THAT-- 59 ANNA
YOU KNOW HOW HARD I'VE TRIED TO KEEP THINGS GOING 123 BEYOND
IN SPITE OF BAD LUCK--
ROB SHUT ME UP WITH ALMOST THE SAME WORDS WHEN I 139 BEYOND
TRIED SPEAKING TO HIM ABOUT IT.
I TRIED SPECULATION. 156 BEYOND
THEN WHEN THE DOCTOR EXAMINED ME, I KNEW--ALTHOUGH160 BEYOND
HE TRIED TO LIE ABOUT IT.
(SLOWLY) I WOULDN'T KNOW HOW TO FEEL LOVE, EVEN 165 BEYOND
IF I TRIED. ANY MORE.
SHE TRIED TO LEND ME HALF A CROWN WHEN I WAS BROKE489 CARDIF
THERE LAST TRIP.
I DON'T S'POSE YOU EVER TRIED THATS 468 CARIBE
WHY, I REMEMBER ONE ARTICLE WHERE YOU ACTUALLY 497 DAYS
TRIED TO PROVE
HE ORGANIZED AN ATHEISTS' CLUB--OR TRIED TO--AND 502 DAYS
ALMOST GOT FIRED FOR IT.
I TRIED TO LOSE MY DREAD IN PRAYER--AND MY GUILT. 507 DAYS
HE HAS TRIED NOBLY TO BE FAIR. 520 DAYS
HE TRIED TO ESCAPE THEM IN WORK. 536 DAYS
I TRIED FUR T' STOP HIM. 233 DESIRE
SHE TRIED T' BE HARD. 237 DESIRE
YOU AIN'T TRIED ME YET. 508 DIFRNT
I TRIED TO MAKE HER GIT BACK TO LAND AT FUST--BUT 515 DIFRNT
SHE WOULDN'T GO.
THERE'S A LOT OF HARD GUYS IN THE ARMY HAVE TRIED 544 DIFRNT
TO GET FUNNY WITH ME TILL I

TRIED (CONT'D.)

AND I TRIED EVERYWHERE TO GET A JOB IN A PLANT BUT461 DYNAMU
NEVER HAD ANY LUCK.
I TRIED YOUR DOOR--BUT YOU HAD LOCKED YOURSELF IN. 16 ELECTR
(SHAKEN--DEFENSIVELY) I TRIED TO LOVE YOU. 31 ELECTR
YOU'VE TRIED TO BECOME THE WIFE OF YOUR FATHER AND 33 ELECTR
THE MOTHER OF ORIN/
I TRIED MY DARNDEST TO PUT HER OFF THE COURSE BY 37 ELECTR
GIVING HER SOME SOFT SOAP--
I TRIED NOT TO HATE ORIN. 55 ELECTR
(TENSELY) AS IF I HADN'T TRIED/ 72 ELECTR
TRIED TO GET HER MOTHER HANGED OUT OF HATRED AND 92 ELECTR
JEALOUSY/
I'VE TRIED TO TRACE TO ITS SECRET HIDING PLACE IN 153 ELECTR
THE MANNON PAST
HE FOUGHT WITH MOTHER LAST NIGHT WHEN SHE TRIED TO173 ELECTR
TALK TO HIM--
WHY HAS HE TRIED TO STEAL CYBEL, AS HE ONCE TRIED 298 GGBROW
TO STEAL MARGARETS
HE TRIED TO APOLOGIZE, BUT I SHUT HIM UP QUICK. 26 HUGHIE
HE FLASHED IT LIKE HE FORGOT AND DEN TRIED TO HIDE583 ICEMAN
IT QUICK.
WHEN THEY TRIED TO MURDER EACH OTHER. 593 ICEMAN
ALTHOUGH SHE'D TRIED TO KID ME ALONG IT WASN'T SG.646 ICEMAN
I TRIED TO WISE DE REST UP DEM UP TO STAY CLEAR OF698 ICEMAN
HIM.
AND KNEW HE'D LAUGH AT ME IF I TRIED THE GOOD 34 JOURNE
ADVICE, OLDER BROTHER STUFF.
IN THAT FILTHY OLD SUIT I'VE TRIED TO MAKE HIM 43 JOURNE
THROW AWAY.
JAMES/ I TRIED SO HARD/ I TRIED SO HARD/ 69 JOURNE
FOR A TIME AFTER MY MARRIAGE I TRIED TO KEEP UP MY104 JOURNE
MUSIC.
I TRIED TO PUNCH HIM IN THE NOSE. 118 JOURNE
BUT I DON'T THINK YOU'VE EVER TRIED TO UNDERSTAND.118 JOURNE
HE'S ALWAYS TRIED TO DO THAT. 119 JOURNE
THAT DRUNKEN LOAFER HAS TRIED TO PICK THE LOCK 121 JOURNE
WITH A PIECE OF WIRE.
I HAVE TRIED TO MAKE ALLOWANCES FOR MYSELF 145 JOURNE
I'VE TRIED TO BE FAIR TO YOU BECAUSE I KNEW WHAT 145 JOURNE
YOU'D BEEN UP AGAINST AS A KID.
I'VE TRIED TO MAKE ALLOWANCES. 145 JOURNE
I'VE TRIED TO FEEL LIKE MAMA THAT YOU CAN'T HELP 145 JOURNE
BEING WHAT YOU ARE
PARTICULARLY THE TIME I TRIED TO COMMIT SUICIDE AT147 JOURNE
JIMMIE THE PRIEST'S.
I CRIED, TOO, THOUGH I TRIED HARD NOT TO. 148 JOURNE
I COULDN'T TOUCH WHAT I TRIED TO TELL YOU JUST 154 JOURNE
NOW.
THE FRON STEPS TRIED TO TRAMPLE ON ME. 155 JOURNE
I'LL BET OLD GASPARD HASN'T TRIED TO KEEP YOU OFF 157 JOURNE
BOOZE.
=SPEAKIN' IN GENERAL, I 'AVE TRIED 'EM ALL, 161 JOURNE
I THINK HE TRIED ONCE TO FIND ME LISTED ON THE 11 MANSNS
PROFIT SIDE OF THE LEDGER.
BUT I HAVE TRIED TO MAKE IT REAL TO MYSELF. 29 MANSNS
I TRIED TO BELIEVE YOUR EXCUSE THAT YOU DIDN'T 83 MANSNS
WANT TO KEEP ME AWAKE.
WHAT HE HAS TRIED TO DO HAS BEEN SO OBVIOUSLY 126 MANSNS
CHILDISH AND FUTILE.
(BEWILDEREDLY) I NEVER BELIEVED PEOPLE--SANE 415 MARCOM
PEOPLE--EVER SERIOUSLY TRIED--
WHEN EVERYONE KNOWS ANY MAN WHO TRIED TO MAKE FREE 19 MISBEG
WITH YOU.
AND THEN YOU SLAPPED THEM GROGGY WHEN THEY TRIED 135 MISBEG
FOR MORE.
NO MATTER HOW I TRIED NOT TO, I'D MAKE IT LIKE ALL140 MISBEG
THE OTHER NIGHTS--
I TRIED TO. 145 MISBEG
YET I TRIED MY BEST TO EDUCATE YOU, AFTER WE CAME 41 POET
TO AMERICA.
AND I TRIED, TOO, BUT-- 41 POET
I HAVE TRIED TO TEACH THE WAITRESS NOT TO SNATCH 98 POET
PLATES FROM THE TABLE
I HAVE TRIED TO MAKE YOU ONE. 114 POET
THOUGH I'D TRIED HARD TO LEAVE IT BEHIND. 143 POET
THAT'S THE WAY HE'S BEEN ALL THE WAY BACK WHEN I 153 POET
TRIED TO PERSUADE HIM.
WHEN HE'D SAID THAT, THE FLUNKY TRIED TO SLAM THE 155 POET
DOOR IN OUR FACES,
YOU KNOW I TRIED TO STOP-- 156 POET
TRIED TO HIDE IT... 24 STRANG
YOU'VE NEVER TRIED TO SEE HIM, NINA/ 27 STRANG
(THINKING GLUMLY) (I WON'T TELL HIM I TRIED FOR 30 STRANG
FLYING SERVICE...
I TRIED HARD TO PRAY TO THE MODERN SCIENCE GOD. 41 STRANG
I HAVE ALWAYS TRIED TO HELP HIM...)) 86 STRANG
NINA HAS TRIED TO TAKE THE CURSE OF OFFENSIVE, 90 STRANG
SHE'S TRIED... 92 STRANG
I TRIED NOT TO THIS TIME--BUT I HAD TO, NINA/ 131 STRANG
I'VE BROKEN WITH HER, RUN AWAY, TRIED TO FORGET 139 STRANG
HER...
DEAR HUSBAND, YOU HAVE TRIED TO MAKE ME HAPPY, 183 STRANG
YOU COULDN'T BE UNFAIR TO ANYONE IF YOU TRIED/ 189 STRANG
I TRIED TO MAKE YOU SEE--THE TRUTH--THAT THOSE 458 WELDED
EXPERIENCES HAD
I TRIED TO FIRE THEM--THOUGHT I HAD--BUT WHEN YOU 467 WELDED
CAME TONIGHT--
(WITH A HARSH LAUGH) ARE YOU FORGETTING WE TRIED 486 WELDED
THAT ONCE TONIGHTS

TRIES

WHICH HE IMMEDIATELY TRIES TO COVER UP WITH A 207 AHWILD
SUPERIOR CARELESSNESS)
BUT AFTER TWO TRIES IN WHICH HE FINDS IT DIFFICULT224 AHWILD
TO LOCATE HIS MOUTH,
(RICHARD TURNS FURIOUSLY AND TRIES TO PUNCH THE 247 AHWILD
BARTENDER.)

TRIES

TRIES (CONT'D.)
(SHE TRIES TO JUMP OUT OF THE BOAT BUT HE HOLDS HER BACK. 284 AHWILD
AS SHE HEARS HIM COMING, ANNA HASTILY DRIES HER EYES; TRIES TO SMILE. 24 ANNA
(HE TRIES TO KISS HER. 52 ANNA
(SHE TAKES THE TICKET FROM HER DRESS AND TRIES TO HOLD IT BEFORE HIS EYES) 71 ANNA
(SHE TRIES TO PUT A FINGER ACROSS HIS LIPS, BUT HE107 BEYOND TWISTS HIS HEAD AWAY.)
(PADDY TRIES TO REACH HIM BUT THE OTHERS KEEP THEM461 CARIBE APART.)
SHE TRIES IN VAIN TO KEEP THE MEN QUIET. 470 CARIBE
IN A VOICE HE TRIES TO MAKE CASUAL BUT WHICH IS 494 DAYS INDEFINABLY SINISTER)
SUDDENLY OVERCOME BY A WAVE OF DROWSINESS HE TRIES555 DAYS IN VAIN TO FIGHT BACK)
(TRIES TO HOLD HIM BACK) YOU CAN'T GO THERE NOW, 560 DAYS JACK.
(TRIES TO BAR HIS PATH) NO/ 563 DAYS
HE LOOKS AROUND FURTIVELY AND TRIES TO SEE--OR 228 DESIRE HEAR--
(HE TRIES TO THROW CABOT ASIDE. 255 DESIRE
(SHE TRIES TO KISS HIM BUT HE PUSHES HER VIOLENTLY256 DESIRE AWAY
AT FUST, CALEB TRIES TO TREAT HER GENTLE AND ARGY 503 DIFRNT WITH HER TO GO BACK,
AND CATCHES UP TO HER AND TRIES TO CLIMB ABOARD. 503 DIFRNT
(HE TRIES TO KISS HER.) 506 DIFRNT
(SHE TRIES TO THROW HER ARMS ABOUT HIM TO STOP HIS543 DIFRNT GOING.
(HE TRIES TO KISS HER.) 433 DYNAMO
SHE RUNS TO HIM AND TRIES TO PUT HER ARMS AROUND 452 DYNAMO HIM)
(HIS FATHER SQUEALS WITH TERROR AND TRIES TO 453 DYNAMO BREAK AWAY FROM HIS HOLD.
(SHE PUTS HER ARMS AROUND HIM PITYINGLY AND TRIES 482 DYNAMO TO HUG HIM TO HER)
HIS EYES POP OUT, HE TRIES TO GET TO HIS FEET AND 194 EJONES FLY, BUT SINKS BACK.
(HE TRIES TO TAKE HER HAND. 24 ELECTR
SHE TRIES TO KEEP HER VOICE INDIFFERENT BUT IT 30 ELECTR TREMBLES A LITTLE.)
AND IF HE TRIES TO STOP ME--/ 38 ELECTR
A PAUSE--THEN HE SAYS IN A VOICE THAT HE TRIES TO 49 ELECTR MAKE ORDINARY)
HE TRIES TO CALL FOR HELP BUT HIS VOICE FADES TO A 62 ELECTR WHEEZY WHISPER)
IN A TONE SHE VAINLY TRIES TO MAKE KINDLY AND 77 ELECTR PERSUASIVE)
(HE TRIES TO FORCE A LAUGH--THEN SHAMEFACEDLY) 83 ELECTR
(SHE TRIES THE DOORKNOB, AND FINDING THE DOOR 100 ELECTR LOCKED,
BUT THIS IS THE MOST IMPORTANT, IF SHE TRIES TO 160 ELECTR MARRY PETER--
(SHE TRIES TO GO BUT LAVINIA KEEPS DIRECTLY 163 ELECTR BETWEEN HER AND THE DOOR.)
(SHE TRIES AWKWARDLY TO SIDLE TOWARD THE DOOR.) 163 ELECTR
HE TRIES TO MAKE CONVERSATION) 262 GGBROW
(HE TRIES CLUMSILY TO KISS HER.) 263 GGBROW
(HE TRIES TO KISS HER BUT SHE JUMPS TO HER FEET 268 GGBROW WITH A FRIGHTENED CRY HOLDING UP
WHICH HE TRIES TO HOLD THROUGHOUT THE SCENE) 294 GGBROW
THE TRIES TO FIGHT BUT IS CLUBBED TO THE PAVEMENT 239 HA APE AND FALLEN UPON.
POST ON THE CORNER AND TRIES TO PULL IT UP FOR A 239 HA APE CLUB.
THE NIGHT CLERK'S FOREHEAD PUCKERS PERSPIRINGLY AS 30 HUGHIE HE TRIES TO REMEMBER.
(HE TRIES OUT A WINK HIMSELF.) 37 HUGHIE
HE TRIES TO BOW TO ME, IMAGINE, 616 ICEMAN
HIS EYES BLINK AS HE TRIES TO KEEP THEM OPEN) 625 ICEMAN
(HE TRIES TO THROW THE DRINK IN HICKEY'S FACE, 686 ICEMAN
(TRIES TO WARD THIS OFF BY POUNDING WITH HIS GLASSTIS ICEMAN ON THE TABLE--
(HE TRIES A WINK AT THE OTHERS. 722 ICEMAN
(HE TRIES TO EMBRACE THEM. 725 ICEMAN
WHO TRIES TO RESIST AND KICKS OUT AT THE BUCKET. 526 INZONE
SMITTY AGAIN TRIES TO BREAK LOOSE BUT HE IS TOO 527 INZONE TIRED
HE TRIES TO LOOK UP IN HER EYES BUT SHE KEEPS THEM 61 JOURNE AVERTED.
EDMUND TRIES TO COPY THIS DEFENSE BUT WITHOUT 71 JOURNE SUCCESS.
(PATS HIS CHEEK AS HE TRIES NOT TO SHRINK AWAY.) 73 JOURNE
(TRIES TO IGNORE THIS.) I HAVE TO GET TOOTH 86 JOURNE POWDER AND TOILET SOAP AND COLD
(OVERWHELMED BY SHAME WHICH HE TRIES TO HIDE, 113 JOURNE FUMBLES WITH HIS WATCH.)
HE TRIES THE DOOR--SEARCHES HIS POCKET.) 6 MANSNS
IT'S LIKE A SPELL THAT TRIES TO COME BETWEEN US. 82 MANSNS
HE TRIES TO REPRESS, WHICH FASCINATES AND AT THE 140 MANSNS SAME TIME HUMILIATES HIM.
(TRIES TO DRAW HER TO HIM.) DARLING/ 146 MANSNS
(TRIES TO TAKE HER TO THE COUCH.) 146 MANSNS
(HE TRIES TO HIDE IT.) 360 MARCOM
TRIES TO STARE INSOLENTLY AT THE KING BUT, AWED IN366 MARCOM SPITE OF HIMSELF,
(TRIES TO SNATCH IT) NO/ 375 MARCOM
TO GLADDEN MY LAST DAYS--(HE NO LONGER TRIES TO 438 MARCOM CONTROL HIS GRIEF.
TRIES TO BE CONTEMPTUOUSLY TOLERANT 60 MISBEG
(HARDER TRIES TO MAKE SOME SORT OF DISDAINFULLY 64 MISBEG DIGNIFIED EXIT.
TRIES TO CORRECT THIS AND LURCHES RIGHT AND BUMPS 80 MISBEG AGAINST HER.
(HE TRIES TO KISS HER, BUT SHE WARDS HIM OFF AND 81 MISBEG STEERS HIM BACK TO THE CHAIR.)

TRIES (CONT'D.)
SHE TRIES TO READ HIS FACE WITHOUT HIS NOTICING. 115 MISBEG
(SHE TRIES TO BE CALCULATINGLY ENTICING) 126 MISBEG
(UNCONSCIOUSLY SHE TRIES TO PULL HER HAND AWAY.) 130 MISBEG
(HE TRIES TO TOUCH BRIMS WITH MELODY'S GLASS, 93 POET
I DEFY YOU OR ANYONE WHO TRIES TO COME BETWEEN US/128 POET
SHE TRIES TO BE MOCKING.) 182 POET
(BENTLEY TRIES TO HIT HIM WITH THE CANE) 584 ROPE
BENTLEY TRIES TO RESIST. 584 ROPE
AND WHEN I COME HOME HE TRIES TO MAKE ME BUMP 598 ROPE OFF--WANTS TO SEE ME A CORPSE--
HIS FACE HAS AN EXPRESSION OF ANXIETY WHICH HE 73 STRANG TRIES TO CONCEAL.
GAWD KNOWS I TRIES TO DO ME BEST FUR YOU. 494 VOYAGE
(HE TRIES TO FORCE HER EYES TO RETURN TO HIS.) 485 WELDED

TRIFLE
LARRY COMES TO THE DOOR AND OPENS IT A TRIFLE-- 13 ANNA
(A TRIFLE IMPATIENTLY) ALL OF YOU SEEM TO KEEP 84 BEYOND HARPING ON MY HEALTH.
IT IS A TRIFLE SPOOKY. 557 CROSS
THIS BEAUTY IS A TRIFLE DIMMED NOW BY TRACES OF 514 DAYS RECENT ILLNESS.
(A TRIFLE IMPATIENTLY) 'COURSE WE DID. 500 DIFRNT
WHICH IS A TRIFLE LOUDER AND QUICKER THAN AT THE 190 EJONES CLOSE OF THE PREVIOUS
I'M JUST A TRIFLE ELATED, NOW THE JOB'S DONE. 316 GGBROW
EYESIGHT A TRIFLE BLURRY, I'M AFRAID. 599 ICEMAN
SHE STILL HAS A YOUNG, GRACEFUL FIGURE, A TRIFLE 12 JOURNE PLUMP.
(A TRIFLE ACIDLY.) I HOPE HE DIDN'T PUT YOU ON TO 15 JOURNE ANY NEW PIECE OF PROPERTY AT
--EVEN IF YOUR NOSE AND MOUTH AND EARS ARE A TRIFLE115 JOURNE TOO LARGE.
LAZARUS TURNS, HIS LAUGHTER GROWN A TRIFLE LOUDER,333 LAZARU AND FACES MARCELLUS.
HER FOREHEAD IS HIGH AND A TRIFLE BULGING, WITH 2 MANSNS SUNKEN TEMPLES.
DRAW YOURSELF BACK UNTIL YOU BECOME NOT THE 3 MANSNS RESPECTABLE, IF A TRIFLE MAD,
YOUR LADY IS A BIT TOO MINERAL, YOUR HEAVEN OF 361 MARCOM LOVE A TRIFLE MONETARY--
DRESSED ONLY A TRIFLE LESS GORGEOUSLY AS 402 MARCOM COMMODORES.
(A TRIFLE WILDLY) OH, YES, YOU HAVE BEEN A MODEL 412 MARCOM GUARDIAN, ADMIRAL DOLIO/
(SHE IS A TRIFLE HECTIC NOW AND HER MANNER HAS 418 MARCOM GROWN WILDER.)
A TRIFLE PUZZLED, AND NOT A LITTLE IRRITATED AS 439 MARCOM HIS THOUGHTS,
A TRIFLE, ONLY. 77 MISBEG
THE NOSE IS DELICATE AND THIN, A TRIFLE AQUILINE, 67 POET
(UNSIDERATELY AND EVEN A TRIFLE CONDESCENDINGLY.) 76 POET
(A TRIFLE DEFENSIVELY) I'M SURE HE WOULD HAVE HAD 9 STRANG A BRILLIANT CAREER.
HER TRAINING HAS ALSO TENDED TO COARSEN HER FIBER 26 STRANG A TRIFLE.
A MARY'S GRIEF SUBSIDES A TRIFLE, HER VOICE IS 26 STRANG HEARD, FLAT AND TONELESS)
(HER FACE BECOMING DEFENSIVE--IN BLUNTED TONES, A 55 STRANG TRIFLE
I HAVE KNOWN A BIT OF HONOR AND A TRIFLE OF SELF- 86 STRANG SATISFACTION...

TRIFLING
IT ALL SEEMS TRIFLING, SOMEHOW. 138 BEYOND
BUT WHO COULD THAT GOD CARE ABOUT OUR TRIFLING 41 STRANG MISERY OF DEATH-BORN-OF-BIRTH$

TRILOGY
(GENERAL SCENE OF THE TRILOGY THE ACTION OF THE 2 ELECTR TRILOGY.

TRIM
WITH A FLAT WHITE TRIM. 28 ELECTR
THE WALLS ARE PLAIN PLASTERED SURFACES, LIGHT GRAY 79 ELECTR WITH A WHITE TRIM.
PRETENDING TO TRIM THE EDGE OF THE LAWN ALONG THE 169 ELECTR DRIVE.
THE HOUSE HAD ONCE BEEN PAINTED A REPULSIVE YELLOW 1 MISBEG WITH BROWN TRIM.
A GOOD IRISH NAME, BUT YOU'RE ENGLISH BY THE TRIM 499 VOYAGE AV YE, AN' BE DAMNED TO YOU.

TRIMLY
(THEY LOWER THE SAIL, AND BEGIN TO TIE IT UP 408 MARCOM TRIMLY.)

TRIMMED
SKY AND TRIMMED WITH SILVER LEAVES/ 261 GGBROW
IT WAS MADE OF SOFT, SHIMMERING SATIN, TRIMMED 115 JOURNE WITH WONDERFUL OLD DUCHESSE LACE,
IS AN OLD-FASHIONED WHITE SATIN WEDDING GOWN, 170 JOURNE TRIMMED WITH DUCHESSE LACE,
OF EVERYTHING BEING METICULOUSLY TENDED AND 95 MANSNS TRIMMED.

TRIMMINGS
WITH WHITE TRIMMINGS. 41 ANNA

TRIMS
NO LONGER TRIMS IT TO HIS PERSONALITY. 66 STRANG

TRINITY
ARE THEY IN ONE PERSON LIKE OUR HOLY TRINITYS 376 MARCOM

TRINK
I COULD TRINK A WHOLE BARREL MINESELF, PY CHIMMINV461 CARIBE CHRISTMAS/
I TRINK/ 470 CARIBE
GIF ME TRINK DERE, YOU/ 208 HA APE
OUT'S NIGGER TRINK. 209 HA APE
BUY ME A TRINK/ 579 ICEMAN
BUY ME A TRINK/ 592 ICEMAN
BUY ME A TRINK/ 634 ICEMAN
AND VE VILL EAT HOT DOGS AND TRINK FREE BEER 635 ICEMAN BENEATH THE VILLOW TREES/

TRINK
(CONT'D.)
(WITH HIS SILLY GIGGLE) VE VILL TRINK VINE 640 ICEMAN
BENEATH THE VILLOW TREES/
DIS VINE IS UNFIT TO TRINK. 658 ICEMAN
VE VILL EAT BIRTHDAY CAKE AND TRINK CHAMPAGNE 658 ICEMAN
BENEATH THE VILLOW TREE/
SOON YOU VILL EAT HOT DOGS BENEATH THE VILLOW 672 ICEMAN
TREES AND TRINK FREE VINE--
I VILL TRINK CHAMPAGNE BENEATH THE VILLOW-- 691 ICEMAN
BUY ME A TRINK/ 694 ICEMAN
BUY ME A TRINK OR I VILL HAVE YOU SHOT/ 695 ICEMAN
BUY ME A TRINK/ 721 ICEMAN
I THINK I HAVE A TRINK NOW, LARRY. 721 ICEMAN
HAVE A TRINK. 722 ICEMAN

TRIP
FOR HER MEMORY OF CERTAIN ASPECTS OF THAT TRIP IS 259 AHWILD
THE OPPOSITE FROM WHAT HE
YOU OUGHT TO HEAR VESTA VICTORIA--YOU REMEMBER 259 AHWILD
THAT TRIP I MADE TO NEW YORK.
MY NERVES IS ON EDGE AFTER THAT ROTTEN TRIP. 16 ANNA
GEE, I HAD AN AWFUL TRIP COMING HERE. 20 ANNA
I'D SURE LIKE A TRIP ON THE WATER, ALL RIGHT. 23 ANNA
I'M ON THIS BARGE BECAUSE I'M MAKING A TRIP WITH 34 ANNA
MY FATHER.
WHAT IS IT YOU DO WHEN YOU'RE NOT TAKING A TRIP 35 ANNA
WITH THE OLD MANS
AND NOW VEN SHE COME ON FIRST TRIP--YOU TANK AY 46 ANNA
VANT HER LEAVE ME 'LONE AGAINS
(AT THIS MENTION OF THE TRIP THEY BOTH FALL 83 BEYOND
SILENT.
WELL, THE TRIP YOU'RE LEAVING ON TOMORROW WILL 83 BEYOND
KEEP YOU MOVING ALL RIGHT.
WHEN I KNOW HOW YOU NEED THIS SEA TRIP TO MAKE A 84 BEYOND
NEW MAN OF YOU--
SPEAK ABOUT YOUR TRIP--UNTIL AFTER YOU'D GONE,. 88 BEYOND
MY MAKING THIS IS ONLY KEEPING THAT PROMISE 89 BEYOND
OF LONG AGO.
(OVERCOME BY A SUDDEN FEAR) YOU WON'T GO AWAY ON 91 BEYOND
THE TRIP.
HE'S BEEN DREAMING OVER THIS TRIP EVER SINCE IT 96 BEYOND
WAS FIRST TALKED ABOUT.
YOU'VE GOT TO SEE HE COMES HOME WHEN THIS TRIP IS 96 BEYOND
OVER.
I TOLD HER I HADN'T BEEN CONSCIOUS OF MY LOVE 100 BEYOND
UNTIL AFTER THE TRIP HAD BEEN
GOD, HOW I ENVY HIM/ WHAT A TRIP/ 125 BEYOND
TELL ME ABOUT YOUR TRIP. 131 BEYOND
IT'S QUITE A TRIP. 137 BEYOND
THE TRIP DID THAT FOR ME, ANYWAY. 138 BEYOND
AN 'LET 'EM KNOW I'D BE LACKIN' A MATE NEXT TRIP 141 BEYOND
COUNT O' YOUR LEAVIN'.
SOMETHING HAPPENED FIVE YEARS BACK, THE TIME YOU 163 BEYOND
CAME HOME FROM THE TRIP.
I'VE WON TO MY TRIP--THE RIGHT OF RELEASE--BEYOND 168 BEYOND
THE HORIZON.
WE SHOULDN'TA MADE THIS TRIP, AND THEN--HOW'D ALL 487 CARDIF
THE FOG GIT IN HERES
SHE TRIED TO LEND ME HALF A CROWN WHEN I WAS BROKE489 CARDIF
THERE LAST TRIP.
THE LAST TRIP HE MADE WAS SEVEN YEARS AGO. 559 CROSS
JIM BENSON WAS MATE WITH YOU THIS LAST TRIP, 500 DIFRNT
WASN'T HE.
WELL, THE WAR WAS OVER, HE WAS WORN OUT, HE'D HAD 70 ELECTR
A LONG, HARD TRIP HOME--
WELL, IT WASN'T A PLEASURE TRIP EXACTLY, 81 ELECTR
WASN'T THE LONG TRAIN TRIP TERRIBLY HARD ON YOU, 81 ELECTR
DEARS
I DON'T BELIEVE WHEN VINNIE RUSHED HIM OFF ON THIS136 ELECTR
TRIP TO THE EAST
ONLY ABOUT THE TRIP. 137 ELECTR
YOUR TRIP CERTAINLY DID YOU GOOD/ 143 ELECTR
TRIP HIM UP/ 232 HA APE
FOR ONE THING, HE LIVED IN BROOKLYN, AND I'D 25 HUGHIE
SOONER TAKE A TRIP TO CHINA.
I'M SORRY WE HAD TO POSTPONE OUR TRIP AGAIN THIS 605 ICEMAN
APRIL, PIET.
I'M SLATED TO LEAVE ON A TRIP. 661 ICEMAN
WHEN I CAME HOME FROM A TRIP. 712 ICEMAN
AS IF I'D JUST COME HOME FROM A BUSINESS TRIP. 713 ICEMAN
(WITH A SIGH) BLIMEY, IT AIN'T NO BLEEDIN' JOKE, 517 INZONE
YER FIRST TRIP.
(GLOOMILY) ITS ME LAST TRIP IN THE BLOODY ZONE, 517 INZONE
GOD HELP ME.
IT'S SUCH A TIRING TRIP UPTOWN IN THE DIRTY OLD 92 JOURNE
TROLLEY ON A HOT DAY LIKE THIS.
DID YOUR TRIP TAKE YOU DOWN AROUND ISPAHAN WAYS 348 MARCOM
BUT WON'T THIS TRIP SO VERY FAR AWAY BE FULL OF 356 MARCOM
DANGERS
WE BETTER READ FROM THE NOTES WE MADE ON OUR LAST 365 MARCOM
TRIP ALL THERE IS TO REMEMBER
FOR I WARN YOU IN ADVANCE THIS IS LIABLE TO BE A 398 MARCOM
MIGHTY LONG TRIP.
THE TERMINATION OF OUR TRIP, PARTICULARLY ON THE 425 MARCOM
LAST DAY.
IT'S A BUSINESS TRIP WITH ME, REALLY... 52 STRANG
BEEN GOING STALE EVER SINCE WE CAME BACK FROM THAT 67 STRANG
TRIP HOME...
THEY 'ARF STARVED THE 'ANDS ON THE LARST TRIP 495 VOYAGE
'ERE.
COME NONE AV YOUR DOG'S THRICKS ON ME THIS TRIP OR496 VOYAGE
I'LL--
PY VINGO, I PITY POOR FALLERS MAKE DAT TRIP ROUND 507 VOYAGE
CAPE STIFF DIS TIME YEAR.

TRIPE
DAT'S ALL TRIPE. 211 HA APE
WHERE D'YU GET DAT TRIPE$ 211 HA APE
WHERE D'YUH GET DAT TRIPE$ 211 HA APE
ALL DAT CRAZY TRIPE ABOUT NIGHTS AND DAYS,. 215 HA APE

TRIUMPHANT

TRIPE
(CONT'D.)
ALL DAT CRAZY TRIPE ABOUT STARS AND MOONS,. 215 HA APE
ALL DAT CRAZY TRIPE ABOUT SUNS AND WINDS, FRESH 215 HA APE
AIR AND DE REST OF IT--
IT PLOUGHS TROU ALL DE TRIPE HE'S BEEN SAYIN'. 215 HA APE
ALL DAT TRIPE YUH BEEN PULLIN'--AW, DAT'S ALL 215 HA APE
RIGHT.
SURE DERE WAS A SKOIT IN IT-BUT NOT WHAT YOUSE 241 HA APE
MEAN, NOT DAT OLD TRIPE.

TRIPLE
I EXPECT HIM TO DOUBLE OR TRIPLE HIS FIRST OFFER. 66 MISREG

TRIPPIN'
DEY'RE WHAT'S BEEN A-TRIPPIN' ME UP AN' BREAKIN' 193 EJUNES
MY NECK.

TRIPPING
LIKE BRIDES JUST TRIPPING OUT OF CHURCH WITH THE 49 STRANG
BRIDEGROOM, SPRING, BY THE ARM.

TRIPS
(MILDRED SLYLY SHOVES HER FOOT OUT SO THAT HE 193 AHWILD
TRIPS OVER IT, ALMOST FALLING.
AIN'T HE SPENT EVERY DURN EVENIN' OF THE TIME HE'S933 DIFRNT
TO HOME BETWEEN TRIPS OVER
SHE TRIPS LIGHTLY TO THE DOOR AND OPENS IT-- 534 DIFRNT
FURCING A LIGHT, CARELESS TONE)
THE EXCUSE YOU'VE MADE FOR ALL YOUR TRIPS THERE 29 ELECTR
THE PAST YEAR,
AND ALL MY TRIPS TO NEW YORK WEREN'T TO VISIT 61 ELECTR
FATHER BUT TO BE WITH ADAM/
I TOLD HIM HOW YOU LIED ABOUT MY TRIPS TO NEW 91 ELECTR
YORK--FOR REVENGE/
WHY DON'T HE GO OFF ON ONE OF HIS OLD TRIPS 138 STRANG
AGAIN...

TRIUMPH
=YESTERDAY THIS DAY'S MADNESS DID PREPARE 261 AHWILD
TOMORROW'S SILENCE, TRIUMPH,
(IN ANGRY TRIUMPH) IT'S THE TRUTH, ANDY MAYO/ 106 BEYOND
(FLOURISHING IT ABOVE HIS HEAD WITH A SHOUT OF 573 CROSS
TRIUMPH)
IN WHOSE LOVE YOURS MAY FIND THE TRIUMPH OVER 508 DAYS
DEATH.
SHE PRETENDS TO DO LIKEWISE BUT GIVES HIM A SIDE 235 DESIRE
GLANCE OF SCORN AND TRIUMPH.)
CABOT STANDS LOOKING DOWN WITH FIERCE TRIUMPH) 256 DESIRE
HER FACE FULL OF TERROR YET WITH AN UNDERCURRENT 259 DESIRE
OF DESPERATE TRIUMPH.
(WITH REVENGEFUL TRIUMPH) SHE'LL NEVER MARRY THE 530 DIFRNT
OLD CUSS--I'LL FIX THAT/
(IN A BOOMING TRIUMPH) =VENGEANCE IS MINE, SAITH 451 DYNAMO
THE LORD/=
THERE IS A FIXED SMILE OF TRIUMPH AND GRATIFIED 468 DYNAMO
VANITY ON HIS LIPS,
AND AN EXPRESSION OF STRANGE VINDICTIVE TRIUMPH 11 ELECTR
COMES INTO HER FACE.)
(LAUGHS WITH A CRAZY TRIUMPH--CHECKS THIS 164 ELECTR
ABRUPTLY--
(THEN WITH TRIUMPH) AT LAST/ 299 GGBROW
(WITH FIERCE TRIUMPH) JEHOVAH IS AVENGED/ 290 LAZARU
THE SENATORS CHEER AND SHOUT AS AT A TRIUMPH.) 320 LAZARU
(WITH SAVAGE TRIUMPH, POINTING) 346 LAZARU
AND THE PRIDE OF A NEW TRIUMPH. 349 LAZARU
I'LL PROVE TO YOU I CAN LEAD THE COMPANY TO A 101 MANSNS
GLORIOUS, FINAL TRIUMPH--
WELL, I AM SURE YOU WISH TO CELEBRATE THIS FAMILY 382 MARCOM
TRIUMPH TOGETHER,
AND ALSO REMEMBER THAT ON EACH OCCASION HE 388 MARCOM
RETURNED IN TRIUMPH,
(WITH A CRY OF TRIUMPH) THANK GOD/ 97 STRANG
(WITH A DEADLY SMILE OF TRIUMPH) 176 STRANG
(WITH A SMILE OF CRUEL TRIUMPH--THINKING) 177 STRANG
(TURNING TO JOE IN TRIUMPH) NAW, WHAT D'YER SAYS 496 VOYAGE
IT'LL BE A TRIUMPH FOR YOU BOTH, WAIT AND SEE. 451 WELDED
(WITH FIERCE TRIUMPH) OH, I MADE HIM BELIEVE/ 468 WELDED
(THEN WITH A QUEER SORT OF SAVAGE TRIUMPH) 475 WELDED
(WITH A PASSIONATE TRIUMPH) LOVE/ 485 WELDED
FIGHT--FAIL AND HATE AGAIN--(HE RAISES HIS VOICE 488 WELDED
IN AN AGGRESSIVE TRIUMPH)

TRIUMPHAL
AT THE MIDDLE OF WHICH IS A TRIUMPHAL ARCH. 326 LAZARU
AS IF THEY WERE HIS OWN (TRIUMPHAL BODY GUARD.) 335 LAZARU

TRIUMPHANT
(WITH TRIUMPHANT MOCKERY) SILENCE/ 565 DAYS
(TRIUMPHANT) YES/ 228 DESIRE
SHE LAUGHS A CRAZY TRIUMPHANT LAUGH) 240 DESIRE
(HIS FACE SUDDENLY LIGHTING UP WITH A FIERCE, 243 DESIRE
TRIUMPHANT GRIN)
HE BECOMES EXCITED, A CRUEL, TRIUMPHANT GRIN COMES253 DESIRE
TO HIS LIPS,
(SUDDENLY TRIUMPHANT WHEN HE SEES HOW SHAKEN EBEN 255 DESIRE
IS)
(WITH TRIUMPHANT MALICE) YES, YOU DO/ 542 DIFRNT
(WITH A TRIUMPHANT GLANCE AT HER FATHER) 442 DYNAMO
THE TOM-TOM BEATS LOUDER, QUICKER, WITH A MORE 199 EJUNES
INSISTENT, TRIUMPHANT PULSATION,)
CHRISTINE BEGINS TO SPEAK IN A LOW VOICE, COOLLY 91 ELECTR
DEFIANT, ALMOST TRIUMPHANT)
(LAVINIA LOOKS AT HIM, FRIGHTENED BY THE 163 ELECTR
TRIUMPHANT SATISFACTION IN HIS VOICE.)
TRIUMPHANT TENDERNESS MINGLED WITH HER GRIEF) 323 GGBROW
(WITH A TRIUMPHANT SMILE) I HAVE IT--BOTH HIS AND220 HA APE
THE CHIEF ENGINEER'S,
AND HIS BEAMING EXPRESSION IS ONE OF TRIUMPHANT 684 ICEMAN
ACCOMPLISHMENT)
(TURNS ON HIM--WITH A STRANGELY TRIUMPHANT, 117 JOURNE
TAUNTING SMILE.)
THAT IT IS LIKE A GREAT BIRD SONG TRIUMPHANT 279 LAZARU
(IN A GREAT TRIUMPHANT VOICE) 293 LAZARU
THE MUSIC STARTS ONCE MORE WITH A TRIUMPHANT CLASH306 LAZARU
OF CYMBALS,

TRIUMPHANT

TRIUMPHANT (CONT'D.)
BECOMING MORE AND MORE INTENSE AND INSISTENT, 318 LAZARU
FINALLY ENDING UP ON A TRIUMPHANT,
BAFFLED, YET FEELING HIS POWER AS CAESAR 348 LAZARU
TRIUMPHANT NEVERTHELESS)
(TRIUMPHANT YET DISAPPOINTED--WITH SCORN AND RAGE)366 LAZARU
(HIS VOICE A TRIUMPHANT ASSERTION OF THE VICTORY 366 LAZARU
OF LIFE OVER PAIN AND DEATH)
(HE LAUGHS WITH A WILD TRIUMPHANT MADNESS AND 370 LAZARU
AGAIN RHETORICALLY,
YOU DON'T HAVE TO LOOK SO TRIUMPHANT, SARA. 46 MANSNS
BOTH THEIR EXPRESSIONS CHANGE TO A TRIUMPHANT 137 MANSNS
POSSESSIVE TENDERNESS.)
WHO *CAN BLARE OUT A TRIUMPHANT MARCH, 428 MARCOM
(TRIUMPHANT FOR A SECOND) YOU MEANT IT/ 119 MISBEG
(WITH STRANGE TRIUMPHANT HARSHNESS) 146 MISBEG
AS A TRIUMPHANT CLIMAX, YOU UNDERSTAND, 83 POET
(SHE PAUSES, A HARD, TRIUMPHANT SMILE ON HER LIPS.160 POET
IT FADES.
(STANDS TENSELY--BURSTS OUT WITH A STRANGE 162 POET
TRIUMPHANT PRIDE.)
(RAISING HER HEAD--THINKING--PROUDLY TRIUMPHANT) 89 STRANG
(THINKING--FIERCELY TRIUMPHANT) 89 STRANG
SHE IS AGAIN THE PREGNANT WOMAN OF ACT THREE BUT 90 STRANG
THIS TIME THERE IS A TRIUMPHANT
(THEN IN A TRIUMPHANT WHISPER) 97 STRANG
A MIXTURE OF LOVE, OF TRIUMPHANT EGOTISM IN 125 STRANG
KNOWING HER LOVER HAS COME BACK TO
(THINKING WITH TRIUMPHANT HAPPINESS) 126 STRANG
LOOKING FROM ONE TO THE OTHER WITH TRIUMPHANT 133 STRANG
POSSESSION)
(WITH A STRANGE TRIUMPHANT CALM) 133 STRANG
(MORE AND MORE STRANGELY TRIUMPHANT) 135 STRANG
(THEN SUPPRESSING AN OUTBREAK OF HYSTERICAL 135 STRANG
TRIUMPHANT LAUGHTER ONLY BY A
(WITH A TRIUMPHANT CRY) MY DEAR GORDON/ 195 STRANG
THERE, FOR SHE CRIES WITH TRIUMPHANT BITTERNESS) 459 WELDED
(WITH A TRIUMPHANT EXCLAMATION OF JOY) 466 WELDED
(THEN UNABLE TO RESTRAIN HIS TRIUMPHANT EXULTANCE)488 WELDED
TRIUMPHANTLY
(THEN TRIUMPHANTLY) BUT THERE IS ONE THING I DID 266 AHWILD
WORK OUT OF HIM--
RAGING TRIUMPHANTLY BEFORE ANNA HAS A CHANCE TO 54 ANNA
GET IN A WORD)
(TRIUMPHANTLY) IT WAS GOD'S PUNISHMENT ON JAMES 114 BEYOND
MAYO FOR THE BLASPHEMIN' AND
(TRIUMPHANTLY) AYE, NOW YE DO/ 568 CROSS
(TRIUMPHANTLY) THEN LOOK OUT IF YE DARE/ 569 CROSS
(TRIUMPHANTLY) AH/ 561 DAYS
(MORE AND MORE TRIUMPHANTLY) 256 DESIRE
(TRIUMPHANTLY) HAVEN'T I ALWAYS SAID, IF THE 449 DYNAMO
TRUTH WERE KNOWN,
(TRIUMPHANTLY) YOU THOUGHT YOU HAD HIM CAUGHT IN 451 DYNAMO
YOUR SNARES, DID YOU/
HE LAUGHS TRIUMPHANTLY) 453 DYNAMO
(HE GLANCES AT HIS MASK TRIUMPHANTLY--IN TONES OF 266 GGBROW
DELIVERANCE)
(HE LAUGHS TRIUMPHANTLY) WELL, BLASPHEMY IS 297 GGBROW
FAITH, ISN'T IT/
(TRIUMPHANTLY, STARING INTO HIS EYES) 298 GGBROW
(POINTING TO THE MASK OF DION--TRIUMPHANTLY) 321 GGBROW
(TRIUMPHANTLY) THERE/ 529 INZONE
(HE BEGINS TO LAUGH TRIUMPHANTLY, STARING DEEP 360 LAZARU
INTO CALIGULA'S EYES)
(PUTS HIS ARM AROUND HER AND HUGS HER TO HIM, HIS 80 MANSNS
FACE TRIUMPHANTLY GRATIFIED--
THEN GLOATING TRIUMPHANTLY BUT MOVED IN SPITE OF 169 MANSNS
HERSELF--
(HER FACE LIGHTS UP TRIUMPHANTLY.) 30 POET
(HAVING SAID THIS, SHE GOES ON TRIUMPHANTLY.) 64 POET
(TRIUMPHANTLY--BETWEEN KISSES) 97 STRANG
NINA LOOKS ACROSS HIM AT DARRELL--TRIUMPHANTLY-- 99 STRANG
THINKING)
(TRIUMPHANTLY) (HOW HIS HAND TREMBLES/... 118 STRANG
(THINKING TRIUMPHANTLY--WITH A CERTAIN CRUELTY) 126 STRANG
(THEN TRIUMPHANTLY AS SHE READS HIM) 126 STRANG
(THINKING--TRIUMPHANTLY MUCKING) 127 STRANG
(THINKING TRIUMPHANTLY) (HE'S TRYING TO INSULT 147 STRANG
ME...
(THINKING TRIUMPHANTLY) (THAT'S RIGHT, SAM... 155 STRANG
(TRIUMPHANTLY THINKING) (THAT MAKES UP FOR HIS 156 STRANG
KISS/...
(SHE HUGS HIM FIERCELY TO HER, TRIUMPHANTLY 156 STRANG
HAPPY.)
(TURNING ON HER TRIUMPHANTLY) 174 STRANG
CAPE CRIES TRIUMPHANTLY) 460 WELDED
(SHE STARES HIM IN THE EYES DEFIANTLY, 485 WELDED
TRIUMPHANTLY.)
TRIUMPHED
HIS LAUGHTER TRIUMPHED OVER ME, BUT HE HAS NOT 351 LAZARU
BROUGHT HER BACK TO LIFE.
TRIUMPHS
THEIR DISEASE TRIUMPHS OVER DEATH--A NOBLE VICTORY352 LAZARU
CALLED RESIGNATION/
TROAT
I'LL DRIVE YER TEET' DOWN YER TRCAT/ 225 HA APE
TROLLEY
I'M GOING TO BEAT IT--JUST TIME TO CATCH THE 199 AHWILD
EIGHT-TWENTY TROLLEY.
YOU KNOW WHAT THEY SAY ABOUT WOMEN AND TROLLEY 216 AHWILD
CARS, AUNT LILY.
SEE HE GETS ON THE TROLLEY ALL RIGHT, ANYWAY. 248 AHWILD
OWNED THE TROLLEY LINE AND LUMBER COMPANY. 710 ICEMAN
I'D RATHER WALK ANY DAY, OR TAKE A TROLLEY. 84 JOURNE
IT'S SUCH A TIRING TRIP UPTOWN IN THE DIRTY OLD 92 JOURNE
TROLLEY ON A HOT DAY LIKE THIS.
WE CAN'T LOCK UP AND GO TO BED TILL JAMIE COMES ON138 JOURNE
THE LAST TROLLEY--

1708

TROLLEY (CONT'D.)
GET ALONG NOW, SO YOU WON'T MISS THE TROLLEY. 7 MISBEG
(HE MOVES) I'LL GRAB THE LAST TROLLEY FOR TOWN. 152 MISBEG
TROLLEYS
(SOOTHINGLY) HE PROBABLY COULDN'T GET A SEAT, THE251 AHWILD
TROLLEYS ARE SO JAMMED.
TROLLOP
OR LIKE THE DREARY TEARS OF A TROLLOP SPATTERING 152 JOURNE
IN A PUDDLE OF STALE BEER ON A
BRAZEN-TROLLOP ACTS
THE DIRTY LITTLE TROLLOP/... 136 MISBEG
TROLLOPS 45 STRANG
I DON'T MEAN TROLLOPS. 642 ICEMAN
TRONK
WHEN HE COMES THERE TRONK/ 675 ICEMAN
LOST ALL HIS MONEY GAMBLING WHEN HE VAS TRONK. 677 ICEMAN
OFTEN WHEN I AM TRONK AND KIDDING YOU I SAY I AM 677 ICEMAN
SORRY I MISSED YOU, BUT NOW,
TROOF
IT'S GAWD'S TROOF, WHAT I TOLE YER. 457 CARIBE
(WITH A GRIN) IT'D BE A GOOD 'AUL, THAT'S THE 496 VOYAGE
TROOF.
MAY GAWD KILL ME IF THAT AIN'T TROOF/ 499 VOYAGE
YOU WOULDN'T THINK IT, BUT IT'S GAWD'S TROOF. 502 VOYAGE
TROOPER
THE CAPTAIN'LL HAVE YOU OUT ON DECK CURSIN' AND 485 CARDIF
SWEARIN' LOIKE A TROOPER
ROARIN' WID RAGE AND CURSIN' LIKE A TROOPER-- 157 POET
LIKE A RUM-SOAKED TROOPER, BRAWLING BEFORE A 158 POET
BROTHEL ON A SATURDAY NIGHT,
TROOPS
(THE TROOPS DO SO EAGERLY. 305 LAZARU
AT THE OPENING OF THE SCENE THERE IS HEARD THE 313 LAZARU
STEADY TRAMP OF DEPARTING TROOPS,
TROPIC
ONE WALK DOWN ONE OF THEIR FILTHY NARROW STREETS 132 BEYOND
WITH THE TROPIC SUN BEATING ON
TROPICS
DEEPLY BRONZED BY HIS YEARS IN THE TROPICS,. 130 BEYOND
THE TROPICS HAVE TANNED HIS NATURALLY PASTY FACE 174 EJONES
WITH ITS SMALL,
HE CAUGHT WHEN HE WAS IN THE TROPICS. 27 JOURNE
(THEN BRIGHTLY) OH, HE'S AFRAID SHE'LL GET FEVER 404 MARCOM
IN THE TROPICS.
HIS SKIN ITS TANNED ALMOST BLACK BY HIS YEARS IN 159 STRANG
THE TROPICS.
DARRELL'S DEEP SUNBURN OF THE TROPICS HAS FADED, 190 STRANG
TROT
A RALE, GOD-FOR-SAKEN SON AV A TURKEY TROT WID 470 CARIBE
GUTS TO UT.
A JERK-SHOULDERED VERSION OF THE OLD TURKEY TROT 471 CARIBE
AS IT WAS DONE IN THE
WAL, I'LL TROT ALONG/ 45 ELECTR
YOU FELLERS TROT ALONG. 134 ELECTR
TROU
DEY SMASH TROU, DON'T DEYS 215 HA APE
IT PLOUGHS TROU ALL DE TRIPE HE'S BEEN SAYIN'. 215 HA APE
WE SPLIT DAT UP AND SMASH TROU--TWENTY-FIVE KNOTS 217 HA APE
A HOUR/
BUT WE DRIVE TROU DAT, DON'T WE5 217 HA APE
I'LL SLAM YER NOSE TROU DE BACK OF YER HEAD/ 225 HA APE
BUT I'LL DRIVE TROU/ 244 HA APE
DRIVIN' TROU--MOVIN'--IN DAT--TO MAKE HER--AND 244 HA APE
CAGE ME IN FOR HER TO SPIT ON/
YOUSE NEEDN'T PUT ME TROU DE TOID DEGREE. 247 HA APE
AND DAT YUH'D WANTER GIVE ME THE ONCE-OVER TROU A 247 HA APE
PEEP-HOLE OR SOMEPIN
I'M TROU-- 254 HA APE
DEY'LL HAVE TO MAKE DE CAGES STRONGER AFTER WE'RE 254 HA APE
TROU/
TROUBADOUR
A QUEER TROUBADOUR- OF-THE-SEA QUALITY ABOUT HIM.1103 ELECTR
TROUBLE
I'M AFEARED THERE'LL BE TROUBLE WITH THE HANDS 539 'ILE
FROM THE LOOK O' THINGS.
BEST NOT HAVE HER ON DECK IF THEY'S GOIN' TO BE 541 'ILE
ANY TROUBLE.
LET THEM MAKE WHAT LAW TROUBLE THEY KIN. 541 'ILE
AND TROUBLE THEY'S GOING TO BE. 541 'ILE
AND TROUBLE I'VE HAD BY LAND AND BY SEA'S LONG AS 541 'ILE
I KIN REMEMBER,
THEY MIGHT MAKE TROUBLE FOR YOU IN THE COURTS WHEN541 'ILE
WE GIT HOME.
(WITH A GRIM SMILE) HERE IT COMES, THE TROUBLE 543 'ILE
YOU SPOKE OF, MR. SLOCUM,
OR HE'LL BE GETTING ME, AND HIMSELF, IN A PECK OF 204 AHWILD
TROUBLE.
YES, IT WON'T DO TO HAVE HIM GETTING ANY DECENT 206 AHWILD
GIRL IN TROUBLE.
DON'T BE MAKING ME LAUGH AND GETTING ME INTO 222 AHWILD
TROUBLE.
IF YOU'RE NOT LOOKING FOR TROUBLE, 247 AHWILD
YOU'LL START NO TROUBLE IN HERE/ 247 AHWILD
YOU 'RE TOO EASY WITH HIM, THAT'S THE WHOLE 253 AHWILD
TROUBLE/
WHAT'S THE TROUBLES 260 AHWILD
THE TROUBLE WITH YOU IS, YOU DON'T UNDERSTAND WHAT274 AHWILD
I LOVE MEANS/
YOU DIDN'T TAKE THE TROUBLE TO SNEAK ANY LETTER TO278 AHWILD
ME, I NOTICE/
THAT'S THE TROUBLE. 291 AHWILD
THINK I'D MAKE TROUBLE, HUH5 11 ANNA
WELL, I GOT YOURS, TOO WITHOUT NO TROUBLE. 15 ANNA
I AIN'T LOOKING FOR TROUBLE. 15 ANNA
WHAT'S TROUBLES 29 ANNA
WHAT'S THE TROUBLES 30 ANNA
I WOULDN'T START NO TROUBLE WITH HIM IF I WAS YOU. 43 ANNA

1709

TROUBLE — TROUSERS

TROUBLE (CONT'D.)
BUT 'TIS NOT TROUBLE I'M LOOKING FOR, AND ME 46 ANNA
SITTING DOWN HERE.
AND A DIVIL TO BE MAKING A POWER OF TROUBLE IF YOU 46 ANNA
HAD YOUR WAY.
IT'S QUARE YOU'D BE THE ONE TO BE MAKING GREAT 47 ANNA
TROUBLE ABOUT HER LEAVING YOU
WHAT'S THE TROUBLES 63 ANNA
YOU'RE TOO EASY GOIN', THAT'S THE TROUBLE. 117 BEYOND
(INDIFFERENTLY) I FORGOT--AND IT'S TOO MUCH 119 BEYOND
TROUBLE THIS WEATHER.
(FROWNING) WHAT'S THE TROUBLE NOW, I WONDERS 123 BEYOND
AND SEE THAT I DO GET IT, OR THERE'LL BE TROUBLE. 125 BEYOND
I WROTE YOU HAD LUNG TROUBLE. 146 BEYOND
I'M USED TO BEARING TROUBLE BY THIS.. 158 BEYOND
TO KEEP TROUBLE AWAY FROM HIM. 165 BEYOND
YOU VANT TO MAKE TROUBLES 458 CARIBE
WANTS TO GIT ME IN TROUBLE. 465 CARIBE
I'LL TROUBLE YOU NOT TO PRY INTO MY AFFAIRS, 468 CARIBE
DONKEYMAN.
WANT TO GET ME IN TROUBLES 471 CARIBE
SO THAT'S THE TROUBLE? 473 CARIBE
YES-PERFECTLY--DON'T TROUBLE. 556 CROSS
(SHE SMILES) THE TROUBLE WITH YOU IS, YOU OLD 523 DAYS
CYNIC,
THAT'S HER TROUBLE AS WELL AS HIS. 557 DAYS
OCEANS O' TROUBLE AN' NUTHIN' BUT WUK FUR REWARD. 226 DESIRE
YE MIGHT'VE TUK THE TROUBLE IV ABUSE ME, ARBLE. 263 DESIRE
MAAL, I'M THANKFUL FUR HIM SAVIN' ME THE TROUBLE. 265 DESIRE
THEY'S TROUBLE ENOUGH IN THE WORLD WITHOUT MAKIN' 508 DIFRNT
MORE.
STORY-BOOK NOTIONS, THAT'S THE TROUBLE WITH YOU. 510 DIFRNT
EMMER.
NOT THAT I DON'T LIKE IT BUT I'D NEVER HAVE GONE 524 DIFRNT
TO THE TROUBLE AND EXPENSE FOR
BUT AS SOON AS HE KNEW HE'D GOT ME INTO TROUBLE HE430 DYNAMO
SPOKE RIGHT UP..."
WHAT'S THE TROUBLE, YOUNG FELLOWS 437 DYNAMO
WHAT'S THE TROUBLES 463 DYNAMO
BUT YOU'SE TOO SHIFTLESS TO TAKE DE TROUBLE. 179 EJONES
DEN, WHEN I SEES TROUBLE COMIN', I MAKES MY 180 EJONES
GETAWAY.
BEFO' I GITS INTO MY LITTLE TROUBLE. 185 EJONES
NURSE GIRL HE'D GOT INTO TROUBLE. 9 ELECTR
BUT I'VE LET IT BE KNOWN THAT HE HAS HEART 39 ELECTR
TROUBLE.
YOU NEEDN'T TROUBLE TO BREAK THE NEWS GRADUALLY, 48 ELECTR
EZRA.
HOW IS THE TROUBLE WITH YOUR HEART, FATHERS 49 ELECTR
HE TOLD ME THE TROUBLE HE HAD WASN'T SERIOUS. 74 ELECTR
I'VE ALREADY TOLD HIM--SO YOU MIGHT AS WELL SAVE 91 ELECTR
YOURSELF THE TROUBLE.
(WITH A NOTE OF PLEADING) PLEASE DON'T TROUBLE. 277 GGBROW
TROUBLE WITH THE COPS PINCHING YOU THERE AND 279 GGBROW
BLAMING ME.
HE ISN'T WORTH THE TROUBLE WE'D GET INTO. 249 HA APE
THAT'S THE TROUBLE WITH KNOWING THINGS. 11 HUGHIE
AND HE WONDERS SADLY WHY HE TOOK THE TROUBLE TO 14 HUGHIE
MAKE IT.)
BUT HE AIN'T MY TROUBLE, PAL. 34 HUGHIE
MY TROUBLE IS, SOME OF THESE GUYS I PUT THE BITE 34 HUGHIE
ON IS DEAD WRONG G'S.
FOLKS IN DE KNOW TELLS ME, SEE DE MAN AT DE TOP, 600 ICEMAN
DEN YOU NEVER HAS TROUBLE.
WITHOUT HER, NOTHING SEEMED WORTH THE TROUBLE. 603 ICEMAN
WHEN I DON'T EVEN GET AN EYE-OPENER FOR MY 610 ICEMAN
TROUBLE.
I CAN TELL YOU'RE HAVING TROUBLE WITH YOURSELF 624 ICEMAN
I AIN'T LOOKIN' FOR NO TROUBLE. 630 ICEMAN
I DON'T WANT NO TROUBLE ON HARRY'S BOITHDAY PARTY.634 ICEMAN
OR YOU AND ME'S GOIN' TO HAVE TROUBLE/ 637 ICEMAN
HIS TROUBLE IS HE WAS BROUGHT UP A DEVOUT BELIEVER643 ICEMAN
IN THE MOVEMENT
I WAS NEVER ONE TO START TROUBLE. 660 ICEMAN
JUST AS I'D DROP OFF ON A CHAIR THERE, DEY'D COME 669 ICEMAN
DOWN LOOKIN' FOR TROUBLE.
(WITH SNEERING DIGNITY) I'S ON'Y SAYIN' YOU DE 673 ICEMAN
TROUBLE, WHITE BOY.
ABOUT THE TROUBLE YOU'RE IN. 679 ICEMAN
YOU GOT IN TROUBLE OUT ON THE COAST, EH$ 679 ICEMAN
(DISAPPOINTEDLY) THEN YOU'RE NOT IN TROUBLE, 679 ICEMAN
PARRITT$
THAT WAS THE TROUBLE. 706 ICEMAN
I TOLD MOLLIE ARLINGTON MY TROUBLE. 710 ICEMAN
THE DIRTY BLACKGUARD/ HE'LL GET ME IN SERIOUS 25 JOURNE
TROUBLE YET.
THAT'S THE TROUBLE WITH YOU. 134 JOURNE
THAT WAS THE TROUBLE. 147 JOURNE
CAN'T, THAT'S THE TROUBLE. 150 JOURNE
AND I THINK YOU WILL HAVE NO TROUBLE CONVINCING 59 MANSNS
HER.
TO TRY AND MAKE TROUBLE BETWEEN YOUR MOTHER AND 78 MANSNS
ME$
THE TROUBLE IS YOU HAVEN'T NOTICED THE CHANGE IN 84 MANSNS
HER.
I'LL NEVER TROUBLE YOU AGAIN/ 188 MANSNS
(THREATENINGLY) GIVE IT TO ME, YOU, OR I'LL MAKE 375 MARCOM
TROUBLE/
(BEWILDEREDLY) WHAT'S THE TROUBLE NOW$ 378 MARCOM
WHO WERE ALWAYS TROUBLE AND GETTING DISCONTENTED. 392 MARCOM
(FAMILIARLY) AND THE TROUBLE WITH ANY SHIP, FOR A 398 MARCOM
MAN OF ACTION,
THAT ONE AT A TIME IS TROUBLE ENOUGH. 405 MARCOM
OH, THERE'S TROUBLE THERE, ALL RIGHT/ 415 MARCOM
IN GENERAL, SHE GAVE BUT LITTLE TROUBLE ON THE 424 MARCOM
VOYAGE.
(HE CHUCKLES) SINCE YOU'VE GROWN UP, I'VE HAD THE 18 MISBEG
SAME TROUBLE.

TROUBLE (CONT'D.)
THAT'S THE TROUBLE. 102 MISBEG
THAT'S THE TROUBLE. 126 MISBEG
OR HE'LL GET IN TROUBLE. 26 POET
I REGRET YOUR HAVING GONE TO SO MUCH TROUBLE. 56 POET
DON'T LOOK FOR TROUBLE BEFORE IT COMES. 79 POET
AND HERE YOUR SIMON STAMMERED SO EMBARRASSEDLY I 110 POET
HAD TROUBLE MAKING HIM OUT--
ALL THE SORROW AND TROUBLE THAT'S COME ON US. 138 POET
WE HAD NO TROUBLE FINDIN' WHERE HARFORD LIVED. 154 POET
AND YOU'LL BE ARRESTED IF YOU MAKE TROUBLE." 155 POET
SHE'LL HAVE SOME TROUBLE, ROOTIN' OUT HIS DREAMS. 173 POET
YE'VE MADE ENOUGH TROUBLE FOR ONE NIGHT/ 597 ROPE
YOU'RE ALWAYS ANTICIPATING TROUBLE. 70 STRANG
ROOT OF HER TROUBLE STILL....)) 80 STRANG
THE TROUBLE IS THERE'S BEEN A DANGEROUS PHYSICAL 102 STRANG
ATTRACTION.
HE'S NEVER MARRIED, THAT'S THE TROUBLE. 156 STRANG
(STARING AT HIM) NED, OLD MAN, WHAT'S THE 181 STRANG
TROUBLES
BUT I WASN'T HOME ENOUGH, THAT'S THE TROUBLE. 185 STRANG

TROUBLED
TROUBLED AND EMBARRASSED) 208 AHWILD
(MOVED IN SPITE OF HERSELF AND TROUBLED BY THIS 38 ANNA
HALF-CONCEALED PROPOSAL--
SHE LOOKS UNHAPPY, TROUBLED, FROWNINGLY 41 ANNA
CONCENTRATED ON HER THOUGHTS.
(DEEPLY MOVED AND TROUBLED--FORCING A TREMBLING 51 ANNA
LAUGH)
HAVE YOU BEEN GREATLY TROUBLED IN SPIRIT BY 507 DAYS
ANYTHING LATELY$
HIS MIND IS PREOCCUPIED, HIS EXPRESSION SAD AND 545 DAYS
TROUBLED.
(WITH AN UNCERTAIN TROUBLED LAUGH) 239 DESIRE
SHE SITS IN ONE OF THE RUCKERS BY THE TABLE, HER 501 DIFRNT
FACE GREATLY TROUBLED.
(AFFECTEDLY TROUBLED) YOU DON'T MEAN TO SAY 220 HA APE
YOU'RE REALLY GOINGS
HIS LARGE TROUBLED EYES, OF A GLAZED GREENISH- 299 LAZARU
BLUES
(TROUBLED--THINKING) (SHE HAS CHANGED... 13 STRANG
TROUBLEDLY
THINKING TROUBLEDLY) 196 STRANG

TROUBLES
(BEAMING NOW THAT HE SEES HIS TROUBLES 11 ANNA
DISAPPEARING)
(SCORNFULLY) IS IT BLAMING THE SEA FOR YOUR 47 ANNA
TROUBLES YE ARE AGAINS
HAVEN'T I GOT MY SHARE OF TROUBLES TRYING TO WORK 122 BEYOND
THIS CURSED FARM
I THINK OUR TROUBLES ARE GETTING YOUR NERVE. 496 DAYS
SO PLEASE DON'T BOTHER YOUR HEAD ABOUT MY 517 DAYS
TROUBLES.
BY ALWAYS COMING TO ME WITH YOUR TROUBLES. 517 DAYS
(WITH A TWISTED SMILE) I THOUGHT WE WEREN'T GOING517 DAYS
TO TALK ABOUT MY TROUBLES/
SHE HAS BEEN SINCERELY MOVED BY THE RECITAL OF HER226 DESIRE
TROUBLES.
BELIEVE ME, PAL, I CAN STOP GUYS THAT START 26 HUGHIE
TELLING ME THEIR FAMILY TROUBLES/
I DON'T WANT TO HEAR YOUR DAME TROUBLES. 26 HUGHIE
EXCEPT TO LEAVE ME OUT OF HIS TROUBLES. 642 ICEMAN
THEN, SOON AS I GOT IN THE DOOR, MAMIE BEGAN 159 JOURNE
TELLING ME ALL HER TROUBLES.
TAKEN YOUR MIND OFF YOUR TROUBLES. 161 JOURNE
WHAT IS IT TROUBLES ME ABOUT HIMS 330 LAZARU

TROUBLING
BEYOND THE FURTHER TROUBLING OF ANY HOPE.) 169 BEYOND
I WANT TO KNOW WHAT'S TROUBLING YOU. 517 DAYS
I KNOW THERE'S SOMETHING THAT'S BEEN TROUBLING YOU529 DAYS
FOR WEEKS--
IT'S SOMETHING UNEASY TROUBLING MY MIND-- 60 ELECTR
IS THAT WHAT'S TROUBLING YOUS 474 WELDED

TROUGH
THAN GETTING ALL FOUR FEET IN A TROUGH OF 543 DAYS
SWILL(HE LAUGHS SARDONICALLY)
WHEN DEY GOT TROUGH DERE WASN'T A CHAIR OR TABLE 234 HA APE
WIT A LEG UNDER IT.
I'M TROUGH WOIKIN'. 700 ICEMAN

TROUPE
AFTER THEM COMES A TROUPE OF YOUNG GIRLS AND BOYS,433 MARCOM

TROUSERS
THE KNEES OF HIS TROUSERS ARE DIRTY, 261 AHWILD
HE IS DRESSED IN GRAY CORDUROY TROUSERS PUSHED 81 BEYOND
INTO HIGH LACED BOOTS,
HE WEARS CORDUROY TROUSERS STUFFED DOWN INTO HIGH 556 CROSS
LACED BOOTS.)
HORNE IS A PARROT-NOSED, ANGULAR OLD MAN DRESSED 571 CROSS
IN GRAY COTTON TROUSERS
(HE PULLS ON HIS TROUSERS TUCKING IN HIS NIGHT 238 DESIRE
SHIRT, AND PULLS ON HIS BOOTS.)
DUNGAREE TROUSERS FADED BY MANY WASHINGS, A BLUE 457 DYNAMO
FLANNEL SHIRT OPEN AT THE NECK.
(HE SCRATCHES A MATCH ON HIS TROUSERS AND PEERS 189 EJONES
ABOUT HIM.
SNEAKERS OVER BARE FEET, AND SOILED WHITE FLANNEL 260 GGBROW
TROUSERS.
(HE REAPPEARS, HAVING CHANGED HIS COAT AND 308 GGBROW
TROUSERS)
HIS TROUSERS ARE HELD UP BY A BRAIDED BROWN 9 HUGHIE
LEATHER BELT WITH A BRASS BUCKLE.
HE WEARS A SHIRT, COLLAR AND TIE, NO COAT, OLD 20 JOURNE
FLANNEL TROUSERS, BROWN SNEAKERS.
(HE BENDS AND SLAPS AT THE KNEES OF HIS TROUSERS.1155 JOURNE
HAD SERIOUS ACCIDENT.
IRISHMAN DRESSED IN PATCHED CORDUROY TROUSERS 582 ROPE
SHOVED DOWN INTO HIGH LACED BOOTS,

TROW

TROW
(THEN WITH EVIDENT ANXIETY) ON'Y TROW IT AWAY IF 15 ANNA
YUH HEAR SOMEONE COMIN'.
TROW IT INTO HER BELLY/ 223 HA APE
DEV'D ON'Y TROW IT AWAY. 580 ICEMAN
BEFORE I'LL TROW IT IN HER FACE SHE WAS A TART. 616 ICEMAN
AND CHUCK AIN'T NEVER GOIN' TO TROW IT IN MY FACE 631 ICEMAN
DAT I WAS A TART, NEIDER.

TROWIN'
TROWIN' IT UP IN MY FACE/ 236 HA APE
SHE'LL BE TROWIN' A FIT. 677 ICEMAN
NOT AFTER HIS TROWIN' IT IN MY FACE I'M A PIMP. 698 ICEMAN

TRUCE
LET US PATCH UP SOME SORT OF ARMED TRUCE. 219 HA APE

TRUCK
IT IS NIGH ON TWO BELLS, MR. STEWARD, AND THIS 539 'ILE
TRUCK NOT CLEARED YET.
I AIN'T NEVER TOUK MUCH STUCK IN THE TRUCK THEM 486 CARDIF
SKYPILOTS PREACH.
YOU AN' ME'D BEST BE GOIN' TO GIVE 'EM A HAND WID 461 CARIBE
THEIR TRUCK.
HE'S A MEAN SKUNK FROM TRUCK TO KEELSON/ 540 DIFRNT
WHY I BECAME A JUDGE AND A MAYOR AND SUCH VAIN 55 ELECTR
TRUCK.
I DON'T WANT NO TRUCK WITH THIS ROTTEN FARM. 599 ROPE

TRUCKIN'
AND TRUCKIN' GROCERIES, AS SAFE FROM A GUN AS YOU 541 DIFRNT
AND ME BE THIS MINUTE.
I HELPED AT TRUCKIN' AND IN DE MARKET. 234 HA APE

TRUCKLOAD
HIM HIDE A TRUCKLOAD IN OUR BARN WHEN THE AGENTS 115 MISBEG
WERE AFTER HIM.

TRUCULENCE
(THE4 WITH DEFENSIVE TRUCULENCE) 585 ICEMAN
(STUNG INTO RECOVERING ALL HIS OLD FUMING 718 ICEMAN
TRUCULENCE)
THEIR MANNER AS THEY ENTER HARDENS INTO A BRAZEN 725 ICEMAN
DEFENSIVE TRUCULENCE.)
ALL THE TRUCULENCE LEAVES THEIR FACES. 725 ICEMAN

TRUCULENT
HE SEEMS BROADER, FIERCER, MORE TRUCULENT, MORE 208 HA APE
POWERFUL.
HE ATTEMPTS TO HIDE HIS DEFENSELESSNESS BEHIND A 576 ICEMAN
TESTY TRUCULENT MANNER.
TRUCULENT SWAGGER AND HIS GOOD-NATURED FACE IS SET636 ICEMAN
IN SULLEN SUSPICION.

TRUCULENTLY
(WALKING TOWARD HIM--TRUCULENTLY) 461 CARIBE
(THEY GLARE AT HIM TRUCULENTLY.) 630 ICEMAN
AND DON'T GIVE ME NO ARGUMENT/ (HE STARES AT ROCKY671 ICEMAN
TRUCULENTLY.
(TURNS ON HIM TRUCULENTLY) YEAHS 682 ICEMAN
(TRUCULENTLY) WHAT'S IT TO YUHS 697 ICEMAN
(HE GLARES TRUCULENTLY AT JOE, WHO IMMEDIATELY 498 VOYAGE
DOWNS HIS BEER.

TRUDGE
TRUDGE ALONG LAST.) 420 MARCOM

TRUE
THERE'S FINE THINGS IN IT, SEEMS TO ME--TRUE 198 AHWILD
THINGS.
I LIKE--BECAUSE IT'S TRUE... 199 AHWILD
(ANGRILY) BY GOD, IF THAT'S TRUE, 205 AHWILD
YES, IT IS TRUE. IF YOU MUST KNOW, AND YOU'D NEVER227 AHWILD
HAVE SUSPECTED IT.
IS THIS TRUE, ESSIE? 227 AHWILD
BUT IT'S A GOOD TRUE STORY FOR KIDS BECAUSE IT 230 AHWILD
ILLUSTRATES THE DANGER OF BEING
IT WAS TRUE FOR TWO YEARS. 18 ANNA
(THINK TO BURKE--FEELINGLY) I KNOW IT'S TRUE, MAT. 51 ANNA
(FORCING OUT THE WORDS) WELL, MAYBE IT'S TRUE, 51 ANNA
MAT.
IT'S TRUE. 53 ANNA
AY GUESS IT'S TRUE YOU VAS IN LOVE WITH HIM ALL 64 ANNA
RIGHT.
IF I COULD HAVE SEEN HOW YOU WERE IN YOUR TRUE 127 BEYOND
SELF--LIKE YOU ARE NOW--
AND NOW THE DREAM IS TO COME TRUE/ 150 BEYOND
(SLOWLY) I THINK I KNOW WHAT YOU'RE DRIVING AT. 162 BEYOND
NOW--AND IT'S TRUE, I GUESS.
IT WAS TRUE--THEN. 164 BEYOND
(INDIGNANTLY) GAWD STRIKE ME DEAD IF IT AIN'T 478 CARDIF
TRUE, EVERY BLEEDIN' WORD OF IT.
TRUE ISN'T IT, DINKS 467 CARIBE
THAT'S TRUE. 469 CARIBE
HIS FACE IS TRANSFIGURED WITH THE ECSTASY OF A 570 CROSS
DREAM COME TRUE.)
THAT'S TRUE. 494 DAYS
WELL, IF IT'S TRUE, YOU CAN HARDLY BLAME HER. 498 DAYS
BUT WITH JOHN I FELT IT WAS ABSOLUTELY TRUE TO 522 DAYS
WHAT I KNEW HE WAS LIKE INSIDE
OUR LOVE COULD MAKE OURS INTO A TRUE SACRAMENT-- 523 DAYS
SACRAMENT WAS THE WORD HE USED--
SO HE MUST HAVE BOTH LIVED TRUE TO IT. 524 DAYS
IT'S NOT TRUE. 529 DAYS
HE WAS NEVER COURAGEOUS ENOUGH TO FACE WHAT HE 535 DAYS
REALLY KNEW WAS TRUE.
I--(HE BLURTS OUT MISERABLY) YES--IT'S TRUE. 549 DAYS
THAT MY PROPHECY IS COMING TRUE--HER END IN MY 554 DAYS
STORY.
HER END IN YOUR STORY IS COMING TRUE. 558 DAYS
(ANGRILY) IT IS MY TRUE SELF--MY ONLY SELF/ 559 DAYS
I KNOW YOU COULDN'T BLASPHEME AT SUCH A TIME--NOT 559 DAYS
YOUR TRUE SELF.
IT HAS COME TRUE SO FAR. 560 DAYS
AT LAST YOU ACCEPT THE TRUE END/ AT LAST YOU SEE 561 DAYS
THE EMPTY PUSHING
MIN'D MAKE A TRUE FAITHFUL HE'PMEET/ 214 DESIRE
HAIN'T IT TRUE$ 257 DESIRE
AN' IT'LL SEEM LIKELY AN' TRUE TO 'EM. 267 DESIRE

TRUE
(CONT'D.)
AN' IT IS TRUE--WAY DOWN. 267 DESIRE
TRUE SONS O' MINE. IF THEY BE DUMB FOOLS-- 268 DESIRE
THAT PART OF IT WAS TRUE ENOUGH 'CAUSE CALEB WAS 503 DIFRNT
ALONE.
IS THAT TRUE$ 508 DIFRNT
WAAL, I GUESS WHAT HE TOLD IS TRUE ENOUGH. 515 DIFRNT
LESS'N I KNOWED IT WAS TRUE$ 540 DIFRNT
YOU OWNED UP YOURSELF THAT WAS TRUE/ 540 DIFRNT
I GOT PROOF IT'S TRUE. 541 DIFRNT
YOU OUGHT TO SEE HIM IN HIS TRUE COLORS SO YOU'D 443 DYNAMO
NOT BE THINKING TOO MUCH ABOUT
OVERWHELMED BY THE CONVICTION THAT WHAT SHE HAS 451 DYNAMO
TOLD HIM IS TRUE.)
BY JINGO, AMOS, IF THAT NEWS IS TRUE, 7 ELECTR
OR DO YOU REMAIN TRUE TO YOUR ONE AND ONLY BEAU, 17 ELECTR
PETERS.
IS THAT TRUE, CAPTAINS 23 ELECTR
(FIERCELY) IT'S NOT TRUE/ 25 ELECTR
SO--IT IS TRUE--YOU ARE HER SON/ 25 ELECTR
THAT'S TRUE ENOUGH, DAMN HIM/ 39 ELECTR
IT ISN'T TRUE, IS IT, FATHER$ 48 ELECTR
IF THAT'S TRUE, SHE OUGHT TO BE PUT IN AN ASYLUM/ 88 ELECTR
SO YOU ARE AFRAID IT'S TRUE/ 97 ELECTR
TELL ME THAT ISN'T TRUE, AT LEAST/ 98 ELECTR
IF THAT'S TRUE, I'LL HATE HER/ 99 ELECTR
IT WAS THE ONLY WAY TRUE JUSTICE COULD BE DONE. 122 ELECTR
A TRUE HISTORY OF ALL THE FAMILY CRIMES, BEGINNING153 ELECTR
WITH GRANDFATHER ABE'S--
(FORCING A LAUGH) PERHAPS THEY'RE TRUE ENOUGH. 276 GGBROW
BUT IT IS TRUE HE HASN'T DONE SO MUCH LATELY SINCE276 GGBROW
WE'VE BEEN BACK.
IS IT TRUE WHAT BILLY TOLD ME--ABOUT YOUR SWEARING301 GGBROW
OFF FOREVER$
CYNICAL ORACLES OF THE ONE TRUE GRAPEVINE. 9 HUGHIE
THAT'S WHAT BARNUM SAID, AND IT'S CERTAINLY TRUE. 19 HUGHIE
ISN'T ITS
AND THIS ONE WAS TRUE, AT THAT. 25 HUGHIE
WOULD YOU MIND TELLING ME IF IT'S REALLY TRUE WHEN 35 HUGHIE
ARNOLD ROTHSTEIN PLAYS POKER,
(THEN INSISTENTLY.) IS IT TRUE WHEN ARNOLD 36 HUGHIE
ROTHSTEIN PLAYS POKER.
YES, I GUESS THAT MUST BE TRUE, LARRY. 588 ICEMAN
AND A BELIEF IN THE ONE TRUE FAITH AGAIN. 589 ICEMAN
IT ISN'T OFTEN THAT MEN ATTAIN THE TRUE GOAL OF 594 ICEMAN
THEIR HEART'S DESIRE--
WITH A SIGN... «SPECTATORS MAY DISTINGUISH THE TRUE599 ICEMAN
BABOON BY HIS BLUE BEHIND.»
BOOZE IS THE ONLY THING YOU EVER TALK ABOUT/ 601 ICEMAN
(SADLY) TRUE.
HICKEY MADE JOKE ABOUT ME, AND THIS LIMEY SAID 650 ICEMAN
YES, IT WAS TRUE/
WELL, I HAVE TO ADMIT THAT'S TRUE, AND I'M DAMNED 660 ICEMAN
SORRY ABOUT IT.
BUT HERE'S THE TRUE REASON, LARRY--THE ONLY 667 ICEMAN
REASON/
(BURSTS OUT WITH HIS TRUE REACTION BEFORE HE 679 ICEMAN
THINKS TO IGNORE HIM)
SHE WAS NEVER TRUE TO ANYONE BUT HERSELF AND THE 680 ICEMAN
MOVEMENT.
AND THEN TELLING HERSELF EVEN IF IT WAS TRUE, HE 712 ICEMAN
COULDN'T HELP IT,
YOU COULDN'T SHAKE HER FAITH THAT IT HAD TO COME 713 ICEMAN
TRUE--TOMORROW/
(WRILY.) THAT'S NOT TRUE, PAPA. 32 JOURNE
IF HE WEREN'T YOUR SON-- (ASHAMED AGAIN.) NO, 36 JOURNE
THAT'S NOT TRUE/
IT WOULD SERVE ALL OF YOU RIGHT IF IT WAS TRUE/ 47 JOURNE
AND YOU'VE LOST YOUR TRUE SELF FOREVER. 61 JOURNE
WHATEVER YOU MEAN, IT ISN'T TRUE, DEAR. 72 JOURNE
IT'S TRUE I'M A BAD CATHOLIC IN THE OBSERVANCE, 77 JOURNE
GOD FORGIVE ME.
THE ONE TRUE FAITH OF THE CATHOLIC CHURCH-- 77 JOURNE
ASKING YOUR PARDON, MA'AM, BUT IT'S TRUE. 98 JOURNE
(THEN, RESENTFULLY.) ANYWAY IT'S TRUE. 111 JOURNE
DON'T SAY THAT/ IT'S NOT TRUE/ 122 JOURNE
(APPROVINGLY.) THAT'S TRUE. 136 JOURNE
IT'S TRUE HE NEVER TOUCHED A DROP TILL HE WAS 137 JOURNE
FORTY.
IT'S NOT TRUE THE WAY YOU LOOK AT IT/ 144 JOURNE
AND IT WAS TRUE/ 150 JOURNE
I TOLD MOTHER I HAD HAD A TRUE VISION WHEN I WAS 175 JOURNE
PRAYING IN THE SHRINE OF OUR
IS IT TRUE TIBERIUS HAS FLED TO CAPRIS 316 LAZARU
I DID NOT KILL HER. IT IS TRUE, BUT I DEPRIVED HER355 LAZARU
OF HER POWER AND SHE DIED.
THE WHORE WAS CAESAR'S DAUGHTER, TRUE-- 356 LAZARU
IT IS TRUE, I AM WELL PRESERVED. 5 MANSNS
I HAVE MY HONOR AND IT'S A TRUE WOMAN'S HONOR THAT 18 MANSNS
YOU'D GIVE YOUR SOUL TO KNOW/
BUT WHAT I'VE SAID IS TRUE ALL THE SAME/ 21 MANSNS
A FRANK STUDY OF THE TRUE NATURE OF MAN AS HE 47 MANSNS
REALLY IS AND NOT AS HE PRETENDS
IS GOOD BECAUSE IT IS TRUE, AND SHOULD, IN A WORLD 47 MANSNS
OF FACTS,
IT'S TRUE YOU HAVE NOTHING IN LIFE, POOR WOMAN, 54 MANSNS
THAT'S NOT TRUE/ 79 MANSNS
THAT'S TRUE ENOUGH. 79 MANSNS
(FROWNS.) YES, IT'S TRUE YOU FEEL HER ALWAYS 84 MANSNS
THERE, WATCHING--
WELL THEN, I KNOW YOU WILL BE WILLING TO BECOME 88 MANSNS
YOUR OLD TRUE SELF AGAIN FOR ME.
IT'S TOO GOOD TO BE TRUE/ 89 MANSNS
IN WHICH ONLY THE FOOLS, WHO ARE FATED TO LOSE 91 MANSNS
REVEAL THEIR TRUE AIMS OR MOTIVES--
YES, THAT IS QUITE TRUE. 96 MANSNS
UNLESS YOU SECRETLY BELIEVE HER TRUE NATURE IS SO 98 MANSNS
GREEDY

1711 TRUST

TRUE (CONT'D.)
BUT ONCE LET HIS ENEMIES SEE HIS TRUE POSITION-- 142 MANSNS
I KNOW YOUR TRUE REASON FOR COMING. 152 MANSNS
I'VE ONLY TO GIVE HIM A HINT OF THE TRUE CONDITION156 MANSNS
OF THE COMPANY.
BUT I DID NOT COME OUT HERE TO DISCUSS MY 172 MANSNS
MEDITATIONS ON THE TRUE NATURE OF MAN.
YOU KNOW HER TRUE NATURE WELL ENOUGH TO REALIZE IT179 MANSNS
WAS SHE WHO MADE ME LAUGH
THE MURDERER POSSESSES THE TRUE QUALITY OF MERCY. 180 MANSNS
IT IS TRUE I HOPED YOU WOULD GUESS WHAT I MEANT. 184 MANSNS
IT NEEDS ONLY A WHISPER OF THE TRUE CONDITION TO 191 MANSNS
TENARD.
THIS TREE IS SACRED TO THE FOUNDER OF THE ONE TRUE349 MARCOM
RELIGION, ZOROASTER,
AND I'LL ALWAYS BE TRUE AND NEVER FORGET OR DO 357 MARCOM
ANYTHING--
EVEN IF THEY ARE TRUE, IT IS TOO MUCH EFFORT TO 359 MARCOM
CONCEIVE THEM.
SMILING YOUR THANKS AS I PROMISE YOU A LARGE 360 MARCOM
FORTUNE IF YOU WILL BE TRUE,
AND GIVE HIM EVERY OPPORTUNITY FOR TRUE GROWTH IF 382 MARCOM
HE SO DESIRES.
(SMILING) BUT I BELIEVE THAT WHAT CAN BE PROVEN 397 MARCOM
CANNOT BE TRUE.
TO CONVERT ME TO WISDOM--IF I COULD FIND THE TRUE 397 MARCOM
ONE/
AND I'VE BEEN TRUE TO HER, TOO. 404 MARCOM
MARCO, THE TRUE RULER OF THE WORLD, WILL HAVE COME426 MARCOM
TO VENICE BY THIS TIME.
AND THE POLOS ARE THE TRUE CHILDREN OF GOD/ 426 MARCOM
BUT YOU WERE TRUE IN SPITE OF THEM, WEREN'T YOU5 430 MARCOM
THE SAME IS TRUE OF HER LEGS. 3 MISBEG
THAT'S TRUE, JOSIE. 7 MISBEG
BUT IT'S TRUE ENOUGH. 19 MISBEG
(WITH ADMIRING AFFECTION) GOD REST HIM, HE WAS A 24 MISBEG
TRUE IRISH GENTLEMAN.
(SERIOUSLY) IT'S TRUE. IF I WAS HIS WIFE, 29 MISBEG
IT'S TOO GOOD TO BE TRUE. 48 MISBEG
AND WHAT I HOPED WOULD HAPPEN, IS TRUE. 175 MISBEG
HE MADE UP HIS MIND HE'D BRING CON UP A TRUE 12 POET
GENTLEMAN.
TRUE, ME FOOT/ 27 POET
IT'S TRUE, JUST THE SAME. 27 POET
THERE WOULDN'T BE A DREAM I'D NOT MAKE COME TRUE/ 27 POET
(APPROVINGLY.) THAT'S THE WAY A TRUE GENTLEMAN 29 POET
WOULD FEEL--
(THEN BOASTFULLY.) BUT IT'S TRUE, IN THOSE DAYS 39 POET
IN PORTUGAL AND SPAIN--
TRUE, HE IS A BIT ON THE SOBER SIDE FOR ONE SO 48 POET
YOUNG.
(RUEFULLY.) IT'S TRUE, MOTHER. 65 POET
THAT IS TRUE, SIR. 74 POET
AND I KNOW THERE'S A TRUE POET IN SIMON. 82 POET
HIS VOICE THE QUAVERING GHOST OF A TENOR BUT STILL 96 POET
TRUE--
A TRUE IRISH HUNTER ME THAT KNOWS AND LOVES ME 102 POET
IF THERE'S TRUE LOVE BETWEEN YOU, 131 POET
OF COURSE IT'S TRUE, MOTHER. 140 POET
(SHE LOOKS RELIEVED.) WELL, IF THE YOUNG LAD SAID140 POET
THAT, MAYBE IT'S TRUE.
AND IT'S A DREAM THAT'S TRUE, AND ALWAYS WILL BE 141 POET
TO THE END OF LIFE.
REMEMBER MEMBER THE BLOOD IN YOUR VEINS AND BE 170 POET
YOUR GRANDFATHER'S TRUE DESCENDAN
(WITH A LAUGH) YE SAID I'D BEEN DRINKIN'--WHICH 585 ROPE
WAS TRUE.
(IAND IT'S TRUE, YOU CONTEMPTIBLE.../I) 11 STRANG
THAT MAY BE TRUE. 20 STRANG
IT IS ALSO TRUE I WAS JEALOUS OF GORDON. 20 STRANG
SOMETIMES I FEEL IT'S TOO GOOD TO BE TRUE... 55 STRANG
(STRUCK--CONFUSEDLY) YES--THAT'S TRUE, ISN'T ITS 62 STRANG
(RELIEVED) WELL, IT'S TRUE. 94 STRANG
YOU WERE MY ONLY TRUE LOVE, NINA. 114 STRANG
AND I THOUGHT YOU WERE ABSOLUTELY TRUE TO ME, 119 STRANG
CHARLIE/.
(THINKING) (IT'S TRUE, TOO/... 119 STRANG
TRUE/... 148 STRANG
TRUE, EVERY WORD OF IT... 149 STRANG
IT'S TRUE HE'S SORT OF LOST HIS GRIP IN A WAY BUT 155 STRANG
HE'S OUR BEST FRIEND.
WHAT A TRUE FRIEND YOU WERE, DARRELL--AND HOW DAMN195 STRANG
MUCH HE LOVED YOU BOTH/
WE SWORE TO HAVE A TRUE SACRAMENT--OR NOTHING/ 448 WELDED
AND EVEN IF IT WERE TRUE, YOU'D FIND IT WAS THEY 456 WELDED
WHO OFFERED THEMSELVES/
(DEATHLY CALM) IT'S TRUE/ 460 WELDED
IT'S TRUE/ 460 WELDED

TRUER
SHE'S A TRUER-BORN, WELL-BRED LADY THAN ANY OF 106 POET
THEIR WOMEN--

TRULL
FAIN TO DRINK DELIGHT OF THAT ENORMOUS TRULL 133 JOURNE

TRULY
TRULY. 103 BEYOND
AN' YE'RE TRULY GOIN' WEST--GOIN' T' LEAVE ME--ALL258 DESIRE
ACCOUNT O' HIM BEING BURNS
BUT I DID TRULY HAVE BEAUTIFUL HAIR ONCE, DIDN'T 28 JOURNE
I, JAMESS
DOES HE TRULY RESEMBLE A GODS 300 LAZARU
REALLY, DEBORAH, I BEGIN TO BELIEVE THAT TRULY YOU 3 MANSNS
MUST BE A LITTLE MAD/
I AM TRULY GRATEFUL. 39 MANSNS
A TRULY DEPLORABLE LOT/ 75 STRANG
YOU'VE GOT TO SHOW ME WHAT'S THE SANE--THE TRULY 84 STRANG
SANE, YOU UNDERSTAND/
(IN SAME TONE) AND THE MAN SHOULD HAVE A MIND 88 STRANG
THAT CAN TRULY UNDERSTAND--

TRUMPET
"THE MOOR, I KNOW HIS TRUMPET." 21 JOURNE
(FOLLOWING A BRAZEN TRUMPET CALL, 319 LAZARU
(THERE IS THE SUDDEN BLARING OF A TRUMPET FROM 331 LAZARU
WITHIN THE PALACE.
WILL INTERRUPT GABRIEL TO SELL HIM ANOTHER 362 MARCOM
TRUMPET/
THERE IS ERE IS THE BLARE OF A TRUMPET, THE 417 MARCOM
REFLECTIONS OF LANTERNS AND TORCHES.
WE HEARD A TRUMPET FROM THE FRENCH LINES AND SAW 97 POET
THEM FORMING FOR THE ATTACK.
GABRIEL'S TRUMPET ITSELF COULDN'T ROUSE HIM. 503 VOYAGE

TRUMPETS
THE BRAZEN TRUMPETS OF THE LEGIONS SOUND FROM 319 LAZARU
BEYOND THE WALL.
(AT THIS SECOND THE BLARING TRUMPETS OF THE 320 LAZARU
LEGIONS ARE HEARD APPROACHING AND

TRUNK
ITS BOW ABOUT TOUCHING THE BANK, EVIDENTLY MADE 275 AHWILD
FAST TO THE TRUNK OF A WILLOW.
A THICK NECK IS JAMMED LIKE A POST INTO THE HEAVY 5 ANNA
TRUNK OF HIS BODY.
FROM BEHIND THE TRUNK OF THE TREE, AS IF HE HAD 200 EJUNES
SPRUNG OUT OF IT.
ITS TRUNK IS A BLACK COLUMN 5 ELECTR
THE TRUNK OF THE PINE AT RIGHT IS AN EBONY PILLAR, 43 ELECTR
ITS BRANCHES A MASS OF SHADE.
I AM TOO CRAZY TRUNK. 672 ICEMAN
I AM SO TRUNK, LARRY, OLD FRIEND, AM I NOT, I 672 ICEMAN
DON'T KNOW WHAT I SAYS
I AM VERY TRUNK. NO, LARRYS 672 ICEMAN
I AM TOO TRUNK NOW. 691 ICEMAN
LARRY VILL TELL YOU I HAF NEVER BEEN SO CRAZY 691 ICEMAN
TRUNK.
BECAUSE I AM SO CRAZY TRUNK/ 692 ICEMAN
I AM NOT TRUNK ENOUGH/ 695 ICEMAN
PLEASE, I AM CRAZY TRUNK/ 695 ICEMAN
I KEPT IT WRAPPED UP IN TISSUE PAPER IN MY TRUNK. 115 JOURNE
IT MIGHT BE IN AN OLD TRUNK IN THE ATTIC, ALONG 152 JOURNE
WITH MAMA'S WEDDING DRESS.
I REMEMBER NOW. I FOUND IT IN THE ATTIC HIDDEN IN1T2 JOURNE
A TRUNK.
ORNAMENTS, TAPERS, HAVE BEEN NAILED ON THE TRUNK 347 MARCOM
OR TIED TO THE BRANCHES.
THE HEAVY LIMBS SPREAD OUT TO A GREAT DISTANCE 347 MARCOM
FROM THE TRUNK.
A BARREL-LIKE TRUNK, STUMPY LEGS, AND BIG FEET. 11 MISBEG
I'LL GET YOUR UNIFORM FROM THE TRUNK. 39 POET
I'LL EVEN HELP YOU GET HIS UNIFORM OUT OF THE 64 POET
TRUNK IN THE ATTIC
(AS THEY GO OUT RIGHT.) I DISREMEMBER WHICH 66 POET
TRUNK--
AND WE'LL GET YOUR FATHER'S UNIFORM OUT OF THE 66 POET
TRUNK.
(HARSHLY.) PUT IT BACK IN THE TRUNK/ 75 POET

TRUNKS
TRUNKS OF THE NEAREST TREES BE MADE OUT, ENORMOUS 187 EJONES
PILLARS OF DEEPER BLACKNESS.
NO MO' BUTTIN' YO' FOOL HEAD AGIN' DE TRUNKS 191 EJONES
(A LARGE CIRCULAR CLEARING ENCLOSED BY THE SERRIED195 EJONES
RANKS OF GIGANTIC TRUNKS OF
THE INTERLOCKED NOPES OF CREEPERS REACHING UPWARD 198 EJONES
TO ENTWINE THE TREE TRUNKS
THE NEAREST TREE TRUNKS ARE DIMLY REVEALED 202 EJONES
PROBABLY IN ONE OF THE OLD TRUNKS IN THE ATTIC. 115 JOURNE

TRUSSING
SOLDIERS WITH DRAWN SWORDS LEAP FORWARD AND SEIZE 379 MARCOM
HIM, TRUSSING HIM UP,

TRUST
I TRUST EMMY ON ORDINARY OCCASIONS, 525 DAYS
(STERNLY AGAIN) I'M SORRY I CAN'T TRUST YOU. 527 DAYS
LUCY,
(WITH A LAUGH) SHOWS YE WHAT TRUST I PUT IN YOU, 496 DIFRNT
EMMA.
YOU CAN TRUST MY WORD FOR THAT. 518 DIFRNT
(STERNLY TO REUBEN) I TRUST YOU MEAN HONORABLY BY438 DYNAMO
HER, YOUNG FELLOW.
HOW CAN I EVER TRUST HERS... 441 DYNAMO
THEN ALL I CAN SAY IS THAT MY BOY I THOUGHT I 446 DYNAMO
COULD TRUST HAS TURNED INTO A LIAR
I DON'T TRUST YOU/ 34 ELECTR
I KNOW I CAN TRUST YOU TO UNDERSTAND NOW AS YOU 85 ELECTR
ALWAYS USED TO.
SAID FATHER WAS NO GOOD ON AN OFFENSIVE BUT HE'D 94 ELECTR
TRUST HIM TO STICK IN THE MUD
ALL I CAN DO IS TRUST YOU. 173 ELECTR
YOU TRUST ME WITH YOUR HAPPINESS/ 176 ELECTR
WOUNDED IN THEIR TRUST OF LIFE/ 176 ELECTR
ISN'T THEIR TRUST--A CONTEMPTS 298 GGBROW
PROMISES ARE ALL RIGHT, BUT--(SHE HESITATES) I 311 GGBROW
DON'T TRUST HIM.
THAT'S THE PRESIDENT OF THE STEEL TRUST, I BET. 242 HA APE
DE STEEL TRUST AND ALL DAT MAKES IT GO. 248 HA APE
PRESIDENT OF THE STEEL TRUST, YOU MEANS 249 HA APE
I KNOW I CAN TRUST YOU. 38 HUGHTE
YES, GENEROUS STRANGER--I TRUST YOU'RE GENEROUS-- 595 ICEMAN
ALWAYS THE WAY. CAN'T TRUST NOBODY. 598 ICEMAN
AIN'T UNCLE SAM OR SAP TO TRUST GUYS LIKE DAT WID 617 ICEMAN
DOUGH/
BUT YOU CAN TRUST ME. 679 ICEMAN
BUT YOU CAN TRUST ME, SO LET'S NOT BEAT ABOUT THE 679 ICEMAN
BUSH.
(HE SIGHS GLOOMILY) DAT KIND OF DAME, YUH CAN'T 698 ICEMAN
TRUST YER.
KNOWING EVERYONE IS SPYING ON ME, AND NONE OF YOU 46 JOURNE
BELIEVE IN ME, OR TRUST ME.
THAT'S CRAZY, MAMA. WE DO TRUST YOU. 46 JOURNE

TRUST

TRUST (CONT'D.)
(BITTERLY.) BECAUSE YOU'RE AFRAID TO TRUST ME 46 JOURNE
ALONE/
OR ARE YOU AFRAID TO TRUST ME ALONE$ 49 JOURNE
FOR GOD'S SAKE, MAMA/ YOU CAN'T TRUST HER/ 116 JOURNE
(WITH A SWEET SMILE OF AFFECTIONATE TRUST.) 171 JOURNE
AND PERSUADE HER TO TRUST ME WITH HER CHILDREN, 39 MANSNS
BECAUSE IF SHE CAN TRUST ME, I CAN LEARN TO TRUST 40 MANSNS
MYSELF AGAIN/
AND IF I COULD TRUST YOU-- 54 MANSNS
YOU CAN TRUST ME NOT TO MAKE THEM, SIMON. 63 MANSNS
NO, NEITHER CAN I--EXCEPT THAT I CAN TRUST YOU TO 73 MANSNS
LISTEN WITHOUT HEARING MUCH,
IT WOULD BE LIKE BREAKING MY PART OF A BARGAIN I'D 85 MANSNS
MADE IN HONOR TO TRUST HER,
I TRUST I HAVE NOT INTRUDED$ 96 MANSNS
I TRUST HER AND I KNOW SHE TRUSTS ME/ 99 MANSNS
IT WAS MEAN OF ME NOT TO TRUST YOU. 124 MANSNS
BUT WE MUST TRUST EACH OTHER AND NEVER LET HIM 135 MANSNS
MAKE US HATE EACH OTHER/
UH, TRUST ME, I CAN ALWAYS THINK OF MORE/ 148 MANSNS
TRUST US TO LOOK AFTER YOUR BEST INTERESTS--AND 381 MARCOM
DECIDED TO--
I CAN TRUST HER. 404 MARCOM
NO, I WOULDN'T THINK IT, BUT MY MOTTO IN LIFE IS 23 MISBEG
NEVER TRUST ANYONE TOO FAR,
WE CAN'T TRUST HIM, 66 MISBEG
TRUST AND BE A SUCKER. 66 MISBEG
TRUST HIMSELF, AND IT'D BE A SIN ON HIS CONSCIENCE 90 MISBEG
IF HE WAS TO SEDUCE YOU.
I--I TRUST YOU WILL OVERLOOK-- 115 POET
AND MAYBE YOU'RE RIGHT NOT TO TRUST ME TOO NEAR 175 POET
THE WHISKEY.
THE GHOST OF AN OLD FAITH AND TRUST IN LIFE'S 53 STRANG
GOODNESS, HOVERS GIRLISHLY,
TRUST... 62 STRANG
AND NED'S THE ONLY ONE I CAN TRUST....) 68 STRANG
IF ONLY SAM DIDN'T TRUST ME/....) 96 STRANG
(CAUSTICALLY) I TRUST I'LL NEVER MAKE THAT KIND 114 STRANG
OF A FOOL OF MYSELF, NINA/.
WHY, HE'D TRUST YOU WITH ANYTHING/ 127 STRANG
HE IS A PERSON ONE CAN TRUST. 127 STRANG
(WINCING--IN A FORCED TONE) AND I'D TRUST SAM 127 STRANG
WITH ANYTHING/
I CAN NEVER TRUST YOU AGAIN/ 130 STRANG
AN' I'D NOT TRUST HIM IN THIS HOLE AS DRUNK AS HE504 VOYAGE
IS,
AND TRUST IN YOUR GOOD INTENTIONS. 467 WELDED
TRUSTED
BUT YOU KNOW VERY WELL SHE CAN'T BE TRUSTED. 498 DAYS
BUT HE STILL TRUSTED IN HIS LOVE. 511 DAYS
A DEITY WHO RETURNED HATE FOR LOVE AND REVENGED 511 DAYS
HIMSELF UPON THOSE WHO TRUSTED
WHEN I TRUSTED HER/... 448 DYNAMO
YOU DON'T GIVE ONE THOUGHT TO FATHER--WHO IS SO 30 ELECTR
GOOD--WHO TRUSTED YOU/
AND THEY'RE NOT TO BE TRUSTED WITH LOVE/ 176 ELECTR
I HAD LOVED AND TRUSTED HIM AND SUDDENLY THE GOOD 295 GGBRDW
GOD WAS DISPROVED IN HIS
HE ALWAYS TRUSTED ME. 38 HUGHIE
GEE, LARRY, THAT'S A HELL OF A WAY TO TREAT ME, 669 ICEMAN
WHEN I'VE TRUSTED YOU,
THEN THEY LIKED YOU, THEY TRUSTED YOU, 711 ICEMAN
ALL THE TIME I WAS AWAY IN BERLIN AND BLINDLY 532 INZONE
TRUSTED YOU.
I HAVE NEVER ENTIRELY TRUSTED HER/ 105 MANSNS
(THINKING IRONICALLY) (TRUSTED TO HIS HONOR 11 STRANG
AGAIN/...
GAVE ME LOVE AND TRUSTED IN ME/ 62 STRANG
TRUSTFUL
THEY'VE ALWAYS BEEN SO TRUSTFUL/ 175 ELECTR
THIS FAMILIAR STRANGER TO WHOM WITH A TRUSTFUL 92 MANSNS
SMILE
THAT SARA HAS NOT BEEN AS BLIND AS YOU HOPED, NOR 98 MANSNS
AS UNSUSPECTINGLY TRUSTFUL.
OF PEACE AND TRUSTFUL FAITH AND HAPPINESS/ 182 MANSNS
OF THEM--WONDERING AND SAD, BUT STILL TRUSTFUL, 169 POET
NOT REPROACHING ME--
TRUSTFULLY
AT THE MOMENT HE ACCEPTS THEM TRUSTFULLY BECOMES 92 MANSNS
ONESELF.
TRUSTFULNESS
AND PITYING SARA FOR WHAT I MISTAKENLY THOUGHT WAS100 MANSNS
HER BLIND TRUSTFULNESS,
TRUSTING
WHY CAN'T ALL OF US REMAIN INNOCENT AND LOVING AND 73 ELECTR
TRUSTING$
BUT THAT MEANS TRUSTING THE MANNON DEAD-- 176 ELECTR
OF SPYING ON HER ALL THE TIME AND NOT TRUSTING 57 JOURNE
HER,
THE SHYLY EAGER, TRUSTING SMILE IS ON HER LIPS AS 175 JOURNE
SHE TALKS ALOUD TO HERSELF.)
WE MUST STAY HERE TOGETHER, TRUSTING EACH OTHER, 170 MANSNS
AND YOU TRUSTING HIM LIKE A POUR SHEEP, AND NEVER 99 MISBEG
SUSPECTING--
HE'S SUCH A TRUSTING FOOL... 100 STRANG
TRUSTS
I TRUST HER AND I KNOW SHE TRUSTS ME/ 99 MANSNS
AND HE TRUSTS ME ABSOLUTELY/....) 96 STRANG
BUT HE TRUSTS HIM MORE/... 154 STRANG
TRUTE
I'D LOIN HIM SOME TRUTE/ 243 HA APE
TRUTH
AIN'T THAT TRUTHS 542 'ILE
HE TELLS THE TRUTH ABOUT REAL LOVE/ 198 AHWILD
DISGRACEFUL WOULD BE NEARER THE TRUTH--AND IT 201 AHWILD
CONCERNS YOUR SON, RICHARD/

TRUTH (CONT'D.)
WELL, IT'LL DO HIM GOOD TO READ THE TRUTH ABOUT 207 AHWILD
LIFE FOR ONCE
AND IT'S GOD'S TRUTH--THERE'D BEEN MUTINY ITSELF 36 ANNA
IN THE STOKHOLE.
SO OUT WITH THE TRUTH, MAN ALIVE. 46 ANNA
BUT YOU KNOW THE TRUTH IN YOUR HEART, 48 ANNA
(PASSIONATELY) AND THAT'S GOD TRUTH, ANNA, AND 51 ANNA
WELL YOU KNOW IT/
AND I WAS ASHAMED TO TELL YOU THE TRUTH-- 59 ANNA
IF I AIN'T TELLING YOU THE HONEST TRUTH/ 73 ANNA
(SLOWLY) IF 'TIS TRUTH YOU'RE AFTER TELLING, I'D 74 ANNA
HAVE A RIGHT, MAYBE,
BUT IT'S THE TRUTH AND I AIN'T SCARED TO SWEAR. 75 ANNA
THAT WAS THE TRUTH. 100 BEYOND
YOU KNOW I'M SPEAKIN' TRUTH--THAT'S WHY YOU'RE 106 BEYOND
AFRAID TO ANGRY
(IN ANGRY TRIUMPH) IT'S THE TRUTH, ANDY MAYO/ 106 BEYOND
THE TRUTH--GOD'S TRUTH/ 107 BEYOND
YOU'RE WRONG, PA, IT ISN'T TRUTH. 107 BEYOND
TELL ME THE TRUTH/ 110 BEYOND
I'M TELLING YOU THE TRUTH WHEN I SAY I'D FORGOTTEN134 BEYOND
LONG AGO.
(STARING AT HIM INTENSELY) ARE YOU TELLING ME THE138 BEYOND
TRUTH, ANDY MAYO$
TELL ME THE TRUTH. 155 BEYOND
THE THINGS HE SAID TO ME HAD TRUTH IN THEM-- 163 BEYOND
IT'S GAWDS TRUTH/ 478 CARDIF
YE SAID NO MORE THAN THE TRUTH, COCKY. 480 CARDIF
I WANT TO GET AT THE REAL TRUTH AND UNDERSTAND 495 DAYS
WHAT WAS BEHIND--
(CONFUSED) WELL, TO TELL THE TRUTH, I HAVEN'T 497 DAYS
GIVEN IT A THOUGHT IN YEARS, BUT--
BOGGED DOWN IN EVOLUTIONARY SCIENTIFIC TRUTH 503 DAYS
AGAIN--
THIS RUNNING AWAY FROM TRUTH IN ORDER TO FIND ITS 504 DAYS
(HE SMILES) TO TELL YOU THE TRUTH, 505 DAYS
IT WOULD KILL FOREVER ALL MY FAITH IN LIFE--ALL 523 DAYS
TRUTH, ALL BEAUTY, ALL LOVE/
WHY DO YOU SUPPOSE I EVER DID IT, EXCEPT FOR HIS 526 DAYS
BENEFIT--IF YOU WANT THE TRUTH$
TO ACCEPT THE ONE BEAUTIFUL COMFORTING TRUTH OF 534 DAYS
LIFE..
ALWAYS ON THE TRAIL OF TRUTH/ 535 DAYS
AND HE FOUND HIS TRUTH AT LAST-- 535 DAYS
THAT THERE IS NO TRUTH FOR MEN, THAT HUMAN LIFE IS535 DAYS
UNIMPORTANT AND MEANINGLESS.
DAMNED BY A FEAR OF THE LIE HIDING BEHIND THE MASK535 DAYS
OF TRUTH.
THE TRUTH IS THAT THIS POOR FOOL WAS MAKING A 538 DAYS
GREAT FUSS ABOUT NOTHING--
BECAUSE THEIR FEAR OF CHANGE WON'T LET THEM FACE 542 DAYS
THE TRUTH.
WHO BY HIS LIFE WILL EXEMPLIFY IT AND MAKE IT A 543 DAYS
LIVING TRUTH FOR US--
WHICH HAD BECOME ALL THE BEAUTY AND TRUTH OF LIFE 549 DAYS
TO ME/
I WANT THE TRUTH/ 556 DAYS
IF YOU WOULD ONLY BE HONEST WITH YOURSELF AND 558 DAYS
ADMIT THE TRUTH IN YOUR OWN SOUL
THE TRUTH YOU ALREADY KNOW IN YOUR HEART. 559 DAYS
BECAUSE I HAVE DECIDED YOU MUST BE TOLD THE TRUTH 559 DAYS
NOW.
WHAT---TRUTHS 559 DAYS
THE TRUTH YOU HAVE YOURSELF REVEALED IN YOUR STORY560 DAYS
LOOK INTO YOUR SOUL AND FORCE YOURSELF TO ADMIT 560 DAYS
THE TRUTH YOU FIND THERE--
THOU ART THE WAY--THE TRUTH-- 566 DAYS
I'LL TELL HIM THE TRUTH 'BOUT THE SON HE'S SO 257 DESIRE
PROUD OF/
HERE'S EMBER TELLIN' YOU THE TRUTH AFTER YOU HAIR-513 DIFRNT
PULLIN' ME ALL THESE YEARS
HE ONLY TOLD ME THE TRUTH, DIDN'T HE$ 515 DIFRNT
I TOLD HIM THE TRUTH, IF THAT'S WHAT YOU MEAN. 528 DIFRNT
(TRIUMPHANTLY) HAVEN'T I ALWAYS SAID, IF THE 449 DYNAMO
TRUTH WERE KNOWN,
CONVINCED NOW OF THE TRUTH AND TRYING TO MAKE 464 DYNAMO
HIMSELF REALIZE IT AND ACCEPT IT)
(SAVAGELY) (INO/...I DON'T OWE HIM THE TRUTH/... 466 DYNAMO
SHE SAW I'D FOUND THE RIGHT PATH TO THE 467 DYNAMO
TRUTH/...
I WON'T EVER BE SATISFIED NOW UNTIL I'VE FOUND THE469 DYNAMO
TRUTH ABOUT EVERYTHING.
TELL HER TO FORGIVE ME, AND TO HELP ME FIND YOUR 474 DYNAMO
TRUTH/
LOVE HIM AND GIVE HIM THE SECRET OF TRUTH 477 DYNAMO
I DON'T WANT TO KNOW THE TRUTH/ 488 DYNAMO
IT'S THE TRUTH, 25 ELECTR
WHEN IT COMES TO FACING THE TRUTH ABOUT 25 ELECTR
THEMSELVES
(APPALLED) NOW SHE KNOWS THE TRUTH/ 25 ELECTR
BUT, BY GOD, YOU'LL HEAR THE TRUTH OF IT, NOW YOU 25 ELECTR
KNOW WHO I AM--
AND I'D HAVE TO KILL HIS SILENCE BY SCREAMING OUT 40 ELECTR
THE TRUTH/
BUT I WAS JEALOUS A MITE, TO TELL YOU THE TRUTH. 53 ELECTR
YOU WANT THE TRUTH$ 61 ELECTR
YOU WANTED THE TRUTH AND YOU'RE GOING TO HEAR IT 61 ELECTR
NOW/
SO NOW YOU KNOW THE TRUTH/ 61 ELECTR
I'LL TELL YOU THE TRUTH, MOTHER/ 86 ELECTR
EVEN WHEN WE WERE LITTLE YOU ALWAYS KNEW I TOLD 96 ELECTR
YOU THE TRUTH, DIDN'T YOU$
I SWEAR BY OUR DEAD FATHER I AM TELLING YOU THE 97 ELECTR
TRUTH/
WE'D HAVE BEEN ARRESTED--AND THEN I'D HAVE TO TELL113 ELECTR
THE TRUTH TO SAVE US.
YOU KNOW THE TRUTH/ 142 ELECTR

TRUTH (CONT'D.)

THE TRUTH, THE WHOLE TRUTH AND NOTHING BUT THE 149 ELECTR
TRUTH/
WHAT WILL THE NEIGHBORS SAY IF THIS WHOLE TRUTH IS149 ELECTR
EVER KNOWN.
ARE YOU SURE YOU WANT THE WHOLE TRUTHS 149 ELECTR
HE MIGHT--IF HE EVER DISCOVERED THE TRUTH/ 173 ELECTR
(VIOLENTLY) WHAT TRUTH, YOU LITTLE FOOL/ 173 ELECTR
OH, GOD, SOMETIMES THE TRUTH HITS ME SUCH A SOCK 286 GGBROW
BETWEEN THE EYES
THAT IS MERELY THE APPEARANCE, NOT THE TRUTH/ 298 GGBROW
WHERE THE FOUNDING FATHERS HAVE GUARANTEED TO EACH243 HA APE
ONE HAPPINESS, WHERE TRUTH,
AIN'T IT THE TRUTH, CHARLIES 29 HUGHIE
TRUTHS 30 HUGHIE
I'M AFRAID I DIDN'T GET--WHAT'S THE TRUTHS 30 HUGHIE
WHAT'S THE MATTER IF THE TRUTH IS THAT THEIR 578 ICEMAN
FAVORING BREEZE HAS THE STINK OF
AS THE HISTORY OF THE WORLD PROVES, THE TRUTH HAS 578 ICEMAN
NO BEARING ON ANYTHING.
TO HELL WITH THE TRUTH/ 578 ICEMAN
AIN'T I TELLING HIM THE TRUTH, COMRADE HUGOS 579 ICEMAN
IT'S DE TRUTH, AIN'T ITS 633 ICEMAN
OH, I KNOW THE TRUTH IS TOUGH AT FIRST. 642 ICEMAN
YOU'VE GOT TO FACE THE TRUTH AND THEN DO WHAT MUST646 ICEMAN
BE DONE FOR YOUR OWN PEACE
BUT THERE'S A LOT OF TRUTH IN SOME OF HIS BULL. 652 ICEMAN
YOU'RE THE ONLY ONE KNOWS THE TRUTH ABOUT THAT. 656 ICEMAN
BUT I'LL BET WHEN YOU ADMIT THE TRUTH TO YOURSELF,657 ICEMAN
THERE'S TRUTH IN THE OLD SUPERSTITION THAT YOU'D 657 ICEMAN
BETTER LOOK OUT WHAT YOU CALL
NO, I GAVE YOU THE SIMPLE TRUTH ABOUT THAT. 658 ICEMAN
AND SHE'D ALWAYS TELL ME THE TRUTH. 667 ICEMAN
IF THE TRUTH WAS KNOWN, YOU WERE MY FATHER. 667 ICEMAN
WHEN IT COMES TO MAKING HIMSELF FACE THE TRUTH. 684 ICEMAN
I'VE SEEN THE DAY WHEN IF ANYONE FORCED ME TO FACE686 ICEMAN
THE TRUTH
YOU'VE FACED THE TRUTH ABOUT YOURSELF. 695 ICEMAN
BEFORE I FACED THE TRUTH AND SAW THE ONE POSSIBLE 705 ICEMAN
WAY TO FREE POOR EVELYN AND
ANY SOTTYLL TELL YOU IF I AIN'T SPEAKIN' TRUTH. 520 INZONE
DIVIL TAKE ME IF I DON'T THINK YE HAVE THE TRUTH 522 INZONE
AV UT, DAVIS.
IF THE TRUTH WAS KNOWN. 522 INZONE
THE TRUTH YOU HAVE COVERED OVER WITH YOUR MEAN 531 INZONE
LIES
BECAUSE YOU KNEW I HAD FOUND OUT THE TRUTH-- 531 INZONE
IT'S THE TRUTH/ 34 JOURNE
I WISH TO GOD WE COULD KEEP THE TRUTH FROM HER, 37 JOURNE
TELL ME THE TRUTH. 45 JOURNE
THE TRUTH IS THERE IS NO CURE AND WE'VE BEEN SAPS 76 JOURNE
TO HOPE--
WHY SHOULDN'T I TELL HARDY THE TRUTHS 80 JOURNE
AND BECAUSE HE'LL KNOW IT ISN'T THE TRUTH-- 80 JOURNE
ALL THE SAME THERE'S TRUTH IN YOUR MOTHER'S 109 JOURNE
WARNING.
WHAT YOU WANT TO BELIEVE, THAT'S THE ONLY TRUTH/ 127 JOURNE
WHERE TRUTH IS UNTRUE AND LIFE CAN HIDE FROM 131 JOURNE
ITSELF.
WHAT LITTLE TRUTH IS IN IT YOU'LL FIND NOBLY SAID 133 JOURNE
IN SHAKESPEARE.
THAT'S THE TRUTH, NO MATTER WHAT SHE SAYS WHEN 142 JOURNE
SHE'S NOT HERSELF.
THAT'S THE TRUTH/ 144 JOURNE
JAMIE SUSPECTED YOU'D CRY POORHOUSE TO HARDY AND 144 JOURNE
HE WORMED THE TRUTH OUT OF HIM.
YOU CAN'T DENY IT'S THE TRUTH ABOUT THE STATE 144 JOURNE
FARM, CAN YOU/
FIFTY CENTS A WEEK/ IT'S THE TRUTH/ FIFTY CENTS 148 JOURNE
A WEEK/
OR MIGHT NOT BE DRUNK ENOUGH TO TELL YOU TRUTH. 165 JOURNE
MAYBE IF THE TRUTH WERE KNOWN, OUR FRIEND THERE 275 LAZARU
NEVER REALLY DIED AT ALL/
SONS OF GOD WHO APPEARED ON WORLDS LIKE OURS TO 289 LAZARU
TELL THE SAVING TRUTH TO EARS
(AFTER A PAUSE--SIGHING) IN TRUTH, THE SENATE IS 315 LAZARU
NOT WHAT IT USED TO BE.
TO SAY THE THING ONE HAS ALWAYS KEPT HIDDEN, TO 354 LAZARU
REVEAL ONE'S UNIQUE TRUTH--
IT IS OUR ONE TRUTH. 358 LAZARU
WHEN I AM CAESAR, I WILL DEVOTE MY POWER TO YOUR 360 LAZARU
TRUTH.
HOW CAN A MAN KNOW ABOUT THE TRUTH OF THE LIES IN 20 MANSNS
A WOMAN'S DREAMS/
TO HIMSELF TO BE--A COURAGEOUS FACING OF THE TRUTH 47 MANSNS
ABOUT HIM--
AND ACCEPT IT AS TRUTH. 91 MANSNS
THE TRUTH IS I HAVE BECOME SUPERSTITIOUS-- 113 MANSNS
AND NOT EVEN THE WHOLE OF YOUR TRUTH. 115 MANSNS
AFTER ALL, THERE IS A GREAT DEAL OF TRUTH IN THAT 115 MANSNS
ASPECT OF IT.
YOUR TRUTH, OF COURSE--NOT SARA'S---NOR MINE. 115 MANSNS
HE SAID I WAS STILL SO BEAUTIFUL TO HIM AND I KNEW133 MANSNS
HE WAS TELLING THE TRUTH.
THE TRUTH IS-- I DIDN'T WANT HIM IN MY GARDEN EVER 134 MANSNS
AGAIN.
THAT A WHISPER, A HINT OF THE TRUTH, 156 MANSNS
TRUTH AMONG YOUR ENEMIES--TO THROW OFF THE BURDEN 157 MANSNS
OF RESPONSIBILITY AND GUILT--
I'VE TOLD YOU THE TRUTH. 167 MANSNS
WHAT THEY DON'T WANT AND BE AFRAID TO CRAVE WHAT 172 MANSNS
THEY WISH FOR IN TRUTH.
I WONDER--I WONDER--OH, GOD HELP ME, I'LL NEVER BE194 MANSNS
SURE OF THE TRUTH OF IT NOW/
(HESITATINGLY) BUT, TO TELL THE TRUTH, I WANT TO 393 MARCOM
RESIGN ANYHOW.
HIS TRUTH ACTS WITHOUT DEEDS. 401 MARCOM
HER TRUTH/ SHE DIED FOR LOVE OF A FOOL/ 437 MARCOM

TRUTH (CONT'D.)

IT WAS THE TRUTH OF POWER. 437 MARCOM
FOR ME THERE REMAINS ONLY--HER TRUTH/ 437 MARCOM
IT WAS THY TRUTH. 437 MARCOM
MY WISDOM, MY TRUTHS 437 MARCOM
WAS IT NOT TRUTHS 437 MARCOM
(AS BEFORE) THY TRUTH. 437 MARCOM
I'LL TELL THE TRUTH THEN. 14 MISBEG
TO TELL THE TRUTH, I NEVER LIKED HIM. 16 MISBEG
BUT TO TELL THE TRUTH, I'M WELL SATISFIED YOU'RE 20 MISBEG
WHAT YOU ARE.
NOW WE'VE COME TO THE TRUTH BEHIND ALL YOUR 30 MISBEG
BLATHER
(TO HARDER, JEERINGLY) COME, TELL US THE TRUTH, 58 MISBEG
ME HONEY.
THERE'S NO USE TELLING THE TRUTH TO A BAD-TEMPERED 80 MISBEG
WOMAN IN LOVE.
THAT'S THE TRUTH BEHIND THE LIES HE TOLD YOU OF 92 MISBEG
HIS CONSCIENCE AND HIS FEAR HE
(KNOWS HE IS TELLING THE TRUTH--SO RELIEVED SHE 132 MISBEG
CAN ONLY STAMMER STUPIDLY)
SO THAT'S--THE TRUTH OF IT. 133 MISBEG
YOU CAN TAKE THE TRUTH, JOSIE--FROM ME. 135 MISBEG
THEN I'LL CONFESS THE TRUTH TO YOU. 136 MISBEG
THAT'S THE TRUTH, JOSIE. 138 MISBEG
AND WHEN THE TRUTH DID COME OUT, WOULDN'T IT MAKE 163 MISBEG
ME
MISERABLY) CAN'T YOU BELIEVE THAT'S THE TRUTH, 175 MISBEG
JOSIE, AND NOT FEEL SO BITTER
AND FACE THE TRUTH THAT YOU LOVED EACH OTHER. 175 MISBEG
I KNOW IT'S THE TRUTH, FATHER. 175 MISBEG
(WITH A GRIN.) MORE THAN YOUR PRAYERS IS THE 10 POET
TRUTH.
THAT'S THE TRUTH, TOO. 12 POET
BUT HE'LL NEVER MAKE ME PRETEND TO HIM I DON'T 24 POET
KNOW THE TRUTH.
TO TELL THE TRUTH, MY STOMACH IS OUT OF SORTS. 36 POET
AND WHAT'S THE LIVING TRUTHS 51 POET
EVEN IF THE TRUTH WAS HER HUSBAND SENT HER TO DO 79 POET
ALL SHE COULD
INURA STARTS TO TELL HER THE TRUTH--THEN THINKS 80 POET
BETTER OF IT.
IF YOU EVER DARED FACE THE TRUTH, YOU'D HATE AND 105 POET
DESPISE YOURSELF/
BUT I DON'T DOUBT YOU'VE MADE YOURSELF THINK IT'S 106 POET
THE TRUTH BY NOW.
WELL, THAT'S NO MORE THAN THE TRUTH. 112 POET
(SHE APPEALS TO ORGAN.) TELL HIM I'M TELLING THE126 POET
TRUTH, JAMIE.
UNTIL I KNEW TONIGHT THE TRUTH OF WHAT YOU SAID 149 POET
THIS MORNING,
BOASTING OF HIS GLORIOUS VICTORY OVER OLD HARFORD,151 POET
WHATEVER THE TRUTH IS/
SO HE'LL HAVE TO FACE THE TRUTH OF HIMSELF IN THAT151 POET
MIRROR.
THE TRUTH--TALAVERA--THE DUKE PRAISING YOUR 178 POET
BRAVERY--AN OFFICER IN HIS ARMY--
YOU THINK ONE CAN LIVE WITH TRUTH. 20 STRANG
I WISH I KNEW THE TRUTH OF WHAT SHE'S BEEN DOING 25 STRANG
IN THAT HOUSE FULL OF MEN...
CAN'T TELL HIM THE RAW TRUTH ABOUT HER 35 STRANG
PROMISCUITY...
I'LL SCREAM OUT THE TRUTH ABOUT EVERY WOMAN/ 40 STRANG
OR EVEN A GOOD MAN PREACHING THE SIMPLE PLATITUDES 41 STRANG
OF TRUTH, THOSE GOSPEL WORDS
HE BELIEVES IF YOU PICK A LIE TO PIECES, THE 41 STRANG
PIECES ARE THE TRUTH/
(THEN BOLDLY) (WELL, THEN, A LITTLE TRUTH FOR 42 STRANG
ONCE IN A WAY/...))
AND MY DUTY AS AN EXPERIMENTAL SEARCHER AFTER 86 STRANG
TRUTH...
TO FACE THE TRUTH... 92 STRANG
(RESENTFULLY) (ISHE CAN'T HELP LETTING THE TRUTH 120 STRANG
ESCAPE HER/.....)
IF I HAD THE COURAGE TO WRITE THE TRUTH.... 120 STRANG
MAKES IT EASIER TO TELL HIM THE TRUTH....)) 128 STRANG
I'LL TELL SAM THE TRUTH NO MATTER WHAT/...)) 129 STRANG
(THINKING) ((I'LL YELL THE TRUTH INTO YOUR EARS 152 STRANG
IF I STAY A SECOND LONGER...
OH, MOTHER GOD, GRANT MY PRAYER THAT SOME DAY WE 156 STRANG
MAY TELL OUR SON THE TRUTH AND
((OH, MOTHER GOD, GRANT THAT I MAY SOME DAY TELL 158 STRANG
THIS FOOL THE TRUTH/...))
SHE TOLD YOU THE TRUTH. 172 STRANG
TRUTH, ISN'T ITS 173 STRANG
TELL SAM THE TRUTH... 173 STRANG
IF THE REAL DEEP CORE OF THE TRUTH WERE KNOWN/ 174 STRANG
I CAN WRITE THE TRUTH/ 177 STRANG
(THINKING VINDICTIVELY) ((I HOPE HE KNOWS THE 193 STRANG
TRUTH, FOR IF HE DOESN'T, BY GOD,
(WITH SUDDEN FURIOUS ANGER) GOD, WHAT I FEEL OF 448 WELDED
THE TRUTH OF THIS--THE BEAUTY/
I TRIED TO MAKE YOU SEE--THE TRUTH--THAT THOSE 458 WELDED
EXPERIENCES HAD
FACE THE TRUTH IN YOURSELF. 469 WELDED
YES--THE TRUTH--IF I CAN. 482 WELDED
YES, I WISH TO TELL YOU THE TRUTH. 482 WELDED
IT'S THE TRUTH, NELLY/ 485 WELDED
YOU ARE THERE--BESIDE ME--ALIVE--WITH YOU I BECOME488 WELDED
A WHOLE, A TRUTH/

TRUTHFUL

WITH YOU THE LIES HAVE BECOME THE ONLY TRUTHFUL 40 STRANG
THINGS.

TRY

AND SEE TO IT THEY DON'T TRY NONE OF THEIR 545 'ILE
SKULKIN' TRICKS.
NOW YOU WILL TRY TO REMEMBER, WON'T YOUS 211 AHWILD

TRY

TRY (CONT'D.)
YOU KIDS GO OUT IN THE YARD AND TRY TO KEEP QUIET 234 AHWILD
FOR A WHILE.
-I HAVEN'T PLAYED THAT IN EVER SO LONG BUT I'LL 257 AHWILD
TRY--
THEN KEEP AWAKE AND TRY AND USE YOUR BRAINS/ 266 AHWILD
AND SHE'D TRY TO GET HIM DRUNK SO-- 267 AHWILD
DON'T TRY TO KID ME. 272 AHWILD
AND SHE'S GOING TO TRY AND SNEAK OUT AND MEET ME 273 AHWILD
TONIGHT.
(PLEADINGLY) YOU TRY FOR NOT HATE ME, ANNA. 65 ANNA
DON'T TRY GETTING TOO CLOSE. 69 ANNA
OH, ROB, I DO WISH SHE'D TRY TO MAKE THE BEST OF 87 BEYOND
THINGS THAT CAN'T BE HELPED.
AND TRY TO FORM A PICTURE OF IT IN MY MIND. 89 BEYOND
PUTS HER HANDS ON HIS SHOULDERS AS THOUGH TO TRY 107 BEYOND
TO PUSH HIM BACK IN THE CHAIR
I'VE GOT TO GET AWAY AND TRY AND FORGET, IF I CAN.110 BEYOND
IT'S A WONDER ROB WOULDN'T TRY TO GET TO MEALS ON 117 BEYOND
TIME ONCE IN A WHILE.
I KNOW YOU DO. BUT LET'S BOTH OF US TRY TO DO 123 BEYOND
BETTER.
(RESENTFULLY) ROB'S TOO GOOD A CHUM TO TRY AND 137 BEYOND
STOP ME
AND DIDN'T HE TRY TO STOP YOU FROM GOINGS 137 BEYOND
I'M GOING TO TRY AND HIRE A GOOD MAN FOR HIM--AN 137 BEYOND
EXPERIENCED FARMER--
SO I THOUGHT I'D TRY TO END AS I MIGHT HAVE--IF 167 BEYOND
I'D HAD THE COURAGE--ALONE--
WE MUST TRY TO HELP EACH OTHER--AND--IN TIME-- 168 BEYOND
HE'LL COME TO KNOW WHAT'S RIGHT--
I TRY. 470 CARIBE
LET ME TRY. 572 CROSS
YOU KNOW I'M DOING IT TO TRY AND EXPLAIN TO 499 DAYS
MYSELF, AS WELL AS TO HER.
AND THEN I DID TRY IT ONCE. 519 DAYS
I TRY NOT TO, BUT--I KNOW IT'S CRAZY, BUT I CAN'T 554 DAYS
HELP BEING AFRAID--
(SUDDENLY) MEBBE YE'LL TRY T' MAKE HER YOUR'N, 214 DESIRE
TOO$
WAAL, HE'D BEST NOT DO NUTHIN' T' TRY ME 'R HE'LL 231 DESIRE
SOON DISKIVER....
(RESENTFULLY) DON'T TRY TO PUT THE BLAME ON JACK.515 DIFRNT
AND TRY TO PUT SOME SENSE BACK INTO HER HEAD. 529 DIFRNT
YOU JUST TRY IT! 530 DIFRNT
I'LL SPILL THE BEANS FOR BOTH OF YOU, IF YOU TRY 530 DIFRNT
TO GUM ME/
(DEFINITELY) YOU JUST TRY IT, THAT'S ALL/ 530 DIFRNT
AND I'LL TRY TO SAVE UP MY PAY AND SEND YOU BACK 532 DIFRNT
ALL I'VE BORROWED NOW AND
I'D LIKE TO SEE YOU TRY IT/ 546 DIFRNT
DOES NOT HIS FOUL RANTING BEGIN TO TRY THY 423 DYNAMO
PATIENCES....
I'D LIKE TO SEE HER TRY TO CATCH MY REUBEN/ 427 DYNAMO
I'LL TRY THAT ON HIM/ 434 DYNAMO
SURE--I'LL TRY, RUBE. 461 DYNAMO
LET DEM TRY DEIR HEATHEN TRICKS. 185 EONES
HOW CAN YOU BE SO VILE AS TO TRY TO USE ME TO HIDE 30 ELECTR
YOUR ADULTERY$
BUT YOU BETTER NOT TRY IT 34 ELECTR
BUT WOULD TRY TO GET LEAVE AT ONCE. 46 ELECTR
I'VE GOT TO EXPLAIN SOME THINGS--INSIDE ME--TO MY 53 ELECTR
WIFE--TRY TO ANYWAY/
I WOULD TRY TO MAKE UP MY MIND EXACTLY WHAT THAT 54 ELECTR
HALL WAS
AND I WOULD TRY TO LOOK AT THEM. 54 ELECTR
(GENTLY) TRY NOT TO THINK OF IT. 72 ELECTR
AND TRY NOT TO THINK ABOUT THINGS. 84 ELECTR
SHE CAN'T BE SO CRAZY AS TO TRY THAT/ 88 ELECTR
TRY AND CONVINCE ORIN OF MY WICKEDNESS/ 92 ELECTR
TRY NOT TO REGRET YOUR SHIP TOO MUCH, ADAM/ 112 ELECTR
YOU OUGHT TO TRY AND SLEEP. 118 ELECTR
TO BE READ IN CASE YOU TRY TO MARRY HIM--OR IF I 156 ELECTR
SHOULD DIE--
(BLURTS OUT) DON'T YOU TRY TO LIVE HERE, VINNIE/ 171 ELECTR
(EMBARRASSED) I'LL TRY, MOTHER. 259 GGBROW
SHE KNOWS I ONLY TRY TO PAINT. 261 GGBROW
I'LL TRY. 270 GGBROW
I WISH YOU'D TRY TO TAKE MORE INTEREST IN THE 270 GGBROW
CHILDREN, DION.
HE DOESN'T TRY TO HAVE AN EXHIBITION ANYWHERE, OR 275 GGBROW
ANYTHING.
(THEN ABRUPTLY) LETS TRY TO NAIL HIM DOWN RIGHT 277 GGBROW
AWAY, MARGARET.
DON'T TRY TO CRAWL OUT/ 281 GGBROW
THEY TRY TO KNOW TOO MUCH. 284 GGBROW
WANTER TRY IT, ANY OF YOUSE$ 211 HA APE
DIDN'T TRY TO GET EVEN WIT 234 HA APE
IT BEATS IT WHEN YOU TRY TO TINK IT OR TALK IT-- 253 HA APE
IT'S WAY DOWN--DEEP--BEHIND--
AND TRY TO SLIP T'IN TO ME. 22 HUGHIE
TAKE MY TIP, PAL, AND DON'T NEVER TRY TO BUY FROM 27 HUGHIE
A DOPE PEDDLER.
SHE WROTE TO DENOUNCE ME AND TRY TO BRING THE 589 ICEMAN
SINNER TO REPENTANCE
I'LL TRY AND MAKE AN HONEST MAN OF YOU, TOO/ 623 ICEMAN
YOU'VE GOT TO TRY AND GET YOUR OLD JOB BACK. 623 ICEMAN
(DRYLY) DON'T TRY TO KID ME, LITTLE BOY. 624 ICEMAN
TRY IT AGAIN. 645 ICEMAN
I USED TO TRY AND GET HER GOAT ABOUT YOU. 647 ICEMAN
(THEN TRY TO RECAPTURE THEIR MOMENTARY ENTHUSIASM)659 ICEMAN
OF COURSE YOU'LL TRY TO SHOW ME/ 660 ICEMAN
AND DON'T TRY TO GET OUT OF IT/ 693 ICEMAN
(GOES ON OBLIVIOUSLY) SOMETIMES I'D TRY SOME JOKE712 ICEMAN
I THOUGHT WAS A CORKER UN
IF YOU WANTS TO TRY YOUR DIRTY SPYIN' TRICKS ON US525 INZONE
TRY TO KICK UT OVER, WUD YES 526 INZONE
I'M NO HAND TO BE READIN' BUT I'LL TRY UT. 529 INZONE

TRY (CONT'D.)
BUT PLEASE DON'T TRY TO TELL ME/ 74 JOURNE
LET'S REMEMBER ONLY THAT, AND NOT TRY TO 85 JOURNE
UNDERSTAND WHAT WE CANNOT UNDERSTAND$
TRY TO GO FOR A DRIVE THIS AFTERNOON. YOU MEANS 85 JOURNE
YOU WON'T EVEN TRYS 85 JOURNE
TO TRY AND THROW YOURSELF OFF THE DOCK/ 86 JOURNE
WE ALL TRY TO LIE OUT OF THAT BUT LIFE WON'T LET 87 JOURNE
US.
FOR GOD'S SAKE TRY AND BE YOURSELF--AT LEAST UNTIL 88 JOURNE
HE GOES/
IF YOU'RE COMING HOME FOR DINNER, TRY NOT TO BE 95 JOURNE
LATE.
YOU MUST TRY TO UNDERSTAND AND FORGIVE HIM, TOO. 117 JOURNE
AND YOU WON'T EVEN LISTEN WHEN I TRY TO TELL YOU 120 JOURNE
HOW SICK--
ALL WE CAN DO IS TRY TO BE RESIGNED--AGAIN. 132 JOURNE
YOU MUST TRY TO SEE MY SIDE OF IT, TOO, LAD. 140 JOURNE
DID TRY OTHER PLAYS, IT WAS TOO LATE. 149 JOURNE
(DEFENSIVELY) OH, PAPA'S ALL RIGHT, IF YOU TRY 157 JOURNE
TO UNDERSTAND HIM--
YOU MUST NOT TRY TO TOUCH ME. 174 JOURNE
YOU MUST NOT TRY TO HOLD ME. 174 JOURNE
WHEN YOU AWAKE TOMORROW, TRY TO REMEMBER/ 323 LAZARU
AND NOW I MUST LIE DOWN AND TRY TO SLEEP/ 356 LAZARU
OH, DON'T TRY TO FOOL ME WITH BLARNEY. 20 MANSNS
AND I SWEAR TO YOU I WILL TRY. 39 MANSNS
I'VE HALF A MIND TO TRY IT/ 47 MANSNS
AND SHE PROMISED SHE WOULD TRY. 62 MANSNS
TO TRY AND MAKE TROUBLE BETWEEN YOUR MOTHER AND 78 MANSNS
ME$
AH, I'D LIKE TO SEE HER TRY--/ 85 MANSNS
(COARSELY SELF-CONFIDENT.) I'D LIKE TO SEE YOU TRY149 MANSNS
TO WANT TO/
I SWEAR BY ALMIGHTY GOD I'LL MURDER YOU IF YOU TRY168 MANSNS
THAT.
I'LL TRY, DONATA. 357 MARCOM
(THEN PLEADINGLY) FOR HEAVEN'S SAKE, TRY AND BE 413 MARCOM
CALM, PRINCESS/
IF YOU WOULD ONLY TRY TO SLEEP A WHILE-- 413 MARCOM
WELL, I WOULDN'T PUT IT PAST THE OLD MAN TO TRY 9 MISBEG
ANY TRICK.
THEN DON'T TRY TO HELP HIM HIDE FROM ME, OR--WHERE 12 MISBEG
IS HE$
BUT DON'T TRY TO CHANGE THE SUBJECT AND FILL ME 14 MISBEG
WITH BLARNEY.
MUST HAVE HAD A TRY AT THAT, AND MUCH GOOD IT DID 21 MISBEG
THEM.
BECAUSE IT'S SO ANCIENT NO ONE WOULD SUSPECT YOU'D 23 MISBEG
TRY IT.
SURE, I'D NEVER TRY TO FOOL YOU. 26 MISBEG
OCH, JIM LOVES TO TRY AND GET YOUR GOAT. 32 MISBEG
DON'T TRY RUNNING AWAY OR MY DAUGHTER WILL KNOCK 61 MISBEG
YOU SENSELESS.
(WITH ANGRY DISGUST) OCH, DON'T TRY-- (THEN 74 MISBEG
CURIOUSLY) WHAT'S HAPPENED$
GOD HELP YOU, IF YOU TRY TO GO UPSTAIRS NOW, 80 MISBEG
YOU'LL END UP IN THE CELLAR.
OR I'LL TRY TO/ 91 MISBEG
I'LL TRY TO CONTROL MY ENVY FOR YOUR BROADWAY 117 MISBEG
FLAMES.
ALL RIGHT, I'LL TRY AND BELIEVE THAT--FOR TONIGHT.129 MISBEG
NOT UNLESS-- I REMEMBER I DID TRY TO GET HIS GOAT. 132 MISBEG
I GAVE IT A TRY--BUT BEFORE I CAME UP HERE. 143 MISBEG
ALL I DID WAS TRY TO EXPLAIN TO MYSELF, +SHE'S 148 MISBEG
DEAD.
DON'T TRY TO FOOL ME, JOSIE. 162 MISBEG
AND TRY TO MAKE YOU, OR ANYTHING LIKE THAT. 173 MISBEG
AKRAH, DON'T TRY TO SCARE ME. 17 POET
WHAT MAKES YOU THINK SHE'LL TRY TO CHANGE HIMS 78 POET
(AFTER A PAUSE--DEFINITELY.) LET HER TRY WHATEVER 80 POET
GAME SHE LIKES.
I DIDN'T SAY SLEEP, BUT I CAN LIE DOWN AND TRY TO 131 POET
REST.
SIMON SAID NO ONE COULD EVER COME BETWEEN US AND 144 POET
HIS MOTHER WOULD NEVER TRY TO.
LET THE POLICE TRY IT/ 147 POET
TRY AND MAKE HIM. 153 POET
I KNOW YOU WON'T TRY RAISIN' THE DEAD ANY MORE. 179 POET
I'LL TRY AND BE LIKE YOU. 182 POET
(HE REACHES UP FOR THE ROPE AS IF TO TRY AND YANK 583 ROPE
IT DOWN.
AN' TRY AN' FIND WHERE IT IS THE AULD MAN HAS THE 586 ROPE
GOLD HID, IF HE HAS IT YET.
HER EYES TRY TO ARMOR HER WOUNDED SPIRIT 26 STRANG
TRY TOMORROW IN MY BEDROOM... 67 STRANG
(GOSH, I OUGHT TO TRY AND GET A NEW START ON THIS 68 STRANG
BEFORE IT'S TIME....))
I MUST TRY... 69 STRANG
I'LL TRY SOON....)) 71 STRANG
OH, I'LL TRY.... 71 STRANG
I MUST TRY TO MAKE HIM FEEL SURE....)) 71 STRANG
(BROKENLY AND EXHAUSTEDLY) I'LL TRY TO MAKE YOU 109 STRANG
HAPPY, SAMMY.
I'LL TRY TO READ....)) 123 STRANG
I'LL TRY, NINA/ 145 STRANG
I TRY TO KNOW YOU AND I CAN'T. 455 WELDED
TRY AND REST. 466 WELDED
AGAIN TONIGHT, WHEN YOU TRY TO GIVE YOURSELF TO ME466 WELDED
OUT OF HATE FOR HIM/
(BROKENLY) WE CAN TRY-- 487 WELDED
TRYIN'
(GRUMBLINGLY) WHAT YUH TRYIN' TO DO, DUTCHY--KEEP 7 ANNA
ME STANDIN' OUT HERE ALL DAYS
A SQUARE-HEAD TRYIN' TO KID MAKTHY OWEN AT THIS 11 ANNA
LATE DAYS
LUUD AND HIM TRYIN' TO HAVE A BIT AV A SLEEP. 479 CARDIF

1715 TRYING

TRYIN' (CONT'D.)
TRYIN' TO LOOK AS WISE AS AN OWL ON A TREE, AND 479 CARDIF
ALL THE TOINE HE NOT
AFTHER HIM TRYIN' TO STICK YOU IN THE BACK, AND 488 CARDIF
YOU NOT SUSPECTIN'.
(SCORNFULLY) DOWN'T BE SHOWIN' YER IGERANCE BE 456 CARIBE
TRYIN' TO
OW, I WAS ON'Y TRYIN' TO EDICATE YER A BIT. 457 CARIBE
TRYIN' T' TELL YERSELF I HAIN'T PURTY T'YE. 229 DESIRE
(DEFIANTLY) HE WAS TRYIN' T' MAKE LOVE T' ME-- 233 DESIRE
WHEN YE HEERD US QUARRELIN'.
SHE TOLD ME YE WAS SNEAKIN' 'ROUND TRYIN' T' MAKE 255 DESIRE
LOVE T' HER
ARE YOU TRYIN' TO JOSH ME, EMMERS 504 DIFRNT
(HE LAUGHS) NO USE DEIR TRYIN'. 179 EJONES
WOODS IS YOU TRYIN' TO PUT SOMETHIN' OVAH ON MES 189 EJONES
TRYIN' TO HOLD ME UP, AIR YER 104 ELECR
(WITH A CYNICAL GRIN) CAN'T YOUSE SEE I'M TRYIN' 210 HA APE
TO T'INKS
CAN'T YOUSE SEE I'M TRYIN' TO TINKS 227 HA APE
WHAT YUH TRYIN' TO DO, KID ME, YUH OLD HARPS 230 HA APE
TRYIN' TO KID ME, YUH SIMP, YUHS 234 HA APE
(AFTER A PAUSE) I WAS TRYIN' TO GIT EVEN WIT 241 HA APE
SOMEONE, SEES
I'M IN DE MIDDLE TRYIN' TO SEPARATE 'EM, 253 HA APE
JEES, IMAGINE TRYIN' TO SLEEP WID DAT ON DE 612 ICEMAN
PHONOGRAPH!
THIS DUMB BROAD WAS TRYIN' TO TELL US YOU'D 619 ICEMAN
CHANGED, BUT YOU AIN'T A DAMNED BIT.
WHAT GETS MY GOAT IS DE WAY HE'S TRYIN' TO RUN DE 631 ICEMAN
WHOLE DUMP AND EVERYONE IN IT.
I DON'T GET NOWHERE TRYIN' TO FIGGER HIS GAME. 669 ICEMAN
HE WAS TRYIN' TO JUMP IN AND DIDN'T HAVE DE NOIVE,699 ICEMAN
I FIGGERED IT.
TRYIN' TO MURRDHER US ALL, THE SCUT/ 526 INZONE
LOOK AT HIM TRYIN' TO GIT LOOSE/ 529 INZONE
IF YE KEPT ON INTERFERIN' AND TRYIN' TO RAISE THE 179 POET
DEAD.
(WEEPING ANGRILY) THAT'S WHAT I GIT FOR TRYIN' TO581 ROPE
BE KIND TO YOU.
I WAS TRYIN' TO GIT HIM HOME BUT HE'S THAT SET I 582 ROPE
COULDN'T BUDGE HIM,.
HE LOOKS LIKE HE WAS TRYIN' TO GRIN,. 595 ROPE
BUT I THOUGHT HE WAS TRYIN' TO KID ME, TOO. 598 ROPE
(KEEPING HER FORCED GRIN) TRYIN' TO KID ME, AIN'T474 WELDED
YOUS

TRYING
(TRYING TO CONTROL HIS CHATTERING TEETH-- 536 *ILE
DERISIVELY)
(TRYING NOT TO WILT BEFORE THE CAPTAIN'S GLANCE 544 *ILE
AND AVOIDING HIS EYES)
(TRYING TO CONCEAL THE FACT THAT HER MEMORIES HAVE548 *ILE
MOVED HIM--GRUFFLY)
(DAZEDLY--TRYING TO COLLECT HIS THOUGHTS) 550 *ILE
THERE MUST BE SOME BOY HE KNOWS WHO'S TRYING TO 196 AHWILD
SHOW OFF AS ADVANCED AND WICKED.
HAVE YOU BEEN TRYING TO HAVE SOMETHING TO DO WITH 206 AHWILD
MURIEL--
(THEN QUICKLY) I'M NOT TRYING TO LEAD YOU ASTRAY,218 AHWILD
UNDERSTAND.
(QUICKLY INTERPOSING, TRYING TO STAVE OFF THE 229 AHWILD
STORY)
(TRYING TO SWITCH THE SUBJECT) 229 AHWILD
I WAS TRYING SO HARD NOT TO--BUT YOU CAN'T HELP 233 AHWILD
IT, HE'S SO SILLY/
AND SHE IS TRYING HARD TO KEEP HER ATTENTION FIXED249 AHWILD
ON THE DOLLY SHE IS DOING.
THAT'S WHAT WE'VE BEEN TRYING TO TELL YOUR MOTHER,254 AHWILD
DON'T TAX YOUR MEMORY TRYING TO RECALL THOSE 254 AHWILD
ANCIENT DAYS OF YOUR YOUTH.
STOP TRYING TO BE SO DARN FUNNY ALL THE TIME/ 255 AHWILD
TRYING TO SEE WHAT THEY COULD GET. 18 ANNA
(HER VOICE RISING ANGRILY) SAY, WHAT'RE YOU 26 ANNA
TRYING TO DO--MAKE THINGS ROTTEN8
A MINUTE AGO, INSTEAD OF TRYING TO KID ME WITH 34 ANNA
THAT MUSHS
(HALF FRIGHTENEDLY--TRYING TO LAUGH IT OFF) 38 ANNA
ARE YOU TRYING TO KID MES 38 ANNA
SAY, LISTEN HERE, YOU AIN'T TRYING TO INSINUATE 42 ANNA
THAT THERE'S SOMETHING WRONG.
(ASTONISHED AND ENCOURAGED--TRYING TO PLEAD 46 ANNA
PERSUASIVELY)
(TRYING TO BE SCORNFUL AND SELF-CONVINCING) 52 ANNA
(TRYING TO KEEP UP HER HARD, BITTER TONE, 59 ANNA
TRYING TO WARD OFF THE BLOW FROM HIS DAUGHTER. 60 ANNA
TRYING DESPERATELY TO BANISH HER THOUGHTS BY 67 ANNA
LOOKING AT THE PICTURES.
(TRYING TO FALL INTO AN EASY, CARELESS TONE) 69 ANNA
ARE YOU TRYING TO ACCUSE ME OF BEING--REALLY IN 73 ANNA
LOVE--WITH THEM
THAT'S WHAT I BEEN TRYING TO TELL YOU ALL ALONG/ 74 ANNA
THOUGH HE'S BEEN TRYING NOT TO SHOW IT. 83 BEYOND
(CONFUSED--LOOKING EVERYWHERE EXCEPT AT ROBERT-- 86 BEYOND
TRYING TO APPEAR UNCONCERNED)
HAVEN'T I GOT MY SHARE OF TROUBLES TRYING TO WORK 122 BEYOND
THIS CURSED FARM
I GAVE UP TRYING FINALLY AND JUST LAID THERE IN 147 BEYOND
THE DARK THINKING.
(TRYING TO RAISE HIMSELF TO A SITTING POSITION AS 167 BEYOND
THEY HASTEN TO HIS SIDE--
(TRYING TO CONCEAL HIS ANXIETY) 485 CARDIF
BUT JUST WHAT IS HE TRYING TO SEES 557 CARDIF
(AS IF TRYING TO CONVINCE HIMSELF--VEHEMENTLY) 563 CROSS
MY GOD, NAT, ARE YOU TRYING TO BRIBE MES 566 CROSS
(TRYING TO SOOTHE HIM) FATHER/ 568 CROSS
(TRYING TO HOLD HIM BACK) NAT--DON'T/ 572 CROSS
I FEEL--(THEN, AS IF DESPERATELY TRYING TO SHAKE 495 DAYS
OFF HIS THOUGHTS)

TRYING (CONT'D.)
WELL, I HOPE YOU REALIZE I'M ONLY TRYING TO 495 DAYS
ENCOURAGE YOU TO MAKE SOMETHING OF
MERELY TRYING TO WORK OUT THE ANSWER TO A PUZZLE--496 DAYS
A HUMAN PUZZLE.
AS IF HE WERE TRYING TO FIGURE SOMETHING OUT. 505 DAYS
THAT YOU WERE UPSET ABOUT SOMETHING AND TRYING TO 517 DAYS
HIDE IT.
FORGIVE ME TRYING TO PUMP YOU. 517 DAYS
I WAS ONLY TRYING TO GET A RISE OUT OF YOU. 524 DAYS
(TRYING TO CONTROL HERSELF) I--I DON'T 538 DAYS
UNDERSTAND.
ARE YOU TRYING THE BOSSY TENDER HUSBAND ON ME, 548 DAYS
JOHNS
(WORRIEDLY, BUT TRYING TO PRETEND TO TREAT IT 550 DAYS
LIGHTLY, REASSURINGLY)
(HIS EYES ARE ON STILLWELL'S FACE, DESPERATELY 554 DAYS
TRYING TO READ SOME ANSWER THERE.
AS IF HE WERE TRYING TO SEE SOME PRESENCE HE FEELS558 DAYS
THERE)
(TRYING TO BREAK FROM HER SPELL--CONFUSEDLY) 229 DESIRE
(TRYING TO REGAIN HER ASCENDANCY--SEDUCTIVELY) 229 DESIRE
(TRYING TO CONCEAL A GROWING EXCITEMENT) 229 DESIRE
(STARES AT HIM SUSPICIOUSLY, TRYING TO MAKE HIM 254 DESIRE
OUT--A PAUSE--
WITH A CRY, ABBIE KNEELS BESIDE HIM, TRYING TO 256 DESIRE
TAKE HIS HEAD ON HER LAP.
(HUSKILY, TRYING TO FORCE A SMILE) 505 DIFRNT
(TRYING TO SMILE) NOTHING. 506 DIFRNT
(TRYING A CONFIDENTIAL TONE) 529 DIFRNT
(TRYING TO CALM HIMSELF A LITTLE AND BE 560 DIFRNT
CONVINCING)
HUTCHINS LIGHT HAS A PAD ON WHICH HE HAS BEEN 422 DYNAMO
TRYING TO MAKE NOTES FOR HIS NEXT
ATTENTION TO HIS TRYING TO RILE YOUS 425 DYNAMO
HE PACES UP AND DOWN TRYING VAINLY TO CALM 426 DYNAMO
HIMSELF)
PLAINLY WORRIED NOW BUT TRYING TO MAKE LITTLE OF 426 DYNAMO
IT)
IT'S LIKE TRYING TO SWIM IN GLUE/ 434 DYNAMO
(GENUINELY FLUSTERED--TRYING TO LAUGH IT OFF) 438 DYNAMO
(THEN WEEPING HYSTERICALLY AND TRYING TO STIFLE 439 DYNAMO
IT)
PUSHES AND PULLS AT IT, TRYING TO FORCE IT OPEN,) 450 DYNAMO
CONVINCED NOW OF THE TRUTH AND TRYING TO MAKE 464 DYNAMO
HIMSELF REALIZE IT AND ACCEPT IT)
(DEEPLY DISTURBED BUT TRYING DESPERATELY TO 465 DYNAMO
CONCEAL IT)
ARE YOU TRYING TO SAY I KILLED HERS 465 DYNAMO
TRYING UNCONVINCINGLY TO REASSURE HIMSELF) 466 DYNAMO
(TRYING TO FORCE A JOKING TONE) 469 DYNAMO
AT THE SAME TIME TRYING TO REASSURE HERSELF) 471 DYNAMO
(HE WALKS AROUND NERVOUSLY) NO USE TRYING TO GO 472 DYNAMO
TO SLEEP...
(THEN TRYING TO PASS IT OFF BY AN ATTEMPT AT 177 EJONES
SCORN)
(TRYING TO FORCE A LAUGH) I WAS ON'Y SPOOFIN' 181 EJONES
YER.
(THEN TRYING TO TALK HIMSELF INTO CONFIDENCE) 193 EJONES
SETH, IN A MOOD OF AGED PLAYFULNESS, IS TRYING TO 7 ELECTR
MAKE AN IMPRESSION ON MINNIE.
(CRUSHED BY THIS BUT TRYING BRAVELY TO JOKE) 14 ELECTR
(AGAIN UNEASY--TRYING TO JOKE IT OFF) 23 ELECTR
(TRYING TO BREAK AWAY FROM HER, HALF PUTTING HER 31 ELECTR
HANDS UP TO HER EARS)
TRYING TO DO EXACTLY WHAT YOU'RE DOING NOW/ 33 ELECTR
(IS EVIDENTLY TRYING TO PULL HIMSELF TOGETHER. 44 ELECTR
AS IF HE WERE TRYING TO COVER UP SOME HIDDEN 48 ELECTR
UNEASINESS.
(THEN TRYING TO CALM HIMSELF STAMMERS) 61 ELECTR
I'VE BEEN TRYING TO GET HER TO BUT SHE WON'T 80 ELECTR
LISTEN TO ME.
CHRISTINE IS DESPERATELY TRYING TO APPEAR CALM. 83 ELECTR
I'M NOT HOME AN HOUR BEFORE YOU'RE TRYING TO MARRY 84 ELECTR
ME OFF/
WHAT ARE YOU TRYING TO DO, ANYWAYS 94 ELECTR
(THICKLY, TRYING TO FIGHT BACK HIS JEALOUS 98 ELECTR
SUSPICION)
(TRYING PITIFULLY TO CHEER HIM) 112 ELECTR
(FRANTICALLY--TRYING TO BREAK AWAY FROM HER) 124 ELECTR
(TRYING TO PUT A BRAVE FACE ON IT) 131 ELECTR
(SETH HURRIES DOWN TO THEM, TRYING TO APPEAR TO 133 ELECTR
SAUNTER.)
ALWAYS TRYING TO TEACH ME MANNERS/ 144 ELECTR
I WAS ONLY TRYING TO SCARE YOU--FOR A JOKE/ 148 ELECTR
BUT YOU'RE ONLY TRYING TO RILE ME--AND I'M NOT 151 ELECTR
GOING TO LET YOU.
(TRYING TO KEEP CALM--TENSELY) 153 ELECTR
(TRYING TO FORCE A LAUGH) WHY, VINNIES 162 ELECTR
(STARTING TO GO, TRYING TO KEEP THE ENVELOPE 163 ELECTR
HIDDEN.
IT'S NO GOOD TRYING ANY MORE/ 177 ELECTR
WHAT ARE YOU SITTING HERE FOR, YOU NUT--TRYING TO 265 GGBROW
GET MORE MOONSTRUCKS
(TRYING NOT TO SHOW HIS ANNOYANCE) 275 GGBROW
(TRYING A BULLYING TONE--ROUGHLY) 281 GGBROW
(TRYING TO GET OJON STARTED) 282 GGBROW
THEY KEEP TRYING TO FIND THE WORD IN THE 284 GGBROW
BEGINNING.
I REALLY BELIEVE YOU WERE TRYING TO AVOID KISSING 308 GGBROW
MES
SHE IS TRYING TO READ A BOOK. 308 GGBROW
HE BLINKS UPWARD THROUGH THE MURK TRYING TO FIND 225 HA APE
THE OWNER OF THE WHISTLE.
UR TRYING TO GET TO SLEEP) 244 HA APE
HIS MIND HAS BEEN TRYING TO FASTEN ITSELF TO SOME 29 HUGHIE
NOISE IN THE NIGHT.
WHO'S THAT GUY TRYING TO CATCH PNEUMONIAS 593 ICEMAN

TRYING

TRYING (CONT'D.)
WHILE HE WAS TRYING TO WRITE A SERMON, 596 ICEMAN
DON'T LOOK AT ME AS IF I WAS TRYING TO SELL YOU A 622 ICEMAN
GOLDBRICK.
NO, BOYS AND GIRLS, I'M NOT TRYING TO PUT ANYTHING624 ICEMAN
OVER ON YOU.
I WAS TRYING TO FIGURE--HAVEN'T WE MET BEFORE SOME624 ICEMAN
PLACE?
HE STIRS ON HIS CHAIR, TRYING TO WAKE UP, 628 ICEMAN
THEY ARE TRYING TO ACT UP IN THE SPIRIT OF THE 629 ICEMAN
OCCASION
WHO'S TRYING YOU. 642 ICEMAN
AS IF HE WERE TRYING TO HAMMER SOMETHING INTO HIS 649 ICEMAN
OWN BRAIN)
WHAT THE HELL YOU TRYING TO DO, YELLING AND 654 ICEMAN
RAISING THE ROOFS
(TRYING TO HIDE HIS DREAD BEHIND AN OFFENDED, 655 ICEMAN
DRUNKEN DIGNITY)
(TRYING TO BRIGHTEN UP) SAY, THAT'S PRETTY. 655 ICEMAN
YOU GOTTAMNED LIMEY--(TRYING TO CONTROL HIMSELF 677 ICEMAN
AND COPY LEWIS' MANNER)
(TRYING NOT TO LISTEN, HAS LISTENED WITH 680 ICEMAN
INCREASING TENSION)
FLATFOOT MICK TRYING TO TELL ME WHERE I GOT OFF/ 681 ICEMAN
THEY FIDGET AS IF TRYING TO MOVE.) 684 ICEMAN
YOU'D THINK I WAS TRYING TO HARM HIM, 690 ICEMAN
HE'S TRYING TO KID HIMSELF WITH THAT GRANDSTAND 700 ICEMAN
PHILOSOPHER STUFF/
TRYING TO FIGURE A WAY TO GET OUT OF HELPING ME/ 701 ICEMAN
ARE YOU TRYING TO MAKE ME YOUR EXECUTIONERS 701 ICEMAN
I'D SEE IN HER EYES HOW SHE WAS TRYING NOT TO 712 ICEMAN
KNOW.
TRYING TO FIGURE SOME WAY OUT FOR HER. 715 ICEMAN
YOU'VE GOT A CRUST TRYING TO TELL US ABOUT HICKEY/718 ICEMAN
BUT TRYING NOT TO LISTEN, IN AN AGONY OF HORROR 721 ICEMAN
AND CRACKING NERVE.)
THERE WAS NO GOOD TRYING TO EXPLAIN TO A CRAZY 724 ICEMAN
GUY, BUT IT AIN'T THE RIGHT TIME.
HE TURNS TO THEM, TRYING HARD TO ASSUME A CARELESS520 INZONE
TONE)
(TRYING TO RESTRAIN HIS GROWING RAGE) 526 INZONE
I KNOW IT'S A WASTE OF BREATH TRYING TO CONVINCE 15 JOURNE
YOU
I'M TRYING TO HELP. 45 JOURNE
OR RATHER HE IS TRYING TO CONCENTRATE ON IT BUT 51 JOURNE
CANNOT.
(GIVES UP TRYING TO IGNORE HER AND GRINS.) 52 JOURNE
YES, IT'S VERY TRYING, JAMIE. 61 JOURNE
YOU DON'T KNOW HOW TRYING. 61 JOURNE
BUT HE STILL CANNOT HELP TRYING TO WARN HIS 67 JOURNE
MOTHER.)
TYRONE'S VOICE, TRYING TO CONCEAL, REVEALS THAT HE 73 JOURNE
IS HEARING BAD NEWS.)
(TRYING TO SPEAK NATURALLY.) 82 JOURNE
(TRYING AGAIN TO GET HIS APPEAL STARTED.) 92 JOURNE
(TRYING TO CATCH HER EYES.) MAMA/ 92 JOURNE
I'M ONLY TRYING TO EXPLAIN-- 93 JOURNE
(FIGHTING THE EFFECT OF HER LAST DRINK AND TRYING 101 JOURNE
TO BE SOBERLY CONVERSATIONAL.)
(HUSKILY, TRYING TO FORCE A SMILE.) 114 JOURNE
NOW PERHAPS YOU'LL GIVE UP TRYING TO REMIND ME, 117 JOURNE
YOU AND EDMUND/
STOP TRYING TO BLAME HIM. 119 JOURNE
YOU'LL FIND WHAT YOU'RE TRYING TO SAY IN HIM-- 131 JOURNE
BUT I WASN'T TRYING TO SAY THAT. 131 JOURNE
WE KNOW WHAT WE'RE TRYING TO FORGET. 132 JOURNE
(TRYING TO CONTROL HIS TEMPER.) 132 JOURNE
I WAS TRYING TO MAKE PLAIN TO YOU-- 147 JOURNE
(THEN DRUNKENLY RESENTFUL.) WHAT ARE YOU TRYING 163 JOURNE
TO DO, ACCUSE ME?
(TRYING TO CONTROL HIS SOBS.) 163 JOURNE
EDMUND HAS LOOKED AWAY FROM HIM, TRYING TO IGNORE 164 JOURNE
THIS TIRADE.)
(TYRONE TURNS AWAY, TRYING TO CONTROL HIS TEMPER.)168 JOURNE
(TRYING TO SHAKE OFF HIS HOPELESS STUPOR.) 174 JOURNE
(TRYING TO CALM HER) SSSHY 284 LAZARU
YOU ARE TRYING TO EVADE DEATH/ 319 LAZARU
YOU ARE TRYING TO SPARE YOUR PEOPLE/ 319 LAZARU
(TRYING TO LAUGH) HA-HA--YES/ 334 LAZARU
TRYING IN VAIN TO ATTRACT HIS OR CAESAR'S 341 LAZARU
ATTENTION.
ARE YOU TRYING TO FOOL ME, HYPOCRITES 359 LAZARU
TRYING FEEBLY TO BE IMPERIAL) 366 LAZARU
FORGIVE ME FOR TRYING TO POISON YOUR HAPPINESS. 17 MANSNS
I REALLY BELIEVE YOU ARE TRYING TO MAKE A GOOD 39 MANSNS
WOMAN OF ME, NICHOLAS/
THEN SARA'S VOICE TRYING TO QUIET THEM AND, FOR 43 MANSNS
THE MOMENT, SUCCEEDING.
BUT WHAT A WAY FOR ME--AND YOU IN YOUR STUDY 44 MANSNS
TRYING TO WRITE/
THERE I WAS AT NIGHT IN MY STUDY TRYING TO 46 MANSNS
CONVINCE MYSELF OF THE POSSIBILITY OF
(INDIGNANTLY.) ARE YOU TRYING TO SAY I'M TO 81 MANSNS
BLAME?
WHAT ARE YOU TRYING TO DO? 99 MANSNS
(TRYING TO CONTROL HERSELF AND BE CASUAL AND 102 MANSNS
INDIFFERENT.)
WHAT ARE YOU TRYING TO DO? 102 MANSNS
I PITY HER WHEN I SEE HIM DELIBERATELY TRYING TO 121 MANSNS
HUMILIATE--
THE CALCULATING COQUETRY OF TWO PROSTITUTES TRYING128 MANSNS
TO ENTICE A MAN.)
YOU'LL BE BETWEEN US, AS YOU'VE BEEN TRYING TO BE.128 MANSNS
THEN TRYING DESPERATELY TO BE CONFIDENTLY MATTER- 131 MANSNS
OF-FACT, AND FORCING A SMILE.)
(SHE PAUSES--TRYING TO REMEMBER.) 135 MANSNS
(TRYING TO TAKE HIS EYES FROM HER.) 141 MANSNS

TRYING (CONT'D.)
(TRYING TO FORCE HIMSELF FROM HIS DAY DREAM-- 145 MANSNS
VAGUELY PLACATING.)
DON'T I KNOW WHAT YOU'RE TRYING TO DO, 155 MANSNS
WHAT ARE YOU TRYING TO DO, EH? 159 MANSNS
I--I WAS TRYING TO CONCENTRATE MY THOUGHTS ON THE 172 MANSNS
FINAL SOLUTION OF THE PROBLEM.
ARE YOU TRYING TO INSINUATE I AM GOING INSANE? 174 MANSNS
CAN'T YOU SEE I AM TRYING TO MAKE CLEAR TO YOU 181 MANSNS
THAT I HAVE CHOSEN YOU.
AS IF SHE WERE TRYING TO CONVINCE A CHILD.) 183 MANSNS
WHAT IS TRYING TO MAKE ME REMEMBERS 187 MANSNS
I WAS ONLY TRYING IT FOR FUN, TO SEE IF I COULD. 361 MARCOM
(TRYING TO HIDE HER PIQUE--FORCING A CYNICAL 368 MARCOM
SMILE)
(MARCO COMES FORWARD, TRYING FEEBLY TO ASSUME A 378 MARCOM
BOLD, CONFIDENT AIR.)
(TRYING TO SOLVE A RIDDLE IN HIS OWN MIND-- 379 MARCOM
MUSINGLY)
(TRYING TO CONCEAL HIS FEAR UNDER A QUAVERING, 380 MARCOM
JOKING TONE)
(TRYING TO RENEW HIS JOKING TONE) 401 MARCOM
WHEN YOU'RE TRYING TO GET SOMETHING DONE. 406 MARCOM
WHEN I FEEL SOMEONE'S TRYING TO STEAL WHAT'S 411 MARCOM
RIGHTFULLY MINE, FOR INSTANCE.
(IN A HURT TONE) I DON'T SEE WHY YOU'RE TRYING TO419 MARCOM
INSULT ME--
I KNOW YOU'RE ONLY TRYING TO MAKE GAME OF ME. 23 MISBEG
(PERSUASIVELY) THERE'D BE NO HARM TRYING IT, 28 MISBEG
ANYWAY.
I'VE BEEN TRYING TO GUESS. 32 MISBEG
I WON'T WASTE WORDS TRYING TO REFORM A BORN CROOK. 62 MISBEG
(TRYING A LIGHT TONE) SURE, THERE'S A LOT OF 78 MISBEG
THOSE IN THE NEIGHBORHOOD.
(TRYING TO EXAMINE HIS FACE WITHOUT HIS KNOWING) 105 MISBEG
TYRONE IS STILL TRYING WITH SHAKING HANDS TO GET 111 MISBEG
HIS CIGARETTE LIGHTED.
TRYING TO GET ME SOUSED, JOSIE? 116 MISBEG
IF YOU'RE SUSPICIOUS I'M TRYING TO GET YOU 116 MISBEG
SOUSED--WELL, HERE GOES.
(TRYING TO READ HIS FACE--UNEASILY) 120 MISBEG
STILL TRYING TO GET ME SOUSED, JOSIE? 124 MISBEG
WAS I TRYING TO RAPE YOU, JOSIE? 138 MISBEG
SURE, I WAS ONLY TRYING TO GIVE YOU HAPPINESS, 141 MISBEG
BECAUSE I LOVE YOU.
TRYING TO WELCH NOW, EH? 146 MISBEG
HE WAS TRYING TO BE BRAVE ENOUGH. 65 POET
TRYING TO HIDE HER APPREHENSION AND ANGER AND 72 POET
SHAME
BY TRYING TO FASCINATE HER WITH YOUR BEAUTIFUL 91 POET
UNIFORM.
(TRYING TO CONTROL HERSELF.) 113 POET
WITHOUT PREJUDICE, TRYING TO BE FAIR TO YOU AND 113 POET
MAKE EVERY POSSIBLE ALLOWANCE--
HE WAS TRYING TO READ A BOOK OF POETRY, 143 POET
TRYING TO MAKE UP SOMEONE WHO COULD MARRY US. 149 POET
SHUT YOUR MOUTH, SARA, AND DON'T BE TRYING TO 156 POET
PLAGUE HIM.
I'M TRYING TO HEAR-- 163 POET
IF YE RAPE ON TRYING TO RAISE THE DEAD/ 176 POET
(TRYING TO ROUSE HER--IN A TEASING TONE.) 182 POET
THE OLD MAN WATCHES HIM WITH EAGER EYES AND SEEMS 596 ROPE
TO BE TRYING TO SMILE.
(SHE COMES INTO THE ROOM AND JUMPS UP, TRYING TO 600 ROPE
GRAB HOLD OF THE ROPE)
YOU SEE, I'M TRYING TO SEE THINGS THROUGH CLEARLY 9 STRANG
AND UNSENTIMENTALLY.
(TRYING TO CONTROL HIS IRRITATION AND TALK IN AN 9 STRANG
OBJECTIVE TONE)
ARE YOU TRYING TO CUT ME DEAD, YOUNG LADYS 13 STRANG
BUT I NEVER QUIT TRYING, ANYWAY/ 29 STRANG
HE'S ALWAYS TRYING TO BULLY HER INTO TAKING BETTER 31 STRANG
CARE OF HERSELF.
TRYING NOT TO DISCOVER WHICH SEX THEY BELONG 34 STRANG
TO/....)
TRYING TO GOAD HERSELF INTO FEELING SOMETHING/ 35 STRANG
WHAT'S HE TRYING TO HIDE... 36 STRANG
(HARSHLY--BUT TRYING TO FORCE A JOKING TONE) 38 STRANG
TRYING TO PULL THE WOOL OVER MY EYES... 38 STRANG
I WAS TRYING TO PRAY. 41 STRANG
(THEN TAKING A SIP OF COFFEE, AND TRYING TO BE 57 STRANG
PLEASANTLY CASUAL)
(REACHING OUT HER HAND TENDERLY, TRYING TO TOUCH 58 STRANG
NINA)
TRYING NOT TO BELIEVE....) 59 STRANG
SHE'S TRYING TO KILL MY BABY/... 59 STRANG
TRYING SO HARD.... 69 STRANG
TRYING TO POUND 69 STRANG
(WITH A SHORT LAUGH) TRYING TO IS RIGHT/ 70 STRANG
I'M TRYING TO PLAY THE GAME.... 71 STRANG
HE SEEMS A PREY TO SOME INNER FEAR HE IS TRYING TO 73 STRANG
HIDE EVEN FROM HIMSELF AND IS
EVANS STAMMERS IN CONFUSION, TRYING AT A 75 STRANG
NONCHALANT AIR)
SHE HAS BEEN TRYING TO READ A BOOK BUT HAS LET 90 STRANG
THIS DROP LISTLESSLY ON HER LAP.
ARGUING WITH HIMSELF, TRYING TO GET UP HIS 92 STRANG
COURAGE)
(TRYING TO OVERCOME HIS GUILTY EMBARRASSMENT) 95 STRANG
(TRYING TO BE MATTER-OF-FACT) 96 STRANG
(UNEASILY TRYING TO FORCE A CASUAL CONVERSATION) 101 STRANG
(AVOIDING LOOKING AT HER, TRYING TO ARGUE 102 STRANG
REASONABLY--COLDLY)
I'M BEGINNING TO THINK WE'VE WRONGED THE VERY ONE 103 STRANG
WE WERE TRYING TO HELP/
THERE'S NO USE TRYING TO THINK OF OTHERS. 103 STRANG
YOU WERE TRYING TO HELP ME, TOO, NED/ 103 STRANG

TRYING (CONT'D.)
(THEN TRYING TO FACE DARRELL WHO KEEPS LOOKING WAY105 STRANG
FROM HIM)
(BEWILDERED AND TERROR-STRICKEN, TRYING FEEBLY TO 107 STRANG
PUSH HIM AWAY--THINKING)
I WAS ONLY TRYING TO MAKE MYSELF THINK SO. 109 STRANG
(TRYING TO BE CALM BUT STAMMERING) 115 STRANG
(THINKING SHAMEFACEDLY) (WHY HAVE I BEEN TRYING 118 STRANG
TO HURT HER$...
(TRYING A BOLD CLOSING STROKE--JOKINGLY) 122 STRANG
(AND USE TRYING TO THINK OUT THAT PLOT TONIGHT... 123 STRANG
IS TRYING TO CONTROL HERSELF, AND IS FRIGHTENED 124 STRANG
NOW)
(TRYING TO MOCK HIS OWN EMOTION BACK--WITH SAVAGE 144 STRANG
BITTERNESS)
(THINKING RESENTFULLY) (IS SHE TRYING TO 147 STRANG
HUMILIATE ME BEFORE HIM$...
(THINKING TRIUMPHANTLY) (HE'S TRYING TO INSULT 147 STRANG
ME...
SHE IS DESPERATELY TRYING TO CONCEAL THE OBVIOUS 158 STRANG
INROADS OF TIME BY AN
(HE STOPS, TRYING TO CONTROL HIMSELF, PANTING, HIS163 STRANG
FACE RED.)
(TRYING TO BE MORE REASONABLE) 167 STRANG
(THEN TRYING TO BE CALCULATING) 167 STRANG
(TRYING TO BE SORROWFUL AND APPEALING) 168 STRANG
I FORGIVE EVEN YOUR TRYING TO TELL MADELINE--YOU 180 STRANG
WANTED TO KEEP GORDON--
(TORTUREDLY--TRYING INCOHERENTLY TO FORCE OUT A 182 STRANG
LAST DESPAIRING PROTEST)
(STARES DOWN AT EVANS--SLOWLY, AS IF TRYING TO 182 STRANG
BRING HER MIND BACK TO HIM)
SHE WAS TRYING TO GET RID OF THE LAST OF THE 188 STRANG
PEOPLE.
(BITTERLY, BUT TRYING TO CONTROL HIMSELF-- 193 STRANG
MEANINGLY)
(TRYING TO SMILE) NO. 502 VOYAGE
(SHE IS ALTERNATELY LOOKING AT JOE AND FEVERISHLY 502 VOYAGE
TRYING TO KEEP OLSON TALKING
TRYING TO CONCEAL HER ACTION, BUT JOE SEES HER. 508 VOYAGE
GLANCING TOWARD ELEANOR, TRYING NOT TO MAKE THE 444 WELDED
SLIGHTEST NOISE.
BUT YOU KEEP TRYING TO ESCAPE AS IF IT WERE A 453 WELDED
PRISON.
(THEN CALMING HIMSELF AND TRYING TO SPEAK MATTER- 464 WELDED
OF-FACTLY)
(STRUGGLES WITH HERSELF, CONFUSED AND IMPOTENT, 465 WELDED
TRYING TO
(TRYING TO CONTROL HERSELF--SELF-MOCKINGLY) 466 WELDED
THEIR LIPS MOVE AS IF THEY WERE TRYING TO SPEAK. 480 WELDED
(TRYING WITH AGONY TO TAKE THIS STOICALLY--
MUMBLING STUPIDLY)
(STARTING UP FROM HIS CHAIR AND TRYING TO TAKE HER485 WELDED
IN HIS ARMS--EXULTANTLY)

TRYST
A LOVER KEEPING A LIFE-LONG PROMISED TRYST$ 30 MANSNS

TRYSTS
AS AN ASSIGNATION PLACE WHERE HE KEEPS PASSIONATE 3 MANSNS
TRYSTS WITH YOU, HIS MISTRESS,

TSEU
BUT WHERE ARE THE HUNDRED WISE MEN OF THE SACRED 378 MARCOM
TEACHINGS OF LAO-TSEU AND

TU'N
AND WHEN I SEES DESE NIGGERS GITTIN' UP DEIR NERVE180 EJONES
TO TU'N ME OUT.

TUB
SHE'S YUST OLE TUB--LIKE PIECE OF LAND WITH HOUSE 21 ANNA
ON IT DAT FLOAT.
WHAT'S THIS TUB$ 31 ANNA
AND I CAN LICK ALL HANDS ON THIS TUB, MAN BE MAN, 32 ANNA
TIRED AS I AM!
FOR I'M THINKING A FINE GIRL THE LIKE OF YOU AIN'T 35 ANNA
LIVING ALWAYS ON THIS TUB.
IT RUNS DIS TUB. 212 HA APE
WHO MAKES DIS OLD TUB RUNS 212 HA APE
WHAT'D THEY WANT PUTTIN' A SPY ON THIS OLD TUB 522 INZONE
FOR$
TWO YEARS ON THIS FOREIGN TUB ARE TOO MUCH. 408 MARCOM

TUBBY
GADSBY IS A SHORT, TUBBY MAN OF FIFTY-SIX, ALMOST 25 MANSNS
COMPLETELY BALD,
BUT WITH YOUR TUBBY JUNKS IT'S JUST AS WELL TO 398 MARCOM
EXPECT THE WORST

TUCK
REMEMBER, IT'S ALL A GAME, AND AFTER YOU'RE ASLEEP288 GGBROW
I'LL TUCK YOU IN.
COME ON TO BED, NOW, AND I'LL HELP YOU UNDRESS AND182 POET
TUCK YOU IN.
TUCK THE PILLOWS BEHIND HER... 31 STRANG
NIP AND TUCK NOW/ 175 STRANG

TUCKERED
I'SE TUCKERED OUT SHO' NUFF. 187 EJONES

TUCKING
(HE PULLS ON HIS TROUSERS, TUCKING IN HIS NIGHT 238 DESIRE
SHIRT, AND PULLS ON HIS BOOTS.)

TUCKS
SHE TUCKS THIS PAPER IN THE SLEEVE OF HER DRESS 35 ELECTR

TUESDAY
AND THEY EXPECT TO BE PAID BACK NEXT TUESDAY, 34 HUGHIE

TUFTY
THE FRINGE OF HAIR AROUND HIS BALDNESS TOUSLED AND256 AHWILD
TUFTY.

TUG
TUG COME AND VE GAT TOWED OUT ON VOYAGE-- 23 ANNA

TUGGING
(TAKING HER HAND AND TUGGING AT IT GENTLY) 280 AHWILD
THE SKIPPING MARY TUGGING AT HER HAND. 143 BEYOND
TUGGING FRANTICALLY AT HIS REVOLVER.) 195 EJONES

TUGGING (CONT'D.)
IN A BOYISH UNEASY WHISPER, TUGGING AT DEBORAH'S 188 MANSNS
HAND.)
TUGGING A SAMPLE CASE IN EACH HAND. 376 MARCOM
(TUGGING AT HIS HAND AND BURSTING AGAIN INTO 584 ROPE
SHRILL LAUGHTER)
(IN AN ANGRY WHINE, TUGGING AT HIS HAND) 591 ROPE

TUGS
(FORGETTING HER GRUDGE, GRABS HER BROTHER'S HAND 256 AHWILD
AND TUGS AT IT.)
(SHE TUGS AT THE HAND ON EBEN'S THROAT) 255 DESIRE
(SHE TUGS AT HIS HAND AND HE FOLLOWS HER UP THE 68 MISBEG
STEPS.

TUK
AN' SHE GOT SCARED--AN' I JEST GRABBED HOLT AN' 214 DESIRE
TUK HER.
I TUK HER. 214 DESIRE
(AGITATEDLY) WHAT'S ALL THIS SUDDEN LIKIN' YE'VE 232 DESIRE
TUK TO EBEN?
FOLKS LAUGHED WHEN I TUK IT. 236 DESIRE
I TUK ANOTHER WIFE--EBEN'S MAW. 237 DESIRE
I TUK HIS MAW'S PLACE. 237 DESIRE
(VAGUELY) I TUK HIS MAW'S PLACE. 248 DESIRE
I WANT YE TUK AWAY, LOCKED UP FROM ME/ 262 DESIRE
YE MIGHT'VE TUK THE TROUBLE T' ROUSE ME, ABBIE. 263 DESIRE

TULIP
(TURNING TO THE LEFT) THIS WAY, ROSE, OR PANSY, 468 CARIBE
OR JESSAMINE, OR BLACK TULIP,

TUMBLE
TUMBLE OVER THE SIDE DAMN QUICK/ 473 CARIBE
ON WHICH CRIMSON AND PURPLE FLOWERS AND FRUITS 284 GGBROW
TUMBLE OVER ONE ANOTHER IN A
ALL THE REST OF THE MEN TUMBLE OUT OF THEIR BUNKS,514 INZONE
STRETCHING AND GAPING.

TUMBLER
(COMES OUT OF THE CABIN WITH A TUMBLER QUARTER- 31 ANNA
FULL OF WHISKY IN HER HAND.
(RETURNING AND POURING OUT A BIG DRINK IN THE 295 GGBROW
TUMBLER)
(JOSIE COMES OUT WITH A BOTTLE AND A TUMBLER) 52 MISBEG
(HANDS TYRONE THE BOTTLE AND TUMBLER) 53 MISBEG
(SHE POURS A TUMBLER HALF FULL OF WHISKEY AND 112 MISBEG
HANDS IT TO HIM)
(SHE POURS THE OTHER TUMBLER HALF FULL.) 112 MISBEG
(HE DRAINS HIS TUMBLER. 119 MISBEG
HE PICKS UP HIS TUMBLER AND POURS A BIG DRINK. 120 MISBEG
SHE IS HOLDING OUT HER TUMBLER BUT HE IGNORES IT.)120 MISBEG
(HE POURS A DRINK INTO HER TUMBLER.) 121 MISBEG
(LOOKS AT THE BOTTLE AND TUMBLER IN HIS HANDS, AS 126 MISBEG
IF HE'D FORGOTTEN THEM--

TUMBLERFUL
(SHE POURS OUT DRINKS AS SHE SPEAKS, A HALF 115 MISBEG
TUMBLERFUL FOR HIM,

TUMBLERS
SHE HAS A QUART OF WHISKEY UNDER HER ARM, TWO 111 MISBEG
TUMBLERS, AND A PITCHER OF WATER.
(HE RELIEVES HER OF THE PITCHER AND TUMBLERS AS 111 MISBEG
SHE COMES DOWN THE STEPS.)
(HE PUTS THE PITCHER AND TUMBLERS ON THE BOULDER 112 MISBEG
AND SHE UNCORKS THE BOTTLE.

TUMBLES
HER HAIR TUMBLES OVER HER SHOULDERS IN DISARRAY, 244 DESIRE
HER FACE IS FLUSHED,

TUMBLIN'
THE STONE WALLS AIR CRUMBLIN' AN' TUMBLIN'/ 221 DESIRE

TUMBRIL
AND I SEE PIERPONT MORGAN BEING DRIVEN BY IN A 195 AHWILD
TUMBRIL/
SO THAT'S WHERE YOU DROVE THE TUMBRIL FROM AND 196 AHWILD
PILED POOR OLD PIERPONT IN IT.

TUMOR
BRAIN TUMOR. 147 MISBEG

TUMULT
THE CURTAIN RISES ON A TUMULT OF SOUND. 207 HA APE
THERE IS A TUMULT OF NOISE-- 223 HA APE
THERE IS A CONFUSED TUMULT OF YELLS, GROANS, 290 LAZARU
CURSES, THE SHRIEKS OF WOMEN,
HIS WORDS ARE NOW HEARD AS THE TUMULT MOMENTARILY 368 LAZARU
DIES DOWN.
(MAKING HIMSELF HEARD ABOVE THE TUMULT) 353 MARCOM

TUNE
(SOFTENED) SEEMS TO ME YOU'VE CHANGED YOUR TUNE A 65 ANNA
LOT.
YE'VE HEARD THE NAMES OF CHANTIES BUT DIVIL A NOTE459 CARIBE
AV THE TUNE ON A LOINE AV THE
TO THE OLD TUNE OF "OH, SUSANNAH"/ 224 DESIRE
WITH STUDIED CARELESSNESS, WHISTLING A TUNE, 187 EJONES
CREW BUT NARY A LICK COULD THEY GIT INTO 'EM TILL 105 ELECTR
I RAISED A TUNE--
I'M THE FINEST CHANTYMAN THAT EVER PUT A TUNE TO 105 ELECTR
HIS LIP/
(AS THE TUNE RUNS OUT, GLANCES AT THE CLOCK, WHICH278 GGBROW
INDICATES MIDNIGHT,
THE SAME SENTIMENTAL TUNE STARTS. 280 GGBROW
PLAY A TUNE. 280 GGBROW
WHICH STARTS UP ITS OLD SENTIMENTAL TUNE. 288 GGBROW
(CHANGING TO A COMIC BASS AND ANOTHER TUNE) 619 ICEMAN
COME ON, JOE, HUM DE TUNE SO I CAN FOLLOW. 644 ICEMAN
I'VE FORGOTTEN DAT HAS-BEEN TUNE. 644 ICEMAN
AND YOU START PLAYING HARRY'S FAVORITE TUNE, CORA.644 ICEMAN
CORA, AT THE PIANO, KEEPS RUNNING THROUGH THE 651 ICEMAN
TUNE, WITH SOFT PEDAL.
BEJEES, THE LEAST YOU COULD DO IS LEARN THE TUNE/ 654 ICEMAN
IT WAS BESSIE'S FAVORITE TUNE. 656 ICEMAN
(SINGS TO HIS SAILOR LAD TUNE) 662 ICEMAN
AND YOU'VE GOT EVERYBODY ELSE SINGING THE SAME 704 ICEMAN
CRAZY TUNE/

TUNE

TUNE (CONT'D.)
THEN SUDDENLY THE TUNE WENT FALSE, THE DANCERS 159 JOURNE
WEARIED OF THE WALTZ..."
(MUSIC BEGINS IN THE ROOM OFF RIGHT, REAR--A 278 LAZARU
FESTIVE DANCE TUNE.
WHISTLIN' A LOVE TUNE TO HIMSELF, DREAMIN' OF 19 MANSNS
ANOTHER WOMAN/
(AN ORCHESTRA VIGOROUSLY BEGINS A FLOWERY, 428 MARCOM
SENTIMENTAL ITALIAN TUNE.
I'LL RAISE A TUNE FOR YOU. 53 POET
I KNOW YOU'D RAISE A BEAUTIFUL TUNE, BUT I HAVE TO 54 POET
GO OUT.
TO THE TUNE OF "BALTIMORUN." 96 POET
HIS VOICE LIKE A FATIGUING DYING TUNE DRONED ON A 16 STRANG
BEGGAR'S ORGAN...
AND WE'LL ROW, ROW, ROW--- REMEMBER THAT OLD 175 STRANG
TUNE--
HE'D BETTER CHANGE HIS TUNE OR I'LL CERTAINLY BE 191 STRANG
TEMPTED TO TELL HIM...
NICK, 'ERE CAN PLAY YER A TUNE, CAN'T YER, NICK$ 499 VOYAGE
(TO NICK) WHERE'S THE TUNE YE WAS PROMISIN' TO 501 VOYAGE
GIVE US$
WE'LL HAVE A TUNE AN' A DANCE IF I'M NOT TOO 501 VOYAGE
DHRUNK TO DANCE.

TUNES
MILDRED KEEPS STARTING TO RUN OVER POPULAR TUNES 259 AHWILD
NOT LIKE THEM SLOW, OLD-TIMEY TUNES. 520 DIFRNT
BUT I GOT 'EM BECAUSE I LIKE THEM JAZZ TUNES 520 DIFRNT
MYSELF.
OF -MOTHER-MAMMY-TUNES. 278 GGBROW
(MUSINGLY) I LOVE THOSE ROTTEN OLD SOB TUNES. 284 GGBROW
MY FEET JUST WON'T GIVE IN TO YOUR TUNES. 403 MARCOM
(CURTLY,) I WANT NONE OF YOUR TUNES. 54 POET

TUNIC
PULLING A CHARIOT IN WHICH LAZARUS STANDS DRESSED 307 LAZARU
IN A TUNIC OF WHITE AND GOLD.

TUNING
THE COMMENCES TUNING UP.) 470 CARIBE
THE MUSICIAN IS TUNING UP HIS FIDDLE, SEATED IN 247 DESIRE
THE FAR RIGHT CORNER.
(TUNING UP) LET'S CELEBRATE THE OLD SKUNK GITTIN'253 DESIRE
(FOOLED/
PATCH RILEY GIVES A FEW TUNING-UP QUAVERS ON HIS 96 POET
PIPES.)

TURBINES
MADE THAT RIVER THAT DRIVES THE TURBINES THAT 477 DYNAMO
DRIVE DYNAMO/

TUREEN
AND NORAH, WHO HAS JUST ENTERED FROM THE PANTRY 222 AHWILD
WITH A HUGE TUREEN OF SOUP IN
(SHE SETS THE SOUP TUREEN DOWN WITH A THUD IN 222 AHWILD
FRONT OF MRS. MILLER
(NORAH, STILL STANDING WITH THE SOUP TUREEN HELD 222 AHWILD
OUT STIFFLY IN FRONT OF HER,

TURF
AND HER ON DE TURF LONG BEFORE ME AND YOU WAS/ 614 ICEMAN

TURKEY
A RALE, GOD-FUR-SAKEN SON AV A TURKEY TROT WID 470 CARIBE
GUTS TO UT.
A JERK-SHOULDERED VERSION OF THE OLD TURKEY TROT 471 CARIBE
AS IT WAS DONE IN THE
(HE STARTS TO FIDDLE "TURKEY IN THE STRAW." 253 DESIRE
MAKE HIM TALK TURKEY AND SAY WHEN IS HE PLANNING 479 DYNAMO
TO MARRY ADA/
HIS COMPLEXION THAT OF A TURKEY. 576 ICEMAN
WHAT A TURKEY/ 428 MARCOM
(THREATENINGLY) AND THEN I'M GOINTER COME AND 589 ROPE
TALK TURKEY TO YOU, SEE$

TURKISH
THIS AIN'T NO TURKISH BATH/ 602 ICEMAN
MOONLIGHT NIGHT IN JULY, 1776, WHILE SOBERING UP 607 ICEMAN
IN A TURKISH BATH.

TURMOIL
THERE IS AN EXPRESSION IN HIS EYES OF WILD MENTAL 68 ANNA
TURMOIL.
(IN A TURMOIL OF GUILT AND FRIGHT) 438 DYNAMO
(HIS MIND IN A TURMOIL) VINNIE/ 177 ELECTR

TURN
THEY'LL LIKELY TURN UGLY, EVERY BLESSED ONE O' 539 'ILE
THEM, IF YOU DON'T PUT BACK.
THE TWO MEN TURN AND LOOK AT HER.) 540 'ILE
(HESITATINGLY) THEN YOU AIN'T GOIN'--TO TURN 341 'ILE
BACK$
TURN BACK$ 541 'ILE
"N YOU WANT TO TURN BACK, TOO. 542 'ILE
IF YOU'VE A HEART AT ALL YOU'VE GOT TO TURN BACK. 547 'ILE
BEST TURN IN, ANNIE, THERE'S A GOOD WOMAN. 547 'ILE
WON'T YOU PLEASE TURN BACK$ 547 'ILE
(NOT HEEDING HER) WILL THE MEN TURN TO WILLIN' OK550 'ILE
MUST WE DRAG 'EM OUTS
THEY'LL TURN TO KILLIN' ENOUGH. 550 'ILE
THEN WE'LL TURN HOMEWARD. 551 'ILE
I CAN'T TURN BACK NOW, YOU SEE THAT, DON'T YES 551 'ILE
YOU TURN EVERYTHING INTO A JOKE. 190 AHWILD
SUSPENDED FROM THE MIDDLE OF THE CEILING AND 210 AHWILD
MANAGES TO TURN ONE LIGHT ON--
WELL, NOTHING TO DO NOW TILL THOSE MEN TURN UP. 217 AHWILD
DETERMINING TO GIVE THE CONVERSATION ANOTHER TURN,228 AHWILD
SAYS TO HIS DAUGHTER)
DICK'LL TURN UP IN A MINUTE OR TWO. WAIT AND SEE/ 260 AHWILD
YOU MARK MY WORDS, THAT BOY'S GOING TO TURN OUT TO290 AHWILD
BE A GREAT LAWYER.
I'M GOING TO TURN OUT THE LIGHT. 298 AHWILD
AND I DON'T EXPECT HE'LL TURN OUT NO BETTER THAN 16 ANNA
THE REST.
(DISGUSTED IN HER TURN) A BARGE$ 17 ANNA
GEE, I KNEW SOMETHING'D BE BOUND TO TURN OUT 17 ANNA
WRONG--ALWAYS DOES WITH ME.

TURN

TURN (CONT'D.)
(ACUTELY EMBARRASSED IN HER TURN) 20 ANNA
DON'T YOU COME TURN IN, ANNA$ 25 ANNA
SO DON'T TURN YOUR BACK ON ME NOW, AND WE 37 ANNA
BEGINNING TO BE FRIENDS.
I'M GOING TO TURN LOOSE ON YOU AND TELL YOU-- 43 ANNA
(WITH A HARD LAUGH) YOUR TURN$ 55 ANNA
IT'S MY TURN NOW. 55 ANNA
AND TURN TO HER IN A STUNNED AMAZEMENT. 50 ANNA
(POINTING TO CHRIS) I'VE BEEN MEANING TO TURN IT 56 ANNA
LOOSE ON HIM EVERY TIME HE'D
(HE STARTS FOR THE DOOR--THEN STOPS TO TURN ON HER 73 ANNA
FURIOUSLY)
AND THEN THEY TELLS THE FISH TO WHISTLE TO 'EM 95 BEYOND
WHEN IT'S TIME TO TURN OUT.
I GUESS IT'S MY TURN TO OFFER CONGRATULATIONS. 101 BEYOND
ISN'T IT$
AND I'LL ALL TURN OUT FOR THE BEST--LET'S HOPE. 109 BEYOND
(WITH KEEN INTEREST) RUTH SAYS ANDY OUGHT TO TURNL15 BEYOND
UP ANY DAY.
BUT THERE IS SOMETHING IN HIS EYES THAT MAKES HER 128 BEYOND
TURN
OH, I COULD GIVE YOU YOUR BELLYFUL OF DETAILS IF I132 BEYOND
WANTED TO TURN LOOSE ON YOU.
AND TURN THIS FARM INTO THE CRACKIEST PLACE IN THE138 BEYOND
WHOLE STATE.
ALL THE MEN TURN AND STARE AT HIM.) 478 CARDIF
WHILE HE IS DOING THIS THE MAN WHOSE TURN AT THE 483 CARDIF
WHEEL HAS BEEN RELIEVED ENTERS.
(THEY ALL TURN AND LOOK UP AT HIM SURPRISED TO 462 CARIBE
HEAR HIM SPEAK.)
I WAS GOIN' TO TURN ONE LOOSE ON THE JAW OF ANY 469 CARIBE
GUY'D COP MY DAME.
WHERE SHE SHAKES OFF HIS HAND LONG ENOUGH TO TURN 470 CARIBE
ON SMITTY FURIOUSLY.)
I THINK I'LL TURN IN. 473 CARIBE
WHY IS IT EVERY ONE DECIDES TO TURN UP WHEN YOU 515 DAYS
LOOK YOUR WORST$
BUT HE IS LOOKING STRAIGHT AHEAD AND THEY TURN 535 DAYS
AWAY AGAIN.)
THEY HAVE ONLY TO OBEY ORDERS FROM OWNERS WHO ARE,542 DAYS
IN TURN, THEIR SLAVES/
(STRANGELY CONFUSED IN HIS TURN--HURRIEDLY) 545 DAYS
(HIS EYES TURN TO THE PRIEST. 551 DAYS
(EXCITED IN HIS TURN) 204 DESIRE
(THEY TURN, STARTLED, AND STARE AT HIM. 205 DESIRE
(THEY TURN, SHOULDERING EACH OTHER, 206 DESIRE
(AMUSED IN TURN, ECHOES HIS BROTHER) 208 DESIRE
(ANGRY IN HIS TURN) 219 DESIRE
THE BROTHERS EDGE AWKWARDLY TO DOOR IN REAR--THEN 220 DESIRE
TURN AND STAND.)
YE'D BETTER TURN HER IN THE PEN WITH THE OTHER 222 DESIRE
SOWS.
(HE LEAPS IN TURN.) 223 DESIRE
THEN I'D TURN FREE. 233 DESIRE
YOU'LL FIND OUT CALEB'LL TURN OUT THE SAME. 512 DIFRNT
THE TURN THE CONVERSATION HAS TAKEN SEEMS TO HAVE 526 DIFRNT
AROUSED A HECTIC,
AND LET YE SEE HOW QUICK HE'D TURN HIS BACK ON YE/543 DIFRNT
(THEN HIS EYES TURN TO HIS MOTHER'S VINDICTIVE 448 DYNAMO
FACE
(MECHANICALLY IN HIS TURN--WITHOUT LIFTING HIS 464 DYNAMO
HEAD)
DE FUSS AND GLORY PART OF IT, DAT'S ONLY TO TURN 177 EJONES
DE HEADS O' DE LOW-FLUNG,
DAT NO-COUNT SMITHERS SAY DEY'D BE BLACK AN' HE 188 EJONES
SHO' CALLED DE TURN.
IF YE LOST 'IS BLOODY WAY IN THESE STINKIN' WOODS 203 EJONES
'E'D LIKELY TURN IN A CIRCLE
LAVINIA DOES NOT TURN OR GIVE ANY SIGN OF KNOWING 45 ELECTR
HER MOTHER IS BEHIND HER.
THE FORCES HIMSELF TO TURN AND, SEEING HER EYES 53 ELECTR
ARE SHUT,
TIME TO TURN IN. 56 ELECTR
SEE YOU TURN IN SOON. 56 ELECTR
AND THEN THEY TURN TO THE STEPS AND THE DOOR IS 67 ELECTR
CLOSED.
SO WHEN IT'S HIS TURN HE CAN HARDLY EXPECT-- 75 ELECTR
SHE MIGHT EVEN GO TO THE POLICE AND--DON'T LET HER 88 ELECTR
TURN YOU AGAINST ME/
(TENDERLY SOOTHING HER) TURN ME AGAINST YOU$ 88 ELECTR
(STARES UP, STARTLED IN HIS TURN AND MOMENTARILY 104 ELECTR
SOBERED--HASTILY)
BUT I'D ADVISE YOU TO TURN IN AND SLEEP IT OFF. 105 ELECTR
(ANGRY IN HIS TURN) WAL, 133 ELECTR
AS THEY ALL TURN TO LOOK, 134 ELECTR
(UNHEEDING--WITH A SUDDEN TURN TO BITTER RESENTFUL140 ELECTR
DEFIANCE)
I GUESS I'M TOO MUCH OF A MANNON, AFTER ALL, TO 145 ELECTR
TURN INTO A PAGAN.
COLLEGES TURN OUT LAZY LOAFERS TO SPONGE ON THEIR 260 GGBROW
POOF OL' FATHERS/
AND YOU'LL LEARN TO BE A BETTER ARCHITECT THAN 261 GGBROW
BROWN'S BOY OR I'LL TURN YOU OUT
TOO WEAK TO DOMINATE HER IN TURN. 296 GGBROW
I'LL TURN THIS RIGHT OVER TO HIM AND INSTRUCT HIM 306 GGBROW
TO CARRY OUT YOUR WISHES.
BROWN HAS JUST TIME TO TURN HIS HEAD AND GET HIS 306 GGBROW
MASK ON.)
AND THEN ALL AT ONCE YOU TURN RIGHT AROUND AND 309 GGBROW
EVERYTHING IS THE SAME AS WHEN WE
(THEY ALL TURN TO AN OLD, WIZENED IRISHMAN WHO IS 209 HA APE
DOZING, VERY DRUNK,
TURN IT OFF/ 212 HA APE
YANK DOES NOT TURN FAR ENOUGH TO SEE HER. 225 HA APE
DEY TURN TINGS ROUND, DO DEY$ 244 HA APE
TURN ALMIGHTY GOD'S REVEALED PLAN FOR THE WORLD 244 HA APE
TOPSY-TURVY.

TURN

(CONT'D.)
I SURE CAN CALL THE TURN ON AGES, BUDDY. 13 HUGHIE
MY BIRTHDAY, TOMORROW, THAT'D BE THE RIGHT TIME TO604 ICEMAN
TURN OVER A NEW LEAF.
I WISH TO HELL HICKEY'D TURN UP. 608 ICEMAN
HICKEY'D NEVER TURN UP DIS TIME OF DE MORNIN'/ 610 ICEMAN
I HOPE HE'LL TURN UP. 610 ICEMAN
ANY TIME YOU THINK I'M TALKING OUT OF TURN, JUST 624 ICEMAN
TELL ME TO GO CHASE MYSELF/
TURN TO HIM WITH EAGER GRINS. 627 ICEMAN
AT ONCE THE LAUGHTER STOPS ABRUPTLY AND THEY TURN 628 ICEMAN
TO HIM STARTLEDLY.)
HE CAN'T MANAGE IT ALONE, AND YOU'RE THE ONLY ONE 642 ICEMAN
HE CAN TURN TO.
I CAN SIZE UP GUYS, AND TURN 'EM INSIDE OUT, 642 ICEMAN
BETTER THAN I EVER COULD.
THEY TURN THEIR BACKS ON EACH OTHER AS FAR AS 650 ICEMAN
POSSIBLE
(THIS TIME HE DOES TURN AWAY.) 656 ICEMAN
(HE STARTS TO TURN AWAY. 656 ICEMAN
YOU'RE THE ONLY ONE IN THE WORLD I CAN TURN TO. 666 ICEMAN
THEY TURN THEIR BACKS ON EACH OTHER. 681 ICEMAN
(THEY BOTH TURN ON HIM RESENTFULLY. 682 ICEMAN
YES, WE KNOW IT'S THE KIND OF RHEUMATISM YOU TURN 684 ICEMAN
ON AND OFF/
AND NOW IT'S YOUR TURN, JIMMY, OLD PAL. 686 ICEMAN
AND NOW IT'S MY TURN, I SUPPOSE$ 688 ICEMAN
(STAMMERS, HIS EYES ON LARRY, WHOSE EYES IN TURN 694 ICEMAN
REMAIN FIXED ON HICKEY)
THE SAME WAY SHE FORGAVE ME EVERY TIME I'D TURN UP713 ICEMAN
AFTER A PERIODICAL DRUNK.
ALL OF THE GROUP TURN TOWARD THE DOOR AS THE TWO 724 ICEMAN
APPEAR.
(THEY TURN TO LOOK. 726 ICEMAN
(THEY TURN AWAY AND FORGET HIM.) 726 ICEMAN
(THEY ALL TURN ON HIM AND HOWL HIM DOWN WITH 727 ICEMAN
AMUSED DERISION.
AN' HE'S LIABLE TO TURN OUT QUEERER THAN ANY OF US516 INZONE
THINK IF WE AIN'T CAREFUL.
AND TURN AS IF THEY WERE GOING TO RUSH FOR THE 523 INZONE
DECK.
LET'S TURN THE DUKE LOOSE, WHAT D'YUH SAYS 528 INZONE
THE OTHERS INSTINCTIVELY TURN AWAY. 528 INZONE
BUT WE'LL TURN 'EM OVER TO THE POLICE WHEN WE 531 INZONE
DOCKS AT LIVERPOOL TO LOOK
GOD STIFFEN US, ARE WE NEVER GOIN' TO TURN IN FUR 532 INZONE
A WINK AV SLEEP$
SMITTY DOES NOT TURN HIS HEAD AROUND 532 INZONE
(WITHOUT CONVICTION.) HE'LL TURN OUT ALL RIGHT IN 18 JOURNE
THE END, YOU WAIT AND SEE.
THEN IT BEGAN TO TURN WHITE. 28 JOURNE
I WANT YOU TO PROMISE ME THAT EVEN IF IT SHOULD 48 JOURNE
TURN OUT TO BE SOMETHING WORSE,
GLAD OF AN EXCUSE TO TURN HIS BACK.) 60 JOURNE
(WITH SHARP IRRITATION.) I TOLD YOU TO TURN OUT 126 JOURNE
THAT LIGHT/
TURN THAT LIGHT OUT BEFORE YOU COME IN. 126 JOURNE
I ASKED YOU TO TURN OUT THAT LIGHT IN THE HALL. 127 JOURNE
YOU LOOK IN THEIR FACES AND TURN TO STONE. 131 JOURNE
NO, SURE NOT. TURN THEM OUT. 151 JOURNE
YOU DON'T MIND IF I TURN THEM OUT, DO YOU$ 151 JOURNE
(HE FUMBLES AT THE CHANDELIER AND MANAGES TO TURN 155 JOURNE
ON THE THREE BULBS.)
(HIS FATHER AND BROTHER BOTH TURN ON HIM FIERCELY,170 JOURNE
AND CANNOT HELP APPEALING PLEADINGLY IN HIS TURN.1173 JOURNE
WILL TURN A LITTLE TOWARD US, SIGHING. 174 JOURNE
JAMIE POURS HIS AND PASSES THE BOTTLE TO EDMUND, 175 JOURNE
WHO, IN TURN, POURS ONE.
AND SISTERS AND KISSES EACH IN TURN ON THE 293 LAZARU
FOREHEAD.
(IN A RAGE) HO, BARBARIAN CUR, TURN ROUND/ 316 LAZARU
JEN, TURN ROUND/ 316 LAZARU
AND THE SENATORS TURN TO RETIRE, HE STOPS THEM ALL322 LAZARU
FOR A MOMENT WITH A
CRY WITH PRIDE, -TAKE BACK, O GOD, AND ACCEPT IN 324 LAZARU
TURN A GIFT FROM ME.
(THEN WITH HIS WRY SMILE) BUT I WILL TURN MY 329 LAZARU
BACK--AND SHUT MY EYES--
TURN ABOUT IS FAIR PLAY. 6 MANSNS
I PROMISE YOU, IN TURN, I NEVER INTEND TO SEE YOUR 21 MANSNS
HUSBAND AGAIN.
(STARING AROUND HIM IN TURN--AS IF FIGHTING 37 MANSNS
AGAINST AN INFLUENCE.)
AND HOW COULD I BE SO CRUEL AND HARD-HEARTED AS TO 55 MANSNS
TURN YOU AWAY.
(AS THEY TURN BACK--INJUREDLY.) 64 MANSNS
(THEY TURN TOWARDS THE DOOR AT REAR, LAUGHINGLY.) 67 MANSNS
HE WANTED TO TURN HIS BACK ON THE DOOR AND GO FAR 111 MANSNS
AWAY.
THE TWO WOMEN TURN TO STARE AT HIM, WITH A 119 MANSNS
STIRRING OF SUSPICION AND RESENTMENT.
(SHE AND DEBORAH SUDDENLY TURN AND STARE AT EACH 129 MANSNS
OTHER WITH DEFIANT,
TO BE ABLE TO BE STILL, OR TO TURN BACK TO REST/ 157 MANSNS
NO COMMON MAN ON THE STREET WOULD TURN TO LOOK AT,166 MANSNS
BUT DEBORAH DOES NOT TURN TO IT AND REMAINS 187 MANSNS
CONFRONTING SARA.)
YOU CAN BET IT ISN'T OLD FOOLS LIKE YOU THAT TURN 367 MARCOM
ME.
(THEY ALL TURN, AND, RECOGNIZING HER, LAUGH WITH 367 MARCOM
COARSE FAMILIARITY.)
(THEN SADLY) BUT NOW YOU IN YOUR TURN MUST LEAVE 386 MARCOM
ME.
FINALLY IT SEEMS TO TURN A CORNER NEARBY, AND A 402 MARCOM
MOMENT LATER,
IMMEDIATELY THE WOMEN ALL TURN WITH ARMS 433 MARCOM
OUTSTRETCHED TOWARD THE CATAFALQUE.

TURNED

(CONT'D.)
WITHOUT ANY REASON YOU CAN SEE, HE'LL SUDDENLY 33 MISBEG
TURN STRANGE, AND LOOK SAD.
I CAN TURN MY BACK, SO THE SIGHT OF HIM DRINKING 52 MISBEG
FREE WON'T BREAK MY HEART/
(THEY TURN BACK TOWARD THE HOUSE. 64 MISBEG
(SHE REACHES OUT TO TURN DOWN THE LAMP.) 76 MISBEG
JOSIE STOPS BY THE TABLE IN THE LIVING ROOM TO 111 MISBEG
TURN DOWN THE LAMP.
THEY TURN MY STOMACH/ 107 POET
MELODY, IN HIS TURN, IS SURPRISED. 116 POET
SHE'S ONLY WATCHING FOR A GOOD EXCUSE TO TURN 127 POET
SIMON AGAINST MARRYING ME.
I WAS A GREAT FOOL TO FEAR HIS MOTHER COULD TURN 142 POET
HIM AGAINST ME.
AND WE'D BE THERE YET IF HARFORD HADN'T MADE THIM 159 POET
TURN US LOOSE.
(HE STARTS TO TURN THE KNOB.) 178 POET
AND STARTS TO TAKE A BRISK TURN ABOUT THE ROOM. 22 STRANG
(COLDLY IN TURN) ON HER EVIDENT CRAVING TO MAKE 36 STRANG
AN EXHIBITION OF KISSING.
ARE YOU STILL WORRYING ABOUT HOW THE DARN OLD 54 STRANG
APPLES ARE GOING TO TURN OUT$
THIS BENCH IN TURN HAS BEEN DRAWN MUCH CLOSER, 66 STRANG
(ANNOYED IN HIS TURN--THINKING) 76 STRANG
(THEN BOTH TURN AWAY IN GUILTY CONFUSION.) 84 STRANG
MY TURN TO BE HAPPY/...)) 124 STRANG
NINA AND DARRELL TURN AND LOOK AT EACH OTHER 130 STRANG
GUILTILY AND FRIGHTENEDLY.
(AS THE THREE TURN TO HER--ANXIOUSLY) 135 STRANG
IT MAKES HIM TURN AGAINST ME/... 142 STRANG
TURN FROM ME TO SAM/)) 142 STRANG
NINA AND DARRELL TURN AND LOOK AT EACH OTHER 164 STRANG
WONDERINGLY, INQUISITIVELY.
TURN ON THE SUN INTO THE SHADOWS OF LIES-- 176 STRANG
HE WILL TURN TO ME FOR COMFORT/... 176 STRANG
(THEN STERNLY IN HER TURN, AS IF SWEARING A PLEDGE183 STRANG
TO HERSELF)
THEY JUMP STARTLEDLY AND TURN AROUND. 188 STRANG
IT'S MY TURN. 195 STRANG
AFRAID TO TURN AND MEET CAPE'S FIERCELY ACCUSING 451 WELDEU
EYES
AT EVERY TURN YOU FEEL YOUR INDIVIDUALITY 453 WELDEU
INVADED--
(BECOMING AWARE IN HIS TURN--HEAVILY) 480 WELDED
SHE DOES NOT TURN BUT REMAINS STARING AT THE DOOR 487 WELDED
IN FRONT OF HER.

TURNED

AND I TURNED AND THERE WAS RED, HIS FACE ALL 230 AHWILD
PINCHED AND WHITE.
EVEN HIS FATHER TURNED ENEMY, HIS FACE GROWING 235 AHWILD
MORE AND MORE REBELLIOUS.
SEA-SICK TINGE, HIS EYES SEEM TO BE TURNED INWARD 261 AHWILD
UNEASILY--
BUT HE ABSOLUTELY GOES ON WHISTLING WITH BACK 278 AHWILD
TURNED.
TURNED OUT TO BE POISON IVY, DIDN'T THEY$ 293 AHWILD
TAWDRY FINERY OF PEASANT STOCK TURNED PROSTITUTE. 14 ANNA
(AT THE SOUND OF HER NAME ANNA HAS TURNED ROUND TO 53 ANNA
THEM.
SNORIN', I SAYS, -I'LL MAKE A NOTE OF WHERE HE'S 95 BEYOND
TURNED IN.
AND RUBBER BOOTS TURNED DOWN FROM THE KNEE.) 568 CROSS
AND AIN'T HE TURNED TRAITOR--MOCKIN' AT ME AND 568 CROSS
SAYIN' IT'S ALL A LIE--
TURNED THE PINT A HALF-HOUR BACK-- 569 CROSS
THEY'D TURNED NAUGHTY SCHOOLBOYS AND WERE THROWING503 DAYS
SPITBALLS AT ALMIGHTY GOD AND
THEN I MARRIED AN' HE TURNED OUT A DRUNKEN SPREER 226 DESIRE
AN' SO HE HAD TO WUK FUR
SHE KEEPS HER FACE TURNED AWAY. 231 DESIRE
(WITH A QUEER SMILE) YE'D BE TURNED FREE, TOO. 233 DESIRE
(SHE HAS TURNED A BLANK FACE, RESENTFUL EYES TO 238 DESIRE
HIS.
I'VE TURNED THE COWS AN' UTHER STOCK LOOSE/ 267 DESIRE
HE WEARS HIGH SEABOOTS TURNED DOWN FROM THE KNEE, 498 DIFRNT
DIRTY COTTON SHIRT AND PANTS.
THE ROOM HAS A GROTESQUE ASPECT OF OLD AGE TURNED 519 DIFRNT
FLIGHTY AND MASQUERADING AS
I S'POSE POOR MA AND PA TURNED OVER IN THEIR 524 DIFRNT
GRAVES WHEN I ORDERED IT DONE.
(WITH A SIGH) I SUPPOSE PA AND MA TURNED OVER IN 535 DIFRNT
THEIR GRAVES.
AND YOU KNOW WHAT A LOW DUG ALF ROGERS TURNED OUT 540 DIFRNT
TO BE.
IN THE BEDROOM ABOVE, REUBEN'S EYES ARE TURNED 422 DYNAMO
TOWARD THE WINDOW.
(THEN, AFTER A PAUSE, HER VOICE TURNED BITTER) 425 DYNAMO
THEN ALL I CAN SAY IS THAT MY BOY I THOUGHT I 446 DYNAMO
COULD TRUST HAS TURNED INTO A LIAR
HIS HAIR HAS, TURNED ALMOST WHITE, HIS MOUTH DROOP5455 DYNAMO
FURLORNLY, HIS EYES ARE DULL.
YES, YER TURNED THE BLEEDIN' TRICK, ALL RIGHT. 178 EJONES
I'VE 'EARD MYSELF YOU 'AD TURNED YER COAT AN' WAS 185 EJONES
TAKIN' UP WITH THEIR BLASTED
(WHILE HIS BACK IS TURNED, 189 EJONES
THE GUARD SEEMS TO WAIT EXPECTANTLY, HIS BACK 195 EJONES
TURNED TO THE ATTACKER.
KEEPING HER BACK TURNED TO PETER.) 15 ELECTR
REALLY, THIS UNCONFIRMED REPORT MUST HAVE TURNED 29 ELECTR
YOUR HEAD--
BUT MARRIAGE SOON TURNED HIS ROMANCE INTO-- 31 ELECTR
DISGUST/
HE WAS WOUNDED IN THE HEAD--A CLOSE SHAVE BUT IT 48 ELECTR
TURNED OUT ONLY A SCRATCH.
TURNED SIDEWAYS TO FACE HER. 51 ELECTR
I TURNED TO VINNIE, BUT A DAUGHTER'S NOT A WIFE. 55 ELECTR

TURNED

TURNED (CONT'D.)		
WHEN I CAME BACK YOU HAD TURNED TO YOUR NEW BABY,	55	ELECTR
DAIN.		
WITH HER FACE TURNED THREE-QUARTERS AWAY FROM HIM.	59	ELECTR
(SHE GETS TO HER FEET BUT KEEPS HER FACE TURNED	59	ELECTR
AWAY FROM HIM.)		
(TURNED AWAY FROM HIM, TAKES A PELLET FROM THE	62	ELECTR
BOX.		
SHE WOULD HAVE TURNED TO ME/	124	ELECTR
(HAS TURNED BACK AND IS STARING FASCINATEDLY AT	143	ELECTR
HER.		
(WITH RESENTFUL BITTERNESS) BUT THEY TURNED OUT	145	ELECTR
TO BE WINNER'S ISLANDS.		
(HIS ANGER TURNED TO GLOATING SATISFACTION)	152	ELECTR
THE LAMP ON THE TABLE IS LIGHTED BUT TURNED LOW.	157	ELECTR
(WHO HAS TURNED AWAY) I'M GOING.	264	GGBORN
ALL THIS HAPPENS QUICKLY WHILE THE MEN HAVE THEIR	225	HA APE
BACKS TURNED.)		
WHILE THE OTHER MEN HAVE TURNED FULL AROUND AND	225	HA APE
STOPPED DUMBFOUNDED BY THE		
HE GLARES INTO HER EYES, TURNED TO STONE.	225	HA APE
(THE NIGHT CLERK SEEMS TURNED INTO A DROOPING WAX-	14	HUGHIE
WORKS, DRAPED ALONG THE DESK.		
I WISH TO HELL HE'D NEVER TURNED UP/	626	ICEMAN
HE HAS TURNED IT SO HE CAN WATCH HER.	629	ICEMAN
THE SITS DOWN WHERE HE WAS, HIS BACK TURNED TO	640	ICEMAN
THEM.)		
YES, IT TURNED OUT IT WASN'T A BIRTHDAY FEAST BUT	665	ICEMAN
A WAKE/		
NOW YOU DON'T HAVE TO BREAK IT, SOON'S MY BACK'S	673	ICEMAN
TURNED.		
TIME I TURNED OVER A NEW LEAF, AND ALL THAT.	675	ICEMAN
(BUT LARRY IS AT THE BAR, BACK TURNED, AND ROCKY	680	ICEMAN
IS SCOWLING AT HIM.		
HE'S TURNED BACK/	689	ICEMAN
A LANTERN IN THE MIDDLE OF THE FLOOR, TURNED DOWN	513	INZONE
VERY LOW.		
I CLAPPED MY EYES SHUT WHEN HE TURNED ROUND.	520	INZONE
(SHE IS SILENT ON THIS, KEEPING HER HEAD TURNED	15	JOURNE
TOWARD THEIR VOICES.		
(HAS TURNED HER HEAD AWAY.) I WILL, DEAR.	29	JOURNE
HAVE TO HUMBLE MY PRIDE AND BEG FOR YOU, SAYING	32	JOURNE
YOU'VE TURNED OVER A NEW LEAF.		
(HER LIPS QUIVER AND SHE KEEPS HER HEAD TURNED	45	JOURNE
AWAY.)		
(STUNG, JAMIE HAS TURNED TO STARE AT HER WITH	60	JOURNE
ACCUSING ANTAGONISM.		
TURNED HALF AWAY FROM HIS MOTHER SO HE DOES NOT	71	JOURNE
HAVE TO WATCH HER.)		
(THE LIGHT IN THE HALL IS TURNED ON AND SHINES	108	JOURNE
THROUGH THE FRONT PARLOR TO FALL		
THE LAMP IN THE FRONT HALL HAS BEEN TURNED OUT,	125	JOURNE
A MOMENT LATER THE HALL LAMP IS TURNED ON.	125	JOURNE
SHE MUST HAVE STARTED DOWN AND THEN TURNED BACK.	139	JOURNE
HIS DRESSING GOWN WET WITH FOG, THE COLLAR TURNED	167	JOURNE
UP AROUND HIS THROAT.		
SUDDENLY ALL FIVE BULBS OF THE CHANDELIER IN THE	169	JOURNE
FRONT PARLOR ARE TURNED ON FROM		
(THEIR FRENZY OF GRIEF TURNED INTO RAGE,	290	LAZARU
TURNED A LITTLE TOWARD FRONT.	363	LAZARU
HER OLIVE COMPLEXION HAS TURNED A DISPLEASING	27	MANSNS
SWARTHY COLOR.		
KEEPING HER FACE TURNED TOWARD SOMETHING FROM	27	MANSNS
WHICH SHE RETREATS.		
BUT SHE KEEPS HER HEAD TURNED SO THAT SHE IS STILL	27	MANSNS
LOOKING BACK		
KEEPING HER BACK TURNED TO DEBORAH, WHILE SHE	137	MANSNS
THINKS.)		
SHE HAS TURNED TO HIM.)	143	MANSNS
THEN HIS GAZE TURNED INWARD, HE MURMURS ALOUD TO	148	MANSNS
HIMSELF.		
(SIMON HAS NOT TURNED, GIVES NO SIGN OF HEARING	154	MANSNS
HIM.		
IT WOULD SERVE HIM RIGHT IF WE TURNED THE TABLES	171	MANSNS
ON HIM, SARA.		
HE KEEPS BEHIND HIS MOTHER, TURNED SIDEWAYS TO	186	MANSNS
SARA.		
THEIR EYES AT ONCE ARE TURNED IN THAT DIRECTION	349	MARCOM
AND.		
BUT SHE SEEMS TURNED TO STONE.	417	MARCOM
WHOSE EYES ARE RIVETED ON THE PRINCESS, WHO HAS	419	MARCOM
TURNED AWAY FROM THEM.		
HE WAS IN THE MEADOW, BUT THE MINUTE I TURNED MY	12	MISBEG
BACK HE SNEAKED OFF.		
EVERY BOULDER ON THE PLACE HAS TURNED TO SOLID	65	MISBEG
GOLD.		
AND I TURNED MY BACK ON HIM AND LEFT THE INN,	86	MISBEG
IT WAS AFTER HE'D TURNED QUEER--EARLY IN THE NIGHT	87	MISBEG
BEFORE SIMPSON CAME.		
HE'S TURNED IN THE GATE WHERE HE CAN HEAR US.	99	MISBEG
(SARA HAS TURNED TO HIM, ALL ATTENTION NOW.)	17	POET
(HIS BACK IS HALF TURNED AS HE HARANGUES O'DOWD	52	POET
AND RILEY.		
WELL, NO ONE CAN SAY OF ME THAT I TURNED AWAY	54	POET
ANYONE I KNEW THIRSTY		
ONE LOT BURNED BLACK AS A NAYGUR WHEN MY BACK WAS	55	POET
TURNED.		
RILEY IS AT FRONT, BUT HIS CHAIR IS TURNED	95	POET
SIDEWAYS SO HE FACES RIGHT.		
HIS BACK TURNED. HE DOES NOT SEE HER GO.	115	POET
THEN, KEEPING HER FACE TURNED AWAY FROM HER	131	POET
MOTHER, TOUCHES HER SHOULDER.)		
AND SIMON LIKED MY COSTUME, IF YOU DON'T, ALTHOUGH143		POET
HE TURNED RED AS A BEET WHEN		
LORD SAKES, SOON 'S EVER MY BACK IS TURNED YOU	579	ROPE
GOES SNEAKIN' OFF AGEN.		
AS THE THIEF COULD TAKE THE FARM FROM US TOMORROW590		ROPE
IF HIMSELF TURNED A LUNATIC.		

TURNED (CONT'D.)		
AND WHEN I TURNED ROUND AND BEAT IT HE SHOUTED	593	ROPE
AFTER ME.		
IT MAY HAVE TURNED HIM AGAINST ME...))	91	STRANG
HE KEEPS HIS TURNED AWAY.)	97	STRANG
(KEEPING HIS BACK TURNED TO HER--ROUGHLY)	103	STRANG
(BUT EVANS HAS TURNED BACK TO HIS PAPER.	114	STRANG
NINA HAS TURNED MINE AND MORE TO ME--	148	STRANG
NINA'S HAIR HAS TURNED COMPLETELY WHITE.	158	STRANG
AND HE'LL BE SO PLEASED WHEN HE KNOWS YOU TURNED	196	STRANG
ME DOWN.		
(HER HEAD HAS BEEN AVERTED SINCE HE TURNED AWAY--	481	WELDED
WITHOUT LOOKING AT HIM)		
(SHE HAS TURNED AWAY FROM HIM.	483	WELDED

TURNER

THE OLD MAN WAS TALKING TO OLD CAPTAIN TURNER.	54	JOURNE
GABBING WITH OLD CAPTAIN TURNER, JAMIE SAYS.	60	JOURNE
CAPTAIN TURNER STOPPED TO TALK AND ONCE HE STARTS	65	JOURNE
GABBING YOU CAN'T GET AWAY		

TURNIN'

HE AIN'T GOT NO EXCUSE FOR NOT TURNIN' BACK FOR	537	'ILE
HOME, THE MEN SAYS.		
AND NOT A SIGN OF HIM TURNIN' BACK FOR HOME/	537	'ILE
YOU AIN'T TURNIN' NO DAMNED SEA-LAWYER, BE YOU,	541	'ILE
MR. SLOCUM?		
I WARN'T THINKIN' OF MYSELF, SIR--'BOUT TURNIN'	542	'ILE
HOME, I MEAN.		
I SEEN 'EM FROM THE BARN DOWN BELOW AT THE	219	DESIRE
TURNIN'.		
AN' TALK O' TURNIN' ME OUT IN THE ROAD.	233	DESIRE
WARN'T YOUR HAIR TURNIN' GRAY LAST TIME I WAS TO	536	DIFNRT
HOME?		
BY TURNIN' IT ALL INTO A JOKE ON HIM FOLKS'D LAUGH135		ELECTR
AT.		
ABOUT TURNIN' OVER A NEW LEAF?	578	ICEMAN
HE'S TURNIN' THIS WAY--HE'S COMIN'/	525	INZONE

TURNING

(TURNING TO HIM--SHARPLY) WAIT/	540	'ILE
(TURNING AND SEEING HIM) DON'T BE STANDIN' THERE	543	'ILE
LIKE A GAWK, HARPOONER.		
(TURNING TO HIS WIFE) ANNIE/	551	'ILE
CHANGES THE SUBJECT ABRUPTLY BY TURNING TO ARTHUR)190		AHWILD
(TURNING BACK--SCORNFULLY) GOSH, HE'S ALWAYS	192	AHWILD
READING NOW--		
(TURNING TO THE OTHERS) MAYBE I BETTER STAY HOME	209	AHWILD
WITH HIM, IF HE'S SICK.		
(AGAIN TURNING TO HER--AGAIN OFFENDEDLY)	225	AHWILD
(TURNING ON SID FURIOUSLY) WILL YOU PLEASE SIT	226	AHWILD
DOWN AND STOP MAKING A FOOL OF		
(TURNING TO HER BROTHER) YOU SILLY GOAT, YOU/	228	AHWILD
(TURNING ON HIM) HAVE WHAT?	229	AHWILD
(TURNING TO NAT) WHAT CAN WE DO TO SAVE HER, NAT?232		AHWILD
(THEN TURNING ON HIM) SAY, HONESTLY, KID, DOES	238	AHWILD
YOUR MOTHER KNOW YOU'RE OUT?		
(HER ANXIETY IMMEDIATELY TURNING TO RELIEVED	253	AHWILD
ANGER)		
(TURNING TO LILY ENTHUSIASTICALLY)	259	AHWILD
(THEN TURNING TO HER HUSBAND)	265	AHWILD
TURNING HIS BACK ON THE PATH, HANDS IN POCKETS,	277	AHWILD
(TURNING TO THEM--ENTHUSIASTICALLY)	296	AHWILD
(TURNING TO GO) SALUD, EHS	5	ANNA
(THEN TURNING TO MARTHY, RATHER	8	ANNA
(THEN TURNING AWAY FROM HIM INDIFFERENTLY)	32	ANNA
(TURNING TO HIM AGAIN--FORCING A SMILE)	37	ANNA
(TURNING AWAY FROM HIM WITH A SHORT LAUGH--	38	ANNA
UNEASILY)		
(TURNING TO HIM, SARCASTICALLY)	42	ANNA
(TURNING ON BURKE REPROACHFULLY)	50	ANNA
(HE GOES AND PICKS UP THE CHAIR, THEN TURNING ON	50	ANNA
THE STILL-QUESTIONING ANNA--		
(TURNING ON HER FATHER ANGRILY)	54	ANNA
(THEN TURNING TO CHRIS) WE'LL BE SEEING WHO'LL	55	ANNA
WIN IN THE END--ME OR YOU.		
(TURNING TO HER IMPATIENTLY)	56	ANNA
(BLAZING OUT--TURNING ON HER IN A PERFECT FRENZY	60	ANNA
OF RAGE--		
(TURNING TO HER EARNESTLY) AND AY'M SORRY FOR YOU	64	ANNA
LIKE HELL HE DON'T COME.		
(TURNING ON HER--OVERCOME BY RAGE AGAIN)	71	ANNA
(TURNING AWAY IN EMBARRASSMENT)	77	ANNA
(JOVIALLY) I'LL BET THAT'S WHAT YOU'VE BEEN	85	BEYOND
TURNING OVER		
(TURNING TO HER QUICKLY, IN SURPRISE--SLOWLY)	88	BEYOND
(SUDDENLY TURNING TO THEM) THERE'S ONE THING NONE	96	BEYOND
OF YOU		
(TURNING TO HIS UNCLE) YOU HAVEN'T ANSWERED BY	104	BEYOND
QUESTION, UNCLE DICK.		
(TURNING TO HIM QUICKLY) ANDY/	104	BEYOND
(TURNING TO HIS FATHER AGAIN)	105	BEYOND
(TURNING TO DOORWAY TO KITCHEN)	125	BEYOND
QUICKLY TURNING AWAY AGAIN FROM THE OTHERS.	140	BEYOND
(TURNING TO LOOK AT ANDREW--IN A TONE OF FIERCE	141	BEYOND
RESENTMENT)		
IT'S THE TURNING POINT, I GUESS.	145	BEYOND
TURNING IT SO SHE CAN FACE HIM,)	154	BEYOND
(TURNING TO HIM) SHUD UP, YOU TAMN FOOL, PADDY/	458	CARIBE
(TURNING TO THE LEFT) THIS WAY, ROSE, OR PANSY,	468	CARIBE
OR JESSAMINE, OR BLACK TULIP,		
THEN HE GOES OVER TO THE TABLE, TURNING THE	562	CROSS
LANTERN VERY LOW, AND SITS DOWN.		
(TURNING TO THE DOOR) I'LL GET OUT.	500	DAYS
(WITHOUT TURNING--QUIETLY) NO.	502	DAYS
(WITHOUT TURNING--QUIETLY) DON'T YOU KNOW, JACK?	503	DAYS
FATHER BAIRD GOES INTO THE HALL, TURNING LEFT TO	541	DAYS
GO UPSTAIRS TO THE STUDY.		
DISAPPEARS IN THE HALL, TURNING RIGHT TOWARD THE	541	DAYS
ENTRANCE DOOR TO THE APARTMENT.		

1721 TWAIN

TURNING (CONT'D.)
TURNING BACK INTO THE STUDY BUT LEAVING THE 561 DAYS
COMMUNICATING DOOR AJAR.
(TURNING TO HER WITH STRANGE PASSION) 238 DESIRE
(SUDDENLY TURNING TO A YOUNG GIRL ON HER RIGHT) 247 DESIRE
(TURNING TO THE FIDDLER) FIDDLE 'ER UP, DURN YE/ 250 DESIRE
(TURNING AWAY FROM HIM--FRIGHTENEDLY) 501 DIFRNT
(TURNING TO HER MOTHER--PLEADINGLY) 511 DIFRNT
(TURNING BACK TO EMMA AGAIN) 513 DIFRNT
(TURNING TO HIS WIFE) WHAT YE GOT TO SAY NOW, MASS13 DIFRNT
WITHOUT TURNING AROUND. 518 DIFRNT
(TURNING TO HER) SAY, YOU'RE A REGULAR FELLER-- 520 DIFRNT
GETTIN' THEM RECORDS FOR ME.
(TURNING IN THE DOORWAY--COQUETTISHLY) 528 DIFRNT
BENNY GOES TO OPEN IT, HIS EXPRESSION TURNING 528 DIFRNT
SURLY AND SULLEN.
(TURNING AWAY FROM HER) AND NOW I'M GOING TO 534 DIFRNT
BLOW.
(TURNING AWAY FROM HER WITH A LOOK OF AVERSION) 544 DIFRNT
(THEN TURNING TO HIS WIFE) 425 DYNAMO
(THEN HIS HORROR TURNING TO A CONFUSED RAGE) 440 DYNAMO
ARE YOU TURNING AGAINST ME--FOR THAT LUMP? 443 DYNAMO
(TURNING TOWARD THE DOOR) KEEP REUBEN HERE. 449 DYNAMO
(THEN PICKING UP HIS BOOKS AND TURNING TOWARD HIS 461 DYNAMO
HOME)
(TURNING TO THE DOOR) WELL, SO LONG. 467 DYNAMO
(TURNING TO MRS. FIFE) YOU STAY HERE/ I'LL BE 481 DYNAMO
BACK.
(TURNING AWAY FROM THEM QUICKLY AND LOOKING DOWN 188 EJONES
AT HIS FEET.
TURNING THEM OVER IN FRANTIC HASTE. 189 EJONES
(TURNING AWAY FROM HIM CONTEMPTUOUSLY) AW/ GARN/203 EJONES
(TURNING ON HIM SHARPLY) WHAT DO YOU MEAN, SETHS. 11 ELECTR
(TURNING DEFIANTLY) WHENEVER YOU WISH. 18 ELECTR
AGITATEDLY SNATCHING HER HAND FROM HIS AND TURNING 21 ELECTR
AWAY FROM HIM.)
(TURNING AWAY--HER VOICE STILL TREMBLING) 34 ELECTR
(TURNING TO STARE AT HIM--SLOWLY) 39 ELECTR
(THEN TURNING AWAY AGAIN) YOU REMEMBER MY TELLING 39 ELECTR
YOU HE HAD WRITTEN
(HALF TURNING TO CHRISTINE) HE GETS THAT FROM 48 ELECTR
YOU.
TURNING TO FACE THE DOOR AS IT OPENS AND LAVINIA 62 ELECTR
APPEARS IN THE DOORWAY.
(TURNING ON HER WITH HATRED) 63 ELECTR
(TURNING TO BORDEN--WITH A SELF-SATISFIED, KNOWING 70 ELECTR
AIR)
(THEN TURNING TO PETER) YOU GO AHEAD IN, PETER. 74 ELECTR
THEN LAVINIA, TURNING HER BACK, 78 ELECTR
(TURNING AWAY AND RESTRAINING A SHUDDER) 81 ELECTR
(TURNING ON LAVINIA WHO STANDS BY THE HEAD OF THE 100 ELECTR
BIER)
(THEN TURNING ON SMALL--SCORNFULLY) 134 ELECTR
(TURNING TO THE HOUSE) LOOK. 136 ELECTR
(SHE TEARS HER EYES FROM THEIRS AND, TURNING AWAY,139 ELECTR
(TURNING TO LOOK AROUND) WHY, HE WAS RIGHT HERE. 144 ELECTR
(TURNING TO PETER AND HOLDING OUT HIS HAND, HIS 148 ELECTR
SMILE BECOMING GHASTLY)
(FORCING A SMILE AGAIN AND TURNING AWAY FROM HIM) 150 ELECTR
(THEN SUDDENLY HER HORROR TURNING INTO A VIOLENT 156 ELECTR
RAGE--
(TURNING TO HAZEL--WITH QUEER FURTIVE EXCITEMENT) 160 ELECTR
(TURNING TO ORIN--SHARPLY) I THOUGHT YOU WERE IN 162 ELECTR
THE STUDY.
(HER CONTROL SNAPPING--TURNING ON HIM NOW IN A 166 ELECTR
BURST OF FRANTIC HATRED AND RAGE)
(TURNING TO HER) YOU'RE LOST IN BLIND ALLEYS, 280 GGBROW
TOO.
(TURNING QUICKLY TO THE DRAFTSMEN) 303 GGBROW
(TURNING AWAY SLOWLY AND PUTTING ON HIS MASK-- 305 GGBROW
DULLY)
(AGAIN TURNING AROUND SCORNFULLY) 210 HA APE
(HE IS TURNING TO GET COAL WHEN THE WHISTLE SOUNDS225 HA APE
AGAIN IN A PEREMPTORY,
AND THERE WAS YANK ROARIN' CURSES AND TURNING 229 HA APE
ROUND WID HIS SHOVEL TO BRAIN HER--
(TURNING TO THE OTHERS, BEWILDERMENT SEIZING HIM 230 HA APE
AGAIN)
(THEN TURNING AWAY, BORED) BUT, AW HELL, WHAT 235 HA APE
GOOD ARE DEYS
(TURNING AROUND ON HIS STOOL) 246 HA APE
BEJEEZ, I'LL BET BESSIE'S TURNING OVER IN HER 615 ICEMAN
GRAVE/
(THEN TURNING AWAY) I DON'T GIVE A DAMN WHAT YOU 649 ICEMAN
DID/
(TURNING TO LARRY WITH A STRAINED LAUGH) 679 ICEMAN
(HE GOES OUT, TURNING RIGHT OUTSIDE.) 685 ICEMAN
(HE GOES OUT, TURNING LEFT OUTSIDE. 685 ICEMAN
TURNING TO HIS RIGHT AND MARCHING OFF OUTSIDE THE 685 ICEMAN
WINDOW AT RIGHT OF DOOR.)
BUNKS, SHOES AND ALL, TURNING THEIR FACES TO THE 532 INZONE
WALL.
THEN TURNING BACK ADDS WITH A CONSTRAINED AIR.) 17 JOURNE
(WITHOUT TURNING--DRYLY.) YOU MEAN ONCE HE STARTS 65 JOURNE
LISTENING.
WITHOUT TURNING, JAMIE SENSES THIS.) 65 JOURNE
(BITTERLY WITHOUT TURNING AROUND.) 72 JOURNE
(TURNING TO EDMUND BUT AVOIDING HIS EYES-- 91 JOURNE
TEASINGLY AFFECTIONATE.)
(HE FINISHES TURNING ON THE LIGHTS.) 128 JOURNE
AND BEGINS TURNING ON THE THREE BULBS IN THE 128 JOURNE
CHANDELIER, WITH A CHILDISH
=THEN, TURNING TO MY LOVE, I SAID, THE DEAD ARE 159 JOURNE
DANCING WITH THE DEAD.
TURNING HIS CHAIR SO HE WON'T LOOK AT JAMIE. 169 JOURNE
(TURNING--UNEASY BUT AFRAID TO GIVE ANY DRASTIC 304 LAZARU
ORDER)
(WITH GENUINE SURPRISE--TURNING TO HER) 327 LAZARU

TURNING (CONT'D.)
CALIGULA SHRUGS HIS SHOULDERS, TURNING AWAY-- 328 LAZARU
LIGHTLY)
(SHAKING HER HEAD AND TURNING AWAY SADLY) 331 LAZARU
(TURNING HIS BACK ON THEM. 332 LAZARU
(TO THE SLAVES WHO ARE TURNING OUT THE FEW 338 LAZARU
REMAINING LAMPS)
(TURNING TO HER--COARSELY) DO NOT WASTE YOUR 341 LAZARU
LUST.
(THEN HIS FEAR TURNING TO RAGE) 341 LAZARU
(SHE DREAMS, HER EYES AGAIN FIXED ON LAZARUS--THEN351 LAZARU
SUDDENLY TURNING TO CALIGULA)
(SUDDENLY--TURNING TO LAZARUS NOW) 351 LAZARU
(TURNING TO HIM AGAIN WITH A SHUDDER OF AGONY-- 364 LAZARU
BESEECHINGLY)
(TURNING AND SCURRYING AWAY-- 369 LAZARU
I THINK LIFE REMEMBERS HE HAD FORGOTTEN ME AND IS 40 MANSNS
TURNING BACK.
(AS IF THE TOUCH OF HIS HAND ALARMED HER--SHRINKS 103 MANSNS
BACK, TURNING AWAY FROM HIM--
(TURNING ON HIM WITH FORCED SCORN.) 113 MANSNS
AGAINST YOU AND MY BROTHER TURNING THIS OFFICE--MY142 MANSNS
FATHER'S OFFICE--INTO A--
(THEN, JUST AS DEBORAH IS TURNING THE KNOB, SHE 165 MANSNS
SPRINGS TOWARD HER.)
(ANGRILY, TURNING TOWARD THE PATH OFF LEFT.) 169 MANSNS
TWISTING AND TURNING HIS LEGS AND FEET, 359 MARCOM
(TURNING ON HIM--GENIALLY) WELL, SON, HERE WE ARE364 MARCOM
IN ISLAM.
YOU'RE LIKE A BAD COIN--ALWAYS TURNING UP. 367 MARCOM
(TURNING TO HAFED) I WIN, UNCLE. 371 MARCOM
(TURNING TO MARCO--CYNICALLY) 371 MARCOM
(TURNING TO THE PRINCESS) 398 MARCOM
(TURNING TO CHU-YIN--HARSHLY) 423 MARCOM
(TURNING HIS ANGER AGAINST HER) 11 MISBEG
(TURNING AWAY) AND IF THAT DIDN'T WORK, 22 MISBEG
(HE PAUSES--THEN WITH GREAT SERIOUSNESS, TURNING 31 MISBEG
TOWARD HER)
(TURNING TO HOGAN) WELL, HOW ABOUT THAT DRINK, 51 MISBEG
PHIL?
(IN THE ACT OF TURNING DOWN THE LAMP, STOPS AND 77 MISBEG
STARES AT HIM,
(TURNING BACK--BITTER ACCUSATION IN HIS TONE NOW) 139 MISBEG
(WITHOUT TURNING TO HER--IN HIS CONDESCENDINGLY 55 POET
POLITE TONE.)
(TURNING AWAY.) I'D BETTER GET BACK. 135 POET
(TURNING BACK TO THE SULKING MARY) 601 ROPE
TURNING THE BAG UPSIDE DOWN, POURS ITS CONTENTS IN601 ROPE
HER LAP.
(TURNING HER EYES TO MARSDEN, HOLDING OUT HER HAND 13 STRANG
FOR HIM TO SHAKE.
(TURNING ON HER FATHER--DETERMINEDLY) 14 STRANG
(TURNING TO MARSDEN--WITH A SUDDEN GIRLISHNESS) 21 STRANG
(TURNING TO MARSDEN) IT'S FOR NINA. 34 STRANG
(AS SOON AS HE IS OUT OF EARSHOT--TURNING ON NINA 95 STRANG
ACCUSINGLY)
(TURNING TO NINA) I THINK I'LL WRITE TO MY SISTER113 STRANG
IN CALIFORNIA AND ASK HER TO
(TURNING OVER A PAGE OF HIS PAPER) 113 STRANG
(THEN WITH SUDDEN ANGER TURNING ON MARSDEN) 127 STRANG
SUPPOSE IT'S THE EXCITEMENT OF NED TURNING UP... 134 STRANG
FLOOR NEAR HER, TURNING OVER THE PAGES OF A BOOK. 137 STRANG
(SUDDENLY TURNING ON HIM) WHEN ARE YOU GOING BACK/40 STRANG
TO THE WEST INDIES, NED?
PICKING UP A MAGAZINE AND TURNING OVER THE PAGES 148 STRANG
AIMLESSLY)
(TURNING TO DARRELL) AND THAT ISN'T FATHER STUFF 162 STRANG
EITHER, NED/
(TURNING BACK TO NINA--RESENTFULLY) 162 STRANG
(TURNING ON HER TRIUMPHANTLY) 174 STRANG
(TURNING TO DARRELL, WHO IS STANDING WITH A SAD 195 STRANG
RESIGNED EXPRESSION)
(TURNING TO JOE IN TRIUMPH) NAW, WHAT D'YER SAYS 496 VOYAGE
(TURNING TO COCKY, WHO IS BLINKING SLEEPILY) 508 VOYAGE
SHE RECOILS FROM IT, TURNING QUICKLY AWAY FROM 490 WELDED
HIM, VISIBLY SHAKEN.
TURNING OVER THE PAGES OF A MAGAZINE) 451 WELDED
(SHE FORCES A SMILE, HALF TURNING AWAY.) 452 WELDED
(IMMEDIATELY TURNING AWAY--SIGNIFICANTLY) 463 WELDED
(TURNING ON HIM DOGGEDELY 484 WELDED
(TURNING TO HER RESENTFULLY) 484 WELDED
(THEN TURNING TO HER--DETERMINEDLY--AFTER A PAUSE) 484 WELDED
(TAKEN ABACK, TURNING AWAY) NO, I SUPPOSE-- 485 WURNIP

TURNIP
OPEN HIM UP AN' YOU'D FIND A DRIED TURNIP/ 106 ELECTR

TURNOVER
AND I MADE A QUICK TURNOVER ON IT FOR A FINE 15 JOURNE
PACFIT.

TURRETED
CONCEIVED ON THE MODEL OF A MEDIAEVAL, TURRETED 139 MANSNS
CASTLE.

TURRIBLE
MUST BE AS TURRIBLE BUGJUICE AS HARRY'S. 616 ICEMAN

TURTLE
YE MAKE A SLICK PAIR O' MURDERIN' TURTLE DOVES/ 267 DESIRE
THIS OLD TURTLE NEVER WINS A RACE, BUT HE WAS AS 25 HUGHIE
FOXY AS TEN GUYS.
I GOT SOME DOUGH RIDIN' ON THE NOSE OF A TURTLE IN 37 HUGHIE
THE 4TH AT SARATOGA.

TURTLES
I DON'T MEAN THEM KIND OF TURTLES. 22 HUGHIE

TUSSLE
THEIR FACES ARE SULLENLY ANGRY, THEIR CLOTHES 650 ICEMAN
DISARRANGED FROM THE TUSSLE.)

TWADDLE
IT'S ALL SILLY TWADDLE, OF COURSE. 942 DAYS

TWAIN
RENT IN TWAIN BY YOUR TEARING GREEDY CLAWS$ 174 MANSNS

TWEED 1722

TWEED
HIS ANCIENT TWEED SUIT HAS BEEN BRUSHED AND HIS 674 ICEMAN
FRAYED LINEN IS CLEAN.
HE IS DRESSED IN A BEAUTIFULLY TAILORED ENGLISH 56 MISBEG
TWEED COAT AND WHIPCORD RIDING
HE IS DRESSED IMMACULATELY IN DARK TWEED.) 111 STRANG

TWEEDS
HE IS A TALL THIN MAN OF THIRTY-FIVE, METICULOUSLY 3 STRANG
WELL-DRESSED IN TWEEDS

TWELVE
RED WAS FOURTEEN, BIGGER AND OLDER THAN ME, I WAS 229 AHWILD
ONLY TWELVE--
I WAS GOING OUT TO LOOK--IF HE WASN'T BACK BY 260 AHWILD
TWELVE SHARP.
SITTING ROOM OF THE FARMHOUSE ABOUT HALF PAST 112 BEYOND
TWELVE IN THE AFTERNOON OF A HOT,
YOU'RE TWELVE YEARS OLDER'N ME, DON'T FORGET, 538 DIFRNT
CALEB--
YOU'D 'AVE TO 'USTLE TO GET THROUGH THAT FOREST IN183 EJONES
TWELVE HOURS.
THE ELDEST IS ABOUT FOURTEEN, THE TWO OTHERS 293 GGBROW
THIRTEEN AND TWELVE.
OR IS IT TWELVES 12 HUGHIE
(WITH A BUSINESS-LIKE AIR) I PICKED TWELVE BUCKS 617 ICEMAN
OFFA HIM.
HE'LL BE GOOD AND RIPE FOR MY BIRTHDAY PARTY 618 ICEMAN
TONIGHT AT TWELVE.
IT WAS GOING ON TWELVE WHEN I WENT IN THE BEDROOM 622 ICEMAN
TO TELL EVELYN I WAS LEAVING.
IT'LL BE TWELVE O'CLOCK AND HARRY'S BOITHDAY 630 ICEMAN
BEFORE LONG.
WELL, WELL, NOT MUCH TIME BEFORE TWELVE. 643 ICEMAN
IT'S TWELVE/ 653 ICEMAN
IF IS ABOUT TEN MINUTES OF TWELVE ON A NIGHT IN 513 INZONE
THE FALL OF THE YEAR 1915.
I WORKED TWELVE HOURS A DAY IN A MACHINE SHOP, 148 JOURNE
LEARNING TO MAKE FILES.
SHE IS A GIRL OF TWELVE, HER FACE PALE AND PRETTY 355 MARCOM
IN THE MOONLIGHT.)
OR PROHIBITING THE PRACTICE OF THE LAWS OF BIOLOGY390 MARCOM
WITHIN A TWELVE-MILE LIMIT.
ABOUT TWELVE FEET LONG BY SIX HIGH, THIS ROOM, 1 MISBEG
WHICH IS JOSIE HOGAN'S BEDROOM,
WHICH EXTENDS AT A HEIGHT OF ABOUT TWELVE FEET 577 ROPE
FROM THE FLOOR AS FAR TO THE
(BITTERLY) MY WORK WAS FINISHED TWELVE YEARS AGO.140 STRANG
IT'S PAST TWELVE-- 454 WELDED

TWENTIES
IT HAS NOT SHAKEN IN THE GREAT HOLLOW BOOM OF THE 7 HUGHIE
TWENTIES.
HE IS A NEAPOLITAN-AMERICAN IN HIS LATE TWENTIES, 577 ICEMAN
SQUAT AND MUSCULAR,
THE OTHER, LIEB, IS IN HIS TWENTIES. 708 ICEMAN
SHE IS A BUXOM IRISH PEASANT, IN HER EARLY 51 JOURNE
TWENTIES.
HE'S DOING REMARKABLE WORK ALREADY, AND HE'S STILL140 STRANG
IN HIS TWENTIES.

TWENTY
IT WAS ON THE TWENTY-FIFTH OF AUGUST WE WERE 548 *ILE
MARRIED, DAVID, WASN'T ITS
I'M GOING TO BEAT IT--JUST TIME TO CATCH THE 199 AHWILD
EIGHT-TWENTY TROLLEY.
BELLE IS TWENTY, A RATHER PRETTY PEROXIDE BLONDE, 236 AHWILD
HE IS A BOYISH, RED-CHEEKED, RATHER GOOD-LOOKING 4 ANNA
YOUNG FELLOW OF TWENTY OR SO.)
SHE MUST BE--LAT ME SEE--SHE MUST BE TWENTY YEAR 9 ANNA
OLD, PY YO/
AFTER ME CAMPIN' WITH BARGE MEN THE LAST TWENTY 11 ANNA
YEARS.
SHE IS A TALL, BLOND, FULLY-DEVELOPED GIRL OF 13 ANNA
TWENTY, HANDSOME AFTER A LARGE,
HE IS A TALL, SLENDER YOUNG MAN OF TWENTY-THREE. 81 BEYOND
HE IS TWENTY-SEVEN YEARS OLD, AN OPPOSITE TYPE TO 82 BEYOND
ROBERT--
SHE IS A HEALTHY, BLONDE, OUT-OF-DOOR GIRL OF 87 BEYOND
TWENTY.
I'VE SAVED TEN THOUSAND FROM THE WRECKAGE, MAYBE 157 BEYOND
TWENTY.
TWENTY MINUTES AFTER I LEAVE HERE I'LL BE BACK IN 558 CROSS
THE CAR.
SHE IS A TALL, SLENDER WOMAN OF TWENTY-FIVE, 562 CROSS
HE IS TWENTY-FIVE, TALL AND SINEWY. 203 DESIRE
SHE'S BEEN PURTY FUR TWENTY YEAR/ 210 DESIRE
(OPENS BAG AND POURS OUT PILE OF TWENTY-DOLLAR 219 DESIRE
GOLD PIECES)
TWENTY-DOLLAR PIECES--THIRTY ON 'EM. 219 DESIRE
I WAS JEST TWENTY AN' THE STRONGEST AN' HARDEST YE236 DESIRE
EVER SEEN--
HE WAS MARRIED TWENTY YEAR. 237 DESIRE
EMMA IS A SLENDER GIRL OF TWENTY, RATHER UNDER THE494 DIFRNT
MEDIUM HEIGHT.
ROGERS IS A HUSKY YOUNG FISHERMAN OF TWENTY-FOUR, 505 DIFRNT
CALEB'S SISTER IS A TALL, DARK GIRL OF TWENTY. 505 DIFRNT
HE IS A YOUNG FELLOW OF TWENTY-THREE, A REPLICA OF519 DIFRNT
HIS FATHER IN ACT ONE.
SHE RESEMBLES SOME PASSE STOCK ACTRESS OF FIFTY 520 DIFRNT
MADE UP FOR A HEROINE OF TWENTY.
TWENTY-THREE YEARS/ 425 DYNAMO
HE GOT TWENTY YEARS FOR IT, 431 DYNAMO
TWENTY YEARS AGO THERE WAS A MAN BY THE NAME OF 440 DYNAMO
ANDREW CLARK LIVED IN THE TOWN
THE JURY SAID IT WAS MURDER IN THE SECOND DEGREE 441 DYNAMO
AND GAVE ME TWENTY YEARS--
HE GOT TWENTY YEARS BUT HE ESCAPED AND RAN AWAY TO447 DYNAMO
CALIFORNIA/
MAYBE I GITS TWENTY YEARS WHEN DAT COLORED MAN 181 EJONES
DIE.
SHE IS TWENTY-THREE BUT LOOKS CONSIDERABLY OLDER. 10 ELECTR

TWENTY (CONT'D.)
HE IS A HEAVILY BUILT YOUNG FELLOW OF TWENTY-TWO. 12 ELECTR
FOR OVER TWENTY YEARS, GIVING MY BODY TO A MAN I-- 31 ELECTR
WE HAVE TWENTY GOOD YEARS STILL BEFORE US/ 55 ELECTR
ALTHOUGH HE IS ONLY TWENTY, HE LOOKS THIRTY. 74 ELECTR
I HAD BEEN A GOOD WIFE TO HIM FOR TWENTY-THREE 77 ELECTR
YEARS--UNTIL I MET ADAM.
SHE IS A STRONG, CALM SENSUAL BLONDE GIRL OF 278 GGBROW
TWENTY OR SO.
TWENTY-FIVE KNOTS A HOUR/ 215 HA APE
WE SPLIT DAT UP AND SMASH TROU--TWENTY-FIVE KNOTS 217 HA APE
A HOUR/
THE FORMER IS A GIRL OF TWENTY, SLENDER, DELICATE,217 HA APE
WITH A PALE,
TWENTY-FIVE KNOTS A HOUR, DAT'S ME/ 231 HA APE
IT MOVES--SPEED--TWENTY-FIVE STORIES UP AND ME AT 238 HA APE
DE TOP AND BOTTOM--MOVIN'/
DERE WAS A MILLION MILES FROM ME TO HER--TWENTY- 241 HA APE
FIVE KNOTS A HOUR.
HELL, I ONCE WIN TWENTY GRAND ON A SINGLE RACE. 36 HUGHIE
THAT'S ACTION/
SINCE HIS WIFE DIED TWENTY YEARS AGO. 594 ICEMAN
(CHUCKLING) GITTIN' DRUNK EVERY DAY FOR TWENTY 601 ICEMAN
YEARS
AND IT'S TWENTY YEARS SINCE 602 ICEMAN
(MOURNFULLY) TWENTY YEARS, 603 ICEMAN
TEN, TWENTY, THIRTY, FORTY, FIFTY, SIXTY, SEVENTY,608 ICEMAN
EIGHTY, NINETY, A DOLLAR,
TEN, TWENTY--THOSE ARE PRETTY SHOES YOU GOT ON, 609 ICEMAN
BESS--
TEN, TWENTY, THIRTY--WHAT'S ON AT THE CHURCH 609 ICEMAN
TONIGHT, BESS/
TEN, TWENTY, THIRTY, FIFTY, SEVENTY, EIGHTY, 609 ICEMAN
NINETY--
TWENTY, THIRTY, FORTY, FIFTY, SIXTY--YOU'RE 609 ICEMAN
COUNTING WITH ME, BESS, AREN'T YOUS
THE TWO GIRLS, NEITHER MUCH OVER TWENTY, ARE 611 ICEMAN
TYPICAL DOLLAR STREET WALKERS,
HE'S HAD FOR TWENTY YEARS. 652 ICEMAN
LOOK HOW HE'S KIDDED HIMSELF FOR TWENTY YEARS/ 655 ICEMAN
MAYBE I THROW A TWENTY-DOLLAR BILL ON DE BAR AND 673 ICEMAN
SAY, DRINK IT UP.
I'VE HAD RHEUMATISM ON AND OFF FOR TWENTY YEARS. 684 ICEMAN
I'M FREE, WHITE AND TWENTY-ONE, AND I'LL DO AS I 687 ICEMAN
DAMNED PLEASE, BEJEES/
TWENTY YEARS IS A LONG TIME. 687 ICEMAN
WASN'T NONE OF THEM AROUND THE LAST TIME, TWENTY 687 ICEMAN
YEARS AGO.
THE DEVIL TAKE THEIR TWENTY-FOIVE PER CENT BONUS--517 INZONE
ENGLAND HAS BEEN LIVIN' THERE FOR TEN, OFTEN AS 521 INZONE
NOT TWENTY YEARS.
YOU'RE A FINE ARMFUL NOW, MARY, WITH THOSE TWENTY 14 JOURNE
POUNDS YOU'VE GAINED.
I'VE KEPT MY APPETITE AND I'VE THE DIGESTION OF A 14 JOURNE
YOUNG MAN OF TWENTY.
AND I WAS ONLY TWENTY-SEVEN YEARS OLD/ 150 JOURNE
AT FRONT, PACING IMPATIENTLY UP AND DOWN, IS A 298 LAZARU
YOUNG ROMAN NOBLE OF TWENTY-ONE,
LAZARUS, LOOKING NO MORE THAN TWENTY-FIVE, HALOED 326 LAZARU
IN HIS OWN MYSTIC LIGHT,
SHE IS TWENTY-FIVE, EXCEEDINGLY PRETTY IN A 1 MANSNS
TYPICALLY IRISH FASHION,
HE IS TWENTY-SIX BUT THE POISE OF HIS BEARING 4 MANSNS
MAKES HIM APPEAR MUCH MORE MATURE.
JOEL HARFORD IS TWENTY-NINE, TALL AND THIN, WITH A 25 MANSNS
SLIGHT STOOP IN HIS CARRIAGE.
HIS BODY HAS PUT ON TWENTY POUNDS OR MORE OF SOLID 69 MANSNS
FLESH,
THAT OF A BEAUTIFUL TARTAR PRINCESS OF TWENTY- 351 MARCOM
THREE,
TWENTY-THREE YEARS EARLIER. 355 MARCOM
KUKACHIN, A BEAUTIFUL YOUNG GIRL OF TWENTY, PALE 384 MARCOM
AND DELICATE,
NOW JUST PICTURE THIS LITTLE BALL MAGNIFIED INTO 395 MARCOM
ONE WEIGHING TWENTY POUNDS OR
AND REMEMBER THEY'VE BEEN GONE TWENTY-ODD YEARS. 427 MARCOM
IT MUST HAVE COST TWENTY LIRE A BOTTLE/ 429 MARCOM
AND ALL THE TWENTY-ODD YEARS I KEPT THINKING OF 430 MARCOM
YOU.
JOSIE IS TWENTY-EIGHT. 3 MISBEG
(MIKE HOGAN IS TWENTY, ABOUT FOUR INCHES SHORTER 3 MISBEG
THAN HIS SISTER.
DON'T FORGET, IF WE HAVE LIVED ON IT TWENTY YEARS, 31 MISBEG
I'VE WANTED TO GO ON THE WAGON FOR THE PAST 45 MISBEG
TWENTY-FIVE YEARS,
TWENTY PIGS AT TWO HUNDRED, THAT'S FOUR THOUSAND. 63 MISBEG
A BLONDE PIG WHO LOOKED MORE LIKE A WHORE THAN 149 MISBEG
TWENTY-FIVE WHORES.
MALOY IS TWENTY-SIX, WITH A STURDY PHYSIQUE AND AN 8 POET
AMIABLE, CUNNING FACE,
SARA IS TWENTY, AN EXCEEDINGLY PRETTY GIRL WITH A 15 POET
MASS OF BLACK HAIR.
AFTER NOT BEIN' AT SUNDAY MEETIN' YOURSELF FOR 580 ROPE
NOREN TWENTY YEARS/
IT WAS IN TWENTY-DOLLAR GOLD PIECES HE GOT IT, I 586 ROPE
REMEMBER MA
HE IS A TALL, STRAPPING YOUNG FELLOW ABOUT TWENTY-587 ROPE
FIVE WITH A COARSE-FEATURED,
FIFTY TWENTY-DOLLAR GOLD PIECES. 602 ROPE
SHE IS TWENTY, TALL WITH BROAD SQUARE SHOULDERS, 12 STRANG
ALTHOUGH HE IS TWENTY-FIVE AND HAS BEEN OUT OF 29 STRANG
COLLEGE THREE YEARS,
HE IS TWENTY-SEVEN, SHORT, DARK, WIRY, HIS 33 STRANG
MOVEMENTS RAPID AND SURE.
ALL THE TWENTY-ODD BOOKS I'VE WRITTEN 176 STRANG
I'M ONLY TWENTY-SIX, HONEST. 474 WELDED
TEN THOUSAND YEARS--ABOUT--ISN'T ITS OR TWENTYS 474 WELDED

TWICE

AND ONCE OR TWICE, TO THROW THE DICE IS A 246 AHWILD
GENTLEMANLY GAME,
(THEN SUDDENLY DEFIANT) AND WHAT IF I DID KISS 286 AHWILD
HER ONCE OR TWICE/
HER SHOULDERS QUIVER ONCE OR TWICE AS IF SHE WERE 52 ANNA
FIGHTING BACK HER SOBS.
(REUBEN FIRES TWICE AND SHE JERKS BACK AND PITCHES488 DYNAMO
SIDEWAYS ON THE STAIRS.)
THERE ARE TWICE AS MANY SKIPPERS AS SHIPS THESE 39 ELECTR
DAYS.
IT WAS LIKE MURDERING THE SAME MAN TWICE. 95 ELECTR
AND WITH THE PISTOL ALMOST AGAINST BRANT'S BODY 114 ELECTR
FIRES TWICE.
I WENT TO SEE HIM TWICE IN THE HOSPITAL. 30 HUGHIE
HE COMES HERE TWICE A YEAR REGULARLY ON A 586 ICEMAN
PERIODICAL DRUNK
ONCE OR TWICE I THOUGHT IT FALTERED-- (HE DRAWS IN357 LAZARU
HIS BREATH WITH AN AVID GASP--
SHE HAS ONLY TALKED TO HIM ONCE OR TWICE EVERY TWO388 MARCOM
YEARS OR SO/
TWICE NOW YOU'VE TREATED MY LOVE WITH THE MOST 468 WELDED
HUMILIATING CONTEMPT--

TWIDDLING

EVANS SITS UNCOMFORTABLY HUNCHED FORWARD, 28 STRANG
TWIDDLING HIS HAT IN HIS HANDS.
(SHEEPISHLY HE GLANCES UP AT CEILING, THEN DOWN AT 33 STRANG
FLOOR, TWIDDLING HIS HAT.)
(OVERCOME, HIS EYES ON HIS SHUFFLING FEET AND 47 STRANG
TWIDDLING CAP)

TWIG

CERTAINLY/ DO YOU NOT KNOW THE LEGEND OF HOW THE 349 MARCOM
HOLY SAKYA PICKED A TWIG

TWILIGHT

THE HUSHED TWILIGHT OF A DAY IN MAY IS JUST 81 BEYOND
BEGINNING.
THE BLUE OF HER WISTFUL WIDE EYES IS FADING INTO A562 CROSS
TWILIGHT GRAY.

TWILIGHT BEGINS. 206 DESIRE
(TWILIGHT OF THE NEXT DAY. 251 HA APE
A BACKGROUND OF TWILIGHT SKY. 275 LAZARU
IT WILL SERVE HER RIGHT TO BE ALONE IN THE 159 MANSNS
TWILIGHT SHE DREADS SO

TWIN

AS IF THEY WERE TWIN BREEDS OF VERMIN/ 387 MARCOM

TWINE

ONE LACED WITH TWINE, THE OTHER WITH A BIT OF 577 ICEMAN
WIRE.

TWINES

SHE TWINES AND UNTWINES THE FINGERS OF HER CLASPEC157 ELECTR
HANDS WITH A SLOW

TWINGE

TWINGE--RHEUMATICS--GETTING OLD, NINA. 44 STRANG
I DON'T FEEL THE SLIGHTEST TWINGE OF JEALOUSY. 175 STRANG

TWINKLE

(A TWINKLE IN HIS EYE) HMM. 194 AHWILD
(WITH A TWINKLE IN HIS EYES) 254 AHWILD
WHO STARES AT HIM WITH A TWINKLE OF MALICIOUS 9 ANNA
HUMOR IN HER EYES.
TAKING IN HIS EMBARRASSMENT WITH A MALICIOUS 11 ANNA
TWINKLE OF AMUSEMENT IN HER EYE.
(WITH A TWINKLE IN HIS EYES) 95 BEYOND
(COMES FORWARD, A TWINKLE IN HIS EYE) 499 DAYS
(A TWINKLE COMING INTO HIS EYE) 501 DAYS
(WITH A TWINKLE IN HIS EYE) NO. 497 DIFRNT
HIS SMALL BLUE EYES TWINKLE. 498 DIFRNT
(A TWINKLE IN HIS EYE) THERE YOU ARE, HARRY. 602 ICEMAN
HIS EYES HAVE THE TWINKLE OF A HUMOR WHICH 618 ICEMAN
DELIGHTS IN KIDDING OTHERS.
PAIN MUST TWINKLE WITH A MAD MIRTH IN A CAESAR'S 358 LAZARU
EYES--MEN'S PAIN--
(THEN WITH A TWINKLE IN HIS EYE) 382 MARCOM
(SUDDENLY HIS EYES TWINKLE AND HE GRINS 15 MISBEG
ADMIRINGLY)
HIS EYES TWINKLE) 43 MISBEG

TWINKLES

BUT THERE STILL TWINKLES IN HER BLOODSHOT BLUE 7 ANNA
EYES A YOUTHFUL LUST FOR LIFE

TWINKLING

TWINKLING WITH A SIMPLE GOOD HUMOR. 5 ANNA
(HIS EYES TWINKLING) 40 MISBEG

TWINS

WE'RE GETTING TO BE LIKE TWINS. 316 GGBROW

TWIRL

FOR A WHILE HE IS TOO DEFEATED EVEN TO TWIRL HIS 30 HUGHIE
ROOM KEY.

TWIRLING

THEY GLANCE UNEASILY AT THE CAPTAIN, TWIRLING 543 'ILE
THEIR FUR CAPS IN THEIR HANDS.)
KICKING AT THE SAND RESTLESSLY, TWIRLING HIS STRAW275 AHWILD
HAT.
HE STARES AT THE FLOOR, TWIRLING HIS ROOM KEY--TO 27 HUGHIE
HIMSELF.)
TWIRLING HIS KEY FRANTICALLY AS IF IT WERE A 28 HUGHIE
FETISH WHICH MIGHT SET HIM FREE.)

TWIST

TO TWIST THEIR BODIES TOWARD AND AWAY FROM EACH 288 LAZARU
OTHER
WRITHE AND TWIST DISTRACTEDLY, SEEKING TO HIDE 349 LAZARU
THEIR HEADS AGAINST EACH OTHER,
(GRASS IT AND TEARS IT FROM HIS HAND WITH ONE 61 MISBEG
POWERFUL TWIST--FIERCELY)
I CAN ALWAYS TWIST HIM ROUND MY FINGER/....)) 118 STRANG

TWISTED

STRAINS ITS TWISTED BRANCHES HEAVENWARDS, BLACK 81 BEYOND
AGAINST THE PALLOR OF DISTANCE.
(WITH A TWISTED GRIN) THINKING AND--(HE INDICATES468 CARIBE
THE BOTTLE IN HIS HAND)

TWISTED (CONT'D.)
(WITH A TWISTED SMILE) YOU FORGET I'M HEIR TO THE566 CROSS
TREASURE, TOO.
(WITH A TWISTED SMILE) I THOUGHT WE WEREN'T GOING517 DAYS
TO TALK ABOUT MY TROUBLES/
THEY SQUIRM UPWARD TOWARD HIM IN TWISTED 190 EJONES
ATTITUDES.
(WITH A TWISTED SMILE) REMEMBER ONLY THAT DEAD 164 ELECTR
HERO AND NOT HIS ROTTING GHOST/
(THEN WITH A TWISTED SMILE) BUT THEY WOULDN'T SEE286 GGBROW
ME.
(WITH A LOOSE, TWISTED SMILE.) 151 JOURNE
OSCAR WILDE'S *READING GAUL* HAS THE THE DOPE 166 JOURNE
TWISTED.
THEN, FORCING A TWISTED GRIN OF SELF-CONTEMPT-- 311 LAZARU
HARSHLY.)
(HE SMILES HIS TWISTED SMILE) 331 LAZARU
WITH A TWISTED ATTEMPT AT A SMILE) 339 LAZARU
HIS THIN LEGS, TWISTED BY RHEUMATISM, 578 ROPE
CHARRED BONES IN A CAGE OF TWISTED STEEL... 5 STRANG
(THEN WITH A STRANGE TWISTED SMILE) 39 STRANG
(FORCING A TWISTED SMILE--WILDLY) 466 WELDED
(WITH A TWISTED SMILE) THAT'S WHAT HE'S DOING 469 WELDED
NOW.
)---(WITH A SUDDEN TWISTED GRIN) 483 WELDED

TWISTING

TWISTING AND TURNING HIS LEGS AND FEET. 359 MARCOM

TWISTS

BUT SIMPLY TWISTS HIS RIGHT HAND BEHIND HIS BACK 49 ANNA
(SHE TRIES TO PUT A FINGER ACROSS HIS LIPS, BUT HE101 BEYOND
TWISTS HIS HEAD AWAY.)
TWISTS HIS HEAD IN THE DIRECTION OF THE SICK MAN) 483 CARDIF
AH WELL, IT'S A ROCKY ROAD, FULL OF TWISTS AND 504 DAYS
BLIND ALLEYS, ISN'T IT, JACK--
HE TWISTS AND WRINGS AND TORTURES OUR LIVES WITH 73 ELECTR
OTHERS' LIVES UNTIL--
I HATE WHAT'S WARPED AND TWISTS AND EATS ITSELF 167 ELECTR
(HE TWISTS ROUND TO FACE MELODY, HOLDS UP HIS 100 POET
GLASS AND BAWLS.)

TWITCH

(HE GULPS AND HIS LIPS TWITCH) 464 DYNAMO
(THEN WITH A TWITCH OF THE LIPS, AS IF SHE WERE 52 ELECTR
RESTRAINING A DERISIVE SMILE)
THE CORNERS OF HER MOUTH TWITCH, 157 ELECTR
HER LIPS TWITCH. 172 ELECTR
HIS HANDS AND MOUTH TWITCH.) 107 MISBEG
AN HYSTERICAL, SNEERING GRIN MAKING HER LIPS 166 POET
QUIVER AND TWITCH.)

TWITCHES

(HIS FACE TWITCHES AND HIS BODY WRITHES IN A FINAL489 CARDIF
SPASM.
SHE MOANS AND HER BODY TWITCHES FOR A SECOND. 558 DAYS
HER MOUTH TWITCHES, HER EYES LOOK DESPERATELY ON 71 ELECTR
ALL SIDES.
TWITCHES A MOMENT ON HIS BACK AND LIES STILL. 114 ELECTR
A GRIM SMILE OF SATISFACTION TWITCHES HIS LIPS 149 ELECTR
HER MOUTH TWITCHES AND DRAWS DOWN AT THE CORNERS 174 ELECTR
AS SHE STIFLES A SOB.
(WILLIE OBAN JERKS AND TWITCHES IN HIS SLEEP AND 580 ICEMAN
BEGINS TO MUMBLE.
(AT THIS QUALIFICATION, A GRIN TWITCHES EDMUND'S 149 JOURNE
LIPS.
(HIS FACE TWITCHES AS IF HE WERE ON THE VERGE OF 10 STRANG
TEARS--HE THINKS DESPERATELY)
MEMORY CROWDS BACK ON HER AND HER FACE TWITCHES 462 WELDED

TWITCHING

(FORCING A SICKLY, TWITCHING SMILE) 256 AHWILD
HIS TWITCHING FINGERS SEEMING TO REACH OUT FOR HER261 DESIRE
THROAT.
HE KEEPS MUTTERING AND TWITCHING IN HIS SLEEP. 577 ICEMAN
(HE TAKES THE BOTTLE WITH BOTH TWITCHING HANDS AND582 ICEMAN
TILTS IT TO HIS LIPS AND
TWITCHING AND QUIVERING AGAIN.) 598 ICEMAN
(HIS MOUTH TWITCHING--FIGHTING AGAINST THE 286 LAZARU
COMPULSION IN HIM--STAMMERS)
HIS BODY SWAYING AND TWITCHING. 304 LAZARU
(WITH A TWITCHING SMILE) IT MUST HAVE BEEN MAD, 90 MISBEG
SURELY.
(GIGGLE GONE TO A TWITCHING GRIN) 14 STRANG

TYPE

THE TYPE OF FOOTBALL LINESMAN OF THAT PERIOD, WITH186 AHWILD
A SQUARE STOLID FACE.
SHE CONFORMS OUTWARDLY TO THE CONVENTIONAL TYPE OF187 AHWILD
OLD-MAID SCHOOL TEACHER,
NOT THE ATHLETIC BUT THE WELL-RAISING SPORT TYPE. 218 AHWILD
SHE KNOWS HIS TYPE BY HEART AND HE KNOWS HERS.) 244 AHWILD
HE IS TWENTY-SEVEN YEARS OLD, AN OPPOSITE TYPE TO 82 BEYOND
ROBERT--
CONVENTIONAL AMERICAN TYPE OF GOOD LOOKS-- 493 DAYS
A PERFECT TYPE OF OUR OLD BEAUTIFUL IDEAL OF WIFE 509 DAYS
AND MOTHER.
THE FIRE HOUSE, A SMALL BROWNISH-TINTED MODERN -0 DYNAMO
STUCCO BUNGALOW TYPE,
LEM IS A HEAVY-SET APE-FACED OLD SAVAGE OF THE 202 EJONES
EXTREME AFRICAN TYPE.
IT IS A LARGE BUILDING OF THE GREEK TEMPLE TYPE 2 ELECTR
THAT WAS THE VOGUE
IN CHARACTER HE IS THE TOWNSFOLK TYPE OF GARRULOUS 6 ELECTR
GOSSIP-MONGER
OF A SIMILAR SCANDAL-BEARING TYPE, HER TONGUE IS 6 ELECTR
SHARPENED BY MALICE.
EAGER-LISTENER TYPE, WITH A SMALL ROUND FACE, 6 ELECTR
ROUND STUPID EYES.
BUT MEN OF HIS TYPE DON'T UNDERSTAND HINTS. 52 ELECTR
HILLS IS THE TYPE OF WELL-FED MINISTER OF A 67 ELECTR
PROSPEROUS SMALL-TOWN CONGREGATION--
THE FATHER IS FIFTY OR MORE, THE TYPE OF BUSTLING,257 GGBROW
GENIAL, SUCCESSFUL,

TYPE

TYPE (CONT'D.)
I CAN IMAGINE HOW THE PLATONIC MUST APPEAL TO 289 GGBROW
DION'S PURE, INNOCENT TYPE/
SHE IS A TYPE EVEN TO THE POINT OF A DOUBLE CHIN 218 HA APE
AND LORGNITES.
THE TYPE OF SMALL FRY GAMBLER AND HORSE PLAYER, 9 HUGHIE
IS A NARROW FIVE-STORY STAUCTURE OF THE TENEMENT 571 ICEMAN
TYPE.
A STRONG RESEMBLANCE TO THE TYPE ANARCHIST AS 574 ICEMAN
PORTRAYED, BOMB IN HAND,
HIS FACE IS ONLY MILDLY NEGROID IN TYPE. 575 ICEMAN
A DUTCH FARMER TYPE. 575 ICEMAN
HER FACE IS DISTINCTLY IRISH IN TYPE. 12 JOURNE
AND YET IT WAS EXACTLY THE SAME TYPE OF CHEAP 74 JOURNE
QUAKER WHO FIRST GAVE YOU THE
EACH PERIOD-TYPE AS PERIOD ONE--TYPE ONE, PERIOD 273 LAZARU
TWO--
THEY ARE ALL SEVEN IN THE SORROWFUL, RESIGNED TYPE274 LAZARU
OF OLD AGE.)
TYPE TWO, AND SO ON UP TO PERIOD SEVEN--TYPE 274 LAZARU
SEVEN--
THERE ARE FORTY-NINE DIFFERENT COMBINATIONS OF 274 LAZARU
PERIOD AND TYPE.
EACH TYPE HAS A DISTINCT PREDOMINANT COLOR FOR ITS274 LAZARU
COSTUMES.
ALL ARE OF THE SIMPLE, IGNORANT TYPE.) 291 LAZARU
THEY ARE ALL OF THE PROUD SELF-RELIANT TYPE, IN 298 LAZARU
THE PERIOD OF YOUNG MANHOOD.
HERE, OF COURSE, THE FOUNDATION OF THE MASK IS THE298 LAZARU
GRECIAN TYPE OF FACE.
IN THE SAME PERIOD AND TYPE AS IN THE PRECEDING 306 LAZARU
SCENES, EXCEPT THAT
HYPOCRITICAL TYPE OF OLD AGE. 312 LAZARU
THEY ARE IN THE PERIOD OF MANHOOD, OF THE SIMPLE, 320 LAZARU
IGNORANT TYPE.
WEARING THE TYPE MASK OF A ROMAN PATRICIAN 332 LAZARU
THREE OF THE FEMALES IN SIMILAR TYPE-PERIOD MASKS.336 LAZARU
IN THE PERIOD OF WOMANHOOD IN THE PROUD, SELF- 336 LAZARU
RELIANT TYPE.
HYPOCRITICAL TYPE, GROUPED ON EACH SIDE OF THE 363 LAZARU
THRONE OF CAESAR ON A LOWER TIER.
EVERY INCH THE TYPE OF CONSERVATIVE, BEST-FAMILY 25 MANSNS
LEGAL ADVISOR,
A FINE ATHLETIC GIRL OF THE SWIMMER, TENNIS 12 STRANG
PLAYER, GOLFER TYPE.
OR IS ABOUT TO TYPE FOR A SHEET OF PAPER CAN BE 66 STRANG
SEEN IN THE MACHINE.
THE ROOM IS A TYPICAL SITTING ROOM OF THE 90 STRANG
QUANTITY-PRODUCTION BUNGALOW TYPE.
AS THOUGH NOW IT DEFINITELY BELONGED TO THE TYPE 111 STRANG
OF PERSON IT WAS BUILT FOR.
WHY, I WAS ONLY PICKING OUT A TYPE I THOUGHT WOULD114 STRANG
BE GOOD FOR YOU, CHARLIE--
QUITE BEAUTIFUL, IF YOU LIKE THAT TYPE. 115 STRANG
HIS TYPE LOGICALLY DEVELOPED BY TEN YEARS OF 159 STRANG
CONTINUED SUCCESS AND ACCUMULATING
JOHN ISN'T THAT TYPE. 456 WELDED
YET SHE IS NOT UGLY--RATHER PRETTY FOR HER BOVINE,471 WELDED
STOLID TYPE--
TYPES
ALL FOUR ARE DISTINCT NEGRO TYPES. 464 CARIBE
THESE LAST THREE ARE TYPES OF TOWNSFOLK RATHER 6 ELECTR
THAN INDIVIDUALS. A
ARE, AS WERE THE AMES OF ACT ONE OF *HOMECOMING,* 67 ELECTR
TYPES OF TOWNSFOLK.
= A CHORUS OF TYPES REPRESENTING THE TOWN AS A 129 ELECTR
HUMAN BACKGROUND
ESPECIALLY CERTAIN TYPES OF WOMEN, IF YOU'LL 289 GGBROW
PARDON ME'S
TYPES OF CHARACTER AS FOLLOWS.. 273 LAZARU
THE SAME FORMULA OF SEVEN PERIODS, SEVEN TYPES, 291 LAZARU
IN SEVEN TYPES OF CHARACTER FOR EACH SEX. 298 LAZARU
SEVEN TYPES IN SEVEN PERIODS, EXCEPT THAT, AS IN 306 LAZARU
THE CHORUS,
MATURING AND OLD AGE ARE REPRESENTED IN THE TYPES 312 LAZARU
OF THE SELF-TORTURED,
IN EACH OF THE THREE TYPES OF THE INTROSPECTIVE, 336 LAZARU
SELF-TORTURED.
THE MALES, IN THE PERIOD OF YOUTH, ONE IN EACH OF 336 LAZARU
THE TYPES REPRESENTED, AND
IN THE PLACING OF ITS PEOPLE AND THE CHARACTERS 369 MARCOM
AND TYPES REPRESENTED.
(HE TYPES A SENTENCE OR TWO, A STRAINED FROWN OF 68 STRANG
CONCENTRATION ON HIS FACE.
TYPEWRITER
LIKE A BEGINNER ON THE TYPEWRITER TOUCHING TWO NEW548 DIFRNT
LETTERS)
A BOX OF TYPEWRITING PAPER, AND A TYPEWRITER AT 66 STRANG
THE CENTER BEFORE THE CHAIR,
AND THE RUBBER COVER FOR THE TYPEWRITER LIKE A 66 STRANG
COLLAPSED TENT.
(TURNS TO HIS TYPEWRITER 67 STRANG
TYPEWRITING
A BOX OF TYPEWRITING PAPER, AND A TYPEWRITER AT 66 STRANG
THE CENTER BEFORE THE CHAIR,
TYPHOON
FORGET A TYPHOONS 131 BEYOND
I'D RATHER GO THROUGH A TYPHOON AGAIN THAN WRITE A131 BEYOND
LETTER.
(WITH EAGER INTEREST) THEN YOU WERE THROUGH A 131 BEYOND
TYPHOON$
IN THE TYPHOON WHEN A WAVE SWEPT ME FROM THE DECK,411 MARCOM
TYPHOONS
THAT IN SPITE OF TYPHOONS, SHIPWRECKS, 411 MARCOM
TYPICAL
HE'S A TYPICAL, GOOD-LOOKING COLLEGE BOY OF THE 218 AHWILD
PERIOD.

TYPICAL (CONT'D.)
A TYPICAL COLLEGE *TART* OF THE PERIOD, AND OF THE236 AHWILD
CHEAPER VARIETY.
A TYPICAL OLD SALT, LOUD OF VOICE AND GIVEN TO 94 BEYOND
GESTURE.
IS A TYPICAL NEW ENGLAND WOMAN OF PURE ENGLISH 67 ELECTR
ANCESTRY, WITH A HORSE FACE.
THE TWO GIRLS, NEITHER MUCH OVER TWENTY, ARE 611 ICEMAN
TYPICAL DOLLAR STREET WALKERS.
HIS MASK IS THAT OF A TYPICAL YOUNG PATRICIAN 326 LAZARU
OFFICER.
THE ROOM IS SMALL, A TYPICAL ROOM OF THE PERIOD, 43 MANSNS
THE ROOM IS A TYPICAL SITTING ROOM OF THE 90 STRANG
QUANTITY-PRODUCTION BUNGALOW TYPE.
TYPICAL TERRIBLE CHILD OF THE AGE... 122 STRANG
TYPICALLY
HIS FEATURES ARE TYPICALLY NEGROID, 175 EJONES
SHE IS TWENTY-FIVE, EXCEEDINGLY PRETTY IN A 1 MANSNS
TYPICALLY IRISH FASHION.
TYPING
HE HAS EVIDENTLY BEEN TYPING, 66 STRANG
(GUILTILY) DID THE NOISE OF MY TYPING BOTHER YOUS 69 STRANG
TYRANNY
DEGENERATED, CORRUPTED BY TYRANNY AND DEBAUCHERY 312 LAZARU
TO AN EXHAUSTED CYNICISM.
TYRANT
THEN HE'D HAVE A HARSH TYRANT TO DEFY. 205 AHWILD
AS MAN, PETTY TYRANT OF EARTH, 309 LAZARU
YOU BLOODY TYRANT/ 61 MISBEG
AS A PIG-MURDERING TYKANT/ 63 MISBEG
TYRANTS
HE WILL LAUGH OUR TYRANTS INTO THE SEA/ 300 LAZARU
DOWN WITH ALL TYRANTS, MALE AND FEMALE/ 72 MISBEG
TZE
FIRST IT WAS CHINA AND LAO TZE THAT FASCINATED 503 DAYS
HIM.
UBER
(CYNICALLY) IGORDON UBER ALLES AND FOREVER/... 29 STRANG
UDDER
REMINDS ME OF DAMN FOOL ARGUMENT ME AND MOSE 584 ICEMAN
PORTER HAS DE UDDER NIGHT.
UGLIER
(CAUTIOUSLY) OH, THE SAME AS IVIR--OLDER AN' 592 ROPE
UGLIER, MAYBE.
UGLINESS
AND THE ROOM IS REVEALED IN ALL ITS PRESERVED 241 DESIRE
UGLINESS.
THE WALLPAPER SO FADED THAT THE UGLINESS OF ITS 421 DYNAMO
COLOR
FIXED ON THE HOUSE TO HIDE ITS SOMBER GRAY 5 ELECTR
UGLINESS.
PAGAN TEMPLE FRONT STUCK LIKE A MASK ON PURITAN 17 ELECTR
GRAY UGLINESS/
ONE OF THOSE ONE-DESIGN DISTRICTS THAT DAZE THE 269 GGBROW
EYE WITH MULTIPLIED UGLINESS.
I WILL FACE CHANGE AND UGLINESS, AND TIME AND 22 MANSNS
DEATH, AND MAKE MYSELF RESIGNED/
A WELL-MANNERED BOW TO AGE AND UGLINESS--GREET 29 MANSNS
THEM AS MY LIFE-END GUESTS--
NOW QUESTION, AND SNEER AND LAUGH AT YOUR DREAMS, 40 MANSNS
AND SLEEP WITH UGLINESS.
IN HIS GARDEN SO HIDDEN FROM THE UGLINESS OF 176 MANSNS
REALITY.
UGLY
D'YOU THINK I'VE NOT SEEN THEIR UGLY LOOKS AND THE539 'ILE
GRUDGIN' WAY THEY WORKED$
THEY'LL LIKELY TURN UGLY, EVERY BLESSED ONE O' 539 'ILE
THEM, IF YOU DON'T PUT BACK.
JOE, THE HARPOONER, AN ENORMOUS SIX-FOOTER WITH A 543 'ILE
BATTERED, UGLY FACE,
THE WALLS ARE PAPERED WHITE WITH A CHEERFUL, UGLY 185 AHWILD
UGLY SIDEBOARD WITH THREE PIECES OF OLD SILVER ON 210 AHWILD
ITS TOP.
I'M NOT SO AWFULLY UGLY, AM IS 240 AHWILD
(WITH AN UGLY SNEER) AND HOW ABOUT HER$ 243 AHWILD
PUT DOWN THAT ORGAN AV YOURS OR ILL BREAK YOUR 481 CARDIF
UGLY FACE FOR YOU.
(A SQUAT, UGLY LIVERPOOL IRISHMAN) 458 CARIBE
I 'OPES ALL THE GELS AIN'T AS BLOOMIN' UGLY AS 461 CARIBE
'ER.
IF YOU'D ALWAYS BEEN A LITTLE INNOCENT, PROTECTED 517 DAYS
FROM ALL UGLY CONTACTS--
A LOOK OF UGLY SATISFACTION COMING INTO HER FACE) 520 DAYS
521 DAYS
(BURSTING OUT) AN UGLY OLD HAKE/ 230 DESIRE
HE'S A DAMN STINGY, UGLY OLD CUSS, IF YOU WANT MY 521 DIFRNT
DOPE ON HIM.
HER SHOULDERS STOOP, AND HER FIGURE IS FLABBY AND 528 DIFRNT
UGLY.
HER FACE IS SET IN AN UGLY, SNEERING EXPRESSION. 450 DYNAMO
FOR YOUR SHIPS OR YOUR SEA OR YOUR NAKED ISLAND 42 ELECTR
GIRLS--WHEN I GROW OLD AND UGLY/
I'VE GROWN OLD IN THE PAST FEW DAYS. I'M UGLY 112 ELECTR
I CAN'T LET MYSELF GET UGLY/ 118 ELECTR
I'M OLD AND UGLY AND HAUNTED BY DEATH/ 118 ELECTR
STARES AT HIM FRIGHTENEDLY, HE SMILES AN UGLY 146 ELECTR
TAUNTING SMILE)
AND I KNEW MY SOBS WERE UGLY AND MEANINGLESS TO 282 GGBROW
HER VIRGINITY.
UGLY/ 314 GGBROW
ALL ARE DRESSED IN DUNGAREE PANTS, HEAVY UGLY 207 HA APE
SHOES.
NOW THAT'S A QUEER WISH FROM THE UGLY LIKE OF YOU,210 HA APE
GOD HELP YOU.
CHUCK WID A SILLY GRIN ON HIS UGLY MAP, DE BIG 614 ICEMAN
BOOB,

UGLY

(CONT'D.)
BEJEES, HICKEY, IT SEEMS NATURAL TO SEE YOUR UGLY,619 ICEMAN
GRINNING MAP.
SO THAT NOW THEY HAVE AN UGLY CRIPPLED LOOK. 12 JOURNE
HOW UGLY THEY ARE! 41 JOURNE
I THOUGHT THAT UGLY MONKEY, SMYTHE, WOULD DRIVE US 98 JOURNE
IN A DITCH OR AGAINST A TREE.
IT'S JUST AN UGLY SOUND. 99 JOURNE
SEE, CATHLEEN, HOW UGLY THEY ARE! SO MAIMED AND 104 JOURNE
CRIPPLED/
HOW MANY TIMES I WAS TO WAIT IN UGLY HOTEL ROOMS. 113 JOURNE
I HAD WAITED IN THAT UGLY HOTEL ROOM HOUR AFTER 113 JOURNE
HOUR.
THE KNUCKLES ARE ALL SWOLLEN. THEY'RE SO UGLY. 171 JOURNE
(SHE POINTS TO MIRIAM) NOT THAT UGLY SLAVES 341 LAZARU
TOO POOR AND TIRED AND UGLY AND OLD TO CARE, TOO 361 LAZARU
SLAVISH--/
AND UGLY HANDS AND DIRTY FINGERNAILS, WERE THEY 9 MANSNS
EVER SO NOBLE-HEARTED/
DO YOU THINK YOU CAN TEMPT ME NOW WHEN I AM AN 36 MANSNS
UGLY,
YOU UGLYS 37 MANSNS
IF YOU KNEW HOW UNHAPPY AND UGLY I'VE FELT SINCE 87 MANSNS
YOU STARTED SLEEPING ALONE--
OH, DARLING, AND I WAS SO AFRAID I'D BECOME UGLY 90 MANSNS
TO YOU AND YOU WERE SICK OF ME.
I FEAR YOU ARE MERELY FLATTERING A POOR UGLY OLD 101 MANSNS
WOMAN.
HE HAD MADE MY BEAUTY GROTESQUELY UGLY BY HIS 122 MANSNS
PRESENCE, BLOATED AND MISSHAPEN--
O'YOU THINK I WANT HER UGLY FACE AROUND& 375 MARCOM
I'D RATHER BE A COW THAN AN UGLY LITTLE BUCK GOAT. 12 MISBEG
YOU KNOW, AND I KNOW, I'M AN UGLY OVER-GROWN LUMP 28 MISBEG
OF A WOMAN.
I'D KISS YOU, JIM, FOR THIS BEAUTIFUL NEWS, IF YOU 51 MISBEG
WASN'T SO DAMNED UGLY.
I'LL PASTE YOUR UGLY MUG ON THE FRONT PAGE OF 63 MISBEG
EVERY NEWSPAPER
TWO UGLY SIDEBOARDS, ONE AT LEFT, THE OTHER AT 71 MISBEG
RIGHT-REAR.
BUT WHEN IT'S A BIG, UGLY HULK LIKE ME-- 92 MISBEG
(AS IF HE HADN'T SPOKEN) WHILE I'M ONLY A BIG, 118 MISBEG
ROUGH, UGLY COW OF A WOMAN.
I SUPPOSE BECAUSE IT SEEMS CRAZY FOR YOU TO HOLD 130 MISBEG
MY BIG UGLY PAW SO TENDERLY.
BECAUSE I'M A GREAT UGLY COW-- 134 MISBEG
BUT SHE HAS LARGE FEET AND BROAD, UGLY HANDS WITH 16 POET
STUBBY FINGERS.
FUN WITHOUT IT WHAT AM I AT ALL BUT AN UGLY, FAT 26 POET
WOMAN GETTIN' OLD AND SICK/
KEEP YOUR THICK WRISTS AND UGLY, PEASANT PAWS OFF 107 POET
THE TABLE IN MY PRESENCE.
AND HIT THE FLUNKY A CUT WITH HIS WHIP ACROSS HIS 155 POET
UGLY MUG THAT SET HIM
YOU UGLY OLD DEVIL! 581 ROPE
SO YOU MIGHT 'S WELL TAKE DOWN THAT UGLY ROPE 581 ROPE
YOU'VE HAD TIED THERE SINCE HE RUN
(RELUCTANTLY MOVES AWAY) IT LOOKS UGLY HANGIN' 583 ROPE
THERE OPEN LIKE A MOUTH.
THE UGLY AND DISGUSTING... 25 STRANG
OF THE UGLY TABLE WITH ITS SET OF STRAIGHTBACKED 48 STRANG
CHAIRS
(HE FALTERS, HIS FACE BECOMES DISTORTED INTO AN 98 STRANG
UGLY MASK OF GRIEF.
I'M UGLY, TOO/ 101 STRANG
(SOOTHINGLY) I KNOW IT'S UGLY, CHARLIE. 101 STRANG
(SUDDENLY WITH AN INSULTING, UGLY SNEER, RAISING 101 STRANG
HIS VOICE)
MY UGLY BODY... 120 STRANG
WE'VE COME TO THE UGLY BITTER STAGE WHEN WE BLAME 144 STRANG
EACH OTHER/
SURE OF OUR LOVE--WITH NO UGLY BITTERNESS FOR 145 STRANG
ONCE!
A-OPENIN' OF YOUR UGLY MOUTH 494 VOYAGE
IF YE CUD SEE YOUR UGLY FACE, 498 VOYAGE
UGLY WALLPAPER, DIRTY, STAINED, CRISS-CROSSED WITH470 WELDED
MATCH-STROKES.
YET SHE IS NOT UGLY--RATHER PRETTY FOR HER BOVINE,471 WELDED
STOLID TYPE--
I'LL BE AS UGLY AS THE WORLD. 474 WELDED

ULCER
(READING) =THIS FIENDISH ORGANIZATION IS A FOUL 243 HA APE

ULCER

ULSTER
(SPEAKING) TO HELL WID ULSTER! 498 VOYAGE

ULTIMATE
BLOOD-STIRRING CALL TO THAT ULTIMATE ATTAINMENT IN318 LAZARU
WHICH ALL PREPOSSESSION WITH

ULTRA
(SHE LAUGHS) OH, I WAS QUITE ULTRA-MODERN ABOUT 523 DAYS
IT/
WITH MANY ULTRA-SENTIMENTAL BARBER-SHOP QUAVERS. 257 GGBROW
(IN HIS ULTRA-PROFESSIONAL MANNER--LIKE AN 85 STRANG
AUTOMATON OF A DOCTOR)

ULULATING
(IN A LONG ULULATING WHISPER) 405 MARCOM

UMBRELLA
HE IS BUTTONED UP TO THE NECK IN AN OLD RAINCOAT 450 DYNAMO
AND CARRIES AN UMBRELLA.)

UNABASHED
(UNABASHED, APPROACHES THE STEPS--WITH A GRIN. 44 ELECTR

UNABLE
(WHO HAS BEEN FIDGITING RESTLESSLY--UNABLE TO BEAR264 AHWILD
THE SUSPENSE A MOMENT LONGER)
(UNABLE TO RESIST FALLING INTO HIS TRAGIC LITERARY279 AHWILD
POSE FOR A MOMENT)
(JUMPING TO HIS FEET--UNABLE TO BELIEVE HIS EARS) 53 ANNA
(UNABLE TO HOLD BACK HIS EXULTATION) 53 ANNA

UNABLE

(CONT'D.)
FINALLY HE IS UNABLE TO BEAR THE THICK SILENCE A 95 BEYOND
MINUTE LONGER, AND BLURTS OUT)
(DUMBFOUNDED--UNABLE TO DOUBT THE DETERMINATION IN105 BEYOND
ANDREW'S VOICE--HELPLESSLY)
(WITH A SIDE GLANCE OF FRANK ENVY--UNABLE TO KEEP 517 DAYS
RESENTMENT OUT OF HER VOICE)
UNABLE TO CONCEAL HIS EMOTION) 218 DESIRE
THEN, EVIDENTLY UNABLE TO KEEP SILENT ABOUT HIS 236 DESIRE
THOUGHTS,
(THEN SUDDENLY, UNABLE TO RESTRAIN HIMSELF ANY 250 DESIRE
LONGER,
(UNABLE TO ENDURE THIS, SPRINGS TO HIS FEET IN A 261 DESIRE
FURY, THREATENING HER,
(UNABLE TO RESTRAIN HIS MIRTH) 502 DIFFNT
(UNABLE TO REPRESS THE GENUINE ADMIRATION OF THE 178 EJONES
SMALL FRY FOR THE LARGE)
(UNABLE TO HOLD BACK ANY LONGER, HE BURSTS FORTH) 85 ELECTR
SHE IS IN A FRIGHTFUL STATE OF TENSION, UNABLE TO 117 ELECTR
KEEP STILL.
(UNABLE TO CONCEAL THEIR EAGERNESS) 323 GGBROW
(UNABLE TO KEEP SILENT LONGER) 519 INZONE
(HE ADDS, UNABLE TO CONCEAL AN ALMOST FURTIVE 36 JOURNE
UNEASINESS.)
(STARTLED AND UNABLE TO CONCEAL AN UPRUSH OF 132 MANSNS
JEALOUS HATE.)
(STARES AT HER, UNABLE TO BELIEVE HER EARS.) 188 MANSNS
(STARES AT HER, UNABLE TO DECIDE WHAT IS BEHIND 82 POET
ALL THIS
(STARTLED--UNABLE TO HIDE A TRACE OF 82 STRANG
DISAPPOINTMENT)
HE IS IN THE LAST STAGE UF INTOXICATION, UNABLE TO503 VOYAGE
MOVE A MUSCLE.
(THEN UNABLE TO RESTRAIN HIS TRIUMPHANT EXULTANCE)488 WELDED

UNADORNED
FIRST IT WAS ATHEISM UNADORNED. 502 DAYS
BUT SHE WEARS IT IN A WAY THAT GIVES A PLEASING 16 POET
EFFECT OF BEAUTY UNADORNED.)

UNAFFECTED
UNAFFECTED CHARM OF A SHY CONVENT-GIRL 13 JOURNE
YOUTHFULNESS SHE HAS NEVER LOST--

UNAFRAID
(UNAFRAID--LOOKING UP INTO HIS EYES--COLDLY) 99 ELECTR

UNALTERABLY
TO INFORM YOU THAT MR. HENRY HARFORD IS 121 POET
UNALTERABLY OPPOSED

UNANIMOUS
THEY ALL JUMP STARTLEDLY AND LOOK AT HIM WITH 634 ICEMAN
UNANIMOUS HOSTILITY.

UNANSWERABLE
THERE IS CERTAINLY SOMETHING ABOUT YOU, SOMETHING 379 MARCOM
COMPLETE AND UNANSWERABLE--

UNASSUMING
AT THE SAME TIME HE WAS SIMPLE, AND KIND, AND 105 JOURNE
UNASSUMING,

UNATTRACTIVE
THE MAN MUST BE SOMEONE WHO IS NOT UNATTRACTIVE TO 88 STRANG
HER PHYSICALLY, OF COURSE.

UNATTRACTIVENESS
AND ITS UNATTRACTIVENESS IS ACCENTUATED BY HER 10 ELECTR
PLAIN BLACK DRESS.

UNAWAKENED
YET WITH A HINT OF SOME UNAWAKENED OBSTINATE FORCE 29 STRANG
BENEATH HIS APPARENT

UNAWARE
HE CARRIES HIS STRAW HAT DANGLING IN HIS HAND, 292 AHWILD
QUITE UNAWARE OF ITS EXISTENCE.)
THEY ARE QUITE UNAWARE OF LOVING'S EXISTENCE, 496 DAYS
AS IF HE WERE UNAWARE OF THEIR PRESENCE. 144 ELECTR
HE IS SEEMINGLY UNAWARE OF THE DARK GLANCES OF 522 INZONE
SUSPICION
SHE TALKS ON AS IF UNAWARE OF THEIR SILENCE.) 109 JOURNE
HE SEEMS ABSOLUTELY UNAWARE OF POMPEIA. 343 LAZARU
WALL AT LIFE WHICH PASSES BY SO HORRIBLY UNAWARE 12 MANSNS
THAT YOU ARE STILL ALIVE/
I--- I AM NOT UNAWARE WHY YOU ARE SO INSISTENT ABOUT141 MANSNS
MY KNOCKING
GOD KNOWS I COULD HARDLY BE UNAWARE OF IT TONIGHT/174 MANSNS
HE APPEARS QUITE UNAWARE OF BEING UNUSUAL 439 MARCOM

UNAWARENESS
IN THEIR DETACHED, MECHANICAL UNAWARENESS.) 236 HA APE

UNBEARABLE
HIS VOICE RINGING MORE AND MORE WITH A TERRIBLE 349 LAZARU
UNBEARABLE POWER AND BEAUTY THAT
THEIR VOICES ATTAIN A PROLONGED NOTE OF UNBEARABLE433 MARCOM
POIGNANCY.
(THIS IS BECOMING UNBEARABLE FOR HER--TENSELY.) 168 POET

UNBEARABLY
TREMULOUS WAIL OF DESPAIR THAT REACHES A CERTAIN 199 EJONES
PITCH, UNBEARABLY ACUTE,

UNBELIEVABLE
UNBELIEVABLE/ 32 MANSNS

UNBELIEVERS
(THEN WITH A SCOWL) THREE DOGS OF UNBELIEVERS, 350 MARCOM
TOO/

UNBENDS
HE UNBENDS, ALTHOUGH HIS TONE IS STILL A BIT CURT.117 POET

UNBLACKED
A BROWN COATING UF RUST COVERS THE UNBLACKED 144 BEYOND
STOVE.

UNBLINKING
AND STARES BACK INTO THE SUN-GLARE WITH 170 ELECTR
UNBLINKING, FROZEN, DEFIANT EYES.)

UNBORN
LAUGHTER, GROWN TOO YOUNG FOR ME, FLEW BACK TO THE345 LAZARU
UNBORN--
BUT A WOMAN MAY FEEL LIFE IN THE UNBORN. 397 MARCOM

UNBOUND

UNBOUND
SO MANY OLD WOUNDS MAY HAVE TO BE UNBOUND, AND OLD188 STRANG
SCARS POINTED TO WITH PRIDE.

UNBROKEN
THE SILENCE IS UNBROKEN EXCEPT FOR THE MEASURED 535 *ILE
TREAD OF SOMEONE WALKING UP AND
IN ITS RHYTHM OF UNBROKEN, ETERNAL CONTINUITY. 486 DYNAMO

UNBUTTONED
DRISCOLL HAS UNBUTTONED HIS STIFF COLLAR AND ITS 496 VOYAGE
ENDS STICK OUT SIDEWAYS.

UNCALLED
LET ME SAY THAT ANY SENTIMENT OF GRATITUDE ON YOUR153 MANSNS
PART IS UNCALLED FOR.

UNCANNY
BUT THE NEXT TIME, HIS VOICE, AS IF UNDER SOME 199 EJONES
UNCANNY COMPULSION,
HE IS DRESSED IN BLACK AND THE RESEMBLANCE BETWEEN149 ELECTR
THE TWO IS UNCANNY.
(SMILING) YOUR LUCK IS UNCANNY. 285 GGBROW
(BLURTS OUT WITH AN UNCANNY, ALMOST LIFELIKE 32 HUGHIE
EAGERNESS.)
AND THE QUALITY OF UNCANNY DETACHMENT IS IN HER 75 JOURNE
VOICE AND MANNER.)
THERE IS AT TIMES AN UNCANNY GAY, FREE 97 JOURNE
YOUTHFULNESS IN HER MANNER.
THE UNCANNY THING IS THAT HER FACE NOW APPEARS SO 170 JOURNE
YOUTHFUL.
(HER VOICE BECOMING A BIT UNCANNY, HER THOUGHTS 18 STRANG
BREAKING THROUGH)
THERE'S SOMETHING UNCANNY/... 188 STRANG

UNCEASING
AN UNCEASING DUEL TO THE DEATH WITH LIFE/ 119 MANSNS

UNCERTAIN
(A BIT BEWILDERED AND UNCERTAIN NOW) 198 AHWILD
HER EYE MISTILY AND RISES TO HIS FEET, MAKING HER 226 AHWILD
A DEEP, UNCERTAIN BOW.
(WHO HAS LISTENED TO HIM WITH A GROWING INTEREST-- 23 ANNA
WITH AN UNCERTAIN LAUGH)
BUT STILL UNCERTAIN, TORN BETWEEN DOUBT AND THE 74 ANNA
DESIRE TO BELIEVE--HELPLESSLY)
SHE SPEAKS IN AN UNCERTAIN VOICE, WITHOUT 112 BEYOND
ASSERTIVENESS.
(WITH AN UNCERTAIN TROUBLED LAUGH) 239 DESIRE
WITH AN UNCERTAIN GLANCE AT THE FROZEN EMMA. 508 DIFRNT
TO HAVE AN UNCERTAIN REALIZATION OF WHAT HE IS 200 EJONES
DOING.
BECAUSE THAT'S THE UNCERTAIN PART. 263 GGBROW
HIS FACE LIGHTED UP FROM WITHIN BUT PAINFULLY 269 GGBROW
CONFUSED--IN AN UNCERTAIN WHISPER)
(WITH A BEWILDERED UNCERTAIN GROWL) 229 HA APE
SHE HESITATES, MISERABLY UNCERTAIN) 683 ICEMAN
SHE IS UNCERTAIN IN HER WALK AND GRINNING 122 JOURNE
WOOZILY.)
(DEALING WITH VERY UNCERTAIN JUDGMENT OF 138 JOURNE
DISTANCE.)
STILL A BIT UNCERTAIN OF ITS FREEDOM, HARSH, 281 LAZARU
DISCORDANT, FRENZIED.
YES, I AGREE THAT IS TOO UNCERTAIN. 179 MANSNS
HIS ATTITUDE A QUEER MIXTURE OF FAMILIARITY AND AN410 MARCOM
UNCERTAIN AWE.)
SHE STANDS LOOKING AT HER MOTHER, AND SUDDENLY SHE136 POET
BECOMES SHY AND UNCERTAIN--
HE HICCOUGHS EVERY NOW AND THEN AND HIS VOICE 594 ROPE
GROWS UNCERTAIN AND HUSKY.)
(THEN VENTURING ON AN UNCERTAIN TONE OF 21 STRANG
PLEASANTRY)
(HIS VOICE GROWS HUSKY AND UNCERTAIN--HE CONTROLS 24 STRANG
IT--STRAIGHTENS HIMSELF)
SOOTHES HER WITH UNCERTAIN TREMBLING WORDS) 43 STRANG
HIS VOICE TAKING ON A PLEADING UNCERTAIN QUALITY) 126 STRANG
(HE STARES TOWARD HER, THEN STOPS--IN A LOW, 463 WELDED
UNCERTAIN VOICE)
TREMBLINGLY UNCERTAIN WHETHER TO RUN AND HIDE 480 WELDED
FROM,

UNCERTAINLY
YOU WOULDN'T DARE--(THEN FINALLY HE SAYS 204 AHWILD
UNCERTAINLY)
TAKES THE LETTER FROM HIM UNCERTAINLY, 208 AHWILD
THEY FILE INTO THE SITTING-ROOM IN SILENCE AND 263 AHWILD
THEN STAND AROUND UNCERTAINLY.
(ENGROSSED BY THE LETTER IN HIS HAND--UNCERTAINLY) 8 ANNA
(HE TURNS THE LETTER OVER IN HIS HANDS 8 ANNA
UNCERTAINLY)
HE MOVES SLOWLY, FEELING HIS WAY UNCERTAINLY, 30 ANNA
BUT MOVED AND PLEASED IN SPITE OF HERSELF--TAKES 34 ANNA
HIS HAND UNCERTAINLY)
(UNCERTAINLY--LOOKING FROM HIM TO HER FATHER) 51 ANNA
(AS SCOTT LOOKS AT HIM UNCERTAINLY) 104 BEYOND
(HIS EYES ROVING FROM ROBERT TO RUTH AND BACK 141 BEYOND
AGAIN--UNCERTAINLY)
THE MEN LOOK UNCERTAINLY AT YANK AS IF UNDECIDED 482 CARDIF
WHETHER TO SAY GOOD-BY OR NOT.)
(UNCERTAINLY) YOU DON'T THINK HE'LL HOLD IT UP 488 CARDIF
AGIN ME--GOD, I MEAN.
(JOHN STARES AT HIM UNCERTAINLY FOR A MOMENT--THEN556 DAYS
OBEDIENTLY LIES DOWN)
(NODDING UNCERTAINLY) AY-EH. 222 DESIRE
(PUZZLED--UNCERTAINLY) WAAL-- 496 DIFRNT
HE LOOKS IN, COUGHS--THEN ASKS UNCERTAINLY) 514 DIFRNT
(AFTER A PAUSE--UNCERTAINLY) 517 DIFRNT
(UNCERTAINLY) OH? 24 ELECTR
(SHE CALLS UNCERTAINLY) OKIN. 76 ELECTR
LOOKS AROUND HER UNCERTAINLY AND SEES SOMEONE 174 ELECTR
COMING FROM OFF LEFT, FRONT--
(HE STOPS UNCERTAINLY, THEN DECIDES TO PLUNGE IN.)276 GGBROW
(THEN UNCERTAINLY) DON'T BE A FOOL/ 289 GGBROW
(UNCERTAINLY) OH--ALL RIGHT--(UNFASTENING DOOR) 300 GGBROW
COME IN.
STANDS OVER IT UNCERTAINLY, CONSIDERING.. 254 HA APE

UNCERTAINLY (CONT'D.)
HE PICKS OUT THE KEY, THEN HESITATES, LOOKING FROM528 INZONE
ONE TO THE OTHER UNCERTAINLY)
(GETS HEAVILY AND A BIT WAVERINGLY TO HIS FEET AND151 JOURNE
GROPES UNCERTAINLY FOR THE
(HE STOPS UNCERTAINLY, BOWING TO LAZARUS, 321 LAZARU
AWKWARDLY)
UNCERTAINLY) 333 LAZARU
(UNCERTAINLY, GLANCING AT SIMON.) 151 MANSNS
SMILES DOWN AT IT UNCERTAINLY, THEN BENDS DOWN TO 366 MARCOM
TAKE HOLD OF ITS HAND.)
(UNCERTAINLY) NO, I SUPPOSE NOT. 381 MARCOM
WELL--(UNCERTAINLY) THAT IS--I DON'T CATCH YOUR 411 MARCOM
MEANING--
SHE GAPES UNCERTAINLY. 429 MARCOM
SHE COMES CLOSER TO HIM AND PEERS INTO HIS FACE-- 581 ROPE
UNCERTAINLY)
(HE MOVES UNCERTAINLY TOWARD THE DOOR.) 26 STRANG
(BUT HIS VOICE BEGINS TO TREMBLE UNCERTAINLY AGAIN 93 STRANG
AS HE CALLS)
MARSDEN TURNS TOWARD IT UNCERTAINLY. 123 STRANG
THEN HE COMES TO HER AND TAKES BOTH OF HER HANDS 130 STRANG
UNCERTAINLY.)
(WALKS A BIT UNCERTAINLY TO NINA'S CHAIR) 175 STRANG
(HE STANDS IN THE DOORWAY UNCERTAINLY. 506 VOYAGE
HE STANDS NEARBY UNCERTAINLY, WATCHING HER. 462 WELDED
(CAPE STARES AT HER UNCERTAINLY, THEN SITS DOWN IN485 WELDED
HIS CHAIR AGAIN.)

UNCERTAINTY
HIS MOVEMENTS HAVE A HAZY UNCERTAINTY ABOUT THEM. 223 AHWILD
IT WAS ONLY THE SILLY UNCERTAINTY THAT HURT. 160 BEYOND
UNCERTAINTY THAT COMPENSATES ITSELF BY BEING 422 DYNAMO
BOUNCINGLY OVERASSERTIVE.
(IN ANGUISHED UNCERTAINTY AGAIN) 99 ELECTR
(SHAKING HER HAND IN AN AGONY OF UNCERTAINTY) 263 GGBROW
(SHAKING HIS HEAD) THIS UNCERTAINTY IS BAD FOR 359 MARCOM
TRADE.
(THEN AS MARCO STARES AT HER UNCERTAINTY, 410 MARCOM
HER, AND OF FEAR AND UNCERTAINTY IN FEELING HER 125 STRANG
NEW PEACE, HER CERTAINTIES,

UNCHANGEABLY
NOTHING REMAINS OF THE STRANGE FASCINATION OF HER 48 STRANG
FACE EXCEPT HER UNCHANGEABLY

UNCHANGED
MRS. FIFE IS UNCHANGED. 476 DYNAMO
THE TWO TABLES ON EITHER SIDE OF THE DOOR AT REAR 695 ICEMAN
ARE UNCHANGED.
THE APPEARANCE OF THE ROOM IS UNCHANGED EXCEPT 24 STRANG
THAT ALL THE SHADES,

UNCLASPING
CLASPING AND UNCLASPING HER HANDS NERVOUSLY. 540 *ILE
SHE SIGHS HOPELESSLY, CLASPING AND UNCLASPING HER 514 DIFRNT
HANDS.

UNCLE
AND IF WE GO TO ANY OF THE OTHER PLACES UNCLE DICK 83 BEYOND
MENTIONS--
UNCLE SAYS YOU'LL BE GONE THREE YEARS. 83 BEYOND
IF I HAD NO OTHER EXCUSE FOR GOING ON UNCLE DICK'S 84 BEYOND
SHIP BUT JUST MY HEALTH,
YOU'D BETTER NOT SAY ANYTHING TO UNCLE DICK 86 BEYOND
BUT THE REALIZATION NEVER CAME 'TIL I AGREED TO GO 91 BEYOND
AWAY WITH UNCLE DICK.
BUT--RUTH--I--UNCLE DICK-- 92 BEYOND
I'M NOT GOING--I MEAN--I CAN'T GO TOMORROW WITH 100 BEYOND
UNCLE DICK--
I CAN'T, UNCLE--NOT NOW. 102 BEYOND
THANKS, UNCLE DICK. 102 BEYOND
YOU'VE BEEN FINE, UNCLE DICK.. AND I APPRECIATE 103 BEYOND
IT.
(FIRMLY) I'M NOT JOKING, UNCLE DICK. 104 BEYOND
(TURNING TO HIS UNCLE) YOU HAVEN'T ANSWERED BY 104 BEYOND
QUESTION, UNCLE DICK.
YOU NEEDN'T WORRY ABOUT THAT SPARE CABIN, UNCLE 104 BEYOND
DICK.
AND IF UNCLE DICK WON'T TAKE ME ON HIS SHIP, I'LL 107 BEYOND
FIND ANOTHER.
(LOOKING THAT WAY) IT'S YOUR UNCLE ANDY. 130 BEYOND
DON'T YOU LIKE UNCLE ANDY--THE MAN THAT CAME 130 BEYOND
YESTERDAY--
IF IT HADN'T BEEN FOR UNCLE DICK BEING SUCH A GOOD131 BEYOND
SKIPPER
I'D HAVE TAKEN IT ON THE SPOT, ONLY I COULDN'T 133 BEYOND
LEAVE UNCLE DICK IN THE LURCH.
WHERE DID UNCLE DICK DISAPPEAR TO THIS MORNING? 135 BEYOND
I COULDN'T LOOK FOR YOU THIS SOON, UNCLE. 141 BEYOND
(EAGERLY) WHAT IS IT, UNCLES 141 BEYOND
COME ON, UNCLE. 142 BEYOND
HOW DID YOU EVER COME TO FALL FOR UNCLE CALEB'S 521 DIFRNT
A BODY'D THINK YOU WERE ACTUALLY JEALOUS OF YOUR 522 DIFRNT
UNCLE THE WAY YOU GO ON.
(PLEASED--CONDESCENDINGLY) YOUR UNCLE CALEB'S AN 522 DIFRNT
OLD MAN, REMEMBER.
UNCLE CALEB LIVIN' NEXT DOOR ALL THESE YEARS AND 522 DIFRNT
COMIN' TO CALL ALL THE TIME.
GOSHY, I WISH PA'D LIVED--OR UNCLE JACK. 522 DIFRNT
I GOT A SWELL CHANCE TELLIN' THAT TO UNCLE CALEB. 523 DIFRNT
UNCLE CALEB'LL BE OVER SOON AND I DON'T WANT HIM 524 DIFRNT
TO CATCH ME HERE--
THAT MEANS UNCLE CALEB HAS COME AND SHE'S TOLD HIM527 DIFRNT
HER STORIES
(ANGRILY) YOUR UNCLE CALEB'LL GIVE YOU A REST 529 DIFRNT
WHEN HE SEES YOU/
YOU'D REMEMBER YOUR UNCLE CALEB'S BEEN IN LOVE 530 DIFRNT
WITH EMMA ALL HIS LIFE AND WAITED
AND I KIN SEE IT'S COME TO THE PYINT WHERE I GOT 530 DIFRNT
TO TELL YOUR UNCLE CALEB EVERY
AND IF MY WORD DON'T HAVE NO INFLUENCE, I'LL TELL 530 DIFRNT
YOUR UNCLE CALEB EVERYTHING.

UNCLE (CONT'D.)
THAT UNCLE CALEB 'D SAID I'D NEVER GET ANOTHER 531 DIFRNT
CENT FROM HIM,
MA AND UNCLE CALEB, THEY'VE CHUCKED ME OUT. 531 DIFRNT
I CAN TALK TO YOUR UNCLE CALEB. 532 DIFRNT
OH, I CAN'T UNDERSTAND YOUR MA AND UNCLE CALEB 532 DIFRNT
BEIN' SO CRUEL/
AFRAID THAT HIS UNCLE MAY BE COMING BACK.) 544 DIFRNT
(COLDLY) I WANTED YOUR UNCLE CALEB, NOT YOU, BUT 547 DIFRNT
YOU'LL HAVE TO DO.
SAY, LISTEN, AUNT EMMER, HE'S HUNG HIMSELF--UNCLE 548 DIFRNT
CALEB--IN THE BARN--HE'S DEAD/
WHEN IT GOT FOUND OUT SHE WAS HIS UNCLE DAVID'S 44 ELECTR
FANCY WOMAN,
AIN'T UNCLE SAM DE SAP TO TRUST GUYS LIKE DAT WID 617 ICEMAN
DOUGH/
DEY FALL FOR YUH LIKE YUH WAS DEIR UNCLE OR OLD 702 ICEMAN
MAN OR SOMETHING.
SURE, DIDN'T IT KILL AN UNCLE OF MINE IN THE OLD 52 JOURNE
COUNTRY.
AND UNCLE AND FATHER ARE PERSONAL FRIENDS OF HIS. 356 MARCOM
AND FATHER AND UNCLE BOTH SAY THERE'S MILLIONS TO 356 MARCOM
BE MADE IN HIS SERVICE IF
THAT'S WHAT FATHER SAYS--AND UNCLE. 356 MARCOM
UNCLE SAYS TAKING CHANCES--NECESSARY CHANCES, OF 356 MARCOM
COURSE--
MAFFEO, MARCO'S UNCLE, IS AROUND THE SAME AGE, 358 MARCOM
(STARES AT HIS UNCLE--THEN MUTTERS FASCINATEDLY) 359 MARCOM
NO--PLEASE, UNCLE. 360 MARCOM
(TURNING TO MAFFEO) I WIN, UNCLE. 371 MARCOM
(GRINNING EAGERLY) WHAT WAS IT, UNCLES 371 MARCOM
(TO HIS UNCLE--IN A WHISPERED CHUCKLE) 372 MARCOM
HIS FATHER AND UNCLE, BOWING. 378 MARCOM
HIS FATHER AND UNCLE MOAN WITH HORROR.) 380 MARCOM
MY FATHER AND UNCLE HAVE TAKEN ME INTO THE FIRM. 382 MARCOM
(HE MAKES A SIGN TO HIS UNCLE AND FATHER. 394 MARCOM
LAST EASTER SUNDAY WHEN FATHER AND UNCLE READ A 394 MARCOM
PRAYER
(HIS UNCLE FIRES THE GUN. 395 MARCOM
MY FATHER AND UNCLE CAN SWEAR-- 396 MARCOM
AND HIS FATHER AND UNCLE, ARE EXPERIENCED MASTERS 397 MARCOM
OF NAVIGATION,
(TO HIS FATHER AND UNCLE) YOU TWO BETTER GET 403 MARCOM
ABOARD YOUR SHIPS
(WITH A GRIN) AND LOOK AT THE OLD MAN AND UNCLE. 403 MARCOM
WHAT, UNCLES 415 MARCOM
(HE SLITS UP THE WIDE SLEEVES OF HIS OWN ROBE, AS 429 MARCOM
DO HIS FATHER AND UNCLE.
AND THEN HE SAID «LOVE SHE'D FEEL FOR AN UNCLE»... 37 STRANG
UNCLE CHARLIE NOW...... 37 STRANG
I MEAN THE SORT OF LOVE SHE'D FEEL FOR AN UNCLE. 37 STRANG
HOW DARE YOU TALK LIKE THAT TO YOUR UNCLE NED/ 142 STRANG
(REBELLIOUSLY) HE'S NOT MY UNCLE/ 142 STRANG
AND DON'T COME NEAR ME AGAIN, DO YOU HEAR, UNTIL 142 STRANG
YOU'VE APOLOGIZED TO UNCLE NED/
UNCLE CHARLIE'S DOWNSTAIRS. 145 STRANG
OUT IN THE KITCHEN WITH UNCLE CHARLIE. 152 STRANG
GOOD-BYE--UNCLE NED. 152 STRANG
WHAT'D YOU GET FROM UNCLE NEDS 153 STRANG
(SURPRISED) YOUR UNCLE NEDS 154 STRANG
THANK YOU, UNCLE CHARLIE/ 188 STRANG
UNCLE'S
I'LL NEED EVERY CENT OF THE WAGES UNCLE'S PAID ME 132 BEYOND
(THEN SEVERELY) YOUR UNCLE'S TO HOME. 528 DIFRNT
UNCLEAN
(IMBECILITIES OF PLEASURE--THE UNCLEAN ANTICS OF 358 LAZARU
HALF-WITTED CHILDREN/
UNCLENCHING
CLENCHING AND UNCLENCHING HER HANDS. 67 ANNA
UNCOMFORTABLE
HE LOOKS DESPERATELY UNCOMFORTABLE, 240 AHWILD
STERN-LOOKING PEOPLE IN UNCOMFORTABLE POSES ARE 493 DIFRNT
HUNG ON THE WALLS.
(MADE MORE AND MORE UNCOMFORTABLE BY THE ARDENT 524 DIFRNT
LOOKS EMMA IS CASTING AT HIM.)
THE THREE STARE ABOUT THEM GAWKILY, AWED AND 8 ELECTR
UNCOMFORTABLE.
THERE IS A SECOND'S UNCOMFORTABLE SILENCE. 45 ELECTR
WITH AN ATMOSPHERE OF UNCOMFORTABLE, STILTED 79 ELECTR
STATELINESS.
(THERE IS AN UNCOMFORTABLE SILENCE. 81 ELECTR
PETER AND HAZEL STAND UP, FEELING UNCOMFORTABLE.) 83 ELECTR
HE LOOKS SLEEPY, HOT, UNCOMFORTABLE AND GROUCHY.) 670 ICEMAN
I KNOW HOW MISERABLY UNCOMFORTABLE YOU MUST BE. 42 JOURNE
ALL ARE DRESSED IN THEIR ILL-FITTING SHORE CLOTHES496 VOYAGE
AND LOOK VERY UNCOMFORTABLE.
UNCOMFORTABLY
(STIRS UNCOMFORTABLY) HMM/ 265 AHWILD
SQUIRMING ABOUT UNCOMFORTABLY ON THE NARROW 275 AHWILD
GUNWALE.
(AFTER A PAUSE--UNCOMFORTABLY) 66 ANNA
AND IS UNCOMFORTABLY SELF-CONSCIOUS AND STIFF 494 DIFRNT
THEREIN.
HE STANDS UNCOMFORTABLY, FUMBLING WITH HIS HAT, 514 DIFRNT
(UNCOMFORTABLY.) AW, YOU'RE KIDDIN'. 524 DIFRNT
(SHE BECOMES UNCOMFORTABLY AWARE OF HIS 536 DIFRNT
EXAMINATION--NERVOUSLY)
(UNCOMFORTABLY) YES, MOTHER. 323 GGBROW
(UNCOMFORTABLY) TOUGH LUCK. 595 ICEMAN
(HE HESITATES--THEN UNCOMFORTABLY.) 35 MANSNS
EVANS SITS UNCOMFORTABLY HUNCHED FORWARD, 28 STRANG
TWIDDLING HIS HAT IN HIS HANDS.
UNCOMPREHENDING
(WITH A SORT OF DUMB, UNCOMPREHENDING ANGUISH) 68 ANNA
(HE LOOKS AT HER UNCOMPREHENDING FACE FOR A 248 DESIRE
SECOND--THEN GRUNTS DISGUSTEDLY)
BEWILDERMENT, A LOOK OF UNCOMPREHENDING HURT. 514 DIFRNT
AN UNCOMPREHENDING HURT IN HER EYES. 270 GGBROW

UNCOMPREHENDING (CONT'D.)
BEWILDEREDLY UNCOMPREHENDING BUT DISTURBED BECAUSE 30 MANSNS
HE SENSE HER DESPAIR,
TRADITIONAL EXPRESSION OF BEWILDERED, 433 MARCOM
UNCOMPREHENDING GRIEF THAT IS LIKE A MASK.
UNCOMPREHENDINGLY
(RUTH LETS HER HANDS FALL FROM HER FACE AND LOOKS 168 BEYOND
AT HIM UNCOMPREHENDINGLY.
HE LIFTS HIS HEAD AND PEERS UNCOMPREHENDINGLY AT 720 ICEMAN
LARRY.
SHE TAKES THE ROSE AUTOMATICALLY, STARING AT HIM 188 STRANG
UNCOMPREHENDINGLY.)
UNCOMPROMISING
BENEATH THE UNCOMPROMISING RIGIDITY OF HIS 70 MANSNS
HABITUAL POISE.
UNCONCEALED
ABBIE SEES HIM AND TURNS AWAY QUICKLY WITH 230 DESIRE
UNCONCEALED AVERSION.
UNCONCERN
(WITH SELF-CONSCIOUS UNCONCERN, IGNORING HIS 269 AHWILD
MUTHER)
UNCONCERNED
(CONFUSED--LOOKING EVERYWHERE EXCEPT AT ROBERT-- 86 BEYOND
TRYING TO APPEAR UNCONCERNED)
UNCONCERNEDLY
WALKING UNDER AN ARM OF THE CROSS UNCONCERNEDLY 327 LAZARU
WITHOUT AN UPWARD GLANCE.
UNCONDITIONALLY
HE WOULD ACCEPT UNCONDITIONALLY IF YOU-- 59 MANSNS
UNCONFIRMED
REALLY, THIS UNCONFIRMED REPORT MUST HAVE TURNED 29 ELECTR
YOUR HEAD---
UNCONSCIOUS
FOR A MOMENT HOPE APPEARS UNCONSCIOUS OF THIS 654 ICEMAN
HANDSHAKE.
SEEMINGLY UNCONSCIOUS OF EVERYTHING. 516 INZONE
BUT THE ACTOR SHOWS IN ALL HIS UNCONSCIOUS HABITS 13 JOURNE
OF SPEECH,
BUT FOR THE MOMENT MARY IS UNCONSCIOUS OF THEIR 108 JOURNE
CONDEMNING EYES.
HOLDING THE WEDDING GOWN IN HIS ARMS WITH AN 172 JOURNE
UNCONSCIOUS CLUMSY,
DRAPING HERSELF UP IN AN UNCONSCIOUS IMITATION OF 81 POET
HER FATHER'S HABITUAL MANNER.
FREDA IS ALREADY BESIDE THE UNCONSCIOUS MAN 508 VOYAGE
ROLLS TO THE FLOOR, AND LIES THERE UNCONSCIOUS.) 508 VOYAGE
UNCONSCIOUSLY
(UNCONSCIOUSLY LOWERING HIS VOICE) 539 'ILE
(UNCONSCIOUSLY SHE SNUGGLES CLOSE AGAINST HIS 90 BEYOND
SIDE
(HE SIGHS UNCONSCIOUSLY) BUT YOU SEE I'VE FOUND--102 BEYOND
A BIGGER DREAM.
(UNCONSCIOUSLY THEY HAVE ALL RAISED THEIR VOICES, 481 CARDIF
UNCONSCIOUSLY THEY BOTH SIGH.) 217 DESIRE
UNCONSCIOUSLY HE STRETCHES OUT HIS ARMS FOR HER 236 DESIRE
AND SHE HALF RISES.
WITH THE UNCONSCIOUSLY MALICIOUS HUMOR OF THE BORN498 DIFRNT
PRACTICAL JOKER.
(UNCONSCIOUSLY HITCHES HER CHAIR NEARER HIS. 526 DIFRNT
UNCONSCIOUSLY HE TAKES THE SAME ATTITUDE AS 36 ELECTR
MANNON, SITTING ERECT,
UNCONSCIOUSLY REPEATING THE EXACT THREAT 156 ELECTR
HER EYES UNCONSCIOUSLY SEEKING THE MANNON 157 ELECTR
PORTRAITS ON THE RIGHT WALL.
UNCONSCIOUSLY HIS HEAD IS INCLINED TOWARD THE 722 ICEMAN
WINDOW AS HE LISTENS.)
AT THE TABLE BY THE WINDOW LARRY HAS UNCONSCIOUSLY724 ICEMAN
SHUT HIS EYES AS HE LISTENS.
NO, AND YUH WON'T HEAR ANY RING, YUH BOOB-- 516 INZONE
(LOWERING HIS VOICE UNCONSCIOUSLY)
(UNCONSCIOUSLY FALLING INTO THE MOOD OF THEIR OLD 60 MANSNS
AFFECTIONATE INTIMACY.)
(UNCONSCIOUSLY SHE SIGHS REGRETFULLY.) 120 MANSNS
(UNCONSCIOUSLY SHE SIGHS REGRETFULLY.) 120 MANSNS
WITH THE SAME STRANGE AIM OF ACTING UNCONSCIOUSLY)122 MISBEG
(UNCONSCIOUSLY SHE TRIES TO PULL HER HAND AWAY.) 130 MISBEG
(UNCONSCIOUSLY HE REACHES OUT FOR THE DECANTER ON 45 POET
THE TABLE--
LOWERING HER VOICE UNCONSCIOUSLY AS IF SHE WERE 81 POET
THINKING ALOUD TO HERSELF.)
MARSDEN UNCONSCIOUSLY TAKES THE PROFESSOR'S PLACE 34 STRANG
BEHIND THE TABLE.
(SMILING) YES, PERHAPS UNCONSCIOUSLY PRESTON IS A166 STRANG
COMPENSATING SUBSTITUTE.
(HE GETS TO HIS FEET, HIS FACE UNCONSCIOUSLY 189 STRANG
BECOMING OLDER AND COLD AND SEVERE.
(UNCONSCIOUSLY HE GRIPS HER TIGHTER, ALMOST 451 WELDED
SHAKING HER.)
THEN, AS IF UNCONSCIOUSLY, FALTERINGLY, WITH 480 WELDED
TREMBLING SMILES.
UNCONTAINED
(THE HOMES WITH FURIOUS, UNCONTAINED LAUGHTER.) 287 LAZARU
UNCONTROLLABLE
(EVERYONE GOES OFF INTO UNCONTROLLABLE LAUGHTER.) 227 AHWILD
THEN LILY GOES OFF INTO UNCONTROLLABLE, HYSTERICAL227 AHWILD
LAUGHTER.
(HER EYES FLASHING--BURSTING INTO UNCONTROLLABLE 126 BEYOND
RAGE)
(SHE IS SHAKEN AGAIN BY A WAVE OF UNCONTROLLABLE 550 DAYS
CHILL, HER TEETH CHATTER--
(SHE BURSTS INTO UNCONTROLLABLE, HYSTERICAL 166 POET
LAUGHTER.
UNCONTROLLED
SHE BREAKS DOWN AND THERE IS THE SOUND OF HER 26 STRANG
UNCONTROLLED SOBBING AND CHOKING.
UNCONVENTIONAL
PROVOKINGLY UNCONVENTIONAL. 26 MANSNS

UNCONVERTED

UNCONVERTED
WHAT WILL YOUR POPE SAY WHEN YOU TELL HIM I'M 396 MARCOM
STILL UNCONVERTED?
UNCONVINCED
(STILL UNCONVINCED) ARE YOU SURE--WILL YOU 138 BEYOND
SWEAR--
(UNCONVINCED--LOOKING AWAY) THE REASON I ASKED-- 507 DAYS
UNCONVINCING
FORCING AN UNCONVINCING ATTEMPT AT HIS NATURAL 654 ICEMAN
TONE)
(STILL PROVOCATIVELY UNCONVINCING, HUGGING HER 80 MANSNS
AGAIN.)
THERE IS AN UNCONVINCING QUALITY ABOUT IT THAT 7 STRANG
LEAVES HIS LARGER AUDIENCE--
UNCONVINCINGLY
TRYING UNCONVINCINGLY TO REASSURE HIMSELF) 466 DYNAMO
(UNCONVINCINGLY) IT MUST BE ANOTHER OF HIS JOKES,625 ICEMAN
HARRY, ALTHOUGH--
UNCORKED
WITH A BOTTLE OF WHISKEY HE HAS JUST UNCORKED. 121 JOURNE
UNCORKS
(HE PUTS THE PITCHER AND TUMBLERS ON THE BOULDER 112 MISBEG
AND SHE UNCORKS THE BOTTLE.
UNCOVERS
THE CROWD NOW ALL JOIN IN WITH HIM, CALIGULA 308 LAZARU
SUDDENLY UNCOVERS HIS FACE,
UNCTION
(CONFIDENTLY--WITH A GENTLE, DRUNKEN UNCTION) 723 ICEMAN
HE DISGUISED HIS GREED WITH SABBATH POTIONS OF 101 MANSNS
GOD-FEARING UNCTION
UNCTUOUS
STOUT AND UNCTUOUS, SNOBBISH AND INGRATIATING, 67 ELECTR
CONSCIOUS OF GODLINESS,
UNCTUOUSLY
(UNCTUOUSLY) HE WAS A GREAT MAN. 69 ELECTR
UNCULTIVATED
THE FIELD IN THE FOREGROUND HAS A WILD 166 BEYOND
UNCULTIVATED APPEARANCE
UNCUT
THIS BOOKCASE IS FULL OF INSTALLMENT-PLAN SETS OF 519 DIFRNT
UNCUT VOLUMES.
MADE OF UNCUT WOOD WHICH STANDS AT CENTER, ITS 173 EJONES
BACK TO REAR.
UND
(TO DRISCOLL) YOU UND ME, VE KEEP DEM QUIET, 458 CARIBE
DRISC.
(TAUNTINGLY) UND I CAN GO HOME TO MY COUNTRY/ 677 ICEMAN
UNDECIDED
THE MEN LOOK UNCERTAINLY AT YANK AS IF UNDECIDED 482 CARDIF
WHETHER TO SAY GOOD-BY OR NOT.)
UNDENIABLY
HER FACE, THOUGH INCLINED TO ROUNDNESS, IS 87 BEYOND
UNDENIABLY PRETTY,
UNDEPENDABLE
AND I'M GOING TO TELL HIM HE CAN'T GO TO YALE, 289 AHWILD
SEEING HE'S SO UNDEPENDABLE.
UNDERBRUSH
A DENSE LOW WALL OF UNDERBRUSH AND CREEPERS IS IN 190 EJONES
THE NEARER FOREGROUND.
(FORGETTING THE PATH HE PLUNGES WILDLY INTO THE 192 EJONES
UNDERBRUSH IN THE REAR AND
THE ONLY SOUNDS ARE A CRASHING IN THE UNDERBRUSH 195 EJONES
AS JONES LEAPS AWAY IN MAD
UNDERCURRENT
AN UNDERCURRENT OF NERVOUS UNEASINESS MANIFESTS 99 BEYOND
ITSELF IN HIS BEARING.)
(AN UNDERCURRENT OF ANGER IN HIS SNEERING) 498 DAYS
THEN QUIETLY, AN UNDERCURRENT OF STERNNESS IN HIS 538 DAYS
VOICE)
(SLOWLY, IN HIS COLD TONE WITH ITS UNDERCURRENT OF540 DAYS
SINISTER HIDDEN MEANING)
(AFTER A WORRIED GLANCE AT HER--AN UNDERCURRENT OF540 DAYS
WARNING IN HIS QUIET TONE)
HER FACE FULL OF TERROR YET WITH AN UNDERCURRENT 259 DESIRE
OF DESPERATE TRIUMPH,
AND HIDING BENEATH A JOKING MANNER AN UNDERCURRENTS25 DIFRNT
OF UNEASINESS)
SHE GOES ON WITH A THREATENING UNDERCURRENT IN HER 17 ELECTR
VOICE)
THEN IN A VOICE THAT BETRAYS A DEEP UNDERCURRENT 47 ELECTR
OF SUPPRESSED FEELING)
BUT WITH A DEEP UNDERCURRENT OF SYMPATHY) 252 HA APE
AN UNDERCURRENT OF NERVOUS IRRITATION AND 629 ICEMAN
PREOCCUPATION.)
(WITH A STRANGE UNDERCURRENT OF 666 ICEMAN
(JOKINGLY BUT WITH AN UNDERCURRENT OF RESENTMENT.) 15 JOURNE
(THEN WITH AN UNDERCURRENT OF LONELY YEARNING.) 44 JOURNE
SUDDENLY A STRANGE UNDERCURRENT OF REVENGEFULNESS 47 JOURNE
COMES INTO HER VOICE.)
TEASING BUT WITH AN INCREASING UNDERCURRENT 120 JOURNE
OF RESENTMENT.)
(PLAYFULLY, BUT WITH A GROWING UNDERCURRENT OF 13 MANSNS
COMPULSIVE
(WITH AN UNDERCURRENT OF TENSE EAGERNESS.) 37 MANSNS
(GAILY--BUT WITH A STRANGE UNDERCURRENT.) 67 MANSNS
(LAUGHINGLY, WITH AN UNDERCURRENT OF TAUNTING 111 MANSNS
SATISFACTION.)
(SHE BLURTS OUT HASTILY WITH AN UNDERCURRENT OF 132 MANSNS
GUILTY DEFIANCE.)
HE GLANCES AT THE PLANS--WITH AN UNDERCURRENT OF 148 MANSNS
MOCKERY.)
IN WHICH THERE IS A STRONG UNDERCURRENT OF 51 POET
ENTREATY.)
AND HOW SHE SHOULD REACT--WITH AN UNDERCURRENT OF 82 POET
RESENTMENT.)
UNDERCURRENTS
TOO MANY UNDERCURRENTS. 557 DAYS

UNDERGOING
WHO HAS STOOD TENSELY WITH HIS EYES SHUT AS IF HE 530 INZONE
WERE UNDERGOING TORTURE DURING
UNDERGONE
HER BEAUTY HAS GROWN MORE INTENSE, HER FACE HAS 407 MARCOM
UNDERGONE A CHANGE,
THE ROOM HAS UNDERGONE A SIGNIFICANT CHANGE. 111 STRANG
UNDERGRADUATE
HIS FOUR UNDERGRADUATE YEARS WILL ALWAYS BE FOR 55 MISBEG
HER THE MOST SIGNIFICANT IN HIS
IS, HE IS ALWAYS MISTAKEN FOR AN UNDERGRADUATE AND 29 STRANG
LIKES TO BE.
UNDERGROUND
IT'S VE THAT'S BLIND--BLIND AS A MOLE UNDERGROUND.254 DESIRE
UNDERGROWTH
STUMBLING AND CRAWLING THROUGH THE UNDERGROWTH. 198 EJONES
UNDERLIES
ALTHOUGH THE RHYTHM OF IRISH SPEECH STILL 75 MANSNS
UNDERLIES IT.
UNDERLINGS
THAT WE ARE UNDERLINGS.= 152 JOURNE
UNDERLININGS
DIDN'T HE SEND ME EVERY ONE WITH BLUE PENCIL 503 DAYS
UNDERLININGS/
UNDERLYING/
AN UNDERLYING, STUBBORN FIXITY OF PURPOSE 87 BEYOND
NERVOUS VITALITY ABOUT ALL HER MOVEMENTS THAT 494 DIFRNT
REVEALS AN UNDERLYING CONSTITUTION
AN UNDERLYING STRENGTH OF WILL, 175 EJONES
THEY WITH AN UNDERLYING DEFENSIVENESS) 600 ICEMAN
(HE CALLS TO HOPE WITH A FIRST TRACE OF UNDERLYING692 ICEMAN
UNEASINESS)
(WITH A SNEER OF SCEPTICISM BUT WITH AN UNDERLYING340 LAZARU
EAGERNESS)
(FLATTERINGLY BUT WITH UNDERLYING SARCASM.) 100 MANSNS
(WITH A SUDDEN UNDERLYING HOSTILITY.) 131 MANSNS
UNDERNEATH
*A BOOK OF VERSES UNDERNEATH THE BOUGH, A JUG OF 199 AHWILD
WINE, A LOAF OF BREAD--
AND I'M TIRED OF PRETENDING I DON'T MIND, TIRED OF519 DAYS
REALLY MINDING UNDERNEATH,
HE SAW THAT UNDERNEATH ALL HIS HYPOCRITICAL 538 DAYS
PRETENSE HE REALLY HATED LOVE.
YOU WERE HATING ME UNDERNEATH, HATING OUR 549 DAYS
HAPPINESS.
I'VE SUSPECTED AT TIMES THAT UNDERNEATH HE WANTS--557 DAYS
SHE IS UNEASY UNDERNEATH, BUT AFFECTS A SCORNFUL 29 ELECTR
INDIGNATION.)
(MOVED) UNDERNEATH, 265 GGBROW
AND I KNOW DAMN WELL, UNDERNEATH YOUR NUTTINESS, 265 GGBROW
YOU'RE GONE ON HER.
YOU'RE A BIGGER KID THAN THEY ARE--UNDERNEATH. 270 GGBROW
UNDERNEATH--I'M BECOMING DOWNRIGHT INFANTILE/ 270 GGBROW
BUT BESS HAD A HEART OF GOLD UNDERNEATH HER 606 ICEMAN
SHARPNESS.
NOW YOU CAN FEEL HER GROWING TENSE AND FRIGHTENED 37 JOURNE
UNDERNEATH.
(SMILINGLY, BUT WITH A THREAT UNDERNEATH.) 92 MANSNS
THEY HAVE EVEN MORE GORGEOUS BLUE ONES UNDERNEATH,428 MARCOM
HE GOES ON QUIETLY, A BITTER, SNEERING ANTAGONISM 60 POET
UNDERNEATH.
MARY DARTS FROM UNDERNEATH AND DASHES OUT THROUGH 578 ROPE
THE DOORWAY.
LOOK OUT HE AIN'T MEANIN' SOME BAD TO YE 595 ROPE
UNDERNEATH.
DIRECTLY UNDERNEATH THE NOOSE OF THE ROPE. 601 ROPE
NO DEPTH, NO DIGGING UNDERNEATH... 34 STRANG
A DOOR UNDERNEATH THE BALCONY IS NOISELESSLY 443 WELDED
OPENED AND MICHAEL COMES IN.
UNDERSHIRT
HAVE NOTHING ON BUT A PAIR OF PANTS AND AN 456 CARIBE
UNDERSHIRT.
ON ACCOUNT OF THE HEAT HE HAS TAKEN OFF EVERYTHING235 DESIRE
BUT HIS UNDERSHIRT AND PANTS.
HE IS STRIPPED TO THE WAIST, HIS COAT, SHIRT, 576 ICEMAN
UNDERSHIRT,
HE WEARS HEAVY BROGANS, FILTHY OVERALLS, AND A 11 MISBEG
DIRTY SHORT-SLEEVED UNDERSHIRT.
UNDERSHIRTS
THEIR UNDERSHIRTS IN SHREDS, BENDING OVER THE 472 CARIBE
STILL FORM OF PADDY,
UNDERSTAND
(DULLY) NO--I DON'T KNOW--I CAN'T UNDERSTAND-- 547 'ILE
A WOMAN COULDN'T RIGHTLY UNDERSTAND MY REASONS. 547 'ILE
IN THE PAST, YOU UNDERSTAND/ 198 AHWILD
(THEN QUICKLY) I'M NOT TRYING TO LEAD YOU ASTRAY,218 AHWILD
UNDERSTAND/
I MEAN I'M AFRAID HE'S A LITTLE BIT--NOT TOO MUCH,223 AHWILD
YOU UNDERSTAND--
WHAT CAN THEY UNDERSTAND ABOUT GIRLS WHOSE HAIR 228 AHWILD
SIZZCHELS.
WELL, I UNDERSTAND THIS MUCH. 271 AHWILD
AH, MA, YOU DON'T UNDERSTAND ANYTHING/ 271 AHWILD
THE TROUBLE WITH YOU IS, YOU DON'T UNDERSTAND WHAT274 AHWILD
LOVE MEANS/
I CAN UNDERSTAND YOUR ATTITUDE, AND PA'S. 84 BEYOND
I'LL HAVE YOU UNDERSTAND THIS IS A FIRST CLASS 86 BEYOND
FARM WITH ALL THE FIXINGS.
(MOODILY) I OUGHT IF YOU'LL UNDERSTAND. 89 BEYOND
YOU'LL HAVE TO, TO UNDERSTAND. 89 BEYOND
(HE TURNS TO HER--SOFTLY) DO YOU UNDERSTAND NOW, 90 BEYOND
RUTH?
I REALIZE HOW IMPOSSIBLE IT ALL IS--AND I 91 BEYOND
UNDERSTAND.
I WANT YOU ALL TO UNDERSTAND ONE THING-- 102 BEYOND
(COLORING) BECAUSE I'M TOO STUPID TO UNDERSTAND 122 BEYOND
THEM.
I DON'T UNDERSTAND YOU. 124 BEYOND
YOU OUGHT TO BE ABLE TO UNDERSTAND WHAT I FEEL. 138 BEYOND

1729 UNDERSTAND

UNDERSTAND (CONT'D.)
I CAN'T UNDERSTAND THE WAY YOU'VE ACTED. 155 BEYOND
THE MAD WAY HE LIVES--UNDERSTAND THAT I WANT YOU 557 CROSS
TO GET ALL THE FACTS--
BUT--I DON'T UNDERSTAND--IS THE SHIP LONG 558 CROSS
OVERDUE--OR WHAT$
AND YOU UNDERSTAND--NEITHER OF US KNOWS ANYTHING 558 CROSS
ABOUT THIS.
THE NEIGHBORS--THEY'RE FAR AWAY BUT--FOR MY 562 CROSS
SISTER'S SAKE--YOU UNDERSTAND.
I WANT TO GET AT THE REAL TRUTH AND UNDERSTAND 495 DAYS
WHAT WAS BEHIND--
CAN'T UNDERSTAND ANY ONE HAVING FEELINGS ANY MORE 497 DAYS
(QUICKLY) BUT NOT THE IGNORANT, BIGOTED SORT, 510 DAYS
PLEASE UNDERSTAND.
DON'T THINK I DON'T UNDERSTAND, BECAUSE I DO. 520 DAYS
HE'LL UNDERSTAND. 533 DAYS
(TRYING TO CONTROL HERSELF) I--I DON'T 538 DAYS
UNDERSTAND.
THEY DON'T WANT TO UNDERSTAND WHAT HAS HAPPENED TO542 DAYS
THEM.
I--I CAN'T UNDERSTAND. 547 DAYS
I UNDERSTAND NOW. 563 DAYS
TO UNDERSTAND HIS CONFLICTING EMOTIONS. 247 DESIRE
AND SHE CAN'T UNDERSTAND THE WAY I FEEL ABOUT 510 DIFRNT
CALEB.
SHE COULDN'T UNDERSTAND ENOUGH ENGLISH FOR ME TO 515 DIFRNT
TELL HER HOW I FELT--
SO'S YOU'D UNDERSTAND. 516 DIFRNT
I THINK I CAN UNDERSTAND--HOW IT HAPPENED--AND 516 DIFRNT
MAKE ALLOWANCES.
IN A LAST EFFORT TO MAKE HIM UNDERSTAND) 516 DIFRNT
(HELPLESSLY) ME 'N' YOU'LL NEVER UNDERSTAND EACH 518 DIFRNT
OTHER, CALEB.
OH, I CAN'T UNDERSTAND YOUR MA AND UNCLE CALEB 532 DIFRNT
BEIN' SO CRUEL/
I SHOULD UNDERSTAND REUBEN'S WEAKNESS AND FORGIVE 435 DYNAMO
HIM....)
DON'T YOU UNDERSTAND I CAN'T--THAT MY FINDING THE 478 DYNAMO
SECRET IS MORE IMPORTANT THAN--
(THEN PLEADINGLY) WHY CAN'T YOU UNDERSTAND$ 482 DYNAMO
OTHERWISE I'D FIND IT DIFFICULT TO UNDERSTAND YOUR 29 ELECTR
SENDING ANNIE TO DISTURB ME
(WITH STRIDENT INTENSITY) YOU WOULD UNDERSTAND 30 ELECTR
SO PLEASE UNDERSTAND THIS ISN'T FOR YOUR SAKE. 32 ELECTR
BUT MEN OF HIS TYPE DON'T UNDERSTAND HINTS. 52 ELECTR
I TORE MY INSIDES OUT FOR YOU--THINKING YOU'D 61 ELECTR
UNDERSTAND/
I DON'T UNDERSTAND. 72 ELECTR
YOU WOULDN'T UNDERSTAND, UNLESS YOU'D BEEN AT THE 75 ELECTR
FRONT.
I CAN'T UNDERSTAND PEACE--HIS END/ 75 ELECTR
BUT I CANNOT UNDERSTAND YOUR ATTITUDE TOWARD ME. 77 ELECTR
I UNDERSTAND HOW YOU FEEL. 83 ELECTR
I KNOW I CAN TRUST YOU TO UNDERSTAND NOW AS YOU 85 ELECTR
ALWAYS USED TO.
YOU DON'T UNDERSTAND, VINNIE. 94 ELECTR
YOU UNDERSTAND I AIN'T SAYIN' THIS TO NO ONE BUT 136 ELECTR
YOU TWO.
MAN'S FEEBLE STRIVING TO UNDERSTAND HIMSELF, 150 ELECTR
ALL OF THE CRIMES, INCLUDING OURS, DO YOU 153 ELECTR
UNDERSTAND$
YOU UNDERSTAND, DON'T YOU$ 171 ELECTR
WHY MUST I HIDE MYSELF IN SELF-CONTEMPT IN ORDER 264 GGBROW
TO UNDERSTAND$
I UNDERSTAND. 272 GGBROW
I'M AFRAID I-- DON'T UNDERSTAND, BILLY BROWN. 276 GGBROW
GENTLY, *AND NOW I AM PERMITTED TO UNDERSTAND AND 292 GGBROW
LOVE YOU, TOO/*
(INTERRUPTING HIM--STIFFLY) I CERTAINLY CAN'T 303 GGBROW
UNDERSTAND--
SHE'LL NEVER UNDERSTAND$ 307 GGBROW
AND SHE'LL UNDERSTAND AND FORGIVE AND LOVE ME/ 307 GGBROW
DID I UNDERSTAND YOU TO SAY THIS WAS YOUR 317 GGBROW
HUSBAND'S DESIGNS
ONLY ARE YOU SURE YOU UNDERSTAND WHAT YOU'VE 247 HA APE
JOINED$
I DON'T REMEMBER NOTHING MUCH ABOUT ERIE, P-A, YOU 14 HUGHIE
UNDERSTAND--OR WANT TO.
NOT THAT I WAS EVER REAL PALS WITH HIM, YOU 18 HUGHIE
UNDERSTAND.
NOTHIN' WITH NO CLASS, YOU UNDERSTAND. 25 HUGHIE
ERIE--BUT DID I UNDERSTAND YOU TO SAY YOU ARE A 32 HUGHIE
GAMBLER BY PROFESSION$
HE'S THE ONE GUY IN THE WORLD WHO CAN UNDERSTAND--587 ICEMAN
*
(WATCHING HIM PUZZLEDLY) UNDERSTAND WHAT$ 587 ICEMAN
I KNEW YOU'D UNDERSTAND. 592 ICEMAN
(CATCHING HIMSELF GUILTILY) YOU CAN UNDERSTAND 615 ICEMAN
HOW I FEEL, CAN'T YOU.
I DON'T UNDERSTAND YOU. 623 ICEMAN
I ONLY DID IT TO MAKE YOU UNDERSTAND BETTER. 648 ICEMAN
I WANT YOU TO UNDERSTAND THE REASON. 648 ICEMAN
AND I KNOW HE'D UNDERSTAND, ALL RIGHT--IN HIS WAY.648 ICEMAN
I DON'T UNDERSTAND YOU. 655 ICEMAN
YOU CAN UNDERSTAND HOW HE'D GO BUGHOUSE 669 ICEMAN
BUT I UNDERSTAND HOW YOU CAN'T HELP STILL 680 ICEMAN
FEELING--
I THINK I UNDERSTAND, LARRY. 680 ICEMAN
BUT HE DOES UNDERSTAND ALL RIGHT/ 701 ICEMAN
ONLY I'VE GOT TO START BACK AT THE BEGINNING OR 709 ICEMAN
YOU WON'T UNDERSTAND.
YOU'RE THE ONLY ONE WHO CAN UNDERSTAND HOW GUILTY 720 ICEMAN
I AM.
I KNEW YOU WERE THE ONLY ONE WHO COULD UNDERSTAND 721 ICEMAN
MY SIDE OF IT.
I DON'T UNDERSTAND WHY YOU SHOULD SUDDENLY SAY 45 JOURNE
SUCH THINGS.

UNDERSTAND (CONT'D.)
HE DOESN'T UNDERSTAND A HOME. 61 JOURNE
(WITH DULL ANGER.) I UNDERSTAND THAT I'VE BEEN A 69 JOURNE
GOD-DAMNED FOOL TO BELIEVE IN
YOU DON'T UNDERSTAND/ 69 JOURNE
YOU DON'T UNDERSTAND/ 69 JOURNE
I UNDERSTAND WHAT A HARD GAME TO BEAT SHE'S UP 76 JOURNE
AGAINST--
LET'S REMEMBER ONLY THAT, AND NOT TRY TO 85 JOURNE
UNDERSTAND WHAT WE CANNOT UNDERSTAND.
YOU DON'T UNDERSTAND/ 88 JOURNE
BUT HOW CAN YOU UNDERSTAND, WHEN I DON'T MYSELF. 93 JOURNE
(STAMMERS PLEADINGLY.) PLEASE DON'T--TALK ABOUT 93 JOURNE
THINGS YOU DON'T UNDERSTAND/
BECAUSE HE CANNOT REALLY UNDERSTAND ANYTHING ELSE.101 JOURNE
IT'S HARD TO UNDERSTAND-- (ABRUPTLY A CHANGE COMES110 JOURNE
OVER HER.
YOU MUST TRY TO UNDERSTAND AND FORGIVE HIM, TOO. 117 JOURNE
BUT I DON'T THINK YOU'VE EVER TRIED TO UNDERSTAND.118 JOURNE
THE VULGAR HERD CAN NEVER UNDERSTAND.* 134 JOURNE
AND ENJOYS PLEASURES *THE VULGAR HERD CAN NEVER 134 JOURNE
UNDERSTAND/
(HASTILY.) I DON'T WANT TO PERSUADE YOU TO 149 JOURNE
ANYTHING, UNDERSTAND.
(DEFENSIVELY.) UH, PAPA'S ALL RIGHT, IF YOU TRY 157 JOURNE
TO UNDERSTAND HIM--
THE VULGAR HERD CAN NEVER UNDERSTAND.* 160 JOURNE
YOU UNDERSTAND. 167 JOURNE
(DULLY) I CANNOT UNDERSTAND. 309 LAZARU
I DO NOT UNDERSTAND THIS. 321 LAZARU
(WITH PUZZELED GOOD NATURE) I DO NOT UNDERSTAND. 322 LAZARU
(WITH A SIGN--MEEKLY) I CANNOT UNDERSTAND. 325 LAZARU
LAZARUS.
I DO NOT UNDERSTAND THIS. 331 LAZARU
TO TELL ME YOU UNDERSTAND AND LAUGH WITH ME AT 346 LAZARU
LAST$
BUT I DO NOT UNDERSTAND THIS-- 352 LAZARU
(THEN DULLY) I DO NOT UNDERSTAND. 352 LAZARU
MEN ARE TOO COWARDLY TO UNDERSTAND/ 352 LAZARU
AND NOT TO LAUGH. YOU UNDERSTAND/ 353 LAZARU
BUT PERHAPS YOU WERE TOO DULL TO UNDERSTAND, 361 LAZARU
CAN'T YOU UNDERSTAND THAT$ 30 MANSNS
I--I DO NOT UNDERSTAND YOU. 38 MANSNS
I UNDERSTAND HER FEELING TOWARD ME. 39 MANSNS
(RESENTFULLY.) I CAN'T UNDERSTAND YOUR MOTHER NOT 45 MANSNS
INVITING YOU TO THE FUNERAL.
(CARELESSLY.) WHY, ALL I UNDERSTAND ABOUT IT IS 55 MANSNS
THAT MY HUSBAND SUGGESTED THAT
AM I TO UNDERSTAND YOU ACCEPT YOUR FATHER'S 58 MANSNS
PROPOSALS
DO YOU UNDERSTAND, SARA$ 62 MANSNS
SO YOU CAN UNDERSTAND WHY I AM WORRIED. 84 MANSNS
(SMILINGLY.) YOU WILL UNDERSTAND WHY WHEN I TELL 97 MANSNS
YOU THE ONE PERSON WHO
MIGHT REORGANIZE YOUR BANKRUPTCY--IF I MAY PUT IT 103 MANSNS
IN TERMS YOU UNDERSTAND.
WE'D UNDERSTAND AND FORGIVE EACH OTHER-- 123 MANSNS
AND I'LL UNDERSTAND WHEN YOU TELL ME-- 132 MANSNS
YOU CAN UNDERSTAND THAT, DEBORAH. 132 MANSNS
(BITTERLY.) YOU SAID YOU'D UNDERSTAND/ 132 MANSNS
WHATEVER IT IS, I WILL REMEMBER IT IS HIS DOING, 132 MANSNS
AND I WILL UNDERSTAND.
YOU CAN UNDERSTAND THAT, CAN'T YOU$ 133 MANSNS
(TENSELY.) I AM MAKING MYSELF UNDERSTAND. 133 MANSNS
YOU PROMISED TO UNDERSTAND. 134 MANSNS
AS A MOTHER, YOU CAN UNDERSTAND THAT, SARA/ 134 MANSNS
(FIGHTING WITH HIMSELF.) I DO NOT UNDERSTAND YOU.143 MANSNS
I DON'T BELIEVE I UNDERSTAND-- (HASTILY FORCING A 152 MANSNS
GOOD-NATURED, GOOD-LOSER AIR.)
I UNDERSTAND. 154 MANSNS
I UNDERSTAND EVERYTHING A WOMAN'S LOVE COULD 192 MANSNS
POSSIBLY COMPEL HER TO DESIRE.
HE MIGHTN'T UNDERSTAND. 359 MARCOM
THAT ONE'S SYMPATHY SHOULD UNDERSTAND ALL THINGS. 372 MARCOM
(WARNINGLY) AND UNTIL I PRONOUNCE YOU GRADUATED, 374 MARCOM
NURSE'S THE WORD. UNDERSTAND/
HE IS STRANGE, PERHAPS, TO PEOPLE WHO DO NOT 387 MARCOM
UNDERSTAND HIM.
YOU DO NOT UNDERSTAND. 400 MARCOM
SO PERHAPS HE DO NOT NEED TO UNDERSTAND. 400 MARCOM
I MYSELF FEEL THERE IS SOMETHING, SOMETHING I 414 MARCOM
CANNOT UNDERSTAND.
IT WASN'T ME YOU UNDERSTAND. 415 MARCOM
ONE MUST HAVE STUPID WRITINGS THAT MEN CAN 423 MARCOM
UNDERSTAND.
I UNDERSTAND NOW. 60 MISBEG
I KNEW YOU'D UNDERSTAND. 141 MISBEG
OR IF YOU DID BELIEVE, YOU COULDN'T UNDERSTAND OR 145 MISBEG
FORGIVE--
(HUGGING HIM TENDERLY) OF COURSE I'LL UNDERSTAND.145 MISBEG
JIM, DARLING.
(UNHEEDING) SHE'D UNDERSTAND AND FORGIVE ME, 151 MISBEG
DIDN'T YOU THINK$
I UNDERSTAND NOW, JIM, DARLING, 152 MISBEG
TO UNDERSTAND AND FORGIVE--AND I DO FORGIVE/ 152 MISBEG
I KNOW YOU'LL UNDERSTAND THE REASON, AND NOT THINK172 MISBEG
I'M TIRED OF YOUR COMPANY.
(GETS UP) OF COURSE, I UNDERSTAND. 172 MISBEG
BUT YOU UNDERSTAND, IT WAS THE LIQUOR TALKING, IF 42 POET
I SAID ANYTHING TO WOUND YOU.
I DON'T UNDERSTAND YOU. 46 POET
(COLDLY.) I DON'T UNDERSTAND YOU. 58 POET
ONE SO BEAUTIFUL MUST UNDERSTAND THE HEARTS OF MEN 71 POET
FULL WELL.
AS A TRIUMPHANT CLIMAX, YOU UNDERSTAND, 83 POET
I DON'T UNDERSTAND YOU. 90 POET
YOU DO NOT UNDERSTAND, MY LASS$ 101 POET
I DON'T UNDERSTAND YOU. 105 POET

UNDERSTAND

UNDERSTAND (CONT'D.)
HAND, BUT HE MUST UNDERSTAND THAT I COULD NOT 110 POET
COMMIT MYSELF UNTIL I HAD TALKED
I CAN UNDERSTAND HIS PHYSICAL INFATUATION. 114 POET
YES, I CAN EVEN UNDERSTAND NOW--A LITTLE ANYWAY-- 150 POET
WHAT SON CAN EVER UNDERSTANDS.... 4 STRANG
I COULDN'T UNDERSTAND HIM.... 4 STRANG
YOU SHOULD UNDERSTAND THIS, FATHER, YOU WHO-- 18 STRANG
RECOGNIZE IT, CHARLIE, LET ALONE UNDERSTAND IT/ 21 STRANG
BUT DO YOU UNDERSTAND NOW THAT I MUST SOMEHOW FIND 21 STRANG
A WAY TO GIVE MYSELF TO
CHARLIE, AND IT'LL BE SO SIMPLE AND EASY TO 21 STRANG
UNDERSTAND THAT I WON'T BE ABLE TO
WELL--I DON'T UNDERSTAND THIS/ 21 STRANG
BUT I DON'T UNDERSTAND ONE WORD OF IT....)) 27 STRANG
DO YOU UNDERSTAND ME, CHARLES 40 STRANG
THEN HE WOULD UNDERSTAND WHY ME, HER CHILDREN, 43 STRANG
HAVE INHERITED PAIN,
I MEAN--I AM, DIDN'T YOU UNDERSTAND ME$ 58 STRANG
I DON'T UNDERSTAND--QUITE. 77 STRANG
CAN'T UNDERSTAND HER NOT HAVING CHILD... 79 STRANG
YOU'VE GOT TO SHOW ME WHAT'S THE SANE--THE TRULY 84 STRANG
SANE, YOU UNDERSTAND/
(IN SAME TONE) AND THE MAN SHOULD HAVE A MIND 88 STRANG
THAT CAN TRULY UNDERSTAND--
I DON'T THINK HE'LL UNDERSTAND, NINA. 101 STRANG
I DON'T UNDERSTAND 126 STRANG
(MISERABLY) BUT I DON'T UNDERSTAND/ 131 STRANG
I UNDERSTAND, I THINK. 179 STRANG
UH, I UNDERSTAND THAT--AND I FORGIVE YOU/ 180 STRANG
BUT HE CAN'T UNDERSTAND ME/... 194 STRANG
BUT YOU UNDERSTAND/ 446 WELDED
(KISSING HIM) I UNDERSTAND. 448 WELDED
(MISERABLY) I--I CAN'T UNDERSTAND/ 452 WELDED
THE OTHER IS ME--OR A PART OF ME--I HARDLY 452 WELDED
UNDERSTAND MYSELF.
WHY CAN'T YOU UNDERSTAND AND BE GENEROUS--BE JUST/453 WELDED
BUT I THOUGHT YOU'D UNDERSTAND--THAT I'D BEEN 458 WELDED
SEARCHING FOR SOMETHING--
(VAGUELY) NO--YOU DON'T UNDERSTAND-- 465 WELDED
(GRAVELY) NO--NOT NOW WHEN I DO UNDERSTAND. 466 WELDED
(WILDLY) AND I MUST BE CONSCIOUS--FULLY 472 WELDED
CONSCIOUS, DO YOU UNDERSTAND$
AND I CAN'T, YOU UNDERSTAND--CAN'T/ 476 WELDED
WHAT I AM, UNDERSTANDS 477 WELDED
UNDERSTANDABLE
(SARCASTICALLY) I'M GLAD IT'S UNDERSTANDABLE/ 75 STRANG
UNDERSTANDIN'
(BITTERLY) PRAY AGEN--FUR UNDERSTANDIN'/ 238 DESIRE
UNDERSTANDING
(AFTER A QUICK UNDERSTANDING GLANCE AT HIM) 196 AHWILD
BY A SMILE OF SHY UNDERSTANDING AND SYMPATHY. 297 AHWILD
BUT WHEN IT COMES TO UNDERSTANDING, 84 BEYOND
YOU'VE ALWAYS WORKED ON IT WITH THAT 105 BEYOND
UNDERSTANDING,.
AND AN EXPRESSION OF AWED UNDERSTANDING COMES OVER490 CARDIF
HIS FACE.
HE HAS TO, YOU SEE, TO KEEP UP HIS POSE OF 526 DAYS
FRIENDLY UNDERSTANDING--
(NODS WITH SAD UNDERSTANDING) 557 DAYS
(AGAIN STARTS--THEN SLOWLY AS IF ADMITTING A 11 ELECTR
SECRET UNDERSTANDING BETWEEN THEM)
(GAZES AT HER WITH UNDERSTANDING) 45 ELECTR
NOT UNDERSTANDING WHAT IS BEHIND THEIR TALK BUT 164 ELECTR
SENSING SOMETHING SINISTER,
(WITH GRIM UNDERSTANDING) AYEH. 178 ELECTR
HER BLINDNESS SURPASSETH ALL UNDERSTANDING/ 271 GGBROW
NOW WITH A GREAT UNDERSTANDING) 320 GGBROW
HE DOESN'T WANT TO BE BOTHERED UNDERSTANDING. 701 ICEMAN
THIS SON LOOKS AT HIM, FOR THE FIRST TIME WITH AN 36 JOURNE
UNDERSTANDING SYMPATHY.
(MOVED, STARES AT HIS FATHER WITH UNDERSTANDING-- 151 JOURNE
SLOWLY.)
ALL THE SAME, I DON'T THINK SHE WAS SO 175 JOURNE
UNDERSTANDING THIS TIME.
UNDERSTANDING SMILE OF SELF-FORGETFUL LOVE, THE 274 LAZARU
LIPS STILL FRESH AND YOUNG.
MAJESTIC FIGURE WHOSE UNDERSTANDING SMILE SEEMS 278 LAZARU
TERRIBLE AND ENIGMATIC TO THEM.)
LAZARUS LOOKS AT HIM, LAUGHING WITH GENTLE 308 LAZARU
UNDERSTANDING.
(SMILES WITH RESPECTFUL UNDERSTANDING. 327 LAZARU
(STILL LAUGHING WITH AN AFFECTIONATE 331 LAZARU
UNDERSTANDING)
(NOT UNDERSTANDING, FIXING HIS EYES ON CALIGULA 339 LAZARU
WITH A MALEVOLENT IRONY)
AND SMILE AT EACH OTHER WITH A RELIEVED 123 MANSNS
UNDERSTANDING.
WITH A SMILE OF GRACIOUS UNDERSTANDING AMUSEMENT.)193 MANSNS
APPEALING FOR A WOMAN'S UNDERSTANDING AND LOVING 70 POET
COMPASSION.)
WITH NO FEAR IN THEM--PROUD, UNDERSTANDING PRIDE--169 POET
LOVING ME--
(THOUGH HE IS MOST LIBERAL--EVEN RADICAL--IN HIS 7 STRANG
TOLERANT UNDERSTANDING
UNDERSTANDING OF ITS REAL SEXUAL NATURE. 33 STRANG
(IN A TONE OF SUPERIOR MANLY UNDERSTANDING, 157 STRANG
(THEY SMILE WITH A QUEER UNDERSTANDING, THEIR ARMS480 WELDED
MOVE ABOUT EACH OTHER,
UNDERSTANDINGLY
HE REGARDS HER UNDERSTANDINGLY.) 18 ELECTR
(STARES AT HER--THEN UNDERSTANDINGLY) 44 ELECTR
(STARES AT HIM--UNDERSTANDINGLY) SURE. I GET IT.584 ICEMAN
(LOOKS AT HIM--AFTER A PAUSE, UNDERSTANDINGLY) 482 WELDED
UNDERSTANDS
(LOOKS AT HIM AND SUDDENLY UNDERSTANDS THAT WHAT 566 CROSS
SHE DREADS HAS COME TO PASS--

UNDERSTANDS (CONT'D.)
AND WHY COULDN'T SOMETHING LIKE THAT THAT NO ONE 472 DYNAMO
UNDERSTANDS YET...
AND HE UNDERSTANDS WHAT I'M REALLY LIKE INSIDE-- 263 GGBROW
AND--
THEN HE UNDERSTANDS--WITH HIS NATURAL TESTY 722 ICEMAN
MANNER)
HE UNDERSTANDS NOTHING/ 74 JOURNE
THE ONLY KIND OF WOMAN HE UNDERSTANDS OR LIKES. 96 JOURNE
BECAUSE SHE ALWAYS UNDERSTANDS, EVEN BEFORE YOU 175 JOURNE
SAY A WORD.
OR HOW WELL SHE UNDERSTANDS--WHAT I WAS. 39 MANSNS
AND BECAUSE YOU'RE THE ONLY WOMAN I'VE EVER MET 145 MISBEG
WHO UNDERSTANDS THE LOUSY ROTTEN
AS SHE LOVES AND UNDERSTANDS AND FORGIVES/ 152 MISBEG
KNOW SHE UNDERSTANDS AND FORGIVES ME, TOO, AND HER153 MISBEG
BLESSING LIES ON ME.
HE UNDERSTANDS SO MUCH... 147 STRANG
OH, HE UNDERSTANDS, HE'D WANT ME TO BE... 189 STRANG
NICK SIGNALS BACK THAT HE UNDERSTANDS.) 497 VOYAGE
UNDERSTOOD
HE NEVER UNDERSTOOD, THAT'S A KINDER WAY OF 134 BEYOND
PUTTING IT.
(INSISTENTLY) YOU UNDERSTOOD ALL I EXPLAINED TO 476 DYNAMO
YOU UP ON THE DAM, DIDN'T YOU$
THEY UNDERSTOOD HER AND KNEW THEIR PARTS AND ACTED284 GGBROW
NATURALLY.
THE GORILLA, AS IF HE UNDERSTOOD, STANDS UPRIGHT, 252 HA APE
I'VE NEVER UNDERSTOOD ANYTHING ABOUT IT, 93 JOURNE
IT TOOK MANY YEARS BEFORE I UNDERSTOOD HIM. 117 JOURNE
WHAT IS UNDERSTOOD AND TO WHAT CANNOT BE 344 LAZARU
UNDERSTOOD/
WE'VE UNDERSTOOD EACH OTHER AND WHAT MIGHT HAVE 124 MANSNS
DEVELOPED INTO A STUPID QUARREL
SHE UNDERSTOOD/ 169 POET
(WHO HAS ONLY HALF-HEARD AND HASN'T UNDERSTOOD, 75 STRANG
SAYS VAGUELY)
SHE HAS KNOWN I HAVE UNDERSTOOD ABOUT HER MERE 148 STRANG
PHYSICAL PASSION FOR DARRELL...
I THOUGHT YOU UNDERSTOOD. 459 WELDED
UNDERSTUDY
AS THOUGH YOU WERE AN UNDERSTUDY LEARNING TO PLAY 92 MANSNS
MY PART.
UNDERTAKER
BUT HERE YOU ARE, ACTING LIKE A LOT OF STIFFS 704 ICEMAN
CHEATING THE UNDERTAKER/
UNDERTAKERS
THE UNDERTAKERS, AND HER BODY IN A COFFIN WITH HER147 MISBEG
FACE MADE UP.
UNDERTONE
(GUILTILY BUT WITH A STRANGE UNDERTONE OF 646 ICEMAN
SATISFACTION)
(SHE CALLS, WITH AN UNDERTONE OF GLOATING 114 MANSNS
MOCKERY.)
UNDERTONES
(HIS MANNER HAS BECOME SECRETIVE, WITH SINISTER 11 HUGHIE
UNDERTONES.
UNDERWEAR
UNDERWEAR. 202 AHWILD
I MUSTN'T FORGET TO MAKE RAMSAY CHANGE TO HIS 429 DYNAMO
SUMMER UNDERWEAR THIS WEEK...
UNDEVELOPED
HER BODY, FORMERLY SO THIN AND UNDEVELOPED, HAS 137 ELECTR
FILLED OUT.
OF GREAT UNDEVELOPED NATURAL RESOURCES, 359 MARCOM
UNDIGNIFIED
MOCKERY OF UNDIGNIFIED AGE SNATCHING GREEDILY AT 520 DIFRNT
THE EMPTY SIMULACRA OF YOUTH.
UNDISTINGUISHED
HIS LONG FACE HAS LARGE, IRREGULAR, 188 AHWILD
UNDISTINGUISHED FEATURES, BUT HE HAS FINE,
UNDO
YOU'VE GOT A CHANCE NOW TO UNDO SOME OF ALL THE 165 BEYOND
SUFFERING YOU'VE BROUGHT ON ROB.
WHATEVER MAGIC THOU DIDST TO ME, DAEMON, I BESEECH343 LAZARU
THEE UNDO IT/
UNDONE
YOU CAN DO TO THE FARM ALL I'VE UNDONE. 161 BEYOND
HANDLE SHALL FINISH WHAT I LEAVE UNDONE/ 425 MARCOM
UNDOUBTEDLY
UNDOUBTEDLY ALL THIS IS WELL KNOWN TO YOU. 595 ICEMAN
UH, THAT'S ALL UNDOUBTEDLY PART OF THE EFFORT 8 STRANG
SHE'S MAKING TO FORGET.
I DID NOT POINT OUT, BUT WHICH GORDON UNDOUBTEDLY 10 STRANG
REALIZED, POOR BOY/
UNDREAMED
FOR THE UNDREAMED-OF MIRACLE/ 38 MANSNS
WITH MY UNDREAMED-OF TALENTS AS A GOOD WOMAN/ 40 MANSNS
UNDRESS
COME ON TU BED, NOW, AND I'LL HELP YOU UNDRESS AND182 POET
TUCK YOU IN.
UNDRESSED
AND I HAD TO GET ALL UNDRESSED AND INTO BED *CAUSE280 AHWILD
AT HALF-PAST HE SENDS MA UP
YOU GETTING DRESSED AND UNDRESSED--AS IF THEY 279 GGBROW
OWNED YOU--
UNDRESSES
(HE STARES AT HER WITH A DELIBERATE SENSUALIST'S 114 MISBEG
LOOK THAT UNDRESSES HER)
UNDRESSING
(SHE GETS UP TO START UNDRESSING. 474 WELDED
UNDULY
I HAVE A PRIDE UNDULY SENSITIVE TO ANY FANCIED 70 POET
SLIGHT.
UNDUTIFUL
LORD GOD O' HOSTS, SMITE THE UNDUTIFUL SONS WITH 227 DESIRE
THY WUST CUSS/
AND THEY ARE GLAD, THESE UNDUTIFUL ONES/ 287 LAZARU

UNEASY

UNDUTIFUL (CONT'D.)
PUT ME OUT OF MY OWN HOME, WILL YOU, YOU UNDUTIFUL100 MISBEG SLUT/

UNE
DE MOON, SHE SHI-I-I-UNE. 6 ANNA

UNEARTHLY
AND SPEAKING WITH A STRANGE UNEARTHLY CALM 279 LAZARU
THEY SAY AN UNEARTHLY FLAME BURNS IN THIS LAZARUS/299 LAZARU
WITH AN UNEARTHLY GLORY. 318 LAZARU
HIS FIGURE RADIANT AND UNEARTHLY IN HIS OWN LIGHT.335 LAZARU
(IN A VOICE OF UNEARTHLY SWEETNESS) 348 LAZARU
AN UNEARTHLY GLOW, LIKE A HALO, LIGHTS UPS THE 352 MARCOM
FACE OF KUKACHIN.

UNEASILY
THE TWO MEN LOOK AT HER UNEASILY.) 541 *ILE
THEY GLANCE UNEASILY AT THE CAPTAIN, TWIRLING 543 *ILE
THEIR FUR CAPS IN THEIR HANDS.)
(GLANCES AT HER UNEASILY, PEEKS SURREPTITIOUSLY AT255 AHWILD
HIS WATCH--
SEA-SICK TINGE, HIS EYES SEEM TO BE TURNED INWARD 261 AHWILD
UNEASILY)
(UNEASILY) WHAT DO YOU MEAN, ANOTHER SIDES 289 AHWILD
(UNEASILY) NO--OF COURSE I AIN'T. 35 ANNA
(TURNING AWAY FROM HIM WITH A SHORT LAUGH-- 38 ANNA
UNEASILY)
(YANK GROANS AND STIRS UNEASILY, OPENING HIS EYES.482 CARDIF
(FROWNING--UNEASILY) WHY? 505 DAYS
(UNEASILY) WHAT DO YOU MEANS 508 DAYS
(UNEASILY) BUT NO. 509 DAYS
(STARING UNEASILY--MECHANICALLY) 524 DAYS
(UNEASILY) OH, YOU MUSTN'T TALK THAT WAY, JOHN. 534 DAYS
ELSA AND FATHER BAIRD START AND STARE AT JOHN 535 DAYS
UNEASILY.
(UNEASILY) WHY DO YOU STARE LIKE THATS 544 DAYS
(STARING AT HIM--UNEASILY) WHAT'D HE MEAN ABOUT 500 DIFRNT
JIM BENSON, CALEBS
(UNEASILY) WHAT'S IT GOT TO WAG ABOUTS 500 DIFRNT
(GLANCING AT EMMA UNEASILY) SSSHH/ 514 DIFRNT
(HE LOOKS AROUND UNEASILY, AFRAID OF WHERE HIS 424 DYNAMO
THOUGHTS ARE LEADING HIM.
(HE LISTENS FOR A MOMENT--UNEASILY) 443 DYNAMO
(STANDS HESITATING--UNEASILY) 444 DYNAMO
IN ALARM AT FINDING THE ROOM DARK AND EMPTY--CALLS445 DYNAMO
UNEASILY)
(HE STARES AT HIS FATHER--UNEASILY) 464 DYNAMO
(UNEASILY) RUBE/ I'M SCARED UP HERE/ 482 DYNAMO
THE STAIRS TO THE LOWER SWITCH GALLERY--SHE CALLS 488 DYNAMO
UNEASILY)
(STARTLED, GLANCES AT HIM UNEASILY) 15 ELECTR
(STARTLED AGAIN--STARING AT HER UNEASILY) 24 ELECTR
(GLANCING UNEASILY AT HER, AS THEY COME TO THE 36 ELECTR
CENTER OF THE ROOM)
HE CHANGES THE SUBJECT UNEASILY) 38 ELECTR
(UNEASILY) HOW DO YOU KNOWS 53 ELECTR
(UNEASILY) BUT I'VE COME BACK. 90 ELECTR
HE SUDDENLY LOOKS AROUND UNEASILY) 108 ELECTR
(UNEASILY) ORIN/ 115 ELECTR
(LOOKING AFTER HIM--UNEASILY) 136 ELECTR
(GLANCES AT HIM UNEASILY-- 138 ELECTR
(SEARCHES HIS FACE UNEASILY--THEN IS APPARENTLY 138 ELECTR
SATISFIED)
(UNEASILY) NOW DON'T BEGIN TALKING NONSENSE 141 ELECTR
AGAIN, PLEASE/
LAVINIA WATCHES HIM UNEASILY AND SPEAKS SHARPLY) 144 ELECTR
SO DOES ORIN WHO UNEASILY COMES TO HAZEL'S 162 ELECTR
RESCUE.)
(UNEASILY) WHAT DID YOU COME FORS 172 ELECTR
(THEN A BIT UNEASILY--FORCING A SMILE) 175 ELECTR
(STARING AT HIM SEARCHINGLY--UNEASILY) 175 ELECTR
(BROWN STIRS UNEASILY) TO BE MERELY A SUCCESSFUL 296 GGBROW
FREAK.
(HE STIRS UNEASILY. 309 GGBROW
(GETTING UP--UNEASILY) I'M AFRAID I-- 315 GGBROW
THEY FIDGET UNEASILY. 323 GGBROW
(ALL AT SEA--UNEASILY) IS THAT SO$ 221 HA APE
(AFTER A GLANCE AT YANKE'S LOWERING FACE--UNEASILY)236 HA APE
(STILL MORE UNEASILY) CALM, NOW. 236 HA APE
(UNEASILY) HICKEY AIN'T OVERLOOKIN' NO BETS, IS 635 ICEMAN
HE$
(UNEASILY) WHAT DO YOU MEANS 642 ICEMAN
(UNEASILY.) OH, DRY UP, JAMIE/ 61 JOURNE
(AGAIN ATTEMPTING UNEASILY TO LOOK UP IN HER 62 JOURNE
EYES.)
(WITH A GLANCE FROM ONE TO THE OTHER, WHICH HIS 63 JOURNE
MOTHER AVOIDS--UNEASILY.)
(THE FRONT DOOR IS HEARD CLOSING AND TYRONE CALLS 108 JOURNE
UNEASILY FROM THE HALL.)
(THEN PROTESTING UNEASILY.) BUT THAT'S MORBID 154 JOURNE
CRAZINESS ABOUT NOT BEING WANTED
(UNEASILY.) SHUT UP/ 165 JOURNE
(NUDGING THE SECOND--UNEASILY) 277 LAZARU
(RAISES HIS HEAD UNEASILY, LOOKS BACK TOWARD THE 335 LAZARU
PALACE.
(HE PAUSES, THEN TURNS TO JOEL UNEASILY.) 27 MANSNS
(UNEASILY.) OH, I MEANT TO HIDE IT. 45 MANSNS
(UNEASILY.) NO, STICK TO YOUR OWN TRADE, SIMON, 48 MANSNS
WHATEVER YOU DO.
(UNEASILY.) YOU MEAN SHE'S INSANES 86 MANSNS
(THEN, AS SHE STARES AT HIM UNEASILY--ABRUPTLY 92 MANSNS
BUSINESS-LIKE.)
(DEBORAH STARTS AND STARES AT HIM UNEASILY.) 98 MANSNS
(UNEASILY AND GUILTILY--FORCING A LAUGH.) 109 MANSNS
(UNEASILY, FORCING A LAUGH.) 109 MANSNS
(THINKING--UNEASILY.) PERHAPS I SHOULD HAVE 120 MANSNS
WAITED--
SIMON STIRS UNEASILY AND HIS EYES CEASE TO FOLLOW 125 MANSNS
THE LINES.
(HESITATES UNEASILY-- 131 MANSNS

UNEASY (CONT'D.)
(UNEASILY.) AND THEY'RE STILL HAPPENING--EVEN IF 136 MANSNS
HE IS LOCKED IN HIS STUDY.
ABRUPTLY FRIGHTENED, SHE TURNS AWAY TO STARE ABOUT163 MANSNS
THE GARDEN UNEASILY.)
(STARTS--STARING AT HIM UNEASILY.) 173 MANSNS
DAZEULY AND UNEASILY.) 187 MANSNS
(TRYING TO READ HIS FACE--UNEASILY) 120 MISBEG
(UNEASILY) WHAT ARE YOU TALKING ABOUTS 122 MISBEG
(UNEASILY) WHY DID YOU TELL ME THIS$ 144 MISBEG
IT AND HE REMAINS UNEASILY SILENT. 159 MISBEG
(UNEASILY) STOP TALKING SO QUEER. 160 MISBEG
(CREGAN GLANCES AT HIM UNEASILY. 10 POET
(PREOCCUPIED--UNEASILY.) DON'T COUNT YOUR 31 POET
CHICKENS BEFORE THEY'RE HATCHED.
UNEASILY AND HESITATES. 80 POET
(THEN UNEASILY.) ONLY, LIKE SIMON'S TOLD ME, 80 POET
(GLANCES UNEASILY AT SARA.) IT WAS THAT. 98 POET
(WATCHING HIM UNEASILY, ATTEMPTS A REASONABLE, 122 POET
PERSUASIVE TONE.)
(GLANCES AT MELODY UNEASILY.) 126 POET
(SHE TAKES HOLD OF HER ARM--WHISPERS UNEASILY.) 130 POET
HE GOES ON UNEASILY.) 161 POET
(UNEASILY) IT'S MARY... 587 ROPE
(UNEASILY) HOW COULD HE$ 590 ROPE
(UNEASILY TRYING TO FORCE A CASUAL CONVERSATION) 101 STRANG
(UNEASILY) NO--I DON'T KNOW. 101 STRANG
(THINKING UNEASILY) 102 STRANG
(SUDDENLY MOVING AWAY FROM DARRELL, LOOKING AROUND145 STRANG
HER UNEASILY)
(MOVING UNEASILY) (STOP IT/... 149 STRANG
(CLEARING HIS THROAT UNEASILY) 196 STRANG
(THINKING UNEASILY) (THEY'RE TALKING ABOUT ME...196 STRANG
(UNEASILY) WON'T YOU HAVE A CIGARETTE, JOHNS 450 WELDED
SHE SITS DOWN, THIS TIME FACING HIM, AND LOOKS AT 455 WELDED
HIM UNEASILY.)
(UNEASILY--WITH A FORCED HEARTINESS) 465 WELDED

UNEASINESS.
AND SHE IS OBVIOUSLY ON TENTERHOCKS OF NERVOUS 249 AHWILD
UNEASINESS.
ALL HER FORMER UNEASINESS COMES BACK ON MRS. 253 AHWILD
MILLER TENFOLD.
(A SUDDEN UNEASINESS SEEMS TO STRIKE HIM) 96 BEYOND
(NOTICES ROBERT'S NERVOUS UNEASINESS) 99 BEYOND
AN UNDERCURRENT OF NERVOUS UNEASINESS MANIFESTS 99 BEYOND
ITSELF IN HIS BEARING.)
(IN THE TOO-CASUAL TONES WHICH BETRAY AN INWARD 556 CRUSS
UNEASINESS)
(WITH INCREASING UNEASINESS) 548 DAYS
AND HIDING BENEATH A JOKING MANNER AN UNDERCURRENT525 DIFRNT
OF UNEASINESS)
(WITH A GREAT PRETENSE OF UNEASINESS) 441 DYNAMO
THERE IS AN EXPRESSION OF PUZZLED UNEASINESS ON 462 DYNAMO
HIS FACE
AND THERE IS A NERVOUS UNEASINESS APPARENT IN HIS 468 DYNAMO
WHOLE MANNER.)
HE GRUMBLES IN A LOUD TONE TO COVER UP A GROWING 188 EJONES
UNEASINESS)
(THEN FILLED WITH UNEASINESS AND RESOLVING HE MUST 22 ELECTR
ESTABLISH HIMSELF UN AN
AS IF HE WERE TRYING TO COVER UP SOME HIDDEN 48 ELECTR
UNEASINESS.
(SENSING HER UNEASINESS--MOCKINGLY) 162 ELECTR
(UNEASINESS CREEPING INTO HER TONE) 162 ELECTR
THEY HAVE ALL FORGOTTEN THEIR UNEASINESS ABOUT HIM627 ICEMAN
NOW AND IGNORE HIM.)
WITH FASCINATED RESENTFUL UNEASINESS.) 639 ICEMAN
THEY ARE AGAIN STARING AT HIM WITH BAFFLED 663 ICEMAN
UNEASINESS.
AND STARES AT HOPE WITH GROWING UNEASINESS) 691 ICEMAN
(HE CALLS TO HOPE WITH A FIRST TRACE OF UNDERLYING692 ICEMAN
UNEASINESS)
(THEN AS HE RECEIVES NO REPLY--WITH VAGUE 722 ICEMAN
UNEASINESS)
(THE OTHERS LIKEWISE BETRAY THEIR UNEASINESS, 519 INZONE
SHUFFLING THEIR FEET NERVOUSLY.)
(HE ADDS, UNABLE TO CONCEAL AN ALMOST FURTIVE 36 JOURNE
UNEASINESS.)
(A DEFENSIVE UNEASINESS COMES INTO HER VOICE 45 JOURNE
AGAIN.)
(SHE PAUSES AND A LOOK OF GROWING UNEASINESS COMES176 JOURNE
OVER HER FACE.
CALLING IN A TONE OF REPRESSED UNEASINESS... 108 MANSNS
STARING AT HIM WITH A FASCINATED UNEASINESS. 177 MANSNS
BUT STILL WITH THE LOOK OF PUZZLED UNEASINESS AT 154 POET
HER FATHER.)

UNEASY
MILLER GIVES AN UNEASY GLANCE AT HIS WIFE AND 250 AHWILD
THEN,
SEARCHES HIS FATHER'S EXPRESSIONLESS FACE WITH 293 AHWILD
UNEASY SIDE GLANCES.
CHRIS WANDERS ABOUT THE ROOM, CASTING QUICK, 41 ANNA
UNEASY SIDE GLANCES AT HER FACE,
WITH AN UNEASY SIDE GLANCE AT JAMES MAYO WHO IS 104 BEYOND
STARING AT HIS ELDER SON AS IF
JOHN FROWNS AND GIVES HIS UNCLE A QUICK UNEASY 505 DAYS
GLANCE.)
(AS IF HIS CONVERSATION HAD RUN DRY, HE FALLS INTO529 DAYS
AN UNEASY SILENCE.
(GIVES JOHN A CURIOUS, UNEASY GLANCE) 536 DAYS
BOTH BECOME TERRIBLY NERVOUS, UNEASY. 239 DESIRE
(PUZZLED AND A BIT UNEASY) SAILORS AIN'T PLASTER 495 DIFRNT
SAINTS, EMMER--
HER MANNER NERVOUS AND UNEASY. 501 DIFRNT
(UNEASY--PERSUASIVELY) MERCY, YOU CAN'T ACT LIKE 511 DIFRNT
THAT, EMMER.
(MORE AND MORE UNEASY) THAT'S ALL YOUR QUEER 512 DIFRNT
NOTIONS,

UNEASY

UNEASY (CONT'D.)
(MADE VISIBLY UNEASY BUT FORCING A MANLY TONE) 439 DYNAMO
(MADE UNEASY BY SOMETHING IN HER TONE-- 447 DYNAMO
INSISTENTLY)
BUT ONE SENSES AN UNEASY WARINESS BENEATH HER 16 ELECTR
POSE)
(AGAIN UNEASY--TRYING TO JOKE IT OFF) 23 ELECTR
SHE IS UNEASY UNDERNEATH, BUT AFFECTS A SCORNFUL 29 ELECTR
INDIGNATION.)
(THEY BOTH STARE AT HIM, LAVINIA IN SURPRISE, 48 ELECTR
CHRISTINE IN UNEASY WONDER.
(SUDDENLY UNEASY AGAIN) DON'T KEEP YOUR EYES SHUT 53 ELECTR
LIKE THAT!
WHAT MAKES YOU SO UNEASY$ 58 ELECTR
IT'S SOMETHING UNEASY TROUBLING MY MIND-- 60 ELECTR
ORIN GIVES HIS MOTHER A SIDELONG GLANCE OF UNEASY 83 ELECTR
SUSPICION.
(IMMEDIATELY UNEASY AGAIN) WHAT LIES$ 86 ELECTR
HE LOOKS AROUND HIM QUICKLY WITH AN UNEASY 104 ELECTR
SUSPICIOUS AIR.
(WITH AN UNEASY GLANCE AT THE HOUSE) 130 ELECTR
(WITH AN UNEASY GLANCE AROUND, REACHING FOR THE 133 ELECTR
JUG)
AND IS IMMEDIATELY FRIGHTENED AND UNEASY AND 139 ELECTR
HURRIES TOWARD THE DOOR, CALLING)
HER FACE FULL OF AN UNEASY BEWILDERMENT. 148 ELECTR
UNEASY LOOK ALTHOUGH HER AIR IS DETERMINED.) 158 ELECTR
(MADE MORE UNEASY AND SUSPICIOUS BY THIS) 176 ELECTR
IN SPITE OF HIMSELF, BROWN IS UNEASY. 295 GGBROW
SHE BECOMES UNEASY) 311 GGBROW
(BUT HE STILL STANDS, EMBARRASSED AND UNEASY.) 247 HA APE
(INTERESTED IN SPITE OF HIMSELF AND AT THE SAME 591 ICEMAN
TIME VAGUELY UNEASY.)
(HE TURNS TO LARRY, AND IS REGARDING HIM NOW 593 ICEMAN
FIXEDLY WITH AN UNEASY EXPRESSION
(LARRY GIVES HIM AN UNEASY SUSPICIOUS GLANCE, THEN$596 ICEMAN
LOOKS AWAY,
BUT IMPRESSED AND DISAPPOINTED AND MADE VAGUELY 620 ICEMAN
UNEASY
THEY ARE STARING AT HIM, UNEASY AND BEGINNING TO 621 ICEMAN
FEEL DEFENSIVE.
THEIR EYES ARE FIXED ON HIM WITH UNEASY 622 ICEMAN
RESENTMENT.
(UNEASY AGAIN) WHAT ARE YOU TALKING ABOUT$ 624 ICEMAN
THEY STARE AT HIM WITH PUZZLED UNEASY 625 ICEMAN
FASCINATION.)
THEY ALL STARE AT HIM, THEIR FACES AGAIN PUZZLED, 628 ICEMAN
RESENTFUL AND UNEASY.)
HAS REVERTED TO UNEASY, SUSPICIOUS DEFENSIVENESS.1659 ICEMAN
THEY STARE AT HIM, BITTER, UNEASY AND FASCINATED. 661 ICEMAN
AND IT'S MADE HIM UNEASY ABOUT HIS OWN. 703 ICEMAN
HIS EXPRESSION IS UNEASY, BAFFLED AND RESENTFUL. 703 ICEMAN
THEY ALL RESPOND WITH SMILES THAT ARE STILL A 722 ICEMAN
LITTLE FORCED AND UNEASY.)
(WITH UNEASY INSISTENCE) WHAT'S MATTER, LARRY$ 723 ICEMAN
(SCRATCHING HIS HEAD IN UNEASY PERPLEXITY) 520 INZONE
THE MEN LOOK FROM ONE TO ANOTHER WITH UNEASY 522 INZONE
GLANCES.
REGARDING HER WITH AN UNEASY, PROBING LOOK. 20 JOURNE
(WITH AN AWKWARD, UNEASY TENDERNESS.) 41 JOURNE
(UNEASY NOW--CHANGING THE SUBJECT.) 66 JOURNE
(WITH AN UNEASY GLANCE THROUGH THE FRONT PARLOR.) 88 JOURNE
THEN HE STARES AT HIS FATHER'S FACE WITH UNEASY 90 JOURNE
SUSPICION.)
EDMUND STARES, IMPRESSED AND UNEASY. 165 JOURNE
(PATHETICALLY UNEASY) YOU FRIGHTEN US, MY SON. 278 LAZARU
(STEPS BACK FROM HIM WITH AN UNEASY SHUDDER) 301 LAZARU
(SUDDENLY BECOMING TERRIBLY UNEASY AT SOME 303 LAZARU
THOUGHT)
(TURNING--UNEASY BUT AFRAID TO GIVE ANY DRASTIC 304 LAZARU
ORDER)
(UNEASY, AS IF ALREADY REGRETTING HER CONSENT.) 55 MANSNS
CREDITORS MAY GROW UNEASY. 60 MANSNS
(STARTLED--RESENTFUL AND UNEASY.) 104 MANSNS
I THOUGHT SHE SOUNDED A LITTLE UNEASY. 108 MANSNS
TO MAKE MYSELF UNEASY--AFTER HE'S PROVED SO 119 MANSNS
CONCLUSIVELY--
BUT HE KNOW HE IS VERY UNEASY NOW, NOT SURE OF 127 MANSNS
HIMSELF AT ALL.
(GIVES WAY TO A FLASH OF JEALOUS, UNEASY ANGER.) 134 MANSNS
(CRUELLY SCORNFUL AND AT THE SAME TIME UNEASY.) 187 MANSNS
IN A BOYISH UNEASY WHISPER, TUGGING AT DEBORAH'S 188 MANSNS
HAND.)
PUZZLED AND UNEASY) 77 MISBEG
SHE BENDS TO GIVE HIM AN UNEASY APPRAISING 102 MISBEG
GLANCE.)
GROWING VISIBLY MORE UNEASY. 158 MISBEG
(WITH AN UNEASY GLANCE AT THE DOOR AT LEFT FRONT.) 30 POET
(SHE SEARCHES HIS FACE, UNEASY NOW, FEELING A 105 POET
THREAT HIDDEN BEHIND HIS COLD,
(ABRUPTLY COMES OUT OF HER PREOCCUPATION, STARTLED148 POET
AND UNEASY.)
(GIVES HER FATHER A PUZZLED, UNEASY GLANCE.) 153 POET
(UNEASY, BUT CONSOLING HER MOTHER.) 159 POET
(GROWING MORE UNEASY BUT SNEERING.) 167 POET
(UNEASY UNDER MARSDEN'S EYES) 29 STRANG
(UNEASY UNDER HIS GLANCE) I'LL HATE THAT 79 STRANG
PROFESSIONAL LOOK IN HIS EYES...
DARRELL REMAINS STANDING AND SEEMS TO BE A LITTLE 165 STRANG
UNEASY.)

UNHAPPY
YOU DON'T GET DRUNK AN' HINSULT POOR GELS WOT 'AS 501 VOYAGE
A 'ARD AN' UNHAPPY LIFE.

UNEQUAL
YOU MEAN CHANGE THE UNEQUAL CONDITIONS OF SOCIETY 248 HA APE
BY LEGITIMATE DIRECT ACTION--

UNEVEN
HIS BIG UNEVEN TEETH ARE IN BAD CONDITION. 8 HUGHIE

UNEVEN (CONT'D.)
LONG TABLE WITH AN UNEVEN LINE OF CHAIRS BEHIND 628 ICEMAN
IT, AND CHAIRS AT EACH END.
HEARING THE FOG DRIP FROM THE EAVES LIKE THE 152 JOURNE
UNEVEN TICK OF A RUNDOWN,

UNEXPECTED
(COLDLY PLEASANT.) THIS IS AN UNEXPECTED 96 MANSNS
PLEASURE, SIMON.
IT IS SUCH AN UNEXPECTED SHOCK--TO FIND SARA HERE 176 MANSNS
WHERE SHE NEVER INTRUDES--
TO WHAT DO I OWE THE HONOR OF THIS UNEXPECTED 391 MARCOM
VISIT$
(THEN ASTONISHED AT THIS UNEXPECTED DOCILITY.) 64 POET
THE UNEXPECTED VISION OF MELODY IN HIS UNIFORM 116 POET
STARTLES HIM

UNFAIR
WELL, I NEVER TOOK UNFAIR ADVANTAGE OF YOU IN THE 506 DAYS
OLD DAYS, DID I$
IT'S AN UNFAIR ADVANTAGE, UNCLE. 506 DAYS
HIM THAT SUCH A PRECIPITATE MARRIAGE WOULD BE 10 STRANG
UNFAIR TO NINA.
YOU TOLD HIM IT'D BE UNFAIR, YOU PUT HIM ON HIS 20 STRANG
HONOR, DIDN'T YOU$
HOW UNFAIR TO ME HE SUDDENLY DECIDED IT WOULD BE/ 20 STRANG
UNFAIR TO ME/ 20 STRANG
OH, I SUPPOSE I'M UNFAIR. 186 STRANG
YOU COULDN'T BE UNFAIR TO ANYONE IF YOU TRIED/ 189 STRANG
BUT I KNEW IT WAS UNFAIR, THAT PEOPLE CAN'T HELP 194 STRANG
LOVING EACH OTHER ANY

UNFAIRLY
YOU'RE ACTING FOOLISHLY, NINA--AND VERY UNFAIRLY. 102 STRANG

UNFAITHFUL
THE FIRST TIME I KNEW HE'D BEEN UNFAITHFUL I DID 519 DAYS
THE CORRECT THING
BUT SUPPOSE JOHN WERE UNFAITHFUL TO YOU-- 522 DAYS
WAS UNFAITHFUL TO HER. 536 DAYS
SO, NATURALLY, SHE WAS UNFAITHFUL. 708 ICEMAN
OH, I'LL NEVER BE UNFAITHFUL TO GORDON... 186 STRANG
(DOES HE MEAN THAT SHE WAS UNFAITHFUL TO HIS 186 STRANG
FATHER$...
DO YOU THINK I WAS EVER UNFAITHFUL TO YOUR FATHER.195 STRANG

UNFAMILIAR
(TOUCHED--EMBARRASSED BY THIS UNFAMILIAR EMOTION) 22 ANNA
NOW, HOWEVER, HE IS VENTURING ON UNFAMILIAR GROUND16 POET

UNFASTENING
(UNCERTAINLY) OH--ALL RIGHT--(UNFASTENING DOOR) 300 GGBROW

UNFAVORABLY
HE APPEARS NOT UNFAVORABLY IMPRESSED BUT HIS TONE 10 HUGHIE
STILL HOLDS RESENTMENT.)

UNFEELING
I KNOW THAT SOUNDS HARD AND UNFEELING, BUT WE'RE 295 AHWILD
TALKING FACTS AND--
HOW CAN YOU BE SO UNFEELING$ 75 ELECTR
THE JEST STRIKES HIM AS BEING UNFEELING-- 132 ELECTR

UNFEELINGLY
UNFEELINGLY--EVEN WITH A HARD CYNICISM--OR 97 JOURNE
ENTIRELY IGNORED.
(IT GETS UNDER MY SKIN TO SEE HIM ACT SO 191 STRANG
UNFEELINGLY TOWARD HIS MOTHER/...

UNFIT
QUITE UNFIT FOR LIFE, I THINK. 531 DAYS
(MOCKINGLY) YES, UNFIT TO LIVE. 531 DAYS
HIS VINE IS UNFIT TO DRINK. 658 ICEMAN
PHYSICALLY UNFIT... 14 STRANG

UNFITNESS
AND MY OWN VERY APPARENT UNFITNESS FOR THE JOB, I 123 BEYOND
WAS GOING TO ADD.

UNFLATTERING
(WITH UNFLATTERING ASTONISHMENT) 196 AHWILD
REALLY, SARA, YOUR HUSBAND'S ATTITUDE IS MOST 66 MANSNS
UNFLATTERING.

UNFLINCHINGLY
THEN STIFFENS REALLY AND RETURNS HIS GAZE 387 MARCOM
UNFLINCHINGLY.
SARA IS TERRIFIED BUT SHE STANDS UNFLINCHINGLY.) 172 POET

UNFOLDS
(SHE UNFOLDS IT AND READS) =I'LL HAVE A MILLION T0375 MARCOM
MY CREDIT

UNFORGIVING
BUT THEY REMAIN STARING AS ONE AT HIM, THEIR EYES 131 MANSNS
HARD AND UNFORGIVING.)
I HAVE JUST BEEN REMINDING SIMON THAT HIS FATHER 82 POET
IS RIGIDLY UNFORGIVING

UNFORTUNATE
I SUSPECT YOU ARE STILL HOLDING AGAINST ME MY 90 POET
UNFORTUNATE BLUNDER
POOR UNFORTUNATE BOY/... 70 STRANG

UNFORTUNATELY
BUT, UNFORTUNATELY, ABSOLUTELY MEANINGLESS/ 545 DAYS
I WAS BORN IN THE PURPLE, THE SON, BUT 595 ICEMAN
UNFORTUNATELY NOT THE HEIR.
BUT UNFORTUNATELY HE LEFT ME TO FACE IT. 59 MANSNS
UNFORTUNATELY, THE TENDENCY TO SPOIL THEM IN THE 9 STRANG
UNIVERSITY IS A POOR TRAINING--

UNFRIENDLY
AND THEN MAYBE YOU WON'T BE SO DISTANT AND 240 AHWILD
UNFRIENDLY, EH$
MAYBE YOU DON'T KNOW OR YOU COULDN'T ACT SO 65 MANSNS
UNFRIENDLY TOWARD HER,

UNGOVERNABLE
HE HAS HIMSELF IN HAND AGAIN AND HIS UNGOVERNABLE 128 POET
FURY HAS GONE.

UNGRATEFUL
AND I'M SUCH AN UNGRATEFUL LITTLE SLUT/ 517 DAYS
HELL, I'M NOT THAT UNGRATEFUL/ 621 ICEMAN

GORDON

COME IN.

UNGRATEFUL (CONT*D.)
(WHAT UNGRATEFUL THOUGHTS ON MY SON'S BIRTHDAY/... 138 STRANG
AND AN EXTREMELY UNGRATEFUL PASSION, I MIGHT ADD/ 457 WELDED

UNGUARDEDLY
(UNGUARDEDLY) YEAH. I*D LIKE TO GIVE HIM ONE 670 ICEMAN
SOCK IN DE PUSS--

UNGUENT
OR AN UNGUENT YOU RUB INTO THE SKIN TO REVITALIZE 354 LAZARU
THE OLD BONES AND TISSUES$

UNHALLOWED
MERCY ON THY POOR CLOD, THY CLOD OF UNHALLOWED 319 GGBROW
EARTH, THY CLAY,

UNHAND
CURSE YOU, JACK DALTON, IF I WON*T UNHAND HER, 246 AHWILD
WHAT THENS

UNHAPPINESS
EVEN THOUGH YOU WISH YOUR OWN UNHAPPINESS. 398 MARCOM
I HAVE STUDIED TO CURE THE BODY*S UNHAPPINESS... 86 STRANG
THAT CAUSE SO MUCH HUMAN BLUNDERING AND 88 STRANG
UNHAPPINESS.

UNHAPPY
SHE LOOKS UNHAPPY, TROUBLED, FROWNINGLY 41 ANNA
CONCENTRATED ON HER THOUGHTS.
A FEELING YOU WERE UNHAPPY, IN SOME GREAT 507 DAYS
SPIRITUAL DANGER.
AND, FOR HEAVEN'S SAKE, DON*T GO TELLING ELSA I*M 513 DAYS
UNHAPPY.
EVEN THOUGH I*D STOPPED CARING FOR HIM AND OUR 520 DAYS
MARRIAGE HAD ALWAYS BEEN UNHAPPY.
AND I DIDN*T APPEAR SO TERRIBLY UNHAPPY THEN, DID 529 DAYS
I$

YOU WOULDN*T WANT ME TO KEEP MY PROMISE TO CALEB 511 DIFRNT
IF YOU KNEW I*D BE UNHAPPY,
IT HAS STARTED ALREADY--HIS BEING MADE UNHAPPY 173 ELECTR
THROUGH YOU/
IT'S ONLY WHEN I*M UNHAPPY THAT IT HURTS--AND I*VE309 GGBROW
BEEN SO HAPPY LATELY, DEAR--
IF YOU KNEW HOW UNHAPPY AND UGLY I*VE FELT SINCE 87 MANSNS
YOU STARTED SLEEPING ALONE--
A HOMELESS, UNHAPPY OUTCAST. 110 MANSNS
YOU WILL RUN NO RISK OF ANYTHING WORSE THAN YOUR 111 MANSNS
PRESENT UNHAPPY EXILE.
I KNOW HOW UNHAPPY YOU FELT. 124 MANSNS
(WITH A SIGH) A QUEEN MAY BE ONLY A WOMEN WHO IS 385 MARCOM
UNHAPPY.
IF IT WILL MAKE YOU UNHAPPY, YOU NEED NOT MARRY 386 MARCOM
ARGHUN KHAN.
I FOUND IT WAS THE UNHAPPY ONES 392 MARCOM
BUT I REMEMBER WHEN SHE WAS ALL RIGHT, SHE WAS 59 STRANG
ALWAYS UNHAPPY.
HE'S UNHAPPY NOW BECAUSE HE THINKS HE ISN*T ABLE 84 STRANG
TO GIVE ME A CHILD.
AND I*M UNHAPPY BECAUSE I*VE LOST MY CHILD. 84 STRANG
(GENTLY) I*M SORRY YOU'RE UNHAPPY, NINA. 167 STRANG

UNARMED
AFTER PASSING UNARMED THROUGH THE WHOLE WAR/ 69 ELECTR
HE WAS BURIED FOUR DAYS AND CAME OUT UNHARMED. 302 LAZARU

UNHEALTHY
AND HAVE AN UNHEALTHY FEVERISH GLITTER. 27 MANSNS
BUT HIS FACE IS STILL GOOD-LOOKING DESPITE ITS 37 MISBEG
UNHEALTHY PUFFINESS
DARRELL IS PALE, THIN, NERVOUS, UNHEALTHY LOOKING.124 STRANG

UNHEARD
AND THAT'S PRACTICALLY UNHEARD OF. 23 JOURNE

UNHEEDING
(UNHEEDING) YOU TO BE WHAT YOU ARE, AND ME TO BE 70 ANNA
MAT BURKE,
(UNHEEDING) YE'VE MADE A FOOL O* ME--A SICK, DUMB257 DESIRE
FOOL.
(UNHEEDING--WITH A SUDDEN OMINOUS CALM) 543 DIFRNT
(UNHEEDING--AS IF THE SCENE WERE STILL BEFORE HIS 26 ELECTR
EYES)
(UNHEEDING) SO YOU MUST HELP ME. 72 ELECTR
(UNHEEDING--WITH A SUDDEN TURN TO BITTER RESENTFUL140 ELECTR
DEFIANCE)
(UNHEEDING) AND THEN MY WIFE CAN BE HAPPY/ 311 GGBROW
(UNHEEDING--GROPING IN HIS THOUGHTS) 241 HA APE
(UNHEEDING) AND NOW YOUR APPEARANCE IS OF ONE 353 LAZARU
YOUNGER BY A SCORE.
(UNHEEDING) SHE*D UNDERSTAND AND FORGIVE ME, 151 MISBEG
DON*T YOU THINKS
(UNHEEDING--ADDRESSES SARA.) 53 POET
(UNHEEDING, CLINGING TO HIM) 172 STRANG
(UNHEEDING) AND WHAT MAKES ME HATE YOU AT THOSE 455 WELDED
TIMES IS THAT I KNOW YOU LIKE
(UNHEEDING) MY PLAYS HAD BEEN WRITTEN. 457 WELDED
(UNHEEDING) BUT THERE WAS SCANDAL ENOUGH ABOUT 458 WELDED
YOU AND HIM,

UNHEEDINGLY.
(UNHEEDINGLY.) 257 DESIRE
(UNHEEDINGLY) HE WAS IMMACULATELY CONCEIVED. 372 MARCOM
(GOES ON, UNHEEDINGLY.) SIMON WAS TERRIBLY ANGRY 145 POET
AT HIS FATHER FOR THAT.
(UNHEEDINGLY) IF HE MARRIES HER, IT MEANS HE*LL 169 STRANG
FORGET ME/
(UNHEEDINGLY) YOU MUST KEEP HIM FROM RUINING HIS 169 STRANG
LIFE.

UNHITCH
THEY UNHITCH THEIR WINGS, KATEY, AND SPREADS 'EM 95 BEYOND
OUT ON A WAVE FOR A BED.

UNHITCHIN*
(BEGINNING TO BE ANGRY) WAAL--LET HIM DO HIS OWN 219 DESIRE
UNHITCHIN*/
(LOOKING OFF TOWARD BARN) THAR HE BE--UNHITCHIN*.220 DESIRE

UNHOLY
AND HE GREETED THAT WITH UNHOLY HOWLS OF GLEE 502 DAYS
I AM AFRAID YOUR HOLY POPE IS A MOST UNHOLY CYNIC.379 MARCOM

UNHOLY (CONT*D.)
HOW LONG HAVE YOU AND I BEEN UNITED IN THE UNHOLY 473 WELDED
BONDS OF--BEDLOCKS

UNHURT
MARY, DISCOVERING SHE IS UNHURT, GLANCES QUICKLY 601 ROPE
AROUND AND SEES THE BAG,

UNICELLULAR
SENSIBLE UNICELLULAR LIFE THAT FLOATS IN THE SEA 198 STRANG

UNIFORM
HE IS DRESSED IN THE SIMPLE BLUE UNIFORM AND CAP 130 BEYOND
OF A MERCHANT SHIP*S OFFICER.)
HE WEARS A UNIFORM SIMILAR TO ANDREW*S. 140 BEYOND
HE IS A TALL, STRONGLY-BUILT MAN DRESSED IN A 472 CARIBE
PLAIN BLUE UNIFORM.)
HE IS DRESSED IN THE KHAKI UNIFORM OF A PRIVATE INS19 DIFRNT
THE UNITED STATES ARMY.
HE WEARS A LIGHT BLUE UNIFORM COAT, SPRAYED WITH 175 EJONES
BRASS BUTTONS,
HIS FACE IS SCRATCHED, HIS BRILLIANT UNIFORM SHOWS191 EJONES
SEVERAL LARGE RENTS)
IS DRESSED IN A PULLMAN PORTER*S UNIFORM AND CAP. 191 EJONES
HIS UNIFORM IS RAGGED AND TORN. 192 EJONES
THEY ARE FOLLOWED BY A WHITE MAN DRESSED IN THE 194 EJONES
UNIFORM OF A PRISON GUARD.
HE WEARS THE UNIFORM OF AN ARTILLERY CAPTAIN IN 13 ELECTR
THE UNION ARMY.)
HE WAS HANDSOME IN HIS LIEUTENANT*S UNIFORM/ 31 ELECTR
DRESSED IN THE UNIFORM OF A BRIGADIER-GENERAL. 46 ELECTR
HE IS DRESSED IN A BAGGY, ILL-FITTING UNIFORM-- 74 ELECTR
IN THE UNIFORM OF AN OFFICER IN WASHINGTON*S ARMY. 79 ELECTR
HIS BODY, DRESSED IN FULL UNIFORM. 93 ELECTR
HE IS DRESSED IN A MERCHANT CAPTAIN*S BLUE 104 ELECTR
UNIFORM.
HE WEARS A LONG CLOAK OVER HIS UNIFORM 109 ELECTR
THINK WE HAD A GOON IN UNIFORM TO OPEN DOORS$ 247 HA APE
OR SOME GUYS IN UNIFORM WILL WALK IN HERE WITH A 33 HUGHIE
BUTTERFLY NET AND CATCH YOU.
IT'S A WONDER HE DIDN*T BORROW A SALVATION ARMY 617 ICEMAN
UNIFORM AND SHOW UP IN THAT/
BEJEES, I*LL HAVE HIM BACK IN UNIFORM POUNDING A 718 ICEMAN
BEAT
HE WEARS OVER HIS MAYOR*S UNIFORM THE REGALIA OF 388 MARCOM
COCK OF PARADISE
OVER HIS GORGEOUS UNIFORM OF MAYOR, 390 MARCOM
WEARING THE SELF-ASSURANCE OF AN IMMORTAL SOUL AND401 MARCOM
HIS NEW ADMIRAL*S UNIFORM/
TO A DEAFENING CLANGOR, MARCO ENTERS, DRESSED IN A402 MARCOM
GORGEOUS ADMIRAL*S UNIFORM.
HE IS DRESSED IN FULL UNIFORM, LOOKING SPICK AND 410 MARCOM
SPAN AND SELF-CONSCIOUS.
DRESSED IN THE FULL MILITARY UNIFORM AND ARMOR OF 421 MARCOM
THE COMMANDER-IN-CHIEF IS
IN A GORGEOUS UNIFORM ENTERS AND STANDS AT 427 MARCOM
ATTENTION AS THE PROCESSION BEGINS.
HE WAS AS STRONG AS AN OX, AND ON A THOROUGHBRED 13 POET
HORSE, IN HIS UNIFORM,
I*LL GET YOUR UNIFORM FROM THE TRUNK, 39 POET
AND YOU*LL WEAR YOUR BEAUTIFUL UNIFORM, 59 POET
I*LL EVEN HELP YOU GET HIS UNIFORM OUT OF THE 64 POET
TRUNK IN THE ATTIC
AND HE*LL GET YOUR FATHER*S UNIFORM OUT OF THE 66 POET
TRUNK.
SARA AND I HAVE YOUR UNIFORM BRUSHED AND LAID OUT 75 POET
ON THE BED.
HE*LL BE ON HIS BEST BEHAVIOR NOW, AND HE*LL FEEL 76 POET
PROUD AGAIN IN HIS UNIFORM.
I GOT HIM TO GO UP AND PUT ON HIS UNIFORM. 77 POET
THANK GOD, IF HE*S PUTTING ON HIS UNIFORM, HE*LL 80 POET
BE HOURS BEFORE THE MIRROR,
BUT I*D LIKE HER TO SEE HIM IN HIS UNIFORM, AT 80 POET
THAT. IF HE WAS SOBER--
HIS OLD UNIFORM OF THE FRENCH REPUBLICAN NATIONAL 83 POET
GUARD.
THE UNIFORM HAS BEEN PRESERVED WITH THE GREATEST 88 POET
CARE.
WEARING THE BRILLIANT SCARLET FULL-DRESS UNIFORM 88 POET
OF A MAJOR
OF THE MAN I WAS WHEN I WORE THIS UNIFORM WITH 89 POET
HONOR.
MY UNIFORM SO INVITINGLY THAT I COULD NOT RESIST 89 POET
THE TEMPTATION TO PUT IT ON
BY TRYING TO FASCINATE HER WITH YOUR BEAUTIFUL 91 POET
UNIFORM.
(ADMIRINGLY.) BE GOD, IT'S THE OLD UNIFORM, NO 92 POET
LESS.
IN HIS BRILLIANT UNIFORM HE PRESENTS MORE THAN 95 POET
EVER AN IMPRESSIVELY COLORFUL
THE UNEXPECTED VISION OF MELODY IN HIS UNIFORM 116 POET
STARTLES HIM
A WORD OF EXPLANATION AS TO WHY YOU FIND ME IN 119 POET
UNIFORM.
HIS SCARLET UNIFORM IS FILTHY AND TORN AND PULLED 152 POET
AWRY.
I THINK THE BOYS IS RIGHT WHEN THEY SAY HE STOLE 170 POET
THE UNIFORM
IN HIS TORN, DISHEVELED, DIRT-STAINED UNIFORM, 175 POET
SHE IS DRESSED IN A NURSE*S UNIFORM WITH CAP, A 26 STRANG
RAGLAN COAT OVER IT.

UNIFORMED
MULTITUDE OF YOUNG STAFF OFFICERS, ALL GORGEOUSLY 421 MARCOM
UNIFORMED AND ARMORED.

UNIFORMS
BOTH ARE DRESSED IN SIMPLE BLUE UNIFORMS.) 484 CARDIF
AND I RECKON NOW THAT IF YOU PUT A COWARD IN ONE 540 DIFRNT
OF THEM THERE UNIFORMS,
IN THEIR DOUBLE MASKS AND GORGEOUS UNIFORMS AND 326 LAZAHU
ARMOR.

UNIFORMS

UNIFORMS (CONT'D.)
A SQUAD OF THE GUARD IN THE SAME UNIFORMS AS THE CHORUS, 326 LAZARU
UNIFORMS OF OUR MODERN KNIGHTS TEMPLAR, OF 390 MARCOM
COLUMBUS, OF PYTHIAS,
SIX IN NUMBER, IN BRILLIANT UNIFORMS) 428 MARCOM
UNIMAGINATIVE
AT THE SAME TIME, ALTHOUGH ENTIRELY AN 184 STRANG
UNIMAGINATIVE CODE-BOUND GENTLEMAN OF HIS
UNIMPORTANT
THAT THERE IS NO TRUTH FOR MEN, THAT HUMAN LIFE IS535 DAYS
UNIMPORTANT AND MEANINGLESS.
MEN ARE ALSO UNIMPORTANT/ 359 LAZARU
BUT I DON'T HESITATE TO STATE THAT ALL THIS 431 MARCOM
ACTIVITY IS RELATIVELY UNIMPORTANT
WITH HIS INCORRUPTIBLE REDEEMER, BUT HE WAS TOO 83 POET
UNIMPORTANT.
UNIMPRESSED
(UNIMPRESSED--WITH A CYNICAL SHRUG OF HER 243 AHWILD
SHOULDERS)
(UNIMPRESSED--SUPERCILIOUSLY) 219 HA APE
UNINFORMATIVE
THAT WALDO EMERSON COMPOSED IT DURING HIS 596 ICEMAN
UNINFORMATIVE PERIOD AS A MINISTER,
UNINTELLIGENT
SHE IS A THIN, PALE-FACED, UNINTELLIGENT-LOOKING 112 BEYOND
WOMAN OF ABOUT FORTY-EIGHT,
UNINTENTIONALLY
UNINTENTIONALLY BURLESQUING GRANDEUR) 301 LAZARU
UNINTERESTED
(WITH A COMPLIANT, UNINTERESTED SMILE.) 10 HUGHIE
UNINTERRUPTEDLY
AND CONTINUES AT A GRADUALLY ACCELERATING RATE 184 EJONES
FROM THIS POINT UNINTERRUPTEDLY
UNION
RED SISK--HIS FATHER KEPT A BLACKSMITH SHOP WHERE 229 AHWILD
THE UNION MARKET IS NOW--
APRONS, THE BUTTON OF THE UNION PINNED 4 ANNA
CONSPICUOUSLY ON THE CAPS
WITH A CURSE BY NIETZSCHE TO BLESS THE UNION. 502 DAYS
WOULD FIND THE COMPLETEST SELF-EXPRESSION IN 524 DAYS
MAKING OUR UNION A BEAUTIFUL THING.
HE WEARS THE UNIFORM OF AN ARTILLERY CAPTAIN IN 13 ELECTR
THE UNION ARMY.)
THAT OF A FIRST LIEUTENANT OF INFANTRY IN THE 74 ELECTR
UNION ARMY.)
THEN YOU CAN TAKE THE UNION CASTLE FROM 605 ICEMAN
SOUTHAMPTON TO CAPE TOWN.
YOU AND CHUCK OUGHT TO HAVE CARDS IN THE BURGLARS'722 ICEMAN
UNION/
HE WISHES MASSACHUSETTS WOULD SECEDE FROM THE 8 MANSNS
UNION.
OH, I'VE BEEN CONSIDERING JOINING THEIR UNION. 42 MISBEG
AND GOD KNOWS I KNOW THE SORDID TRAGEDY OF SUCH A 113 POET
UNION.
UNIQUE
TO SAY THE THING ONE HAS ALWAYS KEPT HIDDEN, TO 354 LAZARU
REVEAL ONE'S UNIQUE TRUTH--
WITH DEEP REGRET FOR THE LOSS OF YOUR UNIQUE AND 393 MARCOM
EXTRAORDINARY SERVICES.
(HOW PERFECTLY THE PROFESSOR'S UNIQUE 4 STRANG
HAVEN/....)
UNISON
AND CLAP THEIR HANDS IN UNISON. 250 DESIRE
UNISON AS IF THEY WERE LAXLY LETTING THEMSELVES 199 EJONES
FOLLOW THE LONG ROLL OF A SHIP
THE OTHERS DO LIKEWISE WITH AS MUCH UNISON AS 224 HA APE
THEIR WEARIED BODIES WILL PERMIT.
(CHANTING IN UNISON) LAUGH/ 311 LAZARU
EVERY MOVEMENT BEING CARRIED OUT IN UNISON WITH A 407 MARCOM
MACHINE-LIKE RHYTHM.
THEY CARRY SILVER CENSERS WHICH THEY SWING IN 433 MARCOM
UNISON TOWARD THE CORPSE OF THE
UNIT
HARD-EARNED PROSPERITY, ENJOYED AND MAINTAINED BY 94 BEYOND
THE FAMILY AS A UNIT.
UNITE
WHY SHOULDN'T THE WORKERS OF THE WORLD UNITE AND 195 AHWILD
RISE!
BROTHERS--LISTEN--WE MUST UNITE--IN ONE CAUSE-- 286 LAZARU
TO--STAMP OUT--THIS ABOMINATION/
THEY UNITE AGAINST THE INVADER-- 129 MANSNS
IT IS ONLY WHEN YOU UNITE TO DISPOSSESS ME 131 MANSNS
UNITED
HE IS DRESSED IN THE KHAKI UNIFORM OF A PRIVATE INS19 DIFRNT
THE UNITED STATES ARMY.
AND STAMPED UPON THE GLORIOUS CONSTITUTION OF 243 HA APE
THESE UNITED STATES/
UNITED BENEATH THE FLAG ON WHICH THE SUN NEVER 599 ICEMAN
SETS.
HAS PRESIDENT JACKSON'S FEUD WITH THE BANK OF THE 29 MANSNS
UNITED STATES
DISCIPLINE MY WILL TO KEEP MYSELF UNITED--ANOTHER 74 MANSNS
SELF REBELS--SECEDES--
THAT WE WERE ONE, UNITED AGAINST--& 105 MANSNS
WE COULD HAVE THE STRENGTH NOW AS WE ARE UNITED 171 MANSNS
AGAIN AS ONE WOMAN.
OF A SENATOR FROM THE SOUTH OF THE UNITED STATES 390 MARCOM
OF AMERICA
THE GUESTS GIVE A NEW UNITED GASP OF ASTONISHMENT)428 MARCOM
IN THE WHOLE UNITED KINGDOM, WITH MY STABLE OF 49 POET
HUNTERS, AND--
HOW LONG HAVE YOU AND I BEEN UNITED IN THE UNHOLY 473 WELDED
BONDS OF--BEDLOCKS
UNITY
A CONFUSED, INCHOATE UPROAR SWELLING INTO A SORT 207 HA APE
OF UNITY, A MEANING---

UNITY (CONT'D.)
I BELONGED, WITHOUT PAST OR FUTURE, WITHIN PEACE 153 JOURNE
AND UNITY AND A WILD JOY.
SOMETIMES I BECOME SO INTENSELY CONSCIOUS OF YOUR 82 MANSNS
UNITY
I THOUGHT THAT YOU BOTH LIVED IN A PERFECT UNITY 82 MANSNS
OF INTERESTS AND DESIRES NOW.
IT REVEALS A BEGINNING IN UNITY THAT I MAY HAVE 488 WELDED
FAITH IN THE UNITY OF THE END/
UNIVERSAL
I LISTEN TO PEOPLE TALKING ABOUT THIS UNIVERSAL 542 DAYS
BREAKDOWN WE ARE IN AND I MARVEL
UNIVERSAL SLOGAN, KEEP MOVING... 122 STRANG
UNIVERSE
ONE OTHER UNIVERSE AMONG INNUMERABLE OTHERS. 41 STRANG
UNIVERSITY
AT THE IVY UNIVERSITY TO WHICH HIS FATHER HAD 55 MISBEG
GIVEN MILLIONS.
THE LIBRARY OF PROFESSOR LEEDS' HOME IN A SMALL 3 STRANG
UNIVERSITY TOWN IN NEW ENGLAND.
UNFORTUNATELY, THE TENDENCY TO SPOIL THEM IN THE 9 STRANG
UNIVERSITY IS A POOR TRAINING--
TWO YEARS IN THE UNIVERSITY, I AM SORRY TO SAY, 17 STRANG
UNJUST
CHRISTINE--I DEEPLY REGRET--HAVING BEEN UNJUST THE 52 ELECTR
KISSES HER HAND IMPULSIVELY--
WHY ARE YOU BOTH SO UNJUSTS 387 MARCOM
SAME OLD UNJUST ACCUSATION/ 79 STRANG
(THEN CONTRITELY) I (OH, I'M UNJUST... 93 STRANG
UNJUSTICE
PERSON AND THE EVIL AND UNJUSTICE OF MAN WAS BORN/295 GGBROW
UNKEMPT
HIS HAIR IS LONG AND UNKEMPT, HIS FACE AND BODY 145 BEYOND
EMACIATED.
A WIDE THIN-LIPPED MOUTH SHADOWED BY AN UNKEMPT 556 CROSS
BRISTLE OF MUSTACHE.
UNKEMPT BLACK BEARD AND MUSTACHE. 102 ELECTR
UNKIND
I DIDN'T MEAN IT IN AN UNKIND WAY. 94 ELECTR
UNKINDLY
(NOT UNKINDLY) NOT YOU, LITTLE KILLER/ 321 LAZARU
UNKNOWABLE
HIS KNOWLEDGE VENERATES THE UNKNOWABLE. 401 MARCOM
UNKNOWN
THE BEAUTY OF THE FAR OFF AND UNKNOWN. 85 BEYOND
IT WAS THE UNKNOWN-- 537 DAYS
SAID, THERE WAS THE UNKNOWN TO RECKON WITH. 538 DAYS
PERHAPS HE NEEDS ME HERE--UNKNOWN, 287 GGBROW
BY THE TERRIFIC IMPACT OF THIS UNKNOWN, ABYSMAL, 225 HA APE
BRUTALITY, NAKED AND SHAMELESS.
HE FEELS HIMSELF INSULTED IN SOME UNKNOWN FASHION 226 HA APE
WHAT BETTER DISGUISE IF HE WISHES TO REMAIN 300 LAZARU
UNKNOWNS
KNOWN AND UNKNOWN/ 344 LAZARU
I HATE THAT UNKNOWN POWER IN YOU WHICH WOULD 453 WELDED
DESTROY ME.
UNLACE
AND, SITTING DOWN IN HIS CHAIR, BEGINS TO UNLACE 298 AHWILD
HIS SHOES)
UNLACES
THE UNLACES THEM AND PULLS THEM OFF-- 196 EJONES
UNLACING
(LAUGHING) WHY DO YOU BOTHER UNLACING YOUR SHOES 298 AHWILD
NOW, YOU BIG GOOSE--
UNLAWFULLY
FOR YOU'LL BE SHIELDING ME UNLAWFULLY BY KEEPING 441 DYNAMO
SILENCE.
UNLEARN
AND ONCE YOU'VE LEARNED A LESSON, IT'S HARD TO 148 JOURNE
UNLEARN IT.
UNLIKE
HIS NOSE IS UNLIKE THAT OF ANY OTHER MEMBER OF THE 19 JOURNE
FAMILY,
UNLINED
BUT HER FACE IS UNLINED AND STILL PRETTY IN A 427 MARCOM
BOVINE, GOOD-NATURED WAY.
UNLOADED
THE SHIP IS UNLOADED AND HER BLACK SIDE RISES NINE102 ELECTR
OR TEN FEET
UNLOADIN'
AND YOU KNOW DURNED WELL HE WAS ONLY IN THE 541 DIFRNT
QUARTERMASTER'S DEPARTMENT UNLOADIN'
UNLOADING
ENGINES OF SOME SHIP UNLOADING NEARBY. 41 ANNA
UNLOADS
THE FOURTH A BANG ON THE GONG AS ONE SLAVE AT EACH400 MARCOM
END LOADS AND UNLOADS.
UNLOCKED
(AS SHE SAYS THIS LAST THE CABIN DOOR IS SILENTLY 18 MANSNS
UNLOCKED AND OPENED AND SARA
UNLOCKING
UNTIL HE FINALLY TRICKS ME INTO UNLOCKING THE 163 MANSNS
DOOR, TAKING HIS HAND--
UNLOCKS
(SETH PRIES OFF THE BOARD DOOR AND UNLOCKS THE 132 ELECTR
INNER DOOR.)
THEN HE UNLOCKS THE DOOR AND COMES BACK TO HIS 149 ELECTR
CHAIR AS LAVINIA ENTERS.
ORIN UNLOCKS THE TABLE DRAWER, PULLS OUT HIS 156 ELECTR
MANUSCRIPT, AND TAKES UP HIS PEN.)
HE COMES QUICKLY TO THE OTHER DOOR AND UNLOCKS 314 GGBROW
IT.)
HE TAKES OUT A SMALL BUNCH OF KEYS AND UNLOCKS THES13 INZONE
SUITCASE.
SHE HASTILY UNLOCKS THE DOOR OF THE CABIN AND 2 MANSNS
CHANGES THE KEY TO THE INSIDE.
NECK--HESITATES FRIGHTENEDLY--THEN UNLOCKS, BUT 164 MANSNS
DOES NOT OPEN THE DOOR.)

1735

UNREMITTING

UNLOCKS (CONT'D.)
HE UNLOCKS THE BARROOM DOOR.) 165 POET

UNLOVED
TO BE UNLOVED BY LIFE/ 296 GGBROW

UNLUCKY
THIS INN, LIKE MYSELF, HAS FALLEN UPON UNLUCKY 69 POET
DAYS.
POOR UNLUCKY DEVIL...)) 82 STRANG
YOU WERE BORN UNLUCKY/ 194 STRANG

UNMARKED
BUT HER FACE IS STILL UNMARKED AND FRESH, HER CALM284 GGBROW
MORE PROFOUND.
(HARDER IS IN HIS LATE THIRTIES BUT LOOKS YOUNGER 55 MISBEG
BECAUSE HIS FACE IS UNMARKED

UNMARRIED
I DID WITH HIM UNMARRIED, 138 POET

UNMASKED
HER UPTURNED UNMASKED FACE LIKE THAT OF A 264 GGBROW
RAPTUROUS VISIONARY.

UNMINDFUL
UNMINDFUL OF THEIR NOISELESS APPROACH, SUDDENLY 194 EJONES
LOOKS DOWN AND SEES THEM.
BUT THE TWO MEN REMAIN UNMINDFUL OF HER PRESENCE. 342 LAZARU

UNMISTAKABLE
THANK GOD, I STILL BEAR THE UNMISTAKABLE STAMP OF 43 POET
AN OFFICER AND A GENTLEMAN.
(HOLDING OUT HIS HAND--WITH UNMISTAKABLE LIKING) 7 STRANG

UNMISTAKABLY
THE STAMP OF HIS PROFESSION IS UNMISTAKABLY ON 13 JOURNE
HIM.
IT IS UNMISTAKABLY HOGAN'S VOICE 71 MISBEG

UNMIXED
(WITH DROWSY CYNICISM--NOT UNMIXED WITH BITTERNESS272 AHWILD
AT THE END)

UNMORAL
IT'S UNMORAL/ 281 GGBROW

UNMOVED
(UNMOVED) THAT'S EVERYBODY'S AFFAIR, WHAT I SAID.468 CARIBE
HE HARDENS HIMSELF, HE REMAINS UNMOVED AND COLD. 259 DESIRE
CHRISTINE IS PREPARED AND REMAINS UNMOVED 50 ELECTR
SHE IS LIKE AN UNMOVED IDOL OF MOTHER EARTH. 284 GGBROW
SHE STARES AHEAD UNMOVED AS IF SHE HADN'T HEARD. 289 GGBROW
BUT THE GENTLEMAN STANDS UNMOVED AS IF NOTHING HAD239 HA APE
HAPPENED.)
BUT HICKEY HAS REMAINED UNMOVED BY ALL THIS 662 ICEMAN
TAUNTING.
(SEEMINGLY UNMOVED BY THIS TAUNT--CALMLY.) 106 POET
(AS SHE CONTINUES TO LOOK AT HIM WITH UNMOVED 103 STRANG
DETERMINATION--PLEADINGLY)

UNMYSTERIOUS
COMMONPLACE AND UNMYSTERIOUS AS A ROOM COULD WELL 245 HA APE
BE.

UNNATURAL
AND SITS IN A SELF-CONSCIOUS, UNNATURAL POSITION. 293 AHWILD
ONLY THIS TIME IT SOUNDED--UNNATURAL, DON'T YOU 163 BEYOND
THINK
YOU UNNATURAL ACCURSED SON/ 465 DYNAMO
HE IS TALKING WITH UNNATURAL EXCITEMENT AS THEY 476 DYNAMO
COME IN.
(WITH A SUDDEN RENEWAL OF HIS UNNATURAL 477 DYNAMO
EXCITEMENT, BREAKS AWAY FROM HER)
(THINKING WITH UNNATURAL EXCITEMENT) 480 DYNAMO
HIS UNNATURAL EXCITEMENT HAS INCREASED, 482 DYNAMO
THAT INDICATES A SOLDIERLY BEARING IS UNNATURAL TO 74 ELECTR
HIM.
(KISSING HER--WITH UNNATURAL EFFUSIVENESS) 117 ELECTR
(WITH UNNATURAL CASUALNESS) GONE HOME. 167 ELECTR
(STARTS AND AT ONCE THE QUALITY OF UNNATURAL 67 JOURNE
DETACHMENT SETTLES ON HER FACE
MARY IS PALER THAN BEFORE AND HER EYES SHINE WITH 97 JOURNE
UNNATURAL BRILLIANCE.
YOU ARE AN UNNATURAL DAUGHTER/ 284 LAZARU
(CONTINUING) --BUT I HAVE NEVER NOTED ANY 425 MARCOM
UNNATURAL CHANGE IN THEM EXCEPT TOWARD
THAT MAKES LIFE SO PERVERTED, AND DEATH SO 42 STRANG
UNNATURAL.
SOMETHING HUMAN AND UNNATURAL IN THIS ROOM/.... 100 STRANG
(SUDDENLY WITH A STRANGE UNNATURAL ELATION-- 133 STRANG
SSSHHH--LISTEN--SOMEONE--(SHE SPEAKS IN AN 449 WELDED
UNNATURAL, MECHANICAL TONE.
(STUNG--BITINGLY) IT'S AN UNNATURAL PASSION 457 WELDED
CERTAINLY--IN YOUR CASE.
WITH AN UNNATURAL PREOCCUPIED CONCENTRATION.) 471 WELDED
THE STARES AT HER WITH UNNATURAL INTENSITY) 473 WELDED

UNNATURALLY
(SHE PAUSES, STARING BEFORE HER WITH UNNATURALLY 105 JOURNE
BRIGHT, DREAMY EYES.
HER MANNER IS UNNATURALLY EFFUSIVE. 108 JOURNE
OR RATHER I SHOULD SAY, UNNATURALLY/ 314 LAZARU

UNNECESSARILY
(RAISING HER VOICE UNNECESSARILY.) 123 JOURNE
FIDDLES AROUND UNNECESSARILY GATHERING UP HER 137 MANSNS
SEWING THINGS.

UNNESHESSARY
UNNESHESSARY INFORMATION NUMBER ONE, EHS 155 JOURNE

UNNOTICED
(WHILE SHE IS TALKING, UNNOTICED BY THEM BOTH, 171 MANSNS
SIMON APPEARS BEHIND THEM,
(WHILE THEY HAVE BEEN SPEAKING, UNNOTICED BY THEM,352 MARCOM
IT HAS GROWN DARK.

UNOBTRUSIVELY
(LOOKING AT HER MEANINGLY) MY LIFE WORK IS TO 140 STRANG
RUST--NICELY AND UNOBTRUSIVELY/

UNOCCUPIED
SHOWING THAT THE HOUSE IS UNOCCUPIED. 129 ELECTR
THE OTHER TWO CHAIRS BEING UNOCCUPIED. 576 ICEMAN
THE OTHER CHAIRS AT THIS TABLE ARE UNOCCUPIED. 95 POET

UNPAID
DEBTS TO THIS ONE AND THAT, TAXES, INTEREST 148 BEYOND
UNPAID/
YOU WERE NEVER INTENDED FOR THE JOB OF SAHA'S 105 MANSNS
UNPAID NURSEMAID.

UNPAINTED
THERE IS A DOOR WITH A FLIGHT OF THREE UNPAINTED 1 MISBEG
STEPS LEADING TO THE GROUND.
AND THAT IS ALL EXCEPT THAT THE WALLS ARE 107 MISBEG
UNPAINTED PINE BOARDS.

UNPARDONABLE
AN UNPARDONABLE SLIGHT, ESPECIALLY AS I AM THE 594 ICEMAN
ONLY INMATE OF ROYAL BLOOD.
THAT WAS UNPARDONABLE. 37 POET

UNPATRIOTIC
HOW COULD WE CONSIDER SUCH AN UNPATRIOTIC IDEA AS 543 DAYS
ANYTHING BUT INSANE, EHS
(HE LAUGHS SARDONICALLY) HOW COULD WE CONSIDER 543 DAYS
SUCH AN UNPATRIOTIC IDEA AS

UNPERTURBABLY
(UNPERTURBABLY--SQUATTING DOWN HIMSELF) 203 EJONES

UNPERTURBED
(UNPERTURBED) SHE DIDN'T MEAN IT. 606 ICEMAN

UNPINNING
AND BEGINS UNPINNING IT FROM THE BOARD--MOCKINGLY)317 GGBROW

UNPINS
UNPINS IT AND HANDS IT TO HER WITHOUT A WORD. 419 MARCOM

UNPLACATED
(UNPLACATED) I'VE BEEN COUNTIN' SURE ON HAVIN' 103 BEYOND
ROBERT FOR COMPANY ON THIS VIGE-

UNPLEASANT
WITH THE AIR OF ONE WHO DETERMINEDLY FACES THE 264 AHWILD
UNPLEASANT)
BUT HIS PERSONALITY IS UNPLEASANT. 585 ICEMAN
HE DOESN'T SEEM ABLE TO AVOID UNPLEASANT TOPICS, DO 137 JOURNE
WE$
THIS IS TAKEN UP BY THE CROWD-- UNPLEASANT, 300 LAZARU
RESENTFUL LAUGHTER.
A NOT UNPLEASANT MAN, AFFABLE, GOOD-LOOKING IN AN 55 MISBEG
ORDINARY
PEOPLE WHO ARE AFRAID TO FACE UNPLEASANT 77 STRANG
POSSIBILITIES UNTIL IT'S TOO LATE

UNPRECEDENTED
FOR THE FISCAL YEAR, AND I KNEW YOU'D BE SO 391 MARCOM
ASTONISHED AT THE UNPRECEDENTED AMOU

UNPREPARED
(TOTALLY UNPREPARED FOR THIS APPROACH-- 293 AHWILD
SHAMEFACEDLY MUTTERS)

UNPRETENTIOUS
HE IS BY NATURE AND PREFERENCE A SIMPLE 13 JOURNE
UNPRETENTIOUS MAN,

UNPRONOUNCEABLE
YOUR PET WITH THE UNPRONOUNCEABLE NAME, FOR 77 JOURNE
EXAMPLE.

UNPROTECTED
HELPLESSLY UNPROTECTED IN ITS CHILDLIKE, RELIGIOUS260 GGBROW
FAITH IN LIFE--

UNPUNISHED
BUT I'D RATHER SUFFER THAT THAN LET THE MURDER OF 97 ELECTR
OUR FATHER GO UNPUNISHED/

UNQUESTIONABLE
SERENELY UNQUESTIONABLE. 488 WELDED

UNQUESTIONED
I, MAFFEO POLO, WHOSE CONSERVATISM IS 381 MARCOM
UNQUESTIONED/

UNQUESTIONING
THE QUALITY OF UNQUESTIONING FAITH IN THE FINALITY294 GGBROW
OF ITS ACHIEVEMENT.
A SECOND'S UNQUESTIONING ACCEPTANCE OF ONESELF, 28 MANSNS

UNQUESTIONINGLY
UNQUESTIONINGLY, AS THOUGH YOU WERE THE MEANEST 153 MANSNS
WORKER IN MY MILLS.

UNREAL
UNDER ITS LIGHT THE ROAD GLIMMERS GHASTLY AND 192 EJONES
UNREAL.
THERE IS SOMETHING STIFF, RIGID, UNREAL, 196 EJONES
MARIONETTISH ABOUT THEIR MOVEMENTS.
GIVING IT AN UNREAL, DETACHED, EERIE QUALITY. 43 ELECTR
EVERYTHING LOOKED AND SOUNDED UNREAL. 131 JOURNE
SO BEAUTIFUL AND SO UNREAL. 109 MANSNS
UNREAL, A GHOST INHUMANLY REMOVED FROM LIVING, 125 MANSNS
BUT IN THE PRESENT STATE OF HER MIND THE REAL AND 11 STRANG
THE UNREAL BECOME CONFUSED--
THERE WAS SOMETHING UNREAL IN ALL THAT HAS 199 STRANG
HAPPENED SINCE YOU FIRST MET GORDON

UNREASONABLE
AND I CAN THROW HIM A LINE OF BULL THAT'LL KID HIM609 ICEMAN
I WON'T BE SO UNREASONABLE
DRISCOLL FLIES INTO AN UNREASONABLE RAGE) 517 INZONE
IT'S UNREASONABLE TO EXPECT BRIDGET OR CATHLEEN TO 72 JOURNE
ACT AS IF THIS WAS A HOME.
CURE HER MIND OF ANY UNREASONABLE IMAGININGS. 405 MARCOM
(WORRIEDLY) PLEASE DON'T BE UNREASONABLE. 412 MARCOM

UNREASONABLY
AND IT EMBITTERS ME TO SEE OTHERS UNREASONABLY 389 MARCOM
HAPPY SO--
IT SEEMS TO ME YOU'RE COMPLAINING UNREASONABLY/ 131 STRANG
BUT I CAN'T HELP REMEMBERING HOW UNREASONABLY 185 STRANG
SHE'S ACTED ABOUT OUR ENGAGEMENT.

UNREGENERATE
HAVE YOU NO RESPECT FOR RELIGION, YOU UNREGENERATE578 ICEMAN
WOPS

UNRELIEVED
AND PUTS UNRELIEVED PRESSURE ON HIMSELF. 43 MANSNS

UNREMITTING
I WISH TO COMMEND THE UNREMITTING ATTENTION TO HIS424 MARCOM
DUTY OF ADMIRAL POLO.

UNREMITTINGLY

UNREMITTINGLY
MILLIONS OF CONTENTED SLAVES LABOR UNREMITTINGLY 431 MARCOM
MILLIONS OF HOURS PER ANNUM
UNRESIGNED
THEIR FACES HAVE A COMPRESSED, UNRESIGNED 204 DESIRE
EXPRESSION.
UNRESTRAINED
THE FAD ELDER AS NATURALLY UNRESTRAINED AS BEASTS 206 DESIRE
OF THE FIELD,
UNRESTRAINEDLY
(SHE SOBS UNRESTRAINEDLY.) 264 DESIRE
UNROLLING
(UNROLLING HIS PLAN) IT'S YOUR PLAN. 306 GGBROW
UNRUFFLED
BRILLIANT AND UNRUFFLED IN THE MOONLIGHT, 199 EJONES
UNRUFFLEDLY
(WITH SATISFACTION--UNRUFFLEDLY) 77 STRANG
(UNRUFFLEDLY-- 173 STRANG
UNRULY
(DESPERATELY PUTTING ON HIS PRIM SEVERE MANNER 15 STRANG
TOWARD AN UNRULY PUPIL)
UNSATISFYING
(SITS AT HIS DESK AGAIN, LOOKING AHEAD IN A NOT 277 GGBROW
UNSATISFYING MELANCHOLY REVERIE.
UNSCARRED
YET YOU SIT HERE, CALM AND BEAUTIFUL AND 517 DAYS
UNSCARRED--/
UNSCIENTIFICALLY
I MUST SAY YOU PROCEEDED VERY UNSCIENTIFICALLY, 82 STRANG
DOCTOR/
UNSCRUPULOUS
HIS EXPRESSION IS ONE OF UNSCRUPULOUS MEANNESS, 174 EJONES
COWARDLY AND DANGEROUS.
WELL, I EXPECTED YOU TO BE LOW AND UNSCRUPULOUS, 18 MANSNS
CONSIDERING YOUR ORIGIN,
SHE WAS JUST AS RUTHLESS AND UNSCRUPULOUS ABOUT 75 MANSNS
DISCARDING YOU
UNTIL I COULD HARDLY RECOGNIZE MY SON IN THE 97 MANSNS
UNSCRUPULOUS GREEDY TRADER,
THAT HE'S GROWN SO GREEDY AND UNSCRUPULOUS AND 133 MANSNS
USED TO HAVING HIS OWN WAY THAT
HER EYES HAVE HARDENED, GROWN CUNNING AND 139 MANSNS
UNSCRUPULOUS.
PERPETRATED BY UNSCRUPULOUS JAPANESE TRADE-PIRATES422 MARCOM
WHO, IN SPITE OF HIS PROTESTS
UNSCRUPULOUSNESS
FINALLY, I WANT TO WARN YOU AGAIN AGAINST THE 71 MANSNS
GROWING UNSCRUPULOUSNESS
UNSEEINGLY
(THEY BOTH STARE AT THEIR CARDS UNSEEINGLY. 138 JOURNE
AND SHE STARES BEFORE HER UNSEEINGLY.) 22 MANSNS
UNSEEMLY
THIS IS ALL MOST UNSEEMLY/ 40 MANSNS
UNSEEN
(A BURST OF HARD, BARKING LAUGHTER COMES FROM THE 240 HA APE
UNSEEN OCCUPANTS OF THE CELLS,
LIKE THE VEIL OF THINGS AS THEY SEEM DRAWN BACK BY153 JOURNE
AN UNSEEN HAND,
SIN IS PRACTICALLY UNSEEN. 393 MARCOM
THIS REVELATION OF AN UNSEEN AUDIENCE STARTLES 58 MISBEG
HARDER.
UNSELFISH
THAT AT BOTTOM HUMAN NATURE IS GOOD AND UNSELFISH. 9 MANSNS
I WANT THE CHANCE TO BE UNSELFISH, 53 MANSNS
I WANT TO MAKE MYSELF AN UNSELFISH MOTHER AND 54 MANSNS
GRANDMOTHER.
AND IT'S ONE OF THOSE UNSELFISH LOVES YOU READ 37 STRANG
ABOUT.
BUT I THINK HIS UNSELFISH LOVE, COMBINED WITH HER 37 STRANG
REAL LIKING FOR HIM,
AMBITION INTO A FELLOW--UNSELFISH AMBITION-- 54 STRANG
PLEASED, IN WHOSE UNSELFISH DEVOTION YOU COULD 81 STRANG
FIND PEACE/
YOU'RE KIND/ YOU'RE UNSELFISH AND FINE/ 466 WELDED
UNSELFISHLY
I ACTED UNSELFISHLY... 11 STRANG
UNSENTIMENTALLY
YOU SEE, I'M TRYING TO SEE THINGS THROUGH CLEARLY 9 STRANG
AND UNSENTIMENTALLY.
UNSETTLED
AND ABOUT HER WHOLE PERSONALITY THE SAME 221 DESIRE
UNSETTLED, UNTAMED,
THERE IS A NEW IMPORT TAX AND TRADE IS VERY 348 MARCOM
UNSETTLED.
UNSHAKABLE
AND ONE GETS IMMEDIATELY FROM HIM THE SENSE OF 500 DAYS
UNSHAKABLE INNER CALM AND
UNSHAKEN
(UNSHAKEN--PLEASANTLY) THAT'S A LIE IN YOUR 46 ANNA
THROAT, DIVIL MEND YOU/
UNSHAVEN
HIS FACE BURNED BY THE SUN AND UNSHAVEN FOR DAYS. 119 BEYOND
HIS UNSHAVEN CHEEKS ARE SUNKEN AND SALLOW. 553 DAYS
HE HAS A ROUND KEWPIE'S FACE--A KEWPIE WHO IS AN 576 ICEMAN
UNSHAVEN HABITUAL DRUNKARD.
(FIERCELY, SHOVING HIS DIRTY UNSHAVEN FACE ALMOST 62 MISBEG
INTO HARDER'S)
UNSLAKED
UNSLAKED BY EIGHTY YEARS OF DEVOURED DESIRES COULD355 LAZARU
KNOW/
UNSPOILED
BUT GORDON WAS ABSOLUTELY UNSPOILED, I SHOULD SAY. 9 STRANG
HE'S A FINE HEALTHY BOY, CLEAN AND UNSPOILED. 38 STRANG
UNSTEADILY
AND WALKS UNSTEADILY INTO BACK ROOM SINGING) 12 ANNA
(AROUSED--GETS UNSTEADILY TO HIS FEET) 13 ANNA
(GETTING UNSTEADILY TO HIS FEET AGAIN--IN A RAGE) 32 ANNA
(STUNG, RISING UNSTEADILY TO HIS FEET 32 ANNA
(HE SCRAMBLES UNSTEADILY TO HIS FEET) 104 ELECTR

UNSTEADILY (CONT'D.)
(THE CHANTYMAN GOES UNSTEADILY OFF LEFT, BETWEEN 107 ELECTR
THE WAREHOUSE AND THE SHIP.
(HE GOES TO THEM UNSTEADILY, OPENING HIS ARMS) 725 ICEMAN
UNSTEADILY--WITH OFFENDED DIGNITY) 80 MISBEG
(SNIRLS UN HIM UNSTEADILY) WHO THE HELL-- 100 MISBEG
(HE WALKS A BIT UNSTEADILY OUT THE DOOR AT LEFT 162 POET
FRONT.)
COCK GETS UNSTEADILY TO HIS FEET AND RAISES HIS 501 VOYAGE
GLASS IN THE AIR.)
UNSTRAPS
(HE UNSTRAPS THEM AND FLINGS THEM AWAY 193 EJONES
DISGUSTEDLY)
UNSTRUNG
(THINKING MORE CLEARLY NOW--AN UNSTRUNG FURY 463 DYNAMO
RISING WITHIN HIM)
I'M ALL UNSTRUNG. 455 WELDED
UNSUBDUED
EACH DAY IS A CAGE IN WHICH HE FINDS HIMSELF 203 DESIRE
TRAPPED BUT INWARDLY UNSUBDUED.
UNSUCCESSFULLY
HIM AND UNSUCCESSFULLY PLOTTING REVENGE. 422 DYNAMO
UNSUITABLE
THIS--THIS IS MOST UNSUITABLE CONDUCT-- 31 MANSNS
UNSUITED
WE'RE ABSOLUTELY UNSUITED TO EACH OTHER/ 103 STRANG
UNSURE
HE BEGINS TO LOOK EXTREMELY UNSURE OF HIMSELF.) 58 MISBEG
UNSUSPECTING
MURDEROUSLY AT THE UNSUSPECTING GUARD. 194 EJONES
IT WOULD PUT HIM AT HIS EASE AND UNSUSPECTING, AND 93 MISBEG
IT'D GIVE YOU COURAGE, TOO,
WHAT A DEVILISH, COWARDLY TRICK TO PLAY ON POOR 124 STRANG
UNSUSPECTING SAM/....))
((BUT I'M NOT UNSUSPECTING/... 124 STRANG
UNSUSPECTINGLY
(UNSUSPECTINGLY--WITH A GRIN) SEND FOR ME TO COME461 DYNAMO
SURE AND BE GOOD/
THAT SARA HAS NOT BEEN AS BLIND AS YOU HOPED, NOR 98 MANSNS
AS UNSUSPECTINGLY TRUSTFUL.
UNSWEPT
THE FLOOR IS UNSWEPT, LITTERED WITH CIGARETTE AND 236 AHWILD
CIGAR BUTTS,
UNTAMED
AND ABOUT HER WHOLE PERSONALITY THE SAME 221 DESIRE
UNSETTLED, UNTAMED,
UNTHINKABLE
OTHERWISE OUR SUFFERING WOULD BE MEANINGLESS--AND 150 BEYOND
THAT IS UNTHINKABLE.
UNTHINKING
THE LONGING FOR A MOMENT'S UNTHINKING PEACE, 28 MANSNS
(WITH AMAZED, UNTHINKING JOY.) 174 POET
UNTHINKINGLY
(UNTHINKINGLY) IT WAS BEFORE I WAS BORN, WASN'T 521 DIFRNT
IT?
UNTIDY
HER BLACK HAIR, STREAKED WITH GRAY, STRAGGLES IN 20 POET
UNTIDY WISPS ABOUT HER FACE.
UNTIE
STRIP OFF THEIR UPPER CLOTHES, UNTIE THE DEAD MEN,353 MARCOM
UNTIES
AND UNTIES THE STRING WHICH IS WOUND TIGHTLY 528 INZONE
AROUND THE TOP.
HIS SHEATH-KNIFE, AND UNTIES THE HANDKERCHIEF OVER532 INZONE
THE GAG.
UNTIL
SEEMS TO ME SHE MIGHT WAIT UNTIL THE FOURTH IS 192 AHWILD
OVER BEFORE BRINGING UP--
UNTIL AT THE END HIS MOUTH DRAWS DOWN AT THE 208 AHWILD
CORNERS,
AND HANG AROUND UNTIL IT'S TIME. 219 AHWILD
YOU PROMISE TO KEEP YOUR FACE SHUT, MID--UNTIL 274 AHWILD
AFTER I'VE LEFT--
NOT UNTIL I WAS DRUNK, I DIDN'T. 276 AHWILD
CAN'T I GO OUT ON THE PIAZZA AND SIT FOR A WHILE--297 AHWILD
UNTIL THE MOON SETS?
SPEAK ABOUT YOUR TRIP--UNTIL AFTER YOU'D GONE. 88 BEYOND
I THINK YOU MIGHT WAIT UNTIL MORNING WHEN HE'S HAD 95 BEYOND
HIS BREAKFAST.
I ASKED YOU TO REMEMBER THAT UNTIL THIS EVENING I 100 BEYOND
DIDN'T KNOW MYSELF.
I DIDN'T KNOW UNTIL THEN. 100 BEYOND
I TOLD HER I HADN'T BEEN CONSCIOUS OF MY LOVE 100 BEYOND
UNTIL AFTER THE TRIP HAD BEEN
=TELL HIM I'LL HOLD THE BERTH OPEN FOR HIM UNTIL 141 BEYOND
LATE THIS AFTERNOON, HE SAYS.
I EXPECTED TO--UNTIL I GOT TO NEW YORK. 156 BEYOND
I BELIEVED UNTIL MY MOTHER'S DEATH. 561 CROSS
AS THE ACTION GOES ON, THE LIGHT IMPERCEPTIBLY 493 DAYS
SPREADS UNTIL,
NO, AS A FAVOR, STAY AROUND UNTIL THE ICE IS 500 DAYS
BROKEN
UNTIL FINALLY HE WROTE ME HE WAS MARRIED. 504 DAYS
I MEAN, UNTIL THE ROAD FINALLY TURNS BACK TOWARD 504 DAYS
HOME.
GOOD-BYE UNTIL THIS EVENING, JACK? 513 DAYS
UNTIL COMPARATIVELY LATE IN LIFE. 514 DAYS
UNTIL I'VE SPRUCED UP ON A BATH AND COCKTAILS. 517 DAYS
LOVING MOVES SILENTLY OVER UNTIL HE IS STANDING 526 DAYS
JUST BEHIND JOHN BUT A STEP
LOVING MOVES UNTIL HE IS STANDING DIRECTLY BEHIND 528 DAYS
HIM.
UNTIL YOU'VE HEARD HOW IT CAME TO HAPPEN. 536 DAYS
BUT I'VE NEVER HAD ANY GOD, YOU SEE--UNTIL I MET 551 DAYS
JOHN.
UNTIL THE BACK OF HIS HEAD IS AGAINST THE FOOT OF 564 DAYS
THE CROSS.

UNTIL

UNTIL (CONT'D.)
(HER REMARK IS REPEATED DOWN THE LINE WITH MANY A 248 DESIRE
GUFFAW AND TITTER UNTIL IT
THE WEASEL,* INCREASING THE TEMPO WITH EVERY VERSE251 DESIRE
UNTIL AT THE END HE IS
EBEN DOES NOT NOTICE HER UNTIL QUITE NEAR.) 252 DESIRE
THE THOUGHT OF THAT GIRL OF HIS NEVER ENTERED MY 426 DYNAMO
HEAD UNTIL A MOMENT AGO--
UNTIL HE COMES TO A SMALL GAP THAT IS ALMOST AT 427 DYNAMO
THE END OF THE HEDGE, FRONT.
UNTIL SHE GIVES UP AND RETURNS HIS KISS-- 459 DYNAMO
I WON'T EVER BE SATISFIED NOW UNTIL I'VE FOUND THE469 DYNAMO
TRUTH ABOUT EVERYTHING.
AND APPROACHES UNTIL HE IS OPPOSITE THE OPEN 473 DYNAMO
DOORWAY.
(HE GOES TO THE DOOR) YOU WAIT UNTIL YOUR 478 DYNAMO
HUSBAND'S GONE HOME.
UNTIL I'D GIVEN UP THE FLESH AND PURIFIED MYSELF/ 478 DYNAMO
HE COMES FORWARD UNTIL HE STANDS BY THE COPING. 482 DYNAMO
FRONT.
AND THE NOISE OF THE DYNAMO DIES UNTIL IT IS THE 488 DYNAMO
FAINTEST PURRING HUM.
AND ALL THE LIGHTS IN THE PLANT DIM DOWN UNTIL 488 DYNAMO
THEY ARE ALMOST OUT
DOES NOT SEE HIM UNTIL IT IS TOO LATE. 174 EJONES
UNTIL SHE IS NOW WITHIN ARM'S REACH OF HER. 16 ELECTR
AND SHE SAID I WAS TO KEEP YOU COMPANY UNTIL SHE 21 ELECTR
RETURNED.
I FORGOT HER UNTIL TWO YEARS AGO WHEN I CAME BACK 26 ELECTR
FROM THE EAST.
YOU WAIT HERE UNTIL I CALL YOU/ 27 ELECTR
(BITTERLY) I LOVED HIM UNTIL HE LET YOU AND YOUR 31 ELECTR
FATHER NAG HIM INTO THE WAR,
WAITING UNTIL SHE HEARS THE SIDE DOOR OF THE HOUSE 35 ELECTR
CLOSE AFTER HER.
THEN YOU MUST WAIT ON THE *FLYING TRADES* UNTIL 40 ELECTR
YOU HEAR FROM ME
UNTIL I GOT HIM WORRIED TOO. 40 ELECTR
(THE CANNON AT THE FORT KEEP BOOMING AT REGULAR 42 ELECTR
INTERVALS UNTIL THE END OF THE
HIS LETTER SAID HE WOULDN'T WAIT UNTIL HIS BRIGADE 46 ELECTR
WAS DISBANDED
(COLDLY) I WOULD PREFER NOT TO DISCUSS THIS UNTIL 50 ELECTR
WE ARE ALONE, EZRA--
SHE DIDN'T GO TO BED UNTIL TWO. 59 ELECTR
TOWARD LEFT FRONT UNTIL THEY ARE BY THE BENCH. 68 ELECTR
(FORCING A NERVOUS LAUGH) IT GETS ON MY NERVES 73 ELECTR
UNTIL I COULD SCREAM/
HE TWISTS AND WRINGS AND TORTURES OUR LIVES WITH 73 ELECTR
OTHERS' LIVES UNTIL--
THAT WE'D GO ON MURDERING AND BEING MURDERED UNTIL 74 ELECTR
NO ONE WAS LEFT ALIVE/
HE WAS THE WAR TO ME--THE WAR THAT WOULD NEVER END 75 ELECTR
UNTIL I DIED.
WAIT UNTIL YOU'VE TALKED TO ME/ 76 ELECTR
I HAD BEEN A GOOD WIFE TO HIM FOR TWENTY-THREE 77 ELECTR
YEARS--UNTIL I MET ADAM.
UNTIL I REALLY BELIEVE SHE WENT A LITTLE OUT OF 86 ELECTR
HER HEAD.
I READ IT AND REREAD IT UNTIL 89 ELECTR
(LAVINIA COMES SLOWLY FORWARD UNTIL SHE IS AT 91 ELECTR
ARM'S LENGTH.
AND HOLD A POSITION UNTIL HELL FROZE OVER/ 94 ELECTR
DIDN'T YOU THINK IT WOULD BE BETTER TO POSTPONE 96 ELECTR
OUR TALK UNTIL--
AND IN BOSTON WE WAITED UNTIL THE EVENING TRAIN 120 ELECTR
GOT IN.
CHRISTINE SHRINKS BACKWARD UP THE STEPS UNTIL SHE 123 ELECTR
STANDS AT THE TOP
AND PASSES IT AROUND UNTIL IT FINALLY REACHES SETH131 ELECTR
AGAIN.
UNTIL SHE STANDS DIRECTLY UNDER THEM IN FRONT OF 139 ELECTR
THE FIREPLACE.
APPROACHES AS IF COMPELLED IN SPITE OF HERSELF 139 ELECTR
UNTIL SHE STANDS DIRECTLY UNDER
I MEAN YOU'VE CHANGED SO--AND WE WEREN'T LOOKING 143 ELECTR
FOR YOU UNTIL--
I CAN'T LEAVE HIM--UNTIL HE'S ALL WELL AGAIN. 147 ELECTR
AND IT PREYED ON HIS MIND UNTIL HE BLAMES HIMSELF 148 ELECTR
FOR HER DEATH.
UNTIL YOU GET SO DEEP AT THE BOTTOM OF HELL THERE 160 ELECTR
IS NO LOWER YOU CAN SINK AND
ORIN FOLLOWS HIM WITH HIS EYES UNTIL HE HEARS THE 160 ELECTR
FRONT DOOR CLOSE BEHIND HIM.)
AND HOW YOU'VE BROODED OVER IT UNTIL YOU BLAME 161 ELECTR
YOURSELF FOR HER DEATH.
YOU SHAN'T LEAVE HERE UNTIL--/ 163 ELECTR
(STARES INTO HER EYES, BENDING HIS HEAD UNTIL HIS 164 ELECTR
FACE IS CLOSE TO HERS--
UNTIL THE CURSE IS PAID OUT AND THE LAST MANNON IS178 ELECTR
LET DIE/
UNTIL AT THE END SHE IS A WIFE AND A MOTHER) 264 GGBROW
UNTIL HE FELT IN THE PAINTING MOOD AGAINS 277 GGBROW
UNTIL AT LAST THROUGH TWO YEARS I WATCHED HER DIE 282 GGBROW
AND HE'LL NEVER LIVE UNTIL HIS LIBERATED DUST 296 GGBROW
QUICKENS INTO EARTH/
IT THRIVE AND BREED AND BECOME MULTITUDES AND EAT 297 GGBROW
UNTIL BROWN IS CONSUMED/
I WAS QUITE FURIOUS UNTIL HE CONVINCED ME IT WAS 310 GGBROW
ALL FOR THE BEST.
UNTIL NOW HE IS INTERRUPTED BY A STORM OF 212 HA APE
CATCALLS, HISSES, BOOS.
UNTIL THEY'RE OLD LIKE ME. 214 HA APE
UNTIL THE EXPECTANT SILENCE CRASHES HIS EARS.) 15 HUGHIE
UNTIL AT LAST IT MUST DIE AND JOIN ALL THE OTHER 19 HUGHIE
LONG NIGHTS IN NIRVANA,
GRADE UNTIL HE WAS TOOK ON AS NIGHT CLERK IN THE 23 HUGHIE
HOTEL THERE.

UNTIL (CONT'D.)
HUGHIE WAS AS BIG A DUPE AS YOU UNTIL I GIVE HIM 25 HUGHIE
SOME INTEREST IN LIFE.
AND WAS IN THE BUCKS FOR A WHILE UNTIL I WAS TOOK 29 HUGHIE
TO THE CLEANERS.
SAWBUCK THERE UNTIL I RAISED IT. 34 HUGHIE
SO I SUPPOSE THEY DIDN'T THINK OF ME UNTIL 588 ICEMAN
AFTERWARD.
THE QUESTIONS MULTIPLY FOR YOU UNTIL IN THE END 590 ICEMAN
IT'S ALL QUESTION AND NO ANSWER.
ONLY TAKE MY ADVICE AND WAIT A WHILE UNTIL 604 ICEMAN
BUSINESS CONDITIONS ARE BETTER.
KEEP THE BALLS COMING UNTIL THIS IS KILLED. 621 ICEMAN
NO, BOYS AND GIRLS, I'VE NEVER KNOWN WHAT REAL 625 ICEMAN
PEACE WAS UNTIL NOW.
UNTIL HE'S A ROTTEN SKUNK IN HIS OWN EYES. 641 ICEMAN
HE'LL KEEP AFTER YOU UNTIL HE MAKES YOU HELP HIM. 642 ICEMAN
UNTIL YOU DON'T GIVE A DAMN FOR HICKEY/ 645 ICEMAN
I MEANT TO WAIT UNTIL THE PARTY WAS OVER. 663 ICEMAN
AND IF YOU'LL ONLY WAIT UNTIL THE FINAL RETURNS 691 ICEMAN
ARE IN.
JUST LEAVE HARRY ALONE AND WAIT UNTIL THE SHOCK 692 ICEMAN
WEARS OFF AND YOU'LL SEE.
HE KEPT HIMSELF LOCKED IN HIS ROOM UNTIL A WHILE 700 ICEMAN
AGO.
UNTIL I'D MADE IT A REAL FINAL TEST TO MYSELF--AND715 ICEMAN
TO HER.
NOT UNTIL WE GET INTO THE WAR ZONE, AT ANY RATE. 514 INZONE
IT WASN'T UNTIL AFTER EDMUND WAS BORN THAT I HAD A 28 JOURNE
SINGLE GREY HAIR.
I DID PUT EDMUND WISE TO THINGS, BUT NOT UNTIL I 34 JOURNE
SAW HE'D STARTED TO RAISE HELL.
SHE HAS CONTROL OF HER NERVES--OR SHE HAD UNTIL 37 JOURNE
EDMUND GOT SICK.
I WAITED UNTIL THEY WENT OUT. 42 JOURNE
SHE WAITS RIGIDLY UNTIL HE DISAPPEARS DOWN THE 42 JOURNE
STEPS.
I REALLY OUGHT TO GO UPSTAIRS AND LIE DOWN UNTIL 49 JOURNE
LUNCH TIME AND TAKE A NAP.
YOU NEVER KNEW WHAT WAS REALLY WRONG UNTIL YOU 57 JOURNE
WERE IN PREP SCHOOL.
AND ONCE THEY'RE DONE THEY MAKE YOU DO OTHER 61 JOURNE
THINGS UNTIL AT LAST EVERYTHING
TELL BRIDGET I'M SORRY BUT SHE'LL HAVE TO WAIT A 62 JOURNE
FEW MINUTES UNTIL MISTER TYRONE
MEDICINE--AND YOU NEVER KNEW WHAT IT WAS UNTIL TOO 74 JOURNE
LATE/
IT IS AS IF THEY WERE WAITING UNTIL SHE GOT 75 JOURNE
UPSTAIRS BEFORE SPEAKING.)
THERE'LL BE THE SAME DRIFTING AWAY FROM US UNTIL 78 JOURNE
BY THE END OF EACH NIGHT--
UNTIL NOW THERE'S NO STRENGTH OF THE SPIRIT LEFT 78 JOURNE
IN HER
I'VE DONE ALL I CAN DO ON THE HEDGE UNTIL YOU CUT 80 JOURNE
MORE OF IT.
AT LEAST, UNTIL ONE OF THE BOYS COMES DOWN. 83 JOURNE
FOR GOD'S SAKE TRY AND BE YOURSELF--AT LEAST UNTIL 88 JOURNE
HE GOES/
YOU'LL ALWAYS BE BROKE UNTIL YOU LEARN THE VALUE-- 89 JOURNE
I LAY AWAKE WORRYING UNTIL I COULDN'T STAND IT ANY 98 JOURNE
MORE.
YOU GO BACK UNTIL AT LAST YOU ARE BEYOND ITS 104 JOURNE
REACH.
MARY WAITS UNTIL SHE HEARS THE PANTRY DOOR CLOSE 106 JOURNE
BEHIND HER.
HE'LL NEVER BE CONTENT UNTIL HE MAKES EDMUND AS 109 JOURNE
HOPELESS A FAILURE AS HE IS.
SHE KEEPS STARING OUT THE WINDOW UNTIL 121 JOURNE
HELL, EVERYONE KEEPS A LIGHT ON IN THE FRONT HALL 126 JOURNE
UNTIL THEY GO TO BED.
I USED TO READ IT EVERY ONCE IN A WHILE UNTIL 152 JOURNE
FINALLY IT MADE ME FEEL SO BAD I
IT'LL PASS THE TIME UNTIL SHE-- 169 JOURNE
THE GREATNESS OF MAN IS THAT NO GOD CAN SAVE HIM--289 LAZARU
UNTIL HE BECOMES A GOD/
I DO NOT EAT NOR DRINK UNTIL YOU HAVE TASTED 301 LAZARU
FIRST.
(YAWNING) THERE WAS A FEAST AT CINNA'S LAST NIGHT314 LAZARU
THAT LASTED UNTIL THIS
ASCENDS THE STEPS UNTIL HE STANDS A LITTLE BELOW 320 LAZARU
LAZARUS.
OVER THE BONES THAT RAISED THEM UNTIL BOTH ARE 330 LAZARU
DUST.
(WALKS TO THE DAIS WHICH SHE ASCENDS SLOWLY UNTIL 342 LAZARU
SHE STANDS BY CAESAR'S COUCH
UNTIL IN THE END THEY DO IT TO AVENGE THEE, FOR 343 LAZARU
THINE HONOR AND GLORY/
UNTIL TONIGHT, WHEN I SPOKE TO YOU OF HOME, I 345 LAZARU
FELT NEW BIRTH--PAINS AS YOUR
GENTLY HE LETS HER BODY SINK UNTIL IT RESTS 347 LAZARU
AGAINST THE STEPS OF THE DAIS.
(HARSHLY) UNTIL I HAVE TESTED HIM WITH HIS OWN 351 LAZARU
LIFE/
AND I STARVED MY MOTHER'S STRENGTH TO DEATH UNTIL 356 LAZARU
SHE DIED.
(PEEKS AFTER HIM UNTIL SURE HE IS GONE-- 357 LAZARU
HAS GRADUALLY MOVED CLOSER TO HIM UNTIL SHE, TOO, 358 LAZARU
IS AT HIS FEET.
UNTIL, AS IT IS FINALLY LOST, HE IS ON TIP-TOES, 371 LAZARU
DREAM YOURSELF BACK UNTIL YOU BECOME NOT THE 3 MANSNS
RESPECTABLE, IF A TRIFLE MAD,
SHUT MY EYES AND FORGET--NOT OPEN THEM UNTIL HE 4 MANSNS
COMES--
UNTIL HE CAN BE EDUCATED TO OUTGROW THEM 8 MANSNS
SPIRITUALLY.
THE DANGER IS THAT YOUR DISCONTENT WILL GROW AND 17 MANSNS
GROW WITH YOUR SUCCESS UNTIL--
SHE ADVANCES NOISELESSLY UNTIL SHE STANDS 18 MANSNS

UNTIL

UNTIL (CONT'D.)

Text	Reference
TURNS AS IT TURNS UNTIL IT FACES TOWARD LEFT-FRONT.	27 MANSNS
AND SCREAM IN SILENCE AND BEAT ON THE WALLS UNTIL YOU DIE OF STARVATION.	40 MANSNS
AND DENY YOURSELF, UNTIL AT LAST YOU FALL IN LOVE WITH MADNESS.	40 MANSNS
YOU MIGHT AT LEAST WAIT UNTIL I HAVE FINISHED EXPLAINING	64 MANSNS
NO, WAIT UNTIL YOU FEEL HER OUT WITH GROWING AMUSEMENT, SHE TIPTOES FORWARD UNTIL SHE STANDS BY HIS TABLE.)	74 MANSNS 75 MANSNS
UNTIL NOTHING IS WHAT IT SEEMS TO BE, AND WE ALL GET SUSPICIOUS OF EACH OTHER.	82 MANSNS
UNTIL FINALLY YOU WILL FIND YOURSELF CAPABLE OF TAKING MY PLACE.	92 MANSNS
UNTIL I COULD HARDLY RECOGNIZE MY SON IN THE UNSCRUPULOUS GREEDY TRADER.	97 MANSNS
UNTIL I SWEAR TO YOU I FELT I COULD BY JUST ONE TINY FURTHER WISH,	102 MANSNS
SHE WOULD SEEM TO STEAL ALL IDENTITY FROM YOU-- UNTIL THERE WAS BUT ONE WOMAN--	105 MANSNS
NOT UNTIL I GIVE YOU PERMISSION TO SPEAK.	115 MANSNS
(THEY BEND CLOSER TO EACH OTHER UNTIL THEIR HEADS ARE ABOUT TOUCHING.	125 MANSNS
UNTIL THEIR FACES TOUCH THE SIDE OF HIS HEAD.	128 MANSNS
UNTIL ONLY ONE OF YOU SURVIVES/	130 MANSNS
I WOULD MAKE HIM PAY FOR ME UNTIL I HAD TAKEN EVERYTHING HE POSSESSED/	133 MANSNS
UNTIL HE GOT SO LOST IN HIS DREAMS HE'D BE NO MORE135 MANSNS A MAN AT ALL.	
BUT OF COURSE I WON'T SIGN THEM UNTIL AFTER-- YOU SAID LATER, BUT I CAN'T GET BACK UNTIL LATE AFTERNOON	146 MANSNS 147 MANSNS
(SHARPLY MATTER-OF-FACT.) I'VE EXPLAINED UNTIL I'M TIRED	147 MANSNS
LET THE COWARDLY OLD WITCH WAIT UNTIL DOMESDAY/	159 MANSNS
GOODBYE UNTIL THIS AFTERNOON.	160 MANSNS
UNTIL NOW HE SEES HER AS THE FILTHY SLUT SHE IS--	162 MANSNS
UNTIL HE FINALLY TRICKS ME INTO UNLOCKING THE DOOR, TAKING HIS HAND--	163 MANSNS
UNTIL WE GET BACK OUR OLD STRENGTH--	170 MANSNS
UNTIL AT LAST WE'D FINALLY BE RID OF HIM.	171 MANSNS
UNTIL--	171 MANSNS
UNTIL MY MIND WOULD BE RIPPED APART/	174 MANSNS
YOU WILL STAY HERE ALONE UNTIL YOU DO WHAT YOU MUST DO TO ESCAPE.	183 MANSNS
HAD IN LEADING SIMON AWAY FROM HIMSELF UNTIL HE LOST HIS WAY	190 MANSNS
IT BEWITCHED EVEN ME UNTIL ALLAH DROVE IT BACK TO 353 MARCOM HELL!	
IT RISES SOFTLY AND AS SOFTLY DIES AWAY UNTIL IT IS NOTHING BUT A FAINT SOUND OF	354 MARCOM
UNTIL THE LOUD LAUGHTER AT THE END OF MAFFEO'S STORY.	370 MARCOM
(WARNINGLY) AND UNTIL I PRONOUNCE YOU GRADUATED, 374 MARCOM MUM'S THE WORD, UNDERSTAND/	
(HURRIEDLY) THERE WAS NO POPE ELECTED UNTIL JUST 378 MARCOM BEFORE--	
UNTIL IT'S TIME TO GO TO BED.	399 MARCOM
UNTIL A SMALL MULTITUDE IS GATHERED STANDING IN SILENCE STARING UP AT THE POOP.	405 MARCOM
I WILL NOT GO UNTIL IT PLEASES ME/	411 MARCOM
YOU KEEP HER FROM DOING ANYTHING RASH UNTIL HE GETS HERE.	417 MARCOM
UNTIL HE BECOMES HIS OWN IDEAL FIGURE, AN IDOL OF 418 MARCOM STUFFED SELF-SATISFACTION/	
LET HIM BE URGED TO EAT AND DRINK UNTIL HE CAN HOLD NO MORE.	418 MARCOM
AGAIN YOUR WISH IS MY WILL, EVEN THOUGH I WILL NOT419 MARCOM LIVE UNTIL I SEE YOU AGAIN/	
WITH THE TRAINED EYE FOR DISPLAY OF WINDOW-DRESSERS, UNTIL THE TABLE,	428 MARCOM
STAY GABBING UNTIL FATHER CAME AND BEAT YOU TO A JELLY, BUT I WON'T.	10 MISBEG
UNTIL YOU REMIND HIM.	33 MISBEG
UNTIL THEY DISCOVERED I WASN'T QUALIFIED	38 MISBEG
I WAS WAITING UNTIL I ARRIVED HERE, KNOWING THAT YOU--	45 MISBEG
NEITHER DID I, BUT HE KEPT ON UNTIL, BE GOD, I SAW 87 MISBEG HE REALLY MEANT IT.	
YOU'LL WALK DOWN TO THE INN WITH ME AND HIDE OUTSIDE UNTIL YOU SEE ME COME OUT	96 MISBEG
UNTIL ONLY A DIM LIGHT REMAINS.	111 MISBEG
HE WOULD NEVER ADMIT IT UNTIL TONIGHT.	135 MISBEG
I COULDN'T BELIEVE THAT UNTIL TONIGHT--BUT NOW I KNOW.	137 MISBEG
(SHE ADDS STRANGELY) NOT UNTIL THE DAWN HAS BEAUTY IN IT.	158 MISBEG
UNTIL LAST NIGHT, I'D NOT SEEN HIDE NOR HAIR OF HIM.	10 POET
UNTIL I SAW IT WAS HOPELESS.	41 POET
KINDLY KEEP HER HERE ON SOME EXCUSE UNTIL I RETURN.	76 POET
UNTIL HE STANDS AT THE END OF THE CENTER TABLE FACING HER.	89 POET
AT ONCE INSTEAD OF WAITING UNTIL EVENING.	89 POET
(WHO HAS BEEN STARING AT HIM WITH SCORN UNTIL HE SAYS THIS LAST--	91 POET
(BEFORE HE THINKS.) BUT I TOLD YOUR MOTHER TO KEEP HER HERE UNTIL--	91 POET
HAND, BUT HE MUST UNDERSTAND THAT I COULD NOT COMMIT MYSELF UNTIL I HAD TALKED	110 POET
UNTIL I KNEW TONIGHT THE TRUTH OF WHAT YOU SAID THIS MORNING.	149 POET
UNTIL SHE IS BESIDE HER MOTHER.)	163 POET
HIS RIGHT HAND GROPING ALONG THE TABLE TOP UNTIL IT CLUTCHES THE DUELING PISTOL.	172 POET

UNTIL (CONT'D.)

Text	Reference
UNTIL HE APPEARS TO HAVE NO CHARACTER LEFT IN WHICH TO HIDE AND DEFEND HIMSELF.	178 POET
(WAITING RESIGNEDLY UNTIL HE HAS FINISHED-- WEARILY)	579 ROPE
UNTIL HE STANDS DIRECTLY UNDER THE ROPE.	587 ROPE
UNTIL IT'S BECOME TOO APPALLINGLY OBVIOUS IN HER WHOLE ATTITUDE TOWARD ME/	10 STRANG
THEY MUST WAIT UNTIL HE HAD COME BACK	11 STRANG
GIVE AND GIVE UNTIL I CAN MAKE THAT GIFT OF MYSELF FOR A MAN'S HAPPINESS WITHOUT	18 STRANG
KISSES UNTIL MY LIPS WERE NUMB--KNOWING ALL THAT NIGHT--	19 STRANG
THAT LAST NIGHT BEFORE HE SAILED--IN HIS ARMS UNTIL MY BODY ACHED--	19 STRANG
I WANTED TO LIVE COMFORTED BY YOUR LOVE UNTIL THE END.	20 STRANG
(SHARPLY) SHE MUST STAY AWAY UNTIL SHE GETS WELL. 21 STRANG OR WAIT UNTIL SHE....)	26 STRANG
DARRELL MOVES BACK AND TO ONE SIDE UNTIL HE IS STANDING IN RELATIVELY THE SAME	39 STRANG
DRIVEN ANIMAL UNTIL ONE NIGHT NOT LONG AGO I HAD A 45 STRANG DREAM OF GORDON DIVING DOWN	
UNTIL HE'D EXPLAINED IT WAS THANKS TO HIS KINDNESS 50 STRANG I DON'T BELIEVE HE EVER MENTIONED HER UNTIL HER	50 STRANG
LETTERS BEGAN COMING OR THAT	
BUT I WASN'T ABLE TO GET TO SLEEP UNTIL AFTER DAYLIGHT SOMEHOW.	57 STRANG
DON'T YOU THINK YOU BETTER WAIT UNTIL SAMMY'S MAKING MORE MONEY'S	57 STRANG
I DIDN'T KNOW ABOUT THE EVANSES UNTIL AFTER I'D MARRIED MY HUSBAND.	59 STRANG
HE DIDN'T TELL ME UNTIL AFTER WE WERE MARRIED.	59 STRANG
AND FROM THEN ON UNTIL HIS FATHER DID REALLY DIE DURING SAMMY'S SECOND YEAR TO	60 STRANG
YOUNG FOLKS DON'T NOWADAYS--UNTIL I'D SEEN YOU AND 61 STRANG TOLD YOU EVERYTHING.	
I(HE'LL BE HAPPY UNTIL HE BEGINS TO FEEL GUILTY AGAIN BECAUSE I'M NOT PREGNANT.	72 STRANG
THAT IS, UNTIL I SAW HIS MOTHER/	75 STRANG
PEOPLE WHO ARE AFRAID TO FACE UNPLEASANT POSSIBILITIES UNTIL IT'S TOO LATE	77 STRANG
YOU'LL NEVER BE REALLY HAPPY UNTIL YOU'VE HAD A BABY, DOCTOR--	81 STRANG
NOT UNTIL AFTER I'M THIRTY-FIVE, AT LEAST/	81 STRANG
(THEN SHE REACHES OUT AND TURNS HIS HEAD UNTIL HIS 88 STRANG FACE FACES HERS BUT HE KEEPS	
AND I'VE WATCHED LOVE GROW IN HIM UNTIL I'M SURE...)	91 STRANG
SHE WAS NEVER SICK A DAY IN HER LIFE UNTIL--(HE TURNS ON DARRELL--COLDLY)	100 STRANG
UNTIL HE IS FORCED TO LOOK INTO HER EYES.)	104 STRANG
KEEP HIDDEN UNTIL BOAT SAILS SO SHE CAN'T REACH ME/...))	105 STRANG
THAT HE'D BE VISITING FRIENDS OUT OF TOWN UNTIL HE108 STRANG SAILED.	
AND DON'T COME NEAR ME AGAIN, DO YOU HEAR, UNTIL YOU'VE APOLOGIZED TO UNCLE NED/	142 STRANG
SHE'LL USE HER BODY UNTIL SHE PERSUADES HIM TO FORGET ME/	169 STRANG
CHORUS AS THE CREWS APPROACH NEARER AND NEARER UNTIL TOWARD THE CLOSE OF THE	176 STRANG
UNTIL OUT AT THE CEMETERY--(HIS VOICE BREAKS.)	184 STRANG
YES--UNTIL STEAMER SAIL FOR STOCKHOLM--IN TWO DAY.506 VOYAGE	
YOU KNOW YOU PROMISED NOT TO RETURN UNTIL YOU DID.445 WELDED	
(GENTLY) NOT UNTIL YOU--	477 WELDED
UNTIL THEY ARE STRETCHED OUT STRAIGHT TO RIGHT AND489 WELDED LEFT, FORMING A CROSS.	
UNTIMELY	
SORROW BECOMES DESPAIR WHEN DEATH COMES TO THE YOUNG, UNTIMELY.	436 MARCOM
UNTO	
*NAY, LET US WALK FROM FIRE UNTO FIRE FROM PASSIONATE PAIN TO DEADLIER DELIGHT--	276 AHWILD
*AN' GOD HEARKENED UNTO RACHEL/	235 DESIRE
AN' GOD HEARKENED UNTO ABBIE/	235 DESIRE
*CAUSE UNTO HIM A--THE HESITATES JUST LONG ENOUGH)248 DESIRE	
*COME UNTO ME ALL YE WHO ARE HEAVY LADEN AND I WILL GIVE YOU REST.	269 GOBRUN
WOE UNTO THEE, JERUSALEM/	292 LAZARU
WOE UNTO US/	292 LAZARU
(IN A GREAT ECHOING CRY) WOE UNTO US/	292 LAZARU
(IN A WAILING CHANT) WOE UNTO ISRAEL/	292 LAZARU
*WOE UNTO US/	579 ROPE
*GIVE THEM SORROW OF HEART, THY CURSE UNTO THEM.	584 ROPE
RENDER UNTO THEM A RECOMPENSE, O LORD, ACCORDING 584 ROPE TO THE WORK OF THEIR HANDS.	
UNTOUCHED	
EBEN SITS BEFORE HIS PLATE OF UNTOUCHED FOOD, BROODING FROWNINGLY.)	216 DESIRE
(HE SITS DOWN, OVERTURNING AS HE DOES SO THE UNTOUCHED CUP OF COFFEE WHICH	517 INZONE
UNTRAINED	
HE HAS A FAIRLY DECENT VOICE BUT HIS METHOD IS UNTRAINED SENTIMENTALITY	257 AHWILD
UNTROUBLED	
SLEEP, UNTROUBLED BY LOVE'S BETRAYING DREAM/	531 DAYS
UNTRUE	
WHERE TRUTH IS UNTRUE AND LIFE CAN HIDE FROM ITSELF.	131 JOURNE
(ANGRILY) YOU KNOW THAT'S UNTRUE.	457 WELDED
UNTRUTHFUL	
THE BLACK OF HER HAIR IS BRAZENLY UNTRUTHFUL.	520 DIFMNT
UNTWINES	
SHE TWINES AND UNTWINES THE FINGERS OF HER CLASPED157 ELECTR HANDS WITH A SLOW	
UNTYING	
(TU DRISCOLL, WHO HAS FINISHED UNTYING THE PACKET)529 INZONE	

UNTYING (CONT'D.)
DRISCOLL COMMENCES UNTYING THE PACKET. 529 INZONE

UNUS
*STETIT UNUS IN ARCEM ERECTUS CAPITIS VICTORQUE AD 23 STRANG SIDERA MITTIT SIDEREOS OCULOS

UNUSED
A BALL OF UNUSED YARN, WITH NEEDLES STUCK THROUGH 113 BEYOND IT.

UNUSUAL
THE FIRST PART IS SO UNUSUAL AND INTERESTING. 533 DAYS
HER FACE IS UNUSUAL, HANDSOME RATHER THAN 9 ELECTR BEAUTIFUL.
IT WAS MY BIRTHDAY AND I'D TAKEN A DROP TOO MUCH--348 MARCOM A VERY UNUSUAL THING FOR ME.
HE APPEARS QUITE UNAWARE OF BEING UNUSUAL 439 MARCOM
BUT SOMETHING UNUSUAL IN HIS ATTITUDE STRIKES HER 58 POET STRUCTURE AND UNUSUAL CHARACTER. 67 POET
COMING BACK SAFE FROM EUROPE ISN'T SUCH AN UNUSUAL 14 STRANG FEAT NOW, IS IT.
SHE IS PRETTIER IN A CONVENTIONAL WAY AND LESS 48 STRANG STRIKING AND UNUSUAL.
BUT THAT'S NOT UNUSUAL IN PERSONS OF HIS BUILD AND170 STRANG AGE.
HIS UNUSUAL FACE IS A HARROWED BATTLEFIELD OF 443 WELDED SUPERSENSITIVENESS.

UNUSUALLY
THEY ARE UNUSUALLY LARGE AND BEAUTIFUL. 12 JOURNE

UNVEIL
UNVEIL IT, BOYS. 640 ICEMAN

UNWANTED
AND SO I AM LEFT ALONE, AN UNWANTED SON, A 73 MANSNS DISCARDED LOVER,

UNWEARIED
(WITH A QUIET SMILE) I SHALL STUDY THIS 379 MARCOM APOTHEOSIS WITH UNWEARIED INTEREST.

UNWELCOME
THE DISTRICT ATTORNEY GAVE HIM SO MUCH UNWELCOME 595 ICEMAN PUBLICITY.
NOT CHARMING COMPANY, BUT A HOSTESS MUST HONOR 29 MANSNS EVEN UNWELCOME GUESTS.

UNWILLING
(GIVING THE UNWILLING MARCO A PUSH) 362 MARCOM

UNWILLINGLY
(UNWILLINGLY) HE'S PRAYING. 362 MARCOM

UNWISE
THAT WAS UNWISE, FOR THUS HE HAS REMAINED A 388 MARCOM STRANGE,

UNWORLDLY
AN INNATE UNWORLDLY INNOCENCE. 13 JOURNE

UNWORRIED
MRS. MILLER'S FACE WEARS AN EXPRESSION OF 288 AHWILD UNWORRIED CONTENT.

UNWORTHY
NO MATTER WHAT AN UNWORTHY FOOL I AM$ 529 DAYS
YOU WOULDN'T DO ANYTHING TO MAKE ME UNWORTHY IN 485 DYNAMO HER SIGHT, WOULD YOU$
HE MASTERS WHAT HE FEELS TO BE AN UNWORTHY PIQUE 275 GGBROW AND TURNS TO HER GENEROUSLY)
YOU JUST TOLD YOUR UNWORTHY OLD MAN I WAS KIDDING. 67 MISBEG
IT IS AN HONOR TO WELCOME YOU TO THIS UNWORTHY 68 POET
(PREENING HIMSELF.) I FLATTER MYSELF I DO NOT 89 POET LOOK TOO UNWORTHY

UNYIELDING
HE REMAINS RIGID AND UNYIELDING. 91 JOURNE

UPHOLD
AND POSSESSIVE AMBITION, AND UPHOLD THE VIRTUE OF 84 POET FREEING ONESELF

UPHOLSTERED
AT LEFT, FRONT, AN UPHOLSTERED CHAIR. 514 DAYS
AN UPHOLSTERED CHAIR IS BESIDE THE FOOT OF THE 553 DAYS BED.
AN UPHOLSTERED CHAIR, COVERED WITH BRIGHT CHINTZ 90 STRANG AT CENTER,

UPLIFTED
THE PEOPLE REMAIN WITH GOBLETS UPLIFTED, STARING 279 LAZARU AT HIM.
THE RODS AND SCOURGES ARE UPLIFTED OVER HIS BACK 348 LAZARU TO STRIKE.

UPPERS
WITH HIS BIG TOES STICKING OUT OF THE UPPERS. 577 ICEMAN

UPPISH
FOLKS THINK HE'S COLD-BLOODED AND UPPISH,-- 7 ELECTR

UPRAISED
WITH ARMS UPRAISED AS IF HIS SHOVEL WERE A CLUB IN194 EJONES HIS HANDS HE SPRINGS
HANDS IN EVERY TENSE ATTITUDE OF STRIKING, 291 LAZARU CLUTCHING, TEARING ARE SEEN UPRAISED.
MARCELLUS STOPS, FROZEN IN MID-ACTION, THE DAGGER 333 LAZARU UPRAISED.
CALIGULA STANDS WITH UPRAISED SWORD BY THE CHAIR 338 LAZARU OF CAESAR.
(SHE LAUGHS, WAVING THE POEM IN HER UPRAISED HAND,375 MARCOM STARING MOCKINGLY)
MUSICIANS, EACH CARRYING ON HIS HEAD OR UPRAISED 428 MARCOM HAND AN ENORMOUS PLATTER ON

UPRIGHT
THEY CAN STAND UPRIGHT ONLY CLOSE TO THE CENTER 212 DESIRE DIVIDING WALL OF THE UPSTAIRS.
(SHE IS SILENT, STARING BEFORE HER WITH HARD EYES, 22 ELECTR RIGIDLY UPRIGHT.
THE LEGS CLOSE TOGETHER, THE SHOULDERS SQUARE, THE 43 ELECTR HEAD UPRIGHT,
HER THIN FIGURE, SEATED STIFFLY UPRIGHT, ARMS 43 ELECTR AGAINST HER SIDES,
THEN SUDDENLY TURNS BACK AND STANDS STIFFLY 115 ELECTR UPRIGHT AND GRIM BESIDE THE BODY AND

UPRIGHT (CONT'D.)
(SHE GOES AND SITS AT THE TOP OF THE STEPS, BOLT 170 ELECTR UPRIGHT.
THEY CANNOT STAND UPRIGHT. 207 HA APE
THE GORILLA, AS IF HE UNDERSTOOD, STANDS UPRIGHT, 252 HA APE
AN OLD UPRIGHT PIANO AND STOOL HAVE BEEN MOVED IN 628 ICEMAN
ALL SIT BOLT UPRIGHT ON THEIR BENCHES AND STARE AT514 INZONE DAVIS.)
(HASTILY) HIS HOLINESS MEANT THAT MARCO, BY 379 MARCOM LEADING AN UPRIGHT LIFE--
HE IS VERY OLD BUT STILL UPRIGHT. 386 MARCOM

UPRIGHTS
THE LINES OF BUNKS, THE UPRIGHTS SUPPORTING THEM, 207 HA APE

UPROAR
THE UPROAR OF SHOUTING, LAUGHING AND SINGING 469 CARIBE VOICES HAS INCREASED IN VIOLENCE.
BRANT IS ALARMED THAT THIS UPROAR WILL ATTRACT 105 ELECTR SOMEONE.
A CONFUSED, INCHOATE UPROAR SWELLING INTO A SORT 207 HA APE OF UNITY, A MEANING---
(FOR THE FIRST TIME SEEMING TO TAKE NOTICE OF THE 209 HA APE UPROAR ABOUT HIM,
IT IS FOLLOWED BY A GENERAL UPROAR OF HARD, 210 HA APE BARKING LAUGHTER.)
(THE UPROAR SUBSIDES. 211 HA APE
HE QUELLS THE UPROAR WITH A SHOUT) 216 HA APE
A GREAT UPROAR OF FRIGHTENED CHATTERING 254 HA APE
(SCEPTICALLY YOU MUST HAVE SHARP EARS TO HAVE 277 LAZARU HEARD HIM LAUGH IN THAT UPROAR/
BEFORE THE CURTAIN, THE CRACKLE OF THE FLAMES AND 363 LAZARU AN UPROAR OF
AND THE UPROAR SUBSIDES OBEDIENTLY. 44 MANSNS
SHUTTING OUT AN UPROAR OF MUSIC AND DRUNKEN 133 POET VOICES.
(THE NOISE IN THE BAR RISES TO AN UPROAR OF 177 POET LAUGHTER

UPROARIOUS
FINALLY MARCO FINISHES TO HIS OWN UPROARIOUS 374 MARCOM AMUSEMENT.)

UPROARIOUSLY
(LOOKS AT HIM A MOMENT, IN ASTONISHMENT--THEN 47 ANNA LAUGHING UPROARIOUSLY)
(HE LAUGHS AGAIN UPROARIOUSLY) 95 BEYOND
(THEY LAUGH UPROARIOUSLY, SLAPPING THEIR THIGHS.) 223 DESIRE
(A ROAR OF LAUGHTER IN WHICH CABOT JOINS 249 DESIRE UPROARIOUSLY.)
(HE WINKS PONDEROUSLY AND GOES OFF LAUGHING 500 DIFRNT UPROARIOUSLY.)
(THEY ALL LAUGH UPROARIOUSLY. 723 ICEMAN
LAUGHING UPROARIOUSLY.) 129 POET

UPRUSH
(STARTLED AND UNABLE TO CONCEAL AN UPRUSH OF 132 MANSNS JEALOUS HATE.)

UPSET
I HATE TO SEE YOU SO UPSET. 215 AHWILD
NOW I THINK OF IT, I'VE FELT UPSET AFTERWARDS 228 AHWILD EVERY DAMNED TIME WE'VE HAD FISH/
AND BE UPSET ALL THE TIME I'M HERE ON MY FOOL 139 BEYOND ACCOUNT.
THAT YOU WERE UPSET ABOUT SOMETHING AND TRYING TO 517 DAYS HIDE IT.
AND YOU WERE AFRAID THAT WOULD UPSET ME$ 529 DAYS
I GAVE HIM A STRONG HINT ON THE STREET TODAY THAT 432 DYNAMO UPSET HIM.
DON'T TAKE IT OUT ON THE GANG BECAUSE YOU'RE UPSET654 ICEMAN ABOUT YOURSELF.
(MISERABLY UPSET) I'M GOINTER 'UP IT AHT ON DECK.520 INZONE
(QUICKLY.) I'M NOT UPSET. 16 JOURNE
WHAT MAKES YOU THINK I'M UPSET$ 15 JOURNE
BUT YOU MUSTN'T LET IT UPSET YOU, MARY. 16 JOURNE
THERE'S NOTHING TO BE UPSET ABOUT. 16 JOURNE
THAT WOULD GET HER MORE UPSET OVER EDMUND. 29 JOURNE
IT'S DAMNABLE SHE SHOULD HAVE THIS TO UPSET HER. 36 JOURNE
IT WOULD UPSET YOU. 47 JOURNE
(MORE UPSET, GRABS EDMUND'S ARM--EXCITEDLY.) 64 JOURNE
WITH NOTHING TO UPSET ME, AND ALL I'VE DONE IS 93 JOURNE WORRY ABOUT YOU.
ALWAYS GETTING UPSET AND FRIGHTENED ABOUT NOTHING 110 JOURNE AT ALL.
(EYEING HIM) (LOOKS DAMNABLY UPSET... 37 STRANG
IT HAS UPSET ME TERRIBLY/... 45 STRANG
SHE SEEMED DREADFULLY UPSET TO SEE CHARLIE WITH 50 STRANG US.

UPSETS
(WIPING HER EYES) IT'S THE HEAT UPSETS HER. 116 BEYOND

UPSETTIN'
UPSETTIN' ALL YOUR PLANS SO SUDDEN/ 100 BEYOND

UPSETTING
AND NEARLY UPSETTING THE TABLE) 498 VOYAGE

UPSIDE
TURNING THE BAG UPSIDE DOWN, POURS ITS CONTENTS IN601 ROPE HER LAP.

UPSTAIRS
I'LL BEAT IT AND LEAVE YOU ALONE--SEE IF THE WOMEN206 AHWILD FOLKS ARE READY UPSTAIRS.
I BETTER GO UPSTAIRS AND GET RIGGED OUT OR I NEVER208 AHWILD WILL GET TO THAT PICNIC.
AND THE STAIRWAY TO THE UPSTAIRS ROOMS. 236 AHWILD
GIRLS ARE ONLY ALLOWED TO SMOKE UPSTAIRS IN THE 239 AHWILD ROOMS, HE SAID.
HONEST, I'M SO STRONG FOR YOU I CAN HARDLY WAIT TO241 AHWILD GET YOU UPSTAIRS/
ARE HAVING UPSTAIRS--WHILE WE SIT DOWN HERE LIKE 241 AHWILD TWO DEAD ONES.
WELL, IF I'M SO NICE, WHY DIDN'T YOU WANT TO TAKE 242 AHWILD ME UPSTAIRS$
THE GUY WHO'S UPSTAIRS WITH MY FRIEND TOLD ME, BUT247 AHWILD I DIDN'T PAY MUCH ATTENTION.

UPSTAIRS

UPSTAIRS (CONT'D.)
UPSTAIRS WE GO/
AND I DIDN'T GO UPSTAIRS WITH HER. 262 AHWILD 276 AHWILD
MURIEL AND I WILL GO UPSTAIRS. 276 AHWILD
FATHER BAIRD GOES INTO THE HALL, TURNING LEFT TO 541 DAYS
GO UPSTAIRS TO THE STUDY.
(FINELY SPEAKS QUIETLY) JACK, EVER SINCE WE CAME543 DAYS
UPSTAIRS.
MARGARET SAYS SHE HEARD SOME ONE GO OUT RIGHT 547 DAYS
AFTER WE CAME UPSTAIRS.
THERE IS A PAUSE AS HE GOES UPSTAIRS. 212 DESIRE
THEY CAN STAND UPRIGHT ONLY CLOSE TO THE CENTER 212 DESIRE
DIVIDING WALL OF THE UPSTAIRS.
THE TWO BROTHERS CLUMP UPSTAIRS TO GET THEIR 219 DESIRE
BUNDLES.
AN' UPSTAIRS--THAT BE MY BEDROOM--AN' MY BED/ 226 DESIRE
YE BETTER COME SMART AN' GIT UPSTAIRS. 245 DESIRE
THE KITCHEN AND THE TWO BEDROOMS UPSTAIRS ARE 247 DESIRE
SHOWN.
(ABEL APPEARS IN THE DOORWAY UPSTAIRS AND STANDS 252 DESIRE
LOOKING IN SURPRISE AND
AN' HIM UPSTAIRS, I'LL RAISE HIM T' BE LIKE ME/ 256 DESIRE
UPSTAIRS, CABOT IS STILL ASLEEP BUT AWAKENS WITH A262 DESIRE
START.
I GOT TO RUN UPSTAIRS AND TIDY MYSELF A LITTLE. 527 DIFRNT
SHE'S UPSTAIRS GETTIN' CALMED DOWN. 529 DIFRNT
(STARTS FROM HIS DREAM BY THE WINDOW UPSTAIRS) 426 DYNAMO
WHO IS UPSTAIRS IN THE BEDROOM PUTTING ON A HEAVY 428 DYNAMO
MAKE-UP OF ROUGE AND MASCARA.
(DREAMING SENTIMENTALLY) (I HEAR ADA UPSTAIRS...429 DYNAMO
I'LL GO UPSTAIRS AND READ THE PAPER. 434 DYNAMO
(LEANS OUT OF THE FRONT WINDOW OF THE BEDROOM 435 DYNAMO
UPSTAIRS)
(I'LL GO UPSTAIRS TO THEM... 443 DYNAMO
(HIS VOICE COMES FROM THE HALL AS HE RUSHES 445 DYNAMO
UPSTAIRS)
HERE--UPSTAIRS. 445 DYNAMO
I WENT UPSTAIRS/ 30 ELECTR
HIDING IN THE HALL UPSTAIRS ON THE CHANCE THAT I'D 90 ELECTR
COME UP
I FOLLOWED THEM UPSTAIRS. 99 ELECTR
UPSTAIRS. 300 GGBROW
YUNO NEVER TINK ALL DESE BUMS HAD A GOOD BED 580 ICEMAN
UPSTAIRS TO GO TO.
GIVE HIM THE BUM'S RUSH UPSTAIRS/ 597 ICEMAN
AND YOU AIN'T EVEN GOT THE DECENCY TO GET ME 602 ICEMAN
UPSTAIRS WHERE I GOT A GOOD BED/
DON'T MAKE ROCKY BOUNCE ME UPSTAIRS/ 607 ICEMAN
I BETTER GO UPSTAIRS. 625 ICEMAN
I'LL GO UPSTAIRS 643 ICEMAN
AND ALL DE GANG SNEAKIN' UPSTAIRS. 665 ICEMAN
OR ELSE DEY'D RAISE HELL UPSTAIRS, LAUGHIN' AND 669 ICEMAN
SINGIN'.
BUT CHUCK HEARS SOMEONE UPSTAIRS IN THE HALL AND 683 ICEMAN
(GRABS CORA'S ARM)
(EDMUND CAN BE HEARD COUGHING AS HE GOES UPSTAIRS. 26 JOURNE
(HE JUMPS UP.) I LEFT MY BOOK UPSTAIRS, ANYWAY. 26 JOURNE
I WAS JUST GOING UPSTAIRS TO LOOK FOR YOU. 42 JOURNE
I REALLY OUGHT TO GO UPSTAIRS AND LIE DOWN UNTIL 49 JOURNE
LUNCH TIME AND TAKE A NAP.
HE SEEMS TO BE LISTENING FOR SOME SOUND FROM 51 JOURNE
UPSTAIRS.
SHE WASN'T ASLEEP WHEN I FINISHED MY WORK UPSTAIRS 53 JOURNE
A WHILE BACK.
UPSTAIRS. 55 JOURNE
SHE'S BEEN UPSTAIRS ALONE ALL MORNING, EH? 56 JOURNE
OR SHE MIGHT START HAVING MOST OF HER MEALS ALONE 56 JOURNE
UPSTAIRS.
AND NOW YOU TELL ME SHE GOT YOU TO LEAVE HER ALONE 57 JOURNE
UPSTAIRS ALL MORNING.
IT IS AS IF THEY WERE WAITING UNTIL SHE GOT 75 JOURNE
UPSTAIRS BEFORE SPEAKING.)
I'M GOING UPSTAIRS FOR A MOMENT, IF YOU'LL EXCUSE 75 JOURNE
ME.
UPSTAIRS.) 79 JOURNE
I MUST GO UPSTAIRS. I HAVEN'T TAKEN ENOUGH. 107 JOURNE
(VAGUELY.) I MUST GO UPSTAIRS. 121 JOURNE
THEN HE STARTS AS HE HEARS A SOUND FROM UPSTAIRS--136 JOURNE
WITH DREAD.)
TYRONE AGAIN LISTENS TO SOUNDS UPSTAIRS--WITH 136 JOURNE
DREAD.)
AND I DON'T WANT TO GO UPSTAIRS, ANYWAY, TILL 138 JOURNE
SHE'S ASLEEP.
THEN TYRONE STOPS, LISTENING TO A SOUND UPSTAIRS.1152 JOURNE
SO I SQUANDERED TWO BUCKS OF YOUR DOUGH TO ESCORT 159 JOURNE
HER UPSTAIRS.
GOT THE IDEA I TOOK HER UPSTAIRS FOR A JOKE. 160 JOURNE
GOD HELP YOU, IF YOU TRY TO GO UPSTAIRS NOW. 80 MISBEG
YOU'LL END UP IN THE CELLAR.
SINCE YOU'VE BEEN PLAYIN' NURSE TO THE YOUNG 16 POET
YANKEE UPSTAIRS.
WHEN YOU WAS UPSTAIRS AT THE BACK TAKING HIM HIS 17 POET
BREAKFAST.
IT'S TIME FOR IT, AND I KNEW YOU'D BE GOING 60 POET
UPSTAIRS.
HARFORD--UPSTAIRS IN BED. 73 POET
(THEY BOTH HEAR A SOUND FROM UPSTAIRS.) 80 POET
NO ONE NOTICED MY RETURN AND WHEN I WENT UPSTAIRS 108 POET
IT OCCURRED TO ME
I'M GOING UPSTAIRS TO BED, MOTHER. 131 POET
AFTER I'D GOT UPSTAIRS IT TOOK ME A WHILE TO GET 142 POET
UP MY COURAGE.
SURE, HE'S ONLY GOIN' UPSTAIRS TO BED. 159 POET
ABOUT NOT MARRYIN' THE YOUNG LAD UPSTAIRS. 179 POET
COME ON UPSTAIRS, CHARLIE, AND HELP ME PACK/ 21 STRANG
(HER VOICE, FRESH AND GIRLISH, CALLS FROM 22 STRANG
UPSTAIRS)
WITH HER FATHER LYING DEAD UPSTAIRS...!) 25 STRANG

UPSTAIRS (CONT'D.)
IS HE UPSTAIRS? 28 STRANG
(HE'S UPSTAIRS ALONE WITH HER... 30 STRANG
THAT'S WHAT SHE'S DOING UPSTAIRS NOW-- 34 STRANG
(WARNINGLY) DO YOU KNOW WHAT I WAS DOING 41 STRANG
UPSTAIRS)
I'LL JUST CARRY NINA UPSTAIRS AND PUT HER ON HER 47 STRANG
BED AND THROW SOMETHING OVER
AND I COULDN'T LEAVE HER UPSTAIRS TO COME AWAY TO 61 STRANG
SEE YOU.
(THEN WITH A GRIM SMILE) WHY, I EVEN LOVE THAT 62 STRANG
IDIOT UPSTAIRS.
I'LL RUN UPSTAIRS. 73 STRANG
NINA'S UPSTAIRS LYING DOWN. 73 STRANG
(EAGERLY) RIGHT UPSTAIRS. 101 STRANG
(FROM UPSTAIRS, HER VOICE STRANGE AND EXCITED) 123 STRANG
(WITH GENTLE BULLYING) YOU'RE GOING UPSTAIRS TO 464 WELDED
BED.
IT'S THE FIRST DOOR UPSTAIRS ON YOUR RIGHT--IF 465 WELDED
YOU'D RATHER GO ALONE.
THE FIRST DOOR TO THE RIGHT--UPSTAIRS-- 465 WELDED
UPSTAIRS--IF I COULD HAVE GONE--I MIGHT HAVE BEEN 469 WELDED
FREE.
YOU'LL WANT TO GO UPSTAIRS AND POWDER YOUR NOSE. 469 WELDED

UPSTART
CURSED YANKEE UPSTART/ 75 POET

UPSTART'S
AND AN ESTATE COMPARED TO WHICH ANY YANKEE 112 POET
UPSTART'S HOME IN THIS COUNTRY

UPSTATE
HE'D COME FROM A HICK BURG UPSTATE. 23 HUGHIE
THEY'RE UPSTATE COUNTRY FOLKS--FRUIT GROWERS AND 38 STRANG
FARMERS, WELL OFF, I BELIEVE.
I WENT UPSTATE AND INVESTIGATED... 149 STRANG

UPSTREAM
THE BOW AND AMIDSHIP OF THE CRUISER ARE OFF RIGHT,158 STRANG
POINTED UPSTREAM.

UPSTREET
I'VE GOT TO GO UPSTREET. 271 AHWILD
I RAN INTO HIM UPSTREET THIS AFTERNOON AND HE WAS 292 AHWILD
MEEK AS PIE.
'CAUSE I SEEN PETER UPSTREET YESTERDAY 11 ELECTR
I'M GOING UPSTREET TO GET THE LATEST NEWS. 35 ELECTR

UPSTRETCHED
ARMS UPSTRETCHED TOWARD THE STARS, THEIR HEADS 290 LAZARU
THROWN BACK.)
AND GRASPS THE NOOSE WITH BOTH HER UPSTRETCHED 601 ROPE
HANDS.

UPSY
UPSY--DAISY/ 130 BEYOND

UPTAKE
SLOW ON THE UPTAKE, AND HAS NO SENSE OF HUMOR. 56 MISBEG

UPTOWN
YOU TALKED TO HIM WHEN YOU WENT UPTOWN YESTERDAY, 30 JOURNE
DIDN'T YOU.
I HAVE TO GO UPTOWN ON BUSINESS, ANYWAY. 73 JOURNE
(ABRUPTLY.) WHAT DO YOU WANT ME TO DO THIS 80 JOURNE
AFTERNOON, NOW YOU'RE GOING UPTOWNS
THEN I'D BETTER GO UPTOWN WITH EDMUND. 81 JOURNE
I'M GLAD JAMIE IS GOING UPTOWN. 82 JOURNE
COME TO THINK OF IT, I DO HAVE TO DRIVE UPTOWN. 86 JOURNE
YOU'LL PROBABLY MEET SOME OF YOUR FRIENDS UPTOWN 90 JOURNE
IT'S SUCH A TIRING TRIP UPTOWN IN THE DIRTY OLD 92 JOURNE
TROLLEY ON A HOT DAY LIKE THIS.
NOW I THINK OF IT, YOU MIGHT AS WELL GO UPTOWN. 94 JOURNE
I WOULD HAVE BEEN LONELY DRIVING UPTOWN ALONE. 102 JOURNE
IT MUST BE MUCH MORE CHEERFUL IN THE BARROOMS 108 JOURNE
UPTOWN.
BESIDES, I WANTED TO TREAT CATHLEEN BECAUSE I HAD 116 JOURNE
HER DRIVE UPTOWN WITH ME.
I THOUGHT YOU'D GONE BACK UPTOWN TO MEET HIM. 129 JOURNE
I HOPE TO GOD HE MISSES THE LAST CAR AND HAS TO 133 JOURNE
STAY UPTOWN/
(CHANGING THE SUBJECT.) WHAT DID YOU DO UPTOWN 158 JOURNE
TONIGHT?

UPTURNED
(KNEELING BESIDE REUBEN, ONE HAND ON THE FOREHEAD 489 DYNAMO
OF HIS UPTURNED FACE)
HER UPTURNED UNMASKED FACE LIKE THAT OF A 264 GGBROW
RAPTUROUS VISIONARY.
(HE MUTTS, HIS FACE UPTURNED--PLEADINGLY) 307 GGBROW
THE COLOR OF RICH EARTH UPTURNED BY THE PLOW. 274 LAZARU
HER FACE UPTURNED, HER LIPS PRAYING. 288 LAZARU

UPWARD
(A TRACE OF AWE IN HIS TONES--HE GLANCES UPWARD) 536 'ILE
UP THE PLATES AND CASTS A QUICK GLANCE UPWARD AT 536 'ILE
THE SKYLIGHT.)
(LOOKING UPWARD AND POINTING) 93 BEYOND
THE FAINT TRACE OF A PATH LEADING UPWARD TO IT 129 BEYOND
FROM THE LEFT FOREGROUND CAN BE
IS BORNE UPWARD FROM THE BEACH BELOW. 555 CROSS
(POINTING UPWARD) UP ON THE POOP. 557 CROSS
AS THEY LOOK UPWARD, THIS SOFTENS.) 204 DESIRE
STEEL WORK, INSULATORS, BUSSES, SWITCHES, ETC. 483 DYNAMO
STRETCHING UPWARD TO THE ROOF.
THEIR SIX CUPPED ARMS STRETCHING UPWARD, 483 DYNAMO
UPWARD IN THE DIMLY LIGHTED GALLERY-- 484 DYNAMO
THEY SQUIRM UPWARD TOWARD HIM IN TWISTED 190 EJONES
ATTITUDES.
THE INTERLOCKED HOPES OF CREEPERS REACHING UPWARD 198 EJONES
TO ENTWINE THE TREE TRUNKS
ANTELOPE HORNS ARE ON EACH SIDE OF HIS HEAD, 200 EJONES
BRANCHING UPWARD.
(LOOKING UPWARD AT THE MOON AND SINGING IN LOW 262 GGBROW
TONE AS THEY ENTER)
(SHE LOOKS UPWARD IN SILENCE. 262 GGBROW
(STAGGERING TO HIS FULL HEIGHT AND LOOKING UPWARD 299 GGBROW
DEFIANTLY)

1741

UTMOST

UPWARD (CONT'D.)

HIS EYES, HIS ARMS, HIS WHOLE BODY STRAIN UPWARD, 319 GGBROW
(SHAKING HIS FIST UPWARD--CONTEMPTUOUSLY) 224 HA APE
HE BLINKS UPWARD THROUGH THE MURK TRYING TO FIND 225 HA APE
THE OWNER OF THE WHISTLE,
(SHAKING ONE FIST UPWARD AND BEATING ON HIS CHEST 232 HA APE
WITH THE OTHER)
AND FOR A TIME AFTER THAT I KEPT ON UPWARD WITH 150 JOURNE
AMBITION HIGH.
THROW YOUR GAZE UPWARD/ 289 LAZARU
GAZING UPWARD INTO THE PALL OF 312 LAZARU
WALKING UNDER AN ARM OF THE CROSS UNCONCERNEDLY 327 LAZARU
WITHOUT AN UPWARD GLANCE.
UPWARD IT SPRINGS LIKE A LARK FROM A FIELD, AND 345 LAZARU
SINGS/
AS IF HE WERE TAKING AN OATH TO LIFE ON HER HEART,349 LAZARU
LOOKS UPWARD AND LAUGHS,
FLARE UPWARE UPWARD AND ARE REFLECTED ON THEIR 367 LAZARU
MASKS IN DANCING WAVES OF LIGHT)
HIS ARMS STRAINING UPWARD TO THE SKY, A TENDER, 371 LAZARU
UPWARDS
KEEP THY HEART FREE AND RAISED UPWARDS TO GOD 291 GGBROW
URBANE
(IMMEDIATELY URBANE AND SMILING) 129 STRANG
URBANELY
(THE SUCCESSFUL ARCHITECT NOW--URBANELY) 306 GGBROW
(HOLDING OUT HIS HAND, URBANELY POLITE) 76 STRANG
URBANITY
BUT HE IMMEDIATELY ASSUMES AN AIR OF GENTLEMANLY 44 POET
URBANITY AND BOWS TO HER.)
URGE
OF ONE WHO LEANS TO EVIL MORE THROUGH WEAKNESS 332 LAZARU
THAN ANY INSTINCTIVE URGE.
NO URGE TO DO ANYTHING EXCEPT SETTLE DOWN ON HIS 55 MISBEG
ESTATE AND LIVE THE LIFE OF A
AND THAT BRINGS ME TO WHAT I WANT YOU TO URGE HER 36 STRANG
TO DO.
URGED
I AS MUCH AS URGED YE T' DO IT/ 266 DESIRE
I URGED THEM TO GO. 118 ELECTR
LET HIM BE URGED TO EAT AND DRINK UNTIL HE CAN 418 MARCOM
HOLD NO MORE,
SAM'S OWN MOTHER URGED ME TO DO IT. 84 STRANG
WITHOUT BEING TOO RUDE, I URGED HIM TO GET BACK TO155 STRANG
HIS WORK,
URGENCY
(SUDDENLY WITH DESPERATE URGENCY) 667 ICEMAN
(WITH A STRANGE FRIGHTENED URGENCY.) 37 MANSNS
(SUDDENLY, MOVED BY A STRANGE URGENCY, HE SPRINGS 111 MANSNS
TO HIS FEET
URGENT
MARRIED, THE MOST URGENT INVITATIONS TO VISIT HER. 50 STRANG
(AS IF UNDER SOME URGENT COMPULSION FROM WITHIN) 185 STRANG
URGENTLY
WHO KEEPS INSISTING URGENTLY) 220 AHWILD
(URGENTLY) DON'T FAIL US, DOCTOR. 562 CROSS
(HE SNAPS HIS FINGERS--THEN URGENTLY) 548 DIFRNT
(THEN URGENTLY) AND NOW YOU MUST GO/ 42 ELECTR
(URGENTLY) LIGHT THE CANDLES/ 653 ICEMAN
SARA SAYS URGENTLY.) 81 POET
URGES
RUTH URGES) WE'LL BE LATE FOR SUPPER, ROB. 93 BEYOND
(SHE URGES HIM TO THE COMPANIONWAY DOOR, 113 ELECTR
(SHE TURNS HIM INTO THE PATH LEADING OFF LEFT AND 194 MANSNS
URGES HIM ALONG IT.)
THE NEXT MINUTE SOMETHING HATEFUL URGES ME TO 94 STRANG
DRIVE HIM INTO DOING IT/...))
URGING
THEN URGING HIMSELF IN WITH MANFUL RESOLUTION) 190 EJONES
(URGING HIM TOWARD THE DOOR) 42 ELECTR
(QUICKLY, URGING HIM ON COMMANDINGLY) 138 ELECTR
URGINGLY
(THEN AS SHE REMAINS SILENT--URGINGLY) 82 STRANG
URN
OUR URN SIDE BY SIDE AND TOUCHING ONE ANOTHER... 148 STRANG
USAGE
WHICH HARD USAGE HAS FAILED TO STIFLE, A SENSE OF 7 ANNA
HUMOR MOCKING,
USEFUL
WE MIGHT AS WELL START MAKING OURSELVES USEFUL. 142 ELECTR
I'VE REFUSED TO BECOME A USEFUL MEMBER OF ITS 591 ICEMAN
SOCIETY.
OUGHT TO BE USEFUL TO 'EM. 522 INZONE
(THEN SOMBERLY) A LITTLE FEAR IS USEFUL EVEN FOR 329 LAZARU
LIONS--
HE'S A CAPABLE BANKER AND CAN STILL BE USEFUL TO 150 MANSNS
US.
USEFULNESS
HE BELIEVES IN WEARING HIS CLOTHES TO THE LIMIT OF 13 JOURNE
USEFULNESS.
USELESS
SO I DON'T FEEL SUCH A USELESS OLD MAID, AFTER 214 AHWILD
ALL.
IT IS USELESS/ 565 DAYS
(TO LARRY) LET US IGNORE THIS USELESS YOUTH, 596 ICEMAN
LARRY.
(THEN DULLY.) I KNOW IT'S USELESS TO TALK. 45 JOURNE
IT'S USELESS TO BE ANGRY NOW. 75 JOURNE
USELESSNESS
(SUBSIDING AS IF REALIZING THE USELESSNESS OF THIS537 'ILE
OUTBURST--SHAKING HIS HEAD--
(SEEING THE USELESSNESS OF STRUGGLING, GIVES WAY 174 EJONES
TO FRANTIC TERROR,
AT FIRST HE STRUGGLES FIERCELY, BUT SEEING THE 525 INZONE
USELESSNESS OF THIS,
USES
(IN HER MOST SEDUCTIVE TONES WHICH SHE USES ALL 225 DESIRE
THROUGH THIS SCENE)

USES (CONT'D.)
(PROUDLY) I GOT BRAINS AND I USES 'EM QUICK, 178 EJONES
AND ONLY USES HIS HOUSE TO SLEEP IN. 302 GGBROW
HE USES ME TO RUN ERRANDS WHEN THERE AIN'T NO ONE 34 HUGHIE
ELSE HANDY.
SHE USES NO ROUGE OR ANY SORT OF MAKE-UP. 12 JOURNE
WHO USES LOVE BUT LOVES ONLY HERSELF, WHO IS 13 MANSNS
ENTIRELY RUTHLESS AND LETS NOTHING
RESIGNATION HAS COME INTO HER FACE, A RESIGNATION 189 STRANG
THAT USES NO MAKE-UP.
USETER
(SADLY) SHE USETER BE AWFUL NICE TO ME BEFORE-- 538 'ILE
I USETER GO TO CHOICH ONCT--SURE--WHEN I WAS A 234 HA APE
KID.
AND CHUCK SOME STONES IN THE OCEAN SAME'S WE 589 ROPE
USETER, REMEMBER?
I USETER SPY ON HIM WHEN I WAS A KID--MAW USED TO 599 ROPE
MAKE ME--
USETH
* BEHOLD, EVERY ONE THAT USETH PROVERBS SHALL USE 579 ROPE
USHER
AN USHER OF THE PALACE COMES QUIETLY TO MARCO 378 MARCOM
USHERS
(HE THROWS OPEN THE DOOR AND USHERS HER INTO HIS 304 GGBROW
PRIVATE OFFICE.)
USTER
IS YOU SELLIN' ME LIKE DEY USTER BEFO' DE WARS 197 EJONES
USUAL
(TARTLY, BUT EVIDENTLY SUPPRESSING HER USUAL SMILE198 AHWILD
WHERE HE IS CONCERNED)
ROBERT'S LATE FOR HIS DINNER AGAIN, AS USUAL. 113 BEYOND
THE STUPID LIVES WE LEAD--AND, OF COURSE, THE 517 DAYS
USUAL FINANCIAL WORRIES.
THAT'S WHAT I HEARS USUAL. 513 DIFRNT
PRAYING AS USUAL-- 462 DYNAMO
WELL, I SUPPOSE THAT'S THE USUAL WAY OF IT. 22 ELECTR
(WITH TIRED SOLICITUDE) I SUPPOSE YOU HAVEN'T 291 GGBROW
EATEN A THING, AS USUAL.
AT RIGHT, THE USUAL NUMBERED TIERS OF MAILBOXES, 7 HUGHIE
AND ABOVE THEM A CLOCK.
BUT HE GOT TOO GREEDY AND WHEN THE USUAL REFORM 594 ICEMAN
INVESTIGATION CAME
DRESSED IN THE USUAL TAWDRY GET-UP. 611 ICEMAN
(THEY ALL JOIN IN WITH THE USUAL HUMOROUS TOASTS.1620 ICEMAN
(WITH A FLASH OF HIS USUAL HUMOR--REBUKINGLY) 651 ICEMAN
IT IS ENTIRELY DIFFERENT FROM THE USUAL IRASCIBLE 654 ICEMAN
BEEFING HE DELIGHTS IN AND
ARMS AND HEAD ON THE TABLE AS USUAL, A WHISKEY 665 ICEMAN
GLASS BESIDE HIS LIMP HAND.
(WARMING UP, CHANGES ABRUPTLY TO HIS USUAL 724 ICEMAN
DECLAMATORY DENUNCIATION)
WELL, I BRINGS IT DOWN HERE SAME AS USUAL 518 INZONE
NOT LIKE THE USUAL BROTHERS/ 35 JOURNE
HE'LL BE LATE, AS USUAL. 60 JOURNE
(FORCING A LAUGH.) ALTHOUGH, AS USUAL, I COULDN'T 68 JOURNE
FIND MY GLASSES.
(TALKS MORE FAMILIARLY THAN USUAL BUT NEVER WITH 98 JOURNE
INTENTIONAL IMPERTINENCE
THEY'LL CUT UNDER OUR PRICES WITH THEIR CHEAP JUNK365 MARCOM
AS USUAL.
OH, HE WAS FULL OF STUPID GAS, AS USUAL, 20 MISBEG
SLAVING AND TOILING AS USUAL, I SEE. 39 MISBEG
(IN A HOARSE WHISPER) MEET ME TONIGHT, AS USUAL, 64 MISBEG
DOWN BY THE PIPPEN.
JIM SAW YOU'D GOT DRUNKER THAN USUAL AND YOU WERE 79 MISBEG
AN EASY MARK FOR A JOKE.
HE DOES NOT APPEAR TO BE DRUNK--THAT IS, HE SHOWS 100 MISBEG
NONE OF THE USUAL SYMPTOMS.
(IN HIS USUAL EASY, KIDDING WAY) 112 MISBEG
NONE OF MY USUAL MORNING-AFTER STUFF-- 171 MISBEG
(FORCING HER USUAL REACTION TO HIS THREATS) 177 MISBEG
AS USUAL, AND YOU'LL WEAR YOUR BEAUTIFUL UNIFORM, 59 POET
AS USUAL, 107 POET
NOT THAT HER FATHER'S DEATH IS A SHOCK IN THE 34 STRANG
USUAL SENSE OF GRIEF.
(MARSDEN COMES IN FROM THE REAR, SMILING, 146 STRANG
IMMACULATELY DRESSED AS USUAL.
(AFFECTIONATELY) I WAS FURGETTING YOU--AS USUAL. 469 WELDED
USUALLY
DO I USUALLY COME WAY BACK HERE FOR DINNER ON A 264 AHWILD
BUSY DAYS
YOU USUALLY DO WHEN SHE AND RUTH COME OVER. 97 BEYOND
WHAT TIME DOES JOHN USUALLY GET HOMES 916 DAYS
USUALLY THE MEN DISCUSSED AREN'T OUR HUSBANDS, AND517 DAYS
AREN'T EVEN GOOD LOVERS.
HE LOATHED SUCH AFFAIRS USUALLY, 537 DAYS
DON'T USUALLY GO IN FOR PSYCHIC NONSENSE. 557 DAYS
YOU USUALLY READ LONG AFTER THAT. 18 ELECTR
USUALLY HE'S LIKE HIMSELF ONLY QUIET AND SAD-- 148 ELECTR
WHICH USUALLY ADORN THE SITTING ROOMS OF SUCH 269 GGBROW
HOUSES.
ERIE USUALLY SPEAKS IN A LOW, GUARDED TONE, 9 HUGHIE
HESS USUALLY HAD BETTER SENSE, BUT SHE WAS IN A 608 ICEMAN
HURRY TO GO TO CHURCH.
TREES, BUT USUALLY THEY BEAR HUMAN FRUIT/ 327 LAZARU
DEAD QUEENS IN THE WEST USUALLY LIE IN STATE. 351 MARCOM
HE USUALLY HAS THE SELF-CONFIDENT ATTITUDE OF 56 MISBEG
ACKNOWLEDGED SUPERIORITY.
HIS MOUTH USUALLY SET IN A HALF-LEERING GRIN. 8 POET
(CONSOLINGLY) WELL, THE SPORT HERO USUALLY 30 STRANG
DOESN'T STAR AFTER COLLEGE.
UTENSILS
KITCHEN UTENSILS HANG FROM NAILS. 206 DESIRE
UTMOST
PUTTING ON EXPRESSIONS OF THE UTMOST CORDIALITY) 365 MARCOM

UTOPIA

UTOPIA
A GREEDLESS UTOPIA, WHILE ALL DAY IN MY OFFICE I 46 MANSNS
WAS REALLY GETTING THE GREATEST

UTTER
HIS FACE IS ONE LARGE, SMILING, HAPPY BEAM OF 221 AHWILD
UTTER APPRECIATION OF LIFE.
HIS FACE IS PALE AND HAGGARD, HIS EXPRESSION ONE 129 BEYOND
OF UTTER DESPONDENCY.
I'VE BEEN AN UTTER FAILURE, AND I'VE DRAGGED YOU 148 BEYOND
WITH ME.
UTTER THEM--FINALLY FINDING HIS VOICE, HE 451 DYNAMO
STAMMERS)
SARA, I WOULD LIKE TO UTTER A WORD OF WARNING--IN 67 MANSNS
MOTHER'S PRESENCE.
(LISTERING IN UTTER CONFUSION, 120 POET
HIS LIPS MOVE CONVULSIVELY AS HE MAKES A 596 ROPE
TACMENDOUS EFFORT TO UTTER WORDS.)
BUT UTTER LONELINESS/.....) 113 STRANG

UTTERLY
AS IF THIS LAST FACT HAD UTTERLY CONDEMNED HIM IN 531 INZONE
THEIR EYES.)
HAVE YOU BECOME SO UTTERLY COARSE THAT YOU FEEL NO 97 MANSNS
SHAME BUT ACTUALLY BOAST

UTTERS
(THEN UTTERS AN EXCLAMATION OF JOY) 540 'ILE
ANNA UTTERS AN EXCLAMATION OF ALARM AND HURRIES TO 39 ANNA
HIS SIDE.)
UTTERS A LOW, CHOKING CRY AND SHRINKS AWAY FROM 226 HA APE
HIM.
SMITTY DRAWS HIS HAND AWAY SLOWLY AND UTTERS A 523 INZONE
SIGH OF RELIEF.)
HIS VOICE UTTERS AND WARMS TO HIS WORK) 431 MARCOM

VACANCY
THERE MAY NOT BE ANOTHER SHIP FOR BUENOS AIRES 141 BEYOND
WITH A VACANCY IN MONTHS.
STARING OFF INTO VACANCY.) 466 CARIBE
THE CLERK'S FACE IS TAUT WITH VACANCY. 29 HUGHIE

VACANT
LEAVING THE MIDDLE ONE (SID'S VACANT) WHILE THEY 221 AHWILD
ARE DOING THIS.
IS THAT THE ONLY ANSWER--TO PIN MY SOUL INTO EVERY279 GGBROW
VACANT DIAPER!
THE NIGHT CLERK REGARDS HIM WITH VACANT, 19 HUGHIE
THERE WOULDN'T BE A SINGLE VACANT CEMETERY LOT 628 ICEMAN
LEFT IN THIS GLORIOUS COUNTRY.
GRAB THE LAST TWO THEMSELVES AND SIT DOWN IN THE 658 ICEMAN
TWO VACANT CHAIRS REMAINING
THE ONE CHAIR BY THE TABLE AT RIGHT, REAR, OF THEM696 ICEMAN
IS VACANT.
HE NODS HIS HEAD IN A NUMBED ACQUIESCENCE, FORCING155 MANSNS
A VACANT SMILE.)
(HE PAUSES, STARING INTO THE MOONLIGHT WITH VACANT143 MISBEG
EYES.)

VACATE
YOU'D TELL HIM YOU'D VACATE THE PREMISES 25 MISBEG

VACATION
IT'S NOT MY IDEA OF HAVING A GOOD TIME IN 192 AHWILD
VACATION.
IT ISN'T FAIR TO ASK YOU--IN YOUR VACATION. 211 AHWILD
YOU NEED VACATION, YES/ 23 ANNA
(A BIT EVASIVELY) OH, I DECIDED A VACATION WAS 506 DAYS
DUE ME.
THAT'S THE REAL REASON I DECIDED TO TAKE MY 508 DAYS
VACATION IN THE EAST, JACK.
DATE PLACE TO COME TO WHEN YOU WAS ON VACATION 525 DIFRNT
FROM THE HORRID OLD ARMY.
AND AFTER THAT I'M GOING TO TAKE A LONG VACATION--304 GGBROW
IS GETTING A BIT QUEER AND IT'S TIME HE TOOK A 311 GGBROW
VACATION.
I WAS LIKE A VACATION, MA'AM. 102 JOURNE
WHEN I CAME HOME FOR EASTER VACATION. 105 JOURNE
(ELATED, EXCITED AS A CROWD OF SCHOOLBOYS GOING ON323 LAZARU
A VACATION.
WOULD MEAN IT WOULD BE THEIR VACATION WITH THEIR 72 MANSNS
MOTHER, NOT MINE WITH MY WIFE.
A VACATION WOULD BE IN ORDER AT SUCH TIMES. 72 MANSNS
EASTER VACATION... 6 STRANG
COULDN'T AFFORD A VACATION... 52 STRANG
AND YOU'LL GET ANOTHER SHIP UP THERE AFTER YOU'VE 502 VOYAGE
'AD A VACATIONS

VAGUE
SHE STARES UP AT HIM WITH A STUPID EXPRESSION, A 551 'ILE
VAGUE SMILE ON HER LIPS.
THEN LOOKS AROUND FROM FACE TO FACE, FIXING EACH 224 AHWILD
WITH A VAGUE, BLURRED,
(HE OPENS HIS EYES AND BLINKS UP AT HER WITH VAGUE 33 ANNA
WONDER.)
(HE GETS TO HIS FEET AND SHAKES ROBERT'S HAND, 101 BEYOND
MUTTERING A VAGUE)
SHADOWY AND VAGUE. 166 BEYOND
CASTING A VAGUE GLOBULAR SHADOW OF THE COMPASS ON 555 CROSS
THE FLOOR.
CABOT WALKS SLOWLY UP FROM THE LEFT, STARING UP AT245 DESIRE
THE SKY WITH A VAGUE FACE.)
HIS FACE IS AS VAGUE AS HIS REACTIONS ARE 251 DESIRE
CONFUSED.
(HE COMES IN AND SHAKES THE HAND SHE HOLDS OUT TO 534 DIFRNT
HIM IN A LIMP, VAGUE,
THE MOONLIGHT IS ALMOST COMPLETELY SHUT OUT AND 198 EJONES
ONLY A VAGUE WAN LIGHT FILTERS
WITH A VAGUE GESTURE OF PUZZLED BEWILDERMENT. 200 EJONES
WHEN HE SPEAKS IT IS JERKILY, WITH A STRANGE, 74 ELECTR
VAGUE, PREOCCUPIED AIR.
(IN A VAGUE MOCKING TONE) SAY, WHERE DO I GO FRUM251 HA APE
HEEE?
THE OTHER CAGES ARE VAGUE, 251 HA APE
(IN THE VAGUE TONE OF A CORPSE WHICH ADMITS IT 18 HUGHIE
ONCE OVERHEARD A FAVORABLE RUMOR
BULGING EYES FULL OF A VAGUE ENVY FOR THE BLIND. 19 HUGHIE

VAGUE (CONT'D.)
(THEN AS HE RECEIVES NO REPLY--WITH VAGUE 722 ICEMAN
UNEASINESS)
(THEY ALL LOOK AT HIM WITH PUZZLED GLANCES FULL OF518 INZONE
A VAGUE APPREHENSION.)
(WITH A VAGUE EXASPERATION AT BEING BROUGHT BACK 106 JOURNE
FROM HER DREAM.)
(A SHADOW OF VAGUE GUILT CROSSES HER FACE.) 114 JOURNE
(SHE LAUGHS--A QUEER, VAGUE LITTLE INWARD LAUGH) 346 LAZARU
AND THERE IS A CERTAIN VAGUE QUALITY IN HIS MANNER100 MISBEG
AND SPEECH.
(TYRONE REGARDS HIM WITH VAGUE SURPRISE.) 101 MISBEG
HE SEEMS TO BE LAPSING AGAIN INTO VAGUE 115 MISBEG
PREOCCUPATION.)
(WITH VAGUE PITY) DON'T CRY. 138 MISBEG
A VAGUE COMPREHENSION COMING INTO HER FACE-- 475 WELDED
SCORNFULLY)

VAGUELY
(VAGUELY--AGAIN PASSES HER HAND OVER HER EYES) 548 'ILE
HE MAKES HIS WAY VAGUELY TOWARD HIS PLACE, 224 AHWILD
(HE BUMPS VAGUELY INTO LILY'S CHAIR AS HE ATTEMPTS224 AHWILD
TO PASS BEHIND HER--
(SINKS BACK INTO PREOCCUPATION--SCANNING THE 250 AHWILD
PAPER--VAGUELY)
CONFIDENTIAL HALF-WHISPER WITH SOMETHING VAGUELY 5 ANNA
PLAINTIVE IN ITS QUALITY.
(VAGUELY) NUTTING--NUTTING. 20 ANNA
(HER VOICE VAGUELY FRIGHTENED, TAKING HER FATHER'S142 BEYOND
HAND)
(VAGUELY) I'LL WRITE, OR SOMETHING OF THAT SORT. 149 BEYOND
(STILL UNDER THE INFLUENCE OF SUNSET--VAGUELY) 206 DESIRE
(NODDING VAGUELY) AY-EH--DOWN TWO WEEKS BACK-- 248 DESIRE
PURTY'S A PICTER.
(VAGUELY) I TUK HIS MAW'S PLACE. 248 DESIRE
(VAGUELY) I'LL BE OVER--IN A MINUTE. 548 DIFRNT
(HAS NOTICED THE NOISE OF MRS. LIGHT'S MOVEMENTS 439 DYNAMO
AND LOOKS DOWN VAGUELY)
(AUTOMATICALLY MAKES A CONFUSED MOTION OF MILITARY122 ELECTR
SALUTE--VAGUELY)
PENITENTLY HE PATS HER HAND--VAGUELY) 270 GGBROW
(TAKING IT--VAGUELY) OHS 275 GGBROW
HE'S PILED ON LAYERS OF PROTECTIVE FAT, BUT 296 GGBROW
VAGUELY,
(HE ADDS VAGUELY,) OR MAYBE IT IS FORTY-FOUR, 13 HUGHIE
AND THE NIGHT VAGUELY REMINDS HIM OF DEATH, AND HE 30 HUGHIE
IS VAGUELY FRIGHTENED.
INTERESTED IN SPITE OF HIMSELF AND AT THE SAME 591 ICEMAN
TIME VAGUELY UNEASY.)
BUT IMPRESSED AND DISAPPOINTED AND MADE VAGUELY 620 ICEMAN
UNEASY
(KNOWS HE IS LYING--VAGUELY.) 40 JOURNE
(VAGUELY.) YOU HAVEN'T SEEN MY GLASSES ANYWHERE, 81 JOURNE
HAVE YOU, JAMES?
(VAGUELY.) THERE IS SOMETHING I WANTED TO SAY. 82 JOURNE
(VAGUELY RESENTFUL.) WELL, HE'S A FINE, HANDSOME,101 JOURNE
KIND GENTLEMAN JUST THE SAME.
VAGUELY.) IT WAS KIND OF YOU TO KEEP ME COMPANY 102 JOURNE
THIS AFTERNOON, CATHLEEN.
(VAGUELY.) YES, HE KNOWS ME. 103 JOURNE
(VAGUELY.) 103 JOURNE
(VAGUELY.) I MUST GO UPSTAIRS. 121 JOURNE
(VAGUELY--HIS VOICE THICK.) IT'S MADNESS, YES. 134 JOURNE
HIS HEAD BOWS AND HE STARES DULLY AT THE CARDS ON 146 JOURNE
THE TABLE--VAGUELY.)
(HE GLANCES VAGUELY AT HIS CARDS.) 150 JOURNE
SHE GLANCES AROUND VAGUELY, HER FOREHEAD PUCKERED 171 JOURNE
AGAIN.)
VAGUELY.) 176 JOURNE
(THEN WITH A GLANCE AT MIRIAM'S BODY AND A 356 LAZARU
SHUDDERING AWAY FROM IT--VAGUELY)
FOR A MOMENT HE STANDS GLANCING ABOUT THE ROOM 140 MANSNS
VAGUELY, HIS GAZE AVOIDING SARA.
PATS HER SHOULDER MECHANICALLY--VAGUELY.) 145 MANSNS
(TRYING TO FORCE HIMSELF FROM HIS DAY DREAM-- 145 MANSNS
VAGUELY PLACATING.)
(VAGUELY) YES. 399 MARCOM
HE STARES VAGUELY AT NOTHING. 102 MISBEG
(VAGUELY SURPRISED BY HER TONE) 106 MISBEG
(STARING AT NOTHING--VAGUELY) 119 MISBEG
(VAGUELY) WHATS 127 MISBEG
(QUICKLY) OH--THAT'S RIGHT--I DID SAY--(VAGUELY) 127 MISBEG
WHAT BLONDES
(PAUSES--VAGUELY) YOU DON'T GET IT, JOSIE. 127 MISBEG
HE MUTTERS VAGUELY, AS IF TALKING TO HIMSELF) 138 MISBEG
(OPENS HIS EYES--VAGUELY) LIKE WHATS 142 MISBEG
(VAGUELY SURPRISED--SPEAKS RAPIDLY AGAIN.) 82 POET
RILEY STUMBLES VAGUELY AFTER THEM. 104 POET
(ANSWERS VAGUELY FROM HER PREOCCUPATION WITH THE 146 POET
PULICE--
(VAGUELY--SHE HAS EVIDENTLY NOT HEARD MUCH OF WHAT 54 STRANG
HE SAID)
VAGUELY.) WELL, I SUPPOSE YOU'VE GOT TO BE CAREFUL 73 STRANG
OF EVERY LITTLE THING WHEN
(WHO HAS ONLY HALF-HEARD AND HASN'T UNDERSTOOD, 75 STRANG
SAYS VAGUELY)
(VAGUELY--WONDERINGLY) (CHARLIE.... 94 STRANG
(VAGUELY) VERY WELL. 101 STRANG
(VAGUELY MAKING TALK) I GOT CHARLIE TO LIE DOWN. 105 STRANG
(VAGUELY IRRITATED--THINKING) 162 STRANG
(VAGUELY TAKING OFF HIS DERBY HAT AND PUTTING IT 497 VOYAGE
ON AGAIN--PLAINTIVELY)
(VAGUELY) NO--YOU DON'T UNDERSTAND-- 465 WELDED
(VAGUELY OFFENDED--IMPATIENTLY) 474 WELDED

VAGUENESS
WONDERING VAGUENESS. 224 AHWILD

VAIN
SHE TRIES IN VAIN TO KEEP THE MEN QUIET. 470 CARIBE

VAIN (CONT'D.)
AND I'M VAIN ENOUGH NOT TO CRAVE ANY MALE VIEWING 517 DAYS
THE WRECKAGE
SUDDENLY OVERCOME BY A WAVE OF DROWSINESS HE TRIES555 DAYS
IN VAIN TO FIGHT BACK)
IN A VAIN EFFORT TO CONCEAL TRACES OF HER TEARS. 505 DIFRNT
WHY I BECAME A JUDGE AND A MAYOR AND SUCH VAIN 55 ELECTR
TRUCK.
NOT A BIT STUCK-UP OR VAIN. 105 JOURNE
I WAS SO PLEASED AND VAIN. 115 JOURNE
NOT FOR VAIN TEARS I WENT UP AT THAT HOUR. 133 JOURNE
TRYING IN VAIN TO ATTRACT HIS OR CAESAR'S 341 LAZARU
ATTENTION.
AND MAKING HIM VAIN AND SPOILING HIM/ 64 MANSNS
(HE DOES NOT SEEM TO HEAR.) STILL SO VAIN AND 128 MANSNS
STUBBORNS
LAUGHING WITH HER TO THINK OF THE PITIABLE 162 MANSNS
SPECTACLE I MAKE WAITING IN VAIN/
HIM, DOES HE, THE VAIN BROADWAY CROOK/ 90 MISBEG
(IN A LIGHT TONE.) FAITH, I SUPPOSE I MUST HAVE 44 POET
LOOKED A VAIN PEACOCK.
DO I HEAR MY NAME TAKEN IN VAINS 197 STRANG
VAINER
THE HEALTHIER AND FATTER YOU GET, THE VAINER YOU 27 JOURNE
BECOME.
VAINLY
IN A VOICE WHICH HE VAINLY ATTEMPTS TO KEEP CALM) 135 BEYOND
AND NOW--(HE STOPS AS IF SEEKING VAINLY FOR WORDS)161 BEYOND
(SEEKING VAINLY FOR SOME WORD OF COMFORT) 486 CARDIF
HE PACES UP AND DOWN TRYING VAINLY TO CALM 426 DYNAMO
HIMSELF)
SEEKING VAINLY TO DISCOVER HIS WHEREABOUTS BY 189 EJONES
THEIR CONFORMATION.)
IN A TONE SHE VAINLY TRIES TO MAKE KINDLY AND 77 ELECTR
PERSUASIVE)
VAIT
LONG TIME AY VAIT FOR YOU. 6 ANNA
SHE GAT TIRED VAIT ALL TIME SVEDEN FOR ME VEN AY 9 ANNA
DON'T NEVER COME.
AND VHEN DEIR BOYS GROW UP, GO TO SEA, DEY SIT AND 28 ANNA
VAIT SOME MORE.
DEY SET AND VAIT ALL 'LONE. 28 ANNA
LONG TIME AY VAIT FOR YOU.= 41 ANNA
YOU VAIT HERE, ANNA'S 62 ANNA
I VAIT TO SAY GOOD-BYE TO HARRY AND JIMMY, TOO. 677 ICEMAN
VAITING
YOU VASN'T VAITING FOR ME, AY BET. 64 ANNA
YOU VAS VAITING, YOU SAYS 65 ANNA
VALET
I'D HIRE OUR DEAR BULLY, HARDER, FOR A VALET. 126 MISBEG
VALIANTLY
(VALIANTLY) I AM NOT SLEEPY/ 252 AHWILD
VALLEY
AND HERE'S OUR CAVALRY BRIGADE IN A VALLEY TOWARD 96 POET
OUR LEFT, IF YOU'LL REMEMBER,
OH, YES, WE WERE WAITING IN THE VALLEY. 97 POET
VALUABLE
BUT HE'S ABOUT THE MOST VALUABLE ADVERTISER I'VE 200 AHWILD
GOT.
TAKE ANYTHING VALUABLE/ 114 ELECTR
(SARCASTICALLY) WELL, GIVE US SOME OF YOUR 248 HA APE
VALUABLE INFORMATION.
THEY WILL MAKE IT MORE VALUABLE. 48 MANSNS
YES, IT IS REALLY A VERY BEAUTIFUL AND VALUABLE 56 MANSNS
PROPERTY, SARA.
TO BELIEVE HUMAN LIVES ARE VALUABLE, AND RELATED 180 MANSNS
TO SOME GOD-INSPIRED MEANING.
YES, A VERY VALUABLE WORLDLY ASSET. 38 MISBEG
LET US PAUSE TO TAKE A LOOK AT THIS VERY VALUABLE 65 MISBFG
PROPERTY.
THAT WOULD HAVE MADE THE PLACE EVEN MORE VALUABLE. 66 MISBEG
VALUE
PLAYING UP ITS SENTIMENTAL VALUE FOR ALL HE IS 258 AHWILD
WORTH.
THE VALUE OF THE PROPERTY--OUR HOME WHICH IS HIS, 564 CROSS
SMITH'S.
A NEW IDEAL TO MEASURE THE VALUE OF OUR LIVES BY/ 542 DAYS
BUT STILL MANAGING TO GET FULL VALUE OUT OF THE 103 ELECTR
CHANTY.)
THAT'LL TEACH HIM THE VALUE OF A DOLLAR/ 260 GGBROW
YOU'VE NEVER KNOWN THE VALUE OF A DOLLAR AND NEVER 31 JOURNE
WILL/
YOU'LL ALWAYS BE BROKE UNTIL YOU LEARN THE VALUE-- 89 JOURNE
YOU'LL LIVE TO LEARN THE VALUE OF A DOLLAR. 128 JOURNE
IT WAS AT HOME I FIRST LEARNED THE VALUE OF A 146 JOURNE
DOLLAR.
(SCORNFULLY) WHAT DO YOU KNOW OF THE VALUE OF A 147 JOURNE
DOLLARS
IT'S ONLY SEVEN DOLLARS A WEEK BUT YOU GET TEN 149 JOURNE
TIMES THAT VALUE.
AND IT'S A POOR WAY TO CONVINCE YOU OF THE VALUE 151 JOURNE
OF A DOLLAR.
I VALUE MYSELF HIGHLY/ 90 MANSNS
SHE MADE ME PAY TWO-FOLD THE VALUE OF EVERY POUND 178 MANSNS
OF FLESH--
VALUED
(WITH BITTER IRONY.) YES, ON PROPERTY VALUED AT A144 JOURNE
QUARTER OF A MILLION.
THIS IS MONEY, LEGALLY VALUED AT TEN YEN'S WORTH 393 MARCOM
OF ANYTHING YOU WISH TO BUY,
VALUES
AND ALL THE HYPOCRITICAL VALUES WE SET ON THE 79 MANSNS
RELATIONSHIP ARE MERE STUPIDITY.
VALUING
VALUING EACH LIFE CONSERVATIVELY AT TEN YEN, 394 MARCOM
VALVE
(SEIZES THIS AS AN ESCAPE VALVE-- 264 AHWILD

VARIANCE

VAMPING
HE LAUGHED TO HIMSELF AT HER CRUDE VAMPING. 537 DAYS
VAMPIRE
AND MAKES THIS TART A ROMANTIC EVIL VAMPIRE IN HIS241 AHWILD
EYES.
VAMPIRES
MADE WHORES FASCINATING VAMPIRES INSTEAD OF POUR, 165 JOURNE
STUPID,
VANDYKE
DOCTOR FAWCETT IS A SHORT, DARK, MIDDLE-AGED MAN 153 BEYOND
WITH A VANDYKE BEARD.
VANISH
ALL THE BITTER HURT AND STEELY RESOLVE TO IGNORE 258 AHWILD
AND PUNISH HIM VANISH IN A
>YET AH, THAT SPRING SHOULD VANISH WITH THE ROSE/ 298 AHWILD
YOU THINK YOU'VE WON, DO YOU--THAT I'VE GOT TO 307 GGBROW
VANISH INTO YOU IN ORDER TO LIVE&
AND OE PIPE DREAM VANISH/ 635 ICEMAN
THEIR CITIES SHALL VANISH IN FLAME, THEIR FIELDS 425 MARCOM
SHALL BE WASTED/
VANISHED
THE CREW HAD VANISHED-- 560 CROSS
AS IF SHE OPENED A DOOR INTO THE PAST IN WHOSE 125 MANSNS
DARKNESS THEY VANISHED
AND MOTHER AND SARA HAVE VANISHED-- 125 MANSNS
(HE VANISHED AS SILENTLY AS HE HAD COME.) 145 STRANG
VANISHES
JOHN'S CORDIAL SMILE VANISHES AND HIS FACE TAKES 526 DAYS
ON A TENSE, HARRIED LOOK.
(WITH LIGHT LEAPS HE VANISHES, HIS HEAD THROWN 318 GGBROW
BACK.
HER SMILE VANISHES AND HER MANNER BECOMES SELF- 20 JOURNE
CONSCIOUS.)
(THE SHADOW VANISHES AND HER SHY, GIRLISH 114 JOURNE
EXPRESSION RETURNS.)
(HIS BODY STIFFENS ON HIS CHAIR AND THE COARSE 171 POET
LEER VANISHES FROM HIS FACE.
THIS VANISHES INTO ONE OF DESIRE AND JOY AS HE 95 STRANG
SEES NINA.
HIS CONFIDENCE VANISHES IN A FLASH. 104 STRANG
VANITY
(NEVERTHELESS, SHE GOES TO THE DESK AT LEFT, REAR,515 DAYS
TAKES OUT A VANITY CASE,
HIS VANITY COULDN'T ADMIT I'D EVER FEEL THE 520 DAYS
SLIGHTEST DISLIKE OUTSIDE OF HIM.
THERE IS A FIXED SMILE OF TRIUMPH AND GRATIFIED 468 DYNAMO
VANITY ON HIS LIPS.
(MOCKINGLY) AREN'T WOMEN LOYAL--TO THEIR VANITY AND287 GGBROW
THEIR OTHER THINGS//
(HIS VANITY PIQUED--TESTILY.) 17 JOURNE
(DISCUSSING AN OLD WOMAN'S VANITY. 6 MANSNS
FATHER, IN HIS BLIND VANITY, OVER-ESTIMATED THE 59 MANSNS
PRESTIGE OF HIS NAME.
OF THE STUPID INSANE IMPULSION OF MAN'S PETTY 179 MANSNS
VANITY
TO CONTEMPLATE IN PEACE THE VANITY OF HIS 384 MARCOM
AUTHORITY.
I KNOW HIS WEAKNESS, AND IT'S HIS VANITY ABOUT HIS 92 MISBEG
WOMEN.
IT'S THE DISGRACE TO HIS VANITY--BEING CAUGHT WITH 96 MISBEG
THE LIKES OF ME--
IT'S HIS VANITY ABOUT WOMEN, 96 MISBEG
I WAS MERELY EXPLAINING MY SEEMING VANITY. 45 POET
(WITH A STRANGE, SCORNFUL VANITY.) 61 POET
(WITH ARROGANT VANITY.) I FLATTER MYSELF SHE WILL 90 POFT
BE GRACIOUSLY PLEASED
AND WOULDN'T IT SHAME THEIR BOASTING AND VANITY 150 POET
IF I'D HAD MORE GUTS AND LESS VANITY, IF I'D HEWN 166 STRANG
TO THE LINE/
THE PROOF OF A GUTLESS VANITY THAT RUINED YOUR 166 STRANG
CAREER--
THAT IT FLATTERS THEIR VANITY 190 STRANG
CHEATING GESTURES WHICH CONSTITUTE THE VANITY OF 487 WELDED
PERSONALITY.
VANT
AY VANT FOR HER STAY WITH ME. 10 ANNA
BUT AY DON'T VANT FOR HER GAT YOB NOW. 10 ANNA
BUT ALL TIME AY HOPE LIKE HELL SOME DAY SHE VANT 12 ANNA
FOR SEE ME AND DEN SHE COME.
AY VANT COME HOME END OF EVERY VOYAGE. 21 ANNA
AY VANT SEE YOUR MO'DER, YOUR TWO BRO'DER BEFORE 21 ANNA
DEY VAS DROWNED,
AY DON'T VANT-- 43 ANNA
VELL--AY DON'T VANT ANNA GAT MARRIED, 46 ANNA
AND NOW VEN SHE COME ON FIRST TRIP--YOU TANK AY 46 ANNA
VANT HER LEAVE ME 'LONE AGAINS
AND AY DON'T VANT SHE EVER KNOW NO-GOOD FALLAR UN 47 ANNA
SEA--
YOU TAL HIM YOU DON'T VANT FOR HEAR HIM TALK, 51 ANNA
ANNA.
YOU VANT FOR MURDER HERS 60 ANNA
(BURSTING OUT ANGRILY) YES, AY VANT/ 61 ANNA
AY DON'T VANT MAKE YOURS DAT WAY, BUT AY DO YUST 65 ANNA
SAME.
AY VANT FOR YOU BE HAPPY ALL REST OF YOUR LIFE FUR 65 ANNA
MAKE UP/
IT MAKE YOU HAPPY MARRY DAT IRISH FALLAR, AY VANT 65 ANNA
IT TOO.
(PLACATINGLY) THROW IT OVERBOARD IF YOU VANT. 67 ANNA
YOU VANT TO MAKE TROUBLES 458 CARIBE
DOES THAT PROVE I VANT TO BE ARISTOCRATS 672 ICEMAN
VAPORING
I HAVE DONE WITH THAT INSANE ROMANTIC VAPORING/ 22 MANSNS
VAPOURS
WHETHER THOU SLEEP, WITH HEAVY VAPOURS FULL, 134 JOURNE
SODDEN WITH DAY, OR,
VARIANCE
IS TOTALLY AT VARIANCE WITH HER HEALTHY OUTDOOR 13 STRANG
PHYSIQUE.

VARIES

VARIES
WHICH VARIES IN KIND ACCORDING TO ITS PERIOD. 274 LAZARU
HER RANGER VARIES BETWEEN AN ALMOST MASCULINE CURTL39 MANSNS
ABRUPTNESS AND BRUTAL.
VARIETIES
RICH FURS OF ALL VARIETIES HANG THERE BATHED IN A 233 HA APE
DOWNPOUR OF ARTIFICIAL LIGHT.
ON WHICH ARE WHOLE PIGS, FOWL OF ALL VARIETIES, 428 MARCOM
ROASTS,
VARIETY
A TYPICAL COLLEGE =TART= OF THE PERIOD, AND OF THE236 AHWILD
CHEAPER VARIETY.
HALF-BARRELS OF CHEAP WHISKY OF THE =NICKEL-A- 3 ANNA
SHOT= VARIETY.
A CHEAP GINMILL OF THE FIVE-CENT WHISKEY, LAST- 571 ICEMAN
RESORT VARIETY
VARIETY'S
YOU KNOW FOR VARIETY'S SAKE. 258 AHWILD
VARIOUS
THE SHRUBS, OF VARIOUS SIZES, ARE ALL CLIPPED INTO 25 MANSNS
GEOMETRICAL SHAPES--
WITH AN IMMENSE MANSION, A CONGLOMERATE OF VARIOUS139 MANSNS
STYLES OF ARCHITECTURE.
YOU HAVE APPLIED TO VARIOUS BANKS FOR A POSITION. 152 MANSNS
A RUSTY PLOW AND VARIOUS OTHER FARMING IMPLEMENTS,577 ROPE
TIME GIVE HAPPINESS TO VARIOUS FELLOW WAR-VICTIMS 35 STRANG
BY PRETENDING TO LOVE THEM.
(MOCKINGLY) DO TELL US ABOUT ALL YOUR VARIOUS 117 STRANG
MISTRESSES IN FOREIGN PARTS.
VARNISHED
THE TABLE AT CENTER IS OF VARNISHED OAK. 519 DIFRNT
THE CARPET HAS GIVEN WAY TO A VARNISHED HARDWOOD 519 DIFRNT
FLOOR.
THE PLUSH-COVERED CHAIRS ARE GONE, REPLACED BY A 519 DIFRNT
SET OF VARNISHED OAK.
A VARNISHED OAK ROCKER WITH LEATHER BOTTOM. 12 JOURNE
VARSITY
WHEN IT'S GORDON'S LAST RACE, HIS LAST APPEARANCE 162 STRANG
ON A VARSITY/
VASE
THE VASE BEING A BIG SCHOONER GLASS FROM THE BAR, 629 ICEMAN
ON TOP OF THE PIANO.
CORA IS ARRANGING A BOUQUET OF FLOWERS IN A VASE, 629 ICEMAN
VASELINE
AND CAME IN TO GET SOME VASELINE. 204 AHWILD
WASN'T
(BREAKING DOWN--WEEPING) AY TANK YOU VASN'T DAT 61 ANNA
KIND UF GEL, ANNA.
YOU VASN'T VAITING FOR ME, AY BET. 64 ANNA
VAST
HE IS AWARE THAT HE IS ALONE IN THE VAST ARENA. 370 LAZARU
SHUT THEE FROM HEAVEN WITH A DOME MORE VAST, TILL 148 MANSNS
THOU AT LENGTH ART FREE.
(SCENE--A SACRED TREE ON A VAST PLAIN IN PERSIA 347 MARCOM
NEAR THE CONFINES OF INDIA.
(IN AN ECHO OF VAST SADNESS) 434 MARCOM
VATCH
ON VATCH. 30 ANNA
PY YESUS, I VISH SOMEPUDY TAKE MY FIRST VATCH FOR 209 HA APE
VAULTED
LEAVE THY LOW-VAULTED PAST/ 148 MANSNS
VEDDER
VE MAKE SLOW VOYAGE--DIRTY VEDDER--YUST FOG, FOG, 7 ANNA
FOG, ALL BLOODY TIME/
VEEK
YOU GO ASHORE ALL TIME, EVERY DAY AND NIGHT VEEK 42 ANNA
VE'VE BEEN HERE.
YOU FORGAT ALL ABOUT HER IN ONE VEEK OUT OF PORT, 47 ANNA
AY BET YOU/
VEGETABLE
FARTHER BACK, IN ORDER, A WINDOW LOOKING OUT ON A 493 DIFRNT
VEGETABLE GARDEN.
VEGETABLES
HUMAN COMES BACK WITH THE VEGETABLES AND 227 AHWILD
DISAPPEARS AGAIN.
VEGETABLES, SALADS, FRUITS, NUTS, DOZENS OF 428 MARCOM
BOTTLES OF WINES.
WHAT VEGETABLES/ 428 MARCOM
VEHEMENCE
IMMENSELY PLEASED BY HER VEHEMENCE--A LIGHT 73 ANNA
BEGINNING TO
(THEN, AS HE SEES THEY ARE SURPRISED AT HIS 636 ICEMAN
VEHEMENCE, HE ADDS HASTILY)
(WITH GUILTY VEHEMENCE.) I DON'T REMEMBER/ 113 JOURNE
VEHEMENT
(GUILTILY VEHEMENT.) NO/ 61 POET
VEHEMENTLY
(VEHEMENTLY) AY AIN'T A SAILOR, ANNA. 26 ANNA
(VEHEMENTLY) ANY GEL MARKY SAILOR, SHE'S CRAZY 28 ANNA
FOOL/
(VEHEMENTLY) I WASN'T MADE FOR IT, MISS. 38 ANNA
(VEHEMENTLY) I SHOULD SAY NOT. 55 ANNA
(VEHEMENTLY) IT MUST/ 150 BEYOND
(AS IF TRYING TO CONVINCE HIMSELF--VEHEMENTLY) 563 CROSS
(VEHEMENTLY) I'D DO ANYTHING' YE AXED, I TELL YE/ 235 DESIRE
(VEHEMENTLY) I WILL LIKE--SAY, WHAT'S COME OVER 504 DIFRNT
YOU, ANYHOW5
(VEHEMENTLY) NO, I DON'T/ 510 DIFRNT
(VEHEMENTLY) I AIN'T JUDGED HIM BY WHAT FOLKS 540 DIFRNT
HAVE TOLD ME.
(SHAKING HER HEAD VEHEMENTLY) 174 EJONES
(VEHEMENTLY) I PRETENDS TO/ 185 EJONES
(HE SUDDENLY BURSTS FORTH VEHEMENTLY, GROWING MORE215 HA APE
AND MORE EXCITED)
(VEHEMENTLY) SURE TING I DO/ 234 HA APE
(TOO VEHEMENTLY.) I DIDN'T THINK ANYTHING/ 47 JOURNE
(TOO VEHEMENTLY.) OF COURSE I BELIEVE IT/ 143 JOURNE

VEHEMENTLY (CONT'D.)
(VEHEMENTLY.) YOU CAN CHOOSE ANY PLACE YOU LIKE/ 148 JOURNE
(SITTING--VEHEMENTLY) THAT'S CHILD'S TALK. 599 ROPE
(VEHEMENTLY) IT'S A LIE/ 456 WELDED
VEIGH!
I COULD DE WHOLE VEIGHT OF IT LIFT/ 676 ICEMAN
VEIL
BLOTTED OUT AND MERGED INTO A VEIL OF BLUISH MIST 199 EJONES
IN THE DISTANCE.
WE CAN DEVOTE THE PROCEEDS TO REHABILITATING THE 237 HA APE
VEIL OF THE TEMPLE.
AND LACE WITH THE ORANGE BLOSSOMS IN MY VEIL. 115 JOURNE
THEN THE HAND LETS THE VEIL FALL AND YOU ARE 153 JOURNE
ALONE, LOST IN THE FOG AGAIN.
LIKE THE VEIL OF THINGS AS THEY SEEM DRAWN BACK BY153 JOURNE
AN UNSEEN HAND.
VEILED
(A VEILED THREAT IN HER TONE) 238 DESIRE
AND ACCOMPLISH ITS VEILED PURPOSE. 192 EJONES
(A WOMAN'S FIGURE DRESSED IN BLACK, HEAVILY 107 ELECTR
VEILED.
THE ORIGIN OF THIS BEAUTIFUL DITTY IS VEILED IN 596 ICEMAN
MYSTERY, LARRY.
(INDIGNANT AT MELODY'S INSULTS TO HIS PROFESSION--119 POET
WITH A THINLY VEILED SNEER.)
VEILS
LINEN DUSTERS, VEILS, GOGGLES, SID IN A SNAPPY 208 AHWILD
CAP.)
NEW APPARELLED, STAND IN GOLD-LACED VEILS OF 134 JOURNE
EVENING BEAUTIFUL.
VEINS
= THAT I COULD DRINK WITH THY VEINS AS WINE, AND 205 AHWILD
EAT THY BREASTS LIKE HONEY.
IS STREAKED WITH INTERLACING PURPLE VEINS. 7 ANNA
THE VEINS OF HIS FOREARMS STAND OUT LIKE BLUE 30 ANNA
CORDS.
YER VEINS IS FULL O' MUD AN' WATER/ 251 DESIRE
FEELING AS THE FLOW OF BLOOD IN HIS OWN VEINS THE 309 LAZARU
PAST RE-ENTER THE HEART OF GOD
AS IF THE IMPERIAL BLOOD IN HIS VEINS HAD BEEN 337 LAZARU
SICKENED BY AGE AND DEBAUCHERY.
HIS LARGE HANDS WITH BLOATED VEINS HANGING 350 LAZARU
LOOSELY.
I SHOULD HAVE OPENED HER VEINS AND MINE, AND DIED 356 LAZARU
WITH HER.
BOILED THE BLOOD BLACK, OUR VEINS HUMMED LIKE 408 MARCOM
BRONZE KETTLES.
WHAT'S IN HIS VEINS, GOD PITY HIM, 138 POET
REMEMBER THE BLOOD IN YOUR VEINS AND BE YOUR 170 POET
GRANDFATHER'S TRUE DESCENDENT.
VELDT
THE VELDT, JAY 605 ICEMAN
THE OLD VELDT HAS ITS POINTS, I'LL ADMIT, BUT IT 605 ICEMAN
ISN'T HOME--
NOR DELIGHTED RELATIVES MAKING THE VELDT RING WITH677 ICEMAN
THEIR HAPPY CRIES--
WOULD HAVE BEEN REMOVED FROM HIS FETID KRAAL ON 723 ICEMAN
THE VELDT
VELT
(GRINS AND SINGS) =DUNNO WHAT TER CALL'IM BUT HE'S189 AHWILD
MIGHTY LIKE A ROSE-VELT.=
VELVET
SHE IS DRESSED IN A GOWN OF GREEN VELVET THAT SETS 45 ELECTR
OFF HER HAIR.
SHE WEARS A GREEN VELVET 149 ELECTR
I COULD FEEL THE NIGHT WRAPPED AROUND ME LIKE A 261 GGBROW
GRAY VELVET GOWN LINED WITH WARM
IF YOU WINS, DAT'S VELVET FOR YOU. 605 ICEMAN
VENEER
BENEATH THE MASK-LIKE VENEER OF HER FACE THERE ARE 71 ELECTR
DEEP LINES ABOUT HER MOUTH.
VENOMOUS
(GIVING HIM A VENOMOUS LOOK OF HATRED) 588 ROPE
VENERABLE
A VENERABLE OLD MAN WITH WHITE HAIR, DRESSED IN A 377 MARCOM
SIMPLE BLACK ROBE.
VENERATES
HIS KNOWLEDGE VENERATES THE UNKNOWABLE. 401 MARCOM
VENETIAN
VENETIAN BLINDS SOFTEN THE LIGHT FROM A BIG WINDOW514 DAYS
AT RIGHT.
FOR HE IS DRESSED AS A VENETIAN MERCHANT OF THE 439 MARCOM
LATER THIRTEENTH CENTURY.
VENETIANS
VENETIANS MAKE THE BEST SWIMMERS IN THE WORLD. 411 MARCOM
VENGEANCE
HIS GOD OF LOVE WAS BEGINNING TO SHOW HIMSELF AS A511 DAYS
GOD OF VENGEANCE, YOU SEE?
(WILDLY) VENGEANCE O' GOD ON THE HULL O' US/ 244 DESIRE
IT'S HER VENGEANCE ON HIM--SO'S SHE KIN REST QUIET244 DESIRE
IN HER GRAVE/
WHEN I WAS LOVIN' YE--AN' I SAID IT T' HIM T' GIT 257 DESIRE
VENGEANCE ON YE/
(RAGINGLY) BUT I'LL GIT MY VENGEANCE TOO/ 257 DESIRE
I'LL LEAVE MAM T' TAKE VENGEANCE ON YE. 260 DESIRE
BUT I'LL TAKE VENGEANCE NOW/ 262 DESIRE
(LOUD) GOD OF RIGHTEOUS VENGEANCE, I THANK 447 DYNAMO
THEE...
(IN A BOOMING TRIUMPH) =VENGEANCE IS MINE, SAITH 451 DYNAMO
THE LORD/=
(WILDLY) VENGEANCE/ 290 LAZARU
DEADLY THY VENGEANCE/ 302 LAZARU
DEADLY THY VENGEANCE/ 302 LAZARU
TO LOVE EVEN YOUR FELLOW MEN WITHOUT FEAR OF THEIR309 LAZARU
VENGEANCE/
AND I BEGAN TO TAKE PLEASURE IN VENGEANCE UPON 356 LAZARU
MEN.
AND PLEASURE IN TAKING VENGEANCE ON MYSELF. 356 LAZARU

VENGEANCE (CONT'D.)
THAT WOULD COMPLETE THE CIRCLE WITH A VENGEANCE/ 158 MANSNS
IS IT MY CUSTOM TO TAKE VENGEANCES 389 MARCOM
THOU HAST SEEN ALL THEIR VENGEANCE AND ALL THEIR 584 ROPE
IMAGINATIONS AGAINST ME---

VENGEFUL
(WITH VENGEFUL PASSION) AN' SOONER'R LATER, I'LL 209 DESIRE
NEEDLE.
(WITH VENGEFUL SATISFACTION) 243 HA APE
(HE GLANCES WITH VENGEFUL YEARNING AT THE DRINK OF671 ICEMAN
WHISKEY IN HIS HAND)

VENGEFULLY
(VENGEFULLY) WAAL--I HOLD HIM T' JEDGMENT/ 207 DESIRE
(VENGEFULLY) JUST LET ME TELL YE A THING OR TWO 233 DESIRE
'BOUT EBEN/
(VENGEFULLY) BUT I'M BEGINNING TO HATE HIM NOW-- 540 DIFRNT
AND I'VE GOOD CAUSE FOR IT/
(VENGEFULLY) DEN I'LL BE DE ONE TO SMASH DE 674 ICEMAN
GLASS.

VENGEFULNESS
(WITH SAVAGE VENGEFULNESS) BY GOD, 89 ELECTR
THERE IS A LOOK OF COOL, MENACING VENGEFULNESS IN 128 POET
HIS FACE.

VENOM
(WITH VENOM) AND FROM WHAT I'VE HEARD 180 EJONES
(HERE CHU-YIN CHUCKLES) BUT I AM AN OLD MAN FULL 389 MARCOM
OF MALICE AND VENOM

VENOMOUSLY
(VENOMOUSLY) WELL, YOU'LL NEED ALL THE BLOODY 180 EJONES
CHARMS YOU 'AS BEFORE LONG,

VENT
BUT HE IS TOO STUNNED AND BEWILDERED YET TO FIND A 58 ANNA
VENT FOR IT.

VENTRILOQUIST
(THEN IN A MOCK-HEROIC FALSETTO, ANSWERING HIMSELF395 MARCOM
LIKE A VENTRILOQUIST)

VENTURE
I WAS PROCEEDING WESTWARD ON A BUSINESS VENTURE, 350 MARCOM
GOOD SIR.
BUT YOU, YOU ARE ON A VENTURE TO THE COURT OF THE 365 MARCOM
GREAT KAAN, WE HEARS
I SHALL NEVER VENTURE FORTH AGAIN TO DO MY DUTY. 86 POET

VENTURED
I HAVE NOT VENTURED FROM MY GARDEN IN MANY YEARS. 86 POET

VENTURES
FINALLY, HE VENTURES IN A GENTLE TONE) 537 DIFRNT
THEN VENTURES ON ANOTHER TACK, MATTER-OF-FACTLY) 277 GGBROW

VENTURING
NOW, HOWEVER, HE IS VENTURING ON UNFAMILIAR GROUND116 MARCOM
(THEN VENTURING ON AN UNCERTAIN TONE OF 21 STRANG
PLEASANTRY)

VENUS
BY THE BREASTS OF VENUS THAT IS A MIRACLE/ 302 LAZARU

VER
SEE HOW GUILTY SHE LOOKS--A VER--VERITABLE 227 AHWILD
LUCRETIA GEORGIA/

VERBAL
AND GAVE ME A VERBAL MESSAGE WHICH HE CAUSED ME TO424 MARCOM
MEMORIZE.
THE EXPERIENCED STRATEGY OF THE HOGANS IN VERBAL 56 MISBEG
BATTLE IS TO TAKE THE OFFENSIVE

VERE
VERE IS YOUR LEEDLE SLAVE GIRLS$ 579 ICEMAN

VERGE
SLAPPING THEM AGAINST HIS SIDES, ON THE VERGE OF 536 'ILE
CRYING.)
(DESOLATELY, ALMOST ON THE VERGE OF TEARS) 251 AHWILD
(ON THE VERGE OF HYSTERIA) OH, I KNOW SOMETHING 260 AHWILD
DREADFUL'S HAPPENED/
(ON THE VERGE OF HUMILIATED TEARS) 278 AHWILD
I WAS ON THE VERGE OF DELIRIUM TREMENS/ 284 AHWILD
CHRIS SEEMS ON THE VERGE OF SPEAKING, HESITATES, 10 ANNA
(ON THE VERGE OF HIS OUTBREAK--STAMMERINGLY) 59 ANNA
(ON THE VERGE OF TEARS) IT'S ALL RIGHT FOR YOU TO 96 BEYOND
TALK.
ANDREW SOOTHES HIS MOTHER WHO IS ON THE VERGE OF 106 BEYOND
TEARS.)
DOLEFUL EXPRESSION OF BEING CONSTANTLY ON THE 112 BEYOND
VERGE OF COMFORTLESS TEARS.
(ON THE VERGE OF TEARS OF WEAKNESS) 148 BEYOND
(ON THE VERGE OF TEARS AT HER INABILITY TO KEEP 471 CARIBE
THEM IN THE FORECASTLE OR MAKE
HE LOOKS ON THE VERGE OF COMPLETE MENTAL AND 553 DAYS
PHYSICAL COLLAPSE.
I'VE BEEN ON THE VERGE--OF A BREAKDOWN--FOR SOME 305 GGBROW
TIME.
I'M SURE HE'S ON THE VERGE OF A BREAKDOWN. 315 GGBROW
(SHE PUTS HER ARM AROUND PEARL--ON THE VERGE OF 654 ICEMAN
TEARS HERSELF)
THERE ARE MANY FIRMS ON THE VERGE OF BANKRUPTCY 48 MANSNS
ALREADY.
THEY WERE ON THE VERGE OF BANKRUPTCY. 76 MANSNS
(TURNS TO HIM--ON THE VERGE OF TEARS-- 387 MARCOM
REBELLIOUSLY)
(ON THE VERGE OF ANGRY TEARS) 74 MISBEG
(TENSELY, ON THE VERGE OF TEARS) 84 MISBEG
(SHE ENDS UP ON THE VERGE OF BITTER HUMILIATED 96 MISBEG
TEARS.)
SHE IS ON THE VERGE OF COLLAPSE HERSELF--BROKENLY)137 MISBEG
(BEWILDEREDLY--ON THE VERGE OF TEARS.) 37 POET
(INSTANTLY ON THE VERGE OF GRATEFUL TEARS.) 39 POET
SARA HIDES HER FACE ON HER SHOULDER, ON THE VERGE 65 POET
OF TEARS.)
SHE LOOKS ON THE VERGE OF COLLAPSE FROM PHYSICAL 133 POET
FATIGUE AND HOURS OF WORRY.
(ON THE VERGE OF DRUNKEN TEARS) 598 ROPE
(HIS FACE TWITCHES AS IF HE WERE ON THE VERGE OF 10 STRANG
TEARS--HE THINKS DESPERATELY)

VERGE (CONT'D.)
SHE'S SEEMED ON THE VERGE ALL DAY... 12 STRANG
(SHE STIFLES ANOTHER LAUGH--THEN ON THE VERGE OF 108 STRANG
FAINTING, WEAKLY)
ON THE VERGE OF TEARS YET STUBBORNLY DETERMINED) 149 STRANG
ON THE VERGE OF TEARS HERSELF) 475 WELDED

VERITABLE
SEE HOW GUILTY SHE LOOKS--A VER--VERITABLE 227 AHWILD
LUCRETIA GEORGIA/

VERITAS
NOT DRUNKEN BULL, BUT *IN VINO VERITAS* STUFF. 165 JOURNE

VERMIN
FOR KILLING VERMIN--/ 181 MANSNS
AS IF THEY WERE TWIN BREEDS OF VERMIN/ 387 MARCOM

VERRY
HE'S BOD, MON, HE'S VERRY BOD. 479 CAMOIF

VERSA
THOSE WITH CRIMSON HAIR ARE DRESSED IN PURPLE, AND336 LAZARU
VICE VERSA.
OR VICE-VERSA...)) 123 STRANG

VERSAILLES
AND YOUR LITTLE WALLED GARDEN OF 3 MANSNS
VERSAILLES,
THE PALACE AT VERSAILLES-- 4 MANSNS
THE PALACE AT VERSAILLES--THE KING AND I WALK IN 22 MANSNS
THE MOONLIT GARDENS--

VERSE
(JUST AS DRISCOLL IS CLEARING HIS THROAT PREPATORY460 CARIBE
TO STARTING THE NEXT VERSE)
THE WEASEL* INCREASING THE TEMPO WITH EVERY VERSE251 DESIRE
UNTIL AT THE END HE IS
SINGING A VERSE OF THE LEGIONARY'S SONG) 357 LAZARU
HE ONLY REMEMBERS ONE VERSE OF THE SONG AND HE HAS 72 MISBEG
BEEN REPEATING IT.)
HE READS THE VERSE WELL, QUIETLY, WITH A BITTER 101 POET
ELOQUENCE.)
SINGS WITH WAILING MELANCHOLY THE FIRST VERSE THATIO2 POET
COMES TO HIS MIND

VERSES
*A BOOK OF VERSES UNDERNEATH THE BOUGH, A JUG OF 199 AHWILD
WINE, A LOAF OF BREAD--

VERSION
A JERK-SHOULDERED VERSION OF THE OLD TURKEY TROT 471 CARIBE
AS IT WAS DONE IN THE
WEAKENED VERSION OF THE DEAD MAN'S. 73 ELECTR

VESPASIAN
AS VESPASIAN REMARKED, THE SMELL OF ALL WHISKEY IS596 ICEMAN
SWEET.

VESSEL
LIKE THE CAPTAIN'S CABIN OF A DEEP-SEA SAILING 555 CROSS
VESSEL.
THE SPACE THUS ENCLOSED IS LIKE THE DARK, NOISOME 198 EJONES
HOLD OF SOME ANCIENT VESSEL.
THE VESSEL LIES WITH HER BOW AND AMIDSHIPS OFF 102 ELECTR
LEFT AND ONLY
THE COMPANIONWAY DOOR ON THE POOP DECK OF THE 104 ELECTR
VESSEL IS OPENED
I'M SKIPPER OF THIS VESSEL 104 ELECTR

VEST
(HE HAS PULLED HIS WATCH OUT OF HIS VEST POCKET-- 250 AHWILD
WITH FORCED CARELESSNESS)

VESTA
YOU OUGHT TO HEAR VESTA VICTORIA--YOU REMEMBER 259 AHWILD
THAT TRIP I MADE TO NEW YORK.

VESTIGE
EACH RETAINS A VESTIGE OF YOUTHFUL FRESHNESS, 611 ICEMAN
AND OF THE CITY OF VENICE NOT ONE VESTIGE SHALL 425 MARCOM
REMAIN.

VETERAN
THE VETERAN IS TOUCHED. 389 MARCOM
HE SHAKES HANDS WITH A ONE-LEGGED VETERAN OF THE 389 MARCOM
MANZI CAMPAIGN

VEXATION
(WITH WEARY VEXATION) IT'S A SHAME FOR HIM TO 118 BEYOND
COME HOME

VEXATIOUSLY
(VEXATIOUSLY) HE'LL KNOW WE'RE IN THIS EARLY, 199 AHWILD
TOO.

VEXED
SHE IS VEXED BY THIS) 145 ELECTR

WHAT'S
WHAT'S TROUBLES 29 ANNA
WHAT'S HAPPENEDS 691 ICEMAN
WHAT'S MATTER, HARRYS 691 ICEMAN

WHEN
AND WHEN DEIR BUYS GROW UP, GO TO SEA, DEY SIT AND 28 ANNA
WAIT SOME MORE.
(WITH A SIGH) AY'M GLAD VHEN VE SAIL AGAIN, TOO. 42 ANNA
VHEN HE COMES THERE TRONK/ 675 ICEMAN
LOST ALL HIS MONEY GAMBLING VHEN HE VAS TRONK. 677 ICEMAN
OFTEN VHEN I AM TRONK AND KIDDING YOU I SAY I AM 677 ICEMAN
SORRY I MISSED YOU, BUT NOW,
VHEN I GET THERE, THEY VILL LET ME COME IN/ 677 ICEMAN
VHEN I LED THE JACKASS MUB TO THE SACK OF 691 ICEMAN
BABYLON,

VHISKY
DOT VHISKY GAT KICK, BY YINGO/ 6 ANNA
VHISKY--NUMBER TWO. 6 ANNA
HE GAT BOTTLE VHISKY AND VE DRANK IT, YUST US TWO. 6 ANNA
VHISKY FUR ME. 8 ANNA
GIVE ME VHISKY HERE AT BAR, TOO. 12 ANNA
YOU FIND VHISKY IN CABIN. 30 ANNA

VI'GE
(THEN INCONSEQUENTIALLY) YOU AIN'T NEEDIN' A 105 ELECTR
CHANTYMAN FUR YOUR NEXT VI'GE,

VI'S
LATELY VI'S GONE ON DRUNKS AND BEEN TOO BOILED TO 159 JOURNE
PLAY,

VIBRATING

VIBRATING
LOW AND VIBRATING.. 184 EJONES
EXULTANT BOOM WHOSE THROBS SEEM TO FILL THE AIR 200 EJONES
WITH VIBRATING RHYTHM.
SO LOUD AND CONTINUOUSLY VIBRATING ARE ITS BEATS. 202 EJONES
VIBRATING THROUGH THE STEEL WALLS AS IF SOME 217 HA APE
ENORMOUS BRAZEN GONG WERE IMBEDUED

VICE
THE SOUND OF MUSIC IN A STRAINED THEME OF THAT 326 LAZARU
JOYLESS ABANDON WHICH IS VICE IS
THOSE WITH CRIMSON HAIR ARE DRESSED IN PURPLE, AND336 LAZARU
VICE VERSA.
THAT HOUSE OF CHEAP VICE... 6 STRANG
OR VICE-VERSA...)) 123 STRANG

VICES
OF INVENTED LUSTS AND ARTIFICIAL VICES. 336 LAZARU
THE CONQUEROR ACQUIRES FIRST OF ALL THE VICES OF 421 MARCOM
THE CONQUERED.

VICINITY
AND SOMEHOW HARDER'S FENCE IN THAT VICINITY HAS A 50 MISBEG
HABIT OF BREAKING DOWN.

VICIOUS
(THER BREAKING INTO A COLD, VICIOUS RAGE) 592 DAYS
FUR HE ADDS REAL SPKY AND VICIOUS.. 210 DESIRE
EDEN HAS A MIXTURE OF SILLY GRIN AND VICIOUS SCOWL212 DESIRE
ON HIS FACE)
(SITTING DOWN ON A BED--WITH VICIOUS HATRED) 213 DESIRE
(HE APPROACHES A LADY--WITH A VICIOUS GRIN AND A 237 HA APE
SMIRKING WINK)
STRONG AS A BULL, AND AS VICIOUS AND 15 MISBEG
DISRESPECTFUL.
THEN HIS FACE GROWS WHITE WITH A VICIOUS FURY) 596 ROPE
PRETTY VICIOUS FACE UNDER CAKED POWDER AND 6 STRANG
ROUGE...
(RESPONDING TO A VICIOUS NUDGE FROM JOE'S ELBOW) 305 VOYAGE

VICIOUSLY
(HE BITES OFF THE END OF THE CIGAR VICIOUSLY. 201 AHWILD
(OPENS THE DOOR AND GOES OUT--TURNS AND CALLS BACK248 AHWILD
VICIOUSLY)
(VICIOUSLY) GOD DAMN THE LUCK/ 248 AHWILD
E FACE WITH ALL HER MIGHT, AND LAUGHS VICIOUSLY. 471 CARIBE
(VICIOUSLY) NO, DAMN YE/ 225 DESIRE
(VICIOUSLY) I DON'T TAKE TYPE, I TELL YE/ 239 DESIRE
(VICIOUSLY) SO YOURE GIVIN' ME THE GATE, TOO, 946 DIFRNT
EH,
LIGHT DRAWS BACK INTO THE ROOM, MUTTERING 425 DYNAMO
VICIOUSLY)
HE RAISES HIS WHIP AND LASHES JONES VICIOUSLY 194 EJONES
ACROSS THE SHOULDERS WITH IT.
(VICIOUSLY) OLD HAG/ 222 HA APE
(VICIOUSLY) G'WAN/ 237 HA APE
BUMPING VICIOUSLY INTO THEM BUT NOT JARRING THEM 238 HA APE
THE LEAST BIT.
(STOMP--TURNS ON HIM VICIOUSLY) 668 ICEMAN
(SPRINGS TO HIS FEET, HIS FACE HARDENED VICIOUSLY)671 ICEMAN
(HE SUDDENLY SLAPS LAZARUS VICIOUSLY ACROSS THE 348 LAZARU
FACE)
(HE ADDS VICIOUSLY) WHERE HE BELONGS, THE OLD 4 MISBEG
HOG/
(WITH A QUICK MOVEMENT HE HITS HER VICIOUSLY OVER 581 ROPE
THE ARM WITH HIS STICK.
(VICIOUSLY) I WAS WISHIN' IT WAS ROUND HIS NECK 590 ROPE
CHOKIN' HIM, THAT'S WHAT I WAS--
(HE STEPS FORWARD AND SLAPS DARELL ACROSS THE 193 STRANG
FACE VICIOUSLY.
(HITS HER VICIOUSLY ON THE SIDE OF THE JAW. 508 VOYAGE
(VICIOUSLY) WHAT NOBLE FAITH/ 498 WELDED

VICIOUSNESS
(WITHOUT LOOKING AT HICKEY--WITH DULL, RESENTFUL 705 ICEMAN
VICIOUSNESS)

VICTIM
HE'S THE KIND THAT'S THE VICTIM OF HIS FRIENDS. 212 AHWILD
A VICTIM OF PARTIAL PARALYSIS FOR MANY YEARS, 113 BEYOND
HIS VOICE IS THE BULLYING ONE OF A SERMONIZER WHO 422 DYNAMO
IS THE VICTIM OF AN INNER
THEY MUST FIND A VICTIM/ 320 GGBROW
A VICTIM OF OVERWORK, TOO. 627 ICEMAN
THEIR ARMS STRETCHED OUT AS IF DEMANDING LAZARUS 288 LAZARU
FOR A SACRIFICIAL VICTIM.
THE LATTER STANDING LIKE A VICTIM) 333 LAZARU

VICTIMS
TIME GIVE HAPPINESS TO VARIOUS FELLOW WAR-VICTIMS 35 STRANG
BY PRETENDING TO LOVE THEM.

VICTOR
(SALUTING LAZARUS) HAIL, VICTOR/ 320 LAZARU
BUT I'LL PROVE TO YOU WHO IS THE FINAL VICTOR 189 MANSNS
BETWEEN US.
HAVING ACCOMPLISHED A TASK--A VICTOR, MORE OR 388 MARCOM
LESS, ACTING THE HERO.

VICTORIA
YOU OUGHT TO HEAR VESTA VICTORIA--YOU REMEMBER 259 AHWILD
THAT TRIP I MADE TO NEW YORK.

VICTORIAN
HOW INCREDIBLY MID-VICTORIAN YOU CAN BE/ 517 DAYS
THERE IS A QUALITY ABOUT HIM OF A PRIM, VICTORIAN 575 ICEMAN
OLD MAID,

VICTORIOUS
(A VICTORIOUS GLEAM IN HER EYE--TAUNTINGLY) 634 ICEMAN
MY FACE OF VICTORIOUS FEAR/ 319 LAZARU
FEELING MY SHOULDER'S VICTORIOUS GLOATING DIE INTO102 MANSNS
BOREDOM AND DISCONTENT--

VICTORQUE
STETIT ONUS IN ARCEM ERECTUS CAPITIS VICTORQUE AD 23 STRANG
SIDERA MITTIT SIDEREOS OCULUS

VICTORY
BUT DOES DEFEAT END IN THE VICTORY OF DEATHS 48 ELECTR
IT'S DREADFUL HE SHOULD DIE JUST AT HIS MOMENT OF 48 ELECTR
VICTORY.

VICTORY (CONT'D.)
ALL VICTORY ENDS IN THE DEFEAT OF DEATH. 48 ELECTR
THE STANDARD OIL MILLIONAIRE, AND WON A GLORIOUS 23 JOURNE
VICTORY.
I TOLD HIM YOU'D BE TICKLED TO DEATH OVER THE 25 JOURNE
GREAT IRISH VICTORY.
THIS IS TOO GLORIOUS A VICTORY FOR YOU, TOO 289 LAZARU
TERRIBLE A LONELINESS/
A VICTORY WREATH AROUND HIS HEAD. 313 LAZARU
(EXULTINGLY) DID THEY NOT LAUGH! THAT WAS THEIR 324 LAZARU
VICTORY AND THEIR GLORY/
THEIR DISEASE TRIUMPHS OVER DEATH--A NOBLE VICTORY352 LAZARU
CALLED RESIGNATION/
(HIS VOICE A TRIUMPHANT ASSERTION OF THE VICTORY 366 LAZARU
OF LIFE OVER PAIN AND DEATH)
CANNOT RECOGNIZE A COMPLETE VICTORY AND A CRUSHING114 MANSNS
DEFEAT WHEN HE SEES THEM/
AND I HAVE WON THE DECIDING VICTORY OVER THEM/ 129 MANSNS
OF HOW INSECURE YOU ARE IN YOUR FANCIED VICTORYS 168 MANSNS
VICTORY OR DEATH/ 395 MARCOM
I DON'T WANT TO BE LEFT OUT ALTOGETHER FROM 113 MISBEG
CELEBRATING OUR VICTORY OVER HARDER.
WOULD I COULD LIVE TO CELEBRATE THAT VICTORY/ 40 POET
BLASTING OF HIS GLORIOUS VICTORY OVER OLD HARFORD,151 POET
WHATEVER THE TRUTH IS/

VICTROLA
HE IS STANDING BY THE VICTROLA ON WHICH A JAZZ 519 DIFRNT
BAND IS PLAYING.
A VICTROLA IS WHERE THE OLD MAHOGANY CHEST HAD 519 DIFRNT
BEEN.
(IADA SAID SHE'D PUT A RECORD ON THE VICTROLA AS 424 DYNAMO
SOON AS SHE WAS FREE...
(FROM THE FIFE HOUSE COMES THE SOUND OF A VICTROLA426 DYNAMO
STARTING A JAZZ RECORD.)
(LISTENING TO THE VICTRULA, FIXES HIS EYES ON HIS 426 DYNAMO
WIFE COMBATIVELY)
A VICTROLA IN THE REAR CORNER, LEFT. 428 DYNAMO

VIDOUT
TOMORROW VIDOUT FAIL/ 602 ICEMAN

VIEW
WELL, IF HE'S REALLY GOT THAT VIEW OF IT DRIVEN 289 AHWILD
INTO HIS SKULL.
THAT I HAD A MENTAL VIEW OF HIM REGARDING HIS 503 DAYS
NAVEL FRENZIEDLY BY THE HOUR AND
IN VIEW OF YOUR HONORABLE INTENTIONS I FEEL BOUND 439 DYNAMO
BY MY CONSCIENCE TO LET YOU
BRACKETS ALONG BOTH WALLS, THERE IS A CLEAR VIEW 473 DYNAMO
OF A DYNAMO, HUGE AND BLACK,
TALL TREES WHOSE TOPS ARE LOST TO VIEW. 195 EJONES
STREET-LIGHTED VIEW OF BLACK HOUSES ACROSS THE 290 GGBROW
WAY.
AS IT HIDES YANK FROM VIEW, 245 HA APE
IN VIEW OF THE COMPANY'S PROGRESS SINCE YOU LAST 93 MANSNS
DREAMED OF IT.
SHUTS OUT ALL VIEW OF THE HARBOR AT THE END OF THE400 MARCOM
WHARF.
A FUGITIVE FROM REALITY CAN VIEW THE PRESENT 3 STRANG
SAFELY FROM A DISTANCE,
(COMES INTO VIEW IN THE HALL, OPPOSITE THE 123 STRANG
DOORWAY, AT THE FOOT OF THE STAIRS--

VIEWING
AND I'M VAIN ENOUGH NOT TO CRAVE ANY MALE VIEWING 517 DAYS
THE WRECKAGE

VIEWPOINT
I WISH TO SAY I SEE YOUR POINT ABOUT POLICY OF 155 MANSNS
BANK--ONLY PRACTICAL VIEWPOINT--
I BEGIN TO APPRECIATE THE PROFESSOR'S 29 STRANG
VIEWPOINT...))

VIFE
(CAJOLINGLY) BIG FALLAR LIKE YOU DAT'S ON SEA, HE 46 ANNA
DON'T NEED VIFE.

VIGE
VIGE. 103 BEYOND
(UNPLACED) I'VE BEEN COUNTIN' SURE ON HAVIN' 103 BEYOND
ROBERT FOR COMPANY ON THIS VIGE--
WHEN I KIN GO OFF ON A TWO-YEAR WHALIN' VIGE AND 496 DIFRNT
LEAVE YOU ALL ALONE
WHY, I WAS THAT ANXIOUS TO BRING BACK YOUR PA'S 497 DIFRNT
SHIP WITH A FINE VIGE THAT'D
MY FUST VIGE AS SKIPPER, YOU DON'T S'POSE I HAD 497 DIFRNT
TIME FOR NO MONKEY-SHININ',
HE WAS TELLIN' ME ALL 'BOUT THEIR VIGE. 501 DIFRNT
THEN IT WAS ON THE VIGE THIS JOKE HAPPENEDS 501 DIFRNT
IT AIN'T RIGHTLY NONE O' YOUR BUSINESS WHAT HE 505 DIFRNT
DOES ON A VIGE.
AND WHEN I COME BACK FROM THE NEXT VIGE AND YOU'VE517 DIFRNT
HAD TWO YEARS TO THINK IT
GOES RIGHT ON MAKIN' VIGE AFTER VIGE TO GRAB MORE 522 DIFRNT
AND NEVER SPENDS A NICKEL
(PERFUNCTORILY) I HOPE HE'S HAD A GOOD VIGE AND 522 DIFRNT
IS IN GOOD HEALTH.
MAKIN' VIGE AFTER VIGE ALWAYS ALONE-- 538 DIFRNT
DON'T--I WAS THINKIN' ALL THIS LAST VIGE--THAT 538 DIFRNT
MAYBE--

VIGE'LL
THIS VIGE'LL MAKE A MAN OF HIM. 96 BEYOND

VIGES
YOU KNOW HOW LITTLE TIME HE'S HAD TO HOME BETWEEN 533 DIFRNT
VIGES.

VIGILANCE
NEVER RELAX MY VIGILANCE-- 119 MANSNS

VIGILANTES
VIGILANTES LOOKIN' HARD AT US$ 487 CARDIF

VIGOR
(STARTS TO DANCE, WHICH HE DOES VERY WELL AND WITH251 DESIRE
TREMENDOUS VIGOR.
RECITE WITH DISCORDANT VIGOR) 435 MARCOM

1747

VINDICTIVENESS

VIGOROUS

I WANTED TO BE BY YOUR SIDE IN THE DANGER AND 545 *ILE
VIGOROUS LIFE OF IT ALL.
HIS BODY IS STILL ERECT, STRONG AND VIGOROUS. 535 DIFRNT
(SHE GIVES HIM A MORE VIGOROUS SHAKE) 165 MISBEG

VIGOROUSLY

BUT MILLER WINKS AND SHAKES HIS HEAD VIGOROUSLY 258 AHWILD
AND MOTIONS HER TO SIT DOWN.)
HE RINGS THIS VIGOROUSLY--THEN STOPS TO LISTEN. 182 EJUNES
AND GOES FROM ONE TO THE OTHER OF THE SLEEPERS AND513 INZONE
SHAKES THEM VIGOROUSLY.
(AN ORCHESTRA VIGOROUSLY BEGINS A FLOWERY, 428 MARCOM
SENTIMENTAL ITALIAN TUNE.
(BENTLEY NODS VIGOROUSLY IN THE AFFIRMATIVE. 596 ROPE

VIKING

VIKING-DAUGHTER FASHION BUT NOW RUN DOWN IN HEALTH 13 ANNA
AND PLAINLY SHOWING ALL THE

VIKINGS

I GUESS I WAS DREAMING ABOUT THE OLD VIKINGS IN 546 *ILE
THE STORY-BOOKS AND I THOUGHT

VILE

THAT WAS SO VILE THEY WOULDN'T EVEN LET IT PLAY INI97 AHWILD
NEW YORK/
NOT VILE AY LIVE/ 52 ANNA
(DULLY) AH, HOW VILE MEN ARE/ 566 CROSS
(THEN BROKENLY) OH, IT'S SUCH A VILE MESS/ 527 DAYS
(WITH A COLD BITTER FURY) YOU VILE--/ 30 ELECTR
HOW CAN YOU BE SO VILE AS TO TRY TO USE ME TO HIDE 30 ELECTR
YOUR ADULTERY&
YOU'VE CALLED ME VILE AND SHAMELESS/ 31 ELECTR
ISN'T BEAUTY AN ABOMINATION AND LOVE A VILE THINGS 45 ELECTR
I SUPPOSE YOU'VE BEEN TELLING HIM YOUR VILE LIES, 100 ELECTR
YOU---
HOW COULD YOU LOVE THAT VILE OLD WOMAN SO& 115 ELECTR
HER LOVE FOR ME MAKES ME APPEAR LESS VILE TO 151 ELECTR
MYSELF/
(THEN WITH A HARSH LAUGH) AND, AT THE SAME TIME, 151 ELECTR
A MILLION TIMES MORE VILE.
HOW CAN YOU STILL LOVE THAT VILE WOMAN SO-- 152 ELECTR
YOU'RE TOO VILE TO LIVE/ 166 ELECTR
HE'D ONLY SPEND IT ON DRINK AND YOU KNOW WHAT A 82 JOURNE
VILE, POISONOUS
VILE JEW, DO YOU DARE THREATEN ME WITH DEATH/ 341 LAZARU
AND ALL OF MEN ARE VILE AND MAD, AND I SHALL BE 370 LAZARU
THEIR MADMAN'S CAESAR/
YOU VILE DEGRADED SLUT/ 136 MANSNS
LET US LEAVE THIS VILE STY OF LUST AND HATRED AND 185 MANSNS
THE WISH TO MURDER/
(ABASHED ONLY FOR A MOMENT) OH, SO THEY'VE SENT 392 MARCOM
THAT VILE SLANDER TO YOU.
IT WOULD BE BENEATH ME TO TOUCH SUCH VILE 123 POET
LICKSPITTLE.
WHAT A VILE THOUGHT/... 33 STRANG
AND VILE TO GIVE MYSELF.... 72 STRANG
NINA COULDN'T BE SO VILE/... 129 STRANG
THEY WOULDN'T BE VILE ENOUGH--FOR HIS BEAUTIFUL 468 WELDED
REVENGE ON ME/

VILENESS

REALIZED THE VILENESS HE HAD BEEN GUILTY OF. 539 DAYS

VILEST

IN THE VILEST, MOST COWARDLY WAY--LIKE THE SON OF 27 ELECTR
A SERVANT YOU ARE/
THAT SHE WILL EVEN ACCUSE ME OF THE VILEST, MOST 85 ELECTR
HORRIBLE THINGS/
-INGRATITUDE, THE VILEST WEED THAT GROWS-/ 33 JOURNE

VILL

YOU COME HELP, VILL YOU& 30 ANNA
YOU SAY THE BUMBOAT VOMAN VILL BRING BOOZE& 450 CARIBE

VILLA

IN THE REAR, THE WALLS OF THE VILLA, 326 LAZARU
SOME DAYS LATER--EXTERIOR OF TIBERIUS' VILLA-- 326 LAZARU
PALACE AT CAPRI.
(FLAVIUS SALUTES AND HASTENS TO THE VILLA, 327 LAZARU
ON THE RIGHT IS A SIDE ENTRANCE OF THE PRETENTIOUS184 STRANG
VILLA.

VILLAGE

ALL MEN IN OUR VILLAGE ON COAST, SVEDEN, GO TO 27 ANNA
SEA.
HE HAIN'T NEVER BEEN OFF THIS FARM 'CEPTIN' T' THE205 DESIRE
VILLAGE IN THIRTY YEAR OR
T' THE VILLAGES 210 DESIRE
THE HULL VILLAGE SAYS. 212 DESIRE
THEN I GOT T' THE VILLAGE AN' HEERD THE NEWS AN' I214 DESIRE
GOT MADDER'N HELL AN' RUN ALL
T' THE VILLAGES 229 DESIRE
HE LOOKS LIKE AN ENLARGED, ELDERLY, BALD EDITION 576 ICEMAN
OF THE VILLAGE FAT BOY--
ABOUT TWO MILES FROM A VILLAGE IN MASSACHUSETTS. 1 MANSNS
LIKE A VILLAGE IDIOT IN A COUNTRY STORE SPITTING 102 MANSNS
AT THE BELLY OF A STOVE--
WHEN I REACHED THE LAST VILLAGE WITH MY CAMELS 351 MARCOM
FOUNDERING,
(SCENE THE DINING ROOM OF MELODY'S TAVERN, IN A 7 POET
VILLAGE A FEW MILES FROM BOSTON.

VILLAGERS

I FOUND THE ACCURSED VILLAGERS 351 MARCOM

VILLOW

'TIS COOL BENEATH THY VILLOW TREES/= 592 ICEMAN
'TIS COOL BENEATH THY VILLOW TREES/= 627 ICEMAN
AND VE VILL EAT HOT DOGS AND TRINK FREE BEER 635 ICEMAN
BENEATH THE VILLOW TREES/
(WITH HIS SILLY GIGGLE) VE VILL TRINK VINE 640 ICEMAN
BENEATH THE VILLOW TREES/
VE VILL EAT BIRTHDAY CAKE AND TRINK CHAMPAGNE 658 ICEMAN
BENEATH THE VILLOW TREE/
SOON YOU VILL EAT HOT DOGS BENEATH THE VILLOW 672 ICEMAN
TREES AND TRINK FREE VINE--
I VILL TRINK CHAMPAGNE BENEATH THE VILLOW-- 691 ICEMAN
ALWAYS THERE IS BLOOD BENEATH THE VILLOW TREES/ 695 ICEMAN

VINDICATIVENESS

(WITH EXTREME VINDICATIVENESS) 175 EJUNES

VINDICTIVE

(WITH A LOOK AT ELSA THAT IS ALMOST VINDICTIVE) 519 DAYS
(COLDLY VINDICTIVE NOW) THAT IS, 530 DAYS
(HIS VOICE WITH SURPRISING SUDDENNESS TAKES ON A 545 DAYS
SAVAGE VINDICTIVE QUALITY)
(THEN WITH SUDDEN VINDICTIVE ANGER) 215 DESIRE
(ENRAGED BEYOND ENDURANCE--WILDLY VINDICTIVE) 233 DESIRE
(THEN HIS EYES TURN TO HIS MOTHER'S VINDICTIVE 448 DYNAMO
FACE
AND AN EXPRESSION OF STRANGE VINDICTIVE TRIUMPH 11 ELECTR
COMES INTO HER FACE.)
(WITH VINDICTIVE PASSION) HE COULD HAVE SAVED 26 ELECTR
HER--AND)
(THEN TO HER FATHER WITH A VINDICTIVE LOOK AT 49 ELECTR
CHRISTINE)
(THEN WITH VINDICTIVE MOCKERY) 120 ELECTR
(SEIZING ON THIS WITH VINDICTIVE RELISH) 657 ICEMAN
(HE LAUGHS WITH A SNEERING, VINDICTIVE SELF- 689 ICEMAN
LOATHING.
CALIGULA FORCES A CRUEL VINDICTIVE SMILE) 324 LAZARU
(WITH VINDICTIVE INSISTENCE) 334 LAZARU
(WITH VINDICTIVE CALCULATION.) 73 MANSNS
(WITH A TRACE OF VINDICTIVE SATISFACTION.) 79 MANSNS
ONE OF VINDICTIVE SATISFACTION AND GLOATING PITY.) 97 MANSNS
(WITH A VINDICTIVE SATISFACTION.) 104 MANSNS
(HE TURNS TO STARE AT HER WITH A VINDICTIVE 120 MANSNS
HOSTILITY.)
(HE STARES AT HER WITH VINDICTIVE HOSTILITY.) 121 MANSNS
(SHE TURNS TO STARE AT HIM WITH VINDICTIVE 122 MANSNS
HOSTILITY.
(WITH A VINDICTIVE SMILE--STRANGELY.) 133 MANSNS
(HE PAUSES--THEN TURNS ON HER WITH A BITTER 184 MANSNS
VINDICTIVE CONDEMNATION.)
(WITH A PERVERSE, JEERING NOTE OF VINDICTIVE 140 MISBEG
BOASTFULNESS IN HIS TONE)
(A LOOK OF VINDICTIVE CRUELTY COMES INTO HIS 107 POET
EYES--QUIETLY.)
(LOOKING UP THE RIVER--WITH VINDICTIVE 171 STRANG
BITTERNESS--THINKING)

VINDICTIVELY

(TOO OCCUPIED WITH HIS OWN THOUGHTS TO HEAR HER-- 125 BEYOND
VINDICTIVELY)
(SLOWLY AND VINDICTIVELY) THAT'S JUST LIKE HIM-- 137 BEYOND
NOT TO.
(VINDICTIVELY) AND NUT HIM, EITHER/ 565 CROSS
(SHE STARTS TO BREAK DOWN, BUT FIGHTS THIS BACK 520 DAYS
AND BURSTS OUT VINDICTIVELY,
(VINDICTIVELY) WALL-- 215 DESIRE
A LONG PAUSE--VINDICTIVELY) 267 DESIRE
(VINDICTIVELY) I PROMISE I WON'T STAND BETWEEN 445 DYNAMO
HIM AND PUNISHMENT THIS TIME/
(GLARING INTO HIS FACE VINDICTIVELY) 447 DYNAMO
SHE STARES AT HIM WITH HATRED AND ADDRESSES HIM 35 ELECTR
VINDICTIVELY,
(VINDICTIVELY) BY GOD/ 38 ELECTR
(VINDICTIVELY) YOU REMEMBER WHAT I'VE GIVEN YOU, 161 ELECTR
HAZEL,
(VINDICTIVELY) GOD STIFFEN HIM/ 223 HA APE
(VINDICTIVELY) I HATE EVERY BITCH THAT EVER 615 ICEMAN
LIVED/
(WHILE HE IS SPEAKING THE FACES OF THE GANG HAVE 662 ICEMAN
LIGHTED UP VINDICTIVELY,
(VINDICTIVELY) LISTEN TO ME, YOU CECIL/ 677 ICEMAN
(VINDICTIVELY) I THINK IT WAS SOMETHING YOU DROVE693 ICEMAN
SOMEONE ELSE TO DO/
VINDICTIVELY) I DON'T GIVE A DAMN WHAT HE DONE TO698 ICEMAN
HIS WIFE,
(WITHOUT LOOKING AT HIM--VINDICTIVELY) 702 ICEMAN
(VINDICTIVELY) BE GOD, 703 ICEMAN
(VINDICTIVELY.) WE WILL GIVE YOU THE FREEDOM YOU J178 MANSNS
USED TO DREAM ABOUT/
(VINDICTIVELY) I'LL PRAY YOU'LL FIND A WAY TO NAB 10 MISBEG
HIM, JOSIE/
(VINDICTIVELY) I'VE NEVER SET FOOT IN A CHURCH 17 MISBEG
SINCE, AND NEVER WILL.
(STARTLED--VINDICTIVELY) SO HE ADMITTED IT, DID 135 MISBEG
HE&
(VINDICTIVELY.) FAITH, 60 POET
(WITH A SUDDEN REVERSAL OF FEELING--ALMOST 77 POET
VINDICTIVELY.)
(THEN VINDICTIVELY.) BUT I'VE TAUGHT HER ONE, 158 PUET
TOO,
(SHE GLARES AT HIM VINDICTIVELY, PAUSING FOR 580 ROPE
BREATH)
(THINKING VINDICTIVELY) (ISERVE HER RIGHT, THE 73 STRANG
OLD SCANDAL-MONGER,
(THINKING VINDICTIVELY) 142 STRANG
(VINDICTIVELY) (BUT SHE WON'T/... 160 STRANG
(THEN VINDICTIVELY) (WELL, SO WOULD I/... 167 STRANG
(BUT SHE CANNOT BEAR THIS THOUGHT--VINDICTIVELY) 168 STRANG
(THINKING VINDICTIVELY) (I HOPE HE KNOWS THE 193 STRANG
TRUTH, FOR IF HE DOESN'T, BY GOD,

VINDICTIVENESS

(TURNS ON HER IN A FLASH OF RESENTFUL 522 DAYS
VINDICTIVENESS)
(GUARDED INTO VINDICTIVENESS.) 142 JOURNE
(WITH SURPRISING VINDICTIVENESS) 284 LAZARU
(WITH AN ALMOST JOYOUS VINDICTIVENESS.) 104 MANSNS
(HIS FACE HARDENS AND A LOOK OF CRUEL 190 MISBEG
VINDICTIVENESS COMES INTO IT--
THERE IS AN INCREASING VINDICTIVENESS IN HIS 112 POET
TONE.)
(SHE LEANS TOWARD HIM AND SPEAKS WITH TAUNTING 171 POET
VINDICTIVENESS,

VINDJAMMER

VINDJAMMER
VEN SHE VAS LITTLE GEL, AY VAS BO'SUN ON 9 ANNA VINDJAMMER.

VINE
WITH VINE LEAVES IN HIS HAIR/= 246 AHWILD
= AND THEN--I WILL COME--WITH VINE LEAVES IN MY 261 AHWILD HAIR/=
WELL, HOW ARE THE VINE LEAVES IN YOUR HAIR THIS 293 AHWILD EVENINGS
DRY EAT GOOD PORT VINE, ANNA. 23 ANNA
(PICKING UP HIS BEER) COME, YOU DRINK VINE. 24 ANNA
GIVE ME DRINK FOR TAKE BACK--ONE PORT VINE FOR 24 ANNA ANNA--
PY GOTT, THERE IS SPACE TO BE FREE, THE AIR LIKE 605 ICEMAN VINE IS,
(WITH HIS SILLY GIGGLE) VE VILL TRINK VINE 640 ICEMAN BENEATH THE VILLOW TREES/
DIS VINE IS UNFIT TO TRINK. 658 ICEMAN
SOON YOU VILL EAT HOT DOGS BENEATH THE VILLOW 672 ICEMAN TREES AND TRINK FREE VINE--
BUT NO MORE VINE/ 694 ICEMAN
MUST HAVE ONCE BEEN UF A ROMANTIC, TENDER, 53 STRANG CLINGING-VINE BEAUTY,

VINEGAR
AND LET THE LOUSY SLAVES DRINK VINEGAR/ 640 ICEMAN

VINEYARD
NOW HE SEEMS AS BROWN AS ONE WHO HAS LABORED IN 276 LAZARU THE EARTH ALL DAY IN A VINEYARD

VINNIE'S
VINNIE'S COMPLETELY KNOCKED OUT, TOO. 80 ELECTR
I RECEIVED ALL OF HAZEL'S LETTERS--AND VINNIE'S. 89 ELECTR
THERE'S NOTHING TO TELL--EXCEPT IN VINNIE'S MORBID 86 ELECTR REVENGEFUL MIND/
IT WAS VINNIE'S FAULT YOU EVER WENT TO WAR/ 87 ELECTR
AND YOU HAVEN'T VINNIE'S EXCUSE/ 88 ELECTR
MY OWN SAKE AND VINNIE'S, TOO, AS WELL AS YOURS-- 89 ELECTR EVEN IF I HAVE--
IF WE DON'T GET OUT OF VINNIE'S REACH RIGHT AWAY 111 ELECTR
VINNIE'S LETTERS HAVEN'T SAID MUCH ABOUT HIM, OR 137 ELECTR HERSELF, FOR THAT MATTER--
(WITH RESENTFUL BITTERNESS) BUT THEY TURNED OUT 145 ELECTR TO BE VINNIE'S ISLANDS,
VINNIE'S BACK SEEIN' TO SOMETHIN', 158 ELECTR
AS LONG AS VINNIE'S TIED DOWN TO HIM WE CAN'T GET 159 ELECTR MARRIED.
(THEN WITH A GRIM PRIDE) BUT VINNIE'S ABLE FUR 170 ELECTR 'EM.

VINO
NOT DRUNKEN BULL, BUT =IN VINO VERITAS= STUFF. 165 JOURNE

VINTAGE
FADED PINK SHIRT AND BRIGHT TIE BELONG TO THE SAME75 ICEMAN VINTAGE.
WHAT A VINTAGE/ 429 MARCOM

VIOLENCE
THE VIOLENCE OF HIS PASSION. 108 BEYOND
(POINTING TO THE BODY--TREMBLING WITH THE VIOLENCE168 BEYOND OF HIS RAGE)
THE UPROAR OF SHOUTING, LAUGHING AND SINGING 469 CARIBE
VOICES HAS INCREASED IN VIOLENCE.
(HE FAINTS WITH THE VIOLENCE OF HIS STRUGGLE AND 311 LAZARU FALLS IN A LIMP HEAP.)
(WITH A SUDDEN STRANGE VIOLENCE) 169 STRANG
(TREMBLING ALL OVER WITH THE VIOLENCE OF HIS 458 WELDED PASSION)

VIOLENT
(HE IS RACKED BY A VIOLENT FIT OF COUGHING 148 BEYOND
(HE TREMBLES WITH VIOLENT PASSION. 149 BEYOND
YES, YES--BUT STILL I DON'T--IS HE LIABLE TO PROVE558 CROSS VIOLENT?
(HE CONTROLS HIMSELF WITH A VIOLENT EFFORT AND 485 DYNAMO
PUSHES HER AWAY FROM HIM KEEPING
(THEN SUDDENLY HER HORROR TURNING INTO A VIOLENT 156 ELECTR RAGE--
IS IT HIS LOOKS--OR BECAUSE HE'S SUCH A VIOLENT 289 GGBROW SENSUALIST--
UHE HAS BUT TO MENTION THE NAME OF JACKSON TO GIVE 8 MANSNS HIM VIOLENT DYSPEPSIA.
(HE PAUSES, THEN BLURTS OUT IN VIOLENT 172 MANSNS ACCUSATION.)
AND MAKES VIOLENT GESTURES TO HIM TO KNEEL DOWN.) 378 MARCOM
(HE GIVES A VIOLENT FIT OF COUGHING.) 382 MARCOM
(KUKACHIN GIVES A VIOLENT START WHICH HE DOES NOT 385 MARCOM NOTICE.
THE LATTER MAKES VIOLENT MOTIONS FOR HIM TO GO ON)596 ROPE
DARRELL GIVES A VIOLENT SHUDDER AS IF HE WERE 174 STRANG COMING OUT OF A NIGHTMARE AND
IVAN GIVES A PARTICULARLY VIOLENT SNORE.) 500 VOYAGE
JOE MAKES VIOLENT SIGNS TO FREDA TO BRING HIM 504 VOYAGE BACK.
(WITH A VIOLENT GESTURE OF LOATHING) 452 WELDED
(HE FLINGS HIMSELF ON THE CHAIR IN A VIOLENT 475 WELDED OUTBURST OF DRY SOBBING.)

VIOLENTLY
BEN IS VIOLENTLY RUBBING OFF THE ORGAN 538 'ILE
(THE SCREEN DOOR IS PUSHED VIOLENTLY OPEN AND 260 AHWILD RICHARD LURCHES IN AND STANDS
(VIOLENTLY) SHE'LL NOT/ 55 ANNA
(VIOLENTLY) WELL, LIVING WITH YOU IS ENOUGH TO 57 ANNA DRIVE ANYONE OFF THEIR NUT.
SHE LEANS OVER IN EXASPERATION AND SHAKES HIM 57 ANNA VIOLENTLY BY THE SHOULDER)
(HE SHAKES HER VIOLENTLY) 128 BEYOND
(VIOLENTLY) OH, HIM AND THE SEA HE CALLS TU/ 564 CROSS
(STARTS VIOLENTLY--STAMMERS) 513 DAYS
(VIOLENTLY) NOT MINE/ 207 DESIRE
(THEN VIOLENTLY) I'LL GO SMASH MY FIST IN HER 211 DESIRE FACE/
(HE PULLS OPEN THE DOOR IN REAR VIOLENTLY.) 211 DESIRE
(BREAKING IN VIOLENTLY) YEW 'N' YEWR GOD/ 227 DESIRE

VIOLENTLY (CONT'D.)
(PUSHING HER AWAY VIOLENTLY) 233 DESIRE
(VIOLENTLY) 233 DESIRE
SHE STARTS VIOLENTLY, LOOKS AT HIM, SEES HE IS NOT236 DESIRE WATCHING HER.
HE FREES HIMSELF FROM HER VIOLENTLY AND SPRINGS TO243 DESIRE HIS FEET.
(SHE TRIES TO KISS HIM BUT HE PUSHES HER VIOLENTLY256 DESIRE AWAY
(VIOLENTLY, BETWEEN SOBS AND GASPS) 256 DESIRE
(VIOLENTLY) I HATE YE, I TELL YE/ 258 DESIRE
SHAKING BOTH FISTS AT HER, VIOLENTLY) 262 DESIRE
(AS SHE DOESN'T ANSWER, HE GRABS HER VIOLENTLY BY 264 DESIRE THE SHOULDER AND SHAKES HER)
(VIOLENTLY) I WANT YOU TO SHET UP/ 505 DIFRNT
(VIOLENTLY) IT'S A SHAME, THAT'S WHAT IT IS/ 528 DIFRNT
(BREAKING OUT VIOLENTLY) NO/ 20 ELECTR
(STARTS VIOLENTLY--IN A STRAINED VOICE) 58 ELECTR
(OVERCOME BY A SENSE OF GUILT--VIOLENTLY 98 ELECTR DEFENSIVE)
(CONTROLS A FURIOUS JEALOUS IMPULSE TO PUSH HER 100 ELECTR VIOLENTLY AWAY FROM HIM--
(SHE POUNDS ON THE DOOR VIOLENTLY.) 100 ELECTR
(TEARS HER HAND AWAY--VIOLENTLY) 124 ELECTR
(AS HE HESITATES, TREMBLING VIOLENTLY, SHE GRABS 142 ELECTR HIS ARM FIERCELY)
(AS HE HESITATES--VIOLENTLY) 163 ELECTR
SHE PULLS VIOLENTLY AWAY. 165 ELECTR
(VIOLENTLY) WHAT TRUTH, YOU LITTLE FOOL/ 173 ELECTR
(PROTESTING VIOLENTLY) NO/ 175 ELECTR
(VIOLENTLY) ROT/ 298 GGBROW
(THERE IS A SOUND OF A DOOR BEING PUSHED VIOLENTLY3 GGBROW OPEN.
(VIOLENTLY) YOU DAMNED FOOL/ 667 ICEMAN
(VIOLENTLY.) IT'S A LIE/ I DID WANT HIM/ 88 JOURNE
(VIOLENTLY.) NO/ 119 JOURNE
(VIOLENTLY.) SHUT UP/ 161 JOURNE
(VIOLENTLY.) NO, I WILL NOT HAVE IT/ 36 MANSNS
(THEN RESISTING MORE VIOLENTLY THAN BEFORE-- 36 MANSNS FURIOUSLY.)
(PULLS HER HAND VIOLENTLY FROM HIS.) 190 MANSNS
WHO HAS STARTED VIOLENTLY AT THE MENTION OF 386 MARCOM MARCO'S NAME--WORRIEDLY) IMPOSSIBLE/
(VIOLENTLY) NO/ 412 MARCOM
(HE SHAKES HIS HEAD VIOLENTLY) 81 MISBEG
HIS HAND IS TREMBLING SO VIOLENTLY HE CANNOT LIGHTILL MISBEG THE CIGARETTE.
(HE PULLS HIS ARMS AWAY SO VIOLENTLY THAT HE 137 MISBEG STAGGERS BACK AND WOULD FALL DOWN
HIS HAND TREMBLES SO VIOLENTLY THAT WHEN HE 35 POET
ATTEMPTS TO RAISE THE GLASS
(VIOLENTLY) SERVE HIM DAMN RIGHT IF I DONE IT. 598 ROPE
(THEN VIOLENTLY) BUT GORDON NEVER POSSESSED ME/ 19 STRANG
(A BIT VIOLENTLY) I TELL YOU IT'D BE A CRIME--A 58 STRANG CRIME WORSE THAN MURDER/
(VIOLENTLY) I DON'T BELIEVE YOU KNOW WHAT YOU'RE 58 STRANG SAYING/
(VIOLENTLY) I THINK YOU'RE HORRIBLE/ 59 STRANG
CRUMPLES IT UP AND THROWS IT VIOLENTLY ON THE 67 STRANG FLOOR.
(CATCHING HIMSELF--VIOLENTLY) 75 STRANG
(VIOLENTLY--ALMOST SHOUTS AT HER) 97 STRANG
(VIOLENTLY) I WAS A FOOL/ 130 STRANG
(BURSTING OUT IN SPITE OF HERSELF--VIOLENTLY) 167 STRANG
(THEN VIOLENTLY) GOD DAMN IT, WHY DID YOU MAKE ME170 STRANG SAY HOPES
(THEN VIOLENTLY) 177 STRANG
(VIOLENTLY) NONSENSE/ 458 WELDED
(VIOLENTLY) YOU DENY THAT I CREATE--S 459 WELDED
(PUSHING HIM AWAY--VIOLENTLY) 485 WELDED
(VIOLENTLY) DON'T BE A FOOL/ 486 WELDED

VIOLET
MY NAME'S BELLA, THIS HERE'S SUSIE, YANDER'S 464 CARIBE VIOLET,
DAVIS AND THE GIRL VIOLET COME OUT OF THE 468 CARIBE FORECASTLE AND CLOSE THE DOOR BEHIND
OR VIOLET, OR WHATEVER THE HELL FLOWER YOUR NAME 468 CARIBE IS.
(DAVIS AND VIOLET COME BACK AND JOIN THE CROWD THE470 CARIBE DUNKEYMEN LOOKS ON THEM ALL
IN WHICH ONLY THE DEEP-SET EYES, OF A DARK VIOLET 9 ELECTR BLUE, ARE ALIVE.
THE SAME PALLOR AND DARK VIOLET-BLUE EYES, 10 ELECTR
I PICKED FAT VIOLET. 159 JOURNE
WELL, THAT MADE ME FEEL SORRY FOR FAT VIOLET, 159 JOURNE
BEEFED HOW ROTTEN BUSINESS WAS, AND SHE WAS GOING 159 JOURNE TO GIVE FAT VIOLET THE GATE.

VIOLET'S
FAT VIOLET'S A GOOD KID. 161 JOURNE

VIOLIN
BUT SHE--SHE HEARD THE VIOLIN, AND LEFT MY SIDE 159 JOURNE AND ENTERED IN.

VIPERISH
(FREUA FAVORS HIM WITH A VIPERISH GLANCE AND SITS 500 VOYAGE DOWN BY OLSON)

VIRGIN
A BURNED, HE-VIRGIN, SKY-PILOTS 513 DIFRNT
SOME DAY WHEN THE BLESSED VIRGIN MARY FORGIVES ME 94 JOURNE AND GIVES ME BACK THE FAITH IN
IN THE CONVENT WHEN YOU USED TO PRAY TO THE 107 JOURNE BLESSED VIRGIN.
(SNEERINGLY.) YOU EXPECT THE BLESSED VIRGIN TO BE107 JOURNE FOOLED
THE BLESSED VIRGIN WOULD NEVER FORGIVE ME, THEN. 121 JOURNE
AND TELL ME TO PRAY TO THE BLESSED VIRGIN, AND 171 JOURNE THEY'LL BE WELL AGAIN IN NO TIME.
THAT I HAD PRAYED TO THE BLESSED VIRGIN TO MAKE ME175 JOURNE SURE, AND TO FIND ME WORTHY.

VIRGIN (CONT'D.)
THAT THE BLESSED VIRGIN HAD SMILED AND BLESSED ME 175 JOURNE
WITH HER CONSENT,
SO I WENT TO THE SHRINE AND PRAYED TO THE BLESSED 176 JOURNE
VIRGIN AND FOUND PEACE AGAIN
OF COURSE, I DON'T MEAN I'VE BEEN ANY HE-VIRGIN. 404 MARCOM
(SCORNFULLY) I'M TO PRETEND I'M A PURE VIRGIN, I 34 MISBEG
SUPPOSES
AND HON'S MY VIRGIN QUEEN OF IRELANDS 41 MISBEG
AND DON'T BE MISCALLING ME A VIRGIN. 41 MISBEG
AND NOW YOU ACT LIKE A NUMBSKULL VIRGIN 80 MISBEG
(HE CHUCKLES) A VIRGIN, NO LESS/ 88 MISBEG
HE THINKS YOU'RE A POOR INNOCENT VIRGIN/ 88 MISBEG
HE BELIEVES YOU'RE A VIRGIN/ 88 MISBEG
YOU'RE A PURE VIRGIN TO HIM, 89 MISBEG
THINKING YOU'RE A VIRGINS 92 MISBEG
BE GOD, I THOUGHT YOU'D STARTED PLAYING VIRGIN 94 MISBEG
WITH ME
TO HAVE ME PRETEND I'M AN INNOCENT VIRGIN TONIGHT.114 MISBEG
I AM A VIRGIN. 134 MISBEG
AND THE DAWN FINDS HER STILL A VIRGIN. 160 MISBEG
(HE ATTEMPTS A JOKING TONE) IS IT YOU WHO'S THE 160 MISBEG
VIRGINS
A VIRGIN WHO BEARS A DEAD CHILD IN THE NIGHT, 160 MISBEG
AND IF HE ONCE HAD ME, KNOWING I WAS A VIRGIN, 164 MISBEG
I'M STILL GORDOM'S SILLY VIRGIN/ 19 STRANG
(CUTTINGLY) OH, SO YOU THINK YOU DESERVE AN 115 STRANG
INNOCENT VIRGIN/.

VIRGINITY
AND I KNEW MY SOBS WERE UGLY AND MEANINGLESS TO 282 GGBROW
HER VIRGINITY.

VIRGINS
I CANNOT CONTEST THE PROFOUND INTUITIONS OF 397 MARCOM
VIRGINS AND MYSTICS.

VIRILE
AN OAF--BUT A HANDSOME, VIRILE OAF. 222 HA APE

VIRTUE
AND ON BOTH SIDES WE WERE ABLE TO KEEP OUR REAL 284 GGBROW
VIRTUE, IF YOU GET ME.
WITH WINE, WITH POETRY, OR WITH VIRTUE, AS YOU 132 JOURNE
WILL.=
DRUNKEN WITH WHATS WITH WINE, WITH POETRY, OR 132 JOURNE
WITH VIRTUE, AS YOU WILL.
(THICKLY HUMOROUS.) I WOULDN'T WORRY ABOUT THE 133 JOURNE
VIRTUE PART OF IT,
WHAT VIRTUE IN KILLING WHEN THERE IS NO DEATHS 322 LAZARU
ALTHOUGH I CANNOT PRETEND TO VIRTUE IN MYSELF 332 LAZARU
I DISCOVERED TO BE A FAT WOMAN WITH A PATIENT 424 MARCOM
VIRTUE.
YOU'VE NEVER CARED ABOUT YOUR VIRTUE, OR WHAT MAN 9 MISBEG
YOU WENT OUT WITH.
THAT WE'LL SUE HIM FOR OUTRAGING YOUR VIRTUES 95 MISBEG
AND POSSESSIVE AMBITION, AND UPHELD THE VIRTUE OF 84 POET
FREEING ONESELF
BOASTING OF HIS VIRTUE/..... 116 STRANG
HE POSSESSES THE RARE VIRTUE OF GRATITUDE. 166 STRANG

VIRTUES
WELL, I KNOW MY FATHER'S VIRTUES WITHOUT YOU 124 MISBEG
TELLING ME.

VIRTUOUS
ARTHUR IS SELF-CONSCIOUSLY A VIRTUOUS YOUNG MAN 263 AHWILD
ARE YOU GOING TO ORDER ME FROM YOUR VIRTUOUS HOME$520 DAYS
HER EXPRESSION IS ONE OF VIRTUOUS RESIGNATION. 422 DYNAMO
(SUDDENLY PRIMLY VIRTUOUS.) I'D NEVER SUGGEST A 52 JOURNE
MAN OR A WOMAN TOUCH DRINK,
HYPOCRITICAL PRETENSES AND VIRTUOUS LIES ABOUT 47 MANSNS
OURSELVES.
DO YOU MEAN TO TELL ME A VIRTUOUS WIFE AND MOTHER 89 MANSNS
LIKE YOU
WHAT IS EVIL IS THE STUPID THEORY THAT MAN IS 172 MANSNS
NATURALLY WHAT WE CALL VIRTUOUS
LET HIM SET AN EXAMPLE OF VIRTUOUS WESTERN MANHOOD363 MARCOM
AND ALL THE LEVITIES OF
YOU'RE VIRTUOUS. 6 MISBEG
YOU'RE SUCH A VIRTUOUS TEETOTALLER-- 93 MISBEG
(RAISING HIS GLASS.) YOUR HEALTH AND 9 POET
INCLINATIONS--IF THEY'RE VIRTUOUS/

VIRTUOUSLY
(VIRTUOUSLY) YOU KNOW I NEVER TOUCH IT. 12 ANNA
(THEN VIRTUOUSLY) BUT I DON'T LIKE TAKING STOLEN 7 MISBEG
MONEY.
BUT HE REPLIES VIRTUOUSLY.) 36 POET

VISAGED
(THE TWO BROTHERS CONGEAL INTO TWO STIFF, GRIM- 221 DESIRE
VISAGED STATUES.
IS ONE OF A GRIM-VISAGED MINISTER OF THE WITCH- 79 ELECTR
BURNING ERA.

VISH
PY YESUS, I VISH SOMEPODY TAKE MY FIRST VATCH FOR 209 HA APE
ME/
AND SO I DO NOT VISH THE DAY COME BECAUSE IT VILL 634 ICEMAN
NOT BE MY DAY.

VISIBLE
A RIM OF MILK VISIBLE ABOUT HIS LIPS. 186 AHWILD
THE INTERIOR OF THE KITCHEN IS NOW VISIBLE. 206 DESIRE
ONLY THE HALF SECTIONS OF THE TWO HOUSES ARE -0 DYNAMO
VISIBLE WHICH ARE NEAREST TO EACH
A SULTRY, HAZY SKY WITH FEW STARS VISIBLE. 468 DYNAMO
THE PART AFT OF THE MIZZENMAST IS VISIBLE WITH THE102 ELECTR
CURVE OF THE STERN AT RIGHT.
AT EXTREME LEFT IS THE MIZZENMAST, THE LOWEST YARDIO2 ELECTR
JUST VISIBLE ABOVE.
AS IF THEY WERE THE VISIBLE SYMBOL OF HER GOD) 157 ELECTR
FOUR WINDOWS ARE VISIBLE WITH A CLOSED DOOR IN THE281 LAZARU
MIDDLE OF THE WALL.
DID I EXPECT DEATH TO OPEN THE DOOR AND ENTER THE 30 MANSNS
ROOM, VISIBLE TO ME,

VISIBLE (CONT'D.)
(MAKING A TREMENDOUS VISIBLE EFFORT HE KISSES HER 473 WELDED
ON THE LIPS.

VISIBLY
THE STEWARD IS VISIBLY FRIGHTENED 539 'ILE
(MADE VISIBLY UNEASY BUT FORCING A MANLY TONE) 439 DYNAMO
SHE HAS VISIBLY WITHDRAWN INTO HERSELF AND IS ON 14 ELECTR
THE DEFENSIVE.
(THEY SHE SEES PETER, WHO IS VISIBLY EMBARRASSED 16 ELECTR
BY HER PRESENCE)
VISIBLY BRACING HERSELF FOR THE ORDEAL OF THE 84 ELECTR
COMING INTERVIEW,
HE STOPS BEFORE THE TWO AND TIPS HIS CAP, VISIBLY 220 HA APE
EMBARRASSED AND ILL-AT-EASE.)
THE OTHERS VISIBLY TREMBLING WITH SUPERSTITIOUS 352 MARCOM
HORROR)
GROWING VISIBLY MORE UNEASY. 158 MISBEG
(HAS BEEN VISIBLY CRUMBLING AS HE LISTENS 178 POET
SHE RECOILS FROM IT, TURNING QUICKLY AWAY FROM 450 WELDED
HIM, VISIBLY SHAKEN.

VISION
THE VISION OF A NEW LIFE OPENING UP AFTER ALL THE 150 BEYOND
HORRIBLE YEARS&
ESPECIALLY IN THE LIGHT OF YOUR RECENT MYSTIC 509 DAYS
VISION/
(STILL IN HIS ECSTATIC MYSTIC VISION--STRANGELY) 566 DAYS
(HE RETREATS BACK BEYOND THE VISION OF THE OLD MAN223 DESIRE
AND TAKES THE BAG OF MONEY
BEATIFIC VISION SWOONS ON THE EMPTY POOLS OF THE 32 HUGHIE
NIGHT CLERK'S EYES.
LIKE A SAINT'S VISION OF BEATITUDE. 153 JOURNE
I TOLD MOTHER I HAD HAD A TRUE VISION WHEN I WAS 175 JOURNE
PRAYING IN THE SHRINE OF OUR
AS IF HIS VISION WERE STILL FIXED BEYOND LIFE. 274 LAZARU
HE MAKES A SLIGHT MOVEMENT, A STIRRING IN HIS 277 LAZARU
VISION.
(SUDDENLY LAUGHING SOFTLY OUT OF HIS VISION, AS IF279 LAZARU
TO HIMSELF,
THEN YOU CAN GO ON--SUCCESSFULLY--WITH A CLEAR 91 MANSNS
VISION--WITHOUT FALSE SCRUPLE--
THE UNEXPECTED VISION OF MELODY IN HIS UNIFORM 116 POET
STARTLES HIM.
ABOVE THE WORLD, BEYOND ITS VISION--OUR MEANING/ 488 WELDED

VISIONARY
HER UPTURNED UNMASKED FACE LIKE THAT OF A 264 GGBROW
RAPTUROUS VISIONARY.
(BURSTING SUDDENLY INTO CHOKING, JOYFUL LAUGHTER--360 LAZARU
LIKE A VISIONARY.)

VISIONS
EVERY DAY THESE EVIL VISIONS POSSESSED HIM. 536 DAYS
AH, BE DAMNED/ HAVEN'T I HEARD THEIR VISIONS A 608 ICEMAN
THOUSAND TIMES&

VISIT
AND AY GO VISIT DEM EVERY TIME AY GAT IN PORT 13 ANNA
NEAR/
I COULD VISIT A WHILE AND REST UP-- 22 ANNA
IT'S LIKE I'D COME HOME AFTER A LONG VISIT AWAY 28 ANNA
SURE PLACE.
ANYWAY, I WANT TO STAY TO HOME AND VISIT WITH YOU 137 BEYOND
FOLKS A SPELL BEFORE I GO.
AND THAT REMINDS ME, I BETTER GO AND PAY MY LITTLE461 DYNAMO
VISIT.
(THEN SUDDENLY) SAY, I THINK I'LL GO AND VISIT 467 DYNAMO
MOTHER'S GRAVE.
WAL, I PROMISED AMOS I'D HELP SHOW YE THE SIGHTS 7 ELECTR
WHEN YOU CAME TO VISIT HIM.
I SUPPOSE ANNIE TOLD YOU I'D BEEN TO VISIT HAZEL 29 ELECTR
AND PETER WHILE YOU WERE AWAY.
YOU DIDN'T VISIT THEM& 29 ELECTR
AND ALL MY TRIPS TO NEW YORK WEREN'T TO VISIT 61 ELECTR
FATHER BUT TO BE WITH ADAM/
I'M AFRAID THIS ISN'T A VERY CHEERFUL HOUSE TO 84 ELECTR
VISIT JUST NOW--
AND TO IMAGINE FOR A MOMENT, IF HE WERE, HE'D EVER 87 ELECTR
COME HERE TO VISIT/
HAD INVITED HIM AND VINNIE TO VISIT THEM OVERNIGHTI08 ELECTR
AT BLACKRIDGE
RETURNING FROM HIS NIGHTLY VISIT TO THE SALOON.) 123 ELECTR
I'M GOING TO MAKE HER LET HIM VISIT US FOR A 159 ELECTR
SPELL.
PERMISSION TO VISIT THE STOKEHOLES 220 HA APE
I USED TO VISIT THEM AND THEY'D VISIT ME IN MY 86 JOURNE
FATHER'S HOME.
(AN AGED, SORROWFUL MAN) AND I USED TO VISIT HIM 276 LAZARU
EVERY DAY.
I INVITED HIM TO VISIT ME IN MY GARDEN NOT LONG 11 MANSNS
AGO--
MAY I ASK TO WHAT I OWE THE HONOR OF YOUR VISIT, 31 MANSNS
GENTLEMEN/
WHY IS IT YOU NEVER COME TO VISIT MOTHERS 73 MANSNS
MOTHER WILL BE CURIOUS ABOUT YOUR VISIT HERE BUT 93 MANSNS
DON'T TELL HER ANYTHING.
SARA HAS PROBABLY TOLD YOU OF HER VISIT TO MY 96 MANSNS
OFFICE THIS MORNING.
WILL YOU DEIGN TO VISIT ME HERE AND COMFORT MY 106 MANSNS
EXILES
(THINKING.) HIS PROPOSAL TO VISIT ME EACH 121 MANSNS
EVENING--
AH, HE'S TAKEN TO PAYING YOUR OLD MOTHER A MORNING140 MANSNS
VISIT
JUST IN TIME FOR MY EVENING VISIT WITH MOTHER. 147 MANSNS
HE'S PAID THE LAST VISIT HERE HE'LL EVER PAY YOU. 166 MANSNS
HIS HONOR, MARCO POLO, MAYOR OF YANG-CHAU, SEEMS 386 MARCOM
ABOUT TO VISIT YOU IN STATE/
TO WHAT DO I OWE THE HONOR OF THIS UNEXPECTED 391 MARCOM
VISITS
I MADE A BET WITH ANOTHER SENIOR I COULD GET A 38 MISBEG
TART FROM THE HAYMARKET TO VISIT

VISIT

VISIT (CONT'D.)
I HAVE ONLY TIME FOR A SHORT VISIT-- 74 POET
(SHE LOWERS HER VOICE.) IT ISN'T JUST TO PAY 78 POET
SIMON A VISIT SHE CAME.
THAN THE ONE WHO PAID US A VISIT THIS MORNING, FOR106 POET
EXAMPLE.
HE WILL VISIT THINE INIQUITY, O DAUGHTER OF EDOM,.579 ROPE
(LOUDLY) *HE WILL VISIT THINE INIQUITY--* 580 ROPE
TO VISIT A FELLOW WHO'D BEEN IN MY OUTFIT I RAN 30 STRANG
INTO HIM AGAIN.
MARRIED, THE MOST URGENT INVITATIONS TO VISIT HER. 50 STRANG
SINCE THAT VISIT HOME... 68 STRANG
HE'S COMING OUT FOR A LITTLE VISIT. 75 STRANG
WHEN WE WENT TO VISIT SAM'S MOTHER 82 STRANG
BUT FROM WHAT I SAW ON THAT VISIT TO HIS HOME, HE 101 STRANG
DOESN'T LOVE HIS MOTHER MUCH.
CHARLIE *TELL COME IN EVERY DAY TO VISIT... 191 STRANG

VISITED
THE TWO TIMES I'VE VISITED THE HOSPITAL SHE'S BEEN 25 STRANG
PLEASANT ENOUGH...

VISITIN'
SHE'S VISITIN' HER FOLKS TO NEW BEDFORD. 130 ELECTR

VISITING
SHE'S BEEN GOING TO NEW YORK ON THE EXCUSE OF 99 ELECTR
VISITING GRANDFATHER HAMEL.
WELL, IF YOU SIMPLY GOT TO BE A REGULAR DEVIL LIKE279 GGBROW
ALL THE OTHER VISITING SPORTS
I'LL BE OUT OF TOWN VISITING. 106 STRANG
THAT HE'D BE VISITING FRIENDS OUT OF TOWN UNTIL HE108 STRANG
SAILED.

VISITOR
JOHN, THERE'S A MYSTERIOUS VISITOR OUTSIDE 499 DAYS
DEMANDING TO SEE YOU.
(HAS BEEN WATCHING THE VISITOR APPROACH) 55 MISBEG

VISITS
I HINTED THAT HIS VISITS WEREN'T WELCOME. 52 ELECTR
I THINK SHE WILL WELCOME VISITS EVEN FROM ME. 91 MANSNS
HE KNOWS THAT HIS VISITS HERE ARE ALL THAT IS LEFT162 MANSNS
ME--
ALONG TO HIS BEDROOM, THERE WAS A DEAL OF GOSSIP 108 POET
ABOUT YOUR VISITS TO HIS CABIN,

VISKEY
SING *VISKEY JOHNNY,* 459 CARIBE
WUT KIND BOOZE DEY BRING--VISKEYS 460 CARIBE

VISTA
FOR BEYOND THE PORTICO NOTHING CAN BE SEEN BUT A 173 EJONES
VISTA OF DISTANT HILLS.

VISUALIZE
CREATIVE IMAGINATION ENOUGH TO VISUALIZE THE 395 MARCOM
ENORMOUS POSSIBILITIES.

VISUALIZED
THE BEGINS TO TELL THE STORY, STARING BEFORE HIM 110 MANSNS
AS IF HE VISUALIZED IT.)

VISUALIZING
AS IF HE WERE VISUALIZING THE SCENE HE IS 544 DAYS
DESCRIBING)

VITAL
BUT ONE SENSES AN INNER TENSE EXCITEMENT, A VITAL 50 MANSNS
EAGER MENTAL ALIVENESS.
AS IF SOMETHING VITAL HAD BEEN STABBED IN HIM-- 51 POET
WITH A CRY OF TORTURED APPEAL.)

VITALITY
THERE IS A FIERCE REPRESSED VITALITY ABOUT HIM. 203 DESIRE
ABBIE IS THIRTY-FIVE, BUXOM, FULL OF VITALITY. 221 DESIRE
NERVOUS VITALITY ABOUT ALL HER MOVEMENTS THAT 494 DIFRNT
REVEALS AN UNDERLYING CONSTITUTION
BULLY-APPEALING VITALITY OF SELF-CONFIDENT YOUTH.505 DIFRNT
THE YOUNGER LOOKING AS IF THE VITALITY OF HER 218 HA APE
STICK HAD BEEN SAPPED BEFORE SHE
BUT I'M AFRAID I HAVE NEITHER THE VITALITY NOR 219 HA APE
INTEGRITY.
HE ALSO LACKS HIS FATHER'S VITALITY. 19 JOURNE
FULL OF HEALTH AND VITALITY, AND RETAINING ITS 2 MANSNS
GRACE DESPITE HER CONDITION.
IT HAS A BULL-LIKE, IMPERVIOUS STRENGTH, A TOUGH 33 POET
PEASANT VITALITY.

VITALS
THE VITALS OF OUR FAIR REPUBLIC-AS FOUL A MENACE 242 HA APE
AGAINST THE VERY LIFE-BLOOD OF

VITTLES
AN' FIX SOME VITTLES. 214 DESIRE
LET HIM GIT HIS OWN VITTLES. 245 DESIRE
YE'VE SWILLED MY LIKKER AN' GUZZLED MY VITTLES 249 DESIRE
LIKE HOGS, HAIN'T YE5
YE GUT ANY VITTLES COOKED? 263 DESIRE
GITTING VITTLES, I CALCULATE. 263 DESIRE

VITUPERATION
SWITCHING SUDDENLY FROM JARRING SHOUTS TO LOW, 56 MISBEG
CONFIDENTIAL VITUPERATION.

VIVACIOUS
SHE IS ALMOST SEVENTEEN, PRETTY AND VIVACIOUS, 262 GGBROW
BLONDE, WITH BIG ROMANTIC EYES,

VIVACITY
SHE HAS VIVACITY AND A FETCHING SMILE. 186 AHWILD

VIVE
VIVE LE SON DES CANONS/* 634 ICEMAN
VIVE LE SON/ 727 ICEMAN
VIVE LE SON/ 727 ICEMAN
VIVE LE SON DES CANONS/ 727 ICEMAN

VIVID
I KNOW YOU HAVE THE MOST VIVID RECOLLECTION OF HIS494 DAYS
TERRIBLE SIN.
(HE GIVES A VIVID IMITATION OF A CAT FIGHT AT THIS507 DIFRNT
LAST.
WHEN THERE IS A VIVID FLASH OF LIGHTNING. 437 DYNAMO
COMMON DINNER BELL WHICH IS PAINTED THE SAME VIVID1B2 EJONES
SCARLET AS THE THRONE.

VIVID (CONT'D.)
IT'S ONE VIVID BLASPHEMY FROM SIDEWALK TO THE TIPS297 GGBROW
OF ITS SPIRES/
VIVID LIFE OF THE SEA ALL ABOUT--- 218 HA APE
HE HAS ON A STRAW HAT WITH A VIVID BAND, 615 ICEMAN

VACATION
I EXPLAINED HOW SURE I WAS OF MY VOCATION, 175 JOURNE

VOCIFEROUSLY
VOCIFEROUSLY AS HE LETS HIM INTO THE APARTMENT. 146 STRANG

VOGUE
IT IS A LARGE BUILDING OF THE GREEK TEMPLE TYPE 2 ELECTR
THAT WAS THE VOGUE

VOICE
(THE SAME TONE OF AWE CREEPING INTO HIS VOICE) 536 *ILE
AND THE QUIET SO THICK YOU'RE AFRAID TO HEAR YOUR 538 *ILE
OWN VOICE.
(UNCONSCIOUSLY LOWERING HIS VOICE) 539 *ILE
(A TOUCH OF RESENTMENT IN HIS VOICE) 540 *ILE
(A TONE OF COMMAND IN HIS VOICE) 540 *ILE
KEENEY'S VOICE IS FULL OF MOCKERY) 544 *ILE
(HIS EYES AND VOICE SNAPPING) 544 *ILE
(HER VOICE BREAKS.) 545 *ILE
AND (HUSHED--(HER VOICE GHOWS TREMULOUS) ALL I 545 *ILE
FIND IS ICE AND COLD--
KITCHEN AGAIN, AND HEAR A WOMAN'S VOICE TALKING TO547 *ILE
ME AND BE ABLE TO TALK TO
(HIS VOICE BETRAYING HIS EMOTION) 549 *ILE
(HIS VOICE SUDDENLY GRIM WITH DETERMINATION) 550 *ILE
AND THE MATE'S VOICE SHOUTING ORDERS.) 550 *ILE
KEENEY'S VOICE TREMBLES) 551 *ILE
THEN MRS. MILLER'S VOICE, RAISED COMMANDINGLY, 186 AHWILD
TOMMY
(HIS FATHER'S VOICE IS HEARD SPEAKING TO HIS 186 AHWILD
MOTHER.
HER VOICE PRESENTS THE GREATEST CONTRAST TO HER 187 AHWILD
APPEARANCE.
(A FLAT BRITTLE VOICE ANSWERS HIM..* 200 AHWILD
(WITHOUT TAKING OFFENSE--IN SAME FLAT, BRITTLE 201 AHWILD
VOICE)
(AGAIN IN HIS FLAT, BRITTLE VOICE, SLOWLY GETTING 203 AHWILD
TO HIS FEET)
(WITH A TRACE OF SHOCKED REPROOF SHOWING IN HIS 205 AHWILD
VOICE)
(A FLUSTERED APPEAL IN HER VOICE) 211 AHWILD
(KISSES HER IMPULSIVELY--HER VOICE HUSKY) 214 AHWILD
(QUOTES FROM *CANDIDIA* IN A HOLLOW VOICE) 216 AHWILD
THEN A MASCULINE VOICE CALLS. 217 AHWILD
THEN AS HE RECOGNIZES THE OWNER OF THE VOICE, 217 AHWILD
(THE NERVOUS WORRIED NOTE IN HER VOICE AGAIN,) 217 AHWILD
BUT SO GREAT IS THE COMIC SPELL FOR HER EVEN IN 220 AHWILD
HER BROTHER'S VOICE,
AS SHE DOES SO, FROM THE FRONT YARD SID'S VOICE IS220 AHWILD
HEARD SINGING *POOR JOHN/*
(RESPECT IN HIS VOICE) THANK YOU, SIR. 239 AHWILD
(THE VOICE OF THE SALESMAN, WHO HAS JUST COME IN 239 AHWILD
THE BAR, CALLS *HEY*
A NEW APPRECIATION FOR HER ESCORT'S POSSIBILITIES 239 AHWILD
IN HER VOICE)
HE STRAIGHTENS ALERTLY AND SPEAKS IN A VOICE THAT,252 AHWILD
IN SPITE OF HIS EFFORT,
AND WHEN I WAS A BOY I HAD A FINE VOICE MYSELF AND255 AHWILD
FOLKS USED TO SAY I'D OUGHT--
(PERKING UP PROUDLY) ARTHUR HAS A REAL NICE 255 AHWILD
VOICE.
ARTHUR, WHAT'S THIS I HEAR ABOUT YOUR HAVING SUCH 255 AHWILD
A GOOD SINGING VOICE
I DON'T KNOW IF MY VOICE-- 256 AHWILD
HE HAS A FAIRLY DECENT VOICE BUT HIS METHOD IS 257 AHWILD
UNTRAINED SENTIMENTALITY
WHY, YOU'VE GOT A SPLENDID VOICE/ 257 AHWILD
MILDRED'S VOICE COMES FROM THE FRONT PARLOR, 257 AHWILD
(SUDDENLY TURNS TOWARD LILY--HIS VOICE CHOKED WITH258 AHWILD
TEARS--
A MELTING DRAWLY VOICE. 277 AHWILD
(HIS EYES ON HER FACE LOVINGLY--GENUINE ADORATION 279 AHWILD
IN HIS VOICE)
(THEN SHOCKED INDIGNATION COMING INTO HIS VOICE) 295 AHWILD
HE SAYS IN A LOW VOICE) 298 AHWILD
NEITHER HIS VOICE NOR HIS GENERAL MANNER DISPEL 3 ANNA
THIS ILLUSION
HIS VOICE, WHEN NOT RAISED IN A HOLLOW BOOM, IS 5 ANNA
TUNED DOWN TO A SLY,
SHE SPEAKS IN A LOUD, MANNISH VOICE. 7 ANNA
SHE SPEAKS HURRIEDLY IN A LOW VOICE) 19 ANNA
AND BY HEARING CHRIS' VOICE) 19 ANNA
(WITH A TRACE OF GENUINE FEELING IN HER VOICE) 20 ANNA
HIS VOICE SEEMING TO PLEAD FOR HER FORBEARANCE) 20 ANNA
WITH A TRACE OF SCORN IN HER VOICE) 21 ANNA
(HIS VOICE TREMBLES) AY'M GETTING OLE. 22 ANNA
(EXULTATION AGAIN IN HER VOICE) 26 ANNA
(HER VOICE RISING ANGRILY) SAY, WHAT'RE YOU 26 ANNA
TRYING TO DO--MAKE THINGS ROTTENS
(A GRIM FOREBODING IN HIS VOICE) 29 ANNA
EXHAUSTED VOICE COMES FAINTLY OUT OF THE FOG TO 29 ANNA
PORT)
THE VOICE IS HEARD AGAIN SHOUTING *AHOY* AND CHRIS 30 ANNA
ANSWERING *DIS VAY.*
CHRIS' VOICE SHOUTS AFTER HIM) 30 ANNA
(IN A SUBDUED VOICE) THEN ALL THE OTHERS WAS 36 ANNA
DROWNEDS
(HURT-- HIS VOICE BREAKING--PLEADINGLY) 39 ANNA
HE CLEARS HIS THROAT AND STARTS TO SING TO HIMSELF 41 ANNA
IN A LOW, DOLEFUL VOICE.**
ANNA CONTINUES SLOWLY, A TRACE OF SADNESS IN HER 44 ANNA
VOICE)
(HALF RISING FROM HIS CHAIR--IN A VOICE CHOKED 49 ANNA
WITH RAGE)
(HER VOICE 53 ANNA

VOICE

VOICE (CONT'D.)
(HER VOICE TREMBLING) THAT KISS WAS FOR GOOD-BY, 53 ANNA MAT.
A TRACE OF RESENTMENT IN HER VOICE) 55 ANNA
WITH FRIGHTENED FOREBODING IN HIS VOICE) 57 ANNA
(WITH A SUDDEN WEARINESS IN HER VOICE) 58 ANNA
(RAISING HER HEAD AT THE SOUND OF HIS VOICE--WITH 59 ANNA EXTREME MOCKING BITTERNESS)
HIS VOICE TREMBLING WITH PASSION) 60 ANNA
(HIS VOICE HIGH PITCHED IN A LAMENTATION THAT IS 60 ANNA LIKE A KEEN)
SHE SPEAKS ALOUD TO HERSELF IN A TENSE, TREMBLING 67 ANNA VOICE)
(IN THE SAME HARD VOICE) WELL, CAN'T YOU TALK? 69 ANNA
(THEN AFTER A PAUSE--IN A VOICE OF DEAD, STONY 71 ANNA CALM)
(HER VOICE BREAKING) OH, FOR GAWD'S SAKE, MAT, 72 ANNA LEAVE ME ALONE/
HE READS ALOUD IN A DOLEFUL, SING-SONG VOICE) 82 BEYOND
(CHARMED BY HIS LOW, MUSICAL VOICE TELLING THE 89 BEYOND DREAMS OF HIS CHILDHOOD)
(CONQUERED BY THIS APPEAL--AN IRREVOCABLE DECISION 92 BEYOND IN HIS VOICE)
A TYPICAL OLD SALT, LOUD OF VOICE AND GIVEN TO 94 BEYOND GESTURE.
(HIS VOICE DIES AWAY AS HE SEES THE PAIN IN 101 BEYOND ANDREW'S EYES.)
(HIS VOICE INDICATES DISBELIEF.) 102 BEYOND
(DUMBFOUNDED--UNABLE TO DOUBT THE DETERMINATION IN105 BEYOND ANDREW'S VOICE--HELPLESSLY)
(HIS VOICE RAISED AND QUIVERING WITH ANGER) 106 BEYOND
(IN A FRIGHTENED VOICE) DON'T YOU ANSWER HIM, 107 BEYOND JAMES.
(THE FIRST TO FIND HIS VOICE--WITH AN EXPLOSIVE 108 BEYOND SIGH)
HE SPEAKS IN A LOW VOICE, FULL OF FEELING) 109 BEYOND
(HIS VOICE BREAKS) THINKING SHE CARED FOR ME. 110 BEYOND
SHE SPEAKS IN AN UNCERTAIN VOICE, WITHOUT 112 BEYOND ASSERTIVENESS.
INTERRUPTED AT INTERVALS BY A WOMAN'S IRRITATED 112 BEYOND VOICE
(BENDING OVER TOWARD HER--IN A LOW VOICE) 115 BEYOND
HIS VOICE CAN BE HEARD FAINTLY AS HE LULLS THE 121 BEYOND CHILD TO SLEEP.
SHE HEARS THE VOICE FROM THE ROOM AND TIPTOES TO 121 BEYOND THE DOOR TO LOOK IN.
(IN A LOUD VOICE) COME ON IN HERE, BEN. 123 BEYOND
SOMETIMES I THINK IF IT WASN'T FOR YOU, RUTH, 126 BEYOND AND--(HIS VOICE SOFTENING) --
(IN A LOW, REPRESSED VOICE--HER EYES SMOLDERING) 126 BEYOND
(HER REPRESSED VOICE TREMBLING) 126 BEYOND
(HIS VOICE RAISED LOUDLY) AND NOW--I'M FINDING 127 BEYOND OUT WHAT YOU'RE REALLY LIKE--
(IN A VOICE OF COMMAND THAT FORCES OBEDIENCE) 128 BEYOND STOP!
THEY HEAR ANDY'S VOICE FROM THE ROAD SHOUTING A 128 BEYOND LONG HAIL--AHOY THERE/A.
(HIS VOICE IS A HARSH SHOUT.) 128 BEYOND
BUSINESS-LIKE BRISKNESS OF VOICE AND GESTURE. 130 BEYOND
(A TRACE OF APPEAL IN HIS VOICE) 135 BEYOND
IN A VOICE WHICH HE VAINLY ATTEMPTS TO KEEP CALM) 135 BEYOND
(BREAKING OUT--IN AN AGONIZED VOICE) 135 BEYOND
(IN A LOW VOICE) YES, ANDY. 135 BEYOND
(HER VOICE SINKS TO A TREMULOUS, TENDER WHISPER AS139 BEYOND SHE FINISHES.)
IN A VOICE HE ENDEAVORS TO KEEP FROM BEING HARSH) 142 BEYOND
HIS VOICE RINGS WITH HOPEFUL STRENGTH AND ENERGY) 142 BEYOND
(HER VOICE VAGUELY FRIGHTENED, TAKING HER FATHER'S142 BEYOND HAND)
COMES AND TAKES MARY'S HAND--IN A DEAD VOICE) 143 BEYOND
(IN A MUFFLED VOICE) I'M COMING, MARY. 143 BEYOND
WHEN SHE SPEAKS HER VOICE IS WITHOUT TIMBRE, LOW 144 BEYOND AND MONOTONOUS.
HE +TENDED+ TO PA AND MA AND--(HIS VOICE BREAKS) 145 BEYOND AND TO--MARY.
(IN A DEAD VOICE) I DON'T KNOW. 147 BEYOND
(HIS VOICE) VOICE IS LOWERED TO A TREMBLING 147 BEYOND WHISPER)
THEN SPEAKS IN A LOW VOICE) 148 BEYOND
HIS VOICE IS SO STRANGE THAT RUTH TURNS TO LOOK AT149 BEYOND HIM IN ALARM)
HIS VOICE TAKES ON A NOTE OF EAGERNESS) 149 BEYOND
(GETTING UP--IN A FRIGHTENED VOICE) 149 BEYOND
HIS VOICE IS MOURNFUL AS HE SPEAKS) 150 BEYOND
(HIS VOICE BREAKING) POOR OLD CHAP/ 154 BEYOND
(GLANCING UP QUICKLY--IN A HARSH VOICE) 154 BEYOND
(SITTING DOWN AND CLEARING HIS THROAT--IN A 157 BEYOND PERFUNCTORY, IMPERSONAL VOICE)
(STOPPING ABRUPTLY AND LOWERING HIS VOICE 157 BEYOND CAUTIOUSLY)
(SHE HESITATES FOR A MOMENT--THEN CONTINUES IN A 158 BEYOND MONOTONOUS VOICE)
YOU'LL HAVE TO SUFFER TO WIN BACK--(HIS VOICE 162 BEYOND GROWS WEAKER AND HE SIGHS WEARILY)
(HIS VOICE FALTERING WITH WEAKNESS) 162 BEYOND
THEN SHE CALLS IN A FRIGHTENED VOICE) 166 BEYOND
(IN A VOICE WHICH IS SUDDENLY RINGING WITH THE 167 BEYOND HAPPINESS OF HOPE)
IN A COMPASSIONATE VOICE) 168 BEYOND
(FACING RUTH, THE BODY BETWEEN THEM--IN A DEAD 168 BEYOND VOICE)
AND NOW--(HIS VOICE TREMBLES AS HE FIGHTS TO 480 CARDIF CONTROL HIS EMOTION)
FROM THE FORECASTLE HEAD ABOVE THE VOICE OF THE 482 CARDIF LOOKOUT RISES IN A LONG WAIL.
(IN A WEAK VOICE) NO. 482 CARDIF
THE CAPTAIN SPEAKS IN A LOW VOICE TO THE MATE) 485 CARDIF
(HIS VOICE BETRAYS GREAT INWARD PERTURBATION.) 488 CARDIF

VOICE (CONT'D.)
(BREAKINGREAKING DOWN--IN A CHOKING VOICE) 484 CARDIF
DRISCOLL LOWERS HIS VOICE IMPRESSIVELY AND 458 CARIBE ADDRESSES THEM ALL)
(OVERHEARING THIS--IN A LOUD EAGER VOICE) 458 CARIBE
(BIG FRANK LEANS OVER AND SAYS SOMETHING TO HIM IN464 CARIBE A LOW VOICE.
(QUICKLY--IN A LOW VOICE) WHO KNIFED HIM$ 472 CARIBE
BROKEN ONOKEN ONLY BY THE HAUNTED, SADDENED VOICE 473 CARIBE OF THE BROODING MUSIC.
HIS VOICE IS LOW AND DEEP WITH A PENETRATING, 556 CROSS HOLLOW, METALLIC QUALITY.
(ANXIOUSLY--LOWERING HIS VOICE) 558 CROSS
HER VOICE IS LOW AND MELANCHOLY. 562 CROSS
IT CREAKS SLIGHTLY AND NAT JUMPS TO HIS FEET--IN A562 CROSS THICK VOICE OF TERROR)
(IN A HARD VOICE) UNLESS WE HAVE--FATHER--TAKEN 564 CROSS
(STARING AT HER--IN A HARD VOICE) 565 CROSS
EXCLAIMING IN A TERRIBLE VOICE) 566 CROSS
COMES FROM ABOVE IN BARTLETT'S VOICE, 569 CROSS
IN A VOICE OF MANNING) 572 CROSS
(LOOKS UP--IN AN ASTONISHED VOICE) 572 CROSS
IN A VOICE HE TRIES TO MAKE CASUAL BUT WHICH IS 494 DAYS INSUFFERABLY SINISTER)
(HIS VOICE SINGULARLY TONELESS AND COLD BUT AT THE494 DAYS SAME TIME INSISTENT)
YOUR HERO'S MANAGED UP TO THE TIME HE IS SNEER 494 DAYS COMES INTO HIS VOICE)
BUT AS HE GOES ON A STRANGE DEFIANT NOTE OF 495 DAYS EXULTANCE COMES INTO HIS VOICE)
(HIS VOICE A MOCKING SNEER) AND WHAT SALVATION 501 DAYS FOR US ARE YOU PREACHING$
WITH A DIRTY SNEER IN HIS VOICE) 501 DAYS
(A STERN NOTE COMES INTO HIS VOICE) 506 DAYS
(QUOTES IN A LOW VOICE BUT WITH DEEP FEELING) 508 DAYS
(A SNEERING TAUNT IN HIS VOICE) 509 DAYS
(HIS VOICE SUDDENLY CHANGES TO HARD BITTERNESS) 510 DAYS
(HIS VOICE SUDDENLY TAKES ON A TONE OF BITTER 511 DAYS HATRED)
(THEN, HIS VOICE BECOMING GUARDED AND PLEASANTLY 513 DAYS CASUAL)
JOHN JUMPS NERVOUSLY--THEN ANSWERS IT IN AN 513 DAYS APPREHENSIVE VOICE.)
(CALLS BACK IN A VOICE WHOSE BREEZINESS RINGS A 515 DAYS BIT STRAINED)
HER VOICE COMES) 515 DAYS
(WITH A SIDE GLANCE OF FRANK ENVY--UNABLE TO KEEP 517 DAYS RESENTMENT OUT OF HER VOICE)
I THOUGHT I HEARD A FAMILIAR VOICE WHEN I CAME IN.525 DAYS
(LOWERING HIS VOICE--HURRIEDLY) 526 DAYS
(QUICKLY, RAISING HIS VOICE TO A CONVERSATIONAL 527 DAYS TONE)
(JOHN LISTENS FASCINATEDLY, AS IF TO AN INNER 531 DAYS VOICE.
(A HOSTILE, REPELLENT NOTE IN HIS VOICE) 534 DAYS
THEN QUIETLY, AN UNDERCURRENT OF STERNNESS IN HIS 538 DAYS VOICE)
(IN A COLD VOICE, AS IF HE WERE PRONOUNCING A 539 DAYS DEATH SENTENCE)
(AN IDEALISTIC EXALTATION COMING INTO HIS VOICE) 542 DAYS
(HIS VOICE HAS TAKEN ON A NOTE OF INTENSE 544 DAYS LONGING.)
(HIS VOICE WITH SURPRISING SUDDENNESS TAKES ON A 545 DAYS SAVAGE VINDICTIVE QUALITY)
THEN FROM ELSA'S BEDROOM JOHN'S VOICE IS HEARD, AS545 DAYS HE LOOKS FOR HER THERE.
JOHN'S VOICE CAN BE HEARD FROM BELOW CALLING 545 DAYS "ELSA."
(THEN A SINISTER NOTE COMING INTO HIS VOICE) 545 DAYS
(WITH LOWERED VOICE TO HIMSELF) 547 DAYS
(CONFUSEDLY REPENTANT--IN A LOW VOICE) 554 DAYS
(BENDS OVER JOHN'S CHAIR AND SPEAKS IN A LOW 554 DAYS CAUTIONING VOICE)
SHARPLY BUT IN A VOICE JUST ABOVE A WHISPER) 555 DAYS
HE SPEAKS TO HIM IN A LOW VOICE) 556 DAYS
(IN A LOW, TENSE VOICE--AS IF HE WERE THINKING 561 DAYS ALOUD)
SAW THERE THE ANSWER TO HIS PRAYER--IN A VOICE 565 DAYS TREMBLING WITH HOPE AND JOY)
(HIS VOICE RISING EXULTANTLY, HIS EYES ON THE FACE566 DAYS OF THE CRUCIFIED)
(IMITATING HIS FATHER'S VOICE) 215 DESIRE
(AS THEY ENTER--A QUEER STRANGLED EMOTION IN HIS 221 DESIRE DRY CRACKING VOICE)
(HER VOICE TAKING POSSESSION) 222 DESIRE
THE VOICE O' GOD SAYIN'.. 237 DESIRE
I GOT AFEERED O' THAT VOICE AN' I LIT OUT BACK T' 237 DESIRE HUM HERE.
THE VOICE O' GOD CRYIN' IN MY WILDERNESS, IN MY 238 DESIRE LONESOMENESS--
THERE IS A SINCERE MATERNAL LOVE IN HER MANNER AND243 DESIRE VOICE--
(RAISING HIS VOICE) BET I KIN TELL YE, ABBIE, 248 DESIRE WHAT EBEN'S DOIN'!
(IN A HARD VOICE) I HAIN'T WANTIN' T' KISS YE 258 DESIRE NEVER AGEN!
(HIS VOICE SHOWING EMOTION IN SPITE OF HIM) 260 DESIRE
(SOMETHING IN HER VOICE AROUSES HIM. 260 DESIRE
(FALLS TO HIS KNEES AS IF HE'D BEEN STRUCK--HIS 261 DESIRE VOICE TREMBLING WITH HORROR)
(SHUDDERS--THEN IN A DEAD VOICE) 263 DESIRE
(HE GOES TO THE DOOR--THEN TURNS--IN A VOICE FULL 265 DESIRE OF STRANGE EMOTION)
(CONSIDERS THIS--A PAUSE--THEN IN A HARD VOICE) 265 DESIRE
(LOWERING HIS VOICE) 'R BEIN' ALIVE WHEN YEW WAS 267 DESIRE DEAD.

VOICE

VOICE (CONT'D.)

I KIN HEAR HIS VOICE WARNIN' ME AGEN T' BE HARD 268 DESIRE AN' STAY ON MY FARM.

(IN A STRAINED VOICE) WELL, AIN'T YOU GOING TO 502 DIFRNT TELL ME?

(HER VOICE TREMBLING) IT'S 'COUNT OF SOMETHING I 504 DIFRNT GOT IN MY OWN HEAD.

(HER VOICE SHOWS THAT SHE HOPES AGAINST HOPE FOR A515 DIFRNT DENIAL.)

(HIS VOICE BETRAYS HIS ANGUISH FOR A SECOND 516 DIFRNT (AS HIS MOTHER'S VOICE IS HEARD MUCH NEARER, 527 DIFRNT CALLING »RENNY!«

(BEFORE SHE CAN REPLY, HARRIET'S VOICE IS HEARD 527 DIFRNT CALLING.)

(HER VOICE FAINTLY HEARD ANSWERING) 531 DIFRNT

HIS VOICE IS THE BULLYING ONE OF A SERMONIZER WHO 422 DYNAMO IS THE VICTIM OF AN INNER

HIS NATURAL VOICE HAS AN ALMOST FEMININE 422 DYNAMO GENTLENESS.

(HEARING HIS FATHER'S VOICE, 424 DYNAMO

(HIS VOICE BOOMING) AND I TELL YOU, AMELIA, IT IS424 DYNAMO GOD'S WILL/

(THEN, AFTER A PAUSE, HER VOICE TURNED BITTER) 425 DYNAMO

FIFE'S VOICE, SARDONIC AND MALICIOUS. 425 DYNAMO

HER VOICE IS SENTIMENTAL AND WONDERING. 428 DYNAMO

(THAT WAS REUBEN'S VOICE?... 437 DYNAMO

(THEN, RAISING HIS VOICE DEFIANTLY) 437 DYNAMO

(FROM HER HIDING PLACE BY THE HEDGE HAS CAUGHT 437 DYNAMO REUBEN'S RAISED VOICE--

(THEN HIS VOICE BOOMING LIKE HIS FATHER'S WITH 438 DYNAMO MORAL SELF-RIGHTEOUSNESS)

THEN GOES ON WITH A GUILTY FURTIVENESS--LOWERING 440 DYNAMO HIS VOICE)

(ANGRILY--HIS VOICE BOOMING DENOUNCINGLY LIKE HIS 442 DYNAMO FATHER'S)

HIS WIFE'S VOICE COMES EXCITEDLY FROM BELOW 445 DYNAMO

(HIS VOICE COMES FROM THE HALL AS HE RUSHES 445 DYNAMO UPSTAIRS)

AND REUBEN'S VOICE CALLING DESPERATELY.) 445 DYNAMO

UTTER THEN--FINALLY FINDING HIS VOICE, HE 451 DYNAMO STAMMERS)

(THEN, AS FIFE'S VOICE IS HEARD CALLING FROM 455 DYNAMO SOMEWHERE IN THE HOUSE)

IN A STRANGE VOICE) 469 DYNAMO

(PITIFULLY--HER VOICE TREMBLING) 469 DYNAMO

AS IF THE SOUND OF HIS VOICE HYPNOTIZED HER 476 DYNAMO

(LOWERING HIS VOICE) D'YOU THINK IT'S HAPPENED 479 DYNAMO BETWEEN THEM--

(HE LOWERS HIS VOICE CAUTIOUSLY AS IF HE DIDN'T 480 DYNAMO WANT THE DYNAMO TO OVERHEAR)

DENOUNCINGLY, HIS VOICE BOOMING LIKE HIS FATHER'S)481 DYNAMO

HIS VOICE IS HEARD EXPLAINING EXCITEDLY AS THEY 482 DYNAMO CLIMB TO THE DAM.

HIS FACE AVERTED FROM HERS--IN A VOICE THAT IS 485 DYNAMO ALMOST SUPPLICATING)

SIMULTANEOUSLY REUBEN'S VOICE RISES 488 EJONES

HE MUTTERS (IN A BEWILDERED VOICE) 189 EJONES

YANKING OUT HIS REVOLVER AS HE DOES SO--IN A 190 EJONES QUAVERING VOICE)

LEFT ARE HEARD AND JONES' VOICE, 191 EJONES

HIS VOICE CATCHES IN A CHOKING PRAYER.) 194 EJONES

AND RAISES HIS CLASPED HANDS TO THE SKY--IN A 196 EJONES VOICE OF AGONIZED PLEADING.)

JONES' VOICE IS HEARD BETWEEN CHATTERING MOANS.) 198 EJONES

HIS VOICE REACHES THE HIGHEST PITCH OF SORROW, OF 199 EJONES DESOLATION.

HIS VOICE SINKING DOWN THE SCALE AND RECEDING 199 EJONES

BUT THE NEXT TIME, HIS VOICE, AS IF UNDER SOME 199 EJONES UNCANNY COMPULSION,

JONES' VOICE IS HEARD FROM THE LEFT RISING AND 199 EJONES FALLING IN THE LONG,

AS HIS VOICE SINKS INTO SILENCE, HE ENTERS THE 200 EJONES OPEN SPACE.

HIS VOICE JOINS IN THE INCANTATION, IN THE CRIES, 201 EJONES

HIS VOICE RISES AND FALLS IN A WEIRD, MONOTONOUS 201 EJONES CROON.

THE WITCH DOCTOR'S VOICE SHRILLS OUT IN 201 EJONES

FROM THE LEFT REAR, A MAN'S VOICE IS HEARD SINGING 5 ELECTR

THE CHANTY »SHENANDOAH«--

THE VOICE GROWS QUICKLY NEARER. 6 ELECTR

(LOWERING HER VOICE ALMOST TO A WHISPER--TO HER 9 ELECTR HUSBAND)

SHE HAS A FLAT DRY VOICE 10 ELECTR

SHE GOES ON WITH A THREATENING UNDERCURRENT IN HER 17 ELECTR VOICE)

THE HAS KEPT HER HAND AND HE DROPS HIS VOICE TO A 21 ELECTR LOW LIVER-LIKE TONE.

STRONG HANDS AND HIS DEEP VOICE.) 21 ELECTR

(DROPPING HIS VOICE TO A REVERENT, HUSHED TONE, 22 ELECTR

(IN A COLD, HARD VOICE) I HAVEN'T FORGOTTEN. 23 ELECTR

HE COMES CLOSER TO HER, DROPPING HIS VOICE AGAIN 24 ELECTR TO HIS LOVE MAKING TUNE)

SHE TRIES TO KEEP HER VOICE INDIFFERENT BUT IT 30 ELECTR TREMBLES A LITTLE.)

(TURNING AWAY--HER VOICE STILL TREMBLING) 34 ELECTR

HE SUDDENLY LEANS OVER TOWARD HER AND, LOWERING 44 ELECTR HIS VOICE ASKS SOBERLY)

(IN A LOW VOICE.) WHAT WAS THAT MARIE BRANTOME 44 ELECTR LIKE, SETH?

(IN A LOW VOICE, AS IF TO HERSELF, STARING AT THE 44 ELECTR HOUSE)

WHEN HE SPEAKS, HIS DEEP VOICE HAS A HOLLOW 46 ELECTR REPRESSED QUALITY.

THEN IN A VOICE THAT BETRAYS A DEEP UNDERCURRENT 47 ELECTR OF SUPPRESSED FEELING)

(PITYINGLY--WITH A TINGE OF SCORN IN HER VOICE) 49 ELECTR

A PAUSE--THEN HE SAYS IN A VOICE THAT HE TRIES TO 49 ELECTR MAKE ORDINARY)

VOICE (CONT'D.)

(LEANS TOWARD HER, HIS VOICE TREMBLING WITH DESIRE 52 ELECTR HE PLODS ON WITH A NOTE OF DESPERATION IN HIS 54 ELECTR VOICE)

(STARTS VIOLENTLY--IN A STRAINED VOICE) 58 ELECTR

IS MY VOICE SO STRANGE TO YOU? 58 ELECTR

THEN MANNON'S VOICE COMES SUDDENLY FROM THE BED, 58 ELECTR DULL AND LIFELESS.)

(THEN A NOTE OF PLEADING IN HIS VOICE) 59 ELECTR

(IN A STIFLED VOICE) LOOK OUT, EZRA/ 60 ELECTR

(THEN ANGER AND HATRED COME INTO HER VOICE) 60 ELECTR

(THEN HER VOICE CHANGES, AS IF SHE HAD SUDDENLY 61 ELECTR RESOLVED ON A COURSE OF ACTION.

(HER VOICE GROWN STRIDENT) DID YOU THINK YOU 61 ELECTR COULD MAKE ME WEAK--

HE TRIES TO CALL FOR HELP BUT HIS VOICE FADES TO A 62 ELECTR WHEEZY WHISPER)

(HER VOICE BECOMES THICK, AS IF SHE WERE DROWSY 63 ELECTR AND FIGHTING OFF SLEEP.

RASPING NASAL VOICE, AND LITTLE SHARP EYES. 67 ELECTR

SHE SPEAKS TO ORIN AND HER VOICE IS TENSELY QUIET 78 ELECTR AND NORMAL)

FROM INSIDE THE HOUSE COMES THE SOUND OF ORIN'S 78 ELECTR VOICE CALLING SHARPLY »MOTHER/

(A JEALOUS RESENTMENT CREEPING INTO HIS VOICE) 81 ELECTR

(HER VOICE TENSE AND STRAINED) 83 ELECTR

(LOWERING HER VOICE TO A WHISPER) 86 ELECTR

(HAS CALMED HERSELF, BUT HER EYES ARE STILL 89 ELECTR TERRIFIED AND HER VOICE TREMBLES)

HIS VOICE BECOMES DREAMY AND LOW AND CARESSING) 89 ELECTR

THE BREAKING OF THE WAVES WAS YOUR VOICE. 90 ELECTR

(IN A FLAT, EMOTIONLESS VOICE) 91 ELECTR

CHRISTINE BEGINS TO SPEAK IN A LOW VOICE, COOLY 91 ELECTR DEFIANT, ALMOST TRIUMPHANT)

(HIS VOICE HAS SUNK LOWER AND LOWER, AS IF HE WERE 95 ELECTR TALKING TO HIMSELF.

(THEN A NOTE OF ENTREATY IN HER VOICE) 98 ELECTR

(HER VOICE COMES THROUGH THE DOOR, FRIGHTENED AND 99 ELECTR STRAINED)

(OBEYING MECHANICALLY--CALLS IN A CHOKED VOICE) 100 ELECTR

HER VOICE BECOMES TERRIFIED) 100 ELECTR

(IN A COLD, GRIM VOICE) IT WAS BRANT WHO GOT YOU 101 ELECTR THIS)

(HE BEGINS TO SING IN A SURPRISINGLY GOOD TENOR 103 ELECTR VOICE.

(HIS VOICE HAS RISEN TO A SHOUT. 105 ELECTR

(AUTOMATICALLY REACTS TO THE VOICE OF AUTHORITY-- 105 ELECTR QUIETLY)

I'D EXPECT A MAN WITH YOUR VOICE WOULD BE IN A 106 ELECTR SALOON, SINGING AND MAKING MERRY/

HE BURSTS AGAIN INTO HIS MOURNFUL DIRGE, HIS VOICE107 ELECTR RECEDING)

(HER VOICE TREMBLING) BUT I'M AFRAID I'M NOT MUCHLI ELECTR TO

(ORIN'S VOICE IS HEARD CALLING FROM THE SITTING- 123 ELECTR ROOM AT RIGHT WHAT'S THAT?/

SETH'S VOICE COMES FROM THE DRIVE, RIGHT, CLOSE AT124 ELECTR HAND.

RUDDY COMPLEXION, AND A SHRILL RASPING VOICE. 129 ELECTR

A FAT, BOISTEROUS MAN, WITH A HOARSE BASS VOICE. 129 ELECTR

SMALL'S EXCITED VOICE CAN BE HEARD RECEDING 134 ELECTR

(HIS VOICE COMES FROM THE DARK HALL) 139 ELECTR

SHE SUDDENLY ADDRESSES THEM IN A HARSH RESENTFUL 139 ELECTR VOICE.)

(IN A STRAINED VOICE) IT'S THE SAME THING--WHAT 146 ELECTR THE WAR DID TO HIM--

(HER VOICE STRIDENT, AS IF HER WILL WERE SNAPPING)151 ELECTR

A TENSE VOICE) 151 ELECTR

(IN A LOW VOICE) YES, THAT IS WHAT I LIVE IN 152 ELECTR TERROR OF--

(HER VOICE TREMBLES AND SHE SEEMS ABOUT TO BURST 159 ELECTR INTO TEARS)

(LAVINIA LOOKS AT HIM, FRIGHTENED BY THE 163 ELECTR TRIUMPHANT SATISFACTION IN HIS VOICE.)

(HANDS HIM THE ENVELOPE--IN A TREMBLING VOICE) 164 ELECTR

IN A FAINT, TREMBLING VOICE) 167 ELECTR

(THEN HER VOICE RISING AS IF IT WERE ABOUT TO 167 ELECTR BREAK HYSTERICALLY--

SHE HOLDS THEM OUT TO SETH AND SPEAKS IN A 170 ELECTR STRANGE, EMPTY VOICE.)

THEN STANDS HER GROUND ON THE TOP OF THE STEPS, 171 ELECTR HER VOICE HARDENING)

IN A STIFLED VOICE BETWEEN HER CLENCHED TEETH) 172 ELECTR

AFTER A PAUSE--IN A TREMBLING VOICE) 173 ELECTR

(A BITTER RESENTFUL NOTE COMING INTO HIS VOICE) 174 ELECTR

(MORE AS IF SHE WERE ANSWERING SOME VOICE IN 175 ELECTR HERSELF THAN HIM--

(IN A DEAD VOICE) I CAN'T MARRY YOU, PETER. 177 ELECTR

(TO THE AIR) I HAD A PRETTY VOICE, WHEN I WAS A 257 GGBROW GIRL.

SUCH POOR VOICE/ 257 GGBROW

AND HIS VOICE BECOMES BITTER AND SARDONIC) 265 GGBROW

(FROM THE END OF THE WHARF, HER VOICE IS HEARD.) 266 GGBROW

DION'S VOICE AT FIRST IN A WHISPER, 267 GGBROW

IN A TREMBLING, EXPIRING VOICE) 272 GGBROW

(HER VOICE BREAKS A LITTLE IN SPITE OF HERSELF.) 276 GGBROW

IN A COARSE, HARSH VOICE) 279 GGBROW

DEEP FAR-OFF VOICE--AND YET LIKE A MOTHER TALKING 288 GGBROW TO HER LITTLE SON)

(IN HER STRANGE VOICE) CYBEL'S GONE OUT TO DIG IN288 GGBROW THE EARTH AND PRAY.

(HER VOICE VERY WEARY) 289 GGBROW

DION'S VOICE CAN BE HEARD, RAISED MOCKINGLY. 294 GGBROW

(IN A STEELY VOICE) I'VE SEEN THE BRAINS/ 297 GGBROW

(HIS VOICE LIKE A PROBE) WHY HAS NO WOMAN EVER 298 GGBROW LOVED HIM?

(HIS VOICE IMITATING DION'S AND MUFFLED BY THE 301 GGBROW MASK)

VOICE (CONT'D.)
EVEN YOUR VOICE IS CHANGED/
FOR A MOMENT, I THOUGHT IT WAS DION, YOUR VOICE SOUNDED SO MUCH.
(HIS VOICE TREMBLING) THEN I HAVE MADE YOU HAPPY--HAPPIER THAN EVER BEFORE--
(HIS VOICE A BIT EXCITED--BUT GUARDEDLY)
(HE RAISES HIS VOICE) COME RIGHT IN, GENTLEMEN.
FINALLY A VOICE SEEMS TORN OUT OF HIM,
THERE IS ABOUT HER MANNER AND VOICE THE SAD BUT CONTENTED FEELING OF ONE WHO
(A VOICE STARTS BAWLING A SONG,)
SUDDENLY CRIES OUT IN A VOICE FULL OF OLD SORROW) 213 HA APE
(HIS VOICE RUNS INTO THE WAIL OF A KEEN, HE ROCKS 213 HA APE BACK AND FORTH ON HIS BENCH,
THROUGH WHICH YANK'S VOICE CAN BE HEARD BELLOWING)216 HA APE
ONE--TWO--THREE--(HIS VOICE RISING EXULTANTLY IN 224 HA APE THE JOY OF BATTLE)
(WITH A GROTESQUE IMITATION OF A WOMAN'S VOICE) 230 HA APE
(AT THE SOUND OF HIS VOICE THE CHATTERING DIES 251 HA APE AWAY INTO AN ATTENTIVE SILENCE.
(HIS VOICE WEAKENING) 254 HA APE
(IN A LOW VOICE OUT OF THE SIDE OF HIS MOUTH) 577 ICEMAN MAKE IT FAST.
(LEANS TOWARD HIM, A COMICAL INTENSITY IN HIS LOW 578 ICEMAN VOICE)
(HE HESITATES--THEN LOWERING HIS VOICE) 583 ICEMAN
(LOWERING HIS VOICE) YES, THAT'S WHAT I WANT, 586 ICEMAN TOO.
(IN A LOWERED VOICE BUT EAGERLY, AS IF HE WANTED 588 ICEMAN THIS CHANCE TO TELL ABOUT IT)
(HIS VOICE FADES OUT AS HE STARES IN FRONT OF HIM,603 ICEMAN
(GLANCES AT JIMMY WITH A CONDESCENDING 604 ICEMAN AFFECTIONATE PITY--IN A HUSHED VOICE)
BUSINESS-LIKE MANNER BUT IN A LOWERED VOICE WITH 612 ICEMAN AN EYE ON HOPE)
(HE YAWNS WITH GROWING DROWSINESS AND HIS VOICE 624 ICEMAN GROWS A BIT MUFFLED)
(IN A LOW CONFIDENTIAL VOICE) 625 ICEMAN
(LEANING TOWARD LARRY CONFIDENTIALLY--IN A LOW 644 ICEMAN SHAKEN VOICE)
(JOE BEGINS TO HUM AND SING IN A LOW VOICE AND 644 ICEMAN CORRECT HER.
(HE BEATS TIME WITH HIS FINGER AND SINGS IN A LOW 645 ICEMAN VOICE)
PARRITT ASKS HIM WITH A SUDDEN TAUNT IN HIS VOICE)646 ICEMAN
ROCKY'S VOICE IS HEARD IN IRRITATED ASTONISHMENT, 650 ICEMAN "WHAT DE HELL--"
(WITH HIS VOICE LEADING THEY ALL SHOUT "HAPPY 653 ICEMAN BIRTHDAY, HARRY,"
AND SHE HAD A BEAUTIFUL VOICE. 656 ICEMAN
(DEEPLY MOVED--HIS VOICE HUSKY) 659 ICEMAN
ROCKY IS THE FIRST ONE WHO CAN VOICE IT.) 660 ICEMAN
(HIS VOICE CATCHING) LISTEN, ALL OF YOU/ 660 ICEMAN
(BENDING TOWARD HIM--IN A LOW, INGRATIATING, 666 ICEMAN APOLOGETIC VOICE)
(GROWS RIGID--HIS VOICE TREMBLING WITH REPRESSED 677 ICEMAN ANGER)
(LOWERING HIS VOICE STILL MORE) 679 ICEMAN
HICKEY'S FACE IS A BIT DRAWN FROM LACK OF SLEEP 684 ICEMAN AND HIS VOICE IS HOARSE FROM
(THEN IN A SUDDEN FURY, HIS VOICE TREMBLING WITH 688 ICEMAN HATRED)
(HIS VOICE BREAKS ON A SOB.) 688 ICEMAN
HOPE SPEAKS TO HIM IN A FLAT, DEAD VOICE) 691 ICEMAN
(LOWERING HIS VOICE--WORRIEDLY TO LARRY) 693 ICEMAN
(STARTS--IN A LOW WARNING VOICE) 698 ICEMAN
(AS CHUCK LOOKS AT HIM WITH DULL SURPRISE HE 698 ICEMAN LOWERS HIS VOICE TO A WHISPER)
(HIS VOICE HARD) I'M WAITIN', BABY. 700 ICEMAN
THEY MUMBLE ALMOST IN CHORUS AS ONE VOICE, 701 ICEMAN
(IN THE VOICE OF ONE REITERATING MECHANICALLY A 704 ICEMAN HOPELESS COMPLAINT)
HE ANSWERS IN A PRECISE, COMPLETELY LIFELESS 707 ICEMAN VOICE.
(IN A LOW VOICE) GUY NAMED HICKMAN IN THE BACK 708 ICEMAN ROOMS
(A TOUCH OF STRANGE BITTERNESS COMES INTO HIS 710 ICEMAN VOICE FOR A MOMENT)
IN A LOW VOICE IN WHICH THERE IS A STRANGE 716 ICEMAN EXHAUSTED RELIEF)
(AT THE TONE OF HIS VOICE, 717 ICEMAN
HICKEY'S VOICE KEEPS ON PROTESTING.) 719 ICEMAN
(LEANS TOWARD HIM--IN A STRANGE LOW INSISTENT 719 ICEMAN VOICE)
HIS QUIVERING VOICE HAS A CONDEMNING COMMAND IN 720 ICEMAN IT)
SAYING TO EACH IN A LOW VOICE. 513 INZONE
(HE LOWERS HIS VOICE AND SPEAKS SLOWLY) 514 INZONE
(LOWERING HIS VOICE--MEANINGLY) 516 INZONE
NO, AND YUH WON'T HEAR ANY RING, YUH BOOB-- 516 INZONE
(LOWERING HIS VOICE UNCONSCIOUSLY)
(LOWERING HIS VOICE) AN' THEN WHAT D'YOU SUPPOSE 519 INZONE HE DIDA
(IN A VOICE MEANT TO BE REASSURING) 520 INZONE
(LOWERING HIS VOICE AND INDICATING SMITTY'S BUNK) 522 INZONE
(HIS VOICE TREMBLING WITH RAGE. 527 INZONE
(READS SLOWLY--HIS VOICE BECOMING LOWER AND LOWER 531 INZONE AS HE GOES ON)
TEACHER SAYS ABOUT HER VOICE, 531 INZONE
(IN A DULL VOICE) WHAT'S THATS 532 INZONE
HER VOICE IS SOFT AND ATTRACTIVE. 13 JOURNE
HIS VOICE IS REMARKABLY FINE, RESONANT AND 13 JOURNE FLEXIBLE.
(HIS VOICE IS SUDDENLY MOVED BY DEEP FEELING.) 17 JOURNE
(LAUGHS AND AN IRISH LILT COMES INTO HER VOICE.) 28 JOURNE
(HIS VOICE GROWS HUSKY AND TREMBLES A LITTLE.) 36 JOURNE
(HER VOICE HAS GROWN BITTER.) 43 JOURNE

301 GGBROW
304 GGBROW

309 GGBROW

311 GGBROW
316 GGBROW
319 GGBROW
323 GGBROW

209 HA APE

VOICE (CONT'D.)
(A DEFENSIVE UNEASINESS COMES INTO HER VOICE 45 JOURNE AGAIN.)
SUDDENLY A STRANGE UNDERCURRENT OF REVENGEFULNESS 47 JOURNE COMES INTO HER VOICE.)
LOWERING HIS VOICE, HURRIEDLY.) 58 JOURNE
AND THERE IS A PECULIAR DETACHMENT IN HER VOICE 58 JOURNE AND MANNER,
(SNEERINGLY.) INTERRUPTING THE FAMOUS BEAUTIFUL 60 JOURNE VOICE/
TYRONE'S VOICE, TRYING TO CONCEAL, REVEALS THAT HE 73 JOURNE IS HEARING BAD NEWS.)
(SHE STOPS TO LISTEN AS TYRONE'S VOICE IS HEARD 73 JOURNE FROM THE HALL.)
AND THE QUALITY OF UNCANNY DETACHMENT IS IN HER 75 JOURNE VOICE AND MANNER.)
(A NOTE OF PLEADING IN HER VOICE.) 82 JOURNE
HER VOICE SEEMS TO DRIFT FARTHER AND FARTHER 87 JOURNE AWAY.)
(SHARPLY, IN A LOW VOICE.) HERE'S EDMUND. 88 JOURNE
HER VOICE BEGINS TO TREMBLE.) 91 JOURNE
(SHE PAUSES--THEN LOWERING HER VOICE TO A STRANGE 93 JOURNE TUNE OF WHISPERED CONFIDENCE.)
(JAMIE'S VOICE IS HEARD FROM THE FRONT HALL.) 94 JOURNE
(TYRONE'S VOICE CALLS.) "COME ON, EDMUND." 95 JOURNE
SHE ADDS IN A CALM, DETACHED VOICE.) 103 JOURNE
(DEEPLY MOVED--HIS VOICE HUSKY.) 112 JOURNE
(HIS VOICE TREMBLES, HIS EYES BEGIN TO FILL WITH 118 JOURNE TEARS.)
LOOKING OUT, A BLANK, FAR-OFF QUALITY IN HER 121 JOURNE VOICE.)
(HIS VOICE QUIVERING.) HUSH, MARY, FOR THE LOVE 122 JOURNE OF GOD/ HE LOVES YOU.
(RAISING HER VOICE UNNECESSARILY.) 123 JOURNE
(EDMUND'S VOICE ANSWERS CURTLY, "YES."= 125 JOURNE
(HIS VOICE THICK.) WHO'S THATS 125 JOURNE
(HE QUOTES, USING HIS FINE VOICE.) 131 JOURNE
(VAGUELY--HIS VOICE THICK.) IT'S MADNESS, YES-- 134 JOURNE
(HE CHOKES HUSKILY. HIS VOICE TREMBLING WITH RAGE,145 JOURNE
(SWAYING AND BLINKING IN THE DOORWAY--IN A LOUD 154 JOURNE VOICE.)
(HIS VOICE FLUTTERS.) I SUPPOSE I CAN'T FORGIVE 162 JOURNE HER--YET.
(IN A LOW VOICE.) THANK GOD HE'S ASLEEP. 167 JOURNE
(HIS VOICE TRAILS OFF. 169 JOURNE
(HIS VOICE TREMBLING, WITH SUPPRESSED FURY.) 170 JOURNE
(IN A STIFLED VOICE.) WHAT'S THAT SHE'S CARRYING,172 JOURNE
EDMUND.
(HER VOICE, RICH WITH SORROW, EXULTANT NOW) 277 LAZARU
GOBLET IN HAND--FORCING HIS VOICE, FALTERINGLY. 278 LAZARU
(SUDDENLY IN A DEEP VOICE--WITH A WONDERFUL 278 LAZARU EXULTANT ACCEPTANCE IN IT)
IN A VOICE THAT IS LIKE A LOVING WHISPER OF HOPE 279 LAZARU AND CONFIDENCE)
(SUDDENLY AGAIN--NOW IN A VOICE OF LOVING 274 LAZARU EXULTATION)
(HIS VOICE HAS RISEN TO A WAILING LAMENT) 285 LAZARU
(HIS VOICE RINGS FROM WITHIN THE HOUSE IN EXULTANT285 LAZARU DENIAL)
LED BY THEIR CHORUS OF OLD MEN, WHOSE JEERING 286 LAZARU HOWLS THEY ECHO AS ONE VOICE)
(HIS VOICE BECOMES A LITTLE BITTER AND MOCKING) 289 LAZARU
HIS VOICE RELEASES HIS OWN DANCERS AND THE MOB 289 LAZARU FROM THEIR FIXED ATTITUDES.
(LEANING OVER THE BALUSTRADE--IN A VOICE OF 290 LAZARU ENTREATY)
A MAN'S VOICE JARRING IN HIGH-PITCHED CRUEL 290 LAZARU LAUGHTER IS HEARD.
FINALLY LAZARUS SPEAKS IN A VOICE OF INFINITE 291 LAZARU DISDAIN)
(LOOKS DOWN UPON THE STRUGGLING MASS AND CRIES IN 291 LAZARU A RINGING VOICE)
(WITHOUT LOOKING AT HIM--HIS VOICE SEEMING TO COME292 LAZARU FROM SOME DREAM WITH HIM)
(IN A GREAT TRIUMPHANT VOICE) 293 LAZARU
(HUMANS AND GREEKS ALIKE AS ONE GREAT VOICE) 305 LAZARU
AT THIS MOMENT THE VOICE OF LAZARUS COMES RINGING 305 LAZARU THROUGH THE AIR
AND CHANT IN A THICK VOICE) 305 LAZARU
HAD FOUND AT LAST ITS VOICE AND A SONG FOR 309 LAZARU SINGING.
(HE LAUGHS AND AGAIN HIS VOICE LEADS AND DOMINATES311 LAZARU THE RHYTHMIC CHORUS OF
THE MIGHTLY VOICE OF THE ROMAN PEOPLE AS LONG AS 313 LAZARU ROME IS ROME.
THE MIGHTY VOICE OF THE ROMAN PEOPLE. 315 LAZARU
HIS VOICE FIGHTS TO OVERCOME THAT OF LAZARUS, 320 LAZARU
(AS IF TAKING AN OATH WITH ONE VOICE) 323 LAZARU
THE TINKLING OF MANY LITTLE BELLS AND YOUR VOICE. 330 LAZARU
(IN A STRAINED VOICE SHAKEN BY APPREHENSION AND 337 LAZARU AWE)
THEN CALIGULA'S VOICE IS HEARD SCREAMING ABOVE THE338 LAZARU CHORUS OF LAUGHTER AS HE
(A PAUSE--THEN IN A LOW VOICE, BENDING DOWN TOWARD340 LAZARU LAZARUS)
(HER VOICE HARDENING) AND HES 342 LAZARU
(HER VOICE CRUEL) HE SHALL NOT LAUGH AT ME/ 342 LAZARU
(HIS VOICE TREMBLES IN SPITE OF HIMSELF) 346 LAZARU
HER WORDS COMING QUICKER AND QUICKER AS HER VOICE 346 LAZARU BECOMES FAINTER AND FAINTER)
(HER VOICE TREMBLING) EVEN IF GOD HAS TAKEN OUR 347 LAZARU LITTLE ONES--
(IN A VOICE OF UNEARTHLY SWEETNESS) 348 LAZARU
HIS VOICE RINGING MORE AND MORE WITH A TERRIBLE 349 LAZARU UNBEARABLE POWER AND BEAUTY THAT
(SUDDENLY, IN A QUIET BUT COMPELLING VOICE) 359 LAZARU
(HIS VOICE TREMBLING A BIT) FAREWELL, BODY OF 362 LAZARU MIRIAM.

VOICE

(CONT'D.)
THIS VOICE COMES, RECOGNIZABLY THE VOICE OF 365 LAZARU
LAZARUS, YET WITH A STRANGE, FRESH,
HA-HA-HA-HA-- (HIS VOICE BREAKS CHOKINGLY.) 366 LAZARU
(HIS VOICE A TRIUMPHANT ASSERTION OF THE VICTORY 366 LAZARU
OF LIFE OVER PAIN AND DEATH)
(HIS VOICE THRILLING WITH EXULTANCE) 366 LAZARU
(HIS VOICE GENTLY REMONSTRATING) 366 LAZARU
(HIS VOICE HAS RISEN TO A PASSIONATE ENTREATY.) 367 LAZARU
(HIS VOICE SPEAKING LOVINGLY, WITH A SURPASSING 367 LAZARU
CLEARNESS AND EXALTATION)
(WITH RESENTFUL JEALOUSY AND RAGE--IN A VOICE 368 LAZARU
RISING TO A SCREAM)
(HIS VOICE IS HEARD IN A GENTLY, EXPIRING SIGH OF 371 LAZARU
COMPASSION.
HER VOICE IS LOW AND MUSICAL. 2 MANSNS
HE SPEAKS QUIETLY, IN A DEEP VOICE WITH A SLIGHT 5 MANSNS
DRAWL.)
BUT STILL KEEPING HER VOICE QUIET.) 18 MANSNS
HIS VOICE IS DRY--PREMATURELY OLD. 26 MANSNS
IN A LOW VOICE THAT HAS LOST ITS OLD MUSICAL 28 MANSNS
QUALITY)
THEN SARA'S VOICE TRYING TO QUIET THEM AND, FOR 43 MANSNS
THE MOMENT, SUCCEEDING.
THEN SARA'S VOICE IS HEARD IN A COMMANDING TONE, 44 MANSNS
FROM THE HALL SIMON'S VOICE IS HEARD EXCLAIMING 50 MANSNS
WITH ASTONISHMENT, «MOTHER!»
AND DEBORAH'S VOICE «SIMON.» 50 MANSNS
DEBORAH'S VOICE AGAIN. 95 MANSNS
AFTER ANOTHER MOMENT THERE IS A LOUDER KNOCK AND 95 MANSNS
SIMON'S VOICE CALLS SHARPLY..
(SARA'S VOICE ANSWERS WITH AN ATTEMPT AT 108 MANSNS
CARELESSNESS..
(FROM THE HOUSE OFF LEFT SARA'S VOICE IS HEARD 108 MANSNS
HE HEARD THE VOICE OF THE ENCHANTRESS SPEAKING 111 MANSNS
FROM THE OTHER SIDE.
(FROM THE HOUSE OFF LEFT COMES SARA'S VOICE... 113 MANSNS
HER VOICE SUDDENLY TAKES ON A RESENTFUL COMMANDIG114 MANSNS
TONE..
(A PAUSE. THEN SARA'S VOICE COMES, HURT AND A 114 MANSNS
LITTLE FORLORN.
(GLANCING AT SIMON RESENTFULLY--LOWERING HER VOICE125 MANSNS
TO A WHISPER.)
(STOPS CRYING INSTANTLY AT THE TONE OF HIS VOICE, 145 MANSNS
HOLDS HIM BY THE SHOULDERS,
(HIS VOICE HAS DROPPED, HE POINTS TOWARD THE 351 MARCOM
COFFIN.
(THEN LOWERING HIS VOICE AS IF AFRAID HE WILL BE 351 MARCOM
OVERHEARD)
(A VOICE WHICH IS KUKACHIN'S AND YET MORE MUSICAL 352 MARCOM
THAN A HUMAN VOICE.
IT WAS THE VOICE OF SOME CHRISTIAN DEVIL YOU 353 MARCOM
SUMMONED/
A FRESH BOY'S VOICE IS HEARD SINGING A LOVE SONG 355 MARCOM
IN A SUBDUED TONE.
BUT IN A VOICE TOO LOW TO BE HEARD. 366 MARCOM
MARKING THE RHYTHM FOR A GROANING, NASAL VOICE, 373 MARCOM
YOU JEST, BUT YOUR VOICE TREMBLES. 380 MARCOM
WHEN THE VOICE FAILS, LISTEN TO SONG. 384 MARCOM
(THEN SUDDENLY IN A STRANGE VOICE) 393 MARCOM
HIS MANNER AND VOICE HAVE BECOME GRAVE AND 394 MARCOM
PORTENTOUS)
(HIS VOICE, HOARSE AND DOMINEERING. 407 MARCOM
MARCO'S VOICE IS AGAIN HEARD, «LOWER THAT 407 MARCOM
MIZZENSAIL/
(AFTER A BROODING PAUSE SHE RISES AND CHANTS IN A 409 MARCOM
LOW VOICE)
(HIS VOICE THRILLING FOR THIS SECOND WITH 415 MARCOM
OBLIVIOUS PASSION)
THE SOUND OF RUNNING ABOUT ON DECK AND MARCO'S 417 MARCOM
VOICE GIVING COMMANDS.
(AFTER A PAUSE--HIS VOICE THRILLING WITH 418 MARCOM
ADMIRATION)
IN A VOICE WHICH IS A FINAL, COMPLETE 420 MARCOM
RENUNCIATION, CALLS)
(HIS VOICE COMES FROM OVER THE WATER CHEERY AND 420 MARCOM
RELIEVED)
MUSIC BRINGS BACK HER VOICE SINGING/ 423 MARCOM
HIS VOICE GROWN HUSKY. 424 MARCOM
I COULD SCARCELY HEAR HER VOICE. 424 MARCOM
MARCO ADDRESSES THE SERVANTS IN A FALSE VOICE.) 428 MARCOM
(IN THE SAME FALSE VOICE) OUR GUESTS LOOK 429 MARCOM
THIRSTY.
(HIS VOICE SOUNDING ABOVE THE HUBBUB) 430 MARCOM
HIS VOICE UTTERS AND WARMS TO HIS WORK) 431 MARCOM
INSTANTLY THERE IS DARKNESS AND FROM HIGH UP IN 432 MARCOM
THE DARKNESS KUBLAI'S VOICE
KUBLAI SPEAKS TO THE PRIESTS IN A VOICE OF COMMAND434 MARCOM
(HIS VOICE APPEARS ABOUT TO BREAK. 435 MARCOM
HE DECLAIMS IN A HIGH WAILING VOICE ACCOMPANIED BY436 MARCOM
THE MUSICIANS
HIS VOICE BREAKS--MORE AND MORE INTENSELY) 438 MARCOM
(HER VOICE HAS SOFTENED, AND SHE BLINKS BACK 7 MISBEG
TEARS.
HIS VOICE IS HIGH-PITCHED WITH A PRONOUNCED 11 MISBEG
BROGUE.)
HE DISAPPEARS ON LEFT, BUT A SECOND LATER HIS 64 MISBEG
VOICE, TREMBLING WITH ANGER,
IT IS UNMISTAKABLY HOGAN'S VOICE 71 MISBEG
(APPEARS DRUNKER, HIS HEAD WAGGING, HIS VOICE 74 MISBEG
THICK, HIS TALK RAMBLING)
AND SAID IN A SICK SHEEP'S VOICE. 82 MISBEG
(HIS VOICE BEGINS TO SINK INTO A DEJECTED 82 MISBEG
MONOTONE)
(LOOKS STRICKEN AND BEWILDERED--HER VOICE 89 MISBEG
TREMBLING)
(HER VOICE TREMBLES) SO THAT WAS HIS REASON-- 90 MISBEG
LOWERING HER VOICE--QUICKLY) 99 MISBEG

(CONT'D.)
(JEERINGLY, BUT HER VOICE TREMBLES) 118 MISBEG
I WANT-- (HIS VOICE TRAILS OFF INTO SILENCE.) 120 MISBEG
HER VOICE TREMBLES WITH SURPRISING MEEKNESS) 121 MISBEG
(HIS VOICE HARD WITH REPULSION) 121 MISBEG
(DEEPLY STIRRED, IN SPITE OF HERSELF--HER VOICE 129 MISBEG
TREMBLING)
(HER VOICE TREMBLES--BUT SHE GOES ON DETERMINEDLY)142 MISBEG
HIS VOICE BECOMES IMPERSONAL AND OBJECTIVE, 146 MISBEG
(SIMPLY) YES, I KNOW SHE--(HIS VOICE BREAKS.) 152 MISBEG
SHE KEEPS HER VOICE LOW, BUT HER TONE IS 157 MISBEG
COMMANDING)
(WITH BITTER VOICE) SO YOU JUST WOKE UP--DID YOU! 159 MISBEG
(RAISING HIS VOICE--WITH REVENGEFUL ANGER) 161 MISBEG
AND FIGHTS DESPERATELY TO CONTROL HIS VOICE AND 173 MISBEG
EXPRESSION)
(LOWERING HIS VOICE.) TELL ME, HAS HE DONE ANY 13 POET
RAMPAGING KID WOMEN HERES
(LOWERING HIS VOICE.) SPEAKIN' AV NORA, YOU NIVIR 13 POET
MENTIONED HER LAST NIGHT.
A GIRL'S VOICE IS HEARD FROM THE HALL AT RIGHT. 15 POET
HER VOICE IS SOFT AND MUSICAL, 16 POET
(SMILES--HER VOICE IS SOFT, WITH A RICH BROGUE.) 20 POET
WITH A TRACE OF GENUINE PITY IN HER VOICE.) 58 POET
THERE IS SEDUCTIVE CHARM IN HIS WELCOMING SMILE 68 POET
AND IN HIS VOICE.)
HIS VOICE TAKES ON A CALCULATED MELANCHOLY 70 POET
CADENCE.
(A COARSE PASSION COMES INTO HIS VOICE.) 71 POET
(SHE LOWERS HER VOICE.) IT ISN'T JUST TO PAY 78 POET
SIMON A VISIT SHE CAME.
(LOWERING HER VOICE.) SHE STARTED TALKING THE 79 POET
SECOND SHE GOT IN THE DOOR.
LOWERING HER VOICE UNCONSCIOUSLY AS IF SHE WERE 81 POET
THINKING ALOUD TO HERSELF.
(A SAD SCORN COMES INTO HER VOICE.) 90 POET
AND HIS VOICE IS FULL OF WELCOMING WARMTH AS HE 92 POET
CALLS.)
HIS VOICE THE QUAVERING GHOST OF A TENOR BUT STILL 96 MANSNS
TRUE--
(SULENLY--BUT CAREFUL TO KEEP HIS VOICE LOW.) 100 POET
A STRONG LILT OF BROGUE COMING INTO HIS VOICE.) 102 POET
HIS VOICE QUIVERS BUT IS DEADLY QUIET.) 114 POET
(CONTROLS HIMSELF--HIS VOICE SHAKING.) 123 POET
IT IS AS IF SHE WERE AFRAID HER VOICE WOULD GIVE 137 POET
HER AWAY.
ROUGHLY, HIS VOICE TREMBLING.) 164 POET
HIS VOICE COARSE AND HARSH.) 166 POET
THEN MELODY'S VOICE IS PLAINLY HEARD IN THE 180 POET
SILENCE AS HE SHOUTS A TOAST..
(HER VOICE TREMBLES.) MAY THE HERO OF TALAVERA 182 POET
REST IN PEACE/
HE LOOKS TOWARD THE SEA AND HIS VOICE QUAVERS IN A579 ROPE
DOLEFUL CHANT)
(LOWERING HIS VOICE) AN' I'VE FOUND OUT WHAT WE 584 ROPE
WAS
A SHRILL BURST OF MARY'S LAUGHTER CAN BE HEARD ANDS87 ROPE
THE DEEP VOICE OF A MAN
AND IRRESPONSIBLE YOUTH IN VOICE AND GESTURE. 587 ROPE
(WITH A THREAT IN HIS VOICE) 588 ROPE
(LOWERING HER VOICE) D'YOU S'POSE HE KNOWS ABOUT 590 ROPE
THE FARM BEIN' LEFT TO HIMS
SWEENEY SPEAKS SUDDENLY IN A STRANGE, AWED VOICE) 590 ROPE
AND ANNIE'S WHINING VOICE RAISED IN ANGRY 594 ROPE
PROTEST.
HE HICCOUGHS EVERY NOW AND THEN AND HIS VOICE 594 ROPE
GROWS UNCERTAIN AND HUSKY.)
(SUDDENLY FINDING HIS VOICE--CHANTS) 594 ROPE
HE'S LETTIN' ON HE'S LOST HIS VOICE AGAIN. 596 ROPE
(HIS VOICE RISES TO A THREATENING ROAR) 597 ROPE
THE SOUND OF A MAID'S VOICE--A MIDDLE-AGED WOMAN-- 2 STRANG
AND HIS AMUSED VOICE RECITES THE WORDS WITH A 4 STRANG
RHETORICAL RESONANCE.)
(HIS VOICE TAKES ON A MUNITIONOUS MUSING QUALITY, 4 STRANG
HIS VOICE HAD WITHDRAWN SO FAR AWAY... 4 STRANG
(HIS VOICE TREMBLES.) 10 STRANG
(HIS VOICE IS SHAKING WITH EMOTION) 11 STRANG
SHE SPEAKS DIRECTLY TO HER FATHER IN A VOICE 13 STRANG
TENSELY COLD AND CALM)
IN HER COOL, PREOCCUPIED VOICE) 13 STRANG
HIS VOICE LIKE A FATIGUING DYING TUNE DRONED ON A 16 STRANG
BEGGAR'S ORGAN...
HER VOICE TREMBLING WITH THE EFFORT TO KEEP IT IN 16 STRANG
CONTROL--ICILY)
(A TOUCH OF ASPERITY IN HIS VOICE) 16 STRANG
(HER VOICE BECOMING A BIT UNCANNY, HER THOUGHTS 18 STRANG
BREAKING THROUGH)
(IN THE SAME VOICE AS BEFORE) 20 STRANG
(HER VOICE, FRESH AND GIRLISH, CALLS FROM 22 STRANG
UPSTAIRS)
(HIS VOICE GROWS HUSKY AND UNCERTAIN--HE CONTROLS 24 STRANG
IT--STRAIGHTENS HIMSELF)
(AS MARY'S GRIEF SUBSIDES A TRIFLE, HER VOICE IS 26 STRANG
HEARD, FLAT AND TONELESS)
INCOHERENT WORDS DROWNING OUT NINA'S VOICE, 26 STRANG
SOOTHING HER.)
(HIS VOICE EMBARRASSED AND HESITATING COMES FROM 28 STRANG
THE HALL)
(IN A QUEER FLAT VOICE) YES, HE'S DEAD--MY 39 STRANG
FATHER--WHOSE PASSION CREATED ME--
(THEN IN A FLAT VOICE) WHAT DO YOU WANT TO BE 44 STRANG
PUNISHED FOR, NINAS
(IN A MUFFLED VOICE, HER SOBBING BEGINNING TO EBB 44 STRANG
AWAY) SIGHS.
IN A YOUNG GIRL'S VOICE) 44 STRANG
(IN HIS FLAT VOICE) YOU MEAN YOU--(THEN 45 STRANG
PLEADINGLY) BUT NOT--DARRELL!
(IN HIS FLAT VOICE) WHY DID YOU DO THIS, NINAS 45 STRANG

VOICE (CONT'D.)
(GOING TO DOOR--IN HIS OWN VOICE NOW) 47 STRANG
HER VOICE 53 STRANG
THEIR VOICES, HIS VOICE EXPLAINING, ARE HEARD, 53 STRANG
(THE SOUND OF EVANS' VOICE AND HIS MOTHER'S IS 53 STRANG
HEARD FROM THE GARDEN.
ASSERTIVENESS, AS IF WHAT SHE SAID THEN WAS MERELY 54 STRANG
A VOICE ON ITS OWN
(SPEAKING MECHANICALLY IN A DULL VOICE) 63 STRANG
(BENDING DOWN FOR ANOTHER SHEET, HIS VOICE 77 STRANG
TREMBLING WITH TERROR)
(HER VOICE SUDDENLY BECOMING FLAT AND LIFELESS) 83 STRANG
(IN A COLD, EMOTIONLESS PROFESSIONAL VOICE, HIS 85 STRANG
FACE LIKE A MASK OF A DOCTOR)
(BUT HIS VOICE BEGINS TO TREMBLE UNCERTAINLY AGAIN 93 STRANG
AS HE CALLS)
(SUDDENLY WITH AN INSULTING, UGLY SNEER, RAISING 101 STRANG
HIS VOICE)
(AT THE FIRST SOUND OF EVANS' VOICE, 104 STRANG
(IN A STRANGE DAZED VOICE-- 104 STRANG
(IN A DETERMINED VOICE) I'VE GIVEN SAM ENOUGH OF 104 STRANG
MY LIFE)
THINKING AS IF SHE WERE REPEATING THE WORDS OF 109 STRANG
SOME INNER VOICE OF LIFE)
(THEN IN A VOICE WHICH SHOWS SHE 123 STRANG
THEN NINA'S VOICE CALLS DOWN THE STAIRS.) 123 STRANG
HIS VOICE TREMBLING A LITTLE WITH SUPPRESSED 123 STRANG
EMOTION)
(FROM UPSTAIRS, HER VOICE STRANGE AND EXCITED) 123 STRANG
HER VOICE/... 124 STRANG
SOUND OF HER VOICE... 125 STRANG
HIS VOICE TAKING ON A PLEADING UNCERTAIN QUALITY) 126 STRANG
EVANS' VOICE IS IMMEDIATELY HEARD, EVEN BEFORE HE 132 STRANG
BOUNDS INTO THE ROOM.
(IN A LOW VOICE) HOW CAN YOU BE SO BITTER, NED-- 141 STRANG
ON GORDON'S BIRTHDAYS
(HIS VOICE SOUNDS FROM THE HALL WITH A STRAINED 145 STRANG
CASUALNESS)
(STARTLED, HER OWN VOICE STRAINING TO BE CASUAL) 145 STRANG
(FROM THE HALLWAY COMES THE SOUND OF MARSDEN'S 146 STRANG
VOICE AND GORDON'S GREETING HIM
(THEN WORRIEDLY) HIS VOICE SOUNDED FUNNY. 146 STRANG
THEN IN A TREMBLING VOICE OF DEEPLY WOUNDED 150 STRANG
AFFECTION)
AND EVANS' HEARTY VOICE.) 151 STRANG
(THAT TONE IN HER VOICE/... 160 STRANG
(THE NOISE OF MADELINE'S EXCITED VOICE CHEERING 174 STRANG
AND CLAPPING HER HANDS,
OF MARSDEN'S VOICE YELLING DRUNKENLY, OF EVANS', 174 STRANG
ALL SHOUTING, "GORDON!"
(SPRINGING TO HER FEET AND FINDING HER VOICE--WITH179 STRANG
DESPAIRING ACCUSATION)
(HE TOUCHES NINA'S ARM--IN A LOW VOICE) 182 STRANG
(HIS VOICE SUDDENLY BREAKING WITH A SINCERE HUMAN 183 STRANG
GRIEF)
(HIS VOICE TREMBLING) I DIDN'T REALLY REALIZE HE 184 STRANG
WAS GONE--
UNTIL OUT AT THE CEMETERY--(HIS VOICE BREAKS.) 184 STRANG
(HIS VOICE TREMBLES. 190 STRANG
LOWED BY HIS VOICE GREETING THEM AND ORDERING 3 T 56
DRINKS. 18
(RAISING HIS VOICE) HO, YOU NICK/ 493 VOYAGE
(IN A LOW VOICE) 'AVE YER GOT THE DROPS$ 495 VOYAGE
(IN A RASPY VOICE) 'ULLO, MATES. 499 VOYAGE
HIS VOICE GROWS WEAKER) 507 VOYAGE
HIS VOICE IS LOW AND CALMING.) 450 WELDED
(AS IF TO HERSELF--IN A STRANGLED VOICE) 460 WELDED
THEN HER VOICE IN A STRAINED, HYSTERICAL PITCH-----462 WELDED
JOHN, I------
THEN HIS VOICE SOOTHINGLY----COME IN/ 462 WELDED
(QUICKLY RECOVERING HERSELF--IN A COLD, HARD 463 WELDED
VOICE) THAT'S--DEAD/
(HIS VOICE QUIVERING) NELLY/ 463 WELDED
(HE STARES TOWARD HER, THEN STOPS--IN A LOW, 463 WELDED
UNCERTAIN VOICE)
(HER VOICE MUFFLED--BETWEEN SOBS) 467 WELDED
HER VOICE IS HEAVY AND SLOW WITH THE STRONG TRACE 470 WELDED
OF A FOREIGN INTONATION,
VOICE--FINALLY BLURTS OUT IN A TONE OF 472 WELDED
DESPERATION)
(IN A QUEER FAR-AWAY VOICE) NO. 487 WELDED
(IN A STRANGLED VOICE) GOOD-BY. 487 WELDED
FIGHT--FAIL AND HATE AGAIN--(THE RAISES HIS VOICE 488 WELDED
IN AGGRESSIVE TRIUMPH)
(PASSIONATELY SURE OF HER NOW--IN A LOW VOICE) 488 WELDED

VOICES
VOICES ARE HEARD IN A CONVERSATIONAL TONE FROM THE185 AHWILD
DINING-ROOM BEYOND THE BACK
(AT THE SOUND OF VOICES FROM THE FRONT PARLOR, 208 AHWILD
THE FRONT SCREEN DOOR IS HEARD SLAMMING AND NAT'S 221 AHWILD
AND SID'S LAUGHING VOICES.
THEN THERE IS A PAUSE--THE MURMUR OF EXCITED 30 ANNA
VOICES--THEN THE SCUFFLING OF FEET.
THE SOUND OF ANDREW'S AND ROBERT'S VOICES COMES 154 BEYOND
FROM THE BEDROOM.
THE OLD VOICES CALLING ME TO COME--(EXULTANTLY) 168 BEYOND
AND THIS TIME I'M GOING/
(UNCONSCIOUSLY THEY HAVE ALL RAISED THEIR VOICES, 481 CARDIF
(A CHORUS OF ASSENTING VOICES) 459 CARIBE
(THE SOUND OF WOMEN'S VOICES CAN BE HEARD TALKING 461 CARIBE
AND LAUGHING.)
THERE IS THE SUBDUED BABBLE OF VOICES FROM THE 466 CARIBE
CROWD INSIDE BUT THE MOURNFUL
THERE IS A ROAR OF VOICES FROM INSIDE. 468 CARIBE
THE UPROAR OF SHOUTING, LAUGHING AND SINGING 469 CARIBE
VOICES HAS INCREASED IN VIOLENCE.
(AS A SOUND OF VOICES COMES FROM LEFT, REAR) 221 DESIRE

VOICES (CONT'D.)
THEIR VOICES AS THEY GO OFF TAKE UP THE SONG OF 224 DESIRE
THE GOLD-SEEKERS
A FAINT STRAIN OF THEIR RETREATING VOICES IS 226 DESIRE
HEARD...
(THEIR VOICES DIE TO AN INTENSIVE WHISPERING. 252 DESIRE
THE NOISE OF STAMPING FEET AND LAUGHING VOICES. 254 DESIRE
THE LIGHT FADES OUT, THE OTHER VOICES CEASE, AND 199 EJONES
ONLY DARKNESS IS LEFT.
THEY TALK IN LOW VOICES.) 8 ELECTR
THERE IS A SOUND OF VOICES FROM INSIDE THE HOUSE, 67 ELECTR
THEN FOOTSTEPS AND VOICES ARE HEARD FROM OFF RIGHT 73 ELECTR
FRONT)
THEIR VOICES ARE HEARD AND A MOMENT LATER THEY 107 ELECTR
ENTER ON THE POOP DECK,
(A WHOLE CHORUS OF VOICES HAS TAKEN UP THIS 211 HA APE
REFRAIN, STAMPING ON THE FLOOR,
TALKING IN TONELESS, SIMPERING VOICES. 236 HA APE
AND THE SOUND OF A MAN'S AND WOMAN'S ARGUING 615 ICEMAN
VOICES.)
SUDDENLY THERE IS A NOISE OF ANGRY, CURSING VOICES650 ICEMAN
AND A SCUFFLE FROM THE HALL.
THE SOUND OF MARGIE'S AND PEARL'S VOICES IS HEARD 724 ICEMAN
FROM THE HALL.
FROM THE DINING ROOM JAMIE'S AND EDMUND'S VOICES 15 JOURNE
ARE HEARD.
(SHE IS SILENT ON THIS, KEEPING HER HEAD TURNED 15 JOURNE
TOWARD THEIR VOICES.
THE BOYS' VOICES ARE AGAIN HEARD AND ONE OF THEM 16 JOURNE
HAS A FIT OF COUGHING.
THEN STOPS IN THE DOORWAY AS SHE HEARS THE SOUND 107 JOURNE
OF VOICES FROM THE FRONT PATH.
THEN THE MUSIC SUDDENLY STOPS AND THE CHANT OF 282 LAZARU
YOUTHFUL VOICES IS HEARD.)
THE VOICES OF ALL HIS FOLLOWERS ECHO HIS LAUGHTER.285 LAZARU
THEIR VOICES SOUND THICK AND HARSH AND ANIMAL-LIKE287 LAZARU
WITH ANGER AS THEY MUTTER AND
(THE MUSIC AND DANCING AND VOICES CEASE. 295 LAZARU
(THEIR VOICES AND THE MUSIC GROWING MORE AND MORE 295 LAZARU
HESITATING AND FAINT)
A BUZZ OF VOICES HUMS IN THE AIR. 298 LAZARU
THE SENATORS BEGIN TO TALK TO EACH OTHER IN LOW 314 LAZARU
VOICES.)
THE VOICES OF HIS FOLLOWERS FROM BEYOND THE WALL, 318 LAZARU
AT FIRST ONE BY ONE,
HEARD ABOVE A CONFUSED DRUNKEN CLAMOR OF VOICES, 326 LAZARU
PUNCTUATED BY THE HIGH,
(AS HE FINISHES SPEAKING ALL THE SOUND OF MUSIC 331 LAZARU
AND VOICES FROM THE HOUSE CEASES
THE FEMALE VOICES ARE HARSH, STRIDENT, MANNISH-- 336 LAZARU
HUMAN VOICES FROM THE MULTITUDE, JEERING, HOOTING,364 LAZARU
HA-HA-HA-- (THEIR VOICES, TOO, BREAK.) 366 LAZARU
TERRIFIED RATS, THEIR VOICES SQUEAKY NOW WITH 369 LAZARU
FRIGHT)
THERE IS A SOUND OF MEN'S VOICES FROM DOWN THE 25 MANSNS
PATH OFF LEFT.
FROM THE HALL AT REAR THE SOUND OF SMALL BOYS' 43 MANSNS
ARGUING VOICES
A CHORUS OF BOYS' EXCITED VOICES, 43 MANSNS
WHAT YOU HEARD WERE THE VOICES OF YOUR OWN MIND. 174 MANSNS
THEN FROM THE DARKNESS AKE THEIR VOICES HEARD IN 357 MARCOM
HUSHED TONES)
(THE SENTIMENTAL SINGING VOICES AND 357 MARCOM
(THE CRIES OF MANY VOICES. 361 MARCOM
THE VOICES ARE INSTANTLY SILENCED. 433 MARCOM
THEIR VOICES RISE TOGETHER IN A LONG, RHYTHMIC 433 MARCOM
WAIL OF MOURNING.
THEIR VOICES ATTAIN A PROLONGED NOTE OF UNBEARABLE433 MARCOM
POIGNANCY.
CRACKED VOICES ACCOMPANYING THE MUSIC IN QUEER, 433 MARCOM
BREAKING WAVES OF LAMENTATION.
(THEIR VOICES DIE AWAY.) 435 MARCOM
(THEIR VOICES DIE INTO SILENCE.) 436 MARCOM
THERE IS THE SAME SOUND OF VOICES FROM THE BAR 66 POET
SLOWLY BECAUSE MELODY, HEARING VOICES IN THE ROOM 88 POET
AND HOPING DEBORAH IS THERE,
SHUTTING OUT AN UPROAR OF MUSIC AND DRUNKEN 133 POET
VOICES.
THEIR VOICES CAN BE HEARD BUT THE WORDS ARE 590 ROPE
INDISTINGUISHABLE.)
(HE GETS TO HIS FEET AS HE HEARS VOICES FROM THE 12 STRANG
RIGHT)
FROM THE FRONT VOICES ARE HEARD, FIRST NINA'S, 26 STRANG
THEN A MAN'S.
THEIR VOICES, HIS VOICE EXPLAINING, ARE HEARD, 53 STRANG

VOICING
(VOICING THE OPINION OF ALL OF THEM) 132 ELECTR

VOID
YOU AKE A BUBBLE PRICKED BY DEATH INTO A VOID AND 309 LAZARU
A MOCKING SILENCE/

VOIGIN
WHAT DE HELL YUH TINK I TINK I'M MARRYIN', A 616 ICEMAN
VOIGIN$
WHAT ARE YOU, A VOIGINS 633 ICEMAN

VOLCANOES
(CHANTING AS HIS MEN WORK) GREAT WERE THE WAVES 408 MARCOM
VOLCANOES OF FOAM

VOLLEY
(SHOUTS FROM THE GARDEN AND A VOLLEY OF SHOTS. 321 GGBROW

VOLTAIRE
VULTAIRE, ROUSSEAU, SCHOPENHAUER, NIETZSCHE, 135 JOURNE
IBSEN/

VOLUBILITY
(WITH A CHILDISH VOLUBILITY) 49 ELECTR

VOLUBLE
(THEN AS IF SEEKING RELIEF FROM THE TENSION IN A 20 ANNA
VULUBLE CHATTER)
(VOLUBLE NOW) DEAD AS A DOOR NAIL/ 548 DIFRNT

VOLUBLY

VOLUBLY

(DETERMINED TO DISGUST HER WITH SEA LIFE--VOLUBLY) 28 ANNA CHRIS STOPS FOR A SECOND--VOLUBLY) 30 ANNA (HOLDING HIM TIGHTER--VOLUBLY) 167 ELECTR AND dEGINS TO TALK VOLUBLY TO DROWN OUT THOUGHT) 167 ELECTR (VOLUBLY.) LUNCH IS READY, MA'AM, I WENT DOWN TO 62 JOURNE MISTER TYRONE,

VOLUME

THERE IS AN INCREASE IN VOLUME OF THE MUFFLED 470 CARIBE CLAMOR FROM THE FORECASTLE AND A THE DYNAMO'S THRUATY METALLIC PURR RISES SLOWLY IN489 DYNAMO VOLUME BUT INCREASED IN VOLUME OF SOUND AND RAPIDITY OF 195 EJONES BEAT.) THEN INCREASING IN VOLUME WITH THE LIGHT, IS 267 GGBROW HEARD) WITH RISING VOLUME) WELL/ WELL// WELL/// (THEY 638 ICEMAN ALL JUMP STARTLEDLY. LIKE CARESSING MUSIC AT FIRST BUT GRADUALLY 318 LAZARU GAINING IN VOLUME. THIS SOUND HAS RISEN TO ITS GREATEST VOLUME AS THE364 LAZARU CURTAIN RISES.) AS THE CURTAIN RISES, DEBORAH IS READING FROM A 95 MANSNS VOLUME OF BYRON'S POEMS. HE SEES THE VOLUME OF BYRON ON THE STEPS. 106 MANSNS THE EXAMINES THE VOLUME--WITH PLEASED BOYISH 107 MANSNS SURPRISE.) BUT GROWING MOMENTARILY IN VOLUME, COMES THE SOUND433 MARCOM OF FUNERAL MUSIC. THE TURNS TO THE BOOKCASE AND PULLS OUT THE FIRST 23 STRANG VOLUME HIS HANDS COME ON AND NO ONE VOLUME IS PLACED WITH ANY RELATION TO THE 66 STRANG ONE BENEATH IT--

VOLUMES

ON THIS SIDE OF THE ROOM ARE ALSO A SMALL BOOKCASE493 DIFRNT HALF FILLED WITH OLD VOLUMES. THIS BOOKCASE IS FULL OF INSTALLMENT-PLAN SETS OF 519 DIFRNT UNCUT VOLUMES. GIBBON'S ROMAN EMPIRE AND MISCELLANEOUS VOLUMES OF 11 JOURNE OLD PLAYS, POETRY, THE WORLD'S BEST LITERATURE IN FIFTY LARGE 11 JOURNE VOLUMES, HUME'S HISTORY OF ENGLAND, THE ASTONISHING THING ABOUT THESE SETS IS THAT ALL 11 JOURNE THE VOLUMES HAVE THE LOOK OF VOLUMES OF THE ENCYCLOPEDIA BRITANNICA MIXED UP 66 STRANG WITH POPULAR TREATISES ON MIND

VOLUNTEERING

I WAS ALWAYS VOLUNTEERING FOR EXTRA DANGER. 95 ELECTR

VOLUPTUOUS

SHE HAS A FINE, VOLUPTUOUS FIGURE AND SHE MOVES 9 ELECTR WITH A FLOWING ANIMAL GRACE. CYBEL HAS GROWN STOUTER AND MORE VOLUPTUOUS, 284 GGBROW (SHE SPEAKS WITH MORE AND MORE VOLUPTUOUS 342 LAZARU SATISFACTION) HER BODY HAS GROWN STRIKINGLY VOLUPTUOUS AND 139 MANSNS PROVOCATIVELY FEMALE. I LIKE THEM TALL AND STRONG AND VOLUPTUOUS, NOW, 43 MISBEG WITH BEAUTIFUL BIG BREASTS.

VUMAN

MY VOMAN--ANNA'S MOTHER-- 9 ANNA YOU SAY THE BUMBOAT VOMAN VILL BRING BOOZES 458 CARIBE

VOMIT

IN MY THROAT LIKE POISONOUS VOMIT AND I LUNG TO 152 ELECTR SPIT IT OUT--AND CONFESS/ YOU'LL BE SAYING SOMETHING SOON THAT WILL MAKE YOU680 ICEMAN VOMIT YOUR OWN SOUL

VORK

AH, AY VORK ON LAND LONG TIME AS YANITOR. 21 ANNA YUU DON'T NEVER HAVE TO VURK AS NURSE GEL NO MORE. 22 ANNA HARD VORK ALL TIME. 28 ANNA UEY ALL VORK AUTTEN YOB ON SEA FOR NUTTING, 28 ANNA DEM FALLARS DAT VORK BELOW SHOVELING COAL VAS DE 43 ANNA DIRTIEST. MIGHT YUST AS VELL VORK ON COAL WAGON ASHORE/ 49 ANNA I AM NOT ASHAMED TO VORK VITH MY HANDS. 676 ICEMAN AND I NEED VURK ONLY LEETLE VHILE TO SAVE MONEY 676 ICEMAN FOR MY PASSAGE HOME.

VORLD

AY GAT NO ONE IN VORLD BUT YOU. 22 ANNA KUUGH GANG OF NO GOOD FALLARS IN VORLD/ 43 ANNA SHE VAS ALL AY GAT IN VURLD. 46 ANNA

NORSE

(FORCIBLY) DAT VAS MILLION TIMES NORSE, AY TAL 43 ANNA YOU/

HE THINKS LIES EVEN VORSE, DAT I-- 634 ICEMAN

VORSEN

WINUYAMMER, AY VAS THROUGH HUNDRED STORMS VORSEN'N 49 ANNA DAT/

VORST

(SPITTING DISGUSTEDLY) FUG'S VORST ONE OF HER 26 ANNA DIRTY TRICKS, PY YINGO/ YES--AND IT'S BAD ON DEM LIKE HELL VORST OF ALL. 28 ANNA YES, AY STOP IT IF IT COME TO VORST. 45 ANNA AY DON'T KNOW--IT'S DAT FUNNY VAY OLE DAVIL SEA DO 78 ANNA HER VURST DIRTY TRICKS, YES.

VUT'S

(PUSHING PADDY BACK) VUT'S THE MATTER VIT YOU, 461 CARIBE PADDY.

VOTE

I OWE HIM A VOTE OF THANKS/ 147 ELECTR A WOMAN AND KIDS--A LOUSY VOTE--AND I'M ALL FIXED 250 HA APE FOR JESUS, HUH? AGAINST JACKSON AND THE DEMOCRATS AND SAYS HE'LL 26 POET VOTE WITH THE YANKEES FOR QUINC. AND I'LL VOTE FOR ANDY JACKSON, THE FRIEND AV THE 178 POET COMMON MEN LIKE ME.

VOTERS

AS VOTERS AND CITIZENS WE KIN FORCE THE BLOODY 229 HA APE GOVERNMENTS--

VOTES

VOTES IS A JOKE, SEE. 236 HA APE VOTES FOR WOMEN/ 236 HA APE THE VOTES OF THE UN-MARCHING PROLETARIANS OF THE 236 HA APE BLOODY WORLD/ (WITH ABYSMAL CONTEMPT) VOTES, HELL/ 236 HA APE

VOTIVE

VOTIVE OFFERINGS, PIECES OF CLOTH TORN FROM 347 MARCOM CLOTHING, BANGLES, ARMLETS,

VOUCH

(SARDONICALLY) YES, INDEED, DARRELL, I CAN VOUCH 127 STRANG FOR THEIR MISSING YOU--

VOUCHSAFED

REUBEN ACCORDING TO THE LIGHT VOUCHSAFED BY GOD. 424 DYNAMO

VOW

I MADE A VOW OF PERPETUAL BACHELORHOOD WHEN YOU 114 STRANG THREW ME OVER IN SAM'S FAVOR/.

VOWED

SO THE POOR FOOL PRAYED AND PRAYED AND VOWED HIS 511 DAYS LIFE TO PIETY AND GOOD WORKS/

VOYAGE

WE'VE GRUB ENOUGH HARDLY TO LAST OUT THE VOYAGE 537 'ILE BACK IF WE STARTED NOW. BUT THIS VOYAGE YOU BEEN ICEBOUND, AN'----- 542 'ILE AY U' THEM SKIPPERS I'VE BEATEN VOYAGE AFTER 542 'ILE VOYAGES REMEMBER, I WARN'T HANKERIN' TO HAVE YOU COME ON 545 'ILE THIS VOYAGE, ANNIE. YOU SEE--I'VE ALWAYS DONE IT--SINCE MY FIRST 547 'ILE VOYAGE AS SKIPPER. VE MAKE SLOW VOYAGE--DIRTY VEDDER--YUST FOG, FOG, 7 ANNA FUG, ALL BLOODY TIME/ DEN VEN HER MUDDER DIE VEN AY VAS ON VOYAGE, 9 ANNA (SLOWLY) AY TANK, AFTER YOUR MODER DIE, VEN AY 21 ANNA VAS AVAY ON VOYAGE, AY VANT COME HOME END OF EVERY VOYAGE. 21 ANNA TUG COME AND VE GAT TOWED OUT ON VOYAGE-- 23 ANNA VE VAS ALL AVAY ON VOYAGE WHEN SHE DIE. 27 ANNA GAT DRUNK, GAT ROBBED, SHIP AVAY AGAIN ON ODER 28 ANNA VOYAGE. AY TANK AY'M DAM FOOL FOR BRING YOU ON VOYAGE, 29 ANNA ANNA. AND THAT'S A LONG VOYAGE ON A SAILING SHIP,. 83 BEYOND I WOULDN'T TAKE A VOYAGE ACROSS THE ROAD 88 BEYOND IT'S A FREE BEGINNING--THE START OF MY VOYAGE/ 168 BEYOND MIDWAY ON THE VOYAGE BETWEEN NEW YORK AND CARDIFF,477 CARDIF (DISGUSTEDLY) NOTHIN' BUT YUST DIRTY WEATHER ALL 481 CARDIF DIS VOYAGE. IT'S HARD TO SHIP ON THIS VOYAGE I'M GOIN' ON-- 489 CARDIF ALONE/ SHIPPED WIV 'IM ONE VOYAGE. 457 CARIBE (GENIALLY) HOPE YOU HAD A NICE VOYAGE. 464 CARIBE WHEN TOM COMES FROM THIS VOYAGE YOU'LL BE MARRIED 564 CROSS AND OUT OF THIS DID YOU HAVE GOOD LUCK THIS VOYAGES 536 DIFRNT SHIPWRECKED MY FIRST VOYAGE AT SEA. 23 ELECTR AND ON THE VOYAGE BACK. 39 ELECTR I'VE A NOTION IF WE'D LEAVE THE CHILDREN AND GO 55 ELECTR OFF ON A VOYAGE TOGETHER--TO THE LEAVE VINNIE HERE AND GO AWAY ON A LONG VOYAGE--TO122 ELECTR THE SOUTH SEAS-- A LONG VOYAGE LIKE THAT WAS THE BEST THING TO HELP137 ELECTR THEM BOTH FORGET. (DULLY NOW) YOU'VE KEPT TALKING ABOUT THEM ALL 140 ELECTR THE VOYAGE HOME. UN THE VOYAGE TO FRISCOS 153 ELECTR AV HOUR AFTER SAILING FROM NEW YORK FOR THE VOYAGE207 HA APE ACROSS. (DECIDEDLY) I DON'T LI-IKE DEES VOYAGE. 515 INZONE A VOYAGE TO FRANCE, SAY--WITH SARA--A SECOND 72 MANSNS HONEYMOON. TO ATTEND ME AND COMMAND THE FLEET ON MY VOYAGE TO397 MARCOM PERSIA/ SUFTLY) PERHAPS ON THE VOYAGE YOU MAY BE INSPIRED399 MARCOM TO WRITE ANOTHER. ON A LONG VOYAGE IN DANGEROUS, ENCHANTED SEAS. 401 MARCOM I WISH TO TAKE THIS VOYAGE. 401 MARCOM YOU ARE AT SOME TIME EVERY DAY OF THE VOYAGE, 404 MARCOM IF HER HUSBAND THINKS AT THE END OF THE VOYAGE 404 MARCOM THAT MY WORK DESERVES A BONUS-- LONG WAS THE VOYAGE/ 408 MARCOM LONG WAS THE VOYAGE/ 409 MARCOM LONG WAS THE VOYAGE/ 409 MARCOM THERE ARE HARBORS AT EVERY VOYAGE-END WHERE WE 410 MARCOM REST FROM THE SORROWS OF THE SEA. THE CLOSE CONFINEMENT OF A LONG VOYAGE, 420 MARCOM IN GENERAL, SHE GAVE BUT LITTLE TROUBLE ON THE 424 MARCOM VOYAGE. SO I BRUNG IT ALONG ON THE VOYAGE. 588 ROPE 'ADO A GOOD VOYAGE. 409 VOYAGE I SPEND ALL MONEY, I HAVE TO SHIP AWAY FOR ANOTHER900 VOYAGE VOYAGE. AND I MEAN ALL TIME TO GO BACK HOME AT END OF 906 VOYAGE VOYAGE.

VOYAGES

THEY'LL BE LONG VOYAGES TOO. 83 BEYOND MORE'N OUR 'ULE BLOODY STOKEHOLE MAKES IN TEN 235 HA APE VOYAGES SWEATIN' IN 'ELL/

VOYAGIN'

WE'LL BE VOYAGIN' ON THE SEA/ 223 DESIRE

VULGAR

(HUFFLING) VULGAR/ 218 HA APE SHE WAS TOO DISTANT A RELATIVE TO BE VULGAR. 218 HA APE THE VULGAR HERD CAN NEVER UNDERSTAND. " 134 JOURNE AND ENJOYS PLEASURES "THE VULGAR HERD CAN NEVER 134 JOURNE UNDERSTAND"/

1757

VULGAR — WAIST

VULGAR (CONT'D.)
THE VULGAR HERD CAN NEVER UNDERSTAND.* 160 JOURNE
NOT THE HUSBAND OF THAT VULGAR IRISH BIDDY, 4 MANSNS
VULGAR, COMMON SLUT/ 21 MANSNS
THAT I SHOULD INVITE THAT VULGAR IRISH BIDDY AND 35 MANSNS
HER BRATS TO LIVE WITH ME?
MERELY A FEMALE, COMMON, VULGAR--A GREEDY HOME- 105 MANSNS
OWNER, DREAMLESS AND CONTENTED/
WILL YOUR VULGAR GREED LEAVE ME NOTHING I CAN CALL111 MANSNS
MY OWN
THE STUPID VULGAR FOOL/ 114 MANSNS
TO BECOME THE VULGAR GRASPING HARLOT YOU WERE BORN136 MANSNS
TO BE/
TOO GARISHLY EXPENSIVE AND LUXURIOUS, IN VULGAR 139 MANSNS
CONTRAST TO THE SOBER,
YOU VULGAR COMMON SLUT/ 166 MANSNS
APPEARS VULGAR AND COMMON, WITH A LOOSE, LEERING 167 POET
GRIN ON HIS SWOLLEN LIPS.)
(HE STRIKES A POSE WHICH IS A VULGAR BURLESQUE OF 176 POET
HIS OLD BEFORE-THE-MIRROR ONE
(THINKING INTENSELY) ((YOU VULGAR BOOR/... 161 STRANG
VULGARITY
THEY WERE THERE IN ALL THEIR VULGARITY, THEIR 521 DAYS
POISONOUS, ENVIOUS TONGUES
VULGARLY
(VULGARLY.) THE BLOW, ME FOOT/ 168 POET
WA'AM
IT'S WA'AM AN' DAT'S A FAC'/ 191 EJONES
WA'M
HER MOUTH'S WA'M, HER ARMS'RE WA'M, SHE SMELLS 211 DESIRE
LIKE A WA'M PLOWED FIELD,
SHE'S LIKE T'NIGHT, SHE'S SOFT 'N' WA'M, HER EYES 211 DESIRE
KIN KINK LIKE A STAR,
MEBBE--BUT THE NIGHT'S WA'M---PURTY-- 211 DESIRE
WHAT DO I CARE FUR HER--'CEPTIN' SHE'S ROUND AN' 214 DESIRE
WA'M,
FEELS LIKE A WA'M FIELD UP THAR. 231 DESIRE
IT'S WA'M DOWN T' THE BARN--NICE SMELLIN' AN' 231 DESIRE
WARM--WITH THE COWS.
WA'NT
RECKON HE WAS JOSHIN', WA'NT HE5 513 DIFRNT
WAD
FOR THE QUANE AV THE CANNIBAL ISLES WAD A DIED AV 478 CARDIF
THE BELLYACHE THE DAY AFTHER
HE'S A TIGHT-WAD AND I HATE FOLKS THAT'RE TIGHT 522 DIFRNT
WITH THEIR COIN.
(HE TAKES A SMALL WAD OF DOLLAR BILLS FROM HIS 585 ICEMAN
POCKET)
(HE GOES TO HIS BUNK AND PULLS OUT A BIG WAD OF 527 INZONE
WASTE AND COMES BACK TO SMITTY.)
WADDLING
HIS GAIT A BIT WADDLING BECAUSE OF HIS SHORT LEGS. 9 HUGHIE
WADING
SHE WAS IN WADING TODAY. 230 AHWILD
WADS
HIS FOLKS AIN'T TIGHT-WADS LIKE MINE. 523 DIFRNT
WADSWORTH
THAT HENRY WADSWORTH LONGFELLOW WOULD HAVE SHOWN A595 ICEMAN
DRUNKEN NEGRESS
WAG
(UNEASILY) WHAT'S IT GOT TO WAG ABOUTS 500 DIFRNT
WAGE
THE WAGE SLAVE GROUND UNDER THE HEEL OF THE 194 AHWILD
CAPITALIST CLASS, STARVING,
THEY DRAGGED US DOWN 'TIL WE'RE ON'Y WAGE SLAVES 212 HA APE
IN THE BOWELS OF A BLOODY SHIP,
BUT ON A BOOKKEEPER'S WAGE-- 33 MANSNS
MOREOVER, THE WAGE WOULD HAVE BEEN INSUFFICIENT 152 MANSNS
WAGED
BECAUSE I'VE NEVER READ MUCH IN A ANY HISTORY 394 MARCOM
ABOUT HEROES WHO WAGED PEACE.
WAGER.
SOME JOKE OF JAMIE'S, I'LL WAGER. 18 JOURNE
(SHE CHUCKLES.) I'LL WAGER MISTER JAMIE WOULDN'T 52 JOURNE
MISS THE TIME TO STOP WORK AND
(WITH ROUGH FAMILIARITY) I WAGER NO ONE WILL MAKE301 LAZARU
THAT COMPLAINT AGAINST YOU
AND I WILL WAGER A MILLION OF SOMETHING OR OTHER 363 MARCOM
MYSELF THAT THE KAAN WILL SOON
(WITH A CUNNING SMIRK) SELLING A BIG BILL OF 365 MARCOM
GOODS HERE-ABOUTS, I'LL WAGER,
YOU DIDN'T GET MUCH THANKS FROM MIKE, I'LL WAGER, 17 MISBEG
FOR YOUR HELP.
I'LL WAGER/ 38 MISBEG
I'LL WAGER HE'S NO DAMNED GOOD TO A WOMAN. 58 MISBEG
I'LL WAGER HE'S LAUGHING TO HIMSELF THIS MINUTE, 83 MISBEG
I'LL WAGER YOU WASN'T AS BRAZEN AS YOU PRETEND. 65 POET
YES, I'LL WAGER MY ALL AGAINST A PENNY THAT EVEN 71 POET
AMONG THE FISH-BLOODED YANKEES
BY THE ETERNAL, I'LL WAGER SHE BELIEVED WHAT I 76 POET
TOLD HER OF TALAVERA
YES, I'LL WAGER THAT'S WHAT SHE'S DONE/ 87 POET
I'LL WAGER SHE WASN'T FOR ALL HER AIRS. 91 POET
I LEFT O'DOWD TO TEND BAR AND I'LL WAGER HE HAS 135 POET
THREE DRINKS STOLEN ALREADY.
I'LL WAGER SIMON NEVER HEARD THE SHOT OR ANYTHING.182 POET
WAGES.
I'LL NEED EVERY CENT OF THE WAGES UNCLE'S PAID ME 132 BEYOND
LET HARRY HIRE A DOORMAN, PAY HIM WAGES, IF HE 637 ICEMAN
WANTS ONE.
AND YOUR FATHER WON'T EVEN PAY THE WAGES THE BEST 61 JOURNE
SUMMER HELP ASK.
OH, I REALIZE HIS WAGES ARE LESS THAN A REAL 84 JOURNE
CHAUFFEUR'S,
AND PAY HIGH WAGES WHETHER HE DRIVES YOU OR NOT. 84 JOURNE
THEY WORK HARD FOR POOR WAGES. 116 JOURNE
THERE'S BEEN SOME DISCONTENT ABOUT OUR LOWERING 146 MANSNS
WAGES

WAGES (CONT'D.)
TELL YOUR CONSCIENCE IT'S A BIT OF THE WAGES HE'S 7 MISBEG
NEVER GIVEN YOU.
WAGGIN'
HE JUST CAN'T KEEP HIS TONGUE FROM WAGGIN', THAT'S500 DIFRNT
ALL'S THE MATTER WITH HIM.
WAGGING
(THEN SUDDENLY, WAGGING AN ADMONISHING FINGER AT 525 DIFRNT
HIM
WAGGING THEM AT THEIR EARS, STICKING OUT THEIR 366 LAZARU
TONGUES, SLAPPING THEIR BEHINDS,
(APPEARS DRUNKER, HIS HEAD WAGGING, HIS VOICE 74 MISBEG
THICK, HIS TALK RAMBLING)
AND I'D FORGET MY LONGING FOR FREEDOM, I'D COME 139 STRANG
WAGGING MY TAIL...
WAGON
MIGHT YUST AS VELL VORK UN COAL WAGON ASHORE/ 49 ANNA
THE CLANGING GONG OF THE PATROL WAGON APPKOACHES 239 HA APE
WITH A CLAMORING DIN.)
I'M ON THE WAGON. 586 ICEMAN
WHO ONCE WORKED FOR A CIRCUS IN THE TICKET WAGON. 594 ICEMAN
I VAS SO TOUGH AND STRONG I GRAB AXLE OF OX WAGON 599 ICEMAN
MIT FULL LOAD
I'LL BE STRAIGHTENED OUT AND ON THE WAGON IN A DAY607 ICEMAN
OR TWO.
THE FIRST NRUBE THAT CAME TO MY WAGON FOR A TICKET 608 ICEMAN
GOSH, THINKING OF THE OLD TICKET WAGON BRINGS 609 ICEMAN
THOSE DAYS BACK.
DEY BEEN DREAMIN' IT FOR YEARS, EVERY TIME CHUCK 614 ICEMAN
GOES ON DE WAGON.
WE OUGHT TO PHONE DE BOOBY HATCH TO SEND ROUND DE 614 ICEMAN
WAGON FOR 'EM.
JEES, WHEN CHUCK'S ON DE WAGON, DEY NEVER LAY OFF 614 ICEMAN
DAT DOPE/
THAT WATER-WAGON BULL-- 621 ICEMAN
I TOLD HIM, "I'M ON DE WAGON FOR KEEPS AND CORA 631 ICEMAN
KNOWS IT."
BY TOMORROW MORNING I'LL BE ON THE WAGON. 644 ICEMAN
DON'T TINK YUH CAN KID ME WID DAT WATER-WAGON 671 ICEMAN
BULL/
SURE I KNOW YOU CARE, JAMIE, AND I'M GOING ON THE 157 JOURNE
WAGON.
BUT WHAT CAN THAT BE ON THE WAGON--LIKE A COFFIN/ 350 MARCOM
OF A TWO-WHEELED WAGON, STAGGER IN, STRAINING 350 MARCOM
FORWARD UNDER THE LASHES
THE CAPTAIN SPRINGS OFF THE WAGON) 350 MARCOM
OF THE CAPTAIN AND A CORPORAL WHO ARE RIDING ON 350 MARCOM
THE WAGON, THE CAPTAIN DRIVING.
LASHED ON THE WAGON IS A COFFIN COVERED WITH A 350 MARCOM
WHITE PALL.)
(THE CHRISTIAN GOES TO THE WAGON 351 MARCOM
THE CAPTAIN AND CORPORALS SPRING UP ON THE WAGON) 354 MARCOM
THE WAGON IS PULLED SWIFTLY AWAY. 354 MARCOM
YOU'VE GONE ON THE WATER-WAGON, I SUPPOSES 45 MISBEG
I'VE WANTED TO GO ON THE WAGON FOR THE PAST 45 MISBEG
TWENTY-FIVE YEARS.
WHEN MAMA DIED, I'D BEEN ON THE WAGON FOR NEARLY 146 MISBEG
TWO YEARS.
WAHT
WAHT DO YOU SAY, DONKS 466 CARIBE
WAIKE
WAIKE UP YOUR FREN'. 500 VOYAGE
WAIL
(A LUNG WAIL IS HEARD FROM THE DECK ABOVE) 551 'ILE
FROM THE HARBOR COMES THE MUFFLED, MOURNFUL WAIL 78 ANNA
OF STEAMERS' WHISTLES.)
FROM THE FORECASTLE HEAD ABOVE THE VOICE OF THE 482 CARDIF
LOOKOUT RISES IN A LUNG WAIL...
DESPAIRING WAIL OF THE 199 EJONES
A SHUDDER OF TERROR SHAKES HIS WHOLE BODY AS THE 199 EJONES
WAIL RISES UP ABOUT HIM AGAIN.
TREMULOUS WAIL OF DESPAIR THAT REACHES A CERTAIN 199 EJONES
PITCH, UNBEARABLY ACUTE.
(HIS VOICE RUNS INTO THE WAIL OF A KEEN, HE ROCKS 213 HA APE
BACK AND FORTH ON HIS BENCH.
THE MONKEYS SET UP A CHATTERING, WHIMPERING WAIL. 254 HA APE
(BUT THE CLERK'S MIND HAS RUSHED OUT TO FOLLOW THE 27 HUGHIE
SIREN WAIL OF A FIRE ENGINE.
THE WALL OF LAMENTATION RISES AND FALLS. 292 LAZARU
A LOW WAIL OF LAMENTATION ARISES FROM THEM. 292 LAZARU
MIRIAM ROCKS TO AND FRO AND RAISES A LOW WAIL OF 320 LAZARU
LAMENTATION.
AND WITH IT THE LAUGHTER OF THE CROWD TURNS TO A 369 LAZARU
WAIL OF FEAR AND LAMENTATION.)
THEIR VOICES RISE TOGETHER IN A LONG, RHYTHMIC 433 MARCOM
WAIL OF MOURNING..
(BREAKS INTO A DIRGELIKE WAIL.) 124 POET
WAILING
(HIS VOICE HAS RISEN TO A WAILING LAMENT) 285 LAZARU
ALL THE NAZARENES DO LIKEWISE, WAILING, RENDING 290 LAZARU
THEIR GARMENTS,
(IN A WAILING CHANT) WOE UNTO ISRAEL/ 292 LAZARU
(WAILING HOPELESSLY NUMB) FORGOTTEN IS LAUGHTER/ 296 LAZARU
WAILING IN THE HOME IN MY HEART THAT YOU HAVE LEFT362 LAZARU
FOREVER/
(THE CHRISTIAN SETS UP A WAILING CRY AND RECEIVES 354 MARCOM
A BLOW.
HE DECLAIMS IN A HIGH WAILING VOICE ACCOMPANIED BY436 MARCOM
THE MUSICIANS
WAILING AN OLD IRISH LAMENT AT THE TUP OF HIS 72 MISBEG
LUNGS.
SINGS WITH WAILING MELANCHOLY THE FIRST VERSE THAT102 POET
COMES TO HIS MIND
WAIST
(THEN REGARDING RICHARD'S ARM ABOUT HER WAIST) 242 AHWILD
HE IS STRIPPED TO THE WAIST, HAS ON NOTHING BUT A 30 ANNA
PAIR OF DIRTY DUNGAREE PANTS.

WAIST

WAIST (CONT'D.)
(WITH A QUICK MOVEMENT HE PUTS HIS ARMS ABOUT HER 33 ANNA WAIST)
HER WAIST AND IS ABOUT TO KISS HER WHEN HE STOPS, 76 ANNA
SHE WEARS A GINGHAM DRESS WITH A SOILED APRON TIED1L6 BEYOND AROUND HER WAIST.)
YANK HAS HIS ARM ABOUT HER WAIST AND IS CARRYING 464 CARIBE HER BASKET IN HIS OTHER HAND.
THE SUDDENLY LAUGHS WILDLY AND PUT HIS ARM AROUND 469 CARIBE HER WAIST AND PRESSES HER TO
AND LEANING AGAINST YANK, WHOSE ARM IS ABOUT HER 470 CARIBE WAIST.
(ELSA PUTS AN ARM AROUND HER WAIST AND THEY GO 528 DAYS BACK TO THE HALL DOORWAY.)
(PUTS AN ARM AROUND ELSA'S WAIST PLAYFULLY) 532 DAYS
HIS ARM IS ABOUT HER WAIST. 494 DIFRNT
(PUTTING HIS ARM ABOUT HER WAIST) 498 DIFRNT
(PUTTING HIS ARM ABOUT HER WAIST AND GIVING HER A 506 DIFRNT SQUEEZE--GRINNING)
A CARTRIDGE BELT WITH AN AUTOMATIC REVOLVER IS 174 EJONES AROUND HIS WAIST.
REVEALING HIMSELF STRIPPED TO THE WAIST) 193 EJONES
NAKED EXCEPT FOR THE FUR OF SOME SMALL ANIMAL TIED200 EJONES ABOUT HIS WAIST.
HE BEATS TIME WITH HIS HANDS AND SWAYS HIS BODY TO201 EJONES AND FRO FROM THE WAIST.
A REVOLVER AND CARTRIDGE BELT ARE ABOUT HIS WAIST. 202 EJONES
SOME WEAR SINGLETS, BUT THE MAJORITY ARE STRIPPED 207 HA APE TO THE WAIST.
A LINE OF MEN, STRIPPED TO THE WAIST, IS BEFORE 222 HA APE THE FURNACE DOORS.
HE IS STRIPPED TO THE WAIST, HIS COAT, SHIRT, 576 ICEMAN UNDERSHIRT,
(HE SINGS--) "OH, HE PUT HIS ARM AROUND HER WAIST,597 ICEMAN BUT SHOWING LITTLE EVIDENCE OF MIDDLE-AGED WAIST 12 JOURNE AND HIPS.
TYRONE'S ARM IS AROUND HIS WIFE'S WAIST AS THEY 14 JOURNE APPEAR FROM THE BACK PARLOR.
SO MY WAIST WOULD BE AS SMALL AS POSSIBLE. 115 JOURNE
WITH FULL BREASTS AND A SLENDER WAIST.) 44 MANSNS
STRIPPED TO THE WAIST, 350 MARCOM
HARNESSED TO EACH OTHER WAIST-TO-WAIST AND TO THE 350 MARCOM LONG POLE.
HER WAIST WIDE BUT SLENDER BY CONTRAST WITH HER 3 MISBEG HIPS AND THIGHS.
TIGHT-FITTING AND DRAWN IN AT THE WAIST, 37 MISBEG
(SHE LEADS HIM BACK, HER ARM AROUND HIS WAIST.) 141 MISBEG
AND A SLENDER WAIST. 16 POET
(GAILY PUTS HER ARM AROUND HER MOTHER'S WAIST.) 66 POET
HER HAIR IS DOWN OVER HER SHOULDERS, REACHING TO 136 POET HER WAIST.
(HE COMES, PUTS HIS ARM ABOUT HER WAIST, KISSES 119 STRANG HER AND THEY GO OUT TOGETHER.)
(HE PUTS HIS ARM ABOUT HER WAIST AND THEY GO OUT 149 STRANG TOGETHER LAUGHINGLY.

WAISTCOAT
STRETCHES ACROSS HIS CHECKED WAISTCOAT. 493 VOYAGE

WAISTED
HE WEARS A LIGHT GREY SUIT CUT IN THE EXTREME, 9 HUGHIE TIGHT-WAISTED, BROADWAY MODE.

WAISTS
THEIR ARMS AROUND EACH OTHER'S WAISTS, THEY 128 MANSNS ADVANCE ON SIMON WITH MOCKING,
THEIR NECKS, WAISTS, AND RIGHT ANKLES LINKED UP BY399 MARCOM CHAINS.

WAIT
(TURNING TO HIM--SHARPLY) WAIT/ 540 'ILE
BEST WAIT FOR A DAY WHEN THE SUN SHINES. 540 'ILE
I DIDN'T WANT TO WAIT BACK THERE IN THE HOUSE ALL 545 'ILE ALONE AS I'VE BEEN DURING
BUT WE CAN'T WAIT FOR THAT/ 546 'ILE
AND THE MEN WON'T WAIT. 546 'ILE
I CAN'T WAIT. 546 'ILE
SEEMS TO ME SHE MIGHT WAIT UNTIL THE FOURTH IS 192 AHWILD OVER BEFORE BRINGING UP--
YOU JUST WAIT TILL YOU SEE WHAT-- 192 AHWILD
WAIT TILL WE GET HIM DOWN TO YALE. 195 AHWILD
WAIT TILL I GET MY HAT, AH?/ 199 AHWILD
(SHOUTS AFTER HER) I CAN'T WAIT. 200 AHWILD
BUT WAIT, WATCH AND LISTEN/ 205 AHWILD
YOU MIGHT AS WELL GO OUT IN THE KITCHEN AND WAIT 211 AHWILD TILL I RING.
DON'T WAIT FOR ME. 223 AHWILD
IF WE WAIT FOR THAT GIRL TO TAKE THEM, WE'LL BE 225 AHWILD HERE ALL NIGHT.
BUT WAIT. 232 AHWILD
HUNG-H, I'M SO STRONG FOR YOU I CAN HARDLY WAIT TO241 AHWILD GET YOU UPSTAIRS/
WAIT/ 246 AHWILD
DICK ONLY SNEAKED OFF TO THE FIREWORKS AT THE 251 AHWILD BEACH, YOU WAIT AND SEE.
DICK'LL TURN UP IN A MINUTE OR TWO, WAIT AND SEE/ 260 AHWILD
BUT YOU WAIT TILL HE COMES BACK TONIGHT/ 270 AHWILD
I'D WAIT A MILLION YEARS AND NEVER MIND IT--FOR 274 AHWILD HER/
YOU WAIT AN SEE IF I CAN'T/ 274 AHWILD
WHAT DO I CARE HOW LONG I WAIT/ 274 AHWILD
IT'S AGES TO WAIT. 274 AHWILD
WAIT/ 284 AHWILD
BUT IT'S SO LONG TO WAIT. 287 AHWILD
WAIT A SECOND. 23 ANNA
WAIT 'N' SEE/ 56 ANNA
(EAGIN') I'LL WAIT 'TILL SHE COMES AND CHOKE HER 68 ANNA DIRTY LIFE OUT.
SO I COME BACK HERE--TO WAIT SOME MORE. 71 ANNA
REGULAR PLACE FOR YOU TWO TO COME BACK TO,--WAIT 77 ANNA AND SEE.
WAIT A MINUTE, ANDY/ 86 BEYOND

WAIT (CONT'D.)
I THINK YOU MIGHT WAIT UNTIL MORNING WHEN HE'S HAD 95 BEYOND HIS BREAKFAST.
I'D HAVE TO WAIT JUST THE SAME TO WASH UP AFTER 122 BEYOND YOU.
WAIT A MINUTE AND I'LL GO LOOK IT OVER. 124 BEYOND
I'LL HAVE TO WAIT FOR A SHIP SAILING THERE FOR 137 BEYOND QUITE A WHILE, LIKELY.
(MEANINGLY) TO WAIT/ 146 BEYOND
EASY NOW. THERE YOU ARE/ WAIT, AND I'LL GET A 199 BEYOND PILLOW FOR YOU.
AND THERE'S NOTHING WE CAN DO BUT SIT AND--WAIT/ 163 BEYOND
(THEY ALL SET THEMSELVES TO WAIT) 458 CARIBE
WAIT. THE RESUMES DELIBERATELY) ONE DAY MY 560 CROSS FATHER SENT FOR ME
HE BUILT THIS CABIN--TO WAIT IN-- 561 CROSS
HE TAUGHT ME TO WAIT AND HOPE WITH HIM--WAIT AND 566 CROSS HOPE--DAY AFTER DAY.
(FRENZIEDLY) WAIT/ 572 CROSS
NO, WAIT. 513 DAYS
IN THE PAUSE WHILE THEY WAIT FOR ELSA TO GET OUT 526 DAYS OF EARSHOT.
AND WHY SHOULD YOU WAIT FOR AN END YOU KNOW WHEN 562 DAYS IT IS IN YOUR POWER TO GRASP
(A PAUSE) WE GOT T' WAIT--TILL HE'S UNDER GROUND.205 DESIRE
(DRYLY) WAIT TILL YE'VE GROWED HIS AGE/ 207 DESIRE
YE WON'T NEVER GO BECAUSE YE'LL WAIT HERE FUR YER 208 DESIRE SHARE O' THE FARM.
WE'LL WAIT ANY SEE. 215 DESIRE
WE'D BEST WAIT AN' SEE THE BRIDE. 215 DESIRE
LET'S WAIT 'N' SEE WHAT OUR NEW MAW LOOKS LIKE. 220 DESIRE
WE GOT T' WAIT. 253 DESIRE
YE MUSTN'T--WAIT A SPELL--I WANT T' TELL YE.... 258 DESIRE
HE SAYS, WAIT 'TILL I GIT DRESSED. 266 DESIRE
WAIT. 269 DESIRE
WAIT. 511 DIFRNT
WAIT. 517 DIFRNT
AND I'LL WAIT FOR YE TO CHANGE YOUR MIND, 518 DIFRNT
I'M GOIN' TO WAIT FOR YOU. 518 DIFRNT
LET HIM WAIT. 528 DIFRNT
WAIT TILL SHE COMES DOWN AND YOU GIT A LOOK/ 529 DIFRNT
I'M GOIN' TO BEAT IT TO THE KITCHEN AND WAIT. 534 DIFRNT
I SAID I'D WAIT THIRTY YEARS--IF NEED BE. 538 DIFRNT
THIRTY YEARS--THAT'S A HELL OF A LONG TIME TO 538 DIFRNT WAIT, EMMER--
ONLY NOT TOMORROW, WE'D BETTER WAIT AND SEE-- 546 DIFRNT
(THEN IN A STRANGE WHISPER) WAIT, CALEB, I'M 549 DIFRNT GOING DOWN TO THE BARN.
WAIT A MINUTE/ 433 DYNAMO
UH-- JUST WAIT/ I TELL HER WHAT I THINK OF 434 DYNAMO HER/....))
WAIT AND SEE/ 442 DYNAMO
(TELL WAIT HERE AND WATCH THE FUN...)) 445 DYNAMO
REUBEN'S PUNISHMENT CAN WAIT. 449 DYNAMO
BUT WAIT/ 452 DYNAMO
(HE STEPS BACK, FROWNING) WAIT TILL LATER, ADA. 468 DYNAMO
(HE GOES TO THE DOOR) YOU WAIT UNTIL YOUR 478 DYNAMO HUSBAND'S GONE HOME.
THE GUARD SEEMS TO WAIT EXPECTANTLY, HIS BACK 195 EJONES TURNED TO THE ATTACKER.
YOU WAIT HERE. 8 ELECTR
AND YOU SAID WAIT TILL THE WAR WAS OVER. 14 ELECTR
WAIT. 19 ELECTR
YOU WAIT HERE UNTIL I CALL YOU/ 27 ELECTR
WAIT/ 34 ELECTR
I WON'T WAIT FOR HIM TO COME HOME/ 35 ELECTR
(SHE MOVES TOWARD THE DOOR TO WAIT FOR HIM. 35 ELECTR
WHEN HE COMES HOME I'LL WAIT FOR HIM 38 ELECTR
YOU SAIL TO BOSTON TOMORROW, TO WAIT FOR CARGOS 40 ELECTR
THEN YOU MUST WAIT ON THE "FLYING TRADES" UNTIL 40 ELECTR YOU HEAR FROM ME
HIS LETTER SAID HE WOULDN'T WAIT UNTIL HIS BRIGADE 46 ELECTR WAS DISBANDED
WAIT/ 59 ELECTR
WAIT/ 60 ELECTR
WAIT. 62 ELECTR
THERE THEY STOP TO WAIT FOR THE MEN WHO STAND AT 68 ELECTR THE FOOT OF THE STEPS WHILE
I WOULD RATHER WAIT FOR ORIN INSIDE. 73 ELECTR
I COULDN'T BEAR TO WAIT AND WATCH HIM COMING UP 73 ELECTR THE DRIVE-- JUST LIKE--
WAIT UNTIL YOU'VE TALKED TO ME/ 76 ELECTR
WAIT. 80 ELECTR
WAIT/ 83 ELECTR
(THEY WAIT, STARING AT THE DOOR. 99 ELECTR
WAIT/ 100 ELECTR
BUT WAIT/ 160 ELECTR
WHY MUST WE WAIT FOR MARRIAGES 176 ELECTR
I'M AFRAID TO WAIT/ 176 ELECTR
I'LL GO DOWN TO THE END OF THE DOCK AND WAIT. 264 GGBROW
YOU JUST WAIT HERE. 300 GGBROW
WAIT/ 307 GGBROW
I MEAN--WAIT A MOMENT, IF YOU PLEASE. 315 GGBROW
(HE SEEMS TO WAIT FOR AN ANSWER-- 319 GGBROW
DEY DON'T WAIT FUR NO ONE. 211 HA APE
SAY, LISTEN TO ME--WAIT A MOMENT--I GOTTER TALK, 215 HA APE SEE--
WAIT A MOMENT/ 216 HA APE
WAIT A MOMENT/ 228 HA APE
I'LL BRAIN HER YET, WAIT 'N' SEE/ 230 HA APE
WAIT AND YER'LL BLOODY WELL SEE-- 234 HA APE
I DON'T WAIT FOR NO ONE. 234 HA APE
DIDN'T I SNEAK ON DE DUCK AND WAIT FOR HER BY DE 235 HA APE GANGPLANKS
WAIT/ 13 HUGHIE
WELL, I'M BETTIN' YOU'LL HAVE A GOOD LONG WAIT. 578 ICEMAN
WAIT A MINUTE, DOUGH. 583 ICEMAN

1759 WAITIN'

WAIT (CONT'D.)
ONLY TAKE MY ADVICE AND WAIT A WHILE UNTIL BUSINESS CONDITIONS ARE BETTER. 604 ICEMAN
WE TOLD DE GUYS WE'D WAIT FOR DEM 'ROUND DE CORNER. 612 ICEMAN
WAIT AND SEE. 639 ICEMAN
WAIT TILL HICKEY GETS THROUGH WITH YOU/ 650 ICEMAN
WAIT, HARRY. 656 ICEMAN
(SHARPLY) WAIT/ (INSISTENTLY--WITH A SNEER) 661 ICEMAN
I MEANT TO WAIT UNTIL THE PARTY WAS OVER. 663 ICEMAN
YOU WAIT AND SEE/ 673 ICEMAN
DAT'S RIGHT, WAIT ON HER AND SPOIL HER, YUH POOR 677 ICEMAN
SAP/
HE CAN'T WAIT ALL DAY FOR YOU, YOU KNOW. 686 ICEMAN
AND IF YOU'LL ONLY WAIT UNTIL THE FINAL RETURNS 691 ICEMAN
ARE IN,
JUST LEAVE HARRY ALONE AND WAIT UNTIL THE SHOCK 692 ICEMAN
WEARS OFF AND YOU'LL SEE.
SO I'LL WAIT, AND WHEN YOU'RE READY YOU SEND FOR 711 ICEMAN
ME AND WE'LL BE MARRIED.
WAIT/ 714 ICEMAN
NO, WAIT, OFFICER/ 717 ICEMAN
I CAN HARDLY WAIT NOW. 718 ICEMAN
(SCOTTY GOES TO THE DOORWAY AND TURNS TO WAIT FOR 516 INZONE
SMITTY.
TO WAIT AN' SEE IF HE'S COMIN' BACK. 518 INZONE
(INTERRUPTING HIM SHARPLY) WAIT/ 530 INZONE
(WITHOUT CONVICTION.) HE'LL TURN OUT ALL RIGHT IN 18 JOURNE
THE END. YOU WAIT AND SEE.
WE CAN'T WAIT ALL DAY/ 62 JOURNE
TELL BRIDGET I'M SORRY BUT SHE'LL HAVE TO WAIT A 62 JOURNE
FEW MINUTES UNTIL MISTER TYRONE
NO, PLEASE WAIT A LITTLE WHILE, DEAR. 83 JOURNE
(DRYLY.) WAIT A MINUTE, PAPA. 89 JOURNE
WOMEN USED TO WAIT AT THE STAGE DOOR JUST TO SEE 105 JOURNE
HIM COME OUT.
TELL BRIDGET I WON'T WAIT. 106 JOURNE
HOW MANY TIMES I WAS TO WAIT IN UGLY HOTEL ROOMS. 113 JOURNE
WAIT/ 284 LAZARU
WAIT/ 318 LAZARU
THEY DID NOT WAIT FOR OUR ATTACK. 321 LAZARU
WAIT/ 323 LAZARU
YOU MAY HAVE TO WAIT. 327 LAZARU
WAIT/ 335 LAZARU
OUR TOMB NEAR OUR HOME, LAZARUS, IN WHICH YOU AND 346 LAZARU
MY CHILDREN WAIT FOR ME.
BECOME YOUR SLAVE, WAIT UPON YOU, GIVE YOU LOVE 361 LAZARU
AND PASSION AND BEAUTY IN
AT YOUR AGE, A WOMAN MUST BECOME RESIGNED TO WAIT 3 MANSNS
UPON EVERY MAN'S PLEASURE.
AM I TO SIT ALL AFTERNOON AND WAIT UPON HIS 4 MANSNS
PLEASURES
WAIT/ 17 MANSNS
(THEN SUDDENLY SUSPICIOUS.) WAIT/ 55 MANSNS
WAIT/ 64 MANSNS
YOU MIGHT AT LEAST WAIT UNTIL I HAVE FINISHED 64 MANSNS
EXPLAINING
WAIT/ 67 MANSNS
WAIT/ 71 MANSNS
NO, WAIT UNTIL YOU FEEL HER OUT 74 MANSNS
WAIT/ 89 MANSNS
WAIT/ 93 MANSNS
WAIT AND SEE, MOTHER/ 101 MANSNS
WAIT/ 111 MANSNS
=WAIT.
I CAN'T WAIT TO TELL HER YOU ARE GOING TO BE WITH 115 MANSNS
ME EACH EVENING.
BUT YOU AND I CAN WAIT TO DISCOVER WHAT THAT IS 115 MANSNS
LATER ON.
WHY DOES HE WAIT$ 119 MANSNS
BUT WAIT TILL YOU HEAR THE REST. 133 MANSNS
WELL, I WON'T WAIT, MY FINE SIMON/ 144 MANSNS
LET TENARD WAIT OUTSIDE THE DOOR FOR A WHILE LIKE 149 MANSNS
THE RUINED BEGGAR HE IS.
WAIT/ 153 MANSNS
YOU'LL REMEMBER YOU PROMISED ME YOU'D FORGET HER 159 MANSNS
AND LET HER WAIT.
LET THE COWARDLY OLD WITCH WAIT UNTIL DOMESDAY/ 159 MANSNS
ALL THEY HAVE TO DO IS TO WAIT TOGETHER AND STAND 173 MANSNS
APART.
YES, WE'VE ONLY TO WAIT AND WE'LL SOON BE FREE OF 173 MANSNS
HIM.
A DAILY APPOINTMENT WITH PEACE AND HAPPINESS IN 180 MANSNS
WHICH WE WAIT DAY AFTER DAY.
WAIT/ 188 MANSNS
WE MUSTN'T WAIT--OR IT MAY BE TOO LATE/ 189 MANSNS
SARA--WAIT--FORGIVE--I WANT TO SAY--MY GRATITUDE--189 MANSNS
WANT TO TELL YOU--
BUT YOU'LL WAIT, WON'T YOU, NO MATTER HOW LONG$ 357 MARCOM
BUT WAIT--A TEST/ 379 MARCOM
WAIT. 399 MARCOM
WAIT. 414 MARCOM
ALL RIGHT, IF YOU'LL PROMISE TO GO AHEAD AND EAT 431 MARCOM
AND NOT WAIT FOR ME.
I HAD TO WAIT TILL HE WENT TO THE PIG PEN. 4 MISBEG
(HER MANNER SOFTENING) WAIT. 6 MISBEG
(HASTILY) WAIT TILL I FINISH AND YOU WON'T BE MAD 10 MISBEG
AT ME.
YOU'D BETTER WAIT. 35 MISBEG
WAIT, NOW/ 59 MISBEG
(SHOUTS) WAIT/ 59 MISBEG
(GRIMLY) WAIT NOW, ME HONEY BOY. 61 MISBEG
WAIT A MINUTE. 65 MISBEG
JIM WON'T HAVE TO WAIT FOR HIS HALF OF THE CASH 84 MISBEG
TILL THE ESTATE'S SETTLED.
WAIT, NOW. 95 MISBEG
WAIT. 97 MISBEG
COMING TO CALL ON YOU, AFTER MAKING YOU WAIT FOR 98 MISBEG
HOURS.

WAIT (CONT'D.)
BUT WAIT TILL I JUIN YOU. 112 MISBEG
HAVE ANOTHER DRINK, AND DON'T WAIT FOR ME. 116 MISBEG
WAIT TILL I GET HOLD OF HIM/ 136 MISBEG
WAIT TILL I'M SURE I'M STILL ALIVE. 166 MISBEG
YOU MEAN YOU--(SUDDENLY) WAIT A MINUTE. 167 MISBEG
(STAMPERS) WAIT, JOSIE/ 174 MISBEG
WAIT AND SEE, NOW. 79 POET
SHE'D MAKE HIM PROMISE TO WAIT. 87 POET
HAPPINESS--BUT THEN SHE'D SAY HE OUGHT TO WAIT AND 87 POET
PROVE HE'S SURE--
AND IT'S THE LAST TIME YOU'LL EVER TAKE 104 POET
SATISFACTION IN HAVING ME WAIT ON TABLE
WAIT/ 107 POET
DID SHE GET HIM TO PROMISE HER HE'D WAITS 110 POET
WAIT/ 112 POET
WHY CAN'T YOU LEAVE IT AT THAT AND WAIT-- 126 POET
YOU'RE GOING TO SIT UP AND WAIT DOWN HERE$ 132 POET
AND THEY'VE ALL COME IN TO WAIT FOR CREGAN AND 134 POET
HIMSELF.
AND SHE ONLY SUGGESTED HE WAIT A YEAR, SHE DIDN'T 144 POET
MAKE HIM PROMISE.
WAIT TILL YOU HEAR, NORA/ 158 POET
WAIT, JAMIE. 165 POET
WAIT TILL THE BOYS HEAR THAT/ 178 POET
NO--EXCEPT WAIT AN' PRAY THAT YOUNG THIEF IS DEAD 986 ROPE
AN' WON'T COME BACK.
BUT I'LL GIT BACK AT HIM AW RIGHT, YUH WAIT 'N 593 ROPE
SEE.
JUST WAIT TILL HE'S ASLEEP AND I'LL SHOW YUH-- 594 ROPE
TERNIGHT.
I'LL WAIT IN HERE, MARY. 4 STRANG
THEY MUST WAIT UNTIL HE HAD COME BACK 11 STRANG
YOU MUST WAIT TILL YOU HAVE A MARRIAGE LICENSE/ 19 STRANG
WAIT, HE TOLD GORDON/ 20 STRANG
WAIT FOR NINA TILL THE WAR'S OVER, 20 STRANG
OK WAIT UNTIL SHE$...) 26 STRANG
WAIT AND SEE/ 54 STRANG
DON'T YOU THINK YOU BETTER WAIT UNTIL SAMMY'S 57 STRANG
MAKING MORE MONEYS
(WAIT... 76 STRANG
IT WAS PRUDENT TO WAIT... 91 STRANG
WAIT A SECOND. 119 STRANG
WAIT TILL I GET MY CHANCE/ 121 STRANG
(WITH A BITTER GRIN) ((WAIT TILL SAM HEARS 125 STRANG
THAT...
WAIT AND SAY GOOD-BY TO SAM. 145 STRANG
WHY WAIT FOR SAM$... 149 STRANG
WE'LL ONLY HAVE A LITTLE WHILE LONGER TO WAIT 175 STRANG
I CAN WAIT. 175 STRANG
(IT WILL NOT HAVE LONG TO WAIT NOW....) 183 STRANG
I'LL GO DOWN TO THE PLANE AND WAIT FOR YOU. 188 STRANG
THEY'LL COME, AN' THEY'LL ALL BE ROTTEN DRUNK. 496 VOYAGE
WAIT AN' SEE.
I WAIT HERE, DRISC. 504 VOYAGE
SO WAIT HERE FOR US, OLLIE. 504 VOYAGE
AN' FUR YOU TO WAIT FUR 'EM$ 505 VOYAGE
WAIT ARF A MO'. 507 VOYAGE
IT'LL BE A TRIUMPH FOR YOU BOTH, WAIT AND SEE. 451 WELDED
NOT NOW--NO--WAIT--YOU MUST WAIT-- 466 WELDED
(FORCING A LIGHT TONE) WELL, I'LL BE RESIGNED TO 467 WELDED
WAIT AND HOPE THEN--
(SUDDENLY GRASPING HIS ARM) WAIT. 469 WELDED

WAIT'LL
WAIT'LL WE SEE THIS COW THE OLD MAN'S HITCHED T'/ 214 DESIRE
WAIT'LL I SEE IF IF I GOT LIGHT ENOUGH AND I'LL 242 HA APE
READ YOU.

WAITED
I WAITED FOR HIM TO WAKE UP BUT HE DIDN'T. 268 AHWILD
YOU'D REMEMBER YOUR UNCLE CALEB'S BEEN IN LOVE 530 DIFNNT
WITH EMMA ALL HIS LIFE AND WAITED
I WON'T-- NOT EVEN IF YOU HAVE WAITED THIRTY 543 DIFNNT
YEARS.
BECAUSE I WAITED OUTSIDE GRANDFATHER'S HOUSE AND 29 ELECTR
FOLLOWED YOU.
AND IN BOSTON WE WAITED UNTIL THE EVENING TRAIN 120 ELECTR
GOT IN.
AND I WAITED TILL DEY WAS ALL GONE TO GIT YUH 252 HA APE
ALONE.
I WAITED UNTIL THEY WENT OUT. 42 JOURNE
I HAD WAITED IN THAT UGLY HOTEL ROOM HOUR AFTER 113 JOURNE
HOUR.
I WAITED, PRAYING HE WOULDN'T. 20 MANSNS
(THINKING--UNEASILY.) PERHAPS I SHOULD HAVE 120 MANSNS
WAITED--
GOD, HOW LONG HAVE I WAITED LIKE THIS--HOURS/ 162 MANSNS
I REMEMBER WHEN I WAITED FOR HIM AT THE CABIN THATI63 MANSNS
AFTERNOON.
I HAVE WAITED EVER SINCE I WAS A LITTLE BOY. 182 MANSNS
IF SHE'D WAITED TILL TOMORROW, EVEN, I'D HAVE GOT 77 POET
HIM TO ASK ME TO MARRY HIM.
BACK AT THE HOTEL I WAITED TILL THEY WERE 6 STRANG
ASLEEP...
I WAITED... 91 STRANG
I'VE WAITED A LIFETIME ALREADY.. 175 STRANG
(SADLY TEASING) IF YOU'VE WAITED THAT LONG, 197 STRANG
CHARLIE,
(STRUNGLY) ALL MY LIFE I'VE WAITED TO BRING YOU 197 STRANG
PEACE.

WAITER
AND GAVE HIM THE GATE TO MARRY A WAITER/ 135 JOURNE

WAITIN'
THERE'S PLENTY OF OTHER GUYS ON OTHER BARGES 11 ANNA
WAITIN' FOR ME.
THAT'S HER IN THERE--YOUR ANNA--JUST COME--AND 19 ANNA
WAITIN' FUR YUH.
FORTUNES LAYIN' JUST ATOP O' THE GROUND WAITIN' T'204 DESIRE
BE PICKED/

WAITIN'

WAITIN' (CONT'D.)
SHE KNEW WHAT IT LAY FUR YEARS, BUT SHE WAS 213 DESIRE
WAITIN'...
I BEEN WAITIN'--MAW TOLD ME. 213 DESIRE
NO. I'M WAITIN' IN HERE A SPELL. 220 DESIRE
(DRYLY) WE'RE WAITIN' T' WELCOME YE HUM--YEW AN' 222 DESIRE
THE BRIDE/
(SLYLY) WE'RE WAITIN' FUR EBEN. 249 DESIRE
AFTER WAITIN' THREE YEARS FOR ME TO GIT ENOUGH 496 DIFRNT
MONEY SAVED--
GIT ABOARD THE SHIP WHERE HE WAS WAITIN' FOR HER 503 DIFRNT
ALONE.
AND HERE I BE WAITIN' IN THE KITCHEN FOR HIM TO 505 DIFRNT
BRING BACK THE THINGS
YOU'LL REMEMBER WHAT I TOLD YE 'BOUT WAITIN', 518 DIFRNT
EPHERS
HE'S WAITIN' TO TALK TO YOU. 528 DIFRNT
WHAT THE 'ELL'S THE GOOD OF WAITIN'S 203 EJONES
THEY'RE ONLY WAITIN' NOW FUR THE NEWS TO BE MADE 11 ELECTR
OFFICIAL
THOSE FOLKS ARE WAITIN' FOR ME. 12 ELECTR
GULLS WAITIN' FOR YOU, HUH? 211 HA APE
WE'RE WAITIN' TO HEAR WHAT THEY LANDED YOU FUR--OR241 HA APE
AIN'T YUH TELLIN'S
WAITIN' AT THE GRAND CENTRAL TO GIVE HIM THE KEY 23 HUGHIE
TO THE CITY.
HE KEEPS ME WAITIN' AND WAITIN', AND 600 ICEMAN
OR DEAT'S A LITTLE IRON ROOM UP DE RIVER WAITIN' 601 ICEMAN
FOR YOU/
KEPT ME DOWN HERE WAITIN' FOR HICKEY TO SHOW UP, 602 ICEMAN
TELL HIM WE'RE WAITIN' TO BE SAVED/ 618 ICEMAN
(HIS VOICE HARD) I'M WAITIN', BABY. 700 ICEMAN
GOD BLESS YOU, NORA. YOU'RE THE ONE I WAS WAITIN' 20 POET
TO SEE.
HAVE I KEPT YOU WAITIN'S 55 POET
WHAT WOULD I BE WAITIN' FOR BUT FOR YOU TO GET 103 POET
THROUGH WITH YOUR BLATHER
I'M SICK WITH WORRY AND I'VE GOT TO THE PLACE 136 POET
WHERE I CAN'T BEAR WAITIN' ALONE,
«REMEMBER, WHEN YOU COME HOME AGAIN THERE'S A ROPE593 ROPE
WAITIN' FOR YUH
THERE'S PLENTY OF 'ANDS LYIN' ABAWT WAITIN' FUR 495 VOYAGE
SHIPS. I SHOULD FINK.

WAITING

ENTERS FROM RIGHT AND STANDS WAITING FOR THE 543 'ILE
CAPTAIN TO NOTICE HIM.)
THESE LAST SIX YEARS SINCE WE WERE MARRIED-- 545 'ILE
WAITING, AND WATCHING, AND FEARING--
EVEN ATTEMPTING TO WHISTLE --WAITING AT THE 208 AHWILD
CHURCH.»
(IN THE FRONT PARLOR, ARTHUR BEGINS TO SING 259 AHWILD
ROLLICKINGLY «WAITING AT THE CHURCH,
YOU'D THINK YOU COULDN'T BEAR WAITING TO PUNISH 268 AHWILD
HIM/
WAITING OUTSIDE THE PLEASANT BEACH HOUSE, 276 AHWILD
WHISTLING WITH INSOUCIANCE « WAITING AT THE 277 AHWILD
CHURCH.»
SHARON AT THE FOOT OF THE PATH, WAITING FOR 278 AHWILD
RICHARD TO SEE HER.
I THOUGHT YOU'D BE WAITING RIGHT HERE AT THE END 278 AHWILD
OF THE PATH.
DON'T FORGET YOUR FATHER'S BEEN WAITING TO TALK T0293 AHWILD
YOU/
YOU'RE WAITING TILL YOU DO BE ASKED, YOU MANES 53 ANNA
I'D BEEN WAITING AND WAITING TILL I WAS SICK OF 64 ANNA
IT.
WHAT AM I WAITING FOR ANYWAYS 68 ANNA
U BEEN WAITING HERE ALL ALONE FOR TWO DAYS, 71 ANNA
THINKING MAYBE YOU'D COME BACK--
HE'S WAITING FOR YOU AT THE ROAD. 135 BEYOND
(BITTERLY) IS THAT WHY YOU'RE WAITING UP ALL 146 BEYOND
NIGHTS
(MOCKINGLY) IS SHE WAITING FOR ANDY, TOOS 147 BEYOND
I'VE BEEN WAITING-- 153 BEYOND
THE OTHERS ARE WAITING FOR YOU. 473 CARBNE
NOW YOU KNOW WHY HE'S MAD--WAITING FUR 561 CROSS
HE'LL FORGET HIS MAD IDEA OF WAITING FOR A LOST 563 CROSS
SHIP
THIS TIME ELIOT COMES IN IMMEDIATELY, WITHOUT 499 DAYS
WAITING FOR AN ANSWER.)
THEN SHE APPEARS IN THE HALL OUTSIDE THE DOORWAY, 515 DAYS
WAITING TO ANSWER THE DOOR.
THE MAN WAS WAITING WHOM I COULD REALLY LOVE. 521 DAYS
WAITING TO CATCH MEN AT ITS MERCY, IN THEIR HOUR 535 DAYS
OF SECURE HAPPINESS--
AND AT HIS DEATH SHE WILL BE WAITING. 544 DAYS
YOU WERE ONLY WAITING FOR THIS CHANCE TO KILL THAT549 DAYS
LOVE.
HER EYES ARE FIXED ANXIOUSLY ON THE OPEN DOOR IN 247 DESIRE
REAR AS IF WAITING FOR SOMEONE.
I WAS WAITING. 266 DESIRE
WAITING FOR HER TO SPEAK OR LOOK UP. 514 DIFRNT
(OFFENDEDLY) WITHOUT WAITING TO SEE MES 531 DIFRNT
(HE COMES BACK TO THE CENTER OF THE ROOM WHERE HE 531 DIFRNT
STANDS WAITING,
WAITING FOR DEATH TO TAKE ME AND NOT ENJOYIN' 536 DIFRNT
ANYTHING.
HE STANDS BY THIS, WAITING NERVOUSLY, PEERING 427 DYNAMO
THROUGH THE GAP AT THE FIRE HOUSE.
RUBE'LL BE WAITING... 430 DYNAMO
I'M LOSING ALL MY NERVE WAITING...) 431 DYNAMO
WAITING TO SCARE SOME FRIEND OF HIS...) 431 DYNAMO
(WITHOUT WAITING FOR AN INTRODUCTION, 436 DYNAMO
BUT I COULDN'T STAND IT ANY MORE, WAITING... 480 DYNAMO
SHE'S WAITING FOR ME/ 482 DYNAMO
MOTIONS WITH HIDEOUS COMMAND TOWARD THE WAITING 201 EJONES
MONSTER.

WAITING (CONT'D.)
THEN SEES SHE HAS NOT NOTICED THEIR PRESENCE, AND 10 ELECTR
STOPS AND STANDS WAITING.
WAITING UNTIL SHE HEARS THE SIDE DOOR OF THE HOUSE 35 ELECTR
CLOSE AFTER HER.
(THEN BRUSQUELY) BRANT IS WAITING OUTSIDE. 35 ELECTR
SO HE'S THE BEAU YOU'RE WAITING FOR IN THE SPRING 46 ELECTR
MOONLIGHT/
THEY ARE EMPTY--WAITING FOR SOMEONE TO MOVE IN/ 60 ELECTR
(A PAUSE--THEN ACCUSINGLY) IS THAT WHAT YOU'RE 60 ELECTR
WAITING FORS
WAITING FOR WHAT TO HAPPENS 60 ELECTR
WHAT WOULD I BE WAITING FORS 60 ELECTR
AS IF SOMETHING IN ME WAS LISTENING, WATCHING, 60 ELECTR
WAITING FOR SOMETHING TO HAPPEN.
YOU ARE WAITING FOR SOMETHING/ 60 ELECTR
I THOUGHT SHE'D SURELY BE WAITING FOR ME. 74 ELECTR
(THEN WITHOUT WAITING FOR A REPLY, BURSTING INTO 76 ELECTR
JEALOUS RAGE)
(THEN ANGRILY) I KNOW WHAT YOU'VE BEEN WAITING 77 ELECTR
FOR--
(SHE PAUSES, WAITING FOR SOME RESPONSE. 77 ELECTR
THERE'S SOMEONE ELSE WAITING WHO WILL BE SO GLAD 77 ELECTR
TO SEE YOU.
(HE STANDS AGAINST THE WAREHOUSE, WAITING FOR THE 104 ELECTR
SWAYING WORLD TO SUBSIDE.
MY NERVES ARE GONE FROM WAITING ALONE HERE 108 ELECTR
SO THIS TIME AT LAST YOU ARE WAITING TO MEET ME 120 ELECTR
WHEN I COME HOME/
WAITING FOR ME IN THERE, WHERE--(TORTUREDLY) BUT 140 ELECTR
SHE WASN'T/
IT'S A SYMBOL OF HIS LIFE--A LAMP BURNING OUT IN ALSO ELECTR
ROOM OF WAITING SHADOWS/
I DIDN'T MIND WAITING. 162 ELECTR
YOU'RE WAITING TO TAKE ME HOME/ 166 ELECTR
DEATH IS AN ISLAND OF PEACE, TOO--MOTHER WILL BE 166 ELECTR
WAITING FOR ME THERE--
MOTHER'S WAITING/ 166 ELECTR
I CAN'T BEAR WAITING--WAITING AND WAITING AND 167 ELECTR
WAITING--/
I'M WAITING FOR PETER. 170 ELECTR
I CAN'T SEE WHY YOU'RE SO AFRAID OF WAITING. 176 ELECTR
(A SECOND'S PAUSE OF WAITING SILENCE-- 265 GGBROW
SHE'S WAITING FOR YOU NOW, DOWN AT THE END OF THE 265 GGBROW
DOCK.
REMEMBER SHE'S WAITING/ 266 GGBROW
(DAZEDLY TO HIMSELF) WAITING--WAITING FOR ME/ 266 GGBROW
(SHE LOOKS AT HIM AS IF WAITING FOR HIM TO REMOVE 279 GGBROW
HIS MASK--
PASS AWAY THE TIME, WHILE ONE IS WAITING--FOR 282 GGBROW
ONE'S NEXT INCARNATION.
AND WITHOUT WAITING FOR AN ANSWER, TURNS THE KNOB.306 GGBROW
OUR WIFE IS WAITING/ 308 GGBROW
MARGARET SITS ON THE SOFA, WAITING WITH THE 308 GGBROW
ANXIOUS/
I'M WAITING FOR THE FOURTH. 221 HA APE
HE'S WAITING FOR US. 222 HA APE
HE WAS ALWAYS WAITING FOR ME TO ROLL IN. 15 HUGHIE
WAITING FOR ANY EXCUSE TO SHY AND PRETEND TO TAKE 576 ICEMAN
THE BIT IN ITS TEETH.
WAITING FOR THE EFFECT.) 583 ICEMAN
SITTING WITH A PARCHED THROAT WAITING FOR HARRY 607 ICEMAN
HOPE TO BUY A DRINK.
BUT I'M WAITING IMPATIENTLY FOR THE END. 611 ICEMAN
IT'S DAMNED TIRING, THIS WAITING FOR THE END. 615 ICEMAN
YOU'RE JUST WAITING IMPATIENTLY FOR THE END--THE 623 ICEMAN
GOOD OLD LONG SLEEP/
AND THE WAITING FOR THE BIG SLEEP STUFF IS A PIPE 641 ICEMAN
DREAM.
I KEPT WAITING. 648 ICEMAN
BUT WHAT ARE WE WAITING FOR, BOYS AND GIRLS$ 657 ICEMAN
SO I IMAGINE THERE WOULD BE NO WELCOMING COMMITTEE677 ICEMAN
WAITING ON THE DOCK,
WAS ONLY WAITING TO SAY GOOD-BYE TO YOU, HARRY, 685 ICEMAN
OLD CHUM.
THERE IS A SUSPENDED, WAITING SILENCE. 711 ICEMAN
SHE'D HAVE BEEN WAITING THERE ALONE, 713 ICEMAN
WHERE PEOPLE HOLD THEIR BREATH, WAITING FOR HIM T0714 ICEMAN
DIE.)
(THEN THEY ALL SIT STILL, WAITING FOR THE EFFECT. 719 ICEMAN
HE PAUSES, AS IF WAITING FOR COMMENT, BUT LARRY 720 ICEMAN
IGNORES HIM)
GENERAL WETJOEN'S, «WAITING AT THE CHURCH». 727 ICEMAN
CATHLEEN MUST BE WAITING TO CLEAR THE TABLE. 15 JOURNE
AND WAS WAITING AT THE GATE TO WELCOME HIM. 24 JOURNE
IT'S A ROTTEN TRICK THE WAY HE KEEPS MEALS 61 JOURNE
WAITING.
WAITING IN THE OVEN, SHE SAID IT SERVED YOU RIGHT, 67 JOURNE
(BUT THEY KEEP ON WITHOUT WAITING FOR HER. 68 JOURNE
IT IS AS IF THEY WERE WAITING UNTIL SHE GOT 75 JOURNE
UPSTAIRS BEFORE SPEAKING.)
(WITH GRIND RESENTMENT.) I HAD IT HERE WAITING 84 JOURNE
FOR YOU
JAMIE'S WAITING. 95 JOURNE
I'VE BEEN WAITING FOR YOU. 108 JOURNE
(WITHOUT WAITING FOR A REPLY SHE DOES SO.) 109 JOURNE
WAITING NIGHT AFTER NIGHT IN DIRTY HOTEL ROOMS FOR141 JOURNE
YOU TO COME BACK
I'LL BE WAITING TO WELCOME YOU WITH THAT «MY OLD 166 JOURNE
PAL» STUFF.
WE ARE WAITING FOR HIM TO SPEAK. 277 LAZARU
WHAT ARE WE WAITING FORS 314 LAZARU
THE LEGIONS ARE WAITING. 317 LAZARU
THICK WALLS SEEM WAITING TO FALL, 330 LAZARU
(HE TURNS HIS BACK ON THEM ALL AND STANDS 332 LAZARU
WAITING.)
I AM WAITING/ 333 LAZARU
AND ALL THE CHILDREN WILL BE WAITING. 346 LAZARU

WAITING (CONT'D.)
YOU HAVE BEEN PLEASED TO KEEP ME WAITING, 5 MANSNS
MONSIEUR,
(WITH COLD CONDEMNATION.) HOW LONG ARE YOU GOING 36 MANSNS
TO KEEP US WAITING HERE
WE ARE WAITING FOR YOUR CONSENT, MOTHER. 36 MANSNS
I'M SORRY TO KEEP YOU WAITING SO LONG, DEBORAH, 61 MANSNS
(WITH SUDDEN DISMAY.) THEN YOU DECIDED IT ALL-- 62 MANSNS
WITHOUT WAITING TO ASK ME/
HE STANDS WAITING. 70 MANSNS
I WOULD HAVE FORGOTTEN HER AND RETURNED TO MOTHER, 74 MANSNS
WAITING FOR ME IN HER GARDEN--
(BITTERLY.) BUT SHE WASN'T WAITING-- 75 MANSNS
AND WOULD ALWAYS REMAIN, WAITING TO SEE IF HE 111 MANSNS
WOULD DARE OPEN THE DOOR.
AS LONG AS YOU DON'T MIND HIS KEEPING YOU WAITING.141 MANSNS
THIS BANKER WHO IS WAITING--HOW HE MUST HATE 142 MANSNS
SIMON--
SORRY TO HAVE KEPT YOU WAITING, MR. TENARD. 151 MANSNS
I'LL BE WAITING AND LONGING-- 158 MANSNS
LAUGHING WITH HER TO THINK OF THE PITIABLE 162 MANSNS
SPECTACLE I MAKE WAITING IN VAIN/
THEN AFTER SUPPER OUT HERE AGAIN--WAITING AGAIN-- 162 MANSNS
WHY DO I
MY POOR HEART WAS TERRIFIED YOU HAD FORGOTTEN I 164 MANSNS
WAS WAITING.
I TOOK PITY ON YOU, KNOWING YOU'D BE KEPT WAITING 165 MANSNS
OUT HERE ALL NIGHT LIKE AN OLD
HE'S WAITING, HOPING TO HEAR I'VE FOUND YOU LOCKED169 MANSNS
INSIDE THERE
I KNOW MY SON IS WAITING FOR AN OPPORTUNITY TO SEE169 MANSNS
ME ALONE.
IT WAS THE STILLNESS THAT FOLLOWS A SHRIEK OF 174 MANSNS
TERROR, WAITING TO BECOME AWARE--
IT'S THE CHILDREN'S BEDTIME AND THEY ARE WAITING 176 MANSNS
FOR YOUR GOODNIGHT KISS.
WHEN YOU DELIBERATELY KEPT ME WAITING HERE HOUR 178 MANSNS
AFTER HOUR--
WITH HER IN HER ARMS TO THINK OF YOU WAITING HERE 179 MANSNS
LIKE AN OLD FOOL--
WHY ARE YOU WAITING, MOTHERS 188 MANSNS
WHY, WHAT IS WAITING TO WELCOME YOU IS MERELY YOUR190 MANSNS
LAST DISDAIN/
(WITHOUT WAITING FOR PERMISSION, 393 MARCOM
SHE'S THERE WAITING FOR ME. 406 MARCOM
IN THE SHADOW OF THE HIGHEST DECK IN REAR HER 407 MARCOM
WOMEN-IN-WAITING ARE IN A GROUP,
THE COURIER IS REVIVED AND GETS TO HIS KNEES, 423 MARCOM
WAITING HUMBLY.)
SITTING ALONE IN A GARDEN, BEAUTIFUL AND SAD, 426 MARCOM
APART FROM LIFE, WAITING--
IMAGINE HER WAITING ALL THIS TIME/ 427 MARCOM
WORTH WHILE YOUR WAITING, EH 430 MARCOM
(RESENTFULLY) AH, I'VE BEEN WAITING FOR THAT. 30 MISBEG
I WAS WAITING UNTIL I ARRIVED HERE, KNOWING THAT 45 MISBEG
YOU--
WITH MY MAD OLD FATHER WAITING FOR HIS DINNER. 68 MISBEG
WAITING HOURS FOR HIM DRESSED UP IN YOUR BEST 78 MISBEG
ANYWAY DON'T THINK BECAUSE HE FORGOT YOU WERE 84 MISBEG
WAITING--
YOU MEAN ME DELIBERATELY, KNOWING I'D BE WAITING-- 89 MISBEG
(FIERCELY) GOD DAMN HIM/
WE'D FIND OUR OWN GHOSTS THERE WAITING TO GREET 135 MISBEG
US--
(HE PAUSES, AS IF WAITING FOR HER TO SAY 130 MISBEG
YOU SAW HOW HURT AND ANGRY I WAS BECAUSE HE'D KEPT163 MISBEG
ME WAITING HERE,
TONE WITH HIM, BUT ALL THE TIME WAITING TO SEE HOW166 MISBEG
MUCH HE WILL REMEMBER)
(AS IF THIS WERE SOMETHING HE HAD BEEN WAITING TO 36 POET
HEAR,
WAITING FOR THE LIQUOR TO TAKE EFFECT, 37 POET
AND I'LL HAVE THE HONOR OF WAITING ON TABLE. 59 POET
I AM SURE MRS. HARFORD IS WAITING TO BE TAKEN TO 74 POET
HER SON.
(SHE TURNS TO THE DOOR.) CATO WILL BE PROVOKED AT 86 POET
ME FOR KEEPING HIM WAITING.
AT ONCE INSTEAD OF WAITING UNTIL EVENING. 89 POET
OH, YES, WE WERE WAITING IN THE VALLEY. 97 POET
WHAT ARE YOU WAITING FOR NOWS 103 POET
(COOLLY.) I AM STILL WAITING FOR YOU TO INFORM ME118 POET
WHO YOU ARE
HE KNOWS WELL HOW TORMENTED I'D BE WAITING. 138 POET
HE KEPT WAITING FOR ME AND WHEN I DIDN'T COME, 143 POET
THE WAITING FOR ME AND THE FEAR HE'D HAD MADE HIM144 POET
FORGET ALL HIS SHYNESS,
(STAMMERS.) NO--NOT JAMIE-- (WILDLY.) OH, I 163 POET
CAN'T BEAR WAITING/
(WAITING RESIGNEDLY UNTIL HE HAS FINISHED-- 579 ROPE
WEARILY)
(LUKE RISES TO HIS FEET AND STANDS, WAITING IN A 594 ROPE
DEFENSIVE ATTITUDE,
MOTHER IS WAITING TEA....) 21 STRANG
MOTHER IS WAITING UP... 45 STRANG
MY MOTHER IS WAITING UP FOR ME. 47 STRANG
STRAIN OF WAITING AND HOPING SHE'D GET PREGNANT... 68 STRANG
WHAT'S SHE WAITING FOR..)) 96 STRANG
AND I SEE MY REAL CHANCE, CHARLIE--LYING RIGHT 121 STRANG
AHEAD, WAITING FOR ME TO GRAB IT--
THAT HE'S WAITING FOR SAM TO DIE/... 139 STRANG
YOUR MOTHER AND I ARE WAITING. 193 STRANG
I'VE GOT TO SAY GOOD-BYE--GOT TO FLY BACK BEFORE 195 STRANG
DARK--MADELINE'S WAITING.
MADELINE IS WAITING/ 195 STRANG
STANDING AT THE HEAD OF THE STAIRS WAITING FOR 466 WELDED
ME--
THE WAITING AND HOPING SEEMED EXCESS LABOR. 467 WELDED
I DON'T MIND WAITING. I'M USED TO IT. 467 WELDED

WAKE

WAITING (CONT'D.)
(MOCKINGLY) WAITING FOR YOUS 482 WELDED
WAITRESS
AND WHERE WAS THE WAITRESS. 18 POET
(RESENTFULLY.) SO SHE ASKED FOR THE WAITRESS, DID 18 POET
SHE$
(WITH BITTER SCORN.) WE CAN'T AFFORD A WAITRESS, 23 POET
SLAVING AS A WAITRESS AND CHAMBERMAID 33 POET
I HAVE TRIED TO TEACH THE WAITRESS NOT TO SNATCH 98 POET
PLATES FROM THE TABLE
LIKE A MAN WHO WOULD PERMIT HIS DAUGHTER TO WORK 118 POET
AS A WAITRESS$
WAITS
GET THE HELL OUT OF HERE--AND NO LONG WAITS/ 248 AHWILD
ROBERT WAITS A MOMENT FOR THEM TO GET AHEAD 143 BEYOND
(SINKS DOWN IN THE CHAIR BY THE TABLE AND WAITS 947 DAYS
TENSELY.
(HE WAITS, STARING AT THE CROSS WITH ANGUISHED 565 DAYS
EYES, HIS ARMS OUTSTRETCHED.
ABBIE WAITS, HOLDING HER BREATH AS SHE LISTENS 228 DESIRE
WITH PASSIONATE EAGERNESS FOR
SHE STOPS ROCKING, HER FACE GROWS ANIMATED AND 228 DESIRE
EAGER. SHE WAITS ATTENTIVELY.
WAITS IN AN ATTITUDE OF STRAINED FIXITY. 239 DESIRE
HE WAITS, LOOKING AT THE DOOR, A GRIN OF MALICIOUS434 DYNAMO
EXPECTANCY ON HIS FACE.
(HE WAITS, HIS BODY STRAINED WITH SUSPENSE, 480 DYNAMO
WHEN I KNOWS DE GAMES UP I KISSES IT GOOD-BY 182 EJONES
WIDOUT NO LONG WAITS.
TIME YOU BEAT IT IN DE WOODS WIDOUT NO LONG WAITS.190 EJONES
(HE WAITS--THEN GOES ON INSISTENTLY) 20 ELECTR
(HE WAITS, HIS FACE UPTURNING--PLEADINGLY) 307 GGBROW
THERE'S A LASS WHO FONDLY WAITS PAKING A HOME FOR 211 HA APE
ME----
THE BLEEDIN' STEWARD AS WAITS ON 'EM, 'E TOLD ME 228 HA APE
ABOUT 'ER.
(HE WAITS FOR APPROVING ASSENT FROM THE NIGHT 15 HUGHIE
CLERK.
HE WAITS FOR IT TO DIE AND THEN GOES ON SADLY) 628 ICEMAN
FROM NOW ON, LARRY WAITS, 721 ICEMAN
SHE WAITS RIGIDLY UNTIL HE DISAPPEARS DOWN THE 42 JOURNE
STEPS.
SHE WAITS FRIGHTENEDLY, SEIZED AGAIN BY A NERVOUS 89 JOURNE
PANIC.
(HE WAITS, FORCING HIS FACE INTO A PLEASANTLY 89 JOURNE
PATERNAL EXPRESSION.
MARY WAITS UNTIL SHE HEARS THE PANTRY DOOR CLOSE 106 JOURNE
BEHIND HER.
THEN HE SITS DOWN AGAIN AND WAITS, HIS EYES 169 JOURNE
AVERTED.
(WAITS TO SEE WHAT LAZARUS WILL SAY-- 344 LAZARU
IN THE ROOM, AN EAVESDROPPING SILENCE THAT WAITS, 117 MANSNS
TOWARD--AND THE SILENCE WAITS--HANDS CLAPPED OVER 120 MANSNS
ITS EARS--
THEN COMES BACK TO THE DESK OPPOSITE SIMON AND 148 MANSNS
WAITS FOR ORDERS.)
THE SONG FINISHED, HE WAITS ANXIOUSLY. 355 MARCOM
(HE WAITS, LOOKS AFTER THEM, PICKS UP THE CRUMPLED363 MARCOM
POEM,
(WAITS) NOS 422 MARCOM
IMPATIENTLY HE WAITS FOR HIS CAR, 439 MARCOM
(HE SITS ON THE BOULDER AND WAITS. 111 MISBEG
SARA SITS AT REAR OF THE CENTER TABLE AND WAITS, 81 POET
CREGAN WAITS FOR MELODY.) 104 POET
(SHE WAITS DEFINITELY, AS IF EXPECTING HIM TO LOSE 105 POET
HIS TEMPER AND CURSE HER.
(HE WAITS, HOPING FOR A WORD OF FORGIVENESS. 115 POET
THIS SAME NIGHT, WITH NO LONG WAITS, EITHER/ 598 ROPE
HE WAITS FOR HER TO SPEAK, NOT KNOWING WHAT TO 462 WELDED
THINK.
WAKE
(WORRIEDLY) SHALL I WAKE UP THE FIRST AND FOURTH,543 'ILE
SIRS
(SHOUTING) HEY, DICK WAKE UP/ 193 AHWILD
(HE'LL WAKE HIM UP/ 194 AHWILD
I WAITED FOR HIM TO WAKE UP BUT HE DIDN'T. 268 AHWILD
I'M SORRY, NAT--BUT HE WAS SOUND ASLEEP AND I 268 AHWILD
DIDN'T HAVE THE HEART TO WAKE HIM.
WAKE UP, YOU OLD POETRY BOOKWORM, YOU/ 133 BEYOND
(SPEAKING WITH AN EFFORT) I WON'T WAKE HER. 145 BEYOND
YOU'LL WAKE HER,. 148 BEYOND
WAKE UP/ 151 BEYOND
WHA' DID YUH WANTA WAKE ME UP FURS 483 CARDIF
YOU THINK IT'S BEST TO WAKE HIM TUNIGHTS 562 CROSS
WAKE UP/ 212 DESIRE
HE'D OUGHT T' WAKE UP WITH A GNASHIN' APPETITE, 263 DESIRE
THE SOUND WAY HE'S SLEEPIN'.
HE HAIN'T NEVER GOIN' T' WAKE UP. 263 DESIRE
THEN SOMETHING HAS TO WAKE YOU UP--AND START YOU 469 DYNAMO
THINKING AGAIN.
WHO DARE WAKE UP DE EMPERORS 176 EJONES
I DIDN'T WANT TO WAKE YOU. 59 ELECTR
IF YOU SEE ME FALLING ASLEEP YOU MUST PROMISE TO 119 ELECTR
WAKE ME/
WAKE UP/ 267 GGBROW
WAKE UP/ 278 GGBROW
I'LL WAKE HIM. 300 GGBROW
AND WHEN I WAKE UP, 322 GGBROW
NIGHTS WHEN THE FOAM OF THE WAKE WOULD BE FLAMING 214 HA APE
MID FIRE,
(ANGRILY) I'LL LOIN YOUSE BUMS TO WAKE ME UP/ 245 HA APE
WELL, YOU CAN HELP TO WAKE 'EM. 246 HA APE
I'D WAKE UP THE WHOLE DAMNED CITY/= 17 HUGHIE
OR HE'D WAKE UP EVERY MORNIN' IN A HOSPITAL. 579 ICEMAN
WAKE UP AND NO LUCK. 583 ICEMAN
YOU WAKE ME UP IF YOU HAS TO BAT ME WID A CHAIR, 586 ICEMAN
AND TAPPED AND TAPPED ENOUGH TO WAKE THE DEAD 597 ICEMAN
HEY, WAKE UP, CECIL, YOU PLOODY FOOL/ 599 ICEMAN

WAKE

WAKE (CONT'D.)
HE STIRS ON HIS CHAIR, TRYING TO WAKE UP, 628 ICEMAN
I HOPE HE MAKES OEM WAKE UP. 631 ICEMAN
WAKE UP, COMRADE/ 634 ICEMAN
REMEMBER DAT, OR YOU'LL WAKE UP IN A HOSPITAL-- 636 ICEMAN
TO WAKE THE DEAD. 638 ICEMAN
BECAUSE HE'LL HELP ME WAKE YOU WAKE UP TO 643 ICEMAN
YOURSELF.
HE'S MADE ME WAKE UP TO MYSELF--SEE WHAT A FOOL-- 645 ICEMAN
IT WASN'T NICE TO FACE BUT--
WAKE UP OUR DEMON BOMB-TUSSER, CHUCK. 658 ICEMAN
YES, IT TURNED OUT IT WASN'T A BIRTHDAY FEAST BUT 665 ICEMAN
A WAKE/
HICKEY DONE ME A FAVOR, MAKIN' ME WAKE UP. 698 ICEMAN
I THOUGHT, GOD, IF SHE'D ONLY NEVER WAKE UP, SHE'D715 ICEMAN
NEVER KNOW/
SHE'D NEVER FEEL ANY PAIN, NEVER WAKE UP FROM HER 715 ICEMAN
DREAM.
(ANGRILY) 'COS DRISC HEARD THE FIRST SEND THE 515 INZONE
THIRD BELOW TO WAKE THE SKIPPER
U'YOU WANT TO WAKE THE WHOLE SHIPS 526 INZONE
AND TEN FOGHORNS COULDN'T WAKE YOU. 20 JOURNE
YOU BETTER WAKE UP/ 104 JOURNE
SEND HERALDS TO WAKE THEM/ 362 LAZARU
YOU'D ONLY WAKE THEM. 63 MANSNS
YOU CAN TRUST ME NOT TO WAKE THEM, SIMON. 63 MANSNS
WAKE UP, DEAR. 127 MANSNS
WAKE UP/ 145 MANSNS
WAKE UP FROM YOUR MAD DREAMS, I'M SAYING/ 165 MANSNS
I'M SORRY IF I HURT YOU, BUT I HAD TO WAKE YOU-- 165 MANSNS
MARCO/ WAKE UP/ 369 MARCOM
YOU'LL THINK YOU'RE THE KING OF ENGLAND AT AN 63 MISBEG
IRISH WAKE/
WITH A DAWN THAT WON'T CREEP OVER DIRTY 153 MISBEG
WINDOWPANES BUT WILL WAKE IN THE SKY
(AS IF TO HERSELF) IT'LL BE BEAUTIFUL SOON, AND 1160 MISBEG
CAN WAKE HIM.
DIDN'T I TELL YOU TO SPEAK LOW AND NOT WAKE HIM/ 161 MISBEG
WAKE UP, JIM. 165 MISBEG
WAKE UP, DO YOU HEAR8 165 MISBEG
WILL YOU WAKE UP, FOR GOD'S SAKE/ 166 MISBEG
WAKE UP. 27 POET
WILL YOU NEVER LET YOURSELF WAKE UP--NOT EVEN NOW 51 POET
WHEN YOU'RE SOBER, OR NEARLY8
WAKE UP, PATCH. 103 POET
AND I'LL NEVER WAKE FROM IT. 141 POET
TRYING TO WAKE UP SOMEONE WHO COULD MARRY US. 149 POET
A CANNON WOULDN'T WAKE HIM. 182 POET
YOU COUNTRY JAY'S OUGHTER WAKE UP AND SEE WHAT'S 593 ROPE
GOIN' ON.
GO ON AND WAKE HER UP/... 92 STRANG
(STAMMERING) I HATE TO WAKE YOU UP BUT-- 93 STRANG
YOU MUST NOT WAKE OUR BABY. 133 STRANG
WAKE UP/ 181 STRANG
AN' WAKE THE TWO GELS WHEN YER GOES HUP. 495 VOYAGE
I'LL WAKE YER IF I WANTS YER. 495 VOYAGE
WAKE UP, YE DIVIL, YE. 503 VOYAGE
OFTEN I WAKE UP IN THE NIGHT-- 488 WELDEO
WAKE/
YOU KNOW IT'S TIME FOR HER NAP AND YOU'LL GET HER 119 BEYOND
ALL WAKED UP.
(THEN RESIGNEDLY) WAAL, LET'S GO HELP EBEN A 219 DESIRE
SPELL AN' GIT WAKED UP.

WAKEFULNESS
HE GOADS HIMSELF INTO A BRIGHT-EYED WAKEFULNESS.) 249 AHWILD

WAKEN
IT WAS ONLY A LOVE TAP TO WAKEN YOUR WITS, SO 5 MISBEG
YOU'LL USE THEM.
=AND BABY'S CRIES CAN'T WAKEN HER IN THE BAGGAGE 111 MISBEG
COACH AHEAD.=
=AND BABY'S CRIES CAN'T WAKEN HER IN THE BAGGAGE 150 MISBEG
COACH AHEAD.=

WAKENED
BUT OUR TALKING HERE HAD WAKENED JONATHAN AND I 61 MANSNS
HAD TO GET HIM BACK TO SLEEP.
I DIDN'T WANT HIM WAKENED-- 157 MISBEG

WAKENS
(HALF WAKENS WITHOUT OPENING HIS EYES--MUTTERS) 165 MISBEG

WAKES
'E'S BOUND TO FIND OUT SOON AS 'E WAKES UP. 175 EJONES
THEN ONE DAY SHE WAKES UP AND FINDS SHE'S GOING TO 15 HUGHIE
HAVE A KID.
BUT NONE OF THEM WAKES UP EXCEPT HOPE.) 581 ICEMAN
IN DE OLD DAYS, PEOPLE CALLS ME =NIGGER= WAKES UP 599 ICEMAN
IN DE HOSPITAL.
(HASTILY) I MEAN, WHEN HE WAKES UP. 625 ICEMAN
SCOTTY WAKES UP AND PEERS AT HIM OVER THE SIDE OF 513 INZONE
THE BUNK.
ALL I HOPE NOW IS THAT WHATEVER HAPPENED WAKES HIM150 POET
FROM HIS LIES AND MAD DREAMS
'E WAKES UP ON BOARD OF 'ER. 508 VOYAGE

WAKING
I WAS A LAD ONLY, AND SHE TOLD ME TO KEEP IT BY ME 75 ANNA
IF I'D BE WAKING OR SLEEPING
ABOUT WAKING UP TO FIND HIM GROANING AND DOUBLED 70 ELECTR
WITH PAIN CONFIRMED IT.
GLAD TO KNOW YOU PEOPLE ARE WAKING UP AT LAST. 246 HA APE
JOE MOTT, THE NEGRO, HAS BEEN WAKING UP.) 583 ICEMAN
FOR FEAR OF WAKING HIM, IS BECOMING TOO MUCH FOR 197 MISBEG
HER.
(IRRITABLY) WHAT'S THE BIG IDEA, WAKING ME UPS 165 MISBEG

WALDO
THAT WALDO EMERSON COMPOSED IT DURING HIS 596 ICEMAN
UNINFORMATIVE PERIOD AS A MINISTER.

WALDORF
WHAT'S SHE TINK DIS IS, DE WALDORFS 670 ICEMAN

WALES

BE THE AIRS 'E PUTS ON YOU'D THINK 'E WAS THE 517 INZONE
PRINCE OF WALES.

WALK
LOOK WHO'S COMING UP THE WALK--OLD MAN MCCUMBER/ 199 AHWILD
AND HE HAD TO WALK HOME. 251 AHWILD
THAT'D BE THE TIME IT'D TAKE HIM TO WALK FROM THE 260 AHWILD
BEACH
(TACEFULLY) I THINK I'LL GO FOR A WALK, TOO. 264 AHWILD
GO OUT AND PLAY IN THE YARD, OR TAKE A WALK, AND 264 AHWILD
GET SOME FRESH AIR.
=NAY, LET US WALK FROM FIRE UNTO FIRE FROM 276 AHWILD
PASSIONATE PAIN TO DEADLIER DELIGHT--
GUESS I'LL TAKE A WALK DOWN TO THE END OF THE DOCK 44 ANNA
FOR A MINUTE AND SEE WHAT'S
I SUPPOSE IT'S NATURAL TO BE CROSS WHEN YOU'RE NOT 87 BEYOND
ABLE TO WALK A STEP.
LITTLE MARY, I'D CHUCK EVERYTHING UP AND WALK DOWN126 BEYOND
THE ROAD
AND WALK SLOWLY INTO THE BEDROOM.) 128 BEYOND
ONE WALK DOWN ONE OF THEIR FILTHY NARROW STREETS 132 BEYOND
WITH THE TROPIC SUN BEATING ON
WALK DOWN WITH ME TO THE HOUSE AND YOU CAN TELL ME142 BEYOND
MORE
(THEY WALK QUICKLY--ALMOST RUN--OFF TO THE LEFT. 473 CARIBE
I SIMPLY WENT FOR A WALK. 549 DAYS
WE KIN WALK. 207 DESIRE
MY FEET FEEL ITCHIN' T' WALK AN' WALK--AN' JUMP 220 DESIRE
HIGH OVER THIN'S--AN'....
HE SCOWLS, STRIDES OFF THE PORCH TO THE PATH AND 228 DESIRE
STARTS TO WALK PAST HER
(HE STARTS TO WALK AWAY.) 229 DESIRE
(HE LAUGHS AND AGAIN STARTS TO WALK AWAY.) 230 DESIRE
JACK COMES UP THE WALK TO THE SCREEN DOOR. 498 DIFRNT
YOU WON'T FIND A MAN IN A DAY'S WALK IS ANY 510 DIFRNT
BETTER'N CALEB--OR AS GOOD.
WHY DON'T WE WALK THE SAME AS-- 433 DYNAMO
WHY COULDN'T WE HAVE GONE FOR A WALKS... 444 DYNAMO
(I THOUGHT I'D WALK AROUND AND THINK UP SOME 444 DYNAMO
LIE...
LET'S TAKE A WALK TONIGHT. 460 DYNAMO
WE'LL WALK OUT TO THE TOP OF LONG HILL. 460 DYNAMO
I'LL GO FOR A WALK.... 472 DYNAMO
HE STARTS TO WALK HESITATINGLY OFF RIGHT-- 478 DYNAMO
I DOES DAT SO'S I KIN TAKE A WALK IN PEACE 179 EJONES
(THEY WALK BACK AROUND THE LEFT OF THE HOUSE AND 11 ELECTR
DISAPPEAR.
THERE'S SOMETHIN' ABOUT HIS WALK CALLS BACK DAVID 20 ELECTR
MANNING, TOO.
NO TIME FOR A WALK, IF YOU ASK ME. 56 ELECTR
I THOUGHT I'D WALK A LITTLE. 56 ELECTR
MRS. BORDEN AND MRS. HILLS WALK TOGETHER 68 ELECTR
I'LL WALK TO THE END OF THE WHARF WITH YOU. 113 ELECTR
THE LONG WALK WE TOOK WITH HAZEL DID YOU GOOD. 151 ELECTR
YOU KNOW VERY WELL SHE HAS TO FORCE HIM TO WALK 158 ELECTR
WITH YOU.
THEY WALK ARM IN ARM, THE MOTHER BETWEEN. 257 GGBROW
(HURRIEDLY) NO,--HE WENT OUT FOR A LONG WALK. 277 GGBROW
(LET'S TAKE A WALK. 280 GGBROW
TOO FAT NOW TO LEARN TO WALK, LET ALONE TO DANCE 296 GGBROW
OR RUN.
THEY WALK TO THE DOOR. 301 GGBROW
WALK) 234 HA APE
(THEY BOTH WALK BACK AND STAND LOOKING IN THE 235 HA APE
JEWELER'S.
I'D RUN YOU IN BUT IT'S TOO LONG A WALK TO THE 251 HA APE
STATION.
I'LL TAKE YOU FOR A WALK DOWN FIF' AVENOO. 254 HA APE
OH SOME GUYS IN UNIFORM WILL WALK IN HERE WITH A 33 HUGHIE
BUTTERFLY NET AND CATCH YOU.
TAKE A WALK AROUND THE WARD, SEE ALL THE FRIENDS 1604 ICEMAN
USED TO KNOW.
SHOW YOU A LITTLE WALK AROUND THE WARD IS NOTHING 621 ICEMAN
TO BE SO SCARED ABOUT.
THAT WALK AROUND THE WARD YOU NEVER TAKE-- 622 ICEMAN
THAT LONG WALK IS BEGINNING TO GET ME. 625 ICEMAN
(WITH AN AIR OF FRANKNESS) YES, AND I OUGHT TO 626 ICEMAN
TAKE A WALK AROUND THE WARD.
YOU COULD WALK ON 'EM FROM HERE TO TEXAS/ 632 ICEMAN
IF HE GETS HIM TO TAKE THAT WALK TOMORROW. 651 ICEMAN
WE'VE HEARD HARRY PULL THAT BLUFF ABOUT TAKING A 652 ICEMAN
WALK EVERY BIRTHDAY
WE'VE HEARD HIS BULL ABOUT TAKING A WALK AROUND 660 ICEMAN
THE WARD FOR YEARS.
THERE IS A DESPERATE BLUFF IN THEIR MANNER AS THEY683 ICEMAN
WALK IN.
I'VE ALWAYS BEEN GOING TO TAKE THIS WALK, AIN'T 687 ICEMAN
I?
TOO DAMNED HOT FOR A WALK, THOUGH, IF YOU ASK ME. 687 ICEMAN
(EGGING HIMSELF ON) I'LL TAKE A GOOD LONG WALK 687 ICEMAN
NOW, I'VE STARTED.
BEJEES, IT AIN'T SAFE TO WALK IN THE STREETS/ 690 ICEMAN
LOOK AT ME PRETENDING TO START FOR A WALK JUST TO 721 ICEMAN
KEEP HIM QUIET.
YESTERDAY WHEN I WENT FOR A WALK I DROPPED IN AT 22 JOURNE
THE INN--
I WON'T WALK OUT IN THIS HEAT AND GET SUNSTROKE. 53 JOURNE
I WAS HALFWAY UP THE WALK WHEN CATHLEEN BURST INTO 54 JOURNE
SONG.
I'D RATHER WALK ANY DAY, OR TAKE A TROLLEY. 84 JOURNE
LOVE HIM DEARLY, FOR ANY FOOL CAN SEE HE WORSHIPS 101 JOURNE
THE GROUND YOU WALK ON.
SHE IS UNCERTAIN IN HER WALK AND GRINNING 122 JOURNE
WOOZILY.)
(STARTS TO WALK AWAY--BLANKLY.) 123 JOURNE
IT'S NOT A NIGHT I'D PICK FOR A LONG WALK. 130 JOURNE
FROM THE GRAVE TO WALK AGAIN WITH A DEVIL INSIDE 285 LAZARU
HIM/

1762

1763

WALK

WALK (CONT'D.)
I WALK WITH THE KING IN THE GARDENS--HE WHISPERS 4 MANSNS
TENDERLY.
(BEWILDEREDLY.) BUT WHY DON'T WE WALK TOGETHER AS 17 MANSNS
FAR AS THE ROADS
THE PALACE AT VERSAILLES--THE KING AND I WALK IN 22 MANSNS
THE MOONLIT GARDENS--
ON THE EDGE OF A NARROW BRICK-PAVED WALK WHICH 25 MANSNS
SURROUNDS A LITTLE OVAL POOL.
AND MAKES HER WALK OFF BESIDE HIM UP THE PATH TO 117 MANSNS
THE HOUSE.)
(SHE STARTS TO WALK AWAY.) 189 MANSNS
WALK TO THE FOOT OF THE THRONE AND KNEEL BEFORE 378 MARCOM
THE KAAN.
I WALK ALONG THE PATH IN WHICH WEEDS HAVE GROWN. 384 MARCOM
TWO PACES BEHIND, SIDE BY SIDE, WALK MAFFEO AND 402 MARCOM
NICOLO.
AS I WAS SAYING, MY THROAT IS PARCHED AFTER THE 44 MISBEG
LONG DUSTY WALK I TOOK JUST FOR
WALK BACK TO THE INN, THEN, AND GIVE IT A GOOD 46 MISBEG
STRAIN.
AND WE WALK IN, AND THERE'S THE TWO OF YOU IN BED, 94 MISBEG
YOU'LL WALK DOWN TO THE INN WITH ME AND HIDE 96 MISBEG
OUTSIDE UNTIL YOU SEE ME COME OUT
YOU OUGHT TO APPRECIATE HIM BECAUSE HE WORSHIPS 124 MISBEG
THE GROUND YOU WALK ON--
I SAID YOU WAS OUT FOR A WALK, AND THE TAVERN 18 POET
WASN'T OPEN YET, ANYWAY.
THE DRIVE IN THE HOT SUN AND THE WALK THROUGH THE 19 POET
WOODS FOR NOTHING.
YOU'D WALK IN THER GLADLY TO BE WITH HIM, AND SING 25 POET
WITH JOY AT YOUR OWN BURNIN',
I'LL TAKE A WALK TO THE STORE AND HAVE A TALK WITH 28 POET
NEELAN.
YES, I DID FIND MY WALK ALONE IN THE WOODS A 86 POET
STRANGELY OVERPOWERING EXPERIENCE.
AND MAKES HIMSELF WALK ABOUT THE ROOM) 5 STRANG
GLAD OF THE CHANCE FOR A WALK. 34 STRANG

WALKED

HE'S AS GOOD AN OLD GUY AS EVER WALKED ON TWO 17 ANNA
FEET.
I WALKED OVER IT THIS MORNING WITH RUTH--AND SHE 133 BEYOND
TOLD ME ABOUT THINGS--
AND SHOOK HIS HEAD, WALKED OUT WIDOUT SAYIN' A480 CARDIF
WORD.
HE FINDS HE HAS WALKED IN A CIRCLE AND IS STANDING544 DAYS
BEFORE THE OLD CHURCH.
YEW WAS T' PUT ALL THE STEPS WE'VE WALKED ON THIS 208 DESIRE
FARM END T' END
AS YOU WALKED BESIDE ME THAT NIGHT WITH YOUR HAIR 24 ELECTR
BLOWING IN THE SEA WIND AND
SO I BEGAN TO LAUGH AND WALKED TOWARD THEIR LINES 95 ELECTR
WITH MY HAND OUT.
WALKING'S BEJEES, DO YOU MEAN TO SAY YOU WALKED6 621 ICEMAN
THAT'S WHY YOU FINALLY WALKED OUT ON HER, ISN'T 647 ICEMAN
IT$
AS IF A FLY HAD WALKED ACROSS HER MIND. 107 JOURNE
I WALKED OUT TO THE BEACH. 129 JOURNE
(THEY DRINK.) IF YOU WALKED ALL THE WAY TO THE 130 JOURNE
BEACH
(HE HAS WALKED TOWARD LAZARUS.) 317 LAZARU
(HE HAS WALKED TOWARD THE THRONE WHILE HE IS 339 LAZARU
SPEAKING.
SHE TOOK SUCH STRICT CARE OF HER OWN, SHE WALKED 100 STRANG
MILES EVERY DAY,

WALKER

FOR SHE'S NO BETTER THAN A STREET WALKER/ 450 DYNAMO
HE MOVES WITH A STRANGE DELIBERATION LIKE A SLEEP-200 EJONES
WALKER OR ONE IN A TRANCE.
(DESCENDING THE STEPS LIKE A SLEEP-WALKER) 366 LAZARU
THE TWO GIRLS, NEITHER MUCH OVER TWENTY, ARE 611 ICEMAN
TYPICAL DOLLAR STREET WALKERS,

WALKIN'

YE MUST LIKE WALKIN'. 213 DESIRE
(THEN SLOWLY) WALKIN' THAR, FUST I FELT 'S IF I'D214 DESIRE
KISS HER.
(WITH A WINK) MEBBE HE'S DOIN' THE DUTIFUL AN' 248 DESIRE
WALKIN' THE KID T' SLEEP.
YE'RE WALKIN' LIKE A BRIDE DOWN THE AISLE, SARAH/ 250 DESIRE
OR MAYBE WORSE, WID YOUR WIFE AND DE ICEMAN 636 ICEMAN
WALKIN' SLOW BEHIND YUH.--
ALL DE WAY WALKIN' TO DE FERRY, 697 ICEMAN
AND I DON'T WANT HIM WALKIN' IN THE MIDDLE OF 518 INZONE
IT.
HE SAID YOU WAS TO KEEP STILL AND NOT GO A-WALKIN'579 ROPE
ROUND.
THEY'LL BE WALKIN' IN IN ARF A MO'. 495 VOYAGE
I BEEN WALKIN' MILES. 471 WELDED

WALKING

THE SILENCE IS UNBROKEN EXCEPT FOR THE MEASURED 535 'ILE
TREAD OF SOMEONE WALKING UP AND
OR I'LL CALL SULLIVAN FROM THE CORNER AND HAVE YOU248 AHWILD
RUN IN FOR STREET-WALKING/
I WAS WALKING PAST HER PLACE JUST NOW WHEN I SAW 273 AHWILD
HER WAVING FROM HER PARLOR
OUT WALKING WITH HER LATEST. 292 AHWILD
I THINK SHE'D GIVE YOU YOUR WALKING PAPERS FOR 294 AHWILD
KEEPS.
IN THROUGH THE SCREEN DOOR. WALKING TOGETHER 298 AHWILD
TOWARD THE FRONT PARLOR
(WALKING UP AND DOWN--DISTRACTEDLY) 70 ANNA
AND YOU CAN HAVE ALL THE SEA YOU WANT BY WALKING A 85 BEYOND
MILE DOWN TO THE BEACH.
(WALKING TOWARD HIM--TRUCULENTLY) 461 CARIBE
(WALKING SLOWLY TOWARD THE TABLE) 556 CROSS
THEY SEE HIM UP THERE WALKING BACK AND FORTH-- 564 CROSS
WAVING HIS ARMS AGAINST THE SKY.

WALKS

WALKING (CONT'D.)
(STARES AFTER HER FOR A WHILE, WALKING TOWARD THE 241 DESIRE
DOOR.
CABOT APPEARS, RETURNING FROM THE BARN, WALKING 253 DESIRE
WEARILY, HIS EYES ON THE GROUND.
WALKING HAND IN HAND TO THE GATE. 269 DESIRE
I'M SICK OF WALKING. 493 DYNAMO
AND STARTS WALKING OFF LEFT--WITH BITTER DEFIANCE)453 DYNAMO
JONES ENTERS FROM THE LEFT, WALKING RAPIDLY. 187 EJONES
HOPE YOU DON'T MIND MY WALKING IN ON YOU WITHOUT 21 ELECTR
CEREMONY.
THAT NIGHT WE WENT WALKING IN THE MOONLIGHT, DU 21 ELECTR
YOU REMEMBER$
HAVE YOU FORGOTTEN THAT NIGHT WALKING ALONG THE 23 ELECTR
SHORES
SHE EVEN WENT WALKING IN THE MOONLIGHT WITH HIM/ 50 ELECTR
I ONLY WENT WALKING ONCE WITH HIM--AND THAT WAS 50 ELECTR
BEFORE--
CHRISTINE IS DISCOVERED WALKING BACK AND FORTH ON 117 ELECTR
THE DRIVE BEFORE THE PORTICO.
SETH APPEARS WALKING SLOWLY UP THE DRIVE FROM 169 ELECTR
RIGHT, FRONT.
FOLLOWING THEM, AS IF HE WERE A STRANGER, WALKING 259 GGBROW
ALONE, IS THEIR SON, DION.
(SHE IS WALKING TOWARD THE END OF THE DOCK, OFF 264 GGBROW
LEFT.)
WALKING'S BEJEES, DO YOU MEAN TO SAY YOU WALKED6 621 ICEMAN
ALL THE TIME I WAS WALKING OVER HERE-- 621 ICEMAN
(AS THEY START WALKING TOWARD REAR--INSISTENTLY) 714 ICEMAN
IT WAS LIKE WALKING ON THE BOTTOM OF THE SEA. 131 JOURNE
WALKING WITH CALIGULA IS CNEIUS CRASSUS, A ROMAN 299 LAZARU
GENERAL--
WALKING UNDER AN ARM OF THE CROSS UNCONCERNEDLY 327 LAZARU
WITHOUT AN UPWARD GLANCE.
IT'S LIKE WALKING A TIGHT-ROPE OVER AN ABYSS-- 156 MANSNS
THE PROSTITUTE, WALKING AWAY, CALLS BACK OVER HIS 375 MARCOM
SHOULDER.
WALKING WITH BURSTING SELF-IMPORTANCE BETWEEN THE 428 MARCOM
FILES OF MUSICIANS.
THAT'S BECAUSE I SOON GET TIRED OF ANY MAN AND 20 MISBEG
GIVE HIM HIS WALKING PAPERS.
LIKE A DEAD MAN WALKING SLOW BEHIND HIS OWN 35 MISBEG
COFFIN.
ONE BIG DRINK, AT LEAST, WHENEVER I STRAIN MY 46 MISBEG
HEART WALKING IN THE HOT SUN.
YOU MUST BE PARCHED AFTER WALKING FROM THE ROAD TO 85 POET
SIMON'S CABIN AND BACK ON
AND THE TWO OF US WOULD BE WALKING AROUND IN THE 149 POET
NIGHT,
(AFTER STARING AT HIM FOR A MOMENT--WALKING AWAY 174 STRANG
FROM HIM--

WALKS

HE JUST WALKS UP AND DOWN LIKE HE DIUN'T NOTICE 536 'ILE
NOBODY--
THE SECOND MATE WALKS SLOWLY OVER TO THE CAPTAIN.1539 'ILE
(SHE TURNS AWAY FROM THEM AND WALKS SLOWLY TO THE 540 'ILE
BENCH ON LEFT.
THEN WALKS SLOWLY TO HER SIDE.) 545 'ILE
(HE TURNS AWAY FROM HER SILENTLY AND WALKS TOWARD 550 'ILE
THE COMPANIONWAY.--
HE WALKS LIKE ONE IN A TRANCE, HIS EYES SHINING 292 AHWILD
WITH A DREAMY HAPPINESS.
HE WALKS WITH A CLUMSY, ROLLING GAIT. 5 ANNA
AND WALKS UNSTEADILY INTO BACK ROOM SINGING) 12 ANNA
THEN HE FORCES HIMSELF TO A BOLD DECISION, PUSHES 20 ANNA
OPEN THE DOOR AND WALKS IN.
(WALKS OVER TO HER SOLICITOUSLY) 25 ANNA
(WALKS AWAY FROM HER TOWARD THE CABIN--THEN COMES 26 ANNA
BACK)
ANNA WALKS BACK TOWARD THE EXTREME STERN 30 ANNA
SHE WALKS TO THE DOORWAY IN REAR--STANDS WITH HER 52 ANNA
BACK TOWARD THEM, LOOKING OUT.
SHE SPRINGS TO HER FEET AND WALKS ABOUT THE CABIN 67 ANNA
DISTRACTEDLY.
(HE WALKS STRAIGHT FOR HER.) 69 ANNA
(HE WALKS OFF DOWN THE ROAD TO THE LEFT. 86 BEYOND
(FINALLY HE GETS UP WITH A SHEEPISH GRIN AND WALKS101 BEYOND
OVER TO ROBERT)
ROBERT WALKS UP THE PATH AND OPENS THE SCREEN DOOR119 BEYOND
QUIETLY
(SHE WALKS AWAY INTO THE KITCHEN.) 121 BEYOND
(HE OPENS THE DOOR AND WALKS OUT AS THE CURTAIN 129 BEYOND
FALLS.)
(HE WALKS OVER AND SITS DOWN ON THE BOULDER BESIDE130 BEYOND
ROBERT
(SHE WALKS TOWARD THE ROCK AND ADDRESSES ROBERT 135 BEYOND
COLDLY)
(STANDS STARING AT HER FOR A MOMENT--THEN WALKS 140 BEYOND
AWAY SAYING IN A HURT TONE)
MARY WALKS BACKWARD TOWARD ROBERT, HER WONDERING 142 BEYOND
EYES FIXED ON HER MOTHER.)
(SHE WALKS OUT LEFT, HER EYES FIXED ON THE GROUND,143 BEYOND
(HE WALKS WEAKLY TO A ROCKER BY THE SIDE OF THE 145 BEYOND
TABLE
(HE WALKS TO HER CHAIR AND BENDS DOWN TO KISS HER 150 BEYOND
SMILINGLY)
(SHE SIGHS AND WALKS TO THE WINDOW IN THE REAR, 152 BEYOND
LEFT.
(HE SPRINGS FROM HIS CHAIR AND WALKS TO THE 163 BEYOND
STOVE.)
(SHE GETS WEARILY TO HER FEET AND WALKS SLOWLY 166 BEYOND
TOWARD THE BEDROOM)
(HE GETS WEARILY TO HIS FEET AND WALKS WITH BOWED 473 CARIBE
SHOULDERS, STAGGERING A BIT,
(HE WALKS OVER TO THEM) GO TO THE CABIN AND GET 473 CARIBE
YOUR MONEY AND CLEAR OFF.
YOU SAY HE ONLY WALKS AT NIGHT--UP THERE$ 557 CROSS
HE ONLY WALKS TO AND FRO--WATCHING-- 562 CROSS

WALKS

WALKS (CONT'D.)
SHE RISES SLOWLY TO HER FEET AND WALKS SLOWLY AND 541 DAYS
WOODENLY BACK PAST HIM AND
OUT--IN THE HOPE THAT IF HE WALKS HIMSELF INTO 544 DAYS
EXHAUSTION,
HE WALKS OUT OF THE CHURCH--WITHOUT LOVE FOREVER 545 DAYS
NOW--
SHE OVERCOMES HER WEAKNESS AND WALKS WOODENLY INTO551 DAYS
HER BEDROOM
(HE TURNS AND WALKS QUICKLY OFF LEFT, REAR, TOWARD217 DESIRE
THE BARN.
(WALKS UP TO HIM--A QUEER COARSE EXPRESSION OF 226 DESIRE
DESIRE IN HER FACE AND BODY--
AND EBEN COMES OUT AND WALKS AROUND TO THE GATE. 244 DESIRE
CABOT WALKS SLOWLY UP FROM THE LEFT, STARING UP AT245 DESIRE
THE SKY WITH A VAGUE FACE.)
(HE WALKS TO THE PORCH--THEN TURNS WITH A GREAT 256 DESIRE
GRIN)
(COMES IN AND WALKS DOWN BESIDE HER CHAIR. 514 DIFFNT
(SHE WALKS TOWARD THE GAP IN THE HEDGE.) 433 DYNAMO
(SHE TURNS HER BACK ON HIM AND WALKS AWAY.) 433 DYNAMO
(HE WALKS TOWARD THE DOOR ON RIGHT.) 443 DYNAMO
(HE WALKS SLOWLY OVER TO WHERE HE HAD STOOD WITH 444 DYNAMO
ADA--DULLY)
(WALKS TOWARD HIM) HOLD YOUR TONGUE/ 448 DYNAMO
(ABRUPTLY HE PUTS DOWN HIS BOOKS AND WALKS UP TO 458 DYNAMO
MRS. FIFE.
(WALKS TOWARD HER, THE SMILE FROZEN ON HIS LIPS, 459 DYNAMO
HIS EYES FIXED ON HERS)
(WITH A SWAGGER AND A COLD SMILE ON HIS LIPS HE 459 DYNAMO
WALKS THROUGH THE GAP JUST AS
(HE WALKS TO THE HEDGE AND THEN, STEALTHILY, 462 DYNAMO
AND A MOMENT LATER WALKS PAST THE FRONT OF THE 467 DYNAMO
HOUSE FROM THE RIGHT.
(HE TURNS HIS BACK ON HER ABRUPTLY AND WALKS OFF 468 DYNAMO
LEFT.
AND WALKS OFF RIGHT TOWARD THE FRONT DOOR OF HIS 470 DYNAMO
HOUSE.)
(HE WALKS AROUND NERVOUSLY) NO USE TRYING TO GO 472 DYNAMO
TO SLEEP--
(HE WALKS SLOWLY OFF RIGHT.) 476 DYNAMO
HE NOW WALKS DELIBERATELY BACK THROUGH THE DOOR TO487 DYNAMO
THE OIL SWITCH GALLERY.
(AS JONES WALKS TOWARD THE DOOR IN REAR-- 186 EJONES
CAUTIONINGLY)
(HE WALKS QUICKLY INTO THE CLEAR SPACE--THEN 192 EJONES
STANDS TRANSFIXED AS HE SEES JEFF--
THE GUARD TURNS HIS BACK ON HIM AND WALKS AWAY 194 EJONES
CONTEMPTUOUSLY.
WALKS OFF TOWARD THE FLOWER GARDEN, 9 ELECTR
(SHE GETS UP AND WALKS TOWARD RIGHT TO CONCEAL HER 15 ELECTR
AGITATION.
(SHE WALKS UP THE STEPS.) 18 ELECTR
(HE WALKS AROUND THE LEFT CORNER OF THE HOUSE. 20 ELECTR
(SHE TURNS HER BACK ON HIM AND WALKS TO THE STEPS 27 ELECTR
TURNS AND WALKS QUICKLY FROM THE ROOM AND CLOSES 42 ELECTR
THE DOOR BEHIND HER.)
HE WALKS UP BY THE LILACS STARTING THE NEXT LINE 43 ELECTR
--"OH, SHENANDOAH--"
(SHE WALKS UP THE STEPS AGAIN.) 45 ELECTR
THEN WALKS STIFFLY DOWN THE STEPS AND STANDS 57 ELECTR
AGAIN.
CLOSING IT BEHIND HER, AND WALKS TO THE HEAD OF 77 ELECTR
THE STEPS.
WALKS SLOWLY AND WOODENLY OFF LEFT BETWEEN THE 78 ELECTR
LILAC CLUMP AND THE HOUSE.
AND WALKS WITH JERKY STEPS FROM THE ROOM LIKE SOME 92 ELECTR
TRAGIC MECHANICAL DOLL.
TURNS, RIGID AND SQUARE-SHOULDERED, AND WALKS 101 ELECTR
WOODENLY FROM THE ROOM.)
(SHE WALKS DOWN THE DRIVE, OFF LEFT, WAVING HER 119 ELECTR
HAND AS SHE DISAPPEARS.
(HE WALKS MECHANICALLY UP THE STEPS--GAZING UP AT 122 ELECTR
THE HOUSE--STRANGELY)
(SHE WALKS UP THE STEPS TO THE PORTICO. 137 ELECTR
SHE WALKS TO THE CLUMP OF LILACS AND STANDS THERE 137 ELECTR
STARING AT THE HOUSE.)
HE WALKS LIKE AN AUTOMATON. 138 ELECTR
AND WALKS TO THE FOOT OF THE STEPS.) 171 ELECTR
HE WALKS SLOWLY, HIS EYES ON THE GROUND-- 174 ELECTR
AND BILLY BROWN WALKS ALONG FROM RIGHT WITH HIS 257 GGBROWN
MOTHER AND FATHER.
HE WALKS QUICKLY TO THE BENCH AT CENTER AND THROWS264 GGBROWN
HIMSELF ON IT.
(SHAKES HIS HAND OFF HIS SHOULDER AND WALKS AWAY 282 GGBROWN
FROM HIM--AFTER A PAUSE)
(JUMPS TO HIS FEET AND WALKS ABOUT EXCITEDLY) 286 GGBROWN
(SHE WALKS AWAY. 290 GGBROWN
(SHE SLAPS HER AUNT INSULTINGLY ACROSS THE FACE 222 HA APE
AND WALKS OFF, LAUGHING GAILY.)
YANK WALKS UP TO THE GORILLA'S 251 HA APE
HE WALKS TO THE DESK WITH A BREEZY, FAMILIAR AIR, 8 HUGHIE
(SMILING AMIABLY) AS FOR YOU, MY BALMY BOER THAT 599 ICEMAN
WALKS LIKE A MAN,
HE WALKS WITH A TOUGH, 636 ICEMAN
(HE PICKS UP HIS DRINK AND WALKS LEFT AS FAR AWAY 637 ICEMAN
FROM THEM AS HE CAN GET AND
(HE WALKS STIFFLY TO THE STREET DOOR--THEN TURNS 673 ICEMAN
FOR A PARTING SHOT--BOASTFULLY)
IT WAS ONE OF THOSE RARE OCCASIONS WHEN THE BOER 676 ICEMAN
THAT WALKS LIKE A MAN--
(MORAN WALKS UP BEHIND HIM ON ONE SIDE, WHILE THE 717 ICEMAN
SECOND DETECTIVE, LIEB,
(HE WALKS TO THE DOOR WITH A CARELESS SWAGGER AND 721 ICEMAN
DISAPPEARS IN THE HALL.
BUT MY OLD BATTLEFIELD COMPANION, THE BOER THAT 723 ICEMAN

WALKS (CONT'D.)
HE SIGHS WITH A PUZZLED EXPRESSION AND GETS UP AND523 INZONE
WALKS OUT OF THE DOORWAY.
HE WALKS LIKE AN OLD MAN. 69 JOURNE
(HE WALKS AWAY FROM HER TO POUR HIMSELF A BIG 69 JOURNE
DRINK.)
(HE WALKS SLOWLY TO WHERE SHE STANDS IN THE 69 JOURNE
DOORWAY.
HE WALKS WEARILY OFF THROUGH THE BACK PARLOR 125 JOURNE
TOWARD THE DINING ROOM.)
(HE WALKS DOWN THE NARROW STAIRS AND, MIRIAM 293 LAZARU
FOLLOWING HIM,
CALIGULA WALKS BEHIND, HIS DRAWN SWORD IN HIS 326 LAZARU
HAND.
WALKS IN A DEEP, DETACHED SERENITY. 327 LAZARU
(WALKS UP THE STEPS TO THE CROSS AND, STRETCHING 329 LAZARU
TO HIS FULL HEIGHT,
(HE WALKS AWAY TO LEFT.) 329 LAZARU
(HE WALKS TO THE DARKNESS AT RIGHT.) 332 LAZARU
(HE TURNS AWAY FROM HIM AND WALKS, LAUGHING, 333 LAZARU
TOWARD THE ARCH IN REAR.
HE WALKS INTO THE BLACK ARCHWAY OF THE DARKENED 335 LAZARU
PALACE.
IN THE SILENCE THAT ENSUES POMPEIA GETS UP AND 341 LAZARU
WALKS OVER TO THE DAIS.
(WALKS TO THE DAIS WHICH SHE ASCENDS SLOWLY UNTIL 342 LAZARU
SHE STANDS BY CAESAR'S COUCH.
(HE WALKS DOWN AND STARTS TO GO OFF, RIGHT--THEN 356 LAZARU
TURNS AND ADDRESSES LAZARUS
HE WALKS AROUND THE DAIS AND CARRIES THE BODY OUT 362 LAZARU
THROUGH THE DOORWAY IN REAR.
(HE WALKS BACK TO HIS DESK.) 94 MANSNS
NO ONE---EXCEPT LIFE, PERHAPS, WHO WALKS AWAY AGAIN162 MANSNS
NOW--
(WALKS SULLENLY OFF TO LEFT. 370 MARCOM
(SHE WALKS OFF LEFT.) 371 MARCOM
(HE WALKS AWAY AND MAKES THE CIRCUIT OF THE 374 MARCOM
FIGURES,
HE WALKS DIRECTLY UP TO THE POLOS AND BOWS 376 MARCOM
DEEPLY.)
(SHE BOWS WITH A PROUD HUMILITY AND WALKS OFF 388 MARCOM
LEFT.
EACH WALKS WITH BENT HEAD READING ALOUD TO HIMSELF434 MARCOM
FROM HIS HOLY BOOK.
AND WALKS IN THE CROWD WITHOUT SELF-CONSCIOUSNESS,439 MARCOM
VERY MUCH AS ONE OF THEM.
(WALKS TOWARD HOGAN--STIFFLY) 56 MISBEG
(HE TURNS AWAY AND WALKS QUICKLY DOWN THE ROAD OFF174 MISBEG
LEFT WITHOUT LOOKING BACK.
THAT'S SINCE YOU BEGAN TO TAKE LONG WALKS BY THE 29 POET
LAKE.
(LAUGHING.) WELL, WHY SHOULDN'T I TAKE WALKS ON 30 POET
OUR OWN PROPERTY?
SHE WALKS PAST SARA INTO THE STREET, TURNS LEFT, 86 POET
AND,
AND YOUR WALKS IN THE WOODS WITH HIM. 108 POET
HE WALKS DAZEDLY TO HIS CHAIR AT THE HEAD OF THE 152 POET
CENTER TABLE.
(HE WALKS A BIT UNSTEADILY OUT THE DOOR AT LEFT 162 POET
FRONT.)
(HE LAUGHS AND WALKS OVER TO ANNIE) 588 ROPE
(HE WALKS OUT AND STANDS, LEANING HIS BACK AGAINST589 ROPE
THE DOORWAY, LEFT.
(SHE TURNS AND WALKS OUT BRISKLY.) 28 STRANG
LIGHTING HIS ALREADY LIGHTED PIPE, WALKS UP AND 67 STRANG
DOWN AGAIN.
(HE JUMPS TO HIS FEET AGAIN--WALKS UP AND DOWN 68 STRANG
AGAIN DISTRACTEDLY)
WALKS SLOWLY AND WOODENLY LIKE A MAN IN A TRANCE 98 STRANG
INTO THE ROOM.
HE WALKS ABOUT. 102 STRANG
(SHE TURNS AND WALKS QUIETLY OUT OF THE ROOM. 136 STRANG
(HE TURNS HIS BACK ON MARSDEN WITH A GLANCE OF 148 STRANG
REPULSION AND WALKS TO THE WINDOW
(HE WALKS UP DEFIANTLY AND CONFRONTS DARRELL WHO 150 STRANG
TURNS TO HIM IN SURPRISE)
(WALKS A BIT UNCERTAINLY TO NINA'S CHAIR) 175 STRANG
HE TURNS AWAY AND WALKS TO THE TABLE. 190 STRANG
(HE WALKS OFF, RIGHT, AND ENTERS THE HOUSE.) 199 STRANG
(HE WALKS TOWARD HIS BAG-- 445 WELDED
FINALLY, MAKING AN EFFORT OF WILL, SHE WALKS BACK 451 WELDED
TO THE TABLE,
(HE WALKS STILL FURTHER AWAY, THEN TURNS TO WATCH 465 WELDED
HER.
SHE WALKS THROUGH THE DOORWAY.) 466 WELDED
SHE WALKS TO HER CHAIR AND SITS DOWN. 480 WELDED
SMILES TO HERSELF AND WALKS BACK TO THE FOOT OF 487 WELDED
THE STAIRWAY.

WALL

IS PLACED AGAINST THE WALL. 535 'ILE
A LONG BENCH WITH ROUGH CUSHIONS IS BUILT IN 535 'ILE
AGAINST A WALL.
EXTENDS ALONG THE REMAINING LENGTH OF WALL. 185 AHWILD
IN THE REAR WALL, LEFT, IS A DOUBLE DOORWAY WITH 185 AHWILD
SLIDING DOORS AND PORTIERES.
IN THE RIGHT WALL, REAR, A SCREEN DOOR IN THIS 185 AHWILD
WALL ARE TWO WINDOWS.
A SOFA WITH SILK AND SATIN CUSHIONS STANDS AGAINST185 AHWILD
THE WALL.
IN THE REAR WALL, LEFT IS THE DOOR TO THE PANTRY. 210 AHWILD
IN THE LEFT WALL, EXTREME FRONT, IS A SCREEN DOOR 210 AHWILD
OPENING ON A SIDE PORCH.
IN THE RIGHT WALL ARE TWO WINDOWS LOOKING OUT ON A210 AHWILD
SIDE LAWN.
IN THE REAR WALL, RIGHT, IS A DOOR LEADING TO THE 236 AHWILD
"FAMILY ENTRANCE."
IN THE MIDDLE OF THE RIGHT WALL IS A WINDOW WITH 236 AHWILD
CLOSED SHUTTERS.

WALL

WALL (CONT'D.)
AT REAR OF DOOR, AGAINST THE WALL, IS A NICKEL-IN-236 AHWILD
THE-SLOT PLAYER-PIANO.
THE HIDEOUS SAFFRON-COLORED WALL-PAPER IS BLOTCHED236 AHWILD
AND SPOTTED.
THE BAR RUNS FROM LEFT TO RIGHT NEARLY THE WHOLE 3 ANNA
LENGTH OF THE REAR WALL.
(THE =AHOY= COMES AGAIN THROUGH THE WALL OF FOG, 29 ANNA
SOUNDING MUCH NEARER THIS TIME.
IN THE REAR WALL, TWO SMALL SQUARE WINDOWS AND A 41 ANNA
DOOR OPENING OUT ON THE DECK
IN THE RIGHT WALL, TWO MORE WINDOWS LOOKING OUT ON 41 ANNA
THE PORT DECK.
STAGGERING BACK AGAINST THE CABIN WALL, WHERE HE 50 ANNA
REMAINS STANDING,
A STRAGGLING LINE OF PILED ROCKS, TOO LOW TO BE 81 BEYOND
CALLED A WALL.
IN THE REAR WALL TO THE RIGHT OF THE SIDEBOARD, 93 BEYOND
IN THE RIGHT WALL, NEAR THE MIDDLE, AN OPEN 93 BEYOND
DOORWAY LEADING TO THE KITCHEN.
AGAINST THE WALL BETWEEN THE WINDOWS, AN OLD- 93 BEYOND
FASHIONED WALNUT DESK.
BLOTCHES OF DAMPNESS DISFIGURE THE WALL PAPER. 144 BEYOND
A PILE OF WOOD IS STACKED UP CARELESSLY AGAINST 144 BEYOND
THE WALL BY THE STOVE.
STRETCHING A HAND OUT TO THE WALL TO SUPPORT 151 BEYOND
HIMSELF.
IN THE RIGHT WALL, FIVE PORTHOLES. 555 CROSS
A COT WITH A BLANKET IS PLACED AGAINST THE WALL TO555 CROSS
THE RIGHT OF THE DOOR.
IN THE REAR WALL, A DOOR LEADING TO THE OUTER 493 DAYS
OFFICES.
IN THE LEFT WALL IS A DOOR LEADING TO THE DINING- 514 DAYS
ROOM.
IN THE MIDDLE OF THE REAR WALL IS A DOORWAY 514 DAYS
LEADING TO THE HALL.
AT LEFT, FRONT, IS THE BED, ITS HEAD AGAINST THE 553 DAYS
LEFT WALL.
IN THE LEFT WALL, REAR, IS THE DOOR TO THE 553 DAYS
BATHROOM.
AT REAR OF THIS DOOR, IN THE MIDDLE OF THE WALL, 553 DAYS
IS A DRESSING TABLE,
WHERE IT MEETS AN END WALL THAT EXTENDS BACK FROM 564 DAYS
RIGHT, FRONT.
A SIDE WALL RUNS DIAGONALLY BACK FROM LEFT, FRONT,564 DAYS
STAINED BY THE COLOR IN THE WINDOWS, FALLS ON THE 564 DAYS
WALL ON AND AROUND THE CROSS.
IN THE MIDDLE OF THE SIDE WALL IS A GREAT CROSS, 564 DAYS
IN THE MIDDLE OF THE END WALL IS AN ARCHED 564 DAYS
DOORWAY.
ON EITHER SIDE OF THIS DOOR, BUT HIGH UP IN THE 564 DAYS
WALL,
THE GRAY WALLS OF THE CHURCH, PARTICULARLY THE 566 DAYS
WALL WHERE THE CROSS IS,
THE SOUTH END OF THE HOUSE FACES FRONT TO A STONE 202 DESIRE
WALL.
THE END WALL FACING US HAS TWO WINDOWS IN ITS 202 DESIRE
UPPER STORY,
IN THE MIDDLE OF THE REAR WALL IS FASTENED A BIG 206 DESIRE
ADVERTISING POSTER WITH A SHIP
AN' HE HAULS UP BY THE STONE WALL A JIFFY. 209 DESIRE
UNTO A STONE WALL, I' WALL IN YER HEART/ 209 DESIRE
THEY CAN STAND UPRIGHT ONLY CLOSE TO THE CENTER 212 DESIRE
DIVIDING WALL OF THE UPSTAIRS.
HER EYES FASTEN ON THE INTERVENING WALL WITH 236 DESIRE
CONCENTRATED ATTENTION.
CONCENTRATES AGAIN ON THE WALL AND PAYS NO 236 DESIRE
ATTENTION TO WHAT HE SAYS)
ABBIE RELAXES WITH A FAINT SIGH BUT HER EYES 236 DESIRE
REMAIN FIXED ON THE WALL.
ABBIE LOOKS AT THE WALL. 236 DESIRE
THEIR HOT GLANCES SEEM TO MEET THROUGH THE WALL. 236 DESIRE
EBEN AND ABBIE STARE AT EACH OTHER THROUGH THE 239 DESIRE
WALL.
ABBIE IS CONSCIOUS OF HIS MOVEMENT AND STARES AT 239 DESIRE
THE WALL.
FINALLY ABBIE GETS UP AND LISTENS, HER EAR TO THE 239 DESIRE
WALL.
CABOT GETS ONE HAND ON HIS THROAT AND PRESSES HIM 255 DESIRE
BACK ACROSS THE STONE WALL.
(SOMEWHAT IMPATIENTLY) WALL, IF HE AIN'T, HE'S A 512 DIFRNT
GOOD MAN JEST THE SAME.
THERE IS A DOOR TO THE HALL IN THE RIGHT WALL, 421 DYNAMO
REAR.
IN THE LEFT WALL IS A WINDOW. 421 DYNAMO
AND AN OLD-FASHIONED BUREAU IN THE MIDDLE OF THE 421 DYNAMO
REAR WALL.
THE MINISTER'S DESK IS PLACED AGAINST THE LEFT 421 DYNAMO
WALL BESIDE THE WINDOW.
THERE IS A DRESSING TABLE WITH A BIG MIRROR 428 DYNAMO
AGAINST THE REAR WALL, RIGHT,
NEAR THE DOOR IN THE LEFT WALL WHICH LEADS TO THE 428 DYNAMO
HALL.
IN THE SAME WALL, TO THE REAR OF THE BED, IS THE 428 DYNAMO
DOOR.
IN THE RIGHT WALL ARE THREE WINDOWS LOOKING OUT ON428 DYNAMO
THE LAWN
THE BED IS AT LEFT, FRONT, ITS HEAD AGAINST THE 428 DYNAMO
LEFT WALL.
(WHEN THE LIGHT COMES ON AGAIN, THE WALL OF THE 435 DYNAMO
FIFE BEDROOM HAS BEEN REPLACED.
WHILE THE WALL OF THE SITTING ROOM HAS BEEN 468 DYNAMO
REPLACED.
ARE IN THE LOWER PART OF THE DYNAMO-ROOM WALL, 473 DYNAMO
BUT IN THE DIM LIGHT OF ONE BULB IN A BRACKET IN 483 DYNAMO
THE LEFT WALL
THIS WALL THEN TURNS AND ASCENDS DIAGONALLY 483 DYNAMO
TOWARD THE LEFT TO THE UPPER

WALL (CONT'D.)
AGAINST THE WALL ON THE RIGHT IS A STAIRWAY THAT 483 DYNAMO
EXTENDS BACKWARD HALF WAY UP
AND A ROW OF GREAT WINDOWS IN THE LEFT WALL. 486 DYNAMO
IN THE RIGHT WALL, CENTER, 173 EJONES
IN THE REAR THE FOREST IS A WALL OF DARKNESS 187 EJONES
DIVIDING THE WORLD.
A DENSE LOW WALL OF UNDERBRUSH AND CREEPERS IS IN 190 EJONES
THE NEARER FOREGROUND,
WITH THE WALL OF THE HOUSE PROPER WHICH IS OF GRAY 2 ELECTR
CUT STONE.
THE WHITE COLUMNS CAST BLACK BARS OF SHADOW ON THE 5 ELECTR
GRAY WALL BEHIND THEM.
THE SOMBER GRAYNESS OF THE WALL, THE GREEN OF THE 5 ELECTR
OPEN SHUTTERS,
SHIMMERING IN A LUMINOUS MIST ON THE WHITE PORTICO 5 ELECTR
AND THE GRAY STONE WALL
ON THE RIGHT WALL IS A PAINTING OF GEORGE 28 ELECTR
WASHINGTON IN A GILT FRAME.
THE WHITE COLUMNS OF THE PORTICO CAST BLACK BARS 43 ELECTR
OF SHADOW ON THE GRAY WALL
A WALL HIDING US FROM EACH OTHER/ 54 ELECTR
I WOULD TRY TO MAKE UP MY MIND EXACTLY WHAT THAT 54 ELECTR
WALL WAS.
I WANT TO FIND WHAT THAT WALL IS MARRIAGE PUT 55 ELECTR
BETWEEN US?
THERE IS NO WALL BETWEEN US. 56 ELECTR
THE HEAD AGAINST THE REAR WALL. 58 ELECTR
FURTHER BACK, AGAINST THE WALL, IS A BUREAU. 58 ELECTR
IN THE LEFT WALL ARE TWO WINDOWS. 58 ELECTR
IN THE RIGHT WALL, FRONT, IS A DOOR LEADING TO THE 58 ELECTR
HALL.
IN THE REAR WALL, CENTER, IS THE DOORWAY GIVING ON 79 ELECTR
THE MAIN HALL AND THE STAIRS.
ARE A WALL TABLE AND CHAIR AND A WRITING DESK AND 79 ELECTR
CHAIR.
A BIG SIDEBOARD STANDS AGAINST THE LEFT WALL, 109 ELECTR
CENTER.
IN THE REAR WALL, AT RIGHT, IS A DOOR LEADING INTO109 ELECTR
THE CAPTAIN'S STATEROOM.
BUILT AGAINST THE RIGHT WALL OF THE CABIN IS A 109 ELECTR
LONG NARROW COUCH, LIKE A BUNK.
THE COLUMNS CAST BLACK BARS OF SHADOW ON THE WALL 129 ELECTR
BEHIND THEM.
THAT WAS EZRA'S PICTURE HANGIN' ON THE WALL, NOT A134 ELECTR
GHOST, YE DURNED IDJUT.
AN' I SEED EZRA'S GHOST DRESSED LIKE A JUDGE 134 ELECTR
COMIN' THROUGH THE WALL--
HER EYES UNCONSCIOUSLY SEEKING THE MANNON 157 ELECTR
PORTRAITS ON THE RIGHT WALL.
(TURNS AND ADDRESSES THE PORTRAITS ON THE WALL 165 ELECTR
WITH A CRAZY MOCKERY)
THE COLUMNS CAST BLACK BARS OF SHADOW ON THE GRAY 169 ELECTR
STONE WALL BEHIND THEM.
THE BACKGROUND IS A BACKDROP ON WHICH THE REAR 269 GGBROW
WALL IS PAINTED
THE BACKGROUND IS A BACKDROP OF AN OFFICE WALL, 274 GGBROW
THE BACKDROP FOR THE REAR WALL IS A CHEAP 278 GGBROW
WALLPAPER OF A DULL YELLOW-BROWN.
THE BLACK WALL DROP HAS WINDOWS PAINTED ON IT WITH290 GGBROW
A DIM,
THE BACKDROP FOR BOTH ROOMS IS OF PLAIN WALL WITH 302 GGBROW
A FEW TACKED-UP DESIGNS AND
THE FORMER IS AT LEFT, THE LATTER AT RIGHT OF A 302 GGBROW
DIVIDING WALL AT CENTER.
FOR IT'S DARK DOWN HERE AND ME OLD MAN'S IN WALL 230 HA APE
STREET MAKING MONEY
A BIG SIGNBOARD IS ON THE WALL AT THE REAR, 245 HA APE
--INDUSTRIAL WORKERS OF THE WORLD--
THEN SEES THE SIGNBOARD ON THE WALL AND IS 246 HA APE
REASSURED.)
LIGHTING COMES FROM SINGLE WALL BRACKETS, TWO AT 573 ICEMAN
LEFT AND TWO AT REAR.
AT REAR, THIS CURTAIN IS DRAWN BACK FROM THE WALL 573 ICEMAN
ARE IN THE LEFT WALL, LOOKING OUT ON A BACKYARD. 573 ICEMAN
IN THE MIDDLE OF THE REAR WALL IS A DOOR OPENING 573 ICEMAN
ON A HALLWAY.
IS AGAINST THE REAR WALL ON EITHER SIDE OF THE 573 ICEMAN
DOOR.
THE RIGHT WALL OF THE BACK ROOM IS A DIRTY BLACK 573 ICEMAN
CURTAIN
AGAINST THE MIDDLE OF THE LEFT WALL IS A NICKEL- 573 ICEMAN
IN-THE-SLOT PHONOGRAPH.
WITH BALKINESS ALWAYS SMOLDERING IN ITS WALL EYES,576 ICEMAN
AND BEGINS PUSHING THE BLACK CURTAIN ALONG THE RUD610 ICEMAN
TO THE REAR WALL.)
AND PROPPED HIM AGAINST A WALL AND GAVE HIM A 617 ICEMAN
FRISK.
AND STAND AGAINST THE WALL AT LEFT, FRONT. 628 ICEMAN
THE BLACK CURTAIN DIVIDING IT FROM THE BAR IS THE 628 ICEMAN
RIGHT WALL OF THE SCENE.
WITH HICKEY TO DO THE WRITING ON THE WALL/ 644 ICEMAN
A THIRD BACK BY THE REAR WALL WITH FIVE CHAIRS, 664 ICEMAN
AND FINALLY,
IN THE RIGHT WALL ARE TWO BIG WINDOWS, 664 ICEMAN
BUT I COULD HEAR HIM THROUGH THE WALL DOING HIS 681 ICEMAN
SPIEL TO SOMEONE ALL NIGHT LONG.
I'D GET SEEING THINGS IN THE WALL PAPER. 712 ICEMAN
WHO HAS GIVEN UP THE FIGHT AND IS PUSHED BACK 526 INZONE
AGAINST THE WALL NEAR THE DOORWAY
AND IS EASILY HELD BACK AGAINST THE WALL.) 527 INZONE
(THEY DO SO AND LEAVE HIM WITH HIS BACK AGAINST 528 INZONE
THE WALL NEAR SCOTTY.
AND HALF TURNS HIS FACE TO THE WALL.) 530 INZONE
(SMITTY TURNS HIS FACE COMPLETELY TO THE WALL.) 531 INZONE
BUNKS, SHOES AND ALL, TURNING THEIR FACES TO THE 532 INZONE
WALL.

WALL

WALL (CONT'D.)
BUT COVERS HIS FACE WITH HIS HANDS AND LEANS 532 INZONE
AGAINST THE WALL.
IN THE LEFT WALL, A SIMILAR SERIES OF WINDOWS 11 JOURNE
LOCKS OUT
IN THE RIGHT WALL, REAR, 11 JOURNE
AGAINST THE WALL BETWEEN THE DOORWAYS IS A SMALL 11 JOURNE
BOOKCASE.
A SMALL WICKER TABLE AND AN ORDINARY OAK DESK ARE 11 JOURNE
AGAINST THE WALL,
AND IT'S SAFER THAN THE STOCKS AND BONDS OF WALL 16 JOURNE
STREET SWINDLERS.
OUTSIDE THE WINDOWS THE WALL OF FOG APPEARS DENSER125 JOURNE
THAN EVER.
THE HARDEST THING TO TAKE IS THE BLANK WALL SHE 139 JOURNE
BUILDS AROUND HER.
A WALL SWITCH, AND A MOMENT LATER SOMEONE STARTS 169 JOURNE
PLAYING THE PIANO IN THERE--
IN THE REAR WALL, RIGHT, A DOOR LEADING INTO THE 273 LAZARU
REST OF THE HOUSE.
FOUR WINDOWS ARE VISIBLE WITH A CLOSED DOOR IN THE281 LAZARU
MIDDLE OF THE WALL.
IN THE CENTER OF THE WALL IS A GREAT METAL GATE. 312 LAZARU
TO THE HIGH WALL OF ROME AT THE EXTREME REAR. 312 LAZARU
SKY BEYOND THE WALL. 313 LAZARU
BUT HOW CAN WE WITNESS AT NIGHT AND THROUGH A 315 LAZARU
WALL?
THE FOLLOWERS OF THIS LAZARUS ENCAMPED OUTSIDE THE315 LAZARU
WALL.
THERE ARE THOUSANDS OF THEM OUTSIDE THE WALL. 316 LAZARU
THE VOICES OF HIS FOLLOWERS FROM BEYOND THE WALL, 318 LAZARU
AT FIRST ONE BY ONE,
MINGLED WITH THE LAUGHING FROM BEYOND THE WALL 318 LAZARU
COMES THE SOUND OF SINGING AND
ARE SUDDENLY HEARD FROM BEYOND THE WALL BEGINNING 319 LAZARU
TO LAUGH THEIR HOARSE,
YOU ON THE WALL? 319 LAZARU
(THE MULTITUDE BEYOND THE WALL, ALL THE SENATORS, 319 LAZARU
(THE BRAZEN TRUMPETS OF THE LEGIONS SOUND FROM 319 LAZARU
BEYOND THE WALL.
(THE GATE IN THE WALL IS CLANGED OPEN. 320 LAZARU
AND ALONG THE REAR WALL ON EITHER SIDE OF THE 335 LAZARU
ARCH.
THEY HOLD THEIR SHIELDS SO THAT THEY FORM A WALL 338 LAZARU
AROUND HIM AND HALF OVER HIM.
THAT TOPS THE WALL THAT ENCLOSES THE ARENA. 363 LAZARU
A WEATHER-BEATEN BENCH STANDS AGAINST THE FRONT 1 MANSNS
WALL, AT LEFT OF THE DOOR.
ANOTHER WINDOW IS IN THE WALL FACING RIGHT. 1 MANSNS
WALL AT LIFE WHICH PASSES BY SO HORRIBLY UNAWARE 12 MANSNS
THAT YOU ARE STILL ALIVE?
AND BEYOND THE WALL THE STEPS OF LIFE GROWIN' 19 MANSNS
PAINTED DOWN THE STREET,
IN THE WALL ABOVE THE DOOR, IN WHICH A LITTLE LAMP 25 MANSNS
BURNS BRIGHTLY.
THE CORNER IS FORMED BY A BRICK ENCLOSING WALL, 25 MANSNS
EIGHT FEET HIGH,
WITH A LINE OF ITALIAN CYPRESSES BEHIND THEM ALONG 25 MANSNS
THE WALL.
THE RIGHT ONE LEADS TO AN ARCHED DOOR, PAINTED 25 MANSNS
GREEN, IN THE WALL AT RIGHT,
THE FOOTSTEPS BEYOND THE WALL. 40 MANSNS
IS IN THE MIDDLE OF THE REAR WALL. 43 MANSNS
THERE ARE TWO WINDOWS IN THE RIGHT WALL, 43 MANSNS
IN THE MIDDLE OF THE LEFT WALL IS A CLOSED DOOR 43 MANSNS
LEADING INTO SIMON'S STUDY.
FARTHER BACK AGAINST THE WALL IS A HIGH DESK WITH 69 MANSNS
A TALL STOOL IN FRONT OF IT.
IN THE REAR WALL RIGHT IS A DOOR LEADING INTO THE 69 MANSNS
HALL.
IN THE LEFT WALL ARE TWO WINDOWS LOOKING OUT ON 69 MANSNS
THE STREET.
AT LEFT OF THIS DOOR, A TALL CABINET STANDS 69 MANSNS
AGAINST THE WALL.
SUDDENLY SHE STOPS, AND LISTENS TO SOMETHING 95 MANSNS
BEYOND THE WALL AT RIGHT.
LATE AFTERNOON SUNLIGHT FROM BEYOND THE WALL AT 95 MANSNS
RIGHT FALLS ON THE POINTED ROOF
AND SHE STARES AT THE DOOR IN THE WALL WITH DREAD. 95 MANSNS
AND THE TREES ALONG THE BRICK WALL AT REAR GLOW IN 95 MANSNS
DIFFERENT SHADES OF GREEN.
I HAVE BECOME SO WEARY OF WHAT THEY CALL LIFE 103 MANSNS
BEYOND THE WALL, MOTHER.
IN THE MIDDLE OF THE REAR WALL IS THE DOOR TO 117 MANSNS
SIMON'S STUDY.
AT EXTREME LEFT-FRONT A SMALL TABLE AGAINST THE 117 MANSNS
WALL.
AGAINST THE RIGHT WALL, TOWARD REAR, ANOTHER 117 MANSNS
TABLE.
AND I TACKED ON THE RIGHT WALL BESIDE HER DESK IS A 139 MANSNS
LARGE ARCHITECT'S DRAWING
IN FRONT OF THE SUMMER-HOUSE AND THE DOOR TO THE 161 MANSNS
STREET IN THE WALL AT RIGHT.
SHE RUSHES OVER, PULLS OPEN THE DOOR IN THE WALL 162 MANSNS
AT RIGHT,
(POINTING TO THE DOOR IN THE WALL AT RIGHT.) 186 MANSNS
SO IT STANDS BACK AGAINST THE WALL. 187 MANSNS
IS SEATED ON A SORT OF THRONE PLACED AGAINST THE 358 MARCOM
REAR WALL.
IN THE REAR IS A SECTION OF THE GREAT WALL OF 373 MARCOM
CHINA WITH AN ENORMOUS SHUT GATE.
THE PEOPLE ON THE OTHER SIDE OF THAT WALL MAY LOOK374 MARCOM
SIMPLE BUT THEY'RE NOT.
(FROM BEHIND THE WALL COMES THE SOUND OF MARTIAL 376 MARCOM
CHINESE MUSIC.
TO MAKE AN EFFECTIVE BREACH IN THIS WALL 394 MARCOM
AND BUILDS THEM INTO A FORTRESS WALL. 394 MARCOM

WALL (CONT'D.)
ON OUR RIGHT, YOU SEE THE FORTRESS WALL OF A 394 MARCOM
HOSTILE CAPITAL.
WHICH KNOCKS A BIG BREACH IN THE WALL OF BLOCKS. 395 MARCOM
GAMBLERS WHO WOULD LIKE TO BE MISTAKEN FOR WALL 37 MISBEG
STREET BROKERS.
A BUREAU AGAINST THE REAR WALL, 71 MISBEG
(SCENE-- THE SAME, WITH THE WALL OF THE LIVING 71 MISBEG
ROOM REMOVED.
(SCENE-- THE LIVING-ROOM WALL HAS BEEN REPLACED 111 MISBEG
BEYOND THE BAR DOOR A SMALL CABINET IS FASTENED TO 7 POET
THE WALL.
HE CATCHES HIS REFLECTION IN THE MIRROR ON THE 43 POET
WALL AT LEFT AND STOPS BEFORE IT.
ONE CANNOT MAKE A DECENT TOILET IN THAT DINGY HOLE 44 POET
IN THE WALL.
RECEDE ALONG THE STREET BEYOND THE HIGH WALL. 86 POET
O'DOWD HAS THE CHAIR AGAINST THE WALL, FACING 95 POET
RIGHT.
FARTHER FORWARD AN OLD CANE-BOTTOMED CHAIR IS SET 577 ROPE
BACK AGAINST THE WALL.
ALL GIVING EVIDENCE OF LONG DISUSE, ARE LYING ON 577 ROPE
THE FLOOR NEAR THE LEFT WALL.
THE RIGHT SIDE OF THE BARN IS A BARE WALL. 577 ROPE
HE LEANS AGAINST THE WALL, IN AN EXTRAORDINARY 594 ROPE
STATE OF EXCITEMENT.
THERE IS ONE ENTRANCE, A DOOR IN THE RIGHT WALL, 3 STRANG
REAR.
A HEAP OF STONES, A MUD IMAGE, A DRAWING ON A 41 STRANG
WALL, A BIRD, A FISH, A SNAKE,
I SEEMED TO FEEL GORDON STANDING AGAINST A WALL 45 STRANG
WITH EYES BANDAGED AND THESE MEN
THE WALL PAPER, A REPULSIVE BROWN, 48 STRANG
IN THE LEFT WALL IS ONE WINDOW WITH STARCHED WHITE 48 STRANG
CURTAINS LOOKING OUT ON A
IN THE RIGHT WALL, A DOOR LEADING TO THE KITCHEN. 48 STRANG
ON THE WALL, A FRAMED PORTRAIT STUDY OF ELEANOR. 462 WELDED
IN THE LEFT WALL, CENTER, A SMALL WINDOW WITH A 470 WELDED
TURN DARK SHADE PULLED DOWN.
WHICH SENDS HIM REELING BACK AGAINST THE WALL) 477 WELDED

WALLED
AND YOUR LITTLE WALLED GARDEN THE GARDEN OF 3 MANSNS
VERSAILLES.
SITTING IN YOUR WALLED-IN GARDEN, DRESSED ALL IN 14 MANSNS
WHITE.
THE COMFORT SHE LOVED, THE PROTECTED PRIVACY, HER 47 MANSNS
FANCIFUL WALLED-IN GARDEN,
IT'S A GRAND MANSION, WITH A BIG WALLED GARDEN 154 POET
BEHIND IT,
HER BIG DARK EYES ARE GRIM WITH THE PRISONER-PAIN 53 STRANG
OF A WALLED-IN SOUL.

WALLER
WHO BUT DICK WALLER, THE LAWYER, THAT I WENT TO 584 ROPE
SEE.
MAYBE WALLER WAS LYIN'. 585 ROPE
WALLER SAID T'WAS NO USE. 586 ROPE
WHAT ELSE DID WALLER SAYS 586 ROPE

WALLET
(HE TAKES A WALLET FROM HIS INSIDE COAT POCKET. 201 AHWILD
(HE TAKES A LETTER FROM HIS WALLET) 203 AHWILD
I KEPT IT IN MY WALLET FOR YEARS. 152 JOURNE

WALLOP
SOME WALLUP/ 471 CARIBE
HE PACKA DA WALLOP, I TELLA YOU/ 209 HA APE
IT DID PACK A WALLOP, ALL RIGHT. 132 JOURNE
IT'S HIT HIM AN AWFUL WALLOP. 171 STRANG

WALLOW
IT HAS LOST ALL MEANING FOR THEM EXCEPT AS A PIG- 542 DAYS
WALLOW.
PURPOSE TO GIVE HIS PIGS A FREE WALLOW. 23 JOURNE
I SHALL SEND HIM HOME TO HIS NATIVE WALLOW. 387 MARCOM
GUZZLE/ GRUNT/ WALLOW FOR OUR AMUSEMENT/ 419 MARCOM
STROLL THROUGH TO WALLOW HAPPILY ALONG THE SHORES 50 MISBEG
OF THE ICE POND.

WALLPAPER
THE WALLPAPER IS NOW A CREAM COLOR SPRAYED WITH 519 DIFRNT
PINK FLOWERS.
THE WALLPAPER SO FADED THAT THE UGLINESS OF ITS 421 DYNAMO
COLOR
THE BACKDROP FOR THE REAR WALL IS A CHEAP 278 GGBROW
WALLPAPER OF A DULL YELLOW-BROWN,
THE BACKGROUND BACKDROP IS BRILLIANT, STUNNING 284 GGBROW
WALLPAPER.
THE LIVING ROOM IS SMALL, LOW-CEILINGED, WITH 71 MISBEG
FADED, FLY-SPECKED WALLPAPER,
UGLY WALLPAPER, DIRTY, STAINED, CRISS-CROSSED WITH470 WELDED
MATCH-STROKES.

WALLS
THE WALLS OF THE CABIN ARE PAINTED WHITE. 535 'ILE
BUT THERE'S NOTHING TO SEE DOWN HERE BUT THESE 540 'ILE
WALLS.
I WON'T STAND IT--I CAN'T STAND IT--PENT UP BY 546 'ILE
THESE WALLS LIKE A PRISONER.
THE WALLS ARE PAPERED WHITE WITH A CHEERFUL, UGLY 185 AHWILD
BLUE DESIGN.
THE WALLS ARE PAPERED IN A SOMBER BROWN AND DARK- 210 AHWILD
RED DESIGN.
A NARROW, LOW-CEILINGED COMPARTMENT THE WALLS OF 41 ANNA
WHICH ARE PAINTED A LIGHT BROWN
BY THE LINES OF STONE WALLS AND ROUGH SNAKE 81 BEYOND
FENCES.
THE WALLS ARE PAPERED A DARK RED WITH A SCROLLY- 93 BEYOND
FIGURED PATTERN.
THEY'RE LIKE THE WALLS OF A NARROW PRISON YARD 126 BEYOND
SHUTTING ME IN
BOOKCASES EXTEND ALONG THE REAR AND RIGHT WALLS. 541 DAYS
THE WALLS ARE OLD GRAY STONE. 564 DAYS

1767 — WANDER

WALLS (CONT'D.)

THE GRAY WALLS OF THE CHURCH, PARTICULARLY THE WALL WHERE THE CROSS IS, 566 DAYS

ITS WALLS ARE A SICKLY GRAYISH, THE GREEN OF THE 202 DESIRE SHUTTERS FADED.

STONES ATOP O' STONES--MAKIN' STONE WALLS--YEAR 204 DESIRE ATOP O' YEARS.

HIM 'N' YEW 'N' ME 'N' THEN EBEN--MAKIN'STONE 204 DESIRE WALLS FUR HIM TO FENCE US IN/.

(BREAKING IN HARSHLY) AN' MAKIN' WALLS--STONE 208 DESIRE ATOP O' STONE

WE BEEN SLAVES T' STONE WALLS HERE. 218 DESIRE

THE STONE WALLS AIR CRUMBLIN' AN' TUMBLIN'/ 221 DESIRE

I PICKED 'EM UP AN' PILED 'EM INTO WALLS. 237 DESIRE

YE KIN READ THE YEARS OF MY LIFE IN THEM WALLS, 237 DESIRE EVERY DAY A HEFTED STONE.

THE CHAIRS, WITH WOODEN BENCHES ADDED, HAVE BEEN 247 DESIRE PUSHED BACK AGAINST THE WALLS.

THE PEOPLE SEATED ALONG THE WALLS STAMP THEIR FEET250 DESIRE

THEY CROWD BACK TOWARD THE WALLS, MUTTERING, 250 DESIRE LOOKING AT HIM RESENTFULLY.)

STERN-LOOKING PEOPLE IN UNCOMFORTABLE POSES ARE 493 DIFRNT HUNG ON THE WALLS.

THE WALLS ARE PAPERED A BROWN COLOR. 493 DIFRNT

ARE HUNG ON THE WALLS AT MATHEMATICALLY- SPACED 519 DIFRNT INTERVALS.

SHE LIFTS DOWN THE FRAMED PICTURES FROM THE WALLS 548 DIFRNT AND PILES THEM ON THE CURTAINS

THE FRONT WALLS OF THESE ROOMS ARE REMOVED TO SHOW -0 DYNAMO THE DIFFERENT INTERIORS.

SEVERAL FRAMED PRINTS OF SCENES FROM THE BIBLE 421 DYNAMO HANG ON THE WALLS.

(WHEN IT GROWS LIGHT AGAIN THE OUTER WALLS OF THE 427 DYNAMO TWO ROOMS IN THE LIGHT HOME

THE WALLS OF THE FIFE AND LIGHT SITTING ROOMS HAVE443 DYNAMO BEEN REPLACED WHILE THE

BRACKETS ALONG BOTH WALLS, THERE IS A CLEAR VIEW 473 DYNAMO OF A DYNAMO, HUGE AND BLACK,

A DEEP BUT NARROW COMPARTMENT WITH RED BRICK 483 DYNAMO WALLS.

THE DYNAMO ROOM IS HIGH AND WIDE WITH RED BRICK 486 DYNAMO WALLS

A SPACIOUS, HIGH-CEILINGED ROOM WITH BARE, 173 EJONES WHITEWASHED WALLS.

RISING SHEER ON BOTH SIDES THE FOREST WALLS IT IN.192 EJONES

INSTANTLY THE WALLS OF THE FOREST CLOSE IN FROM 195 EJONES BOTH SIDES.

AS IF THIS WERE A SIGNAL THE WALLS OF THE FOREST 198 EJONES FOLD IN.

FACING ONE ANOTHER WITH THEIR BACKS TOUCHING THE 199 EJONES FOREST WALLS

THE WALLS ARE PLAIN PLASTERED SURFACES TINTED A 28 ELECTR DULL GRAY

BUT IN THIS WAR I'VE SEEN TOO MANY WHITE WALLS 54 ELECTR SPLATTERED WITH BLOOD

OF THE THREE PORTRAITS ON THE OTHER WALLS, TWO ARE 79 ELECTR OF WOMEN--

THE WALLS ARE PLAIN PLASTERED SURFACES, LIGHT GRAY 79 ELECTR WITH A WHITE TRIM.

PORTRAITS OF ANCESTORS HANG ON THE WALLS. 79 ELECTR

A SMALL COMPARTMENT, THE WALLS NEWLY PAINTED A 109 ELECTR LIGHT BROWN.

BEN USED TO HEAR THINGS CLAWIN' AT THE WALLS AN' 132 ELECTR WINDERS

LIKE SOMETHIN' ROTTIN' IN THE WALLS. 136 ELECTR

AND OF THE OTHER MANNONS ON THE WALLS ON EACH SIDE157 ELECTR OF HIM.

THE PORTRAITS OF THE MANNONS WILL ROT ON THE WALLS171 ELECTR

VIBRATING THROUGH THE STEEL WALLS AS IF SOME 217 HA APE ENORMOUS BRAZEN GONG WERE IMBEDDED

THE WALLS AND CEILING ONCE WERE WHITE, BUT IT WAS 573 ICEMAN A LONG TIME AGO.

A LONG, LOW-CEILINGED, SPARELY FURNISHED CHAMBER, 273 LAZARU WITH WHITE WALLS

THE HOUSE IS LOW, OF ONE STORY ONLY, ITS WALLS 281 LAZARU WHITE.

LIFE IS FOR EACH MAN A SOLITARY CELL WHOSE WALLS 309 LAZARU ARE MIRRORS.

IMMEDIATELY INSIDE THE WALLS OF ROME. 312 LAZARU

THEIR LAUGHTER SEEMS TO SHAKE THE WALLS 321 LAZARU

IN THE REAR, THE WALLS OF THE VILLA, 326 LAZARU

THICK WALLS SEEM WAITING TO FALL. 330 LAZARU

IF FLEEING IN TERROR FROM THE LAUGHTER WHICH NOW 334 LAZARU BEATS AT THE WALLS.)

SMALLER ARCHES IN THE MIDDLE OF THE SIDE WALLS 335 LAZARU LEAD INTO OTHER ROOMS.

LONG COUCHES ARE PLACED ALONG THE WALLS AT RIGHT 335 LAZARU AND LEFT.

THE WALLS AND MASSIVE COLUMNS SEEM TO REVERBERATE 337 LAZARU WITH THE SOUND.

OF CLOSE WALLS OF EARTH BAKED IN THE SUN. 346 LAZARU

IN THE HALF-DARKNESS, THE WALLS ARE LOST IN 350 LAZARU SHADOW, THE ROOM SEEMS IMMENSE.

PICTURES OF AN OLD BUCK GOAT UPON THE WALLS AND 354 LAZARU WRITE ABOVE THEM, CAESARS

LED BY THE CHORUS, THEY POUR DOWN FROM THE BANKED 368 LAZARU WALLS OF THE AMPHITHEATRE AND

ITS WALLS AND POINTED ROOF ENTIRELY COVERED BY 25 MANSNS IVY.

AND SCREAM IN SILENCE AND BEAT ON THE WALLS UNTIL 40 MANSNS YOU DIE OF STARVATION.

ON THE WALLS ARE PICTURES OF WASHINGTON, HAMILTON, 69 MANSNS DANIEL WEBSTER, AND,

AND IVY-COVERED WALLS OF THE SUMMER-HOUSE. 95 MANSNS

THE WALLS AND CEILING ARE WHITE. 117 MANSNS

AND YOU BEAT THE WALLS, SCREAMING FOR ESCAPE AT 163 MANSNS ANY COST/

SQUATTED AGAINST THE SIDE WALLS, 364 MARCOM

WALLS (CONT'D.)

AN IMMENSE OCTAGONAL ROOM, THE LOFTY WALLS ADORNED377 MARCOM IN GOLD AND SILVER.

REMEMBER HOW THAT CHRISTIAN, POLO, INVENTED THE 422 MARCOM ENGINE TO BATTER DOWN WALLS$

I BEGIN TO SEE THROUGH THE WALLS--AH/ 426 MARCOM

THE WALLS TOWER MAJESTICALLY IN SHADOW, 432 MARCOM

ITS WALLS AND SLOPING ROOF ARE COVERED WITH TAR 1 MISBEG PAPER, FADED TO DARK GRAY.

BUT THE WALLS NOW ARE A BLACKENED AND WEATHERED 1 MISBEG GRAY,

AND THAT IS ALL EXCEPT THAT THE WALLS ARE 107 MISBEG UNPAINTED PINE BOARDS.

THE PARTITION IS PAINTED TO IMITATE THE OLD 7 POET PANELED WALLS

WITH HEAVY OAK BEAMS AND PANELED WALLS-- 7 POET

OVER DITCHES AND STREAMS AND STONE WALLS AND 102 POET

THERE IS A DRUNKEN CHORUS OF ANSWERING =HURROS= 180 POET THAT SHAKES THE WALLS.)

THE WALLS ARE LINED ALMOST TO THE CEILING WITH 3 STRANG GLASSED-IN BOOK-SHELVES.

SET BACK AT SPACED INTERVALS AGAINST THE WALLS, 48 STRANG

BY KEROSENE LAMPS PLACED IN BRACKETS ON THE WALLS.493 VOYAGE

WALNUT

AGAINST THE WALL BETWEEN THE WINDOWS, AN OLD- 93 BEYOND FASHIONED WALNUT DESK.

WALPOLE

I FELT AS HORACE WALPOLE DID ABOUT ENGLAND, 590 ICEMAN

WALRUS

A WALRUS MUSTACHE, BLACK EYES WHICH PEER NEAR- 574 ICEMAN SIGHTEDLY

WALTER

WHAT THE DEVIL'S GOT INTO WALTER LATELY, ANYWAYS 498 DAYS

PROBABLY WANTS MY ADVICE ON WHAT TO GIVE WALTER 498 DAYS FOR A BIRTHDAY PRESENT.

AND ALL THE IDIOTIC PARTIES WALTER LETS ME IN FOR.516 DAYS

HOW IS WALTER THESE DAYS$ 517 DAYS

OH, WALTER IS--WALTER. 517 DAYS

I DIDN'T--WHY DON'T I LEAVE WALTER'S 519 DAYS

(INDIGNANTLY) HOW CAN WALTER BE SUCH A BEAST/ 519 DAYS

SO I WENT BACK TO WALTER AND HE DOESN'T KNOW TO 520 DAYS THIS DAY I EVER LEFT HIM.

WALTER WAS DRUNK, PAWING OVER HIS LATEST FEMALE, 521 DAYS AND INSIDE I KEPT SWEARING TO MYSELF THAT I'D SHOW521 DAYS WALTER--

WALTER HAS BEEN TELLING PEOPLE. 526 DAYS

BUT HOW DOES WALTER KNOWS 526 DAYS

AND WALTER WILL HAVE TO TELL THAT TO EVERY ONE, 527 DAYS TOO--TO LIVE UP TO HIS POSE/

WALTER IT WAS I, HIS OLD FRIEND--SO YOU CAN WATCH 527 DAYS HIM SQUIRM SOME MORE/

BUT LET'S NOT TALK ABOUT WALTER. 528 DAYS

WALTER'S

PARTICULARLY SICK OF MYSELF BECAUSE I ENDURE THE 519 DAYS HUMILIATION OF WALTER'S OPEN

I INTENDED TO TELL FATHER I WAS THROUGH AS 519 DAYS WALTER'S WIFE.

IT WAS ONE OF WALTER'S PARTIES. 521 DAYS

GO HOME AND GET ON MY ARMOR FOR ANOTHER OF 524 DAYS WALTER'S PARTIES.

OH, YOU MEAN ON ACCOUNT OF WALTER'S ANTICS$ 528 DAYS

WALTZ

BEGINNING TO WHISTLE =OH, WALTZ ME AROUND AGAIN, 187 AHWILD AND SOMEONE WHISTLING =WALTZ ME AROUND AGAIN, 253 AHWILD WILLIES=)

THE ORCHESTRA AT THE CASINO STRIKES UP A WALTZ) 259 GGBROW

THEN SUDDENLY THE TUNE WENT FALSE, THE DANCERS 199 JOURNE WEARIED OF THE WALTZ...=

WALTZES

THE OPENING OF ONE OF CHOPIN'S SIMPLER WALTZES, 169 JOURNE DONE WITH

WAN

WITH A WAN SMILE) 167 BEYOND

THE MOONLIGHT IS ALMOST COMPLETELY SHUT OUT AND 198 EJONES ONLY A VAGUE WAN LIGHT FILTERS

(FORCING A WAN SMILE) THE HAPPINESS OF SEEING YOU 80 ELECTR AGAIN

HIGH HANGING LAMPS CAST A WAN LIGHT OVER THEIR 312 LAZARU FACES.

WAN FACES AT HOME. 409 MARCOM

THE TWO MAKE A STRANGELY TRAGIC PICTURE IN THE WAN157 MISBEG DAWN LIGHT--

(WITH A WAN, GRATEFUL SMILE) 464 WELDED

WAN'

I WAN' DANCE WITH GIRL. 498 VOYAGE

I WAN' SEE GIRLS--PLENTY GIRLS. 498 VOYAGE

WAN'T

SURE I MIGHT HAVE KNOWN IF I WAN'T A BLOODY FOOL 34 ANNA FROM BIRTH.

WAND

THE WITCH DOCTOR POINTS WITH HIS WAND TO THE 201 EJONES SACRED TREE, TO THE RIVER BEYOND,

THE WITCH DOCTOR PRANCES UP TO HIM, TOUCHES HIM 201 EJONES WITH HIS WAND.

WANDER

WHO DIDST WITH PITFALL AND GIN BESET THE PATH I 198 AHWILD WAS TO WANDER IN--

FREED FROM THE FARM--FREE TO WANDER ON AND ON-- 167 BEYOND ETERNALLY/

HAD BEEN DISPOSSESSED OF HIS REALM AND BANISHED TO110 MANSNS WANDER OVER THE WORLD,

HIS EYES WANDER ABOUT THE ROOM, FINALLY RESTING 397 MARCOM APPEALINGLY ON KUKACHIN.)

I HAD TO GO OUT AND WANDER UP AND DOWN THE TRAIN 149 MISBEG LOOKING FOR COMPANY,

HIS EYES WANDER ABOUT THE ROOM, GREEDILY TAKING IT124 STRANG IN.)

WANDERED

WANDERED
HAS WANDERED OVER TO THE WINDOW AT REAR OF DESK, 199 AHWILD
NIGHT)
IT SEEMS AN IRISHMAN GOT DRUNK IN TANGUT AND 374 MARCOM
WANDERED INTO A TEMPLE

WANDERING
THE NEED OF THE FREEDOM OF GREAT WIDE SPACES, THE 85 BEYOND
JOY OF WANDERING ON AND ON--
(DULLY) HIS MIND WAS WANDERING, I S'POSE. 163 BEYOND
(HIS MIND WANDERING) ARGUING, DID I SAY$ 487 CARDIF
HE BECOMES AWARE HE IS WANDERING, STRAIGHTENS 264 DESIRE
AGAIN.
WHO ARE THOSE PEOPLE I SAW WANDERING ABOUT THE 16 ELECTR
GROUNDS$
HIS WASHED-OUT BLUE EYES HAVE A WANDERING, HALF- 52 POET
WITTED EXPRESSION.
HE LOOKS SAD AND HOPELESS AND BITTER AND OLD, HIS 116 POET
EYES WANDERING DULLY.
(THINKING PITYINGLY) (WANDERING FROM ROOM TO 8 STRANG
ROOM--
HER MIND WAS WANDERING, POOR WOMAN/ 100 STRANG

WANDERINGLY
(WANDERINGLY) DO YOU KNOW WHAT I WAS DOING 41 STRANG
UPSTAIRS$

WANDERS
SHE IS PRETENDING TO READ A NOVEL, BUT HER 249 AHWILD
ATTENTION WANDERS, TOO.
CHRIS WANDERS ABOUT THE ROOM, CASTING QUICK, 41 ANNA
UNEASY SIDE GLANCES AT HER FACE,

WANE
AH, MOON OF MY DELIGHT THAT KNOWEST NO WANE/ 262 GGBROW

WANING
(WHO HAS BEEN REGARDING HIM WITH WANING 28 STRANG
RESENTMENT,

WANLY
ITS MISTY WINDOWS GLOWING WANLY WITH THE LIGHT OF 25 ANNA
A LAMP INSIDE.

WANNA
I WANNA COLLECT DE DOUGH I WOULDN'T TAKE DIS 699 ICEMAN
MORNIN', LIKE A SUCKER,

WANS'T
THAT WANS'T WHAT YOU WAS GOIN' TO SAY, YOU BAD 501 VOYAGE
CUCKY, YOU/

WANTA
WANTA SPILL MY SUDS FOR ME$ 9 ANNA
I WANTA TELL YUH SOMETHIN'-- 19 ANNA
WANTA HAVE A GOOD TIME, KID$ 611 ICEMAN
I SAYS, *HELLO, HANDSOME, WANTA HAVE A GOOD TIME$*616 ICEMAN
BUT I DON'T WANTA BE MARRIED TO NO SOAK. 616 ICEMAN
DON'T LET HICKEY PUT NO IDEAS IN YOUR NUTS IF YOU 631 ICEMAN
WANTA STAY HEALTHY/
D'YUH WANTA GUM HARRY'S PARTYS 632 ICEMAN
WANTA MAKE SOMETHIN' OF IT$ 671 ICEMAN
YUH DON'T WANTA SEE ME GET MARRIED AND SETTLE DOWN671 ICEMAN
LIKE A REG'LAR GUY/
(GRUMPILY) IN DE BACK ROOM IF YUH WANTA DRINK. 708 ICEMAN
I ASK YOU, D'YOU WANTA STAY ALL NIGHTS 472 WELDED

WANTED
I WASN'T 'SPECIALLY ANXIOUS THE MAN AT THE WHEEL 539 *ILE
SHOULD CATCH WHAT I WANTED TO
I WANTED TO BE WITH YOU, DAVID. 545 *ILE
I WANTED TO BE BY YOUR SIDE IN THE DANGER AND 545 *ILE
VIGOROUS LIFE OF IT ALL.
I WANTED TO SEE YOU THE HERO THEY MAKE YOU OUT TO 545 *ILE
BE IN HOMEPORT.
THAT'S ALL I WANTED TO KNOW. 207 AHWILD
AND I WANTED HER TO FACE LIFE AS IT IS. 207 AHWILD
MIND YOUR OWN BUSINESS, KID, AND DON'T BUTT IN 243 AHWILD
WHERE YOU'RE NOT WANTED/
I WANTED TO DIE. 281 AHWILD
SHE WANTED ME TO--BUT I WOULDN'T. 294 AHWILD
AS IF SHE WANTED TO REMAIN AS MUCH ISOLATED AS 30 ANNA
POSSIBLE.
LISTENING TO 'CM BAWLING AND CRYING DAY AND 58 ANNA
NIGHT--WHEN I WANTED TO BE OUT--
I WANTED TO MARRY YOU AND FOOL YOU, BUT I 59 ANNA
COULDN'T.
(THEN WITH A FORLORN LAUGH) IF HE DID COME BACK 64 ANNA
IT'D ONLY BE 'CAUSE HE WANTED TO
YOU SHOULD HAVE GONE BACK TO COLLEGE LAST FALL, 83 BEYOND
LIKE I KNOW YOU WANTED TO.
AND I KNOW HE WANTED THE MONEY TO USE IMPROVING 83 BEYOND
THE FARM.
I COULD HARDLY BACK OUT NOW, EVEN IF I WANTED TO. 88 BEYOND
(AVOIDING HER EYES) I THOUGHT MAYBE ROBERT WANTED 97 BEYOND
TO TONIGHT.
HE ONLY WANTED TO BE POLITE. 97 BEYOND
(HE STANDS BESIDE ROBERT AS IF HE WANTED TO SAY 101 BEYOND
SOMETHING MORE
(EVASIVELY) I'VE ALWAYS WANTED TO GO. 105 BEYOND
GO AND BE A TRAMP LIKE YOU'VE ALWAYS WANTED. 127 BEYOND
OH, I COULD GIVE YOU YOUR BELLYFUL OF DETAILS IF I132 BEYOND
WANTED TO TURN LOOSE ON YOU.
I BEGIN TO FEEL AS IF I'M NOT WANTED AROUND. 140 BEYOND
ANDY'S MADE A BIG SUCCESS OF HIMSELF--THE KIND HE 147 BEYOND
WANTED.
I'VE ALWAYS WANTED TO WRITE. 149 BEYOND
(DULLY) I WANTED TO SEND YOU WORD ONCE, BUT HE 154 BEYOND
ONLY GOT MAD WHEN I TOLD HIM.
I WANTED IT TO COME EASIER, SO LIKE ALL THE REST 156 BEYOND
OF THE IDIOTS.
WHY DO YOU SUPPOSE HE WANTED US TO PROMISE WE'D-- 163 BEYOND
HE WANTED TO MAKE SURE I'D BE ALL RIGHT---AFTER 163 BEYOND
HE'D GONE, I EXPECT.
'TWAS YANK HERE THAT HELD ME DOWN WHEN I WANTED TO482 CARDIF
JUMP INTO THE OCEAN.
ONLY I ALWAYS WANTED TO BE BURIED ON DRY LAND. 489 CARDIF
THEN YOU WANTED TO GO$ 561 CROSS

WANTED (CONT'D.)
MY FATHER WANTED TO GO WITH THEM--BUT MY MOTHER 561 CROSS
WAS DYING.
WANTED YOU. 497 DAYS
AS IF HE WANTED TO START WRITING.) 498 DAYS
I WANTED TO KILL HIM AND HER, BUT I ONLY LAUGHED 521 DAYS
AND HAD SOME MORE TO DRINK.
I WANTED TO TAKE HIS HAPPINESS FROM HIM AND KILL 521 DAYS
IT AS MINE HAD BEEN KILLED/
MY PRIDE WAS SO HURT I WANTED TO REVENGE MYSELF 521 DAYS
IT WAS THE LAST THING I EVER WANTED-- 522 DAYS
YOU LOVED HIM AND YOU WANTED TO BELIEVE. 523 DAYS
AT THESE TIMES HE WANTED ONLY TO DIE. 534 DAYS
HE WANTED TO RUN AWAY FROM HER--BUT FOUND HE 535 DAYS
COULDN'T.
HE WANTED TO DELIVER HIMSELF FROM ITS POWER AND BE538 DAYS
FREE AGAIN.
HE WANTED TO KILL IT/ 538 DAYS
HE WANTED TO KILL IT$ 538 DAYS
HE WANTED TO TELL HIS WIFE AND BEG FOR 539 DAYS
FORGIVENESS--
YE'RE SOLE OWNER--TILL HE COMES--THAT'S WHAT YE 216 DESIRE
WANTED.
I ON'Y WANTED YE FUR A PURPOSE O' MY OWN-- 240 DESIRE
I WANTED T' YELL AN' RUN. 242 DESIRE
NOT THE LIES YE JEST TOLD--BUT 'CAUSE YE WANTED T'262 DESIRE
STEAL AGEN--
IN THE MOONLIGHT--THOUGH IT WAS WARM--AND I WANTED515 DIFRNT
TO WRAP A BLANKET ROUND HER.
AND WANTED TO BE OUT WHERE THERE WAS MORE FUN$ 523 DIFRNT
WHEN I BROKE MY ENGAGEMENT I SAID I WANTED TO STAY$33 DIFRNT
FRIENDS LIKE WE'D BEEN
(COLDLY) I WANTED YOUR UNCLE CALEB, NOT YOU, BUT 547 DIFRNT
YOU'LL HAVE TO DO.
I SURE WAS DUMB WHEN IT CAME TO GUESSING WHAT SHE 458 DYNAMO
REALLY WANTED OR I WOULD HAVE--
AND DIDN'T GET WHAT YOU WANTED AND WAS SO DAMNED 460 DYNAMO
SCARED TO TOUCH YOU.
I NEVER STUCK TO ONE LONG, I WANTED TO KEEP MOVING461 DYNAMO
AND SEE EVERYTHING--
I WANTED TO PUNISH YOU. 466 DYNAMO
BUT--YOU WANTED TO MARRY ME THEN, RUBE. 470 DYNAMO
I'VE ALWAYS WANTED A BOY-- 477 DYNAMO
SHE WANTED TO PROVE I'VE CONQUERED THE FLESH/...)1481 DYNAMO
WOODS NIGGERS RIGHT WHERE I WANTED DEM. 177 EJONES
I WANTED TO BE ALONE--TO THINK OVER THINGS. 16 ELECTR
I'VE FOUND OUT ALL I WANTED TO FROM YOU. 27 ELECTR
HE WANTED MY HELP TO APPROACH YOUR FATHER-- 30 ELECTR
YOU WANTED ADAM BRANT YOURSELF/ 33 ELECTR
BUT YOU WANTED MY ANSWER, DIDN'T YOU$ 34 ELECTR
I WANTED YOU EVERY POSSIBLE MOMENT WE COULD STEAL/ 37 ELECTR
DIDN'T YOU SAY YOU WANTED TO KILL HIM$ 41 ELECTR
IT WAS YOUR DUTY TO TELL HIM FLATLY HE WASN'T 52 ELECTR
WANTED/
I COULD SEE YOU WANTED ME TO GO. 54 ELECTR
NOT FOR WHAT I WANTED MOST IN LIFE/ 55 ELECTR
I WANTED TO GIVE MYSELF/ 61 ELECTR
YOU WANTED THE TRUTH AND YOU'RE GOING TO HEAR IT 61 ELECTR
NOW/
YOU WANTED HIM TO DIE/ 63 ELECTR
AND TO THOSE HE WANTED TO KNOW HE WAS AS PLAIN AND 70 ELECTR
SIMPLE--
AND NOW--WELL, YOU WANTED ME TO BE A HERO IN BLUE, 75 ELECTR
SO YOU BETTER BE RESIGNED/
I WANTED TO DESERT AND RUN HOME--OR ELSE GET 89 ELECTR
KILLED/
I WENT MAD, WANTED TO KILL AND RAN ON, YELLING. 95 ELECTR
PRETEND YOU THINK I'M OUT OF MY MIND, AS SHE 100 ELECTR
WANTED YOU TO.
I KNEW IT--BUT I WANTED TO MAKE SURE. 101 ELECTR
IT GAVE ME THE CHANCE I WANTED TO COME TO YOU. 109 ELECTR
I ONLY WANTED HIM TO DIE AND LEAVE ME ALONE/ 110 ELECTR
I SHOULD HAVE DONE AS I WANTED-- 110 ELECTR
(GRIMLY) YOU WANTED PROOF/ 113 ELECTR
I WANTED TO ASK IF YOU OR PETER HAD HEARD ANYTHING118 ELECTR
FAUM ORIN AND VINNIE.
I WANTED TO TORTURE HER/ 124 ELECTR
THAT'S ALL I WANTED--TO HEAR YOU SAY THAT. 138 ELECTR
AND REMEMBER THIS HOMECOMING IS WHAT YOU WANTED. 141 ELECTR
HE WANTED ME TO, IF YOU REMEMBER. 150 ELECTR
WHEN YOU KNOW ALL SHE WANTED WAS TO LEAVE YOU 152 ELECTR
WITHOUT A THOUGHT AND MARRY THAT--
I SAW HOW YOU WANTED HIM/ 153 ELECTR
AND YOU WANTED HIM/ 154 ELECTR
YOU WANTED WILKINS JUST AS YOU'D WANTED BRANT/ 154 ELECTR
YOU WANTED BRANT FOR YOURSELF/ 154 ELECTR
I WANTED HIM/ 177 ELECTR
I WANTED TO LEARN LOVE FROM HIM--LOVE THAT WASN'T 177 ELECTR
A SIN/
I WANTED TO ASK YOU SOMETHING, TOO. 262 GGBROW
BECAUSE I WANTED TO TELL YOU SOMETHING. 262 GGBROW
HE WANTED TO KNOW WHY YOU'VE NEVER BEEN IN TO SEE 272 GGBROW
HIM.
HE COULD BE ANYTHING HE WANTED TO. 275 GGBROW
HE WANTED WHAT HE THOUGHT WAS MY LOVE OF THE 287 GGBROW
FLESH/
I WANTED CYBEL, AND I BOUGHT HER/ 298 GGBROW
I'VE WANTED TO, MARGARET/ 301 GGBROW
DAT'S WHY I WANTED TO JOIN IN. 247 HA APE
AND DID YOU HAVE ANY SPECIAL JOB IN THAT LINE YOU 248 HA APE
WANTED TO PROPOSE TO US$
HIS FACE'D BE RED AND HE'D LOOK LIKE HE WANTED TO 16 HUGHIE
CRAWL UNDER THE DESK AND HIDE.
HE WANTED ME TO BE THE SHEIK OF ARABY, 28 HUGHIE
HUGHIE WANTED TO THINK ME AND LEGS DIAMOND WAS OLD 29 HUGHIE
PALS.
THAT'S SOMETHING I'VE ALWAYS WANTED TO KNOW MORE 31 HUGHIE
ABOUT, TOO.

WANTED

WANTED (CONT'D.)
I WAS WITH A BUNCH OF HIGH CLASS DOLLS AND I 36 HUGHIE
WANTED TO SEE THEIR EYES POP OUT--
(IN A LOWERED VOICE BUT EAGERLY, AS IF HE WANTED 588 ICEMAN
THIS CHANCE TO TELL ABOUT IT)
MY FATHER WANTED A LAWYER IN THE FAMILY. 595 ICEMAN
STILL COULD HAVE IF I WANTED TO GO OUT AND SEE 600 ICEMAN
THEM.
BESSIE WANTED IT AND SHE WAS SO PROUD. 603 ICEMAN
HELL, IF YOU REALLY WANTED TO DIE, YOU'D JUST TAKE642 ICEMAN
A HOP OFF YOUR FIRE ESCAPE.
CHRIST, YOU'D THINK ALL I REALLY WANTED TO DO WITH645 ICEMAN
MY LIFE
HE WAS ASKING HARRY WHAT HE WANTED TO GO OUT FOR 652 ICEMAN
WHY, ALL THAT EVELYN EVER WANTED OUT OF LIFE WAS 663 ICEMAN
TO MAKE ME HAPPY.
AS IF SHE WANTED TO MAKE UP FOR SOMETHING. 667 ICEMAN
I GOT STUCK ON A WHORE AND WANTED DOUGH TO BLOW IN667 ICEMAN
ON HER AND HAVE A GOOD TIME/
I DON'T STAY WHERE I'S NOT WANTED. 673 ICEMAN
WHEN ALL YOU WANTED WAS TO GET DRUNK IN PEACE. 688 ICEMAN
ALL I'VE WANTED TO DO IS FIX IT SO HE'LL BE 691 ICEMAN
FINALLY AT PEACE WITH HIMSELF FOR
I DON'T WANT TO BE WHERE I'S NOT WANTED. 699 ICEMAN
JEES, IMAGINE ME KIDDIN' MYSELF I WANTED TO MARRY 700 ICEMAN
A DRUNKEN PIMP.
I SAW I COULDN'T DO IT BY KILLING MYSELF, LIKE I 705 ICEMAN
WANTED TO FOR A LONG TIME.
I KNEW EXACTLY WHAT I WANTED TO BE BY THAT TIME. 710 ICEMAN
PRETENDING YOU BELIEVED WHAT THEY WANTED TO 711 ICEMAN
BELIEVE ABOUT THEMSELVES.
THEY WANTED TO BUY SOMETHING TO SHOW THEIR 711 ICEMAN
GRATITUDE.
COULDN'T IF I WANTED TO. 712 ICEMAN
AS IF IT WAS SOMETHING I'D ALWAYS WANTED TO SAY... 716 ICEMAN
I JUST WANTED TO BE SURE. 720 ICEMAN
WE COULDN'T RUN AWAY OR FIGHT IF WE WANTED TO. 516 INZONE
(AS IF SHE WANTED TO DISMISS THE SUBJECT BUT 16 JOURNE
CAN'T.)
IF EDMUND WAS A LOUSY ACRE OF LAND YOU WANTED, THE 31 JOURNE
SKY WOULD BE THE LIMIT/
YOU NEVER WANTED TO DO ANYTHING EXCEPT LOAF IN 32 JOURNE
BARROOMS/
I NEVER WANTED TO BE AN ACTOR. 32 JOURNE
IN LIFE, YOU WANTED TO BELIEVE EVERY MAN WAS A 34 JOURNE
KNAVE WITH HIS SOUL FOR SALE.
SHE STOPPED IN THE HALL TO LISTEN, AS IF SHE 38 JOURNE
WANTED TO MAKE SURE I WAS.
SHE SPRINGS TO HER FEET, AS IF SHE WANTED TO RUN 42 JOURNE
AWAY FROM THE SOUND.
BUT HE'S NEVER WANTED FAMILY FRIENDS. 44 JOURNE
I NEVER WANTED TO LIVE HERE IN THE FIRST PLACE, 44 JOURNE
EVEN IF HE'D WANTED TO, HE COULDN'T HAVE HAD 45 JOURNE
PEOPLE HERE--
I MEAN, YOU WOULDN'T HAVE WANTED THEM. 45 JOURNE
I WANTED TO GIVE HER A CHANCE TO SLEEP. 56 JOURNE
YOU NEVER HAVE WANTED ONE--NEVER SINCE THE DAY WE 67 JOURNE
WERE MARRIED/
(VAGUELY.) THERE IS SOMETHING I WANTED TO SAY. 82 JOURNE
IF HE HEARD YOU HE MIGHT THINK YOU NEVER WANTED 88 JOURNE
HIM.
YOU WANTED TO GET RID OF THEM. 95 JOURNE
I COULDN'T PLAY WITH SUCH CRIPPLED FINGERS, EVEN 104 JOURNE
IF I WANTED TO.
ALL I WANTED WAS TO BE HIS WIFE. 105 JOURNE
MY FATHER TOLD ME TO BUY ANYTHING I WANTED AND 114 JOURNE
NEVER MIND WHAT IT COST.
BESIDES, I WANTED TO TREAT CATHLEEN BECAUSE I HAD 116 JOURNE
HER DRIVE UPTOWN WITH ME.
AND HE WAS HOMESICK FOR IRELAND, AND WANTED TO GO 117 JOURNE
BACK THERE TO DIE.
(STARING BEFORE HIM.) THE FOG WAS WHERE I WANTED 131 JOURNE
TO BE.
THAT'S WHAT I WANTED-- 131 JOURNE
AT THE SAME TIME CRYING POORHOUSE AND MAKING IT 140 JOURNE
PLAIN YOU WANTED A CHEAP ONE/
AND SHE CAME BECAUSE SHE LOVED ME AND WANTED TO BE142 JOURNE
WITH ME.
AND WANTED US OUT OF YOUR WAY/ 142 JOURNE
THERE WAS ALWAYS THE MEMBERS OF MY COMPANY TO TALK142 JOURNE
TO, IF SHE'D WANTED.
NATURALLY, I WANTED HER WITH ME. 142 JOURNE
SHOWING YOU WANTED TO WISH ME ON CHARITY/ 144 JOURNE
I HAD LIFE WHERE I WANTED IT/ 150 JOURNE
(BITTERLY.) WHAT THE HELL WAS IT I WANTED TO BUY,150 JOURNE
I WONDER. THAT WAS WORTH--
AND THEN LIFE HAD ME WHERE IT WANTED ME-- 150 JOURNE
NO, I DON'T KNOW WHAT THE HELL IT WAS I WANTED TO 151 JOURNE
BUY.
IS NOT REALLY WANTED, WHO CAN NEVER BELONG, 154 JOURNE
(THEN PROTESTING UNEASILY.) BUT THAT'S MORBID 154 JOURNE
CRAZINESS ABOUT NOT BEING WANTED
ALL I WANTED WAS A LITTLE HEART-TO-HEART TALK 160 JOURNE
SO I HAD TO SAY I LOVED HER BECAUSE SHE WAS FAT, 160 JOURNE
AND SHE WANTED TO BELIEVE THAT,
AND BECAUSE I ONCE WANTED TO WRITE, 164 JOURNE
WANTED YOU TO FAIL. 165 JOURNE
NEVER WANTED YOU SUCCEED AND MAKE ME LOOK EVEN 165 JOURNE
WORSE BY COMPARISON.
WHAT I WANTED TO SAY IS, 166 JOURNE
BUT I DON'T KNOW WHAT I WANTED IT FOR. 172 JOURNE
I TOLD HER I WANTED TO BE A NUN. 175 JOURNE
THEN IT WAS ONLY MY BODY THAT WANTED A SLAVE. 351 LAZARU
I THOUGHT YOU WANTED TO SEE ME ALONE. 7 MANSNS
YOU WANTED TO PUT DOUBT AND DISGUST FOR HIMSELF IN 20 MANSNS
HIS MIND.
BUT WHAT I WANTED TO SAY IS, YOU DON'T KNOW ME. 20 MANSNS

WANTED (CONT'D.)
(ABRUPTLY.) BUT ALL I WANTED TO TELL YOU WAS MY 47 MANSNS
FINAL DECISION ABOUT THE BOOK.
WHAT I WANTED TO SAY IS-- 65 MANSNS
BECAUSE I WANTED TO CONVINCE MYSELF YOU WERE SURE 67 MANSNS
OF EACH OTHER'S GOOD FAITH.
AND THEN HAVING HAD ALL I WANTED OF HER, DESERTED 74 MANSNS
HER--
TO GET WHAT SHE WANTED. 74 MANSNS
IF I THOUGHT YOU WANTED ANOTHER WOMAN--/ 80 MANSNS
YOU'LL SAY NEXT IT WAS I THAT WANTED YOU TO SLEEP 83 MANSNS
ALONE.
(HUGS HER--PASSIONATELY.) I HAVE NEVER WANTED YOU 91 MANSNS
SO MUCH/
I SIMPLY WANTED TO BE SURE.= 108 MANSNS
HE WANTED TO TURN HIS BACK ON THE DOOR AND GO FAR 111 MANSNS
AWAY.
I WAS A FOOL TO LET HIM SEE I WANTED HIM SO MUCH/ 119 MANSNS
YOU WANTED TO SAY SOMETHINGS 122 MANSNS
AS IF HE WERE DOING ME A FAVOR--I NEVER EVEN 122 MANSNS
WANTED HIM TO BE CONCEIVED--
I THINK YOU COULD TAKE WHAT YOU WANTED FROM ANY 144 MANSNS
ONE OF THEM/
BUT IT WAS YOU--WHAT YOU WANTED ME-- 155 MANSNS
I COULDN'T HAVE KEPT HIM FROM ME IF I'D WANTED/ 166 MANSNS
BECAUSE IT POSSESSED YOU AND YOU WANTED TO BE 183 MANSNS
FREE/
AND THAT'S ALL YOU'VE WANTED, ISN'T ITS 188 MANSNS
THEY COULD NOT KEEP YOU--YOU WERE TOO HOMESICK-- 438 MARCOM
YOU WANTED TO RETURN--
I ONLY THOUGHT YOU WANTED MY OPINION. 22 MISBEG
(MILDLY.) I THOUGHT YOU WANTED MY HONEST OPINION 23 MISBEG
SURE, ALL I WANTED WAS TO GIVE HIM THE FUN OF 26 MISBEG
SEEING THROUGH THEM
OR LET THE EXECUTORS DO IT, EVEN IF THEY WANTED, 31 MISBEG
WHICH THEY DON'T.
I'VE WANTED TO GO ON THE WAGON FOR THE PAST 45 MISBEG
TWENTY-FIVE YEARS,
I'VE ALWAYS WANTED TO OWN A GOLD MINE--SO I COULD 67 MISBEG
SELL IT.
FROM YOUR BRAINS AND GET YOUR HEAD CLEAR WHEN YOU 81 MISBEG
WANTED.
ANYWAY, I WANTED TO FIND OUT WHAT TRICK HE HAD UP 85 MISBEG
HIS SLEEVE,
I THOUGHT YOU WANTED TO MAKE HIM PAY FOR HIS BLACK 94 MISBEG
TREACHERY AGAINST US.
YOU KIDDED THEM TILL YOU WERE SURE THEY WANTED 134 MISBEG
YOU.
THAT WAS ALL YOU WANTED. 134 MISBEG
I WANTED TO CLEAR THINGS UP, THAT'S ALL--FOR 136 MISBEG
PHIL'S SAKE AS WELL AS YOURS.
I'VE WANTED YOU ALL ALONG. 137 MISBEG
DID YOU PROMISE THAT, IF ALL YOU WANTED WAS WHAT 140 MISBEG
ALL THE OTHERS WANT.
NOW LAY YOUR HEAD ON MY BREAST--THE WAY YOU SAID 142 MISBEG
YOU WANTED TO DO--
IT WAS AS IF I WANTED REVENGE--BECAUSE I'D BEEN 150 MISBEG
LEFT ALONE--
HE WANTED TO SLEEP THE WAY HE IS, AND I LET HIM 162 MISBEG
SLEEP.
YOU KNEW I LOVED HIM AND WANTED HIM AND YOU USED 163 MISBEG
THAT.
THE ONE THING YOU TALKED A LOT ABOUT WAS THAT YOU 170 MISBEG
WANTED THE NIGHT WITH ME TO BE
BUT I CAN'T BEAR TO HAVE YOU ASHAMED YOU WANTED MY173 MISBEG
LOVE TO COMFORT YOUR SORROW--
I WANTED YOU TO FIND HAPPINESS-- 175 MISBEG
I WANTED TO SAVE HIM, AND I HOPED HE'D SEE THAT 175 MISBEG
ONLY YOUR LOVE COULD--
AND HE HAD THE CHANCE HE WANTED IN PORTUGAL AND 13 POET
SPAIN WHERE A BRITISH OFFICER
HADN'T STARTS TO GO IN THE BAR, AS IF HE TOO WANTED 15 POET
TO AVOID SARA.
I COULD GIVE ALL OF MYSELF IF I WANTED TO, BUT-- 25 POET
WANTED TO/ 25 POET
HE WANTED TO PROVE HIS INDEPENDENCE BY LIVING 29 POET
ALONE IN THE WILDS,
I'VE TOLD YOU BEFORE HE WANTED TO GET AWAY FROM 29 POET
HIS FATHER'S BUSINESS.
I HAVE WANTED A QUIET CHAT WITH YOU FOR SOME TIME. 46 POET
I WANTED TO LEARN WHAT TRICKS SHE MIGHT BE UP TO, 79 POET
SO I'LL BE ABLE TO FIGHT THEM.
AND SHE HAD SAID ALL SHE WANTED WAS HIS HAPPINESS 109 POET
BUT SHE FELT IN FAIRNESS TO
THAT HE WANTED TO MARRY YOU. 109 POET
HE SAID ALL SHE WANTED WAS FOR HIM TO BE FREE TO 144 POET
DO AS HE PLEASED,
SO I KISSED HIM AND SAID ALL I WANTED IN LIFE WAS 146 POET
HIS LOVE.
IF SHE WANTED REVENGE ON HIM, I'M SURE SHE'S HAD 150 POET
HER FILL OF IT.
HE WANTED TO MAKE SURE THE ROPE WAS STILL HERE. 582 ROPE
YUH WANTED TO SEE ME HANGIN' THERE IN REAL 597 ROPE
EARNEST, DIDN'T YUHS
GURDON WANTED THEIR MARRIAGE TO TAKE PLACE, AND 10 STRANG
NINA CONSENTED.
I HAVEN'T WANTED TO ADMIT IT. 10 STRANG
YOU'RE GOING TO HAVE THE CHILD YOU WANTED, AREN'T 103 STRANG
YOU?
WHAT I WANTED TO BE AND COULDN'T. 120 STRANG
NINA WANTED TO TELL SAM... 124 STRANG
HE WANTED TO WRITE YOU ABOUT THE BABY. 132 STRANG
AND I WANTED TO BOAST ABOUT HOW I WAS GETTING ON/ 133 STRANG
BUT HE HAS ALWAYS WANTED MORE... 138 STRANG
I WANTED TO PUT UP ALL THE MONEY TO BACK SAM WHEN 146 STRANG
HE STARTED.
I WANTED TO DO IT FOR SAM'S SAKE--BUT ESPECIALLY 146 STRANG
FOR MY CHILD'S SAKE.

WANTED

WANTED (CONT'D.)
JUST WHAT I WANTED YOU TO SAY/...)) 155 STRANG
I WANTED TO BRING GORDON AND HIS FRIENDS ON BOARD 161 STRANG
TO CELEBRATE...
AND IT WAS ALWAYS WHAT GORDON HIMSELF WANTED, 167 STRANG
OH--I SUPPOSE YOU WANTED TO MAKE SURE SO YOU COULDN'T2 STRANG
HOPE HE'D GO INSANE!
AND SHE SIMPLY WANTED TO BE REVENGED, I'M SURE. 172 STRANG
I'VE WANTED ALL MY LIFE TO TELL HER/...)) 175 STRANG
I FORGIVE EVEN YOUR TRYING TO TELL MADELINE--YOU 180 STRANG
WANTED TO KEEP GORDON--

WAR
BUT IN THIS WAR I'VE SEEN TOO MANY WHITE WALLS 54 ELECTR
SPLATTERED WITH BLOOD
I CALL TO MIND THE MEXICAN WAR. 54 ELECTR
HE WAS MAYOR OF THE TOWN AND A NATIONAL WAR HERO-- 69 ELECTR
AFTER PASSING UNARMED THROUGH THE WHOLE WAR/ 69 ELECTR
WELL, THE WAR WAS OVER, HE WAS WORN OUT, HE'D HAD 70 ELECTR
A LONG, HARD TRIP HOME--
I CAN'T GRASP ANYTHING BUT WAR, IN WHICH HE WAS SO 75 ELECTR
ALIVE.
HE WAS THE WAR TO ME--THE WAR THAT WOULD NEVER END 75 ELECTR
UNTIL I DIED.
SOMETIME IN SOME WAR 82 ELECTR
THE WAR HAS GOT ME SILLY, I GUESS/ 87 ELECTR
IT WAS VINNIE'S FAULT YOU EVER WENT TO WAR/ 87 ELECTR
FINALLY THOSE ISLANDS COME TO MEAN EVERYTHING THAT 90 ELECTR
WASN'T WAR.
HE BOASTED THAT YOU HAD DONE ONE OF THE BRAVEST 94 ELECTR
THINGS HE'D SEEN IN THE WAR/
FOR HEAVEN'S SAKE, FORGET THE WAR/ 95 ELECTR
I HAD A QUEER FEELING THAT WAR MEANT MURDERING THE 95 ELECTR
SAME MAN OVER AND OVER.
ON BOTH SIDES SUDDENLY SAW THE JOKE WAR WAS AND 95 ELECTR
THEM AND LAUGHED AND SHOOK HANDS/
HE THOUGHT THE WAR HAD MADE A MAN OF YOU/ 98 ELECTR
(IN A STRAINED VOICE) IT'S THE SAME THING--WHAT 146 ELECTR
THE WAR DID TO HIM--
THE ORIN YOU LOVED WAS KILLED IN THE WAR. 164 ELECTR
FOLLOWING THE FIRST WORLD WAR AND PROHIBITION, 7 HUGHIE
BUT THE LAST TIME HE WAS ABLE TO FEEL DESPAIR WAS 17 HUGHIE
BACK AROUND WORLD WAR DAYS
I TELL YOU, PAL, I'D RATHER SLEEP IN THE SAME 21 HUGHIE
STALL WITH OLD MAN O' WAR
WHO LED A COMMANDO IN THE WAR. 593 ICEMAN
IN THE BOER WAR SPECTACLE AT THE ST. LOUIS FAIR 593 ICEMAN
WE MUST FORGET THE WAR. 599 ICEMAN
BEJEES, IF THERE WAS A WAR AND YOU WAS IN IT, 609 ICEMAN
I VAS A FARMER BEFORE THE WAR VEN PLOUDY LIMEY 676 ICEMAN
THIEVES STEAL MY COUNTRY.
I ALSO HAF HEARD RUMORS OF A LIMEY OFFICER WHO, 677 ICEMAN
AFTER THE WAR,
WHEN WE CAN START THE BOER WAR RAGING AGAIN/ 677 ICEMAN
AND BESIDES, YOU'RE OLD WAR HEROES/ 685 ICEMAN
WELL, WE'RE IN THE WAR ZONE RIGHT THIS MINIT IF 514 INZONE
YOU WANTS TO KNOW.
NOT UNTIL WE GET INTO THE WAR ZONE, AT ANY RATE. 514 INZONE
AND THE DIRRTY WORK THEY'RE DOIN' ALL THE WARS 515 INZONE
NOW WE'RE IN THE WAR ZONE. 516 INZONE
THIS WAR ZONE STUFF'S GOT YER GOAT, DRISC-- 517 INZONE
ALL WE KNOW IS HE SHIPS ON HERE IN LONDON 'BOUT A 522 INZONE
YEAR B'FORE THE WAR STARTS.
THIS ONE WAS WRITTEN A YEAR BEFORE THE WAR STARTED53I INZONE
ANYWAY.
NOW WE WANT PEACE TO LAUGH IN--TO LAUGH AT WAR/ 322 LAZARU
WAR, NO MORE/ 323 LAZARU
A WAR--A DUEL TO THE DEATH-- (WITH REVENGEFUL 74 MANSNS
BITTERNESS.)
ALL IS FAIR IN WAR. 152 MANSNS
IT MIGHT MEAN WAR. 386 MARCOM
WAR IS A WASTE OF MONEY WHICH EATS INTO THE 394 MARCOM
PROFITS OF LIFE LIKE THUNDER/
THEN WHY WAR, I ASKED MYSELF/ 394 MARCOM
BUT THIS IS WAR AND NOT A TRAGEDY. 395 MARCOM
LET IT MEAN WAR/ 400 MARCOM
A PRACTICAL WAR OF FEW WORDS, AS THAT POLO YOU 422 MARCOM
ADMIRE WOULD SAY.
AUGUST COMMANDER, IF YOU MUST HAVE WAR, LET IT BE 422 MARCOM
ONE WITHOUT FINE PHRASES--
AND IT WOULD BE A RIGHTEOUS WAR/ 422 MARCOM
LEAD YOUR GALLANT MILLION THERE--AND SEE TO IT 422 MARCOM
YOUR WAR LEAVES ME IN PEACE/
HIS MAJESTY HAS DECLARED WAR/ 422 MARCOM
I REVOKE MY DECLARATION OF WAR--UNLESS YOU LEARN 423 MARCOM
TO DANCE AND BE SILENT/
(SMILING--DISTRACTEDLY) WAR WITHOUT RHETORIC, 423 MARCOM
PLEASE/
SINCE THE WAR WITH THE FRENCH IN SPAIN--AFTER THE 10 POET
BATTLE OF SALAMANCA IN '12.
HE MARRIED HER AND THEN WENT OFF TO THE WAR, 14 POET
IN PENINSULAR WAR DAYS.) 34 POET
GREAT ENOUGH TO CRUSH ENGLAND IN THE NEXT WAR 40 POET
BETWEEN THEM.
HIS WAS A PERSONAL WAR, I AM SURE--FOR PURE 82 POET
FREEDOM.
BUT I SUSPECT THE WAR FOR INDEPENDENCE WAS MERELY 82 POET
I SUPPOSE YOU FOUND EVERYTHING COMPLETELY CHANGED 7 STRANG
SINCE BEFORE THE WAR.
(THE WAR.... 7 STRANG
WELL, THE WAR IS OVER. 14 STRANG
IN THE WAR/ 30 STRANG
AND I THINK NURSING ALL THOSE POOR GUYS KEEPS THE 31 STRANG
WAR BEFORE HER.
TIME GIVE HAPPINESS TO VARIOUS FELLOW WAR-VICTIMS 35 STRANG
BY PRETENDING TO LOVE THEM.
THE WAR KILLED HIM. 35 STRANG
THE WAR HADN'T MAIMED HIM. 45 STRANG

WAR (CONT'D.)
REALLY, THAT THE WAR HAD BLOWN MY HEART AND 45 STRANG
INSIDES OUT/
OF PEACE, AFTER THE LONG INTERLUDE OF WAR WITH 188 STRANG
LIFE.
THE FEATURES AT WAR WITH ONE ANOTHER-- 443 WELDED

WAR-PRAU
A PROPER PROPER WAR-PRAU SUCH AS THE PIRATES USED 560 CROSS
TO USE.

WAR*PRAU
A PROPER WAR*PRAU SUCH AS THE PIRATES USED TO USE.560 CROSS

WAR'S
WAIT FOR NINA TILL THE WAR'S OVER, 20 STRANG

WARD
TRYING TO WARD OFF THE BLOW FROM HIS DAUGHTER, 60 ANNA
(WHO HAS BEEN STARING AT HIM WITH TERROR, RAISING 292 GGBROW
HER MASK TO WARD OFF HIS FACE)
NOMINATION BECAUSE THEY KNEW THEY COULDN'T WIN 603 ICEMAN
THAT YEAR IN THIS WARD.
I KNEW EVERY MAN, WOMAN AND CHILD IN THE WARD, 603 ICEMAN
ALMOST.
TAKE A WALK AROUND THE WARD, SEE ALL THE FRIENDS 1604 ICEMAN
USED TO KNOW.
WHEN BOT' OF 'EM WAS DRAGGED UP IN DIS WARD 614 ICEMAN
SHOW YOU A LITTLE WALK AROUND THE WARD IS NOTHING 621 ICEMAN
TO BE SO SCARED ABOUT.
THAT WALK AROUND THE WARD YOU NEVER TAKE-- 622 ICEMAN
(WITH AN AIR OF FRANKNESS) YES, AND I OUGHT TO 626 ICEMAN
TAKE A WALK AROUND THE WARD.
HARRY'LL MOSEY AROUND THE WARD, DROPPING IN ON 651 ICEMAN
EVERYONE WHO KNEW HIM WHEN.
WE'VE HEARD HIS BULL ABOUT TAKING A WALK AROUND 660 ICEMAN
THE WARD FOR YEARS.
IN--SOMETHING THEY THREW OUT OF THE D. T. WARD IN 713 ICEMAN
BELLEVUE
(TRIES TO WARD THIS OFF BY POUNDING WITH HIS GLASS715 ICEMAN
ON THE TABLE--

WARDED
WAS IT NOT YOUR BRAVE SWORD THAT WARDED OFF THEIR 411 MARCOM
CURVED KNIVES FROM MY BREAST

WARDING
RESOLUTELY WARDING OFF FROM HIS CONSCIOUSNESS. 73 STRANG
PROTECTIVE WARDING OFF AND AT THE SAME TIME A 480 WELDED
SEEKING POSSESSION.

WARDROBE
I FOUND THEM WHERE HE'D HIDDEN THEM ON THE SHELF 192 AHWILD
IN HIS WARDROBE.
THEY WERE ON THE SHELF IN YOUR WARDROBE AND NOW 196 AHWILD
YOU'VE GONE AND HID THEM

WARDS
(SHE WARDS HIM OFF AND STEPS PAST HIM INTO THE 548 DAYS
STUDY.
(HE TRIES TO KISS HER, BUT SHE WARDS HIM OFF AND 81 MISBEG
STEERS HIM BACK TO THE CHAIR.)

WAREHOUSE
HALF IN AND HALF OUT OF THE SHADOW OF THE 102 ELECTR
WAREHOUSE,
ON THE WHARF THE END OF A WAREHOUSE IS AT LEFT 102 ELECTR
FRONT.
(HE STANDS AGAINST THE WAREHOUSE, WAITING FOR THE 104 ELECTR
SWAYING WORLD TO SUBSIDE.
THEN BACK AGAINST THE WAREHOUSE WITH A THUMP. 104 ELECTR
(HE TAKES A STEP BUT LURCHES INTO THE SHADOW AND 104 ELECTR
LEANS AGAINST THE WAREHOUSE)
MOVES STEALTHILY OUT FROM THE DARKNESS BETWEEN THE107 ELECTR
SHIP AND THE WAREHOUSE, LEFT,
AND HE PEEKS DOWN INTO THE SHADOWS OF THE 107 ELECTR
WAREHOUSE)
(THE CHANTYMEN GUES UNSTEADILY OFF LEFT, BETWEEN 107 ELECTR
THE WAREHOUSE AND THE SHIP.
AT THE RIGHT IS A WAREHOUSE, FROM A DOOR IN WHICH 399 MARCOM
A LINE OF HALF-NAKED SLAVES
HE STOLE IT FROM A WAREHOUSE ON FAKED PERMITS. 115 MISBEG

WARILY
(HE DARTS A QUICK GLANCE AT THE CLERK'S FACE AND 36 HUGHIE
BEGINS TO HEDGE WARILY.
(CALIGULA SLINKS DOWN WARILY) 339 LAZARU
(THEN WARILY.) BUT, OF COURSE, IT DEPENDS ON WHAT 56 MANSNS

SIMON--
(COMES OVER TO HER FATHER BUT WARILY KEEPS OUT OF 579 ROPE
RANGE OF HIS STICK)

WARINESS
BUT ONE SENSES AN UNEASY WARINESS BENEATH HER 16 ELECTR
POSE)

WARM
THIS IS A WARM LULU FOR FAIR/ 205 AHWILD
THAT STUFF IS WARM--TOO DAMNED WARM, IF YOU ASK 205 AHWILD
ME/
THE WATER WAS WONDERFUL AND WARM. 228 AHWILD
SOMETHING THAT'LL WARM HIM UP, EHS 238 AHWILD
THIS'LL WARM HIM FOR YOU. 239 AHWILD
TO KEEP THINGS WARM FOR YOU. YOU'RE MISTAKEN. 122 BEYOND
(STARING AT THE STOVE) YOU BETTER COME NEAR THE 145 BEYOND
FIRE WHERE IT'S WARM.
(SHE STRETCHES OUT HER HANDS TO WARM THEM) 152 BEYOND
WE'RE PAYING FOR THE SPELL OF WARM WEATHER WE'VE 153 BEYOND
BEEN HAVING.
SURE YOU'RE WARM ENOUGH$ 533 DAYS
THAT DEATH IS FINAL RELEASE, THE WARM, DARK PEACE 534 DAYS
OF ANNIHILATION.
BUT DEATH IS WHAT THE DEAD KNOW, THE WARM, DARK 562 DAYS
NUMB OF NOTHINGNESS--
IT'S WARM DOWN T' THE BARN--NICE SMELLIN' AN' 231 DESIRE
WARM--WITH THE COWS.
(QUERERLY) DOWN--WHAR IT'S RESTFUL--WHAR IT'S 238 DESIRE
WARM--DOWN IT THE BARN.
IN THE MOONLIGHT--THOUGH IT WAS WARM--AND I WANTED515 DIFRNT
TO WRAP A BLANKET ROUND HER.

WARN

WARN (CONT'D.)
IT'S WARM TONIGHT... 429 DYNAMO
YOU'RE LIKE--DYNAMO--THE GREAT MOTHER--BIG AND 477 DYNAMO
WARM--
THE WARM SAND WAS LIKE YOUR SKIN, 90 ELECTR
THE WARM EARTH IN THE MOONLIGHT, THE TRADE WINDS 112 ELECTR
RUSTLING THE COCO PALMS,
THERE WAS ONLY THIS WORLD--THE WARM EARTH IN THE 147 ELECTR
MOONLIGHT--
BUT THE MOONLIGHT WAS SO WARM AND BEAUTIFUL IN 259 GGBROW
THOSE DAYS,
I COULD FEEL THE NIGHT WRAPPED AROUND ME LIKE A 261 GGBROW
GRAY VELVET GOWN LINED WITH WARM
(SHE STARES UP AT THE SKY) THE MOONLIGHT WAS 261 GGBROW
WARM, THEN,
THE EARTH IS WARM, 322 GGBROW
IT WAS SO WARM AND BEAUTIFUL IN THOSE DAYS. 323 GGBROW
A WARM SUN ON THE CLEAN DECKS, 214 HA APE
A NICE WARM BREEZE-- 221 HA APE
SO AS 'ER AND 'ERS CAN KEEP THEIR BLEEDIN' NOSES 236 HA APE
WARM/
DE SUN WAS WARM, DEY WASN'T NO CLOUDS, AND DERE 252 HA APE
WAS A BREEZE BLOWIN'.
I WAS ACCEPTED SOCIALLY WITH ALL THE WARM 595 ICEMAN
CORDIALITY
TYRONE SPEAKS, AT FIRST WITH A WARM, RELIEVED 126 JOURNE
WELCOME.)
=ALL NIGHT UPON MINE HEART I FELT HER WARM HEART 134 JOURNE
BEAT,
IS THE WARM EARTH SMELLING OF NIGHT 310 LAZARU
IN THE CITY ON A WARM MOONLIGHT NIGHT IN JUNE 25 MANSNS
1836.
CONTENTMENT IS A WARM STY FOR THE EATERS AND 400 MARCOM
SLEEPERS/
A DRINK WILL WARM UP MY WELCOME FOR HIS MAJESTY. 53 MISBEG
IT IS A CLEAR WARM MOONLIGHT NIGHT, AROUND ELEVEN 71 MISBEG
O'CLOCK.
YOU'RE REAL AND HEALTHY AND CLEAN AND FINE AND 118 MISBEG
WARM AND STRONG AND KIND--
AND BEAUTIFUL EYES AND HAIR, AND A BEAUTIFUL SMILE119 MISBEG
AND BEAUTIFUL WARM BREASTS.
IT'S STRONG AND KIND AND WARM--LIKE YOU. 130 MISBEG
AND TAKE OFF HIS SHOES AND SOCKS AND WARM THE 600 ROPE
BOTTOMS OF HIS FEET FOR HIM.
WARM IN HIS ARMS BEFORE THE FIREPLACE... 27 STRANG
WARM IN HIS LOVE, SAFE--DRIFTING INTO SLEEP...= 27 STRANG
FROM THE WINDOW, ALTHOUGH IT IS A BEAUTIFUL WARM 48 STRANG
DAY IN THE FLOWER GARDEN BEYOND
HER TWO HANDS ARE SO WARM/... 88 STRANG
IT'S GOOD 'N' WARM IN THIS DUMP, I'LL HAND IT 471 WELDED
THAT.

WARMED
(GETTING WARMED UP) THE LAND OF THE FREE AND THE 194 AHWILD
HOME OF THE BRAVE/

WARMER
CAN'T YOU LIVEN IT UP, PUT IN SOME DECORATIONS, 306 GGBROW
MAKE IT FANCIER AND WARMER--

WARMIN'
I BEEN WARNIN' A BENCH DOWN TO DE BATTERY--EVER 252 HA APE
SINCE LAST NIGHT.

WARNING
SUN WARMING THE BLOOD OF YOU, 214 HA APE
(WARNING TOWARD THE CLERK.) SAY, NOW I NOTICE, 11 HUGHIE
YOU DON'T LOOK LIKE HUGHIE,
(WARNING TO HIS SUBJECT, SHAKES HIS HEAD SADLY) 627 ICEMAN
(WARMING UP, CHANGES ABRUPTLY TO HIS USUAL 724 ICEMAN
DECLARATORY DENUNCIATION)

WARMINGLY
(WARMINGLY) SHHH/ 370 MARCOM

WARMLY
(WARMLY) A GOOD SHIPMATE HE WAS AND IS, NONE 480 CARDIF
BETTER.
SHE IS WARMLY AROUND ME/ 266 GGBROW
HE GRINS WARMLY AND SAUNTERS CONFIDENTLY BACK TO 36 HUGHIE
THE DESK.)
LEFT, WARMLY WELCOMED BY ALL. 726 ICEMAN
AROUND ME, SOFTLY, WARMLY, AND THE CLOUD DISSOLVED342 LAZARU
INTO THE SKY,

WARMS
HIS VOICE UTTERS AND WARMS TO HIS WORK) 431 MARCOM

WARMTH
WITH HANDS OUTSTRETCHED TO THE WARMTH 144 BEYOND
EVERYTHING THAT WAS PEACE AND WARMTH AND SECURITY. 90 ELECTR
(SOMBERLY) WHEN PAN WAS FORBIDDEN THE LIGHT AND 297 GGBROW
WARMTH OF THE SUN HE GREW
ERIE GOES ON WITH GATHERING WARMTH AND SELF- 36 HUGHIE
ASSURANCE.)
MY HEART LONGS FOR THE WARMTH 345 LAZARU
(CREGAN IS SURPRISED AND PLEASED BY THE WARMTH OF 92 POET
HIS WELCOME.
AND HIS VOICE IS FULL OF WELCOMING WARMTH AS HE 92 POET
CALLS.)

WARN
I WARN YOU BEFOREHAND IF THE ANSWER IS =YES= I'M 206 AHWILD
GOING TO PUNISH YOU AND PUNISH
AND I'VE GOT TO WARN THAT YOUNG IMP TO KEEP HIS 214 AHWILD
FACE STRAIGHT.
I'VE GOT TO WARN THAT TOMMY AGAINST GIVING ME AWAY214 AHWILD
TO NAT ABOUT THE FISH.
OR I WARN YOU SOMETHING'S GOING TO HAPPEN/ 264 AHWILD
I FEEL IT MY DUTY, FATHER, TO WARN YOU THAT JOHN'S504 DAYS
GOT WRITER'S ITCH AGAIN.
THERE'S ONLY ONE THING I'VE GOT TO WARN YOU ABOUT.526 DAYS
I WARN YOU/ 560 DAYS
HE MIGHT WARN FIFE. 449 DYNAMO
I SUPPOSE YOU WANT TO RUN OVER AND WARN YOUR FINE 450 DYNAMO
FRIENDS/
WARN YOU ABOUT WHAT, REUBENS 478 DYNAMO

WARNED

WARN (CONT'D.)
BEFORE THAT SHE USED TO COME ALMOST EVERY NIGHT T0478 DYNAMO
WARN ME.
(MOTHER WOULD WARN ME IF I WAS DOING WRONG... 485 DYNAMO
(THEN SHARPLY) WARN ME4. 12 ELECTR
THERE'S SOMETHIN' BEEN ON MY MIND LATELY I WANT TO 12 ELECTA
WARN YOU ABOUT.
WHAT IS IT ABOUT CAPTAIN BRANT YOU WANT TO WARN ME 18 ELECTR
AGAINST/
I THOUGHT YOU OUGHT TO WARN MOTHER SHE WAS FOOLISH 50 ELECTR
TO ALLOW HIM TO COME HERE.
I WARN YOU SHE'LL DO EVERYTHING SHE CAN TO KEEP 72 ELECTR
HIM FROM MARRYING YOU.
ALL I WANT TO DO IS WARN YOU TO BE ON YOUR GUARD. 76 ELECTR
I'VE GOT TO WARN HIM/ 92 ELECTR
I WARN YOU I WON'T LISTEN/ 96 ELECTR
I WARN YE, SKIPPER/ 106 ELECTR
SO MANY THINGS HAVE HAPPENED I COULDN'T FORESEE--I109 ELECTR
CAME TO WARN YOU--
I HEARD HER WARN HIM AGAINST ME/ 113 ELECTR
I'LL WARN HER. 148 ELECTR
IT'S WISER FOR YOU TO KEEP HAZEL AWAY FROM ME, I 152 ELECTR
WARN YOU.
I--I WARN YOU--I WON'T HEAR IT MUCH LONGER/ 154 ELECTR
I WARN YOU AGAIN/ 155 ELECTR
AND I WARN YOU I WON'T STAND YOUR LEAVING ME FOR 156 ELECTR
PETER/
I RAN HERE TO WARN--SOMEONE/ 320 GGBROW
BUT HE STILL CANNOT HELP TRYING TO WARN HIS 67 JOURNE
MOTHER.)
WANT TO WARN YOU--AGAINST ME. 165 JOURNE
HE IS FAITHFUL TO HIS WIFE, I WARN YOU. LAZARU
(THREATENINGLY) AND I WARN YOU TO ANSWER DIRECTLY)353 LAZARU
IN PLAIN WORDS--
BUT I WILL WARN YOU AGAIN, 358 LAZARU
(SHE SMILES.) I NEED NOT WARN YOU TO SCRUTINIZE 52 MANSNS
IT CLOSELY.
ANYWAY, I WARN YOU FRANKLY THAT I COULD NEVER PLAY 58 MANSNS
FINALLY, I WANT TO WARN YOU AGAIN AGAINST THE 71 MANSNS
GROWING UNSCRUPULOUSNESS
BEFORE YOU OPEN I MUST WARN YOU TO REMEMBER HOW 111 MANSNS
EVIL I CAN BE
I WARN YOU YOUR PRIDE WILL PROBABLY BE IMPELLED TO153 MANSNS
REJECT THEM.
BUT YOU HAD BETTER NOT GO ON WITH YOUR PLOT, 159 MANSNS
BECAUSE I WARN YOU--
SO I HAD TO DO SOMETHING TO WARN YOU, AND I 184 MANSNS
THOUGHT A FAIRY TALE--
WHY DIDN'T YOU WARN ME= 388 MARCOM
FOR I WARN YOU IN ADVANCE THIS IS LIABLE TO BE A 398 MARCOM
MIGHTY LONG TRIP.
(HE GIVES HIM A SHAKE) AND LET ME WARN YOU/ 63 MISBEG
I WARN YOU TO MIND YOUR OWN BUSINESS, MICKEY, 17 POET
I'D BETTER WARN HIM NOT TO SNEER AT THE IRISH 26 POET
AROUND HERE AND CALL THEM SCUM,
SHE SAID SHE'D COME TO WARN SIMON HIS FATHER IS 78 POET
WILD WITH ANGER
BUT I WARN YOU IT IS A QUALITY DIFFICULT FOR A 82 POET
WOMAN TO KEEP ON ADMIRING
EXCEPT PERHAPS, THAT I WISH TO BE FAIR AND WARN 84 POET
YOU-- TOO.
(STIFFENS.) WARN ME ABOUT WHAT, MRS. HARFORDS 84 POET
BUT I WARN YOU IT IS ALREADY WRITTEN ON HIS 85 POET
CONSCIENCE AND--
TAKE CARE, SIR, AND WATCH YOUR WORDS OR I WARN YOU120 POET
YOU WILL REPENT THEM.
THAT THIEF OF A LAWYER WILL WARN HIM-- 128 POET
(WEARILY) I WARN YOU IT ISN'T PRETTY, DOCTOR/ 82 STRANG

WARN'T
I WARN'T 'SPECIALLY ANXIOUS THE MAN AT THE WHEEL 539 'ILE
SHOULD CATCH WHAT I WANTED TO
I WASN'T THINKIN' OF MYSELF, SIR--'BOUT TURNIN' 542 'ILE
HOME, I MEAN.
(WITH SATISFACTION) I WARN'T MUCH AFEARED O' 542 'ILE
THAT, TOM.
REMEMBER, I WARN'T HANKERIN' TO HAVE YOU COME ON 545 'ILE
THIS VOYAGE, ANNIE.
BLOW ME IF THEM WARN'T HER EXACT WOKUS/ 94 BEYOND

WARNED
I WARNED YOU WHAT IT'D BE, ANNIE. 545 'ILE
AND SHE DIDN'T HAVE A CHANCE TO SAY ANYTHING ELSE 273 AHWILD
BECAUSE HER MOTHER WARNED HER
YES--AS I WARNED YOU. 556 CROSS
WHY, WARNED. 556 CROSS
(IN SURPRISE) WARNED ME5 556 CROSS
BUT I WARNED HIM HE'D HUMILIATE ME ONCE TOO 520 DAYS
OFTEN--AND HE DID/
I WARNED YOU IT WAS CLOSING IN/ 528 DAYS
I'VE WARNED YOU YOU'D GO TO PIECES LIKE THIS 559 DAYS
(GLOOMILY) I'VE WARNED YOU OFTEN, AIN'T I, 517 UFRNT
PA AND MA WARNED ME LINESMEN WERE NO GOOD... 430 DYNAMO
AND THEN AGAIN MEBBE I'M RIGHT, AND IF I'M RIGHT, 12 ELECTR
THEN YOU'D OUGHT T'BE WARNED.
I WARNED YOU YOU WOULD HAVE NO CHANCE TO GLOAT/ 46 ELECTR
MOTHER WARNED ME. 96 ELECTR
OH, SHE WARNED ME JUST NOW WHAT TO EXPECT/ 98 ELECTR
SHE WARNED ME OF THAT AND I SEE IT CLEARLY NOW/ 154 ELECTR
I'VE WARNED YOU/ 155 ELECTR
HE SAYS MY HEART IS GONE--BOOZE--HE WARNED ME, 286 GGBROW
NEVER ANOTHER DROP OR--
I WARNED YOU THIS MORNING HE WASN'T KIDDING. 635 ICEMAN
(TENSELY) I'VE WARNED YOU-- 645 ICEMAN
REMEMBER WHAT I WARNED YOU--/ 666 ICEMAN
I'VE WARNED HIM FOR YEARS HIS BODY COULDN'T STAND 33 JOURNE
IT, BUT HE WOULDN'T HEED ME,
HE'D BEEN WARNED IT MIGHT KILL THE BABY. 87 JOURNE
THE DOCTOR THERE HAD WARNED ME I MUST HAVE PEACE 93 JOURNE
AT HOME

WARNED

WARNED (CONT'D.)
I'VE WARNED HIM, ONE DAY I'LL GIVE A CLOUT THAT'LL 99 JOURNE
KNOCK HIM INTO NEXT WEEK.
THAT LYING OLD QUACK? I WARNED YOU HE'D INVENT--/118 JOURNE
REMEMBER I WARNED YOU--FOR YOUR SAKE. GIVE ME 167 JOURNE
CREDIT.
IT'S WHAT I'VE WARNED YOU. 167 JOURNE
BE WARNED AND NEVER FAIL ME IN THIS/ 382 MARCOM
BUT I WARNED YOU, DIDN'T I, IF YOU KEPT ON-- 139 MISBEG
YOUR MOTHER WARNED ME YOU ONLY DID IT TO PROVOKE 45 POET
ME.
SHE WARNED HIM A SUDDEN WEDDING WOULD LOOK 110 POET
DAMNABLY SUSPICIOUS.
I WARNED HIM AND I BEGGED HIM, 150 POET
THAT PIG AV A LAWYER MUST HAVE WARNED HARFORD TO 154 POET
EXPECT US.
I WARNED YOU/ 155 POET
I WARNED YE WHAT YE'D GET 179 POET
(STEPS QUICKLY TO HER SIDE) I'M SORRY, NINA, BUT 179 STRANG
I WARNED YOU NOT TO MEDDLE.

WARNIN'
AFTER ME WARNIN' YOUS 115 BEYOND
AN' RUIN--A WARNIN' T' OLD FOOLS LIKE ME T' B'AR 267 DESIRE
THEIR LONESOMENESS ALONE--
I KIN HEAR HIS VUICE WARNIN' ME AGEN T' BE HARD 268 DESIRE
AN' STAY ON MY FARM.
(WITH A LAUGH) REMEMBER, I'M WARNIN' YOU, EMMER. 496 DIFRNT

WARNING
(WITH A WARNING GLANCE AT TOMMY) 227 AHWILD
RAPE OFF ME NOW. I'M WARNING 49 ANNA
(VERY EARNESTLY) AND I'M WARNING YOU NOW, IF 75 ANNA
YOU'D SWEAR AN OATH ON THIS,
(HUSKILY--IN A TONE OF WARNING) 100 BEYUND
(WHO HAS TAKEN A CHAIR BY HER BROTHER--IN A 570 CRUSS
WARNING WHISPER)
IN A VOICE OF WARNING) 572 CROSS
BUT I WISH HE'D GIVE ME WARNING. 499 DAYS
HE IMAGINED HER SICKNESS WAS A TERRIBLE WARNING TO11 DAYS
HER.
(AFTER A WORRIED GLANCE AT HER--AN UNDERCURRENT OF540 DAYS
WARNING IN HIS QUIET TUNE)
IF THOU DIDST, I WOULD PROCLAIM THE AWFUL WARNING 423 DYNAMO
UP IT ALL OVER AMERICA...
BUT YOUR WARNING WAS NO USE/ 120 ELECTR
I HEARD YOU WARNING HIM AGAINST ME/ 120 ELECTR
GOSH, VINNIE, YOU OUGHT TO HAVE GIVEN US MORE 143 ELECTR
WARNING.
(MAKING A WARNING SIGN TO PETER NOT TO TAKE THIS 144 ELECTR
SERIOUSLY--FORCING A SMILE)
(WITH AN APPREHENSIVE GLANCE AT PETER--PLEADING 146 ELECTR
AND AT THE SAME TIME WARNING)

WARNINGS 222 HA APE
I WAS ONLY WARNING YOU-- 222 HA APE
I'M WARNING YOU, AT THE START, SO THERE'LL BE NO 591 ICEMAN
MISUNDERSTANDING,
(ABRUPTLY HIS TONE SHARPENS WITH RESENTFUL 591 ICEMAN
WARNING)
(HE SPEAKS IN HIS EAR IN CONFIDENTIAL WARNING) 655 ICEMAN
(STARTS--IN A LOW WARNING VOICE) 698 ICEMAN
IN EACH LETTER I'D TELL HER HOW I MISSED HER, BUT 111 ICEMAN
I'D KEEP WARNING HER, TOO.
(HIS FATHER GIVES HIM A SHARP WARNING LOOK BUT HE 27 JOURNE
DOESN'T SEE IT.)
(WITH ANOTHER WARNING GLANCE AT JAMIE--EASILY.) 27 JOURNE
AND I DON'T KNOW WHAT YOU MEAN, WARNING ME TO BE 42 JOURNE
CAREFUL.
COMES THE WARNING RINGING OF BELLS ON YACHTS AT 97 JOURNE
ANCHOR.
IT KEEPS REMINDING YOU, AND WARNING YOU, AND 99 JOURNE
CALLING YOU BACK,
ALL THE SAME THERE'S TRUTH IN YOUR MOTHER'S 109 JOURNE
WARNING.
I HOPE YOU'LL HEED THE WARNING, NOW IT COMES FROM 167 JOURNE
HIS OWN MOUTH.
FEAR OF THIS WARNING OMEN IS WHY THEY NOW MARCH 300 LAZARU
WITH HIM MY LAND.
BUT ACCEPT MY GRATITUDE FOR YOUR WARNING. 317 LAZARU
THANK YOU FOR THE WARNING. 52 MANSNS
SARA, I WOULD LIKE TO UTTER A WORD OF WARNING--IN 67 MANSNS
MOTHER'S PRESENCE.
IN A TONE OF WARNING ADVICE 114 MANSNS
AND MY LIFE/ FOREVER/ THAT IS MY FINAL WARNING/ 130 MANSNS
I WAS ONLY WARNING YOU AGAINST IT. 157 MANSNS
(AS A WARNING TO KUKACHIN TO CONTROL HER EMOTION) 391 MARCOM
HE'S WARNING ME NOT TO GIVE HARDER A BEATING-- 52 MISBEG
(IN A STRANGE WARNING TONE) YOU'D BETTER LOOK 144 MISBEG
OUT, JOSIE.
I'M WARNING YOU/ 177 MISBEG
(SHE SMILES AGAIN.) MY WARNING WAS THE MECHANICAL 82 POET
GESTURE OF A MOTHER'S DUTY,
AND WAS WARNING AND THREATENING ME. 87 POET
(BLURTS OUT) I WOULDN'T DO IT EXCEPT THAT COLE 70 STRANG
GAVE ME A WARNING TO BUCK UP--
WHAT DOES HE MEAN COMING IN ON US WITHOUT 98 STRANG
WARNINGS...)
(HE CHUCKLES PLEASANTLY AND GOES INTO THE HALL-- 129 STRANG
MOCKINGLY WARNING)

WARNINGLY
(THEN WARNINGLY) MIND WHAT I'M SAYING NOW, 217 AHWILD
(AS HE ENTERS--WARNINGLY, IN A LOW TONE) 218 AHWILD
(THEN WARNINGLY TO HER HUSBAND) 264 AHWILD
(WARNINGLY) NOW DON'T BE COMING AT ME AGAIN. 50 ANNA
(WARNINGLY) SSSHHH/ 99 BEYOND
(WARNINGLY) (REMEMBER YE MUST BE QUIET ABOUT UT. 458 CARIBE
YE SCOUTS--
(WARNINGLY, AS HE HEARS THE PANTRY DOOR OPENING) 527 DAYS
(WARNINGLY) MAYBE IT'S GETTIN' TIME FOR YOU TO 181 EJONES
RESIGN--

WARNINGLY (CONT'D.)
(THEN WARNINGLY, MAKING A SURREPTITIOUS SIGNAL AS 45 ELECTR
HE SEES THE FRONT DOOR OPENING
(WARNINGLY) ORIN/ 100 ELECTR
(HEARS A NOISE FROM THE HALL AND COLLECTS 159 ELECTR
HERSELF--WARNINGLY)
(SEES THE ENVELOPE IN PLAIN SIGHT AND CALLS TO HER)63 ELECTR
(WARNINGLY) HAZEL/
ORIN GOES ON WARNINGLY) 163 ELECTR
(WARNINGLY) 302 GBORN
A GIRL'S LAUGH IS HEARD.) (WARNINGLY) NIX/ PIANO/611 ICEMAN
(FROM THE DOORWAY--WARNINGLY) 525 INZONE
(WARNINGLY AS HE HEARS HIS MOTHER IN THE DINING 39 JOURNE
ROOM.)
(WARNINGLY.) SIMON, REMEMBER-- 52 MANSNS
SO YOU HAD BETTER BE SURE OF YOUR COURAGE, THE 111 MANSNS
ENCHANTRESS CALLED WARNINGLY.
(WARNINGLY) AND UNTIL I PRONOUNCE YOU GRADUATED, 374 MARCOM
MUM'S THE WORD, UNDERSTAND/
(WARNINGLY) SSST/ 376 MARCOM
(WARNINGLY) HIS HONOR WISHES TO TALK BUSINESS. 391 MARCOM
PRINCESS.
HE LOOKS UP SUDDENLY INTO HER EYES--WARNINGLY) 126 MISBEG
(WARNINGLY, HIS EYES ON MELODY.) 52 POET
(HEARING A NOISE FROM THE HALL--WARNINGLY) 39 STRANG
(THEN WARNINGLY) I HEAR THEM COMING, DEAR. 132 STRANG
(WARNINGLY) SSSHHH/ 507 VOYAGE
(EXULTANTLY--BUT AS IF TESTING HER, WARNINGLY) 488 WELDED

WARNINGS
I BEGIN TO RESEMBLE CASSANDRA WITH ALL MY 85 POET
WARNINGS.

WARNS
(THEN MUDDILY) BUT ARTER THREE SCORE AND TEN THE 232 DESIRE
LORD WARNS YE T' PREPARE.

WARPED
I HATE WHAT'S WARPED AND TWISTS AND EATS ITSELF 167 ELECTR
BUT RHEUMATISM HAS KNOTTED THE JOINTS AND WARPED 12 JOURNE
THE FINGERS,
HER LONG FINGERS, WARPED AND KNOTTED BY 49 JOURNE
RHEUMATISM,
ARMS REST LIMPLY ALONG THE ARMS OF THE CHAIR, HER 107 JOURNE
HANDS WITH LONG, WARPED,
(SUDDENLY WITH A DISTORTED WARPED SMILE) 300 LAZARU
GRINS HIS WARPED GRIN, 308 LAZARU
THE WHOLE EFFECT OF THESE TWO GROUPS IS OF SEX 336 LAZARU
CORRUPTED AND WARPED,
MADE OF LOGS WITH A ROOF OF WARPED, HAND-HEWN 1 MANSNS
SHINGLES.
AS A CHILD MIGHT, BUT AT THE SAME TIME THERE IS 382 MARCOM
SOMETHING WARPED, DEFORMED--

WARRIOR
ON HIS RIGHT, STANDS A WARRIOR NOBLE, A KNIGHT-- 358 MARCOM
CRUSADER, IN FULL ARMOR,
ON THE RIGHT, THE INEVITABLE WARRIOR--ON HIS LEFT,364 MARCOM
THE INEVITABLE PRIEST--
WARRIOR AND SORCERER TO RIGHT AND LEFT OF HIM. 373 MARCOM
ON HIS RIGHT A MONGOL WARRIOR IN FULL ARMOR WITH 377 MARCOM
SHIELD AND SPEAR,

WARRIORS
FARTHER AWAY, THE NOBLES AND WARRIORS OF ALL 377 MARCOM
DEGREES WITH THEIR WIVES BEHIND

WARS
SINGS HOARSELY AN OLD CAMP SONG OF THE PUNIC WARS,313 LAZARU
POUNDING WITH HIS GOBLET)
COMRADES, MARCH TO THE WARS/ 314 LAZARU
ON, MARCH ON TO THE WARS/ 314 LAZARU
MY MOTHER WAS A DRUNKEN DRABBY OH, MARCH ON TO THE314 LAZARU
WARS/
MY MOTHER WAS A DRUNKEN DRABBY OH MARCH ON TO THE 357 LAZARU
WARS/
THERE ALWAYS HAVE BEEN WARS AND THERE ALWAYS WILL 394 MARCOM
BE, I SUPPOSE,

WARY
HE HAS BECOME WARY NOW, 21 ELECTR
HIS DROOP-LIDDED EYES SUSPICIOUSLY WARY OF 9 HUGHIE
NUERSTEIN EAVESDROPPERS,
THEN TURNS TO THE CLERK, HIS FOOLISHLY WARY, WISE- 19 HUGHIE
GUY EYES DEFENSELESS,
HIS EXPRESSION FREEZING INTO A WARY BLANKNESS. 708 ICEMAN
(HE CHECKS HIMSELF WITH A SUDDEN WARY GLANCE AT 73 MANSNS
JOEL.)
(HE GOES BACK AND CROUCHES AGAIN BEFORE THE 417 MARCOM
PRINCESS, KEEPING A WARY EYE ON HER,

WASH
DON'T STOP TO WASH UP OR ANYTHING. 221 AHWILD
WILL IT WASH OFF--HER KISSES--MAKE YOU FORGET YOU 287 AHWILD
EVER--FOR ALWAYS
WILL WASH THAT BLACK KISS OF YOURS OFF MY LIPS. 61 ANNA
I'VE GOT TO WASH UP SOME AS LONG AS RUTH'S MA IS 86 BEYOND
COMING OVER FOR SUPPER,
I'D HAVE TO WAIT JUST THE SAME TO WASH UP AFTER 122 BEYOND
YOU.
BUT I CAN WASH UP. 122 BEYOND
BUT THERE IS ALWAYS DEATH TO WASH ONE'S SINS 531 DAYS
AWAY--
WITH MY WASH BOWL ON MY KNEE. 224 DESIRE
I'LL WASH UP MY DISHES NOW. 227 DESIRE
EVERY STORM THE WATER'D BEGIN TO DRIP DOWN AND 464 DYNAMO
NO'THER'D PUT THE WASH
THAT'S THE ONLY WAY TO WASH THE GUILT OF OUR 152 ELECTR
MOTHER'S BLOOD FROM OUR SOULS/
THAT OUGHT TO WASH IT CLEAN, DON'T YOU THINKS 221 HA APE
WASH UP/ 227 HA APE
WASH UP/ 227 HA APE
WASH UP, YANK/ 227 HA APE
BETTER WASH UP, YANK. 227 HA APE
HEY, YANK, YOU FORGOT TO WASH. 227 HA APE

1773

WASH

WASH (CONT'D.)
IF I WASH THE ONES I'VE GOT ON ANY MORE, THEY'LL 604 ICEMAN
FALL APART, SOCKS, TOO.
HER HOUSE WOULDN'T BE PROPERLY FURNISHED UNLESS 661 ICEMAN
SHE BOUGHT ANOTHER WASH BOILER.
NOT AFTER I WASH MY FACE. 80 JOURNE
AND RID THE WORLD OF THIS STUPID RACE OF MEN AND 9 MANSNS
WASH THE EARTH CLEAN/
AND DON'T FORGET TO WASH YOUR FACE. 5 MISBEG
GO IN THE HOUSE NOW, AND WASH YOUR FACE, AND TIDY 36 MISBEG
YOUR DRESS.
THAT'S SOMETHING PEOPLE WASH WITH, ISN'T IT? 44 MISBEG
(HE DRINKS HIS WHISKEY AS IF TO WASH A BAD TASTE 129 MISBEG
FROM HIS MOUTH--
FOR GOD'S SAKE, WHY DON'T YOU WASH YOUR HAIRS 42 POET
THERE'S A PILE OF DISHES TO WASH AFTER YOUR GRAND 104 POET
ANNIVERSARY FEAST!
AND I KNOW I'M AN AWFUL WASH-OUT COMPARED TO HIM-- 32 STRANG
DIS ISS ONLY BELLY-WASH, NUS 505 VOYAGE
DATS WHY I DON'T DRINK NUTING TONIGHT BUT DIS-- 506 VOYAGE
BELLY-WASH/

WASHED
THROUGH THE OPEN DOOR TO THE KITCHEN COMES THE 112 BEYOND
CLATTER OF DISHES BEING WASHED,
SEEMING PALE AND WASHED OUT BY CONTRAST. 203 DESIRE
WASHED AND SLICKED UP IN HIS ILL-FITTING BEST.) 505 DIFRIT
TANK HAS NOT WASHED EITHER FACE OR BODY. 226 HA APE
HE AIN'T EVEN WASHED HISSELF. 227 HA APE
HAS THE APPEARANCE OF HAVING NEVER BEEN WASHED. 574 ICEMAN
AND MY POOR MOTHER WASHED AND SCRUBBED FOR THE 148 JOURNE
YANKS BY THE DAY.
HIS WASHED-OUT BLUE EYES HAVE A WANDERING, HALF- 52 POET
WITTED EXPRESSION.
HIS FACE IS WASHED BLANDLY CLEAN OF ALL EMOTION] 22 STRANG

WASHIN'
TO HELL WIT WASHIN'. 227 HA APE
I DO BE WASHIN' IT OFTEN TO PLAZE YOU. 43 POET

WASHING
COOKING AND WASHING DISHES ALL THE TIME. 136 BEYOND
ABBIE IS WASHING HER DISHES.) 228 DESIRE
HE HAS EVIDENTLY BEEN WASHING UP, FOR HIS FACE IS 501 DIFRIT
RED AND SHINY,
WASHING ALL DIRT AND SIN AWAY/ 476 DYNAMO
IT'S AS IF THAT SOUND WAS COOL WATER WASHING OVER 476 DYNAMO
MY BODY/
ROCKY IS BEHIND THE BAR, WIPING IT, WASHING 664 ICEMAN
GLASSES, ETC.

WASHINGS
DUNGAREE TROUSERS FADED BY MANY WASHINGS, A BLUE 457 DYNAMO
FLANNEL SHIRT OPEN AT THE NECK,

WASHINGTON
ON THE RIGHT WALL IS A PAINTING OF GEORGE 28 ELECTR
WASHINGTON IN A GILT FRAME,
I GOT ADMIRING WASHINGTON AND JEFFERSON AND 648 ICEMAN
JACKSON AND LINCOLN.
ON THE WALLS ARE PICTURES OF WASHINGTON, HAMILTON, 69 MANSNS
DANIEL WEBSTER, AND--
IT'S TERRIBLY FAINT BUT--NAVY AND WASHINGTON ARE 168 STRANG
LEADING--GORDON'S THIRD/
LAST I GOT, GORDUN THIRD, NAVY AND WASHINGTON 171 STRANG
LEADING.

WASHINGTON'S
IN THE UNIFORM OF AN OFFICER IN WASHINGTON'S ARMY. 79 ELECTR
ARE MANNION'S WIFE AND THE WIFE OF WASHINGTON'S 79 ELECTR
OFFICER.

WASHSTAND
A WASHSTAND WITH BOWL AND PITCHER IS IN THE LEFT 421 DYNAMO
CORNER, REAR,
IN THE LEFT CORNER, A WASHSTAND. 470 WELDED
(HAVING REMOVED HER HAT AND PUT IT ON THE 471 WELDED
WASHSTAND, TURNS TO HIM IMPATIENTLY)
(HE PUTS IT ON TOP OF THE WASHSTAND AND TURNS TO 474 WELDED
HER--EMBARRASSEDLY)
(HE PUTS TO THE BELL ON THE WASHSTAND) 478 WELDED

WASHY
HIS LITTLE WASHY-BLUE EYES ARE RED-RIMMED AND DART174 EJONES
ABOUT HIM LIKE A FERRET'S.

WASP
(BOUNDING TO HIS FEET AS IF A WASP HAD STUNG HIM) 348 MARCOM

WASPS
AND AS FULL OF RAGE AS A NEST OF WASPS/ 10 MISBEG

WASTE
IT'S JUST A WASTE OF BREATH/ 188 AHWILD
HE'LL WASTE THE MORNING OVER THOSE DARNED BOOKS. 196 AHWILD
JUST THINK OF WASTE EFFORT EATING SOUP WITH 225 AHWILD
SPOONS--
I CAN'T WASTE ALL DAY LISTENING TO YOU/ 266 AHWILD
TOO YOUNG ART THOU TO WASTE THIS SUMMERNIGHT-- 276 AHWILD
YOU SHOULDN'T--WASTE THAT--ON MY HAND. 286 AHWILD
OR ANY OF THE BLACK TRICKS THAT A LANDLUBBER'D 48 ANNA
WASTE HIS LIFE ON.
AND YOU THOUGHT YOURSELF TOO EDUCATED TO WASTE ANY 91 BEYOND
TIME ON ME.
I'LL BET THERE AIN'T NONE OF US'LL LET ANY GO TO 461 CARIBE
WASTE.
(WEAKLY) WHAT D'YE WANT T' WASTE TIME ON HER FUR$230 DESIRE
DON'T WASTE CRYING OVER-- 452 DYNAMO
BUT I AIN'T GOT DE TIME TO WASTE ON NO MORE FOOL 185 EJONES
TALK WID YOU.
(FORCING A JOKING TONE) BUT YOU MUSTN'T WASTE 323 GGBROW
JUNE ON AN OLD WOMAN LIKE ME/
I'M A WASTE PRODUCT IN THE BESSEMER PROCESS--LIKE 219 HA APE
THE MILLIONS.
WAS BECAUSE I DON'T WANT TO WASTE JACK ON NOTHIN' 28 HUGHIE
BUT GAMBLING.
DON'T WASTE YOUR PITY. 594 ICEMAN
I'M A SAP TO WASTE TIME ON YUH. 703 ICEMAN
IT WAS A WASTE OF TIME COMING HERE. 718 ICEMAN

WATCH

WASTE (CONT'D.)
(WITH NO GENTLE HAND SLAPS THE WASTE OVER SMITTY'S527 INZONE
MOUTH)
(HE GOES TO HIS BUNK AND PULLS OUT A BIG WAD OF 527 INZONE
WASTE AND COMES BACK TO SMITTY.)
(JACK HANDS HIM ONE AND HE TIES IT TIGHTLY AROUND 528 INZONE
SMITTY'S HEAD OVER THE WASTE)
I KNOW IT'S A WASTE OF BREATH TRYING TO CONVINCE 15 JOURNE
YOU
YES, IT'S TOO FINE A MORNING TO WASTE INDOORS 40 JOURNE
ARGUING.
IT'D BE A WASTE OF BREATH MENTIONING MODERATION TO 65 JOURNE
YOU.
YOU'LL FIGURE IT WOULD BE A WASTE OF MONEY TO 80 JOURNE
SPEND ANY MORE THAN YOU CAN HELP.
THE SAME OLD WASTE THAT WILL LAND ME IN THE 84 JOURNE
POORHOUSE IN MY OLD AGE/
(IGNORING THIS.) IT WAS ANOTHER WASTE TO HIRE 84 JOURNE
SMYTHE.
(WITH DETACHED CALM.) YES, IT WAS A WASTE OF 84 JOURNE
MONEY, JAMES.
(BITTERLY.) WASTE/ 84 JOURNE
(EXCITEDLY.) IT'S SIMPLY A WASTE OF TIME AND 92 JOURNE
MONEY SEEING HIM.
A WASTE. 141 JOURNE
(MORE BITTERLY.) SO WHY WASTE MONEYS 143 JOURNE
(POURS A DRINK.) A WASTE/ 168 JOURNE
BUT I KNEW IT WAS SIMPLY A WASTE OF TIME. 176 JOURNE
(TURNING TO HER--COARSELY) DO NOT WASTE YOUR 341 LAZARU
LUST.
BUT HOW FOOLISH OF US TO WASTE PRECIOUS MOMENTS 5 MANSNS
AH, I'M A FOOL TO WASTE A THOUGHT ON HER-- 118 MANSNS
AS IF HE'D WASTE HIS TIME IN HER CRAZY GARDEN 137 MANSNS
EVERY EVENING.
DON'T WASTE PITY. 371 MARCOM
WAR IS A WASTE OF MONEY WHICH EATS INTO THE 394 MARCOM
PROFITS OF LIFE LIKE THUNDER/
BUT ALL OF THIS WASTE CAN BE SAVED. 394 MARCOM
OH, MAYBE ONE OR TWO OR SO--BUT I DIDN'T HAVE TIME430 MARCOM
TO WASTE ON FEMALES.
I DON'T WASTE WORDS TRYING TO REFORM A BURN CROOK. 62 MISBEG
I WOULDN'T WASTE YOUR TIME MENTIONING IT, 77 MISBEG
WE'VE NO TIME TO WASTE. 97 MISBEG
AND, BE GOD, THAT'S A WASTE OF BREATH, IF IT DOES 176 MISBEG
DESERVE IT.
(THEN SHARPLY.) BUT YOU NEEDN'T WASTE YOUR DREAMS 50 POET
WORRYING ABOUT MY AFFAIRS.
SHE DIDN'T WASTE MUCH TIME. 80 POET
BECAUSE IT'D BE A MAD THING TO WASTE A GOOD BULLET169 POET
ON A CORPSE/
(SHORTLY AND DRYLY) WE CAN'T WASTE TIME BEING 35 STRANG
SENTIMENTAL, MARSDEN/
DOESN'T WASTE GOOD BEER, DRISC. 500 VOYAGE
WASTEBASKET
OR DROPPING IT IN THE WASTEBASKET. 70 MANSNS
WASTED
(REPROACHFULLY) YOU MIGHT'VE EVEN NOT WASTED TIME 99 BEYOND
LOOKIN' FOR THAT ONE--
HER FACE PALLID AND WASTED. 553 DAYS
AFTER ALL THE MONEY I'VE WASTED ON YOUR EDUCATION, 32 JOURNE
HE THINKS MONEY SPENT ON A HOME IS MONEY WASTED. 61 JOURNE
AND WHEN THE FRIGHTFUL FEVER WASTED ME, 412 MARCOM
THEIR CITIES SHALL VANISH IN FLAME, THEIR FIELDS 425 MARCOM
SHALL BE WASTED/
I'VE WASTED SO MUCH OF THE MORNING AND I HAVE TO 74 POET
RETURN TO THE CITY.
WASTEFUL
IF THEY WANT TO BE WASTEFUL FOOLS, FOR THE SAKE OF126 JOURNE
SHOW, LET THEM BE/
AND YOU BETTER GIVE IN AND AVOID WASTEFUL 395 MARCOM
BLOODSHED.
WASTEPAPER
ON THE FLOOR BESIDE THE TABLE ARE AN OVERFLOWING 66 STRANG
WASTEPAPER BASKET,
WASTIN'
WASTIN' TIME DOIN' EVERYTHING THE WRONG WAY-- 113 BEYOND
THAT LAD'S NOT WASTIN' ANY TOIME. 463 CARIBE
WASTIN' THE 'OLE BLOOMIN' NIGHT 203 EJONES
LIKE A COUPLA STEW BUMS AND WASTIN' OURSELVES. 702 ICEMAN
I COULD HAVE TOLD YOU YOU WAS WASTIN' BREATH. 130 POET
YOU'RE WASTIN' BREATH ANYWAY, THE WAY HE IS. 156 POET
WASTING
THAT IT'S A FOOL YOU ARE TO BE WASTING YOURSELF--A 33 ANNA
FINE, HANDSOME GIRL--
WE'VE NO TIME TO BE WASTING. 56 ANNA
I'M A FOOL TO BE WASTING TALK ON YOU AND YOU 73 ANNA
HARDENED IN BADNESS.
RUB/ DON'T TALK. YOU'RE WASTING YOUR STRENGTH. 167 BEYOND
(FORCING A SMILE) YOU'RE WASTING WORRY. 512 DAYS
BUT YOU'RE WASTING YOUR BREATH. 96 ELECTR
(CALMLY.) I WASN'T WASTING MY PITY. 279 GGBROW
IT'S ONLY BECAUSE WE'RE SUCH OLD PALS--AND I HATE 281 GGBROW
TO SEE YOU WASTING YOURSELF--
YOUR BROTHERS THAT HE'S WASTING HIS COIN YOU 249 HA APE
COULDN'T CATCH A COLD.
SO GO AWAY. YOU'RE WASTING BREATH. 649 ICEMAN
THE GUYS TELL ME THE RUBES ARE WASTING ALL THEIR 724 ICEMAN
MONEY BUYING FOOD
YOU ARE WASTING YOUR TIME, GENTLEMEN. 36 MANSNS
BUT I AM WASTING WORDS. 71 MANSNS
YOU'RE WASTING MY TIME AND I'M SICK OF YOU/ 142 MANSNS
WE'RE WASTING THE DAY, BLATHERING. 35 MISBEG
WASTING KISSES ON MY HAND/ 130 MISBEG
(THEN MATTER-OF-FACTLY) I WAS WASTING MY TIME, 7 STRANG
TOO.

WATCH
HUT WAIT, WATCH AND LISTEN/ 205 AHWILD
I DO WISH YOU'D WATCH--/ 211 AHWILD

WATCH

WATCH (CONT'D.)
(LOOKING AT HER WATCH) QUARTER PAST SIX. 212 AHWILD
HER FACE GROWS SAD AND SHE AGAIN GLANCES NERVOUSLY(2 AHWILD
AT HER WATCH.
WATCH YOUR STEP, KID. 219 AHWILD
I'LL WATCH. 239 AHWILD
YOU HAVE ME REACHING FOR MY WATCH EVERY COUPLE OF 250 AHWILD
MINUTES.
(HE HAS PULLED HIS WATCH OUT OF HIS VEST POCKET-- 250 AHWILD
WITH FORCED CARELESSNESS)
YOU LET ME SEE THAT WATCH? 251 AHWILD
I SUPPOSE HE SNEAKED OFF TO WATCH THE FIREWORKS. 254 AHWILD
(GLANCES AT HER UNEASILY, PEEKS SURREPTITIOUSLY AT259 AHWILD
HIS WATCH--
HE'LL WATCH THE DAWN COME UP LIKE THUNDER OUT OF 288 AHWILD
CHINA/
(WITH A GLANCE AT HIS WATCH) 4 ANNA
I LOVE TO WATCH THE SHIPS PASSING. 44 ANNA
(LOOKING AT HIS BIG SILVER WATCH) 96 BEYOND
(HE LOOKS AT HIS WATCH WITH EXAGGERATED CONCERN) 104 BEYOND
AND WATCH YOU TWO TOGETHER, DAY AFTER DAY--AND ME 110 BEYOND
ALONE.
BUT I'M GOING BACK THERE, YOU BET, AND THEN YOU 133 BEYOND
WATCH ME GET OUT
(GLANCING AT HIS WATCH) I MUST CATCH THE NINE O' 157 BEYOND
CLOCK BACK TO THE CITY.
I SAID A CHANGE OF CLIMATE--(HE LOOKS AT HIS WATCH158 BEYOND
AGAIN NERVOUSLY)
'TWAS ENOUGH TO MAKE A SAINT SHWEAR TO SEE HIM WID479 CARDIF
HIS GOLD WATCH IN HIS HAND,
SOU'WESTERS, SEA-BOOTS, ETC. IN PREPARATION FOR 481 CARDIF
THE WATCH ON DECK.
(AFTER A PAUSE) ISN'T THIS YOUR WATCH ON DECK, 484 CARDIF
DRISCOLL?
(STARES AT HIS WATCH FOR A MOMENT OR SO. 484 CARDIF
(TAKING OUT HIS WATCH AND FEELING YANK'S PULSE) 484 CARDIF
AND YOU TAKE MY WATCH. 489 CARDIF
A BRIDGE TO PACE UP AND DOWN ON--AND KEEP WATCH. 557 CROSS
THEY WATCH THE PAPER BURN WITH FASCINATED EYES AS 567 CROSS
HE TALKS)
WALTER IT WAS I, HIS OLD FRIEND--SO YOU CAN WATCH 527 DAYS
HIM SQUIRM SOME MORE/
AND HE WAS CURIOUS NOW TO WATCH HER REACTIONS. 537 DAYS
THEY WATCH HIM, GRADUALLY BREAKING INTO GRINS. 210 DESIRE
'S IF I COULD, TO MY DYIN' HOUR. I TO SET IT AFIRE 232 DESIRE
AN' WATCH IT BURN--
YO'D COPY TO PLOW AN' SOW AN' THEN SET AN' SMOKE 237 DESIRE
YER PIPE AN' WATCH THIN'S GROW.
THE OTHERS WATCH CABOT SILENTLY WITH COLD, HOSTILE251 DESIRE
EYES.
I'LL SET FIRE T' HOUSE A' BARN AN' WATCH 'EM 267 DESIRE
BURN,
OUT HIS WATCH) 498 DIFRNT
I'D LET YOU MARRY THE SKUNK AND SET AND WATCH WHAT543 DIFRNT
HAPPEN--
WHEN FIFE TOOK OUT HIS WATCH AND SAID IF THERE'S A424 DYNAMO
GUO LET HIM PROVE IT BY
I'LL JUST WATCH HIM AND MAKE SURE... 427 DYNAMO
(I(LOVE TO WATCH LIGHTNING... 444 DYNAMO
I'LL WAIT HERE AND WATCH THE FUN...) 445 DYNAMO
UIU YOU EVER WATCH DYNAMOSS 458 DYNAMO
I MADE MYSELF STAND THERE AND WATCH THE LIGHTNING.460 DYNAMO
AND THEN YOU WATCH ME CONVERT HER OVER FROM THAT 461 DYNAMO
OLD GOD STUFF OF HIS/
DID YOU EVER WATCH DYNAMOSS 461 DYNAMO
UIU YOU EVER WATCH DYNAMOSS 467 DYNAMO
HE SEES THE WOMAN AND STOPS TO WATCH HER 174 EJONES
SUSPICIOUSLY.
(HE PULLS OUT A GOLD WATCH AND LOOKS AT IT) 182 EJONES
YOU WATCH ME, MAN. 183 EJONES
(PUTS HIS WATCH BACK--WITH COOL CONFIDENCE) 183 EJONES
YOU WATCH ME/ 184 EJONES
(STOPS ABRUPTLY TO LOOK AT HIS WATCH--ALERTLY) 185 EJONES
I HOPE SHE DOESN'T HURRY BACK TO STAND WATCH OVER 21 ELECTR
US.
ONLY ENOUGH SO THEY'D BE SUSPICIOUS AND WATCH YOU 35 ELECTR
TOO.
TAKES OUT HIS WATCH MECHANICALLY) 56 ELECTR
I COULDN'T BEAR TO WAIT AND WATCH HIM COMING UP 73 ELECTR
THE DRIVE-- JUST LIKE--
WATCH HER WHEN SHE SEES THAT--IF YOU WANT PROOF/ 100 ELECTR
FOR THE LOVE OF GOD, WATCH OUT FOR VINNIE. 112 ELECTR
ALONG WITH BILLS AND COINS, WATCH AND CHAIN, 115 ELECTR
KNIVES, ETC.
WATCH ME PERISHIN' FUR LACK O' WHISKEY AND YE KEEP130 ELECTR
FROZE TO THAT JUG.
AND YOU WENT TO WATCH THEIR SHAMELESS DANCES 154 ELECTR
(GLANCING AT HIS WATCH) GUSH, I'VE GOT TO HURRY 159 ELECTR
TO THAT DARNED COUNCIL MEETING.
AND I COULDN'T BEAR TO WATCH YOUR EYES GROW BITTER176 ELECTR
AND HIDDEN FROM ME AND
LET'S GO BACK AND WATCH THE YOUNG FOLKS DANCE. 259 GGBROW
I WANT TO WATCH BILLY DANCE. 259 GGBROW
THEY WATCH HIM, WITH QUEER, PUZZLED EYES.) 260 GGBROW
WATCH THE MUSKET IN THE MOON/ 268 GGBROW
(WORRIEDLY) I HOPE THEY'LL WATCH OUT, CROSSING 274 GGBROW
THE STREET.
PUT LIKE UP. I'M DOWN HERE FOR ONE WATCH IN DE 212 HA APE
STOKEHOLE, WHAT'D HAPPENS
AND MID THE DAY DONE, IN THE DOG WATCH, SMOKING ME214 HA APE
PIPE AT EASE,
I'LL NOT REPORT THIS WATCH. 217 HA APE
OUR WATCH, YUH OLD HARP/ 217 HA APE
(LOOKING AT HER WATCH AGAIN) 220 HA APE
(SHE LOOKS AT HER WRIST WATCH) 220 HA APE
YERRA, WILL THIS DIVIL'S OWN WATCH NIVIR ENDS 223 HA APE
WATCH HER SMOKE/ 224 HA APE

WATCH (CONT'D.)
YANK'S WATCH HAS JUST COME OFF DUTY AND HAD 226 HA APE
DINNER.
OUT I'LL GIT SQUARE WIT HER YET, YOU WATCH. 235 HA APE
YOU WATCH MY SMOKE/ 242 HA APE
BACK AT HER YET, YOU WATCH/ 242 HA APE
I KNOW YUH GOT TO WATCH YOUR STEP WIT A STRANGER. 248 HA APE
WATCH DE SMOKE AND SEE IT MOVE/ 249 HA APE
GIMME DE STUFF, UE OLD BUTTER--AND WATCH ME DO DE 249 HA APE
<357
YOU WATCH. 16 HUGHIE
HE WEARS PHONY RINGS AND A HEAVY BRASS WATCH-- 576 ICEMAN
CHAIN--NOT CONNECTED TO A WATCH--.
THEY WATCH HIM. 580 ICEMAN
YOH COULD SET YOUR WATCH BY HIS PERIODICALS BEFORE580 ICEMAN
DIS.
THE SIXTH IS A SQUARE JEWELER'S WATCH BOX. 629 ICEMAN
HE HAS TURNED IT SO HE CAN WATCH HER. 629 ICEMAN
(STUNG) YOU BROADS BETTER WATCH YOUR STEP OR-- 630 ICEMAN
BUT I KNOW WHAT'S GONNA HAPPEN IF HE DON'T WATCH 636 ICEMAN
HIS STEP.
GLANCING AT HIS WATCH) 643 ICEMAN
(HE GLANCES AT HIS WATCH) HALF A MINUTE TO GO. 653 ICEMAN
HICKEY LOOKS UP FROM HIS WATCH) 653 ICEMAN
ONLY WATCH OUT ON THE BOOZE, JIMMY. 655 ICEMAN
AND DERE'S A WATCH ALL ENGRAVED WID YOUR NAME AND 656 ICEMAN
DE DATE FROM HICKEY.
THEN YOU'D BETTER WATCH OUT HOW YOU KEEP CALLING 657 ICEMAN
FOR THAT OLD BIG SLEEP/
BUT I'LL HAVE TO WATCH OUT FOR THE DAMNED 687 ICEMAN
AUTOMOBILES.
TO STAND AND WATCH IN THE ENTRANCE, 716 ICEMAN
WHERE HE CAN WATCH SMITHY WITHOUT BEING SEEN. 913 INZONE
YOU OUT TO WATCH OUT, THAT'S ALL I SAYS. 515 INZONE
BLIMEY IF I DON'T FINK I'LL PUT IN THIS 'ERE WATCH516 INZONE
AHTSIDE ON DECK.
AYE. I'LL WATCH HIM. 518 INZONE
YOU REALLY MUST NOT WATCH ME ALL THE TIME, JAMES. 17 JOURNE
I LOVE TO LIE IN THE SHADE AND WATCH HIM WORK. 49 JOURNE
IT'S A WONDER YOUR FATHER WOULDN'T LOOK AT HIS 51 JOURNE
WATCH ONCE IN A WHILE.
HAVE HIS DROP OF WHISKEY IF HE HAD A WATCH TO HIS 52 JOURNE
NAME/
I MADE THE OLD MAN LOOK AT HIS WATCH. 54 JOURNE
TURNED HALF AWAY FROM HIS MOTHER SO HE DOES NOT 71 JOURNE
HAVE TO WATCH HER.)
YOU'RE WELCOME TO COME UP AND WATCH ME IF YOU'RE 75 JOURNE
SO SUSPICIOUS.
(HE FUMBLES WITH HIS WATCH.) 91 JOURNE
(HE STARES AT HIS WATCH WITHOUT SEEING IT. 113 JOURNE
(OVERWHELMED BY SHAME WHICH HE TRIES TO HIDE, 113 JOURNE
FUMBLES WITH HIS WATCH.)
WHEN I WAS LOOKOUT ON THE CROW'S NEST IN THE DAWN 153 JOURNE
WATCH.
WHY DO YOU COME HERE EVERY NIGHT TO LISTEN AND 282 LAZARU
WATCH THEIR ABOMINATIONS$
(QUEERLY) I LIKE TO WATCH MEN DIE. 301 LAZARU
SO KEEP WATCH/ 331 LAZARU
I NEED TO WATCH YOUR FACE. 341 LAZARU
WHILE I WATCH THEM, ANSWER ME, WHAT CURED THEE OF 341 LAZARU
DEATH$
LIKE A YOUNG SON WHO KEEPS WATCH BY THE BODY OF 350 LAZARU
HIS MOTHER,
AND WATCH CALIGULA COMMANDING LIFE UNDER PAIN OF 360 LAZARU
DEATH TO DO HIS WILL/
NOW I TAKE HIM OUT UNDER THE SKY, WHERE I CAN 360 LAZARU
WATCH HIS MONKEY TRICKS.
AND TO PROVE MY ESCAPE--AS A SYMBOL--WATCH AND 40 MANSNS
BEAR WITNESS, NICHOLAS/
AT FIRST, ALL I WISH YOU TO DO IS TO SIT AND WATCH 92 MANSNS
HOW I DEAL WITH EVERYTHING.
(HE GLANCES AT HIS WATCH.) 92 MANSNS
THAT I HAVE HAD TO WATCH FOR YEARS, 97 MANSNS
IT WILL BE AMUSING TO WATCH. 123 MANSNS
(HE GLANCES AT HIS WATCH.) AND NOW I'LL HAVE TO 158 MANSNS
GO AND CATCH MY TRAIN.
AND WATCH WHILE HE DESTROYS HIMSELF, 173 MANSNS
OUT WITH YOUR EYES TO WATCH I MAY BECOME AT LEAST 418 MARCOM
A SHADOW OF HIS GREATNESS.
SO WATCH YOUR TONGUE. 34 MISBEG
WHILE THEY WATCH THE DISCONCERTING EFFECT OF THIS 58 MISBEG
THEATRICAL MIRTH ON HARDER.)
YOU BETTER WATCH YOUR STEP. 124 MISBEG
IF YOU WON'T WATCH YOUR STEP, I'VE GOT TO. 126 MISBEG
YOU'D LIE AWAKE AND WATCH THE DAWN COME WITH 140 MISBEG
DISGUST,
(PEELING PAST ROCHE TO WATCH MELODY, LEANS ACROSS 100 POET
TO ROCHE--
TAKE CARE, SIR, AND WATCH YOUR WORDS OR I WARN YOU120 POET
YOU WILL REPENT THEM,
THE TWO WOMEN WATCH HIM, NORA FRIGHTENED, 124 POET
SPYIN' TO WATCH ME/ 578 ROPE
YOU BETTER TAKE WATCH ON YOUR HEALTH, PAW, 579 ROPE
COME AND WATCH ME/ 589 ROPE
WATCH ME THROW IT. 589 ROPE
(WITH SUDDEN DECISION) YOU'D BEST LAVE HIM TO ME 590 ROPE
TO WATCH OUT FOR.
HOW WATCH HOW FAR I KIN CHUCK ROCKS. 590 ROPE
(COMPLACENTLY) WELL, YOU WATCH ME AND I'LL LEARN 593 ROPE
YOU WATCH ME/ 593 ROPE
YOU WATCH ME/ 594 ROPE
YOU WATCH ME/ 594 ROPE
YOU WATCH ME/ 594 ROPE
(GRINNING AT SWEENEY) SAY, WATCH THIS. 595 ROPE
YOU JUST WATCH ME, I TELL YUH/ 598 ROPE
YOU WATCH ME/ 598 ROPE
SO YOU WATCH ME/ 599 ROPE

WATCHING

WATCH (CONT'D.)
YOU WATCH ME/ 599 ROPE
YOU WATCH ME/ 600 ROPE
(LOOKS AT HIS WATCH) (IF FIVE-THIRTY JUST... 23 STRANG
THEN HE PULLS OUT HIS WATCH MECHANICALLY AND 25 STRANG
STARES AT IT.
(HE TAKES OUT HIS WATCH MECHANICALLY AND LOOKS AT 25 STRANG
IT)
SHE USED TO LOVE TO WATCH THE FOOTBALL GAMES WHEN 100 STRANG
HE WAS PLAYING.
((I MUST WATCH THEM... 125 STRANG
THEY WATCH HIM SUSPICIOUSLY) 129 STRANG
I'D WATCH HIM AND READ SYMPTOMS OF INSANITY INTO 139 STRANG
EVERY MOVE HE MADE...
NOW I WATCH HIM GROW FAT AND I LAUGH/... 139 STRANG
(PULLING OUT HIS WATCH) SOON BE TIME FOR THE 160 STRANG
START.
(LOOKING AT HIS WATCH AGAIN) 161 STRANG
(THANK GOD, I CAN WATCH HER OBJECTIVELY AGAIN... 161 STRANG
(HE JERKS OUT HIS WATCH AGAIN) 163 STRANG
I'VE GOT TO WATCH HER... 177 STRANG
I MUST WATCH--MY DUTY AS AN ARTIST/ 177 STRANG
I MUST WATCH ALL THIS CAREFULLY/...)) 177 STRANG
((I MUST WATCH THIS... 178 STRANG
WHY DIDN'T YOU COME AND WATCH 178 STRANG
I COULDN'T WATCH HIM. 185 STRANG
I CAN'T BEAR TO WATCH HIM SUFFER ANYMORE/... 194 STRANG
NINA AND DARRELL JUMP STARTLEDLY AND GO TO THE 190 STRANG
REAR OF THE TERRACE TO WATCH THE
AND A GOLD WATCH-CHAIN OF CABLE-LIKE PROPORTIONS 493 VOYAGE
(HE WALKS STILL FURTHER AWAY, THEN TURNS TO WATCH 469 WELDED
HER.

WATCHED
(WHO HAS WATCHED HIM KEENLY WHILE HE HAS BEEN 21 ANNA
SPEAKING--
I'VE WATCHED YOU GROW UP, AND I KNOW YOUR WAYS, 106 BEYOND
AND THEY'RE MY WAYS.
EVERYBODY WATCHED TO SEE HOW I'D TAKE IT. 521 DAYS
BUT I'VE WATCHED HIM GROW UP FROM A BOY AND EVERY 540 DIFRNT
TIME I'VE COME TO HOME
I'VE WATCHED THEM FOR HOURS. 461 DYNAMO
I'VE WATCHED YOU EVER SINCE YOU WERE LITTLE, 33 ELECTR
I'VE WATCHED IT EVER SINCE WE SAILED FOR THE EAST.141 ELECTR
YOU WATCHED HIM STARE AT YOUR BODY THROUGH YOUR 154 ELECTR
CLOTHES, STRIPPING YOU NAKED/
HE SCARES ME AT TIMES--AND VINNIE--I'VE WATCHED 158 ELECTR
HER LOOKING AT YOU.
UNTIL AT LAST THROUGH TWO TEARS I WATCHED HER DIE 282 GGBROW
I'VE WATCHED MANY CASES OF ALMOST FATAL 626 ICEMAN
TEETOTALISM.
IF I'VE WATCHED YOU IT WAS TO ADMIRE HOW FAT AND 17 JOURNE
BEAUTIFUL YOU LOOKED.
(HAS WATCHED THIS PROCEEDING WITH AN AWAKENED 128 JOURNE
SENSE OF HUMOR--
I FOUND MYSELF KNEELING, BUT BETWEEN MY FINGERS I 277 LAZARU
WATCHED JESUS AND LAZARUS.
AS I WATCHED YOU TOGETHER IN THE HOUSE AT NIGHT, 105 MANSNS
WHILE WE WATCHED WITH GRATIFIED WOMANLY PRIDE AND 171 MANSNS
LAUGHED AND GOADED HIM ON/
HAS WATCHED ALL THIS WITH FASCINATED DISGUST WHILE432 MARCOM
CHU-YIN HAS SAT DOWN TO READ
IN HER EYES' MIRROR I WATCHED MYSELF LIVE 437 MARCOM
PROTECTED FROM LIFE BY HER AFFECTION--
I'VE WATCHED YOU MAKING SHEEP'S EYES AT HIM. 9 MISBEG
PROBABLY SNORING, AS YOU WATCHED THE DAWN COME. 124 MISBEG
YOU TALKED ABOUT HOW YOU'D WATCHED TOO MANY DAWNS 171 MISBEG
COME CREEPING GRAYLY OVER
I HAVE WATCHED HAPPY SMILES FORM ON THE LIPS OF 86 STRANG
THE DYING...
AND I'VE WATCHED LOVE GROW IN HIM UNTIL I'M 91 STRANG
SURE...))

WATCHES
BOTH WATCHES. 550 'ILE
MILLER WATCHES HIS SON FROWNINGLY. 206 AHWILD
AS MRS. MILLER WATCHES HER APPREHENSIVELY. 211 AHWILD
MILDRED WATCHES HIM CURIOUSLY--THEN SIGHS 273 AHWILD
AFFECTEDLY)
HE JUST WATCHES EVERY MOVE SHE MAKES. 140 BEYOND
YANK WATCHES THEM FURTIVELY. 485 CARDIF
THE DONKEY MAN WATCHES HIM IMPASSIVELY. 466 CARIBÉ
LOVING WATCHES HIM. 496 DAYS
ELSA WATCHES HER WITH A WORRIED, AFFECTIONATELY 517 DAYS
PITYING LOOK.)
LAVINIA WATCHES HIM. 14 ELECTR
AND WATCHES HIM FROM BEHIND THE CURTAINS AS HE 42 ELECTR
GOES DOWN THE DRIVE.
LAVINIA WATCHES HIM WORRIEDLY.) 49 ELECTR
LAVINIA WATCHES HIM UNEASILY AND SPEAKS SHARPLY) 144 ELECTR
(WATCHES HIM GO--THEN WITH A LITTLE DESPERATE CRY 178 ELECTR
STARTS AFTER HIM)
CYBEL WATCHES THEM BOTH--THEN, BORED, SHE YAWNS) 280 GGBROW
(WATCHES WILLIE, WHO IS SHAKING IN HIS SLEEP LIKE 581 ICEMAN
AN OLD DOG)
ROCKY WATCHES THIS MOVE CAREFULLY.) 613 ICEMAN
(HE WATCHES EXCITEDLY, AS IF IT WERE A RACE HE HAD688 ICEMAN
A BET ON.
SHE WATCHES US WATCHING HER-- 38 JOURNE
EDMUND WATCHES HIM. 116 JOURNE
EDMUND WATCHES WITH AMUSEMENT JAMIE'S WAVERING 154 JOURNE
PROGRESS THROUGH THE FRONT
WITH THE EXCEPTION OF MIRIAM, WHO DOES NOT LAUGH 280 LAZARU
BUT WATCHES AND
LOUIS GIVES ME HIS ARM, WHILE ALL THE COURT 4 MANSNS
WATCHES ENVIOUSLY--
WHILE HE STANDS APART AND WATCHES AND SNEERS AND 171 MANSNS
LAUGHS WITH GREEDY PRIDE
WHO WATCHES OVER THEIR EARTHLY GOODS. 373 MARCOM

WATCHES (CONT'D.)
MARCO WATCHES THIS IMPRESSION AND HURRIES ON WITH 391 MARCOM
AN INJURED DIGNITY)
(WATCHES THE CRACK UNDER JOSIE'S DOOR AND SPEAKS 97 MISBEG
HALF-ALOUD TO HIMSELF.
(WATCHES HIM FOR A SECOND, FIGHTING THE LOVE THAT,141 MISBEG
IN SPITE OF HER,
(HE STOPS AND WATCHES HER FACE WORRIEDLY. 160 MISBEG
SHE WATCHES HIM TENSELY. 172 MISBEG
(WATCHES HER OVER HIS PAPER.) 16 POET
GREGAN WATCHES HIM. 96 POET
THE OLD MAN WATCHES HIM WITH EAGER EYES AND SEEMS 596 ROPE
TO BE TRYING TO SMILE.
SHE WATCHES HIM. 102 STRANG
HE WATCHES WITH CONTENTED EYES THE EVENING SHADOWS200 STRANG
CLOSING IN AROUND THEM.)
JUAN WATCHES HER. 464 WELDED
SHE WATCHES HIM. 471 WELDED

WATCHFUL
BE AS CAREFUL AND WATCHFUL NOW OUTSIDE THE OFFICE 119 MANSNS
AS IN IT--

WATCHIN'
IT WOULDN'A BEEN CLEAR'S A LIGHTHOUSE TO ANY SUB 521 INZONE
THAT WAS WATCHIN'--
AND WON'T HE BE PROUD WATCHIN' HER RISE IN THE 173 POET
WORLD TILL SHE'S A GRAND LADY/

WATCHING
THESE LAST SIX YEARS SINCE WE WERE MARRIED-- 545 'ILE
WAITING, AND WATCHING, AND FEARING--
WATCHING THEM OVER THE SWINGING DOOR. 237 AHWILD
THEN, WATCHING HER, WITH SHOCKED CONCERN) 239 AHWILD
MILDRED AND TOMMY ARE SUBDUED, COVERTLY WATCHING 263 AHWILD
THEIR FATHER.
MA'LL BE COMING BACK SOON AND SHE'LL KEEP WATCHING274 AHWILD
ME LIKE A CAT--
HE IS FACING LEFT, WATCHING THE PATH. 275 AHWILD
(WATCHING HIS SON--AFTER A PAUSE--QUIETLY) 296 AHWILD
(WATCHING HIM INTENTLY--A MOCKING SMILE ON HIS 49 ANNA
LIPS)
(AFTER WATCHING HIM IRRITABLY FOR A MOMENT) 121 BEYOND
WHERE SHE REMAINS WATCHING ROBERT IN A TENSE, 150 BEYOND
EXPECTANT ATTITUDE.
RUTH TURNS AND STANDS WATCHING HIM. 154 BEYOND
IN A DITCH BY THE OPEN ROAD--WATCHING THE SUN 167 BEYOND
RISE.
(AFTER A PAUSE DURING WHICH ALL ARE WATCHING THE 460 CARIBÉ
APPROACHING BOAT)
HE ONLY WALKS TO AND FRO--WATCHING-- 562 CROSS
HE'S UP THERE--WATCHING--AS HE ALWAYS IS. 563 CROSS
AND I SEEMED FOR A MOMENT TO BE WATCHING SOME 522 DAYS
HIDDEN PLACE IN HIS MIND WHERE
YOU COULDN'T RESIST--WATCHING HIM SQUIRM/ 526 DAYS
I WAS WATCHING YOU. 532 DAYS
BOTH ARE WATCHING ELSA WITH ANXIOUS EYES. 553 DAYS
AND THE PRIEST CONTINUES, THE NURSE WATCHING AND 554 DAYS
LISTENING.
WHO IS STILL SITTING IN THE CHAIR BY THE HEAD OF 556 DAYS
THE BED, WATCHING ELSA.
HE SITS, WATCHING HER FACE WORRIEDLY, HIS FINGERS 558 DAYS
ON HER WRIST.
SHE IS WATCHING HIM CAREFULLY) 225 DESIRE
SHE STARTS VIOLENTLY, LOOKS AT HIM, SEES HE IS NOT236 DESIRE
WATCHING HER.
(HE IS WATCHING HER NOW WITH A HORRIBLE 240 DESIRE
FASCINATION.
WATCHING THEIR HOUSE/... 427 DYNAMO
ADA SITS DOWN AT RIGHT, WATCHING HER FATHER WITH A436 DYNAMO
CHALLENGING SMILE.)
BUT I CAN'T MOVE WHILE SHE'S WATCHING...)) 436 DYNAMO
FIFE'S KEEN EYES ARE WATCHING HIM AND HE GRINS 437 DYNAMO
WITH SATISFACTION.)
(LEANING FORWARD IN HER CHAIR AND WATCHING HER 439 DYNAMO
FATHER WORRIEDLY)
(WATCHING FROM HIS WINDOW) (HE'S TALKING TO 451 DYNAMO
FIFE/...
WATCHING THEM ALWAYS HELPS ME SOMEHOW... 472 DYNAMO
DON'T YOU KNOW ALL THIS IS WATCHING--LISTENING-- 484 DYNAMO
THAT SHE KNOWS EVERYTHING?
(WATCHING HIM WITH MALICIOUS SATISFACTION, AFTER A182 EJONES
PAUSE--MOCKINGLY)
WATCHING HER MOTHER AS SHE STROLLS THROUGH THE 10 ELECTR
GARDEN TO THE GREENHOUSE.
AND IS STANDING THERE WATCHING THEM) 18 ELECTR
(WATCHING HER CAREFULLY--KEEPING HIS CASUAL TONE) 22 ELECTR
I'LL BE WATCHING YOU EVERY MINUTE/ 34 ELECTR
I'D NEVER GUESS IT--AND I'VE BEEN WATCHING YOU. 46 ELECTR
(WHO HAS BEEN WATCHING HIM JEALOUSLY--SUDDENLY 49 ELECTR
PULLING HIM BY THE ARM--
AS IF SOMETHING IN ME WAS LISTENING, WATCHING, 60 ELECTR
WAITING FOR SOMETHING TO HAPPEN.
I'LL BE WATCHING YOU/ 156 ELECTR
AWARE THAT LAVINIA IS WATCHING HER SUSPICIOUSLY-- 161 ELECTR
DEFIANTLY TO ORIN)
HC STANDS FOR A MOMENT WATCHING HER, GRIMLY 178 ELECTR
WONDERING.
(WATCHING THEM) AT LEAST I AM LEAVING HER WELL 293 GGBROW
PROVIDED FOR.
WATCHING A DISGUSTING OLD FOOL LIKE ME, EH? 315 GGBROW
(WATCHING HIM PUZZLEDLY) UNDERSTAND WHATS 587 ICEMAN
(WATCHING HIM) YOU SEEM DOWN ON THE LADIES. 615 ICEMAN
(IS WATCHING LARRY'S FACE WITH A CURIOUS SNEERING 623 ICEMAN
SATISFACTION)
(WATCHING LARRY QUIZZICALLY) 639 ICEMAN
CORA GETS HER HANDS SET OVER THE PIANO KEYS, 651 ICEMAN
WATCHING OVER HER SHOULDER.
THINK YOU WAS WATCHING A CIRCUS/ 684 ICEMAN
AND I TIRED OF WATCHING THE STUPID GREED OF THE 689 ICEMAN
HUMAN CIRCUS,

WATCHING

WATCHING (CONT'D.)
THE PAUSES, WATCHING--THEN WORRIEDLY) 689 ICEMAN
HE GETS ANGRY AND STANDS WATCHING HIM AND 708 ICEMAN
LISTENING.)
HE WAS WATCHING. 722 ICEMAN
SHE WATCHES US WATCHING HER-- 38 JOURNE
WATCHING THE DAWN CREEP LIKE A PAINTED DREAM 193 JOURNE
WATCHING LAZARUS WITH FRIGHTENED AWE, TALKING 273 LAZARU
HESITANTLY IN LOW WHISPERS.
WARENESS OF THOUGHT, OR WATCHING ONE ANOTHER WITH289 LAZARU
SUSPICION)
(WATCHING HER.) YES, MOTHER HAS ALWAYS BEEN 82 MANSNS
EXTREMELY GREEDY FOR OTHERS' LIVES.
(FRANKLY) YES, IT'S TRUE YOU FEEL HER ALWAYS 84 MANSNS
THERE, WATCHING--
WATCHING MY WINNINGS PILE UP AND BECOMING CONFUSED102 MANSNS
WITH LOSSES--
OF WATCHING SUSPICIOUSLY EACH CARD I LED TO MYSELF102 MANSNS
FROM ACROSS THE TABLE--
WITHOUT A CARE IN THE WORLD, WATCHING MY SONS GROW148 MANSNS
UP HANDSOME RICH GENTLEMEN,
HOURS SINCE SUPPER EVEN--THE CHILDREN WATCHING, 162 MANSNS
THEIR PRYING EYES SNEERING--
WHEN SHE STANDS FONDLING THE PUPPY AND WATCHING 392 MARCOM
MARCO.)
WATCHING BY MY BEDSIDE LIKE A GENTLE NURSE, 412 MARCOM
SHE KEEPS WATCHING HER FATHER AND DOES NOT NOTICE 10 MISBEG
MIKE'S DEPARTURE)
LOOK AT HIM WHEN HE THINKS NO ONE IS WATCHING, 35 MISBEG
WITH HIS EYES ON THE GROUND.
(ROGAN IS WATCHING THEM BOTH, NOT MISSING ANYTHING 43 MISBEG
IN THEIR FACES.
(WATCHING THEM WITH AMUSEMENT) 48 MISBEG
WATCHING HIM KIDS PAST IN HIS BIG SHINY AUTOMOBILE 51 MISBEG
WITH HIS SNOOT IN THE AIR,
(HAS BEEN WATCHING THE VISITOR APPROACH) 55 MISBEG
IT MAKES ME NERVOUS WATCHING YOU HOLD IT AS IF YOU'24 MISBEG
DIDN'T KNOW IT WAS THERE.
(WATCHING HIM) DRINK UP OR YOU'LL BE ASLEEP 167 MISBEG
AGAIN.
(WATCHING THE SUNRISE--MECHANICALLY) 172 MISBEG
SHE STANDS, WATCHING HIM GO, FOR A MOMENT, 174 MISBEG
SHE DRAWS BACK FOR A MOMENT--THEN STANDS WATCHING 44 POET
HIM CONTEMPTUOUSLY.
(WHO HAS BEEN WATCHING THE DOOR AT LEFT FRONT, 87 POET
PREOCCUPIED BY HER OWN WORRY--
(WHO HAS BEEN WATCHING HIM DISDAINFULLY, REACHES 97 POET
OUT TO TAKE HIS PLATE--
I SUPPOSE SHE DID IT TO FIND OUT BY WATCHING HIM 108 POET
HOW FAR--
WELL, I HAVE BEEN REFLECTING, WATCHING YOU AND 112 POET
EXAMINING YOUR CONDUCT,
(WATCHING HIM UNEASILY, ATTEMPTS A REASONABLE, 122 POET
PERSUASIVE JOKE.)
SHE'S ONLY WATCHING FOR A GOOD EXCUSE TO TURN 127 POET
SIMON AGAINST MARRYING ME,
WITH THAT PALE YANKEE BITCH WATCHING FROM A 157 POET
WINDOW, SNEERING WITH DISGUST!
(WATCHING HIM--THINKING WITH A CONDESCENDING 9 STRANG
AFFECTION)
WATCHING THE BURNING, FROZEN NAKED SWIMMERS DROWN 14 STRANG
AT LAST....)
(THEN WATCHING THE PROFESSOR WITH A PITYING 15 STRANG
SHUDDER)
HE FEELS I'M ALWAYS WATCHING HIM WITH SCORN... 69 STRANG
HOW CAN I HELP WATCHING HIM.... 69 STRANG
(WATCHING HIM--THINKING) (INEAT... 76 STRANG
WATCHING SYMPTOMS.... 79 STRANG
(WATCHING EVANS WITH A CONTEMPT THAT IS ALMOST 95 STRANG
GLOATING--
(WATCHING HIM--SAVAGELY) (I NOW I KNOW/... 124 STRANG
(WHO IS WATCHING THEM KEENLY--THINKING) 126 STRANG
YOU THINK I'LL STAY--TO BE YOUR LOVER--WATCHING 132 STRANG
SAM WITH MY WIFE AND MY CHILD--
DARRELL IS SITTING BY THE TABLE AT LEFT, WATCHING 137 STRANG
NINA.
NINA IS RECLINING ON THE CHAISE LONGUE WATCHING 137 STRANG
GORDON WHO IS SITTING ON THE
(WATCHING HIM--BROODING WITH LOVING TENDERNESS-- 138 STRANG
SADLY)
(WATCHING NINA--SADLY) (I ALWAYS THINKING OF HER 139 STRANG
SON...
JEALOUSY AND RAGE AND GRIEF, WATCHING THEM,) 145 STRANG
(THEY SIT CLOSE, SHE STARING DREAMILY BEFORE HER, 440 WELDED
HE WATCHING HER FACE.)
HE STANDS NEARBY UNCERTAINLY, WATCHING HER, 462 WELDED
JUMP IS WATCHING HER KEENLY NOW. A SAD FOREBODING 465 WELDED
COMING INTO HIS EYES.
HE STANDS IN THE DOORWAY WATCHING EACH MOVEMENT UF471 WELDED
THE WOMAN'S
WATCHMAN
I'M LACKING A WATCHMAN AND I'VE GOT TO KEEP MY 104 ELECTR
WEATHER EYE OPEN.
I FIRED THE WATCHMAN THIS MORNING 107 ELECTR
WATCHMAN'S
NEAR BEAT THE WATCHMAN'S BRAINS OUT/ 105 ELECTR
WATER
HE DON'T WANT TO SEE NO CLEAR WATER. 537 'ILE
THEY'S CLEAR WATER 'S FAR 'S YOU CAN SEE. 537 'ILE
ANY WATER/ 540 'ILE
CLEAR WATER/ 540 'ILE
AND THEY'S PLENTY O' WATER. 541 'ILE
THERE'S CLEAR WATER TO THE SOUTH NOW. 546 'ILE
THERE'S A CLEAR PASSAGE THROUGH THE FLOE, AND 550 'ILE
CLEAR WATER BEYOND,
I USED TO BE A REGULAR WATER RAT WHEN I WAS A BOY.228 AHWILD
THE WATER WAS WONDERFUL AND WARM. 228 AHWILD
FOOLHARDY IN THE WATER-- 230 AHWILD

WATER (CONT'D.)
WHEN I WAS UP TO THE WATER CLOSET LAST-- 253 AHWILD
I LOVE THE SAND AND THE TREES, AND THE GRASS, AND 277 AHWILD
THE WATER AND THE SKY,
HE BACKED WATER AND SAID HE GUESSED I WAS RIGHT. 292 AHWILD
WHICH HAS MADE HIM A PERSONAGE OF THE WATER FRONT. 3 ANNA
I AIN'T BEEN HORN AND DRAGGED UP ON THE WATER 11 ANNA
FRONT FOR NUTHIN'.
I'D SURE LIKE A TRIP ON THE WATER, ALL RIGHT. 23 ANNA
YUST WATER ALL ROUND, AND SUN, AND FRESH AIR, 23 ANNA
A SEA MAN AS DIFFERENT FROM THE ONES ON LAND AS 99 ANNA
WATER IS FROM MUD--
(HE GETS A TIN DIPPER FROM THE BUCKET AND BATHES 483 CARDIF
YANK'S FOREHEAD WITH THE WATER.
GIMME A DRINK OF WATER, WILL YUH, DRISC. 486 CARDIF
(DRISCOLL BRINGS THE DIPPER FULL OF WATER 486 CARDIF
(DRISCOLL GETS HIM A DIPPER OF WATER) 489 CARDIF
(HE GASPS FOR AIR) GIMME A DRINK OF WATER, WILL 489 CARDIF
YUH, DRISC.
(ENTERS, HIS OILSKINS AND SOU'WESTER GLISTENING 490 CARDIF
WITH DROPS OF WATER)
A MELANCHOLY NEGRO CHANT, FAINT AND FAR OFF, 455 CARIBE
DRIFTS, CROONING, OVER THE WATER.
HE IS SITTING ON THE FORECASTLE HEAD LOOKING OUT 456 CARIBE
OVER THE WATER
DON'T BE THROWIN' COLD WATER, LAMPS, 460 CARIBE
THE SINGING FROM SHORE COMES CLEARLY OVER THE 466 CARIBE
MOONLIT WATER.)
THE MELANCHOLY SUNG OF THE NEGROES DRIFTS CROONING473 CARIBE
OVER THE WATER.
THEY'RE DEVILS FOR STAYING UNDER WATER, YOU KNOW--560 CROSS
AND THEY FOUND--IN TWO CHESTS--
WATER-LOGTER-CLOGGED HULK OF A MALAY PRAU-- 560 CROSS
WATER DRIPS FROM THEIR SOAKED AND ROTTEN CLOTHES. 571 CROSS
ALSO A LOAF OF BREAD AND A CROCK OF WATER. 206 DESIRE
HIS FACE SHINES FROM SOAP AND WATER. 228 DESIRE
HER SKIN IS FULL OF MUD AND WATER) 251 DESIRE
AND WE PUT IN AT ONE OF THE ISLANDS FOR WATER. 497 DIFRENT
IT WAS WHEN THEY PUT IN TO GIT WATER AT THEM SOUTH501 DIFRENT
SEA ISLANDS
AND EVEN AFTER THEY'D GOT ALL THE WATER THEY 502 DIFRENT
NEEDED ABOARD,
HAAL, SEEMS LIKE THEY ALL WENT ASHORE ON THEM 502 DIFRENT
ISLANDS TO GIT WATER AND THE
AND WHEN THEY UPS ANCHORS, SHE DIVES IN THE WATER 503 DIFRENT
AND SWIMS OUT AFTER 'EM,
AND FINALLY THEY HAS TO P'INT A GUN AT HER AND 503 DIFRENT
SHOUT IN THE WATER NEAR HER AFORE
I'VE TECHED THAR FOR WATER MORE'N ONCE MYSELF, 513 DIFRENT
EVERYTHING IS DIFFERENT DOWN THERE--THE WEATHER-- 515 DIFRENT
AND THE TREES AND WATER.
(THIS ACTS LIKE A PAIL OF COLD WATER ON EMMA WHO 527 DIFRENT
MOVES AWAY FROM BENNY QUICKLY.)
A SOFT OVERTONE OF RUSHING WATER FROM THE DAM AND 473 DYNAMO
THE RIVER BED BELOW,
AND LISTEN TO THE WATER RUSHING OVER THE DAM/ LIKE476 DYNAMO
MUSIC/
IT'S AS IF THAT SOUND WAS COOL WATER WASHING OVER 476 DYNAMO
MY BODY/
THE OVERTONE OF RUSHING WATER FROM THE DAM SOUNDS 476 DYNAMO
LOUDER BECAUSE OF THE CLOSED
I MUST PUT THESE IN WATER. 17 ELECTR
THAT COUNTED NO MORE THAN DIRTY WATER. 54 ELECTR
(TAKES A SWALLOW OF WATER-- 62 ELECTR
SHE PUTS THE PELLET ON HIS TONGUE AND PRESSES THE 62 ELECTR
GLASS OF WATER TO HIS LIPS)
THEY HOLDS OUT THE PELLET AND A GLASS OF WATER 62 ELECTR
WHICH IS ON THE STAND)
DRIFTS OVER THE WATER FROM A SHIP THAT IS WEIGHING102 ELECTR
ANCHOR IN THE HARBOR.
ON THE SHIP IN THE HARBOR COMES MOURNFULLY OVER 109 ELECTR
THE WATER.
WITH A GLASS AND A PITCHER OF WATER. 109 ELECTR
->SHE'S FAR ACROSS THE STORMY WATER WAY-AY, I'M 124 ELECTR
BOUND AWAY--
AND FILL WATER YOUR GRAVE EVERY SUNDAY AFTER 132 ELECTR
CHURCH,
THEIR FACES AND BODIES SHINE FROM SOAP-AND-WATER 226 HA APE
SCRUBBING BUT AROUND THEIR
AS THE STREAM OF WATER HITS THE STEEL OF YANK'S 245 HA APE
CELL.)
THAT WATER-WAGON HULL-- 621 ICEMAN
I DRINKS DAT OLD BUBBLY WATER IN STEINS/ 640 ICEMAN
LIKE A WATER BUFFALO'S/ 662 ICEMAN
DON'T TINK YUH CAN KID ME WID DAT WATER-WAGON 671 ICEMAN
BULL/
A PITCHER OF WATER. 696 ICEMAN
SEE HIM SITTIN' ON DE DOCK ON WEST STREET, 699 ICEMAN
LOOKIN' AT DE WATER AND CRYIN'/
BRING THE BUCKET OF WATER HERE, JACK, WILL YOUS 524 INZONE
HERE--PUT IT IN THE WATER--EASY/ 524 INZONE
(LOOKING AT THE LOCK ON THE BOX IN THE WATER 527 INZONE
(HE PUTS THE BOX BACK IN THE WATER AND JUMPS TO 527 INZONE
THEIR AID.
(PAUSING--HIS HAND IN THE WATER) 527 INZONE
(HE SELECTS ONE AND GINGERLY REACHES HIS HAND IN 527 INZONE
THE WATER.)
(DRISCOLL TAKES THE DRIPPING BOX FROM THE WATER 527 INZONE
AND STARTS TO FIT IN THE KEY.
WHO AGAIN LIFTS THE BOX OUT OF THE WATER AND SETS 528 INZONE
IT CAREFULLY ON HIS KNEES.
HARBOR AND THE AVENUE THAT RUNS ALONG THE WATER 11 JOURNE
FRONT.
FROM DRINKING THE POISONED WATER. 24 JOURNE
MILLIONAIRE OUGHT TO WELCOME THE FLAVOR OF HOG IN 25 JOURNE
HIS ICE WATER AS AN
SEVERAL WHISKEY GLASSES, AND A PITCHER OF ICE 51 JOURNE
WATER.

1777

WATER

(CONT'D.)
THE GRABS THE BOTTLE AND POURS A DRINK, ADDS ICE 53 JOURNE
WATER AND DRINKS.
AND HERE'S THE WATER YOU'VE BEEN DRINKING. FINE/ 54 JOURNE
THE POURS WATER IN THE GLASS AND SETS IT ON THE 54 JOURNE
TABLE BY EDMUND.)
(HE MEASURES TWO DRINKS OF WATER 54 JOURNE
AND PITCHER OF ICE WATER IS ON THE TABLE, 97 JOURNE
GOD SAVE ME, IT'LL BE HALF WATER. 100 JOURNE
JUST MEASURE A FEW DRINKS OF WATER AND POUR THEM 100 JOURNE
IN.
THE DAMNED STUFF IS HALF WATER/ 116 JOURNE
WITH THE WATER FOAMING INTO SPUME UNDER ME, 153 JOURNE
THE WATER IN THE SMALL OVAL POOL BEFORE THE 95 MANSNS
SUMMER-HOUSE
WHO USED IT TO TAP WATER OUT OF STONES AND FINALLY349 MARCOM
PLANTED IT.
HE GETS UP AND TAKES A GULP OF WATER-- 350 MARCOM
WATER TO REVIVE THEM/ 351 MARCOM
(THE SOLDIERS CARRY AROUND JUGS OF WATER 351 MARCOM
I REASONED, LOVE COMES LIKE THE BREATH OF WIND ON 388 MARCOM
WATER
AND THE BLUE WATER ALONE UNDER A STRANGE SKY AMID 405 MARCOM
ALIEN FLOWERS AND FACES.
I SHALL KNOW THE LONG SORROW OF AN EXILE AS I SAIL405 MARCOM
OVER THE GREEN WATER
SLEEP IN GREEN WATER. 409 MARCOM
IF I WERE ASLEEP IN GREEN WATER, NO PANG COULD BE 409 MARCOM
ADDED TO MY SORROW.
(LONGINGLY) I WOULD BE ASLEEP IN GREEN WATER/ 412 MARCOM
(HIS VOICE COMES FROM OVER THE WATER CHEERY AND 420 MARCOM
RELIEVED)
LIKE WATER OFF A DUCK'S BACK. 33 MISBEG
WATERS 44 MISBEG
IF YOURS IS, MISTER TYRONE, THERE'S A WELL FULL OF 44 MISBEG
WATER AT THE BACK.
YOU'VE GONE ON THE WATER-WAGON, I SUPPOSE 45 MISBEG
PIG IN NEXT SUMMER'S ICE WATER. 51 MISBEG
AND TEN MORE DIED OF CHOLERA AFTER DRINKING THE 63 MISBEG
DIRTY WATER IN IT.
SHE HAS A QUART OF WHISKEY UNDER HER ARM, TWO 111 MISBEG
TUMBLERS, AND A PITCHER OF WATER.
HE POURS WATER IN HER GLASS. 113 MISBEG
I'LL WET A CLOTH IN COLD WATER TO PUT ROUND YOUR 35 POET
HEAD.
HE REACHES OUT WITH HIS RIGHT AND POURS A GLASS OF 35 POET
WATER
TO HIS LIPS THE WATER SLOSHES OVER HIS HAND 35 POET
IT IS AS IF COLD WATER WERE DASHED IN HIS FACE. 103 POET
(SHE THROWS THE DOLLAR AWAY AND BENDS DOWN TO SEE 589 ROPE
IT HIT THE WATER.)
AND BENDS OVER TO SEE THEM HIT THE WATER. 602 ROPE
HIS EYES WATER.) 98 STRANG
BY JOVE, I'LL HAVE TO THROW COLD WATER ON THAT 122 STRANG
FANCY/...))
I SEE A FLASHING IN THE WATER UP THERE/ 175 STRANG
LIFT HER OUT OF THE WATER, SON/ 182 STRANG
PLANE ASCEND FROM THE WATER, STANDING SIDE BY 198 STRANG
SIDE.
THE BAR OF A LOW DIVE ON THE LONDON WATER-FRONT-- 493 VOYAGE

WATER'D

EVERY STORM THE WATER'D BEGIN TO DRIP DOWN AND 464 DYNAMO
MOTHER'D PUT THE WASH

WATER'LL

THE WATER'LL GIT IN AND SPOIL IT. 524 INZONE

WATER'S

SHE SAYS SALT WATER'S THE ONLY THING THAT REALLY 230 AHWILD
HELPS HER BUNION.
THE WATER'S DEEP DOWN THERE, AND YOU'D BE A 589 ROPE
DROWNED RAT IF YOU SLIPPED.

WATERBURY'S

WATERBURY'S NIFTY OLD TOWN WITH THE LID OFF, WHEN 188 AHWILD
YOU GET TO KNOW THE ROPES.

WATERED

WAAL--THE STOCK'D GOT T' BE WATERED. 208 DESIRE
EDMUND AT ONCE REALIZES HOW MUCH THE WHISKEY HAS 111 JOURNE
BEEN WATERED.
LAND THAT'S WATERED WITH THE TEARS OF STARVING 62 MISBEG
WIDOWS AND ORPHANS--

WATERFRONT

FOR THE LIKE OF THEM COWS ON THE WATERFRONT IS THE 34 ANNA
ONLY WOMEN I'VE MET UP WITH
GET THIS AT SOME DRUGGIST'S DOWN BY THE WATERFRONT 40 ELECTR
THE MINUTE YOU REACH THERE.
AND THERE HAVE BEEN A LOT OF WATERFRONT THIEVES 104 ELECTR
AROUND HERE LATELY.
THAT HE WAS KILLED BY WATERFRONT THIEVES. 121 ELECTR
DE BROOKLYN WATERFRONT, DAT WAS WHERE I WAS 234 HA APE
DRAGGED UP.
AN INN LOCAL NEAR THE WATERFRONT, 245 HA APE
FROM THE MARKET PEOPLE ACROSS THE STREET AND THE 594 ICEMAN
WATERFRONT WORKERS.

WATERLOO

WATERWAGON-- WATERBURY-WATERLOO/ 188 AHWILD

WATERPOWER

I SHOVELED SAND ON A BIG WATERPOWER JOB OUT WEST. 461 DYNAMO

WATERS

STRAIN OF MUSIC RECEDING INTO THE SILENCE OVER 324 LAZARU
STILL WATERS.)

WATERWAGON

WATERWAGON-- WATERBURY-WATERLOO/ 188 AHWILD

WATHER

YOU'D BE WANTIN' A DRINK AV WATHER, MAYBES 479 CARDIF
HIS BREATH IS CHOKIN' IN HIS THROAT LOIKE WATHER 479 CARDIF
GURGLIN' IN A POIPE.
AND THE DISH-WATHER THEY DISGUISE WID THE NAME AV 480 CARDIF
TEA/

WAVING

WATHER

(CONT'D.)
WID SCARCELY A DRUP OF WATHER CR A BITE TO CHEW 482 CARDIF
ON.

WAVE

THEN OVERCOME BY A WAVE OF FIERCE TENDERNESS) 20 ANNA
AND WHEN HE HAS RAISED HIGH ON A GREAT WAVE I TOLK 36 ANNA
A LOOK ABOUT
THEY UNHITCH THEIR WINGS, KATEY, AND SPREADS 'EM 95 BEYOND
OUT ON A WAVE FUR A BED.
(SHE IS SHAKEN AGAIN BY A WAVE OF UNCONTROLLABLE 550 DAYS
CHILLS. HER TEETH CHATTER--
SUDDENLY OVERCOME BY A WAVE OF DROWSINESS HE TRIES555 DAYS
IN VAIN TO FIGHT BACK)
WAVE FORM...
(A WAVE OF PASSION COMING OVER HIM, 429 DYNAMO
THAT A GREAT WAVE WID SUN IN THE HEART OF IT MAY 215 HA APE
SWEEP ME OVER THE SIDE SOMETIME.
HE'S GOT HIS REFORM WAVE GUI*' STRONG DIS MORNIN'/665 ICEMAN
ASK UP THE WIND, OR OF THE WAVE, OR OF THE STAR, 132 JOURNE
OR OF THE BIRD,
AND THE WIND, WAVE, STAR, BIRD, CLOCK, WILL ANSWER132 JOURNE
YOU...
WHAT DO YOU THINK I PAID YOU IN ADVANCE FOR--TO 406 MARCOM
WAVE ME GOOD-BYES
IN THE TYPHOON WHEN A WAVE SWEPT ME FROM THE DECK,411 MARCOM
REASSURE HIMSELF ABOUT IT, YET HE IS RIDING THE 53 STRANG
CREST OF THE WAVE.
(SUDDENLY OVERCOME BY A WAVE OF CONSCIENCE-- 156 STRANG
STRICKEN REMORSE AND PITY)
(THEN, WITH A GRIM FATALISM--WITH A FINAL WAVE OF 198 STRANG
HIS HAND AT THE SKY)

WAVED

DO YOU REMEMBER HOW YOU WAVED YOUR HANDKERCHIEF, 82 ELECTR
HAZEL,

WAVER

HER EYES WAVER GUILTILY AND SHE ADDS IN A TONE 60 JOURNE
WHICH BEGINS TO PLACATE.)
SUDDENLY THE FLAMES WAVER, DIE DOWN, 367 LAZARU
FOR A SECOND HIS EYES WAVER AND HE LOOKS GUILTY. 33 POET

WAVERING

STICKS HIS FOOT OUT AND THE WAVERING COUPLE 471 CARIBE
STUMBLE OVER IT
(THEN, SEEING ORIN WAVERING, PITIFULLY) 88 ELECTR
CUNNING, WATCHES WITH AMUSEMENT JAMIE'S WAVERING 154 JOURNE
PROGRESS THROUGH THE FRONT
(SHE TAKES A WAVERING STEP TOWARD THE DOOR, 108 STRANG

WAVERINGLY

(GETS HEAVILY AND A BIT WAVERINGLY TO HIS FEET AND151 JOURNE
GROPES UNCERTAINLY FOR THE

WAVERS

THIS KNEES SAG, HE WAVERS AND SEEMS ABOUT TO FALL. 39 ANNA
THEN SHE WAVERS AND SUDDENLY BOLTS BACK INTO THE 466 WELDED
ROOM, GROPINGLY,

WAVES

HE WAVES HIS HAND AIMLESSLY AND SPEAKS WITH A 224 AHWILD
SILLY GRAVITY.)
(TO THE ACCOMPANIMENT OF THIS LAST HE WAVES HIS 6 ANNA
HAND
NEVER DREAMED WAVES COULD GET SO BIG OR THE WIND 131 BEYOND
BLOW SO HARD.
A DENSE GREEN GLOW FLOODS SLOWLY IN RHYTHMIC WAVES570 CROSS
LIKE A LIQUID IN THE ROOM--
THE BREAKING OF THE WAVES WAS YOUR VOICE. 90 ELECTR
AT HIS EARNEST SOLICITATION--(HE WAVES A HAND TO 152 ELECTR
THE PORTRAIT MOCKINGLY)
FOR A MOMENT THE FAINT SOUND OF THE MUSIC AND THE 259 GGBROW
LAPPING OF THE WAVES IS HEARD.
AGAIN THERE IS SILENCE EXCEPT FOR THE SOUND OF THE262 GGBROW
LAPPING WAVES.
THE SOUND OF THE WAVES AND OF DISTANT DANCE MUSIC.323 GGBROW
(SHE WAVES TO LARRY--AFFECTIONATELY) 615 ICEMAN
HE WAVES HIS HAND IN A LORDLY MANNER TO ROCKY) 619 ICEMAN
ACTION AND JIMMY, WAVES TO WILLIE, LARRY AND 619 ICEMAN
HUGO.
LIKE THE RISING AND FALLING CADENCES OF WAVES ON A303 LAZARU
BEACH)
BEATING WAVES OF SOUND IN THE AIR, 318 LAZARU
HE TAKES OFF HIS HELMET AND WAVES IT) 321 LAZARU
FLARE UPWARE UPWARD AND ARE REFLECTED ON THEIR 367 LAZARU
MASKS IN DANCING WAVES OF LIGHT)
AS SHE EVIDENTLY TURNS TO LOOK BACK AT HIM, HE 371 MARCOM
WAVES HIS HAND AND GRIES--
HE WAVES ONE HAND FOR SILENCE. 389 MARCOM
(CHANTING AS HIS MEN WORK) GREAT WERE THE WAVES 408 MARCOM
VULCA-OES OF FOAM
GREAT WERE THE WAVES/ 408 MARCOM
GREAT WERE THE WAVES/ 408 MARCOM
CRACKED VOICES ACCOMPANYING THE MUSIC IN QUEER, 433 MARCOM
SWEARING WAVES OF LAMENTATION.
AND WAVES HER HAND AT MCCABE AND TURNS BACK, 61 MISBEG
FROM THE ROCKS BELOW THE HEADLAND SOUNDS THE 578 ROPE
MUFFLED MONOTONE OF BREAKING WAVES.
GENTLY WAVES HIS STICK FRANTICALLY IN THE AIR, 583 ROPE
AND GROANS WITH RAGE.)
(SHE WAVES FRANTICALLY.) 198 STRANG
AN 'IS KIDS 'OWLIN' AN' HAVIN' THEIR 463 CARIBE
'ANDKERCHIEFS
DOWN OFF CLACKIN' HIS TONGUE AN' WAVIN' HIS WHIP. 209 DESIRE
WAVIN' A BIG BANKROLL AND WE WAS ALL GOIN' BE 583 ICEMAN
DRUNK FOR TWO WEEKS.

WAVING

I WAS WALKING PAST HER PLACE JUST NOW WHEN I SAW 273 AHWILD
HER WAVING FROM HER PARLOR
(WAVING THEIR PROTESTS ASIDE) 106 BEYOND
(WAVING HER REMARK ASIDE) YOU NEEDN'T DENY IT. 143 BEYOND
WAVING A HAND TOWARD THE LAND) 456 CARIBE
(WAVING A HAND TO ATTRACT HIS ATTENTION) 466 CARIBE

WAVING

WAVING (CONT'D.)
THEY SEE HIM UP THERE WALKING BACK AND FORTH-- 564 CRUSS
WAVING HIS ARMS AGAINST THE SKY.
(WAVING HIS HAND FOR HER TO BE SILENT) 568 CRUSS
WAVING HIS ARMS ABOUT WILDLY) 290 DESIRE
AFTER THAT, MAYBE THEY'D STOP WAVING HANDKERCHIEFS 82 ELECTR
AND GABBING ABOUT HEROES?
(SHE WALKS DOWN THE DRIVE, OFF LEFT, WAVING HER 119 ELECTR
HAND AS SHE DISAPPEARS.
(WAVING HIS PENCIL KNIFE WITH GROTESQUE 311 GGBROW
FLOURISHES)
WAVING THEIR SILLY SWORDS, SO AFRAID THEY COULDN'To77 ICEMAN
SHOW OFF HOW BRAVE THEY WAS/
(DASHES BACK AND-- THEN WAVING HIS BLOODY SPEAR 369 LAZARU
AND RUSHING UP TO THE THRONE
(SHE LAUGHS, WAVING THE POEM IN HER UPRAISED HAND,375 MARCOM
STARING MOCKINGLY)
HE'S WAVING TO US/ 198 STRANG

WAVY
EVEN NOW HER DARK- COMPLETED FACE, WITH ITS RIG 422 DYNAMO
BROWN EYES AND WAVY BLACK HAIR,
IT IS FRAMED BY A MASS OF WAVY WHITE HAIR, 2 MANSNS
FRAMED BY THICK, WAVY, RED-BROWN HAIR. 67 POET

WAX
(THE NIGHT CLERK SEEMS TURNED INTO A DROOPING WAX- 14 HUGHIE
WORK, DRAPED ALONG THE DESK.
THEY ARE LIKE WAX FIGURES, SET STIFFLY ON THEIR 696 ICEMAN
CHAIRS.
HIS FACE HAS A WAX-FIGURE BLANKNESS THAT MAKES IT 707 ICEMAN
LOOK EMBALMED.
MELODY'S FACE IS LIKE GRAY WAX. 164 POET

WAXED
THE SUIT IS OLD AND SHINES AT THE ELBOWS AS IF IT 8 HUGHIE
HAD BEEN WAXED AND POLISHED.
A RUG COVERS MOST OF THE FLOOR OF WAXED DARK WOOD.117 MANSNS

WAXY
STARING BEFORE HER WITH WAXY EYES. 948 DIFRNT

WAYLAY
TOOK ADVANTAGE OF FOG TO WAYLAY ME. 155 JOURNE

WAYS
THAT KIND OF BABY IS DANGEROUS FOR A KID LIKE 267 AHWILD
DICK--IN MORE WAYS THAN ONE.
SO, DARK IT, YOU'VE GOT TO KNOW HOW TO--I MEAN, 295 AHWILD
THERE ARE WAYS AND MEANS--
(THEN HE SMILES) YOU COULDN'T TEMPT HIM, NO WAYS. 97 BEYOND
IT'D BE A GOOD THING FOR ANDY IN MORE WAYS THAN 98 BEYOND
ONE.
I'VE WATCHED YOU GROW UP, AND I KNOW YOUR WAYS, 106 BEYOND
AND THEY'RE MY WAYS.
(SPLUTTERING UP) DOES YOU DO LIKE ME--LITTLE 669? CARIBE
IT'S AN A'MIGHTY WAYS--CALIFORNI-A--BUT IF 207 DESIRE
(WITH A WINK) AND MIGHTY ACCOMMODATIN' IN THEIR 511 DIFRNT
WAYS.
HE'S KIND AT BOTTOM, SPITE OF HIS ROUGH WAYS, AND 521 DIFRNT
HE'S BROUGHT YOU UP.
HE'S SET IN HIS WAYS AND BELIEVES IN BEING STRICT 522 DIFRNT
WITH YOU--
AND LOTS OF WAYS. 526 DIFRNT
WHAT KIND OF WAYS HAVE THEY GOT--THEM FRENCH 526 DIFRNT
GIRLS?
(SMIRKING MYSTERIOUSLY) OH, WAYS OF DRESSIN' AND 526 DIFRNT
DOIN' THEIR HAIR--
LOTS OF WAYS. 526 DIFRNT
YOU'RE SO LIKE YOUR MOTHER IN SOME WAYS. 22 ELECTR
I DON'T LIKE HER AND NEVER DID BUT I CAN IMAGINE 71 ELECTR
WORSE WAYS OF DYING/
DAWNING IN MORE WAYS THAN ONE. 219 HA APE
I SHOWED HIM LOTS OF WAYS HE COULD CROSS HER UP, 16 HUGHIE
BUT HE WAS TOO SCARED.
YOU'RE TOO BUSY THINKING UP WAYS TO CHEAT ME. 982 ICEMAN
TO HELP HIM FIND FRESH WAYS TO EVADE IT. 995 ICEMAN
CONSIDERING IT'S A HELL OF A WAYS, AND I SAT IN 622 ICEMAN
THE PARK FOR A WHILE THINKING.
HELL, IT'S COME TO A PARTING OF THE WAYS NOW, AND 675 ICEMAN
GOOD RIDDANCE.
IF YOU EVER GAVE HIM ADVICE EXCEPT IN THE WAYS OF 34 JOURNE
BITTERNESS,
HE KEPT FINDING WAYS TO MAKE ME LEAVE THEM. 119 JOURNE
YOU ARE SO LIKE HIM NOW, IN MANY WAYS, IT'S 15 MANSNS
ASTONISHING.
HENRY MUST HAVE LOST HIS FAMOUS SHREWDNESS IN MORE 305 MANSNS
WAYS THAN ONE.
AND STOP YOUR SHAMELESS WAYS WITH MEN. 8 MISBEG
SHE'S VERY STRANGE IN HER WAYS. 31 POET
OH, SHE MAY BE DAFT IN SOME WAYS, BUT SHE'S NO 87 POET
FOOL.
HE'S SET IN HIS PROUD, NOBLE WAYS, BUT SHE'LL FIND173 POET
THE RIGHT TRICK/
US COUNTRY FOLKS IS STUPID IN MOST WAYS. 993 ROPE
HE WAS MORTAL'Y OUT LOUD SO YOU COULD HEAR HIM A 947 ROPE
LONG WAYS.
USED TO HELP ME ALONG IN LOTS OF WAYS. 30 STRANG
(WITH A GUILTY TERROR) (IN MORE WAYS THAN ONE, I 67 STRANG
GUESS/....)
THROUGH SEPARATE WAYS LOVE HAS BROUGHT US BOTH TO 477 WELDED
THIS ROOM.

WAYSIDE
BUYING A PIECE OF NOAH'S ARK FROM A WAYSIDE 367 MARCOM
SHARPER.

WE-E-EFORE
WE ARRE ARE THE BYES AV WE-E-EXFORD WHO FOUGHT498 VOYAGE
WID HEARRT AN' HAND/

WE'RE
WE'RE FORGETTING THAT HER FATHER-- 33 STRANG
WE'RE ABSOLUTELY UNSUITED TO EACH OTHER/ 103 STRANG
(TENDERLY) THAT WE'RE GOING TO HAVE A CHILD. 107 STRANG

WE'RE (CONT'D.)
(SOFTLY) IT'S BECAUSE WE'RE GOING TO HAVE A CHILD,109 STRANG
NINA.
OH WE'RE DUE TO HEAR SOME LUSTY HOWLING IN A 119 STRANG
MOMENT.
THAT WE'RE FORCED TO TAKE UP HOBBIES. 140 STRANG
(THEN WITH A HARSH LAUGH) YES, WE'RE TWO BAD 147 STRANG
PENNIES, EH, MARSDENS
WE'RE OLD FRIENDS. 151 STRANG
WE'RE ALL DESERTING HER...!) 161 STRANG
WE'RE OLD. 169 STRANG
(STRANGELY) WE'RE ALWAYS DESIRING DEATH FOR 170 STRANG
OURSELVES OR OTHERS, AREN'T WE--
AFTER WE'RE MARRIED I'M GOING TO WRITE A NOVEL--MY176 STRANG
FIRST REAL NOVEL/
WE'RE NOT IN THE CONGO THAT WE CAN BELIEVE IN EVIL183 STRANG
CHARMS/
SO WE'RE ALONE AGAIN--JUST AS WE USED TO BE. 199 STRANG

WE'S
I TOLD SCHWARTZ, DE COP, WE'S CLOSED FOR DE PARTY.637 ICEMAN

WEAK
BUT MEN ARE WEAK. 212 AHWILD
MILLER LOOKS AROUND AT THEM WITH A WEAK SMILE, HIS227 AHWILD
DIGNITY NOW RUFFLED A BIT.)
IS CHILDISHLY SELF-WILLED AND WEAK, OF AN 5 ANNA
OBSTINATE KINDLINESS.
LET YOU NOT BE THINKING I'M THE LIKE OF THEM THREE 32 ANNA
WEAK SCUTS COME IN THE BOAT
BURKE, WEAK AND TOTTERING, IS CAUGHT OFF HIS 33 ANNA
GUARD.
I'M A DIVIL FOR STICKING IT OUT WHEN THEM THAT'S 36 ANNA
WEAK GIVE UP.
WITH WAN HAND, WEAK AS I AM, 39 ANNA
BE SAYING TO HER, AND I'M THINKING IT'S A POOR 47 ANNA
WEAK THING YOU ARE.
(THEN ANGRILY) 'TIS BECAUSE 'TIS A GREAT WEAK 69 ANNA
FOOL OF THE WORLD I AM,
WEAK-WILLED CRITTER TO BE PERMITTIN' A BOY--AND 102 BEYOND
WOMEN, TOO--
BECOME A WEAK MASK WEARING A HELPLESS, 112 BEYOND
REALLY I'M FINE NOW--ONLY VERY WEAK. 145 BEYOND
THAT MARY'S DEATH WAS DUE TO A WEAK CONSTITUTION 148 BEYOND
INHERITED FROM ME.
(IN A WEAK VOICE) NO. 482 CARDIF
(SHAKING HIS HEAD) I'M AFRAID--HE'S VERY WEAK. 485 CARDIF
MUST BE MY EYES GITTIN' WEAK, I GUESS. 487 CARDIF
BUT SUCIARIA PROVED TOO WEAK--KNEED A MATE, 502 DAYS
RATHER WEAK MOUTH IS DRAWN DOWN BY SHARP LINES AT 515 DAYS
THE CORNERS.
THE FLIPS A BAD THING THE WAY IT LEAVES YOU WEAK 515 DAYS
AFTER.
(SAVAGELY SEIZING ON HIS WEAK POINT) 230 DESIRE
I GOT WEAK--DESPAIRFUL--THEY WAS SO MANY STONES. 237 DESIRE
DID YE THINK I WAS IN LOVE WITH YE--A WEAK THIN' 240 DESIRE
LIKE YEWS
HE IS A LANKY YOUNG FELLOW WITH A LONG, WEAK FACE,247 DESIRE
HE SWALLOWS PAINFULLY SEVERAL TIMES--FORCES A WEAK268 DESIRE
SMILE AT LAST)
ALL THE PASSION DRAINED OUT OF HIM INSTANTLY, 441 DYNAMO
LEAVING HIM WEAK AND PENITENT)
A MOUTH THAT CAN BE STRONG AND WEAK BY TURNS. 21 ELECTR
(SPRINGING UP--WITH WEAK INDIGNATION) 30 ELECTR
I'M SURE EVERYONE KNOWS ABOUT EZRA'S WEAK HEART BY 40 ELECTR
THIS TIME.
THAT YOU'RE A WEAK COWARD LIKE YOUR FATHERS 41 ELECTR
AND THE REACTION WERE TOO MUCH FOR HIS WEAK HEART/ 41 ELECTR
HE'S STILL WEAK. 48 ELECTR
YOU MAKE ME WEAK/ 56 ELECTR
(HER VOICE GROWN STRIDENT) DID YOU THINK YOU 61 ELECTR
COULD MAKE ME WEAK--
I NEVER THOUGHT HIS HEART WAS WEAK. 74 ELECTR
HIS WEATHER-BEATEN FACE IS DISSIPATED, HE HAS A 102 ELECTR
WEAK MOUTH.
SHE SEEMS SUDDENLY WEAK AND FRIGHTENED.) 146 ELECTR
(THEN SUDDENLY HE BREAKS DOWN AND BECOMES WEAK AND155 ELECTR
PITIFUL
ONE MUST HAVE PEACE--ONE IS TOO WEAK TO FORGET-- 167 ELECTR
(HER RAGE PASSES, LEAVING HER WEAK AND SHAKEN. 173 ELECTR
BUT THAT ANCIENT HUMORIST HAD GIVEN ME WEAK EYES, 282 GGBROW
IT MAKES THEM WEAK. 284 GGBROW
YOU'RE NOT WEAK. 285 GGBROW
YOU WEAK TO DOMINATE HER IN TURN. 296 GGBROW
AND IF YOU ARE WEAK AND COWARDLY ENOUGH TO STAND 317 GGBROW
FOR IT, I'M NOT/
OUT HIS WIFE BUTTS IN AND SAYS HE'S WEAK AND HE 30 HUGHIE
MUSTN'T GET EXCITED.
INDECENTLY YES. HARRY HAS ALWAYS BEEN WEAK AND 652 ICEMAN
EASILY INFLUENCED.
I'LL BE A WEAK FOOL LOOKING WITH PITY AT THE TWO 726 ICEMAN
SIDES OF EVERYTHING
MY EYES IS WEAK. 529 INZONE
YOU LOOK WEAK, LAD. 146 JOURNE
(EDMUND HAS STOPPED COUGHING. HE LOOKS SICK AND 146 JOURNE
WEAK.
THEIR EXPRESSION IS SPOILED, PETULANT AND SELF- 299 LAZARU
OBSESSED, WEAK BUT DOMINEERING.
HE WAS STILL WEAK, AS ONE WHO RECOVERS FROM A LONG309 LAZARU
ILLNESS--
YOU ARE TOO WEAK TO KILL YOURSELF. 317 LAZARU
YOU ARE SMALL AND WEAK LIKE OTHER MEN WHEN THE 319 LAZARU
TEST COMES/
THE ONLY MORAL LAW HERE IS THE STRONG ARE 71 MANSNS
REWARDED, THE WEAK ARE PUNISHED.
I HAD BEGUN TO FEEL SO WEAK AND AT THE MERCY OF 124 MANSNS
THE PAST.
BUT THERE IS A STARTLING CHANGE IN HIS MANNER, 140 MANSNS
WHICH NOW SEEMS WEAK, INSECURE,
YOU ARE EVIL BECAUSE YOU ARE WEAK. 152 MANSNS

WEAKNESS

WEAK (CONT'D.)

YOU MUST NOT BE WEAK. 157 MANSNS
WITH SUCH AN INSATIABLE MISTRESS TO INSPIRE ME, 158 MANSNS
HOW COULD I DARE BE WEAK$
WE WOULD BE TOO WEAK. 170 MANSNS
AND OUR WEAK SENTIMENTAL MORAL EVASIONS OF OUR 179 MANSNS
NATURAL SELVES.
A WEAK LAZY BACK AND THE APPETITE OF A DROVE OF 35 MISBEG
STARVING PIGS/
IT WOULD BE FATAL--WITH MY WEAK HEART. 45 MISBEG
SO YOU'VE A WEAK HEART$ 45 MISBEG
HE'S WEAK, WITH ONE FOOT IN THE GRAVE FROM 86 MISBEG
WHISKEY.
WHEN HE'S HERE SICK AND TOO WEAK TO DEFEND 17 POET
HIMSELF.
(HE STARTS GUILTILY, ASHAMED OF BEING CAUGHT IN 58 POET
SUCH A WEAK MOOD.)
WHEN I LEFT FOR THE TOWN HE LOOKED TOO WEAK TO 582 ROPE
LIFT A FOOT.
BUT HIS MOUTH IS WEAK AND CHARACTERLESS,. 587 ROPE
AND THE STOOP TO HIS SHOULDERS OF A MAN WEAK 4 STRANG
MUSCULARLY.
((HOW WEAK HE IS/... 69 STRANG
BECAUSE I HAD MADE HIM WEAK$...)) 139 STRANG
(THINKING CONTEMPTUOUSLY) (INED IS WEAK...)) 154 STRANG
(THEN APPREHENSIVELY)
HE'S SO WEAK. 155 STRANG
EVEN THOUGH HE DOES DO WEAK THINGS SOMETIMES. 160 STRANG
AND THESE ARE MEN AND WOMEN AND SONS AND DAUGHTERS176 STRANG
WHOSE HEARTS ARE WEAK
HIS FACE IS PASTY, HIS MOUTH WEAK, HIS EYES 493 VOYAGE
SHIFTING AND CRUEL.
SO WHAT DOES IT MATTER HOW WEAK I AM$ 469 WELDED
TOO WEAK FOR THE STRONG, TOO STRONG FOR THE WEAK, 476 WELDED
YOU'RE THE PERFECT DEATH--BUT I'M TOO STRONG, OR 476 WELDED
WEAK--
ARE WE WEAK$ 488 WELDED

WEAKEN

WHEN YOU MEDDLE IN MEN'S BUSINESS AND WEAKEN 'EM, 550 'ILE
BEFORE THEY MAKE TOO MANY ENGINES TO WEAKEN THE 422 MARCOM
POWER OF MEN.

WEAKENED

(GUILTILY) WELL--IN HIS WEAKENED CONDITION--I 265 AHWILD
THOUGHT IT BEST--
THE STUBBORN JAW WEAKENED BY A BIG INDECISIVE 422 DYNAMO
MOUTH.
WEAKENED VERSION OF THE DEAD MAN'S. 73 ELECTR
(HAS RECOVERED HIS POISE AS SHE HAS WEAKENED-- 113 MANSNS
CURTLY.)

WEAKENING

(HIS VOICE WEAKENING) 254 HA APE
NO WEAKENING, SO HELP ME GOD/ 116 POET

WEAKENS

HIS IRON SPIRIT WEAKENS AS HE LOOKS AT HER TEAR- 549 'ILE
STAINED FACE.)

WEAKER

(DULLY) HE'S BEEN GETTING WEAKER. 154 BEYOND
YOU'LL HAVE TO SUFFER TO WIN BACK--THIS VOICE 162 BEYOND
GROWS WEAKER AND HE SIGHS WEAKLY)
CAN YOU CONFESS YOURSELF WEAKER THAN HIS 425 MARCOM
STUPIDITY$
HIS VOICE GROWS WEAKER) 507 VOYAGE
I'M THE WEAKER. 476 WELDED

WEAKEST

*AH, FONDEST, BLINDEST, WEAKEST, I AM HE WHOM THOUSO8 DAYS
SEEKEST/

WEAKFISH

HE'S BEEN EATING BLUEFISH FOR YEARS--ONLY I TELL 214 AHWILD
HIM EACH TIME IT'S WEAKFISH.

WEAKLING

SO THAT'S THE POOR WEAKLING YOU REALLY WERE/ 299 GGBROW
WEAKLING/ 348 LAZARU
HE SUSPECTS WHAT I KNOW--THAT I'VE ACTED LIKE A 162 STRANG
COWARD AND WEAKLING TOWARD HIM/
(THINKING IN ANGUISH) ((DAMNED COWARD AND 148 STRANG
WEAKLING/))
(COLDLY) I'M QUITE AWARE MY SON ISN'T A 160 STRANG
WEAKLING--

WEAKLY

AND HE SAYS WEAKLY.. 230 AHWILD
(HE SITS DOWN WEAKLY) YOU'RE ALL IN, YOU MIGHT AS 32 ANNA
WELL OWN UP TO IT.
(SHE COVERS HER FACE WITH HER HANDS AND SINKS 108 BEYOND
WEAKLY INTO MAYO'S CHAIR.
(HE WALKS WEAKLY TO A ROCKER BY THE SIDE OF THE 145 BEYOND
TABLE
LEANING WEAKLY AGAINST IT FOR SUPPORT. 145 BEYOND
(COUGHS AND LIES BACK IN HIS CHAIR WEAKLY--A 148 BEYOND
PAUSE)
(HE SWAYS WEAKLY.) 151 BEYOND
WHERE HE CAN SEE THE SUN RISE, AND COLLAPSES 166 BEYOND
WEAKLY.
ROBERT STAGGERS WEAKLY IN FROM THE LEFT. 166 BEYOND
(HE FALLS BACK WEAKLY. 167 BEYOND
(HE COLLAPSES WEAKLY) ANDY/ 168 BEYOND
(SCORNFULLY) SO HE WEAKLY SURRENDERED-- 539 DAYS
(SHE SWAYS WEAKLY. 551 DAYS
(MORE WEAKLY NOW) HAVE PITY ON ME/ 565 DAYS
(STUMBLES WEAKLY FROM BENEATH THE CROSS) 965 DAYS
(WEAKLY) WHAT D'YE WANT I' WASTE TIME ON HER FUR$230 DESIRE
SHE GETS UP WEAKLY AND GOES TO CABOT.) 252 DESIRE
(HE SUDDENLY BREAKS DOWN, SOBBING WEAKLY.) 256 DESIRE
(SHE STOPS AT THE DOOR WEAKLY, SWAYING, ABOUT TO 262 DESIRE
FALL)
(WEAKLY) EBEN/ 267 DESIRE
(HE LURCHES TO HIS FEET AND LEANS AGAINST THE BACK463 DYNAMO
OF HIS CHAIR WEAKLY.
(HER STRENGTH GONE--SWAYING WEAKLY) 63 ELECTR

WEAKLY (CONT'D.)

UUDOM, THE HAND WITH THE POISON STRETCHED OUT 64 ELECTR
BEHIND HER--WEAKLY)
SHE LEANS AGAINST HIM WEAKLY AND HE SUPPORTS HER 107 ELECTR
WITH HIS ARM AROUND HER)
(WEAKLY) YES--HE DOES--NOW--BUT I DON'T KNOW HOW 109 ELECTR
LONG--
AND WEAKLY BECAUSE THE STRENGTH SHE HAS WILLED 142 ELECTR
INTO HIM HAS LEFT HER EXHAUSTED)
HE BREAKS DOWN, SOBBING WEAKLY AGAINST HER BREAST.142 ELECTR
(SAGS WEAKLY AND SUPPORTS HERSELF AGAINST THE 167 ELECTR
TABLE--
(HE SUBSIDES WEAKLY ON HIS CHAIR, HIS HAND PRESSCO287 GGBROW
TO HIS HEART.)
(SINKING IN HIS CHAIR, MORE AND MORE WEAKLY) 299 GGBROW
(HE KISSES BROWN'S FEET--THEN MORE AND MORE WEAKLY299 GGBROW
AND CHILDISHLY)
(HE SITS DOWN WEAKLY ON LARRY'S RIGHT.) 644 ICEMAN
(SO DISTRACTED HE PLEADS WEAKLY) 649 ICEMAN
(HE SINKS BACK WEAKLY ON A BENCH.) 523 INJONE
(REFUSING TO ADMIT ANYTHING TO HIS BROTHER YET-- 64 JOURNE
WEAKLY DEFIANT.)
(GRABS THE BOTTLE AND POURS HIS GLASS BRIMFULL-- 146 JOURNE
WEAKLY.)
(WEAKLY) DID I FALL$ 283 LAZARU
(SUSPICIOUS LAUGHS WEAKLY WITHOUT TAKING OFFENSE.) 315 LAZARU
(SHE SWAYS WEAKLY AS THOUGH SHE WERE ABOUT TO 19 MANSNS
FAINT--EXHAUSTEDLY.)
YOU COULD REALLY HAVE WON THEN BUT YOU ARE WEAKLY 169 MANSNS
SENTIMENTAL AND PETIFUL.
(DEBORAH WEAKLY LETS HERSELF BE PULLED DOWN BESIDE181 MANSNS
HIM.)
(WEAKLY) MAYBE YOU DID FOOL HIM, FOR ONCE. 131 MISBFG
(FEELING HERSELF BORNE DOWN WEAKLY BY THE SHEER 71 POET
FORCE OF HIS PHYSICAL STRENGTH,
(STUNNED--WEAKLY.) GOD FORGIVE YOU/ 108 POET
(WEAKLY.) I WAS. 148 POET
HIS EYES PEER WEAKLY FROM BENEATH BUSHY, BLACK 578 ROPE
BROWS.
(WEAKLY) SAM/ 107 STRANG
(SHE STIFLES ANOTHER LAUGH--THEN ON THE VERGE OF 108 STRANG
FAINTING, WEAKLY)
WEAKLY STRUGGLING TO SHAKE OFF HER HANDS, WITHOUT 172 STRANG
LOWERING THE GLASSES)
(THINKING--WEAKLY) (EYES, IF IT HADN'T BEEN FUR 173 STRANG
SAM I WOULD HAVE BEEN HAPPY/...
(STRUGGLING WEAKLY--THINKING) 173 STRANG
(HE GETS WEAKLY TO HIS FEET) 508 VOYAGE
(WEAKLY) SSSHH/ 449 WELDED

WEAKNESS

(THEN WITH A TRACE OF SYMPATHY, AS SHE NOTICES HIM 32 ANNA
SWAYING FROM WEAKNESS)
LEANING TO WEAKNESS IN THE MOUTH AND CHIN. 81 BEYOND
(HE POUNDS ON THE TABLE, ATTEMPTING TO COVER UP 103 BEYOND
THIS CONFESSION OF WEAKNESS.)
THE THREE YEARS HAVE ACCENTUATED THE WEAKNESS OF 119 BEYOND
HIS MOUTH AND CHIN.
(ON THE VERGE OF TEARS OF WEAKNESS) 148 BEYOND
(HIS VOICE FALTERING WITH WEAKNESS) 162 BEYOND
IS IT YOUR OLD SECRET WEAKNESS--THE COWARDLY 499 DAYS
YEARNING TO GO BACK--$
(SNEERINGLY) BUT THERE WAS ONE RIDICULOUS 509 DAYS
WEAKNESS IN HER CHARACTER.
FOR THIS COWARDLY GIVING IN TO HIS WEAKNESS IS NUT545 DAYS
THE END)
SHE OVERCOMES HER WEAKNESS AND WALKS WOODENLY INTO551 DAYS
HER BEDROOM
YET THERE IS A WEAKNESS IN IT, A PETTY PRIDE IN 221 DESIRE
ITS OWN NARROW STRENGTH.
YET THERE IS NO HINT OF PHYSICAL WEAKNESS ABOUT 230 DESIRE
HIM--
(THEN SUDDENLY) BUT I GIVE IN T' WEAKNESS ONCE. 237 DESIRE
I'D NEVER SUSPICION SECH WEAKNESS FROM A BOY LIKE 249 DESIRE
YEW/
I KIN SEE HIS HAND USIN' EBEN T' STEAL T' KEEP ME 268 DESIRE
FROM WEAKNESS.
I SHOULD UNDERSTAND REUBEN'S WEAKNESS AND FORGIVE 435 DYNAMO
HIM...))
DEFENSIVE FACE, OBSTINATE TO THE POINT OF STUPID 259 GGBROW
WEAKNESS.
WHY MUST I BE SO ASHAMED OF MY STRENGTH, SO PROUD 264 GGBROW
OF MY WEAKNESS$
YOU'VE GIVEN MY WEAKNESS STRENGTH TO LIVE. 285 GGBROW
YOUR WEAKNESS THE STRENGTH OF MY FLOWERS. 307 GGBROW
ALWAYS LOOKING FOR THE WORST WEAKNESS IN EVERYONE. 61 JOURNE
NEVER MIND HIS WEAKNESS. 101 JOURNE
BUT HE HAD HIS WEAKNESS. 137 JOURNE
OF ONE WHO LEANS TO EVIL MORE THROUGH WEAKNESS 332 LAZARU
THAN ANY INSTINCTIVE URGE.
HE DIED IN PAIN AND WEAKNESS WITHIN A FEW HOURS. 343 LAZARU
IF YOU CAN, DISCOVER HIS WEAKNESS AND THEN USE IT 150 MANSNS
WITHOUT SCRUPLE.
WOULD BEGIN TO BLAME YOU FOR YOUR WEAKNESS. 153 MANSNS
FORGIVE MY WEAKNESS. 386 MARCOM
IT IS A TEST OF MYSELF I WANT TO MAKE AS A PENALTY426 MARCOM
FOR MY WEAKNESS A MOMENT AGO.
KUBLAI REGAINS CONTROL OVER HIS WEAKNESS AND RISES435 MARCOM
TO HIS FEET--
AND HE LOVES TO PICK OUT THE WEAKNESS IN PEOPLE 83 MISBEG
AND SAY CRUEL,
I KNOW HIS WEAKNESS, AND IT'S HIS VANITY ABOUT HIS 92 MISBEG
WOMEN.
DO I HAVE TO TELL YOU HIS WEAKNESS AGAIN$ 96 MISBEG
AND YOU MAKE ME ASHAMED OF MY WEAKNESS. 97 MISBEG
(AGAIN AS IF HE WERE ASHAMED, OR AFRAID HE HAD 105 MISBEG
REVEALED SOME WEAKNESS--
FAITH, I MAY AS WELL CONFESS MY BESETTING WEAKNESS 70 POET

WEAKNESS

WEAKNESS (CONT'D.)
(WITH THE AIR OF ONE FRANKLY ADMITTING A PRAISEWORTHY WEAKNESS.)

A WEAKNESS HE INHERITED FROM ME. I'M AFRAID. 82 POET
THEN HE SAID HE WAS AFRAID MAYBE I'D THINK IT WAS 146 POET
WEAKNESS IN HIM, NOT WISDOM.
THEN I ASKED HIM OUT TO HAVE A DROP O' DRINK, 585 ROPE
KNOWIN' HIS WEAKNESS.

WEAKNESS. 29 STRANG
BUT ONCE HE KISSED ME--IN A MOMENT OF CARNAL 41 STRANG
WEAKNESS/
FROM HIS GENERAL WEAKNESS... 82 STRANG
THIS WEAKNESS COMES FROM HER CONDITION/...)) 108 STRANG
KINDLY BUT LAYING DOWN THE LAW TO WOMANLY 157 STRANG
WEAKNESS/
WEAKNESS, A DEEP NEED FOR LOVE AS A FAITH IN WHICH444 WELDED
TO RELAX.
YOU THINK THAT WEAKNESS. 453 WELDED

WEAKNESSED.
BUT SHE DOESN'T REALIZE THERE ARE FUNDAMENTAL 73 MANSNS
WEAKNESSES IN HER PLAN.

WEALTH
LIKE A FATTED CALF IN THE WAY OF OUR HEALTH AND 311 GGBROW
WEALTH AND HAPPINESS/
OR RATHER, I INHERIT THE ACQUIRED TRAIT OF THE HY-214 HA APE
PRODUCT, WEALTH.
HERE THE ADORNMENTS OF EXTREME WEALTH ARE 233 HA APE
TANTALISINGLY DISPLAYED.
TAKE THE LOSS OF HIS FATHER'S WEALTH SINCE HE TOOK276 LAZARU
OVER THE MANAGEMENT.
COMPETITORS IN THE RACE FOR POWER AND WEALTH AND 46 MANSNS
POSSESSIONS/
HIS PERSONAL WEALTH IN CASH AND JEWELS AND GOODS 359 MARCOM
ALONE.
IT MUST BE A PITIFUL LAND, POOR IN SPIRIT AND 421 MARCOM
MATERIAL WEALTH.
DEFERRED TO BECAUSE OF HIS WEALTH. 56 MISBEG
AND THERE WAS A TIME WHEN I POSSESSED WEALTH AND 112 POET
POSITION.
MAN'S HEAD BECAUSE HIS FAMILY HAPPENS TO POSSESS ALL3 POET
LITTLE WEALTH AND POSITION.
WEALTH, JOVIAL AND SIMPLE AND GOOD-NATURED AS 159 STRANG
EVER.

WEALTHY
IN AN EMINENT, WEALTHY FAMILY LIKE OURS. 179 MANSNS
HAPPY AND WEALTHY... 139 STRANG
OUR BACKING SAM HAS MADE MARSDEN AND ME SO WEALTHY140 STRANG

WEAPON
IT AIN'T OUR WEAPON. 236 HA APE
AS I KNEW SHE MUST, THAT POWERFUL WOMAN WHO BORE 355 LAZARU
ME AS A WEAPON/

WEAPONS
THEY FEEL HIM OVER FOR WEAPONS.) 249 HA APE
THE CROWD HAVE RAISED WHATEVER WEAPONS THEY HAVE 305 LAZARU
FOUND--
NO WEAPONS CAN BE SEEN-- 321 LAZARU

WEAR
CAUSING EVEN INANIMATE OBJECTS TO WEAR AN ASPECT 112 BEYOND
OF DESPONDENT EXHAUSTION.
A GOOD MANY WEAR CAPS. 456 CARIBE
THEY WEAR LIGHT-COLORED. 464 CARIBE
HE IS DRESSED IN AN OLD BAGGY SUIT MUCH THE WORSE 513 DIFRNT
FOR WEAR--
ALL WEAR BROAD PALM-LEAF HATS. 202 EJONES
BRAID WAS SHORT AND EASY ON SHIPS--AND I WOULDN'T 26 ELECTR
WEAR THE NAME OF MANNO.
YOU OUGHT ALWAYS TO WEAR CLEAR. 144 ELECTR
YOU ALWAYS USED TO WEAR BLACK. 144 ELECTR
A SKIN, O GOD, THAT I MUST WEAR ARMOR IN ORDER TO 265 GGBROW
TOUCH OR TO BE TOUCHED&
SHE DOES NOT NEED TO WEAR A MASK NOW. HER FACE 302 GGBROW
HAS
SOME WEAR SINGLETS, BUT THE MAJORITY ARE STRIPPED 207 HA APE
TO THE WAIST.
HUM. YOU'LL EXCUSE ME, MA'AM, BUT ARE YOU 221 HA APE
INTENDING TO WEAR THAT DRESS&
I WILL WEAR THIS VERY DRESS AND NONE OTHER. 222 HA APE
YOU HAVE TO WEAR BLINDERS LIKE A HORSE AND SEE 590 ICEMAN
ONLY STRAIGHT IN FRONT OF YOU.
HER ROUND FACE SHOWING MORE OF THE WEAR AND TEAR 615 ICEMAN
OF HER TRADE THAN THEIRS.
UR WEAR DUTTY CLOTHES. 702 ICEMAN
BE SURE AND WEAR A HAT. 49 JOURNE
WE NEVER HAD CLOTHES ENOUGH TO WEAR, NOR ENOUGH 148 JOURNE
FOOD TO EAT.
MARTHA, MARY AND THE TWO PARENTS ALL WEAR FULL 275 LAZARU
MASKS
COMPOSED ABOUT EQUALLY OF BOTH SEXES, WEAR A MASK 285 LAZARU
THAT.
THEY ALSO WEAR WIRE WIGS BUT OF STRAIGHT HAIR CUT 336 LAZARU
IN SHORT BOYISH MODE.
THEY WEAR ANKLETS AND BRACELETS AND NECKLACES. 336 LAZARU
THESE YOUTHS WEAR FEMALE WIGS OF CURLED WIRE LIKE 336 LAZARU
FRIZZED HAIR OF A YELLOW GOLD.
I WEAR A GOWN OF CRIMSON SATIN AND GOLD, 4 MANSNS
EMBROIDERED IN PEARLS--
THE TWO WOMEN WEAR SEMI-FORMAL EVENING GOWNS, 117 MANSNS
DEMURANS ALL WHITE.
THE WOMEN WEAR COTTON DRAWERS. 365 MARCOM
THEY WEAR THE REGALIA OF OFFICERS IN THE MYSTIC 390 MARCOM
KNIGHTS OF CONFUCIUS
WHICH ONLY GREAT HEROES AND KINGS OF MEN MAY WEAR.419 MARCOM
AND YOU'LL WEAR IT FOR DINNER LIKE YOU'VE DONE 39 POET
EACH YEAR.
YES. I MUST CONFESS I STILL WELCOME AN EXCUSE TO 39 POET
WEAR IT.
AS USUAL, AND YOU'LL WEAR YOUR BEAUTIFUL UNIFORM, 59 POET
I'D WEAR OUT MY LIPS KISSING HIM/ 149 POET

WEAR (CONT'D.)
TO A SHILLING SHE'LL SEE THE DAY WHEN SHE'LL WEAR 173 POET
FINE SILKS.
DUTCH WEAR A MUZZLE, YOU ORT/ 494 VOYAGE

WEARIED
THE OTHERS DO LIKEWISE WITH AS MUCH UNISON AS 224 HA APE
THEIR WEARIED BODIES WILL PERMIT.
THEN SUDDENLY THE TUNE WENT FALSE, THE DANCERS 159 JOURNE
WEARIED OF THE WALTZ..."

WEARILY
(WEARILY) YES, YOU WERE VERY KIND, DAVID. 546 'ILE
(WEARILY) OH, I KNOW IT ISN'T YOUR FAULT, DAVID. 546 'ILE
SHE COMES AND SINKS WEARILY IN A CHAIR BY THE 14 ANNA
TABLE, LEFT FRONT.)
(WEARILY) GEE, I SURE NEED THAT REST/ 16 ANNA
(WEARILY) I AM. 22 ANNA
BURKE SAGS FORWARD WEARILY) 31 ANNA
(WEARILY) GEE. I SURE WISH HE WAS OUT OF THIS 42 ANNA
DUMP AND BACK IN NEW YORK.
(WEARILY) SURE I DO. 67 ANNA
(WEARILY) YOU CAN TELL ME IF YOU WANT TO. 115 BEYOND
SHE SITS IN THE ROCKER IN FRONT OF THE TABLE AND 116 BEYOND
SIGHS WEARILY.
(WEARILY) I S'POSE SO. 117 BEYOND
(SHE WIPES HER MOIST FOREHEAD--WEARILY) 117 BEYOND
(GETTING UP--WEARILY) I'LL GO DOWN RIGHT AWAY. 135 BEYOND
(WEARILY) YOU OUGHTN'T TO TALK ABOUT HIM NOW WHEN152 BEYOND
HE'S SICK IN HIS BED.
(SHE GETS WEARILY FROM THE CHAIR AND PUTS A FEW 152 BEYOND
PIECES OF WOOD IN THE STOVE)
(WEARILY) IT IS SO. 160 BEYOND
YOU'LL HAVE TO SUFFER TO WIN BACK--(HIS VOICE 160 BEYOND
GROWS WEAKER AND HE SIGHS WEARILY)
(SHE SIGHS--WEARILY) IT CAN'T DO NO HARM TO TELL 164 BEYOND
YOU NOW--
(SHE GETS WEARILY TO HER FEET AND WALKS SLOWLY 166 BEYOND
TOWARD THE BEDROOM)
(WEARILY) YES, IVAN. 483 CARDIF
(YANK DOES NOT ANSWER, BUT CLOSES HIS EYES 483 CARDIF
WEARILY.
HE GETS WEARILY TO HIS FEET AND WALKS WITH BOWED 473 CARIBE
SHOULDERS, STAGGERING A BIT.
HOUSE, CREEPS WEARILY IN THROUGH THE PORTHOLES 555 CROSS
WEARILY TO HIS FEET, HIS SHOULDERS BOWED, LOOKING 560 DAYS
TRAGICALLY OLD AND BEATEN--
(HE GOES WEARILY TOWARD THE BARN.) 253 DESIRE
CABOT APPEARS, RETURNING FROM THE BARN, WALKING 253 DESIRE
WEARILY, HIS EYES ON THE GROUND.
(WEARILY) I KNOW THAT, HARRIET. 510 DIFRNT
(WEARILY) HOW LONG I BEEN MAKIN TRACKS IN DESE 191 EJONES
WOODS
(SITS IN THE CHAIR OPPOSITE HIM--WEARILY) 151 ELECTR
(WEARILY) ALL RIGHT. 158 ELECTR
(WEARILY) EVERY DAY OR SO YOU'VE BEEN CASHING 271 GGBROW
CHECKS.
(WEARILY BITTER) I'LL TAKE THE JOB. 281 GGBROW
(WEARILY) SHE WAS LYING ABOUT HER HUSBAND, NOT 281 GGBROW
ME, YOU FOOL/
WEARILY COMES AND SITS DOWN AT HER FEET AND LAYS 285 GGBROW
HIS HEAD IN HER LAP--
(SHE SIGHS WEARILY, TURNS, PUTS A PLUG IN THE 288 GGBROW
PIANO.
(WEARILY REPROVING) THANK GOODNESS I'VE FOUND 291 GGBROW
YOU/
ONLY TO ME WILL THAT POMPOUS FACADE REVEAL ITSELF 313 GGBROW
AS THE WEARILY IRONIC GRIN OF
THE NIGHT CLERK RISES WEARILY. 8 HUGHIE
(IN A TONE OF ONE WHO IS WEARILY RELIEVED 10 HUGHIE
BUT FAILS AND REMAINS WEARILY GLUED TO IT. 27 HUGHIE
HE COMES FORWARD AND DROPS WEARILY IN THE CHAIR AT665 ICEMAN
RIGHT OF LARRY'S TABLE.
(HE FORCES A FEEBLE SMILE--THEN WEARILY) 691 ICEMAN
HE WALKS WEARILY OFF THROUGH THE BACK PARLOR 125 JOURNE
TOWARD THE DINING ROOM.)
(INTONES WEARILY, AS IF UNDER A BORING COMPULSION)313 LAZARU
(WEARILY) A DEGENERATE COWARD. 315 LAZARU
(WITH THE GHOST OF A LAUGH--WEARILY.) 315 LAZARU
(AS BEFORE--WEARILY AS IF UNDER A BORING 315 LAZARU
COMPULSION--INTONES)
(WEARILY) YOUR WORDS ARE MEANINGLESS, LAZARUS. 352 LAZARU
THEN HE SIGHS WEARILY.) 102 MANSNS
THAT RESEMBLES A MODERN SAMPLE CASE, PLODS WEARILY347 MARCOM
TO THE FOOT OF THE TREE.
(WEARILY) I AM BORED WITH YOUR MILLIONS, MESSRS. 359 MARCOM
PULO.
(WEARILY TAKES OUT HIS GUIDE-BOOK 373 MARCOM
(WEARILY PICKS UP THE CASES--THEN GOADING HIMSELF 376 MARCOM
ON)
(WEARILY AND DROWSILY) YOUR WISDOM MAKES ME 402 MARCOM
SLEEP.
(WEARILY) NO. 419 MARCOM
(WEARILY) IT IS MUCH TOO LARGE ALREADY. 421 MARCOM
MY HEART BEATS MORE AND MORE WEARILY. 423 MARCOM
(HIS ANGER PASSING--WEARILY AND BITTERLY, AFTER A 425 MARCOM
PAUSE)
(WEARILY) AND YOUR ANSWER, PRIEST OF ISLAMS 435 MARCOM
(AFTER A PAUSE--WEARILY) LEAVE HER IN PEACE. 436 MARCOM
(SHE SITS AT THE END OF CENTER TABLE RIGHT AND 76 POET
RELAXES WEARILY.
(WEARILY.) LEAVE HIM BE, FOR THE LOVE OF GOD. 80 POET
(WAITING RESIGNEDLY UNTIL HE HAS FINISHED-- 579 ROPE
WEARILY)
(HE LABORIOUSLY CREEPS OVER TO THE BENCH AND SITS 579 ROPE
DOWN WEARILY.
(WEARILY--HER FACE BECOMING DULL AND EMOTIONLESS 581 ROPE
AGAIN)
(THINKING WEARILY) (WHAT HAS CHARLIE DONE... 13 STRANG

70 POET

WEARILY (CONT'D.)
(THINKING WEARILY) (THE FATHERS LAUGH AT LITTLE 14 STRANG DAUGHTER NINA...
HIS TALL, THIN BODY SAGS WEARILY IN THE CHAIR, HIS 24 STRANG HEAD IS SUNK FORWARD,
(WEARILY) I WARN YOU IT ISN'T PRETTY, DOCTOR/ 82 STRANG
(THEN WEARILY) AND YOU'RE NOT. 82 STRANG
LEANING WEARILY TOWARD PEACE...) 187 STRANG
(SHE SITS WEARILY ON THE BENCH. 190 STRANG
BENT OVER WEARILY, HIS SHOULDERS BOWED, HIS LONG 462 WELDED ARMS RESTING ON HIS KNEES,
A PAUSE--THEN THE WOMAN SIGHS AND YAWNS WEARILY-- 471 WELDED BORED)
(AFTER A PAUSE--WEARILY) WE'VE SWORN TO SO MUCH, 485 WELDED
(WEARILY) NOW--FOR A MOMENT. 486 WELDED

WEARIN'
(ARGUMENTATIVELY, AND THERE AIN'T NO CAUSE TO BE 95 BEYOND WEARIN' MOURNING, EITHER,
(STERNLY) THE KIND OF WOMEN I'VE SEEN IN CITIES 536 DIFRNT WEARIN' IT--
WE'RE SICK OF WEARIN' OUT OUR DOGS 669 ICEMAN

WEARINESS
PASSING HER HAND OVER HER EYES WITH A GESTURE OF 548 *ILE PATHETIC WEARINESS)
CABIN, HIS BACK BOWED) HIS HEAD IN HIS HANDS, IN AN 31 ANNA ATTITUDE OF SPENT WEARINESS.)
(WITH A SUDDEN WEARINESS IN HER VOICE) 58 ANNA
(WITH SPENT WEARINESS) OH, WHAT'S THE USE$ 62 ANNA
(HE SIGHS, GIVING WAY FOR A MOMENT TO HIS OWN 557 DAYS PHYSICAL WEARINESS)
SHE SIGHS WITH AFFECTED WEARINESS AND LEANS BACK 53 ELECTR AND CLOSES HER EYES.)
(WITH A BITTER WEARINESS.) YOU OUGHT TO KNOW THAT 57 JOURNE DOESN'T MEAN ANYTHING.
WEARINESS OF THOUGHT, OR WATCHING ONE ANOTHER WITH289 LAZARU SUSPICIONS
(AGAIN WITH BORED WEARINESS AS BEFORE.) 315 LAZARU
GIRLISH MOUTH IS SET IN AN EXPRESSION OF AGONIZED 337 LAZARU SELF-LOATHING AND WEARINESS OF
WITH A SUGGESTION OF WEARINESS AND RESIGNATION NOW 70 MANSNS
IN WHICH IS WEARINESS AND DISBELIEF. 434 MARCOM
(SHE KISSES HIM--THEN SHUTS HER EYES WITH A DEEP 200 STRANG SIGH OF REQUITED WEARINESS)
(THEN WITH A SIGH OF PHYSICAL WEARINESS AS SHE 471 WELDED SITS ON THE SIDE OF THE BED)
SHE SMILES AT HIM AND SPEAKS WITH A TENDER 487 WELDED WEARINESS)

WEARING
EVEN TO WEARING GLASSES. 187 AHWILD
TWO LONGSHOREMEN ENTER FROM THE STREET, WEARING 3 ANNA THEIR WORKING
AND WEARING HIS HEART OUT TO MEET UP WITH A FINE 46 ANNA DACENT GIRL,
BECOME A WEAR MASK WEARING A HELPLESS, 112 BEYOND
(DRISCOLL APPEARS WEARING A BROAD GRIN OF 462 CARIBE SATISFACTION.
(COMING TO HER, HIS FACE WEARING ITS MOST CORDIAL,525 DAYS POKER-FACED SMILE)
WEARING HIS BLACK JUDGE'S ROBE. 28 ELECTR
SHE IS WEARING HER MASK. 300 GGBROW
DRESSED IN DION'S CLOTHES AND WEARING HIS MASK, 301 GGBROW APPEARS AT LEFT.)
HE IS NOW WEARING A MASK WHICH IS AN EXACT 303 GGBROW LIKENESS OF HIS FACE AS IT WAS IN THE
HE IS WEARING THE MASK OF DION. 313 GGBROW
(BROWN ENTERS HIS OFFICE, WEARING THE WILLIAM 314 GGBROW BROWN MASK.
PADDING FEET IN SLIPPERS, AND CYBEL, WEARING 319 GGBROW
WEARING A LIGHT SUIT THAT HAD ONCE BEEN FLASHILY 575 ICEMAN SPORTY
HE SELEVES IN WEARING HIS CLOTHES TO THE LIMIT OF 13 JOURNE USEFULNESS,
WHY ARE YOU WEARING THAT GLOOMY LOOK ON YOUR MUGS 66 JOURNE
CLAD RICHLY, WEARING BEAUTIFULLY WROUGHT ARMOR AND298 LAZARU HELMET,
WEARING THE TYPE MASK OF A ROMAN PATRICIAN 332 LAZARU
GIVES HER THE APPEARANCE OF A GIRL WEARING A 2 MANSNS BECOMING WIG AT A COSTUME BALL.
WEARING THE SELF-ASSURANCE OF AN IMMORTAL SOUL AND401 MARCOM HIS NEW ADMIRAL'S UNIFORM/
IT'S ONLY THE FUNNY PANTS HE'S WEARING. 58 MISBEG
HE DIED WEARING IT. 83 POET
WEARING THE BRILLIANT SCARLET FULL-DRESS UNIFORM 88 POET OF A MAJOR
SARA, WEARING HER WORKING DRESS AND APRON, 95 POET
HE IS WEARING A YACHTING CAP, BLUE YACHTING COAT, 159 STRANG WHITE FLANNEL PANTS.
(WEARING THE SAME GOOD-NATURED GRIN) 498 VOYAGE
(THE WOMEN COME FORWARD TO THE TABLE, WEARING 499 VOYAGE THEIR BEST SET SMILES.)
FOLLOWED BY TWO ROUGH-LOOKING, SHABBILY-DRESSED 506 VOYAGE MEN, WEARING MUFFLERS.

WEARISOME
KITCHEN OF A--BUT THE POSSIBILITIES ARE WEARISOME.218 HA APE

WEARS
HE HAS DISCARDED COLLAR AND TIE, COAT AND SHOES, 249 AHWILD AND WEARS AN OLD, WORN,
MRS. MILLER'S FACE WEARS AN EXPRESSION OF 288 AHWILD UNWORRIED CONTENT.
A CASSOCK WOULD SEEM MORE SUITED TO HIM THAN THE 3 ANNA APRON HE WEARS,
AND WEARS A FADED CAP OF GRAY CLOTH OVER HIS MOP 5 ANNA OF GRIZZLED, BLOND HAIR.
SHE WEARS A MAN'S CAP, DOUBLE-BREASTED MAN'S 7 ANNA JACKET AND A GRIMY CALICO SKIRT.
COAT, PANTS, SOU'WESTER AND WEARS HIGH SEABOOTS.) 25 ANNA
SHE HAS ON A BLACK OILSKIN COAT, BUT WEARS NO HAT. 25 ANNA

WEARS (CONT'D.)
WEARS A CHEAP BLUE SUIT, A STRIPED COTTON SHIRT 45 ANNA WITH A BLACK TIE.
SHE WEARS A HAT, IS ALL DRESSED UP AS IN ACT ONE. 63 ANNA
HE WEARS OVERALLS, LEATHER BOOTS, A GRAY FLANNEL 82 BEYOND SHIRT OPEN AT THE NECK.
SHE WEARS A SIMPLE WHITE DRESS BUT NO HAT.) 87 BEYOND
HE WEARS SPECTACLES. 94 BEYOND
SHE WEARS A GINGHAM DRESS WITH A SOILED APRON TIED116 BEYOND AROUND HER WAIST.)
AND WEARS A BROAD-BRIMMED HAT OF COARSE STRAW 123 BEYOND PUSHED BACK ON HIS HEAD)
HE WEARS A UNIFORM SIMILAR TO ANDREW'S. 140 BEYOND
AND WEARS WORN CARPET SLIPPERS ON HIS BARE FEET.) 145 BEYOND
HE WEARS GLASSES.) 153 BEYOND
HE WEARS CORDUROY TROUSERS STUFFED DOWN INTO HIGH 556 CROSS LACED BOOTS.)
THE SLEEVE ON THAT SIDE OF THE HEAVY MACKINAW HE 556 CROSS WEARS HANGS FLABBILY
SHE WEARS A DARK WRAPPER AND SLIPPERS.) 562 CROSS
HE WEARS A HEAVY, DOUBLE-BREASTED BLUE COAT, PANTS567 CROSS OF THE SAME MATERIAL,
HE WEARS ONLY A BREECHCLOTH. 571 CROSS
SHE WEARS A SIMPLE NEGLIGEE. 514 DAYS
ELSA WEARS A WHITE EVENING GOWN OF EXTREMELY 532 DAYS SIMPLE LINES.
HIS FACE WEARS AN EXPRESSION OF OBSESSED 241 DESIRE CONFUSION.
HIS FACE WEARS A BOLD AND CONFIDENT EXPRESSION, 244 DESIRE
HE WEARS HIGH SEABOOTS TURNED DOWN FROM THE KNEE, 498 DIFRNT DIRTY COTTON SHIRT AND PANTS,
SHE WEARS AN APRON AND HAS EVIDENTLY JUST COME OUT505 DIFRNT OF THE KITCHEN.
SHE WEARS AN APRON 04 WHICH SHE IS DRYING HER 507 DIFRNT HANDS AS SHE ENTERS.
THE WHITE DRESS SHE WEARS IS TOO FRILLY, TOO 520 DIFRNT YOUTHFUL FOR HER.
SHE WEARS AN APRON OVER HER OLD-FASHIONED BLACK 528 DIFRNT DRESS WITH A BROOCH AT THE NECK.
HE WEARS DARK CLOTHES, MUCH THE SAME AS HE WAS 935 DIFRNT DRESSED IN ACT ONE.)
HIS FACE WEARS ITS SET EXPRESSION OF AN 535 DIFRNT EMOTIONLESS MASK
AND IN THE CITIES NOW ALL THE WOMEN WEARS IT. 536 DIFRNT
HE ALWAYS WEARS HIS HEAVIES TOO LONG 429 DYNAMO
SHE WEARS A FADED BLUE WRAPPER 494 DYNAMO
AND WEARS THE COAT UP HIS OLD SUIT. 457 DYNAMO
HER FACE WEARS AN EXPRESSION OF EAGER EXPECTATION.459 DYNAMO
AND WEARS A WHITE CORK HELMET. 174 EJONES
HE WEARS A LIGHT BLUE UNIFORM COAT, SPRAYED WITH 175 EJONES BRASS BUTTONS.
HE WEARS HIS EARTH-STAINED WORKING CLOTHES. 6 ELECTR
SHE WEARS A GREEN SATIN DRESS, SMARTLY CUT AND 9 ELECTR EXPENSIVE.
SHE WEARS HER HAIR PULLED TIGHTLY BACK, AS IF TO 10 ELECTR CONCEAL ITS NATURAL CURLINESS.
HE WEARS THE UNIFORM OF AN ARTILLERY CAPTAIN IN 13 ELECTR THE UNION ARMY.)
HE WEARS A MUSTACHE, BUT HIS HEAVY CLEFT CHIN IS 21 ELECTR CLEAN-SHAVEN.
FRAMED BY COAL-BLACK STRAIGHT HAIR WHICH HE WEARS 21 ELECTR NOTICEABLY LONG.
SHE WEARS SLIPPERS OVER HER BARE FEET 56 ELECTR
HE WEARS A BANDAGE AROUND HIS HEAD HIGH UP ON HIS 73 ELECTR FOREHEAD.
HE WEARS A MUSTACHE SIMILAR TO BRANT'S 74 ELECTR
HE WEARS A LONG CLOAK OVER HIS UNIFORM 109 ELECTR
HE NOW WEARS A CLOSE-CROPPED BEARD IN ADDITION TO 137 ELFCTR HIS MUSTACHE.
HIS FACE WEARS A DAZED EXPRESSION AND HIS EYES 139 ELECTR HAVE A WILD, STRICKEN LOOK.
SHE WEARS A GREEN VELVET 149 ELECTR
THE SAME AS EVER, BUT HAZEL'S FACE WEARS A 158 ELECTR NERVOUS,
THE FATHER WEARS AN ILL-FITTING BLACK SUIT, LIKE A259 GGBROW MOURNER.
THE MOTHER WEARS A CHEAP, PLAIN, BLACK DRESS. 259 GGBROW
(SHE LOOKS HEALTHY AND HAPPY, BUT HER FACE WEARS A314 GGBROW WORRIED,
SHE IS DRESSED IN A BLACK KIMONO ROBE AND WEARS 320 GGBROW SLIPPERS OVER HER BARE FEET.
SHE WEARS HER MASK OF THE PROUD, INDULGENT MOTHER.323 GGBROW
LONG IS DRESSED IN SHORE CLOTHES, WEARS A BLACK 233 HA APE WINDSOR TIE, CLOTH CAP.
HE WEARS AN ILL-FITTING BLUE SERGE SUIT, WHITE 8 HUGHIE SHIRT AND COLLAR, A BLUE TIE.
HE WEARS A LIGHT GREY SUIT CUT IN THE EXTREME, 9 HUGHIE TIGHT-WAISTED, BROADWAY MODE.
LIKE HUGO, HE WEARS THREADBARE BLACK, AND 575 ICEMAN EVERYTHING ABOUT HIM IS CLEAN.
HE WEARS OLD CLOTHES AND IS SLOVENLY. 576 ICEMAN
HE WEARS PRIVY RINGS AND A HEAVY BRASS WATCH- 576 ICEMAN CHAIN--NOT CONNECTED TO A WATCH--
HE WEARS FIVE-AND-TEN-CENT-STORE SPECTACLES WHICH 577 ICEMAN ARE SO OUT OF ALIGNMENT
AND HE WEARS A SOILED APRON. 577 ICEMAN
THE CLOTHES HE WEARS BELONG ON A SCARECROW. 577 ICEMAN
HE WEARS HIS WORKING CLOTHES, SLEEVES ROLLED UP. 664 ICEMAN
AND WEARS A SUNDAY-BEST BLUE SUIT WITH A HIGH 670 ICEMAN STIFF COLLAR.
HE IS SHAVED AND WEARS AN EXPENSIVE, WELL-CUT 674 ICEMAN SUIT, GOOD SHOES AND CLEAN LINEN.
JUST LEAVE HARRY ALONE AND WAIT UNTIL THE SHUCK 692 ICEMAN WEARS OFF AND YOU'LL SEE.
HE WEARS DUNGAREES AND A HEAVY JERSEY.) 516 INZONE
HE WEARS A THREADBARE, READY-MADE, GREY SACK SUIT 13 JOURNE AND SHINELESS BLACK SHOES,
AND WEARS A COLLAR AND TIE. 19 JOURNE

WEARS

WEARS (CONT'D.)

HE WEARS A SHIRT, COLLAR AND TIE, NO COAT, OLD FLANNEL TROUSERS, BROWN SNEAKERS. 20 JOURNE

HER STUPID, GOOD-HUMORED FACE WEARS A PLEASED AND 97 JOURNE FLATTERED SIMPER.

ALMOST SLOVENLY WAY SHE WEARS IT. 97 JOURNE

SHE WEARS THE DRESS INTO WHICH SHE HAD CHANGED FOR 97 JOURNE HER DRIVE TO TOWN, A SIMPLE,

HE WEARS HIS PINCE-NEZ AND IS PLAYING SOLITAIRE. 125 JOURNE

SHE WEARS A SKY-BLUE DRESSING GOWN OVER HER 170 JOURNE NIGHTDRESS.

LAZARUS, FREED NOW FROM THE FEAR OF DEATH, WEARS 274 LAZARU NO MASK.

AS BEFORE THE CHORUS WEARS MASKS DOUBLE THE LIFE 298 LAZARU SIZE OF THE CROWD MASKS.

HE WEARS A HALF-MASK OF CRIMSON, DARK WITH A 299 LAZARU PURPLISH TINGE.

THIS CHORUS WEARS, IN DOUBLE SIZE, THE LAUGHING 306 LAZARU MASK OF LAZARUS' FOLLOWERS.

THE SLAVE WEARS A BLACK NEGROID MASK. 313 LAZARU

SHE WEARS A HALF-MASK ON THE UPPER PART OF HER 336 LAZARU FACE.

HER BODY IS CONCEALED BY THE LOOSE DRESS OF 2 MANSNS MOURNING BLACK SHE WEARS BUT,

DEBORAH WEARS DEEP MOURNING. 50 MANSNS

HE WEARS THEM WELL BUT INDIFFERENTLY. 69 MANSNS

HE WEARS OVER HIS MAYOR'S UNIFORM THE REGALIA OF 388 MARCOM COCK OF PARADISE.

IT IS THE HAND ON WHICH HE WEARS FIVE LARGE JADE 389 MARCOM RINGS.

HE WEARS HIS CHILDISHLY FANTASTIC REGALIA 390 MARCOM WEARS OUT QUICKLY, CAN BE MADE AT VERY SLIGHT 393 MARCOM EXPENSE.

HIS FACE WEARS AN EXPRESSION OF HUMOROUS SCORN. 410 MARCOM

HE WEARS A SIMPLE WHITE ROBE WITHOUT ADORNMENT OF 432 MARCOM ANY SORT.

SHE WEARS A CHEAP, SLEEVELESS, BLUE COTTON DRESS. 3 MISBEG

(MIKE WEARS DIRTY OVERALLS, A SWEAT-STAINED BROWN 4 MISBEG SHIRT.

HE WEARS HEAVY BROGANS, FILTHY OVERALLS, AND A 11 MISBEG DIRTY SHORT-SLEEVED UNDERSHIRT.

BUT SHE WEARS IT IN A WAY THAT GIVES A PLEASING 16 POET EFFECT OF BEAUTY UNADORNED.)

SHE WEARS A FADED OLD WRAPPER OVER HER NIGHTGOWN, 136 POET SLIPPERS ON HER BARE FEET.

HE HAS ON A THREADBARE BROWN OVERCOAT BUT WEARS NO578 ROPE HAT.)

SHE WEARS A SHABBY GINGHAM DRESS. 578 ROPE

SHE WEARS A FADED GINGHAM DRESS AND A TORN 579 ROPE SUNBONNET.

HE WEARS A DARK BLUE JERSEY, PATCHED BLUE PANTS, 587 ROPE ROUGH SAILOR SHOES.

HE STILL WEARS THE LATEST IN COLLEGIATE CLOTHES 29 STRANG AND AS HE LOOKS YOUNGER THAN HE

HE WEARS A SWEATER AND LINEN KNICKERS, COLLEGIATE 53 STRANG TO THE LAST DEGREE.

HE WEARS FLANNEL PANTS, A BLUE COAT, WHITE 159 STRANG BUCKSKIN SHOES.

AND WEARS A MUFFLER AND A CAP. 493 VOYAGE

WEARY

(WITH WEARY SCORN) OH, FOR HEAVEN'S SAKE, ARE YOU 42 ANNA OFF ON THAT AGAIN!

(WITH WEARY VEXATION) IT'S A SHAME FOR HIM TO 118 BEYOND COME HOME

(A WEARY EXPRESSION COMES OVER HIS FACE AND HE 157 BEYOND SIGHS HEAVILY)

HIS SHOULDERS HAVE A WEARY STOOP AS IF WORN DOWN 556 CROSS PEACE FOR THE WEARY-- 496 DAYS

AT WHICH SOMETHING LAUGHS WITH A WEARY SCORN/ 561 DAYS

FOR A MOMENT HE IS OLD AND WEARY. 265 DESIRE

EMMA RISES LIKE A WEARY AUTOMATON AND GOES TO THE 547 DIFRNT DOOR AND OPENS IT.

(HE SIGHS, AFTER LUNCHING, HIS BODY SUDDENLY GONE 477 DYNAMO LIMP AND WEARY.)

(HE SITS IN A WEARY ATTITUDE, LISTENING TO THE 188 EJONES RHYTHMIC BEATING OF THE TOM-TOM)

(AS IF THERE WERE A SHOVEL IN HIS HANDS HE GOES 194 EJONES THROUGH WEARY,

(HER VOICE VERY WEARY) 289 GGBROW

(WITH WEARY BITTERNESS) 219 HA APE

UP A PITYING BUT WEARY OLD PRIEST'S. 574 ICEMAN

(WITH WEARY EXASPERATION) AW, NUTS! 669 ICEMAN

BUT ROCKY ONLY SHRUGS HIS SHOULDERS WITH WEARY 671 ICEMAN DISGUST.

(WITH A DULL, WEARY BITTERNESS) 712 ICEMAN

(HIS ANGER EBBS INTO A WEARY COMPLAINT.) 32 JOURNE

(WITH A DEFENSIVE AIR OF WEARY INDIFFERENCE 34 JOURNE AGAIN.)

MINGLED NOW WITH THE BEGINNING OF AN OLD WEARY, 71 JOURNE HELPLESS RESIGNATION.

HAPPY ROADS IS BUNK. WEARY ROADS IS RIGHT. 161 JOURNE

LOCUS REMARKS WITH A WEARY SMILE) 316 LAZARU

NOW IT IS TOO OLD FOR YOU, A HEART TOO WEARY FOR 345 LAZARU YOUR LOVING LAUGHTER.

I HAVE FELT SO WEARY OF THE GAME-- 102 MANSNS

I HAVE BECOME SO WEARY OF WHAT THEY CALL LIFE 103 MANSNS BEYOND THE WALL, MOTHER.

HE ALSO IS HOT WEARY, AND DUST-COVERED. 347 MARCOM

(WITH A WEARY SMILE) I BEGIN TO THINK KUBLAI IS A359 MARCOM HUMORIST, TOO.

ALL THE POLOS ARE WEARY AND THEIR CLOTHES SHABBY 373 MARCOM AND TRAVEL-WORN.

IT IS APPARENT THE WHOLE COMPANY IS EXTREMELY 374 MARCOM WEARY.

(IRRITABLY) HE IS BEGINNING TO WEARY ME WITH HIS 387 MARCOM GROTESQUE ANTICS.

(WHO HAS BEEN STARING AT THEM WITH WEARY 399 MARCOM AMUSEMENT)

WEARY (CONT'D.)

I AM WEARY/ 419 MARCOM

TRAVEL-STAINED AND WEARY. 423 MARCOM

SHE LOOKS WEARY AND STRICKEN AND SAD. 153 MISBEG

(SHE SINKS ON A CHAIR WITH A WEARY SIGH.) 131 POET

(THINKING WITH WEARY RELIEF) 15 STRANG

(THINKING WITH WEARY SCORN) 15 STRANG

(THINK WITH WEARY HOPELESSNESS) 72 STRANG

I'M SO CONTENTEDLY WEARY WITH LIFE/ 200 STRANG

(AFTER A PAUSE, WITH A GESTURE TOWARD THE DOOR AND469 WELDED A WEARY, BEATEN SMILE)

WEASEL

THE WEASEL,* INCREASING THE TEMPO WITH EVERY VERSE251 DESIRE UNTIL AT THE END HE IS

WEATHER

A RANGY SIX-FOOTER WITH A LEAN WEATHER-BEATEN 539 'ILE FACE.

WEATHER-BEATEN, RED FACE FROM WHICH HIS LIGHT BLUE 5 ANNA EYES PEER SHORTSIGHTEDLY.

WITH A WEATHER-BEATEN, JOVIAL FACE AND A WHITE 94 BEYOND MUSTACHE--

(INDIFFERENTLY) I FORGOT--AND IT'S TOO MUCH 119 BEYOND TROUBLE THIS WEATHER.

THE FOOD IS LUCKY TO BE ABLE TO GET COLD THIS 122 BEYOND WEATHER.

WE'RE PAYING FOR THE SPELL OF WARM WEATHER WE'VE 153 BEYOND BEEN HAVING.

(DISGUSTEDLY) NUTHIN' BUT YUST DIRTY WEATHER ALL 481 CARDIF DIS VOYAGE.

CONTRASTING WITH THE WEATHER-BEATEN LEATHER COLOR 567 CROSS OF HIS FURROWED FACE.

WITH A GREAT, RED, WEATHER-BEATEN FACE SEAMED BY 513 DIFRNT SUN WRINKLES.

EVERYTHING IS DIFFERENT DOWN THERE--THE WEATHER-- 515 DIFRNT AND THE TREES AND WATER.

HIS SKIN IS TANNED AND WEATHER-BEATEN. 457 DYNAMO

HIS WEATHER-BEATEN FACE IS DISSIPATED, HE HAS A 102 ELECTR MEAN MOUTH.

I'M LACKING A WATCHMAN AND I'VE GOT TO KEEP MY 104 ELECTR WEATHER EYE OPEN.

IT ISN'T GOOD FOR YOU STAYING IN THIS STUFFY ROOM 150 ELECTR IN THIS WEATHER.

IT'S ALWAYS FAIR WEATHER, WHEN GOOD FELLOWS GET 619 ICEMAN TOGETHER.

WHAT'S THE WEATHER LIKE OUTSIDE, ROCKYS 687 ICEMAN

IT'S A BETTER WEATHER PROPHET THAN YOU ARE, JAMES. 41 JOURNE

YOU'RE NOT MUCH OF A WEATHER PROPHET, DEAR. 82 JOURNE

A WEATHER-BEATEN BENCH STANDS AGAINST THE FRONT 1 MANSNS WALL, AT LEFT OF THE DOOR.

WE COULD START NOW--WITH SUCH FAVORABLE WEATHER-- 362 MARCOM

WE COULDN'T HOPE FOR BETTER WEATHER. 362 MARCOM

THAT HIS RIVERANCE LIKED WHEN THE WEATHER WAS 96 POET CUWLD.

A WIND FROM THE SOUTH, AND A SKY GRAY WITH 102 POET CLOUDS--GOOD WEATHER FOR THE HOUNDS.

MOTHER IS A BIT UNDER THE WEATHER THESE DAYS. 73 STRANG

WEATHERED

BUT THE WALLS NOW ARE A BLACKENED AND WEATHERED 1 MISBEG GRAY,

WEAVE

THEY BEGIN TO WEAVE IN AND OUT, CLASPING EACH 287 LAZARU OTHER'S HANDS NOW AND THEN.

WEAVED

WHERE I COOKED AND WEAVED AND SANG. 330 LAZARU

WEAVING

(FROM BEHIND THE KEG WHERE HE IS WEAVING DRUNKENLY249 DESIRE

BACK AND FORTH--

LAUGHING, THE FOLLOWERS DANCE TO IT IN WEAVING 285 LAZARU PATTERNS ON THE TERRACE.

TO OBTAIN THE BEST RESULTS IN THE WEAVING AND 431 MARCOM DYEING OF THE FINISHED PRODUCE,

MOVING SLOWLY BACKWARD IN A GLIDING, INTER-WEAVING433 MARCOM DANCE PATTERN.

(HE ENTERS LEFT-FRONT, WEAVING AND LURCHING A BIT. 72 MISBEG

AN EXCUSE FOR WEAVING AMUSING WORDS... 5 STRANG

WEAZENED

(A WEAZENED RUNT OF A MAN. 478 CARDIF

WEB

ONE GETS A GLIMPSE OF THE MATHEMATICALLY ORDERED 473 DYNAMO WEB

WEBSTER

ON THE WALLS ARE PICTURES OF WASHINGTON, HAMILTON, 69 MANSNS DANIEL WEBSTER, AND,

WED

IT'S ONLY ON THE SEA YOU'D FIND RALE MEN WITH GUTS 37 ANNA IS FIT TO WED WITH FINE,

THE LIKE OF YOURSELF, NOW--WOULD BE WILLING TO WED 38 ANNA WITH ME.

WEDDED

AND THAT'S WEDDED TO ME BEFORE NIGHT COMES. 55 ANNA

AND DREAMING DREAMS OF THE FINE LIFE WE'D HAVE 60 ANNA WHEN WE'D BE WEDDED.

WE'LL BE WEDDED IN THE MORNING, WITH THE HELP OF 76 ANNA GOD.

YOU'VE WEDDED TO THE SOIL. 84 BEYOND

THEN IT WAS ATHEISM WEDDED TO SOCIALISM. 502 DAYS

THAT DOESN'T LOOK HOPEFUL FOR FUTURE WEDDED 80 STRANG BLISS/....!)

WEDDIN'

YOU AND CALEB AIN'T HAD A SPAT, HAVE YOU, WITH 506 DIFRNT YOUR WEDDIN' ONLY TWO DAYS OFF.

HERE'S THE WEDDIN' ONLY TWO DAYS OFF, AND 511 DIFRNT EVERYTHIN' FIXED UP WITH THE MINISTER.

A GUY OUGHTA GIVE HIS BRIDE ANYTHING SHE WANTS ON 670 ICEMAN DE WEDDIN' DAY. I SHOULD TINK.

SAY, WHY DON'T ALL YOU BARFLIES COME TO DE 683 ICEMAN WEDDIN'S

1783 WEEP

WEDDING

NO WEDDING BELLS FOR ME/	251	AHWILD
WHAT IS IT THAT'S PREVENTING YOU WEDDING ME WHEN	54	ANNA
THE TWO OF US HAS LOVES		
IF IT WERE, I SAY, THERE'D BE HALF FOR YOU FOR	566	CROSS
YOUR WEDDING PORTION.		
THERE AIN'T GOING TO BE ANY WEDDING.	506	DIFRNT
THEN, JUST BEFORE THE WEDDING, THE OLD MAN FEELS	431	DYNAMO
YOU WERE ALWAYS MY WEDDING NIGHT TO ME--AND MY	31	ELECTR
HONEYMOON/		
THE DAY BEFORE THE WEDDING--I WANT YOU TO MAKE	160	ELECTR
PETER READ WHAT'S INSIDE.		
I'M SURE YOU'VE COMPLETELY FORGOTTEN WHAT MY	114	JOURNE
WEDDING GOWN LOOKED LIKE.		
THAT WEDDING GOWN WAS NEARLY THE DEATH OF ME AND	114	JOURNE
THE DRESSMAKER, TOO/		
DO YOU REMEMBER OUR WEDDING, DEARS	114	JOURNE
WHERE IS MY WEDDING GOWN NOW, I WONDERS	115	JOURNE
IT MIGHT BE IN AN OLD TRUNK IN THE ATTIC, ALONG	152	JOURNE
WITH MAMA'S WEDDING DRESS.		
IS AN OLD-FASHIONED WHITE SATIN WEDDING GOWN,	170	JOURNE
TRIMMED WITH DUCHESSE LACE.		
THE WEDDING GOWN TRAILING ON THE FLOOR.	171	JOURNE
(DULLY,) HER WEDDING GOWN, I SUPPOSE.	172	JOURNE
(SHE REGARDS THE WEDDING GOWN WITH A PUZZLED	172	JOURNE
INTEREST.)		
IT'S A WEDDING GOWN. IT'S VERY LOVELY, ISN'T ITS	172	JOURNE
HOLDING THE WEDDING GOWN IN HIS ARMS WITH AN	172	JOURNE
UNCONSCIOUS CLUMSY,		
HE POURS A DRINK WITHOUT DISARRANGING THE WEDDING	175	JOURNE
GOWN HE HOLDS CAREFULLY OVER		
AND IN THE MEANTIME CAN EASILY AFFORD A BIG	361	MARCOM
WEDDING		
AND IN THE MEANTIME CAN EASILY AFFORD A BIG	375	MARCOM
WEDDING		
(WITH RAGE) SHALL I ASK AS MY FIRST WEDDING	416	MARCOM
PRESENT FROM GHAZAN KHAN THAT HE		
MADEMOISELLE--(HE SEES HER WEDDING RING.) PRAY	69	POET
FORGIVE ME, I SEE IT IS MADAME--		
SHE WARNED HIM A SUDDEN WEDDING WOULD LOOK	110	POET
DAMNABLY SUSPICIOUS		
IT IS OBVIOUS THAT WERE THERE A SUDDEN WEDDING	110	POET
WITHOUT A SUITABLE PERIOD OF		
I'LL START HER ON HER WAY BY MAKING HER A WEDDING	173	POET
PRESENT AV THE MAJOR'S PLACE		
(WITH A SLIGHT SMILE) I'M PRESCRIBING FOR SAM,	38	STRANG
TOO, WHEN I BOOST THIS WEDDING.		
I FELT A BIT SORRY FOR MYSELF AT THEIR WEDDING...	78	STRANG
I WAS ENVIOUS AT HIS WEDDING...	85	STRANG

WEDDINGS

| AND WEDDINGS/ | 188 | STRANG |

WEDGE

(THE SOLDIERS FORM A WEDGE AND CHARGE WITH A	291	LAZARU
SHOUT.		
IT IS SMALL, WITH HIGH CHEEKBONES, WEDGE-SHAPED,	67	POET
NARROWING FROM A BROAD FOREHEAD		

WEE

| JIMMY TOMORROW'S IS =A WEE DOCK AND DORIS=. | 727 | ICEMAN |

WEED

YE'LL NEVER LIVE T' SEE THE DAY WHEN EVEN A	230	DESIRE
STINKIN' WEED ON IT'LL BELONG T' YE/		
=INGRATITUDE, THE VILEST WEED THAT GROWS=/	33	JOURNE

WEEDIN'

| =R WEEDIN'. | 208 | DESIRE |

WEEDS

| I WALK ALONG THE PATH IN WHICH WEEDS HAVE GROWN. | 384 | MARCOM |

WEEK

MAKING GOOD MONEY IN WATERBURY, TOO--THIRTY-FIVE A213	AHWILD
WEEK.		
SEEMS TO ME YOU'VE BEEN INVENTING A NEW SIGNATURE	251	AHWILD
EVERY WEEK LATELY.		
I'D BE ABLE TO HAVE A LITTLE HOUSE AND BE HOME TO	38	ANNA
IT MAN WEEK OUT OF FOUR.		
LAMB EACH NIGHT OF THE WEEK I'D BE IN PORT.	38	ANNA
IT IS AFTERNOON OF A SUNNY DAY ABOUT A WEEK LATER.	41	ANNA
IN THE NEWSPAPERS OF BOSTON A WEEK BACKS	48	ANNA
I BEEN THINKING IT OVER AND THINKING IT OVER DAY	54	ANNA
AND NIGHT ALL WEEK.		
THE MAN FIXED IT ONLY LAST WEEK.	123	BEYOND
I WISH SHE WASN'T LEAVING FOR A WEEK OR SO.	141	BEYOND
IF THIS FOG KEEPS UP, I'M TELLIN' YE, WE'LL NO BE	481	CARDIF
IN CARDIFF FOR A WEEK OR MORE.		
YOU'LL BE HAVIN YOUR PINT OF BEER IN CARDIFF THIS	482	CARDIF
IF THIS HAD ONLY HAPPENED A WEEK LATER WE'D BE IN	485	CARDIF
CARDIFF IN TIME TO--		
BEFORE THE WEEK IS OUT.	485	CARDIF
(AFTER A PAUSE) WE WON'T REACH CARDIFF FOR A WEEK488	CARDIF
AT LEAST.		
IT IS NEARING DAYBREAK OF A DAY ABOUT A WEEK	553	DAYS
LATER.		
IT TOOK 'EM A WEEK TO ROUND UP ALL HANDS FROM	502	DIFRNT
WHERE THEY WAS FOOLIN' ABOUT WITH		
I MUSTN'T FORGET TO MAKE RAMSAY CHANGE TO HIS	429	DYNAMO
SUMMER UNDERWEAR THIS WEEK...		
IT IS AROUND NINE O'CLOCK OF A NIGHT A WEEK LATER.	43	ELECTR
(DISAPPROVINGLY) THIS IS THE SECOND TIME THIS	44	ELECTR
WEEK I'VE CAUGHT YOU COMING HOME		
ANY DAY IN THE WEEK.	133	ELECTR
CYBEL SAID TO TELL YOU SHE'D BE BACK NEXT WEEK,	289	GGBROW
MR. BROWN.		
(WITH FORCED CASUALNESS) YOU'VE BEEN ON THIS TOOT295	GGBROW
FOR A WEEK NOW.		
IN A WEEK OR SO, I HOPE--AS SOON AS I'VE GOTTEN	316	GGBROW
BROWN OFF TO EUROPE.		
THE POOR GUY CROAKED LAST WEEK.	11	HUGHIE
UNE WEEK ON DAT FARM IN JOISEY, DAT'S WHAT I GIVE	670	ICEMAN
YUH/		

WEEK (CONT'D.)

SHE SAYS, =YEAH, BUT AFTER A WEEK YUH'LL BE	671	ICEMAN
TINKIN' WHAT A SAP YOU WAS.		
HERE'S HOPIN' YUH DON'T MOIDER EACH ODDER BEFORE	683	ICEMAN
NEXT WEEK.		
YOU'VE THROWN YOUR SALARY AWAY EVERY WEEK ON	31	JOURNE
WHORES AND WHISKEY/		
I EXPECT A SALARY OF AT LEAST UNE LARGE IRON MAN	40	JOURNE
AT THE END OF THE WEEK--		
WITH WEEK AFTER WEEK OF ONE-NIGHT STANDS, IN	87	JOURNE
TRAINS WITHOUT PULLMANS.		
I'VE WARNED HIM, ONE DAY I'LL GIVE A CLOUT THAT'LL	99	JOURNE
KNOCK HIM INTO NEXT WEEK.		
LEADING PART OF HIS IN A WEEK, AS YOU USED TO DO	136	JOURNE
IN STOCK IN THE OLD DAYS.		
FIFTY CENTS A WEEK/ IT'S THE TRUTH/ FIFTY CENTS	148	JOURNE
A WEEK/		
IT'S ONLY SEVEN DOLLARS A WEEK BUT YOU GET TEN	149	JOURNE
TIMES THAT VALUE.		
BY THE END OF THE WEEK, IS THE RIGHT DOPE.	131	MISBEG
WHY DIDN'T YOU PAY NEILAN THE END OF LAST WEEKS	22	PUET
HAVE TO SETTLE BY THE END OF THE WEEK OR WE'LL GET	22	POET
NO MORE GROCERIES.		
PAID OFF A WEEK AGO--HAD A BUST UP--AND THEN TOOK	588	HUPE
A NOTION TO COME OUT HERE--		
SHE HAS BEEN WRITING SAM REGULARLY ONCE A WEEK	50	STRANG
EVER SINCE SHE'S KNOWN WE WERE		
HE'S ONLY HOME TWO NIGHTS A WEEK...	69	STRANG
DOES SAM WRITE HIS ADS HERE UP A WEEK-END NOWS...	74	STRANG
EVERY WEEK SINCE THEN HE'S BEEN COMING OUT HERE...	91	STRANG
YES, I'M GOING THIS WEEK AND I EXPECT TO BE GONE	147	STRANG
AT LEAST TWO YEARS THIS TIME--		
HED IS SAILING THIS WEEK, CHARLIE.	147	STRANG
LAST TIME I WAS HERE YOU WERE LEAVING FOR THE WEST147	STRANG
INDIES IN A WEEK BUT I SEE		
YOU WROTE NOT TO EXPECT YOU TILL THE END OF THE	444	WELDED
WEEK.		

WEEK'S

| A LANTERN JAW WITH A WEEK'S STUBBLE OF BEARD, | 574 | ICEMAN |

WEEKS

GUESS I DO LOOK ROTTEN--YUST OUT OF THE HOSPITAL	14	ANNA
TWO WEEKS.		
TWO WEEKS AGO.	16	ANNA
YUST OUT OF THE HOSPITAL TWO WEEKS AGO.	22	ANNA
TWO WEEKS OUT WE RAN	35	ANNA
THAT WAS TWO WEEKS AFTER THE STORM.	>56	CROSS
I KNOW THERE'S SOMETHING THAT'S BEEN TROUBLING YOU529	DAYS
FOR WEEKS--		
(ROUSING VAGUELY) AY-EH--BURN TWO WEEKS BACK--	244	DESIRE
PURTY'S A PICTER.		
THEY ONLY GOT THROUGH WITH THE WORK TWO WEEKS AGO.535	DIFRNT
(TWO WEEKS...	464	DYNAMO
TWO WEEKS AGO YESTERDAY.	464	DYNAMO
I SAW IT THERE ONE DAY A FEW WEEKS AGO--	40	ELECTR
THREE WEEKS LATER.	233	HA APE
CHRIST, DAT'S ALL I BEEN DOIN' FOR WEEKS/	241	HA APE
HAVIN' A BIG BANKROLL AND WE WAS ALL GOIN' BE	583	ICEMAN
DRUNK FOR TWO WEEKS.		
I WAS READIN' IN SOME MAGAZINE IN NEW YORK ONT'Y	529	INZONE
TWO WEEKS AGO HOW SOME GERMAN		
SEVERAL WEEKS LATER.	199	MARCOM
AND IN A FEW WEEKS YOU'D HAVE HIP A DIRTY	29	MISBEG
PROHIBITIONIST.		
A TWO WEEKS GROWTH OF STUBBY PATCHES OF BEARD	578	HUPE
COVERS HIS JAWS AND CHIN.		
WITH THE OPENING OF THE NEW TERM ONLY A FEW WEEKS	12	STRANG
OFF...		
(THREE WEEKS NOW...	22	STRANG
NEXT FEW WEEKS NINA COULDN'T BE LOVING ENOUGH...	68	STRANG
AS HE WAS IN THOSE WEEKS AFTER WE'D LEFT HIS	71	STRANG
MOTHER...		
THEN FOR WEEKS HE NEVER EVEN PHONED...	91	STRANG
AND YOUR MOTHER DEAD ONLY TWO WEEKS/...	100	STRANG
(SHORTLY) MY FATHER DIED THREE WEEKS AGO.	125	STRANG
I'VE BEEN FEELING SO LONELY--AND IT'S ONLY BEEN A	445	WELDED
FEW WEEKS, HASN'T ITS		

WEEP

(HE STANDS WRINGING HIS HANDS TOGETHER AND BEGINS	59	ANNA
TO WEEP.)		
(MRS. MAYO BEGINS TO WEEP SOFTLY.	114	BEYOND
(SHE BEGINS TO WEEP SOFTLY.)	261	DESIRE
=BLESSED ARE THEY THAT WEEP, FOR THEY SHALL	322	GGBROW
LAUGH=		
BUT IF I DID IT, YOU KNOW DAMNED WELL WHO'D WEEP	76	JOURNE
AND PLEAD FOR YOU.		
READY FOR A WEEP ON ANY OLD WOMANLY BOSOM.	159	JOURNE
AND THEIR MOTHERS WEEP.	325	LAZARU
(HE BEGINS TO WEEP LIKE A FRIGHTENED BOY, HIS HEAD334	LAZARU
IN HIS HANDS.)		
I SHOULD WEEP FOR HIS DEFEAT/	351	LAZARU
MANY LEAGUES AND YEARS, AND I WEEP THAT NEVER	384	MARCOM
AGAIN SHALL I SEE YOUR FACE.		
YOU ONCE TOLD ME A PRINCESS MUST NEVER WEEP.	386	MARCOM
REMEMBER AGAIN, PRINCESSES MAY NOT WEEP/	390	MARCOM
I HAVE MADE YOU WEEP AGAIN/	400	MARCOM
(IMPULSIVELY) DO NOT WEEP/	400	MARCOM
THE GREAT KAAN, RULER OF THE WORLD, MAY NOT WEEP.	401	MARCOM
WEEP, PRINCESS OF THE WOUNDED HEART,	420	MARCOM
(BOWING--COMPASSIONATELY) THEN WEEP, CLU MAN.	437	MARCOM
BE HUMBLE AND WEEP FOR YOUR CHILD.	437	MARCOM
WEEP FOR ME, KUKACHIN/	438	MARCOM
WEEP FOR THE DEAD/	438	MARCOM
AND WEEP ON YOUR BOSOM, JOSIE.	170	MISBEG
WEEP GREAT TEARS AND APPEAL TO HIS HONOR TO MARRY	171	PUET
YOU AND SAVE YOURS.		
DEAR OLD CHARLIE IS CRYING BECAUSE SHE DIDN'T WEEP	28	STRANG
ON HIS SHOULDER--		
(SHE BEGINS TO WEEP HYSTERICALLY.	61	STRANG

WEEP

WEEP (CONT'D.)
(SHE TAKES HIS HEAD AND PRESSES IT TO HER BREAST 109 STRANG
AND BEGINS TO WEEP.
HELL, I DID WEEP... 190 STRANG
(COMMENCING TO WEEP DOLOROUSLY) 499 VOYAGE

WEEPIN
AH YOU WID A WOMAN AN' CHILDER WEEPIN' FOR YE IN 463 CARIBE
IVORY DIVIL'S POST IN THE WIDE
HER EYES WEEPIN' AN' SLUDGY WITH SMOKE AN' CINDERS209 DESIRE
SAME'S THEY USED T'RE.

WEEPING
HER EYES ARE RED FROM WEEPING AND HER FACE DRAWN 539 'ILE
AND PALE.
KEENLY HEARS HIS WIFE'S HYSTERICAL WEEPING AND 545 'ILE
TURNS AROUND IN SURPRISE--
(SHE RUNS OVER TO HIM AND THROWS HER ARMS AROUND 546 'ILE
HIM, WEEPING.
(SHE THROWS HER ARMS AROUND HIM, WEEPING AGAINST 549 'ILE
HIS SHOULDER.
(BREAKING DOWN--WEEPING) AY TANK YOU VASN'T DAT 61 ANNA
KIND OF GEL, ANNA.
(SHE THROWS HERSELF ON HER KNEES BEFORE HIM, 257 DESIRE
WEEPING)
(SHE FALLS TO WEEPING AGAIN.) 544 DIFRNT
(THEY WEEPING HYSTERICALLY AND TRYING TO STIFLE 439 DYNAMO
IT)
(SHE BREAKS DOWN, WEEPING, AND RUSHES BACK INTO 452 DYNAMO
THE ROOM.)
HER FACE IS SAD AND PALE, HER EYES SHOW EVIDENCE 171 ELECTR
OF MUCH WEEPING.
--THEY ARE OUT LONG, THE WEEPING AND THE LAUGHTER, 130 JOURNE
LOVE AND DESIRE AND HATE--
(HE BEGINS TO SOB, AND THE HORRIBLE PART OF HIS 162 JOURNE
WEEPING IS THAT IT APPEARS
HA-- (THEN FRANTICALLY--HALF-WEEPING WITH 282 LAZARU
MALIGNANT RAGE--TO THE NAZARENES)
(THEY EMBRACE HER, WEEPING) I HAVE NOT KISSED YOU283 LAZARU
SINCE YOU LEFT HOME TO FOLLOW
ARE YOU WEEPING, MARCELLUS? 334 LAZARU
HALF-LAUGHING IN SPITE OF HIMSELF, HALF-WEEPING 369 LAZARU
WITH RAGE)
(HE HIDES HIS FACE IN HIS HANDS, WEEPING) 371 LAZARU
I CAN BEAR HIS CHILDREN, BUT YOU CANNOT FORCE ME 385 MARCOM
TO--(SHE BREAKS DOWN, WEEPING.)
(HE NOTICES SHE IS WEEPING--IN SELF-REPROACH) 400 MARCOM
YOUR EYES ARE RED FROM WEEPING AND YOUR NOSE IS 401 MARCOM
RED.
(HALF SMILING AND HALF WEEPING AT HIS TEASING) 402 MARCOM
(A SOUND OF LOW WEEPING COMES FROM THE CROWD) 405 MARCOM
MY EYES SHALL HE EVER RED WITH WEEPING, MY HEART 405 MARCOM
BLEEDING.
WEEPING HEALS THE WOUNDS OF SORROW TILL ONLY THE 420 MARCOM
SCARS REMAIN
(WEEPING ANGRILY) THAT'S WHAT I GIT FOR TRYIN' T0581 ROPE
BE KIND TO YOU.
WEEPING... 27 STRANG
WEEPING.) 109 STRANG
(SHE'S ACCUSING ME BECAUSE I'M NOT WEEPING... 190 STRANG
WEEPINGLY
(HE COLLAPSES WEEPINGLY, KNEELING AND CLUTCHING 359 LAZARU
LAZARUS' HAND IN BOTH OF HIS.)

WEEPS
RUTH WEEPS HYSTERICALLY) 91 BEYOND
(SHE WEEPS HYSTERICALLY.) 88 ELECTR
(HE SUDDENLY BREAKS DOWN AND WEEPS IN HYSTERICAL 124 ELECTR
ANGUISH.
CALIGULA SUDDENLY DROPS HIS SWORD AND COVERING HIS308 LAZARU
FACE WITH HIS HANDS WEEPS
(HE WEEPS BITTERLY.) 308 LAZARU
HE WEEPS, CAESAR/ 347 LAZARU
FINALLY, AS DEBORAH WEEPS, 169 MANSNS
(SHE BOWS HER HEAD ON THE RAIL AND WEEPS.) 401 MARCOM
(HE WEEPS, HIS TEARS FALLING ON HER CALM WHITE 439 MARCOM
FACE.)
(HE HIDES HIS FACE IN HIS HANDS AND WEEPS SOFTLY) 20 STRANG
(SHE WEEPS WITH BITTER ANGUISH.) 64 STRANG

WEESTLE
I YUST CAN'T SLEEP WHEN WEESTLE BLOW. 481 CARDIF

WEIGHED
(SHE PICKS OFRORAH UP IN HER STRONG ARMS, AS IF 167 MANSNS
SHE WEIGHED NOTHING.
THIS, UNDER THE CIRCUMSTANCES, HAVING WEIGHED THE 46 STRANG
ODDS AND CONS, SO TO SPEAK.

WEIGHING
(AS IF WEIGHING THE MATTER) I DON'T KNOW WHETHER 274 AHWILD
I'LL CONSENT TO KEEP THIS DATE
HIS WIFE IS TALL AND STOUT, WEIGHING WELL OVER TWO426 DYNAMO
HUNDRED.
(HIFTS OVER THE WATER FROM A SHIP THAT IS WEIGHING102 ELECTR
ANCHOR IN THE HARBOR.
IF YOU WOULD NOT FEEL THE HORRIBLE BURDEN OF TIME 132 JOURNE
WEIGHING ON YOUR SHOULDERS AND
NOW JUST PICTURE THIS LITTLE BALL MAGNIFIED INTO 395 MARCOM
WEIGHING TWENTY POUNDS OR

WEIGHS
IS AN INCH TALLER AND WEIGHS LESS, BUT APPEARS 19 JOURNE
SHORTER AND STOUTER
SURE SHE WEIGHS A TON. 159 JOURNE
FIVE FEET ELEVEN IN HER STOCKINGS AND WEIGHS 3 MISBEG
AROUND ONE HUNDRED AND EIGHTY.

WEIGHT
(THEN SOLEMNLY TRAGIC) IT'S ONLY THAT I'VE GOT A 239 AHWILD
WEIGHT ON MY MIND.
AND I THINK YOU'VE BEEN PUTTING ON WEIGHT LATELY, 291 AHWILD
TOO.
(HE DRIVES BACK AT THE DOOR WITH THE WEIGHT OF HIS451 DYNAMO
WHOLE BODY.

WEIGHT

WEIGHT (CONT'D.)
BY SHEER WEIGHT OF NUMBERS HAVE BORNE HIM TO THE 232 HA APE
FLOOR JUST INSIDE THE DOOR.)
IT IS AS IF A HEAVY WEIGHT YOU HAD BEEN CARRYING 300 LAZARU
ALL YOUR LIFE

WEIRD
(LOOKING AROUND HER FRIGHTENEDLY AT THE WEIRD 484 DYNAMO
SHADOWS OF THE EQUIPMENT WRITHING
HIS VOICE RISES AND FALLS IN A WEIRD, MONOTONOUS 201 EJONES
CROON.
A WEIRD CACOPHONY RESULTS FROM THIS MIXTURE 727 ICEMAN

WELCH
TRYING TO WELCH NOW, EH? 146 MISBEG

WELCHIN'
THERE AIN'T GOIN' TO BE NO WELCHIN' ON LITTLE 465 CARIBE
BRIGHT EYES HERE--

WELCOME
AND WELCOME HOME/ 571 CROSS
(FRENZIEDLY) WELCOME HOME, BOYS. 572 CROSS
(DRYLY) WE'RE WAITIN' T' WELCOME YE HUM--YEW AN' 222 DESIRE
THE BRIDE/
(PITIFULLY) YOU'RE WELCOME TO ANYTHING THAT'S 544 DIFRNT
HERE, BENNY.
I HINTED THAT HIS VISITS WEREN'T WELCOME, 52 ELECTR
AND THEY'LL WELCOME ME HOME/ 140 ELECTR
WELCOME, DUMB WORSHIPPERS/ 321 GOBRON
(WITH SATISFACTION) WELCOME TO OUR CITY. 246 HA APE
(WITH A HARD, BITTER LAUGH) WELCOME TO YOUR CITY,251 HA APE
HOURS
WE SAID, "WELCOME TO OUR CITY. 617 ICEMAN
BEJEES, YOU KNOW YOU'RE ALL AS WELCOME HERE AS THE660 ICEMAN
FLOWERS IN MAY/
AND I'LL WELCOME CLOSING MY EYES IN THE LONG SLEEP689 ICEMAN
OF DEATH--
HE'LL WELCOME THE CHAIR/ 703 ICEMAN
WELCOME TO DE PARTY/ 724 ICEMAN
(HIS BLACK BULLET EYES SENTIMENTAL, HIS ROUND WOP 725 ICEMAN
FACE GRINNING WELCOME)
WELCOME HOME/ 725 ICEMAN
AND WAS WAITING AT THE GATE TO WELCOME HIM. 24 JOURNE
MILLIONAIRE OUGHT TO WELCOME THE FLAVOR OF HOG IN 25 JOURNE
HIS ICE WATER AS AN
(FROWNS AT HIM.) JAMIE IS WELCOME AFTER HIS HARD 65 JOURNF
MORNING'S WORK.
YOU'RE WELCOME TO COME UP AND WATCH ME IF YOU'RE 75 JOURNE
SO SUSPICIOUS.
(TOUCHED, RETURNS HIS HUG.) YOU'RE WELCOME, LAD. 90 JOURNE
TYRONE SPEAKS, AT FIRST WITH A WARM, RELIEVED 126 JOURNE
WELCOME.)
I'LL BE WAITING TO WELCOME YOU WITH THAT =MY OLD 166 JOURNE
PAL. STUFF.
YOU WOULD WELCOME HIM THEN, EH, CRY BABYS 303 LAZARU
BUT YOU MUST WELCOME HIM IN CAESAR'S NAME/ 308 LAZARU
I COULD WELCOME MY OWN MURDER AS AN EXCUSE FOR 314 LAZARU
SLEEPING/
CAESAR WISHED ME TO BID YOU WELCOME, TO TELL YOU 333 LAZARU
HOW MUCH REGARD HE HAS FOR YOU.
WELCOME IN THE NAME OF CAESAR, NOW CAESAR IS SLAIN338 LAZARU
AND I AM CAESAR/
I WOULD WELCOME LOSING MYSELF/ 3 MANSNS
I HAVE NEVER BEEN WELCOME HERE. 27 MANSNS
WITH WHAT JOY I WOULD WELCOME IT, THEN/ 38 MANSNS
I THINK SHE WILL WELCOME VISITS EVEN FROM ME. 91 MANSNS
IT IS ONLY ON THAT CONDITION I CAN AGREE TO 113 MANSNS
WELCOME YOU IN MY GARDEN.
DEBORAH PATS THE SOFA ON HER LEFT, SMILING AN 123 MANSNS
AFFECTIONATE WELCOME.)
NO, YOU'RE ENTIRELY WELCOME. 134 MANSNS
WHY, WHAT IS WAITING TO WELCOME YOU IS MERELY YOUR190 MANSNS
LAST DISDAIN
YOU FOLKS ARE A WELCOME SIGHT/ 365 MARCOM
WELCOME TO THAT DEAR OLD MOTHERLAND, MONGOLIA/ 373 MARCOM
I WAS ORDERED TO ARRANGE A WELCOME FOR THEM. 376 MARCOM
SO YOUR WELCOME WILL BE WELCOME, BROTHER. 376 MARCOM
(WITH A SMILE) I BID YOU WELCOME, MASTER MARCO. 378 MARCOM
I BID YOU WELCOME, MESSRS. POLO. 378 MARCOM
(FLATTERINGLY) I BID YOU WELCOME, YOUR HONOR. 391 MARCOM
"WELCOME HOME/" 429 MARCOM
ISN'T ONE OF YOU GOING TO SAY WELCOME HOME? 429 MARCOM
YOUR GENEROUS AND WHOLE-HEARTED WELCOME TOUCHES ME431 MARCOM
PROFOUNDLY.
I BID YOU WELCOME HOME, LITTLE FLOWER/ 438 MARCOM
I BID YOU WELCOME HOME/ 438 MARCOM
OH, WON'T I WELCOME HIM/ 51 MISBEG
A DRINK WILL WARM UP MY WELCOME FOR HIS MAJESTY. 53 MISBEG
I'LL GIVE YOU A WELCOME, IF YOU START CUTTING UP/ 72 MISBEG
AND A SWEET WELCOME HOME IN THE DEAD OF NIGHT. 73 MISBEG
BUT YOU'RE WELCOME TO IT, IF YOU LIKE. 130 MISBEG
WAS WELCOME IN THE GENTRY'S HOUSES. 13 POET
YES, I MUST CONFESS I STILL WELCOME AN EXCUSE TO 39 POET
WEAR IT.
NATURALLY, AN AULD COMRADE IN ARMS WILL BE DOUBLY 59 POET
WELCOME--
THERE IS A CHORUS OF EAGER, THIRSTY WELCOME FROM 63 POET
INSIDE.
IT IS AN HONOR TO WELCOME YOU TO THIS UNWORTHY 68 POET
INN.
HE'D BE WELCOME HERE IF HE NEVER PAID A PENNY-- 74 POET
(CORRIGAN IS SURPRISED AND PLEASED BY THE WARMTH OF 92 POET
HIS WELCOME.
(TO NORA.) HERE HE IS FUR YE, NORA, AND YOU'RE 164 POET
WELCOME, BAD LUCK TO HIM/
A ROAR OF WELCOME IS HEARD AS THE CROWD GREETS HIS165 POET
ARRIVAL.
WELCOME HOME. 13 STRANG
WELCOME, AS THE SAYIN' IS, AN' SIT DOWN. 499 VOYAGE
(SMILING TENSELY) WOULD I STILL BE WELCOME IF I'D463 WELDED
COME--TO STAY?

1785

WETJOEN'S

WELCOMED
LEFT, WARMLY WELCOMED BY ALL. 726 ICEMAN
BECOME A GOOD FAIRY AND OPENED THE DOOR AND 111 MANSNS
WELCOMED HIM HOME
HUNGRY SERPENTS AND WELCOMED YOU INTO THEIR COILS. 83 POET
WELCOMES
WELCOMES THIS OPPORTUNITY FOR DIVERTING ATTENTION.391 MARCOM
WELCOMING
EXPRESSION WHICH IS THE AMERICAN BUSINESS MAN'S 495 DAYS
WELCOMING POKER FACE.
IN A WELCOMING THE-PATRON-IS-ALWAYS-RIGHT GRIMACE. 8 HUGHIE
INTENDED AS A SMILE.
SPECTACLES WITH A WELCOMING GIGGLE.) 618 ICEMAN
SO I IMAGINE THERE WOULD BE NO WELCOMING COMMITTEE677 ICEMAN
WAITING ON THE DOCK.
SHE TURNS TO HIM, HER LIPS SET IN A WELCOMING, 42 JOURNE
MOTHERLY SMILE.)
THE PASSIVE *YES* WELCOMING THE PEACEFUL 171 MANSNS
PROCESSION OF DEMANDING DAYS/
THERE IS SEDUCTIVE CHARM IN HIS WELCOMING SMILE 68 POET
AND IN HIS VOICE.)
AND HIS VOICE IS FULL OF WELCOMING WARMTH AS HE 92 POET
CALLS.)
THERE IS A ROAR OF WELCOMING DRUNKEN SHOUTS, 180 POET
(WITH A RATHER FORCED WELCOMING NOTE) 73 STRANG
WELFARE
SHE NEVER REFUSED TO HEED MY ADVICE FOR HER 424 MARCOM
WELFARE
WELLESLEY
WHEN THE DUKE OF WELLINGTON--LORD WELLESLEY, 38 POET
THEN--
BY THE GREAT DUKE OF WELLINGTON, HIMSELF--SIR 71 POET
ARTHUR WELLESLEY, THEN.
(HIS RAGE WELLING AGAIN, AS HIS MIND DWELLS ON HIS124 POET
HUMILIATION--
WELLINGTON
(JEERINGLY.) THE DUKE OF WELLINGTON, THERE WAS 127 JOURNE
ANOTHER GOOD IRISH CATHOLIC/
WHO SERVED WITH HONOR IN SPAIN UNDER THE GREAT 21 MANSNS
DUKE OF WELLINGTON.
WHEN THE DUKE OF WELLINGTON--LORD WELLESLEY, 38 POET
THEN--
BY THE GREAT DUKE OF WELLINGTON, HIMSELF--SIR 71 POET
ARTHUR WELLESLEY, THEN.
WHO SERVED WITH HONOR UNDER THE DUKE OF WELLINGTON71 POET
IN SPAIN. I AM HE.
AND HE NIVIR FOUGHT UNDER WELLINGTON AT ALL. 170 POET
WELLINGTON'S
AND WASN'T HE AN OFFICER IN THE DUKE OF 24 POET
WELLINGTON'S ARMY--
IN ONE OF WELLINGTON'S DRAGOON REGIMENTS, 88 POET
WELLS
AS HE STOPS, AN AGONIZING TENDERNESS FOR HIM WELLS 90 ELECTR
UP IN HER--
WELSH
BUT HUGHIE LOOKED SO TICKLED I COULDN'T WELSH ON 25 HUGHIE
HIM.
WELSHING
I'VE ALWAYS TOOK A CHANCE, AND IF I LOSE I PAY, 35 HUGHIE
AND NO WELSHING/
WENCH
A YALLER-HAIRED WENCH HAD HER ARM AROUND ME. 106 ELECTR
GOD, WHAT A WENCH/ 53 JOURNE
PEASANT WENCH/ 63 POET
BUT I HONESTLY THOUGHT THAT WENCH WOULD FEEL 6 STRANG
HUMILIATED IF I...
WEPT
I'VE LOVED, LUSTED, WON AND LOST, SANG AND WEPT/ 296 GGBROW
ONLY HE THAT HAS WEPT CAN LAUGH/ 322 GGBROW
SHAUGHNESSY ALMOST WEPT BECAUSE HE HADN'T THOUGHT 25 JOURNE
OF THAT ONE, BUT
I WEPT WHEN HE WAS THROWN IN PRISON-- 105 JOURNE
JESUS WEPT/ 275 LAZARU
MY MOTHER SPOKE TO ME AND SPOKE TO ME AND EVEN 356 LAZARU
WEPT, THAT TALL WOMAN,
WESSEL
WOT'S THE NAME O' THAT WESSEL PUT IN AT THE DOCK 493 VOYAGE
BELOW JEST ARTER NOONS
WEST
HE'S GOT A DAUGHTER SOMEWHERES OUT WEST, I THINK 5 ANNA
HE TOLD ME ONCE.
WHY DIDN'T YOU NEVER COME OUT WEST TO SEE ME$ 21 ANNA
THE FIFTEEN YEARS SHE WAS GROWING UP IN THE WEST. 47 ANNA
(THEN FEARFULLY) IS IT MARRIED TO SOMEONE ELSE 55 ANNA
YOU ARE--IN THE WEST MAYBES
SHE USED TO GET ME OUT OF THE WAY BY PUSHING MY 89 BEYOND
CHAIR TO THE WEST WINDOW AND
AT ANCHOR OFF AN ISLAND IN THE WEST INDIES. 455 CARIBE
(NODDING TOWARD THE SHORE) DON'T YUH KNOW THIS IS457 CARIBE
THE WEST INDIES.
RUM, FOINE WEST INDY RUM WID A KICK IN UT LOIKE A 460 CARIBE
MULE'S HOIND LEG.
SAID HE'D JUST GOT IN FROM THE WEST. 499 DAYS
THE PLAGUE BEGAN RIGHT AFTER I'D HAD TO GO WEST 501 DAYS
(GROWING EXCITED) GOLD IN THE SKY--IN THE WEST-- 204 DESIRE
GOLDEN GATE--CALIFORNIA-/.
THEY'S GOLD IN THE WEST, SIM. 204 DESIRE
GOLDEST WEST/. 204 DESIRE
THEY'S GOLD IN THE WEST. 205 DESIRE
HITCHED UP AN' DRUV OFF INTO THE WEST. 205 DESIRE
I WAS FINISHIN' PLOWIN', IT WAS SPRING AN' MAY AN'209 DESIRE
SUNSET, AN' GOLD IN THE WEST.
SUN'S STARTIN' WITH US FUR THE GOLDEN WEST. 218 DESIRE
THEY'S GOLD IN THE WEST--AN' FREEDOM, MEBBE. 218 DESIRE
SOME WENT WEST AN' DIED. 236 DESIRE
THEY WAS A PARTY LEAVIN', GIVIN' UP, GOIN' WEST. 237 DESIRE

WEST
(CONT'D.)
I'VE KILLED INJUNS IN THE WEST AFORE YE WAS BORN--251 DESIRE
AN' SKULPED 'EM TOO/
AN' YE'RE TRULY GOIN' WEST--GOIN' T' LEAVE ME--ALL258 DESIRE
ACCOUNT O' HIM BEING BURNS
GOLD SUN--FIELDS O' GOLD IN THE WEST/ 262 DESIRE
AN' I'D SUFFER WUSS LEAVIN' YE, GOIN' WEST, 267 DESIRE
THINKIN' OF YE DAY AN' NIGHT,
MEBBE THEY'S EASY GOLD IN THE WEST BUT IT HAIN'T 268 DESIRE
GOD'S GOLD.
THE FAR WEST AND SETTLED DOWN IN INCLUM, 441 DYNAMO
CALIFORNIA.
I SHOVELED SAND UN A BIG WATERPOWER JOB OUT WEST. 461 DYNAMO
HIS PAW MADE HIM GO TO WEST P'INT. R ELECTR
HE COMES FROM OUT WEST. 15 ELECTR
THERE WAS TALK THEY'D GONE OUT WEST, 19 ELECTR
THIS ISN'T THE WEST. 38 ELECTR
AND LET THE BEST MAN COME OUT ALIVE--AS I'VE OFTEN 38 ELECTR
SEEN IT DONE IN THE WEST/
ON A WEST SIDE STREET IN MIDTOWN NEW YORK. 7 HUGHIE
SITUATED ON THE DOWNTOWN WEST SIDE OF NEW YORK. 571 ICEMAN
WORST IS BEST HERE, AND EAST IS WEST, AND TOMORROW600 ICEMAN
IS YESTERDAY.
SEEN HIM SITTIN' ON DE DOCK ON WEST STREET, 699 ICEMAN
LOOKIN' AT DE WATER AND CRYIN'/
AND EDUCATED IN THE BEST CONVENT IN THE MIDDLE 102 JOURNE
WEST.
DEAD QUEENS OF THE WEST USUALLY LIE IN STATE. 351 MARCOM
TO REQUEST THE POPE TO SEND HIM A HUNDRED WISE MEN354 MARCOM
OF THE WEST
(HE LOOKS AROUND) BUT WHERE ARE THE HUNDRED WISE 376 MARCOM
MEN OF THE WEST$
WHICH THE WEST DREAMS LIVES AFTER DEATH--AND MIGHT379 MARCOM
REVEAL IT TO ME$
AND I WILL LISTEN AS TO A HUNDRED WISE MEN FROM 380 MARCOM
THE WEST/
MYSTERIOUS DREAM-KNIGHT FROM THE EXOTIC WEST, 388 MARCOM
NOW IN THE WEST WE'VE LEARNED BY EXPERIENCE 405 MARCOM
WHY DO YOU WANT TO CONQUER THE WESTS 421 MARCOM
BEYOND IT, LIES THE WEST. 421 MARCOM
LET THE WEST DEVOUR ITSELF. 421 MARCOM
YOU HAVE ALREADY CONQUERED THE WEST, I THINK. 422 MARCOM
LEAVE THE WEST ALONE. 422 MARCOM
(WITH A FIERCE CHEER) DOWN WITH THE WEST/ 422 MARCOM
(THEY PERSUASIVELY) THE WEST MAY NOT BE STRONG 422 MARCOM
BUT IT IS CRAFTY.
THE WEST ALREADY INVADES US/ 423 MARCOM
I SHALL CONQUER THE WEST/ 425 MARCOM
OUR LAMENTATIONS ABOUT THE WIND FROM THE WEST. 436 MARCOM
MR. HARFORD SUGGESTS IT WOULD BE ADVISABLE THAT 122 POET
YOU GO WEST--TO OHIO, SAY.
EUROPE HAS *GONE WEST*--SHE SMILES WHIMSICALLY) 7 STRANG
TO AMERICA. LET'S HOPE/.
WHY DOESN'T HE GO BACK TO THE WEST INDIES... 139 STRANG
(SOURENLY TURNING ON HIM) WHEN ARE YOU GOING BACK140 STRANG
TO THE WEST INDIES, NEDS
LAST TIME I WAS HERE YOU WERE LEAVING FOR THE WEST147 STRANG
INDIES IN A WEEK BUT I SEE
WESTERN
IT WAS NOT FOR THE WESTERN SOUL, HE DECIDED, 903 DAYS
STARTED ONE OF THE FUST WESTERN OCEAN PACKET 7 ELECTR
LINES.
FOR THE SLICKEST CHAYTMAN ON THE WESTERN OR ANY 103 ELECTR
OTHER DAMN OCEANS
THAT HENRY HAD BEEN SECRETLY GAMBLING IN WESTERN 31 MANSNS
LANDS.
TO REGAIN A SOUND POSITION BY MAKING A QUICK 32 MANSNS
PROFIT IN WESTERN LANDS.
LET HIM SET AN EXAMPLE OF VIRTUOUS WESTERN MANHOOD363 MARCOM
AMID ALL THE LEVITIES OF
WHICH MARKS THE WESTERN BOUNDARY OF YOUR EMPIRE. 421 MARCOM
WESTWARD
I WAS PROCEEDING WESTWARD ON A BUSINESS VENTURE, 350 MARCOM
GOOD SIR.
WET
(LICKING HIS LIPS) GAWD BLIMEY, I CAN DO WIV A 461 CARIBE
WET.
BUT THE LOWER PART OF HER SKIRT AND HER STOCKINGS 548 DAYS
AND SHOES ARE SOAKING WET.
AN' THAN YE SET CACKLIN' LIKE A LOT O' WET HENS 249 DESIRE
WITH THE PIP/
HIS HAIR WET AND SLICKED IN A PART. 501 DIFRNT
(A PAUSE) AND THEN I WAS AFEERD SHE'D CATCH COLD 515 DIFRNT
GOIN' ROUND ALL NAKED AND WET
AND WHEN I GET A LEAVE TO HOME, EVERYONE TREATS ME523 DIFRNT
LIKE A WET DOG.
(THEN SHAKING HIMSELF LIKE A WET DOG TO GET RID OF188 EJONES
THESE DEPRESSING THOUGHTS)
*AVE A WET? 203 HA APE
DON'T LET ME BE A WET BLANKET, MAKING FOOL 621 ICEMAN
SPEECHES ABOUT MYSELF.
HE'LL OF A FINE WET BLANKET TO HAVE AROUND AT MY 626 ICEMAN
BIRTHDAY PARTY/
THAT'S THE SPIRIT--DON'T LET ME BE A WET BLANKET--628 ICEMAN
YOU MUSTN'T LET THIS BE A WET BLANKET ON HARRY'S 663 ICEMAN
PARTY.
YOU'RE STILL *ET BEHIND THE EARS. 156 JOURNE
HIS DRESSING GOWN WET WITH FOG, THE COLLAR TURNED 167 JOURNE
UP AROUND HIS THROAT.
OUR SOBS STIFLE US, OUR TEARS WET THE GROUND, 436 MARCOM
I'LL WET A CLOTH IN COLD WATER TO PUT ROUND YOUR 35 POET
HEAD.
WET YOUR LIPS, CORPORAL. 98 POET
COME DAWN AND 'AVE A WET WIV YER. 499 VOYAGE
ONE OF THEM BLOKES WANTS YER TO 'AVE A WET WIV 507 VOYAGE
'IM.
WETJOEN'S
GENERAL WETJOEN'S, *WAITING AT THE CHURCH*. 727 ICEMAN

WETS

WETS
SHE CONTINUALLY WETS HER LIPS 526 DIFRNT

WETTED
BLOWN HAIR WETTED AND PLASTERED DOWN IN A PART, 186 AHWILD
AND A SHINY, GOOD-NATURED FACE.

WETTING
(SITS DOWN--WETTING HER LIPS) 526 DIFRNT

WHA'D
AH, WHA'D YOU KNOW ABOUT THATS 528 DIFRNT

WHACK
(GENIALLY) I ALWAYS HIT 'EM A WHACK ON THE EAR 468 CARIBE
A WHACK ON THE EAR'S THE ONLY THING'LL LEARN 'EM. 470 CARIBE

WHACKING
(SHIVING AND WHACKING) BACK/ 300 LAZARU

WHALE
AND THEY'S WHALE HERE, PLENTY OF 'EM. 543 'ILE
THEY'S WHALE I'UTHER SIDE O' THIS FLOE AND WE'RE 550 'ILE
GOING TO GIT 'EM.
IN THE BEDROOM, DIMLY LIGHTED BY A SMALL WHALE-OIL259 DESIRE
LAMP, CABOT LIES ASLEEP.
EVEN A WOMAN'D FIND IT HARD TO GIT JEALOUS OF A 497 DIFRNT
WHALE/
=A DEAD WHALE OR A STOVE BOAT/= 543 DIFRNT
IT AIN'T SO DEEP BUT WHAT I KIN WHALE THE STUFFIN'133 ELECTR
OUT O' YOU
MY OLD MAN USED TO WHALE SALVATION INTO MY HEINIE 622 ICEMAN
WITH A BIRCH ROD.
YES, IT'S LIKE HAVING A SICK WHALE IN THE BACK 17 JOURNE
YARD.
A FOGHORN IS HEARD AT REGULAR INTERVALS, MOANING 97 JOURNE
LIKE A MOURNFUL WHALE IN LABOR,
LIFE DRIFTED BECALMED, A DEAD WHALE AWASH 408 MARCOM

WHALES
SHE WAS SIGHTED BOTTOM UP, A COMPLETE WRECK, BY 558 CROSS
THE WHALER JOHN SLOCUM.
OFF ON A WHALER IN THE INJUN OCEAN, THAT WAS. 132 ELECTR

WHALES
'S IF IT WAS OUR FAULT HE AIN'T HAD GOOD LUCK WITH537 'ILE
THE WHALES.
(IN GREAT EXCITEMENT) WHALES, SIR--A WHOLE SCHOOL951 'ILE
OF 'EM--
(LAUGHING) I WASN'T THINKING OF WHALES, SILLY/ 497 DIFRNT

WHALIN'
AND DAMN THIS STINKIN' WHALIN' SHIP OF HIS, AND 536 'ILE
DAMN ME FOR A FOOL
ON A STINKIN' WHALIN' SHIP TO THE ARCTIC SEAS TO 537 'ILE
BE LOCKED IN BY THE ROTTEN ICE
YOU BEEN WITH ME HIGH ON TEN YEAR AND I'VE LEARNED542 'ILE
YE WHALIN'.
=DAVE KEENEY WHAT BOASTS HE'S THE BEST WHALIN' 542 'ILE
SKIPPER OUT O' HOMEPORT
=WHALIN' AIN'T NO LADIES'= 545 'ILE
I BEEN ALWAYS FIRST WHALIN' SKIPPER OUT O' 547 'ILE
=HOMEPORT, AND=
WHEN I KIN GO OFF ON A TWO-YEAR WHALIN' VIGE AND 496 DIFRNT
LEAVE YOU ALL 'LONE
MOST OF THE WHALIN' MEN HEREABOUT HAVE RUN UP 502 DIFRNT
AGAINST IT IN THEIR TIME.
(JEER.) I'LL TAKE TO WHALIN' 'STEAD O' FISHIN' 510 DIFRNT
AFTER THIS.
AND AS FOR THEM ISLANDS, ALL WHALIN' MEN KNOWS 513 DIFRNT
'EM.
BUT HE'S TO MEAN EVEN YOU RETIRE FROM WHALIN' 522 DIFRNT
HIMSELF--
THAT'S WHY WHEN THE WAR WAS OVER BENNY ENLISTED 541 DIFRNT
AGAIN 'STEAD O' GOIN' WHALIN'
HE SAYS IN WHALIN'-- AND MY BOAT IS STOVE/ 543 DIFRNT
SHE'LL GET A GOOD WHALIN' IF I CATCH HER JUMPIN' 601 ROPE
AT IT.

WHALIN'S
CAPTAIN KEENEY'S CABIN ON BOARD THE STEAM WHALING 535 'ILE
SHIP =ATLANTIC QUEEN=--
THE LAST OF THE WHALING CREW WERE NEVER HEARD FROM559 CROSS
AGAIN--GONE TO THE SHARKS.
MY FATHER WAS A WHALING CAPTAIN AS HIS FATHER 559 CROSS
BEFORE HIM.

WHARF
WITH THE FLOOR OF THE WHARF IN THE FOREGROUND. 102 ELECTR
ABOVE THE LEVEL OF THE WHARF. 102 ELECTR
ON THE WHARF THE END OF A WAREHOUSE IS AT LEFT 102 ELECTR
FRONT.
(THE STERN SECTION OF A CLIPPER SHIP MOORED 102 ELECTR
ALONGSIDE A WHARF IN EAST BOSTON.
HE COMES TO THE RAIL AND STARES EXPECTANTLY UP THE104 ELECTR
WHARF, OFF LEFT.
AND PEERS ANXIOUSLY DOWN THE WHARF. 105 ELECTR
I'LL WALK TO THE END OF THE WHARF WITH YOU. 113 ELECTR
HE'S GOING TO THE END OF THE WHARF. 113 ELECTR
A RAIL ENCLOSES THE ENTIRE WHARF AT THE BACK. 257 GGBROW
(FROM THE END OF THE WHARF, HER VOICE IS HEARD.) 266 GGBROW
THE WHARF EXTENDS OUT, REAR, TO THE RIGHT OF HER. 399 MARCOM
SHUTS OUT ALL VIEW OF THE HARBOR AT THE END OF THE400 MARCOM
WHARF.
MOVES WITH MECHANICAL PRECISION ACROSS THE WHARF, 400 MARCOM
DISAPPEARS INTO THE JUNK.

WHARVES
(SCENE--THE WHARVES OF THE IMPERIAL FLEET AT THE 399 MARCOM
SEAPORT OF ZAYTON--

WHATEVER
(PLAINLY NOT RELISHING WHATEVER IS COMING--TO SID,192 AHWILD
GRUMBLINGLY)
WHATEVER CAN THE OLD FOOL WANT-- 199 AHWILD
WHATEVER THAT IS. 209 AHWILD
YOU DO WHATEVER YOU'VE A MIND TO. 234 AHWILD
YOU'LL PROMISE NOT TO BE ANGRY--WHATEVER IT IS$ 90 BEYOND
WHATEVER--PUT SUCH A FOOL NOTION INTO--INTO YOUR 91 BEYOND
HEAD$

1786

WHATEVER
(CONT'D.)
WHATEVER OF RESEMBLANCE ROBERT HAS TO HIS PARENTS 94 BEYOND
MAY BE TRACED TO HER.
WHATEVER GOT INTO HER OF A SUDDEN$ 100 BEYOND
BUT I KNOW WHATEVER IT IS WHAT COMES AFTER IT 486 CARDIF
CAN'T BE NO WORSE'N THIS.
WHATEVER PAY'S COMIN' TO ME YUH CAN DIVVY UP WITH 489 CARDIF
THE REST OF THE BOYS.
OR VIOLET, OR WHATEVER THE HELL FLOWER YOUR NAME 468 CARIBE
IS.
THAT I WAS TO BLAME FOR WHATEVER WAS HAPPENING TO 507 DAYS
YOU.
(DULLY) WHATEVER YE DONE, IT HAIN'T NO GOOD NOW. 260 DESIRE
WHATEVER OTHER JUNK THEY GOT. 502 DIFRNT
AND WHATEVER YOU THINK IS BEST, SUITS ME. 516 DIFRNT
IT'S KILLED WHATEVER MITE OF DECENCY WAS LEFT IN 540 DIFRNT
HIM.
WITCH DOCTORS, OR WHATEVER THE 'ELL YER CALLS THE 185 EJONES
SWINE.
I DON'T COME ACROSS NO MORE O' DEM, WHATEVER DEY 193 EJONES
IS/
WHATEVER ARE THOSE MEN GOSSIPING ABOUTS 69 ELECTR
THAT YOU'LL ONLY DRAG HIM INTO THIS TERRIBLE 172 ELECTR
THING--WHATEVER IT IS--
I'VE ALWAYS STOOD UP FOR HIM WHATEVER HE'S DONE-- 289 GGBROW
SO YOU CAN BE PERFECTLY FRANK.
AND WHATEVER 'APPENS, YER CAN'T BLAME ME. 237 HA APE
YOU CAN GO BACK AND TELL WHATEVER SKUNK IS PAYING 249 HA APE
YOU BLOOD-MONEY FOR BETRAYING
=LET THIS RIDE ON THE NOSE OF WHATEVER HORSE 22 HUGHIE
YOU'RE BETTING ON TOMORROW.
AND WHATEVER STICKS TO THE CEILING IS MY SHARE/ 582 ICEMAN
BECAUSE THEY I WON'T SUSPECT WHATEVER HE DID ABOUT643 ICEMAN
THE GREAT CAUSE.
IT'S ON YOUR HEAD--WHATEVER IT WAS/ 649 ICEMAN
AND WHATEVER YOU'D LIKE, I CAN'T SPEND MY LIFE 652 ICEMAN
SITTING HERE WITH YOU.
MAKE NO STATEMENTS WHATEVER WITHOUT FIRST 679 ICEMAN
CONSULTING YOUR ATTORNEY.
NO EXCUSE WHATEVER FOR POSTPONING-- 684 ICEMAN
(WITH A TOUCH OF PRIDE.) WHATEVER EDMUND'S DONE, 35 JOURNE
WHATEVER BULL THEY HAND YOU, THEY TELL ME HE'S A 36 JOURNE
PRETTY BUM REPORTER.
WHATEVER YOU MEAN, IT ISN'T TRUE, DEAR. 72 JOURNE
OR OF THE CLOCK, OF WHATEVER FLIES, OR SIGHS, OR 132 JOURNE
ROCKS, OR SINGS, OR SPEAKS.
WITH NO DISHONORABLE INTENTIONS WHATEVER. 160 JOURNE
SHE HAS PAID NO ATTENTION WHATEVER TO THE 171 JOURNE
INCIDENT.
THE CROWD HAVE RAISED WHATEVER WEAPONS THEY HAVE 305 LAZARU
FOUND--
BUT--YOU LIE--WHATEVER YOU ARE/ 308 LAZARU
WHATEVER MAGIC THOU DIDST TO ME, DAEMON, I BESEECH343 LAZARU
THEE UNDO IT/
WHATEVER THE CAUSE BE, IT IS NOT GRIEF. 26 MANSNS
WHATEVER THE COST OF RELEASE-- 31 MANSNS
(UNEASILY.) NO, STICK TO YOUR OWN TRADE, SIMON, 48 MANSNS
WHATEVER YOU DO.
WHATEVER IT IS, I WILL REMEMBER IT IS HIS DOING, 132 MANSNS
AND I WILL UNDERSTAND.
HE HAS TAUGHT US THAT WHATEVER IS IN ONESELF IS 172 MANSNS
GOOD--
THAT WHATEVER ONE DESIRES IS GOOD, THAT THE ONE 172 MANSNS
EVIL IS TO DENY ONESELF.
BUT THE OBVIOUS FACT IS THAT THEIR LIVES ARE 180 MANSNS
WITHOUT ANY MEANING WHATEVER--
WHATEVER THE EXPLANATION BE, 426 MARCOM
JIM PROMISES WHATEVER YOU LIKE WHEN HE'S FULL OF 31 MISBEG
WHISKEY.
WHATEVER MADE YOU TAKE SUCH A SAVAGE GRUDGE 63 MISBEG
AGAINST PIGS$
I KNOW WHATEVER HAPPENED HE MEANT NO HARM TO YOU. 176 MISBEG
SURMISE WHATEVER YOU PLEASE. 47 POET
IF NOTHING ELSE, I CAN ALWAYS GIVE MY NOTE AT HAND 50 POET
FOR WHATEVER AMOUNT--
(AFTER A PAUSE--DEFIANTLY.) LET HER TRY WHATEVER 80 POET
GAME SHE LIKES.
I'LL HAVE TO PRETEND I LIKED HER AND I'D RESPECT 88 POET
WHATEVER ADVICE SHE GAVE HIM.
WHATEVER THE NATURE OF THAT RELATIONSHIP IN THE 121 POET
PAST,
WHICH SPECIFIES THAT YOU RELINQUISH ALL CLAIMS, OF122 POET
WHATEVER NATURE.
WHATEVER THE COST/ 131 POET
THEY'D DRINK, THAT'S SURE, WHATEVER HAPPENED. 141 POET
AND WHATEVER MEANT HAPPINESS TO HIM WOULD BE MY 146 POET
ONLY AMBITION.
AND HE FORGOT WHATEVER SHYNESS WAS LEFT IN THE 147 POET
DARK
THAT A WOMAN CAN FORGIVE WHATEVER THE MAN SHE 149 POET
LOVES COULD DO AND STILL LOVE HIM.
ALL I HOPE NOW IS THAT WHATEVER HAPPENED WAKES HIM150 POET
FROM HIS LIES AND MAD DREAMS.
BOASTING OF HIS GLORIOUS VICTORY OVER OLD HARFORD,151 POET
WHATEVER THE TRUTH IS/
NEWSY, LOVELESS SCRIPTS, TELLING NOTHING WHATEVER 25 STRANG
ABOUT HERSELF...
NECKING, PETTING--WHATEVER YOU CALL IT--SPOONING 36 STRANG
IN GENERAL--
TO MYSELF, NOW THAT I'VE SPENT ONE NIGHT IN IT I 49 STRANG
KNOW THAT WHATEVER SPOOKS THERE
WHATEVER YOU CAN DO TO MAKE HIM HAPPY IS GOOD--IS 64 STRANG
GOOD, NINA/
WELL, WHATEVER IT IS THAT HAS BOUND US TOGETHER, 139 STRANG
IT'S STRONG/...
WHATEVER SUITS YOU. 464 WELDED
WHATEVER'S
WHY, WHATEVER'S THE MATTER WITH YOU, RICHARD$ 208 AHWILD

WHATEVER'S (CONT'D.)
WHATEVER'S GOT INTO YOUS 506 DIFRNT
WHATEVER'S GOT INTO HARRIET LATELYS 531 DIFRNT
HE'S ONLY CLOSE TO WHATEVER'S THE MATTER WITH YOU/ 30 STRANG
WHATEVER
WHATEVER WAS HIS WAS MINE, 480 CARDIF
WHATIVIR
(IRRITABLY) WHATIVIR THEY ARE, THE DIVIL TAKE 457 CARIBE
THEIR CRYIN'.
WHEAT
(AFTER A PAUSE) YOU--A FARMER--TO GAMBLE IN A 161 BEYOND
WHEAT PIT WITH SCRAPS OF PAPER.
IN WHEATS 161 BEYOND
YER BELLY BE LIKE A HEAP O' WHEAT.... 232 DESIRE
WHEEDLING
(CHANGING TO A TONE OF WHEEDLING AFFECTION) 446 DYNAMO
WHEEDLING PLAYFULNESS, AS THOUGH HE WERE TALKING 579 ICEMAN
TO A CHILD)
(HE BREAKS INTO HIS WHEEDLING, BULLYING TONE) 592 ICEMAN
AS THE LAUGHTER DIES HE SPEAKS IN HIS GIGGLING, 627 ICEMAN
WHEEDLING MANNER,
(WITH A QUICK CHANGE OF PACE TO A WHEEDLING 63 MISBEG
CONFIDENTIAL TONE)
WHEEDLINGLY
(WHEEDLINGLY.) YOU KNOW WHAT'S BEST FOR YOU, 159 POET
DON'T YOU, MAJORS
WHEEL
I WARN'T 'SPECIALLY ANXIOUS THE MAN AT THE WHEEL 539 'ILE
SHOULD CATCH WHAT I WANTED TO
(A BIT REPROACHFULLY) WHY DIDN'T YOU WHEEL MRS. 96 BEYOND
HE'S BEEN GONE LONG ENOUGH TO WHEEL THE WIDDER TO 96 BEYOND
HOME, CERTAIN.
MRS. ATKINS IS IN HER WHEEL CHAIR. 112 BEYOND
CONDEMNED TO BE PUSHED FROM DAY TO DAY OF HER LIFELI3 BEYOND
IN A WHEEL CHAIR,
AND STARTS TO WHEEL THE INVALID'S CHAIR TOWARD THELI8 BEYOND
SCREEN DOOR)
HER MOTHER IS ASLEEP IN HER WHEEL CHAIR BESIDE THE145 BEYOND
STOVE TOWARD THE REAR,
(PEREMPTORILY) WHEEL ME IN THERE THIS MINUTE. 153 BEYOND
MY WHEEL. 481 CARDIF
WHILE HE IS DOING THIS THE MAN WHOSE TURN AT THE 483 CARDIF
WHEEL HAS BEEN RELIEVED ENTERS.
A WHEEL COMPASS, BINNACLE LIGHT, THE COMPANIONWAYS57 CROSS
THERE (HE POINTS))
ON THE POOP DECK ABOVE, AT RIGHT, IS THE WHEEL. 102 ELECTR
IS IT A FLESH AND BLOOD WHEEL OF THE ENGINES YOU'D215 HA APE
BES
WHO'S WHEEL IS ITS 516 INZONE
(SULLENLY) MY WHEEL. 516 INZONE
WHEELBARROW
AND I HAVE TO GET THE WHEELBARROW TO COLLECT YOU. 81 MISBEG
WHEELED
I JUST WHEELED MA OVER TO YOUR HOUSE. 87 BEYOND
AND HE'S STILL BEING WHEELED ALONG IN THE 296 GGBROW
PROCESSION.
FLAT WHEELED AND TIRED. 25 HUGHIE
OF A TWO-WHEELED WAGON, STAGGER IN, STRAINING 350 MARCOM
FORWARD UNDER THE LASHES
WHEELING
(WHEELING ABOUT WITH A TERRIFIED GASP) 69 ANNA
WHEELS
(MRS. MAYO WHEELS HER OUT AND OFF LEFT. 118 BEYOND
(RUTH WHEELS HER MOTHER OFF RIGHT. 153 BEYOND
AND MOP UP A COUPLE OF BEERS, THINKING I WAS A 709 ICEMAN
HELL-ON-WHEELS SPORT.
ON SPROCKET WHEELS 399 MARCOM
I GOT IT IN FRISCO--CART-WHEELS, THEY CALL 'EM. 588 ROPE
WHEEZES
(SHE WHEEZES, PANTING FOR BREATH. 11 ANNA
WHEEZILY
(WHEEZILY) PHEW/ 140 BEYOND
WHEEZY
HER BREATH COMES IN WHEEZY GASPS. 7 ANNA
HIS BREATH COMES IN WHEEZY GASPS.) 482 CARDIF
HE TRIES TO CALL FOR HELP BUT HIS VOICE FADES TO A 62 ELECTR
WHEEZY WHISPER)
HE TALKS IN A DRAWLING WHEEZY CACKLE. 129 ELECTR
WHELP
YOU DAMNED WHELP/ 108 BEYOND
DON'T LIE, YE WHELP/ 568 CROSS
WHEN'D
WHEN'D YOU GET INS 450 WELDED
WHEN'S
WHEN'S SHE COMIN', DRISCS 458 CARIBE
WHENCE
(QUOTES BITTERLY) *DRINK FOR YOU KNOW NOT WHENCE 235 AHWILD
YOU COME NOR WHY.
WHENEVER
OF COURSE IT'S A GOOD STORY--AND YOU TELL IT 231 AHWILD
WHENEVER YOU'VE A MIND TO.
HE COMES HERE WHENEVER HE'S IN PORT. 5 ANNA
(RUEFULLY) SEEMS IF I PUT MY FOOT IN IT WHENEVER139 BEYOND
I OPEN MY MOUTH TODAY.
WHENEVER I COME TO HOMES 540 DIFRNT
(TURNING DEFIANTLY) WHENEVER YOU WISH. 18 ELECTR
WHENEVER I REMEMBER THOSE ISLANDS NOW, I WILL 24 ELECTR
ALWAYS THINK OF YOU.
WHENEVER SHE PLEASES/ 98 ELECTR
WHENEVER HE'S COMPLETELY PLASTERED. 593 ICEMAN
WHENEVER I MADE UP MY MIND TO SELL SOMEONE 703 ICEMAN
SOMETHING I KNEW THEY OUGHT TO WANT,
HARDY'S TREATED HIM WHENEVER HE WAS SICK UP HERE, 33 JOURNE
SINCE HE WAS KNEE HIGH.
I HAD TO BE GLAD WHENEVER YOU WERE WHERE YOU 119 JOURNE
COULDN'T SEE ME.
WHENEVER HE CHOOSES HE WILL GATHER A GREAT ARMY 284 LAZARU

WHENEVER (CONT'D.)
SHE IS GOING TO DISCOVER, BEGINNING TODAY, AND 73 MANSNS
SARA, TOO, THAT WHENEVER I WISH,
DON'T I KNOW WHENEVER I WANT, I CAN MAKE HIM MY 129 MANSNS
LOVER AGAIN.
I CAN ALWAYS, WHENEVER I WISH, MAKE HIM MY LITTLE 129 MANSNS
BOY AGAIN.
I KISSED IT SO YOU'D REMEMBER MY KISS WHENEVER YOU375 MARCOM
KISS HER/
AND ALL THE WHILE, WHENEVER HE HAS BEEN WITH ME I 397 MARCOM
HAVE ALWAYS FELT--
THE KHAN PROBABLY MEANT WHENEVER YOU WERE WILLING.411 MARCOM
ONE BIG DRINK, AT LEAST, WHENEVER I STRAIN MY 46 MISBEG
HEART WALKING IN THE HOT SUN.
THE WAY YOU DO, WHENEVER HE TAKES A DRINK, 93 MISBEG
BY SHAKING HIS HAND WHENEVER THEY MEET. 86 POET
WHENEVER HE IS IN HER PRESENCE) 69 STRANG
WHERE'D
WHERE'D HE GO TOS 254 AHWILD
(AFTER A PAUSE) WHERE'D YOU SAY SID AND LILY HAD 291 AHWILD
GONE OFF TOS
WHERE'D YOU GET ITS 6 ANNA
WHERE'D YOU COME FROM, HUHS 14 ANNA
(DISGUSTEDLY) BUT WHERE'D YOU GET THE IDEA HE WAS 17 ANNA
A JANITORS
I SAID, *WHERE'D YOU GRAB THIS DOUGHS 22 HUGHIE
WHERE'D YOU SEE HIM, CORAS 617 ICEMAN
WHERE'LL
WHERE'LL WE GO ON OUR HONEYMOON, DICKS 287 AHWILD
O' SMOKY TEA-KETTLES, THE OLD DAYS IS DYIN', AND 105 ELECTR
WHERE'LL YOU AN' ME BE THENS
WHERE'RE
WHERE'RE YOU GOINGS 23 ANNA
WHEREABOUTS
SEEKING VAINLY TO DISCOVER HIS WHEREABOUTS BY 189 EJONES
THEIR CONFORMATION.)
HOPING YOU MIGHT KNOW THE PRESENT WHEREABOUTS OF 72 POET
MY SON, SIMON.
WHEREAS
WHEREAS IT IS VERY SIMPLE--YOU WANT SARA-- 94 MANSNS
WHEREIN
CITIES ARE PRISONS WHEREIN MAN LOCKS HIMSELF FROM 310 LAZARU
LIFE.
WHEREIN, HAPPINESSS 365 LAZARU
WHEREIN LIES HAPPINESSS 365 LAZARU
WHEREIN LIES HAPPINESSS 365 LAZARU
MY LIFE IS COOL GREEN SHADE WHEREIN COMES NO 187 STRANG
SCORCHING ZENITH SUN OF PASSION AND
WHEREVER
TO BE LAIN/ YOUR COURSE FOR YOU WHEREVER THEY DAMN102 BEYOND
PLEASES.
WHEREVER DID YOU GET HOLD OF THIS STORYS 447 DYNAMO
WHEREVER DID YOU GET THAT SILLY IDEAS 85 ELECTR
I'VE TOLD CATHLEEN TIME AND AGAIN SHE MUST GO 60 JOURNE
WHEREVER HE IS AND TELL HIM.
(STUNG.) I'LL SEND HIM WHEREVER HARDY THINKS 79 JOURNE
BEST/
WHY, WHEREVER HE GOES, IS THERE JOYS 331 LAZARU
HE AUTOMATICALLY TAKES CHARGE WHEREVER HE IS. 152 STRANG
WHIM
I THINK IT'S VERY NATURAL--AND INTERESTING--THIS 556 CROSS
WHIM OF HIS.
I HAVE BEEN ADVISED TO RUN FROM YOU BUT IT IS MY 321 GGBROW
ALMIGHTY WHIM TO DANCE INTO
(BORED) SOME NEW WHIM OF TIBERIUS, NATURALLY-- 314 LAZARU
(WITH A MEANING TITTER) --
IT IS MY WHIM/ 356 LAZARU
I WILL TAKE WHAT MY WHIM DESIRES FROM LIFE, AND 187 MANSNS
LAUGH AT THE COST/
OF COURSE, IF IT WERE MY WHIM-- (HER EYES FALL ON 192 MANSNS
SIMON.
WHIMPER
A LOUD FRIGHTENED WHIMPER SOUNDS FROM THE AWAKENED128 BEYOND
CHILD IN THE BEDROOM. IT CON
(IN A PITIFUL WHIMPER) CALEB/ 543 DIFRNT
TO WHIMPER YOUR FEAR TO HER RESIGNED HEART AND BE 289 LAZARU
COMFORTED BY HER RESIGNATION/
(HIS LAUGHTER SUDDENLY BREAKS OFF INTO A WHIMPER 357 LAZARU
AND
WHIMPERING
(WHIMPERING LIKE A CHILD) ANNA/ 59 ANNA
(WHIMPERING) OH, BENNY, YOU'RE ONLY JOKIN', AIN'T545 DIFRNT
YOUS
WHIMPERING WITH FEAR AS THE THROB OF THE TOM-TON 202 EJONES
FILLS THE SILENCE ABOUT HIM
THE MONKEYS SET UP A CHATTERING, WHIMPERING WAIL. 254 HA APE
AND WHIMPERING COMES FROM THE OTHER CAGES. 254 HA APE
(WHIMPERING LIKE A CHILD.) LET GO/ 165 MANSNS
(MARY RUNS OUT OF THE DOOR, WHIMPERING. 591 ROPE
(HE STEERS THE WHIMPERING, HYSTERICAL BENTLEY TO 597 ROPE
THE DOORWAY)
MARY SPRAWLS FORWARD ON HER HANDS AND KNEES, 601 ROPE
WHIMPERING.
WHIMPERINGLY
WHIMPERINGLY) 226 HA APE
WHIMS
HE SAID I COULD HAVE EQUAL LIBERTY TO INDULGE ANY 520 DAYS
OF MY SEXUAL WHIMS.
ON YOUR PERVERSE WHIMSS 36 MANSNS
(HE MOVES TOWARD HER WITH A SIGH OF HALF- 414 MARCOM
IMPATIENCE WITH HER WHIMS.)
AND I REFUSE TO GIVE UP HIS FRIENDSHIP FOR YOUR 456 WELDED
SILLY WHIMS.
WHIMSICAL
WILLIE INTERPOSES SOME DRUNKEN WHIMSICAL 596 ICEMAN
EXPOSITION TO LARRY)
CAN'T I BE WHIMSICAL, AS OF OLD, IF IT PLEASE MES 17 MANSNS

WHIMSICAL

WHIMSICAL (CONT'D.)
WHIMSICAL AND FANCIFUL. BUT ALWAYS A WELL-BRED 26 MANSNS
GENTLEWOMAN,
TO THE POINT OF WHIMSICAL ECCENTRICITY.) 68 POET
WHIMSICALITY
(THEN WITH A SUDDEN WHIMSICALITY) 363 MARCOM
WHIMSICALLY
EUROPE HAS *GONE WEST*---(HE SMILES WHIMSICALLY) 7 STRANG
TO AMERICA. LET'S HOPE/.

WHINE
(THE THROBBING WHINE OF A MOTOR SOUNDS FROM THE 153 BEYOND
DISTANCE OUTSIDE.)
(IN A COWARDLY WHINE) NO *ARM MEANT, OLD TOP. 176 EJONES
SWAYING ITS HEAD TO THE THIN, SHRILL WHINE OF A 369 MARCOM
GOURD.
SHE TALKS IN A HIGH-PITCHED, SING-SONG WHINE. 579 ROPE
(IN AN ANGRY WHINE, TUGGING AT HIS HAND) 591 ROPE
WHINE, STING, SUCK ONE'S BLOOD... 52 STRANG

WHINER
I'M BECOMING THE DAMNDEST WHINER AND SELF-PITIER. 517 DAYS

WHINEY
THEY'RE ALL TOO DARNED WHINEY. 901 DAYS

WHINING
AND THE PEEVISH WHINING OF A CHILD. 112 BEYOND
(THE WHINING CRYING OF THE CHILD SOUNDS FROM THE 116 BEYOND
KITCHEN.
AH, WHO CAN BLAME YOU FOR WHINING WHEN YOUR 501 DAYS
OMNIPOTENT GOLDEN CALF EXPLODES INTO
BY WHINING THAT THE TIME FOR INDIVIDUALISM IS 542 DAYS
PAST.
FROM WITHIN COMES THE WHINING OF THE FIDDLE AND 253 DESIRE
I'M A DARNED WHINING FOOL/ 82 ELECTR
THE PIANO IS WHINING OUT ITS SAME OLD SENTIMENTAL 284 GGBROW
MEDLEY.
OR HEAR MYSELF WHINING AND PRAYING.. 689 ICEMAN
WHERE HE COULDN'T COME WHINING TO ME THE MINUTE HE 35 JOURNE
WAS BROKE.
IS SWALLOWED AT ONE GULP LIKE A WHINING GNAT BY 358 LAZARU
THE CRETINS'S SILENCE OF
AND BECAME A BEGGAR, WHINING FOR ALMS FROM ALL WHO111 MANSNS
PASSED BY.
(WHINING) MAW/ 583 ROPE
AND ANNIE'S WHINING VOICE RAISED IN ANGRY 594 ROPE
PROTEST.)
(WHINING) I WANTER SWING. 600 ROPE
(STOP WHINING/... 92 STRANG

WHININGLY
(COMMENCING TO CRY WHININGLY) 117 BEYOND
(WHININGLY) YOU GOT TO SEE TO HIM, PAT. IF YOU 594 ROPE
WANT ANY SUPPER.
(AS HE SHAKES HIS HEAD--WHININGLY) 601 ROPE

WHIP
DRUV OFF CLACKIN' HIS TONGUE AN' WAVIN' HIS WHIP. 209 DESIRE
(HE TAPS HER BUNDLE WITH HIS RIDING WHIP 174 EJONES
SIGNIFICANTLY.)
SMITHERS RAISES HIS WHIP THREATENINGLY) 174 EJONES
HE CARRIES A RIDING WHIP IN HIS HAND. 174 EJONES
I CRACKS DE WHIP AND DEV JUMPS THROUGH. 179 EJONES
MAYBE HE HITS ME WID A WHIP AND I SPLITS HIS HEAD 181 EJONES
WID A SHOVEL AND RUNS AWAY AND
THE PRISON GUARD POINTS STERNLY AT JONES WITH HIS 194 EJONES
WHIP.
HE RAISES HIS WHIP AND LASHES JONES VICIOUSLY 194 EJONES
ACROSS THE SHOULDERS WITH IT.
(THE PRISON GUARD CRACKS HIS WHIP--NOISELESSLY-- 194 EJONES
A WINCHESTER RIFLE IS SLUNG ACROSS HIS SHOULDERS 194 EJONES
AND HE CARRIES A HEAVY WHIP.
WHEN CAT GUARD HITS ME WID DE WHIP, MY ANGER 196 EJONES
OVERCOMES ME, AND I KILLS HIM DEAD.
DEREK'S DE DAMN ENGINEER CRACKIN' DE WHIP. 223 HA APE
I'LL TAKE A WHIP. 125 POET
DON'T LET ME FORGET TO STOP AT THE BARN FOR MY 128 POET
WHIP.
HE'LL WHIP THEM BACK TO THEIR KENNELS, THE DIRTY 147 POET
CURS/
AND UGLY THE FLUNKY A CUT WITH HIS WHIP ACROSS HIS 155 POET
UGLY MUG THAT SET HIM
HE'D HAVE HAD ME DOWN ONLY CON BROKE THE BUTT AV 156 POET
THE WHIP OVER HIS BLACK SKULL.
I REMEMBER AT A FAIR IN THE AULD COUNTRY I WAS 161 POET
CLOUTED WITH THE BUTT AV A WHIP

WHIPCORD
HE IS DRESSED IN A BEAUTIFULLY TAILORED ENGLISH 56 MISBEG
TWEED COAT AND WHIPCORD RIDING

WHIPPING
I'LL SHOW HIM WHAT A REAL WHIPPING IS/ 452 DYNAMO

WHIPS
A MOMENT LATER, PRECEDED BY SHOUTS, A CRACKING OF 350 MARCOM
WHIPS,
OF TWO SOLDIERS WHO RUN BESIDE THEM AND THE LONG 350 MARCOM
WHIPS
(WITH A GREAT CRACKING OF WHIPS AND SHOUTS OF PAIN354 MARCOM

WHIRL
THEY WHIRL IN BETWEEN THE SOLDIERS AND CROWD, 306 LAZARU
FORCING THEM BACK FROM EACH OTHER.
(THEY BOTH WHIRL ON HIM WITH STARTLED GASPS OF 172 MANSNS
TERROR
A DERVISH OF THE DESERT RUNS IN SHRIEKING AND 368 MARCOM
BEGINS TO WHIRL.
THERE IS A CONFUSED WHIRL OF EMBRACES, KISSES, 429 MARCOM
BACK-SLAPS.

WHIRLED
CALIGULA HAS WHIRLED AROUND AND STANDS STARING, 333 LAZARU

WHIRLING
(HIS THOUGHTS WHIRLING IN HIS HEAD) 448 DYNAMO
OF HIS DYNAMO-MOTHER WITH ITS WHIRLING METAL BRAIN488 DYNAMO
AND ITS BLANK, OBLONG EYES.)
(WHIRLING ON HIM--DISTRACTEDLY) 151 ELECTR

WHIRLING (CONT'D.)
THE DUST IS WHIRLING WITH THE DUST. 159 JOURNE
THE DANCERS CAN BE SEEN WHIRLING SWIFTLY BY THE 281 LAZARU
WINDOWS.
THE SOUNDS OF BLOWS AS THEY MEET IN A PUSHING, 290 LAZARU
WHIRLING, STRUGGLING MASS
GLANCING OVER HIS SHOULDER AND WHIRLING AROUND 311 LAZARU
(DEBORAH GIVES A FRIGHTENED GASP, WHIRLING TO FACE 18 MANSNS
HER.)

WHIRLS
(WHIRLS ON HIM) WHAT ARE YOU DOING HERE, YOUNG 269 AHWILD
MAN?
(HE WHIRLS HER AROUND THE DECK BY MAIN FORCE. 471 CARIBE
ELECTRICITY OR SOMETHING, WHICH WHIRLS US--ON TO 542 DAYS
HERCULES/
(WHIRLS AROUND AND STANDS STARING AT HER WITH 481 DYNAMO
STRANGE FIXITY FOR A MOMENT.
LAVINIA SENSES HER PRESENCE AND WHIRLS AROUND. 15 ELECTR
HE WHIRLS DEFENSIVELY WITH A SNARLING, MURDEROUS 225 HA APE
GROWL, CROUCHING TO SPRING.
(SWORD IN HAND HE WHIRLS TO CONFRONT LAZARUS, 308 LAZARU
TIBERIUS SUDDENLY WHIRLS AROUND AS IF HE FELT A 340 LAZARU
DAGGER AT HIS BACK.
HE WHIRLS ABOUT, LOOKING AROUND HIM AS IF HE FELT 370 LAZARU
AN ASSASSIN AT HIS BACK.
(WHIRLS ON HIM UNSTEADILY) WHO THE HELL-- 100 MISBEG
(ROCHE WHIRLS AROUND TO FACE MELODY, AND HIS 52 POET
AGGRESSIVENESS OOZES FROM HIM.
(MELODY JUMPS AND WHIRLS AROUND. 68 POET
HE WHIRLS AROUND TO FACE HER--ANGRILY) 103 STRANG
(WHO IS STANDING NEXT TO NED, WHIRLS ON HIM IN A 181 STRANG
FURIOUS PASSION)

WHIRRING
AN IMITATION OF THE WHIRRING PURR OF THE DYNAMO.) 436 DYNAMO
(SHE HUMS HER IMITATION OF A DYNAMO'S WHIRRING 458 DYNAMO
PURR.)

WHISHT
WHISHT, NOW, ME SAIDY/ 33 ANNA
WHISHT, IS ITS 39 ANNA

WHISKER
HIS SHINY WRINKLED FACE IS OBLONG WITH A SQUARE 129 ELECTR
WHITE CHIN WHISKER.

WHISKERED
GRAY-WHISKERED AULD FOOL THE LOIKE AV HIM. 479 CARDIF
GRAY-WHISKERED AULD FOOL, AN THE MATES--AN' THE 463 CARIBE
ENGINEERS TOO, MAYBE.

WHISKERS
THE CAPTAIN IS AN OLD MAN WITH GRAY MUSTACHE AND 484 CARDIF
WHISKERS.
FACING YOURSELF IN THE MIRROR WITH THE OLD FALSE 641 ICEMAN
WHISKERS OFF.

WHISKEY
THEY GULP DOWN THEIR WHISKEY.) 4 ANNA
(JOHNNY SETS TWO GLASSES OF BARREL WHISKEY BEFORE 4 ANNA
THEM.)
GULPS DOWN HIS WHISKEY DESPERATELY AS IF SEEKING 10 ANNA
FOR COURAGE.
YOU'VE HAD TOO MUCH WHISKEY. 45 ELECTR
A BOTTLE OF WINE AND A BOTTLE C' BEER AND A 103 ELECTR
BOTTLE OF IRISH WHISKEY OH/
ON THE TABLE IS A BOTTLE OF WHISKEY, HALF FULL, 109 ELECTR
WATCH ME PERISH! FUR LACK O' WHISKEY AND YE KEEP130 ELECTR
FROZE TO THAT JUG.
AND A BOTTLE OF IRISH WHISKEY OH. 130 ELECTR
(HE GOES AND GETS A BOTTLE OF WHISKEY AND A 295 GGBROW
GLASS.)
A CHEAP GINMILL OF THE FIVE-CENT WHISKEY, LAST- 571 ICEMAN
RESORT VARIETY
BUT TIME AND WHISKEY HAVE MELTED IT DOWN INTO A 576 ICEMAN
GOOD-HUMORED.
BUT IMMEDIATELY RETURNS WITH A BOTTLE OF BAR 577 ICEMAN
WHISKEY AND A GLASS.
NICKEL WHISKEY ON ITS BREATH, AND THEIR SEA IS A 578 ICEMAN
GROWLER OF LAGER AND ALE.
AND, THANKS TO WHISKEY, HE'S THE ONLY ONE DOESN'T 579 ICEMAN
KNOW IT.
GULPS DOWN THE WHISKEY IN BIG SWALLOWS.) 582 ICEMAN
BUT I DISCOVERED THE LOOPHOLE OF WHISKEY AND 595 ICEMAN
ESCAPED HIS JURISDICTION.
(ABRUPTLY TO PARRITT) SPEAKING OF WHISKEY, SIR, 595 ICEMAN
REMINDS ME---
AS VESPASIAN REMARKED, THE SMELL OF ALL WHISKEY 15596 ICEMAN
SWEET.
GOOD WHISKEY, FIFTEEN CENTS, TWO FOR TWO BITS. 601 ICEMAN
HE GOES BEHIND THE BAR AND GETS A WHISKEY BOTTLE 611 ICEMAN
AND GLASSES AND CHAIRS.
ROCKY BEGINS SETTING OUT DRINKS, WHISKEY GLASSES 619 ICEMAN
WITH CHASERS.
(COMING TO HICKEY'S TABLE, PUTS A BOTTLE OF 620 ICEMAN
WHISKEY, A GLASS AND A CHASER ON IT--
BUT IF YOU DRINK A PINT OF BAD WHISKEY BEFORE 626 ICEMAN
BREAKFAST EVERY EVENING,
BOTTLES OF BAR WHISKEY ARE PLACED AT INTERVALS 628 ICEMAN
WITHIN REACH OF ANY SITTER.
A DRINK OF WHISKEY BEFORE HIM. 629 ICEMAN
ARMS ON TABLE, HEAD ON ARMS, A FULL WHISKEY GLASS 629 ICEMAN
BY HIS HEAD.
WHEN THERE WAS PLENTY OF WHISKEY HERE. 652 ICEMAN
WHO STARTS PLAYING AND SINGING IN A WHISKEY 653 ICEMAN
SOPRANO
AND A SHELF ON WHICH ARE BARRELS OF CHEAP WHISKEY 664 ICEMAN
ARMS AND HEAD ON THE TABLE AS USUAL, A WHISKEY 665 ICEMAN
GLASS BESIDE HIS LIMP HAND.
(HE GOES BEHIND THE BAR TO DRAW A GLASS OF WHISKEY670 ICEMAN
FROM A BARREL.)
(HE GLANCES WITH VENGEFUL YEARNING AT THE DRINK OF671 ICEMAN
WHISKEY IN HIS HAND)
(CHUCK SNATCHES A WHISKEY BOTTLE FROM THE BAR 672 ICEMAN

WHISKEY

WHISKEY (CONT'D.)		
HE DELIBERATELY THROWS HIS WHISKEY GLASS ON THE	673	ICEMAN
FLOOR AND SMASHES IT.) HEY/		
WHAT LEETLE BRAIN THE POOR LIMEY HAS LEFT, DOT	676	ICEMAN
ISN'T IN WHISKEY PICKLED.		
(BRUSHING THE WHISKEY OFF HIS COAT--HUMOROUSLY)	686	ICEMAN
SNEAKS TO THE BAR AND FURTIVELY REACHES FOR	686	ICEMAN
LARRY'S GLASS OF WHISKEY.)		
TWO BOTTLES OF WHISKEY ARE ON EACH TABLE, WHISKEY 696		ICEMAN
AND CHASER GLASSES.		
YOU'VE THROWN YOUR SALARY AWAY EVERY WEEK ON	31	JOURNE
WHORES AND WHISKEY/		
HERE'S THE WHISKEY.	51	JOURNE
SEVERAL WHISKEY GLASSES, AND A PITCHER OF ICE	51	JOURNE
WATER.		
HAVE HIS DROP OF WHISKEY IF HE HAD A WATCH TO HIS	52	JOURNE
NAME/		
AND POURS THEM IN THE WHISKEY BOTTLE AND SHAKES IT	54	JOURNE
UP.)		
HE COMES TO THE TABLE WITH A QUICK MEASURING LOOK	65	JOURNE
AT THE BOTTLE OF WHISKEY.		
IT'S BEFORE A MEAL AND I'VE ALWAYS FOUND THAT GOOD	65	JOURNE
WHISKEY,		
HE THOUGHT, LIKE YOU, THAT WHISKEY IS A GOOD	67	JOURNE
TONIC/		
(HER EYES BECOME FIXED ON THE WHISKEY GLASS ON THE	67	JOURNE
TABLE BESIDE HIM--SHARPLY.)		
THE TRAY WITH THE BOTTLE OF WHISKEY HAS BEEN	71	JOURNE
REMOVED FROM THE TABLE.		
THE TRAY WITH THE BOTTLE OF WHISKEY, GLASSES,	97	JOURNE
SHE HOLDS AN EMPTY WHISKEY GLASS IN HER HAND AS IF	97	JOURNE
SHE'D FORGOTTEN SHE HAD IT.		
AND YOU CAN TAKE A BIG DRINK OF WHISKEY TO HER	100	JOURNE
WHEN YOU GO.		
HERE'S THE WHISKEY, DEAR.	108	JOURNE
I'M SURE THEY HONESTLY BELIEVED WHISKEY IS THE	111	JOURNE
HEALTHIEST MEDICINE		
YOUR REMEDY WAS TO GIVE HIM A TEASPOONFUL OF	111	JOURNE
WHISKEY TO QUIET HIM.		
EDMUND AT ONCE REALIZES HOW MUCH THE WHISKEY HAS	111	JOURNE
BEEN WATERED.		
WHO'S BEEN TAMPERING WITH MY WHISKEYS	116	JOURNE
HE'S REALLY ASHAMED OF KEEPING HIS WHISKEY	117	JOURNE
PADLOCKED IN THE CELLAR.		
(TO EDMUND.) I'LL GET A FRESH BOTTLE OF WHISKEY,	117	JOURNE
LADY.		
WITH A BOTTLE OF WHISKEY HE HAS JUST UNCORKED.	121	JOURNE
BUT DESPITE ALL THE WHISKEY IN HIM, HE HAS NOT	125	JOURNE
ESCAPED.		
THE WHISKEY BOTTLE ON THE TRAY IS THREE-QUARTERS	125	JOURNE
EMPTY.		
IF HE'S EVER HAD A LOFTIER DREAM THAN WHORES AND	129	JOURNE
WHISKEY, HE'S NEVER SHOWN IT.		
IT'S A GOOD LIKENESS OF JAMIE, DON'T YOU THINK,	134	JOURNE
HUNTED BY HIMSELF AND WHISKEY.		
BUT, OF COURSE, THAT WAS IN BARROOMS, WHEN I WAS	146	JOURNE
FULL OF WHISKEY.		
(HE GULPS DOWN THE WHISKEY.)	146	JOURNE
(HIS EYES FIX ON THE FULL BOTTLE OF WHISKEY.)	155	JOURNE
AND OFFER HIM A DRINK OF THE GOOD WHISKEY YOU	25	MISBEG
DIDN'T KEEP FOR COMPANY.		
JIM PROMISES WHATEVER YOU LIKE WHEN HE'S FULL OF	31	MISBEG
WHISKEY.		
(IGNORING THIS) AND WHISKEY SEEMS TO HAVE NO	33	MISBEG
EFFECT ON HIM.		
THEN IT MUST BE THE AIR ITSELF SMELLS OF WHISKEY	45	MISBEG
TODAY.		
I WAS JUST GOING TO OFFER YOU A DRINK, BUT WHISKEY	45	MISBEG
IS THE WORST THING--		
WHISKEY, AND THERE'S POISON IVY, AND TICKS AND	63	MISBEG
POTATO BUGS.		
(HE GETS THE BOTTLE OF WHISKEY)	65	MISBEG
YOU DIDN'T GET THE D. T.'S FROM MY WHISKEY, I KNOW	65	MISBEG
THAT.		
(EXASPERATEDLY) WILL YOU STOP YOUR WHISKEY	75	MISBEG
DROOLING AND TALK PLAINS		
AND STOP YOUR WHISKEY GABBLE ABOUT JIM.	79	MISBEG
IT'S THE FIRST TIME I EVER SAW YOU SO PARALYZED	81	MISBEG
YOU COULDN'T SNAKE THE WHISKEY!		
HE WENT TO THE INN AND STARTED DRINKING WHISKEY.	82	MISBEG
HE'S WEAK, WITH ONE FOOT IN THE GRAVE FROM	86	MISBEG
WHISKEY.		
(ANGRILY) AND LOOK AT YOU, YOUR BRAINS DROWNED IN	91	MISBEG
WHISKEY.		
BUT YOU'LL HAVE TO GET A PILE OF WHISKEY DOWN HIM.	93	MISBEG
SHE HAS A QUART OF WHISKEY UNDER HER ARM, TWO	111	MISBEG
TUMBLERS, AND A PITCHER OF WATER.		
(SHE POURS A TUMBLER HALF FULL OF WHISKEY AND	112	MISBEG
HANDS IT TO HIM)		
AND I WON'T TAKE ANY MORE WHISKEY.	122	MISBEG
IF MY POOR OLD FATHER HAD SEEN YOU KNOCKING HIS	123	MISBEG
PRIZE WHISKEY ON THE GROUND--		
(HE DRINKS HIS WHISKEY AS IF TO WASH A BAD TASTE	129	MISBEG
FROM HIS MOUTH--		
IN A KIND OF DAZE, AS IF THE MOON WAS IN YOUR WITS170		MISBEG
AS WELL AS WHISKEY.		
(HE GOES TO THE CUPBOARD AND TAKES OUT A DECANTER	9	POET
OF WHISKEY AND A GLASS.)		
GOD BLESS YOU, WHISKEY, IT'S YOU CAN ROUSE THE	9	POET
DEAD/		
I MUST HAVE SAID MORE THAN MY PRAYERS, WITH THE	10	POET
LASHINGS OF WHISKEY IN ME.		
YOU COULD HAVE ALL THE WHISKEY YOU COULD POUR DOWN	10	POET
YOU.		
HE'S STRONG AS A BULL STILL FOR ALL THE WHISKEY	15	POET
HE'S DRUNK.		
HE, AT LEAST, KNOWS TALAVERA IS NOT THE NAME OF A	57	POET
NEW BRAND OF WHISKEY.		

WHISPER

WHISKEY (CONT'D.)		
I'D RATHER HAVE FREE WHISKEY GO DOWN HIS GULLET	59	POET
THAN THE OTHERS'.		
THEN ABRUPTLY THE SMELL OF WHISKEY ON HIS BREATH	71	POET
BRINGS HER TO HERSELF.		
YOU REEK OF WHISKEY/	72	POET
THE THREE AT THE TABLE HAVE A DECANTER OF WHISKEY.	95	POET
(HE SLOSHES WHISKEY FROM THE DECANTER INTO BOTH	100	POET
THEIR GLASSES.)		
I DIDN'T MEAN--THE WHISKEY TALKING--AS YOU SAID.	107	POET
I DON'T WANT TO LISTEN TO THE WHISKEY IN YOU	107	POET
BOASTING OF WHAT NEVER HAPPENED--		
MY BRAIN IS A BIT ADDLED BY WHISKEY--AS YOU SAID.	115	POET
HE HAS A DECANTER OF WHISKEY AND A GLASS IN HIS	133	POET
HAND.		
A TASTE OF WHISKEY WOULD BRING HIM BACK, IF HE'D	153	POET
ONLY TAKE IT, BUT HE WON'T.		
(HE DOWNS THE WHISKEY, AND POURS OUT ANOTHER--TO	154	POET
NORA AND SARA.)		
AS LONG AS A DRINK OF WHISKEY WAS LEFT IN THE	166	POET
WORLD/		
AND MAYBE YOU'RE RIGHT NOT TO TRUST ME TOO NEAR	175	POET
THE WHISKEY.		
BUT HE'LL SING AND LAUGH AND DRINK A POWER AV	180	POET
WHISKEY AND SLAPE SOUND AFTER.		
AN' THE WHISKEY LOOSENED HIS TONGUE TILL HE'D TOLD985		ROPE
ALL HE KNEW.		
(HE TAKES A FULL QUART FLASK OF WHISKEY FROM THE	587	ROPE
POCKET OF HIS COAT)		
BENTLEY GULPS. THE WHISKEY DRIPS OVER HIS CHIN,	595	ROPE
WHISKEY FOR THE THREE AV US--IRISH WHISKEY/	497	VOYAGE
AN' IRISH WHISKEY FOR THE REST AV US--	500	VOYAGE
WHISKEYS	503	VOYAGE
IRISH WHISKEY, YE SWAB.	503	VOYAGE
(TO JOE) GIVE ME WHISKEY, IRISH WHISKEY/	508	VOYAGE
WHISKIES		
(THEY START AND GULP DOWN THEIR WHISKIES AND POUR	625	ICEMAN
ANOTHER.		
WHISKY		
HALF-BARRELS OF CHEAP WHISKY OF THE =NICKEL-A-	3	ANNA
SHOT= VARIETY.		
GIMME A WHISKY--GINGER ALE ON THE SIDE.	14	ANNA
(DOWNING HER PORT AT A GULP LIKE A DRINK OF	24	ANNA
WHISKY--HER LIPS TREMBLING)		
(COMES OUT OF THE CABIN WITH A TUMBLER QUARTER-	31	ANNA
FULL OF WHISKY IN HER HAND,		
AND I'LL BE DRINKING SLUDS OF WHISKY	61	ANNA
I'LL GET HER SOME WHISKY.	548	DAYS
(HE DOES SO--GETS TWO GLASSES--THEY POUR OUT	217	DESIRE
DRINKS OF WHISKY)		
IS STANDING NEAR THE REAR DOOR WHERE THERE IS A	247	DESIRE
SMALL KEG OF WHISKY		
(HE POURS WHISKY FOR HIMSELF AND FIDDLER.	251	DESIRE
WHISKY, THAT'S THE TICKET/	204	HA APE
SING US THAT WHISKY SONG, PADDY.	209	HA APE
WHISKY/	210	HA APE
WHISKY/	210	HA APE
(AGAIN CHORUS.) =OH, WHISKY DROVE MY OLD MAN MAD/	210	HA APE
=WHISKY JOHNNY= YE WANTS	210	HA APE
OH, WHISKY DROVE MY OLD MAN MAD/	210	HA APE
(THEY ALL JOIN IN ON THIS.) OH, WHISKY IS THE LIFE210		HA APE
OF MAN/		
WHISKY FOR MY JOHNNY/	210	HA APE
WHISKY FOR MY JOHNNY/=	210	HA APE
=OH, WHISKY IS THE LIFE OF MAN/	210	HA APE
WHISPER		
(GOING OVER TO HIM--IN A HALF-WHISPER)	537	'ILE
(SWALLOWING HARD--IN A HOARSE WHISPER, AS IF HE	551	'ILE
HAD DIFFICULTY IN SPEAKING)		
WELL, I DIDN'T NEED ANY LITTLE BIRD TO WHISPER	190	AHWILD
THAT YOU'D BEEN SOME PLACE		
(AT A NOISE FROM THE BACK PARLOR, LOOKS THAT WAY--206		AHWILD
IN A WHISPER)		
YOU NEEDN'T WHISPER, MID.	221	AHWILD
(SUDDENLY IN A HOARSE WHISPER TO HIS MOTHER,	231	AHWILD
(IN A HOARSE, CONFIDENTIAL WHISPER)	232	AHWILD
(IN A WHISPER) IT'S RICHARD--	292	AHWILD
CONFIDENTIAL HALF-WHISPER WITH SOMETHING VAGUELY	5	ANNA
PLAINTIVE IN ITS QUALITY.		
(TO LARRY IN AN ALARMED WHISPER)	10	ANNA
(TO ANNA IN A HURRIED, NERVOUS WHISPER)	19	ANNA
(IN A HALF WHISPER, EMBARRASSEDLY)	23	ANNA
IN A HUSHED WHISPER)	25	ANNA
(SPELLBOUND, IN A WHISPER) YES.	90	BEYOND
(HER VOICE SINKS TO A TREMULOUS, TENDER WHISPER AS139		BEYOND
SHE FINISHES.)		
(HIS VOICE IS LOWERED TO A TREMBLING	147	BEYOND
WHISPER)		
(IN A HUSHED WHISPER) WE'D BEST NOT BE TALKIN'	50478	CARDIF
(IN A HUSHED WHISPER) GAWD BLIMEY/	490	CARDIF
THEY EVEN WHISPER THE HOUSE IS HAUNTED.	564	CROSS
(WHO HAS TAKEN A CHAIR BY HER BROTHER--IN A	570	CROSS
WARNING WHISPER)		
SHE SPEAKS WITHOUT OPENING HER EYES, HARDLY ABOVE	554	DAYS
A WHISPER.		
SHARPLY BUT IN A VOICE JUST ABOVE A WHISPER)	555	DAYS
THE NURSE GETS UP AND HE SPEAKS TO HER IN A	558	DAYS
WHISPER.		
(MISREADING HIS LOOK--IN A FRIGHTENED WHISPER)	563	DAYS
(IN A WHISPER) SEEMS LIKE MAW DIDN'T WANT ME T'	242	DESIRE
REMIND YE.		
(THEN IN A WHISPER, WITH A NUDGE AND A LEER)	248	DESIRE
A WHISPER GOES AROUND THE ROOM.	252	DESIRE
(IN A SNARLING WHISPER) THAT'S RIGHT/	529	DIFRNT
(WITH A SLY GRIN--IN A WHISPER)	529	DIFRNT
(STARING AT HER WITH STUNNED EYES-- IN A HOARSE	542	DIFRNT
WHISPER)		
(FINALLY, IN A SHRILL WHISPER)	544	DIFRNT

WHISPER

WHISPER (CONT'D.)
(IN A FIERCE WHISPER AS HE PASSES EMMA) 547 DIFRNT
(THEN IN A STRANGE WHISPER) WAIT, CALEB, I'M 549 DIFRNT
GOING DOWN TO THE BARN.
IN A HURRIED WHISPER TO REUBEN) SHE'S COMING/ 459 DYNAMO
(HIS STRENGTH FAILING HIM--IN A FALTERING TONE 463 DYNAMO
HARDLY ABOVE A WHISPER)
IN A TERRIFIED WHISPER) 488 DYNAMO
(LOWERING HER VOICE ALMOST TO A WHISPER--TO HER 9 ELECTR
HUSBAND)
(IN AN AWED WHISPER) MY/ 9 ELECTR
(IN A QUICK WHISPER TO MINNIE) 11 ELECTR
HE TRIES TO CALL FOR HELP BUT HIS VOICE FADES TO A 62 ELECTR
WHEEZY WHISPER)
(LOWERING HER VOICE TO A WHISPER) 86 ELECTR
(STARING AT HIM--IN A WHISPER) 89 ELECTR
(IN A QUICK WHISPER) DON'T LET HER KNOW YOU 100 ELECTR
SUSPECT HER.
(IN A WHISPER) ANSWER HER. 100 ELECTR
(IN A FURIOUS WHISPER) LET ME GO/ 113 ELECTR
(HER EYES CAUGHT BY SOMETHING DOWN THE DRIVE--IN ALL9 ELECTR
TENSE WHISPER)
(HARDLY ABOVE A WHISPER) YES. 142 ELECTR
IN A WHISPER AS IF TO HERSELF) 147 ELECTR
(THEN IN AN EXCITED WHISPER, COMING TO THEM) 159 ELECTR
(TEMPTED AND TORTURED, IN A LONGING WHISPER) 165 ELECTR
(IN A PITIFUL PLEADING WHISPER) 166 ELECTR
(WITH A FINAL PLEADING WHISPER) 266 GGBROW
DION'S VOICE AT FIRST IN A WHISPER, 267 GGBROW
HIS FACE LIGHTED UP FROM WITHIN BUT PAINFULLY 269 GGBROW
CONFUSED--IN AN UNCERTAIN WHISPER)
HE SPRINGS LIGHTLY TO THE SIDE OF THE PETRIFIED 318 GGBROW
DRAFTSMEN--IN A WHISPER)
*TIS A DEAD MAN'S WHISPER. 214 HA APE
LARRY ADDS IN A COMICALLY INTENSE, CRAZY WHISPER) 581 ICEMAN
(IN A SARDONIC WHISPER TO PARRITT) 603 ICEMAN
(ALOUD TO HIMSELF--IN HIS COMICALLY TENSE, CRAZY 605 ICEMAN
WHISPER)
IN HIS COMICALLY INTENSE, CRAZY WHISPER) 623 ICEMAN
(THEN IN HIS COMICALLY INTENSE, CRAZY WHISPER) 626 ICEMAN
IN HIS COMICALLY INTENSE, CRAZY WHISPER) 634 ICEMAN
(GIVES A SARDONIC GUFFAW--WITH HIS COMICALLY 677 ICEMAN
CRAZY, INTENSE WHISPER)
(AS CHUCK LOOKS AT HIM WITH DULL SURPRISE HE 698 ICEMAN
LOWERS HIS VOICE TO A WHISPER)
(HIS EYES FULL OF PAIN AND PITY--IN A WHISPER, 719 ICEMAN
ALOUD TO HIMSELF)
(TORTUREDL ARGUING TO HIMSELF IN A SHAKEN 726 ICEMAN
WHISPER)
(IN A WHISPER OF HORRIFIED PITY) 726 ICEMAN
I JUST SAYS=EIGHT BELLS, SMITTY* IN ALMOST A 521 INZONE
WHISPER-LIKE.
(A SIMPLE BOY--IN A FRIGHTENED WHISPER AFTER A 275 LAZARU
PAUSE OF DEAD SILENCE)
IN A VOICE THAT IS LIKE A LOVING WHISPER OF HOPE 279 LAZARU
AND CONFIDENCE)
IN A QUEER WHISPER) 305 LAZARU
(WHO HAS MOVED TO LAZARUS' SIDE DEFENSIVELY--IN A 332 LAZARU
QUICK WHISPER)
(THEN IN A QUEER AWED WHISPER) 334 LAZARU
(NUDGING POMPEIA--WITH A CRAFTY WHISPER) 355 LAZARU
OR WHISPER IT IN THE KISS TO ONE'S BELOVED. 355 LAZARU
(IN THIS WHISPER) THAT IS IT/ 363 LAZARU
GROUP AGAIN, STARING AFTER HIM, AND A WHISPER OF 363 LAZARU
STRANGE, BEWILDERED,
(GLANCING AT SIMON RESENTFULLY--LOWERING HER VOICE125 MANSNS
TO A WHISPER.)
(SLOWLY, HARDLY ABOVE A WHISPER, BUT WITH A 131 MANSNS
TAUNTING,
EVERYONE IS GETTING TO KNOW--TO SMIRK AND WHISPER/142 MANSNS
IT WOULD TAKE ONLY A RUMOR--A WHISPER SPOKEN IN 142 MANSNS
THE RIGHT EAR.
STRICKENLY, IN A GUILTY WHISPER.) 144 MANSNS
THAT A WHISPER, A HINT OF THE TRUTH, 156 MANSNS
I KNOW ONLY TOO WELL HOW TEMPTED YOU ARE TO 157 MANSNS
WHISPER AND START THE RUMOR OF THE
IN A WHISPER.) 160 MANSNS
(IN A SHUDDERING WHISPER.) SIMON/ 179 MANSNS
IN A BOYISH UNEASY WHISPER, TUGGING AT DEBORAH'S 188 MANSNS
HAND.)
IN AN AWED, HORRIFIED WHISPER.) 190 MANSNS
IT NEEDS ONLY A WHISPER OF THE TRUE CONDITION TO 191 MANSNS
TENARD.
THAT REMINDS ME, BEFORE I START THE WHISPER, 191 MANSNS
(STARTS AND STARES AT HER--IN AN AWED WHISPER.) 192 MANSNS
(IN A AWED WHISPER) IN THE PALACE I COMMANDED THE352 MARCOM
COMPANY
(IN A WHISPER) I LOVE YOU. THERE, SILLY/ 356 MARCOM
YOU'LL BE ABLE TO WHISPER TO US IN TIME TO TAKE 381 MARCOM
ADVANTAGE--
(THEN VERY CONFIDENTIALLY--IN A HUMOROUS WHISPER) 399 MARCOM
(IN A LONG ULULATING WHISPER) 405 MARCOM
(IN A WHISPER) DON'T BE AFRAID. 417 MARCOM
WHISPER YOUR SECRET IN MY EAR. 438 MARCOM
(IN AN OMINOUS WHISPER) DID YOU SAY HARDER IS 47 MISBEG
COMING TO CALL ON US, JIM*
(HE TURNS TO JOSIE--IN A WHISPER) 59 MISBEG
(IN A HOARSE WHISPER) MEET ME TONIGHT, AS USUAL, 64 MISBEG
DOWN BY THE PIGPEN.
IN SPITE OF HIMSELF, HE IS STARTLED--IN AN AWED, 158 MISBEG
ALMOST FRIGHTENED WHISPER)
(SEES THE DOOR AT LEFT FRONT BEGIN TO OPEN--IN A 88 POET
WHISPER.)
IN A SNEERING WHISPER.) 100 POET
(IN A WHISPER.) I'VE GOT HIM IN A RIG OUTSIDE, 151 POET
(SHE BEGINS TO TREMBLE--IN A HORRIFIED WHISPER.) 163 POET
IN AN ECSTATIC WHISPER) 43 STRANG
THEN GOD WOULD WHISPER.. 63 STRANG

WHISPER (CONT'D.)
(CONFUSEDLY--IN A HALF-WHISPER) 64 STRANG
(THEN IN A TRIUMPHANT WHISPER) 97 STRANG
IN A WHISPER) 106 STRANG
(THEN IN A STRANGE HALF-WHISPER) 133 STRANG
THEY WHISPER TOGETHER EXCITEDLY.) 504 VOYAGE
(APE STAMMERS IN A FIERCE WHISPER) 949 WELDED
WHISPERED
(FEARFULLY--LIKE A WHISPERED ECHO) 565 CROSS
(STILLWELL GETS UP AND, AFTER EXCHANGING A 554 DAYS
WHISPERED WORD WITH THE NURSE,
FOR A MOMENT AFTER THE CURTAIN RISES THE WHISPERED554 DAYS
PANTOMIME BETWEEN STILLWELL
(SHE PAUSES--THEN LOWERING HER VOICE TO A STRANGE 93 JOURNE
TONE OF WHISPERED CONFIDENCE.)
SHE WHISPERED TO AUGUSTUS AND HE ORDERED ME TO 356 LAZARU
DIVORCE AGRIPINA.
THE POLOS GROUP TOGETHER IN THE FOREGROUND, 362 MARCOM
HOLDING A WHISPERED CONFERENCE.
(THE ALI BROTHERS HAVE SEEN THE POLOS AND A 365 MARCOM
WHISPERED ASIDE.
(TO HIS UNCLE--IN A WHISPERED CHUCKLE) 372 MARCOM
JOE BRINGS THEM THREE BEERS, AND THERE IS A 506 VOYAGE
WHISPERED CONSULTATION.
WHISPERER
THAT'S WHAT I'VE BEEN, NINA--A HUSH-HUSH WHISPERER176 STRANG
OF LIES/
WHISPERIN'
UT HAS TO DO WID THE LADIES SO I'D BEST BE 465 CARIBE
WHISPERIN' UT TO YE MESELF
WHISPERING
(WHISPERING) HOW'S YANKS 483 CARDIF
ENTER FROM THE LEFT, GIGGLING AND WHISPERING TO 464 CARIBE
EACH OTHER.
(FIERCELY) I CAN KEEP UP HIS MAD GAME WITH ME-- 566 CROSS
WHISPERING DREAMS IN MY EAR--
(THEIR VOICES DIE TO AN INTENSIVE WHISPERING. 252 DESIRE
THERE'S A LOT OF WHISPERING IN THE HALL... 436 DYNAMO
(WHISPERING) GEE, HE'S STILL NUTTY. 241 HA APE
(CALCULATINGLY SOLICITOUS--WHISPERING TO HOPE) 608 ICEMAN
(TO JOE, WHO IS STILL WHISPERING INSTRUCTIONS TO 505 VOYAGE
NICK)
WHISPERS
MA, UNCLE SID'S--(SHE WHISPERS IN HER EAR.) 220 AHWILD
(SUE HIDES HER FACE IN HER HANDS--A PAUSE--NAT 564 CROSS
WHISPERS HOARSELY)
HE BENDS OVER AND WHISPERS MOCKINGLY.) 528 DAYS
HE IS CONFERRING IN WHISPERS WITH DOCTOR 553 DAYS
STILLWELL.
(HE WHISPERS TO FATHER BAIRD, HIS EYES ON JOHN. 554 DAYS
AND WHISPERS SOME ORDERS TO THE NURSE.) 564 DAYS
HE WHISPERS) 534 DIFRNT
LOUISA PRODS HER COUSIN AND WHISPERS EXCITEDLY) 8 ELECTR
(BUT HE WHISPERS QUICKLY TO MINNIE) 9 ELECTR
AFTER THE OTHERS DISAPPEAR, HE WHISPERS WITH A 71 ELECTR
MEANING GRIN.)
(SHE WHISPERS LIKE A LITTLE GIRL) 264 GGBROW
MARGIE WHISPERS) YUH SAP, DON'T YUH KNOW ENOUGH 613 ICEMAN
NOT TO KID HIM ON DATS
(MORAN GIVES HIM A CURIOUS LOOK, THEN WHISPERS TO 708 ICEMAN
LIEB.
FORSAKEN EYES AND WHISPERS TO HERSELF.) 95 JOURNE
TYRONE WHISPERS.) 138 JOURNE
WATCHING LAZARUS WITH FRIGHTENED AWE, TALKING 273 LAZARU
HESITANTLY IN LOW WHISPERS.
(SHE WHISPERS IN CAESAR'S EAR AND POINTS TO MIRIAM345 LAZARU
AND THE FRUIT IN HER HAND)
I WALK WITH THE KING IN THE GARDENS--HE WHISPERS 4 MANSNS
TENDERLY...
AND ALL DURING THE FOLLOWING SCENE TALK IN 125 MANSNS
WHISPERS, THEIR EYES FIXED ON SIMON.)
(HE LEANS TOWARD HER AND WHISPERS) 88 MISBEG
(SHE WHISPERS TENDERLY) COME. 137 MISBEG
THEN SHE REALIZES AND WHISPERS SOFTLY) 153 MISBEG
(TURNS ON HER FATHER ANGRILY AND WHISPERS) 161 MISBEG
(SHE TAKES HOLD OF HER ARM--WHISPERS UNEASILY.) 130 POET
(HE KISSES HER AND WHISPERS) 156 STRANG
AND LOVERS WHO AVOID LOVE IN HUSHED WHISPERS/ 176 STRANG
AND COMES UP TO JOE AND WHISPERS IN HIS EAR. 498 VOYAGE
WHISTLE
BEGINNING TO WHISTLE *OH, WALTZ ME AROUND AGAIN, 187 AHWILD
EVEN ATTEMPTING TO WHISTLE *WAITING AT THE 208 AHWILD
CHURCH.*
BUT THE WHISTLE PETERS OUT MISERABLY AS HIS 208 AHWILD
MOTHER,
A LOW WHISTLE COMES FROM JUST OUTSIDE THE PORCH 217 AHWILD
DOOR.
(WITH A WHISTLE) PHEW/ 248 AHWILD
HE ATTEMPTS TO WHISTLE A FEW BARS OF *YOSEPHINE* 10 ANNA
WITH CARELESS BRAVADO.
BUT THE WHISTLE PETERS OUT FUTILELY. 11 ANNA
LARRY LETS A LUNG, LOW WHISTLE ESCAPE HIM AND 24 ANNA
TURNS AWAY EMBARRASSEDLY.)
OR IS IT THINKING I'D BE FRIGHTENED BY THAT OLD 69 ANNA
TIN WHISTLES
AND THEN THEY TELLS THE FISH TO WHISTLE TO 'EM 95 BEYOND
WHEN IT'S TIME TO TURN OUT.
THE BLAST OF THE STEAMER'S WHISTLE CAN BE HEARD 477 CARDIF
ABOVE ALL THE OTHER SOUNDS.
THE STEAMER'S WHISTLE SOUNDS PARTICULARLY LOUD IN 481 CARDIF
THE SILENCE.)
WITH THAT DAMNED WHISTLE BLOWIN' AND PEOPLE 489 CARDIF
SHOUTIN' ALL ROUNDS
WHO DARE WHISTLE DAT WAY IN MY PALACES 176 EJONES
(HE STARTS TO WHISTLE BUT CHECKS HIMSELF ABRUPTLY)191 EJONES
(A WHISTLE IS BLOWN-- 223 HA APE
THEN THE INEXORABLE WHISTLE SOUNDS AGAIN 224 HA APE
HIM AND HIS WHISTLE, DEY 224 HA APE

WHITE

WHISTLE (CONT'D.)
TOIN OFF DAT WHISTLE/
PULLIN' DAT WHISTLE ON ME, HUH$
HE BLINKS UPWARD THROUGH THE MURK TRYING TO FIND
THE OWNER OF THE WHISTLE,
(HE IS TURNING. TO GET COAL WHEN THE WHISTLE SOUNDS225 HA APE
AGAIN IN A PEREMPTORY,
FROM OVERHEAD THE WHISTLE SOUNDS AGAIN IN A LONG, 226 HA APE
ANGRY, INSISTENT COMMAND.)
I WAS BAWLIN' HIM OUT FOR PULLIN' DE WHISTLE ON 230 HA APE
US.

225 HA APE
225 HA APE
225 HA APE

WHISTLED
IT WAS ME WHISTLED TO YER. 176 EJONES

WHISTLES
(HAS BEEN READING THE SLIPS, A BROAD GRIN ON HIS 205 AHWILD
FACE--SUDDENLY HE WHISTLES)
COMES THE SOUND OF STEAMERS' WHISTLES AND THE 41 ANNA
PUFFING SNORT OF THE DONKEY
THE WHISTLES OF STEAMERS IN THE HARBOR CAN BE 63 ANNA
HEARD.
FROM THE HARBOR COMES THE MUFFLED, MOURNFUL WAIL 78 ANNA
OF STEAMERS' WHISTLES.)
HE WHISTLES, GOES THROUGH THE MOTIONS OF DANCING 519 DIFRNT
TO THE MUSIC,
AND WHISTLES SHRILLY WITH HIS FINGERS IN HIS 175 EJONES
MOUTH.
I'M SMOKE AND EXPRESS TRAINS AND STEAMERS AND 216 HA APE
FACTORY WHISTLES,
(MANY POLICE WHISTLES SHRILL OUT ON THE INSTANT 239 HA APE
(THE WHISTLES AND SIRENS FROM THE YACHTS UP THE 176 STRANG
RIVER BEGIN TO BE HEARD.
THE NOISE FROM THE WHISTLES IS NOW VERY LOUD. 180 STRANG

WHISTLIN'
WHAT YO' WHISTLIN' FOR, YOU PO' DOPE/ 191 EJONES
WHISTLIN' A LOVE TUNE TO HIMSELF, DREAMIN' OF 19 MANSNS
ANOTHER WOMAN/

WHISTLING
BUT THERE WAS A STAKE OUT WHERE THE WHISTLING BUOY229 AHWILD
IS NOW, ABOUT A MILE OUT.
AND SOMEONE WHISTLING =WALTZ ME AROUND AGAIN, 253 AHWILD
WILLIE=)
(A MOMENT LATER ARTHUR ENTERS THROUGH THE FRONT 253 AHWILD
PARLOR, WHISTLING SOFTLY.
(THEN, HER LIPS TREMBLING) RICHARD'S ALWAYS 258 AHWILD
WHISTLING THAT.
WHISTLING WITH INSOUCIANCE = WAITING AT THE 277 AHWILD
CHURCH.=
BUT HE RESOLUTELY GOES ON WHISTLING WITH BACK 278 AHWILD
TURNED.
(HE RETURNS TO THE BAR, WHISTLING. 9 ANNA
(A MOMENT LATER ANDREW COMES UP FROM THE LEFT, 130 BEYOND
WHISTLING CHEERFULLY.
WHISTLING IN THE DARK, AND I SEE HE'S STILL ONLY 501 DAYS
OUT OF SHORT PANTS, A WHILE,
WITH STUDIED CARELESSNESS, WHISTLING A TUNE, 187 EJONES
WHISTLING WITH ELABORATE NONCHALANCE.) 132 ELECTR
(SHE SEES SETH APPROACHING; WHISTLING LOUDLY, FROM137 ELECTR
LEFT, REAR,
(THEN WITH A CHUCKLE) LISTEN TO HIM WHISTLING TO 137 ELECTR
KEEP HIS COURAGE UP/
(HE GOES, WHISTLING, SLAMMING THE DOOR.) 288 GGBROW
OPENS IT AT RANDOM AND BEGINS TO READ ALOUD 23 STRANG
SONOROUSLY LIKE A CHILD WHISTLING TO
(HE STROLLS OVER TO THE WINDOW WHISTLING WITH AN 55 STRANG
EXAGGERATEDLY CASUAL AIR,

WHITE
THE WALLS OF THE CABIN ARE PAINTED WHITE. 535 'ILE
THE WALLS ARE PAPERED WHITE WITH A CHEERFUL, UGLY 185 AHWILD
BLUE DESIGN,
AND I TURNED AND THERE WAS RED, HIS FACE ALL 230 AHWILD
PINCHED AND WHITE,
ON THE BEACH, AT CENTER, FRONT, A WHITE, FLAT- 275 AHWILD
BOTTOMED ROWBOAT IS DRAWN UP,
WITH HIS PALE, THIN, CLEAN-SHAVEN FACE, MILD BLUE 3 ANNA
EYES AND WHITE HAIR,
IN THE FAR LEFT CORNER, A LARGE LOCKER CLOSET, 41 ANNA
PAINTED WHITE,
WHITE CURTAINS, CLEAN AND STIFF, ARE AT THE 41 ANNA
WINDOWS.
WITH WHITE TRIMMINGS. 41 ANNA
(HE SINKS SLOWLY BACK IN HIS CHAIR AGAIN, THE 57 ANNA
KNUCKLES SHOWING WHITE
SHE WEARS A SIMPLE WHITE DRESS BUT NO HAT.) 87 BEYOND
WITH A WEATHER-BEATEN, JOVIAL FACE AND A WHITE 94 BEYOND
MUSTACHE--
AN ANDREW SIXTY-FIVE YEARS OLD WITH A SHORT, 94 BEYOND
SQUARE, WHITE BEARD.
IT'S ALL PAINTED WHITE, AN' A BRAN NEW MATTRESS ON1O3 BEYOND
THE BUNK,
GATE IN THE WHITE PICKET FENCE WHICH BORDERS THE 112 BEYOND
ROAD.
ALL THE WINDOWS ARE OPEN, BUT NO BREEZE STIRS THE 112 BEYOND
SOILED WHITE CURTAINS.
NOT THE OLD MAN WITH THE WHITE MUSTACHE--THE 130 BEYOND
OTHERS
SHE IS DRESSED IN WHITE, SHOWS SHE HAS BEEN FIXING135 BEYOND
UP.
(HIS FACE GROWS WHITE AND HIS HEAD FALLS BACK WITH482 CARDIF
A JERK.)
DISTANT STRIP OF CORAL BEACH, WHITE IN THE 455 CARIBE
MOONLIGHT,
TWO SWATE LITTLE SLIPS AV THINGS, NEAR AS WHITE AS462 CARIBE
YOU AN' ME ARE, FOR THAT
THEY'RE ALL THE SAME--WHITE, BROWN, YELLER, 'N' 470 CARIBE
BLACK.
HIS MASS OF HAIR IS PURE WHITE, HIS BRISTLY 567 CROSS
MUSTACHE THE SAME,

WHITE (CONT'D.)
AND A SHREDDED WHITE SAILOR'S BLOUSE, STAINED WITH571 CROSS
IRON-RUST.
HE IS DRESSED IN A DARK SUIT, WHITE SHIRT AND 493 DAYS
COLLAR, A DARK TIE,
WITH THICK WHITE HAIR, RUDDY COMPLEXION. 500 DAYS
ELSA WEARS A WHITE EVENING GOWN OF EXTREMELY 532 DAYS
SIMPLE LINES.
FOR HE COMES BACK AND PUTS ON HIS WHITE SHIRT, 241 DESIRE
COLLAR,
STIFF, WHITE CURTAINS ARE AT ALL THE WINDOWS. 494 DIFRNT
THE WHITE DRESS SHE WEARS IS TOO FRILLY, TOO 520 DIFRNT
YOUTHFUL FOR HER,
IS NOW NEARLY WHITE AND HIS FACE MORE DEEPLY LINED535 DIFRNT
AND WRINKLED.
THE LIGHT HOME, A LITTLE OLD NEW ENGLAND WHITE -0 DYNAMO
FRAME COTTAGE WITH GREEN
HIS HAIR HAS TURNED ALMOST WHITE, HIS MOUTH DROOPS455 DYNAMO
FORLORNLY, HIS EYES ARE DULL,
WHICH IS BRILLIANTLY LIGHTED BY A ROW OF POWERFUL 473 DYNAMO
BULBS IN WHITE GLOBES SET IN
A RED BANDANA HANDKERCHIEF COVERING ALL BUT A FEW 173 EJONES
STRAY WISPS OF WHITE HAIR.
THE FLOOR IS OF WHITE TILES. 173 EJONES
A WIDE ARCHWAY GIVING OUT ON A PORTICO WITH WHITE 173 EJONES
PILLARS,
HE IS DRESSED IN A WORN RIDING SUIT OF DIRTY WHITE174 EJONES
DRILL, PUTTEES, SPURS,
AND WEARS A WHITE CORK HELMET. 174 EJONES
WHICH FAILS TO COVER UP HIS CONTEMPT FOR THE WHITE176 EJONES
MAN)
TALK POLITE, WHITE MAN/ 176 EJONES
LISTENING TO DE WHITE QUALITY TALK, IT'S DAT SAME 178 EJONES
FACT,
(HARSHLY) KEEP YO' HANDS WHAR DY B'LONG, WHITE 179 EJONES
MAN.
IT AIN'T 'EALTHY FOR A BLACK TO KILL A WHITE MAN 180 EJONES
IN THE STATES.
YOU TOLD THE BLACKS 'ERE ABOUT KILLIN' WHITE MEN 180 EJONES
IN THE STATES.
WELL, I TELLS YOU, SMITHERS, MAYBE I DOES KILL ONE180 EJONES
WHITE MAN BACK
WHY, MAN, DE WHITE MEN WENT AFTER ME WID 183 EJONES
BLOODHOUNDS.
(WITH INDIGNANT SCORN) LOUK-A-HEAH, WHITE MAN/ 183 EJONES
(GLOOMILY) YOU KIN BET YO' WHOLE ROLL ON ONE 184 EJONES
THING, WHITE MAN.
IF I FINDS OUT DEM NIGGERS BELIEVES DAT BLACK IS 185 EJONES
WHITE,
G'LONG, WHITE MAN/ 185 EJONES
SO LONG, WHITE MAN/ 186 EJONES
SO LONG, WHITE MAN. 186 EJONES
(HE SEES THE FIRST WHITE STONE AND CRAWLS TO IT 188 EJONES
WITH SATISFACTION)
WHITE STONE, WHITE STONE, WHERE IS YOUS 188 EJONES
HOW COME ALL DESE WHITE STONES COME HEAH WHEN I 189 EJONES
ONLY REMEMBERS ONES
BUT HOW COME ALL DESE WHITE STONES$ 189 EJONES
THEY ARE FOLLOWED BY A WHITE MAN DRESSED IN THE 194 EJONES
UNIFORM OF A PRISON GUARD.
SHOVEL ON THE WHITE MAN'S SKULL, 195 EJONES
I KILLS YOU, YOU WHITE DEBIL, IF IT'S DE LAST 195 EJONES
THING I EVAN DOES/
WHAT YOU ALL DOIN', WHITE FOLKS$ 197 EJONES
THE WHITE PLANTERS LOOK THEM OVER APPRAISINGLY AS 197 EJONES
IF THEY WERE CATTLE,
IN THE OTHER A CHARM STICK WITH A BUNCH OF WHITE 200 EJONES
COCKATOO FEATHERS TIED TO THE
LEM LOOKS UP AT THE WHITE MAN WITH A GRIN OF 203 EJONES
SATISFACTION)
A DRIVEWAY CURVES UP TO THE HOUSE FROM TWO 2 ELECTR
ENTRANCES WITH WHITE GATES.
THE PROPERTY IS ENCLOSED BY A WHITE PICKET FENCE 2 ELECTR
AND A TALL HEDGE.
A WHITE WOODEN PORTICO WITH SIX TALL COLUMNS 2 ELECTR
CONTRASTS
THE WHITE COLUMNS CAST BLACK BARS OF SHADOW ON THE 5 ELECTR
GRAY WALL BEHIND THEM.
BEHIND THE DRIVEWAY THE WHITE GRECIAN TEMPLE 5 ELECTR
PORTICO WITH ITS SIX TALL COLUMNS
IN STRIKING CONTRAST TO THE WHITE COLUMNS OF THE 5 ELECTR
PORTICO.
THE TEMPLE PORTICO IS LIKE AN INCONGRUOUS WHITE 5 ELECTR
MASK
SHIMMERING IN A LUMINOUS MIST ON THE WHITE PORTICO 5 ELECTR
AND THE GRAY STONE WALL
IS AN OLD MAN OF SEVENTY-FIVE WITH WHITE HAIR AND 6 ELECTR
BEARD, TALL,
(DRYLY) =TALL, WHITE CLIPPERS,= YOU CALLED THEM. 23 ELECTR
WITH A FLAT WHITE TRIM, 28 ELECTR
THE PURE WHITE TEMPLE FRONT SEEMS MORE THAN EVER 43 ELECTR
LIKE AN INCONGRUOUS MASK
THE WHITE COLUMNS OF THE PORTICO CAST BLACK BARS 43 ELECTR
OF SHADOW ON THE GRAY WALL.
THAT MADE THE WHITE MEETING-HOUSE SEEM 54 ELECTR
MEANINGLESS--
BUT IN THIS WAR I'VE SEEN TOO MANY WHITE WALLS 54 ELECTR
SPLATTERED WITH BLOOD
THEY WENT TO THE WHITE MEETING-HOUSE ON SABBATHS 54 ELECTR
AND MEDITATED ON DEATH,
THAT WHITE MEETING-HOUSE. 54 ELECTR
ITS WHITE PORTICO LIKE A MASK IN THE MOONLIGHT, AS 67 ELECTR
IT HAD ON THAT NIGHT.
HE IS AROUND SIXTY, SMALL AND WIZENED, WHITE HAIR 67 ELECTR
AND BEARD,
THE WALLS ARE PLAIN PLASTERED SURFACES, LIGHT GRAY 79 ELECTR
WITH A WHITE TRIM.

WHITE

WHITE (CONT'D.)

HE HAS WHITE HAIR AND A WISPY GOAT'S BEARD, BRIGHT129 ELECTR INQUISITIVE EYES,

STILL BATHES THE WHITE TEMPLE PORTICO IN A CRIMSON129 ELECTR LIGHT.

HIS SHINY WRINKLED FACE IS OBLONG WITH A SQUARE 129 ELECTR WHITE CHIN WHISKER.

AND DOWN THE PORTICO STEPS, HIS FACE CHALKY WHITE 134 ELECTR AND HIS EYES POPPING.)

SNEAKERS OVER BARE FEET, AND SOILED WHITE FLANNEL 260 GGBROW TROUSERS.

SHE IS IN A SIMPLE WHITE DRESS. 262 GGBROW

YOU'RE THE ORIGINAL WHITE-HAIRED BOY. 265 GGBROW

AND YOUR BODY IS A YOUNG WHITE BIRCH LEANING 267 GGBROW BACKWARD

STRIPPED NAKED EXCEPT FOR A WHITE CLOTH AROUND HIS319 GGBROW LOINS, IS BROWN.

ALL THE CIVILIZED WHITE RACES ARE REPRESENTED, 207 HA APE

IMPRISONED BY WHITE STEEL. 207 HA APE

PAINTING THEIR WHITE TOPS AND THE CLOUDS FLOATING 214 HA APE BY THEM/

HER SAILS STRETCHING ALOFT ALL SILVER AND WHITE, 214 HA APE NOT A SOUND ON THE DECK,

MILDRED IS DRESSED ALL IN WHITE. 218 HA APE

I HAVE LOTS OF WHITE DRESSES. 221 HA APE

SPECTACLE OF MILDRED STANDING THERE IN HER WHITE 225 HA APE DRESS.

HE SEES MILDRED, LIKE A WHITE APPARITION 225 HA APE

FINE LADY, DRESSED LIKE A WHITE CUANE, 228 HA APE

(SLOWLY) SHE WAS ALL WHITE. 229 HA APE

SHE WAS ALL IN WHITE LIKE DEY WRAP AROUND STIFFS. 230 HA APE

YUH WHITE-FACED BUM, YUH/ 230 HA APE

WHITE AND SKINNY. 231 HA APE

AND HER MUSH, DAT WAS DEAD WHITE, TOO. 231 HA APE

WHERE'S ALL DE WHITE-COLLAR STIFFS YUH SAID WAS 234 HA APE HERE--AND DE SKOIT5--HER KINDS

THE WHITE WINGS GOT SOME JOB SWEEPIN' DIS UP. 234 HA APE

I SEE YUH, ALL IN WHITE/ 238 HA APE

I SEE YUH, YUH WHITE-FACED TART, YUH/ 238 HA APE

SHE WAS DOLLED UP ALL IN WHITE--IN DE STOKEHOLE. 241 HA APE

HER HANDS--DEY WAS SKINNY AND WHITE LIKE DEY 241 HA APE WASN'T REAL BUT PAINTED ON SOMEPIN.

SO YUH'RE WHAT SHE SEEN WHEN SHE LOOKED AT ME, DE 252 HA APE WHITE-FACED TART/

HAVIN' TO STAND FUR 'EM COMIN' AND STARIN' AT 252 HA APE YUH--DE WHITE-FACED,

BUILT IN THE DECADE 1900-10 ON THE SIDE STREETS OF 7 HUGHIE THE GREAT WHITE WAY SECTOR,

HE WEARS AN ILL-FITTING BLUE SERGE SUIT, WHITE 8 HUGHIE SHIRT AND COLLAR, A BLUE TIE.

HIS SHOES ARE TAN AND WHITE, HIS SOCKS WHITE SILK. 9 HUGHIE

UNLESS THE SMALLEST BET YOU COULD MAKE--ONE WHITE 32 HUGHIE CHIP? WAS A HUNDRED DOLLARS.

ONE WHITE CHIP IS--A HUNDRED DOLLARS$ 35 HUGHIE

ONE WHITE CHIP-- 36 HUGHIE

THE WALLS AND CEILING ONCE WERE WHITE, BUT IT WAS 573 ICEMAN A LONG TIME AGO.

HE IS TALL, RAW-BONED, WITH COARSE STRAIGHT WHITE 574 ICEMAN HAIR,

AND HIS WHITE SHIRT IS FRAYED AT COLLAR AND CUFFS,574 ICEMAN

HIS HAIR AND MILITARY MUSTACHE ARE WHITE, HIS EYES575 ICEMAN BRIGHT BLUE.

HARRY HOPE IS SIXTY, WHITE-HAIRED, 576 ICEMAN

YOU HAVE TO SEE, TOO, THAT THIS IS ALL BLACK, AND 590 ICEMAN THAT IS ALL WHITE.

HE'S WHITE, JOE IS/ 599 ICEMAN

YES, SUH, WHITE FOLKS ALWAYS SAID I WAS WHITE. 600 ICEMAN

JOE MOTT'S DE ONLY COLORED MAN DEY ALLOWS IN DE 600 ICEMAN WHITE GAMBLIN' HOUSES.

=YOU'RE ALL RIGHT, JOE, YOU'RE WHITE,= DEY SAYS. 600 ICEMAN

HE KNEW I WAS WHITE. 600 ICEMAN

I SAID YOU WAS WHITE. 600 ICEMAN

SO I OPENS, AND HE FINDS OUT I'SE WHITE, SURE 601 ICEMAN 'NUFF.

HARRY SAYS YOU'RE WHITE AND YOU BETTER BE WHITE 601 ICEMAN

I'LL TREAT YOU WHITE. 605 ICEMAN

=IT'S A BIG WHITE BUILDING ON YOUR RIGHT. 617 ICEMAN

HE'S A WHITE MANS AIN'T HE$ 637 ICEMAN

LISTEN TO ME, YOU WHITE BOYS/ 637 ICEMAN

BEJEES, HICKEY, YOU OLD SON OF A BITCH, THAT'S 659 ICEMAN WHITE OF YOU/

COVERED WITH WHITE MOSQUITO NETTING TO KEEP OFF 664 ICEMAN THE FLIES.

YOU WHITE SONS OF BITCHES/ 672 ICEMAN

I'S SICK AND TIRED OF MESSIN' ROUND WID WHITE MEN.673 ICEMAN

IF I HAS TO BORROW A GUN AND STICK UP SOME WHITE 673 ICEMAN MAN, I GETS IT/

(WITH SNEERING DIGNITY) I'S ON'Y SAVIN' YOU DE 673 ICEMAN TROUBLE, WHITE BOY.

I THEN DEFINITELY BUT IT'S WHITE MAN'S BAD LUCK. 673 ICEMAN

I DON' I LOWER MYSELF DRINKIN' WID NO WHITE TRASH/=673 ICEMAN

= AND LISTEN WHEN DEY ALL PAT ME ON DE BACK AND 673 ICEMAN SAY, = JOE, YOU SURE IS WHITE.=

SO'S NO WHITE MAN SICK ABOUT DRINKIN' FROM DE SAME673 ICEMAN GLASS.

JIMMY'S CLOTHES ARE PRESSED, HIS SHOES SHINED, HIS683 ICEMAN WHITE LINEN IMMACULATE.

I'M FREE, WHITE AND TWENTY-ONE, AND I'LL DO AS I 687 ICEMAN DAMNED PLEASE, BEJEES/

SCUSE ME, WHITE BOYS. 699 ICEMAN

SHE JUST SAID, LOOKING WHITE AND SCARED, =WHY, 710 ICEMAN TEDDY$

DRISCOLL HOLDS THE RUBBER BAG LIMPLY IN HIS HAND 532 INZONE AND SOME SMALL WHITE OBJECT

HER HIGH FOREHEAD IS FRAMED BY THICK, PURE WHITE 12 JOURNE HAIR.

ACCENTUATED BY HER PALLOR AND WHITE HAIR, HER DARK 12 JOURNE BROWN EYES APPEAR BLACK.

WHITE (CONT'D.)

A COLLAR-LESS SHIRT WITH A THICK WHITE 13 JOURNE HANDKERCHIEF.

THEN IT BEGAN TO TURN WHITE. 28 JOURNE

WHITE CURTAIN DRAWN DOWN OUTSIDE THE WINDOWS. 97 JOURNE

MY FATHER EVEN LET ME HAVE DUCHESSE LACE ON MY 115 JOURNE WHITE SATIN SLIPPERS,

ABOUT JAMIE AND THE GREAT WHITE WAY. 133 JOURNE

THE MASTS WITH EVERY SAIL WHITE IN THE MOONLIGHT, 153 JOURNE TOWERING HIGH ABOVE ME.

I DISSOLVED IN THE SEA, BECAME WHITE SAILS AND 153 JOURNE FLYING SPRAY,

THE FAMILY WHITE HOPE/ 163 JOURNE

IS AN OLD-FASHIONED WHITE SATIN WEDDING GOWN, 170 JOURNE TRIMMED WITH DUCHESSE LACE.

HER WHITE HAIR IS BRAIDED IN TWO PIGTAILS WHICH 170 JOURNE HANG OVER HER BREASTS,

A LONG, LOW-CEILINGED, SPARELY FURNISHED CHAMBER, 273 LAZARU WITH WHITE WALLS

THE HOUSE IS LOW, OF ONE STORY ONLY, ITS WALLS 281 LAZARU WHITE,

THE TALL FIGURE OF LAZARUS, DRESSED IN A WHITE 288 LAZARU ROBE,

PULLING A CHARIOT IN WHICH LAZARUS STANDS DRESSED 307 LAZARU IN A TUNIC OF WHITE AND GOLD,

LAZARUS, IN HIS ROBE OF WHITE AND GOLD, 312 LAZARU

ON EACH SIDE, MEMBERS OF THE SENATE ARE SEATED IN 312 LAZARU THEIR WHITE ROBES.

MIRIAM, IN BLACK, HER HAIR ALMOST WHITE NOW, HER 327 LAZARU FIGURE BOWED AND FEEBLE,

HIS SHINY WHITE CRANIUM RISES LIKE A POLISHED 337 LAZARU SHELL ABOVE HIS HALF-MASKED FACE.

PLACED BESIDE THE HEAD OF MIRIAM, SHINES DOWN UPON350 LAZARU THE WHITE MASK OF HER FACE.

PASSING WITH WHITE BODIES SPOTTED BY THE LEPROUS 353 LAZARU FINGERS OF ONE'S LUSTS.

AND THERE A HIGH WHITE FLAME AMIDST THE FIRE--YOU,370 LAZARU LAZARUS/

IT IS FRAMED BY A MASS OF WAVY WHITE HAIR, 2 MANSNS

WHITE TEETH WHEN SHE SMILES. 2 MANSNS

SHE IS DRESSED WITH EXTREME CARE AND GOOD TASTE, 3 MANSNS ENTIRELY IN WHITE.)

SITTING IN YOUR WALLED-IN GARDEN, DRESSED ALL IN 14 MANSNS WHITE,

SHE IS DRESSED ALL IN WHITE.) 28 MANSNS

DRESSED ALL IN WHITE. 95 MANSNS

I CAN SEE YOU SITTING THERE, AS YOU ARE NOW, 109 MANSNS DRESSED ALL IN WHITE,

THE WALLS AND CEILING ARE WHITE. 117 MANSNS

THE TWO WOMEN WEAR SEMI-FORMAL EVENING GOWNS, 117 MANSNS

DEBORAH'S ALL WHITE.

SHE IS DRESSED IN WHITE, AS EVER, 161 MANSNS

HER BEAUTIFUL WHITE HAIR IS PILED UP ON HER HEAD 161 MANSNS

IN CURLS SO THAT IT RESEMBLES

LASHED TILL THE BLOOD RAN DOWN YOUR FAT WHITE 165 MANSNS SHOULDERS/

HE IS A WHITE CHRISTIAN, MIDDLE-AGED, AVERAGE- 347 MARCOM LOOKING.

LASHED ON THE WAGON IS A COFFIN COVERED WITH A 350 MARCOM WHITE PALL.)

A VENERABLE OLD MAN WITH WHITE HAIR, DRESSED IN A 377 MARCOM SIMPLE BLACK ROBE.

HE IS RIDING ON A VERY FAT WHITE HORSE. 388 MARCOM

HE WEARS A SIMPLE WHITE ROBE WITHOUT ADORNMENT OF 432 MARCOM ANY SORT.

HIS EYES ARE FIXED ON A CATAFALQUE, DRAPED IN 432 MARCOM HEAVY WHITE SILK.

ALL ARE DRESSED IN DEEP BLACK WITH WHITE EDGING TO433 MARCOM THEIR ROBES.

DRESSED IN WHITE WITH BLACK EDGING, 433 MARCOM

HER FACE IS WHITE AND CLEAR AS A STATUE'S. 434 MARCOM

(HE WEEPS, HIS TEARS FALLING ON HER CALM WHITE 439 MARCOM FACE.)

AND HER SMILE, REVEALING EVEN WHITE TEETH, GIVES 3 MISBEG IT CHARM.

AND EYEBROWS THAT REMIND ONE OF A WHITE PIG'S. 11 MISBEG

DARK-BROWN MADE-TO-ORDER SHOES AND SILK SOCKS, A 37 MISBEG WHITE SILK SHIRT,

AND BY WAY OF ADORNMENT A WHITE FLOWER IS PINNED 71 MISBEG ON HER BOSOM.

ALL THESE TABLES ARE SET WITH WHITE TABLECLOTHS, 7 POET ETC.

PATCH RILEY IS AN OLD MAN WITH A THATCH OF DIRTY 52 POET WHITE HAIR.

THE MOUTH, WITH FULL LIPS AND EVEN, WHITE TEETH, 67 POET IS TOO LARGE FOR HER FACE.

HER SLENDER, FRAGILE BODY IS DRESSED IN WHITE WITH 68 POET CALCULATED SIMPLICITY.

HIS FACE IS GAUNT, CHALKY-WHITE, FURROWED WITH 578 ROPE WRINKLES.

SURMOUNTED BY A SHINY BALD SCALP FRINGED WITH 578 ROPE SCANTY WISPS OF WHITE HAIR.

THEN HIS FACE GROWS WHITE WITH A VICIOUS FURY) 596 ROPE

IN THE LEFT WALL IS ONE WINDOW WITH STARCHED WHITE 48 STRANG CURTAINS LOOKING OUT ON A

ALL WHITE AND PINKISH AND BEAUTIFUL. 49 STRANG

GORDON STANDS WHITE-FACED, DEFYING HIM. 150 STRANG

NINA'S HAIR HAS TURNED COMPLETELY WHITE. 158 STRANG

SHE IS DRESSED IN A WHITE YACHTING COSTUME. 158 STRANG

HE WEARS FLANNEL PANTS, A BLUE COAT, WHITE 159 STRANG BUCKSKIN SHOES.

HE IS WEARING A YACHTING CAP, BLUE YACHTING COAT, 159 STRANG WHITE FLANNEL PANTS,

BLOODY WINDJAMMER--SKYS'L-YARDER--FULL-RIGGED-- 495 VOYAGE PAINTED WHITE--

WHITECHAPEL

WELL, I HOPE WHITECHAPEL WILL PROVIDE THE NEEDED 219 HA APE NERVE TONIC.

WHITED

THEY'RE APT TO BE WHITED SEPULCHRES--I MEAN, YOUR 295 AHWILD
WHOLE LIFE MIGHT BE RUINED IF-
THE *WHITED* ONE OF THE BIBLE-- 17 ELECTR

WHITENESS

BEHIND, INTENSIFYING THE WHITENESS OF THE COLUMNS, 5 ELECTR
INTENSIFYING THE WHITENESS OF THE COLUMNS, THE 169 ELECTR
DEEP GREEN OF THE SHUTTERS.

WHITER

CAN'T TREAT YOU NO WHITER DAN DAT, CAN IS 605 ICEMAN

WHITES

HIS EYES ARE BROWN, THE WHITES CONGESTED AND 37 MISBEG
YELLOWISH.

WHITEST

WHITEST COLORED MAN I EVER KNEW. 599 ICEMAN

WHITEWASHED

A SPACIOUS, HIGH-CEILINGED ROOM WITH BARE, 173 EJONES
WHITEWASHED WALLS.
IT STUCK IN MY MIND--CLEAN-SCRUBBED AND 54 ELECTR
WHITEWASHED--A TEMPLE OF DEATH/

WHITHER

FLOWING WITH AN INSANE OBSESSION--WHITHERS 385 MARCOM

WHITISH

THE STOOP OF HIS TALL FIGURE IS ACCENTUATED, HIS 159 STRANG
HAIR HAS GROWN WHITISH.

WHITMAN

AND WHITMAN AND POE/ 135 JOURNE

WHOA

WHOA THAR. 131 ELECTR

WHOEVER

(THEN ANGRILY) BY GOD, I'LL MAKE WHOEVER IT WAS 266 AHWILD
REGRET IT/
LEAVIN' MY CLAIM AN' CROPS T' WHOEVER 'D A MIND T'237 DESIRE
TAKE 'EM.
HERE'S HOW, WHOEVER OWNS DIS. 213 HA APE
I SUPPOSE WHOEVER IT WAS MADE A BARGAIN WITH THE 588 ICEMAN
BURNS MEN
I HOPE HIS SOUL ROTS IN HELL, WHOEVER IT IS/ 588 ICEMAN
THE MON THAT OPENED IT MEANT NO GOOD TO THIS SHIP,521 INZONE
WHOEVER HE WAS.
THEY MUST HAVE CASH, WHOEVER THEY ARE. 427 MARCOM
HE SAID HE TOLD THE AGENT TO TELL WHOEVER IT WAS 32 MISBEG
THE PLACE WASN'T FOR SALE.
OR BOTHERING MY HEAD ABOUT HER, ANYWAY, WHOEVER 19 POET
SHE WAS.
BAD LUCK TO THE BLACKGUARD, WHOEVER IT WAS/ 78 POET
WHOEVER IS IN REAL CHARGE DOWN THERE WILL BE ONLY 192 STRANG
TOO GLAD TO ACCEPT IT.

WHOEVER'S

LET YOU NOT BE HIDING FROM ME, WHOEVER'S HERE-- 68 ANNA

WHOLE

(IN GREAT EXCITEMENT) WHALES, SIR--A WHOLE SCHOOL551 'ILE
OF 'EM--
HER WHOLE ATTENTION SEEMS CENTERED IN THE ORGAN. 552 'ILE
AND HER WHOLE ATMOSPHERE IS ONE OF SHY KINDLINESS.187 AHWILD
(RICHARD FOLLOWS HER EXAMPLE AND THEY BOTH DRINK 240 AHWILD
THE WHOLE CONTENTS OF THEIR
YOU'RE TOO EASY WITH HIM, THAT'S THE WHOLE 253 AHWILD
TROUBLE/
(THEN SUDDENLY HIS WHOLE EXPRESSION CHANGES, HIS 261 AHWILD
PALLOR TAKES ON A GREENISH,
I'VE A WHOLE PILE OF THINGS THAT HAVE GOT TO BE 263 AHWILD
DONE TODAY/
THEY'RE APT TO BE WHITED SEPULCHRES--I MEAN, YOUR 295 AHWILD
WHOLE LIFE MIGHT BE RUINED IF-
THE BAR RUNS FROM LEFT TO RIGHT NEARLY THE WHOLE 3 ANNA
LENGTH OF THE REAR WALL.
IT WAS ALL MEN'S FAULT----THE WHOLE BUSINESS. 18 ANNA
WASN'T THE WHOLE STORY OF IT AND MY PICTURE ITSELF 48 ANNA
HE'S NOT AFTER TELLING YOU THE WHOLE OF IT. 50 ANNA
THE WHOLE OF IT'S IN A FEW WORDS ONLY. 51 ANNA
(HIS WHOLE BODY TENSE LIKE A SPRING--DULLY AND 59 ANNA
GROPINGLY)
I'M SICK OF THE WHOLE GAME. 60 ANNA
I'M WISHING THE WHOLE LOT OF THEM WILL ROAST IN 71 ANNA
HELL 'TIL THE JUDGMENT DAY--
THERE IS NO SUGGESTION OF PRIMNESS ABOUT THE 94 BEYOND
WHOLE.
I'M SICK AND TIRED OF THE WHOLE DAMN BUSINESS. 107 BEYOND
OH, THE WHOLE AFFAIR IS SO SENSELESS--AND TRAGIC. 109 BEYOND
TO PUT THE WHOLE RIM OF THE WORLD BETWEEN ME AND 126 BEYOND
THOSE HILLS,
AND TURN THIS FARM INTO THE CRACKIEST PLACE IN THE138 BEYOND
WHOLE STATE.
THE WHOLE ATMOSPHERE OF THE ROOM, CONTRASTED WITH 144 BEYOND
THAT OF FORMER YEARS.
I'LL BET ME WHOLE PAY DAT THERE'S NOT WAN IN THE 459 CARIBE
CROWD 'CEPTIN' YANK HERE,
I COULD TRINK A WHOLE BARREL MINESELF, PY CHIMINY461 CARIBE
CHRISTMAS/
AND THE WHOLE MOB, LED BY DRISCOLL, POURS OUT ON 470 CARIBE
DECK.
AND THAT'S WHAT HIS WHOLE BEING NOW CRIED OUT 539 DAYS
FOR--FORGIVENESS.
HE TAKES IN THE WHOLE FARM WITH HIS EMBRACING 217 DESIRE
GLANCE OF DESIRE)
AND ABOUT HER WHOLE PERSONALITY THE SAME 221 DESIRE
UNSETTLED, UNTAMED,
HE SEES EBEN AND HIS WHOLE MOOD IMMEDIATELY 253 DESIRE
CHANGES.
HIS WHOLE ATTITUDE WOODEN AND FIXED AS IF HE WERE 494 DIFRNT
POSING FOR A PHOTOGRAPH.
YOU'RE WO'TH THE WHOLE PACK OF 'EM PUT TOGETHER. 496 DIFRNT
FOLKS BE ALL CRAZY AND ROTTEN TO THE CORE AND I'M 543 DIFRNT
DONE WITH THE WHOLE KIT AND
SO THE DAMNED IDIOT BLATHERS THE WHOLE STORY 431 DYNAMO
SHE'LL TELL THE WHOLE TOWN I WAS SPYING/... 436 DYNAMO

WHOLE (CONT'D.)

(HE DRIVES BACK AT THE DOOR WITH THE WEIGHT OF HIS451 DYNAMO
WHOLE BODY.
HIS WHOLE FACE IS A MASK OF STRICKEN LONELINESS. 455 DYNAMO
AND A WHOLE LOT OF ME WAS DEAD AND A NEW LOT 460 DYNAMO
STARTED LIVING.
AND THERE IS A NERVOUS UNEASINESS APPARENT IN HIS 468 DYNAMO
WHOLE MANNER.)
AN' OUTPLAY DE WHOLE LOT O' DEM ALL OVAH DE BOARD 184 EJONES
ANY TIME O' DE DAY ER NIGHT/
(GLOOMILY) YOU KIN BET YO' WHOLE ROLL ON ONE 184 EJONES
THING, WHITE MAN.
(THEN WITH A LAUGH) WELL, IF DEY AIN'T NO WHOLE 186 EJONES
BRASS BAND TO SEE ME OFF,
A SHUDDER OF TERROR SHAKES HIS WHOLE BODY AS THE 199 EJONES
WALL RISES UP ABOUT HIM AGAIN.
THE WHOLE SPIRIT AND MEANING OF THE DANCE HAS 201 EJONES
ENTERED INTO HIM,
WHOLE TENSE ATTITUDES IS CLEARLY REVEALED THE 16 ELECTR
BITTER ANTAGONISM BETWEEN THEM.
AFTER PASSING UNHARMED THROUGH THE WHOLE WAR/ 69 ELECTR
WHOLE TOWN COULD HAVE PAID THEIR RESPECTS TO HIM, 69 ELECTR
AND THAT'S THE WHOLE OF THE GREAT CAPTAIN BRANT 87 ELECTR
SCANDAL.
THE WHOLE ISLAND WAS YOU. 90 ELECTR
(THE WHOLE MEMORY OF WHAT HIS MOTHER HAD SAID 96 ELECTR
RUSHES OVER HIM)
THE WHOLE THING IS TOO INSANE/ 97 ELECTR
THE TRUTH, THE WHOLE TRUTH AND NOTHING BUT THE 149 ELECTR
TRUTH/
WHAT WILL THE NEIGHBORS SAY IF THIS WHOLE TRUTH IS149 ELECTR
EVER KNOWN/
ARE YOU SURE YOU WANT THE WHOLE TRUTH/ 149 ELECTR
THAT I'D LIKE TO RUN OUT NAKED INTO THE STREET AND286 GGBROW
LOVE THE WHOLE MOB TO DEATH
AND THIS DESIGN MEANS HIS WHOLE FUTURE/ 304 GGBROW
HIS EYES, HIS ARMS, HIS WHOLE BODY STRAIN UPWARD, 319 GGBROW
LET THE WHOLE WORLD SUFFER AS I AM SUFFERING/ 319 GGBROW
(A WHOLE CHORUS OF VOICES HAS TAKEN UP THIS 211 HA APE
REFRAIN, STAMPING ON THE FLOOR,
TARTS, DAT'S WHAT, DE WHOLE BUNCH OF 'EM. 211 HA APE
ONE OF US GUYS COULD CLEAN UP DE WHOLE MOB WIT ONE212 HA APE
MIT.
STEEL, DAT STANDS FOR DE WHOLE TING/ 216 HA APE
WE RUN DE WHOLE WOIKS. 216 HA APE
BUT US GUYS, WE'RE IN DE MOVE, WE'RE AT DE BOTTOM,216 HA APE
DE WHOLE TING IS US/
HER WHOLE PERSONALITY CRUSHED, BEATEN IN, 225 HA APE
COLLAPSED.
DERE WAS A WHOLE ARMY OF PLAINCLOTHES BULLS 235 HA APE
AROUND.
(THE WHOLE CROWD OF MEN AND WOMEN CHORUS AFTER HER238 HA APE
IN THE SAME TONE OF AFFECTED
AND A WHOLE PLATOON OF POLICEMEN RUSHES IN ON YANK239 HA APE
FROM ALL SIDES.
(HE SHAKES THE BARS OF HIS CELL DOOR TILL THE 244 HA APE
WHOLE TIER TREMBLES.
THE WHOLE IS DECIDEDLY CHEAP, BANAL, 245 HA APE
IT STOPS AND DE WHOLE WOILD STOPS. 250 HA APE
YUH CHALLENGE DE WHOLE WOILD, HUH? 252 HA APE
I'D WAKE UP THE WHOLE DAMNED CITY/* 17 HUGHIE
THAN MAKE THE WHOLE DAMN FOLLIES. 21 HUGHIE
--I MEAN, BIG ENOUGH TO BURN DOWN THE WHOLE DAMN 27 HUGHIE
CITY--
I MEAN, THE WHOLE GODDAMNED RACKET. 33 HUGHIE
TO THE WHOLE MISBEGOTTEN MAD LOT OF US, DRUNK OR 578 ICEMAN
SOBER.
WELL, THAT'S OUR WHOLE FAMILY CIRCLE OF INMATES, 594 ICEMAN
WHAT GETS MY GOAT IS DE WAY HE'S TRYIN' TO RUN DE 631 ICEMAN
WHOLE DUMP AND EVERYONE IN IT.
I COULD DE WHOLE VEIGHT OF IT LIFT/ 676 ICEMAN
YOU DUMBBELL, THAT'S THE WHOLE POINT. 688 ICEMAN
JEES, DERE AIN'T ENOUGH GUTS LEFT IN DE WHOLE GANG699 ICEMAN
TO BATTLE A MOSQUITO/
D'YOU WANT TO WAKE THE WHOLE SHIPS 526 INZONE
CHANGES IN HER WHOLE MANNER 104 JOURNE
(SUDDENLY HER WHOLE MANNER CHANGES. 108 JOURNE
YOU CAN SHOW YOURSELF UP BEFORE THE WHOLE TOWN AS 145 JOURNE
SUCH A STINKING OLD TIGHTWAD/
DON'T YOU KNOW HARDY WILL TALK AND THE WHOLE 145 JOURNE
DAMNED TOWN WILL KNOW/
THE WHOLE LOOK OF HIS FACE HAS CHANGED. 276 LAZARU
(WITH A CRUEL LAUGH) MY GRANDFATHER FREQUENTLY 327 LAZARU
PLANTS WHOLE ORCHARDS OF SUCH
THE WHOLE EFFECT OF THESE TWO GROUPS IS OF SEX 336 LAZARU
CORRUPTED AND WARPED.
LAZARUS CASTS A LUMINOUS GLOW OVER THE WHOLE ROOM 338 LAZARU
AND YET, ON OUR JOURNEY, WHOLE HERDS OF WOMEN-- 341 LAZARU
HIS WHOLE BODY IS NOW RELAXED, AT REST, A DREAMY 342 LAZARU
SMILE SOFTENS HIS THIN,
HIS WHOLE CHARACTER HAS SOMETHING ARIDLY PRIM AND 26 MANSNS
PURITANICAL ABOUT IT.
AND DEED THE WHOLE PROPERTY OVER TO YOU. 56 MANSNS
AND I'LL HAVE THE WHOLE MANAGEMENT AND BE THE 65 MANSNS
MISTRESS.
HE'LL BE OWNING THE WHOLE WORLD IN HIS MIND BEFORE 67 MANSNS
YOU KNOW IT.
THE WHOLE COMPANY TO BE MINE/ 90 MANSNS
YOU CAN GET THE WHOLE COMPANY FROM ME-- 90 MANSNS
AND NOT EVEN THE WHOLE OF YOUR TRUTH. 115 MANSNS
OUR WHOLE COWARDLY MORAL CODE ABOUT MURDER IS BUT 179 MANSNS
ANOTHER EXAMPLE
WHY, I WAS COUNTING ON SELLING HER AND HER HUSBAND349 MARCOM
A WHOLE FLEET OF GOODS/
IT IS APPARENT THE WHOLE COMPANY IS EXTREMELY 374 MARCOM
WEARY.
THE WHOLE PROCESS IS A MAN-POWER ORIGINAL OF THE 400 MARCOM
MODERN DEVICES

WHOLE

1794

WHOLE (CONT'D.)
HER LIPS PART, HER WHOLE BEING STRAINS OUT TO HIM.414 MARCOM
ON WHICH ARE WHOLE PIGS, FOWL OF ALL VARIETIES, 428 MARCOM
ROASTS,
YOUR GENEROUS AND WHOLE-HEARTED WELCOME TOUCHES ME431 MARCOM
PROFOUNDLY.
LAYING ESPECIAL EMPHASIS UPON THE KEYSTONE OF THE 431 MARCOM
WHOLE SILK BUSINESS--
IF HARDER SEES YOU HERE, HE'LL LAY THE WHOLE BLAME 54 MISBEG
ON YOU.
HE'LL SEE THE WHOLE OF BROADWAY SPLITTING THEIR 96 MISBEG
SIDES LAUGHING AT HIM--
EXCEPT I WAS PIE-EYED IN A DRAWING ROOM THE WHOLE 128 MISBEG
FOUR DAYS.
POUR THE WHOLE BOTTLE DOWN YOUR THROAT, IF YOU 138 MISBEG
LIKE/
(SCATHINGLY) I'M SURE YOU'VE MADE UP A WHOLE NEW 163 MISBEG
SET OF LIES AND EXCUSES.
EVEN IF IT IS A GREAT COMPANY THAT TRADES WITH THE 29 POET
WHOLE WORLD IN ITS OWN SHIPS.
IN THE WHOLE UNITED KINGDOM, WITH MY STABLE OF 49 POET
HUNTERS, AND--
ABOUT HER WHOLE PERSONALITY IS A CURIOUS 68 POET
ATMOSPHERE OF DELIBERATE DETACHMENT,
NOT THE WHOLE DIRTY FORCE AV THIM WILL DARE 145 POET
INTERFERE WITH HIM/
AND DON'T PUT ON LADY'S AIRS ABOUT FIGHTING WHEN 156 POET
YOU'RE THE WHOLE CAUSE OF IT.
DIDN'T ME AND JAMIE LICK A WHOLE REGIMENT AV 173 POET
POLICE THIS NIGHT$
SURE, THERE'S DIVIL A MORE LOYAL WIFE IN THE WHOLE174 POET
WORLD--
COURTIN' THAT HARLOT THAT WAS THE TALK O' THE 580 ROPE
WHOLE TOWN/
LEFT YOU--THE SHAME OF THE WHOLE COUNTRY/ 580 ROPE
AND TERMORROW MORNIN', KID, I'LL GIVE YUH A WHOLE 601 ROPE
HANDFUL OF THEM SHINY,
UNTIL IT'S BECOME TOO APPALLINGLY OBVIOUS IN HER 10 STRANG
WHOLE ATTITUDE TOWARD ME/
AND THERE YOU HAVE IT, CHARLIE--THE WHOLE ABSURD 11 STRANG
MESS/
HER WHOLE MANNER, THE CHARGED ATMOSPHERE SHE GIVES 13 STRANG
OFF,
AND I SUPPOSE THAT'S THE LOGICAL CONCLUSION TO THE 40 STRANG
WHOLE EVASIVE MESS, ISN'T IT$
HER WHOLE PERSONALITY SEEMS CHANGED, HER FACE HAS 48 STRANG
A CONTENTED EXPRESSION,
WE NEVER FORGOT TO BE CAREFUL FOR TWO WHOLE YEARS. 60 STRANG
I MIGHT AS WELL GIVE YOU THE WHOLE CASE HISTORY/ 82 STRANG
THE WORLD IS WHOLE AND PERFECT... 91 STRANG
YOU'D BETTER RESIGN FROM THE WHOLE GAME... 92 STRANG
HIS SHOULDERS ARE BOWED, HIS WHOLE FIGURE DROOPS.) 98 STRANG
LITTLE GURDON HAS BECOME MY WHOLE LIFE. 128 STRANG
AND AN WHOLE... 135 STRANG
I'LL YELL OUT THE WHOLE BUSINESS IF I STAY/...) 152 STRANG
WELL, THE WHOLE ESTATE GOES TO YOU AND ME, OF 191 STRANG
COURSE.
SO LET'S YOU AND ME FORGET THE WHOLE DISTRESSING 199 STRANG
EPISODE,
YOU HAD BEST FORGET THE WHOLE AFFAIR OF YOUR 199 STRANG
ASSOCIATIONS WITH THE GORDONS.
THE FIRST IMPRESSION OF HER WHOLE PERSONALITY IS 443 WELDED
ONE OF CHARM, PARTLY INNATE,
I HATE THE WHOLE PLAY/ 451 WELDED
(SHE STROKES HIS HAIR) WE HAVE THE WHOLE NIGHT-- 452 WELDED
HER WHOLE TORTURED FACE EXPRESSES AN ABYSMAL SELF-460 WELDED
LOATHING,
A QUEER STRUGGLE IS APPARENT IN HER FACE, HER 465 WELDED
WHOLE BODY,
REMEMBER KISSING ME ON THE CORNER WITH A WHOLE MOB471 WELDED
PIPIN' US OFF$
HER WHOLE ATTITUDE STRAINED, EXPECTANT BUT 480 WELDED
FRIGHTENED,
YOU ARE THERE--BESIDE ME--ALIVE--WITH YOU I BECOME488 WELDED
A WHOLE, A TRUTH/

WHOLESALE
IN A FLASH A WHOLESALE FIGHT HAS BROKEN OUT AND 472 CARIBE
THE DECK IS A SURGING CROWD OF
HE WAS PROSPEROUS ENOUGH, TOO, IN HIS WHOLESALE 137 JOURNE
GROCERY BUSINESS, AN ABLE MAN.

WHOLESOME
A SWEET, WHOLESOME COUPLE THEY'D MAKE. 98 BEYOND
AND JUST TAKE IT EASY AND ENJOY A GOOD WHOLESOME 398 MARCOM

WHOLLY
MY PLOT, UP TO THE LAST PART, WHICH IS WHOLLY 533 DAYS
IMAGINARY, IS TAKEN FROM LIFE.
YOU SHOULD AWAKEN AND THE DRUNKENNESS BE HALF OR 132 JOURNE
WHOLLY SLIPPED AWAY FROM YOU,
IT IS A STRONG FACE BUT OF A STRENGTH WHOLLY 184 STRANG
MATERIAL IN QUALITY.

WHOOP
FROM THE SIDE ROOM COMES THE SOUND OF AN ACCORDION501 VOYAGE
AND A BOISTEROUS WHOOP FROM

WHOOPING
LISTENING TO MY OLD MAN WHOOPING UP HELL FIRE AND 709 ICEMAN
SCARING THOSE HOOSIER SUCKERS

WHOPPER
ISN'T THIS KID OF MINE A WHOPPER FOR HIS AGE, 152 STRANG
THOUGH/

WHORE
SHE WAS JUST A WHORE. 276 AHWILD
I MEAN THE FARM YEW SOLD YERSELF FUR LIKE ANY 230 DESIRE
OTHER OLD WHORE--
YE'RE A WHORE--A DAMN TRICKIN' WHORE/ 256 DESIRE
YOU--YOU WHORE--I'LL KILL YOU/ 81 ELECTR
YOU--YOU WHORE/ 155 ELECTR
I NEVER WANT TO SEE A WHORE AGAIN/ 594 ICEMAN
AND IMAGINE A WHORE HUSTLIN' DE COWS HOME/ 614 ICEMAN

WHORE (CONT'D.)
I MAY BE A TART, BUT I AIN'T A CHEAP OLD WHORE 632 ICEMAN
LIKE YOU/
(FURIOUSLY) I'LL SHOW YUH WHO'S A WHORE/ 632 ICEMAN
YUH MEAN YOU TINK I'M A WHORE, TOO, HUH$ 633 ICEMAN
I REMEMBER THAT YOU GOT MAD AND YOU TOLD HER, =I 647 ICEMAN
DON'T LIKE LIVING WITH A WHORE,
I GOT STUCK ON A WHORE AND WANTED DOUGH TO BLOW IN667 ICEMAN
ON HER AND HAVE A GOOD TIME/
JUST TO GET A FEW LOUSY DOLLARS TO BLOW IN ON A 680 ICEMAN
WHORE.
SO FORGET DAT WHORE STUFF. 725 ICEMAN
AND EVERY WOMAN WHO WASN'T A WHORE WAS A FOOL/ 34 JOURNE
IN BRIEF, I MARRIED THE WHORE. SHE TORTURED ME, MY356 LAZARU
MOTHER'S SCHEMING PROSPERED--
THE WHORE WAS CAESSAR'S DAUGHTER, TRUE-- 356 LAZARU
THEN I KILLED THAT WHORE, MY WIFE, 356 LAZARU
THEN MY MOTHER MARRIED ME TO A WHORE. 356 LAZARU
BUT A GREEDY, CONTRIVIN' WHORE/ 19 MANSNS
I HAVE DISCIPLINED MY WILL TO BE POSSESSED BY 29 MANSNS
FACTS--LIKE A WHORE IN A BROTHEL/
YES, MY ADVICE TO YOU WOULD BE TO SHUN MARRIAGE 72 MANSNS
AND KEEP A WHORE INSTEAD/
TREATING HIS WIFE AS IF SHE WAS A WHORE HE'D PICK 121 MANSNS
UP ON THE STREET
AND ACTING AS IF I WAS A STREET WHORE-- 133 MANSNS
IF IT'S A WHORE YOU LOVE ME TO BE, THEN I AM IT, 158 MANSNS
BODY AND SOUL.
THERE IS NO NEED-- I HAVE ENCOURAGED HIM TO MAKE A 162 MANSNS
WHORE OF HER--
(WITH A HARD, BRAZEN AIR) BE GOD, IF I'M TO PLAY 95 MISBEG
WHORE, I DESERVE MY PAY/
(A BIT DRUNKENLY) WILL A WHORE GO TO A PICNICS 124 MISBEG
I'M NOT A WHORE. 138 MISBEG
WHORES 139 MISBEG
WHO SAID YOU WERE A WHORES 139 MISBEG
A BLONDE PIG WHO LOOKED MORE LIKE A WHORE THAN 149 MISBEG
TWENTY-FIVE WHORES.
AND I'M THE WHORE ON THE TRAIN TO HIM NOW, NOT-- 166 MISBEG
YOU WHORE/ 128 POET
AND GOT CALLED A PEASANT SLUT AND A WHORE FOR MY 150 POET
PAINS.
LIKE A WHORE/... 40 STRANG
OH, HOW I'D LOVE TO HATE THIS LITTLE WHORE/... 45 STRANG

WHOREHOUSE
I'D GET FEELING IT WAS LIKE LIVING IN A 647 ICEMAN
WHOREHOUSE--
THEN IT DOESN'T TAKE A SOOTHSAYER TO TELL HE'S 129 JOURNE
PROBABLY IN THE WHOREHOUSE.

WHOREMONGERS
WHOREMONGERS AND DEGENERATES/ 135 JOURNE

WHORES
ANYWAY, WE WOULDN'T KEEP NO PIMP, LIKE WE WAS 613 ICEMAN
REG'LAR OLD WHORES.
WAS HINTIN' AND COME RIGHT OUT AND ADMITTED WE WAS633 ICEMAN
WHORES.
WE'RE WHORES. 633 ICEMAN
I'LL BET THIS IS WHAT WILL PLEASE THOSE WHORES 639 ICEMAN
MORE THAN ANYTHING.
=IF WE'RE WHORES WE GOTTA RIGHT TO HAVE A REG'LAR 669 ICEMAN
PIMP
WE'RE WHORES, ARE WE$ 669 ICEMAN
(HE SHAKES HIS HEAD) WHORES GOIN' ON STRIKE/ CAN 670 ICEMAN
YUH TIE DAT$
I'M THROUGH WITH WHORES. 702 ICEMAN
I'LL KNOCK DE BLOCK OFF ANYONE CALLS YOU WHORES/ 725 ICEMAN
(STRIDENTLY) GANGWAY FOR TWO GOOD WHORES/ 725 ICEMAN
YOU'VE THROWN YOUR SALARY AWAY EVERY WEEK ON 31 JOURNE
WHORES AND WHISKEY/
IF HE'S EVER HAD A LOFTIER DREAM THAN WHORES AND 129 JOURNE
WHISKEY, HE'S NEVER SHOWN IT.
CHRIST, I'D NEVER DREAMED BEFORE THAT ANY WOMEN 163 JOURNE
BUT WHORES TOOK DOPE/
MADE WHORES FASCINATING VAMPIRES INSTEAD OF POOR, 165 JOURNE
STUPID,
IT MUST BE A BIG HELP TO YOU, CONVERSING WITH 38 MISBEG
WHORES AND BARKEEPS.
SMALL ALLOWANCE, AND HE LONGS TO GO BACK TO 84 MISBEG
BROADWAY AND HIS WHORES.
AND ALL THE PRETTY WHORES OF BROADWAY HE CAN BUY 85 MISBEG
WITH IT.
DRINKING AND DREAMING OF THE LITTLE WHORES 91 MISBEG
A BLONDE PIG WHO LOOKED MORE LIKE A WHORE THAN 149 MISBEG
TWENTY-FIVE WHORES,
AT HOME, THE ONLY WOMEN HE'D KNOWN WAS WHORES. 13 POET
WITH NO WOMAN'S COMPANY BUT THE WHORES WAS HELPIN' 14 POET
HIM RUIN THE ESTATE.

WHORIN'
I'LL BET RIGHT THEN AN' THAR HE KNEW PLUMB WELL HE215 DESIRE
WAS GOIN' WHORIN',

WHY'D
WHY'D YOU ASK ME SUCH A QUESTION, ANNIE$ 549 'ILE

WICK
HE TURNS UP THE WICK TO GIVE HIM A BETTER LIGHT) 529 INZONE

WICKED
THERE MUST BE SOME BOY HE KNOWS WHO'S TRYING TO 196 AHWILD
SHOW OFF AS ADVANCED AND WICKED,
YOU BAD, WICKED BOY, YOU/ 261 AHWILD
(FORCES A WICKED LEER TO HIS LIPS AND QUOTES WITH 261 AHWILD
PONDEROUS MOCKERY)
BUT THAT'S NOT BECAUSE I THINK IT WAS WICKED OR 270 AHWILD
ANY SUCH OLD-FOGY MORAL NOTION,
IT'S WICKED. 285 AHWILD
YOU KNOW THE KIND I MANE, AND THEY'RE A POOR, 37 ANNA
WICKED LOT, GOD FORGIVE THEM.
THEY'RE NOT AS WICKED AS THAT. 113 BEYOND
I DON'T KNOW ABOUT WICKED, BUT THEY'RE DARNED GOOD526 DIFRNT
SPORTS.

WICKED (CONT'D.)
I'VE HEARD FRENCH GIRLS WAS AWFUL WICKED. 526 DIFRNT
ALL YOU'VE SAID IS A WICKED LIE AND YOU'VE GOT NO 541 DIFRNT
CAUSE--
THAT NASTY WICKED BOY/... 435 DYNAMO
YOU ARE WICKED/ 173 ELECTR
OR THE WICKED WITCH, AND I'D BE ALL GOOSE-FLESH 12 MANSNS
WITH TERROR/
YOUR OLD WICKED WITCHES LED ME ALWAYS TO BE 13 MANSNS
PREPARED FOR THE WORST/
THIS IS MORE WICKED THAN ANY WITCH. 13 MANSNS
YOU WOULD THINK I WAS SOME WICKED OLD WITCH. 66 MANSNS
I WON'T LET YOU SAY SUCH WICKED THINGS. 86 MANSNS
I'LL PLAY ANY GAME WITH YOU YOU LIKE, AND IT WILL 90 MANSNS
BE FUN PLAYING I'M A WICKED,
YOU USED TO INSIST I IMAGINE A NEW ENDING IN WHICH111 MANSNS
THE WICKED ENCHANTRESS HAD
HE WISHED NOW HE HADN'T BEEN SO WICKED--NOW, WHEN131 MANSNS
IT'S TOO LATE.
SURE, EVERYONE SAYS YOU'RE A WICKED OLD TICK, AS 17 MISBEG
CROOKED AS A CORKSCREW.
YOU WICKED, SINFUL GIRL/ 148 POET
IT'S NOT LIKELY THE LORD GOD'LL BE LISTENIN' TO A 582 ROPE
WICKED OLD SINNER THE LIKE OF
AND I DON'T FEEL WICKED... 112 STRANG
BUT AS IT IS I DON'T FEEL GUILTY OR WICKED. 131 STRANG
(CHILDISHLY) SO I HAVEN'T BEEN SUCH AN AWFULLY 180 STRANG
WICKED GIRL, HAVE I, FATHER$
THANK YOU, FATHER--HAVE I BEEN WICKED$ 200 STRANG

WICKEDNESS
TWO BY THAT AWFUL OSCAR WILDE THEY PUT IN JAIL FOR197 AHWILD
HEAVEN KNOWS WHAT WICKEDNESS.
IT ISN'T ENOUGH YOUR WICKEDNESS LAST NIGHT, BUT 270 AHWILD
NOW YOU HAVE TO TAKE TO LYING?
I'M BEGINNING TO THINK YOU'RE HARDENED IN 270 AHWILD
WICKEDNESS, THAT'S WHAT/
AND ME TORMENTED WITH THE WICKEDNESS YOU'D TOLD OF 69 ANNA
YOURSELF,
(THEN WITH A GRIN) YOU'D OUGHT TO BE USED TO THAT494 DIFRNT
PART OF MEN'S WICKEDNESS--
AND I'D LIKE TO SEE YOU PUNISHED FOR YOUR 32 ELECTR
WICKEDNESS/
TRY AND CONVINCE ORIN OF MY WICKEDNESS/ 92 ELECTR

WICKER
A DILAPIDATED WICKER ROCKER, PAINTED BROWN, IS 41 ANNA
ALSO BY THE TABLE.
(JUBILANTLY, AS CHUCK AND ROCKY ENTER CARRYING A 640 ICEMAN
BIG WICKER BASKET)
BENEATH THEM IS A WICKER COUCH WITH CUSHIONS, ITS 11 JOURNE
HEAD TOWARD REAR.
A SMALL WICKER TABLE AND AN ORDINARY OAK DESK ARE 11 JOURNE
AGAINST THE WALL.
THREE OF THEM WICKER ARMCHAIRS, THE FOURTH--AT 12 JOURNE
RIGHT FRONT OF TABLE--
(SHE LAUGHS AND SITS IN THE WICKER ARMCHAIR AT 14 JOURNE
RIGHT REAR OF TABLE.
SHE SINKS DOWN IN ONE OF THE WICKER ARMCHAIRS AT 49 JOURNE
REAR OF TABLE
AND CARRYING A GOLDEN WICKER BASKET, ENTERS. 391 MARCOM
A WICKER TABLE WITH ANOTHER CHAIR IS AT CENTER. 158 STRANG
TWO WICKER CHAIRS ARE AT LEFT AND A CHAISE LONGUE 158 STRANG
AT RIGHT.
A WICKER TABLE AND ARMCHAIR AT LEFT. 184 STRANG

WIDDER
HE'S BEEN GONE LONG ENOUGH TO WHEEL THE WIDDER TO 96 BEYOND
HOME, CERTAIN.
AND BEIN' A WIDDER WITH ONLY A DAUGHTER, AND LAID 98 BEYOND
UP ALL THE TIME TO BOOT, MRS.
LEAVE A WIDDER, DID HE$ 106 ELECTR

WIDE
(HIS EYES GROW WIDE AND FRIGHTENED) 538 'ILE
I USED TO DREAM OF SAILING ON THE GREAT, WIDE, 545 'ILE
GLORIOUS OCEAN.
AND SO SMALL AT THEIR WIDE-CUFFED BOTTOMS 187 AHWILD
IN A ROUND-FACED, CUTE, SMALL-FEATURED, WIDE-EYED 187 AHWILD
FASHION.
"HOP", THEY CRIED, 'THE WORLD IS WIDE, BUT 246 AHWILD
FETTERED LIMBS GO LAME/
THEN, WITH A PUZZLED EXPRESSION, PULLS IT WIDE. 13 ANNA
IN HIS HIGH FOREHEAD AND WIDE, DARK EYES. 81 BEYOND
THE NEED OF THE FREEDOM OF GREAT WIDE SPACES, THE 85 BEYOND
JOY OF WANDERING ON AND ON--
THERE'S WIDE SPACE ENOUGH, LORD KNOWS... 85 BEYOND
IT WAS ALL-WOOL-AND-A-YARD-WIDE-HELL, I'LL TELL 132 BEYOND
YOU.
HE'S GONE/ THE BED'S EMPTY. THE WINDOW'S WIDE 166 BEYOND
OPEN.
AN' YOU WID A WOMAN AN' CHILDER KEEPIN' FOR YE IN 463 CARIBE
IVRY DIVIL'S PORT IN THE WIDE
A WIDE THIN-LIPPED MOUTH SHADOWED BY AN UNKEMPT 556 CROSS
BRISTLE OF MUSTACHE.
(HE FLINGS HIS LEFT ARM IN A WIDE GESTURE SEAWARD)557 CROSS
THE BLUE OF HER WISTFUL WIDE EYES IS FADING INTO A562 CROSS
TWILIGHT GRAY.
(THE DOOR SWINGS WIDE OPEN, REVEALING SUE 562 CROSS
BARTLETT.
STARE FRIGHTFULLY WIDE AT NOTHING. 571 CROSS
A STRAIGHT NOSE AND A SQUARE JAW, A WIDE MOUTH 493 DAYS
THAT HAS AN INCONGRUOUS FEMININE
IF YOU'VE BEEN WIDE AWAKE TO ALL THAT'S HAPPENED 509 DIFRNT
IN THIS TOWN
THE DYNAMO ROOM IS HIGH AND WIDE WITH RED BRICK 486 DYNAMO
WALLS
A WIDE ARCHWAY GIVING OUT ON A PORTICO WITH WHITE 173 EJONES
PILLARS.
(WITH A WIDE LIBERAL GESTURE) 186 EJONES
A WIDE DIRT ROAD RUNS DIAGONALLY FROM RIGHT, 192 EJONES
FRONT, TO LEFT, REAR.

WIDE (CONT'D.)
I CAN'T GET NEAR YOU WAY-AY, I'M BOUND AWAY ACROSS 6 ELECTR
THE WIDE MISSOURI.*
HIS WIDE MOUTH IS SENSUAL AND MOODY-- 21 ELECTR
I'M BOUND AWAY ACROSS THE WIDE MISSOURI. 43 ELECTR
WAY-AY, I'M BOUND AWAY ACROSS THE WIDE MISSOURI/ 103 ELECTR
OH, SHENANDOAH, I CAN'T GET NEAR YOU WAY--AY, I'M 123 ELECTR
BOUND AWAY ACROSS THE WIDE--*
I CAN'T GET NEAR YOU WAY-AY, I'M BOUND AWAY ACROSS169 ELECTR
THE WIDE MISSOURI.
HER COMPLEXION FRESH AND HEALTHY, HER FIGURE FULL-278 GGBROW
BREASTED AND WIDE-HIPPED.
(WITH AN IMPULSIVE MOVEMENT SHE FLINGS HER ARMS 301 GGBROW
WIDE OPEN.
DEY GOT STREAKS A MILE WIDE. 224 HA APE
A GENERAL ATMOSPHERE OF CLEAN, WELL-TIDIED, WIDE 233 HA APE
STREET.
THEY MAKE WIDE DETOURS TO AVOID THE SPOT 237 HA APE
(SURPRISED BUT ADMIRINGLY) YUH MEAN TO SAY YUH 248 HA APE
ALWAYS RUN WIDE OPEN--LIKE DIS$
THIS DULL IN ERIE--DAISY'S HER NAME--WAS ONE OF 14 HUGHIE
THEM DUMB WIDE-OPEN DULLS.
(WITH AN AGGRIEVED AIR.) HUGHIE WAS A WIDE-AWAKE 15 HUGHIE
GUY.
(SUDDENLY HIS EYES OPEN WIDE) 583 ICEMAN
CAPTAIN LEWIS AND GENERAL WETJOEN ARE AS WIDE 598 ICEMAN
AWAKE AS HEAVY HANGOVERS PERMIT.
'CAUSE I RUN WIDE OPEN FOR YEARS AND PAYS MY SUGAR601 ICEMAN
ON DE DOT.
(HOPE IS INSTANTLY WIDE AWAKE AND EVERYONE IN THE 617 ICEMAN
PLACE.
HER NOSE IS LONG AND STRAIGHT, HER MOUTH WIDE WITH 12 JOURNE
FULL, SENSITIVE LIPS.
SHE WAS LYING DOWN IN THE SPARE ROOM WITH HER EYES 53 JOURNE
WIDE OPEN.
TYRONE STARTS TO WIDE-AWAKENESS AND SOBER DREAD, 170 JOURNE
HIS BODY IS BONY AND ANGULAR, ALMOST MALFORMED, 299 LAZARU
WITH WIDE,
WITHIN THE PORTICO ON ROWS OF CHAIRS PLACED ON A 312 LAZARU
SERIES OF WIDE STEPS WHICH ARE
A WIDE DOOR IS FLUNG OPEN AND A STREAM OF REDDISH 331 LAZARU
LIGHT COMES OUT AGAINST WHICH
A WIDE SENSITIVE MOUTH, A FINE FOREHEAD, LARGE 4 MANSNS
EARS, THICK BROWN HAIR,
LIGHT-BROWN EYES, SET WIDE APART, THEIR EXPRESSION 4 MANSNS
SHARPLY OBSERVANT AND SHREWD,
PUSHES THE DOOR BACK AGAINST THE HOUSE, WIDE OPEN, 27 MANSNS
AND FACES FRONT.
AND ANOTHER, A MAN OF WIDE CULTURE, TOLD ME, 387 MARCOM
(HE SLITS UP THE WIDE SLEEVES OF HIS OWN ROBE, AS 429 MARCOM
DU HIS FATHER AND UNCLE.
HER WAIST WIDE BUT SLENDER BY CONTRAST WITH HER 3 MISBEG
HIPS AND THIGHS.
ON HIS HEAD IS AN OLD WIDE-BRIMMED HAT OF COARSE 11 MISBEG
STRAW.
BUT HIS LITTLE PIG'S EYES ARE SHARPLY WIDE AWAKE 157 MISBEG
AND SOBER.

(SUDDENLY ROCKY'S EYES WIDEN) 668 ICEMAN

WIDER
IS MUCH WIDER THAN THE RIGHT SECTION BUT IS A 473 DYNAMO
STORY LESS IN HEIGHT.

WIDOUT
AND SHOOK HIS HEAD, AND WALKED OUT WIDOUT SAYIN' A480 CARDIF
WORD.
WIDOUT NO JEALOUS NIGGER GUNNIN' AT ME FROM BEHIND179 EJONES
DE TREES.
WHEN I KNOWS DE GAME'S UP I KISSES IT GOOD-BY 182 EJONES
WIDOUT NO LONG WAITS.
TIME YOU BEAT IT IN DE WOODS WIDCUT NO LONG WAITS.190 EJONES
I'SE BETTER OFF WIDOUT OLM. 196 EJONES

WIDOW
(THEN BITTERLY) BUT NOW YOU'RE A WIDOW, 84 ELECTR
WHY, YOU COULD BE THE MOST WOOED WIDOW IN THE 37 MANSNS
CITY.
I'D BE HIS LEGAL WIDOW AND GET WHAT'S LEFT. 164 MISBEG
IF HE WERE KILLED, HE WOULD BE LEAVING NINA A 10 STRANG
WIDOW, PERHAPS WITH A BABY,

WIDOW'S
WHICH GOES WITH HER WIDOW'S BLACK. 50 MANSNS

WIDOWED
BUT YOU HAVE AN OLD MOTHER, A WIFE, A WIDOWED 152 MANSNS
DAUGHTER WITH TWO CHILDREN.

WIDOWS
LAND THAT'S WATERED WITH THE TEARS OF STARVING 62 MISBEG
WIDOWS AND ORPHANS--

WIDTH
TWO-THIRDS OF THE WIDTH OF THE STAGE, 364 DAYS
THEN SHE GIVES THE BIG DOOR A PUSH THAT SLIDES IT 479 DYNAMO
OPEN TO ITS FULL WIDTH AND
IT IS OF DOUBLE WIDTH AND EXTENDS OVER THE 483 DYNAMO
SWITCHBOARD ROOM ALSO.
TO THE LEFT OF CENTER SEVERAL LONG TABLES PLACED 273 LAZARU
LENGTHWISE TO THE WIDTH OF THE
HIS FACE IS TOO LONG FOR ITS WIDTH, HIS NOSE IS 4 STRANG
HIGH AND NARROW

WIFE
NOT ABLE TO GO BACK TEACHING SCHOOL ON ACCOUNT OF 545 'ILE
BEING DAVE KEENEY'S WIFE.
AND I'VE ALWAYS BEEN A GOOD WIFE TO YOU, HAVEN'T 549 'ILE
I, DAVID$
I'M YOUR HUSBAND, ANNIE, AND YOU'RE MY WIFE. 549 'ILE
(TURNING TO HIS WIFE) ANNIE/ 551 'ILE
(KEENEY TURNS HIS BACK ON HIS WIFE AND STRIDES TO 552 'ILE
THE DOORWAY.
ALL ABOUT SOMEONE WHO MURDERED HIS WIFE AND GOT 197 AHWILD
HUNG, AS HE RICHLY DESERVED,

WIFE

WIFE (CONT'D.)
MY WIFE DISCOVERED THEM IN ONE OF MURIEL'S BUREAU 201 AHWILD
DRAWERS HIDDEN UNDER THE
AND PLAYING KELLY POOL, THERE WON'T BE MUCH LEFT 213 AHWILD
FOR A WIFE--
HAVE MADE SUCH A WONDERFUL WIFE FOR ANY MAN-- 214 AHWILD
(SITS DOWN BUT BENDS FORWARD TO CALL TO HIS WIFE 223 AHWILD
IN A CONFIDENTIAL TONE)
A JOKE'S A JOKE, BUT---(HE ADDRESSES HIS WIFE IN A 227 AHWILD
WOUNDED TONE)
(IS ABOUT TO TAKE HIS FIRST BITE--STOPS SUDDENLY 227 AHWILD
AND ASKS HIS WIFE)
(WITH A SAD, SELF-PITYING SMILE AT HIS WIFE) 231 AHWILD
(MILLER AND HIS WIFE AND THE CHILDREN ARE ALL 233 AHWILD
ROARING WITH LAUGHTER.
MILLER GIVES AN UNEASY GLANCE AT HIS WIFE AND 250 AHWILD
THEN,
(TO HIS WIFE) IT WON'T KEEP TOMMY AWAKE. 256 AHWILD
--CAN'T GET AWAY TO MARRY YOU TODAY, MY WIFE WON'T 259 AHWILD
LET ME'A
(PUTTING HIS ARM AROUND HIS WIFE) 262 AHWILD
MILLER AND HIS WIFE COME FIRST. 263 AHWILD
MILLER TURNS TO HIS WIFE 264 AHWILD
HIS WIFE IN THE ROCKER AT RIGHT, FRONT, OF TABLE. 288 AHWILD
IS READING A BOOK WHILE HIS WIFE, SEWING BASKET IN288 AHWILD
LAP,
(WITH A NOD AT RICHARD, WINKING AT HIS WIFE) 296 AHWILD
THE OLD MAN OF THE FAMILY, HIS WIFE, AND FOUR 18 ANNA
SONS--
THE LABORS OF A FARMER'S WIFE HAVE BENT BUT NOT 94 BEYOND
BROKEN HER.
JAMES MAYO, HIS WIFE, HER BROTHER, CAPTAIN DICK 94 BEYOND
SCOTT.
MAYO SMILES SLYLY AT HIS WIFE) 99 BEYOND
RUTH'S A FINE GIRL AND'LL MAKE A GOOD WIFE TO YOU.101 BEYOND
AND HUNT UP A WIFE SOMEWHERES FUR THAT SPICK 'N' 104 BEYOND
SPAN CABIN.
HUSBAND AND WIFE LOOK INTO EACH OTHER'S EYES 121 BEYOND
I S'POSE YOU THINK I OUGHT TO BE PROUD TO BE YOUR 127 BEYOND
WIFE--
IT MUST BE GREAT TO HAVE A WIFE, 486 CARDIF
WITH LIFE BEFORE YOU--A CAPTAIN'S WIFE AS YOUR 564 CROSS
MOTHER WAS.
WHY NOT HAVE THE WIFE DIES 494 DAYS
IF HIS WIFE DIED, AND IMAGINE WHAT HE WOULD DO 495 DAYS
WITH HIS LIFE THEN.
AFTER HE HAS LOST HIS WIFE FOREVER-- 498 DAYS
A PERFECT TYPE OF OUR OLD BEAUTIFUL IDEAL OF WIFE 509 DAYS
AND MOTHER.
THE WIFE DIES--OF INFLUENZA THAT TURNS INTO 513 DAYS
PNEUMONIA, LET'S SAY.
I INTENDED TO TELL FATHER I WAS THROUGH AS 519 DAYS
WALTERS'S WIFE.
AND WHEN HE MET THE WOMAN WHO AFTERWARDS BECAME 535 DAYS
HIS WIFE.
HIS WIFE HAD GONE AWAY. 536 DAYS
THIS DAMNED FOOL, WHO LOVED HIS WIFE MORE THAN 536 DAYS
ANYTHING ELSE IN LIFE.
HIS WIFE WAS AWARE OF IT. 537 DAYS
HE THOUGHT OF HIS WIFE--(THE FORCES A LAUGH) BUT, 537 DAYS
AS I'VE
WAS PAVING OVER SOME WOMAN RIGHT UNDER THE NOSE OF537 DAYS
HIS WIFE.
BETWEEN HIS WIFE AND HIM. 538 DAYS
AT THE THOUGHT OF HIS WIFE, SUDDENLY IT WAS AS IF 538 DAYS
SOMETHING OUTSIDE HIM,
(CULLY) NOT WHILE THE WIFE IS ALIVE. 539 DAYS
HE WANTED TO TELL HIS WIFE AND BEG FOR 539 DAYS
FORGIVENESS--
COULD HIS WIFE HAVE FORGIVEN HIM, DO YOU THINKS 539 DAYS
COME ON, JACK, AND GIVE YOUR POOR WIFE A RESPITE 540 DAYS
FROM THE HORRORS OF AUTHORSHIP.
THIS MAN'S WIFE DIES, YOU SAID. 543 DAYS
HE BEGINS TO BELIEVE HIS WIFE IS ALIVE IN SOME 544 DAYS
MYTHICAL HEREAFTER/
HAIN'T I YER LAWFUL WIFE$ 232 DESIRE
I'M YEWR WIFE. 234 DESIRE
WITHOUT LOOKING AT HIS WIFE, HE PUTS OUT HIS HAND 236 DESIRE
AND CLUTCHES HER KNEE.
I TUK ANOTHER WIFE--EBEN'S MAW. 237 DESIRE
I TUK A WIFE. 237 DESIRE
IT'S ONLY TWO DAYS MORE BEFORE YOU AND ME'LL BE 496 DIFRNT
MAN AND WIFE.
(TURNING TO HIS WIFE) WHAT YE GOT TO SAY NOW, MA5513 DIFRNT
(HE SHAKES WITH LAUGHTER AND KISSES HIS WIFE A 513 DIFRNT
RESOUNDING SMACK.)
NO MORE OR BE YOUR WIFE, IT'S JUST THAT I'VE 517 DIFRNT
DECIDED--
WHAT DO I WANT A WIFE FURS 546 DIFRNT
THE REVEREND HUTCHINS LIGHT IS SEATED IN HIS 421 DYNAMO
ARMCHAIR, HIS WIFE IN HER ROCKER.
HIS WIFE IS PRETENDING TO READ, BUT HER THOUGHTS 422 DYNAMO
ARE ACTIVELY ELSEWHERE.
HIS WIFE, AMELIA, IS FIFTEEN YEARS HIS JUNIOR AND 422 DYNAMO
APPEARS EVEN YOUNGER.
(THEN TURNING TO HIS WIFE) 425 DYNAMO
LISTENING TO THE VICTROLA, FIXES HIS EYES ON HIS 426 DYNAMO
WIFE COMBATIVELY)
HIS WIFE IS LYING BACK IN A CHAISE LONGUE THAT SHE428 DYNAMO
HAS PUSHED CLOSE TO THE
HIS WIFE IS TALL AND STOUT, WEIGHING WELL OVER TW0428 DYNAMO
HUNDRED.
(HE TOSSES THE BOOK ON THE TABLE AND SPEAKS TO HIS429 DYNAMO
WIFE)
(AS ADA BEGINS TO READ, HE SPEAKS TO HIS WIFE) 431 DYNAMO
(HE TURNS HIS EXASPERATION ON HIS WIFE) 434 DYNAMO
BARKING MY WIFE AND ADA. 440 DYNAMO
(HE THROWS THE BELT ON THE BED--TO HIS WIFE) 449 DYNAMO

WIFE (CONT'D.)
THE JOKE HAS THROWN HIM--BURSTING INTO A FATUOUS 452 DYNAMO
RAGE--TO HIS WIFE)
AND RUNS PANIC-STRICKEN OFF RIGHT, DRAGGING HIS 453 DYNAMO
MOANING WIFE BY THE ARM.
THEN STOPS WITHOUT LOOKING AROUND HIM AND DOES NOT478 DYNAMO
NOTICE HIS WIFE.)
BEST, AS ARE HIS WIFE AND HER COUSIN, IS A FAT MAN 6 ELECTR
IN HIS FIFTIES.
HIS WIFE, LOUISA, IS TALLER AND STOUTER THAN HE 6 ELECTR
AND ABOUT THE SAME AGE.
CLOSELY FOLLOWING HIM ARE AMOS AMES, HIS WIFE 6 ELECTR
LOUISA, AND HER COUSIN MINNIE.
WHICH IS MURE'N YOU KIN SAY FUR HIS WIFE. 8 ELECTR
I COULDN'T HELP GIVIN' HIM A DIG ABOUT EZRA'S 8 ELECTR
WIFE.
AND IF EZRA'S WIFE STARTS TO RUN YOU OFF FUR 8 ELECTR
TRESPASSIN'
THAT WE HAVE ALREADY SEEN IN THE FACES OF HIS WIFE 28 ELECTR
AND DAUGHTER AND BRANT.
IF YOU WERE THE WIFE OF A MAN YOU HATED/ 30 ELECTR
AND PROMISE TO BE A DUTIFUL WIFE TO FATHER AND 32 ELECTR
MAKE UP FOR THE WRONG YOU'VE DONE
YOU'VE TRIED TO BECOME THE WIFE OF YOUR FATHER AND 33 ELECTR
THE MOTHER OF ORIN/
ALL YOUR OWN--YOUR WIFE/ 42 ELECTR
AS IF AT ATTENTION, STARING AT HIS HOUSE, HIS WIFE 46 ELECTR
AND DAUGHTER.
(REALLY REVELING IN HIS DAUGHTER'S CODDLING BUT 47 ELECTR
EMBARRASSED BEFORE HIS WIFE--
MANNON LOOKS AT HIS WIFE WHO STARES BEFORE HER. 51 ELECTR
I'VE GOT TO EXPLAIN SOME THINGS--INSIDE ME--TO MY 53 ELECTR
WIFE--TRY TO ANYWAY/
THEN ALL THE YEARS WE'VE BEEN MAN AND WIFE WOULD 54 ELECTR
RISE UP IN MY MIND
I TURNED TO VINNIE, BUT A DAUGHTER'S NOT A WIFE. 55 ELECTR
NOT YOUR WIFE/ 60 ELECTR
AND YOU ARE NOT MY WIFE/ 60 ELECTR
YOU ACTED AS IF I WERE YOUR WIFE--YOUR PROPERTY-- 60 ELECTR
NOT SO LONG AGO/
HIS EYES GLARING AT HIS WIFE, 63 ELECTR
HIS WIFE, ABOUT TEN YEARS HIS JUNIOR, 67 ELECTR
THESE PEOPLE--THE BORDENS, HILLS AND HIS WIFE AND 67 ELECTR
DOCTOR BLAKE--
THE CONGREGATIONAL MINISTER, AND HIS WIFE, AND 67 ELECTR
DOCTOR JOSEPH BLAKE,
THE FRONT DOOR IS OPENED AND JOSIAH BORDEN AND HIS 67 ELECTR
WIFE, EVERETT HILLS,
HE IS IN THE FIFTIES, AS IS HIS WIFE, A SALLOW, 68 ELECTR
FLABBY,
SELF-EFFACING MINISTER'S WIFE. 68 ELECTR
NOT BUT WHAT SHE HASN'T ALWAYS BEEN A DUTIFUL 68 ELECTR
WIFE, AS FAR AS ANYONE KNOWS.
MY WIFE ENTIRELY MISUNDERSTOOD ME. 70 ELECTR
MY WIFE SHOULD HAVE REMEMBERED-- 70 ELECTR
ONLY NATURAL BETWEEN MAN AND WIFE-- 71 ELECTR
I HAD BEEN A GOOD WIFE TO HIM FOR TWENTY-THREE 77 ELECTR
YEARS--UNTIL I MET ADAM.
I WOULD HAVE BEEN A GOOD WIFE AGAIN AS LONG AS 77 ELECTR
YOUR FATHER HAD LIVED.
ABE MANNON'S WIFE AND THE WIFE OF WASHINGTON'S 79 ELECTR
OFFICER.
AS NIMS KILLED HIS WIFE WITH A HATCHET--SHE'D 132 ELECTR
NAGGED HIM--
(WITH BITTER HOPELESSNESS--TO HIS WIFE--INDICATING261 GGBROW
THEIR SON)
(THEN MOCKINGLY) ARE MR. ANTHONY AND HIS WIFE 262 GGBROW
GOING IN TO DANCE--
AND I'LL BE MRS. DION--DION'S WIFE-- 264 GGBROW
UNTIL AT THE END SHE IS A WIFE AND A MOTHER) 264 GGBROW
THEN JEERINGLY) SO MY WIFE THINKS IT BEHOVES ME 271 GGBROW
TO SETTLE DOWN AND SUPPORT MY
THEN I ASK MY WIFE TO GO AND ASK BILLY BROWN-- 273 GGBROW
THEN MY POOR WIFE DID A-BEGGING GO/ 281 GGBROW
MY WIFE DRAGGED IN A DOCTOR THE DAY BEFORE 286 GGBROW
YESTERDAY.
I DON'T KNOW WHO MY WIFE IS. 286 GGBROW
I'M JEALOUS OF YOUR WIFE, EVEN THOUGH I KNOW YOU 286 GGBROW
DO LOVE HER.
YOU LOVE HIS WIFE. 289 GGBROW
I ONLY SPOKE AS I DID ON ACCOUNT OF MARGARET--HIS 289 GGBROW
WIFE--
IT WAS THIS LADY--MY WIFE. 293 GGBROW
MY WIFE AND I HAVE BEEN GOING OVER IT AGAIN. 306 GGBROW
OUR WIFE IS WAITING. 308 GGBROW
THAT'S AN AWFUL WAY FOR A WIFE TO FEEL/ 309 GGBROW
(UNHEEDING) AND THEN MY WIFE CAN BE HAPPY/ 311 GGBROW
EXCEPT HIS WIFE AND KIDS, OF COURSE. 11 HUGHIE
HIS WIFE IS A BUM--IN SPADES/ 12 HUGHIE
I'D TELL HIM, «JUST LET THAT WIFE OF YOURS KNOW 16 HUGHIE
YOU'RE CHEATIN'.»
BUT HOW COULD HE WITH HIS WIFE KEEPIN' CASES ON 16 HUGHIE
EVERY NICKEL OF HIS SALARYS
HIS WIFE DEALT HIM FOUR BITS A DAY FOR SPENDING 21 HUGHIE
MONEY.
OH--YOU MEAN MY WIFE$ 24 HUGHIE
HIS WIFE HAD DONE A LOT OF STUFF TO DOLL IT UP. 25 HUGHIE
HUGHIE'S WIFE BUTT IN AND STOPPED ME COLD. 25 HUGHIE
AND HE HAD KIDS AND A WIFE, AND THE FAMILY RACKET 25 HUGHIE
IS OUT OF MY LINE.
HE NEVER DID BEEF TO ME ABOUT HIS WIFE AGAIN. 26 HUGHIE
COME TO FIGGER IT, I'LL BET HE EVEN CHEATED ON HIS 28 HUGHIE
WIFE THAT WAY,
THE FIRST TIME, HIS WIFE WAS THERE AND GIVE ME A 30 HUGHIE
DIRTY LOOK.
BUT HIS WIFE BUTTS IN AND SAYS HE'S WEAK AND HE 30 HUGHIE
MUSTN'T GET EXCITED.

1797

WIFE

(CONT'D.)

REMEMBER HOW HE WORKS UP DAT GAG ABOUT HIS WIFE, 580 ICEMAN
WHEN HE'S COCKEYED.
SINCE HIS WIFE DIED TWENTY YEARS AGO. 594 ICEMAN
(HE CHUCKLES AT A MEMORY) REMEMBER THAT GAG HE 610 ICEMAN
ALWAYS PULLS ABOUT HIS WIFE AND
I JUST GIVE DEM A SLAP, LIKE ANY GUY WOULD HIS 633 ICEMAN
WIFE, IF SHE GOT TOO GABBY.
OR MAYBE WORSE, WID YOUR WIFE AND DE ICEMAN 636 ICEMAN
WALKIN' SLOW BEHIND YUH.»
(EXCITEDLY) D'YOUSE SUPPOSE DAT HE DID CATCH HIS 636 ICEMAN
WIFE CHEATIN'S
COME TO YOU AFTER YOU FOUND YOUR WIFE WAS SICK OF 662 ICEMAN
YOUR
I'M SORRY TO TELL YOU MY DEARLY BELOVED WIFE IS 663 ICEMAN
DEAD.
BUT HIS TELLIN' ABOUT HIS WIFE CROAKIN' PUT DE K. 665 ICEMAN
O. ON IT.
ESPECIALLY SINCE HE TOLD US HIS WIFE WAS DEAD. 666 ICEMAN
YOU NOTICE HE DIDN'T SAY WHAT HIS WIFE DIED OF-. 668 ICEMAN
(TO PARRITT) WHAT D'YOU KNOW ABOUT HICKEY'S WIFE5668 ICEMAN
HENPECKED AND BROWBEATEN BY A NAGGING WIFE. 670 ICEMAN
AND DE FOIST TING I KNOW YUH'LL HAVE ME OUT 671 ICEMAN
HUSTLIN' AGAIN, YOUR OWN WIFE/
(REVENGEFULLY) YOU DROVE YOUR POOR WIFE TO 693 ICEMAN
SUICIDES
(ACCUSINGLY) WHAT DID YOUR WIFE DIE OF& 693 ICEMAN
THEN SLOWLY) NO, I'M SORRY TO HAVE TO TELL YOU MY694 ICEMAN
POOR WIFE WAS KILLED.
I DON'T KNOW NUTTIN', SEE, BUT IT LOOKS LIKE HE 698 ICEMAN
CROAKED HIS WIFE.
WON'T I LOOK SWEET WID A WIFE DAT 698 ICEMAN
VINDICTIVELY) I DON'T GIVE A DAMN WHAT HE DONE TO698 ICEMAN
HIS WIFE.
YUH NEVER EVEN HOID HE HAD A WIFE. 703 ICEMAN
IF SHE'D BEEN THE SAME KIND OF WIFE I WAS A 714 ICEMAN
HUSBAND.
HE'D GONE CRAZY AND CROAKED HIS WIFE. 725 ICEMAN
ALL I WANTED WAS TO BE HIS WIFE. 105 JOURNE
SHE'LL NEVER MAKE A GOOD WIFE.» 114 JOURNE
I HAVEN'T BEEN SUCH A BAD WIFE, HAVE IS 114 JOURNE
TYRONE SCOWLS AND LOOKS AT HIS WIFE WITH SHARP 116 JOURNE
SUSPICION--ROUGHLY.)
KNEELING BESIDE HIM WITH BOWED HEADS ARE HIS WIFE,274 LAZARU
MIRIAM, HIS SISTERS,
HE IS FAITHFUL TO HIS WIFE, I WARN YOU. 341 LAZARU
HAVE YOU NOT A GOOD HOME I MAKE FOR YOU, AND A 347 LAZARU
WIFE WHO LOVES YOUS
(STRANGELY) MY MOTHER WAS THE WIFE OF CAESAR. 352 LAZARU
BUT LOVED HERSELF AS CAESAR'S WIFE. 355 LAZARU
THEN I KILLED THAT WHORE, MY WIFE, 356 LAZARU
POOR WIFE/ 361 LAZARU
BUT DID YOU LOVE HER--OR JUST WOMAN, WIFE AND 361 LAZARU
MOTHER OF MEN&
WIFE OF THE WELL KNOWN MERCHANT, BUT A NOBLE 3 MANSNS
ADVENTURESS OF LOUIS' COURT.
THE OUTIFUL WIFE SAT BY HIS BEDSIDE. 30 MANSNS
GO AND BEG SIMON AND HIS WIFE TO LET YOU LIVE ON 33 MANSNS
CHARITY WITH THEMS
AND WHO WILL TAKE GREAT PLEASURE IN DOING SO-- 35 MANSNS
SIMON'S WIFE/
YOU MAY EVEN FND YOU CAN LIKE HIS WIFE, WHEN YOU 39 MANSNS
KNOW HER.
FORGETTING PREJUDICE, YOU MUST ADMIT SHE HAS BEEN 39 MANSNS
AN ESTIMABLE WIFE AND MOTHER.
IN YOUR HAPPINESS AS MY SON'S WIFE AND HIS 54 MANSNS
HAPPINESS AS YOUR HUSBAND.
WOULD MEAN IT WOULD BE THEIR VACATION WITH THEIR 72 MANSNS
MOTHER, NOT MINE WITH MY WIFE.
IN ORDER TO MAKE OF MY WIFE A SECOND SELF THROUGH 73 MANSNS
WHICH SHE COULD LIVE AGAIN.
MOTHER AND WIFE IN ONE-- 73 MANSNS
BUT NOW NO LONGER NEEDED SINCE THE MOTHER BY 73 MANSNS
BECOMING WIFE
HAS MY FOUR SONS TO SUBSTITUTE FOR ME, AND THE 73 MANSNS
WIFE HAVING THEM,
I CANNOT DISTINGUISH MY WIFE FROM--IT IS A 82 MANSNS
BEWILDERING CONFUSION.
HERE YOU ARE YOURSELF, MY WIFE, MY PARTNER--MY 85 MANSNS
MISTRESS, TOO, I HOPE.
DO YOU MEAN TO TELL ME A VIRTUOUS WIFE AND MOTHER 89 MANSNS
LIKE YOU
THAT'S A NICE WAY TO TALK TO A DECENT WIFE/ 90 MANSNS
SHE WILL BECOME NO MORE THAN THE EMPTY NAME OF 118 MANSNS
WIFE, A HOUSEKEEPER.
TREATING HIS WIFE AS IF SHE WAS A WHORE HE'D PICK 121 MANSNS
UP ON THE STREET
IF YOU THINK I LIKED HIM INSULTING HIS WIFE 133 MANSNS
AND ME YOUR BROTHER'S WIFE. 143 MANSNS
I'M YOUR WIFE AND YOU'RE MINE. 145 MANSNS
YOUR APPOINTMENT IS REALLY WITH MY WIFE. 151 MANSNS
BUT YOU HAVE AN OLD MOTHER, A WIFE, A WIDOWED 152 MANSNS
DAUGHTER WITH TWO CHILDREN.
YOU WERE AFRAID THAT YOUR MOTHER, YOUR WIFE, 153 MANSNS
DAUGHTER,
I'M MOTHER, WIFE, AND MISTRESS IN ONE. 167 MANSNS
DO YOU THINK YOUR HUSBAND WOULD LOVE A WIFE WHO 168 MANSNS
HAD MURDERED HIS MOTHERS
GET BACK TO THE GREASY ARMS OF YOUR WIFE/ 190 MANSNS
WHEN HE CAME TO MANHOOD, RENOUNCED WIFE AND CHILD,372 MARCOM
RICHES AND POWER,
KUKACHIN WILL BE A WIFE. 409 MARCOM
A WIFE MUST NOT SORROW SAVE FOR HER MAN. 410 MARCOM
(WITH A GRIN) WELL, I DON'T MIND A WIFE BEING A 416 MARCOM
BIT PLUMP--
I AM WIFE OF HIS SON, GHAZAN. 423 MARCOM
WILL SOBER HER SPIRIT AND SHE WILL SETTLE DOWN AS 424 MARCOM
A SENSIBLE WIFE SHOULD.

WIFE'S

WIFE (CONT'D.)

I WOULDN'T CALL IT A DIRTY TRICK ON HIM TO GET YOU 24 MISBEG
FOR A WIFE.
(SERIOUSLY) IT'S TRUE, IF I WAS HIS WIFE, 29 MISBEG
HE'D HARDLY GOT SETTLED WHEN HIS WIFE DIED GIVIN' 11 POET
BIRTH TO CON.
HE GOT CAUGHT BY A SPANISH NOBLE MAKING LOVE TO 12 POET
HIS WIFE,
BUT ONCE IN A WHILE THERE'LL BE SOME YANKEE STOPS 13 POET
OVERNIGHT WID HIS WIFE OR
HE MAY AT FIRST, BUT WHEN I'VE PROVED WHAT A GOOD 31 POET
WIFE I'LL BE,
(ADVANCING INTO THE ROOM--BOWS FORMALLY TO HIS 34 POET
WIFE.)
ALTHOUGH HE CANNOT SEE HIS WIFE, HE IS NERVOUSLY 35 POET
CONSCIOUS OF HER.
EVAN'S WIFE, OF COURSE, WAS DRAWN INTO THIS 83 POET
CONFLICT.
IF YOU'RE HIS WIFE--/ 127 POET
OH, BETTER STILL, A WIFE LIKE YOU. 136 POET
HE STARES AT HIS WIFE AND DAUGHTER AS IF HE DID 152 POET
NOT RECOGNIZE THEM.
LET YOU TAKE CARE AV HIM NOW, HIS WIFE AND 165 POET
DAUGHTER/
SURE, THERE'S DIVIL A MORE LOYAL WIFE IN THE WHOLE174 POET
WORLD--
NOW IT'S DEAD--THANK GOD--AND I'LL MAKE A BETTER 180 POET
WIFE FOR SIMON.
YOUR WIFE, INDEED, WITH A CHILD SHE CLAIMED WAS 580 ROPE
YOUR'N.
SWEENEY SPEAKS TO HIS WIFE IN A LOW TONE) 583 ROPE
(TO HIS WIFE) IT'S SOFT-MINDED SHE IS, LIKE I'VE 5898 ROPE
ALWAYS TOLD YOU, AN' STUPID,.
STANDS SHAKING HIS STICK AT SWEENEY AND HIS WIFE) 584 ROPE
(SWEENEY LEANS OVER TO HIS WIFE--INDIGNANTLY) 585 ROPE
DURING THE FOLLOWING CONVERSATION BETWEEN SWEENEY 590 ROPE
AND HIS WIFE
SO AGGRESSIVELY HIS WIFE/.... 5 STRANG
AND HIS WIFE.... 5 STRANG
WIFE/ 9 STRANG
MY WIFE... 9 STRANG
OH, WIFE, WHY DID YOU DIE, YOU WOULD HAVE TALKED 15 STRANG
TO HER,
AS IF SHE'D DETERMINED TO MAKE HERSELF A LOVING 52 STRANG
WIFE--
WORKING FOR HIS WIFE AND NOT JUST HIMSELF-- 54 STRANG
I REMEMBER WHEN I WAS CARRYING SAM, SOMETIMES I'D 63 STRANG
FORGET I WAS A WIFE,.
BEING TIED TO A WIFE WHO'S TOO SICK TO BE A WIFE. 70 STRANG
THE DUTIES OF A WIFE-- 81 STRANG
WHO WOULD BE FOR HIM A LIVING PROOF THAT HIS WIFE 85 STRANG
LOVED HIM.
(THINKING) (I) HAVE A FRIEND WHO HAS A WIFE.... 85 STRANG
WHAT IS IT PRECISELY THAT SAM'S WIFE HAS THOUGHT 85 STRANG
SO MUCH OF DOINGS
(COLDLY) I'VE BEEN CONSIDERING WHAT SAM'S WIFE 86 STRANG
TOLD ME AND HER REASONING IS
YOU MUST GIVE HIS WIFE COURAGE, DOCTOR. 86 STRANG
IT SAVES HIS WIFE.... 86 STRANG
SAM'S WIFE SHOULD FIND A HEALTHY FATHER FOR SAM'S 86 STRANG
CHILD AT ONCE.
OH, DOCTOR, SAM'S WIFE IS AFRAID/ 86 STRANG
CERTAINLY SAM'S WIFE MUST CONCEAL HER ACTION/ 86 STRANG
WIFE SHE CAN'T BEAR THE THOUGHT NOW OF GIVING 88 STRANG
HERSELF TO ANY MAN SHE COULD
I'LL PICK OUT A WIFE FOR YOU--GUARANTEED TO SUIT/,114 STRANG
YOU THINK I'LL STAY--TO BE YOUR LOVER--WATCHING 132 STRANG
SAM WITH MY WIFE AND MY CHILD--
YOUR WIFE IS MINE/... 134 STRANG
SHE'S A WONDERFUL WIFE AND MOTHER....) 134 STRANG
HE HAS A CHARMING WIFE AND A DARLING BOY, 141 STRANG
I SUPPOSE THE THOUGHT OF A WIFE TAKING YOU AWAY 143 STRANG
FROM ME WOULD BE TOO MUCH--
THE WIFE AND MISTRESS IN ME HAS BEEN KILLED BY 149 STRANG
THEM--.
SHE WAS A WONDERFUL WIFE. 185 STRANG
WASN'T IT ENOUGH FOR HIM TO OWN MY WIFE, MY SON, 192 STRANG
IN HIS LIFETIME....
AND I SAW HOW FAIR YOU BOTH WERE TO DAD--WHAT A 199 STRANG
GOOD WIFE YOU WERE, MOTHER--
OWN LITTLE WIFE/ 444 WELDED
(HE PULLS HER TO HER FEET) MY WIFE/ 448 WELDED
MY LOVER/ MY WIFE/ 489 WELDED
WIFE'LL
YOUR WIFE'LL BE WORRIED. 287 GGBROW
WIFE'S
KEENEY HEARS HIS WIFE'S HYSTERICAL WEEPING AND 545 'ILE
TURNS AROUND IN SURPRISE--
(HE STOPS, FEELING HIS WIFE'S EYES FIXED ON HIM, 291 AHWILD
WITH INDIGNANT SUSPICION.)
(LOOKING AT ANDREW OVER HIS WIFE'S SHOULDER-- 107 BEYOND
STUBBORNLY)
AND THE MORE PEACE AND SECURITY HE FOUND IN HIS 536 DAYS
WIFE'S LOVE,
(STARTS--THEN TENSELY) YOU WANT ME TO PUT MYSELF 539 DAYS
IN THE WIFE'S PLACES
YOU CAN IMAGINE THE ANGUISH HE FEELS AFTER HIS 544 DAYS
WIFE'S DEATH--
I WANT TO TALK WITH YOU ABOUT YOUR WIFE'S 555 DAYS
CONDITION.
HIS WIFE'S ROCKER IS AT THE RIGHT OF THE TABLE. 421 DYNAMO
HIS WIFE'S VOICE COMES EXCITEDLY FROM BELOW 445 DYNAMO
THE GRIEF OVER HIS WIFE'S DEATH HAS MADE HIM AN 455 DYNAMO
OLD MAN.
THERE WASN'T NOBODY BUT A COUPLA HIS WIFE'S 31 HUGHIE
RELATIONS.
BY PRETENDING IT WAS MY WIFE'S ADULTERY THAT 707 ICEMAN
RUINED MY LIFE.

WIFE'S

WIFE'S (CONT'D.)
TYRONE'S ARM IS AROUND HIS WIFE'S WAIST AS THEY 14 JOURNE
APPEAR FROM THE BACK PARLOR.
THE MIRACLE COULD NOT REVIVE ALL HIS OLD HUSBAND'S331 LAZARU
LIFE IN MY WIFE'S HEART.
FAITH, I'LL HAVE YOU REPEAT IT FOR MY WIFE'S 97 POET
BENEFIT WHEN SHE JOINS US.
AT LEAST, ONLY THE LOVE OF A FRIEND, NOT A WIFE'S 185 STRANG
LOVE.

WIFELESS
BUT AT THE SAME TIME BY BECOMING SARA, LEAVE ME 73 MANSNS
WIFELESS,

WIFLY
AND I HOPED I HAD AT LAST ESCAPED THE DUNNING OF 36 MANSNS
WIFLY DUTY/

WIG
HER WIG AND DRESS ARE PURPLE. 337 LAZARU
GIVES HER THE APPEARANCE OF A GIRL WEARING A 2 MANSNS
BECOMING WIG AT A COSTUME BALL.

WIGGLE
YOU CAN'T WIGGLE OUT, NOW I GOT ME 'OOKS ON YER. 174 EJONES

WIGGLED
AND WIGGLED YOUR BACKSIDE, 82 MISBEG

WIGS
THEY ALSO WEAR WIRE WIGS BUT OF STRAIGHT HAIR CUT 336 LAZARU
IN SHORT BOYISH MODE.
THESE YOUTHS WEAR FEMALE WIGS OF CURLED WIRE LIKE 336 LAZARU
FRIZZED HAIR OF A YELLOW GOLD.

WILD
(MRS. KEENEY LOOKS AROUND HER IN WILD SCORN) 546 'ILE
(WITH WILD JOY--KISSING HIM) 549 'ILE
YOU NEED REST AFTER TEACHING A PACK OF WILD 212 AHWILD
INDIANS OF KIDS ALL YEAR.
(SHAKING HER HEAD) WILD HORSES COULDN'T DRAG HER 234 AHWILD
THERE NOW.
(WITH A WILD GESTURE OF DEFIANCE--MAUDLINLY 261 AHWILD
DRAMATIC)
RICHARD AND CLEAN FORGOT HOW WILD OLD MCCOMBER WAS292 AHWILD
AGAINST IT.
HIS DARK EYES ARE BLOODSHOT AND WILD FROM 30 ANNA
SLEEPLESSNESS.
THERE IS AN EXPRESSION IN HIS EYES OF WILD MENTAL 68 ANNA
TURMOIL.
(THEN WITH SUDDEN WILD GRIEF) 69 ANNA
(WITH WILD IRONICAL LAUGHTER) 72 ANNA
BUT RUTH WAS SO SPELLED WITH ROBERT'S WILD POETRY 116 BEYOND
NOTIONS
AND HIS EYES LOOKED SO--SO WILD LIKE. 151 BEYOND
(DULLY) HE WAS TALKING--WILD--LIKE HE USED TO-- 163 BEYOND
THE FIELD IN THE FOREGROUND HAS A WILD 166 BEYOND
UNCULTIVATED APPEARANCE
(WITH A WILD LAUGH) AS IF I WERE MADS 567 CROSS
NAT COMES DOWN THE COMPANIONWAY, HIS EYES WILD AND569 CROSS
EXULTING.)
HIS DEFIANT, DARK EYES REMIND ONE OF A WILD 203 DESIRE
ANIMAL'S IN CAPTIVITY.
ROCKING WITH WILD LAUGHTER.) 223 DESIRE
THEN SUDDENLY WILD PASSION OVERCOMES HER. 243 DESIRE
(BOTH HER ARMS AROUND HIM--WITH WILD PASSION) 243 DESIRE
AND SPRINGS TO HER FEET--WITH WILD RAGE AND 264 DESIRE
HATRED)
BEEN RUNS IN, PANTING EXHAUSTEDLY, WILD-EYED AND 265 DESIRE
MAD LOOKING.
IT'LL GIT HIM WILD IF YOU DO THAT. 502 DIFRNT
SHE'S GOIN' WILD. 548 DIFRNT
(AFTER A TENSE PAUSE--WITH A SUDDEN OUTBURST OF 549 DIFRNT
WILD GRIEF)
REUBEN LOOKS UP AND GIVES A WILD LAUGH AS THOUGH 452 DYNAMO
THE THUNDER ELATED HIM.
BUT I AIN'T TALKIN' WILD JUST DE SAME. 179 EJONES
DEY WAS ONLY LITTLE ANIMALS--LITTLE WILD PIGS, I 190 EJONES
RECKON.
WITH SOMETHING FREE AND WILD ABOUT HER LIKE AN 44 ELECTR
ANIMILE.
(CONTROLLING A WILD IMPULSE TO BURST INTO DERISIVE 52 ELECTR
LAUGHTER)
THEN SUDDENLY A WILD LOOK OF TERROR COMES OVER HIS 62 ELECTR
FACE.
HIS FACE WEARS A DAZED EXPRESSION AND HIS EYES 139 ELECTR
HAVE A WILD, STRICKEN LOOK.
AND THE WILD LOOK FADES FROM HIS EYES LEAVING THEM156 ELECTR
GLAZED AND LIFELESS.)
THEN THE OBSESSED WILD LOOK RETURNS TO HIS EYES-- 166 ELECTR
WITH HARSH MOCKERY)
(WITH A WILD BEATEN LAUGH) THE DEAD COMING 176 ELECTR
BETWEEN!
(WITH WILD MOCKERY) ASK HIM IF HE CAN'T FIND AN 273 GGBROW
OPENING FOR A TALENTED YOUNG
OR BECAUSE HE POSES AS ARTISTIC AND 289 GGBROW
TEMPERAMENTAL--OR BECAUSE HE'S SO WILD--
HE IS IN A WILD STATE. 294 GGBROW
A WILD BOAR OF THE MOUNTAINS ALTERED INTO A 296 GGBROW
PACKER'S HOG EATING TO BECOME FOOD--
THE MEN START TO THEIR FEET IN WILD-EYED TERROR 523 INZONE
OUR WILD IRISH LARK/ 54 JOURNE
I WAS WILD WITH AMBITION. 150 JOURNE
(CONTROLLING A WILD IMPULSE TO LAUGH--AGREEABLY.) 151 JOURNE
I BELONGED, WITHOUT PAST OR FUTURE, WITHIN PEACE 153 JOURNE
AND UNITY AND A WILD JOY.
(THIS LAST IN A WILD FRENZY.) 288 LAZARU
THE WILD JOYOUS MUSIC CEASES. 305 LAZARU
HIS ASPECT IS WILD, HIS HAIR DISHEVELED, HIS 368 LAZARU
CLOTHES TORN.
STRANGE WILD MEASURES OF LIBERATED JOY. 368 LAZARU
(HE LAUGHS WITH A WILD TRIUMPHANT MADNESS AND 370 LAZARU
AGAIN RHEIDICALLY
CONSERVATIVE MERCHANT LIKE HENRY KNOW OF SUCH WILD 32 MANSNS
SPECULATIONS

WILD (CONT'D.)
(HE CHECKS HIMSELF, HIS EYES GLEAMING WITH A WILD 159 MANSNS
THREAT.)
WILD HYSTERICAL TEARS. 161 MANSNS
AND THERE IS A WILD LOOK IN HIS EYES CALCULATING 171 MANSNS
AND THREATENING
(WITH WILD DESPAIR PULLS OUT A SMALL DAGGER FROM 415 MARCOM
THE BOSOM OF HER DRESS)
SHE CONFRONTS HIM DEFIANTLY, HER EYES WILD WITH 415 MARCOM
GRIEF AND RAGE.
(GIVES A LAUGH OF WILD IRONY) 419 MARCOM
(WITH WILD LAUGHTER) HA-HA-HA/ 425 MARCOM
(ANOTHER WILD ROUND OF CONGRATULATIONS, KISSES, 430 MARCOM
ETC.)
I TOOK IT FROM HIS LITTLE GREEN BAG, AND WON'T HE 7 MISBEG
BE WILD WHEN HE FINDS OUT/
HE DOESN'T GIVE WILD PARTIES, DOESN'T CHASE AFTER 55 MISBEG
MUSICAL-COMEDY CUTIES.
SHE SAID SHE'D COME TO WARN SIMON HIS FATHER IS 78 POET
WILD WITH ANGER
SUCH A WILD FEELING OF RELEASE AND FRESH 86 POET
ENSLAVEMENT.
SO HE WAS WILD WITH JOY TO SEE ME-- 143 POET
AND ALL THE TIME WE WERE KISSING EACH OTHER, WILD 147 POET
WITH HAPPINESS.
(THINKING WITH WILD AGONY) (DEAR OLD CHARLIE/... 44 STRANG
(NOT HEEDING THIS LAST--WITH WILD MOCKERY) 61 STRANG
(OBLIVIOUS TO DARRELL'S WILD EXPRESSION.) 132 STRANG
(COMES RUSHING OUT IN WILD ALARM) 177 STRANG
WILD JOYOUS PITY) 180 STRANG
(GETTING UP--THINKING WITH A STRANGE, WILD 181 STRANG
PASSION)
(IN WILD PROTEST) NELLY, WHAT ARE YOU OFFERING 452 WELDED
ME--A SACRIFICE?
(WITH A WILD IRONICAL LAUGH) 459 WELDED
(WITH WILD HYSTERICAL SCORN) 460 WELDED
(SHE LAUGHS WITH WILD BITTERNESS) 468 WELDED
HE IS BARE-HEADED, HIS HAIR DISHEVELED, HIS EYES 471 WELDED
WILD.
HIS MIND--WITH A WILD LAUGH) 472 WELDED
(WITH A SUDDEN BURST OF WILD LAUGHTER) 472 WELDED
(STARTING--WITH WILD SCORN) DO YOU THINK I--/ 473 WELDED
YOU,--YOU'RE THE LAST DEPTH--(WITH A STRANGE, WILD473 WELDED
EXULTANCE, LEAPS TO HIS FEET)
(WITH A WILD LAUGH) A FACT? 474 WELDED
(A WILD, IRONICAL LAUGH ESCAPES HIS CONTROL) 483 WELDED

WILDCAT
DOWN TO COMMON SENSE, WITH HIS CRAZY WILDCAT 260 GGBROW
NOTIONS.

WILDE
HIS FATHER WAS IN ENGLAND WHEN THIS WILDE WAS 197 AHWILD
PINCHED--
TWO BY THAT AWFUL OSCAR WILDE THEY PUT IN JAIL FOR197 AHWILD
HEAVEN KNOWS WHAT WICKEDNESS.
THAT IF HE WASN'T FLUNG IN JAIL ALONG WITH WILDE, 198 AHWILD
HE SHOULD HAVE BEEN.
CURING THE SOUL BY MEANS OF THE SENSES, AS OSCAR 271 AHWILD
WILDE SAYS--
POETRY BY SWINBURNE, ROSETTI, WILDE, ERNEST 11 JOURNE
DOWSON, KIPLING, ETC.
THIS DOWSON, AND THIS BAUDELAIRE, AND SWINBURNE 135 JOURNE
AND OSCAR WILDE'S

WILDE'S
(QUOTES WITH GUSTO FROM OSCAR WILDE'S *THE 159 JOURNE
HARLOT'S HOUSE.*)
OSCAR WILDE'S *READING GAOL* HAS THE THE DOPE 166 JOURNE
TWISTED.

WILDER
BUT SHE WON'T LISTEN, SHE GITS WILDER AND WILDER, 503 DIFRNT
EVER WILDER AND WILDER BECOMES HIS FLIGHT, 201 EJONES
(SHE IS A TRIFLE HECTIC NOW AND HER MANNER HAS 418 MARCOM
GROWN WILDER.)

WILDERNESS
AND THOU BESIDE ME SINGING IN THE WILDERNESS-- 199 AHWILD
THE VOICE O' GOD CRYIN' IN MY WILDERNESS, IN MY 238 DESIRE
LONESOMENESS--
A BIT OF FARM LAND NO ONE WOULD WORK ANY MORE, AND 30 POET
THE REST ALL WILDERNESS/

WILDEST
AND HE WAS HANDSOMER THAN MY WILDEST DREAM, 105 JOURNE

WILDLY
(WILDLY) BECAUSE IT'S A STUPID, STUBBORN REASON. 547 'ILE
(WILDLY) THEN DO THIS THIS ONCE FOR MY SAKE, FOR 549 'ILE
GOD'S SAKE--TAKE ME HOME/
SHE SITS DOWN AND STARTS TO PLAY WILDLY AN OLD 551 'ILE
HYMN.
(SHE LAUGHS WILDLY AND HE STARTS BACK FROM HER IN 551 'ILE
ALARM)
AND SHE IS PLAYING WILDLY AND DISCORDANTLY AS THE 552 'ILE
CURTAIN FALLS.)
ANNA LAUGHS WILDLY!) 56 ANNA
(WILDLY) STOP, YOU CRAZY FOOL/ 60 ANNA
(LOOKING UP WILDLY) NOT AFTER HIM/ 61 ANNA
ANNA LOOKS AFTER HIM WILDLY, STARTS TO RUN AFTER 61 ANNA
HIM.
(WILDLY) LOOK OUT, I TELL YOU/ 69 ANNA
(WILDLY) BUT IT'S A LIE, ANDY, A LIE/ 109 BEYOND
AND RUPS WILDLY AT HIS PERSPIRING COUNTENANCE. 140 BEYOND
(WILDLY) NO, AND BE DAMNED TO YOU, YOU'RE NOT. 486 CARDIF
(WILDLY ELATED) HURROO, YE SCUTS/ 460 CARIBE
HIS FACE IS FLUSHED AND HE TALKS RATHER WILDLY) 467 CARIBE
(LAUGHING WILDLY) MY OLD FRIEND IN THE BOTTLE 467 CARIBE
HERE, DONK.
(HE SUDDENLY LAUGHS WILDLY AND PUT HIS ARM AROUND 469 CARIBE
HER WAIST AND PRESSES HER TO
(WILDLY) NO/ 566 CROSS
(HYSTERICALLY--RUNS WILDLY TO THE DOOR IN REAR) 572 CROSS
(THEN WILDLY) OH, JOHN, STOP TALKING/ 590 DAYS

WILDLY (CONT'D.)
(WILDLY) FOR GOD'S SAKE, DON'T SAY THAT/ 556 DAYS
(ENRAGED BEYOND ENDURANCE--WILDLY VINDICTIVE) 233 DESIRE
(WILDLY) MINE 239 DESIRE
(WILDLY) VENGEANCE O' GOD ON THE HULL O' US/ 244 DESIRE
WAVING HIS ARMS ABOUT WILDLY) 250 DESIRE
SUDDENLY LAUGHS WILDLY AND BROKENLY) 255 DESIRE
FLINGS HER ARMS ABOUT HIS NECK AND KISSES HER 259 DESIRE
WILDLY.
(WILDLY) DON'T YE SAY THAT/ 260 DESIRE
(WILDLY) NO/ 260 DESIRE
(SUDDENLY LIFTS HER HEAD AND TURNS ON HIM--WILDLY)263 DESIRE
(HE SUDDENLY IS REMINDED OF SOMETHING--THINKING 450 DYNAMO
WILDLY)
(FORGETTING THE PATH HE PLUNGES WILDLY INTO THE 192 EJONES
UNDERBRUSH IN THE REAR AND
JONES' EYES BEGIN TO ROLL WILDLY. 192 EJONES
HE LOOKS WILDLY ABOUT THE CLEARING WITH HUNTED, 195 EJONES
FEARFUL GLANCES.
LOOKS WILDLY FOR SOME OPENING TO ESCAPE, SEES 197 EJONES
NONE.
(WILDLY) NO/ 33 ELECTR
(PULLS HER HAND AWAY FROM HIM AND SPRINGS TO HER 56 ELECTR
FEET WILDLY)
(WILDLY) STOP/ 98 ELECTR
(STARES AFTER HER WILDLY, THEN HER EYES FASTEN 101 ELECTR
AGAIN ON THE DEAD MAN'S FACE.
SHE LOOKS WILDLY AT LAVINIA'S FROZEN ACCUSING 101 ELECTR
FACE.)
(THEN WILDLY) WHY--WHY DID SHE, VINNIE$ 124 ELECTR
(LAUGHS WILDLY) GHOSTS/ 155 ELECTR
(STARING AT HER WILDLY) WHAT DID SHE TELL$ 161 ELECTR
(THEN SUMMONING HER WILL, SPRINGS TO HER FEET 165 ELECTR
WILDLY)
HE LAUGHS WILDLY) 165 ELECTR
(GROWING MORE DESPERATE--PLEADING WILDLY) 176 ELECTR
MASK ON AND LAUGHS WILDLY AND BITTERLY) 267 GGBROW
(HE LAUGHS WILDLY-- 282 GGBROW
(WILDLY MOCKINGLY) THEY'VE BEEN ACCEPTED--MR. 287 GGBROW
BROWN'S DESIGNS/
(HE LAUGHS WILDLY-- 297 GGBROW
(GRABBING HIS ARM--WILDLY) ARRE YE DAFT, MONS 524 INZONE
(WILDLY) VENGEANCE/ 290 LAZARU
WILDLY--THEN STEPS DOWN FROM THE DAIS AND GOES OFF362 LAZARU
RIGHT, CRYING DISTRACTEDLY)
(MORE AND MORE WILDLY) HOW MUST HE LIVES 365 LAZARU
(SHE RUNS TO HER WILDLY AND GRABS HER ARM-- 169 MANSNS
STAMMERING WITH TERROR.)
(WILDLY.) WELL, I MIGHT HAVE BEEN HOPING. 174 MANSNS
(WILDLY.) NO/ 187 MANSNS
(WILDLY, GRABBING DEBORAH'S SKIRT AGAIN.) 188 MANSNS
PICKS IT UP, CRAMS IT INTO HIS DOUBLET AND RUNS 363 MARCOM
WILDLY OUT THE DOOR.
(WILDLY) NO/ 412 MARCOM
(A TRIFLE WILDLY) OH, YES, YOU HAVE BEEN A MODEL 412 MARCOM
GUARDIAN, ADMIRAL POLO/
(SUDDENLY WILDLY BITTER) I WILL ASSUREDLY/ 412 MARCOM
(THEN WILDLY TO MARCO) I WISHED TO SLEEP IN THE 413 MARCOM
DEPTHS OF THE SEA.
(SHE LAUGHS MORE WILDLY) KNEEL AGAIN/ 419 MARCOM
(STAMMERS.) NO--NOT JAMIE-- (WILDLY.) OH, I 163 POET
CAN'T BEAR WAITING/
HE CRIES WILDLY AND DESPAIRINGLY. 178 POET
(HOPPING UP AND DOWN WILDLY) 587 ROPE
THE OLD MAN STAMPS HIS FOOT AND GESTICULATES 596 ROPE
WILDLY.
(LIFTING HER HEAD--WILDLY) NO/ 61 STRANG
WILDLY, MAKES A MOTION AS THOUGH TO TAKE HER IN 89 STRANG
HIS ARMS.
(HE SEEMS ABOUT TO SOB--THEN ABRUPTLY SPRINGS TO 101 STRANG
HIS FEET WILDLY)
(WILDLY) I'VE GOT TO CALL HIM UP/ 107 STRANG
(THEN SUDDENLY BREAKING FROM HIM--WILDLY) 107 STRANG
(STARING AT HER WILDLY) SAM'S BABY$ 130 STRANG
(WILDLY EXCITED) GORDON'S SPRINTING, ISN'T HE$ 180 STRANG
(WILDLY) NO/ 459 WELDED
(SHE LAUGHS WILDLY) I'D BE SAFE THEN, WOULDN'T 459 WELDED
I--RELIABLE, GUARANTEED NOT TO--
(WILDLY RESENTFUL) WHY DO YOU MAKE ME REMEMBER$ 464 WELDED
(FORCING A TWISTED SMILE--WILDLY) 466 WELDED
(SHE SHUDDERS--THEN SUDDENLY BURSTS OUT WILDLY) 467 WELDED
(WILDLY) AND I MUST BE CONSCIOUS--FULLY 472 WELDED
CONSCIOUS, DO YOU UNDERSTAND$
(HE STAMMERS WILDLY) 475 WELDED
(GLARES AT HER WILDLY) OHO, YOU DON'T DOUBT THAT,484 WELDED
DO YOU$

WILDNESS
HIS WILDNESS DROPS FROM HIM AND HE LOOKS AT 560 DAYS
STILLWELL WITH PLEADING EYES.)
(WITH SUDDEN WILDNESS--TORTUREDELY, SINKING ON HIS 292 GGBROW
KNEES BESIDE HER)

WILDS
ONE AND ORIGINAL--HAIRY APE FROM DE WILDS OF-- 254 HA APE
ALL THE WAY FROM THE WILDS OF DARKEST ASTORIA. 621 ICEMAN
HE WANTED TO PROVE HIS INDEPENDENCE BY LIVING 29 POET
ALONE IN THE WILDS.

WILLED
IS CHILDISHLY SELF-WILLED AND WEAK, OF AN 5 ANNA
OBSTINATE KINDLINESS.
WEAK-WILLED CRITTER TO BE PERMITTIN' A BOY--AND 102 BEYOND
WOMEN, TOO--
SHE'S THAT STUBBORN AND SELF-WILLED. 118 BEYOND
YOU WILL HAVE WILLED FOR YOURSELF THE ACCURSED END560 DAYS
OF THAT MAN--
HER MOUTH AND CHIN ARE HEAVY, FULL OF A SELF- 494 DIFRNT
WILLED STUBBORNNESS.
AND WEAKLY BECAUSE THE STRENGTH SHE HAS WILLED 142 ELECTR
INTO HIM HAS LEFT HER EXHAUSTED)

WILLED (CONT'D.)
(THIS MAN WHO WILLED HIMSELF TO ME/ 299 GGBROW
AS MY PRIDE AND DISDAIN HAVE ALWAYS WILLED I BE/ 190 MANSNS
I LOOKED INTO THE CRYSTAL AND WILLED TO SEE 426 MARCOM
KUKACHIN IN PERSIA AND SHE APPEARED,

WILLIE
WILLIE* AS HE SCANS THE HEADLINES. 187 AHWILD
AND SOMEONE WHISTLING *WALTZ ME AROUND AGAIN, 253 AHWILD
WILLIE*.)

WILLIE'S
(LARRY POURS A DRINK FROM THE BOTTLE ON WILLIE'S 580 ICEMAN
TABLE AND GULPS IT DOWN.
WHO IS STILL CHUCKLING TO HIMSELF OVER WILLIE'S 598 ICEMAN
SONG.
ON WILLIE'S LEFT, AT REAR OF TABLE, IS HOPE. 696 ICEMAN

WILLIES
OR HAD DE WILLIES GETTIN' OVER IT. 618 ICEMAN

WILLIN'
(NOT HEEDING HER) WILL THE MEN TURN TO WILLIN' DR550 *ILE
MUST WE DRAG 'EM OUT$
THEY'LL TURN TO WILLIN' ENOUGH. 550 *ILE
(COCKILY) WAAL, I'M WILLIN' TO LEAVE IT TO THE 499 DIFRNT
GIRLS, TOO.
BUT O' COURSE, IF YOU AIN'T WILLIN' TO TAKE ME THES16 DIFRNT
WAY I BE,
MAYBE THE TIME'LL COME WHEN YOU'LL BE WILLIN' TO 517 DIFRNT
FORGET--
IF HE'S WILLIN' TO DIG IN HIS JEANS FOR SOME REAL 545 DIFRNT
COIN--REAL DOUGH, THIS TIME/
AND SAY, LISTEN, IF HE AIN'T WILLIN' TO COME 546 DIFRNT
ACROSS, I'LL MARRY YOU ALL RIGHT,

WILL'N'NESS
AIN'T NONE OF US DOUBTS YOUR WILLIN'NESS, BUT YOU 102 BEYOND
AIN'T NEVER LEARNED--

WILLING
(STIFFLY) WELL, I HOPE HE FINDS A WOMAN WHO'S 213 AHWILD
WILLING--
HE MIGHT BE WILLING TO STAKE ME TO A ROOM AND EATS 16 ANNA
TILL I GET RESTED UP.
THE ONLY WOMEN YOU'D MEET IN THE PORTS OF THE 37 ANNA
WORLD WHO'D BE WILLING TO SPEAK
THE LIKE OF YOURSELF, NOW--WOULD BE WILLING TO WED 38 ANNA
WITH ME.
IN YOUR PRESENCE IF YOU'RE WILLING. 50 ANNA
WOULD YOU BE WILLING TO SWEAR AN OATH, NOW-- 74 ANNA
AS IF ALL POWER OF WILLING HAD DESERTED HER. 112 BEYOND
(SUSPICIOUSLY) CALEB DIDN'T SEEM WILLING TO TELL 501 DIFRNT
ME MUCH ABOUT THEIR TOUCHING
I'M WILLING. 502 DIFRNT
YOU MEAN--IF HE'S WILLING TO BRIBE YOU WITH MONEY,545 DIFRNT
YOU WON'T MARRY ME TOMORROWS
AND CLARK AND DAWSON WOULD BE WILLING TO SELL THE 39 ELECTR
FLYING TRADES--
I HOPE YOU'RE NOT SUCH A COWARD THAT YOU'RE 98 ELECTR
WILLING TO LET HER LOVER ESCAPE/
(HER EYES ON HIS FACE--AS IF SHE WERE WILLING HER 138 ELECTR
STRENGTH INTO HIM)
THOUGHT YOU'D BE WILLING TO HELP ME ACROSS THE 687 ICEMAN
STREET, KNOWING I'M HALF BLIND.
WILLING TO START AT THE BOTTOM. 36 JOURNE
HE KNOWS IT WAS A CURSE PUT ON YOU WITHOUT YOUR 122 JOURNE
KNOWING OR WILLING IT.
I'D BE WILLING TO HAVE NO HOME BUT THE POORHOUSE 151 JOURNE
IN MY OLD AGE IF I COULD LOOK
OH, TO LOVE I AM A KILLING SLAVE. 7 MANSNS
I AM WILLING TO BEG HER ON MY KNEES TO GIVE ME 39 MANSNS
THIS CHANCE TO BE REBORN/
AND I AM WILLING TO ABIDE BY YOUR DECISION. 66 MANSNS
WHO WAS WILLING TO USE ANY MEANS--EVEN HER 74 MANSNS
BEAUTIFUL BODY--
WELL THEN, I KNOW YOU WILL BE WILLING TO BECOME 88 MANSNS
YOUR OLD TRUE SELF AGAIN FOR ME.
WILLING TO GAMBLE WITH THE HIGHEST POSSIBLE STAKE, 88 MANSNS
ALL SHE HAS,
I'VE TOLD YOU BEFORE I'M WILLING TO LET HER HAVE 147 MANSNS
THE CHILDREN FOR COMPANY AGAIN--
ARE YOU WILLING TO BECOME A CONSCIOUS THIEF AND 154 MANSNS
SWINDLER$
AND YOU'RE WILLING TO DRAG THEM DOWN WITH YOU IN 155 MANSNS
THE GUTTER, TOO/
(HE PULLS HER WILLING HAND DOWN TOWARD HIS LIPS.) 355 MARCOM
THE KHAN PROBABLY MEANT WHENEVER YOU WERE WILLING,411 MARCOM
AND YOU NOT WILLING, WOULD BE CARRIED OFF TO THE 19 MISBEG
HOSPITAL$
NOT EVEN IF I WAS WILLING. 23 MISBEG
LOVE HIM ALL THE MORE AND BE MORE SHAMELESS AND 164 MISBEG
WILLINGS
HENRY HARFORD IS WILLING TO SETTLE ON HIS SON. 111 POET
INQUISITIVE FRIENDLINESS, ALWAYS WILLING TO 4 STRANG
LISTEN, EAGER TO SYMPATHIZE,
SAY YOU'RE WILLING TO GIVE HER A DIVORCE SO SHE 92 STRANG
CAN MARRY SOME REAL GUY WHO CAN
WITHIN A YEAR OR SO THEY'LL BE WILLING TO SELL OUT121 STRANG
CHEAP.
ONCE WHEN YOU WERE WILLING TO ENDURE IT AS THE 468 WELDED
PRICE OF A CAREER--

WILLOW
ITS COOL BENEATH THY WILLOW TREES/ 195 AHWILD
(LEFT OF CENTER) OF THE ROWBOAT IS IN THE DEEP 275 AHWILD
SHADOW CAST BY THE WILLOW.
ITS BOW ABOUT TOUCHING THE BANK, EVIDENTLY MADE 275 AHWILD
FAST TO THE TRUNK OF A WILLOW.
THE TOP OF THE BANK IS GRASSY AND THE TRAILING 275 AHWILD
BOUGHS OF WILLOW TREES EXTEND OUT
YOU'D HAVE BEEN DRINKING OUR BLOOD BENEATH THOSE 658 ICEMAN
WILLOW TREES/
THERE AIN'T ANY COOL WILLOW TREES--EXCEPT YOU GROW691 ICEMAN
YOUR OWN IN A BOTTLE.

WILLOW

WILLOW (CONT'D.)
BENEATH THE WILLOW TREES/ 721 ICEMAN
TIS COOL BENEATH THY WILLOW TREE/ 728 ICEMAN

WILLOWS
AT LEFT, FRONT IS A PATH LEADING UP THE BANK, 275 AHWILD
BETWEEN THE WILLOWS.

WILLS
(THINKS SCORNFULLY) (THE IS ALWAYS SO SURE OF 423 DYNAMO
WHAT GOD WILLS/.
CONSTRAINEDLY, COMPELLED AGAINST THEIR WILLS. 282 LAZARU
WE SHOULD ALL HAVE CLAUSES IN OUR WILLS EXPRESSING180 MANSNS
GRATITUDE TO,
YOUR OPINION IT WILL BE THE NECESSARY PHYSICAL ACT183 MANSNS
BY WHICH YOUR MIND WILLS TO
BELIEVE THAT IF THE MIND WILLS ANYTHING WITH 185 MANSNS
ENOUGH INTENSITY OF LOVE,
DON'T FOLKS BREAK WILLS LIKE HIS'N IN THE COURTS 586 ROPE

WILT
(TRYING NOT TO WILT BEFORE THE CAPTAIN'S GLANCE 944 *ILE
AND AVOIDING HIS EYES)
THOU WILT NOT--DO THAT TO ME AGAIN--WILT THOUS 552 DAYS
THOU WILT NOT--TAKE LOVE FROM ME AGAINS 552 DAYS

WILY
HE'S A WILY SHANTY MICK, THAT ONE. 22 JOURNE

WIMIN
UT'S FAT YE ARE, KATY DEAR, AN* I NEVER CUD ENDURE500 VOYAGE
SKINNY WIMIN.
WHO'D THINK OLLIE'D BE SICH A DIVIL WID THE WIMIN$508 VOYAGE

WIN
BUT HE DOES NOT WIN WHO PLAYS WITH SIN IN THE 246 AHWILD
SECRET HOUSE OF SHAME/*
(THEN TURNING TO CHRIS) WE'LL BE SEEING WHO'LL 55 ANNA
WIN IN THE END--ME OR YOU.
(CALLOUSLY) YOU'D WIN. 64 ANNA
YOU'LL HAVE TO SUFFER TO WIN BACK--THIS VOICE 162 BEYOND
GROWS WEAKER AND HE SIGHS WEARILY)
(JUBILANTLY) BILLY'S GOT THE STUFF IN HIM TO WIN,259 GGBROW
GO ON IN AND WIN/ 265 GGBROW
YOU KEEP GETTING CLOSER, BUT IT KNOWS YOU STILL 285 GGBROW
WANT TO WIN--A LITTLE BIT--
(ELATED.) I WIN. HUHS 13 HUGHIE
WHEN, NO MATTER HOW MUCH HE'D WIN ON A RUN OF LUCK 20 HUGHIE
LIKE SUCKERS HAVE SOMETIMES.
AND I WIN. 23 HUGHIE
AND I'D STOP TO KID HIM ALONG AND TELL HIM THE 23 HUGHIE
TALE OF WHAT I'D WIN THAT DAY,
I'D TELL HIM I WIN TEN GRAND FROM THE BOOKIES, AND 32 HUGHIE
TEN GRAND AT STUD.
AND I'D CUT THE ACE OF SPADES AND WIN AGAIN.* 32 HUGHIE
BUT I DON'T WIN THAT HUNDRED BUCKS. 34 HUGHIE
I DON'T WIN A BET SINCE HUGHIE WAS TOOK TO THE 34 HUGHIE
HOSPITAL.
SINCE HUGHIE GOT TOOK TO THE HOSPITAL. NOT A WIN. 35 HUGHIE
I'D ALWAYS KNOW I'D MAKE A WIN THAT'D FIX IT. 35 HUGHIE
HELL, I ONCE WIN TWENTY GRAND ON A SINGLE RACE. 36 HUGHIE
THAT'S ACTION/
IF THE JOC CAN KEEP HIM FROM JUMPIN' OVER THE 37 HUGHIE
GRANDSTAND, HE'LL WIN BY A MILE.
AND MAY THE BEST MAN WIN AND DIE OF GLUTTONY/ 579 ICEMAN
NOMINATION BECAUSE THEY KNEW THEY COULDN'T WIN 603 ICEMAN
THAT YEAR IN THIS WARD.
IT'S GONNA GET IN A BIG CRAP GAME AND WIN ME A BIG 673 ICEMAN
BANKROLL.
AND HERE'S ANOTHER I'D WIN, 52 JOURNE
YOU WIN THAT ONE. 52 JOURNE
YOU WIN ON THAT. 58 JOURNE
DIDN'T I WIN FIVE DOLLARS FROM YOU ONCE WHEN YOU 136 JOURNE
BET ME I COULDN'T LEARN A
(WITH A CARELESS SHRUG) YOU WILL NOT WIN HIS LOVE342 LAZARU
BY KILLING HER.
THAT TO WIN HER MOTHER LOVE I MUST BECOME CAESAR. 355 LAZARU
I THINK I CAN PROMISE I'LL SOON WIN BACK FOR YOU 57 MANSNS
ALL HIS STUPID FOLLY HAS LOST.
I ALWAYS WIN. 101 MANSNS
(TURNING TO MAFFEO) I WIN, UNCLE. 371 MARCOM
YOU WIN. 40 MISBEG
III MUST WIN CHARLIE OVER AGAIN... 118 STRANG
GORDON IS ALWAYS MEANT--MEANT TO WIN/ 181 STRANG

WINCE
(THEY WINCE AS IF HE HAD SLAPPED THEM, 639 ICEMAN

WINCED
(HAS WINCED WHEN REUBEN WAS HIT--CONSCIENCE-- 448 DYNAMO
STRICKENLY)

WINCES
(WINCES BUT PUTS HER ARM AROUND HER 214 AHWILD
AFFECTIONATELY--GENTLY)
JONES WINCES WITH PAIN AND COWERS ABJECTLY. 194 EJONES
(WILLIE WINCES AND SHRINKS DOWN IN HIS CHAIR. 681 ICEMAN
(SHE WINCES-- 120 JOURNE
(WINCES--PLEADINGLY) JOSIE/ 163 MISBEG
(WINCES) HAVE A HEART. 171 MISBEG
(MELODY WINCES. 61 POET
(SHE WINCES) AT HIS AGE, ONE HAS TO EXPECT--EVEN 168 STRANG
A MOTHER MUST FACE NATURE.

WINCHESTER
A WINCHESTER RIFLE IS SLUNG ACROSS HIS SHOULDERS 194 EJONES
AND HE CARRIES A HEAVY WHIP.

WINCING
(WINCING--FAINTLY) DON'T SAY DAT, ANNA, PLEASE/ 63 ANNA
(WINCING) DON'T/ 526 DAYS
(WINCING AGAIN--STAMMERS HARSHLY) 31 ELECTR
(WINCING AS IF SHE HAD STRUCK HIM IN THE FACE, 177 ELECTR
(WINCING--HER LIPS QUIVERING PITIFULLY.) 45 JOURNE
(AS HE GIVES A WINCING START) 44 STRANG
(WINCING PITIABLY) NO, NOT MUCH MONEY. 70 STRANG
(WINCING BUT FORCING A TEASING AIR) 114 STRANG
(WINCING--THINKING) (ISHE CAN'T BELIEVE ANY WOMAN114 STRANG
COULD POSSIBLY LOVE ME/....))

WINCING (CONT'D.)
(WINCING--IN A FORCED TONE) AND I'D TRUST SAM 127 STRANG
WITH ANYTHING.
(WINCING--THINKING) ((THAT HURTS... 127 STRANG
(REACTING AUTOMATICALLY AND WINCING WITH PAIN-- 200 STRANG
THINKING MECHANICALLY)

WIND
WHAT GOOD WIND BLOWS YOU AROUND ON THIS GLORIOUS 200 AHWILD
FOURTH/
*I HAVE LOVED WIND AND LIGHT AND THE BRIGHT SEA, 82 BEYOND
NEVER DREAMED WAVES COULD GET SO BIG OR THE WIND 131 BEYOND
BLOW SO HARD.
LET ME GET MY WIND FIRST. 140 BEYOND
HAVE IMPORTANT BUSINESS TO WIND UP HERE. 146 BEYOND
BUT WHEN I LANDED IN NEW YORK--I WIRED YOU I HAD 156 BEYOND
BUSINESS TO WIND
MOONLIGHT, WINNOWED BY THE WIND WHICH MOANS IN THE555 CROSS
STUBBORN ANGLES OF THE OLD
IF THE WIND WASN'T SO HIGH YOU'D HEAR HIM NOW-- 557 CROSS
BACK AND FORTH--
IT'S THE WIND AND SEA YOU HEAR, NAT. 570 CROSS
THE SOUND OF THE WIND AND SEA SUDDENLY CEASES AND 570 CROSS
THERE IS A HEAVY SILENCE.
THERE IS NO WIND. 571 CROSS
A SHUTTER IN THE WIND. 571 CROSS
THE WIND AND SEA ARE HEARD AGAIN. 572 CROSS
THERE IS NO WIND AND EVERYTHING IS STILL. 203 DESIRE
A NOISE AS OF DEAD LEAVES IN THE WIND COMES FROM 252 DESIRE
THE ROOM.
THERE'S NO WIND HARDLY AND SHE KIN SWIM LIKE A 503 DIFRNT
FISH
IT MUST BE NICE TO FLOAT IN THE WIND... 444 DYNAMO
THE SOUND OF WIND AND RAIN SWEEPING DOWN ON THE 454 DYNAMO
TOWN FORM THE HILLS IS HEARD.)
A SOMBER MONOTONE OF WIND LOST IN THE LEAVES MOANS187 EJONES
IN THE AIR.
TRADE WIND. 187 EJONES
WID NOTHIN' BUT WIND ON YO' STOMACH, O' COURSE YOU188 EJONES
FEELS JIGGEDY.
HERE IS A GOOD FIELD HAND, SOUND IN WIND AND LIMB 197 EJONES
AS THEY CAN SEE.
BORNE ON THE LIGHT PUFFS OF WIND THIS MUSIC IS AT 5 ELECTR
TIMES QUITE LOUD,
THEN SINKS INTO FAINTNESS AS THE WIND DIES. 5 ELECTR
AS YOU WALKED BESIDE ME THAT NIGHT WITH YOUR HAIR 24 ELECTR
BLOWING IN THE SEA WIND AND
BORNE ON THE WIND THE MELANCHOLY REFRAIN OF THE 102 ELECTR
CAPSTAN CHANTY *SHENANDOAH,
THE TRADE WIND IN THE COCO PALMS--THE SURF ON THE 147 ELECTR
REEF--
ONCE I DREAMED OF PAINTING ON THE SEA AND THE287 GGBROW
SKIMMING FLIGHT OF CLOUD
AND WIND OVER THE MILES OF SHINY GREEN OCEAN LIKE 214 HA APE
STRONG DRINK TO YOUR LUNGS.
OH, TO BE SCUDDING SOUTH AGAIN WID THE POWER OF 214 HA APE
THE TRADE WIND
SUNSHINE ON THE DECK IN A GREAT FLOOD, THE FRESH 218 HA APE
SEA WIND BLOWING ACROSS IT.
WANTER WIND UP LIKE A SPORT *STEAD OF CROAKIN' 253 HA APE
SLOW IN DERE/
IT GOT SO EVERY NIGHT I'D WIND UP HIDING MY FACE 714 ICEMAN
IN HER LAP.
ASK OF THE WIND, OR OF THE WAVE, OR OF THE STAR, 132 JOURNE
OR OF THE BIRD,
AND THE WIND, WAVE, STAR, BIRD, CLOCK, WILL ANSWER132 JOURNE
YOU.
THE WIND LAUGHS/ 280 LAZARU
(EXULTANTLY) ARE YOU A SPECK OF DUST DANCED IN 308 LAZARU
THE WIND/
COME HOME, BRINGING ME LAUGHTER OF THE WIND FROM 347 LAZARU
THE HILLS/
AS IF THE LEAVES WERE TINY HARPS STRUMMED BY THE 352 MARCOM
WIND.
WIND RUSTLING THE LEAVES. 355 MARCOM
A CHILL WIND FROM THE MOUNTAIN BLOWS IN THE 384 MARCOM
GARDEN.
I REASONED, LOVE COMES LIKE THE BREATH OF WIND ON 388 MARCOM
WATER
WHERE THERE IS NEITHER SUN NOR WIND NOR JOY NOR 409 MARCOM
SORROW/
OUR LAMENTATIONS SADDEN THE WIND FROM THE WEST. 436 MARCOM
A WIND FROM THE SOUTH, AND A SKY GRAY WITH 102 POET
CLOUDS--GOOD WEATHER FOR THE HOUNDS.
SO THAT'S HOW THE WIND BLOWS/ 591 ROPE
SQUAT HERE FOR A SPELL AND GIT YOUR WIND. 595 ROPE
WOULD SHE RATHER SEE HER HUSBAND WIND UP IN AN 87 STRANG
ASYLUM$

WINDBAG
EVER SHIPPED ON A WINDBAG/ 49 ANNA

WINDED
GET IT OVER, YOU LONG-WINDED BASTARD/ 711 ICEMAN
HAVE BEEN LONG-WINDED FAIRY TALES FOR GROWN-UPS-- 176 STRANG

WINDERS
BEN USED TO HEAR THINGS CLAWIN' AT THE WALLS AN' 132 ELECTR
WINDERS

WINDIN'
IN WINDIN' SHEETS OR NO SECH LUNATIC DOIN'S. 135 ELECTR

WINDING
AND CAN BE SEEN IN THE DISTANCE WINDING TOWARD THE 81 BEYOND
HORIZON LIKE A PALE RIBBON
WINDING OFF INTO THE DISTANCE, TOWARD THE HILLS, 89 BEYOND
AS IF IT, TOO,
AND WINDING AWAY FROM IT AGAIN TOWARD THE RIGHT. 190 EJONES
HER BODY IS WRAPPED IN A WINDING SHEET OF DEEP 434 MARCOM
BLUE,

WINDJAMMER
WUD BE SAILORS ENOUGH TO KNOW THE MAIN FROM THE 459 CARIBE
MIZZEN ON A WINDJAMMER.

1801

WINDOW

WINDJAMMER (CONT'D.)
NEXT TIME I SHIP ON WINDJAMMER BOSTON TO RIVER 515 INZONE
PLATE,
BLOUDY WINDJAMMER--SKYS'L-YARDER--FULL-RIGGED-- 495 VOYAGE
PAINTED WHITE--

WINDOW
HAS WANDERED OVER TO THE WINDOW AT REAR OF DESK, 199 AHWILD
RIGHT)
IN THE MIDDLE OF THE RIGHT WALL IS A WINDOW 236 AHWILD
CLOSED SHUTTERS.
WHO HAS GONE TO THE WINDOW AT RIGHT AND IS STARING263 AHWILD
OUT FROWNINGLY.
WINDOW, AND I WENT UP AND SHE SAID GIVE THIS TO 273 AHWILD
DICK,
FARTHER BACK, ANOTHER WINDOW. 3 ANNA
ON THE LEFT, FORWARD, OF THE BARROOM, A LARGE 3 ANNA
WINDOW LOOKING OUT ON THE STREET.
THEN STOPPING TO PEER ABSENT-MINDEDLY CUT OF THE 41 ANNA
WINDOW.
HE STANDS LOOKING OUT OF THE WINDOW--MUTTERS-- 44 ANNA
"DIRTY ULE DAVIL, YOU."
SHE USED TO GET ME OUT OF THE WAY BY PUSHING MY 89 BEYOND
CHAIR TO THE WEST WINDOW AND
THERE AT THE WINDOW. 90 BEYOND
A WINDOW LOOKING OUT ON THE ROAD. 93 BEYOND
NEXT TO THE WINDOW A DOOR LEADING OUT INTO THE 93 BEYOND
YARD.
THE SPRINGS TO HIS FEET AND INSTINCTIVELY GOES TO 125 BEYOND
THE WINDOW
(HE GOES QUICKLY TO THE WINDOW IN THE REAR LEFT, 150 BEYOND
(SHE SIGHS AND WALKS TO THE WINDOW IN THE REAR, 152 BEYOND
LEFT,
ON THE LEFT, A WINDOW. 493 DAYS
THE LIGHT FROM THE WINDOW IS CHILL AND GRAY. 493 DAYS
BEFORE IT, A CHAIR, ITS BACK TO THE WINDOW, AND A 493 DAYS
TABLE.
VENETIAN BLINDS SOFTEN THE LIGHT FROM A BIG WINDOW514 DAYS
AT RIGHT.
IN FRONT OF THIS WINDOW IS A TABLE WITH A LAMP. 514 DAYS
AND, OF COURSE, IT BLEW MY PETTY MODERN 524 DAYS
SELFISHNESS RIGHT OUT THE WINDOW.
BEFORE THE WINDOW, RIGHT FRONT, AND STANDS THERE, 525 DAYS
WITHOUT LOOKING AT THEM,
IN THE CHAIR BY THE END OF THE TABLE BEFORE THE 532 DAYS
WINDOW.
EBEN STICKS HIS HEAD OUT OF THE DINING-ROOM 205 DESIRE
WINDOW, LISTENING.)
(LOOKING AT WINDOW) SKYS'S GRAVIN'. 214 DESIRE
(EBEN APPEARS IN THE KITCHEN, RUNS TO WINDOW, PEERS219 DESIRE
OUT,
HIS FACE, LIGHTED UP BY THE SHAFT OF SUNLIGHT FROM220 DESIRE
THE WINDOW.
(IN THE MEANTIME, THE WINDOW OF THE UPPER BEDROOM 224 DESIRE
ON RIGHT IS RAISED
AND PULLS BACK HER HEAD SLOWLY AND SHUTS THE 224 DESIRE
WINDOW.
(THEY BOTH THROW, THE STONES HITTING THE PARLOR 224 DESIRE
WINDOW WITH A CRASH OF GLASS.
EBEN STICKS HIS HEAD OUT OF HIS BEDROOM WINDOW. 228 DESIRE
A LIGHT APPEARS IN THE PARLOR WINDOW. 241 DESIRE
THE WINDOW OF THE PARLOR IS HEARD OPENING AND THE 244 DESIRE
SHUTTERS ARE FLUNG BACK AND
HE LOOKS TOWARD THE WINDOW AND GIVES A SNORT OF 262 DESIRE
SURPRISE AND IRRITATION--
FARTHER BACK, IN ORDER, A WINDOW LOOKING OUT ON A 493 DIFRNT
VEGETABLE GARDEN,
A BLACK HORSEHAIR SOFA, AND ANOTHER WINDOW. 493 DIFRNT
TO THE RIGHT OF IT, IN REAR, A WINDOW LOOKING OUT 493 DIFRNT
ON THE FRONT YARD.
TO THE RIGHT OF THIS WINDOW IS THE FRONT DOOR, 493 DIFRNT
REACHED BY A DIRT PATH
TO THE RIGHT OF DOOR, ANOTHER WINDOW. 493 DIFRNT
THROUGH THE WINDOW AND THE SCREEN DOOR IN THE REAR493 DIFRNT
THE FRESH GREEN OF THE LAWN
THEN SHE GETS TO HER FEET AND GOES FROM WINDOW TO 548 DIFRNT
WINDOW
IN THE LEFT WALL IS A WINDOW. 421 DYNAMO
THE MINISTER'S DESK IS PLACED AGAINST THE LEFT 421 DYNAMO
WALL BESIDE THE WINDOW.
IN THE BEDROOM ABOVE, REUBEN'S EYES ARE TURNED 422 DYNAMO
TOWARD THE WINDOW.
(HE GOES TO THE WINDOW AND LOOKS TOWARD THE FIFE 424 DYNAMO
HOME)
A FAINT FLASH OF LIGHTNING FROM THE DISTANT STORM 424 DYNAMO
FLICKERS THROUGH HIS WINDOW.
(HIS DIGNITY RUFFLED, TURNS HIS BACK ON HER AND 424 DYNAMO
GOES TO THE WINDOW)
(STANDS BY THE WINDOW AND SNIFFS THE AIR) 425 DYNAMO
(TURNS AWAY AND LEANS OUT THE WINDOW STARING INTO 425 DYNAMO
THE NIGHT)
(STARTS FROM HIS DREAM BY THE WINDOW UPSTAIRS) 426 DYNAMO
THERE IS ONE SMALL WINDOW ON THE TOP FLOOR FRONT 427 DYNAMO
OF THE
(SHE GOES TO THE WINDOW, PEERING OUT BUT KEEPING 427 DYNAMO
HER HEAD CAREFULLY INSIDE--
MRS. LIGHT'S HEAD CAN BE SEEN PEERING OUT OF THE 428 DYNAMO
SIDE BEDROOM WINDOW AT REUBEN.
(BENDING OUT OF THE WINDOW IN REUBEN'S BEDROOM-- 431 DYNAMO
(CAN SEE HER NOW FROM THE WINDOW) 433 DYNAMO
(SHE DRAWS BACK QUICKLY FROM THE WINDOW 434 DYNAMO
(LEANS OUT OF THE FRONT WINDOW OF THE BEDROOM 435 DYNAMO
UPSTAIRS)
OH, I WISH I COULD GET CLOSER TO THE WINDOW/ 437 DYNAMO
MRS. FIFE STILL LEANS OUT OF HER BEDROOM WINDOW 443 DYNAMO
AND FIFE STICKS HIS HEAD OUT OF HIS SITTING ROOM 445 DYNAMO
WINDOW
SHE APPEARS AT THE WINDOW NEXT TO HER FATHER. 450 DYNAMO

WINDOW (CONT'D.)
(STILL LEANING OUT OF HIS SITTING-ROOM WINDOW, 450 DYNAMO
CATCHES SIGHT OF LIGHT--
(HE TURNS FROM HER TO THE WINDOW AND LOOKS OUT. 450 DYNAMO
(WATCHING FROM HIS WINDOW) (HE'S TALKING TO 451 DYNAMO
FIFE----
(HE TAKES A FEW STEPS TOWARD THE WINDOW, THEN 452 DYNAMO
STOPS, THINKING BITTERLY)
(HE YELLS AT THE WINDOW) IT'S YOU WHO'RE THE RAT,452 DYNAMO
ADA/
THEN ADA LEANS OUT OF THE WINDOW NEXT TO HER 454 DYNAMO
MOTHER.
(REAPPEARS IN THE WINDOW BESIDE ADA. 456 DYNAMO
ADA APPEARS IN THE WINDOW BESIDE HER MOTHER. 459 DYNAMO
(STICKS HER HEAD OUT OF THEIR SITTING ROOM WINDOW 467 DYNAMO
AS HE PASSES THE LILAC HEDGE.
AND THERE IS A SIMILAR WINDOW IN THE UPPER PART OF473 DYNAMO
THE SECTION ON RIGHT.
AN IMMENSE WINDOW AND A BIG SLIDING DOOR 473 DYNAMO
THROUGH THE WINDOW AND THE OPEN DOOR OF THE DYNAMO473 DYNAMO
ROOM,
THROUGH THE UPPER WINDOW OF THE RIGHT SECTION OF 473 DYNAMO
THE BUILDING.
THE DYNAMO CAN BE PARTLY SEEN THROUGH THE WINDOW. 476 DYNAMO
I'LL KNOCK ON THE WINDOW WHEN I SEE HIM AND GET 480 DYNAMO
HIM TO COME OUT.))
(SHE MOVES CAUTIOUSLY TO THE WINDOW AND PEEKS IN, 480 DYNAMO
BUT CANNOT SEE HIM)
(SHE LOOKS IN THE WINDOW AGAIN.) 480 DYNAMO
FROM WHERE SHE IS LOOKING IN THE WINDOW AND CALLS 481 DYNAMO
TO HIM) RUBE/
THE WINDOW SHUTTERS ARE PAINTED A DARK GREEN. 2 ELECTR
AND GOES TO THE OPEN WINDOW AND CALLS.) 35 ELECTR
CHRISTINE HURRIES FROM THE DOOR TO THE WINDOW 42 ELECTR
(SHE TURNS BACK FROM THE WINDOW. 42 ELECTR
SHE STANDS STARING FASCINATEDLY UP AT THE WINDOW, 57 ELECTR
(THEN LOOKING UP AT THE WINDOW AGAIN--WITH 57 ELECTR
PASSIONATE DISGUST)
(ORIN CLOSES THE SHUTTER HE HAS PUSHED OPEN AND 144 ELECTR
TURNS BACK FROM THE WINDOW.
(SHE SEES HIM AT THE WINDOW) 144 ELECTR
(SHE GOES TO THE WINDOW AND THROWS THE SHUTTERS 151 ELECTR
OPEN AND LOOKS OUT)
SETH LEANS OUT OF THE WINDOW AT THE RIGHT OF THE 179 ELECTR
DOOR
AND GOES TO THE WINDOW AND STARES OUT.) 273 GGBROW
THE JEWELER'S WINDOW IS GAUDY 233 HA APE
(HE TURNS AND SEES THE WINDOW DISPLAY IN THE TWO 235 HA APE
STORES FOR THE FIRST TIME)
AS IF THE SKIN IN THE WINDOW WERE A PERSONAL 236 HA APE
INSULT)
THEN AT A CRY FROM ONE OF THE WOMEN, THEY ALL 238 HA APE
SCURRY TO THE FURRIER'S WINDOW.)
THE CROWD AT THE WINDOW HAVE NOT MOVED OR NOTICED 239 HA APE
THIS DISTURBANCE.
SHE BELONGD IN DE WINDOW OF A TOY STORE, OR ON DE241 HA APE
TOP OF A GARBAGE CAN, SEE/
ON A WINDOW RIGHT OVER HIS HEAD.* 597 ICEMAN
WITH A SPACE BETWEEN IT AND THE WINDOW 664 ICEMAN
(HE GOES TO RIGHT OF DOOR BEHIND THE LUNCH COUNTER677 ICEMAN
AND LOOKS THROUGH THE WINDOW.
LEWIS TAKES UP A SIMILAR STAND AT THE WINDOW ON 677 ICEMAN
THE LEFT OF DOOR.)
HE TURNS LEFT AND DISAPPEARS OFF REAR, OUTSIDE THE685 ICEMAN
FARTHEST WINDOW.)
TURNING TO HIS RIGHT AND MARCHING OFF OUTSIDE THE 685 ICEMAN
WINDOW AT RIGHT OF DOOR.)
DISAPPEARING OUTSIDE THE WINDOW AT RIGHT OF DOOR.1686 ICEMAN
FROM WHAT I'VE SEEN OF 'EM THROUGH THE WINDOW, 687 ICEMAN
(HE GOES TO THE END OF THE BAR TO LOOK THROUGH THE688 ICEMAN
WINDOW--DISGUSTEDLY)
AND AS BLINDLY PAST THE WINDOW BEHIND THE FREE- 688 ICEMAN
LUNCH COUNTER.)
(HOPE PASSES THE WINDOW OUTSIDE THE FREE-LUNCH 689 ICEMAN
COUNTER IN A SHAMBLING,
THE ONE AT LEFT, FRONT, BEFORE THE WINDOW TO THE 695 ICEMAN
YARD, IS IN THE SAME POSITION.
LARRY IS AT LEFT OF IT, BESIDE THE WINDOW, FACING 696 ICEMAN
FRONT.
LISTENING FOR THE SOUND HE KNOWS IS COMING FROM 721 ICEMAN
THE BACKYARD OUTSIDE THE WINDOW.
AT THE TABLE BY THE WINDOW LARRY'S HANDS GRIP THE 722 ICEMAN
EDGE OF THE TABLE.
UNCONSCIOUSLY HIS HEAD IS INCLINED TOWARD THE 722 ICEMAN
WINDOW AS HE LISTENS.)
(AT THE TABLE BY THE WINDOW HUGO SPEAKS TO LARRY 723 ICEMAN
AGAIN.)
AT THE TABLE BY THE WINDOW LARRY HAS UNCONSCIOUSLY724 ICEMAN
SHUT HIS EYES AS HE LISTENS.
(HE HALF RISES FROM HIS CHAIR JUST AS FROM OUTSIDE726 ICEMAN
THE WINDOW COMES THE SOUND OF
OVER BY DE WINDOW, BOSS. 726 ICEMAN
IN HIS CHAIR BY THE WINDOW, LARRY STARES IN FRONT 728 ICEMAN
OF HIM,
TAKE A LOOK OUT THE WINDOW, MARY. 40 JOURNE
(TURNS FROM THE WINDOW--WITH AN ACTOR'S 40 JOURNE
HEARTINESS.)
(SHE TURNS BACK FROM THE WINDOW.) 44 JOURNE
(SHE PAUSES, LOOKING OUT THE WINDOW-- 44 JOURNE
(HE GOES QUICKLY TO THE WINDOW AT RIGHT.) 54 JOURNE
(LOOKING OUT THE WINDOW.) SHE'S DOWN THERE NOW. 60 JOURNE
(JAMIE LOOKS OUT THE WINDOW AGAIN.) 61 JOURNE
JAMIE TURNS TO HER--THEN LOOKS QUICKLY OUT OF THE 61 JOURNE
WINDOW AGAIN.)
(HE TURNS BACK TO THE WINDOW.) 63 JOURNE
(FROM THE WINDOW, WITHOUT LOOKING AROUND.) 64 JOURNE
JAMIE TURNS HIS BACK WITH A SHRUG AND LOOKS OUT 64 JOURNE
THE WINDOW.)

WINDOW 1802

WINDOW (CONT'D.)
HE LIGHTS IT AS HE GOES TO LOOK OUT THE WINDOW AT 71 JOURNE
RIGHT.
(JAMIE GIVES HIM A PITYING GLANCE--THEN LOOKS OUT 73 JOURNE
THE WINDOW AGAIN.
(JAMIE TURNS FROM THE WINDOW. 73 JOURNE
I MIGHT AS WELL HAVE THROWN THE MONEY OUT THE 84 JOURNE
WINDOW.
SHE KEEPS STARING OUT THE WINDOW UNTIL 121 JOURNE
AND A SMALL WINDOW AT LEFT OF DOOR, OVERLOOKS THE 1 MANSNS
LAKE.
ANOTHER WINDOW IS IN THE WALL FACING RIGHT. 1 MANSNS
FARTHER FORWARD, A HIGH WINDOW LOOKING OUT ON THE 117 MANSNS
STREET, THEN A CHAIR,
IS STANDING IN A GONDOLA BENEATH A BARRED WINDOW 355 MARCOM
OF THE HOUSE.
AND HIS FACE IS CLOSER TO THE BARS OF HER WINDOW.)356 MARCOM
(HE GOES TO THE WINDOW AND LOOKS DOWN--WITH 388 MARCOM
IRONICAL BUT INTENSE AMUSEMENT)
(COMING BACK FROM THE WINDOW--IRONICALLY) 389 MARCOM
HE THROWS OPEN THE WINDOW AND CALLS IN A LOUD, 389 MARCOM
COMMANDING TONE)
WITH THE TRAINED EYE FOR DISPLAY OF WINDOW- 428 MARCOM
DRESSERS, UNTIL THE TABLE,
AT RIGHT OF DOOR IS A SMALL WINDOW. 1 MISBEG
CLOSE TO THE HOUSE, UNDER THE WINDOW NEXT TO 1 MISBEG
JOSIE'S BEDROOM,
FRONT, AND ONE WINDOW ON THE FLOOR ABOVE. 1 MISBEG
YOU CAN SIT INSIDE BY MY WINDOW AND TAKE IN 54 MISBEG
EVERYTHING.
WITH THAT PALE YANKEE BITCH WATCHING FROM A 157 POET
WINDOW, SNEERING WITH DISGUST/
(HE LOOKS OUT OF WINDOW, FRONT) 22 STRANG
FROM THE WINDOW, ALTHOUGH IT IS A BEAUTIFUL WARM 48 STRANG
DAY IN THE FLOWER GARDEN BEYOND
IN THE LEFT WALL IS ONE WINDOW WITH STARCHED WHITE 48 STRANG
CURTAINS LOOKING OUT ON A
NINA IS SEATED AT THE FOOT OF THE TABLE, HER BACK 48 STRANG
TO THE WINDOW.
(HE STROLLS OVER TO THE WINDOW WHISTLING WITH AN 55 STRANG
EXAGGERATEDLY CASUAL AIR,
(HE STRAYS OVER TO THE WINDOW AND LOOKS OUT 94 STRANG
LISTLESSLY)
MAYBE I'D BETTER CLOSE THE WINDOWS... 111 STRANG
(HE TURNS HIS BACK ON MARSDEN WITH A GLANCE OF 148 STRANG
REPULSION AND WALKS TO THE WINDOW
IN THE LEFT WALL, CENTER, A SMALL WINDOW WITH A 470 WELDED
TORN DARK SHADE PULLED DOWN.
ON THE WINDOW SHADE FROM SOME STREET LAMP. 470 WELDED

WINDOW'S
HE'S GONE/ THE BED'S EMPTY. THE WINDOW'S WIDE 166 BEYOND
OPEN.

WINDOWLESS
LEADING INTO A DARK, WINDOWLESS, BACK PARLOR. 185 AHWILD
THE OTHER OPENS ON A DARK, WINDOWLESS BACK PARLOR, 11 JOURNE

WINDOWPANES
WITH A DAWN THAT WON'T CREEP OVER DIRTY 153 MISBEG
WINDOWPANES BUT WILL WAKE IN THE SKY
DIRTY WINDOWPANES, WITH SOME TART SNORING BESIDE 171 MISBEG
YOU--

WINDOWS
IN THE RIGHT WALL, REAR, A SCREEN DOOR IN THIS 185 AHWILD
WALL ARE TWO WINDOWS,
BENEATH THE TWO WINDOWS AT LEFT, FRONT, 185 AHWILD
IN FRONT OF THE WINDOWS IS A HEAVY, 210 AHWILD
IN THE RIGHT WALL ARE TWO WINDOWS LOOKING OUT ON A210 AHWILD
SIDE LAWN.
ITS MISTY WINDOWS GLOWING WANLY WITH THE LIGHT OF 25 ANNA
A LAMP INSIDE.
FROM THE HARBOR AND DOCKS OUTSIDE, MUFFLED BY THE 41 ANNA
CLOSED DOOR AND WINDOWS.
IN THE REAR WALL, TWO SMALL SQUARE WINDOWS AND A 41 ANNA
DOOR OPENING OUT ON THE DECK
IN THE RIGHT WALL, TWO MORE WINDOWS LOOKING OUT ON 41 ANNA
THE PORT DECK.
WHITE CURTAINS, CLEAN AND STIFF, ARE AT THE 41 ANNA
WINDOWS.
(A SHADOW CROSSES THE CABIN WINDOWS. 50 ANNA
ON THE LEFT, TWO WINDOWS LOOKING OUT ON THE 93 BEYOND
FIELDS.
AGAINST THE WALL BETWEEN THE WINDOWS, AN OLD- 93 BEYOND
FASHIONED WALNUT DESK.
ALL THE WINDOWS ARE OPEN, BUT NO BREEZE STIRS THE 112 BEYOND
SOILED WHITE CURTAINS.
THE CURTAINS AT THE WINDOWS ARE WORN AND DIRTY AND144 BEYOND
ONE OF THEM IS MISSING.
WINDOWS GRADUALLY FADES TO GRAY. 144 BEYOND
STAINED BY THE COLOR IN THE WINDOWS, FALLS ON THE 564 DAYS
WALL ON AND AROUND THE CROSS.
STAINED-GLASS WINDOWS. 564 DAYS
WHILE THIS IS HAPPENING THE LIGHT OF THE DAWN ON 566 DAYS
THE STAINED-GLASS WINDOWS
THE END WALL FACING US HAS TWO WINDOWS IN ITS 202 DESIRE
UPPER STORY.
BRIGHT SUNLIGHT STREAMS THROUGH THE WINDOWS ON THE493 DIFRNT
LEFT.
STIFF, WHITE CURTAINS ARE AT ALL THE WINDOWS. 494 DIFRNT
ORANGE CURTAINS ARE AT THE WINDOWS. 519 DIFRNT
(FROM THE OPEN, CURTAINED WINDOWS OF THE FIFE 425 DYNAMO
LIVING ROOM
NEAR THE WINDOWS. 428 DYNAMO
IN THE RIGHT WALL ARE THREE WINDOWS LOOKING OUT ON428 DYNAMO
THE LAWN
THESE WINDOWS ARE REPEATED IN THE SAME SERIES IN 428 DYNAMO
THE BEDROOM ABOVE.
WINDOWS ON THE RIGHT SO SHE CAN STARE OUT AT THE 428 DYNAMO
SKY.

WINDOWS (CONT'D.)
MRS. FIFE IS LEANING OUT OF ONE OF THE WINDOWS OF 454 DYNAMO
THEIR SITTING ROOM,
AND A ROW OF GREAT WINDOWS IN THE LEFT WALL. 486 DYNAMO
THERE ARE FIVE WINDOWS ON THE UPPER FLOOR AND FOUR 2 ELECTR
ON THE GROUND FLOOR.
THE WINDOWS OF THE LOWER FLOOR REFLECT THE SUN'S 5 ELECTR
RAYS IN A RESENTFUL GLARE.
ON THE LEFT ARE TWO WINDOWS. 28 ELECTR
ANOTHER ROOM COMES, REVERBERATING, RATTLING THE 42 ELECTR
WINDOWS.
IN THE LEFT WALL ARE TWO WINDOWS. 58 ELECTR
FLANKED BY TWO WINDOWS. 79 ELECTR
ALL THE SHUTTERS OF THE WINDOWS ARE CLOSED. 117 ELECTR
THERE IS A PAUSE IN WHICH PETER CAN BE HEARD 137 ELECTR
OPENING WINDOWS BEHIND THE SHUTTERS
THEN HE GOES TO ONE OF THE WINDOWS 142 ELECTR
THE SHUTTERS OF THE WINDOWS ARE CLOSED. 149 ELECTR
ON THE GROUND FLOOR, THE UPPER PART OF THE 169 ELECTR
WINDOWS, RAISED FROM THE BOTTOM,
THE SHUTTERS ARE ALL FASTENED BACK, THE WINDOWS 169 ELECTR
OPEN.
THE BLACK WALL DROP HAS WINDOWS PAINTED ON IT WITH290 GGBROW
A DIM,
AND MAKES A GESTURE AS IF FLINGING FRENCH WINDOWS 321 GGBROW
OPEN.
IN THE REAR, THE SHOW WINDOWS OF TWO SHOPS, 233 HA APE
TWO WINDOWS, SO GLAZED WITH GRIME ONE CANNOT SEE 573 ICEMAN
THROUGH THEM,
LIGHT COMES FROM THE STREET WINDOWS OFF RIGHT, 574 ICEMAN
AND WHAT LIGHT CAN PENETRATE THE GRIME OF THE TWO 610 ICEMAN
BACKYARD WINDOWS AT LEFT.
COMES FROM THE STREET WINDOWS, OFF RIGHT, 610 ICEMAN
IN THE RIGHT WALL ARE TWO BIG WINDOWS, 664 ICEMAN
BUT IT DOES NOT HIT THE WINDOWS AND THE LIGHT IN 664 ICEMAN
THE BACK-ROOM SECTION IS DIM.
FLANKING THE WINDOWS, 11 JOURNE
IN THE LEFT WALL, A SIMILAR SERIES OF WINDOWS 11 JOURNE
LOOKS OUT
FARTHER FORWARD, A SERIES OF THREE WINDOWS LOOKS 11 JOURNE
OVER THE FRONT LAWN TO THE
SUNSHINE COMES THROUGH THE WINDOWS AT RIGHT. 12 JOURNE
(SHE GETS UP RESTLESSLY AND GOES TO THE WINDOWS AT 17 JOURNE
RIGHT.)
(TYRONE GETS HASTILY TO HIS FEET AND GOES TO LOOK 39 JOURNE
OUT THE WINDOWS AT RIGHT.
AND GOES QUICKLY TO THE WINDOWS AT RIGHT. 42 JOURNE
(SHE TURNS AWAY AND GOES TO THE WINDOWS AT RIGHT. 43 JOURNE
NO SUNLIGHT COMES INTO THE ROOM NOW THROUGH THE 51 JOURNE
WINDOWS AT RIGHT.
(JAMIE GETS UP AND GOES TO THE WINDOWS AT RIGHT, 60 JOURNE
(SHE COMES TO THE WINDOWS AT RIGHT--LIGHTLY.) 82 JOURNE
SHE GOES SWIFTLY AWAY TO THE WINDOWS AT LEFT 89 JOURNE
(SHE RISES FROM THE ARM OF HIS CHAIR AND GOES TO 94 JOURNE
STARE OUT THE WINDOWS AT RIGHT
WHITE CURTAIN DRAWN DOWN OUTSIDE THE WINDOWS. 97 JOURNE
(GOES SLOWLY TO THE WINDOWS AT RIGHT LIKE AN 121 JOURNE
AUTOMATON--
(SHE TURNS QUICKLY AWAY FROM HIM TO THE WINDOWS AT122 JOURNE
RIGHT.
OUTSIDE THE WINDOWS THE WALL OF FOG APPEARS DENSER125 JOURNE
THAN EVER.
WHERE THE ONLY LIGHT CAME THROUGH TWO SMALL FILTHY148 JOURNE
WINDOWS,
THE FURNITURE, THE WINDOWS, 170 JOURNE
SHE MOVES LEFT TO THE FRONT END OF THE SOFA 174 JOURNE
BENEATH THE WINDOWS AND SITS DOWN,
GRAY IN THE FADING DAYLIGHT THAT ENTERS FROM THREE273 LAZARU
SMALL WINDOWS AT THE LEFT.
FOUR WINDOWS ARE VISIBLE WITH A CLOSED DOOR IN THE281 LAZARU
MIDDLE OF THE WALL.
THE DANCERS CAN BE SEEN WHIRLING SWIFTLY BY THE 281 LAZARU
WINDOWS.
THE WINDOWS SHINE BRILLIANTLY WITH THE FLICKERING 281 LAZARU
LIGHT OF MANY CANDLES WHICH
THE LIGHTS IN THE WINDOWS, WHICH HAVE BEEN GROWING295 LAZARU
DIM, GO OUT.
THE WINDOWS OF THE PALACE GLOW CRIMSON-PURPLE 326 LAZARU
THE CRIMSON-PURPLE LIGHTS OF THE MANY WINDOWS OF 334 LAZARU
THE PALACE GO OUT ONE BY ONE AS
THE WINDOWS HAVE BOARDS NAILED ACROSS THEM. 1 MANSNS
THERE ARE TWO WINDOWS IN THE RIGHT WALL, 43 MANSNS
BETWEEN THE WINDOWS IS A DESK WITH A CHAIR. 43 MANSNS
IN THE LEFT WALL ARE TWO WINDOWS LOOKING OUT ON 69 MANSNS
THE STREET.
BETWEEN THE WINDOWS IS A CHAIR. 69 MANSNS
THERE ARE TWO WINDOWS ON THE LOWER FLOOR OF THIS 1 MISBEG
SIDE OF THE HOUSE WHICH FACES
THESE WINDOWS HAVE NO SHUTTERS, CURTAINS OR 1 MISBEG
SHADES.
(JOSIE CAN BE SEEN THROUGH THE WINDOWS, RETURNING 111 MISBEG
FROM THE KITCHEN.
AND ALL WE SEE NOW OF ITS LIGHTED INTERIOR IS 111 MISBEG
THROUGH THE TWO WINDOWS.
I'VE SEEN TOO GODDAMNED MANY DAWNS CREEPING GRAYLY124 MISBEG
OVER TOO MANY DIRTY WINDOWS.
AT REAR ARE FOUR WINDOWS. 7 POET
SUNLIGHT SHINES IN THROUGH THE WINDOWS AT REAR. 8 POET
PASSING BEFORE THE TWO WINDOWS, 86 POET
THIS ROOM IS AT THE FRONT PART OF HIS HOUSE WITH 3 STRANG
WINDOWS OPENING ON THE STRIP OF
GIVING THE WINDOWS A SUGGESTION OF LIFELESS CLOSED 24 STRANG
EYES AND MAKING THE ROOM SEEM
DREAMING INTO THE DARK BEYOND THE WINDOWS... 27 STRANG
WINDOWS ON THE LEFT LOOK OUT ON A BROAD PORCH. 90 STRANG
THE REAR OF THE CABIN WITH BROAD WINDOWS AND A 158 STRANG
DOOR IS AT RIGHT.

WINDOWS (CONT'D.)
THE CRIMSONS AND PURPLES IN THE WINDOWS WILL STAIN197 STRANG OUR

WINDOWS'
THE SMOKE POURED FROM THE WINDOWS' THE NEIGHBORS 346 LAZARU THOUGHT THE HOUSE WAS BURNING/

WINDS
(SUDDENLY HE CAN GO NO FARTHER AND WINDS UP 295 AHWILD HELPLESSLY)
JACK WINDS UP HIS TALE.) 510 DIFRNT
AND WHEN I GITS A CHANCE TO USE IT I WINDS UP 178 EJONES EMPEROR IN TWO YEARS.
THE WARM EARTH IN THE MOONLIGHT, THE TRADE WINDS 112 ELECTR RUSTLING THE COCO PALMS,
ALL DAT CRAZY TRIPE ABOUT SUNS AND WINDS, FRESH 215 HA APE AIR AND DE REST OF IT--
YUH'RE ON'Y DOLLS I WINDS UP TO SEE 'M SPIN. 238 HA APE
LET US GO SEAWARD AS THE GREAT WINDS GO, FULL OF 173 JOURNE BLOWN SAND AND FOAM.
THEIR CLAWS RENDED SAILS INTO RAGS, FIERCE WERE 408 MARCOM THE WINDS/
FIERCE WERE THE WINDS/ 408 MARCOM
FIERCE WERE THE WINDS/ 408 MARCOM
(THE WINDS UP PHILOSOPHICALLY) 410 MARCOM

WINDSOR
LONG IS DRESSED IN SHORE CLOTHES, WEARS A BLACK 233 HA APE WINDSOR TIE, CLOTH CAP.
EVEN HIS FLOWING WINDSOR TIE IS NEATLY TIED. 574 ICEMAN

WINDY
ESPECIALLY WHEN IT WAS WINDY AND THE BREAKERS WERE548 'ILE ROLLING IN,
THE TIME IS AN EARLY HOUR OF A CLEAR WINDY NIGHT 555 CROSS IN THE FALL OF THE YEAR 1900.

WINDYAMMER
WINDYAMMER, AY VAS THROUGH HUNDRED STORMS VORSE'N 49 ANNA DAT/

WINE
-A BOOK OF VERSES UNDERNEATH THE BOUGH, A JUG OF 199 AHWILD WINE, A LOAF OF BREAD--
= THAT I COULD DRINK WITH THY VEINS AS WINE, AND 205 AHWILD EAT THY BREASTS LIKE HONEY.
= A BOTTLE O' WINE AND A BOTTLE O' BEER AND A 103 ELECTR BOTTLE OF IRISH WHISKEY OH/
EVEN JOE NOT IS STANDING UP TO LOOK AT THE WINE 640 ICEMAN WITH AN ADMIRING GRIN.
DERE AIN'T NO WINE GLASSES. 640 ICEMAN
(ROCKY AND CHUCK CARRY THE BASKET OF WINE INTO THE640 ICEMAN BAR.
MY IDEA IS TO USE THE WINE FOR THAT, SO GET IT ALL643 ICEMAN SET.
GET THAT WINE READY, CHUCK AND ROCKY/ 653 ICEMAN
AND GULP HALF THE WINE DOWN, HICKEY LEADING THEM 659 ICEMAN IN THIS.)
THEY ARE NOT LONG, THE DAYS OF WINE AND ROSES-. 130 JOURNE
WITH WINE, WITH POETRY, OR WITH VIRTUE, AS YOU 132 JOURNE WILL.=
DRUNKEN WITH WHATS WITH WINE, WITH POETRY, OR 132 JOURNE WITH VIRTUE, AS YOU WILL.
IT WAS LIKE WINE/ 277 LAZARU
BRING WINE/ 278 LAZARU
WINE IS POURED AND ALL RAISE THEIR GOBLETS TOWARD 278 LAZARU LAZARUS--
THEIR TANNED BODIES AND MASKS DAUBED AND STAINED 298 LAZARU WITH WINE LEES,
OF THE WINE OF LIFE STIRRING FOREVER IN THE SAP 307 LAZARU AND BLOOD AND LOAM OF THINGS.
A SLAVE WITH AN AMPHORA OF WINE CROUCHES ON THE 313 LAZARU STEPS BY HIS CHAIR.
CALIGULA GULPS AT HIS WINE. 314 LAZARU
THERE'S PRETTY GIRLS IN CARTHAGE AND WINE TO SWILL314 LAZARU IN CARTHAGE.
WHAT GOOD IS WINE IF IT CANNOT KILL THOUGHTS 317 LAZARU
OR IS IT A POWDER YOU DISSOLVE IN WINES 354 LAZARU
ME THAN WINE THAT WAY. 406 MARCOM
THE CHAMBERLAIN COMES BACK WITH A CUP OF WINE. 423 MARCOM
LOOK AT THE WINE/ 428 MARCOM
PASS AROUND THE WINE. 429 MARCOM
WITH NAUSEA RETCHING YOUR MEMORY, AND THE WINE OF 140 MISBEG PASSION POETS BLAB ABOUT,
THANK GOD, I STILL HAVE WINE IN MY CELLAR FIT FOR 98 POET A GENTLEMAN.
AND RAISES HIS GLASS OF WINE WITH THE OTHER-- 98 POET IGNORING HER.)
(SMACKING HIS.LIPS.) GOOD WINE, CORPORAL. 98 POET
(IGNORING HER.) NO, I HAVE NO NEED TO APOLOGIZE 98 POET FOR THE WINE.
(HE DRINKS THE REST OF HIS WINE, POURS ANOTHER 100 POET GLASS,

WINES
VEGETABLES, SALADS, FRUITS, NUTS, DOZENS OF 428 MARCOM BOTTLES OF WINES.

WINGS
THEY UNHITCH THEIR WINGS, KATEY, AND SPREADS 'EM 95 BEYOND OUT ON A WAVE FOR A BED.
(LAUGHING EXCITEDLY) I FEEL SO FREE I'D LIKE TO 136 BEYOND HAVE WINGS AND FLY OVER THE SEA.
(SARDONICALLY) IF YE'D GROW WINGS ON US WE'D FLY 213 DESIRE THAT/
THE WHITE WINGS GOT SOME JOB SWEEPIN' DIS UP. 234 HA APE

WINK
(WITH A WINK AT THE OTHERS) WHAT, ARE YOU 190 AHWILD INSINUATING I EVER--?
(WITH A WINK AT RICHARD--JOKINGLY) 198 AHWILD
(WITH A SLY, BLURRY WINK AROUND) 229 AHWILD
(COMING TO THE TABLE--WITH A WINK AT BELLE) 238 AHWILD
(WITH A WINK) I GET YOU. 238 AHWILD
(SETTING THEM DOWN--WITH A WINK AT BELLE) 239 AHWILD

WINK (CONT'D.)
THE BARTENDER NODS TOWARD BELLE, GIVING THE 244 AHWILD SALESMAN A WINK.
(WITH A WINK) HE'S GOING TO MURDER ME. 247 AHWILD
(WITH A WINK AT MARTHY) THIS GIRL, NOW, 'LL BE 9 ANNA MARRYIN' A SAILOR HERSELF,
(COMING UP TO HER--WITH A WINK) 23 ANNA
DIVIL A WINK I'M AFTER HAVING FOR TWO DAYS AND 32 ANNA NIGHTS
(TO ANNA, WITH A WINK) YOU'LL NOT BE LONESOME 77 ANNA LONG.
(WITH A WINK) THEN THERE'S NOTHING TO IT BUT FOR 104 BEYOND YOU TO GET RIGHT OUT
WHIN YE BUY A BOTTLE AV DHRINK OR (WITH A WINK) 463 CARIBE SOMETHIN' ELSE FORBID,
(WITH A WINK AT ELIUT) 501 DAYS
(WITH A WINK AT ELIOT) HE SEEMS TO BE FIXED IN 504 DAYS HIS LAST RELIGION.
SHE'S LIKE T'NIGHT, SHE'S SOFT 'N' WA'M, HER EYES 211 DESIRE KIN WINK LIKE A STAR.
(WITH A WINK AT PETER--DRAWLINGLY) 211 DESIRE
WAAL, I'M A-GOIN' T' STEAL A WINK O' SLEEP. 245 DESIRE
(THEN HE ADDS WITH A WINK) IF YEW HAIN'T, WHO 248 DESIRE WUUDS
(WITH A WINK) MEBBE HE'S DOIN' THE OUTIFUL AN' 248 DESIRE WALKIN' THE KID T' SLEEP.
(WITH A WINK AT THE OTHERS) YE'RE THE SPRYEST 250 DESIRE SEVENTY-SIX EVER I SEES, EPHRAIM/
(WITH A WINK) AND YOU KNOW AS WELL'S ME THAT SOME497 DIFRNT O' THE OTHERS FINDS OUT SOME
(WITH A SLY WINK) OH, IS HE? 502 DIFRNT
(WITH A WINK) BUT I KNOW DAMN WELL WHAT I'D A 503 DIFRNT DONE IN CALEB'S BOOTS.
(WITH A WINK) AND MIGHTY ACCOMMODATIN' IN THEIR 511 DIFRNT WAYS.
(WITH A WINK) I WASN'T BORN YESTERDAY. 525 DIFRNT
(WITH A WINK) OH, BOY/ 526 DIFRNT
(WITH A WINK) CURIOSITY KILLED A CAT/ 527 DIFRNT
(WITH A WINK) YOU OUGHTER SEE HER PERFORM 529 DIFRNT SOMETIMES.
I'M SICK OF THESE FRESH GUYS THAT THINK ALL THEY 430 DYNAMO HAVE TO DO IS WINK AND YOU
(STUNG BUT PRETENDING INDIFFERENCE--WITH A WINK) 176 EJONES
(WITH A WINK AT HAZEL) PETER WILL BE GETTING 81 ELECTR JEALOUS/
(WITH A WINK AT THE OTHERS) HE'S AIMIN' TO GIT SO 130 ELECTR FULL OF INJUN COURAGE
(WITH A WINK AT THE OTHERS) OH, HERS AND A HULL 130 ELECTR PASSEL OF OTHERS.
(WITH A PLAYFUL WINK) YES, 289 GGBROW
(WITH A WINK AT THE OTHERS) SURE I KNOW WHAT'S 227 HA APE THE MATTER.
INTERMITTENT ELECTRIC LIGHTS WINK OUT THE 233 HA APE INCREDIBLE PRICES.
(HE APPROACHES A LADY--WITH A VICIOUS GRIN AND A 237 HA APE SMIRKING WINK)
(WITH A KNOWING WINK) SURE. 247 HA APE
(WITH ANOTHER WINK) AW, DAT'S RIGHT, SEE. 247 HA APE
(HE TRIES OUT A WINK HIMSELF.) 37 HUGHIE
AFFECTIONATE WINK WITH WHICH A WISE GUY REGALES A 38 HUGHIE SUCKER.)
BEJEEZ, CAN'T I GET A WINK OF SLEEP IN MY OWN BACK582 ICEMAN ROOMS
HARRY FUMES) YEAH, GRIN/ WINK, BEJEEZ/ 598 ICEMAN
THEY GRIN HANGOVER GRINS OF TOLERANT AFFECTION AT 598 ICEMAN HIM AND WINK AT EACH OTHER.
(WITH A WINK AT MCGLOIN) YES, YOU CAN'T ASK MORE 602 ICEMAN THAN THAT, HARRY.
(WITH A WINK AT MARGIE--TEASINGLY) 612 ICEMAN
I COULDN'T SLEEP A WINK. 614 ICEMAN
WHAT THE HELL--(THEN WITH A WINK AT THE OTHERS, 620 ICEMAN KIDDINGLY)
(WITH AN AMUSED WINK AT HOPE) 657 ICEMAN
NOT A WINK OF SLEEP. 666 ICEMAN
I DON'T GET A WINK OF SLEEP, SEES 669 ICEMAN
(HE TRIES A WINK AT THE OTHERS. 722 ICEMAN
(WITH A WINK) OUR LITTLE BARTENDER, AIN'T HE, 725 ICEMAN POLL?
B'FORE YOU COULD WINK YOUR EYE. 516 INZONE
GUD STIFFEN US, ARE WE NEVER GOIN' TO TURN IN FUR 532 INZONE A WINK AV SLEEP?
(WITH A WINK) I'LL TELL YOU A GOOD ONE 366 MARCOM
(HE SUDDENLY LOOKS AT MAFFEO WITH A CRAFTY WINK) 381 MARCOM
IT'S LIGHT, EASY TO CARRY,---(THERE HE GIVES A 393 MARCOM PRODIGIOUS WINK)
(WITH A GRIN AND A WINK) NO. 396 MARCOM
BE GOD, I'LL MAKE MYSELF AS SOBER AS A JUDGE FOR 91 MISBEG YOU IN THE WINK OF AN EYE/
(LEERING--WITH A WINK AT NORA.) 177 POET
(PULLS THE BOTTLE FROM HIS COAT POCKET--WITH A 591 ROPE WINK)
(WITH A CUNNING WINK) AW, HE'S GOT IT AW RIGHT. 593 ROPE
NOT A WINK. 51 STRANG
(WITH A WINK) I WAS THINKIN' AS ONE OF 'EM FROM 496 VOYAGE THE GLENCAIRN'D DO--
AND JOE GIVES HIM A SIGNIFICANT WINK AND NODS 497 VOYAGE TOWARD THE DOOR ON THE LEFT.
(WITH A SMIRKING WINK) PRETTY, 'OLESOME GELS THEY499 VOYAGE BE, AIN'T THEY, NICKS
(WITH A WINK) YE HEAR WHAT THE LADY SAYS, OLLIE. 504 VOYAGE
(WITH A MEANING WINK) YE AIN' FREDA WENT AHT 508 VOYAGE T'GETHER 'BOUT FIVE MINUTES PAST.

WINKED
AIN'T I PERTECTED YOU AND WINKED AT ALL DE CROOKED177 EJONES TRADIN' YOU BEEN DOIN'
JAMIE KIDDED HIM ABOUT HOOKING YOU, AND HE WINKED 145 JOURNE AND LAUGHED/

WINKED

WINKED (CONT'D.)
SO HE WINKED AT ME AN' GRINNED--HE WAS DRUNK BY 585 ROPE THIS--AN' SAID.."

WINKER
AND WINKIN' AT WHAT THE BOYS WAS DOIN'. 502 DIFRNT
THEY DOES IT LIKE THAT BY WINKIN' A LIGHT. 521 INZONE

WINKING
(WITH A NOD AT RICHARD, WINKING AT HIS WIFE) 296 AHWILD
(WINKING AT SIMEON) MEBBE COEN'S AIMIN' T' MARRY,214 DESIRE TOO.
THERE IS NO END OF WINKING, OF NUDGING, 247 DESIRE
WHEN THE SKY'D BE BLAZING AND WINKING WID STARS. 214 HA APE

WINKS
(HE WINKS) SEE WHAT I MEAN& 218 AHWILD
(HE WINKS AT ARTHUR, INDICATING WITH HIS EYES AND 256 AHWILD A NOD OF HIS HEAD
BUT MILLER WINKS AND SHAKES HIS HEAD VIGOROUSLY 258 AHWILD AND MOTIONS HER TO SIT DOWN.)
(AS ABBIE DISAPPEARS IN HOUSE--WINKS AT PETER AND 222 DESIRE SAYS TAUNTINGLY)
(HE WINKS AT CALEB WHO GRINS BACK AT HIM.) 499 DIFRNT
THE WINKS PONDEROUSLY AND GOES OFF LAUGHING 500 DIFRNT UPROARIOUSLY.)
(WINKS AT HER CUNNINGLY). 521 DIFRNT
MEBBE YOU COULD TAKE A COUPLE O' WINKS AN' IT'D DO1TO ELECTR YOU GOOD.
(HE WINKS AND CHUCKLES.) 37 HUGHIE
(WINKS AT LARRY) AW, HARRY, ME AND CHUCK WAS ON'Y582 ICEMAN KIDDIN'.
(WINKS AT JOE) SURE, LARRY AIN'T DE ON'Y WISE GUY585 ICEMAN IN DIS DUMP, HEY, JOE&
GUESS I'LL GET BACK IN DE BAR AND CATCH A COUPLA 586 ICEMAN WINKS BEFORE OPENING-UP TIME.
(MUSHER WINKS AT HOPE, SHAKING HIS HEAD, 608 ICEMAN
I'M GOING TO CATCH A COUPLE MORE WINKS HERE 610 ICEMAN
(HE WINKS AT THE OTHERS. 621 ICEMAN
GOT TO GRAB FORTY WINKS--DRINK UP, EVERYBODY--ON 625 ICEMAN ME--
(HE WINKS AROUND AT THE OTHERS. 684 ICEMAN
HE WINKS WITH A KIDDING GRIN.) 21 JOURNE
(HE WINKS AT HER, WITH A DERISIVE GLANCE AT HIS 40 JOURNE FATHER.)
I THINK I'LL CATCH A FEW WINKS. 169 JOURNE
HE WINKS AT JOSIE AND BEGINS IN AN EXAGGERATEDLY 43 MISBEG CASUAL MANNER.)
(WINKS SLYLY.) MAYBE THEY WASN'T LIES. 11 POET
SWEENEY WINKS MYSTERIOUSLY) 584 ROPE
(HE WINKS CUNNINGLY) 585 ROPE

WINNER
SHE'S SURELY A LITTLE WINNER. 140 BEYOND

WINNING
(THEN AS LARRY TURNS TO GO, FORCING A WINNING 14 ANNA SMILE AT HIM)
SHE RELAPSES INTO THE FAMILIAR FORM AND FLASHES 23 ANNA ONE OF HER WINNING TRADE SMILES
BUT IMMEDIATELY PUTS ON HIS MOST POLITE, WINNING 20 ELECTR AIR.
HIS EXPRESSION IS FIXED IN A SALESMAN'S WINNING 618 ICEMAN SMILE

WINNINGS
SO THAT ONE'S WINNINGS HAVE THE SEMBLANCE OF 92 MANSNS LOSSES.
WATCHING MY WINNINGS PILE UP AND BECOMING CONFUSED102 MANSNS WITH LOSSES--

WINNOWED
MOONLIGHT, WINNOWED BY THE WIND WHICH MOANS IN THE555 CROSS STUBBORN ANGLES OF THE OLD

WINS
AND HE WINS/ 21 HUGHIE
THIS OLD TURTLE NEVER WINS A RACE, BUT HE WAS AS 25 HUGHIE FUXY AS TEN GUYS.
WHEN HE GABS ABOUT THE BETS HE WINS AND THE DOLLS 28 HUGHIE HE'S MADE.
HE'LL GAMBLE FOR ANY LIMIT ON ANYTHING, AND ALWAYS 32 HUGHIE WINS.
IF YOU WINS, DAT'S VELVET FOR YOU. 605 ICEMAN
I DON'T CARE WHO WINS--AS LONG AS IT ISN'T GORDON/175 STRANG

WINTER
AND WINTER--IF YOU'RE TOGETHER. 298 AHWILD
AND BEAUTY ENOUGH FOR ANYONE, EXCEPT IN THE 85 BEYONU WINTER.
I'D LOVE TO HAVE A SKUNK-SKIN COAT NEXT WINTER... 439 DYNAMO
IT IS LATE AFTERNOON OF A GRAY DAY IN WINTER. 269 GGBROW
USED TO FOLLOW THE HORSES SOUTH EVERY WINTER. 23 HUGHIE
WHERE YOU ROASTED IN SUMMER, AND THERE WAS NU 148 JOURNE STOVE IN WINTER.
THAT WAS IN THE WINTER OF SENIOR YEAR. 176 JOURNE
IT'S VERY COLD IN WINTER. 365 MARCOM
CAUSE WHEN SPRING IS SMITTEN BY WINTER, WHEN BIRDS436 MARCOM ARE STRUCK DEAD IN FULL SONG,
OF BETTING ON FAVORITES, AND FOLLOW THE HORSES 143 MISBEG SOUTH IN THE WINTER.
COLLEGE. I KEPT HIM AWAY AT SCHOOL IN WINTER AND 60 STRANG CAMP IN SUMMERS AND I WENT TO
AN EVENING EARLY IN THE FOLLOWING WINTER ABOUT 66 STRANG SEVEN MONTHS LATER.
THERE'S JUST ENOUGH WINTER IN THE AIR TO MAKE ONE 456 WELDED ENERGETIC.

WINTHROP
"SIMEON WINTHROP" AT ANCHOR IN THE OUTER HARBOR OF 25 ANNA PROVINCETOWN, MASS.
THE INTERIOR OF THE CABIN ON THE BARGE "SIMEON 41 ANNA WINTHROP" AT DOCK IN BOSTON--

WIPE
YOU SHOULDN'T EVEN WIPE YOUR FEET ON ME/ 258 AHWILD
(HE SHAKES HIS HEAD AND BEGINS TC WIPE THE BAR 677 ICEMAN MECHANICALLY.)
IT'D WIPE IT OUT/ 706 ICEMAN

WIPE (CONT'D.)
I'M NOT WORTHY TO WIPE YOUR SHOES." 710 ICEMAN
IT WOULD BE BETTER TO WIPE OUT THEIR CUNNING NOW 422 MARCOM
PUTTING ON AIRS AS IF HE WAS TOO GOOD TO WIPE HIS 10 MISBEG SHOES ON ME.
I'LL WIPE THE FLOORS WITH HIM, THE LAZY BASTARD/ 11 MISBEG
DON'T COME BACK TILL YOU'VE SLEPT IT OFF, OR I'LL 100 MISBEG WIPE THE FLOOR WITH YOU/

WIPED
DOESN'T MEAN LAST NIGHT IS WIPED OUT. 289 AHWILD
BUT CON WIPED THE SNEER OFF THEIR MUGS 12 POET

WIPES
(AFTER THIS OUTBURST SHE CALMS DOWN AND WIPES HER 545 'ILE EYES WITH HER HANDKERCHIEF.)
(HE WIPES HIS PERSPIRING BROW IN ANGUISH AT THIS 103 BEYOND THOUGHT)
(SHE WIPES HER EYES WITH HER HANDKERCHIEF AND 116 BEYOND SOBS.)
(SHE WIPES HER MOIST FOREHEAD--WEARILY) 117 BEYOND
(SHE WIPES HER EYES QUICKLY AND WITHOUT LOOKING AT143 BEYOND ROBERT.
(RUTH SOBS BROKENLY AND WIPES ROBERT'S LIPS WITH 167 BEYOND HER HANDKERCHIEF.)
HE WIPES HIS FOREHEAD STREAMING WITH SWEAT. 252 DESIRE
(HE WIPES TEARS FROM HIS EYES.) 148 JOURNE
(SHE SOBS AND WIPES HER EYES WITH HER SLEEVE-- 345 LAZARU
THE MAGIAN SETS DOWN HIS BAG AND WIPES HIS BROW.) 347 MARCOM
(HE WIPES HIS BROW WITH A HANDKERCHIEF) 603 MARCOM
(HE WIPES HIS MOUTH ON HIS SLEEVE WITH A SNUFFLE) 598 ROPE
(BLOWS HIS NOSE, WIPES HIS EYES, SIGHS, CLEARS HIS 22 ROPE THROAT.
AND HE PULLS OUT HIS HANDKERCHIEF AND WIPES THEM, 28 STRANG MUTTERING HUSKILY)

WIPING
(SHE TURNS AWAY, WIPING A TEAR FURTIVELY--THEN 214 AHWILD ABRUPTLY CHANGING THE SUBJECT)
(WIPING THE TEARS FROM HER EYES--DEFIANTLY) 227 AHWILD
SATISFACTION, WIPING HER MOUTH WITH THE BACK OF 8 ANNA HER HAND.
(WIPING HER EYES--SIMPLY) JAMES WAS A GOOD MAN. 114 BEYOND
(WIPING TEARS FROM HER EYES WITH HER HANDKERCHIEF)114 BEYOND
(WIPING HER EYES) IT'S THE HEAT UPSETS HER. 116 BEYOND
(WIPING HIS MOUTH) IT WAS LIKE PIZEN ON 'EM. 239 DESIRE
(HE BLINKS BACK ONE TEAR, WIPING HIS SLEEVE ACROSS264 DESIRE HIS NOSE.)
ROCKY IS BEHIND THE BAR, WIPING IT, WASHING 664 ICEMAN GLASSES, ETC.
(WIPING THE BAR--WITH ELABORATE INDIFFERENCE) 683 ICEMAN
HE IS WIPING SWEAT FROM HIS FOREHEAD WITH A 53 JOURNE HANDKERCHIEF.
HASTILY WIPING HER EYES. 122 JOURNE
(WIPING HER LIPS WITH THE BACK OF HER HAND-- 475 WELDED

WIRE
JUST RECEIVED YOUR WIRE. 147 BEYOND
I NEVER DREAMED YOU--WHY DIDN'T YOU WIRE ME YOU 505 DAYS WERE COMING&
ONE LACED WITH TWINE, THE OTHER WITH A BIT OF 577 ICEMAN WIRE.
THAT DRUNKEN LOAFER HAS TRIED TO PICK THE LOCK 121 JOURNE WITH A PIECE OF WIRE.
THEY ALSO WEAR WIRE WIGS BUT OF STRAIGHT HAIR CUT 336 LAZARU IN SHORT BOYISH MODE.
THESE YOUTHS WEAR FEMALE WIGS OF CURLED WIRE LIKE 336 LAZARU FRIZZED HAIR OF A YELLOW GOLD.

WIRED
I WAS CALLING ON NINA WHEN YOUR WIRE CAME. 30 STRANG
BUT WHEN I LANDED IN NEW YORK--I WIRED YOU I HAD 156 BEYOND BUSINESS TO WIND

WIRELESS
AS IF A MYSTERIOUS WIRELESS MESSAGE HAD GONE 617 ICEMAN AROUND.)

WIRES
THIS SECOND GALLERY, DIMLY LIGHTED LIKE THE ONE 483 DYNAMO BELOW, IS A NETWORK OF WIRES,
WHEN ALL THESE SWITCHES AND BUSSES AND WIRES 484 DYNAMO SEEMED LIKE THE ARMS OF A DEVIL
WITH SOMEONE JERKING THE WIRES. 415 MARCOM

WIRY
CABOT IS SEVENTY-FIVE, TALL AND GAUNT, WITH GREAT,221 DESIRE WIRY, CONCENTRATED POWER.
FIFE IS A SMALL WIRY MAN OF FIFTY, OF SCOTCH-IRISH428 DYNAMO ORIGIN.
HE IS A TALL MAN IN HIS EARLY FORTIES, WITH A 28 ELECTR SPARE, WIRY FRAME,
HE IS A THIN, WIRY MAN OF SIXTY-FIVE OR SO, WITH A102 ELECTR TOUSLED MOP OF BLACK HAIR,
SMALL IS A WIRY OLD MAN OF SIXTY-FIVE, A CLERK IN 129 ELECTR A HARDWARE STORE.
THE SAME HEIGHT AS YOUNG BROWN BUT LEAN AND WIRY, 260 GGBROW WITHOUT REPOSE.
A COUPLE OF INCHES TALLER, THIN AND WIRY. 19 JOURNE
HE IS TALL AND LOOSE-JOINTED WITH A WIRY STRENGTH 4 MANSNS OF LIMB.
HE IS TWENTY-SEVEN, SHORT, DARK, WIRY, HIS 33 STRANG MOVEMENTS RAPID AND SURE.

WISDOM
(WITH CALM WISDOM) THAT'S EASY, MA. 254 AHWILD
(THEN WITH A GRIN) YOU SURPRISE ME AT TIMES WITH 291 AHWILD YOUR DEEP WISDOM.
AND THAT'S ENOUGH PHILOSOPHIC WISDOM TO GIVE YOU 578 ICEMAN FOR ONE DRINK OF ROT-GUT.
AND THE PRACTICAL WISDOM OF THE WORLD IN THAT 585 ICEMAN LITTLE PARABLE.
YOU WERE ALL SO BUSY DRINKING IN WORDS OF WISDOM 638 ICEMAN FROM THE OLD WISE GUY HERE,
PUMPING HIM FULL OF WHAT YOU CONSIDER WORLDLY 34 JOURNE WISDOM.
WISDOM FROM THE MOUTH OF BABES. 156 JOURNE

WISDOM

(CONT'D.)

TALK TO THEMSELVES, FOR THEY HAVE REACHED THAT 354 LAZARU HOPELESS WISDOM OF EXPERIENCE

I HAVE HEARD OF WISDOM FROM BABES, BUT WHO COULD 39 MANSNS DREAM OF IT FROM A BACHELOR/

SIT THERE FOR HOURS IN WISDOM-RIDICULING 102 MANSNS CONTEMPLATION OF MYSELF.

MARK MY WORDS, MARCO WILL BE WORTH A MILLION WISE 363 MARCOM MEN--IN THE CAUSE OF WISDOM/

AND AT LAST HE ATTAINED THE WISDOM WHERE ALL 372 MARCOM DESIRE HAS ENDED

(GENTLY) IS INTOLERANCE WISDOMS 388 MARCOM LOVE IS TO WISDOM WHAT WISDOM SEEMS TO LOVE--A 388 MARCOM FOLLY.

TO CONVERT ME TO WISDOM--IF I COULD FIND THE TRUE 397 MARCOM ONE/

I WISH TO BE CONVERTED TO WISDOM, TOO--ONE OR 398 MARCOM ANOTHER--BEFORE I BECOME A NAME.

(WEARILY AND DROWSILY) YOUR WISDOM MAKES ME 402 MARCOM SLEEP.

IN ORDER TO LIVE EVEN WISDOM MUST BE STUPID/ 423 MARCOM WISDOM/ NO, DO NOT READ/ 423 MARCOM IS THIS WISDOMS 425 MARCOM AND--IN THE CAUSE OF WISDOM, SAY--WE MUST SEE WHAT426 MARCOM HE IS DOING NOW.

(TO THE CONFUCIAN) FOLLOWER OF CONFUCIUS, THE 434 MARCOM WISE, HAVE YOU THIS WISDOM

SMILE WITH INFINITE FOREBEARANCE UPON OUR WISDOM, 435 MARCOM TOO BRIEF FOR THE WISDOM OF JOY, TOO LONG FOR THE 436 MARCOM KNOWLEDGE OF SORROW.

(ECHOING SADLY) THY WISDOM. 437 MARCOM IS WAS THE WISDOM OF PRIDE. 437 MARCOM IT WAS THY WISDOM. 437 MARCOM MY WISDOM, MY TRUTHS 437 MARCOM DO NOT WOUND ME WITH WISDOM. 437 MARCOM OH, CHU-YIN, MY WISE FRIEND, WAS THE PRAYER I 437 MARCOM TAUGHT THEM WISDOMS

FOR ALL HIS BROADWAY WISDOM ABOUT WOMEN, 87 MISBEG AND KEEP HIS WISDOM, 146 POET THEN HE SAID HE WAS AFRAID MAYBE I'D THINK IT WAS 146 POET WEAKNESS IN HIM, NOT WISDOM.

WISE

(THEN CONSIDERING) CAN YOU FIX IT SO YOUR FOLKS 219 AHWILD WON'T GET WISE8

STUPID FACE AND A CYNICALLY WISE GRIN, STANDS JUST236 ICEMAN INSIDE THE BAR ENTRANCE.

DO YOU KNOW THE LOBSTER AND THE WISE GUY-8 246 AHWILD WHY DIDN'T YOU PUT ME WISE, YOU LOUSY TRAMP YOU/ 248 AHWILD I'M WISE TO WHAT'S IN BACK OF YOUR NUT, DUTCHY. 11 ANNA I'M WISE TO THE GAME, UP, DOWN, AND SIDEWAYS. 11 ANNA TRYIN' TO LOOK AS WISE AS AN OWL ON A TREE, AND 479 CARDIF ALL THE TOIME HE NOT

WISE-CRACKING AT EVERYTHING WITH ANY DECENT HUMAN 521 DAYS DIGNITY AND WORTH.

YOU'D GET WISE TO SOMETHING THEN. 529 DIFRNT (WHY DID THE POOR BOOB LET POP GET WISE HE WAS 438 DYNAMO SCARED OF LIGHTNINGS...)

I'M WISE TO YOUR DIRTY GAME--AND I WON'T STAND FOR484 DYNAMO IT/

THEY MAKE ME WISE TO PEOPLE. 284 GGBROW AND IT'S ALL I CARE ABOUT IS PLAYING. 285 GGBROW NOW YUH'RE GETTIN' WISE TO SOMEP'N. 217 HA APE (PHILOSOPHICALLY) IT WOULD TAKE A WISE MAN TO TELL228 HA APE ONE FROM THE OTHER.

(WITH GROWING ANGER) BUT ONE TING I'M WISE TO, AW231 HA APE RIGHT/

I'M WISE TO WHERE DEY HANGS OUT NOW. 242 HA APE I'M WISE TO DAT. 247 HA APE YOU SEEM TO BE WISE TO A LOT OF STUFF NONE OF US 247 HA APE KNOWS ABOUT.

I'M WISE TO DE GAME. 248 HA APE SAY, YOUSE UP DERE, MAN IN DE MOON, YUH LOOK SO 250 HA APE WISE, GIMME DE ANSWER, HUH8

SHE WASN'T WISE DAT I WAS IN A CAGE, TOO--WORSER*N252 HA APE YOURS--SURE--A DAMN SIGHT--

IN MANNER, HE IS CONSCIOUSLY A BROADWAY SPORT AND 9 HUGHIE A WISE GUY--

ONE OF THEM FRESH WISE PUNKS. 10 HUGHIE I'D WISE THEM UP TO KID HIM ALONG AND PRETEND 16 HUGHIE THEY'D FELL FOR HIM.

THEN TURNS TO THE CLERK, HIS FOOLISHLY WARY, WISE- 19 HUGHIE GUY EYES DEFENSELESS,

AND HE'D NEVER WISE UP HE WAS TOOK. 20 HUGHIE (HE LAUGHS.) YOU'DA THOUGHT HUGHIE WOULDA GOT 20 HUGHIE WISE SOMETHING WAS OUT OF ORDER

ERIE, HAVING SOOTHED RESENTMENT WITH HIS WISE- 25 HUGHIE CRACKS,

OH, I WAS WISE I WAS KIDDIN' MYSELF. 29 HUGHIE I WAS WISE I WAS TAKIN' A CHANCE. 35 HUGHIE SAY, CHARLIE, WHY DIDN'T YOU PUT ME WISE BEFORE, 36 HUGHIE YOU WAS INTERESTED IN GAMBLING8

AFFECTIONATE WINK WITH WHICH A WISE GUY REGALES A 38 HUGHIE SUCKER.)

DON'T WANT DE BOSS TO GET WISE WHEN HE'S GOT ONE 578 ICEMAN OF HIS TIGHTWAD BUNS ON.

DE OLD ANARCHIST WISE GUY DAT KNOWS ALL DE 579 ICEMAN ANSWERS/

I'M WISE TO YOU AND YOUR SIDEKICK, CHUCK. 582 ICEMAN (WINKS AT JOE) SURE, LARRY AIN'T DE ON'Y WISE GUY585 ICEMAN IN DIS DUMP, HEY, JOE8

I GOT WISE IT WAS ALL A CRAZY PIPE DREAM/ 592 ICEMAN OH, I KNOW THERE WAS JEALOUS WISE GUYS SAID THE 603 ICEMAN BOYS WAS GIVING ME THE

WISE, HELL/ A DAMNED OLD FOOL ANARCHIST I-WON'T- 605 ICEMAN WORKER/

THE OLD WISE GUY/ 605 ICEMAN HELLO, OLD WISE GUY, AIN'T YOU DIED YETS 611 ICEMAN

WISER

WISE (CONT'D.)

JEES, I'M WISE YUH HOLD OUT ON ME, BUT I KNOW IT 613 ICEMAN AIN'T MUCH, SO WHAT THE HELL,

HELLO, OLD WISE GUY/ 615 ICEMAN SAY, CORA, WISE ME UP. 616 ICEMAN YOU DON'T HAVE TO ASK ME, DO YOU, A WISE ULD GUY 623 ICEMAN LIKE YOUS

(SNEERING) DE OLD WISE GUY/ 635 ICEMAN YOU WERE ALL SO BUSY DRINKING IN WORDS OF WISDOM 638 ICEMAN FROM THE ULD WISE GUY HERE,

YOU DIDN'T THINK I WAS, WISE ABOUT YOU AND HER. 646 ICEMAN THEN HE GRINS AND SAYS, NEVER MIND, LARRY'S 646 ICEMAN GETTING WISE TO HIMSELF.

I'VE BEEN WISE, EVER SINCE I CAN REMEMBER, TO ALL 646 ICEMAN THE GUYS SHE'S HAD.

I'M WISE TO YOU/ 671 ICEMAN A GANG OF GANG WISE8 698 ICEMAN I TRIED TO WISE DE REST OF DEM UP TO STAY CLEAR UF698 ICEMAN HIM,

I'D HELP YUH AND WISE YUH UP TO DE INSIDE DOPE ON 702 ICEMAN DE GAME.

IT'D BE A PIPE FOR YUH, 'SPECIALLY WID ME TO HELP 702 ICEMAN YUH AND WISE YUH UP.

SO I TINKS, DEYS'E MY PALS AND I OUGHT TO WISE UP 702 ICEMAN TWO GOOD GUYS LIKE DEM TO PLAY

EVERYONE GOT WISE TO ME. 709 ICEMAN WHERE'S THE OLD WISE GUYS 726 ICEMAN I DID PUT EDMUND WISE TO THINGS, BUT NOT UNTIL I 34 JOURNE SAW HE'D STARTED TO RAISE HELL,

BUT I WAS WISE TEN YEARS UR MORE BEFORE WE HAD TO 57 JOURNE TELL YOU.

(WITH DEFENSIVE DRYNESS.) PERHAPS IT WOULD BE 135 JOURNE WISE TO CHANGE THE SUBJECT.

CAN THE WISE STUFF, KID. 156 JOURNE DON'T PLAY THE WISE GUY WITH ME/ 163 JOURNE NEVER FORGET THE FIRST TIME I GOT WISE. 163 JOURNE MY PUTTING YOU WISE SO YOU'D LEARN FROM MY 165 JOURNE MISTAKES,

THE FORMER SQUATTING ON HIS HAMS, MONKEY-WISE, AND311 LAZARU BROODING SOMBERLY.)

YES TO THE STUPID AS TO THE WISE/ 343 LAZARU LAZARUS' FEET, BLINKING UP AT HIS FACE MONKEY- 358 LAZARU WISE.

SHE'S A WISE WOMAN AND KNOWS IT'D DO NO GOOD FOR 45 MANSNS HER TO INTERFERE--

TO REQUEST THE POPE TO SEND HIM A HUNDRED WISE MEN359 MARCOM OF THE WEST

I HAVE NO HUNDRED WISE MEN--NOR ONE/ 363 MARCOM MARK MY WORDS, MARCO WILL BE WORTH A MILLION WISE 363 MARCOM MEN--IN THE CAUSE OF WISDOM/

INDIFFERENT ATTITUDE OF THE WORLDLY-WISE. 370 MARCOM (HE LOOKS AROUND) BUT WHERE ARE THE HUNDRED WISE 376 MARCOM MEN OF THE WESTS

AND HE HAD NO WISE MEN, ANYWAY. 378 MARCOM BUT WHERE ARE THE HUNDRED WISE MEN OF THE SACRED 378 MARCOM TEACHINGS OF LAO-TSEU AND

(SMILING) ARE YOU HIS HUNDRED WISE MENS 379 MARCOM WASN'T THAT JUST A JOKE, YOUR ASKING FOR THE WISE 379 MARCOM MEN

HE SAID I'D BE WORTH A MILLION WISE MEN TO YOU. 379 MARCOM RIGHT SET AN EXAMPLE THAT WOULD ILLUSTRATE, BETTER379 MARCOM THAN WISE WORDS,

AND I WILL LISTEN AS TO A HUNDRED WISE MEN FROM 380 MARCOM THE WEST/

EVEN A HUNDRED WISE MEN COULD BES 381 MARCOM AND I AM TOO OLD, IF NOT TOO WISE, TO AFFORD 386 MARCOM ANYTHING BUT OPTIMISM/

MR. CHU-YIN OUGHT TO BE WISE ENOUGH TO 397 MARCOM ACKNOWLEDGE--

THE WISE MAN IGNORES ACTION. 401 MARCOM THE GENTLE ONE, THE GOOD, THE KIND, THE PITIFUL, 422 MARCOM THE MERCIFUL, THE WISE.

WHAT GOOD ARE WISE WRITINGS TO FIGHT STUPIDITYS 423 MARCOM (TO THE CONFUCIAN) FOLLOWER OF CONFUCIUS, THE 434 MARCOM WISE, HAVE YOU THIS WISDOMS

OH, CHU-YIN, MY WISE FRIEND, WAS THE PRAYER I 437 MARCOM TAUGHT THEM WISDOMS

ALL THE STUDENTS WERE WISE AND I HAD THEM ROLLING 39 MISBEG IN THE AISLES AS I SHOWED

THAT'S WISE DOPE, PHIL. 66 MISBEG AND HIS BROADWAY PRIDE HE'S SO WISE NO WOMAN COULD 96 MISBEG FOOL HIM,

PHIL IS WISE TO YOU, OF COURSE, BUT ALTHOUGH HE 135 MISBEG KNEW I KNEW,

BUT I NEVER SUSPECTED YOU WERE A WISE WOMAN TOO, 149 POET THANK YOU KINDLY BUT I'VE ALREADY TAKEN YOUR WISE 171 POET ADVICE, FATHER.

YUH OUGHTER GET WISE TO YOURSELF. 592 ROPE NO, BUT THERE'S THE OTHER PLACE, AND HE NEVER KNEW599 ROPE I WAS WISE TO THAT.

MUSTN'T LET HER GET WISE I GOT HIM TO COME TO LOOK 68 STRANG HER OVER...

IT'S A WISE FATHER WHO KNOWS HIS OWN CHILD, YOU 117 STRANG KNOW/.

I WISED YOU UP ABOUT WOMEN, SO YOU'D NEVER BE A 164 JOURNE FALL GUY,

WISELY

I DID WISELY TO STAND HIM IN MY PLACE. 340 LAZARU LIFE IS PERHAPS MOST WISELY REGARDED AS A BAD 402 MARCOM DREAM BETWEEN TWO AWAKENINGS,

WE'VE TALKED ABOUT OUR CHILD WISELY, 91 STRANG DISPASSIONATELY...

WISER

THE SECOND MATE AFTHER HIM NO WISER THAN HIMSELF, 480 CARDIF AIR YE ANY THE WISER FUR ALL I'VE TOLD YES 238 DESIRE IT'S WISER FOR YOU TO KEEP HAZEL AWAY FROM ME, I 152 ELECTR WARN YOU.

WISER

WISER

WISER (CONT'D.)
WELL, THAT'S WHY I QUIT THE MOVEMENT, IF IT LEAVES5VO ICEMAN
YOU ANY WISER.
AN' NO ONE THE WISER. 524 INZONE
DID THEIR POPE MEAN THAT A FOOL IS A WISER STUDY 381 MARCOM
FOR A RULER OF FOOLS
I WOULD BE BOTH WISER AND HAPPIER 70 POET
(DISAPPOINTEDLY) BUT FOR ALL THE GOOD IT DOES US 585 ROPE
WE MIGHT AS WELL BE NO WISER

WISH

I ONLY WISH I DIDN'T HAVE TO BE PLEASANT WITH THE 200 AHWILD
OLD BUZZARD--
I WISH WE STILL BELONGED TO ENGLAND/ 209 AHWILD
I DO WISH YOU'D WATCH--/ 211 AHWILD
I DO WISH YOU WOULDN'T ENCOURAGE THAT STUPID GIRL 223 AHWILD
BY TALKING TO HER,
OH, I DO WISH RICHARD WOULD COME HOME/ 250 AHWILD
BUT I WISH HE WAS HOME. 254 AHWILD
(SIGHS WORRIEDLY AGAIN) I DO WISH THAT BOY WOULD 255 AHWILD
GET HOME/
(DOLEFULLY) YES--BUT I WISH HE WOULDN'T SING SUCH258 AHWILD
SAD SONGS.
I WISH YOU'D STOP JUMPING TO CONCLUSIONS/ 263 AHWILD
(GIVING IN TO HER WORRY) I WISH YOU WOULDN'T SAY 271 AHWILD
THOSE TERRIBLE THINGS--
GOSH, I WISH SHE'D COME/ 275 AHWILD
DARK IT, I WISH SHE'D SHOW UP/.. 276 AHWILD
I WISH I COULD WRITE POETRY. 277 AHWILD
I WISH YOU WERE DEAD/ 284 AHWILD
I ONLY KNOW I WISH I WAS DEAD/ 285 AHWILD
(PASSIONATELY) I'M THINKING I'D RATHER BE FRIENDS 34 ANNA
WITH YOU THAN HAVE MY WISH
(WEARILY) GEE, I SURE WISH HE WAS OUT OF THIS 42 ANNA
DUMP AND BACK IN NEW YORK.
I WISH YOU COULD HAVE SEEN THE LITTLE HOME IN THE 43 ANNA
COUNTRY
OH, RUN, I DO WISH SHE'D TRY TO MAKE THE BEST OF 87 BEYOND
THINGS THAT CAN'T BE HELPED.
(REBELLIOUSLY) WELL, I DO WISH HE WASN'T/ 96 BEYOND
(HER LIPS TREMBLING) I WISH ROBBIE WEREN'T GOING. 96 BEYOND
(FIERCELY) I CAN WISH YOU AND RUTH ALL THE GOOD 109 BEYOND
LUCK IN THE WORLD, AND I DO.
(WRINGING HER HANDS) OH, I WISH I COULD TELL IF 138 BEYOND
YOU'RE LYING OR NOT/
I WISH SHE WASN'T LEAVING FOR A WEEK OR SO. 141 BEYOND
(WITH SUDDEN EXASPERATION) OH, I WISH YOU'D NEVER152 BEYOND
MARRIED THAT MAN/
I WISH I DIDN'T HAVE TO. 157 BEYOND
I WISH THE STARS WAS OUT, AND THE MOON, TOO. 489 CARDIF
I WISH THIS WAS A PINT OF BEER. 489 CARDIF
I WISH THEY'D STOP THAT SONG. 459 CARIBE
I WISH YOU JOY. 564 CROSS
THE WISH IS FATHER TO THAT THOUGHT, EH5 494 DAYS
BUT I WISH HE'D GIVEN ME WARNING. 499 DAYS
I ONLY WISH I COULD HAVE YOU STAY WITH US, BUT 506 DAYS
THERE'S NO ROOM.
I WISH I DIDN'T LOOK SO LIKE A SICK CAT. 515 DAYS
I HOPE SHE'S A SHE-DEVIL THAT'LL MAKE HIM WISH HE 215 DESIRE
WAS DEAD
I WISH I WAS DEAD ALONG WITH YE AFORE THIS COME/ 257 DESIRE
I WISH I'D NEVER SOT EYES ON HIM/ 257 DESIRE
(TORTUREDLY) I WISH HE NEVER WAS BORN/ 257 DESIRE
I WISH YE WAS DEAD/ 257 DESIRE
I WISH HE'D DIE THIS MINIT/ 257 DESIRE
(SOFTLY) I DO WISH YOU WOULDN'T SWEAR SO AWFUL 494 DFRNT
MUCH, CALEB.
(SIGHING HAPPILY) GOSH, I WISH WE COULD SIT THIS 494 DFRNT
WAY FOREVER/
GOSH, I WISH I'D BEEN THERE/ 503 DFRNT
(A PAUSE) I WISH YOU COULD SEE THEM ISLANDS, 515 DFRNT
EMMA, AND BE THERE FOR A TIME.
(AFTER A PAUSE--GROPINGLY) I WISH I COULD EXPLAIN516 DFRNT
MY SIDE OF IT--
(AFTER A PAUSE--INTENSELY) OH, I WISH I COULD 516 DFRNT
MAKE YOU SEE--MY REASON.
GOSH, I WISH PA'D LIVED--UR UNCLE JACK. 522 DFRNT
I WISH SHE'D HURRY UP.... 425 DYNAMO
I WISH TOWNSEND WOULDN'T GO FORCING HIS BOOKS ON 429 DYNAMO
ME.
(GOSH, I WISH ADA'D HURRY UP... 431 DYNAMO
I-- WISH THIS COURAGE FAILS HIM--LAMELY) 433 DYNAMO
OH, I WISH I COULD GET CLOSER TO THE WINDOW/ 437 DYNAMO
(II WISH I'D NEVER COME HERE/... 438 DYNAMO
I WISH THEY'D HUNG HIM/...) 442 DYNAMO
I WISH I COULD TELL HER... 446 DYNAMO
I WISH THAT LIGHT BOY WOULD COME BACK. 454 DYNAMO
(AS SHE TURNS TO GO) I WISH YOU'D MAKE IT UP WITH455 DYNAMO
YOUR POP, ADA.
I WISH SHE'D GET TO KISSING HER POP AGAIN THAT 456 DYNAMO
WAY...
(II WISH HE'D STOP CRYING...)) 464 DYNAMO
HOW I WISH I'D NEVER READ THEM/...)) 465 DYNAMO
(II WISH SHE HADN'T DIED... 467 DYNAMO
GOD, HOW I WISH THE MIRACLE WAS OVER AND WE 482 DYNAMO
COULD--/
(TURNING DEFIANTLY) WHENEVER YOU WISH. 18 ELECTR
I WISH TO GOD HE WAS/ 27 ELECTR
I WISH YOU WOULDN'T TALK LIKE THAT, EZRA. 59 ELECTR
SHE SAYS IT WAS EZRA'S WISH HE'D OFTEN EXPRESSED 69 ELECTR
(TENSELY) I WISH YOU WOULDN'T TALK OF DEATH/ 83 ELECTR
WELL, YOU CAN GO AHEAD NOW AND TELL ORIN ANYTHING 91 ELECTR
YOU WISH/
(IN TENSE DESPERATION) I WISH ORIN AND VINNIE 119 ELECTR
WOULD COME/
BUT I DON'T WISH TO CONVEY THAT HE APPROVES OF ALL153 ELECTR
I'VE SET DOWN--
I'LL WISH YOU HAPPINESS--YOU AND ADAM/ 166 ELECTR
I WISH YOU WERE DEAD/ 166 ELECTR

WISH (CONT'D.)

I WISH DION WOULD KISS ME AGAIN/ 263 GGBROW
I WISH YOU'D TRY TO TAKE MORE INTEREST IN THE 270 GGBROW
CHILDREN, DION.
AND, BY JINGO, I WISH HE WAS/ 277 GGBROW
WE'D MAKE HIM WISH HE HADN'T/ 300 GGBROW
HE'S STILL WITH ME BUT FOR REASONS OF HIS OWN, 306 GGBROW
DOESN'T WISH IT KNOWN.
NOW THAT'S A QUEER WISH FROM THE UGLY LIKE OF YOU,210 HA APE
GOD HELP YOU.
I WISH HUGHIE WAS HERE. 28 HUGHIE
(WITH MOURNFUL LONGING,) CHRIST, I WISH HUGHIE 32 HUGHIE
WAS ALIVE AND KICKIN'.
AS IF AVOIDING SOMETHING HE DOES NOT WISH TO SEE,1596 ICEMAN
I WISH TO HELL HICKEY'D TURN UP. 608 ICEMAN
I WISH TO HELL HE'D NEVER TURNED UP/ 626 ICEMAN
(THEN ANGRILY) I WISH DE LOUIE NEVER SHOWED UP/ 631 ICEMAN
I DON'T CARE WHERE HE IS, EXCEPT I WISH IT WAS A 636 ICEMAN
THOUSAND MILES AWAY/
I WISH--(THE CHORES UP.) 656 ICEMAN
BUT I WISH I WAS DRUNK RIGHT NOW, BECAUSE IF I 671 ICEMAN
WAS,
AS A MATTER OF FACT, ROCKY, I ONLY WISH A POST 676 ICEMAN
TEMPORARILY.
I WISH TO GOD THEY WERE/ 679 ICEMAN
(TEARFULLY INDIGNANT) AIN'T YUH GOIN' TO WISH US 683 ICEMAN
HAPPINESS,
I WISH THEY WERE ALL IN JAIL--OR DEAD/ 702 ICEMAN
I WISH YOU'D GET RID OF THAT BASTARD, LARRY. 706 ICEMAN
I WISH IT WAS DECIDED FOR ME. 719 ICEMAN
I WISH TO GOD WE COULD KEEP THE TRUTH FROM HER, 37 JOURNE
I WISH I'D GRABBED ANOTHER DRINK. 58 JOURNE
I WISH THE OLD MAN WOULD GET A MOVE ON. 61 JOURNE
(BITTERLY) ONLY I WISH SHE HADN'T LED ME TO HOPE 78 JOURNE
THIS TIME.
WHY, YES, IF YOU WISH ME TO, 85 JOURNE
HAVE ANOTHER DRINK YOURSELF, IF YOU WISH, 100 JOURNE
CATHLEEN.
I WISH IT WAS ALWAYS THAT WAY. 102 JOURNE
I WISH TO GOD I DIDN'T/ 120 JOURNE
SHOWING YOU WANTED TO WISH ME ON CHARITY/ 144 JOURNE
(HEAVILY.) I WISH TO GOD SHE'D GO TO BED SO THAT 169 JOURNE
I COULD, TOO.
YOU WISH TO FORGET/ 289 LAZARU
I HEARD YOU WISH FOR DEATH, LUCIUS. 317 LAZARU
MY DUTY, IF I WISH TO BECOME CAESAR, IS TO CAESAR.328 LAZARU
I WISH WE WERE HOME, LAZARUS. 329 LAZARU
OR PEACHERS OF LAUGHTER IF THEY WISH TO LAUGH 329 LAZARU
LONG/
I HAVE NO WISH TO DIE/ 329 LAZARU
I WISH WE WERE HOME, LAZARUS. 330 LAZARU
AT THE FOOT OF THE DAIS WITH THEIR CONCENTRATED 347 LAZARU
DEATH WISH.)
IS ONE, AND I CLING TO THESE CERTAINTIES--AND I D0353 LAZARU
NOT WISH TO DIE/
OR DID SHE KNOW NO HAPPY MAN WOULD WISH TO BE 356 LAZARU
CAESAR?
FOR I COULD WISH TO LOVE ALL MEN, AS YOU LOVE 358 LAZARU
THEM--
I CAN STILL BE A CONVINCING ACTRESS IF I WISH/ 14 MANSNS
YOU'VE THE WISH FOR LIFE BUT YOU HAVEN'T THE 19 MANSNS
STRENGTH EXCEPT TO RUN AND HIDE
I WISH I COULD FORGET. 27 MANSNS
HOW MANY TIMES I WISH TO PINCH YOU TO DISCOVER IF 33 MANSNS
YOU'RE STUFFED/
FATHER DID NOT WISH TO APPEAR IN THE MATTER. 34 MANSNS
SIMON WILL NOT WISH YOU TO BE RUINED, MOTHER. 35 MANSNS
THAT IS MY WISH TOO. 52 MANSNS
IT WAS YOUR FATHER'S WISH THAT YOU DECIDE THIS 52 MANSNS
MATTER
ALL I WISH IS A PEEK AT THEM, 56 MANSNS
I TOLD YOU IT IS MY WISH 58 MANSNS
BEFORE I GO-- YOU WILL, OF COURSE, WISH ME TO 60 MANSNS
RESIGN FROM MY POSITION--
I CAN STILL BACK OUT, IF YOU WISH. 64 MANSNS
WELL, PERHAPS I AM--NOW--WITH GOOD REASON--BUT IF 66 MANSNS
I AM, WHOSE WISH WAS IT--S
I CANNOT SEE WHY YOU WISH TO DISCUSS SUCH MATTERS 72 MANSNS
WITH ME.
SHE IS GOING TO DISCOVER, BEGINNING TODAY, AND 73 MANSNS
SARA, TOO, THAT WHENEVER I WISH,
GOD KNOWS I'VE AS HAPPY A LIFE AS A WOMAN COULD 77 MANSNS
WISH
YOU MUST HAVE HAD THE WISH-- 80 MANSNS
THAT SHE'D LIKE ME TO HAVE NO WISH BUT HER WISH, 82 MANSNS
AT FIRST, ALL I WISH YOU TO DO IS TO SIT AND WATCH 92 MANSNS
HOW I DEAL WITH EVERYTHING.
(PULLING AWAY.) I WISH YOU WOULDN'T TALK AS IF 93 MANSNS
LOVE--
IF YOU WISH, 99 MANSNS
UNTIL I SWEAR TO YOU I FELT I COULD BY JUST ONE 102 MANSNS
TINY FURTHER WISH,
WE DO NOT REALLY WISH SUCH NONSENSE. 103 MANSNS
I DO NOT WISH YOU TO BE TOO LONELY, 106 MANSNS
AND THE WISH IN HIS HEART TOLD HIM HIS QUEST WAS 111 MANSNS
ENDED.
YOUR WISH MY LAW, MADAME. 113 MANSNS
(THINKING--FROWNING.) I CONTROL THE GAME NOW AND 119 MANSNS
CAN HAVE IT PLAYED AS I WISH--
I CAN ALWAYS, WHENEVER I WISH, MAKE HIM MY LITTLE 129 MANSNS
BOY AGAIN.
I ONLY WISH TO SAY--I'VE QUITE DECIDED TO SELL MY 143 MANSNS
INTEREST IN THE BUSINESS--
THEY WOULD NEVER WISH ME-- 155 MANSNS
I WISH TO SAY I SEE YOUR POINT ABOUT POLICY OF 155 MANSNS
BANK--ONLY PRACTICAL VIEWPOINT--
WHEN MY ONE WISH ABOUT HER IS TO DRIVE HER AWAY 159 MANSNS
FOREVER

1807 WISHIN'

WISH (CONT'D.)
THAT I CAN FIND IT IN MYSELF TO WISH HE WERE NOT 171 MANSNS
HERE.
WHAT THEY DON'T WANT AND BE AFRAID TO CRAVE WHAT 172 MANSNS
THEY WISH FOR IN TRUTH.
I WILL DO ANYTHING YOU WISH/ 174 MANSNS
AND THEN TO HEAR OF YOUR RECONCILEMENT--BUT IT IS 176 MANSNS
MY DEAREST WISH--
I WISH TO GO IN AND JOIN SARA. 178 MANSNS
SO HOW COULD I WISH TO REMEMBER YOU& 178 MANSNS
I WISH TO BE FREE, MOTHER/ 182 MANSNS
LET US LEAVE THIS VILE STY OF LUST AND HATRED AND 185 MANSNS
THE WISH TO MURDER/
YES, AND I CAN EVEN WISH YOU TO BE HAPPY SO YOU 188 MANSNS
CAN MAKE HIM HAPPY/
I CAN WISH HIM HAPPINESS WITHOUT ME, AND MEAN IT/ 188 MANSNS
I WISH I DIDN'T HAVE TO GO AWAY. 356 MARCOM
I WISH, TOO/ 356 MARCOM
BUT I WISH YOU WEREN'T GOING FOR SO LONG. 357 MARCOM
I WISH TO BE ALONE/ 362 MARCOM
I CAN START YOU UPON ANY CAREER YOU WISH. 380 MARCOM
WELL, I AM SURE YOU WISH TO CELEBRATE THIS FAMILY 382 MARCOM
TRIUMPH TOGETHER.
THIS IS MONEY, LEGALLY VALUED AT TEN YEN'S WORTH 393 MARCOM
OF ANYTHING YOU WISH TO BUY.
WHEN YOU HAVE TIME, I WISH YOU'D LOOK THIS OVER. 395 MARCOM
I WISH TO BE CONVERTED TO WISDOM, TOO--ONE OR 398 MARCOM
ANOTHER--BEFORE I BECOME A NAME.
EVEN THOUGH YOU WISH YOUR OWN UNHAPPINESS. 398 MARCOM
(REBELLIOUSLY) YET I WISH SOME POWER COULD GIVE 400 MARCOM
ME ASSURANCE
I WISH TO TAKE THIS VOYAGE. 401 MARCOM
YOUR WISH IS MY WILL/ 419 MARCOM
AGAIN YOUR WISH IS MY WILL, EVEN THOUGH I WILL NOT419 MARCOM
LIVE UNTIL I SEE YOU AGAIN/
YOU WISH ME TO BE HAPPY, DO YOU NOT& 423 MARCOM
I WISH TO COMMEND THE UNREMITTING ATTENTION TO HIS424 MARCOM
DUTY OF ADMIRAL POLO.
WHAT WOULD BE HER WISH& 425 MARCOM
(PROTESTINGLY) WHY DO YOU WISH TO HURT YOURSELF 426 MARCOM
FURTHER&
I WISH YOU ALL THE LUCK IN THE WORLD, MIKE. 7 MISBEG
I WAS GOING TO SAY I WISH YOU LUCK WITH YOUR 10 MISBEG
SCHEMING, FOR ONCE.
I WISH TO HELL I COULD STAY HERE// 39 MISBEG
BUT AT THE SAME TIME ARE ABLE TO PULL THEMSELVES 72 MISBEG
TOGETHER WHEN THEY WISH AND BE
I WISH I'D BEEN THERE TO LAUGH UP MY SLEEVE. 90 MISBEG
WISH I COULD BELIEVE IN THE SPIRITUALISTS' BUNK. 151 MISBEG
THE DAMNED SICK REMORSE THAT MAKES YOU WISH YOU'D 171 MISBEG
DIED IN YOUR SLEEP SO YOU
MAY YOU HAVE YOUR WISH AND DIE IN YOUR SLEEP SOON,177 MISBEG
JIM, DARLING.
YOUR HAPPINESS, MY DEAR, AND WHAT I WISH TO 46 POET
DISCUSS MEANS HAPPINESS TO YOU.
SIMON'S FATHER OR HIS LEGAL REPRESENTATIVE WILL 50 POET
WISH TO DISCUSS WITH ME.
I WISH TO BE ALONE IN QUIET WITH MY MEMORIES. 57 POET
I DO NOT WISH TO DISCUSS IT. 62 POET
I WISH JAMIE CREGAN WOULD COME. 66 POET
WHAT DOES THE LADY WISH& 72 POET
BECAUSE SHE DOES NOT WISH TO CREATE FURTHER 74 POET
EMBARRASSMENT.)
EXCEPT PERHAPS, THAT I WISH TO BE FAIR AND WARN 84 POET
YOU, TOO.
I WISH TO SPEAK TO MY DAUGHTER. 104 POET
ALL I WISH IS TO RELATE SOMETHING WHICH HAPPENED 106 POET
THIS AFTERNOON.
HIS FATHER WILL WISH TO DO THE FAIR THING BY HIM. 111 POET
BUT IF YOU WISH TO SEE MAJOR CORNELIUS MELODY, 117 POET
AND WHY YOU SHOULD WISH TO SEE ME. 118 POET
I WISH NO QUARREL WITH YOU, SIR. 121 POET
I WISH HE WAS-- 162 POET
AS IF SHE'D LOST ALL DISCRIMINATION OR WISH TO 8 STRANG
DISCRIMINATE.
I WISH I HADN'T COME HERE TODAY/...) 20 STRANG
I WISH I WERE OUT OF THIS/... 20 STRANG
IS THAT WHAT YOU WISH ME TO SAY& 20 STRANG
I WISH I KNEW THE TRUTH OF WHAT SHE'S BEEN DOING 25 STRANG
IN THAT HOUSE FULL OF MEN...
BUT I CAN WISH YOU GOOD LUCK. 33 STRANG
I WISH TO GOD IT WERE/ 34 STRANG
I WISH HE WOULDN'T TELL ME/...) 35 STRANG
BUT THERE MIGHT BE MANY REASONS WHY HE'D WISH TO 36 STRANG
GET RID OF HER...)
(EAGERLY) ANYTHING YOU WISH, NINA--ANYTHING/ 44 STRANG
((I WISH SHE HADN'T TOLD ME THIS... 45 STRANG
I WISH HER FATHER WERE ALIVE...- 46 STRANG
AND THEN I USED TO WISH I'D GONE OUT DELIBERATE IN 63 STRANG
OUR FIRST YEAR.
(SIGHING) I WISH THAT COULD BE SAID OF MORE OF 80 STRANG
US--(THEN QUICKLY)--
OH, NED, HOW I WISH/...) 118 STRANG
WOULD I WISH TO&... 119 STRANG
WELL, IN THIS ADOLESCENT COUNTRY, WHAT GREATER 120 STRANG
BLESSING COULD ME WISH FOR&...)
((I WISH DARRELL'D GET OUT OF HERE/... 138 STRANG
I'LL GO--THIS MINUTE IF YOU WISH/ 145 STRANG
I WISH I KNEW MORE ABOUT IT. 147 STRANG
YES, SO DO I WISH YOU DID, MARSDEN/ 147 STRANG
I WISH I THOUGHT THAT. 163 STRANG
(THINKING KEENLY) ((THERE'S A DEATH WISH... 163 STRANG
I WISH SHE WOULDN'T TOUCH ME... 172 STRANG
AND I'LL HAVE TO WISH THEM GOOD LUCK. 186 STRANG
((OH, I WISH NED WOULD GO AWAY AND STAY AWAY 194 STRANG
FOREVER.

(THEN FORLORNLY) BUT I WISH I DID LOVE YOU, NED/ 196 STRANG
YES, I WISH TO TELL YOU THE TRUTH. 482 WELDED

WISH (CONT'D.)
AS YOU WISH. 486 WELDED
YES--IF YOU WISH. 486 WELDED
ISN'T OUR FUTURE AS HARD AS YOU COULD WISH& 489 WELDED
WISHED
AS IF HE WISHED IT WERE MCCUMBER'S HEAD, AND SITS 201 AHWILD
DOWN OPPOSITE HIM.)
WHEN YOU READ THROUGH THAT LITERATURE YOU WISHED 207 AHWILD
ON HIS INNOCENT DAUGHTER&
I WISHED I HAD SOME OF YOUR FACULTY FOR BUSINESS. 133 BEYOND
AND EVERY TIME I THOUGHT OF HOME I WISHED IT 224 DESIRE
WASN'T ME/
YE SAID YE HATED HIM AN' WISHED HE WAS DEAD-- 261 DESIRE
WISHED I OWNED IT/ 269 DESIRE
(FROM THE NEXT ROOM) GOSH, I WISHED I'D BEEN 510 DIFRNT
THERE/
SHE DOES IT NOW AS IF SHE WISHED SHE WAS A 456 DYNAMO
MOSQUITO WITH A STINGER...
WHAT I'VE ALWAYS WISHED I COULD HAVE BEEN MYSELF/ 258 GGROW
I WISHED IT'D KNOCKED HER BLOCK OFF/ 231 HA APE
(FURIOUSLY) I WISHED IT'D BANGED HER/ 231 HA APE
BUT I DID FEEL A LITTLE HURT WHEN YOU WISHED YOU 112 JOURNE
HADN'T COME HOME.
HE WISHED FOR DEATH/ 276 LAZARU
CAESAR WISHED ME TO BID YOU WELCOME, TO TELL YOU 333 LAZARU
HOW MUCH REGARD HE HAS FOR YOU.
BUT I FEEL THAT WAS NOT ALL OF IT, THAT MY MOTHER 356 LAZARU
WISHED TO KEEP ME TORTURED
IF I WISHED--IF I HAD THE OPPORTUNITY--NO. 21 MANSNS
SHE KNEW FATHER WOULDN'T HAVE WISHED ME TO COME 45 MANSNS
AND PRETEND GRIEF
YOU WISHED HER TO SIGN. 97 MANSNS
THAT IS WHAT I WISHED TO DO/ 109 MANSNS
IT MIGHT BE ANY DOOR, BUT IF HE WISHED TO FIND IT 111 MANSNS
WITH ALL HIS HEART,
HE WISHED TO TELL YOU AND MADE ME PROMISE I 131 MANSNS
WOULDN'T.
AND I WOULD REVENGE MYSELF BY BECOMING WHAT HE 133 MANSNS
WISHED ME TO BE/
I PRESUME YOU WONDER WHY I WISHED TO SEE YOU, MR. 151 MANSNS
TENARD.
TO TAKE ANYTHING FROM LIFE YOUR HEART WISHED FOR/ 158 MANSNS
AS IF YOU WISHED-- 182 MANSNS
I WISHED I HAD NEVER BEEN BORN/ 184 MANSNS
I WISHED YOU DEAD/ 184 MANSNS
AND HOW CAN YOU ADMIT YOU HATED YOUR MOTHER AND 184 MANSNS
WISHED HER DEAD/
IT MUST HAVE BEEN A MESSAGE SHE WISHED ME TO TAKE 352 MARCOM
BACK TO MARCO POLO/
(THEN WILDLY TO MARCO) I WISHED TO SLEEP IN THE 413 MARCOM
DEPTHS OF THE SEA.
THERE MUST BE SOMETHING HE WISHED YOU TO FIND. 414 MARCOM
I WISHED TIME TO REFLECT ON A FURTHER ASPECT OF 112 POET
THIS PROPOSED MARRIAGE.
I BELIEVE I HAVE SAID ALL I WISHED TO SAY TO YOU. 115 POET
THERE'S NOT A DAY PASSED I'VE NOT WISHED HIM IN 599 ROPE
HIS GRAVE.
I KNOW HOW MUCH YOU'VE WISHED FOR IT, 106 STRANG
IT'S THE LAST THING I'D WANT WISHED ON A BOY OF 141 STRANG
NINE--
WISHES
I'LL TURN THIS RIGHT OVER TO HIM AND INSTRUCT HIM 306 GGROW
TO CARRY OUT YOUR WISHES.
BEGINNING TO ACHE AND HE WISHES 492 WOULD STOP 13 HUGHIE
TALKING AND GO TO BED SO HE CAN
EVEN THOUGH I KNOW SHE WISHES NO. I WAS DEAD/ 703 ICEMAN
INSTANTLY EDMUND WISHES HE COULD TAKE BACK WHAT HE120 JOURNE
HAS SAID.
WHAT BETTER DISGUISE IF HE WISHES TO REMAIN 300 LAZARU
UNKNOWN&
ONE GETS OLD, ONE BECOMES TALKATIVE, ONE WISHES TO1354 LAZARU
CONFESS.
HE WISHES MASSACHUSETTS WOULD SECEDE FROM THE 8 MANSNS
UNION.
CERTAIN LAST WISHES OF YOUR FATHER'S, AND A 52 MANSNS
BARGAIN HE PROPOSES.
WHO WISHES TO DESTROY YOUR CLAIM TO HER REALM, 111 MANSNS
AND WISHES NOW HE HADN'T BEEN SO WICKED--NOW, WHEN131 MANSNS
IT'S TOO LATE.
(WARNINGLY) HIS HONOR WISHES TO TALK BUSINESS, 391 MARCOM
PRINCESS.
GOOD-BYE, YOUR MAJESTY--AND ALL BEST WISHES FOR 420 MARCOM
LONG LIFE AND HAPPINESS/
(DISDAINFULLY) TO HELL WITH THE LIMEY'S GOOD 48 MISBEG
WISHES.
WISHFUL
(WITH A FORCED GAYETY) IT IS WISHFUL FOR HEAVEN 483 CARDIF
YE ARE&
'TIS ONLY WHEN I'M DEAD TO THE WORLD I'D BE 210 HA APE
WISHFUL TO SING AT ALL.
I'M NOT WISHFUL TO DISCOURAGE YE, BUT-- 593 ROPE
WISHIN'
BILL TINKER WAS WITH ME AND WE WAS BOTH WISHIN' WE525 DIFRNT
HAD A DRINK.
BUT TERE'S WISHIN' YER LUCK JUST THE SAME. 186 EJONES
AIN'T I WISHIN' MYSELF YOU'D BRAINED HER& 230 HA APE
DON'T BE WISHIN' HIM HARM, FOR IT'S THIRSTY WE'D 100 POET
BE WITHOUT HIM.
WISHIN' TO KNOW. 589 ROPE
(VICIOUSLY) I WAS WISHIN' IT WAS ROUND HIS NECK 590 ROPE
CHUKIN' HIM, THAT'S WHAT I WAS--
I WAS ALMOST WISHIN'--(HE HESITATES.) 590 ROPE
WASN'T WISHIN' HERSELF TO SEE IT OR I'D HAVE ASKED592 ROPE
YE SOONER.
IT'S TO SEE YOU HANG YOURSELF HE'S WISHIN', THE 596 ROPE
AULD FIEND/

WISHING

WISHING
I WAS ONLY WISHING THIS HADN'T COME UP--JUST AT 264 AHWILD THIS PARTICULAR TIME.
YOU'D BE WISHING ANNA MARRIED TO A FAMER, SHE TOLD 48 ANNA ME.
YOU ARE, 'TIL I'M AFTER WISHING I WAS NEVER BORN 69 ANNA AT ALL/
(IN A FRENZY) OH, I'M WISHING I HAD WAN OF THEM 71 ANNA PUNISHED ME THIS MINUTE
I'M WISHING THE WHOLE LOT OF THEM WILL ROAST IN 71 ANNA HELL 'TIL THE JUDGMENT DAY--
AND HERE'S WISHING YOU EVERY HAPPINESS, YOU AND 101 BEYOND RUTH.
YOU WERE WISHING IN YOUR HEART THAT I WOULD DIE/ 550 DAYS I'M SURE HE'S BEEN WISHING FOR A LONG TIME THAT 456 DYNAMO LIGHT BOY'D COME HOME
SO HERE'S WISHING YOU ALL THE SUCCESS AND 263 GGBROW HAPPINESS IN THE WORLD, MARGARET--
(THEN, WISHING TO LEAVE ON A PLEASANT CHANGE OF 305 GGBROW SUBJECT--FORCING A SMILE)
IS IT TO BELONG TO THAT YOU'RE WISHINGS 214 HA APE HERE'S WISHING YOU ALL THE LUCK THERE IS, HARRY, 659 ICEMAN AND LONG LIFE AND HAPPINESS/
THEY SEEMED TO BE WISHING I WAS DEAD/ 714 ICEMAN I KEPT WISHING I'D PAID OVER THE BET WITHOUT 136 JOURNE MAKING YOU PROVE IT.
I DON'T WANT YOU HUGGING ME WHEN MAYBE YOU'RE 81 MANSNS WISHING IT WAS ANOTHER--
SU--THEN I'M THE MISTRESS YOU WERE WISHING FOR/ 90 MANSNS BUT WISHING TO EMBARRASS HIM FURTHER WITH TALK OF 111 POET MONEY.

WISHT
I WISHT I HAD NUTHIN' BLACKER THAN THAT ON MY 488 CARDIF SOUL.
I WISHT HE WAS DEAD/ 266 DESIRE I WISHT I WAS. 697 ICEMAN I ONLY WISHT I'D A MOTHER ALIVE TO CALL ME OWN. 498 VOYAGE (SADLY) WISHT I 'AD/ 502 VOYAGE

WISP
A PALE, DELICATE WISP OF A THING WITH BIG EYES. 18 POET

WISPS
A RED BANDANA HANDKERCHIEF COVERING ALL BUT A FEW 173 EJONES STRAY WISPS OF WHITE HAIR.
WISPS OF HAY STICK TO HIS CLOTHES AND HIS FACE IS 157 MISBEG SWOLLEN AND SLEEPY.
HER BLACK HAIR, STREAKED WITH GRAY, STRAGGLES IN 20 POET UNTIDY WISPS ABOUT HER FACE.
SURMOUNTED BY A SHINY BALD SCALP FRINGED WITH 578 ROPE SCANTY WISPS OF WHITE HAIR.
STRAGGLY WISPS FROM THE PILE OF RANK HAY FALL 601 ROPE SILENTLY TO THE FLOOR
DRIFTED AWAY OVER THE GRASS, WISPS OF MIST BETWEEN 49 STRANG THE APPLE TREES.

WISPY
HE HAS WHITE HAIR AND A WISPY GOAT'S BEARD, BRIGHT129 ELECTR INQUISITIVE EYES.

WISTFUL
THE BLUE OF HER WISTFUL WIDE EYES IS FADING INTO A562 CRUSS TWILIGHT GRAY.
AND STARES UP AT THE MOON WITH A WISTFUL, RESIGNED323 GGBROW SWEETNESS)

WISTFULLY
(WISTFULLY) I'D LIKE TO HAVE MY OLD JOB ON THE 607 ICEMAN FORCE BACK.
(SHE KISSES HIM--WISTFULLY) WILL YOU LET ME ROT 197 STRANG AWAY IN PLACES

WISTFULNESS
(WITH A STRANGE PATHETIC WISTFULNESS) 667 ICEMAN

WIT
NOR ALL YOUR PIETY NOR WIT SHALL LURE IT BACK TO 199 AHWILD CANCEL HALF A LINE,
AND STARING AT THE DYNAMOS AND HUMMING LIKE A 479 DYNAMO HALF-WIT/
ME FUH SOMEP'N WIT A KICK TO IT/ 209 HA APE T'HELL WIT HOME/ 211 HA APE WHAT D'YUH ANT WIT HOMES 211 HA APE TO HELL WIT 'EM. 211 HA APE WHAT'S DEM SLOBS IN DE FOIST CABIN GOT TO DO WIT 212 HA APE US?
ONE OF US GUYS COULD CLEAN UP DE WHOLE MOB WIT ONE212 HA APE MIT.
I MOVE WIT IT. 215 HA APE WHAT'S TINKIN' GOT TO DO WIT ITS 217 HA APE AW, TO HELL WIT HIM/ 224 HA APE TO HELL WIT WASHIN'. 227 HA APE AND DERE SHE WAS WIT DE LIGHT ON HER/ 230 HA APE UP IN BACK OF ME, AND I HOPPED ROUND TO KNOCK HIM 230 HA APE DEAD WIT DE SHOVEL.
TINK I'M GOIN' TO LET HER GIT AWAY WIT DAT STUFF? 231 HA APE I COULDA TOOK HER WIT JUST MY LITTLE FINGER EVEN, 231 HA APE AND BROKE HER IN TWO.
NO ONE AIN'T NEVER PUT NOTHIN' OVER ON ME AND GOT 231 HA APE AWAY WIT IT, SEE!
YOUSE ALL KIN GO! YOUR SHUITS I'LL GIT EVEN WIT 231 HA APE HER.
I'LL GIT SQUARE WIT HER/ 232 HA APE I RUNNED AWAY WHEN ME OLD LADY CROAKED WIT DE 234 HA APE TREMENS.
WHEN DEY GOT TROUGH DERE WASN'T A CHAIR OR TABLE 234 HA APE WIT A LEG UNDER IT.
DIDN'T I TRY TO GET EVEN WIT 234 HA APE BUT I'LL GIT SQUARE WIT HER YET, YOU WATCH. 235 HA APE SHE TINKS SHE KIN GET AWAY WITH MOIDER--BUT NOT 235 HA APE WIT ME/
I' HELL WIT DE STARVIN' FAMILY/ 235 HA APE T' HELL WIT YOUSE/ 237 HA APE (AFTER A PAUSE) I WAS TRYIN' TO GIT EVEN WIT 241 HA APE SOMEONE, SEE!

WIT (CONT'D.)
AND IF I CAN'T FIND HER I'LL TAKE IT OUT ON DE 242 HA APE GANG SHE RUNS WIT--
HOLDIN' ME DOWN WIT HIM AT DE TOP/ 244 HA APE DEN YUH SURE GOT YOUR NOIVE WIT YOUSE/ 248 HA APE I KNOW YUH GOT TO WATCH YOUR STEP WIT A STRANGER. 248 HA APE (BOLDLY) SURE, I'LL COME OUT WIT IT. 249 HA APE AW, TO HELL WIT 'EM/ 250 HA APE BUT ME, I BELONG WIT 'EM--BUT I DON'T, SEES 253 HA APE KNOCK 'EM DOWN AND KEEP BUSTIN' 'EM TILL DEY 253 HA APE CROAKS YUH WIT A GAT--WIT STEEL/
BUT I KIN MAKE A BLUFF AT TALKIN' AND TINKIN'-- 253 HA APE A'MOST GIT AWAY WIT IT--A'MOST!
YUH DON'T BELONG WIT 'EM AND YUH KNOW IT. 253 HA APE DEY DON'T BELONG WIT ME, DAT'S WHAT. 253 HA APE I' HELL WIT IT/ 253 HA APE WE'LL KNOCK 'EM OFFEN DE OITH AND CROAK WIT DE 254 HA APE BAND PLAYIN'.
CROAK WIT YOUR BOOTS ON/ 254 HA APE THE WOMEN WHO HATE ME FOR MY WIT AND BEAUTY, 4 MANSNS BY HER WIT AND CHARM-- 13 MANSNS IF THIS IS WHAT IS KNOWN AS IRISH WIT-- 120 POET

WIT'
DAT HICKEY, HE GETS MY HEAD ALL MIXED UP WIT' 637 ICEMAN CRAZINESS.

WITCH
NO, YE DURNED OLD WITCH/ 227 DESIRE WITCH DOCTORS, OR WHATEVER THE 'ELL YER CALLS THE 185 EJONES SWINE.
THE FIGURE OF THE CONGO WITCH DOCTOR APPEARS. 200 EJONES (THE WITCH DOCTOR SPRINGS TO THE RIVER BANK. 201 EJONES THE WITCH DOCTOR SWAYS, STAMPING WITH HIS FOOT, 201 EJONES THE WITCH DOCTOR POINTS WITH HIS WAND TO THE 201 EJONES SACRED TREE, TO THE RIVER BEYOND,
THE WITCH DOCTOR PRANCES UP TO HIM, TOUCHES HIM 201 EJONES WITH HIS HAND.
THE WITCH DOCTOR'S VOICE SHRILLS OUT IN 201 EJONES THE WITCH DOCTOR SPRINGS BEHIND THE SACRED TREE 202 EJONES AND DISAPPEARS.
IS ONE OF A GRIM-VISAGED MINISTER OF THE WITCH- 79 ELECTR BURNING ERA.
OR THE WICKED WITCH, AND I'D BE ALL GOOSE-FLESH 12 MANSNS WITH TERROR/
THIS IS MORE WICKED THAN ANY WITCH. 13 MANSNS YOU WOULD THINK I WAS SOME WICKED OLD WITCH, 66 MANSNS HAUNTED BY TERRIBLE GHOSTS AND RULED OVER BY A 111 MANSNS HIDEOUS OLD WITCH.
SHE IS REVENGEFUL AND EVIL--A CANNIBAL WITCH WHOSE126 MANSNS GREED WILL DEVOUR/
I MUST BE GOING DAFT--AS DAFT AS THAT MAD OLD 144 MANSNS WITCH IN HER GARDEN.
LET THE COWARDLY OLD WITCH WAIT UNTIL DOMESDAY/ 159 MANSNS CAN'T YOU RID OUR LIFE OF THAT DAMNED GREEDY EVIL 160 MANSNS WITCH
THE IMPRESSION OF BEING BODILESS, A LITTLE, 161 MANSNS SKINNY, WITCH-LIKE, OLD WOMAN,
I MIGHT JUST AS WELL HAVE IMPORTED SOME WITCH 100 STRANG DOCTORS FROM THE SOLOMON ISLANDS/

WITCHES
YOUR OLD WICKED WITCHES LED ME ALWAYS TO BE 13 MANSNS PREPARED FOR THE WORST/
(SHE LAUGHS.) EVIL OLD WITCHES/ 83 POET

WITHDRA
OF COURSE, IT WOULDN'T DO TO WITHDRAW THAT MUCH 93 MANSNS CAPITAL NOW.

WITHDRAWAL
MORE FIXED IN ITS RESOLUTE WITHDRAWAL FROM LIFE. 269 GGBROW

WITHDRAWING
(WITHDRAWING HER HAND) I WAS SERIOUS. 270 GGBROW (WITHDRAWING HER HAND, COLDLY) 276 GGBROW KUBLAI SITS BACK ON HIS CUSHIONS AGAIN, 436 MARCOM WITHDRAWING INTO CONTEMPLATION.
AND WITHDRAWING FROM YOU. 144 STRANG (WITHDRAWING HER HANDS FROM HIS WITH A QUICK 457 WELDED MOVEMENT--SARCASTICALLY)

WITHDRAWN
(HIS HEAD IS WITHDRAWN AND HE CAN BE HEARD 551 'ILE SHOUTING ORDERS.)
SHE HAS VISIBLY WITHDRAWN INTO HERSELF AND IS ON 14 ELECTR THE DEFENSIVE.
SETH COMES FORWARD FROM WHERE HE HAD WITHDRAWN 18 ELECTR AROUND THE CORNER OF THE HOUSE.
(TERRIBLY WOUNDED, WITHDRAWN INTO HIS STIFF 56 ELECTR SOLDIER ARMOR--
AS IF SHE WERE A LITTLE WITHDRAWN FROM HER WORDS 58 JOURNE AND ACTIONS.)
IT IS HURRIEDLY WITHDRAWN. 355 MARCOM HIS VOICE HAD WITHDRAWN SO FAR AWAY... 4 STRANG MORE WITHDRAWN FROM LIFE THAN BEFORE. 24 STRANG

WITHDRAWS
THEN WITHDRAWS BACK INTO THE ROOM. 228 DESIRE (INSTINCTIVELY SHE WITHDRAWS HER HAND FROM 132 MANSNS SARA'S.)

WITHER
I BUT HER EYES ARE FIXED ON HIS SO BURNINGLY THAT 240 DESIRE HIS WILL SEEMS TO WITHER
CENTURIES WITHER INTO TIRED DUST. 417 MARCOM POSSESSION TO WITHER THE HEART WITH BITTER 187 STRANG POISONS...

WITHERED
THE THIRTY YEARS HAVE TRANSFORMED EMMA INTO A 519 DIFRNT WITHERED,
STINKING BIT OF WITHERED OLD FLESH WHICH IS MY 689 ICEMAN BEAUTIFUL LITTLE LIFE/
YOU HARP ON AGE AS THOUGH I WERE A WITHERED OLD 3 MANSNS HAG/
AS ELDERLY SUITORS FOR MY BODY, ROUES IN THEIR 29 MANSNS BORED, WITHERED HEARTS.

WITHERED (CONT'D.)
HER WITHERED LIPS ARE ROUGED AND THERE IS A 161 MANSNS
BEAUTY-SPOT ON EACH ROUGED CHEEK.

WITHERING
(GIVES SID A WITHERING LOOK--THEN IS OFF AGAIN) 229 AHWILD
LAUGHING WITH WITHERING CONTEMPT)
HE SUMMONS UP STRENGTH FOR A WITHERING CRACK.) 265 DESIRE
(FIXING HIM WITH A WITHERING LOOK) 27 HUGHIE
SHE SNATCHES HER HAND FROM HIS AND SPEAKS WITH 529 INZONE
WITHERING CONTEMPT.) 72 POET

WITHERINGLY
(WITHERINGLY) AW, JOIN DE SALVATION ARMY/ 229 HA APE

WITHERS
THE LAST CHRYSANTHEMUM WITHERS BESIDE THE DESERTED384 MARCOM
SUMMERHOUSE.

WITHHOLDING
AS IF HE WERE CONTINUALLY WITHHOLDING EMOTION FROM 46 ELECTR
IT.

WITHIN
HIS FACE BETRAYS THE TREMENDOUS STRUGGLE GOING ON 549 'ILE
WITHIN HIM.
BETRAYS THE CONFLICT GOING ON WITHIN HIM) 92 BEYOND
(CLUTCHING AT HIS THROAT AS THOUGH TO STRANGLE 565 CROSS
SOMETHING WITHIN HIM--HOARSELY)
NOT SLAVERY OR BOREDOM BUT FREEDOM AND HARMONY 524 DAYS
WITHIN OURSELVES--AND HAPPINESS.
IN WHICH THERE LOVE WILL GO ON FOREVER WITHIN THE 544 DAYS
ETERNAL PEACE AND LOVE OF GOD/
(MECHANICALLY) DUST WITHIN DUST. 562 DAYS
DUST WITHIN DUST TO SLEEP/ 562 DAYS
EVERY SOUND WITHIN THE HOUSE. 228 DESIRE
FROM WITHIN COMES THE WHINING OF THE FIDDLE AND 253 DESIRE
(ARGUING TORMENTEDLY WITHIN SELF) 422 DYNAMO
(UGH, I'LL GIT HUTCHINS TO BEAT HIM WITHIN AN INCH439 DYNAMO
OF HIS LIFE/...)
(THINKING MORE CLEARLY NOW--AN UNSTRUNG FURY 463 DYNAMO
RISING WITHIN HIM)
HE STRETCHES OUT HIS ARMS AND CALLS TO SOME GOD 201 EJONES
WITHIN ITS DEPTHS.
UNTIL SHE IS NOW WITHIN ARM'S REACH OF HER. 16 ELECTR
(THEN AS IF THE WORDS STIRRED SOMETHING WITHIN HIM165 ELECTR
HIS FACE LIGHTED UP FROM WITHIN BUT PAINFULLY 269 GGBROW
CONFUSED--IN AN UNCERTAIN WHISPER)
YET LIGHTED FROM WITHIN BY A SPIRITUAL CALM AND 284 GGBROW
HUMAN KINDLINESS.
THEN STOPS. FIGHTING SOME QUEER STRUGGLE WITHIN 215 HA APE
HIMSELF--
YANK CAN BE SEEN WITHIN, 239 HA APE
WITHIN, KNOCKS CAREFULLY. 246 HA APE
WITHIN ITSELF CALLED ARNOLD ROTHSTEIN.) 32 HUGHIE
WE ARE ALL BROTHERS WITHIN THE EMPIRE 599 ICEMAN
BOTTLES OF BAR WHISKEY ARE PLACED AT INTERVALS 628 ICEMAN
WITHIN REACH OF ANY SITTER.
HE IS OBVIOUSLY FRIGHTENED AND SHRINKING BACK 654 ICEMAN
WITHIN HIMSELF.
(BEGINNING TO COLLAPSE WITHIN HIMSELF--DULLY) 691 ICEMAN
AROUND THE TABLE WITHIN READING-LIGHT RANGE ARE 12 JOURNE
FOUR CHAIRS.
SHE HAS HIDDEN DEEPER WITHIN HERSELF AND FOUND 97 JOURNE
REFUGE AND RELEASE IN A DREAM
OUT OF A MISTY DREAM OUR PATH EMERGES FOR A WHILE,130 JOURNE
THEN CLOSES WITHIN A DREAM.=
IT FELT DAMNED PEACEFUL TO BE NOTHING MORE THAN A 131 JOURNE
GHOST WITHIN A GHOST.
NIGHT-LONG WITHIN MINE ARMS IN LOVE AND SLEEP SHE 134 JOURNE
LAY.
ANY PLACE YOU LIKE--WITHIN REASON. 149 JOURNE
I BELONGED, WITHOUT PAST OR FUTURE, WITHIN PEACE 153 JOURNE
AND UNITY AND A WILD JOY.
WITHIN SOMETHING GREATER THAN MY OWN LIFE, OR THE 153 JOURNE
LIFE OF MAN, TO LIFE ITSELF/
ANYTHING WITHIN REASON. 158 JOURNE
WITHIN REASON, OF COURSE. 158 JOURNE
(SHE LETS HIM TAKE IT. REGARDING HIM FROM 172 JOURNE
SOMEWHERE FAR AWAY WITHIN HERSELF,
THEIR GAZE TURNS WITHIN, OBLIVIOUS TO THE LIFE 274 LAZARU
OUTSIDE.
THAT STRANGE LIGHT SEEMS TO COME FROM WITHIN HIM/ 275 LAZARU
FROM WITHIN COMES THE SOUND OF FLUTES AND DANCE 281 LAZARU
MUSIC.
(FROM WITHIN THE HOUSE) LAUGH/ 282 LAZARU
THE MUSIC CONTINUES TO COME FROM WITHIN. 285 LAZARU
(HIS VOICE RINGS FROM WITHIN THE HOUSE IN EXULTANT285 LAZARU
DENIAL)
THE MUSIC BEGINS TO PLAY AGAIN WITHIN THE HOUSE, 289 LAZARU
VERY SOFT AND BARELY AUDIBLE.
WITHIN THE PORTICO ON ROWS OF CHAIRS PLACED ON A 312 LAZARU
SERIES OF WIDE STEPS WHICH ARE
(THERE IS THE SUDDEN BLARING OF A TRUMPET FROM 331 LAZARU
WITHIN THE PALACE.
HE DIED IN PAIN AND WEAKNESS WITHIN A FEW HOURS. 343 LAZARU
BELIEVE IN THE LAUGHING GOD WITHIN YOU/ 360 LAZARU
THE FACE OF A METHODICAL MEDIOCRITY, WHO WITHIN 25 MANSNS
HIS NARROW LIMITS IS
IT COULD BE THE CHANCE FOR A NEW LIFE--ESCAPE FROM 39 MANSNS
THE DEATH WITHIN MYSELF.
COMPLETE INDEPENDENCE AND FREEDOM WITHIN ITSELF/ 102 MANSNS
AS THOUGH THAT OPPONENT WITHIN HAD SPAT AN 102 MANSNS
EXTINGUISHING POISON OF DISDAIN--
WHOSE LIVES HAVE MEANING ONLY IN SO FAR AS THEY 118 MANSNS
LIVE WITHIN MY LIVING--
A CONSPIRACY WITH HER TO DRIVE ME BACK FURTHER AND163 MANSNS
FURTHER WITHIN MYSELF--
GIVE ME YOUR HAND AND LET US GO WITHIN, SIRE-- 164 MANSNS
WITHIN THE FAMILY PARTICULARLY, 172 MANSNS
IF THE CONFLICTING SELVES WITHIN A MAN ARE TOO 172 MANSNS
EVENLY MATCHED--

WITHOUT

WITHIN (CONT'D.)
FOR ALL THE CONFUSION IN OUR MINDS, THE CONFLICTS 172 MANSNS
WITHIN THE SELF,
FREE OF ONE OF MY TWO SELVES, OF ONE OF THE 182 MANSNS
ENEMIES WITHIN MY MIND,
(SHE TURNS TO FACE THE DARKNESS WITHIN THE 189 MANSNS
DOORWAY.)
(STARTLED BY A NOISE FROM WITHIN) 357 MARCOM
IN THE FAR REARWALL, WITHIN A DEEP RECESS LIKE THE377 MARCOM
SHRINE OF AN IDOL,
READY TO SAIL FOR PERSIA WITHIN TEN DAYS. 388 MARCOM
OR PROHIBITING THE PRACTICE OF THE LAWS OF BIOLOGY390 MARCOM
WITHIN A TWELVE-MILE LIMIT,
HE CAN MOBILIZE ONE MILLION HORSEMEN ON THE DANUBE421 MARCOM
WITHIN A MONTH.
CONTAIN THE HARMONY OF WOMB AND GRAVE WITHIN YOU/ 435 MARCOM
HER FACE BETRAYS THE CONFUSED CONFLICT WITHIN HER 114 MISBEG
OF FRIGHT, PASSION, HAPPINESS,
THEY SAID THE ESTATE WOULD BE OUT OF PROBATE 131 MISBEG
WITHIN A FEW DAYS.
HE SEEMS TO SHRINK BACK GUILTILY WITHIN HIMSELF. 89 POET
(AS IF LISTENING FOR SOMETHING WITHIN HER-- 90 STRANG
JOYFULLY)
I AM LIVING A DREAM WITHIN THE GREAT DREAM OF THE 91 STRANG
TIDE...
WITHIN A YEAR OR SO THEY'LL BE WILLING TO SELL OUT121 STRANG
CHEAP.
(AS IF UNDER SOME URGENT COMPULSION FROM WITHIN) 185 STRANG
IT IS AS IF NOW BY A SUDDEN FLASH FROM WITHIN THEY487 WELDED
RECOGNIZED THEMSELVES.

WITHOUT
(WITHOUT TAKING OFFENSE--IN SAME FLAT, BRITTLE 201 AHWILD
VOICE)
NO DAY IS COMPLETE WITHOUT IT. 232 AHWILD
YOU CAN HAVE IT WITHOUT--I MEAN, I'LL BE GLAD TO 242 AHWILD
GIVE--
(BUT RICHARD ONLY GLOWERS AT HIM GLOOMILY WITHOUT 246 AHWILD
ANSWERING)
(THEN WITHOUT GIVING HIM A CHANCE TO ANSWER) 259 AHWILD
(ACCUSINGLY) YOU DON'T MEAN TO TELL ME YOU'RE 263 AHWILD
GOING BACK WITHOUT SEEING HIM.
WHEN YOU'RE YOUNG YOU CAN STAND ANYTHING WITHOUT 265 AHWILD
IT FEAZING YOU.
SID WITHOUT OPENING HIS EYES, SPEAKS TO HIM 271 AHWILD
DROWSILY.)
HE WENT BACK TO THE OFFICE WITHOUT SEEING ME. 272 AHWILD
I AM TOO YOUNG TO LIVE WITHOUT DESIRE, 276 AHWILD
WITHOUT HAVING SEEN HER/. 277 AHWILD
(WITHOUT LOOKING AT HIM) I'M NEVER GOING TO, PA. 295 AHWILD
WE COULD USE A LOT OF MONEY RIGHT HERE ON THE FARM 85 BEYOND
WITHOUT HURTING IT ANY.
YOU CAN GO ANYWHERE YOU'RE A MIND TO WITHOUT 85 BEYOND
PAYING FARE.
IT'LL BE HARDER FOR ME WITHOUT ANYONE. 88 BEYOND
IN THE SUN LIKE A SLAVE WITHOUT GETTING A WORD OF 107 BEYOND
THANKS FOR IT.
SHE SPEAKS IN AN UNCERTAIN VOICE, WITHOUT 112 BEYOND
ASSERTIVENESS,
SAID HE DIDN'T KNOW HOW HE'D PULL THROUGH 'TIL 115 BEYOND
HARVEST WITHOUT IT.
(ABSENT-MINDEDLY, WITHOUT TAKING HIS EYES FROM THE122 BEYOND
BOOK)
(HE PICKS UP HIS KNIFE AND FORK AND BEGINS TO EAT 122 BEYOND
GINGERLY, WITHOUT APPETITE.)
WITHOUT YOUR ADDING TO THEM 122 BEYOND
(WITHOUT RESENTMENT) YES, AND'LL SEE THE RIGHT 125 BEYOND
THING TO DO IN A JIFFY.
I CAN GET ALONG WITHOUT YOU, DON'T YOU WORRY. 127 BEYOND
(SHE WIPES HER EYES QUICKLY AND WITHOUT LOOKING AT143 BEYOND
ROBERT.)
WHEN SHE SPEAKS HER VOICE IS WITHOUT TIMBRE, LOW 144 BEYOND
AND MONOTONOUS.
(WITHOUT A TRACE OF FEELING) 146 BEYOND
(WITHOUT FEELING) I DON'T HATE YOU. 148 BEYOND
(WITHOUT LOOKING AT HIM) MARY'S BETTER OFF--BEING148 BEYOND
DEAD.
YOU CAN'T DENY THAT WITHOUT HELP I'VE SUCCEEDED 148 BEYOND
IN--
(WITHOUT INTEREST) YES. 153 BEYOND
WITHOUT ANYONE TO ATTEND TO HIM BUT A COUNTRY 154 BEYOND
QUACK!
(WITHOUT EMOTION) A LETTER TAKES SOME TIME TO GET155 BEYOND
WHERE YOU WERE--
HE KNOWS VERY WELL I'D NATURALLY LOOK AFTER YOU 163 BEYOND
WITHOUT--ANYTHING LIKE THAT.
I'D GOT TO THE END OF BEAKING THINGS--WITHOUT 164 BEYOND
TALKING.
(PITEOUSLY) HE WAS SO HAPPY WITHOUT MY LYING TO 168 BEYOND
HIM.
WITHOUT THAT--THEY BECOME DREAMS UP HERE--DREAMS, 557 CROSS
DOCTOR.
OLD SMITH TOLD ME I COULD LIVE HERE INDEFINITELY 565 CROSS
WITHOUT PAYING--AS CARETAKER--
(WITHOUT LOOKING UP, CALLS) COME IN. 496 DAYS
(HIS EYES PASS OVER LOVING WITHOUT SEEING HIM. 496 DAYS
I CAN REMEMBER WHEN I COULDN'T PICK UP AN 497 DAYS
ADVANCED-PRIMER ORGAN WITHOUT KUNNING
THIS TIME ELIOT COMES IN IMMEDIATELY, WITHOUT 499 DAYS
WAITING FOR AN ANSWER.)
FATHER BAIRD SAYS QUIETLY, WITHOUT ANY SIGN OF 501 DAYS
TAKING OFFENSE)
(WITHOUT TURNING--QUIETLY) NO. 502 DAYS
(WITHOUT TURNING--QUIETLY) DON'T YOU KNOW, JACK4 503 DAYS
(WITHOUT LOOKING AT HIM) THINKING OF IT--TO PASS 505 DAYS
THE TIME.
YOU'VE NEVER LET A LETTER PASS WITHOUT SOME PIOUS 507 DAYS
REMINDER OF MY FALL--
AND HE WAS LEFT ALONE--WITHOUT LOVE. 510 DAYS

WITHOUT

1810

WITHOUT (CONT'D.)
YOU CAN'T LIVE THERE WITHOUT BECOMING LIKE THE 521 DAYS
REST OF THE CROWD/
(DEEPLY MOVED--WITHOUT LOOKING AT ELSA, TAKES HER 524 DAYS
HAND AND SQUEEZES IT--HUSKILY)
BEFORE THE WINDOW, RIGHT FRONT, AND STANDS THERE, 525 DAYS
WITHOUT LOOKING AT THEM.
I HOPE ELSA WILL FEEL I'M ONE OF THE FAMILY AND 533 DAYS
TREAT ME WITHOUT CEREMONY.
HE FELT LOST WITHOUT HER--FEARFUL, DISINTEGRATED. 536 DAYS
WITHOUT LOVE. 536 DAYS
(WITHOUT RAISING HIS HEAD) YES. 537 DAYS
(WITHOUT LIFTING HIS EYES--QUIETLY) 539 DAYS
(QUIETLY, WITHOUT EVASION, 542 DAYS
ONCE WE HAVE ACCEPTED IT WITHOUT EVASION, 542 DAYS
WITHOUT HIS KNOWING HOW HE GOT THERE, 544 DAYS
HE WALKS OUT OF THE CHURCH--WITHOUT LOVE FOREVER 545 DAYS
NOW--
(PULLS THEM AWAY FROM HIM--COLDLY, WITHOUT LOOKING548 DAYS
AT HIM)
YOU HAVE ENOUGH ON YOUR CONSCIENCE ALREADY-- 551 DAYS
WITHOUT MURDER/
SHE SPEAKS WITHOUT OPENING HER EYES, HARDLY ABOVE 554 DAYS
A WHISPER.
(WITHOUT TOUCHING HIM, MAKES A MOTION OF PUSHING 563 DAYS
HIM ASIDE)
BUT ALWAYS WITHOUT TOUCHING HIM, ENDEAVORS TO KEEP564 DAYS
FROM ENTERING THE CHURCH.
ADDRESSING THE CROSS NOT WITHOUT A FINAL TOUCH OF 566 DAYS
PRIDE IN HIS HUMILITY)
EDEN PICKING AT HIS FOOD WITHOUT APPETITE, 206 DESIRE
SIMEON AND PETER SHOULDER IN, SLUMP DOWN IN THEIR 206 DESIRE
CHAIRS WITHOUT A WORD.
(CUNNINGLY) WHAR YEW WON'T NEVER FIND IT WITHOUT 213 DESIRE
ME.
WITHOUT SEEMING TO SEE THE TWO STIFF FIGURES AT 221 DESIRE
THE GATE)
(GRIMLY--WITHOUT LOOKING UP) 224 DESIRE
(SHE LAUGHS A LOW HUMID LAUGH WITHOUT TAKING HER 229 DESIRE
EYES FROM HIS.
WITHOUT LOOKING AT HIS WIFE, HE PUTS OUT HIS HAND 236 DESIRE
AND CLUTCHES HER KNEE.
THEY COVETED THE FARM WITHOUT KNOWIN' WHAT IT 238 DESIRE
MEANT.
(EBEN TURNS AWAY WITHOUT ANSWERING. 254 DESIRE
(KISSES HER WITHOUT EMOTION--DULLY) 260 DESIRE
(WITHOUT MOVING) NO. 263 DESIRE
WITHOUT LOOKING BEHIND HIM, 263 DESIRE
DIFFICULTLY OUT OF THE CORNERS WITHOUT MOVING HIS 494 DIFRNT
HEAD.)
BUT LOTS AND LOTS OF THE OTHERS DOES THE SAME 497 DIFRNT
THING WITHOUT THINKING NOTHING
THEY'S TROUBLE ENOUGH IN THE WORLD WITHOUT MAKIN' 508 DIFRNT
MORE.
(FROM OUTSIDE THE DOOR WHICH HE HAS APPROACHED 513 DIFRNT
WITHOUT THEIR NOTICING HIM--
WITHOUT TURNING AROUND. 518 DIFRNT
WITHOUT A NICKEL IN MY JEANS AND JUST SPONGIN' ON 523 DIFRNT
HIM.
(OFFENDEDLY) WITHOUT WAITING TO SEE MES 531 DIFRNT
(AT SOME NOISE HE HEARS FROM WITHOUT, HE STARTS 534 DIFRNT
FRIGHTENEDLY)
NOT WITHOUT A TRACE OF MALICE) 535 DIFRNT
SHE DOES ALL THIS WITHOUT A TRACE OF CHANGE IN HER548 DIFRNT
EXPRESSION.
LIGHTNING GETS ON A LOTS OF PEOPLE'S NERVES 424 DYNAMO
WITHOUT THEIR BEING AFRAID OF IT.
A MASS OF HEAVY COPPER-COLORED HAIR IS PILED 428 DYNAMO
WITHOUT APPARENT DESIGN AROUND HER
IT'S ME WHO FIXES IT WITHOUT ANY THEORY/.....) 429 DYNAMO
(RAISES HERSELF TO HER FEET PLACIDLY, WITHOUT A 434 DYNAMO
TRACE OF RESENTMENT)
(WITHOUT WAITING FOR AN INTRODUCTION, 436 DYNAMO
I'LL GO WITHOUT A MOTHER RATHER THAN HAVE YOUR 450 DYNAMO
KIND/
(MRS. FIFE DISAPPEARS MEEKLY WITHOUT ANOTHER WORD.455 DYNAMO
AND IT IS APPARENT THAT HE HAS NOT GROWN ITS 457 DYNAMO
DEFENSIVE CALLOUSNESS WITHOUT A
SOMETIMES I'VE GONE WITHOUT EATING TO BUY BOOKS-- 458 DYNAMO
AND OFTEN I'VE READ ALL NIGHT--
BECAUSE I CAN'T STAY ON HERE WITHOUT A JOB. 461 DYNAMO
(MECHANICALLY IN HIS TURN--WITHOUT LIFTING HIS 464 DYNAMO
HEAD)
WHEN EYES THAT SEE YOU WITHOUT SEEING YOU... 474 DYNAMO
THEN STOPS WITHOUT LOOKING AROUND HIM AND DOES NOT476 DYNAMO
NOTICE HIS WIFE.)
(WITHOUT LOOKING AT HER--DULLY) 485 DYNAMO
PASSING BEHIND THE LILAC CLUMP WITHOUT HAVING 9 ELECTR
NOTICED AMES AND THE WOMEN.)
(WITHOUT LOOKING AT LAVINIA. 17 ELECTR
(WITHOUT LOOKING AT HER--GULLY) 17 ELECTR
AND SINCE WHEN HAVE YOU THE RIGHT WITHOUT 17 ELECTR
CONSULTING ME$
I AIN'T BEEN WITH THE MANNONS FOR SIXTY YEARS 19 ELECTR
WITHOUT LEARNING THAT.
HOPE YOU DON'T MIND MY WALKING IN ON YOU WITHOUT 21 ELECTR
CEREMONY.
HOW YOU SAY THAT--WITHOUT ANY SHAME/ 30 ELECTR
SQUARE-SHOULDERED AND STIFF, WITHOUT A BACKWARD 35 ELECTR
GLANCE.
(SLOWLY--WITHOUT LOOKING AT HIM) 37 ELECTR
(CALCULATING--WITHOUT LOOKING AT HIM) 39 ELECTR
(SHE GOES UP THE STEPS PAST HER MOTHER WITHOUT A 51 ELECTR
LOOK.
TO GO ON DOGGEDLY WITHOUT HEEDING ANY 53 ELECTR
INTERRUPTION)
(FEELING HIS DESIRE AND INSTINCTIVELY SHRINKING-- 53 ELECTR
WITHOUT OPENING HER EYES)

WITHOUT (CONT'D.)
(WITHOUT OPENING HER EYES) WHY ARE YOU TALKING OF 54 ELECTR
DEATH$
WELL, IT ONLY GOES TO SHOW HOW YOU CAN MISJUDGE A 68 ELECTR
PERSON WITHOUT MEANING TO--
(THEN WITHOUT WAITING FOR A REPLY, BURSTING INTO 76 ELECTR
JEALOUS RAGE)
IT IS A NEAR ROOM WITHOUT INTIMACY, 79 ELECTR
(WITHOUT LOOKING AT HER) 84 ELECTR
IF YOU KNEW HOW HORRIBLY LONELY I'VE BEEN WITHOUT 84 ELECTR
YOU--
WHO TOOK IT INTO HIS SILLY HEAD TO CALL HERE A FEW 87 ELECTR
TIMES WITHOUT BEING ASKED.
HIS MOTHER BROUGHT DISGRACE ENOUGH ON OUR FAMILY 87 ELECTR
WITHOUT--
LOOKING OVER THE HEAD OF LIFE WITHOUT A SIGN OF 94 ELECTR
RECOGNITION--
I'M JUMPY ENOUGH WITHOUT--THEN AS SHE TURNS AND 94 ELECTR
LUCKS THE DOOR BEHIND HER--
I HAD ACTED WITHOUT ORDERS, OF COURSE-- 95 ELECTR
(THEN, WITHOUT GIVING HER TIME TO ANSWER HIS 108 ELECTR
QUESTION.
(WITHOUT CONVICTION) YES. 137 ELECTR
YOU KNOW I'M GLAD TO SEE YOU WITHOUT ANY POLITE 144 ELECTR
PALAVER.
THE NATIVES DANCING NAKED AND INNOCENT--WITHOUT 147 ELECTR
KNOWLEDGE OF SIN/
(SOMBERLY) DARKNESS WITHOUT A STAR TO GUIDE US/ 151 ELECTR
WHEN YOU KNOW ALL SHE WANTED WAS TO LEAVE YOU 152 ELECTR
WITHOUT A THOUGHT AND MARRY THAT--
(LAVINIA GIVES A LITTLE BITTER LAUGH WITHOUT 173 ELECTR
OPENING HER EYES)
(WITHOUT OPENING HER EYES--STRANGELY, AS IF TO 174 ELECTR
HERSELF)
(WITHOUT OPENING HER EYES--LONGINGLY) 174 ELECTR
(WITHOUT OPENING HER EYES--STRANGELY) 174 ELECTR
(WITHOUT LOOKING AT HIM, PICKING UP THE WORDS OF 178 ELECTR
THE CHANTY--
THE SAME HEIGHT AS YOUNG BROWN BUT LEAN AND WIRY, 260 GGBROW
WITHOUT REPOSE.
IN THE GUTTER WITHOUT A PENNY/ 261 GGBROW
WHY WAS I BORN WITHOUT 264 GGBROW
PRIDE WITHOUT WHICH THE GODS ARE WORMS/ 272 GGBROW
(WITHOUT LOOKING AT HIM--IN A COMFORTING, MOTHERLY273 GGBROW
TONE)
THINGS HAVE COME MY WAY WITHOUT MY DOING MUCH 275 GGBROW
ABOUT IT.
AS IF GOD HAD LOCKED HER IN A DARK CLOSET WITHOUT 282 GGBROW
ANY EXPLANATION.
BECAUSE HER HANDS ALONE HAD CARESSED WITHOUT 282 GGBROW
CLAIMING.
(WITHOUT TAKING OFFENSE) CUT IT/ 285 GGBROW
AND THEY KEEP RIGHT ON MOVING ALONG AND DYING 286 GGBROW
WITHOUT MY HELP ANYWAY.
WITHOUT YOUR STAYING AWAY AND WORRYING US TO 291 GGBROW
DEATH/
WITHOUT IT LOOKING LIKE THE FIRST SUPERNATURAL 297 GGBROW
BANK/
HE'S GOT TO BE ABLE TO WORK WITHOUT DISTRACTIONS. 304 GGBROW
AND WITHOUT WAITING FOR AN ANSWER, TURNS THE KNOB.306 GGBROW
AND STARES WITHOUT MOVING INTO THE EYES OF DION'S 307 GGBROW
MASK.
WE MUST DIE WITHOUT HIM (THEN--ADDRESSING THE 319 GGBROW
MASK--HARSHLY)
(COMES JUST INTO SIGHT AT LEFT AND SPEAKS FRONT) 323 GGBROW
WITHOUT LOOKING AT THEM--
HIS NOSE IS LARGE AND WITHOUT CHARACTER. 8 HUGHIE
(HE IS WELL WOUND UP NOW AND GOES ON WITHOUT 22 HUGHIE
NOTICING
AND IS ASKING, WITHOUT CURIOSITY, 26 HUGHIE
SOME NIGHTS I'D COME BACK HERE WITHOUT A BUCK, 29 HUGHIE
I MUST HAVE CAUGHT SOME OF IT WITHOUT MEANING TO.» 30 HUGHIE
WITHOUT HOPE OF A LISTENER.) 30 HUGHIE
ALWAYS BEFORE THIS I'VE BEEN ABLE TO HEAR WITHOUT 31 HUGHIE
BOTHERING TO LISTEN.
WITHOUT MALICE, FEELING SUPERIOR TO NO ONE, A 576 ICEMAN
SINNER AMONG SINNERS.
(WITHOUT CORDIALITY) WHAT'S UP$ 585 ICEMAN
(PARRITT TURNS STARTLEDLY AS HUGO PEERS MUZZILY 592 ICEMAN
WITHOUT RECOGNITION AT HIM.
WITH AN ABSURD STRAINED ATTENTION WITHOUT 600 ICEMAN
COMPREHENDING A WORD)
WITHOUT HER, NOTHING SEEMED WORTH THE TROUBLE. 603 ICEMAN
I THINK WE SHOULD APPOINT HIM HOUSE PHYSICIAN HERE627 ICEMAN
WITHOUT A MOMENT'S DELAY.
AT RIGHT, FRONT, IS A TABLE WITHOUT CHAIRS. 628 ICEMAN
(WITHOUT ENTHUSIASM) SURE, IT'S AW RIGHT BY ME. 630 ICEMAN
WITHOUT FEELING ASHAMED. 641 ICEMAN
I HOPED YOU--(BITTERLY) AND YOU COULD BE, TOO, 646 ICEMAN
WITHOUT IT HURTING YOU.
NOT WITHOUT KILLING HIMSELF.» 647 ICEMAN
HARDLY THE DECENT THING TO POP OFF WITHOUT SAYING 677 ICEMAN
GOOD-BYE TO OLD HARRY.
MAKE NO STATEMENTS WHATEVER WITHOUT FIRST 679 ICEMAN
CONSULTING YOUR ATTORNEY.
WITHOUT LOOKING AT HIM. 700 ICEMAN
THEN SHOVES IT IN HIS POCKET WITHOUT A WORD OF 700 ICEMAN
ACKNOWLEDGMENT.
(WITHOUT LOOKING AT HIM--VINDICTIVELY) 702 ICEMAN
WITHOUT A SINGLE DAMNED HOPE OR LYING DREAM LEFT 704 ICEMAN
TO TORMENT YOU/
(WITHOUT LOOKING AT HICKEY--WITH DULL, RESENTFUL 705 ICEMAN
VICIOUSNESS)
WITHOUT HAVING TO FEEL REMORSE OR GUILT, 705 ICEMAN
WITHOUT ANYTHING DISTINCTIVE TO INDICATE WHAT THEY708 ICEMAN
DO FOR A LIVING.)
WHAT I'D WANT WAS SOME TRAMP I COULD BE MYSELF 712 ICEMAN
WITH WITHOUT BEING ASHAMED--

1811 — WITHOUT

WITHOUT (CONT'D.)
(DULLY, WITHOUT RESENTMENT) YEAH. 713 ICEMAN
(AT FIRST WITH THE SAME DEFENSIVE CALLOUSNESS-- 717 ICEMAN
WITHOUT LOOKING AT HIM)
NO ONE ELSE IN THE WORLD COULD WITHOUT DYING OF 14 JOURNE
INDIGESTION.
(WITHOUT CONVICTION.) HE'LL TURN OUT ALL RIGHT IN 18 JOURNE
THE END. YOU WAIT AND SEE.
BUT ON THE RARE OCCASIONS WHEN HE SMILES WITHOUT 19 JOURNE
SNEERING.
GOD, PAPA, THIS OUGHT TO BE ONE THING WE CAN TALK 37 JOURNE
OVER FRANKLY WITHOUT A BATTLE.
(WITHOUT LOOKING UP FROM HIS BOOK.) 51 JOURNE
WITHOUT HER CONSENT.) 51 JOURNE
SHE'S ALWAYS ON TIME WITHOUT ANY CALLING. 52 JOURNE
(WITHOUT LOOKING AT HER.) NOTHING. 59 JOURNE
WHY DON'T YOU GO AHEAD WITHOUT HIM? 62 JOURNE
(FROM THE WINDOW, WITHOUT LOOKING AROUND.) 64 JOURNE
(WITHOUT TURNING--DRYLY.) YOU MEAN ONCE HE STARTS 65 JOURNE
LISTENING.
WITHOUT TURNING, JAMIE SENSES THIS.) 65 JOURNE
SHE FEELS THEM AND TURNS SHARPLY WITHOUT MEETING 68 JOURNE
HIS STARE.)
(BUT THEY KEEP ON WITHOUT WAITING FOR HER. 68 JOURNE
EDMUND TRIES TO COPY THIS DEFENSE BUT WITHOUT 71 JOURNE
SUCCESS.
(BITTERLY WITHOUT TURNING AROUND.) 72 JOURNE
YES, HE'LL BE IN WITHOUT FAIL. 73 JOURNE
(HE ADDS CAUSTICALLY.) IF YOU CAN WITHOUT MAKING 81 JOURNE
IT AN EXCUSE TO GET DRUNK/
SHE COMES FORWARD, ADDRESSING HER HUSBAND WITHOUT 81 JOURNE
LOOKING AT HIM.)
WITH WEEK AFTER WEEK OF ONE-NIGHT STANDS, IN 87 JOURNE
TRAINS WITHOUT PULLMANS.
HE'S FEELING BAD ENOUGH ALREADY WITHOUT-- 88 JOURNE
SIMPLY AND WITHOUT SELF-CONSCIOUSNESS, THE NAIVE, 97 JOURNE
HAPPY,
(SHE DRINKS WITHOUT BOTHERING ABOUT A CHASER.) 100 JOURNE
EDMUND HAS ALSO HAD MORE THAN A FEW DRINKS WITHOUTIO8 JOURNE
MUCH APPARENT EFFECT.
(WITHOUT WAITING FOR A REPLY SHE DOES SO.) 109 JOURNE
(HE STARES AT HIS WATCH WITHOUT SEEING IT. 113 JOURNE
(TO HIS MOTHER, WITHOUT LOOKING AT HER.) 116 JOURNE
HOW DARE DOCTOR HARDY ADVISE SUCH A THING WITHOUT 119 JOURNE
CONSULTING ME/
I HOPE, SOMETIME, WITHOUT MEANING IT, I WILL TAKE 121 JOURNE
AN OVERDOSE.
HE KNOWS IT WAS A CURSE PUT ON YOU WITHOUT YOUR 122 JOURNE
KNOWING OR WILLING IT.
I KEPT WISHING I'D PAID OVER THE BET WITHOUT 136 JOURNE
MAKING YOU PROVE IT.
(HE GOES ON DULLY, WITHOUT RESENTMENT.) 146 JOURNE
I BELONGED, WITHOUT PAST OR FUTURE, WITHIN PEACE 153 JOURNE
AND UNITY AND A WILD JOY.
* THAT'S A PART HE CAN PLAY WITHOUT MAKE-UP. 158 JOURNE
(HE ADDS, SMILING WITHOUT RESENTMENT.) 158 JOURNE
WHAT IS A MAN WITHOUT A GOOD WOMAN'S LOVES 159 JOURNE
GREAT PART IN IT YOU CAN PLAY WITHOUT MAKE-UP. 168 JOURNE
(MUMBLES GUILTILY, WITHOUT RESENTMENT.) 171 JOURNE
WITHOUT RECOGNITION, WITHOUT EITHER AFFECTION OR 172 JOURNE
ANIMOSITY.)
HE POURS A DRINK WITHOUT DISARRANGING THE WEDDING 175 JOURNE
GOWN HE HOLDS CAREFULLY OVER
(WITHOUT LOOKING AT HIM--HIS VOICE SEEMING TO COME292 LAZARU
FROM SOME DREAM WITH HIM)
WITHOUT KNOWING IT SUDDENLY WERE LIFTED. 300 LAZARU
WITHOUT THEIR KNOWING IT. 304 LAZARU
TO LOVE EVEN YOUR FELLOW MEN WITHOUT FEAR OF THEIR309 LAZARU
VENGEANCE/
(SULPICIUS LAUGHS WEAKLY WITHOUT TAKING OFFENSE.) 315 LAZARU
WALKING UNDER AN ARM OF THE CROSS UNCONCERNEDLY 327 LAZARU
WITHOUT AN UPWARD GLANCE.
(SMILING WITHOUT BITTERNESS--WITH A SAD 328 LAZARU
COMPREHENSION)
HE PASSES UNDER THE CRUCIFIED LION WITHOUT A 331 LAZARU
GLANCE--
(FROM WITHOUT) LAUGH/ 337 LAZARU
(NOT WITHOUT DREAD HIMSELF) THAT IS THE MAN, 338 LAZARU
CAESAR.
(WITHOUT LOOKING AT HER) HE IS NO MAGICIAN. 341 LAZARU
(IMPATIENTLY) DO YOU THINK I WOULD BELIEVE 343 LAZARU
WITHOUT GOOD EVIDENCE.
THEN DARE TO LOVE ETERNITY WITHOUT YOUR FEAR 352 LAZARU
DESIRING TO POSSESS HER/
AND I DEMAND AN EXPLANATION FOR THE CAUSE WITHOUT 353 LAZARU
MYSTIC NONSENSE OR EVASION.
HEARING ONLY CALIGULA'S WORDS WITHOUT THEIR 355 LAZARU
MEANING)
WITHOUT PAIN THERE IS NOTHING-- 358 LAZARU
YOU WHO ARE NEITHER A MAN NOR A GOD BUT A DEAD 361 LAZARU
THING WITHOUT DESIRE/
(HE STANDS SALUTING HIMSELF WITH A CRAZY INTENSITY370 LAZARU
THAT IS NOT WITHOUT GRANDEUR.
NOT WITHOUT DETERMINATION AND A RIGID INTEGRITY, 26 MANSNS
FURNISHED WITHOUT NOTICEABLE GOOD OR BAD TASTE. 43 MANSNS
(BITTERLY.) UNLESS SHE THOUGHT I WOULDN'T LET YOU 45 MANSNS
GO WITHOUT ME.
REASSURINGLY.) YOU KNOW THAT I WILL MAKE NO 52 MANSNS
DECISION WITHOUT YOUR CONSENT.
(WITH SUDDEN DISMAY.) THEN YOU DECIDED IT ALL-- 62 MANSNS
WITHOUT WAITING TO ASK ME/
NOW AFTER YOU'VE GONE AHEAD AND AGREED WITHOUT 64 MANSNS
CONSULTING ME AT ALL/
AS JOEL STARES IN COLD SURPRISE WITHOUT MAKING ANY 71 MANSNS
MOVE, HE BURSTS OUT ANGRILY.)
NO, NEITHER CAN I--EXCEPT THAT I CAN TRUST YOU TO 73 MANSNS
LISTEN WITHOUT HEARING MUCH.

WITHOUT (CONT'D.)
AN OUTCAST WITHOUT MEANING OR FUNCTION IN MY OWN 73 MANSNS
HOME BUT PLEASANTLY TOLERATED
THEN YOU CAN GO ON--SUCCESSFULLY--WITH A CLEAR 91 MANSNS
VISION--WITHOUT FALSE SCRUPLE--
WITHOUT SCREAMING SCORNFUL LAUGHTER AT MYSELF. 102 MANSNS
SIMON, WITHOUT LOOKING AT HER, BEGINS TO SPEAK 103 MANSNS
AGAIN.
SHE KNOWS WITHOUT THEM I SHALL BE LOST AGAIN/ 105 MANSNS
YOU DIDN'T WANT TO ADMIT I COULD LIVE, EVEN FOR A 110 MANSNS
MOMENT, WITHOUT YOU.
WITHOUT GIVING HIM ANY SENSIBLE REASON-- 110 MANSNS
AND, AS I KNEW HOW LONELY I WOULD BE IN THE FUTURE134 MANSNS
WITHOUT THE CHILDREN--
THEIR CLASPED HANDS, WITHOUT THEIR BEING AWARE, 136 MANSNS
LET GO AND DRAW APART.
HOW DARE YOU COME IN HERE WITHOUT KNOCKINGS 140 MANSNS
WITHOUT A CARE IN THE WORLD, WATCHING MY SONS GROW148 MANSNS
UP HANDSOME RICH GENTLEMEN,
IF YOU CAN, DISCOVER HIS WEAKNESS AND THEN USE IT 150 MANSNS
WITHOUT SCRUPLE.
SIMON DOES NOTHING WITHOUT MY CONSENT, MR. TENARD.151 MANSNS
(BREAKS IN--WITHOUT ANY HINT OF APOLOGY.) 151 MANSNS
LEAVING ME WITHOUT A KISS? 158 MANSNS
IF YOU THINK I WILL BEAR YOUR INSULTS WITHOUT 162 MANSNS
RETALIATING/
AS ONE, ON THE OTHER BENCH, STARING AT HIM, 175 MANSNS
EXHAUSTED AND WITHOUT FEELING.)
BUT THE OBVIOUS FACT IS THAT THEIR LIVES ARE 180 MANSNS
WITHOUT ANY MEANING WHATEVER--
(TURNS HIS HEAD TO STARE AT SARA WITHOUT 186 MANSNS
RECOGNITION.
I CAN WISH HIM HAPPINESS WITHOUT ME, AND MEAN IT/ 188 MANSNS
(SHE TURNS TO GO OFF LEFT--BROKENLY, WITHOUT 189 MANSNS
LOOKING AT SIMON.)
YOU KNOW--WITHOUT MY SAYING IT. 356 MARCOM
(WITHOUT WAITING FOR PERMISSION, 393 MARCOM
AND I WOULD BE LOST WITHOUT YOU/ 393 MARCOM
THEY'VE HAD IT UNDER THEIR NOSES FOR YEARS WITHOUT395 MARCOM
A SINGLE SOUL EVER HAVING
HIS TRUTH ACTS WITHOUT DEEDS. 401 MARCOM
I'LL DO WHAT'S RIGHT BY HER WITHOUT CONSIDERING 404 MARCOM
FEAR OR FAVOR.
(DISGUSTEDLY) THEY WOULD HAVE COME WITHOUT NOISE.405 MARCOM
(LETTING THE PAPER SLIP FROM HER HAND WITHOUT A 410 MARCOM
GLANCE--DULLY)
MY LIPS SPOKE WITHOUT ME SAYING A WORD. 415 MARCOM
UNPINS IT AND HANDS IT TO HER WITHOUT A WORD. 419 MARCOM
AUGUST COMMANDER, IF YOU MUST HAVE WAR, LET IT BE 422 MARCOM
ONE WITHOUT FINE PHRASES--
(SMILING--DISTRACTEDLY) WAR WITHOUT RHETORIC, 423 MARCOM
PLEASE/
WHICH CREATES AND DESTROYS WITHOUT OTHER PURPOSE 426 MARCOM
I CAN TELL WITHOUT BITING IT. 427 MARCOM
HE WEARS A SIMPLE WHITE ROBE WITHOUT ADORNMENT OF 432 MARCOM
ANY SORT.
WHICH IS THE GREATEST EVIL, TO POSSESS OR TO BE 434 MARCOM
WITHOUT$
AND WALKS IN THE CROWD WITHOUT SELF-CONSCIOUSNESS,439 MARCOM
VERY MUCH AS ONE OF THEM.
(HE ADDS, NOT WITHOUT MORAL SATISFACTION) 8 MISBEG
NOT WITHOUT YOU TO GIVE HIM THE GUTS AND HELP HIM, 13 MISBEG
HE CUTS THE PLUG AND STUFFS HIS PIPE--WITHOUT 15 MISBEG
RANCOR)
CARRYING ON WITH MEN WITHOUT A MARRIAGE LICENSE. 18 MISBEG
WITHOUT IT THERE'D BE NO POPULATION. 28 MISBEG
WITHOUT ANY REASON YOU CAN SEE, HE'LL SUDDENLY 33 MISBEG
TURN STRANGE, AND LOOK SAD.
(RESENTFULLY) I WON'T HAVE YOU SUSPECTING JIM 34 MISBEG
WITHOUT ANY CAUSE, D'YOU HEAR ME/
BUT WHEN HE SMILES WITHOUT SNEERING. 37 MISBEG
WITHOUT BEING SNEERED AT BY HIS RICH LANDLORDS 40 MISBEG
WITHOUT THEIR NOTICING, JOSIE APPEARS IN THE 40 MISBEG
DOORWAY BEHIND TYRONE.
(WHO HAS BEEN TAKING EVERYTHING IN WITHOUT SEEMING 42 MISBEG
TO)
YOU WOULDN'T GO WITHOUT A WORD OF GOOD-BYE TO ME, 64 MISBEG
WOULD YOU, DARLIN'S
LIKE A POOR SHEEP WITHOUT PRIDE OR SPIRIT-- 79 MISBEG
(WITHOUT LOOKING AT HER--ENTHUSIASTIC AGAIN) 96 MISBEG
(TRYING TO EXAMINE HIS FACE WITHOUT HIS KNOWING) 105 MISBEG
AND THIS ACT FOLLOWS THE PRECEDING WITHOUT ANY 111 MISBEG
LAPSE OF TIME.
SHE TRIES TO READ HIS FACE WITHOUT HIS NOTICING. 115 MISBEG
WELL, I KNOW MY FATHER'S VIRTUES WITHOUT YOU 124 MISBEG
TELLING ME.
(GOES ON WITHOUT REAL INTEREST, TALKING TO KEEP 132 MISBEG
FROM THINKING)
(SHE HAS DRAWN AWAY FROM HIM AS FAR AS SHE CAN 150 MISBEG
WITHOUT GETTING UP.
BECAUSE I KNEW I WAS LOST, WITHOUT ANY HOPE LEFT--150 MISBEG
SHE GOES ON IN THE SAME TONE, WITHOUT LOOKING AT 157 MISBEG
HIM)
(STILL WITHOUT OPENING HIS EYES) 165 MISBEG
(HALF WAKENS WITHOUT OPENING HIS EYES--MUTTERS) 165 MISBEG
AS IF I'D HAD A SOUND SLEEP WITHOUT NIGHTMARES. 167 MISBEG
(HE TURNS AWAY AND WALKS QUICKLY DOWN THE ROAD OFF174 MISBEG
LEFT WITHOUT LOOKING BACK.
I KNEW THAT THE BASTARD WOULD NEVER LOOK AT A 176 MISBEG
PIECE OF ICE AGAIN WITHOUT
BUT I KNOW ALL ABOUT IT WITHOUT YOU TELLING ME. 13 POET
MICKEY CAN'T PUT TWO AND TWO TOGETHER WITHOUT 26 POET
MAKING FIVE.
FOR WITHOUT IT WHAT AM I AT ALL BUT AN UGLY, FAT 26 POET
WOMAN GETTIN' OLD AND SICK/
I WANT TO LOVE HIM JUST ENOUGH SO I CAN MARRY HIM 31 POET
WITHOUT CHEATING HIM,
AND HE DOWNS IT WITHOUT MUCH DIFFICULTY. 37 POET

WITHOUT

WITHOUT (CONT'D.)
(CONTEMPTUOUSLY--WITHOUT BROGUE NOW.) 46 POET
THAT I WOULD GIVE YOU AWAY WITHOUT A PENNY TO YOUR 50 POET
NAME
(WITHOUT TURNING TO HER--IN HIS CONDESCENDINGLY 55 POET
POLITE TONE.)
(THEN GALLANTLY BUT WITHOUT LOOKING AT HER.) 59 POET
I'VE ENOUGH TO WORRY ME WITHOUT BOTHERING ABOUT 88 POET
HIM.
AND BUYS FOOD THAT ONE CAN EAT WITHOUT DISGUST. 98 POET
DON'T BE WISHIN' HIM HARM, FOR IT'S THIRSTY WE'D 100 POET
BE WITHOUT HIM.
WITHOUT GRAVELY COMPROMISING YOUR REPUTATION. 108 POET
IT IS OBVIOUS THAT WERE THERE A SUDDEN WEDDING 110 POET
WITHOUT A SUITABLE PERIOD OF
WITHOUT PREJUDICE, TRYING TO BE FAIR TO YOU AND 113 POET
MAKE EVERY POSSIBLE ALLOWANCE--
WITHOUT KNOWING HOW IT HAPPENED, 144 POET
OR SLEEP IN THE GRASS OF A FIELD WITHOUT A ROOF TO146 POET
OUR HEADS,
(HE PUSHES HER AWAY WITHOUT LOOKING AT HER. 152 POET
(WITHOUT LOOKING UP OR ANY CHANGE IN HIS DAZED 157 POET
EXPRESSION.
(SUDDENLY SPEAKS, WITHOUT LOOKING UP, IN THE 166 POET
BROADEST BROGUE.
HE SPEAKS WITHOUT BROGUE, NOT TO THEM BUT ALOUD TO169 POET
HIMSELF.)
(FURIOUSLY) FLIPPIN' AWAY DOLLARS, THE DIRTY 590 ROPE
THIEF, AN' US WITHOUT--
GIVE AND GIVE UNTIL I CAN MAKE THAT GIFT OF MYSELF 18 STRANG
FOR A MAN'S HAPPINESS WITHOUT
SCRUPLED, WITHOUT FEAR, WITHOUT JOY EXCEPT IN HIS 18 STRANG
JOY/
(WITHOUT LOOKING AT HIM, HER EYES ON HER 19 STRANG
FATHER'S--INTENSELY)
(HIS THOUGHTS AT EBB, WITHOUT EMPHASIS, SLUGGISH 24 STRANG
AND MELANCHOLY)
GORDON WENT AWAY WITHOUT--WELL, LET'S SAY MARRYING 35 STRANG
HER.
WITHOUT ONE BACKWARD GLANCE OF REGRET OR 49 STRANG
RECOLLECTION.
I FEEL IT HAS LOST ITS SOUL AND GROWN RESIGNED TO 49 STRANG
DOING WITHOUT IT.
I GOT THE FEELING THE GHOSTS HAD ALL DESERTED THE 51 STRANG
HOUSE AND LEFT IT WITHOUT A
AND YET I DESERVE IT'S A GORGEOUS MORNING WITHOUT, 51 STRANG
THE FLOWERS ARE FLOWERING,
YOU CAN'T LIVE WITH THEM AND CAN'T LIVE WITHOUT 51 STRANG
THEM.
WITHOUT HUMAN EMOTION TO INSPIRE IT.) 54 STRANG
HE SAID HE LOVED ME SO MUCH HE'D HAVE GONE MAD 59 STRANG
WITHOUT ME.
WHAT REASON COULD I GIVE, WITHOUT TELLING HIM 61 STRANG
EVERYTHING
AND MAYBE MY HUSBAND WOULD FEEL WITHOUT EVER 63 STRANG
KNOWING HOW HE FELT IT,
WITHOUT MY HUSBAND KNOWING, AND PICKED A MAN, A 63 STRANG
HEALTHY MALE TO BREED BY,
AND YET I'VE GIVEN MYSELF TO MEN BEFORE WITHOUT A 72 STRANG
THOUGHT
WITHOUT LOVE OR DESIRE... 72 STRANG
DAMN IT, YOU'RE CONDEMNING HER WITHOUT--/ 77 STRANG
WITHOUT SEEING ME...) 79 STRANG
ALTHOUGH HE MIGHT, WITHOUT HARM TO ANYONE, DESIRE 88 STRANG
HER.
I'D DIE WITHOUT HER/...] 92 STRANG
(INDIFFERENTLY) HE'LL PROBABLY COME WITHOUT 94 STRANG
BOTHERING TO WRITE.
WHAT DOES HE MEAN COMING IN ON US WITHOUT 98 STRANG
WARNINGS...!)
I KNEW THAT YOU'D NEVER COME TO REALLY LOVE ME 109 STRANG
WITHOUT THAT.
I CAN'T TELL HIM WITHOUT NED TO HELP ME/. 109 STRANG
I CAN GIVE MYSELF WITHOUT REPULSION... 112 STRANG
HE ASKED FOR MORE MONEY AND THEY GAVE IT WITHOUT 113 STRANG
QUESTION...
WITHOUT PAIN/...) 113 STRANG
I DON'T KNOW WHAT I'D DO WITHOUT YOU/. 119 STRANG
(WITHOUT LOSING ANY CONFIDENCE--WITH A GRIN) 122 STRANG
AND AS LONG AS WE CAN LOVE EACH OTHER WITHOUT 132 STRANG
DANGER TO HIM,
PROUD WITHOUT BEING PROUD ENOUGH/... 138 STRANG
WITHOUT MY HAVING TO TELL HIM...) 147 STRANG
SHE KNOWS THAT I LOVE HER WITHOUT MY TELLING... 148 STRANG
WITHOUT A GLANCE AT DARRELL.) 149 STRANG
WITHOUT BEING TOO RUDE, I URGED HIM TO GET BACK TO159 STRANG
HIS WORK,
(WITHOUT LOWERING THE GLASSES) 160 STRANG
(WITHOUT LOWERING THE GLASSES FROM HER EYES-- 160 STRANG
THINKING GOOD-NATUREDLY)
SEEMS TO ME YOU COULD SHOW A LITTLE MORE INTEREST 162 STRANG
WITHOUT IT HURTING YOU,
WITHOUT DESIRE OR JEALOUSY OR BITTERNESS... 165 STRANG
I'LL SEND YOU A COUPLE OF MILLION CELLS YOU CAN 170 STRANG
TORTURE WITHOUT HARMING
(WITHOUT LOWERING GLASSES--DRYLY) 172 STRANG
WEAKLY STRUGGLING TO SHAKE OFF HER HANDS, WITHOUT 172 STRANG
LOWERING THE GLASSES)
(WITHOUT LOOKING AT HIM--TO THE AIR) 180 STRANG
(THINKING IN AMAZEMENT, BUT NOT WITHOUT A QUEER 186 STRANG
SATISFACTION)
HE'S LEAVING ME WITHOUT A BACKWARD LOOK/ 198 STRANG
(WITHOUT LOOKING AT HIM--MECHANICALLY) 449 WELDED
AS IF IN SPITE OF HIMSELF, WITHOUT A WORD.) 450 WELDED
WITHOUT APPEARING TO NOTICE, JOHN SCRUTINIZES 450 WELDED
THEIR FACES KEENLY.
(CAPE NODS WITHOUT SPEAKING. JOHN GOES TO THE 451 WELDED
DOOR, ELEANOR ACCOMPANYING HIM)

WITHOUT (CONT'D.)
YES, BECAUSE I CAN'T LIVE WITHOUT YOU/ 453 WELDED
I SUPPOSE YOU THINK THAT WITHOUT YOUR WORK I-- 457 WELDED
I WAS HAPPY--THAT IS, AS HAPPY AS I EVER CAN BE 457 WELDED
WITHOUT YOU.
IS POSSIBLE FOR A WOMAN WITHOUT HER BEING LOW. 459 WELDED
AND YOU WAS BEATIN' IT LEAVIN' YOUR MONEY THERE-- 477 WELDED
WITHOUT NOTHIN'.
(HER HEAD HAS BEEN AVERTED SINCE HE TURNED AWAY-- 481 WELDED
WITHOUT LOOKING AT HIM)
(WITHOUT LOOKING AF HER HE REACHES OUT AND CLASPS 482 WELDED
HER HAND.)
(MOVEL, WITHOUT LOOKING AT HIM, REACHES AND CLASPS483 WELDED
HIS HAND)

WITNESS
I WANT YOU TO BE A WITNESS/ 477 DYNAMO
BUT HOW CAN WE WITNESS AT NIGHT AND THROUGH A 315 LAZARU
WALLS
LET THE PEOPLE WITNESS/ 362 LAZARU
BUT YOU MUST BEAR WITNESS, WON'T YOU, NICHOLAS, 37 MANSNS
AND TO PROVE MY ESCAPE--AS A SYMBOL--WATCH AND 40 MANSNS
BEAR WITNESS, NICHOLAS/
IF YOU COULD ONLY BRING FORWARD ONE RELIABLE 396 MARCOM
WITNESS.
I WILL BEAR WITNESS HE HAS A SOUL. 397 MARCOM
SURE, HIS LAWYER WOULD HAVE ALL YOUR OLD FLAMES IN 95 MISBEG
THE WITNESS BOX,
THERE'S NOTHING FOR THEM TO WITNESS THAT-- 159 MISBEG
TO PARIS TO WITNESS THE EMPEROR'S CORONATION. 84 POET
I'LL WANT YOU FOR A WITNESS. 124 POET
TO BEAR WITNESS WE ARE LIVING/...) 165 STRANG

WITNESSES
LET'S GIT OUR BET SET OUT PLAIN AFORE WITNESSES. 131 ELECTR
AND WHAT PART DO WE PLAY--OFFICIAL WITNESSES? 315 LAZARU
I HAVE HAD THEM TAKE THE STATEMENTS OF MANY 343 LAZARU
WITNESSES.
MAYBE HE THINKS IF HE CAUGHT YOU WITH JIM AND HAD 9 MISBEG
WITNESSES TO PROVE IT,
WITH WITNESSES AND A SHOTGUN, AND CATCH HIM THERE. 22 MISBEG
YOUR PART IN IT IS TO COME AT SUNRISE WITH 92 MISBEG
WITNESSES AND CATCH US IN--
ALL WE WANT IS A PAPER SIGNED BY HIM WITH 94 MISBEG
WITNESSES THAT HE'LL SELL THE FARM TO
I COME AT SUNRISE WITH MY WITNESSES, AND YOU'VE 94 MISBEG
FORGOT TO LOCK YOUR DOORS,
THEN YOU CAN SNEAK IN THE INN YOURSELF AND PICK 96 MISBEG
THE WITNESSES TO STAY UP WITH
(GUILTILY) WITNESSES? 158 MISBEG
WHERE'S YOUR WITNESSES? 158 MISBEG
(FINALLY HAS TO BLURT OUT) SURE, IF I'D BROUGHT 159 MISBEG
THE WITNESSES,

WITOUT
IT CAN'T MOVE WITOUT SOMEP'N ELSE, SEES 216 HA APE

WITS
IS IT LOSING THE SMALL WITS YE IVER HAD, HE ARES 31 ANNA
I'M CLUMSY IN MY WITS WHEN IT COMES TO TALKING 37 ANNA
PROPER WITH A GIRL THE LIKE OF
I'M THINKING THIS OUT OF YOUR WITS YOU'VE GOT WITH 48 ANNA
FRIGHT OF THE SEA.
AND SCARED ME NEAR OUT OF MY WITS? 151 BEYOND
SHE'S FRIGHTENED OUT OF HER WITS/ 99 ELECTR
I WAS SCARED OUT OF MY WITS RIDING BACK FROM TOWN. 98 JOURNE
(WITH SATISFACTION, AS IF THIS WAS A PERPETUAL 121 JOURNE
BATTLE OF WITS WITH HIS ELDER SON
DO YOU WANT TO LOSE WHAT LITTLE WITS YOU'VE LEFTS 186 MANSNS
IT WAS ONLY A LOVE TAP TO WAKEN YOUR WITS, SO 5 MISBEG
YOU'LL USE THEM.
WELL, GOD GRANT SOMEONE WITH WITS WILL SEE THAT 16 MISBEG
DUPEY GANDER AT THE DEPOT AND
IT'S YOUR HAPPINESS I'M CONSIDERING WHEN I 27 MISBEG
RECOMMEND YOUR USING YOUR WITS TO
(EAGERLY) BE GOD, NOW YOU'RE USING YOUR WITS. 30 MISBEG
I'LL LISTEN, NOW I SEE YOU HAVE HOLD OF YOUR WITS. 82 MISBEG
(GIVES HIM A SHAKE) KEEP HOLD OF YOUR WITS 83 MISBEG
(SHE GIVES HIM A SHAKE) GET YOUR WITS ABOUT YOU 91 MISBEG
AND ANSWER ME THIS:
(ANGRILY) DIDN'T YOU TELL ME TO GET HOLD OF MY 93 MISBEG
WITS?
IN A KIND OF DAZE, AS IF THE MOON WAS IN YOUR WITS170 MISBEG
AS WELL AS WHISKEY.
WHERE'S YOUR WITS, PATCH? 53 POET
AND THE NEXT TIME I'LL KEEP MY WITS. 65 POET
SURE, IT'D TAKE MORE THAN A FEW CLUBS ON THE HEAD 168 POET
TO DARKEN MY WITS LONG.
IT'S THE CURSE IS IN THE WITS OF YOUR FAMILY, NOT 583 ROPE
MINE.
FUR IF HE SEEN HIM SUDDIN IT'S LIKELY THE LITTLE 590 ROPE
WITS HE HAS LEFT WOULD LEAVE
HE'S BORE TO PRETIND HE'S LOONY, BUT HE'S HIS WITS592 ROPE
WITH HIM ALL THE TIME.

WITS'
I'VE HEARD RUMORS THE MANAGEMENT WERE AT THEIR 604 ICEMAN
WITS' END

WITTED
IMBECILITIES OF PLEASURE--THE UNCLEAN ANTICS OF 358 LAZARU
HALF-WITTED CHILDREN/
HIS WASHED-OUT BLUE EYES HAVE A WANDERING, HALF- 52 POET
WITTED EXPRESSION.
I SPOSE I'M A BIGGER FOOL THAN YOU BE TO ARGY 581 ROPE
WITH A HALF-WITTED BODY.

WITTICISM
(THE WITTICISM DELIGHTS HIM AND HE BURSTS INTO A 606 ICEMAN
SHRILL CACKLE.

WITTY
THE DANDIES POINT WITH THEIR FINGERS AND MAKE 197 EJONES
WITTY REMARKS.
A CHARMING HOSTESS, WITTY AND GAY--AND BEAUTIFUL. 26 MANSNS
HE'S GETTING TOO WITTY/ 374 MARCOM

1813

WOMAN

WITTY (CONT'D.)
ABOUT DEAR OLD LADIES AND WITTY, CYNICAL BACHELORS176 STRANG
AND QUAINT CHARACTERS WITH

WIVES
FARMERS AND THEIR WIVES AND THEIR YOUNG FOLKS OF 247 DESIRE
BOTH SEXES
THEY GROW IT ON THEIR WIVES. 9 ELECTR
AND ALL THE MOTHERS AND WIVES AND SISTERS AND 82 ELECTR
GIRLS DID THE SAME/
AT THE RULER'S FEET HIS WIVES CROUCH LIKE SLAVES. 364 MARCOM
THE KINGS HAVE FIVE HUNDRED WIVES APIECE. 370 MARCOM
FARTHER AWAY, THE NOBLES AND WARRIORS OF ALL 377 MARCOM
DEGREES WITH THEIR WIVES BEHIND
ON THE LEFT, THE WIVES AND CONCUBINES OF THE KAAN,377 MARCOM
WHY DO WIVES HIDE IT FROM THEIR HUSBANDS... 53 STRANG
WITH NO ONE TO SPEAK TO EXCEPT SAM'S BUSINESS 143 STRANG
FRIENDS AND THEIR DEADLY WIVES.
OH, I KNOW WHAT WIVES CAN DO/ 169 STRANG

WIZARD
AFTER HER AND NOT YOU, Y' OLD WIZARD/ 580 ROPE

WIZENED
(A WIZENED RUNT OF A MAN WITH A STRAGGLING GRAY 456 CARIBE
MUSTACHE--
HE IS WIZENED AND OLD. 200 EJONES
HE IS AROUND SIXTY, SMALL AND WIZENED, WHITE HAIR 67 ELECTR
AND BEARD.
(THEY ALL TURN TO AN OLD, WIZENED IRISHMAN WHO IS 209 HA APE
DOZING, VERY DRUNK,
WHEN OUT OF YOUR MAD DREAMS YOU'RE ONLY A POOR 166 MANSNS
LITTLE WIZENED OLD WOMAN
(DONATA ENTERS ON THE ARM OF HER FATHER, A CRAFTY,427 MARCOM
WIZENED OLD MAN.
CUCGY, A WIZENED RUNT OF A MAN WITH A STRAGGLING 496 VOYAGE
GRAY MUSTACHE,

WO'TH
YUH'RE WO'TH THE WHOLE PACK OF 'EM PUT TOGETHER. 496 DIFRNT
CALEB'S A MAN WO'TH EN O' MOST AND, SPITE O' HIS 513 DIFRNT
BEIN' ON'Y A BOY YIT,

WOBBLIES
WOBBLIES! 242 HA APE
IF YOU WANT TO GET BACK AT THAT DAME, YOU BETTER 242 HA APE
JOIN THE WOBBLIES.
HERE'S WHERE HE GITS DOWN TO CASES ON THE 243 HA APE
WOBBLIES.

WOBBLY
WHICH GIVES HER A SHUFFLING, WOBBLY GAIT.) 7 ANNA
WHERE THEY'D NEVER LOOK FOR A WOBBLY, PRETENDING 1588 ICEMAN
WAS A SPORT.

WOE
FACE IN HANDS, HIS ROUND EYES CHILDISHLY WOUNDED 258 AHWILD
AND WOE-BEGONE.
I GET THE SAME TALE OF WOE FROM EVERY ONE IN OUR 501 DAYS
PART OF THE COUNTRY.
WOE UNTO THEE, JERUSALEM/ 292 LAZARU
WOE UNTO US/ 292 LAZARU
(IN A GREAT ECHOING CRY) WOE UNTO US/ 292 LAZARU
(IN A WAILING CHANT) WOE UNTO ISRAEL/ 292 LAZARU
WOE TO US, WOE/ 293 LAZARU
(BESIDE THE BODIES) WOE TO US, WOE/ 293 LAZARU
BUT WOE/ 295 LAZARU
WOE TO US, WOE/ 295 LAZARU
*WOE UNTO US/ 579 ROPE

WOID
ON DE WOID OF A HONEST BARTENDER/ 722 ICEMAN

WOIDS
YUH GOT WHAT I WAS SAYIN' EVEN IF YUH MUFFED DE 252 HA APE
WOIDS.

WOIK
WAY HE GRABS, YUH'D TINK IT WAS HIM DONE DE WOIK. 613 ICEMAN
AND MAKE SOMEONE ELSE WOIK FOR YUH, IS DERE$ 702 ICEMAN
ON'Y SUCKERS WOIK. 702 ICEMAN

WOIKIN'
LETTIN' HER KID ME INTO WOIKIN'. 697 ICEMAN
I'M TROUGH WOIKIN'. 700 ICEMAN
NOT DAT I BLAME YUH FOR NOT WOIKIN'. 702 ICEMAN

WOIKS
WE RUN DE WHOLE WOIKS. 216 HA APE
I'LL SHOOT DE WOIKS FOR YOUSE. 247 HA APE
I MEAN BLOW UP DE FACTORY, DE WOIKS, WHERE HE 249 HA APE
MAKES DE STEEL.
TELL ME WHERE HIS WOIKS IS, HOW TO GIT THERE, ALL 249 HA APE
DE DOPE.
REMEMBER HOW HE WOIKS UP DAT GAG ABOUT HIS WIFE, 580 ICEMAN
WHEN HE'S COCKEYED,
HE'S EVEN GIVE HUGO DE WOIKS. 635 ICEMAN

WOILD
DE NOISE AND SMOKE AND ALL DE ENGINES MOVIN' DE 216 HA APE
WOILD, DEY STOP.
EVERYTING ELSE DAT MAKES DE WOILD MOVE, SOMEP'N 216 HA APE
MAKES IT MOVE.
I START SOMEP'N AND DE WOILD MOVES/ 216 HA APE
DEY'RE ALL DEAD TO DE WOILD. 246 HA APE
TO BLOW UP DE STEEL, KNOCK ALL DE STEEL IN DE 249 HA APE
WOILD UP TO DE MOON.
IT STOPS AND DE WHOLE WOILD STOPS. 250 HA APE
NOW I AIN'T STEEL, AND DE WOILD OWNS ME. 250 HA APE
STEEL WAS ME, AND I OWNED DE WOILD. 250 HA APE
YUH CHALLENGE DE WHOLE WOILD, HUH$ 252 HA APE
YUH'RE DE ON'Y ONE IN DE WOILD DAT DOES, YUH LUCKY253 HA APE
STIFF/

WUILDS
YOUSE WOULDN'T FOR WOILDS. 247 HA APE

WOIST
TAKIN' ALL DE WOIST PUNCHES FROM BOT' OF 'EM. 253 HA APE
HE'D HAVE BEAT HER UP AND DEN GONE ON DE WOIST 636 ICEMAN
DRUNK HE'D EVER STAGED.

WOITH
HE AIN'T WOITH A PUNCH. 213 HA APE

WOKE
SEEMS TO ME YOU WOKE UP PRETTY QUICK--JUST AFTER 269 AHWILD
YOUR PA LEFT THE HOUSE/
(WITH ASPERITY) AND IS THAT ALL YOU WOKE ME OUT 151 BEYOND
OF A SOUND SLEEP FUR,
I WOKE HIM UP. 266 DESIRE
HE WOKE UP. 458 DYNAMO
I WOKE UP AND SAW HER STANDING BESIDE MY BED-- 477 DYNAMO
IT WOKE ME UP-- 62 ELECTR
SHE WOKE UP CHUCK AND DRAGGED HIM OUTA DE HAY TO 613 ICEMAN
GO TO A CHOP SUEY JOINT.
(BITTERLY) JEES, EVER SINCE HE WOKE UP, YUH CAN'T630 ICEMAN
HOLD HIM.
IT WAS HER PULLING SHERRY FLIPS ON ME WOKE ME UP. 697 ICEMAN
'TWAS JUST THAT MOMENT I WOKE AND SPIED HIM. 519 INZONE
HE LOOKS ROUND TO SEE IF ANYONE'S WOKE UP--- 520 INZONE
I WOKE UP AND HEARD HER MOVING AROUND IN THE SPARE 38 JOURNE
ROOM.
BUT I'M SURE I FIXED MY HAIR AGAIN WHEN I WOKE UP. 68 JOURNE
I CAN REMEMBER THAT TEASPOONFUL OF BOOZE EVERY 111 JOURNE
TIME I WOKE UP WITH A NIGHTMARE.
AND BY THE TIME I WOKE UP TO THE FACT I'D BECOME A149 JOURNE
SLAVE TO THE DAMNED THING AND
THE MOMENT AFTER YOU'VE WOKE UP FROM THE OLD/ 47 MANSNS
(IRONICALLY) YOU ALSO WOKE UP THE PRINCESS. 403 MARCOM
I JUST WOKE UP. 159 MISBEG
(WITH BITTER VOICE) SO YOU JUST WOKE UP---DID YOU$ 159 MISBEG
YOUR--SO THAT'S WHY I WOKE UP IN YOUR ARMS. 167 MISBEG
DON'T THINK I WOKE YOU JUST TO ADMIRE THE SUNRISE.172 MISBEG
IT WOULD SERVE CON RIGHT IF I TOOK THE CHANCE NOW 138 POET
AND BROKE MY PROMISE AND WOKE
SEEMED STARING OUT OF HIS EYES WITH A BURNING 45 STRANG
PAIN, AND I WOKE UP CRYING.

WOLF
HE'S NO WOLF IN SHEEP'S CLOTHING, 78 MISBEG

WOMAN
WHO BUT A MAN THAT'S MAD WOULD TAKE HIS WOMAN--AND$37 'ILE
AS SWEET A WOMAN AS EVER WAS--
SHE IS A SLIGHT, SWEET-FACED LITTLE WOMAN DRESSED 539 'ILE
IN BLACK.
A WOMAN COULDN'T RIGHTLY UNDERSTAND MY REASONS. 547 'ILE
BEST TURN IN, ANNIE, THERE'S A GOOD WOMAN. 547 'ILE
(THINKING TO HUMOR HER) 'TIS NO FIT PLACE FUR A 548 'ILE
WOMAN, THAT'S SURE.
(STERNLY) WOMAN, YOU AIN'T ADOIN' RIGHT 550 'ILE
WOMAN, WHAT FOOLISH MOCKIN' IS THIS$ 551 'ILE
A SHORT STOUT WOMAN WITH FADING LIGHT-BROWN HAIR 187 AHWILD
SPRINKLED WITH GRAY.
OH, HE'D GIVE UP ALL THAT--FOR THE RIGHT WOMAN. 213 AHWILD
(STIFFLY) WELL, I HOPE HE FINUS A WOMAN WHO'S 213 AHWILD
WILLING.
YOU'RE A GOOD WOMAN, LILY--TOO GOOD FOR THE REST 214 AHWILD
OF US.
CAN IT BE THIS WOMAN HAS BEEN SLOWLY POISONING YOU227 AHWILD
ALL THESE YEARS$
SIDNEY, SHE SAID,*NEVER MARRY A WOMAN WHO 232 AHWILD
DRINKS/
SO FINE A WOMAN UNCE--AN NOW SUCH A SLAVE TO RUM/ 232 AHWILD
(HE RECITES SCORNFULLY) *FOR A WOMAN'S ONLY A 245 AHWILD
WOMAN,
HERE'S A NOTE A WOMAN LEFT WITH ONE OF THE BOYS 266 AHWILD
DOWNSTAIRS AT THE OFFICE THIS
AW, WHO EVER HEARD OF A WOMAN EVER BEING ON TIME. 277 AHWILD
(WITH A CHUCKLE) SERVE YE RIGHT, YE OLD DIVIL-- 10 ANNA
HAVIN' A WOMAN AT YOUR AGE/
AND WHAT IS A FINE HANDSOME WOMAN THE LIKE OF YOU 31 ANNA
DOING ON THIS SCOWS
YOU'RE NOT THE OLD SQUARE-HEAD'S WOMAN, I SUPPOSE 32 ANNA
YOU'LL BE TELLING ME NEXT--
BUT DIVIL A WOMAN IN ALL THE PORTS OF THE WORLD 34 ANNA
HAS IVER MADE A GREAT FOOL OF ME.
THIS IS THE FIRST TIME I'VE HAD A WORD WITH A 37 ANNA
RALE, DACENT WOMAN.
SHE'S THE WAN WOMAN OF THE WORLD FOR ME, AND I 47 ANNA
CAN'T LIVE WITHOUT HER NOW,
WHERE I'D BE GIVING A POWER OF LOVE TO A WOMAN IS 60 ANNA
THE SAME AS OTHERS YOU'D MEET
WAS THERE EVER A WOMAN IN THE WORLD HAD THE 60 ANNA
ROTTENNESS IN HER THAT YOU HAVE,
(BEWILDEREDLY) AND ME TO LISTEN TO THAT TALK FROM 70 ANNA
A WOMAN LIKE YOU AND BE
THAT I MAY NEVER SEE ANOTHER WOMAN TO MY DYING 73 ANNA
HOUR/
WHAT KIND OF WOMAN YOU'D BEEN IN THE PAST AT ALL. 74 ANNA
AND WOMEN, TOO, MAYBE, AND I'M THINKING I'D CHANGE 74 ANNA
YOU TO A NEW WOMAN ENTIRELY.
'TIS MY OLD WOMAN HERSELF WILL BE LOOKING DOWN 75 ANNA
FROM HIVIN ABOVE,
(CHUCKLING) AND THAT MISSION WOMAN, 94 BEYOND
RATHER PRIM-LOOKING WOMAN OF FIFTY-FIVE WHO HAD 94 BEYOND
ONCE BEEN A SCHOOL TEACHER,
THEY'RE LIABLE AS NOT TO SUSPICION IT WAS A WOMAN 103 BEYOND
I'D PLANNED TO SHIP ALONG,
SHE IS A THIN, PALE-FACED, UNINTELLIGENT-LOOKING 112 BEYOND
WOMAN OF ABOUT FORTY-EIGHT,
NO, THEY THINK I'M A CRAZY, CRANKY OLD WOMAN, HALF113 BEYOND
DEAD A'READY,
NO WOMAN COULD. 164 BEYOND
NO WOMAN COULD. 164 BEYOND
LIKED YOU/ WHAT KIND OF A WOMAN ARE YOU$ 164 BEYOND
THIS IS YOUR DOING, YOU DAMN WOMAN, YOU COWARD, 168 BEYOND
YOU MURDERESS/
DIVIL TAKE ME IF I'M NOT STARTIN' TO BLUBBER LOIKE480 CARDIF
AN AULD WOMAN,
AIN' THAT BLASTED BUMBOAT NAYGUR WOMAN TOOK HER 457 CARIBE
OATH SHE'D BRING BACK KUM ENOUGH
SAY ORISC, HUW VE PAY DIS WOMAN FUR BOOZE$ 463 CARIBE

WOMAN

WOMAN (CONT'D.)
A** YOU WID A WOMAN AN' CHILDER KEEPIN' FUR YE IN 463 CARIBE
IVIRY DIVIL'S POKE IN THE WIDE
THE SILLY LAUGHTER OF A WOMAN IS HEARD.) 463 CARIBE
SHE IS A TALL, SLENDER WOMAN OF TWENTY-FIVE, 562 CROSS
THAT LETTER WAS FULL OF MORE ARDENT HYMNS OF 504 DAYS
PRAISE FOR A MERE LIVING WOMAN THAN
SHE WAS A WONDERFUL WOMAN. 509 DAYS
TO A WOMAN WHO LOVES AND IS LOVED. 514 DAYS
SHE IS STILL AN EXTREMELY ATTRACTIVE WOMAN BUT, IN515 DAYS
CONTRAST TO ELSA,
WHAT EVERY WOMAN DREAMS OF HEARING HER LOVER SAY, 524 DAYS
I THINK.
AND WHEN HE MET THE WOMAN WHO AFTERWARDS BECAME 535 DAYS
HIS WIFE
WAS PAWING OVER SOME WOMAN RIGHT UNDER THE NOSE OF537 DAYS
HIS WIFE.
HE HAD NOT THE SLIGHTEST DESIRE FOR THIS WOMAN. 537 DAYS
THE WOMAN WITH HIM COUNTED ONLY AS A MEANS. 538 DAYS
THE NURSE IS A PLUMP WOMAN IN HER LATE THIRTIES. 554 DAYS
JENN. MY WOMAN, SHE DIED. 204 DESIRE
(JEERINGLY) THE SCARLET WOMAN/ 210 DESIRE
THAT'S WHAT THE WOMAN LIVED-- 213 DESIRE
A HUMP'S GOT IT HEY A WOMAN. 222 DESIRE
AN' HAPE YER NEW WOMAN/ 223 DESIRE
YE'RE ON'Y A WOMAN. 234 DESIRE
WILL YE EVER KNOW ME---'R WILL ANY MAN 'R WOMAN'S 236 DESIRE
SHE WAS A GOOD WOMAN. 237 DESIRE
A CHANGE HAS COME OVER THE WOMAN. 241 DESIRE
AND I GUESS HE AIN'T THE CUSSED OLD WOMAN YOU 503 DIFFRNT
MAKES HIM OUT.
HEATHEN WOMAN THAT AIN'T NO BETTER'N A NIGGER$ 504 DIFFRNT
SHE IS A LARGE, FAT, FLORID WOMAN OF FIFTY. 506 DIFFRNT
IS IT THAT STORY ABOUT CALEB AND THAT HEATHEN 508 DIFFRNT
BROWN WOMAN YOU'RE TALKING ABOUT$
(WITH EMPHASIS) I AIN'T NEVER GUIN' TO MARRY NO 518 DIFFRNT
WOMAN BUT YOU, EMMER.
SCRAWNY WOMAN. 520 DIFFRNT
(SEVERELY) AND I HOPE YOU KNOW THE KIND OF WOMAN 525 DIFFRNT
SHE IS AND HAS BEEN
HE'D TEASE AN OLD WOMAN TO GET MONEY OUT OF HER, 528 DIFFRNT
AND HER ALONE IN THE WORLD.
CAN'T I CARE FOR HIM SAME AS ANY WOMAN CARES FOR A542 DIFFRNT
MAN$
DON'T HURT HIM-- JUST BECAUSE YOU THINK I'M AN OLD543 DIFFRNT
WOMAN AIN'T NO REASON--
(THEN AMUSEDLY) (WELL, SHE'S A DAMN FUNNY 430 DYNAMO
WOMAN. . . .
WHO AM I TO CAST THE FIRST STONE AT REUBEN IF HE 435 DYNAMO
DESIRES A WOMAN$. . .
NO, LIKE A WOMAN. . . . 474 DYNAMO
A NATIVE NEGRO WOMAN SNEAKS IN CAUTIOUSLY FROM THEL73 EJONES
ENTRANCE ON THE RIGHT.
(THE WOMAN KEEPS SULLENLY SILENT. 174 EJONES
THE WOMAN LOOKING BACK OVER HER SHOULDER 174 EJONES
CONTINUALLY.
HE SEES THE WOMAN AND STOPS TO WATCH HER 174 EJONES
SUSPICIOUSLY.
ME OLD WOMAN. 175 EJONES
THE OLD WOMAN SPRINGS TO HER FEET AND RUNS OUT OF 175 EJONES
THE DOORWAY, REAR.
HER COUSIN, MINNIE, IS A PLUMP LITTLE WOMAN OF 6 ELECTR
FORTY, OF THE MEEK,
(CHRISTINE MANNON IS A TALL STRIKING-LOOKING WOMAN 8 ELECTR
OF FORTY
I ONLY KNOW OF ONE OTHER WOMAN WHO HAD IT. 22 ELECTR
YOU SAID YOU LOVED THEM MORE THAN YOU'D EVER LOVED 23 ELECTR
A WOMAN.
OR I'LL FORGET YOU'RE A WOMAN--NO MANNON CAN 25 ELECTR
INSULT HER WHILE I--
I ASKED THE WOMAN IN THE BASEMENT. 30 ELECTR
I'M TALKING TO YOU AS A WOMAN NOW, NOT AS MOTHER 31 ELECTR
TO DAUGHTER/
HE'LL STILL BE IN HIS PRIME WHEN YOU'RE AN OLD 34 ELECTR
WOMAN WITH ALL YOUR LOOKS GONE/
SHE'S AS BEAUTIFUL A SHIP AS YOU'RE A WOMAN. 39 ELECTR
IF IT WAS A QUESTION OF SOME WOMAN TAKING YOU FROM 41 ELECTR
ME.
WHEN IT GOT FOUND OUT SHE WAS HIS UNCLE DAVID'S 44 ELECTR
FANCY WOMAN.
BEFORE I KNEW HE'S THE KIND WHO CHASES AFTER EVERY 50 ELECTR
WOMAN HE SEES.
IT SEEMS TO ME A LATE DAY, WHEN I AM AN OLD WOMAN 51 ELECTR
WITH GROWN-UP CHILDREN,
IS A TYPICAL NEW ENGLAND WOMAN OF PURE ENGLISH 67 ELECTR
ANCESTRY, WITH A HORSE FACE,
(HARSHLY) I CAN'T ABIDE THAT WOMAN/ 68 ELECTR
SHE'S A DAMNED HANDSOME WOMAN AND HE'D BEEN AWAY A 71 ELECTR
LONG TIME.
(SHE FORCES A LAUGH) YOU DON'T SEEM TO REALIZE 87 ELECTR
I'M AN OLD MARRIED WOMAN
I WON'T TALK TO A CRAZY WOMAN/ 97 ELECTR
FOUGHT WITH EZRA MANNON AS TWO MEN FIGHT FOR LOVE 110 ELECTR
OF A WOMAN/
HOW COULD YOU LOVE THAT VILE OLD WOMAN SO$ 115 ELECTR
I'LL COMFORT YOUR OLD WOMAN-- 132 ELECTR
SHE SEEMS A MATURE WOMAN, SURE OF HER FEMININE 139 ELECTR
ATTRACTIVENESS.
HOW CAN YOU STILL LOVE THAT VILE WOMAN SO-- 152 ELECTR
I WAS HIS FANCY WOMAN/ 177 ELECTR
THE MOTHER IS A DUMPY WOMAN OF FORTY-FIVE. 257 GGBROW
THE MOTHER IS A THIN FRAIL FADED WOMAN. 259 GGBROW
(HE KISSES HER) I TAKE THIS WOMAN--*' 268 GGBROW
(TENDERLY JOKING) HELLO WOMAN/ 268 GGBROW
TO BE A GENEROUS HERO AND SAVE THE WOMAN AND HER 273 GGBROW
CHILDREN/
STILL HARDLY A WOMAN. 274 GGBROW

WOMAN (CONT'D.)
U WOMAN--MY LOVE--THAT I HAVE SINNED AGAINST IN MY292 GGBROW
SICK PRIDE AND CRUELTY--
STARING FROM THE WOMAN ON THE BENCH TO THEIR 293 GGBROW
FATHER, ACCUSINGLY.)
SAVING MY WOMAN AND CHILDREN/ 297 GGBROW
(HIS VOICE LIKE A PROBE) WHY HAS NO WOMAN EVER 298 GGBROW
LOVED HIM$
(FORCING A JOKING TONE) BUT YOU MUSTN'T WASTE 323 GGBROW
JUNK ON AN OLD WOMAN LIKE ME/
ME OLD MAN AND WOMAN, DEY MADE ME. 234 HA APE
A WOMAN AND KIDS--A LOUSY VOTE--AND I'M ALL FIXED 250 HA APE
FOR JESUS, HUH$
(JOCOSELY) GOD PITY YOUR OLD WOMAN/ 251 HA APE
THE LITTLE WOMAN HAS, TOO. 24 HUGHIE
HOW D'YOU AND YOUR LITTLE WOMAN HIT IT OFF, 24 HUGHIE
BROTHERS.
WELL, THE ONE WOMAN THEY PINCHED, ROSA PARRITT, 15584 ICEMAN
HIS MOTHER.
I'D NEVER HAVE THOUGHT SHE WAS A WOMAN WHO'D KEEP 589 ICEMAN
LETTERS.
I TOLD HER, *YOU'VE ALWAYS ACTED THE FREE WOMAN, 591 ICEMAN
AND NOW THE INFLUENCE OF A GOOD WOMAN ENTERS OUR 597 ICEMAN
MARINER'S LIFE.
A SWEETER WOMAN NEVER DREW BREATH. 603 ICEMAN
I KNEW EVERY MAN, WOMAN AND CHILD IN THE WARD, 603 ICEMAN
ALMOST.
HASN'T HE BEEN MIXED UP WITH SOME WOMAN'S 642 ICEMAN
THAT ISN'T WHAT'S GOT HIM STOPPED. IT'S WHAT'S 643 ICEMAN
BEHIND THAT. AND IT'S A WOMAN.
THAT WAS A SILLY STUNT FOR A FREE ANARCHIST WOMAN,646 ICEMAN
WASN'T IT.
I REMEMBER HER PUTTING ON HER HIGH-AND-MIGHTY 647 ICEMAN
FREE-WOMAN STUFF.
AND YOU THOUGHT A WOMAN YOU LOVED WAS A PIECE OF 647 ICEMAN
PRIVATE PROPERTY YOU OWNED.
MORE BITTER SORROW THAN LOSING THE WOMAN ONE 657 ICEMAN
LOVES BY THE HAND OF DEATH--
THINKING OF ALL THE WRONG I'D DONE TO THE SWEETEST714 ICEMAN
WOMAN IN THE WORLD
THAT IT ISN'T HUMAN FOR ANY WOMAN TO BE SO PITYING714 ICEMAN
AND FORGIVING.
THAT NO WOMAN COULD HAVE STOOD ALL SHE STOOD AND 714 ICEMAN
STILL LOVED ME SO MUCH--
SPY IN PARIS WAS WRITIN' LOVE LETTERS TO SOME 529 INZONE
WOMAN SPY IN SWITZERLAND WHO SENT
AND EVERY WOMAN WHO WASN'T A WHORE WAS A FOOL/ 34 JOURNE
SHE'S A DIFFERENT WOMAN ENTIRELY FROM THE OTHER 37 JOURNE
TIMES.
OR EVEN AN AFTERNOON, SOME WOMAN FRIEND I COULD 46 JOURNE
TALK TO--
(SUDDENLY PRIMLY VIRTUOUS.) I'D NEVER SUGGEST A 52 JOURNE
MAN OR A WOMAN TOUCH DRINK.
THERE WAS THE SCANDAL OF THAT WOMAN WHO HAD BEEN 86 JOURNE
YOUR MISTRESS, SUING YOU.
THE ONLY KIND OF WOMAN HE UNDERSTANDS OR LIKES. 94 JOURNE
I MEAN, WITH ANY OTHER WOMAN. NEVER SINCE HE MET 105 JOURNE
ME.
HE'S A FINE GENTLEMAN AND YOU'RE A LUCKY WOMAN. 106 JOURNE
AND IS AN AGING, CYNICALLY SAD, EMBITTERED WOMAN.1107 JOURNE
AND JAMIE NEVER LOVED ANY CYNARA, AND WAS NEVER 134 JOURNE
FAITHFUL TO A WOMAN IN HIS LIFE,
A FINE, BRAVE, SWEET WOMAN. 148 JOURNE
I'LL BE THE LOVER OF THE FAT WOMAN IN BARNUM AND 160 JOURNE
BAILEY'S CIRCUS/
THE MASK IS THE PURE PALLOR OF MARBLE, THE 274 LAZARU
EXPRESSION THAT OF A STATUE OF WOMAN,
MIRIAM IS A SLENDER, DELICATE WOMAN OF THIRTY-- 274 LAZARU
FIVE, DRESSED IN DEEP BLACK.
THE MOTHER IS TALL AND STOUT, OVER SIXTY-FIVE, A 275 LAZARU
GENTLE, SIMPLE WOMAN.
EASIER TO FORGET, TO BECOME ONLY A MAN, THE SON OF289 LAZARU
A WOMAN.
SHE APPEARS OLDER, A WOMAN OVER FORTY-FIVE.) 307 LAZARU
(TO MIRIAM) YOU, WOMAN/ 329 LAZARU
YOU ARE A WOMAN. 342 LAZARU
SO HE LOVES THAT WOMAN$ 342 LAZARU
TO TALK LIKE A GARRULOUS OLD WOMAN, 346 LAZARU
AND LAUGHING DUST, BORN ONCE OF WOMAN ON THIS 348 LAZARU
EARTH, NOW FREE TO DANCE/
AND NOW THAT HAG IS DEAD HE WILL NEED A WOMAN, 351 LAZARU
YOUNG AND BEAUTIFUL.
(THEN HE TURNS AWAY) MY MOTHER, LIVIA, THAT 355 LAZARU
STRONG WOMAN, GIVING BIRTH TO ME,
(HARSHLY) I HATED THAT WOMAN, MY MOTHER, AND I 355 LAZARU
STILL
HOW CRUEL ONLY THAT PASSIONATE, DEEP-BREASTED 355 LAZARU
WOMAN
AS I KNEW SHE MUST, THAT POWERFUL WOMAN WHO BORE 355 LAZARU
ME AS A WEAPON/
MY MOTHER SPOKE TO ME AND SPOKE TO ME AND EVEN 356 LAZARU
WEPT, THAT TALL WOMAN.
THEN THAT PROUD WOMAN, MOTHER, SAW MY HAPPINESS. 356 LAZARU
THAT SUBTLE AND CRAFTY WOMAN/ 356 LAZARU
BELIEVE THAT ONE MAN OR WOMAN IN THE WORLD KNEW 358 LAZARU
AND,
MY BODY, MY HEART--ME, A WOMAN--NOT WOMAN, WOMEN/ 361 LAZARU
POOR WOMAN/ 361 LAZARU
AS YOU LOVED THAT WOMAN THERE (SHE POINTS TO 361 LAZARU
MIRIAM)
AND I LOVE YOU, WOMAN. 361 LAZARU
BUT OLD YOU LOVE HER--OR JUST WOMAN, WIFE AND 361 LAZARU
MOTHER OF MEN$
A WOMAN HAS THROWN HERSELF IN THE FLAMES, CAESAR/ 367 LAZARU
AT YOUR AGE, A WOMAN MUST BECOME RESIGNED TO WAIT 3 MANSNS
UPON EVERY MAN'S PLEASURE.
TEAR, MAY BECOME A WOMAN WHILE SHE'S YOUNG. 5 MANSNS

WOMAN

WOMAN (CONT'D.)
WHO PAYS A DUTY CALL ON A WOMAN OF WHOM HE 11 MANSNS
DISAPPROVES--
WHISTLIN' A LOVE TUNE TO HIMSELF, DREAMIN' OF 19 MANSNS
ANOTHER WOMAN/
AS THE WOMAN ONE HAS ALWAYS DESIRED TO BE. 28 MANSNS
MADE MYSELF A DECENTLY RESIGNED OLD WOMAN. 29 MANSNS
HAS THIS ALIEN WOMAN GONE COMPLETELY INSANE$ 30 MANSNS
RESIGNED OLD WOMAN WHOSE LIFE IS ONLY IN THE MIND$ 36 MANSNS
AS A WOMAN OF BREEDING AND HONOR, YOU HAVE NO 37 MANSNS
POSSIBLE CHOICE.
NOR COULD ANY OTHER WOMAN. 37 MANSNS
I REALLY BELIEVE YOU ARE TRYING TO MAKE A GOOD 39 MANSNS
WOMAN OF ME, NICHOLAS/
WITH MY UNDREAMED-OF TALENTS AS A GOOD WOMAN/ 40 MANSNS
SHE'S A WISE WOMAN AND KNOWS IT'D DO NO GOOD FOR 45 MANSNS
HER TO INTERFERE--
YOU LOOK AN OLD WOMAN NOW. 53 MANSNS
I AM AN OLD WOMAN, SARA. 53 MANSNS
IT'S TRUE YOU HAVE NOTHING IN LIFE, POOR WOMAN. 54 MANSNS
DON'T BE A FRIGHTENED OLD WOMAN/ 70 MANSNS
TO MERGE AND BECOME ONE WOMAN-- 73 MANSNS
A SPIRIT OF WOMAN MADE FLESH AND FLESH OF HER MADE 73 MANSNS
SPIRIT,
WHOSE GREED CAN BE USED TO BRING IN MONEY TO 73 MANSNS
SUPPORT WOMAN/
GOD KNOWS I'VE AS HAPPY A LIFE AS A WOMAN COULD 77 MANSNS
WISH
ALMOST ANY FOOL OF A WOMAN CAN HAVE A SON, 79 MANSNS
IF I THOUGHT YOU WANTED ANOTHER WOMAN--/ 80 MANSNS
IF ANY WOMAN THINKS SHE CAN TAKE YOU FROM ME, 81 MANSNS
THAT YOU APPEAR AS ONE WOMAN TO ME. 82 MANSNS
THE POOR WOMAN/ 86 MANSNS
A FASCINATING GAME--RESEMBLING LOVE, I THINK A 91 MANSNS
WOMAN WILL FIND.
AH, POOR WOMAN. 93 MANSNS
WHERE SHE HAD SEEMED A PREMATURELY OLD, MIDDLE- 95 MANSNS
AGED WOMAN THEN,
POSSESSES THE QUALIFICATIONS I DESIRE IS A YOUNG 97 MANSNS
AND VERY BEAUTIFUL WOMAN.
I WILL NOT HAVE YOU PUT SUCH THOUGHTS IN MY MIND 98 MANSNS
ABOUT A WOMAN TO WHOM I OWE AN
I FEAR YOU ARE MERELY FLATTERING A POOR UGLY OLD 101 MANSNS
WOMAN.
SHE WOULD SEEM TO STEAL ALL IDENTITY FROM YOU-- 105 MANSNS
UNTIL THERE WAS BUT ONE WOMAN--
NOW I WON'T HAVE A SEPARATE MAN'S LIFE FREE OF 120 MANSNS
WOMAN EVEN THERE/
(THINKING--RESENTFULLY.) POOR WOMAN/ 122 MANSNS
TO REAPPEAR AS ONE WOMAN--A WOMAN RECALLING MOTHER125 MANSNS
BUT A STRANGE WOMAN--
THEN YOU ARE THE WOMAN HE BOASTED HE WAS LIVING 132 MANSNS
WITH AS A--
BUT--YOU APPEALED TO ME AS A WOMAN, DIDN'T YOUS 133 MANSNS
YOU'RE A WOMAN, TOO. 133 MANSNS
IF I REFUSED HIM, HE'D ONLY BUY ANOTHER WOMAN. 133 MANSNS
TELL YOU, AS WOMAN TO WOMAN, 135 MANSNS
I DO NOT SEE WHY YOU SHOULD LAUGH--LIKE A COMMON 143 MANSNS
STREET WOMAN.
IT WAS ONLY WHAT EVERY WOMAN THINKS AT TIMES IN 144 MANSNS
HER HEART--
BUT I CANNOT ANSWER A WOMAN--I KNOW IT MUST BE 154 MANSNS
YOUR HUSBAND WHO--
AND LIVE LIKE A DECENT, HONEST WOMAN WORKING IN 156 MANSNS
THE EARTH/
I'VE THE GRANDEST, STRONGEST LOVER THAT WAS EVER 158 MANSNS
OWNED BY A WOMAN/
THE IMPRESSION OF BEING BODILESS, A LITTLE, 161 MANSNS
SKINNY, WITCH-LIKE, OLD WOMAN,
PUSH ME INSIDE ALONE WITH THAT MAD WOMAN I LOCKED 163 MANSNS
IN THERE--
WHEN OUT OF YOUR MAD DREAMS YOU'RE ONLY A POOR 166 MANSNS
LITTLE WIZENED OLD WOMAN
WE COULD HAVE THE STRENGTH NOW AS WE ARE UNITED 171 MANSNS
AGAIN AS ONE WOMAN.
SISTER AND SISTER, ONE WOMAN AND ANOTHER, WITH THE171 MANSNS
WAY SO CLEAR BEFORE US,
GOOD HEAVENS, WHAT WOMAN WOULDN'T BE DISGUSTED 178 MANSNS
WITH THE GREEDY,
ABOUT A WOMAN WHO LOVES YOU SO DEEPLY. 178 MANSNS
MY LOVE, YOU NO LONGER REMEMBER THIS WOMAN, DO 186 MANSNS
YOUS
THIS IS LONG BEFORE ANY OTHER WOMAN. 187 MANSNS
YOU KNOW NO WOMAN COULD LOVE A MAN MORE THAN WHEN 188 MANSNS
SHE GIVES HIM UP TO SAVE HIM/
(BUT NEITHER WOMAN SEEMS TO HEAR.) 188 MANSNS
YOU THE NOBLE LOVING WOMAN/ 189 MANSNS
(REASSURED AND PLEASANT.) I AM NOT MAJESTY, MY 192 MANSNS
POOR WOMAN.
AH, GOD PITY HER, THE POOR WOMAN/ 192 MANSNS
WHY, THANK YOU, GOOD WOMAN. 193 MANSNS
WHERE HE MISTOOK ONE OF THE FEMALE STATUES FOR A 374 MARCOM
REAL WOMAN AND--
BUT, NEVER MIND, ARGHUN OF PERSIA IS A HERO NO 385 MARCOM
WOMAN COULD FAIL TO LOVE.
BUT A WOMAN MAY FEEL LIFE IN THE UNBORN. 397 MARCOM
IT IS THE FACE OF A WOMAN WHO HAS KNOWN REAL 407 MARCOM
SORROW AND SUFFERING.
HE SHALL LOOK INTO MY EYES AND SEE THAT I AM A 414 MARCOM
WOMAN AND BEAUTIFUL/
SEE MY EYES AS THOSE OF A WOMAN AND NOT A 414 MARCOM
PRINCESS/
(AGAIN CLUTCHING A HOPE) A GIRL--A WOMAN--YOU SAW416 MARCOM
IN ME$
IN THIS CONTEMPLATION LIVES THE WOMAN. 417 MARCOM
I DISCOVERED TO BE A FAT WOMAN WITH A PATIENT 424 MARCOM
VIRTUE.
SHE IS ALL WOMAN. 3 MISBEG

WOMAN (CONT'D.)
SHE IS SO OVERSIZE FOR A WOMAN THAT SHE IS ALMOST 3 MISBEG
A FREAK--
THAT'S NICE TALK FOR A WOMAN. 8 MISBEG
I NEVER YET LAID HANDS ON A WOMAN--NOT WHEN I WAS 15 MISBEG
SOBER--
A SWEET WOMAN. 18 MISBEG
I'M AFRAID YOU WERE BORN TO BE A TERRIBLE WANTON 20 MISBEG
WOMAN,
YOU KNOW, AND I KNOW, I'M AN UGLY OVER-GROWN LUMP 28 MISBEG
OF A WOMAN,
MAYBE HE'D LIKE A FINE STRUNG HANDSOME FIGURE UF A 28 MISBEG
WOMAN FOR A CHANGE,
MAYBE YOU HAD NO WOMAN IN BED WITH YOU, FOR A 41 MISBEG
CHANGE.
I'LL WAGER HE'S NO DAMNED GOOD TO A WOMAN. 58 MISBEG
THERE'S NO USE TELLING THE TRUTH TO A BAD-TEMPERED 80 MISBEG
WOMAN IN LOVE.
WILL YOU STOP BLATHERING LIKE AN OLD WOMAN AND 83 MISBEG
TELL ME PLAINLY WHAT HE'S DONE/
AND HIS BROADWAY PRIDE HE'S SO WISE NO WOMAN COULD 96 MISBEG
FOOL HIM.
(AS IF HE HADN'T SPOKEN) WHILE I'M ONLY A BIG, 118 MISBEG
ROUGH, UGLY COW OF A WOMAN.
YOU'RE THE ONLY WOMAN I CARE A DAMN ABOUT. 129 MISBEG
AND BECAUSE YOU'RE THE ONLY WOMAN I'VE EVER MET 145 MISBEG
WHO UNDERSTANDS THE LOUSY ROTTEN
THIS BIG SORROWFUL WOMAN HUGGING A HAGGARD-FACED, 157 MISBEG
WHAT WOMAN DOESN'T SORROW FOR THE MAN SHE LOVED 161 MISBEG
WHO HAS DIED$
MIND YOU, I'M NOT SAYING ANYTHING AGAINST POOR 14 POET
NURA. A SWEETER WOMAN NEVER LIVE
YOU'RE WORSE THAN AN OLD WOMAN FOR GOSSIP. 17 POET
YOU'RE A STRANGE WOMAN, MOTHER. 25 POET
AND A GRAND WOMAN/ 25 POET
FOR WITHOUT IT WHAT AM I AT ALL BUT AN UGLY, FAT 26 POET
WOMAN GETTIN' OLD AND SICK/
YOU'RE SO HANDSOME IN IT STILL, NO WOMAN COULD 39 POET
TAKE HER EYES OFF YOU.
YOU'RE A SWEET, KIND WOMAN, NURA--TOO KIND. 42 POET
SURE YOU WAS THAT HANDSOME, NO WOMAN COULD RESIST 61 POET
YOU.
IGUESSES AT ONCE THIS MUST BE THE WOMAN MICKEY HAD 72 POET
TOLD HER ABOUT.
DAMNED FOOL OF A WOMAN/ 75 POET
WHAT WOMAN WOULD WANT HER SON TO MARRY THE 77 POET
DAUGHTER OF A MAN LIKE--
BUT I WARN YOU IT IS A QUALITY DIFFICULT FOR A 82 POET
WOMAN TO KEEP ON ADMIRING
IF YOU'D LEFT THE SPANISH WOMAN ALONE AND NOT 99 POET
FOUGHT THAT DUEL.
SHE IS A WOMAN OF THE WORLD. 108 POET
(WITH AFFECTED CASUALNESS.) A PRETTY YOUNG WOMAN.118 POET
BE QUIET, WOMAN/ 125 POET
(SUFFLY.) YES, THE HONOR OF HER LOVE TO A WOMAN. 139 POET
HERE I'D GONE TO HIS ROOM WITH MY MIND MADE UP TO 144 POET
BE AS BOLD AS ANY STREET WOMAN
I WAS ONLY AN IGNORANT, SILLY GIRL BOASTING, BUT 147 POET
I'M A WOMAN NOW, MOTHER.
I KNEW NOTHING OF LOVE, UR THE PRIDE A WOMAN CAN 147 POET
TAKE IN GIVING EVERYTHING--
THAT A WOMAN CAN FORGIVE WHATEVER THE MAN SHE 149 POET
LOVES COULD DO AND STILL LOVE HIM.
SURE, I'VE ALWAYS KNOWN YOU'RE THE SWEETEST WOMAN 149 POET
IN THE WORLD, MOTHER.
BUT I NEVER SUSPECTED YOU WERE A WISE WOMAN TOO, 149 POET
SINCE THEY BROUGHT HIM TO--ABOUT THE HARFORD 158 POET
WOMAN--
(STARES AT HER--MOVED.) YOU'RE A STRANGE, NOBLE 182 POET
WOMAN, MOTHER.
SHE IS A THIN, SLOVENLY, WORN-OUT-LOOKING WOMAN OF579 ROPE
ABOUT FORTY WITH A DRAWN,
BUT THE THOUSAND DOLLARS PAW GOT FOR THE MORTGAGE 585 ROPE
JUST BEFORE THAT WOMAN RAN
THE MAN AND WOMAN STARE AT HIM IN PETRIFIED 587 ROPE
AMAZEMENT.)
THE SOUND OF A MAID'S VOICE--A MIDDLE-AGED WOMAN-- 3 STRANG
SHE'S A WOMAN NOW.... 5 STRANG
AND I COULDN'T SHARE A WOMAN--EVEN WITH A GHOST/ 39 STRANG
I'LL SCREAM OUT THE TRUTH ABOUT EVERY WOMAN/ 40 STRANG
TO MAKE GOD A WOMAN/ 42 STRANG
NOT WOMAN.... 43 STRANG
HE'D EVER HAVE COME TO SEE THE POOR WOMAN IF I 50 STRANG
HADN'T INSISTED.
CHARLIE'S LIKE A FUSSY OLD WOMAN ABOUT HIS CAR, 50 STRANG
IT'S AMAZING HOW A LITTLE SHE IS LIKE HIM A STRANGE 50 STRANG
WOMAN
PECULIAR WOMAN.... 53 STRANG
HIS MOTHER IS A TINY WOMAN WITH A FRAIL FIGURE, 53 STRANG
HER HEAD AND FACE,
SHE IS AGAIN THE PREGNANT WOMAN OF ACT THREE BUT 90 STRANG
THIS TIME THERE IS A TRIUMPHANT
HER MIND WAS WANDERING, POOR WOMAN/ 100 STRANG
(WINCING--THINKING) (SHE CAN'T BELIEVE ANY WOMAN14 STRANG
COULD POSSIBLY LOVE ME/...))
I COULDN'T RESPECT A WOMAN WHO HADN'T RESPECTED 115 STRANG
HERSELF,
NO WOMAN LIKES TO LOSE A MAN EVEN WHEN SHE NO 116 STRANG
LONGER LOVES HIM....)
I'M SURE HE NEVER EVEN DARED TO KISS A WOMAN 117 STRANG
EXCEPT HIS MOTHER/....)
(THINKING--TORMENTEDLY) ((THE THOUGHT OF THAT 117 STRANG
WOMAN/...
LIKE A WOMAN.... 124 STRANG
WHAT DO I CARE ABOUT THAT WOMAN$...)) 127 STRANG
I SHOULD BE THE HAPPIEST WOMAN IN THE WORLD/...)) 135 STRANG
((WHY, I SHOULD BE THE PROUDEST WOMAN ON EARTH/...135 STRANG
AT FORTY A WOMAN HAS FINISHED LIVING... 136 STRANG

WOMAN

WOMAN (CONT'D.)
NO WOMAN CAN MAKE A MAN HAPPY WHO HAS NO PURPOSE 139 STRANG
IN LIFE/...
THE DAMNED OLD WOMAN/ 146 STRANG
WHAT WOMAN COULD BE EXPECTED TO LOVE SAM 148 STRANG
PASSIONATELY...
HE THINKS I'M AN OLD WOMAN/ 175 STRANG
I KNOW YOU'RE THE BEST WOMAN THAT EVER LIVED--THE 195 STRANG
BEST OF ALL/
TO A HONEST WOMAN WHAT AIN'T NEVER DONE YOU NO 494 VOYAGE
HARM.
Y'SEE MY OLE MAN WOMAN COME 'ERE TO ENGLAND 502 VOYAGE
WHEN I WAS ON'Y A BABY AN' THEY
SHE IS A WOMAN OF THIRTY. 443 WELDED
IS POSSIBLE FOR A WOMAN WITHOUT HER BEING LOW. 459 WELDED
A PAUSE--THEN THE WOMAN SIGHS AND YAWNS WEARILY--- 471 WELDED
BORED)
THE WOMAN IS FAIRLY YOUNG. 471 WELDED
THE WOMAN INSISTS DULLY) 472 WELDED
(STARING AT HER INTENTLY--SUDDENLY DEEPLY MOVED) 475 WELDED
POOR WOMAN/
(HE SPRINGS UP, HIS FACE DISTURTED, AND CLUTCHES 475 WELDED
THE WOMAN FIERCELY IN HIS ARMS)
YES--SHE WAS A WOMAN. 485 WELDED
(WITH BITTER CYNICISM) A WOMANS 485 WELDED
WOMAN'D
EVEN A WOMAN'D FIND IT HARD TO GIT JEALOUS OF A 497 DIFRNT
WHALE/
WOMAN'S
ON THE SIDEBOARD, A WOMAN'S SEWING BASKET. 535 'ILE
YE'VE BEEN BELOW HERE GOSSIPIN' OLD WOMAN'S TALK 539 'ILE
WITH THAT BOY.
AND "YOU BETTER STAY TO HUME WHERE YOU'VE GOT ALL 546 'ILE
YOUR WOMAN'S COMFORTS."
KITCHEN AGAIN, AND HEAR A WOMAN'S VOICE TALKING TO547 'ILE
ME AND BE ABLE TO TALK TO
(HE RECITES SCORNFULLY) "FOR A WOMAN'S ONLY A 245 AHWILD
WOMAN."
IT'S A WOMAN'S HANDWRITING--NOT SIGNED, OF COURSE.267 AHWILD
LOOKS LIKE A WOMAN'S WRITING, TOO, THE OLD DEVIL/ 5 ANNA
HE LET THEM COUSINS OF MY OLD WOMAN'S KEEP ME ON 18 ANNA
THEIR FARM.
AIN'T THAT JUST LIKE A FOOL WOMAN'S QUESTIONS 94 BEYOND
AIN'T THAT A WOMAN'S WAY U' SEEIN' THINGS FOR YOUS 95 BEYOND
WELL, MAYBE A WOMAN'S EYES IS SHARPER IN SUCH 98 BEYOND
THINGS, BUT--
INTERRUPTED AT INTERVALS BY A WOMAN'S IRRITATED 112 BEYOND
VOICE
A WOMAN'S GOT T' HEV A HUM/ 222 DESIRE
BEIN' MARRIED TO ALF ROGERS FOR FIVE YEARS'D 539 DIFRNT
PIZEN' ANY WOMAN'S LIFE.
HOUND LIKE A WOMAN'S. 474 DYNAMO
A*' ALL DAT OLE WOMAN'S TALKS 185 EJONES
(A WOMAN'S FIGURE DRESSED IN BLACK, HEAVILY 107 ELECTR
VEILED,
SHE DOESN'T WANT ME NOW--A COWARD HIDING BEHIND A 107 ELECTR
WOMAN'S SKIRTS/
(DERISIVELY) "YOU LIKE YOUR BOTTLE 'CEPTIN' WHEN 130 ELECTR
YOUR OLD WOMAN'S GOT HER EYE ON
I'D LET EZRA'S WOMAN'S GHOST SET ON MY LAP. 130 ELECTR
(WITH A GROTESQUE IMITATION OF A WOMAN'S VOICE) 230 HA APE
OUTA THE LITTLE WOMAN'S PURSE, HUGHIE 22 HUGHIE
WELL, ANYWAY, HUGHIE SNEAKED THE TWO BUCKS BACK IN 22 HUGHIE
THE LITTLE WOMAN'S PURSE
AND THE SOUND OF A MAN'S AND WOMAN'S ARGUING 615 ICEMAN
VOICES.)
WHAT IS A MAN WITHOUT A GOOD WOMAN'S LOVES 158 JOURNE
TO BLESS ME WITH HER WOMAN'S LOVE. 159 JOURNE
DISCUSSING AN OLD WOMAN'S VANITY. 6 MANSNS
WELL, A WOMAN'S LOVE IS JEALOUSLY POSSESSIVE--OR 7 MANSNS
SO I HAVE READ--
I HAVE MY HONOR AND IT'S A TRUE WOMAN'S HONOR THAT
YOU'D GIVE YOUR SOUL TO KNOW/
HOW CAN A MAN KNOW ABOUT THE TRUTH OF THE LIES IN 20 MANSNS
A WOMAN'S DREAMS?
THAT I MIGHT HAVE FOUND ANOTHER WOMAN'S BODY 80 MANSNS
I UNDERSTAND EVERYTHING A WOMAN'S LOVE COULD 192 MANSNS
POSSIBLY COMPEL HER TO DESIRE.
SURE, THAT'S EVERY WOMAN'S SCHEME SINCE THE WORLD 28 MISBEG
WAS CREATED.
(DIMLY CONSCIOUS UP A WOMAN'S BODY--CYNICALLY) 165 MISBEG
WITH NO WOMAN'S COMPANY BUT THE WHORES WAS HELPIN' 14 POET
HIM RUIN THE ESTATE.
APPEALING FOR A WOMAN'S UNDERSTANDING AND LOVING 70 POET
(COMPASSION.)
I SHOULD GRANT IT IS A PRETTY WOMAN'S PRIVILEGE TO 76 POET
BE ALWAYS RIGHT
SOME WOMAN'S SICKNESS... 67 STRANG
THIS WOMAN'S DUTY IS TO SAVE HER HUSBAND AND 87 STRANG
HERSELF
SHE'S JUST PASSED THROUGH A CRUCIAL PERIOD IN A 178 STRANG
WOMAN'S
HE HAS BECOME THAT STRANGER, ANOTHER WOMAN'S 190 STRANG
LOVER....)
THEN THE DOOR IS OPENED AND A WOMAN'S FIGURE IS 470 WELDED
SILHOUETTED
HE STANDS IN THE DOORWAY WATCHING EACH MOVEMENT OF471 WELDED
THE WOMAN'S
WOMANHOOD
NOR AT THE OUTRAGING OF DEFENSELESS WOMANHOOD. 244 HA APE
BOYHOOD--OR GIRLHOOD--, YOUTH, YOUNG MANHOOD--OR 273 LAZARU
WOMANHOOD--,
MANHOOD--OR WOMANHOOD--, MIDDLE AGE, MATURITY AND 273 LAZARU
OLD AGE,
OR WOMANHOOD--, 285 LAZARU
IN THE PERIOD OF WOMANHOOD IN THE PROUD, SELF- 336 LAZARU
RELIANT TYPE.
YOUTH, AND YOUNGMANHOOD--OR WOMANHOOD-- 336 LAZARU

1816

WOMANHOOD (CONT'D.)
NINA IS THIRTY-FIVE, IN THE FULL BLOOM OF HER 137 STRANG
WOMANHOOD.
WOMANLESS
YOU'RE GHOSTLESS AND WOMANLESS--AND AS SLEEK AND 52 STRANG
SATISFIED AS A PET SEAL/
WOMANLY
READY FOR A WEEP ON ANY OLD WOMANLY BOSOM. 159 JOURNE
WHILE WE WATCHED WITH GRATIFIED WOMANLY PRIDE AND 171 MANSNS
I LAUGHED AND GOADED HIM ON/
KINDLY BUT LAYING DOWN THE LAW TO WOMANLY 157 STRANG
WEAKNESS)
WOMB
BUT DEATH IS WHAT THE DEAD KNOW, THE WARM, DARK 562 DAYS
WOMB OF NOTHINGNESS--
THEN IT GREW YOUNGER AND I FELT AT LAST IT HAD345 LAZARU
RETURNED TO MY WOMB--
OH, IF MEN WOULD BUT INTERPRET THAT FIRST CRY OF 352 LAZARU
MAN FRESH FROM THE WOMB
LIKE THE FLIGHT OF HIS SOUL BACK INTO THE WOMB OF 371 LAZARU
INFINITY)
THE LIGHT PASSED INTO THE WOMB OF MAYA, AND SHE 372 MARCOM
BORE A SON WHO,
CONTAIN THE HARMONY OF WOMB AND GRAVE WITHIN YOU/ 435 MARCOM
WOMEN
NOW, YOU WOMEN STOP PICKING ON SID. 190 AHWILD
I'LL BEAT IT AND LEAVE YOU ALONE--SEE IF THE WOMEN200 AHWILD
FOLKS ARE READY UPSTAIRS.
(HE AND THE TWO WOMEN MOVE OFF THROUGH THE FRONT 210 AHWILD
PARLOR.)
HIS TAKING UP WITH BAD WOMEN. 213 AHWILD
TO BE GOOD MEN AND WOMEN. 214 AHWILD
YOU KNOW WHAT THEY SAY ABOUT WOMEN AND TROLLEY 216 AHWILD
CARS, AUNT LILY.
THAT'S ALL YOU WOMEN THINK OF/ 216 AHWILD
AND EGGS HIM ON AND RUINS HIS LIFE--LIKE ALL WOMEN235 AHWILD
LOVE TO RUIN MEN'S LIVES--
BUT I LEARNED ABOUT WOMEN FROM HER.= 244 AHWILD
OH, I KNOW HE'S BEEN WITH ONE OF THOSE BAD WOMEN, 262 AHWILD
I KNOW HE HAS---MY RICHARD/
YOU KNOW, I WAS AFRAID HE'D BEEN WITH ONE OF THOSE266 AHWILD
BAD WOMEN.
DAMN WOMEN, ANYWAY/ 266 AHWILD
ABOUT WOMEN AND ALL THOSE THINGS. 267 AHWILD
AGAIN, (THE MISQUOTES CYNICALLY) =WOMEN NEVER KNOW274 AHWILD
WHEN THE CURTAIN HAS FALLEN.
IF WOMEN ARE TOO SURE OF YOU, THEY TREAT YOU LIKE 277 AHWILD
SLAVES.
SO I SAID TO MYSELF, I'M THROUGH WITH WOMEN. 282 AHWILD
IF HE'D ONLY CHOOSE SOME OTHER SUBJECTS BESIDES 288 AHWILD
LOOSE WOMEN.
WELL, THERE ARE A CERTAIN CLASS OF WOMEN-- 295 AHWILD
I NEVER HAD ANYTHING TO DO WITH SUCH WOMEN, 295 AHWILD
THE TWO WOMEN SIZE EACH OTHER UP WITH FRANK 14 ANNA
STARES.
(HEN HASTILY) BUT SAY--LISTEN--DID ALL THE WOMEN 28 ANNA
OF THE FAMILY MARRY SAILORS?
FUR THE LIKE OF THEM COWS ON THE WATERFRONT IS THE 34 ANNA
ONLY WOMEN I'VE MET UP WITH
(EARNESTLY) THIS IS LET I'M TELLING YOU ABOUT THE 34 ANNA
WOMEN)
THE ONLY WOMEN YOU'D MEET IN THE PORTS OF THE 37 ANNA
WORLD WHO'D BE WILLING TO SPEAK
YOU A KIND WORD ISN'T WOMEN AT ALL. 37 ANNA
ALL THE WOMEN HAVE MARRIED SAILORS, TOO. 37 ANNA
I'M THINKING YOU'RE THE LIKE OF THEM WOMEN CAN'T 55 ANNA
MAKE UP THEIR MIND TILL THEY'RE
AND WOMEN, TOO, MAYBE, AND I'M THINKING I'D CHANGE 74 ANNA
YOU TO A NEW WOMAN ENTIRELY,
WEAK-WILLED CRITTER TO BE PERMITTIN' A BOY--AND 102 BEYOND
WOMEN, TOO--
BOTH WOMEN ARE DRESSED IN BLACK. 113 BEYOND
(THE TWO WOMEN SIT IN SILENCE FOR A MOMENT. 116 BEYOND
(THE TWO WOMEN REMAIN SILENT FOR A TIME STARING 152 BEYOND
DEJECTEDLY AT THE STOVE.)
SHE'LL BE BRINGIN' SOME BLACK WOMEN WITH HER THIS 456 CARIBE
TIME.
(THE FOUR WOMEN 463 CARIBE
(POMPOUSLY) GENTLEMEN DON'T HIT WOMEN. 468 CARIBE
BELLA IS THE ONLY ONE OF THE WOMEN WHO IS 470 CARIBE
ABSOLUTELY SOBER.
BUT THE LITTLE GROUP OF WOMEN ON THE HATCH.. 472 CARIBE
THE WOMEN SHRIEK AND TAKE REFUGE ON TOP OF THE 472 CARIBE
HATCH.
THE MATE LOOKS UP AND SEES THE WOMEN ON THE HATCH 473 CARIBE
FOR THE FIRST TIME.)
(TO THE WOMEN, HARSHLY) YOU NEEDN'T GO TO THE 473 CARIBE
SKIPPER FOR ANY MONEY.
NOT TO MENTION ALL HIS AFFAIRS WITH WOMEN. 498 DAYS
THEY ARE LIKE EXHAUSTED WOMEN 202 DESIRE
BEING SEA-FARING MEN, AWAY FROM THEIR WOMEN FOLKS 495 DIFRNT
MOST OF THE TIME.
ONY--WOMEN FOLKS AIN'T GOT TO KNOW EVERYTHING, 501 DIFRNT
HAVE THEY&
THEM NIGGER WOMEN. 502 DIFRNT
NATIVE BROWN WOMEN, ALL NAKED A'MOST, COME ROUND 502 DIFRNT
TO MEET YEH
WHY, THEM KIND O' WOMEN AIN'T WOMEN LIKE YOU. 504 DIFRNT
FROM WHAT I HEARS OF THEM BROWN WOMEN, 510 DIFRNT
AND THEM NATIVE WOMEN--THEY'RE DIFFERENT. 515 DIFRNT
A MAN DON'T THINK OF 'EM AS WOMEN--LIKE YOU. 515 DIFRNT
(STERNLY) THE KIND OF WOMEN I'VE SEED IN CITIES 536 DIFRNT
--HEARIN' IT--
AND IN THE CITIES NOW ALL THE WOMEN WEARS IT. 536 DIFRNT
THREE MEN OF DIFFERENT AGES, TWO WOMEN, ONE WITH A197 EJONES
BABY IN HER ARMS, NURSING.
PASSING BEHIND THE LILAC CLUMP WITHOUT HAVING 9 ELECTR
NOTICED AMES AND THE WOMEN.)

WOMEN (CONT'D.)

YOU SAID THEY WERE LIKE BEAUTIFUL, PALE WOMEN TO 23 ELECTR YOU.

WOMEN ARE JEALOUS OF SHIPS. 23 ELECTR

THE NAKED NATIVE WOMEN. 24 ELECTR

(THE THREE MEN JOIN THE WOMEN BY THE BENCH, BORDEN 69 ELECTR TALKING AS THEY COME)

OFF LEFT, HILLS GOING WITH THE TWO WOMEN. 71 ELECTR

WOMEN IMMEDIATELY WANT TO MOTHER HIM. 74 ELECTR

OF THE THREE PORTRAITS ON THE OTHER WALLS, TWO ARE 79 ELECTR OF WOMEN--

THEY OUGHT TO MAKE THE WOMEN TAKE THE MEN'S PLACE 82 ELECTR FOR A MONTH OR SO.

THEY ONLY MADE ME SICK--AND THE NAKED WOMEN 145 ELECTR DISGUSTED ME.

PROBABLY HE'D LIVED WITH ONE OF THE NATIVE WOMEN/ 154 ELECTR (MOCKING) AREN'T WOMEN LOYAL--TO THEIR VANITY AND287 GGBROW THEIR OTHER THINGS//

WHAT IS IT THAT MAKES DION SO ATTRACTIVE TO 289 GGBROW WOMEN--

ESPECIALLY CERTAIN TYPES OF WOMEN, IF YOU'LL 289 GGBROW PARDON ME$

THE WOMEN ARE ROUGED, CALCIMINED, DYED, 236 HA APE OVERDRESSED TO THE NTH DEGREE.

VOTES FOR WOMEN/ 236 HA APE

THEN AT A CRY FROM ONE OF THE WOMEN, THEY ALL 238 HA APE SCURRY TO THE FURRIER'S WINDOW.)

(THE WHOLE CROWD OF MEN AND WOMEN CHORUS AFTER HER238 HA APE IN THE SAME TONE OF AFFECTED

AND BUMS AND FREE WOMEN PLOT TO OVERTHROW OUR 649 ICEMAN GOVERNMENT.

MY PLAYING AROUND WITH WOMEN, FOR INSTANCE. 712 ICEMAN

YOU'RE TAKIN' MORE THAN A PAIR AV AULD WOMEN 518 INZONE WOULD BE STANDIN' IN THE ROAD,

ATTRACTIVE TO WOMEN AND POPULAR WITH MEN. 19 JOURNE

IF THEY ARE TO BE GOOD CHILDREN, AND WOMEN NEED 88 JOURNE HOMES.

WOMEN USED TO WAIT AT THE STAGE DOOR JUST TO SEE 105 JOURNE HIM COME OUT.

BLESSED ART THOU AMONG WOMEN.= 107 JOURNE

THEY'RE INNOCENT WOMEN, ANYWAY, WHEN IT COMES TO 138 JOURNE THE WORLD.

CHRIST, I'D NEVER DREAMED BEFORE THAT ANY WOMEN 163 JOURNE BUT WHORES TOOK DOPE/

I WISED YOU UP ABOUT WOMEN, SO YOU'D NEVER BE A 164 JOURNE FALL GUY.

WHERE THERE IS A CROWD OF WOMEN. 273 LAZARU

AND ALL THE WOMEN SCREAMED/ 277 LAZARU

THE CROWDS OF MEN AND WOMEN ON EACH SIDE PUSH INTO278 LAZARU THE ROOM TO STARE AT HIM.

EACH IS COMPOSED ABOUT EQUALLY OF MEN AND WOMEN, 282 LAZARU FORTY-NINE IN EACH.

THERE IS A CONFUSED TUMULT OF YELLS, GROANS, 290 LAZARU CURSES, THE SHRIEKS OF WOMEN,

(FROM EACH SIDE MEN AND WOMEN COME FORWARD TO 292 LAZARU IDENTIFY AND MOURN THEIR DEAD.

WOMEN HAVE LOVED HIGH-FLIERS AND WE ARE EAGLES OF 314 LAZARU ROME/

STACCATO LAUGHTER OF WOMEN AND YOUTHS. 326 LAZARU

NOT GO TO SUCH PAINS TO FRIGHTEN WOMEN. 328 LAZARU

RECLINING ON THE COUCHES ON THE RIGHT ARE YOUNG 336 LAZARU WOMEN AND GIRLS.

THE WOMEN ARE DRESSED AS MALES IN CRIMSON OR DEEP 336 LAZARU PURPLE.

AND YET, ON OUR JOURNEY, WHOLE HERDS OF WOMEN-- 341 LAZARU

MY BODY, MY HEART--ME, A WOMAN--NOT WOMAN, WOMEN/ 361 LAZARU

THE WOMEN WHO HATE ME FOR MY WIT AND BEAUTY. 5 MANSNS

AH, YES, IF ONLY MEN--AND WOMEN--WERE NOT MEN AND 9 MANSNS WOMEN/

WITH MEN AND WOMEN WHAT THEY ARE. 46 MANSNS

WHAT DO YOU KNOW OF WOMEN$ 65 MANSNS

AS IF I REALLY DESIRED TWO DAMNED POSSESSIVE WOMEN 74 MANSNS

THE TWO WOMEN WEAR SEMI-FORMAL EVENING GOWNS, 117 MANSNS DEBORAH'S ALL WHITE.

I AM WHERE I BELONG BETWEEN THEM--TWO WOMEN-- 118 MANSNS OPPOSITES--

THE TWO WOMEN TURN TO STARE AT HIM, WITH A 119 MANSNS STIRRING OF SUSPICION AND RESENTMENT.

THE TWO WOMEN SIT WITH CLASPED HANDS, THEIR FACES 124 MANSNS RELIEVED.

YOU'RE PRETENDING TO LOVE YOUR WOMEN AND CHILDREN 154 MANSNS BUT BE FORCED TO COME BACK AFTER HE'D FACED HIS 155 MANSNS WOMEN AGAIN.

THE FACES OF THE TWO WOMEN HAVE HARDENED INTO A 172 MANSNS DEADLY ENMITY.)

(HE BEGINS TO SOB EXHAUSTEDLY--THE TWO WOMEN SIT 174 MANSNS TOGETHER.

(THE TWO WOMEN SPRING TO THEIR FEET. 176 MANSNS

THE WOMEN WEAR COTTON DRAWERS. 365 MARCOM

THE WOMEN DO ALL THE BUYING AND SELLING. 373 MARCOM

WITH THEIR WOMEN BESIDE THEM. 377 MARCOM

(WITH A SIGH) A QUEEN MAY BE ONLY A WOMEN WHO IS 385 MARCOM UNHAPPY.

MUST WOMEN, INCLUDING KUKACHIN, LOVE CHILDREN-- 389 MARCOM AND ALL WOMEN MUST TAKE ACTING SERIOUSLY IN ORDER 389 MARCOM TO LOVE AT ALL.

(PROUDLY AND FUSSILY) YOU CAN'T HAVE WOMEN AROUN0406 MARCOM

IN THE SHADOW OF THE HIGHEST DECK IN REAR HER 407 MARCOM WOMEN-IN-WAITING ARE IN A GROUP.

A HERO IS MERCIFUL TO WOMEN. 410 MARCOM

THE WOMEN COME OUT TO ATTEND THE PRINCESS. 417 MARCOM

I BE ALLOWED TO REMAIN ON BOARD ALONG WITH MY 419 MARCOM WOMEN$

(THEN JEALOUSLY) BUT I KNOW ALL THE HEATHEN WOMEN430 MARCOM

(THEN WORRIEDLY) YOU SAID THERE WERE ONE OR TWO 430 MARCOM WOMEN$

THEY ARE FOLLOWED BY THE CHORUS OF NINE SINGERS, 433 MARCOM FIVE MEN AND FOUR WOMEN.

WOMEN (CONT'D.)

WITH ONE MOTION, THE WOMEN THROW THEMSELVES 433 MARCOM PROSTRATE ON THE FLOOR.

THESE ARE MASKED, THE MEN WITH A MALE MASK OF 433 MARCOM GRIEF, THE WOMEN WITH A FEMALE.

IMMEDIATELY THE WOMEN ALL TURN WITH ARMS 433 MARCOM OUTSTRETCHED TOWARD THE CATAFALQUE.

A MUFFLED SOUND OF SOBBING COMES FROM THE 435 MARCOM PROSTRATE WOMEN.

THEY ARE FOLLOWED BY THE NOBLES AND OFFICIALS WITH437 MARCOM THEIR WOMEN COMING AFTER.

IT IS HIS HUMOR AND CHARM WHICH HAVE KEPT HIM 37 MISBEG ATTRACTIVE TO WOMEN.

BECAUSE YOUR FANCY IS FOR DAINTY DOLLS OF WOMEN$ 42 MISBEG

FOR ALL HIS BROADWAY WISDOM ABOUT WOMEN, 87 MISBEG

I KNOW HIS WEAKNESS, AND IT'S HIS VANITY ABOUT HIS 92 MISBEG WOMEN.

IT'S HIS VANITY ABOUT WOMEN. 96 MISBEG

DIFFERENT FROM ALL THE OTHER NIGHTS YOU'D SPENT 171 MISBEG WITH WOMEN.

IT'S NO NEWS ABOUT HIS WOMEN. 12 POET

AT HOME, THE ONLY WOMEN HE'D KNOWN WAS WHORES. 13 POET

(LOWERING HIS VOICE.) TELL ME, HAS HE DONE ANY 13 POET RAMPAGIN' WID WOMEN HERE$

YOU'D NIVIR DOUBT ANY BOAST HE MAKES ABOUT 13 POET FIGHTIN' AND WOMEN.

THEY KNOW NOTHING OF WOMEN. 63 POET

I'VE KNOWN TOO MANY WOMEN-- (IN A RAGE.) =ABSURD 75 POET PERFORMANCE,= WAS ITS

THE HARTFORD PURSUIT OF FREEDOM IMPOSED UPON THE 83 POET WOMEN WHO SHARED THEIR LIVES.

I NEVER HAD AN EYE FOR SKINNY, PALE SNIPS OF 90 POET WOMEN.

AND WOMEN, TOO/ 102 POET

SHE'S A TRUER-BORN, WELL-BRED LADY THAN ANY OF 106 POET THEIR WOMEN--

THE TWO WOMEN WATCH HIM, NORA FRIGHTENED, 124 POET

HIS MANNER IS BASHFUL WITH WOMEN 28 STRANG

THERE IS A QUALITY ABOUT HIM, PROVOKING AND 33 STRANG DISTURBING TO WOMEN.

ATTRACTIVE TO WOMEN, I DARE SAY....) 33 STRANG

OF COURSE, WOMEN WOULD SEE HIM THAT WAY. 42 STRANG

ALL I MEANT WAS THAT GHOSTS REMIND ME OF MEN'S 51 STRANG SMART CRACK ABOUT WOMEN.

ALL THE OTHER WOMEN IN THE WORLD AREN'T WORTH YOUR 70 STRANG LITTLE FINGER/

I HAVE EXPERIENCED PLEASURE WITH A NUMBER OF WOMEN 86 STRANG I DESIRED BUT NEVER LOVED...

AS IF WOMEN LOVED YOU FOR THAT/...... 116 STRANG

I DON'T WANT NINA TO THINK I'VE HAD NO EXPERIENCE$116 STRANG WITH WOMEN.....))

WOMEN LIKE ME... 120 STRANG

OTHER WOMEN... 129 STRANG

OTHER WOMEN--THEY ONLY MADE ME LOVE YOU MORE/ 130 STRANG

TOO MANY WOMEN... 134 STRANG

IT USED TO BE DRINK AND WOMEN, NOW IT'S TO THE 143 STRANG STATION.

(GRINNING) NEVER MIND THE WOMEN, GORDON. 154 STRANG

WHAT IDIOTS WOMEN MAKE OF THEMSELVES ABOUT THESE 168 STRANG GORDONS/...

AND THESE ARE MEN AND WOMEN AND SUNS AND DAUGHTERS176 STRANG WHOSE HEARTS ARE WEAK

(THE TWO WOMEN, FREDA AND KATE, ENTER FROM THE 499 VOYAGE LEFT.

THE WOMEN COME FORWARD TO THE TABLE, WEARING 499 VOYAGE THEIR BEST SET SMILES.)

(IVAN SEEMS TO SEE THE WOMEN FOR THE FIRST TIME 500 VOYAGE AND GRINS FOOLISHLY.)

JOE, NICK, AND THE WOMEN LOOK AT THE MONEY WITH 500 VOYAGE GREEDY EYES.

THE WOMEN GIGGLE. 500 VOYAGE

WHY, MY WOMEN USED TO BE--DEATH MASKS. 449 WELDED

THAT JOHN HAD TO BRIBE WOMEN TO LOVE HIM. 456 WELDED

THE OTHER WOMEN HE HELPED COULD HARDLY CLAIM HE 456 WELDED HAD REMAINED--

NOW I KNOW WHY THE WOMEN IN YOUR PLAYS ARE SU 459 WELDED HIDDEN/

HE'S GONE TO ONE OF THOSE WOMEN HE LIVED WITH 468 WELDED BEFORE-- (LAUGHING HARSHLY) NO/

WOMEN'S

(THE SOUND OF WOMEN'S VOICES CAN BE HEARD TALKING 461 CARIBE AND LAUGHING.)

WHAT THE HELL DO I KNOW O' WOMEN'S FIXIN'S ANYHOW$537 DFRNT

(JEERINGLY) YOUR HELL AND GOD MEAN NO MORE TO ME 442 DYNAMO THAN OLD WOMEN'S NONSENSE WHEN

MAYBE THAT'S JUST OLD WOMEN'S NONSENSE, LIKE FIFE 444 DYNAMO SAYS.

THEY ARE DRESSED IN WOMEN'S ROBES OF PALE 336 LAZARU HELIOTROPE.

WHAT MADE THEIR PETTY SENTIMENTAL WOMEN'S WORLD 120 MANSNS

AS HIS THOUGHTS HAVE PROGRESSED THE EXPRESSIONS ON126 MANSNS THE TWO WOMEN'S FACES

(THE TWO WOMEN'S FACES GROW COLD AND HOSTILE AND 130 MANSNS DEFIANT.

WON

OH, I WON ALL RIGHT/ 156 BEYOND

I'VE WON TO MY TRIP--THE RIGHT OF RELEASE--BEYOND 168 BEYOND THE HORIZON/

AS SHE SEES HE IS DEFINITELY WON OVER NOW. 42 ELECTR

I'VE LOVED, LUSTED, WON AND LOST, SANG AND WEPT/ 296 GGBROW

YOU THINK YOU'VE WON, DO YOU--THAT I'VE GOT TO 307 GGBROW VANISH INTO YOU IN ORDER TO LIVE$

THE ARTIFICIALITIES THAT ENERGY HAD WON FOR ITSELF218 HA APE IN THE SPENDING.)

I AIN'T WON NOTHIN' SINCE HUGHIE WAS TOOK TO THE 18 HUGHIE HOSPITAL.

YOU WON THE MONEY GAMBLING, I SUPPOSE-- 34 HUGHIE

WON

WON (CONT'D.)
BUER AND BRITON, EACH FOUGHT FAIRLY AND PLAYED THES99 ICEMAN
GAME TILL THE BETTER MAN WON.
I WOULD HAVE WON THE ELECTION EASY, TOO. 603 ICEMAN
LUVE ALWAYS WON. 713 ICEMAN
THE STANDARD OIL MILLIONAIRE, AND WON A GLORIOUS 23 JOURNE
VICTORY.
AND I HAVE WON THE DECIDING VICTORY OVER THEM/ 129 MANSNS
YOU COULD REALLY HAVE WON THEN BUT YOU ARE WEAKLY 169 MANSNS
SENTIMENTAL AND PITIFUL.
(DULLY.) WE HAVE WON, SARA. 175 MANSNS
YOUR SKIN IS LIKE SILVER IN THE MOON YOUR EYES ARE360 MARCOM
BLACK PEARLS. I HAVE WON.
I HAVE WON A CONVERT. 402 MARCOM
I PLAYED MY SYSTEM, BUT I FOUND I DIDN'T CARE IF 1143 MISBEG
WON OR LOST.
SHE WON/... 97 STRANG
SO THAT WHEN THE RACE WAS OVER AND THEY'D WON 153 STRANG
GORDON FAINTED
HE'S WON/ 182 STRANG
HE'S WON/ 182 STRANG
HE'S WON/ 182 STRANG
HE'S WON/ 182 STRANG
I KNEW I HAD FINALLY WON--THROUGH YOUR WORK/ 447 WELDED

WONDER
'TIS A GOD'S WONDER WE'RE NOT A SHIP FULL OF 538 'ILE
CRAZED PEOPLE--
BUT THIS LOOKS--I WONDER IF HE IS HANGING AROUND 205 AHWILD
HER TO SEE WHAT HE CAN GET&
(THEN SUDDENLY) MY GOODNESS, I WONDER WHAT TIME 271 AHWILD
IT'S GETTING TO BE.
WHO COULD IT HAVE BEEN, I WONDERS 272 AHWILD
AND I WONDER IF MURIEL WOULD THINK YOU WERE SO 294 AHWILD
FINE.
SHE IS STARING OUT INTO THE FOG ASTERN WITH AN 25 ANNA
EXPRESSION OF WONDER.
I DON'T WONDER YOU ALWAYS BEEN A SAILOR. 26 ANNA
(HE OPENS HIS EYES AND BLINKS UP AT HER WITH VAGUE 33 ANNA
WONDER.)
NO WONDER HE WAS MAD. 51 ANNA
WONDER YOU WASN'T PULLED IN. 70 ANNA
(MUSINGLY) I WONDER IF YOU DO, REALLY. 84 BEYOND
AND I USED TO WONDER WHAT THE SEA WAS LIKE, 89 BEYOND
I WONDER IF I OUGHT TO/ 90 BEYOND
WONDER WHAT'S HAPPENED TO ROBERTS 96 BEYOND
(AFTER A PAUSE) WHAT'S COME OVER ANDY TONIGHT, I 97 BEYOND
WONDERS
(MUSINGLY) I WONDER IF HE'S CHANGED MUCH. 115 BEYOND
IT'S A WONDER ROB WOULDN'T TRY TO GET TO MEALS ON 117 BEYOND
TIME ONCE IN A WHILE.
(FROWNING) WHAT'S THE TROUBLE NOW, I WONDERS 123 BEYOND
I WONDER IF THE OLD CHUMP'S CHANGED MUCHS 125 BEYOND
FROM ALL THE FREEDOM AND WONDER OF LIFE/ 126 BEYOND
IT WOULD SICKEN YOU FOR LIFE WITH THE -WONDER AND 132 BEYOND
MYSTERY- YOU USED TO DREAM OF.
HUM'D HE COME TO GET BACK SO SOON, I WONDERS 140 BEYOND
WHAT TIME IS IT NOW, I WONDERS 142 BEYOND
NO WONDER HE'S DYING/ 164 BEYOND
I WONDER NOW, DO THEY CALL THAT KEENIN' A SONG& 456 CARIBE
I'M AFRAID SHE MIGHT BEGIN TO WONDER-- 494 DAYS
NOW I WONDER WHAT HIDES BEHIND THAT SOMEWHERE& 499 DAYS
BUT I DID WONDER A LITTLE AT YOUR SUDDEN COMPLETE 516 DAYS
IGNORING OF OUR EXISTENCE.
THE OLD PERFECT MARRIAGE THAT'S BEEN THE WONDER OF516 DAYS
US ALL, EH&
BUT DO YOU KNOW ANY ONE, I WONDERS 517 DAYS
WHY DID I HAVE TO TELL YOU, I WONDERS 522 DAYS
WONDER IF HE KNOWED WE WAS WANTIN' FUR CALIFORNI- 210 DESIRE
A&
(A PAUSE--RESTLESSLY) SPEAKING O' MILK, WONDER 218 DESIRE
HOW EBEN'S MANAGIN'S
WONDER WHAT EBEN'S A-DOIN'S 248 DESIRE
AND A SNEAK, AND I DON'T WONDER YOU FEEL GUILTY IN446 DYNAMO
GOD'S SIGHT/
NO WONDER YOUR SON IS A SAP/ 451 DYNAMO
WHAT IS DEATH, LIKE, I WONDERS 454 DYNAMO
POOR RUBE/...WHAT'S HE BEEN DOING ALL THIS TIME, 1455 DYNAMO
WONDERS...)
WELL, IT'S A DAMN WONDER WE DIDN'T ALL DIE OF IT 464 DYNAMO
YEARS AGO, LIVING IN THIS DUMP/
NO WONDER HE'S SICK OF ME/... 480 DYNAMO
I WONDER IF DEY'S STARTIN' AFTER MES 188 EJONES
WONDER DEY WOULDN'T GIT SICK O' BEATIN' DAT DRUM. 188 EJONES
WHAT TIME'S IT GITTIN' TO BE, I WONDERS 191 EJONES
I DON'T WONDER YOU'RE SURPRISED/ 32 ELECTR
THAT'S WHAT I WONDER/ 48 ELECTR
(THEY BOTH STARE AT HIM, LAVINIA IN SURPRISE, 48 ELECTR
CHRISTINE IN UNEASY WONDER.
I DON'T WONDER SHE-- 73 ELECTR
NO WONDER HE'S DEAD/ 88 ELECTR
SO DO YOU WONDER I LAUGH/ 96 ELECTR
WHO WITS IT, I WONDERS 106 ELECTR
I WONDER HOW ORIN IS. 137 ELECTR
NO WONDER ORIN KILLED HIMSELF--GOD, I--I HOPE 177 ELECTR
YOU'LL BE PUNISHED--I--/
WHERE IS ORIN NOW, I WONDERS 263 GGBROW
I WONDER IF ODIN--I SAW HIM LOOKING AT ME AGAIN 263 GGBROW
TONIGHT--OH, I WONDER.../
NO WONDER YOU HID/ 299 GGBROW
WONDER WHAT'S GOT INTO HIM THE LAST MONTHS 302 GGBROW
ALL HE'D SAY WAS -GOSH, ERIE, NO WONDER YOU TOOK 20 HUGHIE
UP GAMBLING.
I DON'T WONDER YOU NEVER WORRY ABOUT MONEY, WITH 21 HUGHIE
YOUR LUCK--
(HE CHUCKLES.) NO WONDER HE LIKED ME, HUHS 28 HUGHIE
(HE LAUGHS) I WONDER WHAT'S HAPPENED TO HIM. 580 ICEMAN
(ALOUD TO HIMSELF, WITH A MUZZY WONDER) 598 ICEMAN

WONDER (CONT'D.)
(ALOUD TO HIMSELF MORE THAN TO PARRITT--WITH 608 ICEMAN
IRRITABLE WONDER)
IT'S A WONDER HE DIDN'T BURRY A SALVATION ARMY 617 ICEMAN
UNIFORM AND SHOW UP IN THAT/
WHAT MADE ME SAY THAT, I WONDER. 680 ICEMAN
CURA SPEAKS WITH A TIRED WONDER AT HERSELF RATHER 700 ICEMAN
THAN RESENTMENT TOWARD HIM)
(LOOKING DOWN AT THE BOX) HOW'LL WE BE OPENIN' 525 INZONE
THIS, I WONDERS
WHY DID THE BOYS STAY IN THE DINING ROOM, I 15 JOURNE
WONDERS
WHAT'S THE JOKE, I WONDERS 18 JOURNE
IT'S A WONDER YOUR FATHER WOULDN'T LOOK AT HIS 51 JOURNE
WATCH ONCE IN A WHILE.
NO WONDER MY FEET KILL ME EACH NIGHT. 53 JOURNE
NO WONDER--/ 113 JOURNE
WHERE IS IT NOW, I WONDERS 119 JOURNE
WHERE IS MY WEDDING GOWN NOW, I WONDERS 115 JOURNE
I WONDER WHERE I HID ITS 115 JOURNE
HE SAID IT WAS A WONDER I HADN'T GONE MAD/ 118 JOURNE
WHY IS IT FOG MAKES EVERYTHING SOUND SO SAD AND 121 JOURNE
LOST, I WONDERS
(HE LAUGHS.) YOU'RE A WONDER, PAPA. 128 JOURNE
CHRIST, IS IT ANY WONDER SHE DIDN'T WANT TO BE 141 JOURNE
CURED.
I WONDER WHAT THEY THOUGHT OF YOU WHEN THEY HEARD 144 JOURNE
YOU MOANING POORHOUSE AND
(BITTERLY.) WHAT THE HELL WAS IT I WANTED TO BUY,150 JOURNE
I WONDER. THAT WAS WORTH--
WHERE IS IT NOW, I WONDERS 152 JOURNE
HOW DOES THAT JEW MAKE THAT LIGHT COME FROM HIM, 1314 LAZARU
WONDERS
BUT ARE YOU, I WONDERS 9 MANSNS
WITH AN INSTINCTIVE GRATEFUL WONDER. 20 MANSNS
GOOD GOD, YOU WONDER I WAS TEMPTED TO OPEN THAT 30 MANSNS
DOOR AND ESCAPE/
AND YOU WONDER WHY I HATE YOU/ 102 MANSNS
(THINKING.) WHAT IS HE THINKING, I WONDERS 119 MANSNS
AND MURMURS DROVSILY IN GENTLE WONDER.) 129 MANSNS
I PRESUME YOU WONDER WHY I WISHED TO SEE YOU, MR. 151 MANSNS
TENARD.
IT'S A WONDER IF YOU HAVEN'T CAUGHT YOUR DEATH 170 MANSNS
ALREADY--
I WONDER--I WONDER--OH, GOD HELP ME, I'LL NEVER BE194 MANSNS
SURE OF THE TRUTH OF IT NOW/
IT CAN DO NO HARM--AND IT IS A VERY GREAT WONDER/ 351 MARCOM
IN THE MEANTIME, MARCO HAS SLIPPED OFF, FULL OF 366 MARCOM
CURIOSITY AND WONDER.
WITH QUEER APPALLED WONDER THAT PUZZLES HIM 395 MARCOM
WILL DONATA KNOW MARCO, I WONDERS 427 MARCOM
YES, MY WONDER BOY/ 430 MARCOM
MEETING HIS EYES, WHICH ARE REGARDING HER WITH 113 MISBEG
PUZZLED WONDER,
AND THAT DRIVEL HE TALKED ABOUT OWING ME ONE--WHAT132 MISBEG
GOT INTO HIS HEAD, I WONDER.
YOU'RE STIFF AND CRAMPED, AND NO WONDER. 166 MISBEG
YOU'RE A WONDER, JIM. 169 MISBEG
SMALL WONDER. YOU'D THE DIVIL'S OWN LOAD WHEN YOU 8 POET
LEFT AT TWO THIS MORNING.
IF YOU'D SEEN HIM THEN, YOU WOULDN'T WONDER. 13 POET
(BITTERLY.) I HAD FORGOTTEN MYSELF AND NO WONDER. 38 POET
I DO NOT WONDER YOUR INN ENJOYS SUCH MEAGER 72 POET
PATRONAGE.
WHY ARE YOU SO JEALOUS OF THE MARE, I WONDERS 107 POET
(RESENTFULLY.) IT'S A WONDER SHE WOULDN'T HAVE 135 POET
MORE THOUGHT FOR YOU
SMALL WONDER HE DID/ 143 POET
NO WONDER SHE BROKE DOWN... 5 STRANG
(I WILL SHE FEEL ANY REAL GRIEF OVER HIS DEATH, I 25 STRANG
WONDERS...
HE SURE WAS A WONDER, WASN'T HES 29 STRANG
I WONDER IF SHE CAN REALLY LIKE HIM... 52 STRANG
(GLOOMILY) (I) WONDER WHY..... 55 STRANG
(THINKING) (I) WONDER IF THERE'S A DRAFT IN THE 111 STRANG
BABY'S ROOMS...
WONDER WHAT HE'D SAY IF I PROPOSED THAT HE BACK 113 STRANG
ME&...
HOW SOON, I WONDERS...) 140 STRANG
I WONDER IS OUR OLD GARDEN THE SAMES 199 STRANG

WONDERFUL
LATER, AT SCHOOL, HE LEARNED OF THE GOD OF 510 DAYS
PUNISHMENT, AND HE WONDERED.
HE HAD OFTEN WONDERED IF SHE CARED, 537 DAYS
THAT I WONDERED WHERE I HAD MET THAT MAN BEFORE. 282 GGBROW
I'VE OFTEN WONDERED WHY A MAN THAT LIKES FIGHTS AS 19 MISBEG
MUCH AS YOU DIDN'T GRAB AT
YOU'VE PROBABLY WONDERED WHY I OBJECTED. 178 STRANG

WONDERFUL
HAVE MADE SUCH A WONDERFUL WIFE FOR ANY MAN-- 214 AHWILD
THE WATER WAS WONDERFUL AND WARM, 228 AHWILD
(KISSING HIM AGAIN) JUST THINK OF THE WONDERFUL 241 AHWILD
TIME EDITH AND YOUR FRIEND WINT
GOSH, MURIEL, IT SURE IS WONDERFUL TO BE WITH YOU 279 AHWILD
AGAIN/
YOU LOOK WONDERFUL/ 281 AHWILD
IT FELT WONDERFUL--EVEN TO HAVE YOU BITE/ 286 AHWILD
(THEN AFTER A PAUSE) WON'T IT BE WONDERFUL WHEN 287 AHWILD
WE'RE MARRIEDS
(HAZILY, BUT HAPPILY) THAT'LL BE WONDERFUL, WON'T288 AHWILD
ITS
FAR-OFF WONDERFUL PLACE/ 288 AHWILD
WITH SUCH A WONDERFUL MOON. 296 AHWILD
IT WAS WONDERFUL--DOWN AT THE BEACH--(HE STOPS 296 AHWILD
ABRUPTLY, SMILING SHYLY.)
YES, I'LL BET THOSE MUST HAVE BEEN WONDERFUL 297 AHWILD
NIGHTS, TOO.
AND I THINK IT'S WONDERFUL AND SINCERE. 84 BEYOND

WONDERFUL

WONDERFUL (CONT'D.)
SONGS THAT TOLD OF ALL THE WONDERFUL THINGS THEY 90 BEYOND
HAD
SOMETHING I DISCOVERED ONLY THIS EVENING--VERY 99 BEYOND
BEAUTIFUL AND WONDERFUL--
ALL THE WONDERFUL FAR PLACES I USED TO DREAM 125 BEYOND
ABOUT/
SHE WAS A WONDERFUL WOMAN, 509 DAYS
YOU LOOK WONDERFUL. 517 DAYS
YOU'VE BEEN THE MOST WONDERFUL FRIEND. 517 DAYS
I USED TO HAVE THE MOST WONDERFUL DREAMS ABOUT 89 ELECTR
YOU.
OH, MOTHER, IT'S GOING TO BE WONDERFUL FROM NOW 90 ELECTR
ON.
OH, WON'T IT BE WONDERFUL, PETER-- 167 ELECTR
HE'S ALWAYS BEEN SUCH A WONDERFUL SON BEFORE--AND 173 ELECTR
BROTHER.
(FONDLY) YOU OUGHT TO MAKE A WONDERFUL ARCHITECT.261 GGBROW
DION.
(TO THE MOON) DION IS SO WONDERFUL/ 262 GGBROW
IT SOUNDS WONDERFUL, DOESN'T IT$ 268 GGBROW
WONDERFUL THING ABOUT YOU, HARRY, YOU KEEP YOUNG 604 ICEMAN
AS YOU EVER WAS.
I'M DOING IT BECAUSE IT'S BEEN SO WONDERFUL HAVING 45 JOURNE
YOU HOME THE WAY YOU'VE BEEN.
WHAT IS SO WONDERFUL ABOUT THAT FIRST MEETING 107 JOURNE
BETWEEN A SILLY ROMANTIC
THEY PREDICTED A WONDERFUL FUTURE FOR HIM 110 JOURNE
IT WAS MADE OF SOFT, SHIMMERING SATIN, TRIMMED 115 JOURNE
WITH WONDERFUL OLD DUCHESSE LACE,
HER WONDERFUL HOME WAS ORDINARY ENOUGH. 137 JOURNE
(SUDDENLY IN A DEEP VOICE--WITH A WONDERFUL 278 LAZARU
EXULTANT ACCEPTANCE IN IT)
OR THE POOR ABUSED LITTLE PRINCESS--THAT WAS 12 MANSNS
WONDERFUL.
THAT GOT SUCH WONDERFUL RESULTS IS SIMPLICITY 392 MARCOM
ITSELF.
ANOTHER AT THE MOON, AND EACH TIME HE SAID THAT 397 MARCOM
NATURE WAS WONDERFUL/
WHAT IS THAT WONDERFUL GLITTERING BEAST$ 419 MARCOM
YOU'VE A WONDERFUL WAY WITH ANIMALS, GOD BLESS 14 MISBEG
YOU.
YOU'RE A WONDERFUL FIGHTER. 14 MISBEG
(CHUCKLES) YOU DID IT WONDERFUL. 25 MISBEG
SURE, LOVE IS A WONDERFUL MAD INSPIRATION/ 153 MISBEG
GOD HELP YOU, IT MUST BE A WONDERFUL THING TO LIVE 50 POET
IN A FAIRY TALE
AND HELP COUSIN JAMIE CELEBRATE OUR WONDERFUL 175 POET
SHINDY WID THE POLICE.
HIS WONDERFUL ATHLETE'S BODY... 5 STRANG
I NEVER THINK OF HER--THAT WAY--SHE'S TOO 32 STRANG
BEAUTIFUL AND WONDERFUL--
HOW PROUD I AM YOU'RE DOING SO WONDERFUL WELL/ 54 STRANG
OH, IT'D BE WONDERFUL, NINA/ 71 STRANG
(THINKING ADMIRINGLY) (WONDERFUL-LOOKING AS 79 STRANG
EVER...
OUR WONDERFUL AFTERNOONS OF HAPPINESS/... 91 STRANG
HOW WONDERFUL THAT IS/...)) 102 STRANG
DEAR WONDERFUL AFTERNOONS OF LOVE WITH YOU, MY 110 STRANG
LOVER...
BUT SAM MAKES A WONDERFUL FATHER... 112 STRANG
AND A WONDERFUL COOK AND HOUSEKEEPER-- 114 STRANG
THIS IS A WONDERFUL SURPRISE/ 126 STRANG
WONDERFUL FATHER... 128 STRANG
(AS BEFORE) YES, SAM MAKES A WONDERFUL FATHER, 128 STRANG
NED.
SHE'S A WONDERFUL WIFE AND MOTHER...)) 134 STRANG
IT'S ALWAYS SO WONDERFUL WHEN YOU FIRST COME BACK.143 STRANG
BUT YOU ALWAYS STAY TOO LONG--
DEAREST, IT'S WONDERFUL OF YOU TO SAY THAT/ 145 STRANG
BUT SHE'S KEPT HER WONDERFUL BODY/...) 168 STRANG
BUT SHE'S KEPT HER WONDERFUL BODY... 169 STRANG
HE WAS SO WONDERFUL AND SWEET TO ME. 184 STRANG
SHE WAS A WONDERFUL WIFE. 185 STRANG
(CONSOLED--PROUDLY) YES, SHE SURE WAS WONDERFUL 185 STRANG
TO HIM, ALL RIGHT/
(MADELINE'S WONDERFUL/...
THOSE WERE WONDERFUL AFTERNOONS LONG AGO/ 189 STRANG
AFTER A PAUSE) YOU CAN'T IMAGINE HOW WONDERFUL 196 STRANG
IT'S BEEN UP IN THE COUNTRY. 456 WELDED
HE HAS A WONDERFUL IMAGINATION. 468 WELDED
WONDERFULLY
YOUR PENMANSHIP IS IMPROVING WONDERFULLY. 250 AHWILD
WE ALL KNOW HOW WONDERFULLY HAPPY YOU AND JOHN 524 DAYS
ARE.
LIVING FLESH BUT A WONDERFULLY LIFELIKE PALE MASK, 9 ELECTR
BUT THEN, BILLY IS DOING SO WONDERFULLY WELL, 275 GGBROW
EVERYONE SAYS.
HE'S PAINTING WONDERFULLY/ 275 GGBROW
YOU ARE WONDERFULLY SHREWD AND FAR-SIGHTED, 101 MANSNS
MOTHER.
YOU HAVE WONDERFULLY IMPROVED AND I THINK IT MOST 16 STRANG
ILL-ADVISED IN THE HOTTEST
OF A WONDERFULLY MADE, LIFELIKE DOLL. 53 STRANG
SHE'S BEEN WONDERFULLY NICE. 185 STRANG
WONDERIN'
ALL I'M WONDERIN' IS, HAS HE GOT TEN DOLLARSS. 133 ELECTR
DAT'S WHAT WE'RE ALL WONDERIN'. 617 ICEMAN
WONDERING
WONDERING LOOK, AS IF SOME DEEP PUZZLE WERE 224 AHWILD
CONFRONTING HIM.
WONDERING VAGUENESS. 224 AHWILD
FINALLY HE LOOKS UP AND REGARDS HIS SISTER AND 224 AHWILD
ASKS WITH WONDERING AMAZEMENT)
AND WONDERING IF HE HASN'T DROWNED HIMSELF OR 251 AHWILD
SOMETHING.
LIGHT-BROWN HAIR, BIG NAIVE WONDERING DARK EYES, 4277 AHWILD
ROUND DIMPLED FACE,

WONDERINGLY

WONDERING (CONT'D.)
SLEEP, WONDERING HOW I WAS EVER GOING TO SEE YOU 284 AHWILD
AGAIN AND CRYING MY EYES OUT.
WE WERE WONDERING WHEN HE'D GET HOME. 117 BEYOND
MARY WALKS BACKWARD TOWARD ROBERT, HER WONDERING 142 BEYOND
EYES FIXED ON HER MOTHER.)
(THOUGHTFULLY) I'VE BEEN WONDERING WHAT THE GREAT161 BEYOND
CHANGE WAS IN YOU.
YES, SHE HAS BEEN WONDERING WHY SHE HASN'T HEARD 513 DAYS
FROM YOU IN SO LONG.
(TAKEN ABACK, GIVES JOHN A WONDERING LOOK--THEN 534 DAYS
APOLOGETICALLY)
HER VOICE IS SENTIMENTAL AND WONDERING. 428 DYNAMO
(HE SHUDDERS, FLINGING OFF THE MEMORY--THEN 456 DYNAMO
WONDERING BITTERLY)
I WAS WONDERING WHEN I WAS GOING TO SEE YOU. 16 ELECTR
(THEN AS HE STARES, DUMBFOUNDED AND WONDERING, 124 ELECTR
I'VE BEEN THINKING OF YOU ALL THE WAY HOME AND 143 ELECTR
WONDERING--
ARE YOU WONDERING WHAT IT WAS DRIN WROTES 175 ELECTR
HE STANDS FOR A MOMENT WATCHING HER, GRIMLY 178 ELECTR
WONDERING.
(HAS BEEN STARING INTO HIS EYES WITH A FASCINATED 641 ICEMAN
WONDERING DREAD)
WONDERING IF HIS BROTHER CAN REALLY MEAN THIS. 59 JOURNE
(WITH WONDERING AWE) DO YOU REMEMBER HIM, 276 LAZARU
NEIGHBORS, BEFORE HE DIED$
THERE IS SOMETHING OF SHY WONDERING CHILD ABOUT 308 LAZARU
HIS ATTITUDE NOW.
I WAS WONDERING IF YOU WOULD BRING HER WITH YOU 7 MANSNS
TODAY.
SIMON WILL BE WONDERING WHERE I HAVE GONE. 21 MANSNS
IN HIS EYES AND JOEL'S A WONDERING ALARM. 30 MANSNS
AS IF YOU WERE WONDERING WHAT WAS MY BUSINESS 81 MANSNS
THERE.
SARA MUST BE WONDERING WHAT IS KEEPING ME, NOW THE102 MANSNS
SUN IS SETTING.
WONDERING WHAT WE WILL DECIDE TO DO ABOUT HIM. 127 MANSNS
JUST AS I WAS WONDERING WHY YOU EVER CONSENTED TO 151 MANSNS
COME--UNDER THE CIRCUMSTANCES.
(RAISES HIS HEAD, A CONFUSED, DREAMY WONDERING 175 MANSNS
PEACE IN HIS FACE--DAZEDLY.)
WHAT MADE IT DO THAT, YOU'RE WONDERINGS 395 MARCOM
(WITH WONDERING BITTERNESS) THE EYE SEES ONLY ITS397 MARCOM
OWN SIGHT.
(GHAZAN, FASCINATED, YET WITH A WONDERING GLANCE, 419 MARCOM
THEN ADDS WITH STRANGE, WONDERING SINCERITY) 103 MISBEG
YOU LOOK AS IF YOU'D DRAWN A BLANK AND WERE 166 MISBEG
WONDERING HOW YOU GOT HERE.
WONDERING HOW YOU GOT HERE. 168 MISBEG
(CANNOT HELP BEING IMPRESSED--LOOKS AT HER MOTHER 25 POET
WITH WONDERING RESPECT.)
(THEN, SEEING THE LOOK OF WONDERING HURT IN THE 54 POET
OLD MAN'S EYES,
(STARES AT HIM STARTLED AND WONDERING. 157 POET
OF THEM--WONDERING AND SAD, BUT STILL TRUSTFUL, 169 POET
BUT REPROACHING ME--
MOTHER MUST BE WONDERING WHAT KEEPS ME SO LONG... 21 STRANG
PRESTON MUST BE WONDERING IF I'VE DESERTED 190 STRANG
HIM....))
(THEN WITH A WONDERING SADNESS) 190 STRANG
CAPE STOPS TWO STEPS BELOW HER--IN A LOW, 489 WELDED
WONDERING TONE)
WONDERINGLY
(STARES AT HIM WONDERINGLY FOR A MOMENT, 297 AHWILD
(AS CHRIS MAKES NO COMMENT BUT A HEAVY SIGH, SHE 29 ANNA
CONTINUES WONDERINGLY)
(WONDERINGLY) AH-- 558 CROSS
(WONDERINGLY) BUT IF HE'S HITCHED AGEN-- 213 DESIRE
STANDS BAREFOOTED LOOKING ABOUT HIM IN 241 DESIRE
BEWILDERMENT, MUTTERS WONDERINGLY)
(THEN AFTER A SECOND'S THOUGHT--WONDERINGLY) 203 EJONES
(WONDERINGLY) CAN MARGARET STILL LOVE DION 291 GGBROW
ANYTHING$
(HE SAYS THIS MECHANICALLY BUT THE LAST TWO WORDS 299 GGBROW
AWAKEN HIM--WONDERINGLY)
(SHE STARES WONDERINGLY AT HIM AND HE AT HER. 301 GGBROW
REACHES OUT AND SHAKES THE BARS--ALOUD TO HIMSELF, 240 HA APE
WONDERINGLY) STEEL.
(THEN WONDERINGLY) BUT DEN WHAT KIND OF A SAP IS 584 ICEMAN
HE
(WONDERINGLY) WHAT THE HELL WAS THATS 726 ICEMAN
(ALL ARE STARTLED AND LOOK AT HIM WONDERINGLY.) 514 INZONE
MECHANICALLY DRISCOLL LEANS OVER AND PICKS IT UP, 532 INZONE
AND LOOKS AT IT WONDERINGLY.)
(WONDERINGLY SHE LEAVES LAZARUS' SIDE AND FOLLOWS 330 LAZARU
HIM.
STARING AT LAZARUS, WONDERINGLY) 340 LAZARU
CALIGULA GOES ON WONDERINGLY) 342 LAZARU
WONDERINGLY.) 353 LAZARU
(STARES AT HIM WONDERINGLY--SLOWLY.) 34 MANSNS
(WONDERINGLY) IS HE CRAZYS 369 MARCOM
(WONDERINGLY) THERE MAY BE HOPE--AFTER ALL. 406 MARCOM
(STARES AT HER--WONDERINGLY.) 141 POET
(STARING AT HIM WONDERINGLY) 10 STRANG
(WONDERINGLY) YOU DON'T MEAN TO TELL ME SHE HAS 11 STRANG
ACCUSED YOU OF ALL THIS$
(VAGUELY--WONDERINGLY) (CHARLIE... 94 STRANG
BUT GLANCING WONDERINGLY AT EVANS AND NINA. 111 STRANG
(STARING AT EVANS WONDERINGLY) 113 STRANG
NINA AND DARRELL TURN AND LOOK AT EACH OTHER 104 STRANG
WONDERINGLY, INQUISITIVELY,
(WONDERINGLY) GORDON/ 186 STRANG
(HE STARES UP AT HER WONDERINGLY. 452 WELDED
(WONDERINGLY--NOT LOOKING AT HER) 481 WELDED
(WONDERINGLY) YOU-- 483 WELDED
(TURNS AND STARES AT HER--A PAUSE--THEN HE ASKS 484 WELDED
WONDERINGLY, EAGERLY)

WONDERMENT   1820

WONDERMENT
MILDRED STARES AT HIM IN PUZZLED WONDERMENT, 195 AHWILD
(KUBAL LOOKS AT HER WITH A SAD WONDERMENT, CHU- 397 MARCOM
KLIN SMILINGLY,
(WITH A SORT OF DULL STUPID WONDERMENT) 62 STRANG

WONDERS
THAT ALL THE WONDERS OF THE WORLD HAPPENED ON THE 90 BEYOND
OTHER SIDE OF THOSE HILLS.
AND HE WONDERS SADLY WHY HE TOOK THE TROUBLE TO 14 HUGHIE
MAKE IT.)
(THE CLERK WONDERS WHAT HORSES HAVE TO DO WITH 22 HUGHIE
ANYTHING--
WONDERS WILL NEVER CEASE/ 40 JOURNE
WILL WONDERS NEVER CEASE. 108 JOURNE
(SUDDENLY) MANY WONDERS HAVE COME TO PASS IN 368 MARCOM
THESE REGIONS.
(FLATTERINGLY) YES, YOU'VE DONE WONDERS IN THE 121 STRANG
PAST YEAR.

WONDROUS
HERE'S A WONDROUS FAIR CAPITOL/ 313 GGBROW

WONT
(THINKING.) THEY DO NOT SIT TOGETHER ON THE SOFA 118 MANSNS
AS HAS BEEN THEIR WONT--
SHE COMES MORE NEARER THAN SHE WAS WONT, AND MAKES151 MISBEG
MEN MAD."

WOOD
A PILE OF WOOD IS STACKED UP CARELESSLY AGAINST 144 BEYOND
THE WALL BY THE STOVE.
(SHIVERING IRRITABLY) FOR GOODNESS' SAKE PUT SOME152 BEYOND
WOOD ON THAT FIRE.
(SHE GETS WEARILY FROM THE CHAIR AND PUTS A FEW 152 BEYOND
PIECES OF WOOD IN THE STOVE)
THIS IS THE LAST OF THE WOOD. 152 BEYOND
AN EXCEPTIONALLY FINE PIECE OF WOOD CARVING. 564 DAYS
MADE OF UNCUT WOOD WHICH STANDS AT CENTER, ITS 173 EJONES
BACK TO REAR.
THAT DURNED NIGGER COOK IS ALLUS ASKIN' ME TO 10 ELECTR
FETCH WOOD FOR HER/
A MOMENT LATER THERE IS THE SOUND OF SPLINTERING 114 ELECTR
WOOD
LOAD WITH WOOD ONLY SO IT FLOAT, BY GOLLY/ 515 INZONE
CLOSE BY THE LEFT AND REAR OF THE CABIN IS THE 1 MANSNS
WOOD--
THE ROOM IS SMALL, WELL-PROPORTIONED, PANELLED IN 69 MANSNS
DARK WOOD.
A RUG COVERS MOST OF THE FLOOR OF WAXED DARK WOOD.117 MANSNS
THE CROSS OUR LORD WAS CRUCIFIED ON WAS MADE OF 349 MARCOM
THIS WOOD.
(HE SHOWS THEM A PIECE OF WOOD) 364 MARCOM
LOVER IN THE WOOD PILE OR TO BELIEVE IN AN 75 STRANG
IMMACULATE CONCEPTION....
ONLY I BETTER KNOCK WOOD....)) 135 STRANG

WOODBIN
THE FIRST OF THESE IS USED AS A WOODBIN AND IS 577 ROPE
HALF FULL OF PILED-UP CORDWOOD.

WOODED
WHICH SURROUND THE HOUSE, A HEAVILY WOODED RIDGE 2 ELECTR
IN THE BACKGROUND.

WOODEN
IN THE BACK ROOM ARE FOUR ROUND WOODEN TABLES WITH 3 ANNA
FIVE CHAIRS GROUPED ABOUT
IN FRONT OF THE BUNKS, ROUGH WOODEN BENCHES. 477 CARDIF
DIRECTLY UNDER THEM, A WOODEN BENCH. 555 CROSS
WITH A WOODEN GATE AT CENTER OPENING ON A COUNTRY 202 DESIRE
ROAD.
FOUR ROUGH WOODEN CHAIRS, A TALLOW CANDLE ON THE 206 DESIRE
TABLE.
THE CHAIRS, WITH WOODEN BENCHES ADDED, HAVE BEEN 247 DESIRE
PUSHED BACK AGAINST THE WALLS.
HIS WHOLE ATTITUDE WOODEN AND FIXED AS IF HE WERE 494 DIFRNT
POSING FOR A PHOTOGRAPH.
(HE LOWERS HIMSELF CAREFULLY TO A WOODEN POSTURE 514 DIFRNT
ON THE EDGE OF A ROCKER NEAR
A WHITE WOODEN PORTICO WITH SIX TALL COLUMNS 2 ELECTR
CONTRASTS
HER MOVEMENTS ARE STIFF AND SHE CARRIES HERSELF 10 ELECTR
WITH A WOODEN,
HIS MOVEMENTS ARE EXACT AND WOODEN AND HE HAS A 46 ELECTR
MANNERISM OF STANDING AND
(TENSELY.) I KNOW VERY WELL IT IS A WOODEN DOOR--183 MANSNS
BUT TO CONNECT THE DOOR AND THAT SILLY TALE WITH 183 MANSNS
THE ACTUAL WOODEN DOOR--
NOW I KNOW WHY THE WOMEN IN YOUR PLAYS ARE SO 459 WELDED
WOODEN/

WOODENLY
SHE RISES SLOWLY TO HER FEET AND WALKS SLOWLY AND 541 DAYS
WOODENLY BACK PAST HIM AND
SHE OVERCOMES HER WEAKNESS AND WALKS WOODENLY INTO551 DAYS
HER BEDROOM
WOODENLY ERECT AND SQUARE-SHOULDERED.) 27 ELECTR
(WOODENLY) I DIDN'T FEEL SLEEPY. 56 ELECTR
WALKS SLOWLY AND WOODENLY OFF LEFT BETWEEN THE 78 ELECTR
LILAC CLUMP AND THE HOUSE.
TURNS, RIGID AND SQUARE-SHOULDERED, AND WALKS 101 ELECTR
WOODENLY FROM THE ROOM.)
HE CARRIES HIMSELF WOODENLY ERECT NOW, LIKE A 137 ELECTR
SOLDIER.
(HE OBEYS WOODENLY. 138 ELECTR
ORIN STRAIGHTENS WOODENLY TO A SOLDIERLY 145 ELECTR
ATTENTION.
LAVINIA PIVOTS SHARPLY ON HER HEEL AND MARCHES 179 ELECTR
WOODENLY INTO THE HOUSE.
THE LATTER MOVES HALTINGLY AND WOODENLY. 152 POET
(COLLECTING HIMSELF--WOODENLY) 20 STRANG
(WOODENLY) LET US SAY THEN THAT I PERSUADED 20 STRANG
MYSELF IT WAS FOR YOUR SAKE.
WALKS SLOWLY AND WOODENLY LIKE A MAN IN A TRANCE 98 STRANG
INTO THE ROOM.

WOODIN'
'N THEY WAS WOODIN' T' DO. 208 DESIRE

WOODLAND
ON A GRAND ESTATE AV STATELY WOODLAND AND SOFT 173 POET
GREEN MEADOWS AND A LAKE.

WOODLANDS
UP AS FINE PASTURE AND WOODLANDS AS YOU'D FIND 49 POET

WOODS
AN' I'LL KICK YE BOTH OUT IN THE ROAD--T' BEG AN' 257 DESIRE
SLEEP IN THE WOODS--
I CUT ACROSS THE FIELDS AN' THROUGH THE WOODS. 266 DESIRE
I'VE DRUV 'EM INTO THE WOODS WHAR THEY KIN BE 267 DESIRE
FREE/
FELLOW, BUT SHE LOVED CLARK AND USED TO MEET HIM 440 DYNAMO
IN THE WOODS.
WOODS NIGGERS RIGHT WHERE I WANTED DEM. 177 EJONES
LOW-FLUNG, WOODS NIGGERS/ 182 EJONES
ONCE IN DE WOODS IN DE NIGHT, DEY GOT A SWELL 183 EJONES
CHANCE O' FINDIN' DIS BABY/
MY GOODNESS, LOOK AT DEM WOODS, WILL YOUS 188 EJONES
WOODS IS YOU TRYIN' TO PUT SOMETHIN' OVAH ON MES 189 EJONES
WOODS--ALL DE NIGHTS 189 EJONES
TIME YOU BEAT IT IN DE WOODS WIDOUT NO LONG WAITS.190 EJONES
(WEARILY) HOW LONG I BEEN MAKIN TRACKS IN DESE 191 EJONES
WOODS$
DESE WOODS IS SHO' FULL O' DE QUEEREST THINGS AT 193 EJONES
NIGHT.
(EXASPERATEDLY) WELL, AIN'T YER GOIN' IN AN' 'UNT203 EJONES
'IM IN THE WOODS$
IF 'E LOST 'IS BLOODY WAY IN THESE STINKIN' WOODS 203 EJONES
'EE LIKELY TURN IN A CIRCLE
YOUSE CAN SIT AND DOPE DREAM IN DE PAST, GREEN 253 HA APE
WOODS,
OUT INTO THE WOODS/ 310 LAZARU
(SCENE A LOG CABIN BY A LAKE IN THE WOODS 1 MANSNS
THE CLEARING IS PARTLY IN SUNLIGHT, PARTLY 1 MANSNS
SHADOWED BY THE WOODS.
SHE COMES STEALTHILY TO THE EDGE OF THE WOODS AT 2 MANSNS
LEFT-FRONT,
AND PEERS UP A PATH WHICH LEADS FROM THE CLEARING 2 MANSNS
INTO THE WOODS.
(THERE IS A SOUND FROM UP THE PATH AT LEFT-FRONT, 4 MANSNS
THROUGH THE WOODS.
AT RIGHT-REAR, THROUGH A FIELD OF HAY STUBBLE TO A 1 MISBEG
PATCH OF WOODS.
AND DISAPPEARS ALONG THE PATH TO THE WOODS, RIGHT- 10 MISBEG
REAR.
ALONG THE PATH TO THE WOODS) 11 MISBEG
THE DRIVE IN THE HOT SUN AND THE WALK THROUGH THE 19 POET
WOODS FOR NOTHING.
YES, I DID FIND MY WALK ALONE IN THE WOODS A 86 POET
STRANGELY OVERPOWERING EXPERIENCE.
AND YOUR WALKS IN THE WOODS WITH HIM. 108 POET

WOOED
WHY, YOU COULD BE THE MOST WOOED WIDOW IN THE 37 MANSNS
CITY/

WOOL
IT WAS ALL-WOOL-AND-A-YARD-WIDE-HELL, I'LL TELL 132 BEYOND
YOU.
A DYED-IN-THE-WOOL MECHANIST. 503 DAYS
I KIN ALLUS PULL THE WOOL OVER HIS EYES. 245 DESIRE
HE'S A DYED-IN-THE-WOOL DOC. 30 STRANG
TRYING TO PULL THE WOOL OVER MY EYES$... 38 STRANG

WOOLEN
AND A WOOLEN CAP WITH EAR-FLAPS. 535 'ILE

WOOLLY
MY HEAD HAS GONE WOOLLY. 551 DAYS

WOOS
WHILE YOU ARE STILL BEAUTIFUL AND LIFE STILL WOOS 12 MANSNS
YOU,
DEATH WOOS ME. 423 MARCOM

WOOZILY
SHE IS UNCERTAIN IN HER WALK AND GRINNING 122 JOURNE
WOOZILY.)

WOOZY
HE IS VERY DRUNK AND WOOZY ON HIS LEGS. 154 JOURNE

WOP
SHUT UP, WOP/ 209 HA APE
HAVE YOU NO RESPECT FOR RELIGION, YOU UNREGENERATE578 ICEMAN

WOPS
DAMNED BOURGEOIS WOP/ 579 ICEMAN
FOR HARRY'S SAKE, NOT YOURS, YUH LITTLE WOP/ 634 ICEMAN
THAT AUTOMOBILE, YOU DUMB WOP/ 690 ICEMAN
DON'T ASK QUESTIONS, YOU DUMB WOP/ 694 ICEMAN
HE LOOKS NOW LIKE A MINOR WOP GANGSTER. 697 ICEMAN
(HIS BLACK BULLET EYES SENTIMENTAL, HIS ROUND WOP 725 ICEMAN
FACE GRINNING WELCOME)

WORDLESS
RISING AND FALLING IN A WORDLESS CHANT. 373 MARCOM

WORDS
(DRAGGING OUT THE WORDS WITH AN EFFORT) 549 'ILE
THEM ARE MIGHTY STRONG WORDS. 194 AHWILD
EVER HEAR THOSE WORDS TO IT, KIDS 237 AHWILD
(FINALLY SURVEYS THE TWO WORDS SHE HAS BEEN 249 AHWILD
WRITING AND IS SATISFIED WITH THEM)
MILDRED SITS AT THE DESK AT RIGHT, FRONT, WRITING 249 AHWILD
TWO WORDS OVER AND OVER AGAIN.
YOU MARK MY WORDS, THAT BUY'S GOING TO TURN OUT TO290 AHWILD
BE A GREAT LAWYER.
HIS LIPS MOVING AS HE SPELLS OUT THE WORDS. 8 ANNA
(GRINNING) YE TAKE THE WORDS OUT OF MY MOUTH. 33 ANNA
AFRAID THERE MAY BE SOME HIDDEN INSINUATION IN HIS 35 ANNA
WORDS.
CHRIS, WHO HAS BEEN LISTENING TO BURKE'S LAST 40 ANNA
WORDS WITH OPEN-MOUTHED AMAZEMENT
(SCOWLING AND FORCING OUT THE WORDS) 44 ANNA
(FORCING OUT THE WORDS) WELL, MAYBE IT'S TRUE, 51 ANNA
MAT.

WORDS

WORDS (CONT'D.)
THE WHOLE OF IT'S IN A FEW WORDS ONLY. 51 ANNA
YOU HEARD THE WORDS FROM HER OWN LIPS. 52 ANNA
AY--HE FIGHTS FOR WORDS TO EXPRESS HIMSELF, BUT 67 ANNA
FINDS NONE--MISERABLY--
(HANGING ON HIS WORDS--BREATHLESSLY) 74 ANNA
(AFTER AN INWARD STRUGGLE--TENSELY--FORCING OUT 74 ANNA
THE WORDS WITH DIFFICULTY)
BLOW ME IF THEM WARN'T HER EXACT WORDS! 94 BEYOND
AND RUNNIN' AWAY'S THE ONLY WORDS TO FIT IT. 106 BEYOND
MOB SHUT ME UP WITH ALMOST THE SAME WORDS WHEN I 139 BEYOND
TRIED SPEAKING TO HIM ABOUT IT.
AND NOW--(HE STOPS AS IF SEEKING VAINLY FOR WORDS)161 BEYOND
(THE DOOR CLOSES BEHIND THEM, CUTTING OFF HIS 166 BEYOND
WORDS AS THE CURTAIN FALLS.)
HE--(BUT RUTH, IF SHE IS AWARE OF HIS WORDS, GIVES169 BEYOND
NO SIGN.
WORDS DO YE KNOW. 459 CARIBE
WHERE THE CROSS IS MADE THE GULPS AND THE WORDS 566 CROSS
POUR OUT INCOHERENTLY)
JOHN NERVOUSLY WRITES A FEW WORDS ON A PAD-- 494 DAYS
HIS LIPS PART AND WORDS COME HALTINGLY, AS IF THEY551 DAYS
WERE FORCED OUT OF HIM.
MAKE HIM SEE THAT THOU, ALONE, HAST THE WORDS OF 558 DAYS
ETERNAL LIFE.
SHORN OF YOUR BOASTFUL WORDS, 561 DAYS
WORDS/ 565 DAYS
(HOLDING HIS EYES AND PUTTING ALL HER WILL INTO 240 DESIRE
HER WORDS
CABOT, ALTHOUGH HE HASN'T HEARD THE WORDS, 249 DESIRE
KEEPING HIS WORDS IN THE RHYTHM OF THE MUSIC AND 250 DESIRE
INTERSPERSING THEM WITH JOCULAR
(STANDS LOOKING AT HER DAZEDLY--A PAUSE--FINDING 264 DESIRE
HIS WORDS WITH AN EFFORT--
(AFTER A PAUSE--FORCING THE WORDS OUT SLOWLY) 504 DIFRNT
(WITH THE CALCULATING GLANCE TO SEE WHAT EFFECT 523 DIFRNT
HIS WORDS ARE HAVING--
(DAZEDLY--AS IF SHE COULD NOT REALIZE THE 545 DIFRNT
SIGNIFICANCE OF HIS WORDS)
(A MOMENT LATER HURRIES IN EXCITEDLY, HER WORDS 445 DYNAMO
POURING OUT)
SO THAT FOR A MOMENT HIS LIPS MOVE, FORMING WORDS,450 DYNAMO
BUT HE CAN'T
HER LAST WORDS/... 456 DYNAMO
THAT HER LAST WORDS WERE HIS WORDS... 466 DYNAMO
HER LAST WORDS WERE THE VERY WORDS YOU HAD WRITTEN466 DYNAMO
HER.
HER LAST WORDS/... 466 DYNAMO
RATHER THAN THE MEANING OF THE WORDS.) 476 DYNAMO
AND A HABIT OF SNAPPING OUT HER WORDS LIKE AN 10 ELECTR
OFFICER GIVING ORDERS.
HER LIPS MOVE AS IF SHE WERE GOING TO SPEAK, BUT 27 ELECTR
SHE FIGHTS BACK THE WORDS,
TEARS OFF A LIP OF PAPER AND WRITES TWO WORDS ON 35 ELECTR
IT.
I MEAN--WHAT IS THE GOOD OF WORDS$ 56 ELECTR
THE WORDS SHATTER HER MERCIFUL NUMBNESS AND AWAKEN122 ELECTR
HER TO AGONY AGAIN.
SHE CALLS SHAKENLY AS IF THE WORDS WERE WRUNG OUT 123 ELECTR
OF HER AGAINST HER WILL)
(SHE STOPS ABRUPTLY, TERRIFIED BY HER OWN WORDS.) 156 ELECTR
(THEN AS IF THE WORDS STIRRED SOMETHING WITHIN HIM165 ELECTR
(WITHOUT LOOKING AT HIM, PICKING UP THE WORDS OF 178 ELECTR
THE CHANTY--
(HE SAYS THIS MECHANICALLY BUT THE LAST TWO WORDS 299 GGBROW
AWAKEN HIM--WONDERINGLY)
IT WAS JUST TOO DISGUSTING FOR WORDS TO HEAR HIM/ 311 GGBROW
TOO FUNNY FOR WORDS/ 315 GGBROW
HE STAMMERS GROPINGLY AMONG THE ECHOES OF ERIE'S 24 HUGHIE
LAST WORDS.)
AND JONATHAN EDWARDS WAS THE AUTHOR OF BOTH WORDS 597 ICEMAN
AND MUSIC.
YOU WERE ALL SO BUSY DRINKING IN WORDS OF WISDOM 638 ICEMAN
FROM THE OLD WISE GUY HERE,
OF THE LETTER THEY SEES ON'Y THE WORDS WHAT TELLS 529 INZONE
THEM WHAT THEY WANTS TO KNOW.
AS IF SHE WERE A LITTLE WITHDRAWN FROM HER WORDS 58 JOURNE
AND ACTIONS.)
A STREAM OF WORDS THAT ISSUES CASUALLY, 71 JOURNE
THEN AS IF HER WORDS HAD BEEN AN EVOCATION WHICH 104 JOURNE
CALLED BACK HAPPINESS SHE
BY A LYING DOPE FIEND RECITING WORDS/ 107 JOURNE
I MADE THE MANAGER PUT DOWN HIS EXACT WORDS IN 152 JOURNE
WRITING.
SURELY SHE, SHE TOO, REMEMBERING DAYS AND WORDS 174 JOURNE
THAT WERE,
FOLLOWING HIS WORDS THE LAUGHTER OF LAZARUS IS 306 LAZARU
HEARD,
(SHE STARES AT LAZARUS, HER WORDS CHALLENGING 343 LAZARU
HIM.)
HER WORDS COMING QUICKER AND QUICKER AS HER VOICE 346 LAZARU
BECOMES FAINTER AND FAINTER)
AND HER WORDS ONLY THE LAST DESIRE OF HER LOVE TO 350 LAZARU
COMFORT YOU, LAZARUS$
(WEARILY) YOUR WORDS ARE MEANINGLESS, LAZARUS. 352 LAZARU
(HIS WORDS ARE LIKE A BENEDICTION HE PRONOUNCES 353 LAZARU
UPON THEM.
(THREATENINGLY) AND I WARN YOU TO ANSWER DIRECTLY353 LAZARU
IN PLAIN WORDS--
HEARING ONLY CALIGULA'S WORDS WITHOUT THEIR 355 LAZARU
MEANING)
HIS WORDS ARE A THICK BABBLE I COULD NOT HEAR. 357 LAZARU
OH, HOW HIS SOOTHING GRAY WORDS MUST HAVE PECKED 361 LAZARU
AT THE WOUND IN YOUR HEART LIKE
HIS WORDS ARE NOW HEARD AS THE TUMULT MOMENTARILY 368 LAZARU
DIES DOWN)
(SLOWLY--AS IF FORCING THE WORDS OUT IN SPITE OF 38 MANSNS
HERSELF.)

WORK

WORDS (CONT'D.)
BUT I AM WASTING WORDS. 71 MANSNS
MARK MY WORDS, MARCO WILL BE WORTH A MILLION WISE 363 MARCOM
MEN--IN THE CAUSE OF WISDOM/
MIGHT SET AN EXAMPLE THAT WOULD ILLUSTRATE, BETTER379 MARCOM
THAN WISE WORDS,
A PRACTICAL WAR OF FEW WORDS, AS THAT POLU YOU 422 MARCOM
ADMIRE WOULD SAY.
A SILENT MAN GIVEN TO DEEDS, NOT WORDS--(HERE HE 431 MARCOM
FALTERS FITTINGLY) AND SO NOW--
FORGIVE MY EMOTION--WORDS FAIL ME-- 431 MARCOM
WON'T YOU ADDRESS A FEW WORDS TO YOUR OLD FRIENDS 431 MARCOM
AND NEIGHBORS
MARCO BEGINS AGAIN BUT THIS TIME THE CLAMOR IS TOO432 MARCOM
GREAT, HIS WORDS ARE LOST.
CAN WORDS RECALL LIFE TO HER BEAUTY$ 434 MARCOM
PRAYER IS BEYOND WORDS/ 435 MARCOM
YOUR WORDS ARE HOLLOW ECHOES OF THE BRAIN. 437 MARCOM
I WON'T WASTE WORDS TRYING TO REFORM A BORN CROOK. 62 MISBEG
(MANAGES TO GET IN THREE SPUTTERING WORDS) 63 MISBEG
(SHE BITES HER WORDS BACK, ASHAMED.) 32 POET
MUSICAL FLOW OF WORDS, AS SHE STRAINS TO GRASP THE 84 POET
IMPLICATION FOR HER.
AND I CONTINUE TO STAND HERE BORING YOU WITH 85 POET
WORDS.
TAKE CARE, SIR, AND WATCH YOUR WORDS OR I WARN YOU120 POET
YOU WILL REPENT THEM,
AS IF SHE HEARD NORA'S WORDS BUT THEY HAD NO 137 POET
MEANING FOR HER.
HE SPEAKS SLOWLY, WITH DIFFICULTY KEEPING HIS 171 POET
WORDS IN BROGUE.)
THEIR VOICES CAN BE HEARD BUT THE WORDS ARE 590 ROPE
INDISTINGUISHABLE.)
HIS LIPS MOVE CONVULSIVELY AS HE MAKES A 596 ROPE
TREMENDOUS EFFORT TO UTTER WORDS.)
AND HIS AMUSED VOICE RECITES THE WORDS WITH A 4 STRANG
RHETORICAL RESONANCE)
AN EXCUSE FOR WEAVING AMUSING WORDS... 5 STRANG
FIND THE RIGHT WORDS/... 15 STRANG
DEAD WORDS DRONING ON.... 15 STRANG
HIS WORDS ARISING FROM THE TOMB OF A SOUL IN PUFFS 16 STRANG
OF ASHES...))
INCOHERENT WORDS DROWNING OUT NINA'S VOICE, 26 STRANG
SOOTHING HER.)
(IRONICALLY) THAT'S THE OTHER SIDE OF IT YOU 27 STRANG
COULDN'T DISSECT INTO WORDS FROM
(THEN SHARPLY DRIVING HIS WORDS IN) 35 STRANG
IT'S BECAUSE I'VE SUDDENLY SEEN THE LIES IN THE 40 STRANG
SOUNDS CALLED WORDS.
WE POOR MONKEYS HIDE FROM OURSELVES BEHIND THE 40 STRANG
SOUNDS CALLED WORDS/
OR EVEN A GOOD MAN PREACHING THE SIMPLE PLATITUDES 41 STRANG
OF TRUTH, THOSE GOSPEL WORDS
SO MANY MANY WORDS HAVE JAMMED UP INTO THOUGHTS IN 41 STRANG
MY POOR HEAD/
THEY'RE ONLY WORDS, REMEMBER/ 41 STRANG
SOOTHES HER WITH UNCERTAIN TREMBLING WORDS) 43 STRANG
(IN HER BLUNT FLAT TONES--WITH A MECHANICAL 57 STRANG
RAPIDITY TO HER WORDS)
AND POUNDS OUT A FEW WORDS WITH A SORT OF AIMLESS 67 STRANG
DESPERATION--
(REPEATS HIS WORDS AS IF SHE WERE MEMORIZING A 71 STRANG
LESSON)
(THE WORDS AND THE TONE SHOCK HIS PRIDE TO LIFE. 99 STRANG
THINKING AS IF SHE WERE REPEATING THE WORDS OF 109 STRANG
SOME INNER VOICE OF LIFE)
(THEN IN A FLOOD OF WORDS) OH, IT'S BEEN HELL, 130 STRANG
NINA/
IT'S TOO IDIOTIC FOR WORDS/ 168 STRANG
SHE LOOKS UP AT JOHN AND FORCES THE WORDS OUT 462 WELDED
SLOWLY)
ALTHOUGH THE WORDS ARE CLEARLY ENOUGH DEFINED. 471 WELDED
(HE CHUCKLES SARDONICALLY AT HIS OWN PLAY ON 473 WELDED
WORDS.)
FINALLY THEIR LIPS FORCE OUT WORDS.) 480 WELDED
(EXALTED BY HIS EXULTATION RATHER THAN BY HIS 488 WELDED
WORDS)

WORE
YOU'RE ALL WORE OUT CRYIN' OVER WHAT CAN'T BE 548 'ILE
HELPED.
YOU DON'T WANT TO BE ALL WORE OUT WHEN THE 151 BEYOND
SPECIALIST COMES, DO YOU$
I'M WORE OUT WITH YOU STEPPIN' ON MY TOES, YOU 471 CARIBE
CLUMSY NICK.
DON'T YE GIT WORE OUT/ 252 DESIRE
AND HE WORE A COLORED HANDKERCHIEF ROUND HIS NECK 430 DYNAMO
JUST LIKE A COWBOY...
THE KINDEST, BIGGEST-HEARTED GUY EVER WORE SHOE 722 ICEMAN
LEATHER.
OF THE MAN I WAS WHEN I WORE THIS UNIFORM WITH 89 POET
HONOR.
HE'D OUGHT TO BE SHAMED HE IVIR WORE THE BLOODY 100 POET
RED AV ENGLAND.

WORK
INSTEAD OF DOIN' YOUR RIGHTFUL WORK, 539 'ILE
WE AIN'T AGOIN' TO WORK NO MORE 'LESS YOU PUTS 544 'ILE
BACK FOR HOME,
-WURK AND PRAY WHILE YOU MAY. 233 AHWILD
WELL, GET IT OFF YOUR MIND AND GIVE SOMETHING ELSE239 AHWILD
A CHANCE TO WORK.
INTENSELY CONCENTRATED ON HER WORK. 249 AHWILD
(RESENTFULLY) I SEE THIS IS GOING TO WORK AROUND 265 AHWILD
TO WHERE IT'S ALL MY FAULT/
THAT'S THE TIME PA AND MA COME UP TO BED, AS 280 AHWILD
REGULAR AS CLOCK WORK.
I DON'T SEE BUT WHAT IT MIGHT WORK OUT REAL WELL. 290 AHWILD
(CURIOUSLY) WHAT DOES SHE WORK AT, YOUR ANNA$ 10 ANNA
AND WORK ME TO DEATH LIKE A DOG. 18 ANNA

WORK

WORK (CONT'D.)
YOU WORK TOO HARD FOR YOUNG GEL ALREADY. 23 ANNA
GEE, I'D YUST LOVE TO WORK ON IT, HONEST I WOULD, 26 ANNA
IF I WAS A MAN.
(HE LAUGHS) ALL IN THE DAY'S WORK, DARLIN'. 31 ANNA
YOU DID SOME HARD WORK, DIDN'T YOUS 36 ANNA
(SURPRISED) WORK ON LAND, IS ITS 37 ANNA
HE IS SILENT, HIS FACE AVERTED, HIS FEATURES 59 ANNA
BEGINNING TO WORK WITH FURY.
RETURNING FROM HIS WORK IN THE FIELDS. 82 BEYOND
INSPIRED BY THE SAME LOVE, WILL TAKE UP THE WORK 84 BEYOND
WHERE HE LEAVES OFF.
BUT AS A PLACE TO WORK AND GROW THINGS, YOU HATE 84 BEYOND
IT.
THIS FARM IS HIS LIFE-WORK, AND HE'S HAPPY IN 84 BEYOND
KNOWING THAT ANOTHER MAYO,
WITH PLENTY O' ROOM TO WORK IN. 98 BEYOND
AND THE MEN WHAT DID THE WORK ON IT--WHAT'LL THEY 103 BEYOND
THINK
YOU CAN EASILY GET A MAN TO DO MY WORK. 105 BEYOND
NOTICE RIGHT NOW WHEN WE'RE UP TO OUR NECKS IN 105 BEYOND
HARD WORK.
I'VE DONE MY SHARE OF WORK HERE. 107 BEYOND
I COULDN'T TAKE INTEREST IN THE WORK ANY MORE, 110 BEYOND
WORK WITH NO PURPOSE IN SIGHT.
AND ANXIOUS TO GET HOME AND SETTLE DOWN TO WORK 115 BEYOND
AGAIN.
AT ANY RATE IT WAS GOD'S WORK--AND HIS WILL BE 116 BEYOND
DONE.
AND YOU DOIN' THE WORK/ 117 BEYOND
(SHORTLY) YOU'VE GOT TO GET BACK TO YOUR WORK, I 119 BEYOND
S'POSE.
AND BESIDES, YOU'VE GOT YOUR OWN WORK THAT'S GOT 122 BEYOND
TO BE DONE.
HAVEN'T I GOT MY SHARE OF TROUBLES TRYING TO WORK 122 BEYOND
THIS CURSED FARM
(SPITEFULLY) WORK YOU'LL NEVER GET DONE BY 122 BEYOND
READING BOOKS ALL THE TIME.
BUT WHY ARE YOU QUITTING NOW, BEN, WHEN YOU KNOW 124 BEYOND
I'VE SO MUCH WORK ON HANDS
'TWASN'T WORK, ANYHOW. 124 BEYOND
TWO OF THE CREW ARE DOWN WITH FEVER AND WE'RE 126 BEYOND
SHORT-HANDED ON THE WORK.
TO WORK AND DO THINGS LIKE OTHER PEOPLE. 127 BEYOND
WELL, THERE WAS SO MUCH DIRTY WORK GETTING THINGS 131 BEYOND
SHIP-SHAPE AGAIN I MUST HAVE
TO WORK THE PLACE ON A SALARY AND PERCENTAGE. 137 BEYOND
WHAT DECENT PERSON'D WANT TO WORK ON A PLACE LIKE 152 BEYOND
THISS
BUT THAT'S A POOR SHOWING FOR FIVE YEARS' HARD 157 BEYOND
WORK.
AND THE KIND UF REST I NEED IS HARD WORK IN THE 157 BEYOND
OPEN--
PLENTY O' WORK AND NO FOOD--AND THE OWNERS RIDIN' 480 CARDIF
AROUND IN CARRIAGES/
JUST ONE SHIP AFTER ANOTHER, HARD WORK, SMALL PAY,486 CARDIF
AND BUM GRUB.
AND KIDS TO PLAY WITH AT NIGHT AFTER SUPPER WHEN 486 CARDIF
YOUR WORK WAS DONE.
THAT IT WOULD BE INTERESTING TO WORK OUT YOUR 495 DAYS
HERO'S ANSWER TO HIS PROBLEM,
MERELY TRYING TO WORK OUT THE ANSWER TO A PUZZLE--496 DAYS
A HUMAN PUZZLE.
THAT'S THE HARDEST JOB WE HAVE NOW, FATHER-- 501 DAYS
KEEPING UP THE PRETENSE OF WORK.
HIS WORKS 523 DAYS
BUT IT IS--AND THAT'S ENTIRELY JOHN'S WORK, NOT 523 DAYS
MINE.
I WANT TO DO A LITTLE MORE WORK ON MY PLOT. 530 DAYS
HE TRIED TO ESCAPE THEM IN WORK. 536 DAYS
SIMEON AND PETER COME IN FROM THEIR WORK IN THE 203 DESIRE
FIELDS.
THEIR SHOULDERS STOOP A BIT FROM YEARS OF FARM 204 DESIRE
WORK.
ME COOKIN COOKIN'--DOIN' HER WORK--THAT MADE ME 209 DESIRE
KNOW HER, SUFFER HER SUFFERIN'--
BY THE ETERNAL, I KIN BREAK MOST O' THE YOUNG 234 DESIRE
FELLERS' BACKS AT ANY KIND O' WORK
WAAL--YE BETTER GIT T' WORK. 246 DESIRE
AN' HE KIN DO A GOOD NIGHT'S WORK, TOO/ 249 DESIRE
HE KIN DO A DAY'S WORK A'MOST UP T' WHAT I KIN-- 249 DESIRE
HE KIN WORK DAY AN' NIGHT TOO, LIKE I KIN, IF NEED249 DESIRE
BE/
I COULDN'T WORK TODAY. 267 DESIRE
EVEN THIS DIDN'T WORK. 503 DIFRNT
YOU GOT TO PLAY THIS JOKE ON HIM YOURSELF OR IT 504 DIFRNT
WON'T WORK.
I TOLD HER TO CUT THE ROUGH WORK AND BEHAVE--AND 4525 DIFRNT
NICE TIME WAS HAD BY ALL.
I'LL BET I KIN WORK IT, TUG/ 531 DIFRNT
THEY ONLY GOT THROUGH WITH THE WORK TWO WEEKS AGO.535 DIFRNT
BUT HE DOES HIS WORK GOOD...TOO DAMNED GOOD/... 478 DYNAMO
STEEL WORK, INSULATORS, BUSSES, SWITCHES, ETC. 483 DYNAMO
STRETCHING UPWARD TO THE ROOF.
THAT'S PART OF THE DAY'S WORK. 176 EJONES
YOU DIDN'T LET ME IN ON YO' CROOKED WORK OUT O' NO177 EJONES
KIND FEELIN'S DAT TIME.
I DONE DE DIRTY WORK FO' YOU--AND MOST O' DE BRAIN177 EJONES
WORK, TOO, FO' DAT MATTER--
IT DON'T GIT ME NOTHIN' TO DO MISSIONARY WORK FOR 185 EJONES
DE BAPTIST CHURCH.
AND AT THAT SIGNAL ALL THE CONVICTS START TO WORK 194 EJONES
ON THE ROAD.
SETH BECKWITH, THE MANNONS' GARDENER AND MAN OF ALL 6 ELECTR
WORK.
(HE TURNS AWAY ABRUPTLY) WAL, CALC'CLATE I BETTER 20 ELECTR
GIT BACK TO WORK.
NOT ABLE TO WORK, NOT KNOWING WHERE TO REACH ME, 26 ELECTR

WORK (CONT'D.)
THE WORK ON THE =FLYING TRADES= IS ALL FINISHED, 40 ELECTR
ISN'T ITS
THEN I MADE UP MY MIND I'D DO MY WORK IN THE WORLD 55 ELECTR
HE DID THE WORK AND LET OTHERS DO THE SHOWING-OFF. 69 ELECTR
MANY'S A TIME I'VE SEED A SKIPPER AN' MATES 105 ELECTR
SWEATIN' BLOOD TO BEAT WORK OUT OF A
(SHE STARTS TO WORK. 142 ELECTR
HE IS INTENT ON HIS WORK. 149 ELECTR
(SHARPLY) YOUR WORKS 150 ELECTR
WHAT WORKS 150 ELECTR
AND I FIND ARTIFICIAL LIGHT MORE APPROPRIATE FOR 150 ELECTR
MY WORK--
I WANT TO BE ALONE--TO FINISH MY WORK. 156 ELECTR
SETH, YOU GO WORK IN BACK, PLEASE/ 171 ELECTR
IF HE'LL ONLY WORK HARD ENOUGH. 259 GGBROW
(DUTIFULLY) I'LL WORK HARD, DAD. 259 GGBROW
THEY TALK AS THEY WORK. 302 GGBROW
THEY WORK SILENTLY.) 302 GGBROW
THEY WORK.) 302 GGBROW
THEY WORK.) 302 GGBROW
HE'S GOT TO BE ABLE TO WORK WITHOUT DISTRACTIONS. 304 GGBROW
DION IS HARD AT WORK ON HIS DESIGN FOR THE NEW 304 GGBROW
STATE CAPITOL.
(THEY WORK.) 304 GGBROW
DON'T WORK DION TO DEATH/ 305 GGBROW
I'VE GOT TO DO SOME WORK. 310 GGBROW
(DISAPPOINTEDLY) WHAT, HAS THAT OLD BILLY BROWN 310 GGBROW
GOT YOU TO WORK AT HOME AGAIN,
I'VE GOT TO WORK. 312 GGBROW
HE STARES AHEAD, THEN SHAKES OFF HIS THOUGHTS AND 312 GGBROW
CONCENTRATES ON HIS WORK--
OUR BEAUTIFUL NEW CAPITOL CALLS YOU, MR. DION/ TO 312 GGBROW
WORK/
(THE TWO DRAFTSMEN IN THE NEXT ROOM HAVE STOPPED 313 GGBROW
WORK AND ARE LISTENING.)
(HE BENDS OVER HIS WORK.) 313 GGBROW
THE TWO DRAFTSMEN HAVE BENT OVER THEIR WORK. 314 GGBROW
CROSS EACH OTHER LIKE THE STEEL FRAME-WORK OF A 207 HA APE
CAGE.
WORK--AYE, HARD WORK--BUT WHO'D MIND THAT AT ALLS 214 HA APE
SURE, YOU WORKED UNDER THE SKY AND 'TWAS WORK WID 214 HA APE
SKILL AND DARING TO IT.
IT TAKES A MAN TO WORK IN HELL. 215 HA APE
AFTER EXHAUSTING THE MORBID THRILLS OF SOCIAL 219 HA APE
SERVICE WORK ON NEW YORK'S EAST
SEE DE STEEL WORKS 238 HA APE
WE GOT PLENTY OUT OF WORK. 247 HA APE
WHAT WE NEED IS MEN WHO CAN HOLD THEIR JOBS---AND 247 HA APE
WORK FOR US AT THE SAME TIME.
YOU OUGHT TO SEE THE DOLLS GET SORED UP WHEN I 13 HUGHIE
WORK IT ON THEM/
AFTER GRAMMAR SCHOOL, MY OLD MAN PUT ME TO WORK IN 14 HUGHIE
HIS STORE.
(THE NIGHT CLERK SEEMS TURNED INTO A DROOPING WAX- 14 HUGHIE
WORK, DRAPED ALONG THE DESK.
AND IT DIDN'T WORK OUT SO BAD. 25 HUGHIE
BUT I'M A BARTENDER AND I WORK HARD FOR MY LIVIN' 580 ICEMAN
IN DIS DUMP.
THE TWO OF THEM WHEN THEY CAME HERE TO WORK 593 ICEMAN
DON'T ASK ME WHAT HIS TWO PALS WORK AT BECAUSE 594 ICEMAN
THEY DON'T.
WE'LL MAKE IT NEXT YEAR, EVEN IF WE HAVE TO WORK 605 ICEMAN
AND EARN OUR PASSAGE MONEY, EH$
SURE, IT'S HOT, PARCHING WORK LAUGHING AT YOUR 606 ICEMAN
JOKES/
(DISTURBED--ANGRILY) YOU BUGHOUSE I-WON'T-WORK 626 ICEMAN
HARP,
AND NEVER WORK IF YOU CAN HELP IT, YOU MAY LIVE TO626 ICEMAN
A RIPE OLD AGE.
(MUSINGLY) YOU CAN'T BE TOO CAREFUL ABOUT WORK. 626 ICEMAN
AS IF HE HATED HIMSELF FOR EVERY WORK HE SAID, AND660 ICEMAN
YET COULDN'T STOP/
AS THE CURTAIN RISES, ROCKY FINISHES HIS WORK 665 ICEMAN
BEHIND THE BAR.
DON'T EXPECT US TO WORK TONIGHT, 'CAUSE WE WON'T, 669 ICEMAN
SEE/
I HAVE THE GREAT STRENGTH TO DO WORK OF TEN 676 ICEMAN
ORDINARY MENS.
(HE PATS JIMMY ON THE BACK) GOOD WORK, JIMMY, 684 ICEMAN
(SPIRITLESSLY) GOOD WORK. 691 ICEMAN
ALONE WITH A BOTTLE OF BOOZE, BUT HE COULDN'T MAKE700 ICEMAN
IT WORK/
AND THE DIRTY WORK THEY'RE DOIN' ALL THE WARS 515 INZONE
HIS REAL ESTATE BARGAINS DON'T WORK OUT SO WELL. 15 JOURNE
SO KEEP UP THE GOOD WORK, MARY. 17 JOURNE
YOU MUSTN'T MAKE EDMUND WORK ON THE GROUNDS WITH 29 JOURNE
YOU, JAMES, REMEMBER.
I WAS HOPING HE'D FOUND THE WORK HE WANTS TO DO AT 36 JOURNE
LAST.
WELL, IF WE'RE GOING TO CUT THE FRONT HEDGE TODAY, 39 JOURNE
WE'D BETTER GO TO WORK.
DID I ACTUALLY HEAR YOU SUGGESTING WORK ON THE 40 JOURNE
FRONT HEDGE, JAMES/
WELL, IF YOU'RE GOING TO WORK ON THE HEDGE WHY 41 JOURNE
DON'T YOU GOS
THE WAY TO START WORK IS TO START WORK. 41 JOURNE
I LOVE TO LIE IN THE SHADE AND WATCH HIM WORK. 49 JOURNE
(SHE CHUCKLES.) I'LL WAGER MISTER JAMIE WOULDN'T 52 JOURNE
MISS THE TIME TO STOP WORK AND
SHE WASN'T ASLEEP WHEN I FINISHED MY WORK UPSTAIRS 53 JOURNE
A WHILE BACK.
YOU, WHO, THANKS TO HIM, HAVE NEVER HAD TO WORK 60 JOURNE
HARD IN YOUR LIFE/
(FROWNS AT HIM.) JAMIE IS WELCOME AFTER HIS HARD 65 JOURNE
MORNING'S WORK.
IT'S FOR THE LADY I WORK FOR, MRS. 103 JOURNE

1823 — WORKED

WORK (CONT'D.)

IF YOU CAN CALL IT WORK WHEN YOU DO SOMETHING YOU 103 JOURNE

LOVE.
THEY WORK HARD FOR POOR WAGES. 116 JOURNE
YOUR FATHER HAD TO GO TO WORK IN A MACHINE SHOP 117 JOURNE
WHEN HE WAS ONLY TEN YEARS OLD.
AND FOUND OUT WHAT HARD WORK FOR LITTLE PAY WAS, 145 JOURNE
OH, I KNOW YOU HAD A FLING OF HARD WORK WITH YOUR 146 JOURNE
BACK AND HANDS,
YOU TALK OF WORK/ 148 JOURNE
MADE FUN OF WORK AS SUCKER'S GAME. 165 JOURNE
WHEN I SAID IN KINDNESS, - YOU MUST GO BACK TO 286 LAZARU
WORK,- THEY LAUGHED AT ME/
THEY COME TO HIM AND WORK FOR NOTHING/ 287 LAZARU
(THE SOLDIERS WORK WITH A WILL. 304 LAZARU
SURE, WHAT MAN DOESN'T COMPLAIN OF HIS WORK, AND 20 MANSNS
PRETEND HE'S A SLAVE$
YOU KNOW I'VE NEVER BELIEVED YOUR DREAM WOULD 46 MANSNS
WORK.
BUT YOU WOULD SEND ME INTO MY STUDY TO WORK ON IT 46 MANSNS
LIKE A REGULAR SLAVE-DRIVER/
I WILL GO BACK TO MY WORK. 71 MANSNS
(GETS UP FROM HIS CHAIR.) IF YOU HAVE DONE, MAY I 74 MANSNS
GO BACK TO MY WORK$
WELL, I WANT YOU TO WORK WITH ME HERE IN THE 89 MANSNS
COMPANY
YOU WILL START YOUR WORK HERE TOMORROW MORNING. 92 MANSNS
YES, THAT PART WILL WORK ITSELF OUT ACCORDING TO 94 MANSNS
PLAN.
ON YOUR RETURN FROM WORK, I KNOW THE CHILDREN 103 MANSNS
WOULD BE PLEASED TO SEE YOU.
SARA IS PRETENDING TO WORK ON A PIECE OF NEEDLE- 117 MANSNS
POINT.
(THINKING.) SHE IS ONLY PRETENDING TO WORK ON HER118 MANSNS
NEEDLE-POINT--
I WORK LIKE A SLAVE ALL DAY TO STUFF YOUR 130 MANSNS
INSATIABLE MAWS
HE GOT ME TO AGREE TO WORK WITH HIM AT HIS OFFICE 132 MANSNS
FROM NOW ON.
AND HE ASKED ME WOULDN'T I PLEASE HELP HIM WITH 132 MANSNS
HIS WORK AND SHARE--
FINALLY, SEEING SHE IS APPARENTLY ABSORBED IN HER 140 MANSNS
WORK,
(HARSHLY.) GET BACK TO YOUR WORK/ 142 MANSNS
YOU CAN GO BACK TO WORK ON YOUR PLANS FOR THE 148 MANSNS
ESTATE.
AND THE BOYS WILL WORK WITH ME. 191 MANSNS
THEY DID A LOT OF WORK FOR HIM. 356 MARCOM
YOU'RE NOT AFRAID OF WORK AND KEEP AWAKE TO 357 MARCOM
OPPORTUNITY.
THAT'S THE WORK OF A MERE HANDFUL OF RADICALS-- 392 MARCOM
I'VE APPOINTED FIVE HUNDRED COMMITTEES TO CARRY ON393 MARCOM
MY WORK AND I RETIRE
ALL PLAY AND NO WORK MAKES JACK A DULL BOY. 398 MARCOM
NOW IF I HAD THE KIND OF SHIPS WE BUILD IN VENICE 398 MARCOM
TO WORK WITH
AFTER A GOOD DAY'S WORK IN WHICH YOU KNOW YOU'VE 398 MARCOM
ACCOMPLISHED SOMETHING.
IF HER HUSBAND THINKS AT THE END OF THE VOYAGE 404 MARCOM
THAT MY WORK DESERVES A BONUS--
(CHANTING AS HIS MEN WORK) GREAT WERE THE WAVES 408 MARCOM
VOLCANOES OF FOAM
HIS VOICE UTTERS AND WARMS TO HIS WORK) 431 MARCOM
WHEN HE'S NOTHING BUT A DRUNKEN BUM WHO NEVER DONE 10 MISBEG
A TAP OF WORK IN HIS LIFE.
I DO MY WORK AND I EARN MY KEEP AND I'VE A RIGHT 19 MISBEG
TO BE FREE.
AS IF THAT WOULD EVER WORK. 21 MISBEG
(TURNING AWAY) AND IF THAT DIDN'T WORK, 22 MISBEG
I NEED HARD WORK IN THE SUN TO CLEAR IT. 35 MISBEG
I'LL GO TO THE MEADOW AND FINISH MIKE'S WORK. 35 MISBEG
I'LL DO NO MORE WORK/ 64 MISBEG
WELL, THE AGENT DID A LITTLE DETECTIVE WORK AND HE 65 MISBEG
DISCOVERED IT CAME FROM
AND BEFORE HE FINISHED I TAKE MY OATH I BEGAN TO 87 MISBEG
HOPE YOU COULD REALLY WORK
THE BOOZE AT THE INN DIDN'T WORK TONIGHT. 106 MISBEG
WELL, THIS'LL WORK. 106 MISBEG
IT MIGHT WORK-- 124 MISBEG
I KNOW HOW YOU FEEL, AND IF I COULD GIVE YOU 140 MISBEG
HAPPINESS--BUT IT WOULDN'T WORK.
BUT IT DIDN'T WORK. 143 MISBEG
BUT IT DIDN'T WORK. 145 MISBEG
BUT NOT BEFORE YOUR LIE HAD DONE ITS WORK-- 163 MISBEG
YOU CAN LIVE ALONE AND WORK ALONE YOUR CUNNING 164 MISBEG
SCHEME ON YOURSELF.
AND IT'S TIME FOR ME TO START WORK, NOT GO TO BED.172 MISBEG
WELL, I'LL RUN ALONG AND LET YOU DO YOUR WORK. 173 MISBEG
BE THE SAINTS, THERE'S A BLACKSMITH AT WORK ON IT/ 8 POET
I CAME TO THESE PARTS LOOKING FOR WORK. 9 POET
AND BUILD HIS OWN CABIN, AND DO ALL THE WORK, AND 29 POET
SUPPORT HIMSELF SIMPLY,
A BIT OF FARM LAND NO ONE WOULD WORK ANY MORE, AND 30 POET
THE REST ALL WILDERNESS/
I SEE WORK ON THE RAILROAD AT BALTIMORE IS 40 POET
PROGRESSING.
THE THIRD DRINK BEGINS TO WORK AND HIS FACE 43 POET
BECOMES ARROGANTLY SELF-ASSURED.
ABOUT LOVIN' HORSES, AND GIVE ME A CHANCE TO 103 POET
FINISH MY WORK$
LIKE A MAN WHO WOULD PERMIT HIS DAUGHTER TO WORK 118 POET
AS A WAITRESS$
AND WORK OUR HANDS TO THE BONE, OR STARVE ITSELF, 146 POET
SURE, I'M NOT IN LOVE WITH WORK, I'LL CONFESS, 174 POET
«RENDER UNTO THEM A RECOMPENSE, O LORD, ACCORDING 584 ROPE
TO THE WORK OF THEIR HANDS.»
AN' WE'D BOTH WORK HARD WITH A MAN OR TWO TO HELP,587 ROPE
(JOVIALLY) GOOD WORK/ 591 ROPE

WORK (CONT'D.)

LET'S GIT TO WORK. 600 ROPE
WE GOT WORK TO DO FIRST. 601 ROPE
I MUST START WORK TOMORROW... 5 STRANG
HOW I COULD WORK THEN/...)) 31 STRANG
AND I'LL WORK MY WAY UP FOR HER--I KNOW I CAN/ 32 STRANG
ONCE HE GROWS UP AND BUCKLES DOWN TO WORK. 38 STRANG
YOU WORK WITH THEM. 40 STRANG
YOU'LL WORK YOURSELF INTO-- 42 STRANG
NOW THAT YOU'VE GOT THE CHANCE YOU'VE ALWAYS 49 STRANG
WANTED TO DO RESEARCH WORK.
THAT'S BEEN THE WORK OF MY LIFE, KEEPING HIM FROM 60 STRANG
KNOWING.
BUT SIMPLY GOT TO WORK OUT SOMETHING OR... 67 STRANG
I KNOW IT ISN'T PLEASANT FOR YOU HAVING ME DRAG MY 69 STRANG
WORK OUT HERE.
NEED ALL MY MIND ON MY WORK... 78 STRANG
HONESTLY, NINA, I'VE BEEN SO RUSHED WITH WORK 80 STRANG
DAMN IT, MY MIND WON'T WORK/... 85 STRANG
FORGET HER IN WORK/... 105 STRANG
BUCKLE DOWN TO WORK NOW/ 106 STRANG
(I MUST GET BACK TO WORK/..... 112 STRANG
HOW QUEERLY THINGS WORK OUT/.... 112 STRANG
IT HAS GOT TO BE DONE SYMPATHETICALLY OR I WON'T 113 STRANG
BE ABLE TO WORK.....
AND FOR YOUR WORK. 115 STRANG
THEY CAN'T PILE ON THE WORK FAST ENOUGH. 121 STRANG
IF IT'S A CASE OF WORK, GO TO IT/ 122 STRANG
WORK.... 125 STRANG
(LOOKING AT HER MEANINGLY) MY LIFE WORK IS TO 140 STRANG
RUST--NICELY AND UNOBTRUSIVELY/
YOU KNOW BETTER THAN TO CALL THAT WORK. 140 STRANG
AND WHEN I'M DOWN THERE I DO WORK HARD, HELPING 140 STRANG
PRESTON.
HE'S DOING REMARKABLE WORK ALREADY, AND HE'S STILL140 STRANG
IN HIS TWENTIES.
I DON'T SEE HOW YOU CAN AFFORD TO LEAVE YOUR WORK 140 STRANG
FOR SUCH LONG PERIODS.
(BITTERLY) MY WORK WAS FINISHED TWELVE YEARS AGO.140 STRANG
EVEN IF I CALL YOU BACK BEFORE THEN--AND WORK THIS145 STRANG
TIME, REALLY WORK$
(HIS WORK.... 147 STRANG
TWO YEARS OF HARD WORK. 147 STRANG
WITHOUT BEING TOO RUDE, I URGED HIM TO GET BACK TO155 STRANG
HIS WORK,
WORK/ 165 STRANG
IN THAT WAY I FEEL I'VE PAID MY DEBT--THAT HIS 166 STRANG
WORK IS PARTLY MY WORK.
THEN I CAN GO BACK TO WORK.... 190 STRANG
TO STEAL MY WORK/...)) 192 STRANG
A HALF-MILLION FOR YOUR STATION TO BE USED IN 192 STRANG
BIOLOGICAL RESEARCH WORK.
I'M GOING BACK TO WORK. 196 STRANG
YUST WORK, WORK, WORK ON SHIP. 502 VOYAGE
I GOT ALL SEA I WANT FOR MY LIFE--TOO MUCH HARD 502 VOYAGE
WORK FOR LITTLE MONEY.
WORK ON FARM. 503 VOYAGE
(GRINNING) NO MORE SEA, NO MORE BUM GRUB, NO MORE503 VOYAGE
STORMS--YUST NICE WORK.
I WORK ON FARM TILL I AM EIGHTEEN. 503 VOYAGE
I LIKE IT, TOO--IT'S NICE--WORK ON FARM. 503 VOYAGE
ROTTEN GRUB AND DEY MAKE YOU WORK ALL TIME-- 507 VOYAGE
OH, I'M GOING TO WORK SO HARD, MICHAEL/ 445 WELDED
I KNEW I HAD FINALLY WON--THROUGH YOUR WORK/ 447 WELDED
YOUR WORK SAVED MINE. 447 WELDED
EVEN MY WORK MUST EXIST ONLY AS AN ECHO OF YOURS. 453 WELDED
SOLITUDE AND WORK. 457 WELDED
THE WORK WAS DONE. 457 WELDED
(SHARPLY) YOU IMAGINE I'M JEALOUS OF YOUR WORK$ 457 WELDED
I SUPPOSE YOU THINK THAT WITHOUT YOUR WORK I-- 457 WELDED
YOUR APPEARANCE IN THE WORK OF OTHER PLAYWRIGHTS--457 WELDED
AS FOR MY WORK, YOU'VE ACKNOWLEDGED A MILLION 457 WELDED
TIMES--
THEY DIDN'T WANT YOUR WORK, YOU KNOW IT/ 458 WELDED
(FURIOUSLY) GOOD GOD, HOW DARE YOU CRITICIZE 459 WELDED
CREATIVE WORK, YOU ACTRESS/
NOTHING MEANT ANYTHING THEN BUT A CHANCE TO DO MY 459 WELDED
WORK--YES, I AGREED--
IT WILL GIVE YOU PEACE FOR YOUR WORK--FREEDOM-- 486 WELDED
I'LL WORK FOR YOU/ 486 WELDED

WORK'S

I THOUGHT YOU WERE A REAL FIND, BUT YOUR WORK'S 67 STRANG
FALLEN OFF TO NOTHING....))

WORKABLE

THERE'S ONLY ONE WORKABLE WAY AND THAT'S TO 394 MARCOM
CONQUER EVERYBODY ELSE IN THE WORLD

WORKED

KEEP US ALL HERE AFTER OUR TIME IS WORKED OUT 537 'ILE
D'YOU THINK I'VE NOT SEEN THEIR UGLY LOOKS AND THE539 'ILE
GRUDGIN' WAY THEY WORKED$
EXCUSE ME, RUTH, FOR GETTING WORKED UP OVER IT... 88 BEYOND
YOU LOOK ALL WORKED UP OVER SOMETHING, ROBBIE. 99 BEYOND
YOU'VE ALWAYS WORKED ON IT WITH THAT 105 BEYOND
UNDERSTANDING...
I HAVEN'T GOT IT FINALLY WORKED OUT. 497 DAYS
THE END ISN'T CLEARLY WORKED OUT YET. 530 DAYS
THAT WOULD BE VERY INCONSIDERATE AFTER HE'S WORKED550 DAYS
OUT SUCH A CONVENIENT END FOR
I'VE WORKED FOR ELECTRICIANS. I'VE GONE OUT 461 DYNAMO
HELPING LINESMEN,
GETTIN' THEIR COURAGE WORKED UP B'FORE THEY STARTS184 EJONES
AFTER YOU.
HE SANK DOWN AND DOWN AND MY MOTHER WORKED AND 25 ELECTR
SUPPORTED HIM.
SHE'S WORKED HERSELF INTO SUCH A STATE OF GRIEF 80 ELECTR
WOULD YOU BELIEVE IT THAT SHE HAS WORKED IT ALL 87 ELECTR
OUT THAT

WORKED

WORKED (CONT'D.)
I'VE SAILED ON MANNUN HOOKERS AN' BEEN WORKED T' 106 ELECTR DEATH
HE'S WORKED LIKE A DOG-- 317 GGBROW
SURE, YOU WORKED UNDER THE SKY AND 'TWAS WORK WID 214 HA APE SKILL AND DARING TO IT.
WORKED ALONG SHORE. 234 HA APE
WHO ONCE WORKED FOR A CIRCUS IN THE TICKET WAGON. 594 ICEMAN
BESIDES, I STILL WORKED THEN, AND THE CIRCUS 608 ICEMAN SEASON WAS GOING TO BEGIN SOON.
I GOT ALL WORKED UP, SHE WAS SO PRETTY AND SWEET 710 ICEMAN AND GOOD.
YOU'RE GETTING YOURSELF WORKED UP OVER NOTHING. 46 JOURNE
BUT HE'S WORKED HARD ALL HIS LIFE. 60 JOURNE
YOU WORKED HARD BEFORE YOU TOOK ILL. 89 JOURNE
I WORKED SO HARD AT MY MUSIC IN THE CONVENT-- 103 JOURNE
AND WORKED IN WITH THE FOLDS THAT WERE DRAPED 115 JOURNE ROUND
YOU'VE GOT YOURSELF WORKED UP OVER NOTHING. 146 JOURNE
I WORKED TWELVE HOURS A DAY IN A MACHINE SHOP, 148 JOURNE LEARNING TO MAKE FILES.
I'D WORKED LIKE HELL. 150 JOURNE
HE USED TO BE PALE EVEN WHEN HE WORKED IN THE 276 LAZARU FIELDS.
WHO ONCE WORKED UNDER HIS FATHER AND KNOWS THE 34 MANSNS BUSINESS,
--HAVE WORKED TOO HARD ON THIS RAILROAD DEAL-- 131 MANSNS
YOUR OWN PLANTATIONS WORKED BY YOUR OWN SLAVES-- 157 MANSNS
FOR HIS OLD MAN WHO'D WORKED UP FROM NOTHING TO BE 24 MISBEG RICH AND FAMOUS
AND THEN CAME SNEAKING HERE TO SEE IF THE SCHEME 159 MISBEG BEHIND YOUR SCHEME HAD WORKED/
YOU WORKED IT SO IT WAS ME WHO DID ALL THE DIRTY 163 MISBEG SCHEMING--
WHERE HE WORKED FOR A YEAR AFTER HE GRADUATED FROM 29 POET HARVARD COLLEGE,
AND NOT GET SO WORKED UP OVER WHAT I SHOULD SAY IS 12 STRANG A COMBINATION OF IMAGINATION
IT'S A PRETTY IDEA BUT IT HASN'T WORKED OUT. 36 STRANG
HE HAS WORKED HIMSELF INTO A REAL ANGER.) 191 STRANG

WORKER
WISE, HELL/ A DAMNED OLD FOOL ANARCHIST I-WON'T- 605 ICEMAN WORKER/
UNQUESTIONINGLY, AS THOUGH YOU WERE THE MEANEST 153 MANSNS WORKER IN MY MILLS.
I'M VERY MUCH A WORKER IN THE RANKS. 165 STRANG

WORKERS
WHY SHOULDN'T THE WORKERS OF THE WORLD UNITE AND 195 AHWILD RISE?
DID HE SIGN FOR HINSULTS TO OUR DIGNITY AS 'ONEST 228 HA APE WORKERS
CALLING THEMSELVES THE INDUSTRIAL WORKERS OF THE 242 HA APE WORLD.
EIGHT OR TEN MEN, LONGSHOREMEN, IRON WORKERS, AND 245 HA APE THE LIKE.
A BIG SIGNBOARD IS ON THE WALL AT THE REAR, 245 HA APE -INDUSTRIAL WORKERS OF THE WORLD--
FROM THE MARKET PEOPLE ACROSS THE STREET AND THE 594 ICEMAN WATERFRONT WORKERS,
FOR THE BENEFIT OF THEIR WORKERS PRINCIPALLY, 149 JOURNE

WORKIN'
THERE AIN'T A SQUARE-HEAD WORKIN' ON A BOAT MAN 11 ANNA ENOUGH TO GIT AWAY WITH THAT.
WELL, YOU'RE STILL WORKIN' ON IT, AIN'T YOU. 21 ANNA
YOU AIN'T BEEN WORKIN' HERE FOR NO HIRE, ANDY, 105 BEYOND
WHAT GOOD'S WORKIN' HARD IF IT DON'T ACCOMPLISH 114 BEYOND ANYTHING, I'D LIKE TO KNOWS
THEY WAS LAUGHIN' AT ME FOR WORKIN' FOR YOU, 124 BEYOND THAT'S WHAT/
(IRRITABLY) IF I AIN'T A SAP TO LET CHUCK KID ME 665 ICEMAN INTO WORKIN' HIS TIME
-I AIN'T NEVER TAKEN YOUR DOUGH 'CEPT WHEN I WAS 671 ICEMAN DRUNK AND NOT WORKIN'/*
YUH AIN'T GOT YOUR SEA-LEGS WORKIN' RIGHT. 595 ROPE
AND WORKIN' MYSELF TO DEATH ON SHIPS AND THINGS-- 598 ROPE

WORKING
(SUDDENLY GETS UP FROM HER CHAIR AND STANDS 233 AHWILD RIGIDLY, HER FACE WORKING--JERKILY)
IS WORKING INDUSTRIOUSLY ON A DOLLY. 288 AHWILD
TWO LONGSHOREMEN ENTER FROM THE STREET, WEARING 3 ANNA THEIR WORKING
IF THAT AIN'T A SWELL JOB TO FIND YOUR LONG LOST 15 ANNA OLD MAN WORKING AT/
WORKING AT/ 17 ANNA
SHRIVELED SWABS DOES BE WORKING IN CITIES& 48 ANNA
(HIS FACE WORKING WITH RAGE, HIS HAND GOING BACK 49 ANNA TO THE SHEATH-KNIFE ON HIS HIP)
ANDY HAS BEEN WORKING. 115 BEYOND
WON'T THEY LAUGH AT YOU JUST THE SAME WHEN YOU'RE 124 BEYOND WORKING FOR TIMMS$
AND ALWAYS READING YOUR STUPID BOOKS INSTEAD OF 127 BEYOND WORKING.
HE FINISHED WORKING WHERE HE WAS. 135 BEYOND
IF WORKING HARD AND A DETERMINATION TO GET ON CAN 138 BEYOND DO IT--
(WORKING HERSELF INTO A FIT OF RAGE) 152 BEYOND
WE CAN GET THE FARM WORKING ON A SOUND BASIS ONCE 156 BEYOND MORE.
WELL, MAYBE IT WAS THE BOOZE WORKING. 522 DAYS
HE IS DRESSED IN HIS WORKING CLOTHES. 244 DESIRE
* PARALLEL WORKING*... 429 DYNAMO
THEN LOOKS DOWN AT HIS FEET, WORKING HIS TOES 196 EJONES INSIDE THE SHOES--WITH A GROAN)
HE WEARS HIS EARTH-STAINED WORKING CLOTHES. 6 ELECTR
I FINISHED WHAT I WAS WORKING ON. 162 ELECTR
IT WOULD BE SUCH FUN FOR ME WORKING THERE/ 272 GGBROW
(A PAUSE--EMBARRASSEDLY) IS HE WORKING AT 275 GGBROW ANYTHING THESE DAYS$

WORKING (CONT'D.)
(DIFFIDENTLY) I THOUGHT HE MIGHT BE SENSITIVE 277 GGBROW ABOUT WORKING FOR--
IF YOU'D HEARD HER DEFEND YOU, LIE ABOUT YOU, TELL281 GGBROW ME HOW HARD YOU WERE WORKING,
WE MUST GET OUT PLOT TO WORKING/ 307 GGBROW
THE TWO DRAFTSMEN ARE BENT OVER THEIR TABLE, 313 GGBROW WORKING.
BROWN, AT HIS DESK, IS WORKING FEVERISHLY OVER A 313 GGBROW PLAN.
I THINK YOU'RE WORKING HIM TO DEATH. 315 GGBROW
MR. ANTHONY'S IS HE WORKING HERE AGAINS 317 GGBROW
MURDERERS AND CUTTHROATS WHO LIBEL ALL HONEST 242 HA APE WORKING MEN
BUT HELL, I ALWAYS KEEP MY NOGGIN WORKING, BOOZE 12 HUGHIE OR NO BOOZE.
IT'S STAYING SOBER AND WORKING THAT CUTS MEN OFF 626 ICEMAN IN THEIR PRIME.*
HE WEARS HIS WORKING CLOTHES, SLEEVES ROLLED UP. 664 ICEMAN
I EARN MY BOARD AND LODGING WORKING ON THE 32 JOURNE GROUNDS.
WORKING HIS WAY ALL OVER THE MAP AS A SAILOR AND 35 JOURNE ALL THAT STUFF,
HOW HE HATES WORKING IN FRONT WHERE EVERYONE 43 JOURNE PASSING CAN SEE HIM.
THAT'S WHAT I HATE ABOUT WORKING DOWN IN FRONT. 54 JOURNE
OH, I'D FORGOTTEN YOU'VE BEEN WORKING ON THE FRONT 59 JOURNE HEDGE.
I'VE BEEN WORKING IN THE DAMNED DIRT UNDER THE 68 JOURNE HEDGE ALL MORNING.
NEVER LEARNING A NEW PART, NEVER REALLY WORKING 150 JOURNE HARD.
(WORKING HIMSELF INTO A RAGE) 319 LAZARU
THE MENTAL STRAIN OF A MAN WHO HAS BEEN WORKING 43 MANSNS TOO HARD
WORKING WITH A RULER AND DRAFTING INSTRUMENTS ON A139 MANSNS PLAN.
AND LIVE LIKE A DECENT, HONEST WOMAN WORKING IN 156 MANSNS THE EARTH/
IT IS A WORKING MODEL OF A CLUMSY CANNON. 394 MARCOM
HE SEES YOU'RE NOT WORKING. 10 MISBEG
DIDN'T I OFTEN SEE HIM WORKING ON HIS GROUNDS 24 MISBEG
HER EVERYDAY WORKING DRESS IS OF CHEAP MATERIAL, 16 POET
CRACKED WORKING SHOES, RUN DOWN AT THE HEEL, ARE 20 POET ON HER BARE FEET.
SARA, WEARING HER WORKING DRESS AND APRON, 95 POET
(WORKING HERSELF TO REBELLION AGAIN.) 138 POET
WORKING FOR HIS FATHER HE HAS THE ABILITY FOR 146 POET TRADE, THOUGH HE HATES IT.
WORKING FOR HIS WIFE AND NOT JUST HIMSELF-- 54 STRANG
(WITH ANGRY DISGUST) IF ONLY THAT DAMNED RADIO 162 STRANG WAS WORKING/
(WITH A FORCED AIR) HE'S BEEN WORKING TOO HARD. 450 WELDED
WHEN YOU'RE WORKING I MIGHT DIE AND YOU'D NEVER 457 WELDED KNOW IT.
HER FEATURES ARE WORKING CONVULSIVELY. 460 WELDED

WORKS
AND EVERYTHING WORKS OUT ALL RIGHT IN THE END. 215 AHWILD
(MORE IRRITABLY) HELL, THAT GUMS THE WORKS FOR 218 AHWILD FAIR/
YOU CAN'T SAY BUT ROBERT WORKS HARD, SARAH. 114 BEYOND
SO THE POOR FOOL PRAYED AND PRAYED AND VOWED HIS 511 DAYS LIFE TO PIETY AND GOOD WORKS/
AND HER CRAZINESS ALL WORKS OUT IN HATRED FOR ME/ 86 ELECTR
AS HE WORKS, HE CHUCKLES WITH MALICIOUS GLEE-- 313 GGBROW
HOW THE OTHER HALF LIVES AND WORKS ON A SHIP, 220 HA APE
DE ANARCHIST HE NEVER WORKS. 394 ICEMAN
AW, IT AIN'T GOT NO WORKS, SO IT AIN'T NO BOMB, 528 INZONE I'LL BET.
STENDHAL, PHILOSOPHICAL AND SOCIOLOGICAL WORKS BY 11 JOURNE SCHOPENHAUER, NIETZSCHE, MARX,
(HIS FACE WORKS AND HE BLINKS BACK TEARS--WITH 112 JOURNE QUIET INTENSITY.)
IT'S THE SAME POWDER THEY'VE BEEN USING HERE IN 395 MARCOM CHILDREN'S FIRE WORKS.
BUT IT STILL WORKS NOW AND AGAIN, I'M TOLD, 22 MISBEG

WORL'
WANT ALL DE WORL' TO HEAH YOUS 191 EJONES

WORLD
I WAS OFF IN ANOTHER WORLD. 193 AHWILD
RELUCTANTLY CALLED BACK TO EARTH FROM ANOTHER 193 AHWILD WORLD.
YOU THINK THERE'S NOTHING IN THE WORLD BESIDES 195 AHWILD YALE.
WHY SHOULDN'T THE WORKERS OF THE WORLD UNITE AND 195 AHWILD RISE$
HERE I AM, THANKS TO YOUR AND NAT'S KINDNESS, WITH214 AHWILD THE BEST HOME IN THE WORLD.
ALL'S RIGHT WITH THE WORLD. 221 AHWILD
UHO, THEY CRIED, *THE WORLD IS WIDE, BUT 246 AHWILD FETTERED LIMBS GO LAME/
WHAT WOULD YOU LIKE BEST IN THE WORLD$ 273 AHWILD
HE THINKS THE WORLD OF YOU, HONEST HE DOES. 19 ANNA
(DECIDEDLY) I'D RATHER HAVE ONE DROP OF OCEAN 27 ANNA THAN ALL THE FARMS IN THE WORLD/
YOU BELONG ON A REAL SHIP, SAILING ALL OVER THE 27 ANNA WORLD.
THERE'S NOT A MAN IN THE WORLD CAN SAY THE SAME AS 33 ANNA YOU.
THAT HE SEEN MAT BURKE LYING AT HIS FEET AND HIM 33 ANNA DEAD TO THE WORLD.
FOR ANYTHING ELSE IN THE WORLD. 34 ANNA
BUT DIVIL A WOMAN IN ALL THE PORTS OF THE WORLD 34 ANNA HAS IVER MADE A GREAT FOOL OF ME
THE ONLY WOMEN YOU'D MEET IN THE PORTS OF THE 37 ANNA WORLD WHO'D BE WILLING TO SPEAK
STORM AND FOG TO THE MAN SPOT IN THE WORLD WHERE 39 ANNA YOU WAS/

1825 WORLD

WORLD (CONT'D.)

YOU'RE HER OLD MAN AND I'D NOT RAISE A FIST TO YOU 39 ANNA FOR THE WORLD.

YOU'RE THE GIRL OF THE WORLD AND WE'LL BE MARRYING 39 ANNA SOON

AND HOW IS THE WORLD TREATING YOU THIS AFTERNOON, 45 ANNA ANNA'S FATHERS

SHE'S THE WAN WOMAN OF THE WORLD FOR ME, AND I 47 ANNA CAN'T LIVE WITHOUT HER NOW,

TIS ONLY ON THE SEA HE'S FREE, AND HIM ROVING THE 48 ANNA FACE OF THE WORLD.

WAS THERE IVER A WOMAN IN THE WORLD HAD THE 60 ANNA ROTTENNESS IN HER THAT YOU HAVE,

AND WAS THERE IVER A MAN THE LIKE OF ME WAS MADE 60 ANNA THE FOOL OF THE WORLD.

WORLD WHERE I'LL NEVER SEE YOUR FACE AGAIN/ 61 ANNA (THEN ANGRILY) 'TIS BECAUSE 'TIS A GREAT WEAK 69 ANNA FOOL OF THE WORLD I AM,

AND ME WANTING TO DRIVE YOU A BLOW WOULD KNOCK YOU 70 ANNA OUT OF THIS WORLD WHERE I

THAT YOU'D NEVER HAD LOVE FOR ANY OTHER MAN IN THE 74 ANNA WORLD BUT ME--

SWEAR I'M THE ONLY MAN IN THE WORLD IVIR YOU FELT 75 ANNA LOVE FOR.

I'D BE KILLING THE WORLD-- (HE SEIZES HER IN HIS 76 ANNA ARMS AND KISSES HER FIERCELY.)

YOU'VE SEEN A BIT OF THE WORLD, ENOUGH TO MAKE THE 84 BEYOND FARM SEEM SMALL,

AND I WOULDN'T HAVE YOU MISS THIS CHANCE FOR THE 84 BEYOND WORLD.

FOR THE BEST OPPORTUNITY IN THE WORLD OF THE KIND 88 BEYOND PA THINKS OF.

(WITH A SMILE) THERE WAS ALL THE MYSTERY IN THE 89 BEYOND WORLD TO ME THEN ABOUT THAT--

THAT ALL THE WONDERS OF THE WORLD HAPPENED ON THE 90 BEYOND OTHER SIDE OF THOSE HILLS.

I WOULDN'T MISS IT FOR ANYTHING IN THE WORLD UNDER102 BEYOND ANY OTHER CIRCUMSTANCES.

I FEEL I OUGHT'NT TO MISS THIS CHANCE TO GO OUT 106 BEYOND INTO THE WORLD AND SEE THINGS,

YOU AIN'T GOT NO LIKIN' IN THE WORLD TO GO. 106 BEYOND (WITH BITTER SCORN) SO--YOU WANT TO GO OUT INTO 106 BEYOND THE WORLD AND SEE THIN'S$

(FIERCELY) I CAN WISH YOU AND RUTH ALL THE GOOD 109 BEYOND LUCK IN THE WORLD, AND I DO...

TO PUT THE WHOLE RIM OF THE WORLD BETWEEN ME AND 126 BEYOND THOSE HILLS.

IT SHOULD ME THE WORLD IS A LARGER PROPOSITION 138 BEYOND OF COURSE I'LL STAY FOR DINNER IF I MISSED EVERY 142 BEYOND DAMNED SHIP IN THE WORLD.

WHY, I LOVE ROB BETTER'N ANYBODY IN THE WORLD AND 165 BEYOND ALWAYS DID.

TRAVELIN' ALL OVER THE WORLD AND NEVER SEEIN' NONE486 CARDIF OF IT.

MAKE A MOCK O' ME WHAT HAS SEEN MORE O' THE WORLD 457 CARIBE THAN YESELF EVER WILL.

WHAT IN THE WORLD BRINGS YOU-- 500 DAYS

YOU SOMEHOW MANAGED TO LIVE IN SOME LOST WORLD 517 DAYS AND OTHERS I WOULDN'T HURT FOR ANYTHING IN THE 521 DAYS WORLD--IF I WAS IN MY RIGHT MIND.

I WOULDN'T HAVE BELIEVED IT OF ANOTHER MAN IN THE 522 DAYS WORLD.

ONLY REMEMBER, THE WORLD IS FULL OF SPITEFUL LIARS524 DAYS

WHO WOULD DO ANYTHING TO

THEY'S WORSE'N HIM IN THE WORLD, I'LL BET YE/ 214 DESIRE I'M NOT THE WUST IN THE WORLD--AN' YEW AN' ME'VE 226 DESIRE GOT A LOT IN COMMON.

BETTER'N EVERYTHIN' ELSE IN THE WORLD/ 259 DESIRE I'LL DO ANY CUSSED THING IN THE WORLD YOU WANT ME 496 DIFRNT TO, AND YOU KNOW IT/

(WITH A MAN-OF-THE-WORLD- ATTITUDE OF CYNICISM) 506 DIFRNT THEY'S TROUBLE ENOUGH IN THE WORLD WITHOUT MAKIN' 508 DIFRNT MORE.

MEN IS MEN THE WORLD OVER, I RECKON. 512 DIFRNT I KNEW YOU'D KNOW, BEING GROWED TO A MAN OF THE 520 DIFRNT WORLD NOW

SOME JAZZ, I'LL TELL THE WORLD/ 520 DIFRNT HE'D TEASE AN OLD WOMAN TO GET MONEY OUT OF HER, 528 DIFRNT AND HER ALONE IN THE WORLD.

IN INTERCOURSE WITH THE WORLD, HOWEVER, 422 DYNAMO THEY'RE ALWAYS SINGING ABOUT EVERYTHING IN THE 436 DYNAMO WORLD....)

HE'S THE KINDEST MAN IN THE WORLD...!) 439 DYNAMO (CLINGING TO HER) (I LOVE MOTHER BETTER'N 446 DYNAMO ANYTHING IN THE WORLD...

WHEN I LOVED HER BETTER THAN ANYONE IN THE 448 DYNAMO WORLD/...))

IT'S YOU WHO ARE THE KINDEST IN THE WORLD. 456 DYNAMO THEY KNOW. LIKE I DO, THAT HE'S REALLY THE KINDES7456 DYNAMO MAN IN THE WORLD.

((SINGING ALL THE TIME ABOUT EVERYTHING IN THE 458 DYNAMO WORLD*...

THEY'RE SINGING ALL THE TIME ABOUT EVERYTHING IN 458 DYNAMO THE WORLD/

WHEN YOU KISS ME LIKE THAT NOTHING IN THE WORLD 469 DYNAMO MATTERS BUT YOU/

ALWAYS SINGING ABOUT EVERYTHING IN THE WORLD*... 474 DYNAMO I TELLS 'EM DAYS * CAUSE I'M DE ON'Y MAN IN DE 179 EJONES WORLD BIG ENUFF TO GIT ME.

IN THE REAR THE FOREST IS A WALL OF DARKNESS 187 EJONES DIVIDING THE WORLD.

HE'S SAILED ALL OVER THE WORLD--HE LIVED ON A 15 ELECTR SOUTH SEA ISLAND ONCE, SO HE SAYS.

(THEN WITH INTENSITY) I LOVE FATHER BETTER THAN 22 ELECTR ANYONE IN THE WORLD.

BETWEEN US FOR THE WORLD. 23 ELECTR ONCE HE FELT THE WORLD LOOKED DOWN ON HIM. 25 ELECTR THEN I MADE UP MY MIND I'D DO MY WORK IN THE WORLD 55 ELECTR

WORLD (CONT'D.)

OTHER SIDE OF THE WORLD--FIND SOME ISLAND WHERE WE 56 ELECTR COULD BE ALONE A WHILE.

I BROUGHT YOU INTO THE WORLD. 77 ELECTR (WITH A TENDER SMILE) WE HAD A SECRET LITTLE 89 ELECTR WORLD OF OUR OWN IN THE OLD DAYS,

HE HATED YOU BECAUSE HE KNEW I LOVED YOU BETTER 86 ELECTR THAN ANYTHING IN THE WORLD/

BUT WE'LL MAKE THAT LITTLE WORLD OF OUR OWN AGAIN, 86 ELECTR WON'T WES

YOU ARE ALL I HAVE IN THE WORLD, DEAR/ 88 ELECTR I LOVE YOU BETTER THAN ANYTHING IN THE WORLD AND-- 89 ELECTR THIS WAS THE MOST BEAUTIFUL ISLAND IN THE WORLD-- 90 ELECTR AS BEAUTIFUL AS YOU, MOTHER/

I'LL SHOW YOU THE WORLD AS A DAUGHTER WHO 91 ELECTR DESIRED HER MOTHER'S LOVER AND THEN

(HE STANDS AGAINST THE WAREHOUSE, WAITING FOR THE 104 ELECTR SWAYING WORLD TO SUBSIDE.

YOU'RE ALL I HAVE IN THE WORLD/ 140 ELECTR BUT WHAT IN THE WORLD/ 147 ELECTR THERE WAS ONLY THIS WORLD--THE WARM EARTH IN THE 147 ELECTR MOONLIGHT--

I HAVE NO RIGHT IN THE SAME WORLD WITH HER. 151 ELECTR IT WILL BE THE BEST THING IN THE WORLD FOR HIM. 163 ELECTR SO HERE'S WISHING YOU ALL THE SUCCESS AND 263 GGBROW HAPPINESS IN THE WORLD, MARGARET--

ALL THE WORLD LOVES A LOVER, GOD LOVES US ALL AND 266 GGBROW *E LOVE HIM/

LET GO YOUR CLUTCH ON THE WORLD/ 267 GGBROW ACKNOWLEDGES NO WOUND TO THE WORLD. 274 GGBROW YOU KNOW DARN WELL I'D DO ANYTHING IN THE WORLD TO276 GGBROW HELP YOU--OR DION.

IT TAKES ALL KINDS OF LOVE TO MAKE A WORLD/ 285 GGBROW TO WHOM THE AFFAIRS OF THIS WORLD DO NOT--BELONG/ 290 GGBROW LEARN NOW TO DIE TO THE WORLD THAT THOU MAYST 290 GGBROW BEGIN TO LIVE WITH CHRIST/

IS THE MASK OF THE BRAVE FACE SHE PUTS ON BEFORE 291 GGBROW THE WORLD TO HIDE HER SUFFERING

STRENGTH TO LOVE IN THIS WORLD AND DIE AND SLEEP 307 GGBROW AND BECOME FERTILE EARTH,

LET THE WHOLE WORLD SUFFER AS I AM SUFFERING/ 319 GGBROW (SHE STANDS LIKE AN IDOL OF EARTH, HER EYES 323 GGBROW STARING OUT OVER THE WORLD.)

'TIS ONLY WHEN I'M DEAD TO THE WORLD I'D BE 210 HA APE WISHFUL TO SING AT ALL.

I WOULD LIKE TO BE OF SOME USE IN THE WORLD. 219 HA APE 'E MAKES ARF THE BLOODY STEEL IN THE WORLD/ 228 HA APE THE VOTES OF THE ON-MARCHING PROLETARIANS OF THE 236 HA APE BLOODY WORLD/

I CALL THEM THE INDUSTRIOUS WRECKERS OF THE 242 HA APE WORLD/

CALLING THEMSELVES THE INDUSTRIAL WORKERS OF THE 242 HA APE WORLD..

NATION THE WORLD HAS EVER KNOWN, WHERE ALL MEN ARE243 HA APE BURN FREE AND EQUAL,

TURN ALMIGHTY GOD'S REVEALED PLAN FOR THE WORLD 244 HA APE TOPSY-TURVY,

A BIG SIGNBOARD IS ON THE WALL AT THE REAR, 245 HA APE +INDUSTRIAL WORKERS OF THE WORLD--

YUH'RE DE CHAMP OF DE WORLD. 253 HA APE FOLLOWING THE FIRST WORLD WAR AND PROHIBITION, 7 HUGHIE BUT THE LAST TIME HE WAS ABLE TO FEEL DESPAIR WAS 17 HUGHIE BACK AROUND WORLD WAR DAYS

HE SAYS, +THEY'RE THE MOST BEAUTIFUL THINGS IN THE 21 HUGHIE WORLD. I THINK--

AWAKE WHEN EVERYONE ELSE IN THE WORLD IS ASLEEP, 29 HUGHIE EXCEPT ROOM 492.

AS THE HISTORY OF THE WORLD PROVES, THE TRUTH HAS 578 ICEMAN NO BEARING ON ANYTHING.

SO I SAID TO THE WORLD, GOD BLESS ALL HERE, 579 ICEMAN A SHREWD BUSINESS MAN, WHO DOESN'T MISS ANY 580 ICEMAN OPPORTUNITY TO GET ON IN THE WORLD.

AND THE PRACTICAL WISDOM OF THE WORLD IN THAT 585 ICEMAN LITTLE PARABLE.

HE'S THE ONE GUY IN THE WORLD WHO CAN UNDERSTAND--587 ICEMAN

I'VE GOTTEN BEYOND THE DESIRE TO COMMUNICATE WITH 589 ICEMAN THE WORLD--

I COULDN'T GO ON BELIEVING FOREVER THAT GANG WAS 592 ICEMAN GOING TO CHANGE THE WORLD BY

HE HAS NO NEED OF THE OUTSIDE WORLD AT ALL. 594 ICEMAN EVERYONE IN THE WORLD KNOWS-- 595 ICEMAN OF THE LATE WORLD-FAMOUS BILL OBAN, KING OF THE 595 ICEMAN BUCKET SHOPS.

I THOUGHT EVERYONE IN THE WORLD-- 595 ICEMAN STONE COLD SOBER AND DEAD TO THE WORLD/ 626 ICEMAN HE WAS POSITIVELY THE ONLY DOCTOR IN THE WORLD WHO626 ICEMAN CLAIMED THAT RATTLESNAKE

HE'S STARTED A MOVEMENT THAT'LL BLOW UP THE WORLD/634 ICEMAN THEY'RE THE BEST LITTLE SCOUTS IN THE WORLD. 639 ICEMAN I'VE ALWAYS BEEN THE BEST-NATURED SLOB IN THE 641 ICEMAN WORLD.

I HAVEN'T A SINGLE FRIEND LEFT IN THE WORLD. 646 ICEMAN I SAW IT WAS THE BEST GOVERNMENT IN THE WORLD, 648 ICEMAN AMUSEDLY) YES, WE'VE ALL HEARD YOU TELL US YOU 656 ICEMAN THOUGHT THE WORLD OF HER,

BIGGEST-HEARTED GUY IN THE WORLD/ 659 ICEMAN YOU'RE THE ONLY ONE IN THE WORLD I CAN TURN TO. 666 ICEMAN AND I'D GET BLIND TO THE WORLD NOW 680 ICEMAN OH, I KNOW I USED TO HATE EVERYONE IN THE WORLD 705 ICEMAN WHO WASN'T AS ROTTEN A BASTARD

THAN ANYTHING IN THE WORLD. 711 ICEMAN THINKING OF ALL THE WRONG I'D DONE TO THE SWEETEST714 ICEMAN WOMAN IN THE WORLD

NO ONE ELSE IN THE WORLD COULD WITHOUT DYING OF 14 JOURNE INDIGESTION.

THE MOST BEAUTIFUL IN THE WORLD/ 28 JOURNE

WORLD 1826

WORLD (CONT'D.)
SNEER AT MY PROFESSION, SNEER AT EVERY DAMNED 32 JOURNE
THING IN THE WORLD--
IT WAS IN HER LONG SICKNESS AFTER BRINGING HIM 39 JOURNE
INTO THE WORLD THAT SHE FIRST--
THEY'RE THE SWEETEST HANDS IN THE WORLD. 41 JOURNE
I HAVE ALL THE PITY IN THE WORLD FOR HER. 76 JOURNE
MORE THAN ANYTHING IN THE WORLD/ 88 JOURNE
WHEN SHE SEES NO ONE IN THE WORLD CAN BELIEVE IN 94 JOURNE
ME EVEN FOR A MOMENT ANY MORE,
IT HIDES YOU FROM THE WORLD AND THE WORLD FROM 98 JOURNE
YOU.
ALL THE PEOPLE IN THE WORLD COULD PASS BY AND I 102 JOURNE
WOULD NEVER KNOW.
HE WAS DIFFERENT FROM ALL ORDINARY MEN, LIKE 105 JOURNE
SOMEONE FROM ANOTHER WORLD.
THEN FROM THE WORLD OUTSIDE COMES THE MELANCHOLY 107 JOURNE
MOAN OF THE FOGHORN.
BECAUSE I WAS SO AFRAID TO BRING YOU INTO THE 111 JOURNE
WORLD.
TO BE ALONE WITH MYSELF IN ANOTHER WORLD 131 JOURNE
THEY'RE INNOCENT WOMEN, ANYWAY, WHEN IT COMES TO 138 JOURNE
THE WORLD.
SHE WAS NEVER MADE TO RENOUNCE THE WORLD. 138 JOURNE
ABOUT MYSELF AND ALL THE OTHER POOR BUMS IN THE 159 JOURNE
WORLD.
THE HAPPY ROADS THAT TAKE YOU O'ER THE WORLD.* 161 JOURNE
I'D LIKE TO SEE YOU BECOME THE GREATEST SUCCESS IN166 JOURNE
THE WORLD.
AND ALL THE WORLD IS BITTER AS A TEAR. 173 JOURNE
IS NOT ONE WORLD IN WHICH YOU KNOW NOT HOW TO LIVE279 LAZARU
ENOUGH FOR YOUR
THE WORLD IS MY ENEMY. 301 LAZARU
LIKE A NUN WHO ASKS MERCY FOR THE SINS OF THE 313 LAZARU
WORLD.
THAT THEIR PASSING MAY BE A SYMBOL TO THE WORLD 318 LAZARU
THAT THERE IS NO DEATH/
THIS WOMAN WORLD IS FULL OF EVIL. 329 LAZARU
IT IS A WORLD DEADLY TO YOUR JOY, LAZARUS. 330 LAZARU
BELIEVE THAT ONE MAN OR WOMAN IN THE WORLD KNEW 358 LAZARU
AND
THIS MAN HAS MADE YOU A FOOL BEFORE ALL THE WORLD/362 LAZARU
AND RID THE WORLD OF THIS STUPID RACE OF MEN AND 9 MANSNS
WASH THE EARTH CLEAN/
TO HAVE LOVE AND HOLD IT AGAINST THE WORLD, NO 18 MANSNS
MATTER HOW/
YOU WOULDN'T HOPE YOU COULD USE HIS OLD DREAM OF A 20 MANSNS
BOOK THAT'LL CHANGE THE WORLD
I KNOW WHAT HE REALLY LIKES--THE WORLD AS IT IS. 20 MANSNS
GREAT ENOUGH TO DESTROY ALL THE GREED IN THE 20 MANSNS
WORLD.
IS GOOD BECAUSE IT IS TRUE, AND SHOULD, IN A WORLD 47 MANSNS
OF FACTS,
I AM DETERMINED TO LIVE WITH A WORLD THAT EXISTS, 61 MANSNS
SIMON, AND ACCEPT IT AS GOOD.
HE'LL BE OWNING THE WHOLE WORLD IN HIS MIND BEFORE 67 MANSNS
YOU KNOW IT.
JUST BECAUSE SHE HAPPENED TO BEAR ME INTO THE 79 MANSNS
WORLD/
DON'T I LOVE YOU MORE THAN ALL THE WORLDS 81 MANSNS
AND THERE'S NO ONE ELSE IN THE WORLD, AND I'M 89 MANSNS
YOURS AND YOU'RE MINE,
=I HAVE NOT LOVED THE WORLD, NOR THE WORLD ME. 107 MANSNS
HAD BEEN DISPOSSESSED OF HIS REALM AND BANISHED TO110 MANSNS
WANDER OVER THE WORLD.
HE MUST SEARCH THE WORLD FOR A CERTAIN MAGIC DOOR.110 MANSNS
WHAT MADE THEIR PETTY SENTIMENTAL WOMEN'S WORLD 120 MANSNS
WITHOUT A CARE IN THE WORLD, WATCHING MY SONS GROW140 MANSNS
UP HANDSOME RICH GENTLEMEN,
AND PLAN YOUR BOOK THAT WILL SAVE THE WORLD 191 MANSNS
HE'S THE RICHEST KING IN THE WORLD 356 MARCOM
I WANT TO TRAVEL AND SEE THE WORLD AND ALL THE 356 MARCOM
DIFFERENT PEOPLE.
HE'S THE RICHEST KING IN THE WORLD. 359 MARCOM
WHICH RELIGION IN THE WORLD IS BEST. 359 MARCOM
ABOUT THIS CORNER OF THE WORLD. 365 MARCOM
LARGEST SHEEP IN THE WORLD. 370 MARCOM
THE GREAT KAAN, LORD OF THE WORLD, SENT ME-- 376 MARCOM
FOR KUKACHIN, AND HER GRANDFATHER, THE SON OF 388 MARCOM
HEAVEN AND RULER OF THE WORLD/
THERE'S ONLY ONE WORKABLE WAY AND THAT'S TO 394 MARCOM
CONQUER EVERYBODY ELSE IN THE WORLD
YOU CONQUER THE WORLD WITH THIS-- 396 MARCOM
THE GREAT KAAN, RULER OF THE WORLD, MAY NOT WEEP. 401 MARCOM
(PROUDLY) THE BEST LITTLE GIRL IN THE WORLD/ 406 MARCOM
RIDGE AFTER RIDGE TO THE RIM OF THE WORLD/ 408 MARCOM
MORE THAN ANY ONE IN THE WORLD, I CAN APPRECIATE 411 MARCOM
YOUR DEVOTION TO DUTY/
VENETIANS MAKE THE BEST SWIMMERS IN THE WORLD. 411 MARCOM
NOR BELIEVE AGAIN IN ANY BEAUTY IN THE WORLD. 424 MARCOM
MARCO, THE TRUE RULER OF THE WORLD, WILL HAVE COME426 MARCOM
TO VENICE BY THIS TIME.
SOVEREIGN OF THE WORLD/ 435 MARCOM
SOVEREIGN OF THE WORLDS 435 MARCOM
THEN I COMMAND THE WORLD TO PRAY/ 435 MARCOM
HER SMILE MADE ME FORGET THE SERVILE GRIN OF THE 437 MARCOM
FACE OF THE WORLD.
WHO IS SURE OF HIS PLACE IN THE WORLD. 439 MARCOM
AND SO IS ONE OF THE ELITE OF THE ALMIGHTY GOD IN 4 MISBEG
A WORLD OF DAMNED SINNERS
AND HIM WAY UP IN THE WORLD, A NOBLE SERGEANT OF 5 MISBEG
THE BRIDGEPORT POLICE.
I WISH YOU ALL THE LUCK IN THE WORLD, MIKE. 7 MISBEG
YOU MEAN HE'S RUN OFF TO MAKE HIS OWN WAY IN THE 13 MISBEG
WORLD
AND GAPE AT HIM AND TELL HIM HE WAS THE HANDSOMEST 25 MISBEG
MAN IN THE WORLD.

WORLD (CONT'D.)
SURE, THAT'S EVERY WOMAN'S SCHEME SINCE THE WORLD 28 MISBEG
WAS CREATED.
SAVING MONEY IS THE ONLY THING IN THE WORLD, 33 MISBEG
THE WORLD MUST BE FULL OF LIARS. 45 MISBEG
SURE, WHO IN THE WORLD CARES WHO THE HELL YOU ARE$ 57 MISBEG
YOU HAVE THE MOST BEAUTIFUL BREASTS IN THE WORLD, 68 MISBEG
DO YOU KNOW IT, JUSSIE$
IF THERE WASN'T A JIM TYRONE IN THE WORLD. 79 MISBEG
THINKING IT'S THE CUTEST JOKE IN THE WORLD, THE 83 MISBEG
FOOLS HE'S MADE OF US.
(CHUCKLING) BE JAYSUS, IT WAS THE MADDEST THING 90 MISBEG
IN THE WORLD.
BE GOD, YOU'LL MAKE HIM THE PRIZE SUCKER OF THE 95 MISBEG
WORLD/
GREATEST LIAR IN THE WORLD/ 119 MISBEG
WE CAN KID THE WORLD BUT WE CAN'T FOOL OURSELVES, 135 MISBEG
I LIKE MOST PEOPLE.
I THOUGHT THEY WERE THE MOST BEAUTIFUL THINGS IN 143 MISBEG
THE WORLD.
AND I'M PROUD YOU CAME TO ME AS THE ONE IN THE 152 MISBEG
WORLD YOU KNOW LOVES YOU ENOUGH
TO PRETEND TO THE WORLD WE BELIEVE THAT LIE, 24 POET
IT'S WHEN YOU DON'T GIVE A THOUGHT FOR ALL THE 25 POET
IF'S AND WANT-TO'S IN THE WORLD/
AND WRITE A BOOK ABOUT HOW THE WORLD CAN BE 29 POET
CHANGED SO PEOPLE WON'T BE GREEDY TO
EVEN IF IT IS A GREAT COMPANY THAT TRADES WITH THE 29 POET
WHOLE WORLD IN ITS OWN SHIPS.
IT'S MY CHANCE TO RISE IN THE WORLD AND NOTHING 31 POET
WILL KEEP ME FROM IT.
WITH ME TO HELP HIM WE'LL GET ON IN THE WORLD. 32 POET
YOU HAVE THE KINDEST HEART IN THE WORLD, NORA. 39 POET
=I HAVE NOT LOVED THE WORLD, NOR THE WORLD ME. 43 POET
I SUPPOSE IT WOULD BE DOWNRIGHT SNOBBERY TO HOLD 48 POET
TO OLD-WORLD STANDARDS.
LOST IN A WORLD OF HIS OWN FANCY, OBLIVIOUS TO 52 POET
WHAT IS GOING ON.)
AND IT'LL GIVE HER A CHANCE TO RISE IN THE WORLD. 63 POET
=I HAVE NOT LOVED THE WORLD, NOR THE WORLD ME. 67 POET
BE GOD, IT'S YOU CAN BATE THE WORLD AND NEVER LET 94 POET
IT CHANGE YOU/
SHE IS A WOMAN OF THE WORLD. 108 POET
IN MY OPINION, THE LADY DISPLAYED MORE COMMON 109 POET
SENSE AND KNOWLEDGE OF THE WORLD
=I HAVE NOT LOVED THE WORLD, NOR THE WORLD ME. 116 POET
HE'LL APOLOGIZE, OR HE'LL FIGHT, OR I'LL BRAND HIM125 POET
A CRAVEN BEFORE THE WORLD/
YOU'LL NOT LET A DUEL OR ANYTHING IN THE WORLD 131 POET
KAPE YOU FROM EACH OTHER,
I'M THE ONLY ONE IN THE WORLD HE KNOWS NIVIR 138 POET
SNEERS AT HIS DREAMS/
HE KNOWS MY LOVE IS ALL HE HAS IN THE WORLD TO 139 POET
COMFORT HIM.
AS IF THERE WASN'T A CARE IN THE WORLD, WHILE YOUR140 POET
POOR FATHER--
I HAD THE BEST IN THE WORLD. 142 POET
SO I KISSED HIM AND TOLD HIM HE WAS THE HANDSOMEST145 POET
IN THE WORLD, AND HE IS.
SURE, I'VE ALWAYS KNOWN YOU'RE THE SWEETEST WOMAN 149 POET
IN THE WORLD, MOTHER,
AS LONG AS A DRINK OF WHISKEY WAS LEFT IN THE 166 POET
WORLD/
SO REMEMBER IT'S TO HELL WID HONOR IF YE WANT TO 170 POET
RISE IN THIS WORLD.
AND WON'T WE BE PROUD WATCHIN' HER RISE IN THE 173 POET
WORLD TILL SHE'S A GRAND LADY/
SURE, THERE'S DIVIL A MORE LOYAL WIFE IN THE WHOLE174 POET
WORLD--
=I HAVE NOT LOVED THE WORLD, NOR THE WORLD ME. 176 POET
BE CHRISTI, IF HE WASN'T THE JOKE AV THE WORLD, THE177 POET
MAJOR.
I WAS GREEN AS GRASS WHEN I LEFT HERE, BUT BUMMIN'593 ROPE
ROUND THE WORLD.
SUPERIOR MANNER OF THE CLASSROOM TOWARD THE WORLD 6 STRANG
AT LARGE.
AND BEGUN TO ESTABLISH HIS POSITION IN THE WORLD. 11 STRANG
WHAT CAN I EXPECT WHEN THE FIRST WORD YOU EVER 14 STRANG
SPOKE IN THIS WORLD WAS AN INSULT
DEAFEN THE WORLD WITH LIES... 14 STRANG
YOU KNOW I'D GLADLY CONSENT TO ANYTHING IN THE 16 STRANG
WORLD TO BENEFIT YOU, BUT--
UH, CHARLIE, YOU'RE ALL I'VE GOT LEFT IN THE 27 STRANG
WORLD....
THE WORLD IS ADOPTING YOU/-- 34 STRANG
AND TO GIVE LOVE--ONESELF--NOT IN THIS WORLD/ 45 STRANG
=GOD'S IN HIS HEAVEN, ALL'S RIGHT WITH THE WORLD/= 51 STRANG
GUILTY OF CONTINUING LIFE, OF BRINGING FRESH PAIN 53 STRANG
INTO THE WORLD....)
SHE HASN'T A CARE IN THE WORLD. 59 STRANG
YOU GOT TO GIVE ONE EVANS, THE LAST ONE, A CHANCE 62 STRANG
TO LIVE IN THIS WORLD/
BUT THE GLASS SEPARATING THEM FROM THE WORLD IS 66 STRANG
GRAY WITH DUST,
ALL THE OTHER WOMEN IN THE WORLD AREN'T WORTH YOUR 70 STRANG
LITTLE FINGER/
WHY DOES EVERYONE IN THE WORLD THINK THEY CAN 74 STRANG
WRITE...
THE WORLD IS WHOLE AND PERFECT... 91 STRANG
WHAT DO I CARE FOR ANYTHING IN THE WORLD BUT 97 STRANG
YOU....
SAM THINKS I'M FINEST FELLOW IN WORLD... 105 STRANG
HE HAS MATURED, FOUND HIS PLACE IN THE WORLD. 111 STRANG
AS IF I WERE THE LAST ONE IN THE WORLD HE COULD 114 STRANG
IMAGINE....)
YOU COULD HAVE TOLD HIM WHAT A WORLD-BEATER WE'VE 118 STRANG
GOT/.

1827

WORRIED

WORLD (CONT'D.)
YOU'RE THE ONLY PERSON IN THE WORLD--EXCEPT NINA 133 STRANG
AND CHARLIE--
I SHOULD BE THE HAPPIEST WOMAN IN THE WORLD/...) 135 STRANG
NOT THE SLIGHTEST BIT IN THE WORLD/ 141 STRANG
(MOCKINGLY) MY DEAR BOY, I WOULDN'T MAKE FUN OF 142 STRANG
YOUR FATHER FOR THE WORLD/
YOU'VE GOT TO KNOW HOW TO FIGHT TO GET ON IN THIS 154 STRANG
WORLD.
HE IS MAKING HIS NAME WORLD-FAMOUS. 166 STRANG
((THAT IS ON ANOTHER PLANET, CALLED THE WORLD... 187 STRANG
(FORCING A TORTURED SMILE) NOT FOR ANYTHING IN 196 STRANG
THE WORLD/
THAT MAY DO VERY WELL WITH THE COMMON LOVES OF THE446 WELDED
WORLD--BUT OURS--/
I'D GIVE ANYTHING IN THE WORLD TO LIVE THOSE DAYS 447 WELDED
OVER AGAIN/
IF I HAVE--BUT PLEASE REMEMBER THERE ARE OTHER 457 WELDED
PLAYWRIGHTS IN THE WORLD/
I'LL BE AS UGLY AS THE WORLD. 474 WELDED
IN A BLACK WORLD, ALONE IN A HUNDRED MILLION YEARS488 WELDED
OF DARKNESS.
ABOVE THE WORLD, BEYOND ITS VISION--OUR MEANING/ 488 WELDED
WORLD'S
THE WORLD'S FULL O'MEN IF THAT'S ALL I'D WORRY 12 ANNA
ABOUT/
OUTWARD EVIDENCES OF BELONGING TO THE WORLD'S 13 ANNA
OLDEST PROFESSION.
THE SECRET THAT CALLED TO ME FROM OVER THE WORLD'S 92 BEYOND
RIM.
WHAT WOULD I BE IN THE WORLD'S EYES$ 38 ELECTR
THE WORLD'S BEST LITERATURE IN FIFTY LARGE 11 JOURNE
VOLUMES, HUME'S HISTORY OF ENGLAND,
I WAS SAYING AGAIN DOC HARDY ISN'T MY IDEA OF THE 40 JOURNE
WORLD'S GREATEST PHYSICIAN.
(THEN SUDDENLY--CONSOLED) WELL, IT'S A NEW 359 MARCOM
WORLD'S RECORD, ANYWAY.
AND THEY'RE THE WORLD'S FOREMOST, AS EVERYONE 412 MARCOM
KNOWS.
AND TO POSSESS, AND ROAM ALONG, THE WORLD'S TIRED 101 POET
DENIZEN,
I WOULD HAVE BEEN THE WORLD'S GREATEST 173 STRANG
NEUROLOGIST/...
WORLDLY
AS HISTORY PROVES, TO BE A WORLDLY SUCCESS AT 590 ICEMAN
ANYTHING, EXPECIALLY REVOLUTION,
PUMPING HIM FULL OF WHAT YOU CONSIDER WORLDLY 34 JOURNE
WISDOM.
I'LL AGREE TO PAY WITH ALL MY WORLDLY GOODS. 90 MANSNS
INDIFFERENT ATTITUDE OF THE WORLDLY-WISE. 370 MARCOM
YES, A VERY VALUABLE WORLDLY ASSET. 38 MISBEG
WORLDS
SONS OF GOD WHO APPEARED ON WORLDS LIKE OURS TO 289 LAZARU
TELL THE SAVING TRUTH TO EARS
WORM
'TWOULD BE LIKE HITTING A WORM. 539 'ILE
(THEN TRIUMPHANTLY) BUT THERE IS ONE THING I DID 266 AHWILD
WORM OUT OF HIM--
DID YOU WORM OUT OF HIM WHO IT WAS$ 266 AHWILD
NOW MANAGES TO WORM HERSELF BETWEEN THEM--SHARPLY) 47 ELECTR
YOUTHS AND THE OLD LECHER HOPES HE CAN WORM THE 302 LAZARU
SECRET OUT OF HIM--
JOEL HAS BECOME A CONFIRMED LEDGER-WORM. 10 MANSNS
WORMED
JAMIE SUSPECTED YOU'D CRY POORHOUSE TO HARDY AND 144 JOURNE
HE WORMED THE TRUTH OUT OF HIM.
WORMS
PRIDE WITHOUT WHICH THE GODS ARE WORMS/ 272 GGBROW
AND SO THE WORMS OF THEIR LITTLE FEARS EAT THEM 352 LAZARU
AND GROW FAT AND TERRIBLE AND
THERE ARE CONSTANTLY EMPLOYED MILLIONS UPON 431 MARCOM
MILLIONS OF MILLIONS OF WORMS/
I REFER TO THE BREEDING OF WORMS/ 431 MARCOM
WORMWOOD
IT MADE ME BITTER 'N WORMWOOD. 238 DESIRE
WORN
HE HAS DISCARDED COLLAR AND TIE, COAT AND SHOES, 249 AHWILD
AND WEARS AN OLD, WORN,
ALL THE EFFERVESCENCE OF HIS JAG HAS WORN OFF. 256 AHWILD
HER FACE IS PALE, LOOKS TERRIBLY TIRED AND WORN, 63 ANNA
YOU OUGHT TO HAVE WORN YOUR COAT A SHARP NIGHT 99 BEYOND
LIKE THIS, ROBBIE.
HE LOOKS ALL WORN OUT, RUTH. 137 BEYOND
THE CURTAINS AT THE WINDOWS ARE WORN AND DIRTY AND144 BEYOND
ONE OF THEM IS MISSING.
AND WEARS WORN CARPET SLIPPERS ON HIS BARE FEET.) 145 BEYOND
HIS SHOULDERS HAVE A WEARY STOOP AS IF WORN DOWN 556 CROSS
YOU'VE SEEMED WORN RAGGED LATELY. 496 DAYS
THEN HIS MOTHER, WORN OUT BY NURSING HIS FATHER 511 DAYS
AND BY HER GRIEF, HAS TAKEN ILL.
I GUESS BECAUSE I'M TOO WORN OUT TO HAVE THE GUTS.519 DAYS
IF YOU FIND YOURSELF FEELING AT ALL WORN-OUT, 533 DAYS
SHE LOOKS HORRIBLY OLD AND WORN OUT. 547 DIFRNT
HE IS DRESSED IN A WORN RIDING SUIT OF DIRTY WHITE176 EJONES
DRILL, PUTTEES, SPURS,
IN THE CENTER IS A BIG, DEAD STUMP WORN BY TIME 195 EJONES
WELL, THE WAR WAS OVER, HE WAS WORN OUT, HE'D HAD 70 ELECTR
A LONG, HARD TRIP HOME--
YOU MUST BE WORN OUT. 80 ELECTR
YOU CAN SEE HOW WORN OUT HE IS/ 83 ELECTR
YOU'RE ONLY TERRIBLY WORN OUT. 118 ELECTR
GOWN SIMILAR TO THAT WORN BY CHRISTINE IN ACT 150 ELECTR
THREE OF =HOMECOMING.=
YOU LOOK TERRIBLY WORN OUT. 174 ELECTR
(THEN SOLICITOUSLY) BUT YOU MUST BE WORN OUT. 301 GGBROW
WORN LONG AND RAGGEDLY CUT. 574 ICEMAN
HIS WORN CLOTHES ARE FLASHY. 576 ICEMAN

WORN (CONT'D.)
ALTHOUGH THE GAME IS BEGINNING TO GET THEM AND 611 ICEMAN
GIVE THEM HARD, WORN EXPRESSIONS.
I WAS SO WORN OUT FROM LAST NIGHT. 68 JOURNE
(CAUSTICALLY.) I DON'T NOTICE YOU'VE WORN ANY 77 JOURNE
HOLES IN THE KNEES OF YOUR PANTS
I--I BEG YOUR PARDON FOR BEING RUDE--I AM WORN OUT130 MANSNS
I HAVE WORN IT LATELY OVER MY HEART. 164 MANSNS
SHE LOOKS WORN OUT AND DISSIPATED, WITH DARK 164 MANSNS
CIRCLES UNDER HER EYES.
OF THE THIRTEENTH CENTURY ARE TRAVEL-WORN. 347 MARCOM
SOME OF THE FRESHNESS OF YOUTH HAS WORN OFF. 369 MARCOM
ALL THE FOLDS ARE WEARY AND THEIR CLOTHES SHABBY 373 MARCOM
AND TRAVEL-WORN.
HE IS DRESSED NEATLY BUT IN OLD, WORN CLOTHES. 8 POET
BUT SHE HAS BECOME TOO WORN OUT TO TAKE CARE OF 20 POET
HER APPEARANCE.
FINELY TAILORED CLOTHES OF THE STYLE WORN BY 34 POET
ENGLISH ARISTOCRACY
(SHE PAUSES--HER TIRED, WORN FACE BECOMES SUDDENLY181 POET
SHY AND TENDER.)
CARROTY HAIR WORN IN A PIGTAIL. 578 ROPE
SHE IS A THIN, SLOVENLY, WORN-OUT-LOOKING WOMAN OF579 ROPE
ABOUT FORTY WITH A DRAWN,
AN EXPRESSION OF OVERWHELMING JOY SUFFUSES HIS 595 ROPE
WORN FEATURES.)
AND MORE WORN-OUT BY CONTRAST. 158 STRANG
WURRD
I'LL SKIN HER BLACK HOIDE OFF AV HER IF SHE GOES 460 CARIBE
BACK ON HER WURRD,
UP HAVIN' A WURRD WID THE SKIPPER, 462 CARIBE
WORRIED
(WORRIED BY HER STRANGE TUNE AND THE FAR-AWAY LOOK547 'ILE
IN HER EYES)
(LILY LOOKS WORRIED, AND SIGHS. 212 AHWILD
(THE NERVOUS WORRIED NOTE IN HER VOICE AGAIN.) 217 AHWILD
BUT HIS MIND IS PLAINLY PREOCCUPIED AND WORRIED, 249 AHWILD
MRS. MILLER WHO HAS AGAIN SUNK INTO WORRIED 256 AHWILD
BROODING.
OH, I'M GETTING WORRIED SOMETHING DREADFUL, NAT/ 259 AHWILD
(A TIRED, HARASSED, DEEPLY WORRIED LOOK ON HIS 262 AHWILD
FACE--SOOTHING HER)
MRS. MILLER'S FACE IS DRAWN AND WORRIED. 263 AHWILD
(FROWNINGLY) YEP--AND THAT'S JUST WHAT'S GOT ME 267 AHWILD
WORRIED.
I'D HAVE WORRIED MY HEART OUT IF SHE HADN'T, 289 AHWILD
(LOOKING QUEERLY AT HIM, PERPLEXED AND WORRIED, 34 ANNA
LET YOU NOT BE WORRIED AT ALL. 50 ANNA
WHEN SHE'S WORRIED NEAR OUT OF HER SENSES BY HIS 114 BEYOND
GOIN'S-ON,
AND NOT BE WORRIED THINKING ONE OF US MIGHT HAVE 139 BEYOND
THE WRONG NOTION.
(WORRIED BY HIS EXCITEMENT) YES, YES, OF COURSE, 150 BEYOND
ROBB, BUT YOU MUSTN'T--
(WITH A WORRIED LOOK AT HIM) 569 CROSS
I'M NOT WORRIED BY OUR ARGUMENTS. 512 DAYS
ELSA WATCHES HER WITH A WORRIED, AFFECTIONATELY 517 DAYS
PITYING LOOK.)
(AFTER A WORRIED GLANCE AT HER--AN UNDERCURRENT OF540 DAYS
WARNING IN HIS QUIET TUNE)
FATHER BAIRD'S FACE GROWS MORE WORRIED. 547 DAYS
I'VE BEEN SO DAMNED WORRIED. 547 DAYS
(HIS FACE WORRIED AND ANGRY) 500 DIFRNT
HIS FACE IS SET EMOTIONLESSLY BUT HIS EYES CANNOT 514 DIFRNT
CONCEAL A WORRIED
(WORRIED BY THE FINALITY IN HER TONE--PLACATINGLY)529 DIFRNT
PLAINLY WORRIED NOW BUT TRYING TO MAKE LITTLE OF 426 DYNAMO
IT)
SHE LOOKS WORRIED AND RUN DOWN, 480 DYNAMO
(WORRIED ABOUT HIM HAS COME DOWN FROM THE PLATFORM8R DYNAMO
AND IS BEGINNING TO DESCEND
I PRETENDED TO BE DREADFULLY WORRIED, 39 ELECTR
UNTIL I GOT HIM WORRIED TOO. 40 ELECTR
SHE'S WORRIED ALREADY ABOUT HIS HEART. 41 ELECTR
(WORRIED AND PLEASED AT THE SAME TIME) 80 ELECTR
BUT SINCE YOU'VE GONE SHE HAS WORRIED AND BROODED 86 ELECTR
HE MUSTN'T BE WORRIED, HE SAID-- HE NEEDS REST ANDO1 ELECTR
PEACE--
I--I MUST CONFESS I'M WORRIED--AND FRIGHTENED. 118 ELECTR
AND YOU GET ME SO WORRIED WITH YOUR INCESSANT 151 ELECTR
BROODING OVER THE PAST.
WORRIED, APPREHENSIVE EXPRESSION ABOUT THE NOSE 270 GGBROW
AND MOUTH--
YOUR WIFE'LL BE WORRIED. 287 GGBROW
(SHE LOOKS HEALTHY AND HAPPY, BUT HER FACE WEARS A314 GGBROW
WORRIED.
OH, YOU NEEDN'T LOOK WORRIED, 314 GGBROW
DON'T BE WORRIED, DEAR. 316 GGBROW
I'M WORRIED ABOUT YOU. 316 GGBROW
I AIN'T WORRIED. 18 HUGGIE
HE LOOKS SLEEPY, IRRITABLE AND WORRIED. 665 ICEMAN
(GAZES WITH WORRIED KINDLINESS AT HOPE) 695 ICEMAN
I'M JUST WORRIED ABOUT YOU, WHEN YOU PLAY DEAD ON 704 ICEMAN
ME LIKE THIS.
I'M ONLY WORRIED ABOUT YOU. 707 ICEMAN
SO DON'T LET YOURSELF GET WORRIED-- 16 JOURNE
(HE GIVES HER A QUICK, WORRIED LOOK.) 16 JOURNE
(SHE GOES TO THE BACK-PARLOR DOORWAY, THEN TURNS, 29 JOURNE
HER FACE WORRIED AGAIN.)
YOU LIKE TO GET US WORRIED SO WE'LL MAKE A FUSS 42 JOURNE
OVER YOU.
I'VE BEEN SO WORRIED EVER SINCE YOU'VE BEEN SICK. 48 JOURNE
JAMIE GLANCES AT HIM WITH WORRIED PITY. 58 JOURNE
(WITH A WORRIED LOOK AT HIM--PUTTING ON A FAKE 65 JOURNE
HEARTINESS.)
I'M SO WORRIED ABOUT EDMUND/ 69 JOURNE
I'M WORRIED ABOUT YOU, EDMUND. 72 JOURNE

WORRIED

WORRIED (CONT'D.)
(CHECKS HIMSELF GUILTILY, LOOKING AT HIS SON'S 89 JOURNE
SILK FACE WITH WORRIED PITY.)
(WORRIED AGAIN.) THE MASTER'S SURE TO NOTICE 100 JOURNE
WHAT'S GONE FROM THE BOTTLE.
I MEAN, DEEPLY WORRIED. 101 JOURNE
I CAN TELL THE MASTER IS WORRIED ABOUT HIM. 101 JOURNE
AND MR. TYRONE NEVER IS WORRIED ABOUT ANYTHING, 101 JOURNE
HOW I FUSSED AND WORRIED/ 114 JOURNE
YOUR FATHER IS MUCH TOO WORRIED ABOUT WHAT 10 MANSNS
PRESIDENT JACKSON WILL DO OR SAY
SO YOU CAN UNDERSTAND WHY I AM WORRIED. 84 MANSNS
(THEY ALL STARE AND BEGIN TO GROW WORRIED.) 349 MARCOM
(WORRIED NOW--LOOKS AT CHU-YIN HOPEFULLY) 397 MARCOM
(WORRIED AGAIN) PERHAPS IT'S BRAIN FEVER. 413 MARCOM
(WORRIED--SOOTHINGLY) THERE/ 416 MARCOM
(SHE GLANCES AT TYRONE PROVOKINGLY--THEN SUDDENLY 54 MISBEG
WORRIED AND PROTECTIVE)
I'D BE SERIOUSLY WORRIED. 67 MISBEG
HER MANNER CHANGES TO WORRIED SOLICITUDE 68 MISBEG
(REALLY WORRIED NOW) HOW IS IT ALL SETTLED$ 81 MISBEG
NOT WORRIED ABOUT ME ANY MORE. 147 MISBEG
(WORRIED AGAIN.) MAYBE YOU OUGHT TO HAVE TOLD HER 19 POET
HE'S HERE SICK TO SAVE HER
GIVES HER MOTHER AN IMPATIENT BUT AT THE SAME TIME 21 POET
WORRIED GLANCE.
I'M WORRIED ABOUT YOUR FATHER. 26 POET
BUT HE COULDN'T HE WAS THAT WORRIED HOPING I'D 143 POET
COME TO SAY GOODNIGHT,
HE LOOKS WORRIED... 9 STRANG
(THINKING SELF-MOCKINGLY BUT A BIT WORRIED ABOUT 12 STRANG
HIMSELF)
(A BIT WORRIED HIMSELF NOW--PERSUASIVELY) 41 STRANG
HE'S WORRIED NOW... 69 STRANG
MOTHER IS RATHER DIFFICULT TO LIVE WITH THESE 74 STRANG
DAYS. GETTING ME WORRIED TO DEATH,
SHE'S TERRIBLY WORRIED. 77 STRANG
HE WENT TO SEE YOU AND TOLD YOU HOW WORRIED HE WAS 82 STRANG
ABOUT ME AND ASKED YOU OUT TO
WORRIEDLY
(WORRIEDLY) SHALL I WAKE UP THE FIRST AND FOURTH,543 'ILE
SIRS
(MORE WORRIEDLY) I THOUGHT HE WAS REALLY STUCK ON2O5 AHWILD
HER--
(IMMEDIATELY SENSING SOMETHING «DOWN» IN HIS 208 AHWILD
MANNER--GOING TO HIM WORRIEDLY)
(STARES AFTER HIM WORRIEDLY--THEN SIGHS 209 AHWILD
PHILOSOPHICALLY)
(WORRIEDLY) CAREFUL/ 210 AHWILD
(WORRIEDLY) NOW, LILY, NOW YOU MUSN'T TAKE ON SO.233 AHWILD
(LOOKS AFTER HER WORRIEDLY FOR A SECOND--THEN 248 AHWILD
SHRUGS HIS SHOULDERS)
(STARING BEFORE HER--SIGHS WORRIEDLY) 250 AHWILD
(SIGHS WORRIEDLY AGAIN) I DO WISH THAT BOY WOULD 255 AHWILD
GET HOME/
(WORRIEDLY) NOW YOU KEEP YOUR TEMPER, NAT, 266 AHWILD
REMEMBER/
(WORRIEDLY IMPRESSED BY THIS THREAT--BUT 271 AHWILD
PRETENDING SCORN)
(STARING AT HIM WORRIEDLY) HELLO, RICHARD. 292 AHWILD
(CHRIS FIDGETS FROM ONE FOOT TO THE OTHER 26 ANNA
WORRIEDLY.
(WORRIEDLY) I DON'T KNOW. 142 BEYOND
(SUBMITTING TO HIS KISS--WORRIEDLY) 150 BEYOND
ELSA LOOKS AT HIM WORRIEDLY. 529 DAYS
(WORRIEDLY--GRASPING HER HAND) 533 DAYS
(GETS UP--WORRIEDLY) BUT WHY DIDN'T YOU TELL ME$ 540 DAYS
(WORRIEDLY, BUT TRYING TO PRETEND TO TREAT IT 550 DAYS
LIGHTLY, REASSURINGLY)
HE SITS, WATCHING HER FACE WORRIEDLY, HIS FINGERS 558 DAYS
ON HER WRIST.
(WORRIEDLY) OH, LAND SAKES/ 547 DIFRNT
MRS. LIGHT THINKS WORRIEDLY) 427 DYNAMO
(OBSERVING REUBEN--WORRIEDLY) 438 DYNAMO
(LEANING FORWARD IN HER CHAIR AND WATCHING HER 439 DYNAMO
FATHER WORRIEDLY)
(LOOKS AT HER WORRIEDLY--WITH A SIGH) 454 DYNAMO
(HE TAKES A STEP FORWARD, THEN STOPS--WORRIEDLY) 191 EJONES
LAVINIA WATCHES HIM WORRIEDLY.) 49 ELECTR
(WORRIEDLY) PERHAPS ORIN GOT SO SICK HE WASN'T 119 ELECTR
ABLE TO.
I SUPPOSE IT WAS--BUT-- (SHE STOPS AND SIGHS--THEN137 ELECTR
WORRIEDLY)
HAZEL LOOKS AFTER HIM WORRIEDLY. 160 ELECTR
(STANDS HOLDING THE FLOWERS AND REGARDING HER 170 ELECTR
WORRIEDLY)
SETH STARES AT HER WORRIEDLY, SHAKES HIS HEAD AND 171 ELECTR
SPITS.
HE LOOKS AT HER WORRIEDLY. 174 ELECTR
(WORRIEDLY) I HOPE THEY'LL WATCH OUT, CROSSING 274 GGBROW
THE STREET.
(STOPS CRYING--BUT STILL WORRIEDLY) 312 GGBROW
(THEN WORRIEDLY) SAY, ED, WHAT THE HELL YOU 610 ICEMAN
THINK'S HAPPENED TO HICKEYS
(HE PAUSES, WATCHING--THEN WORRIEDLY) 689 ICEMAN
(WORRIEDLY) JEES, LARRY, HUGO HAD IT RIGHT. 692 ICEMAN
(LOWERING HIS VOICE--WORRIEDLY TO LARRY) 693 ICEMAN
MARY LISTENS WORRIEDLY. 16 JOURNE
(WORRIEDLY.) YOU SHOULDN'T DRINK NOW, EDMUND. 22 JOURNE
(WORRIEDLY, TAKING HIS ARM.) 42 JOURNE
(GETS UP WORRIEDLY AND PUTS HIS ARM AROUND HER.) 46 JOURNE
(GOES WORRIEDLY TO EDMUND AND PUTS HER ARM AROUND 58 JOURNE
HIM.)
(THEN, WORRIEDLY.) WHAT TIME IS IT, MA'AMS 99 JOURNE
WHO HAS STARTED VIOLENTLY AT THE MENTION OF 386 MARCOM
MARGOT'S NAME--WORRIEDLY) IMPOSSIBLE/
(WORRIEDLY) PLEASE DON'T BE UNREASONABLE. 412 MARCOM
(WORRIEDLY, SUDDENLY REACHES OUT TO TAKE HER HAND)412 MARCOM

WORRIEDLY (CONT'D.)
(THEN WORRIEDLY) YOU SAID THERE WERE ONE OR TWO 430 MARCOM
WOMEN$
(WORRIEDLY) WHAT$ 158 MISBEG
(HE STOPS AND WATCHES HER FACE WORRIEDLY. 160 MISBEG
HUGAN LOOKS AT HER SAD FACE WORRIEDLY-GENTLY) 176 MISBEG
(WORRIEDLY NOW.) I HOPE YOU DIDN'T INSULT HER 18 POET
WITH YOUR BAD MANNERS.
(A PAUSE--WORRIEDLY.) NEILAN SENT ROUND A NOTE TO 21 POET
ME ABOUT HIS BILL.
(DRIES HER EYES--AFTER A PAUSE SHE SIGHS 26 POET
WORRIEDLY.)
BUT TURNS TO STARE AT HIM WORRIEDLY AGAIN. 35 POET
SHE LOOKS AT HIM WORRIEDLY.) 55 POET
NORA GOES ON WORRIEDLY AGAIN.) 137 POET
(THINKING WORRIEDLY) (I HOPE SHE WON'T MAKE A 12 STRANG
SCENE.--
(WORRIEDLY) NINA, WHY DON'T YOU LIE DOWNS 41 STRANG
(THINKING WORRIEDLY) (SLIPPING BACK INTO THAT 51 STRANG
MORBID TONE...
(WORRIEDLY THINKING) (HAVE I EVER BEEN HAPPYS... 86 STRANG
(WORRIEDLY) SIT DOWN, CHARLIE. 99 STRANG
(THINKING--WORRIEDLY) (WHAT'S CHARLIE TALKING 129 STRANG
ABOUT$...
(THEN WORRIEDLY) HIS VOICE SOUNDED FUNNY. 146 STRANG
WORRIEDLY) 505 VOYAGE
(STARTING TO GET UP--WORRIEDLY) 507 VOYAGE
(WORRIEDLY, BUT GIVING IN TO HER AT ONCE) 464 WELDED
(GLANCING AT HER WORRIEDLY) WON'T YOU LIE DOWN 466 WELDED
HERE$
WORRIES
(THEN EVASIVELY) OH, WELL--YES, MAYBE, IF YOU MEANSOT DAYS
BUSINESS WORRIES.
THE STUPID LIVES WE LEAD--AND, OF COURSE, THE 517 DAYS
USUAL FINANCIAL WORRIES.
YOU JUST PUT YOUR MIND ON THAT AND FORGET YOUR 530 DAYS
SILLY WORRIES.
HE NEVER WORRIES IN HARD TIMES BECAUSE THERE'S 594 ICEMAN
ALWAYS OLD FRIENDS FROM THE DAYS
THAT'S WHAT WORRIES ME ABOUT YOU, GOVERNOR. 695 ICEMAN
YOU KNOW HOW SHE WORRIES. 51 STRANG
WORKK
AN' HOW SHE HOPES HE'LL SETTLE DOWN TO RALE WORRK 530 INZONE
AN' NOT BE SKYLARKIN' AROUND
'TIS HARRD WORRK, THIS. 503 VOYAGE
WORKIN'
AN' HOW GLAD SHE IS THAT HER SIDNEY BYE IS 531 INZONE
WORKIN' HARRD
WURRLD
WORRLD, IF WE CAN BELIEVE YOUR OWN TALE AV UT. 463 CARIBE
«I LOVE YOU BETTHER THAN ANYTHIN' IN THE WORRLD. 530 INZONE
MY UNE REMAININ' HOPE IS THAT NIVIR IN GOD'S 532 INZONE
WORRLD WILL I IVIR SEE YOUR FACE
WORRLD'LL
ANY MAN IN THE WORRLD'LL STAND UP TO ME FACE TO 524 INZONE
FACE,
WORRY
YOU MUSN'T WORRY ABOUT ME. 215 AHWILD
(GOING TO HIM) BUT I DO WORRY ABOUT YOU. 215 AHWILD
DON'T WORRY ABOUT THAT. 219 AHWILD
ALWAYS AIM AT HIS HEAD, REMEMBER--SO AS NOT TO 226 AHWILD
WORRY US.
NAT MILLER, YOU'RE TELLING ME A FIB, SO'S NOT TO 250 AHWILD
WORRY ME.
DON'T YOU WORRY ABOUT HIM. 250 AHWILD
AN, DON'T LET HIM WORRY YOU, MA. 251 AHWILD
ESSIE, YOU MUSN'T WORRY SO/ 260 AHWILD
(GIVING IN TO HER WORRY) I WISH YOU WOULDN'T SAY 271 AHWILD
THOSE TERRIBLE THINGS--
(REASSURINGLY, STOICAL NOW) YOU NEEDN'T WORRY, MA.271 AHWILD
YOU DON'T WANT TO WORRY ME TO DEATH, DO YOUS 271 AHWILD
AND I DON'T THINK WE'LL EVER HAVE TO WORRY ABOUT 297 AHWILD
HIS BEING SAFE--FROM HIMSELF--
THE WORLD'S FULL O'MEN IF THAT'S ALL I'D WORRY 12 ANNA
ABOUT/
YOU NEEDN'T WORRY ABOUT THAT SPARE CABIN, UNCLE. 104 BEYOND
DICK,
I CAN GET ALONG WITHOUT YOU, DON'T YOU WORRY. 127 BEYOND
DON'T WORRY ABOUT IT. 134 BEYOND
WELL, YOU NEEDN'T WORRY ABOUT THAT NO MORE-- 139 BEYOND
YOU'RE SILLY TO WORRY. 150 BEYOND
(FORCING A SMILE) YOU'RE WASTING WORRY. 512 DAYS
AH, YOU NEEDN'T WORRY, MADAME. 515 DAYS
FORGIVE YOU FOR NOT WANTING TO WORRY MES 529 DAYS
AND NOW PROMISE ME YOU'LL FORGET IT AND NOT WORRY 530 DAYS
ANY MORE$
PLEASE DON'T WORRY ABOUT ME. 533 DAYS
TELL HIM HE MUSTN'T WORRY. 563 DAYS
(ROUGHLY) YOU NEEDN'T WORRY. 522 DIFRNT
BUT A MINISTER'S SON HAS REASON TO WORRY, MAYBE, 437 DYNAMO
DON'T WORRY ABOUT ME. 437 DYNAMO
I WON'T TELL THE POLICE, YOU NEEDN'T WORRY. 442 DYNAMO
I SHOULD WORRY ABOUT THAT POUR FISH/ 443 DYNAMO
BUT YOU NEEDN'T WORRY ANY MORE, ADA. 460 DYNAMO
YOU WOULDN'T HAVE TO WORRY ABOUT COMMANDS OR 39 ELECTR
UNKERS-FAVORS THEN.
YOU NEEDN'T WORRY. 49 ELECTR
THE DOCTOR GAVE ME ORDERS TO AVOID WORRY OR ANY 49 ELECTR
OVER-EXERTION OR EXCITEMENT.
DON'T LET ANYTHING WORRY YOU, FATHER. 51 ELECTR
THEN THERE'S NOTHING TO WORRY ABOUT. 118 ELECTR
I'LL HAVE TO RUN HOME AND TELL MOTHER, SO SHE 119 ELECTR
WON'T WORRY.
YOU NEEDN'T WORRY BUT YOU'LL HAVE PLENTY O' 130 ELECTR
COMPANY.
DON'T WORRY, VINNIE/ 146 ELECTR
AND NOW DON'T YOU WORRY ANY MORE ABOUT HIM. 148 ELECTR

WORRY

WORRY (CONT'D.)
YOU MUSTN'T WORRY--YOU MUST START YOUR BEAUTIFUL 272 GGBROW
PAINTING AGAIN--
BELIEVE ME, BROTHER, I NEVER BEEN A GUY TO WORRY, 17 HUGHIE
BUT THEY SAY MOST OF THE THINGS WE WORRY ABOUT 18 HUGHIE
NEVER HAPPEN.
"WHAT I ALWAYS TELL JESS WHEN SHE NAGS ME TO WORRY 19 HUGHIE
ABOUT SOMETHING.."
I DON'T WONDER YOU NEVER WORRY ABOUT MONEY, WITH 21 HUGHIE
YOUR LUCK..
BUT EVEN THAT AIN'T MY BIG WORRY, CHARLIE. 35 HUGHIE
I WOULDN'T NEVER WORRY ABOUT OWING GUYS, LIKE I 35 HUGHIE
ONE THEM GUYS.
MY BIG WORRY IS THE RUN OF BAD LUCK I'VE HAD 35 HUGHIE
NO ONE HERE HAS TO WORRY ABOUT WHERE THEY'RE GOINGS87 ICEMAN
NEXT.
(SARDONICALLY) SHE DIDN'T, DON'T WORRY. 589 ICEMAN
(DARKLY) DON'T WORRY ABOUT MY NOT FORCING THE D. 607 ICEMAN
A. TO REOPEN YOUR CASE.
FIRST TIME I EVER HEARD YOU WORRY ABOUT SLEEP. 620 ICEMAN
OH, HELL, MAC, WE'RE SAPS TO WORRY. 652 ICEMAN
YOU'LL BE IN A TODAY WHERE THERE IS NO YESTERDAY 661 ICEMAN
OR TOMORROW TO WORRY YOU.
YOU'RE BEGINNING TO WORRY ME, GOVERNOR. 695 ICEMAN
YUH WOULDN'T HAVE TO WORRY WHERE DE NEXT DRINK'S 702 ICEMAN
COMIN' FROM.
(GOES ON QUIETLY NOW) DON'T WORRY ABOUT THE 706 ICEMAN
CHAIR, LARRY.
(CALLS AFTER HIM) DON'T WORRY, HICKEY/ 719 ICEMAN
TWO OR THREE ECHO HOPE'S "DON'T WORRY, HICKEY." 719 ICEMAN
JEES, I WAS BEGINNIN' TO WORRY ABOUT YUH, HONEST/ 725 ICEMAN
YUH NEEDN'T WORRY. 520 INZONE
JUST WHEN SHE NEEDS PEACE AND FREEDOM FROM WORRY. 36 JOURNE
IT WOULD BE LIKE A CURSE SHE CAN'T ESCAPE IF WORRY 39 JOURNE
OVER EDMUND--
YOU MUSTN'T WORRY SO MUCH ABOUT EDMUND. 41 JOURNE
AND YOU WON'T WORRY YOURSELF SICK, AND YOU'LL KEEP 48 JOURNE
ON TAKING CARE OF YOURSELF--
AND THERE'S NO HOUSEKEEPING TO WORRY ABOUT. 72 JOURNE
WITH NOTHING TO UPSET ME, AND ALL I'VE DONE IS 93 JOURNE
WORRY ABOUT YOU.
DON'T WORRY ABOUT BRIDGET. 100 JOURNE
(HE SEES HIS FATHER STARING AT HIM WITH MINGLED 131 JOURNE
WORRY AND IRRITATED DISAPPROVAL.
(THICKLY HUMOROUS.) I WOULDN'T WORRY ABOUT THE 133 JOURNE
VIRTUE PART OF IT.
DO NOT WORRY YOUR HEAD ABOUT LAZARUS. 284 LAZARU
DON'T WORRY, SARA. 114 MANSNS
(EASILY) DON'T WORRY ABOUT THEM. 536 MARCOM
IF SHE WERE A MILLION YEN WORTH OF SILK OR SPICES,403 MARCOM
I WOULDN'T WORRY AN INSTANT.
WE WERE BOTH TOO BUSY CURSING ENGLAND TO WORRY 26 MISBEG
OVER THE RENT.
BY WORRY, AMBITION, OR ANY OF THE COMMON HAZARDS 55 MISBEG
OF LIFE.
AND DON'T WORRY I CAN'T DO MY PART OF THE TRICK. 94 MISBEG
SO DON'T WORRY-- 96 MISBEG
SO DON'T WORRY I'LL PASS OUT AND YOU'LL HAVE TO 113 MISBEG
PUT ME TO BED.
FREE FROM WORRY. 147 MISBEG
(GENTLY) DON'T WORRY ABOUT ME, FATHER. 176 MISBEG
BUT YEARS OF OVERWORK AND WORRY HAVE MADE HER LOOK 19 POET
MUCH OLDER.
I DON'T MIND AT ALL, IF I CAN SAVE YOU A BIT OF 28 POET
THE WORRY THAT'S KILLING YOU.
SO HE NEEDN'T WORRY. 60 POET
HE'D HAVE WRITTEN YOU HE WAS SICK, BUT HE DIDN'T 75 POET
WANT TO WORRY YOU.
AND HE'S GONE TO SEE HIS LAWYER--BUT THAT DOESN'T 78 POET
WORRY ME.
(WHO HAS BEEN WATCHING THE DOOR AT LEFT FRONT, 87 POET
PREOCCUPIED BY HER OWN WORRY--
I'VE ENOUGH TO WORRY ME WITHOUT BOTHERING ABOUT 88 POET
HIM.
THERE, MOTHER, DON'T WORRY. 125 POET
BUT I'LL NOT WORRY THIS TIME, AND LET YOU NOT, 130 POET
EITHER.
AND THE SAME WORRY AND SORROW. 130 POET
SHE IS SUNK IN MEMORIES OF OLD FEARS AND HER 131 POET
PRESENT WORRY ABOUT THE DUEL.
SHE LOOKS ON THE VERGE OF COLLAPSE FROM PHYSICAL 133 POET
FATIGUE AND HOURS OF WORRY.
SHE WAS DROPPIN' WITH TIREDNESS AND DESTROYED WITH135 POET
WORRY.
I'M SICK WITH WORRY AND I'VE GOT TO THE PLACE 136 POET
WHERE I CAN'T BEAR WAITIN' ALONE.
DON'T TELL ME NOT TO WORRY. 137 POET
LET YOU NOT WORRY, ALLANAH. 167 POET
I'M ALL HERE, YUH NEEDN'T WORRY. 595 ROPFE
A PLEASED RELIEVED EXPRESSION FIGHTING THE 6 STRANG
FLURRIED WORRY ON HIS FACE.
AND THERE'S NOT THE SLIGHTEST REASON TO WORRY 17 STRANG
ABOUT ME.
IN A FEW YEARS YOU WON'T HAVE TO WORRY ONE WAY OR 54 STRANG
ANOTHER
HELP WORRYING OVER HIS WORRY BECAUSE OF WHAT IT 69 STRANG
MIGHT LEAD TO...
WELL, IT ISN'T A JOB TO WORRY MUCH ABOUT LOSING, 70 STRANG
IS IT.
HE IS STOUTER, THE HAGGARD LOOK OF WORRY AND SELF-111 STRANG
CONSCIOUS INFERIORITY HAS GONE
IT'S NOTHING TO HOPE--I MEANT, TO WORRY OVER/
DON'T WORRY YOUR PRETTY HEAD/ 170 STRANG
DON'T WORRY, OLE BIRD, I'M ORF. 175 STRANG
505 VOYAGE

WORRYIN'
DON'T BE WORRYIN', YANK. 482 CARDIF
IT'S GOT TO DO WITH WHAT'S WORRYIN' YOU--THAT IS, 12 ELECTR
IF THERE'S ANYTHIN' IN IT.

WORSE

WORRYIN' (CONT'D.)
HE NEEDN'T DO NO WORRYIN' NOW. 33 HUGHIE
DON'T BE WORRYIN' NOW. 133 POET
I'M GLAD TO SEE YOU ROUSED FROM YOUR WORRYIN'. 135 POET
WORRYIN' MY HEART OUT FOR A MAN WHO--IT ISN'T ONLY138 POET
FEAR OVER THE DUEL.

WORRYING
BUT SHE INSISTS ON WORRYING HER HEAD OFF. 254 AHWILD
I'VE A NOTION TO GIVE HIM HELL FOR WORRYING US ALL260 AHWILD
LIKE THIS.
STOP WORRYING. 269 AHWILD
I MEAN, IF THEY'RE WORRYING I'M OFF LIKE LAST 274 AHWILD
NIGHT.
AND HE NEEDN'T BE WORRYING HIMSELF TO DEATH ANY 137 BEYOND
MORE.
SOMETHING YOU'RE KEEPING BACK BECAUSE YOU'RE 529 DAYS
AFRAID OF WORRYING ME.
YOUR HUSBAND WAS HALF OUT OF HIS MIND WORRYING 548 DAYS
ABOUT WHAT HAD HAPPENED TO YOU.
SHE'S MAKING HERSELF SICK WORRYING. 478 DYNAMO
AREN'T YOU HER MOTHER, AND DON'T YOU SEE SHE'S 479 DYNAMO
WORRYING HER HEART OUT!
(STIFFLY) THERE'S NOTHING WORRYING ME. 12 ELECTR
TO KEEP US FROM WORRYING. 49 ELECTR
WORRYING ABOUT FATHER AND ORIN AND---YOU. 52 ELECTR
I KNOW SOMETHING IS WORRYING YOU--AND I DON'T WANT160 ELECTR
TO SEEM PRYING--BUT
(JOKINGLY) I'D SAY IT WAS A BIT EARLY TO BE 282 GGBROW
WORRYING ABOUT THAT.
WITHOUT YOUR STAYING AWAY AND WORRYING US TO 291 GGBROW
DEATH/
I'LL JUST LIE THERE WORRYING-- 17 HUGHIE
SO QUIT WORRYING/ 654 ICEMAN
I LAY AWAKE WORRYING UNTIL I COULDN'T STAND IT ANY 98 JOURNE
MORE.
SOMETIMES, I GO MAD WORRYING/ 142 MANSNS
I CAN'T SLEEP, WORRYING/ 156 MANSNS
WHAT'S WORRYING YOU, THEN$ 31 MISBEG
BUT WE'RE NOT WORRYING YOU'D EVER FORGET YOUR 66 MISBEG
PROMISE TO US FOR ANY PRICE.
HE STARTED TALKING ABOUT YOU, AS IF YOU WAS ON HIS 87 MISBEG
MIND, WORRYING HIM--
WHAT'S WORRYING YOU NOW$ 27 POET
(THEN SHARPLY.) BUT YOU NEEDN'T WASTE YOUR DREAMS 50 POET
WORRYING ABOUT MY AFFAIRS.
NORA IS WORRYING AND HASN'T LISTENED. 150 POET
ARE YOU STILL WORRYING ABOUT HOW THE DARN OLD 54 STRANG
APPLES ARE GOING TO TURN OUT$
I USED TO BE A GREAT ONE FOR WORRYING ABOUT WHAT'S 64 STRANG
GOD AND WHAT'S DEVIL.
HELP WORRYING OVER HIS WORRY BECAUSE OF WHAT IT 69 STRANG
MIGHT LEAD TO...

WORSE
BETTER MEN THAN YE ARE HAVE EATEN WORSE. 544 'TLE
AND SAID WORSE HIMSELF, I BET/ 195 AHWILD
I'VE HEARD WORSE THAN ANYTHING UNCLE SID SAYS. 195 AHWILD
PUTTING THE CURB BIT ON WOULD MAKE HIM WORSE. 205 AHWILD
(KINDLY) OH, THERE'S LOTS WORSE THAN YOU AROUND, 268 AHWILD
SO DON'T TAKE TO BOASTING.
I WAS WORSE LATER. 283 AHWILD
IF I'D REFUSED, IT WOULD ONLY HAVE MADE EVERYTHING286 AHWILD
WORSE.
RICHARD COULD DO WORSE. 290 AHWILD
ALWAYS LOOKING FOR AN EXCUSE TO--YOU'RE WORSE THAN299 AHWILD
TOMMY/
AND THEY TREATED ME WORSE THAN THEY DARE TREAT A 18 ANNA
HIRED GIRL.
ONLY WORSE. 36 ANNA
WHERE DO YOU COME IN BUTTING IN AND MAKING THINGS 54 ANNA
WORSE$
SHE NEVER SEEMS TO GET ANY BETTER OR ANY WORSE. 87 BEYOND
YOU'RE ONLY MAKING IT WORSE. 107 BEYOND
AND THAT WOULD'VE BEEN WORSE, FOR RUTH WOULD'VE 110 BEYOND
SUFFERED THEN.
AND HE'S GETTIN' WORSE 'STEAD OF BETTER. 114 BEYOND
AND YOU CAN'T DENY THAT THINGS HAVE BEEN GOIN' 114 BEYOND
FROM BAD TO WORSE
THINGS MIGHT BE WORSE. 114 BEYOND
STILL, I THINK IT'D BE WORSE IF-- 135 BEYOND
THINGS KEPT GETTING WORSE, THAT'S ALL--AND RUB 155 BEYOND
DIDN'T SEEM TO CARE.
THEY MIGHT BE MUCH WORSE. 157 BEYOND
AND MANY'S THE TOIME IT'D A BEEN ON THE BEACH OR 480 CARDIF
WORSE, BUT FOH HIM.
IT STILL HURTS, SIR, WORSE THAN EVER. 484 CARDIF
AND ONLY MADE HIM WORSE. 502 DAYS
AND YOU--YOU'RE WORSE--WITH YOUR HYPOCRITICAL LIES513 DAYS
ABOUT YOUR GREAT HAPPINESS/
OH, HE'S NO WORSE THAN A LOT OF OTHERS. 519 DAYS
IT MAKES ME OUT WORSE THAN YOU EXPECTED, EH$ 522 DAYS
I'VE SEEN MANY WORSE CASES WHERE THE PATIENT 557 DAYS
PULLED THROUGH.
IS SHE--WORSE$ 558 DAYS
DON'T YOU TWO GIT TO FIGHTIN'--TO MAKE THINGS 510 DIFRNT
WORSE.
HE IS DRESSED IN AN OLD BAGGY SUIT MUCH THE WORSE 513 DIFRNT
FOR WEAR--
(FORCING A SMILE) I GUESS THERE'S WORSE THINGS 517 DIFRNT
THAN BEING AN OLD MAID.
YOU'D ONLY MAKE IT WORSE AND GET YOURSELF IN DUTCH532 DIFRNT
WITH HIM, TOO/
IT'S MADE HIM WORSE/ 540 DIFRNT
ON'Y WORSE/ 540 DIFRNT
OR IT'LL BE THE WORSE FOR YOU/ 438 DYNAMO
DON'T MAKE MATTERS WORSE BY LYING/ 446 DYNAMO
SHE HATED US WORSE THAN POISON/ 454 DYNAMO
WELL, MAYBE YOU'D BE WORSE 455 DYNAMO
WORSE ONES. 9 ELECTR

WORSE

WORSE (CONT'D.)
BUT HE HATED HER WORSE THAN ANYONE 44 ELECTR
I DON'T LIKE HER AND NEVER DID BUT I CAN IMAGINE 71 ELECTR
WORSE WAYS OF DYING/
YOU AND I, WHO ARE INNOCENT, WOULD SUFFER A WORSE 97 ELECTR
PUNISHMENT THAN THE GUILTY--
AND AS FUR ME BEIN' AN OLD FOOL, YOU'RE OLDER AN' 133 ELECTR
A WORSE FOOL.
IF IT WASN'T FOR ORIN--HE'S GETTING WORSE. 158 ELECTR
LIVING ALONE HERE WITH THE DEAD IS A WORSE ACT OF 178 ELECTR
JUSTICE THAN DEATH OR PRISON/
YOU'RE WORSE OFF THAN HUGHIE WAS. 12 HUGHIE
"THAT'S WORSE," I SAID, "NO GUY CAN BEAT THAT 22 HUGHIE
RACKET."
UH MAYBE WORSE, WID YOUR WIFE AND DE ICEMAN 636 ICEMAN
WALKIN' SLOW BEHIND YUH...
THE KIND THAT LEAVES THE POOR SLOB WORSE OFF 641 ICEMAN
ONLY WORSE, BECAUSE SHE DIDN'T HAVE TO MAKE HER 647 ICEMAN
LIVING--
HE'S A WORSE PEST THAN HICKEY. 668 ICEMAN
AND I HAD TO FACE A WORSE BASTARD IN MYSELF THAN 685 ICEMAN
ANY OF YOU WILL HAVE TO IN
REJECTS, YOU'RE A WORSE GABBER THAN THAT NAGGING 692 ICEMAN
BITCH, BESSIE, WAS.
IT'S WORSE IF YOU KILL SOMEONE AND THEY HAVE TO GO706 ICEMAN
ON LIVING.
I'M MUCH WORSE NOW. 707 ICEMAN
YOU KNOW WHAT I DID IS A MUCH WORSE MURDER. 720 ICEMAN
IT ONLY MAKES THEM WORSE TO CROSS THEM. 723 ICEMAN
(TURNS ON JAMIE.) AND YOU'RE WORSE THAN HE IS, 26 JOURNE
ENCOURAGING HIM.
WHICH MAKES HIS COLD WORSE. 27 JOURNE
IT WILL O WILL ONLY MAKE THE SHOCK WORSE WHEN SHE 29 JOURNE
HAS TO FACE IT.
IT COULDN'T HAVE COME AT A WORSE TIME FOR HIM. 36 JOURNE
WHAT MAKES IT WORSE IS HER FATHER DIED OF 37 JOURNE
CONSUMPTION.
I WANT YOU TO PROMISE ME THAT EVEN IF IT SHOULD 48 JOURNE
TURN OUT TO BE SOMETHING WORSE,
WHAT'S WORSE, THEY'LL SELL YOURS, 74 JOURNE
AND SOME OF THE POEMS YOU'VE WRITTEN YOURSELF ARE 90 JOURNE
EVEN WORSE/
THEY'RE WORSE THAN THE FOGHORN FOR REMINDING ME-- 104 JOURNE
NEVER WANTED YOU TO SUCCEED AND MAKE ME LOOK EVEN 165 JOURNE
WORSE BY COMPARISON.
WORSE AND WORSE/ 10 MANSNS
YOU HATE ME WORSE THAN POISON. 20 MANSNS
YOU WILL RUN NO RISK OF ANYTHING WORSE THAN YOUR 111 MANSNS
PRESENT UNHAPPY EXILE."
THEN I'LL HAVE TO STEAL IT, AND THAT'S A WORSE 355 MARCOM
SIN.
POETRY ACTS WORSE ON 405 MARCOM
TO MAKE MATTERS WORSE, A ONE-STORY, 1 MISBEG
YOU'RE WORSE THAN DECENT. 6 MISBEG
I'VE FELT WORSE. 41 MISBEG
BUT IT WOULD BE A MILLION TIMES WORSE AFTER-- 140 MISBEG
GOT RAPIDLY WORSE. 147 MISBEG
I'M WORSE FROM HOLDING YOU. IF THAT'S ANY COMFORT.166 MISBEG
YOU'RE WORSE THAN AN OLD WOMAN FOR GOSSIP. 17 POET
HE'S GETTING WORSE. 24 POET
AND THIS YEAR, NOW JAMIE CREGAN HAS APPEARED, 58 POET
YOU'VE AN EXCUSE TO MAKE IT WORSE.
YOU'LL HAVE NO CHANCE TO MAKE BAD WORSE 91 POET
IF THEY DO HATE CON MELODY, HE'S IRISH, AND THEY 134 POET
HATE THE YANKS WORSE.
BUT IF WE'RE MARKED, THERE'S OTHERS IS MARKED 154 POET
WORSE AND SOME AV THIM IS POLICE/
THERE ARE WORSE THINGS THAN BEING A TRAINED 22 STRANG
NURSE...
(A BIT VIOLENTLY) I TELL YOU IT'D BE A CRIME--A 58 STRANG
CRIME WORSE THAN MURDER/
WORSE/... 123 STRANG
TO KILL HAPPINESS IS A WORSE MURDER THAN TAKING 133 STRANG
LIFE/...
BUT IT ONLY MAKES HIM WORSE/... 142 STRANG
INSTEAD OF THAT IT'S GOT WORSE.... 160 STRANG
(THINKING FURIOUSLY.) (IT'S WORSE... 192 STRANG
HE SAID HE'D KILL OUR LOVE AS I HAD--WORSE-- 468 WELDED
WORSE'N
I HATED HIM WORSE'N HELL AND HE KNEW IT. 57 ANNA
BUT I KNOW WHATEVER IT IS WHAT COMES AFTER IT 486 CARDIF
CAN'T BE NO WORSE'N THIS.
THERE'S WORSE'N HIM IN THE WORLD. I'LL BET YE/ 214 DESIRE
THERE'S MANY A LETTER IS WORSE'N ANY BOMB. 529 INZONE
WURSER
HER AND CALEB IS WORSER AT SPOONIN' THAN WHAT WE 506 DIFRNT
ARE.
WORSER'N
IS WORSER'N GOIN' ALOFT TO THE SKYS'L YARD IN A 140 BEYOND
BLOW.

WORSHIP

THEY'LL KNEEL AND WORSHIP THE IRONIC SILENUS WHO 297 GGBROW
TELLS THEM THE BEST GOOD IS
(THE NIGHT CLERK DREAMS, A RAPT HERO WORSHIP 32 HUGHIE
TRANSFIGURING HIS PIMPLY FACE..
THEY WILL BEGIN TO WORSHIP IN FILTHY IDOLATRY THE 283 LAZARU
SUN AND STARS AND MAN'S BODY--
MOB IS THE SAME EVERYWHERE, EAGER TO WORSHIP ANY 302 LAZARU
NEW CHARLATAN/
THEY WORSHIP LIFE AS DEATH/= 309 LAZARU
THEY WORSHIP LIFE AS DEATH/ 310 LAZARU
IF FOOLS KNEEL AND WORSHIP ME BECAUSE THEY FEAR 352 LAZARU
ME, SHOULD I BE PROUD?
--NOR CRIED ALOUD IN WORSHIP OF AN ECHO.= 107 MANSNS
WE'RE NOW PASSING THROUGH KINGDOMS WHERE THEY 365 MARCOM
WORSHIP MAHMET.
THEY RELATE THAT IN OLD TIMES THREE KINGS FROM 368 MARCOM
THIS COUNTRY WENT TO WORSHIP A

WORSHIP (CONT'D.)
THEIR EYES ARE KEPT ON HIM WITH THE ARDENT 433 MARCOM
HUMILITY AND RESPECT OF WORSHIP.
NOR CRIED ALOUD IN WORSHIP OF AN ECHO.. 43 POET
NOR CRIED ALOUD IN THE WORSHIP OF AN ECHO.. 67 POET
NOR CRIED ALOUD IN WORSHIP AV AN ECHO.. 176 POET
(WITH ADMIRATION AMOUNTING TO HERO-WORSHIP) 29 STRANG
WORSHIPED
SHE WORSHIPED HIM AND SHE'S NEVER FORGOTTEN. 37 JOURNE
WORSHIPER
(TO THE BUDDHIST PRIEST) WORSHIPER OF BUDDHA, 434 MARCOM
HE WENT TO FRANCE AND BECAME A RABID JACOBIN, A 83 POET
WORSHIPER OF ROBESPIERRE.
WORSHIPING
THEN MARGARET COMES IN, FOLLOWED BY THE HUMBLE 262 GGBROW
WORSHIPING BILLY BROWN.
WORSHIPPER
(THINKING CYNICALLY) ((THIS GORDON WORSHIPPER 30 STRANG
MUST BE THE APPLE OF NINA'S
WORSHIPPERS
WELCOME, DUMB WORSHIPPERS/ 321 GGBROW
WORSHIPS
HE JUST WORSHIPS THEM/ 276 GGBROW
LOVE HIM DEARLY, FOR ANY FOOL CAN SEE HE WORSHIPS 101 JOURNE
THE GROUND YOU WALK ON.
YOU OUGHT TO APPRECIATE HIM BECAUSE HE WORSHIPS 124 MISBEG
THE GROUND YOU WALK ON--
WORST
THE WORST IS YET TO COME/ 205 AHWILD
(INDIGNANTLY) AND DON'T YOU DESERVE THE WORST I'D 72 ANNA
SAY, GOD FORGIVE YOUS
I REMEMBER THINKING ABOUT YOU AT THE WORST OF IT, 132 BEYOND
AND SAYING TO MYSELF..
WHY IS IT EVERY ONE DECIDES TO TURN UP WHEN YOU 515 DAYS
LOOK YOUR WORST?
YOU'RE THE WORST OF 'EM ALL. 506 DIFRNT
YOU'RE ALWAYS SO READY TO BELIEVE THE WORST OF 426 DYNAMO
HIM.
CHEER UP, NIGGER, DE WORST IS YET TO COME. 188 EJONES
YOU KNOW YOU DESERVE THE WORST PUNISHMENT YOU 32 ELECTR
COULD GET.
HE'S THE TOWN'S WORST OLD GOSSIP. 40 ELECTR
(THEN HURRYING ON) BUT I HAVEN'T TOLD YOU THE 87 ELECTR
WORST YET.
IT'S THE WORST THING FOR YOUR HEALTH. 151 ELECTR
KEEPING HIM SHUT UP HERE IS THE WORST THING VINNIE158 ELECTR
COULD DO.
NOBODY KISSES ME--SO YOU CAN ALL BELIEVE THE 315 GGBROW
WORST/
AS STUPIDLY GREEDY FOR POWER AS THE WORST 588 ICEMAN
CAPITALIST THEY ATTACK.
WORST IS BEST HERE, AND EAST IS WEST, AND TOMORROW600 ICEMAN
IS YESTERDAY.
YOU'VE BEEN THE WORST INFLUENCE FOR HIM. 34 JOURNE
BY GOD, NOW YOU CAN LIVE WITH A MIND THAT SEES 36 JOURNE
NOTHING BUT THE WORST MOTIVES
ALWAYS LOOKING FOR THE WORST WEAKNESS IN EVERYONE. 61 JOURNE
DON'T YOU KNOW IT'S THE WORST THINGS 67 JOURNE
WHETHER SHE'S DOING HER BEST OR HER WORST. 72 JOURNE
WHAT THEY SEE FULFILLS THEIR WORST EXPECTATIONS. 108 JOURNE
HE BECAME A STEADY CHAMPAGNE DRINKER, THE WORST 137 JOURNE
KIND.
AND THE IDEA SHE MIGHT HAVE BECOME A NUN. THAT'S 138 JOURNE
THE WORST.
SHE THINKS I ALWAYS BELIEVE THE WORST, BUT THIS 162 JOURNE
TIME I BELIEVED THE BEST.
HOPING FOR THE WORST, 163 JOURNE
ALWAYS SUSPECTED OF HOPING FOR THE WORST, 163 JOURNE
AND WORST OF IT IS, I DID IT ON PURPOSE. 165 JOURNE
HE LOVES TO EXAGGERATE THE WORST OF HIMSELF WHEN 167 JOURNE
HE'S DRUNK.
YOUR OLD WICKED WITCHES LED ME ALWAYS TO BE 13 MANSNS
PREPARED FOR THE WORST/
THAT WOULD BE THE WORST/ 153 MANSNS
BUT WITH YOUR TUBBY JUNKS IT'S JUST AS WELL TO 398 MARCOM
EXPECT THE WORST
I WAS JUST GOING TO OFFER YOU A DRINK, BUT WHISKEY 45 MISBEG
IS THE WORST THING--
YES, IT'S THE WORST GHOST OF ALL, YOUR OWN. 112 MISBEG
I DON'T THINK I'LL NEED IT BUT IF THE WORST COMES 115 POET
TO THE WORST I PROMISE YOU
THE DAMNED THIEVES OF THE LAW DID THEIR WORST TO 118 POET
ME MANY YEARS AGO IN IRELAND.
=(IT'D BE A SIN, ADULTERY, THE WORST SIN/= 63 STRANG
(ANGRILY) I KNOW DAT DAMN SHIP--WORST SHIP DAT 507 VOYAGE
SAIL TO SEA.
WORTH
PLAYING UP ITS SENTIMENTAL VALUE FOR ALL HE IS 258 AHWILD
WORTH.
I WAS DESPERATE, UNCLE--EVEN IF SHE WASN'T WORTH 272 AHWILD
IT.
I'LL CATCH HELL WHEN I GET BACK, BUT IT'LL BE 275 AHWILD
WORTH IT....
WELL, IF YOU MEANT WHAT WAS IN THE LETTER, YOU 282 AHWILD
WOULDN'T HAVE BEEN WORTH IT,
AND, ANYWAY, I THOUGHT TO MYSELF, SHE ISN'T WORTH 282 AHWILD
IT.
ONE OF HIS FINGERS IS WORTH ALL THE HUNDREDS OF 44 ANNA
MEN I MET OUT THERE--INLAND.
WAN OF THEM IS WORTH ANY TEN STOCK-FISH-SWILLING 49 ANNA
SQUARE-HEADS.
IT AIN'T WORTH MUCH, BUT IT'S ALL I'VE GOT. 489 CARDIF
IT'S NOT WHAT IT'S WORTH. 565 CROSS
WHY, OVER AND ABOVE THE MORTGAGE IT'S WORTH-- 565 CROSS
WISE-CRACKING AT EVERYTHING WITH ANY DECENT HUMAN 521 DAYS
DIGNITY AND WORTH.
THEY AIN'T WORTH NOTICE FROM A CHRISTIAN. 510 DIFRNT
UH, NOTHIN' WORTH TELLIN'. 539 DIFRNT

WORTH

WORTH (CONT'D.)

YOU AIN'T WORTH IT-- AND HE AIN'T-- AND NO ONE 543 DIFRNT
AIN'T, NOR NOTHIN'.
AIN'T I WORTH ITS 544 DIFRNT
AIN'T I WORTH A MILLION PLAYED-OUT OLD CRANKS LIKE544 DIFRNT
HIM.
IT'S WORTH TAKIN' A STAB AT, DAMNED IF IT AIN'T. 545 DIFRNT
FORCED HIM TO SELL FOR ONE-TENTH ITS WORTH, YOU 25 ELECTR
MEAN?
THAT DIDN'T APPEAR WORTH A THOUGHT ONE WAY OR 54 ELECTR
ANOTHER.
IT'S WORTH IT A MILLION TIMES/ 111 ELECTR
I NEVER COULD MEMORIZE POETRY WORTH A DARN. 262 GGBROW
SHE AIN'T BLEEDIN' WELL WORTH IT. 231 HA APE
HE ISN'T WORTH THE TROUBLE WE'D GET INTO. 249 HA APE
I'D BE WORTH TEN MILLION DOLLARS. 20 HUGHIE
BUT LIKE HE COULDN'T THINK OF NOTHIN' ABOUT 23 HUGHIE
HIMSELF WORTH SAYING.
IT SURE WAS WORTH IT TO GIVE HUGHIE THE BIG SEND- 35 HUGHIE
OFF.
WITHOUT HER, NOTHING SEEMED WORTH THE TROUBLE. 603 ICEMAN
I SAID TO MYSELF, I DON'T CARE HOW MUCH IT COSTS, 639 ICEMAN
THEY'RE WORTH IT.
IF I WASN'T ABSOLUTELY SURE IT WILL BE WORTH IT T0661 ICEMAN
YOU IN THE END,
AFTER SHE'D GONE, I DIDN'T FEEL LIFE WAS WORTH 688 ICEMAN
LIVING.
IT'S MORE THAN YOU'RE WORTH, AND YOU COULDN'T GET 31 JOURNE
THAT IF IT WASN'T FOR ME.
AS YOU'LL FIND EVERYTHING ELSE WORTH SAYING. 131 JOURNE
HARDY AND THE SPECIALIST KNOW WHAT YOU'RE WORTH. 144 JOURNE
A DOLLAR WAS WORTH SO MUCH THEN. 148 JOURNE
YES, MAYBE LIFE OVERDID THE LESSON FOR ME, AND 149 JOURNE
MADE A DOLLAR WORTH TOO MUCH.
(BITTERLY.) WHAT THE HELL WAS IT I WANTED TO BUY,150 JOURNE
I WONDER, THAT WAS WORTH--
HE IS NOT WORTH IT/ 284 LAZARU
LOVE IS WORTH EVERYTHING/ 17 MANSNS
YOU DON'T THINK MY LOVE IS WORTH ITS 141 MANSNS
AND TO MYSELF--HOW MUCH YOU ARE WORTH TO ME$ 146 MANSNS
A DOLLAR IN CASH IS WORTH A HUNDRED TO YOU NOW. 157 MANSNS
MARK MY WORDS, MARCO WILL BE WORTH A MILLION WISE 363 MARCOM
MEN--IN THE CAUSE OF WISDOM/
HE SAID I'D BE WORTH A MILLION WISE MEN TO YOU. 379 MARCOM
WHAT IS IT WORTH$ 393 MARCOM
THIS IS MONEY, LEGALLY VALUED AT TEN YEN'S WORTH 393 MARCOM
OF ANYTHING YOU WISH TO BUY.
IT'S WORTH TEN YEN. 393 MARCOM
IF YOU MAKE THE PEOPLE BELIEVE IT'S WORTH IT, IT 394 MARCOM
IS/
IF SHE WERE A MILLION YEN WORTH OF SILK OR SPICES,403 MARCOM
I WOULDN'T WORRY AN INSTANT,
THEY MUST BE WORTH MILLIONS. 428 MARCOM
LAVISH/ THEY MUST BE WORTH MILLIONS/ 428 MARCOM
THEY MUST BE WORTH MILLIONS/ 429 MARCOM
WORTH WHILE YOUR WAITING, EH$ 430 MARCOM
I DON'T MIND TELLING YOU, DONATA, I'M WORTH OVER 430 MARCOM
TWO MILLIONS/
I KNEW WHEN YOU'D CALMED DOWN YOU'D THINK IT WORTH 16 MISBEG
SIX DOLLARS TO SEE THE LAST
SURE, THREE IS ALL IT'S WORTH AT MOST. 84 MISBEG
DON'T I LOOK TEN THOUSAND DOLLARS' WORTH TO ANY 98 MISBEG
DRUNKS
BUT NOT A PENNY'S WORTH OF CREDIT. 10 POET
YOU WAS WORTH ANY TEN MEN IN THE ARMY THAT DAY/ 93 POET
YOU'RE WORTH A HUNDRED AV THIM. 136 POET
HE WAS WORTH TWO MEN, LETTIN' OUT RIGHT AND LEFT, 157 POET
WILL GRADUALLY GIVE HER BACK A SENSE OF SECURITY 37 STRANG
AND A FEELING OF BEING WORTH
IT'S YOU WHO OUGHT TO HAVE MARRIED SOMEONE WORTH 70 STRANG
WHILE, NOT A POOR FISH LIKE ME/
ALL THE OTHER WOMEN IN THE WORLD AREN'T WORTH YOUR 70 STRANG
LITTLE FINGER/
WELL, IT'S WORTH A BET, ANYWAY... 113 STRANG
THERE'S NOTHING IN LIFE WORTH GRIEVING ABOUT, I 175 STRANG
ASSURE YOU, NINA/
I NEVER COULD ROW WORTH A DAMN/ 182 STRANG

WORTHLESS

YOU'RE A WORTHLESS LOAFER, BENNY ROGERS, SAME AS 529 DIFRNT
YOUR PA WAS.
SHE USED TO TELL ME, «I DON'T KNOW WHAT YOU CAN 608 ICEMAN
SEE IN THAT WORTHLESS, DRUNKEN,
MY DEATH IS WORTHLESS TO TIBERIUS. 316 LAZARU

WORTHY

TO PROVE OURSELVES WORTHY OF A FINER REALIZATION. 150 BEYOND
SHE WANTS SOME ONE MAN TO LOVE HER PURELY AND WHEN477 DYNAMO
SHE FINDS HIM WORTHY SHE WILL
SHE DIED TO TELL ME SHE HAD AT LAST FOUND ME 478 DYNAMO
WORTHY OF HER LOVE.
THAT DYNAMO WOULD NEVER FIND ME WORTHY OF HER 478 DYNAMO
SECRET
YOU MUST PRAY THAT SHE MAY FIND ME WORTHY. 485 DYNAMO
I'M NOT WORTHY TO WIPE YOUR SHOES.» 710 ICEMAN
I KNEW I'D PROVED BY THE WAY I'D LEFT EUGENE THAT 88 JOURNE
I WASN'T WORTHY TO HAVE
THAT I HAD PRAYED TO THE BLESSED VIRGIN TO MAKE ME175 JOURNE
SURE, AND TO FIND ME WORTHY.
LORD, I AM NOT WORTHY/ 362 MARCOM
AND HE SAID HE WASN'T WORTHY BECAUSE HE HAD SO 145 POET
LITTLE TO OFFER.
I'M NOT WORTHY OF YOUR LOVE/... 156 STRANG
AND MADE WORTHY TO BLEACH IN PEACE. 199 STRANG
ISN'T HE AS WORTHY OF LOVE--AS YOU ARE$ 456 WELDED

WOULDN'T

I WOULDN'T GIVE A DAMN IF YOU EVER DISPLAYED THE 32 JOURNE
SLIGHTEST SIGN OF GRATITUDE.

WOUND

WELL, IT WAS THE BUSINESS THAT WOUND ME UP/ 157 BEYOND

WRANGLING

WOUND (CONT'D.)

LUCKY IT'S ONLY A FLESH WOUND. 472 CARIBE
(THE MATE ROLLS PADDY OVER AND SEES A KNIFE WOUND 472 CARIBE
ON HIS SHOULDER.)
THEY'S A ARRER WOUND ON MY BACKSIDE I C'D SHOW YE/251 DESIRE
MY WOUND IS HEALED AND I'VE GOT ORDERS TO LEAVE 13 ELECTR
TOMORROW.
OF COURSE, THE JOKE WAS ON ME AND I GOT THIS WOUND 95 ELECTR
IN THE HEAD FOR MY PAINS.
ACKNOWLEDGES NO WOUND TO THE WORLD. 274 GGBROW
(HE IS WELL WOUND UP NOW AND GOES ON WITHOUT 22 HUGHIE
NOTICING
ON HIS LOWER LEFT SHOULDER IS THE BIG RAGGED SCAR 576 ICEMAN
OF AN OLD WOUND.
AND UNTIES THE STRING WHICH IS WOUND TIGHTLY 528 INZONE
AROUND THE TOP.
AND HE WOUND UP BY SAYING THAT HE HAD TO PUT UP 24 JOURNE
WITH POISON IVY, TICKS,
THEY WELL FROM HIS LIPS LIKE CLOTS OF BLOOD FROM A357 LAZARU
REOPENED WOUND.
OH, HOW HIS SOOTHING GRAY WORDS MUST HAVE PECKED 361 LAZARU
AT THE WOUND IN YOUR HEART LIKE
DO NOT WOUND ME WITH WISDOM. 437 MARCOM
BUT YOU UNDERSTAND, IT WAS THE LIQUOR TALKING, IF 42 POET
I SAID ANYTHING TO WOUND YOU.

WOUNDED

AS HE READS HIS FACE GROWS MORE AND MORE WOUNDED 208 AHWILD
AND TRAGIC.
A JOKE'S A JOKE, BUT--(HE ADDRESSES HIS WIFE IN A 227 AHWILD
WOUNDED TONE)
(PLEASED, BUT STILL NURSING WOUNDED DIGNITY) 255 AHWILD
FACE IN HANDS, HIS ROUND EYES CHILDISHLY WOUNDED 258 AHWILD
AND WOE-BEGONE.
(ARTHUR GOES OUT WITH A STIFF, WOUNDED DIGNITY.) 264 AHWILD
I WAS WOUNDED TO THE HEART. 272 AHWILD
WOULD YOU BRING HER TIRED SOUL BACK TO HIM AGAIN 565 CROSS
TO BE BRUISED AND WOUNDED$
NOT TO DELIBERATELY DISFIGURE MYSELF OUT OF 521 DAYS
WOUNDED PRIDE AND SPITE.
(WOUNDED) OH/ 515 DIFRNT
A WOUNDED LOOK OF BEWILDERED HURT.) 535 DIFRNT
(WOUNDED TO THE QUICK-- FURIOUSLY) 542 DIFRNT
YOU ROTTEN SON OF A--(THE CHOKES IT BACK--THEN 465 DYNAMO
HELPLESSLY, WITH A WOUNDED LOOK)
I KNOW THAT, BUT--YOU DON'T THINK HE'S BEEN 13 ELECTR
WOUNDED, DO YOU, VINNIE$.
WOUNDED/ 48 ELECTR
ORIN WAS WOUNDED. 48 ELECTR
HE WAS WOUNDED IN THE HEAD--A CLOSE SHAVE BUT IT 48 ELECTR
TURNED OUT ONLY A SCRATCH.
(TERRIBLY WOUNDED, WITHDRAWN INTO HIS STIFF 56 ELECTR
SOLDIER ARMOR--
WOUNDED IN THEIR TRUST OF LIFE/ 176 ELECTR
BRUNO STAGGERS BACK AND FALLS ON THE FLOOR BY THE 321 GGBROW
COUCH, MORTALLY WOUNDED.)
(HE SITS DOWN IN HIS OLD PLACE AND SINKS INTO A 669 ICEMAN
WOUNDED, SELF-PITYING BROODING.)
(WITH AN EXPRESSION OF WOUNDED HURT) 707 ICEMAN
TEN DEAD AND MORTALLY WOUNDED LIE ON THE GROUND, 291 LAZARU
OF BEING WOUNDED AND DESERTED AND LEFT ALONE IN A 184 MANSNS
LIFE IN WHICH THERE WAS NO
WEEP, PRINCESS OF THE WOUNDED HEART, 420 MARCOM
BEING WOUNDED TO THEIR DEPTHS AND MADE DEFIANT AND 13 STRANG
RESENTFUL BY THEIR PAIN.
HER EYES TRY TO ARMOR HER WOUNDED SPIRIT 26 STRANG
I HAVE WOUNDED EVERYONE.... 148 STRANG
I FEEL HOW LIFE HAS WOUNDED HIM... 148 STRANG
THEN IN A TREMBLING VOICE OF DEEPLY WOUNDED 150 STRANG
AFFECTION)
EVEN «WOUNDED, ON ONE'S KNEES 476 WELDED
(WOUNDED) DON'T/ 482 WELDED
(WOUNDED, TURNS AWAY FROM HER) 485 WELDED
(WOUNDED) YOUR FAITH$ 487 WELDED

WOUNDEDLY

(DEEPLY OFFENDED, RICHARD DISDAINS TO REPLY BUT 216 AHWILD
STALKS WOUNDEDLY TO THE SCREEN
(THEN HE IS STRUCK BY WHAT SHE SAID ABOUT HIS 86 ELECTR
FATHER--(WOUNDEDLY)
(THINKING WOUNDEDLY) (I) HOPED SHE WOULD THROW 27 STRANG
HERSELF IN MY ARMS...

WOUNDS

BUT THE WOUNDS ARE ALL HEALED--COMPLETELY HEALED. 517 DAYS
HEAD WOUNDS ARE NO JOKE. 80 ELECTR
SHOWING OFF YOUR WOUNDS/ 602 ICEMAN
WOUNDS, NO MORE/ 323 LAZARU
WEEPING HEALS THE WOUNDS OF SORROW TILL ONLY THE 420 MARCOM
SCARS REMAIN
SO MANY OLD WOUNDS MAY HAVE TO BE UNBOUND, AND OLD188 STRANG
SCARS POINTED TO WITH PRIDE,
(TORTUREDLY) WOUNDS/ WOUNDS/ 458 WELDED
(IN A BLAND, ABSENT-MINDED TONE WHICH WOUNDS HIM) 467 WELDED
(A PAUSE) AN END OF LOATHING--NO WOUNDS, NO 476 WELDED
MEMORIES--SLEEP/

WOVEN

A FOREST OF MASTS, SPARS, SAILS OF WOVEN BAMBOO 400 MARCOM
LATHS,

WRAITH

IT IS THIN AND AGED, THE WRAITH OF WHAT MUST ONCE 6 ELECTR
HAVE BEEN A GOOD BARITONE.
SETH'S THIN WRAITH OF A BARITONE
FAVORITE MOURNFUL «SHENANDOAH»,
IN HIS AGED PLAINTIVE WRAITH OF A ONCE-GOOD 169 ELECTR
BARITONE, THE CHANTY «SHENANDOAH»..

WRANGLING

(IRRITABLY) AND IT'S WHERE YOUR EVERLASTING 255 AHWILD
WRANGLING GIVES ME A PAIN, YOU TWO/

WRAP

WRAP

IN THE MOONLIGHT--THOUGH IT WAS WARM--AND I WANTED515 DIFRNT
TO WRAP A BLANKET ROUND HER.
SHE WAS ALL IN WHITE LIKE DEY WRAP AROUND STIFFS. 230 HA APE

WRAPPED

A HEAVY SHAWL IS WRAPPED ABOUT HER SHOULDER, 144 BEYOND
WRAPPED UP IN A BLANKET. 145 BEYOND
ABBIE IS SITTING IN A ROCKING CHAIR, A SHAWL 247 DESIRE
WRAPPED ABOUT HER SHOULDERS.
AND WHAT'S DAT IN BOX O' GRUB I HID ALL WRAPPED 189 EJONES
UP IN OIL/
I COULD FEEL THE NIGHT WRAPPED AROUND ME LIKE A 261 GGBROW
GRAY VELVET GOWN LINED WITH WARM
SHE IS WRAPPED IN A GRAY CLOAK. 323 GGBROW
A BLOOD-STAINED BANDAGE IS WRAPPED AROUND HIS 240 HA APE
HEAD.)
HIDDEN IN UNDER HIS DUDS AN' WRAPPED UP IN 'EM, IT519 INZONE
WAS--
I KEPT IT WRAPPED UP IN TISSUE PAPER IN MY TRUNK. 115 JOURNE
JUST AS HE APPEARED IN THE OPENING OF THE TOMB, 277 LAZARU
WRAPPED IN HIS SHROUD--
(THREATENINGLY) GIVE ME WHAT WAS WRAPPED UP IN 375 MARCOM
THAT'S D'YOU HEAR?
(HE PULLS THE PIECES OF THE MINIATURE WRAPPED IN 430 MARCOM
THE HANDKERCHIEF
MOTIONLESS, WRAPPED IN CONTEMPLATION. 432 MARCOM
HER BODY IS WRAPPED IN A WINDING SHEET OF DEEP 434 MARCOM
BLUE.
I FEEL HER IN THE MOONLIGHT, HER SOUL WRAPPED IN 152 MISBEG
IT LIKE A SILVER MANTLE, AND I

WRAPPER

SHE WEARS A DARK WRAPPER AND SLIPPERS.) 562 CROSS
SHE WEARS A FADED BLUE WRAPPER) 454 DYNAMO
SHE IS DRESSED AS AT THE END OF ACT THREE, IN 62 ELECTR
NIGHTGOWN, WRAPPER AND SLIPPERS.
SHE WEARS A FADED OLD WRAPPER OVER HER NIGHTGOWN, 136 POET
SLIPPERS ON HER BARE FEET.

WRAPPERS

143 POET
IN YOUR BARE LEGS WITH ONLY YOUR NIGHTGOWN AND 143 POET
WRAPPER TO COVER YOUR NAKEDNESS/

WRAPS

(SHE FLINGS HERSELF ON HER KNEES AND WRAPS HER 543 DIFRNT
ARMS AROUND HIS LEGS IN
WITH A SPRING HE WRAPS HIS HUGE ARMS AROUND YANK 254 HA APE
IN A MURDEROUS HUG.

WRATH

(CHOKING WITH WRATH) O GOD OF THE SOMBER HEAVENS/425 MARCOM
AN' YOU CURSIN' AN' CALLIN' DOWN THE WRATH O' GOD 583 ROPE
ON HIM BY DAY AN' BY NIGHT.

WRATHFULLY

WRATHFULLY, AT THE TOP OF HIS LUNGS) 526 INZONE
(WRATHFULLY.) THE PADLOCK IS ALL SCRATCHED. 121 JOURNE

WREATH

A FUNERAL WREATH IS FIXED TO THE COLUMN AT THE 67 ELECTR
RIGHT OF STEPS.
ANOTHER WREATH IS ON THE DOOR. 47 ELECTR
A VICTORY WREATH AROUND HIS HEAD. 313 LAZARU

WREATHED

HE IS A BIT BREATHLESS FROM HASTE BUT HIS FACE IS 386 MARCOM
WREATHED IN SMILES.)

WREATHS

THERE WASN'T NU FLOWERS BUT A COUPLA LOUSY 31 HUGHIE
WREATHS.
ALL HAVE WREATHS OF IVY IN THEIR HAIR 306 LAZARU

WRECK

YOU TELL ME ABOUT YOURSELF AND ABOUT THE WRECK. 35 ANNA
TELL ME ABOUT THE WRECK, LIKE YOU PROMISED ME YOU 35 ANNA
WOULD.
SHE WAS SIGHTED BOTTOM UP, A COMPLETE WRECK, BY 558 CROSS
THE WHALER JOHN SLOCUM.
THEIR DAMN LIE O' THE MARY ALLEN BEIN' A WRECK. 568 CROSS
WRECK YOUR HAPPINESS AND DRAG YOU DOWN TO THEIR 524 DAYS
LEVEL--WHAT I WAS DOING.
WHICH MIGHT WRECK BOTH OUR LIVES, DOES NOT EXIST 530 INZONE
FOR YOU.
A WRECK, A DRUNKEN HULK, DONE WITH AND FINISHED/ 168 JOURNE
HOLY JOSEPH, I'M A WRECK ENTIRELY. 166 MISBEG

WRECKAGE

I'VE SAVED TEN THOUSAND FROM THE WRECKAGE, MAYBE 157 BEYOND
TWENTY.
AND I'M VAIN ENOUGH NOT TO CRAVE ANY MALE VIEWING 517 DAYS
THE WRECKAGE
OR A PIECE O' WRECKAGE FROM SOME SHIP THEY'VE SENT523 INZONE
TO DAVY JONES.
AND BEGINS PICKING UP THE WRECKAGE IN HIS 418 MARCOM
HANDKERCHIEF.

WRECKED

DEIR STEAMER GAT WRECKED. 30 ANNA
HIS SHIP HAD BEEN WRECKED IN THE INDIAN OCEAN. 559 CROSS
THOSE FOOLS LIED ABOUT HER BEING WRECKED. 570 CROSS
WRECKED MY LOIFE AS YOU HAVE WRECKED YOUR OWN. 532 INZONE
THERE IS A LOOK OF WRECKED DISTINCTION ABOUT IT, 34 POET
OF BROODING, HUMILIATED PRIDE.

WRECKERS

I CALL THEM THE INDUSTRIOUS WRECKERS OF THE 242 HA APE
WORLD/

WRECKERS, DAT'S DE RIGHT DOPE/ 243 HA APE

WRECKS

ANOTHER ONE OF HIS WRECKS/ 564 CROSS
HOLDS THE WRECKS OF THE SHOES IN HIS HANDS AND 196 EJONES
REGARDS THEM MOURNFULLY)
HIS SHOES ARE EVEN MORE DISREPUTABLE, WRECKS OF 577 ICEMAN
IMITATION LEATHER.

WRENCH

THE FLOOR LIKE A MONKEY'S, HE GIVES A GREAT WRENCH244 HA APE
BACKWARDS.

WRENCHES

SHE GIVES A SMOTHERED GASP, WRENCHES HER EYES FROM 27 MANSNS
THE DARKNESS INSIDE.

WRENCHES (CONT'D.)

HE WRENCHES OPEN THE DOOR AND FLINGS HIMSELF INTO 143 MANSNS
THE BOOKKEEPER'S ROOM.
(HE WRENCHES OPEN THE DOOR AND FLINGS HIMSELF INTO155 MANSNS
THE HALL, SLAMMING THE DOOR.
(HE STARTS TO SOB BUT WRENCHES HIMSELF OUT OF IT 169 POET
AND SPEAKS IN BROAD

WRENCHING

(ABRUPTLY WRENCHING HIS EYES FROM HERS--GRUMBLES 37 MANSNS
IRRITABLY TO HIMSELF.)

WRESTING

SPRINGS FORWARD AND WRESTING THE DAGGER FROM HER 415 MARCOM
HAND, FLINGS IT OVER THE SIDE.

WRESTS

(HE WRESTS THE CANE FROM THE OLD MAN'S HANDS) 584 ROPE

WRETCH

SO THAT'S WHY HE WANTS FATHER SENT AWAY, THE 565 CROSS
WRETCH/

WRETCHES

THE HARNESSED WRETCHES IN THE EXHAUSTED ATTITUDES 352 MARCOM
OF SLEEP,

WRIGGLES

(COCKY WRIGGLES AWAY FROM HIM) 463 CARIBE
AND I'M INTERESTED IN THAT GERM WHICH WRIGGLES 296 GGBROW
LIKE A QUESTION MARK OF

WRIGGLING

(PLEASED BUT STILL MORE CONFUSED--WRIGGLING HIS 501 VOYAGE
FEET)

WRINGING

(HE STANDS WRINGING HIS HANDS TOGETHER AND BEGINS 59 ANNA
TO WEEP.)
(WRINGING HER HANDS) OH, I WISH I COULD TELL IF 138 BEYOND
YOU'RE LYING OR NOT/
(WRINGING HER HANDS) OH, NAT, BE STILL/ 573 CROSS
(WRINGING HER HANDS--DESPERATELY) 513 DIFRNT
WRINGING HER HANDS IN A PITIFUL DESPERATION.) 57 ELECTR
WRINGING HER HANDS TOGETHER IN STRICKEN ANGUISH. 121 ELECTR
SHE STARES BEFORE HER, WRINGING HER HANDS AND 121 ELECTR
MOANING.
WRINGING MOVEMENT WHICH RECALLS HER MOTHER IN THE 157 ELECTR
LAST ACT OF «THE HUNTED.»

WRINGS

HE TWISTS AND WRINGS AND TORTURES OUR LIVES WITH 73 ELECTR
OTHERS' LIVES UNTIL--

WRINKLE

DAT'S HICKEY'S WRINKLE, TOO. 630 ICEMAN

WRINKLED

HE IS DRESSED IN A WRINKLED, ILL-FITTING DARK SUIT 5 ANNA
OF SHORE CLOTHES,
(AN OLD GRAY-HEADED MAN WITH A KINDLY, WRINKLED 458 CARIBE
FACE.
IS NOW NEARLY WHITE AND HIS FACE MORE DEEPLY LINED535 DIFRNT
AND WRINKLED.
HIS SHINY WRINKLED FACE IS OBLONG WITH A SQUARE 129 ELECTR
WHITE CHIN WHISKER.
THIS MASK ACCENTUATES HIS BULGING, PREMATURELY 299 LAZARU
WRINKLED FOREHEAD,

WRINKLES

THERE ARE WRINKLES ABOUT HER EYES, AND HER SMALL, 515 DAYS
FULL,
WITH A GREAT, RED, WEATHER-BEATEN FACE SEAMED BY 513 DIFRNT
SUN WRINKLES.
HIS FACE IS SQUARE, RIBBED WITH WRINKLES, THE 422 DYNAMO
FOREHEAD LOW, THE NOSE HEAVY,
(SHE WRINKLES HER FOREHEAD AGAIN.) 115 JOURNE
WITH ONLY THE FIRST TRACING OF WRINKLES ABOUT THE 2 MANSNS
EYES AND MOUTH.
DO YOU MEAN TO SAY YOU DON'T SEE ALL THE WRINKLES/ 5 MANSNS
HER SMALL, DELICATE, OVAL FACE IS HAGGARD WITH 161 MANSNS
INNUMERABLE WRINKLES.
HIS FACE IS GAUNT, CHALKY-WHITE, FURROWED WITH 578 ROPE
WRINKLES,

WRINKLING

(SHE PAUSES, WRINKLING HER BROW IN AN EFFORT OF 115 JOURNE
MEMORY.)

WRIST

HE SITS, WATCHING HER FACE WORRIEDLY, HIS FINGERS 558 DAYS
ON HER WRIST.
STILLWELL REACHES FOR HER WRIST IN ALARM, 563 DAYS
I THOUGHT YOU WOULD SPRAIN YOUR WRIST/ 82 ELECTR
(SHE LOOKS AT HER WRIST WATCH) 220 HA APE
(STERNLY--GRABBING HER BY THE WRIST) 178 STRANG
NINA LETS GO OF HER WRIST AND STARES AFTER THEM IN178 STRANG
A SORT OF STUNNED STUPOR)

WRISTS

WRISTS AND ANKLES. 200 EJONES
(THEY RUN TO HER SIDE, KNEEL AND RUB HER WRISTS. 293 GGBROW
(HE NODS TO LIEB, WHO SLIPS A PAIR OF HANDCUFFS ON717 ICEMAN
HICKEY'S WRISTS.
(SHE BEGINS TO CHAFE HIS WRISTS AND TURNS TO STARE190 MANSNS
AT THE SUMMER-HOUSE--
KEEP YOUR THICK WRISTS AND UGLY, PEASANT PAWS OFF 107 POET
THE TABLE IN MY PRESENCE,
(LETTING HER WRISTS DROP--APPALLED--STAMMERS) 108 STRANG
HE CHAFES HER WRISTS) 108 STRANG

WRIT

IT'S WRIT DOWN PLAIN IN YOUR EYES. 542 'ILE
«THE MOVING FINGER WRITES, AND HAVING WRIT, MOVES 199 AHWILD
ON.»
I'VE HAD IT WRIT OUT AN' READY IN CASE YE'D EVER 213 DESIRE
GO.

WRITE

OR PRETENDING TO WRITE ONE. 192 AHWILD
HER OLD MAN MADE HER WRITE IT. 273 AHWILD
I WISH I COULD WRITE POETRY. 277 AHWILD
BUT YOU MIGHT HAVE KNOWN I'D NEVER WRITE THAT 281 AHWILD
UNLESS--

1833 WRITING

WRITE (CONT'D.)
WHY DIDN'T YOU HAVE MORE SENSE THAN TO LET HIM 286 AHWILD
MAKE YOU WRITE ITS
YOU OUGHT TO HAVE KNOWN HE STOOD RIGHT OVER ME AND286 AHWILD
TOLD ME EACH WORD TO WRITE.
(HE DRINKS) AY NEVER WRITE FOR HER TO COME, 12 ANNA
THIS WAS ALWAYS THE ONLY ADDRESS HE GIVE ME TO 16 ANNA
WRITE HIM BACK.
SPITE OF ALL YOU USED TO WRITE ME ABOUT HATING IT. 21 ANNA
DIDN'T I WRITE YOU YEAR AFTER YEAR HOW ROTTEN IT 57 ANNA
WAS
AND WRITE YOU A LETTER 'BOUT IT.- 95 BEYOND
I'D RATHER GO THROUGH A TYPHOON AGAIN THAN WRITE A131 BEYOND
LETTER.
(VAGUELY) I'LL WRITE, OR SOMETHING OF THAT SORT. 149 BEYOND
I'VE ALWAYS WANTED TO WRITE. 149 BEYOND
I MEANT TO WRITE OFTENER. 160 BEYOND
EACH GIRL'LL HAVE A SLIP AV PAPER WID HER AN' WHIN463 CARIBE
YOU BUY ANYTHIN' YOU WRITE UT
IF YE CAN'T WRITE HAVE SOME ONE WHO CAN DO UT FOR 463 CARIBE
YE.
YE MUST WRITE DOWN TOBACCY OR FRUIT OR SOMETHIN' 463 CARIBE
THE LOIKE AV THAT.
THEN I'LL WRITE IT FOR YUH. 465 CARIBE
(SULLENLY) I CAN'T WRITE ME NAME. 465 CARIBE
HE COULDN'T WRITE. 561 CROSS
OH, I'LL PROBABLY NEVER WRITE IT, BUT IT'S AMUSING497 DAYS
TO DOPE OUT.
YOU CERTAINLY SHOWED YOU COULD WRITE IN THE OLD 497 DAYS
DAYS--ARTICLES, ANYWAY.
WHY SHOULDN'T YOU WRITE ITS 497 DAYS
EVEN IF HE DIDN'T WRITE YOU LETTERS. 502 DAYS
I NEVER GAVE HER MY ADDRESS BECAUSE I THOUGHT 465 DYNAMO
SHE'D ONLY WRITE BAWLING ME OUT.
YOU'LL DO AS I SAY AND NOT FORCE ME TO WRITE MY 27 ELECTR
FATHER.
IF HE ISN'T, I'LL WRITE FATHER AGAIN. 35 ELECTR
THAT'S WHY I FELT IT MY DUTY TO WRITE YOU. 50 ELECTR
AND ALL ON ACCOUNT OF A STUPID LETTER VINNIE HAD 51 ELECTR
NO BUSINESS TO WRITE.
(THEN WITH AN EFFORT) I'LL WRITE CLARK AND DAWSONILL ELECTR
TONIGHT
HE CAN PAINT BEAUTIFULLY AND WRITE POETRY 263 GGBROW
PLEASE FORGIVE MY INTRUSION, AND REMEMBER ME TO 290 GGBROW
CYBEL WHEN YOU WRITE.
(HALF TO HIMSELF) AND I'LL WRITE HER A LETTER 249 HA APE
WRITE IT IN DE BLOTTER. 251 HA APE
WHILE HE WAS TRYING TO WRITE A SERMON. 596 ICEMAN
I PLANTED IT IN YOUR MIND THAT SOMEDAY YOU'D 164 JOURNE
WRITE/
AND BECAUSE I ONCE WANTED TO WRITE, 164 JOURNE
HELL, I USED TO WRITE BETTER STUFF FOR THE LIT 164 JOURNE
MAGAZINE IN COLLEGE/
PICTURES OF AN OLD BUCK GOAT UPON THE WALLS AND 354 LAZARU
WRITE ABOVE THEM, CAESARS
TELL ME, SIMON, DO YOU EVER THINK NOW OF THE BOOK 8 MANSNS
YOU WERE SO EAGER TO WRITE
AND YOU REALLY SHOULD WRITE IT. 8 MANSNS
I'LL WRITE MY BOOK THEN. 16 MANSNS
WRITE ME FRANKLY OF YOUR DISCONTENTS. 17 MANSNS
I HEARD YOU, WHEN HE SAID HE'D RETIRE TO WRITE HIS 20 MANSNS
BOOK WHEN WE HAD ENOUGH,
OR EVEN WRITE TO HIM. 21 MANSNS
BUT WHAT A WAY FOR ME--AND YOU IN YOUR STUDY 44 MANSNS
TRYING TO WRITE/
AS FOR HER HAVING JOEL WRITE ME HE WAS DEAD 45 MANSNS
INSTEAD OF WRITING ME HERSELF,
AND FOR THE LAST COUPLE OF YEARS, WHO HAS BEEN 45 MANSNS
ENCOURAGING ME TO WRITE ITS
AND YOU CAN WRITE POETRY AGAIN OF YOUR LOVE FOR 191 MANSNS
ME.
(HESITATINGLY) WILL YOU WRITE ME--A POEMS 357 MARCOM
AND YOU'LL WRITE ME& 357 MARCOM
I'LL HAVE TO WRITE DONATA ALL ABOUT THIS. 369 MARCOM
(ABASHED AND FURIOUS) I DIDN'T WRITE THAT. 375 MARCOM
SOFTLY) PERHAPS ON THE VOYAGE YOU MAY BE INSPIRED399 MARCOM
TO WRITE ANOTHER.
WRITE ME WHEN YOU REACH PERSIA. 401 MARCOM
AND TELL THE KAAN--ANYTHING HE WANTS--WRITE ME-- 407 MARCOM
JUST VENICE--
AND I WAS ALWAYS INTENDING TO WRITE-- 430 MARCOM
AND WRITE A BOOK ABOUT HOW THE WORLD CAN BE 29 POET
CHANGED SO PEOPLE WON'T BE GREEDY TO
THAT THE POETRY HE HOPED THE PURE FREEDOM OF 81 POET
NATURE WOULD INSPIRE HIM TO WRITE I
FOR EXAMPLE, THIS BOOK SIMON PLANS TO WRITE TO 84 POET
DENOUNCE THE EVIL OF GREED
I DO NOT EVEN BELIEVE SIMON WILL EVER WRITE THIS 85 POET
BOOK ON PAPER.
JUST ENOUGH TO BE COMFORTABLE, AND HE'D HAVE TIME 146 POET
OVER TO WRITE HIS BOOK.
COULDN'T WRITE A LINE THERE... 5 STRANG
AND I CAN WRITE/... 5 STRANG
I COULDN'T WRITE A LINE. 7 STRANG
THOSE SOUNDS OUR LIPS MAKE AND OUR HANDS WRITE. 40 STRANG
THEN I WANTED TO WRITE TO YOU BUT I WAS SCARED HE 61 STRANG
MIGHT READ IT.
WHY DOES EVERYONE IN THE WORLD THINK THEY CAN 74 STRANG
WRITES...
DOES SAM WRITE HIS ADS HERE OF A WEEK-END NOWS... 74 STRANG
(A BIT EMBARRASSEDLY) I'VE REALLY MEANT TO WRITE. 79 STRANG
BUT PERHAPS SHE CAN WRITE HIM OUT OF HER 81 STRANG
SYSTEM....)
BUT I SUPPOSE HE'S STILL TOO BROKEN UP OVER HIS 94 STRANG
MOTHER'S DEATH TO WRITE.
(INDIFFERENTLY) HE'LL PROBABLY COME WITHOUT 94 STRANG
BOTHERING TO WRITE.
I WAS PROUD TO BE ABLE TO WRITE HER THAT... 112 STRANG

WRITE (CONT'D.)
(TURNING TO NINA) I THINK I'LL WRITE TO MY SISTER113 STRANG
IN CALIFORNIA AND ASK HER TO
I MUST WRITE TO JANE... 113 STRANG
IF I HAD THE COURAGE TO WRITE THE TRUTH... 120 STRANG
WE WANTED TO WRITE YOU ABOUT THE BABY. 132 STRANG
THEN YOU MIGHT WRITE MORE ABOUT LIFE 147 STRANG
WHY DON'T YOU WRITE A NOVEL ABOUT LIFE SOMETIME, 148 STRANG
MARSDENS
YOU MAY REMEMBER I USED TO WRITE YOU ABOUT HIM 166 STRANG
WITH ENTHUSIASM.
AFTER WE'RE MARRIED I'M GOING TO WRITE A NOVEL--MY176 STRANG
FIRST REAL NOVEL/
I CAN WRITE THE TRUTH/ 177 STRANG
I'LL WRITE THE BOOK OF US/ 177 STRANG
I WRITE BACK ALWAYS I COME SOON. 506 VOYAGE
MY BROTHER HE WRITE SAME TING TOO. 506 VOYAGE
I WRITE ONCE IN A WHILE AND SHE WRITE MANY TIME,. 506 VOYAGE
AND MY BROTHER HE WRITE ME, TOO. 506 VOYAGE
I WRITE TO HER FROM BUENOS ERES BUT I DON'T TELL 506 VOYAGE
HER I COME HOME.

WRITER
OR A GREAT DOCTOR, OR A GREAT WRITER, OR-- 290 AHWILD
NO WRITER IS OUTSIDE OF HIS BOOKS... 35 STRANG

WRITER'S
I FEEL IT MY DUTY, FATHER, TO WARN YOU THAT JOHN'S504 DAYS
GOT WRITER'S ITCH AGAIN.

WRITES
=THE MOVING FINGER WRITES, AND HAVING WRIT, MOVES 199 AHWILD
ON..
(HE TAKES THE PAPER FROM PEARL AND WRITES) 465 CARIBE
JOHN NERVOUSLY WRITES A FEW WORDS ON A PAD-- 496 DAYS
TEARS OFF A SLIP OF PAPER AND WRITES TWO WORDS ON 35 ELECTR
IT.
AND NINA--WRITES OF GORDON AS IF HE HAD BEEN A 75 STRANG
DEMI-GOD....
HE NEVER WRITES TO HER, DOES HE& 101 STRANG

WRITHE
HIS MUSCLES WRITHE WITH HIS LIPS 319 GGBROW
WRITHE AND TWIST DISTRACTEDLY, SEEKING TO HIDE 349 LAZARU
THEIR HEADS AGAINST EACH OTHER,

WRITHEN
WITH A GRIM WRITHEN SMILE) 178 ELECTR

WRITHES
SIDE AND WRITHES ON THE THIN MATTRESS OF HIS BUNK.484 CARDIF
(HIS FACE TWITCHES AND HIS BODY WRITHES IN A FINAL489 CARDIF
SPASM.

WRITHING
(WRITHING) I KNOW, PA. 294 AHWILD
(WRITHING) DON'T/ 549 DAYS
(LOOKING AROUND HER FRIGHTENEDLY AT THE WEIRD 484 DYNAMO
SHADOWS OF THE EQUIPMENT WRITHING
MIRIAM'S BODY IS SEEN TO RISE IN A WRITHING 348 LAZARU
TORTURED LAST EFFORT.)
(WRITHING--THINKING) (IIT HURTS NOW/... 152 STRANG

WRITIN'
PAUL, MINNESOTA--AND A LADY'S WRITIN'. 8 ANNA
SPY IN PARIS WAS WRITIN' LOVE LETTERS TO SOME 529 INZONE
WOMAN SPY IN SWITZERLAND WHO SENT

WRITING
WITH A WRITING DESK AND A CHAIR BETWEEN THEM. 185 AHWILD
I'LL BET HE'S OFF SOMEWHERE WRITING A POEM TO 192 AHWILD
MURIEL MCCCOMBER, THE SILLY/
NOT UNLESS YOU APOLOGIZE IN WRITING AND PROMISE TO203 AHWILD
PUNISH--
(FINALLY SURVEYS THE TWO WORDS SHE HAS BEEN 249 AHWILD
WRITING AND IS SATISFIED WITH THEM)
MILDRED SITS AT THE DESK AT RIGHT, FRONT, WRITING 249 AHWILD
TWO WORDS OVER AND OVER AGAIN.
I'VE BEEN PRACTICING A NEW WAY OF WRITING MY NAME.250 AHWILD
WHAT ARE YOU IN TRAINING FOR--WRITING CHECKS& 251 AHWILD
LOOKS LIKE A WOMAN'S WRITING, TOO, THE OLD DEVIL/ 5 ANNA
YUH KEPT RIGHT ON WRITING HIM W'EN HAS A NURSE GIRL 19 ANNA
STILL.
JOHN IMMEDIATELY PRETENDS TO BE WRITING. 495 DAYS
AS IF HE WANTED TO START WRITING.) 498 DAYS
YES. I REMEMBER HIS WRITING TO BOAST ABOUT THAT. 502 DAYS
AT REAR OF DOOR, A WRITING DESK. 514 DAYS
THAT'S WHAT I KEPT WRITING HER.... 466 DYNAMO
ORIN NOT WRITING DOESN'T MEAN ANYTHING. 13 ELECTR
HAZEL FEELS BAD ABOUT ORIN NOT WRITING. 14 ELECTR
ARE A WALL TABLE AND CHAIR AND A WRITING DESK AND 79 ELECTR
CHAIR.
WRITING BY THE LIGHT OF A LAMP. 149 ELECTR
AS HE STOPS WRITING AND READS OVER THE PARAGRAPH 149 ELECTR
HE HAS JUST FINISHED.
YOU'LL DAMN SOON STOP YOUR TRICKS WHEN YOU KNOW 152 ELECTR
WHAT I'VE BEEN WRITING/
I'VE BEEN WRITING THE HISTORY OF OUR FAMILY/ 152 ELECTR
ONE IS WRITING A LETTER. 245 HA APE
(WRITING) ROBERT SMITH. 246 HA APE
WITH MICKEY TO DO THE WRITING ON THE WALL/ 644 ICEMAN
HE SAID HE'D INCLUDE IT IN A LETTER HE'S WRITING 26 JOURNE
TO HARKER.
WRITING IT TO A DUMB BARMAID, WHO THOUGHT HE WAS A135 JOURNE
POOR CRAZY SOUSE.
I MADE THE MANAGER PUT DOWN HIS EXACT WORDS IN 152 JOURNE
WRITING.
AS FOR HER HAVING JOEL WRITE ME HE WAS DEAD 45 MANSNS
INSTEAD OF WRITING ME HERSELF,
THEN, SHAKING AWAY THIS INTERRUPTION, BENDS TO HIS359 MARCOM
WRITING AGAIN.)
I'M ONLY WRITING SOMETHING. 360 MARCOM
WHAT ARE YOU WRITING, SONS 360 MARCOM
THEN IF I MIGHT ASK YOU A FAVOR, THAT YOU PUT IN 412 MARCOM
WRITING ALL YOU'VE JUST SAID IN
WRITING A PRESCRIPTION.... 33 STRANG
WRITING A LETTER. 48 STRANG

WRITING

WRITING (CONT'D.)
SHE HAS BEEN WRITING SAM REGULARLY ONCE A WEEK 50 STRANG
EVER SINCE SHE'S KNOWN WE WERE
WHOM IS SHE WRITING TO$...)) 50 STRANG
I'M WRITING TO NED DARRELL. 51 STRANG
I KEPT WRITING SAMMY TO BRING YOU HERE RIGHT OFF, 61 STRANG
(ISEF THE OLD MAN TURNS OVER IN HIS GRAVE AT MY 67 STRANG
WRITING ADS IN HIS STUDY...
WHY DIDN'T YOU TELL ME IF I WAS INTERRUPTING--YOUR 75 STRANG
WRITING/
(HE HAS PULLED OUT HIS PEN AND A CARD AND IS 77 STRANG
WRITING.
WRITINGS
ONE MUST HAVE STUPID WRITINGS THAT MEN CAN 423 MARCOM
UNDERSTAND.
WHAT GOOD ARE WISE WRITINGS TO FIGHT STUPIDITYS 423 MARCOM
WRITTEN
IT'S ONE OF THE GREATEST NOVELS EVER WRITTEN/ 197 AHWILD
THE BALLAD OF READING GAOL, ONE OF THE GREATEST 197 AHWILD
POEMS EVER WRITTEN.
IF YOU HADN'T WRITTEN THAT LETTER-- 284 AHWILD
HADN'T YOU WRITTEN ME YOU WERE$ 286 AHWILD
BUT I MUST HAVE WRITTEN YOU ALL THIS. 131 BEYOND
IT'S WRITTEN HERE IN HIS HANDWRITING.. 573 CROSS
HE'D EVER WRITTEN BEFORE ABOUT ANY OF HIS GREAT 504 DAYS
SPIRITUAL DISCOVERIES.
YOU'VE WRITTEN ME YOU WERE HAPPY, AND I BELIEVED 512 DAYS
YOU..
HER LAST WORDS WERE THE VERY WORDS YOU HAD WRITTEN466 DYNAMO
HER.
SHE'D SUNK HER LAST SHRED OF PRIDE AND WRITTEN TO 26 ELECTR
YOUR FATHER ASKING FOR A LOAN.
OH, I'D WRITTEN TO HER NOW AND THEN AND SENT HER 26 ELECTR
MONEY WHEN I HAPPENED TO HAVE
(THEN TURNING AWAY AGAIN) YOU REMEMBER MY TELLING 39 ELECTR
YOU HE HAD WRITTEN
AND TAKES OUT THE SLIP OF PAPER SHE HAD WRITTEN 40 ELECTR
ON)
I'VE WRITTEN SOMETHING HERE. 40 ELECTR
VINNIE MUST HAVE WRITTEN YOU THE SAME NONSENSE SHE 85 ELECTR
DID YOUR FATHER.
SO LONELY YOU'VE WRITTEN ME EXACTLY TWO LETTERS IN 85 ELECTR
THE LAST SIX MONTHS/
(TENSELY) WHAT HAVE YOU WRITTEN$ 152 ELECTR
TELL ME WHAT YOU'VE WRITTEN/ 152 ELECTR
(AGHAST) DO YOU MEAN TO TELL ME YOU'VE ACTUALLY 153 ELECTR
WRITTEN--
MOST OF WHAT I'VE WRITTEN IS ABOUT YOU/ 153 ELECTR
AND COME TO WHAT I'VE WRITTEN ABOUT YOUR 154 ELECTR
ADVENTURES ON MY LOST ISLANDS.
I'M GOING TO PUT THIS CONFESSION I'VE WRITTEN IN 156 ELECTR
SAFE HANDS--
HAVE YOU GIVEN HER WHAT YOU'VE WRITTEN$ 163 ELECTR
I HAVEN'T WRITTEN HER IN A COUPLE OF YEARS--OR 589 ICEMAN
ANYONE ELSE.
IT WAS WRITTEN ALL OVER HER FACE, SWEETNESS AND 714 ICEMAN
LOVE AND PITY AND FORGIVENESS.
THE NAME THAT'S WRITTEN IS SIDNEY DAVIDSON, WAN 530 INZONE
HUNDRED AN'--
THIS ONE WAS WRITTEN A YEAR BEFORE THE WAR STARTED531 INZONE
ANYWAY.
SOME OF THE POEMS AND PARODIES HE'S WRITTEN ARE 36 JOURNE
DAMNED GOOD.
AND SOME OF THE POEMS YOU'VE WRITTEN YOURSELF ARE 90 JOURNE
EVEN WORSE/
I READ ALL THE PLAYS EVER WRITTEN. 150 JOURNE
THERE'S THE BOOK THAT OUGHT TO BE WRITTEN-- 47 MANSS
SURELY IT CANNOT BE A SONG HE HAS WRITTEN$ 360 MARCOM
THAT'S WRITTEN IN THE BIBLE. 368 MARCOM
SEE TEN YEN WRITTEN ON IT, DON'T YOUS 393 MARCOM
THEY'VE NOT WRITTEN ME IN YEARS. 7 MISBEG
WHY, I REMEMBER TELLING HIM TONIGHT I'D EVEN 133 MISBEG
WRITTEN MY BROTHER
SHE HAD PARLOR HOUSE WRITTEN ALL OVER HER-- 149 MISBEG
(SHE SMILES COQUETTISHLY.) ALL HE'S WRITTEN THE 29 POET
LAST FEW MONTHS ARE LOVE POEMS.
HE HASN'T WRITTEN ANY OF IT YET, ANYWAY--ONLY THE 29 POET
NOTES FOR IT.
HE'D HAVE WRITTEN YOU HE WAS SICK, BUT HE DIDN'T 75 POET
WANT TO WORRY YOU.
OF COURSE, IT IS SOME TIME SINCE HE HAS WRITTEN. 81 POET
BUT I WARN YOU IT IS ALREADY WRITTEN ON HIS 85 POET
CONSCIENCE AND--
AND SAID HE MEANT ALL THE BOLD THINGS HE'D WRITTEN147 POET
IN THE POEMS I'D SEEN.
HIS NOVELS JUST WELL--WRITTEN SURFACE... 34 STRANG
HAVE YOU WRITTEN ANOTHER NOVEL LATELY$ 40 STRANG
(READING WHAT SHE HAS JUST WRITTEN OVER TO 49 STRANG
HERSELF)
WRITTEN AFTER WE READ OF YOUR APPOINTMENTS 49 STRANG
(THINKING AMUSEDLY) ((IF HE KNEW WHAT I'D JUST 50 STRANG
WRITTEN...
I'VE WRITTEN ON THE MARGINS. 74 STRANG
WHY HASN'T NED EVER WRITTEN$ 112 STRANG
NOT A LINE WRITTEN IN OVER A YEAR/.... 112 STRANG
I'VE WRITTEN HIS MOTHER I'M MAKING HIM HAPPY... 112 STRANG
I SUPPOSED HE'D WRITTEN YOU. 115 STRANG
((OH, NED, WHY HAVEN'T YOU WRITTEN$... 116 STRANG
IS THAT WHY HE'S NEVER WRITTEN$....)) 116 STRANG
ALL THE TWENTY ODD BOOKS I'VE WRITTEN 176 STRANG
(UNHEEDING) MY PLAYS HAD BEEN WRITTEN. 457 WELDED
THE ONE YOU PLAYED IN FIRST WAS WRITTEN THREE 457 WELDED
YEARS BEFORE.
WRONG
I KNOW THEY IS AND I AIN'T NEVER GONE WRONG YIT. 543 'ILE
WELL, SHE'S GOT THE TABLE ALL WRONG. 211 AHWILD
ARRAH, WHAT HAVE I DONE WRONG$ 211 AHWILD

WRONG (CONT'D.)
DON'T PASS THE PLATES ON THE WRONG SIDE AT DINNER 211 AHWILD
TONIGHT.
AND EVERYTHING COMES OUT ALL WRONG IN THE END/ 215 AHWILD
AM I RIGHT OR WRONG$ 225 AHWILD
ALWAYS WRONG--BUT HEART OF GOLD, HEART OF PUREST 225 AHWILD
GOLD.
I KNEW SOMETHING WAS WRONG WHEN HE CAME HOME.. 234 AHWILD
(THEN SINCERELY CONCERNED) I HOPE YOU'RE WRONG. 267 AHWILD
NAT.
(THEN SUDDENLY FEELING THIS ENTHUSIASM BEFORE 273 AHWILD
MILDRED IS ENTIRELY THE WRONG NOTE
IT'S WRONG TO SAY THAT. 287 AHWILD
IT'S WRONG MAYBE, BUT WHAT CAN YOU DO ABOUT IT$ 295 AHWILD
AIN'T NOTHING WRONG WITH ME. IS THERE$ 15 ANNA
GEE, I KNEW SOMETHING'D BE BOUND TO TURN OUT 17 ANNA
WRONG--ALWAYS DOES WITH ME.
I DIDN'T GO WRONG ALL AT ONE JUMP. 18 ANNA
AND GIVING ME THE WRONG START. 18 ANNA
YUH'RE ALL WRONG ABOUT HIM, KID. 19 ANNA
MORE WRONG NOTIONS. 34 ANNA
'TIS ONLY THE IGNORANCE OF YOUR KIND MADE ME SEE 34 ANNA
YOU WRONG.
SAY, LISTEN HERE, YOU AIN'T TRYING TO INSINUATE 42 ANNA
THAT THERE'S SOMETHING WRONG
IT'S ALL WRONG ANYWAY, AND YOU MIGHT AS WELL GET 56 ANNA
CURED THAT WAY AS ANY OTHER.
YOU'RE ALL WRONG. SEE$ 56 ANNA
THE YOUNGEST SON--PAUL--THAT STARTED ME WRONG. 57 ANNA
TORMENTED WITH THOUGHTS OF MAT BURKE AND THE GREAT 61 ANNA
WRONG YOU'VE DONE HIM/
WE'RE POOR NUTS, AND THINGS HAPPEN, AND WE JUST 65 ANNA
GET MIXED IN WRONG. THAT'S ALL.
AY'M SORRY FOR EVERYTANG AY DO WRONG FOR YOU, 65 ANNA
ANNA.
DON'T GET THE WRONG IDEA, MA. 105 BEYOND
YOU'RE WRONG, PA, IT ISN'T TRUTH. 107 BEYOND
WASTIN' TIME DOIN' EVERYTHING THE WRONG WAY-- 113 BEYOND
(DULLY) SOMETHING MUST HAVE GONE WRONG AGAIN. 117 BEYOND
SOMETHING'S ALWAYS GOING WRONG THESE DAYS, IT 117 BEYOND
LOOKS LIKE.
(SIGHING) I S'POSE IT ISN'T ROB'S FAULT THINGS GO118 BEYOND
WRONG WITH HIM.
SAY A WORD OF ENCOURAGEMENT ONCE IN A WHILE WHEN 123 BEYOND
THINGS GO WRONG.
BUT I'VE KEPT ON TELLING MYSELF THAT I MUST BE 127 BEYOND
WRONG--LIKE A FOOL.
AND NOT BE WORRIED THINKING ONE OF US MIGHT HAVE 139 BEYOND
THE WRONG NOTION.
THEN, BEFORE THINGS BROKE, I LEFT--I WAS SO 156 BEYOND
CONFIDENT I COULDN'T BE WRONG.
IT'S TOO BAD--THINGS SEEM TO GO WRONG SO. 157 BEYOND
I GUESS THIS GUY WENT DOWN THE WRONG WAY AN' THEY 456 CARIBE
GOT INDIGESTION.
NOT THAT I AIN'T HAD MY SHARE OF THINGS GOIN' 467 CARIBE
WRONG.
BUT YOU'RE WRONG, YOU SEE. 469 CARIBE
BUT YOU'RE WRONG ABOUT THIS GIRL. 469 CARIBE
(PLACATINGLY) YOU'RE WRONG, FATHER. 568 CROSS
AND I DON'T WANT HER TO GET THE WRONG ANGLE ON MY 512 DAYS
PLOT.
THERE'S NOTHING WRONG, EXCEPT WHAT SEEMS TO BE 517 DAYS
WRONG WITH EVERY ONE.
OF COURSE, THAT'S WRONG-- 545 DAYS
(LAUGHING) LEAVE IT TO MEN FOLKS TO STICK UP FOR 499 DIFRNT
EACH OTHER, RIGHT OR WRONG.
WRONG$ 500 DIFRNT
NO, NOTHIN' A MAN'D RIGHTLY CALL WRONG. 500 DIFRNT
I AIN'T DONE NOTHING WRONG. HAVE YOUS 500 DIFRNT
WHAT YOU TOLD ONLY GOES TO PROVE I WAS WRONG ABOUT504 DIFRNT
IT.
BESIDES, YOU DON'T KNOW THEY WAS NOTHIN' WRONG 509 DIFRNT
HAPPENED.
I AIN'T CLAIMING SHE'S WRONG. 510 DIFRNT
YOU'D OUGHT TO REMEMBER ALL HE'S BEEN TO YOU AND 512 DIFRNT
FORGET THIS ONE LITTLE WRONG
IT AIN'T EVEN THAT I THINK YOU'VE DONE NOTHING 516 DIFRNT
TERRIBLE WRONG.
(CARELESSLY) WELL, DON'T THINK NOTHING WRONG-- 525 DIFRNT
'CAUSE THERE WASN'T.
IT'S ALL YOUR FOOL FAULT THAT'S GOT ME IN WRONG. 546 DIFRNT
HE STARES BEFORE HIM WITH THE RESENTFUL AIR OF ONE422 DYNAMO
BROODING OVER A WRONG DONE
WHEN ANYTHING GOES WRONG AT THE PLANT 429 DYNAMO
THEY WERE WRONG ABOUT RAMSAY... 430 DYNAMO
I SAID, WHY IS IT WRONG WHEN I LOVE HIM$... 430 DYNAMO
FOLKS'D THINK HE WAS WRONG TO ARGUE WITH YOU/ 437 DYNAMO
MOTHER'LL GUESS SOMETHING IS WRONG AS SOON AS SHE 444 DYNAMO
LOOKS AT ME...
((SOMETHING'S ALL WRONG HERE... 462 DYNAMO
((MOTHER WOULD WARN ME IF I WAS DOING WRONG... 485 DYNAMO
(MALICIOUSLY) BUT S'POSIN' SOMETHIN' 'APPENS 184 EJONES
WRONG ANY THEY DO HAS YERS
I KNOWS I DONE WRONG, I KNOWS IT/ 196 EJONES
I DONE WRONG/ 196 EJONES
I DONE WRONG/ 196 EJONES
I DONE WRONG/ 196 EJONES
AND PROMISE TO BE A DUTIFUL WIFE TO FATHER AND 32 ELECTR
MAKE UP FOR THE WRONG YOU'VE DONE
I FELT THERE WAS SOMETHING WRONG THE MOMENT I SAW 37 ELECTR
HER.
BUT LISTEN, ME AS YOUR HUSBAND AND BEING KILLED, 54 ELECTR
THAT SEEMED QUEER AND WRONG--
THAT'S WHERE YOU'RE WRONG. 68 ELECTR
(CRUSHED) I DIDN'T MEAN ANYTHING WRONG, DOCTOR. 70 ELECTR
(GRIMLY) I WAS GOING TO GIVE THEM A FIGHT FOR 108 ELECTR
IT--IF THINGS WENT WRONG.
THERE'S SOMETHING GONE WRONG/ 108 ELECTR

1835

WRONG

WROTE

WRONG (CONT'D.)
I WANT TO TELL YOU WHAT'S WRONG WITH ORIN--SO YOU 148 ELECTR
AND HAZEL CAN HELP ME.
I FEEL THERE'S SOMETHING AWFULLY WRONG--SOMEHOW. 158 ELECTR
(BITTERLY MOCKING) DEAD WRONG/ 281 GORDON
YUH'RE ALL WRONG. 212 HA APE
YER BEEN LOOKIN' AT THIS 'ERE 'OLE AFFAIR WRONG. 235 HA APE
(DISGUSTEDLY) AW, YUH'RE ALL WRONG/ 241 HA APE
THINKS HE MAY HAVE GOTTEN IN THE WRONG PLACE. 246 HA APE
(MORE EASILY) I TOUGHT I'D BUMPED INTO DE WRONG 246 HA APE
DUMP.
STILL, SOME GUYS GET A WRONG SLANT ON US. 247 HA APE
IT'S ALL WRONG/ 250 HA APE
DEY'RE IN DE WRONG PEW--DE SAME OLD BULL--SOAP- 250 HA APE
BOXES AND SALVATION ARMY--
IT'S ALL WRONG, AIN'T IT$ 252 HA APE
(EARNESTLY.) DON'T GET THE WRONG IDEA, PAL. 29 HUGHIE
MY TROUBLE IS, SOME OF THESE GUYS I PUT THE BITE 34 HUGHIE
ON IS DEAD WRONG G'S.
HELL, I GOT YOU ALL WRONG, PAL. 36 HUGHIE
YOU'VE COME TO THE WRONG HOUSE. 582 ICEMAN
WELL, YOU'RE ALL WRONG. 585 ICEMAN
DON'T GET ME WRONG. 590 ICEMAN
BUT DON'T GET ME WRONG. 621 ICEMAN
DON'T GET NO WRONG IDEA-- 634 ICEMAN
YOU'VE GOT ME ALL WRONG. 638 ICEMAN
I'VE HAD A BELLYFUL OF IT IN MY TIME, AND IT'S ALL641 ICEMAN
WRONG.
LISTEN, LARRY, YOU'RE GETTING ME ALL WRONG. 641 ICEMAN
(SNEERINGLY) AND YOU'RE THE BOY WHO'S NEVER 643 ICEMAN
WRONG/
YOU THINK I'M ON THE WRONG TRACK AND YOU'RE GLAD 1643 ICEMAN
AH.
BUT YOU'RE ALL WRONG ABOUT PARRITT. 643 ICEMAN
UNLESS I'M WRONG, GOVERNOR, AND I'M BETTING I'M 655 ICEMAN
NOT.
(BITTERLY) DIS IS ALL WRONG. 656 ICEMAN
BUT YOU'RE GETTING THE WRONG IDEA ABOUT POOR 663 ICEMAN
EVELYN, AND I'VE GOT TO STOP THAT.
YOU'RE STILL GETTING ME ALL WRONG. 663 ICEMAN
IT'S LIKE I WAS DOING WRONG TO HER MEMORY. 688 ICEMAN
YOU KNOW WHAT I TOLD YOU ABOUT THE WRONG KIND OF 690 ICEMAN
PITY.
(DULLY) WHAT'S WRONG WITH THIS BOOZE$ 692 ICEMAN
THE WRONG KIND/ 703 ICEMAN
WE'VE GOT TO GET BUSY RIGHT AWAY AND FIND OUT 705 ICEMAN
WHAT'S WRONG.
IT'S ALL WRONG/ 708 ICEMAN
THINKING OF ALL THE WRONG I'D DONE TO THE SWEETEST714 ICEMAN
WOMAN IN THE WORLD
YOU'VE GOT ME ALL WRONG, OFFICER. 718 ICEMAN
AH, THE DAMNED PITY--THE WRONG KIND, AS HICKEY 726 ICEMAN
SAID/
YOU MUST HAVE GOTTEN OUT OF THE WRONG SIDE OF THE 22 JOURNE
BED THIS MORNING.
THERE'S NOTHING WRONG WITH YOUR HAIR. 27 JOURNE
I THINK IT'S THE WRONG IDEA TO LET MAMA GO ON 29 JOURNE
KIDDING HERSELF.
I WAS ALL WRONG. 37 JOURNE
I'VE JUST SAID I WAS ALL WRONG. 38 JOURNE
IT WAS WRONG FROM THE START. 44 JOURNE
AND IT WOULD BE WRONG DOPE TO KID YOURSELF. 55 JOURNE
(PERSUASIVELY.) YOU'RE ALL WRONG TO SUSPECT 56 JOURNE
ANYTHING.
YOU NEVER KNEW WHAT WAS REALLY WRONG UNTIL YOU 57 JOURNE
WERE IN PREP SCHOOL.
IT'S WRONG TO BLAME YOUR BROTHER. 64 JOURNE
SOMETHING IS ALWAYS WRONG. 84 JOURNE
I'M WRONG TO TREAT YOU. YOU'VE HAD ENOUGH 129 JOURNE
ALREADY.
(AGGRESSIVELY.) WELL, WHAT'S WRONG WITH BEING 132 JOURNE
DRUNK$
IT WAS YEARS BEFORE I DISCOVERED WHAT WAS WRONG. 141 JOURNE
THERE'S NOTHING WRONG WITH LIFE. 152 JOURNE
BUT DON'T GET THE WRONG IDEA, KID. 166 JOURNE
YOU ARE WRONG TO THINK MY PRESENT FEELING IS ONE 61 MANSNS
OF ANTAGONISM.
UNLESS MY MEMORY IS ALL WRONG/ 85 MANSNS
IT'S MEAN AND WRONG OF ME TO SUSPECT HER. 83 MANSNS
(RESENTFULLY) YOU'RE ALL WRONG/ 349 MARCOM
STILL, THAT'S WRONG. 394 MARCOM
THERE'S NOTHING SERIOUSLY WRONG. 413 MARCOM
TO REVENGE EQUALLY THE WRONG OF AN EQUAL PERHAPS, 425 MARCOM
BUT THIS--$
YOU'LL SOON LAUGH FROM THE WRONG END OF YOUR 78 MISBEG
MOUTH/
I'M WRONG TO BOTHER YOU. 81 MISBEG
SOME OF IT WENT DOWN THE WRONG WAY. 113 MISBEG
IF I SAID ANY WRONG OF CON MELODY-- 11 POET
BUT IT'S WRONG OF YOU TO THINK BADLY OF SIMON. 32 POET
YOU MUST HAVE RISEN THE WRONG SIDE OF THE BED THIS 45 POET
MORNING.
WHAT'S WRONG WITH YOU, FATHERS 58 POET
EVEN WHEN SHE IS WRONG. 76 POET
"MAYBE I'M WRONG," SAYS HE, "BUT I DOUBT THAT 102 POET
YOU'LL BE AS GAY TOMORROW.
"ANYWAY, YOU'VE COME TO THE WRONG DOOR," HE SAYS, 155 POET
SHE'LL SOON SNEER FROM THE WRONG SIDE OF HER 158 POET
MOUTH/
"O LORD, THOU HAST SEEN MY WRONG.. 584 ROPE
(HE'S ON THE WRONG TACK WITH HIS PROFESSOR'S 15 STRANG
MANNER...
(HE CHUCKLES--THEN HASTILY) BUT DON'T GET ME 30 STRANG
WRONG ABOUT HIM.
(I DON'T WANT HIM TO GET THE WRONG IDEA OF NED... 31 STRANG
I MUST HAVE BEEN WRONG... 36 STRANG
(WRONG AGAIN.... 37 STRANG
(THINKING BAFFLEOLY) (WRONG AGAIN/... 39 STRANG

WRONG (CONT'D.)
THERE IS SOMETHING WRONG WITH ITS PSYCHE, I'M 49 STRANG
SURE.
(THINKING APPREHENSIVELY) (I DC HOPE I'M 54 STRANG
WRONG/...
HOPE IT'S NOTHING WRONG... 55 STRANG
I'VE GOT TO KNOW WHAT'S WRONG... 68 STRANG
WAS I WRONG IN THINKING HE HAD STUFF IN HIMS... 78 STRANG
WHAT DO YOU SUSPECT IS WRONG WITH THE PATIENT NOW, 79 STRANG
DOCTOR$
WAS I REALLY WRONG ON EVERY POINT, NINA$ 81 STRANG
(ALL WRONG, WHAT I THOUGHT... 82 STRANG
SO OF COURSE I HAD TO AGREE IT WOULD BE WRONG--AND 83 STRANG
I HAD AN OPERATION.

WRONG/
THAT SEEMS TO HER SO RIGHT AND THEN SO WRONG/ 87 STRANG
IT'S WRONG. 87 STRANG
(HASTILY) OF COURSE, I MIGHT BE WRONG. 185 STRANG
(THEN BURSTING OUT) NO, I'M NOT WRONG/ 185 STRANG
(CONFUSED) YOU WAS WRONG, MISS FREDA. 501 VOYAGE
I TANK SOMETING GO WRUNG WITH DRISC AND COCKY. 507 VOYAGE
(WITH SUDDEN PASSION) IT'S WRONG, NELLY. 446 WELDED

WRONGDOING
AFTER READING THOSE PAPERS, TO CLAIM YCUR SON WAS 202 AHWILD
INNOCENT OF ALL WRONGDOING/

WRONGED
AND HIS FACE GROWS FLUSHED WITH HUMILIATION AND 208 AHWILD
WRONGED ANGER.
RICHARD STANDS FOR A SECOND, BITTER, HUMILIATED, 235 AHWILD
WRONGED.
AT LAZARUS WHEN I FIND HIM FEELING WRONGED BECAUSE328 LAZARU
MEN ARE MEN/
I'M BEGINNING TO THINK WE'VE WRONGED THE VERY ONE 103 STRANG
HE WERE TRYING TO HELP/

WRONGING
(ANGRILY.) I WON'T HAVE YOU WRONGING HIM, MOTHER. 32 POET

WRONGLY
I WAS, PERHAPS WRONGLY, REFERRING TO MRS. MANNUN. 70 ELECTR

WROTE
YOU KNOW, NAT, THE ONE WHO WROTE A PLAY ABOUT-- 197 AHWILD
WELL, NEVER MIND--
ANYWAY MURIEL'S CONFESSED TO ME HE WROTE THEM. 202 AHWILD
(LAUGHING) IS THAT WHAT HE WROTE TO MURIEL$ 228 AHWILD
LET ME SEE WHAT YOU WROTE, MID. 252 AHWILD
WHEN THEY COME TO "SENT AROUND A NOTE, THIS IS 259 AHWILD
WHAT SHE WROTE.
HE'S THE KID THAT WROTE THE BOOK/ 262 AHWILD
AM I SURE SHE WROTE NINE$ 275 AHWILD
HE WROTE ME HE WAS HIMSELF. 17 ANNA
WAS THAT ALL A BLUFF YUH PUT UP WHEN YUH WROTE 18 ANNA
HIM$
AND YOU WROTE ME YOU WAS YANITOR OF A BUILDING. 21 ANNA
BUT ONE THING I NEVER WROTE YOU. 57 ANNA
I LIED WHEN I WROTE YOU--I WAS IN A HOUSE, THAT'S 58 ANNA
WHAT--
HE'S HEAD OFFICER ON DICK'S BOAT, HE WROTE ROBBIE.115 BEYOND
(CALLOUSLY) I ONLY WROTE WHAT DOCTOR SMITH TOLD 146 BEYOND
ME.
I WROTE YOU HAD LUNG TROUBLE. 146 BEYOND
YOU WROTE ROB YOU WAS COMING BACK TO STAY THIS 156 BEYOND
TIME.
I WAS WHEN I WROTE THEM. 156 BEYOND
AND WROTE ME HE'D FOUND A CONGENIAL HOME AT LAST 502 DAYS
IN THE BOSOM OF KARL MARX.
UNTIL FINALLY HE WROTE ME HE WAS MARRIED. 504 DAYS
I NEVER WROTE, EXCEPT SOME POSTCARDS TO MOTHER I 461 DYNAMO
SENT TO GET HER GOAT--AND HIS.
SHE BLAMED HERSELF FOR YOUR RUIN AND SHE WROTE 465 DYNAMO
LONG LETTERS BEGGING YOUR
(THEN HARSHLY) WHERE ARE THOSE LETTERS SHE WROTE$465 DYNAMO
I WROTE TO FATHER AND ORIN AS SOON AS I GOT BACK 35 ELECTR
FROM NEW YORK/
VINNIE WROTE ME YOU'D HAD COMPANY. 50 ELECTR
FATHER'S BEEN SICK FOR THE PAST YEAR, AS I WROTE 52 ELECTR
YOU.
WHAT WAS THAT STUFF YOU WROTE ABOUT SOME CAPTAIN 76 ELECTR
BRANT COMING TO SEE MOTHER$
SHE WROTE HIM$ 85 ELECTR
BUT I WROTE YOU MUCH MORE/ 85 ELECTR
I MEAN THE CAPTAIN BRANT I WROTE YOU ABOUT/ 98 ELECTR
ARE YOU WONDERING WHAT IT WAS ORIN WROTE$ 175 ELECTR
WAS THERE ANYTHING IN WHAT ORIN WROTE THAT WOULD 176 ELECTR
STOP US FROM--
(THEN SUSPICIOUSLY) IS IT--WHAT ORIN WROTE$ 177 ELECTR
SHE WROTE TO DENOUNCE ME AND TRY TO BRING THE 589 ICEMAN
SINNER TO REPENTANCE
UNLESS YOU CAN CALL WHAT HEINE WROTE IN HIS POEM 591 ICEMAN
TO MORPHINE AN ANSWER.
I'M THE GUY THAT WROTE THE BOOK. 621 ICEMAN
I'M THE GUY THAT WROTE THE BOOK. 623 ICEMAN
I WROTE THE BOOK. 686 ICEMAN
WROTE HER A KIDDING LETTER, I REMEMBER, 710 ICEMAN
BECAUSE YOU WROTE TELLING ME YOU MISSED ME AND 87 JOURNE
WERE SO LONELY,
YOU CAN IMAGINE HOW EXCITED I WAS WHEN MY FATHER 105 JOURNE
WROTE ME HE AND JAMES TYRONE
THEY WROTE US HOW SORRY THEY WERE, 110 JOURNE
WHO WROTE IT$ 133 JOURNE
(GRINS PROVOCATIVELY.) HE ALSO WROTE A POEM 133 JOURNE
I'D HARDLY CALL THE LETTERS SHE ONCE WROTE ME 45 MANSNS
INTERFERING.
I CROSSED IT OFF AND I WROTE ON THE STATUTE BOOKS 392 MARCOM
I ONCE WROTE A POEM MYSELF... 399 MARCOM
YOU KNOW WHAT KIPLING WROTE.. 66 MISBEG
"SLEEPLESS WITH PALE COMMEMORATIVE EYES," AS 135 MISBEG
ROSSETTI WROTE.
D'YOU NOT REMEMBER THE LETTER SHE WROTE TELLIN' 586 ROPE
HIM HE COULD SUPPORT LUKE ON THE

WROTE 1836

WROTE (CONT'D.)
OF ALL THE ENGLISH AUTHORS WHO WROTE WHILE S WAS STILL LIKE AN F AND A FEW SINCE 3 STRANG
I WROTE TO HIM AND HE ANSWERED THAT HE'LL GLADLY ARRANGE IT. 17 STRANG
MY DUTY TO GORDON, SHE WROTE... 161 STRANG
WHEN I HEARD YOU WERE BACK I WROTE YOU BECAUSE I NEED A FRIEND. 165 STRANG
FROM THINGS SHE WROTE ME BEFORE SHE DIED, 172 STRANG
YOU WROTE NOT TO EXPECT YOU TILL THE END OF THE WEEK. 444 WELDED

WROUGHT
(MORE AND MORE WROUGHT UP) I WON'T HEAR OF NO SUCH THING. 532 DIFRNT
CLAD RICHLY, WEARING BEAUTIFULLY WROUGHT ARMOR AND298 LAZARU HELMET.
THERE IS A WROUGHT-IRON LANTERN HANGING FROM A BRACKET 29 MANSNS

WRUNG
SHE CALLS SHAKENLY AS IF THE WORDS WERE WRUNG OUT 123 ELECTR OF HER AGAINST HER WILL)

WRY
(WITH A WRY ATTEMPT AT A SMILE) 88 BEYOND
(MAKING A WRY FACE) I CAN GUESS. 136 BEYOND
(WITH A WRY SMILE) WE'D ALL FORGOTTEN HE'S DEAD, 81 ELECTR HADN'T WE$
(THEN FORCING A WRY SMILE) I'LL GIVE UP THE SEA. 112 ELECTR
(WITH A WRY IRONICAL SADNESS.) 152 JOURNE
(THEN WITH HIS WRY SMILE) BUT I WILL TURN MY BACK--AND SHUT MY EYES-- 329 LAZARU
(TYRONE DRINKS AND MAKES A WRY FACE.) 53 MISBEG
(HE SMILES WITH A WRY AMUSEMENT FOR A SECOND--THEN 25 STRANG BITTERLY)
(SMILING WITH A WRY AMUSEMENT AT HERSELF) 138 STRANG
(WITH A WRY SMILE) IT'S POSSIBLE. 146 STRANG
HE SWALLOWS HALF HIS GLASS OF GINGER BEER AND 507 VOYAGE MAKES A WRY FACE.)
(WITH A WRY GRIN) YOU MUST HAVE BEEN DISAPPOINTED446 WELDED IF YOU EXPECTED DON JUAN.
(WITH A WRY SMILE) THAT ISN'T ME. 466 WELDED
(THEN CHECKING HIS ANGER AND FORCING A WRY SMILE) 468 WELDED
(WITH THE SAME WRY SMILE) WHILE I BEGIN TO 469 WELDED SUSPECT THAT IN A WAY I'M LUCKY--
(WITH A WRY SMILE) STUDY YOUR PART. 469 WELDED
(WITH A WRY GRIN) NO. 484 WELDED

WRYLY
(HE GRINS WRYLY.) WAS THAT A LAUGH/ 22 HUGHIE
(WRYLY.) THAT'S NOT TRUE, PAPA. 32 JOURNE
(HE GRINS WRYLY.) IT WAS A GREAT MISTAKE, MY 153 JOURNE BEING BORN A MAN.
(SHE SMILES WRYLY.) THERE. 39 MANSNS

WRYNESS
(SMILING WITH A STRANGE WRYNESS) 516 DAYS

WU'TH
AND I WAS WU'TH MONEY TO YOU, DAT'S DE REASON. 177 EJONES

WUK
AN' TILL HE COMES, LET'S YEW 'N' ME NOT WUK A LICK. 215 DESIRE
NARY A TOIL 'R SPIN 'R LICK O' WUK DO WE PUT IN/ 216 DESIRE
(PEREMPTORILY) YE BETTER GIT T' WUK. 217 DESIRE
(COMMANDINGLY) YE GIT T' WUK/ 222 DESIRE
OCEANS O' TROUBLE AN' NUTHIN' BUT WUK FUR REWARD. 226 DESIRE
THEN I MARRIED AN' HE TURNED OUT A DRUNKEN SPREE'R 226 DESIRE AN' SO HE HAD TO WUK FUR
HUMS, DOIN' OTHER FOLKS' WUK TILL I'D MOST GIVE UP226 DESIRE HOPE O' EVER DOIN' MY OWN WUK
ON'Y I DISKIVERED RIGHT AWAY ALL I WAS FREE FUR 226 DESIRE WAS T' WUK AGEN IN OTHER FOLKS'
I WAS A ORPHAN EARLY AN' HAD T' WUK FUR OTHERS IN 226 DESIRE OTHER FOLKS' HUMS.
(THEN QUICKLY) WHY HAIN'T YE T' WUKS 227 DESIRE
I CAN'T WUK IT ALL ALONE. 227 DESIRE
I HOPE EBEN'S T' WUK. 263 DESIRE
I'LL GIT T' WUK. 265 DESIRE
AIN'T DAT WUKS 179 EJONES

WUKED
WE'VE WUKED. 204 DESIRE
SHE WUKED HARD. 237 DESIRE

WUKIN'
LET HIM SEE WE HAIN'T WUKIN'/ 216 DESIRE
AIN'T THAR NOBODY ABOUT--'R WUKIN'--R' NUTHIN'S 222 DESIRE
(EXPLODING) WHY HAIN'T YE WUKIN'S 222 DESIRE
WAS OVERSEER OVAH US WHEN WE'RE WUKIN' DE ROAD. 181 EJONES
MAKING A BLUFF DEY WAS WUKIN' ALL DE TIME. 182 EJONES

WURRA
I'M NOT LIKE YOU, OWNING UP I'M BEATEN AND CRYING 91 MISBEG WURRA-WURRA LIKE A COWARD AND

WURRK
GOOD WURRK FOR YE, DAVIS, YE SCUT/ 524 INZONE

WUSSER'N
IT MUST HEV SOUNDED WUSSER'N I MEANT. 233 DESIRE

WUST
I'M NOT THE WUST IN THE WORLD--AN' YEW AN' ME'VE GOT A LOT IN COMMON. 226 DESIRE
LORD GOD O' HOSTS, SMITE THE UNDUTIFUL SONS WITH 227 DESIRE THY WUST CUSS/

WUTH
WUTH A GUY WITH NO HARD FEELIN'S. 12 ANNA
I'M WUTH TEN O' YE YIT, OLD'S I BE/ 227 DESIRE
-THIS HAIN'T WUTH NOTHIN' T' ME. 237 DESIRE
HE HAIN'T WUTH HANGIN' FUR--NOT BY A HELL OF A SIGHT/ 256 DESIRE

WUTHLESS
THAT EVERY WUTHLESS DRUNK IN THE COUNTRY HAS.... 230 DESIRE

Y'ARE
HERE Y'ARE, GRAFIER/ 613 ICEMAN

Y'R
MIND Y'R OWN BUSINESS. 224 AHWILD

Y'UNDERSTAND
Y'UNDERSTAND. 36 HUGHIE

YACHT'S
HE CARRIES A SMALL, EXPENSIVE YACHT'S MODEL OF A 149 STRANG SLOOP WITH THE SAILS SET.

YACHTING
SHE IS DRESSED IN A WHITE YACHTING COSTUME. 158 STRANG
HE IS WEARING A YACHTING CAP, BLUE YACHTING COAT, 159 STRANG WHITE FLANNEL PANTS.

YACHTS
COMES THE WARNING RINGING OF BELLS ON YACHTS AT ANCHOR. 97 JOURNE
THE AFTERDECK OF THE EVANS' MOTOR CRUISER ANCHORED158 STRANG IN THE LANE OF YACHTS NEAR
(THE WHISTLES AND SIRENS FROM THE YACHTS UP THE 176 STRANG RIVER BEGIN TO BE HEARD.
THIS GROWS MOMENTARILY LOUDER AS ONE AFTER ANOTHER176 STRANG OTHER YACHTS JOIN IN THE

YAHOOS
MORE THAN ONE CAN SAY OF THESE MODERN SEX- YAHOOS/..... 5 STRANG

YAIL
I WAS CAGED IN, I TELL YOU--YUST LIKE IN YAIL-- 58 ANNA

YALE
YOUR EDUCATION IN KICKING A FOOTBALL AROUND YALE 192 AHWILD
(WITH HIGH SCORN) OH, YALE/ 195 AHWILD
YOU THINK THERE'S NOTHING IN THE WORLD BESIDES YALE. 195 AHWILD
WAIT TILL WE GET HIM DOWN TO YALE. 195 AHWILD
AFTER ALL, WHAT IS YALE$ 195 AHWILD
A CLASSMATE OF ARTHUR'S AT YALE. 218 AHWILD
AND IF I DIDN'T KNOW YOU WERE COMING DOWN TO YALE 219 AHWILD NEXT YEAR.
WE'LL TAKE THAT OUT OF YOU WHEN WE GET YOU DOWN TO261 AHWILD YALE/
YOU BETTER DO WHAT YOUR PA THINKS BEST--AND I'D 287 AHWILD LIKE YOU TO BE AT YALE.
PERHAPS I NEEDN'T GO TO YALE. 287 AHWILD
AND I'M GOING TO TELL HIM HE CAN'T GO TO YALE, 289 AHWILD SEEING HE'S SO UNDEPENDABLE.
I GUESS HE CAN GO TO YALE/ 289 AHWILD
(UP IN ARMS AT ONCE) NOT GO TO YALE/ 289 AHWILD
THEN YOU'LL GO TO YALE AND YOU'LL STAY THERE TILL 296 AHWILD YOU GRADUATE.
WELL, I'D THOUGHT OF TELLING YOU YOU COULDN'T GO 296 AHWILD TO YALE--
BUT, OF COURSE, THAT IS A YALE HYMN, 595 ICEMAN

YALLER
AND I WAS AGOIN' HOME LIKE A YALLER DOG/ 550 'ILE
SHE'D HAIR LONG'S A HOSS' TAIL--AN' YALLER LIKE 204 DESIRE GOLD.
THAT YALLER-HAIRED PIG WITH THE PINK DRESS ON/ 104 ELECTR
A YALLER-HAIRED WENCH HAD HER ARM AROUND ME. 106 ELECTR

YANDER'S
MY NAME'S BELLA, THIS HERE'S SUSIE, YANDER'S 464 CARIBE VIOLET,

YANITOR
HE'S YANITOR OF SOME BUILDING HERE NOW--USED TO BE 16 ANNA A SAILOR.
AH, MY VORK ON LAND LONG TIME AS YANITOR. 21 ANNA
AND YOU WROTE ME YOU WAS YANITOR OF A BUILDING. 21 ANNA
WELL, WHEN I MADE UP MY MIND TO COME TO SEE YOU, I 22 ANNA THOUGHT YOU WAS A YANITOR--

YANK
YANK/ 479 CARDIF
(WITH A GREAT SOB) YANK/ 490 CARDIF
CAN YOU LEAVE YANK FOR ARF A MO' AND GIVE ME A 'AND$ 490 CARDIF
WHEN SOME YANK IN WHOSE HOUSE MOTHER HAD BEEN 148 JOURNE SCRUBBING GAVE HER A DULLAR EXTRA
(THEY DO SO WITH ENTHUSIASM AND YANK GADSBY FROM 123 POET HIS CHAIR.)
YOU SHOULD HAVE SEEN THE YANK/ 129 POET
(HE REACHES UP FOR THE ROPE AS IF TO TRY AND YANK 583 ROPE IT DOWN.

YANK'S
(HE GETS A TIN DIPPER FROM THE BUCKET AND BATHES 483 CARDIF YANK'S FOREHEAD WITH THE WATER.
(TAKING A THERMOMETER FROM HIS PUCKET AND PUTTING 484 CARDIF IT INTO YANK'S MOUTH)
(TAKING OUT HIS WATCH AND FEELING YANK'S PULSE) 484 CARDIF
THEN TAKES THE THERMOMETER FROM YANK'S MOUTH AND 485 CARDIF GOES TO THE LAMP TO READ IT.
(HE BREAKS DOWN LAMELY BEFORE YANK'S STEADY GAZE) 485 CARDIF
THEN COMES BACK AND PUTS A TREMBLING HAND ON 490 CARDIF YANK'S CHEST
PEARL DRINKS FROM YANK'S BOTTLE EVERY MOMENT OR 470 CARIBE SO, LAUGHING SHRILLY.
YANK'S RIGHT. 213 HA APE
(PADDY FROM THE START OF YANK'S SPEECH HAS BEEN 216 HA APE TAKING ONE GULP AFTER ANOTHER
THROUGH WHICH YANK'S VOICE CAN BE HEARD BELLOWING)216 HA APE
YANK'S WATCH HAS JUST COME OFF DUTY AND HAD 226 HA APE DINNER.
(AFTER A GLANCE AT YANK'S LOWERING FACE--UNEASILY)236 HA APE
(RUSHING UP AND GRABBING YANK'S ARM) 237 HA APE
HE IS IN THE CELL NEXT TO YANK'S. 242 HA APE
AS THE STREAM OF WATER HITS THE STEEL OF YANK'S 245 HA APE CELL,
(HE COMES CLOSER AND LAUGHS MOCKINGLY IN YANK'S 249 HA APE FACE)

YANKEE
YANKEE BLUFF DONE IT. 179 EJONES
A LONG YANKEE FACE, WITH INDIAN RESEMBLANCES, 4 MANSNS SWARTHY, WITH A BIG STRAIGHT NOSE.
YOU THINK IN YOUR YANKEE PRIDE IGNORANCE, 21 MANSNS
HIS LARGE-FEATURED YANKEE FACE LOOKS HIS THIRTY- 43 MANSNS ONE YEARS.

1837 YEAR

YANKEE (CONT'D.)
BUT ONCE IN A WHILE THERE'LL BE SOME YANKEE STOPS 11 POET
OVERNIGHT WID HIS WIFE OR
IT, FOR ALL THEIR MODERN YANKEE AIRS. 13 POET
THE DAMNED YANKEE GENTRY WON'T LET HIM COME NEAR 13 POET
THEM,
SINCE YOU'VE BEEN PLAYIN' NURSE TO THE YOUNG 16 POET
YANKEE UPSTAIRS,
AND A YANKEE LADY GOT OUT AND CAME IN HERE. 17 POET
I DON'T LIKE YANKEE AIRS ANY MORE THAN YOU. 18 POET
LIKE ONE OF THE YANKEE GENTRY, WHEN YOU KNOW WHAT 26 POET
HE CAME FROM.
BUT I DON'T LIKE YOU BEGGIN' TO A YANKEE. 28 POET
WHAT ABOUT HIS FINE YANKEE FAMILY? 31 POET
THERE IS A ROMANTIC TOUCH OF THE POET BEHIND HIS 48 POET
YANKEE PHLEGM.
APPARENTLY, HIS FATHER IS A GENTLEMAN--THAT IS, BY 48 POET
YANKEE STANDARDS,
AND ALL THE SLAVE-DRIVIN' YANKEE SKINFLINTS LIKE 52 POET
YOU/
TAKE HIS MILK TO OUR YANKEE GUEST, AS YOUR MOTHER 60 POET
SUGGESTS.
CURSED YANKEE UPSTART/ 75 POET
(HE CHUCKLES.) THE DEVIL OF IT IS, I CAN NEVER 90 POET
GET USED TO THESE YANKEE LADIES.
THE DAMNED YANKEE YOKELS SHOULD FEEL FLATTERED 106 POET
LITTLE YANKEE CLIQUE, THERE WOULD BE NO QUESTION 110 POET
OF A HASTY MARRIAGE,
AND AN ESTATE COMPARED TO WHICH ANY YANKEE 112 POET
UPSTART'S HOME IN THIS COUNTRY
(HE SPRINGS TO HIS FEET.) BUT FIRST, YOU YANKEE 122 POET
SCUM, I'LL DEAL WITH YOU/
(RAGING.) THAT DAMNED, INSOLENT YANKEE BITCH/ 127 POET
AND WHAT CHANCE WILL THIS AULD STICK AV A YANKEE 130 POET
HAVE AGAINST HIM
THE YANKEE DIDN'T APOLOGIZE OR YOUR FATHER'D BEEN 137 POET
BACK HERE LONG SINCE.
AND HE'D HAVE DRAGGED AULD HARFORD FROM HIS BURROW156 POET
AND TANNED HIS YANKEE HIDE
WITH THAT PALE YANKEE BITCH WATCHING FROM A 157 POET
WINDOW, SNEERING WITH DISGUST/
YOU MUST MAKE THE YOUNG YANKEE GINTLEMAN HAVE YOU 171 POET
IN HIS BED.
ONE AV THE YANKEE GINTRY HAS STOPPED TO BE SEDUCED172 POET
BY MY SLUT AV A DAUGHTER/
AND SHE'LL LIVE IN A YANKEE MANSION, AS BIG AS A 173 POET
CASTLE,
I'M TOO PROUD TO MARRY A YANKEE COWARD'S SON/ 178 POET
THE LOVE OF GOD, CLOUT THE DAMNED YANKEE, MAJOR/ 2 T 41
12

YANKEES
AGAINST JACKSON AND THE DEMOCRATS AND SAYS HE'LL 26 POET
VOTE WITH THE YANKEES FOR QUINC
IF I HAD NOT BEEN A CREDULOUS GULL AND LET THE 40 POET
THIEVING YANKEES SWINDLE ME
WHEN IT COMES TO MAKING LOVE THE YANKEES ARE 62 POET
CLUMSY, FISH-BLOODED LOUTS.
YES, I'LL WAGER MY ALL AGAINST A PENNY THAT EVEN 71 POET
AMONG THE FISH-BLOODED YANKEES
AND HIS SHOWIN' OFF BEFORE THE YANKEES, AND THIM 168 POET
LAUGHIN' AT HIM,
THE LAND THE YANKEES SWINDLED HIM INTO BUYIN' FOR 173 POET
HIS AMERICAN ESTATE,

YANKING
YANKING OUT HIS REVOLVER AS HE DOES SO--IN A 190 EJONES
QUAVERING VOICE)

YANKS
(REACHES IN UNDER A BUNK AND YANKS OUT A PAIR OF 481 CARDIF
SEA-BOOTS, WHICH HE PUTS ON)
(YANKS WILLIE BY THE ARM) COME ON, BUM. 597 ICEMAN
(AT THE SAME MOMENT CHUCK GRABS WETJOEN AND YANKS 677 ICEMAN
HIM BACK.)
AND YANKS HIS ARM) 718 ICEMAN
AND MY POOR MOTHER WASHED AND SCRUBBED FOR THE 148 JOURNE
YANKS BY THE DAY.

YAP
IF YUH OPENED YOUR YAP, I'D KNOCK DE STUFFIN' OUTA671 ICEMAN
YUH/*

YAPPING
TREE--(A TERRIFIC CHORUS OF BARKING AND YAPPING.) 243 HA APE

YARD
THE LILACS WILL BE ALL IN BLOOM IN THE FRONT 548 *ILE
YARD--
YOU TAKE YOUR CRACKERS OUT IN THE BACK YARD, YOU 189 AHWILD
HEAR ME/
AS SHE DOES SO, FROM THE FRONT YARD SID'S VOICE IS220 AHWILD
HEARD SINGING *POOR JOHN/*
YOU KIDS GO OUT IN THE YARD AND TRY TO KEEP QUIET 234 AHWILD
FOR A WHILE,
GO OUT AND PLAY IN THE YARD, OR TAKE A WALK, AND 264 AHWILD
GET SOME FRESH AIR.
I WAS SO SCARED, AND THEN I SNEAKED OUT THROUGH 281 AHWILD
THE BACK YARD,
NEXT TO THE WINDOW A DOOR LEADING OUT INTO THE 93 BEYOND
YARD.
(THE DOOR FROM THE YARD OPENS, AND ROBERT ENTERS. 99 BEYOND
THROUGH IT THE YARD CAN BE SEEN. 112 BEYOND
THEY'RE LIKE THE WALLS OF A NARROW PRISON YARD 126 BEYOND
SHUTTING ME IN
IT WAS ALL-WOOL-AND-A-YARD-WIDE-HELL, I'LL TELL 132 BEYOND
YOU.
IS NORSER'N GOIN' ALOFT TO THE SKY5'L YARD IN A 140 BEYOND
BLOW.
HE MUST HAVE CRAWLED OUT INTO THE YARD/ 166 BEYOND
COMIN' OUT T' THE YARDS 220 DESIRE
TO THE RIGHT OF IT, IN REAR, A WINDOW LOOKING OUT 493 DIFRNT
ON THE FRONT YARD.

YARD (CONT'D.)
AT EXTREME LEFT IS THE MIZZENMAST, THE LOWEST YARD0102 ELECTR
JUST VISIBLE ABOVE,
TREE SQUARE A DAY, AND CAULIFLOWERS IN DE FRONT 250 HA APE
YARD--EKAL RIGHTS--
DE BOOZE DEY DISH OUT AROUND DE BROOKLYN NAVY YARD616 ICEMAN
DE GANG IS EXPECTIN' YUH WID DEIR TONGUES HANGIN' 617 ICCMAN
OUT A YARD LONG.
WHAT THE HELL'S TO BE SCARED OF, JUST TAKING A 687 ICEMAN
STROLL AROUND MY OWN YARDS
THE ONE AT LEFT, FRONT, BEFORE THE WINDOW TO THE 695 ICEMAN
YARD, IS IN THE SAME POSITION.
YES, IT'S LIKE HAVING A SICK WHALE IN THE BACK 17 JOURNE
YARD.
ON THE RIGHT, ANOTHER DOORWAY LEADING TO THE YARD 273 LAZARU
(FROM THE YARD, OFF LEFT FRONT, THERE IS THE 162 POET
MUFFLED CRACK OF A PISTOL SHOT
SOMEONE'S AT THE YARD DOOR. 163 POET

YARDER
AND SHIPPED JOB ON A SKYSAIL-YARDER ROUND THE HORN,487 CARDIF
BLOODY WINDJAMMER--SKYS'L-YARDER--FULL-RIGGED-- 495 VOYAGF
PAINTED WHITE--
I SAIL ON HER ONCE LONG TIME AGO--THREE MASTS, 507 VOYAGE
FULL RIG, SKYS'L-YARDERS

YARDS
AND A ROW OF TALL MAPLES IN THE BACKGROUND BEHIND -0 DYNAMO
THE YARDS AND THE TWO HOUSES.
THEY'D SEE HIM A-SETTIN' ON THE YARDS AND HEAR HIM132 ELECTR
MOANIN' TO HIMSELF.
COUNTY HIGHWAY (ABOUT A HUNDRED YARDS OFF LEFT) 1 MISBEG

YARK
LEND ME FOUR BOB IN NOO YARK, 'E DID. 480 CARDIF

YARN
A BALL OF UNUSED YARN, WITH NEEDLES STUCK THROUGH 113 BEYOND
IT
SPIN DAT YARN, COCKY. 457 CARIBE

YAW
I HIT HIM SMASH IN YAW, PY GOTT/ 208 HA APE

YAWN
(HE IS OVER COME BY A JAW-CRACKING YAWN.) 253 AHWILD
(WITH ANOTHER YAWN) 'COURSE ME DOES. 265 AHWILD
(A PAUSE. BOTH YAWN) LET'S GIT T' BED. 211 DESIRE
(WITH A BONE-CRACKING YAWN.) 169 JOURNE
(WITH A BORED YAWN) NO DOUBT. 359 MARCOM
(MOCKINGLY--WITH A YAWN) YOUTH WILL HAVE ITS 374 MARCOM
LAUGH/
(THEY YAWN AND PREPARE TO LIE DOWN.) 374 MARCOM
IN AN AISLE SEAT IN THE FIRST ROW A MAN RISES, 439 MARCOM
CONCEALS A YAWN IN HIS PALM,
(PRETENDS TO YAWN BOREDLY) MAYBE NOT. 42 MISBEG

YAWNIN'
AN' UP HE GETS YAWNIN' 521 INZONE

YAWNING
CLOSING HIS EYES AND YAWNING.) 586 ICEMAN
ROCKY APPEARS FROM THE BAR AT REAR, RIGHT, 597 ICEMAN
YAWNING.)
(YAWNING--TOO SLEEPY TO BE AROUSED BY ANYTHING-- 514 INZONE
CARELESSLY)
(YAWNING) THERE WAS A FEAST AT CINNA'S LAST NIGHT314 LAZARU
THAT LASTED UNTIL THIS
DO I HEAR GRAVEYARDS YAWNING FROM THEIR SLEEP-- 51 STRANG
(YAWNING) BLIMEY IF BIZNESS AIN'T 'ARF SLOW 493 VOYAGE
TONIGHT.

YAWNS
OF TABLE AND IMMEDIATELY YAWNS) 264 AHWILD
WHILE SID YAWNS DROWSILY AND BLINKS HIS EYES) 269 AHWILD
SHE YAWNS) 245 DESIRE
CYBEL WATCHES THEM BOTH--THEN, BORED, SHE YAWNS) 280 GOBROW
(HE YAWNS WITH GROWING DROWSINESS AND HIS VOICE 624 ICEMAN
GROWS A BIT MUFFLED)
(HE YAWNS AGAIN) GOD, I'M SLEEPY ALL OF A SUDDEN.625 ICEMAN
(ROCKY SHRUGS HIS SHOULDERS AND YAWNS SLEEPILY.) 666 ICEMAN
(HE YAWNS) I'M ALL IN. 666 ICEMAN
(SMITHY YAWNS LOUDLY WITH A GREAT PRETENSE OF 514 INZONE
HAVING BEEN DEAD ASLEEP.
A PAUSE--THEN THE WOMAN SIGHS AND YAWNS WEARILY-- 471 WELDED
BORED)
(SHE YAWNS) YOU BETTER LET ME GO TO BED AND COME 473 WELDED
YOURSELF.
SHE YAWNS. 473 WELDED

YE'
INTO SOMETHIN' ELSE--TILL YE' BE JINED WITH IT-- 229 DESIRE
AN' IT'S YOUR'N--

(MORE KINDLY) WHERE WAS IT YE'VE BEEN ALL O' THE 536 *ILE
TIME--THE FO'C'S'TLES
YE'VE BEEN BELOW HERE GOSSIPIN' OLD WOMAN'S TALK 539 *ILE
WITH THAT BOY.
YE'VE HEARD THE NAMES OF CHANTIES BUT DIVIL A NOTE459 CARIBE
AV THE TUNE OK A LOINE AV THE

YEAH
YEAH. 433 DYNAMO

YEAR
IN THE AFTERNOON OF A DAY IN THE YEAR 1895. 535 *ILE
HOLDIN' US IN FOR NIGH ON A YEAR--NOTHIN' TO SEE 536 *ILE
BUT ICE--
FUR NIGH ON A YEAR, 537 *ILE
YOU BEEN WITH ME NIGH ON TEN YEAR AND I'VE LEARNED542 *ILE
YE WHALIN'.
IT'S NEVER BEEN SO BAD BEFORE IN THE THIRTY YEAR 1543 *ILE
BEEN ACOMIN' HERE.
YOU NEED REST AFTER TEACHING A PACK OF WILD 212 AHWILD
INDIANS OF KIDS ALL YEAR,
AND THEN THERE ARE ALL THE BOYS AND GIRLS I TEACH 214 AHWILD
EVERY YEAR,
AND IF I DIDN'T KNOW YOU WERE COMING DOWN TO YALE 219 AHWILD
NEXT YEAR,

YEAR

1838

YEAR	(CONT'D.)		

FOURTH OF JULY IS LIKE CHRISTMAS--COMES BUT UNCE A223 AHWILD YEAR.

OUT NEXT YEAR I'LL BE ALLUVED--THAT IS, PIPES AND 239 AHWILD CLEARS.

AY DUN'T GAT LETTER FROM ANNA--MUST BE A YEAR. 8 ANNA SHE MUST BE--LAT ME SEE--SHE MUST BE TWENTY YEAR 9 ANNA OLD. PY YOU

AY NEVER GAT HOME ONLY FEW TIME DEM YEAR. 9 ANNA IN SVEDEN FIVE YEAR JLO. 9 ANNA SHE STAY UN DEM COUSINS' FARM 'TIL TWO YEAR AGO. 10 ANNA AY DUN'T KNOW, ANNA, VHY AY NEVER COME HOME SVEDEN 21 ANNA IN OLD YEAR.

DIS UNE TIME BECAUSE VE MEET AFTER MANY YEAR. 23 ANNA (MOUSLY) AY'VE DONE DAT MANY YEAR, ANNA, WHEN AY 27 ANNA VAS DAM FULL.

AY DUN'T SEE ANNA FOR FIFTEEN YEAR. 46 ANNA GEE, YOU MUST TAKE ME FOR A FIVE-YEAR-OLD KID. 54 ANNA DIDN'T I WRITE YOU YEAR AFTER YEAR HOW ROTTEN IT 57 ANNA WAS

I SUPPOSE IT'S THAT YEAR IN COLLEGE GAVE YOU A 82 BEYOND LIKING FOR THAT KIND OF STUFF.

I WAS TOO PROUD TO LET YOU SEE I CARED BECAUSE I 91 BEYOND THOUGHT THE YEAR YOU HAD AWAY

(DISGUSTEDLY) GOD ALMIGHTY, KATE, YOU TREAT 99 BEYOND ROBERT AS IF HE WAS ONE YEAR OLD/ CARRYING IN HER ARMS HER TWO-YEAR-OLD DAUGHTER, 116 BEYOND MARY.

IS HE SEASONIN' HIS HAY WITH RAIN THIS YEAR, SAME 124 BEYOND AS LASTS= THEY SHOUTS.

(CONFIDENTLY) I CAN MAKE IT UP IN A YEAR OR SO 157 BEYOND DOWN THERE--

I SOLD OUT LAST YEAR. 161 BEYOND 'APPEARED TEN YEAR AGO COME CHRISTMAS. 478 CARDIF AND HE NOT DEAD AT ALL, BUT GOIN' TO LIVE MANY A 480 CARDIF LONG YEAR YET. MAYBE.

THIS LAST YEAR HAS SEEMED ROTTEN, AND I'VE HAD A 487 CARDIF HUNCH I'D QUIT--

THE TIME IS AN EARLY HOUR OF A CLEAR WINDY NIGHT 555 CRUSS IN THE FALL OF THE YEAR 1900.

THE CABOT FARMHOUSE IN NEW ENGLAND, IN THE YEAR 202 DESIRE 1850.

IT IS SUNSET OF A DAY AT THE BEGINNING OF SUMMER 203 DESIRE IN THE YEAR 1850.

STONES ATOP OF STONES--MAKIN' STONE WALLS--YEAR 204 DESIRE ATOP O' YEAR--

(SUDDENLY) EIGHTEEN YEAR AGO. 204 DESIRE HE HAIN'T NEVER BEEN OFF THIS FARM 'CEPTIN' T' THE205 DESIRE VILLAGE IN THIRTY YEAR OR

YEAR AFTER YEAR IT'S SKULKED IN YER EYE-- 208 DESIRE SOMETHIN'.

SHE'S BEEN PURTY FUR TWENTY YEAR/ 210 DESIRE (PAUSE. WITH YEARNING) MEBBE A YEAR FROM NOW 211 DESIRE WE'LL BE IN CALIFORNI-A.

WAAL--EVERY THIRTY YEAR O' ME BURIED IN YE--SPREAD218 DESIRE OUT OVER YE--

ANY DAY O' THE YEAR/ 234 DESIRE AUT BUT WHAT I HAIN'T A HARD NUT T' CRACK EVEN 234 DESIRE YET--AIN' FUR MANY A YEAR T' COME/

WHEN I COME HERE FIFTY OUD YEAR AGO-- 236 DESIRE HE WAS MARRIED TWENTY YEAR. 237 DESIRE 'TWAS AFTER I'D BEEN HERE TWO YEAR. 237 DESIRE (A NIGHT IN LATE SPRING THE FOLLOWING YEAR. 247 DESIRE I HAIN'T SLEPT THIS LATE IN FIFTY YEAR/ 263 DESIRE IT IS MID-AFTERNOON OF A FINE DAY IN LATE SPRING 493 DIFRNT OF THE YEAR 1890.

WHEN I KIN GU OFF ON A TWO-YEAR WHALIN' VIGE AND 496 DIFRNT LEAVE YOU ALL 'LONE

AND THEN, S'FAR AS PORTS GU, WE DIDN'T TECH AT ONE497 DIFRNT THE LAST YEAR--

AND I TELLS YOU, AFTER A YEAR OR MORE ABOARD SHIP,514 DIFRNT IT IS LATE AFTERNOON OF A DAY IN THE EARLY SPRING 519 DIFRNT OF THE YEAR 1920.

FOR HER YEAR AFTER YEAR HOPIN' IN THE END SHE'D 530 DIFRNT CHANGE HER MIND AND MARRY HIM.

SHE'D BEEN PINING AWAY FOR ALMOST A YEAR. 465 DYNAMO AND DIED THAT SAME YEAR 8 ELECTR IT'S WHAT YOU ASKED ME A YEAR AGO WHEN YOU WERE 14 ELECTR MORE ON LEAVE. ISN'T IT'.

HE SEEMS TO HAVE BEEN SICK SO MUCH THIS PAST YEAR. 17 ELECTR THE EXCUSE YOU'VE MADE FOR ALL YOUR TRIPS THERE 29 ELECTR THE PAST YEAR.

SHE SAID YOU HAD COME THERE OFTEN IN THE PAST 30 ELECTR YEAR.

FATHER'S BEEN SICK FOR THE PAST YEAR, AS I WROTE 52 ELECTR YOU.

ON THE EVENING OF A CLEAR DAY IN SUMMER A YEAR 129 ELECTR LATER.

YOU'VE KEPT UP THE HARD DRINKING AND GAMBLING YOU 271 GGBROW STARTED THE LAST YEAR ABROAD.

ONE OF THESE 'ERE WOULD BUY SCOFF FOR A STARVIN' 235 HA APE FAMILY FOR A YEAR/

HE COMES HERE TWICE A YEAR REGULARLY ON A 586 ICEMAN PERIODICAL DRUNK

HUMILIATION BECAUSE THEY KNEW THEY COULDN'T WIN 603 ICEMAN THAT YEAR IN THIS WARD.

I MET DICK TRUMBULL ON THE STREET A YEAR OR TWO 604 ICEMAN AGO.

WE'LL MAKE IT NEXT YEAR, EVEN IF WE HAVE TO WORK 605 ICEMAN AND EARN OUR PASSAGE MONEY, EH'

BUT THIS LAST YEAR THERE WAS ACTUALLY ONE NIGHT I 627 ICEMAN HAD SO MANY PATIENTS.

ALL RIGHT, I'S EARNED ALL DE DRINKS ON HIM I COULD637 ICEMAN DRINK IN A YEAR FOR

IT IS ABOUT TEN MINUTES OF TWELVE ON A NIGHT IN 513 INZONE THE FALL OF THE YEAR 1915.

HE'S BEEN ON SHIP NEAR TWO YEAR, AIN'T HE' 520 INZONE

YEAR (CONT'D.)

ALL WE KNOW IS HE SHIPS UN HERE IN LONDON 'BOUT A 522 INZONE YEAR B'FORE THE WAR STARTS.

THIS ONE WAS WRITTEN A YEAR BEFORE THE WAR STARTED531 INZONE ANYWAY.

SO EVERY YEAR I HAVE STUPID, LAZY GREENHORNS TO 61 JOURNE DEAL WITH.

HE CLAIMS THAT IN SIX MONTHS TO A YEAR EDMOND WILL 117 JOURNE BE CURED, IF HE OBEYS ORDERS.

A YEAR OR SO AFTER THEY CAME TO AMERICA. 117 JOURNE YOU'LL BE CURED IN SIX MONTHS OR A YEAR AT MOST. 143 JOURNE AND THEN IF AFTER A YEAR OR TWO I STILL FELT SURE,175 JOURNE THAT WAS IN THE WINTER OF SENIOR YEAR. 176 JOURNE IT IS EARLY MORNING IN MID-SUMMER OF THE FOLLOWING139 MANSNS YEAR, 1894.

I AM FULLY AWARE OF THE MEANS YOU HAVE USED IN THE141 MANSNS PAST YEAR.

I WASN'T MORE THAN A YEAR OLD AT THE TIME. 145 MANSNS FOR THE FISCAL YEAR, AND I KNEW YOU'D BE SO 391 MARCOM ASTONISHED AT THE UNPRECEDENTED AMOU

AND YOU'D GET A LETTER SAYING HIS AGENT TOLD HIM 24 MISBEG YOU WERE A YEAR BEHIND IN THE

THE MOST EXCITING EPISODE OF EACH YEAR FOR HIM, 55 MISBEG YOU CAME BACK FROM THE COAST ABOUT A YEAR AGO 128 MISBEG AFTER-- (SHE CHECKS HERSELF)

I'LL NEVER GET IT CLEAR IN MY HEAD WHAT HE'S BEEN 28 POET DOING THERE THE PAST YEAR.

WHERE HE WORKED FOR A YEAR AFTER HE GRADUATED FROM 29 POET HARVARD COLLEGE,

AND YOU'LL WEAR IT FOR DINNER LIKE YOU'VE DONE 39 POET EACH YEAR.

AND THIS YEAR, NOW JAMIE CREGAN HAS APPEARED, 58 POET YOU'VE AN EXCUSE TO MAKE IT WORSE.

SHE MENTIONED A YEAR, I BELIEVE. 109 POET AND SHE ONLY SUGGESTED HE WAIT A YEAR, SHE DIDN'T 144 POET MAKE HIM PROMISE.

ONLY TO MEET HER END AT THE HANDS OF GOD A YEAR 580 ROPE AFTER--

IT IS ABOUT NINE O'CLOCK OF A NIGHT IN EARLY FALL, 24 STRANG OVER A YEAR LATER.

THEN ABOUT A YEAR AGO WHEN I WENT TO THE HOSPITAL 30 STRANG ABOUT NINE O'CLOCK IN THE MORNING OF A DAY IN LATE 48 STRANG SPRING OF THE FOLLOWING YEAR.

AND FROM THEN ON UNTIL HIS FATHER DID REALLY DIE 60 STRANG DURING SAMMY'S SECOND YEAR TO

AND THEN I USED TO WISH I'D GONE OUT DELIBERATE IN 63 STRANG OUR FIRST YEAR.

PHYSICALLY HERSELF THROUGH YEAR AFTER YEAR OF 87 STRANG DEVILLING HERSELF AND HIM'

SEE YOU AGAIN IN A YEAR OR SO. 106 STRANG (VERY HURRIEDLY) YES--GOING TO STUDY OVER THERE 106 STRANG FOR A YEAR OR SO.

HE'S GOING OVER FOR A YEAR OR SO TO STUDY. 107 STRANG A YEAR OR SO/ 107 STRANG

THE SAME--AN EVENING A LITTLE OVER A YEAR LATER. 111 STRANG NOT A LINE WRITTEN IN OVER A YEAR/.... 112 STRANG HE'S BECOME A NEW MAN IN THE PAST YEAR.... 112 STRANG WITHIN A YEAR OR SO THEY'LL BE WILLING TO SELL OUT1Z2 STRANG CHEAP.

(FLATTERINGLY) YES, YOU'VE DONE WONDERS IN THE 121 STRANG PAST YEAR.

I ONLY INTENDED TO STAY A YEAR, AND IT'S OVER THAT126 STRANG SINCE--

LAST TIME HE WAS GONE MORE'NA YEAR.... 138 STRANG IF I HADN'T HE'D SIMPLY HAVE HUNG AROUND ME YEAR 139 STRANG AFTER YEAR, DOING NOTHING....)

ANY TWO-YEAR MEN TO BE PAID OFF' 494 VOYAGE FOUR TWO-YEAR MEN PAID OFF WIT THEIR BLOODY 495 VOYAGE POCKETS FULL O' SOVEREIGNS--

MUST BE MORE THAN TEN YEAR. 506 VOYAGE PY TINGO, I PITY POOR FELLERS MAKE DAT TRIP ROUND 507 VOYAGE CAPE STIFF DIS TIME YEAR.

YOU AND I--YEAR AFTER YEAR-TOGETHER--FORMS OF OUR 448 WELDED BODIES MERGING INTO ONE FORM..

FOR THE LAST YEAR OR SO YOU'VE BEGUN TO ACT MORE 456 WELDED AND MORE AS YOU DID WHEN WE

YEAR'S

YOU'VE A YEAR'S GROWTH SCARED OUT OF ME. 69 ANNA YOU SCARED HER OUT OF A YEAR'S GROWTH. 231 HA APE JEES, HICKEY, YUH SCARED ME OUTA A YEAR'S GROWTH, 638 ICEMAN SNEAKIN' IN LIKE DAT.

SCARED ME OUT OF A YEAR'S GROWTH/ 690 ICEMAN NURA WAS AS PRETTY A GIRL AS YOU'D FIND IN A 14 POET YEAR'S TRAVEL.

I GO BACK WITH TWO YEAR'S PAY AND BUY MORE LAND 503 VOYAGE YET..

YEARLING

HE'S AS SPRY ON HIS STUMPY LEGS AS A YEARLING-- 10 MISBEG

YEARNING

IS IT YOUR OLD SECRET WEAKNESS--THE COWARDLY 499 DAYS YEARNING TO GO BACK--'

(PAUSE. WITH YEARNING) MEBBE A YEAR FROM NOW 211 DESIRE WE'LL BE IN CALIFORNI-A.

(WITH BITTER YEARNING) IF I COULD ONLY BELIEVE 39 ELECTR THAT, ADAM'

(WITH A BITTER, HOPELESS YEARNING) 112 ELECTR (YEARNING FOR THE REALIZATION OF A DREAM) 258 GGBROW (SENTIMENTALLY, WITH REAL YEARNING) 605 ICEMAN (HE GLANCES WITH VENGEFUL YEARNING AT THE DRINK OF671 ICEMAN WHISKEY IN HIS HAND)

THEN WITH AN UNDERCURRENT OF LONELY YEARNING.) 44 JOURNE (WITH A GREAT YEARNING) IF MEN WOULD REMEMBER/ 323 LAZARU TO HAVE BEEN DREAMING GREAT YEARNING DREAMS 370 LAZARU (GLANCING AROUND THE GARDEN--WITH A TONE OF 99 MANSNS NOSTALGIC YEARNING.)

(THINKING--WITH A MINGLING OF FASCINATED DREAD AND129 MANSNS AN ANGUISHED YEARNING.)

YEARS

YEARNING (CONT'D.)
(HE IS STARING BEFORE HIM WITH A FASCINATED 157 MANSNS
YEARNING.)
(THEN WITH A REAL, LONELY YEARNING.) 66 POET
(LOOKING AT MARSDEN WITH A STRANGE YEARNING) 197 STRANG
ME, LEAVING AN ETERNAL YEARNING TO BECOME ONE LIFE448 WELDED
AGAIN.
YEARNINGLY
(YEARNINGLY) THAT'S ALWAYS BEEN MY DREAM--SOME 39 ELECTR
DAY TO OWN MY OWN CLIPPER/
(YEARNINGLY) BUT THE NIGHTS NOW ARE SO MUCH 323 GGBROW
COLDER THAN THEY USED TO BE.
(EYES THE BOTTLE YEARNINGLY BUT SHAKES HIS HEAD-- 674 ICEMAN
DETERMINEDLY)
(YEARNINGLY.) OH, IF I ONLY HAD THE COURAGE/ 139 POET
(LOOKING DOWN AT HIM--THINKING YEARNINGLY) 183 STRANG

YEARS
TWO YEARS O' THIS DOG'S LIFE, AND NO LUCK IN THE 537 'ILE
FISHIN'.
THE TWO YEARS WE ALL SIGNED UP FOR ARE DONE THIS 537 'ILE
DAY.
THE TWO YEARS THEY SIGNED UP FOR IS UP TODAY. 539 'ILE
AND THE TWO YEARS THEY SIGNED ON FUR IS UP TODAY. 541 'ILE
THESE LAST SIX YEARS SINCE WE WERE MARRIED-- 545 'ILE
WAITING, AND WATCHING, AND FEARING--
TWO YEARS/ 547 'ILE
COULD THERE BE AUGHT BUT LOVE BETWEEN US AFTER ALL549 'ILE
THESE YEARS$
YEARS--BOOKS THE FAMILY REALLY HAVE READ. 185 AHWILD
WHICH HAS RECEDED A BIT FROM THE EXTREME OF 186 AHWILD
PRECEDING YEARS, BUT STILL RUNS TO
BUT IS ENTIRELY BALD, AND LOOKS TEN YEARS OLDER. 201 AHWILD
IT'S BEEN SIXTEEN YEARS SINCE I BROKE OFF OUR 213 AHWILD
ENGAGEMENT.
HE'S BEEN EATING BLUEFISH FOR YEARS--ONLY I TELL 214 AHWILD
HIM EACH TIME IT'S WEAKFISH.
YOU'VE EATEN BLUEFISH FOR YEARS AND THRIVED ON IT 227 AHWILD
CAN IT BE THIS WOMAN HAS BEEN SLOWLY POISONING YOU227 AHWILD
ALL THESE YEARS
THOUGH I'D BE RUSTY, NOT HAVING BEEN IN ALL THESE 228 AHWILD
YEARS.
FORTY-FIVE YEARS AGO--WASN'T A SINGLE HOUSE DOWN 229 AHWILD
THERE THEN--
I'VE TAKEN DOWN THE DISTANCE EVERY TIME YOU'VE 230 AHWILD
SAVED BEDY'S LIFE FOR THIRTY YEARS.
IN EVERY THOUSAND YEARS--BUT, DEARIE ME, HOW HE 231 AHWILD
DOES ENJOY IT/
WELL, IT'S ONLY A COUPLE OF YEARS OLD/ 237 AHWILD
I'VE BEEN SMOKING FOR THE LAST TWO YEARS--ON THE 239 AHWILD
SLY.
I'D WAIT A MILLION YEARS AND NEVER MIND IT--FOR 274 AHWILD
HER/
FIRST TIME HE'S DONE THAT IN YEARS. 297 AHWILD
(SURPRISED) YOU'VE NOT SEEN HER IN FIFTEEN YEARS 9 ANNA
AFTER ME CAMPIN' WITH BARGE MEN THE LAST TWENTY 11 ANNA
YEARS.
YOU'RE ME FORTY YEARS FROM NOW. 15 ANNA
(EVASIVELY) SEEN HIM ABOUT FOR YEARS. 17 ANNA
IT WAS TRUE FOR TWO YEARS. 18 ANNA
IT'S GOOD--FOR SEE YOU--AFTER ALL DEM YEARS, ANNA. 20 ANNA
NO, HE WAS BO'SUN ON SAILING SHIPS FOR YEARS. 36 ANNA
(STOUTLY) YES, THANK GOD, THOUGH I'VE NOT SEEN A 37 ANNA
SIGHT OF IT IN FIFTEEN YEARS.
IF I'D BEEN LUCKY ENOUGH TO 'VE MET HIM FOUR YEARS 44 ANNA
AGO--OR EVEN TWO YEARS AGO--
WHEN YOU NEVER LAID EYES ON HER ONCE IN ALL THEM 47 ANNA
YEARS.
THE FIFTEEN YEARS SHE WAS GROWING UP IN THE WEST. 47 ANNA
IN OLE YEARS WHEN AY WAS ON 48 ANNA
TWAS YOURSELF KNEW IT ONCE, AND YOU A BO'SUN FOR 48 ANNA
YEARS.
YOU--KEEPING ME SAFE INLAND--I WASN'T NO NURSE 58 ANNA
GIRL THE LAST TWO YEARS--
AND YOU TAKING UP WITH THIS ONE AND THAT ONE ALL 73 ANNA
THE YEARS OF YOUR LIFE$
HE IS TWENTY-SEVEN YEARS OLD, AN OPPOSITE TYPE TO 82 BEYOND
ROBERT--
UNCLE SAYS YOU'LL BE GONE THREE YEARS. 83 BEYOND
YOU DON'T REALIZE HOW I'VE BUCKED UP IN THE PAST 84 BEYOND
FEW YEARS.
I'VE LOVED YOU ALL THESE YEARS, 91 BEYOND
HE IS FIFTY-EIGHT YEARS OLD. 94 BEYOND
AN ANDREW SIXTY-FIVE YEARS OLD WITH A SHORT, 94 BEYOND
SQUARE, WHITE BEARD.
SUN-BAKED DAY IN MID-SUMMER, THREE YEARS LATER. 112 BEYOND
A VICTIM OF PARTIAL PARALYSIS FOR MANY YEARS, 113 BEYOND
AND YOU'VE GOT YEARS AND YEARS BEFORE YOU. 113 BEYOND
EVER SINCE YOUR HUSBAND DIED TWO YEARS BACK. 114 BEYOND
(SNAPPILY) HE'S HAD THREE YEARS TO LEARN, 114 BEYOND
(WITH A SIGH) THREE YEARS/ 115 BEYOND
THE THREE YEARS HAVE ACCENTUATED THE WEAKNESS OF 119 BEYOND
HIS MOUTH AND CHIN.
I'M ONLY SAYING WHAT I'VE BEEN THINKING FOR YEARS.127 BEYOND
DEEPLY BRONZED BY HIS YEARS IN THE TROPICS.. 130 BEYOND
THE DAYS WERE LIKE YEARS. 132 BEYOND
IN A COUPLE OF YEARS DOWN THERE, I'LL MAKE MY 138 BEYOND
PILE$ SEE IF I DON'T.
SO'S WE THREE CAN BE TOGETHER SAME'S YEARS AGO, 139 BEYOND
FROM THE JOVIAL BOOMING PERSON HE WAS THREE YEARS 140 BEYOND
BEFORE.
AS IF IT HAD NOT BEEN USED IN YEARS. 144 BEYOND
THE WHOLE ATMOSPHERE OF THE ROOM, CONTRASTED WITH 144 BEYOND
THAT OF FORMER YEARS,
TOWARD THE END OF OCTOBER FIVE YEARS LATER. 144 BEYOND
(WITH BITTER MOCKERY) FIVE YEARS/ IT'S A LONG 146 BEYOND
TIME.
IT'S ONLY RIGHT FOR SOMEONE TO MEET HIM AFTER HE'S146 BEYOND
BEEN GONE FIVE YEARS.

YEARS (CONT'D.)
(AFTER A PAUSE) YES, THESE YEARS HAVE BEEN 147 BEYOND
TERRIBLE FOR RUTH OF US.
OF HOW HARD THESE LAST YEARS MUST HAVE BEEN FOR 147 BEYOND
YOU.
ONE KISS--THE FIRST IN YEARS, ISN'T IT$ 150 BEYOND
THE VISION OF A NEW LIFE OPENING UP AFTER ALL THE 150 BEYOND
HORRIBLE YEARS$
I JUDGE FROM THEM YOU'VE ACCOMPLISHED ALL YOU SET 160 BEYOND
OUT TO DO FIVE YEARS AGO$
I'M PROUD ENOUGH OF THE FIRST FOUR YEARS. 161 BEYOND
AFTER TWO YEARS I HAD A SHARE IN IT. 161 BEYOND
YOU'VE SPENT EIGHT YEARS RUNNING AWAY FROM 161 BEYOND
YOURSELF.
SOMETHING HAPPENED FIVE YEARS BACK, THE TIME YOU 163 BEYOND
CAME HOME FROM THE TRIP.
EVERYBODY KNEW IT--AND FOR THREE YEARS I'D BEEN 164 BEYOND
THINKING--
AND YOU'VE LIVED TOGETHER FOR FIVE YEARS WITH THIS165 BEYOND
BETWEEN YOU$
FIVE YEARS, AND MORE OF IS SINCE FIRST I SHIPPED 480 CARDIF
MID HIM,
FIVE YEARS AND MORE, SURR. 485 CARDIF
NEVER--FOR THE PAST THREE YEARS. 550 CRUSS
HE APPEARS MUCH OLDER THAN HIS THIRTY YEARS. 556 CROSS
LOST IN A HURRICANE OFF THE CELEBES WITH ALL ON 558 CROSS
BOARD--THREE YEARS AGO/
THE LAST TRIP HE MADE WAS SEVEN YEARS AGO. 559 CROSS
IT WAS FOUR YEARS BEFORE WE SAW HIM AGAIN. 559 CROSS
HE EXPECTED TO BE GONE TWO YEARS. 559 CROSS
THE SHIP HE'S STILL LOOKING FOR--THAT WAS LOST 561 CROSS
THREE YEARS AGO$
I'VE CARRIED IT ABOUT FOR YEARS. 566 CROSS
THINKIN' IT FOR THE PAST THREE YEARS, YE BIN-- 568 CROSS
I'VE BEEN DROWNED FOR YEARS/ 570 CROSS
(CONFUSED) WELL, TO TELL THE TRUTH, I HAVEN'T 497 DAYS
GIVEN IT A THOUGHT IN YEARS, BUT--
IF YOU KNEW WHAT A BURDEN HE MADE MY LIFE FOR 501 DAYS
YEARS WITH HIS PREACHING.
I KNOW YOU'D HARDLY DO THAT WITH ME, AFTER ALL 516 DAYS
THESE YEARS.
I'VE NOTICED IT GROWING ON YOU FOR THE PAST FEW 519 DAYS
YEARS.
JUST BECAUSE YOU'VE PAMPERED ME SO TERRIBLY THE 529 DAYS
PAST FEW YEARS/
AND IN AFTER YEARS, EVEN AT THE HEIGHT OF HIS 535 DAYS
RATIONALISM,
HE HAD KNOWN HER FOR YEARS. 537 DAYS
GIVE OUR YEARS. 204 DESIRE
THEIR SHOULDERS STOOP A BIT FROM YEARS OF FARM 204 DESIRE
WORK.
SHE KNEW WHAT IT LAY FUR YEARS, BUT SHE WAS 213 DESIRE
WAITIN'.
(A PAUSE) I LOST COUNT O' THE YEARS. 237 DESIRE
YE KIN READ THE YEARS OF MY LIFE IN THEM WALLS, 237 DESIRE
EVERY DAY A HEFTED STONE.
ODD YEARS, SHE DIED. 238 DESIRE
EVEN AFTER WE'RE MARRIED YEARS AND YEARS, 495 DIFRNT
AFTER WAITIN' THREE YEARS FUR ME TO GIT ENOUGH 496 DIFRNT
MONEY SAVED--
AND I NEVER DOUBTED YOU THEM TWO YEARS. 497 DIFRNT
SIXTY YEARS OLD BUT STILL IN THE PRIME OF HEALTH 513 DIFRNT
AND STRENGTH.
HERE'S EMMER TELLIN' YOU THE TRUTH AFTER YOU HAIR-513 DIFRNT
PULLIN' ME ALL THESE YEARS
AND WHEN I COME BACK FROM THE NEXT VIGE AND YOU'VES17 DIFRNT
HAD TWO YEARS TO THINK IT
AND TWO YEARS CAN'T MAKE NO CHANGE IN ME--THAT 517 DIFRNT
WAY.
THIRTY YEARS IF IT'S NEEDFUL/ 518 DIFRNT
I DON'T GIVE A DURN HOW LONG IT'LL TAKE--TILL I'M 518 DIFRNT
SIXTY YEARS OLD/
IN THIRTY YEARS WE'LL BOTH BE DEAD AND GONE, 518 DIFRNT
PROBABLY.
(SCENE--THIRTY YEARS AFTER--THE SCENE IS THE SAME 519 DIFRNT
BUT NOT THE SAME.
THE THIRTY YEARS HAVE TRANSFORMED EMMA INTO A 519 DIFRNT
WITHERED,
A TOO-APPARENT EFFORT TO CHEAT THE YEARS BY 520 DIFRNT
APPEARANCES.
UNCLE CALEB LIVIN' NEXT DOOR ALL THESE YEARS AND 522 DIFRNT
COMIN' TO CALL ALL THE TIME
SHE'S BEEN GETTIN' FLIGHTY THE PAST TWO YEARS. 529 DIFRNT
(COVLY) I HAVEN'T GIVEN HIM THE SLIGHTEST REASON 533 DIFRNT
TO HOPE IN THIRTY YEARS.
HERE WITH YOU--FOR THE LAST THIRTY YEARS/ 533 DIFRNT
IN APPEARANCE, HE HAS CHANGED BUT LITTLE IN THE 535 DIFRNT
THIRTY YEARS. SAVE THAT HIS HAIR
IT WAS THIRTY YEARS AGO THIS SPRING. 537 DIFRNT
NOW WHEN THE THIRTY YEARS ARE PAST--I WAS THINKIN'538 DIFRNT
THAT MAYBE--
THIRTY O' THE BEST YEARS OF A MAN'S LIFE OUGHT TO 538 DIFRNT
BE PROOF ENOUGH
I SAID I'D WAIT THIRTY YEARS--IF NEED BE. 538 DIFRNT
THIRTY YEARS--THAT'S A HELL OF A LONG TIME TO 538 DIFRNT
WAIT, EMMER--
D'YOU REMEMBER WHAT HAPPENED THIRTY YEARS BACKS 538 DIFRNT
YOU'RE TWELVE YEARS OLDER'N ME, DON'T FORGET, 538 DIFRNT
CALEB.
(IGNORING HER QUESTION) I SEED WHAT HE WAS COMIN'540 DIFRNT
TO YEARS BACK.
WHEN YOU'VE BEEN A'MOST AS MUCH A MOTHER TO HIM 542 DIFRNT
FOR YEARS AS HARRIET WAS$
I WON'T-- NOT EVEN IF YOU HAVE WAITED THIRTY 543 DIFRNT
YEARS.
THIRTY O' THE BEST YEARS OF MY LIFE FLUNG FUR A 543 DIFRNT
YELLER DOG LIKE HIM TO FEED ON.

YEARS

1840

YEARS (CONT'D.)
HIS WIFE, AMELIA, IS FIFTEEN YEARS HIS JUNIOR AND 422 DYNAMU
APPEARS EVE+ YOUNGER.
TWENTY-THREE YEARS/ 425 DYNAMO
SHE IS ABOUT FORTY YEARS OLD. 428 DYNAMO
THERE WAS A MAN IN OHIO MANY YEARS BACK 431 DYNAMO
HE GOT TWENTY YEARS FOR IT. 431 DYNAMO
TWENTY YEARS AGO THERE WAS A MAN BY THE NAME OF 440 DYNAMO
ANDREW CLARK LIVED IN THE TOWN
THE JURY SAID IT WAS MURDER IN THE SECOND DEGREE 441 DYNAMU
AND GAVE ME TWENTY YEARS--
HE GOT TWENTY YEARS BUT HE ESCAPED AND RAN AWAY TO447 DYNAMO
CALIFORNIA/
IT IS MUCH OLDER THAN HIS YEARS. 457 DYNAMO
WELL, IT'S A DAMN WONDER WE DIDN'T ALL DIE OF IT 464 DYNAMU
YEARS AGO, LIVING IN THIS DUMP/
(WITH PRIDE) FROM STOWAWAY TO EMPEROR IN TWO 177 EJONES
YEARS/
AND WHEN I GITS A CHANCE TO USE IT I WINDS UP 178 EJONES
EMPEROR IN TWO YEARS.
(REMINISCENTLY) IF DEY'S ONE THING I LEARNS IN 178 EJONES
TEN YEARS ON DE PULLMAN CA'S
YOU AIN'T NEVER LEARNED ARY WURD ER IT, SMITHERS, 179 EJONES
IN DE TEN YEARS YOU BEEN HEAH.
MAYBE I GITS TWENTY YEARS WHEN DAT COLORED MAN 181 EJONES
DIE.
THE THREE PLAYS TAKE PLACE IN EITHER SPRING OR 5 ELECTR
SUMMER OF THE YEARS 1885-1886.)
THEY'VE BEEN TOP DOG AROUND HERE FOR NEAR ON TWO 8 ELECTR
HUNDRED YEARS
I AIN'T BEEN WITH THE MANNONS FOR SIXTY YEARS 19 ELECTR
WITHOUT LEARNING THAT.
I FORGOT HER UNTIL TWO YEARS AGO WHEN I CAME BACK 26 ELECTR
FROM THE EAST.
IS A LARGE PORTRAIT OF EZRA MANNON HIMSELF, 28 ELECTR
PAINTED TEN YEARS PREVIOUSLY.
FOR OVER TWENTY YEARS, GIVING MY BODY TO A MAN I-- 31 ELECTR
DON'T FORGET YOU'RE FIVE YEARS OLDER 33 ELECTR
WELL, YOU CAN'T SAY I DIDN'T DO MINE ALL THESE 45 ELECTR
YEARS)
IF YOU'D SEEN AS MUCH OF DEATH AS I HAVE IN THE 49 ELECTR
PAST FOUR YEARS,
THEN ALL THE YEARS WE'VE BEEN MAN AND WIFE WOULD 54 ELECTR
RISE UP IN MY MIND
WE HAVE TWENTY GOOD YEARS STILL BEFORE US/ 55 ELECTR
I LOVED YOU THEN, AND ALL THE YEARS BETWEEN, AND I 55 ELECTR
LOVE YOU NOW.
MAKE ME FORGET ALL THE YEARS& 61 ELECTR
HE'S WHAT I'VE LUNGED FOR ALL THESE YEARS WITH 61 ELECTR
YOU--A LOVER/
HIS WIFE, ABOUT TEN YEARS HIS JUNIOR. 67 ELECTR
I HAD BEEN A GOOD WIFE TO HIM FOR TWENTY-THREE 77 ELECTR
YEARS--UNTIL I MET ADAM.
(WITH A STRANGE CRUEL SMILE OF GLOATING OVER THE 178 ELECTR
YEARS OF SELF-TORTURE)
SCENE--SEVEN YEARS LATER. 269 GGBROW
WELL, FOR FIVE YEARS IT KEPT US LIVING ABROAD IN 271 GGBROW
PEACE.
AND SHE PLAYED MOTHER AND CHILD WITH ME FOR MANY 282 GGBROW
YEARS IN THAT HOUSE
SCENE--CYBEL'S PARLOR--ABOUT SUNSET IN SPRING 284 GGBROW
SEVEN YEARS LATER.
YOU'VE BEEN ASKING ME THAT FOR YEARS. 285 GGBROW
WE'VE BEEN FRIENDS HAVEN'T WE, FOR SEVEN YEARS& 285 GGBROW
WE DIMLY REMEMBER SO MUCH IT WILL TAKE US SO MANY 291 GGBROW
MILLION YEARS TO FORGET/
DRAWN AND CAREWORN FOR ITS YEARS, AND SAD, 291 GGBROW
RESIGNED, BUT A BIT QUERULOUS.)
IN THE YEARS SINCE WE SETTLED DOWN HERE. 292 GGBROW
ONE DAY WHEN I WAS FOUR YEARS OLD, 295 GGBROW
TO GO TO EUROPE FOR A COUPLE OF YEARS-- 304 GGBROW
WHY, BILLY-- I SIMPLY WON'T BELIEVE--AFTER ALL 305 GGBROW
THESE YEARS.
SCENE--FOUR YEARS LATER. 323 GGBROW
MUST HAVE BEEN TEN YEARS AGO--YES, EDDIE, THE 12 HUGHIE
OLDEST, IS ELEVEN NOW--
IN ALL THE YEARS I KNOW HIM, HE NEVER BET A BUCK 16 HUGHIE
ON NOTHIN'.
THE SCOWS,) I'VE BEEN CAMPIN' HERE, OFF AND ON, 17 HUGHIE
FIFTEEN YEARS.
IT IS YEARS SINCE HE CARED WHAT ANYONE CALLED HIM. 24 HUGHIE
JOE MUTT IS A NEGRO, ABOUT FIFTY YEARS OLD, BROWN-574 ICEMAN
SKINNED, STOCKY,
HIS MOTHER AND I WERE FRIENDS YEARS AGO ON THE 583 ICEMAN
COAST.
I GUESS I GOT TO FEEL IN THE YEARS YOU LIVED WITH 588 ICEMAN
US
THAT WAS ELEVEN YEARS AGO. 589 ICEMAN
I HAVEN'T WRITTEN HER IN A COUPLE OF YEARS--OR 589 ICEMAN
ANYONE ELSE.
WHAT HAVE YOU BEEN DOING ALL THE YEARS SINCE YOU 591 ICEMAN
LEFT THE COAST, LARRY&
HE HAD THE GUTS TO SERVE TEN YEARS IN THE CAN IN 593 ICEMAN
HIS OWN COUNTRY
SINCE HIS WIFE DIED TWENTY YEARS AGO. 594 ICEMAN
BUT AS I BECAME BURDENED WITH YEARS, 601 ICEMAN
'CAUSE I RUN WIDE OPEN FOR YEARS AND PAYS MY SUGAR601 ICEMAN
OA DE OUT.
(CHUCKLING) GITTIN' DRUNK EVERY DAY FOR TWENTY 601 ICEMAN
YEARS
AND IT'S TWENTY YEARS SINCE 602 ICEMAN
TOOK 'EM YEARS TO LICK A GANG OF DUTCH HAYSEEDS/ 602 ICEMAN
(MOURNFULLY) TWENTY YEARS. 603 ICEMAN
THEY WILL NOT KNOW ME, IT IS SO MANY YEARS. 605 ICEMAN
DEY BEEN DREAMIN' IT FOR YEARS, EVERY TIME CHUCK 614 ICEMAN
GOES ON DE WAGON.
CORA IS A THIN PEROXIDE BLONDE, A FEW YEARS OLDER 615 ICEMAN
THAN PEARL AND MARGIE.

YEARS (CONT'D.)
ONLY EIGHTY YEARS OLD WHEN HE WAS TAKEN. 627 ICEMAN
EACH FOR TEN YEARS. 630 ICEMAN
HE ROTTED TEN YEARS IN PRISON FOR HIS FAITH/ 641 ICEMAN
HE'S HAD FOR TWENTY YEARS. 652 ICEMAN
LOOK HOW HE'S KIDDED HIMSELF FOR TWENTY YEARS/ 655 ICEMAN
EACH FOR TEN YEARS, EH& 656 ICEMAN
WE'VE HEARD HIS BULL ABOUT TAKING A WALK AROUND 660 ICEMAN
THE WARD FOR YEARS.
I'VE HAD RHEUMATISM ON AND OFF FOR TWENTY YEARS. 684 ICEMAN
TWENTY YEARS IS A LUNG TIME. 687 ICEMAN
WASN'T NONE OF THEM AROUND THE LAST TIME, TWENTY 687 ICEMAN
YEARS AGO.
AND THAT WAS YEARS AGO. 707 ICEMAN
IT WAS THE SAME OLD STORY, OVER AND OVER, FOR 713 ICEMAN
YEARS AND YEARS.
YOU'VE KNOWN OLD HICKEY FUR YEARS/ 716 ICEMAN
WE'VE KNOWN HIM FOR YEARS, 718 ICEMAN
ENGLAND HAS BEEN LIVIN' THERE FOR TEN, OFTEN AS 521 INZONE
NOT TWENTY YEARS,
JAMES TYRONE IS SIXTY-FIVE BUT LOOKS TEN YEARS 13 JOURNE
YOUNGER.
EDMUND IS TEN YEARS YOUNGER THAN HIS BROTHER, 19 JOURNE
YOU'D THINK YOU WERE THE ONE TEN YEARS OLDER. 21 JOURNE
WILL YOU LISTEN TO YOUR FATHER, JAMIE--AFTER 29 JOURNE
THIRTY-FIVE YEARS OF MARRIAGE/
I'VE WARNED HIM FOR YEARS HIS BODY COULDN'T STAND 33 JOURNE
IT, BUT HE WOULDN'T HEED ME.
WHAT HAD I TO DO WITH ALL THE CRAZY STUNTS HE'S 35 JOURNE
PULLED IN THE LAST FEW YEARS--
BUT I WAS WISE TEN YEARS OR MORE BEFORE WE HAD TO 57 JOURNE
TELL YOU.
HEAVEN KNOWS I OUGHT TO AFTER ALL THESE YEARS. 74 JOURNE
I'VE PRAYED TO GOD THESE MANY YEARS FOR HER. 77 JOURNE
IT'S HARD FOR A STRANGER TO TELL, BUT AFTER 83 JOURNE
THIRTY-FIVE YEARS OF MARRIAGE--
I'VE LOVED HIM DEARLY FOR THIRTY-SIX YEARS. 101 JOURNE
I HAVEN'T TOUCHED A PIANO IN SO MANY YEARS. 104 JOURNE
THIRTY-SIX YEARS AGO, BUT I CAN SEE IT AS CLEARLY 105 JOURNE
AS IF IT WERE TONIGHT/
AND IN ALL THOSE THIRTY-SIX YEARS, 105 JOURNE
DURING THE TWO YEARS HE LIVED BEFORE I LET HIM DIE110 JOURNE
THROUGH MY NEGLECT.
YOU REMEMBER, JAMES, FOR YEARS AFTER HE WENT TO 110 JOURNE
BOARDING SCHOOL,
I DIDN'T KNOW HOW OFTEN THAT WAS TO HAPPEN IN THE 113 JOURNE
YEARS TO COME.
YOUR FATHER HAD TO GO TO WORK IN A MACHINE SHOP 117 JOURNE
WHEN HE WAS ONLY TEN YEARS OLD.
IT TOOK MANY YEARS BEFORE I UNDERSTOOD HIM. 117 JOURNE
IT WAS YEARS BEFORE I DISCOVERED WHAT WAS WRONG. 141 JOURNE
BECAUSE I WAS THE MAN OF THE FAMILY. AT TEN YEARS148 JOURNE
OLD/
I'D LOST THE GREAT TALENT I ONCE HAD THROUGH YEARS150 JOURNE
OF EASY REPETITION,
AND I WAS ONLY TWENTY-SEVEN YEARS OLD/ 150 JOURNE
BUT A FEW YEARS LATER MY GOOD BAD LUCK MADE ME 150 JOURNE
FIND THE BIG MONEY-MAKER.
I KEPT IT IN MY WALLET FOR YEARS. 152 JOURNE
TOLD ME YEARS AGO TO CUT OUT BOOZE OR I'D SOON BE 164 JOURNE
DEAD--AND HERE I AM.
IN APPEARANCE LAZARUS IS TALL AND POWERFUL, ABOUT 274 LAZARU
FIFTY YEARS OF AGE,
IT WAS THE FIRST TIME I HAD SEEN HIM SMILE IN 276 LAZARU
YEARS.
YES, OF LATE YEARS HIS LIFE HAD BEEN ONE LONG 276 LAZARU
MISFORTUNE.
AS ONE WHO FROM A DISTANCE OF YEARS OF SORROW 277 LAZARU
REMEMBERS HAPPINESS.
HE SEEMS TEN YEARS YOUNGER, AT THE PRIME OF FORTY.288 LAZARU
THIRTY YEARS& YEARS OF DISCIPLINE AND I--HALT, 311 LAZARU
TRAITOR/
UNSLAKED BY EIGHTY YEARS OF DEVOURED DESIRES COULD355 LAZARU
KNOW/
AND MANY YEARS PASSED IN BEING HERE AND THERE, IN 356 LAZARU
DURING THIS AND THAT,
THE CABIN GIVES EVIDENCE OF HAVING BEEN ABANDONED 1 MANSNS
FUR YEARS.
DREAM THEM AWAY AS YOU HAVE ALL THE OTHER YEARS 3 MANSNS
SINCE SIMON DESERTED YOU&
I STILL HAVE YEARS BEFORE ME. 3 MANSNS
(SHE SITS DOWN, AND WHAT WILL YOU DO WITH THESE 3 MANSNS
YEARS, DEBORAH&
WITH FOUR YEARS MORE OF MR. 8 MANSNS
FOUR YEARS IS A LONG «LATELY.» 16 MANSNS
DEBORAH NOW SEEMS MUCH OLDER THAN HER FORTY-NINE 27 MANSNS
YEARS.
SO ALL DAY FOR YEARS I HAVE LIVED WITH THEM. 29 MANSNS
IT APPEARS HE HAD OVERREACHED HIS RESOURCES DURING 32 MANSNS
THE PAST FEW YEARS--
I TELL YOU I SWORE TO MYSELF YEARS AGO 36 MANSNS
WHAT AMBIUSH THOUGHTS FOR A MAN OF MY YEARS AND 37 MANSNS
PROFESSION/
HIS LARGE-FEATURED YANKEE FACE LOOKS HIS THIRTY- 43 MANSNS
FIVE YEARS.
AND FOR THE LAST COUPLE OF YEARS, WHO HAS BEEN 45 MANSNS
ENCOURAGING ME TO WRITE ITS
AS FOR YOU AND ME, WE HAVE NOT EVEN CORRESPONDED 58 MANSNS
IN YEARS.
HE HAS CHANGED GREATLY IN THE FOUR YEARS 69 MANSNS
IN THE FACE OF ALL I'VE ACCOMPLISHED IN FOUR 70 MANSNS
YEARS/
SHE HAS NOT CHANGED MUCH IN THE FIVE YEARS. 75 MANSNS
IT WILL BE PLEASANT TO FIND MYSELF IN HER GARDEN 94 MANSNS
AGAIN AFTER ALL THESE YEARS.
THAT I HAVE HAD TO WATCH FOR YEARS, 97 MANSNS
A FEW YEARS OF HIS LIFE. 150 MANSNS

YELLING

YEARS (CONT'D.)
SHE LOOKS BEAUTIFUL AND SERENE, AND MANY YEARS 191 MANSNS
YOUNGER.)
TWENTY-THREE YEARS EARLIER. 355 MARCOM
AFTER SPENDING NINE YEARS AT THE COURT OF THE 356 MARCOM
GREAT KAAN
TWO YEARS IN SESSION/ 359 MARCOM
ABOUT FIFTEEN YEARS HAVE ELAPSED. 384 MARCOM
MANY LEAGUES AND YEARS, AND I WEEP THAT NEVER 384 MARCOM
AGAIN SHALL I SEE YOUR FACE.
SHE HAS ONLY TALKED TO HIM ONCE OR TWICE EVERY TWO388 MARCOM
YEARS OR SO/
THEY'VE HAD IT UNDER THEIR NOSES FOR YEARS WITHOUT395 MARCOM
A SINGLE SOUL EVER HAVING
IN THE HARBOR OF HORMUZ, PERSIA--A MOONLIT NIGHT 407 MARCOM
SOME TWO YEARS LATER.
TWO YEARS ON THIS FOREIGN TUB ARE TOO MUCH. 408 MARCOM
AND REMEMBER THEY'VE BEEN GONE TWENTY-ODD YEARS. 427 MARCOM
I'D NEVER HAVE REMAINED SINGLE ALL THESE YEARS IN 430 MARCOM
THE EAST/
AND ALL THE TWENTY-ODD YEARS I KEPT THINKING OF 430 MARCOM
YOU.
GRAND THRONE ROOM IN THE IMPERIAL PALACE AT 432 MARCOM
CAMBALUC, ABOUT TWO YEARS LATER.
THEY'VE NOT WRITTEN ME IN YEARS. 7 MISBEG
DON'T FORGET, IF WE HAVE LIVED ON IT TWENTY YEARS, 31 MISBEG
LIKE OUR BEAUTIFUL NEIGHBOR, HARDER, THE STANDARD 32 MISBEG
OIL THIEF, DID YEARS AGO.
NO ONE EVER HAS IN ALL THE YEARS-- 32 MISBEG
IT'S A TERRIBLE THING TO BREAK THE HABIT OF YEARS. 41 MISBEG
I'VE WANTED TO GO ON THE WAGON FOR THE PAST 45 MISBEG
TWENTY-FIVE YEARS.
I'VE PINED TO HAVE A QUIET WORD WITH MR. HARDER 51 MISBEG
FOR YEARS.
HIS FOUR UNDERGRADUATE YEARS WILL ALWAYS BE FOR 55 MISBEG
HIM THE MOST SIGNIFICANT IN HIS
(WITH A FIXED SMILE) YOU'D THINK I'D BEEN GONE 111 MISBEG
YEARS.
WHEN MAMA DIED, I'D BEEN ON THE WAGON FOR NEARLY 146 MISBEG
TWO YEARS.
TO SEE ABOUT SELLING A PIECE OF PROPERTY THE OLD 147 MISBEG
MAN HAD BOUGHT THERE YEARS AGO.
THE TAVERN IS OVER A HUNDRED YEARS OLD. 7 POET
AND FOR SOME YEARS NOW THE TAVERN HAS FALLEN UPON 7 POET
NEGLECTED DAYS.
BUT YEARS OF OVERWORK AND WORRY HAVE MADE HER LOOK 19 POET
MUCH OLDER.
SURELY YOU'RE NOT ASHAMED BEFORE ME, AFTER ALL 46 POET
THESE YEARS.
LOST IN MEMORIES OF A GLORIOUS BATTLE IN SPAIN, 58 POET
NINETEEN YEARS AGO TODAY.
I HAVE NOT VENTURED FROM MY GARDEN IN MANY YEARS. 86 POET
THE DAMNED THIEVES OF THE LAW DID THEIR WORST TO 118 POET
ME MANY YEARS AGO IN IRELAND.
YOU'LL HAVE A THOUSAND YEARS IN HELL, I WOULDN'T 149 POET
CARE.
(FRIGHTENEDLY.) I'VE NEVER HEARD HIM TALK LIKE 160 POET
THAT IN ALL THE YEARS--
AND HIM ONLY FIVE YEARS OLD/ 580 ROPE
(INTERRUPTING) AND THE CARRYIN'S-ON YOU HAD THE 580 ROPE
SIX YEARS AT HOME AFTER I'D
AFTER NOT BEIN' AT SUNDAY MEETIN' YOURSELF FOR 580 ROPE
MORE'N TWENTY YEARS/
(JEALOUSLY) YOU WAS FOND ENOUGH OF HIM ALL THEM 581 ROPE
YEARS--
IT'S FIVE YEARS HE'S BEEN GONE, AND NOT A SIGHT OF583 ROPE
HIM.
SO I BET ON I WAS ONLY PAYIN' A FRIENDLY CALL, 585 ROPE
HAVIN' KNOWN HIM FOR YEARS.
THE AULD LOON MUST HAVE HAD CASH WITH HIM THEN, 586 ROPE
AN' IT'S ONLY FIVE YEARS BACK.
AN' IF HE DIDN'T COME BACK BY SIVIN YEARS FROM 586 ROPE
WHEN HE'D LEFT--
AN' HIMSELF RUININ' IT YEARS AGO 586 ROPE
TWO YEARS FROM NOW, THAT'D BE-- 586 ROPE
AN' IN A FEW YEARS WE'D BE RICH,. 587 ROPE
AH, WELL, I'LL SAVE WHAT I CAN AN' AT THE END OF 587 ROPE
TWO YEARS,
BACK AFTER FIVE YEARS OF BUMMIN' ROUND THE ROTTEN 588 ROPE
OLD EARTH IN SHIPS AND THINGS.
I'M HARBORING NO GRUDGE AGEN YOU THESE PAST YEARS.591 ROPE
CARPENTRYIN' THESE FIVE YEARS PAST. 592 ROPE
'TIS DEAD AGAINST IT HE'S BEEN THESE FIVE YEARS 595 ROPE
PAST.
(LOOKING AT THE BOOKS NOW) (HE HASN'T ADDED ONE 4 STRANG
BOOK IN YEARS...
SEEMS IMPOSSIBLE SHE'S BEEN DEAD SIX YEARS... 5 STRANG
THAT SIX MONTHS AGO THE DOCTORS THOUGHT IT MIGHT 16 STRANG
BE YEARS BEFORE--
TWO YEARS IN THE UNIVERSITY, I AM SORRY TO SAY, 17 STRANG
ALTHOUGH HE IS TWENTY-FIVE AND HAS BEEN OUT OF 29 STRANG
COLLEGE THREE YEARS.
REALLY ONLY SINCE SHE'S BEEN AT THE HOSPITAL, 29 STRANG
ALTHOUGH I MET HER ONCE YEARS AGO
I THOUGHT OF A MILLION LIGHT YEARS TO A SPIRAL 41 STRANG
NEBULA--
IN A FEW YEARS YOU WON'T HAVE TO WORRY ONE WAY OR 54 STRANG
ANOTHER.
SHE LIVES ON THE TOP FLOOR OF THIS HOUSE, HASN'T 59 STRANG
BEEN OUT OF HER ROOM IN YEARS.
WE NEVER FORGOT TO BE CAREFUL FOR TWO WHOLE YEARS. 60 STRANG
I'VE TAKEN CARE OF HER SO MANY YEARS, LIVED HER 62 STRANG
LIFE FOR HER WITH MY LIFE.
I'M CERTAINLY GLAD TO SEE YOU AGAIN--AFTER ALL 79 STRANG
THESE YEARS/
AND SAM'S FATHER HAD LOST HIS MIND FOR YEARS 83 STRANG
BEFORE HE DIED.

YEARS (CONT'D.)
SHE MUST BE AT LEAST TEN YEARS OLDER THAN YOU, 114 STRANG
LARGE AND MATRONLY AND PLACID.
(IN ANGUISH) IT DEAR OLD ROVER, NICE OLD DOGGIE, 120 STRANG
WE'VE HAD HIM FOR YEARS.
I COULDN'T HAVE SAID THAT TWO YEARS AGO--AND 121 STRANG
BELIEVED IT.
NEARLY ELEVEN YEARS LATER. 137 STRANG
WHAT HAS BOUND US TOGETHER ALL THESE YEARS$... 138 STRANG
FIVE YEARS MORE.... 138 STRANG
(BITTERLY) MY WORK HAS FINISHED TWELVE YEARS AGO.140 STRANG
(THEN SERIOUSLY) AND WILL YOU PROMISE TO STAY 145 STRANG
AWAY TWO YEARS--
YES. I'M GOING THIS WEEK AND I EXPECT TO BE GONE 147 STRANG
AT LEAST TWO YEARS THIS TIME--
TWO YEARS OF HARD WORK. 147 STRANG
AND MADE HIM PROMISE ME HE WOULDN'T RETURN FOR TWO155 STRANG
YEARS.
AND HE'LL BE GONE TWO YEARS/... 155 STRANG
LATE AFTERNOON IN LATE JUNE, TEN YEARS LATER-- 158 STRANG
HE LOOKS HIS FIFTY-ONE YEARS, PERHAPS, BUT NOT A 159 STRANG
DAY MORE.
HIS SKIN IS TANNED ALMOST BLACK BY HIS YEARS IN 159 STRANG
THE TROPICS.
HIS TYPE LOGICALLY DEVELOPED BY TEN YEARS OF 159 STRANG
CONTINUED SUCCESS AND ACCUMULATING
THESE LAST THREE YEARS HAVE FINALLY DONE 161 STRANG
IT...
I HAVEN'T LOVED HER IN YEARS/...) 162 STRANG
AFTERNOONS OF HAPPINESS PAID FOR WITH YEARS OF 165 STRANG
PAIN...
HOW MANY YEARS SINCE... 169 STRANG
THEN YOU'VE LIVED ALL THESE YEARS--WITH THIS 180 STRANG
HORROR?
HE KEPT COMING BACK EVERY COUPLE OF YEARS. 186 STRANG
COME TO SEE ME ONCE IN A WHILE IN THE YEARS TO 195 STRANG
COME?
I REMEMBER FUIVE OR SIX YEARS BACK 496 VOYAGE
PARTLY IMPOSED BY YEARS OF SELF-DISCIPLINE. 443 WELDED
DO YOU MEAN TO SAY YOU STILL READ THEM OVER--AFTER444 WELDED
FIVE YEARS OF ME?
IT BEGAN WITH THE SPLITTING OF A CELL A HUNDRED 448 WELDED
MILLION YEARS AGO INTO YOU AND
(AFTER A PAUSE--SOMBERLY) YOU MENTIONED OUR YEARS455 WELDED
TOGETHER AS PROOF.
WHY, YOU'VE TOLD ME YOURSELF HE WAS IN LOVE WITH 455 WELDED
YOU FOR YEARS.
(WITH A SHORT LAUGH) I SHOULD THINK AFTER FIVE 455 WELDED
YEARS--
WHAT OF THE YEARS THAT PRECEDED$ 455 WELDED
(BITINGLY) YOU WERE ON THE STAGE SEVEN YEARS 457 WELDED
BEFORE I MET YOU.
THE ONE YOU PLAYED IN FIRST WAS WRITTEN THREE 457 WELDED
YEARS BEFORE.
THEN ALL THESE YEARS YOU'VE REALLY BELIEVED--$ 458 WELDED
TEN THOUSAND YEARS--ABOUT--ISN'T ITS OR TWENTY$ 476 WELDED
YOU SAID THAT YEARS AGO YOU HAD OFFERED YOURSELF--484 WELDED
TO HIM--
IN A BLACK WORLD, ALONE IN A HUNDRED MILLION YEARS488 WELDED
OF DARKNESS.
LIFE GUIDES ME BACK THROUGH THE HUNDRED MILLION 488 WELDED
YEARS TO YOU.
YEARS'
BUT THAT'S A POOR SHOWING FOR FIVE YEARS' HARD 157 BEYOND
WORK.
AT THE END OF THIRTY YEARS' DEVOTION TO THE CAUSE,590 ICEMAN
THAT I WAS NEVER MADE FOR IT.
YEARS'D
BEIN' MARRIED TO ALF ROGERS FOR FIVE YEARS'D 539 DIFRNT
PIZEN' ANY WOMAN'S LIFE.
YEARTH
REPEATS ONE WORD OF IT, I ENDS YO' STEALIN' ON DIS181 EJONES
YEARTH MIGHTY DAMN QUICK/
YELL
AND A LOUD YELL OF PAIN.) 472 CARIBE
I'LL YELL 'EM AT THE TOP O' MY LUNGS. 209 DESIRE
I WANTED T' YELL AN' RUN. 242 DESIRE
SHE WANTS TO HEAR ME YELL...) 448 DYNAMO
JONES LOOKS DOWN, LEAPS BACKWARD WITH A YELL OF 190 EJONES
TERROR.
(HE IS INTERRUPTED BY A MUFFLED YELL OF TERROR 134 ELECTR
FROM THE HOUSE.
WE HEARD SOMEONE YELL. 293 GGBRWN
DEN SHE'D YELL --DAT'S A SWEET WAY TO TALK TO DE 671 ICEMAN
GUIL YUH'RE GOIN' TO MARRY.#
WE'LL SHOVE A RAG IN HER MOUTH SO'S SHE CAN'T 600 ROPE
YELL.
(THINKING) (I'LL YELL THE TRUTH INTO YOUR EARS 152 STRANG
IF I STAY A SECOND LONGER....
I'LL YELL OUT THE WHOLE BUSINESS IF I STAY/...) 152 STRANG
NOW I'M GOING TO GIVE AN HONEST HEALTHY YELL-- 176 STRANG
THE PEOPLE HAVE TO YELL AND SCREAM TO MAKE 181 STRANG
THEMSELVES HEARD.)
YELLED
PA YELLED TO GET OUT. 430 DYNAMO
THE POOR PIGS, SHAUGHNESSY YELLED, HAD CAUGHT 24 JOURNE
THEIR DEATH OF COLD.
YELLER
THEY'RE ALL THE SAME--WHITE, BROWN, YELLER, 'N' 470 CARIBE
BLACK.
THIRTY O' THE BEST YEARS OF MY LIFE FLUNG FOR A 543 DIFRNT
YELLER DOG LIKE HIM TO FEED ON.
YELLIN'
SHE KEEPS SWIMMIN' ROUND AND YELLIN' FOR CALEB. 503 DIFRNT
YUH'LL COME RUNNIN' IN HERE SOME NIGHT YELLIN' FOR670 ICEMAN
A SHOT OF BOOZE
YELLING
DEN VE DON'T HEAR DOT YELLING. 459 CARIBE

YELLING

1842

YELLING (CONT'D.)

I WENT MAD, WANTED TO KILL AND RAN ON, YELLING. 95 ELECTR
I AGREE TO ANYTHING--EXCEPT HUMILIATION OF YELLING281 GGBROW
SECRETS AT THE DEAF/
(SCARED NOW--YELLING OFF LEFT) 245 HA APE
WHO'S THAT YELLINGS 581 ICEMAN
WHAT THE HELL YOU TRYING TO DO, YELLING AND 654 ICEMAN
RAISING THE ROOF$
MA*SUEN APPEARS SWAYING IN THE CABIN DOORWAY 174 STRANG
YELLING = GORDON/*
OF MASSDEN'S VOICE YELLING DRUNKENLY, OF EVANS', 174 STRANG
ALL SHOUTING =GORDON/=

YELLOW

A YELLOW, DRUNKEN BUM/ 250 AHWILD
BUT I HAVEN'T--I'M YELLOW, TOO/ 258 AHWILD
SHE HAD YELLOW HAIR--THE KIND THAT BURNS AND 283 AHWILD
STINGS YOU/
HIS LARGE MOUTH, OVERHUNG BY A THICK, DROOPING, 5 ANNA
YELLOW MUSTACHE,
HE IS DRESSED IN YELLOW OILSKINS-- 25 ANNA
WHERE ELSE'D YOU GET THAT FINE YELLOW HAIR IS LIKE 34 ANNA
A GOLDEN CROWN ON YOUR HEADS
OH, GOD HELP ME, I'M A YELLOW COWARD FOR ALL MEN 70 ANNA
TO SPIT AT/
AND A YELLOW SOU'WESTER PUSHED JAUNTILY ON THE 498 DIFRNT
BACK OF HIS HEAD,
I'D SHIP HER OFF AS FEMALE MISSIONARY TO THE 514 DIFRNT
DAMNED YELLOW CHINKS.
AND IF I DUN'T SHOW HIM UP YELLOW 432 DYNAMO
HE ISN'T YELLOW. 432 DYNAMO
SO YOU DON'T BELIEVE THAT LAD'S YELLOW, DON'T YOU$432 DYNAMO
OH, IF YOU'D ONLY MAKE A PRIZE JACKASS OF THAT 432 DYNAMO
YELLOW NANCY SON OF HIS/
GEE, HE IS YELLOW ALL RIGHT/....) 442 DYNAMO
HE'S YELLOW/ 449 DYNAMO
BUT YOU'RE YELLOW, TOO. 449 DYNAMO
AND I'M YELLOW. 449 DYNAMO
YOU'RE A YELLOW RAT/ 451 DYNAMO
POP TOLD YOU TO PROVE YOU WERE YELLOW/ 451 DYNAMO
AND HE WAS YELLOW, WASN'T HE$... 455 DYNAMO
SHE CALLED ME A YELLOW RAT--AND SHE HAD THE RIGHT 458 DYNAMO
DOPE.
SHE'LL FIND OUT IF I'M YELLOW NOW/....) 459 DYNAMO
EVEN WHEN YOU WERE BAWLING ME OUT FOR A YELLOW 460 DYNAMO
RAT.
I'M NOT YELLOW ABOUT YOU OR GOD OR ANYTHING ELSE/ 460 DYNAMO
SHARP FEATURES TO A SICKLY YELLOW. 174 EJONES
BACKDROP FOR THE REAR WALL IS A CHEAP 278 GGBROW
WALLPAPER OF A DULL YELLOW-BROWN.
HER YELLOW HAIR HANGS DOWN IN A GREAT MANE OVER 320 GGBROW
HER SHOULDERS.
YELLOW, DAT'S YOU. 212 HA APE
YUH'RE YELLOW, DAT'S WHAT. 212 HA APE
YUH'RE YELLOW, DAT'S YOU. 212 HA APE
YELLOW/ 213 HA APE
HE'S YELLOW, GET ME$ 224 HA APE
ALL DE ENGINEERS IS YELLOW. 224 HA APE
COME DOWN OUTA DERE, YUH YELLOW, BRASS-BUTTONED, 225 HA APE
BELFAST BUM, YUH/
YUH LOUSY, STINKIN', YELLOW MUT OF A CATHOLIC-- 225 HA APE
MURDERIN' BASTARD/
YUH'RE YELLOW, DAT'S WHAT. 236 HA APE
(GLARING AT HIM) OR A HAIRY APE, YUH BIG YELLOW 245 HA APE
BUM/
DE BLACK HAND, DEY'RE A LOT UF YELLOW BACK- 248 HA APE
STICKIN' GINEES.
BUT I'D SWEAR THERE COULDN'T BE A YELLOW STOOL 588 ICEMAN
PIGEON AMONG THEM.
A LOUD SUIT, TIE AND SHIRT, AND YELLOW SHOES. 615 ICEMAN
HE'S YELLOW, HE AIN'T GOT THE GUTS, HE'S SCARED 660 ICEMAN
HE'LL FIND OUT--
HE'S A YELLOW OLD FAKER/ 666 ICEMAN
(SNEERINGLY) I'D TAKE THAT HUP OFF YOUR FIRE 668 ICEMAN
ESCAPE YOU'RE TOO YELLOW TO TAKE,
I KNOW HOW DAMNED YELLOW A MAN CAN BE 684 ICEMAN
SHOW THE OLD YELLOW FAKER UP/ 689 ICEMAN
AND LET ME STILL CLUTCH GREEDILY TO MY YELLOW 689 ICEMAN
HEART THIS SWEET TREASURE,
HE WAS YELLOW. 699 ICEMAN
(WITH ANGRY SCORN) AH, SHUT UP, YOU YELLOW FAKER/706 ICEMAN
(SNAPPING) GOD DAMN HIS YELLOW SOUL, IF HE DOESN'T726 ICEMAN
SOON.
THESE YOUTHS WEAR FEMALE WIGS OF CURLED WIRE LIKE 336 LAZARU
FRIZZED HAIR OF A YELLOW GOLD.
YELLOW OUT/ 366 LAZARU
THE HOUSE HAD ONCE BEEN PAINTED A REPULSIVE YELLOW 1 MISBEG
WITH BROWN TRIM.
LEAVING HIS SKIN A MONGOLIAN YELLOW. 190 STRANG
AGAINST THE DIM YELLOW LIGHT OF A HALL. 470 WELDED

YELLOWISH

HIS YELLOWISH BROWN EYES ARE SLY. 129 ELECTR
HIS EYES ARE BROWN, THE WHITES CONGESTED AND 37 MISBEG
YELLOWISH.

YELLOWLY

IT IS LATE AFTERNOON BUT THE SUNLIGHT STILL BLAZES173 EJONES
YELLOWLY BEYOND THE PORTICO

YELLS

I YELLS =WHAR YE GOIN', PAWS= 209 DESIRE
(HE YELLS AT THE WINDOW) IT'S YOU WHO'RE THE RAT,452 DYNAMO
ADA/
DON I YELLS IT OUT LOUDER 'N DEIN LOUDEST. 185 EJONES
FOLLOWED A SECOND LATER BY SAVAGE EXULTANT YELLS. 203 EJONES
(SUDDENLY YELLS IN HIS NIGHTMARE) 581 ICEMAN
PEARL YELLS) HEY, ROCKY/ FIGHT IN DE HALL/ 649 ICEMAN
PEARL YELLS) 650 ICEMAN
THE YELLS AT CORA WHO HAS STOPPED SINGING 654 ICEMAN
THERE IS A CONFUSED TUMULT OF YELLS, GROANS, 290 LAZARU
CURSES, THE SHRIEKS OF WOMEN,

YELPING

YELPING) 370 LAZARU

YEN

THE OLD BOOZE YEN GOT ME. 147 MISBEG

YEN'S

THIS IS MONEY, LEGALLY VALUED AT TEN YEN'S WORTH 393 MARCOM
OF ANYTHING YOU WISH TO BUY,

YEOMAN

AND EVEN BROKEN HEARTS MAY BE REPAIRED TO DO 318 GGBROW
YEOMAN SERVICE/

YEP

(FROWNINGLY) YEP--AND THAT'S JUST WHAT'S GOT ME 267 AHWILD
WORRIED.
YEP. 298 AHWILD
YEP. 531 DIFRNT

YER

=BEDELIA, I'D LIKE TO FEEL YER.= 237 AHWILD

YER'D

GIV'T YOUR MATE THERE WAS ARSKIN' FUR GELS AN' I 499 VOYAGE
THURGHT AS 'OW YER'D LIKE 'EM TO

YER'LL

WAIT AND YER'LL BLOODY WELL SEE-- 234 HA APE
THEN YER'LL SEE IT'S 'ER CLARSS YER'VE GOT TO 235 HA APE
FIGHT, NOT 'ER ALONE.
YER'LL SEE 'EM IN ARF A MO', WHEN THAT CHURCH LETS235 HA APE
OUT.
YER'LL 'AVE THE BLOODY COPPERS DOWN ON US. 237 HA APE

YER'VE

THEN YER'LL SEE IT'S 'ER CLARSS YER'VE GOT TO 235 HA APE
FIGHT, NOT 'ER ALONE.

YERRA

(CONTEMPTUOUSLY) YERRA, DON'T BE BOASTING. 48 ANNA
YERRA, GOD HELP ME/ 60 ANNA
YERRA, MAT BURKE, 'TIS A GREAT JACKASS YOU'VE 68 ANNA
BECOME AND WHAT'S GOT INTO YOU AT
YERRA, WHAT'S THE DIFFERENCES 78 ANNA

YERSELVES

ENJOY YERSELVES. 252 DESIRE

YESTERDAY

WHY, SEEMS TO ME IT WAS ONLY YESTERDAY HE WAS 217 AHWILD
STILL A BABY.
*YESTERDAY THIS DAY'S MADNESS DID PREPARE 261 AHWILD
TOMORROW'S SILENCE, TRIUMPH,
AND I AIN'T SPOKE A WORD WITH NO ONE SINCE DAY 15 ANNA
BEFORE YESTERDAY.
DON'T YOU LIKE UNCLE ANDY--THE MAN THAT CAME 130 BEYOND
YESTERDAY--
HE CAME YESTERDAY AND TALKED WITH ME. 563 CROSS
(WITH A WINK) I WASN'T BORN YESTERDAY. 525 DIFRNT
TWO WEEKS AGO YESTERDAY. 464 DYNAMO
'CAUSE I SEEN PETER UPSTREET YESTERDAY 11 ELECTR
WHERE WAS YOU GALLIVANTIN' NIGHT AFORE LAST AND 11 ELECTR
ALL YESTERDAYS.
IT SEEMS ONLY YESTERDAY WHEN I USED TO FIND YOU IN 90 ELECTR
YOUR NIGHTSHIRT
I MENTIONED IT YESTERDAY AND SHE GAVE ME SUCH A 159 ELECTR
LOOK/
MY WIFE DRAGGED IN A DOCTOR THE DAY BEFORE 286 GGBROW
YESTERDAY.
HIM YESTERDAY, ME OR YOU TOMORROW, AND WHO CARES, 38 HUGHIE
AND WHAT'S THE DIFFERENCES
YESTERDAY HE SELLS DE RUM ONE BACK TO SOLLY FOR 581 ICEMAN
FOUR BITS
THE MUGS AT JOE'S JOE HERE HAS A YESTERDAY IN THE 594 ICEMAN
SAME FLUSH PERIOD.
WORST IS BEST HERE, AND EAST IS WEST, AND TOMORROW600 ICEMAN
IS YESTERDAY.
ISN'T A PIPE DREAM OF YESTERDAY A TOUCHING THINGS 603 ICEMAN
YOU'LL BE IN A TODAY WHERE THERE IS NO YESTERDAY 661 ICEMAN
OR TOMORROW TO WORRY YOU.
YESTERDAY WHEN I WENT FOR A WALK I DROPPED IN AT 22 JOURNE
THE INN--
YOU TALKED TO HIM WHEN YOU WENT UPTOWN YESTERDAY, 30 JOURNE
DIDN'T YOUS
(SUFFLY.) I REMEMBER, DEAR, AS CLEARLY AS IF IT 107 MANSNS
WERE YESTERDAY.
FATHER FLYNN STOPPED ME ON THE ROAD YESTERDAY AND 26 POET
TOLD ME
SURE I SEE IT AS CLEAR AS YESTERDAY/ 96 STRANG
AS SICKENINGLY CLEAR AS IF IT WERE YESTERDAY.... 6 STRANG
THINK YOU'D JUST SEEN CHARLIE YESTERDAY/ 14 STRANG
I HAD A TALK OVER THE PHONE WITH APPLEBY 95 STRANG
YESTERDAY.
A PLOT CAME TO ME YESTERDAY... 112 STRANG

YESTERDAYS

WITH A FEW HARMLESS PIPE DREAMS ABOUT THEIR 587 ICEMAN
YESTERDAYS AND TOMORROWS,

YESUS

PY YESUS, I VISH SOMEPODY TAKE MY FIRST VATCH FOR 209 HA APE
ME/

YIELDED

BURROWED TOO FREELY, AND THEN YIELDED TO THE 32 MANSNS
TEMPTING

YIELDING

WHICH HE RESPONDS TO WITH AN INSTANT GRATEFUL 141 MISBEG
YIELDING.)
YIELDING FINGERS THAT LET YOU FALL BACK INTO 79 STRANG
YOURSELF....)

YIELDS

THE CRINGING ENVY IN THEIR EYES THAT ONLY YIELDS 309 LAZARU
TO FEAR/
AND YIELDS ENORMOUS PROFIT. 393 MARCOM

YIMINY

PY YIMINY/ 8 ANNA
(MOUSED) PY YIMINY, AY FORGAT. 9 ANNA
AY BET ALL MEN SEE YOU FALL IN LOVE WITH YOU, PY 20 ANNA
YIMINY/
YOU REST ALL YOU WANT, PY YIMINY/ 22 ANNA

1843

YOUNG

YIMINY (CONT'D.)
(SNORTS SCORNFULLY) PY YIMINY, YOU GO CRAZY, AY 44 ANNA
TANK/

YIMMINY
AND DAT 'S VAY IT HAPPEN NOW, PY YIMMINY/ 12 ANNA
(BURSTING WITH JOY) BY YIMMINY CRICKENS, AY 13 ANNA
CALABRATE DAT/

YINGER
YINGER ALE--SAS'PRILLA, MAYBE. 23 ANNA
DEN GIVE ME A LITTLE YINGER BEER--SMALL ONE. 505 VOYAGE

YINGO
DOT VHISKY GAT KICK, BY YINGO/ 6 ANNA
PY YINGO, AY GAT DAT MARTHY SHORE OFF BARGE BEFORE 10 ANNA
ANNA COME/
AY KEEP MY WORD, PY YINGO/ 21 ANNA
(SPITTING DISGUSTEDLY) FOG'S VORST ONE OF HER 26 ANNA
DIRTY TRICKS, PY YINGO/
NO MAN DAT LIVE GOING TO BEAT HER, BY YINGO/ 66 ANNA
PY YINGO, WE HAVE ONE HELL OF A TIME/ 458 CARIBE
PY YINGO, I SEE SIX IN BOAT, YES, SIR. 460 CARIBE
PY YINGO, WE DON'T PAY SO MUCH. 462 CARIBE
YOU GAT HEADACHE, PY YINGO/ 210 HA APE
PY YINGO, I PITY POOR FALLERS MAKE DAT TRIP ROUND 507 VOYAGE
CAPE STIFF DIS TIME YEAR.

YO'SE
NOW YOU SEES WHAR YO'SE GWINE. 191 EJONES

YO'SELFS
COOL YO'SELFS. 188 EJONES

YOB
SHE GAT SICK ON YOB IN ST. 8 ANNA
DAN SHE GAT YOB NURSE GEL IN ST. 10 ANNA
BUT AY DON'T VANT FOR HER GAT YOB NOW. 10 ANNA
AY DON'T GAT YOB ON SEA, ANNA, IF AY DIE FIRST. 21 ANNA
AND, ANNA, DIS AIN'T REAL SAILOR YOB. 21 ANNA
YOB ON HER AIN'T SEA YOB. 21 ANNA
YUST SHORT TIME AGO AY GOT DIS YOB CAUSE AY VAS 21 ANNA
SICK, NEED OPEN AIR.
AND DON'T YOU TALK NO MORE ABOUT GATTING YOB. 22 ANNA
DEY ALL VORK ROTTEN ON SEA FOR NUTTING. 28 ANNA
BUT AY LIKE FOR YOU MARRY STEADY FALLAR GOT GOOD 43 ANNA
YOB ON LAND.
THAT WAS WHAT MADE ME GET A YOB AS NURSE GIRL IN 58 ANNA
ST.
AND YOU THINK THAT WAS A NICE YOB FOR A GIRL, TOO, 58 ANNA
DON'T YOUS
AY GAT MY OLE YOB--BO'SUN. 65 ANNA

YOE
HEY, YOE/ 505 VOYAGE

YOHNNY
HELLO, YOHNNY/ 6 ANNA
AY TALK TO YOHNNY. 7 ANNA

YOHNSON
GO GAT ODER FALLAR, YOHNSON. 30 ANNA

YOKEL
WHICH ONLY THE DRUNKEST YOKEL FROM THE STICKS 571 ICEMAN

YOKELS
THE DAMNED YANKEE YOKELS SHOULD FEEL FLATTERED 106 POET

YOKOHAMA
YOU KNOW THE =SUNDA= SAILS AROUND THE HORN FOR 83 BEYOND
YOKOHAMA FIRST.

YONAH
DAT OLE DAVIL, SEA, SHE MAKE ME YONAH 65 ANNA

YONDER
I'VE HEARD ABOUT HIM FROM ALL SIDES SINCE I FIRST 557 CROSS
CAME TO THE ASYLUM YONDER.
(POINTING) YONDER ATOP O' THE HILL PASTURE, YE 205 DESIRE
MEANS

YORK
SCENE---JOHNNY-THE-PRIEST'S= SALOON NEAR SOUTH 3 ANNA
STREET, NEW YORK CITY.
I NEVER BEEN IN NEW YORK BEFORE, YOU KNOW, AND--- 20 ANNA
(WEARILY) GEE, I SURE WISH WE WAS OUT OF THIS 42 ANNA
DUMP AND BACK IN NEW YORK.
I WENT ASHORE TO GET A TRAIN FOR NEW YORK. 64 ANNA
I WAS GOING TO NEW YORK. 71 ANNA
I'LL GO TO NEW YORK TOMORROW. 72 ANNA
(OPENING IT) NEW YORK. 146 BEYOND
BUT WHEN I LANDED IN NEW YORK--I WIRED YOU I HAD 156 BEYOND
BUSINESS TO WIND
I EXPECTED TO--UNTIL I GOT TO NEW YORK. 156 BEYOND
MIDWAY ON THE VOYAGE BETWEEN NEW YORK AND CARDIFF.477 CARDIF
IT TELLS YOU I'SE SAFE'S 'F I WAS IN NEW YORK CITY.186 EJONES
AN HOUR AFTER SAILING FROM NEW YORK FOR THE VOYAGE207 HA APE
ACROSS.
ON A WEST SIDE STREET IN MIDTOWN NEW YORK. 7 HUGHIE
HE HAS BEEN A NIGHT CLERK IN NEW YORK HOTELS SO 8 HUGHIE
LONG
I'VE BEEN A NIGHT CLERK IN NEW YORK ALL MY LIFE, 37 HUGHIE
ALMOST.
SITUATED ON THE DOWNTOWN WEST SIDE OF NEW YORK. 571 ICEMAN
WHEN SAINT PATRICK DROVE THE SNAKES OUT OF IRELAND718 ICEMAN
THEY SWAM TO NEW YORK AND
I WAS READIN' IN SOME MAGAZINE IN NEW YORK ON'Y 529 INZONE
TWO WEEKS AGO HOW SOME GERMAN
WELL, IT'S BETTER THAN SPENDING THE SUMMER IN A 44 JOURNE
NEW YORK HOTEL, ISN'T IT?
HE KNEW HIM AND LITTLE OLD NEW YORK JUST THE SAME.133 JOURNE
THE DINING ROOM OF THE EVANS' HOMESTEAD IN 48 STRANG
NORTHERN NEW YORK STATE--
KNOW WHEN I GO TO NEW YORK... 50 STRANG
IN A SEASHORE SUBURB NEAR NEW YORK. 90 STRANG
THE SITTING ROOM OF THE EVANS' APARTMENT ON PARK 137 STRANG
AVENUE, NEW YORK CITY--
STAGE A PARTY IN NEW YORK... 161 STRANG

YORK'S
AFTER EXHAUSTING THE MORBID THRILLS OF SOCIAL 219 HA APE
SERVICE WORK ON NEW YORK'S EAST

YORKER
BUT I'VE LIVED HERE IN THE BIG TOWN SO LONG I 14 HUGHIE
CONSIDER MYSELF A NEW YORKER NOW.
MARGIE HAS BROWN HAIR AND HAZEL EYES, A SLUM NEW 611 ICEMAN
YORKER OF MIXED BLOOD.

YORKSHIRE
IS AS OBVIOUSLY ENGLISH AS YORKSHIRE PUDDING 575 ICEMAN

YOSEPHINE
= MY YUSEPHINE, COME BOARD DE SHIP. 6 ANNA
HE ATTEMPTS TO WHISTLE A FEW BARS OF =YOSEPHINE= 10 ANNA
WITH CARELESS BRAVADO.
=MY YOSEPHINE, COME BOARD DE SHIP--= 12 ANNA
=MY YOSEPHINE, COME BOARD DE SHIP--= 13 ANNA
MY YOSEPHINE, COME BOARD DE SHIP. 41 ANNA

YOU'SELF
YOU BEEN IN JAIL YOU'SELF MORE'N ONCE. 177 EJONES

YOUNG
NONE O' YOUR LIP, YOUNG 'UN, OR I'LL LEARN YE. 536 TILE
NEVER YOU MIND ROBESPIERRE, YOUNG MAN/ 196 AHWILD
WITH DELIBERATELY ATTEMPTING TO CORRUPT THE MORALS201 AHWILD
OF MY YOUNG DAUGHTER, MURIEL.
THE CONTAMINATION OF A YOUNG MAN WHOSE MIND, 202 AHWILD
ELDERS AND HIS GIRL AND BUY FRIENDS TO SHOW OFF 202 AHWILD
WHAT A YOUNG HELLION HE IS/
(THEN FROWNING) I'VE GOT TO DO SOMETHING ABOUT 204 AHWILD
THAT YOUNG ANARCHIST
THAT THEY'RE HARDLY FIT READING FOR A YOUNG GIRL. 207 AHWILD
BEAMINGLY GOOD-NATURED YOUNG IRISH GIRL--A 210 AHWILD
=GREENTHORN.=
AND I'VE GOT TO WARN THAT YOUNG IMP TO KEEP HIS 214 AHWILD
FACE STRAIGHT.
UNE MORE SOUND OUT OF YOU, YOUNG MAN AND YOU'LL 229 AHWILD
LEAVE THE TABLE/
YOU'RE AS YOUNG AS YOU EVER WERE. 231 AHWILD
LISTEN HERE, YOUNG MAN/ 235 AHWILD
THE BARTENDER, A STOCKY YOUNG IRISHMAN WITH A 236 AHWILD
FOXILY CUNNING,
(HE CALLS ENCOURAGEMENT) THAT'S SWELL DOPE, YOUNG245 AHWILD
FELLER.
BUT IF I WERE IN YOUR BOOTS I'D GIVE THIS YOUNG 247 AHWILD
SOUSE THE GATE.
IT'S BAD ENOUGH FOR BOYS, BUT FOR A YOUNG GIRL 250 AHWILD
SUPPOSED TO HAVE MANNERS--
(THEN SHARPLY TO TOMMY) YOU HEARD WHAT I SAID, 252 AHWILD
YOUNG MAN/
ARTHUR IS SELF-CONSCIOUSLY A VIRTUOUS YOUNG MAN 263 AHWILD
YOUNG MAN, I'VE NEVER SPANKED YOU YET, BUT THAT 264 AHWILD
DON'T MEAN THAT I NEVER WILL/
WHEN YOU'RE YOUNG YOU CAN STAND ANYTHING WITHOUT 265 AHWILD
IT FEAZING YOU.
(WHIRLS ON HIM) WHAT ARE YOU DOING HERE, YOUNG 269 AHWILD
MAN$
I AM TOO YOUNG TO LIVE WITHOUT DESIRE, 276 AHWILD
TOO YOUNG ART THOU TO WASTE THIS SUMMERNIGHT--- 276 AHWILD
SO LONG AGO, WHEN YOUR MOTHER AND I WERE YOUNG AND297 AHWILD
PLANNING TO GET MARRIED.
THERE HE IS--LIKE A STATUE OF LOVE'S YOUNG DREAM. 298 AHWILD
HE IS A BOYISH, RED-CHEEKED, RATHER GOOD-LOOKING 4 ANNA
YOUNG FELLOW OF TWENTY OR SO.)
DIS AIN'T GOOD PLACE FOR YOUNG GEL, ANYWAY. 22 ANNA
AY DON'T TANK DEY GOT MUCH FANCY DRINK FOR YOUNG 23 ANNA
GEL IN DIS PLACE, ANNA.
YOU WORK TOO HARD FOR YOUNG GEL ALREADY. 23 ANNA
DO YOU THINK THAT'S A GOOD PLACE FOR A YOUNG GIRL 23 ANNA
LIKE ME--UN A COAL BARGE$
THE DECKHAND, JOHNSON, A YOUNG BLOND SWEDE, 30 ANNA
FOLLOWS HIM.
DAT AIN'T NICE FOR YOUNG GEL, YOU TANKS 42 ANNA
YOU WAS YOUNG FOOL/ 48 ANNA
HE IS A TALL, SLENDER YOUNG MAN OF TWENTY-THREE. 81 BEYOND
I'VE HEARD THERE ARE GREAT OPPORTUNITIES FOR A 85 BEYOND
YOUNG FELLOW WITH HIS EYES OPEN
AN I B'LIEVE IN LETTIN' YOUNG FOLKS RUN THEIR 98 BEYOND
AFFAIRS TO SUIT THEMSELVES.
AND I AIN'T PRETENDIN' I CAN REG'LATE LOVE FOR 102 BEYOND
YOUNG FOLKS.
DRAT THAT YOUNG UNE/ 116 BEYOND
HE IS A HULKING, AWKWARD YOUNG FELLOW 123 BEYOND
WHO'S THIS PRETTY YOUNG LADY$ 130 BEYOND
(GOING OVER TO MARY) AND WHO'S THIS YOUNG LADY I 130 BEYOND
FIND YOU ALL ALONE WITH, EH$
BUT THERE'S NO DENYING SHE'S YOUR YOUNG ONE, 140 BEYOND
EITHER.
WE'RE YOUNG YET. 149 BEYOND
(A DARK YOUNG FELLOW) HO-HU/ 478 CARDIF
THE SEAMAN WHO HAS BEEN ON LOOKOUT, SMITTY, A 483 CARDIF
YOUNG ENGLISHMAN,
SEA-FARIN' IS ALL RIGHT WHEN YOU'RE YOUNG AND 487 CARDIF
DON'T CARE.
(A YOUNG ENGLISHMAN WITH A BLOND MUSTACHE. 456 CARIBE
A PRETTY YOUNG MAIDEN I CHANCED FOR TO MEET, 460 CARIBE
A PRETTY YOUNG MAIDEN I CHANCED FOR TO MEET, 460 CARIBE
A PRETTY YOUNG MAIDEN I CHANCED FOR TO MEET, 460 CARIBE
WOULD YOU SADDLE YOUR YOUNG HUSBAND WITH A MADMAN 564 CROSS
AND
JIMMY IS A TALL, SINEWY, BRONZED YOUNG KANAKA. 571 CROSS
OH, HE WAS A REMARKABLY SUPERSTITIOUS YOUNG FOOL/ 510 DAYS
IT DROVE THE YOUNG IDIOT INTO A PANIC OF 511 DAYS
SUPERSTITIOUS REMORSE.
BY THE ETARNAL, I KIN BREAK MOST O' THE YOUNG 234 DESIRE
FELLERS' BACKS AT ANY KIND O' WORK
FARMERS AND THEIR WIVES AND THEIR YOUNG FOLKS OF 247 DESIRE
BOTH SEXES
HE IS A LANKY YOUNG FELLOW WITH A LONG, WEAK FACE.247 DESIRE
(SUDDENLY TURNING TO A YOUNG GIRL ON HER RIGHT) 247 DESIRE
(HE STARTS TO FIDDLE =LADY OF THE LAKE= FOUR YOUNG250 DESIRE
FELLOWS AND FOUR GIRLS FORM
BEATIN' THE YOUNG 'UNS LIKE I ALLUS DONE/ 251 DESIRE
THE YOUNG FOLKS GET UP TO DANCE.) 253 DESIRE

YOUNG 1844

YOUNG (CONT'D.)

AN' FUR YOUNG FOOLS LIKE YE T' HOBBLE THEIR LUST. 267 DESIRE FOR ALL THE YOUNG FELLERS IN TOWN TO MAKE EYES AT.ARAY HE IS A HULKING, STOCKY-BUILT YOUNG FELLOW OF 25. 498 DIFRNT ROGERS IS A HUSKY YOUNG FISHERMAN OF TWENTY-FOUR, 505 DIFRNT HE IS A YOUNG FELLOW OF TWENTY-THREE, A REPLICA OF519 DIFRNT OF HIS FATHER IN ACT ONE. I WAS YOUNG AND FOOLISH AND GOT ENGAGED TO HIM--- 521 DIFRNT I WAS FORGETTING I GOT A BONE TO PICK WITH YOU, 525 DIFRNT YOUNG MAN/ (WITH A SILLY LAUGH) YOU'RE TOO YOUNG. 527 DIFRNT NOW IT'S LIGHT AND AIRY AND YOUNG-LOOKING, DON'T 535 DIFRNT YOU THINK? YOU'VE GOT UP IN THEM THINGS LIKE A YOUNG GIRL 537 DIFRNT GOIN' TO A DANCE. (STIFFLY) A BODY'S AS OLD AS THEY FEELS---AND I 538 DIFRNT FEEL RIGHT YOUNG. AND WHAT DO YOU SUPPOSE THAT YOUNG SKUNK DOES? 431 DYNAMO AND MIND YOU BEAR THAT IN MIND, YOUNG LADY, 431 DYNAMO WHEN YOU'RE FOOLING WITH THAT YOUNG ASS NEXT DOOR/432 DYNAMO (THEN HASTILY) NOT THAT IT'S ANYTHING IN MY YOUNG432 DYNAMO LIFE. I AIN'T A DAMNED SERIOUS TALK WITH YOU, YOUNG MAN/ 436 DYNAMO SO YOU'RE YOUNG MR. LIGHT, ARE YOUS 436 DYNAMO WHAT'S THE TROUBLE, YOUNG FELLOW? 437 DYNAMO (STERNLY TO REUBEN) I TRUST YOU MEAN HONORABLY BY438 DYNAMO HER, YOUNG FELLOW. I'LL HAVE NO YOUNG SPARK SEDUCING MY DAUGHTER-- 438 DYNAMO SOLEMNLY) YOUNG MAN, I'LL BE HONEST WITH YOU. 439 DYNAMO CHIEFLY YOUNG BELLES AND DANDIES WHO HAVE COME 196 EJOINES HE IS A HEAVILY BUILT YOUNG FELLOW OF TWENTY-TWO, 12 ELECTR HE WENT TO SEA WHEN HE WAS YOUNG AND WAS IN 15 ELECTR CALIFORNIA FOR THE GOLD RUSH. I NOTICE YOU DIDN'T MENTION THAT IN YOUR LETTER, 50 ELECTR YOUNG LADY/ (EMBARRASSED---IRRITABLY) THOUGHT YOU'D GONE TO 56 ELECTR BED, YOUNG LADY/ I'M NOT FIT COMPANY FOR A YOUNG GIRL, I'M AFRAID. 118 ELECTR DID YOU SEE YOUNG ANTHONY STRUTTING AROUND THE 258 GGBROW BALLROOM IN DIRTY FLANNEL PANTS? LET'S GO BACK AND WATCH THE YOUNG FOLKS DANCE. 259 GGBROW THE SAME HEIGHT AS YOUNG BROWN BUT LEAN AND WIRY, 260 GGBROW WITHOUT REPOSE. GAVIN, SCOFFING AND SENSUAL YOUNG PAN. 260 GGBROW TAKES HIS PLACE AT THE RAIL, WHERE YOUNG BROWN HAD260 GGBROW STOOD. BEING SALUTED BY THE YOUNG MASTER---THEN ADDS 261 GGBROW (LIGHTLY) AND YOUR BODY IS A YOUNG WHITE BIRCH LEANING 267 GGBROW BACKWARD I WANT TO HAVE A SERIOUS TALK WITH YOU, YOUNG MAN/271 GGBROW (WITH WILD MOCKERY) ASK HIM IF HE CAN'T FIND AN 273 GGBROW OPENING FOR A TALENTED YOUNG HER FACE IS CONCEALED BEHIND THE MASK OF THE 274 GGBROW PRETTY YOUNG MATRON. TWO DRAFTSMEN, A MIDDLE-AGED AND A YOUNG MAN, BOTH302 GGBROW STOOPSHOULDERED. SHE LOOKS YOUNG AND HAPPY. 308 GGBROW BUT ME, I'M YOUNG/ 215 HA APE WELL, I'M GLAD THEY FIRED THAT YOUNG SQUIRT THAT 215 HUGHIE TOOK ON WHEN HUGHIE GOT SICK. SAY, LARRY, HOW 'BOUT DAT YOUNG GUY, PARRITT, 583 ICEMAN WONDERFUL THING ABOUT YOU, HARRY, YOU KEEP YOUNG 604 ICEMAN AS YOU EVER WAS. ALL YOU NEED IS A BRILLIANT YOUNG ATTORNEY TO 607 ICEMAN HANDLE YOUR CASE. SAY, LARRY, WHERE'S DAT YOUNG FRIEND OF YOURS 636 ICEMAN DISAPPEARED TO? IT'S A SHOCK, BUT HE'S YOUNG AND HE'LL SOON FIND 643 ICEMAN ANOTHER DREAM JUST AS GOOD. THIS GABBY YOUNG PUNK WAS TALKING MY EAR OFF, 668 ICEMAN THAT'S ALL. HE IS A YOUNG AMERICAN WITH A TOUGH, GOOD-NATURED 515 INZONE FACE. SHE STILL HAS A YOUNG, GRACEFUL FIGURE, A TRIFLE 12 JOURNE PLUMP. I'VE KEPT MY APPETITE AND I'VE THE DIGESTION OF A 14 JOURNE YOUNG MAN OF TWENTY. YOU'RE YOUNG YET. YOU COULD STILL MAKE YOUR MARK. 33 JOURNE WHEN HE WAS TOO YOUNG TO SEE THAT YOUR MIND WAS SO 34 JOURNE POISONED BY YOUR OWN FAILURE. WHOSE HELLISH BEAUTY MAKES ME YOUNG AGAIN. 134 JOURNE YOU INSOLENT YOUNG CUB/ 141 JOURNE YOUNG ACTORS WITH THE GREATEST ARTISTIC PROMISE IN150 JOURNE AMERICA. «THAT YOUNG MAN IS PLAYING OTHELLO BETTER THAN I 150 JOURNE EVER DID.» (WITH THE SHY POLITENESS OF A WELL-BRED YOUNG GIRL172 JOURNE TOWARD AN ELDERLY GENTLEMAN BOYHOOD---OR GIRLHOOD---, YOUTH, YOUNG MANHOOD---OR 273 LAZARU WOMANHOOD--- UNDERSTANDING SMILE OF SELF-FORGETFUL LOVE, THE 274 LAZARU LIPS STILL FRESH AND YOUNG. MARK IS YOUNG AND PRETTY, NERVOUS AND HIGH-STRUNG.275 LAZARU OUR YOUNG PEOPLE ARE CORRUPTED/ 286 LAZARU THEY ARE ALL OF THE PROUD SELF-RELIANT TYPE, IN 298 LAZARU THE PERIOD OF YOUNG MANHOOD. AT FRONT, PACING IMPATIENTLY UP AND DOWN, IS A 298 LAZARU YOUNG ROMAN NOBLE OF TWENTY-ONE. HIS MASK IS THAT OF A TYPICAL YOUNG PATRICIAN 326 LAZARU OFFICER. RECLINING ON THE COUCHES ON THE RIGHT ARE YOUNG 336 LAZARU WOMEN AND GIRLS. IT IS YOUNG. 339 LAZARU LAUGHTER, GROWN TOO YOUNG FOR ME, FLEW BACK TO THE345 LAZARU UNBORN--- LIKE A YOUNG SON WHO KEEPS WATCH BY THE BODY OF 350 LAZARU HIS MOTHER,

YOUNG (CONT'D.) AND NOW THAT HE IS DEAD HE WILL NEED A WOMAN, 351 LAZARU YOUNG AND BEAUTIFUL. YOU ARE YOUNG. 353 LAZARU SHE POISONED PRINCE MARCELLUS AND YOUNG GAIUS AND 355 LAZARU LUCIUS THAT THE WAY MIGHT BE AND IN HIS PLACE YOU WILL BE BLESSED WITH THE 357 LAZARU BEAUTIFUL YOUNG GOD, CALIGULA/ WITH THE SLENDER IMMATURE FIGURE OF A YOUNG GIRL. 2 MANSNS YOU'RE AS YOUNG AND PRETTY AS EVER. 5 MANSNS TEARS MAY BECOME A WOMAN WHILE SHE'S YOUNG. 5 MANSNS THE MOST TALENTED OF ITS YOUNG MERCHANTS. 15 MANSNS YOU'RE BECOMING THE YOUNG NAPOLEON OF TRADE HERE 76 MANSNS IN THE CITY. POSSESSES THE QUALIFICATIONS I DESIRE IS A YOUNG 97 MANSNS AND VERY BEAUTIFUL WOMAN. THERE WAS ONCE UPON A TIME A YOUNG KING OF A HAPPY110 MANSNS LAND WHO. TAKE A POSSESSIVE GRATIFICATION IN TEASING A YOUNG128 MANSNS BASHFUL SON. AND ONE DAY SOON I WILL BE HATING HER YOUNG BODY 181 MANSNS AND HER PRETTY FACE. TWO CHILDREN PLAYING A GAME, A YOUNG GIRL AND A 364 MARCOM YOUNG MAN IN A LOVING EMBRACE. WELL, THERE WAS AN OLD JEW NAMED IKEY AND HE 366 MARCOM MARRIED A YOUNG GIRL NAMED REBECCA. (GRINNING TEASINGLY) YOU'RE TOO YOUNG. 371 MARCOM YOUNG MAN. HE IS NOW NEARLY EIGHTEEN, A BRASH, SELF-CONFIDENT373 MARCOM YOUNG MAN. (HESITANTLY) MY SON, MARCO, YOUR MAJESTY---STILL 378 MARCOM YOUNG AND GRACELESS. GIVE HIM MY HUMBLE ADVICE---HE IS YOUNG--- 380 MARCOM YOU YOUNG SCAMP/ (LAUGHING) HA-HA/ GOOD BOY, 381 MARCOM MARK/ KUKACHIN, A BEAUTIFUL YOUNG GIRL OF TWENTY, PALE 384 MARCOM AND DELICATE. (SMILING BACK LIKE A BOY) YES, I DID TOO, WHEN I 399 MARCOM WAS YOUNG AND FOOLISH. HERE NOW, YOUNG LADY/ 412 MARCOM GHAZAM IS A YOUNG MAN, NOT HANDSOME BUT NOBLE AND 418 MARCOM MANLY LOOKING. MULTITUDE OF YOUNG STAFF OFFICERS, ALL GORGEOUSLY 421 MARCOM UNIFORMED AND ARMORED. AFTER THEM COMES A TROUPE OF YOUNG GIRLS AND BOYS,433 MARCOM THE YOUNG BOYS AND GIRLS PLACE THEIR SMOKING 434 MARCOM CENSERS ABOUT THE CATAFALQUE. OUR PRINCESS WAS YOUNG AS SPRING, SHE WAS 436 MARCOM BEAUTIFUL AS A BIRD OR FLOWER. SORROW BECOMES DESPAIR WHEN DEATH COMES TO THE 436 MARCOM YOUNG, UNTIMELY. FINALLY THE YOUNG BUYS AND GIRLS TAKE UP THEIR 437 MARCOM CENSERS. THE NIGHT'S YOUNG YET, AND WE'LL HAVE IT ALL TO 103 MISBEG OURSELVES. I LOOKED YOUNG AND PRETTY LIKE SOMEONE I 147 MISBEG REMEMBERED MEETING LONG AGO. SINCE YOU'VE BEEN PLAYIN' NURSE TO THE YOUNG 16 POET YANKEE UPSTAIRS. IT'S HARD TO TELL, BUT SHE'S TOO YOUNG FOR HIS 18 POET MOTHER, I'D SWEAR. IT'S EASY TO TELL YOUNG MASTER HARFORD HAS A TOUCH 30 POET AV THE POET IN HIM--- YOUNG HARFORD SEEN'S A DACENT LAD. 31 POET YOUNG SIMON IS IN LOVE WITH YOU. 47 POET YOUNG HARFORD IS, I AM CONVINCED, AN ESTIMABLE 47 POET YOUTH. HOW IS OUR PATIENT, YOUNG SIMON HARFORD, THIS 47 POET MORNING? TRUE. HE IS A BIT ON THE SOBER SIDE FOR ONE SO 48 POET YOUNG. OH, YES, YOUNG SIMON'S FAMILY. 49 POET I SUPPOSE I MAY EXPECT THE YOUNG MAN TO REQUEST AN 49 POET INTERVIEW WITH ME. HERE'S THE MILK THE DOCTOR ORDERED FOR THE YOUNG 59 POET GENTLEMAN. THE POOR YOUNG DEVIL HASN'T A CHANCE TO ESCAPE 60 POET AS IF YOU THOUGHT SHE'D BE UP TO ANYTHING TO CATCH 62 POET YOUNG HARFORD. (THEN QUICKLY.) NOT THAT I DON'T APPROVE OF YOUNG 63 POET HARFORD. MIND YOU. I WAS ABOUT TO TELL YOU OF THE TALK I HAD THIS 107 POET AFTERNOON WITH YOUNG HARFORD. THE POINT IS, MY BASHFUL YOUNG GENTLEMAN FINALLY 109 POET BLURTED OUT THERE WAS ANOTHER REASON WHY I TOLD YOUNG HARFORD 112 POET WHOSE ONLY THOUGHT IS MONEY AND WHO HAS 113 POET SHAMELESSLY THROWN HERSELF AT A YOUNG I HOLD YOUNG HARFORD IN TOO HIGH ESTEEM. 113 POET YOUNG HARFORD NEEDS TO BE SAVED FROM HIMSELF. 114 POET (WITH AFFECTED CASUALNESS.) A PRETTY YOUNG WOMAN,119 POET DO YOU HAPPEN BY ANY CHANCE TO REPRESENT THE 119 POET FATHER OF YOUNG SIMON HARFORD? SHE MUST HAVE FALLEN ASLEEP LIKE THE YOUNG CAN. 135 POET ARRAH, SAVE YOUR BLARNEY FOR THE YOUNG GIRLS/ 136 POET THE DIVIL TAKE YOUNG GIRLS. 136 POET (SHE LOOKS RELIEVED.) WELL, IF THE YOUNG LAD SAID140 POET THAT, MAYBE IT'S TRUE. YOU MUST MAKE THE YOUNG YANKEE GINTLEMAN HAVE YOU 171 POET IN HIS BED. BE GOD, HE'LL NIVIR RESIST THAT, IF I KNOW HIM, 171 POET FOR HE'S A YOUNG FOOL. THE YOUNG LAD WANTS TO MARRY HER AS SOON AS CAN 172 POET BE, SHE TOLD ME. WHERE HE LET HER YOUNG GINTLEMAN BUILD HIS CABIN---173 POET ABOUT NOT MARRYIN' THE YOUNG LAD UPSTAIRS. 179 POET WHAT WOULD THE YOUNG LAD THINK OF YOUS 182 POET NO---EXCEPT WAIT AND PRAY THAT YOUNG THIEF IS DEAD 386 ROPE AN' WON'T COME BACK..

1845

YOUTHFULNESS

YOUNG (CONT'D.)

HE IS A TALL, STRAPPING YOUNG FELLOW ABOUT TWENTY-587 ROPE FIVE WITH A COARSE-FEATURED,

(MOCKING BITTERLY) (=NOTHING HALF SO SWEET IN 6 STRANG LIFE AS LOVE'S YOUNG DREAM,

ARE YOU TRYING TO CUT ME DEAD, YOUNG LADYS 13 STRANG YOU ARE YOUNG. 20 STRANG PARTICULARLY THAT SELF-IMPORTANT YOUNG ASS OF A 25 STRANG DOCTOR/...

(THINKING SNEERINGLY) ((AMUSING, THESE YOUNG 33 STRANG DOCTORS/...

DID YOU EVER KNOW A YOUNG SCIENTIST, CHARLIES 41 STRANG IN A YOUNG GIRL'S VOICE) 44 STRANG IS FOR YOU TO MARRY THAT YOUNG EVANS. 46 STRANG AND YOU'RE ON YOUR HONEYMOON, AND OLD AGE IS 56 STRANG ALWAYS SAD TO YOUNG FOLKS.

YOUNG FOLKS DON'T NOWADAYS--UNTIL I'D SEEN YOU AND 61 STRANG TOLD YOU EVERYTHING.

THEN YOU GO RIGHT TO BED, YOUNG LADY/ 136 STRANG TO THE YOUNG DOCTOR WE HAD SEEN AT THE HOUSE OF 158 STRANG NINA'S FATHER IN ACT TWO.

YOU'VE GOT YOUNG EYES. 159 STRANG (YOUNG EYES... 160 STRANG HE SEES LOVE IN HER YOUNG EYES/... 160 STRANG (NINA HATES THIS YOUNG LADIE... 161 STRANG HOW WELL AND YOUNG HE LOOKS... 165 STRANG (WITH A FRIENDLY SMILE) I HAVEN'T SEEN YOU LOOK 165 STRANG SO YOUNG AND HANDSOME SINCE I

THERE'S A YOUNG LADY WHO SEEMS TO CARE A LOT 168 STRANG WHETHER GORDON COMES IN LAST OR

AND WHY AM I TAKING THIS YOUNG GORDON'S PARTS... 168 STRANG (STARING BEFORE HER AS IF SHE WERE IN A TRANCE-- 179 STRANG SIMPLY, LIKE A YOUNG GIRL)

((BAH, WHAT HAS THAT YOUNG MAN TO DO WITH MES... 191 STRANG AT ONE OF THE TABLES, FRONT, A ROUND-SHOULDERED 493 VOYAGE YOUNG FELLOW IS SITTING.

UT'S LATE FOR WAN SO YOUNG TO BE OUT IN THE NIGHT.504 VOYAGE THE WOMAN IS FAIRLY YOUNG. 471 WELDED

YOUNG'S

SO I TOOK THEM OVER TO MRS. YOUNG'S TO PLAY. 270 GGBROW AND STOP AT MRS. YOUNG'S AND ASK THE CHILDREN TO 273 GGBROW HURRY RIGHT HOMES

YOUNGER

SHE IS THIRTY-FIVE BUT LOOKS MUCH YOUNGER. 514 DAYS RATHER HE LOOKS MORE ROBUST AND YOUNGER. 230 DESIRE (HAPPILY) WHY I SEEM TO GET FEELIN' YOUNGER AND 536 DIFRNT MORE CHIPPER EVERY DAY.

HIS WIFE, AMELIA, IS FIFTEEN YEARS HIS JUNIOR AND 422 DYNAMO APPEARS EVEN YOUNGER.

HE SPEAKS TIMIDLY AND HESITATINGLY, AS A MUCH 422 DYNAMO YOUNGER BOY MIGHT.

BUT SHE APPEARS YOUNGER. 9 ELECTR YOU'RE YOUNGER. 52 ELECTR (FORCES A LAUGH) YOUNGER AND MORE BEAUTIFUL/ 82 ELECTR YOU'RE YOUNGER, TOO, SOMEHOW. 82 ELECTR IT ACTUALLY SOUNDS YOUNGER, DO YOU KNOW ITS 301 GGBROW THE YOUNGER DRAFTSMAN IS THE FIRST TO RECOVER.) 318 GGBROW THE YOUNGER LOOKING AS IF THE VITALITY OF HER 218 HA APE STUCK HAD BEEN SAPPED BEFORE SHE

JAMES TYRONE IS SIXTY-FIVE BUT LOOKS TEN YEARS 13 JOURNE YOUNGER.

EDMUND IS TEN YEARS YOUNGER THAN HIS BROTHER, 19 JOURNE AND FACIAL EXPRESSION, SHE LOOKS YOUNGER. 105 JOURNE AND MY OLDER SISTER SEWED, AND MY TWO YOUNGER 148 JOURNE STAYED AT HOME TO KEEP THE HOUSE.

HE SEEMS TEN YEARS YOUNGER, AT THE PRIME OF FORTY.288 LAZARU BUT THEN IT GREW YOUNGER AND I FELT AT LAST IT HAD345 LAZARU RETURNED TO MY WOMB--

AND EVER YOUNGER AND YOUNGER-- 345 LAZARU EVER YOUR LAUGHTER HAS GROWN YOUNGER, LAZARUS/ 345 LAZARU (UNHEEDING) AND NOW YOUR APPEARANCE IS OF ONE 353 LAZARU YOUNGER BY A SCORE.

REVERSED THE NATURAL PROCESS AND GROWS YOUNGERS 354 LAZARU DEBORAH IS FORTY-FIVE BUT LOOKS MUCH YOUNGER. 2 MANSNS APPEARS ACCOMPANIED BY DEBORAH'S YOUNGER SON, 25 MANNS JOEL.

SHE LOOKS BEAUTIFUL AND SERENE, AND MANY YEARS 191 MANSNS YOUNGER.)

I WAS YOUNGER THEN. 385 MARCOM (HARDER IS IN HIS LATE THIRTIES BUT LOOKS YOUNGER 55 MISBEG BECAUSE HIS FACE IS UNMARKED

HE STILL WEARS THE LATEST IN COLLEGIATE CLOTHES 29 STRANG AND AS HE LOOKS YOUNGER THAN HE

MAKING HER APPEAR A YOUNGER, PRETTIER PERSON FOR 79 STRANG THE MOMENT.

HE LOOKS YOUNGER, CALM AND CONTENTED. 187 STRANG YOUNGER. 190 STRANG

YOUNGEST

TURNS AND FIXES HIS YOUNGEST SON WITH A STERN 264 AHWILD (FORBIDDING EYE)

IT WAS ONE OF THE SONS--THE YOUNGEST--STARTED ME-- 18 ANNA WHEN I WAS SIXTEEN.

THE YOUNGEST SON--PAUL--THAT STARTED ME WRONG. 57 ANNA AND ROBBIE MY YOUNGEST, TOO. 96 BEYOND THE YOUNGEST AND BEST-LOOKING COMES LAST. 464 CARIBE SHE'S ALONE NOW THAT HER YOUNGEST DAUGHTER IS 113 STRANG MARRIED.

YOUNGMANHOOD

YOUTH, AND YOUNGMANHOOD--UR WOMANHOOD-- 336 LAZARU

YOUNGSTER

DARNED YOUNGSTER/ 189 AHWILD THAT HAPPENED WAY BACK WHEN I WAS A YOUNGSTER. 9 ELECTR HE WAS A BOY THEN, BUT HE WAS CRAZY ABOUT HER, 44 ELECTR TOO, LIKE A YOUNGSTER WOULD BE.

YOUNGSTERS

(GRINNING) THERE'S NO SPIRIT IN THE YOUNGSTERS 371 MARCOM NOWADAYS I'LL BET HE WON'T.

YOUTH

DON'T TAX YOUR MEMORY TRYING TO RECALL THOSE 254 AHWILD ANCIENT DAYS OF YOUR YOUTH.

IN THE BEST OF YOUR YOUTH DO THE LIKE OF WHAT I 48 ANNA DONE IN THE STORM AND AFTER.

HER FACE HAS LOST ITS YOUTH AND FRESHNESS. 116 BEYOND BUT UNDER THIS HER DESIRE IS DIMLY AWAKENED BY HIS225 DESIRE YOUTH AND GOOD LOOKS.

BOLDLY-APPEALING VITALITY OF SELF-CONFIDENT YOUTH.505 DIFRNT THE MUST EMPTY-HEADED YOUTH. 519 DIFRNT MOCKERY OF UNDIGNIFIED AGE SNATCHING GREEDILY AT 520 DIFRNT THE EMPTY SIMULACRA OF YOUTH.

YOU SHOULD HAVE YOUTH AND BEAUTY AND FREEDOM 118 ELECTR AROUND YOU.

SHE HAS GROWN MATURE AND MATERNAL, IN SPITE OF 270 GGBROW YOUTH.

REGAINED THE SELF-CONFIDENT SPIRIT OF ITS YOUTH, 303 GGBROW HER EYES SHINE WITH HAPPINESS.)

OH, TO BE BACK IN THE FINE DAYS OF MY YOUTH, 213 HA APE OCHONE/

(TU LARRY) LET US IGNORE THIS USELESS YOUTH, 596 ICEMAN LARRY.

BOYHOOD--OR GIRLHOOD--, YOUTH, YOUNG MANHOOD--OR 273 LAZARU WOMANHOOD--,

(A HAPPY YOUTH--WITH REASSURING CONVICTION) 275 LAZARU THE PERIOD OF ALL THESE MASKS IS ANYWHERE BETWEEN 285 LAZARU YOUTH AND MANHOOD--

(BUT AT THIS MOMENT A NAZARENE YOUTH, EXHAUSTED BY290 LAZARU GRIEF AND TEARS,

YOUTH, AND THE OLD LECHER HOPES HE CAN WORM THE 302 LAZARU SECRET OUT OF HIM--

YOUTH, AND YOUNGMANHOOD--UR WOMANHOOD-- 336 LAZARU THE MALES IN THE PERIOD OF YOUTH, ONE IN EACH OF 336 LAZARU THE TYPES REPRESENTED, AND

YOU WILL CONCLUDE THE OLD LECHER DESIRES YOUTH FOR354 LAZARU HIS LUSTS/

WHAT WAS IT RESTORED YOUR YOUTHS 354 LAZARU I WANT YOUTH AGAIN BECAUSE I LOATHE LUST AND LONG 354 LAZARU FOR PURITY/

PERHAPS YOU ASK YOURSELF, WHAT WOULD TIBERIUS DO 354 LAZARU WITH YOUTHS

(THEN WITH ALMOST A CRY) I WANT YOUTH, LAZARUS, 355 LAZARU AND IT IS MY COMMAND THAT YOU REVEAL THE SECRET OF356 LAZARU YOUR YOUTH TO ME WHENI

MUST I EXPLAIN TO YOU WHY I WANT YOUTHS 356 LAZARU HE GREATLY RESEMBLES A YOUTH I SAW BACK ON THE 367 MARCOM ROAD.

SOME OF THE FRESHNESS OF YOUTH HAS WORN OFF. 369 MARCOM (MOCKINGLY--WITH A YAWN) YOUTH WILL HAVE ITS 374 MARCOM LAUGH/

COULD HE BELIEVE THIS YOUTH POSSESSES THAT THING 379 MARCOM CALLED SOUL

ARE YOU AFRAID TO DIE, IMMORTAL YOUTHS 380 MARCOM IN THE SPRING WE SANG OF LOVE AND LAUGHED WITH 384 MARCOM YOUTH BUT NOW WE ARE PARTED BY

(THEN SPECULATIVELY) YOUTH NEEDS SO MUCH SLEEP 402 MARCOM AND OLD AGE SO LITTLE.

OH, THAT HER BEAUTY COULD LIVE AGAIN, THAT HER 436 MARCOM YOUTH COULD BE BORN ANEW.

AND AN EXTREMELY IRRITATING YOUTH TO HAVE AROUND.) 4 MISBEG YOUNG HARFORD IS. I AM CONVINCED, AN ESTIMABLE 47 POET YOUTH.

BUT MY DAUGHTER HAS THE LOOKS, THE BRAINS-- 63 POET AMBITION, YOUTH--SHE CAN GO FAR.

AND IRRESPONSIBLE YOUTH IN VOICE AND GESTURE. 587 ROPE (THEN FORCING A SMILE) SO TELL ME WHAT FOUNTAIN 165 STRANG OF YOUTH YOU'VE FOUND.

YOUTH MUST KEEP DECENTLY AWAY... 188 STRANG

YOUTH'S

THAT YOUTH'S SWEET-SCENTED MANUSCRIPT SHOULD 298 AHWILD CLOSE/=

YOUTHFUL

BUT THERE STILL TWINKLES IN HER BLOODSHOT BLUE 7 ANNA EYES A YOUTHFUL LUST FOR LIFE

HER YOUTHFUL FACE IS ALREADY HARD AND CYNICAL 13 ANNA BENEATH ITS LAYER OF MAKE-UP.

TOO YOUTHFUL AND EXTREME IN STYLE. 516 DAYS THE WHITE DRESS SHE WEARS IS TOO FRILLY, TOO 520 DIFRNT YOUTHFUL FOR HER.

HE IS THE IDEAL OF THE STILL-YOUTHFUL, GOOD- 288 GGBROW LOOKING, WELL-GROOMED,

EACH RETAINS A VESTIGE OF YOUTHFUL FRESHNESS, 611 ICEMAN THE UNCANNY THING IS THAT HER FACE NOW APPEARS SO 170 JOURNE YOUTHFUL.

HER FACE LOOKS EXTRAORDINARILY YOUTHFUL AND 175 JOURNE INNOCENT.

THEN THE MUSIC SUDDENLY STOPS AND THE CHANT OF 282 LAZARU YOUTHFUL VOICES IS HEARD..

HE HAS GROWN MORE YOUTHFUL. 317 LAZARU HE SEEMS MORE YOUTHFUL STILL NOW, 350 LAZARU HER FACE IS SMALL, ASTONISHINGLY YOUTHFUL, 2 MANSNS AND BY CONTRAST WITH HER FACE, YOUTHFUL. 28 MANSNS SHE NOW HAS THE LOOK OF A SURPRISINGLY YOUTHFUL 95 MANSNS GRANDMOTHER.

HE STILL HAS THE GHOST OF A FORMER YOUTHFUL, 37 MISBEG IRRESPONSIBLE IRISH CHARM--

SHE IS SMALL, A LITTLE OVER FIVE FEET TALL, WITH A 67 POET FRAGILE, YOUTHFUL FIGURE.

YOUTHFULLY

HER FACIAL EXPRESSION INTELLIGENT BUT YOUTHFULLY 262 GGBROW DREAMY,

MARCU PULU, A BOY OF FIFTEEN, YOUTHFULLY HANDSOME 355 MARCOM AND WELL MADE.

YOUTHFULNESS

HIDDEN IN THE FRANKLY-APPEALING CHARM OF HER FRESH 87 BEYOND YOUTHFULNESS.

UNAFFECTED CHARM OF A SHY CONVENT-GIRL 13 JOURNE YOUTHFULNESS SHE HAS NEVER LOST--

YOUTHFULNESS

YOUTHFULNESS (CONT'D.)
THERE IS AT TIMES AN UNCANNY GAY, FREE 97 JOURNE
YOUTHFULNESS IN HER MANNER,
WHICH BY CONTRAST WITH THE YOUTHFULNESS OF HER 2 MANSNS
FACE

YOUTHS
STACCATO LAUGHTER OF WOMEN AND YOUTHS. 326 LAZARU
THOSE OF THE YOUTHS AFFECTED, LISPING, EFFEMINATE.336 LAZARU
ON THE LEFT, YOUTHS OF AN EQUAL NUMBER. 336 LAZARU
THESE YOUTHS WEAR FEMALE WIGS OF CURLED WIRE LIKE 336 LAZARU
FRIZZED HAIR OF A YELLOW GOLD.
(HER LAUGHTER IS CAUGHT UP BY ALL THE GIRLS AND 362 LAZARU
YOUTHS OF THE PALACE. WHO,
THE CHORUS AND YOUTHS AND GIRLS MAKE WAY FOR HIM 362 LAZARU
IN AWED SILENCE--

YUH'D
WHERE YUH'D BE SAFE--GAWD/ 17 ANNA
WAY IN THE MIDDLE OF THE LAND WHERE YUH'D NEVER 486 CARDIF
SMELL THE SEA OR SEE A SHIP.
(GETTING UP) YUH KNOW WHAT HE SAID YUH'D GET IF 457 CARIBE
YUH SPRUNG ANY OF THAT LYIN'
CHRIST, YUH'D OUGHTER SEEN HER EYES/ 241 HA APE
AND LAT YUH'D WANTER GIVE ME THE ONCE-OVER TROU A 247 HA APE
PEEP-HOLE ON SOMEP'N

YUH'LL
TAKE A SLANT IN THE MIRROR AND YUH'LL SEE. 11 ANNA
YUH'LL BE PASSIN' DE HAT TO ME NEXT. 235 HA APE
YUH'LL STICK TO UE FINISH/ 253 HA APE

YUH'RE
(GRINNING) YOU AIN'T CHANGED, THAT'S SURE--UN'Y 588 ROPE
YUH'RE HOMELIER'N EVER.
TO GIT ALL THE DIRTY THINGS YUH'RE THINKIN' ABOUT 589 ROPE
ME OFF YOUR CHEST.
YUH'RE SLOW. 592 ROPE
THEN YUH'RE SIMPLE.. 593 ROPE
YUH'RE LETTIN' HIM KID YUH. 593 ROPE
S'POSE YUH'RE TICKLED TO PIECES TO SEE ME--LIKE 594 ROPE
HELL/
(DISAPPROVINGLY) YUH'RE STILL SPOUTIN' THE ROTTEN595 ROPE
OLD WORD U' GOD SAME'S EVER,

YUH'VE
BECAUSE YUH'VE ALWAYS BEEN A GRAND GUY. 636 ICEMAN

ZACTLY
(-ZACTLY LIKE/
(HE QUOTES FROM THUS SPAKE ZARATHUSTRA.) 78 JOURNE

ZAYTON
(SCENE--THE WHARVES OF THE IMPERIAL FLEET AT THE 399 MARCOM
SEAPORT OF ZAYTON--

ZEAL
I ENJOYED A LONG INTERVAL OF PEACE FROM HIS 504 DAYS
MISSIONARY ZEAL.

ZENITH
MY LIFE IS COOL GREEN SHADE WHEREIN COMES NO 187 STRANG
SCORCHING ZENITH SUN OF PASSION AND

ZEST
(HE SINGS WITH A MAUDLIN ZEST.) 103 ELECTR

ZEUS
HE MUST BE THE FIRE-BORN, THE SON OF ZEUS/ 299 LAZARU

ZIEGFELD
NOT THAT SHE WAS NOTHIN' ZIEGFELD WOULD WANT TO 25 HUGHIE
GLORIFY.

ZIGZAG
(AS THEY ZIGZAG UP TO THE BAR) 503 VOYAGE

ZION
=THE PUNISHMENT OF THINE INIQUITY IS ACCOMPLISHED,579 ROPE
O DAUGHTER OF ZION.

ZOLA
WITH A PICTURE OF SHAKESPEARE ABOVE IT, CONTAINING 11 JOURNE
NOVELS BY BALZAC, ZOLA,
YOUR DIRTY ZOLA/ 135 JOURNE

ZONE
WELL, WE'RE IN THE WAR ZONE RIGHT THIS MINIT IF 514 INZONE
YOU WANTS TO KNOW.
NOT UNTIL WE GET INTO THE WAR ZONE, AT ANY RATE. 514 INZONE
WHEN WE FETCHED THE ZONE--'BOUT FIVE BELLS, IT 515 INZONE
WAS.
BUT YOU KNOW THEY'RE NOT PASTING UP BULLETINS TO 515 INZONE
LET THE CREW KNOW WHEN THE ZONE
NOW WE'RE IN THE WAR ZONE. 516 INZONE
THIS WAR ZONE STUFF'S GUT YER GOAT, DRISC-- 517 INZONE
(GLOOMILY) 'TIS ME LAST TRIP IN THE BLOODY ZONE, 517 INZONE
GOD HELP ME.

ZOO
CAGED IN BY STEEL FROM A SIGHT OF THE SKY LIKE 214 HA APE
BLOODY APES IN THE ZOO/
SURE, 'TWAS AS IF SHE'D SEEN A GREAT HAIRY APE 230 HA APE
ESCAPED FROM THE ZOO/
I TOUGHT I WAS IN A CAGE AT DE ZOO-BUT DE APES 240 HA APE
DUN'T TALK, DUDEY&
DIS IS DE ZOO, HUH& 240 HA APE
(MOCKINGLY) THE ZOOS 240 HA APE
THE MONKEY HOUSE AT THE ZOO. 251 HA APE
WE SHOULD HAVE TAKEN YOU TO THE LONDON ZOO 599 ICEMAN
STRAIGHT TO THE BABOON'S CAGE AT THE LONDON ZOO, 723 ICEMAN
A CONTRIBUTION TO YOUR ZOO--FROM YOUR MOST HUMBLE 391 MARCOM
SERVANT/

ZOROASTER
THIS TREE IS SACRED TO THE FOUNDER OF THE ONE TRUE349 MARCOM
RELIGION, ZOROASTER,

ZYBSZKO
SAY--DEY OUGHTER MATCH HIM--WITH ZYBSZKO. 254 HA APE